DICTIONARY OF WORLD HISTORY

GENERAL EDITOR G·M·D HOWAT

ADVISORY EDITOR A·J·P TAYLOR

NELSON

Thomas Nelson and Sons Ltd

36 Park Street London W1Y 4DE
PO Box 18123 Nairobi Kenya

Thomas Nelson (Australia) Ltd
171–5 Bank Street South Melbourne
Victoria 3205

Thomas Nelson and Sons (Canada) Ltd
81 Curlew Drive Don Mills Ontario

Thomas Nelson (Nigeria) Ltd
PO Box 336 Apapa Lagos

First published 1973

0 17 144005 6

Printed in Great Britain by
Butler & Tanner Ltd., Frome and London

CONTENTS

Editorial Structure

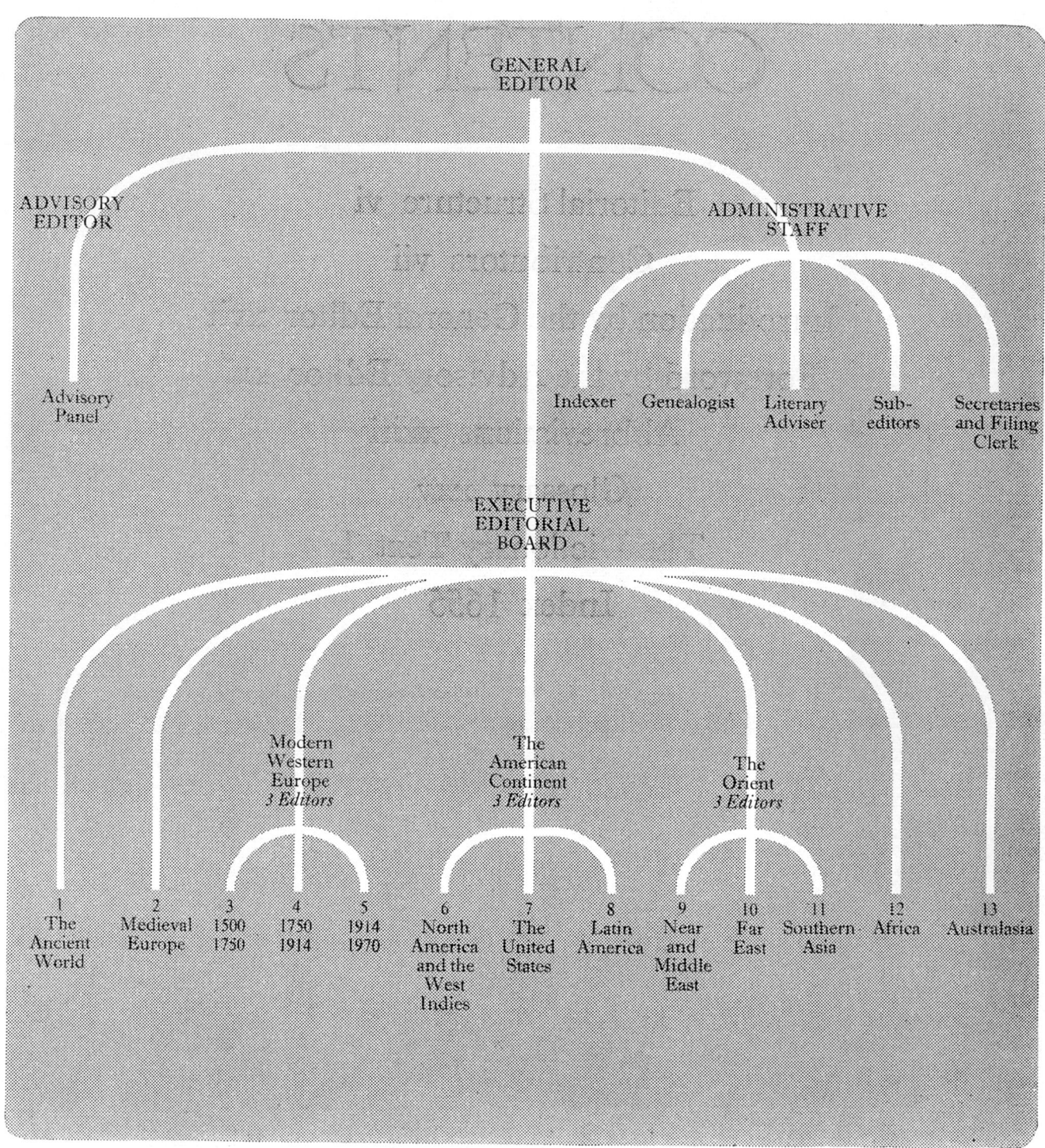

GENERAL EDITOR

ADVISORY EDITOR

ADMINISTRATIVE STAFF

Advisory Panel

Indexer Genealogist Literary Adviser Sub-editors Secretaries and Filing Clerk

EXECUTIVE EDITORIAL BOARD

Modern Western Europe
3 Editors

The American Continent
3 Editors

The Orient
3 Editors

1 The Ancient World

2 Medieval Europe

3 1500 1750

4 1750 1914

5 1914 1970

6 North America and the West Indies

7 The United States

8 Latin America

9 Near and Middle East

10 Far East

11 Southern Asia

12 Africa

13 Australasia

CONTRIBUTORS

General Editor
G M D Howat BLITT MA FRHISTS

Author of *From Chatham to Churchill*, 1966; *Essays to a Young Teacher*, 1966; *The Story of Health*, 1967; *Documents in European History, 1789–1970*, 1972; *Stuart and Cromwellian Foreign Policy*, 1973; 'The Duke of Devonshire' in *The Prime Ministers*, 1973

The Executive Editorial Board

D K Adams AM MA DPHIL
Professor of American Studies and Director of the David Bruce Centre for American Studies, at the University of Keele. Author of *America in the Twentieth Century*, 1967; *An Atlas of North American Affairs*, 1969 (with H B Rodgers)

EXECUTIVE EDITOR, THE UNITED STATES

F Alexander CBE BA MA LITTD
Professor-Emeritus of Modern History in the University of Western Australia. Sometime Visiting Professor of Commonwealth History and Institutions at the Indian School of International Studies, New Delhi. Chairman of the Library Board of Western Australia. Author of *Australia and the United States*, 1941; *Moving Frontiers*, 1947; *The Commonwealth Story*, 1958; *Adult Education in Australia*, 1959; *Canadians and Foreign Policy*, 1960; *Campus at Crawley*, 1963; *Australia Since Federation*, 1972; Editor of *Documents and Readings in Australian History*, 1972

EXECUTIVE EDITOR, AUSTRALASIA

Basil Davidson MC
Sometime Visiting Professor at the University of Ghana, at the University of California at Los Angeles and the University of Edinburgh. Author of *Old Africa Rediscovered*, 1959; *Black Mother*, 1961; *The African Past*, 1964; *A History of West Africa, 1000–1800*, 1965; *A History of East and Central Africa to the late 19th century*, 1967; *Africa in History*, 1968; *A History of West Africa, 1000–1800*, 1968 (with F K Buah); *The Africans: an Entry to Social and Cultural History*, 1969; *The eye of the storm: Angola's people*, 1972

EXECUTIVE EDITOR, AFRICA

E B Fryde MA DPHIL FRHISTS
Professor of History, University College of Wales, Aberystwyth. Author of *Wool Accounts of William de la Pole*, 1964; *Some Business Transactions of York Merchants, 1336–49*, 1966; (with E Miller) *Historical Studies of English Parliament to 1603*, 1970. Contributor to *Cambridge Economic History, vol. iii*, 1963; Editor (with Sir Maurice Powicke) of *Handbook of British Chronology*, 1961; Editor of *Book of Prests of the King's Wardrobe for 1294–5*, 1962

EXECUTIVE EDITOR, MEDIEVAL HISTORY

Advisory Editor
A J P Taylor MA DCL DUNIV FBA

Author of *The Course of German History*, 1945; *The Struggle for Mastery in Europe, 1848–1918*, 1954; *Bismarck*, 1955; *The Trouble-Makers: Dissent over Foreign Policy, 1792–1939*, 1957; *The Origins of the Second World War*, 1961; *The First World War: an Illustrated History*, 1963; *English History, 1914–45*, 1965; *From Sarajevo to Potsdam*, 1966; *Max Aitken, Lord Beaverbrook*, 1972

Betty Kemp MA FRHISTS FSA
Fellow of St Hugh's College, Oxford and Tutor in Modern History. Author of 'The Stewardship of the Chiltern Hundreds' in *Essays Presented to Sir Lewis Namier*, 1956; *King and Commons, 1660–1832*, 1957; 'Pledges, Patriotism and the People' in *A Century of Conflict. Essays for A. J. P. Taylor*, 1966; *Sir Francis Dashwood: An Eighteenth-century Independent*, 1967; *Votes and Standing Orders of the House of Commons: the beginning*, 1972

EXECUTIVE EDITOR, BRITISH AND EUROPEAN HISTORY, 1750–1914

Wilfrid Knapp MA
Fellow of St Catherine's College, Oxford and Tutor in Politics. Author of *A History of War and Peace, 1939–45*, 1967; *Unity and Nationalism in Europe since 1945*, 1969; *Tunisia*, 1970; *France, 1934–6*, 1972

EXECUTIVE EDITOR, BRITISH AND EUROPEAN HISTORY, 1914–70

M J Macleod MA PHD
Associate Professor of Latin American History in the University of Pittsburgh. Author of 'The Novel of Social Protest, the Chaco War and the Revolution' in *Beyond the Revolution: Bolivia since 1952*, 1971; 'The Audiencia of Guatemala', in *Historical Literature of Latin America*, 1971; *Spanish Central America: a socio-economic History, 1520–1720*, 1972; *The Pen and the Sword: the Bolivian Novel of Social Protest*, 1973

EXECUTIVE EDITOR, LATIN AMERICA

R. J. Moore MA PHD
Professor of History, Flinders University of South Australia. Author of *Sir Charles Wood's Indian Policy, 1853–66*, 1966; *Liberalism and Indian Politics, 1872–1922*, 1966; 'Imperialism and Free Trade in India, 1853–5' in *Great Britain and the Colonies, 1815–65*, 1970; 'The Making of India's Federation, 1927–35' and 'British Policy and the Indian Problem, 1936–40', in *The Partition of India*, 1970

EXECUTIVE EDITOR, SOUTH ASIA

R C Reinders BA MA PHD
Senior Lecturer in American Studies in the University of Nottingham. Author of *End of an Era: New Orleans, 1850–60*, 1964

EXECUTIVE EDITOR, COLONIAL NORTH AMERICA, CANADA AND THE WEST INDIES

T T B Ryder MA PHD
Reader in Classics in the University of Hull. Sometime
Visiting Professsor in History, Michigan State University.
Author of *Koine Eirene: General Peace and Local Independence
in Ancient Greece*, 1965

EXECUTIVE EDITOR, ANCIENT HISTORY

J H Shennan BA PHD FRHISTS
Reader in History in the University of Lancaster. Author of
The Parlement of Paris, 1968; *Government and Society in
France, 1461–1661*, 1969

EXECUTIVE EDITOR, BRITISH AND EUROPEAN HISTORY, 1500–1750

R B Smith BA PHD
Reader in the History of South East Asia at the School of
Oriental and African Studies in the University of London.
Author of *Vietnam and the West*, 1968; *Land and Politics in
the England of Henry VIII*, 1970

EXECUTIVE EDITOR, THE FAR EAST

M E Yapp BA PHD
Lecturer in History, and Chairman of the Centre for Near
and Middle East Studies at the School of Oriental and
African Studies in the University of London

EXECUTIVE EDITOR, THE NEAR AND MIDDLE EAST

Associate Editors

W J Gardner MA
Reader in History in the University of Canterbury. Author of
The Amuri, a County History, 1956; Editor of *A History of
Canterbury*, vols i and ii, 1965, 1972; Editor (with
W D McIntyre) of *Speeches and Documents on New Zealand
History*, 1971

ASSOCIATE EXECUTIVE EDITOR, AUSTRALASIA

J O Hunwick BA
Associate Professor of History in the University of Ghana.
Author of *The History of Islam in West Africa*, 1972; Editor
of *The Transactions of the Historical Society of Ghana*

ASSOCIATE EXECUTIVE EDITOR, AFRICA

Assistant Editor

Anne Summers Johnson BA BPHIL

ASSISTANT EDITOR, BRITISH AND EUROPEAN HISTORY, 1914–70

Advisory Panel

Max Beloff BLITT MA LLD FRHISTS
Gladstone Professor of Government and Public
Administration in the University of Oxford, and Fellow of
All Souls College. Sometime Member of the Institute for
Advanced Study at Princeton. Author of *The United States
and the Unity of Europe*, 1963; *The Future of British Foreign
Policy*, 1969; *Imperial Sunset* (vol. i), 1969; *The American
Federal Government*, 1969; *The Intellectual in Politics*, 1970

Asa Briggs MA BSC DSC DLITT LLD FRHISTS
Professor of History and Vice-Chancellor of the University of
Sussex. Sometime Member of the Institute for Advanced
Study at Princeton and Visiting Professor at the University
of Chicago and the Australian National University. Author
of *Victorian People*, 1954; *The Age of Improvement*, 1959;
The Birth of Broadcasting, 1961; *Victorian Cities*, 1963;
The Golden Age of Wireless, 1965; *The War of Words*, 1970

G R Elton MA PHD LITTD FRHISTS FBA
Professor of English Constitutional History in the University
of Cambridge, and Fellow of Clare College. Sometime
Visiting Professor at the University of Pittsburgh. Author
of *England under the Tudors*, 1955; *The Tudor Constitution*,
1960; *The Practice of History*, 1967; *Political History:
Principles and Practice*, 1970; *Policy and Police: the
enforcement of the Reformation in the age of Thomas Cromwell*,
1972; *Reform and Renewal: Thomas Cromwell and the Common
Weal*, 1973. Editor of *The New Cambridge Modern History*,
vol. ii, 1958

Don E Fehrenbacher MA PHD DHL
Coe Professor of American History in Stanford University,
California. Sometime Harmsworth Professor of American
History in the University of Oxford. Author of *Chicago
Giant: A Biography of 'Long John' Wentworth*, 1957;
Prelude to Greatness: Lincoln in the 1850's, 1962; *The Era of
Expansion, 1800–1848*, 1969

J A La Nauze MA LITTD
Professor of History in the Institute of Advanced Studies
at the Australian National University, Canberra, and
Chairman of the Editorial Board, *The Australian Dictionary
of Biography*. Author of *Political Economy in Australia*, 1949;
Alfred Deakin, A Biography, 1965; *The Making of the
Australian Constitution*, 1971

C H Philips MA PHD DLITT LLD
Professor of Oriental History, and Director of the School of
Oriental and African Studies in the University of London.
Author of *India*, 1949; *Handbook of Oriental History*, 1951;
The Evolution of India and Pakistan, 1962; *Politics and Society
in India*, 1963; *The Partition of India*, 1970; *Lord William
Bentinck in India*, 1973

R W Southern MA DLITT FBA FRHISTS
President of St John's College, Oxford. Sometime Chichele
Professor of Modern History in the University of Oxford.
Author of *The Making of the Middle Ages*, 1953; *Western
Views of Islam in the Middle Ages*, 1962; *St Anselm and his
Biographer*, 1963; *Medieval Humanism and other Studies*, 1970;
Western Society and the Church in the Middle Ages, 1970

Sir Ronald Syme MA LITTD DLITT DÈSLETTRES FBA
Sometime Camden Professor of Ancient History in the
University of Oxford, and Fellow of Wolfson College.
Author of *Tacitus*, 1958; *Colonial Elites*, 1958; *Sallust*,
1964; *Ammianus and the Historia Augusta*, 1968; *Emperors
and Biography*, 1970

The biographical notes make reference to the major books and
editorial work undertaken by editors and advisers. They do not
include articles published in learned journals.

List of Contributors

As a general principle, contributors have their current or past appointment set beside their names. In some cases authorship has been quoted instead. The preposition 'of' has been omitted in all references to Universities. The initials used below appear under entries of more than 300 words.

AA **Anthony Atmore** BA
Lecturer in the History of Africa,
School of Oriental and African Studies and
Secretary, Centre of International Studies,
London University

AB **Anthony Brook** BA MA FRGS
Lecturer in American Geography,
Keele University

ABG **A Boyce Gibson** BA MA DLITT
Emeritus Professor of Philosophy,
Melbourne University

ABri **Asa Briggs** MA BSC DSC DLITT LLD FRHISTS
Vice-Chancellor and Professor of History,
Sussex University. Advisory Panel,
Dictionary of World History

AC **Arnold Cook** AM PHD
Senior Lecturer in Economics,
Western Australia University

A de QR **The Rev A de Q Robin** BA MA THL
Author, *Charles Perry*

AFCR **A F C Ryder** MA DPHIL FRHISTS
Professor of History, Ibadan University

AGA **A G Austin** MC BA MED
Professor of Education, Melbourne University

AGLS **A G L Shaw** MA
Professor of History, Monash University, Australia

AHMK-G **A H M Kirk-Greene,** MBE MA
Senior Research Fellow in African Studies,
St Antony's College, Oxford

AHW **A H Wood** OBE MA DD FACE
Sometime President-General,
Methodist Church of Australia

AJH **A J Hill** MBE ED BA MA MACE
Senior Lecturer in History,
Royal Military College, Duntroon

AJN **A J Nicholls** MA BPHIL
Fellow of St Antony's College, Oxford

AJPT **A J P Taylor** MA DCL DUNIV FBA
Fellow of Magdalen College, Oxford.
Honorary Director,
The Beaverbrook Library, London.
Advisory Editor, *Dictionary of World History*

AJR **Captain A J Robertson** DSC
Royal Australian Navy

AJS **Alan J Sharp** BA

AJSR **Anthony Reid** MA PHD
Fellow in Pacific History,
Australian National University

AJT **A J Tyrrell** MA
Lecturer in American Studies,
Didsbury College of Education, Manchester

AK **A Kirilloff** BA
Lecturer in Russian,
University College of Wales, Aberystwyth

AKMcI **Archibald K McIntyre** BSC MB BS DSC FAA
Professor of Physiology, Monash University

AM **Arthur Marsh** MA
Fellow of St Edmund Hall, Oxford

AMCGH **Anne Howat** MB CHB
Author, *The Story of Health*

AP **Antony Polonsky** BA DPHIL
Lecturer in East European History,
Glasgow University

APa **Allen Paterson** MED NDH
Curator, Chelsea Physic Garden, London

ASJ **Anne Summers Johnson** BA BPHIL
Assistant Editor, *Dictionary of World History*

AV **Adriano Vincentalli** MA
Tutor in Italian,
University College of Wales, Aberystwyth

AW **Alan Walton** BA
History Master,
Harrogate Grammar School, Yorkshire

AWi **Alistair Wisker** MA

BB **Beverly Bazler** MA

BD **Basil Davidson** MC
Visiting Professor at Ghana University,
California University at Los Angeles
and Edinburgh University.
Author, *Old Africa Rediscovered; The Africans*.
Executive Editor, *Dictionary of World History*

BDav **Bryan Davies** BA BSC(ECON)
Principal Lecturer in Politics and Modern History,
Enfield College of Technology, London

BEP **Brian Porter** BSC PHD
Senior Lecturer in International Politics,
University College of Wales, Aberystwyth

BFH **Barbara F Harvey** MA BLITT FRHISTS
Fellow of Somerville College, Oxford

BFR **Brynley F Roberts** MA PHD
Senior Lecturer in Welsh Language
and Literature,
University College of Wales, Aberystwyth

BH **Brian Harrison** MA DPHIL
Fellow of Corpus Christi College, Oxford

BHW **B H Warmington** MA
Reader in Ancient History, Bristol University

BJW **Beryl J Williams** BA
Lecturer in History, Sussex University

BK **Betty Kemp** MA FRHISTS FSA
Fellow of St Hugh's College, Oxford. Executive
Editor, *Dictionary of World History*

BK de G **Brian Kelvin de Garis** MA DPHIL
Lecturer in History, Western Australia University

BM **Bruce Mazlish** MA PHD
Professor of History,
Massachusetts Institute of Technology

BMor **Brian Morgan** BA
Sometime Head of History Dept.,
Calder High School for Girls, Liverpool

BMos **Ben Moskowitz** BS MA
Instructor in History,
Community College of Allegheny County,
Pittsburgh

BOO **B. Olatunji Oloruntimehin** BA PHD
Lecturer in History, Ibadan University

CC **Chris Cook** MA
Senior Research Officer and Director of the
Political Archives Investigation,
London School of Economics

CCB **C C Bonwick** MA PHD
Lecturer in American History, Keele University

CCD **C Collin Davies** MA PHD FRHISTS
Reader Emeritus in Indian History,
Oxford University

CFB **Christopher F Black** BA BLITT
Lecturer in Modern History, Glasgow University

CHC **Clive H Church** BA PHD
Lecturer in French History, Lancaster University

CHP **C H Philips** MA PHD DLITT
Professor of Oriental History and Director of the
School of Oriental and African Studies,
London University.
Advisory Panel, *Dictionary of World History*

CJ **C J Jones** BA MA MLITT
Assistant Librarian,
Institute of Historical Research,
London University

CJM **Carol J Morgan** BA PHD

CRB **C R Bawden** MA PHD
Professor of Mongolian,
School of Oriental and African Studies,
London University

CRBa **Colin R Badger** MA
Sometime Director,
Council of Adult Education, Victoria

DAG **The Rt Rev David A Garnsey** BA MA THD
Bishop of Gippsland

DB **David Birmingham** BA PHD
Senior Lecturer in History,
Dar es Salaam University

DBe **Deirdre Beddoe** BA PHD
Lecturer in History,
Glamorgan College of Education, Barry

DBS **D B Swinfen** MA DPHIL
Lecturer in History, Dundee University

DBSm **D B Smith** BA
Lecturer in History,
University College of Swansea,
University of Wales

DCE **D C Earl** MA PHD
Reader in Roman Politics, Leeds University

DEF **D E Fehrenbacher** MA PHD DHL
Coe Professor of American History,
Stanford University, California.
Advisory Panel, *Dictionary of World History*

DHP **Dewey H. Palmer** BA MA
Senior Lecturer in American Studies,
Didsbury College of Education, Manchester

DJF **Doris J Frazee**
Sometime Librarian,
Contra Costa County, California

DJM **D J Mosley** MA PHD
Senior Lecturer in Classics and Ancient History,
Sheffield University

DJND **Donald J N Denoon** BA PHD
Lecturer in History,
Makerere University, Uganda

DJR **D J Ratcliffe** MA BPHIL
Lecturer in Modern History, Durham University

DKA **D K Adams** AM MA DPHIL
Professor of American Studies and Director of
the David Bruce Centre for American Studies,
Keele University.
Executive Editor, *Dictionary of World History*

DKW **David K Wyatt** AB MA PHD
Associate Professor of Southeast Asian History,
Cornell University

DL **Diana Lary** MA PHD
Associate Professor of History,
York University, Toronto

DM **David Mossenson** MA BED PHD
Director of Secondary Education,
Western Australia

DMK **Diana Mary Knox** MA BLITT
Head of History Dept.,
Sydenham School, London

D MCK **Derek McKay** B A
Lecturer in International History,
London School of Economics

DP **David Pong** B A PHD
Associate Professor of History,
Delaware University

DPK **D P Kirby**
Senior Lecturer in History,
University College of Wales, Aberystwyth

DS **D Slay**
Senior Lecturer in English,
University College of Wales, Aberystwyth

DWM **David W Morgan** B A B PHIL D PHIL
Associate Professor of History,
Wesleyan University, Middleton, Connecticut

DWRR **D W R Ridgway** B A
Lecturer in Archaeology, Edinburgh University

EAA **Emmanuel Ayankanmi Ayandele** B A PHD
Senior Lecturer in History, Ibadan University

EBF **E B Fryde** M A D PHIL FR HIST S
Professor of History,
University College of Wales, Aberystwyth.
Executive Editor, *Dictionary of World History*

EFAL **Edward F A Lamont,** B A M A
Visiting Lecturer in History,
Aston University, Birmingham

EJA **E J Alagoa** B A PHD
Research Fellow, Institute of African Studies,
Ibadan University

ES **Elissa Speizman**

FA **Frederick Alexander** CBE B A M A LITT D
Professor-Emeritus of Modern History,
Western Australia University.
Executive Editor, *Dictionary of World History*

FPB **Frederick P Bowser** M A PHD
Assistant Professor of History,
Stanford University

FPK **Frank P King** B A M A

FSVD **F S V Donnison** CBE M A
Sometime Chief Secretary to the Government
of Burma and Historian at the Cabinet Office,
London

GAC **Sir George Alexander Currie** B SC D SC D LITT
LL D
Sometime Vice-Chancellor
of New Zealand University

GAJR **G A J Rogers**

GAS **George Shepperson** M A
Professor of Commonwealth
and American History,
Edinburgh University

GBR **G B Rattray** B SC A ICT A
Head of Science Dept.,
Culham College of Education, Oxfordshire

GCB **G C Bolton** M A D PHIL FR HIST S
Professor of Modern History,
Western Australia University

GD **Gareth Davies** B SC (ECON)
Lecturer in Modern History, Glasgow University

G de B **Sir Gavin de Beer** FRS FSA M A D SC SCD D-ÈS-L
D DEL'UNIV
Sometime Director,
The British Museum (Natural History)

GFO **Giles Francis Oakley**

GHRK **Graham H R Kent** B A

GJO **George James Odgers** M A

GLL **G Lindsay Lockley** M A BD PHD
Principal of Cromwell College,
Queensland University

GMDH **G M D Howat** B LITT M A FR HIST S
General Editor, *Dictionary of World History*

GNB **Geoffrey Blainey** M A
Professor of Economic History,
Melbourne University

GNU **G N Uzoigwe** B A D PHIL
Associate Professor of History,
Michigan University, Ann Arbor

GRE **G R Elton** M A PHD LITT D FBA FR HIST S
Fellow of Clare College, Cambridge University and
Professor of English Constitutional History.
Advisory Panel, *Dictionary of World History*

GSC **Geoffrey Scholefield** B A PHD
Lecturer in Medieval History,
Trinity College, Dublin

G Se **G Seddon** B A M SC PHD
Senior Lecturer in the Philosophy of Science,
Western Australia University

GSP **G S Parsonson** BEM M A
Associate Professor of History,
Otago University, Dunedin, New Zealand

GSR **G S Reid** B COM PHD
Professor of Political Science,
Australian National University

GSt **Graham Stephenson** M A B LITT
Head of the History Dept.,
Sherborne School, Dorset

HDS **Harold D Sims** B A M A PHD
Associate Professor of History,
Pittsburgh University

HMD **Helen Margaret Davies** M A

HNBM **H N B Morgan** B A
Senior Lecturer in History,
St Martin's College of Education, Lancaster

HPH **H P Heseltine** B A M A PHD
Associate Professor of English,
New South Wales University

HRT **Howard Reed Temperley** BA MA PHD
Senior Lecturer in American History,
East Anglia University

HTN **H T Norris** BA MA PHD
Lecturer in Arabic,
School of Oriental and African Studies,
London University

ICP **I C Purchase** BA MA PHD
Visiting Lecturer in History,
Aston University, Birmingham

ID **Irvine Douglas**
Author, *Opportunity in Australia*

IP **The Rev Rabbi Israel Porush** OBE PHD
Chief Minister, The Great Synagogue, Sydney,
President, Australian Jewish Historical Society

ISM **I S McLean** BA BPHIL
Lecturer in Politics,
Newcastle upon Tyne University

JALaN **J A La Nauze** MA LITTD
Professor of History,
Research School of Social Sciences,
Institute of Advanced Studies,
Australian National University, Canberra.
Advisory Panel, *Dictionary of World History*

JAM **J A Merritt** MA PHD
Lecturer in History,
Western Australia University

JAMil **J A Miller** AB MPHIL PHD
Lecturer in History, Warwick University

JAT **J. A Thompson** BA PHD
Lecturer in American History,
University College, London

JB **James Bynon** DOCTEN LING
Lecturer in Berber, School of Oriental and
African Studies, London University

JBW **J Bertin Webster** BA MA PHD
Professor of African History,
Makerere University College

JC **Jane Caplan** MA

JCB **J C Browning** BED
Visiting Lecturer in American History,
Culham College of Education, Oxfordshire

JDL **J D Legge** MA DPHIL
Professor of History, Monash University

JDLee **John D Lees** BA MA PHD
Senior Lecturer in American Government,
Keele University

JDS **J D Smart** MA
Lecturer in Classics, Leeds University

JEL **J E Lavers** BSC MSC
Lecturer in African History,
Ahmadu Bello University, Kano, Nigeria

JES **J E Shiroya** BA MA PHD
Lecturer in History,
Makerere University, Uganda

JFAA **J F Ade Ajayi** BA PHD
Professor of History, Ibadan University

JGdeC **J G de Casparis** DLITT PHD
Reader in the History of
South and South East Asia,
School of Oriental and African Studies,
London University

JHS **J H Shennan** BA PHD FRHISTS
Reader in History, Lancaster University.
Executive Editor, *Dictionary of World History*

JHWGL **J H W G Liebeschuetz** BA PHD
Lecturer in Classics, Leicester University

JJCS **J J C Smart** MA BPHIL
Professor of Philosophy, Adelaide University

JKG **J K Gillespie** BA JP
Sometime History Mistress,
Sandfield School, St Albans

JLD **J L Davies** BA
Lecturer in Archaeology,
University College of Wales, Aberystwyth

JLG **J L Grassi** MA DPHIL
Principal Lecturer in History,
Trinity and All Saints Colleges of Education,
Leeds

JKL **J K Leverson** BSC

JM **J Matthews** MA DPHIL
Fellow of Corpus Christi College, Oxford

JMac **J P Mackintosh** MA AM DLITT MP
Author, *The British Cabinet*

JMF **J M Freeland** DFC MARCH DTRP FRAIA
Professor of Architecture,
New South Wales University

JMK **Joseph Michael Kitch** AB MA
Lecturer in History,
School of Slavonic and East European Studies,
London University

JMR **J M Roberts** MA DPHIL FRHISTS
Fellow of Merton College, Oxford

JMS **J M Soper** MA PHD
Principal Scientific Officer,
United Kingdom Atomic Energy Authority,
Harwell

JMSa **Josefa M Saniel** BSE AM PHD
Professor in East Asian Studies, Asian Centre,
The Philippines University

JOF **James O Fairfax** MA

JOH **J O Hunwick** BA
Associate Professor of History,
Ghana University.
Associate Executive Editor,
Dictionary of World History

JP **June Philipp** MA PHD
Senior Lecturer in History,
La Trobe University, Victoria

JPa **Rev James Parkes** MA DPHIL DHL DLITT
Author, *A History of the Jewish People;
A History of Palestine: 135 to 1948*

JPY **J P Young** BA MA PHD
Associate Professor of Political Science,
New York State University

JR **John Ramsden** BA

JRey **John Reynolds**
Chairman of Directors,
Orieco Mining Company, Tasmania

JRA **Roy Avery** MA FRSA
Headmaster,
Harrow County School for Boys, London

JRCW **Jonathan Wright** MA DPHIL
Student of Christ Church, Oxford

JRLS **John Southam** MA
Barrister-At-Law,
Legal Adviser to the Gas Council, London

JRMM **JRM Murdoch** MA PHD

Jsh **J Shearer** BA MSC FINSTP FAIP
Sometime Reader in Experimental Physics,
Western Australia University

JSK **J S Kirkman** OBE MA PHD FSA
Curator, Fort Jesus Museum, Mobasa, Kenya

JSM **John Stanley Martin** MA BED PHD
Lecturer in Old Icelandic and Swedish,
Melbourne University

JW **J White** BA MA
Lecturer in American Studies, Hull University

JWHL **J W H Lugg** PHD DSC DIC FRIC FRACI
Professor of Biochemistry,
Western Australia University

KEB **K E Beazley** BA MA MP

KHJG **K H J Gardiner** BA PHD
Author, *The Early History of Korea*

KJC **K J Cable** MA
Associate Professor of History,
Sydney University

KM **Keith Mallinson** BA
History Master, Royal Grammar School,
Newcastle upon Tyne

KR **The Rt Rev Keith Rayner** BA PHD
Bishop of Wangaratta

LB **Lucia Beier** MPHIL

LFF **L F Fitzhardinge** MA BLITT
Reader in Australian History,
Australian National University, Canberra

LGRN **Leonard G R Naylor** MA
Sometime Vice Principal,
Culham College of Education, Oxfordshire.
Genealogical Adviser, *Dictionary of World History*

LMB **L M Brown** MA PHD FRHISTS
Senior Lecturer in History,
London School of Economics

LR **Lloyd Ross** MA LLB DLITT FRECONS
Author, *William Lane and the
Australian Labor Movement*

LRM **L R Marchant** BA MA
Senior Lecturer in History,
Western Australia University

LS **L Statham** BA

LWB **L W Barnard** MA PHD
Lecturer in Church History, Leeds University

MANL **M A N Loewe** MA PHD
Fellow of Clare Hall, Cambridge

MBel **Max Beloff** BLITT MA LLD FRHISTS
Fellow of All Souls College and
Gladstone Professor of Government and
Public Administration, Oxford University.
Advisory Panel, *Dictionary of World History*

MB **Michael Brett** BA PHD
Lecturer in History,
School of Oriental and African Studies,
London University

MCo **Margaret Corris** MA
Fellow of Monash University

MC **Michael Cannon**
Author, *The Land Boomers*

MCR **M C Ricklefs** BA
Lecturer in South-East Asian History,
School of Oriental and African Studies,
London University

ME **Modris Eksteins** BPHIL DPHIL
Associate Professor of History, Toronto University

MEB **Muriel E Burton** MA
Senior Lecturer in History,
Culham College of Education, Oxfordshire

MEH **Mary Hodges** MA
Head of History Dept.,
Lady Spencer-Churchill College of Education,
Oxford

MEY **M E Yapp** BA PHD
Lecturer in History and Chairman of the Centre for
Near and Middle East Studies,
School of Oriental and African Studies,
London University.
Executive Editor, *Dictionary of World History*

MF **Maryellen Fullam** BA

MH **Michael Hughes** BA PHD
Lecturer in History,
University College of Wales, Aberystwyth

MHe **Muriel Heppell** MA PHD
Lecturer in the Medieval History of
Orthodox Eastern Europe,
School of Slavonic and East European Studies,
London University

MJB **M J Bennett** BSC PHD DIC ARCS
Senior Scientific Officer,
United Kingdom Atomic Energy Authority,
Harwell

MJH **M J Heale** BA DPHIL

MJM **Murdo J Macleod** MA PHD
Associate Professor of Latin American History,
Pittsburgh University.
Executive Editor, *Dictionary of World History*

MKS **Margaret K Shennan** BA
Visiting Lecturer in History,
St Martin's College of Education, Lancaster

ML **Mollie Lukis** BA FLAA
Archivist and Librarian,
Battyl Library, Perth, Western Australia

MM **M Mills** MA DPHIL
Senior Lecturer in English,
University College of Wales, Aberystwyth

MMR **M M Reese** MA
Author,
Tudors and Stuarts; The Cease of Majesty

MN **Michael Newman** B.A.

MNA **Mervyn Neville Austin** MA BD
Head of Classics and Ancient History Dept.,
Western Australia University

MP-D **Michael Pinto-Duschinsky** MA
Fellow of Pembroke College, Oxford

MR **M Robinson** MA AM
Head of History Dept.,
Radley College, Berkshire

MRB **M R Buckley** MA

MRH **M R Heafford** MA BLITT
Lecturer in Education,
Hockerill College of Education, Bishops Stortford

MS **Margaret Shinnie**
Author, *Ancient African Kingdoms*

MT **Merab Tauman** MA PHD
Sometime Senior Lecturer in Economics,
Western Australia University

MW **Margaret Walsh** MA AM PHD
Lecturer in History, Birmingham University

MWM **Michael W Moss** BA ALA
Assistant Librarian, Keele University

OA **Omoniyi Adewoye** BA MA PHD
Lecturer in History, Ibadan University

OI **Obaro Ikime** BA PHD
Lecturer in History, Ibadan University

OMR **Michael Roe** MA PHD
Reader in History, Tasmania University

OWF **O W Furley** MA BLITT
Senior Lecturer in History,
Makerere University, Uganda

NB **Nicolas Bentley** FSIA
Artist, Author, *The Victorian Scene*
Literary adviser, *Dictionary of World History*

ND MCL **Noel David McLachlan** MA PHD
Reader in History, Melbourne University

NFS **Neville F Stanley** DSC
Professor of Microbiology,
Western Australia University

NRB **Nicholas R Bomford** MA
Head of General Studies, Wellington College,
Berkshire

PAMT **P A M Taylor** MA PHD
Senior Lecturer in American Studies,
Hull University

PBi **P Bibine** BA
Lecturer in Old Norse, St Andrews University

PBO **Peter Boyce** MA PHD
Reader in Political Science, Tasmania University

PBR **P B Richardson** MA
Headmaster, Reading Blue Coat School, Berkshire

PCP **Paul C Palmer** BA MA
Professor of History, Texas A & I University

PD **Philip Denwood** BA
Lecturer in Tibetan,
School of Oriental and African Studies,
London University

PDob **The Rev Peter Doble** MA
Senior Lecturer in Religious Studies,
Culham College of Education, Oxfordshire

PDP **Sir Philip David Phillips** CMG MA LLB QC
Lecturer in Law, Melbourne University

PDR **P D Reeves** MA PHD
Lecturer in History,
School of African and Asian Studies,
Sussex University

PF **Peter Figueroa** PHD
Lecturer in Education, West Indies University

PGB **Peter G Boyle** MA PHD
Lecturer in American Studies,
Nottingham University

PGW **P G Walsh** MA PHD
Professor of Humanity, Glasgow University

PJBD **P J B Dallard** BA

PJP **Peter J Parish** BA
Lecturer in American History,
Glasgow University

PJO'F **P J O'Farrell** MA PHD
Associate Professor of History,
New South Wales University

PLB **P L Brown** BA
Editor, *The Narrative of George Russell*

PM **Philip Mackinnon** BA MA

PMH **Paul M Hayes** BA

PMW **Philip M Williams** MA
Fellow of Nuffield College, Oxford

PP **Paul Preston** MA

PRH **Sir Peter Richard Heydon** CBE BA LLB

1400 letters with those concerned in the project while directives on policy numbered over 90 pages supported by a monthly 'bulletin'. There was also a *Dictionary's Dictionary* giving guidance on the various terminology used in its organization, while a *Mini-Dictionary* was prepared giving sample entries as a guide to contributors.

For editorial purposes all entries were designated 'long', 'medium', or 'short'. Editors were presented with an algebraic formula which indicated the proportion of the lengths of the entries they might have within their divisions.

The filing of the manuscript entries required 240 drawers, as well as three large cabinets.

It might be thought that as many words were being written on the administration of the *Dictionary* as would eventually appear in it. In retrospect, this seems defensible in the setting up of a structure involving five years of editorial work before production even began and employing the literary services of over 300 people.

We would describe this book as a British-based work of scholarship. A large number of those involved in its compilation work in British educational institutions. At the same time, we realized at the outset the importance of incorporating into our planning a major contribution from overseas scholars. Five of our Executive Editorial Board work overseas in Africa, Australasia, or the United States, while our advisory panel has a representative from both Australia and the United States. Our contributors are drawn from many parts of the world and include professors and lecturers from over 50 universities and higher education institutions.

Acknowledgements

Not least among the personal pleasures which I, as General Editor, have enjoyed has been the close contact I have been able to have with both the Executive Editorial Board and the Advisory Panel, all of whom have been in the British Isles at some time during the preparation of the *Dictionary*. I must declare my appreciation of their whole-hearted co-operation in this enterprise. In taking 'everlasting leave of an old and agreeable companion', I must also record my particular thanks to many other people. Mr A J P Taylor has been an exemplar as a colleague whose advice and guidance have always been prompt and dependable. Mr Nicolas Bentley and I have been in constant touch throughout the entire period. He read every page of the *Dictionary*, saving it from many infelicities of style and acting as a link between the historians and the publishers. Both Mr Taylor and Mr Bentley might have claims themselves to be subjects in the *Dictionary*: the one as a major historian of our generation, the other as artist, illustrator, novelist, satirist, and historian. My administrative staff deserve my warmest thanks: my successive secretaries, Mrs Carole Gilbert and Mrs Angela Griffiths; my successive sub-editors, Mrs Penelope Brading and Mr Vernon Robinson; the indexer, Mrs Brenda Hall; the genealogist, Mr L G R Naylor; the alphabetical filing clerk, Mrs Antonia Beard, and the metrication adviser, Mr D B Howat. Mr Brian Seyer also has my gratitude for answering numerous questions of a library nature.

Finally, I would thank the publishers, Thomas Nelson and Sons Ltd, and in particular, Mr James Shepherd, and the printers, Butler and Tanner Ltd, with whom I have enjoyed a cordial relationship.

And so, if, with Samuel Johnson, we have turned 'over half a library to make one book', we take refuge with him for our mistakes: 'Ignorance, madam, pure ignorance.'

North Moreton
Berkshire
England

G M D Howat

FOREWORD
by A J P Taylor

A dictionary of history is a collection of facts—about people, about happenings, about beliefs. Facts are not history just as a skeleton is not a man. They are the raw material which the historian shapes into a pattern. Facts limit the range within which the historian works. No doubt he, too, is an imaginative writer, but—unlike the novelist or the poet—he cannot conjure up facts at will. This is why Samuel Johnson dismissed the writing of history as a mechanical operation.

The facts of history were not chosen for the historian's benefit, at any rate not until very recently. The historical facts are merely those which happened to survive, sometimes by chance, often because men centuries ago attached importance to things which no longer seem important to us—and the other way round. The *Dictionary* gives us evidence of this: too many kings and queens; too many battles. But these were the things which seemed important to our ancestors. Or to put it another way, those who recorded the facts often wrote to please monarchs or warriors. Dynasties provided the historian's calendar until just the other day. They even gave their names to cultures. We almost imagine that the Ming emperors produced all the porcelain or Louis XIV all the furniture of the time. There is one group of men who have proved even more memorable than monarchs. These are the leaders or founders of religions. We have all heard of Buddha even though we cannot recall the name of a single ruler of ancient India. Zoroaster counts for more than the rulers of Persia. Jesus Christ and Mohammed still influence the destinies of mankind, and the Roman emperors who were their contemporaries do not.

History, it has been said, is the record of the victors. Theirs is the record that survives. The conquered have no memorial. Thus we know how the Spaniards conquered South America. We knew little until recently about the Incas or the Aztecs who were conquered. We know even less about the mass of people who did not belong to the ruling class except when they attempted to rebel. The poor have no memorial. Anatole France said that the biography of most men could be expressed in three sentences: 'He was born. He suffered. He died.' Yet throughout this miserable record men have remained cheerful. They have continued to hope in the most hopeless circumstances. The cargoes of slaves hoped to reach America and some did. The soldiers in the trenches hoped to find Homes fit for Heroes, and maybe some did. At the present time men all over the world go lightheartedly about their business, confident that they will somehow survive a nuclear war. We are entitled to be gloomy about man's past. Those who lived through it were less gloomy than we are.

The starting point for every historian is the question: how do we know? Facts lie at the basis of his claims, although until recently all our historical records were what one man reported about other men or sometimes what a man reported about himself. Previously our facts were hearsay. The evidence that an event happened has come only with the camera and the television set, and even that can be twisted or manufactured.

Yet these facts call the historian to order. They limit his speculations and dictate the development of his argument. According to Sir Thomas Browne, 'What song the Syrens sang, or what name Achilles assumed when he hid among women, though puzzling questions, are not beyond conjecture.' Did St Brendan discover America? Do not ask. Was the false Dimitri the son of Ivan the Terrible? Better not to enquire. Was the Tichborne claimant a butcher from Wapping? A question interesting only for the stir it aroused. The information collected in this *Dictionary* is the stock that chroniclers have handed down to us. The historian tries to make sense of this smudged record. For the true historian is not a chronicler. In a sense he 'makes' history. He creates a version that satisfies contemporaries until a better one comes along.

The essence of history is that it moves. Events do not happen at random. They occur one after another in a more or less orderly sequence. This idea of development grew up, I think, only in the nineteenth century. Sir Walter Scott was the first to appreciate that the past was different from the present—different in spirit and in outlook and not merely happening earlier.

This appreciation is what differentiates the historian from the chronicler. The one records; the other narrates. The story, we must remember, is very short even when told on the most expanded scale. History begins and prehistory ends only when men learnt to write and could leave written records. That was a mere four thousand years ago. This is nothing when compared with the thousands of millions of years that the Earth has existed or even with the hundred thousands of years that man has lived upon it. History is the tiny venture of a single species.

At the end, when we have chewed over the facts and added our surmises, what have we achieved? Some men, anxious to enhance the prestige of historians, claim that we learn from history. I myself learn from history that most rulers are vain, incompetent, and greedy for power; that there is little limit to human credulity; and that men have always displayed a desire for general destruction that only their relative impotence has until recently kept within bounds. Against this, we can set the devotion of a few inspired leaders and the patience of the nameless multitude. To my mind, history helps us to understand the past better, no more and no less. If this *Dictionary* provides material towards that understanding, it will have achieved its purpose.

The General Editor, Mr Gerald Howat, has done a magnificent job. The *Dictionary* deserves world-wide recognition on the shelves of public and academic libraries, and private homes.

Beaverbrook Library
London

A J P Taylor

ABBREVIATIONS

COUNTRIES OF THE WORLD

Britain
Hunts	Huntingdonshire
Lancs	Lancashire
Lincs	Lincolnshire
Notts	Nottinghamshire
Salop	Shropshire
Staffs	Staffordshire
Yorks	Yorkshire

Canada
Alta	Alberta
BC	British Columbia
Man.	Manitoba
NB	New Brunswick
Nfld	Newfoundland
NS	Nova Scotia
Ont.	Ontario
PEI	Prince Edward Island
Que.	Quebec
Sask.	Saskatchewan
NWT	North West Territories
YT	Yukon Territory

Australia
ACT	Australian Capital Territory
NSW	New South Wales
NT	Northern Territories
Qld	Queensland
Tas.	Tasmania
SA	Southern Australia
Vic.	Victoria
WA	Western Australia

United States
AL	Alabama
AK	Alaska
AZ	Arizona
AR	Arkansas
CA	California
CZ	Canal Zone
CO	Colorado
CT	Connecticut
DE	Delaware
DC	District of Columbia
FL	Florida
GA	Georgia
GU	Guam
HI	Hawaii
ID	Idaho
IL	Illinois
IN	Indiana
IA	Iowa
KS	Kansas
KY	Kentucky
LA	Louisiana
ME	Maine
MD	Maryland
MA	Massachusetts
MI	Michigan
MN	Minnesota
MS	Mississippi
MO	Missouri
MT	Montana
NB	Nebraska
NV	Nevada
NH	New Hampshire
NJ	New Jersey
NM	New Mexico
NY	*New York
NC	North Carolina
ND	North Dakota
OH	Ohio
OK	Oklahoma
OR	Oregon
PA	Pennsylvania
PR	Puerto Rico
RI	Rhode Island
SC	South Carolina
SD	South Dakota
TN	Tennessee
TX	Texas
UT	Utah
VT	Vermont
VA	Virginia
VI	Virgin Islands
WA	Washington
WV	West Virginia
WI	Wisconsin
WY	Wyoming

Personal Titles
Abp	Archbishop
Bp	Bishop
Capt.	Captain
C.-in-C.	Commander-in-Chief
Col.	Colonel
Dr	Doctor
Gen.	General
Gov.	Governor
Mlle	Mademoiselle
Mme	Madame
Rev.	Reverend
Ven.	Venerable
St	Saint

*New York retained when referring to the city

General List
Word	Meaning
AD	*anno Domini* = after Christ
AH	*anno Hegirae* = Mohammedan era
BC	before Christ
c.	*circa* = about
eg	*exempli gratia* = for example
ie	*id est* = that is
etc.	etcetera
vol.(s)	volume(s)

Months
Jan.	January
Feb.	February
Aug.	August
Sept.	September
Oct.	October
Nov.	November
Dec.	December

Ancient Roman
praenomen: first name
A.	Aulus
C.	Caius (Gaius)
Cn.	Cnaeus (Gnaeus)
D.	Decimus
Fl.	Flavius
L.	Lucius
M.	Marcus
M'.	Manius
P.	Publius
Q.	Quintus
S.	Sextus
T.	Titus

ORGANIZATIONAL
Abwehr	'defence' = Espionage, Counter-espionage, and Sabotage Service of the German High Command
AEG	Allgemeine Electrizitats-Gesellschaft = General Electric (Company)
AFO	Anti-Fascist Organization
AFPFL	Anti-Fascist People's Freedom League
AICC	All-India Congress Committee
AIHRL	All-India Home Rule League
BBC	British Broadcasting Corporation
BBTC	Bombay Burmah Trading Corporation
BEA	British European Airways
BEF	British Expeditionary Force
BNA	Burmah National Army
BOAC	British Overseas Airways Corporation
BVP	Bayerische Volkspartei = Bavarian People's Party
CDU	Christian Democratic Union
CEDA	Confederacion de Derechas Autonomous
CENTO	Central Treaty Organization
CGOC	Confederacion General de Obreros Campesinos
CGT	Confédération générale du travail
CGTU	Confédération générale du travail unitaire
CODER	Council of Regional Economic Development of Brittany
CPGB	Communist Party of Great Britain
CPI	Communist Party of India
CPSU	Communist Party of the Soviet Union
CSP	Congress Socialist Party
DDP	Deutsche Demokratische Partei = German Democratic Party
DK	Dravida Khazaqan = Dravidian Federation

DMK	Dravida Munnetra Khazaqan = Dravidian Progressive Federation
DNVP	Deutsche National-Volkspartei
DVP	Deutsche Volkspartei
ECSC	European Coal and Steel Community
EEC	European Economic Community
EFTA	European Free Trade Association
GATT	General Agreement on Tariffs and Trade
GCBA	General Council of Burmese Associations
GCMG	(Knight or Dame) Grand Cross of St Michael and St George
Gestapa	Geheime Staatspolizeiamt its successor being:
Gestapo	Geheime Staatspolizei
HMS	His/Her Majesty's Service/Ship
IAS	Indian Administrative Service
ICS	Indian Civil Service
IHRL	Indian Home Rule League
ILO	International Labour Organization
ILP	Independent Labour Party
IMF	International Monetary Fund
IMRO	Internal Macedonian Revolutionary Organization
INA	Indian National Army
JP	Justice of the Peace
Kadet	Constitutional Democrat (Russ.)
KGB	Komitet Gosudarstvennoi Bezopastnosti = Foreign Directorate of the Soviet Committee of State Security (its predecessors carrying the initials CHEKA, GPU, MVD, NKGB, NKVD, OGPU)
KMPP	Kisan Mazdoor Praja Party
KNDO	Karen National Defence Organization
KNU	Karen National Defence Union
KPD	Kommunistische Partei Deutschlands = Communist Party of Germany
KPP	Komunistyczna Partia Poliski = Communist Party of Poland also: Krishnak Praja Party
KPRP	Komunistyczna Partia Robotnicza Polski = Communist Workers' Party of Poland
KSC	Komunisticka Strana Ceskoslovenska = Czechoslovak Communist Party
MCA	Malayan Chinese Association
MCP	Malayan Communist Party
MLN	Mouvement de Libération National
MP	Member of Parliament
MRP	Mouvement Républicain Populaire
MSR	Mouvement Social Révolutionnaire
MSZMP	Magyar Szocialista Munkaspart = Hungarian Socialist Workers' Party
NATO	North Atlantic Treaty Organization
NEP	Novaya Ekonomicheskaya Politika = New Economic Policy
NLF	National Liberation Federation

NSDAP	Nationalsozialistische Deutsche Arbeiter Partei = National Socialist German Workers' Party (Nazi Party)
NWFP	North West Frontier Province
OECD	Organization for Economic Co-operation and Development
ORI	Integrated Revolutionary Organization
PAP	People's Action Party
PCC	Communist Party of Cuba
PCE	Partido Comunista de España
PCF	Parti Communiste français
PMIP	Pan-Malayan Islamic Party
POUM	Partido Obrero de unificacíon
PPF	Parti populaire français
PPR	Pilska Partia Robotnicza
PPS	Polska Partia Socjalisttyczna
PSP	Praja Socialist Party
PSU	Parti Socialiste Unifié
PZPR	Polska Zjednoczona Partia Robotnicza
RAF	Royal Air Force
RFC	Royal Flying Corps
RNAS	Royal Naval Air Service
RPF	Rassemblement du peuple français
RSDLP	Russian Social Democratic Labour Party
RSHA	Reichssicherheitshauptamt = Central Security Department of the (Third) Reich
RSS	Rashtriya Swayamsevak Sangh = National Volunteer Group, Cultivators' and Tenants' Party
SA	Sturmabteilungen = Stormtroopers
SCF	Scheduled Caste Federation
SD	Sicherheitsdienst = Security Service
SEATO	South-East Asia Treaty Organization
SFIO	Section française de l'internationale ouvrière
SGPC	Shiromain Gurdwara Parbandhak = Committee for the Management of Sikh Holy Places
SHAPE	Supreme Headquarters Allied Powers, Europe
SKJ	Savez Komunista Jugoslavije = Communist Party of Yugoslavia
SPD	Sozialdemokratische Partei Deutschlands = Social Democrat Party of Germany
SR	Social Revolutionary
SS	Schutzstaffel
TISCO	Tatar Iron and Steel Company
TUC	Trades Union Congress
UDSR	Union démocratique et Socialiste de la Résistance
UMNO	United Malays' National Organization
UN(O)	United Nations (Organization)
UNIA	Universal Negro Improvement Association
UNRRA	United Nations Relief and Rehabilitation Administration
US(A)	United States (of America)
USPD	Unabhängige Sozialdemokratische Partei Deutschlands = Independent Social Democrat Party of Germany
USSR	Union of Soviet Socialist Republics

GLOSSARY

ABITURIENTENEXAMEN school leavers' examination
ADIGAR minister
AERARIUM Roman official state treasury
AHL AL-DHIMMA people with a compact
AIDES tax
ALCABALA sales tax
ALCALDE mayor
ALE Earth Goddess
ALMAMI head of Muslim community
AMIR AL-UMARA chief of chiefs
ANJUMAN secret society
ANNÉE PROPÉDEUTIQUE preparatory year of university studies
ANNLOMA caste determined by husband or wife
ANNONAE FOEDERATICAE annual subscription
APELLA assembly
APELLA, GERONSIA, KRYPTEIA secret police
APPARATCHIKI full-time party bureaucrats
ARIKI chief
ARTEL workshop
ASANTEHENE ruler
ASHIGARU foot soldier
ASHRAM hermitage, community
ASHTA PRADHAN Council of Eight
ASIENTO contract
ASKIA title of Songhay rulers 1493–1591
ASTROLABE instrument for measuring the stars
ATABAK AL-ASAKIR marshal of the armies
ATELIER workshop
AUDIENCIA high court
AUKATI border
AVOCAT-GÉNÉRAL solicitor-general
AWQAF pious foundations
AYLLU extended family or clan

BAB coastal outlet
BACCALAURÉAT matriculation
BAGHLA East African sailing craft
BAILLI bailiff
BAKSHI paymaster

BAKUFU Shogun's government
BALAMA title of military commander of Kabara (Niger port of Timbukitu) in the 15th–16th centuries
BALISE beacon
BALLISTA and MANGONEL projectiles
BALLISTAE spring guns
BARANGAY head of kinship group
BASILEUS king
BAST sanctuary
BEGLERBEG chief of chiefs
BEGLERBEGLIK governorship
BEGLIK lordship
BEGS military chiefs
BELCHAH spade
BENDAHARA prime minister
BHADRALOK literary classes
BHIKKHU monk
BHOODAN land-gift
BLANCOS conservatives
BODHISATTVA enlightened being (Buddhism)
BOKWAI the 'seven' true Hausa states
BOQAR strict order of precedence amongst nobles
BOROROJE pastoralists
BOUCAN dried meat
BOULE council of 500
BOYAR Russian gentry
BRACCIANTI landless labourers
BRETWALDA overlord
BUNDESTAG federal diet
BUNGA EMAS gold and silver trees sent as tribute
BURH fort
BURSCHENSCHAFTEN German leagues of students
BUSHI provincial mounted warriors
BUTI sailing craft in East Africa

CABALLERO Spanish noble
CABILDO governing body
CACIQUISMO electoral management
CAID military and administrative title used in N. Africa
CALIPH supreme sovereign (Islam)
CAMARILLA small group of courtiers
CANCELLA king's seal

CANCELLARIUS chancellor
CAPELLANUS king's chaplain
CAPITULA MISSORUM royal envoys
CAPITULUM clause; pl. CAPITULATIO
CAPUCHE pointed hood
CARBONARI charcoal burners
CARTA CARITATIS rule of charity
CASTES exclusive social groupings among Hindus
CAUDILLISMO personalist government
CAUDILLO leader
CHAKRA wheel
CHANGAMINE king
CHAUTH quarter of the revenue levied by Marathas on Mughal provinces
CHEF-LIEU departmental capital
CHIN-SHIH examination laureate (China)
COMARCAS large districts
CONDOTTIERI commanders of mercenary troops
CONNUBIO alliance, marriage
CONQUISTADORES conquerors
CONSILLADO guild and mercantile court
CONSULARDO council of commerce
CORTES legislature
CORVÉE forced labour
CORVUS boarding-plank
CRIOLLOS Creoles
CRISTERO religious zealot
[CURIA REGIS,] BARONES SCACCARII barons of the exchequer
CURSUS SCACCARII practice of the exchequer

DAIMYŌ lord
DAMEL ruler
DAR-AL-HARB land of war
DĀRUNĀ 'our land'
DAU Swahili: small sailing vessel
DÉCIME tax
DECURIONES local councillors in the *municipia*
DEFFUFA mound
DEMES local resident groups
'DEMOCRISTIANI' Christian Democrats

DENUNCIA formal title
DERI BAN sacred grove
DÉROGEANCE exercise of non-noble occupations
DERVISH Muslim ascetic
DESHBANDHU 'friend of the country'
DESHMUKHI levy of one-tenth
DEVARAJA cult of royalty
DHIMMI Christians, Jews, Zoroastrians
DIA traditional royal title of early Songhay (Gao) kings
DIASPORA migrations of the Jews
DICASTERIA popular courts
DÎME ROYALE royal tithes
DIOLKOS slipway for passage of ships over land (Gk)
DIVUS god
DIWAN council of state, tribunal
DIWANI power to collect revenues
DOAB land between two rivers (Ganges and Jumna)
DON GRATUIT free gift
DONATÁRIOS recipients of captaincies
DUBASH secretary
DVORIANE lesser gentry, nobles
DVORYANSTVO holders of Pomestie estates; the nobility

ECCLESIA assembly
ÉCU obsolete French coin
ÉLECTIONS financial administrative units
ENCOMIENDA system of grants
ENGANZI prime minister
ENOSIS separation
ENPATRIDAE hereditary aristocrats
EPARCH civil ruler
EQUITES cavalry
ETAPPENSTRASSEN military roads
EYALET province

FASCES 'bundle', 'group'
FEDAYIN Palestine guerrillas
FÉDÉRÉS allies
FEE free heritable tenement in medieval England

FIDA'IS the faithful
FIEF feudal land holding
FINANCIERA development bank
FOLKMOOT court of a county or its subdivision
FREIKORPS irregular troops
FUDA'I religious devotee
FUEROS municipal rights based on common law
FÜRSTENBUND league of princes

GABELLE salt tax
GADI judge
GAEKWAR rulers of Baroda
GALON fabulous bird
GANA republican tribe
GÉNÉRALITÉS financial and administrative divisions
GEROUSIA council
GOTRA exogamous clans
GRAGN 'left-handed'
GRAND CONSEIL great council
GRANDES ÉCOLES professional academies (Napoleonic foundation)
GRENIERS administrative areas
GURDWARA Sikh shrine
GURU teacher
GUTSHERRSCHAFT creation of vast arable estates

HABEAS CORPUS (that) you have the body
HACENDADO landowner
HACIENDA plantation
HADITH sacred traditions
HAMSA mythical goose
HANS feudal domains (Japan)
HARAKIRI ceremonial suicide (and see SEPPUKU)
HARIJANS people of god
HECTEMOROI sixth-partners
HEGEMON leader (Gk)
HEPETAI counts
HETMAN Polish supreme army commander
HIJRA emigration
HIPPEIS over 300 (measures)
HOFKAMMER exchequer
HOFKRIEGSRAT Viennese imperial war council
HOMENS BONS leading citizen
HONGI fleets
HOSPODARS Turkish office
HUI Chinese secret society
HUTOR smallholdings

IBTIDA TIMARI 'beginner's fief'

IJTIHAD speculative understanding
IKHWAN brothers
IMAM Islamic leader, rulers of Yemen
INDELNINGSVERK apportionment of Crown land for the maintenance of soldiers and sailors
INSEI 'cloister government'
INTENDANT administrative officer
IQTA grant of land
ISMA'ILI followers of Ismail

JACQUERIES peasants' risings
JAGIR land tenure carrying the right to revenues
JAHAZI large East African sailing ship
JATI caste by social group
JAYANTI 2500th anniversary of the Buddha's enlightenment
JEBELU proportionate number of soldiers
JEFE MÁXIMO supreme leader
JIHAD holy war
JITO stewards
JIZYA poll-tax
JUIZES ORDINARIO presiding officers
JUNKERS nobility

KAISAR-I-HIND Emperor of India
KALAM method of argument
KAOMAN force of deeds in the present and past lives as determinants of the shape and quality of the next
KAPELLMEISTER conductor of choir or orchestra
KARMA burden of fate arising from deeds (Buddhism)
KARŌ house elder
KHADDAR, KHADI hand-spun and hand-woven cloth
KHALIFA sultan's vice-regent
KHAN Turkish and Mongol princely title
KHANEDAN families
KHEL exogamous group
KILIS sword
KOFUN 'ancient tomb'
KOLKHOZ collective farm
KULTURKAMPF fight for secular civilization
KUMARA sweet potato
KURUCOK Hungarian patriots in exile
KUSTI thread-girdle

LAKSAMANA admiral
LANDSKNECHT German mercenary soldier
LANDTAG provincial diet or estates
LATIFUNDIA private estates
LATIFUNDISMO semi-servile labour
LAWAGETAS commander-in-chief
LEGATUS officer
LETTRE DE CACHET arbitrary warrant of arrest
LEVÉE EN MASSE general recruitment
LITS DE JUSTICE king's court
LLANERO a plainsman
LLANOS lowlands of Venezuela
LOGOTHETE chancellor
LUBA province
LUMPENPROLETARIAT lowest social class
LUSTRUM five-year period

MACEHUAL pre-conquest commoner
MADHHAB 'school' of Islamic law
MAGISTRI EQUITUM cavalry officers
MAHA chief, great
MAHA MUDALIYAR chief native officer
MAHAVAMSA 'Great Chronicle'
MAHDI Islamic Messiah
MAI king
MAIDAN parade ground near a town
MAIESTAS treason
MAÎTRE DES REQUÊTES lawyer
MAJLIS national assembly
MAKUTI sailing craft in East Africa
MANA prestige
MANDALA cosmological or mystic circle (Hinduism)
MANSABDAR military title in Mughal empire
MANUFACTURES ROYALES royal factories
MARK march
MASTABA ancient Egyptian tomb
MAUND Indian, Middle Eastern, measure of weight
MBARI cult with its associated house in Onitsha area, eastern Nigeria
MESTA guild of sheep-owners
MESTIŌO Indian–European origin

MESTIZAJE racial mixture
MESTIZO mixed parentage
MESTNICHESTRO strict order of procedure among the nobility
MÉTIS person of mixed race
MILICE French political police
MINAR turret
MIR peasant commune
MISL branch of the Sikh confederacy
MISSI royal envoys
MOHUR gold coin
MTEPE East African sailing vessel of ancient type
MUHAJARIN pilgrims
MUJAHIDDUN those who fight the Holy War
'MUR D'ARGENT' financial circles

NAGARI village republic
NA'IB deputy
NARKOMINDEL foreign office
NAURUZ Persian new year
NAYAK deputy
NEMBUTSU calling on Buddha's name
NEODAMODEIS liberated helots
NGALAWA East African coastal canoe
NIEN-HAO reign period
NIRVANA supreme bliss
NOVA star
NZIMA Akan-speaking group of SW Ghana

OBERSCHULKOLLEGIUM permanent central administrative body to supervise university entrance
OFFICIALITES ecclesiastical courts
OFO ancestral stick
OKPARA lineage heads
OMNGABE king
OOSTHOEK 'east hook'
OPRICHNIKI officials of:
OPRICHNINA—'private court'
OSTRAKON potsherd
OTIOSI men of leisure

PA fort
PAN domain
PANCHAYAT court, council
PARLEMENT court, assembly
PATRES original senators
PATRIMONIUM emperor's private wealth
PATTA rent-roll
PAYS D'ÉTAT provinces of France

PENTACOSIOMEDIMNI over 500 measures
PETRONEL horse-pistol
PHALANX close formation
PHRATOLIES kinship groups
PHYLE tribe
PLEBEIANS ordinary people
PODESTA high judicial and military office
POGLAVNIK leader
POGROM massacre
POMESTIE personal and conditional ownership of land
PRAETOR leader
PRASADA storied or terraced construction
PRAVOSLAVNAYA TSERKOV Russian Orthodox Church
PRAZOS estates held by Portuguese-speaking families
PRESIDENT À MORTIER chief justice
PRIMOS cousins
PROBOULOS special commissioner
PROCURADOR procurator
PROCUREUR-GÉNÉRAL attorney-general
PRŌTOSYMBOULOS first councillor
PUROS liberals

QADI judges
QANUN set of regulations
QIBLA facing towards Mecca
QUAESTOR magistrate
QUARANTA GIORNI isolated for 40 days

RAIYAT peasant cultivator
RAIYATWARI revenue system in Madras
RAJA MUDA viceroy
RAJAKARIYA compulsory service
RANGATIRA chief
RASKOLNIK (adj.) Russian Orthodox Church
RAZNOCHINTSY social origins
REALSCHULE non-classical secondary school
RÉGALE king's right to revenue of vacant bishopric
REGNUM temporal authority
REICHSKAMMERGERICHT imperial court

REICHSRITTER knights
REICHSWEHR national army
REITER German horsemen
RENTES state investments
REPARTIMIENTO a sharing out
RIKSDAG Swedish Estates
RISHI saint, sacred bard
RISORGIMENTO rising
ROBE gown worn by lawyers
ROTURIERS tenant farmers
RUBA'IS quatrain

SABHA place of meeting
SACERDOTIUM priesthood
SACHSENSPRIEGEL German legal code
SADAR military commander
SAEIMA parliament
SALADERO establishment for the preparation of salt beef for export
SAMARERA novices
SAMBUK sailing vessel
SAMSARA transmigration
SAMURAI Japanese feudal warrior
SANAD grant or charter
SANATANIST orthodox
SANGATHAN reform movement
SANGHA monkhood (Buddhist)
SANJAK BEGLIK district officership
SANKHA shell
SANS-CULOTTES French revolutionary crowd
SAR one fourth
SARKAR revenue district
SARO Sierra Leone immigrants
SARVODAYA welfare for all
SATI, SUTTEE ritual self-immolation by widows
SATYAGRAHA passive resistance
SCABINI permanent doomsmen
SEJM national assembly
SENAPATI commander-in-chief
SEPPUKU ceremonial suicide
SHARI'A the holy law of Islam
SHEHU sheikh
SHIKKEN Hojo regents
SHŌEN estate
SHOGUN military ruler
SHUDDHI Muslim

SHUGÓ constables
SIPAHISI or SIPAHI Ottoman feudal cavalryman
SOCII allies
SOLIDUS gold unit of currency
STAATSRAT Council of State
STADTHOLDER head of state
STRATEGOI directly elected generals
STRAGEGOS Byzantine office
STRELTSKY Russia royal guards
STUPA Buddhist reliquary
SUBAH province
SUDREH sacred shirt
SUFI mystic
SUNNI orthodox form of Islam
SWADESHI Indian-made goods, boycott of foreign products
SWAYAMSEVAK volunteer
SZLACHTA Polish landowning nobility

TAGUS leader
TAILLE poll tax
TALUK division of a province
TALUKDAR holder of a Taluk
TAQLID imitation
TARAI forested foothills of the Himalaya
TARIGA Muridiyya fraternity
TARIKA dervish order
TARIQA a Sufi order or craft guild
TAUTININKAI nationalist bloc
TELESTAI barons
TELESTERION hall of initiation
TERAKKI additions
TERMO hinterland
THAGI system of robbery
THEGNS lower-rank nobles
THEME province
THETES under 200 measures
TIERS ÉTAT third estate
TIMAR feudal
TOHUNGA priest
TOURNELLE court of criminal justice
TRAITANTS tax-gatherers
TRASFORMISMO denigration of party political distinctions
TRIMURTI Hindu Trinity
TUMANDAR chief

TURCO Arabic-speaking immigrant

UJI local ruling family
ULAMA traditional religious classes
UMARA chiefs
UPARAJA deputy king
UPSAKA Buddhist laymen

VAINE PÂTURE common grazing rights
VAIVODA governor
VARNA fourfold division of Indian society
VECINOS principal property-holders
VEDANTA Indian philosophical system
VEREADORES aldermen
VERNUNFTREPUBLIKANER republican by national decision
VIGILES watchmen
VILAYET province in Ottoman empire
VIZIER, WAZIR minister
VOTCHINA allodial estates

WAGHNAKH tiger's claw
WAKA ancestral 'cause' group
WAQ'A'- NUWIS official historiographer
WAQF religious endowment
WERGELD blood prince
WHANAU extended family

YAMEN office and residence of an official in Imperial China
YURT appanage or landholder

ZAIBATSU Japanese industrial combine
ZAMINDAR landowner
ZAWIYA lodge
ZEMSTVO Russian elected provincial assemblies
ZENANA womenfolk, female apartments
ZEUGITAE over 200 measures
ZILA PARISHAD district
ZIQQURAT stepped temple
ZU'AMA (horsemen holding an Ottoman military fief)

A

AACHEN (AIX-LA-CHAP-ELLE), probably Charlemagne's birthplace and his chief place of residence in his later years. From 813 to 1531 it was the traditional place for the sacring of the German kings. The central portion of the cathedral, modelled by Charlemagne on the San Vitale at Ravenna, survives as it was rebuilt in 983.

AAHMES (c. 1575–1550 BC), Egyptian King of the XVIIIth dynasty, who completed the expulsion of the Hyksos and reconquered Kush and part of Nubia. He reorganized the administration and resumed building operations and trading contacts lost during the Hyksos period.

AALTO, ALVAR (1898–), Finnish architect who has been prominent among Scandinavian architects in emphasizing the human dimensions of buildings. His most notable works include the Turun Sanomat plant, Turku (1930), the Senila plant near Kotka (1936–9), the Vipurii Library (1935), an MIT dormitory (1939), and the Vuoksenniska church (1955).

AARGAU, part of the valley of the Aare river in north-west Switzerland. This rich agricultural region, containing many castles, including the Habsburg, was conquered by the Swiss confederate army in 1415 and became the first truly Swiss area, being held in common by all the cantons. Its capture closed the last gap in the cantons' defences against the Habsburgs.

AASEN, IVAR ANDREAS (1813–96), Norwegian philologist of peasant origins who travelled throughout Norway collecting old dialects which he gathered together to form the 'country language' (landsmaal) and to reflect the traditions and heritage of Old Norse, and of the independent Norway of the early Middle Ages. His work had both literary and political importance in contributing to the movement for complete Norwegian independence, attained in 1905.

ABA, important commercial and industrial city in eastern Nigeria which grew rapidly after the building of the Port Harcourt–Kano railway in the 1920s. In 1929 it was the centre of the 'Women's Riots', when thousands of women throughout south-eastern Nigeria conducted violent demonstrations against the colonial authorities, fearing they were to be taxed like their menfolk.

ABADAN, site of a major oil refinery on the Persian Gulf which was nationalized by the Iranian government in May 1951, under the premiership of Dr Musaddiq. The refinery was constructed by the Anglo-Persian Oil Co. between 1910 and 1913, following the discovery, at Masjid-i-Sulaiman in 1908, of a major oilfield some 209 kms from the sea.

Up to the outbreak of the Second World War Persian oil accounted for two-thirds of the Middle East's output, and before the development of the shipping of crude oil to refineries in Europe Abadan was of vital importance. The Persian oil industry, including the Abadan refinery, expanded rapidly to meet the needs of the British navy during both World Wars. Between 1939 and 1946 the output from Abadan doubled, to reach 17 million tons a year; by 1950 it had risen to 24 million. The refinery extended over 1·6 kms and employed 38,000 men. A town had been constructed on what was once a barren island; but although the conditions of pay and service for the AP Co.'s Persian employees were superior to the general level in the rest of the country, the top management remained in British hands, inevitably giving the company an imperialistic reputation.

At the end of the Second World War the Persian government pressed for a revision of the 1933 agreement (extending the concession and establishing a new schedule of payments to the government, with the company, especially in regard to the distribution of profits, along the lines of a 50–50 agreement that had been negotiated between the Saudi–Arabian government and Aramco. The company offered two new agreements designed to meet the government's demands, but this action was overtaken by a mounting tide of nationalist resentment against foreign exploitation of Persian oil. On 1 May 1951 the shah signed a nationalization law, proposed by Musaddiq as prime minister and passed by the Majlis.

Nationalization provoked a two-year-long dispute between the company and the government which had political repercussions of major importance. The company's British staff were expelled and the refinery taken over; but the newly established National Iranian Oil Co. lacked the resources to ship or market oil and the refinery came to a standstill. The effect of this on the Persian economy, the nationalist fervour which Dr Musaddiq evoked, and the activity of the Tudeh (Communist) Party created a grave threat to the western position in Iran at the time of the Korean war and the Cold War in Europe.

Negotiations (in which the US government and American oil consultants played a prominent part) failed to produce a settlement. In Aug. 1953 the shah and the army, with the support of British and American Intelligence, ousted Musaddiq, who was placed under house arrest. The way now became open for the negotiation of an agreement, known as the Consortium Agreement (Oct. 1954), which placed the industry in the hands of a consortium of the major oil companies—Anglo-Iranian (which later became British Petroleum) receiving a 40 per cent share.   WFK

ABAKA (d. 1282), second of the Mongol Il-Khans to rule over Persia. His reign (1265–82) saw conflict between the Mongols in Persia and the Mamluks of Syria and Egypt. Abaka sought to establish relations with the Christians of Europe, his ambassadors appearing at Lyons (1274) and Rome (1277).

ABBADIE, ANTOINE THOMSON D' (1810–97), French explorer and scholar, who travelled extensively in Ethiopia (1838–48).

ABBAS I (reg. 1587–1629), Safawid Shah of Persia, who came to the throne when Persia was involved in a long war (1578–90) with the Ottoman empire. Threatened through the advance of the Uzbeg Turks into north-eastern Persia (Khurasan) in 1588, Shah Abbas made peace with the Ottomans in 1590, ceding to them large territories in Azerbayjan and in the Caucasus. After ten years of conflict (1588–98), Abbas was able to drive the Uzbegs from Khurasan. His attempt to bring Balkh under Safawid control ended, however, in failure in 1602. During these years the shah reduced to obedience, inside Persia, the ill-disciplined Turcoman chieftains who supplied him with the bulk of his forces. At the same time, he strengthened the slave regiments recruited from the Georgians and the Circassians of the Caucasus.

Abbas also made use of foreign experts like Robert Sherley to reorganize his armies and to introduce, on a more effective scale than heretofore, the use of cannon and firearms. The shah, eager to find allies against the Ottoman Turks, sent Anthony Sherley, the brother of Robert, to Europe in 1599 as his ambassador; and in 1607 Robert Sherley himself set out for Europe as the shah's representative. These missions met with no real success. In 1603 Abbas began a new war against the Ottomans, then engaged in a great conflict on the Danube and also involved in attempts to repress serious rebellion in Asia Minor. Within a few years the shah regained the territories yielded in 1590. Peace was made between the Ottomans and the Safawids in 1612 and again in 1618. In 1623 another conflict broke out, this time for the possession of Iraq. Shah Abbas did not live to see the end of this war, which lasted until 1639.

ABBAS II (*reg.* 1642–66), Safawid Shah of Persia. During his reign the Safawid forces regained control of Kandahar and the adjacent territories from Shah Jahan, Mughal Emperor of Delhi.

ABBAS HILMI (1874–1944), Khedive of Egypt (1892–1914), who unsuccessfully opposed British domination in Egypt. He was deposed (1914) for supporting the Ottoman empire against the entente.

ABBAS MIRZA (1789–1833), son of Fath Ali Shah Qajar, whom he predeceased, and heir-apparent to the Iranian throne. As governor of Azerbayjan, he was the first Iranian leader to begin the modernization of the Iranian army upon European lines and to send students to Europe.

ABBASID, a Muslim dynasty ruling in the Middle East (750–1258). The year 750 saw the fall of the Umayyad caliphate—a fall arising from a recrudescence of tribal feuds among the Arabs, from the opposition of the Shi'is, who believed that the caliphate should be vested in the House of Ali, and from the discontent of the Mawali, the new converts to Islam, who, as Muslims, expected to have, but did not receive, an equal status with the Arab warrior class dominant within the empire. A mechanism of revolution was to hand in the form of the Hashimiyya, an extremist religious sect, the control of which had fallen to the Abbasids. A suitable theatre of revolution was Khurasan, a frontier province located far from the central regime and possessed of a war-like population, many of whom had been converted to the Muslim faith. The architect of revolution was Abu Muslim, a member of the Hashimiyya, who brought together all the elements hostile to the Umayyads and used them to raise the House of Abbas to the caliphate.

The Abbasids held the caliphate for a little over 500 years, a span of time which can be divided into three main periods. The first of these (750–*c.* 850) saw the golden age of the caliphate. The true founder of the new regime was the Caliph al-Mansur (754–5), who founded Baghdad. Also to this period belong the reign of Harun al-Rashid, later to be celebrated in *The Thousand and One Nights*, and the reign of Al-Ma'mun, when the transmission into Arabic, from Greek and Syriac, of the philosophic and scientific heritage of the Ancient World was in full progress. It was, moreover, a time of great material wealth, of rich manufacturing enterprises, and of a flourishing international trade extending to India, China, Africa, and Europe. These commercial and industrial developments led to the growth of an elaborate system of banking, making use of such devices as cheques and letters of credit.

The second period (*c.* 850–*c.* 1050) was one of political disintegration. It witnessed the rise of autonomous dynasties all over the empire, *eg*, the Aghlabids in Ifriqiyya or the Tahirids in Khurasan. It also saw the subjection of the Abbasid caliphate to the Shi'i regime (945–1055) of the Buwayhids and, in addition, the establishment in Egypt of a Fatimid anti-caliphate (969–1171).

The last period of Abbasid rule (*c.* 1050–1258) can be described as an age of barbarian invasion—of the Seljuk Turks, who captured Baghdad in 1055, of the Latin Crusaders, who conquered much of Syria after 1096, and, at the close of the period, of the Mongols, who, overrunning Persia in 1255 and taking Baghdad in 1258, brought the Abbasid caliphate to an end, although a line of nominal Abbasid caliphs continued in Egypt until 1517.			VJP

ABBEY THEATRE, founded in Dublin (1904), became the centre of the Irish literary revival at the beginning of the 20th cent., and of the nationalist movement associated with it, to the development of which the theatre made an important contribution.

ABBOTT, SIR JOHN (1821–93), prime minister of Canada (1891) and one of the signatories of the annexation manifesto (1849), he raised the 'Argenteuil Rangers' for the government in 1861. He was Dean of the Faculty of Law at McGill University (1855–65) and Hugh Allan's solicitor in negotiating the charter of the Canadian Pacific Railroad. Documents taken from his files were instrumental in the 'Pacific Scandal' (1873).

ABBOTT, LYMAN (1835–1922). Born into a distinguished New England family, Abbott became a Congregational minister in 1860. He edited the *Christian Union*, later renamed *Outlook*, with Henry Ward Beecher, whom he succeeded at Plymouth Congregational Church, Brooklyn (1887). A prolific author and preacher, he made *Outlook* an influential, progressive journal.

ABC POWERS, abbreviation for Argentina, Brazil, and Chile. An entente existing between these three nations from the turn of the century until the First World War gave rise to the term.

ABD AL-AZIZ II IBN SA'UD (*c.* 1880–1953), refounder of Saudi power in Arabia. In 1902 he recovered Riyahd from the Rashidis and became leader of the Saudi party, although his father, Imam Abd al-Rahman ibn Faisal ibn Sa'ud (1850–1928), remained nominal head of the household until his death. Abd al-Aziz extended his power over Nejd, Al-Hasa (1913), Hail (1921), the Hijaz, of which he was proclaimed king (Jan. 1926), and Asir (1926). His realm became known as the 'Kingdom of Saudi Arabia' in 1934. His remarkable success in consolidating his kingdom was clouded in the last decade of his reign by his failure to modernize Saudi institutions to cope with the enormous new flow of oil riches.

ABD AL-ILAH (1913–58), Crown Prince and Regent of Iraq during the minority of his nephew, Faisal II (1939–53), and son of King Ali of the Hijaz. As regent he pursued policies of alliance with Britain and support for the creation of a Fertile Crescent Union by union with Syria. He was murdered during the July 1958 revolution.

ABD AL-KADER b. MUHIJI AL DIN, the Amir (1808–83), principal leader of Algerian resistance to French invasion and occupation. Of Rif origins, he spent his youth in Koranic learning under the influence of a pious father, and made the pilgrimage in 1828–9. Taking over military leadership from his father after the loss of Algiers (1830), he was proclaimed sultan by the Hashim of his native district of Mascara and then recognized as Amir al-Muminin (Commander of the Faithful) also by the French, who were still restricted to Algiers and other ports they had seized (1835).

The young amir settled on the site of the ancient Ibadi city of Tahert, in central Algeria, and, after renewed fighting, was again able to secure a treaty with the French—with Bugeaud in 1837—which kept wide areas under his control. As French intrusions continued, there came fresh resistance as well as revolts in areas now enclosed by France. These reached a climax in 1846. Only a major military effort by the French at last enabled them to shatter the amir's forces. He himself tried for refuge in Morocco; failing to find it, and increasingly the victim of local hostility, he surrendered to the French in 1847. They interned him for five years in France before they eventually fulfilled the terms of his surrender, and allowed him to reside freely in the Middle East.

He settled first in Brusa, Turkey, and then, in 1855, took up permanent residence in Damascus. Reconciled with his old enemies, in 1860 he saved the French consul and several thousand Christians from an acute threat of massacre by Druses, for which France gave him a medal with the words: 'Amir of North Africa: Defender of Arab Nationality: Protector of Oppressed Christians'.

ABD AL-KARIM (c. 1882–1963), Emir of the Rif, led the Rif tribes in rebellion against Spanish occupation, and threatened to reunify Morocco. He was put down with French assistance (1926).

His rebellion, like that of Abd al-Kader in Algeria, represented the opposition of a society unchanged by the colonial process; nevertheless he stands at the beginning of Moroccan nationalism which arose from that process. He was detained on Ascension for 20 years, but found asylum in Egypt (1947).

ABD AL-MALIK IBN MARWAN (647–705), 5th—and perhaps the greatest—caliph (685–705) of the Umayyad line. He came to the throne at a moment of grave danger for his house. Rebellion was aflame in the empire, most of which had given allegiance, at least in name, to Abdallah ibn al-Zubayr. A struggle was in progress against the Khawarij in Arabia and above all in Persia. The Shi'i elements supporting the claims of the descendants of Ali to the caliphate opposed the Umayyads in Iraq. The Arab armies which dominated the empire had been much weakened through a recrudescence of tribal feuds. In 689 Abd al-Malik had to deal with a serious revolt in Syria, the centre of Umayyad power. Also in 689 the caliph made a truce with Byzantium, agreeing to pay tribute to Constantinople. With freedom of action restored to him, Abd al-Malik crushed the pro-Shi'i forces at the battle of Maskin in 691. Mecca fell to his troops, under the command of Al-Hajjaj, in 692, his rival Abdallah ibn al-Zubayr being killed in the fighting. The years after 692 saw the defeat of the Khawarij in Arabia (692–3) and of the Khawarij in Persia (695–7). Further trouble arose in 700, when Abd al-Rahman ibn Muhammad ibn al-Ash'ath began a rebellion in north-eastern Persia (Khurasan) and then invaded Iraq— only to be routed at Dayr al-Jamajim and at Maskin in 701. The year 702 witnessed the foundation of Wasit (between Kufa and Basra), ie, of a new garrison centre reserved for the Syrian forces of the Umayyads and intended to maintain firm control over the troublesome province of Iraq. Abd al-Malik also did much to centralize the admininstration of the empire, making Arabic the official language of the state and introducing a new Islamic gold coinage (the dinar).   VJP

ABD AL-MU'MIN (d. 1163), 1st Almohad caliph and founder of the empire. From Ibn Tumart's death (1129) he pursued the struggle against the Almoravids by strategic occupation of high ground which culminated in a campaign from Tlemcen to Marrakesh, extinguishing their dynasty (1146). Acknowledged in Andalus, he turned to take the central Maghrib (1151) and Ifriqiyya (1160), evicting the Sicilian Normans from Mahdiyya. Thereafter till his death he prepared the subjugation of Andalus. A stranger to the High Atlas Berbers forming the Almohad community, he rose above the sect to make his power hereditary in a typical Andalusian sultanate.

ABD AL-RAHMAN III (912–61), greatest Umayyad emir, who made Andalus a major power in the Mediterranean. Assuming the caliphate (929) against Fatimid pretensions, he dominated Morocco while reckoning with new Christian states in Spain.

ABD AL-RAHMAN AL-DAKHIL (d. 788), entered Spain, escaping Abbasid persecution, to become the first Andalusian Umayyad emir (756). He dominated the Arab and Berber factions, and consolidated the north against the Christians aided by Charlemagne (778).

ABD AL-RAHMAN IBN MUHAMMAD IBN AL-ASH'ATH (d. 704) served, in 695–6, against the Khawarij of Mesopotamia. The Umayyad governor of Iraq, Al-Hajjaj, sent him thereafter to Sijistan in Persia and, setting at his disposal a splendid force (known in the chronicles as the Army of the Peacocks), ordered him to conquer the region of Afghanistan. Ibn al-Ash'ath rose in rebellion against Al-Hajjaj in 700 and marched into Iraq, but was routed there in 701 at the battles of Dayr al-Jamajim and Maskin. He continued the revolt for some time in Persia. There was, however, little prospect of success and Ibn al-Ash'ath, with his cause now far in decline, killed himself.

ABD AL-RAHMAN KHAN (c. 1844–1901), Emir of Afghanistan (reg. 1880–1901), son of Afzal Khan, and grandson of Dost Muhammad Khan. After exile in Turkestan following the defeat of his party in the Afghan civil war (1863–8), he returned to become emir with British support towards the end of the second Anglo-Afghan war. An able though autocratic ruler, he greatly increased the central authority by suppressing tribal opposition. The present frontiers of Afghanistan were established during his reign. Although he received a British subsidy, he retained considerable independence and his activities on India's north-west frontier, by provoking tribal unrest, were a source of much embarrassment to the British–Indian government.

ABD AL-WADD, dynasty arising from Berber nomads employed as auxiliaries by the Almohads in the central Maghrib, became independent at Tlemcen (1235). This city, at the crossing of the main route from Fez to Tunis with a second from Sijilmasa to Andalus, was of great strategic and commercial importance. The Banu Abd al-Wadd confirmed it as a political centre, and maintained themselves between the Marinids of Morocco and the Hafsids of Ifriqiyya until the political pattern of the medieval Maghrib collapsed in the 16th cent. with the arrival of Spaniards and Turks.

The history of the Abd al-Wadd divides in the mid-14th cent., when Tlemcen twice fell to the Marinids. Previously they had progressed from a patriarchal regime under their founder, Yaghmurasan, towards a typical sultanate relying on varying combinations of nomad allies. Fez was the main enemy, kept at bay by alliances with Granada and Castile, and stubborn resistance to a blockade of Tlemcen (1299–1307). Abu Tashfin (1318–37) profited from Marinid quiescence to attempt to win Bougie and Constantine from the Hafsids. The Hafsid sultan appealed to Fez, and Tlemcen fell to the Marinid Abu'l-Hasan (1337).

After the final Moroccan retreat (1359), the new sultan, Abu Hammu II (1359–89), placed more formal reliance on nomad tribes, while the vizier tended to become a major-domo of the palace. Later Moroccan attempts to establish puppet rulers yielded before the imposition of Hafsid suzerainty in the 15th cent. In the 16th cent. stability was lost when Tlemcen became an object of competition, changing hands between Spaniards, Turks, and Moroccans until it fell to the Turks in 1550 and the dynasty closed.

ABD AL-WAHHAB, MUHAMMAD IBN (1703–92), founder of the religious movement known as the Wahhabiyya, who studied in the Hijaz, in Iraq, and in Persia. He returned to his birthplace, Uyaina, in Arabia, and there began to preach the doctrines associated with his name, ie, insistence on the worship of Allah, opposition to the cult of saints, and disapproval of bida' (innovation) in the Muslim faith. Expelled from Uyaina, he found refuge and aid at Dar'iya with the local chieftain, Muhammad ibn Sa'ud. From 1747 the Wahhabiyya began to gain ground by force under the able leadership of Ibn Saʻud and of his son, Abd al-Aziz. With the fall of Riyadh in 1773 most of the Nijd came under Wahhabi control. Abd al-Wahhab died with the empire of the Wahhabis still in the course of expansion.

ABDALLAH IBN AL-ZUBAYR (624–92) took part in the campaigns of Arab conquest in North Africa and in Persia. He was a member of the commission which the Caliph Uthman created to prepare the official recension of the Koran and fought at the Battle of the Camel against the Caliph Ali in 656. Not long after the death of the Umayyad Yazid I (683) he proclaimed himself caliph, winning recognition (more nominal than real) throughout almost all of the Arab empire, except Syria. The troops of the Umayyad Caliph Abd al-Malik besieged Mecca in 692 and Ibn al-Zubayr was killed in the fighting which led to the fall of the town after a siege of six months.

ABDUL FATAH, SULTAN AGENG, also known as Sultan Tirtajasa, ruler of Bantam, West Java (*reg.* 1651–82). His title was said to have come from Mecca, and he was known as an enemy of the infidel Dutch, then established at their post in Batavia, with whom he fought a series of wars. His rule has been described as a golden age for Bantam. It ended in dissensions within the royal house and the intervention of the Dutch East India Co., which thus gained a monopoly of trade with Bantam to the exclusion of other foreigners. In 1682 Sultan Ageng attempted an unsuccessful flight from the Dutch forces, supporting his son and rival, Sultan Hadji (*reg.* 1682–7), but was forced to submit to the latter in 1683. He died in Batavia in 1695.

ABDUL GHAFFAR KHAN, KHAN (1891–), political leader of North-West Frontier Province, India, known as the 'Frontier Gandhi'. Active in social welfare work from 1912, Abdul Ghaffar formed the *Khudai Khidmatgar* or 'Servants of God', popularly called 'Red Shirts', in 1929 to act as both a welfare organization and a force of political 'volunteers'. He later linked the *Khudai Khidmatgar* with the Indian National Congress and adopted Gandhi's technique of *satyagraha* (lit. 'truth force'; in effect, non-violent non-co-operation). As a result of this alliance, NWFP was the only Muslim majority province controlled by Congress after 1937. Both Congress ministries (1937–9, 1946–7) were led by Abdul Ghaffar's elder brother, Dr Khan Sahib.

The closeness of the link with Congress, and their boycott of the referendum (July 1947) on the accession of NWFP to Pakistan, caused difficulties for the Khan brothers and the *Khudai Khidmatgar* in Pakistan. Abdul Ghaffar's demand for an independent Pathan state, Pakhtunistan, was seen as disloyalty and he was imprisoned twice (1948, 1956) and at other times held in detention. Released in 1964 on account of ill-health, he went into exile in Afghanistan.

ABDUL RAHMAN PUTRA, TUNKU (1903–), first prime minister of independent Malaya, and later of Malaysia. A prince of Kedah educated at Cambridge, he remained a civil servant until being thrust into the leadership of the United Malays' National Organization (UMNO) in 1951. He rebuilt the party in opposition to the more multi-racial approach of its original leader, Dato Onn. After securing his position as chief spokesman for the Malay community, however, he made his own accommodation with Chinese leaders in the form of the tripartite Alliance Party. He led the alliance in pressing for an elected majority in the 1955 Legislative Council. After a victory in this election he became chief minister, and negotiated with Britain for the independence of Malaya on 31 Aug. 1957. As prime minister (1955–70) and foreign minister of the new country, he was primarily responsible for its cautious, pragmatic conservatism in close co-operation with Britain. Abdul Rahman's easy-going, genial image became an important focus for national unity, his most important single achievement being the merger of Malaya, Singapore, Sarawak, and North Borneo into the new Malaysia (16 Sept. 1963). Although his leadership of these diverse territories was at first consolidated by the common threat from Indonesia, he eventually felt it necessary to sever the link with Singapore in 1965, for fear of growing politico-racial tension. He resigned on 21 Sept. 1970.

ABDUL RAZAK BIN HUSSEIN, TUN (1922–), Malaysian politician and prime minister of Malaysia after Sept. 1970. He had supported Tunku Abdul Rahman since his London student days (1947–50) and became, in turn, deputy president of UMNO (1951–70) and deputy prime minister (1957–70), holding concurrently the portfolios of defence and rural development. He held effective power as chairman of the emergency national operations council following the May 1969 riots, but remained loyal to the Tunku until the latter's voluntary retirement.

ABDÜLAZIZ (1830–76), 32nd Ottoman Sultan (*reg.* 1861–76), son of Mahmud II, who succeeded his brother, Abdülmecid (1861). During his reign the Tanzimat reform programme continued, especially in administration, law, and education, although the tendency of government was towards greater autocracy. In the latter part of his reign the despotic and capricious ruler was held partly responsible for the worsening condition of the empire, demonstrated by financial bankruptcy, internal revolts (notably in Bulgaria), and foreign pressures. He was deposed on 30 May 1876.

ABDÜLHAMID II (1842–1918), 36th Ottoman Sultan (*reg.* 1876–1909), son of Abdülmecid, who succeeded his brother Murad V (1 Sept. 1876). Abdülhamid quickly removed the constitutionalists who had brought him to the throne, dismissed the Constituent Assembly, and established a system of despotic government which, assisted by an extensive spy system, endured until he was forced to restore the constitution in 1908. His bloody repression of opposition, especially among Christians, earned him the European soubriquet of 'The Red Sultan'. More positively his reign was significant for developments in communications and education and for his encouragement of Pan-Islamism, both to help to bind the Ottoman empire together and to attract the support of Muslims elsewhere. He was deposed in 1909.

ABDULLAH, SHEIKH MUHAMMAD (1905–), Kashmiri nationalist, prime minister of Kashmir, and founder of the Kashmir Muslim Conference (1927), which he later renamed the National Conference. Abdullah was the leader of the campaign for constitutional government and civil liberties in the state. Sentenced to nine years' imprisonment in the 'Quit Kashmir' campaign (1946), he was released (July 1947) to head the Emergency Administration and organize his followers as a Peace Brigade during the crisis over accesssion to India. He was prime minister until 1953, when, impatient at the deadlock between India and Pakistan over Kashmir, he advocated Kashmiri independence. Dismissed and imprisoned or detained almost continually since 1953, he was released in 1964, had talks with Nehru, and was allowed to visit Pakistan, but was then detained (1965) on new charges of anti-Indian activities. Finally released in Dec. 1967 on account of ill-health, he has maintained his demand for Kashmiri self-determination.

ABDULLAH BIN ABDULKADIR ('MUNSHI') (1797–1854), first Malayan author to write in modern style for the printing press. Of mixed parentage, Abdullah was a proficient linguist and worked as a language teacher and translator for English missionaries and officials in the Straits Settlements. His major works, *Kesah Pelayaran Abdullah* (1837) and *Hikayat Abdullah* (1840–3), are autobiographical.

ABDULLAH IBN AL-HUSAYN (1882–1951), Emir of Transjordan and first King of Jordan. As the second son of Husayn of Mecca he played an important role in the Arab revolt (1916). In 1921, while marching to the support of his brother,

Faysal, in Syria, he established himself in British-mandated territory in Transjordan, where he was given recognition, a subsidy, and assistance in building up the Arab Legion. In 1948 he intervened in Palestine and gained extensive territories on the west bank of the Jordan, including Jerusalem. His wider aims contemplated the establishment of a Greater Syria to include Syria, Lebanon, Transjordan, and Palestine (including Israel). His policies made him the object of the particular hatred of Arab revolutionaries, by whom he was assassinated.

ABDULLAH IBN MUHAMMAD FUDI (1776–1829), commonly known as Abdullahi dan Fodio, scholar, poet, military leader, and administrator. From the outset of his brother Uthman's *jihad* movement in Hausaland (now northern Nigeria) 1804, Abdullah was a close collaborator and soon assumed the position of chief vizier. He was given charge of the western provinces of the emerging Muslim state (1812) and set up his headquarters at Bodinga. On the death of Uthman (1817) he hoped to succeed him, but leadership of the community passed to Uthman's son, Muhammad Bello. Abdullah moved his headquarters to Gwandu and from there further expanded the western domains, but always in allegiance to his nephew.

He was a prolific author in Arabic and also wrote poetry in Fulani. His account of the *jihad*, *Tazyin al-Waragat*, with specimens of his Arabic verse, has been translated into English by M. Hiskett (1963).

ABDULLAH IBN YASIN (d. 1057), Gazula Berber from the Moroccan Sus, was the religious teacher who inspired the militant Almoravid movement in the western Sahara during the 11th cent. When Yahya ibn Ibrahim of the Gudala sought a religious teacher to accompany him to the Sahara, Abdullah went with him. After the Gudala rejected his strict teachings he found solace in the active support of the ruling families of the Lamtuna, among whom he preached his doctrines.

The Lamtuna thereupon converted or reduced their Sanhaja brethren, the Massufa, and their foes, the Gudala. Abdullah established his headquarters at a town he founded called Aretnanna. Having captured and sacked ancient Ghana (1054) and Sijilmasa (1055), he continued the conquest of Morocco, but died fighting there.

ABDÜLMECID (1823–61), 31st Ottoman Sultan, son of Mahmud II, whom he succeeded (1 July 1839). During his reign, the programme of reform known as the Tanzimat was launched. Abdülmecid sought to stem the decline of the Ottoman empire by seeking European help against Muhammad Ali of Egypt and the assistance of Britain and France against Russia during the Crimean War. Abdülmecid was noted for his broad outlook, being the first Ottoman sultan to speak a European language (French), and for his intelligence, although he lacked the ruthless determination which characterized his father and his son, Abdülhamid.

ABE, MASAHIRO (1819–57), Japanese political leader in the Tokugawa period. After a rapid rise to dominance of the *bakufu* ruling council, he was faced (1853) with America's demand for the opening of Japan. With great skill he succeeded not only in satisfying Commodore Perry without making any far-reaching concessions, but also in stemming criticism of *bakufu* weakness within Japan by broadening the base of Tokugawa power to include elements which had traditionally been excluded. His policy of moderate reform, however, was considered injurious to Tokugawa authority by other *fudai daimyo*s and in 1856 Abe was obliged to retire.

A'BECKETT, SIR WILLIAM (1806–69), London lawyer, and the first of a long line of a'Becketts who figured prominently at the bar and on the Victorian bench. After migrating to NSW (1837), he became solicitor-general there, then a judge of the Supreme Court and later (1846) resident judge in the Port Phillip district. In 1853 he was appointed first Chief Justice of Vic. Ill-health caused his retirement and return to England in 1863. He was the author of several legal biographies and other works.

ABELARD, PETER (1079–1142), most famous teacher and logician of the Middle Ages, who was largely responsible for the intellectual supremacy of the schools at Paris in the 12th cent. His treatise *Sic et Non* (*Yes and No*), deliberately juxtaposing conflicting texts from the Bible and other Christian authorities, and then offering a method of reconciling them, was a masterpiece of medieval dialectic. After studying at Paris under William of Champeaux, Abelard started teaching there, first at Mont St Genevieve and then (*c.* 1113) at Nôtre Dame. At this time he began an association with Heloïse, the niece of Fulbert, a canon of Nôtre Dame. Although they married when Heloïse became pregnant, the outraged Fulbert had Abelard castrated. After a period of retirement, Abelard returned to teach at Paris until the condemnation of his theological opinions by the council of Soissons in 1121. He then retired to Nogent-sur-Seine, but his pupils discovered his whereabouts and a school grew up around him. He used the lands given him there to found an abbey, the Paraclete, with Heloïse as its first abbess. Abelard returned to Paris in 1136, but his teaching aroused the hostility of St Bernard of Clairvaux, who obtained its condemnation in 1141. Abelard began a journey to Rome to appeal to the pope, but was persuaded by Peter the Venerable to remain at Cluny until his death.

ABEOKUTA, chief town of the Egba branch of the Yoruba on the Ogun river 65 miles (104 kms) north of Lagos; it was founded about 1830 by Egba migrants dislodged from their forest home by Oyo and Ife raiders. In this rocky fortress (Abeokuta means under the rocks) about 153 townships, each with many chiefs, welded themselves into an urban agglomeration under the titular headship of the Alake. In 1839 liberated Egba in Sierra Leone colony began to arrive in Abeokuta and were followed by Christian missions. By 1860 thousands of *Saro* (Sierra Leone immigrants) were in Abeokuta, which became a citadel of Christianity and British influence. The British occupation of Lagos in 1861 strained Anglo-Egba relations and European missionaries and traders were expelled from Abeokuta in 1867. But it remained the chief centre of missionary endeavour in Yorubaland till the turn of the century.

ABERCROMBY, JAMES (1706–81), Scotsman who entered the British army as an infantry officer and rose to take command of British forces in North America (1758). In the autumn of that year he launched a frontal attack on Fort Ticonderoga, which was garrisoned by 3000 troops under the French general Montcalm. The British force was defeated and Abercromby was recalled to England. He was appointed deputy governor of Stirling Castle (1772).

ABERCROMBY, SIR RALPH (1734–1801), British general and MP. He fought in the Seven Years War and the French Revolutionary War. After successfully capturing several West Indian islands, including Trinidad (1797), he served in the Mediterranean, and died of wounds received at Aboukir Bay.

ABERDARE, HENRY AUSTIN BRUCE, 1st Baron (1815–95) and British Liberal MP (1852–73), who, as home secretary (1868–73), passed important measures regulating mines and trade unions, but had to withdraw his ambitiously restrictive Licensing Bill (1871). Even his modest Licensing Act (1872) damaged the Liberal Party at the 1874 election. His political career ended in that year, but he was prominent thereafter in philanthropy and in the founding of the University of Wales.

ABERDEEN, GEORGE GORDON, 4th Earl of (1784–1860) Conservative statesman and diplomatist. He was prime minister of the coalition government under which Britain entered the Crimean War (1854). His main interests were diplomatic. He was a signatory of the treaty of Paris (1814) and foreign secretary in Wellington's ministry (1828–30), a period which saw the treaty of Adrianople and the recognition by Britain of Louis Philippe. He was secretary for war and colonies in Peel's first ministry (1834–5) and foreign secretary in his second ministry (1841–6), when he worked for the restoration of the Anglo-French entente. After Peel's death he led the Peelites, and after a period of ministerial instability became prime minister of a Whig–Peelite coalition (1852–5). Critics have suggested that his indecisive handling of the Eastern Question led Britain into the Crimean War.

ABERDEEN, JOHN CAMPBELL HAMILTON GORDON, 7th Earl and 1st Marquis of (1847–1934), lord lieutenant of Ireland (1886 and 1905–15) and Governor General of Canada (1893–8). While in Canada he earned the Conservatives' enmity by refusing to approve certain appointments submitted by the Conservative leader who had shortly before been defeated in Parliament.

ABERDEEN, UNIVERSITY OF, which originated in 1494 with the founding of the King's College by William Elphinstone, Bp of Aberdeen. Marischal College was added in 1593. The buildings of both colleges are architecturally fine.

ABERHART, WILLIAM (1878–1943), Canadian politician and prime minister of Alta (1935–43). He was born in Huron Co., Ont., and educated at Queen's University, and was principal of Crescent Heights School, Calgary (1915–35). He formed the Social Credit Party, aimed at redistributing purchasing power and providing every citizen with £5 a month. In 1935 the party won the election in Alta, but federal government action in 1937 prevented implementation of the party's programme.

ABERNETHY, JOHN (1764–1831), assistant surgeon at St Bartholomew's hospital (1787–1827) and full surgeon (1827–1831). His reputation rests on his teaching skill and on his defence of the work of John Hunter, rather than on original work.

ABERNON, EDGAR VINCENT D', Viscount (1857–1941), British financier and diplomat. In 1882 he was appointed British representative on the Council of the Ottoman public debt, and seven years later governor of the Imperial Ottoman Bank (1889–97). In 1899 he was elected Conservative MP for Exeter. Defeated in 1906, he stood as a Liberal for Colchester in 1910. From 1920 to 1926 he served as Britain's first ambassador to the Weimar Republic. The high point of his career came with the signing of the Locarno treaty (1925), since D'Abernon had worked hard to restore Germany to the concert of Europe.

ABETZ, OTTO (1903–   ), German propagandist, who became ambassador to the Vichy government of France. Born at Karlsruhe, he became a drawing teacher, and took part in activities dedicated to Franco-German reconciliation. In 1937 he joined the Nazi movement and established a reputation for himself as an expert on France, from where he was expelled in 1939. Appointed ambassador to France in 1940, he tried unsuccessfully to pursue a semi-independent policy of co-operation with the Pétain government. In 1944 he advocated Hitler's resignation, but was not involved in the 20 July plot. He was sentenced to 20 years' hard labour by a French military court (July 1949).

ABHAYAGIRI, name of one of the three great ancient dagobas (tower-like monuments in which relics of Lord Buddha were enshrined; also called *stopa*s) in Anuradhapura, Ceylon, founded in the 1st cent. BC. Its diameter at the base is 99 metres (325 ft) and its height 107 metres (350 ft), making it one of the most impressive monuments of the island. The adjacent monastery, whose monks played an important part

in early missionary activity, soon became a centre of dissident Buddhist views opposed by the Mahāvihāra until the Buddhist community was reunited in the 12th cent.

ABIDJAN, capital of the Ivory Coast, has been the nucleus of one of the strongest economies in West Africa. Its population grew from 10,000 in 1931 to about 180,000 in 1960, and is of mixed ethnic origins.

ABJURATION ACTS (1581 and 1702). The first of these acts was a formal and revolutionary declaration (July 1581) of the deposition of Philip II of Spain as sovereign of the Netherlands by the Calvinist alliance of the Union of Utrecht. Holland and Zeeland accepted William of Orange as their count, while the Duke of Alençon became sovereign of the other states. The act put into practice the concepts expounded in the *Vindiciae contra Tyrannos*, which asserted that a prince who ruled as a tyrant could be deposed by his subjects, who were free to choose another ruler.

The second act was passed by parliament in retaliation for Louis XIV's recognition of the Old Pretender as James III of England. Though it was passed by a Whig-dominated parliament, the Tories were equally anxious to dissociate themselves from the Jacobites by supporting the act. The Abjuration Act imposed the test of a new and stricter oath for all MPs, clergymen, and office-holders. The compromise of the Revolution Settlement whereby Tories could recognize William III as king 'in fact' now ended, as the oath stressed that William III and afterwards Anne, were 'lawful and rightful' monarchs, and that the Pretender and his heirs had no right to the throne. Thus the Tories were forced to accept the Revolution Settlement as final and turn their backs on the principle of divine-right monarchy.

ABLEMAN v. BOOTH, 21 Howard 506 (1859). US Supreme Court case resulting from a violation by WI of the Fugitive Slave Act (1850). Booth, having assisted in the escape of a fugitive slave, was convicted in the federal district court (1854). The WI supreme court issued a writ of *habeas corpus*, freed Booth, declared his conviction illegal and the 1850 act void. Ableman, a US District Marshal, obtained a writ of error in the Supreme Court to review the WI court decision.

Chief Justice Taney's opinion contained a strong defence of national supremacy. He denied the state judiciary the right to interfere in federal cases, upheld the supremacy of the national constitution and the role of the federal judiciary as the final arbiter of constitutional opinions, and briefly affirmed the constitutionality of the 1850 act. The WI supreme court refused to receive notice of the writ and ignored the subsequent review decision.

ABNAKI INDIANS, American Indian confederacy of Algonquian tribes, centred in the present state of ME. The name Abnaki was used by the Algonquian tribes to designate their numbers living in the northern region of the Atlantic seaboard. The Abnaki, early friends of the French, fought the English until the decline of French power, when some tribes withdrew to Canada and others made peace with the English. All subsequently dwindled to insignificance.

ABO, TREATY OF (1743), ended the war begun by Sweden against Russia in 1741. The Russians restored most of the Finnish territory conquered during the war, in return for acceptance by the Swedish Estates of Adolphus Frederick as heir to the throne. Although Finland lost one-tenth of its population, the treaty confirmed the Hat Party in power.

ABOLITION ACTS (1807–38), laws passed by the British parliament and overseas possessions dealing with slavery. The Abolition Act of 1807 made it illegal for British subjects to engage in the slave trade and allowed the British navy to seize slave ships of other nationals. In 1811 slave trading was made a felony—the 1807 Act provided merely for fines and seizure—and in 1824 became a capital offence. William

Wilberforce, MP, played a leading role in abolishing the slave trade and after the 1807 act agitated for the abolition of slavery. He was a founder of the Anti-Slavery Society (1823) and was supported by such humanitarians as Thomas Fowell Buxton, Zachary Macaulay, Thomas Clarkson, and Lord Brougham. Unsuccessful resolutions for the abolition of slavery were introduced into parliament (1823, 1830), but under Grey's ministry (1830–4) the Slavery Abolition Act was passed (1833). The law provided for a four- to six-year apprenticeship period, after which slaves were completely emancipated and slave owners compensated. Conditions of apprentices were improved by an amendment to the act (1838). Colonies were free to act before the apprenticeship period lapsed and the governments of the Leeward Islands and Bermuda abolished slavery in 1834. In 1838 the remaining slave colonies ratified the Slavery Abolition Act of 1833.

W. L. Mathieson, *British Slavery and Its Abolition 1823–1838* (London, 1926).   RCR

ABOLITIONISM, term used in the US to describe the radical doctrines of William Lloyd Garrison, Theodore Dwight Weld, and other anti-slavery militants (1830–65). It is sometimes loosely applied to anti-slavery activity in general, but many who opposed slavery also opposed the abolitionists.

During the colonial period the Quakers were the most notable group to oppose slavery. Individual Quakers, as is shown by Benjamin Lay's *All Slave-Keepers Apostates* (1737), adopted attitudes similar to those of the later abolitionists. But Enlightenment thought, although critical of slavery, discouraged this sort of extremism. When the first anti-slavery societies were formed in the latter part of the century (the earliest was established in Philadelphia in 1775) less radical ideas prevailed. These were years which saw many social changes in America. By 1810 slavery had virtually disappeared from the North, and in the South too large numbers of Negroes were freed. Another major achievement was the outlawing of the African slave trade by Congress in 1807.

The abolition movement of the 1830s differed in many respects from this post-Independence movement. Hitherto much of the anti-slavery activity had been in the South; the abolition movement was exclusively Northern. Where the earlier movement had been concerned with means, the abolitionists stressed ends. Above all they emphasized the sinful nature of the institution of slavery and of those who supported it. Evils, in their view, could be mitigated gradually, but sins needed to be eradicated immediately, totally and without regard to consequences.

This intransigent doctrine resulted from a combination of factors: the failure of the anti-slavery movement after 1810 to achieve anything of consequence; the growing conviction that nothing could be achieved through ordinary political channels; the success of the British in abolishing slavery in the West Indies, and the teachings of the evangelist Charles Grandison Finney, who preached 'disinterested benevolence' as the ultimate manifestation of religious experience. Abolitionists were much influenced by evangelical Christianity, a fact which has led some later observers to claim that they were concerned less with slavery than with their own psyches.

Despite the hostile reactions they inspired, in the North as well as the South, abolitionists did much to alter attitudes towards slavery. Such works as Weld's *American Slavery as It Is* (1839) and Harriet Beecher Stowe's *Uncle Tom's Cabin* (1852), had an enormous impact. During the 1830s the movement was largely controlled by the American Anti-Slavery Society (1833), but in 1840 this body was captured by a radical minority led by Garrison. Thereafter there was much disagreement between rival factions. Control passed to individual state organizations, which expressed their views through the Liberty and Free Soil parties and also in local grass-roots politics. Abolitionists were continually being charged with trying to destroy the Union, and when the Civil War broke out there were many who held them responsible. Although it was not due to their efforts alone,

the ultimate triumph of the abolitionists came with the abolition of slavery in the US by the 13th Amendment to the Constitution (1865).

Dwight L. Dumond, *Antislavery: the Crusade for Freedom in America* (Ann Arbor, 1961).
John L. Thomas (ed.), *Slavery Attacked: the abolitionist crusade* (Englewood Cliffs, NJ, 1965).   HRT

ABOLITIONIST MOVEMENT IN WEST AFRICA. Inspired from Britain, this began in 1787 with the founding of Sierra Leone settlement and continued into the second half of the 19th cent. The movement involved several agencies and thousands of individuals; of the former, the West African Squadron of the British navy, Thomas Fowell Buxton's Society for the Extinction of the Slave Trade, and Christian missions should be noted, as should the efforts of British secular agents, explorers, and traders.

The much-criticized West African Squadron which patrolled West African waters from 1810 to 1867 consisted of scarcely more than 25 small ships manned by about 3000 men. Although the area patrolled was too large for this force to have a substantial effect, and the number of slaves taken from West Africa to the New World increased from 85,000 annually in the 18th cent. to 135,000 in the first half of the 19th cent., the success of the squadron should be judged from the number of slavers captured and the thousands of liberated Africans deposited in Sierra Leone Colony.

The influence of the Society for the Extinction of the Slave Trade (formed 1839) was short but dramatic. It was through its efforts that the disastrous expedition of 1841 to the Niger was organized by the British government. But its 'Bible and the Plough' programme was endorsed and sponsored by Christian missions. As Buxton had argued, missionaries were potentially the most effective abolitionists: it was through their work that the old society built upon slavery and the slave trade would be destroyed and another based upon Christianity, Commerce, and Civilization, erected in its place.

Also important was the role of explorers in exposing the nature and extent of the trans-Saharan slave traffic in the savannah belt of West Africa and the pleadings these explorers made to African rulers to abandon the traffic in favour of legitimate trade. Among these explorers were Denham, Clapperton, Oudney, and James Richardson.

British secular agents, too, achieved a great deal in the abolition movement, largely because they were able to employ physical force to compel African chiefs within the reach of the gunboat to put an end to the trans-Atlantic trade. Through persuasion, some African chiefs in the Niger Delta signed abolition treaties, but others (Kosoko of Lagos and the kings of Dahomey) refused to accept treaties; Kosoko, whose kingdom was within the reach of the gunboat, was removed from the throne, but Gezo and Gelele in far-away Abomey could only be vilified. Through establishment of informal empire, the trans-Atlantic slave trade was ended in some parts of West Africa.

By and large, the abolitionist movement was confined to the Atlantic seaboard. The internal traffic went on until the end of the 19th cent., and the vast majority of African chiefs were not taken into full partnership. The refusal of several of them to accept abolition treaties cannot be explained in terms of their aversion to the anti-slave trade clauses alone; their awareness of the political implications of such treaties should also be taken into account. Finally, military expeditions and the consolidation of colonial rule helped to put an end to the slave traffic and the institution of slavery.

The abolition movement yielded benefits to both Britain and West Africa. Although the movement cost Britain a great deal in terms of men and money (the squadron alone cost between £150,000 and £1 million yearly), Britain reaped considerable rewards. The movement was a cornerstone of its empire in West Africa, and West Africa itself also gained. Her sylvan resources were developed, and there grew up, along the Atlantic littoral, educated elite communities whose social and political aspirations were to be adopted in the colonial and post-independence eras. EAA

ABORIGINAL, THE AUSTRALIAN. The Australoid is no palaeolithic survival, but essentially 'modern man'. Current evidence suggests early south-east Asian associations, with possible entry points being Cape York and Arnhem Land. Specific conditions led to development of regional types and cultures, during some 30,000 years' occupancy. As semi-nomadic hunters and food-collectors, their technology was simple but ensured the maximum use of their environmental resources. Their complex and varied way of life emphasized links between religion and land, with elaborate symbolic systems, and an oral literature which equalled the world's finest.

Numbering some 300,000 when the British first settled in Australia, the Aborigines were to feel increasingly the effects of this European incursion into their areas. Divided into some 500 major socio-linguistic groupings, with no continent-wide communications or some form of common identity, they lacked political and military organization, as well as technical equipment with which to defend their territories. By the early 20th cent. their traditional life survived only in areas that were inhospitable, inaccessible, or not immediately needed for development, while many Aborigines had become stranded in the 'poverty zones' of cities and country towns.

During the first 150 years of European settlement, government programmes fluctuated between protection and destruction, not only of Aboriginal cultures, but even of Aboriginal lives. Neglect, disease, and deliberate killings caused depopulation, while the new population that grew out of miscegenation became not a bridge but a barrier. In some areas mission and government centres mitigated the worst features and, though earlier attempts at absorption were largely unsuccessful, an undetermined percentage of the physically less conspicuous gradually merged into the wider Australian community. Government policies before the mid-1930s were based on the conviction that the disappearance of the Aborigines was inevitable; these policies therefore favoured protection-through-segregation in outlying areas and assimilation (absorption) in the closely settled south. Thus, in the late 1930s large reserves were established.

By the 1940s both full-blooded and part-Aboriginal populations were increasing, their growth rates accelerating in the post-war decades. Public and anthropological interest increased also and by 1967 discriminatory legal restrictions had been lifted and the Aborigines' status as citizens reaffirmed. A nation-wide referendum authorized the Commonwealth to legislate on their behalf—without removing that power from the states. Official policies thereafter became fairly uniform, with assimilation, as redefined, allowing at least nominal choice in retaining or rejecting surviving aspects of traditional life.

The response of the Aborigines—estimated 1970 total about 80,000 more than half Aboriginal—varied, many wanting to be identified as Aborigines while retaining access to the wider society. This intermediate ambition had political and social implications. Though the Aborigines' future remained uncertain, the inevitability of their extinction had been abandoned; the Aboriginal past had won some recognition, although reluctantly accorded, as a vital part of the general Australian heritage.

R. M. and C. H. Berndt, *The World of the First Australians* (Sydney and London, 1964–8).
D. J. Mulvaney, *The Prehistory of Australia* (London, 1969).
  RMB

ABRAHAMS, JOSEPH (1855–1938), Rabbi of Melbourne Hebrew Congregation (1883–1922), chairman of its ecclesiastical court (Beth Din), and principal of Melbourne Hebrew School until its dissolution. An impressive personality and a scholar, he was sought after as a speaker inside and outside the Jewish community. Though broad-minded, he stood firmly by the principles of Traditional Judaism and opposed Reform.

ABS, HERMANN (1901–   ), influential German banker who contributed to the recovery of Western Germany after the Second World War. He joined the board of the Deutsche Bank in 1937, became its chairman in 1939, was detained for three months by the British in 1945, then returned to the bank. In 1968 he was appointed chairman of Krupps after it was forced to become a public company.

ABSALON (1128–1201), bishop of Roskilde from 1158 and archbishop of Lund from 1177, he was prominent in Danish state affairs. He effectively founded Copenhagen by fortifying its harbour and waged war successfully against Baltic pagans.

ABSOLUTISM. Theory of kingship, usually associated with Louis XIV, which stressed both the vast powers of the ruler and his subordination to certain controls in the exercise of power. It is not to be confused with either tyranny or enlightened despotism. In an absolutist state, power was vested in a hereditary monarch, but was limited by vaguely defined concepts of natural law, tradition, the social order, and especially of responsibility to God. The monarch was seen as the representative of God on earth, and was therefore endowed with divine authority and responsibility. It was well summarized by the Marquis d'Argenson when he said that 'France is an absolute monarchy where despotism is tempered by reason and justice, which suggest to the monarch the need to seek aid and counsel from those he is pleased to choose amongst the three orders of his state'. Louis himself recognized the constraints of fundamental law and of his responsibilities towards God and his subjects. He described the condition of kingship as being hard and rigorous because kings owed what he called 'a public account to all the universe and to all the centuries'. This conception marks a move away from the more personal monarchy of the early modern period and towards that of constitutional monarchy, and was made possible by the destruction of the old intermediary bodies in the course of the 17th cent.

ABU ABDALLAH AL-SHI'I (d. 911), made propaganda, from 893, on behalf of the Isma'ili movement among the Kutama Berbers in North Africa and, overthrowing with their aid the dynasty of the Aghlabids, established there a caliphate under the Fatimid Iman Ubayd Allah al-Mahdi. Al-Mahdi, fearing the influence of Abu Abdallah, had him executed.

ABU BAKAR BIN IBRAHIM, modernizing ruler of Johor state, Malaya (1862–95). As Temenggong of Johor by inheritance, he effectively controlled the state. He was educated in Singapore English schools, visited England six times, and ruled his state efficiently with the help of British advisers. In return, Britain supported his assumption of the title Maharaja in 1866 and Sultan of Johor in 1885, despite the claims of the original dynasty. Although he assisted the British to install Residents in the neighbouring Malay states, he retained personal control over his own state.

ABU BAKR (d. 634), the 1st Caliph (*reg.* 632–4), was born soon after 570. He was converted to Islam some time before the Hijra of 622 and became the trusted confidant of the Prophet. His daughter A'isha was the wife of Muhammad. Abu Bakr, during most of his short reign, was preoccupied with 'Al-Ridda', the War of Apostasy, ie, with the effort to bring once more under Muslim control the Arab tribes who, on the death of the Prophet in 632, threw off their allegiance to Mecca and Medina. The battles of Al-Buzakha and of Aqraba in 632–3 restored the influence of the Muslim state in central Arabia. Moreover, subordinate operations were soon to reduce the peripheral regions of Bahrayn, Oman, the

Mahra, the Hadhramaut, and the Yemen to dependence on the Muslim regime. Out of the Ridda war came the great campaigns of Arab conquest in Syria and Iraq. Abu Bakr died not long after the first great Muslim success at the battle of Ajnadayn in southern Palestine (634).

ABU BAKR IBN UMAR (*fl.* 11th cent.), leader of the southern Almoravid armies after the death of his brother Yahya at the battle of Tebferilla (1056–7). Following the death of Ibn Yasin (1057) he became the leader of the movement and played a major role in the founding of Marrakesh (*c.* 1068). After pacifying the Gudala in the southern Sahara (1071–2) he returned to Marrakesh to find that his deputy, Yusuf ibn Tashufin, had become virtually independent. To avoid strife he acknowledged Yusuf's position and returned south. There he led the campaign which overran the Soninke state of Ghana (1076) and was later killed in an encounter in the Mauretanian Adrar (1087–8).

ABU HANIFA AL-NU'MAN IBN THABIT (*c.* 699–767), theologian and jurist, the founder of the Hanafi School of Muslim law. He wrote nothing on law himself, hence his teaching has to be gathered from the works of his disciples, *eg,* Abu Yusuf and Al-Shaybani. He did much to systematize legal studies and to elaborate the techniques of legal analysis.

ABU MUSLIM (d. ?754), architect of the revolution which brought the House of Abbas to the caliphate. It is probable that he was a slave of Persian origin. The Abbasid Imam Ibrahim ibn Muhammad sent him to Khurasan in 745–6. Here he created the coalition of discontented elements, Arab and Persian alike, which overthrew the Umayyad regime, the decisive battle occurring on the Great Zab river in 750. Abu Muslim, in 754, crushed the dangerous revolt, in northern Syria, of another member of the Abbasid house, Abd Allah ibn Ali, soon after the accession of the second Abbasid caliph, Al-Mansur. The power of Abu Muslim was, however, so great that Al-Mansur had him killed not long afterwards. The name of Abu Muslim remained alive in Khurasan and contributed to the continuing disaffection there, *eg,* in the great revolt of Al-Muqanna' during the reign (775–85) of the Caliph al-Mahdi.

ABU SA'ID (1305–35), 9th Mongol Il-Khan of Persia, succeeded his father Uljaytu in Dec. 1316. The dominant figure during the first ten years of his reign was the Emir Coban, who acted as regent until 1327. Abu Sa'id renounced the Shi'i doctrines that Uljaytu had favoured and gave his allegiance to the Sunni (*ie,* orthodox) form of Islam. His death, without heir, in 1335, led to the breakdown of the Il-Khanid regime.

ABU SIMBEL, site on the Nile in Lower Nubia where the Egyptian King Rameses II (*c.* 1304–1247 BC) had two temples cut in the rock. The temples were raised mechanically (1963–8) to avoid inundation by the Nile after the building of the Aswan High Dam.

ABU YAZID (*c.* 885–947), itinerant Zenata Berber, remembered as 'the man on a donkey', who shook Fatimid power in Ifriqiyya in the 10th cent. At a time when the Fatimid governors were forcing economic development, to the benefit of the towns, and multiplying taxation and labour-services at the cost of the peasants, Abu Yazid roused the hinterland in a revolt under the banners of Kharijite dissent. He carried the countryside with him in 943, but in 947 failed to capture Mahdiya, the Fatimid capital of Ifriqiyya, and was hunted to death. The Fatimids survived, but dissent remained.

ABU'L FAZL, SHEIKH (1551–1602), was the second son of Sheikh Mubarak of Nagor and brother of Sheik Faizi, the leading Persian poet during Akbar's reign. These three formed an intellectual eclectic group, and influenced Akbar in his estrangement from orthodox Islam in the years after his introduction to court (1574). He was the chief exponent of Akbar's religious cult, the *Din Illahi* or Divine faith, which borrowed from Zoroastrianism, Christianity, Hinduism, and Jainism. From this time he remained at court as a secretary in the emperor's confidence until his murder at the hands of Akbar's son, Prince Salim, who resented and feared his influence with Akbar. Abu'l Fazl was a polished Persian scholar and a subtle philosopher with an encyclopedic mind. His two principal works were the *Akbarnama*, or history of Akbar's reign, and the *Ain-i-Akbari*, an encyclopedia of the contemporary Mughal empire.

ABU'L-HASAN AL-MARINI (d. 1351), most famous Marinid sultan of Fez. On his accession (1331) he inherited a Hafsid alliance against the Banu Abd al-Wadd which led to his capture of Tlemcen (1337). Tempted to intervene in Andalus against a renewed Castilian offensive, he recovered Algeciras (1333), but his defeat at Tarifa (1340) ended Maghribi intervention in Spain. In 1347 he exploited the Hafsid alliance to invade Ifriqiyya. Defeated by nomads belonging to the Hafsid political system, he remained in Tunis for a year. Meanwhile, his son, Abu Inan, had seized power in Fez. Returning alone by sea and land, he died in the High Atlas.

ABUSHIRI BIN SALIM (d. 1889), leader of the revolt which bears his name. In 1888, when German colonial officials occupied Pangani, Abushiri led a resistance movement which spread throughout the Arab coastal communities of Tanganyika, and attracted some African assistance. He was hanged by the Germans in Dec. of the following year.

ABWEHR. German military intelligence service which came into conflict with the rival Nazi (SS) intelligence service, the Sicherheitsdienst (SD) under Heydrich, and then Kaltenbrunner, by which it was destroyed in 1944. On 31 Dec. 1934 Gen. von Blomberg dismissed Conrad Patzig, its director, on the grounds that the Abwehr had collected information on the Maginot Line without notifying the minister in charge. Patzig was succeeded by Admiral Wilhelm Canaris.

Increasing friction between the Abwehr and the SD forced Canaris to accept the '10 commandments agreement' from 12 Dec. 1936, which barred the Abwehr from collecting 'political' information. Conditions worsened for the Abwehr when on 11 Nov. 1938 Hitler legalized the SD as 'intelligence organization for State and Party'. This ended the Abwehr's pre-eminence, and led to chaos in intelligence. The Prague agreement between Canaris and Heydrich from May 1942— a few weeks before the latter's assassination—legalized the SD's activities also in military affairs.

In Feb. 1944 Hitler ordered the Abwehr to merge with the SD. This process was speeded up by the participation of several members of the Abwehr in the plot against Hitler.

ABYSSINIAN SLAVES were frequently employed by the chiefs of Muslim India, specially in the Deccan. They were valued not only for their physical prowess, but frequently for their ability and lack of personal ties which might encourage disloyalty. The most famous of these slaves were Malik Ambar of Ahmadnagar, who defied the Mughals for many years, and the Sidis of Janjira in western India. They commanded the fleet of the Bijapur sultan, defying the Marathas, until 1670, when they transferred their allegiance to the Mughal Emperor Aurangzeb.

ACADÉMIE DE PEINTURE ET DE SCULPTURE. Set up to advance the cause of painters in France (1648), the académie was taken over by the Crown (1655) and established in the Louvre. It still exists in the guise of the Académie des Beaux Arts (1795).

ACADÉMIE ROYALE DES SCIENCES, association of leading French scientists which had its roots in an informal gathering of scientists in the circle of Mersenne (1635) and was placed under royal patronage in 1666. In 1795 it became part of the *Institut National*. It attracted men like Cassini as members and carried out a large amount of scientific and educational work. It flourished in the 19th cent., and now consists of 68 full members and 65 section members, there being sections for each branch of science.

ACADEMIES, DISSENTERS',

in England. The rise of the dissenters' academies dates from the Act of Uniformity of 1662, which required schoolmasters and private tutors to assent to the Book of Common Prayer and led to the expulsion of many university and grammar schools teachers. The law, however, was not strictly enforced and those who were expelled were able to set up academies of their own. These became more securely established after the Toleration Act of 1689, and in the 18th cent. tended to concentrate on education for different denominations of the ministry. Some academies, particularly at the beginning of the century, provided teaching of very high quality, and attracted pupils who were not dissenters. Secker, later Abp of Canterbury, was learning algebra, geometry, conic sections, and reading Locke at Bowes's Academy in Bishopsgate Street, London, in 1710, and later, at Gloucester, studied Greek, Latin, Hebrew, Chaldee, and Syriac. Warrington Academy, where Priestley was educated, was run by rational dissenters, and was notable in the later 18th cent. for its scientific education.

ACADEMY OF SCIENCE,

Russian institution founded in St Petersburg (1725) to stimulate an interest in science and to train native scientists. A secondary school for boys was also founded as an adjunct to the academy. Though it was established shortly after his death, the academy owes its existence to Tsar Peter the Great, who first outlined his plans in discussions with the German philosopher Leibnitz in 1711. Initially the academicians came from Germany and Switzerland, but in 1742 the first Russian, Lomonosov, was appointed. During the following two decades he did important work in physics, chemistry, and applied science. The new institution made an immediate and effective contribution through its support of the second Bering expedition (1733–1743), which crossed Siberia and reached the coasts of Alaska and Japan, and through its encouragement of technical education which resulted in a number of important inventions, including the first Russian steam engine (1766). The academy continued to grow during the 19th cent. and by the eve of the First World War it embraced a number of affiliated scientific institutions and learned societies, historical and philological as well as scientific. In the Soviet period it has become the country's leading scientific research centre, at the same time incorporating an ever-increasing number of research institutes, in a variety of fields.

ACADEMY, ROYAL

(1768), was founded by a group of artists including Sir Joshua Reynolds, PRA (1723–92), Sir William Chambers, and Benjamin West, to improve professional standards of British painting and sculpture. From the beginning it held annual exhibitions, the profits of which helped to defray the expenses of its teaching schools.

ACADEMY, RUSSIAN,

founded (1783) in St Petersburg by Princess Dashkova, a friend of Catherine II, to encourage the development of Russian as a literary language. It published a dictionary (1789–94) and was incorporated into the Academy of Science in 1841.

ACADIA,

former French colony in North America within present NS, NB, and ME, for which the French and the British contended (1613–1713). Its history dates from a visit by the Cabots (1497), but there were no attempts at colonization until a century later. Early French expeditions, like those of Champlain (1603) and De Monts (1604), were made for the purpose of trading with the Indians. Religious and commercial zeal combined to foster deeper consolidation based on the modern sites of Annapolis and St Croix. Despite expulsion by English forces from Virginia (1613), the French continued to assert claims to Acadia and for 100 years there were continuous squabbles between English and French fur traders and grantees. Acadia was twice conceded to France, by the treaties of St Germain-en-Laye (1632) and Breda (1667), but France relinquished its claim to NS by the treaty of Utrecht (1713). However, the French in Que. still tried to exercise authority over the Acadians living in boundary areas. New England regarded NS as the key to its security and demanded an oath of allegiance to the English Crown from the Acadians. Under pressure from priests from St Lawrence, particularly the Abbé le Loutre, and the Micmac Indians, they refused the demand and were consequently expelled in 1755, dispersing themselves among English colonies along the Atlantic seaboard. Many also went to LA, where they were granted lands along the Bayon Teche. They afterwards made a distinct contribution to LA life, maintaining their own *cajun* culture. Their ruthless expulsion by the British inspired Longfellow's narrative poem, 'Evangeline: a tale of Acadia'.

J. B. Brebner, *New England's Outpost: Acadia before the conquest of Canada* (New York, 1927).
G. F. Clarke, *Too Small a World: the story of Acadia* (Fredricton, NB, 1958).   GFO

ACAPULCO,

principal port of the south-western region of Mexico, from which Spanish *galeónes* sailed for the Philippines and China (1565–1815). Oriental fabrics and spices were sold at the Acapulco fair following the return of the Manila *galeón* each year. Smuggling characterized Acapulco's trade throughout the colonial era. In spite of royal prohibitions, much of the merchandise arriving at the port was shipped to Peru.

ACCADEMIA DEL CIMENTO

(1653–61), scientific body, consisting of nine members, set up by the Grand Duke of Tuscany to perform experiments. After making several detailed observations it was suppressed because of political and religious opposition to its objectives. Its transactions were later published.

ACCADEMIA DEL LINCEI,

scientific body, established by Prince Federico Cesi (1603), to which Galileo belonged. It ceased to be on Cesi's death (1653), but was revived in the 18th cent. (1745–55) and again in the 19th, when it became first a papal and then a national body (1944), equivalent to the Académie Française.

ACCADEMIA DEL SCIENZA,

originally founded as a private scientific society in Turin in 1757, by G. B. Beccaria (1716–81), J. L. Lagrange (1736–1813), and others, with the title *Philosophico-Matematica Società Privata Taurinensis*. Beccaria, elected a fellow of the Royal Society in 1755, is known for his study of atmospheric electricity, and Lagrange, who had connections with the political theorist Saint-Simon, for his general and analytical mechanics. The society became the *Società Reale* in 1761 and the *Regia Accademia della Scienze* in 1783.

ACCADEMIA DELLA CRUSCA

(1552), Florentine literary academy, the most famous of some 700 such academies founded in Italy during the 16th cent. It was specifically devoted to the study of the Italian language, and the *Vocabulario della Crusca*, which it published in 1612, helped to establish Tuscan speech as the basis of the Italian literary language.

ACCADEMIA FISICO-MATEMATICO,

17th-cent. scientific society in Rome. One member was the engineer C. J. Meijer, from Amsterdam, who produced plans (1676) for draining the Pontine marshes.

ACCADEMIA SECRETORUM NATURAE

(1560), one of the earliest of the societies formed to discuss natural philosophy.

It was founded in Naples by Giambattista della Porta (1538–1615), the author of a popular book, *Magiae Naturalis*, which contained a mixture of physics, alchemy, and magic, and probably reflects the discussions of the members of the society—the *Otiosi*, or men of leisure.

ACCESSORY TRANSIT COMPANY, headed by Commodore Cornelius Vanderbilt, a US railroad magnate, ferried CA-bound gold prospectors across Nicaragua (1849).

ACCURSIUS, FRANCISCUS (d. 1263), a former student of the law school of Bologna, was the most important of the commentators or glossators on Roman civil law. His comprehensive work, the *Accursiana*, was known simply as 'The Gloss' and replaced even the *Corpus Juris Civilis* in law courts as the ultimate authority.

ACHAEAN LEAGUE, Greek federal association of city-states in the Peloponnese. First created perhaps in 5th cent. BC, it lasted until *c.* 323, when Alexander the Great suppressed it. Revived *c.* 281, it expanded until in the 2nd cent. it included almost all the Peloponnese, having a common central administration, army, coinage, and weights and measures. Aratus of Sicyon directed the league's first major expansion after 250 when it gained most of Arcadia, but opposition from Cleomenes III of Sparta ended this. As a Macedonian satellite the League opposed Rome in the First Macedonian War, but led by Philopoemen and Aristaenus it joined Rome during the Second Macedonian War and shared the Roman victory. This led directly to the League's second major expansion, conducted by Philopoemen and Diophanes, in which it absorbed almost all the Peloponnese. Misinterpretation of the League's relationship with Rome led eventually to the Achaean War (146), after which Rome dissolved it.

ACHAEMENID, Iranian dynasty (*c.* 559–330 BC) which derives its name from Achaemenes, although his descendant, Cyrus II (*reg. c.* 559–530 BC), founded the empire. Cyrus and his early descendants, Cambyses II (*reg. c.* 530–522), Darius I (*reg. c.* 522–486) and Xerxes I (*reg. c.* 486–465) conquered and ruled an empire which, at its height, included Mesopotamia, Egypt, Asia Minor, the Greek cities and islands, Syria, parts of India, and the entire Iranian plateau. Each of the early Achaemenids thought of himself as 'king of kings', bringing peace and unity to a great variety of peoples. No attempt to enforce uniformity was made and ancient cultures were preserved and encouraged, sometimes at the expense of stability. Government was centralized and bureaucratic, the empire being divided into 20 units known as satrapies. Greatly improved roads and sea routes connected the different parts of the empire. Surveys were made and taxes levied systematically. The Achaemenid period seems to have been one of growing economic prosperity. Agriculture remained the main occupation, but large building schemes demanded increased quarrying and, in the towns, clothes, shoes, metal goods, jewellery, and furniture were manufactured. With improved roads, standardized coinage, and the establishment of private banks, trade increased throughout the empire and beyond. It was a period of extensive building, especially at the cities of Susa, Pasargadae, Ecbatana, and Persepolis. Huge palaces and halls, with splendid reliefs, were built. As a result of the employment of artisans from different parts of the empire, a handsome and distinctive style emerged. Great public works were undertaken. Subterranean canals were built for irrigation and ports with quays were constructed for the first time. The later Achaemenids, although wealthy and apparently powerful, suffered from frequent revolts within the empire and every succession led to family assassinations. In 330, when faced with a determined enemy—Alexander the Great—the empire quickly collapsed.   JKG

ACHESON, DEAN GOODERHAM (1893–), US secretary of state, and one of the authors of the post-war policy of containment of communism. A brilliant lawyer who once worked for Louis D. Brandeis, he was appointed undersecretary of the treasury in May 1933, but resigned in Nov. because he regarded F. D. Roosevelt's monetary policies as unsound. He joined the state department as assistant secretary in 1941, later becoming under-secretary (1945–7). An advocate of the development of the western alliance, he helped to formulate the Truman Doctrine (1947) and the Marshall Plan (1948). As secretary of state (1949–53), he secured ratification of the North Atlantic treaty (1949) and the commitment of US troops to NATO (1951). His Asian policy made him the object of mounting Republican disapproval, and he was criticized for the outbreak of war in Korea (1950).

ACHESON, EDWARD GOODRICH (1856–1931), US industrial chemist who in 1891 discovered silicon carbide ('carborundum'). He manufactured this widely employed abrasive commercially, after 1895, using the cheap hydroelectric power of Niagara Falls. Acheson used the electric furnace also, in 1899, to make synthetic graphite, which has had invaluable industrial applications, *eg*, as lubricants and electrodes.

ACHIMOTA, educational institution in Ghana, founded (1927) by Sir Gordon Guggisberg, offering an education that is African in content and practical in outlook.

ACHOLI, a Luo people of about a quarter of a million, most of whom live in northern Uganda, the rest in southern Sudan. They occupied their Ugandan homeland between 1500 and 1750.

ACILIUS GLABRIO, M', Roman consul (191 BC), a *novus homo* who probably owed his advancement to the Scipios. His victory at Thermopylae in 191 drove Antiochus III of Syria from Greece.

ACKIA, BATTLE OF (1736), fought in north-western MS, when Chickasaw Indians repulsed a combined French and Choctaw force under Bienville.

ACOMA, American Indian tribe and pueblo (town) of the Keresan linguistic group, in NM. Acoma is the oldest inhabited settlement in the US and was first visited by Coronado's army in 1540. The Acoma participated in the Pueblo rebellion against Spanish dominion in 1680, but were reconquered.

ACOSTA, JOSÉ DE (*c.* 1539–1600), Spanish Jesuit missionary and author of the *Historia natural y moral de las Indias* (1590). He made a famous 17-year trek from Peru to Mexico (1570–87).

ACRAGAS (mod. Agrigento), Greek city in southern Sicily, founded by Gela and Rhodians (*c.* 580 BC). It flourished under the tyrants Phalaris (*c.* 550) and Theron (488–472) and many imposing Doric temples were built. In 480 it joined Syracuse in defeating the Carthaginians at Himera. After the establishment of democracy (471) the tyrants' building programme was continued. Destroyed by the Carthaginians in 405, the city was resettled by Timoleon (*c.* 340). It suffered badly during the Punic Wars (264–201), but by the 1st cent. had recovered its agricultural prosperity and continued to flourish throughout antiquity.

ACRE (AKKA), on the seaboard of Palestine, fell to the crusaders in 1104. In 1187 it was captured by Saladin. The forces of the Third Crusade, led by Richard Cœur de Lion and by Philippe Auguste of France, retook the town after a memorable siege (1189–91). Acre surrendered to the Mamluks of Egypt and Syria in 1291, an event which marked the end of the crusading presence in Syria. The town flourished once more, after 1746, under Sheikh Zahir al-Umar and, after

1775, under Ahmed al-Jazzar. Napoleon besieged Acre without success in 1799, his assault failing to overcome the resistance of Al-Jazzar and of a small naval force under Sir Sidney Smith. Ibrahim Pasha, the son of Muhammad Ali of Egypt, captured Acre in 1832 and razed its defences.

ACRE TERRITORY. Brazil obtained Acre from Bolivia by the treaty of Petropolis (1903) following a brief war. Brazil paid Bolivia £2 million in compensation. The Acre territory is in western Brazil, adjacent to the Bolivian and Peruvian borders.

ACTE ADDITIONEL (1815), constitution issued by Napoleon at the beginning of the Hundred Days (1815). Similar in general character to Louis XVIII's constitution of 1814, it provided for representative government with a chamber of deputies and a senate, freedom of the press and of religion, and an independent judiciary.

ACTION FRANÇAISE (1898). The Comité de l'Action Française was a right-wing group led by Charles Maurras. It was royalist, Catholic, anti-Semitic, and virulent in its attacks on its enemies. It became prominent in the attacks on supporters of Dreyfus. The movement's newspaper, also called *Action Française*, was edited by Léon Daudet, and published daily after 1908. The movement was disowned by the French pretender and condemned (1914) by Pius X, although the condemnation was only made public in 1926 by Pius XI.

ACTION GROUP, Nigerian political party founded by Chief Obafemi Awolowo and launched in April 1951. In that year the party was elected to power in the House of Assembly in Western Nigeria. From being a predominantly Yoruba party it soon began to reconstruct itself on a national basis and played a major role in achieving political independence for Nigeria. A split in the party in 1962, with consequent crisis in the government of the Western Region, which it had controlled since 1951, and the subsequent trial and imprisonment of Chief Awolowo and some of his supporters, proved a turning point in the post-independence history of Nigeria.

ACTION NATIONALE, French-Canadian nationalist magazine (1933–present). In the 1930s it supported the 'Jeune-Canada' movement and embraced the 'Program of Social Restoration' of the École Social Populaire. Strongly affirming its dedication to Catholicism and French traditions, it has become increasingly racist and anti-Semitic in tone and since World War II has supported Quebec separatism.

ACTION RÉPUBLICAINE ET SOCIALE, group of French deputies who broke away from the Gaullist RPF Party in 1952, after voting for the installation of the conservative Pinay government against the wishes of De Gaulle. Although the ARS deputies were about a quarter of the Gaullist strength, they were mostly men who had sat as orthodox conservatives before being elected as Gaullists in 1951, and were returning to their natural allegiance. They were later absorbed into the existing conservative groups.

ACTIUM, BATTLE OF (2 Dec. 31 BC), sea battle which decided the fate of the Roman world. It was fought off the promontory of Actium, north of the gulf of Ambracia in Greece, between the fleets of Octavian, commanded by Agrippa, and those of Antony and Cleopatra. The preceding campaign is badly reported and the course and purpose of the final battle obscure. It is not known whether Antony fought for victory or to escape blockade or whether his fleet refused to fight or was defeated, but Cleopatra broke away for Egypt and Antony followed with 40 ships, leaving Octavian supreme.

ACTON OF ALDENHAM, JOHN EMERICH EDWARD DALBERG ACTON, 1st Baron (1834–1902), British historian and moralist. By his writings in the 1850s he became a leader of those Roman Catholics who desired to bring the teaching and organization of the Church into line with modern thought and science, being an unflinching opponent of absolutism and an advocate of freedom of conscience. In the mid-1860s he became a close friend of Gladstone and influenced the development of his religious ideas, but he later attacked Gladstone's *Vatican Decrees in their bearing on civil allegiance*. Acton became regius professor of modern history at Cambridge (1895) and planned the *Cambridge Modern History*, published after his death.

ACUNA, ANTONIO DE (d. 1526), warrior-prelate of Castile who helped to lead the *Communeros* revolt (1520–1). Originally a diplomatic agent in Rome, he persuaded Pope Julius II to appoint him Bp of Zamora in Castile. After the collapse of the revolt (1521), he was captured, imprisoned in Simancas, and condemned to death in 1526 for attempting to escape.

ACUNA, HERNANDO DE (d. 1580), Spanish poet, whose sonnet addressed to Philip II anticipated that his reign would bring to Spain 'one monarch, one empire, and one sword'.

ADAB, Sumerian city (mod. Tell Bismaya), which had one king, Lugal-anne-mundu, recognized as suzerain of Sumeria.

ADAD-NIRARI II (*c.* 911–891 BC), Assyrian king, who inaugurated a period of expansion by a series of campaigns against Babylonia, the Aramaeans settled in the Tigris valley, and the small kingdoms in the north and west of Assyria.

ADAD-NIRARI III (*c.* 810–783 BC), Assyrian king, who lost north-western territories to Urartu, but defeated a coalition of Syrian states and forced them to accept his suzerainty.

ADALBERON, archbishop of Rheims at the time of the death of the last Carolingian ruler of France, Louis V. He took the lead in securing the election as king of Hugh Capet, Duke of Francia, who became the founder of the Capetian dynasty, and whom he crowned in 987.

ADALBERT, Saint (*c.* 950–97), a Czech prince and Bp of Prague, who promoted the alliance of his friend Emperor Otto III and Boleslaw I of Poland. Adalbert needed Polish support for the conversion of the heathen Prussians, who killed him in 997. He was buried by Boleslaw at Gniezno, which Otto III accepted in 1000 as the seat of the first independent Polish archbishopric.

ADAM OF BREMEN (d. *c.* 1081), author of a history of the archbishops of Hamburg-Bremen, chiefly valuable for its reference to contemporary German ecclesiastical and political affairs, but also containing a description of Scandinavia based largely on oral reports and including the earliest reference to the Vikings' discovery of Vinland (ie, America).

ADAM, JOHN (1779–1825), official of the East India Co. who acted as governor-general of India for nine months in 1823. He encouraged native education, put an end to the discreditable transaction of the Palmer Co. in Hyderabad, and restricted the freedom of the press in Bengal.

ADAM, ROBERT (1728–92), Scottish-born architect, son of William Adam, who designed some fine houses and country mansions in the early 18th cent. With his brother, William, he exploited the classical revival which had been stimulated in the 1740s and 1750s by British travellers to Athens, Palmyra, and Baalbek, and by his own visit to the ruins of Diocletian's palace at Spalato (Split). His work was distinguished by its highly inventive use of apses, arcades, and classical motifs in interior decoration, and he was probably the first to create decorative schemes as a whole, furniture, carpets, and ceilings being, as at Osterley, designed to relate to one another. He was at the height of his influence in the 1760s and 1770s. The bulk of his work related to country mansions, the most notable perhaps being Kedleston, Derbyshire; he also designed the Adelphi, London, and the Old Quadrangle at Edinburgh University, where he had been a student.

ADAMAWA, emirate of the Sokota caliphate in Nigeria. Founded by *Modibo* Adama (*c.* 1820), it was essentially an association of *Fulani* emirates owing allegiance to Sokoto through Yola. It was partitioned between Britain and Germany after 1884.

ADAMITES, radical Hussite sect in Bohemia, who believed that society could be redeemed if man could return to the biblical paradise of Adam and enjoy a pastoral life in which there was social and economic equality.

ADAMJEE JUTE MILLS, pioneer enterprise of the jute mill industry in Pakistan. The partition of India (1947) left the jute mills in India and the jute-growing areas in Pakistan. The first Adamjee jute mill started production in Narayan-gang, near Dacca, in Dec. 1951.

ADAMNAN, abbot of Iona (679–704), author of a life of St Columba, a work of fundamental importance in the early history of Scotland. Adamnan was in touch with Bede's monastery and tried unsuccessfully to win Iona over to the Roman Easter. In the 690s he persuaded the Irish Church to adopt the Roman date.

ADAMS, BROOKS (1848–1927), US historian, son of Charles Francis Adams. Seeking, like his brother Henry, a theory of historical development that would explain the rise and fall of civilizations, he came to a mixed mechanistic and Darwinist interpretation revolving round a 'law of centralization'. Once dispersion of peoples had been replaced by concentration, he found an inherent tendency towards stagnation, leading to renewed dispersion. Reinvigoration could come through imperial expansion, and he saw the US and Russia engaged in a struggle for empire over China. A staunch nationalist, Adams believed that militarism could be a useful antidote to the self-destructive tendencies of commercialism. After *The Emancipation of Massachusetts* (1887), a case study of a specific civilization, he developed his general theory in *The Law of Civilization and Decay* (1895), *America's Economic Supremacy* (1900), and *The New Empire* (1902). He exerted considerable influence over the intellectual life of his time.

ADAMS, CHARLES FRANCIS (1807–86), US minister to Britain during the American Civil War. The son and grandson of US presidents John and John Quincy Adams, he was the father of three distinguished sons, Charles Francis Jr, Brooks, and Henry. His anti-slavery views made him a founder and vice-presidential candidate of the Free-Soil Party (1848), and then led him into the Republican Party. A member of the House of Representatives (1859–61), he was sent by President Lincoln as minister to London (1861–8). There, his determination, patience, and skill, especially in the crises over the *Trent*, the *Alabama*, and the *Laird Rams*, did much to safeguard the international position of the US during the war. He led the US commission at the tribunal which settled the dispute with Britain over the *Alabama* claims (1871–2).

ADAMS, SIR GRANTLEY HERBERT (1898–   ), Barbados political leader, born in Barbados, educated at Oxford, and called to the bar (1923). He returned to Barbados in 1934 and was elected to the House of Assembly. As the leading lawyer in Barbados, he defended Clement Payne, leader of the labour riots of 1937. Adams was chosen president of the Progressive League (1939), which in 1942 became the Barbados Labour Party. He was the first president (1941–53)

of the Barbados Workers Union. Adams led the Barbados Labour Party to victory in 1951 and with constitutional changes became first prime minister of Barbados (1954–8). He was founder of the loosely organized Federal Labour Party and became prime minister of the West Indies (1958–62). In 1966 he became leader of the opposition in the Barbados House of Representatives.

ADAMS, HENRY BROOKS (1838–1918), US historian and man of letters. Born in Boston, MA, son of Charles Francis Adams, his New England and family background moulded his view of history and influenced his concept of civilization. After graduating from Harvard (1858), he studied in Berlin and Dresden and afterwards served as his father's secretary in London (1861–8). He was editor of the *North American Review* (1870–6) and also taught at Harvard (1870–7), where he introduced German seminar methods and pursued research in American history that resulted in *The Life and Writings of Albert Gallatin* (1879) and a *History of the United States during the Administrations of Jefferson and Madison* (9 vols, 1889–91). He moved to Washington DC, where his house became the centre of a famous literary circle. In addition to his historical works, Adams wrote the novels *Democracy* (1880) and *Esther* (1884), elegantly ironic commentaries on contemporary life. After 1885 he travelled widely and began the study of medieval European culture that increasingly obsessed him. Seeking a philosophy of history and intrigued by the 'unity' of the Middle Ages, symbolized by the Virgin, he came to see his own time as an age of 'multiplicity' controlled by the laws of physics and dominated by a modern symbol, the Dynamo. His sentimental and yet sceptical intellectual pessimism is expressed in *Mont-Saint-Michel and Chartres* (1904) and the autobiographical *Education of Henry Adams* (1907).

ADAMS, JOHN (1735–1826), US statesman and second president. Born in Braintree, MA, educated at Harvard, a schoolteacher and then a lawyer, he was active in colonial resistance to British policy, condemned the Stamp Act (1765), and published anonymous articles in the *Boston Gazette* (1765), which appeared in England as *A Dissertation on the Canon and Feudal Law* (1768). Later he served in the MA colonial legislature (1770–1) and defended a British officer, Capt. John Preston, on charges arising from the Boston Massacre (1770). He approved of the Boston Tea Party, condemned the Intolerable Acts, and was a prominent delegate to the first Continental Congress (1774). His *Novanglus* letters (1775), written while he was a member of the MA provincial congress, argued that although parliament could regulate trade, it had no authority within the colonies.

At the second Continental Congress he urged the necessity for confederation, was active in promoting independence, served on the committee that drafted the Declaration of Independence, and fought for its adoption in Congress. His *Thoughts on Government* (1776) had considerable influence on the making of early state constitutions. He served as a commissioner to France (1778–9) and was principal author of the MA state constitution (1779–80). Although a successful minister to Holland (1780–5) and a US commissioner at the Paris peace negotiations (1780–3), as envoy to Britain (1785–8) his relations with the British government were cool and frustrating.

As US vice-president (1789–97) Adams was again frustrated, for the office lacked power, but he none the less performed useful service supporting Washington's foreign policy and Alexander Hamilton's financial programme. A conservative often accused of monarchical tendencies, he was horrified by the aftermath of the French Revolution, which also exacerbated his difficulties when he succeeded Washington as president (1797–1801). Although a devoted federalist, he sought to improve deteriorating relations with France, but the XYZ affair (1798) threatened to turn existing naval hostilities into full-scale war. Adams resisted this pressure and, learning that the French were prepared to reopen negotiations, averted war by concluding a Franco–American convention (1800). His foreign policies made him widely unpopular and he was also held responsible for the undemocratic Alien and Sedition Acts (1798). With Alexander Hamilton openly working against him, he was narrowly defeated for re-election (1800) and spent the rest of his life in retirement.

Vain, irritable, and often pompous, Adams was critical of all men, including himself, but also capable of deep emotion. A major American political thinker, he was concerned with the implementation of principles rather than speculative thought, and advocated a system which would check men's ambitions by balancing them against each other.

Gilbert Chinard, *Honest John Adams* (Boston, 1933).
John R. Howe, *The Changing Political Thought of John Adams* (Princeton, NJ, 1966).

ADAMS, JOHN QUINCY (1767–1848), US statesman, son of John Adams. Born at Braintree, MA, he was educated largely in Europe, served as secretary to Francis Dana in Russia (1781–3), and attended his father at the Paris peace negotiations. After serving as minister to Holland (1794–7) and Prussia (1797–1802), he became a federalist senator from MA (1803–8). He pursued an independent policy, approving the purchase of LA, though not the method of acquisition, and generally supported Republican foreign policy. After participating in the caucus which nominated James Madison for the presidency, he was forced to resign his seat. He was minister to Russia (1809–14), and a delegate at the Ghent negotiations (1814) which ended the War of 1812. After a period as minister to Britain (1815–17), he became James Monroe's secretary of state (1817–25).

With a vision of a great continental nation Adams made a major contribution to American expansion. He negotiated the boundary with Canada along the 49th parallel from the Great Lakes to the Rockies and a ten-year joint occupation with Britain of the OR country (1818). He also supported Andrew Jackson's raids in FL and negotiated the Adams–Onis Treaty with Spain (1819). Later, he encouraged Monroe to recognize the independence of the Spanish South American colonies (1822), and assisted him in formulating the Monroe Doctrine (1823). As a presidential candidate in 1824, Adams obtained 84 votes in the electoral college compared with Jackson's 99, William Crawford's 41, and Henry Clay's 37. As no candidate received an overall majority, the election was determined by the House of Representatives, in accordance with the provisions of the constitution. Here, Clay's support gave Adams the election. Clay was later appointed secretary of state, leading to the charge by Jackson's supporters of a corrupt bargain.

As president, Adams's proposal to use federal authority to promote extensive internal improvements provoked opposition among northern strict constructionists and southern slave-holders, who feared an extension of federal power. Inhibited from forming his own group of supporters by belief that it was his duty to serve the national interest independent of faction, Adams was defeated by Jackson in the bitter presidential campaign of 1828. Refusing to retire completely, he continued to pursue an independent line as a congressman from MA (1831–48). Although not a true abolitionist, he was prominent in the fight against slavery and its extension into the territories, pointing out that the institution had deleterious effects on the entire nation. He condemned the 'gag rule' and helped to keep slavery perpetually in the public eye. Honest, vigorous of mind, and with a grand vision of America's future, he aroused hostility through his lack of political finesse. The diaries he kept not only reveal his character, but provide valuable insights into the history of his time.

S. F. Bemis, *John Quincy Adams and the Foundations of American Foreign Policy* (New York, 1949).
S. F. Bemis, *John Quincy Adams and the Union* (New York, 1956).

ADAMS, SAMUEL (1722–1803), US politician, born in Boston, and cousin of John Adams. After graduating from Harvard (1740), he was involved in a number of unsuccessful business ventures, but devoted his life to politics, playing a major role in the American Revolution.

A prominent member of the popular party and a leader of the Sons of Liberty in Boston, Adams exploited the Sugar and Stamp Acts (1764–5) to attack the conservative party in MA and assumed leadership of the radical majority in the colonial legislature (1765–74). He controlled opposition to the Townshend Acts, assisted in co-ordinating the Non-importation Association, and drafted the legislature's Circular Letter to other colonies (1768). Later, he exploited the Boston Massacre (1770), and wrote polemical newspaper articles to ensure that colonial hostility towards Britain did not die out. Boston's appointment of a committee of correspondence and adoption of a declaration of rights at Adams's instigation (1772) are often considered the origin of revolutionary government in MA. Adams was also largely responsible for the publication of compromising letters written by Gov. Hutchinson to friends in England (1773). A prime mover in the Boston Tea Party (1773), he led resistance to the Intolerable Acts by means of a non-intercourse policy (1774) and after some hesitation urged that MA should participate in the First Continental Congress at Philadelphia (1774). Believing that although colonial legislatures were subject to parliament they were not subordinate, he was equally convinced that their duties included the protection of the Americans' natural rights, and after 1768 may have envisaged complete independence. Adams and his cousin left overt leadership to the Virginians, preferring for tactical reasons to work behind the scenes. Instrumental in summoning a convention in Suffolk County, MA, Adams secured approval of Resolves proposing vigorous resistance to British policy, rejection of Joseph Galloway's Plan of Union, and adoption of the Continental Association for boycotting trade with Britain. Avoiding arrest by British troops, he became a delegate to the Second Continental Congress (1775), where he advocated immediate independence and recommended that interested states should form a confederation (Jan. 1776). He signed the Declaration of Independence (July 1776).

Thereafter, Adams played only a lesser role. He served in Congress until 1781, was a member of the MA Constitutional Ratifying Convention (1779–80), and president of the state senate (1781). Initially he opposed the US Constitution, but came to accept it. Unable to secure election to Congress, he served as lieutenant-governor (1789–93) and governor (1793–7) of MA. A brilliant polemicist and radical organizer, he was not, however, a constructive statesman.

John C. Miller, *Sam Adams: pioneer in propaganda* (Stanford, CA, 1936).

ADAMSON ACT (1916), US legislation establishing an eight-hour work day on all interstate railroads, and extra pay for overtime. The first federal act on this subject, its constitutionality was upheld by the Supreme Court in *Wilson v. New*, 243 US 332 (1917).

ADAMS–ONIS TREATY (1819), negotiated between the US and Spain, sometimes called the Transcontinental treaty. Spain ceded east FL and renounced claims to west FL, the US renounced claims to TX and assumed financial claims of its citizens against Spain. Definition of the western boundary of the Louisiana Purchase removed any Spanish title to the Pacific north-west.

ADASHEV, ALEXSEI (d. 1560), boyhood friend of Tsar Ivan IV (the 'Terrible') and subsequently one of the members of his 'Chosen Council' which advised the tsar during the first part of his reign. Adashev was of comparatively humble origin and owed his influential position to Ivan's personal trust. He lost favour in 1560 and was demoted to a command in Livonia.

ADAT, complex collection of largely pre-Islamic Indonesian customary laws and practices. In certain areas the prescriptions of *adat* law have been in conflict with those of formal Islamic law (*hukum*), particularly on questions of family law. This has sometimes led to considerable social tension and conflict, notably in Sumatra. The dichotomy is often less sharp, however, and both *adat* law and *hukum* have often influenced one another.

ADDAMS, JANE (1860–1935), pioneer US social worker. Born in IL and a graduate of Rockford College (1882), her studies at the Women's Medical College, Philadelphia, were interrupted by illness and during a visit to England (1887–8) she became committed to social work. One of the founders of Hull-House, in the Chicago slums, she instituted a highly successful settlement house pattern that not only emphasized immediate relief but also inaugurated educational, vocational, and recreational programmes designed to give the poor a renewed sense of personal dignity. She exerted great influence over the progressive movement for social reform and her ideas can be traced in parts of the New Deal in the 1930s. Her account of her early work, *Twenty Years at Hull-House* (1910), is a classic. Devoted to the cause of world peace, she became chairman of the Women's Peace Party (1915) and later president of the Women's International League for Peace and Freedom, sharing the Nobel Peace Prize (1931) with Dr Nicholas Murray Butler.

ADDIS ABABA (lit. 'New Flower'), capital and most important city of Ethiopia. First established in 1885 by Menelik II, then King of Shoa, the town was named by his consort, Taitu, in 1887. After Menelik's coronation as Emperor of all Ethiopia, Addis Ababa replaced the earlier capital of Entoto in 1891, and then developed as the country's largest market and the site of modern innovations. With a present population of over 500,000 it has become an important centre of African diplomacy, being the headquarters of both the Economic Commission for Africa and the Organization of African Unity.

ADDISCOMBE COLLEGE, military school near Croydon, England (1809–61), for the education of cadets for the East India Co.'s engineers and artillery in India. From 1816 cadets were admitted for the infantry also. With the end of the company after the Mutiny of 1857, the Indian army was completely reorganized. On 1 April 1862 the Bengal, Bombay, and Madras Engineers were amalgamated with the Royal Engineers. Thereafter, engineers intended for India came from the Royal Military Academy at Woolwich and received a specialized training at the School of Military Engineering, Chatham. In 52 years about 3600 cadets passed out from Addiscombe. Among the distinguished engineers it produced were Napier of Magdala, Henry Durand, Richard Strachey, 'Buster' Browne, and Thomas Holdich.

ADDISON, CHRISTOPHER, 1st Viscount (1865–1951), British Liberal and later Labour statesman. Addison's career fell into two parts. He became under-secretary to Lloyd George at the ministry of munitions in 1915, and, as his closest ally in the House of Commons, was responsible for ascertaining the probable extent of support for Lloyd George as prime minister among the Liberals in Dec. 1916. Addison again became minister of munitions in 1916, minister of reconstruction (1917–19), and president of the local government board (1919–21). In this last post he was responsible for the housing programme. A policy of generous Exchequer grants when materials and labour were scarce led to excessive rises in building costs, and in response to a public outcry Lloyd George made Addison the scapegoat and dismissed him. Shortly afterwards he joined the Labour Party and was minister of agriculture (1930–1). He entered the House of Lords in 1937, and in the Labour administrations of 1945–51 was Commonwealth secretary (1945–7) and lord privy seal (1947–51).

ADDISON, JOSEPH (1672–1719), British poet and journalist. Born in Wiltshire, son of a rector, Addison was educated first at Charterhouse, where he met Richard Steele, and then at Queen's College, Oxford. Here Addison became skilled in Latin verse; his first English poem was not published until 1693.

In 1695 Addison was introduced to Somers (lord chancellor) and Montague (chancellor of the exchequer), who persuaded him to write his 'Poem to His Majesty' (1695) and a Latin poem on the peace of Ryswick (1697), by doing which he secured himself a pension. Between 1699 and 1703 Addison travelled abroad as tutor to Edward Wortley Montague. On his return, with the Whigs out of office, he was short of work until Godolphin needed a poet to celebrate Marlborough's victory at Blenheim, for which he wrote 'The Campaign' (1704).

Politically Addison's fortunes now began to rise. He was made under-secretary of state (1706) and secretary to the lord lieutenant of Ireland, Wharton (1708–10). In 1708 he entered parliament for Lostwithiel and after 1710 retained Malmesbury, a seat under Wharton's influence, until his death.

Addison, however, was not a politician and never spoke in parliament. It is far more as a literary man that he is remembered. He tried his hand at opera (*Rosamond*, 1707, a failure) and drama (*Cato*, 1713, far more successful), but his greatest contributions were as a journalist. From 1709 he helped his friend Steele with *The Tatler*, a thrice-weekly periodical. In 1713 he contributed to Steele's *Guardian* and in 1711–12 and 1714 the two men wrote *The Spectator*. Addison's aim in *The Tatler*, and more so in *The Spectator*, was at a publication free of malevolent party politics and showing a greater concern for literary content. He hoped thereby to make the paper acceptable to most shades of opinion, and indeed *The Spectator* was the first paper to have some concern for women's tastes.

On the death of Queen Anne and the Whigs' triumph, Addison returned to politics. He was appointed a commissioner of the treasury (1716) and secretary of state (1717). By this time, however, Addison was a sick man. His last publications were in 1719, when, roused by Steele's attack on the Peerage Bill, Addison wrote two articles defending the bill in *The Old Whig*.

W. Graham (ed.), *The Letters of Joseph Addison* (London, 1941).   AW

ADDLED PARLIAMENT (1614), second parliament of James I. A new one had been consistently opposed by the pro-Spanish faction at court, headed by the Earl of Northampton. However, the need for money became so urgent that James I decided to call a parliament. The election caused much excitement owing to the activities of some self-appointed 'undertakers', who, in exchange for promises of court favour, hoped to secure the return of members likely to support the court. Rumours magnified the matter into a conspiracy to procure a nominated parliament. Consequently court candidates met with resistance almost everywhere, while opponents of the royal policy over impositions and the ecclesiastical settlement—the two burning issues left over from the dissolution of James's first parliament in 1611—were easily elected. The friends of the king in the Commons (headed by the attorney-general, Sir Francis Bacon, and the chancellor of the exchequer, Sir Julius Caesar) were few in number. All the leaders of the earlier opposition were elected, *eg*, Sir Edwin Sandys, William Hakewill, James Whitelock, and Thomas Wentworth. The most striking fact about the membership of the Commons was that 300, *ie*, nearly two-thirds of the whole House, were new members. This was a major cause of the 'addling' of the parliament. When conflict came with the king and the House of Lords over impositions, this inexperienced assembly degenerated into a mob. Leadership did not come from Sir Ralph Winwood, the newly appointed principal **secretary**

of state (29 March 1614), whose job it was. He, like many members, had never sat in parliament before.

The session opened (5 April) with a speech by James calling for support for the maintenance of religion, for the provision of the succession to the throne, and for the granting of supplies. These were moved for by Winwood on 11 April, but members raised grievances over impositions and ecclesiastical matters. Supplies were postponed until the undertakers' activities were looked into, and until impositions were settled to the Commons' satisfaction. Later investigations involving the undertakers proving fruitless, these were dropped. The Commons then decided to ask the Lords for a conference on impositions, but by a vote of 39 to 30 (24 May) the Lords refused to agree. The majority vote included 16 bishops and the two Scots in the House, *ie*, the Earls of Somerset and Richmond. Later, Bp Neile of Lincoln made a speech vilifying the Commons which led to uproar in the House the next day, the Commons refusing to consider other business until they were satisfied. Neile apologized, but the Commons strayed into trifling accusations against him. At this James's patience ran out and he sent word that unless parliament proceeded forthwith to discuss supplies, he would dissolve it (3 June). The Commons then complained about royal favourites, pensions, and the influence of Scots. On 7 June the parliament was dissolved without a single bill receiving the royal assent. Several members were sent to the Tower and papers concerning the proposed conference were burnt. The dissolution left the pro-Spanish faction supreme at court.

S. R. Gardiner, vol. 1, *History of England 1603–1642* (London, 1885).

T. L. Moir, *The Addled Parliament of 1614* (Oxford, 1958). CJ

ADEL, Muslim province of eastern Ethiopia. Formerly an independent Muslim sultanate, it was often a threat to the emperors of Ethiopia in the Middle Ages.

ADELAIDE, QUEEN (1792–1849), daughter of George, Duke of Saxe-Coburg Meiningen. She married the Duke of Clarence, later William IV of England, in 1818. During the Reform Bill agitation (1830–2) she became unpopular with radicals, being suspected of unduly influencing the king.

ADELANTADO, official possessing military, civil, and judicial authority who was charged with advancing the frontiers of the Spanish empire in the days of the conquest. The title originated in Old Spain, where an official with similar powers had been active during the wars against the Muslims.

ADELARD OF BATH (*fl. c.* 1100–50), pioneer student of Arabic science, extensively travelled and well educated. The future Henry II of England was his pupil for a time. Adelard is best known for his *Astrolabe*, which describes the uses of the Arabic astrolabe, an instrument for observing the stars.

ADENAUER, KONRAD (1876–1967), first chancellor of the German Federal Republic and founder and leader of the Christian Democratic Union. Adenauer dominated the politics of West Germany and was responsible for the policy of integrating West Germany into a strong European and Atlantic framework in which the reconciliation of France and Germany was a central part. He also insisted on Germany's recognition of its responsibilities towards the Jews.

He was born in Cologne, the son of an official in the Cologne law courts. He studied law, became a member of the Catholic Centre Party, and entered municipal politics. In 1917 he was appointed Chief Burgomaster of Cologne, an office which he held until 1933 and in which he distinguished himself by his leadership in civic improvement, including the building of a new river harbour, a part in the construction of the first autobahn from Cologne to Bonn, and above all in the revival of Cologne University.

A bitter opponent of Nazism, he was summarily dismissed from office in March 1933, and lived in retirement (interrupted by two brief periods in prison, in 1934 and 1944) until June 1945, when he was reinstated as mayor by the American Military Government, only to be deprived of office once again by the British, when they took over their zone of occupation.

Soon afterwards he became chairman of the CDU, and when the German Federal Republic was established in 1949 was elected its first chancellor. His party was successful in the federal elections of 1949, 1953, and 1957; its failure to win an overall majority in 1961 led to prolonged negotiations for the establishment of a coalition government. Adenauer's style of government was strongly personal and the coalition cabinets which he formed owed their cohesion to his dominance rather than to political bargaining.

He was thus able to exercise a decisive influence over the development of Western Europe and the western alliance in the 20 years following the Second World War. His proposals for Franco-German co-operation anticipated those of the Schuman plan, and he gave full support both to plans for European union and to German participation in western defence under NATO. He did not believe in the possibility of concessions being made by the Soviet government and therefore resisted any policy of concession from the west, maintaining that the best hope for German reunification lay in the establishment of a strong West Germany fully integrated in a strong Western Europe. He negotiated Germany's entry into the European Coal and Steel Community; secured the ratification of the European Defence Community—being his own foreign minister (1951–5) at a time when French policy was hesitant—and, on the question of the Saar, hostile to German interests; and strongly supported the development of the European Economic Community.

In the autumn of 1955 he visited Moscow, and signed an agreement providing for an exchange of ambassadors and the return of German prisoners of war; but he and his government opposed the establishment of diplomatic relations with countries which recognized the German Democratic Republic. He also resisted concessions to the east in the Berlin crisis of 1958–61.

The constancy of his policy in the 1950s, in contrast to the weakness of France and the isolation of Britain from the European Community, led to a close working relationship with the American secretary of state, John Foster Dulles. Subsequently Adenauer established a close *rapport* with President de Gaulle, which contributed to the signature of the Franco-German treaty of 1963 and the hopes based thereon of close co-operation between European heads of state.

Adenauer retired from the chancellorship in Oct. 1963, after a period in which he tried unsuccessfully to prevent Erhard succeeding him. He retired from the chairmanship of the Christian Democratic Union in March 1966.

R. Hiscocks, *Germany Revived* (London, 1966).

P. Weymar, *Konrad Adenauer* (London, 1957). WK

ADER, CLEMENT (1841–1925). French aircraft inventor whose *Avion* (1897) failed to fly.

ADHEMAR DE MONTEIL (d. 1098), French noble and Bp of Le Puy. He was appointed in 1095 by Pope Urban II as the legate in charge of the First Crusade. His wisdom, tact, and integrity played a decisive part in preventing quarrels among the crusading leaders from breaking up the crusade and in achieving the capture of Antioch.

ADIGAR, principal officer of the kingdom of Kandy, Ceylon, which kept its independence till it was extinguished by the British (1815). Two or three in number, the adigars exercised military, judicial, and administrative powers. They invariably came from high caste families.

ADIL, AL (*c.* 1145–1218), Al-Malik al-Adil Abu Bakr Muhammad ibn Ayyub, Sultan of Egypt and Syria (*reg.* 1200–18), was the brother and confidant of the great Salah al-Din (Saladin), founder of the Ayyubid regime. Al-Adil, an able politician and administrator, had a large share in the peace negotiations between Saladin and Richard Cœur de Lion which brought the Third Crusade to an end in 1192. After the death of Saladin in 1193, Al-Adil sought to mediate between the sons of the dead sultan. Their continuing quarrels led him in 1200 to take on himself the office of sultan. After 1207 his own sons ruled under his supervision —Al-Kamil in Egypt, Al-Mu'azzam in Syria, Al-Ashraf in Diyarbakr, and Al-Awhad in Al-Jazira.

ADIL SHAHI DYNASTY (1489–1686), so called after its founder, Yusuf Adil Shah. It controlled the state of Bijapur in the Deccan after breaking away from the Bahmani kingdom, which collapsed following the murder of Mahmud Gawon (1481). Yusuf was a Georgian slave who rose by his ability in the Bahmini service to be governor of Bijapur until he declared its independence. He was said by Ferishta to have been a son of Sultan Murad of Turkey smuggled from Persia when his life was endangered. He proved to be an able man, consolidating his kingdom as one of the two principal successor states of the Bahmini empire. He introduced the Shia form of Islam, but practised general toleration. Goa, on the west coast, the port of entry for the horse trade from the Middle East, was a favourite residence of his. When the Portuguese took it by surprise (1510) he recovered it by a great effort, but died soon after, when it was lost again during succession disputes.

During the early years of their rule the Adil Shahis had to face attacks from the other Deccan sultanates, which were repelled partly owing to friendly relations with the Hindu state of Vijayanagar. After 1558, however, a breach occurred which led to a coalition of the four Muslim Deccan states of Bijapur, Golkonda, Bidar, and Ahmadnagar against Vijayanagar. At the battle of Talikota (1565) the issue was decided by the capture and execution of the Hindu leader Ramraja. Vijayanagar was sacked and the empire collapsed.

The most distinguished sultan of the 17th cent. was Ibrahim Adil Shah II (*reg.* 1579–1626). He enlarged his dominions to the border of Mysore, and was noted as a skilful and equitable administrator and as a patron of the arts. He reverted to the Sunni form of Islam, but maintained a generous toleration which included Christians as well as Shias and Hindus.

Thereafter Bijapur was overshadowed by the Mughal empire. Its increasing weakness enabled Sivaji, the son of a Bijapur *jagirdar*, to revolt and to repel a serious attempt under the general Afzal Khan to repress him. The Mughals, under Prince Aurangzeb, were already pressing Bijapur hard when the illness of Shah Jahan in 1657 diverted him from his campaign to seize the throne. Later operations were carried on desultorily by Aurangzeb's son Muazzam, who would have preferred compromise. In 1685 Aurangzeb himself attacked Bijapur, which surrendered in the following year. For all its later feebleness, the Adil Shahi dynasty left behind it a memory of tolerance, cosmopolitan culture, and patronage of the arts. The monuments of the Adil Shahi kings are some of the finest in India.

T. W. Haig, *Historic Landmarks of the Deccan* (Allahabad, 1907).   TGPS

ADKINS v. CHILDREN'S HOSPITAL, 261 US 525 (1923), US Supreme Court case concerning the constitutionality of a District of Columbia minimum wage law enacted by Congress (1918). In a 5 to 3 decision the statute was declared void as violating the due process of law clause of the Fifth Amendment. The majority opinion by Justice Sutherland gave unprecedented scope to the doctrine of free contract, asserting such freedom to be the general rule, and restraint the exception. He defined four categories of permissible restraint, but as minimum wage legislation did not fall into any of these, it was unconstitutional as well as socially and economically unsound. Dissenting opinions attacked the manifest 'legislative' character of the majority opinion.

The case, a classic instance of identification of laissez-faire economics with constitutional rights, became a precedent for broad interpretations of the scope of free contract and the striking down of several state minimum wage laws.

ADLECTIO, technical term under the Roman Principate for admission to the Senate by act of the censors or emperor instead of by holding a magistracy. *Adlectio* was also used to accelerate a senator's career by enrolling him in a higher rank in the senatorial hierarchy than that to which the magistracy he had held entitled him, *eg*, an ex-quaestor thus deemed of praetorian rank could stand directly for the consulship. Much used by Julius Caesar, but only sparingly by the early emperors, the right of adlection became a normal imperial prerogative after Domitian. After Diocletian and Constantine, even adlection to consular rank became common.

ADMIRAL OF FRANCE, high office of state investing the holder both with overall control of French naval forces and with certain judicial and fiscal rights. The office originated in the Middle Ages but was abolished by Richelieu in 1627. It was re-established as a purely honorific title in 1699 and finally disappeared in 1830.

ADMIRALTY, COURT OF. This formerly exercised an independent jurisdiction in British maritime affairs, trying both civil and criminal cases. The majority of such cases have since been transferred to other courts.

At least by the reign of Edward III the lord high admiral, or a judge whom he appointed, had jurisdiction over piracy and crimes at sea and also over civil disputes in which mariners and merchants were involved. In criminal cases the court was often ineffective because its procedure was based on civil law, but it was strengthened by an act of 1536 which caused all offences on the high seas to be tried by common law judges. Civil issues continued to be determined to some extent by international law and the recognized customs of the sea.

The growth of piracy, trade, and exploration in the Tudor period extended the work and responsibilities of the court, and this excited the jealousies and apprehensions with which any prerogative court was regarded by the common lawyers. But it was not until the 19th cent. that the Admiralty court gradually lost its special powers. The Central Criminal Court (1834) was empowered to decide all criminal cases occurring within Admiralty jurisdiction, and the Naval Offences Act (1866) transferred its authority over naval discipline to naval courts martial. Some of its civil jurisdiction was transferred to county courts, although in these matters it continued to be a court of appeal. In 1857 its civil powers were brought under the authority of the same judges who sat in cases of probate and divorce, and the Judicature Act (1873) set up a single Admiralty, probate, and divorce division of the high court. In the event of war a separate authority was to be issued for the establishment of an Admiralty prize court.

Civil jurisdiction in naval affairs is now concerned with disputes about salvage, seamen's wages, bottomry, and damages arising from collisions and alleged negligence at sea.

W. S. Holdsworth, *History of English Law*, vol. 1 (London, 1922–38).   MR

ADMONITION TO PARLIAMENT (1572), tract written by two British Puritan ministers, Field and Wilcox, to influence debates on religion in the House of Commons. It demanded the abolition of bishops and the government of the Church by the Presbyterian system of ministers, elders, and deacons.

A second tract, coarsely attacking 'Popish abuses', was widely circulated and the authors were imprisoned.

ADOBE WALLS, BATTLE OF (June 1874), fought on the north side of the Canadian river in the Texas panhandle at a buffalo hunters' base camp. Comanche, Kiowa, Cheyenne, and Arapaho Indians, led by Quanah Parker, laid siege to 29 whites in a stockade but were driven off after three days. This was the last big battle waged by the Comanches against the whites.

ADOLPHUS FREDERICK (1710–71), Duke of Holstein-Gottorp and King of Sweden. He was elected heir to the Swedish throne in 1743, married Louisa Ulrika, sister of Frederick II of Prussia (1744), and as king (1751–71) resisted the party-rule of 'Hats' and 'Caps', but without lasting success.

ADOWA, BATTLE OF (1 March 1896), decisive victory of the Ethiopian Emperor Menelik over the Italians. In 1889 Menelik and Italy had signed the Uccialli treaty, the Italian version of which differed from the Amharic and was the basis for Italy's claim to a protectorate over Ethiopia. Menelik denounced the treaty, and war began in Jan. 1895, when the Italians occupied Tigre province. Later in the year the emperor drove them back. At the battle of Adowa the Italians had 17,000 men and 56 cannon, Menelik 100,000 riflemen and 40 cannon. Such fire-power combined with popular support gave him a resounding victory, whereupon Italy withdrew its claim to a protectorate.

ADRIAN I (*reg.* 772–95), Pope, whose appeal for help against the Lombards brought Charlemagne into Italy (773–4) and began the intervention of the Frankish kings in the affairs of the papacy. Charlemagne gave the papal territories the boundaries which they were to retain without much change until the 19th cent.

ADRIAN IV (*c.* 1110–59), Pope. Born near St Albans and the only English pope. His short pontificate (*reg.* 1154–9) is notable for the bull *Laudabiliter*, which sanctioned the invasion and conquest of Ireland by Henry II. He crowned Frederick Barbarossa as emperor, but began later to drift into a conflict with him which developed into an open struggle under Adrian's protégé and successor, Alexander III.

ADRIAN (1627–1700), last patriarch of the Russian Church before the abolition of the office by Peter the Great in 1721. Adrian was an ignorant man and a supporter of the Church's obscurantist tradition which opposed change of any kind. He condemned Peter's hostility to the wearing of beards as a fundamental assault upon Russian orthodoxy and the tsar refused to appoint another patriarch after Adrian's death.

ADUD AL-DAWLA (936–83), Buwayhid, Amir al-umara, who became the ruler of Fars in 944. In 967 he extended his influence to Oman in north-eastern Arabia. Thereafter, he gained control of Kirman (968) and of the Makran (971–2). He took Baghdad from his cousin Bakhtiyar (978–9). Most of Persia, Iraq, and Mesopotamia thus came under his domination. The rule of Adud al-Dawla, no doubt the greatest of the Buwayhid amirs, was notable for the firmness of his administration, for the building of public works, and for the patronage of literature and learning.

ADULIS, main port of the Aksumite empire, situated on the Red Sea coast of Africa some 50 kms south of modern Massawa.

ADULLAMITES (1866). A small group of the British Liberal Party who were united in opposing Gladstone's Reform Bill of 1866. They were so nicknamed by Bright after the biblical cave of Adullam in which collected 'everyone that was in distress and everyone that was discontented' in the reign of David. They included Lord Elcho and Lord Grosvenor, and their most prominent member was Robert Lowe. Outside parliament they were supported by Delane of *The Times*, and represented the Palmerstonian element in the Liberal Party. By voting with the Conservatives they defeated Gladstone's bill and enabled Derby and Disraeli to take office.

ADVENTURERS' ACT (1642). This assigned 2½ million acres (10,000 sq. kms) of Ireland to subscribers as security for loans they would 'adventure' to raise forces for the suppression of the Irish rebellion. The lands were to be assigned by lot as soon as parliament declared the rebellion at an end. The scheme did not prove to be as popular as was expected. Much of the money raised was used in the Civil War in England.

ADVISORY COUNCIL FOR ITALY, set up by the Council of Foreign Ministers (Oct. 1943), included Russian and French (as well as British and US) representatives. It lacked power, which remained with the purely Anglo-American Control Commission set up at the same time. The Russians pressed vigorously for a part in the administration of Italy after the armistice and the council was created to meet their demands. It has been argued that the Soviet government took the Italian arrangement as a precedent in reverse for its own control of the defeated German satellites in south-eastern Europe.

ADWALTON MOOR, BATTLE OF (1643), fought near Bradford, Yorkshire, in the English Civil War. On 30 June the parliamentary forces under Lord Ferdinando Fairfax and his son, Sir Thomas, were defeated by the royalists under William Cavendish, Earl of Newcastle. As a result, the royalists controlled all Yorkshire, except Hull.

ADWERT ACADEMY, 16th-cent. north European society of humanists devoted to learned discussion.

AEDILES, magistrates of ancient Rome. Initially (494 BC) the aediles were two plebeians who assisted the plebeian tribunes; later they formed, with the two patrician curule aediles, an executive board. These four officials, elected annually, exercised jurisdiction in four civil spheres—markets (supervising measures and prices); streets and buildings (maintaining the fabric and controlling traffic); health and morals in baths and taverns; and certain public games, in which private funds were often invested to win popularity and further office. Tenure came between quaestorship and praetorship, but was not essential for higher advancement. In 44 BC two more aediles were created for corn-supply duties. Augustus made the office—or the plebeian tribunate—essential for non-patrician aspirants to higher magistracies, but later it became progressively less important and disappeared under Alexander Severus in the 3rd cent. AD.

AEDUI, Gallic tribe settled in Burgundy, whose alliance with Rome, dating from 121 BC, was used by Julius Caesar as pretext for his attack on the Helvetii (58). They joined Vercingetorix' revolt (52), but submitted after his capture and in the 1st cent. AD became rapidly Romanized.

AEGATES ISLANDS, BATTLE OF THE (March 241 BC), final engagement in the First Punic War. The Romans, under Lutatius Catulus, defeated the Carthaginian fleet off western Sicily as it tried to relieve Hamilcar on Mt Eryx.

AEGEAN ISLANDS, situated in the Aegean Sea between modern Greece and Turkey. They were overrun by the Ottoman Turks in the decade following the conquest of Constantinople (1453) and remained within the Ottoman empire until the 19th cent.

AEGINA, ancient Greek island state in the Saronic gulf, the neighbour and rival of Athens. After Mycenean settlements had been overrun by the Dorians, it became a centre of trade from the 7th cent. BC and was probably the first homeland city to introduce coinage; its prosperity is attested by the fine ruins of the temple of Athena Aphaea (c. 490). The Aeginetans' threat to Medize in 491 out of hostility to Athens was met by the Spartan Cleomenes' intervention, and, after suspending the quarrel with Athens (481), they fought well against the Persian invasion of 480–479. They remained outside the Delian League, but were attacked and subjected by Athens in the First Peloponnesian War (457). Athenian treatment of the Aeginetans was an issue in the crisis before the second war, and at its start (431) they were expelled. Restored after Athens' defeat (404), they continued to oppose Athens in the 4th cent.

AEGOSPOTAMI, BATTLE OF (Sept. 405 BC), in the Hellespont (Dardanelles), the final and decisive naval victory of the Spartans in the Second Peloponnesian War, which led to the siege and surrender of Athens (404). After five days in which the two fleets watched one another without fighting, the Spartan admiral, Lysander, attacked the Athenian fleet beached for the night and captured 160 of its 180 ships, only Conon with a small squadron escaping to Cyprus.

AELFRIC, abbot of Eynsham (c. 955–?), the outstanding literary figure of the 10th-cent. West Saxon renaissance. He translated several books of the Bible into Anglo-Saxon, and composed *Homilies*, saints' *Lives*, and *Pastoral Letters* in the vernacular. He was educated at Winchester under Aethelwold.

AELIUS ARISTIDES (d. AD 189), Greek sophist (professional orator) in the Roman empire, active in Asia Minor and Rome. Of his ceremonial speeches in elaborate style on various topics, 55 survive, the best known being a panegyric on Rome and its rule.

AELRED OF RIEVAULX, Saint (c. 1110–67), one of the most famous of Cistercian monks, second in his order only to St Bernard of Clairvaux. A member of a noble Northumbrian family, he spent the greater part of his youth at the court of David I of Scotland before becoming a monk at the Cistercian abbey of Rievaulx (c. 1134), whose second abbot he became in 1147. Aelred was a man of great charm, celebrated in his own time as preacher, historian, and spiritual writer. He was an influential figure in Anglo-Scottish affairs. One of the most famous medieval biographies, the *Vita Aelredi*, written by Walter Daniel, for many years a monk under him at Rievaulx, preserves the details of his life and work.

AEMILIUS LEPIDUS, M., Roman senator and consul in 187 BC. As ambassador he formally declared war on Philip V in 200 BC. He gave his name to the Via Aemilia (between Ariminum and Placentia), and to the Basilica Aemilia Fulvia, built in his censorship in 179.

AEMILIUS LEPIDUS, M., Roman aristocratic revolutionary, consul in 78 BC. Of patrician family, he perhaps served as military tribune under Cn. Pompeius Strabo in the Social War and may have captured Norba for Sulla in the Civil War (82–81). Elected consul after governing Sicily oppressively (80), he quarrelled with his colleague over Sulla's funeral honours, proposed to rescind some of Sulla's measures, and finally raised a revolt. Defeated by Pompey (77) he was pursued through Etruria, but escaped to Sardinia, where he died.

AEMILIUS LEPIDUS, M. (d. 12 BC), colleague of Antony and Octavian in the Second Triumvirate. Son of the consul of 78, he was a close associate of Julius Caesar and after Caesar's death was, with Antony, one of the two potentially most powerful men in Rome. His relations with the Senate deteriorated and as governor of Narbonese Gaul and Nearer Spain he joined Antony against the Senate, and with him and Octavian established the Second Triumvirate (Nov. 43). As consul in 42 he controlled Rome while Octavian and Antony waged the campaign of Philippi. On Octavian's return to Rome (41) he became governor of Africa. After co-operating with Octavian in the war against Sextus Pompey (36), he attempted to seize Sicily. Octavian won over his army, expelled him from the Triumvirate, and sent him away to Circeii, where he lived until his death, retaining the office of Pontifex maximus in which he succeeded Julius Caesar.

AEMILIUS PAULLUS, L. (d. 216 BC), Roman consul in 219 and 216 BC. In 219 he destroyed the piratical power of Demetrius of Pharos and the Illyrians. He was defeated and killed at Cannae. A biased version in the histories exonerates him and vilifies his plebeian colleague, Terentius Varro.

AEMILIUS PAULLUS MACEDONICUS, L., Roman general, consul in 182 BC and 168, and censor in 164. After military experience in Spain (190–189) and against the Ligurians (181), he achieved his greatest triumph by winning the Third Macedonian War, defeating Perseus at Pydna in June 168. Though the settlement imposed by Paullus and the senatorial commission, which divided Macedonia into four republics and Illyria into three, was politically successful, it was accompanied by brutal repression of anti-Roman elements, for which Paullus became notorious. Executions in Aetolia, deportations from Achaea, the pillaging of 70 towns, and the enslavement of 150,000 people in Epirus document the fate of those who resisted Rome. At home, Paullus was associated with the policies of the Scipios. His name was a byword for financial integrity.

AEMILIUS SCAURUS, M., Roman aristocrat who, although of impoverished and politically obscure family, became consul in 115 BC, censor in 109, *princeps senatus* in 115–89, and was in the late 2nd and early 1st cents the director of senatorial policy.

AENEAS, Trojan hero and legendary founder of Rome. In Homer as Dardanian leader he is a mainstay of Troy, with no hint of later departure. Later Greek writers, beginning c. 600 BC with Stesichorus, chronicle the western voyage to Italy. Early Roman poets depict him as grandfather of Romulus and Remus. Virgil reflects the synthesis of Greek legends and native traditions. Aeneas bears the household gods to Thrace, Delos, and Crete successively, but portents force him onward. En route to Italy from Sicily, he is blown to Carthage, where his divinely directed desertion of Dido symbolizes Rome's future wars with that city. In Latium he defeats the Rutulian Turnus and builds Lavinium. The gap between the fall of Troy and the now canonical date of Rome's foundation is filled by the insertion of kings of Alba Longa, the parent city of Rome, who are depicted as descendants of his son Iulus (Ascanius).

AEOLIANS, Greek ethnic group, many of whom were displaced (c. 1100 BC) from Boeotia and Thessaly by northern intruders, subsequently settling on Lesbos and the adjacent coast from the Troad to Smyrna. From an original league of 12 mainland cities, including Cyme, Smyrna was lost c. 700 to the Ionians. The mainland Aeolians remained secluded and agricultural, sharing only in the emergence of oral epic poetry (c. 1000–800). The Lesbians, however, joined the Ionians in developing sea-borne trade in the 7th cent. and c. 600 Sappho and Alcaeus produced lyric poetry of high quality. From c. 550 onwards, being of little political importance, the Aeolians were controlled in turn by the Persians, the Athenians, more loosely by the Hellenistic kingdoms, and finally by the Romans.

AEQUI, ancient Italian mountain people dwelling in the central Appenines on the eastern borders of Latium. Their raids from the forward base of Mt Algidus, which caused

Rome and the Latin league to reconcile their differences in the 5th cent. BC, ended with the capture of that strategic height by Rome *c.* 430. Hostilities continued sporadically for another century, till Rome finally subdued the Aequi *c.* 300, establishing Latin colonies at Alba Fucens and Carsioli.

AERARIUM. The Roman state treasury. Situated in the temple of Saturn in the Forum below the Capitol, it was controlled by the quaestors assisted by a permanent bureaucracy supervised by the Senate. Julius Caesar found in it 15,000 bars of gold, 30,000 bars of silver, and 30 million sesterces in 48 BC; but Augustus four times bailed out the treasury from his own pocket and under the empire its income was very small compared with that of the emperor. With financial control concentrated in the hands of the emperor and his financial officers, the aerarium declined in importance until it became merely the city treasury of Rome.

AERARIUM MILITARE. The Roman military treasury established by Augustus in AD 6 with an initial gift of 170 million sesterces from his own fortune. It provided cash gratuities for discharged soldiers and was maintained by two new taxes, a sales tax and death duties levied only on the estates of Roman citizens.

AERENTHAL, LEXA, Baron von (1854–1912), an Austro-Hungarian foreign minister, who died in office. He was appointed (1906) in an attempt to achieve closer relations with Russia, but his policy in fact led to a complete deterioration in relations between the two powers. He had envisaged a partition of the Balkans with Russia which would have left Austria in control of the western half with Serbia as a client state. To effect this he was prepared to use deceit towards his allies as well as his enemies, as was shown in the annexation of Bosnia-Herzegovina (1908).

AERONAUTICAL SOCIETY OF GREAT BRITAIN, founded (1866) for the advancement of aerial navigation. It encouraged scientific and technical experiments and its importance in the 19th cent. far outweighed its tiny membership. It expanded with the development of powered flight and in 1918 received a royal charter. Its publications, examinations, lectures, archives, exhibitions, and technical surveys (*eg*, on Stressed Skin Structures) have made a significant contribution to 20th-cent. aeronautics. In its centenary year it had a world-wide membership of 11,000.

AERSCHOT, PHILIPPE DE CROY, Duke of (1526–95), member of the great Walloon house of Croy, knight of the Golden Fleece and councillor of state, appointed by Philip II in 1565. He wholeheartedly supported the Spanish crown against the rebellious nobles led by Orange and Egmont until Alva's repressive measures aroused in him a *politique* reaction and he came to believe that national unity in the Netherlands was preferable to religious uniformity. After Requesens' death (1576) Aerschot and his *politique* friends in Brussels seized the initiative and summoned a states general of all the provinces to protect the country from the mutinous Spanish soldiery and to reach an agreement with the rebellious provinces of Holland and Zeeland. The peace of the Duke of Aerschot (1576) between the Calvinist and Catholic provinces was the high point of his career and he was made *stadtholder* of Flanders by the states general. The ensuing Calvinist revolution in the cities of Brabant and Flanders and renewed personal rivalry with Orange destroyed the common front against Spain. The secession of the Walloon provinces followed. Aerschot made his personal peace with Philip II's new governor, the Duke of Parma (1579), though he became the leader of the southern Netherlands once again in the 1590s, protesting against the harsh policy of Fuentes, Alva's brother-in-law.

AESCHINES. 4th-cent. BC Athenian politician who, displaying flexibility and unflamboyant eloquence, rose from humble origins to influence. As envoy to Megalopolis (348) he realized the inevitability of negotiating with Philip II of Macedon and was envoy for the peace of Philocrates (346). Following its unsatisfactory implementation, Aeschines, charged with diplomatic misconduct by his co-envoy Demosthenes, was acquitted (343) after countercharging Demosthenes' associate Timarchus. At the Amphictyonic Council (339), by brilliantly defending Athenian conduct and ensuring Amphissa's condemnation, he was indirectly responsible for Philip's intervention in central Greece, which led to his victory at Chaeronea. He retired into exile (330), politically discredited after failing in prosecuting Ctesiphon for unconstitutionally proposing civic honours for Demosthenes.

AESCHYLUS (525–456 BC), first of the three great Athenian tragedians and author of 90 plays, of which seven survive. He is regarded as the true originator of Greek tragedy in its final form. By employing a second actor he introduced dramatic dialogue and by adopting stage dress and mechanical devices gave the drama a greater sense of realism. Grand themes from mythology and concern with order and morality and divine punishment of insolence, such as occurs in the Prometheus legend, interested him, as did the fatality of destiny and the heredity of crime and its absolution, as in the Oresteia trilogy. *Persae* (472), his only extant tragedy on a contemporary subject, relates the theme of insolence and punishment to the failure of the Persian invasion of Greece (480–479), and some of his other plays seemingly reflect current Athenian political controversies.

AETHELBERT (*c.* 565–*c.* 618), King of Kent, first Christian king among the Anglo-Saxons. He married a Frankish Christian princess and in 597 received missionaries sent by Pope Gregory the Great led by Augustine of Canterbury. Aethelbert established himself as the overlord (*bretwalda*) of the southern English.

AETHELFLAED (d. 918), daughter of Alfred the Great and wife of Aethelred, *ealdorman* of West Mercia, she ruled alone in Mercia after the latter's death in 910. In collaboration with her brother, King Edward the Elder of Wessex, she attacked the Danish army bases in the east Midlands and built her own network of *burh*s or forts across Mercia, preparing the way for the unification of England under the house of Wessex.

AETHELRED I (*reg.* 865–71), King of Wessex, son of Aethelwulf, King of Wessex. His accession coincided with the first serious Danish invasion of England. Together with his brother and successor Alfred, he won a considerable victory at Ashdown in 871. But Wessex was still under sustained Viking attack when Aethelred died.

AETHELRED II (*c.* 967–1016), King of England who succeeded (*reg.* 978–16) on the murder of his half-brother Edward the Martyr. Aethelred's nickname '*unraed*', meaning 'evil counsel', was a pun on his name, which means 'noble counsel'. The Scandinavian attacks on England began again in 981 and gradually increased in severity. Vast sums were levied in taxation and paid as danegeld to secure temporary truces. In 1013 Swein, King of Denmark, conquered all England and Aethelred fled to his wife's relatives in Normandy. Swein's death necessitated a second invasion by his son Cnut (1015), which ended in a complete Danish conquest. His reign witnessed considerable legislative activity.

AETHELWEARD (d. *c.* 998). A descendant of Aethelred I, King of Wessex, and *ealdorman* of west Wessex. A patron of Aelfric of Eynsham, he was a scholarly layman who translated into Latin a text of the *Anglo-Saxon Chronicle* to 973, which preserves readings not otherwise extant.

AETHELWOLD, bishop of Winchester (963–84). Most austere of the leaders of the Benedictine monastic reform movement in England. A disciple of Dunstan at Glastonbury, Aethelwold rebuilt Abingdon monastery and, as Bp of Winchester, replaced the cathedral clergy by monks. He revived the fenland monasteries of Ely, Peterborough, and Thorney.

AETIUS (390–454). One of the greatest Roman generals in the last age of the Western empire. He lived for some years as a hostage among the Huns and repeatedly recruited Hun mercenaries. With their support he was able for 20 years (433–53) to impose his will on the imperial family in Italy. His greatest achievement was his resistance in 451 at Châlons to an invasion of Gaul by Attila, King of the Huns, which was followed in 453 by Attila's death and the end of the Hunnish menace. No longer needed, Aetius was murdered by the Emperor Valentinian III.

AETOLIAN LEAGUE, federal association of Aetolian communities in western central Greece, first known in 4th cent. BC. Gaining control of Delphi (c. 300), it won great prestige by defending the shrine against Celtic invaders (278). Continually hostile to Macedon, the league spread during the 3rd cent. over central and western Greece, where its anti-Macedonian attitude gained it adherents. In the First Macedonian War (215–205) it became Rome's first Greek ally. It offended Rome by making a separate peace with Macedon (206), but in the Second Macedonian War (200–197) again fought alongside Rome. Annoyed at the slight reward it gained for this, it urged Antiochus III of Syria to invade Greece (193) and joined him against Rome. Finally defeated in 189, the league never regained power or importance.

AFDAL IBN BADR AL-JAMALI, AL, ABU'L-QASIM SHAHINSHAH (c. 1066–1121), succeeded his father as vizier of the Fatimid caliph of Egypt in March–April 1094. On the death of the caliph at Mustansir in the same year, Al-Afdal raised to the throne not Nizar, the eldest son of the dead prince, but a younger, who ruled thereafter (1094–1101) as the Caliph Al-Musta'li. This change in the succession to the throne led to a schism in the Isma'ili movement. Al-Afdal was unable to prevent the First Crusade from taking Jerusalem in 1099. He did, however, maintain in southern Palestine a bridgehead, centred round the fortress of Ascalon, which served to protect the approaches to Egypt and to the Hijaz. The son of Al-Musta'li, the caliph Al-Amir, brought about the death of Al-Afdal in 1121, after he had dominated the affairs of Egypt with great skill for some 27 years.

AFFAIRE DU BONNET, dispute over precedent and procedure between the magistrates of the *parlement* of Paris and the peers. The central issue was whether or not the first president of the *parlement* should remove his official hat or *mortier* when addressing the peers in the court and whether or not the latter should remove their hats before replying. The dispute raged fiercely but inconclusively after the death of Louis XIV (1715), each side producing a series of memoranda and pamphlets to argue its case.

AFFONSO I (*reg. c.* 1506–43). King of Kongo, who attempted to gain Portuguese support in modernizing his kingdom, but his efforts were largely in vain, and his reign ended in serious economic and political decline.

The earliest contacts between Kongo and Portugal were established in the reign of Affonso's predecessor Nzinga Nkuwu (João I), who received Portuguese ambassadors, preachers, educationists, masons, and even printers who hoped to impart scholarly and spiritual aspects of European culture to the peoples of Kongo. Kongo found difficulty in paying for the goods and services thus received. Resentment at the challenge to traditional values of law and religion was also strong, and by the end of João's reign the kingdom was split between the traditionalists and the modernizers. Affonso defeated the traditionalists to gain the kingship and for about 40 years maintained a court which was outwardly Christian.

Despite his success in maintaining control over the people of his large kingdom, he was increasingly frustrated by the failure of Portuguese support. The missionaries and teachers that he required to introduce European education were never supplied in numbers adequate to make more than a small impact on the people of the capital. Portuguese sent to the kingdom rapidly found that they could make good profits by privately engaging in the slave trade, which increasingly became the only product of Kongo in which Portugal was interested.

The key to Portuguese domination in its partnership with Kongo was its possession of sea-going ships. Affonso never succeeded in participating even in the carrying trade to the off-shore island of São Thomé, let alone in the international trade of the Atlantic. The Portuguese allowed him to establish tenuous relations with the papacy, and his son Henrique was appointed a bishop by Leo X; but relations with other European nations were prevented.

By the time of his death he had succeeded in maintaining the unity of his kingdom despite the pressures of a rapidly changing society, but had failed to build up any economic alternative to dependence on the export of labour, and this rapidly proved disastrous in the years after his death.

J. Vansina, *Kingdoms of the Savannah* (Madison, 1966).
G. Balandier, *Daily Life in the Kingdom of Kongo* (London, 1968). DBB

AFFRY, LOUIS, Comte d' (1743–1810), Swiss noble in command of the Swiss troops in French pay until their dissolution (1792). Napoleon later appointed him (1803) his main agent in controlling the Swiss Confederation.

AFGHAN WARS. The First Anglo-Afghan War (1839–42) arose from British fears of the establishment of Russo-Persian influence on the British Indian borders and took the form of the replacement of the existing Barakzay rulers of Kabul and Kandahar by a pro-British ruler, Shah Shuja'al-Mulk, supported by British and Indian troops and advised by a British envoy, Sir W. H. Macnaghten. Frequent risings took place against this unpopular government, culminating in a major revolt (Nov. 1841), in which the British garrison from Kabul was destroyed while retreating to Jalalabad. Although Kabul was later recovered, British troops were then evacuated.

The Second Anglo-Afghan War (1878–81) arose from fears of Russian influence in Afghanistan. A British force occupied Kabul, expelled Amir Shir Ali, and made the treaty of Gandamak (1879) with his son and successor, Yaqub, establishing British control of Afghan foreign relations and a British Resident, Sir Louis Cavagnari, in Kabul. Cavagnari was murdered and a new anti-British rising took place. Afghanistan was reconquered after campaigns which included a British defeat at Maiwand by Ayub Khan and General Roberts's famous march from Kabul to relieve the garrison at Kandahar. British forces were eventually withdrawn following an agreement with a new amir, Abd al-Rahman, to exclude Russian influence.

The Third Anglo-Afghan War (1919) arose from the wishes of the new King of Afghanistan, Amanullah, to throw off British control and divert attention from domestic problems. Amanullah's attack on British territory was easily repulsed, but at the treaty of Rawalpindi (1919), Britain abandoned her attempt to control Afghan foreign relations. MEY

AFRICA, ASSOCIATION FOR PROMOTING THE DISCOVERY OF THE INTERIOR PARTS OF, founded in 1788 in England. It sponsored Mungo Park's exploration in search of the Niger and that of Frederick Horneman (1798), who died in Nupe after travelling overland from Cairo in Muslim disguise. In 1830 the association became the Royal Geographical Society.

AFRICA. ROMAN. The province formed by the Romans after the destruction of Carthage in 146 BC, which ultimately covered roughly the area of modern Tunisia. Numidia was added by Julius Caesar, but later administered separately, and Mauretania was annexed and formed into two separate provinces by Claudius.

Governed from Carthage, and refounded as a Roman colony by Augustus, it received many Italian immigrants and became proverbial for its agricultural prosperity. There were several large imperial and private estates in the province and also a notable density of towns, both Roman settlements, *eg*, Thuburto Maius and Veneria Sicca, and native communities which became Romanized, *eg*, Thugga and Maktar. Corn, olive oil, marble, timber, and animals were important exports. Many Africans achieved high rank in the imperial administration. Christianity spread more rapidly than elsewhere in the west, producing such notable figures as Tertullian, Cyprian, and Augustine. Roman Africa was conquered by the Vandals in the 5th cent.

AFRICAN BRONZE OR BRASS SCULPTURE has been known in West Africa for over 1000 years, and examples of a variety of styles are found in the Ivory Coast, Ghana, Dahomey, Nigeria, Chad, and Cameroons. The most ancient and remarkable bronzes or brasses have been those of Nigeria, where the sculptural arts of Benin and Ife rank as among the best in the world.

Knowledge of metallurgy may have entered West Africa from two directions: down the Nile valley by way of Meroe; and from North Africa (possibly through Carthage) across the western Sahara by the routes marked by the pictures of chariots on desert rocks, for Ife and Benin archaeologists have noted the northern provenance of such cultural associations as horses, impluvia, and potsherd pavements, better known in Africa north of the Sahara or above the forest belt.

Iron-working preceded the knowledge of metal sculpture in sub-Saharan Africa. Thus while the iron-working culture of Nok in central Nigeria may have received iron by 500 BC, the earliest dated bronzes of Igbo-Ukwu in east-central Nigeria have extreme terminal dates of AD. 560–1130. The bronzes of Benin (stated by oral tradition to be derived from the art of Ife) date from about the mid-13th cent. or earlier; small bronze finds at Daima, Bornu, belong to stratigraphical levels dated to the 10th cent. and earlier. Most other West African and Nigerian bronzes (such as those of the Tsoede group of the Niger/Benue confluence, and in the Niger delta) have been found on the surface or at secondary sites, and undated.

Spectrographic analyses have shown significant variations in the metallic composition of West African bronzes. Igbo-Ukwu bronzes divide into two groups: those of copper, and those of lead and tin. Most Benin sculptures are of brass (copper, zinc, lead) or bronze (copper, lead, tin) with more lead than tin. Ife bronzes are of copper or heavily leaded brass with varying proportions of zinc, lead, and tin. The Sao bronzes from Chad and finds from Dawu, Ghana, are also of mixed brass and copper with differing proportions of other minerals (including iron, nickel, arsenic, and manganese).

The variations in the alloy were apparently not always the result of chance or of ignorance of metallurgy; the differences in composition suggest different sources of supply. The most ancient West African bronzes are believed to have been made out of metal from the Sahara or North Africa; later supplies to the guild of Benin bronze-casters were brought from the Congo by the Portuguese in the form, mainly of manillas. The most significant technique in West African bronze sculpture was the process of casting by the *cire perdue* or 'lost wax' method.

West African bronze sculpture was essentially a 'court'

art, serving mainly commemorative, ritual, and ceremonial functions. Thus the large and impressive collections of Ife and Benin belonged to the forest kingdoms at these centres, and the Igbo-Ukwu bronzes possibly to a divine king or *Eze Nri*.

Bronze sculpture was an integral part of African artistic tradition going back through antiquity to the terracottas of Nok, and to the wood and stone sculptures of other localities and times. Neither the naturalism of Ife nor the stylization of other schools have been proved to derive from outside Africa.

Thurstan Shaw, *Excavation in Dawu* (London, 1961).
Frank Willett, *Ife in the History of West African Sculpture* (London, 1967). EJA

AFRICAN INSTITUTION (1807), founded in London after the abolition of the slave trade to work for the civilizing of Africa and the Africans, and to watch for evasions of the Abolition Act. Its real importance was that it held together the anti-slavery movement at a time when it might have disintegrated.

AFRICAN NATIONAL CONGRESS, founded in 1912, as the South African Native National Congress. It united a number of regional political associations among Africans. The leaders were mainly western-educated, Christian, and middle-class. Their objectives were to unite African opinion and bring their disabilities to the attention of whites through deputations, overseas delegations, and demonstrations. They believed that constitutional advance could be achieved through rational argument, on the model of 19th-cent. Britain. Although there was always an activist strain with congress, reasoned moderation was its hallmark until 1948. By then, however, it was clear that its protests against specific grievances, such as the Natives Land Act (1913), the Native Representation Act (1936), and the Pass Laws, went unheeded. With the rapid urbanization of Africans during the 1930s and 1940s, a more militant mood began to permeate congress, manifested by the formation of the left-wing Youth League. In 1949, the Youth League nominated its candidate for the presidency of congress and its programme of action was adoped. These changes, and the onslaught of the Nationalist government on Africans after 1948, brought congress mass support for the first time. The 1950s witnessed a series of passive resistance campaigns unprecedented in South Africa, notably the defiance campaign of 1951, undertaken jointly with the Indian National Congress, and the Congress of the People (1955), which brought together all the resistance movements and formulated a 'Freedom Charter'. This co-operation with non-African movements led to a split in 1958; those who felt the Africans should 'go it alone' then formed the Pan-African Congress. After growing disturbances, congress was banned in 1960 and its leaders forced underground or into exile.

AFRICAN ROCK ART is to be found in many parts of the continent and is often associated with Stone Age cultures, though it is a form of art which has survived until today. The best known paintings are at Tassili in the Sahara and those of the Bushmen in South Africa. They are painted on rock faces, sometimes in caves, and natural ochre colours are used, the outline sometimes being incised into the rock for greater permanence. Another method is the pecking out of chips of rock within an outline, the picture in this case being left uncoloured. Apart from their interest as examples of art, often skilled both in design and in expressive line showing a high degree of artistic competence, they are most informative, often showing animals in areas where they no longer exist, and the kind of life that led.

The rock paintings at Tassili and other rocky outcrops in the Sahara span a long period of time, the earliest having an assumed date of *c.* 6000 BC, and the later ones after *c.* 200 BC, for they show the camel, which did not come into Africa until about this time. Among this fine series of paintings men and women are shown leading their lives as hunters or cattle owners, in battle, and on domestic and social occasions, and a study of the pictures gives a fairly detailed impression of how the Saharan peoples lived. The same is true of the Bushmen paintings, which are more numerous, and show every aspect of life from hunting and fishing to meetings and other social events. The wealth of detail is such that their appearance, daily life and activities, social attitudes and organizations can all be inferred, and, in this sense, rock paintings are historical evidence as well as works of art.

MS

AFRIDIS, a large and powerful Pathan tribe on the north-west frontier of Pakistan inhabiting the northern half of Tirah and the Khyber pass. They constantly attacked Mughal troops and caravans passing through the Khyber to Kabul and later raided the settled districts of British India. The most contumacious of their clans were the Zakka Khels. In 1881, in return for allowances, the Afridis accepted responsibility for the safety of the Khyber route. In 1898 the Khyber Rifles were placed under British officers. Afridi raids on the British borders led to a punitive expedition in 1908. The danger of an Afridi rising during the First World War was averted by doubling their allowances. After the Third Afghan War (1919), the Khyber Rifles were disbanded. Their allowances were increased during the construction of the Khyber railway. Since 1947 the government of Pakistan has been responsible for the control of the Afridis.

AFRIKAANS, language derived from the Dutch of the original white settlers in South Africa. It retains much Netherlandic vocabulary, but the grammar has been greatly modified.

AFRIKANER PEOPLE. Numbering about 57 per cent of the 3,800,000 whites in South Africa, the Afrikaners are descended from the Dutch, German, and French Huguenot settlers who immigrated to the Cape between 1652 and the end of the 18th cent. By the time Britain occupied the Cape during the Napoleonic Wars, the cattle ranchers, or Boers, had moved into the interior, a process accelerated by the Great Trek (1835–7). By the end of the 19th cent. Afrikaners were a minority of the white population only in Natal.

Afrikaner nationalism was a reaction to British domination, and a response to the opposition of Africans to white settlement. In the Cape the Afrikaner Bond, the first real political party in South Africa, was founded in 1880. The Boer War became a nationalist struggle against British imperialism, and the loss of republican independence, and certain features of the war, such as the British concentration camps for women and children, provided a great impetus for Afrikaner sentiment, which became more extreme in the 1930s under the impact of the Depression and, to some extent, of European fascism. Not until 1948, however, was the first wholly Afrikaner government voted into power.

The political manifestations of Afrikaner nationalism are intertwined with the cultural. Both have a solid base in the Dutch Reformed Church, which provides a theological assurance in determinism and a social in elitism. Afrikaner culture is a compound of Calvinism, a love of the language, which has produced some fine literature, and a sense of history so distorted as to be almost mythical. Africans can participate in this civilization only as inferiors, and can never be full members of the *volk*. There is much that appears implausible and naive in Afrikaner nationalist culture, the product of a people who have developed in a special historical environment, and who believe themselves to be unique. It is difficult to conceive that this culture could thrive anywhere but in South Africa.

Sheila Patterson, *The Last Trek* (London, 1957).
F. A. van Jaarsveld, *The Awakening of Afrikaner Nationalism* (Cape Town, 1961). AEA

AFRIQUE FRANÇAISE, COMITÉ DE L'. Founded in 1890 under the presidency of Prince d'Aremberg, this was a society formed to promote African exploration. It was an imperialist pressure group, intended to counteract official inertia, and was particularly interested in the attempt to unite French Saharan colonies with the French Congo.

AFZAL KHAN (d. 1659), title of Abdullah Bhatari, general in the service of the Adil Shahi dynasty of Bijapur. He distinguished himself in campaigns against the Mughals and in 1659 was sent with an army to subdue the rising Maratha chief, Sivaji. Preferring negotiations to fighting, he agreed to an interview with only one attendant on each side. In a scuffle which followed, he was killed by Sivaji's use of the steel device known as the *waghnakh* or tiger's claw. This incident was later glorified by the nationalist Maratha politician Tilak, and became a fruitful source of Hindu–Muslim ill-feeling.

AGA KHAN III, AGA SULTAN MUHAMMAD SHAH (1875–1957), head of the Khoja Ismaili community, Indian politician, and diplomat. Wealthy and well educated, he was able to move between influential circles in India and Europe and thus to play an important part in representing Muslim political interests, although he was limited in the policies that he was prepared to espouse. In his first period of political activity in India (1902–13), he was active in the Muhammadan Educational Conference, sat on the Viceroy's Legislative Council (1902–4), led the Muslim deputation to Lord Minto (1 Oct. 1906), which asked for separate representation for Muslims in the legislatures, helped in the formation of the All-India Muslim League (1906) and acted as its permanent president (1907–13). He resigned as its president in 1913 because of the nationalist tendency within the League and played little part in its affairs during the period of Congress–League rapprochement and Khilafat activity. He reappeared as president of the conservative All Parties Muslim Conference (Dec. 1928) and in a second period of Indian activity, led the Muslim delegation to the Round Table Conferences (1930–2), where he was instrumental in securing agreement on representation among the minorities on which the Communal Award (1932) was based and which secured Muslim separate electorates. He was leader of the Indian delegation to the League of Nations in the mid-1930s, and was elected president of the Assembly (1937–8).

AGADE, capital of Akkad under its founder, Sargon (c. 2334—2279 BC). Its location is unknown.

AGADÈS, chief town of the Aïr region of the central Sahara. It was founded c. 1413 as a seat for the Tuareg sultans of Aïr at a vital commercial crossroads between Egypt and the Niger Bend and between North Africa and the Hausa States. At the height of its prosperity it may have had 10,000 inhabitants but now has fewer than half that number.

AGADIR CRISIS (1911). One of the international crises which led to the strengthening of the Anglo-French entente before 1914. In 1911 the French occupied Fez in Morocco, and Kaiser William II, arguing that this action nullified the Algeciras Act, sent a gunboat, the *Panther*, to Agadir to protect the interest of German nationals. This proved to be the opening move of a bargaining proposal whereby Germany offered to leave France free in Morocco but claimed compensation for this in the Congo. Britain strongly supported France. In the end Germany withdrew, disclaiming interest in the coast of Morocco and also reducing her claims in the Congo.

AGAJA (1679–1740), fourth ruler of the West African kingdom of Dahomey founded c. 1620. Dynamic and inventive, he greatly extended the territorial power of Dahomey, strengthened peace at home, and effectively regulated relations with European traders on his seaboard. He is remembered as the originator of new policies and tactics in a political system which became famous for its strongly centralized power. His intelligence service was unusually good, and his army partly professional. Thus equipped, he moved on his coastal neighbours and rivals in 1724, first conquering Allada (Ardrah) and then Ouidah (Whydah). This breakthrough to the coast provoked strong reprisals from the alafin or king of the empire of Oyo, who was accustomed to regard himself as suzerain of the territory which became Dahomey; and Abomey, the kingdom's capital, was burned down four times during Oyo invasions. Relations continued to be hostile, but Agaja and his successors remained supreme along their seaboard, first attempting to reduce the export of captives sold into slavery, and then to control this export for their own benefit.

AGAMEMNON, son of Atreus and King of Mycenae *c.* 1200 BC. Oral epic tradition first recorded in the 8th cent., as in Homer's *Iliad*, told in poetic and unhistorical detail of his leadership of the Achaean (*ie*, Greek) host against Troy.

AGAMENTICUS, English settlement in Maine, US (1624). It was the first municipal corporation in America (1642).

AGASSIZ, JEAN LOUIS RODOLPHE (1807–73), Swiss-born zoologist and geologist. He emigrated to the US (1846), was appointed to the chair of Natural History at Harvard (1848), and founded the Museum of Comparative Zoology (1859). His reputation suffered when he became a leading opponent of Darwin's evolutionary theories.

AGATHOCLES, tyrant of Syracuse (317–289 BC), first Sicilian Greek leader to take the war with Carthage into Africa and the last to play an independent role in Mediterranean politics. Winning power with the support of the masses, he maintained it by the violent suppression of the wealthy, earning the hostility of their friends in other cities, who called in Carthage. Confined to Syracuse, his reply (310) was to invade Africa, where he captured Utica and harassed Carthage, until peace was made (306), enabling him to subdue his Greek enemies. Thereafter he ruled moderately and Syracuse and other cities, *eg*, Gela, achieved new prosperity.

AGBEBI, MOJOLA (1860–1917). For many years Agbebi played a significant role in the social, religious, literary, and political life of Yorubaland in particular, and of West Africa in general, during the colonial period. First and foremost an evangelist, he saw in Christianity both a means of salvation for Africans and of opposition to colonial rule. Connected with the Native Baptist Church, the first breakaway African Church in Nigeria, over which he presided till his death, he evolved a theology and a liturgy related to the Nigerian milieu without sacrificing the tenets of Christianity.

Agbebi believed that religious independence by Africans, through independent churches, would automatically result in political independence. A gifted orator and eloquent debater, an author of pamphlets, and editor of all contemporary Lagos newspapers at one time or another, his talents and activities were admired throughout English-speaking West Africa and the US, where 11 Oct. was named Agbebi Day by Negroes in gratitude for his activities. He was a vice-president of the Lagos Auxiliary of the Aborigines Protection Society (1910–1913), and the first president of the Yoruba Association (1914–17), nucleus of the Nigerian Baptist Convention.

AGE OF CONSENT ACT (INDIA), 1891, forbade the consummation of marriage before the wife had attained the age of 12. It was passed despite the violent opposition of Hindu orthodoxy led by Tilak in Poona and the Hindus of Calcutta, who contended that the act was contrary to Hindu religion and customs.

AGE OF GREATNESS in Sweden (1611–1718), period in which the Swedes built up and defended a Baltic empire. Apart from the strength of their national army, ably led by soldier kings, their chief resource was their copper and high-grade iron industry. By 1700 Sweden–Finland contained only one-half of the population of the Swedish empire, which was therefore almost bound to succumb to the pressure of more populous neighbours.

AGE OF REASON, term used to describe the Enlightenment, or less commonly the intellectual life of the age of Descartes. Most authorities stress the metaphysical elements in the latter era and prefer to use the term for the succeeding age. Reason is seen as a key concept in the Enlightenment, although the meaning then given to it was rather different from that which is current today. Reason was held to be a built-in faculty of man rather than an analytical method, and in fact much of the 'reason' of the Enlightenment consisted of a priori ideas. Moreover, the emphasis on rationality was increasingly called into question during the later 18th cent.

AGENCY FOR INTERNATIONAL DEVELOPMENT, established (1961) as an agency of the US department of state to promote economic development and raise living standards in underdeveloped friendly countries. Loans for long-term development are supported by a programme of grants for educational projects, and by investment guaranties to encourage participation by private enterprise.

AGESILAUS. King of Sparta (*reg.* 398–360 BC), the most assertive for a century, whose career immensely damaged Sparta and Greece. Winning the disputed succession to his brother, Agis II, with Lysander's help, he quickly discarded him after taking over the war in Asia Minor against the Persians (396). There he achieved some success and may have hoped to conquer the hinterland, but was recalled, when the Persians retaliated by stirring up the Corinthian War in Greece. Defeating the Thebans on his way home at Coronea (394), he subsequently campaigned inconclusively around Corinth (391–390). Opposed perhaps to the surrender of the Asiatic Greeks to Persia in the King's Peace (387), he readily enforced its terms on Sparta's enemies and then supported interference in Mantinea, Phlius, and Olynthus and the treacherous capture of Thebes (382). When Thebes broke free, he fought unsuccessfully in Boeotia and after Sphodrias' raid on Attica favoured his acquittal, which provoked Athens to war (378). At the peace conference of 371 he wrangled with the Theban Epaminondas, striking the Thebans from the treaty; the result was the Theban victory over the Spartans at Leuctra and the end of Spartan supremacy in the Peloponnese. In his old age Agesilaus helped to rally Spartan resistance to Thebes, but was defeated by Epaminondes at Mantinea (362) and died after leading a mercenary army to Egypt.

AGESIPOLIS. Spartan king (*reg.* 395–380 BC), son of Pausanias and colleague of Agesilaus, whose aggressive foreign policy he opposed in the period after the King's Peace (? 387). Sent to take over the siege of Olynthus in 381, he died before its conclusion.

AGGREY, JAMES EMMANUEL KWEGYIR (1875–1927), Ghanaian educationist, orator, and man of letters. Born at Anomabu, the son of a gold-taker, he obtained a higher education in the US, and afterwards served on the two Phelps–Stokes Commissions (1920–1 1924–5), sponsored in the US for enquiry into the conditions of education for Africans in West, East, and South Africa. He urged an African cultural renaissance, and argued for black–white co-operation on a basis of equality of rights and respect.

AGHA (with the general meaning of 'lord, master'), title given, in the Ottoman empire, to numerous officials, most of them belonging to the household and to the armed forces of the sultan, *eg, Kapi Aghasi* (the Agha of the Gate, *ie*, the Chief of the White Eunuchs) or *Yeniceri Aghasi* (the Agha of the Janissaries). The term also occasionally signifies 'eunuch'.

AGHA MUHAMMAD SHAH (1742–97), founder of the Qajar dynasty in Persia. Becoming chief of the Qajar Turcomans on the death of his father in 1758, Agha Muhammad was engaged, from 1779, in a long conflict with the princes descended from Karim Khan, the Shah of Persia. By 1785, when Tehran became the centre of his power, Agha Muhammad controlled most of central and northern Persia. He crushed Lutf Ali Khan, the last descendant of Karim Khan, in 1794, restored Persian influence over Georgia in 1795, became Shah of Persia in 1796, and then seized Khurasan from Shahrukh, the grandson of Nadir Shah. Agha Muhammad was an able statesman and soldier, but also cruel and vindictive in temperament. He was killed by an assassin.

AGHLABIDS, dynasty ruling Ifriqiyya in the 9th cent., which typified the crisis of the Abbasid empire in the west. The first provincial governors to become independent, they imitated the Abbasids, provoking similar distrust from the religious as a civilian Muslim society arose. On the Muslim frontier, they raided in the central Mediterranean, undertaking a slow conquest of Byzantine Sicily. Continually threatened by a disaffected *jund*, the hereditary Arab army, they abolished it, thereby exposing themselves to the workings of the Isma'ili revolution on the unassimilated Berbers to the west. A Kutama rising ended the dynasty and ushered in the Fatimids (909).

AGIADS, senior of the two Spartan royal houses. Its 6th-cent. BC kings Anaxandridas and Cleomenes were active and powerful, but after the disgrace of Pausanias (*c.* 470) the house was eclipsed for two centuries by the junior Eurypontids.

AGINCOURT, BATTLE OF, fought on 25 Oct. 1415, when a huge French army intercepted Henry V's smaller force of under 6000 on its march from Harfleur to Calais. The heavily armoured French, in attempting to advance in congested masses over a sodden ploughed field, were decimated by the English archers, their losses including many leading French nobles. English losses were probably under 300. Agincourt had no immediate strategic effect, but it gave the English a military ascendancy over the French which lasted until the time of Joan of Arc.

AGIS II, Spartan king (*reg.* 427–399 BC), son of Archidamus I. Censured for failing to press home a well-planned attack on Argos in 418, he restored his prestige with victory at Mantinea. In 413 he organized the fortification of Decelea and frequently led Spartan armies in Attica, joining with Lysander in the siege of Athens (405–404).

AGIS IV (*c.* 262–241 BC), Eurypontid king of Sparta from 244, an ambitious idealist who aimed to restore Spartan power by cancelling mortgages and redistributing land, measures which, invoking tradition, he called a return to Lycurgus' constitution. Though well intentioned, he treated opposition in cavalier fashion, even deposing the conservative board of ephors in 242 and causing the other king, Leonidas, to flee. Such revolutionary methods provoked violent reaction, and Agis perished when Leonidas returned in force and seized power. His ideas lived on, even at Sparta, since his widow Agiatis married Cleomenes III and persuaded him to adopt Agis' plans.

AGNADELLO, BATTLE OF, major defeat of the Venetians on 14 May 1509 by the French under Louis XII near the River Adda in northern Italy. The battle resulted in the loss to France and her allies in the League of Cambrai of most of the subject-towns in northern Italy belonging to Venice.

AGNELLI, Turin family largely responsible for making FIAT one of Italy's greatest industrial complexes. Giovanni Agnelli (1866–1945) abandoned a military career in 1892, and in 1899 helped found the Fabbrica Italiana Automobili Forino (FIAT) company. Under his administration the company diversified its production to include buses, taxis, marine, aero and diesel engines, and ball-bearings (RIV company). Having survived the 1907–8 slump and a law suit (1909–12), in which Agnelli was acquitted of financial malpractices, the company was adapted to military needs, eclipsing all its rivals during the Second World War. Agnelli became president of FIAT in 1920, and in 1923 became a senator. Under Agnelli's autocratic but paternalistic rule FIAT led the way in workers' welfare, which helped his policy of subduing militant unionism after the 1920 occupation of the factories. He helped to finance pro-fascist newspapers and in 1925 bought Turin's *La Stampa*. Sometimes consulted by the regime, he influenced policies on monopolies and protectionism. His son, Giovanni (b. 1921), is partly responsible for recent expansion in southern Italy, and for Russian contracts, but does not exercise his grandfather's autocratic influence.

AGOBARD (769–840), archbishop of Lyon and an influential ecclesiastical statesman during the reign of the Emperor Louis the Pious. He tried to combat the primitive superstitions rampant among the Christians and was the leader of a movement to abolish the use of ordeals and judicial duels in the procedure of both ecclesiastical and secular courts, though these practices were not finally prohibited by the Western Church until 1215.

AGOSTA, BATTLE OF (1676), indecisive naval engagement off the coast of Sicily between the French and ships of the Dutch–Spanish alliance in the Dutch War. The French, commanded by Duquesne, had superior numbers and the allied admiral, De Ruyter, was mortally wounded.

AGRARIAN PARTY in Czechoslovakia, founded at the beginning of the 20th cent., a vigorous peasant party which gave impetus to the Czech national movement before the First World War. In 1925 (by then known as the Czechoslovak Agrarian Party) it became the strongest party in the Czechoslovak state and remained dominant in parliament and government until 1938.

Having achieved its aim of moderate land reform in 1920, the party became increasingly inflexible in protecting the peasant small-holder. After the onset of the depression, by adopting a high tariff policy to protect agriculture, the party weakened the state. Trade was carried out through bilateral agreements, and by barring the Czechoslovak market to agricultural states (through the tariff system), Czechoslovakia caused those states to close their markets to Czechoslovak-manufactured exports in return. This entailed suffering for the German minority in Czechoslovakia, who were dependent on industry; this increased their hostility to the state and thus made Hitler's path easier. At the same time, the anti-communism of the Agrarians served to undermine the validity of Beneš' Soviet alliance (1935)—an alliance which might have guaranteed Czechoslovak security.

In 1945 the majority parties in the coalition government allowed the Communist Party to disband the Agrarian Party, which they regarded as partly responsible for the country's downfall in 1938, and hoped that peasant support would be transferred to their own parties. In fact, the peasant vote was chiefly responsible for the Communist victory in May 1948.

AGRARIAN REFORM ISSUE IN LATIN AMERICA, a socioeconomic issue which first arose after the early 19th-cent. independence movements in Spanish America. The reforms with which it was concerned failed to start, however, until the Mexican Revolution of 1910. In the 20th cent. vigorous attacks were made by reformist and leftist elements on 19th-cent. *latifundismo, ie*, the policy of using semi-servile labour to work large underdeveloped land holdings. Limited land ownership was generally extended following independence.

In Argentina the vast Pampa was divided in the early 19th cent. The 1850s witnessed the beginnings of the attack on *latifundismo*, particularly on corporate (church and village) ownership.

Mexico launched an attack on *latifundismo* in 1910. Land reform would mean freedom from debt peonage to the *latifundistas*. Article 27 of the Mexican constitution of 1917 provided for the redistribution of communal land to villages, rather than as private holdings. This solution was attempted until 1940, when continuing grants were made to individual villagers. The *ejidol* (communal) solution had failed to solve the problems of the farmers. By 1940 lands totalling roughly 283,000 sq. kms had been allotted to villages containing in all over 2 million heads of families. By 1967 over 50 per cent of the productive land of Mexico had been distributed among 20,000 new *ejidos*, or village communal holdings. One-fifth of the latter were being worked collectively. Though population growth had kept ahead of land reform, Mexico was cited as a model throughout Latin America of how to implement a land reform programme.

The revolutionary path was also pursued in Bolivia, where armed farmers seized lands (1952) and were subsequently granted titles by a reformist regime. The Cuban revolution of 1958–9 promised land reform also and two extensive reorganizations of agriculture were carried out. The first (1959) parcelled out lands seized from foreigners and Cuban *latifundistas*, and the second (1962) created states farms. The change was far too rapid and agricultural production declined radically. The Cuban example has stirred more lethargic regimes into action. Since 1960 Venezuela, Colombia, Brazil, Chile, and Peru have begun gradual, non-revolutionary land reform programmes.

HDS

AGRARIAN UNION (Bulgaria), the political organization of the Bulgarian peasantry. Founded in 1900 by Dimitar Dragiev, it steadily gained strength before the First World War to emerge as the strongest party in the elections of Aug. 1919, from which a government was formed under Alexander Stambuliski in Oct. 1919. The Agrarian government followed the party's programme, redistributing land, initiating legal and fiscal reforms, and pursuing a peaceful foreign policy. But Stambuliski's regime fell foul of the army and the International Macedonian Revolutionary Organization (IMRO) over its Macedonian policy and was ousted by a violent coup on 9 June 1923, although its popular support had been confirmed in the April elections. The party split in two. Followers of Stambuliski fled to Belgrade and returned in 1933 to form the liberal faction, called *Pladne* (*Mid-day*), after their journal. A conservative faction grouped itself round Dimitar Gichev, and participated in the National Bloc government (1931–4), but the *Pladne* group remained in opposition. In 1942 the group joined the Fatherland Front and in Sep. 1944 both factions entered the government, though the conservatives were quickly expelled. The Agrarian Union, now led by Nikola Petkov of the *Pladne* group, became the chief opponents of communism. The communists used a faction of the Agrarians led by Alexander Obbov, also of the *Pladne* group, to undermine the party. Petkov, however, kept the support of the electorate and enjoyed the protection of the Allies. In 1945–6 the Soviet government blocked efforts made by the Bulgarian Communist Party to reach agreement with Petkov's Agrarians. Meanwhile, Petkov's criticism of the communists grew more outspoken. Finally, Petkov and his supporters were arrested, tried, and executed (Sept. 1947). Although Obbov's group remained in the government, the Agrarian Union had been eliminated from politics.

'AGREEMENT OF THE PEOPLE' (1647), pamphlet by John Lilburne asserting the Levellers' doctrines of the sovereignty of the people, universal manhood suffrage, and religious toleration. It was supported by agitators in Cromwell's army, and although he punished the ringleaders, he was afterwards committed to a more radical programme that included the execution of Charles I. Lilburne reissued the 'Agreement' in 1649 in protest against the Rump Parliament.

AGRICOLA (AD 40–93), distinguished Roman governor who completed the conquest of northern Britain (78–84), known chiefly from a memoir by Tacitus, his son-in-law. Earlier experience in Britain as military tribune during Boudicca's revolt (60) and as legionary commander (70–73) fitted him for the governorship after his consulate (77). After mopping up resistance in Wales he subjugated the Brigantes and completed his campaigns by crushing native resistance in Scotland, led by Calgacus at Mons Graupius (84). Recalled for triumphal honours at Rome, he retired in ill-health and died without further appointment. His military strategy involved building 1300 miles of roads and was characterized by shrewd topographical sense and co-ordinated action by land and sea. His administration was noted for integrity and encouraging Romanization.

AGRICOLA, GEORG BAUER (1490–1555), German scholar and mineralogist whose *De re Metallica* (1556) was an early masterpiece of technological writing of a descriptive nature, reflecting the late medieval tradition in applied science. In this he discussed mining methods, described the assaying of ores, the processes of preparing and smelting them, and the testing of base metals for gold and silver. He wrote in good Latin, using copious classical quotations. It was this work which Newton consulted when investigating the chemistry of metals. Agricola also wrote on other scientific subjects, *eg*, *On the Nature of Fossils*. His knowledge of industrial chemistry was acquired when he worked as a physician in the mining towns of Joachimsthal in Bohemia and Chemnitz in Saxony.

AGRICULTURAL ADJUSTMENT ACTS (1933 and 1938). The 1933 act was part of an early US New Deal programme designed to alleviate distress in the agricultural community by restricting output through the raising of prices. Farmers were authorized to enter into agreements for the reduction of acreage, and farm incomes were to be re-established on a parity with industrial incomes by subsidies paid from a processing tax. The Agricultural Adjustment Administration, set up within the Department of Agriculture, was the supervisory authority. The slaughter of 9 million pigs and the ploughing under of growing crops in order to raise prices during the interim period before the quota system came into effect aroused an outcry from those who misunderstood or would not accept the economic principles involved. The act was declared unconstitutional by the Supreme Court in *US v. Butler* (1936).

The act of 1938 was designed to replace the 1933 act. Farmers participating in soil conservation programmes were to receive payments out of general revenue, and marketing quota criteria were established, as part of the 'ever-normal granary' programme to stockpile surplus commodities until market factors raised prices.

AGRICULTURAL DEPRESSION (1870s). The basic reason for the depression is to be found in foreign competition, itself the result of improved transport facilities. In the pre-railway age the movement, at competitive prices, of bulky goods such as wheat could only come from areas close to water transport. The ending of the American Civil War and the opening of the Middle West by railways made the cheap export of wheat to western Europe possible. At the same time there was development of exports from eastern Europe, from South America, and from Australia. Import of frozen meat from Argentina was made practicable by the use of refrigeration. The depression was to some extent common to western Europe, Germany suffering from eastern European competition, and France and Britain from American. France and Germany used their tariffs to meet the threat, but in Britain the tradition of free trade was too firmly established to allow for such a solution.

The extent of the depression in Britain is uncertain. The effect on wheat was severe, prices falling from an average of £2·80 (56s) a quarter in 1867–71 to £1·36 (27s 3d) in 1894–8, but the effect on other cereals was rather less. Prices of home-produced meat and dairy produce fell by about 10 per cent in the last 20 years of the century, while milk prices remained stable. Many factors must be taken into account in assessing the effects on agriculture. Cheaper cereals reduced the cost of feeding stuffs and thus reduced the cost of dairy produce. The increasing population, the reduced amount which people needed to spend on bread, and the rising real wages of the end of the 19th cent. combined to stimulate the demand for a better and more varied diet. More money was being spent on meat, milk, eggs, fruit, and vegetables. It has been suggested that, from the repeal of the Corn Laws (1846) onwards, arable farming had tended to be less profitable than pasture farming, and that the depression of the 1870s accentuated this trend.

Nevertheless, in parts of England the depression had marked effects. It encouraged the conversion of farms from arable to pasture. It meant farming bankruptcies, reductions of rents, and loss of income to landowners. It did not lead in general to the break-up of landed estates, but it was probably one of a number of factors leading to a decline in political influence of the landed aristocracy. It also had effects in Ireland in intensifying agrarian unrest and providing the basis of the Home Rule movement.

Christabel S. Orwin and Edith H. Whetham, *History of British Agriculture, 1846–1914* (London, 1964).   LMB

AGRICULTURAL GUIDANCE AND GUARANTEE FUND, established under the EEC, is financed by levies on imported foodstuffs and by contributions from national governments and is disbursed in order to compensate for the effects of common agricultural prices and to provide for agricultural improvement. The fund, an integral part of the common agricultural policy, touches two politically sensitive areas—the regulation of agriculture, and the degree of financial control in the hands of the community rather than national governments. In consequence it has always been the subject of intensive bargaining, of which the most important sessions were in Dec. 1963 (when the fund came into operation retrospectively from 1962) and in Jan.–Feb. 1966. Its operation was partially suspended following the devaluation of the franc in Aug. 1969.

AGRICULTURAL MARKETING ACT, 1931, formed part of the restrictionist economic policies of the British government in the 1930s. It authorized producers to fix prices and market their products, and to impose their regulations on dissenting producers.

AGRICULTURAL SOCIETIES, FRANCE. These were founded for the promotion of scientific agriculture, the earliest (1739) by the estates of Brittany. From 1761 they were promoted by the central government. As Arthur Young showed in his *Travels in France* (1792), they had little influence, the peasants, generally speaking, lacking capital for improvements, and the wealthier classes, unlike their English counterparts, being unwilling to invest in agriculture.

AGRIPPA, M. VIPSANIUS (*c.* 63–12 BC), leading general and *éminence grise* of the Augustan Principate at Rome. Of unknown parentage and origin, Agrippa was the same age as Augustus, with whom he returned to Italy from Apollonia after Julius Caesar's murder. In the wars by which Augustus won supreme power (44–30) the strategy, tactics, and field command were Agrippa's. Closely associated with Augustus in his public works programme and in the constitutional settlements of 27 and 23, he became in 18 almost co-regent with Augustus, divorcing his second wife, Marcella, to marry Julia, Augustus' daughter, by whom he had five children, including Gaius and Lucius Caesar, subsequently adopted by Augustus as his intended heirs. In 13 Agrippa went to Pannonia to complete the conquest of Illyricum, but died the next year in Italy.

AGRIPPA POSTUMUS (12 BC–AD 14), third and youngest son of Agrippa and Julia, adopted by Augustus in AD 4 after the death of Gaius Caesar. He was banished in 7, perhaps to clarify Tiberius' position as Augustus' successor, and murdered immediately after Augustus' death.

AGRIPPINA THE ELDER (*c.* 14 BC–AD 33), daughter of Marcus Agrippa and Julia, daughter and only child of the Emperor Augustus. In AD 5 she married Germanicus, nephew of the later Emperor Tiberius, by whom she had six sons and nine daughters. After the death of Germanicus (19) she and her family were involved in political struggles at Rome about the succession to Tiberius. Accused of treason and banished (29), she starved to death in 33. Nevertheless, her youngest son Gaius (Caligula) became emperor in 37.

AGRIPPINA THE YOUNGER (*c.* AD 16–59), eldest daughter of Agrippina the Elder and Germanicus, and mother of Nero. She married Cn. Domitius Ahenobarbus (28) and their son was born in 37. Exiled in 39 by her brother Caligula on charges of adultery and conspiracy, she was recalled by Claudius (41) and, already twice widowed, induced him to marry her (49). Beautiful and ambitious, she persuaded Claudius to adopt Nero (50) and was generally believed to have poisoned Claudius (54) to ensure her son's succession. She attempted to dominate Nero's principate, but was prevented by Seneca and Burrus, and in 59 Nero had her murdered because of her attempts to interfere in the government and his private life.

AGROGOROD (agro-town), proposed institutional arrangement for Soviet agriculture put forward by Khrushchev in 1949, under which farm workers would live in apartment blocks as in cities, with their private plots grouped together in a large common area. The proposal was attacked in *Pravda* and at the XIXth Party Congress, after which it was dropped, to be revived by Khrushchev in 1958. The plan had been tried, notably in the Ukraine, under a different name.

AGUASCALIENTES, CONVENTION OF, meeting of Mexican revolutionaries in Oct. 1914 to heal the split within the constitutionalist movement. Venustiano Carranza and Pancho Villa (Doroteo Arango), who headed the disputing factions, were not personally present. Eulalio Gutiérrez was named provisional president. He chose Villa as commander-in-chief, since the convention was a captive of the latter. The convention failed to resolve major differences and civil war followed when Carranza refused to accept the consequences.

AGUESSEAU, HENRI-FRANÇOIS D' (1668–1751), statesman, scholar, and the leading French jurist of his age. D'Aguesseau became the *avocat-général* in the *parlement* of Paris in 1690 and *procureur-général* in 1700. He played a leading role in the religious disputes of the last years of Louis XIV's reign, resolutely opposing the king's attempts to browbeat the *parlement* into an unqualified acceptance of the papal bull *Unigenitus* which condemned the tenets of Jansenism. He was willing to risk personal disgrace to defend what he considered to be the correct legal position, an attitude which he maintained throughout his career. In 1717 d'Aguesseau became chancellor, an office bestowed for life, so that although he resigned the seals in 1750 he remained chancellor until his death in Feb. 1751.

For 60 years d'Aguesseau played an important political role, especially in the protracted financial and religious quarrels between the government and the *parlement* during the Regency (1715–23) and under the regime of Cardinal Fleury (1726–43). He was a prolific writer on politics and law, his collected works extending to 13 volumes. He was also a great bibliophile and his enormous library acquired a European reputation.

AGUINALDO, EMILIO FAMY (1869–1964), president of the short-lived first Philippine Republic inaugurated in 1899. He was educated at a Dominican school for boys and later by private tutors. He engaged in trade before being elected in 1894 as *Capitan Municipal* of his home town, Kawit, in Cavite province. A few months later he was inducted into the *Katipunan* by its head, Andres Bonifacio, whose leadership of the Philippine revolutionary movement Aguinaldo soon assumed. In 1897 Aguinaldo was elected president of the revolutionary government at the Tejeros Convention. Pursued by the Spanish army to Biak-na-Bato, in Bulacan province, he there reorganized his revolutionary government. On the basis of the new constitution of Biak-na-Bato, he was again elected president. He then negotiated the pact of Biak-na-Bato with Pedro A. Paterno, a Filipino lawyer representing the Spanish colonial administrators: in exchange for a promise by the Spanish colonial government of a money settlement and an amnesty for the revolutionists, he and other revolutionary leaders voluntarily exiled themselves to Hong Kong. There Aguinaldo met the Americans, who arranged for his return to the Philippines after the battle of Manila Bay (May 1898), allegedly with the promise of American recognition of Philippine independence. On 12 June 1898 he formally proclaimed Philippine independence at Kawit. He restored the revolutionary government, replacing the dictatorship he had established after his arrival in Manila. The Malolos Congress, which he called to draft the constitution creating the first republic of the Philippines, ratified the proclamation of independence. Shortly after his inauguration as president the Philippine–American war broke out. Again Aguinaldo led the Filipino resistance movement, until he was captured (1901) at Palanan, Isabel province. He ran for the presidency of the Commonwealth of the Philippines in 1935, but otherwise spent the rest of his life looking after the welfare of veterans of the Philippine revolution.

Aguinaldo y Famy, Emilio, *A Second Look At America* (New York, 1957).

JMSa

AGUIRRE CERDA, PEDRO (1879–1941), president of Chile during the Popular Front (1938–41), minister of the interior on three occasions, and a federal senator. Aguirre Cerda was head of the Radical Party.

AGUIRRE Y LECUBE, JOSE ANTONIO (1904–60), Basque nationalist leader, president of the Basque autonomous government (1936) and of the Basque government-in-exile in France until his death. He came from a Carlist, middle-class family and practised as a lawyer. Lecube commanded the support of the broad spectrum of Basque nationalists, and endeavoured to maintain unity between Catholics and the proletarian movement, being elected to the presidency of the Basque republic (Euzkadi) by a nearly unanimous vote on 7 Oct. 1936. After the fall of Bilbao (June 1937) he led the Basque resistance in Santander, but in the face of further defeat, escaped to France by air in August. There he sought to safeguard the interests of the Basques by diplomacy and arranging evacuation.

AGUIYI-ARONSI, JOHNSON THOMAS UMUNAKWE (1924–66), major-general, first Nigerian GOC of the Nigerian army (1965). He headed the military government following Maj. Nzeogwu's abortive coup (Jan. 1966), but was assassinated during the coup which brought Gen. Gowon to power (29 July 1966).

AGUSTIN I (1783–1824), Emperor of Mexico (*reg.* 1822–3). Agustin de Iturbide came from the creole landowning class, and detested the radicalism and Indianism of the Hidalgo and Morelos revolts, in which he fought on the Spanish side. He was sent to crush the forces of Vicente Guerrero, but entered into negotiations with him. The result was the Plan of Iguala (1821), a compromise whereby Mexico was to become independent, but remain a Bourbon monarchy. After independence was achieved, Iturbide's supporters staged a demonstration as a result of which he was raised to the status of Emperor of Mexico. His rule was arbitrary, and bitterly resented by the republican leaders of the struggle for independence, and in 1823 he was overthrown and exiled to Europe. The following year, misinformed about the extent of his support in Mexico, he returned to seek to regain his position. The Mexican authorities tried him for treason and he was shot.

AHALYA BAI, RANI (*reg.* 1765–95), widowed daughter-in-law of the Maratha chief Malhar Rao Holkar (*reg.* 1728–65), the founder of the Maratha state of Indore. She assumed the government on the death of her son, using a clansman, Tukoji, as the commander of her armies. Her rule was a by-word for justice and benevolence in a period of much turbulence and violence.

AHD, AL (The Covenant), secret society founded in Istanbul (1913) by Aziz Ali al-Misri, and including several officers of Iraqi origin, to work for greater independence for the Arab provinces of the Ottoman empire.

AHL AL-KITAB, 'the people of the book', *ie*, having a book of scripture. The term was employed, in Muslim usage, to denote above all the Christians and the Jews, but also other religious communities such as the Sabaeans and the Zoroastrians.

AHMAD AL-MANSUR AL-DHAHABI (d. 1603) (the 'golden'), greatest Sa'dian sultan of Morocco, acceded in the moment of his victory over Portuguese invaders at Al-Qasr al-Kabir (1578). Wealthy from Portuguese ransoms and careful of commerce and industry, he was able with his makhzen, or retinue of military tribes, to levy taxes and control the whole of Morocco, restraining in particular the marabouts. Against Spain he cultivated an English alliance. Rival of the Ottomans in Algeria, he perhaps envisaged a caliphate of the African west. Southwards he pacified Mauretania (1583), ravaged Tuwat-Gurara (1583–6), and finally overthrew the Askias of Songhay (1591) after a quarrel over ownership of the salt-mines of Taghaza. An unstable pashalik was established in Timbuctoo and some gold was obtained.

AHMAD BABA IBN AHMAD (1556–1627), great-great-grandson of Muhammad Aqit. He received his education in Timbuctoo from his father and other relatives, though his chief mentor was the Dyula scholar Muhammad Baghayogho. He rapidly achieved distinction in the Islamic sciences and gathered a circle of pupils. In 1593 he was exiled to Marrakesh by the Moroccan Pasha of Timbuctoo together with other members of the Aqit family.

After two years in detention there he was released but confined to the city, where he taught large and enthusiastic audiences and pronounced legal rulings. He was allowed to return to Timbuctoo in 1608 and taught there until his death. A prolific author, Ahmad Baba wrote over 40 books on Islamic law and theology, Arabic grammar, history, and the words and deeds of the Prophet (*hadith*), many of which are still studied in Morocco and West Africa. His biographical dictionary, the *Nail al-Ibtihaj*, gives precious details of the scholarly life of Timbuctoo in the 15th–16th cents.

AHMAD BAMBA (*c.* 1850–1927), the Wolof saint and founder of the Muridiyya fraternity (*tariqa*), born in Senegal. By the age of 30 he had acquired a considerable reputation for piety and learning. In 1895 the French authorities, fearing he might foment trouble for them, exiled him to Gabon for seven years. On his return he became a focus of popular devotion and his followers showered him with gifts.

A year later he was again exiled, this time to Boutilimit

in Mauritania, where he was able to pursue further studies with his master Sheikh Sidiya. In 1907 he was allowed to return to Senegal under surveillance and again became a focus of pilgrimage and gifts. In 1912 he was allowed to live at Diourbel, where his Murid movement was consolidated. His movement led to the conversion to Islam of almost a third of the Wolof population of Senegal. His descendants and their followers still play an important role in Senegalese religious and political life.

AHMAD GRAGN (1506–43), a Muslim leader of Harar and temporary conqueror of Ethiopia. Ahmad ibn Ibrahim El Ghazi, nicknamed by the Ethiopians *gragn*, or 'left-handed', married Bati Del Wanbara, daughter of the Amir of Zeila, and soon afterwards succeeded in making himself master of the trading centre of Harar. In 1527 he proclaimed a holy war against the Christian empire of Ethiopia, and, making effective use of muskets and cannon, then novelties in this area, succeeded with the help of Turkish volunteers in overrunning most of the country. In 1541, however, the Portuguese sent 400 musketeers to aid Emperor Galawdewos, whose army defeated and killed Gragn.

AHMAD IBN FARTUA (*fl.* 1580). Chief Imam of Bornu in northern Nigeria, a scholar, warrior, and author of *The Kanem Wars* and *The First Twelve Years of the Reign of Mai Idris Aloma*.

AHMAD LOBBO (1775–1844), known as Seku Ahmadu, a militant Fulani scholar from Masina. After a traditional Muslim education he travelled widely and was in Hausaland in 1805 when Uthman ibn Fudi was embarking on his *jihad*. From the latter he received authority to pursue his own *jihad* in Masina (1818). Within a year he had taken Jenne and built himself a capital, which he named Hamdullay, and over the next 25 years constructed an Islamic state along the axis Jenne–Timbuctoo. After his death his son Ahmad ruled (1844–52), and was followed by his son, Ahmad III. In 1862 Ahmad III was defeated by the rising power of *al-hajj* Umar and the theocratic state created by Seku Ahmadu was swallowed up in his larger empire.

AHMAD LUTFI AL-SAYYID (1872–1963), Egyptian lawyer and journalist, known as 'the philosopher of the generation'. As editor of *al-Jarida* (1907–15), he was the most articulate advocate of liberal, secular Egyptian nationalism.

AHMAD SHAH ABDALI (or DURRANI) (*c.* 1722–73), last of the great Central Asian conquerors and founder of the Durrani empire in Afghanistan and northern India in the second half of the 18th cent. An adventurer who first rose to influence as commander of Nadir Shah's Afghan bodyguard, he established his own rule at Kandahar after Nadir's murder in 1747. He raided into Khurasan and northern India, where he established his supremacy over the Marathas at Panipat (1761). Subsequently his authority over outlying parts of his empire relaxed and declined rapidly under his successors.

AHMADABAD, capital city of the modern state of Gujarat in the Indian Union. The present city owes its origin to Sultan Ahmad Shah of Gujarat (1411–43), who built it as his capital on the site of the Hindu city of Ashaval. It was strengthened and adorned by successive sultans of Gujarat, in particular Mahmud Shah Begara (1459–1511). After the Mughal conquest in 1572, the city became the capital of a Mughal *subah*, but fell into Maratha hands during the 18th cent. In 1818 it passed from the control of the Peshwa to that of the British.

Ahmadabad, now an important centre of the Indian cotton industry, was formerly famous for handicrafts of all kinds, and as the centre of a prosperous and fertile region was one of the leading cities of India during the 16th and 17th cents. It is notable for the mosques and tombs erected by the Gujarat sultans. The local Hindus and Jains were also vigorous builders and the fusion of the two traditions produced a unique Hindu–Muslim style, in which the large conceptions of the Muslims were enriched by the exquisite detail of the Hindu craftsmen.

AHMADIYYA, Islamic revivalist movement (regarded by most orthodox Sunni Muslims as heretical) launched in Qadiyan, east Punjab, in 1889 by Ghulam Ahmad (*c.* 1839–1908). In 1914 the Ahmadi movement split. One group, which accepted Ghulam Ahmad as a divinely inspired prophet, developed into the great proseletysing Ahmadiyya or Qadiyani movement throughout the Muslim world, but especially in Pakistan, India, and West Africa, under the leadership of the founder's son, Mahmud (b. 1889), and claiming a membership of over 1 million. The second, smaller group which regarded Ghulam Ahmed only as a reformer, established its headquarters at Lahore, West Pakistan, under the leadership of Maulana Muhammad Ali (d. 1951), working for Muslim reform and also engaging in missionary work.

AHMADNAGAR, state founded by and named after Ahmad Nizam Shah, when, as governor of the district for the Bahmani sultans of the Deccan, he broke away to found his own kingdom (1490). It maintained itself through the 16th cent. by constant local wars. Half of the state was overrun by Akbar (1600), and, despite a revival by Malik Ambar, the remainder was annexed by Shah Jahan (1635). The Emperor Aurangzeb died in the city (1707). It passed in turn into the hands of the Marathas (1759) and the British (1818).

AHMED I, 14th Ottoman Sultan (*reg.* 1603–17). The year 1603 saw the beginning of a Persian offensive which soon regained for Shah Abbas all the territories that, in 1590, he had yielded to the Ottoman Sultan in Azerbayjan and in the Caucasus. At Zsitva-Torok in Nov. 1606 the long war begun in 1593 against Austria came to an end. The sultan now recognized the emperor as his equal. Austria was also freed from the payment of tribute to the Ottomans. These years witnessed in Asia Minor a series of revolts suppressed only by the ruthless measures of Kuyuju Murad Pasha after 1606. Peace was made with Persia in 1612 and again in 1618 after a brief renewal of warfare. Ahmed I, in 1612, granted trade privileges (capitulations) to the Dutch in the Ottoman empire. He was responsible also for the construction (1609–1616) of the famous mosque which bears his name at Istanbul.

AHMED II (?1642–95), son of Sultan Ibrahim and 21st Ottoman Sultan (1691–5) in succession to his brother Süleyman II.

AHMED III (1673–1736), son of Mehmed IV and 23rd Ottoman Sultan (1703–30) in succession to Mustafa II. His reign saw victory over Russia (Pruth, 1711), disastrous defeat by Austria (Passarovitz, 1718), an ultimately inconclusive war with Iran (1723–30), and the beginnings of Europeanization in the Tulip Era (1718–30).

AHMED AL-JAZZAR (d. 1804), Pasha of Acre (Akka). Of Bosnian origin, he became governor of the *eyalet* (province) of Sidon (including Acre) in 1775. In 1799, with the aid of a small naval force operating under the command of Sir Sidney Smith, he defended Acre successfully against Napoleon.

AHMED IBN HANBAL (780–855), celebrated theologian and jurist, the founder of one of the four recognized schools (Hanafi, Shafi'i, Maliki, and Hanbali) of Muslim law. He opposed the doctrines of the Mu'tazila in the time of the caliph at Ma'mun. The most famous of his works is a large collection of the sacred traditions (*hadith*). Through his disciple Ibn Taymiyya his thought was to have a strong influence on Abd al-Wahhab, the founder of the Wahhabiyya movement in 18th-cent. Arabia.

AHMED IBN TULIN (835–84), founder of the Tulunid dynasty (868–905) in Egypt. His father, Tulun, of Turkish descent, had risen to be captain of the personal guard of the caliph. In 868 Ahmed was sent out to govern Egypt in the name of Bakbak, his stepfather, a Turkish general whom the caliph had appointed to that province. Using the wealth of Egypt to recruit a strong army and to retain, through lavish gifts, the favour of the caliph, Ibn Tulun was able to establish himself in firm command at Cairo and also to extend his control over much of Syria. The fact that the government in Iraq was involved in a sustained effort to suppress the revolt (869–83) of the Negro slaves known as the Zanj helped him greatly in the realization of his aims.

AHMED RIZA (1859–1930), Ottoman Young Turk revolutionary and positivist who, while in exile in Paris from 1889, published *Meshveret*, a newspaper advocating Ottoman reform under central control.

AHOMS, Shan tribes of the Thai race, who overran Assam between 1228 and 1826. Their leading families kept *buranjis* (historical chronicles) written in the Ahom language on strips of bark. Their religion was animistic until Hinduized. Ahoms criminal law countenanced mutilations and more terrible punishments. They were divided into exogamous groups or *khel*s and were heavy drinkers of rice beer. Their octagonal silver coinage is well executed. From 13th to 16th cent. they were consolidating their power in the Brahmaputra valley and adjusting their relationships with the neighbouring principalities of Kamata (Cooch Behar), Cachar, Jayantia, Darrang, Chutia, and Kamrup. During the 17th cent. they set a limit to the eastward expansion of the Mughal emperors. Towards the end of the 18th cent. their power declined and their territories were occupied by the Burmese until they were expelled by the British (1824–6).

AHUMA, S. R. B. ATTOCH (1864–1921), influential Gold Coast (Ghana) journalist, author, and nationalist. Educated at the Wesleyan High School, Cape Coast, and trained for the ministry at Richmond College, London, in 1888 he joined the Methodist Mission, but soon resigned. After a brief stay in England and the US he returned to the Gold Coast, where he became secretary of the Gold Coast Aborigines' Rights Protection Society, founded in 1897 to promote nationalist objectives. With Egyir Assam he founded the *Gold Coast Aborigines* as the society's organ. His books on nationalist themes include *Memoirs of West African Celebrities* (1903) and *Gold Coast Nation and Consciousness* (1911).

AIDAN, bishop of Lindisfarne (*c.* 635–?651), Irishman, or Scot, who led the first effective Scottish mission into England, being sent from Iona to convert Northumbria under King Oswald, the latter at first acting as interpreter for him. Aidan was a model bishop and travelled extensively throughout Northumbria.

AIDES, French indirect tax originating in the 14th cent. as a 5 per cent tax on all goods sold in the north and centre of the kingdom. From the reign of Louis XI (1461–83) the number of commodities subject to the tax was greatly reduced and the area over which it was levied was extended. Increasingly the *aides* were levied only on the sale of fish, meat, wood, and, principally, wine. A number of separate *aides* were added to the original in 1531, 1632, 1640, and 1680. None of these was enforced uniformly throughout the country and certain privileged groups, including clerics and noblemen, enjoyed exemption in so far as the products of their estates were concerned.

AIDHAB, ancient port on the Red Sea coast of the Sudan which flourished from 9th to 15th cent. AD. It was of importance for the Far East trade and for the Mecca pilgrimage. In 1183 it was sacked by the Crusaders and never recovered its former wealth, being ultimately replaced by Suakin further south.

AIDIT, DIPA NUSANTARA (1923–65), leader of the Indonesian Communist Party (PKI) from 1951 to 1965. He built the party into Indonesia's strongest political movement, only to see it collapse in a massacre of its members following the coup of Oct. 1965. Aidit was born in North Sumatra, where his father was a minor official, and was active in radical youth groups in Djakarta during the Second World War. He joined the PKI in 1946, rising rapidly to membership in its politburo, but fled to China following the party's defeat in the Madiun Affair of 1948, returning in 1950. In 1951 he and his close associates, Njoto and M. H. Lukman, seized control of the party and worked to transform it into a mass movement with a strongly nationalist orientation. The PKI expanded rapidly under Aidit's leadership to a claimed 3 million members in 1965. It presented a public image of efficiency and social concern, by which Aidit hoped to bring it to power peacefully on the basis of broad popular support. For protection he relied on Sukarno's favour, which proved a fatal mistake, for when Sukarno's power was broken by the coup of Oct. 1965 the PKI was defenceless against the onslaught of the military-backed right. Aidit was summarily shot by the army; his policies were later rejected as 'revisionist' by PKI leaders reorganizing underground.

AIGUES MORTES, NEGOTIATIONS. These were conducted personally between Charles V and Francis I during the truce in the Italian wars which had been negotiated at Nice (June 1538). As a result of the negotiations the two adversaries agreed to take co-ordinated action against heretics in their own lands.

AIGUILLON, EMMANUEL ARMAND, Duc d' (1720–88), French general and foreign secretary. While military governor of Brittany (1753–66), his attempt to implement government financial measures brought him into conflict with the local estates. As a public opponent of the estates and *parlements* he was drawn into the government with Terray and Maupeou (the *Triumvirate*) at the fall of Choiseul (1771), being made foreign secretary. He supported his colleagues in the temporary destruction of the *parlements*, but as foreign secretary was ineffective and fell with the death of Louis XV.

AIKEN, HOWARD HATHAWAY (1900–   ), collaborated with IBM (1939) in constructing the first electronic computer, the Automatic Sequence Controlled Calculator. Although this machine was largely mechanical, electric motors and electric switches were used. It operated until the 1950s and produced a large number of mathematical tables still in use (1970).

AILLEBOUST DE COULANGE ET D'ARGENTENAY, LOUIS D' (1612–60), third governor-general of New France (1648–1651). Born in France, he is believed to have landed with the founders of Montreal in 1642. His governorship coincided with the savage Iroquois raids which destroyed the Huron nation. He failed to achieve a commercial and defensive alliance with MA, but reorganized the local militia.

AILLY, PIERRE DE (1350–1420), Parisian scholar and a cardinal (1411), who tried to bring about the end of the Great Schism through a general council. He was one of the foremost theorists of the conciliar movement which resulted in the Council of Constance. His geographic writings (1410–13) were accepted as authoritative and a copy owned and profusely annotated by Christopher Columbus before his voyages has survived. Ailly taught that the earth was spherical and that the sea between Europe and Asia could not be large.

AINU, a race, possibly Caucasian in origin, which has inhabited northern Japan since prehistoric times. They were once believed to have been Japan's original inhabitants, but this view is no longer held, though the date and circumstances of their arrival in Japan remain obscure. They lived by hunting and fishing and had their own language and literature. After many hard campaigns they were pushed back to the extreme north of Japan, where, from the 11th cent., they lived in relative harmony with the Japanese. Though now somewhat intermixed racially, their abundant hair still distinguishes them from the Japanese. Their numbers have declined (1970) to little more than 15,000.

AÏR, or Abzen, massif in the central Sahara, now in the republic of Niger. In early times it was inhabited by Gobirawa Hausa cultivators and herdsmen, probably centred on Asode, but in the 11th cent. the first Tuareg groups, the Itesan, moved into the area. Further Tuareg immigration led to confrontation with the Gobirawa who, by the 15th cent., had been driven out to their present home north of Sokoto. Later immigrations, notably of the Kel Ewi in the 17th cent., led to inter-Tuareg wars in the 18th and 19th cents.

Aïr lay astride important trade routes from North Africa and Egypt, and its neighbours, Songhay, Kebbi, Katsina, and Bornu, dominated it for varying periods during the 16th and 17th cents. A Tuareg 'Sultanate of Aïr' was founded in the early 15th cent. chiefly to arbitrate in internal disputes, but there was no 'state' as such. It still existed when the French incorporated Aïr into their *Colonie du Niger* (1906), though serious revolts in 1917 led the French to expel most of the Tuareg to the southern plains of Damergu, a policy later reversed.

AIR FORCE, ROYAL. Before the First World War air branches of the two senior services existed as the Royal Naval Air Service and the Royal Flying Corps. Their function in the war, beginning with reconnaissance and artillery spotting, developed into aerial fighting. This led to claims for independence which resulted in the formation of the Royal Air Force in 1918. At the outbreak of war the two aerial wings had under 2000 men between them; at its conclusion there were over a quarter of a million serving in the RAF. The first chief of staff, Hugh Trenchard, was a great advocate of the role of air-power.

Between the two World Wars RAF numbers never reached 100,000. Despite political and economic restrictions, the RAF made considerable technical advances, including pioneer work in radar, and participated in attacks upon world speed records. The significance of this was seen at the outbreak of the Second World War. The RAF, small in comparison to the German Air Force, saved Britain from defeat in 1940, Spitfire and Hurricane aircraft accounting respectively for high-flying German fighters and for bombers. The RAF later participated in the bombing of German shipping and cities, and as part of the Allied 2nd Tactical Air Force in the invasion of Europe (1944).

After the Second World War the RAF was re-equipped with Hunters and supersonic Lightning fighters. Its transport aircraft included Comet, VC10, Hercules, and Belfast. The Nimrod, which was developed from the Comet, replaced the Shackleton in maritime operations. The Vulcan and Victor remained the original 'V' Bomber force and the ubiquitous Canberra served in roles from interdictor to photographic reconaissance. The RAF played a vital role in troop movements to troubled areas throughout the world in the 1950s and 1960s.

AIR FORCE, ROYAL AUSTRALIAN, formed 31 March 1921 as the Australian Air Force, was one of the earliest in the world to have separate command from naval and military forces. Organized military flying began at Point Cook in Aug. 1914 and a small Australian force of airmen gained Australia's first experience of air war in the Mesopotamian campaign (1915). Later, four squadrons of the Australian Flying Corps fought elsewhere. On its formation in 1921, the RAAF of 150 men was equipped with First World War aircraft and grew slowly to 3300 in 1939. During the Second World War,

with its peak strength at more than 182,000 men and women by 1944, it was equipped largely with Australian-manufactured aircraft. RAAF squadrons or individuals served in all major war theatres, in which 10,562 of them died. Post-war activities included the Berlin airlift and tasks in Malaya, Korea, Thailand, and Vietnam.

AIR FORCE, ROYAL NEW ZEALAND, was established in 1923 under army control, became a separate arm in 1937. Its two bomber squadrons served with the RAF (1939–45), and new Pacific units were formed from 1942. After 1945, the RNZAF maintained (at various times) bases in Fiji, Japan, Cyprus, Malaya, and Thailand. Its strength in the 1960s was about 4500.

AIR PACT PROJECT (1936). In Dec. 1935 Hitler was threatening to reoccupy the Rhineland because the Franco-Soviet rapprochement was, he considered, a violation of the Locarno Pact. To forestall this action, the British foreign minister, Eden, reformulated a proposal for an air pact which had made little progress in conjunction with Anglo-French security proposals in Feb. 1935. On 6 March 1936 Eden proposed an Air Pact of Mutual Guarantee between the Locarno Powers, limiting indiscriminate bombing, but not the size of air forces. He hoped this would lead to wider security discussions. However, on 7 March Hitler invaded the Rhineland.

AIRLANGGA (1000–50), king in ancient Indonesia (*reg.* 1016–c. 1050), belonging to a Balinese branch of the East Javanese royal family. In 1016 he was married to the Javanese crown princess, daughter of King Dharmawangsa Teguh. A few days later, however, the capital (in the Brantas delta) was completely destroyed by a raid and Dharmawangsa, with most members of his family, was killed. The attacking army, probably acting by order of the kingdom of Sri Vijaya, withdrew shortly afterwards, leaving Java in chaos and division. Airlangga fled to the forest with a few companions and obtained shelter in a hermitage where he led the life of an ascetic and thus acquired, by his concentration, the spiritual force that would enable him to overcome his enemies. Starting from a small basis near present Pasuruhan he first consolidated his position, then, from 1028 to 1035, defeated his enemies one after the other and re-established a great Javanese empire. His success is no doubt partly connected with the temporary eclipse of the power of Sri Vijaya owing to a raid by the South Indian Cholas in c. 1024. Airlangga's reign marks the beginning of a long period of balance of power, with Sri Vijaya remaining in control of western Indonesia (including West Java and the Malay peninsula), and East Java as a predominating power in eastern Indonesia. This political stability favoured an unprecedented development of Javanese culture, particularly literature, in the 12th cent. In the last part of his career Airlangga lived in retirement as a royal ascetic while, according to a later tradition unsupported by reliable documents, he divided the kingdom between his two sons.

AIR-PUMP, device used in laboratories for pumping water out of vessels, adapted from the common well-pump by Otto von Guericke (1602–86).

A'ISHA (c. 614–78), the favourite wife of the Prophet Muhammad and the daughter of the first caliph, Abu Bakr. Defeated, with her allies Talha and Al-Zubayr, at the battle of the Camel against the Caliph Ali (656), she was sent into retirement at Mecca, where she spent the rest of her life.

AISIN GIORO, the Golden Tribe, an aristocratic Chinese clan which held the hereditary chieftainship of a Jürched tribe from the 15th cent. From the middle of the Sungari river the Jürched tribes moved gradually southwards and, in the 16th cent., the Aisin Gioro established itself at the head-waters of the Hun river. It was here, under the leadership of

Nurhachi (1559–1626), that the clan rose rapidly to power and challenged Chinese suzerainty. In 1635, it imposed the name Manchu on all the Jürched tribes, and established the Manchu (Ch'ing) dynasty (1644–1911).

AISLABIE, JOHN (1670–1742), chancellor of the exchequer (1718–21), who was accused of receiving bribes of shares from the South Sea Co. With the bursting of the South Sea Bubble, Aislabie was forced to resign as chancellor, and later (1721) was expelled from the House of Commons.

AISNE, BATTLE OF THE, fought in April 1917 under the direction of Gen. Nivelle, achieved results comparable in gains and casualties to other Western Front offensives, but is regarded as a catastrophe because of the high expectations which Nivelle had created. The battle led to his dismissal, and was followed by mutinies in the French army, making a further offensive in 1917 impossible. Nivelle's failure discredited the idea of a supreme command over British and French armies, which he had been given.

AIX-LA-CHAPELLE, CONGRESS (1818). Congress of the four powers, Austria, Russia, Prussia, and Britain, summoned to discuss the post-war settlement of France. It marked the first divergence of Britain from the legitimist policies of her wartime allies. In 1818 the British Cabinet proposed that the army of occupation be withdrawn to the Low Countries in order to improve the standing of the restored Bourbon regime. This withdrawal was agreed by the allies, and France was invited to join the congress. Discussions about future meetings of the powers raised misgivings in the British cabinet, which feared that future meetings might give support to governments to which British public opinion was hostile. In particular, Castlereagh, the British representative at the congress, refused to accept a proposal by Alexander I of Russia whereby each sovereign would be guaranteed his throne and territory.

AIX-LA-CHAPELLE, TREATIES OF (1668, 1748). The first treaty was between France and Spain ending the War of Devolution. Louis XIV, in pursuance of a claim based upon his wife's rights as a Spanish infanta, invaded the Spanish Netherlands in May 1667, and later Franche-Comté. The Grand Pensionary of Holland, John de Witt, fearing for the safety of the United Provinces, pursuaded the signatories of the Triple Alliance, England, Holland, and Sweden, to mediate in the conflict. Fearing that Spain would gain support from the alliance, Louis agreed to discuss terms. The preliminary conditions were settled at St Germain-en-Laye between the French foreign minister, Lionne, and the Dutch and English ambassadors, van Beuningen and Trevor, on 15 April, and were confirmed by a conference of the powers at Aix-la-Chapelle on 2 May. The terms were advantageous to Louis, who retained most of the towns he had occupied in Flanders and Brabant, though he restored Franche-Comté. Spain was guaranteed her remaining possessions in the Netherlands by the Triple Alliance powers. The treaty rankled with Louis and he vowed the destruction of the Dutch republic. In 1748, at the end of the War of the Austrian Succession, a second treaty was signed by France, England, Holland, Sardinia, Spain, and Austria. It largely restored the status quo. It was partly a peace of exhaustion and has its roots in earlier diplomatic conversations (1745–6) which were held up by the death of Philip V of Spain and by Austrian victories in Italy. They were resumed after Saxe's invasion of Holland, when the fall of the Comte d'Argenson and the final French defeat in Italy made the latter willing to treat. Plenipotentiaries were appointed in Jan. 1748 and met in April. An Anglo-Dutch-French agreement was initialled at the end of the month, and in May and June the Austrians and Spaniards were forced to accept it.

The terms of the treaty (a) guaranteed Silesia and Glatz to Prussia (which did not participate in the congress), albeit in rather loose terms; (b) restored Savoy and Nice, which had been overrun by France, to Sardinia, together with Upper Novara and the Vivegano, which were ceded by Austria; (c) restored the southern Netherlands to Austria, with the exception of the Barrier forts, which remained garrisoned by the Dutch, in return for Parma, Piacenza, and Guastella, which were made over to Don Philip of Spain. Austria also had to return Modena to its duke, and territories in Bavaria to the Elector; (d) provided for French recognition of George II and the Hanoverian succession, and for demolition of the seaward defences of Dunkirk. The French also exchanged Madras for Louisburg as part of a return to the status quo in the colonies and recognized both the Pragmatic Sanction and the election of Francis of Lorraine as Holy Roman emperor; and (e) provided for Spanish implementation of the commercial clauses of the treaty of Utrecht, so as to aid English trade, and confirmed Naples and Sicily in the possession of Don Carlos.

The treaty averted Russian entry into the war, and when confirmed by the treaty of Arunjuez (1750), settled the balance of power in Italy for a generation. It also ended Holland's role as a battlefield, and marked further points in the rise of Sardinia, Prussia, and England. However, in the short term it did not solve the underlying animosities and was merely a breathing space in both the colonial and the European struggles.

R. Lodge, *Studies in Eighteenth-Century European Diplomacy, 1740–1748* (London, 1930).   CJ

AJAMI literature. A term used to describe the writings of West African Muslim scholars in African languages using the Arabic script. It is now becoming clear that this mode of expression was much more common and is probably older than has been generally supposed. Kanembu, an archaic language of the Chad region, was being written in Arabic characters in the 18th cent. for the purposes of Koranic exegesis and there are indications that the tradition of *ajami* literature may antedate this by two and a half centuries.

The first specimens of written Fulani literature appear at the end of the 18th cent. in the form of religious poetry by Uthman ibn Fudi and it is now known that an extensive Fulani verse literature exists from areas as widely separated as Futa Jallon and Adamawa. Hausa *ajami* literature traditionally begins with Isa, son of Uthman ibn Fudi, who translated some of his father's verse into Hausa, though its origins may well be older. Other languages which have produced their own *ajami* literature, albeit less extensive than Fulani and Hausa, include Mandinka, Dagbane, Nupe, and Yoruba. Nowadays the Arabic script is rapidly giving way to the use of Roman characters for writing all these languages.

AJANTA, CAVES AND FRESCOES, group of 27 caves in a narrow valley about 60 miles (96 kms) north of Aurangabad, Maharashtra, India. The caves vary considerably in size, the largest measuring 87 ft square (8·08 sq. ms) with 28 columns. All the caves are Buddhist and are of two basic types. The first, called *caitya* or 'assembly hall', comprises a rectangular portico and nave with side aisles in the form of an apse at the end. The second, *vihara* or 'monastery', consists of a square hall surrounded by rows of cells on three sides. Both types are richly decorated with sculpture and frescoes. The latter are of unique value for our knowledge of ancient Indian painting, for aspects of the history of Buddhism, and, above all, for scenes of daily life in the ancient Deccan. The dating of the caves is based on an analysis of style and technique as well as on the palaeography of the numerous inscriptions recording pious gifts. As a result, the caves have been dated at being between the 2nd or 1st cent. BC and the 7th cent. AD, with the highest achievements datable to the Gupta period (5th–6th cents).

AJIT SINGH, RAJA (1679–1724), posthumous son of Raja Jaswant Singh of Marwar (Jodhpur), who died in 1678. After many adventures, he was recognized as chief (1707). He played an active part under a series of Mughal emperors until his murder, said to have been instigated by his own son. Ajit Singh was one of the last Rajput chiefs to give a daughter in marriage to a Mughal emperor (Farrukhsiyar), and was notable for his habit of changing sides in the court politics of the day.

AJIVIKAS, sect of wandering naked ascetics founded in northern India *c.* 6th cent. BC. Their principal tenet was a belief in blind fate as the moving force of the universe. They apparently flourished during the reign of Ashoka, who made donations to them, but little is heard of this sect in north India after that time. In south India, however, the presence of Ajivikas is attested as late as the 15th cent.

AJNADAYN (634), battle won by the Muslims, led by Khalid ibn al-Walid against the Byzantine forces defending Palestine under the command of Theodorus, the brother of the Emperor Heraclius. The success of the Muslims left Palestine defenceless before them.

AK KIRMAN (KERMAN), Cetatea Albă (Rumanian), the 'White Town', lies at the mouth of the Dniester. It was under Mongol rule after 1241. The Genoese and then the Moldavians held it in the 14th and 15th cents. In 1484 it fell to the Ottoman Turks, who yielded it to Russia in 1812.

AK KOYONLU, the 'White Sheep', a powerful confederation of Turcoman tribes originating in the region of Diyarbakr. The Ak Koyonlu had as their rivals the Kara Koyunlu or 'Black Sheep' Turcomans located in the area north of Lake Van. The fortunes of the Ak Koyonlu prospered under the guidance, after 1453, of their famous chieftain, Uzun Hasan, who defeated the last of the Kara Koyunlu princes in 1467 and then overran much of Persia. After the death of Uzun Hasan in 1478 and of his son, Ya'kub Beg, in 1490, dynastic quarrels brought about the collapse of the Ak Koyonlu domination. The end came in 1499–1503, when the Safawids defeated the last of the Ak Koyonlu begs and established a new regime in Persia.

AKALI DAL, the main political organization of the Sikh community in the Punjab, India. The first Akalis were late 17th-cent. Sikh zealots who took upon themselves the role of censors of the community. The modern 'army of the Akalis' began in the early 1920s as the militants in a campaign to reclaim the Sikh shrines of *gurdwara*s from the Hindu priests, who had gained hereditary control of them and their wealth. Their sacrifices in this agitation gave the Akalis great authority within the community and the Dal has dominated from the beginning the Shiromani Gurdwara Parbandhak Committee, a popularly elected committee to control the shrines for the community, which the Punjab government established (1925) in response to the Akali agitation. The Dal's control of the SGPC has been the result of the skilful leadership of Master Tara Singh (1885–1967), who has dominated Akali affairs from 1930.

In the 1930s there was co-operation between the Akali Dal and the Congress, but the Dal always gave priority to Sikh communal interests. Following the rise of the Pakistan movement, the Dal formulated a scheme (1944) for a Sikh homeland in the central Punjab. After partition, this was altered to a demand for a language-based 'Punjabi Suba', which was granted (1966).

AKAN, group of peoples who form about 40 per cent of the population and are culturally the dominant group of Ghana, occupying the area between the Black Volta and the coast. They comprise the Asante, Fante, Akyem, Kwahu, Akwapim, Wassa, Denkyira, Twifu, Assin, Gomoa, and Nzima peoples. They share a seven-day week and a 40-day calendar, common religious beliefs and ceremonies, and the same matrilineal system of inheritance. They speak the Twi language or mutually intelligible dialects of it. Membership of their clans

cuts across tribal and political boundaries. Thus, an Asante who belongs to the Oyoko clan regards an Akyem belonging to the same clan as his blood brother or sister, with whom he shares a number of things in common and whom he cannot marry.

The hypothesis that there was a connection between the Akan peoples and the ancient kingdom of Ghana cannot be entirely dismissed. Many Akan traditions can be interpreted as indicative of north–south migration. It may be that when the ancient Ghana kingdom was declining (AD 1076–1240), refugees from that kingdom settled in existing Akan kingdoms. Despite the scepticism of many historians, the Gold Coast assumed the name of Ghana upon becoming independent.

What is not in doubt is the historical role of the Akan peoples. In the coastal districts of present-day Ghana, the Akan met the Guan peoples, the ancestors of the Kyerepong, Anum, Bassa, Breku, Afutu, Etsii, and the Asebu peoples of today. The Akan eventually assimilated them wholly or totally. By the middle of the 18th cent. the multifarious kingdoms in the southern districts of Ghana had been subsumed within the political systems of the two leading Akan peoples, the Fante and the Asante. In this way was brought about the cultural unity of most of the peoples of southern Ghana.

AKBAR II (1760–1837), second son of the Emperor Shah Alam, succeeded as emperor under British protection as 'King of Delhi' (Nov. 1806). After some attempt to assert his position and influence, he settled down to the role of a mediatized prince. Bp Heber described his court on a visit in 1824–5, depicting him as a mild and cultured prince. He employed Ram Mohan Roy, to whom he gave the title of Raja, to represent his case for an increased pension to the East India Co. in London, which achieved partial success.

AKBAR, PRINCE (1657–1706), third son of the Emperor Aurangzeb, who at one time preferred him to his brothers because he was born of a Muslim wife. He was employed by his father in his Rajput campaign to annex Marwar and Mewar (1679–81). He experienced a number of reverses and suffered much censure from his father on this account. Being transferred from the Mewar to the Marwar sector, he impulsively joined his opponents and proclaimed himself emperor (Jan. 1681). Aurangzeb at Ajmir was in grave danger, for his troops were scattered, but Akbar's dilatoriness enabled him to call up reinforcements and undermine the opposition. The Rajputs deserted Akbar, who fled to the court of the Maratha chief Sambhaji, the successor to Sivaji. From there he fled to Persia, where he died a few months before his father. Akbar's rebellion had the effect of saving Mewar from the threat of conquest.

AKBAR SHAH, THE GREAT (1542–1605), the 3rd Mughal Emperor of India, born at Umarkot in Sind, the eldest son of the Emperor Homayun, who was in flight from the Afghan chief Sher Shah. He returned to India with his father in 1555 and the next year became emperor at the age of 13 on his father's sudden death. For the next four years he was under the tutelage of Bairam Khan, a loyal but imperious Turkish nobleman. In 1560 Bairam was dismissed, but for two more years Akbar remained under the influence of his foster-mother and Adham Khan devoting himself to sport. In 1562 he personally had Adham Khan hurled over the battlements after the Khan had murdered Akbar's chief minister. His real reign begins from this time and lasted for 43 years. It was Akbar's success and versatility in many fields which earned him the title 'Great'. He was the real founder of the Mughal empire in India.

Akbar may be seen first in the orthodox character of a conqueror. At his death he left an empire extending across the whole of northern India to Kabul and Badakshan and as far south as Ahmadnagar and Surat. Malwa had been taken by Adham Khan. Akbar defeated the Rajput chiefs in successive sieges at Chitor and Ranthambor (1567-9), thus neutralizing the chief rivals to the Mughals. In 1573 he seized the rich province of Gujarat and the port of Surat in a lightning campaign; he followed this up by the conquest of fertile Bengal (1576). Later acquisitions included Sind, Kashmir, and parts of the Muslim kingdoms in the Deccan.

But Akbar was much more than a conqueror. Following his defeat of the Rajputs, he virtually took them into partnership; Rajputs commanded armies, governed provinces, and sat on his privy council. Their support balanced the Muslim chiefs and made the empire Indian rather than purely Muslim. He later abolished the *jizya* or tax on non-Muslims, thus establishing both toleration and partnership. This bi-communal policy gave the empire stability for a century.

Akbar's followers contained Turkish and Afghan chiefs, Persians, and Indian Muslims as well as Rajputs. To bind these together he organized the empire into twelve *suba*s or provinces divided into *sarkar*s or districts. Control was exercised by an imperial service of 33 graded ranks known as the *mansabdar*s. These officers were strictly controlled, and thus was created both a path of honour for the ambitious and a curb of discipline for the unruly. Also, through his Hindu revenue minister, Todar Mal, Akbar reorganized the whole land system of northern India on lines still traceable when the British took over. There was measurement of land, classification of soils, and rules for assessment.

From 1582 Akbar started a new religious cult, known as the Divine Faith and centred on himself. Though ridiculed at the time and abandoned at his death, it had the effect of surrounding with sanctity the office of emperor and attracting to it the ready devotion of the Indian people.

Akbar was a generous and perceptive patron of literature, music, painting, and architecture, and was the real founder of the exquisite Mughal school of miniature painting. Fatehpur-Sikri remains a monument to his architectural flair.

V. Smith, *Akbar, the Great Mogul* (Oxford, 1927).
L. Binyon, *Akbar* (London, 1832).   TGPS

AKCHE ('small and white'), Ottoman silver coin, known to the Europeans as the asper (*cf.* Greek *aspron*). In the course of time the word came to have the more general sense of 'money'. The akche continued to be minted until the reign of Sultan Mahmud II (1808-39).

AKHI, term used in Asia Minor to denote associations of young men (*yiğit*) recruited mainly from the craftsmen in the towns. The Akhis organized themselves into guilds with a strong attachment to religion and to the ideals of the *futuwwa*. Their influence was great in the Asia Minor of the 13th–14th cents.

AKHMATOVA, ANNA ANDREYEVNA (1888–), Russian poetess, associated with Nicholas Gumilëv and Osip Mandelshtam in a literary group calling themselves 'Acmeists' (1911) in opposition to symbolism. She wrote lyrical poetry before the Revolution, and remained silent for the greater part of the Stalinist period, but was attacked by Zhdanov in 1946 and expelled from the Writers Union. After Stalin's death she published translations from Jewish poets shot in 1912.

AKIGA (*c.* 1898–), member of the million-strong Tiv people of the central Nigeria. He became the first African evangelist of the Dutch Reformed Church Missions which introduced Christianity into Tivland in 1911, serving his people in various secular capacities in Northern Nigeria, first as editor of a Tiv newsheet, then as member of the Northern House of Assembly. He is best known as the author of *Akiga's Story*, translated from the vernacular by Dr Rupert East, which is of great value for an understanding of pre-colonial Tiv society.

AKINTOLA, CHIEF SAMUEL LADOKE (1910–66), Nigerian journalist, lawyer, and politician. A prominent member of the Action Group, he was prime minister of Western Nigeria (1960–6). Later, he founded the United Peoples' Party, which became the Nigerian National Democratic Party.

AKKAD, Semitic kingdom in central Mesopotamia, founded by Sargon (*c.* 2334–2279 BC) around the city of Agade. Semitic people had lived in the area for many years, but Sargon and his followers may have been newcomers from Syria. He appears to have founded the city of Agade and proceeded to build his empire round it, conquering all Mesopotamia, Elam, Syria, and Lebanon. It was the largest empire yet formed in ancient Mesopotamia and Sargon's successors, Rimus (*reg. c.* 2278–2270), Manistusu (*reg. c.* 2269–2255), Naram-Sin (*reg. c.* 2254–2218), Shar-Kali-Shari (*reg. c.* 2217–2193), Igigi, Nanijum, Imi, and Elulu (*reg. c.* 2192–2190), Dudu (*reg. c.* 2189–2169), and Su-Turnul (*reg. c.* 2168–2154), were engaged in continual efforts to defend it against internal revolts and outside attacks. By the reign of Shar-Kali-Shari, the last of Sargon's dynasty, the empire was already breaking up, though it did not finally disappear until *c.* 2159, when the Gutians seized control. The government of the empire was centralized in the hands of the king. Akkadian governors usually ruled alongside the native rulers in conquered territories. The distribution of land to government officials and supporters resulted in the acquisition of private property and wealth, contradicting the Sumerian conception of property as belonging to the city god. The most lasting effect of the empire was the spread of the Akkadian language at the expense of Sumerian. Used along with Sumerian for official inscriptions, it gradually became the spoken language of the whole area. Having adopted cuneiform writing, the Akkadians transmitted it to other peoples of north Mesopotamia, and the Lullubi, the Hurrians, and the Elamites.

AKKERMAN, CONVENTION OF (1826), concluded between Russia and Turkey on 7 Oct. after a Russian ultimatum threatening invasion. Although it did not provide a solution to the critical Greek question, it seemed to have achieved a settlement elsewhere in the Balkans by the restoration of privileges to the Danubian Provinces and the granting of others to Serbia. In addition Russian merchant shipping was to be allowed to use Turkish waterways. Sultan Mahmud II looked on the convention only as a temporary measure and repudiated it in the following year.

AKOSOMBO DAM, Ghana, built (1960–5) as the major part of a scheme to provide cheap and plentiful electric power from the Volta river, and linked to other economic projects, notably aluminium-smelting.

AKSHAK, early Sumerian city, about 30 miles (48 kms) south of Baghdad.

AKSUMITE EMPIRE, important semi-maritime power of north-east Africa during much of the first millennium AD. The Aksumite state, called after its capital, Aksum, originated in a migration, perhaps around 500 BC, from south Arabia to the highlands of northern Ethiopia, of the Sabaeans, an agricultural and trading people who spoke a Semitic language written in a script related to the Phoenician. On settling in Africa they developed a distinctive civilization. They practised an advanced form of agriculture, and traded widely through the port of Adulis with Egypt, Arabia, Persia, and India, exporting ivory, gold, and slaves in return for textiles and other manufactured goods, as described in the *Periplus of the Erythraean Sea*, an Egyptian–Greek document. The Aksumites also proved themselves good architects and builders in stone, producing monolithic stelae and imposing palaces and temples. Their coins circulated from the 3rd to *c.* the 10th cent. AD. The Aksumites, whose rulers erected a number of inscribed stelae to record their victories, evolved a new language, Geez, as well as a special script, both based on, but substantially different from, the earlier Sabaean. Greek also had some limited use, being found on both inscriptions and coins, while the *Periplus* states that the ruler of Aksum was 'acquainted with Greek literature'.

The Aksumites were originally pagans; the sun and moon are depicted on many of their coins and several obelisks, while some inscriptions pay homage to the gods of ancient Greece. In the 4th cent., however, the Emperor Ezana embraced Christianity, which became the official religion; but this did not prevent a subsequent Aksumite ruler, Armah, from giving refuge, perhaps for reasons of statecraft, to some of the early followers of Islam. Ezana and several rulers who followed him did much to expand the borders of the realm, which at its zenith covered a large part of the northern Ethiopia plateau. On at least two occasions, the second (*c.* AD 525) during the reign of Kaleb, the Aksumites also extended their rule to parts of south Arabia.

R. Pankhurst, *An Introduction to the Economic History of Ethiopia* (London, 1961).
J. Doresse, *Ethiopia* (London, 1959).   RP

ALA AL-DIN KAYKOBAD I, Seljuk Sultan of Rum (1219–1237). Ala al-Din defeated the Khwarazm Shah Jalal al-Din near Erzinjan in 1230. His reign saw the Sultanate of Rum at the height of its splendour. Ala al-Din spent much of his revenue on new buildings, *eg* at Konya, Siwas, and Alaya.

ALA UD-DIN RIAYAT SHAH AL-KAHAR (*reg. c.* 1539–71) Sultan of Atjeh, was the major enemy of the Portuguese in Malacca, which he twice attacked (1547, 1568). He established relations with Turkey (1561–8), which sent him military assistance.

ALA-AD-DIN KHILJI (d. 1316) was the nephew of Jalal-ad-din Firoz Shah, first ruler of the Khilji dynasty of Delhi sultans. Ala-ad-din first distinguished himself by the capture of Bhilsa, then went on a plundering raid against the Raja of Deogir which ended in the city of Ellichpur surrendering to him. Financed by loot, Ala-ad-din organized treason, and having slain his uncle after enticing him to an interview, became sultan (1296). Ala-ad-din's reign was a period of unrestrained imperialism and unexampled success. The Mongol danger was now receding and the sultans were free to turn their attention to internal expansion. In 1297 there was an attack on Gujarat, which was annexed and great spoils secured. The most valuable asset was Malik Kafur, a young eunuch of outstanding ability. The Rajput princes were a standing threat to the Delhi empire, and the southern states of India, with their reputed wealth, a standing temptation. First Ala-ad-din attacked the Rajputs. In 1301 he took Ranthambor, the raja committing *jauhar* (putting his family to death and killing himself). In 1303 he took Chitor amid similar tragic scenes. Malwa, including Mandu and Ujjain, was also annexed. Ala-ad-din then turned his attention to the south. In a series of raids led by Malik Kafur, his army penetrated as far as Madurai. Meanwhile, the Mongols were held at bay on the frontier by Ghazi Malik, who, as Ghyas-ad-din Tughluq Shah I, later replaced the Khilji dynasty with his own.

Ala-ad-din's administration was severe and oppressive. Delhi enjoyed a fictitious prosperity from the spoils of Kafur's campaigns, but the high military expenses led to severe revenue exactions and general discontent. Ala-ad-din marked his successes by sumptuous building. He doubled the size of the Qutab mosque, added an ornate gateway, which remains his chief visible monument, and started to build a *minar* (turret) which was to be twice the height of the original. He also built a new royal citadel at Siri.

Ala-ad-din's health collapsed under the strain of activity and excess. On his death Malik Kafur placed Ala-ad-din's youngest son on the throne, but was himself killed by the partisans of the third son, Mubarak Shah. After a short and ill-starred reign, the dynasty ended with his murder by Khusrav Khan.

Ishwari Prasad, *History of the Qaraunch Turks* (Allahabad, 1936).   TGPS

ALABAMA, name of a Liverpool-built Confederate blockade-runner during the American Civil War. Under Captain Semmes she destroyed or captured over 60 Union vessels before being sunk off Cherbourg (1864). The ship caused Anglo-American relations to deteriorate during the war and later gave rise to the case known as the '*Alabama* Claims'. The US sought damages from Britain on the grounds that, by allowing the building and fitting out of the *Alabama* and similar vessels, Britain had abused her neutral status. The treaty of Washington (1871) set up an international arbitration tribunal, and the dispute was settled by the subsequent British payment of $15,500,000.

ALABAMA, 22nd member state of the US. After first being explored by the Spaniards, the AL region was settled (1702) by the French, who exported furs, rice, and indigo from Mobile. France lost the area to England (1763), and northern AL, as part of GA, passed to the US in 1783, the southern portion being transferred to Spain. Mobile was captured from Spain (1813), defeat of the Creek Indians (1814) resulted in the acquisition of Indian lands, and in the Adams–Onis treaty (1819) Spanish claims were finally abrogated. A territory (1817) and a state (1819), AL, with a plantation economy, seceded from the Union in Jan. 1861. Its capital, Montgomery, became the first capital of the Confederacy. Following the defeat of the South in the Civil War, AL was re-admitted to the Union (1868) and since Reconstruction its political, economic, and racial history has followed the Southern pattern, compounding progressivism with extreme conservatism.

ALAIN, pen name of Émile Chartier (1868–1951), French writer on philosophy and politics, often regarded as the official philosopher of French radicalism. He did much to form the attitudes of French democrats for several decades through his *Propos* (begun in 1903), essays published in periodicals and later collected in books. He wrote on a great variety of topics, but will be remembered primarily for his political views. These are well summarized by the title of one of his books, *Le Citoyen Contre Les Pouvoirs* (1926). Alain was a democrat of a strongly individualist kind, suspicious of the state and of all forms of power. He became a pacifist after service in the First World War. His concept of liberty has been criticized as essentially negative, but may be seen as characteristically French in its emphasis on the 'small man' and his rights. Alain spent his life as a school teacher, and, true to his own views, refused all promotion and honours.

ALAIS (or ALÈS), PEACE OF (1629), treaty between Richelieu and the Huguenots signed in July at the end of the latter's rebellion against the Crown. It abolished all the Huguenots' political privileges, but was tolerant of them, subject to their good behaviour.

ALALIA, BATTLE OF (*c.* 535 BC), fought at sea off Corsica between Phocaean settlers at Alalia and the combined Carthaginian and Etruscan fleet. Though victorious, the Phocaeans had to evacuate Corsica and move to southern Italy. The battle marked the end of Greek expansion westwards.

ALAMÁN, LUCAS (1792–1853), monarchist politician and mine-owner of Mexico, secretary of state (1823, 1830–2), and noted historian of the independence era. Alamán sought unsuccessfully to revive the mining industry and to encourage the growth of home manufacturing following independence. His most notable legislative achievement was the immigration act of 1830, which attempted to bar North Americans from

Texas. Before his death Alamán helped Santa Anna to become dictator of Mexico. His monumental *Historia de México* (5 vols, 1849–52) is regarded as a classic.

ALAMEIN, BATTLE OF (23 Oct.–4 Nov. 1942), decisive battle of the Second World War, fought between the Allied and the Axis powers, resembling in the artillery bombardment which preceded the attack the battles of the First World War. It opened the way for the advance of Montgomery's army along the North African coast to Tunis. (Defeat would have left Alexandria, 96 kms to the west, defenceless and given Rommel control of Egypt.) The advantages which Montgomery enjoyed were that the Qattara depression on his left and the sea on his right enabled his preparations to proceed unimpeded by flank attacks; Rommel's communications across the Mediterranean were hazardous and he lost command of the air. German and Italian losses were some 10,000 casualties, 30,000 prisoners, and 500 tanks destroyed.

ALAMGIR II (1688–1759), the title of Prince Aziz-ad-din, second son of the Emperor Jahandar Shah (*reg.* 1712–13) and his Hindu wife Anup Bai. He was raised to the throne in June 1754 by the Vizier Imad-ul-Mulk, after the overthrow of the Emperor Ahmad Shah, but remained a puppet of the vizier with only nominal power, and, being of a pious disposition, spent much of his time with religious men. Chafing at the vizier's control, he attempted to secure the support of the Rohilla chief Najab Khan, but was murdered on Imad-ul-Mulk's orders while visiting a dervish in Firoz Shah's fort near Delhi.

ALAMO, fortified mission building in San Antonio, TX, which was held for 13 days by nearly 200 men under James Bowie and William Travis against 3000 Mexicans led by Santa Anna. The mission fell on 6 March 1836, and 'Remember the Alamo' became the rallying cry of TX revolutionaries.

ALAMUT, fortress in the Alburz mountains, north-east of Qazwin in Persia. Hasan-i Sabbah, founder of the Isma'ili order of the Assassins, made it the centre of his power in 1090. The Mongols took Alamut in 1257.

ALANBROOKE, ALAN FRANCIS BROOKE, 1st Viscount (1883–1963), British commander in the Second World War. Born and educated on the continent, he joined the army in 1902 and in the First World War served in the Royal Artillery. His career between the wars was concerned chiefly with military training.

During the Second World War he commanded the 2nd Army Corps of the British Expeditionary Force. His contribution to the success of the Dunkirk evacuation was recognized when the BEF was reconstituted and thrown in to support Weygand's continuing resistance. Here Brooke was seen at his most brilliant as a field commander. The gradual collapse of French resistance, however, soon compelled a second evacuation in mid-1940. To meet a possible invasion, Brooke was then entrusted with the organization of an army from what forces remained.

In 1941 he became chief of the Imperial General Staff. His solid practical sense and strategic imagination sometimes acted as a counterweight to Churchill's ambitious though not always practicable schemes. The Allied invasion of Europe took place through Italy in 1943 and by 1944 the invasion of France seemed imminent. Brooke appeared an obvious choice as its commander but the American contribution to the war was now predominant, and the appointment went to Eisenhower. This aroused much controversy, and Brooke, though bitterly disappointed, continued to lend his great abilities to the war effort until his retirement in 1946.

ÅLAND ISLANDS, archipelago between Sweden and Finland, with a Swedish-speaking population. With Finland, it was ceded unconditionally by Sweden to Russia in 1809. Retro-cession was held out to Sweden as an inducement to join Britain and France in the Crimean War, in which they captured the half-completed Russian fortress of Bomarsund. Sweden having stayed neutral, the Åland Convention and treaty of Paris (1856) required Russia only to demilitarize the islands. This situation lasted until the First World War, although Sweden failed to secure its express confirmation in the Baltic treaty of 1908.

ALANS. A non-Germanic barbarian people originally settled in southern Russia, some of whom joined in the great migration urged westwards by the Huns, ultimately crossing into Spain in 409. Thereafter this section of the Alans lost their separate identity, merging with the Vandals and associated tribes.

AL-ANSAR, 'the helpers', the name given to those elements at Medina who supported the Prophet Muhammad. After the great Arab conquests the Ansar declined in importance.

ALARIC (d. 411), King of the Visigoths encamped in the Balkans. He first menaced Constantinople, but in 401 moved towards Italy. Avoiding the destruction that overwhelmed other Germanic bands in 405, he bided his time until there was no effective opponent in Italy. His first siege of Rome was raised on payment of heavy compensation. In 410 he captured and sacked the city, but did not destroy it. This event reverberated throughout the Roman world. St Augustine was at pains to prove that it was not a visitation on the Eternal City by the pagan gods in punishment for the spread of Christianity.

ALASKA BOUNDARY DISPUTE, conflict between Canada and the US concerning the extreme southern portion of AK. In 1867 the US purchased AK from Russia. The boundaries were those defined by an Anglo-Russian treaty of 1825 because the coast had not been surveyed. Precise definition was not thought necessary until the Klondike Gold Rush (1896). Jurisdiction was sought on whether the boundary should go over or round the indentations of the coast. This would decide whether Canadians would be liable for American Customs duties. When in 1897 a joint High Commission failed to settle the dispute, the British Government suggested it should go to arbitration, but it was not until 1903 that the US agreed. A commission of six 'impartial jurists' decided in favour of the US. The British chief justice, Lord Alverstone, voted with the Americans, causing widespread resentment in Canada. It was felt that Canadian interests had been sacrificed for Anglo-American friendship. The award has since come to be regarded as a reasonable compromise.

ALASKA HIGHWAY, all-weather military highway built as a result of agreement between Canada and the US during the Second World War. It was constructed (1942) to link AK with supply bases in the US and Canada in case control of sea routes should be lost to the enemy.

ALASKA, PURCHASE OF (1867). AK was bought by the US from Russia for $7,200,000 primarily as a commercial and naval foothold on the Pacific. Although originally referred to as 'Seward's Icebox', it was later found to contain vast mineral wealth and in 1959 became the 49th of the United States.

ALAUNGPAYA (1714–60), King of Ava (*reg.* 1752–60), established the last Burmese dynasty. After driving the Mons back to Lower Burma, he turned north to deal with enemies in Manipur and the Shan States. In 1756–7 he resumed operations against the Mons, which were interrupted by a second campaign in Manipur (1758–9). He invaded Siam (late 1759), but in May 1760 was mortally wounded by the explosion of one of his own cannon while besieging Ayuthia. Alaungpaya was no administrator, but his war-like energy united Burma for only the second time in her history.

ALAWIDS, the present (1970) royal family of Morocco, which arose in the second half of the 17th cent. Claiming descent from the Prophet and aided by the Ma'qil Araba, Mulay al-Rashid, from the Tafilalt and Taza, overran Morocco from Fez to Marrakesh between 1666 and his death (1672), suppressing the regional authorities of marabouts.

Mulay Isma'il (*reg.* 1672–1727) tried to unite the country in recognition of the sharifs as descendants of Muhammad. Suppression of the marabout authorities, however, deprived the mountain regions of leadership without substituting any central control. A division was established between the *bilad al-makhzan*, the plains under the government, and the *bilad al-siba*, the unsubdued remainder. After Isma'il's death there followed 30 years of anarchy. While family and soldiery fought over the succession, the *bilad al-siba* expanded. Sidi Muhammad (*reg.* 1757–90) restored order in the *bilad al-makhzan* while negotiating recognition from a much-enlarged remainder. European trade was governed by agreements. This was the pattern for the 19th cent. Without problems of succession, four competent sultans managed the country on limited resources from a limited territory. *Harka*s (military expeditions) were made into the *bilad al-siba* to obtain homage in return for independence.

After 1894 conditions changed. Weak government coincided with international competition. To exclude Germany, France established a protectorate in 1912, while Spain took the Rif. The dynasty took on new life after 1927 with Muhammad V. While the French, having gained control of the *bilad al-siba*, came to rely on its Berber tribes for support, the king became the focus of a growing nationalism centred on the former *bilad al-makhzan*. Independence was achieved in 1956.

ALAWITE, extremist Shiite sect, also called Nusayri, founded by Ibn Nuwayr in 9th cent. and centred in mountainous Lataqiya area of northern Syria. Separately governed under French mandate, the Alawis, through their predominance in the army, came to play the dominant role in Syrian politics in the 1960s.

ALBA IULIA, RESOLUTIONS OF (1918), united Transylvania with the Rumanian kingdom. On 1 Dec. 1918 a national assembly of the Rumanians of Transylvania gathered at Alba Iulia and voted for the union of all Rumanians in a single state. This was to take place on the basis of (*a*) full national liberty for all peoples; (*b*) complete autonomy for all regions; (*c*) general, direct, equal, and secret elections; (*d*) freedom of press, assembly, and association; (*e*) extensive redistribution of landed property; and (*f*) equitable conditions for industrial workers.

ALBA LONGA, ancient Latin city on the site of modern Castel Gandolfo, predating Rome and peopled by the same ethnic stock. The account of its foundation by Iulus (Ascanius), son of Aeneas, and of an era of Trojan occupation there before the foundation of Rome, are the merest legend. Livy's story of its dismantling by Tullus Hostilius, and the translation of its population to Rome, is imaginative elaboration, but archaeology confirms the decline of the city during the Roman regal period.

ALBANIAN NATIONAL MOVEMENT. Before 1878 occasional disturbances in Albania were directed against Ottoman centralization rather than being nationalist manifestations. In 1878 northern Albanians began to assert nationalist claims in opposition to other Slav demands (Albanian League, 1878). Later, Catholic Albanians from the Shkodär (Scutari) area and Orthodox Albanians from the south demanded some administrative autonomy although central Albanian Muslims opposed these demands. Albanian nationalism first acquired a linguistic aspect through the activities of Albanian émigrés, especially in Italy, in the later 19th cent., and this was extended

within Albania after the 1908 revolution through the establishment of Albanian clubs, schools, and newspapers and discussion about the adoption of an Albanian alphabet. This movement conflicted with Young Turk centralization and considerable unrest developed (1910–12). More far-reaching demands were formulated by Albanians under the leadership of Isma'il Kemal (Gerche Programme, 1911). Still the movement affected only a minority of Albanians, who were themselves deeply divided on religious and social grounds, and went no further than a demand for autonomy within the Ottoman empire. In the First Balkan War (1912) most Albanians fought for the Ottomans, and only when it became apparent that Ottoman rule in Europe was collapsing and the choice between partition amongst other Balkan states or an independent Albania become clear, did Isma'il Kemal and a number of nationalists, with Austrian support, proclaim Albanian independence (28 Nov. 1912).

ALBANIAN RISINGS (1908–12), revolutionary movement among Albanian nationalists which brought the country independence from Turkey. An attempt was made to overcome local religious differences and to form a provisional government at Monastir (1908), which pressed the Turks for some autonomy. Refusal was followed by widespread revolt (1910), culminating in the occupation of Scopje (1912). However, it was only on Austrian insistence that this incipient national state was given independence and not absorbed by Serbia, Montenegro, and Greece.

ALBANIAN–ITALIAN AGREEMENTS (9 March 1936), a series of financial, trade, and economic agreements signed between King Zog and Mussolini, supplementing the political pacts of 1925 and 1927. Close economic ties dated back to 1925, when the National Bank of Albania was founded in Rome, and the Italian State Railways obtained shares in southern Albanian oil wells. Yugoslavia, Italy's chief rival in this area, tacitly endorsed Italy's position in the Italo-Yugoslav settlement of March 1937, and took no action when Italy annexed Albania (7 April 1939).

ALBANY, titular Countess of (1753–1824), wife of Prince Charles Edward, the Stuart 'Young Pretender', whom she married in 1772.

ALBANY, ROBERT STEWART, 1st Duke of (Scottish) (*c.* 1340–1420), effective ruler of Scotland for nearly 30 years. After the death of his father, King Robert II, in 1390, he became regent for his enfeebled brother, King Robert III (d. 1406), and murdered in 1402 the latter's heir, David. Because the king feared the same fate for his younger son James, he sent him to France in 1406, but the boy was captured at sea by the English and remained in captivity in England until 1424. Albany continued in power as 'governor' for his absent nephew after Robert III's death, but never dared usurp the Crown because he lacked firm control over other Scottish magnates. His son Murdoch succeeded him as 'governor', but was executed in 1425 by the re-established King James I.

ALBANY, JOHN STUART, 4th Duke of (Scottish) (1481–1536), Stuart claimant to the throne of Scotland, who lived for some time in France before being sent back to his native country by Francis I in order to stir up trouble for Henry VIII. Albany overthrew the government, which was in the hands of Henry's sister, Margaret, widow of James IV, replacing her as regent (1515). He returned to France shortly after and was detained there (1517) by Francis, now anxious to conciliate England. With the imminent renewal of Anglo-French hostility (1522), Francis released Albany, who again returned to Scotland to create a diversion (1523), but he failed to take advantage of the weakness of the English defences and finally retired to France (1524). He accompanied Francis I on the Pavia campaign (1525) and later visited Rome several times as French ambassador. He helped to negotiate the marriages of his wife's niece, Catherine de Medici, to Henry,

Duke of Orleans, and James V of Scotland to Marie de Bourbon.

ALBANY, HENRY STUART (LORD DARNLEY), 6th Duke of (Scottish) (1545–67), cousin and second husband (1565) of Mary Queen of Scots, their son becoming James VI of Scotland (1567) and James I of England (1603). The marriage, although strengthening Mary's claim to the English succession, was unhappy and Mary began to show favour to the Catholic party in Scotland, in particular to Rizzio, her Italian secretary. With other disaffected nobles, Darnley had Rizzio murdered in Mary's presence; despite a pretended reconciliation, she did not forgive him. He fell ill and she had him moved from Glasgow to a lonely house at Kirk o'Field, Edinburgh, where he was murdered. Mary's suspected complicity provoked a rebellion which removed her from the throne and drove her in flight to England.

ALBANY PLAN OF UNION (1754), Benjamin Franklin's proposal that the British colonies should federate under a general council and a president. It was adopted at a congress of colonial delegates in Albany, NY, but rejected by the colonies, which were unwilling to concede the necessary powers.

ALBANY REGENCY, political group in NY (1820s–1830s) dominated by Martin Van Buren. Operating a sophisticated political machine, it aided the growth of the Democratic Party, but collapsed as a result of the economic crisis (1837) and growing factionalism within the state.

ALBASIN, key fortress on the Amur river in south-eastern Siberia during a series of disputes between Russian and Chinese forces which extended from the mid-17th cent. to the signing of the treaty of Nerchinsk (1689).

ALBEMARLE, GEORGE MONCK, 1st Duke of (1608–70), English soldier and sailor, who at the beginning of King Charles I's reign, entered upon a military career, his first active service being on the ill-fated Cadiz Expedition (1625). During the 1630s he fought mainly for the Dutch, but by 1640 was back in England for the Second Bishops' War. A brief spell in Ireland to fight against the rebels was followed by his participation in the First Civil War on the royalist side. After the war he threw in his lot with the king's opponents and once more went to Ireland, where he concluded an armistice with Owen Roe O'Neill. He served in the New Model Army under Oliver Cromwell, and fought at Dunbar (1650). His pacification of Scotland thereafter was one of his notable achievements. Most of his time in the 1650s was spent there, apart from a period at sea during the first Anglo-Dutch war, when he won the battles of the Gabbard and Scheveningen (1653). Subsequently he resumed his command in Scotland and was named by Oliver Cromwell to sit in the upper chamber after the presentation of the Humble Petition and Advice, though he did not attend its debates. It was in the critical period after Cromwell's death (1658) that Monck played a temporary but crucial role when the fabric of state was disintegrating. At the beginning of 1660 he marched several thousand troops from Scotland into England, occupied London, and kept law and order while the Restoration (1660) was accomplished without bloodshed. It was the most striking episode of his life. He was rewarded with the title of Duke of Albemarle and the appointment of captain-general of the forces, but made no effort to cling to power otherwise. Only three times afterwards did he attract much public attention: when he lost the Four Days' Battle in the Second Anglo-Dutch War; when he was keeping order in London after the Great Fire; and when he improvised shore defences against the Dutch attack on the Medway.

ALBEMARLE, ARNOLD JOOST VAN KEPPEL, 1st Earl of (1669–1718), Dutch courtier and later a soldier who accompanied William III to England. Keppel came with William as companion page, but when William became attached to him his advancement was rapid. In 1695 he was created an earl and given land grants in Ireland, a gift which aroused resentment in England. In the later years of William's reign Keppel rivalled Bentinck as his most trusted adviser. Keppel also received advancement in the army, becoming a major-general in 1701. On the death of William, Keppel returned to the United Provinces, where he resumed his career in the army, becoming a general of horse. He served in Flanders, being present at Ramillies and Oudenarde, and commanded the allied detachment at Denain, where he was defeated and captured.

ALBERDI, JUAN BAUTISTA (1810–84), Argentinian writer born at Tucuman, whose ideas were to be the basis of the durable constitution of 1853. His influential view of the proper government for Argentina included a federal system with a strong executive. He conceived of federalism as granting virtual autonomy to the provinces. A firm believer in immigration, he coined the phrase 'To govern is to populate'. Alberdi feared the ambitions and monarchical institutions of Brazil. His book *El imperio del Brasil ante la democracia de América* (1869) included a denunciation of Negro slavery. Alberdi is generally considered to have been Latin America's most original political philosopher. His best known work was *Bases y puntos de partida para la organización de la República Argentina*. His final days were spent in Paris.

ALBERIC, Senator and Prince of the Romans (d. 954), member of a leading Roman noble family who became a palace official and faction leader. By violent means he replaced his mother Marozia as the ruler of Rome and manipulated five popes, of whom one, John XII, was his son. His rule as senator marked the re-establishment of landowning noble predominance in the city, which was only ended after Alberic's death by the deposition of John XII by the German King Otto I in 963.

ALBERONI, GIULIO (1664–1752), Spanish–Italian cardinal and statesman of European importance during the years 1715–19. His ambitious reforms and dynastic foreign policy almost dragged the European powers into a general war which none of them wanted.

Alberoni, the son of a vine dresser, was born in Parma, Italy. Though he became a priest, he preferred diplomacy and during the War of the Spanish Succession went to Spain as an agent of the Duke of Vendôme. After the war he remained in Spain as diplomatic agent of the Duke of Parma, successfully arranging the marriage of the duke's daughter, Elizabeth Farnese, to Philip V (1714). It was to Elizabeth Farnese that Alberoni owed his importance, for although he never held any recognized Spanish administrative post or title, his influence over the queen made him the leading personality in Spain for a time.

His absorbing interest was in foreign affairs; in particular, he wanted to replace Austrian by Spanish influence in Italy. His task was made easier by the fact that both Spain and the emperor, Charles VI of Rome, were dissatisfied with the terms of the treaty of Utrecht and technically they were still at war. Alberoni's plans went further; he planned, in the event of the death of Louis XV of France, to assert the claims of Philip V to the French throne, Philip being a grandson of Louis XIV, in spite of the renunciation at Utrecht. This brought Spain into conflict with France, ruled by the regent and heir-apparent, Orléans. In addition, Alberoni wished to restore the Stuarts to the English throne.

Alberoni built up Spanish resources (1715–17). He was aided by Patinol who revitalized the army and rebuilt the navy. In July 1717 Philip V declared war on the emperor. Sardinia was quickly won and, while Austrian resources were tied down by a war with the Turks, Alberoni attacked Sicily, the territory of the neutral King of Savoy.

Spain was now faced by a coalition of hostile powers who

were determined not to allow a general war. They—Britain especially—also feared a revitalized Spain since Spanish naval power threatened British domination in the Mediterranean. To distract his opponents, Alberoni encouraged the Turks in their war against the emperor, the Hungarian rebels, and the enemies of the French regent, and revived Jacobite intrigues, going so far as to support an abortive invasion. However, his diplomacy was in vain. The emperor concluded peace with the Turks, and the great powers joined together in the Quadruple Alliance to halt Spanish aggression.

Spain's new empire depended on sea power, and when Alberoni's new fleet was destroyed by the British navy off Cape Passaro, the whole structure collapsed. Alberoni was finally discredited when a French army invaded Spain. He fled and resumed his career in the Church, becoming Legate of Ravenna (1735) and Bologna (1740).

E. Armstrong, *Elizabeth Farnese* (London, 1892).   AW

ALBERT OF AUSTRIA, Archduke (1559–1621), brother of Emperor Rudolph II and the archdukes Matthias and Ernest and nephew of Philip II of Spain. After serving as governor of Portugal, he was designated by Philip as governor of the Low Countries in 1595 on the recall of the Count of Fuentes. Albert had the difficult task of organizing the military campaigns in the Netherlands and against France on slender financial resources. Under him the Spanish army captured Calais in 1596 and Amiens in 1597.

After Spain's conclusion of peace with France (1598), Philip made over the Netherlands to the Archduke Albert and his wife, Philip's favourite daughter, the Infanta Isabella Clara Eugenia, and they ruled nominally as sovereign princes (1598–1621). Although never free from ultimate Spanish control, the independence of 'the archdukes' helped to remove the stigma of Spanish domination from the Catholic Netherlanders. An ardent Catholic, Albert did much to revive the Church in the impoverished southern Netherlands and as a keen patron of the arts he recognized the genius of Rubens. When he died without issue, the Low Countries reverted to the Spanish Crown.

ALBERT III, Duke of Austria (*reg.* 1365–95), one of the builders of the territorial power of the Austrian principality. A man of modest talents but highly developed dynastic ambitions, he considerably expanded the possessions of the Habsburgs, acquiring Trieste and lands in south-western Germany. His other main achievement was the organization of Vienna University, founded by his brother Rudolph IV.

ALBERT, Elector of Mainz (1490–1545). As Prince Albert of Brandenburg, he became Abp of Magdeburg and administrator of the see of Halberstadt in 1513 at the age of 23, and soon afterwards Abp of Mainz, and primate of Germany. He was at the centre of the indulgence controversy which provoked the Lutheran revolt. The pope had demanded an extra payment for Albert's extraordinary pluralism in addition to the normal annates. He proclaimed the collection of an indulgence to help Albert raise the additional assessment which was to be used towards the rebuilding of St Peter's, Rome. When Luther made his famous protest against indulgences he sent a copy of his 95 theses to Albert, who forwarded them to Rome, asking that Luther should be silenced. He later became a member of the Catholic League of Nuremberg (1538) which challenged the Protestant Schmalkaldic League.

ALBERT I (1875–1934), King of Belgium (*reg.* 1909–34) and commander-in-chief of the Belgian army during the First World War. After his government had rejected the German demand for a free passage through Belgium, despite the country's neutrality, the king conducted its defence in person and led a rapid retreat into northern France. After the war he acted as a strictly constitutional monarch except for a period

of six months (1926), when he was given dictatorial powers during a financial crisis. He died in a climbing accident.

ALBERT I (*reg.* 1298–1308), King of the Romans, son of Emperor Rudolph I. In 1298 he deposed King Adolph of Nassau by force and was elected in his place. Albert's attempt to revive the power of the German kingship and vest it permanently in the Habsburg dynasty was cut short by his untimely death. After a reign of troubles and considerable achievement, he was murdered in a private quarrel. His death ended the attempt to secure the hereditary succession for his family, but he was able to establish his House even more firmly in the Austrian lands.

ALBERT THE BEAR, Margrave of Brandenburg (1134–70), one of the main promoters of the German expansion eastwards across the Elbe. He worked in close co-operation with the Church and brought in Dutch and Flemish settlers. His house ruled in Brandenburg (1134–1319).

ALBERT, PRINCE CONSORT (1819–61), second of the two sons of Ernest, Duke of Saxe-Coburg-Gotha, and husband of Queen Victoria, whom he married in 1840. He helped to steer the monarchy away from partisan involvement towards a mediating role in British politics and greatly improved the management of the British monarchy's revenues and estates. Despite formidable opposition, he was powerfully instrumental in the creation of the Great Exhibition (1851). In the early 1850s, he strongly supported Victoria in her struggle with Palmerston to be kept properly informed on foreign affairs. He was created Prince Consort in 1857. In his last illness he modified the tone of a despatch on the Trent dispute, thus helping to avert war with the US. He died of typhoid fever, and is commemorated by the Albert Hall (1867) and Albert Memorial (1876).

Albert, by tact and extremely hard work, helped to align the royal family behind middle-class ideals of domestic virtue and philanthropy, thus reaping unpopularity with certain sections of the aristocracy and the working class. He also deserves high praise for raising the standard of public taste in music, for struggling to improve British technology and design, and for his half-successful crusade against British philistinism and chauvinism.

ALBERT THE GREAT, Saint (*c.* 1200–80), the teacher of St Thomas Aquinas. A German noble, he joined the Dominican order (*c.* 1223) as a student at Padua. While lecturing in Paris (*c.*1241–8) he read the newly translated works of Aristotle and began an attempt to present the whole of human knowledge in Aristotelian form, a work which occupied him for 20 years, during which period he also founded Cologne University. His writings are one of the greatest intellectual achievements of the Middle Ages, and his works on the natural sciences established these as a respectable branch of study and had a profound influence on Roger Bacon and the Renaissance scientists.

ALBERT, ALEXANDRE MARTIN (1815–95), known popularly as Albert 'the worker', a minor member of the French provisional government formed in February 1848. He followed his fellow republicans and socialists, Louis Blanc and Auguste Blanqui, in organizing the unsuccessful rising of 15 May 1848 against a government which was showing little genuine desire to satisfy the economic grievances of the Parisian lower classes. He had far less political significance than his fellow conspirators, but nevertheless spent the next 11 years in prison for his part in the rising.

ALBERTA, westernmost of the provinces of Canada, lying between BC and Sask., created in 1905. It was originally part of the Hudson's Bay Co's territory granted by the charter of 1670, but not until the last quarter of the 18th cent. did the Northwest Co. and the Hudson's Bay Co. penetrate it for trading purposes. The area was transferred from the Hudson's Bay Co. to the new Dominion of Canada in 1869, and the Northwest Territories Act (1875) set up territorial government. Canadian immigration policy and the completion of the Canadian Pacific Railway (1885) led to an increasing influx of settlers from eastern Canada, the US and Europe. The province created in 1905 was based on that administrative district set up in the south-westerly section of the Northwest Territories in 1882, named after Queen Victoria's daughter Princess Louise Alberta. With a single-chamber elective legislature and a lieutenant-governor appointed by the federal ministry, the province immediately had the status conferred by the British North America Act of 1867. To facilitate further settlement, public lands remained under federal control until 1930. Railway expansion encouraged further immigration, particularly of farmers from the US, and although government was at first conducted by parties on the conventional conservative and liberal models, farmer movements played an increasingly important part in political and economic life. As inhabitants of a wheat-growing area, Alberta farmers favoured low tariffs and cheap freight rates and by the end of the First World War were determined to gain these ends by political action. The 1921 federal and provincial elections showed the strength of agrarian discontent and the United Farmers of Alberta formed the provincial government (1921–35). The Prairie provinces were all hard hit by the Depression in the early 1930s, partly as a result of over-cultivation of wheat and soil impoverishment, and people were greatly influenced by the radio broadcasts of William Aberhart, the founder of the Social Credit Party. Aberhart formed a government after the election of 1935 and tried to establish a new currency system, with the idea that economic troubles could be cured by a redistribution of wealth through 'social dividends' and price controls, but the bills passed by the provincial legislature were disallowed by the Supreme Court of Canada. Other measures failed and the 1937 provincial budget showed a huge deficit. Resorting to more orthodox policies, the Social Credit Party was returned to power after the 1940 election. The growth of the oil and mining industries after the Second World War considerably strengthened the economy and some Social Dividends were paid in 1957–8 (Citizen's Oil Royalties). But after that Alberta directed its surplus funds into a five-year anti-recession programme. Increased and diversified industry superseded farming as the dominant economic activity. While the population of the province rose from 73,000 (1901) to 1,300,000 (1961), the farm population dropped more than 40 per cent (1931–61), with the trend towards larger and more mechanized farms. The increased population was absorbed into the growing urban centres.

John Blue, *Alberta, Past and Present, Historical and Biographical* (1924).
Kenneth E. Liddell, *Alberta Revisited* (Toronto, 1960).
GFO

ALBERTI, LEONE BATTISTA (1404–72), Italian painter, philosopher, poet, musician, and architect. He was one of the recreators of interest in classical architecture and restorers of its style. His *De Re Aedificoria* describes architecture of buildings and of gardens. His horticultural recommendations derive clearly from the Younger Pliny, but have none the less much that is personal and of his time.

ALBIGENSIANS, name given by outsiders to the adherents of an heretical movement prevalent in the late 12th cent. in southern France, with one of its centres being at Albi near Toulouse. These heretics called themselves Cathars, or 'pure'. They rejected the humanity of Christ and other essential Catholic beliefs. The counts of Toulouse and other rulers of the south refused to persecute them since persecution on a wide scale would have depopulated and impoverished their territories, and some of the southern aristocracy were friendly to them. The acceptance of the Cathar movement was one of the features of a sophisticated and original civilization in southern France, more akin to that of Italy than of northern France. The assassination in 1208 of a papal legate in charge of reconverting the Albigensians, provided a pretext for the launching of a crusade against them. King Philip Augustus of France encouraged it and crusaders were mainly northern French nobles led by Philip's vassal, Simon de Montfort. By 1229, after 20 years of warfare, the heresy was destroyed and the south of France and its civilization were ruined. The way was prepared for the annexation of Languedoc by the French Crown.

ALBIZZI FAMILY, leading Florentine family of cloth merchants and bankers who headed the oligarchy governing Florence after the defeat of the popular revolution of the Ciompi in 1378. The Albizzi expanded the evil practices of exiling all rivals and shamelessly manipulating the Florentine electoral system. Under Maso degli Albizzi, Florence successfully resisted serious threats from Milan and Naples and conquered Pisa in 1406. Maso's son Rinaldo was driven out in 1434 by the supporters of Cosimo de Medici, who inaugurated the 60 years of Medici pre-eminence in Florence.

ALBOIN (d. 573), King of the Lombards, whom he led from the Danube valley into Italy in 568. His state comprised the north Italian plain and much of Tuscany. It broke up after his death into some 30 'duchies', each under a duke, which quarrelled fiercely among themselves.

ALBORNOZ, GIL ALVAREZ DE (d. 1367), Spanish cardinal sent to Italy in 1353 to restore papal authority in the papal states. Through his skill both as a soldier and a politician he succeeded and enabled the papacy to return to Rome from Avignon, by assuring for the popes a sufficient revenue from their Italian territories and a possibility of residing there securely. He promulgated in 1357 an important code of law for the papal territories (*constitutiones Aegidiane*).

ALBRET, ARNAUD AMANIEU (d. 1401), one of the most powerful vassals of Edward, the Black Prince, in Aquitaine. In 1368 Albret and his uncle, the Count of Armagnac, refused to allow Edward to collect a tax from their tenants and appealed against it to King Charles V of France. Charles's acceptance of their appeal in Dec. 1368 amounted to a resumption of the war with England and fighting began (Jan. 1369), leading to the reconquest by the French of most of the English lands in France. Albret, by committing himself to the French cause, started his family on a path that led his descendant, Henry of Navarre, to become King Henry IV of France.

ALBRET, CHARLES, Lord of (d. 1415), important southern French noble and constable of France, who led the French army, though three times as large as the English, to the massive defeat of Agincourt (25 Oct. 1415). He was among the 7000 French who died at the hands of the English archers.

ALBUERA, BATTLE OF (16 May 1811), fought near Spain's southern frontier with Portugal. A British army under Beresford defeated a French one under Soult.

ALBUQUERQUE, FRANCISCO FERNANDEZ DE LA CUEVA, 7th Duke of (d. 1637), viceroy of Catalonia, who was appointed in 1616 by Philip III of Spain to restore law and order to that province. He suppressed banditry and curtailed Catalan liberties.

ALBUQUERQUE, AFFONSO D' (1453–1515) followed Vasco da Gama, who discovered the sea route to India (1497), and Francisco d'Almeida, the first viceroy, as governor of the Portuguese in India. Within six years he had founded the sea empire of the Portuguese in the east. In 1510 he took Goa from the Sultan of Bijapur and made it the capital of the Portuguese empire. By marrying his soldiers to the widows of the Muslim garrison he established a resident Portuguese population and founded the modern Goan Luso–Indian race. In 1511 he captured Malacca, the entrepôt for trade between the Far East and south Asia, and in 1515 Ormuz, which dominated the entrance to the Persian Gulf. He failed to take Aden, but secured Socotra as a base for controlling the Red Sea. He hoped by these means to ruin the Muslim power in Egypt and Turkey. He succeeded in establishing a Portuguese supremacy over the south Asian seas which was exercised by means of a system of licences, and gave the European spice trade to the Portuguese. He was recalled, but died at Goa.   TGPS

ALCABALA (or 'tenth penny'), a 10 per cent sales tax on all commodities, was introduced into Spain in 1341 and lingered on until the Napoleonic occupation (1808). It was remunerative to the Crown, but had a hampering effect on trade, since the tax was chargeable four times, on the raw material and again when the finished article passed from the manufacturer to the wholesaler, the retailer, and the consumer. Alva's proposal to introduce the *alcabala* into the Netherlands (1569) was so bitterly resisted that he was obliged to postpone it for two years. When it was imposed, it led to a virtual cessation of trade and was one of the main reasons for the defection of the commercial classes.

An *alcabala* of 2–6 per cent on all commercial transactions was introduced in all the Spanish-American colonies between 1575 and 1591. Indians, however, were generally exempt from this tax.

ALCAEUS, Greek aristocrat and lyric poet of Mytilene (*c.* 600 BC). His numerous political poems directed against both the short-lived tyrants at Mytilene and their opponent, Pittacus, give valuable insight into the general revolutionary atmosphere of Greece *c.* 600.

ALCALÁ GALIANA, ANTONIO (1789–1865), Spanish writer and liberal politician. After taking part in the liberal revolution of 1820 he gradually became more radical when the change of government did not bring him the expected professional advancement. But by the mid-1830s he had once more become a moderate with a great admiration for the English system of government. He believed that Spanish liberalism should aim at a union of the educated upper and middle classes against the Carlist one of Crown, Church, and peasantry.

ALCALA ZAMORA, NICETO (1877–1949), Catholic conservative, who was president of the Spanish republic (Dec. 1931–May 1936). He was elected to the Cortes in 1905 and later became minister of works (1917) and minister of war (1922). In Aug. 1930 he became chairman of a revolutionary committee which united Spanish republicans and the Catalan left, although his conversion to republicanism was but a year old and he was known for his hostility to Catalan nationalism. In April 1931 he negotiated the removal from Spain of the king (who had refused to abdicate) and the assumption of power by a provisional government which he headed. The Constituent Cortes elected in June was, however, too radical to support his premiership, and he resigned in Oct. rather than accept the church settlement embodied in the new constitution. He was then (Dec.) elected to the presidency, although neither his views nor his political skills suited the growing extremism of the period. He was deposed by an overwhelming vote (238–5) of the Cortes in April 1936.

ALCALA UNIVERSITY, at Alcala de Henares, near Madrid, was founded (*c.* 1510) by Cardinal Ximenes and was famous for the publication of the Complutensian Polyglot Bible (1514–17), Complutum being the old Roman name for the town. The university's principal building was the college of San Ildefonso, completed in 1583. Known all over Europe for its courses in classics and philosophy, Alcala became a rival to the older 13th cent. foundation at Salamanca, and at one time it had 7000 students. In 1836 the university was transferred to Madrid and its buildings were later used for storing state archives and the records of the Inquisition.

ALCALDE, Spanish judicial officer, a post of ancient origin which came to acquire political and administrative authority and carried with it the chairmanship of the town council. The post, which was also introduced into Spain's New World settlements, gradually lost its political powers, which in 1870 were removed altogether.

ALCARAZ, PEDRO RUIZ DE, Spanish mystic, condemned by the Inquisition (1525) for claiming insights allegedly based on direct communion with God. Fearing the spread of heresy in Spain, the Inquisition stamped on all pretensions to a personal way of salvation.

ALCAZAR OF TOLEDO. Half-fortress and half-palace, the Alcazar (Arab., 'castle') dominates the city of Toledo and the Tagus river. It acquired a legendary character during the Spanish Civil War, when Nationalist forces withstood a 70-day siege until they were relieved on 27 Sept. 1936. Their resistance was made possible by the incapacity of the Republican militia to mount a proper offensive. The relief of the Alcazar delayed the arrival of the Nationalist army in Madrid, thereby perhaps depriving it of a speedy victory.

ALCHEMY, the transmutation of metals in the belief that baser metals have the same constituents as gold and may be restored to their elemental form by the removal of impurities. Although discredited by its natural appeal to fanatics and charlatans, alchemy has been practised by many learned and honest men and may not unreasonably be regarded as the beginning of scientific chemistry.

ALCIBIADES (*c.* 450–404 BC), brilliant but unstable public figure at Athens in the great Peloponnesian War, who was brought up by Pericles and associated with Socrates. Elected general in 420, by political intrigue at Athens and diplomacy in Argos he precipitated the failure of the peace of Nicias, but the Argive alliance led to defeat at Mantinea (418). A strong advocate of the expedition to Sicily (415) in opposition to Nicias, he was elected commander with him and Lamachus. Before its departure he was implicated in the scandal of the mutilation of the Hermae, but despite his pleas notice of trial was not served until he reached Sicily. He then fled to the Spartans and gave them invaluable advice to send a general to Syracuse and fortify Decelea as a base in Attica. Subsequently discredited at Sparta, he joined the Persian satrap Tissaphernes and promised the Athenians Persian aid if they would substitute oligarchy for democracy. But when the oligarchs seized power at Athens (411), he rejoined the democratic Athenian fleet at Samos and helped to prevent civil war, and after defeating the Spartans at Cyzicus returned to Athens (407). He was elected to an extraordinary command, but after the defeat of his deputy at Notium (406) he retreated into exile in the Chersonese, where he gave unheeded advice to the Athenians before their defeat at Aegospotami (405). He was assassinated in Phrygia.

ALCMEONIDAE, Athenian aristocratic family well connected abroad and powerful at Athens in the 6th cent. BC. Cursed and banished from Athens after Megacles' sacrilege against Cylon (*c.* 632), the family soon returned. Megacles' son, Alcmeon, supported Delphi in the First Sacred War (*c.* 590) and his son, also called Megacles, led the 'men of the coast' in the regional faction preceding Peisistratus' tyranny. Banished by Peisistratus (*c.* 546), the family returned under Hippias (*c.* 527), only to be banished again after Hipparchus' murder (514). It used its influence at Delphi to hasten the Spartan expulsion of Hippias (510). Worsted in subsequent aristocratic intrigue, the Alcmeonid Cleisthenes won popular support by his democratic reforms (508). Subsequently the family's influence declined and prominent Alcmeonids, suspected of treachery at Marathon (490), were ostracized in the 480s. Both Pericles and Alcibiades were related to the family through their mothers.

ALCOHOL INTERESTS in France have formed one of the main political pressure groups in the 20th cent. The lobby consists of (*a*) over 3 million *bouilleurs de cru*, farmers permitted to distil alcohol for home consumption tax free, and (*b*) wine-growers and beet-growers benefiting from the guaranteed government purchase of surplus alcohol, dating from 1916. This policy has burdened the taxpayer and encouraged the overproduction of alcohol, which has been disposed of at times by adding it to petrol. The social evils of alcoholism have been another motive for reform, but for many years the alcohol lobby had enough political influence to frustrate attempts, notably those of Mendès-France (1954), to limit its privileges. Since 1960, the governments of the Fifth Republic have had more success.

ALCOTT, LOUISA MAY (1832–88), US writer who enjoyed life-long success after the publication of *Little Women* (1868). A campaigner for such causes as female suffrage and temperance, her work is characteristically concerned with moral edification.

ALCUIN (d. 804), Northumbrian, educated at York, who became master of the cathedral school. In 782 he joined the court of Charlemagne and emerged as one of the leading figures of the Carolingian Renaissance. He played a prominent part in bringing about the imperial coronation of Charlemagne in 800. He corrected the Vulgate text of the Bible, producing the standard version used subsequently in the Middle Ages.

ALDEN, JOHN (1599–1687), *Mayflower* pilgrim and original settler of Duxbury, MA, who became a friend and neighbour of Miles Standish and deputy governor (1664). Longfellow's version of his marriage to Priscilla Mullins in 'The Courtship of Miles Standish' has no historical foundation.

ALDHELM (d. 709) outstanding West Saxon literary figure, who wrote verse and prose in an obscure and ornate Latin style. First entering the monastery of Malmesbury under its Irish founder Maidulf, he went on to study at Canterbury under Theodore and Hadrian. In 705 he became Bp of Sherborne. His writings, a product of the earliest schools in England, are essential for the understanding of 7th-cent. culture.

ALDINE PRESS, a printing house founded at Venice by Aldo Manuzio, the inventor of italic type. Its first publication was Musaeus' *Hero and Leander* (1494). The press, later transferred to Rome, was important in Renaissance scholarship for its many editions of the classics.

ALDO MANUZIO (TEOBALDO MANUCCI) (*c.* 1450–1515). The introduction of printing made possible the publication of scholarly standard editions. Aldo was one of the first European humanists to grasp the technical possibilities of such publication. Settling at Venice in 1490, he secured the financial support of a princely humanist for founding the Aldine Press. Using some of the best scholars, he edited a series of Greek, Latin, and Italian classics. His Greek editions were particularly famous. The beautiful printing type devised by him was generally adopted by European publishers for Greek texts.

ALDRICH, NELSON WILMARTH (1841–1915). US financier and politician, leader of the Republican 'Old Guard' in the Senate. He began his political career on the common council of Providence, RI (1869–74), later becoming a state legislator (1875–6), US congressman (1879–81), and finally US senator (1881–1911). From humble origins as a grocery clerk he became a millionaire. Admitted into the inner circle of the Senate, sometimes called the 'millionaires' club', he became a prominent member of the finance committee and spokesman for big business. Under presidents Theodore Roosevelt and Taft his leadership in the Senate was challenged by progressive Republicans. The clash came to a head over the Payne–Aldrich high tariff (1909), which contributed to the party-split for a decade.

ALDRINGER, JOHANN VON, Count (1588–1634), Imperialist soldier, for 25 years in the Spanish army before serving under Tilly at Breitenfeld (1631) and the Lech (1632). He was made a count of the Holy Roman Empire and, after Tilly's death, helped to overthrow Wallenstein, then took command of the army of the Catholic League. He was killed at the defence of Landshut.

ALEANDER, JEROME (1480–1542), Italian scholar and humanist who from 1508 became famous for his lectures on Greek and Latin authors at Paris University, where he taught Guillaume Budé and Richard Croke. He later became an important papal diplomat and cardinal, and from the Diet of Worms (1520) became increasingly conservative and a determined opponent of Lutheranism.

ALEGRÍA, CIRO (1909–67), Peruvian novelist, whose novels of social protest (*eg*, *La serpiente de oro* (1935), *El mundo es ancho y ajeno* (1941)) portrayed the plight of the Peruvian Indian.

ALEJANDRINO, CASTO (1911–) Philippine Communist leader, who was deputy commander-in-chief of the *Hukbo nang Bayan Laban sa Hapon* (*Hukbalahap*) or People's Army against Japan, launched in 1942, and later chief of staff of the *Hukbong Magpapalaya nang Bayan* or People's Liberation Army; Alejandrino, a member of a comparatively wealthy family of Arayat, Pampanga, one of the seedbeds of social unrest in Luzon, began to show concern for the plight of the peasants in 1928. As a high school graduate, he organized the *Aguman Kapatiran Ding Magsasaka* or Brotherhood Association of Farmers, which agitated for agrarian reforms. This later merged with similar associations, which, in 1938, together joined forces with a national leftist party, the *Partido Frente Popular* or Popular Front Party, at the time when the Philippines' Communist Party joined ranks with the Socialist Party. Alejandrino became a member of the Friends of China, one of the Communist Party's subsidiary organizations. He was mayor of Arayat (1940–1) until Japanese occupation of the Philippines (1941). In 1942 he helped to found the anti-Japanese *Hukbalahap*, a guerrilla organization. When the Americans returned to the Philippines (1945), he was arrested by the Central Intelligence Corps and imprisoned at Iwahig penal colony. Released in 1946, he managed the *Hukbalahap's* campaign of the Nacionalista Party in Pampanga. Soon after, he again took to the hills, but was captured in 1960 by Philippines government agents, charged with subversion under the 1957 Anti-Subversion Law, and imprisoned.

ALEKSANDROV, GEORGIY FËDOROVICH (1908–), Russian communist philosopher, author of *A History of West European Philosophy in the Nineteenth Century* (1944). Head (1934–47) of Agitprop (the agitation and propaganda department of the Central Committee of the CPSU), he was then dismissed, following attacks made on him by Zhadov, but was not disgraced and in 1954 was appointed minister of culture by Malenkov, being dismissed when the latter fell in 1955.

ALEKSEYEV, MIKHAIL VASIL'YEVICH (1857–1918), commander-in-chief on the Russian western front (1915), chief of staff to Nicholas II, and supreme commander under the provisional government. In 1918 he organized an anti-Bolshevik volunteer army in the south, but died in the same year.

ALEMÁN VALDÉS, MIGUEL (1902–), president of Mexico (1946–52), the first civilian executive since Madero. Born in Sayula, Veracruz, he began his political career as a lawyer in Mexico City, became a justice of the superior court of Veracruz, then a senator and governor of Veracruz (1936–1940). He served as minister of the interior (1940–5).

Alemán inherited the Institutional Revolutionary Party (PRI) which was sharply divided between its agrarian, labour, and 'popular' (business and professional) sectors. His administration was characterized by the emergence of a business elite in politics and a decline in the political importance of labour and agriculture. Corruption multiplied and student unrest degenerated into violence. Alemán's answer was to construct elaborate new campuses on the fringes of the capital. Vast irrigation projects were also undertaken at government expense. Foreign money was attracted by the industrial expansion policies of the central government and a pro-US foreign policy was vigorously pursued.

ALEMBERT, JEAN LE ROND D' (1717–83), mathematician and one of the most influential writers of the French Enlightenment. He co-operated with Diderot in the founding of the *Encyclopédie* and contributed articles to it himself on literature and the sciences, emphasizing the need for an empirical approach to science. Both Frederick the Great and Catherine the Great tried, unsuccessfully, to tempt him away from France to be their court philosopher.

ALENÇON, HERCULE-FRANÇOIS, Duc d' (1554–84), youngest son of Catherine de Medici and Henry II of France who played a stormy and sinister role in the later stages of the Wars of Religion. A small, tubercular, and unattractive personality, he first attracted attention as a candidate for the hand of Elizabeth of England (1570–3). Given command of a royal army in Brittany, he conspired to kidnap Charles IX, but was betrayed by his fellow conspirators (1574). He then conspired with Henry of Navarre against Henry III (1575–6) and negotiated the peace of Monsieur (1576) between Catholics and Protestants, thereby earning himself the duchy and appanage of Anjou. Subsequently he continued to pay court to Elizabeth (1579 and 1581) and negotiated with the Dutch to become their ruler. He led two forays into the Netherlands (1577, 1582), on the second of which he attempted to seize Antwerp, but was driven out.

ALESIA (mod. Alise-Sainte-Reine), town in central Gaul where Julius Caesar besieged the Gallic leader Vercingetorix, who surrendered after Caesar had beaten off a large relief force (52 BC).

ALESSANDRI PALMA, ARTURO (1868–1950), president of Chile (1920–4; 1925; 1932–8), born in Linares. As a liberal politician, Alessandri served as minister of industry and public works (1908), of finance (1913), and as prime minister (1918). He came to be known as the 'first president of the Chilean people'. When congress blocked his reform legislation, Alessandri resigned the presidency (Sept. 1924). Recalled in 1925, he obtained a new constitution which established popular government. Again he resigned (1925) and exiled himself to Italy. Following his subsequent re-election (1932), Alessandri displayed more conservative tendencies.

ALESSANDRIA, town in western Lombardy. Originally founded by an imperial supporter, the Marquis of Monferato, and called Cesaria, it was rebuilt as a fortress town in 1168 by the Lombard League as part of its preparations for war against Emperor Frederick Barbarossa, and renamed Alessandria in honour of Frederick's great opponent, Pope Alexander III. Its strategic position enabled it to disrupt the communications of the imperialists and it was besieged for six months by Frederick (1174–5).

ALEUADAE, aristocratic family, members of which, as rulers of Larisa, were powerful in Thessaly in the 6th–4th cents. BC.

Descendants of Aleuas, alleged organizer of the Thessalian confederacy, they supported the Persian invasion of Greece in 480–479, perhaps through self-interest, and afterwards frustrated a Spartan attempt to remove them. Praised by Pindar for stable government, they preserved their position against rivals at Pharsalus and Pherae through the Peloponnesian and subsequent wars, despite Spartan hostility, until Jason of Pherae's domination (c. 375–370). Later, they called in Philip II of Macedon against Pherae and his victory ended Thessalian independence.

ALEUT INDIANS, branch of the Esquimauan family, living in the Aleutian Islands and the north side of the Alaska peninsula. They were first visited by the Russians in 1741, against whose firearms they pitted their darts. They were soon under the power of the Russian traders, who exploited their skill as hunters, and whose brutality greatly reduced their numbers. From 1794, intervention by the Russian government and missionaries partially improved their situation. In 1867 the Aleuts, with the rest of the population of Alaska, came under the control of the US.

ALEXANDER OF TUNIS, RUPERT HAROLD LEOFRIC GEORGE ALEXANDER, 1st Earl (1891–1969), British field marshal. Alexander spent the First World War in France. In 1919 he commanded Baltic German anti-communist troops in northern Russia. During the 1930s he took part in frontier actions in northern India and was promoted to major-general (1937). In the Second World War (1940) he commanded a rearguard in the British withdrawal from Dunkirk and early in 1942 the retreat of the British and Indian armies from Burma. He became C.-in C. Middle East (Aug. 1942), when German forces were threatening Alexandria. Under his command the 8th army, under Gen. Montgomery, won the battle of El Alamein. As deputy Allied supreme commander, he commanded the 1943 campaign in Tunisia, and directed the Allied invasions of Sicily and Italy; in Nov. 1944 he was appointed supreme Allied commander in the Mediterranean. His advance through Italy was delayed by priority being given to the invasion of France. He was governor-general of Canada (1946–52) and minister of defence (1952–4) in the Conservative administration.

ALEXANDER THE GREAT (356–323 BC), Persian emperor, son and successor of Philip II of Macedon, one of the great conquerors of history, and a military genius who in ten years overran the Persian empire, marching to Egypt, Turkestan, and India, and initiated the second great outward expansion of Greek civilization. Tutored by Aristotle, he was brought up by his father to rule and when only 18 was prominent in the victory at Chaeronea. He succeeded Philip after his assassination (336) and soon showed his decisiveness in defeating Macedon's northern neighbours and quelling unrest in Greece, tempering severity towards Thebes, which he destroyed (335), with mercy towards Athens, where he spared his enemies. Resuming Philip's planned invasion of Asia (334), he probably aimed from the first to conquer the Persian empire and within four years had overrun Asia Minor, Syria, Egypt, Babylonia, and the Persian homeland, enforcing several difficult sieges, eg, at Tyre, and defeating Darius III's satraps at the Granicus (334) and Darius himself at Issus (333) and Gaugamela (331), and proclaimed himself Great King. Eager to explore as well as conquer, he pressed eastwards, inspiring his small army to perform marvels in action and on the march, until, after defeating the Indians at the Hydaspes (326), his troops refused to go further. Despite a nearly disastrous return journey, he was planning further conquests in Europe when he died. Though ruthless with suspect supporters, eg, Parmenio, and capable of savage outbursts, eg, in killing Cleitus, he showed remarkable mercy to defeated Persians, associating them from an early stage in governing his empire. Some of his native satraps proved unreliable and his adoption of oriental manners and encouragement of intermarriage between his soldiers and Asiatics offended

Greek and Macedonian sentiment; yet his plans for uniting his empire could well have succeeded but for his death. As it was, his empire broke up through the quarrels of his generals rather than through native uprisings, and much of it remained part of the Greek world for centuries.

Tarn, W. W., *Alexander the Great*, 2 vols (Cambridge, 1948).
Griffith, G.T. (ed.), *Alexander the Great: the main problems* (Cambridge, 1968).   TTBR

ALEXANDER I (1777–1825), Emperor of Russia (*reg.* 1801–1825). The great event of his reign was the war of 1812. Son of Paul I, he was educated by his grandmother Catherine II, with the republican La Harpe as tutor. Brought up between the enlightenment of Catherine's court and the military discipline of his father's establishment, his contradictory but forceful character was influenced by both. Under Paul I he was military governor of St Petersburg and connived at Paul's overthrow, if not his murder (1801).

His accession was greeted with enthusiasm and was expected to inaugurate a reforming era. In the early years of his reign he was assisted by his Unofficial Committee of four liberal advisers (1801–3). Peter I's collegiate system of central government was replaced (1802) by eight ministries nominally under the senate. A council of state was established (1810), but no cabinet system developed. Torture was abolished, and there were far-reaching reforms in education and government encouragement of literature and science. Constitutional projects, mainly associated with Speransky, however, were not implemented, and, except for the freeing of serfs without land in the Baltic Provinces, and the encouragement of individual nobles to grant emancipation, serfdom was untouched.

Alexander joined the war of the Third Coalition (1805), but after defeat at Austerlitz he made peace with Napoleon at Tilsit (1807). Disputes over Napoleon's economic and dynastic policy led the French to invade Russia (1812). This war was conducted by his generals, but Alexander led the army himself in the war of the Fourth Coalition and entered Paris (1814). He was a leading figure at the Congress of Vienna, and gained acceptance for his 'Holy Alliance'. The 'sacred mission' of uniting the Christian sovereigns against republicanism occupied much of the rest of his reign.

The post-war years are associated with the reactionary policies of Arakcheyev and Alexander's own scheme for military colonies. A riot in the Semenovsky regiment (1820) and the revolutionary situation in Europe stopped all talk of further reform and reversed many earlier measures. Madame Krudener and Archimandrite Photius encouraged Alexander's growing religious mysticism.

The Napoleonic wars resulted in the annexation of Finland (1808) and Poland (1815). To them, though not to Russia, Alexander granted a constitution. The Russo–Turkish War (1806–12) gained Bessarabia, and after the voluntary annexation of Georgia (1801), wars with Persia resulted in the acquisition of the Caucasus by the treaty of Gulistan (1813).

Alexander died unexpectedly at Taganrog on 1 Dec. 1825. Rumours of his continued existence as Feodor Kuzmitch, a hermit, were widely believed.

L. I. Strakhovsky, *Alexander I of Russia: The Man who defeated Napoleon* (New York, 1947).
M. Raeff, *Michael Speransky, Statesman of Imperial Russia, 1772–1839* (The Hague, 1957).   BJW

ALEXANDER II (1818–81), Emperor of Russia (*reg.* 1855–81). His reign was marked by a series of reforms which began the modernization of Russian society, and inaugurated a period of social change based on railway development, industrialization, and financial reform. As Tsarevich he had shared Nicholas I's military tastes, but received a liberal education and had experience of affairs of state.

An amnesty and relaxation of the censorship led the intelligentsia to hope for a liberal policy, on his accession, and defeat in the Crimea made some reform inevitable. The greatest of the reforms, the Emancipation of the Serfs (1861), which gave Alexander the title of the Tsar Liberator, ironically began the period of disillusionment. Alexander had in 1856 declared his intention to abolish serfdom from above before it abolished itself from below, and fear of a peasant revolt was mixed with the tsar's humanitarian principles. The statute was immensely complicated, and involved a series of commissions associated especially with the names of Grand Duke Constantine and Rostsovtsev. Alexander's determination was vital to its passage. Though a considerable achievement, in granting personal freedom with land, it failed to satisfy either party or to solve the agrarian problem.

A European judicial system with trial by jury, an independent judiciary, justices of the peace, and public proceedings was established, although tempered by the right of administrative arrest. Military reform (1874) which established conscription and reduced service from 25 to 6 years had more lasting results. Educational reform opened universities to all classes and inaugurated a short-lived period of university autonomy. Zemstovs, local self-governing bodies elected from all classes, were established (1864) with corresponding City Dumas (1870).

Liberal gentry pressed for a national assembly but, although projects for limited constitutional reform were discussed, and Alexander actually signed one on the day of his death, he remained a firm believer in autocratic government. After student unrest, the 1863 Polish rebellion, and an assassination attempt (1866), Alexander became disillusioned and restricted the development of earlier reforms. More reactionary policies under Counts P. Shuvalov and D. Tolstoy and Gen. Trepov were paralleled by the spread of revolutionary groups known as Populists. 1873–4 saw the 'going to the people' movement and the end of the 1870s an increase in terrorism, culminating in the assassination of Alexander by the 'People's Will' on 1 March 1881.

The chief focus of Alexander's foreign policy was the Balkans. He himself was not a Panslavist but his vacillating and expansionist policy led to the Russo–Turkish War (1877–8). Russian troops reached the outskirts of Constantinople, but the Congress of Berlin restricted Russian gains. Nevertheless, Russian influence, especially in Bulgaria, where Alexander allowed a constitution, increased. In Central Asia the khanates of Khiva, Bokhara, and Samarkhand were conquered in the 1860s and the treaties of Aigun (1858) and Peking (1860) gave Russia the left bank of the Amur and the Maritime Province, and Vladivostok was founded.

E. M. Almedingen, *The Emperor Alexander II* (London, 1962).
W. E. Mosse, *Alexander II and the Modernization of Russia* (New York, 1958).   BJW

ALEXANDER III (1845–94), Emperor of Russia (*reg.* 1881–94). His reign was marked by a policy of Russification, reaction, and political repression. Trained as a soldier, he became heir on the death of his elder brother (1865), succeeded after the assassination of his father (1881), and after a short period of conflict between reforming and reactionary ministers replaced the remaining liberal advisers of Alexander II with conservatives. D. Tolstoy was promoted to minister of the interior (1882), but Alexander's chief adviser throughout the reign was the Procurator of the Holy Synod, Pobedonostsev.

The emergency powers given to governors of provinces and the ministry of the interior reversed many of the legal reforms of Alexander II, and justices of the peace but not juries were abolished. Zemstvo powers were drastically cut, Land captains were established (1889) in the rural areas to control the peasantry, and the educational system was run on lines of strict discipline, reactionary syllabuses, and social exclusiveness. University autonomy was abolished, and press censorship made very severe. Attempts to restore noble authority by measures like a noble land bank in 1885 failed and the reign saw the development of a huge and stifling bureaucracy. Despite Alexander's bluff identification with the peasant masses and the establishment of a peasants' land bank (1882), agriculture stagnated into famine by 1891.

Under Alexander and Pobedonostsev, Russification became an official policy, with the Russian language and culture forced on non-Russian minorities, including the Poles and Baltic Germans. Rigid restrictions on Jews from 1882 led to pogroms and increasing numbers of Jews joining revolutionary movements. Non-Orthodox religions also suffered persecution. The revolutionary movement was driven underground and the action of the 1870s was replaced by philosophical debates between the populists and the new marxist groups. An attempt on the tsar's life (1887) involved Lenin's elder brother.

Alexander did, however, encourage the industrialization and railway development which marked his reign and are especially associated with Witte. The tsar authorized the starting of the Trans-Siberian railway in 1891. The rise of a proletariat was one result of the development of heavy industry.

Despite his autocratic principles Alexander was unable to maintain the *Dreikaiserbund* with Germany and Austria after the Bulgarian crisis (1885–6), and his reign saw the development of the Franco-Russian alliance (1892). Alexander's repressive reign, though a period of peace abroad and apparent stability, bequeathed many problems to his heir.

H. Seton-Watson, *The Russian Empire* (Oxford, 1967).
K. P. Pobedonostsev, *Reflections of a Russian Statesman* (London, 1898).   BJW

ALEXANDER (1888–1934), Regent of Serbia (1914–18) and of Yugoslavia (1918–21), King of Yugoslavia (*reg.* 1921–34). Alexander was the son of Peter I and acted as regent for his father during the First World War. As regent he was implicated in the Salonika affair (June 1917) in which Dimitriević and other leaders of the Black Hand were tried and executed for an alleged attempt against Alexander's life. Alexander declared for the Yugoslav ideal in 1916, became prince-regent (Dec. 1918), and took the oath to the constitution on 28 June 1921. In Jan. 1929, at the height of tension between Serbs and Croats, he abolished the constitution and proclaimed a royal dictatorship. Under his regime the White Hand, a group of army officers who superseded the Black Hand after the Salonika affair, rose to prominence. Authoritarian and unyielding, Alexander disdained the particularism which was undermining the Yugoslav ideal. He forbade the use of national designations and changed the name of the state to Yugoslavia (from the Kingdom of the Serbs, Croats, and Slovenes). His dictatorship was confirmed by a new constitution adopted in 1931. In 1934 he visited France, but his political intentions in doing so were obscure. He was assassinated alongside Louis Barthou by a Macedonian terrorist at Marseilles on 9 Oct.

ALEXANDER III (*reg.* 1249–86), King of Scotland, last of the native Scottish dynasty. In 1278 Alexander did homage to his brother-in-law, Edward I. In 1265 the Norwegians sold Alexander the Hebrides and the Isle of Man. The death of his heiress, Margaret, in 1290 led to a disputed succession and an Anglo-Scottish war in 1295.

ALEXANDER I (OBRENOVIĆ) (1869–1903), King of Serbia, succeeded on the abdication of his father (1889), although until 1893 he was subject to a regency and then to his father's influence from behind the scenes. His ten years' personal rule was arbitrary and became increasingly unpopular with all political parties, especially Serbian nationalist groups, who resented his subservience to Austria-Hungary and wanted him to pursue a pro-Russian foreign policy. On 10 June 1903 he was murdered with his equally unpopular wife by a group of army officers. His death brought a change of dynasty and a rapid deterioration in relations between Serbia and Austria-Hungary.

ALEXANDER III (*reg.* 1159–81), Pope, one of the ablest and most influential medieval popes. A distinguished lawyer, trained at Bologna, he became the effective organizer of a centralized judicial system for the whole of Catholic Europe. Preliminary proceedings would be entrusted to local ecclesiastics acting as papal delegates, while the settlement of cases could at every stage be referred to the papal court. Alexander's rulings on numerous important matters determined the principles of Canon Law for centuries. Emperor Frederick Barbarossa opposed Alexander's election to the papacy and Alexander subsequently played a leading part in destroying Frederick's chances of dominating Italy. After the murder of Thomas à Becket, Alexander negotiated a statesmanlike compromise at Avranches (1172) which substantially settled Anglo-papal relations for a long period.

ALEXANDER VI (1431–1503), a Spaniard who was created cardinal by his maternal uncle, Pope Calixtus III (1455–8) and was himself Pope (*reg.* 1492–1503). At a conclave of 1492 he successfully purchased his own election and thereafter used the papacy to advance the Borgia fortunes, especially those of his notorious son, Cesare. The French invasion of Italy (1494–5) threatened the pope's position, which he sought to safeguard by forming a league and even seeking aid from the Sultan of Turkey. Ruthless and treacherous in his dealings with the Italian magnates, he at first showed forbearance in face of the denunciations of the Florentine reformer Savonarola, but later sanctioned his condemnation. In 1493 he partitioned the New World between Spain and Portugal. In his moral character he was probably the worst of all the popes, although little different from his secular contemporaries. His reign marks the ultimate point in the secularization of the papacy.

ALEXANDER VII (1599–1667). Pope (*reg.* 1655–67). For most of his pontificate he was in conflict with the French monarchy over the Gallican articles, which denied that the Church was an absolute monarchy under the pope and asserted the king's independence in all temporal affairs. As papal nuncio at the negotiations leading to the peace of Westphalia he had already crossed Cardinal Mazarin, and French hostility to him as pope eventually led to clashes in Rome between the French embassy and the papal guard, and to the French invasion of the papal city of Avignon, which was not returned in the humiliating treaty of Pisa (1664).

A reconciliation of expediency occurred when the king, Louis XIV, demanded the assistance of the pope against the Jansenist heresy, but although Alexander took the opportunity to emphasize the impotence of the French king and bishops to deal with the heresy, Gallican claims were strongly pressed after the pope's death.

He secured the restoration to Venice of the Jesuits, exiled in 1606, and received Queen Christina of Sweden into the Roman Church.

He failed to maintain his initial determination to rid the papal court of its notorious nepotism, but improved the architecture of Rome.

ALEXANDER VIII (1610–91), Pope, elected (1689) when an octogenarian. In gratitude for the old man's inactivity, Louis XIV restored to him the papal city of Avignon, occupied by the French during their quarrel with Alexander VII. Thereupon the pope declared the Declaration of Gallican Liberties null and invalid, and in the papal brief *Inter multiplices* condemned the competence of the Assembly of Clergy to make such a declaration. Ottoboni was the son of a chancellor of the Republic of Venice, and it was at the request of the Republic that he had been made a cardinal by Innocent X in 1652. He helped Venice in the war against the Turks by payment of subsidies. His generous nature was revealed by a reduction of taxes in the papal states for the benefit of the poor, and by the distribution of riches for the benefit of his relations.

ALEXANDER I (BATTENBURG) (1857–93), first prince of the semi-independent state of Bulgaria (1879–86). Although a German, he was expected to be a Russian puppet, since he was a relation of Tsar Alexander II and had fought in the Russian army. However, he was determined to throw off his country's political dependence on Russia. In 1883 he dismissed the Russian generals in his government and tried to rule through a parliament with a nationalist and anti-Russian majority. When Eastern Rumelia broke away from Turkey and demanded union with Bulgaria (1885), his acceptance inevitably met with Russian opposition and led to an international Bulgarian crisis (1885–6). His failure to follow up his military victory over the Serbs (1885), because of Austrian pressure, produced disappointment at home and support for a Russian-inspired *coup d'état* by army officers, who forced him to abdicate in Sept. 1886.

ALEXANDER (CUZA) (1820–73), elected prince of the two autonomous provinces of Moldavia and Wallachia (1859), which he ruled as the unified state of Rumania. He came from a Moldavian noble family and had been elected as a compromise choice, but he immediately showed unexpected political ability and progressive views. As well as trying to unite the two provinces and to shake off their legal dependence on Turkey, Alexander aimed at destroying the power of the large landowners and improving the position of the peasantry. In 1864 he staged a *coup d'état*, dissolved the land-owner-dominated assembly, abolished serfdom, and began a redistribution of land among the peasants. But the landowners and their army sympathizers struck back (1866), kidnapped the prince, and forced him to abdicate.

ALEXANDER NEVSKY, Saint (1220–63), best known for the victories he won as Prince of Novgorod. He defeated the Swedes on the Neva river (1240) and the Teutonic Knights on Lake Peipus (1242), drawing them on to the ice, where, weighed down by their own and their horses' armour, they drowned. He always accepted the predominance of the Mongols, who recognized him as Grand Prince of Vladimir in 1252 because of his loyalty to them. He made himself responsible for the collection of the tribute due from the Russian princes to the Mongols. Alexander's patient strategy preserved for the future an independent centre of Russian power. After his death he became the object of a popular cult and he was officially canonized by the Orthodox Church in 1547.

ALEXANDER OF HILLESBOROUGH, ALBERT VICTOR ALEXANDER, 1st Viscount (1885–1965), British Labour politician, first lord of the admiralty in Churchill's wartime government (1940–5) and again (1945–6) under Attlee; minister of defence (1947–50). Born of working-class parents, Alexander, who had an elementary education, became a Baptist lay preacher and was commissioned in the First World War. He entered politics as a Co-operative Party MP (1922–1931; 1935–50). In the first Labour government he was parliamentary secretary to the board of trade and in the second, first lord of the admiralty. In 1931 he opposed Ramsay MacDonald over cuts in unemployment benefits and over the formation of the National Government.

ALEXANDER, SAMUEL (1859–1938), philosopher, was born in Sydney and educated at Wesley College, Melbourne. After a year at Melbourne University, he went to Balliol College, Oxford (1878) and, though not alienated from his native country, never returned there. His work in Oxford, apart from the teaching in which he delighted and excelled, was summed up in his book *Moral Order and Progress* (1889), in which he displayed the unusual combination, which later made him famous, of philosophical comprehensiveness and respect for empirical fact. He was also concerned with experimental psychology.

He became a professor at Owens College, Manchester (1893–1924), and played a large part in the process whereby it became a university. His greatest philosophical achievement was *Space-Time and Deity* (1920). In this he expounded a realist theory of knowledge together with a reinterpretation of evolution and the concept of deity. In 1930 he was awarded the OM. He had a keen interest in literature, and much of his later writing was in the field of criticism and aesthetics.

Alexander was a religious Jew and an early supporter of Zionism.

He impinged on Australian cultural history at two points. At his Gifford Lectures in Glasgow (1916–18), he captured the imagination of John Anderson, who was later to become professor of philosophy at Sydney University and was to transmit British empirical realism to generations of Australian students.

ALEXANDRA, QUEEN (1844–1925), wife of Edward VII (*reg.* 1901–10), whom she married as Prince of Wales in 1863. She was the daughter of Christian IX of Denmark, and sister of the Empress Marie, wife of Alexander II of Russia.

ALEXANDRA FYODOROVNA, Empress (1872–1918), daughter of the Grand Duke of Hesse and grand-daughter of Queen Victoria, who married Nicholas II of Russia (1894) and was murdered with him by the Bolsheviks. Her influence on Nicholas was strong and politically unfortunate (*eg,* promotion of Rasputin), and she was wrongly suspected of pro-German feeling (1914–17).

ALEXANDRETTA, partly Turkish-speaking area included in the French mandate for Syria, following the Franklin–Bouillon agreement (1921), but placed under separate administration. It became the Hatay republic (1938) and was annexed by Turkey (1939).

ALEXANDRIA (Greek) in Egypt. One of the great cities of the ancient world, a centre of Greek, Jewish, and Christian thought, captured by the Arabs in AD 642. Founded by Alexander the Great (331 BC), it became the capital of the Ptolemies, who built the Pharos lighthouse and established the Museum and Library, which attracted outstanding mathematicians, astronomers, literary scholars, geographers, and doctors. After 30 BC the city became the residence of the Roman Prefect of Egypt. By then a city of 300,000 free inhabitants, it was torn by the rivalry of Greeks with Jews, who eventually revolted, unsuccessfully, in AD 115, though the Septuagint and the writings of Philo (30 BC–AD 45) effectively combine Greek and Jewish learning. Christianity, appearing after 200, flourished through Clement and Origen, heads of a catechetical school, and the heretic Arius and his opponent Athanasius (328–73), eventually became the dominant creed. After 451 the city was monophysite. Schools of philosophy continued into the 6th cent.

ALEXANDRIA, BATTLE OF (1801). This led to the fall of the port to a British force after the defeat of the remnants of Napoleon's Egyptian expeditionary force.

ALEXANDRIA, CRUSADE OF, the last crusade aimed directly at the reconquest of Palestine by the Christians. It was organized by King Peter of Cyprus (*reg.* 1359–69), who intended to capture Alexandria, the chief Egyptian port, in order to exchange it for Jerusalem. Alexandria was captured by surprise (9–11 Oct. 1365), but the Crusaders, in defiance of Peter, sacked it, 'making its exchange for Jerusalem impossible', and then insisted on departing with loot, dooming the expedition to futility.

ALEXANDRIA, DONATIONS OF, Mark Antony's gift in the autumn of 34 BC to Cleopatra and her children of parts of the Roman empire. Antony proclaimed that Caesarion was the legitimate son of Julius Caesar and Cleopatra, thus implying that Octavian, Caesar's adopted son, was a usurper; Caesarion and Cleopatra were to be joint rulers of Egypt and Cyprus and Antony's children by Cleopatra were to govern other parts of the east, including Roman provinces and client-kingdoms. His action alienated sympathy at Rome and afforded Octavian good propaganda material.

ALEXANDRIA RIOTS (11 June 1882), Egyptian demonstrations against Europeans in Alexandria in which some 50 Europeans and 300 non-Europeans were killed. The riots provided one motive for the subsequent British occupation.

ALEXANDRINE WAR (48–47 BC), Julius Caesar's hard-fought campaign in Egypt against Ptolemy, brother of Cleopatra, and his supporters after the defeat of Pompey, narrated in the *Bellum Alexandrinum* (once wrongly ascribed to Caesar).

ALEXANDROV, TODOR (1881–1924), a leader of the Internal Macedonian Revolutionary Organization (IMRO). In the early 1920s Alexandrov sought to associate IMRO with other revolutionary elements, particularly the communists. He signed a protocol with Bulgarian communists in April 1924 which envisaged a Balkan federation of which Macedonia would form a constituent part. Alexandrov's policy divided the IMRO leadership. While travelling to a meeting to explain his actions, Alexandrov was assassinated. His murder caused a wave of terror inside and outside IMRO.

ALEXANDROVSKAYA SLOBODA, village near Moscow to which Tsar Ivan IV retired in Dec. 1564, apparently as an act of abdication, but in reality to gain support for his *oprichnina* policy which he launched shortly afterwards.

ALEXIS MIKHAILOVICH (1629–76). 2nd Romanov Tsar (*reg.* 1645–76) and father of Peter the Great. Alexis was a relatively enlightened, if somewhat passive, ruler. Early in his reign he was faced with a serious riot in Moscow (1648) and was forced to issue a code of laws to satisfy, in particular, the new nobility (*dvorianstvo*). This code gave final confirmation to the establishment of serfdom. Subsequently, however, Alexis showed himself sympathetic to reform, notably in spiritual and educational matters, surrounding himself with reforming ministers like Nikon, Polotsky, Rtishchev, Ordin-Nashchokin, and Matveev. He supported the Patriarch Nikon in his attempt to destroy the obscurantist introspection of the Russian Church, by restoring its links with Greek Orthodoxy, though his relations with the patriarch later deteriorated, largely because of Nikon's over-bearing and arrogant personality. The tsar was also sympathetic to western culture, especially enjoying the theatre in his later years, thereby helping to undermine his predecessors' policy of isolation from the west. Indeed, Alexis was willing to take a new initiative in foreign policy. On Ordin-Nashchokin's advice he attempted and failed to break through to the Baltic and seize the port of Riga from Sweden (1656–8). Relations with the traditional enemy, Poland, reached a decisive point during his reign, for by the peace of Andrussovo (1667) Muscovy acquired the eastern Ukraine and the key cities of Kiev and Smolensk and was thus made vulnerable to powerful Greek and western influences.

> V. O. Kliuchevsky, *A Course in Russian History: The seventeenth century* (ed. A. J. Rieber, Chicago, 1968).
>
>   JHS

ALEXIS PETROVICH (1690–1718), Peter the Great's son and the father of Tsar Peter II. Alexis opposed the radical reforms of his father and in 1716 fled to Vienna. He was persuaded to return to Russia, where he renounced his claim to the throne (1718). However, his involvement in a plot to oust his father, reverse his policies, and move the Russian capital from St Petersburg back to Moscow, led to his arrest and death sentence. He died shortly before the hour fixed for his execution.

ALEXIUS I (1048–1118), member of one of the leading families of Byzantine military aristocracy and a statesman and diplomat of a high order. He became Byzantine emperor in 1081, when the empire seemed on the brink of ruin and, with Venetian help, he managed to repulse the Normans who from their southern Italian realm had thrust deep into the Balkans. With the aid of the Kumans he defeated the Petchenegs in 1091, then attacked Constantinople. To drive back the Turks, who since 1071 had overrun most of Asia Minor, Alexius appealed to Western Europe for help. The answer was the First Crusade, which became a threat to Alexius, since there was a fear that the Crusaders would be diverted into an attack on the Byzantine empire itself. It did, however, help to defeat the Turks and restore to Byzantine control much of Asia Minor. His achievements are chronicled in the *Alexiad* of his daughter Anna Comnena.

ALEXIUS, Saint (*c.* 1298–1378), Metropolitan of Moscow. Member of the eminent Muscovite family of Pleshchev, and highly educated according to the standards of his day, Alexius became metropolitan of Moscow in 1353. He is a rare example in Russian history of a statesman-ecclesiastic, a man of sincere piety and founder of a number of monasteries, and at the same time an able politician. As guardian and later adviser of Dimitri Oonskoy, he did much to consolidate the power of the Muscovite princes and thus contributed to the unification of the Russian land under their rule.

ALFARO, ELOY (1842–1912), president of Ecuador (1895–1901; 1906–11), born in Montecristi. As a leader of the liberals he was exiled until 1875, when Garcia Moreno was assassinated. He remained a conspirator until 1895, when the liberals of Guayaquil united themselves behind his banner and over-threw the conservative regime. Alfaro was the arbiter of power for 16 years. His government enforced the constitution of 1897, which granted religious toleration and reversed the principal provisions of the clerical constitution of 1884. Though a liberal, Alfaro centralized the government and personally selected all provincial governors. In 1906, as his second term began, he promulgated a second constitution which further attacked clerical institutions. He succeeded in having the president of his choice elected in 1911, but the new president died soon after. Alfaro then tried unsuccessfully to recapture the presidency, but was arrested and imprisoned. A mob dragged him from the gaol and killed him.

AL-FATAT (Young Arab Association). Arab secret society, founded in Paris (1911) by Syrian Arabs to advocate greater autonomy for the Arab provinces of the Ottoman empire.

ALFONSO V THE MAGNANIMOUS (1396–1458), King of Aragon (*reg.* 1416–58), devoted himself to increasing Spanish influence in the Mediterranean and conquered the kingdom of Naples in 1435. There he established his court for the rest of his reign and became a major patron of Renaissance humanism. While temporarily at war with the papacy, he encouraged his secretary Lorenzo Valla to write a treatise proving that the Donation of Constantine on which the popes based their claims to territorial power was a forgery.

ALFONSO VI (*c.* 1042–1109), King of Castile (*reg.* 1072–1109), reunited the kingdoms of Galicia, León, and Castile, which had been divided at his father's death. In 1085 he captured Toledo from the Arabs, which made possible the permanent Christian settlement of large areas of northern Spain. Confronted with the problem of incorporating Christian, Muslim, and Jew into a viable community, he adopted the humane solution of granting each creed its own privileges. He was responsible for the introduction of Roman liturgy into Castile in place of the liturgy of the Visigothic Church.

ALFONSO VIII (1155–1214), King of Castile (*reg.* 1170–1214), was single-minded in pursuit of war against Muslim Spain. His major military achievement was the victory of Navas de Tolosa (1212), which gave Castile control of Estremadura and broke Almohad power in Spain.

ALFONSO X THE WISE (1221–84), King of Castile (*reg.* 1252–84), son of St Ferdinand. Primarily an intellectual and a scholar, he lacked the ability to realize his vision of a centralist government based on legal uniformity and the curtailment of aristocratic privilege. Besides being a poet, Alfonso supervised teams of scholars in various enterprises, including the production of legal treatises, a history of Spain, and the compilation of a set of astronomical tables which in a revised form was in wide use during the later Middle Ages.

ALFONSO HENRIQUES (*c.* 1112–85), King of Portugal (*reg.* 1128–85), grandson of Alfonso VI of Castile. In 1128 he seized control of the virtually autonomous County of Portugal. He obtained its recognition as an independent kingdom from Castile in 1143, and thus became first King of Portugal. In 1147 he captured Lisbon from the Moors with the aid of English and German crusaders.

ALFONSO V, THE AFRICAN (1432–81), King of Portugal (*reg.* 1438–81). On the death of Henry IV of Castile, Alfonso married Henry's daughter Joanna in an unsuccessful attempt to secure the throne of Castile, which went to Isabella the Catholic. His reign saw the early stages of the Portuguese exploration of Africa under his uncle Prince Henry the Navigator.

ALFONSO XIII (1886–1941), King of Spain (*reg.* 1902–31), was noted for his pretensions to power and political manœuvring, which had the effect of discrediting and enfeebling Spanish parliamentary institutions. Forced by defeat in Morocco to accept the dictatorship of Primo de Rivera, he had neither support nor sympathy when the latter was overthrown. His education was restricted and conservative; he was not sent abroad, and had little understanding of the political and social problems of his country. He enjoyed the power his throne gave him, but it was largely negative. In a political system where parties were half-formed and lacked cohesion, he could deny to ministers the dissolution they needed to form a majority, but could not govern effectively himself. His skill was in the manipulation of a limited political class and the first 21 years of his reign saw 33 different governments. His regime was threatened by the outburst of Catalan nationalism after the First World War; but the massacre of a Spanish army, in an engagement with Abd el-Krim at Annal in Morocco (July 1921), for which he was known to be largely responsible, resulted in his subordination to de Rivera, as the army and the king shielded each other from the consequences of their shortcomings. When de Rivera was overthrown Alfonso tried for 15 months to restore his authority, but was confronting overwhelming opposition expressed in municipal elections. He was also no longer considered indispensable by the conservatives as a safeguard against the Revolution, and had lost the support of the army. He was forced from the throne, refusing to abdicate, and left Spain in April 1931. He was rehabilitated by Franco and his property restored, but he remained abroad. In Jan. 1941 he abdicated in favour of his son Don Juan and died on 28 Feb.

ALFRED (*reg.* 871–99), King of Wessex, son of Aethelwulf, King of Wessex (*reg.* 839–58). By 875 Alfred was the only surviving native Anglo-Saxon king. In 878 he was driven into hiding at Athelney, but in the spring of the same year he gained a decisive victory over the Danes at Edington. England was partitioned in 886 along the line of Watling Street and Alfred took advantage of a period of relative peace to extend his influence into Mercia. When the Danish wars began again in 892, he was powerful enough to receive the uneasy submission of the Northumbrian and East Anglian Danes and the North Welsh. He developed the West Saxon fleet and began the construction of the earthwork *burgh*s or forts. Alfred codified West Saxon, Mercian, and Kentish law and is particularly distinguished by his concern for the revival of learning in England. He himself learned to read Latin. Translations into English of major late Roman writings (and of Bede's *Ecclesiastical History*) were produced at his court. In the *Boethius* and the *Soliloquies of St Augustine* Alfred included his own reflections on the meaning of life. The *Anglo-Saxon Chronicle* was probably put together in the form we have it to 892 at the king's command. Alfred's energetic defence of Wessex against the Danes and his deep interest in the spiritual well-being of his subjects have justly earned him—alone of English kings—the epithet Great.

ALGECIRAS CONFERENCE (1906), international meeting called to discuss the internal government, particularly the police, of Morocco. It was significant as the first testing of the Anglo-French entente. From the 1890s the nominally independent empire of the Sultan of Morocco was in decay and both France and Spain were anxious to intervene in the internal running of the country and open it for economic development. The conference agreed, in the Algeciras Act, on a joint Franco–Spanish police force, under a Swiss inspector-general. In negotiation France found herself supported by Italy, Britain, and Russia against Germany. It had been thought that the accession of the British Liberal ministry of 1905 might weaken the entente with France. But the conference proved the reverse, and Grey, the British foreign secretary, opened military and naval staff conversations with France in Jan. 1906.

ALGER, HORATIO (1834–99), US writer of boys' stories. He graduated from Harvard Divinity School (1860) and was ordained a Unitarian minister (1864), but after two years left New England to pursue a literary career in New York. Inspiration came from his close connection with the Newsboys' Lodging House, a home for street urchins, and the lives of these boys, idealized and sentimentalized, formed the subject-matter of many of his most successful works, beginning with *Ragged Dick* (1867). A prodigious worker, he completed 119 novels with the theme that virtue and persistent endeavour are always rewarded by wealth and honour. This 'rags to riches' theme accurately captured the optimism and hope of American society.

ALGERIA (2,382,000 sq. kms), north African state, independent since 1962, formerly under French rule. The population (1970) of 12,041,000 includes 130,000 French settlers. Under the 1962 constitution, a president and parliament are elected by adult suffrage from one party, the National Liberation Front.

ALGERIAN FRONT OF LIBERATION, nationalist organization which arose immediately after Nasser's rise to power in Egypt (1952–3), by which it was considerably influenced. Its purpose was to fight for Algeria's national independence, which began (1 Nov. 1954) when young nationalists, who had broken away from the reformism of Messali Hadj and his followers, proclaimed the need for a structural revolution if a free Algeria were to stand on its own feet. The FLN (Front de Libération Nationale) gradually built up political and military power inside the country, and launched its basic political programme at a clandestine congress held in the valley of the Soummam (Aug. 1956).

In Oct. 1956, Ben Bella and four other FLN leaders were seized by the French while travelling by air from Morocco to Tunisia and imprisoned for the rest of the war. But the revolt was now well under way and in Sept. 1958 a provisional government of the Algerian republic was formed in Tunisia. At the same time, the FLN's armed forces were strengthened by the formation, also in Tunisia, of a regular army. This was used to infiltrate the eastern frontier, but produced political complications at the end of the war which led to Ben Bella's removal from the presidency by an army coup under Col. Boumedienne, who became president in Ben Bella's stead (1965).

ALGERIAN WAR OF INDEPENDENCE (1954–62), began in the Aures mountains, and ended when the armies of the Fourth French Republic, though numbering upwards of a million men, had proved unable to destroy the armed forces of the Algerian Front of Liberation (FLN), or to break the will of a large majority of the Arabic-speaking population for further resistance against French rule. This resistance, initiated by a small group of young nationalists, among whom Ben Bella emerged as the principal leader, originated from the repeated French refusal, motivated chiefly by European settlers in Algeria, to grant to indigenous nationalism the same concessions that France was already in the course of making in Tunisia and Morocco. The war demonstrated the Algerians' capacity to organize a united front, and on the French side an extremist military response. Rather than admit defeat, a number of French senior officers even tried to unseat the government in Paris. Their revolt was crushed by Gen. de Gaulle, who resumed command of the state in 1958 and ended the war with the recognition of Algerian independence. Ben Bella became Algeria's president.

ALGIDUS, Mt, scene of a Roman military disaster in 458 BC suffered by the consul Minucius at the hands of the Aequi, which caused Cincinnatus to be appointed dictator.

ALGIERS, regency, the origin of modern Algeria. With Ottoman help, the corsairs Barbarossa and succeeding *beys* during the 16th cent. built a dominion in the central Maghrib from their base at Algiers. In 1588 it became an Ottoman province, though its pashas lost power in rivalry between corsairs and janissaries until the *bey* was recognized head of state (1711). With piracy in decline, this elected officer was chosen by the militia, directly controlling the province of Algiers, elsewhere appointing three plenipotentiary *beys*. After 1800 insurrection under marabout leadership disturbed the system. With the declining power of the Ottoman empire and the rise to power of Muhammad Ali in Egypt, Algiers lay open to French expansion. In 1829–30 the French government, under Polignac, made more than one proposal for a joint attack, with Muhammad Ali, on Algiers. Muhammad Ali rejected these proposals as he knew they would incur British hostility. The French alone captured Algiers in June 1830 at a time when Britain was preoccupied with the constitutional crisis which followed the death of George IV. The July revolution in France made no difference to the policy of penetration of Algeria, which continued under Louis-Philippe (1830–48).

ALGONQUIAN INDIANS, linguistic group of American Indian tribes, formerly occupying more territory than any other group in North America. The tribes ranged from the Atlantic coast to the Rocky Mountains, and through most of Canada. Tribes included the Cheyenne, Arapaho, Chippewa, Algonkin, Abnaki, and Sauk groups; and several confederacies and groups south of Maine to the Carolinas. The first French, Dutch, and English settlements were in Algonquian lands, making these tribes the first north of the Gulf of Mexico to come into contact with Europeans. Generally sedentary and agricultural, the Algonquian tribes cultivated maize as their staple food, which they supplied on several occasions to colonists who were short of food in New England and Virginia. Relations between the Algonquian tribes and the French were as a rule friendly, but the English were frequently involved in border wars with tribes attempting to hold their lands against advancing settlements. The eastern tribes from Maine to the Carolinas were defeated and their tribal organization broken. Some withdrew to Canada; others became extinct. After the American War of Independence, many crossed the Allegheny mountains to join first the French, then the British, in an attempt to keep the Ohio river as the boundary of Indian lands. Alliances between the tribes were usually temporary and without cohesion, making united resistance to the advancing settlements difficult. The exceptions were the Virginia Indians

under the chief Powhatan, which resisted virtually to the death. In 1795, the Indians acknowledged defeat and signed a treaty ceding the first lands west of the Ohio river.

The Sewanee chief Tecumseh once more roused the tribes, but defeat at Tippecanoe in 1811 and his death in 1813 broke the resistance. In 1815, Algonquians who had fought against the US in the War of 1812 made peace. During the next 30 years, the Algonquians signed a series of treaties ceding their lands east of the Mississippi river, and moved to the west. Another factor in the decline of the Algonquian was the rise of the powerful Iroquoian confederacy, which pushed the Algonquian tribes westward during the 17th cent. until the French came to their aid. Western tribes such as the Cheyenne and the Arapaho were subdued and confined to reservations during the 19th cent.

F. W. Hodge (ed.), *Handbook of American Indian Tribes North of Mexico*, vol. 1 (Washington, DC, 1907).   MF

ALI, CHAUDHURI MUHAMMAD (1905–   ), prime minister of Pakistan (1955–6). An experienced civil servant, he made possible Muslim League effectiveness in the Interim Government (1946–7) by helping Liaquat Ali Khan control the finance department. He had great influence after partition as secretary-general of the Pakistan civil service, establishment secretary, and also cabinet secretary (1947–51). From minister of finance (1951–5) he became prime minister (Aug. 1955) and piloted Pakistan's first constitution through the Assembly (23 March 1956), but resigned because of shifting party alignments (Sept. 1956).

ALI, MAULANA MUHAMMAD (1878–1931), leader of the Khilafat movement in India. He served in the states of Rampur and Baroda (1902–10), began political writing, and became involved in the politics of Aligarh College. He founded *Comrade*, an English-language weekly, in Calcutta (1911), then moved it to Delhi (1912), where he acquired an Urdu daily paper, *Hamdard* (1913). These newspapers, which took the lead in expressing Pan-Islamic views, were the foundation of his influence and reputation. His reputation increased through his being interned, with his brother Shaukat, in 1915, and when they were released (Dec. 1919) Ali was able to assume leadership of the newly formed Khilafat Conference. The Ali brothers co-operated closely with the Congress during the Khilafat movement (1919–24), were imprisoned in 1921 as a result of a Khilafat resolution, which called upon Muslims to refuse to serve in the army, and in 1923 Muhammad Ali was elected president of Congress.

The abolition of the caliphate (1924) undermined the Khilafat movement, and although the Conference continued for some time, it was only one of a number of Muslim political groups, none of which could gain overwhelming support. Muhammed Ali restarted *Comrade* and *Hamdard*, but they were now less influential. At the National Convention (Dec. 1928) he clashed with Hindu delegates over the question of constitutional safeguards for Muslims; thereafter he involved himself with purely communal organizations. He died during a session of the first Round Table Conference (1930–1), to which he was a Muslim delegate.

ALI, MAULANA SHAUKAT (1873–1938), Indian political organizer, elder of the 'Ali brothers'. Prominent first in politics at Aligarh College, he organized the *Anjuman-i-Khuddam-i-Kaaba* (1913) to give Indian support to Muslim struggles in the Middle East. He was interned (1915–19), and became one of the organizers of the Khilafat movement (1919–24), during which he was imprisoned. He diverged from the Congress in the late 1920s, played an important part in reorganizing Muslims in the United Provinces in the 1930s, and was elected to represent United Provinces' Muslims in the central Legislative Assembly (1934).

ALI BEY (d. 1773), a Mamluk of Caucasian origin, made himself the master of Egypt (1760–8) and of Syria (1770–1).

Opposed by another Mamluk grandee, Muhammad Abu'l-Dhahab, Ali Bey was wounded and captured at Salihiyya in May 1773, and died at Cairo a few days later.

ALI DINAR IBN ZAKARIYYA (d. 1916) Sultan of Darfur (Sudan), recognized as independent after the battle of Omdurman (1898) by the Anglo-Egyptian administration, but deposed and killed after his revolt (1916).

ALI GAJI (d. 1503), *mai* of Bornu (1470–1503), brought to an end the internecine strife between the lineages of the Saifawa, establishing the supremacy of the Idrisids. Ngazargamu was founded *c.* 1484 as the new capital, whence Ali directed a number of campaigns against the Kororofa and Bulala. His long reign saw the laying of the foundations of a stable political and economic base, developed by his successors into the empire of Bornu.

ALI GOLOM, provincial governor in the Mali empire, said to be a son of the 16th *dia* of Songhay, Assibai. In *c.* 1275 he became independent of Mali and founded a new Songhay dynasty known as the Sunnis.

ALI IBN ABI TALIB, 4th Caliph (656–61) and a cousin of the Prophet Muhammad. He married Fatima, the daughter of the Prophet, who bore him two sons, Al-Hasan and Al-Husayn. On the murder of the Caliph Uthman, Ali himself succeeded to the throne. A'isha, the wife of the Prophet, with Talha and Al-Zubayr, then raised the standard of rebellion at Basra. Ali sought support at Kufa, also in Iraq, and crushed his enemies at the battle of the Camel (Dec. 656). More serious was the opposition of Mu'awiya, the Umayyad governor of Syria, who demanded vengeance for the murder of his kinsman Uthman. The forces of Ali and Mu'awiya met in battle at Siffin (657). The battle led to a formal arbitration at Adhruh (659), an arbitration which reduced Ali from the status of a caliph to the level of a candidate, like Mu'awiya, for that office. Among the supporters of Ali were some who believed that he should not have accepted the arbitration. At Nahrawan in 658 Ali was obliged to use force against these people, henceforth to be known as the Khawarij. It was a Khawarijite who killed Ali. The reign of Ali revealed that power in the empire resided no longer in the Hijaz, but in the provinces like Syria and Iraq, where the armies of the conquest era had their cantonments, as at Kufa and Basra. Out of the career and death of Ali was to arise the Shi'at Ali, a movement which claimed that the caliphate should of right be vested in the descendants of Ali, and which was to evolve into the most famous of all the heterodox versions of Islam.

ALI PASHA OF JANINA (*c.* 1744–1822), rebellious Ottoman governor in Lower Albania whose unsuccessful attempts to aggrandize himself helped to pave the way for the Greek Revolt.

ALI PASHA MEHMED AMIN (1815–71), a shopkeeper's son who became foreign minister and grand vizier and one of the leading Ottoman statesmen of the Tanzimat. His principal efforts were directed to obtaining European diplomatic support for the Ottoman empire.

ALI SUAVI (1838–78), prominent Young Ottoman critic of Ottoman government and editor of *Muhbir*, who broke with his colleagues and was killed in an attempted coup.

ALIANZA OBRERA, an attempt, led by Largo Caballero (1869–1946), in Oct. 1934, to form an alliance of Spanish working-class parties which enjoyed partial success only in Asturias, where it was joined by the anarchist Confederación Nacional de Trabajo (CNT) and, a few days before the rising, the communists. Elsewhere the CNT refused to join and the Alianza embraced only small left-wing groups.

ALIBAMU INDIANS, American Indian tribe of the Creek confederacy which the French found living on the shores of Mobile Bay in 1701–2. Little is known of the Alibamu except that they were war-like. They grew some crops and raised stock.

ALIBERT, RAPHAËL (1887–1963), one of the architects of the Vichy regime in France and its first minister of justice (1940–1). In the 1930s, Alibert was a leader of the right-wing movement *Redressement français* and the political adviser of Pétain, a role which he continued when Pétain became prime minister. With Laval, Alibert engineered the transfer of full powers to Pétain, and his own social ideas were the basis of the regime's 'National Revolution'.

ALIEN AND SEDITION ACTS (1798), US legislation threatening freedom of speech and of the press. When war against France seemed imminent, Federalists in Congress passed the acts to harass Republican opponents whom they feared were plotting to introduce Jacobinism into America. The Alien Act authorized the president to deport aliens regarded as dangerous to public safety. The Alien Enemies Act authorized him to arrest, imprison, or deport enemy aliens in time of war. The Sedition Act penalized both 'unlawful' combinations opposing execution of federal law and 'false, scandalous, and malicious' utterances against the government or its officers. The associated Naturalization Act extended the period of residence necessary for naturalization from 5 to 14 years.

The acts caused considerable alarm among opponents of the government, but helped to rally the Republicans, inspired the Virginia and Kentucky Resolutions (1798), and aided Jefferson's bid for the presidency (1800). Aliens were especially affected by the Naturalization Act. The Alien Act was not enforced, but the Sedition Act was used as a political weapon during the presidential election (1800). The Alien and Sedition Acts expired in 1800, the Naturalization Act was repealed (1802), but the Alien Enemies Act is still valid.

ALIENS ACT (1705), passed in retaliation for the Scots' Act of Security. The act gave the Scots the choice of some measure of union with England, or a ban on Scottish exports and alien status for Scots in England. The act was repealed later in 1705 to aid union negotiations.

ALIGARH COLLEGE, Muhammadan Anglo-Oriental college at Aligarh in Uttar Pradesh, founded (1875) in order to provide Muslims with an education which would enable them to retain their traditional Islamic culture and at the same time compete with western-educated Hindus. Sir Sayyid Ahmad Khan (1817–98), seeing the disastrous results to the Muslim community from neglecting English education, became convinced that Islamic culture could be harmonized with western learning. He believed that the Muslims' continuing devotion to the Koran and Islamic learning would result in their being unable to compete with the Hindus, who had taken their place in courts and offices of the administration, where English and the vernacular had been substituted for Persian. Closely connected with Sir Sayyid were the poet Khwaja Altaf Husain Hali of Panipat (1837–1914); the novelist and lecturer Maulvi Nazir Ahmad of Bijnor (1836–1912); and the scholar and traveller Maulvi Shibli Numani of Azamgarh (1857–1914). Among the English educationalists connected with Aligarh were Theodore Beck, the first principal; Sir Theodore Morison; and Sir Thomas Arnold, the Arabic scholar. Beck was chosen as principal at the early age of 24 because he had had experience of a residential university at Cambridge. The debating union of Aligarh became one of the chief college debating societies in India. English games such as cricket were encouraged. Dining in hall was compulsory, for, being a Muslim institution, there were no caste or exclusive dining customs and a distinctive Muslim dress was evolved. Religious instruction was regarded as of great importance, but it remained free from any theological bias, and various schools of thought (Shiah and Sunni) were given free scope. The college was not devoted entirely to the education of Muslims, and students (who included Hindus, Christians, and Parsis) came from all parts of India and the Islamic world. The college had a profound influence on the intellectual and political progress of Indian Muslims. In 1920 it became the Aligarh Muslim University.   CCD

ALIMENTA, Latin term for a method of providing maintenance for the children of the poor in the towns of ancient Italy. Under Trajan (AD 98–117) the financing of most alimentary schemes passed to the imperial treasury. Designated landowners took up (apparently compulsorily) loans of about 8 per cent of the value of their land, paying interest of 5 per cent in perpetuity to their nearest town for the support of the children, boys receiving 16 sesterces a month, and girls 12. The aim was to raise the Italian birth rate, which was stagnant or falling. The schemes may have had some success at first, but were ruined in the 3rd cent. by inflation.

ALIMUD DIN (d. *c.* 1789), Sultan of Sulu (1735–73), who afterwards abdicated in favour of his son, Muhamad Israel. He was better known among the people of Sulu as Amirul Mu'minim or 'Prince of the Faithful', and is referred to in various historical accounts as Alimuddin I, Azim ud-Din, and Ferdinand I of Sulu. To stem off the increasing depletion of Sulu's resources and isolation from other Muslim principalities which had fallen under the colonial control of western powers, Alimud Din introduced reforms aimed at strengthening the sultanate and other Islamic institutions, and entered into commercial and political relations with Spain, China, and the British East India Co. His reforms included an attempt to establish a uniform currency under the supervision of the sultanate, a necessary innovation towards attracting foreign traders to Sulu. Under the treaty of 1737, concluded by his emissaries with the colonial administrators in Manila, Alimud Din granted the request of King Philip V, ten years later, to allow Jesuit missionaries in Sulu. This arrangement and his other reforms were opposed by members of the Sulu aristocracy led by Datu Bantilan, his younger brother. In order to retain his ascendancy, Alimud Din sought the help of the Spanish governor in Zamboanga (1748), then of the governor-general at Manila, where he was welcomed the following year. While he was away, Bantilan dissolved the regency which Alimud Din had created, and proclaimed himself Sultan Mu'izzudin. Between then and his reinstatement as sultan in 1764, Alimud Din remained a virtual prisoner of the Spanish authorities in Manila. He was baptized as a Roman Catholic Christian and given the name of Fernando. But during the British occupation of Manila (1762–4) he requested their help in restoring him to his position in Sulu. The British officials complied, in exchange for a grant to the British East India Co. of trading rights within Fernando's territory, and the cession of all the territories of the sultanate in North Borneo and southern Palawan and the adjacent islands of Tulayan and Balambagan, which were soon occupied and garrisoned by British forces.

N. Saleeby, *The History of Sulu* (Manila, 1963).   JMSa

ALINAGAR, TREATY OF, was concluded by Clive (7 Feb. 1757) after his recovery of Calcutta from the Nawab of Bengal, Siraj-ud-daula. By this treaty Calcutta was restored to the East India Co., its privileges renewed, and permission given to fortify the town and to coin money. It was the prelude to Clive's plot to overthrow the nawab.

ALIVARDI KHAN (*c.* 1678–1756), an officer in the Mughal service who rose to be the deputy governor of Bihar under the Nawab Shuja-ad-din of Bengal. In 1740 he overthrew Shuja's son and successor, Sarfaraz Khan, and became ruler of the three Mughal provinces of Bengal, Bihar, and Orissa.

This achievement encouraged others to follow his example and much of his time was spent dealing with rebellions. In 1741 the Marathas invaded Bengal, inflicting much misery before they withdrew (1751), their price being the cession of Orissa and an annual payment of 12 lakhs of rupees. Alivardi was virtually independent of Delhi. He was a strong ruler, but the manner of his rise meant that he was never really secure. He promoted Hindu officers to balance the Muslims and it was these men who helped to bring down his heir and grandson in 1757.

ALJUBARROTA, BATTLE OF (1385), military encounter between two claimants to the Portuguese throne, John of Avis and John I of Castile. John of Avis's victory, with the aid of English troops, destroyed the power of the conservative nobility and, by ensuring the presence of the mercantile urban classes in the new power structure of Portugal, paved the way for Portuguese trade and conquest overseas.

ALKALAWA, capital of the Habe state of Gobir. Its capitulation, after a short siege (3 Oct. 1808), marked a turning point in the *jihad* of Uthman ibn Fudi.

ALL THE TALENTS (1806), nickname of the ministry which took office on the death of Pitt, and included Fox, Grenville, and Addington. In fact, its policies were those of the Foxites. The Talents attempted, unsuccessfully, peace negotiations with Napoleon (1806), abolished the slave trade (1807), and revived the Catholic emancipation question, proposing a bill enabling Roman Catholics to hold army commissions in England. This incurred the hostility of George III, and lost them the support of Sidmouth (formerly Addington). The members of the ministry offered to drop the bill, provided they could continue to press for its general principles. George III required a written promise that they would never raise the matter again. The Talents thereupon resigned and were replaced by the followers of Pitt, now under the leadership of Portland. The fall of the Talents is important as showing the political power which could still be wielded by the monarch, and as the sole Foxite or Whig administration between 1784 and 1830.

ALLAHABAD, TREATY OF (1765). By this agreement, which was from the Mughal point of view a concession or grant, Robert Clive, on behalf of the East India Co., regulated relations with the fugitive Mughal Emperor Shah Alam II. Shah Alam was given the districts of Korah and Allahabad for his maintenance, with an annual grant of 26 lakhs of rupees from the Bengal revenues. On his part, he granted the *diwani*, or revenue-collecting power, in Bengal to the company. It thus became, with Mughal sanction, a virtually independent territorial power in Bengal.

ALLAL AL-FASI, pan-Arab Moroccan nationalist and Islamic reformer. Active from 1926, he was imprisoned abroad, (1937–46), exiled in Egypt (1947–56), but returned at independence, and was president of the Istiqlal Party founded (1943) by Balafrej.

ALLEN OF HURTWOOD, REGINALD CLIFFORD ALLEN, 1st Baron (1889–1939), British pacifist and Labour politician, born in Wales, the son of a draper, and educated at Bristol University and Peterhouse, Cambridge, where he was chairman of the university Fabian society. He was general manager of the first Labour daily newspaper, the *Daily Citizen* (1911–15).

In Nov. 1914 he was founder and chairman of the No Conscription Fellowship and refused to serve in the armed forces or do any alternative service which contributed towards the war effort. He was three times imprisoned between 1916 and 1917 and went on hunger strikes from which he almost died.

In 1920 he visited the Soviet Union with a delegation of the Independent Labour Party and was chairman (1922–6)

of both the party and its journal, the *New Leader*. He wrote several books on socialism and on the political future of Labour in Britain.

In 1931 he broke with the left wing of the Labour movement after supporting Ramsay MacDonald in the crisis which split the Labour Party. For his support of the National Government he was given a peerage in 1932. He incurred further criticism from the left by visiting Hitler and Göring in 1935 in a quest for peace, which later led him to break with the Labour movement. He became a close political collaborator of Harold Macmillan and the 'next five years' group, which advocated a mixed economy, and interested himself in progressive co-education.

ALLEN, ETHAN (1738–89), American frontiersman and soldier, born in CT. Allen acquired land in the New Hampshire Grants (now Vermont), where he organized an irregular militia, the Green Mountain Boys (1771), to protect VT from the claims of New York. The militia, in a surprise attack, captured the key British post of Fort Ticonderoga. Allen himself was captured in the American attack on Canada (1775). On being released (1778), he returned to VT. With his brothers Ira and Levi he was implicated in attempts to negotiate a treaty with Britain favourable to VT (1780–3).

ALLEN, SIR JAMES (1855–1942), NZ political leader. As defence minister (1915–19) and acting prime minister in Massey's absences (1916–17, 1919), Allen dealt ably and fairly with difficult problems of administration during the First World War.

ALLEN, JOHN (1476–1534), archbishop of Dublin. He attracted the attention of Cardinal Wolsey, and rose under his favour to be Abp of Dublin and chancellor of Ireland (1528). After Wolsey's fall he was tried for offences against the statutes of provisions and *praemunire*, but received a pardon (1532). He was murdered in the Fitzgerald rebellion.

ALLEN, WILLIAM (1532–94), cardinal and Catholic controversialist, who trained missionaries for the recovery of England from Protestantism. Formerly principal of St Mary Hall at Oxford, he fled to the Continent shortly after the accession of Elizabeth I and in 1568 established at Douai a college where Catholic refugees from England were trained as seminary priests and sent back, at the risk of their lives, to attempt the work of conversion. The college was later transferred to Rheims, and similar establishments were founded in other cities. Allen worked in close association with the Jesuits, who began their mission to England in 1580. His *Admonition to the People of England* (1588) urged them to accept the excommunication of Elizabeth and support the Spanish invasion on behalf of Philip II.

ALLENBY OF MEGIDDO, EDMUND HENRY HYNMAN ALLENBY, 1st Viscount (1861–1936), British field marshal, who commanded the Cavalry Division (1914) and the 3rd army during the battles of the Somme (1916) and Arras (1917). He was appointed c.-in-c. in Palestine (1917–19), where he directed the campaigns against the Turks. As special high commissioner in Egypt (1919–25), he was largely responsible for the British decision to end the protectorate.

ALLENSTEIN PLEBISCITE (11 July 1920) was held under the terms of the Versailles treaty in the district of Allenstein in East Prussia, where the population was predominantly Polish, but had long been subjected to German rule and influence. The result was 363,209 votes for union with East Prussia and 7980 for union with Poland. The area was assigned to Germany.

ALLIANCE DÉMOCRATIQUE, French conservative party, at the height of its influence in the inter-war years, though founded in 1901. It was more a loose grouping of individuals than a disciplined party, and its members sat in parliament under various designations. But they were united by their belief in economic liberalism and their hostility to socialism, state intervention, and high taxation. They were distinguished from other conservatives by their anti-clericalism. Among political leaders who belonged to the party were Poincaré, Barthou, Flandin, Reynaud, and Pinay. It was especially associated with Flandin, and was compromised and divided by his support of the Vichy regime. It survived into the Fourth Republic, but never regained its former strength.

ALLIANCE FOR PROGRESS, ten-year programme (1961–71) of co-operation between the governments of the US and Latin America (except Cuba), aimed at altering the socioeconomic structure of the Latin American communities. Reform was to be elicited from their governments by the offer of extensive aid, more than half of it pledged by the US in low-interest, long-term loans. A suggested minimum of $20 million in aid was to be dispensed during 1961–71. The funds not directly allocated by the US were to be solicited from international agencies, Western Europe and private capital.

The key to socio-economic progress was said to reside in Latin American promises of reform. The objectives of a charter signed at Punta del Este, Uruguay (Aug. 1961), included six years' schooling for all, literacy for the roughly 50 million illiterate, eradication of malaria, public housing, and potable water for all. The Inter-American Economic and Social Council, which would administer the programme, was to receive plans for development from the participating governments.

During the first year plans were submitted by five nations and reform laws were passed by seven. The conservative elite reacted vigorously, however, and trade problems resulting from falling prices in the world market wiped out the meagre gains initially reported. This was to be the story of the *Alianza*, coupled with the gradual withdrawal of US aid as the commitments of the latter shifted to Asia. US investors heeded the call, however, and US foreign policy returned to military intervention in hemispheric relations in 1965.

The Alliance came under greater Latin American supervision, but progress remained below expectations. Economists generally saw little hope (1970) for either the continuation of the *Alianza* or the realization of its minimal goals by 1971.

ALLIANCE PARTY, governing party in Malaya, and later Malaysia, since independence in 1957. It has succeeded in a multiracial electorate by federating three autonomous communal parties—in order of strength, the United Malays' National Organization (UMNO), the Malayan Chinese Association (MCA), and the Malayan Indian Congress (MIC) —which can appeal to voters in their own communal terms, and yet still form a government through accommodation between the leaders of the constituent parties. The alliance began as a purely ad hoc vote-winning device in 1952, but had assumed permanent organizational form in time for the first parliamentary elections (1955). It won 51 of the 52 elected seats on a programme of rapid independence. In post-independence elections for the 104 Malayan seats, the alliance won 74 in 1959, 89 in 1964, and 66 in 1969. Since the formation of Malaysia (1963), various local parties in Sarawak and Sabah have also joined the alliance, which has thereby been able to form the state governments. In Singapore it had no success. Although the most important Malayan inter-communal bargaining has been within the alliance, differences have mostly been resolved on a basis of mutual trust between a few of the leaders. Alliance policies have been pragmatic, socially conservative, and anti-communist.

ALLIED CONTROL COUNCIL FOR GERMANY, four-power (Britain, France, US, USSR) council set up at the end of the Second World War for the administration of Germany. Representatives on the council were the commanders of the occupied zones. Conflicting policies over reparations, economic administration, and the setting up of German administrative departments hindered its working and made unanimity unattainable, with the result that these questions were referred to the Council of Foreign Ministers. It broke up when Marshal Sokolovsky walked out (20 March 1948) during the conflict which led to the Berlin blockade.

ALLIED COUNCIL FOR AUSTRIA, four-power (Britain, France, US, USSR) council set up at the end of the Second World War to supervise the establishment of an Austrian administration and government—a task which proved relatively simple as a result of the four-power acceptance of the provisional government of Karl Denmer. In June 1946 the Austrian government became virtually independent of the council, although the latter remained in existence until the Austrian treaty was signed (1955).

ALL-INDIA MUSLIM LEAGUE, the major political organization of Indian Muslims in the 20th cent., founded in 1906. Its history falls into three main phases (1906–13, 1913–37, 1937–47). At first (1906–13), the league was a loosely controlled organization, lacking effective secretarial services until 1910 and having as its 'permanent president' the Aga Khan, who was too itinerant a leader to give it more than a semblance of continuity. It was an elitist conference, proclaiming Muslim support for the British government in India in return for a protected place for Muslims in the political institutions of the country. The grant of separate electoral representation in 1909 vindicated the league's early policy.

As it became the nation-wide spokesman of Muslims, pressures developed within the league for a policy of co-operation with the Indian National Congress. In 1913 its emphasis upon 'loyalty to the government' was replaced by its espousal of the cause of self-government, and in 1920 it became pledged to the attainment of *swaraj* (self-rule) for India. However, it was bedevilled by the need to find a formula by which Muslim representation could be secured to the satisfaction of both Hindus and Muslims. In 1916 the Lucknow Pact secured Congress acceptance of Muslim separate electorates, but it proved an embarrassment to the league. The pact entailed the deliberate sacrifice of the position of Bengali and Punjabi Muslims, who were given under-representation as compared to their majority position in their provinces, in order to provide 'weightage' or over-representation for Muslim minority provinces. The league's problems were intensified by the fact that it was not the sole voice of the community in the 1920s. The Khilafat movement overshadowed it after the war to the extent that there was no meeting of the league (1922, 1923), and even when the league re-emerged (1924), no single leader was able to gain general agreement on a policy for Muslim representation. When constitutional discussions began (1927–8), the league divided into two sections, led by M. A. Jinnah and Sir Muhammad Shafi, which supported, respectively, joint electorates with reserved seats for Muslims in return for concessions in the Muslim provinces of Sind and the North-West Frontier, and separate electorates with weightage. The confusion increased with the emergence of a conservative All Parties Muslim Conference (1928) under the Aga Khan, the continuation of the rump Khilafat Conference, led by the Ali brothers, and the formation of the Nationalist Muslim Party (1929) by Dr Ansari. In the event, Jinnah was forced from the field, the Nationalists made no headway, and the Shafi League, Khilafatists, and APMC combined to secure Muslim separate electorates. In 1934 Jinnah returned to India to reorganize the league, and by 1937, under his leadership, it assumed a controlling influence in Muslim affairs in the minority provinces, although regional parties in Bengal, Punjab, and North-West Frontier Province resisted its advance.

In the last phase (1937–47), the league became again an organization concerned exclusively with Muslim interests, but now as a mass party. From 1940 Muslim interests were seen in terms of 'Pakistan'. Jinnah, who dominated the league throughout this period, came to accept partition as the only means of securing Muslim interest in the event of a transfer of power. The majority provinces were not brought behind this demand until the mid-1940s, but in 1946 the league confirmed its command of the Muslim vote. Congress Muslims challenged the league in the elections (1946), but were beaten everywhere except in the NWFP. After partition (Aug. 1947) the league was dissolved (Dec. 1947) and separate Muslim leagues were established for Pakistan and the Indian Union. They continued to operate into the 1960s.

S. R. Mehrotra, *India and the Commonwealth, 1855–1929* (London, 1965).
Khalid Bin Sayeed, *Pakistan: The Formative Phase* (London, 1968).   PDR

ALLOBROGES, Gallic tribe of Roman times living in modern Dauphiné and Savoy. Annexed by Rome in 121 BC, they refused to co-operate in Catiline's conspiracy (63), revolted, and were crushed in 61 and took no part in Vercingetorix' rising (52). The name disappeared in the early Roman empire.

ALLOUEZ, CLAUDE JEAN (1622–89), French Jesuit missionary to New France. Born at St Didier, he entered the Society of Jesus at Toulouse and was ordained as a priest in 1655. He was sent to Quebec (1658) and was stationed at settlements along the St Lawrence river until he was appointed vicar-general of the north-west in 1663, where no missions had then been founded. He travelled extensively from 1665, when he established a mission to the Hurons and Ottawas. Despite many dangers and privations he went to the furthest limits of Lake Superior and then turned back to Sault Ste Marie, where he founded an enduring mission. On Lake Michigan he worked among the Indians at Green Bay (1669) and by the time of his death near the site of Niles, MI, he had taught 100,000 Indians and baptized 10,000. He had been called the founder of the Catholic Church in western Canada.

ALLSTEDT, little town in Saxony, the scene of Thomas Munzer's experiments with the vernacular liturgy (1523–4).

ALMA, BATTLE OF THE (1854), victory of the allies in the Crimean War (1854–6), shortly after their landing. It left Sebastopol, only partly fortified, in danger, but the allies failed to exploit their advantageous position.

ALMAGRO, DIEGO DE (1475–1538), Spanish conquistador in Peru and Chile. He joined Pizarro on his expedition from Panama into South America (1524–5) and was a leader in the conquest of Peru (1533), which involved the march on Cuzco. Almagro led the expedition against Chile (1535–6) and, upon his return, laid claim to Cuzco. Civil war followed among the Spaniards and Almagro was defeated by the Pizarro brothers and executed. His half-breed son Diego (1520–42) took up the cause, which led to the murder of Francisco Pizarro (1541). Diego was defeated and executed by royalists at the battle of Chupas (1542).

ALMANZA, BATTLE OF (1707), in the War of the Spanish Succession, in which a Franco–Spanish force of 25,000–30,000, commanded by the Jacobite Duke of Berwick, defeated a mixed force of English, Dutch, Huguenots, and Portuguese, commanded by the Huguenot Earl of Galway. The battle was hard-fought until Galway's Portuguese allies fled, leaving 8000 to face the total Franco–Spanish force. Though about half of these troops escaped, Galway's army was ruined. The defeat at Almanza meant that the allies were forced to commit more and more of their resouces to the Peninsula. However, they never recovered the initiative and the Archduke Charles lost his chance of becoming King of Spain. Yet the war was to linger on and the allied war aim of victory in Spain was to prevent peace until 1713.

ALMOHADS, 'unitarians'. The last sect in the medieval Maghrib to create a dominion, they completed its Islamization. The founder, Ibn Tumart, employed the theology of his time to denounce the Almoravids as crudely heretical. He himself was unorthodox in his claim to be the Mahdi, in which capacity he organized the Berber tribes of the High Atlas into a strict religious community on para-military lines. The tribes, each with officers, were graded into an army. Leadership was provided by a group around the Mahdi, with a council of sheikhs for wider reference. The Almoravids of Marrakesh were defied until, after Ibn Tumart's death (1129), his caliph, Abd al-Mu'min, led the community towards victory over the Almoravids (1146) and the conquest of the Maghrib and Andalus during the following 20 years.

Possession of an empire emphasized the ethnic character of the community, which became a ruling elite under the leadership of sheikhs such as Abu Hafs Umar and his descendants. Its distinction from the caliphate was established when the office became hereditary in the family of Abd al-Mu'min. The sovereigns Abu Ya'qub Yusuf and Abu Yusuf Ya'qub resided in Andalus, gaining control of the eastern portion from the rebel Ibn Mardanish (1172) and defending it from the Reconquista to the victory of Alarcos (1196). They were associated with a civilization of great artistic and intellectual achievement.

Under Nasir after 1200 the empire began to fall apart. The Hafsids became independent in Ifriqiyya. In the west, Andalus was lost after defeat by the Christians at Las Navas de Tolosa (1212). Driven back on Morocco, the caliphs were obliged to readmit the influence of the Almohad sheikhs. Control was gradually lost until both dynasty and community were extinguished by the Marinids (1269).

ALMOJARIFAZGO, export–import duty of 5–10 per cent collected in both Spain and America during the colonial period on goods departing from or arriving at the ports. The methods used for assessing the tax varied greatly from one era to another.

ALMON, JOHN (1737–1805), London journalist and bookseller, an associate of John Wilkes, and an important figure in the history of the freedom of the press. He began his political career by writing in the *Gazetteer* in support of the elder Pitt and Temple, and against Bute's and Grenville's administrations. In 1763 he set up as a bookseller, specializing in political pamphlets. He was prominent as a critic of general warrants, the Stamp Act, and government persecution of journalists, being prosecuted himself in 1765. From 1768 he was a pioneer in the daily reporting of parliamentary proceedings.

ALMORAVID MOVEMENT (11th–12th cents). Its founder, Abdullah ibn Yasin, was schooled in the orthodox Muslim tradition of Qairawan and the judicial schools of Muslim Spain. He preached an ascetic and puritan reformist Islam among the Berber nomads of the western Sahara, who, inspired by his teaching and united politically under princes of the Lamtuna Sanhaja, conquered ancient Ghana, Morocco, and a large part of Spain. It is said that the title *Al-Murabitun*, 'men of the *ribat*', was given by Abdullah to his followers because they had shared his temporary exile in a fortified island of retreat in Senegal or Mauritania. But it is not unlikely that the original title indicated an orthodox Muslim brotherhood whose members 'bound' their services to the propagation of true Islam, as they saw it, whether by study or teaching, or by death on the battlefield.

The dynasty established by the Lamtuna family of Abu Bakr ibn Umar and Yusuf ibn Tashfin and their descendants, in the Sahara and Morocco respectively, was short-lived. In Spain it lasted from 1090 to 1147, and was bitterly resisted by the Christians, particularly the Cid, who occupied Valencia (1094). The Almoravids destroyed much, but they were also patrons of the arts and poetry. The luxury of Spanish life was one of the principal reasons for their rapid decline and the triumph of their successors, the Almohads, Masmuda Berbers who were traditional enemies of the Sanhaja Lamtuna. The Almoravid empire spanned the western Sahara, and their founding of the towns of Marrakesh and Aghmat was to have important political and cultural consequences in later Moroccan history.

J. Spencer Trimingham, *A History of Islam in West Africa* (Oxford, 1962). HTN

ALODIA, or Alwah, the southern Christian kingdom of the Sudan with its capital at Soba. It flourished from the 6th cent. until the early 16th cent.

ALOISI, POMPEO (1875–1949), leading Italian and League of Nations diplomat. As director of naval intelligence he eliminated (Feb. 1917) the Austro-Hungarian spy network organized from Zürich. For this and services at the peace talks he was made a baron in 1919. A strong supporter of international co-operation, especially with Britain and France, and of League of Nations activities, in early 1923 he served as the league's commissioner to Memel, where he restored order, was president of the Council in 1933, and headed a commission to the Saar (1934–5). In 1920 while in Copenhagen he facilitated the resumption of Russo-Italian diplomatic relations, and in 1926–7 was instrumental in developing Italo-Albanian economic co-operation. Aloisi ran the diplomatic service (1932–61), with Mussolini as his own foreign minister. He led delegations to the disarmament conferences, then to the league to defend Italy's conquest of Ethiopia, being personally disappointed at Franco-British opposition. His influence declined with the new pro-German policy and he retired in 1939.

ALP ARSLAN (*c.* 1030–73), 2nd Great Seljuk Sultan (1063–1073). Alp Arslan succeeded his uncle, Tughril Beg, on the throne. He undertook campaigns against Armenia (1064), capturing Ani and Kars, and against Georgia (1068). The great event of his reign was the defeat inflicted by him on the Byzantine Emperor Romanus IV at the battle of Mantzikert (1071). This decisive encounter made possible the future Turkish conquest of Asia Minor. Alp Arslan was killed while on campaign against the Karakhanids in Turkistan.

ALPHAND, HERVÉ (1907–), leading French diplomat. A career official, Alphand resigned from the diplomatic service in 1941 to join de Gaulle, and occupied important posts in his provisional administrations. After the war, he headed the French delegations to the OEEC, NATO, and UNO, and was ambassador in Washington (1956–65). In 1965 he became secretary-general of the foreign ministry.

ALPHONSE VI OF BRAGANZA (1643–83), King of Portugal, son of John IV of Portugal, succeeded to the throne in 1656. Alphonse being physically and mentally abnormal, Portugal was ruled by the Count of Castelo Melhor until Alphonse's French wife, Marie Françoise, secured their marriage annulment and his abdication (1668).

ALPHONSE OF POITIERS (d. 1271), brother of King Louis IX of France and one of his most loyal collaborators, especially in preparing the incorporation into France of western Languedoc, where he ruled after 1249. He died without issue and his counties of Auvergne, Poitou, and Toulouse passed to the King of France.

ALPINE PASSES, natural passes through the Alps in Switzerland and Austria, the most important being, from west to east, Mont Cenis, St Bernard, Simplon, St Gotthard, Lukmanier, San Bernardino, Splügen, Septimer, and Brenner. There is evidence that all except the St Gotthard and Septimer have been used since the Late Bronze Age and for long they were the shortest and most economic route between north and south Europe. Many towns, of which the most notable are Basle, Geneva, and Zürich, owed their importance to their position with relation to these nodal points of long-distance communications. From about 1237 the newly opened St Gotthard became the most important pass and the opening of this route brought the central Swiss area into the main stream of European communications. In the 15th cent. the Swiss tried to expand their control over both sides of the system and this led to the appearance of Swiss armies of mercenaries in northern Italy.

ALPUJARRAS, REVOLTS OF (1499–1500 and 1568–70), two risings occurring in the bandit-infested mountain slopes of the Sierra Nevada region of Granada, Spain. The first was prompted by the forcible conversion of the Moors to Christianity by Abp Ximenes, the second by the government's enforcement of the pragmatic of 1566–7, confirming anti-Morisco decrees.

ALSACE, key province lying between the Rhine river and the Vosges mountains. It played a significant part in the long struggle between French and German rulers for control of the west bank of the Rhine.

Originally part of the middle kingdom of the Holy Roman empire, it was inherited by the German emperors, but re-assumed significance in the French encroachment under Philip the Fair upon imperial territory, which was only checked by the Hundred Years War and the rise of Burgundy. From the mid-15th cent., and especially in the reign of the Emperor Maximilian I (1493–1519), the French renewed their threat to Alsace, which became part of the inheritance of Ferdinand I when the Habsburg possessions were divided (1555). Coveted by Spain during the Thirty Years War for its strategic position on the overland route from Italy to the Netherlands, most of Alsace was granted to France by the treaty of Munster (1648). Louis XIV consolidated French power in Alsace by annexing Strasbourg (1681) under his *réunion* policy, describing the province as 'a passage for our troops to Germany'. Total French control was established during the French revolutionary wars, but the restitution of Alsace to Germany in 1871 reopened 50 years of bitterness, ultimately settled by its final restoration to France after the Second World War.

ALSACE-LORRAINE (1871–1914), former French province taken by Germany after the Franco-Prussian War (1870). It proved the major source of embittered Franco-German relations (1871–1914). The area had originally been German, but had been acquired by France—Alsace by Louis XIV, and Lorraine by Louis XV. Prussia had failed to obtain them at the Congress of Vienna (1815). The French deputies from the area protested against annexation in 1871, but the area tended to be separatist rather than pro-French in feeling while under German rule. Alsace-Lorraine was returned to France by the treaty of Versailles (1919).

ALTAN KHAN (1507–82), ruler of the Tumet Mongols, and the most influential of the various Mongol princes who succeeded to the declining power of the Mongol emperors in the 16th cent. The earlier years of his reign were devoted to the establishment of his realm and to armed raids into China which were intended to force the opening of frontier markets. In later life he embraced Buddhism, and was responsible for the penetration from Tibet into southern Mongolia of the Yellow Sect of Lamaism. He patronized the translation of Buddhist scriptures and is notable for having built, at Köke Qota, the first permanent Mongol city of modern times.

ALTENBURG DISPUTATION (1568), public disputation held at Altenburg in the presence of Duke John William of Saxony, who also took part. This occasion illustrated the divisions which had developed among the Lutherans of the empire, especially between the supporters of Philip of Hesse in Wittenburg and the Gnesiolutherans at Jena.

ALTGELD, JOHN PETER (1847–1902), German-born US lawyer and politician. His *Our Penal Machinery and its Victims* (1884) expressed concern with justice for the poor. He was a judge on the Cook County superior court (1886–91), and Democratic governor of IL (1893–7). He worked with Chicago progressives, and supported Jane Addams in sponsoring legislation to regulate child labour. His opposition to President Cleveland's sending of federal troops to Chicago during the Pullman strike (1894) led to his being called a radical and to vicious attacks from conservatives. He was a supporter of 'free silver' in the Democratic presidential campaign (1896) and lost his own bid for re-election.

ALTHINGI. The annual general assembly of free men in Iceland (930–1264), the *Althingi* was a legislature and judicature without an administration, controlled by a self-perpetuating oligarchy of 36 (later 48) chieftain-priests under the merely formal authority of a law-speaker elected by the chieftains.

ALTMARK, TRUCE OF (1629), between Sweden and Poland, negotiated near Marienburg, East Prussia, chiefly by French mediation. The Swedes, represented by Axel Oxenstierna, secured possession of Livonia and the towns of Elbling, Frauenburg, Braunsberg, and Memel. An ancillary agreement with Danzig (Feb. 1630) provided for the sharing of the valuable import and export duties. Although the truce had only a six-year term—it was later prolonged to 32 years—on its expiration Gustavus Adolphus was ready to enter the war in Germany.

ALTONA, CONVENTION OF (1689), resulted from a congress summoned by the Emperor Leopold I in 1687. Sweden in alliance with Lüneburg compelled Denmark to restore the lands and rights of the Duke of Holstein-Gottorp, whose position was guaranteed by England and the Netherlands. This seriously weakened Denmark and was a cause of the Great Northern War.

ALTRANSTÄDT, TREATY OF (1707), was imposed by Charles XII of Sweden upon the Emperor Joseph I; it required the renewal and extension of the toleration partly conceded to Silesian Protestants in 1648. The treaty, which was guaranteed by England and the Netherlands, marked the zenith of Charles's influence in Europe and the last achievement of Sweden as a champion of Protestantism.

ALTRINCHAM, EDWARD WILLIAM GRIGG MACLEAY, 1st Baron (1879–1955), British journalist and politician who was private secretary to Lloyd George, as prime minister, and subsequently a Liberal MP (1922–5). After a term of office as governor of Kenya Colony (1925–31), he became a National Conservative MP for Altrincham. As a strong imperialist, he criticized the government's India and defence policies, and was not given office until 1940. He then occupied several minor governmental positions, ending the Second World War as minister resident in the Middle East.

ALUM TRADE. Alum was a mineral indispensable in medieval leather and textile industries, especially in fixing dyes and producing certain essential colours (*eg*, black and blue). It formed the mainstay of Genoese trade, the best supplies coming after 1275 from Genoese-owned mines in Asia Minor. The first regular sea voyages from the Mediterranean to north-western Europe were organized by Benedetto Zaccaria in the late 13th cent. to market this alum. The Genoese alum importers played a vital part in the development of the English cloth industry in the 14th cent. and were pioneers in selling its products in the Mediterranean region. In 1462 alum was discovered at Tolfa in Italy within the papal states and its exploitation rapidly became one of the mainstays of papal finances, contributing to the artistic patronage of the Renaissance popes.

ALVA, FERDINAND ALVAREZ DE TOLEDO, Duke of (1507–82), a brilliant soldier, but a ruthless and tyrannical statesman, who served as military commander-in-chief to the Emperor Charles V and his son, Philip II of Spain.

Charles V relied heavily on Alva during the frequent military campaigns of the 1540s and the 1550s between the imperialist armies and the forces of France and the German princes. The duke defeated the army of the Elector of Saxony at the battle of Muhlberg (1547).

Alva's name is associated with the Spanish attempt to crush the revolt of the Netherlands. An advocate of merciless suppression by military force, he was sent by Philip II to the Low Countries in 1567 to assist the Governor, Margaret of Parma, in eliminating opposition to the centralizing policy of the Spanish government. Alva ordered the arrest of Counts Egmont and Hoorne. He set up a new court, the Council of Blood, to try suspected rebels, which resulted in the condemnation of some 12,000 people. Continued opposition in the province of Groningen caused Alva to retaliate (June 1568) with the execution in Brussels of 20 nobles, including Egmont and Hoorne. He then tried to levy a 10 per cent sales tax, the Tenth Penny, upon all financial transactions. This failed because of the refusal of the local authorities to implement his orders and it brought the influential burgher class into alignment with the feudal opposition. Alva continued to rule the Netherlands with an iron grip, allowing the Spanish soldiery to perpetrate brutal reprisals upon resisting citizens. While defending the southern Netherlands from an anticipated invasion by the combined forces of Charles IX of France and Louis of Nassau, Alva was unable to prevent the Sea Beggars from retaking the coastal provinces of Zeeland and Holland during 1572. This successful campaign by the Netherlands privateers marked the turning point in the revolt and Alva was recalled to Spain in Dec. 1573.

In 1580 Alva redeemed his military reputation. When Philip II claimed the kingdom of Portugal on the extinction of the royal line, Alva successfully secured its annexation by the swift capture of Lisbon and Oporto. MKS

ALVAR, 'the Profound', term applied to 12 ancient Tamil sages who, according to tradition, laid the foundations of Vaishnavism in south India. The 'Four Thousand Hymns', in Tamil *Nalayirappirabandangal*, are attributed to them. Though traditionally relegated to a remote antiquity, it seems that at least one of them may have lived as late as the 9th cent. AD.

ALVARADO Y MESÍA, PEDRO DE (*c.* 1485–1541), Spanish conquistador in Mexico, Central America, and northern South America, born in Badajoz. He was Hernan Cortés's chief collaborator in the conquest of Mexico (1519–21). Cortés sent Alvarado to Guatemala (1523), which he brought under Spanish control, as he did El Salvador. Soon afterwards Alvarado ventured south with roughly 500 Spaniards and 2000 Indian allies to attempt the conquest of Quito. After crossing the Andes, he met the forces of Francisco Pizarro and Diego de Almagro. Alvarado sold his supplies and 'rights' for 100,000 gold pesos and returned to New Spain, where he died in a battle with Indians.

ALVAREZ DEL VAYO, JULIO (1891–   ), Spanish socialist politician and writer who had an important influence in the alliance between socialists and communists during the Spanish Civil War, and was of decisive importance in the collapse of the Caballero government in May 1937. Appointed, together with his brother-in-law, Araquistain, as adviser to Largo Caballero (leader of the Socialist Party), he strengthened the left of the party at a time when Caballero was predisposed to move to the left to compete with the anarchists in the perod 1931–3. After the outbreak of the Civil War, he was appointed foreign secretary (Sept. 1936) and pleaded the Republican government's case at the League of Nations. In May 1937, following the Barcelona rising, he

(with Giral, Irujo, Prieto, and Negrín) provoked Caballero's resignation and prevented his re-forming the government by insisting on communist participation. He retained office in the subsequent Negrín cabinet, and continued to represent Spain at the League. In March 1939, following Casado's coup against Negrín and the communists, he fled to France; he was expelled from the Socialist Party because of his communist relationship.

ALVARO I (d. 1587), King of Kongo (*reg.* 1568–87), who lost his kingdom to the invading Jaga (1569), but regained it with the help of Portuguese troops.

ALVEAR, MARCELO TORCUATO DE (1868–1942), president of Argentina (1922–8) and Radical party politician of Buenos Aires. He took part in the Radical revolts of 1890, 1893, and 1905. Alvear attempted unsuccessfully to regain the presidency (1937).

AMADEO I (1845–90), constitutional King of Spain (*reg.* 1870–3). A son of Victor Emmanuel II of Italy, he was persuaded to come to Spain by the provisional government under Gen. Prim, and was the nominee of the Spanish generals who had been in control of Spain since the deposition of Queen Isabella (1868). On the day that he reached Spain, Prim was shot dead. Handicapped by being a foreigner and with no political party of his own within Spain, Amadeo struggled for two years to rule constitutionally. The combined opposition of the Carlists and Republicans made his task hopeless. Perpetual ministerial crises and his personal isolation finally drove him to abdicate. He left Spain in 1873.

AMALFI, port on the south-western coast of Italy. In the 10th and 11th cents it was one of the chief intermediaries in the trade between Byzantine and Moslem lands, ranking in Italy as second in importance after Venice. The capture of Amalfi by the Normans in 1073 ended its Byzantine connections and its autonomy. Its rivals, the Pisans, sacked it in 1135–7 and its harbour was destroyed by a storm in 1343.

AMALIA ELIZABETH (1602–51), Landgravine of Hesse-Cassel. After the death of her consort, William V, she was appointed regent (1637) and virtually saved the state from extinction in the Thirty Years War. With French and Swedish help she made a truce with the emperor (1639) and afterwards preserved her neutrality by subsidies and temporary agreements. At Westphalia (1648) she received the prince-abbacy of Hersfeld as compensation for her losses during the war. She was also victorious in a long dispute with Hesse-Darmstadt about the succession to Marburg.

AMALRIC I (*reg.* 1162–74), King of Jerusalem. Most of his reign was spent in conflict with the Zangid prince, Nur al-Din, for the possession of Egypt. The factions at Cairo offered an ample pretext for armed intervention. On three occasions (1164, 1167, and 1168) Amalric invaded Egypt. At length (Jan. 1169), Shirkuh, the general of Nur al-Din, took over the Fatimid state. Amalric, aware that the loss of Egypt to the Zangids endangered the whole future of the crusading states, turned for aid to Byzantium. A Byzantine fleet came to the assistance of the king when he attacked Damietta, though without success (Oct.–Dec. 1169). Amalric sought to strengthen the entente with Byzantium still further and in 1171 visited the Emperor Manuel Commenus at Constantinople. Amalric, an able soldier and statesman, died at Jerusalem.

AMAND, Saint (d. 675), most important and best-known of the missionaries who converted the Netherlands. He was active from *c.* 625, especially in Flanders and eastern Belgium, where he gained the patronage of the early Carolingians.

AMANGKURAT (or Mangkurat), name of four rulers of the central Javanese kingdom of Mataram, in the 17th and 18th cents. The first was Susuhunan Amangkurat I (Sunan Seda Tegal-Arum, *reg.* 1645–77), whose troubled reign ended with his death in mid-flight from his court, which had fallen to the rebel Trunadjaja. His son, Amangkurat II (Sunan Kartasura, *reg.* 1677–1703), who had had a hand in the rebellion, established a new court at Kartasura, and ruled in times no less troubled than those of his father. His dislike of the Dutch led him to become involved in the rebellion of Surapati. Amangkurat III (Sunan Mas) contested authority (1703–8) over the kingdom with Susuhunan Pakubawana I, but was eventually captured by the Dutch and exiled to Ceylon, where he died in 1737. Susuhunan Amangkurat IV (Sunan Djawa, *reg.* 1719–27) succeeded his father Pakubuwana I amid intrigues within the royal family, which shortly led to rebellion.

AMANISHAKHETE, Meroitic queen of the 1st cent. BC, possibly the queen (*Candace*) mentioned by Strabo as sending an expedition against the Roman garrison at Aswan.

AMANULLAH (1890–1959), third son of Habibullah and King of Afghanistan (*reg.* 1919–29). During his reign he freed Afghanistan from British control of its foreign relations and inaugurated a modernization programme, which led to tribal risings culminating in the capture of Kabul (1929) by a Tajik bandit, Bacca-i Saqaw (Habibullah Khan), and Amanullah's exile.

AMAR SINGH THAPA, Gurkha general during the Anglo-Nepalese War (1814–16). In 1790 his forces captured Almora. Between 1805 and 1809 he failed to take the Sikh fortress of Kangra. During the war with the British he defended Malaun fort with great bravery, but was forced to surrender to Gen. Ochterlony (1815).

AMARAPURA, capital of Burma (1837–57), on the Irrawaddy, and only a few miles from Ava and Mandalay. Like these, it owes its location on the river to the proximity of the fertile Kyaukse rice lands. Amarapura was the centre of the silk-weaving industry, but its importance and prosperity declined when the monarchy and court were dissolved by the British in 1886.

AMARAVATI, ancient site on the Kistna river in the state of Andhra Pradesh, India, some 60 miles (96 kms) from the coast. The great Buddhist *stupa* (*thope* or pagoda: monument built originally to enshrine relics of Lord Buddha) that once stood there was completely demolished in the 18th cent., but numerous carved marble reliefs and other components were brought to safety. The richest collections gradually found their way to museums in and outside London, especially Madras and the British Museum. The numerous brief inscriptions on the relief panels are of great value in determining the date of the monument, as palaeography often permits more precise conclusions than stylistic analysis. On this basis the monument has been dated back to the 2nd–3rd cents AD, although the original dome may have been very much older. In the vicinity of Amaravati lay the ancient capital Dhanyakataka, a port from which Buddhism and other elements of Indian civilization spread to parts of South-East Asia in the early cents AD.

Amaravati is also the name of a region in ancient Champa in the present Quang-nam province of Viet-nam. Some of the most important archaeological sites of Champa, such as Mi-son and Dongduong, are in this area.

AMATI FAMILY, Italian violin-makers who first evolved the flat shallow form which was the original of the modern instrument. Andrea Amati (d. 1578) founded the Cremona school of violin making, continued by his two sons until 1635. His grandson Nicolo (1596–1684) was the master under whom Stradivari and Guarnieri learned the craft.

AMAURY I (*reg.* 1162–74), King of Jerusalem, an able man, who succeeded his more gifted brother Baldwin III. His reign was the last period during which the Christian conquest of Egypt might have been possible, but Amaury's attempts to achieve this failed and in 1171 Saladin, the greatest of the Muslim leaders, emerged as the new ruler of Egypt. Amaury's son, Baldwin IV (*reg.* 1174–85), proved an able ruler but was soon incapacitated by leprosy, and the effective rule of the kings of Jerusalem ended with him.

AMBAR, MALIK (*c.* 1547–1626), Abyssinian slave who rose to eminence in the service of the Nizam Shahi sultans of Ahmadnagar. He continued resistance after the Mughals had taken the capital city. Confusion at the time of Akbar's death enabled him to regain much lost ground. He eventually came to terms with Prince Khurram (later Shah Jahan) and died in possession of his territories. He was famous both for his military talents and his revenue measures, which rivalled those of Todar Mal in northern India.

AMBASSADORS, resident accredited representatives of individual countries whose diplomatic activity indicated the emergence of the modern territorial nation. Special ambassadors had been used in the later Middle Ages for specific missions, but resident ambassadors first appeared in the Italian states in the 14th cent. By the later 15th cent. they had established the traditions and acquired the professional techniques which were to be copied by the rest of Europe in the 16th cent.

Ambassadors were the agents through whom rulers replaced sheer military force by diplomatic pressure to achieve their ends. Their purpose was to supply useful information to their sovereign which could advance their country's policies, to conduct personal negotiations, and to maintain their ruler's dignity and prestige abroad. This last function led to frequent diplomatic clashes over precedence, aggravated by diplomatic immunity, especially in the 17th cent.

The Emperor Maximilian (1493–1519) sent ambassadors to England, Rome, France, and Spain but starved them financially. His grandson Charles V (1519–56), inheriting the system, was the first to build up a reliable imperial diplomatic network. The French diplomatic service evolved when Franco-Habsburg rivalry was at its height in the later years of Francis I's reign. Henry VII, from the end of the 15th cent., maintained resident ambassadors in Rome to glean diplomatic gossip. However, parsimony and limited ambition stopped him from forming a complete network, though he maintained one resident ambassador, John Stile, in Spain from 1505. Henry VIII, more ambitious than his father, developed the English network, though he was hampered by a dearth of English diplomats and relied at first on Italians. The system improved considerably under Wolsey and by the early 1520s England was served by several skilled and impressive ambassadors in the major European states.

With the diplomatic system developed the chanceries in which the records of ambassadors, the dispatches and transcripts of relevant documents, were stored. Apart from regular dispatches, the ambassadors also sent reports and relations. The ambassador's report was a carefully drawn up assessment of the political situation within his sphere of appointment. The 'relation' was the final report, originally given orally, which a diplomat drew up on the completion of his mission. Once the ambassadors had established their intelligence systems, the practice of ministerial interference with dispatches developed, which led to the widespread use of ciphers and code names. Ciphers were often simple to break and some less astute ambassadors used the same ciphers for many years.

G. Mattingly, *Renaissance Diplomacy* (Boston, 1955; London, 1962).   MKS

AMBEDKAR, BHIMRAO RAMJI (1893–1956), Indian 'untouchable' political leader. Profoundly suspicious of all attempts by caste Hindus, including Gandhi, to organize the 'untouchables' for political purposes, Ambedkar worked during the 1920s to create welfare and political organizations led by 'untouchables' themselves, in his own province of Bombay and nationally in the All-India Depressed Classes Conference. At the Round Table Conferences he joined in the Minorities Pact, which recognized separate electorates for Depressed Classes in the provincial legislatures, and these were accepted in the Communal Award (1932). Gandhi forced him to accept a compromise, the 'Poona Pact' (1932), which gave the Depressed Classes larger representation, but only by reserving seats within general constituencies. He led an Independent Labour Party in the Bombay legislature (1937), and in 1942 formed a Scheduled Castes Federation, which fared badly in elections (1946, 1952). In 1956 he tried to establish a Republican Party which would give the Depressed Classes broader basis of political support, but died before the party was organized. He did see, however, the start of the campaign of mass conversion of 'untouchables' to Buddhism. Ambedkar's political career reached its peak in the 1940s, when he served as Labour member of the viceroy's executive council (1942–6) and as minister of law (1947–51) in the first independent government, with special responsibility for piloting the constitution of the new republic through the Constituent Assembly.

AMBER ROUTE, trade-route of the European Bronze Age, which started from West Jutland and crossed Germany to reach the Po and the head of the Adriatic. The trade implied by its existence was probably controlled by merchants in central Europe who could barter metal for amber, which they passed eastwards to the Aegean and westwards to France, the Iberian peninsula, and Britain. It is therefore no coincidence that close British parallels exist for certain Bronze Age amber finds from Crete and the mainland of Greece. In the Iron Age, amber was conveyed by a slightly different route from the east Baltic to Picene territory, on the east coast of Italy, where a native amber-carving industry flourished in the 6th cent. BC.

AMBHI (or Omphis in Greek). King of Taksasila or Taxila (*fl.* 4th cent. BC), who concluded a treaty with Alexander of Macedonia during the latter's invasion of India (327 BC). His principal motive was probably that of gaining some advantage over his rival Puru or Poros.

AMBOINA 'MASSACRE' (1623). The murder of ten British merchants and nine Japanese mercenaries belonging to the declining English factory in the spice islands. They were in fact executed on the orders of the local Dutch governor and council, after confessing under torture to a plot against the Dutch. The incident inflamed anti-Dutch feeling in England, and was one of the causes of the Anglo-Dutch Wars.

AMBOISE, GEORGE, Cardinal d' (1460–1510), leading minister and churchman under Louis XII of France. Son of a royal chamberlain, he rose rapidly in the ecclesiastical hierarchy, becoming archbishop, first of Narbonne (1492) and then of Rouen (1493). As almoner to Charles VIII he fell into disgrace because of his support for the Duke of Orléans, but was restored to favour and served in Italy. When Orléans was crowned as Louis XII (1498) Amboise became virtual prime minister and proved himself as able an administrator and statesman as he had been a churchman. He played a significant role in the diplomacy of the Italian Wars, and also became both a cardinal (1499) and papal legate (1501). He was at one stage a candidate for the papacy (1503) and remained popular and influential until his death.

AMBOISE, CONSPIRACY OF (1560), attempted *coup de force* against Francis II of France which helped to spark off the Wars of Religion. On the death of Henry II (1559) power was seized by the Guise faction, who continued the persecution of Huguenots in Paris. As the King of Navarre, the first prince of the blood, failed to exercise his rights, the Prince de Condé began to plot against the Guise. His agent was

Jean de Barry, Seigneur de la Rénaudie, a Perigordin who had contacts among the Parisian Huguenots. He raised a force of provincial gentry and mercenaries and planned to seize Francis and the Guise, so that Condé could forcibly plead for the restoration of good government and the exclusion of the Guise faction from power. The plot was betrayed and the conspirators ambushed by the Guise, who killed la Rénaudie and many others. Condé denied his complicity, but the incident rankled in the minds of many and helped to raise the political temperature.

AMBOISE, EDICT OF (19 March 1563), treaty which ended the first Religious War in France. Its terms were that prisoners on both sides should be released and that the Crown would pay off the Huguenot army. By its religious provisions liberty of conscience was recognized, but liberty of worship was restricted. Nobles were allowed to worship freely in their own homes, but public worship was limited to one town in each bailiwick, and even there churches could only be built in the suburbs. Both parties found fault with the edict and it failed to pacify religious passions.

AMBRIS, ALCESTE DE (1874–1934), Italian syndicalist leader. He drafted the first programme for Mussolini's Fascist Movement (1919), though never a *fascio* member. Becoming D'Annunzio's adviser in Fiume (1920), he produced the Charter of Carnero, proposing a democratic, syndicalist republic. He opposed Mussolini's links with industrialists (1922), and settled in France as journalist and publisher.

AMBROSE, Saint (AD 340–95), forceful and learned Bp of Milan and persistent opponent of Arianism. Pressed by popular acclamation to take the bishopric when serving as provincial governor, he accepted reluctantly (374), routing the Arians at the Council of Acquileia (381) and in 386 refusing to surrender one of his churches in Milan for their use. He later forced the Emperor Theodosius to revoke an order compelling the Bp of Callinicum to repair a synagogue (388) and to perform public penance after the massacre of Thessalonica (390). A fine preacher, he strongly influenced the young Augustine; and with Ambrose's encouragement, Milan became a noted centre of Christian philosophical studies.

AMBROSIAN REPUBLIC (1447–50), named after St Ambrose, the patron saint of Milan. It was established on 14 Aug. 1447 by a spontaneous movement of the people of Milan after the death without heir of Duke Filippo Maria Visconti. It was destroyed by Filippo's best general, Francesco Sforza. The episode left a profound impression in Italy, demonstrating the impossibility of re-establishing a republic after 200 years of despotism.

AMBUILA, BATTLE OF (1665), in which Portuguese-led forces defeated and killed António I of Kongo and destroyed the power and unity of the Kongo kingdom.

AMBUR, BATTLE OF (1749), fought between the Nawab Anwar-ad-din, the nizam's nominee as Nawab of the Carnatic, and the nizam's rival Muzaffar Jung, supported by the late nawab's son-in-law, Chanda Sahib, and French troops despatched by the French governor of Pondicherry, Dupleix. The discipline and fire-power of the French decided the issue, and opened the eyes of Indian princes to the potential value of European military aid, with immense political results.

AMDA TSEYON (*reg.* 1314–44), a warrior Emperor of Ethiopia, who conquered the Muslim sultanates to the east of the country.

AMEGIAL, BATTLE OF (1663), in the Portuguese War of Independence. Charles II, after his Portuguese marriage

(1662), sent 2000 foot and 1000 horse to Portugal under the Comte de Schomberg. The gallantry of these English auxiliaries was responsible for the disastrous defeat sustained by the Spanish army under Don John of Austria at the hands of the Portuguese on 8 June. The victory helped to secure independence for Portugal (1668).

AMEN, PRIESTS OF, ancient Egyptian priests serving the god Amen at Thebes. In due course they accumulated enormous wealth and power. From the time of the priest Herihor (*c.* 1085 BC) until *c.* 950, the high priests ruled southern Egypt independently, while another dynasty ruled the north from Tanis. Both series of rulers together form the XXIst dynasty. The rule of the priests of Amen corresponded to a theocratic dictatorship, but they lacked adequate power to enforce their authority and, as a result, lost control of Nubia and internal disorders became general in Upper Egypt.

AMENDE HONORABLE, a punishment in pre-revolutionary French law necessitating a degrading public ritual as a sign of the victim's guilt. In its most severe form the guilty person, guarded by the public executioner, was forced to kneel in a prominent place, dressed only in a long shirt with a rope around his neck and a lighted candle in his hand.

AMENEMHAT I (AMMENEMES) (*c.* 1991–1962 BC), Egyptian King, founder of the XIIth dynasty, and previously vizier to Mentuhetep IV. He reorganized the kingdom, restoring to the nobility their ancient powers, yet retaining control of its members. He defeated the Libyans and built a defence against Asian invaders, but otherwise his reign seems to have been a period of peace and prosperity.

AMENEMHAT III (AMMENEMES) (*c.* 1842–1797 BC), Egyptian King of the XIIth dynasty. His reign was a period of prosperity. Large quantities of gold came in tribute from Nubia, and commerce was carried on with Punt (Somali coast), Syria, and Greece. He is noted for his public works, especially the reclamation of the Fayyum by building earthworks to control the waters of Lake Moeris. He started intensive mining, especially in Sinai, and built a pyramid and the Labyrinth at Hawarah.

AMENHETEP I (AMENOPHIS) (*c.* 1550–1528 BC), Egyptian King of the XVIIIth dynasty, who extended control of Nubia further south and may have campaigned in Syria and Palestine. He spent lavishly on the priesthood of Amen and buildings at Karnak.

AMENHETEP III (AMENOPHIS) (*c.* 1405–1367 BC), Egyptian King of the XVIIIth dynasty, whose reign marked the zenith of Egyptian civilization. In and around the capital of Thebes he built palaces, temples, and colonnades and lived in great luxury. Commerce flourished, gold being exchanged for copper from Cyprus and horses and lapis lazuli from Babylonia. Diplomatic correspondence, some of which has been found at Al-Amarna, was conducted with neighbouring rulers. An early invasion of Nubia was his only military expedition and Egyptian control of western Asia weakened.

AMENHETEP IV (AMENOPHIS or AKHENATEN) (*c.* 1367–1350 BC), Egyptian King of the XVIIIth dynasty, whose reign is sometimes called the Amarna Period. He developed the worship of one god, Aton, suppressing the worship of other Egyptian gods. The court was moved to Al-Amarna, where he built palaces, mansions, and temples in which he acted as high priest. He lived luxuriously, encouraging art, while social unrest grew and Egyptian control of west Asia passed to the Hittites.

AMER, ABD AL-HAKIM ALI (1919–67), Gamal Abd al-Nasir's principal deputy in the Free Officers' movement in Egypt before 1952 and, subsequently, war minister and first vice-president. He commanded Arab forces in the June 1967 war, resigned after defeat, and committed suicide after suspected complicity in a projected coup.

AMERICA FIRST COMMITTEE (1940–2) in the US, organization based in Chicago, that focused opposition to US participation in the Second World War in Europe. Emphasizing hemispheric defence as the key to American security, the committee was supported by a number of prominent Americans, including Charles A. Lindbergh and US senators Gerald P. Nye, Burton K. Wheeler, and Bennett Champ Clark. It conducted a vigorous public opinion campaign until the Japanese attack on Pearl Harbor (Dec. 1941) and was finally dissolved on 22 April 1942.

AMERICAN ANTI-SLAVERY SOCIETY, the first attempt (1833) to create a national organization among the abolitionists. Claiming 1350 affiliated societies by 1838, but plagued by financial problems, internal dissensions, and competing claims of state and local societies, the society eventually fell under the control of William Lloyd Garrison and his supporters (1840).

AMERICAN CIVIL LIBERTIES UNION (1920–), US organization for the defence of individual liberties against both private and governmental infringement. Founded at a time when fears of anarchism and communism bred intolerance of diversity, the ACLU became widely known after the Sacco and Vanzetti trial. Since then it has fought racial segregation and arbitrary police powers.

AMERICAN CIVIL WAR (1861–5), also known as the War between the States, and the War of the Rebellion. There was a widening gap between the expanding urban-industrial democratic society of the North and the predominantly agrarian South, with its plantation aristocracy and large Negro slave population. The North was outstripping the South in population, economic growth, and expansion into the west. Slavery was the conspicuous sign of Southern distinctiveness, and under mounting moral censure from Northern abolitionists, Southerners increasingly defended it as a positive good, and sought constitutional protection in the doctrine of states' rights. The pressing political issue was not slavery where it already existed, but its extension into the western territories. Two sectional compromises had been achieved (1820, 1850) and the Kansas–Nebraska Act (1854) sought to leave the issue to the local inhabitants. But as sectional antagonisms intensified, constitutional restraints and the party system gave way under the strain. A new Northern sectional Republican Party emerged (1854), and when its candidate, Abraham Lincoln, was elected president (1860) on a platform of opposition to slavery's extension, seven states of the deep South seceded from the Union (1860–1) and formed the Confederate States of America, with Jefferson Davis as president. They were joined by four more states after the Civil War began (April 1861). The Confederacy had a population of only 9 million, (including 3½ million Negroes), the Union almost 23 million, and the economic disparity between the two sides was even greater. But the South, which expected to receive help from Europe, needed only to survive to establish its independence.

The land war was fought in two main theatres. In the east the heaviest concentrations of troops fought on a narrow front between the rival capitals, Washington and Richmond. Here, for two years, the Confederate army enjoyed considerable success, with two victories at Bull Run, the defeat of McClellan's peninsular campaign, and further victories at Fredericksburg and Chancellorsville. But Lee's army was defeated at Antietam (1862) and when he again invaded the North he was heavily defeated at Gettysburg (1863). This crucial Northern victory coincided with another Union triumph in the west, where Grant's capture of Vicksburg (1863) re-established Union control of the Mississippi. In the western theatre, on a wider front and with greater room for manœuvre, the North had been successful since early 1862; now, after Vicksburg, and another victory by Grant at Chattanooga (1863), Sherman was able to advance south-east to Atlanta and then to march across Georgia to the sea (1864). Meanwhile, Grant, now commander-in-chief of all Union armies, kept up a relentless pressure on Lee in Virginia, and at last, after evacuating Richmond, Lee surrendered at Appomattox (1865). Numerical and material superiority, naval supremacy, Lincoln's leadership, and Southern inability to win recognition or support abroad, all contributed to the Union's victory.

This, the greatest war between 1815 and 1914, in its implications and results, cost over 600,000 lives. Its scale, methods, and technology foreshadowed the warfare of the 20th cent. The Union had been saved and slavery abolished (Emancipation Proclamations 1862, 1863, 13th amendment to the constitution, 1865) but the problems of race and colour remained, and a new legacy of hate obstructed the integration of black and white America.

J. G. Randall and D. Donald, *The Civil War and Reconstruction*, 2nd ed. (Boston, 1961).

B. Catton, *The Penguin Book of the American Civil War* (London, 1966). PJP

AMERICAN COLONIZATION SOCIETY (1818–1912) aided manumission of slaves and the deportation of free Negroes to Liberia. Before the Civil War, its activities, hampered by slave-owners and abolitionists, achieved only limited success. After 1865 it was mainly concerned with sustaining its Liberian settlements.

AMERICAN EXPRESS COMPANY was originally concerned with the rapid transportation of parcels, but expanded into banking and travel. The original company (1850), directed by Henry Wells, William G. Fargo, and Johnston Livingston, was an eastern and central concern with a western associate in Wells, Fargo and Co.

AMERICAN FEDERATION OF LABOR (founded 1886), US organization of craft unions. The Federation of Organized Trades and Labor Unions (1881) included both craft unions and the Knights of Labor, but continued divisions between the two groups resulted in an open rift (1886), and representatives of the craft unions founded the American Federation of Labor, with Samuel Gompers as president. Under his leadership, the AF of L was committed to a policy of moderation and an acceptance of the basic principles of capitalism. The organization avoided identification with political parties and with extreme reform groups, and concentrated on labour's immediate objectives of higher wages, shorter hours, and improved working conditions. AF of L members rejected the concept of mass unionization and were proud of their status as skilled working men. Keeping within limited perspectives, and inhibited by the strength of employers' associations and by the willingness of the courts to apply anti-trust laws against labour, Gompers tried to avoid direct confrontation between labour and capital. Membership of the federation grew slowly from some 150,000 in 1886 to 868,500 in 1900. Aided by progressive state and federal legislation in the early 20th cent., the AF of L began to achieve some of its objectives and the passage of the Clayton Act (1914) freed it from legal injunction as an illegal combination in restraint of trade. Membership continued to increase, and by 1914 stood at 2,020,671.

During the First World War, membership grew more rapidly and by 1921 had reached almost 4 million. The prosperous 1920s, however, were a decade of labour weakness, when employers established company unions and enforced 'yellow dog' contracts prohibiting workers from joining outside unions. By 1929 AF of L membership had dropped to 2,961,096. During the New Deal, a changed attitude of government towards labour resulted in legislation affirming the right of labour to bargain collectively through represen-

tatives of its own choosing (Section 7(a) of the National Industrial Recovery Act (1933)), and stronger government protection for unions through the National Labor Relations Act (1935) and the Fair Labor Standards Act (1938). Total non-company union membership increased from some 3 million during the Depression (1933) to 4,700,000 in 1936 and to 8,200,000 in 1939. Much of the growth of organized labour in the late 1930s, however, stemmed from the activities of industrial unions and the new industrial union organization of the Committee (after 1938 Congress) for Industrial Organization. The AF of L, under the leadership of William Green, continued to reject the principle of mass unionization.

Uneasy relations between the two organizations, and a series of strikes in the early and mid-1940s, contributed to a hardening of public and political attitudes. The Taft–Hartley Act (1947) effectively limited some of the newly won power of the unions. In an effort to retrieve their position, both the AF of L and the CIO attempted to eliminate corrupt practices and purge communists from union offices. They began moving closer together in the early 1950s and in 1955 merged to form the AF of L–CIO, with over 17 million members. This merger, however, was more an establishment of links between parallel structures than an organic union, and the general distinction between AF of L craft unions and CIO industrial unions remains.

Philip Taft, *The AF of L in the time of Gompers* (New York, 1957).

Philip Taft, *The AF of L from the Death of Gompers to the Merger* (New York, 1959). DKA

AMERICAN HORSE (Wasechum-tashunka) (*c.* 1859–1907), Oglala Sioux minor chief, who served as the tribe's spokesman before the Sioux Commission of 1887. He was the white-supported leader of the 'progressive' faction of the Sioux and headed a delegation from Pine Ridge Reservation to Washington, DC (1891).

Also the name of a Sioux chief killed in the battle of Slim Buttes (1875), a Southern Cheyenne Indian policeman, and a Northern Cheyenne chief of about the same period.

AMERICAN INDIAN CONGRESS, also known as the National Congress of American Indians, an organization of some 80 member tribes founded (1944) at Denver, CO. It represents some 500,000 tribal Americans.

AMERICAN LEGION, organization of US war veterans founded in 1919. As well as advancing its members' interests, it has acted as a powerful pressure group on behalf of national security. A nationalist and patriotic organization, the Legion has consistently opposed diplomatic recognition of communist China.

AMERICAN LIBERTY LEAGUE (1934–40), US organization of conservatives opposed to the New Deal. Dominated by businessmen and industrialists, its membership was drawn from both major political parties and included many of President F. D. Roosevelt's political rivals, notably Alfred E. Smith.

AMERICAN LOANS TO BRITAIN. These were made necessary by the exceptional circumstances of Britain's involvement in debilitating world wars with the support and alliance of the US, whose economy did not suffer to the same extent. The settlement of terms for debt repayment after the First World War created a minor political storm in Britain when Stanley Baldwin, as chancellor of the exchequer, was accused of agreeing to (and publicly announcing) an unnecessarily harsh settlement, so that Bonar Law, the prime minister, had to be persuaded not to resign. To recoup, the British government (having failed in its plea for the abandonment of all debts and reparations) took a tougher line on the payment of reparations. When the latter were virtually abandoned at the Lausanne Conference (1932), they renounced their debt to America (1933). In the US the recollection of loans made during the First World War reinforced isolationist sentiment in the 1930s.

Lend-lease obviated any similar problem after the Second World War. But the abrupt ending of lend-lease and British insolvency led to the Anglo-American loan of 1946 ($3,750 million at 2 per cent). The arrangement of the loan coincided with the establishment of the International Monetary Fund and the World Bank, and in both series of negotiations the British government was in a weak position in arguing its case on international liquidity. It accepted a commitment to the free convertibility of sterling in 1947, and the attempt to honour this commitment caused the next of the major financial crises of the post-war years.

AMERICAN PEACE SOCIETY, founded (1828) by William Ladd, and the leading US group working for the maintenance of world peace until it lost ground to newer organizations after the First World War.

AMERICAN PHILOSOPHICAL SOCIETY. The first American scientific society, founded (1743) by Benjamin Franklin in Philadelphia.

AMERICAN POPULAR REVOLUTIONARY ALLIANCE (Peru), *Alianza Popular Revolucionaria Americana* or the Aprista Movement, founded by Víctor Raúl Haya de la Torre (1924). APRA's stated purpose was to end foreign imperialism in Spanish America and to bring about Indian integration throughout Indo-America. The APRA programme at first included a call for the nationalization of land and industry and the internationalization of the Panama Canal. It was also opposed to Marxist communism. Haya de la Torre, who has been the perennial presidential candidate of APRA, has never succeeded in becoming president.

To avoid the possibility, APRA was outlawed (1933) and the elections of 1936 and 1942 took place without APRA participation. The party re-emerged as *Partido Popular* (1945) and began its current policy of contracting alliances with other groups—a strategy which increased its political influence but resulted in a decline in its popular support. From 1945 APRA enjoyed considerable influence, until it withdrew its support from the government (1947). An unsuccessful revolt (1948) was attributed to APRA, resulting in a new persecution of the party which again became illegal. Until 1954, Haya de la Torre remained hidden in the Colombian embassy. APRA re-emerged in 1956 to support a former enemy, Manuel Prado, who legalized its existence (1957). The Cuban Revolution divided the party (1960), APRA *Rebelde* moving to the left and APRA remaining hostile to Castro. Haya de la Torre stood for election again (1962), but the required majority was not forthcoming and the decision was thrown into congress. The military intervened, annulled the election, and called new elections (1968). Again APRA was defeated. Late in 1968 the military removed the civilian government.

AMERICAN REVOLUTION. Thirteen of the British North American colonies (NH, MA, RI, CT, NY, NJ, PA, DE, MD, VA, NC, SC, GA) were mature though discrete societies by 1760, more homogeneous in class structure but ethnically more variegated than Britain. Theoretically subject to imperial authority, they were, in practice, internally self-governing and increasingly resented British regulation of their trade. The collapse of the French empire in North America in the Seven Years War reduced their feeling of dependence on Britain, although they still valued their membership of the empire. British efforts to reinvigorate the Old Colonial System [Proclamation Line (1763), Sugar Act (1764), Stamp Act (1765), Declaratory Act (1766)] aroused vigorous opposition. Exacerbated by the Townshend Duties (1767), the posting of British troops in Boston (1768), and the Boston Massacre (1770), tension reached a crucial stage when the Boston Tea Party (1773) provoked the British

government under Lord North to impose the 'Intolerable Acts' on Massachusetts (1774). At the first Continental Congress (1774) the colonists rejected Joseph Galloway's Plan of Union, and advocated preparations for resistance and a trade embargo. Concurrently they argued that colonial legislatures were not subordinate to parliament, but enjoyed a direct relationship with the Crown.

After the failure of North's Conciliatory Plan (Feb. 1775), skirmishes at Lexington and Concord (19 April 1775) were followed by a Pyrrhic British victory at Bunker Hill (June 1775). The second Continental Congress established the Continental army with George Washington as commander-in-chief, and issued a Declaration of the Causes and Necessities of Taking Up Arms; its conciliatory 'Olive Branch Petition' was ignored by George III (July 1775). Irreconcilable attitudes on both sides stimulated American demands for complete separation from Britain, and resulted in the Declaration of Independence (4 July 1776).

In the war that followed Britain enjoyed naval and military superiority, but was faced with the difficulty of conducting distant campaigns in generally hostile territories and suffered weakness in leadership. Gen. Burgoyne's surrender at Saratoga (1777) ended British attempts to divide the Americans along the Hudson. Washington succeeded in keeping his army intact and the US, rejecting Carlisle's peace commission, concluded an alliance with France (1778). The entry of Spain (1779) and Holland (1780) completed British isolation in a world conflict. The surrender of a British army under Lord Cornwallis at Yorktown (1781) effectively ended the war. In the treaty of Paris (1783) Britain, acknowledging the collapse of her first empire, recognized the independence of the United States.

Internally the Revolution resulted in the emigration of many Loyalists, an increase in social mobility, a generally broader franchise, progress towards the abolition of slavery, and in some states the disestablishment of religion. In their new constitution the states, asserting legislative supremacy over executive authority and the necessity of safeguarding individual rights, emphasized the responsibility of government to the people. An approach towards implementation of these principles at national level was made in the first US constitution, the Articles of Confederation (1781).

John R. Alden, *A History of the American Revolution* (New York, 1969).
Gordon S. Wood, *The Creation of the American Republic, 1776–1787* (Chapel Hill, NC, 1969).

AMERICAN SYSTEM, name given by Henry Clay, of KY, to a domestic programme for the US aimed at stimulating economic growth and removing dependence on foreign markets. In a speech on the tariff in the US House of Representatives (30–31 March 1824), Clay advocated high import duties in order to encourage industrial development, for thriving local industry would provide a strong domestic market for American primary products. Surplus revenues from the tariff could be used to keep land prices low, so encouraging western settlement, and also to pay for 'internal improvements' in interstate transportation. Clay, a nationalist, saw the System as a unifying programme that would mitigate increasing sectionalism, but, whilst satisfying Northern and Western interests, it threatened those of the South. Adoption of the American System by the Whigs, and later by the Republicans, represented the end of Calhoun's dream of an agrarian political alliance between South and West and, together with the dominant issue of slavery, contributed to the isolation of the South.

AMERICAN TELEPHONE AND TELEGRAPH COMPANY (founded 1885), a privately owned, though publicly regulated, utility company. Gaining a near monopoly of telephone services on acquiring the Bell companies (1899), it has combined profitability with high standards of service and technical innovation.

AMERICAN TEMPERANCE UNION (1836), federal union of North American temperance societies. Active at state level since 1808, the temperance movement, stirred by the crusade of Lyman Beecher, founded the American Society for the Promotion of Temperance (1826). This national organization sponsored the Temperance Union.

AMERICANS FOR DEMOCRATIC ACTION, US organization founded (1947) by liberal Democrats to ensure the survival of New Deal principles in post-war America. ADA has provided a forum for non-communist liberals and has sought to influence the Democratic Party's policies and its choice of candidates for political office.

AMERIND, a term derived from the first syllables of 'American' and 'Indian', suggested by lexicographers in 1899 to designate native American tribes. The term was proposed to a meeting of the Anthropological Society of Washington in 1899, during a discussion of various schemes of ethnological classification and nomenclature. Advocates of the word argued that there was no useful term to designate native tribes, misnamed 'Indian' by Columbus. They held that 'American' was unsatisfactory because it was generally used to refer to the Caucasian population of the Western Hemisphere. Other descriptions, such as 'Red Men', were considered misleading. Besides being incorrect, the word 'Indian' was connotive rather than denotive. The term was proposed as a designation of all the aboriginal tribes of the American continent and its adjacent islands, including the Eskimo. This designation was approved by most of the working ethnologists in the Anthropological Society of Washington and its officials. The term was also accepted by the officials of the Bureau of American Ethnology. It was the subject of further discussion at the International Congress of Americanists in New York in 1902, and subsequently found its way into both scientific and non-scientific literature.

F. W. Hodge (ed.), *Handbook of American Indians North of Mexico*, vol. 1 (Washington DC, 1907).

AMERY, LEOPOLD (1873–1955), British Conservative statesman and imperialist, and a life-long supporter of Joseph Chamberlain's policy of imperial preference. He was MP for South Birmingham, and later for Sparkbrook from 1911, but was unseated in 1945. He served as under-secretary to Milner at the Colonial office (1919–21), parliamentary and financial secretary to the admiralty (1921–3), colonial secretary (1924–9), and dominions secretary (1925–9). Baldwin's refusal to adopt Protection tended to alienate Amery from the Conservatives, and his strong imperialism excluded him from the National Government (1931). In the 1930s he became, with Churchill, a strong critic of appeasement and the failure to rearm adequately. He was thus well placed for a return to office in the coalition government (May 1940), when he became secretary of state for India and Burma (1940–5). Although Amery, unlike Churchill, had supported the Government of India Act (1935), his imperialist reputation made it hard for him to handle India's affairs at a time when India was opposed to participation in the war.

AMES, FISHER (1758–1808), US conservative spokesman. He condemned Shays' Rebellion (1786) and promoted ratification of the US Constitution (1787–8). A prominent Federalist congressman from MA (1789–97), he bitterly resisted the extension of democracy, preferring rule by an aristocracy of talent and wealth.

AMETHYST INCIDENT (1949), involving the British frigate *Amethyst* and Chinese communist forces. Shortly before the communist crossing of the Yangtse, at a crucial stage in the Communist–Kuomintang Civil War, *Amethyst* came under Chinese fire while sailing between Shanghai and Nanking. She was badly damaged and driven aground, and her commander and 17 men were killed. For three months the ship remained aground, her acting commander, Kerrans, holding out against communist demands that the British should assume responsibility for the incident. Eventually *Amethyst* made a dramatic escape and limped back to Shanghai. In British eyes her escapade demonstrated the prowess of the navy, but in China it represented a psychological victory for the communists, who had successfully crippled a ship of a navy whose ships had sailed China's coastal and inland waters unchallenged for a century.

AMHARA, major ethnic group of northern Ethiopia which has given its name to Amharic, the present official and literary language of Ethiopia.

AMHERST OF ARRACAN, WILLIAM PITT AMHERST, 1st Earl (1773–1857), British soldier, who was sent to China in 1816 to represent to the emperor the wrongs which British merchants were suffering under his rule, but was treated with great discourtesy. As governor-general of India (1823–1828), he was forced by Burmese aggression to declare war (1824). After a badly managed campaign, the British dictated terms in the treaty of Yandabo (1826). Amherst also had difficulties with the state of Bharatpur, where a disputed succession and the anti-British activities of Durjan Sal led to the capture of the fort of Bharatpur by Lord Combermere (Jan. 1826). Amherst inaugurated Simla as the summer residence of the governor-general (1826).

AMHERST OF HOLMESDALE AND MONTREAL, JEFFREY AMHERST, 1st Baron (1717–97), British general and governor in North America. Amherst's first important military operation was as commander of the forces which captured Louisbourg from the French (1758). Appointed by Pitt as commander-in-chief of the British troops in North America (1759), he captured Ticonderoga and Crown Point (1759) and Montreal (1760). He became governor-general of the British possessions in North America (1760–3) and held this position until he was made nominal governor of VA, although he never went there (1763–8).

AMI DU PEUPLE, radical newspaper founded by the French Revolutionary extremist Jean-Paul Marat in Sept. 1789. Its denunciations of the Revolution's enemies gave it great influence.

AMICABLE LOAN, forced loan levied (1525) by Wolsey in the form of a tax on every man's property in order to pay for a proposed invasion of France. Because of successive taxes levied since 1522 this misnamed 'loan' met with so much opposition that Henry VIII abandoned both it and the invasion.

AMIENS, PEACE OF (27 March 1802), signed by Britain and France. Together with the treaty of Lunéville (1801), it followed Napoleon's defeat of the Second Coalition and left an uneasy stalemate in Europe. Under the terms of the peace Britain returned her overseas conquests and France agreed to evacuate central and southern Italy and provide compensation for the House of Orange, expelled from Holland. The peace was rapidly undermined by French expansion in Holland and Italy and by evidence of massive French naval preparations against England. Britain declared war again on France in May 1803.

AMIN, MUHAMMAD, AL-, (787–813), Abbasid Caliph (809–13), son of Harun al-Rashid and Zubayda, a niece of Al-Mansur. His father had the oath of allegiance (*bay'a*) given to Al-Amin in 792 and in 799 arranged that another of his sons, Al-Ma'mun, should succeed Al-Amin. This settlement was confirmed in 802, Al-Amin recognizing the almost independent position of Al-Ma'mun as vice-gerent of the caliph over the eastern lands of the Abbasid empire. After the death of Harun al-Rashid (809) a civil war broke out between the two brothers. In 811 the troops of Al-Ma'mun invaded

Iraq from Khurasan under the command of Tahir ibn al-Husayn and Harthama ibn A'yan. Baghdad fell after a long siege (812–13), Al-Amin being killed while attempting to escape.

AMINA (*fl.* 14th–15th cent.), Queen of Zaria, northern Nigeria, who waged war throughout Hausaland. Remains, particularly city walls, associated with Amina are scattered from Katsina to the Niger river.

AMINI COMMISSION (1776–8), appointed by Warren Hastings to collect information for a new settlement of the land revenues of Bengal. It failed to ascertain the real value of the lands and the rents that the landholders collected from the cultivators.

AMIR, Arabic term meaning 'lord', 'prince'. In Abbasid times the title was given to the governors of provinces. Some of the amirs established dynasties which limited their relations with the Caliphate to the acceptance of a decree (*ahd*) confirming them in their office, to the reading of the caliph's name in the *khutba* or Friday prayer, and to the inscription of that name on their coins (*cf* the Aghlabids). Other amirs shared the attributes of power with the caliph, adding their own names in the khutba and on the coinage (*cf* the Tahirids). At Baghdad itself, in 935, there came into being a 'lord of lords', or *amir al-umara*, this title underlining the pre-eminence of the amir who controlled the caliph and the capital of the empire. Under the Seljuks, the Ayyubids and the Mamluks of Egypt and Syria, the title was accorded to a wide range of appointments, most of them military in character. The title *amir al-mu minin* (Commander of the Faithful) was, from the time of the Caliph Umar (634–44), applied almost exclusively to the caliphs themselves or to other Muslim rulers claiming independent political authority.

AMIR ALI, SAYYID (1849–1928), Indian jurist and Islamic leader. Called to the bar at the Inner Temple (1873), he became a member of Bengal's legislative council (1878–83) and an additional member of the governor-general's council (1883–5), chief presidency magistrate (1879), judge of the Calcutta high court (1890–1904), and, after retirement to England, the first Indian member of the judicial committee of the privy council. He worked for the benefit of Muslims through the Central National Muhammadan Association (1876–90) and was a strong advocate of English education and the education of Muslim women, for he regarded Indian nationalism as a cloak for Hindu domination. He wrote enthusiastically on the glories of Islamic culture. His *Spirit of Islam* (1891) was a detailed apologia for Islam which probably had more influence in the west than in the east. He also wrote a *History of the Saracens* (1899).

AMIR BASHIR II (1767–1851), Shihabi ruler of Mount Lebanon (1788–1840), who dominated the mountain and, in alliance with Muhammad Ali of Egypt, made himself independent of the Ottoman government, until Egyptian power in Syria was destroyed.

AMIR IBN AL-AS (*d.* 663) had a pre-eminent role in the Arab campaigns of conquest which followed the death of the Prophet in 632. He fought in the battles of Ajnadayn (634) and the Yarmuk (636). His most famous achievement was the conquest of Egypt, taken from the Byzantines (639–42). Amir associated himself with the Umayyad governor of Syria, Mu'awiya, against the Caliph Ali between 656 and 661. He was present at the battle of Siffin (657), brought Egypt over to Mu'awiya (658), and acted as the representative of Mu'awiya at the Arbitration of Adhruh (659). An able soldier and an astute politician, Amir spent the last years of his life as governor of Egypt, dying at an advanced age.

AMIR KHUSRU (1253–1325) was the son of a Turkish immigrant to India at the time of the Mongol invasions. As such, he was associated with the princes who sought refuge with the Slave Kings of Delhi. He lived at the court of Ala-ad-din Khilji and was considered the best of the Persian poets of the pre-Mughal period. His free use of Hindi words was a step in that process of literary integration which produced the Urdu language. He was a disciple of the *sufi* Nizam-ad-din Auliya, and his poems were admired for their mystical fervour.

AMIR-I KABIR (the Great Amir), the title by which the outstanding Iranian statesman and reformer Mirza Taqi Khan (d. 1852), minister of Nasir al-Din Shah, was best known.

AMIRS OF SIND, the ruling chiefs of Sind, the area of India straddling the lower course of the Indus from near Shikarpur, during the early British period. Sind was a Mughal province (1591–1750) until it passed to the rising Afghan ruler, Ahmad Shah Abdali. In 1783 Mir Fath Ali Khan Talpura overthrew the last Kalora chief, and thereafter his clan gradually asserted its independence of the declining Afghan power. There were three main branches, Mir Fath Ali, holding central Sind from Hyderabad; the Mirpur family, ruling from Mirpur; and the Sohrabanis at Khairpur. On Mir Fath Ali's death (1802) his territory was divided into four portions among his relatives, one of whom received nominal allegiance as chief. The Afghans were too distracted to assert their supremacy and the amirs too suspicious and indolent to unite. Sind was thus parcelled out into a number of petty principalities, whose chiefs were notable for suspicion, faction, and backwardness. Trade was neglected and the country poor.

Serious British interest in Sind developed as they approached the Sutlej river and the north-west (1803). Absorbed with the French danger, Lord Minto, the governor-general of India, induced the amirs to undertake to resist the French (1809). Interest sharpened from 1818 when the British frontier marched with that of the Sikh chief Ranjit Singh. In 1831 a mission was sent up the Indus with a gift of carthorses to Ranjit. In 1832 a treaty between Lord William Bentinck, the governor-general and the amirs threw the Indus open to commerce, but gave them protection from Ranjit and a virtual guarantee of independence. This treaty was violated when the next governor-general, Lord Auckland, made Sind a base for his operations in Afghanistan (1838). A new treaty was imposed, compelling the amirs, under threats of annexation, to pay a subsidy for an auxiliary force.

The Afghan adventure having ended in disaster, the new governor-general, Lord Ellenborough, turned his attention to Sind. New demands were made and the amirs goaded to resistance by Sir Charles Napier. They were defeated at Miani (1843) and their territories, except that of the Mir of Khairpur, annexed.

H. T. Lambrick, *Sir Charles Napier and Sind* (Oxford, 1952).
TGPS

AMIS DES NOIRS (1787), French anti-slavery society founded in imitation of the British abolitionist movement. Its members included Siéyès, Condorcet, Mirabeau, and Lafayette.

AMMIANUS MARCELLINUS (*c.* AD 330–400), the outstanding historian of the later Roman empire. Born at Antioch, he travelled widely on military service under Constantius II and Julian, whom he accompanied on the Persian invasion of 363. Returning to Antioch, he later (*c.* 383) visited Rome, where he was giving recitations from his history in 392. The complete work, covering the period from Nerva (96–8) to 378, was probably published soon after 392, but only books XIV–XXXI, covering 353–378, survive. The history is rightly seen as a masterpiece, distinguished for its completeness of information and by the sanity and honesty of its judgement. It is no less remarkable for being composed in Latin by a man whose native tongue was Greek.

AMMON, ancient Semitic state, north-east of the Dead Sea, established *c.* 1200 BC, conquered by the Hebrews (*c.* 1000) and later tributary to Assyria. It was a pastoral and agricultural community with several fortified towns.

AMMURIYYA (AMORION), famous Byzantine stronghold in Phrygia, on the great road from Constantinople to Cilicia. The Arabs attacked it in 666, 669, 708, and 716. Its defences were strengthened thereafter in the time of Leo III (717–41). After resisting further attacks in 779 and 792, Amorion fell to the Caliph al-Mu'tasim in 838.

AMNESTY QUESTION, Canadian political dispute. Hoping to settle the Red River Rebellion (1869–70) peacefully, the Canadian government promised amnesty to the rebels, led by Louis Riel. But the situation was confused by the summary execution of Thomas Scott by the Métis, which English-speaking Canadians regarded as murder. Trivial in itself, the controversy revealed the weakness of Canadian racial unity and problems of imperial constitutional relations. The prime minister, Alexander Mackenzie, unable to satisfy both French and English Canadians, referred the case to the colonial office in England. But they refused to relieve the Canadians of their constitutional responsibility. The problem was resolved in 1875 by the governor-general, Lord Dufferin, who acting on his own responsibility, commuted the death sentence passed on Ambrose Lepine in 1873 for heading Scott's court-martial. Later, passions cooled sufficiently to allow for the enactment of legislation similar to the Amnesty Act of 1849.

AMO, ANTON WILHELM (d. *c.* 1753), a Nzima of Axim in south-west Ghana (Gold Coast), who lived in Germany (1707–47) and studied at Halle, Wittenberg (where he was awarded a Ph.D), and Jena universities. Amo was among the first Africans to make an academic career in Europe.

AMORITES, ancient Semitic people, originally nomads of Syria, known from early times to the Sumerians, who had fought them on the frontiers. In *c.* 2030 BC they broke into Mesopotamia, where they founded kingdoms (including Mari, Isin, and Larsa), the first dynasty of Babylon (*c.* 1894–1594), and the first Assyrian empire. They adopted the Akkadian language and assimilated Sumero-Akkadian culture and religion, but the former city-states disappeared and the power of the temples and priests declined as the Amorite chiefs gave away land and encouraged the ownership of private property. Their rule was ended by the Hittites (*c.* 1594). They appear also to have been a ruling class in Syria–Palestine, where they were organized in small states, the most important being Carchemish, Aleppo, and Qatna.

AMPÈRE, ANDRÉ MARIE (1775–1836), French mathematician who was the first to propound the electro-dynamic theory. The unit of electric current is named after him.

AMPHICTYONIC LEAGUE, or Council, a religious association of ancient Greek states, notably that centred on Delphi, composed predominantly of central and northern communities. Though chiefly concerned with the Delphic shrine's administration, the league was sometimes used for political ends. It declared the First Sacred War (*c.* 590 BC) on Delphi's neighbour, Crisa, which was destroyed, but its development as a political body was retarded by the comparative backwardness of its chief members and later by their Medism in the Persian Wars. In 355 the league was induced by Thebes to declare the Third Sacred War on the Phocians, whose prolonged resistance enabled Philip II of Macedon to enter central Greece on the league's behalf and, after crushing them, to acquire their two votes and the council's chairmanship. In 339 Philip used a dispute between the league and Amphissa to invade central Greece again and defeat Athens and Thebes at Chaeronea.

AMPHIPOLIS, Athenian colony on the Strymon river, three miles from its mouth. It was founded in 437–436 BC after at least one earlier attempt to establish the colony had failed. It was important because of its local minerals, for the transport of ship-timber from the hinterland, and for its position on the land route to the Hellespont (Dardanelles). Probably resented at first by Athens' local allies, Amphipolis went over to the Spartan Brasidas without a fight (424). In 422 Cleon and Brasidas were killed in an unsuccessful attempt to recover the colony. Though conceded to Athens in the peace of Nicias (421), it refused to agree and resisted coercion. Later, after failing to capture Amphipolis between 369 and 358, the Athenians allowed Philip II of Macedon to take it, but he did not hand it over as agreed (357), and himself exploited the gold-mines of Mt Pangaeus nearby and founded Crenides, later Philippi, which in time overshadowed it.

AMRITSAR, city in the modern Indian state of the Punjab, founded (1574–81) by the fourth Sikh *guru,* Ram Das. From the early 18th cent. it became the centre of the Sikh community. On an island in a lake arose the chief Sikh shrine, the Golden Temple.

AMRITSAR MASSACRE (13 April 1919), incident which arose from an agitation created by Gandhi in protest against the Rowlatt Acts. The Punjab government under Sir Michael O'Dwyer refused to allow Gandhi to enter the Punjab in connection with this campaign and serious disorders resulted in Amritsar, where several people, including five Europeans, were killed. Gen. Reginald Dyer, commanding troops at Jullundur, was ordered to take charge in the city following these disturbances. He assumed control on 11 April and proclaimed a ban on meetings, declaring that, if necessary, they would be dispersed by force. On the same day it was announced that a meeting would be held on April 13 at Jallianwala Bagh. Although Dyer knew of this, he took no steps to forestall the meeting. Instead, he went with 50 armed men to the Bagh, an enclosed square with narrow entrances, at which he posted his men, then ordered them, without preliminaries, to fire into the crowd. As a result, 379 people were killed and over 1200 wounded. The Punjab government supported Dyer's action, but it was disowned by the British government and he was removed from active service (1920).

Report of the Committee appointed to investigate disturbances in the Punjab (Cmd. 681, 1920).   PDR

AMRITSAR, TREATIES OF (1809, 1846). By the treaty of April 1809, the British frontier was advanced from the Jumna to the Sutlej and the cis-Sutlej Sikhs were protected from Ranjit Singh. By the treaty of March 1846 with the British, Gulab Singh acquired Kashmir, Ladakh, Gilgit, and Chamba for 75 lakhs of rupees.

AMSTERDAM, town on the canalized Amstel river which, after the building of a sea wall in the 13th cent., developed rapidly from a small fishing port. Originally a fief of Utrecht, in 1296 it became part of the county of Holland and was first chartered in 1300. Occupying an outlet of the Rhine to the North Sea, it grew in the 15th cent. into a major shipping and commercial centre of northern Europe, specializing in the import of grain and timber for the rest of the Netherlands. By the 16th cent. it had replaced Antwerp as the most important commercial and banking centre of the Netherlands, a position enhanced by the closing of the Scheldt river (1648). In the 19th and 20th cents improvements in inland communications, through canal construction and the building of docks, helped to develop Amsterdam as a key industrial centre. It has a State (1632) and Free (1880) university and possesses some of the greatest examples of Dutch art.

AMSTERDAM BANK, the Wisselbank, founded in 1609 on the model of the Bank of Venice to provide means for the efficient handling of metallic currency. Thus, unlike the

Bank of England, the Bank of Amsterdam never issued currency, but was used simply for depositing and transferring payments, although it also later lent money to trading organizations, eg, the Dutch East India Co.

The bank, together with the exchange, symbolized the precedence which Amsterdam had by 1600 established over Antwerp in the financial and business world of western Europe.

AMSTERDAM, TREATY OF (1717), between Russia, France, and Prussia. It was promoted by Peter the Great, who wished to conclude a Russo–French alliance to ensure his conquests in the Baltic during the Great Northern War. Peter visited Paris in 1717 in an effort to gain such an alliance, but found France loyal to her traditional ally Sweden. Peter had to be satisfied with an innocuous and ineffective treaty of friendship signed at Amsterdam. However, the treaty constituted a further recognition of Russia's new status as a European power.

AMYNTAS III (*reg. c.* 393–369 BC), King of Macedon, whose involvement in Greek politics foreshadowed Philip II's expansionism. After encouraging the Spartans to dissolve the Chalcidian League (382), he made an agreement with Athens (375), but later allied himself with Jason of Pherae.

AN LU-SHAN (703–57), of Sogdian origin, served as an officer on China's northern borders, attaining command of a large body of troops and administrative control of wide areas of territory, and enjoying the favouritism of the T'ang Emperor Hsüan-tsung. In 755 he rebelled against the central government, captured the capital city, and declared himself emperor, but was murdered by his son. The series of rebellions which he started was crushed only in 763, and by then the government had been obliged to call on the Uighurs for help. The rebellions resulted in the irreparable disruption of the government and economy of the T'ang empire, despite the survival of the dynastic house until 906.

ANABAPTISTS, members of radical religious sects of the 16th cent. who rejected infant baptism. The term, which means rebaptism, was first used as a form of abuse by Zwingli, from whose reformed Protestant community at Zürich the first true Anabaptists separated themselves in 1523.

Rejecting all the externals of religion as well as civil magistracy, and all authority except that of the inner spirit, the Anabaptist sects can hardly be classified as a movement, although the activities of some leading spirits created a certain practical cohesion. Some beliefs were held by all groups, the fundamental one, separating them from Lutherans and, later, Calvinists, being the belief in free will. Characteristics most widely shared were expressed in the Schleitheim Confession (1527), the articles of which included adult baptism, the celebration of the Lord's Supper in a strictly memorial sense, and the exclusion from it of any who were in error or sin.

The Swiss Brethren, a minority at Zürich led by Balthasar Hubmaier and Conrad Grebel, were banished after failing to convince the Council in 1525 of the necessity of refusing baptism for their children.

Anabaptist settlements survived in Moravia because they were well organized by Jakob Hutter, and they were sufficiently strong to contribute to the migrations to North America, where their descendants are still known as Hutterites.

In the states of north Germany the Anabaptists suffered the reflected notoriety of Thomas Muntzer (c. 1490–1525), a Saxon priest who defected from Luther at Wittenberg in 1521, preaching social revolution of a violent and apocalyptic kind. He was captured and killed after taking part in the Peasants' War, which he regarded as Christ's second coming.

Many leading Anabaptists met at Strasbourg until the city condemned them in 1534. In that year hundreds of radical Anabaptists, who with refugees from the Low Countries, led by Jan Matthys, had taken control of Munster in Westphalia, and driven out Catholics and Lutherans, were massacred there after a siege by the city's prince-bishop. In extremity they had experimented with polygamy and primitive communism.

To a certain extent Anabaptism was a response to accelerating economic hardship during the 16th cent. In northern Europe it was saved from extinction under persecution by the moderate organizer Menno Simons, who though a fugitive managed to impose rigid discipline on the sects, so that his teaching survived into the 17th cent.

Despite their contribution to the idea of liberty of conscience, the Anabaptists' influence on their own times was rather to persuade the Protestant reformers to embrace the assistance of the godly magistrate in defence of doctrinal and social order.

N. Cohn, *The Pursuit of the Millennium* (London, 1957).

HNBM

ANACONDA COPPER COMPANY, chief US producer in Chile, where it operates Chuquicamata, the largest surface mine in the world.

ANADYR, north-eastern Siberian river flowing into the Pacific Ocean. By sailing from the Kolyma river on the Arctic coast of Siberia to the mouth of the Anadyr (1648), the cossack Dezhnev made the first recorded voyage through the north-eastern passage.

ANAESTHESIA (the word was suggested by Oliver Wendell Holmes), was discovered in several places more or less simultaneously. In the US Crawford Lang and William Morton used ether (1842 and 1846) and Horace Wells used nitrous oxide, 'laughing gas' (1844). The first operation under ether in Britain was in 1846. Chloroform had been prepared in the US, France, and Germany, but was first used by Prof. James Young Simpson in Scotland (1847). Its popularity for the next 50 years was partly due to Dr John Snow, who administered it twice to Queen Victoria.

ANAGNI, OUTRAGE OF (Sept. 1303). Anagni was the native town of Pope Boniface VIII who was surprised there by a band of French soldiers led by Nogaret, one of the chief advisers of King Philip IV of France. The attack was designed to forestall the expected excommunication of Philip by Boniface. Nogaret's allies, members of the Roman family of the Colonna, who were Boniface's personal enemies, manhandled the pope. He was soon rescued by the townspeople, but died of shock within a few weeks.

ANALECTS OF CONFUCIUS (*Lun-yü*), one of the Four Books of the Chinese Classics. There are 20 chapters, which include sayings attributed to Confucius and dialogue exchanged between him and his pupils; the text was probably compiled by his pupils' disciples. The aphorisms stress the responsibilities of human beings for each other's well-being; the value of social discipline, education, established modes of conduct, social distinctions; and the proper place in government of men endowed with qualities suitable for governing.

ANALOG COMPUTER, machine for performing mathematical operations upon physical quantities, *eg*, electric currents, which themselves are proportional to the numerical values of the input data. Analog (corruption of 'analogue') computers have their uses in certain scientific applications, but had not, by 1970, become as widely used as digital computers because of the relative complexity of design and manufacture.

ANALYTICAL GEOMETRY, or co-ordinate geometry, founded by Descartes (1596–1650), differs from pure or Euclidian geometry in achieving solutions by algebraical methods. Its basic principles is a pair of axes, called the x and y axes, and a point has x and y co-ordinates (the Cartesian co-ordinates) which fix its position uniquely.

ANANDA MAHIDOL (1925–46), King of Siam, was only ten years old when he succeeded his uncle (1935). The eighth king of the Chakri dynasty, he was the eldest son of Prince Mahidol (1892–1929) and grandson of King Chulalongkorn by Queen Sawangwatthana. He returned to Bangkok to assume his constitutional duties only in 1946, and, on 9 June, was found dead of a gunshot wound. The mystery of his death was never satisfactorily solved, and it contributed to the decline of parliamentary government and the return to power of Phibunsongkhram.

ANANDA RANGA PILLAI (1709–61), diarist and *dubash* or secretary of Jean François Dupleix, governor of French India at Pondicherry (1742–54). The surviving portions of the diary, which is a day-to-day account of events in Pondicherry (1736–late 1760), by a man with a deep admiration for Dupleix, is a recognized classic of its kind.

ANARCHISM as a political philosophy can be traced back to William Godwin's *Enquiry Concerning Political Justice* (1793), in which he postulated a peaceful distribution of wealth among the needy, the ending of the state, and the creation of a society of self-governing communities. The more influential Pierre Proudhon, who claimed in the 1840s that 'property is theft' and demanded the abolition of the state and of private property, also believed in peaceful change. But Proudhon influenced a generation of revolutionaries in the 1860s and 1870s, including Bakunin, who began to maintain that change could only come through violence. While agreeing with the Marxists on the need to overthrow the existing state and capitalism and replace them by a communist system, the anarchists rejected their authoritarian ideas and also claimed that the peasants throughout Europe were as much revolutionary material as the industrial proletariat. Their belief was borne out in Spain and Italy, where large anarchist parties of workers and peasants existed until the success of Franco and Mussolini. While the moderate anarchist movement in the last years of the 19th cent. followed the idealism of Prince Kropotkin, the more extreme undertook individual acts of violence against public figures, causing the deaths of President Carnot of France, the American president, William McKinley, the Empress Elizabeth of Austria, and King Humbert I of Italy. Perhaps their greatest success, however, was in France, where, influenced by Kropotkin and Georges Sorel, the anarchists, or syndicalists, penetrated the trade unions and largely controlled them in the decade before the First World War.

ANARCHISM IN SPAIN, owed its origins to Giuseppe Fanelli, who introduced it in 1868. Fanelli was a pupil of the Russian, Bakunin. By 1873 there were 50,000 anarchists who adhered to Bakuninist notions of the tyranny of wealth, authority, and religion. The 1874 Catalonist revolt added to anarchism the ideas of Proudhon and Pi y Margall, who advocated free federations of autonomous communes.

Anarchism was strongest in rural Andalusia. Its religious tone, its denunciation of riches, and its promise of an earthly utopia appealed to primitive labourers. The 'idea' was carried from village to village by austere wandering anarchists. Action took the form of peasant jacquerie, crop-burnings, and attacks on rural guards. Repression followed and apathy took over. Development was thus cyclical. Without organization, anarchism relied on the triumph of isolated violence. In 1883 the Civil Guard discovered the Black Hand conspiracy to murder all Andalusian landlords. Evidence of its existence was probably faked and it provoked savage repression. In 1892 a peasant army occupied Jerez.

Meanwhile, immigrant labour from the south and cramped slum conditions in Barcelona encouraged the growth of Catalan anarchism. In the 1890s this took the form of 'propaganda by deed': bomb-throwing and terrorism. Police repression and torture were met by reprisals which included the assassinations of three prime ministers. However, the need for industrial action promoted the growth of more moderate syndicalism, whose history is that of the CNT. The older terrorist traditions were kept alive by the FAI.

For a brief period after the outbreak of the Spanish Civil War the 'idea' saw reality. Industry in Barcelona was collectivized and rural communes were set up in Aragon and Andalusia. The needs of war, together with communist hostility, curtailed the experiment. The Nationalist victory in 1939 killed anarchism, except for its persistence among a few heroic diehards who waged guerrilla war on Franco's Spain until 1948.   PP

ANASTASIA ROMANOVNA (d. 1560) first wife of Tsar Ivan IV (the 'Terrible'). She died 53 years before her family became the ruling dynasty in Muscovy.

ANASTASIUS I (440–518), Eastern emperor (491–518) and the last Byzantine ruler to support the Monophysite sect in Egypt and Syria. The abandonment of his tolerant policy under his successors paved the way for the speedy conquest of these provinces by the Arabs.

ANATOMY, branch of morphology concerned with the study of human structure by dissection. Its advance was for long obstructed by inhibitions about the desecration of the dead, and in later times mercenary criminals like Burke and Hare made a useful contribution to scientific progress. Dissection was carried out in the schools of Alexandria and Bologna. The pioneer of the modern science was the Fleming Vesalius (1514–64), professor at Padua, who introduced objective experimental methods to discredit traditional notions about the structure of the body. Latterly radiography has revolutionized anatomy by enabling the body to be studied during life.

ANAWRAHTA (*reg.* 1044–77) King of Pagan, by a series of conquests, united for the first time virtually the whole of Burma. To the west he controlled part of Arakan. To the north and east he pushed his frontiers to the mountains, and imposed suzerainty over some of the Shan states beyond. To the south he conquered the Mon kingdom of Thaton. But he was not only a man of war. In his capital he built temples, so initiating Burma's 200-year golden period of architecture. He brought from Thaton a purer form of Buddhism and the beneficent cultural influence of the Mons, notwithstanding their political subjugation.

ANAXAGORAS (fl. mid-5th cent. BC), Greek physicist and rational philosopher from Clazomenae, who taught at Athens and became the friend and tutor of Pericles, whose political enemies almost certainly secured his exile (of uncertain date, 450–431) for impiety, probably on the grounds that he denied the divinity of the sun, moon, and stars.

ANAXANDRIDAS (*reg. c.* 560–520 BC), Agiad, King of Sparta, who joined unwillingly in Chilon's foreign policy. After the ephors had obliged him to take a kinswoman of Chilon, subsequently mother of Cleomenes, as his second wife, his previously childless first wife gave birth to Dorieus, Leonidas, and Cleombrotus.

ANAXILAS (d. 476 BC), Tyrant of Rhegium (494–476 BC) and supporter of the Carthaginians during their attack on Greek Sicily in 480. After persuading Samian exiles to seize Zancle (493), he later expelled them, replacing them with new settlers, including Messenians, and renaming it Messana. In 484–483 he joined his father-in-law, Terillus, tyrant of Himera, in an appeal to Carthage for help against Gelon of Syracuse and Theron of Acragas, but is not heard of in the subsequent campaign and Carthaginian defeat at Himera, though his fleet probably barred the straits to Gelon. He then probably acknowledged Gelon's supremacy, and ruled Rhegium and Messana until his death.

ANCESTOR CULT, CHINESE. From earliest times the Chinese believed in the survival of the souls of the dead. By serving these spirits with due respect, by ceremonies and material offerings, it was hoped to secure their blessing for current activities and to prevent their malevolent interference in the world of the living. These beliefs and practices have promoted social stability and family unity throughout Chinese history.

ANCIEN RÉGIME. The social and political system of pre-revolutionary France. This usage is not universally accepted, some authorities using the term to denote either the period of European history preceding the Revolution or the general European system of government at this time. The phrase in both its revolutionary origins and in the hands of 19th-cent. historians such as Taine and de Tocqueville signified a set of French institutions, and this is the sense in which most historians have used it. The *ancien régime* is usually seen as coming into being in the late 16th cent., and as having lasted until the Revolution of 1789. Some of its institutions, such as the *taille* and venality of offices, have their origins in the Middle Ages, just as others lasted into the 19th cent., but the period from Henry II to Louis XVI is that with which the *ancien régime* is associated. And although there are parallels in other European countries, the close relationship of state and society and the limitations which this placed on the monarchy are peculiar to France. In France the *ancien régime* was not a unitary and unchanging organism. It was composed of many elements and was subject to considerable changes under pressure of events. It was initially a response to the problems of the religious wars, was developed in the course of the early 17th-cent. crises, reached a peak under Louis XIV, and gradually ossified during the following cent. In its maturity it was an extremely complex interrelationship of society and politics, in which all social classes were controlled by, or attached to, the administrative structure of the absolute monarchy. The mechanisms involved were not merely feudalism or centralization, but were much more complex. The *ancien régime* was a traditional, hierarchical, and corporative society, catholic and socially unjust, in which groups were attached to the intricate and ramshackle administration of an absolute monarchy which was both personal and administrative, and which was also both dynastic and *étatist* in its outlook. The nobles were linked to the structure by tax privileges, feudal dues, and political preferment, the middle classes by venality of offices, artisans by the gild system, and the Church by tax exemptions. This process has been described as the *mainmise* of the state over society, but in the long run it was the state which was subsumed in society. Louis XIV and the cardinals sought to combat social and military crises by buying support and in the long run this meant that the absolute monarchy was hamstrung by the many groups who thereby acquired a vested interest in the status quo. It was unable to modernize itself or to cope with the problems of the 18th cent., and crumbled in the face of noble reaction and revolution.

C. B. A. Behrens, *The Ancien Régime* (Library of European Civilization) (London, 1967).
J. MacManners and J. M. Wallace-Hadrill (eds), *France: Government and Society* (London, 1957).   JHS

ANCIENTS AND MODERNS, controversy about the respective merits of classical and modern literature, started in France (*c.* 1670) by Desmarets de Saint-Sorlin, who attacked Homer and Virgil and argued that Christian themes were the only appropriate subjects for heroic poetry. While Boileau and Racine defended the traditional view, Charles Perrault, author of *Cinderella*, urged contemporary writers to excel the ancients instead of slavishly imitating them, and Fontenelle dismissed much classical writing as ignorance and superstition. In England Sir William Temple defended classical literature (*Reflections upon Ancient and Modern Learning*, 1694), but his argument rebounded when the *Letters of Phalaris*, which he had incautiously praised, were shown by the classical scholar, Richard Bentley, to have been a forgery. The dispute was treated satirically in Swift's *Battle of the Books* (1704), the advantage resting slightly with the ancients.

ANCÓN, TREATY OF (Oct. 20, 1883), between Peru and Chile, ending the War of the Pacific. Peru surrendered Tarapaca and Chile gained the right to occupy Tacna and Arica until a plebiscite could be held in ten years. The plebiscite was never held, and the existence of the two areas caused friction between Chile and Peru. In 1929 Chile agreed to return Arica to Peru, but retained Tacna.

ANCRUM MOOR, BATTLE OF (1545), Scottish ambush of an English raiding party under Sir Ralph Evers in retaliation for the latter's attack on Jedbergh and Melrose Abbey. Ancrum Moor halted the English raids, revived Scottish spirits and caused Henry VIII to recall Hertford from France to take command in the Scottish border campaign.

ANCUS MARCIUS (*reg.* 642–617 BC), traditionally the fourth Roman king, to whom is ascribed the Roman conquest of Ostia, and the building of the Pons Sublicius, perhaps to facilitate exploitation of the Ostian salt-beds.

ANCYRA (mod. Ankara), capital of the Roman province of Galatia, famous for the *monumentum Ancryanum*, a text in Greek and Latin of the Emperor Augustus' record of his achievements inscribed on the ruins of the temple of Rome and Augustus.

ANDAGOYA, PASCUAL DE (1495–1548), Spanish conquistador who headed an expedition down the coast of Colombia (1522). He was appointed governor of the region (1539) and later wrote a *Relación* concerning his experiences.

ANDALUS, AL-, word of uncertain but possibly Vandal origin, was used by Muslims for Muslim Spain from the earliest times of their conquests there, early in the 8th cent. AD. At first under governors formally loyal to the Ummayyad caliphate in Damascus, Al-Andalus emerged as a separate entity and a variant of Muslim civilization under Abd al-Rahman I (AD 756–822). By the 9th cent. Al-Andalus included most of the Iberian peninsula. With its capital at Cordoba, a distinctive, tolerant, and often brilliant culture flourished under the Western Ummayyad caliphate (AD 912–1031). Craft industries and agriculture prospered; cities were embellished with splendid buildings; long-distance trade linked Al-Andalus with northern and western Africa, with the central and eastern Mediterranean, and to some extent with northern Europe. After a period of disintegration, a certain unity was restored under Almoravid leaders in the 12th cent., and again under Almohad rulers in the early 13th. But Christian conquest was now in course, and was completed late in the 15th cent.

ANDALUSIA, territory in Spain, guarded by the Sierra Morena to the north and the Sierra Nevada to the south, is made up of arid rolling countryside. A generally poor dry soil is devoted to wheat, olive, or vine monoculture, although there are fertile areas of intensive cultivation—the *vegas* around Granada, Cordoba, and the wine area of Jerez, and cotton growing near Seville.

The system of land-tenure in the south has made Andalusia the classic land of class hatred, anarchism, and *caciquismo*. It is the area of the *latifundia*—huge estates—often run by overseers on behalf of absentee landlords, some surviving from feudal times, others acquired during the break-up of Church and common lands in the 19th cent. These estates were worked by landless day labourers, half starving, earning a pittance, and unemployed for more than six months of the year. The *latifundia* aggravated the problem of supporting a large population on a dry soil, especially as rich landowners often did not cultivate the best land, perhaps reserving it for bull-breeding.

The vast differences between rich and poor turned the agricultural proletariat to anarchism, although the power of the *caciques* ensured the election of right-wing deputies. Movements for agrarian reform had been blocked since the 18th cent. in Andalusia and during the Second Republic agrarian discontent erupted into violent uprisings and strikes. There was constant revolutionary disorder throughout Andalusia before the Spanish Civil War, although Andalusia, with the exception of Malaga, fell rapidly to the Nationalist forces in the early stages of the war.   PP

ANDAMAN ISLANDS, group of islands in the Bay of Bengal, used as a penal colony for British India (1858–1942). It began as a settlement for 773 prisoners from the Mutiny (1857–8). It was occupied by the Japanese (1942–5), and was not reopened for convicts after the war.

ANDERSON, SHERWOOD (1876–1941), US writer. After a variety of occupations, including service in the Spanish–American War, writing advertising copy, and managing his own paint-manufacturing company in Ohio, Anderson suddenly left his family and went to Chicago to become a writer. His first novel, *Windy McPherson's Son* (1916), describes a similar pattern of success and renunciation. *Winesburg, Ohio* (1919), with its searching examination of small-town Midwestern America, established his reputation. He continued to explore this theme in *Poor White* (1921), and later novels, essays, and stories. A Naturalistic writer, the frustrated, puzzled characters whose minds he probed in *Winesburg* are characteristic of those portrayed throughout his work. Anderson gave early encouragement to William Faulkner. His general influence on the American novel has probably been underestimated.

ANDERSONVILLE PRISON, GA, a Confederate camp for Union prisoners in the later stages of the American Civil War. It held over 30,000 prisoners in appalling conditions (1864), and thousands died. Its commandant, Henry Wirz, although not altogether to blame for the camp's horrors, was the only important Confederate officer executed after the war.

ANDOCIDES (*c.* 440–391 BC). Athenian politician and one of the ten great Attic orators. Surviving speeches concern his banishment (415), his return (403) and subsequent legal proceedings, the challenge to his status (399), and his embassy to Sparta in the Corinthian War (392–391), after which he failed to persuade the Athenians to accept the terms offered and anticipated capital sentence by flight.

ANDRADE E SILVA, JOSÉ BONIFACIO DE (1765–1838), prime minister of the independent Empire of Brazil (1822–3). Educated in Portugal, he became a scientist and was also the intellectual advocate in São Paulo of Brazilian independence. So great was his popularity that Pedro I had him and his two brothers exiled (1823). He had opposed freedom of the press and the masonic lodges. After his return from France, he exercised considerable influence as the tutor of young Pedro II.

ANDRÁSSY, GYULA, Graf (1823–90), Hungarian prime minister (1867) and Austro-Hungarian foreign minister (1871), who laid the foundations of the Dual Monarchy's foreign policy of co-operation with Germany and hostility towards Russia. Although he had been one of Kossuth's supporters in the revolution of 1848–9, by the time of the *Ausgleich* (1867) he agreed with Deák on the advisability of accepting the Habsburg dynasty, if it in return accepted the existence of the Hungarian nation and abandoned its centralizing and federative policies. Owing to the pressure of Deák and the Austrian foreign minister, Beust, Andrássy was made the first prime minister of an autonomous Hungary. The new Austria-Hungary, based on a working alliance between the Germans and Hungarians at the expense of the Slavs, was exactly what he wanted.

Andrássy was above all interested in diplomacy and especially in the need for the Dual Monarchy to assert its position in Europe, which he believed, depended on co-operating with Bismarck's Germany. By opposing Beust's wish to intervene on the French side in the Franco-Prussian War, Andrássy was appointed foreign minister of Austria–Hungary at Beust's resignation (1871). Although on occasions he was ready to co-operate with Russia, he was determined to resist any increase in Russian power in the Balkans, as was shown in his policy during the Eastern Crisis, which developed in 1875 and culminated in the Congress of Berlin (1878). At this congress, although he did not wish to see any more Slavs within the monarchy, he insisted on the occupation of Bosnia-Herzegovina to prevent worse alternatives. Just before his resignation (1879) he was able to persuade Bismarck to sign the Dual Alliance, which gave Austria-Hungary protection from possible Russian aggression.

ANDREW OF SUZDAL (*c.* 1111–74), a grandson of Vladimir Monomakh. In 1157 he became Prince of Rostov and Suzdal, and in 1169 master of the city of Kiev, which he sacked; but he preferred to live in Suzdalia, leaving Kiev in the hands of a puppet-prince. He made his capital the city of Vladimir-in-Suzdal, which he enlarged and beautified. He was the first Russian prince to try to establish a centralized Russian state under the absolute power of the ruler, but his attempt was unsuccessful. In 1174 he was assassinated by a conspiracy of boyars, whose power he had tried to curtail.

ANDREW OF WYNTOUN (d. *c.* 1424), Scottish ecclesiastic and writer of a vernacular *orygynale cronykil of Scotland*.

ANDREWES, LANCELOT (1555–1626), English bishop. The son of a merchant, he became master of Pembroke College, Cambridge (1589–1605), chaplain to Abp Whitgift and chaplain in ordinary to Elizabeth I, Bp of Chichester and king's almoner (1605), Bp of Ely (1609), and of Winchester (1619). He was also a privy councillor of England (1609) and Scotland (1617). His political activity was negligible but, like Hooker, he did a great deal to reconcile Catholic ceremonies with Protestant beliefs, and thus he helped to establish the characteristic Anglican position.

ANDREWS, CECIL ROLLO PATON (1870–1951), Australian educational pioneer, who went to Western Australia from Battersea Training College in 1902, as the first principal of Claremont Training College. As head of the state education department (1903–29), he established Perth Modern School and other state high schools, provided rural schools throughout the newly pioneered agricultural districts, and helped to found the University of WA (1911).

ANDREYEV, ANDREY ANDREYEVICH (1895–   ), member of the CPSU and the Soviet government with special responsibility for agriculture. He is responsible also, as first secretary, for collectivization in the North Caucasus, and, as commissar for agriculture (1943–6), was responsible for increasing agricultural production during the war. As chairman of the Council for Collective Farms (1946–53), he sought to reverse the wartime liberalization of the *kolkhoz* system without diminishing agricultural production.

ANDRIC, IVO (1892–   ), contemporary Serbian writer and winner of the Nobel Prize for literature (1961). Andric was born in Bosnia and educated at Zagreb, Graz, and Vienna. He was interned by the Austro-Hungarian authorities during the First World War for his Yugoslav nationalism. He wrote short stories while pursuing a career as a diplomat; in 1940 he was appointed ambassador in Berlin. During the Second World War he remained in occupied Belgrade. Andric's approach to life centres upon the isolation of the individual, an isolation conditioned by fear of both external disaster and internal anxiety. Much of his work is set in Bosnia. His best-known novels are *Bosnian Story, The Bridge on the Drina*, and *The Woman from Sarajevo*.

ANDRONICUS I COMNENUS (1120–85), Byzantine Emperor (1183–5). A relative of the ruling Comneni emperors, he had an eventful career filled with conspiracies and largely spent in exile. He returned to Constantinople in 1182 as the leader of the anti-Latin party and became emperor (1183), murdering his predecessor, the young Alexius II. Andronicus was an enemy of the landed aristocracy and tried to promote reforms, but this, and the terroristic nature of his rule, aroused much hatred. He was eventually killed during a tumult in Constantinople.

ANDRONICUS II PALAEOLOGUS (1260–1332), became (1282) the second Byzantine Emperor of the Palaeologus dynasty. During his reign the Ottoman Turks overran most of western Asia Minor. A force of Catalan mercenaries enlisted by Andronicus won some success against the Turks, but the political ambitions of the Catalan leader, Roger de Flor, terrified the Byzantines, who assassinated him in 1305. Thereupon the Catalans revolted and, after fearful ravaging, established an independent principality at Thebes and Athens in Greece. Andronicus was deposed by his grandson Andronicus III in 1328.

ANDRONICUS III PALAEOLOGUS (1296–1341), Byzantine Emperor (1328–41), made war on his grandfather, Andronicus II in 1320, became co-emperor in 1325, and forced Andronicus II to abdicate in 1328. Most of his reign was spent in opposition to the Turks in Asia Minor and to the Serbs, under Stephen Dushan, in the Balkans.

ANDROS, SIR EDMUND (1637–1714), English governor in America. In 1674 the Duke of York appointed him governor of his territories, which included NY, NJ, and parts of ME and CT. When England decided to unite all of New England into one colony, Andros became governor of New England (1686–9) and of NY and NJ (1688). He ruled without local assemblies, and this and his interference in their affairs irritated the colonists so much that they rebelled and returned him to England as a prisoner. Later, he was appointed governor of VA (1692–9).

ANDRUSSOVO, TREATY OF (1667), signed between Muscovy and Poland. The treaty signified a decisive shift in the balance of power from the latter to the former. War had broken out in 1654 when Tsar Alexis accepted the allegiance of the Ukrainian cossacks. It ended with an agreement to divide the Ukraine between the two powers, a settlement which brought Muscovy to the Dnieper river and gave her the important towns of Kiev and Smolensk.

ANEIRIN (*fl.* late 6th cent.), Welsh poet named, together with Taliesin, by Nennius. His putative work, the *Gododdin*, is extant in a 13th-cent. copy. It is a long series of brief laments for the members of a band of north British warriors killed in a raid.

ANEITYUM, small island in the southern New Hebrides which played an important role in the early history of the group. Its Melanesian inhabitants rejected Europeans (the *Alpha*, 1830), but accepted Samoan teachers from the London Missionary Society (1841). These were followed by European missionaries (Roman Catholic and Presbyterian), and the islanders split into two sectarian groups, which generated strife culminating in the attempted murder of John Geddie, a Presbyterian missionary. The Catholic priests withdrew to New Caledonia (1852), and with the establishment of a second Presbyterian mission the islanders accepted Christianity, though nearby islanders rejected the faith until the 20th cent. Epidemics gradually decimated the island's population of 3500; 1100 died of measles in 1860–1, and by 1900 only 170 inhabitants remained.

ANFU CLIQUE (active *c.* 1917–20), major war-lord faction in early Republican China. The clique, led by Tuan Ch'i-jui, rose to power in 1917. It packed the Chinese parliament through massive bribery. During the 4 May Movement (1919) the clique's pro-Japanese attitude brought it into disrepute, and the following year it was defeated by the Chihli Clique.

ANG CHAN (*reg.* 1516–66), last great King of independent Cambodia. After spending the years 1508–16 in exile at Ayudhya, because of a conflict about the succession, he returned home to reunify the country and establish its capital at Lovek, north of Phnom Penh. He was later involved in wars with Ayudhya, in which the city of Khorat was lost to the Thai (1560), but was recovered (1566). In 1563 he endowed a Buddhist monastery at Angkor Wat. He received the first European visitor to Cambodia, a Portuguese Dominican, in 1556. One other Cambodian king bore the same name (*reg.* 1806–34). By the latter period, the country had suffered encroachments by both Siam and Viet-nam, and its kings had to send tribute both to Bangkok and to Huê.

ANG DUONG (*reg.* 1845–59), King of Cambodia in the period when Viet-namese and Thai pressure on that country reached its peak. The Viet-namese, who had occupied Phnom Penh in 1836, and annexed the whole of Cambodia in 1841, were driven out by a rebellion in 1845, and Ang Duong, in exile in Bangkok, returned to control the country with Thai support. By agreement between the Viet-namese and the Thai, he ruled as virtually their vassal, recognizing a sort of joint suzerainty. An appeal to France in 1853 for some kind of recognition that might save Cambodia from extinction at the hands of its neighbours did not bear fruit until after his death.

ANGAS, GEORGE FIFE (1789–1879), Australian philanthropist, company promoter, banker, and early settler, known as 'Father and Founder' of the colony of SA. An ardent Baptist, with whom commerce and Christianity went hand in hand, he supported missionary enterprise in British Honduras, where his family's timber interests prepared the way for his early association with SA.

Though his South Australia Co. (SAC) failed to obtain the charter it sought in 1832, and he held aloof from the South Australian Association which secured the passage of the Foundation Act (1834), Angas still wished to provide 'a place of refuge for distressed Dissenters', as well as to improve the spiritual state of Australian Aborigines. In 1838 he sent a party of German Lutheran missionaries to the colony under Pastor Kavel. The SAC, with Angas as its moving spirit, provided capital and gave the young colony a backing in London through the Bank of South Australia, which it established in 1836. Angas himself moved to Adelaide 14 years later and was for 16 years a member of the colony's legislative council, displaying there a conservatism which contrasted with his earlier radical enterprise.

ANGELICO, FRA GIOVANNI (1387–1455), Florentine painter and a friar of the Dominican convent of San Marco in Florence. In 1449–52 he acted as prior of the convent in Fiesole. Most of his surviving work, including the murals for the cells of the brothers and the Annunciation in San Marco, is in these convents. His work, which displays great delicacy and spirituality, also reflects contemporary Florentine developments in the techniques of perspective. In 1447 Pope Nicholas V commissioned him to decorate his private chapel in the Vatican.

ANGKOR, centre of the Khmer (Cambodian) kingdom from the 9th to 15th cents, following the establishment of a new capital in that region by Jayavarman II in 802. His successors, Jayavarman III (*reg.* 850–77) and Indravarman (*reg.* 877–89), ruled at Roluos, east of Angkor, where the latter built two major Hindu temples. The capital was established at Angkor itself by Yasovarman I (*reg.* 889–900), and apart from a short period in the 9th cent. Angkor remained the dominant Khmer centre down to the early 15th cent. The history of that period is recorded in a number of Sanskrit inscriptions, and reflected in the series of Hindu temples which has made Angkor one of the major tourist attractions of Asia in the 20th cent.

The most famous of the temples, and the best preserved, are Angkor Wat, built by Suryavarman II (*reg.* 1113–50), and the Bayon, dating from the late 12th cent., the latter, with its faces of the Bodhisattva Lokeshvara, stands at the centre of the capital of Angkor Thom, built by Jayavarman VII (*reg.* 1181–c. 1219); the gates of the city, part of the royal palace, and a number of Buddhist temple-monasteries also survive from his reign. Many of the temples fell into ruin after Angkor ceased to be the capital and owe their present state to reconstruction by French archaeologists. Another feature of the ancient city revealed by archaeological research was an extensive hydraulic system, begun by Yasovarman I and elaborated by Suryavarman II. Its function was to ensure a plentiful supply of water for irrigation.

Angkor dominated the lower Mekong basin for several cents, and at certain periods controlled an even wider area. In the period 1128–36, Suryavarman II conducted unsuccessful campaigns against the Viet-namese of Dai-Viet, and in 1145 subdued Champa. The Chams recovered, and sacked Angkor in 1177, but were again dominated by the Khmers under Jayavarman VII, who also conquered a large part of present-day Thailand. After his death, Khmer power declined, and by the 14th cent. Angkor was threatened by the Thai, who had moved into the Menam basin, from *c.* 1200. For long it was believed that Angkor held out until 1432, was sacked by the Thai (of Ayudhya) in that year, and shortly afterwards was abandoned. It has now been shown that the Khmer capital was sacked by the Thai in 1369, and again in 1389, though it was not finally abandoned till *c.* 1440. Even then, it remained a centre of Theravada Buddhism in the 16th cent. and later. The first European to visit Angkor was Henri Mouhot, in 1859.

L. P. Briggs, *The Ancient Khmer Empire* (Philadelphia, 1951).
B. P. Groslier, *Indochina, Art in the Melting Pot of Races* (London, 1962).
RBS

ANGLES, one of the continental Germanic tribes to invade Britain in the 5th cent. The Angles came from Angeln in southern Denmark, and settled predominantly in midland and northern England, giving rise to the kingdoms of Northumbria, Mercia, and East Anglia.

ANGLESEY, HENRY WILLIAM PAGET, 1st Marquis of (1768–1854), lord lieutenant of Ireland (1828–9 and 1830–3), field marshal (1846), and master general of ordnance (1846–1852). He commanded the cavalry in the Peninsular War and at Waterloo. He held office in Ireland during the critical years in which Catholic emancipation was introduced and O'Connell was at the height of his political power. Anglesey was sympathetic to Catholic claims in Ireland, and pressed vigorously for the tithe and educational reform, and for the introduction of a poor law, but he was naive and impetuous, and became a liability to both the governments he served. Wellington recalled him in 1829, and in 1833 he resigned after embarrassing the Whigs by quarrelling with O'Connell.

ANGLICANISM, the organization and doctrine of the Church of England and other Churches in communion with it, which took its present form in the religious struggles of the 16th cent.

Legally this Church was the creation of Crown and parliament, its powers, structure, and beliefs being defined by statute. Doctrinally it has always been in dispute whether at the Reformation the Crown restored a true Catholic Church, purged of the errors and abuses that had accumulated under the papal supremacy, or whether it created an entirely new Church in sympathy with Protestant opinions. The crucial issue was episcopacy, which in one view exists through an apostolic succession divinely ordained, and in the other is at best an optional and possibly convenient form of ecclesiastical government.

When Henry VIII rejected papal authority, but in other respects preserved Catholic doctrine and organization, he claimed to be merely restoring the rights and purity of an ancient Church. But for many reformers this was only an initial stage in the establishment of a Church derived from the indisputable authority of the Bible and the worship of the early Christians. These views were blessed under Edward VI, when many Catholic practices were irrevocably swept away, but, after the brief reaction under Mary, Elizabeth I imposed a settlement that was to be a test of loyalty rather than a formulation of religious truth. Retaining vestments and many of the traditional forms of worship, it was designed as a compromise, and its adherents were able to hold conflicting opinions upon such matters as the Eucharist and the validity of the episcopal office.

Although the settlement was disliked by the extremists of both parties, it came to be identified with the struggle for national unity and survival, and it was in this reign that Anglicanism achieved its character as something peculiarly English, standing aloof from partisan passion and willing to accommodate reasonable men of any shade of moderate opinion. It found its first great apologist in Hooker, whose *Ecclesiastical Polity* (1594–7) justified the Church not merely as a political expedient but as a philosophical system firmly grounded in reason, tradition, and scriptural truth.

Having survived the struggles of the 17th cent., when it was threatened by the High Church party as well as by the Presbyterians and the Cromwellian sects, Anglicanism lost some of its balance and inclusiveness when dissenting groups like the Methodists and Congregationalists broke away to form their own independent Churches. In the 19th cent. its legal and political basis was challenged by the Tractarians, who declared the Church to be a more than human institution, possessing a ministry and sacraments directly ordained by Christ. Some Tractarians inevitably found refuge in Roman Catholicism, but in general the Church of England has been able to embrace, and even to some extent to reconcile, Christians of very divergent views, whether Anglo-Catholics, Low Churchmen still cherishing the old ideas of plenary inspiration, or Modernist theologians who reject the literal interpretation of many of its fundamental beliefs. The recent discussions on reunion with the Methodists suggest that the ideals of Hooker have not lost their potency.

J. R. H. Moorman, *A History of the Church of England* (London, 1953).
MMR

ANGLO-AMERICAN CARIBBEAN COMMISSION, established (1942) by Britain and the US to co-ordinate regional development in the Caribbean. France and the Netherlands joined (1945) when the title changed to the Caribbean Commission. It was reconstructed in 1959 as the Caribbean Organization.

ANGLO-AMERICAN COMMITTEE ON PALESTINE, was established (1945) to examine the position of Jewish refugees in Europe and Jewish immigration into Palestine, which recommended (April 1946) the admission of 100,000 Jewish immigrants into Palestine, contrary to official British policy.

ANGLO-AUSTRIAN AGREEMENT (6 June 1878), concluded secretly immediately after the Russo-Turkish peace of San Stefano, which had provided for the creation of a large Bulgarian state stretching as far south as the Aegean Sea. It was fairly obvious that the new state would be dominated by Russia and this provided a community of interests between

Britain and Austria-Hungary in checking Russian expansion in the Balkans. The agreement provided for diplomatic co-operation to achieve a smaller Bulgaria, without access to the Aegean, and for Austrian occupation of Bosnia-Herzegovina.

ANGLO-DUTCH WAR (1780–4) broke out during the War of American Independence, when Britain was already involved with France and Spain. In an attempt to stop the Dutch from profiting by neutrality and furnishing supplies to the rebel American colonists, Britain declared war on the Dutch republic in Dec. 1780. The war saw little significant action, although Dutch trade suffered heavily. Peace terms were agreed in Sept. 1783, but only signed in the following May, when the Dutch were forced to surrender Negapatam in Ceylon and to acknowledge freedom of navigation in the Dutch East Indies.

ANGLO-DUTCH WARS in the 17th cent. permanently damaged the commercial and maritime power of Holland. After the first war (1651–4) the Dutch recognized the regicide government in England, accepted the Navigation Acts, and paid belated compensation for the massacre of Amboina (1623). In the second (1664–7), England was weakened by the Great Plague and the Fire of London, and de Ruyter sailed up the Medway as far as Chatham, but the Dutch surrendered New Amsterdam (renamed New York) and other settlements in North America. The third war (1672–4) followed the treaty of Dover, in which Charles II agreed to join Louis XIV in an attack on Holland; but England withdrew from the fighting and under the leadership of William of Orange the Dutch saved their country by cutting the dykes. In 1677 William married Mary, Charles II's niece, and in 1688 they became joint-sovereigns of England.

ANGLO-EGYPTIAN AGREEMENT ON SUDAN (12 Feb. 1953), an important agreement in which Egypt consented to self-determination for the Sudan, so ending a major dispute between Britain and Egypt and hastening the achievement of Sudanese independence.

ANGLO-EGYPTIAN TREATIES (1936 and 1954). The first was an agreement ending the abnormal situation existing since the unilateral British declaration of Egyptian independence (1922) and providing for the abolition of the Capitulations, the postponement of the question of the Sudan, a British base in the Canal Zone, and use of Egyptian facilities in wartime. The conclusion of the agreement was influenced by the Italian threat to Egypt and its existence was of great value to Britain in the Second World War. The second treaty provided for British evacuation of the Suez Canal base, so ending the last pillar of British military influence in Egypt.

ANGLO-FRENCH COMMERCIAL TREATIES IN THE 17TH AND 18TH CENTS. The treaty of 1713 was intended to end the economic war between the two countries. French tariffs were to revert to the level of 1664, and France was to be given 'most favoured nation' treatment, except in manufactured goods, sugar, salted fish, and whaling products, where the economic rivalry of the two countries was keen.

However, a parliamentary bill was needed to alter British custom arrangements, and the treaty met opposition. The Whigs were traditionally protectionist and they received support from others with vested interests in high tariffs, particularly those in industries that would be hit by French competition. After a pamphlet controversy the tariff clauses of the treaty were thrown out by parliament and the chance of resuscitating Anglo-French trade was lost. Over a century of commercial competition lay ahead, though the Eden treaty of 1786 sought to put into practice the free trade ideas of Adam Smith, although it is doubtful if the negotiators were consciously following his ideas. The pressure for the treaty, which was signed on 26 Sept., came from the French foreign secretary, Vergennes, who had abandoned the pro-

tectionist policy of his predecessors. French wines were allowed into England at the same favourable tariff applying to those from Portugal, and English textiles benefited from a 12 per cent tariff. Because of the bad effect of the treaty on the underdeveloped French textile industry it was very unpopular in France and was denounced at the outbreak of war (1793).

From 1840 onwards a further treaty was under discussion, but negotiations failed, chiefly on account of the opposition of the French iron and textile industries. Finally, the Cobden treaty (1860) allowed British manufactured goods and coal to enter France at rates of duty not exceeding 30 per cent, and reduced British duties on French wines and brandy. Napoleon III, conscious of the insecurity of his position, was anxious for an entente with Britain, and realized that a commercial treaty would be popular with powerful free trade interests there. He was also influenced by Michel Chevalier, who negotiated the treaty on the French side, and believed that lower import duties would stimulate French industries. On the English side a rapprochement between Cobdenites, Peelites, and Whigs in 1859 had increased support for this commercial treaty.

ANGLO-FRENCH CONVENTION (1899) settled the dispute which had come to a head at Fashoda (1898). It demarcated the British and French spheres of interest in East Africa, and confirmed Britain's control of the Upper Nile. It had become clear to the French foreign ministry that France could not risk simultaneous enmity with Britain and Germany, and that the disputes with Germany, notably the question of Alsace-Lorraine, were more serious than colonial rivalry on the Upper Nile.

ANGLO-FRENCH ENTENTE (1841–6). The Near Eastern crisis (1839–41) had seriously damaged Anglo-French relations. When Guizot replaced Thiers in France (1840) and Aberdeen replaced Palmerston in Britain (1841) the way was opened for an improved understanding. Both statesmen represented a moderate conservatism, and both believed that their countries, as liberal states with wide overseas interests, had common interests against the autocracies of eastern Europe. The entente was not free of friction. Disagreement arose on the question of Tahiti, and Guizot was anxious to avoid the appearance of subservience to Britain. Palmerston's handling of the Spanish marriages, after the fall of the Peel administration (1846), finally broke the entente.

ANGLO-FRENCH ENTENTE (1904), the first step in the process of British alignment with France and against Germany before the First World War. France c. 1900 was anxious that the Mediterranean powers should recognize her special interests in Morocco. Agreement was reached with Italy (1900) but in negotiations with Spain (1902) the latter asked for the agreement of Britain also, as the power occupying Gibraltar. The Russo-Japanese War (1904–5) entailed a risk of collision between their respective allies, France and Britain. In addition, British attempts to negotiate with Germany were inconclusive, and Britain, increasingly anxious about the growth of the German fleet, was anxious for an entente with France, the other Mediterranean naval power. The entente, which was assisted by an exchange of state visits between Edward VII and President Loubet (1903), was signed in April 1904. It took the form of three conventions settling outstanding matters of dispute in Newfoundland, West Africa, Egypt, Morocco, and South-East Asia. It envisaged no alliance or military commitment.

ANGLO-FRENCH UNION, proposed after the fall of France (June 1940). Britain wished to make her consent to a French armistice with Germany conditional on the sailing of the French fleet to British ports. It was felt that some positive offer should accompany this stipulation. On 14 June, a meeting took place in London between, among others, Vansittart, the foreign secretary's chief diplomatic adviser, Monnet, head of the Anglo-French co-ordinating mission in

London, and Gen. de Gaulle to arrange for the conveyance of the French government and army to North Africa. The next day, Vansittart and Corbin, the French ambassador, outlined to Churchill a proposal for Anglo-French Union, designed to keep France in the war.

On 16 June, de Gaulle reported to the British war cabinet a telephone conversation with Reynaud, the French prime minister. Reynaud was convinced that the proposal would dissuade the French cabinet, due to meet that day, from concluding an armistice. The British cabinet drafted a proclamation of union whose text was immediately communicated to Reynaud by telephone.

The 'Franco-British Union's' constitution provided for joint defence, foreign and economic policies, joint citizenship, and associated parliaments. France would keep her available forces in the war. There would be a single war cabinet, and resources would be pooled for peacetime reconstruction. The union appealed to America to increase economic and material assistance.

Campbell, the British ambassador, was instructed to withdraw two previous telegrams to the French government demanding inter-government consultations and the sailing of the fleet to British ports. The French cabinet, meeting to discuss an armistice, and Britain's conditions, were confused by the unexpected union proposal. It was condemned, especially by Pétain and his supporters, who suspected British designs to subordinate France and her empire. Without discussing arrangements with Britain, the cabinet voted for an armistice and Reynaud resigned.

W. S. Churchill, *The Second World War*, vol. II (London, 1949).   ASJ

ANGLO-GERMAN NAVAL AGREEMENT was embodied in an exchange of notes on 18 June 1935, during a visit of German naval experts to London. Germany was permitted to build its fleet to 35 per cent of the British Commonwealth's strength, and to construct submarines to 100 per cent of Commonwealth tonnage, although submarine construction would not exceed 45 per cent of the Commonwealth total without prior notice to Britain. Germany reserved the right to consult further with Britain if any 'exceptional construction' by other powers disturbed 'the general equilibrium of naval armaments'.

In the Stresa declaration a month earlier, Britain, France, and Italy had censured German rearmament. Britain's encouragement of German infringements of the Versailles Treaty incensed France. France also feared that the agreement, concluded between Germany and the Commonwealth as a whole, would reduce Britain's relative naval effectiveness around the European continent. Britain described the agreement as contributing to European peace, and stressed Germany's willingness to recognize the rules of the 1930 London Naval Treaty governing submarine warfare, but France was not conciliated.

The agreement originated in Britain's imperial rather than European considerations. By the end of 1934, only Britain fully upheld the ratio system established between national fleets by the Washington and London conferences. The admiralty anticipated an increasing strain on imperial defence if new agreements could not be initiated, particularly as the growing air force was reducing the naval proportion of the national defence budget.

In Jan. 1935 Hitler had mentioned a possible naval agreement to Lord Allen of Hurtwood and Lord Lothian. When the foreign minister, Sir John Simon, and Anthony Eden visited Hitler in March, they invited German naval experts to London. Until Dec. 1938, when he launched a new naval programme, Hitler constantly referred to the agreement as demonstrating his dedication to world peace. He denounced it in April 1939.

ANGLO-GUATEMALA CONVENTION of 1859. By this convention Guatemala recognized UK sovereignty over British Honduras and the British government agreed to provide £50,000 for the construction of a road from the coast to the interior of Guatemala. Britain's failure to honour the agreement is the basis of the claim that British Honduras should be returned to Guatemala.

ANGLO-INDIAN LAW CODES. The enactment of these measures resulted in the codification and simplification of the law, one of the greatest benefits of British rule in India. Under the East India Co. the administration of both criminal and civil justice was unsatisfactory and confused. Under Hindu and Muhammadan law there was no definite law of procedure, criminal or civil, no law of torts, and no public and constitutional law. The law of contract was primitive. Muhammadan criminal law was one of barbarous severity and the law of evidence grossly unfair to non-Muslims. The Charter Renewal Act (1833) provided for the appointment of a body of experts, the Indian Law Commission, the most important member of which was Macaulay, the first law member of the governor-general's council. It met in 1834 and the work of codification began. Its most important achievement was the drafting of a Penal Code, chiefly the work of Macaulay, which did not become law until 1860. Its provisions were based upon the criminal law of England adapted to suit Indian circumstances. It was also influenced by the French *Code pénal* and the Louisiana Code. It repressed crimes common to all countries and abated crimes peculiar to India such as *thagi*, *sati* (*suttee*), professional sodomy, the dedicating of girls to a life of temple-harlotry, human sacrifice, the exposing of infants, and the burying of lepers alive. In 1853, when the Company's Charter was renewed, a second commission was appointed and sat in England. It resulted in the enactment of Macaulay's Penal Code, with some revision, and the Codes of Civil and Criminal Procedure (1859 and 1861 respectively). A third commission was convened in 1861, but its members resigned in 1870 because of the opposition to their recommendations. Thereafter, until 1879, the work of codification was carried on by the law member in India, Sir James Stephen, who was thus responsible for a new Limitation Act (1871) and a revised Criminal Procedure Code (1872). There were revised Criminal Codes in 1882 and 1898. The Civil Procedure Code of 1859, after four amending acts in the next four years, further amendments in 1877, and substantial revision in 1879, was replaced by revised codes in 1882 and 1908. Still, codification untouched many of the essentials of private law. Hindus retained their family law regulating marriage, adoption, the joint family, partition, and inheritance. Muslims preserved their law of marriage, of testamentary and intestate succession, and that relating to religious endowments.

Whitley Stokes (ed.), *The Anglo-Indian Codes*, 2 vols and supplements (Oxford, 1887–91).
Cambridge History of India, vol. vi, ch. xxi (Cambridge, 1932).   CCD

ANGLO-INDIANS, persons of mixed European and Asian descent. Because of the stigma attached to the term 'Eurasian' in both British and Indian circles, the more euphemistic expression 'Anglo-Indian' was officially recognized in 1911. No reliable census statistics are available, for many returned themselves as Europeans. They found employment chiefly in the railway, telegraph, postal, police, customs, medical, and nursing services. The Anglo-Indian community has suffered much from the attitude adopted towards it by both Indians and Europeans, which fostered a sense of racial inferiority. Some steps were taken by the British to see that their interests were not prejudicially affected by Indianization. Although their problems seem to be more economic than constitutional, special seats in the legislatures were preserved for them by the Government of India Acts of 1919 and 1935 and by the Indian Constitution.

ANGLO-IRANIAN WAR (1856). While Anglo-Iranian relations were suspended following a quarrel (Nov. 1855)

between the Iranian chief minister and the British minister, the Hon. Charles Murray, Iran attacked Herat (March 1856). Britain, in reply, occupied Kharg and Bushir (Dec. 1856). In March 1857 British forces under Sir James Outram occupied Muhummerah (Khurramshahr). By the treaty of Paris (4 March 1857) Iran agreed to recognize the independence of Herat.

ANGLO-IRAQI TREATIES (1922, 1930). In 1922 a treaty provided sanction for British mandated authority and, through accompanying military and financial agreements, secured British preponderance in Iraq. It was modified in 1923, 1926, and 1927, and replaced in 1930 with an alliance, enabling British administrative and military control to be ended, and leaving only air bases at Shu'ayba and Habbaniya. The treaty, accompanied by a judicial agreement, led to the ending of the Mandate and the admission of Iraq to the League of Nations (3 Oct. 1932).

ANGLO-IRISH AGREEMENTS (April 1938) provided a settlement of Irish land amenities and other payments by British acceptance of a single lump sum of £10 million (as against total claims of some £100 million) and a continuance of the annual payment by Ireland of £250,000 for damages during the Irish rebellion. British rights to the use of the 'treaty ports', agreed in the treaty of 1921, were renounced, this last provision being vigorously attacked by Winston Churchill in the House of Commons.

ANGLO-ITALIAN AGREEMENTS (2 Jan. 1937, 16 April 1938). In 1937 there was a 'gentleman's agreement' by which both sides declared their interest in maintaining the status quo in the Mediterranean. Anglo-Italian rivalry had been exacerbated when Britain reinforced her Mediterranean fleet during the Abyssinian crisis, and Italy set up a base in the Balearic Islands shortly after Mussolini's intervention in the Spanish Civil War. Britain wished to enforce the principle of non-intervention in the war by outside powers. However, the agreement committed Italy to respect only the territorial integrity, and not the independence, of Spain. By 1938 the conflict between Britain and Italy had sharpened. In Sept. Italian ships torpedoed British merchant vessels provisioning the Spanish Republicans. In the new agreement, Britain promised to facilitate the recognition of Italy's sovereignty over Ethiopia, and assured Italy that the Suez Canal would not be closed against her. Italy promised to respect the Mediterranean status quo, implying that no air or naval bases would be maintained in the Balearic Islands. Italy also agreed to withdraw her 'volunteer' troops from Spain. The British foreign minister, Eden, considered the agreement an unnecessary appeasement, and resigned.

ANGLO-JAPANESE ALLIANCE (1902), the first major departure from the traditional British policy of diplomatic isolation. The Boer War had shown Britain to be isolated in Europe. In the Far East, where Britain, Germany, Japan, and Russia had been battling for concessions, there were particular fears of Russian encroachment in Manchuria. The Japanese also were in need of an ally and believed they had to choose between Britain and Russia. They opened negotiations with both powers, and received a prompt response from Britain which, more than any other western European power, appreciated the strength of Japan as a military power. The treaty, to last for five years, provided that each should recognize the other's special interests in China, and that Britain should recognize Japan's interest in Korea. Should either be attacked by two powers the other should come to its aid, but should either be attacked by a single power the other should remain neutral. Thus Britain remained neutral in the Russo-Japanese War (1904–5).

ANGLO-OTTOMAN WAR (1807–9), an undeclared war terminated by the peace of the Dardanelles (1809), in which Britain sought unsuccessfully to counter French influence in the Ottoman empire by a naval attack on the Dardanelles under Admiral Duckworth (Feb. 1807) and an occupation of Egypt.

ANGLO-PERSIAN AGREEMENT (1919), a treaty providing for British administrative, technical, financial, and military assistance to Iran, which aroused intense nationalist opposition in Iran, hostility in France and the US, and was abandoned (May 1920) without being ratified.

ANGLO-PERSIAN OIL COMPANY, formed (1909) to exploit the 1901 D'Arcy concession area. The British government acquired a majority shareholding for £2 million (May 1914). A new concession valid until 1993 was signed (1933), but an attempt to negotiate a new agreement after the Second World War failed and Iran nationalized the oil industry. In 1954 a new agreement gave the company a 40 per cent share in a new Consortium formed to operate the oilfields of South-west Iran and the Abadan refinery. In 1955 the company, which had previously changed its name to Anglo-Iranian Oil Co. (1935), became British Petroleum (a name previously borne by a marketing company).

ANGLO-POLISH ALLIANCE, Aug. 1939, followed the British guarantee to Poland of 31 March. On 6 April, after conversations in London with Beck, the Polish prime minister, the details of the guarantee were formally expanded, and it became reciprocal. However, a formal alliance was not concluded until 25 Aug. On 1 Sept. Hitler invaded Poland, and on 3 Sept. France and Britain declared war.

Chamberlain's declaration was prompted by rumours in March that Rumania and Poland were threatened with invasion by Hitler. Chamberlain attempted to negotiate a joint declaration involving Russia, on Polish and Rumanian independence, but was defeated by Poland's refusal to admit Soviet troops on her territory. Chamberlain was strongly criticized in England for accepting Poland's objections, which made the guarantee almost impossible to fulfil. He assumed that Russia would ultimately find it in her own interest to defend Poland against Germany.

Britain did little to supply Poland with war material after March 1939, and continually urged Beck to negotiate with Germany over Danzig and the Polish Corridor. It is possible that Britain's guarantee was primarily intended to deter Hitler from further aggression by threatening him with war on two fronts. A formal alliance was concluded only after the Nazi-Soviet Pact was announced. This convinced Britain that Hitler's aggression would be directed against the west. After 29 Aug. Britain ceased to urge Poland to negotiate with Hitler.

The alliance supplemented Poland's existing agreements with France. It pledged reciprocal support against both direct aggression, and aggression in a sphere of security including Danzig, Belgium, and Holland. There was no agreement to defend Rumania. The accompanying protocol, in veiled terms, reserved Britain's right to conclude an agreement with Russia.

ANGLO-PORTUGUESE DECLARATION (1899), alternatively known as the treaty of Windsor, reaffirmed the guarantee by each power to support the other in case of attack. In 1898 Britain had signed a secret convention with Germany dividing the Portuguese colonies should Portugal wish to sell them.

ANGLO-RUSSIAN ALLIANCE (1805), signed in St Petersburg on 11 April, formed the basis of the Third Coalition against Napoleon I. In the previous Nov., Alexander, disgusted by the execution by Napoleon of d'Enghien and by French encroachments in Germany and Italy, had sent Novosiltsev to London to negotiate an alliance. Pitt's government was suspicious when Alexander spoke about self-government for the oppressed peoples of Europe, and there were also difficulties over Malta, but they finally agreed to an alliance which contained secret articles providing for the reduction of France to her prerevolutionary frontiers and the setting up of an enlarged Holland and Piedmont.

ANGLO-RUSSIAN CONVENTION (1801) ended the conflict between Britain and Russia caused by Tsar Paul's forming the Armed Neutrality with the Scandinavian powers against Britain's interpretation of her maritime rights. The new Tsar, Alexander I, worked out a compromise with Britain, which was agreed to by Denmark and Sweden and signed on 17 June. They agreed that only effective blockades of enemy ports, and not paper blockades, were legal and that any contraband of war and enemy property carried in neutral ships could be confiscated.

ANGLO-RUSSIAN ENTENTE (1907) continued the process of grouping the powers which were ultimately to fight against Germany in 1914. Russia was the ally of France and, in spite of the treaty of Björkö (1905), had co-operated with the entente powers at Algeciras, and, after defeat by Japan (1905), was anxious to improve relations with Britain. The convention removed longstanding causes of friction. Persia, an independent state, was to remain so, but was divided into British and Russian spheres of interest. Afghanistan was recognized as being of special interest to Britain. It was also agreed that Tibet should be maintained as a buffer state under Chinese suzerainty.

ANGLO-RUSSIAN TRADE AGREEMENT (16 March 1921) raised the blockade against Russia, reopened Russian ports to British ships, and regulated the admission of British commercial and official representatives. Each country pledged to refrain from hostile propaganda against the other, and to release each other's subjects from detention. Russia recognized in principle its liability to pay compensation wherever goods and services supplied to Russia remained unpaid.

These terms were Britain's essential conditions for a *de jure* recognition of Soviet Russia, for which the agreement was described as a preliminary. The agreement was indicative of Lenin's new policy of encouraging capitalist investment and commerce in Russia.

ANGLO-SAXON CHRONICLE, chronological account of mainly West-Saxon events, first put together in the form we have it (*c.* 892) at the court of Alfred, King of Wessex. This is one of the most important sources of early English history and was continued until as late as 1155.

ANGLO-SOVIET TREATY (1942) provided for mutual assistance in the war against Germany and excluded a separate peace; and (in a second part valid for 20 years) provided for post-war co-operation and eschewed territorial aggrandizement. The USSR had pressed for recognition of Russia's incorporation of the Baltic states and a new Russo-Polish boundary. The British government accepted the former and rejected the latter, but all mention of territorial claims in the treaty was dropped under pressure from the US, together with the prospect of a second front in 1942.

ANGLO-SOVIET-PERSIAN TREATY (1942), agreement formed to legitimize the Anglo-Soviet invasion of Iran (Aug. 1941) and the subsequent occupation to ensure Allied control of Iranian resources during the Second World War.

ANGLO-SPANISH CRISIS (1568–9), the first serious threat of hostility between these two countries, which had been allied since the marriage of Prince Arthur to Catherine of Aragon (1501). Many factors contributed to the deterioration in Anglo-Spanish relations after the death of Mary Tudor. Elizabeth's accession brought renewed religious division. The flight of Mary Queen of Scots to England (May 1568) ended the danger of a Franco-Scottish bloc under Guise control, a major factor in Philip II's alliance with England. In Dec, 1568 Elizabeth made the first gesture of open hostility

by ordering the confiscation of a large shipment of bullion earmarked to pay Alva's soldiers in the Netherlands. The treasure ships had taken refuge in English ports to evade capture by Huguenot pirates and Elizabeth was able to 'borrow' the bullion, which was still legally owned by Genoese bankers. On the advice of De Spes, the Spanish ambassador, Alva replied with an embargo on English trade, while Cecil ordered the seizure of Spanish property in England (Jan. 1569). Meanwhile the attacks of English seamen upon the Spanish American colonies culminated in the retaliatory counter-attack on Hawkins and Drake at San Juan de Uloa (Sept. 1568), news of which reached England at this critical point (Jan. 1569). With heavy commitments elsewhere, Philip was reluctant to launch Spain into another conflagration and his final act in this cold war was to foment the northern rising and the Ridolfi Plot (1569).

ANGLO-SPANISH WAR (1625–30), over the invasion of the Palatinate and the failure of Charles I's marriage negotiations. Since the peace of 1604, James I had pursued a pro-Spanish policy, but after the expulsion of the Elector, James's son-in-law, from the Palatinate, in 1620, public opinion and parliament had been violently anti-Spanish. James, however, was still anxious for an alliance and for the marriage of his son to an infanta, the negotiations for which had dragged on inconclusively since 1615. Consequently, the future Charles I and the Duke of Buckingham went to Madrid, but their mission failed over the Palatinate. They returned in favour of war, and were supported by parliament. A French marriage was speedily negotiated, and after James's death (1625) an alliance was signed. The expedition against Spain, for which parliament had failed to grant the expected subsidies, was a disastrous failure. The war dragged on for four years, but hostilities were practically confined to private enterprise. The Dunkirk privateers took the opportunity to cripple English commerce, and hostilities broke out with France in 1627. In 1629 Charles's determination to rule without parliament made peace essential. The treaty of Madrid (5 Nov. 1630) ended the war; Charles had to accept the situation in the Palatinate.

ANGLO-SPANISH WAR (1655–9), colonial and naval war against Spanish claims in the New World which restored England's prestige in Europe. After Spain had refused the offer of an alliance in 1654, Cromwell turned to the idea of a raid on the Spanish colonies, hoping to ape the successes of Queen Elizabeth. An expedition under William Penn and Robert Venables sailed in 1654. It was ill-equipped and badly led. An attack on San Domingo was called off, but Jamaica was occupied. In April 1656 Charles II allied England with Spain in exchange for promised assistance in his restoration. Consequently, the war took on a more serious nature, involving the survival of the domestic regime. Cromwell in reply allied himself with France (March 1657). In the war at sea England proved conspicuously successful. Richard Stayner intercepted a treasure fleet off Cadiz with an enormous loss to Spain of specie and ships. Throughout the winter of 1656–7 Admiral Blake maintained a blockade of the Spanish coast, and inflicted crippling losses on it at the battle of Santa Cruz (20 April 1657). This victory left England indisputably supreme at sea. The French army, with an English contingent, campaigned in Flanders, and the English occupied Mardyke (1657) and Dunkirk, after the battle of the Dunes (14 June 1658). In the spring of 1659 France and Spain signed a truce, ratified by the treaty of the Pyrenees (Nov. 1659), both deserting their English allies.

ANGLO-SPANISH WAR (1762–3) began largely because of Charles III's fears that Britain was about to achieve an unacceptable colonial supremacy by her victories over France in the Seven Years War. Pitt, having realized that Spain would soon enter the war, had resigned (1761) when his ministerial colleagues had refused to declare war first. Although Spain's losses in the short war were catastrophic (Florida, Cuba, and the Philippines), at the peace of Paris

(1763) they were restricted to Florida because of France's determination to keep her as an ally at the cost of greater losses on her own part.

ANGLO-THAI TREATY (1909) marked the first step towards the abolition of extra-territoriality in Siam by submitting British subjects to the jurisdiction of the Thai courts; but in order to gain this concession to national sovereignty the Thai government was required to cede the four northern Malay states of Kelantan, Trengganu, Kedah, and Perlis. The treaty involved secret protocols and letters barring the cession or lease of any of the Thai portion of the Malay peninsula to a third power, and providing for the loan of funds to the Thai government to construct its portion of the Bangkok–Singapore railway.

ANGOLA (1,246,000 sq. kms), west-central African 'overseas province' or colony of Portugal. Kongo, Mbundu, Tchokwe, and Lunda predominate in a population of about 5 million which includes 300,000 Portuguese and some white settlers. Though formally represented by seven members elected to the Lisbon Assembly, Angola is ruled by the autocratic system of the Estado Novo introduced by Dr Salazar. African nationalist risings, aimed at independence, began in 1961.

ANGOLAN WARS (16th–17th cent.). After their failure to gain control of the Kongo kingdom and develop it as an economically viable allied nation, the Portuguese in central-west Africa turned to setting up a white settlement colony independent of any African political power. They chose the Kwanza valley, thinking that it would lead them, with a minimum of military opposition, to the fertile highlands of Angola, and possibly to rich mineral deposits.

Opposition by the kings of Angola proved effective and wars of conquest lasted intermittently from 1580 to about 1680. The original kingdom of Angola was first destroyed in the 1620s, then resurrected in alliance with the Portuguese, only to be destroyed again in the 1670s. Some of the Mbundu peoples of Angola, under the leadership of Queen Nzinga, retreated to form a new kingdom called Matamba. They eventually succeeded in establishing commercial and diplomatic relations with the Portuguese colony without submitting to its political authority. The Dutch intervened (1641–8), capturing the port and capital of Luanda. They and Queen Nzinga kept the Portuguese confined to the fortress town of Massangano in the interior until, seven years later, Brazilian forces effected the restoration of Portuguese power.

During these wars about 1 million slaves were shipped from Angola to the Americas. Some were prisoners of war captured during campaigns, others were retainers of conquered chiefs driven to pay them as political tribute to the European authorities; others were sold by independent African states to raise foreign exchange to buy imported consumer goods. By the later 17th cent. the concept of colonial expansion, and of warfare as a means of obtaining slave labour, was in decline. Trade became the major activity, punctuated by short wars to recover runaway slaves or curb the excesses of highway robbers.

D. B. Birmingham, *The Portuguese Conquest of Angola* (London, 1965).
D. B. Birmingham, *Trade and Conflict in Angola* (London, 1966). DBB

ANGOSTURA, CONGRESS OF, met on 15 Feb. 1819 in liberated Venezuela to elect Simón Bolívar commander-in-chief of the revolutionary army, as well as president of the newly declared republic of Venezuela. In Dec. the congress formally called into existence Gran Colombia, to be composed of Venezuela, New Granada, and the presidency of Quito. The last-named region had not been wrested from Spanish control as yet. Bolívar was named president of the consolidated region.

ANGOULÊME, TREATY OF (SETTLEMENT OF) (1619), agreement negotiated by Richelieu between Louis XIII of France and the Queen Mother, Marie de Medici, after the latter had escaped from captivity. It failed to resolve the differences between them and a further agreement had to be negotiated at Angers in the following year.

ÅNGSTRÖM, ANDERS JONAS (1814–74) a Swedish physicist whose work in spectroscopy made a vital contribution to the measurement of light. The Ångström unit, named after him, is a measure of the wavelength of light, being one ten-millionth of a metre.

ANGUILLA, West Indian island probably sighted by Columbus (1493). It was colonized by the English (1650) and governed from the island of St Kitts. In 1967 Anguilla became part of the Associated State of St Kitts–Nevis–Anguilla, though considerable dissatisfaction was shown by the Anguillans in 1967–8.

ANGUS MAC FERGUS (*reg.* 729–61), King of the Picts, rose to power in Pictland by overthrowing Nechtan mac Derile, King of the Picts, and several other rivals. In 741 he conquered Dalriada (Argyllshire), but in 750 was defeated by the Strathclyde Britons. He is probably the King Angus who figures in the legend of the founding of the Church of St Andrews.

'ANIAN', STRAIT OF, hypothetical western passage through central America to the eastern seas, sought by the Spanish as an alternative to the Portuguese-controlled route around the Cape of Good Hope.

ANKARA, BATTLE OF (July 1402), where to the north of the town, Timur Beg defeated the Ottoman Sultan Bayezid I. The battle led to the dislocation of the Ottoman state and to an interregnum of ten years (1403–13) before Sultan Mehmed I was able to reunite the Ottoman lands.

ANKOLE, a district in Southern Uganda. In common with other interlacustrine Bantu societies, Banyankole (the people of Ankole) traditionally considered themselves as divisible into three social categories: the Hinda ruling clan, Hima pastoral clans, and Iru agricultural clans, in that order of precedence. The distinction probably reflects different ethnic origins, though in pre-colonial times the Hinda were perceived as a unifying force, and the division of labour between Hima and Iru was useful as well as customary. Banyankole assert that the states which now comprise the district were separatist successors to the Abachwesi rulers of Kitara. During the 1890s the British established cordial relations with Nuwa Mbaguta, the *enganzi* (prime minister) of Kaaro-Karuagi, one of these states. As a result, most of the states in the area were absorbed into that kingdom, whose name—Nkore—became the name of the district, Ankole, and whose *omugabe* (king) Kahaya ruled over the other states as well. The monarchy was abolished in 1967 by the Uganda government.

ANNA COMNENA (1083–1148), daughter of the Emperor Alexius I. A gifted princess, Anna wrote the *Alexiad*, an account of her father's life, embracing the years 1069–1118. It is a valuable source, portraying well the character of Byzantine life and thought and depicting vividly the confrontation between the Byzantines and the Latins at the time of the First Crusade.

ANNA IVANOVNA (1693–1740), Empress of Russia (*reg.* 1730–40), niece of Peter the Great and a former Duchess of Courland. Anna's reign was unpopular in Russia because of the predominance of German advisers at her court. She received the throne on condition that she governed with the advice and guidance of the Supreme Secret Council of boyars. She quickly overcame this limitation, but tended subsequently to turn to foreigners for advice. Chief among these was her former secretary, Biron, who held no political office but was considered to be the power behind the throne. Anna entrusted the administration of government to a cabinet of three, two Russians and a German, Ostermann, who was its head. Although the period of the *Bironovshchina* aroused much resentment, there are no grounds for believing that Russia's interests were sacrificed to foreign considerations, nor that there were substantially more foreigners in Russia during Anna's reign than either before or afterwards. Neither Anna nor Biron were attractive personalities. Biron prompted the revival of a spy system, Peter's secret chancellery, and brutal methods were employed to extract taxation. The basic cause of their unpopularity, however, was to be found in the hostility aroused against foreigners by the westernizing reforms of Peter the Great. Anna inherited his interest in education and it was under her auspices that the second Bering expedition made its valuable scientific contributions. Her reign also witnessed the establishment of the Russian ballet. Her record in foreign affairs was, broadly speaking, successful. Russia and Austria together succeeded in establishing their candidate, Augustus III of Saxony, upon the Polish throne (1733) and the same allies fought an inconclusive four-year war against the Ottoman empire, which ended with the treaty of Belgrade (1739). As a result of these two adventures Russia's military reputation was greatly enhanced.

H. Rogger, *National Consciousness in Eighteenth Century Russia* (Harvard, 1960).   JHS

ANNA LEOPOLDOVNA OF BRUNSWICK (1718–46), regent (1740–1) for her infant son, Tsar Ivan VI of Russia. The wife of the Duke of Brunswick, she represented the interest of the German court party which had been powerful during the preceding reign (1730–40) of her aunt, the Empress Anna. She replaced Anna's former favourite, Biron, as regent in Nov. 1740, but in Nov. 1741 Elizabeth Petrovna, the daughter of Peter the Great, seized the throne and Anna was imprisoned.

ANNALES MAXIMI, name given to the outline of Roman history collected into 80 books by P. Mucius Scaevola shortly before 115 BC. The information was gathered from the *tabulae pontificum,* the white boards affixed each year to the residence of the pontifex maximus. Names of magistrates and priests, sacral information, and probably military and political events were shown. Entries survive only indirectly in the literary sources; those after 300 BC are acknowledged to be accurate, but the reliability of those of the 5th and 4th cent. is disputed.

ANNAM, originally the Chinese name for Viet-nam, coined in the T'ang period (618–907) and meaning 'Pacified South'. It was later used by Europeans. From 1885 the French, having created a colony of Cochin-China and a Protectorate of Tongking, used the term Protectorate of Annam to refer exclusively to the provinces of central Viet-nam.

ANNAPOLIS CONVENTION (Sept. 1786), called by VA and attended by delegates from five US states to discuss matters relating to interstate trade. Delegates included Alexander Hamilton and James Madison. Their recommendation that federal powers should be strengthened encouraged Congress to summon the Philadelphia Convention (1787).

ANNAPOLIS ROYAL, port of entry for Nova Scotia. Founded as Port Royal (1604), it was the capital of Acadia. The name was changed in honour of Queen Anne when the English captured it from the French in 1710. Ceded to Britain by the treaty of Utrecht (1713), it remained the seat of government in Nova Scotia until 1749.

ANNATES, STATUTES OF (1532 and 1534), in England, legislation of Henry VIII's reign directed against an old grievance of the church in western Europe, *ie*, the annates,

or payments made by the bishops to the pope on succession to their sees, reckoned at a third of one year's income.

The 1532 statute constituted the first direct attack made by the Henrician reformation upon the power of Rome. It struck a double-edged blow at the papacy by abolishing annates, thus removing the main source of papal revenue in England, and challenging the pope's spiritual authority by providing for the consecration of bishops by English authority. The act also contained a delaying clause, requiring confirmation by letters-patent and giving the opportunity for negotiation with the curia. It was not, in fact, put into effect until July 1533, by which time the pope had already been deprived of his temporal authority in England.

A second act of 1534 confirmed the prohibition on the payment of annates and laid down the procedure for the election of bishops.

ANNE (1665–1714), Queen of Great Britain (*reg.* 1702–14), second daughter of James Stuart and his first wife Anne Hyde, and the last Stuart to rule the British Isles. Although James was a Roman Catholic, with his permission and on the suggestion of Charles II, Anne was given a Protestant education. Anglicanism was to have a profound influence on her life, even outweighing her loyalty to her father in the Revolution of 1688.

In 1683 Anne married Prince George of Denmark and remained devoted to him. The couple had 17 children, though only Prince William survived childhood, to die in 1700, aged 12. Anne was greatly influenced by favourites; Sarah Churchill and Marlborough until they quarrelled in 1710, and after that by Abigail Hill.

Anne ascended the throne in 1702 and her reign coincided with a growth in the influence of political parties. She favoured the Tories, though she was not dominated by them; indeed, some of her ministries were controlled by the Whigs. For a long time Anne was regarded by historians as a political nonentity who had preferred to delegate her power to favourites. It is true that she did not control political life in the manner of her predecessor, but in a time of violent party warfare even William III had found his position increasingly difficult. Though Anne did allow her ministers to rule for her, they remained her ministers ruling in the manner she wanted. Her importance can be seen in the way she ousted the Marlborough–Godolphin coalition in 1710, replacing it with a ministry more favourable to her own views. Similarly, by a mass creation of peers (1712) she was able to force a policy she supported—the ending of the war—through a hostile House of Lords.

In foreign affairs her reign was dominated by the War of the Spanish Succession and by the threat of a Jacobite invasion. However, the latter did not materialize, and by the treaty of Utrecht (1713) her country emerged as a strong power with most gains from the war. Her reign also saw the union of the parliaments of England and Scotland (1707).

In later life Anne's health, which had never been good, began to break down. When she died the country was in a state of uncertainty, peacefully resolved by the prompt action of the Hanoverian supporters and the inaction of the Jacobites.

G. M. Trevelyan, *England under Queen Anne,* 3 vols (London, 1930–4).
G. S. Holmes, *British Politics in the Age of Anne* (London, 1967).   AW

ANNE OF AUSTRIA (1601–66), mother of Louis XIV of France, and possibly the wife of Mazarin. As part of Marie de Medici's reconciliation with Spain, she herself, being a daughter of Philip III of Spain, married Louis XIII (1615). Their relationship was cool and Richelieu excluded her from authority because of her Spanish connections, forcing her into intrigues with the Duchess de Chevreuse and the Duke of Buckingham (1625–6). Although she eventually gave Louis two children (1638 and 1640), her powers as regent on Louis's death (1643) were severely limited. She set aside his will and assumed full powers, which she then entrusted to Mazarin, although adhering to Richelieu's aims. While Mazarin was in exile during the Fronde (1648–52) she carried on the government. In her last years she became very pious and was much respected by Louis XIV.

ANNE OF BEAJEU (d. 1522), the ablest child of Louis XI of France. During the minority of her younger brother, Charles VIII, she controlled the government. In 1483–4 she weathered a dangerous reaction against the late regime of her father, crushed a rising led by her brother-in-law, Louis of Orleans, and successfully forced Brittany into union with the Crown.

ANNE BOLEYN (1507–36), Queen, second wife of King Henry VIII of England whose infatuation for her precipitated his determination to have annulled his marriage to his barren Queen Catherine of Aragon. She was the daughter of Sir Thomas Boleyn, Earl of Wiltshire, and Henry decided during the winter of 1526–7 that she should bear him a legitimate male heir, although it was not until six years later that their marriage took place, the ceremony being performed in secret. During this time the great constitutional preparations were made for the final break with Rome, which coincided with Anne's coronation. The birth of a daughter, the future Elizabeth I, to Anne in Sept. 1533 sealed her fate. After she had miscarried in 1536 Henry planned to marry again; meanwhile Cromwell collected evidence to support a charge of treason against her. She was beheaded on 19 May 1536.

ANNE OF CLEVES (1515–57), Queen of England and fourth wife of Henry VIII, the choice of Thomas Cromwell, who wanted to win the support of the German Lutheran princes for the Henrician reformation. The marriage was disastrous from the beginning, not only because Anne proved to be even plainer than her Holbein portrait suggested, but also because Henry realized that his political interests did not lie in a Lutheran alliance. Henry's divorce from Anne coincided with Cromwell's execution, after which she lived in England on an income provided by Henry until her death in Chelsea 17 years later.

ANNEXATION ACT (1587) in Scotland, resumed for the Crown all the temporalities belonging to abbacies and prelacies, bringing wealth to an impoverished government, but as it was directed only at 'possessors of great benefices', leaving them with little but the houses they lived in, and exempted the manses and glebes of the lesser clergy, it undermined the episcopal structure which the Crown was anxious to support.

ANNEXATION MANIFESTO (1849), a call for annexation of Canada to the US. Signed by and circulated among Montreal merchants, it was primarily a reaction to losses sustained when Britain abolished colonial preferential duties and adopted Free Trade. The signatories were accused of disloyalty, but many of them, *eg* John Abbott and A. T. Galt, later performed distinguished service for Canada after the issue subsided.

ANNUAL REGISTER in Britain, year book reviewing home and foreign political events of the preceding year; a useful historical source, particularly for 18th-cent. events. The *Annual Register* also contained literary and miscellaneous essays and book reviews.

ANNUAL SHIP, right of the English South Sea Co., acquired in 1713 with the *asiento*, to send one shipload of general merchandise annually to Portobello fair. This small limitation upon the Spanish trading monopoly led to Spanish hostility and English fraud and ended with the financial failure of the company.

ANONYMOUS OF YORK, name given to the author of several tracts written in the late 11th cent., displaying great independence and subtlety of argument. Their writer saw nothing wrong in clerical marriage and he vindicated the divine right of secular authorities to share in the appointment of clergy and bishops. They survived in a unique copy rescued by Parker, the first Anglican Abp of Canterbury of Queen Elizabeth I.

ANSA SASRAKU (d. c. 1689), King of Akwamu, under whom the kingdom became a coastal power on the Gold Coast (Ghana). In 1677 he successfully attacked Accra and annexed the remaining coastal areas of Accra kingdom (1679–81). He thus controlled the Accra trading centre and strengthened the economic power of Akwamu. Economically secure, Ansa embarked upon further expansion. By the time of his death Akwamu had expanded through conquest and diplomacy to the east, north, and west.

ANSARI, AL- (1005–89), was born, and died, at Herat in modern Afghanistan. He was famous for his devotion to the doctrines of Ibn Hanbal, for his learning in the religious sciences, and for the mystical experiences which he enshrined in his *Munajat*.

ANSARI, MUKHTAR AHMAD (1880–1936), a Muslim leader within the Indian National Congress. A Delhi physician, he led a medical mission which organized relief for Turkish forces (1912) and took a leading part in the Khilafat movement (1919–24). Unlike the Ali brothers, Ansari remained with Congress after the collapse of Khilafat, became president of the Congress (1927), and attempted to rally Congress Muslims in the All-India Nationalist Muslim Party (1929).

ANSCHLUSS, the incorporation of Austria in the German Reich (1938). Hitler's invasion began on 11 March; in a plebiscite on 10 April, 99·75 per cent of Austrians voting approved the union, prohibited under the 1919 peace settlement.

Since attaining power in Germany, Hitler had denounced the Austrian government for repressing local Nazi activities. The attempted Nazi putsch of 1934 worsened relations, but Hitler's appointment of the Catholic politician von Papen as ambassador in Vienna resulted in the Austro-German Agreement of 1936.

The agreement's practical results disappointed the Austrian Nazis. The governing coalition's objections prevented the chancellor, Schuschnigg, from appointing active Nazis to government posts. Hitler himself, wishing to avoid antagonizing the Western powers, especially Italy, preferred the 'National Opposition's' legal tactics to those of the Austrian Nazis. By Sept. 1937, however, when Mussolini visited Germany, Italy's commitments in Spain clearly limited Mussolini's power to protect Austria. At his policy conference of 5 Nov. 1937, Hitler envisaged military solutions for Austrian and Czechoslovak questions.

Following this conference, Hitler dismissed his war and finance ministers. Shortly afterwards, von Papen was recalled. On 5 Feb. 1938, he flew to see Hitler to salvage his career and Schuschnigg's current negotiations with the 'National Opposition', on developing military, political, and economic ties with Germany, and increasing 'National' participation in the government. He returned with an invitation for Schuschnigg to visit Hitler, whose recent dismissals reflected domestic difficulties from which the prospect of success in Austria offered a distraction.

On 12 Feb. Schuschnigg and his foreign minister met Hitler and several generals at Berchtesgaden. During the morning Hitler threatened military action to enforce his demands. These were formulated that afternoon by Hitler, Ribbentrop, and Austrian Nazi representatives. At first Schuschnigg declined on constitutional grounds to appoint 'National' ministers of finance and the interior, or to institute Austro-German staff conversations. Finally, he signed Hitler's protocol, agreeing to its ratification within three days.

Hitler was outraged to learn, on 9 March, that Schuschnigg

planned a plebiscite on national independence for 13 March. On 10 March he approved plans to invade Austria. The next morning, the 'National' minister of the interior, Seyss-Inquart, received Hitler's order to obtain by noon, on pain of invasion, Schuschnigg's postponement of the plebiscite and an improvement of Nazi electoral representation. An enclosed draft telegram entreated German intervention. At 1.00 p.m., receiving no answer, Hitler signed the first invasion directive, to be enforced only if all else failed.

At 2.45 p.m., Seyss-Inquart telephoned Göring, announcing the plebiscite's cancellation. After conferring with Hitler, Göring demanded Schuschnigg's resignation, and Seyss-Inquart's formation of a government. President Miklas refused Seyss-Inquart the necessary authorization. Göring set a new ultimatum for 7.30 p.m.; the invasion order was finally issued at 7.45 p.m. for daybreak. Miklas subsequently capitulated; Seyss-Inquart tried, unsuccessfully, to halt the invasion.

Hitler arrived in Austria on 12 March. By 13 March he had decided to incorporate Austria rather than set up a satellite government. After a cabinet meeting, Seyss-Inquart presented Hitler with a law whose first clause declared Austria a province of the German Reich.

J. Gehl, *Austria, Germany and the Anschluss 1931–38* (London, 1963).
A. Bullock, *Hitler, a Study in Tyranny* (London, 1963).

ASJ

ANSEI TREATIES, signed by Japan in the fifth year of the Ansei period (1858) with the United States, Holland, Russia, Britain, and France. They marked the real end of Japan's exclusion policy, and were obtained only because the Tokugawa *bakufu* feared Western naval power. The treaties opened the ports of Nagasaki, Kanagawa, and Hakodate to unimpeded trade from 1859, with Niigata, Edo, Hyogo, and Osaka to follow, and established moderate tariffs, which were reduced to 5 per cent in 1866. Legations were permitted and a system of extra-territorial jurisdiction by consuls provided for. These concessions played an important part in the downfall of the *bakufu*. After the Meiji Restoration they were regarded as harmful and humiliating, and until 1894 treaty revision was the major task of Japanese diplomacy.

ANSELM (*c.* 1033–1109), archbishop of Canterbury. A great deal is known about Anselm from the writings of his contemporary but partisan biographer, Eadmer. Born in Piedmont, Anselm took monastic vows at Bec in Normandy, and became abbot in 1078. His theological writings, which place him among the greatest of medieval scholastics, were largely concerned with the relationship in Christian thought between reason and faith. Though he continued his studies after his appointment to Canterbury (1093)—his *Why God became Man* was not completed until 1098—he was increasingly involved in political disputes. Ill-informed on the latest papal views and totally lost in the world of court diplomacy and intrigue, as archbishop he was not a great success. An old man when appointed, he found himself, under William Rufus, the prey to petty frustrations and became convinced that Rufus was deliberately persecuting him. He received almost no support from the English bishops and, when he went into exile, none from the papacy, which needed the support of Rufus against an anti-pope. Returning on the accession of Henry I, Anselm quarrelled with the king over the investiture of prelates with the symbols of office by the lay power. In 1107 Henry felt it wise to come to terms with Anselm and the papacy, and surrendered the symbols of investiture, but not his power to control Church appointments.

R. W. Southern, *St Anselm and his Biographer* (Cambridge, 1963). DPK

ANSHAN, ancient city and district of Iran, probably in the north of Elam. It came under the control of the Achaemenid Persians (*c.* 675 BC), whose kings bore the title King of Anshan until the accession of Darius I (*c.* 522).

ANSKAR (801–65), archbishop of Hamburg, later Hamburg-Bremen (831–65). A pious, brave, and persuasive Frank, he worked for the conversion of the northern lands, in part by frequent visits to the Danes and two personal missions to the Swedes. Churches were established at Hedeby (Slesvig), Ribe, and Birka (Lake Mälar).

ANSON, GEORGE ANSON, 1st Baron (1697–1762), British admiral, who entered the fleet in 1712. He led a squadron of six ships to raid Spanish commerce in the Pacific (1740–4), during which he captured a treasure galleon, and after circumnavigating the globe returned with a single ship. He served in the admiralty and as MP for Hedon, Yorks (1745–1747). Promoted vice-admiral (1746), he defeated a French fleet off Cape Finistere (1747). As first lord of the admiralty (1751–6, 1757–62), he made major reforms in naval construction, armaments, and administration.

ANTALCIDAS (d. 367 BC), Spartan diplomat of the early 4th cent. BC, who went on several missions to Persia. In 391, in the Corinthian War, his terms for a Spartan–Persian settlement impressed the satrap Tiribazus, though Persia's Greek allies rejected them, but then Tiribazus was replaced by King Artaxerxes. In 387 Antalcidas persuaded Artaxerxes himself to support a Spartan fleet, which he commanded, and thus to impose on Greece the King's Peace (or Peace of Antalcidas) which established Spartan supremacy. Later, after the Spartan defeat at Leuctra and the loss of Messenia, he failed to obtain Persian backing when Artaxerxes favoured the Theban Pelopidas (367), and committed suicide.

ANTEIMORO, migrants who settled in south-eastern Madagascar in the 16th cent. They developed a script of mixed Arabic and Malagasy. Their origins are disputed—Arabia, Ethiopia, and the Swahili coast have been suggested.

ANTHEMIUS (*reg.* 467–72), the last effective Western emperor. Chosen by the Eastern Emperor Leo, he was at first accepted by the Burgundian Ricimer, who commanded the army in Italy. Anthemius attempted unsuccessfully to reconquer Gaul from the Visigoths. Ricimer killed him in 472.

ANTHONY, SUSAN BROWNELL (1820–1906), US crusader for temperance, abolitionism, and woman's rights. A leader of the radical New York wing of the movement, she became identified with campaigns for female suffrage and liberal divorce laws, and was president of the National American Woman Suffrage Association (1892–1900).

ANTHRACITE COAL STRIKE (1902), US labour dispute significant because of presidential intervention. Coal mine owners rejected demands from the United Mine Workers for improved conditions and union recognition. President Theodore Roosevelt offered federal mediation and, this being rejected, threatened to take over the mines. Many union demands were then granted, except recognition.

ANTI-CLERICALISM. As a movement in modern European history against the influence of the Church in society and the state, anti-clericalism largely developed out of the ideas of the French Enlightenment, finding its first success in the expulsion of the Jesuits from all Catholic states by 1773. At the same time Catholic rulers, especially Joseph II of Austria, brought the Church closely under the control of the state. As this had already largely been achieved in Protestant countries in the 16th cent., anti-clericalism tended to affect the Catholic Church alone. It reached its peak in the French Revolutionary and Napoleonic era, but there was then a reaction in the generation after the Vienna settlement (1815).

In France Catholicism allied itself very closely to the restored Bourbon monarchy and aristocracy, so that the liberals and republicans tended to be anti-clerical. Although the Orleanist monarchy and the Second Empire saw a continual struggle to remove clerical influence from the state and education, the fiercest conflict came under the Third Republic, when the clericals were closely associated with those monarchical and right-wing groups which wished to overthrow the Republic. Under Ferry (1880–2) and then Combes (1902–5), legislation was passed which largely removed the clerical danger. In Spain anti-clericalism was advocated by a similar group of liberals, republicans, and socialists against the alliance of Crown, Church, and aristocracy. But in Italy the situation was somewhat different. Republicans and liberals were joined in their opposition to the Church and desire for Italian unification by the monarchy of Piedmont-Sardinia after 1848. The opposition of the papacy to Italian unity led to an estrangement between the new kingdom of Italy and the papacy which was not resolved until the time of Mussolini. Perhaps the most determined onslaught on the Catholic Church in the 19th cent. came in Germany under Bismarck. During his period of co-operation with the National Liberals (1871–8) he undertook his *Kulturkampf* against the Catholic Church and the doctrine of papal infallibility.

E. E. Y. Hales, *Revolution and the Papacy, 1769–1846* (London, 1960).

A. R. Vidler, *The Church in an Age of Revolution; 1789 to the Present Day* (London, 1961).   D MCK

ANTI-COMINTERN PACT (25 Nov. 1936), by which Germany and Japan announced their co-operation in defensive measures against the communist menace. The negotiations for the pact had taken over a year, and Britain, France, and Russia rightly suspected a military alliance and an agreement to partition spheres of influence in the Pacific.

The Japanese foreign ministry announced that the pact was not a German alliance, and that Japan was willing to co-operate on similar terms with other powers. At the same time, it attempted, without success, to placate Russia. The pact was advocated by the army, and by Yosuke Matsuoka. The navy opposed it, being willing to confront Russia but not, as Germany demanded, Britain as well.

Japan intended the pact to strengthen her against China, which she invaded in 1937. The German army and foreign office were reluctant to lose the German interest in China, and retained a military mission there until April 1938. The pact was largely the work of Ribbentrop, who is said to have kept some of its clauses secret from Hitler himself. After its signature, Ribbentrop declared that the world would now be defended against communism by Japan in the Far East, Germany in central Europe, and Italy in the Mediterranean. However, Italy did not join the pact until a year later (6 Nov. 1937).

The German-Japanese understanding survived the Nazi–Soviet Pact, and in Sept. 1940 the Tripartite Pact was signed between Italy, Germany, and Japan. The Anti-Comintern Pact itself was renewed in Nov. 1941.

ANTI-CONFEDERATION LEAGUE, Nova Scotian movement which threatened the peace of the province, led by Joseph Howe against the Confederation of Canada after 1865. By tactful negotiations Howe was induced to accept confederation (1869) based on 'better terms' in the annual dominion subsidy to the province. The league, thus robbed of its leader, lost its force.

ANTI-CORN LAW LEAGUE (1839), outstanding example of an extra-parliamentary pressure group in England in the early 19th cent. There had been criticism of the Corn Laws since 1815, and the league was founded, at a time of industrial depression and high bread prices, to agitate for repeal. Its leaders were R. Cobden, J. Bright, J. B. Smith, and George Wilson. It mobilized vast resources by the standards of the time, collecting £116,000 in 1845. It operated by means of paid lecturers, distribution of pamphlets, public debates, and parliamentary petitions. It also attempted to influence electors by establishing known supporters in £2 freeholds. The core of its support came from cotton merchants and manufacturers, and for this reason it was suspected by the working classes, though with the Chartist decline after 1842 this suspicion declined also. It was never successful in rural districts. The extent of its influence is debatable, since in 1845 Peel decided on repeal without testing opinion at a general election. Yet the public's deep opposition to agricultural protection for almost a century after 1846 may have owed something to league propaganda. Its organization was also influential on many later 19th-cent. agitations.

ANTIETAM, BATTLE OF (17 Sept. 1862), known by the Confederates as Sharpsburg, the bloodiest battle of the American Civil War, involving 25,000 casualties. Lee's first attempt to invade the North was abandoned after this defensive struggle against George B. McClellan's much larger forces 50 miles (80 kms) north-west of Washington. Northern success encouraged Lincoln to issue his first Emancipation Proclamation.

ANTI-FASCIST PEOPLES FREEDOM LEAGUE (AFPFL), emerged in Burma in 1945 out of the Anti-Fascist Organization (AFO), a Marxist nationalist movement formed in 1944 under Japanese occupation. When the British returned, the AFPFL claimed the status of a provisional government. This was refused and the AFPFL went into opposition, forcing a great acceleration of the British programme for independence. After the British left, the AFPFL ruled Burma for ten years despite bitter guerrilla opposition from communists. In 1958 internal dissensions broke up the league and in 1962 the military seized power.

ANTIFEDERALISTS, those who opposed ratification of the US Constitution (1787–8). Unlike the promoters of the constitution, who took the title 'Federalist', they were a heterogeneous body of men without organization or a common platform. There were no sharp socio-economic divisions between them and the federalists but, while federalists generally came from the cities and commercial farming areas, antifederalists were often from the back country. They probably formed a substantial majority in some states, such as NY, NC, SC, RI, and a narrow majority in MA and VA. Prominent antifederalists included Richard Henry Lee, George Mason, Patrick Henry, George Clinton, and James Winthrop.

Acceptance of many basic federalist premises put the antifederalists always on the defensive. They agreed on the necessity for union, republicanism, government by consent and limitation on government powers, but differed over the proposed methods of implementing these in the new constitution. Believing that republican government could only be effective in a small area, they advocated a weak federal administration. They condemned the consolidating and centralizing tendency of the new government because it might lead to despotism, and criticized the method of representation, which they feared would lead to an irresponsible, self-seeking Congress; they also demanded annual elections which would make the legislature directly responsible to the electorate. Their most effective demand was for a Bill of Rights.

In spite of their numbers the antifederalists were outmanoeuvred. The constitution was approved by men of outstanding national prestige, such as Washington and Franklin, and federalists controlled most of the newspapers. Antifederalist diversity brought with it ill-co-ordinated attacks on the constitution, and conflicting and diverse proposals for changes. The federalists trumped their demand for a Bill of Rights by conceding the point and many antifederalists, accepting that the central government needed strengthening, could only argue that the constitution went too far. Ultimately they were reduced to recommending continuation of the Articles of Confederation, or the appointment of a second constitutional convention. Political divisions took new forms after ratification of the constitution.

Jackson Turner Main, *The Antifederalists: Critics of the Constitution, 1781–1788* (NC, 1961).

ANTIGONISH MOVEMENT, influential programme of social rehabilitation for depressed areas, based on adult education and co-operatives, inspired by Father James J. Tompkins, of St Francis Xavier University, Antigonish, NS.

ANTIGONUS DOSON (*c.* 263–221 BC), guardian (229) of Philip V of Macedon, who called himself King after 227. His expedition against Ptolemaic possessions in Caria achieved little lasting success (227), but in Greece he re-established Macedonian influence in the Peloponnese through exploiting the Achaean League's danger from Cleomenes III of Sparta. He regained Corinth, organized his allies into a league whereby he hoped to control them more easily and less obviously, and defeated Cleomenes at Sellasia (222).

ANTIGONUS GONATUS (*c.* 320–239 BC), King of Macedon from 276, whose interest in philosophy seemed, to those Greeks who suffered from his aggressions, inadequate compensation for his constant attempts to reassert waning Macedonian control and for his autocratic method of ruling. Although the death of his father, Demetrius Poliorcetes (? 284), fired his ambition to rule Macedon, he was not recognized as king until 276. Thereafter, with Macedon behind him, he fought with sporadic success for control of Greece against Pyrrhus, Ptolemy II, and the many Greek states who thought their interests better served by independence than by subservience to Macedon.

ANTIGONUS MONOPHTHALMUS (*c.* 381–301 BC), the most active and finally least successful of Alexander the Great's successors. Antigonus exploited the political chaos after Alexander's death, allying himself with Antipater, who then controlled Macedon. By 315 he had become dominant in the Asiatic section of Alexander's empire. Aiming to become the sole successor of Alexander, he opposed Cassander, who now controlled Macedon, Lysimachus, who held Thrace, and Ptolemy, who held Egypt. His propagandist claim, that he brought freedom to the Greeks, had some success under his energetic son Demetrius Poliorcetes, and he and Demetrius were the first of the successors to call themselves kings (307). But he failed to dislodge any of his opponents, while Seleucus after 311 detached the eastern part of his empire. He was finally defeated by a coalition of Lysimachus, Cassander, Seleucus, and Ptolemy and was killed at Ipsus.

ANTIGUA, West Indian island discovered by Columbus (1493) and colonized by the English (1632) under Sir Thomas Warner, after failures by the Spanish (1520) and French (1629). In early years the island suffered from raids by Carib Indians and from 1665–7 was occupied by the French. A plantation economy—tobacco and sugar—was based on labour drawn from prisoners of the English Civil War and African slaves. As the only British West Indian possession with an excellent harbour, Antigua was an important naval post until the closure of the dockyard (1854). In 1967 Antigua and the nearby islands of Barbuda and Redonda became an Associated State of the United Kingdom.

ANTI-JAPANESE WAR (1937–45), China's name for the war launched by Japan against China. The war followed six years of gradual Japanese encroachment upon China. By 1939 the Kuomintang government had been forced to abandon all the eastern provinces of China to the Japanese. Japanese troops behaved with extreme brutality in China and civilian as well as military casualties ran into many millions. This brutality acted as a catalyst in awakening Chinese nationalism. After 1941 the Kuomintang government followed a policy of waiting for the US to win the Pacific War, and benefited very little from the new nationalism, but the communists were active in organizing resistance to the Japanese and won massive support before the end of the war. This stood them in good stead in the civil war which followed.

ANTI-MASONIC PARTY, earliest US third party movement. Founded on popular suspicion of secret societies, it devised the national nominating convention as a method of selecting presidential candidates (1832). The party had merged with the Whigs by 1838.

ANTINOUS OF BITHYNIA (*fl.* 2nd cent. AD), favourite of the Roman Emperor Hadrian, whose life and death by drowning on Hadrian's voyage up the Nile (130) brought him legendary fame and deification, especially at Antinopolis, Egypt, founded by Hadrian in his memory.

ANTIOCH (mod. Antakiya, Turkey), on the Orontes, 24 kms from the sea, the great metropolis of the Roman east, founded as his royal seat by Seleucus I in 300 BC with Greek settlers, natives, and Jews and from 64 BC capital of Roman Syria. It was the home of the earliest gentile Christian community, whose Bp Ignatius was martyred in 116. Though captured by the Persians in 256 and 260, and by the Palmyrenes in 261, it recovered in the 4th cent. to reach a population of *c.* 200,000, and became a centre of intellectual activity, both pagan (*eg*, Libanius) and Christian (*eg*, John Chrysostom), but after the Council of Chalcedon (451) it was divided by the Monophysite movement and declined in the 6th cent. through fire, earthquakes, and Persian invasions. It was occupied by the Arabs (637–8), though ultimately recovered by the Crusaders, being the first major obstacle encountered by the First Crusade on its advance into Syria. Divisions among the Moslem powers paralysed two successive attempts to relieve Antioch. To forestall a third, most menacing attempt by Kerbogha of Mosul, the crusaders managed through treason within Antioch to enter the city (3 June), being besieged, in turn, by Kerbogha (7 June). A crusading sortie crushed Kerbogha on 28 June. In 1099 Antioch was the base for the successful march on Jerusalem.

Antioch became the earliest of the Latin principalities created as the result of the First Crusade. Tancred, who effectively controlled Antioch (1100–12), was the real founder of its great power in the first half of the 12th cent. Subsequently, it gradually lost its eastern territories as the result of successive Muslim conquests, but the city of Antioch remained one of the wealthiest Christian centres until its capture by Baibars of Egypt in 1268.

ANTIOCHUS III ('The Great') (*reg.* 223–187 BC), King of Syria, son of Seleucus II Callimachus. After achieving military successes against the Parthians and Bactrians (212–205), which secured his eastern frontier, he allied himself with Philip V of Macedon, and wrested southern Syria and Palestine from Egypt (201–200), before arranging a dynastic marriage between his daughter and the Egyptian Ptolemy V. His attempt to regain his hereditary possessions in Asia Minor and Thrace (197–196) alarmed the Romans, who were fighting Philip V; Thrace was to be his final conquest, but they saw it as his bridge into Greece, especially when Hannibal fled to his court. Diplomacy achieved a respite (the Romans withdrew from Greece in 194), but in 192 Antiochus accepted an Aetolian invitation to cross to Greece. Routed at Thermopylae (191), he was again defeated at Magnesia in Asia in 189 by L. Scipio. The harsh terms imposed in the treaty of Apamea spelled the end of a strong Syria, making possible future Roman predominance.

ANTIOCHUS IV Epiphanes (*reg.* 175–164 BC), King of Syria. He temporarily revived the fortunes of his country by a successful attack on Egypt (170–168), capturing Ptolemy VI, investing Alexandria, and seizing Cyprus, but meekly obeyed the Romans' peremptory instruction to evacuate Egypt and Cyprus, underlining Syria's subservient role in the eastern Mediterranean.

ANTI-PARTY GROUP, name given to Khrushchev's opponents in the conflict for power which came to a head in June 1957. They included Malenkov, Kaganovitch, Molotov, Bulganin, Saburov, Pervukhin, and Voroshilov, all members of the Presidium of the Central Committee, and the candidate member, Shepilov. The group resisted the growing dominance of Khrushchev and also opposed his policy of partial destalinization (his secret speech to the XXth party congress the preceding year had sparked off the risings in eastern Europe), as well as his economic policies. They succeeded in outvoting Khrushchev in the Presidium, but he convened an extraordinary plenary session of the Central Committee (which, as first secretary, he had been able to reconstruct with his own supporters) and appealed to it against the Presidium. The entire Central Committee of 309, except Molotov, who abstained, was reported as voting in his support. He appears to have owed much to the support of Marshal Zhukov, as is borne out both by the latter's promotion to the Presidium and by his removal, as a dangerous rival, a few months later (Oct. 1957).

The 'anti-party group' was then removed from power, although Bulganin and Voroshilov retained their posts for the time being. Bulganin was demoted in stages during 1958, in a process reminiscent of Stalinism, but from which terror and execution were absent.

'Anti-party group' was in part a misnomer, since its members lacked the cohesion of a single group; and while it is true that Khrushchev's power base was within the party (in contrast, for example, to ministries) he would have failed without the support of the army. The epithet had an obvious political value.

ANTIPATER (d. 319 BC), Macedonian noble and one of Philip II's generals, who, after Philip's assassination, supported Alexander the Great's succession and was left by him to govern Macedonia and Greece, when he invaded Asia. Ignoring treaty obligations to support his friends in Greece, he failed to reconcile its enemies with Macedonian rule, but he prevented trouble and defeated Sparta (331). After Alexander's death he crushed Athens and her allies in the Lamian War (323–322), abandoning the pretence that the Greeks were Macedon's free allies, and in the struggle for power among his generals he allied himself with Antigonus Monophthalmus and Ptolemy I and was briefly regent for the idiot Philip III and the infant Alexander IV. His death ended the hope of Alexander's empire being peacefully held together.

ANTIPHON (c. 480–411 BC), earliest of the ten greatest Attic orators. Renowned as a teacher of rhetoric, he was the first professional speech writer for litigants, specializing in murder cases. While adopting a plain and austere style, he emphasized balance in the composition of sentences and speeches. Despite his skill in developing rhetoric for political purposes, his first public speech was not delivered until 411, when he emerged as a leader of the revolution of the Four Hundred at Athens and subsequently made an eloquent but fruitless defence against a charge of treason, on which he was executed.

ANTIQUARIES OF LONDON, SOCIETY OF. A group of antiquaries began to hold weekly meetings in London in 1707. The society was formally constituted in 1717, receiving a royal charter in 1751. It publishes *Archaeologia*, the *Antiquaries Journal*, and Research Report. The Society of Antiquaries of Scotland, founded in 1780, obtained a royal charter in 1783.

ANTI-SALOON LEAGUE, founded (1893) in Oberlin, Ohio, by the Rev. H. H. Russell, to prohibit the sale of intoxicating liquor in the US. The 'Ohio Plan' was adopted in other states and the Anti-Saloon League of America established (1895). Under the leadership of Wayne B. Wheeler the league mobilized the sentiment of evangelical protestantism and by the turn of the century had developed into a powerful political lobby. Pressure at state and federal level was eventually rewarded by passage of the Eighteenth Amendment (Dec. 1917, ratified Jan. 1919). The league continued to strive for the rigid enforcement and maintenance of Prohibition, but faced increasing public animosity until the Eighteenth Amendment was repealed (1933).

ANTI-SEMITISM. The late 18th cent. brought religious toleration and civil emancipation for the Jews after almost universal persecution and ostracism in the Middle Ages and early modern period. The French National Assembly gave them equal citizenship (1791) and French conquests brought similar emancipation throughout western Europe. In the mid-19th cent., however, they were to come under attack from three quarters: from their old enemies, the clericals, who now equated them with liberals and rationalists; from nationalist movements, who viewed them as an alien and international force; and from the socialists and anti-capitalists, who resented their involvement in the world of business. In an age of increasing nationalism and anti-capitalism the Jews appeared the natural enemy for very different groups. The years after 1870 saw the growth of political parties advocating anti-Semitic policies. In Austria-Hungary Georg von Schönerer's pan-German German National Party preached rabid anti-Semitism, but far more successful was Karl Lueger's Christian Socialist Party, built on an alliance of clericals, peasantry, and the Viennese lower middle-class, which was directed against liberalism, socialism, and Jewish capitalism. In France anti-Semitism was closely linked with the clerical, monarchist, and right-wing groups and came to a head with the Dreyfus Affair. Although Bismarck had been contemptuous of Jews as inferiors, and Adolf Stöcker's anti-Semitic Christian Socialist Party had some success in Germany in the early 1890s, anti-Semitism was not a serious influence there before the First World War. The most virulent form of anti-Semitism in the late 19th and early 20th cents was in Russia, where Jews were confined to the towns and an area of western Russia known as the 'Pale'. The orthodox and nationalist tsarist autocracy pursued an official anti-Jewish policy, encouraging attacks on Jews' property and frequent massacres (pogroms), which led to widespread Jewish emigration to central and western Europe and America. One response of the Jews to actual or threatened persecution was the Zionist movement.

P. G. J. Pulzer, *The Rise of Political Anti-Semitism in Germany and Austria* (New York, 1964).   D MCK

ANTI-SLAVERY SOCIETY in Britain. Its foundation (1823) marks the beginning of effective agitation against slavery, as opposed to the slave trade (abolished 1807). The society's membership, which included a royal duke as president, and five peers and 14 MPs as committee members, showed the greatly enhanced standing of the abolitionists. Having fulfilled its purpose as a pressure group, the society was disbanded in 1833.

ANTI-TRINITARIANISM, the belief that God is One Person, was preached in the 3rd cent. by Sabellius and Arius, and although the unitarian doctrine was condemned at the Council of Nicaea (325), it was never wholly suppressed. At the Reformation it was taught in Poland and Hungary by George Blandrata and was more widely spread by the followers of Faustus Socinus, who said that Jesus had no existence before being miraculously born as man. The Trinity was denied by some of the Protestant sects in England.

ANTOFAGASTA, northern Chilean province, rich in nitrates and copper, exploited by Chile after 1866 under treaties with

Bolivia. Chilean victory in the War of the Pacific (1879–83) forced Bolivia to cede the area.

ANTONELI, GIOVANNI (*fl.* 16th cent.), Italian engineer, who was sent by Philip II to the Caribbean to advise on the defence of the Spanish colonies against English attack (1586–7).

ANTONELLI, GIACOMO (1806–76), conservative and corrupt Italian cardinal, who acted as secretary of state (1850–1876) to Pius IX. Following his disillusionment with liberalism after the revolutions of 1848, Pius left the government of the papal states largely in Antonelli's hands. Here he opposed all constitutional experiment and did his best to maintain the pope's secular position during the period of Italian unification. In his style of living, his personal wealth, and his illegitimate children, Antonelli resembled a Renaissance prelate.

ANTONESCU, ION (1882–1945), dictator of Rumania (1940–1944). Antonescu forced Carol II's abdication in 1940 after the territorial losses to the USSR and Hungary. At first, Antonescu and the Iron Guard shared power in the National-Legionary state (Sept. 1940–Jan. 1941). After three days of bitter fighting in Jan. 1941 the army, with German backing, eliminated the Iron Guard and established a military dictatorship, with Antonescu calling himself *Conducator* (*Führer*). Bound to a pro-Axis policy, he participated in the war against the USSR and resisted an armistice to the end. Unlike most of Germany's satellites, Antonescu always commanded Hitler's respect. The regime was overthrown by a coup on 23 Aug. 1944 and Antonescu was taken in custody by Soviet occupation forces. In May 1945 he was tried and executed.

ANTONESCU, MIHAI (1904–45), deputy prime minister and foreign minister in the Rumanian military regime (1940–4). He sought to bring Germany's allies together, withdraw from the war, and make a separate peace. The Germans learnt of his intrigues and pressed for his dismissal, but he held his place in the government. He was captured in 1944 and in May 1945 was tried and executed with Ion Antonescu (no relation).

ANTONINE WALL, Roman frontier in Scotland on the Forth–Clyde isthmus, built of turf (*c.* AD 140) to replace Hadrian's Wall. After assault and reconstruction (*c.* 158), it was occupied simultaneously with Hadrian's Wall, but was abandoned after further assault and reconstruction (*c.* 184–5).

ANTONINO PIEROZZI, Saint (1389–1459), Dominican who in 1435 secured for the stricter (Observant) branch of his order the convent of St Marco at Florence, where he established the first 'public library' and commissioned the religious frescoes of Fra Angelico. He became Abp of Florence in 1446 and, by his independence, moral fervour, and practical wisdom, epitomized all that the Florentines most admired.

ANTONINUS PIUS (AD 86–161), Roman emperor (*reg.* 138–161). Descended from wealthy provincial families on both sides, he had a distinguished career as a senator before becoming a member of Hadrian's privy council. Adopted by Hadrian in 138, he succeeded him in the same year. His reign was one of benevolent paternalism and appears to have been popular with all sections of the empire. Although deferential to the Senate, he allowed it no increase in power. Firm control of the imperial administration was exercised without the expensive tours of inspection favoured by Hadrian, and his legislation was relatively humane. Troubles on the frontiers were minor and he adhered in general to Hadrian's non-expansive policy, though Roman control in Britain was pushed northwards into Scotland to the so-called Antonine Wall. However, notwithstanding Rome's peace and

apparent prosperity during his reign, there were some signs of economic stagnation and social difficulties.

ANTONIUS FELIX, ex-slave who, as procurator of Palestine from AD 52, kept St Paul in prison for two years and ruthlessly suppressed Jewish Messianic revolts, though he could not stamp out the Messianic movement.

ANTONOV UPRISING, the most important of a series of rural riots which broke out as the Red Army was demobilized in the autumn of 1920. They were led by Antonov (a Socialist Revolutionary since 1905) in Tambor province, and were contemporaneous with the Kronstadt mutiny (March 1921). The movement had some 20,000–50,000 supporters and resisted repressive measures under the command of Tukachevsky. It finally subsided in 1924 as a result of the New Economic Policy.

ANTONY, MARK (*c.* 82–30 BC), a leading figure in the final collapse of the Roman republic, a member of the Second Triumvirate, and Octavian's rival for supremacy. As a member of Julius Caesar's staff in Gaul, he defended him in the Senate (Jan. 49), serving in his campaigns in Italy and Greece in the Civil War. After Pharsalus (48) he returned to Italy, becoming Caesar's magister equitum and colleague in the consulship of 44. After Caesar's murder his attempts to control affairs alienated the Senate and he was defeated at Forum Gallorum and Mutina (April 43) when trying to seize Cisalpine Gaul from Decimus Brutus. Retreating to Narbonese Gaul, he joined forces with Aemilius Lepidus, was reconciled with Octavian, and with them formed the Second Triumvirate (Nov. 43). After defeating Brutus and Cassius at Philippi (42), he undertook the settlement of the East and by the treaty of Brundisium (40) recognized Octavian's control of Italy and the West and married his sister, Octavia, later supporting Octavian against Sextus Pompey. His invasion of Parthia (36) ended in disaster and his alliance with Cleopatra alienated sympathy at Rome. Octavian gradually outmanoeuvred him, persuading the Senate to deprive him of his authority and to declare war on Cleopatra (32). Antony was decisively defeated at the battle of Actium, failed to defend Egypt against Octavian, and committed suicide before the capture of Alexandria.

ANTRAIGUES, EMMANUEL LOUIS, Comte d' (1755–1812), French counter-revolutionary propagandist. Although he entered the French Estates-General as an enthusiastic reformer, he soon went to the opposite extreme and left France at the beginning of 1790. From then until his assassination he encouraged foreign intervention against the Revolution and Napoleon.

ANTUN SA'DA (1904–49), Greek Orthodox Christian of Brazilian–Lebanese origin, who founded (1932) in Beirut the militant and authoritarian *Parti Populaire Syrien*, which advocated the establishment of a Syrian national state including Syria, Lebanon, Palestine, and eventually Iraq and Cyprus. Sa'da was executed in Lebanon after an armed insurrection, although his party remained a dynamic force in Syria and Lebanon.

ANTWERP, SACK OF (1576), occurred when Spanish troops mutinied (the 'Spanish Fury') through lack of pay and captured several cities in the southern Netherlands. Antwerp was plundered and devastated and never regained its former wealth and importance. This led to the temporary union of all the Netherlands provinces in the Pacification of Ghent.

ANTWERP, SIEGES OF (1583–5), by France and Spain. A French force under the Duke of Anjou besieged the city in 1583, but was repulsed by William of Orange with heavy losses. In the confusion following William's assassination (1584) Parma captured several Flemish towns and marched on Antwerp, which surrendered after a 14-month siege.

ANTWERP, TRUCE OF (1609), concluding the struggle for Dutch independence of Spain. Although the Dutch had virtually achieved independence by 1598, they were excluded from the peace of Vervins between Spain and France, and desultory fighting continued until a 12-year truce was agreed in 1609. When it expired Spain was engaged in the Thirty Years War, and Dutch independence was formally recognized at Westphalia (1648).

ANURADHAPURA, capital city of Ceylon (3rd cent. BC or earlier–11th cent. AD), situated in the present North Central Province. Among its most prominent features are the three huge ancient *dagoba*s (tower-like monuments in which relics of the Lord Buddha were enshrined; also called *stupa*s), namely the Ruvanvaliseya, Abhayagiri, and Dakkhina, countless ruins of other Buddhist foundations and four immense irrigation tanks. The city and surrounding area became depopulated after the 11th cent., but have more recently been developed into an important centre.

ANVERS, TREATY OF (BARRIER TREATY) (1715), between Britain, the United Provinces, and the Holy Roman emperor, to overcome difficulties in the Austrian Netherlands. The Dutch were to garrison the barrier fortresses at the emperor's expense while the emperor agreed to keep the Scheldt closed, condemning Antwerp to economic stagnation.

ANVILLE, JEAN-BAPTISTE LOUIS, Duc d' (1709–46), French nobleman and admiral. In 1746 he became commander of a French fleet and was ordered to recapture Louisburg, but the fleet was becalmed off the Azores. Owing to illness and food and water shortages, followed by a storm which scattered much of the fleet, 2300 men died—d'Anville himself on 15 Sept. 1746 at Halifax, NS—and only six ships returned to France.

ANWAR-AD-DIN KHAN (d. 1749), a soldier of fortune who rose to distinction serving the family of the Nizam-ul-mulk in the Deccan. In 1743 he was appointed nawab or governor of the Carnatic. On the nizam's death (1748) the claimant to the Deccan, Muzaffar Jung, with French help defeated and killed him at Ambur (1749), favouring a relation of the previous nawab. His second son, Muhammad Ali, retired to Trichinopoly and received British support. This incident began the second phase of the Anglo-French struggle in southern India.

AN-YANG, a bronze-age archaeological site on the north bank of the Yellow River. The site includes tombs of the Shang kings (*c.* 1400–1100 BC); it has yielded some of the earliest specimens of Chinese writing and highly decorated bronze vessels, thus testifying to the high cultural standard of the age.

ANZA EXPEDITION (1775), Spanish expedition led by Gen. Juan Bautista de Anza (1735–88) from Arizona to found the *presidio* of San Francisco.

'ANZAC', code name officially used from Jan. 1915 for the Australian and New Zealand Army Corps in Egypt. It came to be applied to all who served at Gallipoli, then, more specifically, to Australian and NZ forces there. A national day of remembrance, Anzac Day (25 April), subsequently commemorated the exploits of all Australian and NZ servicemen who fought overseas.

ANZIO, bridgehead and battle (Jan.–May 1944) in the Second World War. On 21 Jan. 1944 a sea-borne assault was launched from Naples to capture a bridgehead further north and thus accelerate the advance of the allied armies towards Rome. The bridgehead was established and held, but the prolonged defence by the German armies at Monte Cassino involved its maintenance for four months until a junction was made with the main army from the south on 25 May.

APACHE INDIANS, group of American Indian tribes comprising the most southern branch of the Athapascan linguistic family, first encountered by the Spanish in New Mexico and west Texas. From the Spanish colonization until 1900 they were known for their hostility to Indian and white settlements alike. From 1870 to 1886, the Apache were in constant conflict with the US government, which attempted to confine them to reservations. Raiders under the chiefs Cochise, Victorio, Nana, and Geronimo terrorized settlers in Arizona, New Mexico, and northern Mexico. Geronimo, the last of the raider chiefs, surrendered in 1886, but a number of Apache remained in the mountains, and as late as 1900 were attacking Mormon settlers in northern Mexico. The main Apache tribal groups were the Querechos, the Coyoteros, the Arivaipa, the Gila, and the Tontos.

APALACHE MASSACRE (1704), an action by James Moore in west Florida in which he defeated Spaniards and Indians under Capt. Mexia and captured about 1400 Indians.

APAMEA, TREATY OF, settlement imposed by Rome on Antiochus III of Syria in 188 BC, after his defeat at Magnesia. The king was stripped of possessions outside Syria, and of his warships and elephants, and ordered to pay indemnities to Rome and to Pergamum. His Asia Minor territories were divided between Rome's allies, Pergamum and Rhodes, though the Greek towns of the western seaboard remained mostly free. The settlement demonstrated the Romans' intention to use their allies rather than maintain a presence in Asia, but it made Syria too weak to defend her eastern possessions, which were soon lost to Greek civilization.

APARTHEID (lit. 'apartness') is South Africa's traditional policy of racial segregation, elevated, since 1948, to a political philosophy and given legislative force. It has two facets: total or ideal apartheid, formulated by Afrikaner intellectuals partly to meet world criticism of South Africa's racial policies, and practical or restrictive apartheid, aimed at ensuring continued white domination.

Exponents of ideal apartheid believe that the complete territorial, social, and political separation of black and white will prevent friction and protect the ethnic heritage of all groups. In exchange for their loss of rights within the so-called 'white areas', Africans will be granted opportunities 'to develop along their own lines' on lands set aside for their sole occupation. There are, however, grave practical difficulties in the way of this scheme. These 'reserved' lands constitute about 11 per cent of the land total of the republic for over two-thirds of its population. Under half the African population actually lives on them, and the large capital expenditure and long-term planning necessary, if they are to hold their present population, let alone those expelled from the 'white areas', have not materialized. So far, even the most advanced of these areas politically, the Transkei, has little more than limited local self-government subject to white control.

In the case of the substantial coloured and Asian (Indian) minorities, the difficulties of applying 'separate development' have been even greater. Neither group possesses a territorial 'homeland', and culturally the coloured group is virtually indistinguishable from its white forebears. Nevertheless, each group has been granted separate institutions, including representative councils, with limited powers of community legislation.

If ideal apartheid has had only a very limited application, restrictive apartheid legislation, often based on earlier precedents, has been extended to govern every aspect of daily life and thousands of lives have been dislocated as a result. Despite all such attempts to keep the races apart, the economic expansion of South Africa in the last 20 years has integrated more Africans than ever before into the money economy. Within the 'white areas' non-whites without rights form the majority in every important town and industrial complex, and there is little sign that whites can or will do without their black labour in the interests of total apartheid. Bitter opposition to the policies of apartheid from the non-white masses, as well as from a handful of whites, has led to increasingly severe restrictions of freedom in South Africa.

G. M. Carter, *The Politics of Inequality: South Africa since 1948* (New York, 1959).

C. R. Hill, *Bantustans, The Fragmentation of South Africa* (Oxford and London, 1964). SM

APEDEMEK, lion-headed war god of Meroe. He is known from numerous temple reliefs, where his role as a warrior is made clear. The religion of Kush was initially of Egyptian origin, and the principal Egyptian gods Amun, Osiris, and Isis continued to be worshipped throughout Meroitic history. Only in the later periods were Apedemek and other local gods included in the pantheon. Temples dedicated to them are found in the southern part of Kush, mainly in the 'Island of Meroe', and were built at a time when this had become the heart of the kingdom. By then the local gods appear to have become as important as those of Egypt.

APELLA, sovereign assembly of full Spartan citizens meeting regularly every month from the 7th cent. BC onwards. Its presidents were at first the kings, later (5th cent.) the ephors. It elected by acclamation ephors and members of the *gerousia* and similarly decided questions of war, peace, and foreign alliance.

APELLES, the most renowned Greek painter of the 4th cent. BC, born probably at Colophon in Ionia. Famous for his portraits, whose subjects included Alexander the Great in allegorical representation and Aphrodite, he also developed new colouring techniques.

APIAN, PETER (1495–1552), German astronomer and mathematician, favoured by Emperor Charles V. He published *Astronomicum Caesareum* (1540).

APOLOGY OF THE COMMONS (1604), statement and defence of British parliamentary privileges and proceedings. It arose after parliament had proposed another, larger revenue to replace that obtained from the anachronistic court of wards, and had received a reprimand from James I. The commons asserted the privileges of free elections, freedom from arrest during parliamentary sessions, and freedom of speech. The apology was never formally presented to the king.

APOTHECARIES, SOCIETY OF, granted by James I (1606) a monopoly for the buying and selling of drugs, and established the right to treat patients as well as to supply medicines (1704). An act of 1815 authorized the society to examine and license all practising pharmacists, and this raised the standard of medical practice by leading to the regular teaching of students at principal hospitals.

APPA SAHIB (d. 1840), appointed regent of the Maratha state of Nagpur (Berar) on the death of Raghuji Bhonsla II (March 1816). He entered into a subsidiary alliance with the British, but attacked the Resident's troops and was defeated at Sitabaldi (Nov. 1817). After fresh intrigues (March 1818) he fled to the Punjab.

APPALACHIA, mountain system of eastern North America, extending from Nfld to central AL. Densely forested summits rise to uniform heights, but important water-gaps traverse the ridge and valley topography. During the colonial period Appalachia acted as a barrier to westward expansion, and so promoted dense occupation of the eastern seaboard. Settlers infiltrated the fertile interior valleys in the late 18th cent., but became isolated after the frontier finally crossed the Appalachians. The first commercial oil well in North America was drilled in western PA (1859), and coal mining had become important in the Allegheny plateau of PA and WV by the end of the century. Now dependent upon subsistence farming and declining sectors of the coal industry, Appalachia has come to epitomize regional poverty. It has recently been designated as a Redevelopment Area (1961), and been given large-scale federal aid.

APPARENTEMENT, in French politics, an electoral alliance between parties. It is used specifically of an arrangement introduced in 1951 for the election of that year whereby, under the Fourth Republic's system of proportional representation in multi-member constituencies, parties which formed an *apparentement* counted as a single party and so could claim more seats. If the alliance had an absolute majority, it took all the seats in the constituency. *Apparentement* was designed to benefit the moderate parties of the centre at the expense of the communists and Gaullists, and it did have this effect, although it failed to lead to more stable government, as had been hoped.

APPEAL COMME D'ABUS, judicial complaint to the French *parlement* against ecclesiastical judges who were accused of exceeding their powers.

APPEAL EN CAS DE SAISINE ET NOUVELLETE, legal channel in prerevolutionary French law, through which clerics could seek redress in royal courts.

APPEAL, JUDICIAL. A private person in England could bring a charge, known as a judicial appeal or appeal of felony, against another private individual. The issue was decided by private combat and a defeated defendant, if not killed outright, was immediately punished. By a writ of 1219, the defendant could make the appeal a matter for trial by jury, on the grounds that the appeal was made maliciously. The jury's competence very rapidly widened into the right of deciding upon the actual issue of the appeal, and private prosecutions became a matter for trial in a court of law, although the judicial appeal by combat was not formally abolished (together with the judicial duel) until 1819.

APPEAL TO THE CHRISTIAN NOBILITY OF THE GERMAN NATION, polemical tract written by Martin Luther in Aug. 1520, in which he called upon the German ruling classes to repudiate the theocratic nature of the Catholic Church and to lead the reforming movement by which the Church would be stripped of its excessive wealth.

APPEALS, STATUTE OF (1533), one of the major parliamentary acts of the Henrician reformation. It enabled the annulment of Henry VIII's marriage to Catherine of Aragon to be expedited and his marriage to Anne Boleyn, two months earlier, to be recognized as lawful.

Prepared by Thomas Cromwell in the autumn of 1532, the bill to restrain appeals to Rome became law in March 1533. It extended the concepts of Richard II's statute of *praemunire*, prohibiting the transference of appeals in matrimonial cases from the courts of the English archbishops to the papal curia. Thus, in May 1533 Cranmer, appointed Abp of Canterbury in the previous Jan., was able to declare Henry's marriage to Catherine void.

The act also contained in its preamble a declaration of supreme importance. It stated that 'this realm of England is an empire . . . governed by one Supreme Head and King', thus expounding as accepted fact that England was a sovereign national state and the monarch was its supreme head, both in secular and ecclesiastical matters. The measure indicated the way in which government policy was being enunciated through statute.

APPEASEMENT. After the First World War the conviction was widespread that war could have been prevented, and must be in future. It was felt that mutual discussion and compromise could have restrained national rivalries, and appeased a situation which had become inflamed.

The 1919 peace settlement was widely criticized both in Germany and the victorious states, especially Britain. The advocates of appeasement feared that the withdrawal of German territory and the demand for reparations would create national resentments leading to another war. Keynes's *Economic Consequences of the Peace* (Dec. 1919) supplied their most telling arguments.

Other sentiments reinforced appeasement. It was felt that France had dragged Britain into the war, and would do so again, by pressing punitive claims. Germany appeared an ideological and geographical bulwark against Bolshevism. There was some sympathy with German claims to racial superiority over the Poles and Czechs governing former German nationals.

The policy of redressing understandable national grievances acquired the connotation of making unjustifiable concessions only in the 1930s. The 1935 Hoare–Laval plan to acquiesce in Mussolini's Abyssinian conquest was popularly denounced in France and Britain, and abandoned. However, when Hitler reoccupied the Rhineland in 1936, violating the Versailles Treaty and the Locarno Pact, there was little objection in England to Hitler's invading 'his own back garden'. Appeasement was acquiring a pro-German aspect.

Paradoxically, several French and British politicians in this period hoped, by appeasing aggressive expansion in Italy, to check similar tendencies in Germany. They hoped particularly that Italy would protect Austria against Germany. This morally inconsistent policy was chiefly blocked by Britain and France's reluctance to admit Italy into their respective Mediterranean and Danubian spheres of influence.

Appeasement of Hitler reached a climax in 1938. Hitler's *Anschluss* with Austria, and demand for the German districts of Czechoslovakia, seemed understandable national objectives to the British prime minister, Chamberlain. The Munich conference made it clear that neither Britain nor France would risk war in such a cause.

Hitler's invasion of Czechoslovakia (March 1939) jarred with accepted notions of necessary treaty revisions, and hardened British opinion on the merits of Hitler's territorial dispute with Poland. The Anglo-Polish alliance did not deter Hitler from invading Poland on 1 Sept., thus inaugurating the Second World War.

The contemporary opponents of appeasement, particularly Churchill, Eden, and Reynaud, condemned the policy as being dishonourable and leading directly to war: a vigorous resistance at an early stage to Hitler's challenges to the peace settlement, coupled with adequate rearmament measures, would have deterred him from aggression. However, after the Second as after the First World War, it has proved difficult to draw unequivocal conclusions from a study of the origins of the conflict. Doubtful analogies with the Hitler period led Eden into the Suez debacle, and contributed to the institution of the Cold War. Appeasement came to have most currency as a moral criticism, denoting a refusal to act against, and defend the victims of, unjustified aggression.

M. Gilbert, *The Roots of Appeasement* (London, 1966).
Lord Avon, *Facing the Dictators* (London, 1962).   ASJ

APPELLANT, LORDS, the nobles who seized power from King Richard II in 1386, attacked his policies, and in 1388 executed some of his friends. Richard recovered control of the government in 1389 and took his revenge in 1397–8. The Duke of Gloucester was murdered, the Earl of Arundel executed and his brother, Abp Arundel, deprived of Canterbury. The others were banished. The return of one of them, Henry of Lancaster, in 1399, led to Richard's deposition.

APPERT, NICHOLAS (1752–1841), French inventor, the 'father of canning', who was trained as a cook. In 1795 the French Directoire, faced with difficult problems of food supplies for sailors, soldiers, and civilians, offered a prize for a practical method of preservation. Appert eventually devised a method of heating and sealing which he applied successfully to a large range of foods. He used the prize (1810) to open the first commercial cannery, from which the modern industry, using essentially the same methods, is derived.

APPIA, VIA, famous Roman highway constructed in 312 BC between Rome and Capua by the censor Appius Claudius. Later it was extended through Calatia and Caudium to Beneventum, and finally through Venusia and Tarentum to Brundisium.

APPIUS CLAUDIUS (*fl.* 5th cent. BC), great social reformer in early Rome and chairman of commissions of ten appointed in 451 and 450 BC, which codified the law in the Twelve Tables. A tendentious tradition alleged that Appius tyrannically clung to power, until deposed by popular action.

APPLESEED, JOHNNY, the nickname of MA-born John Chapman (1774–1847), a legendary North American frontier horticulturist. He supplied settlers passing through the Ohio valley between 1801 and 1847 with apple-seeds and saplings grown in his PA nursery.

APPOMATTOX, 60 miles (96 kms) west of Richmond, VA, the scene of Gen. Lee's surrender to Gen. Grant (9 April 1865), which virtually ended the American Civil War, although minor engagements continued for over a month.

APPRENTICE SYSTEM, labour system in British West Indian colonies based on the Emancipation Act (1833) which required freed slaves, exclusive of children, to serve an apprenticeship of four to six years for their masters. It provided a transitional period of quasi-slavery before complete emancipation.

APRAXIN, STEPHEN (*fl.* 17th–18th cent.), governor of Kazan during the reign of Tsar Peter the Great. He went to extraordinary lengths to extract money from the inhabitants of his territory in order to satisfy the growing demands of the central treasury.

APRIL REVOLUTION (1960), only successful popular revolution in Korean history, led by students, which overthrew the government of Syngman Rhee. Before the elections of 15 March, students had organized groups dedicated to opposing Rhee's illegal election methods. Police brutality in Masan resulted in rioting there and demonstrations in Seoul, which by the government's vindictive reaction on 18–19 April were turned into a revolution that caused Rhee's resignation. The success of the Korean students provided an example to those of other countries, particularly Turkey, and has an important place in the development of 'student power' in the 1960s.

APRIL THESES, enunciated by Lenin in speeches and in *Pravda* on his return to Russia through Germany in April 1917 and constituting his most decisive intervention in the Revolution. He rejected the notion of 'double power' (shared between the Provisional Government and the Soviets), urged 'all power to the Soviets', and rejected any co-operation with or support for the Provisional Government. He did not now advocate immediate peace, but stressed the need for anti-war propaganda. He said that estates should be confiscated immediately and land transferred to the peasantry; that his party should change its name to Communist; and a new militant international be set up which would exclude all but his own followers. He conjured a vision of a proletarian dictatorship without police, bureaucrats, or standing army.

His speeches were at first received with stupefaction by his supporters, while his rivals believed they meant his political demise. But his moral and intellectual dominance brought their acceptance before the month was out, so that the Bolsheviks were now distinguished from the Mensheviks (as they had not been before Lenin's arrival) by their readiness to carry through the Revolution, for which the April Theses provided the slogans.

AQIT, dynasty of scholars and judges in Timbuctoo. The Aqit family, which belonged to the Massufa clan of the Sanhaja confederation, settled in Timbuctoo in the mid-15th cent. under the headship of Muhammad Aqit. His son Umar married Sitta, daughter of the judge (*qadi*) Anda-Ag Muhammad, and the next three generations of these two families provided the *qadi*s of Timbuctoo and the *imam*s of its Sankore mosque for over a century. Celebrated among Umar's sons were Mahmud (*qadi*, 1498–1548) and Ahmad (d. 1535), a noted peripatetic teacher. After Mahmud's death, three of his sons held the post of *qadi* in succession; Muhammad (1548–65), Al-Aqib (1565–83), and Umar, from 1583 until his exile to Morocco in 1594. Most celebrated of all the Aqit family was Ahmad Baba (d. 1627), the jurist and author, grandson of Ahmad ibn Umar Aqit. His works are still studied.

AQRABA, in the Yamama region of north-east Arabia, was the scene, in 633, of a defeat of the Banu Hanifa, led by Musaylama, by the Muslims under Khalid ibn al-Walid. The fighting was so severe that it earned for the site of the main encounter the name of 'the garden of death' (hadiqat al-mawt).

AQUAE SEXTIAE, BATTLE OF (102 BC), Marius' victory in southern Gaul over the Germanic Ambrones and Teutones, who were attempting with the Cimbri and Tigurini to invade Italy.

AQUAVIVA, FATHER RUDOLFO (1550–83), a younger son of the Duke of Atri in the kingdom of Naples. He joined the Jesuit order, went to India, and was noted for his piety and austerity. He headed the first Jesuit mission to Akbar's court in 1580; he returned to Goa, disappointed, in 1582, where he was shortly afterwards murdered by a Hindu crowd.

AQUILEIA, 'Latin' colony founded by the Romans near the head of the Adriatic (181 BC) for defence and the exploitation of neighbouring gold-mines. Important under the empire, especially for the amber trade, it was destroyed by Attila (AD 452) and its inhabitants fled to the lagoons of Venice.

AQUINAS, THOMAS, Saint (c. 1225–74), greatest and most influential of all medieval theologians and philosophers. Son of a southern Italian noble, he became a Dominican while studying at Naples. The order sent him to Paris, where he studied under Albert the Great. In 1252, on Albert's recommendation, he became regent (master) in the Dominican school at Paris and was embroiled in the controversy between the secular masters of the university and the mendicant Dominican and Franciscan masters. In 1256 he was appointed professor in the university and had to be protected by royal troops when delivering his inaugural lecture. He died, perhaps accidentally, on his way to the general church council at Lyons. He was canonized in 1323.

The importance of Aquinas is hard to overstate. His output of works was prodigious. He first gave convincing evidence of the compatibility of Christian philosophy and theology. Despite severe opposition, including a temporary ban on lectures on Aristotle's works in Paris, to the acceptance of Aristotelianism, Aquinas' influence led to its becoming the basis of virtually all later medieval philosophic thought. In theology, his *Summa Theologiae*, begun in 1245 and left uncompleted on his death, and other works have had, if anything, an even more profound influence. Adapting and adopting many of Aristotle's ideas and using Aristotle's method, the *Summa* became the fundamental tenet of Roman Catholic theology. Popes from John XXII (d. 1334) to Pius XII (d. 1958) have affirmed the primacy of Thomist theology.

ARAB BUREAU, organization of Middle Eastern experts under Commander D. C. Hogarth established in Cairo (Feb. 1916) and important in moulding and executing British policy towards the Arabs.

ARAB CONQUESTS. Having overcome the desert tribes which, after the death of the Prophet Muhammad in 632, had thrown off allegiance to Mecca and Medina, the Muslim forces turned outward from Arabia and began a series of campaigns against Byzantium and Sasanid Persia. The battle of Ajnadayn (634) laid all Palestine open to the Arabs. Damascus yielded in 635, and in 636, on the Yarmuk river, the Byzantine forces, gathered for a counter-offensive, met with an irremediable defeat. All Syria came now under Muslim rule. It was not long before Egypt also had to face the Arab assault. Al-Farama (Pelusium) fell in 640 and, in the summer of that year, the Muslims routed the Byzantine troops in Egypt at 'Ayn Shams. Babylon was taken in 641 and Alexandria in 642. The Byzantines re-took Alexandria in 645, but lost it again the next year. Egypt was now definitely under Muslim domination. Meanwhile, the Arab armies had been campaigning with notable success in Iraq. After losing the 'Battle of the Bridge' (634), fought near Al-Hira, the Muslims overcame the Sasanids at Buwayb in 635 and won a decisive battle against them at Al-Qadisiya, not far from Al-Hira (637). The Sasanid capital in Iraq, Ctesiphon, now fell to the victorious warriors of Islam. The Arabs won a further success at Jalula (637), which cleared the Sasanids from northern Iraq. Mosul was captured in 641 and in the same year the last major force available to the Sasanid Shah was routed at Nihawand. Thereafter, against a stiff local resistance, the Muslims brought one province of Persia after another under their own control. Istakhr (Persepolis) was conquered in 649–50, but it was not until the reign of the Caliph Mu'awiya (661–80) that the great province of Khurasan in north-east Persia was reduced to obedience.

A second age of Muslim conquest occurred during and after the reign of the Caliph al-Walid I (705–15). Qutayba b. Muslim, appointed governor of Khurasan in 704, conquered Balkh (705), Bukhara (706–9), and Samarkand (710–12). A further extension of Muslim influence was to be carried out from Khurasan towards Farghana and Tashkent in the years after 738. The reign of Al-Walid I saw also Muslim forces under Muhammad b. al-Qasim engaged in the subjugation of Sind and of the southern Punjab in India (711–13). In North Africa the Arabs had established themselves at Kayrawan in 670. Byzantine Carthage fell to the Muslims in 698. Soon afterwards, the great campaigns began which led to the conquest of most of the Spanish peninsula. Tariq b. Ziyad crushed the Visigoths at Wadi Bakkah in 711. In the same year Toledo was taken. In 713 Musa b. Nusayr reduced Seville. Muslim forces crossed the Pyrenees into France during 717 or 718. This penetration north-westward was to be halted, however, at the battle of Tours in 732, although Muslim raids continued on a considerable scale until the Christian recapture of Narbonne (759).   VJP

ARAB HIGHER COMMITTEE, a Palestinian Arab organization under the Mufti of Jerusalem established (1936) to organize the Arab general strike. It became the principal expression of Palestine Arab political opinion. Declared illegal (1937), it was reconstituted (1945) and merged into the Arab Higher Executive in 1946.

ARAB LEAGUE, regional organization established (Alexandria Protocol 1944) by the Lebanon, Egypt, Iraq, Syria, and Transjordan and subsequently joined by other Arab states. Its constitution (Pact of the League of Arab States) was drafted in 1945, and in 1950 its then seven members gave it a military aspect with the Arab Collective Security Pact. Originating, with British support, in Iraqi proposals for a Greater Syria, it inevitably came under predominantly Egyptian influence. A loose co-ordinating body without coercive powers, the league became an important arena for inter-Arab disputes, as well as an agency for co-ordinating policies, especially against Israel (*eg*, the economic boycott).

ARAB LEGION, force raised originally (1920) by Lieut.-Col. G. F. Peake, from Transjordanian villagers for protection against Bedouins. Completely reorganized after 1930 under Maj. (later Gen.) J. G. Glubb with Bedouin recruits, British officers and substantial subsidies, the legion, expanded to 8000 during the Second World War, became in 1948 the most effective Arab military force in Palestine. The legion was Jordanized after the dismissal of Gen. Glubb (1 March 1956).

ARAB NATIONALISM, political and cultural movement with various manifestations all characterized by a consciousness that Arabs were linked by a common factor of Arabness. Before the 19th cent. the word 'Arab' was usually employed only to describe Arabian nomads. Most inhabitants of what is now called the Arab world thought of themselves primarily as belonging to a particular religious community, tribe, village, town, or occupation and had no particular consciousness of any Arab bond. During the 19th cent. this situation began to change with the influx of new European ideas of nationalism, the development of modern literary Arabic, the spread of education, and the centralizing policy of the Ottoman government. Early manifestations of a new consciousness occur among Lebanese Christians and are associated with the aspirations of various Christian communities, although often phrased in terms of Lebanese or Syrian nationalism and the accentuation of Arab links. The most extreme formulation of these ideas is found in the writings of Negib Azoury. Muslim Arabs, however, remained largely unaffected before 1908, apart from certain individuals (*eg*, Abd al-Rahman al-Kawakibi). After 1908 disappointment with the results of the Young Turk Revolution and increasing hostility towards the centralizing policy of the Young Turks led a small minority of educated Muslim Arabs, especially in Syria, to demand greater administrative autonomy for the Arab provinces of the Ottoman empire. Various societies (*eg*, Al-Qahtaniyya, Al-Ahd, Al-Fatat, the Beirut Reform Committee, the Ottoman Decentralization Society) were founded. The movement remained a minority one until the destruction of the Ottoman empire compelled Arabs to seek new forms of political organization. The creation of a plurality of Arab states after 1918 often channelled this search into local nationalisms, but the idea of a wider Arab nationalism was kept alive by various factors, including Hashemite ambitions and Arab sympathies for each other's struggles, particularly for the resistance of Palestinian Arabs to Zionism. In 1944 popular sympathies were reinforced by an alliance of Arab governments, including Egypt, which had hitherto remained aloof, in the Arab League. Since then, Arab political unity has remained an aspiration largely subordinated to the pull of loyalties to individual state systems and strongest among those Arabs who felt alienated from their own particular state system. Philosophically, Arab thinkers have been preoccupied with defining an Arab, and at various times history, religion (Islam), culture, common aspirations, and language have been held to be the principal determinants. In recent years, especially in the writings of Sati-al-Husri, language has come to predominate as the emblem of Arabism.

A. Hourani, *Arabic Thought in the Liberal Age* (Oxford, 1967).
Sylvia Haim, *Arab Nationalism* (California, 1962).   MEY

ARAB REVOLT, anti-Ottoman movement in the Hijaz proclaimed (10 June 1916) by Sharif Husayn of Mecca. The troops were Hijazis and Bedouins, many of the officers were Iraqis, and financial assistance and contingents were supplied by Britain and France. The northern forces under Faysal, accompanied by Col. T. E. Lawrence, captured Akaba (6 July 1917) and took part in the Syrian campaigns under Allenby in 1917–18.

ARABI PASHA (1839–1911), Col. Ahmad Arabi, son of a village headman, who was educated at Al-Azhar, came to prominence in 1881 as the leader of an Egyptian army mutiny against the Turco-Circassian administration, and subsequently became minister of war and one of the dominant figures in the nationalist government of 1882.

ARABIA, EGYPTIAN CONQUEST. At the instigation of the Ottoman government, Muhammad Ali of Egypt undertook the conquest of Arabia to end Wahhabi raids. He defeated the Wahhabis in a bitter struggle (1811–18) and founded an Egyptian empire in Arabia which collapsed after 1840.

ARABIAN-AMERICAN   OIL   COMPANY,   originally California-Arabian Standard Oil Co. (1933–44), renamed ARAMCO (1944) and widened to include most major US oil groups (1947). Granted oil concession in Saudi Arabia (1933), the company discovered oil (Dharan, 1935) and became (1952) the greatest oil-producing company in the world and remarkable for its extensive ancillary work.

ARAB-ISRAELI WAR (1947–9). Following UN approval of the partition of Palestine (29 Nov. 1947) fighting began between Palestinian Arabs, who rejected partition, and Jews, in which the former were aided by volunteers from neighbouring Arab states. On the ending of the British mandate (15 May 1948) the war entered a new stage with the entry into Palestine of the armies of Iraq, Transjordan, Syria, Lebanon, and Egypt with a Saudi Arabian contingent. At the first truce (11 June) neither side had the advantage, but resumed fighting (9 July) was characterized by striking Israeli gains. A second truce (18 July) was broken (15 Oct.) and, in the last campaigns, punctuated by further truces, Israel occupied the Negev to the Gulf of Akaba. Armistices were arranged at Rhodes (Jan.–July 1949).

ARAB-ISRAELI WAR (1967) (The Six-Day War). Palestine guerrilla raids against Israel in 1966 provoked Israeli retaliation against their bases in Jordan. To avert a similar retaliation against Syria (May 1967), Egypt moved troops towards the Israeli border, removing the UN expeditionary force and recovering control of Sharm al-Shaykh, covering the entrance to the Gulf of Akaba and threatening to prevent Israel's access to her port of Eilath. On 30 May Jordan signed a defence agreement with Egypt. Confronted by a ring of apparently hostile Arab states and the possibility of the closure of Eilath port, Israel struck (5 June). Pre-emptive air strikes destroyed Arab air forces, while ground troops seized the Sinai peninsula, the West Bank of the Jordan, including Jerusalem, and the Golan Heights before the final cease fire (10 June).

ARAGO, DOMINIQUE FRANÇOIS JEAN (1786–1853), French scientist and republican politician, who acted as minister of war and marine under the 1848 Republic.

ARAGON, formerly an independent kingdom in the northeast of the Iberian peninsula, which, with its component states of Catalonia and Valencia, became united with the wealthier kingdom of Castile in 1479. Aragon itself was a poor country, with a population of only 270,000 in 1495, and it remained economically subordinate to Castile through its exclusion from the American trade. Arid and treeless, Aragon produced only hemp and saffron, but through its ancient union with Catalonia (from 1137) it had developed an export trade in wool and a strong maritime tradition. As a result of Aragon's natural outlook towards the Mediterranean Sea, the kingdom had acquired Sardinia, Sicily, and the Balearic Isles, and the interest which successive Spanish monarchs showed towards Italy, the Levant, and North Africa reflected this Aragonese tradition.

The government of the united state of Castile-Aragon, from which the kingdom of Spain emerged, remained a loose confederation, in which royal authority in Aragon was limited in practice by such factors as the inefficiency of the bureaucracy, the survival of seigneurial jurisdiction, and traditional privileges or *fueros*. From the reign of Ferdinand II, Aragon was ruled through a viceroy, and from 1494 the king drew on the advice of the Council of Aragon, consisting of a president and five councillors, all Aragonese subjects. Royal jurisdiction was also challenged by the court of the *Justicia*, which existed to protect the people of Aragon from public as well as private injustice. Finally, the general *cortes* of Aragon, Catalonia, and Valencia, with its four estates of the nobility, gentry, clergy, and the towns, possessed rights of procedure, taxation, and legislation which rendered the Crown less absolute in Aragon than in the rest of Spain.

ARAGON, CRUSADE OF (1285), a Holy War against the Infidel and an attempt, instigated by the pope, to conquer the kingdom of the Christian King of Aragon, Peter III. He had aroused the wrath of the pope by supporting the Sicilians after their rising of 1282 against the pope's ally, Charles of Anjou. For this Pope Martin IV declared Peter to be deposed and Philip III of France was entrusted with the conquest of Aragon, which he invaded in January 1285. Peter's great admiral, Roger de Loria, destroyed the French fleet. The army, bereft of supplies, had to withdraw. Philip III died during the retreat and the shock of this disaster played an important part in determining his successor, Philip IV (the Fair), never to act in future in papal rather than French interests.

ARAI, HAKUSEKI (1657–1725), Japanese scholar and political figure of the Tokugawa period. As adviser to two *shoguns*, he sought to revive Confucian values. He is especially noted for his historical writings.

ARAKAN, the coastal strip of Burma outside the western mountains. The Arakanese are Burmese Buddhists with an admixture of Indian blood. They arrived during the 10th cent. and established a stable kingdom. In the 16th cent. the Portuguese gained a footing, making common cause with Arakanese pirates and slave raiders. Arakan was annexed by the Burmese King Bodawpaya (1782–1819). Plots by Arakanese fugitives in British India caused frontier incidents which ultimately led to the First Anglo-Burmese War (1824–1826). Arakan was the scene of bitter fighting in the Second World War.

ARAKCHEYEV, ALEKSEY ANDREYEVICH, Count (1769–1834), Russian soldier, statesman, and favourite of Alexander I. The term 'Arakcheyevshchina' is often used to describe the reactionary, militaristic, internal regime of Alexander's last years. Starting his career as an artillery drill-master he became chief military adviser to Paul I and was war minister (1808–10) under Alexander I. He resigned after a conflict with Speransky but remained close to the emperor, and as deputy to the president of the Committee of Ministers (1814–25) was, in practice, the centre of government.

An unattractive and cruel personality, his disciplinarian ideas made him unpopular, but he was an able and honest organizer. His name is chiefly associated with the hated military colonies initiated by Alexander after 1815 where soldiers combined farming and craft industries with military drill.

ARAMAEANS, Semitic nomads of mixed origin who first settled on the fringes of Syria in the second millennium BC and at the end of the 13th cent. invaded Syria, Palestine, and Mesopotamia. They took up sheep farming, agriculture, and international caravan trading, being most powerful in Mesopotamia in the 10th cent. and in Syria in the 8th cent. Their language, with its alphabetic script, was adopted, probably first by other nomads and then by the older populations and gradually became the common tongue of the entire area and remained so until the Arab conquest (7th cent. AD).

ARAMAYO, CARLOS VICTOR (1889–), one of three tin-mining magnates to be expropriated in 1952 following the Bolivian revolution. Aramayo had served in several diplomatic posts while directing the Aramayo Mining Co.

ARANDA, PEDRO PABLO, Conde de (1719–98), Aragonese nobleman and leading minister of the Spanish enlightened despot, Charles III. Before becoming a minister he had spent a varied career as an administrator and as ambassador to Poland, and was also an unsuccessful general in the Spanish campaign against Portugal (1762). His extensive travels brought him into contact with the *philosophes* and their work. Knowing him to be a supporter of royal absolutism, Charles III made him president of the Council of Castile (1766) and from this position he acted as the true head of Charles's government till 1773. Although his colleagues, Campomanes and Floridablanca, have usually been looked on as more important in the formulation of royal policy in these years, he was probably the most radical of the three ministers. He was above all a determined opponent of the Jesuits and carried through their expulsion from Spain and her colonies (1767) with military ruthlessness. The universities, freed from Jesuit control, were put under the state. Parallel with this anti-clerical move was an attack on rural poverty under Aranda's auspices. Landless peasants were given surplus land and the state encouraged the colonization of underpopulated areas. At the same time, an attempt was made to solve Spain's shortage of cereal by rearing fewer sheep and growing more corn.

Aranda's radicalism and quarrels with his ministerial colleagues made Charles III decide to employ him outside Spain. He was sent as ambassador to France (1773), where till 1787 he conducted a successful policy, raising the value of the connection with Spain in French eyes. For a few months (1792) he was again chief minister under the new king, Charles IV, and pursued a more friendly policy towards the French Revolution, relaxing government censorship. But in Nov. 1792 the queen's favourite, Godoy, replaced him and reversed his policy. On the outbreak of war with France, Aranda became an advocate of peace, which led to his exile (1794).

R. Herr, *The Eighteenth-Century Revolution in Spain* (Princeton, 1958). DMCK

ARAPAHO INDIANS, American Indian tribe of the Algonquian family, which formed a permanent alliance with the Cheyenne. They were famous as raiders on the western plains and were involved in numerous battles with the US army, including the Washita Massacre and the Little Big Horn. About 1840, they made peace with the Sioux, Kiowa, and Comanche tribes, but remained at war with the Shoshone, Ute, and Pawnee until they were confined to reservations. During the 19th cent. the Arapaho divided into Northern and Southern groups, but the Northern Arapaho in WY were considered the nucleus, and retained the sacred tribal articles. By the Medicine Lodge Treaty (1867), the Southern Arapaho were placed on a reservation in OH, and in 1876 the Northern Arapaho were confined to a reservation in WY.

ARAQUISTAIN QUEVEDO, LUIS (1886–1959), Spanish journalist and intellectual, who joined the Socialist Party before the First World War and was one of a group of intellectuals who supported the Allied cause. He was editor of Caballero's newspaper *Claridad*. Influenced by events in Germany and Austria, he advocated a policy of left-wing militancy. After the outbreak of the Spanish Civil War he was appointed ambassador to Paris (1936–7). In contrast to his associate and brother-in-law, Alvarez del Vayo, he became bitterly anti-communist.

ARATUS OF SICYON (271–213 BC), Greek statesman and general, who led the Achaean League's major expansion after Sicyon joined it (250), his chief acquisitions being Corinth,

Megalopolis, and Argos. An energetic guerrilla leader against Macedonian domination, he failed to defeat Cleomenes III of Sparta and paradoxically turned to Achaea's old enemy, Macedon, with an invitation to Antigonus Doson to defend it (224). Doson's successor, Philip V, at first accepted advice from Aratus, but not for long. Aratus could not then disguise Macedon's domination which, after his 25 years' resistance, his own invitation to Doson had re-established. His *Memoirs*, though lost, were apologetic and have distorted the accounts of our extant sources.

ARAUCANIANS, war-like Indian tribal group of Chile who remained unconquered during the colonial period. The Araucanians had successfully avoided conquest by the Incas. Pedro de Valdivia attempted to conquer them, pushing south of the Maule river (1551). But the Araucanians, led by Lautaro, drove the Spaniards back across the Maule (1553). War continued under Caupolicán, who was captured and executed by the Spaniards (1558). Eventually, the Araucanians were pushed southward beyond the Bío Bío river, but they regained the Bío Bío (1593) and there the dividing line remained for 300 years. The Chileans finally conquered the Araucanians in the 1880s.

ARAUSIO, BATTLE OF (105 BC), disastrous Roman defeat in southern Gaul by the Cimbri and Teutones, caused by the refusal of the consul Cn. Mallius and the proconsul Q. Servilius Caepio to co-operate.

ARAVIDU DYNASTY, the fourth and last dynasty of the south Indian empire of Vijayanagar. It was founded by Tirumala, brother of the minister and real ruler, Ram Raja, after the latter's death at the battle of Talikota (1565). Vijayanagar was abandoned in favour of Penugonda in the Anantapur district. The capital was later moved to Chandragiri. One of the last princes granted the site of Madras to the East India Co.

ARAWAKS, in pre-conquest times the largest linguistic group in the Caribbean and South America. Their language was spoken from Florida to Argentina. By 1492 they were being driven from the southern Antilles, the Guianas, and Venezuela by the cannibalistic Carib Indians. The Arawaks of the Antilles were peaceful and skilled in agriculture and crafts. Remnants of Arawak tribes exist today in Guyana and the Guianas, Venezuela, Colombia, Brazil, and even Bolivia.

ARBENZ GUZMÁN, JACOBO (b. 1914), president of Guatemala (1951–4). As a lieutenant-colonel he took part in the revolt of 1944 and joined the revolutionary government which followed as minister of war. He took office as president (March 1951) and embarked immediately upon a programme of social and economic reform which worried both the US investors in Guatemala and their government in Washington. Arbenz's nationalism led him to seek aid from the Soviet Union in order to stave off threats from conservative exiles and the US. Land distribution and labour organization followed policies which threatened the United Fruit Co. Arbenz was overthrown by the exile Col. Castillo Armas with US arms (June 1954). The Guatemalan army had abandoned the regime to its enemies. From Cuba Arbenz continued to campaign against the weak conservative governments of Guatemala.

ARBITRISTAS, group of Spaniards, including González de Cellorigo, Sancho de Moncada, and Fernández Navarrete, who analysed the social disillusionment and the economic crisis affecting Castile at the end of the 16th cent., which was reflected in Cervantes' *Don Quixote*. The *arbitristas* campaigned for widespread social and economic reform and proffered much advice to Philip III's government which went unheeded until the regime of Philip IV's favourite, Olivares.

ARBUTHNOT, JOHN (1667–1735), Scottish physician and writer. He was educated at St Andrews and settled in London, where he became the friend of Swift and Pope and physician in ordinary to Queen Anne. He was an early advocate of the union of England and Scotland. In 1712 he advocated the end of the war with France in a series of pamphlets collected into *The History of John Bull*, in which he created the burlesque figure of the typical Englishman. Arbuthnot was the principal author of the satirical *Memoirs of Martinus Scriblerus* (1741). He was also a poet and the author of medical works.

ARBUTHNOT AND AMBRISTER, two British traders accused by Gen. Andrew Jackson of actively leading the Seminole Indians of Florida against the US in 1818. Both were court-martialled and executed.

ARCADIA CONFERENCE (Dec. 1941–Jan. 1942), Anglo-American conference held in Washington, DC, on the initiative of Winston Churchill. When the Japanese attack brought the US into the war, Churchill was anxious that the American effort should flow in directions most beneficial to his strategic views, and travelled to Washington with Beaverbrook, as minister of supply, and the service chiefs. The two most important results of the conference were the Allies Declaration of Jan. 1942 and the establishment of the Anglo-American Combined Chiefs of Staff Committee. US strategy, as was clear from the start of the conference, gave priority to the war in Europe, and beyond that Churchill was unable to secure support for his strategic views.

ARCADIAN LEAGUE, ancient Greek federation of non-Dorian communities in the central Peloponnese, formed in 370 BC after the defeat at Leuctra of the Spartans, who had frustrated earlier attempts at unity. Organized by Lycomedes of Mantinea, it was an interesting federal experiment with primary assembly and representative council meeting at the newly built capital, Megalopolis, and an annually elected chief magistrate. Its appeal to the Thebans against Sparta enabled them to invade the Peloponnese (370–369), but it soon resented Theban leadership, allied itself with Athens (366), and split in 362, Megalopolis and Tegea supporting and Mantinea opposing Thebes at the battle of Mantinea. The two parts remained separate, both claiming to represent Arcadia, but with little effect on subsequent history.

ARCADIUS (*reg.* 395–408), Eastern Emperor. His father, Theodosius I (d. 395), was the last Roman emperor to rule over the undivided empire. In partitioning it before his death he gave the elder son Arcadius the eastern part. The first years of Arcadius' reign witnessed the menace of a Gothic conquest of Constantinople, but after 401 the Visigothic leader Alaric turned his attention chiefly to Italy and the Eastern empire was allowed to survive.

ARCH, JOSEPH (1826–1919), English pioneer leader of agricultural trade unionism, whose puritanism and belief in self-help and in the dignity of his class naturally attached him to Gladstonian Liberalism. Hedgecutter, Primitive Methodist lay-preacher, and bane of squire and parson, he was, in his own words, 'a nonconformist by nature and by conviction'. He formed the Warwickshire Agricultural Labourers' Union (1872) and was a Liberal MP (1885–6, 1892–1902).

ARCHANGEL, town on the White Sea coast founded in 1584 to handle trade reaching Muscovy in English and Dutch ships. For more than a century it remained Muscovy's only port, though an inadequate one since its harbour was ice-free only during three summer months and was remote from the chief Russian trading areas. Nevertheless, it became the focal point for Muscovy's contacts with western Europe and a great fair was held there annually to encourage trade. After the foundation of St Petersburg (1703), Archangel's overall importance diminished, though it remained a busy and prosperous port throughout the 18th cent. It retains its importance as one of the USSR's four leading ports in foreign overseas trade, timber being its chief export product.

ARCHIBALD, SIR ADAMS GEORGE (1814–92), Canadian statesman. Born in Truro, NS, and trained as a lawyer, Archibald was elected to the Nova Scotia house of assembly as a Liberal (1851). He became solicitor-general (1856), attorney-general (1860), and Liberal Party leader (1863). He supported the passage of the 1864 Education Act, which laid the foundations for the province's public school system. He also advocated confederation and Dominion status and was a delegate to the Charlottetown (1864) and London (1866) conferences. He was appointed secretary of state of the Dominion of Canada (1867–70) and served as the first lieutenant-governor of Manitoba and the North West Territories (1870–3). He opened up lands for settlement by negotiating treaties with the Indians and sent Sir William Francis Butler to investigate health conditions in fur-trading posts and missions. Archibald was appointed lieutenant-governor of NS (1873–83) and was a member of the House of Commons (1888–91).

ARCHIDAMUS I (*reg. c.* 468–427 BC), King of Sparta, successor to his exiled grandfather Leotychidas. As a young man he distinguished himself during the Helot revolt (465–464). He is given by Thucydides a leading role in the debate at Sparta before the great Peloponnesian War (431), arguing against immediate warfare on the grounds of Sparta's unpreparedness. In the war he led the Peloponnesian invasions of Attica in 431, 430, and 428, and in 429 began the blockade of Plataea, after failing to win it peacefully and then by assault.

ARCHILOCHUS (*fl.* mid-7th cent. BC) Greek iambic and elegiac poet of Paros. He shared in the colonization of Thasos and perhaps served as a mercenary soldier. His poems reflect the break with tradition and growing individualism in 7th-cent. Greece.

ARCHIMEDES (287–212 BC), Sicilian mathematician, inventor, and courtier of Hiero of Syracuse. His contrivances helped to delay the Romans' capture of Syracuse which led to his death. He is said to have invented the pulley, the screw, and a form of pump. Amongst his mathematical discoveries were the method of calculating circumference from radius, the relation between cylinder and sphere, and the law that a body dipped in water loses weight equivalent to that of the water displaced. He also constructed an orrery to demonstrate the movements of the heavenly bodies.

ARCHITECTS, ROYAL INSTITUTE OF BRITISH (1834). The purpose of the institute was not at first clearly defined. It awarded prizes and provided a centre for the profession. In 1862 it introduced a voluntary examination for associate membership (ARIBA), which was made compulsory in 1882, and became the accepted professional qualification for architects.

ARCHON. 'Ruler' or chief magistrate in Athens and other Greek cities. By the 7th cent. BC there were nine in Athens, elected annually: the *eponymus* archon had authority over property and the family, the *basileus* archon over religion, the *polemarch* over war, and six *thesmothetae* exercised general jurisdiction. Ex-archons joined the Areopagus. Solon (594) extended eligibility from the aristocracy to members of his upper two income groups. In 487 the lot was introduced into the election and soon after Ephialtes' reforms (462) all but the poorest citizens became eligible to serve (458). By 450 the archons' original political, judicial, and military powers had passed to the popular council (*boule*), the popular courts (*dicasteria*), and ten directly elected generals (*strategoi*).

ARCHPOET (*fl. c.* 1165), one of the best Latin poets of the Middle Ages. His name and the details of his personal life are not known. He was a member of the entourage of Frederick Barbarossa's chancellor, Rainald von Dassel, on whose patronage he depended and for whom he wrote propaganda poems and hymns to the emperor, frequently embodying the ideal of emperor as world ruler. He was also an outstanding member of the Goliardic school of poets, a group of wandering clerks, who composed roistering poems, love lyrics, and drinking songs of irreverently secular character.

ARCOS RAID, carried out by British police (May 1927) on the premises of the Soviet trading organization in London. It failed to produce any evidence of subversive activity, but was followed in March 1929 by the severance of diplomatic relations with the USSR.

ARCOT, now a small town about 70 miles (112 kms) east-south-east of Madras in the Madras state. In 1712 the Mughal Nawab of the Carnatic made it his capital, and it remained so until the Anglo-French wars in the mid-century. In 1751 its capture and successful defence against the nawab's army with French support was Clive's most brilliant feat of arms and turned the scale in the war.

ARCY, WILLIAM KNOX D' (1849–1917), British financier who made a fortune in Australian gold mining. In 1901 he obtained an oil concession in Persia which, after the discovery of oil at Masjid-i Sulayman (1908), became the foundation of the Iranian oil industry.

ARDASHIR I (*reg. c.* 224–240), first Sasanian King of Iran. As King of Persis, he defeated the surrounding'princes and subsequently the last Arsacid King, Artabanus V. A coalition led by Armenia was defeated and the Iranian frontier extended. The fortresses of Nisibis and Carrhae were won back from the Romans. Ardashir built a new Iranian empire, based on centralized government and a powerful army and extending from the Euphrates to Seistan and Herat.

ARDENNES OFFENSIVE ('Battle of the Bulge', 1944), last major German offensive of the Second World War. In the autumn of 1944 Hitler, hoping to repeat his success of 1940, ordered von Rundstedt to break through the Ardennes and seize Antwerp. This would have had the effect of cutting the Allied armies in two. The attack, on 16 Dec., caught the Allies by surprise. By the end of Jan. 1945, however, the Germans were back behind their own frontiers. Hitler, by throwing away his last reserves, had only hastened his own downfall.

ARDO, Fulani title meaning 'chief', used by the 19th cent. rulers of Masina and the emirs of Adamawa.

ARDRES, PEACE OF (June 1546), concluded between Henry VIII and Francis I, ended the last bout of Anglo-French hostility (1543–6) before their deaths. In 1544 Henry had launched an invasion of France from Calais, led by the old Dukes of Norfolk and Suffolk, who had captured Boulogne. They then faced the need to defend the town from French naval operations launched from the Channel. By 1546 both sides were glad to withdraw from a costly and indecisive war. By the terms of the peace, England retained Boulogne until 1554, when the French redeemed it.

AREOPAGUS, COUNCIL OF, oldest council of ancient Athens, which met on Areopagus hill. Originally composed of nobles and advisory to the *basileus*, it controlled Athens after the introduction of archons (8th cent. BC) until Solon made his upper two income groups eligible for membership and limited its powers in favour of the popular assembly (*ecclesia*) and a second council (594). Subsequently subservient to the Peisistratids (*c.* 546–510), the council was further weakened by Cleisthenes' strengthening of the *ecclesia* and establishment of a new popular council (*boule*). Though it retained some unknown supervisory powers, the prestige of the Areopagus declined after archons were elected by lot (487) and it was finally stripped of all political power by Ephialtes (462). Thereafter it retained limited religious jurisdiction, particularly in cases of murder, and all but the poorest citizens became eligible for membership (458).

ARETINO, PIERRO (1492–1556), scabrous and prolific writer, established at Venice (1527), who was feared by many sovereigns because of his satirical pen.

ARÉVALO BERMEJO, JUAN JOSÉ (b. 1904), president of Guatemala (1946–51), Arévalo, a symbol of democratic aspirations to Guatemalans during the Ubico dictatorship, returned from Argentine exile (1945) and was elected president. He took office forcibly (1946) and completed his term (1951), having retained press censorship and accomplished little in the way of reform. Arévalo supported the election of Col. Jacobo Arbenz (Nov. 1950). Since the counter-revolt of 1954, Arévalo has lived in exile. His threat to return (1963) contributed to the coup against President Fuentes. His writings include *The Shark and the Sardines*, a scathing attack on the Latin American policy of the US.

ARGALL, SIR SAMUEL (1572–1626), English soldier and adventurer. In 1609 he went to Virginia, where he was alleged to have kidnapped the famous Pocahantes (1612). He was commissioned by the colonial government in 1613 to attack the French settlements of Acadia (NS) and destroyed the Jesuit mission at Mount Desert, ME, and the settlement at Port Royal (Annapolis Royal). He served as deputy governor of VA (1617–19), but was removed for questionable conduct. He later cleared himself and in 1625 became an admiral and served as a member of the New England Royal Council.

ARGAON, BATTLE OF (29 Nov. 1803), during the Second Maratha War (1803–5). The army of the Bhonsla Raja of Berar was defeated by Arthur Wellesley. By the treaty of Deogaon (17 Dec. 1803) the raja ceded Cuttack and Balasore to the British, as well as all his territories west of the Warda river.

ARGENLIEU, GEORGES THIERRY D' (1899–1964), Frenchman who combined a naval with a monastic career. After serving in the First World War, he joined the Carmelite order in 1920, was recalled to the navy in 1939, and was one of the first officers to join de Gaulle (1940), who gave him various missions, including that of commanding the Free French naval forces (1943). As high commissioner in Indo-China, he advocated a more uncomprising policy towards the Viet-minh than that of the government he represented and took independent action, notably in the establishment of a separatist Viet-namese government in Cochin-China independent of Hanoi, which added to the difficulties of a compromise with Ho Chi Minh (if such a compromise was possible). Following the outbreak of war at the end of 1946 he was replaced (March 1947). He then returned to monastic life.

ARGENSON, MARC RENÉ VOYER D' (1652–1721), French politician and administrator under Louis XIV and one of the founders of the French police service. He was trained as a lawyer, and subsequently rose rapidly in royal service, becoming a master of requests (1695) and finally lieutenant-general of police in Paris (1697), a post which he made more powerful and important than ever before.

ARGENSON, RENÉ LOUIS VOYER D' (1694–1757), French statesman and memorialist of the mid-18th cent. He became a councillor of state (1720) and *intendant* of Hainault (1721), where his reputation was that of a sympathetic administrator. He also emerged as a thinker through his friendship with Voltaire and his membership of the *Club d'Entresol*. His career moved forward under the patronage of Chauvelin,

but the latter's fall (1737) led to his own eclipse, and he did not return to power until he became minister for foreign affairs on the fall of Amelot (1744). In the interim he kept a diary of political events and formulated a powerful critique of French government (1739). As minister he supported the Prussian alliance and had visions of an Italian federation, but his policies were not successful and led to his fall (1747).

ARGENTIA CONFERENCE (9–12 Aug. 1941), secret meeting between President F. D. Roosevelt and Winston Churchill off the coast of Nfld. They established cordial personal relations and, although the US was still technically neutral, issued the statement of joint aims that became known as the Atlantic Charter.

ARGHUN, fourth of the Mongol Il-Khans to rule over Persia, had been governor of Khurasan in the reign (1265–1282) of his father, Abaka. He rose in rebellion against his uncle Tekudar (Ahmad) in 1284 and wrested the throne from him. Arghun was much under the influence of the Buddhists, but was also well disposed towards the Christians. His reign (1284–91) saw a continuation of the attempts, begun under Abaka, to establish with the pope and with the princes of Christendom a common front against the Mamluks of Egypt and Syria.

ARGINUSAE, BATTLE OF (Aug. 406 BC), last Athenian naval victory of the Peloponnesian War, fought to the south-east of Lesbos in the Aegean. When Callicratidas, who had superseded Lysander as Spartan commander, was blockading Conon in Mytilene with 170 ships, the Athenians melted down temple-treasures and enrolled metics and slaves to man a relieving fleet. In the ensuing battle Callicratidas was killed and 69 Spartan ships lost, but the Athenians failed to exploit their new command of the sea, rejecting peace overtures and condemning their eight admirals for failing to rescue survivors.

ARGISTIS I (c. 785–755 BC), Urartian king, who annexed the district around Lake Urmiah and extended his control over most of eastern Asia Minor.

ARGONAUTS, legendary crew of the *Argo*, led by Jason of Iolcus, who sailed (c. 1300 BC) to Colchis to win the Golden Fleece. The journey was the subject of early Greek oral poetry and is variously recorded in later sources, principally by the 3rd-cent. Greek poet Apollonius Rhodius. It is possible that the story owes something to both Mycenaean (14th–13th-cent.) and later (7th-cent.) Greek trading voyages to the Black Sea.

ARGOS, ancient Greek city-state in the north-east Peloponnese. After Mycenean civilization collapsed, Argos outshone neighbouring Mycenae and Tiryns, reaching its zenith in the 7th cent. BC under Pheidon's rule, and was the strongest Peloponnesian city until it was eclipsed by Sparta's rise in the 6th cent. After defeat by Sparta at Sepeia (494), Argos remained neutral during the Persian Wars, but the sympathy of Argive and Athenian democracy led to ineffective alliances against Sparta in 461 and 420. Argos joined Sparta's enemies in the Corinthian War (395), but an attempted federation with Corinth was dissolved at the King's Peace (386). Later it assisted the anti-Spartan movement in the Peloponnese after 370, but only occasionally played any significant role before passing with the rest of Greece under Roman rule (146).

ARGÜEDAS, ALCIDES (1879–1946), Bolivian novelist of the Indianist social protest movement. In 1919 he published his best-known work, *Raza de bronce* (*Race of Bronze*). His most famous sociological work is *Pueblo enfermo* (*A Sick People*).

ARGÜELLES, AGUSTIN (1776–1844), Spanish liberal and the most eloquent of the leaders of the Cortes of Cadiz

(1810–13) who played a major role in the liberal revolution of 1820.

ARGYLL, JOHN CAMPBELL, 2nd Duke of (Scottish) (1678–1743). An experienced soldier and leader of the old Scottish court party, he was a supporter of the Protestant succession in Scotland. With inferior numbers he defeated the Jacobite forces of the Earl of Mar at Sheriffmuir on 13 Nov. 1715, saving Scotland for the Hanoverian government. Ambitious and arrogant, he was a mediocre politician and antagonized George I and his English ministers (1716). He cultivated the friendship of the Prince of Wales and with his brother, the Earl of Islay, enjoyed great influence in Scotland during Walpole's administration. After the Porteous riots of 1736 relations between Argyll and Walpole deteriorated and in the 1741 elections Argyll's prestige helped to bring about the election of a large hostile bloc of Scottish members of parliament.

ARGYLL, ARCHIBALD CAMPBELL, 3rd Duke of (1682–1761), an able politician, who became a keen supporter of Walpole and exploited the British government's anxiety for a stable administration in Scotland, emerging as a superb political organizer. After Walpole's downfall he was reconciled with the powerful Pelham group and from 1743 until his death he became indispensable as the manager of Scottish affairs for successive ministries.

ARGYLL, ARCHIBALD CAMPBELL, 9th Earl of (Scottish), (1629–85), a Scottish nobleman ruined at the instigation of James, Duke of York (1681) for refusing to take the test oath wholeheartedly, though in fact he was neither a covenanter nor a presbyterian. The Duke of York was encouraged by the earl's many enemies, especially the royalist Macleans, who were jealous of his vast Argyll estates, which had been restored to him in 1669. The earl was sentenced to death for treason, but escaped to the United Provinces, where he joined the other leaders of English and Scottish opposition. In May 1685 Argyll led an attempted revolt against James II, but the rising failed, Argyll being captured and executed.

ARGYLL, ARCHIBALD CAMPBELL, Marquis of (Scottish) (1598–1661), soldier and politician who generally opposed Charles I by concurring in the abolition of episcopacy in Scotland (1638), leading forces into England in the Civil War, and fighting against the royalist, Montrose. In the closing years of the conflict, his own position became less certain. He invited Oliver Cromwell to Edinburgh, but opposed the execution of Charles I. He participated in the Scottish coronation of Charles II, but later accepted the Commonwealth. His vacillation proved his undoing, and he was executed for treason at the Restoration.

ARIOSTO, LUDOVICO (1474–1533), Italian poet, author of *Orlando Furioso* (1516, revised 1532), a romantic epic about the wars of Charlemagne against the Saracens. The poem, translated by Sir John Harrington (1591), inspired much of the romantic verse of the period. Ariosto also wrote Horatian satires, a prose tract on the science of medicine, and several plays. His comedy *I Suppositi* was adapted in Gascoigne's *Supposes* (1566), the earliest surviving prose comedy in English, and was one of Shakespeare's sources for *The Taming of the Shrew*.

ARISTAGORAS of Miletus (*fl.* 5th cent. BC), leader of the Greeks at the beginning of the Ionian Revolt against Persia (499–494 BC). He succeeded his father-in-law, Histiaeus, as the Persian-backed tyrant of Miletus, but after failing with the Persians to capture Naxos (500), he decided to exploit the growing discontent of the Ionian Greeks and, after resigning his autocratic power, went to Greece for assistance, failing at Sparta, but obtaining some help from Athens and Eretria. In 496 he abandoned the Greek cause and was killed in Thrace.

ARISTARCHUS of Samos (*c.* 310–230 BC), Greek scientist and thinker, whose rejection of current geocentric views of the universe and suggestion that the earth and the planets revolved round the stationary sun was in turn rejected by Hipparchus of Nicaea, Archimedes, and others.

ARISTARCHUS of Samothrace (*fl.* 2nd cent. BC), Greek scholar and head of the Ptolemaic library at Alexandria (*c.* 153–145 BC), famous for his work in establishing the disputed texts of the early Greek poets, especially Homer.

ARISTIDES (d. *c.* 468 BC), Athenian statesman of aristocratic birth and democratic sympathies, who achieved international repute for his integrity. During the Persian Wars he served as a general at Marathon (490) and as archon (?489). Because of domestic political conflict with Themistocles he was ostracized (?483), but in the second Persian invasion he returned to co-operate with Themistocles and held commands at Salamis (480) and Plataea (479). After Spartan leadership of the Greeks became discredited, he played a major role in organizing the Delian Confederacy under Athenian leadership against Persia, and for his fair assessment of allied war contributions was known as Aristides the Just.

ARISTOPHANES (*c.* 450–385 BC), the greatest Athenian comic dramatist. Of his works some 40 titles are known and 11 plays survive. In the period of the 'Old Comedy' he achieved fame by exploiting topical events, ideas, and personalities for frequently coarse and farcical humour. Conservative in social and political outlook, he portrayed Socrates, Euripides, and democratic leaders such as Cleon unfavourably. Throughout the Peloponnesian War he maintained consistently anti-war themes, especially in the *Lysistrata*. In his last two plays, typical of 'Middle Comedy', the *Ecclesiazusae* (391) and the *Plutus* (388), the interest is rather in the comic situation than in topicalities.

ARISTOTELIANISM represented the acceptance of the philosophical and ethical ideas (which were empirical, as opposed to the idealism of Plato) and of the intellectual method of Aristotle by later generations. Aristotelianism flourished in the eastern Roman empire and thence passed into Islamic thought. In the early Middle Ages knowledge of Aristotle in western Europe was limited to the scientific works, later known as the *Vetus Corpus* (ancient body), and his philosophical and ethical ideas were known only through the medium of the works of Boethius, which were a synthesis of Aristotelianism and Platonism. Aristotelianism proper began in the west with the reception of the *Novum Corpus* (recent body). The *Posterior Analytics* and part of the *Metaphysics* were translated from Arabic versions into Latin in the 12th cent. and the *Nichomachaean Ethics*, the *Poetics*, and a number of lesser works in the 13th cent., especially by William of Moerbecke, whose translations became the standard medieval versions. The reception of these works revolutionized medieval thought and scholarship. They provided both an encyclopedia of knowledge and a model of how to reason. Later medieval theology was Aristotelian, especially in the case of Aquinas and his followers. So likewise was 14th-cent. science. During the Renaissance there came a reaction. The Aristotelian texts used by the medieval scholastics were shown by humanists to be corrupt. The revival of the study of commentaries on Aristotle, written in Antiquity, revealed that he could not be used to justify Christian doctrines (eg, the doubts of Pomponazzi). Aristotelian science, because of its lack of interest in mathematics, was discredited by Galileo.

ARISTOTLE (384–322 BC), Greek philosopher, polymath, and encyclopedist, pupil of Plato, and tutor of Alexander the Great. His speculations were based rather upon material observation than upon abstract contemplation. His practical and analytical approach is seen in his *Ethics* and *Politics*. In the *Metaphysics*, his 'forms' and 'ideas' are a part of, not apart from, physical manifestations. He collected scientific data and created scientific interest in astronomy, meteorology, psychology, and, especially, biology. Besides a handbook on rhetoric he wrote the earliest surviving work on literary and dramatic criticism, the *Poetics*. Interested in correct argumentation, he developed syllogistic reasoning. At Athens he founded a private library and a school, the Lyceum, noted for peripatetic instruction. His methods of criticism, research, and tabulation influenced the founding of the Museum at Alexandria.

ARISTOV, AVERKI BORISOVICH (1903–), Russian Communist Party official and diplomat who gained short-lived importance as a supporter of Khrushchev. He joined the party (1921) and held a number of district posts before becoming a member of the central committee of the CPSU (1952) and of the presidium (1952–3, 1957–61). He backed Khrushchev in the leadership struggle (1957), but his importance declined from the time of the U2 incident (1961). He lost his place in the presidium (Oct. 1961) and was appointed ambassador to Warsaw.

ARIZONA, 48th member state of the US. The first European impact on this region was by Spanish explorers in search of gold (1539) and by missionaries trying to convert the Indians. In the 18th cent. a loose pattern of settlement grew up round the Missions. Although forming part of the Spanish empire in North America, AZ was virtually abandoned to the Indians during the Mexican war for independence (1811–22), after which it became a province of Mexico. Acquired by the US in the treaty of Quadalupe Hidalgo (1848), it became part of the Territory of New Mexico (1860) and a separate Territory (1863). As an important link in communications with the Pacific coast, its position was strengthened by the Gadsden Purchase (1853), which made the Gila valley available for the construction of a transcontinental railroad. Despite mineral resources AZ gained only limited population and did not become a state until 1912. New technology and the climatic attractions of the state as a retirement area have recently stimulated growth.

ARK ROYAL, name of a warship perpetuated in the British and Royal navies from the reign of Elizabeth I to the present day. The original was called the *Ark Raleigh* and was bought by the Crown in 1588 on the eve of the Spanish Armada. The ships carried the flag of the lord high admiral of England, Charles Howard of Effingham. The last, an aircraft carrier, was completed in 1955. Its immediate predecessor, also an aircraft carrier, was sunk by a German U-boat off Gibraltar in Nov. 1941.

ARKANSAS, 25th member state of the US. Originally explored by de Soto (1541), Marquette (1673), and La Salle (1682), early European settlements had little success. Acquired by the US in the Louisiana Purchase (1803) AR became a Territory (1819) and in 1836 its inhabitants drafted a state constitution and successfully applied for admission as a state of the Union. The economic crisis of 1837 stimulated trans-Mississippi migration and this, together with the discovery of coal (1840), and AR's role in east–west communications modified its simple economy based upon cotton, hides, lumber, and Mississippi river traffic. Although a slave state, AR resisted secession until Lincoln's call for troops propelled it into the Confederacy (May 1861). AR underwent military and Republican rule before the Democrats 'redeemed' the government after a factional war (1874). Railroad construction (1860s–90s) opened the way for agricultural diversification and exploitation of the state's rich mineral resources, but until recently industrial development has been slow.

ARKWRIGHT, SIR RICHARD (1732–92), British inventor of the water frame (patented 1769). This invention necessitated the gathering of cotton spinners in a factory organization, and Arkwright established mills at Cromford, Derby, and elsewhere. He made a large fortune and, unlike many early industrialists, became a prominent public figure, being knighted (1786) and appointed high sheriff of Derbyshire (1787).

ARLES, COUNCIL OF (1 Aug. AD 314), summoned by the Emperor Constantine to deal with the Donatist schism. This was the most impressive body of clergy which had ever met in the West and included 33 bishops (3 from Britain), the Donatists and the Caecilianists being represented by 10 each. The council followed the Caecilianists, condemning the African insistence on the rebaptism of reconciled heretics, but its more liberal approach was not accepted by the Donatists; they appealed again to the emperor, who ordered their recalcitrant leaders to be sent to his court. The council also passed 22 canons dealing with abuses resulting from the persecutions.

ARLINGTON, HENRY BENNET, Earl of (1618–85), British secretary of state and a member of the Cabal. While in exile during the Civil War, he formed a friendship with Charles II, which was to prove the basis of his future power. Charles appointed him resident in Spain (1658–61), and though his mission was a failure it provided him with diplomatic skills and an anti-French outlook, which affected his future foreign policy. In 1661 he was recalled to England, where he soon became the centre of opposition to Clarendon. In 1662 he became secretary of state and in 1665 Baron Arlington, and was the principal person concerned with foreign policy even before Clarendon's fall (1667). He was responsible for the Triple Alliance with Sweden and the Netherlands (1668), and controlled the reorganized committee on foreign affairs of the privy council—the Cabal. He and Clifford were the only ministers in Charles's confidence over the secret treaty of Dover (1670), which Arlington personally opposed. In 1672 he became an earl. An attempt by the Commons to impeach him (1674) failed, but with the rise of Danby he lost influence and resigned his secretaryship (Sept. 1674). He was appointed lord chamberlain, which office he retained until his death, though it carried no influence.

ARLINGTON NATIONAL CEMETERY, burial place of many famous Americans, established (1864) as a military cemetery of an estate once owned by the Washington and Lee families. It overlooks Washington, DC, across the Potomac river.

ARMA, name derived from the Arabic word for 'musketeers' and applied to the descendants of the Moroccan military force which conquered Timbuctoo in 1591 and ruled it for the next 150 years. Many were mercenaries of European origin. Their present-day descendants, now physically scarcely distinguishable from other Songhay, form a 'noble' class in Timbuctoo.

ARMADA DE BARLAVENTO, Spanish fleet first established in the 16th cent., the purpose of which was to patrol the approaches to the Caribbean to protect Spanish traders from Dutch and English marauders. Its existence was, however, intermittent owing to the Spanish Crown's permanent shortage of money.

ARMADA, SPANISH (1588), Philip II's attempted invasion of England, would have sailed in the previous year but for Drake's destruction of about 30 ships in Cadiz harbour. A large fleet was ready by the following spring, manned by 8500 sailors and carrying 20,000 soldiers. It consisted of 130 ships, of which about 50 were men-of-war, heavy, high-structured galleons designed for the old kind of sea-fighting in which the object was to lock with an enemy ship and fight a miniature military engagement. The armada was commanded by the Duke of Medina Sidonia, a mild man with no naval experience and further handicapped by his master's specific instructions that he was to attempt no landing until he had sailed up the Channel and made contact with Parma's troops waiting in the Netherlands.

The English, commanded by Lord Howard of Effingham, the lord high admiral, had approximately the same number of ships, but the majority were merchantmen and fishing-boats unequipped for naval fighting. The regular ships of the navy, about 50 in number, were lighter and faster than the Spaniards, and superior in long-range gunnery, but this force had to be divided into two sections, one based on Plymouth to guard the western approaches and the other, under Lord Edward Seymour, stationed off the Downs to keep watch on Parma.

The armada was sighted off the Lizard on 19 July, advancing in a compact crescent formation which negatived the English tactic of line-ahead sailing aimed at concentrating superior power on individual ships. But to keep formation its progress had to be slow, and for nine days there was a running battle up the Channel, with larger engagements off Portland and the Isle of Wight. Forbidden to try to capture an English harbour, Medina Sidonia could only keep steadily on his way, and he anchored off Calais on 27 July with his fleet virtually intact. The Spaniards' discipline and seamanship were of a high order, and the English had been able to make little impression on them.

The fatal flaw in the Spanish plan was that Parma had no friendly harbour where the armada could take refuge, and no armed ships to reinforce it. On the night of the 28th, Howard, joined now by Seymour's division and able for the first time to achieve parity of forces, prepared for the decisive action. At midnight he sent in fire-ships to dislodge the enemy, break their formation, and force them out to sea. The crucial battle was fought off Gravelines on the following day. For eight hours the Spaniards were battered by the English guns, and squalls threatened to drive them on to the Flemish coast. At the end of the battle the armada had virtually ceased to exist as a fighting force.

Medina Sidonia could only make for home. He dared not venture another passage of the Channel, and with the wind now backing to the south-west he attempted to make his way round the north of Scotland. Howard, after pursuing him as far as the Firth of Forth, fell back through lack of provisions and ammunition, and once in the open sea the Spanish ships were shattered by the Atlantic gales and thrown on to rocky coasts. Less than half got home.

The defeat of the armada was not the end of the war, still less the end of Spain as a fighting power. The conquered learned their lesson so well that in the next decade they were able to deny the English any substantial success at sea. Naval tactics would never again consist of short-range gunnery as a prelude to boarding and hand-to-hand fighting on deck.

G. Mattingly, *The Defeat of the Spanish Armada* (London, 1959). MR

ARMAGH, BOOK OF, illustrated volume, compiled in 807 by Ferdomach, containing the New Testament and materials connected with Armagh and St Patrick. It is less ornate than the Book of Kells, but beautifully decorated and written.

ARMAGNACS. One of the factions contending for power in the French civil war in the early 15th cent. They were the followers of the Duke of Orléans. Louis, the first duke, was the younger brother of the mad king, Charles VI (1380–1422), and was the effective ruler of France until his cousin John, Duke of Burgundy killed him (1407). In the ensuing civil war the leadership of resistance to the Duke of Burgundy was assumed by Bernard VII, Count of Armagnac, father-in-law of Charles, the second Duke of Orléans, hence the name of the Armagnacs assumed by the anti-Burgundian party. The English took advantage of this situation to invade France, but even this did not heal the rift between the warring French factions, though a token truce was made at Arras in 1413. At the crucial battle of Agincourt against the English (1415) John of Burgundy kept the bulk of his forces aloof from the battlefield. Although the Armagnacs retained control of Paris after Agincourt, the essential advantage was henceforward enjoyed by John of Burgundy, who collaborated with the English invaders and captured Paris in 1418, killing Bertrand of Armagnac. In 1419 John himself was killed by the heir to the Crown, the future King Charles VII (1422–61), and the Armagnac factions was merged with Charles's pro-royalist followers.

ARMED NEUTRALITIES. In 1691 the first armed neutrality was formed between Sweden and Denmark–Norway in retaliation against English and Dutch naval attempts to prevent Sweden from trading with France during the War of the League of Augsburg.

In 1780 and 1800 leagues of neutral powers were organized by Russia on two occasions against the British challenge to their naval supremacy during their wars with France. Catherine the Great of Russia formed the first league (1780) during the American War of Independence, persuading the Scandinavian and remaining neutral powers, Austria, Prussia, and Portugal, to join it. Russia's aim was to break the British control of her foreign trade. Realizing that the British depended for their naval stores on supplies from the Baltic, Catherine hoped that by excluding them from it she would force the British to accept the neutrals' interpretation of their 'maritime rights'. The league demanded freedom to sail along the coasts of belligerent powers, to enter their ports, and to carry belligerents' goods in their ships. It also sought to ban the British practice of 'paper' blockades, claiming that only 'effective' ones could be regarded as legal. The British had infringed all these 'rights' and were unlikely to admit them without complete naval defeat. In practice this first league had little effect on British attitudes or actions.

The second league, formed by Tsar Paul towards the end of the War of the Second Coalition (1800), had identical aims, although only the Scandinavian powers and Prussia joined it. This time the effects on Britain were most serious, causing food riots. But the league broke up after a year, when the British forced an entry into the Baltic, destroying the Danish fleet at Copenhagen (April 1801), a week after the assassination of Tsar Paul. The new tsar, Alexander I, was eager to come to terms with Britain, and an Anglo-Russian convention was signed in June.

ARMENIA, kingdom situated in mountainous country southeast of the Black Sea. Previously subjects of the Seleucids, the natives declared their independence after the Roman victory over Antiochus III (189 BC), but the expansionist Tigranes II was defeated by Lucullus and Pompey (72–64 BC) and Armenia became a buffer state between Romans and Persians (Parthians). Nero recognized Tiridates (AD 66) of the Persian royal family, the Arsacids, who ruled to the end of Armenian independence (387), balancing the two powers. After Tiridates III's conversion to Christianity (c. 290), a national church was established. Conquered by the Arabs in 654, Armenia again flourished under vassal Bagratid kings (885–1080).

ARMENIAN MASSACRES. In 1894–6 demands for better treatment led to massacres of Armenians in eastern Asia Minor (estimated dead, 50,000–350,000) by Kurdish irregulars and Ottoman troops. These were stopped by the major European powers, but in 1915–16 Ottoman suspicions of Armenian loyalty led to further massacres and deportations (estimated dead, 1,500,000).

ARMENIAN NATIONALISM began as a cultural movement in the 18th cent., but took on a radical, political aspect in later 19th cent., following major educational advances in the Armenian communities of Russia and the Ottoman empire. Sporadic Armenian revolts against Ottoman power took place and émigré Russian Armenian revolutionaries formed societies (Hunchak, 1887; Dashnak, 1890) advocating an armed struggle for Armenian autonomy within the Ottoman Empire. Dashnak also resisted Russification in Russian Armenia

(1903–5). Most Armenians within the Ottoman empire remained uninterested until they were inevitably drawn into the conflict through the activities of the revolutionaries and the suspicions of the Ottoman government, especially after 1914, when massacres and deportations almost obliterated the Armenian community in Asia Minor. In 1918–19 Armenians demanded an independent Armenia from the Mediterranean to the Caspian. The allies accepted a much attenuated form of this proposal at Sèvres (1920), but the US refused the mandate and the Turkish nationalists regained control of Asia Minor and crushed the Armenian Republic, which passed under Soviet control (1920).

ARMFELDT, CHARLES, Baron d' (1666–1736), Swedish general who fought the Russians in Finland after Poltava. He was defeated by Apraxin's army at Storkyvo (1714) and after Nystadt (1721) he returned to Finland to reorganize the troops of this province.

ARMINIUS, JACOB HERMANDZOON (1560–1609), Dutch scholar and founder of the Arminian Church, who first seriously challenged Calvinism. He was trained at Geneva under Beza and ordained as a minister at Amsterdam in 1588, where he was called upon by the Church to refute the ideas of Coornaert, who had criticized the orthodox Calvinist doctrine of predestination. Arminius came to sympathize with rather than condemn Coornaert's views and the dispute between Arminius and Peter Plancius and his Calvinist supporters caused a great stir. In 1603 Arminius was appointed professor of theology at Leyden, a controversial choice opposed by Francis Gomar. Arminius defended his beliefs at a special meeting of the states general at the Hague in 1608.

After his death Arminianism survived, his followers being known as Remonstrants, from their presentation of a remonstrance to the states general in 1610. Arminianism became an inflammatory political issue, complicated by the rivalry between Maurice of Nassau and John of Oldenbarneveldt, a member of the Remonstrant party. The Synod of Dort (1618) condemned Arminianism, Oldenbarnevelt was executed, and Grotius, another Arminian, imprisoned.

ARMISTICE, 1918. The most important negotiations bringing the First World War to an end were those leading to an armistice between Germany on the one side and Britain, France, and the US on the other. They were opened by a German note on 3 Oct. appealing to President Wilson for an armistice—a note which resulted from Ludendorff's fear of imminent military collapse. The note, signed by Prince Max of Baden, as imperial chancellor, accepted as a basis for peace negotiations Wilson's speech of 8 Jan. 1918 (which included his fourteen points) and his subsequent pronouncements, especially the speech of 27 Sept. Before consenting to open discussions with the Allies, Wilson sought assurances from the German government on their acceptance of the Fourteen Points and on the military terms of the armistice. These assurances were given in the German note of 20 Oct. There then followed a period of discussion within and between the governments of Britain, France, and the US, in which the two former agreed, under the threat of a separate peace, to negotiate on the basis of the Fourteen Points (of which House, as presidential adviser, had given an accommodating interpretation) subject to reservations of the freedom of the seas and claims to reparations. At the same time, the military terms were agreed. They were designed both to prevent a renewal of German capability to wage war and to shape the main lines of a peace settlement; they were agreed, with minor concessions, with the German envoys at Réthondes and the armistice, signed at Compiègne at 5.12 a.m. on 11 Nov., came into force at 11 a.m. The terms required German withdrawal from Belgium, France, Luxemburg, and Alsace-Lorraine within 15 days and a further withdrawal east of a Rhineland neutral zone within 31 days; the surrender of stipulated equipment; occupation by Allied troops up to the Rhine, and bridgeheads across the Rhine at Mainz, Coblenz,

and Cologne; the surrender of all German submarines and the internment in neutral or Allied ports of six battle cruisers, ten battleships, eight light cruisers, and fifty destroyers; and finally, the continuation of the blockade.

Ludendorff had recommended that the negotiation of the armistice should be undertaken by civilians and that the German government should be given a wider and more democratic character. By the time the armistice was signed the Kaiser had been forced to abdicate and popular movements threatened to break through control by the government.

The German armistice was the decisive event in the conclusion of the war, after the withdrawal of Russia. The surrender of Austria–Hungary had already taken place at Villa Giusti, being effective from 4 Nov.; Austro-Hungarian troops were to be demobilized and the victors were given full and free accesss to Austro-Hungarian means of communication. The capitulation of the Ottoman empire had occurred at the end of Oct. and an armistice was signed at Mudros on 30 Oct.

ARMISTICE, FRANCO-GERMAN (22 June 1940), signed in the same railway carriage at Compiègne as had been used for the armistice of 1918. The agreement provided for the occupation of the greater part of France, including the whole of the Channel and Atlantic coasts, leaving an unoccupied zone in the south. The French army was to be disarmed and demobilized under German supervision in French ports— a provision which alarmed the British, who had hoped that it would escape German control, and led to the incident of Mers el-Kébir. France agreed to pay the costs of the army of occupation and French prisoners were to be kept in Germany until the conclusion of peace—conditions which gave Germany an unforeseen hold over France in the ensuing years of the war.

ARMOUR, MEDIEVAL. Various types of 'soft' armour— leather or quilted garments—were in use throughout western Europe in the medieval period, being worn especially by footsoldiers, but in the period c. 600–1250 armour as such consisted of a sleeved mail shirt (hauberk) with or without a mail hood (coif), and mail leggings. A conical metal helmet with a nasal guard was in common use from the 10th to the mid-13th cent., but after c. 1200 the most popular headpieces were the steel skull-cap or bascinet, frequently worn under the coif, and the kettle hat. Contemporary illustrations of plate defences for the shins, knees, thighs, and elbows appear c. 1250, but plate was not universally adopted until c. 1330, possibly because it could stop high-velocity arrows at a time when archery was beginning to make significant advances on the battlefield. A leather or cloth garment lined with metal plates and known as a coat of plates became increasingly common after c. 1320 and this, together with a rudimentary breast plate, complete plate leg-harness, and part-plate arm defences and gauntlets, became the most widely used body defence of the 14th cent. Effigies and brasses show the rapid dissemination of this style of armour. The visored helm and bascinet were the main types of headpiece at this time. The second decade of the 15th cent. saw the completely developed 'white' armour, in which mail was scarcely used at all, and which gave exceptionally good protection, with the sallet, a lighter headpiece. Thereafter two great schools of armourers emerged, in northern Italy and Germany, which developed their own distinctive styles. The period 1410–1500 saw the flowering of the armourers' craft and some of the armour produced to order for the nobility and used in the joust or on the battlefield are superb works of craftsmanship.

ARMS TRADE CONVENTION (1925), drawn up at the International Conference on the Control of International Trade in Arms, Munitions, and Implements of War (May– June 1925). It described categories of armaments whose export to specified areas was to be restricted and controlled by a licence system. Unless requested by the power exercising sovereignty or a protectorate, no arms other than warships could be exported to Africa or the Middle East, except for South Africa, Abyssinia, French and Spanish North Africa, and Egypt. The convention expanded the League of Nations' provisions for mandated territories. Partly owing to America's abstention, it failed to bring arms traffic under league control.

ARMSTRONG, LOUIS (1900–), US jazz trumpeter, singer, and band leader. His professional career began in New Orleans (1917) and after playing with leading Chicago and New York bands he formed his own group (1925). An important soloist and innovator, he has exerted considerable influence on the development of jazz.

ARMSTRONG, NEIL (1930–), first man on the moon. He joined NASA in 1955, and performed the first orbital docking manœuvre (1962). As commander of Apollo 11, he set foot on the moon on 21 July 1969, being followed by Edwin Aldrin (1930–).

ARMY, THE NEW ZEALAND. British regiments bore the brunt of the Maori Wars, but various colonial forces were raised to assist them: district militia, a small regular force, soldier-settlers, ranger companies, and, later, an armed constabulary. After the wars, district volunteer corps continued rather ineffectually until 1910, when compulsory training was introduced. A territorial force of 30,000 was raised, and formed the core of NZ's expeditionary force (1914–18). This system became a casualty of the Depression, but by 1939 11,000 volunteers were in training. Conscription (1940) raised 80,000 troops for service overseas by the end of the Second World War. Since 1961 there has been universal registration and selection by ballot of an annual intake of about 3000. In the middle 1960s, NZ aimed to maintain a field force, including a battalion in Malaysia and a small detachment in Viet-nam, and a static support force (about 16,000).

ARMY REFORMS (CARDWELL). Reform of the British army had been actively under discussion at least since the time of the Crimean War, but had been blocked partly by the opposition of the Duke of Cambridge as commander-in-chief and by vested interests within the army, and partly by the tradition of fiscal economy. Reform was at last vigorously tackled by Cardwell, secretary for war in Gladstone's first ministry. He abolished flogging in time of peace (1868), shortened the period of service from 12 years to 6 with the colours and to 6 with the reserves, thus vastly improving conditions of service and the quality of recruits, and making a trained reserve possible. He reorganized the regiments on a territorial basis, that is into the county regiments of today, and introduced the system of linked battalions, whereby one battalion was at the depot while the other was on foreign service. Greater obstacles were presented by the reform of the higher command. Cardwell succeeded in subordinating the commander-in-chief to the secretary for war (1870) and was then able to reorganize the war office. The decisive struggle came over the abolition of purchase of commissions. This time-honoured system was defended fiercely, and Cardwell's Army Regulation Bill was defeated in the House of Lords (1871). Purchase was abolished in the same year by royal warrant. The combined effect of these reforms was seen in the greatly improved efficiency of the colonial campaigns of the later 19th cent.

ARNALDO DA BRESCIA (d. 1155), religious reformer and scholar. He was involved in the condemnation of Abelard for unorthodox teaching in 1140, and also in the Roman revolution against the papacy (1145). His forceful preaching, ascetic life, and religious idealism gained him a large following. When Rome was reconquered for the pope by the Emperor Frederick Barbarossa, Arnaldo was executed.

ARNAULD, ANGÉLIQUE (1591–1661), French nun, appointed an abbess at the age of seven. She was converted to a strict view of her duties (1609), passed under the influence of St Cyran (1636), and played an important role in Jansenist organization and controversy.

ARNAULD, ANTOINE (1612–94), the leading French theologian of the first phase of Jansenism. The youngest son of the 20 children of Antoine Arnauld the elder, he was noted for his piety from an early age. He was trained as a lawyer, but turned to theology in the Sorbonne (1635). Assailed by doubts about his vocation, he consulted St Cyran, who confirmed him in his resolve and as a result he became a priest, and a doctor of the Sorbonne (1641). On the death of St Cyran (1640) he became the animator of the Jansenists and wrote *De la fréquente communion* (1643), which soon became a source of controversy and led to his exclusion from the Sorbonne (1656). He went into retirement and gave himself up to writing and teaching grammar, and although he helped Pascal, he came out in favour of signing the Formulary. He later renewed his controversies with the Jesuits (1668) and eventually had to retire to the Spanish Netherlands (1677), only returning to France after the solution of the *régale* dispute. His last years were given over to attacks on Calvinism. A man of great integrity and fervour, he gave Jansenism much of its harsh and rigid character.

ARNAULD, HENRI (1597–1692), elder brother of Antoine, who, although nominated to a canonry, served as a diplomatic agent in Italy until he was elected Bp of Angers (1649). A saintly bishop, he became a leading Jansenist and held out against accepting the Formulary until Sept. 1668.

ARNAULD DE POMPONNE, SIMON NICOLAS (1618–99), French diplomat and minister of foreign affairs under Louis XIV. Son of Arnauld d'Andilly, he made his debut as a writer and only later did he enter royal service (1643), through the patronage of Le Tellier, serving as *conseiller d'état* (1644), military *intendant*, and envoy in Italy (1654). He fell into disfavour (1662) because he married Fouquet's cousin and was recalled and sent as ambassador first to Sweden (1666), then to Holland (1667–8), then to Sweden again (1670). He was raised to ministerial rank and entrusted with the direction of foreign affairs (1672), in which he pursued a policy of moderation which eventually led Louvois to secure his dismissal (1678). He remained influential and was recalled to office on the death of Louvois (1690).

ARNE, THOMAS AUGUSTINE (1710–78), British composer, whose works include 'Rule Britannia', 'Judith' (the first oratoria in England for women's voices), and Shakespearian songs, *eg*, 'Where the bee sucks'.

ARNESON, NICHOLAS (*c.* 1145–1225), Norwegian cleric who held political control of Oslo during a period of weak monarchical rule.

ARNHEM, scene of a Second World War battle (Sept. 1944) which developed from an attack launched by a British airborne division to capture the Arnhem bridge over the Rhine. The attack was defeated by the slowness of its advance from the drop to the bridge and the rapidity with which Gen. Model organized the German defence, with reserves stronger than the British had estimated. The strong resistance encountered by the relieving army coming from Nymwegen contributed to the British difficulties. The failure of the attack finally dispelled any hope of victory before the winter; Arnhem was taken in April 1945.

ARNIM, HANS GEORG VON (1581–1641), mercenary general in the Thirty Years War. A native of Brandenburg and a deeply religious Protestant, he rose to become one of Wallenstein's best commanders and was largely responsible for Wallenstein's victorious Silesian campaign (1627). He left the imperial service after the Edict of Restitution and became commander of the Saxon forces, resigning after the peace of Prague (1635).

ARNOLD, BENEDICT (1741–1801), American turncoat. With Ethan Allen he captured Fort Ticonderoga on Lake Champlain, but failed to take Que. (1775). After successfully defending Ticonderoga (1776) he relieved Fort Stanwix and with Horatio Gates defeated the British at Saratoga (1777). Although enjoying Washington's confidence his promotion was slow. This, and attacks on his conduct in Canada, he much resented, and when given command in Philadelphia he began passing military information to the British (1779). Being deeply in debt, he arranged for his transfer to West Point, and then offered to surrender this key position for £20,000. The plot being discovered, he fled to the British (1780) and as a British officer led raids in CT and VA. He left for England in 1781 and in the US his name became a byword for treachery.

ARNOLD, MATTHEW (1822–8), poet and critic, and son of Thomas Arnold. He strongly criticized, particularly in *Culture and Anarchy* (1869), the vulgar and commercial culture of his day. While sceptical of the literal inspiration of the Bible, and of much religious dogma, he valued the 'sweetness and light' of Christian culture.

ARNOLD, THOMAS (1795–1842), schoolmaster and historian. As headmaster of Rugby (1828–42), he initiated educational reforms in school organization, ethical standards, and curriculum. He gave a status to modern history, while remaining himself a distinguished ancient historian. His lectures at Oxford as regius professor of modern history (1841–2) discussed research techniques and the nature and philosophy of history, ultimately influencing history teaching in universities and schools in the late 19th cent.

ARNULF THE GREAT, Count of Flanders (*reg.* 918–65), a ruthless warrior who had his enemies assassinated, and consolidated the principality created by his father, Baldwin II. His most important success was the acquisition of several territories to the south of Flanders, including Artois, annexed in 932.

ARNULF, King of Germany (*reg.* 887–99), Emperor (*reg.* (896–9). Grandson of King Louis the German. He won renown by defeating the Vikings near Louvain in 891, but his encouragement of the Hungarian attack on the Slavonic state of Great Moravia opened up western Europe to disastrous Hungarian raids.

ARO CHUKU ORACLE, or Chuku Ibinokpabi or 'Long Juju', the leading Ibo Oracle, also consulted by non-Ibos from the Lower Niger delta and Cross river for arbitration, particularly in disputed cases. The oracle was destroyed by the Aro Field Force, 1901–2, but continued to wield influence for some time.

AROOSTOOK WAR, a series of bloodless clashes between Americans and Canadians (Feb.–May 1839) in the disputed border area between ME and NB along the Aroostook river. A truce was arranged by General Winfield Scott (US) and Sir John Harvey, lieutenant-governor of New Brunswick (1839). The dispute ended when the boundary was settled by the Webster–Ashburton treaty of 1842.

ARPÁD DYNASTY, first and only native Hungarian dynasty descended from Arpád, who led his people into modern Hungary in 895–6. His descendants ruled Hungary until the death of Andrew III (1301). Perhaps the greatest Arpád was St Stephen, patron saint of Hungary and king from 997 to 1038. Stephen was recognized as Christian king by the pope in 1000, after which Hungary was accepted among the kingdoms of Europe. Stephen's more able successors, notably Bela III, Stephen II, Andrew II, and Bela IV, were able to achieve a gradual expansion of territory into surrounding areas, making Hungary the strongest state in south-eastern Europe. In two centuries the area of Hungary almost doubled with the absorption of Transylvania, Slavonia, and Croatia. But the kings had to tolerate the growth of a strong magnate class, and after the last two Arpáds (1273–1301) the country was in the grip of a noble clique.

ARQUEBUS, forerunner of the rifle, the first hand-gun requiring only one man to fire it. It was operated by a mechanical lock that applied the match to the priming-pan. Its first use in England was by German mercenaries at St Albans (1461). It was effective up to about 50 yards and was the standard infantry weapon until the 17th cent.

ARQUES, BATTLE OF (21 Sept. 1589), resulted in victory for Henry IV of France over the Duke of Mayenne and the larger army of the Catholic League near Dieppe. After repulsing Mayenne's assault on his entrenchments, Henry was able to resume his advance on Paris.

ARRAPKHA (mod. Kirkuk), Assyrian garrison town and strategic province east of the Tigris. Nearby, at Nuzi, were found tablets giving important information on Assyria and Mitanni in the 14th cent. BC.

ARRAS, *chef-lieu* of the *Pas de Calais*, historic French town in northern France. It was a tribal capital in Roman times and a Flemish town until 1180. In the later Middle Ages it was noted for its money-lenders, its production of high-quality light-weight cloth, and its tapestries. Later it fell into decline and passed under Burgundian rule. Its walls were razed by Louis XI (1477), after which it became a Spanish possession (1492). It was recaptured for France by Louis XIII (1640), was the scene of fighting during the Fronde, and was recognized as French by the peace of the Pyrenees (1659).

ARRAS, BATTLES OF. A battle fought on 24–5 Aug. 1654 was a victory for the French under Turenne over Condé and the Spaniards, when the former broke through the Spanish lines, forcing them to withdraw and abandon their projected invasion of France. A second battle (April 1917) during the First World War was a preliminary to the Nivelle offensive and one of the most successful, if costly, British Commonwealth engagements on the Western Front. Canadian troops captured Vimy Ridge, and this was to be of vital importance in holding the German offensive of March 1918. British Commonwealth casualties were 84,000, German 75,000.

Thirdly, in 1940, an engagement during the Second World War between the Germans and a British armoured brigade at Arras may have contributed to the delay in the German advance, which in turn made possible the evacuation from Dunkirk.

ARRAS, UNION OF (Jan. 1579), alliance of the Walloon provinces of the southern Netherlands formed in self-defence against the Calvinist revolution in the cities of Flanders and Brabant. In June the nobility of the union concluded a treaty with Philip II of Spain, renewing their allegiance and promising to re-establish Catholicism in return for the restoration of their ancient provincial and aristocratic privileges. The Union of Arras forced the northern provinces to react by forming their own defensive union.

ARRAY, COMMISSIONS OF. Beginning with the Assize of Arms (1181) and developed fully by the Statute of Winchester (1285), this was the system of levying, county by county, men at arms below the rank of knight, who were used to fight against rebellion in or invasion of England.

ARRET, formal judicial decision in French law. Before 1789 the sovereign's judicial power was exercised through a variety of corporate bodies and individuals whose official verdicts, whether on legal, administrative, or political matters, all took this form.

ARRETS OF MARLY (1711), French royal decrees intended to encourage emigration to Canada by liberalizing land tenure and modifying the seigneurial system.

ARRIAN (*fl.* 2nd cent. AD), Greek historian whose *Anabasis*, derived from Ptolemy and another contemporary, Aristobulus, is the most substantial and best source of information on the conquests of Alexander the Great.

ARROW CROSS, largest of the Hungarian National Socialist parties, which came into existence in the 1930s. The Arrow Cross's founder and leader was the nationalist, Ferencz Szalasi, who developed the idea of 'Hungarism', calling for the restitution of the frontiers of the old kingdom and a dominant position for the Magyar race. Support for the Hungarist idea was strengthened by several factors—the territorial loss resulting from the treaty of Trianon, the Jewish domination of industry and finance, the anti-communism of the middle class, and the need for social reform all played their part. By 1938, the Arrow Cross's agitation had reached alarming proportions and the government decided to arrest Szalasi. This served only to make him a martyr. In the elections of 1939 his party polled 750,000 out of a possible 2 million votes (although allowance must be made for the fact that the illegal Communist Party had advised its supporters to vote for the Arrow Cross). During the war, many grew to suspect the party of serving German interests and membership fluctuated widely. In 1944 Szalasi was placed in power by the Germans after Horthy had requested an armistice. By this time, however, Soviet troops were already on Hungarian soil. The Arrow Cross held office for only a few months as a vehicle for German rule. The party had enjoyed widespread support, but had always suffered from internal division, and, but for the Germans, would never have come to power.

ARROW INCIDENT (8 Oct. 1856), the *casus belli* of the Second Sino-Foreign War (1856–60), occurred when the lorcha *Arrow*, anchored at Canton, was boarded by Chinese officers and all its crew were arrested on suspicion of an act of piracy. Although the *Arrow* was owned by a Chinese and had a Chinese crew, its captain was British, it was registered at Hong Kong, and flew the British flag. Harry S. Parkes, British consul at Canton, protested to Yeh Ming-ch'ên, the governor-general, that the crew was entitled to British protection and that the Union Jack had been hauled down. He demanded the release of the crew and an apology for insulting the British flag. Yeh delivered 9 of the crew of 12 to the British consulate on 14 Oct., explaining that 3 were detained for further examination, but he made no apologies, the Chinese claiming that the Union Jack was not hoisted at the time of the incident. Parkes refused to accept the 9 sailors and on 22 Oct. Yeh, under pressure, delivered all the crew. But again they were rejected by Parkes because they were not handed over in the manner which he had prescribed. Five days later, Parkes ordered the British navy to fight its way to Canton and bombarded Yeh's yamen with one gun at ten-minute intervals, but to no avail. The British government thereupon decided to send an expeditionary force, and were joined by the French, who found a *casus belli* in the execution of a missionary for travelling in the interior of China, which he had had no right to do.

The aims of the expedition went beyond the settlement of the *Arrow* affair. The American treaty of Wanghia (1844) had provided for the revision of China's treaties with the Powers. This Yeh had persistently refused. Furthermore, the Cantonese vehemently denied Westerners entry into the walled city of Canton, as provided for by the treaty of Nanking (1842). The *Arrow* incident and the execution of the French missionary thus provided the cause for insisting on improved relations with China on Western terms. The expeditionary forces took Canton on 29 Dec. 1857 and then proceeded directly to Tientsin, where they secured the treaty of Tientsin (June 1858). A year later, the British and French ministers were refused passage to Peking for the treaty's ratification, and in 1860 a second expedition was despatched. The British and French troops took Peking in Oct. of that year and the treaty of Tientsin was finally ratified.

H. B. Morse, *The International Relations of the Chinese Empire*, 3 vols (London, 1910–18). DP

ARSACID, dynasty which ruled Iran during the Parthian period (*c.* 240 BC–AD 224). The dynasty was founded by the chief of the Parni tribe, Arsaces, but the real founder of the empire was Mithridates I (171–140 BC), who ruled an area extending from India in the east to Mesopotamia in the west. At first, the Arsacid kings remained nomadic, depending on the Parthian nobility and existing institutions, mostly Greek, for government. They were content to accept tribute and homage from conquered rulers. Similarly, they tolerated religions other than their own and the Jews regarded them as protectors. The lack of centralized government limited the king's authority and gradually the nobility became the real power in the land. Towards the end of the period, perhaps as a reaction to constant wars with Rome and the dominance of the Kushans in the east, Iranian influences revived and replaced Greek. The dynasty ended with Artabanus V, who was defeated by the Sasanian, Ardashir, in 224.

'ARSENAL OF DEMOCRACY', a phrase used by President F. D. Roosevelt (29 Dec. 1940) to describe the role that a non-belligerent US could play in the Second World War. Following Roosevelt's statement that he hoped to be able to 'eliminate the dollar sign' in British–American trade (17 Dec. 1940), it foreshadowed the policy of Lend-Lease (March 1941).

ARSENAL OF VENICE, shipbuilding yard operated by the Venetian state. It had seemed so dark, noisy, and filthy to Dante that he compared it to a chasm of Hell filled with pitch. About 1500 it was the largest industrial enterprise in Europe, employing up to 2000 men.

ARSUF, BATTLE OF (7 Sept. 1191). After its capture of Acre on 12 July 1191 the Third Crusade advanced southwards to menace Jerusalem, constantly harassed by Saladin's army. At Arsuf, where the ground particularly favoured him, Saladin attacked but was repelled. The battle ended all serious danger to the Crusaders but was otherwise inconclusive and the Third Crusade ended in 1192 without any other lasting achievement.

ARTABANUS V (*reg. c.* 213–24), last Parthian King of Iran, who twice defeated the Romans and re-established the Iranian frontier on the Euphrates, but was defeated and killed in battle by the Sasanian, Ardashir.

ARTAGNAN, CHARLES DE BATZ-CASTELMORE D' (*c.* 1610–73), French captain of guards under Louis XIV and the prototype of Dumas's hero. As a member of a poor Armagnac family, he came to Paris to seek his fortune (1640), entered the army and served in Flanders, later being transferred to the Royal Musketeers (1644). He became attached to Mazarin (1646) and emerged as one of his most trusted lieutenants during the Fronde, for which he was rewarded by a captaincy in the Royal Guards (1655). He served Louis XIV in the same capacity and was responsible for the arrest of Fouquet (1662).

ARTAPHERNES (Artaphrenes) (*fl.* 5th cent. BC), commander, with Datis, of the Persian expedition against Eretria and Athens, which was defeated at Marathon (490 BC), after winning over Naxos and other Aegean islands and sacking Carystus and Eretria. Artaphernes' father-in-law (of the same name), brother of Darius I and satrap at Sardis during the Ionian Revolt (499–494), was responsible for its suppression and the subsequent settlement.

ARTAXERXES I (*reg. c.* 465–424 BC), Achaemenid King of Iran, whose reign saw the first indications of the break-up of the empire. He began by quelling a revolt led by one of his brothers in Bactria and killing all of them. A rebellion in Egypt was only suppressed with difficulty. In Greece Artaxerxes followed a policy, not always successful, of provoking enmity between Athens and Sparta. In Babylonia, the land and administration came increasingly into Iranian hands. He continued to allow the Jews to return to Judah.

ARTAXERXES II (*reg. c.* 404–359 BC), Achaemenid King of Iran. At the start of his reign he defeated a rebellion by his brother, Cyrus. He bribed Sparta, Athens, and Thebes to fight each other and forced the submission of the Ionian Greeks. A successful revolt in Egypt during his reign resulted in that province establishing its temporary independence of Achaemenid authority, but an Egyptian-assisted revolt of the satraps of Asia Minor collapsed when Egyptian support was withdrawn.

ARTAXERXES III (*reg. c.* 359–338 BC), Achaemenid King of Iran, who started his reign by murdering all his siblings and quelling a revolt of the satraps. A Phoenician revolt was ended with the destruction of Sidon and he then invaded and conquered lower Egypt, but the Egyptian king retained control of the south. The last years of his reign were occupied with intrigues between Iran, Athens, and the growing power of Macedonia. He was eventually murdered.

ARTAXIAS (*fl.* 2nd cent. BC), King of Armenia Major. He was considered the founder of historical Armenia and became king after the battle of Magnesia (189 BC), when the Romans defeated the Seleucid King, Antiochus III, and founded Armenia Major and Minor. An attempt by Artaxias to unite the two parts failed (165 BC).

ARTEMISIUM, BATTLE OF (480 BC), the first naval action of the Persian invasion of Greece. While the army held Thermopylae, the Greek fleet under Eurybiadas waited in narrow waters off Cape Artemisium in northern Euboea, to protect the army's flank and perhaps in hope of a decisive victory. Some details of Herodotus' narrative are obscure, but, though the actual fighting was inconclusive, the Persians, forced first to sail along the Thessalian coast to the bay of Pagasae, then to attempt to envelop the Greeks from the south, lost many ships through storms. When the Persian army penetrated Thermopylae, the Greek fleet withdrew to Salamis, more confident of eventual victory.

ARTHASHASTRA, basic ancient Indian text on statecraft, written in Sanskrit and ascribed to Kautilya or Canakya, chief minister of King Chandragupta Maurya (*c.* 320–290 BC). It has been demonstrated, however, that at least the major part of the present text, though undoubtedly based on an earlier prototype, must be a few centuries younger. The text gives, often in a rather pedantic manner, advice on how a king, naturally bent upon increasing his power, should rule his kingdom. Many sections deal with related topics, such as social and political institutions, or give information about, *eg*, ancient Indian technology. In many cases, however, it is difficult for the historian to distinguish between what actually existed at the time when the text was composed and what was deemed desirable.

ARTHUR III, Duke of Brittany (1393–1458), younger member of the Breton ducal house, who is known as Arthur de Richemont. For a period he sided with England in the Hundred Years War, but in 1425 he became Charles VII's constable of France. He was instrumental in bringing about the reconciliation between France and Burgundy in 1435 which ensured France's ultimate victory over England, and he was also largely responsible for a reorganization of the French army (1444–5), which contributed vitally to that victory. Through the death of his relatives he became, unex-

pectedly, near the end of his life Duke of Brittany (1457) but reigned for only 15 months.

ARTHUR, Prince (1486–1502), eldest son of Henry VII of England and Elizabeth of York. His betrothal to Catherine of Aragon, daughter of Ferdinand and Isabella, was negotiated by a treaty of 1489. However, Arthur died suddenly in 1502, five months after his marriage, leaving the succession to his younger brother Henry.

ARTHUR (d. *c.* 537), 6th-cent. British leader against the Anglo-Saxons. Celtic fairy story and chivalric romance combined in the 12th cent. to produce the legendary Arthur, King of Britain. The legend was developed in France and England, notably in Malory's *Morte d'Arthur* in the 15th cent. and Tennyson's *Idylls of the King* (1842–85).

ARTHUR OF BRITTANY (1187–1204), son of Constance, heiress to the duchy of Brittany, and Geoffrey, elder brother of King John of England. Arthur, who was both the symbol of Breton independence and a threat to John, was captured by William de Braose in 1202 and handed over to John, who probably had him murdered in 1204.

ARTHUR, CHESTER ALAN (1830–86), US president (1881–4). Before his election as Republican vice-president (1880) he was a collector at the New York custom house. He succeeded to the US presidency on the death of James Garfield. His administration was honest and efficient, if unexceptional, and he was not renominated in 1884.

ARTHUR, SIR GEORGE (1784–1854), British army officer, colonial administrator, and governor of the penal settlement in Van Diemen's Land (1825–38). He was appointed lieutenant-governor of Upper Canada, the last to hold this post, at the end of the rebellion of 1837. By severe measures and by calling out the militia to discourage sympathetic Americans from crossing the border, he eradicated armed opposition in Canada.

ARTICLES OF CONFEDERATION, first constitution of the US (1781–9). The concept of union between the 13 colonies had received intermittent expression at least since 1754, and the Continental Congress began to exercise de facto governmental powers before independence, but the states continued to act independently of each other for several years. Following a proposal in Congress (7 June 1776) by Richard Henry Lee, a committee under the chairmanship of John Dickinson proposed a draft constitution providing for a strong central government (July 1776). Although the states were to retain control over their internal affairs, all other powers, except the right to levy taxes and customs duties, were implicitly granted to Congress. Debate on this draft constitution continued until 1777.

The final version differed radically from the draft in that each state was to retain its 'sovereignty, freedom, and independence', and 'every power, jurisdiction, and right' not expressly delegated to Congress. Other provisions gave the states equal voting rights in Congress, and required each state to give 'full faith and credit' to the judicial proceedings of other states. But despite the grant of numerous powers to Congress, this constitution, the Articles of Confederation, contained crucial weaknesses. Congress was not authorized to establish its own judicial system, except in maritime affairs. It lacked the power to tax and depended for revenue on appropriations from the states. It had no authority to regulate commerce. No provision was made for the establishment of a separate executive. Above all, unanimous consent of the states was necessary for amendment of the constitution. Although the Articles of Confederation asserted that a perpetual union had been established, it was little more than a 'league of friendship' between the states. The powers granted to Congress were essentially only those it already exercised and the states remained supreme.

The articles had been ratified by most states by 1779, but did not come into effect until 1781, as Maryland refused ratification until control of the western lands had been transferred from the states to Congress. The weaknesses of the articles became apparent during the Critical Period, but they probably represented the strongest form of union that could have been achieved during the early years of independence.

M. Jensen, *Articles of Confederation* (Madison, WI, 1941).

ARTICLES OF RELIGION, various formularies of the Church of England defining the government of the Church and the faith as it was to be observed at different times. The first articles were ten in number (1536) and provided a compromise between the old Catholic faith and the reforming ideas of Cranmer. In 1538 13 articles were issued, attacking images and pilgrimages and ordering the reading of the English Bible. In the following year, under the influence of the conservative majority in the Church, Henry VIII accepted the Act of Six Articles which restated Catholic doctrine, but the articles were never fully enforced and were repealed in Nov. 1547 after Henry's death.

The 42 articles of 1553, produced by Cranmer, were a compromise between the Lutheran and Calvinist creeds and together with the 1552 prayer book and the 1550 ordinal established the Edwardian reformation.

Under Elizabeth the 42 articles were modified. The 39 articles of 1563, which have remained the basis of the established Church, attempted to conciliate the Catholic viewpoint by deliberate vagueness. The growing Puritan wing of the Church was attacked by Abp Whitgift in the 24 articles of 1583.

ARTICLES OF WAR (1527), composed by Ferdinand I, King of Bohemia and later Emperor. These constituted an important code of wartime conduct in a year made memorable by the sack of Rome by imperialist forces. The code attempted to enforce some discipline upon soldiers and to provide for compensation for the state, as well as regulating that for individuals. The articles forbade plundering without permission, which was to be properly given by signal. Artillery, ammunition, and military stores were to be reserved for the emperor and captured cities were not to be looted.

ARTICULI HENRICIANI, conditional promises for constitutional reform presented to Henry of Valois when he was elected King of Poland (1573–5). The king was to summon parliament for an ordinary session once every two years and was not to wage war or levy taxes without its consent, thus accepting clearly defined limitations upon his own authority. Henry was crowned King at Cracow in Jan. 1574, but refused to confirm the *articuli* in his coronation oath, thereby arousing opposition in some areas of his kingdom; but his reign was cut short by his hasty return to Paris in that same year to assume the French Crown.

ARTIFICERS, STATUTE OF (1563), important piece of English paternalistic legislation of Elizabeth I's reign, which attempted to stabilize society and deal with the growing problem of pauperism and unemployment. The act restricted the movement of labour by insisting that men were to live and work in the milieu into which they were born. The regulations governing apprenticeship in all trades were enforced and justices of the peace empowered to fix wages. The act was designed to protect the lower classes of society against the capitalists and farmers, but the traditional attitude to social and economic matters embodied in its clauses presented no new solution to these problems.

ARTIFICIAL ISLANDS (MELANESIA), a series of lagoon villages in eastern Melanesia, the most easterly of which, Mele in the New Hebrides, and Taumako in the Duff group (described by Quiros in 1606) probably date from the 14th–15th cents. The numerous islets in the Lau and Langalanga lagoons off Malaita (Solomon Islands) are derivative, the earliest, Fouenda, being founded by Polynesians (long since assimilated) in the early 17th cent. Those off Port Moresby (New Guinea) are later again, after Torres's visit in 1606. Built on stilts (Port Moresby) or on loose coral mounds, Tongan style, they represent an effective solution to the problem encountered by late Micronesian and Polynesian migrants of living on malarious coastlines in Melanesia.

ARTIGAS, JOSÉ GERVASIO (1764–1850), gaucho leader of the movement for autonomy in the Banda Oriental (1811–20). Artigas led the unsuccessful struggle for the removal of the Spanish from Montevideo (1811–12). Buenos Aires desired control over the Banda Oriental and Artigas was forced to confront the Porteños militarily (1815). He defeated the Argentines and declared Uruguay independent. During the years 1816–20, Artigas led the struggle against the Portuguese, who wished to annex Uruguay to Brazil. He was forced to seek exile in Paraguay (1820), where he lived for the rest of his life. He is considered to have been the father of Uruguayan independence.

ARTILLERY, MEDIEVAL. Whereas Roman artillery could be extensively employed on the battlefield (under the early empire a legion had a complement of 60 easily portable *ballistae* or spring guns), that of the medieval period is most often associated with the art of the siege. The most important types of medieval siege engines were the catapult and the *ballista*. These machines worked on the principle of torsion and tension to provide the force for missile propulsion. The missiles themselves consisted largely of stones of various sizes or, less frequently, spears or large arrows. A machine called a 'springal' was used, chiefly in naval engagements, to hurl firebrands. The only machine actually developed during the course of the medieval period was the trebuchet, which used the principle of counterpoised weights to hurl large stones. It gradually replaced the *ballista*. Even after technological improvements from the mid-14th cent. onwards with the introduction of cannon, the early engines were still extensively employed to reduce fortifications.

ARTOIS, ROBERT, Count of (d. 1302), led the French armies in two victories in 1297, over the English in Gascony and over England's Flemish allies in southern Flanders. But faced in 1302 with a host of Flemish townsmen and peasants, he underestimated them and was destroyed with most of his army at Courtrai.

ARTS, MANUFACTURES, AND COMMERCE, SOCIETY FOR THE ENCOURAGEMENT OF (1754), now known as the Royal Society of Arts, had from its foundation an important influence on public interest and taste, and had 2500 members in 1762. But its success in stimulating invention by the award of prizes and medals was perhaps limited, because inventions submitted for award became the property of the society. Thus inventors such as Arkwright or Watt preferred to preserve their monopolies by patent.

ARTS, SEVEN LIBERAL. This division of secular learning was first made by Cassiodorus. In his *Institutes of Divine and Secular Literature* (c. 550), he arranged his subjects into one group of three (*trivium*), consisting of grammar, rhetoric, and dialectic, and a second group of four (*quadrivium*), comprising arithmetic, geometry, astronomy, and music. This formed the basic syllabus of medieval schools and of the earliest university courses.

ARTUKIDS, Turkish dynasty, composed of several branches, which ruled over the region of Diyarbakr. Mardin came under their control in 1097, Hisn Kayfa in 1102, Kharpert in 1113–15, and Mayyafarikin in 1118. Amid was acquired, with the aid of Salah al-Din, in 1183, but the great sultan occupied Mayyafarikin in 1185 and thus strengthened his influence over the Artukid lands. Amid and Hisn Kayfa fell to the Ayyubid Sultan al-Kamil in 1232–3, leaving only Mardin to the Artukids. Their rule endured there until 1409.

ARUBA, West Indian island, occupied by the Spanish (1527), but a Dutch possession since 1634. It was a centre for the slave trade. In the 20th cent. oil refineries were established and provided the only basis of the island's economy.

ARUNACHALAM, SIR PONNAMBALAM (1853–1924), the first Tamil to gain a place in the Ceylon civil service in open competition. He rose to be registrar-general. Later, he entered politics and did much to promote the Ceylon National Congress, which he afterwards quitted owing to dissatisfaction with the representation of the Tamil community in the Legislative Council under the 1924 constitution.

ARUNDEL, THOMAS (1352–1414), archbishop of York after 1388 and of Canterbury in 1397 and 1399–1414, four times chancellor of England. Younger brother of the appellant Earl of Arundel and strong political partisan, he played an important part in the deposition of Richard II. He was a vigorous opponent of Lollardy, being responsible for intensified persecution and for the prohibition of the reading of the English Bible without episcopal licence.

ARUSHA DECLARATION, (Feb. 1967), issued by the Tanzanian government, as President Nyerere's blueprint for Tanzanian socialism. It eliminates most of the earlier ambiguity in Nyere's socialist thought, without demolishing his initial premises—that 'Socialism is an attitude of mind. The basis of socialism is a belief in the oneness of man and the common historical destiny of mankind. The justification of socialism is man; not the state, not the flag.'

ARVAD (Aradus), Phoenician city which prospered at the beginning of the first millennium BC as a port serving the Aramaean kingdoms of Syria.

ARVALES, Roman religious college of 12 dedicated to the cult of Dea Dia (?Acca Larentia). Marble tablets discovered at their meeting-place, 8 kms from Rome, reveal that in imperial times the office of priest was held by the reigning emperor, who with his colleagues offered vows for the imperial house.

ARYA SAMAJ, religious and social movement founded in 1875 by Swami Dayanand Saraswati, whose aim was to restore the paramount authority of the Vedas by purging away subsequent accretions. It repudiated the hereditary caste system and untouchability, opposed infant marriage, and also aimed at improving the lot of Hindu widows. Its greatest achievement was in the educational field, and the Dayananda colleges in various parts of India were an attempt to conduct Indian schools independent of the influence and support of the British government. Its activities were chiefly confined to western and northern India, but its branches extended to Burma and East Africa. It developed missions and sought to counteract the influence of Christianity. Its leaders figured conspicuously in anti-British propaganda in the Punjab and the United Provinces. They were the leaders of the Rawalpindi riots (1907), especially Lala Lajpat Rai and Ajit Singh, who were arrested and deported.

ARYABHATA (*fl.* 6th cent. AD), Indian astronomer and mathematician. His principal merit lies in his numerous corrections to the earlier basic astronomical text, the *Suryasiddhanta*. Aryabhata apparently had a clear idea of the rotation of the earth.

ARYANS. The Sanskrit word *arya*, from which the term derives, has a wide range of connotations. It is used in the sense of 'noble', either to refer to the ruling classes or to ose that have attained a certain level of spiritual achievement

(notably in Buddhism). More specifically it is used with reference to the three highest 'twice-born' castes, *ie*, Brahmins, Kshatriyas, and Vaishyas. On the other hand, the English usage, as well as that of corresponding words in other Western languages, frequently carries racial overtones. With reference to India the term is generally used for the tribes, related to the Iranians and Armenians, as well as nearly all the European peoples, that invaded the Indo-Pakistani sub-continent from the west or north-west probably in the latter half of the 2nd millennium BC and gradually merged with the earlier settled populations. According to widely accepted but rightly challenged views these invaders made an end to the Indus Valley Civilization and introduced into India both the horse and the use of iron. In addition, but usually in the form Indo-Aryan, it is applied to a vast group of languages used mainly in the Indo-Gangetic basin and the northern Deccan as well as by the Sinhalese in Ceylon. This group also includes the classical languages Sanskrit and Pali.

ARYAVARTA, lit. 'Realm of the Aryas', Sanskrit term used to indicate the Indo-Gangetic basin or, more widely, the Indian sub-continent north of the Vindhya–Satpura range. It is distinct from Daksinapatha, *ie*, the Deccan. Though Indo-Aryan languages are spoken all over Aryavarta thus defined, the present border between Indo-Aryan and Dravidian languages runs far south of the Vindhya–Satpura range.

ASAF JAH, NIZAM-UL-MULK (1671–1748), the founder of Hyderabad state. He was the son of a distinguished Turkish noble in the Mughal service and himself served under Aurangzeb. He took little part in the two succession contests (1707 and 1712). In 1713, as a reward for deserting the Emperor Jahandar Shah, he was given charge of all the Deccan provinces and the title of Nizam-ul-mulk (Regulator of the Kingdom). He took part in the overthrow of the Sayyid brothers and for a time was the vizier or chief minister of the Emperor Muhammad Shah. Disgusted with the obstacles placed in his way, he retired to the Deccan (1726) and until his death ruled it as a virtually independent state. He enlarged his dominion through the coastal Carnatic nearly to Madurai. He was the ablest Mughal noble of his time and stood for the code of duty of Aurangzeb's time. After his death his family continued to control the state through various vicissitudes until Hyderabad became the leading Indian state in the British Indian empire.

ASAF KHAN (1571–1641), the title of Abu'l Hasan, by which he is commonly known. He was the son of Jahangir's visier, Itim-ad-daula, and the brother of Nur Jahan, Jahangir's famous wife. He succeeded his father as vizier and managed the succession of Shah Jahan, who had married his daughter, Mumtaz Mahal, of the Taj Mahal.

ASAF-UD-DAULAH, ruler of Oudh, 1775–97, succeeded his father Shuja-ud-daulah as nawab-vizier of this important buffer state to the rising British power in Bengal. He was an incapable ruler who spent his time in riotous living. By the treaty of Faizabad (1775) the hostile majority on Warren Hastings's council raised the subsidy he paid for the use of a British subsidiary force and compelled him to cede Benares, Jaunpur, and Ghazipur to the British in full sovereignty. By the treaty of Chunar (1781) Hastings attempted to reform his administration and reduced the number of British troops in Oudh. Hastings's share in the resumption of the *jagir*s and in the sequestration of the treasures of the begams of Oudh formed one of the charges brought against him at the time of his impeachment.

ASBJÖRNSEN, PETER CHRISTEN (1812–85), Norwegian writer who collaborated with Bp Jorgen Engebretsen Moe (1813–82) in collecting folk-tales which gave Norwegians a national cultural heritage, were translated (1859) into English, and were a stimulus to the social and political aspirations of the Norwegian peasantry.

ASBURY, FRANCIS (1745–1816), first Methodist bishop in America. Born in Birmingham, Asbury emigrated to America, where he was appointed Methodist superintendent by John Wesley (1772). When Thomas Ranklin was sent to take over this position (1773), Asbury was unco-operative and was ordered back to England (1775), but he refused, and in 1778 became a citizen of Delaware. A founder of the Methodist Episcopal Church in America, he was named superintendent at a conference in Baltimore (1784), but soon began referring to himself as bishop (1785). He believed in the circuit rider system and himself rode thousands of miles. He established churches in the more settled parts of the country and sent preachers to the frontier.

ASCALON, BATTLE OF (12 Aug. 1099). Jerusalem was stormed and captured during the First Crusade on 15–16 July 1099 in an attempt to forestall a huge relieving army advancing from Egypt. On 12 Aug. the crusaders massacred the Egyptians outside the fortress of Ascalon, ensuring the survival of their newly created Latin state of Jerusalem.

ASCENSION ISLAND (90 sq. kms) in the South Atlantic has (1970) a population of around 500. It was discovered by the Portuguese on Ascension Day 1501, but remained unoccupied until the British secured it after the Napoleonic Wars because of its proximity to St Helena. Until 1922, when the colonial office assumed responsibility, it was administered by the British admiralty. During the Second World War it had an air base, built by the US.

ASCHAM, ROGER (1515–68), English scholar, tutor to Elizabeth I. His *Toxophilus* (1546), a treatise on archery, stressed the importance of exercise in education, and he discussed education in a wider sense in the posthumous *Schoolmaster* (1570), in which he deplored excessive discipline.

ASEN, the first ruling house of the second Bulgarian empire. In 1186–7 two brothers, Asen and Peter Belgun, the former soon to become tsar as Ivan Asen I (d. 1196), rose in revolt against the Byzantines and, with the aid of the Kumans, took over most of northern Bulgaria, the capital of the new state being at Trnovo. The Tsar Kaloyan (1197–1207) extended Asen control into Serbia. He was also involved in war against the Latins at Constantinople, defeating the Emperor Baldwin at Adrianople in 1205. It was a son of Kaloyan—Ivan Asen II (1218–41)—who raised the Bulgarian state to the height of its power, taking over much of Macedonia, Epirus, and Albania after the battle of Klokotnitsa, which he won against Theodorus, the Despot of Epirus, in 1230. The years 1241–57 saw the Asenid regime fall into a rapid decline. With the brief reign (1279–80) of Ivan Asen III the Asen line came to an end.

ASHANTI (ASANTE) EMPIRE, founded late in the 17th cent., which grew out of unco-ordinated migrations by a variety of Twi-speaking peoples into the region of present-day Kumasi. These migrations were given political and military direction by Osei Tutu, the first well-known ruler of the emergent Asante state, who founded a capital at Kumasi.

During the military campaigns which marked the era of consolidation of the empire, a number of leading men established their own settlements known as *amanto*, prominent among which were Mampon, Juaben, and Kokofu. The empire thus began as a confederation of Kumasi and the largely autonomous *amanto*. At this stage the relationship of the 'king' in Kumasi to the *amanhene* (sing., *omanhene*) or rulers of the *amanto* was one of *primus inter pares*. While the *amanto* continued to enjoy a large measure of autonomy throughout Asante history, Kumasi gradually became supreme. This was due to the transformation of the confederation into a large

empire through military conquests. The Asantehene in Kumasi acquired more powers by his direction of these conquests, and by the provision of an appointed rather than a hereditary bureaucracy to handle the increasingly complex government of the empire. In the institution of the Golden Stool, which was believed to represent the soul of the Asante nation, and of which the Asantehene was custodian, he found supernatural sanction to confirm his political pre-eminence.

Throughout its history the empire depended heavily on its military strength. The maintenance of an uninterrupted supply of arms and ammunition thus constituted one of the cornerstones of Asante policy. Tied up with this was state-controlled trade in gold, slaves, kolanuts, and other commodities both with its coastal neighbours and the European traders and, through inland routes, with other African states such as the Hausa states, Timbuctoo, and Jenne.

Despite wars with the Fante and other groups in Ghana, Asante maintained its military, political, and economic primacy. Its collapse at the end of the 19th cent. was the result both of internal strains and the intervention of British imperial power. The internal strains had to do with the semi-autonomous status of the *amanto* which enabled them to organize rebellion against Kumasi. The British began to exploit this weakness in the Asante 'constitution'. Kumasi also had to deal with her Fante and other southern neighbours who sought to exclude Asante from the coastal trade. Asante was able to deal successfully with these southern neighbours, but found it increasingly difficult to contain the aggressive imperialism of the late 19th cent., when the British began to ally themselves with the Fante. In a series of campaigns the British ultimately succeeded in breaking the military might of the empire and establishing a protectorate over it.

K. A. Busia, *The Position of the Chief in the Moden Political System of Ashanti* (London, 1951).
W. Tordoff, *Ashanti Under the Prempehs* (Oxford, 1965).

OI

ASHANTI (ASANTE) WARS can be divided into two categories: wars of conquest (c. 1650–1750) and wars of survival (19th cent.). The former were the result of Asante determination to found an empire and control the trade and trade routes from their capital of Kumasi to the coast. These wars saw the incorporation of the Gonja, Dagomba, Akyem, Wassa, Akwamu, and others into the Asante empire. The second category of wars resulted from Asante confrontation with the Fante and their British allies. This arose from Asante determination to maintain direct trading links with the European traders at the coast and to preserve their empire intact, and Fante desire to exclude the Asante from the coastal trade and shake off Asante military and political domination. As British imperial interests increasingly coincided with Fante interests, the former threw in their military might against Asante and, in a series of wars in 1806, 1824, 1826, 1874, and 1896, overthrew Asante power.

ASH 'ARI, ABU' L-HASAN, AL- (d. 935–6), famous Muslim theologian born at Basra ?873. Abandoning the Mu'tazila he gave his allegiance (c. 912–13) to the orthodox tradition, to the defence of which he applied the rational methods of argument (*kalam*) characteristic of the Mu'tazila. In general he adhered to the teaching of Ibn Hanbal.

ASHIDA, HITOSHI (1887–1959) Japanese politician and prime minister (March–Oct. 1948), when the emphasis of Occupation policy was being changed from democratization to reconstruction.

ASHIKAGA SHOGUNATE, government set up by Ashikaga Takauji in Kyoto in 1338, after the overthrow of the Kamakura shogunate; it survived until 1573, but never enjoyed real strength. Its first half-century was dominated by civil war between rival claimants to the Imperial Throne, while during the century following the Onin War (1467–77) the Ashikaga *shogun*s were unable to control even the provinces around the capital. In the intervening years their authority rested on an uneasy coalition of great *daimyo* families, notably the Hosokawa, the Shiba, and the Hatakeyama, who filled in succession the office of *shogun*'s deputy. Rivalries among these families weakened even such able *shogun*s as Yoshimitsu, Yoshimochi, and Yoshinori, and the Ashikaga regime was further undermined by changes taking place in the provinces. Frequent warfare led to encroachment on the estates which still remained outside the feudal system, and to the rise of independent local *samurai* and new *daimyo*s. There was a corresponding decline in the authority of the provincial constables, who generally represented both the great families and the central government, and were frequently drawn into Kyoto politics or involved in succession disputes as a result of the tendency towards primogeniture. Against this political instability, the great economic and cultural advance which the 14th and 15th cents witnessed owed much to the *shogun*s who encouraged trade with China and were lavish patrons of the arts.

ASHTA PRADHAN (lit. Council of Eight), the name given to the Council of State formed by the Maratha leader, Sivaji. It was an advisory council presided over by the raja, and had more the status of the privy Council of Tudor England than that of a modern European cabinet. The cabinet of the American president is perhaps the nearest modern equivalent. The council included the *Mukha Pradhan* or peshwa, who held the seal and was the chief administrative officer, the commander-in-chief (*senapati*), a financier, a foreign and a chief religious officer. Sivaji's innovation consisted in giving these officers a corporate existence. The council was abolished by Sivaji's son, Sambhaji. After Aurangzeb's death the Maratha state was reformed by Sivaji's grandson Shahu. He found himself surrounded by military chiefs supported by land revenue grants. In 1714 he appointed Balaji Vishvanath Bhat as peshwa and soon after made the office hereditary in his family. The brilliance of successive Bhat peshwas gradually transferred power to themselves and made them, by the time of Shahu's death (1750), the heads of a Maratha military confederacy.

ASHTI, BATTLE OF, fought on 20 Feb. 1818 during the Third Maratha War (1817–19) between the English East India Co. and Baji Rao II, the Maratha peshwa. The peshwa's army was defeated, his bravest general, Gokhale, killed, and the Raja of Satara captured. The peshwa surrendered in June 1818.

ASHURBANIPAL (*reg.* 668–627 BC), an Assyrian king, who twice quelled revolts in Egypt, but lost the province in 655. After 12 years of friction with Babylonia, where his brother was king, Ashurbanipal attacked and conquered it (648). After repeated indecisive clashes, he invaded Elam (642), devastated it, and destroyed the capital, Susa. His conquests made Assyria rich and, apparently, never stronger, but 15 years after his death the empire was destroyed. A huge library of literary, religious, and scientific writings from the time of Ashurbanipal has been found at Nineveh.

ASHURNASIRPAL II (*reg.* 884–859 BC), Assyrian king who appears to have been energetic, ruthless, and cruel. On raids and campaigns he extended Assyrian power in northern Mesopotamia, conquered the Aramaean kingdom of Bit-Adini, and reached the Mediterranean, claiming tribute from cities and rulers. In the south he fought the emerging power of the Chaldeans. He founded the city of Nimrud, which became the military capital of the empire.

ASHUR-RESH-ISHI (*c.* 1133–1116 BC), Assyrian king, who successfully defended the country against the Aramaeans, by whom the north-western trade routes, the Guti and Lullubi in the east, and Babylonia in the south, were threatened.

ASHWANDER V. TENNESSEE VALLEY AUTHORITY, 297 US 288 (1936). The US Supreme Court having upheld the validity of a contract between the TVA and the Alabama Power Co. for the sale of 'surplus power' generated by the Wilson Dam, Chief Justice Hughes argued that the dam had been built for national defence and the improvement of navigation. Both objectives were clearly within the scope of federal authority, and the right of the federal government to dispose of property legally acquired could not be denied. A concurring opinion by Justice Brandeis is of particular significance to constitutional lawyers as an exposition of the rules he felt should apply to the Court's consideration of constitutional questions.

ASIA, CENTRAL, RUSSIAN CONQUEST OF. Russian political and economic interest in Central Asia increased during and after the Napoleonic wars. After the failure of the 1839 Khivan expedition, steady advances were made from the posts of Orenburg and Semipalatinsk. In 1864 the two lines of advance were united to encircle the Kazakh steppe, claimed by Russia since early in the 18th cent. Conflicts followed with the Turkestan Khanates of Khiva, Bukhara, and Kokand, of which local Russian commanders took advantage. Tashkent was occupied (June 1865) by Gen. M. G. Cherniaev and Samarkand (May 1868) by Gen. Kaufmann. Protectorates were established over Kokand (1866), Bukhara (1868), and Khiva (1873), Kokand being later annexed (1876), after an uprising. In Transcaspia, Krasnovodsk was occupied (1869) by forces from the Caucasus and became the base for campaigns against the Turkmen, whose resistance was broken by Gen. Skobolev (Geok-Tepe, 1881). The conquest was completed by the annexation of Merv (1884) and the Pamir region (1895). It owed its success to the superiority of Russian discipline and arms over the irregular Turkish cavalry.

ASIA, ROMAN, one of the richest provinces of the Roman empire, bequeathed to the Romans by Attalus III of Pergamum in 133 BC. Embracing Nysia, Lydia, Ionia, Caria, and Phrygia, it was divided into city territories, *eg*, Ephesus, Pergamum, Smyrna, Miletus, and Sardes. Exploited by Roman tax farmers and Italian business men, of whom 80,000 were massacred in 80 BC, it suffered from the Civil Wars, but recovered under the empire, as a senatorial province ruled by proconsuls, its prosperity witnessed by inscriptions and remains and its loyalty by its worship of Rome and Augustus. Christianity, introduced by St Paul, made steady progress against occasional popular opposition. After Gothic invasions in the 3rd cent. it became a mainstay of the eastern empire.

ASIATIC SOCIETY OF BENGAL, founded at Calcutta (1784) by the Welsh orientalist Sir William Jones, for the purpose of enquiry into the history, antiquities, arts, sciences, and literatures of Asia. It provided accommodation for a library and museum and collected manuscripts in many oriental languages. In 1787 it started a publication called *Asiatic Researches* and in 1839 began to publish its famous *Journal*. It edited texts and translations of oriental works in a series known as the *Bibliotheca Indica*. Between 1914 and 1919 it sponsored a bardic and historical survey of Rajputana. It was an important centre for the use of scholars, with a valuable library of books and manuscripts and a collection of coins, medals, pictures, and busts. From 1858 to 1947 it was known as the Royal Asiatic Society of Bengal.

ASIENTO, or *asiento de negros*, the contracts granted by the Spanish government (1517–1713) for the shipment of a specified number of African slaves to America by foreign persons or nations. In exchange for the exclusive privilege to import slaves, the slave trader (*asentista*) agreed to pay a specified sum to the Crown, which limited the legitimate number of Africans who could be introduced into the colonies.

Asientos were seldom sufficient to supply the labour requirements of the colonists and illegal participation in the slave traffic by foreigners resulted.

The first *asiento* was granted to a Genose company (1517) for the delivery of 1000 African slaves to the Spanish colonies within eight years. The second *asiento* was purchased by two Germans (1528) who agreed to supply 4000 African slaves to the colonies for 45 ducats each at the port of entry. They received a four-year *asiento* in exchange for 20,000 ducats. *Asientos* were issued on seven additional occasions (1552, 1595, 1609, 1615, 1696, 1701, and 1713).

The final *asiento* was granted to the English South Sea Co. as a consequence of the treaty of Utrecht. The English company was authorized to provide 4800 African slaves per year for 30 years. Though none can say exactly how many Africans were introduced into the colonies under the *asientos*, an estimated 3000 slaves per year were authorized (1600–1750).   HDS

ASIR, area in western Arabia, which, under the leadership of Sayyid Muhammad ibn Ali al-Idrisi (d. 1923), gained its independence from the Ottomans in the First World War, but eventually came under Saudi Arabia (1926).

ASKE, ROBERT (d. 1537), English leader of the Pilgrimage of Grace. He organized a formidable revolt in Yorkshire but after meetings with the Duke of Norfolk he disbanded his army on the assurance that the rebels' grievances would be considered. Despite the promise of a free pardon he was hanged at York.

ASKIA, dynasty of Songhay (1493–1591). In 1493 Muhammad ibn Abi Bakr, a Songhay provincial governor of Tukolor extraction, rebelled against the ruler of Songhay, Sunni Baro, and established himself ruler with the new title of Askia, which was used by his nine successors until the dynasty was overthrown by the Moroccans in 1591.

With the Askia dynasty the Songhay empire entered upon its greatest period of expansion and power. For a short period in the early 16th cent. its subject territories extended from the Senegal river to Hausaland and halfway across the Sahara. The capital was at Gao and the empire was administered by provincial governors and tax-collectors with a number of ministers at the centre charged with special responsibilities. A central army included a camel cavalry corps, and regional governors also raised their own forces. A royal fleet of barges made strategic use of the Niger river as a means of communication.

Eight of the nine Askias were sons or grandsons of the founder and rivalries among them were a major cause of instability. As each Askia came to power he reallocated the major state offices among his most trusted brothers and other relatives and sought to eliminate those considered a threat to his power. No Askia stayed in office for more than ten years, except the sixth, Dawud (*reg.* 1549–83), who combined the same qualities of military energy and Islamic piety which had characterized his father, the founder of the dynasty.

Shortly before the death of the eighth Askia, Muhammad Bani (*reg.* 1586–8), there was a rebellion in the western provinces and the combined armies of several governors marched on Gao. A force under the new Askia, Ishaq II (*reg.* 1588–91), defeated the rebels, but a severe blow had been struck at the Songhay state. Before Ishaq had recovered, he was faced with a new threat from Morocco.

For 50 years there had been a running dispute with Morocco over the ownership of the central Saharan salt mines at Taghaza, controlled by the Askias. Its salt was an important source of revenue, as well as being the chief barter item of the merchants who obtained gold from the forest regions to the south and south-west of the Niger Bend, much of which was exported to North Africa and thence to Europe. In 1591 3000 soldiers of the Moroccan sultan, mainly renegades and mercenaries, crossed the Sahara and defeated Ishaq's forces at Tondibi near Gao. Their use of firearms against the Songhay

lances and arrows was the decisive factor. Ishaq fled and although resistance continued for many years, the power of the Askias was broken. The new Moroccan administration, based on Timbuctoo, appointed puppet Askias, while the free Songhay withdrew down the Niger to Dendi, where they continued to appoint their own Askias and govern a small and impoverished state.

E. W. Bovill, *The Golden Trade of the Moors* (London, 1968). J. F. Ajayi and M. Crowder, *A History of West Africa* (London, 1970).   JOH

ASLANDAZ (31 Oct.–1 Nov. 1812), decisive victory by Russians under Gen. de Rtishchev over Persians under Abbas Mirza which sealed the fate of Persian Transcaucasia.

ASOKA (*reg.* 268–231 BC), one of the greatest rulers of ancient India. He was a son of Bindusara and grandson of Chandragupta, the founder of the Maurya dynasty. At his accession Asoka already had considerable experience in government having served as a viceroy in several provinces during his father's reign. The empire that he inherited comprised the major part of the Indo-Pakistani sub-continent. Initially Asoka ruled like Indian kings before him, but after a campaign against Kalinga (mod. Orissa), followed by his conversion to Buddhism at some later time, he initiated an entirely new policy based upon a particular concept of *Dharma*, 'Righteousness', which was to become the norm of conduct for all his subjects.

Although the principle of *Dharma* was apparently laid down at an early stage the actual contents gradually developed and were elaborated into over 25 different edicts, most of which are extant in numerous copies written down on rocks and pillars all over the sub-continent. These inscriptions, the only strictly contemporary sources for Asoka's reign, are of unique value to the historian. They are written in Brahmi script except for a few inscriptions in the north-western area, which are in Kharosthi. The language used is Prakrit, presumably the official language of Asoka's court at ancient Pataliputra (mod. Patna, in Bihar), but adapted to local speech in different areas. A few inscriptions in Taxila and Kandahar, however, are in Aramaic and Greek. After more than a century of intensive research the correct reading and translation of the edicts are now firmly established but there still remain serious differences of opinion among scholars concerning the precise interpretation of terms. Some of these entail direct implications for our assessment of Asoka's personality and the effects of his rule. Most scholars now agree that Asoka's policies were neither anti-Brahmanic nor aimed at the disruption of the earlier social order. An older view that Asoka, inspired by absolute non-violence, should have disbanded the army now finds little support, although some still hold Asoka responsible for the decline of the Maurya empire that began some time after his death. The present tendency both in and outside India is to regard Asoka above all as a humane ruler who successfully controlled a huge empire and attempted to give it a sense of common purpose, based upon the highest achievements of Indian civilization. His profound concern for the material and spiritual welfare of his subjects is unique for the age in which he lived. Although the Maurya empire did not survive him by less than 50 years (and may have started to disintegrate soon after his death) it seems that the empire remained an ideal to which later rulers tried to give shape. Above all, the more intensive interrelations following the centralization of government may have contributed to the growth of a common consciousness that lent India its proper identity.

Romila Thapar, *Asoka and the Decline of the Mauryas* (Oxford, 1961).   JGdeC

ASPASIA (*fl.* 5th cent. BC), famous courtesan of cultural and intellectual attainment from Miletus. As the companion of the Athenian statesman Pericles, whose son she bore, she became a butt of the comedians and the target of his political opponents, but was successfully defended by him on a charge of impiety (431).

ASPELTA (*reg.* 6th cent. BC), King of Kush. It may have been during his reign that the capital was moved from Napata to Meroe, where his name is the earliest found, though he was buried at Nuri near Napata. In 591 BC Pharaoh Psammetichus II attacked Kush and caused much destruction at Napata, where remains of broken royal statues, of which the latest was that of Aspelta, have been found. This, together with the finding of his name at Meroe, indicates the possibility that it was Aspelta who moved the capital from Napata.

ASPERUCH (d. 701), ruler of the Hunnish Bulgars, who led his tribe from southern Russia into the Danube valley, defeated the Byzantines in 679, and created the Bulgarian state, comprising modern Rumania, Bulgaria, and Macedonia, ruling over numerous subject Slavs. This state endured until its destruction by the Byzantines in 1018.

ASSAM, eastern-most state of the republic of India, comprising a large part of the Brahmaputra valley and the neighbouring hill ranges between East Pakistan and Burma. Under British rule it was divided into Assam proper, *ie,* the five districts of Kamrup, Darrang, Nowgong, Sibsagar, and Lakhimpur, with the Sadiya and Balipara frontier tracts; Goalpara, including the Eastern Duars; Cachar, Sylhet and Jaintia; and the hill districts of the Garo, Khasi, Nagar, and Lushai. Most of Sylhet became part of Pakistan in 1947. Its early history is obscure, but lower Assam came under Hindu influence before the Christian era. The Chinese pilgrim Hiuen Tsang, who visited the valley *c.* AD 640 reported that Hinduism was the state religion. The region also became a centre of the bloody human sacrifices and licentious orgies inculcated in the Tantras. Its true history begins with the Ahom invasions in the 13th cent. According to the Ahom *buranjis* (chronicles), the Ahoms first crossed the Patkai mountains into Assam under their leader Sukapha in 1228 and gradually became masters of the whole Brahmaputra valley, which they ruled over for some 600 years. During the reign of Suhungmung (1497–1539) the Ahom dominions were extended in all directions. He suppressed the Nagas, Kacharis, and Chutiyas and repulsed three Muslim invasions. In 1637 the Muslims temporarily drove the Ahoms out of Kamrup, but under Rudra Singha (1696–1714) the Ahoms finally repulsed the Muslim invaders and were in possession of practically the whole valley. In 1780 Gaurinath Singh succeeded to the throne, but had to face a formidable rising of the Moamarias, a Vaishnavite sect. In 1792 he appealed for British help and Lord Cornwallis sent a detachment under Capt. Welsh to restore order. In the early 19th cent. the Burmese occupied Assam until they were driven out by the British during the war of 1824–6. For a time the British left certain tracts under local chiefs, but after 1838 gradually extended their administration over the area. Until 1874, when Assam became a separate province under a chief commissioner, it was administered as part of Bengal. On the partition of Bengal in 1905 Eastern Bengal and Assam were formed into a new province under a lieutenant-governor, but in 1912 Assam once more became a separate administration under a chief commissioner until 1921, when it became a governor's province. The most important commercial crop is tea. The largest rainfall measured in India in one year was 905 inches in 1861 at Cherrapunji in the Khasi hills. The British experienced great difficulty in controlling the unruly tribes on Assam's north-eastern frontier, the Abors, Akas, Daflas, Khamptis, Miris, Mishmis, Singphos, and more especially the Nagas. Since the British withdrawal this problem has become more complicated.

E. A. Gait, *A History of Assam* (Calcutta, 1906).
S. K. Bhuyan, *Anglo-Assamese Relations, 1771–1826* (Gauhati, 1949).   CCD

ASSASSINS, *ie,* **HASHISHIYAN,** 'those who eat hashish' (*Cannabis indica*) in order to induce ecstatic visions. The name is applied to the Isma'ili movement centred around Hasan-i Sabbah at Alamut. It denotes also the adherents of Hasan-i Sabbah, who, at the time of the Crusades, occupied various hill fortresses in northern Syria, *eg,* at Hisn al-Masyad (Masyaf) in 1140–1. The head of these Syrian Hashishiyan was known as the Sheikh al-Jibal (the Christian 'Old Man of the Mountain'). Of these sheikhs the most famous was Rashid al-Din Sinan, who held office for 30 years (1163–93). It was the Mamluk Sultan Baybars (1260–77) who set a term to the activities of the Assassins in Syria.

ASSAYE, BATTLE OF, fought on 23 Sept. 1803, when Arthur Wellesley defeated the combined Maratha forces of Sindhia and Berar. Wellesley has been criticized for dividing his forces in the presence of the enemy and because of the heavy casualties, but it was a golden rule in Maratha warfare to attack even although heavily outnumbered.

ASSEMBLIES OF THE CLERGY, general meetings of deputies elected from the various ecclesiastical provinces of France, held every five years in Paris. The assemblies were regulated by the contract of Poissy (1561) and were summoned by the king to obtain revenue, not in the form of taxation but as a donation freely voted. In this way the clergy preserved their privilege of freedom from direct taxation, but contributed to the financial needs of the state to a limited extent.

ASSEMBLIES, PROVINCIAL, short-lived bodies erected by the government of Louis XVI of France to rationalize its administrative and fiscal organs. Calonne originally proposed a reorganization of French local government to accompany his financial reforms (1786). He wanted a hierarchy of local assemblies, starting at a parochial level, rising to a district one and culminating in provincial assemblies, which would cover an area equivalent to that administered by the *intendants.* The assemblies were to be made up of substantial landowners, with no distinction on the basis of class for voting purposes, as in the existing estates. Their main purpose was to be the assessment and allocation of Calonne's proposed general land tax, but they were also to be responsible for poor relief and public works. The intention was not to give the local notables more say in their affairs, nor to carry out decentralization. The assemblies were to be merely consultative bodies, closely controlled by the local *intendants.* They would increase centralization and royal control of the provinces. Consequently the noblesse opposed them, when Calonne's critic and successor, Brienne, set up the assemblies (1787).

ASSEMBLY OF NOTABLES, consultative body of leading nobles and officials called by French kings at irregular intervals. It originated as just another meeting of the basic royal council and before the 17th cent. is often hard to distinguish from the latter. It had no representative element, and its membership rarely included members of the Third Estate. Its members were summoned by *lettre de cachet,* presented no *cahiers,* met informally, and usually debated one or two major items of royal policy. Its powers were much more restricted than the states general, so that kings preferred to summon it as it represented less of a slur on royal sovereignty. The meetings usually accepted as constituting an Assembly of Notables are those at Tours (1470), which discussed the Burgundian question; Tours again (1506), which debated the Breton marriage; Paris (1527), which discussed how to deal with the imprisonment of Francis I; Paris again (1557–8), which was called to obtain financial aid; Rouen (1596), where Henry IV secured approval of his financial policies; Rouen again (1617) and Paris (1627), where noble plans for reform were debated; and finally the crucial meetings at Versailles (1787–8), where the plans of Calonne and others to reform the financial system were rejected and preparations made for the calling of the states general.

ASSIGNATS, paper money issued by successive French revolutionary governments. In Dec. 1789 the French Constituent Assembly had tried to solve the country's financial crisis by issuing bonds bearing an interest of 5 per cent on the security of the nationalized church lands. The following year these bonds, or *assignats*, were turned into actual currency notes, which relieved both the financial difficulties of the government and also compensated for the shortage of coin in France. Every French government printed more *assignats*, leading to rapid inflation until the decision in 1797 to abolish paper currency.

ASSIMILATION, FRENCH POLICY OF. The assimilation, politically and culturally, of the colonies to metropolitan France had its roots in the revolutionary doctrines of equality and popular sovereignty. Under it, colonists would be equal French citizens, sending deputies to the Chamber on equal terms with French constituencies. Local government would be organized in the same way as in France. Colonies would pay the same taxes and be subject to French law. French would be the official language and medium of instruction. This policy may be contrasted with the British preference for indirect rule, that is, the maintenance and support of native systems of government as far as possible.

Assimilation, which if fully applied would reconcile overseas possessions with democracy, had practical shortcomings and was not applied in all territories. It respected the equality of all citizens, but presupposed the superiority of French culture and institutions. It was generally applied in those colonies possessed by France in 1870. The West Indian and Indian territories, Senegal, and Algeria elected deputies to the Chamber. The defects of the system might be seen in Algeria, where the deputies for the departments of Oran, Algiers, and Constantine were elected by the French settlers and, after the Cremieux decree (1870), by Algerian Jews. Arabs were eligible for citizenship if they renounced Muslim law and accepted monogamy, but were in practice disfranchised. The same policy was carried a stage further in Algeria by the policy of 'attachment', whereby separate colonial administration was abandoned in favour of direct administration by the ministries in Paris. The governmental and fiscal situation of Algeria proved very different from that of the average French department, and the system was abandoned in 1896.

The same policy of direct rule without reference to pre-existing political traditions was applied in Cochin-China, which elected deputies from 1881, and in Tonkin. In other parts of the empire an indirect system of government prevailed, particularly if French influence had been established by treaty with rulers, rather than, as in Tonkin or Algeria, by outright conquest. Thus the Bey of Tunis, the Sultan of Morocco, the Emperor of Annam, the rulers of Madagascar, and the Emperor of Cambodia continued to exercise authority under French protection (1970).

S. H. Roberts, *History of French Colonial Policy*, 2 vols (London, 1928). LMB

ASSINIBOIN INDIANS, large nomadic American Indian tribe of the Sioux family, living in the northern Great Plains. They were in constant conflict with other tribes. While the buffalo abounded, they were noted for the quality of their pemmican, which they bartered to explorers and traders for liquor, tobacco, and firearms.

ASSIZES OF HENRY II. The name 'assizes' applied to the decrees issued by the king and his council which, taken as a whole, mark a major development in English law and justice and replaced judicial duels with trial by a jury.

(a) *Assize Utrum* (1164) determined whether land was in the jurisdiction of the secular or the ecclesiastical court.

(b) *Assize of Clarendon* (1166) generalized the jury of presentment, which brought charges against suspected criminals and was the origin of the grand jury.

(c) *Assize of Northampton* (1166) instituted the actions of

Mort d'Ancestor, which safeguarded an heir's rights of succession, and *Novel Disseisin*, which safeguarded the rights of possession, though not of ownership, against forceful dispossession.

(d) *Grand Assize* (1179) offered a legal alternative, the writ of right, to the judicial duel as a means of settling disputes over land ownership.

(e) *Assize of Darrein Presentment* (after 1179) dealt with rights of advowson.

(f) *Assize of Arms* (1181) defined and renewed the obligations of every free man to perform military service.

ASSOCIATE STATES, in French Indochina. Following the collapse of the Indochinese Union in 1945, the French only gradually recovered control of their former colony, and it became clear that at the very least they would grant some measure of internal autonomy. In 1949, they created, by agreement with their future governments, three Associate States: Viet-nam, ruled by the ex-Emperor Bao-Dai; Cambodia, under King Norodom Sihanouk; and Laos, under King Sisavang Vong. Although recognized by some Western powers, the Associate States remained within the French Union, with France controlling their defence and foreign relations, and were held together by a French-imposed customs union. Only after the Geneva Agreements of 1954 did the French allow the states full independence, and their Associate status came to an end.

ASSOCIATED PRESS, US news agency which developed out of the New York Associated Press (1827). Successfully surviving the development of the telegraph (1844), the agency had absorbed most of its rivals by the 1860s. Reorganized after congressional charges of monopoly (1900), it remains a leading US press service.

ASSOCIATION, English device of extra-parliamentary political agitation recommended at the end of the 18th cent. by parliamentary reformers such as John Cartwright, Obadiah Hulme, and James Burgh, and put into practice notably in the 1780s, in the Society for Constitutional Information and the Society for Commemoration of the Glorious Revolution. Associations were intended to be nation-wide and to include all classes. By the 1830s they had become a familiar method of bringing public opinion to bear upon parliament.

ASSOCIATION, ACT ON (1585), gesture of loyalty to Queen Elizabeth I of England, promoted by the parliament of 1584–5. Stimulated by a voluntary association which sprang up throughout the country in defence of the queen's life (1584), this act modified the language of the association's oath and aimed at preventing any attempt on her life. Its main victim was Mary Queen of Scots.

ASSOCIATION, ISLAND OF, West Indian isle settled by an English company of Puritans in Charles I's reign, which was seized by the Spanish to prevent its being used as a base for attacks on their treasure fleets.

ASSOCIATION CATHOLIQUE DE LA JEUNESSE FRANÇAISE, one of the earliest youth movements organized by Catholic laymen in France, which made an important contribution to the Catholic revival of the 20th cent. Founded in 1886 by the monarchist Albert de Mun, it was originally a conservative and middle-class movement aimed at spreading Catholic influence among the governing elite. The ACJF widened its appeal from about 1900 and took a more radical standpoint on social questions. It helped to train many leaders of the Christian Democrat movement. From the late 1920s it was eclipsed by the growth of specialized youth movements for Catholic workers, peasants, etc., and in recent years has acted simply as a co-ordinating organization for these. An attempt to revivify it in the 1950s caused much dissension.

ASSOCIATORS (Nov. 1747–8), American league of volunteer soldiers organized by Benjamin Franklin to defend Philadelphia. After the peace of Aix-la-Chapelle the league was dissolved.

ASSUR (mod. Qal 'al Sherqat), ancient city on the Tigris commanding important routes to the south and east. It was the early capital of the kingdom of Assyria.

ASSYRIA, kingdom of northern Mesopotamia, founded around its early capital, Assur. Its first kings were nomadic chiefs. It had temporary importance under Sargon of Akkad (c. 2334–2279 BC) and during the 20th and early 19th cents, but first became powerful under an Amorite dynasty founded by Shamshi-Adad (c. 1813–1781) which conquered Mari and controlled nearly all northern Mesopotamia. A long period of Mitannian domination followed until (c. 1363–1330) the reign of Ashur-uballit marked the beginning of a period of Assyrian power. He and his successors, who included Adad-Nirari I (c. 1307–1275), Shalmaneser I (c. 1274–1245), and Tukulti-Ninurta I (c. 1244–1208), subdued Urartu, the Guti, and Hurrians and conquered Carchemish, Elam, and Babylon. Mass invasions of nomads, particularly Aramaeans, brought a period of chaos to the area, so that by the end of the 10th cent. Assyria was reduced to a narrow strip of land on the Tigris. Adad-Nirari II ushered in (c. 911) the great period of Assyrian supremacy. The Aramaeans were expelled and all northern Iraq brought under Assyrian domination. Under Shalmaneser III (c 858–824) tribute was collected from people living as far away as Armenia and the Taurus mountains, Til-Barsip (Tell-Ahmar) was conquered, and Babylon subdued. There followed almost a century of stagnation until Tiglathpileser III (c. 745–727) conquered parts of Syria, Palestine, and Armenia and annexed Babylonia. At first, annual raids were made for the purpose of frontier defence, in search of booty, or to collect tribute, but these raids developed into wars of conquest. Tiglathpileser's administrative reforms brought the kingdom under royal control and conquered lands became provinces with Assyrian rulers. The army was reconstructed and a policy of mass deportations from conquered territories inaugurated. At its height under a series of outstanding kings, Sargon III (c. 721–705), Sennacherib (c. 704–681), Esarhaddon (c. 680–669), and Ashurbanipal (c. 668–627), the empire stretched from the Persian Gulf to the Mediterranean and included parts of Iran, Asia Minor, and Egypt. The empire under Ashurbanipal had never seemed stronger, but despite this a period of internal disorder and probable military failures from c. 639 led to the break-up of the empire and the conquest of Assyria by the Medes and Babylonians in 609.

G. Roux, *Ancient Iraq* (London, 1964).
A. L. Oppenheim, *Ancient Mesopotamia* (Chicago, 1964).
JKG

ASSYRIAN ADMINISTRATION. Government in Assyria was largely in the hands of the king, assisted by advisers, of whom only the commander-in-chief had a defined post. There were provincial administrative officials and probably there was considerable local independence.

ASSYRIAN ARMY. This was originally recruited in north Iraq, but Tiglathpileser III (c. 745–727 BC) created a standing army, levied by provincial governors. Scythian mercenaries were later used. The army was composed of cavalry, infantry, chariots, and engineers for siege work. Its success resulted from superior weapons (being the first army entirely equipped with iron), efficient organization, and a number of capable leaders.

ASSYRIAN MASSACRES (Aug. 1933). These occurred during an Iraqi army campaign with Kurdish and Arab support, which crushed the dissident Christian minority Assyrian community after an attempt by Assyrian émigrés to return to Iraq from Syria.

ASSYRIANS, ancient people of northern Mesopotamia, an area occupied in early times by people of the Halaf and Ubaid cultures. To the north and east of Assyria were mountains from which fierce nomads continually threatened the area, while to the south lay Babylonia, an attractive prize, a frequent enemy, and a strong cultural influence. The most important Sumerian deities followed the Assyrian god Ashur in the Assyrian pantheon, and Babylonian scribal traditions were adopted by the Assyrians. Likewise, the Assyrian law was basically the common law seen in Hammurabi's Code, but with stronger retributive punishments. The Assyrians spoke an Akkadian dialect, called Assyrian, until they adopted Aramaean about the 8th cent BC. West of Assyria lay the plain of Jazirah, site of important trade routes and the path for Assyrian expansion towards the Mediterranean, but also giving easy access to invaders and nomads. Particularly in the second millennium, Assyria was greatly affected by movements of Amorites, Hurrians, and Aramaeans.

There were four main classes in Assyrian society, the nobility, professional men (merchants, scribes, and bankers), workers, and slaves, of whom successful wars brought increasing numbers. Agriculture was the main occupation, but there were vigorous trading activities during prosperous periods. Urbanization was encouraged as in the rest of Mesopotamia, both for defence and for easier government control. New cities were founded by the kings, eg, at Nimrud and Nineveh, and built on a new rectangular plan. Artistically, the most distinctive achievement of the Assyrians was their splendid development of relief sculpture, usually depicting scenes of war and hunting. Of the minor arts, work in metal and ivory and textiles may have been mostly done by foreign artisans. The Assyrians have retained a reputation as fierce, cruel soldiers and they certainly seem to have used terrorism and deportation as instruments of war, but the records and possessions they have left behind show them to have been also cultured and civilized.

Bibliography. See Assyria. JKG

ASTON, FRANCIS WILLIAM (1877–1945), British scientist, who began his career as a brewery chemist. In 1901 he went to the Cavendish Laboratory, Cambridge, where he developed the mass spectrograph and discovered many isotopes. He received the Nobel Prize for Chemistry in 1922.

ASTOR, NANCY WITCHER ASTOR, Viscountess (1879–1964), first woman MP of the British House of Commons, born in America and married to William Waldorf Astor, an American millionaire who became a British subject. Lady Astor succeeded her husband as Unionist member for Plymouth in 1919 and remained a member of parliament until 1945. She was a Christian Scientist and a temperance advocate and in 1923 piloted through parliament a bill preventing the sale of liquor to persons under 18. She sought the right of women to have equal guardianship of their children, which was secured by the Guardianship of Infants Act (1925), and also advocated the raising of the school-leaving age, the provision of proper nursery school education, and the improvement of conditions under which women worked in the catering and distributive trades. She was an active political hostess and during the 1930s her house at Cliveden was an influential centre for those who supported appeasement in foreign affairs.

ASTOR, JOHN JACOB (1763–1848), German-born American fur trader. Already established in the fur trade, he benefited from Jay's Treaty (1794) by concluding a direct importation agreement with the British North West Co. Similarly he exploited the Louisiana Purchase and by 1807 was competing with British interests in the upper Mississippi valley. Astor incorporated the American Fur Co. (1808) and his plan to ship furs directly to China led to the creation of the Pacific Fur Co. (1810) and the foundation of Astoria (1811) at the mouth of the Columbia river. Astor also speculated heavily in

New York City real estate which, after he sold his fur interests (1834), became his main concern. One of the first American multi-millionaires, worth over $20 million, he followed philanthropic precedents by endowing the Astor Library in New York City. His descendants played a part in British public life.

ASTRAKHAN, Tatar Khanate in area of lower Volga, established as one of the successor states of the Golden Horde (1466). Conquered by Russia (1554), the Khanate was incorporated into Russia in 1556.

ASTROLOGY, 'judicial' as opposed to 'natural' astronomy, a pseudo-science claiming that the position of the planets, in relation to each other and to the fixed stars and constellations, is an indication of the divine will whereby it is possible to predict events on earth. As it was evident that the sun sustained life on earth, many believed the other planets similarly were sources of divine energy and might influence human affairs. Astrology had considerable importance in the ancient world and during the Middle Ages, but it was largely discredited when its elaborate theoretical structure was thrown out of balance by the discovery of new planets.

ASTRONOMY, the scientific study of the heavenly bodies. It was practised in ancient times by the Chinese, Chaldaeans, Hindus, and Babylonians, all of whom have left records of their attempts to plot and measure celestial phenomena. It was first brought to an exact science by the Greeks, despite their lack of instruments. Thales (*fl.* 600 BC) predicted a solar eclipse and recognized that the stars were fiery bodies and the earth a sphere. The mathematician Pythagoras (*fl.* 530 BC) believed, 2000 years before it was generally acknowledged, that the earth and the other planets revolved round the sun. Aristotle's speculations on astronomy have not survived, but Eudoxus of Cnidos (406–350 BC) estimated the length of the year at $365\frac{1}{4}$ days, and Hipparchus of Rhodes (*c.* 160–120 BC) took the science as far as it could go without the use of the pendulum and the telescope. He was the inventor of trigonometry, and among other discoveries he postulated the procession of the equinoxes and the elliptical motion of celestial bodies. The work of the Greek astronomers was summarized in the *Almagest* (*c.* AD 150) of the geographer Ptolemy, who discovered the 'evection' of the moon and gave his name to the Ptolemaic system of planetary motion.

In the Dark Ages astronomy gave way to the pseudo-sciences of alchemy and astrology, but it was kept alive by the Arabs and was revived in Europe by the renewed study of Greek thought. The *Almagest* was translated in the 13th cent., and modern astronomy began with Copernicus, who aroused clerical hostility by teaching that the planets revolved round the sun and that the apparent movement of the stars was an illusion due to the rotation of the earth in a contrary direction. Tycho Brahe (1546–1601) made important deductions from the observation of a new star in Cassiopeia. He denied the traditional belief that the planets moved in crystal spheres, but believed that the earth was stationary, with the other planets, including the sun, orbiting round it.

Galileo (1564–1632), who had already studied the uses of the pendulum, advanced the whole nature of astronomy by constructing a telescope (1609). This enabled him to discover the satellite moons of Jupiter, and from the observation of sun-spots he concluded that the sun rotated on its own axis. From this he deduced that the earth did likewise, and, like Jupiter, carried its own moon. Kepler (1571–1630) stated three laws of planetary motion to the effect that the planets describe ellipses round the sun, whose centre is a focus. The sun's attraction holds the planets in their orbits, so that its relative distance from them may be calculated. Kepler conceived a theory of gravitation to be confirmed a generation later by Newton.

All the heavens now lay open to discovery. Greenwich Observatory was founded in 1675, and English astronomers like Flamsteed, Hadley, and Herschel enlarged the size and range of the telescope until it was possible to survey and record the whole surface of the sky. With this great advance in observational astronomy, other scientific aids were presently brought to the study of the universe, among them photography, spectroscopy, and astro-physics, which is the analysis of the physical composition of the stars and their atmospheres.

In the present century astronomy has been brought into a wider cosmological context by the great English astronomer Sir Arthur Eddington (1882–1944), whose observations enabled him to confirm Einstein's theory of relativity.

H. Macpherson, *Makers of Astronomy* (London, 1933).
S. S. Eddington, *The Mysterious Universe* (London, 1933).
MMR

ASTURIAS RISING in Spain, (Oct. 1934), the only rising of what might have been a nation-wide leftist revolution, and a prelude to the Spanish Civil War. The elections of Nov. 1933 were marked by the success of the Catholic electoral confederation of Gil Robles (the CEDA) and followed by the inclusion of CEDA members in Lerroux's cabinet. The revolution of the following Oct. was the leftist reaction to this supposed capture of the republic by the right, but it was a fiasco in Madrid, and in Catalonia was rendered futile by the indifference of the Confederación Nacional de Trabajo (CNT).

In Asturias, by contrast, a prototype Popular Front of left-wing parties was formed and some 70,000 miners rose, occupying Oriedo and Gijon. Isolated as it was, the rising was doomed from the start and was suppressed in an action in which the Foreign Legion and Moroccan troops played the most important part. Some 3000 people were killed and 7000 wounded, the majority being workmen.

The rising evoked panic on the right. The action of the revolutionaries in executing some 20 persons and burning several churches was distorted into widespread stories of atrocities against persons and property. The use of Moorish troops against Spaniards was unprecedented. On the left, the unity which made the rising possible, the resistance of the miners, and the hardship of the subsequent repression, both contributed to the formation of the Popular Front and helped engender the mystique of left-wing resistance to fascism, especially outside Spain.

ASWAN DAM, storage dam for Nile irrigation, built (1898–1902), and heightened (1910–12 and 1936). A new high dam for irrigation and hydro-electric power was constructed from 1960 onwards with Soviet financial aid.

ATABEG (ATABAK), Turkish title given under the Seljuks to high officials appointed to act as guardians of the young princes of the blood. Some of the Atabegs, taking advantage of domestic strife amongst the Seljuk princes, established local dynasties of their own—eg, the Zangids at Mosul.

ATAHUALPA (1500–33), the de facto ruler of Peru when the Spaniards arrived at Cajamarca (1532). Atahualpa was the son of a union between the Inca emperor Huayna Capac and the daughter of the ruler of Quito. Recently victorious over his half-brother Huáscar in a civil war, Atahualpa was confident that the Spaniards represented no threat. He was quickly captured, held for ransom, then assassinated by order of Pizarro (29 Aug. 1533).

ATAIDE, LUIS DE (*fl.* late 16th cent.), viceroy of Portuguese India. His brilliant defence of Chaul and Goa against the Sultans of Birjapur and Golconda earned him the reputation of a military genius.

ATASI, AL-, HASHIM (1869–1960), Sunni Muslim landlord and politician from Homs in Syria. An Ottoman official before 1918, he became the leading nationalist under the French mandate and president of the Syrian republic (1936–1939, 1950–1, 1954–5).

ATHANASIUS (c. AD 295–373), bishop of Alexandria from 328 and defender of the Nicene faith against Arianism. First prominent as deacon of Alexander at the Council of Nicaea, he was exiled five times when bishop because of his views, but retained the support of the Alexandrian Christians as well as the monks. In later years he became more conciliatory to those who refused to use the Nicene language. His extensive theological works are mostly concerned with the controversies of his age and with vindicating the Nicene faith. The most famous, *On the Incarnation*, was an early work, written some time before 318.

ATHAPASCAN INDIANS, the most widely distributed of all Indian linguistic groups of North America, originally extending from the Arctic coast into northern Mexico; from the Pacific to the Hudson Bay at the north; and from the Rio Colorado to the mouth of the Rio Grande at the south. Athapascan languages are sharply distinguished from other American languages, but clearly related to each other. Athapascan speakers showed wide differences in physical type and culture, owing to their geographic separation. Because members of this family tended to adopt the culture of neighbouring peoples, it is difficult to determine or describe any distinctive Athapascan culture. The most representative culture is probably that of the tribes of the northern group, such as the Chippewa. A certain amount of cultural and linguistic uniformity was found among the southern tribes, which included the Apache and Navajo.

ATHELSTAN (*reg.* 924–39), King of Wessex, son of King Edward the Elder, was a great ruler and a cultured patron of learning. His overlordship of the principal kings in Britain, acknowledged in 927, was challenged in 937 by a coalition of Britons, Scots, and Scandinavians which Athelstan defeated at Brunanburh.

ATHENS, capital of modern Greece, the most splendid and best known of the ancient Greek city-states, renowned for its democratic government, its courageous opposition to the Persian invasions, and the intellectual and artistic achievements of its people.

First settled in the neolithic period, it was a Mycenean centre, though insignificant in the Homeric poems, and, with Attica, remained free of the Dorian invaders (c. 1100–1000 BC), archaeology showing a continuity of culture and tradition telling that Ionians fled from the Peloponnese to Attica and thence crossed the Aegean to Asia Minor. In the Geometric period (c. 1050–750) its pottery was outstanding, but thereafter Dorian states developed faster, chiefly through the fruits of colonial enterprises (in which Athens took no part), Corinthian pottery dominating in the Orientalizing and early Black-Figure periods. By 600 aristocratic oppression and economic stringency, threatening the peasants with permanent serfdom, had brought Attica near to revolution, but Solon's reforms (594) freed the serfs, laying the foundations of economic expansion and of democracy. Though fine Attic Black-Figure pottery began to fill foreign markets, further political strife enabled Peisistratus to seize power, but the Peisistratid tyranny (546–510), by interrupting aristocratic faction and strengthening national spirit, hastened Athens' development at home and abroad. At its end, Spartan intervention was frustrated and Cleisthenes' reforms (508) confirmed the end of local rivalries, vesting authority in the primary assembly (*ecclesia*) and representative popular council (*boule*). Thebes and Chalcis were defeated and, though some were ready to give way, the first Persian invasion was repulsed at Marathon (490). Thereafter Themistocles silenced potential partisans for Persia and prepared a fleet, so that, when the Persians invaded again (480), the Athenians contributed greatly to Greek survival with their ships at Artemisium and Salamis and their readiness to fight on when Athens and Attica were overrun.

After the Persian withdrawal, Athens took over the leadership of the Aegean and Asiatic Greeks, organized the Delian League, which kept the area free from Persian interference for 65 years, and, under vigorous leaders, *eg*, Cimon and Pericles, rapidly became wealthier and more powerful than any other Greek state. In the century after 480 it produced its most brilliant literature and art, the world's first great dramatic tragedies by Aeschylus, Sophocles, and Euripides, and comedies by Aristophanes, the finest Red-Figure pottery, the sculpture of Pheidias, and the Parthenon, Erectheum, and other buildings; and it was the centre of the new rationalism, exemplified in Thucydides, the historian, and Socrates and in the many Sophists drawn to Athens from other cities. Its political eminence was, however, resented by many allies, some of whom were forcibly coerced, *eg*, Euboea (446) and Samos (440-439), and by mainland Greeks, *eg*, Sparta, Corinth, and Thebes.

After a first indecisive war with the Spartan alliance (459–445), the second great Peloponnesian War (431–404) ended in Athens' total defeat. This was due as much to the inability of its leaders, *eg*, Nicias and Alcibiades, to hold the democracy to a consistent use of predominant naval power, and to internal disputes, *eg*, the revolution of the Four Hundred (411), as to the disastrous plague (430–426), the Spartans' military superiority, and the eventual intervention of Persia. Athens' political and economic resurgence was remarkable. Recovering full independence in the Corinthian War (395–387), it was influential after 378, in rallying opposition to Sparta in the Second Athenian Confederacy, but, though Sparta was humbled, the victory was the Thebans' and subsequent failures against them and defeat in the Social War (357–355) weakened the Athenians' resistance to the expansion of Macedon under Philip II. Urged on by Demosthenes, they refused to compromise with him, though ill-supported by other Greeks and themselves reluctant to pay the price of effective warfare. But the coalition eventually organized by Demosthenes was defeated at Chaeronea (338) and Greece passed under Macedonian control.

Intellectually Athens was still supreme. In this century academies were established, by Isocrates concentrating on oratory, the practice of which reached its high point with Demosthenes, and on a wider basis by Plato and Aristotle, whose philosophical writings form the foundation of much western thought. Partly because of this cultural distinction Athens was well treated by Philip and Alexander the Great, but after the Lamian War democracy was suppressed and a Macedonian garrison installed (322–307); an experience repeated after 295 and after the Chremonidean War between 262 and 228, as Hellenistic rulers allowed anxiety to secure Athens' position to outweigh respect for its brilliance. In the third century, though outshone by Alexandria in many fields, Athens remained supreme in philosophy, the Stoic Zeno and Epicurus founding their schools. Sympathetic to Roman intervention (c. 200), it became a centre of learning in the new Greco-Roman world, even after Sulla sacked it for supporting Mithridates VI of Pontus (86 BC). Later Athens was much favoured by certain emperors, *eg*, Hadrian, who completed the temple of Zeus begun in the 6th cent., its professors being paid from the imperial treasury from the 2nd cent. AD, surviving Alaric's occupation (395) and Theodosius I's edicts, until Justinian prohibited the study of philosophy (529).

Rarely mentioned in the Byzantine chronicles, Athens declined in the Middle Ages, until it fell to the Turks (1458). Its monuments suffered severely during Venetian attacks in 1687-8, especially when a Turkish powder magazine in the Parthenon was exploded, and in the Greek War of Independence, when the Greeks captured the city in 1821, losing it again between 1827 and 1833. It then became the capital of the new kingdom, growing rapidly in population from about 5000 in 1834 to 1,837,041 (greater Athens) in 1961 and surviving the fighting of the Second World War and subsequent disturbances without serious damage.

Burn, A. R., *Pericles and Athens* (London, 1948).
Hill, I. T., *The Ancient City of Athens* (London, 1953).

TTBR

ATHLONE, GODARD VAN REEDE, 1st Earl of (Irish) (1644–1703), soldier and favourite of William III. He came to England with William and served him in Ireland, where he was in command (1691) until the cessation of fighting, and in Flanders. Promoted field marshal and created an earl (1692), he was appointed second-in-command to Marlborough in 1702.

ATHOLL, WALTER STEWART, 19th Earl of (Scottish) (c. 1360–1437), paternal uncle of James I, in whose assassination he was implicated (Feb. 1437). His motives included a desire to rid Scotland of an effective but unpopular king, and his own ambition to secure the crown. He and his fellow-assassins were executed in March 1437.

ATHOS, a peninsula of Chalcidice, long famous as a centre of monastic life within the Greek Orthodox Church. It is an autonomous republic forming part of Greece. There are 20 monasteries at Athos and also 12 hermitages. A Synod comprising one member from each establishment sits at Kariai.

ATISHA (d. 1054), Buddhist scholar and preacher who, in 1042, at a mature age, left eastern India to settle in Gu-ge (south-western Tibet) and later moved to Nye-thang near Lhasa, where he stayed till his death. His principal achievement is that of making Mahayana Buddhism the dominant religion in Tibet.

ATJEH (or ACHIN), sultanate and Islamic centre in northern Sumatra. The state was born out of the Muslim counter-attack against the Portuguese in Asia, when Sultan Ali Mughayat (d. 1530) drove the Portuguese from Pidië (1521) and Pasai (1524). The various competing port-states of Sumatra's north coast were thereby united, and were gradually welded into a distinct ethnic and linguistic group. The Muslim trade which left Malacca at the Portuguese conquest (1511) began to focus on the Atjehnese capital, and a new Muslim spice route was established directly between Atjeh and the Red Sea, avoiding Portuguese bases in India. Atjeh established relations with Constantinople in the 1560s, and several of the six attacks it launched against Portuguese Malacca (1537–1629) were in concert with other Muslim powers. The strongest of Atjeh's sultans, Iskandar Muda (1607–36), centralized government and conquered as far afield as Pahang (1618). But the aristocracy of *ulèëbalang*s reacted after his death by successively putting four women on the throne (1641–99), and limiting their direct authority to the capital. Meanwhile, the profitable dependencies producing pepper in western Sumatra and tin in Malaya fell under Dutch control. The sultanate continued to decline under later Arab (1699) and Bugis (1727) dynasties. After 1786 British Penang replaced Atjeh as the local entrepôt port. But the contemporary revival of pepper cultivation made Atjeh the world's biggest supplier (c. 1790–1873). In the 19th cent. Atjeh successfully kept the colonial powers at bay, while renewing its links with Turkey (1850, 1868, 1873). Following a treaty of mutual defence which Raffles had signed with Atjeh (1819), Britain included a guarantee of Atjehnese independence in her 1824 convention with Holland. The Dutch, however, increasingly regarded Atjeh as the 'Achilles' heel' of their position in the Archipelago, and persuaded Britain to abandon this guarantee in return for commercial concessions (1871). Holland soon attacked Atjeh (1873) and began the ruinous 40-year 'Atjeh War'. Effective Dutch control began only in 1898, and guerrilla fighting led by the *ulama* continued until 1912. Having abolished the sultanate (1874), the Dutch based their administration entirely on the *ulèëbalang* class. This left the *ulama* as the popular spokesmen for peasant discontents. Organized in Daud Beureu'eh's PUSA, they led an anti-Dutch uprising on the eve of the Japanese invasion (1942), a successful anti-*ulèëbalang* purge during the early independence struggle (1945–6), and an abortive revolt against Djakarta aiming at an Islamic state (1953–9).

A. Reid, *The Contest for North Sumatra: Atjeh, the Netherlands and Britain, 1858–1898* (Kuala Lumpur, 1969).

AJSR

ATKINS, RICHARD (1745–1820), son of an English baronet, Sir William Bowyer, assumed the surname Atkins on inheriting a legacy. He exploited the standing of his family to secure various official appointments, rising to be judge-advocate, in New South Wales, to which he migrated in 1791. Dissolute, financially distrusted, and judicially ineffective, he nevertheless retained office at the trial of his creditor, John Macarthur (1808), when his presence on the bench contributed to the Bligh mutiny. Shortly after this he was recalled to England, where he died insolvent.

ATKINSON, SIR HARRY ALBERT (1831–92), prime minister and treasurer of NZ during the 1870s and 1880s. Born in England, Atkinson emigrated (1853) to Taranaki, NZ, where he set up as small farmer. He joined Weld's ministry (1864–1865), advocating 'self-reliance' in defence. As colonial treasurer from 1875, he sought to moderate Vogel's 'leaps and bounds' policy into one of 'prudence'. Treasurer and/or prime minister for most of the period to 1891, Atkinson gained an unrivalled reputation in public finance, the House of Representatives turning to him after the extravagances of Macandrew (1879) and Vogel (1887). Labelled a Conservative by self-styled Liberal opponents, Atkinson sometimes called himself a radical, but his politics were pragmatic. His state insurance and leasehold bills (1882–3) were rejected as too advanced. His greatest work was to give the colony an adequate customs revenue (1888), thus also reassuring British bondholders. He became involved (1890–81) in dubious manœuvres to handicap his successor, John Ballance.

ATLANTA, BURNING OF (1864), controversial incident during the American Civil War. Sherman occupied Atlanta, GA (1 Sept.), and before starting on his march to the sea in November, most of the civilian population was expelled and much of the city burned.

ATLANTIC, BATTLE OF (1940–3), German attacks on shipping in the Atlantic during the Second World War. The German strategy aimed at cutting off Britain's supply of food and munitions, primarily by submarine. It was not until the last quarter of 1943 that the tide turned. Asdic and radar, combined with the 260 destroyers supplied by the US in 1943, meant that U-boat sinkings were running at a rate greater than that at which they could be replaced, while by 1944 American and British shipbuilding exceeded the losses of merchant ships.

Year	British loss (net of new British construction)		U-boats sunk
	000 tons	(metric tons)	
1940	3627	3684	22
1941	3479	3533	35
1942	6402	6503	85
1943	1410	1432	237

ATLANTIC CHARTER (1941), declaration of common objectives by President F. D. Roosevelt and the British prime minister, Winston Churchill, after a secret meeting off Argentia, Nfld (Aug. 1941), almost four months before the US entered the Second World War. They disclaimed any desire for territorial aggrandizement and announced agreement on the principles that should underlie the post-war settlements. Most of these, such as self-determination for all peoples, equal access to trade and raw materials for all nations, disarmament, and freedom of the seas, paralleled Woodrow Wilson's Fourteen Points (1918). Although serving as the ideological basis for Allied co-operation during the war, there was considerable disagreement about interpretation and application of specific clauses and the ultimate objectives of the charter were never realized.

ATLANTIC MONTHLY (1857–), US literary magazine also devoted to politics and the arts. Very influential in the 19th cent. under the editorship of James Russell Lowell, William Dean Howells, and others, its contributors included most of the leading intellectuals of the day.

ATLANTIC NUCLEAR FORCE, counter-proposal of the British Labour government of 1964 to the Multilateral Force proposal of the US. It provided for a nuclear naval and air force composed of British, US, and French elements, together with a mixed-manned and jointly owned element in which the non-nuclear European powers would take part. Designed, like the MLF, to satisfy hypothetical German aspirations to nuclear status while preventing the dissemination of nuclear weapons, it was a still-born proposal whose only effect was to increase doubts on the continent of Europe as to the seriousness of Britain's 'European' commitment.

ATLANTIC TRIANGLE describes the pattern of Anglo-American trade in the 18th cent. Britain exported manufactured goods to West Africa, receiving in exchange cargoes of slaves. These were paid for in the West Indies by exports of sugar and rum to Britain. At the same time, the American colonies exported provisions and raw materials to the West Indies, receiving in exchange rum from the colonies and manufactures from Britain.

ATLASOV, A. (*fl.* 17th cent.) cossack leader who led the conquest of Kamchatka, the eastern peninsula of Siberia, in 1697, thereby completing the expansion of Muscovy to the Pacific.

ATOMIC ENERGY COMMISSION, US governmental agency controlling the domestic development of atomic energy. It was established by the Atomic Energy Act (1946), which provided for control to be vested in civilian rather than military hands.

ATONISM, ancient Egyptian worship of the god Aton, of whom the visible aspect was the sun, developed by Amenhetep IV (*c.* 1367–1350 BC), who suppressed the worship of other gods and centred the worship of Aton at Amarna. Soon after his death, Atonism was suppressed.

ATTAINDER, ACT OF. British act of parliament registering a person's conviction for treason and declaring the forfeiture of his property to the Crown. Attainder also deprived the convicted man's heirs of lands in tail and was thus used by successive victors in the civil wars of the 15th cent. to acquire the property of their defeated rivals. It was first used in 1459 against Richard, Duke of York, and his baronial supporters. Under the Tudor and early Stuart monarchs it remained a powerful but arbitrary weapon by which parliament could dispose of embarrassing individuals without a trial, *eg,* Thomas Cromwell, Strafford, and Laud, whose alleged crimes were insufficient to be proved treasonable in a court of law or by process of impeachment. As a supplementary legal procedure attainder lost credit under the later Stuarts and with the development of constitutional monarchy and ministerial responsibility this vicious and irrelevant parliamentary process disappeared.

ATTALUS I (*reg.* 241–197 BC), King of Pergamum, first of the Attalid dynasty, who raised his kingdom to its greatest power and was instrumental in bringing the Romans into the Greek world. After early victories over the Galatians and the Seleucids, he supported the Aetolians in Greece against Philip V of Macedon, whose ambitions he feared, and allied himself with the Romans in the First Macedonian War (211–205). In 201, after more aggression by Philip, he joined

Athens and Rhodes in seeking Roman help, co-operating with the Roman fleet in the subsequent Second Macedonian War.

ATTALUS III (*reg.* 138–133 BC), last Attalid King of Pergamum, whose kingdom, bequeathed to the Romans, became the province of Asia.

ATTERBURY, FRANCIS (1662–1733), bishop of Rochester and dean of Westminster and one of the most prominent High Church Tories in Queen Anne's reign. Consecrated bishop in 1713, he was a friend of Oxford and Bolingbroke, and on the queen's death urged his extreme Tory colleagues, led by Bolingbroke, to overthrow the Act of Settlement, proclaim James III at the royal exchange, and request immediate help from Louis XIV. Atterbury believed that the legitimacy of the Stuart line was in conscience more important than a Protestant monarchy and that adequate safeguards for the Church could be secured from James Edward.

　　Remaining a devoted Jacobite, he became associated in 1722 with a plot to seize power from George I. In August he was arrested, but his involvement was never proved. Despite his own eloquent speech of defence, the bill of pains and penalties depriving him of his preferments and sentencing him to perpetual banishment was passed by the Lords in May 1723 with a majority of 40. Atterbury went into exile.

ATTICUS, T. POMPONIUS (109–32 BC), Roman banker and patron of literature. Though intimate with Cicero, whose letters to himself he published, he took no part in politics, but was careful to be a friend to all parties.

ATTILA (d. 453), King of the Huns. Known to contemporaries as 'the Scourge of God', between 445 and 450 he ravaged the provinces of the eastern empire, thereafter sweeping west in attacks on Gaul and Italy. In 451 a joint army of Romans and Visigoths under Aetius inflicted a decisive check on the Huns at Châlons. Two years later Attila was dead and the Hunnish threat to the west melted away. He does not seem to have been the savage of popular imagination and had considerable gifts of military leadership. However, he created no stable institutions and the year after his death the Hunnic dominion collapsed (454).

ATTLEE, CLEMENT RICHARD ATTLEE, 1st Earl (1883–1967), leader of the British Labour Party (1935–55) and prime minister from July 1945 to Oct. 1951. Attlee, the son of a solicitor, was called to the bar in 1906, but abandoned legal practice in 1909. In 1907 he began doing social work in the East End of London, where he lived until 1922.

　　Unlike many of his associates, Attlee was not a pacifist and served with distinction during the First World War. In 1919 he returned to social work in the East End, and became mayor of Stepney, and in 1922 was elected MP for Limehouse, which he represented until 1950; then till 1955 he was member for West Walthamstow.

　　He gained administrative experience as under-secretary of state for war in the first Labour government (1924). In 1927 he was appointed to the Statutory Commission for India, in 1930 became chancellor of the duchy of Lancaster, and in 1931 postmaster-general. He reacted strongly against MacDonald's formation of the National Government (1931). He became deputy leader of the Labour Party, and in 1935 succeeded to the leadership of the parliamentary party after Lansbury's resignation. Attlee had been one of the few Labour leaders to retain his parliamentary seat in the election of 1931, and though after 1935 attempts were made by those returning to parliament to replace him as leader, they were unsuccessful.

　　Under Attlee the Labour Party was moderately reformist in domestic policy and sought to oppose fascism in Europe, not by building up national defences, but by collective defence through the League of Nations. Attlee supported the decision to declare war in 1939, but his refusal to serve under Chamberlain in a national government was instrumental in the latter's replacement by Winston Churchill. Attlee, alone with Churchill, served in the war cabinet throughout the coalition government. As well as being deputy prime minister, he was lord privy seal (1940–2), secretary of state for the dominions (1942–3), and lord president of the council (1943–5).

He led the Labour Party in the electoral victory of 1945. His government was responsible for a series of measures, notably the creation of a national health service, and the extension of national insurance, which came to be regarded as establishing a 'Welfare State'. The actions of his government in which he was most closely involved personally were the grant of independence to India and Pakistan (in which he had a longstanding interest) and the decision to make the atom bomb (because of the secrecy involved). His government's foreign policy included the containment of the Soviet Union in close association with the US, and the refusal to enter the negotiations which led to the establishment of European Coal and Steel Community.

In Feb. 1950 the government's majority was reduced to six and the government itself weakened by a dispute over rearmament and social expenditure, which led to the resignation of Bevan and Wilson. In Oct. 1951 the Labour Party won a popular majority over the Conservatives but lost its parliamentary majority, and Attlee was subsequently criticized for his tactics in these two elections. In opposition he fought for the unity of the party against Bevanite opposition over German rearmament. He retired from the leadership in 1955. He published two volumes of memoirs, *As it happened* (1954), and (with Francis Williams) *A Prime Minister Remembers* (1961).

ATTOLICO, BERNARDO (1880–1942), Italian career diplomat. As ambassador to Moscow (1930–5), he negotiated economic agreements and a pact of friendship (1933). As ambassador to Berlin (July 1935–April 1940), he prepared the Axis agreement of Oct. 1936. He subsequently sought to prevent firm Italian commitments to Hitler, though his valuable information and intuitions about German policies towards Czechoslovakia, Russia, and Poland went largely unheeded by Mussolini. He facilitated Chamberlain's Munich settlement and helped forestall an early Italian entry into the war in 1939.

ATTWOOD, THOMAS (1783–1856), British radical politician and currency reformer. He was a banker and ironmaster who first became publicly known through his opposition to the resumption of cash payments after 1819, which brought deflation in its train. Birmingham industries, he argued, had been severely hit by the ending of the Napoleonic War, and a period of moderately rising prices was essential to the restoration of prosperity. This he wished to achieve through a carefully regulated issue of banknotes. Attwood has attracted attention in recent years as one who foreshadowed modern monetary theory.

As a politician he is important for his foundation of the Birmingham Political Union (Dec. 1829). He was elected MP for Birmingham (1832). He supported the Chartists and presented the first Chartist petition to the House of Commons (1839), though he later quarrelled with O'Connor.

AUBREY, JOHN (1626–97), British antiquary, author, and foundation fellow of the Royal Society. His most famous work is his *Brief Lives* of 17th-cent. figures, first published as *Lives of Eminent Men* in volume 2 of *Letters written by Eminent Persons in the 17th and 18th Centuries* (1813). His *Monumenta Britannica* (never published in full) contains the first reference to Stonehenge and the Druids.

AUCHINLECK, SIR CLAUDE JOHN EYRE (1884–), British field marshal and army commander during the Second World War. He began his career in the Indian army and in the First World War served in the Middle East.

He commanded the British army in Norway (1940), was appointed commander-in-chief of the Indian army (1941), and was in command of the Middle East front (1941–2). The defeat of the British army in Libya and his subsequent reluctance to mount a counter-offensive led to his removal and replacement by Gen. Alexander. Auchinleck returned to his command of the Indian army, but held no further frontline command. He was responsible for the armed services in India during the period of the transfer of power and partition.

AUCKLAND, GEORGE EDEN, Earl of (1784–1849), president of the board of trade and master of the mint in Grey's reform ministry (1830), first lord of the admiralty under Melbourne (1834), and successor to Bentinck as governor-general of India (1836–42). He favoured the promotion of English education in India, but not at the expense of oriental studies and institutions, and he patronized the educational institutions of the missionaries, but refused to countenance their religious activities. He was interested in famine relief and the amelioration of slavery, but became involved in the disastrous First Afghan War (1838–42). Though responsibility for the war must be shared by the British government, Auckland was unduly influenced by his advisers, especially Macnaghten and Wade. His greatest error was to wage war after the siege of Herat had been raised. He was recalled by Peel in Feb. 1842.

AUCKLAND, CITY OF, selected by Gov. Hobson as NZ's second capital (1840) because of its fine harbour, position among Maori settlements, and agricultural possibilities, Auckland was the seat of the General Assembly (1854–65). For a time (mid-1860s–mid-1880s) eclipsed by Dunedin as NZ's largest city, greater Auckland was from the early 1930s NZ's principal port and had a population of a half-million by 1970.

AUCKLAND, PROVINCE OF. Not 'Wakefieldian' in origin and with most Maoris, Auckland stood apart from the southern settlements of NZ. Settled largely before 1840 from NSW, it was by 1853 the largest and most populous province, losing primacy to Otago in the 1860s, but regaining it by 1901. As bush-clad areas were cleared, Auckland dairy farming leapt ahead of Taranaki, especially after 1918, when poorer pumice land was broken in and conifer forests planted. Together with Auckland city, some secondary centres (*eg*, Hamilton, Gisborne, Whangarei) grew rapidly after 1945, and by the early 1960s the former Auckland province accounted for over 40 per cent of NZ's population and over 70 per cent of its Maoris.

AUCTORITAS, Roman political term denoting the prestige and authority of a man who was an *auctor* ('originator') of public policy and who could thus influence decisions and events through the deference paid to his opinions. It referred to the Senate as the policy-making body in republican Rome and to senior senators as individuals who directed and controlled the Senate's deliberations. Augustus used the term to describe the basis of his pre-eminence and under the Roman empire it became the prerogative of the emperors as being the originators of all policy.

AUDIENCIA, highest court of colonial Spanish America, combining judicial, administrative, and legislative powers. It served as a court of appeals directly below the Council of the Indies in the colonial hierarchy, and as a consultative council to the viceroy or captain general. The Crown authorized the establishment of the first *audiencia* in Spanish America at Santo Domingo (1511). Its jurisdiction included the entire Caribbean region. The first *audiencia* on the mainland was established at Mexico City (1527), with jurisdiction over New Spain. An *audiencia* was authorized for Lima, Peru (1542), with jurisdiction over all of continental South America. Central America was charged to an *audiencia* established in Guatemala (1543). By the late 18th cent. the number of *audiencias* had grown to 13.

The *audiencia* was usually the second most powerful governing institution in the colonies after the viceroy. A strong *audiencia* could at times exert a greater influence over local affairs than a viceroy or captain general. In the absence of the local governor, the *audiencia* assumed power.

Internal dissension often divided the *audiencia*, sapping its effectiveness. Conflicts with viceroys were common throughout the colonial era. The *audiencia* was authorized to hear cases brought against viceroys by individuals.

Audiencias varied in size according to time and location. The *audiencia* at Mexico City consisted initially of four judges (*oidores*) and a president (the viceroy). Ten judges sat on the tribunal by the 18th cent., while less prominent *audiencias* consisted of three to five judges. Both civil and criminal cases were tried and, normally, two days each week were set aside for cases involving Indians.   HDS

AUDUBON, JOHN JAMES (1785–1851), Haiti-born artist and naturalist. He studied in Paris under J.-L. David and travelled widely in the US before publishing *The Birds of America* (1827–38). Although sometimes scientifically inaccurate, his depictions are extraordinarily alive. Work on *The Viviparous Quadrupeds of North America* was unfinished at his death.

AUGHRIN, BATTLE OF (12 July 1691), bloody engagement fought near Athlone between the Protestant forces of William III's general, Ginkel, and a combined Franco-Irish army under St Ruth during the Irish campaign of 1689–91. The French were confident of victory, but the delay between St Ruth's death and Sarsfield's assumption of command enabled the British to slaughter the Irish.

AUGMENTATIONS, COURT OF, English revenue court modelled on that of the duchy of Lancaster and established by statute in 1536 to deal with the disposal of monastic properties with an income of less than £200 dissolved in that year. The buildings, land, plate, and jewels were surveyed by officers of the court in the king's name, who took possession of them and then resold or leased them. The court, one of the six financial departments of state reorganized by Thomas Cromwell, was served by civil servants, *eg*, Sir Walter Mildmay, and performed its task reasonably efficiently and humanely, taking care to rehouse or pension off the monks affected by the dissolution.

In 1547 the court was fused with that of general surveyors and this new court of augmentations administered all the Crown lands except those of the duchy of Lancaster. It was abolished seven years later (1554), its work being transferred to the exchequer.

AUGSBURG, free imperial city on the Lech river, originally a Roman site. The Magyar invasions of Bavaria in the 9th cent. gave the impetus for its resettlement, the city becoming a refuge. It enjoyed great commercial prosperity, mainly as an entrepôt for Italian (particularly Venetian) trade. In the late 15th and 16th cents it was a leading German financial and cultural centre, the home of the Fugger family, Germany's richest bankers.

AUGSBURG, CONFESSION OF (1530), statement of Lutheran doctrine composed by Melanchthon and the humanist Spalatin as the basis of discussion for reunion at the Diet of Augsburg. Moderate and conciliatory in tone, it dissociated the Lutherans from the Anabaptists and preserved the concept of the eucharist. The Catholic negotiators, however, could not accept any deviation from Catholic doctrine and the confession, far from providing the means of religious reunion, became, in its revised form (1551), the basis of the Lutheran Church.

AUGSBURG, DIETS OF (1525, 1530, 1547–8, 1555). Various meetings at Augsburg of the imperial diet or the body of representatives of the states within the Holy Roman empire,

summoned by the Emperor Charles V to discuss the major problem of his reign, the Lutheran revolt and its consequences.

At the first Diet (1525), the emperor temporized on the question of Lutheranism, preoccupied as he was with the Peasants' War. Despite the condemnation of Luther by the Edict of Worms, support for him grew among the German princes. At the second Diet (1530), therefore, Charles, in trying to tackle the Lutheran problem, faced a well-entrenched religious and economic movement. The dissenters were asked to prepare statements of their belief as a basis for discussion, the most prominent of which was Melanchthon's Confession of Augsburg. Despite the latter's moderate tone, the Diet failed in its objective of restoring unity by compromise. At the next Diet (1547–8), after the Protestant collapse in the War of the Schmalkaldic League, the representatives reluctantly accepted an Interim (30 June 1548) with a Catholic bias. This was soon repudiated by both Catholics and Protestants and the struggle continued until the Diet of 1555 forged a compromise settlement known as the peace of Augsburg.

AUGSBURG, PEACE OF (1555), compromise settlement reached by Catholic and Protestant representatives at the Diet of Augsburg, which ended the German phase of the Reformation. The peace is best known for its advocacy of the principle of *cuius regio eius reliqio*, by which the religion of the prince determined the faith of his subjects. This emphasis on religious uniformity and condemnation of dissent was characteristic of the 16th cent.

The settlement gave half a century of peace to the German states by permitting Catholic and Lutheran princes to live together in a degree of mutual tolerance. By excluding the Calvinists from the compromise, however, it merely postponed a further religious conflict. The peace proved unenforceable with regard to the continuing process of secularization of ecclesiastical property. When the Catholic and Protestant camps were reinforced by the extreme forces of the Jesuit order on the one hand and the Puritan and Calvinist groups on the other, the uneasy settlement of Augsburg was submerged in the wider European strife of the Thirty Years War (1618–48).

AUGSBURG, WAR OF THE LEAGUE OF (1689–97), also known as the Nine Years War. This was the first European conflict in which Louis XIV's ambitions were successfully checked by a great alliance of powers.

Louis XIV's *réunion* policy had provoked the formation of the League of Augsburg (1686), a defensive alliance of some of the German states, headed by Bavaria and Brandenburg, and including Sweden. While the Holy Roman emperor was involved with Turkey and William of Orange was preoccupied with James II's declining popularity in England, Louis felt that a swift assault upon the empire was the best means of defending himself against the league. In 1688 the French army invaded the Palatinate and part of the electorate of Cologne to back up prepared dynastic claims. Shortly after, he declared war on the United Provinces, while simultaneously William invaded England (Nov. 1688), allowing James II to flee for refuge to France. In May 1689 the Dutch and the emperor joined in an anti-French alliance, to which England, united with the Dutch under one effective ruler, later acceded, to be followed in 1690 by Spain and Savoy. Thus Louis XIV found himself encircled by enemies.

The war was the first major conflict in modern times in which sea power was a decisive factor. At first the French navy, built up by Colbert, successfully challenged English and Dutch control of the Channel, enabling James II to launch his invasion of Ireland. The French naval victory under Tourville off Beachy Head (1690) emphasized the danger of a Catholic invasion of England and undermined Anglo-Dutch commerce. However, the battle of La Hogue (1692) forced the French navy back into its traditional subsidiary role and for the duration of the war French naval activity was confined to the attacks of privateers under royal licence upon English and Dutch shipping. Meanwhile, the defeat of James II's army at the Boyne (1690) saw the effective end of the danger to England's flank, and Louis XIV was forced back upon defensive continental campaigns.

Militarily, the war was marked by a series of unspectacular French successes in Flanders under the Duke of Luxembourg, *eg*, Fleurus (1690), the capture of Mons (1691) and Namur (1692), and the battles of Steinkirk (1692) and Neerwinden (1693). Elsewhere, Marshal Catinat conquered Savoy and Nice (1691) and Vendôme Barcelona (1697), but English naval power in the Mediterranean prevented Louis from exploiting his land victories in that area. William's recapture of Namur (1697) exemplified this war of siege and counter-siege and produced a stalemate ended in 1697 by the treaty of Ryswick.   MKS

AUGURS, Roman religious college allegedly founded by Romulus, but in fact established later under Etruscan influence. The complement, originally 3, rose to 16 by the end of the republic; vacancies were initially filled by the college, but after 104 BC by popular election. Its members' religious duties, laid down in the *libri augurales*, were chiefly to man permanent observation-posts round Rome, and by observation of the flight of birds to decide whether it would be expedient to conduct official business.

AUGUSTENBURG, FREDERICK, Duke of (1829–80), claimant to Schleswig-Holstein in 1863. The son of Duke Ernest, he revived with his father's connivance the claim under the Salic law which the latter had formally abandoned (1852). He was well received in Holstein and supported by the German Diet, but discarded by Bismarck.

AUGUSTINE, archbishop of Canterbury (597–*c.* 604). Having been chosen by Pope Gregory the Great to lead the first Roman mission to the pagan Anglo-Saxons, Augustine converted Aethelbert, King of Kent. As the first Abp of Canterbury he continued to act on papal instructions. He failed to establish friendly relations with the aloof British clergy.

AUGUSTINE OF HIPPO, Saint (354–430), was born in North Africa of a pagan father and a Christian mother, St Monica. He studied at Carthage, where he became a Manichee, but growing dissatisfied with the sect after nine years, he moved to Milan in 384. There he came into contact with Neoplatonism, the work of St Paul, and with the bishop, St Ambrose. This was the turning point of his life; while reading St Paul in 386 he underwent a dramatic conversion. He was baptized by Ambrose in 387 and retired to a monastery which he founded (388–9) at Tagaste in Africa. He became a priest by popular demand and succeeded as Bp of nearby Hippo in 395. He remained at Hippo for the rest of his life, dying during the siege of the city by the Vandals in 430. The details of his life are to be found in his *Confessions*, written between 397 and 401, the first known autobiography.

Augustine was the greatest and most original of all the Latin Church fathers; in political thought and philosophy as well as in theology he dominated western Christendom for a millennium. His greatest work was *The City of God*, inspired by the fall of Rome in 410. Theologically, this had an influence on the development of western thought second only to the Bible; medieval political thought was dominated by it and medieval philosophy given a strongly Platonic cast by it until at least the time of Aquinas.

AUGUSTINIAN ORDER. The Hermits of St Augustine, commonly called Austin friars, claim descent for their rule from that given by St Augustine to the monastery he founded at Tagaste in 388–9. The Augustinian order proper dates from the 'Great Union' in 1256 of a number of minor orders. The order was strongly papalist; ironically, it subsequently produced Martin Luther.

AUGUSTINUS, THE (1640), posthumous Latin treatise by Cornelius Jansen, Bp of Ypres, on St Augustine's writings and theories of grace. Hostile to the Jesuit position on grace, it was condemned by the Sorbonne and the papacy but became the basis of Jansenist thinking.

AUGUSTUS (63 BC–AD 14), formerly Octavian, the first Roman Emperor and founder of the Roman imperial system. Son of C. Octavius and Atia, niece of Julius Caesar, he was adopted by Caesar in his will. On Caesar's death (44) he returned with Agrippa to Rome and accepted the adoption, becoming C. Julius Caesar Octavianus. Playing on Caesar's name, he commended himself to the urban mob and the legionary veterans and obtained the rank of propraetor from the Senate. He co-operated in defeating Antony at Mutina, but then used his army to extort the consulship and with Antony and Lepidus formed the Second Triumvirate, obtaining Africa, Sicily, and Sardinia as his provinces. After Philippi he returned to Italy, where he defeated L. Antonius in the Perusine War (41). After a new agreement and distribution of provinces at Brundisium (Oct. 40), he turned against Sextus Pompey, finally defeating him in 36 and depriving Lepidus of his authority. Next he outmanœuvred Antony in a propaganda campaign and decisively defeated him at Actium (31). Octavian then established a popular despotism behind republican forms with an act of legitimization on 17 Jan. 27, when he received the name Augustus. Subsequent constitutional adjustments in 23 and 19–18 made no difference to the foundation of his power, the enrolment of the inhabitants of Rome and the empire in his personal clientele. He secured Rome's frontiers in the north by conquest (16–9) and in the east by diplomacy, established a proper system of provincial administration and secured internal peace and stability through his long reign.

Donald Earl, *The Age of Augustus* (London, 1968).   DCE

AUGUSTUS II (1670–1733) King of Poland, Elector of Saxony (1694). He was elected King of Poland in 1697, but could not establish himself against a rival candidate, Stanislas Lesczynski, until 1709, when he was supported with military assistance from his ally, Peter the Great of Russia. Lesczynski's opposition continued to render Augustus's position insecure and it was Russian mediation which established political and economic stability by the treaty of Warsaw, an agreement between Augustus and the Polish nobility. After 1717 Augustus turned increasingly to Austria to avoid dependence on Russia, and the treaty of Vienna, which he concluded with the emperor and George I, guaranteed Poland's frontiers. After 1720 his efforts were concentrated on securing the Saxon succession in Poland, while the nobility worked for Lesczynski's election.

Known as 'the Strong', Augustus failed to undertake constitutional reform, neglected Poland's interests in his foreign policy, and led scandalous private life.

AUGUSTUS III (1696–1763), King of Poland, Elector of Saxony (1733). He was elected King of Poland in 1733 with Austrian and Russian backing, thus provoking the War of the Polish Succession, since his candidature was challenged by Stanislas Lesczynski, the French protégé. He took possession of his kingdom with the help of a Russian army in 1736 and his succession was confirmed by the treaty of Vienna (1738). Siding with Austria against Prussia in the War of the Austrian Succession, he lost Saxony to Frederick II (1745), but regained it in 1746. In the Seven Years War his electorate was invaded and his army captured by Frederick (1756), so Augustus retired to Poland, which was continuously occupied by the troops of Russia, Austria, and Prussia.

A devout Catholic, whose only passion was hunting, he subordinated Poland to the interests of Saxony and failed to carry out much-needed internal reforms. He married Maria Josepha, a niece of the Emperor Charles VI, in 1720.

AULD ALLIANCE, longstanding friendship, cemented by many formal treaties, between Scotland and France, dating from the 12th cent. and continuing until the mid-18th cent. The alliance was founded on their common hatred for England and survived the religious differences created by the Reformation to become a major factor in English policy from Henry VIII's reign to the collapse of the 1745 Jacobite rebellion. The union of England and Scotland eventually undermined the traditional alliance with France.

AULNAY-CHARNISAY, CHARLES DE MENOU, Sieur d' (1604–50), French soldier and administrator. After service in the French navy he went, in 1632, to the settlements in Acadia (NS) as assistant to the governor, Isaac de Razilly. On de Razilly's death in 1635 Aulnay-Charnisay proclaimed himself governor. His authority was challenged by Charles La Tour and Nicolas Denys. After 20 years of argument and warfare Aulnay-Charnisay eliminated his opponents by seizing their fortress headquarters. He established new settlements and trading posts in Acadia at great financial cost to himself.

AULUS PLAUTIUS SILVANUS (*fl.* 1st cent.), the first Roman governor of Britain (AD 43–7). Chosen, after success in Pannonia, by the Emperor Claudius to command the Roman invasion of Britain (43), he landed unopposed with 40,000 men. After routing Caractacus and Togodumnus in Kent, he forced a crossing of the Medway and proceeded to the Thames near London, where he waited for Claudius to lead the crossing before marching to Camulodunum. Having substantially conquered Britain south and east of the Exeter–Lincoln axis, he returned to Rome for the last known *ovatio* granted by an emperor.

AUNEAU, BATTLE OF (1587), victory of the forces of the Catholic League under the Duke of Guise over the Swiss and German troops of the Baron von Dohna, who had crossed into Lorraine in Aug. 1587 to join the Protestant forces of Navarre. As a result of his victory Guise was widely acclaimed by Catholic France, and the reputation of Henry III was undermined.

AUNG SAN (1917–47), Burmese nationalist leader. Born in Taungdwingyi, he went to Rangoon University, where he encouraged student agitation (1936) and was president of the Students' Union. He became general secretary of the Thakin Party, a youthful, communist, ultra-nationalist organization that was proscribed after the outbreak of war in Europe. Aung San and a companion escaped, but were intercepted on their way to China by the Japanese and taken to Tokyo. Thirty Burmese, led by Aung San, were given military training and accompanied the Japanese to raise Burmese guerrillas when they invaded Burma (1941–2). They grew into the Burma National Army (BNA), which Aung San commanded. In March 1945 the BNA deserted the Japanese and came over to the British. Aung San arrived in May and claimed the Anti-Fascist People's Freedom League (AFPFL) as the provisional government of Burma. The BNA usurped administrative functions behind the advancing British forces. As operations ceased, the British sought to disband the BNA or absorb it into regular forces, but Aung San preserved a private army in the new People's Volunteer Organization, ostensibly recruited for social work, but actually engaged in military training. When the British government returned, Aung San entered politics. His terms for joining the governor's Executive Council were incompatible with the British policy of rehabilitating Burma before handing over responsibility. There followed an 11-month struggle, in which the AFPFL opposed the constitution, and the British authorities decided first that they would, then that they would not, prosecute Aung San for the murder of a British-appointed headman in 1942. This struggle culminated in a strike of the police force, government employees, and other workers in the face of which the government was powerless. Aung San and

the AFPFL were brought into the executive council on their own terms. Real power was now in the hands of the AFPFL, which kept up the pressure on the government. In Jan. 1947 Aung San headed a delegation to London. The principle of independence was conceded and he returned in triumph. In April 1947 the AFPFL gained an overwhelming victory at the elections for a constituent assembly. Work began at once on a constitution, but on 19 July Aung San and seven other members of the executive council were murdered.

Hugh Tinker, *The Union of Burma* (London, 1961).
Frank N. Trager, *Burma from Kingdom to Republic* (London, 1966).   FSVD

AUPHAN, GABRIEL (1894–   ), French admiral who played a minor political role in the Vichy regime. Minister of marine (1942), he resigned because he opposed the collaboration of Laval. After the Allied landings (1944) Pétain sent him to establish contact with de Gaulle with a view to maintaining political continuity, but de Gaulle refused to receive him.

AURANGZEB (1618–1707), 6th Mughal Emperor, and third son of the Emperor Shah Jahan, with the regnal title of Alamgir. His mother was Mumtaz Mahal, in whose memory the Taj Mahal was built. Well-educated, serious-minded, and able, he held a series of official appointments, but tension developed between him and his eldest brother, Dara Shekoh. When Shah Jahan fell ill in 1657, Dara, whom he favoured, controlled the central government at Agra. Aurungzeb defeated Dara and imprisoned his father with the aid of his brother Murad, whom he then also imprisoned. Later Dara was defeated again and executed, and his surviving brother, Shuja, driven into Arakan. Though ruthless in seizing power (1658), Aurangzeb was conscientious in exercising it.

During the first part of his reign (until *c.* 1680) Aurangzeb was a highly competent and successful ruler in the regular Mughal tradition. He safeguarded his frontiers in the northwest, and through his Rajput general Jai Singh was able to curb the ambitions of the Maratha chief Sivaji. However, an attempted reconciliation with Sivaji (1666) failed. Aurangzeb, always an orthodox Sunni Muslim, began in 1679 to transform the empire from a secular state ruled by Muslims into an Islamic state. The reimposition of the *jizya* tax on non-Muslims (1679) was followed by a Rajput revolt, in which Aurangzeb's youngest son Akbar joined.

The second part of the reign (*c.* 1680–1707) was marked by four major developments. The first was an increasing religiosity which led Aurangzeb to become a benevolent and bewildered devotee. The second was a drive southwards to overthrow the kingdoms of Bijapur (1686) and Golkonda (1687), the latter becoming the centre of the Mughal power in the Deccan. Mughal influence was extended down the Carnatic coast until the French and English companies intervened in the mid-18th cent. The third development was Aurangzeb's effort to destroy the Maratha state. Sivaji's son Sambhaji was captured and killed (1689) and the Marathas resorted to guerrilla warfare, which undermined Mughal morale and prosperity. The fourth was a deepening economic crisis, with peasant revolts in various parts of India, often taking a religious form. Aurangzeb bequeathed a series of problems that his successors found insoluble.

Sin J. Sarkar, *Aurangzeb*, 5 vols (Calcutta, 1912–25).
                                                                                                                      TGPS

AURELIAN, L. DOMITIUS (d. 275), one of the great Illyrian emperors of the later 3rd cent., who devoted himself to the work of military restoration. Raised to the throne at Sirmium by a military *pronunciamento* (270), he repelled barbarian invasions in Pannonia (270) and in northern Italy (271), and suppressed usurpations by Zenobia in Syria and in Gaul. He fortified Rome with the defensive wall which still stands, but was obliged to evacuate to the Goths the trans-Danubian province of Dacia. Assassinated, he was succeeded by Tacitus.

AURIOL, VINCENT (1884–1966), French socialist politician and first president of the Fourth Republic (1947–54). The son of a baker, Auriol was trained as a lawyer, and became active in socialist politics at an early age. He entered parliament in 1914, and became a specialist in financial questions. As minister of finance in Blum's Popular Front government (1936–7), Auriol failed to cope with the financial crisis which caused its collapse. In 1940, he was arrested and imprisoned for a time, but in 1942 joined the Resistance in the *maquis*. In 1943 he escaped to London to join de Gaulle, and after the Liberation re-entered parliament and was president of the two Constituent Assemblies. He was one of the principal founders of the Fourth Republic, whose constitution was based largely on his own ideas. Auriol was a successful president of the republic, giving the office a more positive role than had been expected. The instability of the political situation gave him considerable initiative in the choice of governments, and he took a direct interest in foreign affairs. After his retirement from office, Auriol did not return to active politics, but supported the recall of de Gaulle in 1958.

AUSGLEICH (1867). The 'compromise' reached between the Austrian Emperor Francis Joseph and his Hungarian (Magyar) subjects for a dualistic constitution for the Habsburg monarchy. Since the suppression of the Hungarian revolution by force (1849), the Magyars had remained in sullen opposition to the monarchy, especially to the 'Bach system' of the 1850s, the object of which was to try to destroy their local autonomy and privileges. The monarchy emphatically rejected the Magyar claim to be a historic kingdom with its own constitution and control of the subject races of Slovakia, Transylvania, and Croatia. After the failure of various federative projects in the early 1860s, Francis Joseph was trying to come to terms with the Magyars when the Austro-Prussian War broke out (1866).

Austrian defeat made a settlement with the Magyars more likely, as it lowered the emperor's prestige. His foreign minister, Beust, was determined on a settlement to strengthen Austria's external position, and, as an outsider from Saxony, found it easier to negotiate with the Magyar leaders than did the emperor. He soon had an understanding with the younger Andrássy and Deák, who were prepared for an autonomy which would give them control of their subject Slavs. By Jan. 1867 a settlement had been reached acceptable to Francis Joseph and the Magyars.

This *Ausgleich* divided the monarchy at the Leitha river: the eastern half became a separate Hungarian kingdom with Francis Joseph as king, ruling through a Hungarian ministry and parliament at Budapest on the basis of the 1848 constitution. With Andrássy as prime minister, Hungary was to have complete home rule, although it was to be associated with the rest of the empire. The two halves were to have a common ruler and common foreign, financial, and war ministers. A crown council of these common ministers and the two prime ministers was to act as a de facto common cabinet. An annual meeting of 'delegates' drawn equally from both halves was to vote on common problems, including a customs union between them.

Almost as an afterthought the western half of the monarchy was also given a new settlement. Andrássy and Beust had insisted on the calling of a parliament, or *Reichsrat*, there to confirm the settlement. Francis Joseph was induced to make this a permanent parliament and to yield far-reaching concessions to the German liberals, who were taken into the ministry. The Habsburg monarchy, or Austria-Hungary as it was now called, had been divided between the Magyars in the east and the Germans in the west. Despite the many justified criticisms, the *Ausgleich's* effectiveness was above all shown by its 50-year duration.

C. A. Macartney, *The Habsburg Empire, 1790–1918* (London, 1968).
A. J. P. Taylor, *The Habsburg Monarchy* (London, 1964).

DMCK

AUSONIUS, DECIMUS MAGNUS (*c.* AD 310–95), poet and politician from Bordeaux, who became praetorian prefect of Gaul (378) and consul (379). His poetry, which displays technical virtuosity and occasional lyric warmth, but little profundity, is important as a mirror of contemporary Gallic society.

AUSTEN, JANE (1775–1817), English novelist. Within the confines of her own upper-middle-class and clerical upbringing she portrayed with precision the manners, conventions, and emotions of her contemporaries. *Sense and Sensibility* (1811), *Pride and Prejudice* (1813), *Mansfield Park* (1814), and *Emma* (1816) were published in her lifetime. *Northanger Abbey* and *Persuasion* appeared posthumously. Sir Walter Scott admired her, but she had little influence on other 19th-cent. novelists. Her work has attracted wide-ranging literary criticism in the 20th cent.

AUSTERLITZ, BATTLE OF (2 Dec. 1805). Napoleon's most impressive victory, fought in Austrian Moravia. He decisively defeated an Austro-Russian army and forced Austria's immediate withdrawal from the Third Coalition.

AUSTIN, JOHN (1790–1859), English jurist and professor of jurisprudence, University College, London (1826–32). He was a friend and neighbour of Bentham and the Mills but, unlike them, never adopted political radicalism. In *The Province of Jurisprudence Determined* (1832, 2nd ed., full text, 1861), he introduced ideas derived partly from Bentham, partly ultimately from Hobbes. His intention was to define positive law so as to free it from confusion with the precepts of religion and morality which had been encouraged by natural law theorists and exploited by opponents of legal reform. Law he defined as 'the command of a superior' and a superior as one who can compel others to obey through the use of sanctions. Positive law is that which can be enforced in the courts; positive morality contains those man-made rules which are not enforceable in the courts. Austin, though comparatively neglected in his own day, became a dominant influence on jurisprudence in the later 19th cent.

AUSTIN, STEPHEN FULLER (1793–1836), one of the founders of Texas. He established a colony (1822), under a grant from the Mexican government, took part in the Texas Revolution (1835–6) and, when defeated by Sam Houston for the presidency of the 'Lone Star Republic', accepted the post of secretary of state.

AUSTRALIA, HIGH COURT OF, for which express provision was made in the Commonwealth Constitution, was constituted in 1903 with an original membership of three, increased to five in 1906, and subsequently to seven. The court (1970) has a role similar to that of the US Supreme Court in interpreting the constitution but unlike that court is a general court of appeal from state courts on matters of state law and also has a comparatively extensive original jurisdiction, though most of its work is done as an appeal court.

The extent of the high court's jurisdiction demands very broad legal skills of the members of the bench who, for the most part, have been distinguished and successful practitioners at the bar. The court's constitutional work occupies only a comparatively small part of its time and energies, and it has made significant and learned contributions to many branches of law and jurisprudence and has earned a very high regard in the common law world.

In interpreting the constitution, the high court has played a role of major importance, giving the constitution enacted in 1900 a necessary adaptability to changing conditions. Interpretations have also varied in their emphases. In the earliest years the majority in the court leaned against broad interpretations of central powers. For a decade or so after 1920, the influence of Isaac Isaacs was strong and there was a much greater emphasis on national power. Since then, the court has swung back somewhat to interpretations which emphasize the federal character of the constitution. The style of the court's work and judgments is precise and careful and reflects the background of its members as working lawyers.

zc

AUSTRALIA, NEW ZEALAND'S RELATIONS WITH. Missionaries and traders, based on Sydney, paved the way for the annexation of NZ as part of NSW (1840). NZ's first sheep-runs were founded on Australian flocks and experience. The colony's goldfields (1860s), especially Westland, were briefly a Victorian frontier. During its classic 'Australasian' period (1870s–1890s), NZ shared the Australian colonies' attempts at fiscal reciprocity and political union, and joined in an Australasian consensus against non-European immigration. By 1892, NZ had withdrawn from the federal movement: Australia was an economic competitor; UK markets were expanding. The Anzac campaign in Gallipoli (1915) forged limited and commonly exaggerated links. After 1918, trans-Tasman trade further dwindled, but after 1945 Australian manufactured exports to NZ rose steeply. The 1965 NZ–Australian Free Trade Agreement (NAFTA) aimed to balance and increase trade. Australia followed a more 'Pacific' policy than NZ (1939–45), but post-war events brought the two countries much closer in foreign policy.

AUSTRALIAN CAPITAL TERRITORY, THE, transferred from NSW to the Commonwealth (1911) and containing the federal capital, Canberra. It comprises 911 sq. miles (2359 sq. kms), and is approximately 200 miles (322 kms) south-west of Sydney. Little developed before Parliament House was opened (1927); Canberra's population was still below 25,000 in 1951. Subsequent rapid expansion and concentration of government departments, and Canberra's popularity as a national headquarters for non-government organizations, as well as a growing university, produced five-fold increase by 1970. The ACT includes the Duntroon Royal Military College and Jervis Bay (28 sq. miles; 72 sq. kms) (transferred 1915), a port for the territory, and a site of a Royal Naval College.

AUSTRALIAN IMPERIAL FORCE, THE. In August 1914 Australia raised a volunteer force of one infantry division and a light horse brigade for service in Europe. It was named the AIF by its first commander, Maj.-Gen. W. T. Bridges, and fought at Gallipoli and in France, Flanders, Egypt, Palestine, and Syria. Under Gen. Sir W. Birdwood the AIF grew to five infantry divisions, five light horse brigades, and four squadrons of the Australian Flying Corps. It remained a volunteer force throughout the war.

The initial campaigns of the 2nd AIF were fought in North Africa, Greece, Crete, and Syria (1940–2). After the capture of the 8th Division at Singapore (1942), the 6th, 7th, and 9th Divisions defeated the Japanese in New Guinea and other south-west Pacific islands, finally landing in Borneo in 1945. The 2nd AIF also was a volunteer force.

AUSTRALIAN NATIVES' ASSOCIATION, patriotic and friendly society founded (1871) in Melbourne, which quickly spread to all Australian colonies. Membership was originally restricted to native-born Australians, the ANA's central aim being cultivation of national sentiment. Divisive sectarian and partisan issues were eschewed. The ANA was closely associated with the movement for federation; subsequently it pressed for an Australian navy and compulsory military training. Other questions in which the ANA took a continuing interest included educational and constitutional reform, the 'White Australia' policy, and the promotion of Australian-made products. By the mid-20th cent. its political influence had diminished, but it remained an important friendly society.

AUSTRALIAN WORKERS UNION, THE, largest trade union in Australia. Founded (1886) as the Amalgamated Shearers

Union, it grew by incorporating numerous other small unions of primarily unskilled and semi-skilled workers. The bulk of its members (160,000 in 1970) are in rural areas, though some are in mining and others in urban occupations. The AWU is notable for its adherence to industrial arbitration; its influential position in the affairs of the Australian Labor Party; and, despite its early radicalism, a firmly right-wing labour stance.

AUSTRIAN NETHERLANDS, the former Spanish Netherlands and part of the territorial compensation granted to the Emperor Charles VI on the division of the Spanish empire in 1713–14. The Netherlands constituted a rich but defenceless part of the Habsburg possessions and were overrun by the French in 1744–7. They retained strong local traditions and institutions, with which the Empress Maria Theresa was careful not to tamper. Her successor, Joseph II, however, anxious to create a strong central state, considered exchanging the Netherlands for Bavaria. After this plan failed, he tried to introduce his modernizing reforms into the Netherlands and in particular to reduce the power of the Catholic Church there. From 1787 the provinces were in open revolt and in 1789 the Netherlands Estates repudiated Joseph's authority. Ghent and Brussels were taken by the Belgian patriots, who on 10 Jan. 1790 declared the Republic of the United Belgian States.

AUSTRIAN SUCCESSION, WAR OF THE (1740–8), the result of Frederick II of Prussia's seizure of the Habsburg state of Silesia in Dec. 1740, shortly after the succession to the Habsburg possessions of the Archduchess Maria Theresa. The war was the first phase in the struggle between Austria and Prussia for the mastery of the German states. Frederick coveted the mineral resources and territorial protection which Silesia would afford to Brandenburg-Prussia, but Maria Theresa was determined to defend Habsburg territorial integrity embodied in the Pragmatic Sanction, despite the impoverished condition of her inheritance.

When Austria's old enemies, Bavaria and Spain, united against Maria Theresa by the treaty of Nymphenburg (May 1741), she appealed to her ally, Britain, but George II, fearful of Hanover's safety, negotiated its neutrality (July 1741). Meanwhile, France made a military alliance with Prussia (June 1741).

The war was notorious for the ineffectiveness of its military campaigns and the instability of its alliances. Frederick II defeated the Austrians at the battle of Mollwitz (April 1741), but later suspended military operations and made the Convention of Klein-Schnellendorf with Maria Theresa (Oct. 1741). This enabled the Austrians to expel Prussia's allies, France and Bavaria, from Upper Austria and to invade Bavaria itself. Frederick resumed hostilities, but in June 1742 again abandoned his allies, making peace with Maria Theresa, who agreed to the cession of most of Silesia (Preliminaries of Breslau) in the expectation of Anglo-Dutch assistance against France. The allied force, known as the 'Pragmatic Army', defeated the French at Dettingen (June 1743). Relations between the allies were strained, however, by Dutch unwillingness to act and British insistence on the Austrian cession of part of Milan to Charles Emmanuel of Sardinia, who agreed by the treaty of Worms to defend Italy against Spain and France (Sept. 1743).

These Habsburg successes alarmed Frederick II, who re-entered the war, renewed his alliance with France (June 1744) and invaded Bohemia. However, the death of Charles Albert of Bavaria (Jan. 1745) removed one threat to Maria Theresa, who revived Habsburg prestige by securing the election of her husband, Francis, as emperor. Further military defeats by Prussia at Hohenfriedberg and Soor forced Maria Theresa to recognize Prussian control of Silesia by the treaty of Dresden (Dec. 1745).

The Austrian Netherlands had meanwhile become the main area of conflict. The French under Marshal Saxe won several victories against the Pragmatic Army, eg. Fontenoy

(1745), Rocoux (1746), Lauffeldt (1747), and the capture of Bergen-op-Zoom, which opened the way for an invasion of the United Provinces. The war in the Mediterranean also reached a stalemate as the military successes of the Franco-Spanish forces in 1745 were counterbalanced by British command of the sea. Philip V's death in 1746 halted Spanish involvement in Italy.

Since 1744 the war had developed from a German conflict into a great colonial struggle between Britain and the Franco-Spanish bloc. Anglo-Spanish hostility had existed since the War of Jenkins' Ear, but in 1744 France declared war on Britain. The attack on Portobello by Admiral Vernon and Louisburg's capture by the English settlers in America (June 1745) were offset by the French seizure of Madras, the East India Co. trading post.

The war ended with the treaty of Aix-la-Chapelle (Oct.–Nov. 1748).   MKS

AUSTRIAN TREATY (May 1955) recognized the re-establishment of Austria as a sovereign independent and democratic state, its frontiers being those of 1 Jan. 1938. At the conclusion of the Second World War Austria was treated by the victors as a victim, not an accomplice, of German aggression, except that the Soviet government instituted a claim for the payment of reparations. But the negotiation of a treaty, the terms of which provided no major obstacle, was repeatedly delayed by the USSR, so that the occupation of the country by small detachments of British, French, US, and Soviet forces continued. The signature of the treaty in 1955 formed part of a new flexibility in Soviet foreign policy. It prohibited *Anschluss* between Austria and Germany and was followed by an Austrian constitutional law 'declaring of her own free will her perpetual neutrality'. The USSR surrendered appropriated German assets and received instead a payment of $150 million in Austrian goods. Navigation on the Danube was declared free and open for the nationals, vessels of commerce and goods of all states. The treaty was followed by the withdrawal of the occupying troops.

AUSTRO-FRENCH AGREEMENT (12 June 1866), secret pact by which Napoleon III promised that France would remain neutral in the imminent Austro-Prussian War. In return, Austria agreed to cede Venetia to Italy, whether Austria was defeated or not. In the case of Austrian victory, Napoleon was ready to agree to Austria's rearranging Germany as it wished, although France was still to be consulted. Verbal assurances were also given that France would be allowed to create a client buffer state on the Rhine similar to Napoleon I's Confederation of the Rhine.

AUSTRO-GERMAN AGREEMENT (11 July 1936). By this 'gentleman's agreement', Austria acknowledged herself 'a German state', implicitly renouncing her previous dependence on Italy. The signatories, by ending reciprocal trade restrictions and press hostilities, established the principle of non-interference in each other's internal affairs, with particular reference to the Nazi Party in Austria. Secret clauses, however, bound Schuschnigg, the Austrian chancellor, to admit the 'National Opposition' to government posts and greater political participation. The agreement, facilitated by Mussolini's rapprochement with Hitler after his conquest of Abyssinia, was foreshadowed in May 1936, when Mussolini's protégé, the Heimwehr leader Starhemberg, was dismissed from the Austrian coalition government.

AUSTRO-GERMAN ALLIANCE (1879), signed secretly on 7 Oct. It was to last initially for five years and was intended by the German chancellor, Bismarck, to give Austria security from Russia and to prevent her from coming to an agreement with Britain and France. The terms were that if Russia attacked Germany or Austria, either would immediately come to the other's aid; in the case of attack by any other power, the other should only have to maintain benevolent neutrality. Bismarck had regarded the alliance as a temporary

expedient, but it was to become one of the bases of German policy until 1914.

AUSTRO-GERMAN CUSTOMS UNION. This project, announced on 21 March 1931, was conceived as much to enhance mutual national prestige as to alleviate economic difficulties, as both the Brüning government in Germany and the Schober government in Austria faced extreme nationalist opposition.

The treaties of Versailles and St Germain prohibited encroachments on Austrian independence. Following the League of Nations' loan to Austria, the 1922 Geneva Protocol extended this prohibition to economic independence. Although Austria and Germany stipulated that no common administrative bodies were envisaged, and that they favoured similar arrangements with other countries, France condemned the customs union as contravening existing international agreements. France's foreign minister, Briand, also considered the project inimical to his proposals for European union.

The British foreign minister, Henderson, requested the submission of the project to the League Council, which on 19 May decided to refer it to the Permanent Court of International Justice. By 11 May, the Austrian *Creditanstalt* faced failure. A government loan issue required the consent of the guarantor states of the 1922 loan. France and Czechoslovakia tried to make their consent conditional on Austria's abandoning the customs union, but were defeated by Britain. On 16 June Austria requested a French loan; France's renewed demands for renunciation of the project were countered when the Bank of England advanced Austria 150 million *schillings*. Later in June, France attempted, again unsuccessfully, to exercise similar pressure on Germany during the Hoover Moratorium negotiations. By July, however, Austria's resistance was weakening, while the financial crisis reached German and, to a lesser extent, British banks. On 3 Sept. Schober and Curtius announced the renunciation of the customs union. Two days later, the Permanent Court condemned the project. In June 1932, in return for the Lausanne loan, Austria was again pledged not to compromise her independence.

AUSTRO-ITALIAN WAR (1859) broke out in April after Cavour, prime minister of Piedmont-Sardinia, had bluffed Austria into declaring war. Assured by Napoleon III of French help through the pact of Plombières, Cavour looked forward to the rapid expulsion of the Austrians from the Italian provinces of Lombardy and Venetia. French and Sardinian troops won decisive victories in June at Magenta and Solferino, although these were not completely disastrous defeats for Austria. To Cavour's disgust Napoleon III then decided to call a halt and insisted on making preliminaries of peace with Austria at Villafranca in July. Austria was forced only to cede Lombardy to France for transfer to Sardinia. The war was none the less the signal for risings throughout Italy which were to lead to almost complete Italian unification in the next two years.

AUSTRO-PRUSSIAN ALLIANCE, signed secretly in May 1851. It provided for mutual defence for three years. The alliance sealed Prussia's humiliation at Olmütz in the previous year. Aimed primarily at preventing the spread of revolution in Europe, it gave Austria guarantees for her possessions in Italy without giving Prussia similar guarantees for her territories in the Rhineland. The refusal of Tsar Nicholas I to join prevented it from becoming a revival of the Holy Alliance. Three years later the alliance was renewed (1854) immediately after the Franco-British declaration of war against Russia and the opening of the Crimean War. The parties agreed to oppose any extension of Russian power into the Balkans, although Prussia had no intention of opposing such a move by force. The alliance gave security to Austria so that she could put pressure on Russia to evacuate the Danubian provinces.

AUSTRO-PRUSSIAN WAR (1866), 'the Seven Weeks War', began on 14 June and resulted in the exclusion of Austria from Germany and the erection of the North German Confederation under Prussian leadership. Bismarck had provoked Austria into war by demanding the dissolution of the German Confederation and Austrian exclusion. Most of the German states sided with Austria, but the new Italian state took this opportunity to attack Austria. Although the Italians were defeated at Custozza, the decisive campaign was in Bohemia. Using railways and the telegraph to advantage, the Prussians overwhelmingly defeated the Austrian army at Sadowa (Königgrätz) and forced the Emperor Francis Joseph to peace at Prague in August. Besides agreeing to the reorganization of Germany, he was also forced to cede Venetia to Italy.

AUSTRO-RUSSIAN ALLIANCE (1726), result of a chain of diplomatic and political manœuvres precipitated by the rapprochement between Spain and the empire in 1725. Disillusioned with the conduct of his allies at the Congress of Cambrai, the Emperor Charles VI not only received Ripperda's overtures, but sought an understanding with Russia or Sweden. The British minister, Townshend, answered this threat by ordering a squadron to the Baltic in 1726, which persuaded Sweden to reject the emperor's friendship in favour of the Anglo-French alliance of Hanover (1725). Russia, however, reacted by joining the Austro-Spanish alliance in August 1726, guaranteeing the Pragmatic Sanction. Austro-Russian friendship survived the Diplomatic Revolution of the mid-18th cent.

AUSTRO-RUSSIAN ENTENTE (1897), made at St Petersburg during their visit to Russia by the Emperor Francis Joseph and his foreign minister, Goluchowski, on 30 April. By this agreement the two powers came to an understanding which had the effect of 'putting the Balkans on ice'. Goluchowski had hoped for more, but the Russians refused to commit themselves to allowing Austria-Hungary to annex Bosnia-Herzegovina or to erect an independent Albanian state.

AUSTRO-SARDINIAN WAR (1848–9), unsuccessful attempt on the part of King Charles Albert of Sardinia, in alliance with the revolutionary movements in northern and central Italy, to expel the Austrians from Lombardy and Venetia. After the revolutionaries in Milan had appealed for help, Sardinia declared war, but suffered a humiliating defeat at Custozza in July 1848. Forced to accept an armistice in Sept., Charles Albert broke it in March 1849, only to suffer another defeat at Novara in the same month. This second humiliation caused Charles Albert's abdication, and it was left to his son, Victor Emmanuel II, to make peace in Aug. on the payment of a large indemnity.

AUSTRO-TURKISH WAR (1716–18) started when the Emperor Charles VI renewed his alliance with Venice in 1716. The Turks had declared war on Venice two years earlier and had occupied Venetian territory in Crete and the Morea. Charles VI demanded Turkish evacuation of the Balkans, to which the Porte reacted by declaring war on Austria. Prince Eugene with an army of 62,000 men met the advancing Turkish force of 150,000 at Petrovaradin and inflicted a crushing defeat upon them (1716). The Turks retreated to Belgrade, while the Austrians recaptured Temesvar and relieved the whole of south-eastern Hungary. The following year the reinforced Austrian army took Belgrade after a fortnight's siege. This war, the only successful military operation of Charles VI's reign, ended in July 1718 with the treaty of Passarovitz.

AUTOMATIC DATA PROCESSING (ADP), the use of automatic machine systems to provide from a mass of information those elements relevant to a particular operation, or to a particular purpose. Typically, an electronic computer processes the input material, and controls subordinate electro-mechanical machines that receive, hold, and issue the output information.

AUTOMATION. In spite of the frequency with which it is used (or perhaps because of it), the word automation has (1970) no single, widely accepted definition. It is applied to many of the more recent and complex stages in the evolution of mechanization. These usually fall into one or more of three categories: (*a*) substantial but straightforward increases in mechanization; (*b*) automatic control of a machine or of a system of machines; (*c*) data processing.

The first is more aptly termed 'mechanization'. The second category, of automatic controls, appears very early in the Industrial Revolution with the introduction of the governor on steam-engine valves. This is an example of *feedback* in which the control of the system is made to depend on the output (here the speed of the drive shaft) in such a way that the latter is stabilized at some desired value. Feedback is an essential feature of many modern developments in automation; eg, rolling mills are controlled by measuring the thickness of the rolled product, and 'homing' missiles. A second early example of automatic control was the Jacquard loom (1801). This used punched cards, read one after another, to control the lifting of the individual warp threads on each pass of the shuttle, and could be easily 'programmed' to produce weaving patterns of any desired degree of complexity. Numerically controlled machine tools are modern examples of this type of automation.

The third category, of data processing, covers the collection, storage, analysis, and use of *information*. Its basic tool is the digital computer, most of whose principles were discovered by Charles Babbage in the 1820s. Their full implementation, however, did not occur until the 1950s, and the last two decades have produced developments at a rate unrivalled in any other field. Computers can choose their courses of action according to the data presented to them, or any other quantifiable criterion, and so can follow easily (and at great speed) the appropriate path through sets of instructions that may be logically very complex indeed. This ability, together with their huge 'memories' and the possibility of communicating directly with them over great distances, is bringing about a very high degree of automation in many white-collar jobs that involve the keeping and use of records and accounts, eg, banking, and airline ticket reservations.

In the early days of automation predictions of unprecedented unemployment among unskilled and semi-skilled workers were common. These have not been fulfilled, largely because the fact was overlooked that while the very *last* stage of automation might eliminate the need for labour altogether (except for some highly skilled maintenance staff), this stage is almost never reached, for reasons both technical and economic. Most *intermediate* stages, on the other hand, actually *reduce* the degree of skill required by an operative, eg, as in the motor industry. This goes a long way towards maintaining the balance between skilled and unskilled labour requirements, and it would seem that the social consequences of this new Industrial Revolution may not prove as disastrous as once appeared likely.   JMS

AUTONOMY BILLS. Bills introduced into the Canadian parliament in 1905 to create the Canadian provinces of Saskatchewan and Alberta from the North West Territories. The focal point of controversy in these bills was the proposal to establish a dual English-speaking Protestant, French-speaking Catholic state school system. Although this system had been authorized by the North West Territories Act of 1875 the majority in the two provinces wanted a non-parochial system. By the ordinances of 1892 and 1901 a uniform school system had been established. The controversy led to the resignation of Clifford Sifton, minister of the interior and administrator of the North West Territories. Finally, a face-saving compromise was devised which largely conceded the position to the unified system advocates. This compromise reiterated the 1875 Act, but recognized the legal validity of the 1892 and 1901 ordinances.

AUTOS DA FÉ, literally, acts of faith, the ceremony in which sentence was delivered after a supposed offender had been examined by the Inquisition. Priests and accused went in procession to the cathedral, where Mass was celebrated, oaths repeated, and after a sermon the sentence was read. The first *autos da fé* took place when Torquemada (1420–98) was inquisitor-general.

AUXILIA, auxiliary troops in the Roman army. From *c.* 200 BC units of specialist light armed infantry soldiers, *eg,* Balearic slingers, and cavalry, *eg,* Numidians, were raised outside Italy to supplement the powerful but relatively inflexible heavily armed legions. Under Augustus, auxilia, still raised from non-Romans, formed a permanent and increasingly important part of the Roman military establishment; Gaul, Spain, Illyria, and Syria all provided large numbers. Auxiliary units were organized in *alae* or cohorts 1000 or 500 strong. On discharge, auxiliary soldiers received Roman citizenship. From the 3rd cent. the legions declined in importance and in the 4th auxilia of Gallic or German origin were elite units.

AVA, four times a capital city (1364–1555, 1635–1752, 1765–1783, and 1823–37), a distinction owed to its position on the Irrawaddy, Burma's main line of communication, and within easy reach of the fertile Kyaukse rice lands. Between the unifications of Burma under Anawrahta and Alaungpaya, Upper Burma came to be known as the Kingdom of Ava, whether or not the capital was in fact at Ava, and Lower Burma as the Kingdom of Pegu. Ava is now an unimportant village with few relics of its former splendour.

AVACHA BAY, natural harbour on the eastern coast of Siberia containing the port of Petropavlovsk, which was established by the second Bering expedition in 1741 before it set sail from the harbour in search of North America.

AVANTI, an ancient kingdom in Malwa (India), its capital being Ujjayini (Ujjain). The oldest historical references date back to the age of the Buddha when the aggressive Pradyota (Pajjota) Mahasena was ruling the country.

AVARS, a nomad people from Central Asia who irrupted into eastern Europe in the middle of the 6th cent., starting a fresh wave of tribal migrations. They created a large empire of subject Asiatic and Slavonic peoples with its centre in the Danube valley, in modern Hungary and Austria, splitting up the Slavonic tribes and gradually pushing the southern Slavs south of the Danube, while the Germanic Lombards fled in 568 to Italy. The resultant Slavonic settlement of much of the Balkans and the Lombard conquests in north and central Italy deprived the eastern empire of most of its Latin-speaking subjects and made it into a Greek state. The Avar empire was destroyed by Charlemagne in the last decade of the 8th cent. and the ensuing rebellions of the tribes subject to them led to their complete extermination.

AVATARA, lit. 'descent', especially of a divinity, mostly Vishnu, into a human or animal form. In early medieval India, from *c.* 10th or 11th cent., the system of ten *avataras* of Vishnu, including even Lord Buddha, was particularly popular. In this system the god descended on earth to deliver mankind from certain scourges in different ages. Nine of these are referred to the past whereas the tenth, that of Kalkin, is foreseen at a future time of chaos. In addition to these ten complete *avataras,* Hinduism acknowledges also partial *avataras* by which a portion of the divine essence descended into a human being. This doctrine enabled some rulers, such as those of Java in the 12th cent., to assert semi-divine status.

AVAUX, JEAN DE MESMES, Count of (1640–1704), son of Claude de Mesmes, a French diplomat. Avaux also entered the diplomatic service, under Louis XIV, and was twice ambassador to the Hague (1676–92, 1701–4) and also to Sweden (1692–1701).

AVELLANEDA, NICOLÁS (1837–85), Argentine president (1874–80). Domingo F. Sarmiento, a previous president, appointed him to carry out an ambitious programme of public instruction. As president Avellaneda concerned himself with economic reform and the destruction of the southern Indians.

AVENTINUS, JOHANN TURMAIR (1477–1534), Bavarian chronicler, whose *Annales Boiorum,* printed in 1554, were a landmark in the development of German historiography.

AVERESCU, ALEXANDRU (1859–1938), Rumanian military and political leader. Born into a Bessarabian peasant family, Averescu joined the army as a private soldier and rose through the ranks. He commanded units charged with suppressing the peasant rebellion of 1907 and in 1913 became chief of the general staff. Averescu commanded the Rumanian forces in the First World War, masterminding the successful defensive actions at Marasesti and Marasti in the summer of 1917. He resigned from the army in 1920 and entered politics as leader of the People's League. As prime minister (1920–2) he promulgated the land reform law and suppressed revolutionary activities.

AVERROES (1126–98), Arab philosopher, born in Spain, whose major contributions to philosophy were his commentaries on the works of Aristotle and his attempt to define how far the revealed truths of religion were compatible with the reasoned truths of philosophy. About this, Averroes was more pessimistic than was acceptable to Christian theologians. Averroes' work, translated into Latin, was a challenge to Thomas Aquinas and was thus an important influence on medieval European philosophy.

AVESTA, collection of oral traditions compiled by the disciples of Zoroaster in the Sasanian period (3rd–7th cents) in Iran. An original collection was reputed to have been destroyed by Alexander the Great.

AVIGNON, ANNEXATION OF (1791), by the French constituent assembly at the request of the local population, so ending the independence of this papal enclave.

AVIGNONESE PAPACY. The papacy was settled at Avignon (1308–77) in southern France. This resulted from the humiliation of Boniface VIII at Agnani and the renewed strife in Italy between Guelf and Ghibelline, which was intensified by the election of the anti-papal Emperor Henry VII in 1307. The move to Avignon was never intended to be permanent, but the political climate in Italy made the return to Rome too hazardous to attempt. Later popes were too hard pressed—partly through their own extravagance—for money and the state of Rome was too anarchic for them to move, but the work of Cardinal Albornoz enabled Urban V (*reg.* 1362–70) to attempt to do so in 1367. The reluctance of the cardinals, the hostility of the Roman populace, and his own desire to mediate between England and France forced him to return to Avignon. His successor, Gregory XI (*reg.* 1370–8), finally accomplished the move to Italy in 1377.

AVILA, PEDRO ARIAS DE (d. 1531), first Spanish governor of Darién, famous for his cruelty and energy and called by his contemporaries '*furor domini*'. Avila's main rival in Darién was the conquistador Balboa, who had already explored the isthmus of Panama. Appointed in 1513 to administer the new colony on behalf of the Crown, Avila continued Balboa's work of exploration and settlement for 16 years, but gave up his policy of conciliation towards the natives. He engineered the trial of Balboa on a charge of treason for which the latter was executed (1519). Later Avila clashed with Cortés, the conqueror of Mexico, whose expedition met a party of Avila's men exploring northwards from Darién (1523).

ÁVILA CAMACHO, MANUEL (1897–1955), president of Mexico (1940–6), born in Tezuitlán, Puebla. He rose to the rank of general following the revolution (1914–17). Ávila Camacho served as minister of war (1932–4) and secretary of national defence (1939). He was supported by the official party of the Mexican Revolution (PRM) (1940). The general's administration bridged the gap between the agrarian reform years under Lázaro Cárdenas and the subsequent business retrenchment under Miguel Alemán.

AVISO SHIPS. Some eight vessels dispatched yearly after 1720 to New Spain and the isthmus, by the Spanish Council of Commerce (*consulado*), in order to improve communications between Spain and the Indies, especially concerning marketing conditions.

AVNOJ, Anti-Fascist Council for the National Liberation of Yugoslavia, the political and administrative arm of the Partisan movement and basis of the provisional government and parliament. AVNOJ was constituted at Bihac in Bosnia on 26–7 Nov. 1942 after the Allies had resisted Partisan efforts to form a provisional government. Communists were supreme, but non-communist elements participated. Dr Ivan Ribar was elected president. An executive council was established to deal with non-military affairs and officials were placed in charge of education, public health, social welfare, and religion in the liberated territories. People's councils were set up as institutions of local government and their activities were co-ordinated by AVNOJ. At the second meeting of AVNOJ at Jajce in Bosnia (29 Nov. 1943), the National Liberation Committee was formed as the provisional government of Yugoslavia under the premiership of Marshal Tito. By the Tito–Subasic agreements (June and Nov. 1944) AVNOJ was enlarged and raised to the position of a provisional parliament. On 10 Aug. 1945 AVNOJ formally became the National Provisional Parliament of Yugoslavia.

AVOCAT-GÉNÉRAL, the office of royal barrister, whose chief task was to present the king's case in the French *parlements*. The *avocat* and the *procureur-général* were known collectively as the *gens du roi* or the *parquet*.

AVOGADRO, AMEDEO (1776–1856), Italian physicist who was responsible for the hypothesis known later as Avogadro's Law. The law distinguished between atoms and molecules and is one of the basic concepts of modern chemistry.

AVON, ROBERT ANTHONY EDEN, 1st Earl of (1897–   ), British Conservative politician and prime minister. After serving in the First World War and securing a 'First' in Oriental languages at Oxford, he became MP for Leamington (1923–57). He spent seven years in junior government posts before succeeding Sir Samuel Hoare as foreign secretary (1935). He had already worked closely with the League of Nations and was now brought into direct confrontation with the challenge of Germany and Italy to European peace. He resigned (Feb. 1938) after disagreement with the appeasement policy of Neville Chamberlain, the prime minister. On the outbreak of the Second World War he returned to office as secretary for dominions (1939–40) and for war (1940), until Winston Churchill restored him to the foreign office (1940–1945). He was associated with Churchill's overseas visits and conferences, and his diplomatic skill was invaluable in negotiations with allied and neutral powers. He was leader of the House of Commons (1942–5) and deputy leader of the opposition during the Labour administration (1945–51). In the post-war years he advocated the identification of Britain with the French Schuman plan for European co-operation in coal and steel production.

The Conservatives' return to power (1951) brought Eden's third tenure of the foreign secretaryship (1951–5). His involvement in Far Eastern affairs contributed to the Korean armistice (1953) and the setting up of the South-East Asia Treaty Organization (1954). He was also chairman of the Organization of European Economic Co-operation (OEEC) during this period (1952–4).

In 1955 he succeeded Churchill as prime minister (1955–7). During his premiership Britain became embroiled in the Middle East crisis created by the nationalization of the Suez Canal by Nasser in 1956. Eden, in conjunction with the French government, decided to attack Egypt and overthrow Nasser. A successful air bombardment and the capture of Port Said (Nov. 1956) was followed by a cease-fire in the face of world-wide hostility, endorsed by economic threats. The US, Russia, and the Afro-Asian bloc all deplored what seemed a revival of 19th-cent. British imperialist policies. Public opinion in Britain was sharply divided on Suez. Henceforth Britain was not to act again independently in the Middle East while Eden himself resigned a few weeks later (Jan. 1957), largely on health grounds. Eden had dominated British foreign policy for a quarter of a century. As prime minister his main interests continued to lie in that direction. Thus the brevity of his tenure of office, the controversy the Suez crisis aroused, and the absence of domestic legislation associated with his name, must make his premiership an unfruitful end to a distinguished career.

Avon, Earl of, *Eden Memoirs* (London, 1960, etc.).
G. McDermott, *The Eden Legacy and the Decline of British Diplomacy* (London, 1969). GMDH

AVRANCHES, COUNCIL OF (1172), the council at which Henry II of England, in the presence of the pope, Alexander II, was reconciled to the Church after the murder of Thomas à Becket. The main concession made by Henry was the recognition of freedom of appeals to Rome in all judicial and religious matters.

AVVAKUM (*c.* 1615–81), Russian archpriest and religious leader who opposed the Church reforms introduced by the Patriarch Nikon in the mid-17th cent. Avvakum believed that Russian orthodoxy alone retained the true Christian heritage and that even changes in ritual would destroy its unique position. He was arrested in 1653 and exiled to Siberia, though after Nikon's fall he was allowed to return to Moscow. However, his uncompromising attitude led to his excommunication at the Church council of 1666–7. Subsequently the Russian Church remained in a state of schism. The Old Believers, as Avvakum's followers came to be called, were cruelly persecuted and Avvakum himself was burnt at the stake.

AWDAGHUST, oasis town and caravan terminus in southeastern Mauritania. It was originally ruled by Sononke princes and contained a sizeable Muslim Berber and Arab community. It was destroyed by the Almoravids in 1054–5. Its site is possibly at Tagdaost.

AWOLOWO, OBAFEMI (1909–   ), Nigerian political leader, of Yoruba origin. He was educated at Anglican and Methodist schools and at Wesley College, Ibadan. In the late 1930s he organized the Nigerian Produce Traders' Association and other bodies while continuing his part-time studies. In 1940 he became secretary of the Ibadan branch of the Nigerian Youth Movement, an emergent nationalism body, and in 1944 went to London, where he wrote *Path to Nigerian Freedom*, and founded the Yoruba cultural society, Egbe Omo Oduduwa.

Returning to Nigeria in 1947, after qualifying in law, he entered national politics and with Bode Thomas founded the Action Group (1950–1). He was minister of local government of the Western Region of Nigeria (1951–4), when he became leader of the opposition in the federal parliament. In 1962 he was arrested by the federal government on charges of treasonable policy, and sentenced to ten years' imprisonment, but was pardoned and released in 1966 following the military coups of that year. Since then, Chief Awolowo has taken a leading part in federal politics.

AYACUCHO, BATTLE OF (1824), last important military action in the Spanish-American drive for independence. The 5000 men under Gen. Antonio José de Sucre defeated 9000 royalists of the viceroy, La Serna, thus securing the independence of Peru.

AYALA, PLAN OF, issued by the Mexican revolutionary Emiliano Zapata (1911; reissued in 1914). The plan called for small farmers to have restored to them the lands of which they had been dispossessed during the Porfirian era (1876–1911) and offered an indemnity of one-third of the value of estates willingly surrendered. The property of those who resisted was to be expropriated without indemnity. The plan became, in effect, part of the Mexican revolutionary programme. Article 27 of the constitution of 1917 embodied the agrarian demands emanating from the *Zapatista* movement.

A'YAN, Arabic word meaning 'notables', used to denote the powerful local dignitaries and officials prominent in the Ottoman empire's Balkan territories during the 18th and 19th cents. The a'yan—*eg*, Bayrakdar Mustafa Pasha—wielded great influence in the reigns of Selim III (1789–1807) and Mustafa IV (1807–8). It was Sultan Mahmud II (1808–39) who, in the first half of his reign, reduced the a'yan to obedience.

AYBAK, IZZ AL-DIN, 1st Mamluk Sultan of Egypt (1250–57). After the murder of the last Ayyubid Sultan, Turan Shah, in 1250, Aybak acted as the *atabeg* of Shajar al-Durr, the widow of the Ayyubid Sultan Al-Malik al-Salih Ayyub (d. 1249). He soon became sultan and in order to strengthen his hold on the throne, married Shajar al-Durr. Aybak did much to bring the nascent Mamluk regime in Egypt through the difficult years, when there was danger from the Ayyubid princes still controlling Syria and from the Crusaders under Louis IX of France, then in Palestine (1250–54). Shajar al-Durr, fearing that Aybak intended to renounce her, had him killed in 1257, only to lose her own life soon afterwards.

AYLESBURY CASE (1700–4), party dispute and later British constitutional crisis over a question of privilege. In the parliamentary election of 1700, the Tory mayor of Aylesbury, White, prevented some Whig supporters from voting. Such incidents were not uncommon, but Lord Wharton, attempting to build an interest in Aylesbury, persuaded one such supporter, Ashby, to bring an action against White for deprivation of franchise. Ashby won his case in the local assize court. The Tories appealed to the court of Queen's Bench, where three judges declared that election disputes were matters for the Commons, not the courts. However, a fourth judge, Holt, argued that a vote was a piece of property and so subject to the common law. His decision was upheld by the House of Lords, where Ashby next took the case. Party dispute was followed by a crisis between the House of Commons and the House of Lords, the former fearing that the decision would give the latter control over the Commons' membership. The constitutional deadlock was broken only by the prorogation of parliament, when the affair subsided, though a formal solution was never reached.

AYLLU, the fundamental clan unit of the Indo-Andrean area and for the communal village governmental and social organization which distributed lands among its members. Ethno-historians disagree about its exact function, some emphasizing a kinship basis for the Ayllu, others claiming that the communal village is the essential element.

AYLMER, JOHN (1521–94) bishop of London, and an able Elizabethan scholar and administrator who was preceptor to Lady Jane Grey. He helped Fox with his *Acts and Monuments* and defended England against John Knox's *Blast Against the Government of Women* (1559). After being consecrated Bp of London (1576), he tried to prevent the spread of prophesying within his diocese, which was one of the centres of Puritanism.

AYMARAS, indigenous group of Peru and Bolivia who, before their consolidation into the Inca empire in the 15th cent., had created an advanced civilization to the south of Lake Titicaca. The Ayllu, held by some to be an extended family, or clan, was the basis of their governmental, social, and economic organization. Under Spanish rule, they were sent to the silver mines, where their numbers diminished greatly. They rose unsuccessfully against the Spaniards for the last time in 1780. During the 19th cent. the remaining Aymaras suffered repeated losses of lands which had been theirs for centuries.

AYN JALUT, BATTLE OF (Sept. 1260) in which the Mamluks of Egypt, led by Sultan Kutuz, defeated the Mongol forces operating in Syria under Kitbugha Noyon. The importance of the battle has perhaps been overestimated. No doubt the death of the Great Khan Möngke (Sept. 1259) did much to halt the Mongol offensive. None the less, Ayn Jalut did in fact mark the furthest limit of the Mongol advance within the lands of Islam.

AYRAULT, PIERRE (*fl.* 16th cent.), legal commentator who was one of the first to criticize the French criminal procedure, regarding both its secrecy and the overwhelming advantage it allowed to the prosecution.

AYUB KHAN, MUHAMMAD (1907–), president of Pakistan (Oct. 1958–March 1969), commander-in-chief of Pakistan's armed forces (1951), and minister of defence (1954–6). After a *coup d'état* (7 Oct. 1958), he was appointed supreme commander and chief administrator under martial law by President Iskander Mirza. He then ousted Mirza (27 Oct.) and assumed the presidency (Jan. 1960), securing approval of his action through the electoral college of Basic Democracies which he had created (1959).

He instituted a series of economic, agrarian, and political reforms and tried to improve relations between east and west Pakistan. In 1962 he promulgated a new constitution with a strong president and provincial and national assemblies elected by the electoral college of Basic Democrats. Martial law was then abrogated and political parties were permitted. In the presidential election (Nov. 1964), Ayub Khan defeated a Combined Opposition Parties candidate, Miss Fatima Jinnah, sister of Muhammad Ali Jinnah, but the vote showed the relative weakness of his position in the major cities and in East Pakistan. After the war with India (1965), the armed forces declined to support him as popular agitation grew for a return to parliamentary government. On 25 March 1969 he resigned and Gen. Yahya Khan, the commander-in-chief, took charge as the head of a new martial law regime.

AYUBALE, BATTLE OF (14 Dec. 1703), clash at the Spanish mission in Ayubale, FL, between the Spaniards and Indians on one side and English colonists and Indians, led by James Moore of SC, on the other. Moore defeated the Spanish and laid waste the surrounding countryside.

AYUDHYA, KINGDOM OF (1350–1767), principal predecessor of modern Thailand (Siam). Ayudhya was founded on an island in the Chaophraya river by a Thai prince from the west at a time when Cambodian domination of the area was weakening. Within two decades Ayudhya mounted a successful attack on Angkor, the Cambodian capital, and by the middle of the 15th cent. had forced its abandonment. The kingdom took shape in the same century under King Borommatrailokanat, expanding north at the expense of the earlier kingdom of Sukhothai. Its institutions and culture owed much to the creative adaptation of Cambodian models, on which classical Thai civilization was built. From its foundation it was a trading port, with connections to the Persian Gulf and China and Japan. Its commerce and firm administrative institutions gave it a strength which withstood the sack of the city by the Burmese in 1569, the first major battle in a conflict which lasted through the rest of the 16th cent. During the 17th cent. Ayudhya was an important post of the Dutch and English East India companies; and it was against Dutch domination of the kingdom's external trade in the 1670s and 1680s that King Narai attempted to balance French power, which brought about the overthrow of his dynasty and the expulsion of the French in 1688. The Phlu Luang dynasty (1688–1767) was increasingly insecure on the throne against the pressure of the nobility. It came to an end with the capture and sack of the capital by an invading Burmese army in 1767, following which the city was abandoned. Its ruined temples remain as an important archaeological site.

AYUTLA, PLAN OF, revolutionary proclamation issued in 1854 by the Mexican liberals in the state of Guerrero. The dictator, Antonio López de Santa Anna, supported by the conservatives, was directed to resign and hand over the government to a convention which would draft a new constitution. The outcome was a victory for the liberals and defeat and exile for the dictator in 1855. The plan rallied the support of liberals in all parts of Mexico and made possible the emergence of Benito Juárez and the new political leadership of the reform period.

AYYUBIDS, dynasty ruling over Egypt and Syria (1169–1250). The Ayyubids came from the region of Dwin in Armenia and belonged to the Rawwadi clan of the Kurdish tribe of Hadhbani. Ayyub, with his brother Shirkuh, entered the service of the Atabeg of Mosul, Zangi, in 1138. Shirkuh, high in the favour of Nur al-Din, the son of Zangi, made three expeditions to Egypt (1164, 1167, and 1168), the third of which brought the country into the possession of the Zangids. Shirkuh died in March 1169, leaving Egypt under the control of his nephew, Salah al-Din. It was he who now (1169–93) fashioned a great Ayyubid state embracing Egypt, Syria, and Al-Jazira. The Ayyubid concept of power was a familial one. Power rested with the ruling house as a whole and not with one member alone. The sons of a sultan received great appanages. Subordinate lines of the Ayyubid house ruled over lesser principalities, as at Hama. Moreover, in Al-Jazira, local dynasties (Zangid and Artukid) survived as vassals of the sultan at Cairo. On the death of Salah al-Din (1193), the empire was divided among his sons. Their ineptitudes and discords led the brother of Salah al-Din, Al-Adil, to assume control, as sultan, in 1200. After 1218 the sons of Al-Adil ruled in Egypt and Syria. It was left to the able Sultan Al-Kamil (1218–38) to attempt the reduction of the subordinate regimes and to replace them with a more unified form of rule. Al-Kamil died in 1238 before his task was complete. Power, after his death, resided with the slave troops (mamluks), who formed the core of the Ayyubid armies. The recruitment of such troops was intensified under Al-Malik al-Salih Ayyub (1240–9). In 1250 the Mamluks killed the last Ayyubid sultan, Turan Shah, and established, first in Egypt and then in Syria, a famous slave regime which was to last until 1517.   VJP

AZAD, MAULANA ABUL KALAM (1888–1958), Muslim leader of the Indian National Congress. His extreme Pan-Islamic articles in his newspaper, *Al-Hilal* (*The Crescent*), led to his internment in 1915. On his release (Jan. 1920) he joined the Khilafat movement (1919–24). He presided over a special session of the Congress (1923) and was elected president in 1940. Because of the Second World War, he remained president until 1946, conducting important negotiations with Cripps (1942) and, after being imprisoned (1942–5), with Wavell (1945). He became minister of education in the government of India (1947–58).

AZAÑA Y DIAZ, MANUEL (1880–1940), prime minister and president of the Spanish republic, a man of unusual intellectual purity, personally unambitious, dedicated to a republic radical in its religious policy, but moderate in its social legislation, and responsible for an important series of reforms from 1931 to 1933. Overtaken by the events of the civil war, he died in exile. Born (like Cervantes) in Alcalá de Henares, he was educated at the Augustinian college of the Escorial (where he lost his faith) and in Paris. A civil servant and a writer, he was drawn into politics and in 1931 was elected president of the Ateneo, the foremost literary club of Madrid. He led the Republican Action group in the constituent Cortes and was appointed first minister for war (July) then, following the resignation of Alcalá Zamora, prime minister (Oct.). He was responsible for the reform of the army, for anti-clerical constitutional legislation, the agrarian law, and the Catalan statute. In spite of his achievements his coalition became increasingly unpopular, being zealous enough to provoke a reaction from the right, but too moderate to satisfy the left. Azaña resigned (Sept. 1933), and in the election which followed (Nov.) the left was defeated.

Following the rising of Oct. 1934 Azaña was arrested in Barcelona, but his trial collapsed through lack of evidence (his part had in fact been an attempt to restrain the Esquerra). He then took a leading part in the organization of the Popular Front, whose unity brought success in the elections of Feb. 1936. As a result, Azaña became prime minister. Then, after the deposition of Alcalá Zamora, he was elected president (May 1936). His response to the nationalist rising of the following July was to seek a compromise solution, notably through the appointment of Martínez Barrio to the premiership. But as this policy failed he became no more than a figurehead during the civil war. He escaped to France (Jan. 1939).   WFK

AZAVEDO, DON JERONIMO, Portuguese captain-general of Ceylon (1594–1612) and viceroy (1612–18). After the Portuguese had suffered a disastrous defeat by the army of the King of Kandy, he recovered all the lost territory, invaded Kandy and burnt it. As ruler he committed many cruelties. After his return to Portugal he was accused of peculation and died in prison.

AZEGLIO, MASSIMO TAPARELLI, Marchese d' (1798–1866), a leading figure in the Italian Risorgimento and prime minister of Piedmont-Sardinia. He achieved prominence in the 1830s in Piedmont through his historical novels, which contrasted Italy's past glory with the existing foreign domination of the peninsula. The novels caused trouble with the Piedmontese censor because of their thinly veiled attacks on Austrian control of northern Italy. But not only the Austrian presence distressed Azeglio. His extensive travels throughout Italy made him a bitter opponent of the papal secular state, which he criticized in a pamphlet, 'On the Recent Events in the Romagna' (1846). Because of his essentially aristocratic outlook he would have nothing to do with Mazzini's ideas or secret revolutionary societies. Like Balbo, he believed that the Italian governments, especially that of Piedmont, stood the best chance of achieving Italian unity.

After Piedmont's defeat by Austria (1848–9), the new king, Victor Emmanuel II, retained the liberal constitution and appointed Azeglio premier, with the task of rebuilding the state and the monarchy's prestige. The constitution came under fierce attack from the clericals, whom Azeglio treated with easy tolerance until the admission of Cavour into his cabinet (1850). Pressure from Cavour and public opinion persuaded him to carry through the anti-clerical Siccardi Laws (1850), which abolished ecclesiastical jurisdiction and excessive landholding by the Church. In Oct. 1852 Azeglio resigned and was replaced by Cavour as prime minister, after a year of mounting difficulties between them, caused by Cavour's wish to increase the tempo of reform in alliance with the liberals. Despite this, Azeglio gave generous support to Cavour's Italian policy, especially the decision to annex the papal states, although he was opposed to the annexation of Naples and Sicily, believing they should form a kingdom independent from the rest of Italy.

AZERBAYJAN CRISIS (1946). During their occupation of north-west Iran (1941–6) the USSR encouraged a separatist movement in the Turkish-speaking area of Azerbayjan. In Nov. 1945 a communist-dominated government under Ja'far Pishevari was established. Contrary to the 1942 agreement, Soviet troops were not evacuated and the Iranian government was prevented from reasserting control. A diplomatic crisis resulted and eventually the USSR withdrew its troops (May 1946), after skilful Iranian diplomacy under Qavam al-Sultaneh and in return for an oil concession which was never ratified. In Nov.–Dec. 1946 Persian forces restored control over Azerbayjan.

AZERBAYJAN REPUBLIC, Muslim republic in Soviet Transcaucasia proclaimed on 28 May 1918, given de facto recognition by Allied Supreme Council (Jan. 1920) and overthrown by Bolshevik forces (April 1920).

AZHAR, AL- ('the brilliant one'), famous mosque built at Cairo in the reign of the Fatimid caliph Al-Mu'izz. Begun in 970 and inaugurated in 972, Al-Azhar was destined to become a renowned centre of Muslim learning. It has undergone, in the 19th and 20th cents, a series of reforms designed to meet the demands of modern education.

AZIKIWE, BENJAMIN NNAMDI (1904–), Ibo president of the Federal Republic of Nigeria (1963–6). In 1925, 'Zik'—as he came to be called—went to the US, where he worked his way through Lincoln and Howard universities, being much influenced by the condition of black Americans. A forceful polemicist in periodicals partly or entirely of his own foundation, he launched the *West African Pilot* as an organ of nationalist expression (1937) and gave a powerful thrust to African political life.

In 1952 he became chief minister and then prime minister of the Eastern Region, and was later involved in much political and personal controversy. Having led an alliance between the National Convention of Nigerian Citizens (NCNC) and the Northern People's Congress (NPC), he became president of the newly formed federal senate in 1959, then governor-general and later president of the independent federation proclaimed in 1960. In the secession war (1967–70), he took the Biafran side.

AZILIA, MARGRAVATE OF, territory comprising what is now Georgia (US), advertised by Sir Robert Montgomery, Aaron Hill, and Amos Kettleby as a settlers' paradise. The land was granted to Montgomery in 1717, but there was little enthusiasm and the settlement failed.

AZIM-UD-DAULAH (d. 1819), was made titular nawab of the Carnatic by Lord Wellesley on the death of his uncle, Umdat-ul-umara (1801). The civil and military administration of the Carnatic was transferred to the East India Co., and the nawab was granted a pension, arrangements being made for the liquidation of his private debts.

AZIM-ULLAH KHAN, Muslim agent of the notorious Nana Sahib. He visited England (1853–6), but failed to get the directors of the East India Co. to continue the ex-peshwa's pension to Nana and returned to report that England was no longer powerful. Azim-Ullah was one of the advisers responsible for the atrocities committed by Nana at Cawnpore.

AZIZ, AL- (reg. 975–96), the 5th and perhaps the most able caliph of the Fatimid line. Much of his reign was devoted to a sustained attempt, not without some measure of success, to bring Syria under Fatimid rule. Al-Aziz was able to gain control of Damascus in 982–3. His efforts to capture Aleppo in 983 and in 991–5 ended in failure, not least because the Byzantines, from their strong base at Antioch, cast their protection over the town. In Egypt itself Al-Aziz enjoyed the services of the able Ya'qub ibn Killis, who held the office of vizier until 991. The caliph was tolerant towards the Christians and the Jews—indeed, he had a Christian wife. His reign saw a large recruitment of Turks into the armed forces of the Fatimid state. Al-Aziz died while he was preparing a new campaign against Aleppo.

AZIZ ALI AL-MISRI (b. c. 1879), Ottoman officer of Circassian origin and Egyptian birth, who was prominent in the early history of Arab nationalism, although personally sympathetic to maintenance of an Ottoman connection. In the Second World War he was dismissed from his post as chief of the Egyptian General Staff because of his pro-Axis sympathies.

AZM, AL-, name of a powerful family which, in the 18th cent., rose to prominence at Damascus, extending its influence also to Tripoli, Sidon, and even, at times, to Aleppo. The most important members of the Azm line to hold office as Pasha of Damascus were Isma'il (1725–30), Sulayman (1733–8, 1741–3), As'ad (1743–57), and Muhammad (1771–83, with a short interval in 1772–3).

AZO (d. c. 1230), one of the outstanding members of the law school of Bologna, second only to Accursius as a commentator on Roman civil law. His *Summae* remained the standard introduction to Roman Law throughout the Middle Ages.

AZORES (2280 sq. kms), nine islands in the Atlantic Ocean which fall into three geographical groups with a population of 333,000. Although probably known to Arab traders, they were fully discovered by the Portuguese in the 15th cent. and have been administered by them ever since.

AZORES, BATTLE OF (1582), between France and Spain. A Spanish fleet routed a French expedition sailing to support a claimant to the throne of Portugal, which had been annexed by Spain in 1580. At the same time, the French made an unsuccessful invasion of the Netherlands, both expeditions being encouraged, though not actively supported, by Elizabeth I.

AZOURY, NEGIB (d. 1916), Syrian Christian, founder of *Ligue de la Patrie Arabe* (1904) and author of *Le Réveil de la nation arabe* (1905), who advocated an independent Asian–Arab confederation of Arabs outside Egypt.

AZOV, stronghold controlling the mouth of the Don river and access to the Sea of Azov. It was seized briefly from the Turks by the Don Cossacks (1637–42), regained by Peter the Great in 1696, relinquished in 1711, and destroyed in 1739, following the treaty of Belgrade between Russia, Austria, and the Ottoman empire. The area was incorporated into the Russian state during the reign of Catherine the Great (1762–96).

AZOV, SEA OF, an almost land-locked sea in southern Russia, connected to the Black Sea by the Straits of Kerch and dominated by Russia since 1792, when, following the treaty of Jassy with Turkey, she acquired the Crimea and stretches of the Black Sea's northern shores.

AZPILCUETA, MARTÍN DE (1493–1586), Spanish economist, and professor at Salamanca University, whose *De usuris* (1556) attributed 16th-cent. inflation to the influx of precious metals.

AZTECS, Indian tribe which ruled the central valley of Mexico and neighbouring areas when the Spaniards arrived (1519). The Aztecs had entered the valley of Anahuac in the 12th cent. and by 1325 were constructing their capital city, Tenochtitlán, on an island in Lake Texcoco. From there, this war-like people extended their control over neighbouring kingdoms for the purpose of collecting tribute and victims for sacrificial altars. The relationship between a religion which sanctioned ritual murder and the prevalence of warfare suggests over-population in the central valley.

Aztec society was complex but technologically less advanced than its neighbours, from whom it borrowed heavily. Government was directed by a chieftain and a tribal council which represented the cities' 20 clans. The council elected the chieftain from among members of the ruling family. The land was owned by the clan rather than the individual, except in the case of the nobility. Serfs cultivated the land of the nobility, which was a military caste. A brave soldier could rise into the nobility by feat of arms and his sons could inherit his status.

Though slavery existed, the mainstay of society was the numerous *macehual*, or pre-conquest commoners, who performed much of the necessary labour and paid most of the taxes. The armies of Hernán Cortés defeated the Aztecs and destroyed the city of Tenochtitlán (1521).

AZUCHI–MOMOYAMA PERIOD, term used mainly by Japanese cultural historians to denote the age of Nobunaga and Hideyoshi. Their castles at Azuchi and Momoyama displayed a new grandeur, reflecting both the new rulers' power and their less refined taste.

AZUELA, MARIANO (1873–1952), Mexican novelist of the Revolution, who portrayed the disillusionment of the educated participants in the revolutionary struggle in the north after 1910. His best-known novel was *Los de abajo* (1916).

BA MAW, Dr (1897–), Burmese nationalist, of Christian parentage and probably partly Armenian. He studied law in the west and appeared for the defence in the trials (1932) following Saya San's rebellion. Ba Maw entered politics and formed the *Sinyètha Wunthan* Party, and became first minister for education (1934) and the first prime minister (1937–9). After being imprisoned for anti-war propaganda (1940), he was made chief executive of the Japanese-sponsored administration (1942) and head of state (1 Aug. 1943). Later, he escaped to Japan, where he was interned by the Allies. He returned to Burma (1946), formed the *Maha Bama* Party, and was interned twice again (1947–8, 1966–8). His grasp of world affairs was unmatched by that of any of his Burmese contemporaries.

BA PE, U (b. 1885), Burmese politician, editor of *Sun* and leader of the United General Council of Burmese Associations (GCBA) Party. He was a cunning politician, but, lacking a private political army, was worsted by Dr Ba Maw and U Saw. He was minister for forests (1930–2, 1934–6) and for home affairs (1939). Ba Pe did not collaborate with the Japanese. He was a member of the Anti-Fascist People's Freedom League (AFPFL) and became a member of the Governor's Council in 1946, but was dismissed on suspicion of corruption. Eventually, he was imprisoned (1954–8) for alleged conspiracy against the government in 1949.

BAALBEK, ancient Heliopolis, in Lebanon, famous for the ruins of a temple complex begun by the Emperor Antoninus Pius (138–61) and completed under Caracalla in honour of Jupiter Heliopolitanus, identified, probably, with the Semitic Hadad.

BABAD, generic Javanese term for 'chronicle'. Normally written in verse, *babad*s may concern individuals, kingdoms, or particular events. The most famous chronicle is *Babad Tanah Djawi*, known in many versions. It begins with the first man, Adam, followed by a genealogy including the first, semi-mythical rulers of ancient Java. The early history of Java is largely mythical, but the sections from the 17th cent. onwards became progressively more reliable as historical documentation. These chronicles, like those of other lands, were often written not primarily as historical narratives but as legitimate documents for the ruler and his kingdom; their use as historical material thus requires caution.

BABAK, adherent of the Khurrami sect, began in 816–17 a formidable revolt in the mountainous region of Arran, in Azerbayjan. The Caliph Al-Mu'tasim sent Al-Afshin, a Turkish soldier, against the rebels. He brought the revolt to an end in 837.

BABBAGE, CHARLES (1792–1871). English scientist who designed a difference engine (1822) for the automatic computation and printing of mathematical tables. In 1833 he planned the analytical engine, which was to have been controlled by perforated cards and anticipated the 20th-cent. computer. But engineering techniques of the day were inadequate and, despite treasury aid, the project failed.

BABENBERG DYNASTY, a family powerful in Austria and Switzerland and at the height of its importance one of the richest houses in the empire. They ruled Austria from 976 to 1246, raising a small weak margravate into a powerful state.

BABEUF, FRANÇOIS NOEL ('Gracchus') (1760–97), French communist conspirator, whose ideas and example influenced nearly all 19th-cent. egalitarian movements. After imprisonment (Feb. 1795) for attacks on the Thermidorians in his paper *Le Tribun du Peuple*, Babeuf, with his disciple Buonarotti, formed a secret Society of Equals. They planned a coup for 11 May 1796, but were arrested beforehand. Babeuf was executed and his plot gained little popular support. But his ideas for a 'Republic of Equals' and the organization of society on communist lines were spread in the next century by Buonarotti, as was his advocacy of revolution through a tight knot of dedicated, professional conspirators.

BABINGTON, ANTHONY (1561–86), Catholic conspirator, who was page to Mary Queen of Scots and plotted to release her and assassinate Elizabeth. The conspiracy was discovered by Walsingham's spies, and, as it was shown that Mary knew of it, her life was forfeit under the statute that followed the Bond of Association. Babington and his associates were executed (1587), as was Mary a few months later.

BABISM, messianic Iranian religious movement founded by Sayyid Ali Muhammad Shirazi (1819–50), who was known as the Bab (gate), and crushed with extreme severity by the Iranian government after an attempt on the shah's life (1852).

BABUR, ZAHIR-AD-DIN MUHAMMAD (1483–1530), 1st Mughal Emperor of India, was fifth in descent from the Turkish conqueror Taimur. As a member of a younger branch, he succeeded (1494) only to the small Kingdom of Fargana beyond the Hindu Kush, but as a Timurid, among whom succession was settled by the sword, he regarded himself as a king by profession and entitled to possess himself of all Taimur's dominions. His ambition was to recover the ancestral capital of Samarkand, but he found himself threatened by the rising power of Persia on the one hand and the Uzbegs on the other. After several unsuccessful attempts to recover Samarkand, he established himself at Kabul (1504), but finding that Shia Persian aid won him victories but lost him the support of his Sunni subjects, he gave up his ancestral ambition (1513) and turned his eyes towards India. Raids revealed discontent in the Afghan sultanate of Delhi against the Sultan Ibrahim, and, encouraged by an invitation from the Punjab governor, he staged an invasion. At Panipat (21 April 1526) he defeated a superior Indian army with the aid of Turkish artillery and the wheeling tactics of his cavalry, coupled with Afghan disaffection. Ibrahim was killed and Babur secured Delhi and Agra. In 1527, at Kanwaha, he faced a coalition of Rajput chiefs led by Rana Sanga. The same tactics as before, reinforced by Rajput clan jealousies, gave his small army a second victory in a critical situation. His enemies were now divided and he was able to extend his empire as far as the borders of Bengal.

Babur's empire was a loosely knit personal kingship over a variety of chiefs from Kabul to the borders of Bengal and was held together by his ability and leadership. It was left to his grandson Akbar to organize the real Mughal empire. Nevertheless, his own achievement was remarkable and influenced later developments. His personal magnetism created a tradition of loyalty, and his love of all forms of

Persian culture, especially of gardens, set a pattern for the empire-to-be. His first act on reaching Agra was to lay out a garden.

In person Babur, who loved sport and good living, was versatile and attractive and he was a Turki poet and prose writer of distinction, his *Memoirs* being a classic of their kind.

The Memoirs of Babur, tr. by J. Leyden and W. Erskine, 2 vols (London, 1921).
S. M. Edwardes, *Babur, Diarist and Despot* (London, 1926).
TGPS

BABYLON, ancient city and kingdom of Mesopotamia, on the left bank of the Euphrates, 70 miles (112·7 kms) south of Baghdad and near modern Hilla. It enjoyed two great periods, at the beginning and at the end of its history. The first Babylonian dynasty (1894–1595 BC) was founded by the Amorite, Sumuabum, its most famous king being Hammurabi (*c.* 1792–1750). During his reign Akkad and Sumer were conquered and Assyria and part of Syria came under his control. The Akkadian language and religion were adopted, except that the former god, Enlil, was replaced by Marduk. It was a period of change in the area, when royal power grew and the status of the temple declined, when there appeared a class of free people, attached neither to the temple nor the king, and there was extensive private ownership of land. The first dynasty was ended by a brief Hittite invasion (*c.* 1594), followed by the Kassite conquest, which lasted about 400 years. Little is known about either this period or the 500 years which followed, except that Elam was briefly conquered by Nebuchadnezzar I (*c.* 1124–1103). Babylonia seems to have been politically unimportant, finally being conquered by the Assyrians. During this period also, the Chaldean tribes settled in Babylonia and in 625 the Chaldean chief, Nabopolassar, founded the last great dynasty of Babylon. Under his successor, Nebuchadnezzar II (*c.* 605–562), Babylon conquered all the old Assyrian lands of Mesopotamia, Syria, and Palestine. During the Chaldean period the city of Babylon was rebuilt and fortified with massive walls. Nebuchadnezzar built a splendid palace with five courts, a great temple to Marduk, and a huge ziqqurat, and in his reign the city became a scientific and literary centre. This period of glory was again short-lived and Babylon finally lost its sovereignty to the Persian king, Cyrus II, in 539.

H. W. F. Saggs, *The Greatness that was Babylon* (London, 1962).
A. Leo Oppenheim, *Ancient Mesopotamia* (Chicago, 1964).
JKG

BABYLONIA, ancient kingdom of Mesopotamia, founded by Sumuabum (*c.* 1894–1881 BC). The term is also used to denote the southern part of Mesopotamia (from Akkad in the north to Sumer in the south), even for the period before the kingdom of Babylon existed.

BABYLONIAN EXILE. In 597 and 587 BC Babylon conquered the southern Hebrew state of Judah and deported the ruling classes to an area between the Tigris and Euphrates, where they may have been joined by the descendants of Hebrews from Samaria (conquered 721 BC) who had earlier been deported from Assyria. They were allowed to return to Judea in 538 after the conquest of Babylon by Cyrus, but many remained and developed an outstanding centre of Jewry in Iraq.

BABYLONISH CAPTIVITY OF THE CHURCH (1520–1), radical tract composed by Martin Luther attacking Catholic teaching on the sacraments. In it he enunciated his belief in the supremacy of faith and asserted that the sacraments should be reduced from five to two, the Lord's Supper and baptism.

BACCHIADS, members of a dominant Dorian aristocratic family at Corinth *c.* 750–650 BC, who monopolized political office and exploited Corinth's rapid commercial growth. Their power was eventually broken (*c.* 650) by the tyrant Cypselus.

BACH, name of a Thuringian family of musicians active in the 17th and 18th cents, of which evidence is found before the Reformation. Its most illustrious member was Johann Sebastian (1685–1750), director of music (Cantor) at the Thomaskirche, Leipzig, from 1723 until his death. During his life he was known principally as an organist; but he composed in most of the forms then current, and some of his works are now considered among the finest masterpieces.

Of his sons, Wilhelm Friedmann (1710–84) was also famed as an organist; Carl Philipp Emanuel (1714–88) was a prolific composer, and author of a famous keyboard method (1759); and Johann Christian (1735–82) was an opera composer long resident in England, where he was music teacher to the queen.

BACH, ALEXANDER VON (1813–93), Austrian minister of the interior and instigator of the 'Bach system' of extreme centralization and bureaucratic control of the Habsburg empire. His father was a peasant, but Bach was trained as a lawyer and became one of the young radicals in Metternich's Vienna. His impatience with the monarchy's inefficiency made him join the bourgeois opposition, which took control in the revolution of March 1848. He did not share the interest in German unity of many of his colleagues, but wanted a strong and German-dominated Austrian empire. In June 1848 he was made minister of justice in the liberal provisional government, but when the revolution became more radical in Oct. he fled to the court. He was one of the few liberals willing to serve under the reactionary Schwarzenberg, largely because he believed co-operation was the only way of preventing the return of the old privileged and feudal society.

In June 1849 he became minister of the interior and gradually took over the direction of the monarchy's internal policy. The revolution had swept away many of the monarchy's provincial differences and privileges, including the diets and estates, and had set up a centralized ministry. The counter-revolution in its turn ensured that no representative assembly was set up, so that the government had the opportunity to institute a far-reaching autocracy. Bach took this opportunity to return to the centralizing policies of Joseph II, employing a German bureaucracy to bring the whole of the empire under the control of Vienna. Although his system was bitterly attacked, it was beneficial to the peasants because of the large-scale redistribution of land which accompanied it. The Magyars above all objected to the system, and it was largely because of the danger of another Magyar rising that the Emperor Francis Joseph dismissed Bach (1859) after the monarchy's defeat in the Italian war. Francis Joseph's personal confidence in him ensured Bach a post as minister at the Vatican before a long retirement.

C. A. Macartney, *The Habsburg Empire, 1790–1918* (London, 1968).
A. J. P. Taylor, *The Habsburg Monarchy* (London, 1964).
DMcK

BACHELOR'S WALK, Dublin street in which, in July 1914, British troops shot 3 and wounded 38 in a riot which developed from an attempt by the Irish Volunteers to land a cargo of rifles. The incident was contrasted with the highly successful landing of rifles and ammunition by the Ulster volunteers at Larne in April, and added one further obstacle to the negotiation of an Irish settlement.

BACON, SIR NICHOLAS (1509–79), father of Francis Bacon and brother-in-law of Burghley, was lord keeper (1558–79) with a special responsibility for influencing the Commons in support of government policies. He also exercised the jurisdiction of lord chancellor, delivering some notable judgments in equity. Bacon played an important part in the discussions leading to the religious compromise of 1559. Himself a sincere Protestant, he subsequently upheld the doctrines and disciplines of the Church against Puritan criticism, and he continuously advised strong measures against Mary Queen of Scots, presiding at the enquiries held when she fled to England in 1568. Bacon, who was enriched by the dissolution of the monasteries, built a magnificent house at Gorhambury, in Hertfordshire (1563-8).

BACON, ROGER (c. 1216-92). The popular concept of Bacon as a progressive thinker imprisoned and persecuted by an obscurantist church is without foundation, but he was a scholar of exceptional independence of mind and some of his criticisms of his most distinguished contemporaries were justified. He lectured on the arts in Paris (1245-7), where he became interested in experimental science. He joined the Franciscans and was at their house at Oxford. At the request of Pope Clement IV (1265-8), he began to attempt a synthesis of all the natural sciences. The attempt failed, but resulted in his three major works, the *Opus Maior*, *Opus Minor*, and *Opus Tertium*. His title of *doctor mirabilis* is deserved for his work on optics and his place as an early Aristotelian.

BACON'S REBELLION (1675-6), uprising led by a young Virginia colonist, Nathaniel Bacon, against Gov. William Berkeley. Berkeley failed to support the farmers and frontiersmen against depredations by the Susquehannah Indians. There were suspicions that Berkeley had an interest in the fur trade with the Indians, so a group of 300 men under Bacon attacked the Indians without Berkeley's approval. While they were away, Berkeley instituted governmental reforms to attract popularity, but upon his return Bacon marched on Jamestown and burned it, whereupon Berkeley fled. The new burgesses, with Bacon as a member, passed more reform legislation. After a few months in Jamestown Bacon died (Oct. 1676) and the rising collapsed. Berkeley returned and dealt so severely with many of Bacon's followers that he was recalled to England.

BAD AXE, BATTLE OF (Aug. 1832), waged at the junction of Mississippi river with Bad Axe river in WI. Black Hawk's band was caught between US troops under Gen. Henry Atkinson and a gunboat. The Indians' flag of truce was ignored and one of the bloodiest tragedies in American–Indian relations occurred. The battle ended the Indians' attempt to return to their homeland in the Rock River valley of IL.

BADAJOZ, Spanish fortress-town on the Portuguese border which was in both French and British hands at different times during the Peninsular War. Its ultimate capture by Wellington (1812) made possible the British capture of Madrid and the end of Napoleon's influence in Spain. During the Spanish Civil War Badajoz remained Republican, finally falling to Nationalist forces (Aug. 1936).

BADAN CHANDRA, the Ahom governor of Gauhati who, in 1810, quarrelled with Purnananda, the chief minister, and fled to Bengal. Failing to get British help, he persuaded the Burmese king to reinstate him (1816). His oppressive policy led to his assassination and the Burmese conquest of Assam (1819).

BADARIAN CULTURE, Egyptian predynastic culture of which settlements and cemeteries have been excavated. The people were among the earliest Egyptian farmers, growing grain, keeping herds of cattle and sheep, hunting and fishing. They made very fine pottery, stone tools, and cloth, and became skilled in the use of copper. Unlike their immediate forebears, who depended only on local materials, they engaged in trade, since foreign woods, notably cedar and juniper, and beads made of non-local materials have been found among their possessions. Although much of prehistoric Egyptian culture seems to have originated in Asia, that of the Badarians is probably of African origin.

BADEN, TREATY OF (1714), one of 11 separate treaties (1713-14) ending the War of the Spanish Succession. That of Baden was a formal ratification, by the Imperial Diet of the Holy Roman empire, of the clauses of the treaty of Rastadt relating to Germany which had been concluded by France and the emperor earlier in the year. The Electors of Bavaria and Cologne were reinstated, while France retained Alsace with Strasbourg and Landau, but restored all other conquests on the right bank of the Rhine.

BADENI, CASIMIR FELIX, Graf (1846-1909), Polish noble and Austrian statesman, who made an unsuccessful attempt to solve the nationality problem in the Austrian half of the Habsburg monarchy. He was appointed prime minister (1895) at a moment of crisis for the empire, after a succession of coalition ministries had failed to solve the vital questions of extending the franchise and resolving the disputes between the Czechs and Germans in Bohemia. His service as governor of Galicia indicated that he was the strong man needed. Although he effectively dealt with the franchise issue (1896), he fell from power in Nov. 1897, when his language ordinances, by which he had tried to conciliate the Czechs by putting Czech on an equal footing with German for administrative purposes in Bohemia and Moravia, provoked widespread German nationalist riots, reaching revolutionary proportions in Vienna.

BADEN-POWELL, ROBERT STEPHENSON SMYTH BADEN-POWELL, 1st Baron (1857-1941), soldier and founder of the Boy Scout and Girl Guide movements. After distinguished army service in various campaigns in the late 19th cent. he won fame in defending Mafeking in the Boer War.

BADOGLIO, PIETRO (1871-1956), Italian field commander, who made his reputation in the Libyan war (1911-12), but was an indecisive politician as successor to Mussolini. In the First World War, after successfully planning the attack on Monte Sabotino (1916), he saved his reputation in the Caporetto breakthrough (Oct. 1917) by defensive moves, became deputy to Gen. Diaz, and was a major architect of the Vittorio Veneto victory. In 1919 he became a senator, and in 1925 succeeded Diaz as chief of the general staff, and in 1926 was raised to the rank of marshal. He was largely responsible for the reconquest and harsh colonization of Libya (1929-34), and the conclusion of the Ethiopian campaign (though he had opposed the venture). He was appointed Duke of Addis Ababa and, briefly, viceroy in May 1936. Badoglio opposed Italy's entry into the war and the Greek invasion, but did not resign until after the military defeats in Dec. 1940. The king, wishing to avoid a political rupture, chose him, as a loyal friend, to succeed Mussolini as prime minister (25 July 1943). General distrust of Badoglio and his own hesitancy hampered the negotiations for an armistice and the subsequent declaration of war against Germany (13 Oct.), which left Rome and northern Italy in Nazi hands. The suspicion of the Allies and of anti-fascist elements rendered ineffectual Badoglio's government, based first at Brindisi and then Salerno. With the abdication of King Victor Emmanuel he was replaced by Bonomi (June 1944).

BADR, BATTLE OF (624), to the south-west of Medina, where the Prophet Muhammad attacked a rich caravan returning from Syria to Mecca under Abu Sufyan, the head of the clan of the Umayya. This battle, the first success of the Prophet in the field, did much to increase the prestige of the Muslims.

BADR AL-DIN MAHMUD (1358-1416), sufi (mystic) and Ottoman officer who was exiled after the fall of his patron, Musa Chelebi (1413), to Iznik (Nikaea), where, with his disciple Bürklüje Mustafa, he organized a formidable rebellion (1416) which spread from western Asia Minor to the Balkans, before the defeat of Badr al-Din near Edirne, his capture and execution (Dec. 1416).

BADR AL-JAMALI (d. 1094), celebrated vizier of the Fatimid Caliph Al-Mustansir (1036–94). Under Al-Mustansir the Fatimid state was on the verge of collapse. In Egypt there was famine and also violent conflict between the Turkish and the Sudanese troops of the caliph. There was danger, too, from the advance of the Seljuks in Syria. Of Armenian origin, Badr al-Jamali began his career as a slave of the amir Jamal al-Dawla ibn Ammar. He rose to be governor of Damascus and also of Acre. His pre-eminence rested on the strong force of Armenians which he recruited into his service. Summoned to Egypt in 1073, he crushed the dissension prevailing there in four years of ruthless endeavour (1073–7). Meanwhile, in Syria, Damascus fell to the Seljuks (1076). The attempts (1078–9, 1085–6, 1088–90) of Badr al-Jamali to restore Fatimid control in Syria met with little success, but he was able to maintain a firm hold on southern Palestine. Not the least of his achievements was his success in ensuring that, on his own death, the office of vizier should go to his able son, Al-Afdal Shahinshah.

BAD-TIBIRA, ancient city of Sumeria, probably situated at modern Tell-Medineh. It had, according to the Sumerian King List, three kings who ruled for an alleged 108,000 years.

BAEDEKER, KARL (1801–59), German author and publisher, whose guide to the Rhine (1839) began a pioneering and much-used series of guide books in German, French, and English.

BAEKELAND, LEO HENDRICK (1863–1944), founder of the plastics industry. He was born and educated in Ghent, and in 1889 went to the US, where he manufactured a new photographic paper with enormous success. In 1905 Baekeland was looking for a substitute for shellac in the resinous products of the reaction between phenol and formaldehyde. Failing to dissolve the hard residue, he decided to put its inertness to good use and developed 'Bakelite', the first thermo-setting plastic, a substance of major importance in manufacturing developments during the first half of the 20th cent.

BÁEZ, BUENAVENTURA (1810–84), president of the Dominican Republic five times and leader of the political faction known as the 'Reds'. Early in his career he was the political rival of Gen. Pedro Santana. Because of his fear of invasion from Haiti, Báez negotiated with President Grant for the Republic's admission to the Union. Grant supported the idea, but it was dismissed by the US Congress (1870).

BAFFIN, WILLIAM (1584–1622), English explorer and a member of the Danish expeditions to Greenland (1612) and Spitzbergen (1613, 1614). Baffin, serving under Robert Bylot, piloted Arctic voyages (1615, 1616) to discover the North-West Passage. They mapped the north shore of Hudson's Bay Strait and discovered Mill Island, Lancaster Sound, Smith Sound, Baffin Bay, and Baffin Island. The 1616 expedition reached the entrance to the North-West Passage without realizing they had done so. Baffin's accounts of the Arctic voyages were disbelieved and his charts ignored until their accuracy was reaffirmed by the explorations of John Ross (1818) and Edward Parry (1821).

BAGEHOT, WALTER (1826–77), English journalist, writer and literary critic. He edited *The Economist* from 1860 till his death, while also managing the London agency of his father's banking business. His *English Constitution* (1867) depicts the contemporary workings of British politics, just as his *Lombard Street* (1873) exposes the real workings of the Victorian money-market.

Bagehot's conservative Liberalism lent him an objectivity which set a new standard in political and economic analysis, though it also set him apart from the radicals and working men who were capturing the Liberal Party in his day. His combination of scholarship and common sense flourished on his unique synthesis of the contemplative and the active life.

BAGHDAD PACT (1955), a mutual co-operation agreement of which the nucleus was a pact signed between Turkey and Iraq (24 Feb.) later adhered to by Britain (5 April), Pakistan (23 Sept.), and Iran (25 Oct.). The pact accorded well with the defence interests of Turkey against the USSR and with the western orientation and interests of Nuri as-Said's government in Iraq; it also met the British need to maintain a defensive line (of which the airbases in Iraq were the essential link) in the Middle East and provided a means of reforming the 1930 treaty with Iraq after the collapse of the treaty of Portsmouth (1948). The pact was vigorously opposed by the Egyptian government, as a breach of Arab solidarity, a strengthening of its traditional rival, Iraq, and a continuation of British bases in the Middle East. The US government had favoured the negotiation of defensive alliances in the Middle East, but gave primacy to its Egyptian policy and so did not join the pact, concentrating on the establishment of a 'northern tier' alliance with Turkey, Iran, and Pakistan (and negotiating the supply of arms to Iraq). The diplomacy surrounding the Baghdad Pact thus divided the Middle East. The British attempt to secure the adherence of Jordan provoked a major political crisis and ended in failure; the pact was also an issue in Syrian politics, where the balance in the end swung decisively towards Egypt. In 1956 the pact was virtually destroyed as far as the Arab states were concerned by the Anglo-French attack on Egypt; the *coup de grâce* was given by the Iraqi revolution of July 1958. The pact then survived in truncated form and was the base of the Central Treaty Organization

The terms of the pact, which were less important than its political results, provided for co-operation for security and defence, a commitment to the principles of the UN Charter, accessibility to members of the Arab League, and the establishment of a Permanent Council at ministerial level.   WFK

BAGHDAD RAILWAY, projected German-financed railway from Konya to Baghdad with an extension to the Persian Gulf. The concession (granted 1899, confirmed 1903) aroused considerable Russian and British hostility, both of whom sought to restrict the railway's extension towards their spheres of influence. However, agreements (1911–14) provided for the settlement of disputes, although the line was still uncompleted in 1914.

BAGHIRMA, unstable state east of Lake Chad, founded by Kenga immigrants in the 16th cent. and superficially Islamized. After Rabih's invasion (1897) it came under French protection.

BAGODA (10th–11th cents), first Kutumbawa ruler of Kano, northern Nigeria, who was a grandson of Bayajida of Daura and one of the sons of Bawo.

BAGRATID, family of considerable prominence in Armenian history from the 3rd cent., which spread into Georgia in the 8th cent. and gradually established its position as the ruling family, attaining the apogee of its power in the 11th–13th cents under David IV the Builder (1089–1125) and Queen Tamar (1184–1213). The Bagratids maintained local power after the subordination of Georgia to the Mongols, and later the Ottomans and Iranians, and ruled until the 1801 confirmation of the Russian annexation of Georgia and, in Imeretia, until 1808, being probably the longest-ruling dynasty in history.

BAGYIDAW (*reg.* 1819–37), King of Burma, seventh ruler of the Alaungpaya dynasty, personally benevolent, but publicly a despot. He appointed the ambitious and war-like Bandula as governor of Assam, so precipitating frontier incidents that led to the First Burmese War. The treaty of Yandabo ended the war, but much resentment remained against the British. Maj. Henry Burney, the British envoy, succeeded in gaining the confidence of Bagyidaw, but the king became liable to recurring fits of insanity and was deposed (1837) by his younger brother, Tharraweddy Min. The British mission was eventually withdrawn.

BAHADUR SHAH I (1643–1712), (Mughal Emperor (*reg.* 1707–12), second son of the Mughal Emperor Aurangzeb, whom he succeeded in 1707 after defeating his younger brother, Prince Azam, at the battle of Jajau. In his short reign he made peace with the Marathas, conciliated the Rajputs, and defeated the Sikhs.

BAHADUR SHAH II (*reg.* 1837–58), last Mughal Emperor of Delhi. Because of his complicity in the Mutiny of 1857 he was deposed (1858) and the Crown took over the government of India from the East India Co. He died in exile at Rangoon (1862).

BAHAISM, syncretic religious movement founded by Baha'ullah (1817–92) as an offshoot of Babism. Centred on Mt Carmel, it became a world religion, although most widespread in Iran.

BAHAMAN REBELLION, in Pahang, Malaya (1891–5). A sporadic guerrilla war against British control of Pahang, established in 1888, was led by Bahaman, a chief of Semantan, upper Pahang. Siam increased its control over Kelantan and Trengganu by skilfully 'exiling' Bahaman at Britain's request after he had fled from Pahang.

BAHAMAS, an archipelago (700 islands) betwen FL and Cuba. San Salvador (Waitling's Island) in the Bahamas may have been Columbus's first landfall (1492). Spaniards removed the Indians to work in Cuban mines, but made no settlement. The Bahamas were granted to an Englishman, Sir Robert Heath (1629), and colonized by the Company of Elutherian Adventurers (1649). Settlers formed a government and elected a House of Assembly. In 1670 the islands were granted to six of the Carolina Proprietors and surrendered to the Crown in 1717. The islands were, before 1717, a centre for pirate activity and were subject to raids by Spaniards (1680, 1684, 1781–3), French (1703), and Americans (1776). The American War of Independence led to an influx of loyalists and their slaves from the American mainland. The end of slavery (1838) marked the economic decline of the Bahamas, except for blockade running in the American Civil War (1861–5) and bootlegging during the prohibition era in the US (1920–33). Since the Second World War the Bahamas have become a major tourist attraction and because of a lenient tax structure an important centre for international business operations. In 1964 internal self-government was granted to the islands and in 1967 the power of the white merchant clique ('Bay Street Boys') was limited by the election as prime minister of Lynden O. Pindling, who represented a predominantly black, working-class movement.

BAHMANI DYNASTY, of the Deccan, so called because its founder claimed descent from the Persian King Bahman. He was Hasan Zafar Khan, an officer of the Tughluq dynasty of the Delhi sultanate, who proclaimed his independence from Sultan Muhammad Tughluq in 1347, and took the title of Ala-ad-din. He established his capital in Gulbarga and during the 11 years of his reign built up a dominion from the Penganga river in the north to the Krishna river in the south, and including the port of Goa. With the Tughluq empire declining in the north, he had chiefly to deal with the Hindu kingdoms of Warangal to the north-east and the rising empire of Vijayanagar in the south. His successor, Muhammad Shah I (1358–1373), carried on ferocious wars against Vijayanagar

and Warangal, but also gave administrative shape to his kingdom by creating a council of eight ministers, by yearly tours of supervision and inspection, and by raising a royal bodyguard or standing army. The state was a military ascendancy of mainly Turkish Muslim nobles, with some reinforcement of Afghans, Persians, Arabs, and Abyssinians. It was held together by vigorous military leadership, achieved by bitter struggles leading to frequent assassinations and blindings. In this way the divided Hindu chiefs were held in check, while the ever-present menace of Vijayanagar provided a focus for Muslim sentiment and an antidote to aristocratic factionalism. The court life was brilliant and brittle; the cultural climate was Persian. As time went on, the intolerance of the earlier sultan was replaced by intellectual and religious eclecticism, which became a characteristic of the Deccan Muslim kingdoms. The Bahmani dynasty was also notable for its public buildings, at first at Gulbarga and from the reign of Ahmad Shah (1422–35) at the new capital at Bidar. These characteristics in general were passed on to the five successor kingdoms, the last of which was conquered by the Mughals in 1687.

The Hindu kingdom of Warangal was extinguished in 1424–5, but the wars with Vijayanagar continued with no decisive result. In the mid-15th cent. the state was governed by the famous minister Mahmud Gawan, who served both Homayun (1457–62) and Muhammad III (1463–82). During this period the kingdom attained its largest size. His death on the order of Muhammad (1481) followed by that of the sultan led to the break-up of the kingdom into five successor kingdoms. The Bahmanis lingered on at Bidar until 1526, when they were replaced by Amir Barid. The other four kingdoms were Bijapur, which absorbed Bidar after 1620, Golkonda, Ahmadnagar, and Berar.

J. S. King, *History of The Bahmani Dynasty* (London, 1900).
                                                                    TGPS

BAHOL, PHYA (*Phraya* Phahonphonphayuhasena, personal name, Phot Phahonyothin) (1888–1947), prime minister of Siam from June 1933 to Sept. 1938, during the early years of the constitutional regime. He received a military education in Germany and rose rapidly in the artillery corps of the Thai army to the rank of colonel in 1931. His nomination as prime minister signalled the ascendency of the military group among the promoters of the revolution of 1932. He was pushed aside after a vote of no-confidence in 1938, in favour of Phibunsongkhram.

BAIAN, leader of the Avars, who entered the Danube valley in the sixties of the 6th cent., destroyed the Gepids, and drove the Lombards into Italy (568). Baian became the first ruler of a vast Avar empire.

BAIF, LAZARE DE (1532–89), French humanist poet, patronized by Francis I. He was a friend of Ronsard and a member of the circle of poets known as the *Pléiade.* An academy with which he was associated was founded for the practice of the arts of poetry, music, and dance. It had some effect on the development of the court ballet and royal festivals organized by Catherine de Medici, and ultimately on French opera.

BAILLI, medieval French royal official in evidence from the late 12th cent. in northern France. He was the chief royal representative in a district, exercising royal justice, supervising the revenues, and commanding the local forces. The *bailli* received a good salary and might be promoted to higher posts in the royal central government. By the late Middle Ages the *bailli* was almost always a noble and only his military and police functions continued to be of importance.

BAILLIE, ROBERT (1599–1662), moderate Scottish Presbyterian leader in the general assembly at Glasgow (1638), who was sent by the Covenanting Lords to London to draw up accusations against Laud (1640). He attended Charles II at the Hague when he was proclaimed king in Scotland (1649). His last years were spent as Principal of Glasgow University.

BAILLIEU, WILLIAM LAWRENCE (1859–1936), Australian financier and member of the Legislative Council of Vic. (1901–22). He was associated with city and rural development and with some of the larger mining, manufacturing, and trading companies, and was minister for public works and health (1909), minister in various Vic. cabinets (1912–17), financial adviser to wartime governments, and a pioneer of employee profit-sharing.

BAILLY, JEAN SYLVAIN (1736–93), eminent French astronomer who achieved prominence in the first years of the Revolution. He was elected president of the Third Estate and was one of those chiefly responsible for the Tennis Court oath. A constitutional monarchist, Bailly acted as mayor of Paris (July 1789–Nov. 1791), but had to resign because of his unpopular decision to order the National Guard to disperse the Champs de Mars demonstration. After being accused of trying to restore the monarchy, he was executed.

BAINES, EDWARD (1774–1848), British journalist, proprietor, from 1801, of the *Leeds Mercury*, which he made into one of the foremost provincial Liberal journals. As MP for Leeds (1834–41), he supported the Anti-Corn Law League and opposed state control of education.

BAIRAM KHAN (c. 1524–61), the appointed guardian of Akbar when the latter became Mughal emperor at the age of 13 (Jan. 1556) on the death of his father, Homayun. A Turkish nobleman of distinguished ancestry, his loyalty and talents enabled the Mughals to survive the crisis in their fortunes which followed. Bairam defeated a Sur claimant at Sirhind, and the much greater challenge of the Hindu general Hemu at Panipat in Nov. 1556. Bairam, as Akbar's chief minister, added Malwa and Jaunpur to the empire before Akbar asserted himself to dismiss him (1561). He was murdered by an enemy on his way to Mecca.

BAIRD, JOHN LOGIE (1888–1946), Scottish inventor and television pioneer. He pursued his researches as an amateur and by 1924 had produced a crude outline form of television apparatus. In 1926 he demonstrated the first true television to the Royal Institution in London, and in 1929 provided the apparatus for the first experimental television broadcasts for the BBC, and later for some of the first regular BBC broadcasts, which started in 1936. His competitors in this latter service were EMI Marconi, and in 1937 their system was chosen exclusively in preference to Baird's. Baird also pioneered colour television and a form of stereoscopic television.

BAJI RAO I (1698–1740), second of the hereditary peshwas of the Bhat family of Chitpavan Brahmins. He succeeded his father in 1720 and turned Maratha energies to northward expansion through raids with fast-moving Maratha cavalry to secure the grant of *chauth* (quarter of the revenue from Mughal provinces). As the Mughal power waned, this was converted into outright cession. The policy of raids was increasingly backed by regular armies containing many besides Marathas. Military chiefs thus became powerful, and three of them (Gaekwar, Holkar, and Sindhia) founded dynasties. Baji Rao's father had secured the *chauth* of the six Deccan provinces. Denied further progress there by the nizam, the Marathas entered Malwa and Gujarat. After a series of campaigns which included a raid on Delhi, the Marathas obtained the outright cession of Malwa in 1738. This was the springboard for their further northern expansion.

BAJI RAO II (*reg.* 1796–1818), last Maratha peshwa, a weak and treacherous ruler who spent most of his time in gross debauchery. He alienated his subjects by a reign of terror and had the brother of Holkar crushed to death under the feet of an elephant. In 1799 his territories were disturbed by internecine warfare which was aggravated by the death of Nana Fadnavis (1800). Defeated by Holkar, he fled to Bassein, where he entered into a subsidiary alliance with the English Co. (31 Dec. 1802). This made war with the Marathas inevitable because Sindhia and Berar disliked the provision for British arbitration in their internal disputes. During the governor-generalship of Lord Hastings, Baji Rao continued to plot against the British and plundered the British Residency. After his defeat, the peshwaship was abolished (1818) and he was granted a pension. He died at Bithur in 1851.

BAKELITE, forerunner of a vast range of plastics, was developed in the US by L. H. Baekeland, in 1909. It had many industrial uses and was particularly valuable as an insulator, but its brittleness led to its being replaced by tougher and more flexible materials.

BAKER, NEWTON DIEHL (1871–1937), US politician and lawyer. City solicitor in Cleveland, OH (1902–12), he was a prominent member of Mayor Tom Johnson's progressive reform group. Baker was mayor (1911 and 1913), and one of the country's most respected municipal officials. As a supporter of Woodrow Wilson, he served as secretary of war (1916–21) and shared Wilson's enthusiasm for the League of Nations. He was appointed to the Permanent Court of International Justice at the Hague (1928) and was one of F. D. Roosevelt's rivals for the Democratic party presidential nomination (1932).

BAKER, RAY STANNARD (1870–1946), US journalist and scholar. A 'muckraking' writer for *McClure's Magazine*, he attacked the trusts and wrote a pioneer study of race relations, *Following the Color Line* (1908). His best-known work was the *Life and Letters of Woodrow Wilson* (8 vols, 1927–39).

BAKER, SHIRLEY WALDEMAR (1836–1903), British Wesleyan missionary, who emigrated to Australia and later went to Tonga (1860), where he became George Tupou's lieutenant in a programme of modernization aimed at averting foreign annexation. In 1876 he was accused by local Europeans of malpractice and oppression and the High Commissioner sought his removal, but, ignoring a demand for his recall by the Australian Wesleyan Conference (1879), he left the mission and was installed as prime minister (1881). The establishment of a Free Church (1885) completed the breach. An attempt on his life (1887) disturbed the balance of his mind and he was removed (1890).

BAKER v. CARR, 369 US 186 (1962). In this case the US Supreme Court asserted for the first time its authority and duty to pass on matters concerning the apportionment of legislative representation. The case was brought by citizens of Nashville, TN, whose state legislature had not reapportioned since 1901.

In departing from the traditional reluctance of the court to accept that they had jurisdiction over such cases, Justice Brennan (supported by five other justices) considered only the specific, narrow issues of the case. A citizen could sue in a federal court; federal courts had jurisdiction over the subject-matter of cases concerning legislative apportionment and hence could give decisions on such cases. This assertion that individuals could seek relief from the federal courts opened the way for further cases challenging malapportionment in state legislatures.

BAKEWELL, ROBERT (1725–95), British sheep breeder. His New Leicesters were bred to fatten quickly and to yield a fleece of reasonable quality. He also produced an improved breed of shire horse. Bakewell's importance is sometimes exaggerated, for he was the best known of a number of equally successful stock-breeders.

BAKEWELL HALL, or Blackwell Hall, the London centre in the 16th and 17th cents for the buying and selling of cloth. Situated near the Guildhall, it was a warehouse as well as a market and was supervised by the wool staplers, who were sometimes accused of abusing their privileges by blending the best wool with inferior strains.

BAKHTIYARI, Iranian tribe in the Isfahan region which played an important role in the restoration of the constitution (1909) and dominated Iranian politics (1911–14).

BAKHUIZEN, LUDOLF (1631–1708), 17th-cent. Dutch painter of shipping and the sea. He was also a naval architect and made technical drawings of ships for Tsar Peter the Great.

BAKI (1526–1600), one of the greatest of Ottoman poets, a master of form and language whose *chef d'œuvre* is the famous lament that he wrote on the death (1566) of the sultan, Süleyman the Magnificent.

BAKR SIDQI (d. 1937), Iraqi general of Kurdish origin, who suppressed Assyrian and Shiite revolts (1933–5) and, with Hikmet Sulayman, led the first Iraqi army coup (28 Oct. 1936).

BAKRI, AL-, ABU UBAID ABDULLAH (*c.* 1040–94), Arab author born into a family long settled in Spain. He spent most of his life in Cordoba and Almeria and is best known for his *Kitab al-Masalik wa'l-Mamalik*, a major source of geographical and historical information about contemporary Africa.

BAKUFU, term meaning 'tent-government', applied to successive feudal governments in Japan. It originally referred to the headquarters of the commander of the imperial guard in Kyoto, but after Minamoto Yoritomo was appointed to this post (1190) it became associated with his Kamakura regime. When the Ashikaga shogunate was established the term continued to be used, and after the fall of the Ashikaga it was revived to describe the Tokugawa shogunate. By the time feudal government came to an end in 1868, the *bakufu* had evolved into a vastly more elaborate governmental machine than those of earlier periods.

BAKUNIN, MIKHAIL ALEKSANDROVICH (1814–76), Russian revolutionary and theorist of anarchism. His influence was due more to his flamboyant personality than to his unsystematic writings or limited achievements. He was the eldest son of a noble landowner. After resigning from the guards in 1834, he studied German philosophy in Moscow, and came to Europe in 1840.

His pamphlet 'Reaction in Germany' (1842) and his revolutionary ideas led to his permanent exile. In 1848 he played an enthusiastic part in the revolutions in Paris and eastern Europe and attended the Slav Congress in Prague. His *Appeal to the Slavs* called for a federation of free Slav states and a working-class revolution to destroy state power, and expressed faith in the revolutionary potential of the Russian peasant commune.

Arrested in Dresden (1849), he was returned to St Petersburg, where he wrote from prison his *Confession* to Nicholas I. After exile to Siberia, he escaped to Japan and, now a European legend, joined Herzen in London (1861). The cautious Herzen found Bakunin's revolutionary enthusiasms anachronistic and their association lapsed. Bakunin attempted to aid the Polish rebellion (1863) and the Lyons revolt (1870). He encouraged revolutionary groups in Russia, started several semi-imaginary secret societies, and in 1869 urged the Russian intelligentsia to 'go to the people'. The years 1867–1872 saw the height of his influence. Joining the first

International (1868), he founded an International Social-Democratic Alliance and his challenge to Marx's domination of the International and his influence in the Jura, Spain, and Italy led Marx to split the movement by expelling him (1872).

His emotional commitment to spontaneous peasant rebellion and destruction, his individualism and anarchism, his belief in a society of free federations—all opposed Marx's dictatorship of the proletariat. However, he also believed in dictatorship, secret elite revolutionary organizations, and was joint author of the unsavoury Nechaev's *Revolutionary Catechism* on revolutionary discipline. Although his ideas influenced the Russian populists, it was on the anarchist movements of Spain and Italy that he had lasting influence.

E. H. Carr, *Michael Bakunin* (London, 1937).
E. Lampert, *Studies in Rebellion* (London, 1957).   BJW

BALACLAVA (1854), battle in the Crimean War, the occasion of the charge of the Light Brigade. It left the Russians in occupation of the allied supply route, thus aggravating the sufferings of the British army in the winter of 1854–5.

BALAJI BAJI RAO (1721–61), the third member of the Bhat family to become a Maratha peshwa, was the eldest son of Baji Rao I and succeeded (1740) both because he had won the favour of Raja Shahu and because his chief rival, Raguji Bhonsla of Berar, was away on an expedition in the Carnatic. This expedition was in opposition to the peshwa's policy of northward expansion, and though suspended while Raguji challenged Balaji at Satara, it inaugurated large-scale Maratha intervention in the south which lasted for the rest of the 18th cent. In 1744 Balaji bought off his rival by allowing him a free hand in Bengal. There followed an attack on Alivardi Khan and the eventual occupation of Orissa by the Marathas. Raguji established himself at Nagpur.

In 1749 Shahu's death involved Balaji in a struggle for power with Tara Bai, grandmother of Ramraja, Shahu's successor, who called in the Gaekwar from Gujarat. His victory left the peshwas as heads of the Maratha state, with their seat, Poona, as the capital. The descendants of Sivaji were kept in seclusion at Satara, though all state documents were sent to them for signature. The peshwas' usurpation of effective power meant that a Brahmin supremacy had replaced joint Brahmin–Maratha rule, and a military confederacy a loosely knit national monarchy. The Marathas gained in immediate strength, but hastened their ultimate disintegration.

The struggle with Tara Bai prevented Balaji from taking advantage of the death of the nizam in 1748. When he was able to move, the French general de Bussy's troops stood in the way. When de Bussy was recalled, Balaji defeated Salabat Jung (1760). This might have been fatal but for developments in the north, where the Mughal empire was disintegrating and suffering from the raids of Ahmad Shah the Afghan. The Marathas were called by the rival parties and eventually against the Afghans. Balaji was committed to the north and saw himself as succeeding to the throne of the Mughals. A Maratha army took Lahore in 1758, only to lose Delhi early in 1760. A grand army was then sent to the north under the peshwa's cousin, the Bhao Sahib. A classic campaign ended in defeat at Panipat (14 Jan. 1761), when both the Bhao Sahib and Balaji's heir were killed. Balaji himself died in June, thus ending the peshwa's dream of Indian empire.

Balaji was a good administrator with a handsome appearance and gracious manner. But he lacked the ability and high character of his father and grandfather and towards the end of his life became indolent and sensual.

N. G. Ranade, *Rise of the Maratha Power* (Poona, 1900).
C. A. Kincaid and D. B. Parasnis, *History of the Maratha People* (London, 1931).   TGPS

BALAJI VISVANATH (*c.* 1662–1720), founder of the Bhat dynasty of peshwas in Maharashtra, who came from a

Chitpavan Brahmin family in the service of the Maratha royal house. He rose to eminence in the troubles following the death of Aurangzeb, when the authority of Shahu, the grandson of Sivaji, newly returned from the Mughal court, was disputed by Tara Bai, regent for her infant son (and Shahu's nephew) Sivaji. Balaji attached himself to Shahu, whose forces prevailed largely through his skill. In 1714 he was appointed peshwa by Shahu, who later made the office hereditary in his family. Balaji's great achievements were the consolidation of Shahu's authority in Maharashtra, the conciliation of the chief Angria, who received the title of admiral of the Maratha fleet and held the coast for them, and the grant by the Mughals of *chauth* (one-fourth) and *sar-desh-mukki* (one-tenth) of the revenues of the six Deccan provinces. This provided a war chest with which Balaji's son organized his later conquests.

BALAMBANGAN, the south-eastern projection of Java, adjacent to the island of Bali, often called *oosthoek* (the 'east hook') by the Dutch. The area was troublesome and rebellious, controllable neither by the Dutch nor the Javanese rulers, and it remained true in many ways to the pre-Islamic religious traditions of Java, until finally subdued by Dutch forces in 1777.

BALANCE, long used in assaying. Its wider functions as an invaluable research tool for the chemist were recognized from the 17th cent.

BALANCE OF POWER. The policy of maintaining an equilibrium between states so that no one state or grouping should predominate has throughout history been one of the guiding principles of diplomacy. Whatever its defects, it has been realistic in acknowledging power as a determining factor in international relations, and it has sought equilibrium as the most satisfactory form of accommodation to disagreeable facts.

A balance of power was sought by the city-states of Greece, as in the defensive leagues against Athens and later against Sparta and Thebes, and it might be said that its breakdown in the Mediterranean area helped to establish the Roman empire. It was consciously pursued in Renaissance Italy, *eg*, in the efforts of the papacy to preserve its temporal power during the foreign invasions, and its importance increased as the loose feudal organization gave way to the sovereign state. By the 17th cent. it had become a cardinal principle of European diplomacy that no state or alliance should be allowed to achieve a dominating position, and on several occasions this principle was strong enough to override the religious or economic interest of individual nations. The combinations against Charles V, Louis XIV, and Napoleon, the chessboard settlements of Westphalia, Utrecht, and Vienna, even Canning's demagogic claim to have called a new world into existence to redress the balance of the old, are all evidence of its continuing vitality. David Hume justified it by detailed reference to historical precedents (*Essays and Treatises*, 1752), and the Swiss jurist Emeric de Vattel regarded Europe as a loose federation based on a fundamental identity of interest, so that nations had not merely a right but a duty to intervene if the balance were in danger (*Le Droit des Gens*, 1758). Vattel held that Britain's occasional interventions in continental affairs were caused by her desire to preserve this equilibrium.

The balance of power rested on the view that the policies and interests of dynastic states did not materially alter, but in the 19th cent. new factors emerged in the development of the US as an independent power, Britain's relative withdrawal from Europe during her great colonial period, and the nationalist and liberal revolutions in Europe which often gave a new direction to the policies of the nations involved. Thus the continental pacts engineered by Bismarck, obviously traditional in intent, were too slowly countered by the traditional methods. It is arguable that Britain's 'splendid isolation' was one of the major causes of the First World War,

in that her reversion to a policy of balancing ententes was too late to be convincing or effective.

The horrors of this war led to a widespread feeling that they must not be allowed to happen again, and the US, in the person of President Wilson, denounced the old diplomacy of 'power politics'. The League of Nations was set up to arbitrate in international disputes, and at the same time the Russian Revolution stimulated the hope that socialist ideals would cross frontiers and bury national pride and animosities in the universal brotherhood of man.

But in the absence of effective international policing, which would appear to be the only credible alternative, the balance of power was invoked, although once again too late, against the preponderant strength of the Italo-German axis. At the present time, despite the existence of the United Nations, it seems to be the principle underlying the formation of bodies like NATO, the manœuvres of 'the cold war', and the constant striving for parity in missile strength.   MMR

BALBAN, GHIYAS-AD-DIN (1207–87), Turkish slave sold to the Sultan Iltutmish of Delhi. By degrees he rose in the royal service until he became the chief minister of Sultan Nasir-ad-din Mahmud (1246–66), whom he succeeded as sultan. He was noted for his sternness as well as his ability. His great achievement was to keep at bay the Mongols, then at the height of their power under Hulugu, grandson of Chinghiz Khan.

BALBO, CESARE, Conte (1789–1853), Italian political writer with great influence on the moderate movement for national unity. He began his adult life in the Napoleonic administration of Italy and this kept him out of office at the restoration of the Piedmontese ruling family (1814) despite his loyalty to it. In his writings he favoured a federal solution to the question of Italian unity and recognized that the Austrians could only be expelled by military and diplomatic action. When King Charles Albert of Piedmont-Sardinia granted a constitution (1848), Balbo acted for a few months as prime minister.

BALBOA, VASCO NUÑEZ DE (1475–1519), Spanish adventurer, who, with a band of followers, left Hispaniola and became the first of the conquistadores of the American mainland. He founded the settlement of Darién and crossed the tropical forests of the isthmus of Darién to discover the Pacific Ocean on 25 Sept. 1513. Balboa's discovery revealed the narrowness of the land which separated the Atlantic Ocean and the 'South Sea' and gave great encouragement to those seeking a western passage to the East Indies. He later fell foul of the vicious and unscrupulous governor of Darién, Pedro Arias de Avila, who plotted Balboa's execution on a charge of treason (1519).

BALBUS, L. CORNELIUS, native of Gades (Cadiz) who served under Pompey against Sertorius, received Roman citizenship (72 BC), and became closely associated with Julius Caesar. He later supported Octavian and became BC Rome's first foreign-born consul.

BALDUS DE UBALDIS (*c.* 1320–1400), pupil of Bartolo di Sassoferrato, who taught law at Siena, Bologna, Perugia, and Pavia and was one of the greatest commentators on Roman law.

BALDWIN (1172–1205), Count of Flanders (1194) and of Hainaut (1195), the first Latin Emperor of Constantinople, was raised to the throne after the Fourth Crusade had captured the Byzantine capital (April 1204). His reign saw the extension of the Latin conquests in Thrace, Macedonia, and Greece. A revolt in Thrace led to hostilities with Bulgaria. At the battle of Adrianople (April 1205) the Latins suffered a serious reverse, Baldwin being captured and killed soon afterwards.

BALDWIN OF BEWDLEY, STANLEY BALDWIN, 1st Earl (1867–1947), three times British prime minister, and a formative influence on the Conservative Party between the two World Wars. As the son of a Bewdley ironmaster, he always owed more to his provincial origins than to his social status. He became an MP in 1908. As president of the board of trade (1921) he came to detest the cynicism of the Coalition cabinet and in a speech at the Carlton Club (Oct. 1922) helped deprive the coalition of Conservative support.

His rise was rapid: chancellor of the exchequer (1922–3) and Conservative prime minister (1923–4, 1924–9). In standing for 'safety first' and integrity, he deliberately reacted against Lloyd George's political style. He was quick to sense the mood of parliament and of the public, and no politician of his generation was more skilled as a broadcaster.

Baldwin associated with Labour MPs and encouraged them to think of themselves as an alternative government. He loathed the continental theories which attracted left-wing intellectuals, and preferred the party's trade unionist wing. He adopted a Disraelian policy of blurring incipient class conflict with soothing phrases. At the same time, Baldwin guided his party away from a purely sectarian defence of wealth and privilege. He always saw himself as a national rather than a party figure, and the old-fashioned paternalism of his own business experience separated him from contemporary commercial attitudes. His actions over tariff reform suggest that there was never any direct relation between business pressure and Baldwin's conduct. His fair-minded broadcasts helped to avoid violence during the General Strike (1926).

In subsequent months, his leadership was undoubtedly lacking. Baldwin allowed the miners to be starved into submission, failed to get the coal industry reorganized, allowed restrictive legislation against the trade unions, and gave insufficient backing to Neville Chamberlain's social reform schemes. A Conservative prime minister was not, of course, free to ignore backbench opinion, but his conduct also stemmed from a tendency to relapse into inertia after a crisis, a distaste for administrative detail, and a reluctance to take difficult decisions. Yet he defeated his extreme right wing when they favoured out-and-out resistance to the British Labour movement and to Indian nationalism and overcame Beaverbrook and Rothermere when they tried to dictate Indian policy through their newspapers.

Baldwin was less decisive about rearmament. As lord president of the council (1931–5) and prime minister (1935–7), he could have accelerated it considerably, but his conduct does seem to have sprung from a combination of deference to public opinion, from defects in character, and from deliberate policy. Nobody could have been more concerned to avoid war, but Baldwin knew too well the strength of pacifist opinion. He disliked foreigners and lacked interest in foreign policy while Sir Edward Grey's failure made him sceptical of seeking peace through strength.

Baldwin's mature judgement featured prominently in the 1936 Abdication Crisis, and after his resignation in May 1937 he was created Earl Baldwin.

G. M. Young, *Stanley Baldwin* (London, 1952).
K. Middlemass and T. Barnes, *Baldwin* (London, 1969).

BHH

BALDWIN I (*reg.* 1100–18), King of Jerusalem, younger brother of Godfrey de Bouillon, leader of the German Crusaders, who became, on Godfrey's death in 1100, the crusading commander in Jerusalem. He foiled the plans of the patriarch, Daimbert, to become the ruler of the crusading state and ensured that it became a secular kingdom with himself as its first monarch. His reign was spent assuring the sea communications of his kingdom through the successive capture of the Palestinian and Syrian harbours and he successfully asserted his overlordship over the other Latin principalities. By his conquests and internal policies he was the effective creator of the Latin kingdom of Jerusalem.

BALDWIN II (*reg.* 1118–31), King of Jerusalem and Count of Edessa (1100–18), on the important route linking northern Syria with Mesopotamia and Iraq, which was under constant pressure from the Muslims. He was a prisoner in Muslim hands and (1104–8) was often engaged in warfare against the forces of Mosul and Mardin, as in 1110 and in 1114–15. As King of Jerusalem he routed Mardin's troops at Danith in 1119. Captured again by the Muslims (1123–4), he won a notable success against them at the battle of Azaz (1125), but his attempt (1129) to seize Damascus failed. During his reign the great religious Orders of the Hospital and of the Temple began to assume a prominent position in the defence of the Crusading states.

BALDWIN III OF JERUSALEM (1130–62), the first Latin King of Jerusalem, born in Palestine. His brief personal rule (1152–62) established him as the most gifted member of his able dynasty. The alliance with the Byzantine empire was the cornerstone of his policies and under him the kingdom reached the height of its prosperity.

BALDWIN IV (1161–85), King of Jerusalem (*reg.* 1174–85), was an able prince, though a leper. He defeated the forces of Salah al-Din at Montgisard in 1177. A truce made in 1180 was of brief duration. The great Christian fortress of Karak threatened the routes running from Egypt to Syria and to the Hijaz. The lord of Karak, Renaud de Chatillon, attacking the Muslim caravans and also launching naval raids into the Red Sea, did much to bring about a resumption of hostilities. Baldwin IV was able to beat off a Muslim assault against Karak in 1183.

BALDWIN, ABRAHAM (1754–1807), US statesman and one of the founders of Georgia University. He was the state's member of the Continental Congress and a delegate to the Constitutional Convention. In the US House of Representatives (1790–9) and the US Senate (1799–1807) he supported Jefferson.

BALDWIN, JAMES ARTHUR (1924–   ), US Negro writer, born in Harlem. The publication of *Go Tell It on the Mountain* (1953) brought him fame. His later works include *Giovanni's Room* (1956), *Another Country* (1963), and the play *Blues for Mister Charley* (1964).

BALDWIN, ROBERT (1804–58), Canadian statesman, son of William Warren Baldwin. After being called to the bar (1825), he served for short periods in the Upper Canada legislature (1829–30) and on the executive council (1836). Baldwin favoured a policy of Canadian self-government and on a visit to England (1836) he influenced Lord Durham, secretary of state for the colonies, to favour moderate changes in the Canadian governmental structure. Baldwin attempted, unsuccessfully, to mediate between the governor, Sir Francis Head, and William Lyon Mackenzie during the rebellion of 1837. In 1842–3 Baldwin joined forces with Louis Lafontaine, with whom he formed a ministry. In 1848 they again combined in the 'Great Ministry', which established Toronto University, laid the basis of municipal government in Canada West, stimulated railroad building (Railway Guarantee Act), and in the Amnesty Act pardoned those sentenced for their part in the rebellion of 1837. Baldwin resigned (1851) after being defeated over a bill to establish a Chancery court. In 1854 he helped organize a coalition of reformers in the Liberal-Conservative party, the forerunner of the modern Conservative Party.

BALDWIN, WILLIAM WARREN (1775–1844), Canadian reformer. The father of Robert Baldwin, he came to Upper Canada from Ireland in 1798. In 1828 he was the first leading Canadian to advocate a greater degree of local control over domestic affairs. He served in the House of Assembly (1824–1830), where he was leader of the reform group. In 1836 he became the president of the Constitutional Reform Society.

He was elected to the Assembly of unified Canada in 1841 and appointed to the legislative council in 1843.

BALEARIC ISLANDS

BALEARIC ISLANDS (4900 sq. kms), formed part of the medieval Catalan empire. These western Mediterranean isles, Majorca, Minorca, Iviza, and Formentera, assumed considerable importance from the 16th cent. as fortified defence posts of the Spanish Habsburgs against Turkish incursion into Spanish waters. Lost to Spain when the British seized Minorca in 1708, the Balearic islands became a significant pawn in the 18th-cent. struggle between Britain and the Franco-Spanish alliance for control of western Mediterranean trade. The main naval base of Port Mahon on Minorca was captured by France in 1782, returned to Spain by the treaty of Versailles (1783), and recaptured by the British in 1798.

BALFOUR, ARTHUR JAMES BALFOUR

BALFOUR, ARTHUR JAMES BALFOUR, 1st Earl (1848–1930), British statesman and philosoper, famous for his announcement, on behalf of the British cabinet, of the Balfour Declaration (1917).

He was a nephew of Lord Salisbury, and his early career gained much from his aristocratic connections. He entered parliament as a Conservative in 1874 and was a member of the Fourth Party (1880). He was a skilful administrator rather than a strong political leader and his reputation was made as chief secretary for Ireland (1887–91), where he firmly repressed disorders and began to put into effect land purchase and allied policies. He succeeded Salisbury as prime minister in 1902. Notable landmarks of his ministry were the Education Act (1902), military reorganization, the creation of the Committee of Imperial Defence (1902), and, in foreign affairs, the creation of the Anglo-French Entente (1904). The weakness of the Conservatives lay in their division over free trade and protection, which Balfour's attempt at a compromise solution did little to repair.

The general election of 1906 resulted in a Liberal landslide. The Conservatives, reduced to a handful in the Commons, began to use their predominance in the Lords to block unpalatable measures. For this line of action, which led to the Parliament Act crisis (1910–11), Balfour must be held responsible, though Lansdowne may have provided the driving force behind it. After the crisis a 'Balfour must go' campaign developed, blame being laid upon him for the electoral defeat of 1906 and for subsequent failures. He resigned the leadership and was replaced by Bonar Law.

In the coalition government of 1915 he became first lord of the admiralty, replacing Churchill. He took no part in the manœuvres which ousted Asquith but neither did he resist them. He held office continuously under Lloyd George (1915–22) and, as foreign secretary, made the announcement (1917) that promised Palestine to the Jews as their homeland. He participated in the Versailles settlement (1919) and in the Washington naval conference (1922). He retired from politics in 1922 but returned to serve as foreign secretary under Baldwin (1925–9), playing a major part in the negotiations which led, just after his death, to the Statute of Westminster (1931).

Balfour's political services spanned over half a century. In the early years of his life he made a contribution to philosophy in his *A Defence of Philosophical Doubt* (1879) and *Foundations of Belief* (1895).

Kenneth Young, *Arthur James Balfour* (London, 1963).

LMB

BALFOUR DECLARATION

BALFOUR DECLARATION (2 Nov. 1917) took the form of a letter from Balfour, as British foreign secretary, to Lord Rothschild (who held no office either in the English Zionist Federation or the World Zionist Organization, but was nevertheless a potent force in British Jewry) and provided a diplomatic basis for the Jewish colonization of Palestine and the establishment of a Jewish state. Together with the MacMahon letter and the Sykes–Picot agreement, it established thrice mutually conflicting commitments in British Middle East policy. The letter included the following statement:

His Majesty's Government view with favour the establishment in Palestine of a national home for the Jewish people, and will use their best endeavours to facilitate the achievement of this object, it being clearly understood that nothing shall be done which may prejudice the civil and religious rights of existing non-Jewish communities in Palestine, or the rights and political status enjoyed by Jews in any country.

The declaration was immediately made public, but excited little immediate reaction. It represented the successful culmination of persistent attempts by the Zionists, since the turn of the century, to secure the protection of a dominant power—first the Ottomans, then Britain—for Jewish settlement in the Middle East, partly as a refuge from anti-Semitism, partly to satisfy nationalist ambitions. The achievement was attributable to the skill and diplomacy of Chaim Weizmann. Zionist pressure evoked a response within the British government from those who were susceptible to Zionist ideals and those who attached importance to the support which the Jewish community might give to Britain during the war.

BALFOUR NOTE

BALFOUR NOTE (1 Aug. 1922), addressed by the British government (in which Lord Balfour was foreign secretary) to the representatives in London of the Allied Powers owing war debts to Britain, proposing the abandonment of the debts and reparations under a 'general settlement [which] would, in their view, be of more value to Mankind than any gains that could accrue even from the most successful enforcement of legal obligations'. The note brought no tangible result; indeed, it aroused the suspicions both of the American government (which refused to admit the connection between war debts and reparations) and of the Allies.

BALI

BALI. Among the oldest important remains of this Indonesian island is a bronze kettle-drum belonging to the so-called Dongson culture (*c.* 3rd cent. BC) when Bali was already in contact with mainland South-East Asia. According to tradition, some isolated villages in eastern Bali, called Bali-aga (original Bali), cling to ancient culture, relatively little touched by later influences. The earliest written sources are clay tablets inscribed with the Buddhist 'credo' (the *ye-te* formula) datable to the 7th–8th cents AD. Relations with China may go back slightly earlier if the identification of Po-li with Bali—once generally upheld but now mostly rejected—is followed. From the 9th cent. onwards there are a large number of inscriptions on stone and, more frequently, bronze plates. These are charters dealing with immunities and privileges granted to people and institutions, often hunting and fishing rights. They testify to the existence of a well-ordered society in parts of southern Bali and yield information on names of rulers and on some aspects of administration. The earlier inscriptions are in Old Balinese (related to, but clearly distinct from, Old Javanese). Javanese influence, however, gradually increased and from the end of the 10th cent. almost all charters are in Old Javanese. Among the most interesting are those issued by the parents of King Airlangga, who ruled together in southern Bali. In spite of strong cultural Javanese influence the island remained politically independent until the end of the 13th or the middle of the 14th cent., when it was for some time under the authority of a brother-in-law of the King of Majapahit. When in the 15th–16th cents Islam spread over nearly the whole of Java and Majapahit disintegrated, some circles closely associated with the court apparently sought refuge in Bali and strengthened the already present Javanese influences. This led, in the kingdom of Gelgel, to a remarkable renaissance of Old Javanese pre-Islamic culture. Old Javanese works were copied, recited, and explained, and new works in the same tradition were added. Although Bali became politically divided from the 17th cent. the cult of Old Javanese letters remained, combined with a form of religion which, though essentially Balinese, was strongly influenced by Hinduism. In this period Bali extended its authority also over easternmost Java (Balambangan) and parts of Lombok.

The first contacts with the Dutch date back to 1596, but did not, for over 200 years, lead to a settlement of the Netherland East India Co. In 1639 Sultan Agung of Mataram in central Java, after conquering Balambangan, invaded Bali, but had to retreat after fierce resistance. The Balinese often supplied soldiers to the Dutch company. The best known of these was Suropati who, at the beginning of the 18th cent., after deserting from the Dutch army, raised a resistance movement against the Dutch. The first Dutch expedition against Bali took place in 1841 and resulted in the occupation of a small area in the north of the island. A later expedition at the beginning of the 20th cent. led to a protracted war, lasting till 1911. The whole island was then occupied after the rulers had committed suicide. The Dutch then made Bali, together with Lombok, into a residence. Measures were taken to protect Bali's unique cultural heritage and to promote the continuing development of Balinese culture.

JG de C

BALITUNG (*reg. c.* 900–10), King in ancient Indonesia who, by marriage or conquest, succeeded in bringing central and eastern Java under his authority. His relatively numerous inscriptions in Old Javanese testify to his concern for good and safe communications between various parts of his kingdom.

BALKAN CONFERENCES (1930–3). These were aimed at greater co-operation between the Balkan states with a view to the establishment of a Balkan federation. Four conferences were held: Athens (5–13 Oct. 1930); Istanbul (20–6 Oct. 1931); Bucharest (22–9 Oct. 1932); Salonika (2–11 Nov. 1933). Politicians, trade unionists, civil servants, and scholars attended these conferences from Greece, Turkey, Yugoslavia, Bulgaria, and Rumania. Permanent commissions were established to handle economics, communications, public health, and education. Political achievements were slight. A non-aggression pact was drafted, but never implemented, as Bulgaria refused to accept the territorial status quo on which it was based. The failure of the Balkan conferences to resolve political questions led to the formation of the Balkan Entente, a defensive alliance between Greece, Yugoslavia, Rumania, and Turkey signed at Belgrade on 9 Feb. 1934.

BALKAN LEAGUE (1912), a union of Montenegro, Serbia, Greece, and Bulgaria, which aimed at the partition of the remains of Turkey's empire in Europe and provoked the First Balkan War.

BALKAN PACT (9 Feb. 1934). Greece, Yugoslavia, Rumania, and Turkey agreed to guarantee each other's frontiers, and to consult together before taking any action concerning any Balkan state outside the pact. The pact gave mutual guarantees of resistance to Bulgaria, which had irredentist claims on all four states. It originated in the fears of Greece, Rumania, and Turkey that a growing Bulgaria–Yugoslav rapprochement might focus Bulgarian hostility on them alone. The pact was concluded after Bulgarian objections had doomed to failure a project initiated by the Rumanian foreign minister Titulescu for a non-aggression pact between all the Balkan states.

BALKAN WARS (1912–13). These reduced the Ottoman empire in Europe to Constantinople and eastern Thrace. At the outbreak of the wars the Ottoman empire still included territory stretching from the Adriatic to the Aegean, roughly equivalent to modern Albania, northern Greece, and southern Yugoslavia. The central area, Macedonia, was made up of a mixture of Balkan nationalities, Serbs, Bulgars, and Greeks, as well as Macedonians. The Young Turk revolution (1908) had resulted in attempts to bring this area under direct control, causing revolutionary nationalism among the native population and a desire for intervention by the independent Balkan states.

Largely through the encouragement of the Russian ministers in Bulgaria and Serbia, these two states swallowed their differences and allied themselves against Turkey (March 1912), taking advantage of her involvement in war with Italy in North Africa. Greece and Montenegro had joined this alliance (the Balkan League) by October. Montenegro declared war on 8 Oct. and the other states attacked Turkey. The Turks suffered complete defeat within two months, being confined to a small area round Constantinople when an armistice was made on 3 Dec.

Meanwhile, the European powers, surprised by the rapid success of the allies, opened the London Conference. Through Austrian pressure the powers forced the Balkan League to agree to the establishment of an independent Albania, which served the purpose of denying Serbia access to the sea. Nothing was settled by the conference about the division of the rest of the territory taken from Turkey. Barred from the Adriatic, Serbia was determined to increase her share of Macedonia at the expense of Bulgaria, which was already at loggerheads with Greece over Salonika.

Bulgaria tried to steal a march on her former allies by attacking Serbia and Greece on 29 June 1913, thus beginning the Second Balkan War. The Bulgars were rapidly defeated, both Rumania and the defeated Turks taking the opportunity to declare war against them. The treaty of Bucharest (Aug. 1913), which produced a territorial settlement of both Balkan Wars, consequently hit Bulgaria almost as hard as Turkey, which actually improved its position at Bulgaria's expense.

M. S. Anderson, *The Eastern Question*, 1774–1923 (London, 1966).

DMCK

BALLANCE, JOHN (1839–93), NZ Liberal prime minister, was a Radical from Birmingham, who became a newspaper editor in Wanganui before entering the House of Representatives in 1873. As colonial treasurer (1878–9) in the Grey ministry, he introduced a mild land tax, but his private land speculations led to a breach with Grey. Advanced in theory, but more cautious in administration, Ballance advocated land nationalization but as minister of lands (1884–7) hardly got beyond establishing village settlements. As opposition leader in 1890, he put forward a moderate programme of taxation and land reform. Unexpected reaction against Atkinson turned him into prime minister (1891); he then welded a diverse following into a strong Liberal Party. Opposition and press denounced Ballance's 'socialism', and the upper house threw out some bills, but these actions merely strengthened his hand. A depressed colony approved his mild, limited reforms, but was unimpressed by his radical advocacy. Ballance commanded respect in both wings of his party; his death in office precipitated a Liberal crisis.

BALLINGER–PINCHOT CONTROVERSY (1909–11), dispute over US conservationist policies which intensified the breach between President Taft and Theodore Roosevelt. Richard A. Ballinger (1858–1922), Taft's secretary of the interior, was unsympathetic to the national conservation policies begun during Roosevelt's administration. Gifford Pinchot (1865–1946), chief forester of the US, friend of Roosevelt's, and a leading conservationist, attacked Ballinger for returning water-power sites to the national domain, so making them available for purchase by private interests, and for obstructing investigation of allegedly fraudulent land claims in AK. Pinchot's dismissal (1910) was interpreted by some progressives as further evidence of Taft's conservatism, and despite Ballinger's replacement by a conservationist in 1911 the split in the Republican Party widened significantly. Pinchot became a leading member of Roosevelt's Progressive Party in 1912.

BALLIOL, JOHN (*c.* 1250–1313), King of Scotland. Chosen as King of Scotland by English and Scottish commissioners, presided over by Edward I of England, Balliol swore fealty (1292) to Edward and did homage for his kingdom. Edward chose to put a strict interpretation on his overlordship of Scotland. Balliol was summoned to appear before English courts and even called on to bring troops to fight in Edward's wars. Balliol was no match for Edward. In 1295 the Scottish nobles therefore thrust on him a council, which was really to rule, and allied themselves with Edward's enemy, France. In 1296 Edward conquered Scotland and deposed Balliol.

BALLISTICS, branch of dynamics, the field of applied mathematics, which was one of the main areas of scientific study in the 17th cent. The science of ballistics was stimulated by Tartaglio's application of the impetus theory, and it contributed to greater efficiency in the development of firearms.

BALLOT ACT (1872). This substituted secret for open voting at British parliamentary elections. Demand for the ballot was included in the programme of some 18th-cent. and most post-1832 radicals. It was one of the Six Points of the People's Charter (1836) and George Grote introduced six motions for it into the Commons (1833–9). Lord John Russell persuaded the Whig cabinet to make the ballot an open question in 1839 (when Grote's motion received 216 votes), but the fate of later motions showed that it could not prevail unless it became a Whig government measure. Russell probably favoured this in 1866, and Gladstone's change of mind after the enquiries into corruption at the general election of 1868, and Bright's presence in his cabinet, ensured its adoption.

BALMACEDA FERNÁNDEZ, JOSÉ MANUEL (1840–91), diplomat, Liberal Party leader, and president of Chile. His presidential term (1886–91) benefited from the prosperity of the country at that time, but ended in disaster. The theme of his administration was construction, especially public works. Roads, railways, schools, and hospital services were all expanded.

Towards the end of his term Balmaceda quarrelled with his party and with congress over the budget. Civil war broke out in 1891. The government forces were defeated, looting in Santiago and Valparaiso causing great damage, and Balmaceda was forced to seek asylum in the Argentine embassy. Two weeks later he committed suicide.

BALOCHPUR, BATTLE OF (1623), was fought to the south of Delhi, between Mahabat Khan, general of the Emperor Jahangir, and Raja Vikramajit, acting for Jahangir's rebellious son Khurram, later Shah Jahan. Vikramajit was defeated and killed and Khurram driven back into the Deccan. It was an early move in a complicated war of succession which ended with Jahangir's death in 1627.

BALTA–LIMAN CONVENTION (1 May 1849), signed between Russia and Turkey in an attempt to solve their quarrel over the Danubian Provinces.

BALTIC ENTENTE (12 Sept. 1934). Latvia and Estonia, after expanding and renewing their 1927 bilateral alliance, admitted Lithuania to a 'Baltic Entente'; they stipulated that they should not be embroiled in Lithuania's territorial disputes with Germany and Poland. The pact originated in the 1934 Franco-Soviet negotiations for an Eastern Locarno, which Russia wished to encompass the Baltic states as well as France's east European allies. The Baltic states disliked this plan. Those forming the 'Entente' nevertheless extended their existing non-aggression treaties with Russia until 1945.

BALTIC PACT (1934), agreement between Lithuania, Estonia, and Latvia which followed from the initiative of Lithuania, provoked into a more co-operative attitude towards its Baltic neighbours by the German–Polish Pact of Jan. 1934. The

pact (signed in Sept.) provided for co-operation by means of regular meetings between foreign ministers, but (Article 3) safeguarded Estonia and Latvia from being drawn into Lithuania's quarrels with Poland over Vilna and with Germany over Memel.

BALTIC STORES, timber, tar, pitch, and hemp, natural products of the Baltic countries, which were essential naval requirements in the 16th–19th cents. England was deficient in these commodities and the need to import naval stores and to deprive her rivals, first the Dutch and then the French, of their supply, dominated England's attitude to bullion and her diplomacy and naval strategy. In 1715, 1716, and 1726 a British fleet was sent to the Baltic to protect British merchant ships and to keep open the supply of naval stores. British interference occasionally stimulated Baltic hostility, which coalesced into the alliances of the Armed Neutrality of 1691, 1780, and 1800.

BALTIMORE, GEORGE CALVERT, 1st Baron (Irish) (c. 1580–1632), British secretary of state under James I. Calvert became an MP and secretary of the privy council, but was forced to resign his post because of his conversion to Catholicism. The king elevated him to the peerage, and gave him a charter to lands in Nfld, where attempts were made to establish a colony at Avalon; but, because of the rigorous climate, Baltimore asked for land further south. Colonists objected to a settlement of Catholics in VA but Charles I issued a charter (1632) to lands in south VA to the second Lord Baltimore, Cecilius Calvert, who founded the colony of Maryland (named after Henrietta Maria) as a haven for persecuted Catholics from England (1634).

BALUCHISTAN, frontier tract of West Pakistan extending from the Gomal Pass on the north-east to the coast of Mekran in the south, and from the borders of Iran and Afghanistan to Sind and the Punjab. The term Baluchistan (land of the Baluch) is a misnomer, for it is also inhabited by large numbers of Pathan and Brahui tribes. The ethnic boundary between Pathan and Baluch runs roughly from Chaudhwan in Dera Ismail Khan through Thal-Chotaili and Sibi to Chaman. North of this live the Pathan tribes, the Kakars, Tarins, Panis, and Sheranis. There is evidence of agricultural communities in Baluchistan c. 3000 BC. Mekran was inhabited by people of the Kulli culture, who burnt their dead. In the Brahui hills were the people of the Nal culture, who appear to have practised fractional burial. There is a clearly defined similarity between the Kulli culture and that of Elam and Mesopotamia.

Excavations at Mohenjo-Daro in Sind, and at Harappa in the Punjab and elsewhere in Baluchistan, prove that about 5000 years ago civilized urban communities flourished in these areas. Most of the great invaders and conquerors of northern India passed through one of the five main mountain passes between Peshawar and Quetta. Baluchistan (Gedrosia) was a satrapy of the Persian empire until the invasion of Alexander the Great, who appears to have retreated through the Mulla Pass to Kandahar. Part of Gedrosia was ceded to Chandragupta Maurya by Seleucus Nikator in the 3rd cent. BC. It formed part of the Kushan empire. During the Arab conquest of Sind (AD 712) Baluchistan served as a line of communication. Kuzdar to the south of Kalat and Mekran paid tribute to Mahmud of Ghazni. Baluchistan was annexed to the Mughal empire in 1594.

The British connection began in 1839, when it was traversed by British troops during the First Afghan War. The proposal to occupy Quetta dates back to 1856, but the occupation did not take place until 1877. This was of great strategical importance in the British scheme of north-west frontier defence. British relations with the Khan of Kalat were regulated by the treaty of 1854. Because of internecine struggles in Kalat the British agent was recalled (1873) and the subsidy stopped. Robert Sandeman's mission (1876) led to the Mastung agreement and the treaty of Jacobabad, which marked the end of non-intervention on this frontier. Sandeman was appointed agent to the governor-general, with his headquarters at Quetta, from where, by a system of allowances, he controlled the tribes through their *tumandars* (chiefs). By the treaty of Gandamak (1879), Pishin and Sibi were handed over to the British by Yakub Khan, but they were not declared British territory until 1887. Under British rule communications were developed, irrigation schemes taken in hand, and arrangements made for the collection of the land revenues. Baluchistan became part of Pakistan in 1947.

T. H. Thornton, *Sir Robert Sandeman* (London, 1895).
C. C. Davies, *The Problem of the North-West Frontier* (Cambridge, 1932).   CCD

BAMBATHA REBELLION, Natal (1906), called after Chief Bambatha, the leader. The imposition of a poll tax in 1905, and the government's handling of the first indications of disaffection, provoked some 12,000 Africans, already restless over white land and labour policies, into revolt. Nearly 4000 Africans and 24 colonists were killed.

BAMFORD, SAMUEL (1788–1872), weaver, poet, and prominent Lancashire radical who withdrew from politics after being imprisoned for his part in Peterloo (1819). From 1826 he was a London newspaper correspondent, and maintained a life-long interest in the Lancashire dialect and customs. His *Passages in the Life of a Radical* (1844) and *Early Days* (1848) make him 'the greatest chronicler of early nineteenth-century Radicalism' (E. P. Thompson, *The Making of the English Working Class*), though his Lancashire radicals are portrayed as being more respectable and less conspiratorial than they really were.

BAN ET ARRIÈRE-BAN, procedure by which all French noblemen were summoned to serve for 40 days a year in the king's army, and for three months if they remained in France. Those who could not attend in person were expected to depute a substitute or pay taxes instead. With the appearance of mercenary troops the *ban et arrière-ban* became anachronistic, though the feudal host was still being summoned by this means in the reign of Louis XIV. However, the host was by that time a highly inefficient force and the *ban et arrière-ban* was employed for the last time in 1697.

BANA, Sanskrit writer (1st half of the 7th cent.), who was long associated with Harshavardhana's court at Kanauj. Of his works, written in ornate Sanskrit, the *Harshacharita*, 'Deeds of Harsha [vardhana]' is of special interest to the historian, not primarily for the historical 'facts' but rather for the elaborate descriptions which give us some idea of social and religious life in northern India in the 7th cent.

BANAT (18,800 sq. kms), bounded by the Mures river in the north, the Danube to the south, and the Transylvanian Alps in the east. Originally part of Hungary, the Banat became a Turkish *pashalik* in 1552. By the treaty of Passarowitz (1718) it was ceded to Austria by the Porte. Until 1751 the Banat was governed as a military province from Vienna. Civil administration was introduced in 1751 and in 1779 the Banat was incorporated into Hungary. Rich in natural resources, the Banat has attracted colonists throughout its history and consequently has a mixed population. The western Banat is heavily Serb, the eastern portions predominantly Rumanian; Magyar and German communities are sprinkled throughout the province. During the First World War the Banat was contested by the Serbian and Rumanian governments and by the treaty of Trianon (1920) was partitioned between Yugoslavia and Rumania. On the outbreak of the Second World War both Hungary and Rumania claimed the entire Banat. Avoiding a choice between his allies, Hitler kept the Banat under German administration.

After the war the Trianon frontier between Yugoslavia and Rumania was restored.

BANCROFT, EDWARD (1744–1821), diplomat and inventor. Though born in MA, Bancroft settled in England and served as double agent during the American War of Independence. He wrote on American affairs and invented textile dyes.

BANCROFT, GEORGE (1800–91), US historian, diplomat, and politician, whose *History of the United States* (10 vols 1834–74) is a landmark in American historiography. A New Englander and a Harvard graduate, who also studied extensively in Germany, he was a prominent figure in the scholarly and literary circles of Boston and New York, and an active Jacksonian Democrat in politics. As secretary of the navy in Polk's administration (1845–6), he established the US Naval Academy at Annapolis, MD. He was US minister to Great Britain (1846–9) and to Germany (1867–74). In both his scholarly and his political activities, he was an eloquent and enthusiastic champion of American democracy.

BANCROFT, RICHARD (1544–1610), archbishop of Canterbury, and a vigorous and uncompromising opponent of Puritanism. As chaplain to Abp Whitgift (1592) he took a prominent part against the Puritans. He became Bp of London (1597), and, because Whitgift's infirmities rendered him incapable of discharging his office, virtually primate of England. He was present at the death of Elizabeth I (1603) and joined in the proclaiming of James I. His hostility to the Puritans at the Hampton Court conference (1604) was so great that it provoked a rebuke from James. As president of the convocation of Canterbury on the death of Whitgift, he was responsible for drawing up a coercive set of canons which was denounced by parliament. In Nov. 1604 he was appointed Abp of Canterbury, and came into conflict with the civil courts over his Articles of Abuses, which aimed at rendering ecclesiastical courts independent of the law. He also succeeded in forcing non-conforming clergy out of the Church of England by the *ex animo* form of subscription. In 1608 he became chancellor of Oxford University.

BANDA, HASTINGS KAMUZU (1906–), president of Malawi. Born in Kasungu and educated at Livingstonia, he worked in the South Africa mines before obtaining a higher education in the US. After qualifying as a doctor at Meharay Medical College, Nashville, he requalified at Glasgow and Edinburgh universities and afterwards became an elder of the Church of Scotland.

While practising medicine in London, Banda organized opposition to the Federation of the Rhodesias and Nyasaland (1953–63). From 1953–5 he lived at Kumasi in Ghana, but remained in touch with his home country. In 1958 he returned to Nyasaland at the invitation of the National Congress, so as to lead it. A year later he was imprisoned at Gwelo, Southern Rhodesia, for aiding and abetting political disturbances, but was released in 1960. In 1963 his forceful leadership brought an end to the Federation and, a year later, independence to his country.

BANDA ORIENTAL, or eastern bank of the Uruguay river. Now roughly the Republic of Uruguay, this area was a bone of contention between the Spanish and Portuguese empires during the 17th and 18th cents.

In 1679 the Portuguese established Colônia do Sacramento, a smuggling depot on the Plata estuary. In spite of Spanish attacks, Colônia remained Portuguese for nearly a century. As Buenos Aires grew in importance during the late 18th cent., new efforts were made to expel the Portuguese from the Banda Oriental. Côlonia fell (1777) and soon all Portuguese had been driven out.

During the Latin American Wars of Independence the region was the scene of a three-sided struggle. Montevideo was a Spanish stronghold, José Artigas led local patriots and federalist provinces against the centralists of Buenos Aires, and the Brazilians asserted the old Portuguese claims. For a time the Brazilians were dominant. In 1817 Montevideo was taken, and in 1821 they annexed the entire province. Artigas, unwelcome in Buenos Aires, withdrew to Paraguay.

With the help of the United Provinces of the Río de la Plata, local patriots soon reacted, and in April 1825 the famous 'Thirty-three' raised the standard of revolt. Montevideo fell to them and was blockaded by the Brazilian navy. Britain's annoyance at the disruption of trade in the Plata estuary led to her interference in the struggle. Her diplomatic intervention, plus the unpopularity of the war in Brazil and the United Provinces, led to a compromise whereby both nations abandoned claims to the Banda Oriental and agreed to guarantee the independence of a new buffer state, the Eastern Republic of the Uruguay. For years Uruguay was to remain a quasi-protectorate of Great Britain.

BANDARANAIKE, MRS SIRIMAVO (1916–), widow of S. W. R. D. Bandaranaike and daughter of a high caste Kandyan chief. Though convent-educated, she was a Buddhist. During her husband's lifetime she took little part in politics. After his murder (1959) his party fell into confusion, and the government, defeated in the House of Representatives by one vote, resigned. In the following general election (March 1960) the United National party failed to obtain an overall majority and though Dudley Senanayake, its leader, formed a government it was almost immediately defeated in parliament. Mrs Bandaranaike was induced to lead her late husband's Sri Lanka Freedom Party (SLFP) and won a resounding victory, partly because of sympathy on account of the manner of her husband's death. She became prime minister, being the first woman ever to hold such office, and a seat was found for her in the Senate.

She carried out her duties ably and was no mere figurehead. She announced that she intended to follow her husband's policies of neutrality, moderate socialism, and Sinhalese nationalism, but went a good deal further by nationalizing the denominational schools—an action which provoked bitter indignation in the considerable Christian community—life insurance, and the distribution of petrol and oil. This last measure annoyed the US authorities over the matter of compensation, and American aid to Ceylon was withdrawn. Many restrictions were placed on the import of commodities, and travel abroad was severely restricted, the island's economy having deteriorated since 1956.

The government was unable to cope with the financial situation and a coalition with a Trotskyist group caused a split in the party, which was losing its popularity in the country. At the 1963 general election Mrs Bandaranaike's party was defeated, and she became leader of the opposition in the House of Representatives.

S. A. Pakeman, *Ceylon* (London, 1964).　　　　SAP

BANDARANAIKE, SOLOMON WEST RIDGEWAY DIAS (1899–1959), the son of Sir Solomon Dias Bandaranaike, *maha mudaliyar* (chief native officer) of Ceylon, was educated at a Christian college in Colombo, and at Oxford University. On returning to Ceylon, he became a Buddhist and founded a party, the Sinhala Maha Sabha, to promote the interests of the majority community. He was elected to the State Council (1931) and to be minister of local administration (1936). When, as the result of the Soulbury Commission's report, a new constitution came into being, he merged his party with the United National Party and was appointed minister of health and local government, and leader of the House of Representatives (1947). In 1951, finding himself out of sympathy with his cabinet colleagues, he resigned and founded the Sri Lanka Freedom Party, taking with him eight other members. At the 1952 general election his party secured only a few seats, but before the next election he campaigned for greater attention to be given to the Sinhalese language and culture and to the Buddhist religion, all of which, he claimed, had hitherto been neglected. He formed a coalition (Mahajana Eksath Peramuna) with a Trotskyist group led by Philip Gunawardena and an extremist Sinhalese party. At the election this coalition won by a sweeping majority, and Bandaranaike became prime minister.

He put his election promises into practice by an act making Sinhalese the official language—a cause of bitter resentment among the Tamil community. He laid down a foreign policy of neutrality and a home policy of moderate socialism and unilaterally repudiated the defence agreement with Britain (1947), under which the British had been allowed the continued use of Trincomali harbour and Katunayake airfield as naval and air bases. This he had a right to do under the agreement. He nationalized public transport and the main activities of the port of Colombo. Intercommunal antagonism erupted into severe riots (1958) in which hundreds of Tamils and some Sinhalese lost their lives. Bandaranaike wavered, but was induced to declare a state of emergency and Sir Oliver Goonetilleke, the governor-general, took over and restored order with the aid of the small army and navy.

Bandaranaike found it difficult to satisfy his supporters in the cabinet, in parliament, and in the country. In Sept. 1959 he was assassinated by a Buddhist monk with a private grievance.

E. F. C. Ludowyk, *Modern History of Ceylon* (London, 1966).　　　　SAP

BANDARANAIKE–CHELVANAYAKAM PACT. After the passing of the 'Sinhala only' act (1956) by the Ceylon parliament, the prime minister came to some agreement with Chelvanayakam, leader of the Tamil Federal party, regarding the 'reasonable use' of the Tamil language in administration, but under pressure from extremist Sinhalese repudiated it a few months later (1957). This was one cause of the severe communal riots the next year.

BANDE MATARAM, 'Hail to the Mother', the opening words of a poem in Bankim Chandra Chatterjee's novel, *Anandamatha*. During the agitation against the partition of Bengal it became the patriotic song of the revolutionary party. It was also the name of an anti-British newspaper published between 1906 and 1908.

BANDEIRANTES, members of Brazilian exploring bands in the 17th cent. Leaving the coastal areas, mainly around São Paulo, these bands hunted for Indian slaves, gold, and precious stones. As a result of their activities much of the interior of South America was first explored. Their slave raiding and discoveries of precious metals had a great impact on the speed of Brazilian development.

Pioneers of mixed blood, renowned for their ferocity and lawlessness, they were viewed with both admiration and disdain by the Portuguese settlers of other areas. Local church men repeatedly condemned them for their immorality and slave raiding. Their destruction of the Jesuit missions among the Guarani Indians along the Parana river (1628–32) has blackened their historical reputation.

BANDJERMASIN, major commercial and political centre of southern Borneo. It was established as a Muslim sultanate in the mid-16th cent. with help from Muslim Demak, near the site of the ancient Hindu Martapura. Its polyglot population of Javanese, Malay, and Bugis immigrants and indigenous Ngadjus was gradually welded into a distinct ethnic group, the Bandjerese, all adopting Islam and accepting the sultan's authority. The sultanate prospered in the 17th cent. through its exports of pepper. Chinese were the most important buyers, and Dutch attempts to obtain a monopoly were successfully repulsed until 1747. Dutch control only became effective as a result of the 'Bandjermasin War' (1859–62), during which the sultanate was abolished.

BANDULA (d. 1 April 1825), Burmese general and governor of Assam, who, when he was transferred to Arakan in 1824, prepared to invade Chittagong. He was recalled to repel the British amphibious invasion of Rangoon, but failed to do so and was killed in action at Danubyu.

BANDUNG CONFERENCE (April 1955), the first major neutralist conference, produced little concrete result, but opened the promise of a major role in international affairs for that group of states variously described as 'neutralist', 'developing', and 'third world'—a promise which was largely unfulfilled. The conference had its origin in the initiative of the Colombo powers (Burma, Ceylon, India, Indonesia, and Pakistan) and brought together Afghanistan, Cambodia, China, Egypt, Ethiopia, the Gold Coast, Iraq, Japan, Jordan, Laos, Lebanon, Liberia, Libya, Nepal, Persia, the Philippines, Saudi Arabia, Siam, Sudan, Syria, Turkey, North and South Viet-nam, and the Yemen. The Central African Federation was invited, but declined: neither South Africa nor Israel was invited.

The communiqué which followed the conference gave a good indication of its proceedings. It pressed for the elimination of nuclear weapons under international control and set out such principles of political conduct as 'respect for the sovereignty and territorial integrity of all nations; recognition of the equality of all races and of the equality of all nations large and small'. It also expressed support for the participating states against those not represented (eg, Indonesia against Holland over West Irian), but omitted reference to the conflicts of interest between participants.

The nature of the Chinese participation suggested that the communist government would pursue a policy of active, though relatively traditional, diplomacy as a leader of the 'third world', though this expectation was unfulfilled. The conference enhanced the status of neutralism as a policy and a slogan.

BANER, JOHANN (1595–1641), Swedish marshal of an ancient noble family, who, after Gustavus Adolphus's death, commanded a Swedish army in the Thirty Years War. He defeated the Saxons near Chemnitz (1639). An ambitious careerist, he hoped to acquire considerable estates from the empire and in 1640 married the daughter of the Margrave of Baden.

BANERJEA, SIR SURENDRANATH (1848–1925), Indian platform orator, newspaper editor, and political organizer, intimately associated with the Indian National Congress from its inception. Born to an orthodox Kulin Brahman family of Calcutta, he entered the Indian civil service (1869) and was posted (1871) to Sylhet as assistant magistrate and collector, but was dismissed for irregularities. Because of this he was excluded from the English bar. He became professor of English at the Metropolitan Institution, Calcutta, and at the Free Church College, and principal of Ripon College, Calcutta, which he founded. He lectured on Mazzini and on Indian unity and took up the cause of the Indianization of the services. He was an active member of the Indian Association, founded in 1876, and editor and proprietor of the *Bengalee*, an influential journal. He opposed Lytton's Vernacular Press Act (1878) and supported the Ilbert Bill of 1883, when he was sentenced to two months' imprisonment for contempt of court. He was prominent in the founding at Calcutta of the All-India National Conference (1883), which, after 1885, was merged in the India National Congress, and he was president of the 11th and 18th sessions of the Congress (Poona, 1895, and Ahmadabad, 1902). As a member of the Bengal Legislative Council (1893–1901) he opposed Curzon's bill for reforming the Calcutta Corporation (1899). He led the opposition to the partition of Bengal and supported the boycott of British goods as a weapon to procure its reversal.

Banerjea was inspired by the political philosophy of the British Liberal Party and was never an extremist. His writings and speeches awakened political interest among the educated classes of Bengal. He did not believe in violence or in India's separation from England and played an important part at the Surat Congress (1907) in preventing the extremists from dominating the congress, though they eventually won the day (1916). He accepted the Government of India Act of 1919 and this led to a breach with Congress. His attempt to form a new organization, the Liberal Federation, failed to secure popular support. He accepted ministerial office in Bengal after the introduction of the Montagu–Chelmsford reforms (1921), but was defeated at the second general election (1923). Knighted in 1921, he lived to be denounced by his countrymen as a hireling of the British government. In his memoirs (*A Nation in Making*, 1925), he retaliated by expressing his contempt for the violence and intolerance of the non-co-operators.   CCD

BANERJEE, KRISHNAMOHAN (1813–85), Indian scholar and linguist and president of the Indian Association. As a student of Derozio at the Hindu College, Calcutta, he was converted to Christianity and ordained an Anglican clergyman. He was a professor at Bishop's College, Calcutta (1852–68), and published in Bengali and English the *Vidyakalpadrum*, an encyclopedia in 13 volumes.

BANERJEE, W. C. (1844–1906), president of the Indian National Congress (1885, 1892), and a member of the Calcutta High Court bar. He represented Calcutta University on the Bengal Legislative Council. He retired from the Calcutta bar in 1901 and settled in England, where he continued to promote the cause of the Congress.

BANGORIAN CONTROVERSY (1717–20), theological-political dispute arising from the publication of a pamphlet by Benjamin Hoadly, Bp of Bangor, which stated that civil government had no jurisdiction over ecclesiastical affairs, except when these constituted a national danger, eg, when the clergy who refused allegiance to William III were deprived of their benefices.

BANISTER, JOHN (1650–92), first North American botanist. Banister was born in England and settled in Virginia (1678) after a few years in the West Indies. He catalogued Virginian plant life and published many works on plant and animal life in Jamaica and Virginia.

BANK ACT (1871), first general Bank Act of the Dominion of Canada. Mainly the work of Sir Francis Hincks, the finance minister, it began the practice of decennial revision of the Bank Act. Banks required a parliamentary charter for which rigid conditions were prescribed.

BANK CHARTER ACT (1844), last of a series of important statutes regulating the position of the Bank of England as central banker. In the early 19th cent. the bank had a number of functions. It made advances and held deposits, including those of many country bankers. It issued notes, as did many other banks on a much smaller scale, and its notes, since the resumption of cash payments (1819) were convertible to gold on demand. It carried out large-scale foreign exchange transactions. Finally, it acted as lender of last resort in time of commercial crisis, without which support small country banks would be threatened with collapse. These functions could be incompatible. It was to the bank's advantage to lend out at interest as large a proportion of its reserves as possible. On the other hand, the need to support the general banking system in time of crisis, and the need to pay out large amounts of bullion, especially in years of heavy wheat imports, made necessary the maintenance of adequate reserves.

These problems gave rise to extended discussion in the 1830s. Horsley Palmer, then governor of the bank, stated to a select committee (1832) that it was the bank's policy to hold a specie reserve equal to one-third of notes and deposits. However, in the later 1830s the bank's credit was increasing while reserves were declining, and a foreign exchange crisis in 1839 led to public anxiety and the appointment of the select committee on banks of issue (1840), of which Peel was a member. It was argued, especially by Samuel Jones Loyd, that the solution lay in the separation of the functions of note issue, which should be regulated strictly, and the handling of notes and deposits, in which the bank should have the same freedom as any other bank.

These ideas formed the basis of the Bank Charter Act. Under it the bank was divided into separate banking and issue departments, each with its own reserves. Note issue was regulated by law so that, apart from a fiduciary issue of £14 million, notes had to be backed, pound for pound, by specie in the issue department's reserve. At the same time, the note issue of other banks was strictly regulated. The commercial crisis of 1847 subjected these arrangements to strain. The bank then received many calls for support from banking and commercial houses, and the government, faced with a choice between widespread bankruptcies or the temporary suspension of the act, decided on the latter course and allowed the bank to transfer some of its reserves from the issue to the banking department. A similar procedure was adopted in subsequent crises.

The Bank Charter Act is one of the pieces of economic and social legislation passed by Peel's administration (1841–6) which were of fundamental importance in the 19th cent. It remained in force until the First World War.

F. W. Fetter, *Development of British Monetary Orthodoxy, 1797–1875* (Cambridge, MA, 1965).　　　　　　　LMB

BANK FOR INTERNATIONAL SETTLEMENTS was established (May 1930) to provide an agency for reparations payments and for co-operation between central banks. The board of directors was composed of the governors of the five central banks (of Belgium, France, Germany, Britain, and Italy) and the nominees of the two banking groups (Japanese and US) which together guaranteed the original subscription of 500 million gold francs. The ending of reparations payments after 1932 deprived the bank of part of its function and it remained relatively inactive until the Second World War. Thereafter it became banking agent for OEEC, OECD and certain functions of OECD. Its governors resumed their annual meetings and the bank became a centre for research and consultation.

BANK HOLIDAY ACT (1871), promoted by Sir John Lubbock, provided four statutory holidays (Boxing Day, Easter Monday, Whit Monday, and the first Monday in August) for bank clerks in England. Initially, bank holidays were observed by banks in the city of London, but not generally. Alterations in the specific days appointed as bank holidays have since been made by proclamation. The Whit Monday holiday is now officially known as the Spring bank holiday.

BANK NATIONALIZATION BILL, THE AUSTRALIAN (1947), introduced by the Labor prime minister, J. B. Chifley, to nationalize the private trading banks, following his failure to force local authorities to bank with the government-owned Commonwealth Bank. The bill passed both houses despite one of the most vigorous publicity campaigns in Australian history, but the high court declared it unconstitutional (Aug. 1948) and this decision was upheld by the judicial committee of the privy council. Feelings aroused by the controversy were among the chief reasons for Labor losing the 1949 general election.

BANK OF ENGLAND, incorporated company founded in 1694 as the first joint stock bank which was allowed to issue notes and discount bills. It was instituted in order to raise £1,200,000 as an 8 per cent interest loan to the government from the public. The money was raised in 12 days and the bank's loan to the government had no need to be fully repaid provided that the interest was always guaranteed. The bank

was one of the highly successful expedients conceived by Charles Montagu, Lord Halifax, to finance the war of the League of Augsburg. It was the origin of the funded national debt, which stood at £14 million by the end of that war (1697).

BANK OF FRANCE (1800), founded by Napoleon during the Consulate as an independent body, although closely tied to the government through its floating of state loans. It received the monopoly of issuing notes (1803) and managed the issue of a new, stable gold currency, the franc (1804). The bank survived Napoleon's fall and has since played a similar role in France to that of the Bank of England.

BANK OF IRELAND (1783), first incorporated bank in the country. Its charter, modelled on that of the Bank of England's, forbade the issue of notes by any bank having more than six partners. Because of the limited character of Irish 18th-cent. commerce, the Bank of Ireland did not deal in foreign exchange, nor act as a clearing bank for provincial banks. Its policies were therefore of less general importance than those of the Bank of England.

BANK OF NORTH AMERICA, first private commercial bank in the US. Organized by Robert Morris in Philadelphia, it received a charter from Congress (1781) and provided valuable financial services to the national government in the 1780s.

BANK OF PRUSSIA (1765), formed by Frederick the Great as a state discount bank on the model of the Bank of England.

BANK OF THE UNITED STATES, FIRST AND SECOND banks chartered by the federal government for national purposes. The first Bank of the United States (1791) was an integral component of Alexander Hamilton's financial programme. Modelled on the Bank of England and established in Philadelphia, it was intended to perform many functions of a central bank and to provide a circulating medium through the issue of bank notes. It received government deposits and handled the financial business of the government, encouraged the growth of capital, and assisted in attracting the support of the commercial classes to the federal government. The bank was opposed by agrarian democrats, such as John Taylor of Caroline, who feared not only its possible effects on state institutions but the growth of a self-perpetuating aristocracy with power based on paper, rather than 'real', wealth. In his famous opinion on the constitutionality of the bank Jefferson denied that the federal government had any constitutional authority to charter a bank, but Hamilton, by eloquently enunciating the constitutional doctrines of broad construction and implied powers, convinced President Washington of the bank's legality. One-fifth of its capital of $10 million was subscribed by the government, the rest by private investors. It was authorized to issue up to $10 million in circulating notes and to conduct normal commercial business. Although Presidents Jefferson and Madison later came to appreciate the bank's role, its charter was not renewed (1811).

After an unsatisfactory period of reliance on state banks, the second Bank of the United States was granted a similar charter (1816), its permitted capital was increased to $35 million and the federal government was authorized to appoint 5 of the 25 directors. Its constitutionality was affirmed by Chief Justice Marshall in *McCulloch v. Maryland* (1819). Badly managed by William Jones, it was put on a sound basis by Langdon Cheves (1819–23) and his successor, Nicholas Biddle. As the largest bank in America, with branches in most states, it exercised a powerful and generally restraining influence over other banks. It also appeared to be politically partial and although its charter ran to 1836 the Whigs persuaded Biddle to seek early renewal as a means of attacking President Jackson. The bill passed Congress, but Jackson vetoed it (1832), arguing that the government had no right to charter such a bank, and that in doing so it had granted special privileges to a select body of stockholders. His secretary of the treasury, Roger Brooke Taney, removed government deposits from the bank to a number of state, or 'pet', banks (1833). When the charter lapsed the bank continued to operate under a Pennsylvania charter until it collapsed (1841).

B. Hammond, *Banks and Politics in America: from the Revolution to the Civil War* (Princeton, 1957).

BANKING IN AUSTRALIA. The first Australian trading bank, the Bank of New South Wales, established in 1817 by Gov. Lachlan Macquarie to overcome the colony's currency problems (due mainly to excessive loss of coins to pay for imports), survived to become the largest private trading bank in Australia. With banks similarly founded in other Australian colonies, in many cases with large injections of British capital, a high proportion of advances was to farmers and graziers and in periods of financial crisis, caused by poor seasons or low export prices, there were bank failures or amalgamations.

In the second half of the 19th cent. Australian banks tended to make advances to enable farmers and graziers to obtain clear titles to their land and in the early 1890s there was a consequential liquidity crisis. Falls in prices of exported primary products and rising land values caused a lack of confidence in land companies and land 'banks'. This spread to the trading banks, which had financed much of the speculative land boom; a five-day moratorium was declared for banks in Victoria in May 1893 and major reconstruction of the Australian banks was required before confidence was restored.

With federation the Australian constitution gave the Commonwealth parliament power over money and banking, but not over state-owned banks and, in 1911, the Fisher Labor government established the Commonwealth Bank, a Commonwealth-owned trading bank and savings bank under a governor, Sir Denison Miller. The bank gave considerable assistance to the Commonwealth government as its wartime financial adviser and agent and 1924 legislation, introduced by the Bruce–Page government, gave control of the note issue to the Commonwealth Bank under a board of eight members.

With the onset of depression towards the end of 1929, the bank commandeered all available stocks of gold and exercised a powerful and largely conservative influence on the economy, the Scullin Labor government being unable to get the Commonwealth Bank to carry out the expansionist monetary policy favoured by its leading members.

A royal commission on the Australian monetary and banking system reported in 1937, but none of its recommendations to strengthen central banking had been applied by 1939. Under wartime national security regulations, however, the Commonwealth Bank was converted into a strong central bank, able to call into special accounts any percentage it wanted of increased assets of each trading bank.

By its 1945 banking legislation the Chifley Labor government confirmed the peacetime position of the Commonwealth Bank as a central bank and restored single governor control, but Chifley failed in his 1947 attempt to nationalize the private banks. The new Menzies coalition government restored Commonwealth Bank Board control in 1951 and, in 1953, modified the special accounts system. In 1959 banking legislation completed separation of the central bank, now the Reserve Bank of Australia, from the Commonwealth Trading Bank.

During the 1960s, however, there was a gradual development towards greater co-operation between the central bank and the major trading banks, which had been reduced by amalgamation to seven, the Commonwealth Trading Bank and six private trading banks with branches spread over the six states and in New Zealand and Papua/New Guinea.

AC

BANKING IN NEW ZEALAND was principally Australian in origin, and began with the Union Bank of Australia (1840). Many Australian practices and institutions for financing land transactions and development were adopted. Later, however, four of six trading banks, including the locally founded Bank of NZ (1861), had their headquarters in London. NZ banks were involved in the somewhat speculative financing of the later 19th cent., and in the Australasian crisis of the early 1890s. The Bank of NZ was saved by swift government aid in 1894, and absorbed the moribund Colonial Bank of NZ (1895). Criticism of bank policies on credit and exchange rate led to the establishment of the NZ Reserve Bank in 1933. Both this bank (1936) and the Bank of NZ (1945) became state-owned. In 1966, NZ had 13 trustee savings banks, of which Auckland (1847) was the oldest.

BANKING, MEDIEVAL. Because of the multiplicity and unreliability of medieval coinages, money changers were active at all the business centres and the earliest banks of deposit were kept by them. Where, as at Bruges *c.* 1360, all the local money changers had accounts with each other, an efficient system of money transfers could be organized. At leading centres, like Bruges and Venice, most people of means had bank accounts to avail themselves of these facilities. The leading commercial firms, especially in Italy, accepted deposits on which they paid interest in order to accumulate large capital resources. This has been done on a huge scale since the 13th cent. Using their network of branches and correspondents in different parts of Europe, these firms provided international transfer facilities, specializing in the financing of trade. All medieval banks were private enterprises and were very vulnerable to panics among depositors; only at Venice did the state protect the latter. The extension of credit beyond the banks' real assets was rightfully regarded by some medieval rulers as an infringement of their princely monopoly to mint money and in some medieval states deposit banking was at times discouraged or even prohibited for this reason, though such regulations could never be effectively enforced.

BANKRUPTCY IN SPAIN in the 17th cent., a contributory factor in the decline of Spain and her empire, was the result of the three-fold decline in Castile's economic primacy (1590–1620), upon which Spain's 16th-cent. imperial greatness had been founded. First, her population declined by 25 per cent in the 17th cent., producing a manpower crisis; second, productivity declined as wealth was transferred into attractive but unproductive areas of investment (*eg*, government bonds) and as she became economically and technologically more backward; third, there was a drastic reduction in the value to the Spanish Crown of Castile's overseas possessions. In 1597 it was clear for the first time that the American market was overstocked with European goods. The colonies began to develop their own agriculture and industry. From the last quarter of the 16th cent. to the last quarter of the 17th, the tonnage of ships plying between Spain and the Indies fell by some 75 per cent, and in the latter period trade had virtually passed into the hands of foreigners, who supplied five-sixths of the cargoes of outbound fleets. Foreigners had begun to take over Spanish industry from the 1550s. They also ran the Crown's finances and controlled the Castilian economy. From 1601 Spanish silver prices declined and remittances began to fall off (1610–20). Eventually Seville's trading system with the New World collapsed (1639–41). In addition, Spain's continuing imperialistic attitude and the revival of Castilian nationalism under Olivares led to expensive and exhausting wars with France for most of the 17th cent. and the revolts of Portugal and Catalonia in the 1640s.

BANKS, SIR JOSEPH (1743–1820), president of the Royal Society (1778–1820), and the outstanding scientific figure of his time. He accompanied Captain Cook as scientific observer in the *Endeavour* (1768–71) and was instrumental in the founding of Australia. Banks was director of Kew Gardens

(1772–1820) and was the first to develop its scientific work, sending out collecting expeditions to many parts of the world. He also organized the introduction of Spanish merino sheep, establishing a flock for George III.

BANKS, NATHANIEL PRENTISS (1816–94), US politician, who served in the House of Representatives (1853–7, 1865–1873, 1875–7, 1889–91), was elected speaker (1856) after a protracted struggle, and governor of MA (1858–60). One of the least successful Civil War 'political generals', he was humiliated by Stonewall Jackson in the Shenandoah valley campaign (1862) and fared little better in the west (1863–4).

BANNERET, medieval military rank accorded to the leader of a troop of four or five knights and at least ten or twelve troopers serving under his banner in war. During the performance of his military obligations to his lord he received a higher fee than an ordinary knight. The king's bannerets ranked as magnates in 14th-cent. England.

BANNOCKBURN, BATTLE OF (24 June 1314). Fought near Stirling, this was the greatest defeat ever inflicted on the English by the Scots. It ensured the independence of Scotland, confirmed Robert Bruce as king, and led to a series of invasions of northern England during the next generation, and to the invasion of Ireland by Edward Bruce (1318).

BANQUE GÉNÉRALE, was founded originally in Paris in May 1716 by the Scots financier John Law as a private bank. It was converted into a royal bank in Dec. 1718 after two years of highly successful activity. Law won concessions from the regent, Orléans, in the form of trading monopolies with Louisiana, the West Indies, and Canada, for which he founded a subsidiary company. Later he won for his company the right of farming taxes and finally he took over the national debt. In 1720 the bank and the company were officially merged, despite widespread opposition in financial circles. The collapse of Law's bank in the Mississippi bubble (1720) strengthened French distrust of paper money and hindered the development of credit banks in France.

BANQUETING HOUSE at the royal palace of Whitehall, the first English building in the Palladian style, was built by Inigo Jones for James I. The ceiling has panels painted by Rubens. From one of the windows Charles I stepped on to the scaffold erected for his execution (1649).

BANTAM (Banten), the western portion of the island of Java, known during the first years of European activity in the area as the major port for trade, especially in pepper. The Dutch gained a monopoly of trade in the late 17th cent. as they gained control over the sultan himself. The rulers of Bantam were known as pious Muslims, descended (according to traditional texts) from Sunan Gunung Djati (d. *c.* 1570), as was also the ruling house of Tjeribon.

BANTING, SIR FREDERICK GRANT (1891–1941), Canadian scientist who, with Charles H. Best, was the first to extract the hormone insulin from the pancreas. Their work showed that the hormone was specific in the treatment of diabetes.

BANTRY BAY, BATTLE OF (1689), fought off Ireland's south-west coast in the war of the Grand Alliance. On 11 May an English fleet under Arthur Herbert (later Earl of Torrington) attacked a French fleet attempting to land reinforcements for the former James II, who had landed in Ireland on 14 March. The attack was beaten off and the reinforcements landed, but they were not sufficient to turn the tide in favour of James.

BANTU, term used to describe the languages of most peoples of central, eastern, and southern Africa from Cameroun to Natal. Unlike the languages of the sub-Saharan belt, the Bantu languages show a notable degree of affinity. M. Guthrie's study of Bantu language classification suggests that the most likely explanation of this affinity is a linguistic colonization of Africa south of the equator, originating possibly in the southern Congo savannah. Historians have tried to associate this theory of linguistic spread with archaeological data on the spread of agriculture, pot-making, and metal working. These food-producing Iron Age cultures, possibly in association with a diffusion of Bantu languages, reached nearly all parts of the sub-continent except the dry southwest, where Khoi-speaking hunter–gatherers survived until and even beyond the 17th-cent. advent of Europeans.

The dating of this spread is as yet only partially known, though it is clear that the Iron Age had reached much of East Africa and the Zambezi basin by the 3rd cent. AD. In some of the forests of central Africa, Pigmy peoples did not adopt food-producing cultures and may only recently have acquired Bantu languages. In South Africa the Iron Age spread rapidly from about the 10th cent. AD, probably in association with the Bantu languages, although the earliest purely linguistic evidence is from Portuguese sources; these merely indicate that Bantu speakers occupied the eastern half of South Africa before the 16th cent.

BANTU EDUCATION ACT (1953), an essential part of the South African policy of 'separate development'. Its aim is 'to train and teach people [*ie*, Africans] in accordance with their opportunities in life according to the sphere in which they live'. The act places the education of Africans, previously in the hands of missions, churches, and provincial councils, under the specially created Bantu Education division of the Department of Bantu Administration. Africans, who say it provides 'education for barbarism', non-Afrikaner educationists, and almost all the churches, have consistently opposed the act.

BANTUSTANS, South African colloquialism for areas set aside for African occupation and limited local self-government. Eight are envisaged, although as yet only the Transkei has its own regional parliament (1963).

BANU HASSAN, nomads originally from the Arabian peninsula, who migrated from southern Morocco in the 14th and 15th cents to the western Sahara, where they eventually subdued the largely Berber population. Their dialect, of Arabic 'Hassaniyya', has become the lingua franca of the whole western Sahara.

BANU HILIL, group of Arab tribes, Ibn Khaldun's 'swarm of locusts', said to have been sent from Egypt (1051) to punish the Zirid Mu'izz, and held responsible for subsequent desiccation of the Maghrib. In fact, they entered some time previously, representative of a westward drift of Arab nomads (10th–14th cents), including also Banu Qurra and Sulaim, to be militarily employed by Mu'izz. After a quarrel leading to conflict at Hidaran (1052), which precipitated the disintegration of the Zirid dominion, they provided forces for dynasties of the region, helping develop the *makhzan* system of government through military tribes. Moving westwards partly through such employment, and amalgamating with local tribes, their descendants lost their identity, at the same time contributing to the Arabization of the countryside. The charge of their ruining the economy by destroying agriculture cannot be sustained.

BAO-DAI, last Emperor of Viet-nam (*reg.* 1925–45). Born in 1911, only son of the Emperor Khai-Dinh (*reg.* 1916–25), he was educated in France (1922–32), and did not reign effectively until 1933. After an abortive attempt to establish a genuinely constitutional regime he accepted his role as a French pawn. In April 1945, at the behest of the Japanese, who then controlled Viet-nam, he abrogated the treaties which had established French rule in Viet-nam, and formed a supposedly independent government. In Aug., following the seizure of Hanoi by the Viet-minh, he abdicated and as

Mr Vinh-Thuy accepted the role of adviser to Ho Chi-minh. Later he moved to Hong Kong, and in 1948 accepted a French invitation to head the Associate State of Viet-nam, a position he held until 1955, when he was deposed by Ngo Dinh-diem. By then he was already in exile in France, where he remains (1968).

BAPTISTS, religious sect founded by Menno Simons (1492–1559) as a modification of Anabaptism. He and his followers believed that the church was a voluntary association of believers, distinct from the state and open to all who wished to seek salvation and united in a pacifist attitude towards mankind. They discarded the baptism of infants in favour of adult baptism after the profession of faith. Beginning in the northern provinces of the Netherlands, the Baptist sect soon spread throughout the Western world.

BAPTIST WAR (1831–2), Jamaican slave insurrection. Led by Negro Baptists and aroused by emancipation movements in Britain, slaves in the Montego Bay area burned plantations and killed about 12 whites. The Jamaican government declared martial law, arrested white Baptist ministers, and killed and executed 500 blacks. Planters burned Wesleyan and Baptist chapels. The slave revolt led British opinion to favour abolition.

BAR, CONFEDERATION OF (1768), brought together a large section of the Polish nobility and gentry in opposition to the increasing influence of Russia in Poland. Russia had recently used this influence to force the Polish diet to grant toleration to protestant and orthodox dissenters. The confederation, led by Joseph Pulaski and Bp Krasinski, aimed to maintain the exclusive position of the Catholic Church and uphold the anarchic Polish constitution by an armed revolt against King Stanislas and his Russian supporters. With French help the confederation was able to turn their movement into a national revolt, but it was suppressed by 1772 through Russian troops and the help of those Polish families, including the powerful Czartoryski, who had refused to support it. The immediate consequence of the revolt was the First Partition of Poland.

BAR HEBRAEUS (Ibn al-Ibri, also known as Abu'l-Faraj) (1226–86), a Jacobite Catholic of Tagrit (1264–86). He wrote numerous works (philosophical, religious, medical, etc.), mostly in Syriac, but some in Arabic. His great achievement was a universal chronicle which made use of sources written in Arabic and Persian.

BARA, pastoralists of the southern plateau of Madagascar. They were first mentioned by Europeans in the 16th cent. Their ruling group is thought to have come from the mainland of Africa.

BARANGÉ, *loi* (1951), a controversial French law allowing state subsidies to be paid to private—mostly Catholic—primary schools. It provided an allowance for each pupil, paid to the parents' associations of the schools. Although the sums involved were not large, the law was bitterly contested by anti-clericals as a departure from the republican tradition of state neutrality in religious matters. The law was politically significant because it destroyed the alliance between the Christian Democrat (MRP) and socialist parties which had been the basis of the government coalition before 1951. The accompanying *loi Marie* made private school pupils eligible for state scholarships.

BARANTE, AMABLE-GUILLAUME-PROSPER-BURGIERE, Baron de (1782–1866), French statesman. He began his career as an administrator under Napoleon, being successively *intendant* of the occupied territory of Danzig (1806–7), sub-prefect of Bressuire, and prefect of Loire-Inférieur. After 1815 he supported the Bourbon regime and became a liberal deputy in the Chamber, secretary-general of the Ministry of the Interior, and a peer (1819). Under the July Monarchy he was ambassador at Turin (1830) and at St Petersburg (1835), where he was regarded as an able and insistent advocate of French interests. His political career ended with the revolution of 1848.

BARBADOS, Caribbean island, possibly discovered by Columbus (1498) and a landfall for several Portuguese, Spanish, and English mariners in the 16th and early 17th cents. The first settlement on Barbados was made by Henry Powell (1627), an employee of Sir William Courteen. The island was granted by Charles I to James Hay, Earl of Carlisle (1628), which led to conflict with Courteen interests. Barbados was leased to Lord Francis Willoughby (1647), who served as governor until 1667, except for the years when the island was occupied by Cromwell's forces (1652–60). The English Crown assumed control over Barbados in 1661. A plantation economy was based on tobacco in the 17th cent. and sugar in the 18th cent., English indentured servants providing the original labour force, followed by extensive use of African slaves. Slavery was abolished in 1835. With a legislative council dating from 1627 and a House of Assembly from 1637, Barbados has the second oldest constitution in the British Commonwealth. Political control rested with a plantation aristocracy until manhood suffrage was granted in 1954. Under the leadership of Sir Grantly Adams, Barbados entered the West Indian Federation (1958–62) and attempted to form an Eastern Caribbean Federation (1962). Barbados became an independent state in 1966.

BARBADOS CONSOLIDATED SLAVE ACT (1797) required Anglican clergy to give religious instruction to slaves, but made it illegal to teach reading and writing. It was the first such law passed in British West Indies.

BARBADOS PROGRESSIVE LEAGUE, founded (1938) by Hope Stevens. The name was changed to the Barbados Labour Party (1942) and under the leadership of Sir Grantly Herbert Adams became the majority party (1951–66).

BARBARO, ERMOLAO (c. 1453–93), Venetian humanist who revolutionized the study of Aristotle's writings by relying exclusively on Greek commentators writing in Antiquity, some of whose works he published. His work on a critical edition of Pliny's *Natural History* was a model of humanist scholarship.

BARBAROSSA, ie, Khair ed-Din (d. 1546), known to the Christians as Barbarossa, a famous Turkish corsair. At first he served under his brother Aruj, who, from c. 1504, operated as a corsair from Tunis and Jerba. Aruj occupied Algiers in 1516, but was killed during a campaign against Tlemcen (c. 1517–18). Barbarossa then placed himself under the protection of the Ottoman Sultan Selim I. By 1529 he had established a powerful corsair state at Algiers. In 1534 he was made Kapudan (High Admiral) of the Ottoman fleet. Khair ed-Din took Tunis in 1534, but the Emperor Charles V captured it in 1535; a campaign which the emperor led against Algiers in 1541 ended, however, in failure. At Prevesa in 1538 Barbarossa defeated the naval forces of Spain and Venice, thus winning for the Ottomans an initiative at sea which endured until Lepanto in 1571. The last major campaign of Khair ed-Din came in 1543, when he ravaged the Italian coastlands and took Nice.

BARBARY, corsairs and states. The Maghribi association of piracy with *jihad* dates from the 8th cent. In the 16th cent. Levantine corsairs made this piracy a weapon in the Ottoman struggle with Spain. Collaborating with Turkish regulars, they established bases notably at Algiers, Tunis, and Tripoli, which became capitals for new Ottoman provinces, origins of modern political divisions. In the 17th cent. these provinces became independent, while piracy as an economic activity increased, expanding in Morocco with Andalusian refugees at Salé, and serving, in the Mediterranean economy, to undercut prices by supplying cheap goods to Europe. In the 18th cent. piracy declined as Europe developed. The Napoleonic Wars increased commercial and naval possibilities, but also brought French invasion in their wake, and, in 1830, the conquest of Algiers.

BARBED WIRE, first marketed in the US by J. F. Glidden (1874), and a major factor in the decline of the American Cattle Kingdom. The wire provided cheap mass-produced fencing on the treeless plains and was extensively used by homesteaders. Cattlemen also benefited, for closed ranges provided opportunities for improving livestock quality.

BARBESIEUX, LOUIS FRANÇOIS MARIE LE TELLIER, Marquis de (1668–1701), fourth son of the Marquis de Louvois, Louis XIV's war minister. He succeeded his father in that post.

BARBIANO, ALBERICO DE (*fl.* 15th cent.), Italian soldier who was one of the first prominent native *condottieri* (military adventurers) and founder of the Company of St George, of which many *condottieri* who later became well known were members. He contributed to the development of the art of war in Italy and to the organization of Italian armies as mercenary enterprises. He failed to create a territorial state for himself, but set an example for his more successful followers by his attempts to obtain Bologna and other cities.

BARBIER, E. J. F. (1689–1771), barrister in the *parlement* of Paris, who kept an informative diary of his times which was subsequently published under the title of *Chronique de la Régence et du Règne de Louis XV* (1718–63).

BARBOSA, RUY (1848–1923), Brazilian statesman and lawyer. He gained prominence under the monarchy as an advocate of the abolition of slavery and of republicanism. Barbosa helped to write the first republican constitution, promulgated in 1891. As a minister in the government of Manoel Deodoro da Fonseca he was less successful, and his later career was devoted to diplomacy and international law. He was a presidential candidate in 1910, and served on the Permanent Court of International Justice.

BARBOUR, JOHN (*c.* 1316–95), vernacular Scottish poet. His patriotic poem *The Bruce* is an important source for the history of Scotland in the 14th cent.

BARBUDA, Caribbean island, colonized by the English (1628) and granted to the Codrington family (1680). It reverted to the Crown in the 19th cent.

BARCELONA, Spanish industrial city which grew up in the early 19th cent. Both as a bustling sea-port and centre of the textile industry it was well suited to be the capital of Catalonia. In the 20th cent. Barcelona has been the scene of violent political conflict. Close ties with France made it receptive to both Republicanism and anti-clericalism. The large industrial proletariat of the city, cramped into sordid slums and faced by intransigent employers, was often ready to resort to violent methods to improve conditions. Barcelona was thus the great stronghold of anarcho-syndicalism. Another factor in the situation was the fervent Catalan nationalism of the city's bourgeoisie, who resented losing their profits in taxes to Madrid.

These factors combined to bring political chaos to the city. In the 1890s there began a series of bomb outrages, attributed to the anarchists, but probably the work of government *agents-provocateurs* intending to give Madrid an excuse to declare martial law—a move against Catalan nationalism. Barcelona remained a political hot-bed until 1909, when, after a military disaster in Morocco, the government called up the Catalan reserves. All the city's social and political tensions erupted into a week of rioting and church burning—the Tragic Week. The disturbances were repressed with brutal severity.

The city was relatively quiet (1909–19), especially during the First World War. The Barcelona Employers' Federation decided to rid itself of working-class militants by declaring lock-outs and hiring professional gunmen to attack anarchist leaders. The CNT retaliated in kind and until the coming of the dictatorship there was gang warfare in the streets.

During the Second Republic Barcelona was the great Republican city. CNT opposition to a bourgeois republic was the cause of constant strikes and occasional shootings. A major crisis came in Oct. 1934 when Companys declared a separate Catalan state. It was suppressed on the same day.

On July 19–20 1936 Barcelona was the scene of hard fighting between armed workers and the military insurgents. Thereafter, it witnessed a widespread anarchist collectivization of industry, then a power struggle between the anarchists and communists. After the battle of the Ebro, Barcelona fell to the Nationalists on 24 Jan. 1939, its industrial plant being handed over unharmed.   PP

BARCELONA, TREATY OF (1529), between the Emperor Charles V and Pope Clement VII. After Charles V's troops had sacked Rome in 1527, he decided that he needed the pope's friendship, since a lasting enmity would weaken his anti-Lutheran campaign in Germany and his hold on Italy. The pope (formerly Giulio de' Medici) was absorbed with dynastic interests and the restoration of the papal states. The result was the treaty of Barcelona, signed on 29 June. By it the emperor gave the papal states back to the pope and undertook to restore Florence to the Medici by force of arms. Further, as a pledge of friendship, the emperor gave his illegitimate daughter, Margaret, to Alessandro de' Medici, the pope's nephew. The imperial coronation was to take place in Italy, and the pope recognized Ferdinand, the brother of Charles V, as King of Bohemia and Hungary. Clement crowned Charles emperor on 25 Feb. 1530 at Bologna, and on 12 Aug. Florence fell to imperial troops. The republican constitution of the town was formally annulled (27 Aug. 1532) and Alessandro de' Medici was proclaimed Duke of Florence.

BARCLAY, WILLIAM (1546–1608), Scottish jurist who emigrated to France (1571), studied at Paris and Bourges, and became professor of civil law at Angers university. He was also a councillor of state and master of requests. His most important work was *De regno et regali potestate* (1600).

BARCLAY DE TOLLY, Prince (1761–1818), Russian general, commander in Finland (1808–9), and minister of war (1810–1813). He commanded the first army against Napoleon. After his policy of retreat had lost Smolensk (1812), he was replaced by Kutuzov, but was reinstated the next year and fought at Leipzig.

BARDOLI, a highly successful no-tax campaign (12 Feb.–4 Aug. 1928) in Bardoli *taluka*, Surat district, Bombay. Led by Sardar Vallabhbhai Patel and using *satyagraha* techniques, the campaign called for an impartial enquiry into the enhancement of land revenue by 22 per cent. A committee appointed (Aug. 1928) reported in March 1929 that the enhancement was excessive and recommended a nominal increase of 6¼ per cent.

BAREBONE'S PARLIAMENT (1653), nominated assembly of Puritan notables installed by Oliver Cromwell to rule the Commonwealth of England. Its name, acquired from Praise-God Barebone, one of the members for the City of London, was not given contemporaneously. The Rump of the Long Parliament was expelled on 20 April 1653. It was a hasty and unpremeditated act and Cromwell had no plan for a new government. He decided on a broad and respectable body which would consist of 'persons of approved fidelity and honesty . . . called from the several parts of this Commonwealth to the supreme authority'. The council of officers kept close control over the choosing of members. Suggestions for membership were received from the gathered churches, but they were generally prepared to leave the choice to Cromwell and his officers. Most of the members were nominated by the latter without consultation. The people looked to for membership were friends, kinsmen, old comrades, faithful members of the Rump, and any gentry faithful to the Commonwealth. Only three categories of people were disqualified: serving army officers; practising lawyers; practising 'accomptants' (ie, those who handled public funds). The total membership of 144 included five for Scotland, six for Ireland, and five co-opted members, including Cromwell and Harrison.

The assembly was addressed by Cromwell on 4 July, when he devolved the supreme authority on it till 3 Nov. 1654. On 5 July it assembled at Westminster and elected Francis Rous as speaker and co-opted the five members. On 6 July the members resolved to assume the name Parliament and established an executive council of state. Soon a division appeared in the membership and two parties formed over the question of the abolition of tithes on 15 July. The moderates defeated the radicals by 68 to 43. The former were not against ending tithes, but they wished to provide lay-improprietors with compensation for their loss of property. This fear for the safety of property was the main cause of the rift. Other factors were that the moderates detested the low social background of many of the radicals; that the radicals undertook measures which hit the army, eg, reducing pay, transferring officers, and abolishing the monthly assessment; that they tried to reduce, simplify, and codify the laws, eg, on 5 Aug. the Court of Chancery was abolished; and that they attempted to abolish another form of property—church patronage. The moderates began to fear a universal assault on traditional institutions. Cromwell, though he had lost patience by August with the parliament's attempt to frustrate the peace negotiations with the Dutch, tried to avoid taking sides.

On 2 Dec. the committee on tithes reported on a proposed scheme. On 10 Dec. the first clause was defeated by the radicals 56 to 54. Consequently, on the next day in private consultations, probably unbeknown to Cromwell, a group of moderates decided on a parliamentary abdication. They went early to the House on 12 Dec., and after a short debate the speaker and 40 members went to Whitehall and resigned their authority to Cromwell. The minority left at Westminster were ejected by soldiers. Cromwell, though surprised, accepted the resignation.

S. R. Gardiner, *History of the Commonwealth and Protectorate*, vol. 2 (London, 1897). CJ

BAREL CASE (1953), important decision of the French *Conseil d'État* under the Fourth Republic. Barel and four other students were refused permission to sit for the entrance examination of the *École Nationale d'Administration*. They appealed to the *Conseil d'État*, which ruled that the exclusion had been decided on political grounds rather than on merit, and overruled the government's decision.

BARENTS, WILLIAM (d. 1597), early Dutch navigator and explorer who sought a north-east passage to the Indies. In 1596 he discovered Bear Island and Spitzbergen before sailing east to winter in Novaya Zemlya. Here, by their ingeniousness, he and his associates survived the hardships of the Arctic conditions, but though his companions returned safely to Amsterdam in the summer of 1597, Barents died on the voyage.

BARÈRE DE VIEUZAC, BERTRAND (1755–1841), French Revolutionary politician and member of the Committee of Public Safety, who began his career in the National Assembly as a constitutional monarchist, but moved with the Revolu-

tion as it became more extreme. Barère's main achievement was his survival: he had responsibility for foreign affairs in the Committee, but deserted Robespierre at the crucial moment of his overthrow.

BARGHASH BIN SAID (reg. 1870–88), Sultan of Zanzibar, son of Said bin Sultan. He encouraged the expansion of trans-continental trade, which reached Uganda and the Congo. He replanted the clove plantations, ruined by a hurricane, and continued the policy of his father and brother of dependence on and, in the last resort, of submission to the will of Britain. In 1872 he was obliged to prohibit the slave trade. In 1885, abandoned by Britain, he was forced to surrender large areas of the mainland, over which he had exercised a paramount authority, to Germany, and in 1887 he handed over the administration of what was later to be the Kenya coast to the Imperial British East Africa Co.

BARGHAWATA, people of the Moroccan coast south of Salé, in the 8th–12th cents, characterized by an heretical religion with its own prophet and a Berber 'Koran'. They may have arisen from a Kharijite revolt (739–42), but the religion's spread dates from Yunus's headship (842–85). Its antecedents—Christian, Jewish, or Muslim—are uncertain. The Barghawata were considered infidels, coming under attack from Muslim neighbours from the late 10th cent. After being largely suppressed by the Almoravids, they disappeared with the Almohads' victory c. 1150.

BARI, town on the southern Adriatic coast of Italy much used for travel to Greece and the Levant. Until 1071 it was the Byzantine capital in southern Italy. Its commercial prosperity was hampered by lack of political autonomy. It rose unsuccessfully against the Byzantines in 1009 and rebelled repeatedly against the Normans, who conquered it in 1071 and temporarily destroyed it as a punishment for rebellion in 1156. Incorporated in a succession of aggressive territorial states, it could never henceforth rival the prosperity of the autonomous cities of central and northern Italy.

BARING, SIR FRANCIS (1740–1810), London merchant and founder of the merchant house of Baring.

BARISAN SOSIALIS (SOCIALIST FRONT), Singapore opposition party. Formed by pro-communist defectors from the ruling Peoples' Action Party in 1961, it seemed likely to gain control until being out-manœuvred by Lee Kuan Yew on the merger with Malaysia, which it opposed. It held 13 of the 51 Legislative seats until deciding to boycott the 1968 election in protest against the arrest of its main leadership.

BARKLY, SIR HENRY (1815–98), English colonial administrator, governor successively of British Guiana (1848–53), Jamaica (1853–56), Victoria (1856–63), Mauritius (1863–70), and Cape of Good Hope Colony (1870–77).

BARKUK, Mamluk Sultan of Egypt and Syria (1382–9, 1390–9), was bought as a slave in the Crimea. He rose (1377) to be *atabak al-asakir* (marshal of the armies) and in 1382 became sultan. He had to face a serious rebellion in Syria led by the powerful amirs Yilbugha and Mintash. Barkuk, defeated before Damascus and, again, outside Cairo in 1389, was deposed and imprisoned in Karak. He escaped and was able to regain the throne in 1390. His reign was the time when pre-eminence within the Mamluk regime began to pass from the Turks to the Circassians.

BARLOW, SIR GEORGE (1762–1847), servant of the English East India Co. He was in the revenue department under Cornwallis at the time of the Permanent Settlement of Bengal (1793) and as chief secretary to the government under Shore and Wellesley, until being made a member of the Supreme Council (1801). As acting governor-general (1805–1807), he continued Cornwallis's policy of non-intervention and even withdrew British protection from their former allies, the Rajput chiefs, who were sacrificed to the Marathas. As governor of Madras (Dec. 1807 until his recall in 1812), he suppressed the mutiny of the Madras officers and made himself unpopular because of his repellent manner. His career is one of many examples of a capable departmental officer not being a successful head of government.

BARMAK, name of a distinguished family high in the service of the first Abbasid caliphs. The most important members of the family were Khalid ibn Barmak (d. 781–2), prominent in the reigns of Al-Saffah and Al-Mansur as an administrator, and as the governor of Fars, of Tabaristan, and of Mosul; Yahya ibn Khalid, who was tutor and vizier to Harun al-Rashid, with full control over the affairs of the empire; and the sons of Yahya, Al-Fadl, and Ja'far, who assisted their father in the conduct of government. Yahya and his sons held office until 803, when the Barmak family fell into disgrace, Ja'far being executed in that year at the command of Harun al-Rashid and Yahya (d. 805), with Al-Fadl (d. 808), being imprisoned at Al-Rakka.

BARNABITES, order of the Clerks Regular of St Paul, founded in Milan by Antonio Zaccaria (1530), so-called because they met in the church of St Barnabas. They pledged themselves to monastic obligations and the study of Paul's epistles. Later there were about 20 Barnabite colleges in Europe, chiefly engaged in educational and missionary work.

BARNARD, CHRISTIAAN (1922–   ), South African surgeon who performed (1967) the first successful heart-transplant operation.

BARNARDO, THOMAS JOHN (1845–1905), British philanthropist. As a medical student in London from 1866, he became convinced by his spare-time work for evangelical organizations and ragged schools that London's destitute children must be cared for. He therefore abandoned his aim of becoming an overseas missionary and in 1867 opened the first of his famous children's homes at Stepney.

BARNAVE, ANTOINE PIERRE (1761–93), French protestant lawyer and one of the outstanding figures in the first stage of the French Revolution. Although he described himself as a constitutional monarchist, he wanted strict control of the monarch by denying him the right to veto legislation. He played a large part in carrying the Civil Constitution of the Clergy. After the Flight to Varennes, Barnave became less radical and actually negotiated secretly with the queen. It was the discovery of this correspondence which led to his execution.

BARNBURNERS, radical group of New York Democrats (1844–54), so-called because their conduct was held to be like that of the farmer who burnt his barn to kill the rats. Clashing with the national party over slavery, they helped create the Free-Soil Party (1848) and many joined the Republicans in 1854.

BARNES, SIR EDWARD (1776–1838), governor of Ceylon (1820–1, 1824–31), departed from his predecessor's, Maitland's, military policy of numerous fortresses and had roads built into the formerly almost inaccessible kingdom of Kandy, notably the Colombo–Kandy road. As well as for their military effectiveness, these roads proved essential for the transport of coffee, whose introduction Barnes encouraged.

BARNES, ROBERT (1495–1540), Franciscan theologian and leading English Lutheran reformer of the 1530s. He wrote the *Lives of the Popes* (1536) and was burnt for heresy shortly after the downfall of his patron, Thomas Cromwell.

BARNES, THOMAS (1785–1841), editor of *The Times* (1817–41). The paper already had the lead over others by reason of the superiority of its foreign news. Barnes, the first professional journalist to become editor, built it up to its predominant position as a paper independent of political groups, the proprietor, John Walter II, giving him a free hand as editor.

BARNET, BATTLE OF (13 April 1471), first of two disasters which ruined the cause of the Lancastrians in 1471. Their defeat was partly caused by division in their ranks between the followers of the Earl of Warwick (the Kingmaker) and Lancastrians of older standing. The treacherous Duke of Clarence, who had deserted his brother Edward IV for Warwick, rejoined him just before the battle. Warwick was confused by bad visibility, outflanked, and killed while retreating. It only remained for Edward to administer the final defeat to the Lancastrians at Tewkesbury (1471).

BAROCHE, PIERRE JULES (1802–70), French politician who won fame as a lawyer under the July monarchy and became one of Odilon Barrot's closest collaborators in opposition to Guizot's ministry. During the Second Republic he moved steadily to the right, becoming minister of the interior and then minister for foreign affairs (1851). A partisan of Napoleon III, he was made president of the council of state and helped build up the servile government majority in the legislature.

BAROMETER, instrument for measuring atmospheric pressure, invented by the Italian Torricelli, a pupil of Galileo, who found, with the aid of a mercury barometer, that the air exerts a definite pressure. Blaise Pascal, a Frenchman from Clermont, carried a barometer to the top of a mountain and showed that atmospheric pressure falls as altitude increases. These experiments developed the chief uses of the barometer, to enable seamen and meteorologists to foretell the weather, and pilots and mountaineers to calculate their height above sea-level.

BARONS' WARS, THE (1263–5). In 1263 civil war broke out in England between the barons, led by Simon de Montfort and Gilbert Earl of Gloucester, and King Henry III. Henry's misgovernment, favouritism of foreigners, and expensive continental entanglements had led to opposition in 1258, when he had submitted to baronial demands. Later he obtained papal release from his oath. In 1263 open war broke out, but by victory at the battle of Lewes (1264) Montfort gained control of England. He ruled from 1264 to 1265, calling a parliament which for the first time contained not only magnates but also representatives of shires and boroughs. But in 1265, having quarrelled with Gloucester, Montfort was killed and his army defeated at Evesham by Henry's son, Edward.

BARONY (English). The term was not originally a technical or well-defined one, but by the early 13th cent. a barony was beginning to be regarded as a particular form of feudal tenure with particular obligations. It consisted of a complex of estates, regarded as forming a single unit and dependent upon a key estate, known as the *caput*. The complex was said to be held *per baroniam*, a form of feudal tenure which seems to have implied that the feudal services due from the individual estates of the barony were treated as if due from the barony as a whole. In *Magna Carta* the relief paid on a barony was made equal to those of 20 knights. From the time of Edward I, it became increasingly accepted that the holding of a recognized barony made a baron and gave him the right to individual summons to the upper house of parliament. From 1387 baronies could be created by writ.

BAROQUE ARCHITECTURE, picturesque and emotive style of the 17th and 18th cents, was a revolt against the rigidities of Palladianism. It flourished chiefly in Roman Catholic countries and corresponded emotionally to the softening of the early austerities of the Counter-Reformation.

As it became less militant, the Counter-Reformation needed instinctively to enlarge its appeal to the mystical and non-rational elements in mankind, to demonstrate the glories of the faith in ways that were aesthetic and dramatic rather than intellectual. In its decadence baroque became wilful and eccentric, as in the unrestrained exuberance of José de Churriguera, but essentially it employed classical methods to achieve a controlled and harmonious effect. As in Gothic, the parts cannot be separated from the whole. Painting, sculpture, and structural design worked together to delight, astonish, and overwhelm. The interiors of baroque churches give an impression of continuous dramatic movement directed towards the altar as a stage lit by paintings, richly coloured marble, and groups of sculptured figures. 'By the splendour of the arts we honour a king.'

The first artist to experiment with baroque was Michelangelo, whose dome at St Peter's shows his occasional impatience with the orthodoxy of his time; but the movement really began at Rome during the pontificate of Urban VIII (1623–44). Its inspiration was the nave and facade designed for St Peter's by Carlo Maderna, whose greatest successors were Bernini, Borromini, and Cortona. These men were painters and sculptors as well as architects, and in their work, secular as well as religious, the freedom of the baroque conception was always disciplined by the obligation of all the arts to contribute to an indivisible unity.

For more than a century baroque was a dominant style in Italy, Spain, and especially southern Germany (where a fine example is Johann Neumann's church of Vierzehnheiligen in Franconia), but it had much less impact in the protestant areas to the north, where the universal character of art was giving way to the aristocratic idea that it belonged only to a handful of the educated and wealthy. In England, however, Wren introduced occasional baroque variations, and much of the work of Vanbrugh, Hawksmoor, and Thomas Archer was in this style.

In painting baroque is recognizable by the clever patterning of light and shade and colour, the flowing draperies, the character borne on tufted clouds, a massed impression of euphoric but slightly unhealthy podginess. Baroque was never afraid of seeming somewhat unreal, because that was how it achieved its effects. First popularized in Rome by Cortona and Lanfranco, it found a painter of genius in Rubens. He had numerous imitators in Italy, but in Spain the cool realism of Velasquez was a restraining influence on the softer expansiveness of Murillo and his school. Nor did baroque painting ever become very fashionable in France or England.

N. Pevsner, *An Outline of European Architecture* (London, 1963).
R. Wittkower, *Art and Architecture in Italy: 1600–1750* (London, 1958).   MMR

BAROQUE MUSIC, term used in connection with works produced between the end of the 16th cent. and the middle of the 18th cent. Opera was an early development, principally through the efforts of the Florentine *camerata* (1600), who revived what they considered to be the principles of declamation in the classical Greek theatre; baroque music paid greater attention than that of the Renaissance to the expression of emotion, both melodically and harmonically.

An essential characteristic of the period is the thoroughbass, which requires a player to improvise harmonies over a given bass part; the practice was mentioned as early as 1553. Equal importance was given to the melodic part, thus continuing a development seen in the later madrigals; but polyphony survived throughout the period.

BARRACKPORE, MUTINIES AT (1824 and 1857). In Oct. 1824 the 47th Bengal Native Infantry, who had been ordered to Burma, became discontented because they feared that they would be sent by sea and thus lose caste. There were also rumours that the British had suffered serious reverses in

Burma. On 1 Nov. they mutinied on parade. A battery of European artillery opened fire on the mutineers, who suffered heavy casualties. The regiment was disbanded.

In 1857 the sepoy army was disturbed by rumours that they would lose caste by using greased cartridges and that they were to be forcibly converted to Christianity. On 29 March, Mangal Pande, a sepoy of the 34th Native Infantry, attempted to kill the European adjutant. He was tried by court-martial and hanged and the regiment was disbanded.

BARRAS, PAUL FRANÇOIS, Vicomte de (1755–1829), French politician who was largely responsible for Napoleon's rise to power. He had been a Jacobin, but led the troops who arrested Robespierre. On 1 Nov. 1795 he became one of the Directors and remained as such until Napoleon's *coup d'état* of *Brumaire*. He first gave Napoleon prominence by giving him command of the troops who suppressed the royalist rising of *Vendémiaire* (1795). He encouraged him to marry Josephine, and had him appointed commander of the army in Italy (1796). Barras connived in the *Brumaire* coup but was immediately pushed out of political life. His notorious financial and moral corruption made him too much of a liability for Napoleon to employ him.

BARRICADES, DAYS OF THE (1588 and 1648). In 1588, during the French wars of religion, Henry III and his mercenary troops were driven out of Paris by the duc de Guise and his supporters in the Catholic League, who mistrusted the king's willingness and capacity to maintain the pre-eminence of the Catholic faith in France. In 1648 another episode marked the beginning of the civil disturbances in France known as the Fronde. Two of the government's most outspoken critics, Broussel and Blancmesnil, magistrates in the *parlement* of Paris, were arrested, and this precipitated a riot of the poorer people of the capital in their support. Paris was in a state of disorder and confusion between 26 and 28 Aug., and, only with the magistrates' release was order temporarily restored.

BARRIENTOS ORTUÑO, RENÉ (1920–69), Bolivian air force officer and president. While vice-president under Victor Paz Estenssoro, he withdrew to Cochabamba and led a successful revolt from there in 1964. In 1966 he called elections and emerged as president, in which capacity he favoured the army and attacked the tin miners.

BARRIER FORTRESSES, line of fortresses in the Spanish (later Austrian) Netherlands garrisoned by Dutch troops and providing an advanced line of defence for the United Provinces. The fortresses, maintained from local rates, were of great commercial value to the Dutch, but as a defensive chain proved militarily unsound, as was shown by Saxe in 1745. However, their original purpose was not as a protective chain on foreign soil, but to hold up and denude an invading army allowing the Republic time to build up an army of defence. Viewed in this light, the fortresses were militarily satisfactory.

BARRIER TREATIES (1709 and 1713). In 1709 there was a mutual guarantee of certain war aims between the Whig government of Britain and the United Provinces. The Dutch obtained British agreement to their occupation of a line of fortresses in the Spanish Netherlands and in return guaranteed the Protestant Succession in England. In 1713 a replacement treaty was forced on the Dutch by the new Tory government. The Dutch again guaranteed the Protestant Succession in England, but the number of fortresses for their occupation was far fewer than that agreed in the earlier treaty.

BARRINGTON OF ARDGLASS, WILLIAM WILDMAN, 2nd Viscount (Irish) (1717–93), British secretary at war during the American War of Independence, having been appointed in 1765 at the wish of George III. The secretary at war was responsible for the equipment and training of troops, but not for strategy or for the overall strength of the army. Barrington was throughout pessimistic of the possibility of winning the war on land because of shortage of troops. He was blamed for sending untrained German mercenaries to America.

BARRIOS, JUSTO RUFINO (1835–85), Guatemalan general and Liberal president. Barrios ruled the nation strictly for 12 years (1873–85). Noted for his anti-clericalism, he expropriated Catholic Church property and prohibited clerical participation in education. Barrios believed in the fostering of export crops to achieve national prosperity, and stimulated the growing of coffee, cotton, rice, and other staples. His desire to reunite the defunct Central American Confederation caused him to interfere in the affairs of Honduras and El Salvador in favour of Liberals.

BARROS ARANA, DIEGO (1830–1907), Chilean historian, lawyer, and educator. Twice rector of Chile University, and a political exile for long periods. His most famous work is his multi-volume *Historia general de Chile*.

BARROT, CAMILLE-HYACINTHE-ODILON (1791–1873), French statesman and moderate monarchist, prominent in the period 1830–49. In 1830 he discouraged Lafayette from proclaiming a republic, and thus may be considered one of the founders of the July Monarchy. He was prefect of the Seine in the 1830s and a deputy, but only held office during the ministries of Thiers. In the revolution of 1848 he argued unsuccessfully for another monarchical constitution, and formed the first ministry of Louis Napoleon's presidency (Dec. 1848). After supporting the French expedition against the Roman republic (1849), he was dismissed from office. He resisted Louis Napoleon's *coup d'état* of 1851 and thereafter lived in retirement.

BARROW, HENRY (d. 1593), radical Puritan, who, with John Greenwood, the probable author of the Marprelate Tracts, led the Separatist or gathered church in London until 1587. The Separatists, like the Puritans, wanted to purge the Elizabethan Church of forms which remained in it as a compromise with the past, particularly the episcopacy and the use of vestments and words of eucharistic significance, but for Barrow the complete separation of independent congregations from the civil power was only a regrettable necessity in the face of Abp Whitgift's determined conservatism and the inquisitorial procedure of the ecclesiastical commission. He applied his learning to the composition of tracts, and after six years of imprisonment, and examinations before the High Commission, he and Greenwood were executed.

BARROW, ISAAC (1630–77), English theologian and mathematician, wrote mathematical works that were admired by his pupil Newton and sermons that excited Coleridge by their 'verbal imagination'. In addition to treatises on optics and geometry, Barrow wrote *Euclidis Elementa* (1655) and *Archimedis Opera* (1675). In theology his principal work was an *Exposition of the Creed, Decalogue and Sacraments* (1669). His posthumous discussion of *The Pope's Supremacy* (1680) contended that the authority of St Peter was personal to him alone and was not transmitted, and that the early bishops of Rome had no supreme jurisdiction. Barrow became Master of Trinity College, Cambridge, in 1672 and when vice-chancellor of the university (1675–6) he wished to build a theatre, schools, and library 'by which we may come nearer in beauty to our dear and beautiful sister, Oxford'. Frustrated in this, he founded the famous library at his own college.

BARROW, SIR JOHN (1764–1848), second secretary of the admiralty (1804–6) and secretary (1807–45). As second secretary he used his influence and planning ability to further exploration of the Arctic and the search for the North-West Passage, particularly the voyages of David Buchan and John

Ross. He was disappointed by the results obtained by the latter and remained convinced that Lancaster Sound was not landlocked, an opinion shared by Ross's second-in-command Edward Parry, who discovered (1819) the main east–west passage through the Arctic islands between the Lancaster and Viscount Melville Sounds and named the central section Barrow Straits. He was Sir James Graham's right-hand man in putting through the naval reforms of the 1830s. He wrote summaries of Arctic exploration in 1818 and 1846.

BARRY, SIR CHARLES (1795–1860), English architect, much of whose work was in an Italian Renaissance style, *eg*, the Travellers' and Reform Clubs, Cliveden, and Harewood House. His best-known work is the exterior of the Houses of Parliament (1840–60).

BARRY, SIR REDMOND (1813–80), Irish barrister, who settled in Melbourne. As first solicitor-general in the separated colony of Victoria (1851) and on the bench of its new supreme court (1852), he was conservative and a severe, though conscientious, judge, presiding dispassionately over the Eureka riot trials and that of Ned Kelly (1880). Barry's reputation rested mainly on his social, cultural, and philanthropic activities, which included his work as a founder and first chancellor of Melbourne University and as president of the trustees of the Public Library.

BARSBY, Mamluk Sultan of Egypt and Syria (1422–38), who launched a successful expedition to assert his suzerainty over Cyprus (1426) and a disastrous campaign against Iraq (1433).

BARTENSTEIN, JOHANN CHRISTOPHE (1690–1766), Austrian secretary or *Referendar* to the privy council under the Emperor Charles VI and later Maria Theresa. He was the effective head of the Austrian administration, though non-noble by birth. He did not believe in the centralization of the scattered Habsburg lands and allowed each component to keep its own institutions. He was superseded by Haugwitz.

BARTH, HEINRICH (1821–65), German scholar and explorer. In 1849, having travelled extensively in North Africa and the Near East, Barth joined a British mission of exploration to central Africa, led by James Richardson and in the company of Dr Vogel. During a journey lasting nearly six years he travelled from Tripoli through Aïr, Bornu, and the Hausa states to Timbuctoo, surviving numerous deprivations and illnesses, as well as the death of his two companions.

The five-volume account of his *Travels and Discoveries*, published in both German and English (1857, reprinted, London, 1967), gives the history and culture of the peoples through whose territories he passed. His *Central African Vocabularies* gave Europe its first serious knowledge of several African languages.

BARTHÉLEMY, AUGUSTE MARSEILLE (1796–1867), French political satirist. Contemporaries looked on him as a political chameleon, since his satirical poems oscillated between support for and opposition to the regimes of both Charles X and Louis Philippe. After 1848, however, he remained a constant supporter of the Bonapartist cause.

BARTHÉLEMY, JEAN JACQUES, Abbe (1716–95), French scholar and antiquarian, particularly interested in mid-18th-cent. discoveries in Italy (*eg*, at Herculaneum). His *Voyage du jeune Anacharsis en Grèce* (1779), a reconstruction of life in 4th-cent. Greece, was translated into several languages, as were his letters describing his own travels in Italy.

BARTHÉLEMY, JOSEPH (1874–1945), minister of the Vichy regime in France, and an example of its 'respectable' supporters. Barthélemy was a distinguished authority on constitutional and international law who had sat as a conservative in the parliament of the Third Republic. As minister of justice (1941–3), he was noted for his persecution of communists. Arrested in 1944, he died while awaiting trial.

BARTHOU, LOUIS-JEAN-FIRMIN (1862–1934), French right-wing statesman closely associated with Poincaré. Barthou became prominent as minister of public works under Sarrien and Clemenceau (1906–9) and served as minister of justice under Briand (1909–10 and 1913). On the fall of Briand, he formed his own ministry, which was notable for raising, against strong left-wing opposition, the term of military service to three years. He entered Painlevé's ministry as foreign minister (1917), was minister of war under Briand (1921), and of justice under Poincaré, both in 1922 (when he led the French delegation to the Genoa conference), and again in 1926–9. Barthou returned to office in Doumergue's government as foreign minister. The renewed threat from Germany made him anxious to revive the Franco-Russian alliance and the Little Entente. He was assassinated with Alexander of Yugoslavia at Marseilles (Oct. 1934), when the latter was on a diplomatic visit connected with this policy.

BARTOLO DI SASSOFERRATO (1313–57), teacher of law at Pisa and Perugia, who developed a system of applying the principles of Roman civil law according to scholastic method, thus founding the school of jurists known as Bartolists.

BARTOLOMMEO DI PAGHOLO, Fra (1475–1517), Florentine painter, who was one of the first to use the lay figure. He influenced Italian art by his insistence on symmetrical composition, later developed by Raphael, and his skilful use of light and shade and rich impasto colouring.

BARTON, SIR EDMUND (1849–1920), first prime minister of the Australian Commonwealth, was born in Sydney. Called to the bar in 1871, he entered the colonial parliament in 1879 as a protectionist and was Speaker of the Legislative Assembly (1883–7). His vigorous advocacy of federation made him the undisputed leader of the movement throughout Australia, notably at the 1897–8 federal convention. This prompted his eventual selection as the first prime minister. During two years of significant, formative legislation he presided with tact and skill over a 'cabinet of giants' who had all held high office in the federating colonies. On the formation of the High Court of Australia in 1903, he became second justice of the court under Sir Samuel Griffith. His abilities showed to the full when he was challenged by a great cause, such as federation.

BARTON, ELIZABETH (1506–34), 'the nun of Kent', a servant-girl subject to epileptic trances in which she delivered prophecies. Her supposed inspiration was exploited by opponents of Henry VIII's 'divorce', and after she had prophesied his death if he married Anne Boleyn she and four associates were executed.

BARTRAM, JOHN M. (1699–1777), American naturalist, called by Linnaeus 'the greatest natural botanist in the world'. Bartram conducted the first experiments in hybridization in the New World (1728), and established what was probably the first botanical garden in America. He was a prolific and ubiquitous naturalist, as well as an ornithologist, archaeologist, anthropologist (in his study of the American Indian), geologist, and lepidopterist. He explored the east coast of the US and published an account of his travels (1751). He became (1765) botanist to King George III, the stipend from which post allowed him to continue his explorations. He passed on his love of nature to his son, William Bartram (1793–1823), and together they explored central Florida (1765–66). William also explored the south-east part of America (1773–7). William later joined his brother in running the botanical garden inherited by their father, and continued his work there.

BARUCH, BERNARD MANNES (1870–1965), US financier, political adviser, and public servant. Before he was 30, he acquired great wealth and fame as a speculator on the New York Stock Exchange. Thereafter he became one of the most influential private citizens in the US. During the First World War he served as a member of the advisory committee of the Council of National Defense, and as chairman of the war industries board (1918), which mobilized the economy for war. As one of President Wilson's leading advisers, he attended the Paris peace conference and was a member of the supreme economic council in Paris. In Oct. 1919 he served as chairman of the president's National Industrial Conference in Washington. During the 1920s and 1930s Baruch continued to be an unofficial aide, confidant, friend, and patron of financial, business, and political leaders. He was often consulted by F. D. Roosevelt, and during the Second World War his influence was considerable as an adviser on strategic materials and manpower for industrial mobilization. At the age of 75 he returned to government service as a member of the US delegation to the UN Atomic Energy Commission (1945–6).

BARUCH PLAN (14 June 1946), US proposal for international control of nuclear weapons and the sources of atomic energy. Based on the earlier Acheson–Lilienthal plan, and named after Bernard M. Baruch, the plan provided for international inspection of atomic energy establishments and suspension of the veto power in the UN Security Council. No action was taken by the UN Atomic Energy Commission after objections by the USSR, Britain, and others.

BÄRWALDE, TREATY OF (1631), culmination of the long-projected alliance between France and Sweden, by which Richelieu hoped to secure the safety of France in her dynastic conflict with the Habsburgs. Gustavus II Adolphus was to keep an army of 30,000 foot and 600 horse in Germany, part of the expense being borne by France. Richelieu was to pay a twice-yearly subsidy, in exchange for which Gustavus promised freedom of worship for Catholics in Germany, and agreed not to make a separate peace for five years.

BARWELL, RICHARD (1741–1804), son of William Barwell, governor of Bengal. He was appointed a member of the Bengal Council under the Regulating Act of 1773, and supported Warren Hastings against the hostile majority. In 1780 he retired with an enormous fortune and bought an estate at Stanstead, Sussex. A typical nabob, he was detested by the local gentry.

BARWICK, SIR GARFIELD EDWARD JOHN (1903–), Chief Justice of the High Court of Australia (1964–), was called to the NSW bar in 1927. The most prominent practising barrister in Australia during the late 1940s and 1950s, Barwick appeared in the Bank Nationalization and Communist Party Dissolution cases. A Commonwealth MP (1958–64), he was attorney-general (1958–63) and also minister for external affairs (1961–4). He was responsible for the introduction of notable legislation including the Matrimonial Causes and Marriage Acts, and was also charged with the difficult task of conducting Australia's relations with Indonesia during the West Irian and Malaysian confrontation disputes.

BASCIO, MATTEO DA (c. 1495–1552), Italian monk from Urbino, the founder and first vicar-general of the Capuchins. He decided that the Franciscans of his time had departed in some respects from the rule of their founder, notably in no longer wearing a pointed hood (capuche), and Clement VII authorized him to institute an order obedient to the rigid Franciscan observance (1528).

BASCO Y VARGAS, JOSE (1731–1805), Spanish sailor, who became governor-general of the Philippines (1778–87). He embarked on a major project for economic development and strengthened the colony's fortifications and defences. He undertook military expeditions to subjugate ethnic minorities, and conquered the Batanes islands, north of Luzon. He also organized the Chinese communities outside the city gates of Manila and settled some of them in Pampanga. He improved the schools and encouraged the study of the Spanish language. In the economic field, he provided incentives to agriculturists as well as those prospecting for and mining minerals, and encouraged the establishment of factories. On his recommendation a royal decree of 1781 created the Economic Society of Friends of the Country, to be funded by merchants from a percentage of the galleon rights. Another significant innovation of Basco's administration was the establishment of government monopolies as a source of income, the most lucrative—but the most odious to the people—being the tobacco monopoly established in 1782. It lasted for a century, and not only balanced the colony's budget, but also reversed the flow of revenue from the Philippines to Spain. A decree of 1785 created the Royal Co. of the Philippines. Despite his achievements, there was opposition to Basco's reformist policies and resentment against the monopolies resulted in sporadic uprisings. Basco resigned his governorship in 1787 and returned to Spain, where he was promoted to be commodore of the Spanish royal navy, ennobled, and made governor of Cartagena. His career in the Philippines paved the way towards accelerated agricultural, commercial, and industrial developments in the 19th cent.

H. de la Costa, *Readings in Philippine History* (Manila, 1965).

JMS

BASHKIR, Turkish people of southern Urals, conquered by Russia during the 17th–18th cents. After an unsuccessful attempt to reassert their independence (1918–20), the Bashkirs were integrated in the Soviet Union, especially in the Bashkir ASSR.

BASIC DEMOCRACY, system of councils established in Pakistan by order of President Ayub Khan (Oct. 1959) to act both as local government units and as an electoral college for Pakistan. The 8000 local councils each had ten members, elected by adult suffrage. Above these were councils up to provincial level, each composed equally of chairmen of lower councils and nominated officials and experts. Local councils were expected to maintain village police and registration facilities with local funds and all were expected to promote developmental activities. The system was used as an electoral college in presidential elections (1960, 1964) and in elections for the national and provincial assemblies (1962). The system, dominated by influential local notables, forced such men to seek popular support and, therefore, although they did not provide a solution to Pakistan's constitutional problems or a means of dispensing with political parties, the councils made possible some local political development in Pakistan in the early 1960s.

BASIL I (*reg.* 867–86), Byzantine Emperor and founder of the Macedonian line which held the imperial throne for almost two centuries (867–1056). He rose to prominence through the favour of Michael III, whom he killed in order to seize the throne. His reign saw the destruction of Tephrike, the centre of the Paulician sect, in Asia Minor and also the reassertion of Byzantine influence in the south Italian lands. His most remarkable achievement, however, was to initiate a programme of legal reform which was realized in full during the reign of his son, Leo VI.

BASIL II (958–1025), called Bulgaroctonus ('Slayer of the Bulgars'), Byzantine Emperor (*reg.* 963–1025). At first he had to share power with powerful co-emperors, Nicephorus Phocas and John Tzimisces, and was not completely master of the empire until 989. He was able to maintain Byzantine influence in the north Syrian marchlands against the armies of the Fatimid caliphate in Egypt and Syria and to incorporate into the Byzantine empire portions of Armenia. The great achievement of his reign was the conquest of Bulgaria (986–1018). Under Basil II, one of the greatest of the soldiers and statesmen to rule at Constantinople, the Byzantine empire attained the summit of its medieval greatness.

BASIL, Saint (c. 330–79), Bp of Caesarea in Cappadocia, whose energies were devoted to winning support for Catholic orthodoxy under the Arian regime of the Emperor Valens (364–78), and to monastic organization, of which he was an early champion.

BASILEUS, Greek 'king'. The hereditary *basileus* and his council constituted the normal government of Greek states in the Geometric Period (c. 1000–750 BC). With the emergence of the city-state and the introduction of elected aristocratic magistrates (c. 700) hereditary kings generally disappeared. Except at Sparta and in the more backward areas of northern Greece, *eg*, Thessaly and Macedonia, only the title '*basileus*' remained to describe an elected magistrate particularly concerned with matters of state religion. The Macedonian domination of Greece and conquest of Persia (338–325) restored hereditary kingship to the Greek world in the form of the *basileus* of the Hellenistic kingdoms.

BASIN, THOMAS, bishop (1412–91), Bp of Lisieux and councillor of Charles VII. After being exiled in 1465 by Louis XI, he wrote valuable histories of the reigns of these two kings. Though marred by hostility to Louis, they form a major source for the history of France in the 15th cent.

BASKERVILLE, SIR THOMAS (d. 1597), English soldier, who so gallantly defended Sluys that he was embraced by the victorious Parma after its capitulation (1587). He served under Willoughby in supporting Henry IV (1589) and later commanded the English contingent in Brittany and Picardy (1594–5). In 1595–6 he was general of 'the Indian Armada', an unsuccessful raid on the Caribbean, and brought the fleet home after the two naval commanders, Drake and Hawkins, had died at sea.

BASLE, COUNCIL OF (1431–49), a general council of the church which marked both the culmination of the Conciliar Movement and the greatest pre-Reformation challenge to papal supremacy. The extremism of the council lost it general support and the papal initiative which led to the nominal reunion of the Greek and Roman churches at the council of Ferrara-Florence (1438–9) ensured its failure.

BASLE, PEACE OF (1795), brought the withdrawal of Prussia and Spain from the First Coalition against Revolutionary France. The war had become of secondary importance to Prussia. Her military defeats, and increasing anxiety that Catherine the Great of Russia intended to absorb all Poland, meant that Prussia had no qualms over deserting her Austrian and English allies. In return for Prussia's accepting the Rhine frontier, France agreed in the peace (5 April) to the neutralization of northern Germany under Prussian guarantee. A few months later (22 July) Spain also made peace, merely ceding to France her half of the island of St Domingo.

BASMACHI MOVEMENT, Muslim anti-Bolshevik guerrilla revolt with nationalist elements which began in Farghana (1918) and spread throughout Soviet Central Asia. In 1921 Enver Pasha became the leader, but after his defeat and death (1922) the movement disintegrated, although persisting for some years in isolated areas.

BASQUE PROVINCES of Spain, Vizcaya, Guipúzcoa, Álava, and Navarre during the 1920s and 1930s formed a centre of important political and economic activity. Before the First World War the iron foundries of the Vizcayan port of Bilbao and nearby cement and paper works made the region the scene of rapid expansion in industry and banking. The national economic programmes of Primo de Rivera (1923–30) involved principally Basque finance. The iron foundry workers made Bilbao an early centre of Spanish socialism; the Vizcayan miners, with those of Asturias, were the nascent Communist Party's main strength after 1921. The Church and small farmers supported Basque separatism. Large industrialists had participated in founding the separatist party (PNV) in 1894; their subsequent association with the central government diminished their interest in the cause. The PNV, claiming the *fueros*, self-governing privileges lost during the 19th cent. as the penalty for supporting Carlism, never won Navarre, the least industrialized province, from the Carlist allegiance.

The PNV was at first antagonized by the anti-clericalism of the Second Republic. In 1931 and 1933 it formed an electoral bloc with Catholic and right-wing parties, including the Carlists. However, Basque nationalism diverged from Navarrese Carlism in June 1932, when, at Pamplona, delegates of all the Basque provinces except Navarre approved the government's proposed statute of autonomy. In 1936 the PNV voted with the Popular Front. When the Civil War broke out, Vizcaya, Guipúzcoa, and Álava allied themselves with the Republic, which granted them autonomy in Oct. 1936. The nationalists conquered the provinces in 1937. German aircraft bombed Guernica, the ancient Basque capital, in April; Bilbao surrendered to Gen. Mola shortly afterwards; and in Sept. Guipúzcoa was overrun from Navarre by Falangist and Carlist militias. ASJ

BASS, GEORGE (1771–*c*. 1803), born in Lincolnshire, served a surgeon's apprenticeship, and at 18 joined the Royal Navy. In 1794–5 he sailed aboard *Reliance* to NSW and contributed to Australian exploration by both sea and land. In 1797 he indicated the existence of what became known as Bass Strait, proof of which came in 1798–9, when he and Matthew Flinders circumnavigated Van Diemen's Land. After returning to England, Bass sailed back to Australia in 1801 to exploit the commercial resources of the Pacific. He left Sydney in 1803, seeking piratical trade with Spanish America, and was heard of no more.

BASSEIN, TREATY OF (31 Dec. 1802), between Lord Wellesley and Baji Rao II, the peshwa or titular head of the Maratha confederacy. Wellesley's efforts to persuade each member of the confederacy to subscribe to a separate subsidiary alliance ended in failure, as did his earlier effort to form a similar alliance with the peshwa. Dissensions in the confederacy were followed by the flight of the peshwa to Bassein (1802), where he entered into a subsidiary alliance with the English Co. He agreed to maintain a subsidiary force inside his dominions; to exclude all Europeans hostile to the company; to relinquish all claims on Surat; to recognize engagements between the Gaekwar and the company; to abstain from negotiations or hostilities with other states; and to accept British arbitration in disputes with the nizam and the gaekwar. This made war inevitable between the British and the Raja of Berar and Daulat Rao Sindhia.

BASTIAT, FRÉDÉRIC (1801–50), economic writer and chief of the classical economists in France. A strong free trader, he hoped to organize a movement in France similar to the Anti-Corn Law League, but was unsuccessful.

BASTID, PAUL (1892–), French radical politician, journalist, and expert on constitutional law. As a member of parliament (1924–40 and 1946–51) he took a special interest in international questions, and represented France at the League of Nations. He was minister of commerce in Blum's Popular Front government (1936–7), and active in the Resistance.

BASTIDE, JULES (1800–79), French left-wing politician and journalist, involved in the July revolution (1830). After

taking part in a rising at Grenoble (1834) he spent two years' exile in London. He returned to France in 1836 and founded, with Buchez, the *Revue Nationale*. In the republic of 1848 he was foreign minister under Lamartine and Cavaignac. When Louis Napoleon became president he went into opposition.

BASTILLE, FALL OF (1789), marks the symbolic opening of the French Revolution. The Parisian lower classes stormed this former prison on 14 July and for the first time significantly changed the course of the revolution.

BASUTO PEOPLE, fleeing from the wars of the Mfecane in the 1820s in South Africa, were led by Moshweshwe to form the nation of Lesotho. They came into conflict with the Free State Boers, to whom they lost much land, and passed under British protection in 1868. The Basuto won the Gun War (1880–1), against the Cape government, and from 1884 were ruled directly by Britain. Lesotho regained political independence in 1966, although it is economically dependent upon South Africa, which surrounds it geographically.

BATAVI, early German tribe living in the Rhine delta, their name surviving in the district of Betuwe. They became effectively subject to Rome under Augustus, supplying auxiliary troops to the Roman army, but remaining free from tribute. They raised a formidable revolt (AD 69–70) along the Rhine under Julius Civilis, which was suppressed with difficulty. Subsequently, they became unimportant and in the 4th cent. ceased to have an independent existence, merging with the Franks.

BATAVIA (mod. Djakarta), capital of Indonesia, founded (30 May 1619) as the headquarters of the Dutch East India Co. by Jan Pieterszoon Coen, a commercial agent and administrator, who became governor-general of Batavia (1627).

Batavia was also the name of a Dutch merchant ship wrecked on the Abrolhos islands off Western Australia (June 1629). Leaving the surviving passengers and crew on the islands, the master, Pelsaert, sailed in an open boat to Java for aid. During his absence some of the crew massacred others and seized the *Batavia*'s treasure. Survivors contacted Pelsaert on his return and the mutineers were executed or otherwise punished. Two, marooned on the mainland, were the first white settlers in Australia.

BATAVIAN REPUBLIC (1795–1806), set up by the Dutch 'patriots' after the French occupation of the Dutch republic (Jan. 1795). It was the first of France's five satellite 'sister republics' and the most difficult to control. On the whole, the constitutions of the republic followed the changes in France, although the Dutch held longer to a democratic system. Napoleon forced a new constitution on them (1801) after its rejection by a plebiscite. Throughout its existence the republic had to support a French occupation force and contribute militarily and financially to France's war effort. In the course of the war they rapidly lost their remaining colonies to England. The republic disappeared when Napoleon abolished it (1806) and made his brother, Louis, king in an attempt to associate the country more closely with his economic isolation of England.

BATES, DAISY (née O'Dwyer Hunt) (1861–1951), known as Kabbarli ('grandmother') by Australian Aborigines, among whom she spent much of her life, emigrated in 1884 and travelled extensively in the outback of NSW and western Qld with her Australian husband and, later, in western and central parts of the continent. As a journalist in England (1884–9), she was sent by the London *Times* to report on alleged maltreatment of WA Aborigines and, following her husband's death, became increasingly involved in Aboriginal welfare work. Sometimes enjoying official status from WA or SA governments, though more frequently under her own auspices, Daisy Bates gained national recognition through her 16 years' residence with Aborigines on the Nullarbor plain at Ooldea. At this siding on the trans-continental railway, she tended the sick, the young, and the aged; respected tribal customs; and collected valuable material now in the National Library, Canberra. She published a commentary on her life and experiences, *The Passing of the Aborigines* (1938).

BATE'S CASE (1606), in which an English merchant, John Bate, refused to pay customs duty or imposition on currants, which he believed to be illegal. Chief Baron Fleming in the court of exchequer ruled that the duties were newly levied by the king, without parliamentary authority, in order to augment his revenue; that the king's power was both ordinary, *ie*, subject to parliament, and absolute, *ie*, governed by rules of policy; and that customs duties were part of foreign trade, all foreign affairs being part of the king's absolute power. Thus he found that impositions were rightly levied by this extraordinary prerogative, so long as they were used to regulate foreign commerce and not solely for purposes of taxation.

BA'TH PARTY, Arab political party, founded (1943) by Michel Aflaq and Salah al-Din al-Bitar, centred in Syria, but with branches in other Arab countries, especially Iraq, and advocating Arab unity, socialism, and neutralism.

BATHORY, STEPHEN (1532–86), elected Prince of Transylvania (1571) and King of Poland (1575). A highly intelligent and cultured man, his interest in humanism sprang from his education at Padua. He was also a gifted soldier and a powerful monarch. Under his leadership (1576–86) Poland enjoyed both military glory and political prestige. Although an ardent Roman Catholic, he showed remarkable tolerance, believing that the Tridentine reforms should be imposed by example, not by force. To divert Poland's energies from religious quarrels he embarked upon war against the traditional enemy, Muscovy. In 1578 he routed the forces of Ivan the Terrible at Wenden, and after four years of military success forced him to accept a humiliating truce (1582), ceding all non-Swedish Livonia to Poland. Muscovy's eclipse, accelerated by the death of Ivan in 1584, left Poland supreme in eastern Europe. Meanwhile, Stephen became involved in a grandiose crusade against Turkey to enable Poland to unite with Hungary and Muscovy in a vast eastern empire, but he died before it was launched.

BATHS, ROMAN. The public bath buildings were important features of both the architecture and the social life of many cities of the Roman empire. Providing facilities for exercise and leisurely converse, as well as hot and cold bathing, they were often lavishly constructed, and the ruins of those built in Rome by Caracalla and Diocletian are impressive examples of Roman brickwork on the grand scale, their vaulted main halls foreshadowing the naves of later basilicas and medieval cathedrals. Important ruins elsewhere are at Antioch (Antakiya, south-eastern Turkey), Aquae Sulis (Bath, Britain), Leptis Magna (Tripolitania), Pompeii, and Augusta Treverorum (Trier, Germany).

BATHURST, HENRY BATHURST, 2nd Earl (1714–94), British MP and lord chancellor. Until the death of Frederick, Prince of Wales, Bathurst had been a member of his opposition group. The Pelhamite government made him a judge of the common pleas (1754). To most people's surprise he was brought into Lord North's ministry as lord chancellor (1771). Though totally unfitted for the post, he retained it till 1778, when he was made lord president of the council.

BATHURST, HENRY BATHURST, 3rd Earl (1762–1834), British Tory statesman. He was president of the board of trade (1807–9), foreign secretary (1809–12), secretary for war and colonies (1812–27), and lord president of the Council (1828–30). At the board of trade he introduced the policy of Orders in Council. As secretary for war and colonies he was

responsible for the campaign in the Peninsula, and improvement in the conduct of the war coincided with his appointment. In Wellington's administration (1828–30) he was sympathetic to Catholic Emancipation.

BATHURST, capital of British settlements in the Gambia, founded in 1816 on St Mary's island at the estuary of the Gambia river, soon replaced Fort James, the earlier centre of British trade upstream. The population of St Mary's island comprised people who had migrated there from various parts of the Gambia river, liberated Africans from Sierra Leone, and descendants of immigrants from the neighbouring French colonies of Saint Louis and Gorée, who had arrived during and after the Napoleonic wars. The main significance of Bathurst lay in its commercial potentialities. It was the main centre of the Gambia's mercantile activities, of the ground-nut trade with Europe, and of the shipping carrying the trade of the Gambia to other parts of Africa, especially Sierra Leone. Today Bathurst is the capital of the independent state of Gambia, surrounded by the republic of Senegal.

BATISTA Y ZALDÍVAR, FULGENCIO (1901–), Cuban president and army officer. Batista joined the army in 1921 and began to participate in politics as an opponent of the dictator Gerardo Machado. After the fall of Machado, Batista was a leader of the *coup d'état* which placed Ramón Grau San Martín in the presidency. Because of his role in this coup, Batista rose quickly through the ranks and assumed the role of king-maker. Between 1933 and 1940 presidents governed only with his permission. In 1940 he won the presidential election and ruled for four years. Batista's career dimmed in 1944 when his candidate for president was defeated. His political recovery began in 1948 with his election to the senate, but his failure to win the presidential election of 1952 caused him to resort once more to the *coup d'état*. Installed in power as provisional president, he called elections (1954), which his enemies later claimed were fraudulent, and was elected for a four-year term (1955–9). This term was characterized by authoritarianism and brutal repression of all opposition. Guerrilla activity in the mountains and cities led by Fidel Castro Ruz and others undermined the internal coherence and confidence of the regime which became increasingly associated with corruption. US criminal interests took over much of the famous night-life of Havana and bribery and theft of public funds became commonplace.
On 1 Jan. 1959 Batista resigned and he and his closest associates abandoned Cuba. Since that date he has lived in exile, mostly in Spain.

BATLLE Y ORDÓNEZ, JOSÉ (1856–1929), journalist, politician, and twice president of Uruguay. A member of the Colorado Party, he was an early leader in an attempt to transform it into a modern, mass-based organization. He founded the newspaper *El Día* (1886) as a means of publicizing his views. After several years in the senate he was elected to the presidency (1903). His first term saw little innovation and was disturbed by civil war and the constant threat of *coups d'état*. Towards the end of this term he began a programme of governmental reorganization based on European welfare-state ideas. He travelled widely (1907–11), paying particular attention to the collegiate form of government in Switzerland. Re-elected to the presidency (1911–15), he sponsored measures which turned Uruguay into a welfare state. Public ownership of utilities was extended, workman's compensation, the eight-hour day, state insurance and pensions, and the abolition of capital punishment were all passed. His most controversial proposal was the plural or collegiate form of executive. Shaken by his first-term experience, and convinced that authoritarian, personalist government (*caudillismo*) was a threat to the nation, he called a constitutional convention in 1917. As a result, a new National Council of Administration gave both major parties a voice in the government, and the presidency of the body rotated among its members. Its supporters claimed that this system, since abandoned, ended authoritarian government. Batlle served twice as the president of the National Council which he had helped to create, and during his later years assumed the role of elder statesman of Uruguay.

BATMAN, JOHN (1801–39), pioneered settlement on Port Phillip Bay, Australia, as field manager of the Tasmanian-based Port Phillip Association. The son of a respected Protestant ticket-of-leave settler at Parramatta, near Sydney, he left in 1821 for Tasmania. By mid-1828 he was a literate, self-reliant, practical bushman and farmer, on rugged Ben Lomond, near Launceston; courageous and understanding in handling both bushrangers and Aboriginals, he was at ease with all social ranks, although just married to a convict-girl. In 1827, he and a legal friend, J. T. Gellibrand, had vainly sought official encouragement to depasture across Bass Strait; but in May 1835, six months after the Hentys settled at Portland, Batman entered Port Phillip in the chartered schooner *Rebecca*. On 6 June he bargained with native elders for 600,000 acres (2500 sq. kms) north and west of the bay, promising an annual tribute in two deeds of feoffment prepared by Gellibrand. Back in Tasmania, 'the greatest landowner in the world', Batman was formally constituted the agent-partner of a dozen leading colonists. He supported his holding party at Indented Head, organized occupation, and in April 1836 established his family on the Yarra river. But the government would not countenance his transaction with the Aboriginals, and his Association dwindled. His bid for fortune brought poverty to his dependents and earned him an unwarranted reputation as knave or hero. But the city of Melbourne stands upon Batman's 'place for a village'.

BATTA means literally an allowance. It was the term used to cover officers' expenses when on field duty. The practice began in south India with the Anglo-French wars of the mid-18th cent. Clive regularized the grant in Bengal. Officers in cantonments drew half-batta, those on field service in Bengal full batta, and outside double batta.

BATTAL, *ie,* Sayyid Battal Ghazi, an Arab chieftain who fought against Byzantium in the Umayyad period and later became the heroic central figure of a famous Turkish epic.

BATTLE-AXE CULTURE, one of a complex of cultures representing the progress of migrants (most probably from the south Russian steppes) north-westwards over much of east and central Europe as far as the Rhine and the Low Countries in the late third millennium BC. Their language was probably within the Indo-European group; their material culture marks a distinct break with the long-established Danubian tradition of peasant villages, and is symptomatic of the future importance of a 'heroic' warrior caste.

BATTLE HYMN OF THE REPUBLIC, US patriotic hymn written (1861) by Julia Ward Howe to the tune of 'John Brown's Body'. The song enjoyed wide popularity throughout the Union during the Civil War.

BATU KHAN (d. *c.* 1255), founder of the Mongol regime known as the Altin Ordu, *ie,* the Golden Horde. On the death of his father Jochi, the eldest son of Chingiz Khan, Batu received as his *yurt* (appanage) the regions of Khwarazm and the Dasht-i Kipchak, north-east of the Black Sea. As a result of the great campaigns that he led in 1236–41 he became the master of a new Mongol state in southern Russia.

BAUDIN, THOMAS (1754–1803), French naval officer and explorer, who made the most comprehensive scientific survey of Australia in his day. Previous experience commanding scientific voyages for Austria (Indian Ocean, 1792) and France (West Indies, 1796) prompted his appointment to lead the Australian expedition for Napoleonic France. Baudin's rich collection of reports, maps, illustrations, and samples, made during more than two years' scientific surveying in *Géographe* and *Naturaliste,* with a complement of 'savants', still provides material for scholarly research. There were continual confrontations on the voyage, with 'savants', 'revolutionary egalitarians', seamen, and scientists. These adversely affected the expedition's programme and tarnished Baudin's reputation. But there is no basis for the charge that his published maps were based on the missing charts of Matthew Flinders.

BAUDOUIN, PAUL (1894–1964), French foreign minister when the armistice was signed by Pétain's government (1940). A banker and financial expert, he had been brought into politics earlier in 1940 by Reynaud and served as a minister under the Vichy regime until 1941.

BAUDRILLART, HENRI JOSEPH (1821–94), French economist, who first became interested in social problems because of the revolution of 1848, and from this turned to political economy. Under the Second Empire he held the chair of political economy at the Collège de France (1866) and was then made inspector-general of libraries (1869). His writings dealt mainly with the economic problems of rural France.

BAUHIN, JEAN (1541–1631), Swiss physician and botanist, whose *Historie planatarum universalis* listed 5000 plants, to many of which he gave a generic and specific name. This highly significant system, with which Linnaeus is generally credited, thus antedates his work by more than a century.

BAUTZEN, BATTLE OF (20–1 May 1813), although Napoleon could claim a tactical victory, he was unable to prevent the Russo-Prussian forces retreating in good order, and thus rendering the battle indecisive.

BAVARIAN SUCCESSION, WAR OF (1778–9), nicknamed the 'plum and potato war' because the opposing Prussian and Austrian troops spent more time looking for food than fighting. The war was a classic case of the 18th cent. war of manœuvre, and it considerably reduced Frederick the Great's military prestige. It began through an attempt by the Austrian co-ruler, the Emperor Joseph II, to annexe most of Bavaria and thereby increase direct Austrian influence in Germany by a deal with the new Bavarian elector, Charles Theodore. Posing as the defender of German liberties and the rights of Charles Theodore's heirs, Frederick tried to prevent by force this increase in Austrian power. The military stalemate was resolved by Russia and France's mediating peace at Teschen (1779), which gave Austria the small Innviertel and left the rest of Bavaria intact.

BAVIN, SIR THOMAS RAINSFORD (1874–1941), NZ-born Australian lawyer and politician, who became prime minister of NSW (1927–30) and, subsequently, a supreme court judge. Political apprenticeship as private secretary to the first two Australian prime ministers, followed by experience at the Sydney bar, were insufficient preparation for the rigours of the NSW premiership during the economic depression. Bavin's lack of tough party convictions and failing health combined to enforce his political retirement (1932).

BAWANDIDS, princes of Iranian origin, ruling (665–1349) in the mountainous region of Tabaristan. There were, in fact, three branches of the House of Bawand—the Kayusiyya (665–1006), the Ispahbadiyya (1073–1210), and the Kinakhwariyya (1237–1349).

BAXTER, RICHARD (1615–91), English Puritan minister. He was ordained in the Church of England (1638), but by 1640 he was in alliance with the puritans in their opposition to episcopacy. He was minister at Kidderminster (1641–60), with several interruptions), and his preaching became famous. He had two objects in his sermons: conversion to a life of faith in God, and a life of Christian discipline and obedience.

He epitomized the Puritan concern for pastoral ministry. He served for a short time as a chaplain to the parliamentary army. He also helped to bring about the Restoration, fighting for toleration of moderate dissent in the Church of England. He failed and was persecuted for over 20 years, being vindicated only after the revolution of 1688. His autobiography, *Reliquiae Baxterianae* (1696), shows him as a typical mainstream English Puritan, austere but not bigoted or fanatical, and not over-concerned with the controversy over church government. He was neither a Presbyterian nor an Independent and had a horror of sectarianism, and during the Civil War and Commonwealth he was successful in forming Associations of Ministers of different sects up and down the country.

BAY OF PIGS (17 April 1961), abortive attempt by American-trained Cuban exiles to invade Cuba and overthrow Fidel Castro. The US provided very limited air support, but no troops, mistakenly assuming that the exile force of 1500 would be sufficient to promote a mass uprising. Although planned during the Eisenhower administration, the invasion was carried out with President Kennedy's consent and constituted an unpromising beginning to his efforts to identify the US with anti-colonialism. Its failure intensified criticism of the Central Intelligence Agency, which had organized the invasion. Within Cuba, Castro's support was consolidated.

BAY PSALM BOOK (1640), first complete book printed in North America, published for the Massachusetts Bay Co. by Stephen Day (Daye). Eleven copies of the book remain extant.

BAY STREET BOYS, white clique which has controlled Bahamas economy and politics for centuries. The victory of the largely black Progressive Labour Party (1968) was the first limitation on its power.

BAYBARS (1223–77), Mamluk Sultan of Egypt and Syria (*reg.* 1260–1277), was of Kipchak Turkish origin and had been a slave of the Ayyubid Sultan al-Malik al-Salih Ayyub (d. 1249). Baybars distinguished himself in the operations against the Crusade of Louis IX of France to Egypt (1249–50). He had a share also in the murder of the last Ayyubid sultan, Turan Shah, in 1250. After the battle of Ayn Jalut in 1260 Baybars had Sultan Kutuz killed and ascended the throne himself. The great achievement of his reign was to bring under Mamluk rule most of the territories still remaining to the Crusaders in Syria. In a series of well-organized campaigns he conquered Caesarea (1265), Arsuf and Safad (1266), Jaffa, Beaufort, and Antioch (1268), Safitha and Crac des Chevaliers (1271). In 1272 he made a ten-year truce with the Latins. Baybars also undertook several campaigns against the Christian kingdom of Lesser Armenia, a state which served as a link between the Crusaders in Syria and the Mongols in Persia. At Darbsak in 1266 Sultan Baybars routed the Armenian forces and ravaged much of Cilicia. He attacked Lesser Armenia again in 1275 and in 1277 marched against the Mongol forces in Asia Minor, advancing as far as Kayseri. It was Baybars who, after the Mongol capture of Baghdad (1258) and after his own accession to the throne of Egypt and Syria (1260), sought to legitimize the Mamluk regime in the eyes of the Muslims and, to this end, summoned an Abbasid prince to Cairo, establishing him there as a kind of 'shadow caliph'.

BAYEUX SPEECH (1946), speech made by de Gaulle setting out his ideas on constitutional reform. These ideas differed markedly from those being proposed at the time for the constitution of the Fourth Republic, and foreshadowed de Gaulle's attacks on the Republic after he founded the RPF movement in 1947. In the Bayeux speech, de Gaulle emphasized the need for a strong state and the dangers of party faction. He called for a separation of powers, with a strong executive independent of 'political contingencies' and a government drawing its authority from the chief of state rather than from parliament. This 'Bayeux constitution' contains the principles on which the constitution of the Fifth Republic was based.

BAYEUX TAPESTRY, woven within living memory of the events of 1066, measures 23 ft by approximately 20 inches (7 m. × 50 cms) wide. It depicts the Norman version of events leading to the victory of William of Normandy at Hastings and provides valuable evidence about contemporary life.

BAYEZID I (1354–1403), Ottoman Sultan (*reg.* 1389–1403), known as Yildirim ('the Thunderbolt'). The first years of his reign saw the occupation of the rival Turkish principalities (Aydin, Sarukhan, Menteshe, Hamid, Germiyan) in western Asia Minor and the repulse of a hostile coalition embracing Qastamonu, Karaman, and Siwas. Trnovo, the old capital of Bulgaria, fell to the Ottomans in 1393 and Thessaloniki in 1394. The sultan, also in 1394, began a blockade of Constantinople which was to last seven years. At Nikopolis on the Danube, in Sept. 1396, Bayezid I defeated a powerful Christian crusade. He carried out a punitive campaign against Karaman in 1397 and in 1398 extended his influence in Asia Minor to include the regions of Janik and Siwas. This eastward advance brought him into conflict with Timur Beg. At Ankara in 1402 Timur crushed the Ottoman forces. Bayezid died at Ak Shehir as the captive of Timur Beg.

BAYEZID II (*c.* 1447–1512), Ottoman Sultan (*reg.* 1481–1512). On the death of Mehmed II in 1481 there was a violent conflict for the throne between his two sons, Jem and Bayezid. Jem, defeated in 1482, took refuge with the Knights of St John at Rhodes and remained thereafter, until his death in 1495, a captive in the hands of the Christians. The reign of Bayezid saw the Ottomans engaged in an inconclusive war (1485–91) with the Mamluks of Syria and Egypt for the control of Cilicia; and also in a conflict with Venice (1499–1503), which meant, for the Signoria, the loss of important territories in southern Greece and on the eastern shore of the Adriatic. During the last years of his reign Bayezid had to meet a dangerous crisis arising from the growth of Safawid influence in Asia Minor and from the dissension amongst his sons over the succession to the throne. Bayezid abdicated (April 1512) in favour of his youngest son, Selim, and died in May of the same year.

BAYINNAUNG, Burmese king of the Toungoo dynasty (*reg.* 1551–81), who conquered Pegu and Ava (1555) and waged war successfully against Siam (1564 and 1569). A model king in Buddhist eyes, he undertook many religious works of merit.

BAYLE, PIERRE (1647–1706). French philosopher and historian whose rationalism was a fundamental influence upon the *philosophes*, particularly on Voltaire. More important than Fontenelle, he ranks in stature with John Locke. Bayle was the son of a Calvinist minister and was converted to Catholicism, reconverted to Protestantism, and ended by becoming a religious sceptic. Forced to flee from France, he took refuge in Rotterdam, where he was professor of philosophy (1681–1693). His *Pensées diverses sur la comète* (1680) attacked popular superstition and in the *Nouvelles de la République de Lettres*, a critical periodical which he started in 1684, he advocated free thought and toleration. He condemned Louis XIV's folly in sacrificing national harmony for the sake of religious unity. Bayle's most famous work was the *Dictionnaire Historique* (1697–9). As a historian he would only accept rational evidence and he regarded the Bible as an inaccurate source. Although a sceptic, his philosophy was never totally negative. He rejected the criterion of religious dogma, but always accepted what could be explained by the rational observation of scientific data.

BAYLEN, BATTLE OF (20 July 1808), fought during the Peninsular War, when a French force under Dupont was forced to surrender by the Spanish regular army and a body of guerrillas.

BAYONET, infantry weapon in the form of a blade attached to the muzzle of a musket or rifle. Developed at Bayonne in France, it supplanted the pike in the 17th cent. It was of great practical use while firearms were single-shot weapons and hand-to-hand fighting the basic battle tactic, and its morale value remained high as late as the Second World War.

BAZAINE, ACHILLE (1811–88), French marshal, who first came to international notice as commander of the French during the disastrous French expedition to Mexico (1862–7). He was made commander-in-chief of the French army (1870) after the initial defeats in the Franco-Prussian war and made the tactical error of trying to defend Metz, where his army was surrounded. The attempt by Napoleon III and Mac-Mahon to relieve him led to the decisive French defeat at Sedan and his own surrender soon afterwards.

BAZARD, SAINT-ARMAND (1791–1832), French socialist thinker. With Enfantin and other members of what came to be known as the St Simon school, Bazard developed St Simon's belief in the need to extend industrial production into the necessity of making society and industry subservient to improving the condition of the masses. They expounded their ideas in the collective *Exposition de la Doctrine de Saint-Simon* (1828–30) and tried to practise them by forming a society of their own, known as the 'Family', with strange religious trappings. After a quarrel with Enfantin over the role of women in their society, Bazard left the 'Family' (1831) and died shortly afterwards.

BEACHY HEAD, BATTLE OF (1690), fought in the English Channel in the war of the Grand Alliance. On 10 July a French fleet of 70 ships under the Comte de Tourville engaged an Anglo-Dutch fleet of 56 ships under Arthur Herbert, Earl of Torrington. Though Torrington had the advantage of the wind, he lost 12 ships; the French lost none. He was court-martialled for withdrawing to the Thames, but was acquitted on enunciating the concept of maintaining a 'fleet in being' to safeguard England from invasion.

BEACONSFIELD, BENJAMIN DISRAELI, Earl of (1804–81), British prime minister, novelist, and wit, was a principal founder of the modern Conservative party. His lively imagination inspired his early radicalism and helped him to portray the miseries of early Victorian working-class urban life in *Sybil* (1845), while at the same time he venerated England's ancient institutions (monarchy, Church, and squirearchy) and, with his 'Young England' friends, dreamt of investing them with new beneficent roles.

As Tory MP from 1837, Disraeli was mortified when he was passed over for office (1841), and became increasingly critical of Peel's business-like, empirical policies. With Lord George Bentinck, he led the Protectionist squires in their opposition to Corn Law repeal (1846), and his attacks drove Peel from office, denuded the shaken Tories of talent, and made Disraeli himself acceptable to the Protectionist majority. By 1849 he was effectively their leader in the Commons. In the 1850s, convinced that opposition to Free Trade was no longer realistic, he jettisoned Protection. With equal adroitness he persuaded the country gentlemen to 'shoot Niagara' by enfranchising male householders in the boroughs (1867).

Although chancellor of the exchequer in Derby's administrations (1852, 1858–9, 1867), Disraeli was an indifferent financier. He disliked the grind of preparing and presenting legislation, and is remembered not for a body of well-drafted reforms, but for a number of brilliant *tours de force*, *eg*, the Reform Act (1867), the purchase of 40 per cent of the Suez Canal shares (1875), and the treaty of Berlin (1878).

After Derby's resignation (Feb. 1868), Disraeli became prime minister, but remained in office for only ten months. In his second ministry (1874–80), his home secretary, Richard

Cross, introduced useful social reforms, *eg*, a Trade Union Act, the consolidating Public Health Act (1875), and the Artisans Dwellings Act. The ten-hour factory day was also achieved. Disraeli himself, who was created Earl of Beaconsfield in 1876, took more interest in foreign affairs. His ministry pursued a forward policy in Afghanistan and Zululand, having annexed the Transvaal in 1877. In spite, or because, of his Jewish origins, Disraeli was a patriot in the Palmerstonian mould. He took a strongly pro-Turkish line in the Eastern crisis (1876–8). His triumphant return from the Congress of Berlin was the climax of his career.

Disraeli's policy statements were impressionistic, and his government's domestic actions often, ironically, Peelite in temper; yet he created a Conservative image which his party and a large section of the nation could recognize and accept.

R. Blake, *Disraeli* (London, 1966).   MRB

BEAGLEHOLE, JOHN CAWTE (1901–   ), NZ-born historian and leader in many NZ cultural fields. His editing of Cook's *Journals* (1955–   ) is generally regarded as NZ's outstanding contribution to historical scholarship.

BEALE, ROBERT (1541–1601), Elizabethan civil servant, diplomat, and antiquarian. Compelled by religion to leave Marian England, he became secretary to Walsingham when the latter was ambassador in Paris. Later he acted as secretary of state in Walsingham's absence, served with Leicester in the Netherlands (1587), and negotiated with the United Provinces (1589) and Spain (1600).

BEAR FLAG REPUBLIC (1846), short-lived Californian republic, so called because its standard included a grizzly bear. The incident was no more than a minor prelude to the US conquest of California during the war with Mexico.

BEAR-BAITING. A sport in which a bear was chained by the leg or neck to a stake and harassed by dogs. It was popular in England for several hundred years, but after the late 17th cent. was permanently outlawed by Act of Parliament in 1835. The exhibitions usually took place in arenas popularly called bear gardens.

BEARD, CHARLES AUSTIN (1874–1948), US political scientist and historian, whose emphasis upon the importance of economic factors in American history challenged traditional interpretations of the American past. His early reputation was made by the critically received *An Economic Interpretation of the Constitution of the United States* (1913) and *The Economic Origins of Jeffersonian Democracy* (1915), in which he stressed the interplay of economic groups and issues rather than abstract political ideals. He resigned from his post at Columbia University in protest against the dismissal of alleged pacifists during the First World War, and helped to found the New School for Social Research in New York. In *The Rise of American Civilisation* (with Mary R. Beard, 4 vols, 1927–43) he offered a broad synthesis of American history focused on the conflict between rival socio-economic concepts. In *The Idea of National Interest* (1934) he reiterated his thesis of the continuing battle between Jeffersonian agrarianism and Hamiltonian commercial capitalism. In a series of books on foreign policy including *The Open Door at Home* (1934), *A Foreign Policy for America* (1940), *American Foreign Policy in the Making 1932–1940* (1946), and *President Roosevelt and the Coming of the War, 1941* (1948) he urged the avoidance of overseas commitments that might lead to war and advocated the building of national strength at home as the best way to serve the national interest. His passionate concern to preserve American integrity in a world in conflict, and his fear that a devious president was committing the US to foreign ventures that were irrelevant to the interests of the nation, led him into polemic that damaged his reputation. He was the author of some 50 books, with a circulation of millions. Both his interpretations and his use of evidence have been successfully challenged but he remains a towering figure in American historiography.   DKA

BEATON, DAVID, cardinal (*c.* 1494–1546), Abp of St Andrews and champion of French interests in Scotland. As chancellor, during the minority of Mary Queen of Scots, he weakened English influence and had the treaty of Greenwich repudiated (1543). In religious matters his condemnation of the Protestant, George Wishart, led to his murder.

BEATTY, DAVID BEATTY, 1st Earl (1871–1936), British Admiral, who commanded the battle cruiser squadron of the British Grand Fleet at the battle of Jutland (31 May 1916). Beatty, who joined the navy at the age of 13, was widely acclaimed as a war hero with a reputation for tactical daring. Having been in action against the Dervishes on the Nile, at Lord Kitchener's request he took part in the Omdurman campaign. He also saw active service during the Boxer rebellion in China. He was promoted captain at the age of 29 and rear-admiral (1910), being the youngest flag officer for over 100 years. In 1912, he was chosen by Winston Churchill as his naval secretary. In the same year he took over the battle cruiser squadron and in 1916, against the express recommendation of the former commander, Sir John Jellicoe, became commander of the fleet. He directed the anti-submarine campaign of 1917–18, and was first sea lord (1919–27). He fought to preserve British cruiser strength at the Washington Conference (1921) and was a strong advocate of a powerful base at Singapore.

BEAUFORT, HENRY (*c.* 1375–1447), second son of John of Gaunt, Duke of Lancaster, by his mistress Katherine Swynford. He was thus a half-brother to King Henry IV, but from a branch of the royal family debarred from the succession to the throne. He was Bp of Lincoln after 1398 and of Winchester after 1405, and became in 1417 a cardinal. He was the leading figure in the affairs of both state and church, especially during the minority of Henry VI after 1422, when he became the chief opponent of the King's uncle, Humphrey, Duke of Gloucester, for control of England. Beaufort's immense wealth made him the chief banker of the royal government and he helped to finance the defence of the English conquests in France.

BEAUHARNAIS, EUGÈNE DE (1781–1824), viceroy of Italy and stepson of Napoleon I through his marriage to Josephine. He was a competent and loyal administrator and general.

BEAUHARNOIS, CHARLES DE LA BOISCHE (1670–1749), naval officer and, later, governor of New France (1726–47). His quarrels with the *intendant*, Dupuy, especially over ecclesiastical affairs, led to the latter's recall in 1728. Beauharnois was much interested in the fur trade and western exploration. Fort Beauharnois, a trading post, was established on Lake Pepin, WI, in 1727 and re-established in 1731, after the defeat of the Fox Indians in 1728, but was later abandoned. Beauharnois supported the expeditions of La Verendrye, father and son, but failed, in 1731 and 1734, to persuade Louis XV to sponsor them further. He returned to France in 1747, consequent upon the fall of Louisbourg, and was appointed lieutenant-general of the naval forces.

BEAULIEU, E. DE (*fl.* 1536), French anti-royalist, who criticized the repressive religious policy of Francis I towards the Protestants in the later years of his reign.

BEAUMANOIR, PHILLIPPE DE (d. *c.* 1296), notable royal official who served as seneschal and *bailli* in various parts of France. His *Coutumes de Clermont en Beauvaisis* describes the legal system of his native Picardy. It forms an invaluable source for the study of French government and law in the later 13th cent.

BEAUMARCHAIS, PIERRE AUGUSTIN CARON DE (1732–1799), French dramatist whose comedies *Le Barbier de Séville* and *Le Mariage de Figaro* satirized French society of the *ancien régime*, and provided libretti for Rossini's and Mozart's operas of the same name.

BEAUMONT, CHRISTOPHE DE, archbishop of Paris from 1749, and a violent enemy of the Jansenists. He excommunicated and deprived of the last sacraments those of his flock who had not a ticket to prove that their confessor accepted the papal bull *Unigenitus*, which had condemned Jansenist doctrine in 1713. His action provoked the intervention of the *parlements* in favour of those accused of Jansenism.

BEAUMONT, SIR FRANCIS (1584–1616), English dramatist, who went to London to study law, met Jonson, Drayton, and other poets, and after writing *Salmacis and Hermaphroditus*, an Ovidian romance (1602), worked mainly for the theatre. Of a dozen plays in collaboration with John Fletcher, his best known is *The Knight of the Burning Pestle* (1609).

BEAUMONT, JEAN-BAPTISTE-AMAND-LOUIS-LÉONCE ÉLIE DE (1798–1874), French geologist. He was engineer-in-chief of mines (1833–47), and inspector-general (1847–61).

BEAUREGARD, PIERRE GUSTAVE TOUTANT (1818–93). Louisiana-born Confederate general in the American Civil War. He was in command at Charleston when Fort Sumter was attacked, and also fought at Bull Run (1861), Shiloh (1862), and around Petersburg (1864–5).

BEAUVAIS, VINCENT OF (*c.* 1190–*c.* 1264), Dominican writing under the patronage of King Louis IX of France. His main work, *Speculum Maius*, is an encyclopedia of all knowledge available to a western Christian scholar of his time.

BEAVERBROOK, WILLIAM MAXWELL AITKEN, 1st Baron (1879–1964), British newspaper proprietor and champion of imperial unity, who grew up in Newcastle, NB. His father was a minister of the Church of Scotland in Canada, who had migrated from Scotland. Aitken became a financier in 1900 and was a millionaire by 1910. In that year he became a Unionist MP in the British parliament and the intimate friend of Bonar Law, whom he helped to make Unionist Leader in 1911. He was Canadian eye witness, records officer and military representative on the Western front (1915–17), and played a principal part in the overthrow of Asquith and the elevation of Lloyd George to the premiership in Dec. 1916. He received a peerage in 1917 and was minister of information and chancellor of the duchy of Lancaster in 1918.

He had acquired financial control of the *Daily Express* in 1916 and assumed active control at the end of 1918, when he also founded the *Sunday Express*. In 1923 he bought the *Evening Standard* and in 1929 founded the *Scottish Daily Express*. His papers aimed at a mass readership and also advocated imperial unity. Though a Unionist, Beaverbrook championed freedom for Ireland, a capital levy, and high wages. In 1930 he launched the Empire Crusade and attempted to force this policy on the Conservative Party. In 1931 he opposed the economy programme of the National government. In 1936 he attempted to avert the abdication of Edward VIII.

Throughout the 1930s Beaverbrook advocated isolation from Europe, coupled with heavy armaments. Though he opposed entry into the Second World War, he joined Churchill's government and was a member of the war cabinet (1940–2). As minister of aircraft production (1940–1), he played the chief part in providing the aircraft which won the Battle of Britain. He was minister of supply (1941–2) and, briefly, minister of war production (1942). He organized supplies for Russia and largely inspired American production. He left the government in order to preach the Second Front and returned as lord privy seal (1943–5).

After the war he continued to support the cause of empire and applauded the Conservative government's policy over Suez in 1956. He opposed successfully the institution of bishops in the Church of Scotland, which had been debated in the 1958 General Assembly. He also opposed (1962–3) British entry into the European Economic Community.

His writings are a unique contribution of personal memoirs and detached history.

Lord Beaverbrook, *My Early Life* (NB, 1965).
Lord Beaverbrook, *The Decline and Fall of Lloyd George* (London, 1963).
AJPT

BEBEL, FERDINAND AUGUST (1840–1913), German politician, co-founder and leader for nearly 40 years of the German Social Democratic Party. He co-operated with Liebknecht in forming the Marxist Social Democratic Workingmen's Party (1869). Bismarck's anti-socialist policy in the 1870s induced Bebel to merge his party with the non-Marxist Lassalleans (1875), the followers of Ferdinand Lassalle (1825–64) as the Social Democratic Party supporting the Gotha programme. The SDP accepted Marx's ideas of the class struggle, but aimed at maintaining the conflict by parliamentary means. Despite persecution and imprisonment Bebel continued as leader of German Social Democracy inside and outside the Reichstag, insisting on patience and constitutional action. After the dropping of Bismarck's anti-socialist laws (1890), Bebel's party went from strength to strength under his direction until it had become (1912) the largest party in the Reichstag, with 110 members, and the most effective socialist party in Europe.

BECCARIA, CESARE BONESANA, Marchese (1738–94), Italian economist and the first modern criminologist. His major work, *On Crimes and Punishments*, first appeared anonymously (1764) and owed much to the influence of Montesquieu, the Encyclopaedists, and Helvétius. He argued that prevention was better than punishment and that the danger of arrest was a greater deterrent than barbarous retribution. He pointed out that imposing the death penalty for theft merely led to the murder of victims to prevent future detection. This utilitarian approach to the problem of crimes had some influence on Jeremy Bentham. The Austrian administration of Beccaria's native Milan under the 'Enlightened Despots', Joseph II and Leopold II, adopted reforms suggested by him, as did the French Constituent Assembly and Catherine the Great of Russia.

BECHUANALAND, country of the Tswana people, which became a British protectorate in 1884, and achieved independence as the republic of Botswana in 1966.

BECK, JÓZEF (1894–1944), Polish politician and diplomat. He was born in Warsaw and studied at the Lvov Polytechnic and the Vienna Export Academy. Through his father he was associated with the insurrectionist movement for Polish independence. In Aug. 1914 he joined Pilsudski's Legions and quickly established a close relationship with him. After the achievement of independence, Beck occupied military and diplomatic posts in Bucharest, Budapest, and Brussels. He also worked for a time in the Intelligence Department of the Polish General Staff. In Jan. 1922 he became Polish military attaché in Paris, but was forced to resign in the summer of 1923, when the French, suspecting him of working for German Intelligence, declared him *persona non grata*. He rejoined the Polish army, and was assigned first to the Military Academy and later to the Operations Division of the General Staff. As one of Pilsudski's most trusted confidants, he played a major role in organizing military preparations for the armed demonstration which led to the May coup of 1926 and Pilsudski's return to power. After the coup, Beck was one of Pilsudski's principal advisers, and his role became more important as the conflict with parliament grew more intense from 1928 onwards. He first held the post of *chef de cabinet* to the minister of war (1926–1930), then joined the cabinet briefly at the height of the clash with parliament (Aug.–Nov. 1930). From Dec. 1930

until Nov. 1932 he was under-secretary in the foreign ministry, and finally became foreign minister, holding this office until the Polish collapse in Sept. 1939. After Poland's defeat he escaped to Rumania, where he was interned and died.

As foreign minister, Beck was responsible for the implementation of Pilsudski's principle that Poland should 'balance' between her two powerful neighbours, Russia and Germany. After Pilsudski's death, Beck's attempts to remain on good terms with Hitler made Poland seem to the rest of Europe almost an ally of Nazi Germany. This was particularly true in 1938 during the Czech crisis. Although attempts have been made to defend this policy on the grounds that Western appeasement left him no alternative, there seems little doubt that Beck bears a major responsibility for the Polish catastrophe.
ABP

BECK, LUDWIG (1880–1944), German army chief of staff (1933–8). Beck, who was connected with the anti-Hitler opposition (1938–44), served on the General Staff during the First World War and by 1927 had reached the rank of colonel. At first he was a supporter of the National Socialist movement, openly celebrating the election victory of Sept. 1930. By 1938, however, he had become an opponent of Hitler's plans for aggression and attempts to destroy the independence of the army, and in August of that year he resigned his commission. Although later Beck's objections to the Nazi regime were to broaden, at this stage they were purely professional. During 1938–44 he was connected with several anti-Hitler plots. If the July 1944 plot had succeeded, he was to have become interim president of the Reich, but after its failure he was arrested and forced to commit suicide.

BECKER, JOHANN JOACHIM (1635–82), German chemist, natural philosopher, author of *Physicae Subterranae* (1669), and founder of the cameralist school in Vienna.

BECKET, THOMAS (*c.* 1118–70), archbishop, was the son of a London merchant, who, after being educated at Paris, entered the household of Abp Theobald of Canterbury. On Theobald's recommendation, Henry II appointed Becket chancellor in 1154, in which post he became Henry's intimate adviser and friend. When Theobald died, Henry insisted, despite Becket's reluctance, that he become Abp (1162). Becket saw it as his duty to safeguard the rights of the Church, but Henry saw this attitude as a personal betrayal. Their difference came to a head at the Council of Westminster (1163), when the bishops, led by Becket, resisted Henry's demands that they accept royal control over the Church. These demands were repeated in the constitutions of Clarendon (1164). Becket once again refused to accept them. Henry determined to break Becket and, at the council of Northampton (Oct. 1164), charged him with treason. Becket fled the country. During the next six years all attempts at reconciliation failed, but the coronation, in flagrant defiance of the rights of Canterbury, of Henry's eldest son (June 1170) by the Abp of York and two other bishops, forced Henry to a reconciliation and Becket returned in triumph (Dec. 1170). The continued enmity of the three prelates led Becket to excommunicate them. The news of this action reached Henry in France, and he was provoked to utter the rash words which led four knights to go to Canterbury Cathedral and there, on 29 Dec., murder Becket before the high altar. Becket was canonized in 1173 and his shrine at Canterbury became the most popular object of pilgrimage in western Europe until it was destroyed by Henry VIII in 1538.

BECKFORD, WILLIAM (1709–70), West India merchant, and father of William Beckford, author of *Vathek*. Beckford was an outstanding figure in metropolitan politics, being MP for the City of London (1754–74) and lord mayor (1763 and 1770). In the 1760s he and Sawbridge became widely known as Wilkes's strongest supporters. As a West India merchant, he believed that his business was threatened by the peace of Paris (1763). He left a vast fortune to his son.

BECQUEREL, ANTOINE HENRI (1852–1908), French scientist, who discovered radioactivity (1896). In 1903 he was awarded a Nobel Prize jointly with Marie and Pierre Curie.

BEDCHAMBER CRISIS (1839) gave a public demonstration of Queen Victoria's preference for Whigs over Tories. In May 1839, Melbourne, who had had a very small majority since the general election of 1837, resigned. Peel, as leader of the Conservatives, was invited to form a government. In order to have a demonstration of the queen's support, he asked her to substitute Tory for Whig ladies of the bedchamber. The queen, mainly for personal reasons, refused. Melbourne, who had a very strong influence over her, did not attempt to persuade her. Peel abandoned the attempt to form a government after this rebuff, and Melbourne returned to office till 1841. The crisis illustrates that, in spite of the Reform Act, the notion of the neutrality of constitutional monarchy was by no means accepted. The queen made no attempt to hide her partisanship, and Melbourne and Peel both regarded royal support as necessary to a stable ministry.

BEDE, Venerable (673–735), most outstanding scholar of the early Middle Ages. He was a monk at the Northumbrian double monastery at Monkwearmouth and Jarrow and wrote a valuable history of its abbots. Though primarily interested in theology and biblical study, he also wrote on grammar, versification, natural history, and chronology. His other historical writings included a life of St Cuthbert and the *Ecclesiastical History of the English Nation*, completed in 731, which has no literary parallel in early medieval Europe. It describes the conversion of the Anglo-Saxons and the organization of the Church by Theodore and his successors. Though handicapped by the limitations of oral tradition on which he largely drew, Bede maintained a critical attitude to his evidence and tried to write the truth. He was translating the Fourth Gospel into Anglo-Saxon when he died.

BEDFORD, JOHN, Duke of (1389–1435), English regent in France after the death in 1422 of his brother King Henry V. The maintenance of English rule in northern France depended chiefly on him. His prolonged success rested on his good relations with his brother-in-law, Duke Philip of Burgundy.

BEDFORD, JOHN RUSSELL, 7th Duke of (4th of 4th creation) (1710–71). British politician and head of one of the aristocratic groups which dominated politics in the mid-18th cent. He was in opposition for most of the 1750s, but accepted office as lord privy seal in 1760. He strongly advocated peace with France, and as ambassador negotiated the preliminaries of peace (Oct. 1762). He was lord president of the council in successive ministries (1763–7), and was attacked by Burke for his attachment to office rather than political principle, though he was in reality not much different from the leaders of other groups.

BEDLAM, strictly Bethlem, London hospital for the insane. Founded in Bishopsgate as a priory (1247), it came under the protection of the City (1346) and by 1400 was a hospital for lunatics. It was incorporated as a royal foundation (1547) and transferred to Moorfields (1676) and later to Lambeth (1815). In the 18th cent. it was the only London hospital caring for the insane. Its management has become notorious, though contemporaries (eg, Dr Thomas Bond of the Pennsylvania Hospital) were impressed by the number of its cures. Sightseers were admitted at 1d or 2d a head, inmates were treated by regular and indiscriminate bleedings and purgings, and many were kept in permanent restraint. By 1815 more enlightened standards brought a public enquiry and reformed methods.

BEECHAM, SIR THOMAS (1879–1961), British musical conductor who revived and promoted the performance of opera in Britain, made known the works of Delius, and raised the standards of musical performance. He founded (1919) the British Opera Company, the Imperial League of Opera (1927), and the London Philharmonic Orchestra (1932).

BEECHER, HENRY WARD (1813–87), US nonconformist minister, son of Lyman Beecher, and brother of Harriet Beecher Stowe. After eight years as pastor of a Presbyterian church in Indiana, he moved to Plymouth Congregational Church, Brooklyn, NY (1847). A vital, emotional man, his sentimental sermons violently denounced all forms of vice, and he was an ardent champion of anti-slavery, lecturing in England during the American Civil War to support the Union cause. An unsuccessful adultery suit brought by Theodore Tilton (1874) overshadowed his later career. Apart from his sermons, Beecher's best-known works include *The Life of Jesus, the Christ* (1871), and *Evolution and Religion* (1885).

BEECHER, LYMAN (1775–1863), New England Presbyterian clergyman and reformer, father of a notable family that included Henry Ward Beecher and Harriet Beecher Stowe. He was active in the temperance movement, the anti-slavery crusade, the establishment of the American Bible Society, and the promotion of education, especially in the western states, and became first president of Lane Theological Seminary in Cincinnati (1832–50). His turbulent career included a fierce campaign against the alleged menace of Roman Catholicism in the American West, and a dispute at Lane Seminary over the slavery issue, which caused many of its students to move to the more liberal Oberlin College. Accusations of heresy and hypocrisy brought against Beecher by conservative Presbyterians contributed to the split in the Presbyterian Church (1837–8).

BEECKMAN, ISAAC (1588–1637). Dutch physicist and philosopher, who was influenced by Galileo's work on mechanics. He and Descartes further examined the concept of motion.

BEECROFT, JOHN (1790–1854), British merchant, explorer, and administrator who began his mercantile and administrative career in Fernando Po (1829). He explored the Lower Niger (1835, 1840, 1845) and was first British consul in the Bights of Benin and Biafra (1849). He intervened in a Lagos dynastic dispute between Kings Kosoko and Akitoye in the latter's favour (1852) and in 1854 deported King Pepple V of Bonny, following further dynastic disputes. Other consuls in the Bight of Biafra up to 1880 were less influential.

BEERBOHM, SIR MAX (1872–1956), British caricaturist and satirist, more especially of the English literary scene of the 1890s. He was a contributor to the famous *Yellow Book* (1894–7) and succeeded Bernard Shaw as dramatic critic of *The Saturday Review*. His output, which was small, was characterized by his fastidious taste and his ironical style.

BEETON, MRS ISABELLA MARY (1836–65), English culinary expert, whose *Household Management* (1861), a combined cookery book and treatise on domestic economy, was one of the great best sellers of the Victorian era and initiated the perennial fashion for books about cookery.

BEG, a Turkish word meaning 'lord' (cf the Arabic *amir*). It often occurs in titles, eg, *sanjak begi* (the governor of an Ottoman sanjak or province) and in personal designations, eg, Timur Beg. The Ottoman title of *beglerbegi* (lord of lords) corresponds in its literal meaning with the Arabic *amir al-umara*.

BEGGAR'S OPERA, THE (1728), by John Gay, with music from popular contemporary tunes (English, Scottish, French, and German), was produced in London by John Rich after Swift had suggested 'a Newgate pastoral'. The principal characters were Peachum, a receiver, and Macheath, a libidinous highwayman. It was so successful that Italian opera temporarily went out of favour in London, but its outspoken satire led to a tightening of the censorship, and a successor, *Polly*, was refused a licence. Brecht's *The Threepenny Opera* (1928), satirizing the Weimar Republic, was an adaptation.

BEGHO, important West African trading centre, near the Black Volta (mod. Ghana) and of 15th-cent. Mande foundation, being established as a vital link for exchanges between the Central Sudan and the Guinea forest lands.

BEGUIN, JEAN (1559–1620), French scientist, whose recipe book on chemistry, *Tyrocinium Chymicum* (1610), was the pattern of all later textbooks. He regarded chemistry as an auxiliary to medicine.

BEHAINE PIGNEAU, PIERRE DE (1741–99), French Catholic missionary in Viet-nam and Bp of Adran, who left France in 1765 and spent most of his career in south-east Asia or at Pondicherry. In 1777 he gave protection to the young Viet-namese prince Nguyen Anh, with whose struggle to reconquer Viet-nam he was associated for the rest of his life. He helped to secure a Franco–Viet-namese treaty at Versailles in 1787, and when it broke down, he attracted a number of French mercenaries to the support of Nguyen Anh.

BEHANZIN (*reg.* 1889–94), King of Dahomey during a period of French colonial wars in West Africa. As crown prince, Behanzin had shown courage and ability in defending Dahomey against the French. In Nov. 1889 he refused French demands—based on treaties allegedly concluded in 1868 and 1878, but which he disputed—that Dahomey should surrender Cotonou to the French. From then onwards Behanzin led his people in a series of military campaigns against French armies under Dr Bayol and then Col. (later Gen.) Dodds, but was finally defeated. The French occupied Cotonou on 22 Feb. 1890, Abomey in Nov. 1892, and in 1894 deposed Behanzin, who is remembered in Dahomey today as a national hero.

BEHISTAN INSCRIPTION, a panel relief and account in Persian, Elamite, and Akkadian, of the ancestry of Darius I (*c.* 522–486 BC) and the rebellion he crushed at the beginning of his reign. It is carved on a rock above the road between Kermanshah and Hamadan, Iran.

BEHN, MRS APHRA (1640–89), English playwright and novelist, was brought up in Surinam, the background of *Oroonoko* (1678), her best-known novel. During her marriage to a wealthy Dutch merchant, Charles II employed her as a government spy in Antwerp. In widowhood she was perhaps the first Englishwoman to earn a living by her writing. Her plays, mostly coarse comedies of contemporary life, were still popular in the 18th cent.

BEHRING, EMIL ADOLF VON (1854–1917), German scientist whose studies in the treatment of infectious diseases led him to pioneer immunization, particularly in relation to diphtheria.

BEIRUT, AMERICAN UNIVERSITY OF, inaugurated as Syrian Protestant College (1866) by US missionaries. It became a university in 1920 and the major Middle Eastern centre for education of a western type and the training of Arab intellectuals.

BEIT, ALFRED (1853–1906), German-born financier in the South African diamond- and gold-mining industries. He was a friend of Cecil Rhodes, with whom he was associated in various enterprises and whose political views he shared. He bequeathed much of his fortune to education, hospitals, and railway development, and established a chair of colonial history at Oxford.

BEKBULATOVICH, SIMEON (*fl.* 16th cent.), Tatar prince mockingly nominated by Tsar Ivan (the 'Terrible') to rule over half the country during the violent years of the *oprichnina*, the tsar's brutal scheme for land reallocation. He survived Ivan, but was later blinded, apparently on the orders of Tsar Boris Godunov.

BEKTASHIYYA, famous dervish order (*tarika*) which took its name from a certain Hajji Bektash Wali (13th cent.), who would seem to have been a disciple of Baba Ishak. The *tarika* assumed its definitive form in the 15th and 16th cent. Its teaching embraced a disregard for the formalities of Muslim ritual, an acceptance of doctrines associated with the moderate form of Shi'ism (the 'Twelver Shi'a') and an emphasis on 'popular' forms of mysticism. It also welcomed ideas deriving from the cabbalistic speculations of the Hurifi sect and from the Christian faith (*eg*, the confession of sin to a spiritual head and the bestowing of absolution). The order acknowledged as its 'Grand Master' a Chelebi resident at Hajji Bektash, situated between Kir Shehir and Kayseri. The political importance of the *tarika* arose from its connection with the Ottoman janissaries, among whom the Bektashi influence was strong from the time of Sultan Mehmed II (1451–81) onwards. Though outlawed in 1826, the order was subsequently revived, but dissolved again by Mustafa Kemal (1925).

BELA IV (*reg.* 1235–70), King of Hungary, one of the best Arpád kings of Hungary, whose reign saw the first Tatar invasion (1241). After defeat he fled, and the country was occupied and ravaged for a year. Bela's great achievement was in reconstructing Hungary after the Tatars had left.

BELFORT, town in Alsace celebrated for having successfully withstood three sieges (1814, 1815, 1870–1). Belfort is of great strategic importance because it commands the 'Belfort gap' leading from the Rhine valley to south-eastern France. In 1870–1 it held out for 103 days under the command of Denfert-Rochereau, and this resistance was one reason why Belfort was not handed over to Germany in 1871 with the rest of Alsace. Since then the 'territory of Belfort' has formed a separate French department.

BELGAE, Gallic people formed in the 2nd cent. BC by a coalition of German and Celtic tribes on the lower Rhine and, in Julius Caesar's time, living north and east of the Seine and Marne. In 57 BC, after the defeat of Ariovistus, they rose against Caesar, who defeated them on the Aisne, but they joined Vercingetorix' rising and continued to give trouble for nearly 30 years. A group which migrated to Britain (*c.* 75) developed into the kingdom of Cassivellanus in the south-east, and another, arriving *c.* 50, spread westwards, perhaps as far as the Bristol Channel.

BELGIAN REVOLUTION (1830), the first major departure from the Vienna settlement, establishing a state with a liberal constitution, and the first occasion on which Palmerston played a decisive role in foreign affairs. In 1815 Belgium had, under William I, been united to Holland as a bulwark against France. In the 1820s friction grew over the position of Belgian Catholics and the economic difficulties of the industrial workers of eastern Belgium, for which they blamed the Dutch government, particularly its tariff policy, and over Belgian under-representation in the states general. Demands for concessions after 1827 (though not yet the independence) were strengthened by the alliance of liberal industrial workers with Belgian clericals, but received no response. The July Revolution in France precipitated a rising in Brussels (Aug. 1830), and William I failed to reassert control.

The future of the new state depended on the attitudes of the European powers. A conference met in London (Nov.) shortly before Palmerston became foreign secretary. The British feared that an independent Belgium would fall under French influence. The legitimist powers of eastern Europe wished to support William I, but the July Revolution had removed much of the British suspicion of France, and Palmerston initiated the policy, repeated later elsewhere, of allying Britain with France to keep her in check. The conference proposed that Belgium should be established under perpetual guarantees of neutrality and inviolability. The choice of sovereign presented a problem, the French candidate being acceptable to the Belgians, but not to Britain; finally, Leopold of Saxe-Coburg-Gotha was chosen. As William I was unwilling to accept the settlement, the Dutch were finally ejected from Belgium (1831) by a combined Anglo-French action. The Belgian–Dutch frontier remained in dispute, and the definitive five-power treaty, under which Britain went to war in 1914, was not signed until 1839.

Sir Charles Webster, *The Foreign Policy of Palmerston, 1830–1841* (London, 1951).   LMB

BELGIANS IN CENTRAL AFRICA.

In 1908 King Leopold handed over the Congo Independent State to Belgium, which thereupon became one of the major colonial powers in Africa and remained a key influence in the continent even after the independence of the Congo republic (1960). In 1919, at the time of the parcelling out of the old German colonies in Africa, Belgium also acquired the small territories of Rwanda and Burundi as a mandate of the League of Nations.

As a colonial power, Belgium adopted an attitude even more paternalistic and exploitative than other colonial regimes. A large share of the Congo economy was in the hands of giant companies such as the Union Minière du Haut Katanga, whose prime concern was the extraction of minerals with maximum efficiency and minimum investment. To achieve this, Belgium adopted a policy of providing extensive primary and technical education for its African subjects. Literacy and manual skills were encouraged in order to increase industrial productivity. Higher levels of learning were not introduced, however, and all managerial, administrative, and financial matters remained in European hands.

After the Second World War, when colonial subjects in British and French colonies began campaigning for a degree of self-government, Belgium hoped to prevent the spread of such demands to the Congo. When this proved futile Belgium reversed its policy overnight and offered immediate political independence to its colonies, although no background in education, political training, democratic process, or responsible government had been introduced. It is likely that Belgium hoped to retain effective, or at least financial, control over the Congo despite the grant of independence, but during the 1960s it appeared to experience more difficulty than either France or even Britain in maintaining influential relations with its former subjects.

R. Slade, *King Leopold's Congo* (London, 1962).
R. Anstey, *King Leopold's Legacy* (London, 1966).   DBB

BELGIUM: ANGLO-FRENCH DECLARATION (24 April 1937).

This released Belgium from her security obligations under the Locarno Pact, breached by Hitler's reoccupation of the Rhineland, and from engagements undertaken immediately after the reoccupation. Britain and France maintained their own undertakings to assist Belgium under these instruments, on the understanding that Belgium would maintain her own defences, remain faithful to the League of Nations Covenant, and refuse to lend her territory to purposes of aggression against other states. There was, however, no explicit reference to Article 16 of the Covenant, which permitted the passage of troops of league states executing military sanctions against an aggressor.

BELGIUM: GERMAN DECLARATION (13 Oct. 1937).

After the Anglo-French declaration regarding Belgium, Germany demanded that Belgium should clarify her position on the right of passage across her territory. On 13 Oct. Belgium accepted Germany's declaration of respect for her inviolability and integrity, subject to Belgium's preventing the use of her territory for an attack on any other country, and absten-tion from military action against Germany if Germany were to become involved in armed conflict. Germany would support Belgium if she were attacked or invaded. Spaak, Belgium's foreign minister, subsequently declared that Belgium's League of Nations undertakings remained unaltered.

BELGIUM: NEUTRALITY (1936).

Germany's reoccupation of the Rhineland (March 1936) strengthened domestic critics of Belgium's policy of alliances. The foreign minister, Spaak, agreed to joint general staff conversations with France and Britain, but hinted that Belgium was considering a purely defensive military policy; her sole contribution to European security should lie in guaranteeing her own independence. King Leopold's cabinet address to this effect (14 Oct.), published to counter opposition to the government's defence programme, surprised Britain and France more than Germany. Spaak insisted that Belgium would honour her existing engagements, including those with the League of Nations.

BELGRADE,

situated at the confluence of the Sava and the Danube, was known to the Ottoman Turks as the *Dar al-Jihad* (the Abode of Sacred War). The Ottomans attacked it without success in 1456. It fell to Sultan Suleiman in 1521. Here, in 1717, Prince Eugène won a famous battle against the Ottomans. The fortress was twice in Austrian hands (1688–90, 1718–39). Belgrade became the capital of Serbia in 1867 and, since 1918, has been the capital of Yugoslavia.

BELGRADE, TREATY OF (1739),

concluded three years of war by Austria and Russia against the Ottoman empire. Russia had sought access to the Black Sea since the time of Peter the Great, but had failed in that direction since the peace of Constantinople (1700), at which she yielded her conquests on the Don. At an abortive peace conference in 1737 the Russians demanded all the land between the Kuban and the Dniester, but at Belgrade they were forced to relinquish everything except Azov. Not until Kuchuk-Kainardji (1774) were the hopes of 1737 fulfilled. For Austria and the Ottoman empire, Belgrade established a frontier along the line of the Danube and the Save, which lasted until 1914. Austria's loss thereby of those parts of Bosnia, Serbia, and Wallachia which had been won in 1718 was, for the Ottomans, a corresponding recovery.

BELGRANO, MANUEL (1770–1820),

Argentine general and independence leader. After an equivocal career as a revolutionary general with monarchist sympathies, Belgrano was replaced as leader of the patriot armies (1814) by José de San Martín. He then turned to civil and diplomatic affairs. His reform proposals embraced agriculture, manufacturing, trade, and education.

BELINSKY, VISSARION GRIGORIEVICH (1811–48),

Russian journalist, literary critic, and a founder of Russian radical thought. The son of an army doctor, he was an early example of non-noble intelligentsia, a member of Stankevich's circle and, in the 1840s, a leader of the Westernizers against the Slavophils. Influenced by Hegel and, later, Feuerbach, he opposed serfdom and the Church and stressed the importance of the individual and the need to adapt Western civilization to Russia.

His journalistic writings in *The Notes of the Fatherland* and *The Contemporary* and his *Letter to Gogol* (1847) had enormous influence on two generations of Russian radicals. A gifted literary critic, his conviction that good art will and should reflect social issues started a belief in the use of literature as a weapon of social criticism which was to dominate later Russian writing.

BELISARIUS (c. 494–565),

one of the ablest generals in Byzantine history, especially distinguished as a commander of heavy cavalry, which in weight of armour and type of equipment foreshadowed the knights of medieval warfare. Belisarius was the greatest of Justinian's generals and remained loyal to him despite much provocation. He saved Justinian's life and throne in 532 by putting down the circus uprising in Constantinople. He started Justinian's conquests by destroying, in 533, the Vandal state in North Africa, and began in 535 the reconquest of Italy from the Ostrogoths, winning repeated victories despite inadequate backing from Justinian. His favour with the emperor ended in 548 on the death of the Empress Theodora, who was his chief supporter, and the final conquest of Italy (552–4) was accomplished by others. In 559, however, Belisarius was reinstated and successfully defended Constantinople against a sudden attack by the Huns.

BELIZE, capital and chief port of British Honduras, lying on the Caribbean coast approximately 900 miles (1450 kms) south of New Orleans. The derivation of the name may arise from the ancient Maya name for the river on which the town stands, or from the French *balise* (beacon), or from a mispronunciation of Wallace, the Scottish pirate who founded the settlement, traditionally in 1603, but more probably in 1638. The community was joined by shipwrecked sailors, and an influx of disbanded soldiers followed the British capture of Jamaica from Spain (1655). Spain ceded the area to Britain by the treaty of Madrid (1670), although a Spanish attempt to recapture the town was beaten off by the inhabitants (1697). Belize, built almost at sea-level, suffered serious damage in hurricanes (1931, 1961), and plans were made after the last one to resite the town inland.

BELL, ALEXANDER GRAHAM (1847–1922), Scottish-born inventor of the telephone. His father was a pioneer of speech education for the deaf, and the two worked together (1868–70). Bell was appointed professor of Vocal Physiology in Boston, MA (1873). His telephone was successfully demonstrated at the Centennial Exposition (1876) at Philadelphia to mark the hundredth anniversary of the American Declaration of Independence, and soon became an instrument of everyday use. Bell also helped to improve the phonograph, and his interest in aviation led to the foundation in the US of the Aerial Experiment Association (1907).

BELL, SIR FRANCIS DILLON (1822–98), a NZ company agent and Maori land purchaser (1843–50). Later, he became native minister (1862–3) and Maori land commissioner (1880). Bell was a key figure in NZ's relations with Britain as agent-general in London (1880–91), promoting British loans and investments and helping to ease tensions over Pacific islands.

BELL, GEORGE KENNEDY ALLEN (1883–1958), Anglican bishop of Chichester (1929–58), leader of the ecumenical movement, and an outspoken opponent of Nazism, who led an abortive attempt to start peace negotiations in the Second World War. He was dean of Canterbury (1924–9), where he began the practice of broadcasting religious services. During the 1930s he secured asylum in Britain for refugees from Germany.

He had close contact with the German Confessional Church and in 1942 travelled to Sweden, where German emissaries from the opposition to Hitler asked Bell whether Britain would negotiate a peace should they succeed in overthrowing the Führer. The British government instructed Bell to give no answer. After the War Bell became chairman and then president of the World Council of Churches.

BELL, HENRY (1767–1830), Scottish shipbuilder, who conceived the idea of using steam to propel marine-craft, and built the first practical steamboat, the *Comet* (1812).

BELL, JOHN (1797–1869), US politician from Tennessee. As congressman (1827–41) and US senator (1847–59), Bell was a high-minded moderate and a leader of the Southern Whigs. With the realignment of political groups in 1860,

Bell became presidential candidate of the Constitutional Union Party and carried Tennessee, Kentucky, and Virginia.

BELL, SIR ROBERT (d. 1577), English judge, MP, and speaker of the House of Commons (1572–6). He supported Peter Wentworth in his defence of MPs' right of free speech. He became chief baron of the exchequer (1577).

BELL MISSION, US economic survey mission headed by Daniel W. Bell, president of the American Security and Trust Co. at Washington, DC, sent to the Philippines in 1950 by President Truman at the request of President Quirino. The mission surveyed the contemporary crisis of Philippine society and recommended measures to meet it. Its report was divided into two parts: the first covered the economic difficulties of the Philippines, *eg*, in agriculture, industry, internal and external finance, domestic and foreign trade, as well as in public administration; the second part dealt with development problems and policies concerning the immediate measures recommended by the mission to help raise production and living standards in the Philippines. The report was submitted in Oct. 1950 to President Quirino with nine technical memoranda and an assurance that there was no compulsion on the Philippines to accept the plan suggested by the mission. The year 1950 marked a turning point for US policy in Asia. Threats of communism in South-East Asian countries aroused strong currents of disapproval in America against foreign aid and 'give away' to emerging countries. Consequently, the mission suggested that American aid should be extended to the Philippines only if steps were taken to implement the reforms it recommended. President Quirino therefore created a seven-man committee, headed by J. Yulo, to study the Bell report and make recommendations for its implementation. Yulo also co-ordinated all eight sub-committees, referred to as the Eight Bell Study Groups. After the submission of the Study Committee's report, the Philippine government undertook to implement the acceptable recommendations of the Bell Mission.

The Bell Report. US Economic Survey Mission's Report with the Recommendations in the Hardie Report (Manila, 1950).
JM Sa

BELL REBELLION (1531), popular revolt which broke out in Bergslagen and Dalarna against Gustavus Vasa's anti-clerical decree that one bell in every church throughout Sweden should be contributed to the exchequer. The rebels were encouraged by Christian II of Denmark's attack on Norway, but by 1533 they had been ruthlessly suppressed.

BELLAMY, EDWARD (1850–98), US journalist and author concerned mainly with social and economic problems. His *Looking Backward: 2000–1887* (1888) was a utopian romance advocating a mild form of socialism disguised as nationalism. It contained a theory of state capitalism that has had considerable influence. Bellamy, or Nationalist, clubs were founded to discuss the book's social implications, and Bellamy established the *Nationalist* (1889–91) and the *New Nation* (1891–4) to advance his theories.

BELLARMINE, ROBERT (1542–1621), French cardinal and writer. He lectured at Louvain University (1570–6), but spent nearly all the rest of his life in Rome as a professor of theology at the Jesuit College and later as a theological adviser to the papal curia, where he was involved in the trial of Galileo. His career is the prime example of the tendency in Catholic theology to concentrate on anti-Protestant dialectic. His ultramontane attitude towards the secular power aroused great animosity, particularly among French Gallicans. The assassination of Henry IV (Nov. 1610) was felt by many in France to be a dangerous illustration of this attitude, expressed in the *Tractatus de potestate summi pontificis* (1610).

BELL-BEAKER CULTURES (2nd millennium BC), so named from a pottery vessel so highly standardized as to be indicative of a significant drink, such as beer or milk. From what at present appears to be an original nucleus in the Iberian peninsula, Bell-Beakers spread rapidly eastwards and northwards over Europe. Their distribution extends from the British Isles in the west to a dense concentration in central Europe as far as the Vistula river in the east. Considerable local exploitation of copper and gold resources must be attributed to the makers of Bell-Beakers, who took their knowledge of elementary metallurgy to regions that were still largely stone-using.

BELLE ISLE, island off southern Brittany taken (1761) by a British naval and military force. It was returned to France in 1763.

BELLEAU WOOD, BATTLE OF (6–21 June 1918), one of the first major battles in the First World War involving the American Expeditionary Force in France. The US 2nd Division and 4th Marine Brigade cleared the wood, pushed back the German line, and strengthened the Allied position around Château-Thierry.

BELLINI, GIOVANNI (*c.* 1430–1516), the most famous of a family of Tuscan painters who settled in Venice. He was strongly influenced by Flemish painting and its Italian exponent Antonello da Messina. Bellini was one of the first Italian artists to paint in oils and on canvas. The result was a mellow and luminous quality which strongly influenced his followers, Giorgione and Titian, as did his interest in the painting of landscape. He excelled as a portrait painter, his most famous portrait being that of Leonardo Loredan, doge of Venice.

BELLO LÓPEZ, ANDRÉS (1781–1865), Venezuelan educator and writer. Bello taught the young Bolívar, and served the Venezuelan independence movement in London. He left Venezuela (1829) and lived in Chile until his death. His career was devoted to the construction of the Chilean educational system. He headed the National University and wrote many of the textbooks and regulations for the primary and secondary schools. He was also the author of a new Chilean civil code. A man of great erudition, Bello's works included poetry, essays, law, and politics. His Spanish grammar is still (1970) widely used.

BELLOC, HILAIRE (1870–1953), poet, essayist, historian, and a leader of intellectual Roman Catholicism in Britain. Born in France, the son of a French father and an English mother, Belloc was educated in Birmingham and at Balliol College, Oxford. He was naturalized in 1903 and in 1906 was elected Liberal MP for South Salford. He left politics in 1910 to devote his time to writing. Among his historical works are *Danton* (1899), *Robespierre* (1901), *Richelieu* (1929), and a *History of England* (1925–31). He will probably be best remembered, however, for his essays and light verse.

BELLORI, GIOVANNI PIETRO (1615–96), Italian antiquary. He published his *Admiranda Romanarum Antiquitatum*, which typified the 17th-cent. interest in classical Rome, in 1693.

BELMONT, AUGUST (1816–90), German-born US financier and Democratic politician. Though widely distrusted as an agent of the Rothschilds, he was a key figure in the Democratic Party and struggled to preserve both his party and the Union during the American Civil War. His European contacts helped to prevent recognition of the Confederacy.

BELVEDERE PALACE, at Vienna, built for Eugène of Savoy by the German architect Hildebrandt (1724). With its massive spatial effects, the cunning perspectives of its staircases, and its decorative mouldings and gables, it is the consummation of German Baroque.

BELZÚ, MANUEL ISIDORO (1808–66), Bolivian president, general and revolutionary. Belzú, after seizing power (1848), governed with the support of the urban poor until his resignation in 1855. Both his presidential terms saw revolts followed by brutal repression. His second presidency (1865–66) ended in his being overthrown and murdered. Since the Bolivian Revolution (1952) Belzú's reputation has undergone a revision. Some claim he was a forerunner of the revolution, and fought for justice for the poor.

BEMBA, people of north-eastern Zambia whose military and commercial skills helped them to create an important state during the 19th cent.

BEN GURION, DAVID (1886–), first Israeli prime minister (1948–53, 1955–63) and the leading figure in Jewish politics in Palestine. He was chairman of the Jewish Agency (1935–48) and leader of the Mapai Party.

BENALCÁZAR, SEBASTIÁN DE (1495–1550), Spanish conquistador, born, like many of them, in Estremadura. Benalcázar took part in the campaigns in Panama and Nicaragua before joining in the conquest of the Inca domains. He commanded the expedition to the northern area (roughly modern Ecuador). Benalcázar disposed of a challenge by Pedro de Alvarado by buying him off, then defeated the local chieftain, Rumiñahui. He established his headquarters at Quito (1533). Continuing north, he met two other conquistador bands, led by Gonzalo Jiménez de Quesada and Nicolás Federmann at Bogotá. After a jurisdictional quarrel Benalcázar was awarded the governorship of Popayan.

BENARES, TREATY OF (7 Sept. 1773), between Shuja-ud-daulah of Oudh and Warren Hastings. The ruler of Oudh agreed to pay two lakhs 10,000 rupees per month for a British subsidiary brigade. He also agreed to purchase Kora and Allahabad for 50 lakhs of rupees.

BENARES HINDU UNIVERSITY. Schemes for a Hindu university were put forward by Pandit Madan Mohan Malaviya (1905), Mrs Besant of the Theosophical Society, and the Maharaja of Darbhanga (1907), but it was Malaviya who brought the schemes to fruition. He gained the support of the others for the Hindu University Society (1911), which raised, chiefly from the princes, the funds to endow the institution. In 1913 the Central Hindu College, Benares, founded by the Theosophical Society (1898), agreed to amalgamate with the new university when it began. Inaugurated (1916) as a teaching and residential university under the government of India, it had over 9000 students by 1970.

The university has a clear Hindu denominational basis in the composition of its governing body, the Court, and in its declared intention to foster studies in Hindu culture and learning. It has also made special efforts to promote scientific and technical studies to foster indigenous industrial development. Both aspects reflect Malaviya's influence, as founder and as vice-chancellor (1919–39). The other notable vice-chancellor was Prof. S. Radhakrishnan (1939–48), philosopher and later president of India.

BENAVIDES, OSCAR RAIMUNDO (1876–1945), general and conservative president of Peru (1933–6), who participated in the revolt of 1914. He was re-elected (1936) for three more years after the APRA-dominated elections were annulled by the conservative Constituent Assembly.

BENBOW, JOHN (1653–1702), British admiral who fought at Beachy Head and La Hogue, and commanded fireships at St Malo (1693) and Dunkirk (1694). In 1701 he was sent to the West Indies, where, on the outbreak of war, he fought a running battle with an inferior French force off Santa Marta. Four of Benbow's seven ships refused to obey signals to attack, their captains having a personal feud with Benbow. The French squadron escaped and the recalcitrant captains were court-martialled, two of them afterwards being shot. The episode illustrates the indiscipline of many naval officers at this time.

BENBURB, BATTLE OF (1646), incident in the extraordinarily complex rebellion in Ireland. At that time there were five armies in the field, each representing a different political interest. On 5 June the Ulster Scots, under Gen. Robert Monro, were defeated by the Irish Confederates under Owen Roe O'Neill. The victory greatly increased O'Neill's prestige in Ireland.

BENCOOLEN (or BENGKAHULU), in south-west Sumatra, site of the principal British East India Co's base in the East Indies (1685–1824). The company, after its expulsion by the Dutch from the Bantam pepper-market (1682), hoped a factory at Bencoolen would tap the surrounding pepper-growing districts. Fort Marlborough was later constructed (1714–19) on a nearby headland, and ranked briefly as an independent presidency (1763–1802), then reverted to Bengal. But it was too far from the main Malacca Straits route to China, and its system of monopoly drove the centres of pepper production and marketing elsewhere. Raffles was its last British lieutenant-governor (1818–24) before it became a Dutch residency, but he was unable to accomplish much beyond ending slavery and forced cultivation.

BENDA, JULIEN (1867–1956), French writer, remembered chiefly for his controversial pamphlet 'La Trahison des clercs' (1927), in which he condemned French intellectuals for abandoning their independent position and surrendering to political passions, especially nationalism. His chief targets were Barres, Maurras, and Bergson. Benda was associated briefly with Péguy's *Cahiers de la Quinzaine*, but he cannot be identified with any particular school. Faith in the power of reason and the importance of intellectual independence were his central ideas.

BENDER, town in Bessarabia. It prospered in the 14th and 15th cents as a result of its location on the trade route running from Ak Kirman to Lvov in Poland. The Ottomans seized Bender in 1484 and, later (c. 1570), made it the centre of a *sanjak beglik* (district officership). It was at Bender that Charles XII of Sweden found refuge (1709–13) after the battle of Poltava. The Russians took Bender in 1770, 1789, and 1806, acquiring the town as a permanent possession at the peace of Bucharest in 1812.

BENEDEK, LUDWIG AUGUST, RITTER VON (1804–81), Austrian general who commanded the army defeated at Sadowa. He spent his early career in the Italian campaigns (1848–9, 1859), in which he was the only Austrian commander to show any real competence. In the Austro-Prussian War (1866) he was given charge of the defence of Bohemia instead of being left to fight the Italians, whose terrain he knew.

BENEDETTI, VINCENT, Comte (1817–1900), French ambassador at Berlin (1864–70) before the outbreak of the Franco-Prussian War. In 1870 he was given the task of requesting King William I of Prussia to confirm his decision to withdraw the Hohenzollern candidature to the Spanish Crown. William's refusal was turned by Bismarck into the provocation for the famous Ems telegram.

BENEDICT XII (*reg.* 1334–42), Pope, who was the third of the Avignon popes. His pontificate was associated with reforms and education, while in his political aims he sought, without avail, to keep England and France at peace.

BENEDICT XIII (1649–1730), Pope (*reg.* 1724–30), a conscientious Dominican, but one lacking in political and administrative skill. The internal administration of his papacy was delegated to the corrupt Niccolò Coscia, under whom it

deteriorated rapidly. Benedict tried to enforce the Tridentine decrees to raise the standards of the clergy, and induced the Abp of Paris to accept the bull *Unigenitus*. His extension to the Universal Church of the Office of Gregory VII offended several European courts.

BENEDICT XIV (1675–1758), Pope (*reg.* 1740–58), who allowed the clergy of Spain to be taxed at the same rate as the laity, and by the Concordat of 1753 gave up to the Spanish Crown the right of appointment to all but 52 specified benefices in exchange for a payment calculated to yield the same annual income. He also yielded to the King of Portugal extended rights of patronage and the additional title 'Most Faithful'. Similar concessions were made to Naples and Sardinia, while to the imperial court was offered a diminution of appointed holidays. He also reconstituted the Roman nobility as a closed cast of 187 families.

BENEDICT XV (1854–1922), Pope (*reg.* 1914–22). His career began in the papal diplomatic service and he was Abp of Bologna at the time of his election.

His first encyclical called for peace, and throughout the war he refused to condemn any particular belligerent, disappointing French and Belgian Catholics as well as Italian interventionists. The Italian state Law of Guarantees was silent on Vatican diplomatic rights, and communications with the Universal Church, during the war. Benedict hoped that strict neutrality would lead to international guarantees of Vatican independence in peacetime. However, in 1915, the Italian government made the pope's exclusion from the peace conference a condition of Italy's intervention in the war.

The German Catholic politician, Erzberger, visited Italy and the Vatican in 1915, to try to prevent Italy's intervention. This somewhat compromised Benedict's neutrality, although he did not respond to Erzberger's schemes for reinforcing Vatican independence.

Benedict hoped to save the Habsburg empire from disintegration, encouraging Habsburg concessions in territorial and nationality disputes with Italy and the subject provinces. These were mentioned in his famous note to the belligerents of 15 Aug. 1917, which otherwise proposed peace on a basis of pre-war frontiers, with special provision for Belgian damages. This initiative proved unsuccessful: Austria refused to compromise with Italy; Germany would not reveal her designs for Belgium; the US had recently entered the war, and made German defeat a precondition for peace.

Benedict's peace policy created unwonted harmony between Italian clericals and socialists. In 1919 he withdrew his *non expedit* which had restrained Catholics from voting, and Catholics formed the Italian Popular Party. His papacy significantly improved Vatican-state relations. In his last years the creation of a sovereign Vatican City was under discussion. His was the first papal death since 1870 officially acknowledged by the Italian government.

C. Seton-Watson, *Italy from Liberalism to Fascism* (London, 1967).
J. A. Thayer, *Italy and the Great War* (Wisconsin, 1964).

ASJ

BENEDICT OF ANIANE, Saint (c. 750–821). Born of a noble family, he used his inheritance to found the Abbey of Aniane (779), of which he was the first abbot. He became the confidant and religious adviser of the Emperor Louis the Pious. Under Benedict's guidance, Louis in 817 made the 6th cent. Rule of St Benedict binding on all monks in his dominions, thus making Benedictinism virtually synonymous with monasticism in western Europe.

BENEDICT BISCOP (d. 690) a Northumbrian, who made several journeys to the continent and Rome, bringing back with him books and works of art. He founded the double monastery at Monkwearmouth (674) and Jarrow (685) (where Bede was a monk), and became its first abbot.

BENEDICT OF NURSIA, Saint (*c.* 480–547), the father of western monasticism. Very little is known of his life, and that only from the *Dialogues* of Pope Gregory I the Great, written *c.* 594. Born of a patrician family, Benedict studied at Rome before living as a hermit. His fame spread and several groups of hermits gathered around his cave. After dissension and an attempt to poison Benedict, they moved (*c.* 529) to Cassino, where he founded a monastery, for which he presumably wrote his *Rule* (*c.* 540). Doubts have been cast on Benedict's authorship of the *Rule*, but most scholars accept it as his work. It is closely based on the earlier anonymous *Regula Magistri*. The great virtues of Benedict's *Rule* are that, although it is short, it is remarkably comprehensive and of such simplicity, moderation, clarity, and wisdom that it became universally accepted and virtually synonymous with western monasticism.

BENEDICTINE ORDER was not in the Middle Ages, strictly speaking, a monastic order, each of its houses being autonomous. There were no constitutional links between the houses, the only real link being the acceptance of the Benedictine rule of Benedict of Nursia (d. 547). The most important stage in the history of the order began with the move of the monks to Rome from the monastery of Monte Cassino on its destruction by the Lombards (*c.* 577). The future Pope Gregory I, himself a monk as well as an influential Roman notable, patronized them. After he became pope he fostered the spread of the order by dispatching St Augustine to England to convert the Anglo-Saxons (596–7). The order was introduced into Germany by Anglo-Saxon missionaries, especially by St Boniface in the 8th cent., and was established in France with the foundation of Fleury (*c.* 672). Major reforms of the order were initiated in the Carolingian empire by St Benedict of Aniane, in 10th-cent. England by St Dunstan, and, above all, by Cluny (911). Cluny introduced a measure of organization with each Cluniac house dependent ultimately upon Cluny itself for discipline. In 1215 the Lateran Council tried to bring the houses of a province into a legislative and disciplinary union, and the 15th cent. saw the rise of 'congregations', which grouped abbeys together for disciplinary purposes, though it was not until the Council of Trent that the congregational system became universal. Medieval Europe owed an incalculable debt to the Benedictines and for several centuries monasticism was virtually synonymous with Benedictinism. Scholarship and learning were wholly dependent upon, and all religious and spiritual vitality came from, them.

BENEFIT OF CLERGY, medieval privilege, surviving into the 18th cent., by which members of the clergy (in practice, those people able to read) could plead for less stringent treatment than ordinary felons.

BENELUX, customs union established by agreement between the wartime governments of Belgium, Holland, and Luxemburg. It came into effect in Jan. 1948, when customs duties between the three states were abolished and a uniform tariff established on imported goods. The union thus established was carried further in 1955 with an agreement to harmonize agricultural policies and the establishment of an Interparliamentary Council. In 1954 the movement of capital between the three countries was freed and in 1956 a common labour market established. In Feb. 1958 a treaty establishing the Benelux Economic Union was signed (within the provisions of Article 223 of the European Economic Community Treaty and Article 202 of the Euratom Treaty). The union has a series of institutions, similar to those of the EEC, of which the Council of the Economic Union has the function of a board of management.

BENEŠ, EDUARD (1884–1948), Czech statesman; member of the National Socialist (centre) Party, foreign minister (1918–1935), president (1935–8, 1946–8). He was born of peasant stock in north-west Bohemia, and educated at Prague and

Dijon universities and the Sorbonne. In 1915 he joined Thomas Masaryk in his efforts to mobilize world opinion against the Habsburg regime. On the formation of the Czech National Council in 1916 Beneš was appointed its secretary general. The National Council gradually evolved into the basis of the government of the embryo Czechoslovak state and on 14 Oct. 1918 the Allies recognized the National Council as the Provisional Government of Czechoslovakia. Beneš was appointed foreign minister of the new republic and in 1919 he headed the Czechoslovak delegation to the Versailles Conference. He was the leading figure in the formation of an alliance of the successor states against Hungarian revisionism (the 'Little Entente' between Czechoslovakia, Rumania, and Yugoslavia was completed in 1921) and, subsequently, their connection with France (Franco-Czech treaties, 1924; 1925). He was elected a member of the League council (1923), and was one of the main architects of the Geneva Protocol, which attempted to make arbitration between members compulsory. At Geneva Beneš became the most famous spokesman of the small nations and was elected president of the League (1935).

At the end of the same year he succeeded Masaryk as president. Beneš faced growing Nazi activity among the Sudeten Germans, who were supplied with funds by Germany. In 1935 their party, the Sudetendeutsche Partei, became the third largest Czech party. After the Anschluss (March 1938) the local SP leader, Henlein, and Hitler stepped up the propaganda campaign. Henlein claimed that he only sought a greater degree of autonomy from Prague, but in effect his demands repudiated the principles of the Czech state. Beneš had supplemented the Franco-Soviet Pact of May 1935 with a Czech-Soviet Pact. Under the terms of this agreement the Russians would only act if France acted first. Beneš conducted negotiations with Henlein with dignity and skill, but was under pressure from the British and French governments to concede to German demands. Following the Munich settlement (Sept. 1938) he resigned (5 Oct.).

During the Second World War Benes headed the Czech government in exile which was formed in London (1940). He believed that he could achieve an understanding with Stalin and in Dec. 1943 he travelled to Moscow, where he signed a treaty of friendship and alliance. He returned to Czechoslovakia after the war and was elected president (19 June 1946). In the following year the communist minister of the interior intensified his policy of appointing communists in the police force. In protest, 11 non-communist ministers resigned (20 Feb.). Under pressure from the communist prime minister, Gottwald, supported by the mobilization of communist organizations throughout the country, Beneš agreed to the formation of a new government which proved to be a communist dictatorship. Rather than accept the new constitution, however, he resigned (7 June).

Eduard Beneš (tr. P. Selver), *My War Memoirs* (London, 1928).
E. B. Hitchcock, *Beneš, the Man and the Statesman* (London, 1940).   RE

BENÉT, STEPHEN VINCENT (1898–1943), US author and poet. Great faith in the American nation, coupled with a deep interest and insight into American history, pervades his work. Best-known is his American Civil War epic poem, 'John Brown's Body' (1928).

BENEVENTO, BATTLE OF (26 Feb. 1266), the decisive victory of Charles of Anjou, the papal candidate for the crown of Sicily, over the ruling king, Manfred, son of the Emperor Frederick II, who was regarded by the papacy as a mortal threat to its independence. Charles had invaded Manfred's lands in a surprise winter campaign. At Benevento, Manfred was at first victorious, but the indiscipline of his troops, led to their defeat and Manfred's death.

BENEZET, ANTHONY (Antoine) (1713–1784), American abolitionist. Born of Huguenot parents in St Quintin (France),

D W H—G

Benezet emigrated with his family to Holland (1715), then to Philadelphia (1731). He became a Quaker and supported freedom for slaves and rights for American Indians. After a business career, Benezet opened a school for girls (1755), where he taught. He was a prolific writer on the evils of slavery. He eventually endowed a school for the education of Negroes in Philadelphia.

BENGAL, rich alluvial region watered by the Ganges and the Brahmaputra and their tributaries, and stretching from Bihar on the west to Assam and the Bay of Bengal on the east, and from the foothills of the Himalayas on the north to Orissa in the south. It comprises (since 1947) West Bengal, a state of India with its capital at Calcutta, and East Pakistan, with its capital at Dacca. East Pakistan contains the Dacca and Chittagong divisions of the former British province and most of the Sylhet district of Assam. West Bengal comprises the rest of the old province and the state of Cooch Bihar (merged with West Bengal in 1950). Bengal is the Anglicized form of the ancient 'Banga' or 'Vanga'. In the 3rd cent. BC it formed part of Asoka's extensive empire. It was annexed to the Gupta empire of Samudragupta in the 4th cent. AD. In the first half of the 7th cent. Harsha extended his frontiers to the borders of Kamarupa, so as to include Pundravardhana, Karnasuvarna, and Samatata. The Palas were the ruling power in the 9th cent., but had great difficulty in maintaining their independence, threatened as it was by the Gurjara-Pratiharas to the north-west. In the 11th cent. the Senas were the chief power until Qutb-ud-din's general, Muhammad Bakhtyar, overran Bihar and Bengal at the end of the 12th cent. It formed part of Muhammad bin Tughluq's empire in the 14th cent., but became independent in 1341 under Afghan rulers, until it was conquered by Akbar (1576). With the decline of the Mughal empire in the 18th cent. the provincial governors began to assert their independence. From Alivardi Khan, a Muslim adventurer, descended the *nawab nazims* of Bengal with whom Clive came into contact. After Clive's victory at Plassey (1757) the British were the de facto rulers of Bengal. For a time they attempted to exert control by means of puppet *nawabs*, but, after Munro's victory at Buxar (1764), they were the unchallenged rulers of the province. By the *diwani* grant of 1765 the British obtained the right to collect and administer the revenues of Bengal, Bihar, and Orissa. Under the Regulating Act of 1773 Warren Hastings became the first governor-general of Bengal. By Cornwallis's Permanent Settlement (1793) the land revenue demand was fixed in perpetuity and the *zamindars* (formerly landholders) became the landowners. In 1854 the administration of Bengal was placed under a lieutenant-governor. In 1874 Assam was placed under a separate chief-commissioner. Curzon's partition of Bengal (1905) produced constant agitation until it was revoked (1912), when Bengal was placed under a governor, Bihar and Orissa under a lieutenant-governor, and Assam under a chief commissioner. In 1937 Bengal became an autonomous province until the partition of the sub-continent (1947).

R. C. Majumdar, *The Early History of Bengal* (Dacca, 1925). J. Sarkar (ed.), *The History of Bengal, Muslim Period* (Dacca, 1948).   CCD

BENIN, city in mid-western Nigeria, historically the capital of an important state whose origins can be traced to the 14th cent. Its government was based on a complex structure of hierarchically ordered societies through which all subjects were integrated into the state. The prestige of its semi-divine monarchy and an efficient military organization enabled Benin to expand greatly in the 15th and 16th cents. It lost ground in the 19th cent. and was conquered by the British in 1897. Europeans traded intermittently with Benin from 1485, exporting slaves, pepper, cloth, ivory, and gum. The brasswork produced over many centuries to decorate the royal palace and shrines has become world-famous for its artistry and craftsmanship.

BENJAMIN, ASHER (1773–1845), US carpenter and architect. In *The Country Builder's Assistant* (1797), *The Rudiments of Architecture* (1814), and many other manuals for the small-town builder, Benjamin helped to popularize and disseminate the 'Federal' style of architecture.

BENNELONG (*c.* 1764–1813), a captured Australian Aboriginal, through whom Phillip the first governor of NSW, sought to improve knowledge and understanding of Aborigines. He readily adopted white habits, good and bad. Taken to England by Phillip (1792), he was presented to King George III but died in relative obscurity after his return.

BENNETT, RICHARD BEDFORD BENNETT, Viscount (1870– 1947). Canadian prime minister, who was elected Conservative MP for Olds in the territorial legislative (1898), but was defeated in the first general election in the new province of Alberta (1905), then re-elected in 1909. He resigned in 1911 and was returned to the Canadian House of Commons by Calgary East. During the First World War he was director-general of national service until 1917. He was minister of justice and attorney-general in Arthur Meighen's short administration (1921) and minister of finance under Meighen (July–Oct. 1926), succeeding him as Conservative leader (Oct. 1927). He led the party to victory at the 1930 election on a programme of national effort to combat the effects of the Great Depression. Bennett acted as his own finance minister and foreign secretary. He negotiated a St Lawrence Seaway treaty with the US (1932), which was rejected by the American Senate. In Jan. 1935 Bennett, in a series of radio broadcasts, outlined his Canadian version of the New Deal. Five of his reforming measures (the Minimum Wages, Limitation of Hours of Work, Weekly Rest in Industrial Undertakings, Unemployment Insurance, and the Natural Products Marketing Acts) were declared *ultra vires* of the federal parliament by the courts (1937), but formed the basis for later legislation after a revision of the constitution. The Conservatives, split between Bennett and H. H. Stevens, lost the 1935 election, but Bennett continued to lead the party until his retirement (1938), when he moved to Britain (1939).

Ernest Watkins, *R. B. Bennett: a biography* (Toronto, 1963).
                                                                     AJS

BENOIST-MÉCHIN, JACQUES (1901–), advocate of Franco-German collaboration under the Vichy regime in France. A writer and journalist, he had been an admirer of Germany in the 1930s and a member of the fascist *Parti populaire français*. As a minister (1941–2), he was responsible for Franco-German relations. After the war he was tried and imprisoned.

BENT, ELLIS (1783–1815) and **JEFFERY HART** (1781–1852), brothers who were active in the administration of justice in New South Wales during the governorship of Lachlan Macquarie. Ellis sailed to NSW in 1809 and in his early years, as judge-advocate in succession to Richard Atkins, worked harmoniously with Macquarie, making recommendations for reform of the colony's judicial system. These were only partially adopted (1814), Ellis retaining criminal and other restricted jurisdiction, but being passed over for his brother Jeffery, who arrived from England in July 1814, as judge of a 'Supreme Court of Civil Judicature'. Jeffery was perpetually at loggerheads with Macquarie, notably on the admission of emancipist attorneys, and increasingly influenced his brother. Eventually, the governor recommended that both brothers should be removed from office. Ellis died before news of the decision to remove them reached NSW. Jeffery returned to England and some years later was variously employed by the colonial office, as chief justice in Grenada, puisne judge in Trinidad, chief judge of St Lucia, and chief justice of British Guiana—in most of which posts he lived up to his NSW reputation as a troublemaker with local authorities.

BENTHAM, JEREMY (1748–1832), English philosopher, who developed Utilitarianism in England. Though a major figure in the history of political thought, for much of his life Bentham kept apart from politics. He was educated as a lawyer and his first efforts were directed to legal reform. He attacked the law's obscurity and devious procedures, and held that the theories of natural rights and separation of powers supported by Blackstone involved much practical injustice. Bentham became converted to the need for parliamentary reform *c.* 1807, partly by James Mill, the father of John Stuart Mill, and partly because the government would not adopt his scheme for a model prison, the Panopticon. After 1815 he became increasingly a recluse, but he was surrounded by a group of disciples, including Grote, Chadwick, Bowring, James and John Stuart Mill, who edited his works for publication and through whom his ideas became influential after 1832, particularly in penal reform, public health, and poor law administration.

Utilitarianism, as elaborated by Bentham, holds that men pursue pleasure and avoid pain, and that the prudent legislator will so govern as to produce the greatest happiness of the greatest number. Bentham produced an elaborate 'felicific calculus' with which to calculate the effect of actions. His theory can lead both to laissez-faire and, as expounded by Chadwick, to greater central government control. Bentham's best-known works are *A Fragment on Government* (1776) and *Introduction to the Principles of Morals and Legislation* (1780).

BENTINCK, LORD WILLIAM CAVENDISH (1774–1839), governor-general of India. As governor of Madras (1803–7), whence he was recalled because of his attitude towards the Vellore Mutiny (1806), he laid it down as a principle that British greatness was founded on Indian happiness. He saw military service in Portugal and commanded a brigade at Corunna. He was appointed envoy to the court of Sicily and as commander-in-chief of the British forces on the island (1811), he led an expeditionary force against Genoa (1814). He became governor-general of Bengal (July 1828–Nov. 1834) and first governor-general of India (Nov. 1834–March 1835), in which post he carried out policies of retrenchment and reform. The directors of the British East India Co. insisted on economy because of the heavy debt incurred in the Burmese War. He stopped the 'half-*batta*' or field allowance enjoyed by the European officers of the company's army in addition to their pay, and gave the sepoys increased pay after long service. He abolished flogging in the sepoy army, but retained it for European troops, and gave increased employment to educated Indians in the judicial and administrative service, thus reversing Cornwallis's policy of non-Indianization. It is a fallacy that he initiated the change by which collectors of revenue became magistrates also, for Regulation IV of 1821 enabled the governor to confer the powers of a magistrate on any collector, and this had already been done in Kumaon, and in the Delhi, Saugor, and Nerbudda territories. An improved land revenue settlement was carried out by R. Bird in the North-Western Provinces.

BENTINCK, LORD WILLIAM GEORGE CAVENDISH (1802–1848), British politician who led the protectionists against Peel's repeal of the Corn Laws (1846). The attack on repeal was initiated by Disraeli, but Bentinck, with his greater social standing, was accepted as leader of the movement, although a poor speaker. A strong believer in the value of the territorial aristocracy, he felt that Peel had betrayed them. He was a firm friend to Disraeli, and in effect made possible his career as a leader of the country gentry.

BENTLEY, RICHARD (1662–1742), English classical scholar, the first to use scientific textual criticism which combined philological with historical knowledge. Educated at Cambridge, he took deacon's orders in 1690. He was the first Boyle lecturer (1692) and in 1693 was appointed keeper of the Royal Library.

Bentley became involved in the controversy concerning the comparative merits of ancient and modern learning. His *Dissertation upon the Epistles of Phalaris* (1699) showed these letters, praised by Sir William Temple, to have been spurious, through both geographical and linguistic anachronisms. The controversy was satirized by Swift in his *Battle of the Books*.

In 1700 he was appointed master of Trinity College, Cambridge, and was involved in a 30-year feud with the fellows over college reforms, from which he emerged victorious. In 1717 he became regius professor of divinity. He produced many revisions of the texts of classical authors, *eg*, Horace, Terence, and Manlius, combining learning with critical acuteness.

BENTON, THOMAS HART (1782–1858), US Senator from Missouri, and a leading figure in American politics for nearly 40 years. He was a champion of westward expansion, a prosettler in land policy, and advocated hard money (hence the nickname 'Old Bullion'), Jacksonian democracy, and the preservation of the Union. Born in North Carolina, he moved west, first to Tennessee, then to Missouri territory, which he helped to statehood (1821). He was the first senator to serve for 30 consecutive years (1821–51), and later served a term in the House of Representatives (1853–5). He wrote two works of great historical value, his autobiography, *Thirty Years View* (1854–6), and an *Abridgment of the Debates in Congress from 1789 to 1856* (1857–61).

BEOWULF, epic Anglo-Saxon vernacular pre-Viking poem (in MS form *c.* 1000), containing a wealth of heroic detail and traditional folklore. It describes the legendary adventures of Beowulf of the Geats against a mere-monster and a fire-dragon and is set in the Sweden and Denmark of the 6th cent.

BERAR, district in central India lying between the Tapti river and the Satpura range to the north and the Penganga river to the south. It was anciently known as Vidharba and is now incorporated in the Indian state of Maharashtra. In the 14th cent. it became a part of the Muslim Bahmini kingdom, but in 1940 broke away to become independent. In 1575 it was conquered by Ahmadnagar, but in 1596 it passed to the Mughals and from them to the Nizams of Hyderabad (1724). Berar was constantly harassed and overrun by the Marathas until it was formally restored by the British to the nizam (1803). Through being claimed and alternately mulcted by the Marathas and the nizam, it lost its former prosperity. In 1853 Berar was 'assigned' to the East India Co., its revenue being used to defray the cost of the Hyderabad contingent, a charge on the nizam's government under the treaty of 1804. In 1902 Lord Curzon turned the assignment into a perpetual lease and made other changes, which the nizam resented as being extorted under duress. In 1926 his last attempt at redress was rejected by the British government.

BERBERS. When the conquering Arabs, freshly converted to Islam, arrived in North Africa in the closing years of the 7th cent. AD they found that in addition to the Byzantines of the coastal towns and the region corresponding to the former province of Africa, it was peopled by independent tribesmen speaking a distinctive language of their own. For this language the Arabs adopted the term Berber (*barbarīya*) and referred to its speakers as Berbers (*al-barbar, barābira*), which would appear to derive ultimately from the Greek *barbaroi* and be pejorative in origin. But, while these are the terms which have come to be employed generally by outsiders for the indigenous inhabitants of North Africa and for their language, they are practically unknown to the Berbers themselves, who usually employ local tribal names and, when they wish to generalize, refer to themselves as *Imazighn*, 'the lords, the masters', and to their language as *Tamazight*.

In the centuries succeeding the Islamic conquest, and more particularly from the 11th cent. onwards, following the invasion of the Beni Hilal, many of these Berber speakers became linguistically and at least to some extent culturally

Arabized while others, notably those inhabiting the mountainous and desert retreat areas, although they embraced the new religion, clung to their ancient language and customs. The linguistic pattern thus presented by North Africa today is that of a number of Berber-speaking enclaves separated from each other by intervening zones of Arabic. The importance of these Berber-speaking areas increases from Siwa Oasis in Egypt (perhaps a few hundreds of speakers) towards Morocco on the Atlantic seaboard (nearly half the population, covering an even larger proportion of the territory). Although Berber is not normally a written language, the Tuareg tribes of the central and southern Sahara have retained the use of a script called *tifinagh*; this shows a close affinity with that employed in the so-called Ancient Libyan inscriptions found throughout North Africa. More than a thousand of these have so far been discovered and, with the aid of bilingual inscriptions, the values of the symbols and even the meanings of some of the texts have been satisfactorily determined. While certain of the words used have clear cognates in the modern language, the linguistic evidence is not yet such as to permit a firm statement that the language in which these inscriptions are written is the direct ancestor of modern Berber. The grouping together of Berber and Ancient Libyan under the label of Libyco-Berber remains therefore, for the time being at least, no more than the expression of a useful working hypothesis.

The more distant connections of Ancient Libyan and Berber are naturally even less certain, but probably most linguists now accept the likelihood that, together with Semitic and Ancient Egyptian (and perhaps Cushitic and Chadic), they are members of a larger Hamito-Semitic language family, the proto-language of which presumably broke up and spread into approximately its present area at some time soon before the 3rd millennium BC. The case of Guanche, the extinct language of the Canary Islanders, stated to have been related to Berber, is equally unresolved. In spite of all these linguistic uncertainties, and notwithstanding a certain influx of Arab and Negro genes over the years, the great mass of the present-day population of North Africa is probably constituted by the direct descendants of those peoples, referred to by the classical authors under such various titles as Libyans, Numidians, Mauretanians, Getulians, Garamantians, Nasamonians, Psylli, Machlyans, Maxyans, etc.

A. Basset, *La Langue berbère*, in *Handbook of African Languages* (Oxford, 1952).
H. Basset, *Essai sur la litterature des Berbères* (Algiers, 1920).
JB

BERBICE, easternmost county of three comprising former British Guiana, now part of Guyana. The colony was founded by the Dutch (1627), captured by the British (1803), ceded to Britain (1814), and incorporated into British Guiana (1831).

BERCHTESGADEN, Hitler's mountain home in Bavaria. On 15 Sept. 1938, when Britain and France feared that the situation in Bohemia-Moravia might lead to a German–Czech conflict which might become general, Chamberlain, the British prime minister, made a dramatic flight to see Hitler at Berchtesgaden. It proved impossible to bargain with him on such points as a plebiscite in the Sudetenland. Hitler demanded its secession from Czechoslovakia on the principle of national self-determination. Chamberlain agreed to return for a second meeting after cabinet discussions. On 18 Sept. Britain and France formulated proposals for secession which they forced on an unwilling Czechoslovakia.

BERCHTOLD, LEOPOLD, Graf (1863–1942), foreign minister of Austria-Hungary at the outbreak of the First World War. He became foreign minister in 1912 and conducted a vacillating policy during the two Balkan Wars. He was, however, able to force Serbia to agree to the establishment of an independent Albania, a move which denied Serbia access to the Adriatic (1913). Under the army's influence, Berchtold

came to believe that Serbia should be crushed. When an opportunity came, with the murder of the Austrian heir-apparent in June 1914, his remaining doubts were resolved by pressure from Austria-Hungary's ally, Germany. Berchtold sent an ultimatum to Serbia, so worded as to be unacceptable and inevitably to result in war. He did this knowing full well that an Austro-Serbian conflict would probably develop into a European war.

BERENGAR II (*reg.* 950–61), King of Italy, grandson of the Emperor Berengar (915–24), who provoked the intervention in Italy of the German King Otto I. Otto's first Italian expedition in 951 led to the freeing of Berengar's captive, Adelaid, the widow of the former king, whom Otto married. Berengar's attack on Pope John XII led to Otto's second Italian venture in 961, Berengar being deposed. In 962 Otto received the imperial crown from the pope.

BERENGUER IV, Count of Barcelona (d. 1162), united Catalonia and Aragón by marrying the daughter of Ramiro II of Aragón. He established the principle that Catalonia and Aragón should respect each other's autonomy, thus determining the future constitutional form of the Crown of Aragón as a federation of autonomous states.

BERGEN, TOWN OF. The principal harbour of medieval Norway. Founded by a Norwegian king *c.* 1070–5, it became from *c.* 1200 the main centre for the German (Hanseatic) trade in Norway. The Hansards chiefly exported cod and supplied corn and textiles. This traffic was declining by *c.* 1500.

BERGEN-OP-ZOOM, key fortress town and centre of the Netherlands cloth trade, situated just north of the mouth of the Scheldt river in the Dutch-speaking province of Brabant.

BERGERAC, PEACE OF (1577), negotiated by the secretary of state, Villeroy, between Henry III and the Huguenots under Henry of Navarre during the French Wars of Religion. The peace of Monsieur (1576), which granted favourable terms to the Huguenots, provoked a bitter reaction from the Catholic nobility, who formed an extremist and anti-royalist Holy League. To protect himself, Henry III ousted Guise from the leadership of the league, though he received little help from the Catholic party in the renewed conflict with the Huguenots. The king's forces achieved some success against the Huguenots, which forced Navarre to negotiate again with Henry III. The peace of Bergerac, known as the 'King's Peace', deprived the Huguenots of their recently gained concessions, *ie*, the free exercise of their religion, but the development of the Catholic party was also arrested by the declaration that all leagues were henceforth illegal.

BERGH, WILLEM COUNT VAN DEN (1538–86), nobleman of Gelderland, who in 1556 married Maria of Nassau, sister of William the Silent. He became *stadtholder* of Gelderland for the states in 1581, but was deposed in 1583 on suspicion of collusion with the Duke of Parma.

BERGSON, HENRI (1859–1941), French humorist and philosopher. Two central notions dominate Bergson's philosophy: (*a*) that of '*durée réelle*'—real duration; (*b*) that of '*élan vital*'—vital impulse. From the first arises Bergson's theory of time and from the second his theory of evolution. He contributed important work on the notion of humour in *Le Rire* (1900) and on the meaning of social structure in *Les deux sources de la morale et de la religion* (1932).

BERIA, LAVRENTI PAVLOVICH (1899–1953), head of the Soviet Secret Police (1938–53), and originator of much Stalinist distortion of history. Born in Georgia of poor peasant stock, Beria joined the Communist Party in 1917. Four years later he joined the Cheka and rose rapidly in the secret police hierarchy. In 1938 Stalin used him to liquidate

Yezhov, thus ending the Great Purge. On the outbreak of war (June 1941) Beria was appointed to the State Defence Committee and entrusted with raising arms production. His control over the security networks made him one of the most powerful men in Russia. After the death of Stalin he attempted to increase his power by strengthening his hold over the secret police and at the same time courting popularity. On 10 July 1953 an official announcement denounced Beria as an enemy of the people and would-be restorer of capitalism. His rivals in the struggle for power after Stalin's death recognized the threat to themselves of his police empire and he was executed.

BERING, VITUS (1681–1741), Danish sea captain, from 1704 in the service of Russia, who, during the first half of the 18th cent., led two important expeditions to the Russian Far East. His first expedition in Peter the Great's navy began in 1725 with the aim of proving that a north-eastern sea passage separated Russia from America. In the summer of 1728 Bering sailed north from the eastern shore of Siberia and passed the most easterly tip of Asia. Though he believed he had sailed through the straits separating Asia and America, the expedition had not sighted the American shore, and as a result Bering was criticized on his return to St Petersburg (1730). He therefore proposed a second expedition. This was backed by the Empress Anna and the newly established Academy of Sciences, and grew into a great scientific venture. Besides the quest for a north-east passage, Bering was made responsible for establishing the exact position of Japan, organizing the exploration and charting of the Arctic coast, transporting settlers to the Far East, and supervising the establishment of industrial, educational, and farming enterprises. Bering was joined by the historian Müller, members of the Academy of Sciences, including the botanist Gmelin, the natural historian Steller, and the astronomer de Lisle. The expedition yielded valuable scientific and geographical information and unearthed a cache of old documents in Yakutsk, among them the charts of the Cossack Dezhnev, who, unknown to the rest of the world, had sailed through the north-east passage almost 100 years before (1648). Japan was located, and in July 1741 an Alaskan peak observed. This was Mount St Elias, named after the saint on whose feast-day the sighting was made. Landfall was made on an off-shore island, though not on the mainland itself. The expedition then sailed westwards, its crew suffering from scurvy and lack of water, and eventually drifted on to the shore of what is now Bering Island, some 200 miles northeast of its home port, Petropavlovsk.

G. A. Lensen (ed.), *Bering's Voyages*, 2 vols (New York,
   1922–5).   JHS

BERING STRAITS, north-eastern passage between the tip of Siberia and Alaska, named after the Danish sailor Vitus Bering, who sailed through the straits in 1728.

BERKE (d. 1266), 2nd Khan of the Golden Horde (1257–66) and a brother of Batu Khan, who ascended the throne in 1257. During the years 1261–3 he made an entente with the Mamluk Sultan of Egypt and Syria, Baybars, against the Mongol Il-Khan Hulagu, then ruling in Persia. Berke Khan was converted to Islam, perhaps before 1251, but some 50 years were to pass before the Muslim faith became dominant within the Golden Horde.

BERKELEY OF STRATTON, JOHN BERKELEY, 1st Baron (c. 1606–78), English soldier and public servant. He fought in the Civil War as a royalist, attempting mediation between Charles I and Oliver Cromwell and accompanying the king to Carisbrooke Castle. After the king's execution (1649) he went abroad. He returned at the Restoration (1660) to become commissioner of the navy (1660–4), lord lieutenant of Ireland (1670–2), and ambassador extraordinary at the Nymwegen treaty discussions (1676–7). Charles II's brother,

the Duke of York, gave him a share in holdings in the American colonies, Berkeley gaining interests between the Hudson and Delaware rivers in New Jersey, which he had financially disposed of by 1674.

BERKELEY, GEORGE (1685–1753), bishop of Cloyne, philosopher, theologian, and social reformer, who published most of his philosophical works at an early age. His three main doctrines were 'nominalism', 'immaterialism', and 'acquired visual perception'. In 1713 he went to England, where he was appointed chaplain to Lord Peterborough. Later he returned to Ireland and in 1721 became successively dean of Dronmore and then of Derry. In 1723 he inherited a fortune from Esther Vanhomrigh (Swift's 'Vanessa'), but caring nothing for riches he devoted his wealth to promoting a college at Bermuda to train missionaries for the Indians, and to reform the morals and manners of American colonists. The scheme failed and he returned to Ireland, where he became Bp of Cloyne (1734). He remained there until his retirement (1752), devoting himself to reforming social conditions in Ireland.

BERKELEY, SIR ROBERT (1589–1656), English judge whose support for the royal prerogative in Hampden's case on ship money is remembered for his assertion: 'I never read nor heard, that *lex* was *rex*; but it is common and most true, that *rex* is *lex*, for he is "*lex loquens*", a living, speaking, an acting law.'

BERKELEY, SIR WILLIAM (1606–77), colonial governor of Virginia. After having been commissioner to Canada (*c.* 1632), Berkeley returned to become a member of privy council under Charles I. In 1642 he was sent to succeed Sir Francis Wyatt as governor of the Virginia colonies. He exercised a unifying and strengthening influence in the colony, suppressing Indian uprisings and encouraging an increase in agricultural endeavours. He remained a Royalist after 1640, managing to avoid trouble with the Roundheads by mustering support for his beliefs in the colony. He was relieved of his office in 1652, but regained it at the Restoration. After 1660, his governance was marked by conflicts with Quakers and backwoodsmen.

BERLAYMONT, CHARLES, Count of (1510–78). An impecunious Walloon nobleman of an old Catholic family, member of the ancient order of the Golden Fleece, and president of the Council of Finance in the Netherlands in 1559, he was one of the few native councillors of state to be trusted by Philip II of Spain. When the noble rebels presented the Brussels petition to the governess, Margaret of Parma, in 1566, Berlaymont referred contemptuously to them as 'these beggars [*gueux*]', from which the rebel nickname 'Sea Beggars' was later derived. Berlaymont became a member of Alva's Council of Blood, and in 1576 was arrested and imprisoned for his loyalty to the Spanish Crown, later rallying to the support of Don John of Austria, the governor of the Spanish Netherlands.

BERLAYMONT, GILLES DE (d. 1579), Baron of Hierges, eldest son of Charles, Count of Berlaymont, and like him, Knight of the Fleece and a Spanish loyalist in the Dutch revolt. In 1572 he was appointed *stadtholder* of Friesland, Overysel, and Gelderland, and acting in a similar capacity over the provinces of Holland, Zeeland, and Utrecht from 1574, took part in the Spanish military advance of 1575. He captured Buren, Oudewater, Schoonhaven, and the fortifications near Krimpen on the Lek. Later, in the hope of obtaining his father's release from prison, Hierges aligned himself with the Duke of Aerschot and the states general movement in opposition to Spanish rule; but after his father's release he returned to the pro-Spanish Catholic party under Don John of Austria.

BERLIET. French motor manufacturers founded at Lyons in 1894 by Marius Berliet (1866–1949). It specializes in commercial vehicles, of which Berliet was a pioneer. The firm was sold to Citroën in 1967.

BERLIN BLOCKADE (1948–9), major incident in the Cold War and in the division of Germany between east and west. Under the occupation arrangements Berlin was in the Russian zone, but was itself divided into four zones, although both Germany and Berlin were to be administered by the four powers acting together. This arrangement soon broke down, the Soviet zone being closed to all normal trade and exchange with the west. The British, US and, later, French governments therefore merged their zones and promoted economic and political development. This posed the question of the relation of their zones in Berlin to the western zone, and the problem became critical over the question of currency reform, a necessary part of economic recovery. In the gathering crisis the Soviet delegate left the Control Council for Germany (March 1948) and currency reform was introduced into the western zone (18 June). The Russians then stopped passenger trains and road traffic to Berlin, introduced their own form of currency into Berlin, and stopped all remaining road and rail traffic (23 June 1948).

The western powers then supplied Berlin by air, initially to gain time for discussion and then (when the airlift succeeded beyond their expectations) as a means of holding on to their position. An interview between Stalin and a US journalist (Jan. 1949) opened the possibility of fresh negotiations, and these led to an ending of the blockade (May 1949) and the much less important counter-blockade which the western powers had instituted.

By this time it was however too late to halt development towards a German government in the west. The basic law establishing the German Federal Republic was signed in the same month, and the German Democratic Republic followed in the east (Oct. 1949). Berlin was divided. Two municipal governments had come into existence there during the blockade; west Berlin now became a *Land* under the German Federal Republic (with representation but not votes in the Bundestag) while east Berlin became the capital of the German Democratic Republic.   WFK

BERLIN, CONGRESS AND TREATY OF (1878) settled the eastern crisis of the 1870s by negotiation. After the Turks had suppressed revolts in Bosnia (1875) and Bulgaria (1876) with great brutality, pan-Slav circles in Russia forced the tsar, Alexander II, to intervene (April 1877). Russia's victory over Turkey was halted by the dispatch of the British fleet to the Straits early in 1878. None the less, at the treaty of San Stefano, Turkey had to agree to the creation of a large independent Bulgaria stretching from the Aegean into Macedonia. Seeing the new state as a cover for Russian control of the Balkans, the Austro-Hungarian foreign minister, Andrássy, and the British prime minister, Disraeli, demanded a European congress to revise the treaty. The German chancellor, Bismarck, was anxious to avoid conflict between his Russian and Austrian allies. Playing the part of 'the honest broker', he persuaded the Russians to come to a European congress at Berlin. The congress sat for a month (13 June–13 July) and assembled a brilliant group of negotiators, Andrássy, Disraeli, Salisbury, and the Russians Gorchakov and Shuvalov. Most of the congress's decisions had in fact been worked out in secret agreements beforehand. The chief decision was to reduce Bulgaria's size and to make it a semi-independent state. The southern part—Eastern Rumelia—was returned to Turkey as an autonomous province, and Macedonia was returned unconditionally. Rumania had to cede southern Bessarabia to Russia, but she received the Dobrudja from the Bulgarians in compensation. The congress also provided for Austria's occupation of Bosnia-Herzegovina and the Sanjak of Novibazar, as well as Britain's occupation of Cyprus, although all of these provinces were to remain under Turkish suzerainty. The congress managed to produce a compromise among the powers without war: the San Stefano treaty was torn up, but on the other hand little was left

of the Ottoman empire in Europe. Russo-German relations were harmed by the congress since the Russians resented Bismarck's genuine impartiality.   DMCK

BERLIN CRISIS (1958–63), fresh crisis, after that of 1948–9, which arose over the future of Berlin. It opened when the Russian leader, Khrushchev, proposed (Nov. 1958) a revision of the Potsdam agreement to 'renounce the remnants of the occupation regime in Berlin and thereby make it possible to create a normal situation in the capital of the German Democratic Republic'. The proposal had the character of an ultimatum, since Khrushchev suggested handing over to the East German authorities the functions hitherto exercised by the Soviet agencies (thereby creating a dilemma over the recognition of the German Democratic Republic) and said that if agreement were not reached within six months the Soviet Union would make a separate agreement with the GDR.

The Soviet Union and the GDR acted in concert in the diplomacy which followed, although their interests were not identical. It seems reasonable to assume that Khrushchev, in spite of his brusque methods, hoped for a settlement of the Berlin question as a prelude to some more general detente in Europe; but the GDR was beset with a more urgent problem in the vast outflow of refugees through Berlin to the west (of whom, according to the German Federal Republic, there were 200,000 in 1960).

This may explain the alternation of tension and detente which characterized the crisis, although account must also be taken of the fact that Eisenhower was succeeded as US president by Kennedy (Jan. 1961) and the anxieties which the latter felt about Khrushchev's intentions as a result of their meeting in Vienna (June 1961). Thus the expiry of Khrushchev's 'ultimatum' produced, not a heightening of crisis, but a period of negotiation, when Khrushchev visited the US and plans were laid for a summit meeting in Paris. In contrast, the summit meeting (May 1961) was broken up by the U2 incident. The return of tension increased to the climactic point of the construction of a concrete wall along the zonal boundary between east and west Berlin (Aug. 1961), preventing all movement of Germans across the city, and the confrontation of Soviet and US tanks at 'check-point Charlie' (Oct. 1961).

Thereafter the crisis abated, and at the 22nd Congress of the CPSU (Oct. 1961) Krushchev ended the pressure he had built up by denying that there was any urgency for a settlement. The existence of the wall and even more the Cuban crisis (Oct. 1962) kept up an atmosphere of tension in Berlin, while negotiation for a German settlement made no progress. However, the peaceful visit of Kennedy and Khrushchev to west and east Berlin respectively (June 1963) marked the end of the crisis. In the following year the first of a series of agreements was signed providing for limited visits by Germans across the wall at Christmas and Easter.   WFK

BERLIN MEMORANDUM (1876). Largely the work of the Austro-Hungarian foreign minister, Andrássy, it provided for an armistice between Turkey and her rebels in Bosnia-Herzegovina.

BERLIN PUTSCH (1938), abortive attempt to remove Hitler. In Sept. 1938 a group of conspirators planned to seize him as soon as he gave the order to attack Czechoslovakia. Among those involved were von Witzleben (commander of the 3rd Military District, which included Berlin), Goerdeler (Reich price controller), Oster (chief assistant to Canaris at the Abwehr), and Beck. Subsequently, the conspirators claimed that the Munich Agreement, by eliminating the risk of general war, undermined their position. It is more likely, however, that Brauchitsch's equivocal position was primarily responsible for the failure of the putsch.

BERLIN REVOLUTION (1848). This failed to give Prussia a permanent liberal or radical constitution. Rapid population growth in the countryside, accompanied by famine and cholera (1847), subjected Berlin, like most European cities, to an influx of unemployed peasants. Berlin had more industry and a larger working class than the majority of cities, but it was still inadequate to absorb the pool of unemployed. Added to this economic discontent among the lower classes were the grievances of the Berlin middle class against the autocratic government of Frederick William IV of Prussia.

News of revolution in other European cities led to street fighting between the workers and Prussian troops (15–18 March), which Frederick William ended by withdrawing the soldiers and trying to come to terms with the revolutionaries. Hoping to lead the revolution and effect his own ideas for uniting Germany, the king appointed a ministry of middle-class liberals under Camphausen, called a Prussian parliament, and declared that 'from henceforth Prussia is merged in Germany'.

From this high point the revolution gradually collapsed. When the parliament met in May, it proved far more radical than the liberal ministry, which was determined to make no concessions to Berlin's lower classes, although determined to destroy the privileges of the *Junkers*. Squeezed between the intransigence of the *Junkers* and the demands of the radicals in parliament, the Camphausen ministry was reduced to impotence. By Oct. Frederick William had recovered his nerve and realized that the united Germany envisaged by the Prussian parliament and by the all-German parliament at Frankfurt was very different from his concept. Turning to the army, which had remained intact and loyal throughout, he dismissed his ministry and ordered the parliament out of Berlin, which was completely under military control on 10 Nov. A month later the king dissolved the parliament and promulgated the first stage of a more reactionary constitution.

W. Carr, *A History of Germany, 1815–1945* (London, 1969).

D McK

BERLIN, TREATY OF (1745), between Maria Theresa, the Habsburg ruler, and Frederick II of Prussia during the War of the Austrian Succession. Maria Theresa's main aim in the war was the recovery of Silesia from Prussia. To this end, in 1745 she made peace with the new Elector of Bavaria and tentative proposals of territorial concessions to France. Frederick counter-attacked, defeating the Austro-Saxon forces at Hohenfriedberg and Soor. Since Maria Theresa was still reluctant to make peace, Frederick struck a further blow at Austria's ally, Saxony, invading the electorate and capturing Dresden. Meanwhile, the French rebuffed Austrian suggestions of abandoning the Prussian alliance, and with Saxony suing for peace Maria Theresa had no alternative but to conclude the treaty of Berlin, reaffirming the terms of the Breslau settlement of 1742, *ie*, Prussian possession of Lower Silesia, Glatz, and most of Upper Silesia was guaranteed. This was later confirmed by the treaty of Aix-la-Chapelle (1748) at the end of the war.

BERLIN, UNIVERSITY OF (1809), founded during Humboldt's ministry to replace the Halle University, lost to the French. It broke away from the traditional role of training civil servants and professional men and became a centre of learning. Among its first staff were Fichte, Schleiermacher, and Nieburr.

BERLIN, WEST AFRICA CONFERENCE (1884–5), met on Bismarck's initiative to solve the Congo problem by international agreement. Bismarck intended to enlist French support against Britain's supposed ambitions to annex the Congo. In fact, trade, not annexation, had been Britain's aim, and she was able to take advantage of the conference to ensure France's exclusion from the Congo as well. The conference above all benefited King Leopold of the Belgians, whose International Association of the Congo was turned into the Congo Free State under him, although the new state was thrown open to free trade.

BERMUDA, group of some 300 small islands in the Western Atlantic, comprising in all 20½ sq. miles (52 sq. kms) of land, and known officially as the Somers Islands. They were named after a Spanish sea captain, Juan de Bermudez, who had apparently twice visited them by 1515. Admiral Sir George Somers was forced to put into the islands after a hurricane (1609) with a ship-load of colonists bound for North America, and Bermuda, hitherto uninhabited, became British by occupation. The pleasant climate and favourable reports of Somers's party led the Virginia Co. to have its charter extended to cover the islands (1612) and a colonizing expedition was dispatched. The City of London bought the concession for £2000 (1615), but the Crown assumed responsibility for the colony (1684). Self-government in the colony began very early (1620) and the settlers lived mainly by trade (their 'Bermuda-rigged' vessels outstripping French and Spanish privateers) and the produce of their salt ponds. The islands proclaimed Charles II their king (1649) and only reluctantly accepted Oliver Cromwell when Barbados was captured (1651). During the American War of Independence Bermuda remained loyal to the Crown despite the great suffering caused by the loss of their major food supplier. The islands were a centre for cotton blockade-runners during the American Civil War. During the Second World War, as part of 'lend-lease', America was granted a 99-year lease for naval and air bases. The colony was governed by the governor, the Executive and Legislative Councils, all appointed by the Crown, and 36 elected members of the House of Assembly. The 1968 Constitution gave the Assembly complete control over internal affairs.

BERNADOTTE MISSION, UN mission under the leadership of Count Folke Bernadotte, appointed (May 1948) to mediate between Israel and the Arabs. It produced the Bernadotte Plan (16 Sept. 1948). Bernadotte was assassinated (17 Sept.) and succeeded by his assistant, Ralph Bunche.

BERNARD, SIR CHARLES (1837–1901), chief commissioner of British Burma before the Third Burmese War (1885). At first an opponent of British intervention in Upper Burma, he changed his views when negotiations between the Burmese and the French brought danger of French control of Mandalay. The Third Burmese War followed. Bernard discarded the possibility of retaining Upper Burma as a protected state because there was no person or body with sufficient authority. He became first chief commissioner of all Burma, with responsibility for pacifying and establishing an administration in Upper Burma.

BERNARD OF CLAIRVAUX, Saint (1090–1153), member of a noble Burgundian family, whose entry into the Abbey of Citeaux (1112) began the transformation of the puny Cistercian order into a religious giant. In 1115 he was sent to found the Abbey of Clairvaux, which, under him, became the leading monastery in Europe. He was a man of extraordinarily powerful personality, irresistible charm, and puritanical zeal, qualities that made him one of the greatest religious and spiritual forces of medieval times. He was primarily responsible for the great growth of the cult of the Virgin Mary and was an opponent of Abelard and others of heterodox views, the leading figure in avoiding a schism in the Western Church (1131) and the preacher of the Second Crusade (1146). His sermons on the Song of Songs are a landmark in the development of western mystical theology.

BERNARD, SAMUEL, 17th-cent. French banker, of a bourgeois family, who twice made a fortune financing Louis XIV's wars. His son, Bernard de Rieux, reached *parlementaire* rank, inheriting 7 million livres from his father; his grandson, Bernard de Boulainvilliers, was also a counsellor in the *parlement* of Paris.

BERNARD OF SAXE-WEIMAR (1604–39). Protestant general during the Thirty Years War. As the 11th son of the

Duke of Weimar, he was without hereditary prospects and tried to win a principality by military service. From 1622 he fought under various Protestant colours against the imperial armies, and in 1631 joined Gustavus II Adolphus. Bernard clinched the victory of Lützen (1632) by assuming command of the Swedish army on the king's death. With the Swedish general Horn, he invaded south Germany and acquired the Duchy of Franconia as a Swedish fief (1633). In 1634 he suffered heavy reverses owing to incessant quarrels with the Swedish leaders, and was defeated with Horn at Nördlingen (Sept. 1634) by Ferdinand III and Matthias Gallas. This cost Bernard his duchy. By the treaty of St Germain-en-Laye (Oct. 1635) he entered the French service, tempted by a promise of the Duchy of Alsace. A series of victories followed in Lorraine and the upper Rhine, culminating in the fall of Breisach. On his death, his army and conquered territories were taken over by France.

BERNARDINO (ALBIZZESCHI), Saint (1380–1444), a Sienese noble, who joined the austere order of the Observant Franciscans, whose vicar-general he became in 1437. His sincere and eloquent preaching all over Italy promoted a temporary religious revival, but had no enduring effect. He was canonized in 1450.

BERNE, capital city of Switzerland, originally a free imperial city, founded (1191) by Count Berchtold IV of Zähringen. It grew to prominence as a centre of government and military conquest rather than as a seat of trade and industry. Profiting from the disappearance of strong princes in the 13th cent., it was able to snap up many neighbouring lordships, making itself supreme on the central Swiss plateau. A growing share of east–west trade brought it additional financial strength. It first joined the Swiss Confederation in 1353, but did not become a permanent member until early in the 15th cent.

BERNE CONFERENCE (Sept. 1924). The British, French, Belgian, and German ministers of labour discussed the ratification of the Washington Convention of 1919. This stipulated an eight-hour working day. It had not been ratified by any leading industrial country, mainly because of Germany's abandonment of the eight-hour day in 1923. At the conference Brauns, the German delegate, agreed to secure the ratification of the convention by his government, but this subsequently proved impossible.

BERNIER, FRANÇOIS (1620–88), standard European authority on Mughal India. After receiving a medical training under the philosopher Gassendi, Bernier engaged in travel and reached India about the end of 1658. He was physician to Danishmand Khan (1660–5), a nobleman at the Mughal court of Aurangzeb. He returned to France in 1669 and in 1670 published his *Travels*, which are notable for their accurate observation and clear descriptions.

BERNINI, GIOVANNI LORENZO (1598–1680), Italian sculptor and architect, one of the masters of Roman Baroque, who, for much of his life, was papal architect and director of public buildings. His first important work was the *baldacchino* over the high altar at St Peter's, and after the death of Maderna (1629) he was chiefly responsible for completing the building. He also continued Maderna's work in the Palazzo Barberini, where he constructed the facade and staircase. At the Vatican he designed the Scala Regia, fronted by an equestrian statue to the Emperor Constantine. This is the main entrance to the palace, and Bernini constructed it with the exaggerated perspectives that give an illusion of depth to theatrical settings. His churches, fountains, and private buildings all enriched the beauty of Rome, his masterpiece being the chapel of S. Teresa (1646). Instead of the usual painting, the centrepiece of the altar is a niche containing a sculptured group of the saint rising in ecstasy into the arms of an angel.

Bernini's fame was international, and he was invited to submit designs for the completion of the Louvre, but patriotic motives prevailed, and the work was given to Claude Perrault.

N. Pevsner, *An Outline of European Architecture* (London, 1963).
R. Wittkower, *Bernini* (London, 1955).   MMR

BERNSTORFF, ANDREAS GOTTLIEB, Baron von (1649–1726), Hanoverian minister of King George I of England. Bernstorff was a nobleman from Mecklenburg–Schwerin, where he had large estates, a fact which often influenced his policies. He took service with George William of Zell, uncle of George Lewis, and later transferred his service to Hanover. In 1714 Bernstorff accompanied George I to England and soon became the power behind the throne, meddling in British affairs. Bernstorff's foreign policy was one of friendship with the emperor and of hostility towards Denmark and Prussia. However, Stanhope, as secretary of state, advocated a coalition of Baltic German powers co-operating with Sweden against Russia. Stanhope was hindered by the mutual dislike of the rulers of Hanover and Prussia and by a land dispute in Mecklenburg between Bernstorff and the King of Prussia. In 1719 Stanhope supplanted Bernstorff and induced George I to ally Britain with Prussia. He also obtained the king's promise to exclude Bernstorff from British affairs.

BERNSTORFF, ANDREAS PETER (1735–97), Danish statesman. He was the nephew of J. H. E. Bernstorff, and was dismissed with him by Struensee in 1770. He became foreign minister (1773), signed the Gottorp treaty, and followed a policy of peace. When Denmark nevertheless joined the Armed Neutrality of the North (1780), he balanced this by a secret agreement with Britain about 'contraband', which put him out of office for four years. He restricted Denmark's activities in the Russo-Swedish War (1788–90), and opted out of the alliances against revolutionary France. He also conducted a liberal domestic policy, *eg*, the emancipation of the serfs.

BERNSTORFF, JOHANN HARTWIG ERNST (1712–72), Danish statesman, a Hanoverian by birth, who served as a Danish envoy in Germany and France until 1751, when he became foreign minister. He avoided taking part in the Seven Years War until the attack threatened by Peter III of Russia in Holstein caused him to invade Mecklenburg. He negotiated the treaty with Catherine the Great (1767) by which Denmark acquired the long-disputed lands of Holstein-Gottorp, and was then created a count. He was dismissed by Struensee in September 1770.

BERRY, SIR GRAHAM (1822–1904), Australian politician and radical-protectionist leader in Victorian colonial politics of the 1870s. He was three times prime minister and chief secretary. A storekeeper with little education, he emigrated to Australia in 1852 and strengthened his political aspirations by suburban and country journalism. After entering the Legislative Assembly of Victoria in 1860, he figured prominently in its struggles against the conservative Legislative Council and championed land taxation and payment of MPs. His importance declined in the 1880s, when he served as agent-general in London, as speaker of the Legislative Assembly (1897), and as member of the federal conventions of 1891 and 1897–8.

BERTHELOT, PHILIPPE (1866–1934), French diplomat, who helped to shape France's foreign policy in the 1920s. As head of the foreign service, he was at the height of his influence from 1924 until his retirement (1933), and was closely associated with Briand's policy of reconciliation with Germany.

BERTRAN DE BORN (*c.* 1140–*c.* 1215). Provençal warrior, politician, and troubadour. As a poet he is best known for his satirical and bellicose *sirventes*; two of these, urging the eldest son of Henry II of England to persist in his quarrel with his father and his brother Richard, helped to secure for Bertran a place among Dante's 'sowers of schism' in the *Inferno*.

BERTRAND, HENRI GRATIEN, Comte de (1773–1844), Napoleon's military engineer and companion in exile on Elba and St Helena.

BERULLE, PIERRE (1575–1629), French theologian and founder of the Congregation of the Oratory (1611), one of the new orders of the Counter-Reformation. He was created cardinal (1627) and minister of state by Louis XIII, but retired because of Richelieu's jealousy.

BERWICK, JAMES FITZJAMES, Duke of (1670–1734), Jacobite soldier. Berwick was the illegitimate son of James, Duke of York, later James II, and Arabella Churchill, the elder sister of John Churchill, later Duke of Marlborough. He was educated in France as a Roman Catholic, and before returning to England saw military service in Hungary against the Turks. On his return to England (1687) he was created a duke. In 1688 he accompanied his father to France and in the following year went with him to Ireland as nominal commander of the Jacobite adherents. He was defeated at the battle of the Boyne, and on returning to France was commissioned in the French army. He fought in Flanders under Luxembourg, and was captured at Landen (1695). On the death of his father (1701), he became chief adviser to his half-brother, the Old Pretender. However, his advice, though usually sensible and intelligent, was often ignored. On the outbreak of the War of the Spanish Succession he was sent to command the French forces in Spain. After the loss of Gibraltar (1704) he quarrelled with the Spanish court and was recalled. In France he stamped out the Huguenot Revolt of the Camisards in the Cevennes (1705–6) and in 1706 was appointed marshal of France and once again sent to Spain. At the battle of Almanza (1707) he met a smaller allied force under Galway and almost annihilated it. It was this battle that gave Berwick his military reputation, since it saved Spain for Philip.

In 1708 Berwick saw service on the Rhine, where he entered into secret correspondence with Marlborough. Though Marlborough was never committed to the Jacobites, this correspondence went on until the accession of George I. In 1709–10 Berwick successfully defended the south-eastern frontiers of France against the larger forces of the Duke of Savoy. He finished the war in Spain, where he ended Catalan independence by taking Barcelona (1714). Though an ardent Jacobite, Berwick did not take part in either the invasion attempt of 1708 or the rising of 1715. Indeed, his experiences in Ireland gave him a low opinion of an invasion dependent on Scottish and Irish Jacobites. In 1733 Berwick was appointed commander-in-chief of the French armies. He was killed during the siege of Philippsburg.

W. S. Churchill, *Marlborough*, 4 vols (London, 1933–8).
                                                                                        AW

BERWICK, TREATIES OF. Berwick, on the Anglo-Scottish borders, was the only Scottish town permanently retained by King Edward III of England after his attempted conquest of Scotland (1333). It formed, henceforth, the main English base during all the Anglo-Scottish wars and gave its name to three treaties between the two countries. In 1357 a treaty procured the release of David II of Scotland, captured by the English at the battle of Neville's Cross (1346). There was to be a truce for ten years and a ransom of 100,000 marks (£66,666) to be paid in annual instalments during that time. Two centuries later (1560) the English, represented by the Duke of Norfolk, made a treaty with the Scottish Lords of the Congregation at the instigation of Maitland of Lethington. England was to provide further military assistance

against the Queen Regent, Mary of Guise, and the French forces entrenched around Leith. As a result of the treaty, an English army under Lord Grey de Wilton joined the Scottish in the siege of Leith. The event marked the end of centuries of Franco-Scottish friendship and the beginnings of an Anglo-Scottish alliance at a time when factional strife in Scotland was at a peak. James VI's main concern was to retain his Scottish throne and to secure the English succession, while Elizabeth I was anxious to undermine French influence and to safeguard her own and her kingdom's safety.

In July 1586 James VI made a treaty with Elizabeth I by which the two countries were to give each other specified help in the event of invasion. Elizabeth promised an annual subsidy of £4000 to Scotland and was to do nothing derogatory to James's succession prospects, but refused both to give official recognition to that claim and to confer on him an English peerage. On her death (1603), the two crowns were united in the person of James VI of Scotland and I of England.

BERYTUS (mod. Beirut), Phoenician city, and Roman colony from 15 BC. It later became famous for its school of Roman law, which made possible the preservation of classical legal thought in the Justinianic compilation. Occupied by the crusaders (1100–87), it flourished as a port through medieval and Ottoman times.

BESANT, MRS ANNIE (1847–1933), Englishwoman who left her husband in 1873 and, after losing her religious faith, joined Bradlaugh's secularist movement. In the 1880s she joined the Social Democratic Federation and organized the match girls' strike (1888), the first example of a women's strike. She became interested in Theosophy (*c.* 1893) and went to India, where she played a part in the growth of the Indian nationalist movement.

BESS OF HARDWICK (1518–1603), Elizabeth Talbot, Countess of Shrewsbury, daughter and co-heir of John Hardwick of Hardwick, Derbyshire. She married four times, one of her husbands being the 6th Earl of Shrewsbury, and inheriting the fortunes of her four husbands had an estimated annual income of £60,000. Her daughter married Charles Stuart, younger brother of Lord Darnley, and Arabella Stuart was her granddaughter.

BESSARABIA was disputed between Russia and Rumania from 1878. Rumanians were in 1917 the largest single national group in Bessarabia, forming, however, less than half of its population. The status of Bessarabia after the Russian revolution was disputed between its different nationalities. In Dec. 1917 the local council declared a 'Moldavian Democratic Republic' within Russia. In Jan. 1918, when the Bolsheviks entered Kishinev, the Rumanian group appealed for Rumania's military assistance. After fighting between Russian and Rumanian troops, Rumania in March agreed to evacuate Bessarabia, but did not withdraw. In April and Nov. 1918 the Bessarabian Council voted for union with Rumania.

In March 1920 the Allied Supreme Council acquiesced in the union. The US objected that the Russian case had not been heard. The union was never recognized by Russia, and later Soviet diplomatic initiatives left the question unresolved. Bessarabia's status was not defined in the 1929 Litvinov Protocol signed with Rumania, Poland, Latvia, and Estonia. In 1933, in a series of pacts with her neighbours, including Rumania, it was understood that although Russia would not commit aggression against the *de facto* occupier, there would be no *de jure* renunciation of Bessarabia.

In concluding the Nazi–Soviet Pact (1939), Hitler recognized Bessarabia as part of the Russian sphere. Rumania hoped that Germany would prevent the Russian invasion she feared, and Germany did in fact attempt to persuade Russia to restrict the area of invasion. However, on 26 June 1940, Rumania was forced to surrender Bessarabia and North Bukovina.
                                                                                        ASJ

BESSARION, Cardinal (*c.* 1403–72), a Greek Abp of Nicaea, who supported the union between the Greek and the Catholic churches at the Council of Florence (1439). He became the leading patron of Greek learning in Italy and helped especially to promote interest in Plato.

BESSEMER, SIR HENRY (1813–98) inventor of the Bessemer process for making steel which, by driving an air blast through molten pig-iron (1856), greatly cheapened the cost of manufacture.

BESTUZHEV-RYUMIN, ALEKSEI PETROVICH (1693–1768), Count, Russian statesman who became chancellor in 1744 during the reign of the Empress Elizabeth. He served the Elector of Hanover before achieving power in Russia after the *coup d'état* of Elizabeth Petrovna in 1741. Subsequently, he became a leading figure in European diplomatic circles, favouring an anti-Prussian policy. In 1755 he negotiated the Russo-British subsidy treaty which contributed to the diplomatic revolution of the following year.

BETANCOURT, RÓMULO (b. 1908), leader of the Democratic Action Party (AD) and president of Venezuela. After being exiled to Costa Rica by the dictator Juan Vicente Gómez, he briefly joined the Communist Party. He was a founder of his party, and president of the ruling junta (1954–8). During the regime of Marcos Pérez Jiménez he was again exiled. When Pérez Jiménez fell Betancourt returned and won the presidential elections of 1958. New programmes proliferated in spite of unrest and guerrilla activity. In 1964 he handed over to his successor, Raúl Leoni.

BÉTHENCOURT, JEAN DE (*c.* 1360–1422), a Norman noble with Spanish connections, who attempted in 1402 to conquer and colonize the Canary islands and became a vassal of the king of Castile. In the 15th cent. the islands produced a fresh source of sugar for western Europe.

BETHLEHEM STEEL CORPORATION, US company, and world's second largest steel producer. Organized (1904) with original plant in the Lehigh valley of eastern Pennsylvania, its Sparrows Point works in Maryland is the world's largest single steelmill, with an annual capacity of over 8 million tons.

BETHMAN-HOLLWEG, THEOBALD VON (1856–1921), German chancellor before and during the First World War. A moderate conservative, he intended, on becoming chancellor (1909), to maintain the authoritarian character of the German empire, although willing to accept moderate electoral reforms. In 1917 he believed Germany's survival depended on a democratization of the regime. This attitude, and his pessimism over Germany's ability to win the war, led to the army's forcing his resignation (July 1917). His pre-war foreign policy had aimed unsuccessfully at ending the naval race with Britain and ensuring British neutrality. In July 1914 he decided to encourage Austria to undertake a localized war against Serbia. He was ready to face the consequences of this developing into a general European war, because he believed that Germany had more chance of winning in 1914 than in 1917, when Russia's military reforms would be complete.

BETHUNE, JOHN ELLIOT DRINKWATER (1801–51), British legislator and educationist. Appointed legal member of the Supreme Council of India (1848), he was partly responsible for the revision of Macaulay's Penal Code and he established the Bethune Girls' School at Calcutta for Indian upper-class girls, which developed into the Bethune College for women.

BEUST, FRIEDRICH FERDINAND, Graf (1809–86), Saxon, and later Austrian, foreign minister, who was largely responsible for the *Ausgleich*. On being made foreign minister of Saxony (1849), he called in Prussian troops to suppress the revolutionary movement there; but as minister of the interior in the 1850s he followed a liberal economic policy and a consistently anti-Prussian line in the German Confederation. When Austria and Saxony were defeated by Prussia (1866), the Austrian Emperor Francis Joseph appointed him foreign secretary, with the intention of pursuing an anti-Prussian policy in the future, which he did until Beust's resignation (1871). To Austria he brought a foreigner's insight and saw it was essential to buy off the Magyars. Largely through his influence Francis Joseph agreed to the *Ausgleich* (1867) and to the liberal reforms in the Austrian half of the monarchy afterwards.

BEUVE-MÉRY, HUBERT (1902–), director (ret. Dec. 1969) of the influential French newspaper *Le Monde*. In the 1930s he was an official at the French Institute in Prague, and a correspondent of *Le Temps* until he resigned because the paper supported the Munich agreement. He was director of studies at the Uriage training school for youth leaders set up by the Vichy regime, and when this was closed because of its Resistance tendencies, he joined the *maquis* (1942). *Le Monde* was founded in 1944, and under Beuve-Méry's direction has gained a high reputation for seriousness, independence, and international coverage. His own contributions appeared under the pen-name 'Sirius'.

BEVAN, ANEURIN (1897–1960), British Labour politician and minister, responsible for the enactment of the national health service. Bevan, son of a coal miner, was born in Wales and began life as a miner. He became an active trade unionist, entered local politics, and in 1929 was elected MP for Ebbw Vale. He was on the left wing of the Labour Party during the 1930s and because of his association with Sir Stafford Cripps's United Front movement was expelled from the party for a period during 1939, when he opposed conscription, and also strikes in essential industries, and challenged Churchill's conduct of the war in parliamentary debate.

As minister of health in Attlee's government in 1945, Bevan was responsible for housing and for the introduction of the free health service after tough negotiations with the medical profession. He was associated with the Keep Left movement of 1947 and after the outbreak of the Korean war became increasingly opposed to rearmament at the expense of the social services. In Jan. 1951 he became minister of labour, but resigned in April over a dispute concerning an increase in the defence budget and the decision to introduce charges for some items in the health service.

In the mid-1950s a dissident group within the Labour Party formed around him as he challenged the leadership. The central issues of the dispute were German rearmament and nuclear defence. In the election for a Labour Party leader in 1955, Bevan was defeated by Gaitskell but was reconciled to his leadership and became shadow foreign minister. He became deputy-leader of the party after the 1959 election. He published *In Place of Fear* in 1952.

BEVERIDGE, ALBERT JEREMIAH (1862–1927), US historian, politician, and associate of Theodore Roosevelt. As a well-known orator in Indiana, he attracted national attention as an imperialist with his speech 'The March of the Flag' (1898). He was a Republican Senator (1899–1911), but became estranged from his party's inner councils because of his support for regulation of the trusts and sponsoring the Meat Inspection Act (1906). He failed to secure re-election in 1910 largely because he joined the 'Insurgent' Republicans in opposing the Payne–Aldrich tariff (1909). He became a leading member of the Progressive Party (1912), but later rejoined the Republican Party (1916) and opposed US involvement in the First World War and the League of Nations.

BEVERIDGE, WILLIAM HENRY BEVERIDGE, Baron (1879–1963), British economist whose report on social insurance was decisive in shaping and winning public support for subsequent legislation. Beveridge was born in India and educated at

Oxford, after which he became the sub-warden of a settlement house in the East End of London, where he derived his interest in the causes of unemployment and in possible remedies to end it. In 1909 he published *Unemployment: a problem of Industry*, which looked to the proper organization of industry as the means to combat unemployment. He was asked by Winston Churchill, as president of the board of trade, to work on the creation of labour exchanges and on a scheme for compulsory unemployment insurance. He was Director of Labour Exchanges (1909–16) and in 1919 permanent secretary of the ministry of food.

He then left the civil service and was appointed director of the London School of Economics (1919–37). There he sought to reduce the element of a priori theory in the social sciences and to direct them towards empirical investigations. His fact-finding approach aroused much controversy in the school and led to a bitter clash with Harold Laski. In 1933 Beveridge established a fund to give help to German academics persecuted by the Nazis.

Beveridge was made chairman of the Unemployment Insurance Statutory Committee (1934–44) and in 1937 became Master of University College, Oxford, where Harold Wilson worked for him as a research assistant. In 1940 he was brought by Bevin into the ministry of labour and in 1941 headed an enquiry into social insurance. His report on its results was published in Dec. 1942. In 1945 he published *Full Employment in a Free Society*, a work much influenced by Keynesian economics. He was a liberal MP for six months in 1945.   MC

BEVERIDGE REPORT on social insurance and allied services was presented to the British government in Nov. 1942. It was expected to be merely a technical document, but took the character of a declaration of human rights. The report aimed at establishing a system of social security which would create freedom from want, which Beveridge defined as the lack of income to obtain the means of healthy subsistence— adequate food, shelter, clothing, and fuel. It proposed a comprehensive social security system and insisted on benefits payable to all as a right without a means test; it recommended flat-rate, not graduated, contributions, and advocated the establishment of a national health service and a system of family allowances, and assumed the implementation of a policy of full employment. Its major recommendations became law under Attlee's first administration (1945–50).

BEVIN, ERNEST (1881–1951), British trade unionist responsible for the creation of the Transport and General Workers' Union, wartime minister of labour and foreign secretary in the Labour government of 1945. Bevin began life as a farm labourer. After moving to Bristol as a carter, he joined the Dockers' Union in 1910 and by 1920 was its assistant general secretary. He won prominence by the way in which he presented the dockers' case for a guaranteed wage to the Shaw Court of Enquiry and led the Council of Action (Aug. 1920) against possible British support for Poland in the war with Russia. In 1921, his activities were decisive in bringing about the amalgamation of the transport unions into the Transport and General Workers' Union of which he was general secretary, and which became the largest trade union in Britain. As a member of the general council of the Trades Union Congress in 1925 he was responsible for the organization of the General Strike (1926) and the negotiation of its conclusion. Thereafter he worked to ensure that the trade union movement maintained its active role in political matters and its interest in general economic policy. In 1928–9 he took part in the Mond–Turner talks, and was a leading member of the TUC's Economic Committee, and in 1930 served on the Macmillan Committee on finance and industry. He was critical of the Labour government's failure to combat unemployment and in 1931 refused to support the National government. During the 1930s he resisted communist influence in the trade union movement. The international connections of his union gave him an appreciation of the dangers

of fascism and he led the Labour Party's move towards sanctions and rearmament, forcing Lansbury's resignation by his attack at the party conference in 1935.

In 1936–7 he was chairman of the General Council of the TUC. In May 1940 Churchill appointed him minister of labour and national service, with membership of the war cabinet, and he was brought into parliament as MP for Central Wandsworth (having twice stood unsuccessfully, in 1918 and 1931).

In 1945 Bevin became foreign secretary. He was an architect of the policy of containing the Soviet Union and regarded US participation in the recovery of Europe as essential to this aim. His response to the Marshall offer was decisive in its success and he took the lead in creating the Brussels Treaty Organization and NATO. But he was cool towards plans for European federation and rejected the Schuman plan. In the Middle East his attempt to rebuild good relations with the Arab states and his dislike of Zionist methods led him to oppose increased Jewish immigration to Palestine. Throughout his period of office he was hampered by Britain's financial weakness, but he inspired the Colombo plan for mutual help in Asia. He resigned in March 1951 because of ill-health, and remained in the cabinet as lord privy seal until his death a month later.

A. Bullock, *Ernest Bevin*, vol. 1, 1881–1940 (London, 1954); vol. 2, 1940–5 (London, 1967).
F. Williams, *Ernest Bevin* (London, 1952).   MC

BEXLEY, NICHOLAS VANSITTART, Baron (1766–1851), British politician and economic expert. He supported the younger Pitt and Addington, holding office as secretary to the treasury (1801–4, 1806–7) and chief secretary for Ireland (1805). In 1812, when the Sidmouth group joined Liverpool's government, Vansittart became chancellor of the exchequer. In 1816 his proposal to continue income tax after the end of the war was defeated, largely by the efforts of Brougham. Vansittart was a competent and conscientious chancellor at a time of great difficulty, and one of the ablest of Sidmouth's group. He held office until 1813, when Liverpool brought in the Caningites, and he then became chancellor of the Duchy of Lancaster (1823–8).

BÉZA, THEODORE (1519–1605), French Protestant reformer. He was Catholic prior of Longjumeau until he became converted (1548). During ten years spent as professor of Greek at Lausanne, he made a Latin translation of the New Testament and negotiated on behalf of the oppressed Protestants of the Vaud. In 1559 he joined Calvin at Geneva and led the Protestant delegation at the Colloquy of Poissy (1561). After Calvin's death (1564), Béza was acknowledged as his successor and leader of the French and Swiss reformed churches. He was one of the Huguenots' principal spokesmen during the religious wars in France and is often credited with having converted the Bourbon family of Navarre to Protestantism. With advancing years Béza became less disputatious and agreed with Henry IV that what France chiefly needed was peace, although in Geneva itself Calvin's stern regime was not conspicuously relaxed. To the Huguenots he left a psalter and the definitive version of their Bible.

BHADRALOK, small land-holding, professional, and clerical classes of Bengal. With a passion for English education, they established Anglo-vernacular schools in towns and villages on a scale unknown elsewhere in India. Because of increasing competition for employment they became discontented. An attempt (1902) by the brothers Barindra Kumar and Arabindo Ghosh to spread revolutionary ideas among the *bhadralok* met with little response. However, Curzon's Universities Bill (1904), which was regarded as an attempt to limit the number of Indians educated in English, and the Partition of Bengal (1905) favoured their efforts. They started a newspaper, the *Jugantar*, and a revolutionary society, the *Anusilan Samiti*, and began making arms and explosives. This was followed (1905–16) by acts of brigand-age and terrorism by *bhadralok* youths. The details can be read in the *Sedition Committee Report* (Calcutta, 1918).

BHAGAT SINGH, SARDAR (1907–31), Indian revolutionary. He was active in the non-co-operation (1920–2) and *gurdwara* agitations (1922–4), a founder and the first secretary of the Naujawan Bharat Sabha or Indian Youth Association (1925) in Lahore, and played an important part in the formation of the combined north Indian revolutionary group, the Hindu-stan Socialist Republican Association (Sept. 1928). On 17 Dec. 1928 Singh was in an HSRA group which murdered J. P. Saunders, a Lahore police officer, in retaliation for the death of Lala Lajpat Rai from injuries inflicted by the police during a demonstration against the Simon Commission. In April 1929 Singh and Batukeshwar Datta made a bomb attack in the Indian Legislative Assembly as a protest against the government's legislation to deal with revolutionary activities. They were arrested and later the HSRA's organization and bomb arsenals were seized by the police. Singh and Datta were sentenced to life transportation, then Singh was arraigned with his Lahore colleagues for Saunders's murder. They went on hunger strike in order to force the government to treat them as political prisoners (as a result of which one of them died), which led to the adoption of a Special Tribunal procedure, with no right of appeal. Bhagat Singh and two others were executed (23 March 1931). Their deaths evoked widespread sympathy in Indian political circles, but also marked the end of an effective terrorist movement in India.

BHAGAVAD GITA (lit. 'the Lord's Song'), a basic Indian religious text within, or rather incorporated into, the *Mahabharata*. On the eve of the great battles between the 5 Pandavas with their allies and the 100 Kavravas (cousins of the Pandavas who had taken possession of the latters' kingdom) Arjuna, one of the Pandavas, is reluctant to pro-ceed. Krishna, however, in truth an incarnation of the god Vishnu acting as Arjuna's charioteer, convinces the hero that it is his duty to fight. In doing so he gives an elaborate and profound exposition of a form of devotional Hinduism with strong emphasis upon living in accordance with the caste into which one is born, as well as upon complete sur-render to a merciful god. The influence of the *Gita* on Indian thought and society cannot be overrated.

BHAGAVATAS, THE, one of the earliest theistic sects in ancient India, fully developed in the 2nd cent. BC. The principal doctrines are based upon some later Vedic texts, notably the Upanishads, as well as on the *Bhagavad Gita* and the *Bhagavata Purana*. Salvation, which in India was mainly viewed as deliverance from the cycle of rebirths, could be attained by a righteous life and complete surrender to the will and mercy of Lord Krishna (Vishnu). One of the earliest known Bhagavata devotees was a Greek, Heliodoros, envoy of the Indo-Greek ruler Antialcidas at the Shunga court in the second half of the 2nd cent. BC. To demonstrate his faith he had a high pillar erected, with an inscription in Prakrit in Brahmi script and crowned with a representation of the Garuda, the mythical bird associated with the god Vishnu. This column still stands at Besnagar (ancient Vidisha) in Malwa. The Bhagavatas and the sects based upon their doctrines have remained important in India until modern times.

BHAKTI, in Indian religion: 'intense devotion' to an omnipo-tent and merciful god, most often Vishnu, especially in his form of Krishna. *Bhakti* is distinct from, though sometimes combined with, other forms of worship such as asceticism, ritual, and the quest for transcendental knowledge. It is commonly associated with offerings of fruit and flowers, the burning of incense, and, in later times, communal chant-ing of hymns. Though its roots can be traced back to the Vedas, it had become a prominent feature of some Indian religions by the 2nd cent. BC and influenced all the others,

including Buddhism, in later times. It is generally held that the increasing emphasis upon image worship from about the beginning of our era is connected with the growth of *bhakti*.

BHAKTI MOVEMENT AND CULT. The Sanskrit word *bhakti* signifies 'loving devotion'. It was applied to a cult, the basis of which was loving devotion to a personal god as a way of personal salvation, and emphasizes the oneness of God though under different names, and the brotherhood of man. In consequence it was liberal in matters of caste and favoured local languages rather than Sanskrit. Under its inspiration versions of the Hindu epics, like Tulsi Das's *Ramayana* in Hindi, were produced.

The *bhakti* movement can be traced back at least as far as Ramanuja, the 10th-cent. Indian thinker. It was probably influenced by—and influenced—Islam, tending to draw the two together in the worship of one God. The *bhakti* were the Hindu analogue of the Muslim *sufis*. Kabir, the poet-weaver of Banaras, illustrates this tendency. There was a succession of *bhakti* 'saints' in Maharashtra from the late 13th cent., of whom the greatest was Tukaram. Other out-standing figures were Chaitanya of Bengal, who started the Vaishnavite movement there and popularized Brindaban as the traditional birthplace of the God Krishna, and Guru Nanak, founder of the Sikh religion. His movement began, like others, as an effort to unite in one worship Hinduism and Islam.

BHARATAVARSHA, old name for the Indo-Pakistani sub-continent, also called Jambudvipa. It is often subdivided into Aryavarta, the Indo-Gangetic basins and adjoining areas, and Dakshinapatha, the Deccan plateau.

BHARATPUR, city and district of the modern Indian state of Rajasthan. The founders of the Jat state of Bharatpur were Badan Singh and his adopted son, Suraj Mal, who rose to power during the decline of the Mughal empire. During the Second Maratha War (1803–5) its ruler, who had a friendly alliance with the British, joined their enemies the Marathas. Lord Lake laid siege to the fort (3 Jan.–22 Feb. 1805) and attempted four unsuccessful assaults with an inadequate siege train and no skilled engineers. British casualties were 3203 killed and wounded, of whom 103 were European officers. Thereafter the state remained friendly until the succession war of 1824. In 1826 a force under Lord Combermere captured the fortress, but the victory was marred by his rapacity for prize-money.

BHARHUT *STUPA*, one of the oldest known *stupas* (ie, thopes or pagodas: stone monuments built to enshrine relics of Lord Buddha or other Buddhist saints, later also to enshrine holy texts, usually engraved in gold) which once stood at Bharhut in Bundelkhand, about 100 miles (161 kms) south-west of Prayaga (former Allahabad). Hardly anything re-mains of the site, but important carved fragments of the railing (2nd–1st cent. BC) have found their way into museums (especially the Indian Museum in Calcutta). These show some of the oldest examples of genuine Indian art, uninflu-enced by the Persians or Greeks.

BHASKARACHARYA (*fl.* 12th cent. AD), one of the best-known ancient Indian mathematicians.

BHAVABHUTI (*fl.* 8th cent. AD), Indian playwright. His plays, such as the Uttararamacarita, 'The later Deeds of Rama', excel in the ornate, often somewhat pathetic, ex-pression of noble sentiments. Though based on mythical or pseudo-historical traditions, they are of interest to the his-torian in that they illustrate the significance of the remote past for Indians in the early medieval period.

BHAVE, ACHARYA VINOBA (1895–), Gandhian social worker, founder of the *Sarvodaya*, 'Welfare for all', and

Bhoodan, 'land-gift', movements. Vinoba joined Gandhi's *ashram* in Gujarat in June 1916 and was associated mainly with constructive and village uplift work. He moved to Wardha, Central Provinces, in 1921. Gandhi sent him to lead the Vaikom temple *satyagraha* (non-violence) in Travancore–Cochin (1924) and to be the first of the individual *satyagrahi*s protesting at India's involvement in the war (1940). Bhave formed the *Sarvodaya Samaj* (1948) to work among refugees, then in 1951 began the *bhoodan* movement to collect 50 million acres (200,000 sq. kms) of land for redistribution to landless villagers. In the late 1950s he saw *gramdan* (the gift of the entire cultivable land of a village to a joint council of villagers) as a more effective programme. By 1967, 4·25 million acres (17,200 sq. kms) had been donated under *bhoodan*, but only 1 million acres (4000 sq. kms) had been distributed because of the shift of interest to *gramdan*, in which 37,520 villages had been given (1967). Bihar had more than one-third of all *gramdan* villages and was also the largest state for *bhoodan* donations.

BHILS, aboriginal Indian tribes of the hilly country of Mewar, Malwa, Khandesh, and Gujarat, whose language has disappeared. They were treated with great cruelty by the Marathas, but under British rule a policy of reclamation was attempted by Outram after 1825. The Mewar Bhil Corps remained loyal during the Mutiny of 1857.

BHOPAL, city and state in central India. Bhopal state extended over nearly 7000 sq. miles (17,800 sq. kms) lying to the west of Indore and bounded on the south by the Narbada river. It was the second largest Muslim state in India and was founded by an Afghan adventurer, Dost Muhammad Khan, who came to the court of the Mughal Emperor Bahadur Shah I seeking employment (1708). He obtained a grant of Bhopal and in the years which followed Bahadur Shah's death, made himself an independent chief with the title of nawab. During the 18th cent. the family fortunes underwent many vicissitudes from the attacks of Marathas and Pindaris and from internal disputes. The nawab's minister assisted Col. Goddard on his march from Bengal to Bombay in 1778. The state revived in the 19th cent. under British protection and was notable for a succession of princesses who ruled the state with great ability. The last ruling nawab played an active part in Indian state politics, being for some years the chancellor of the Chamber of Princes. The state survived until 1956, when it was absorbed into the state of Madhya Pradesh. Bhopal city is the capital of the new state.

BHRIGU, one of the (traditionally) mythical ancient Indian sages (*rishi*) and supposed founder of the Brahmanic Bhargava clan (*gotra*).

BHUTAN, independent state in the Himalayas between Tibet and India, bounded on the east by the tribal tracts of the Abhors and Mishmis and on the west by Sikkim and Darjeeling. The name is a contraction of the Indian term 'Bhotanta', meaning the end of Bhot, that is, Tibet. The inhabitants are known as Bhotias and are of Tibetan origin. Their language is a dialect of Tibetan with local variations. They profess a form of Buddhism similar to the Lamaism of Tibet, but as in Tibet, it seems to have been superimposed on the animistic creeds and devil worship which preceded Buddhism. Both men and women in Bhutan have close-cropped hair and do not wear pigtails, which distinguishes them from the Bhotias of Tibet and Sikkim. Although the directors of the East India Co. in London wished to foster friendly commercial relations with Bhutan and Tibet, nothing had been done before Warren Hastings assumed control of Bengal (1772). One of his first tasks was to protect the company's possessions from Bhutanese aggression when they invaded Cooch Behar. This prompted the Tashi (Panchen) Lama, who was regent of Tibet and guardian of the infant Dalai Lama, to intercede on behalf of the Bhutanese. Hastings seized the opportunity

to dispatch George Bogle to Bhutan (1774) and thence to the court of the Tashi Lama at Tashilhunpo. A further attempt to promote friendly commercial relations was Samuel Turner's mission (1783), but little intercourse took place until the British occupation of Assam (1826). The annexation of the Assam Duars (mountain passes) by Bhutan and constant raids into British territory led to Pemberton's unsuccessful mission (1838). Finally, in 1841, the Duars became British territory. Bhutan was to be paid an annual subsidy provided she ceased raiding the British frontier districts. But Bhutanese aggression continued. In 1863, Sir Ashley Eden, sent as envoy to Bhutan, was grossly insulted. A British army invaded Bhutan (1865) and forced her to cede all the Duars of Bengal and Assam. In return, by the treaty of Sinchula (11 Nov. 1865), Bhutan was granted a yearly allowance, provided they kept the peace. From this time, British relations with Bhutan remained friendly. During the 1904 Tibet mission, Bhutan assisted in the negotiations with the Tibetan authorities. By a treaty in 1910, the British increased the annual allowance from Rs 50,000 to Rs 100,000, and Bhutan agreed to be guided by the advice of the British in regard to her external relations. China then claimed Bhutan as a feudatory state, but was told that the British would not tolerate any Chinese interference. After India became independent, the government of India raised the annual subsidy to Rs 500,000 and ceded the territory known as Dewangiri to Bhutan, whose foreign relations were to be controlled by India.

C. U. Aitchison (ed.), *Treaties, Engagements and Sanads*, vol. 14 (Calcutta, 1929).   CCD

BIBULUS, M. CALPURNIUS (d. 48 BC), Roman noble. Although a leading opponent of Julius Caesar, he was unable, as his colleague in the consulship of 59, to thwart him. He governed Syria (51) and commanded Pompey's fleet in the Civil War (49–48).

BICOCCA, BATTLE OF (1522), fought on the northern plains of Italy between the imperialist forces and a Franco-Swiss army under Lautrec. The latter was severely defeated, the Swiss mercenaries suffering enormous losses in the face of the imperialist artillery.

BIDAULT, GEORGES (1899–), French Resistance leader and politician of the Fourth Republic who became a bitter opponent of de Gaulle's Algerian policy. A teacher by profession, Bidault made his name in the 1930s as an activist in the Christian Democrat movement, being associated with the Popular Democrat Party and the newspaper *l'Aube*. A prisoner of war in 1940, he was released in 1941 and joined the Resistance movement *Combat* in Lyons. He was a member of the *Conseil National de la Resistance* (CNR), and became its chairman after the capture of Jean Moulin (1943).

At the Liberation, Bidault had a claim to power as a leader both of the Resistance and of the MRP, the new Christian Democrat Party shortly to enjoy great electoral success. There was some tension between the CNR and de Gaulle, but Bidault co-operated with the latter and was foreign minister in his provisional government (1944). He occupied this post with one short break until 1948, trying to apply de Gaulle's policy of keeping Germany divided and economically weak, against the wishes of the other western allies. He was foreign minister again in 1953–4, and twice prime minister (1946, 1949–50).

After the French withdrawal from Indo-China (1954), Bidault was increasingly preoccupied with the colonial question, attacking the concessions made to nationalism in North Africa. In the last years of the Fourth Republic, he was a leader of the 'Algeria lobby' whose destruction of successive governments on this issue helped bring the Republic down. In 1958 he broke with the MRP and founded his own party, *Démocratie chrétienne*. He supported the recall of de Gaulle (1958), but joined the right-wing opposition to him when it became clear that his policy would lead to Algerian independence. He headed the '*comité de Vincennes*', a body dissolved by the government in 1961.

Charged with conspiracy against the state, Bidault went into exile (1962). He returned to France in 1968, and campaigned against de Gaulle in the 1969 referendum. He has defended his political activity in *Resistance, the Political Autobiography of Georges Bidault* (New York, 1967).

BIDDLE, NICHOLAS (1786–1844), third president of the Second Bank of the US, whose struggle with President Jackson over the re-charter of the bank was a major public issue of the 1830s. As president of the bank (1822–39), Biddle, a cultivated man, an able financier, and a resourceful intriguer, pursued conservative financial policies designed to foster confidence and stability. But he aroused opposition from western state banks, New York banking interests, and supporters of inflation and opponents of chartered privilege, and —most notably—from President Jackson. When Biddle, partly for political reasons, sought a new charter for the bank (1832) four years before the expiry of the old one, Jackson vetoed the bill. After 1836 the bank lost its special position, but continued under a charter from the State of Pennsylvania until 1841.

BIDWELL, MARSHAL SPRING (1799–1872), politician and lawyer. Bidwell, an American by birth, was a member of the Assembly of Upper Canada (1825–36) and was twice speaker (1829, 1835). He fled from Canada after the 1837 rebellion, although he was not implicated, and thereafter lived in New York.

BIELFELD, JACOB FRIEDRICH, Freiherr von (1717–70), inspector-general of Prussian universities, whose *Institutions Politiques* (1760) showed the combined influence of the French Enlightenment and Prussian bureaucracy.

BIENVILLE, JEAN BAPTISTE LE MOYNE, Sieur de (1680–1768), governor of Louisiana and founder of New Orleans, who took the title Bienville on the death of an elder brother, François (1691). He joined the navy and accompanied another brother, Iberville, on an expedition against the English Hudson Bay settlements, taking part in the second capture of Fort Nelson (1697). He again sailed with Iberville (1698–1699) to found the colony of Louisiana, acting as administrator for his brother, who was appointed governor in 1703. Iberville died in 1706 and Bienville succeeded him as governor. He was removed from office and reinstated in 1707, and then served either as governor or as administrator to a series of governors sent from France until his appointment to the chief office (10 Oct. 1717). During this period he established a reputation for his successful Indian policy and built (1710) Fort Louis on the present site of Mobile. As governor, with the increasing numbers of colonists attracted by John Law's Mississippi ventures, Bienville established the settlement of New Orleans (1718), which became capital of the colony in 1722. He captured (1719) the Spanish fort at Pensacola, but in 1724 was recalled to give an account of his administration to the French government. Despite a forceful defence, he was deprived of his offices. He lived quietly in Paris until 1732, when the threatened ruin of Louisiana, which faced trouble with the Natchez Indians and was burdened by an incompetent governor, caused the government to reappoint him royal governor. Bienville returned to America in 1733, but the Indian troubles continued. An expedition against the Chickasaw (1736) ended in disaster, and another (1739–40) led only to an inconclusive peace. He requested his own recall and left Louisiana for the last time in 1743. In 1766, when Jean Millet came from Louisiana to protest against its proposed cession to Spain, Bienville joined his fruitless mission to the French government, but the colony was nevertheless surrendered.

Grace King, *Jean Baptiste le Moyne, Sieur de Bienville* (New York, 1892).   AJS

BIERUT, BOLESLAW (1892–1956), Polish communist. From 1918 he was an important member of the underground Communist Party of Poland (KPP). He was imprisoned for his activities (1933–9) by the Polish authorities and thus was not affected by Stalin's purge of Polish communists, which culminated in the dissolution of the KPP (1938) and the liquidation of most of its leaders.

In 1943 Bierut was flown back from Russia to reorganize the Communist Polish Workers' Party (PPR), formed in Jan. 1942, and remained on its central committee throughout the war. He was chairman of the pro-communist National Council established in Jan. 1944 to replace the government-in-exile in London, and was also involved in forming the Polish Committee of National Liberation in Lublin (July 1944). When this committee declared the presidency vacant (Sept. 1944), the functions of that office were assigned to Bierut. In Dec. 1944 the committee declared itself the provisional government of Poland and was recognized as such by the Big Three at Yalta (Feb. 1945). Bierut formally became president in Feb. 1947, and also (Aug. 1948) secretary-general of the central committee of the PPR, and later first secretary of the United Workers' Party (PZPR), formed by the union of the PPR and the Polish Socialist Party (Dec. 1948).

As leader of the 'Muscovites', as the Moscow-trained group in the PPR was called, Bierut clashed with Gomulka, who argued for a more independent line towards the USSR. Gomulka was stripped of his party functions in Nov. 1949. A further formal concentration of power in Bierut's hands took place in Nov. 1952, when he became prime minister, at the same time relinquishing the presidency.

The extent to which Bierut controlled political life in this period remains unclear. He deputed much of his control of the PZPR to his *éminence grise*, Jakub Berman, and it is fairly well established that many key decisions were in fact dictated by Soviet security 'advisers'. Though a firm believer in the pre-eminent role of the Soviet Union, Bierut attempted to avoid the worst excesses of Stalinism. Show trials, for instance, were less a feature of Polish life at this time than in Czechoslovakia or Hungary.

Stalin's death (March 1953) considerably weakened Bierut's position. In March 1954 he ceased to be prime minister and his control of the party became increasingly ineffective. At the time of his death the Stalinist system in Poland was collapsing in the face of economic difficulties and demands for intellectual freedom and more independence from the Soviet Union. Bierut's removal from politics just before the crisis broke was one of the principal reasons why events in Poland in Oct. 1956 did not take such a violent course as in Hungary.

M. K. Dziewanowski, *The Communist Party of Poland. An outline of history* (Cambridge, MA, 1959).
R. Hiscocks, *Poland, Bridge or Abyss?* (Oxford, 1963).

AP

BIG HOLE, BATTLE OF (Aug. 1877), bitterly fought battle lasting 24 hours, which took place in the Bitteroot mountains, MT. Col. John Gibbon led a surprise attack against a camp of Nez Perces Indians, whose resistance was weakened through the loss of some of their greatest warriors.

BIG STICK, US term used to describe the diplomatic stance of President Theodore Roosevelt (1901–9). Taken from an African proverb that the president was fond of quoting ('Speak softly and carry a big stick, you will go far'), it underlined his belief that foreign policies had to be sustained by measurable national power.

BIGGAR, JOSEPH (1829–90), Irish nationalist, who introduced an obstructionist policy in the parliament of 1874–80, delaying the work of the house by long speeches, numerous questions, or motions for adjournment, to draw attention to the wrongs of Ireland. He thereby incurred the opposition of the more moderate Butt, but attracted the interest of Parnell. Biggar was elected a treasurer of the extremist Land League (1879).

BIGGE, JOHN THOMAS (1780–1843), Englishman who was the author of three reports on conditions in the colony of New South Wales towards the close of the governorship of Lachlan Macquarie. Following colonial experience as chief justice of Trinidad (1815–18), he was sent to NSW (1819) as a commissioner with extraordinary powers. As a mediator between the governor and his many critics, Bigge failed, but his accounts of the convict system, the judicial organization, and the economic life of the colony provided a mine of information for the authorities at home and for historians. His mercantilist mistrust of the colonial manufacture of clothing, blankets, and hats, and his prejudices made him insensitive to the social changes inevitable in the developing NSW community. Some of his proposals were nevertheless embodied in the Judicature Act (1823), though he opposed the immediate introduction of trial by jury and discounted the prospect of political progress in what he regarded as primarily a convict settlement.

BIGO. Large Iron Age earthworks in central Uganda, credited to the Chwezi rulers. Their isotopic date (AD 1350–1500) corresponds with that of oral tradition.

BIGOD, HUGH (d. 1268). Brother of the Earl of Norfolk and chief justiciar of England, he combined excellently the headship of the royal council with the functions of a chief justice and instituted important enquiries into administrative abuses.

BIGOT, FRANÇOIS (1703–*c.* 1777), *intendant* of New France. Born in France of a well-connected family, Bigot became a lawyer and civil servant. It is probable that his misappropriation of defence funds while paymaster at Louisbourg (1739–44) led to his fall. He returned to France (1745) and obtained the position of *intendant* of New France (1748). Through La Grande Compagnie, Bigot and his accomplices (who included high officials in France and Canada) defrauded the province of vast sums. When the British captured Canada, assisted by the discontent he had created, Bigot returned to France (1760), where he was imprisoned (1761) for 11 months in the Bastille, then forced to restore 1,500,000 livres and banished.

BIHAR, state of modern India occupying the valley of the Ganges from Nepal to Orissa, bounded on the west by Uttar Pradesh and Madhya Pradesh, and on the east by West Bengal. From very early times Videha or Mithila, to the north of the Ganges, was a great seat of Sanskrit learning. In the 6th cent. BC this area was the home of republican clans, the most important of whom were the Licchavis of Vaisali. The district of Saran was at one time part of the great Kosala kingdom of Oudh. The eastern districts of Monghyr, Bhagalpur, and Purnea belonged to the ancient kingdom of Anga. Patna, Gaya, and Shahabad to the south of the Ganges comprised the kingdom of Magadha. It was here that the Buddha developed his religion. The term Bihar is thought to be derived from *vihara*, the name for a Buddhist monastery. Here also Mahavira founded the Jain religion. When Buddhism arose there was no paramount power in northern India. It was Chandragupta Maurya who overthrew Nanda, the Sudra king of Magadha, and annexed it to his famous empire. In the 4th cent. AD it formed part of the Gupta empire and remained so until the end of the 5th cent., when that empire was overrun by the Hunas. In the first half of the 7th cent. it was included in Harsha's dominions. Gopala, the founder of the Pala dynasty, built the famous Buddhist monastery at Udantapura. The Palas ruled over both Bihar and Bengal in the 9th cent. until Mahendrapala I (885–*c.* 910) extended the Pratihara kingdom at the expense of the Palas. Pala rule was further weakened by the rise of the Sena dynasty in Bengal, but at the close of the 12th cent. both the Palas and the Senas were overthrown by Muslim invaders. Bihar was one of the 23 provinces of Muhammad bin Tughluq's extensive empire in the first half of the 14th cent. In 1397 it was annexed to the kingdom of Jaunpur. On the eve of Babur's invasion it once more formed part of the sultanate of Delhi, but was annexed by Babur (1529). When Akbar re-established Mughal rule in northern India (1556), Bihar and Bengal were under an Afghan ruler, Sulaiman Kararani, until they became incorporated as *suba*s (provinces) into the Mughal empire. With the decline of Mughal rule, the provincial governors threw off their allegiance to the central government. In 1740, Sarfaraz Khan, viceroy of the three provinces of Bengal, Bihar, and Orissa, was overthrown by Ali Vardi Khan, a subordinate official in charge of Bihar. This led to the rise of the independent dynasty of *nawab-nazim*s of Bengal with whom Clive came into contact. During the Hindu period, Bihar was a great cultural centre. In modern times it has become an industrial centre with vast mineral resources of coal, copper, iron, manganese, and mica.

J. Houlton, *Bihar The Heart of India* (London, 1949).

CCD

BIITO DYNASTY in Buganda, founded by Kato Kimera, twin brother of King Rukidi of Kitera (*c.* 1500). Under this dynasty Buganda became the most powerful kingdom in the lacustrine region. It was abolished in 1967. Some authors question whether this dynasty was of Ababiito origin.

BIITO DYNASTY in Bungoro, was probably of mainly Luo origin. Between 1450 and 1550 the Biito took over and remodelled the Chwezi's system of kingship in central and southern Uganda. Their kingdom lasted until 1967, when it was abolished by Uganda's Republican Constitution.

BIJAPUR, headquarters of the Bijapur district of the present Mysore state in the Union of India. It was formerly the seat of the Adil Shahi dynasty of Muslim kings, who ruled as independent sovereigns and successors to the Bahmani kingdom of the Deccan (1489–1686). Bijapur was the most important of these successor states and Sultan Ibrahim II has the distinction of commissioning the historian Ferishta to write his classic history.

Under this dynasty Bijapur was a centre of the arts and particularly architecture, the most notable examples of which are the Ibrahim Rauza, or tomb and mosque of Ibrahim II (1580–1626), and the Gol Gumbaz, or tomb of Muhammad Adil Shah (1626–56).

BIKANIR state was founded by Bika, a younger son of the ruling Rajput of Marwar in the late 15th cent. The Bikanir chief was given the title of Raja by the Mughal Emperor Akbar, who married his daughter (1570). Raja Rai Singh (1571–1611) rose high in the Mughal service and married his daughter to Akbar's son and successor, Prince Salim. He also built the main Bikanir fortress-palace. In the 18th cent. there was much fighting with the parent state of Marwa until both states came under British protection (1818). Early in the 20th cent. Maharaja Ganga Singh (*reg.* 1887–1943) was active in British Indian politics. He was the first chancellor of the Chamber of Princes (1921–6), and his Round Table Conference speech (1930), advocating an Indian federation in which the princes would join, helped to give a new direction to Indian politics.

BILGRAMI, SYED HUSSAIN, Nawab Imad-ul-Mulk (1844–1926), first Muslim member of Council of India, London (1907). In the service of the Nizam of Hyderabad (1873–1907), he became a member of the Indian Legislative Assembly (1902) and was a member of the Indian Education Commission (1902). He assisted in the drawing up of the Muslim memorandum for Minto (1 Oct. 1906) and in organizing the Muslim League.

BILHAPUR, BATTLE OF (1 April 1731), fought between the Maratha Peshwa, Baji Rao I, and his rival Trimbak Rao, the Senapati or commander-in-chief, between Baroda and Dhaboi in western India. The battle confirmed the supremacy of the Bhat family of peshwas among the ministers of the Maratha Raja Shahu.

BILL OF RIGHTS (1689), in England, in which was embodied the Declaration of Rights drawn up by the Convention (in the absence of a 'valid' parliament) to solve certain problems raised by the 'Revolution' of 1688. It represented an attempt to solve the immediate difficulties facing the country after the Revolution. It was left deliberately vague, so as to satisfy as many as possible from both parties.

The immediate problem was the settlement of the succession. Few Tories believed that James II could be allowed to return, and yet Toryism was strongly legitimist. The Whigs had no belief in the divine right of kings, but wished to press the idea of a contract between king and nation, represented by parliament. Thus the deposition of James II was left vague and inaccurate, with the claim that James had 'abdicated' the throne and not fled from rebellion, and that the throne was vacant, James's infant son being ignored. The act made the throne temporarily elective and offered the Crown jointly to William of Orange and his wife, Mary. They were recognized as sovereigns de facto, no attempt being made to prove them rightful and lawful king or queen.

The Bill of Rights also made provision for the succession in the future. In the event of William and Mary dying childless, the Crown was to pass to Anne and her heirs, and failing this to any children of William by a second marriage. In addition, in the future no Roman Catholic or any person marrying a Roman Catholic was to be allowed to stand in line for the succession.

The bill tried to settle 'the religion, laws and liberties of the kingdom' so that they could never again be subverted as they had been under James II. Most of the practices referred to, *eg*, the use of the Ecclesiastical Commission, the suspending power, denying the right to petition the Crown, and raising finances without parliamentary consent, were already illegal, but the act also declared illegal the dispensing power 'as used of late' and the raising of a standing army in peacetime, both of which previously had been legal.

There was a definition of parliament's position. It was stressed that parliament ought to meet frequently, that there ought to be freedom of speech and of debates in parliament, and that the election of MPs ought to be free from Crown interference.

Finally, the bill attempted to ensure a diminution of Crown control over the law, and attacked the Crown's tampering with juries, excessive bail and fines, fines before conviction, and prosecutions in King's Bench which ought to be in parliament.

Though the Bill of Rights was an answer to certain immediate problems, it was seen as a definition of the Revolution Settlement and of a balanced constitution. Thus, for over a century it was the basis for all constitutional changes and reforms.

In Scotland events were similar. A Convention prepared a Claim of Right and offered the Crown to William and Mary. James was declared to have 'forefaulted' the Crown. A major distinction in the implications of the Revolution in Scotland was the rejection of Episcopacy and the establishment of the state church as Presbyterian in government. This largely arose because the Scottish bishops (unlike most of their English counterparts) refused to accept William.

E. N. Williams, *The Eighteenth Century Constitution* (Cambridge, 1960).   AW

BILL OF RIGHTS (1791), the first ten amendments to the US constitution, intended to protect individual rights from infringement by the federal government. Following the lead of VA, most states incorporated Bills of Rights in their first constitutions, grounding them on doctrines of natural law and of natural rights. Sensitivity to such doctrines had been heightened by the events leading to the Revolution. Americans argued that the liberty of the individual could best be protected by restrictions on government and explicit declarations of the rights of the citizen.

There was little discussion of a Bill of Rights at the Constitutional Convention (1787), but the question became a major issue during the debates over ratification. Supporters of the constitution argued that a Bill of Rights was superfluous, since the constitution granted only enumerated powers to the federal government. Furthermore, to specify certain rights might imply that the citizen enjoyed those rights and no others. Critics, however, continued to demand the inclusion of a Bill of Rights and several states, including the crucial MA, VA, and NY ratified the constitution, only with the proviso that one be added.

James Madison, who had originally opposed the proposal, led the movement for a Bill of Rights in the First Congress, wishing to incorporate it at appropriate points in the constitution. Congress rejected this suggestion and recommended 12 amendments. The states ratified ten. The first eight gave specific protection to individual rights. By Article I Congress was prohibited from either establishing any form of religion or preventing its free exercise, from abridging freedom of speech or the press, and from restricting the right of assembly and petition for the redress of grievances. Article II proclaimed the citizen's right to bear arms. Article III severely regulated the quartering of soldiers in private houses. Article IV protected the citizen's property and person from unreasonable searches and seizure, and from general warrants. Article V gave him the protection of the due process of law, and Articles VI, VII and VIII specified his rights in criminal and civil proceedings, especially the right to trial by jury and protection against excessive bail and cruel or unusual punishments. Article IX answered Federalist arguments by stating that enumeration of certain rights did not exclude others. The Xth Article referred to relations between federal and state governments, declaring that powers not delegated to the US, nor prohibited to the states, were reserved to the states, or to the people.

The Bill of Rights, like the rest of the US constitution, has subsequently been modified by additional constitutional amendments, by congressional acts, and by judicial interpretations.

BILL OF RIGHTS, SOCIETY OF SUPPORTERS OF (1769), in England, was founded by Westminster and Middlesex friends of John Wilkes, to defend the liberty of the subject and support Wilkes's position. It put forward some radical ideas on parliamentary reform, but never escaped from its primary concern with Wilkes's affairs. It paid many of his debts, staged riots before and after his expulsion from parliament (Feb. 1769), and was active in the petitioning campaign which followed his expulsion and the Commons declaration of his incapacity to be re-elected.

BILLING, NOEL PEMBERTON (1880–1948), British independent MP and an early advocate of a strong air policy, including that of bombing civilian populations. He successfully challenged the party truce during the First World War and was elected MP for East Hertfordshire (1916–21), being known as the 'member for air'. He founded *Aerocraft*, which he edited (1908–10).

BILLOTTE, PIERRE (1906–), French general and Gaullist politician. Billotte joined de Gaulle after escaping to Russia from a prisoner-of-war camp, and fought in the 1944 campaign. In 1951 he resigned from the army to enter parliament, and has occupied posts in the government and the Gaullist party. Billotte is one of the leading left-wing Gaullists.

BILLOUX, FRANÇOIS (1903–), French communist leader. Billoux was one of the three communist ministers dismissed from office in 1947. The son of a peasant, he joined the French Communist Party on its foundation in 1920, and has served it as a full-time official, being a member of the party secretariat since 1954. Billoux entered parliament in 1936, and was imprisoned during the war (1939–43). He was a member of de Gaulle's provisional assembly at Algiers (1943) and of his provisional government (1944). In 1946 he was minister of reconstruction and minister of defence when dismissed from Ramadier's government. Billoux has represented Marseilles in parliament since 1945.

BILLY THE KID, the alias of William H. Bonney (1854–81), an infamous outlaw of the American South-West. With 12 companions, he became a wholesale cattle thief and personally committed 21 murders before being shot by Sheriff Pat Garrett at Fort Sumner, NM.

BILTMORE PROGRAMME (1942), programme adopted by a meeting of the American Zionist Emergency Council at the Biltmore Hotel in New York. It urged that:

the gates of Palestine be opened; that the Jewish Agency be vested with control of immigration into Palestine and with the necessary authority for the upbuilding of the country, including the development of its unoccupied and uncultivated lands; and that Palestine be established as a Jewish Commonwealth integrated into the structure of the new democratic world.

The conference at which the programme was adopted marked the succession of Ben Gurion to leadership of the Zionist movement in place of Chaim Weizmann; it was also an important step in the dominance of Zionism within American Jewry, which had traditionally been markedly assimilationist.

BIMBISARA (reg. 6th cent. BC), King of Magadha (mod. Bihar). He is clearly a historical figure who, from humble beginnings, created an important state which was to remain the political and cultural centre of ancient India for most of the following 1000 years. He was a contemporary of the Buddha, who frequently visited his court, as well as of the Jina Mahavira. According to a somewhat suspect tradition he died while being imprisoned by his son Ajatashatru.

BINET, ALFRED (1857–1911), French psychologist, who developed the concept of assessing individual 'mental age' from which evolved the 'Binet scale' of measurement (1908).

BINH-XUYEN SOCIETY, a Viet-namese (and partly Chinese) secret society which became prominent in Saigon and Cholon in the period 1945–55. It created for itself a powerful position during the Indo-Chinese War, and in 1955 presented a serious threat to the power of Ngo Dinh Diem. In May 1955 the latter forced Binh-Xuyen elements to withdraw from the South Viet-namese capital after street-fighting, and they have not operated under that name since.

BIO-BIO RIVER, after 1557 the frontier of Spanish occupation in Chile for some three centuries. The opposition of the Araucanian Indians prevented expansion to the south.

BIONDO FLAVIO (1392–1463), one of the pioneers of humanist historiography, distinguished by his critical spirit and his use of a wide range of sources, such as remains of buildings, coins, and inscriptions, as well as official documents. His most important works were the *Decades*, a history of Rome and its successors (412–1443); *Italia illustrata*, containing a historical and geographical account of the regions of Italy and serving as a model for later humanist works describing other countries; and *Roma Triumphans*, the first scholarly attempt to reconstruct the topography of ancient Rome.

BIRD, GEORGE (d. 1857), was the first to open up high land in Ceylon for the planting of coffee, and to introduce labour from southern India to work on the plantations. He received strong support from the governor, Sir Edward Barnes. The planting of coffee, which was succeeded by tea-planting, laid the foundations of Ceylon's economic prosperity in the 19th cent.

BIRD, ROBERT MERTTINS (1788–1853), joined the Bengal civil service (1808), became commissioner of revenue in the Gorakhpur Division (1829), and a member of the Board of Revenue, North-Western Provinces (1832). He was in charge of the settlement of the land revenues of this area (1833–41), on which he wrote an elaborate report. Bird's settlement embraced an area of 72,000 sq. miles (184,000 sq kms) with a population of 23 million. The standard land revenue demand was reduced to two-thirds of the net rental. A cadastral survey was carried out with a demarcation of boundaries and a definition of rights and privileges. The settlement was made for 30 years. Under this system the supersession of the *taluqdar* class was pressed forward with great severity. In 1842 he returned to England, where he became an active member of the Church Missionary Society.

BIRGER, JARL (reg. 1250–66), King of Sweden. His reign was of great importance in the history of Sweden for its promotion of the ideal of a united kingdom and for its legislation. Birger is the real founder of the city of Stockholm and, after 1249, of the Swedish hegemony in Finland. Under him German influence began to be strongly felt in Swedish towns.

BIRINGUCCIO, VANOCCIO (1480–c. 1538), author of *Pirotechnia* (1540), an account of every aspect of mining and metal manufacture, derived from practical experience and observation, which heralded the expansion of the new chemical industry.

BIRKA, fortified Swedish island town on Lake Mälaren (west of modern Stockholm), with access to the Baltic. It was among the most important trade centres in Scandinavia in the 9th and 10th cents. Its 2000 graves have revealed great wealth and far-reaching and varied trade, especially with the Volga region. Ansgar, the 'Apostle of the North', preached there in 830.

BIRKBECK, GEORGE (1776–1841), British founder of the mechanics' institutes. He began lectures on elementary science for working men in Glasgow (1800) and took a leading part in the foundation of the London Mechanics' Institute (1823), now Birkbeck College, making it a substantial loan. He was a radical, associated in politics with Brougham and Burdett, and was a member of the council of University College, London (1827).

BIRKENHEAD, FREDERICK EDWIN SMITH, 1st Earl of (1872–1930), British politician, lawyer, and lord chancellor (1919–22) who became a Conservative MP in 1906 and made a great reputation as an excellent speaker capable of great satire, wit, and invective. He played a prominent part in the battles against the Parliament Act (1911) and the inclusion of Ulster in the Home Rule Bill. He became solicitor-general in the Coalition Cabinet (May 1915) then followed Sir Edward Carson as attorney-general. At 46 he became lord chancellor, an outstanding member of Lloyd George's postwar coalition, whose greatest achievement was the Law of Property Act (1922), a much-needed reform which greatly simplified the conveyance of land. He took a leading part in the Irish negotiations and on being reconciled to the official Conservatives became secretary of state for India (1924–8) under Baldwin.

BIRMINGHAM POLITICAL UNION, in England, founded Dec. 1829 by Thomas Attwood and others to promote parliamentary reform. It was a union of middle- and working-class radicals and was primarily concerned with organizing mass demonstrations. Political unions on the Birmingham model spread rapidly to other towns, and form a distinctive feature of the Reform Bill crisis (1830–2). It has been argued that joint middle- and working-class action was easily achieved in Birmingham because, by reason of the predominance of small-scale workshop organization in the metal trades, there was no sharp social distinction between masters and men. The union withered away in the revived prosperity of 1834, but was formally reconstituted in the depression of 1837, and for a short period was one of the constituent elements in Chartism.

BIRNEY, JAMES GILLESPIE (1792–1857), Kentucky-born slave-holder, who became a leader of the anti-slavery movement in the US. He moved from uneasy acceptance of slavery through a belief in gradual emancipation and Negro colonization abroad to a much more direct anti-slavery position, especially after he freed his own slaves and moved north in the mid-1830s. He worked for the American Anti-Slavery Society for a time, but his advocacy of political action within constitutional limits was at variance with the more extreme position of William Lloyd Garrison and his supporters. He was twice the presidential candidate of the anti-slavery Liberty Party (1840, 1844), but polled only a handful of votes in his first campaign, though his modest vote in 1844, especially in NY, may have cost Henry Clay the election. An accident in 1845 ended his active work in the anti-slavery movement.

BIRON, CHARLES DE GONTAUT, Duke of (1562–1602), son of a leading *Politique*, an able soldier, governor of Burgundy, and a former royal favourite. He was created admiral (1592) and marshal of France (1594). Biron became implicated in various plots and in 1602 was associated in a clumsy conspiracy to assassinate Henry IV, which also involved the king's mistress, Henrietta d'Entragues, Philip III of Spain, the Duke of Savoy, and several princes of the blood. He was betrayed, arrested, imprisoned in the Bastille, and then executed (July 1602). The failure of the conspiracy served to strengthen the house of Bourbon and encouraged the king and his chief minister, Sully, to accelerate the reduction of the great nobles' power.

BIRON, ERNST JOHANN (1690–1772), Duke of Courland and favourite of the Russian Empress Anna (1730–40). Biron was a Baltic German nobleman, detested in Russia because of the harsh fiscal policy associated with his regime and the predominantly German influence which he established at court and in government. There is no evidence, however, to suggest that he pursued a policy disadvantageous to Russia. His influence ended abruptly with Anna's death, though he was restored to favour by Catherine II and spent the last nine years of his life from 1763 administering his duchy of Courland.

BIRTH CONTROL, temporary prevention of conception, as distinct from other methods of population control such as infanticide, abortion, and male or female sterilization. It includes the prevention of implantation by mechanical means (the inter-uterine coil or loop—IUD), the prevention of fertilization by chemical or mechanical means (spermicidal substances, diaphragms, or sheaths), the prevention of ovulation by chemical means (a hormonal 'birth pill'), *coitus interruptus* and celibacy. It has been practised to maintain the physical or mental health of parents or children, and to allow agricultural, social, and industrial developments to keep pace with the population growth, thus maintaining the standard of living.

Egyptian papyri (1850 and 1550 BC) contained recipes for contraceptives. Both physical and chemical means were used by the more sophisticated Greek and Roman families according to Soranus of Ephesus (AD 98–138). Interest in making contraceptive knowledge more widespread throughout the social classes was aroused in several countries, *eg*, Britain, the US, and Holland, in the 1830s after Malthus had pub-

lished his theories on population growth. He himself disapproved of artificial family limitation.

In Britain Francis Place wrote handbills, *Illustrations and Proofs of Principle of Population* (1822), which were distributed to married working men and women. They described techniques for contraception and gave economic and medical reasons for using them. Charles Knowlton's *The Fruits of Philosophy* (1832), first published in the US, was later published in Britain (1834). It led to the trial of Mrs Annie Besant and of Charles Bradlaugh (1877). After their vindication the Malthusian league was founded.

The first birth-control clinic was opened by Dr Aletha Jacobs in Holland in 1881. Mrs Margaret Sanger founded the first US clinic in Brooklyn in 1916. It was closed as a public nuisance, but was later legalized for treatment on medical grounds. The movement spread, developed into the Planned Parenthood Federation of America (1942), and later into the International Planned Parenthood Federation (1952). The first British clinic was opened by Marie Stopes (1921), and was soon followed by one run by the Malthusian League. Local authorities were allowed to set up clinics from 1930 for giving help and advice in cases where 'further pregnancy would be detrimental to health'. Their scope was further increased in 1934. Most British clinics were affiliated to the Family Planning Association (founded in 1930) which works closely with the Marriage Guidance Council (founded in 1938).

In spite of reappraisals in the 1960s since the widespread use of anovulant pills, the Roman Catholic Church maintained its opposition to artificial contraception. The rhythm method, however, was formally approved by Pope Pius XI (1930). The Anglican communion, which had opposed birth control as late as 1920, supported responsible parenthood at the Lambeth Conference of 1958. Other major religions did not (1970) prohibit contraceptive methods. Where the duty to found a family is not ignored, both health and economic reasons are accepted by Jews. The eastern faiths for differing reasons allow contraception, while forbidding abortion.

In many countries government attitudes towards birth control have shifted from opposition to permissiveness and then to active support under the pressure of preventing high abortion rates and population increases, and in order to promote health. The Swedish government was the first to give assistance in family planning in the 1930s. Federal aid was given by the US in 1942, though separate states vary in their approach. In India aid was given in the 1950s, in Korea from 1961, in China from 1960. Abortion laws have fluctuated in USSR since 1920, but recently contraception has been encouraged. Chile was the first predominantly Roman Catholic country to give state aid (1963). The subject was first debated by the United Nations Assembly in 1962, and technical aid granted in 1965.

E. Jay, *Population and Family Planning* (London, 1969).
C. E. Curran, *Contraception: authority and dissent* (London, 1969).   A MCG H

BIRTHS, MARRIAGES AND DEATHS REGISTRATION ACT (1836), in Britain. Civil registration had a two-fold purpose. It was intended to ease English Dissenters' disabilities, and a bill making marriages in licensed chapels in the presence of the registrar legal was introduced at the same time. Registration was also an indispensable tool of social administration. The restriction of children's working hours was hard to enforce without proof of age, and evidence of the ages and causes of death in different areas was essential to the study of public health. By the 1830s it was generally recognized that the information provided by parish registers was too incomplete to be of use for these purposes.

BIRUNI, AL- (b. 973), one of the most profound and original of all Muslim scholars, well versed in the mathematical, astronomical, and physical sciences, and also distinguished as a geographer, historian, and linguist. After 1017 he accompanied Sultan Mahmud of Ghazna on several of his campaigns to India. Al-Biruni died some time after 1050.

BISHOPS' BOOK (1537), in England, called *The Institution of a Christian Man*, a primer circulated by the authority of Henry VIII in defence of Catholic orthodoxy against Protestant innovation. It asserted the seven sacraments and the need for justification by works.

BISHARA AL-KHURI (1890–1964), Lebanese Maronite lawyer, politician, and president of the Lebanon (1943–52), who was one of the principal architects of Christian–Muslim co-operation against the French mandate, expressed in the National Pact.

BISHOPS' WARS (1639–41), between England and Scotland over Charles I's attempt to impose Anglicanism on Scotland. In 1637 Charles had attempted to impose the Book of Common Prayer, and had aroused a patriotic fervour and the fear of popery. The Scots retaliated by establishing a permanent body of commissioners and producing a covenant signed by almost the whole of the population, which bound them to resist innovations in religion. Charles would not withdraw the book, but allowed a general assembly to meet (Nov. 1638). When the bishops refused to acknowledge its authority, the assembly was dissolved by the royal commissioner, the Marquis of Hamilton. But it continued to sit, abolishing not only the book, but episcopacy as well, and re-establishing Presbyterianism. War followed. The Scots had a well-trained army under Alexander Leslie; Charles had to rely on an irregular force of noblemen and trained bands. He could not risk a battle and the first Bishops' War ended with the treaty of Berwick (June 1639). The Scots were to disband their army and all ecclesiastical and civil matters were to be decided by the assembly and a Scottish parliament. Rapid and radical reforms followed. Charles decided to renew the war. He called parliament to provide money, but the Short Parliament refused until its grievances had been discussed, and was therefore dissolved (5 May 1640). Charles's motley army was ill-paid and disaffected. The Scots dispersed the English with a cannonade at Newburn-on-the-Tyne. The treaty of Ripon (Oct. 1640), whereby the Scots remained in possession of Northumberland and Durham and were to be paid £850 a day until matters were settled, virtually ended the second war, though negotiations dragged on into 1641.   CJ

BISMARCK, OTTO, PRINCE VON (1815–98), creator and first chancellor of modern Germany. A masterly tactician who used circumstances to his own advantage, this Prussian *Junker* achieved notoriety by his violent reactionary attitude in domestic politics and his advocacy, while Prussian representative at the Frankfurt Diet (1851–9) and ambassador to Russia (1859–62) of a revolutionary solution to the German problem through the destruction of Austrian influence in Germany. In 1862 he was appointed Prussian prime minister in a desperate attempt by King William I to solve the deadlock between him and the liberal majority in parliament over an increase in the army. Bismarck solved the problem by ignoring parliament and collecting taxes regardless.

His chief interest was in foreign affairs and deciding whether Austria or Prussia should dominate the collection of German states. He was thinking in terms of some kind of political unity, in which Prussia should play a predominant role and from which Austria should be excluded. Unlike the liberals of 1848, he believed this would not be achieved 'by speeches and majority votes . . . but by blood and iron'—by military force. He was helped in his policy of aggression towards Austria by the passivity of France and Russia.

After persuading Austria to collaborate with him in the war against Denmark over Schleswig-Holstein (1864), Bismarck used a quarrel over the settlement as an excuse for war against Austria herself (1866). By annexing the North

German states Prussia was expanded into the North German Confederation, with William I as president and Bismarck as chancellor. The Germans in the confederation were given a Reichstag, elected by universal suffrage, in which a liberal majority was prepared to forgive Bismarck's past and enthusiastically support a policy which amounted to trying to achieve German unification. But Bismarck, an authoritarian conservative, allowed the Reichstag no real control over his policies.

The absorption of the South German states completed the unification of the German empire, proclaimed on 18 Jan. 1871 at Versailles, after the defeat of France in the Franco-Prussian War, a war which Bismarck welcomed, although possibly did not consciously plan. The political institutions of the empire were similar to those of the confederation and enabled Bismarck to juggle with the parties in the Reichstag to maintain his own complete control. He believed the main danger to the empire at home came from the Catholics and Social Democrats, which led him to wage a vigorous campaign against both. Ultimately his power rested on the confidence of the emperor, and when this was lost under William II, he resigned (1890).

Abroad he regarded his policy after 1871 as one of safeguarding and consolidating Germany's position. France had to be kept isolated and co-operation maintained with the conservative powers, Austria and Russia (*Dreikaiserbund*, 1873, 1884). The greatest danger to his policy came from a possible war between Austria and Russia over the Balkans, which might involve Germany. His alliance system, the Dual Alliance with Austria (1879) and the Reinsurance Treaty with Russia (1887), was designed to avoid this danger, although he was finding it increasingly difficult to control towards the end.

A. J. P. Taylor, *Bismarck: The Man and the Statesman* (London, 1955).
W. N. Medlicott, *Bismarck: and Modern Germany* (London, 1965).   D McK

BISMARCK, German battleship of the Second World War, sister ship of the *Tirpitz*. The *Bismarck* was launched in 1939 and became operational early in 1941. She was the most powerful battleship of her time, displacing 50,000 tons and with a main armament of eight 15-inch guns; like all German capital ships of the period, she was employed mainly on commerce raiding in the Atlantic. For this purpose she and the cruiser *Prinz Eugen*, under the command of Admiral Lutjens, left Gdynia in the Baltic on 18 May 1941. The two vessels were spotted at anchor in Kors Fjord near Bergen by an aircraft of RAF Coastal Command, but they immediately took advantage of bad weather and headed for the Atlantic via the Denmark Strait between Greenland and Iceland. A massive search operation was mounted by the Home Fleet under Admiral Tovey and by Coastal Command. The two ships were eventually sighted by the cruisers *Norfolk* and *Suffolk* patrolling the Denmark Strait, and Tovey directed the brand-new battleship *Prince of Wales* and the old battle cruiser *Hood* to intercept them. In a brief engagement on 24 May, the *Hood* was blown up but the *Prince of Wales* inflicted some damage to Bismarck's fuel tanks. Lutjens detached the *Prinz Eugen* and decided to make for a French port for repairs; subsequently she shook off the shadowing *Suffolk*. After a further search, a Catalina of Coastal Command spotted the *Bismarck*, by which time the Home Fleet from Scapa Flow, Force H from Gibraltar, and the battleship *Ramillies*, detached from convoy protection duties, were closing in on her. A torpedo attack delivered by Swordfish from the carrier *Ark Royal* damaged her steering gear, and in this crippled condition she was pounded to destruction by the guns and torpedoes of the Home Fleet on 27 May. Her loss led to a change in the German policy of using surface ships for commerce raiding.

BITHYNIA, independent kingdom in north-west Asia Minor (297–74 BC) left by Nicomedes IV to the Romans, organized as a province by Pompey, who divided its land among cities, notably Nicaea, Nicomedia, Prusa, and Apamea. After senatorial administration under the early empire, Trajan and Hadrian sent, respectively, Pliny and Julius Severus to prevent financial mismanagement in a province crossed by essential civil and military communications. The letters of Pliny and speeches of Dio Chrysostom tell of social tension, and rivalry between cities. Annually ravaged by Arabs (AD 663–78) and settled with Slav military small-holders by Justinian II (685–711), it was organized as the Opsikion Theme of the Byzantine empire.

BITONTO, BATTLE OF (1734), one of a series of Austrian defeats in Italy by the French and Spanish armies during the War of the Polish Succession. In the ensuing peace the Habsburgs lost Naples and Sicily to Spain, receiving instead the smaller states of Parma, Piacenza, and Tuscany.

BIZONIA, amalgamation (Sept. 1947) of the British and US zones of occupation in Germany, following the initiative of the US government. The agreement provided for the establishment of German boards to lay down policies for the economic administration of the combined zones (the purely economic nature of the joint administration being stressed in order to avert Russian charges of creating political divisions in Germany). Costs were divided between the US and Britain, and a Joint Export-Import Agency established to promote German exports.

BJÖRKÖ, TREATY OF (1905), unsuccessful attempt to undermine the Franco-Russian alliance. It was negotiated personally by the kaiser and the tsar, and provided that if either signatory were attacked by a European power, the other would support it in Europe. The treaty was attacked by Bülow in Germany because it entailed a risk from Russo-British tension in India, and by Lamsdorff in Russia because it would antagonize France. The tsar then proposed that the treaty should not apply to France, and this being rejected by Germany, the treaty was still-born.

BJØRNSON, BJØRNSTJERNE MARTINIUS (1832–1910), Norwegian author and political leader. He wrote many dramas, novels, and lyrics (including the Norwegian national anthem), and also handled contemporary problems in speeches and letters to the world's press. He was an eloquent liberal, and pleaded for the separation of the Norwegian Crown from Sweden and the freeing of oppressed European nations, such as the Slovaks.

BLACK, HUGO LA FAYETTE (1886–), associate justice of the US supreme court, to which he was appointed (1937) by President Roosevelt. As US senator from AL (1927–37), he was associated with much New Deal legislation. His judicial opinions have been characterized by concern for social welfare and civil liberties.

BLACK AND TANS, name popularly applied, because of their makeshift uniforms, to recruits sent from Britain to strengthen the Royal Irish Constabulary from March 1920. In addition, a force of 'auxiliaries' was recruited from ex-army officers. Relations between Britain and Ireland had been deteriorating throughout 1919; the Sinn Fein victory in southern Irish constituencies in the 1918 election had led to the formation of a southern Irish parliament (Dail Eireann) in Dublin, and 1919 saw a struggle between British and Sinn Fein administrations for control of the countryside. In Sept. 1919 the British authorities in Dublin outlawed Dail Eireann, but because of popular sympathy with Sinn Feinn the British administration steadily lost control. The 'Black and Tans' were introduced to help to bolster the shattered strength and morale of the Irish police (Royal Irish Constabulary) and for 18 months there was guerrilla war between the Black and Tans and the Irish Republican Army (the military wing of Sinn Fein). Supporters of each side condemned the other's atrocities, but undoubtedly the 'Tans' were the more undisciplined force. Growing revulsion of liberal opinion in Britain, and increasing concern overseas, caused Lloyd George to open negotiations in Oct. 1921 with the Irish leaders, and in Dec. 1921 the treaty which established the Irish Free State was concluded.   ISM

BLACK BALL LINE (1818–78), US company providing the first scheduled monthly transatlantic packet from New York. The service, organized by a group of New York merchants, was instituted by the *Courier*, sailing from Liverpool, England, and the *James Monroe* from New York City. The line, named after the black disc carried on the fore topsail and flag, started with four ships, which were later increased to eight and a semi-monthly service in 1822. It continued until 1878, by which time 43 different ships had been used.

BLACK CARIBS. Descendants of African Negro slaves brought to the West Indies, who escaped to the island of St Vincent and intermarried with the native Carib Indians. By 1763, when England annexed the island, it was estimated that there were ten times as many Black Caribs as original inhabitants, and they had developed a distinct society. During the American War of Independence, the French, in order to frustrate the English war effort, helped the Black Caribs regain control of St Vincent, but by 1783 the English had reasserted dominion. In 1795, again at French instigation, the Black Caribs declared war against the English, led by the Carib Chatoyé. They were overwhelmed in 1796 and exiled, 5000 strong, to the island of Roatán, in the Gulf of Honduras.

BLACK CODES, southern US state legislation regulating the conduct of Negroes immediately after the Civil War. Before Emancipation, white control of the Negro slave had been effected by plantation custom and the slave codes. The Black Codes represented an attempt by the defeated South to impose restrictions on the freed Negro. Definition of his position included the legalization of Negro marriages and the freedman was entitled to hold property and entertain civil actions. However, Negro participation in 'white' cases was limited, many of the criminal provisions of the old codes re-enacted, and inter-racial marriages prohibited. The Negro's right to hold property was restricted. Vagrancy and apprenticeship laws and restrictive contracts were designed to safeguard the labour supply. Although some regulation may have been necessary to prevent complete social disintegration, the penal aspects of the codes aroused resentment in the North, as well as amongst southern Negroes, and helped to create an emotional climate that influenced Radical Reconstruction.

BLACK DEATH (1348–52), most virulent of a series of plague epidemics, brought to Europe from Central Asia via trade routes, and spread by refugees and by drifting infected ships. The name derived from black skin patches, and treatment of both pneumonic and bubonic forms was unavailing. Late preventive measures led to quarantine (1377) whereby ships arriving from the east were isolated for 40 days (*quarante giorni*). An estimated quarter of the population died, causing complete disruption in agriculture, a weakening of the Feudal System, and a wave of anti-Semitism, since Jews were accused of poisoning the wells. The last plague epidemic in England (1665) centred on London, where trade came to a standstill and one-fifth of the inhabitants died. Until the 18th cent. epidemics continued to flare up sporadically in France and Italy. The causative bacillus was discovered in 1894.

BLACK DRAGON SOCIETY, name by which the *Kokuryukai*, or Amur River Society, the most important of Japan's ultra-nationalist organizations, was generally known in other countries. The society was founded in 1900 by Uchida Ryohei, at a time when Japan was primarily concerned with

Russia's ambitions, but its subversive activities in almost every other part of eastern Asia inclined foreigners to adopt the more literal and sinister reading of the characters comprising its name. It was most influential at about the time of the Russo-Japanese War, when it was in contact with nationalists such as Sun Yat-sen, who saw in Japan a liberating force for Asia.

BLACK DRIVE, THE (1830), first serious attempt to deal with the native problem in Van Diemen's Land (Tasmania) which followed the decision of Gov. Arthur to enforce a policy of segregation. Some 3000 men were employed on a great round-up of natives which, however, made insufficient allowance for their superior bushcraft. The haul, costing £30,000, netted only one native woman and a boy. More tactful approaches, including those of George Augustus Robinson, a bricklayer who devoted his leisure to religious and social work, eventually produced agreement for the surviving blacks to transfer to Flinders Island. There they gradually dwindled in numbers until, in 1847, survivors were brought back to Oyster Bay, near Hobart, where the last pure-blooded male Tasmanian black died in 1869.

BLACK FLAGS. In 1865, remnants of the Taiping and Panthay rebels, some 200 in number, fled with their leader Liu Yung-fu across the Chinese border into north Viet-nam. Because of their opposition to the Miao tribesmen, who presented a serious threat to Viet-namese authority in this area, the Black Flags, as these outlaws were called, found favour with the Viet-namese government. Their number soon increased to 2000 enabling them to block French economic expansion up the Red River. During the Sino-French War of 1883–5 the Black Flags co-operated with the Chinese, their former enemies, to resist French expansion in Tongking. After China's defeat, the Black Flags were withdrawn into south China. They made their last appearance in the 1890s, when they were sent to guard Taiwan against the Japanese.

BLACK HAND (SERBIA) (1911), revolutionary secret society aimed at the liberation of, and union with, Serbia, of the South Slavs, still in the Austro-Hungarian and Turkish empires. Formed by army officers and intimately connected with members of the Serbian government, its head was Col. 'Apis' Dimitriević, chief of the Serbian general staff's intelligence department. The society's weapons were terror and the assassination of political opponents, and its main successes were in Austrian Bosnia, where, on 28 June 1914, young Bosnians, trained and directed from Serbia, assassinated the Austrian Archduke Franz Ferdinand and his wife at Sarajevo. This was the immediate cause of the First World War. Later, the society was broken up (1917) by the Serbian government because of its attempt to control Serbia's war policy.

BLACK HAND TRIALS (1883–4), broke up a Spanish anarchist society, the Black Hand, which was said to have had 50,000 members and had terrorized the landlords of Andalusia. The society was a revolutionary offshoot of the Regional Federation of Spain, which advocated rural anarchism. The Spanish government was determined to repress and imprison the anarchists, although there was some doubt about their guilt.

BLACK HAWK WAR (1832), campaign to prevent settlement of lands in the US traditionally held by the Sauk and Fox Indians, led by Chief Black Hawk, and fought in what is now IL and WI. By treaty in 1804, the Sauk and the Fox had surrendered all their lands east of the Mississippi river. When settlers began to arrive after the War of 1812, Black Hawk refused to leave, maintaining that he had been deceived by the terms of the treaty. During the winter of 1831–2, he attempted to rally other tribes to his cause. Although few joined him, he scored initial successes in raids on frontier

settlements during the spring of 1832 owing to the ineffectiveness of the army. He was defeated in three decisive encounters with militia (July, Aug. 1832) and although he escaped, he was later captured by Winnebago Indians and turned over to military authorities.

BLACK HILLS. Broken hills rising from the Great Plains in SD, US, scene of the gold-rush of 1875, which gave rise to the famous mining camps of Deadwood and Custer City and led to war with the Sioux. On one of the hills, Mt Rushmore, are carved massive profiles of four American presidents.

BLACK KETTLE (d. 1697), American Indian chief of the Onondaga tribe, called Chaudière Noire by the French. He was involved in numerous campaigns against the French, including an attack which he led on Montreal (1692). In 1697, he concluded a peace settlement with the French, but was killed by some Algonquian Indians while hunting near a French fort.

The name also belonged to another chief (c. 1803–68) who led the Southern Cheyenne, an American Indian tribe of the Algonquian family. After leading his warriors in a resistance against advancing white settlements, Black Kettle made a pact with US military authorities (1864), and settled his band at Sand Creek, CO. In Nov. 1864, a Colorado militia regiment attacked the settlement, slaughtering women and children. Black Kettle and his family escaped. Although some of his tribe sought revenge, Black Kettle accepted a new treaty and reparation for the massacre. In 1867, he signed the Medicine Lodge Treaty, binding his people to a reservation. He was killed in 1868, when the 7th US Cavalry attacked his village in the Washita valley.

BLACK LEGEND, or *Leyenda Negra,* term coined to identify a tendency to characterize Spanish conquest and imperialism in the New World as cruel and inhuman in all its aspects. The opposite tendency, sometimes referred to as 'the white legend', sees Spanish imperialism as the bringer of Christianity, enlightenment, and Hispanic culture to previously benighted peoples. Both are, of course, exaggerations.

The Black Legend had its origins in the international politics and pamphleteering of 16th cent.-Europe. The Dominican friar Bartolomé de las Casas had written about the brutality of the conquistadors towards the Indians in an attempt to convince the Spanish authorities of the need for reform. His writings, particularly the *Brief Account of the Destruction of the Indies*, were seized upon by Dutch and English propagandists and used as justification for intrusions upon Spanish possessions in America. Lurid tales about the New World Inquisition, and the fate of captured pirates, added to the legend. The novels of Charles Kingsley and others carried it to the 20th-cent. schoolboy.

Both the Black Legend and its opposite persist because of the massive amount of selected evidence which can be presented for either case. Neither view is now considered respectable in scholarly circles.

BLACK MUSLIMS, US Negro nationalist sect, whose members form the all-black Nation of Islam led by the so-called The Honourable Elijah Muhammad. This primarily religious movement, which began in the early 1930s, achieved national prominence 30 years later when Malcolm X, a protégé of Muhammad, challenged many of the integrationist goals of the civil rights movement.

BLACK POWER, contemporary phenomenon whose roots in the US can be traced back to the period of Negro slavery. In emphasizing black nationalism and black pride, its exponents reiterate some of the arguments used by earlier black leaders eg, W. E. B. Dubois and Marcus Garvey. The slogan Black Power, coined by Adam Clayton Powell (1965), was popularized by Stokely Carmichael in Mississippi (1966) while campaigning for support for groups discontented with the relative failure of the civil rights movement to obtain significant civil rights legislation through non-violent direct action alone.

Black Power contains diverse and often conflicting elements of withdrawal, separation, racial solidarity, and collective self-help, racial identity and pride, violent rhetoric, and acceptance of a resort to force in self-defence. It has become the rallying-cry of a racially oriented mass movement led by young blacks who, having been treated in the past as a dependent group of low cultural status, have now resolved to free themselves from psychological and social inferiority. While Garvey dreamt of a return to Africa, Black Power leaders seek to create independent Afro-Americas in city ghettos, like Harlem in New York and Watts in Los Angeles, as autonomous black communities bargaining with other communities for black-defined ends. The colour line defines the group and dictates strategy, and where blacks are in the majority they must dominate and control political, social, and economic activity.

Some of the rhetoric of Black Power at times owes more to Frantz Fanon and Che Guevara than Dubois or Garvey, and conscious attempts have been made to link the American Black Power movement with revolutionary movements in the Third World, but the significance of Black Power within the US has been to signal a concerted shift in black protest from demands for radical integration to claims more akin to nationalist separation. Black critics have condemned this development, both for destroying the possibility of further advances in civil rights and for concealing behind a rhetoric of revolution and violence a substantive retreat to policies limited to black social reform and conservative nationalism. While the movement has spawned distinctive offshoots, such as the Black Panthers and the Peace and Freedom party of Eldridge Cleaver, there remains an implicit admission that perhaps what most black Americans really want to possess is the economic security characteristic of middle-class white America.

F. B. Barbour (ed.), *The Black Power Revolt* (Boston, 1968).
S. Carmichael and C. V. Hamilton, *Black Power: The politics of liberation in America* (New York, 1968).   JDL

BLACK SEA CLAUSES (1856–71), contained in the treaty of Paris (1856) after the Crimean War, confirmed the 1841 Straits Convention and neutralized the Black Sea, which was closed to all warships, but opened to all commercial traffic. Arsenals and naval dockyards along its shores were prohibited. The clauses were aimed exclusively at Russia, who took the opportunity of the Franco-Prussian War to renounce them in Oct. 1871. A conference of the powers in London the following January confirmed this move, but also allowed the Turks to open the Straits to the warships of other powers in peacetime, if the remaining clauses of the treaty of Paris were at risk.

BLACK WATCH, THE, famous Scottish highland regiment raised by General Wade in accordance with the act for disarming the highland clans. Wade originally raised four companies, but in 1739 they were increased to eight, after which they fought at the battle of Fontenoy (1745). The regiment distinguished itself in both World Wars.

BLACKET, EDMUND THOMAS (1817–83), British draughtsman and surveyor, who migrated to Australia (1842) with letters to Bp Broughton and others. These aided his appointment as inspector of teaching and building in Anglican schools in NSW and, later (1849–54), as colonial architect. As founder of the architectural firm of Blacket and Son he made many pseudo-Gothic contributions to churches, schools, and the first buildings of Sydney University, but his standing and influence among contemporaries was greater than the quality of his architectural work.

BLACK-FIGURE POTTERY, style of Greek painted pottery characterized by black figures with incised detail on an un-painted ground. It was first developed at Corinth (c. 700 BC), perfected at Athens (c. 600), and became the most popular fine pottery of the 6th-cent. Greek world.

BLACKHEATH, BATTLE OF (1497), climax of the Cornish rebellion against Henry VII's arbitrary levying of taxes for a Scottish invasion. The 15,000 rebels, led by a nobleman, James Lord Audley, a blacksmith, Joseph, and a lawyer, Flamank, reached Blackheath near London before being crushed by the artillery and cavalry of Henry and his commander, Daubeny.

BLACKLOISTS, group of English Catholics who, under the temporary relaxation of the penal legislation during the Cromwellian period, favoured an understanding with the papacy, which would permit the expulsion of the Jesuits and the ending of the papacy's temporal claims over England.

BLACKSTONE, SIR WILLIAM (1723–80), English constitutional writer and author of *Commentaries on the Laws of England* (1765). The *Commentaries* are chiefly notable for their elaborate description of the checks and balances in the British constitution of the 18th cent. Blackstone was criticized for his tendency to glorify the existing state of affairs and, by his great contemporary influence, to erect barriers against fundamental change.

BLADENSBURG, BATTLE OF (24 Aug. 1814), British victory during the War of 1812. General Ross's regulars landed in Chesapeake Bay, moved up the Patuxent river, and, after defeating the American militia at Bladensburg, MD, sacked Washington, DC, and burned the White House.

BLAINE, JAMES GILLESPIE (1830–93), US politician, statesman, journalist, newspaper owner, and founder of the Republican Party in Maine. He first became nationally prominent as a member of the US House of Representatives (1863–76). After a meteoric success within the Republican Party, he became speaker of the house (1869–75) and nearly gained the Republican nomination for president on the first ballot (1876), but lost to Rutherford B. Hayes, charges of corruption having been circulated. He then won election to the US Senate (1876–81). His second attempt to secure the Republican nomination (1880) failed, but in 1884 he succeeded, narrowly losing the presidential election to Grover Cleveland after party dissidents (the 'Mugwumps') refused to support him.

Despite the frustrations of his presidential aspirations, Blaine succeeded in building a solid record as secretary of state. During his first term (March–Dec. 1881), cut short by the assassination of President Garfield, he generated several new policies but the new administration failed to implement them. In his second term as secretary of state (1889–92), however, many of Blaine's earlier ideas came to fruition. He called together in Washington what later became known as the first Pan-American conference (1889), at which he proposed the establishment of arbitration machinery for the settling of disputes between American states, the creation of a low tariff zone, and the construction of a railway to run the length of the American hemisphere.

BLAIR, FRANCIS PRESTON (1791–1876), US journalist and politician. On being summoned to Washington (1830) to establish the Jacksonian Washington *Globe*, Blair became a leading member of President Jackson's 'Kitchen Cabinet'. Later he became a Free-Soiler, left the Democratic Party, joined the Republicans, and supported Abraham Lincoln's nomination for the presidency (1860).

BLAIR, JAMES (1656–1743). Scottish episcopal clergyman, sent as missionary to Virginia (1685), and later appointed Deputy for Virginia by the Bp of London (1689). He established the College of William and Mary in Williamsburg, VA (1693), and was its first president. He moved from

Jamestown to Middle Plantation (then Williamsburg) in 1710 as rector of Bruton Parish, a post he held until his death.

BLAKE, EDWARD (1833–1912), Canadian lawyer and politician. Elected (1867) as a Liberal to both the Canadian House of Commons and the Legislative Assembly of Ontario, Blake became prime minister of Ontario (1871), but chose national politics when his own government abolished dual representation (1872). He was briefly minister without portfolio in Alexander Mackenzie's government (1873), but resigned and declared at Aurora for the new 'Canada First' nationalist party (1874). He returned to liberalism, however, and became minister of justice (1875–7) and president of the council (1877–8) under Mackenzie, whom he succeeded as leader of the Liberal Party (1879–87). In 1890 he withdrew from Canadian politics, and although elected as an Irish Nationalist to the British House of Commons (1892–1907) made little impact there.

BLAKE, ROBERT (1599–1657), English admiral who fought for parliament in the English Civil War and reorganized the Commonwealth navy. The son of a merchant, he was elected for Bridgwater to the Short Parliament (1640) and to the Long Parliament (1645–53), and for Somerset to Barebone's Parliament (1653). In the First Civil War he distinguished himself as a general, particularly at the defence of Lyme (1644). In Feb. 1649 he was appointed a general at sea, and fought royalist squadrons in Ireland, Portugal, the Mediterranean, and the Scilly Isles (1649–51). On the outbreak of the First Dutch War (1652) he was appointed to command the Channel fleet, and several times engaged de Ruyter and Tromp, particularly in the battles of the Kentish Knock and Dungeness (1652), and Portland (1653). In Nov. 1654 Blake was given command of the Mediterranean fleet and was victorious against the corsairs of Tunis. In the war with Spain he blockaded the Spanish coast in the winter of 1656–7, and on 20 April 1657 gained a great victory at Santa Cruz. However, his health deteriorated and he died as his fleet was about to reach Plymouth.

BLAMEY, SIR THOMAS ALBERT (1884–1951), Australian soldier, was born in NSW, and entered the Australian army in 1906. He was chief of staff to Gen. Sir John Monash during the First World War, and chief commissioner for police for Victoria (1922–36). In 1939 he was appointed to command the 6th Division, 2nd AIF, and by 1942 had become commander-in-chief Australian Military Forces and commander Allied Land Forces, South-West Pacific Area. In 1950 he became the first Australian to reach the rank of field marshal.

BLANC, LOUIS (1811–82), French socialist writer and politician. In his *Organisation du Travail* (1839), an important event in the development of socialist thought, he proposed a scheme whereby industries should be financed by the state. They would be run on communal lines, profits being divided into wages, the support of the sick and aged, and payment for capital equipment or interest to outside bodies. Blanc became prominent in the revolution of 1848, which occurred at a time of industrial unemployment in Paris. He was made head of an industrial commission, but his proposal for national workshops organized on the lines described above degenerated into inadequate doles for the unemployed. Blanc went into exile in England (1849–70) on the rise of Louis Napoleon. He then returned in triumph to Paris and was elected deputy (Feb. 1871).

BLANCHE OF CASTILE (d. 1252), Spanish wife of King Louis VIII of France, who became regent for her son, Louis IX, upon Louis VIII's death in 1226. The minority was a highly dangerous period for the Capetian monarchy. The French nobility, resenting the growth in royal power under Philip Augustus and Louis VIII, sought to check this development by rebellion. This was the most serious threat the Capetian monarchy had to face in the 13th cent. and Blanche showed great ability in crushing the rising. By 1230 the leaders had submitted and King Henry III of England had been repelled. Blanche ruled France firmly until Louis came of age in 1234. She again acted as regent in his absence on a crusade. Her great achievement was to preserve the power of the French Crown during the dangerous years of Louis's minority.

BLANCMESNIL, NICOLAS POTIER DE NOVION DE (1618–97), president in the *Enquêtes*, a chamber of the *parlement* of Paris, who was arrested with Pierre Broussel (26 Aug. 1648) on the orders of Anne of Austria for leading *parlementaire* opposition to royal edicts. Their arrest precipitated the Days of the Barricades and the first phase of the Fronde.

BLANCO PARTY in Uruguay. Much of 19th- and early 20th-cent. Uruguayan history was disturbed by the struggle between the Blancos (whites) and Colorados (reds). Today the Blancos are considered to be more conservative and less anti-clerical than their traditional rivals.

BLAND, RICHARD (1710–78), Virginian statesman. He was born in Berkeley (now near Norfolk), VA, educated at William and Mary, and served in the Virginia House of Burgesses for over 30 years. He was an early advocate of individual liberties and home rule, and in 1766 published *An Inquiry into the Rights of the British Colonies*, perhaps the first colonial document of any importance on the colonists' attitude towards parliamentary taxation practices.

BLAND–ALLISON ACT (1878), US legislation requiring the secretary of the treasury to make monthly purchases of not less than 2 million and not more than 4 million dollars' worth of silver for coinage of dollars at full legal tender value. It failed to provide for the unlimited coinage of silver urged by inflationist groups.

BLANKETEERS (1817), English protest group which united the sophisticated pressure-group techniques of English provincial radicalism with the primitive popular conviction that monarchs can single-handedly protect their subjects from distress. Post-war economic distress revived militant radicalism in the north of England, which in 1817 evoked repressive legislation from a frightened government. On 10 March 1817 several hundred blanket-carrying working men, mostly weavers, left Manchester for London. Their petitions to the Prince Regent recounted the local distress, repudiated repression, and urged parliamentary reform—but they were intercepted by the authorities. For contemporary Tories and for some modern historians the march was part of an ambitious radical conspiracy, but few of the marchers were clear in their objectives, and the Hammonds found it 'difficult enough to understand how the authorities could connect this pathetic and futile outcry with any "traitorous conspiracy"'.

BLANQUI, JÉROME ADOLPHE (1798–1854), French economist, who produced social surveys of the living conditions of the lower classes in French industrial towns in the 1840s. His studies led him to demand government intervention on behalf of the working class.

BLANQUI (LOUIS), AUGUSTE (1805–81), French revolutionary socialist, whose ideas on revolutionary elites influenced Lenin. A follower of Buonarotti, he preached the separation of society into poor and rich, revolution and counter-revolution. He believed that revolution itself would purify society and act as a creative force. Blanqui spent half his life in prison and the rest plotting insurrection. Under Louis Philippe his Society of the Seasons failed to begin a revolution through an unsuccessful plot (1839), but during the 1848 Revolution he was the leader of a largely working-class and socialist Central Republican Party, which took part in the abortive rising of 15 May. He remained active under Napoleon III with periodic spells in prison. His success was shown in 1871, when probably a third of the Paris Commune was made up of his supporters, although he himself was under arrest at the time.

BLATCHFORD, ROBERT (1851–1943), British socialist and journalist, who founded the *Clarion* at Manchester (1891). He began his career on a sporting paper, and, by his flair for mixing entertainment and progressive politics, made a success of the *Clarion*. Blatchford was an important influence in the formation of the Independent Labour Party (1893).

BLATHWAYT, WILLIAM, secretary at war under William III, a trusted and industrious royal servant, who served as secretary of state on some of William's continental campaigns.

BLAXLAND, GREGORY (1778–1853) and **JOHN** (1769–1845), were among Australia's first English 'gentlemen settlers', as Gov. Macquarie contemptuously termed them. Gregory, younger son of an old Kentish family whose interest in Australia was inspired by friendship with Sir Joseph Banks, arrived in NSW in 1806, his brother John a year later. The brothers devoted themselves chiefly to cattle-breeding. Gregory's participation in the passage of the Blue Mountains in 1813, with William Lawson and W. C. Wentworth, is better known than the steady contribution of the two men to the pastoral industry. Despite recurring difficulties with governors Bligh and Macquarie, the brothers prospered. Their headquarters were on the Parramatta, but their sons pressed westward beyond the legal limits of the counties. Gregory was associated with the movement for trial by jury and representative government in the late 1820s and John, though never really interested in politics, became a legislative councillor (1829–44). Despite their considerable contributions to the colony, neither man was easy to get on with.

BLED AGREEMENTS signed by Tito and Dimitrov at Bled in Slovenia on 1 Aug. 1947, which constituted a tentative step towards a Bulgarian–Yugoslav federation. By these agreements frontier travel barriers were removed and a future customs union was envisaged. An attempt was made to settle the Macedonian problem. Yugoslavia pressed for the cession of Pirin Macedonia, but Bulgaria said this must follow federation. However, the Bulgarians did consent to grant the Pirin Macedonians opportunities for 'free cultural development' and 'spiritual union' with the Vardar Macedonians in Yugoslavia. The agreements were a measure of Yugoslavia's burgeoning power in the Balkans and caused added disquiet in Moscow, contributing to the Yugoslav–Soviet split the next year.

BLEDISLOE COMMISSION (1939) reported on closer association between Southern and Northern Rhodesia and Nyasaland. The Hilton Young Commission (1929) had recommended that Northern Rhodesia and Nyasaland should join a proposed union of east African colonies. Whites in the two Rhodesias objected, although those in Southern Rhodesia rejected union with South Africa. The Depression hit the settlers hard, and they coveted the Copper Belt. The British government's Bledisloe Commission favoured amalgamation of the three territories, but emphasized that African opposition was 'a factor that cannot be ignored'. Nevertheless, it was ignored when the Central African Federation was established in 1953.

BLEEDING KANSAS, an event that became a curtain-raiser to the American Civil War. Disorders broke out in the Kansas territory of the US following passage of the Kansas–Nebraska Act (1854). Rivalry between supporters and opponents of slavery reached a peak of violence and lawlessness (1856) with the sacking of Lawrence by pro-slavery 'border ruffians', and the 'Potawatomie massacre', a reprisal raid by the anti-slavery group under John Brown. Events in Kansas,

and exaggerated reports of them, kept feelings at fever pitch in North and South, especially when Charles Sumner was severely beaten by the southerner Preston Brooks after his 'Crime against Kansas' speech in the Senate (1856).

BLENHEIM, BATTLE OF (1704), first major encounter of the War of the Spanish Succession. It was fought on the left bank of the Danube river (13 Aug. 1704), and was won by the allied commanders Marlborough and Eugène, assisted by Prince Louis of Baden, against the French Marshal Tallard and the elector of Bavaria. Marlborough had moved the bulk of his troops from the Maas valley across the Rhine into Germany to prevent the French and Bavarians from capturing Vienna and thereby detaching the Holy Roman emperor from the Grand Alliance. The Allies had 52,000 troops, the French and Bavarians about 54,000. Marlborough deluded Tallard into thinking that his main effort was to be directed against the French right flank posted in strength in the village of Blenheim, but launched his principal attack across the Nebel river, a tributary of the Danube, against the enemy centre. Tallard was captured, and nearly half of his men were killed, injured, or taken prisoner. This was the first great battle to be won by an English general on the continent since Agincourt, and the first to be lost by the French during Louis XIV's reign.

BLENHEIM PALACE, in England, designed by Sir John Vanbrugh, built at Woodstock, Oxon, between 1705 and 1722 at the nation's expense and presented to the Duke of Marlborough in gratitude for his military achievements. The gift was later criticized by Marlborough's Tory opponents as a waste of government money.

BLÉRIOT, LOUIS (1872–1936), French aviator, who made the first flight across the English Channel (July 1909).

BLEUS, nickname given *c.* 1850 to supporters of Louis H. Fontaine, the French-Canadian reformer.

BLIGH, WILLIAM (1754–1817), British sailor, and the central figure in the famous mutiny on the *Bounty* (1789). He was born in Cornwall, entered the navy at the age of eight, and served under James Cook in HMS *Resolution*, before being appointed to command *Bounty* on a voyage to Tahiti (1787). The extent of his responsibility for the mutiny has been the subject of much controversy, despite evidence of his harsh treatment of officers and men during the voyage. Yet he showed great courage and navigational skill in directing a party of 18, set adrift with him near the Friendly Islands, in a voyage across nearly 4000 miles of almost unknown sea, through Torres Strait to Timor.

After returning to England in 1790, another voyage to Tahiti, and active service against Napoleon, Bligh, sponsored by Sir Joseph Banks, succeeded Philip Gidley King as governor of NSW (1805). His tactlessness and ill-temper often prevented him from carrying out a policy that was in itself in many respects commendable. He returned to England after the mutiny of 1808 against his administration.

BLIGH MUTINY, THE (1808), was directed against the 'tyranny' of William Bligh, governor of NSW, who was deposed by Lieut-Col. George Johnston (1764–1823), commanding the NSW Corps. Bligh's autocratic manner brought him into conflict with John Macarthur when Bligh tried to end the rum traffic and the corrupt practices of the officer-traders of the corps. His arraignment of Macarthur before a court presided over by the latter's known enemy, Judge Advocate Richard Atkins, led the officers of the corps (to which Macarthur had once belonged) to uphold the accused's objection to its president. Thereupon Bligh ordered Macarthur's imprisonment. To prevent an insurrection, Johnston, as lieutenant-governor, released Macarthur and arrested Bligh, leaving administration of the colony to the officers of the corps, with Macarthur as 'colonial secretary'. Those responsible for the 'mutiny' gained little. Johnston was cashiered, Macarthur exiled for eight years, and Macquarie's administration was no less autocratic, though more efficient, than Bligh's. The disbanding of the NSW Corps as a result of the mutiny was not only a defeat for its officers, but also a step towards constitutional government.

BLITZ, THE (German *blitzkrieg*, 'lightning war'), sustained aerial onslaught by German bombers on selected cities, ports, and industrial centres of Britain between Sept. 1940 and May 1941 during the Second World War. Raids were often made on the same target areas on several consecutive nights, compounding the damage done in earlier attacks. In London alone 375,000 people were made homeless, thousands were killed or wounded, and well over a million houses damaged. Public services, industry, trade, and business were violently disrupted, as much by fire as by high-explosive bombs, and day-to-day existence became completely haphazard. But for the government's policy of evacuating children, invalids, and the elderly, which was brought into force at the beginning of the war, the loss of life would have been far greater than it was. Thanks to a well-organized system of civil defence, to arrangements for sheltering the population underground and rehabilitating those who lost their homes, total chaos was avoided, though civilian life became disorganized on a gigantic scale.

Among the worst-hit areas outside London were Birmingham, Bristol, Clydeside, Coventry—where more than 1000 people died in raids on two successive nights—Manchester, and Merseyside. Such were the Germans' losses, and the capacity of the British to survive the worst the Luftwaffe could do, that the blitz was eventually called off.

A renewal of the attacks came in June 1944, when flying bombs, and in Sept. V2 rockets, were launched against London and the southern counties. Though more sporadic and less damaging to property than the massive conflagrations of the Blitz, these missile attacks, which lasted seven months, caused more than 2500 deaths and severely injured well over 6000 people.

BLITZKRIEG. The idea stemmed from the British military theorist Liddell Hart's concept of an 'expanding torrent' theory, which he had developed as a preventive against the static warfare of 1914–18. The idea was taken further by the German Heinz Guderian, particularly in his prophetic work *Achtung Panzer*. The tactics of the blitzkrieg consisted of the use of armoured columns in a deep thrust on a narrow front. This was followed by linking or sweeping movements, which enveloped large pockets of enemy forces. These were dealt with by troops moving up in the wake of the fast-moving armour. The whole operation was supported by extensive air cover. For Germany the blitzkrieg represented a calculated risk: the belief the war could be won quickly without the need for a full war economy. After the attack on Russia the deficiencies of the German war economy became all too clear. The blitzkriegs against Poland and France, however, were triumphs of military planning and co-ordination.

BLOC NATIONAL, alliance of the victorious centre and right-wing parties in the French election of 1919. Its principal leaders were Millerand, Briand, and Poincaré, and anti-bolshevism and the assertion of French interests against Germany were the main themes of the campaign. The governments of the bloc found the financial and international problems of the period intractable, and their most lasting achievement was perhaps the appeasement of religious conflict within France. By the 1924 election, the alliance had broken down, and the right was defeated.

BLOC POPULAIRE, attempt (1944) to unite French Canada's radical nationalist groups. The bloc, which opposed French-Canadian participation in the Second World War and the use of foreign capital for the industrialization of Quebec, won four seats in the provincial elections of 1944, but owing to lack of cohesion dissolved shortly after the election.

BLOCKADE, form of naval warfare which played an important role in the strategy of the naval belligerents in both World Wars. Blockade of an enemy's coast can have two broad objectives: military, to contain enemy fleets in their ports; and economic, to cripple an enemy's potential to wage war by denying him the ability to trade in war materials or food. Its effectiveness is dependent on the degree to which the nation concerned relies on sea-borne trade. By the time of the First World War, the development of the submarine, aircraft, and long-range artillery had led to the abandoning of the old 'close' blockade in favour of the 'open' type, in which surveillance is exercised by ships at a greater distance, reinforced by extensive minefields. Since the 1856 Congress of Paris, blockade has been subject to complex international law to safeguard the rights of neutrals. In the First World War both sides sought to blockade each other, the British exploiting their geographical advantage by using their fleet to close the exits from the North Sea, the Germans by using the submarine to counter British superiority in surface ships. The British overcame the problem of neutral traffic with the Central Powers by firm but tactful diplomacy, but the Germans fatally antagonized the US by their excursions into unrestricted submarine warfare, the first briefly in 1915, when American lives were lost in the sinking of the British liner *Lusitania*, the second from 31 Jan. 1917, which led to the American intervention in the war on the Allied side. The British blockade of Germany was highly successful and played a major part in bringing about the social and economic collapse of Germany in Oct. and Nov. 1918. The German blockade of Britain, on the other hand, was less effective, despite Britain's total reliance on sea-borne trade; British losses at sea had become so great by 1917 that the admiralty were forced to reintroduce the age-old but discarded method of convoy and escort for their merchant shipping, which decisively curtailed the successes of the U-boats.

In the Second World War the British again attempted to blockade the Axis powers, but Germany's overrunning of Norway and France in 1940 enabled her both to outflank the British fleet and to operate her U-boats from bases which gave her extensive range into the Atlantic. On 17 Aug. 1940 Germany declared unrestricted submarine warfare against Britain, though after many vicissitudes Britain, by mid-1943, had gained the upper hand in the battle of the Atlantic. Germany's control of the greater part of continental Europe made her relatively invulnerable to any Allied blockade. The most effective blockade of the war was that imposed on Japan by America: like Britain, Japan relied heavily on sea communications for her livelihood, but by the time of the dropping of the atomic bombs in Aug. 1945 American submarine action had almost annihilated her merchant marine and had brought her economy to the brink of collapse.   NRB

BLOIS, ORDINANCE OF (1579), one of the series of great reforming ordinances promulgated by French monarchs, the first dating from the reign of St Louis (1226–70). This ordinance of 365 articles included sections on the reorganization of justice in the kingdom, the confirmation of rules governing the royal domain, regulations concerning the purchase of noble land, the reformation of French universities, the rights of parents over their children, and a statement of the chief disciplinary decisions of the Council of Trent.

BLOIS, TREATIES OF (1504–5), diplomatic manœuvres in the dynastic struggle between the Emperor Maximilian and Louis XII of France. Louis, after being defeated in Naples by a Spanish army, was sensitive about possible Habsburg encirclement. He therefore concluded a bargain with Maximilian (Sept. 1504) which gave Milan to France for 200,000 ducats in return for Louis's undertaking not to interfere in imperial affairs. Successive treaties having provided for the marriage of Louis's daughter, Claude, to Maximilian's grandson, Charles, arrangements were made for Charles's succession to Milan, Blois, and Brittany should Louis die without male heirs.

Shortly after this, Isabella of Spain died (Nov. 1504), leaving her daughter, Joanna, and Joanna's husband, Archduke Philip, as her successors. Isabella's husband, Ferdinand of Aragon, seeking a male heir who could challenge this Habsburg succession to Spain, approached his old enemy, Louis XII. A second treaty of Blois (1505) repudiated the first treaty and Louis's niece, Germaine de Foix, married Ferdinand. This treaty failed in its objective. The second marriage produced no heir, while the death of Philip (1506) and the madness of Joanna left Charles heir to all Spain.

BLOIS, TREATY OF (1572), defensive alliance marking a rapprochement between England and France, which was to have been cemented by the marriage of Elizabeth I to the Duke of Anjou, Catherine de Medici's second son. The treaty was the result of Catherine's desire to unite a divided France by encouraging traditional anti-Spanish feeling. Elizabeth wanted French friendship to prevent a union of the Catholic powers which would implement the papal bull of 1570. Elizabeth therefore sent Walsingham to negotiate with Catherine, and the treaty was signed in April 1572. Apart from providing for mutual defence against Spain, the treaty was to transfer the English cloth staple from Antwerp to Rouen.

The massacre of St Bartholomew (Aug. 1572) seriously undermined the treaty. The marriage scheme, long regarded by Elizabeth as a mere diplomatic weapon, was dropped, as was the clause concerning the staple. Elizabeth sent secret aid to the Huguenots of La Rochelle on the renewal of the French religious wars. Despite the treaty's renewal by Henry III (1575) it remained a dead letter.

BLOMBERG, WERNER VON (1879–1946), German soldier and politician, who was Hitler's first minister of defence (1933–8). He was a known sympathizer with the aims of National Socialism, and was President Hindenburg and Von Papen's military candidate for the Hitler–Papen cabinet in 1933. His position became complicated in 1934 with the appointment to the government of Roehm, head of the paramilitary SA, who was jealous of the army's autonomy. By April 1934 Blomberg reached an implicit bargain to support Hitler as the ailing Hindenburg's successor in return for Hitler's reduction of the SA. As the SA became increasingly restive and revolutionary, Blomberg hinted to Hitler on 21 June that Hindenburg might take the initiative against them by establishing martial law. The army did not intervene on 30 June 1934 when Roehm and the SA cadres were massacred. On 1 July Blomberg's Order of the Day to the army expressed full support for Hitler. On Hindenburg's death, Blomberg prepared a new military oath of loyalty to his successor Hitler, replacing the old oath to the state.

Blomberg subsequently disagreed with Hitler's foreign policy. Although in May 1935 he had issued directives preparing for the military reoccupation of the Rhineland, he opposed Hitler's orders to this effect in March 1936, and then, believing that England and France would retaliate, begged Hitler to withdraw the troops which had crossed the Rhine. In a conference of 5 Nov. 1937 recorded in the Hossbach Memorandum, Blomberg was one of several officers querying Hitler's plans to find *Lebensraum* in Czechoslovakia and Austria.

In Jan. 1938 Blomberg married his secretary, who was subsequently revealed to have been a prostitute. His rival officers insisted to Hitler that Blomberg be dismissed for dishonouring the army. Hitler announced Blomberg's resignation on 4 Feb., together with other personnel changes consolidating Hitler's personal command of all the armed forces. Blomberg subsequently lived in obscurity in Bavaria.

ASJ

BLOMFIELD, CHARLES (1786–1857), bishop of London (1828–57). He became unpopular because of his opposition to the Reform Bill (1832) and his chairmanship of the Whig Poor Law Commission (1834). He was outstanding among contemporary bishops for drive and administrative ability, being described as an 'ecclesiastical Peel'. He established (1836) a building fund for metropolitan churches, principally in slum districts, and was an energetic member of the Ecclesiastical Commission. He was hostile to the tractarians, who suspected him for his enthusiasm for sweeping reform of church organization. In the 1850s he led the movement to legislate for Sunday observance.

BLOODY ASSIZES (1685), judicial aftermath of the unsuccessful Monmouth rising. Early in July 1685 the Duke of Monmouth and his supporters had been defeated at the battle of Sedgemoor. Two days later James II appointed a commission of five, including Lord Chief Justice Jeffreys, to hear the cases of those accused of involvement in the uprising. The judges sat at Winchester, Salisbury, Dorchester, Exeter, Taunton, Wells, and Bristol. During the course of the assizes, some 300 persons are believed to have been sentenced to death, and about 800 to transportation, although the exact figures are not known. But there is little doubt that the trials were conducted sadistically and that the sentences imposed were extremely harsh. Even if they were not criticized immediately, the proceedings of the Bloody Assizes were roundly condemned after the Glorious Revolution.

BLOODY KNIFE (*c.* 1839–76), Arikara warrior and chief, who served as an army scout with Gen. Stanley on the Yellowstone expedition (1873) and with Custer in the Black Hills (1874). He was killed fighting with Reno's force at the battle of the Little Big Horn (1876).

BLOODY MARSH, BATTLE OF. One of a series of battles at St Simon's Island, GA, in July 1740, between Sir James Oglethorpe's settlers and soldiers, and a much larger Spanish force from Cuba and the St Augustine settlement. By a ruse, Oglethorpe convinced the Spanish he had superior arms and manpower, thus causing their withdrawal to Florida and assuring the safety and growth of the English settlement.

BLOODY SUNDAY (13 Nov. 1887), in London was the culmination of a series of meetings of the Social Democratic Federation in Trafalgar Square, which the Metropolitan Police were anxious to end. The meeting was held in defiance of police prohibition and was broken up by baton charges. One hundred people were injured and two died, and two SDF leaders, John Burns and Cunninghame Graham, were arrested and imprisoned. Bloody Sunday may be regarded as the climax of the SDF movement. With improving trade in the late 1880s, socialist activity turned towards trade union organization.

BLOODY SUNDAY (Jan. 1905), in St Petersburg. A procession of workers led by Gapon marched on the Winter Palace in St Petersburg to present a petition to the tsar. Troops fired on the crowd, causing several hundred casualties, and the resulting protest movement turned into the 1905 revolution.

BLOOMSBURY, district of London containing the British Museum and a major part of the university, which gave its name to a set of literary, artistic, and aesthetic attitudes that flourished in the first quarter of the 20th cent. Bloomsbury was the social centre of the London literary world, and the name was associated with a socially exclusive, intellectual, and unconventional way of life. The group centred around the Stephens sisters, Vanessa and Virginia, the novelist and, later, the wife of the Fabian socialist Leonard Woolf. Most of the men had been strongly influenced by philosophers such as G. E. Moore and Bertrand Russell, and also included among its members the art critic Roger Fry, who did much to introduce French Impressionist painting to Britain. On the fringe of the group were the poet T. S. Eliot and the economist Lord Keynes. The group's beliefs can be summed up in Moore's dictum that 'The supreme values of life are the states of consciousness involved in human relations and in the appreciation of beauty.' Their intellectual influence faded when political questions began to dominate literary circles in the 1930s.

BLOW, JOHN (1649–1708), English musician, teacher of Henry Purcell. At various times Blow was a chorister, choirmaster, and organist of the Chapel Royal, and organist also at Westminster Abbey, both preceding and following his illustrious project. He is considered to have been the first recipient of a Lambeth doctorate in music.

BLÜCHER, GEBHARD LEBERECHT VON, Prince of Wahlstadt (1742–1819), Prussian field marshal, who acted as commander-in-chief in the final stages of the Napoleonic wars. He played a decisive part in the allied campaigns in Germany in 1813 and during the 100 Days was Prussian commander in Belgium. Although he was wounded and defeated by Napoleon's army at Ligny (16 June 1815), he appeared at a crucial moment in the battle of Waterloo two days later, though whether his intervention was decisive for Wellington's victory is debatable.

BLUE MOUNTAINS, NSW. The crossing in 1813 of this picturesque but rugged barrier plateau some 30 miles (48 kms) west of Port Jackson by Gregory Blaxland, William Lawson, and William Charles Wentworth led to the exploration of the interior of the first Australian colony. It opened the way for occupation of inland plains and development of sheep farming, though settlers did not move over the mountains in significant numbers until the 1820s.

BLUE WATER POLICY. Strategic concept to limit war expenses, expounded by extreme Tories in Britain during the War of the Spanish Succession. They proposed that Britain should concentrate on a naval war to gain an empire and trade, and act only as an auxiliary to other nations in the land aspects of the war.

BLUEFIELDS, town in Nicaragua on the Caribbean coast at the mouth of the Escondido river. It was founded as a trading centre with the Moskito Indians (1634) by Samuel Axe and his Dutch companion Blauveldt, who gave his name to the settlement. British control was maintained over the town until 1860, when Bluefields passed to Nicaragua.

BLUELICKS, BATTLE OF (Aug. 1782), was one of the last conflicts in the American War of Independence. A British and Indian raiding party, led by Capt. William Caldwell and Alexander McKee, trapped and defeated an American militia force in Kentucky.

BLUES, musical style originating in Negro areas of the southern US, developing from the spirituals and work songs of 19th-cent. share-croppers and prison gangs. In the early 20th cent. itinerant singers spread the blues throughout the south, and the music was carried north to Chicago and other industrial cities by the massive migration of Negroes in search of work during the First World War. The peak of its popularity came with the Depression.

BLUM, LÉON (1872–1950), French socialist leader in the inter-war years, and as head of the Popular Front government (1936–7) France's first socialist prime minister. Born into a rich Jewish family, Blum first made his mark in the literary world, especially as a theatre critic. The Dreyfus affair helped shape his socialist convictions, and brought him into contact with the socialist leader Jaurès, whose disciple he became. Like Jaurès, he tried to combine Marxist socialism with the democratic traditions of the French Revolution. Blum became more active in politics after Jaurès's assassination (1914), and entered parliament in 1919. He was the

man chiefly responsible for rebuilding the Socialist Party after the socialist-communist split (1920). In the following years he established his ascendancy over the party through his intellectual ability, integrity, and idealism. His newspaper, *Le Populaire*, was the main organ of his influence.

After being kept from office for many years by the socialist policy of non-participation in 'bourgeois' governments, Blum was the obvious choice as prime minister after the electoral victory of the Popular Front (1936). This was an alliance of socialists, communists, and Radicals, but Blum's government did not include communist ministers.

Blum's task was difficult. The Popular Front's victory aroused great hopes, and set off a wave of strikes. Blum was able to end these by the 'Matignon agreements', promising higher wages, but his long-term economic policy, based on the Keynesian idea of reviving the economy by creating purchasing power, failed because of inflation and financial crisis. In 1937 Blum resigned when the Senate refused to approve his emergency financial measures.

His government was more successful in its social reforms, and its permanent achievements included paid holidays and the 40-hour week for workers, some nationalization, and the public control of the Bank of France. In foreign affairs, Blum began French rearmament, but the Anglo-French policy of non-intervention in the Spanish Civil War, of which Blum was the real author, alienated his communist allies.

Blum was briefly prime minister again in 1938, but the Popular Front experiment was really over by 1937. It remains a controversial episode, and some of Blum's critics blame its failure partly on his own lack of political ruthlessness. At the time, the Popular Front left a legacy of disillusion and national division. Blum himself was detested by the right, and was the target of violent, often anti-semitic, press attacks.

He was arrested by the Vichy government, and accused at the 'Riom trial' (1942) of neglecting France's interests when in power. He defended himself so effectively that the trial was suspended. He was then imprisoned in Germany (1942–1945). After the war, he did not re-enter parliament, but acted as elder statesman of the Socialist Party, and headed a brief caretaker government (1946–7). Among his numerous writings, *For All Mankind* forms a sort of political testament.

L. E. Dalby, *Léon Blum, Evolution of a Socialist* (New York, 1963).
J Colton, *Léon Blum, Humanist in Politics* (New York, 1966).
RDA

BLYDEN, EDWARD WILMOT (1832–1912), Liberian author, politician, and diplomat, and an outstanding figure among the West African elite from 1851 to 1912. Born of Hausa parents on the island of St Thomas, he was denied admission to a college in the US on racial grounds, and moved to Liberia, where he served in various capacities for the next 60 years, being Liberian secretary of state (1864–6) and ambassador in London (1872 and 1892). His erudition, particularly in the classics, and knowledge of languages impressed his audiences in West Africa, England, and the US. For the educated elite he exemplified mental attributes which exposed the anti-Negro prejudice of racist pseudo-anthropologists, who asserted that blacks were biologically inferior to whites. In his writings and speeches he urged Europeanized Africans to be proud of being Africans and to renounce alien culture.

BOARD, PETER (1858–1945), country schools' inspector in NSW when the state's educational reform movement reached its peak (*c.* 1900). His brief *Report on Primary Education* (1904) stimulated other NSW educational institutions, including Sydney University and the Workers' Educational Association.

BOARD OF AGRICULTURE (1793–1822), British society created by enthusiasts for improved agriculture to focus public energy and help spread new practices. It had an unusual constitution, being an upper-class voluntary society with a government grant and some government membership. Its most valuable work was a pair of surveys of the farming and the landowning structure of the country, undertaken county by county. After the death of its original secretary, Arthur Young, it became involved with the Agricultural Association, a body representing the extreme landed interest demand for higher protection, and this led the government to destroy it by stopping its grant. The later Board of Agriculture, founded in 1889, was entirely different, being a government department carrying on work previously developed by the agricultural department of the privy council.

BOARD OF CONTROL, body of commissioners for Indian affairs established by Pitt's India Act (1784). Avowedly a compromise aimed at combining the vested interest of the East India Co. with the prerogatives of monarchy, it greatly extended the control of the state over the company. There were to be six unpaid commissioners, consisting of the chancellor of the exchequer, one of the principal secretaries of state, and four other privy councillors appointed by the king and holding office during his pleasure. There was to be a quorum of three and the president had a casting vote. They were empowered to superintend, direct, and control all matters relating to the civil and military government and revenues of the British possessions in the East Indies. The board had no patronage, nor did it interfere in commercial affairs. The right of appointing the company's servants was retained by the directors, except that the governor-general, the members of council, and the commander-in-chief were chosen subject to the Crown's veto. The board had full access to all papers of the company and the directors were required to deliver to the board copies of all their minutes and of dispatches sent by or received by them or their committees. The board could approve, disapprove, or modify any dispatches sent by the directors. There was to be a secret committee of three directors, appointed by the court of directors, through which all important secret orders of the board were to be transmitted to India without the other directors being informed. The court of proprietors lost the right of revoking or modifying any proceedings of the directors which had received the approval of the board. This was because the court had recently overruled a resolution of the directors for the recall of Warren Hastings. The Board of Control was obviously based on Fox's seven commissioners, but it was not an independent executive body, as it was linked with the government of the day. Under Dundas, its first president, the board exemplified all the defects urged against Fox's bill (1783), and Dundas occupied a position similar to the later secretary of state for India. Pitt's India Act was modified with typical Pitt-like caution and his board had no control over commerce. This was the sacrifice Pitt made to secure Leadenhall Street support. Under Dundas the company gained little from Pitt's compromise. In 1793 the Board of Control was somewhat remodelled and the two junior members no longer had to be privy councillors. Provision was also made for the payment of the members and staff of the board out of Indian revenues. The board was abolished in 1858 when the powers of the company were transferred to the Crown and its place was taken by the Council of India under the newly-appointed secretary of state for India.

C. H. Philips, *The East India Company 1784–1834* (Manchester, 1940). CCD

BOARD OF REVENUE, a term loosely used by contemporary and later writers for various revenue committees of the East India Co. after the *diwani* grant of 1765 entitled them to collect and administer the revenues of Bengal, Bihar, and Orissa. This had been left to local officials until the directors decided to 'stand forth as *diwan*' (1772) and through their own servants control the revenue system. Warren Hastings and his council at Calcutta were established as a committee or board of revenue. After 1781 the term 'board of revenue' was used to indicate the Supreme Council when sitting to hear revenue appeal cases from the committee of revenue. Strictly speaking, the term dates from 1786, when a board of revenue replaced the existing committee of revenue. Under Cornwallis the board was ordered (1787) to make a decennial revenue settlement, which was made permanent in 1793.

BOARD OF TRADE AND PLANTATIONS, established (1674) by King Charles II of England as the Council for Trade and Plantations. It was reorganized after the Revolution of 1688. During the War of the Grand Alliance (1689–97) the Commons became dissatisfied with the defence of commerce, and moved to establish a parliamentary committee for trade with executive powers. To preserve his prerogative, William III set up a board of trade, which consisted of eight paid members, as well as, nominally, the great officers of state, with a staff who together formed a government department. The board's function was to guard England's overseas interests. It was a policy-making group concerned with the security and welfare of the colonies, and colonial life, including the management of servants, slaves, and (in North America) the Indians. Because it failed to adjust itself to changes in the colonies it was a major cause of the War of American Independence. It was abolished by the British parliament in 1782, and reconstituted by Pitt, as prime minister, in 1786, though only as an advisory body.

BOBADILLA, NICHOLAS (d. 1590), one of Ignatius Loyola's disciples, who studied with him at Paris University (1528–1535). He and eight others joined with Loyola in taking the famous vow at the chapel of Saint-Denis, Montmartre (15 Aug. 1534), dedicating themselves to poverty and chastity and their lives to God's purpose, either in missionary activity in the Holy Land or through their service to the pope. During the 1540s Bobadilla visited a number of German states, studying the problem of Protestantism and advising Catholic princes, lay and ecclesiastical. He witnessed the battle of Muhlberg (1547) where the Catholic imperialist forces triumphed over the Protestant Elector of Saxony.

BOBRIKOV, NIKOLAI IVANOVICH (1839–1904), governor-general of Finland (1898–1904), where he intensified the Russification policy, enforcing service in the Russian army and precedence for Russian laws, language, and trade. His suspension of the constitution guaranteeing Finnish autonomy (1903) led to his assassination by a nationalist group (June 1904).

BOCCACCIO, GIOVANNI (1313–75), one of the most famous medieval writers. He was a Florentine, though long resident at Naples. His best-known work, *The Decameron*, a collection of 100 novels, is one of the great works of world literature. His friendship with Petrarch and personal religious experiences eventually turned Boccaccio towards serious scholarship. He found one of the most important manuscripts of Tacitus and he was one of the pioneers of humanist scholarship. He wrote the earliest commentary on Dante and was the first to lecture on Dante's *Divine Comedy*.

BOCCHUS I (*reg.* 118–81 BC), King of Mauretania at the time of the war against Jugurtha. He first allied himself with the latter, who was his son-in-law, but finally delivered him into the hands of the Romans in exchange for a treaty of friendship.

BOCCHUS II (*fl.* 1st cent. BC), King of Eastern Mauretania during Caesar's war in Africa. Together with Bogud, King of Western Mauretania, he helped Caesar in his defeat of Juba I and the Pompeians.

BOCKELSON, JAN (d. 1535), native of Leyden, prominent Anabaptist and friend of Jan Matthys, the sect's leader in the Netherlands. He fled from persecution in Holland to Munster, where, on Matthys's death, he took control (1533). He later discredited the sect by allowing polygamy (1535). In that year the city was captured by Catholic forces and Bockelson was executed.

BOCSKAY, STEPHEN (1557–1606), *vaivoda* (or governor) of Transylvania, who disliked the Habsburg policies, which were designed to diminish the power of the Hungarian estates and the rights of the Hungarian Protestants. During the last years of the war (1593–1606) between the Ottoman empire and Austria he made common cause with the Turks. In 1605 the estates of Transylvania elected him to be their *vaivoda*, a choice which the Ottoman Sultan Ahmed I hastened to approve. He negotiated an agreement with Austria which ensured to the Hungarians their political and religious privileges and to himself formal recognition as *vaivoda* of Transylvania. The agreement was confirmed at the peace of Zsitvatorok in 1606.

BODAWPAYA (*reg.* 1782–1819), King of Ava and sixth ruler of the Alaungpaya dynasty. His reign began with ruthless massacres, but later he proved an enlightened ruler. He invaded Arakan and Assam and made war inconclusively against Siam.

BODH-GAYA, site of Lord Buddha's Enlightenment near the town of Gaya (South Bihar, India). The most important monuments there are the Mahabodhi temple, which may go back to an Ashokan prototype, but has been restored, enlarged, and rebuilt several times (once in *c.* AD 1100 by the efforts of the Burmese King Kyanzittha), and, especially, the Bôtree under which the Buddha attained Enlightenment. Though destroyed by fire the tree is reported to have miraculously risen from its ashes. In the 3rd cent. BC a branch of the Bô-tree is reported to have been transferred to Ceylon, where it soon grew into a full tree.

BODICHON, BARBARA (born Barbara Leigh Smith) (1827–1891), English champion of women's rights. She was a founder of Girton College (1869) and contributed largely to its endowment. She was a close friend of George Eliot, and is believed to be the model for the heroine of *Romola*.

BODIN, JEAN (*c.* 1530–96), French political theorist of the 16th cent. He was born at Angers and trained as a lawyer at Angers and Toulouse universities. In 1576 he produced his most important work, *The Six Books of the Republic*. Bodin was actively concerned with the political implications of the Wars of Religion, and as the elected deputy for Vermandois he attended the meeting of the estates general at Blois (1576), where he adopted a moderate *politique* attitude. His *Republic* was itself an attempt to support and strengthen the king's position. It was widely read by contemporaries and has retained its place as the most original work to come out of that troubled epoch. Bodin's idea of sovereignty is the most important element of his political writing. He defined it as supreme power in the state unrestrained by law, and the originality of his concept lies in the implicit assumption that sovereignty is man-made, whereas the contemporary theory of divine-right monarchy was based on the belief that power was derived from God alone. In later life, disillusioned with King Henry III, Bodin joined the Catholic League when it took over the town of Laon, where he was living (1588), though his action indicated passive acceptance rather than active support. He repudiated the league in 1593.

BODLEY, SIR THOMAS (1545–1613), English diplomat, whose missions took him to Denmark (1585), France (1588), and to the United Provinces, as a resident diplomat (1589–1596). He also refounded the Bodleian Library, Oxford (1598), which was created from the earlier libraries of Cobham and Humphrey, Duke of Gloucester. The library increased from 2000 volumes in 1602 to 16,000 by 1620 and continued to benefit from later bequests. By 1970, with its dependent libraries, *eg*, Radcliffe Camera (1749), New Library (1746), it contained over two-and-a-half million books.

BODMER, CHARLES (1809–93), Swiss painter, whose atlas was published with Prince Maximilian von Wied-Neuwied's *Travels in the Interior of North America* (1839), and contained the first detailed topographical paintings of the Missouri valley.

BOËL, BARON RENÉ (1899–   ), Belgian industrialist who took an active part in the movement for European unity, being president of the European League of Economic Co-operation and a member of the Executive Bureau of the European Movement.

BOENECHEA, DOMINGO DE (d. 1775), Spanish sailor, who was sent in the *Aguila* from Peru to David's Land and Tahiti (1772, 1774) to secure Spanish rights against English intrusion. On his second voyage he landed Catholic missionaries at Tahiti, where he died. Don Cayetana de Langana y Huarte removed the mission on *Aguila's* third voyage (1775–6).

BOER WAR (SOUTH AFRICAN WAR) (1899–1902). The discovery of gold on the Witwatersrand in 1886 made the Transvaal the economic centre of South Africa. By the end of the 1890s over 50,000 foreign whites, the *Uitlanders*, were on the Rand. President Kruger's refusal to grant the *Uitlanders* full political rights was the immediate *casus belli*, but the underlying reason was the intention of the British government and of the Rand capitalists to control the richest part of South Africa, and the reluctance of the Transvaalers to countenance this.

Rhodes attempted on his own account to storm the fortress in 1895, when his colleague Jameson launched his disastrous raid from Bechuanaland. Thereafter Kruger used revenue from the gold mines to buy armaments, and British troop reinforcements were sent to South Africa in 1899. War broke out on 11 Oct. 1899.

Until Feb. 1900 the Afrikaners were successful on several fronts, including the northern Cape, where many farmers rebelled against the British. By March British weight of numbers had worn down the republican armies. Generals Roberts and Kitchener drove north, capturing Bloemfontein and Johannesburg, and relieving Mafeking. But the Afrikaner commandos continued guerrilla fighting. To combat this, Kitchener resorted to a scorched-earth policy, and interned women and children in concentration camps. The war finally ended with the treaty of Vereeniging (31 March 1902), by which the republics lost their independence, but were promised eventual self-government.

The Boer War, one of the longest and bloodiest wars fought south of the Sahara in modern times, was a war between rival white groups. Africans, when they participated at all, did so only as auxiliaries. They witnessed at first hand the destructive potential of European warfare. Although Milner, the British high commissioner, had precipitated the war, it was not the short combat he envisaged. The length of the war and the great cost in men and money made it impossible for him to take over the Transvaal economy intact, as he had hoped. The Transvaal and the Orange Free State had to be reconstructed, and this could only be achieved with the co-operation of the Afrikaners, the majority white group. When the two ex-republics were granted self-government (1906–7), Africans living in them were not given political rights. This was in accordance with the terms of the peace treaty, which left it to the whites to decide whether or not to extend the franchise to Africans. The real losers of the war were the African inhabitants of South Africa.

J. Selby, *The Boer War* (London, 1969).
G. H. L. Le May, *British Supremacy in South Africa, 1899–1907* (Oxford, 1965).   **AEA**

BOERHAVE, HERMAN (1668–1738), Dutch chemist, author of *Elementa Chemiae* (1732) and professor at Leyden University, the leading medical school in Europe. From here Boerhave's influence spread to the medical schools at Vienna and Edinburgh.

BOETHIUS, ANICIUS MANLIUS SEVERINUS (*c.* 480–524). His work may be regarded as a bridge between classical culture and medieval Christian scholarship. He belonged to a distinguished senatorial family from Italy and was consul in 510. He was long imprisoned by the Ostrogothic king, Theodoric, and finally executed. His most influential work was *The Consolation of Philosophy*, written in prison. It was an attempt to show the essential agreement of the philosophical ideas of Plato and Aristotle and until the 12th cent. provided the bulk of the information available to western Europe about these thinkers.

BOGAZKOY, modern site, in Anatolia, of Hattusas, the capital of the Hittites (*c.* 1650–1215 BC), first excavated by Dr Hugo Winckler from 1906.

BOGLE, GEORGE (1746–81), servant of the East India Co., sent by Warren Hastings to the court of the Tashi Lama of Tibet to foster trade and friendly relations (1774). A later attempt to renew this intercourse was frustrated by the departure of the Tashi Lama for Peking.

BOGLE, PAUL (d. 1865), leader of an unsuccessful insurrection at Morant Bay, Jamaica (Oct. 1865), in which over 600 persons died. The rising collapsed after Bogle's capture and execution.

BOGOMILS, members of a religious sect which flourished in the Balkan lands during the 10th–15th cents. It arose in Bulgaria as the result of a fusion between neo-Manichaean doctrines imported from the East and Slavonic aspirations towards reform within the local Greek Orthodox Church. The Bogomil faith rested on a dualism between good and evil, the material world being the creation of the devil. Animated, at least in its earlier manifestations, by an austere code of behaviour and belief, Bogomilism spread far and wide in the 11th–12th cents. In a modified form (the Patarene faith) it won the allegiance of the princes and nobles of Bosnia and also exerted a strong influence on the Albigensian movement. With the advance of the Ottoman Turks into the Balkans during the 14th–15th cents. a large number of the Bogomils became Muslim.

BOGOMOLOV, ALEKSANDR YEFREMOVICH (1900–69), plenipotentiary representative of the USSR in France (1941–1943), then representative at the French Committee for National Liberation in Africa and ambassador to France from the time of the Liberation through the early days of the Cold War (1944–50). He returned to Moscow in 1950 for two years and was then ambassador to Czechoslovakia (1952–4) and Italy (1954–7).

BOGOTÁ, CONFERENCE OF, ninth Pan-American Conference, held in March 1948. During the conference the Colombian Liberal leader Jorge Gaitán was assassinated and rioting broke out, massive damage being done.

BOHEMIA, east European kingdom (1198–1918), an upland plateau forming a distinct geographical unit and separated by mountains from the neighbouring states of Saxony, Austria, Hungary, and Poland. It was largely populated by Czech-speaking Slavs, but there was also a strong German minority dating from the 12th cent. By the 16th cent. these 'lands of the crown of St Wenceslas' included the kingdom of Bohemia, the margravate of Moravia, several duchies of Polish-German Silesia, Upper and Lower Lusatia, and the minor lordships of Eger, Glatz, Elbogen, and Troppau. From *c.* 1415 the majority of Czechs belonged to the schismatic Hussite national Church of the Utraquists, though from the Reformation there were minority groups of Lutherans, Calvinists, and Bohemian Brethren until the Counter-Reformation reimposed Catholicism.

Rich in lead, copper, and silver, Bohemia was for centuries the mining centre of Europe. Its crown was coveted by the Austrian Habsburgs because of its mineral wealth and its electoral vote in the imperial college. In 1526 the ruling Polish Jagiellon dynasty ended and the Archduke Ferdinand of Austria was elected King of Bohemia and Hungary, thus beginning the long period of Habsburg control.

Bohemia's constitution provided for an elective monarchy largely subservient to the nobility, the most important estate in both the central and provincial diets. Under the Habsburgs, monarchical government became slowly stronger. The expulsion of the native aristocracy during the Thirty Years War (1618–48) and the reforms of Haugwitz (1740s) and Joseph II (1780s) marked stages in this process.

BOHEMIA, DIRECTORS OF, government of 13 appointed by the assembly of Protestant deputies after the defenestration of Prague (May 1618), to exercise the executive functions of the imperial governors. The Directorate ended with its submission to the Emperor Ferdinand after the battle of the White Mountain (Nov. 1620).

BOHEMIA-MORAVIA, formerly part of the Habsburg empire, was awarded to the new Czechoslovak state at the Paris Peace Conference (1919). Over 3 million Germans, one-third of Bohemia-Moravia's population, passed under Czechoslovak rule. The German settlement was not compact, comprising groups of differing backgrounds, scattered along the mountainous frontier. Before 1919, the area of settlement was only rarely designated the Sudetenland.

The German population was engaged predominantly in light industry, commerce, and administration. Germans controlled local government in areas with a German-speaking majority; however, many lost pre-war government posts through the new Czech language requirement. Post-war economic crises affected Germans more than the less industrialized Czechs of central Bohemia-Moravia. That government contracts appeared to foster developing Czech industries rather than German concerns was an additional grievance.

The Weimar Republic subsidized German institutions in Czechoslovakia, and encouraged moderate German parties to join the government in 1925. The 1931 Depression worsened Czech–German relations, German light industry suffering from the contraction in world trade, and recovering more slowly than Czech heavy industry. National extremism increased, especially after Hitler's accession to power in Germany.

In Oct. 1933, after the local Nazi Party was suppressed, Konrad Henlein founded the *Sudetendeutsche Heimatfront* (SHF) with Reich financial support. Renamed *Sudetendeutsche Partei* (SdP), it received over 60 per cent of all German votes in the 1935 elections. In Feb. 1937 the government promised to redress outstanding German grievances; Henlein, unappeased, told Hitler in Nov. that his party desired incorporation in the Reich. After the *Anschluss*, SdP activities exacerbated tensions between Hitler and Czechoslovakia. Hitler occupied the Sudetenland on 1 Oct. 1938, following the Munich agreement. He continued to champion the German minority remaining in central Bohemia-Moravia, which contained important munition works, and which he occupied on 14 March 1939, establishing a protectorate two days later.

E. Wiskemann, *Czechs and Germans* (London, 1938).
R. Luža, *The Transfer of the Sudeten Germans* (London, 1964.)   ASJ

BOHEMOND (1058–1111), ablest but most treacherous of the leaders of the First Crusade. Son of Robert Guiscard, the Norman ruler of southern Italy, he participated in

Robert's attempt to conquer the Byzantine lands in the Balkans (1080–5). His participation in the First Crusade dismayed the Eastern emperor, Alexius I. The successful march of the crusaders through Asia Minor and the capture of Antioch (1097–8) were largely due to Bohemond, but the Byzantine suspicions were justified when he refused to restore Antioch to Alexius. The consequent hostility of the Byzantines placed the Crusaders in grave danger and Bohemond refused to join in their final march on Jerusalem, preferring to safeguard his new principality of Antioch. In 1107–8 he organized a fresh western crusade against Byzantium but was defeated by Alexius.

BÖHM-BAWERK, EUGEN VON (1851–1914), Austrian economist and statesman. He is best known for his theory of capital productivity, to which he applied the concept of marginal utility, expounded in his *Positiv Theorie des Kapitalzinses* (1893). He was Austro-Hungarian minister of finance, a privy councillor, and one of the chief planners of the important fiscal reform of 1896.

BOHR, NIELS HENRIK DAVID (1885–1962), Danish physicist, who in 1913 formulated the first consistent theory explaining the electronic structure of the atom. Bohr was among the first to recognize the implications of nuclear bombs. He played a major scientific role during the formulation of atomic policy in 1944–5, advocating, unsuccessfully, international openness and co-operation. He was awarded a Nobel Prize in 1922.

BOIGNE, BENOIT DE (1751–1830), Savoyard soldier of fortune who entered the service of the Indian Maratha chief, Mahadaji Sindhia, in 1784. He trained Sindhia's battalions on European lines and won for him the battles of Patan (1790), Merta (1791), and Lakheri (1793). He returned to his native Savoy in 1796 with a fortune.

BOII, Celtic people from Transalpine Gaul, a wave of whom migrated about 400 BC to settle in eastern Italy between the Po and the Apennines. After over a century of sporadic hostilities with the Romans, they were provoked by their expansion along the Adriatic to join the gathering of Gallic invaders defeated by Rome at Telamon (225). Roman colonies at Placentia and Cremona, and the outpost at Mutina, reinforced their hostility, and during the Second Punic War they allied themselves with Hannibal. Tepid as allies, they fought more fiercely against Rome after Hannibal's departure, and with the Insubres captured Placentia (200). But after the reduction of the Insubres they were isolated, and decisively defeated by Scipio Nasica (191). Thereafter they were gradually absorbed into the Roman state, though a century elapsed before Gallia Cisalpina became a province.

BOILEAU-DESPREAUX, NICOLAS (1636–1711), French classical poet famous for his satire, whose *Art poétique* (1674) was the manifesto of a new school of writers including Fontaine, Molière, and Racine. Boileau was appointed historiographer to Louis XIV jointly with his friend Racine and was admitted to the Académie Française in 1683. His concise and rhythmic poems give a vigorous picture of society and his system of aesthetics was adopted by the great French writers of the 17th cent.

BOISGUILBERT, PIERRE LE PESANT DE (1646–1714), military governor of Rouen, but better known as an economist and writer of treatises on the reform of the tax system under Louis XIV. His name is often linked with that of Vauban, but his thought was more original. He is regarded as a forerunner of the Physiocrats. Boisguilbert believed that the wealth of a state depended on its capacity to exchange and that money was useful only as a means of facilitating exchange. He criticized the onerous nature of French taxation, especially the fact that huge sums were levied by tax collectors for their own, rather than the state's, benefit to the detriment of the peasantry in particular.

BOK, EDWARD WILLIAM (1863–1930), Dutch-born US editor and philanthropist. He received a Pulitzer prize (1921) for his autobiography, *The Americanization of Edward Bok* (1920). Best known for his successful editing of the *Ladies Home Journal* (1889–1919), he was also an enthusiast for progressive reform and world peace.

BOKI (d. 1829), minor Hawaiian chief, who epitomized the shallow impact of 19th-cent. Christianity in the Pacific. As governor of Oahu (Hawaii) under Kamehameha I, he accompanied Kamehameha II on his fatal London visit (1823–1825). On his return Boki drifted into dubious commercial ventures and finally broke with Christianity. He disappeared at Rotumah while on a sandalwood expedition to the New Hebrides.

BOLESLAW I, The Mighty, Prince of Poland (*reg.* 992–1025), son of Mieszko I, who ultimately broke with his father's policy of being an ally of the German emperors. By his conquests at the expense of all the neighbours of Poland, Boleslaw created the most powerful Slavonic state of his time. His friend, St Adalbert, prepared the way for the creation in 1000 of the Polish metropolitan see at Gniezno, where Boleslaw had himself crowned king a second time (1025), profiting from the divisions in Germany after the death of Emperor Henry II. His successors lost most of his conquests and a pagan reaction inside Poland threatened to disrupt it altogether, a much-reduced Christian principality being restored only with German help.

BOLESLAW II (*reg.* 1058–81), King of Poland, succeeded his father, Casimir I, as ruler of Poland. Boleslaw became the leading ally in eastern Europe of Pope Gregory VII. Profiting from the papal excommunication of Emperor Henry IV in Feb. 1076, Boleslaw crowned himself king at Christmas 1076. A great warrior but a despotic ruler, he aroused the opposition of Polish magnates, and the execution of Bp Stanislaw of Cracow for pro-imperialist conspiracy encouraged revolts. In 1079 Boleslaw had to flee to Hungary, where he died.

BOLESLAW III (Wrymouth) (d. 1138), Prince of Poland (1102–38), who conquered and converted the pagan Pomeranians, thus gaining for Poland access to the sea. But his partition of Poland among his sons initiated a period of division lasting nearly two centuries, during which several territories bordering on Germany were permanently lost.

BOLÍVAR, SIMÓN (1783–1830), patriot and revolutionary hero of the Latin American Wars of Independence. Born in Caracas, Venezuela, to a wealthy Creole family, Bolívar received his early education from tutors. Two of them, Simón Rodríguez and Andrés Bello, were to become well-known revolutionaries. Bolívar married while visiting the Spanish court in Madrid, but his wife died within a year. He travelled widely and became impressed with the idea of the 'man of destiny'. Napoleon became one of his heroes. He was also caught up in the thinking which lay behind the French revolutionary slogan of 'Liberty, Equality, Fraternity'. In Rome (1805) he took an oath to liberate his homeland from Spanish rule.

In Venezuela Bolívar became an active supporter of the patriot cause and joined Francisco de Miranda's uprising against the local Spanish army. After Miranda's defeat, Bolívar believed that Miranda had betrayed the revolutionary cause, and he and others permitted Miranda to be captured by the Spaniards.

After Miranda's capture, Bolívar became the leader of the Venezuelan independence movement. Early defeats meant exile in Curaçao, Cartagena, and later Jamaica and Haiti. In 1816 he re-entered Venezuela and after a two-year campaign managed to defeat the Spaniards and establish the region's independence. He then pushed the wars into Colombia and

Ecuador, and helped to organize the new nation of Gran Colombia, (roughly Colombia, Venezuela, and Ecuador), of which he became first president.

Bolívar then turned his attention southward. After a controversial and unsuccessful meeting with Gen. José de San Martín in Guayaquil, he and his second-in-command, Gen. José Antonio de Sucre, campaigned for two years in Peru and Bolivia, freeing these areas from Spanish rule. On his return to Gran Colombia his centralist, authoritarian opinions met with federalist opposition. His dreams of a closer Pan-American relationship also found lukewarm support, and in spite of his efforts Venezuela and Ecuador left the federation of Gran Colombia. Disillusioned, he resigned (1830) and died.

His career revealed both high idealism and personal aggrandizement. He was a *caudillo* and a liberator.

G. Masur, *Simón Bolívar* (Albuquerque, NM, 1948).   MJM

BOLIVIAN NATIONAL REVOLUTION. The Chaco War between Bolivia and Paraguay (1928–35) emphasized problems which had been troubling Bolivian society. Returning war veterans formed associations and political parties varying from extreme right to extreme left, but all proposing revolutionary solutions. After several short-lived regimes, the National Revolutionary Movement (MNR) emerged as the strongest of these new parties, though it was opposed by the old ruling elites and especially by the three great tin magnates, Patino, Hochschild, and Aramayo. The MNR demanded greater social justice for the Indian, nationalization of the tin mines, redistribution of the nation's agricultural land, and diversification of the country's economy to free it from dependence on the world price of tin.

The MNR first came to power as a junior partner of some reformist elements of the army. This arrangement was unsatisfactory, and when President Gualberto Villarroel was overthrown and murdered (July 1946), the MNR was forced to go underground and many of its members, including the leader, Victor Paz Estenssoro, fled abroad.

After several abortive uprisings the MNR participated in the elections of 1951. Paz emerged as the leader in the voting, but was prevented from taking power by a military junta. In April 1952 the MNR led a popular revolution and Victor Paz Estenssoro became the first revolutionary president. The government embarked on a series of sweeping reforms. The mines were nationalized and the franchise extended to illiterates (which meant most of the Indian population). Land reform, accompanied by some peasant invasions of large estates, was begun, and the Cochabamba–Santa Cruz paved highway, the first real link between highlands and lowlands, was finished. At the end of Paz's term (1956) his vice-president, Hernan Siles Suazo, was elected in his place. He was more conservative than Paz, and embarked on a monetary stabilization programme to try to halt inflation. The tin mines being largely worked out, production dropped drastically. In June 1960 Paz was re-elected to the presidency, which caused a severe split in the MNR's ranks. His programme for economic development relied heavily on US aid and his regime began to lose support, whereupon he amended the Bolivian constitution to allow for his immediate re-election (1964), splitting the party still further. The growing personal ambitions of his vice-president, Rene Barrientos Ortuno, led to his overthrow that same year. Barrientos favoured the army and suppressed the miners by force. He called elections (1966) and won them. His death in a plane crash (1969) renewed MNR hopes of a return to power, but the army, led by Gen. Ovando Candia, seemed to be in control.

The Bolivian National Revolution has transformed the nation's economy and social structure. Much of its programme is now accepted by all parties, but the future course of the revolution remains uncertain. The MNR is hated and feared by large sections of the dominant army.

R. J. Alexander, *The Bolivian National Revolution* (New Brunswick, NJ, 1958).

BOLLANDISTS, THE, 17th-cent. Jesuit fathers in the southern Netherlands, called after John Bolland, one of the greatest of their company. They undertook the immense task of collecting and editing the materials for the history of the Christian saints, called the *Acta Sanctorum*.   MJM

BOLOGNA, CONCORDAT OF (1516), agreement between King Francis I of France and Pope Leo X, which regulated the affairs of the French Church. The old system of electoral self-government for bishoprics, abbeys, and priories, confirmed by the Pragmatic Sanction of Bourges (1438), was abolished and the principle of royal nomination and papal appointment was substituted. In addition the pope's claim to exact money from the holders of benefices in France in the form of annates was accepted, though it had been denied in the Pragmatic Sanction. After 1516, Francis I controlled some hundred archbishoprics and bishoprics and about 500 abbeys. Henceforth the king's nomination would be much more important than the pope's confirmation, though the latter was not entirely discounted. Thus the concordat confirmed the king's authority over the French Church. It remained in force until the end of the *ancien régime*, despite the opposition of clerics and lawyers, who continued to demand the restoration of the Pragmatic Sanction on the grounds that it enshrined the traditional liberties of the French Church.

BOLOGNA, UNIVERSITY OF, perhaps the oldest university of western Europe, antedating that of Paris by half a century. It existed before 1100, was granted privileges by Frederick Barbarossa in 1158, and papal incorporation in 1219. Bologna was the chief centre of legal study in Europe. In the 13th cent. it was also famous as a school of medicine. Bologna was a student university, *ie*, one in which the student organizations elected the rector and chose the masters. This greatly influenced the organization of other universities, especially in Italy, Germany, and Scotland.

BOLOTNIKOV, IVAN (1584–1613), peasant leader who led a revolt in southern Russia during the Time of Troubles. Taking advantage of the confused political situation, he defeated the forces of Tsar Vasili Shuisky and made a victorious march on Moscow. He attracted to his banner the dispossessed, the poor, and the serfs and waged war increasingly on the rich and the privileged. Consequently, he was deserted by powerful elements of the gentry class, whose interests he no longer represented, and was defeated and killed by the tsar's troops (1607).

BOLSHEVIKS, the left wing of the Russian Social Democratic Labour Party, led by Lenin, which seized power in Russia (Nov. 1917). The name, meaning 'majority men', as distinct from the Mensheviks (or 'minority men'), followed from the division in the party which took place at the second congress, in London (1903), when the withdrawal of the delegates from the Bund gave Lenin a majority. The issue on which the congress divided concerned the direction and organization of the party, which it was the task of the congress to define in statutes and membership rules. In his pamphlet, 'What Is To Be Done' (1903), Lenin had already expounded his belief that the party should be a tightly disciplined party of professional revolutionaries, leading the working class from outside and not relying on 'spontaneity'. In spite of the temporary advantage which he gained at the congress, the Bolsheviks, modelled on Lenin's precepts, remained a minority faction within the Russian Social Democratic Labour Party. They played a relatively minor role in the revolution of 1905, since Lenin was in exile, and Trotsky (who had initially sided with the Mensheviks) was in Petrograd. In 1912 they formed a separate party of their own. Increasingly they became a party of revolutionary action, while the Mensheviks continued to believe that a bourgeois democratic revolution must precede any attempt by the Social Democrats to take power.

Lenin's disciplined party organization was suited to the

circumstances of 1917. Following his return (April) to Russia, the Bolsheviks, with the support of the Petrograd Soviet and the Red Guards (organized by Trotsky, who had now joined Lenin), seized power against Menshevik opposition. Consolidating their power after the revolution, they emerged in the 1920s as the sole party in the Soviet Union. In 1918 they changed their name to Communist Party (Bolsheviks); in 1952 the word Bolshevik was dropped.

L. Schapiro, *The Communist Party of the Soviet Union* (London, 1960).
J. Keep, *The Rise of Social Democracy in Russia* (London, 1963).   BJW

BOLSHEVIK REVOLUTION IN CENTRAL ASIA. Owing to difficulties of communications and peculiar local conditions, the Bolshevik revolution in Central Asia took a different form from elsewhere. Russian soldiers and railway workers, organized as the Tashkent Soviet, seized power (Sept. 1917) and held it against counter-revolutionary movements in Transcaspia (which received some British help, 1918–19) and in Tashkent (Osipov Mutiny, 1919). Official Bolshevik policy notwithstanding, the Tashkent Soviet was hostile to Muslim aspirations for independence and suppressed such movements in Kokand and Turkmenia. With help from European Russia, the Tashkent Bolsheviks procured revolution in Bokhara and Khiva (1920), suppressed the Basmachis (1922), and brought about the incorporation of Central Asia into the USSR.

BOLTON, CHARLES PAULET, 3rd Duke of (1685–1754), British Whig politician who was lord chamberlain in 1715, lord lieutenant of Ireland (1717–20) and governor of the Isle of Wight. During the South Sea Bubble crisis he lost a fortune. He joined the opposition to Walpole over the Excise Bill (1733) and though a member of the Lords, used his political influence in the Commons to ensure the bill's defeat.

BOMBAY, capital of the modern Indian, Marathi-speaking state of Maharashtra, and the most populous Indian city (pop. of greater Bombay exceeds 4 million). Since 1818 it has been the principal port and industrial centre of western India. Bombay was an island until it became joined in the 19th cent. to the larger island of Salsette by a causeway and irrigation works. It is notable for its fine natural harbour, its cosmopolitan character, and especially for the enterprising Parsi community. Bombay island was first settled by Raja Bhima of Mahim (c. 1294), as a result of Muslim attacks on the mainland. Muslims from Gujarat conquered it (1348) and their ruler ceded it to the Portuguese (1534), who built churches and allotted the land to religious orders, but their intolerance hindered its growth as a rival port to Surat. Ceded to Charles II of England in 1661 as part of the dowry of his queen, Catherine of Braganza, Bombay was the first independent British territory in India. It then had about 10,000 inhabitants. In 1668 it was transferred to the East India Co., but its real founder was Gerald Aungier (1669–77), who attracted settlers and trade and left Bombay with a population of 50,000. It then relapsed, but after a dockyard was established (1736) by the Parsi Lowji, it enjoyed modest prosperity, limited however by Portuguese hostility in Salsette and Maratha control of the mainland. In the late 18th cent. Bombay was much concerned with Maratha politics at Poona, which led on the one hand to the capitulation of Wadgaon, and on the other to profitable acquisitions in Gujarat. Bombay also controlled the spice stations on the Malabar coast.

The annexation of the peshwa's dominions (1818) gave Bombay for the first time a large hinterland, settled with great skill by Mountstuart Elphinstone. It provided an outlet for cotton as well as an intake for European goods, especially after 1853 with the construction of railways. The American Civil War (1861–5) boosted the economic life of Bombay by stimulating cotton exports. In spite of a post-war slump, the £81 million extra wartime profit gave Bombay a new life through engineering and reclamation schemes and the beginning of a machine-cotton industry. From 1880 the number of cotton mills increased to make Bombay the first great centre of an industry which both captured the internal Indian cotton market and extended the Indian cotton trade to East Africa, the Middle East and South-East Asia.

The Bombay Presidency included Sind from 1843 until it became a separate province (1936). After independence it continued as before for some years. Now Gujarat has been separated from it and the boundaries of the remainder redrawn to make the state Maharashtra.

Firoz Malabari, *Bombay in the Making* (London, 1910).
                                                                                                                                         TGPS

BONAPARTE, JEROME (1784–1860), youngest brother of Napoleon I and King of Westphalia. His early years were spent in the navy and in America, but in 1807 his marriage to an American was annulled by Napoleon, who required his services. He proved an undistinguished ruler (1807–14). He lived in exile in Italy until Napoleon III made him president of the Senate.

BONAPARTE, JOSEPH (1768–1844), Napoleon's elder brother and King of Naples (*reg.* 1806–8) and of Spain (*reg.* 1808–13). He owed his position to his brother and in the last resort was dependent on him. As King of Naples he showed administrative ability, carrying out social and political reform on similar lines to those in France, although his efforts were nullified by local brigandage and Napoleon's military exactions. In Spain he never had the chance to rule. The country was in revolt before he arrived and his position depended entirely on the fortunes of the French army. When the French were driven from Spain (1813) he abdicated, never having had his brother's confidence throughout his reign.

BONAPARTE, LOUIS (1778–1846), King of Holland (*reg.* 1806–10) and a younger brother of Napoleon I who fought in the Napoleonic War. Rather than identify himself with the Continental blockade, and cause distress to his subjects, he abdicated. He married Napoleon's stepdaughter, Hortense de Beauharnais, their younger son becoming the Emperor Napoleon III.

BONAVENTURE, Saint (*c.* 1220–74), an Italian who became a Franciscan while a student in Paris (*c.* 1234). There he became a friend of Thomas Aquinas. He was elected superior general of his order (1257) and gave it a revised and definitive set of constitutions. He was created cardinal (1273) and died while attending the Council of Lyon. Bonaventure is to the Franciscans what Aquinas is to the Dominicans; he is the 'seraphic doctor' as Aquinas is the 'angelic doctor'. One of the greatest medieval mystics, he was founder of the Franciscan school of theologians and his place in the history of the Franciscans is second only to that of St Francis.

BONCERF, PIERRE-FRANÇOIS (1745–1811), French writer on agricultural economics. His *Les inconvenients des droits feodaux* (1774) proposed the commutation of feudal dues.

BOND, THOMAS (1712–84). American physician who was one of the founders of the Pennsylvania Hospital (1752) in Philadelphia. His lectures at the hospital inaugurated a new method in medical education. He was one of the original founders of Pennsylvania University Medical School, and of the American Philosophical Society (1768).

BOND, THE, unilateral declaration of 1844 by nine chiefs of Fante, Denkyira, and Assin in the southern Gold Coast (Ghana), by which they gave certain civil rights to the British.

BOND OF ASSOCIATION (1584), in England, to protect the life of Elizabeth I after the Somerville and Throckmorton plots and the alarm caused by the assassination of William of Orange (1584). Thousands of signatories pledged themselves to demand the death of any person who might profit from further conspiracies against Elizabeth I. The implications of this led to the execution of Mary Queen of Scots (1587) after the Babington plot.

BONDFIELD, MARGARET GRACE (1873–1953), the first woman to enter the British cabinet and to be sworn as a privy councillor. Miss Bondfield had a long career as a trade unionist. She was assistant secretary of the Shop Assistants' Union (1898–1908), a national officer of the General and Municipal Workers' Union (1908–38) and in 1923 was the first woman to be elected chairman of the General Council of the Trades Union Congress. She was a Labour MP (1923–4, 1926–31). In 1924 she was parliamentary secretary to the minister of labour and was minister of labour (1929–31). Miss Bondfield opposed the General Strike and in 1927 supported the lowering of unemployed insurance benefits. Her policy in office was attacked by the left of the party. She supported Ramsay MacDonald in 1931, and thus ruined her political future.

BONGAJA (BONGGAYA) TREATY (18 Nov. 1667), between the Dutch East India Co. and various chiefs of South Celebes. The treaty stipulated a Dutch trade monopoly, the expulsion of the Portuguese and English from Makassar, and the fragmentation of the former Makassar kingdom into a number of small states accepting Dutch suzerainty. It was in force from the final defeat of Makassar (1669) until 1905.

BONHAM, FRANCIS ROBERT (1775–1853), British Conservative Party agent during the whole period of Peel's leadership. He was the central figure in the electoral organization of the party after its debacle between 1830 and 1832. The substantial Conservative gains in the general elections of 1835 and 1837 were usually credited in part to his superior party organization.

BONIFACE VIII (c. 1235–1303), Pope (reg. 1294–1303). Under Boniface the papacy was embroiled in political affairs. His deepest entanglement, which led to his ruin, was with Philip IV, the Fair, of France. England and France were at war and both monarchs applied pressure on the Church to obtain increased taxes from it. Boniface issued the bull *Clericis Laicos* (1296) forbidding such taxation, but he was unable to prevail against the two strongest monarchs in Europe and the bull *Etsi de Statu* (1297) virtually annulled *Clericis Laicos*. The quarrel with France broke out again in 1301 and in 1303 Boniface issued the most famous of all bulls, *Unam Sanctam*, which asserted papal supremacy over temporal princes. Philip's reply was a campaign of vilification against Boniface and the dispatch of Guillaume de Nogaret to Italy to forestall a possible excommunication. On 7 Sept. 1303 Nogaret broke into the papal palace at Anagni and seized Boniface. Although he was forced to release him after three days, the 'outrage of Anagni' caused the physical and mental collapse of Boniface, who died a month later. Boniface was a great lawyer. The sixth book (the *Sext*) which he added to the *Corpus Juris Canonici* is a landmark in the development of Canon Law.

BONIFACE, Saint (680–754), whose native English name was Winfrid, was educated at Exeter. In 719 he received from Pope Gregory II a commission to preach the gospel to all the tribes in Germany. His considerable success in Hesse and Thuringia led Pope Gregory III to appoint him Abp of Germany in 732 and papal legate in 739. He directed reform of the Frankish Church in the 740s and played a part in the consecration as king of Pepin, first of the Carolingian rulers of Gaul. Boniface was martyred among the Frisians in 754. His vigorous letters still survive. He was in close touch with the Church in England and he inspired a generation of Anglo-

Saxon missionaries, who continued his work in Germany in the second half of the 8th cent.

BONIFACIO, ANDRES (1863–97), often referred to as the Father of the Philippine Revolution, was born in Tondo, then a comparatively prosperous suburb of Manila, where his parents lived in the slums. He had only a brief formal education, but read Western books and is said to have been greatly influenced by the French Revolution. Reforms demanded by Philippine intellectuals, such as the right of the country to be represented at the Spanish Cortes as a Spanish province, failed to materialize, so Bonifacio and his followers, who believed that the ills of Philippine society could be corrected only by separation from the mother country, organized a secret association (1894) known as the *Kataastaasang Kagalanggalangang Katipunan nang manga Anak nang Bayan*, or *Katipunan* ('Most High and Most Revered Association of the Sons of the Nation'). In Aug. 1896 its members symbolically ended their allegiance to Spain by tearing up their *cedula* certificates at Balintawak, soon after the betrayal of the *Katipunan* to the Spanish authorities by one of its members. Bonifacio might have continued at the helm of the revolutionary movement but was eclipsed by Emilio F. Aguinaldo, who had defeated Spanish military forces during the first phase of the revolution. A split within the revolutionary organization developed and attempts to reunify the movement at the Tejeros Convention (1897) failed. This failure led to the execution of Bonifacio and his brother, Procopio, by their fellow revolutionaries.

Teodoro A. Agoncillo, *The Revolt of the Masses: the story of Bonifacio and the Katipunan* (Quezon City, 1965). JMSa

BONNEFOUS, ÉDOUARD (1907–), French politician and a leading figure of the Centre. After activity in the Resistance, Bonnefous entered parliament in 1946, sitting for the small UDSR Party. He was a minister several times under the Fourth Republic, and entered the Senate in 1959.

BONNER, EDMUND (1500–69), bishop of London (1540–59). He approved of the early stages of the repudiation of papal authority in England, but his continued belief in transubstantiation kept him a Catholic in doctrinal issues. Originally one of Wolsey's chaplains, he was employed by Henry VIII on diplomatic business, but under Edward VI he was deprived and imprisoned for rejecting the royal injunctions and refusing to enforce the new prayer book. He was restored by Mary and was active in the religious persecutions of her reign, but he was again deprived under Elizabeth I and died in prison.

BONNET, GEORGES (1889–), French foreign minister at the time of the Munich agreement (1938), and one of its authors. Bonnet entered parliament as a Radical in 1924, and held numerous ministerial posts. As minister of finance, he created the National Lottery (1933). He represented France at various international conferences, and was ambassador at Washington (1936–7). He was foreign minister from 1938 until the outbreak of war. Bonnet's policy of postponing or preventing war by 'appeasement' was undoubtedly widely supported at the time, but it has been harshly judged since. The Munich agreement in particular has been condemned as a shameful episode in view of France's obligations to Czechoslovakia.

Bonnet did not support the Vichy regime, and in 1943 fled from France to escape arrest. After the war, he returned to parliament (1956–68), but not to office.

BONNEVAL, CLAUDE ALEXANDRE, Comte de (1675–1747), renegade French nobleman who lived in Turkey, where he was known as Bonneval Pasha. He influenced Turkish foreign policy, encouraging its strong pro-French bias, and in the 1730s made limited improvements in the Turkish army.

BONNY (IBANI), commercial, administrative, and missionary centre in south-eastern Nigeria (now Rivers State). Earlier, it was a city-state under the Pepple (Perekule) dynasty and, during the 19th cent., a principal commercial port for slaves and palm-oil. Its commercial importance was lost to Port Harcourt after 1913, but partially recovered, from 1958, as a Shell-BP oil terminal.

BONO, EMILIO DE (1866–1944), Italian general, monarchist, and organizer of the fascist 'March on Rome' (1922). He was chief of police (1922–4), but was dismissed after being implicated in Matteotti's murder, and was first head of the militia (1923–4). He commanded the opening campaign in Ethiopia (1935). De Bono was executed for voting against Mussolini in July 1943.

BONOMI, IVANOE (1873–1952), Italy's first socialist prime minister. Having been deputy since 1909, he was expelled from the Socialist Party at the 1912 congress for advocating reformist socialist policies, and helped to form the small but influential Reformist socialist party. As a supporter of war intervention, he served in the Boselli cabinet (1916–17). While minister of war (1920–1) and prime minister (June 1921–Feb. 1922) he tried unsuccessfully to curb fascist violence. He lost his seat in the 1924 election.

In 1942 he became co-ordinator of anti-fascist resistance. On becoming head of the central Committee for National Liberation, he critized Badoglio's government for indecisiveness, but when prime minister himself (June 1944–June 1945) he similarly suffered from the contradictory demands of allied officials, military, anti-fascist party, and partisan leaders. He successfully postponed major constitutional decisions until the war was over. He was an unsuccessful candidate for the presidency of the republic, but served as president of the Senate (1948–52).

BONUS ARMY, in US, 17,000 unemployed First World War veterans, led by William Waters, who marched on Washington, DC (May–July 1932), and camped on Anacostia Field. They lobbied Congress unsuccessfully for immediate payment of their veterans' bonuses, but were dispersed by troops under Gen. MacArthur. This episode helped to discredit the Hoover administration.

BONYTHON, SIR JOHN LANGDON (1848–1939), editor and sole proprietor from 1893 of the South Australian newspaper the *Advertiser*, the staff of which he had joined in 1864. Bonython, who was born in London, migrated with his parents to Adelaide, where he was educated. He was a SA member of the Commonwealth House of Representatives (1901–6) and gave benefactions to Adelaide University and to the South Australian School of Mines and Industry, for the founding of which he was largely responsible.

BOOK OF COMMON PRAYER, liturgy of the Church of England, first issued in 1549 to impose a uniform order of service in place of older service-books like the Sarum Use. It was written by Abp Cranmer and was Lutheran in tendency, especially in replacing Latin by the vernacular. A second book (1552) was more decisively influenced by Protestant thought and changed the Eucharist into a commemorative sacrament. Elizabeth's Prayer Book (1559), which followed the Marian reaction, sought a middle path between the rival dogmas, and there were few changes in a further revision (1662) which established the liturgy that remained substantially in use for the following centuries. All these books were imposed on the Church and people by direct state action and were accompanied by Uniformity Acts to compel their use. By 1970 certain revisions had been proposed and introduced into Anglican dioceses.

BOOK OF THE DEAD. Ancient Egyptian lists of information believed to be necessary for the after-world, written on papyrus or leather, and buried in the tombs of wealthy people.

BOOLE, GEORGE (1815–64), English mathematician and logician, wrote *The Laws of Thought* (1854), in which he treated the basic logic arguments required for any process of logical deduction. A systematic process for treating a particular argument was founded, known as Boolean Algebra, which is widely used (1970) in analysing and simplifying electronic digital logic circuits.

BOONE, DANIEL (1734–1820), American frontiersman and legendary hero. The Boone myth, enlarged by Byron in *Don Juan* and still popular, distorted his real, but limited, achievements. Although, contrary to myth, he did not discover Kentucky, he largely pioneered its settlement, arriving at what became Boonesborough in 1775. A great Indian fighter, he helped to defend it against Indian attacks. Although virtually illiterate, he was well known for his practical common sense, held a number of public offices in KY, and was elected to the state legislature (1783). After a series of law suits beginning in 1785, which lost him his land holdings in KY, he moved to WV and later to MO.

BOONEN, JACOB (1573–1655), archbishop of Mechlin (1621–55), who, with the Duke of Aerschot, sought the help of the estates general of the northern provinces in an unsuccessful attempt to establish an independent south Netherland republic (1632).

BOOTH, CHARLES (1840–1916), British shipowner, statistician, and sociologist, whose social survey, *Life and Labour in London* (17 vols, 1891–1903), was conducted at his own expense, and revealed the extent of London's poverty despite all that had been attempted in the 19th cent. It profoundly influenced later British and American social surveys, but English academic sociology did not follow Booth's empirical lead. Many of his approaches were later adopted by the Chicago school of urban sociologists.

BOOTH, JOHN WILKES (1838–65), American actor, who assassinated Abraham Lincoln (14 April 1865) in Ford's Theatre, Washington, five days after Lee's surrender at Appomattox. He was himself killed by his pursuers two weeks later. The theory that Booth's deed was part of a wider conspiracy has never been substantiated.

BOOTH, JOSEPH (1851–1932), British Christian missionary. He influenced African nationalists in central and southern Africa (1892–c. 1915), especially John Chilembwe, the Malawi insurrectionist.

BOOTH, WILLIAM (1829–1912), British evangelist and founder of the Salvation Army. His zeal for outdoor evangelism took him out of ordinary denominational work and into independent evangelism in London. It was this that led to his founding of the Army (1878). Booth's grim theology and puritanism did not prevent him from advocating, in his *In Darkest England and the Way Out* (1890), home- and overseas-colonization as remedies for poverty. Edward VII encouraged Booth's work.

BOOTHBY, ROBERT JOHN GRAHAM, Life Baron (1900–), British Conservative MP for East Aberdeenshire (1924–58). In the 1920s he advocated greater state intervention in economic affairs; in the 1930s he opposed appeasement, voting against Chamberlain (1940). He was parliamentary secretary to the ministry of food (1940–1), and prominent in the European movement after 1945. Boothby opposed the Suez expedition, and advocated reform of the law on homosexuality.

BOOTLEGGING. American term to describe the sale of illicit liquor, especially associated with the prohibition era (1919–33). The expression probably derived from the earlier practice of Indian traders who smuggled illicit bottles of alcohol in their boots. During prohibition, bootlegging developed into an organized and profitable business. It provided the main source of income for gangs such as that of Al Capone, which terrorized Chicago in the 1920s.

BORAH, WILLIAM EDGAR (1865–1940), US politician and lawyer. During his long career as a Republican senator from Idaho (1907–40), he was especially influential and well known in the area of foreign affairs. He was chairman of the Senate committee on foreign relations (1924–33), but declined the secretaryship of state in Hoover's administration (1929). Borah, considered a maverick by many, was in some ways a typical western progressive and nationalist. He supported social and economic reform, but feared the over-extension of federal powers. He was one of the strongest opponents of American entry into the League of Nations and the World Court (1919), one of the prime movers behind the Washington disarmament conference (1921–2), and an early, unfashionable champion of diplomatic recognition of the USSR, Philippine independence, and American non-interference in South American affairs. As a bitter opponent of repeal of the Neutrality Act (1939), he consistently and adamantly resisted efforts to use economic or military sanctions as instruments of foreign policy.

BORDEAUX. One of the finest natural French harbours on the Atlantic seaboard. A Roman provincial capital, it became the capital of the medieval duchy of Aquitaine and from 1154 to 1453 was ruled by the kings of England. Its great medieval prosperity rested on its huge exports of Gascon wine.

BORDEN, SIR ROBERT LAIRD (1854–1937), Canadian prime minister, born in Grand Pré, NS. He was elected to parliament in 1896 and in 1901 chosen as leader of the Conservative Party. Having devised a new platform and strengthened the party, he led it to victory (1911). Under his premiership (1911–20) the government established the Canadian National Railways, instituted the income tax, expanded industrialization, and transformed Canada into a creditor nation. During the First World War he introduced conscription (1917) and enlarged the naval forces. As a result of his insistence upon an independent voice for his country in the conduct of the war, Canada secured a place in the Imperial War Cabinet, separate representation at the Peace Conference, became a founding member of the League of Nations, and thus gained an international role in world affairs. Borden retired from active political life in 1920, but represented Canada at the Washington disarmament conference (1921–2) and acted for Great Britain in arbitration with Peru (1922).

BORDER STATES, term commonly used to describe those US slave states bordering on the north before the Civil War. Their geographic position, economic ties with the north, and the relative decline of slavery within their boundaries, divided their loyalties between the Union and the Confederacy. Their spokesmen were prominent in attempts to find a compromise between North and South (1860–1), and provided the main support for the Crittenden Compromise. When compromise failed, MO, MD, and DE remained within the Union, as did KY after trying for a time to remain neutral; VA joined the Confederacy, and her western portion was separated and admitted to the Union as the free state of West Virginia (1863). All the border states contributed large numbers of soldiers to the Confederacy. In political, social, and economic terms the border states still mark a transition zone between northern and southern attitudes.

BORELLI, GIOVANNI ALFONSO (1608–79), Italian mathematician and friend of Galileo, who contributed to the evolution of the modern theory of gravitation. He applied his knowledge of mathematics and mechanics to the study of muscular movement in *On the Motion of Animals* (1681).

BORGES, JORGE LUIS (1899–), Argentine poet, essayist, thinker, and a leader of contemporary Latin American literature.

BORGU, area of north Dahomey inhabited by the Bariba people, whose territory extends eastwards to the Niger river. The region, which lay on the important Kano–Gonja trade route, was attacked by Songhay several times in the 16th cent., but never subdued.

BORIS I OF BULGARIA (d. 907), Khan of Bulgaria since 852. He was responsible for converting it in 865 to Christianity according to the eastern rite. This made him the supreme ruler over all his subjects, Slav and Bulgar (Hunnish) alike. The Bulgar military aristocracy, who regarded the khan as but a superior noble, rose in revolt against Christianity and was partly exterminated. Boris relied on the Slavs, who formed the majority of his subjects and for whom a special Slavonic church liturgy was devised. In 889 he abdicated and retired to a monastery, but this encouraged an aristocratic and pagan reaction which he crushed and then abdicated again, this time leaving Christianity permanently established.

BORIS III (1894–1943), King of Bulgaria (*reg.* 1918–43). The coup carried out by Zveno and the Military League on 19 May 1934 anticipated Boris's own plans to assume control of the government. However, by April 1935 Boris had successfully undermined the new regime and reasserted his authority. He ruled as royal dictator until his death. Boris was drawn to the Axis, but limited Bulgaria's commitment and refused to participate in the Russian campaign despite severe pressure. After the battle of Stalingrad he made overtures to the Allies and died in mysterious circumstances following a meeting with Hitler.

BORMANN, MARTIN (1900–), German politician and member of the Nazi hierarchy, who achieved prominence during the course of the Second World War. In 1941 he succeeded Hess as deputy leader of the Nazi Party, and head of the party chancery. He consolidated his position in 1942 by decreeing that he alone should handle the party's share in state legislation and the appointment of party members within state organizations. As far as possible he obstructed contact between party offices and the supreme Reich offices. His chief agents were the *Gauleiters*, who by 1943 controlled the whole civilian war effort. His chief rival was the SS chief, Himmler, who became (1943) minister of the interior. Himmler was, however, unable to undermine Bormann's position, which became stronger in April 1943, when he was officially recognized as Hitler's personal secretary.

Bormann was present in Hitler's bunker during his last days. He was named as executor of Hitler's personal will, and in his political will and testament was appointed party minister, Goebbels being named as chancellor. Bormann remained obsessed with his rivalry with Himmler and dispatched missions to murder him and Goering. He witnessed both the marriage and funeral of Hitler and Eva Braun in April 1945. He was said by some witnesses to have been killed in May 1945 in the mass attempt at escape from the bunkers around the Chancellery, but doubt has always surrounded accounts of his death. Of all the missing Nazi personalities, Bormann was still, in the 1960s, the most frequently reported to be alive and in South America.   ASJ

BORNEO COMPANY, the sole European company allowed by the ruling Brooke family to trade in Sarawak, from its foundation in 1856 until the 1920s. Its biggest profits, however, were made in Malaya, Siam, and Java.

BORNHOLM, Danish island in the Baltic Sea, 40 kms from Scania. It was captured by the Swedes in 1645 and restored the same year, but was ceded to Sweden in the Dano-Swedish peace treaty of 1658. The population rebelled, and the island was finally returned to the Danish Crown in exchange for property in Scania (1660).

BORNHÖVED, BATTLE OF (1227), defeat of King Waldemar II of Denmark at the hands of an alliance of north German princes and the Hanseatic cities Lübeck, Hamburg, and Bremen. It resulted in the loss of Denmark's German possessions, ended the dreams of a Danish Baltic empire, and opened the Baltic to German exploitation by the Hanseatic League.

BORNU, former state, now (1970) a province of northern Nigeria, stretching from the shores of Lake Chad to the plains of Hausaland and inhabited by a mainly sedentary population, speaking dialects of Kanuri, and by the former tributary peoples, such as the Bedde, Bolewa, and Babur, who speak languages of the Chadic group. In addition, there are groups of nomadic Fulbe, Shuwa Arabs, and Tubu. It was partitioned by the colonial powers and is (1970) divided between the states of Nigeria, Niger, and Cameroon.

BOROBUDUR (also spelt Barabudur), name, the meaning of which is uncertain, of one of the greatest Buddhist monuments, in Central Java, Indonesia, about 20 miles (32 kms) north-west of Jogdjakarta. It was probably built in the 1st half of the 9th cent. by order of the Shailendra King Samaratungga (c. 792–824, or later). The monument covers a small natural hill and consists of a huge pyramid-like basis, topped with three round terraces and crowned with a terminal *stupa* (Buddhist reliquary). The basis comprises a broad platform for circumambulation and four closed galleries. These are decorated with an enormous number of carved relief panels on either side, depicting basic Buddhist texts, and crowned with niches with meditating Buddha images. The round terraces each have a circle of perforated *stupa*s also containing seated Buddhas. The terminal *stupa* no doubt once contained a deposit which has, however, vanished.

Although the precise meaning of most constituent parts has gradually been ascertained, there is still great uncertainty about the meaning of the monument as a whole. It has been interpreted as basically a *stupa*, ie, a monument to enshrine relics of Lord Buddha or his disciples, but this fails to explain the relative preponderance of the basis. Others have thought of a combination of a *stupa* and a *prasada* (storied or terraced construction), of a monument built primarily to glorify the kings of the Shailendra dynasty identified with bodhisattvas at different stages of perfection, or of a huge *mandala* to assist the pious worshippers to concentrate their minds upon the transcendental truth. Whatever the explanation, the Borobudur is a closed world in which the pilgrim, finding his way along the galleries, gradually feels himself detached from the impermanence and suffering of this world. For the historian the monument is of particular significance for the many scenes depicting aspects of daily life in ancient Java, for house types, ships, dress, and ornaments.

N. J. Krom, *Barabudur, Archaeological Description*, 2 vols (The Hague, 1927).   JGdeC

BORODIN, MIKHAIL MARKOWICK (1884–1953), Soviet revolutionary and Comintern activist, best known for his work in China (1923–7). Borodin (born Grusenberg) was educated in the US, and did not return to Russia until 1917. His acquaintance with foreign countries led to his assignment to Comintern work. He carried out missions in Turkey, Mexico, Spain, and Scotland, before being sent to Canton in south China (1923), as the chief of a group of Soviet advisers who were to supervise the modernization and reorganization of the Kuomintang Party and army. This group came to China as a result of the Sun–Joffe Agreement (1923), which opened the way for Soviet–Kuomintang co-operation. Under the guidance of Borodin and other civilian advisers, the Kuomintang Party was remoulded on Leninist lines and took on an autocratic, centralized structure which it still retains, though it has been bitterly anti-communist since 1927. Military advisers, led by General Bluecher (known in China as Galin), went to the military academy at Whampoa, and helped to train the nucleus of a modern army. All aspects of Kuomintang policy were tightened up, and plans were laid for expansion away from the base in Canton. For some time, the Soviet advisers exercised great influence over the Kuomintang, which took on a strong left-wing flavour, but after Chiang Kai-shek emerged as the Kuomintang's strong man (1926), their influence waned. Their influence over the Chinese Communist Party, then in alliance with the Kuomintang, was still strong, but when policy towards China became a key issue in the Stalin–Trotsky struggle in Moscow, they frequently found instructions being issued over their heads from Moscow. A series of misguided orders from Stalin played the Chinese Communists into Chiang Kai-shek's hands when he turned against them (April 1927). Borodin was forced to leave China soon afterwards, and returned to Moscow in disgrace. The last advisers to leave China fled after the Canton Commune (Dec. 1927) had collapsed, after many of their comrades in Canton had been murdered.

BORODINO, BATTLE OF (7 Sept. 1812), fought 112 kms west of Moscow. It was Napoleon's last opportunity, which he lost, to surround and defeat the Russians under Kutuzov.

BOROMMAKOT (reg. 1733–58), King of Siam. His reign was a period of relative peace following a long period of disputed successions and internecine warfare, and preceding the long wars which brought an end to the kingdom of Ayudhya. As such, Borommakot's reign has always been looked back upon as a 'golden age' of classical Thai civilization. It was, however, a period of weakness and inattention to provincial administration, during which the nobles at court stood unchallenged in their ministries and grew rigid and complacent.

BOROMMATRAILOKANAT (reg. 1448–88), King of Siam, sometimes called Trailok. A great legislator, Trailok was primarily responsible for systematizing and formalizing Siam's administrative and social institutions. He divided the administration on functional lines, creating a military division and a civil division, the latter consisting of separate departments (krom) with responsibilites for local government, land and agricultural affairs, finance, and justice, and the royal household. His 'Palatine Law' (1468) made clearer the lines of succession to the throne; and the cumulative effect of his laws was to elaborate in all-encompassing fashion the structure of Thai society.

BORROMEO, CHARLES, Saint (1538–84), cardinal-archbishop of Milan (1560–84). A great pastoral bishop, personally caring for the plague-stricken populace (1567–8), and responsible for energetic diocesan reforms. He attacked the problem of clerical immorality and established three seminaries in Milan. He also concerned himself with the education of the laity and founded the Confraternity of Christian Doctrine, which provided 40,000 pupils with 3000 teachers in 740 schools. His reforms met with opposition, however, from vested interests. He fell foul of the religious order of the Humiliati and of the lax clergy whom he rigorously disciplined, and also of the Duke of Albuquerque, governor of Milan, who resented his interference in civil matters.

BOSCAWEN, EDWARD (1711–61), British admiral, who commanded a fleet sent to the East Indies in 1747. After passing the French island of Mauritius, he failed in an attempt to take Pondicherry, the capital of the French East India Co. He held various other commands, and became a Lord of Admiralty.

BOSCH, JOHANNES VAN DEN (1780–1844), governor-general of the Dutch East Indies (1830–3), initiator of the Culture System. He was born in Herwijnen, Netherlands. During his administration, the powers of the governor-general were expanded vis-à-vis those of the Council of the Indies (Raad van Indie). Upon his return to the Netherlands he was made minister of the colonies (1834), a post he held until 1839.

BOSCH, JUAN (1909–), Dominican intellectual and novelist, president of the Dominican Republic (Feb.–Sept. 1963). Bosch has spent much of his life in exile from the dictatorial regime of Trujillo, and helped to found the Dominican Revolutionary Party (PRD), a social democratic group. After Trujillo's assassination (1961) Bosch returned to the Dominican Republic and campaigned for the presidency, which he won in 1962. His tenure of office was brief. The army and former associates of Trujillo combined with the anti-communist middle class to overthrow him and he returned to exile in Puerto Rico. Attempts to restore Bosch to power brought about civil war in 1965. After an unsolicited intervention by the US and mediation by the OAS, new elections were called in 1966. Bosch again ran for president, but did little campaigning. He claimed that his life was in danger. He was defeated by a former Trujillo official, Joaquín Balaguer, and left the country once more. He has argued since that the US played a part in his party's defeats, and that the US armed forces are responsible for a new kind of imperialism, defined as Pentagonism.

BOSE, ANANDA MOHAN (1847–1906), Indian politician, educationist, and religious reformer, educated at the Presidency College, Calcutta, and Cambridge University, of which he was the first Indian wrangler. He was called to the bar in 1874. He drafted the constitution of the *Sadharan Brahma Samai* (1878), which broke away from the *Brahma Samaj*, and he worked with Surendranath Banerjea to interest the young men of Bengal in political affairs. He founded and was the first president of the Students Association of Calcutta, and was also secretary of the Indian Association. He helped to convene the first session of the Indian National Conference (1883), and presided over its 14th session (Madras, 1898). He opposed the Partition of Bengal and played an important part in the *swadeshi* movement. The Ananda Mohan College at Mymensingh bears witness to his work as an educationist.

BOSE, SIR JAGDISH CHANDRA (1858–1937), Indian physicist and plant physiologist, professor of physical sciences at Calcutta (1885–1915), director of the Bose Research Institute, Calcutta (1917–37), and the first Indian to be made a fellow of the Royal Society. He published a large number of erudite works.

BOSE, SUBHAS CHANDRA (1897–1945), Indian nationalist leader, organizer of the Indian National Army during the Second World War, known as *Netaji*, 'the leader'. Bose passed into the Indian civil service (1920), but did not take up an appointment. He returned instead to Bengal to work under Chittaranjan Das in the non-co-operation movement and the Swaraj Party, managed the Calcutta newspaper, *Forward*, for Das (1922–4), then became chief executive officer of the Calcutta corporation (1924), when Congress captured that valuable political prize. He was placed under detention in Mandalay (1925–7).

After his return, he gained importance in wider Congress circles, joined Nehru in opposition to Congress' avowal of its objective as dominion status for India (1928), and with him formed an Independence League to work for complete independence. He took part in civil disobedience (1930) but became increasingly dissatisfied with Gandhian methods and strategy because he felt that insistence upon non-violence as a determinant of strategy rather than a tactic had inhibited nationalist activity and weakened the Congress. He called for a more sustained and aggressive nationalist party based on a disciplined, revolutionary mass movement, and believed that only in a combination of fascism and communism could the ideological foundations for a truly revolutionary party and state be ensured.

As president of Congress (1938) he established a National Planning Committee to provide a framework for future state planning of economic development, but his views brought him into open conflict with other leaders of the 'high command'. He won election for a second term as president (1939)

against the wishes of Gandhi, and the Gandhians forced him to resign by withdrawing their support from his Working Committee. He then left Congress and formed the Forward Bloc as a new militant nationalist party, but it achieved very little.

When war came he escaped from detention (Jan. 1941) and made his way to Germany, where the government allowed him to establish an Indian National Army from among Indian prisoners of war, and to broadcast to India. In 1943 he was taken by submarine to Singapore, where an Indian Independence League was formed and a new Indian National Army (*Azad Hind Fauj*) was created from among prisoners taken by the Japanese. In Oct. 1943 he proclaimed the formation of a Provisional Indian government with himself at the head. The INA moved into the Burma campaign and reached as far as Kohima in Manipur state before the Japanese retreat forced them to withdraw. Bose, flying to Japan, was killed in a plane crash.

S. C. Bose, *The Indian Struggle, 1920–42* (London, 1964).
S. C. Bose, *Crossroads: Being the works of S. C. Bose, 1938–40* (London, 1962).   PDR

BOSELLI, PAOLO (1838–1932), centre-right Italian deputy (1870–1921), and minister, widely respected as an administrator. A strong advocate of Italy's participation in the war, he formed a broad coalition government in June 1916 which declared war on Germany and resisted Allied proposals for a separate peace with Austria-Hungary (April 1917). But he lacked sufficient force to deal with inflation, food shortages, riots, diminishing military morale, and quarrelling colleagues. The coalition was voted out (25 Oct. 1917) before news of the Caporetto breakthrough arrived.

BOSNIA. A region of modern Yugoslavia between Serbia to the north-east and the Adriatic Sea to the west. During the 6th–7th cents the Slavs settled in Bosnia and the adjacent lands. At various times in the following centuries Bosnia was dependent on the Bulgars, the Byzantines, and the Serbs. The Patarene faith, a modified form of Bogomilism, became established in Bosnia during the 12th–13th cents. Under able princes like Stephen Kotroman (1287–1316), Stephen Kotromanic (1322–53), and Tvrtko I (1353–91), Bosnia extended its domination over Herzegovina, Dalmatia, and Croatia. Tvrtko raised Bosnia to the height of its medieval splendour. After his death internal dissension and also conflict with the Hungarians and the Ottoman Turks contributed to the decline of the Bosnian state. In 1463–4 the Ottomans overran Bosnia, most of the Bogomil nobles became Muslims and served thereafter, during the 15th–17th cents, as the most famous of the border warriors defending the northern frontiers of the Ottoman empire. Austria occupied Bosnia and Herzegovina in 1878 and annexed these territories in 1908. After the First World War (1918) the two provinces became absorbed into Yugoslavia.

BOSNIA-HERZEGOVINA, annexation of (7 Oct. 1908), by Austria-Hungary, produced one of the most dangerous international crises before the outbreak of the First World War. At the Congress of Berlin (1878) the European powers had agreed to Austria's occupation of the two provinces, although they remained formally part of the Ottoman empire. The population of the provinces was Serbo-Croat and after 1903 was becoming increasingly attracted by the Pan-Serb policies of independent Serbia. Austria-Hungary was therefore looking for an opportunity to annex Bosnia-Herzegovina, not only to regularize her position there, but to end all chance of their being united with Serbia. The Austro-Hungarian foreign minister, Aerenthal, intended to annex them at the first opportunity. He was in any case forced to move in July 1908, when a Young Turk revolution in Constantinople inaugurated attempts to reassert Turkish sovereignty in the provinces. Aerenthal hoped to achieve the annexation through a preliminary agreement with Russia, offering Austrian support for Russian policy at the Straits in return. After meeting the Russian foreign minister, Izvolsky, at Buchlau, he went ahead with the annexation unilaterally.

Izvolsky had expected that Aerenthal would first get the consent of the powers to the annexation and to the changes Russia wanted at the Straits. He therefore felt cheated, and with the support of Serbia, France, and Britain called for an international conference to discuss this breach of the treaty of Berlin. The German chancellor, Bülow, was prepared to use the crisis to achieve a diplomatic victory over Russia, who had just made an entente with Britain. Bülow therefore backed Austria-Hungary completely and refused to have a conference. Under the virtual threat of war from Germany, Russia was forced to back down and agree to the annexation (March 1909), having received only lukewarm support from her French ally. Relations between Russia and Germany never recovered from this crisis.

BOSNIAN WAR, 1875, socio-agrarian revolt of Christian peasants against Muslim landlords which developed into a major diplomatic problem through attempts by European powers, especially Russia, to induce the Ottoman government to introduce reforms.

BOSSU, MAXIMILIEN DE HENNIN, Count of (1542–79), member of a Catholic royalist family of Hainaut, who was appointed *stadtholder* of Holland, Zeeland, and Utrecht by Alva (1567), and when commanding the Spanish forces in the Holland campaign (1572–3) was captured on the Zuider Zee (1573). Later (1577), he was appointed commander-in-chief of the army of the states general.

BOSSUET, JACQUES BENIGNE (1627–1704), court preacher, master of French prose, and the leader of the French clergy under Louis XIV. Bossuet was already famous for his sermons when he came to Paris in 1659 at the age of 32. In 1670, when he was Bp of Condom, he was appointed tutor to the Dauphin, for whom he wrote *La Politique Tirée de l'Écriture Sainte*, in which he proclaimed the divine right of kings, a doctrine which became semi-official as a result of Bossuet's close association with the king and the court. As a reward for his 10 years' service to the dauphin's education, he received the bishopric of Meaux in 1681. He approved Louis's decision to repeal the Edict of Nantes in 1685, the final step in the war against Protestantism in France, though his own attitude was one of magnanimity. His unyielding Gallican orthodoxy also led him into controversy with his famous contemporary, Fénelon, who had supported the views of the quietist, Mme de Guyon, views which Bossuet considered heretical (1695–99). Earlier, in 1682, it had led him to draft the four Gallican articles in defence of the king's interpretation of the right of *régale*. He carried on a long correspondence with the German philosopher Leibnitz, beginning in 1678 and only ending in 1702, two years before his death. Bossuet never wavered in his loyalty to the Gallican Church, though he possessed a generosity of spirit which transcended the formal intolerance of his official position.

BOSTON MASSACRE (5 March 1770), event leading up to the American War of Independence. A mob of 60, aroused by the presence of British troops in Boston, threw snowballs at a squad of redcoats on Boston Common. Someone ordered the soldiers to fire on the mob and three men were killed and eight wounded; two more died later. Samuel Adams, denouncing the attack, demanded that Gov. Thomas Hutchinson should withdraw the British regiments from Boston, which he did. Capt. Preston and the British soldiers, who were defended by John Adams and Josiah Quincy, were acquitted of a charge of manslaughter, but two were branded on the hand. Although Boston citizens were partly to blame for the fracas, Samuel Adams, Paul Revere, and others used the incident to foment anti-British feeling and arouse the colonists to take a stand for American independence.

BOSTON POLICE STRIKE (Sept. 1919), in US, by police over their right to affiliate with the American Federation of Labor. Gov. Coolidge's action in calling out the militia gained him the credit for restoring law and order, and gave him the Republican vice-presidential nomination (1920).

BOSTON TEA PARTY (16 Dec. 1773). The Tea Act, passed by the British parliament, in 1773 gave the East India Co. a monopoly on all tea exported to the colonies and raised the tax on tea. American colonists, resentful of the tax and the monopoly, seized shipments of tea. Everywhere in the colonies British tea was boycotted. In Boston, Sons of Liberty dressed as Mohawk Indians, boarded ships in the harbour, broke open 342 chests of tea, and threw them into the sea. The British government, in retaliation, passed the Boston Port Act, which closed the port and ruined its trade, and troops under Gen. Thomas Gage were dispatched to the city. This was one of four legislative measures of a punitive nature against the colonies.

BOSWELL, JAMES (1740–95), Scotsman who moved in London literary circles. His friendship and travels with Dr Samuel Johnson provided material for *Journal of a Tour in the Hebrides* (1785) and *The Life of Samuel Johnson* (1791). Discoveries in the 20th cent. of Boswell's mss have enhanced his place in literature.

BOSWORTH, BATTLE OF (22 Aug. 1485), made Henry Tudor King of England in place of the Yorkist Richard III. Richard's army was inferior to Henry's, partly through the desertion of Thomas, Lord Stanley, Henry's stepfather, and his brother Sir William Stanley. Richard's defeat and death allowed Henry to proclaim himself king and march unopposed to London.

BOTANY BAY, 5 miles (8 kms) south of Sydney, was the scene of James Cook's first landing on Australian soil (1770). Called Sting-ray Harbour in his log, the 'Botany Bay' of his *Journal* recalled the flora collected there by Joseph Banks, who later suggested the site as being suitable for a convict settlement (1788). Though Phillip preferred Port Jackson, the name became synonymous with the destination of transported convicts.

BOTHA, LOUIS (1862–1919), South African prime minister, who was born in Natal and lived in the Transvaal. He was a Boer general during the Anglo-Boer war, and became leader of the Afrikaner party Het Volk, after the war. He was first prime minister of the Transvaal (1907) and first prime minister of the New Union (1910–19).

BOTHMAR, JOHANN CASPAR (1656–1732), Hanoverian envoy to the Hague and London and later minister of George I. He went as envoy to the Hague (1708) during the time of the peace negotiations with Louis XIV, and in 1710 moved to London as envoy, remaining there until the accession of George I. In 1711 Bothmar caused a diplomatic crisis by publishing George Lewis's views on the Tory peace negotiations. Thenceforth Bothmar collaborated closely with the Whigs, informing his master about Jacobite plots. On the arrival of George I (1714), he became a leading Hanoverian minister, overshadowed only by Bernstorff, and exercised great influence over diplomacy, especially in the Baltic, until the Hanoverian ministers were supplanted by British ministers (1719).

BOTHWELL, JAMES HEPBURN, 4th Earl of (Scottish) (*c.* 1535–78), third husband of Mary Queen of Scots, hereditary lord high admiral, and a powerful nobleman who was involved in political intrigues. He was suspected of complicity in the murder (Feb. 1567) of Lord Darnley, the queen's second husband. Three months later he had abducted Mary, divorced his wife, Lady Jane Gordon, and married the queen (May 1567). A month later, Mary having surrendered to the

Scottish nobles at Carberry, Bothwell escaped to Denmark, where he was kept in prison. The marriage contributed to Mary's abdication, flight to England, and 20-year imprisonment (1567–87).

BOTHWELL BRIG, BATTLE OF (22 June 1679), defeat by an army of royalist troops under the Duke of Monmouth of a force of conventiclers at Bothwell Bridge on the Clyde. The rebels were divided between moderates and extreme covenanters, interfering clergy hindering their command. After their defeat they were generously treated by Monmouth.

BOTSWANA (712,000 sq. kms), independent Commonwealth republic in the south-western interior of Africa, and until 1966 a British Protectorate. The Tswana are the principal group in a population of 576,000. A president and a national assembly are elected by adult suffrage.

BOTTA, Marquis de (1688–1745), Austrian ambassador at St Petersburg, who was accused of being involved in a plot to overthrow the Empress Elizabeth by the French faction, who wished to discredit the longstanding friendship between Austria and Russia (1741). De Botta was recalled and his alleged co-conspirators, including the Bestuzhevs, were cruelly punished.

BOTTGER, JOHANN FRIEDRICH (1682–1719), German alchemist and inventor of hard-paste porcelain (1708–9). He was kept a virtual prisoner by the elector of Saxony, Augustus the Strong, under whose patronage he started the Dresden faïence factory in 1708, where he invented the hard red stoneware which bears his name. He also produced white kaolinic porcelain of the Chinese type and in 1709 discovered a glaze for it. In 1710 the elector founded the Meissen factory under Bottger's direction.

BOTTICELLI, SANDRO (ALESSANDRO DEI FILIPPI, known as) (1444–1510), an influential Renaissance painter. He worked at first in the studio of Filippo Lippi and although he developed a highly individual technique he remained close to his master in style. His earlier paintings, commissioned by several members of the Medici family, dealt mainly with mythological and secular subjects, the Primavera, the Birth of Venus, and Mars and Venus, being three of the most famous. In 1481–2, together with other artists, he helped to decorate the Sistine Chapel in the Vatican. In the mid-1490s came a change. He was strongly influenced by Savonarola, lost his Medici patrons, and all secular subjects disappear from his work.

BOTTOMLEY, HORATIO (1860–1933), British journalist and financier, who was involved in spectacular financial scandals. He became a Liberal MP (1906), but resigned his seat in 1912, after the first of numerous bankruptcies. He made and lost two fortunes and enjoyed huge popularity as a jingoistic orator. In 1918 he was again elected an MP, but was expelled (1922) on being convicted of fraud, and imprisoned.

BOUCHER, PIERRE (1622–1717), French-Canadian colonial governor. Indian interpreter and author. While governor of Trois-Rivières (1653–9, 1663–7), he influenced the royal decision to turn New France into a crown colony (1663). He wrote *Histoire véritable et naturelle des mœurs et productions du pays de la Nouvelle-France, vulgairement dite le Canada* (Paris, 1664).

BOUCHETTE, ROBERT ERROL (1863–1912), French-Canadian civil servant and writer, a pioneer of economic independence for French Canada. Among his books are *L'Évolution économique du Canada* (1901) and *L'Indépendance économique du Canada français* (1906).

BOUDICCA (or BOADICEA) (d. AD 62), Queen of the Iceni, who, on the death of her husband, Prasutagus, led the British revolt (AD 60) against Roman brutality and exploitation. Widespread destruction resulted in the east and south-east before Suetonius Paulinus regained control. On her defeat she committed suicide.

BOUDINOT, ELIAS (1803–39), American Indian of the Cherokees and editor of the first Cherokee newspaper. He wrote a book in Cherokee characters and also translated some of the New Testament. He was murdered for supporting the surrender of Cherokee lands to the US government.

BOUFFLERS, LOUIS-FRANÇOIS, (1644–1711), marshal of France. His career included service in Africa (1664), Holland (1672), and Flanders (1667, 1702–11). In 1701 Boufflers, after agreement with the governor of the Spanish Netherlands, the Elector of Bavaria, expelled the Dutch garrisons from the Barrier Fortresses, though at that time no state of war existed between France and the United Provinces. During the early years of the War of the Spanish Succession, Boufflers faced Marlborough and was continually outmanœuvred and out-fought by him. However, Boufflers did defeat Opdam and a Dutch detachment in a minor engagement at Eckeren (1703). His greatest fame came late in the war. In 1708 he defended Lille, unsuccessfully but heroically, against a protracted siege lasting over four months. He was also present, as a volunteer, at the battle of Malplaquet (1709), where he supervised the withdrawal of the French army after Villars had been wounded.

BOUGAINVILLE, LOUIS-ANTIONE, Comte de (1729–1811), French mathematician, explorer, and military commander, who won international recognition for his *Traité de calcul intégral* (Paris, 1751), and was elected to the Royal Society (1756). In the same year he went to Canada as aide-de-camp to Montcalm, and distinguished himself in the battles of Forts Oswego and William Henry. After returning to France (1761), he joined the French navy (1763) and undertook to found, at his own expense, a colony in the Falkland Islands, which he occupied (1764) as a bar to British expansion in the eastern Pacific until Spain intervened. Sent (1766–9) in search of Quiros's continent, he visited Tahiti and discovered Samoa, Espiritu Santo, Orangerie Bay (New Guinea), the Louisiades and New Ireland, and (like Carteret) passed unawares through the lost Solomons. The account of his discoveries given in his *Voyage autour du monde* (1771) stimulated French interest in the Pacific. Later, Bougainville became secretary to Louis XV, was in North America during the American War of Independence as commodore of the French fleet (1779–82), and was subsequently given the rank of a field marshal (1782) and a vice-admiral (1791).

BOUILLE, FRANÇOIS-CLAUDE-AMOUR, Marquis de (1739–1800), French general. After service in the Seven Years War, Bouille was appointed governor of Guadaloupe (1768) and later governor-general of the Windward Islands (1777). During the American War of Independence his troops and ships seized Dominica (1778), Tobago (1781), St Eustatius (1781), and St Kitts (1782). On his return to France, Bouille held military commands in eastern France (1785–90). At first, he supported the French Revolution, but in 1790 used his troops in an unsuccessful effort to secure the escape of Louis XVI. Bouille emigrated to Luxembourg and (1790–3) served in German and English armies. He made two voyages to the Antilles (1796–7).

BOUKMAN (?–1791), Jamaica-born slave who led an unsuccessful insurrection in Santa Domingo (1791). He was captured and executed.

BOULAINVILLIERS, Comte de (1658–1722), French historian, courtier, and critic of Louis XIV's system of government. He attacked Louis's despotism and the system of taxation which preserved privilege and crushed the peasantry, at the same time arguing for the resurrection of the old federal constitution of France. In his *Lettres sur les anciens Parlements de France* and *Essais sur la Noblesse de France* he argued that the conquering Franks were the ancestors of the 17th-cent. nobility, and since kings were elected by the nobles under the Frankish system of government Louis had no right to make laws and edicts without the support of the estates.

BOULANGER, GEORGES-ERNEST-JEAN-MARIE (1837–1891), French general. His popularity in 1887–9, which suggested a revival of Bonapartist sentiment, threatened to overturn the Third Republic. He had been a reforming and popular minister of war in the ministries of Freycinet and Goblet, but was forced out of office in 1887 and became the figurehead both of extreme right and extreme left.

BOULE (Greek, 'council'), in particular at Athens the 'Council of 500' established by Cleisthenes (508 BC) in place of Solon's council and, after Ephialtes' reforms (462), successor to the Areopagus Council as the chief deliberative and executive body. It was composed of 500 citizens elected annually by lot, 50 from each of the ten Attic tribes. The *boule* prepared the agenda for the popular assembly (*ecclesia*), effected its decisions, and supervised the magistrates. Each tribal group of 50 sat continually in turn for one-tenth of the civil year as a standing committee for the day-to-day conduct of state business. The provision that no citizen could serve more than twice ensured extensive citizen participation in government. The *boule* survived the oligarchic revolutions of 411 and 404 and, with some changes in composition and function, the later loss of Athens' independence to the Macedonians and the Romans.

BOULOGNE, TREATY OF (1550), between England and France. King Henry VIII's Scottish campaign (1542) and his continental involvements (1543–6), which brought about the English capture of Boulogne (1544), had depleted his treasury. In March 1550 the Duke of Northumberland negotiated the surrender of Boulogne to King Henry II of France for the sum of 400,000 crowns and the release of those Protestant Scots, including John Knox, captured by the French at the siege of St Andrews castle (1547). The withdrawal of English troops from Scotland also followed.

BOULTON, MATTHEW (1728–1809), British industrialist. He established the Soho Manufactory, Birmingham (1761), making buttons, buckles, ormolu, etc., which was the first large-scale factory organization in Birmingham. He entered partnership with James Watt in 1774, and the combination of Watt's engineering skill, Boulton's business experience, and the inventiveness of their foreman and, later, partner, William Murdoch, established steam-engine manufacture on a firm foundation.

BOUN OUM (1912–), Prince of the House of Champasak in southern Laos and leader of the popular resistance to the Japanese early in 1945. Reluctantly agreeing in 1946 to the incorporation of the south in a unified Laos under the House of Luang Phrabang, he was granted for life the title of inspector-general of the kingdom, yielding precedence only to the king. He served as prime minister (1949–50) and headed a pro-Western coalition in 1960–2.

BOURASSA, JOSEPH-NAPOLEON-HENRI (1868–1952), French-Canadian nationalist leader and journalist. He was co-founder, with Olivier Asselin, of La Ligue Nationaliste (1903), a founder of *Le Devoir*, a Montreal French-language newspaper (1910), and a member of parliament (1896–9, 1900–1907, 1925–35). He supported French-Canadian opposition to Canada's participation in the First World War. In the 1920s he tempered his nationalist views and was forced to resign the editorship of *Le Devoir*. He withdrew from public life but returned in 1944 to assist in the formation of the Bloc Populaire.

BOURBON, CHARLES, Duke of (1490–1527), constable of France, who claimed the inheritance of his wife, Suzanne of Beaujeu, in defiance of Francis I (1521). Bourbon joined the service of Charles V (1523), leading an invasion of southern France (1524). By the treaty of Madrid (1526) Francis was forced to pardon his act of treason and to restore his lands, but after Bourbon's death the settlement was renounced by the treaty of Cambrai (1529).

BOURBON, ARMAND DE, Prince de Conti (1629–66), soldier, younger son of Henry II de Bourbon, Prince de Condé, and brother of the Great Condé. He took part in the Fronde of the princes, later retiring to write on theology.

BOURBON, FRANÇOIS-LOUIS DE, Prince de Conti (1664–1709), elected King of Poland (June 1697), but was opposed by the candidature of Frederick Augustus, Elector of Saxony, who was crowned before Bourbon's arrival in Poland.

BOURBON, LOUIS I DE, Prince de Condé (1530–69), younger brother of King Anthony of Navarre and leader of the revolutionary Huguenot party in France. On the death of Henry II he claimed the right to participate in the Guise-dominated government of Francis II, demanding a regency under his elder brother, the heir to the House of Valois. He was arrested in March 1560 as a result of the Conspiracy of Amboise, but was released on Charles IX's accession (1560) and religious liberty was later granted to the Huguenots (1562). When the first Religious War broke out (1562) Bourbon took command of the Huguenots centred on Orléans, and negotiated for help from Elizabeth of England in return for Le Havre. He was taken prisoner at Dreux by the Catholic party (19 Dec. 1562) and agreed to the Pacification of Amboise. Renewed mistrust of the religious intentions of Catherine de Medici caused Bourbon and Coligny to make another attempt to capture the king (1567), which provoked further outbreaks of fighting. The Huguenots were defeated at the battle of Jarnac (13 March 1569) and Bourbon was killed, leaving Coligny in sole command.

BOURBON, LOUIS II DE, Prince de Condé, Duc d'Enghien (1621–86), succeeded to the title of his father, Henry II, Prince de Condé, in 1646. He was known as 'the Great Condé' and made his name as a soldier. While still the Duc d'Enghien, he defeated the Spaniards at the battle of Rocroi (19 May 1643) and two years later was the victor of Nordlingen. On returning to France after victory in the Thirty Years War, he sided with the court in the Fronde of the *parlement*, blockading Paris on behalf of the regent (1648). Condé, however, became jealous of the influence of Mazarin upon royal policies; as the first prince of the blood, he felt entitled to be Louis XIV's counsellor. In Jan. 1650 Mazarin ordered the arrest of Condé, Conti, his brother, and Longueville, his brother-in-law, for treasonable conspiracy. This was a signal for rebellion in the provinces and the Princesse de Condé set up a rebel government in Bordeaux. By 1651 Mazarin was forced to release the princes, and fled abroad. Condé entered the service of Philip IV of Spain and fought with varying success against the court party, commanded by Turenne (1652–5). He remained exiled from the court until 1659, when, with the conclusion of peace with Spain, he was restored to his former dignities. Condé's last battle was at Seneff (1674), when he defeated the Prince of Orange.

BOURBON, CHARLES, Cardinal of (d. 1590), Catholic claimant to the French throne on the death of the Duke of Anjou (1584) and a pawn of the Guise family. He challenged the claim of the Protestant Henry of Navarre and headed the revived Catholic League, backed by Philip II of Spain.

BOURBON, HOUSE OF, dynasty which ruled France from 1589, when Henry IV came to the throne, until the 1830 revolution, which deposed Charles X, with the exception of the years 1793–1814. The first Duke of Bourbon was Louis

(1279–1341), son of Robert, Count of Clermont, sixth son of Louis IX. His descendant, Anthony de Bourbon, Duke of Vendôme (1518–62), who married Jeanne d'Albret, heiress to the kingdom of Navarre, was the father of Henry of Navarre, who as Henry IV was the first Bourbon prince to become the ruling sovereign of France. His succession in 1589, which occurred during the Wars of Religion, was the result of the assassination of Henry III, the last of the Valois.

In Henry IV (1589–1610) and his grandson Louis XIV (1643–1715), son of Louis XIII (1610–43), the house of Bourbon produced two of the most able kings of France, during whose reigns the long-standing rivalry between the French royal family and the Spanish Habsburgs came to a climax. Under Louis XIV's successors, his great-grandson Louis XV (1715–74) and the latter's grandson, Louis XVI (1774–93), the monarchy's prestige underwent a steady decline. With Louis XVI's deposition (1791) and subsequent execution (1793) the dynasty was interrupted, giving way to successive republics and the Napoleonic empire, although royalists recognized the succession of the young Louis XVII (1793–5).

The Bourbons were restored in 1814 in the person of Louis XVIII (1814–24), brother of Louis XVI, and continued with his youngest brother, Charles X (1824–30). After the revolution of 1830 the elder branch of the house of Bourbon ceased to rule, although Charles X's grandson, the Duke of Bordeaux, was proclaimed Henry V by the legitimist party and continued to be a claimant to the throne from his exiled court in London.   MKS

BOURGEOIS, LÉON VICTOR AUGUSTE (1851–1925), French statesman and representative in the League of Nations. He was prime minister of the first Radical government, which collapsed after less than a year (1895–6) over the failure of its major financial reforms. Bourgeois continued, however, to play a major political role as a minister in subsequent governments. He was a strong advocate of the Hague peace conferences before the First World War and of the League of Nations afterwards.

BOURGEOYS, MARGUERITE (1620–1700), founder of the Sisters of the Congregation of Notre-Dame, the first religious order to originate in Canada. She inspired the settlers to build the church of Notre-Dame-de-Bon-Secours in Montreal (1657) and was responsible for the founding of seven schools in French Canada. She was beatified (1950).

BOURGES, PRAGMATIC SANCTION OF (1458), statute passed in an assembly of the French Church, convened by the king, which virtually abolished papal rights in episcopal appointments in France and of receipt of revenues from the French Church. It created the 'Gallican Church', virtually ruled by the French monarchy.

BOURGÈS-MAUNOURY, MAURICE (1914–), French Radical politician, active under the Fourth Republic. After a distinguished Resistance career, Bourgès-Maunoury entered parliament (1946), and was a minister in several governments. As prime minister in 1957, he was defeated over the Algerian question. In 1958, he opposed de Gaulle's return to power and retired from active politics. His business interests include the famous Radical newspaper *La Dépêche du Midi* of Toulouse.

BOURGET, IGNACE (1799–1885), Roman Catholic bishop of Montreal (1840–76), who reintroduced the Jesuit order to Canada (1842) and was instrumental in the founding of many religious communities, charitable institutions, and colleges. His administration was marked by suppression of liberalism and the participation of the Church in political affairs.

BOURGUIBA, HABIB (1903–), president of Tunisia, who became involved in nationalist politics (1927) and in 1934 broke with the established Destour party and formed the Néo-Destour faction vowed to activist policies. He was imprisoned in France (1938–42) by the Nazis, who released him in the hope of winning his collaboration, which he refused. Arrested again by the French in 1952, he was released after France had recognized Tunisia's right to independence, and returned in triumph in 1955 to head a Néo-Destour government. He became prime minister in 1956 and president of the republic of Tunisia.

BOURKE, SIR RICHARD (1777–1855), general, Dublin-born and English-educated kinsman of Edmund Burke, who combined the role of country gentleman with military service under Wellington and colonial administration in the Cape (1826–8) and NSW (1831–7). Bourke, a liberal-minded Whig governor, tried to conciliate Kaffirs in the Cape and to soften 'exclusive'–'emancipist' intolerance in Sydney. He extended the jury system in NSW, planned the liberalization of its legislative council (actually introduced 1842), promoted economic development, and encouraged expansion of settlement, notably at Port Phillip.

BOURNE, HUGH (1772–1852), English founder of the Primitive Methodists. For most of his life he was a carpenter and builder. He began as a Wesleyan minister, but was expelled in 1808 for using revivalist techniques. Thereafter he travelled widely in the hope of restoring Methodism to its primitive simplicity, but unintentionally found himself creating a new Methodist sect.

BOURNE, WILLIAM (d. 1583), English mathematician, whose description of the log in his book *A Regiment for the Sea* helped to improve the English sailor's knowledge of longitude.

BOUTHILLIER, YVES (1901–), French minister of finance under the Vichy regime (1940–2). After a career as a civil servant, Bouthillier became one of the 'technocrats' who supported Vichy. As minister he tried to limit German economic exactions, and resigned when Laval returned to power. He was later imprisoned by the Germans.

BOUVINS, BATTLE OF (27 July 1214), defeat of the coalition forces of John of England, Emperor Otto IV, his nephew, and various Belgian princes by the smaller French army of King Philip Augustus. The French won because their enemies blundered into the battle in separate detachments which were destroyed piecemeal. The king's success ensured his predominance in western Europe.

BOVES, JOSÉ TOMÁS (c. 1770–1814), Spanish soldier and mercenary of the Venezuelan wars of independence. Boves's sphere of activity was the *llanos*, the Orinoco lowlands of Venezuela. He recruited an army of wild plainsmen to fight for the Spanish cause. Noted for his ruthlessness, he proved more than a match for Bolívar's patriot armies. After his death his army was brought over to the patriot cause by José Antonio Páez.

BOW, implement used for hunting and war from very early times. The first clear representation comes from North Africa in the Upper Paleolithic period (30,000–15,000 BC). The first evidence of its use in war is from Egypt and the Middle East, by infantry and charioteers and, later, in what became its characteristic form, by light cavalry. The mounted archer, using a composite bow, was the dominant element in warfare in Mongolia, Central Asia, the Middle East, and surrounding areas, from the 3rd cent. BC until the use of firearms became widespread. In Europe the bow never acquired the same military significance. Its most important use was in England, where the technically inferior long bow, of south Wales origin, adopted under Edward I, was employed primarily as a defensive infantry weapon. The crossbow is claimed to be a Chinese innovation of the early 4th cent. BC. There is evidence of its use by Greeks and Carthaginians.

The Romans used large winch-operated crossbows and derivations, rather than the hand crossbows which were developed in Europe in the 10th cent. Despite its condemnation at the 1139 Lateran Council, the crossbow became the principal European missile weapon until the development of firearms, its useful career being extended by the introduction of steel bows in the late 14th cent. The bow retained its importance in Asia long after its decline in Europe and crossbows continued to be used by Chinese armies as late as 1860.

BOWDOIN, JAMES (1726–90), American statesman, who inherited a mercantile business from his father, the richest merchant in New England. Bowdoin graduated from Harvard College (1745), was elected to the General Court (1753), and served for 20 years on the governor's advisory council (1757–77). He presided at the state constitutional convention (1779) and was governor of Massachusetts (1785–7), during which time he put down Shay's Rebellion. He was a founder and first president of the American Academy of Arts and Sciences (1788–90), to which he bequeathed his library. He also founded Bowdoin College at Brunswick, ME, as a liberal arts college.

BOWELL, SIR MACKENZIE (1823–1917), Canadian prime minister, Grand Master of the Orange Association and its spokesman in parliament, where he sat as a Conservative member (1867–92). Bowell was appointed to the senate (1892) and became prime minister in 1894. After the Conservative defeat of 1896 he led the opposition in the senate until 1906.

BOWERY, street east of Broadway in lower Manhattan, New York, once a fashionable residential district. By 1860 it was largely populated by German immigrants. Other ethnic groups followed. In recent decades it has become a resort of derelicts and alcoholics.

BOWLEY, SIR ARTHUR LYON (1869–1957), British statistician and economist who played an important part in the development of the application of sampling techniques in the social sciences at the London School of Economics. Bowley was professor of mathematics at Reading University (1907–1913) and of statistics at London University (1919–36).

During the Second World War he acted as director of the Oxford University Institute of Statistics. He wrote widely on unemployment, poverty, the economic effects of war, and foreign trade.

BOWORADET, Prince (1877–1953), assumed the leadership of a royalist rebellion against the newly established constitutional regime in Siam in Oct. 1933, in the suppression of which Phibunsongkhram first gained national prominence.

BOWRING TREATY (1855) between Siam and Britain opened Siam to foreign trade and ushered in an era of open intercourse with the West, which ultimately was to assure the kingdom's survival. Negotiated by Sir John Bowring and Chaophraya Si Suriyawong (Chuang Bunnag), the treaty yielded extra-territorial jurisdiction over British subjects to their consul, abolished the Thai government's monopolistic trading practices, and fixed *ad valorem* duties on imports at 3 per cent and rates averaging 5 per cent on exports from Thailand. It served as the model for numerous subsequent treaties between the Siamese government and Western powers.

BOXER MOVEMENT (1898–1900), anti-foreign peasant movement aimed at ridding China of the presence and influence of Europeans. Despite the efforts made during and after the T'ung-chih Restoration (1862–74) to revitalize the dynasty, the Ch'ing government was unable to curtail Western intrusion. China's defeat by the traditionally despised Japanese in 1895 brought about widespread discontent and social disorder. Economic depression, the influx of de-

mobilized troops, refugees from the southern provinces driven north by drought, floods, and famines, and the flooding of the Yellow river, were all blamed on the Westerners and their religion, as well as on the incompetence of the Manchu government. One of the provinces most affected was Shantung, where the Boxer Rising began (1898). The members of the movement were known as 'Boxers', because they went in for a system of callisthenic exercises not unlike boxing, which were aimed at harmonization of the mind and muscles in preparation for combat. This was supported by spiritualist rituals which they claimed induced invulnerability to sword-cuts and bullets. Their organization, 'Righteous and Harmonious Society' (*I-ho T'uan*), had an endemic existence among the lower classes in north China. Despite its anti-dynastic nature, it had managed to survive sporadic government suppression, particularly in the provinces of Shantung and Chihli. The Boxers' slogan, 'Overthrow the Ch'ing; destroy the foreigner', summarized their aim; missionaries and Chinese converts became their first victims. The court at Peking, which had become reactionary and anti-foreign after the 'Hundred Days' Reform' decided to turn the Boxer Rising to its advantage. The Boxers, unable to cope with two enemies at once, accepted the government's overtures. By early 1900, they were roaming the metropolitan province of Chihli, killing foreigners and converts and destroying their property. Foreign diplomats at Peking protested in vain. Military help was sent for, but the arrival of a small force of 426 marines of different nationalities early in June only served to heighten existing tensions. The climax of the Rising came with a siege of the diplomatic quarters in Peking which lasted 55 days. The siege, which was raised by troops of the powers on 14 Aug., was followed by several months of plundering. The episode ended with the Boxer Protocol (1901), which formally closed the Boxer episode and was signed between China, six European powers, the US, and Japan. It was virtually a dictated settlement; negotiation was a matter for the Western powers and Japan, and only jealousy prevented a more severe punishment of the Chinese. It required the execution of 10 high officials and the punishment of 100 others; suspension of examinations in 45 cities where foreigners were killed or cruelly treated, thus depriving the gentry class (leaders in anti-foreign incidents) of the chance of high office; formal apologies; destruction of 25 Chinese forts, and the right of foreign nations to station troops at a dozen points to guarantee access from the sea to Peking; extension of the legation quarter to 0·81 sq. kms (200 acres), to make it a defensible fortress within the city of Peking; and a huge indemnity to be paid over a period of 39 years at a high rate of interest.

P. Fleming, *The Siege at Peking* (London, 1959).
C. Tan, *The Boxer Catastrophe* (New York, 1955).   DP

BOXHEIM PAPERS, secured by the government of Hesse in Nov. 1931, being the record by Werner Best (later Reiches commissioner of occupied Denmark) of discussions among local Nazis at Boxheimer Hof. They included detailed plans of a Nazi counter-coup against a hypothetical communist rising. Hitler denied knowledge of them (probably genuinely). The Reich government refused to act against the Nazis, and thereby assisted Hitler's 'legal' rise to power.

BOYACÁ, BATTLE OF (7 Aug. 1820), fought between patriots and Spanish troops near the Boyacá river, Colombia. It was won by Simón Bolívar and Francisco Santander, their victory assuring the fall of Bogotá and thus the liberation of New Granada from Spanish rule.

BOYARS, the old Russian nobility, dating back to the 11th cent., when for the first time native slavs began to join the prince's retinue. The boyars were gradually weakened as a class during the reigns of Ivan III of Moscow and of his son and grandson, Vasili III and Ivan IV (1462–1584), when a new service nobility was created. By the end of the 17th cent.

the boyars had become indistinguishable from the new nobility as they too accepted the obligation to provide service.

BOYARS' DUMA, council of boyars which had an advisory role in government, though on occasion, *eg,* during the minority of Ivan the Terrible, it wielded executive power. Its importance steadily diminished during the 17th cent. and it was replaced in 1711 when Peter the Great instituted the Senate.

BOYD OF MERTON, ALAN TINDAL LENNOX-BOYD, Viscount (1904–), British politician who held office in Conservative administrations as minister of transport (1952–1954) and colonial secretary (1954–9).

BOYD, ARTHUR (1920–), Australian painter, potter, and ceramic sculptor, mainly self-taught. Boyd's most important paintings include early Wimmera landscapes and Breughel-inspired religious works of the 1940s.

BOYD FAMILY, family of Scottish magnates who seized the 14-year-old King James III (1466) and exercised undisputed power until 1469. They used their position to obtain the earldom of Arran and to marry into the Scottish royal family. They fell when the Estates of Scotland declared their lands forfeit (1469).

BOYD, MASSACRE OF (1809), took place at Whangaroa, NZ. Maori sailors on the *Boyd* from Sydney, aggrieved at shipboard punishment, instigated the killing and eating of nearly all the ship's complement of 70.

BOYD-ORR, JOHN BOYD-ORR, 1st Baron (1880–), British nutritionist and agricultural scientist. His book, *Food, Health and Income* (1936), formed the basis of the wartime system of food-rationing, with which he was closely connected. He was director-general of the UN Food and Agriculture Organization (1954–8). In 1949 he received the Nobel Peace Prize.

BOYER, ABEL (1667–1729), editor and historian. Boyer, a Huguenot, was French tutor to William of Gloucester (1692–1700). He published a famous English–French dictionary (1702), and also edited the *Post Boy* (1705–9), reported parliamentary debates, and wrote histories of the reigns of William III and Anne, the latter published in annual volumes.

BOYER, JEAN PIERRE (1776–1850), Haitian revolutionary leader and president. Born a free mulatto and educated in France, he played a leading role in the Haitian wars of independence. Upon the death of Pétion (1818), Boyer took control of the southern part of Haiti, and when the leader of the north, Henri Cristophe, committed suicide two years later, Boyer brought the whole country under his control. In 1822 he annexed the Spanish-speaking eastern part of the island.

His government was anti-clerical, conservative, mulatto, and elitist. His purchase of French recognition for the new country brought an indemnity which long hampered Haitian development. Boyer was less of an autocrat than Cristophe or Dessalines, but by his *Code Rural* (1826) he tried to restore a form of share-cropping. Economic instability caused political unrest and he was overthrown by a *coup d'état* (1843). He lived in exile in France until his death.

BOYER, SIR RICHARD JAMES FILDES (1891–1961), Australian pastoralist and publicist, who began his career as a Methodist minister. After serving in the First World War, he became a grazier in Queensland. From 1935, he was prominent as the woolgrowers' spokesman, advocating low tariffs. He served from 1940 as a member, and from 1945 until his death as chairman, of the Australian Broadcasting Commission. Widely respected as an idealist and inter-

nationalist, and for his integrity and approachability, he frequently defended the ABC against political pressures and oversaw the introduction of television to Australia.

BOYLE, SIR EDWARD CHARLES GURNEY (1923–), British Conservative politician. Boyle held a series of posts (1951–62) and became minister of education (1962), where his three years of office were marked by his liberal views, in particular his attitude to the new experiments in comprehensive education. He remained as an authority upon educational matters until, in Nov. 1969, he resigned from political office in order to become Vice-Chancellor of Leeds University.

BOYLE, ROBERT (1627–91), English chemist and natural philosopher. Son of Robert, 1st Earl of Cork, Boyle was educated at Eton. During a trip round Europe (1638–44) he underwent a religious conversion at Geneva and studied the work of Galileo in Rome. Thus were born his two great interests, religion and empirical science. On his return to England he became a member of the 'Invisible College', a group concerned in experimental enquiries. In 1654 he settled in Oxford. With Robert Hooke he devised an improved version of the air pump and began experiments on the properties of air, publishing his results in 1660. While answering objections to his findings he enunciated the relationship between the elasticity and pressure of gases, which is known as 'Boyle's law'. In 1663 the 'Invisible College' became the Royal Society and Boyle was a member of its first council. He also worked on theological subjects and supported projects for the diffusion of scriptural knowledge. At one point Clarendon solicited him to take Holy Orders, but he refused, having no inner calling. He also refused the provostship of Eton (1665) and repeatedly declined a peerage. In 1668 he moved to London, and in 1680 was elected president of the Royal Society, but declined to act because of a scruple about the oath. Voluminous writings on a multitude of subjects earned him an immense reputation throughout Europe. He virtually demolished the Aristotelian doctrine of the four elements, replacing it with a tentative principle of a 'mechanical philosophy' based on the atomic hypothesis, *ie,* there is one universal kind of matter, and diversity of substance results from different groupings and manners of movement of atoms. Because he believed that matter was capable of transmutation by rearrangement of particles, he still believed in the alchemistic transformation of gold and was instrumental in obtaining the repeal of the statute of Henry IV against multiplying gold (1689). In his will he founded the Boyle lectures for the defence of Christianity.   CJ

BOYNE, BATTLE OF THE (1690), in Ireland, where the Protestant forces of William III crossed the Boyne river and defeated the forces of James II. It is regarded by Irish Protestants as the decisive event which kept Ireland under English and Protestant domination, hence their celebration of its anniversary (12 July).

BOZEMAN TRAIL, pioneered 1863–5, the most direct emigrant route in the US from the Oregon Trail to the MT goldfields. It was temporarily abandoned in 1868 after attacks from the Sioux, but later became an important cattle trail from TX to WY and MT.

BRABANT, DUCHY OF, leading medieval Belgian principality owing its military power to its position at the centre of the Netherlands. In 1106 the title of duke of Lower Lotharingia was conferred by Henry V of Germany on Godfrey I, of the dynasty of the Counts of Louvain, who were descended from the Carolingians. The hereditary right of Godfrey's descendants to the ducal title became recognized in the course of the 12th cent. and after 1235 they styled themselves Dukes of Brabant, as their main possessions lay within that region. The duchy was merged in the Burgundian state in 1428.

BRABANT, LINES OF, continuous line of fortification constructed by Vauban and stretching from Antwerp to Namur. The lines were formed partly by river barriers, but mostly by extensive earthworks, and were considered extremely formidable. However, they were stormed with slight loss by Marlborough in 1705.

BRABAZON OF TARA. JOHN THEODORE CUTHBERT MOORE-BRABAZON, 1st Baron (1884–1964), British aviation pioneer, who became in 1907 the first man to hold a British pilot's licence. He was noted for his exploits in pre-war aviation and in the First World War pioneered aerial photography. Turning to politics after the war, he was a notable propagandist for British aviation. He became minister of transport in 1941, and was later minister of aircraft production (1941–2).

BRACEROS, seasonal agricultural labourers from Mexico imported to the south-western US (1942–64) under formal contracts. Less fortunate were the 'wetbacks', or illegal Mexican immigrants, so called because many waded or swam across the Rio Grande. Since they had no legal status many were exploited by their employers.

BRACKEN, BRENDAN BRACKEN, Viscount (1901–58), British Conservative politician. He became MP for North Paddington in 1929. A close friend and supporter of Churchill during the 1930s, he played a key part in persuading him of Labour support for his premiership in 1940. He was parliamentary private secretary to Churchill (1940–1), minister of information (1941–5), and first lord of the admiralty in 1945.

BRACKENRIDGE, HUGH HENRY (1748–1816), US jurist and author. Having settled in Pennsylvania, he practised law in Pittsburgh, where he established the first newspaper and bookshop, later becoming justice of the Pennsylvania supreme court (1799–1816) and a leading champion of the federal Constitution. His novel, *Modern Chivalry* (1792–7), was a satire exposing the follies of the uneducated and the mediocre striving for political and social advancement.

His son, Henry Marie Brackenridge (1786–1871), a lawyer and author, assisted in drafting the Louisiana judicial system and served as state deputy attorney-general and district judge. In 1817 he published a pamphlet, 'South America, A Letter on the Present State of That Country', in which he recommended an American foreign policy later embodied in the Monroe Doctrine. His *Recollections of Persons and Places in the West* (1834) is a valuable source of the study of the West.

BRACTON, HENRY DE (*c.* 1200–68), English jurist, known in his day as 'Bratton', held the Assizes for the south-western counties (1248–68) and other judicial commissions from time to time; he was archdeacon of Barnstaple and prebend and chancellor of Exeter. His incomplete treatise, *On the Laws of England*, shows the then abiding influence of Roman law on the development of the Common Law, as well as the native elements of restriction of rights by the express wording of the writs or 'forms of action' and the citation of decided cases as precedents. For the last purpose he compiled a 'Note Book' of annotated cases from the rolls of Common Bench and others. His views on the high responsibility of judges and the subordination of the Crown to the Law influenced later generations of common lawyers.

BRADDOCK, EDWARD (1695–1755), British major-general in the Coldstream Guards, who was appointed commander-in-chief of British forces in America in 1754. He distrusted the provincial troops and persisted in using European military tactics. With 1400 British regulars and 700 provincials under Lieut.-Col. George Washington, he set out to attack Fort Duquesne (later Pittsburgh), and succeeded in cutting the first road across the Alleghenies, which later became the highway of western expansion. In the battle of the Wilderness (9 July 1755) Braddock's forces met, and were defeated by, 900 French and Indians, the general being mortally wounded; Washington led the remnant of the forces back to Fort Cumberland. Braddock's defeat left the western frontier exposed to hostile Indians and marked the first battle in the French and Indian War.

BRADDON, SIR EDWARD NICHOLAS COVENTRY (1829–1904), prime minister of Tasmania, was born in Cornwall. From the Indian civil service he retired to Tasmania in 1878, was prime minister (1894–9), and a member of the federal convention (1897–8). The 'Braddon clause' of the Constitution, moved by him, restricted the Commonwealth's financial powers until 1911. He sat in the Commonwealth parliament (1901–4).

BRADEN, SPRUILLE (1894–   ), US diplomat and assistant secretary of state of affairs of American Republics (1945–7). He opposed the Argentinian dictator Juan Perón. The Blue Book on Argentina, issued by the state department at Braden's instigation, denounced Perón as a Nazi sympathizer and annoyed Argentine nationalists and increased Perón's support.

BRADFORD, WILLIAM (1590–1657), Pilgrim leader, born in Bradford, England, who went to Leyden with the Pilgrims and sailed in the *Mayflower* (1620) to the New World. He helped to draw up the Mayflower Compact. As governor of Plymouth Colony, he was a strong administrator, guiding the colonists through famine, skirmishes with the Indians, and internal dissension. In 1627, Bradford with seven other Pilgrims and four London merchants assumed the debt to the original merchant adventurers who had financed the colonial venture. He maintained Plymouth Colony as a compact settlement separate from Massachusetts Bay Colony, but co-operated with other New Englanders in the Pequot War and the New England Confederation. His *History of Plymouth Plantation* is a valuable source book for historians.

BRADFORD, WILLIAM (1663–1752), London printer who emigrated with William Penn to Pennsylvania (1682). He established the first printing press in Philadelphia (1685), and the first paper mill in the New World at Roxboro (1696). He became official printer to the colony of New York (1695) and established its first newspaper, *The New York Gazette*, in 1725.

William Bradford (1722–91), grandson of the above, was called the 'patriot printer of 1776'. He was a printer, journalist, bookseller, and keeper of a coffee house in Philadelphia. His press issued works on politics, religion, and literature, and continued for 80 years as one of the principal publishing houses in the country. He was the official printer of the First Continental Congress.

BRADLAUGH, CHARLES (1833–91), English secularist, president of the London Secular Society (1859), and founder and editor of the *National Reformer* (1861). In the early 1870s he published republican propaganda, and in 1877 was prosecuted, with Mrs Besant, for disseminating information on birth control. They were convicted, but their sentences were quashed on appeal. Bradlaugh was elected Radical MP for Northampton (1880) and on entering the House asked to affirm instead of taking the oath. The question was referred by the Speaker to a select committee, which decided against affirmation. Bradlaugh then asked to take the oath in the normal form. The opposition, led by Lord Randolph Churchill, was anxious to embarrass the new Liberal government and raised a storm by denying the right of an atheist to take a religious oath, and presenting the case as one of parliamentary privilege. Bradlaugh was three times declared ineligible and three times re-elected at Northampton. He was finally allowed to take his seat as of right in 1886, the new Speaker, Peel, refusing to allow members to interfere between individuals and the oath.

BRADLEY, JAMES (1693–1762), English astronomer-royal at Greenwich (1742). He has been called the founder of modern observational astronomy. He discovered the law of the 'constant of aberration' and 'mutation' of the earth's axis.

BRADLEY, OMAR NELSON (1893–), US general in the Second World War, who fought in North Africa (1943) and led US ground forces in the Normandy invasion (1944). After serving as chief of staff, US army (1948–9), he became the first chairman of the newly combined Joint Chiefs of Staff (1949–53).

BRADMAN, SIR DONALD GEORGE (1908–). Australian cricketer and probably the greatest batsman in cricket history. He was also a brilliant fieldsman and a shrewd captain. In first-class cricket he scored 28,067 runs, played in 52 test matches, and in 80 innings made a total of 6996 runs at an average of 99·94.

BRADSHAW, ROBERT LLEWELLYN (1916–). West Indian trade union leader and politician. Born in St Kitts, Bradshaw emerged as a labour leader in the 1930s and in 1946 founded the St Kitts Labour Party. He served as chief minister of St Kitts and minister of finance in the West Indian Federation. After the formation of St Kitts, Nevis, and Anguilla as an associated state of the United Kingdom (1967) Bradshaw became prime minister. He opposed secessionist movements in Anguilla (1968–9).

BRADSTREET, JOHN (1711–74), Canadian soldier and colonial administrator. He distinguished himself during the capture of Louisbourg (1745), Fort Frontenac (1758), and Detroit (1764). He was lieutenant-governor of St John's, ND (1746), and was later appointed deputy quartermaster-general of British forces in America (1757).

BRADSTREET, SIMON (1603–97), leader in Massachusetts Bay Colony. He emigrated from England to New England (1630), and until 1690 was continually in public service as secretary of Massachusetts Bay Colony, deputy governor, and governor until 1692. He helped to organize the New England Confederation and was a commissioner for 33 years. He was also a large landowner and engaged in land speculation and trading on the frontier.

His first wife, Anne Dudley Bradstreet, was the first American poetess and was widely read in the colonies. Her early poems were didactic and strongly Puritan, but her later work was simpler, depicting the life of New England.

BRADWARDINE, THOMAS (*c.* 1290–1349), eminent member of the school of mathematicians at Merton College, Oxford, and a distinguished theologian, who wrote against William Ockham. He was the confessor of King Edward III and was elected Abp of Canterbury (1348), but died of the plague shortly after his consecration.

BRADY, MATTHEW (*c.* 1823–96), American photographer whose pictorial record of the Civil War has done much to convey the impression that this was the first modern war. He and his assistants took some 3500 pictures of civil and military leaders, common soldiers, and battlefield scenes.

BRAGANZA FAMILY, younger branch of the Portuguese royal family descended from John I (1357–1433), whose son Alphonso was the first Duke of Braganza. On the expulsion of Philip IV of Spain from the kingdom of Portugal, John, Duke of Braganza, became ruler of Portugal as John IV (1640–56). The house of Braganza retained the throne until the flight and abdication of Manuel II (1910) and the declaration of a republic.

BRAGG, SIR WILLIAM HENRY (1862–1942), British scientist, who held chairs in Australia and England before becoming director of the Royal Institution and of the Davy Faraday research laboratory. His work in radioactivity at Adelaide won him his FRS; thereafter, his most notable achievements were in X-rays and crystal structure. Bragg's Australian-born son, Sir William Lawrence (1890–), shared with his father the 1915 Nobel Prize for Physics and also became director of the Royal Institution (1954–66).

BRAHE, PER, Count (1602–80), Swedish soldier, administrator and chamberlain to Gustavus Adolphus. He fought in his Polish wars and subsequently in the Thirty Years War in Germany. On the king's death (1632) he turned to politics and was president of the Swedish Diet, a senator, and one of the regents of the kingdom during the minorities of Christina and Charles XI. He also made his mark as governor-general of Finland (1637–40, 1648–54), where he stimulated trade and agriculture, created a postal system, founded 10 new towns, and established Abo University.

BRAHE, TYCHO (1546–1601), Danish astronomer, who was probably the greatest of all observers before the invention of the telescope. Born at Knudstrup (southern Sweden, then Danish) of a noble family, Brahe was educated at Copenhagen and in Germany. He first came to prominence with his work on the very bright new star (*nova*) that appeared in 1572, and in 1576 was granted a pension by King Frederick II of Denmark, together with funds, for building a large observatory and the island of Hveen on which to build it. These privileges were withdrawn in 1597 by Christian IV (1597).

Brahe's best-known single pieces of work are those on the *nova* of 1572 and on the great comet of 1577, both of which posed difficulties for the Aristotelian system; in spite of this, he held all his life to a version of the Ptolemaic earth-centred view of the universe. His real importance lies, however, in the mass of accurate observational work he carried out, using new methods and instruments of his own invention. The young Johannes Kepler joined him in Prague in 1600 and on his death inherited both his post and this great mass of data. From the latter Kepler was able to deduce his laws of planetary motion.

BRAHMA, one of the principal Hindu gods, conceived of as the creator of the universe, especially as part of the Hindu Trinity (*Trimurti*), where Brahma figures together with Vishnu, the Preserver, and Shiva, the Destroyer. In the Upanishads and in the philosophical systems based thereon Brahma is the Absolute for union with whom all souls yearn. Brahma, has, however, enjoyed little worship as an independent deity. If so, he is represented in sculpture as four-headed, riding the *hamsa* (a mythical goose) and escorted by his spouse Sarasvati, the goddess of learning.

BRAHMA MOVEMENT. A development of the Brahma Sabha, a theistic organization founded (1828) in Calcutta by Ram Mohan Roy, who believed in the unity of God and discarded the worship of images. While rejecting the divinity of Christ, he accepted the importance of his ethical teachings. Roy advocated certain social reforms, like *sati*, but his idea was to reform Hinduism, not abandon it. Later leaders of this early reforming movement deny that it was more than a *sabha* or place of meeting and contend that the Brahma (Anglice Brahmo) Samaj was the work of his successors. After Roy's departure for England (1830) the society languished until 1842, when it was revised by Maharshi Devendranath Tagore (1817–1905), the father of Rabindranath Tagore. Under Tagore it became a movement based on a pure monotheistic form of Hinduism, its followers regarding the Vedas as divine revelation and therefore infallible. Tagore propagated its principles through the *Tattva Bodhini Patrika*, a Bengali newspaper edited by Akshoya Kumar Datta. Not wishing to cut himself entirely adrift from Hindu society, Tagore opposed social reforms like the abolition of caste and inter-caste marriages. In 1857 the movement was joined by Keshab Chandra Sen (1838–84). Thereafter it suffered from fissiparous tendencies as the younger members, led by Datta and Sen, questioned the infallibility of the Vedas and demanded the abolition of caste restrictions and the disuse of the Brahmanical thread in devotion. This was too much for Tagore, who dismissed Sen and his followers. There followed a great schism. Tagore and a small body of followers formed the Adi Brahma Samaj, which stood for a pure monotheistic form of Hinduism, while the younger members, under Sen, formed themselves into the Bharatvarshiya Brahma Samaj or the Brahma Samaj of India, whose adherents were interested in social and other reforms. It was Keshab Chandra Sen who was the real founder of the Brahma Samaj. Extracts from the scriptures of many religions—Christian, Hindu, Buddhist, Muhammadan, Zoroastrian, and Confucian—were read at their services. They also sought to emancipate women by means of education. Missionaries were sent out to various parts of India and Sen was received by Queen Victoria on his visit to England (1870). All went well until 1878, when a further schism followed the marriage of Sen's daughter at an immature age to the Maharaja of Kuch Behar in contravention of the Samaj's condemnation of child marriage. The younger members then formed themselves into the Sadharan Samaj, which had definite anti-Christian tendencies and professed a broad theism. Sen sought to counter this by forming the Nava Bidhana, which was extremely eclectic. The Brahma movement was not confined to Bengal, but spread to Uttar Pradesh, the Punjab, and Madras. In Maharasthra, where one of its chief leaders was M. G. Ranade, it was known as the Prarthana Samaj.

Sibnath Sastri, *History of the Brahmo Samaj*, 2 vols (Calcutta, 1911–12).   CCD

BRAHMANAS, a particular type of ancient Indian prose text in archaic Sanskrit (*c* 800–600 BC), recording traditions among the Brahmans on various topics associated with the Vedic hymns, including not only speculation on the meaning of sacrificial ritual, but also cosmological myths and discourses on the origin and essence of social institutions. Though not true historical sources, they illustrate some aspects of social and cultural history of ancient India during a particularly dark period.

BRAHMANISM, imprecise term, sometimes used to describe the social order of ancient and medieval India (but after the period of the Vedic hymns) when the Brahmans imposed their standards of social order and culture upon society. In some cases, however, the term is especially used in opposition to Buddhism.

BRAHMANS, one of the four classes (*varna*), usually considered the highest, into which the entire population of India has been divided since very early times. The Brahmans do not constitute a real caste, as they comprise numerous endogamous groups. According to a different classification the Brahmans are divided into a number of exogamous clans (*gotra*), each of which is traced back to one particular primeval saint (*rishi*). Originally a priestly class, the Brahmans specialized in learning and usually occupied influential posts as ministers and other advisers of the kings. In addition, quite a few royal dynasties of ancient India belonged to the Brahman class. The Brahmans, especially in the early medieval period, were usually rewarded with land for their services, often in perpetual ownership and with all kinds of immunities. They thus became a major landowning class in many parts of India. They played a leading part in organizing the freedom movement. On the public life of India they still exert an influence out of proportion to their numbers, in the legislatures, the administrative services, and the judiciary, though many Brahmans are now engaged in humble occupations.

BRAHMI SCRIPT, ancient Indian script of unknown origin, first found used in the inscriptions of Ashoka of the middle of the 3rd cent. BC. It is remarkably systematic in the rendering of all the Sanskrit (or Prakrit) phonemes. All later scripts of South and South-East Asia (excluding Arabic and Latin script) can be traced back to Brahmi.

BRAINS TRUST (1932–3), in US, popular name for an early group of F. D. Roosevelt's advisers. After Gov. Roosevelt announced his candidacy for the presidency (22 Jan. 1932), Raymond Moley, professor of government and public law at Columbia University, with the guidance of Roosevelt's adviser Samuel I. Rosenman, and his former law partner D. Basil O'Connor, began to assemble a group of intellectuals to prepare background papers and assemble speech material for the campaign.

Prof. Moley became chairman of the group that had as its nucleus his Columbia colleagues Adolf A. Berle and Rexford G. Tugwell. Depending on the issues being discussed, the most regular members were Robert M. Lovett, Francis Perkins, Gen. Hugh S. Johnson, Robert K. Straus, Charles W. Taussig, Joseph D. McGoldrick, James W. Angell, Lindsay Rogers, Schuyler Wallace, and Howard Lee McBain. In addition to writing speeches and providing an intellectual forum for discussion with Roosevelt, the Brains Trust began to produce memoranda on a broad variety of topics, from agriculture to presidential war powers. Even when subjects were given out to specialists who were nonmembers of the trust, its members stood behind the accuracy of the data.

Although the Brains Trust was highly successful in its creation and formulation of many New Deal policies, the group began to disintegrate shortly after the election, when its principals took up salaried positions in the new administration (March 1933). Moley went to the department of state, Tugwell to the department of agriculture, and Berle to the Reconstruction Finance Corporation. By this time, President Roosevelt, pressed by a new diversity of problems, had informally established numerous and scattered subsidiary study groups composed of people both in and outside the government. Ironically, by the time the term 'Brains Trust' began to be a household and journalistic commonplace, the original group had ceased to exist. Eventually, however, it became popular to call any non-governmental presidential adviser a member of the Brains Trust.   FPK

BRAMAH, JOSEPH (1748–1814), British inventor and toolmaker whose inventions included a hydraulic press, a machine for printing serial numbers on bank notes, and the ball-cock on water-closets. He also designed machine tools to achieve greater precision.

BRAMANTE (LAZZARI) (*c.* 1444–1514), Renaissance architect who made his reputation at Milan (1476–99) and was a pioneer in introducing the Renaissance style into Rome, being the original designer and first builder (after 1506) of St Peter's cathedral.

BRANDEIS, LOUIS DEMBITZ (1856–1941), lawyer and associate justice of the US Supreme Court. He abandoned a successful career as a corporation lawyer in Massachusetts to fight for social justice, and through factual briefs such as that in *Muller v. Oregon* (1908) sought to convince the courts that economic and social data are as relevant as legal precedents in determining the validity of social legislation. A close adviser of President Wilson, he became the first Jewish member of the US Supreme Court (1916–39), where he was a firm exponent of the belief that judges have a creative role to play in moulding constitutional law to meet the needs of social change. A strong supporter of the 'new liberalism', which called for the use of governmental powers to protect individual liberties and the welfare of the community, he had reservations about some of the early New Deal legislation.

BRANDENBURG, DUCHY OF, frontier province or *mark* (march) wooded and marshy, colonized by German settlers from the 10th cent. In the hands of the Ascanian dynasty and especially under the margrave Albrecht 'the Bear' (1134–70), the march of Brandenburg was consolidated between the rivers Elbe and Oder. With the extinction of the Ascanian line (1319) the Wittelsbachs seized Brandenburg (1324), which was later acquired by the Emperor Charles IV (1347–1378). The struggles for its possession played into the hands of the estates and the aristocracy, whose power reached its peak in the reign of the Emperor Sigismund (1410–37). In 1415 Sigismund appointed Frederick of Hohenzollern, burgrave of Nuremberg and his lieutenant in the march, as Elector of Brandenburg, thus establishing the dynasty which was to control the duchy until and after its union with Prussia.

The rise of the duchy of Brandenburg under the Hohenzollerns is a story of tenacity and opportunism. In 1608 the Calvinist elector, Sigismund (1609–19), by his marriage with Anne of Prussia, added to his dominions the Polish fief of Prussia and the march of Cleves-Julich. He succeeded to the latter in 1614 and the former in 1618. Under the policy of neutrality pursued by his successor, George William (1619–1640), during the Thirty Years War, the Lutheran people of Brandenburg suffered greatly, but through the skilful diplomacy of the next elector, Frederick William I (1640–88), known as 'the Great Elector', the duchy acquired East Pomerania and the bishoprics of Magdeburg, Minden and Halberstadt and Kammin (1648), as well as total sovereignty in Prussia (1657).

Until 1648 Brandenburg was a second-class German state subordinate to the Palatinate, and despite its growing prestige remained inferior to Bavaria and Saxony until the 18th cent. For services to the emperor against the French in 1701 the elector, Frederick of Brandenburg-Prussia (1688–1713), was recognized as King of Prussia, from which point the history of the duchy of Brandenburg was merged in that of the new kingdom.   MKS

BRANDENBURG CONTRIBUTION, ancient taxes levied upon the towns and peasantry of Brandenburg, usually in the form of a uniform land tax and poll tax, to raise the ordinary revenue. Under the Great Elector (1640–88) the towns were subject to the excise and the contribution was confined to rural society.

BRANDT, WILLY (1913–   ), first Social Democrat chancellor of Germany (Oct. 1969) since the resignation of Hermann Muller in March 1930. Brandt had previously been mayor of West Berlin (1957–66); SPD candidate for the chancellorship (1961, 1965); and, from Dec. 1966, foreign minister in the CDU–SPD coalition.

He was born Karl Herbert Frahm and, as a young man, was an ardent socialist and an active opponent of the Nazis. On Hitler's accession to power he went into exile in Norway, where he changed his name and (having been deprived of German citizenship) adopted Norwegian nationality. When Norway was occupied he moved to Sweden. Brandt returned to Germany after the war and readopted German nationality. He quickly gained prominence in West Berlin politics and in Oct. 1957 was elected mayor (1958). In 1960 he was chosen to lead the SPD campaign against the 85-year-old chancellor Adenauer's Christian Democrat Party. Although Adenauer was re-elected, Brandt made a considerable impact during the campaign and was described as the 'German Kennedy'. He again led the SPD in the 1965 elections. The party failed to win a majority, but the disenchantment of the CDU with their allies, the Free Democrats, led to the formation of a new 'Grand Coalition', between the CDU and the SPD (Nov. 1966). Brandt became vice-chancellor and foreign minister under Kiesinger, the chancellor. The coalition was possible because of the changes in SPD leadership and policies which had taken place since the late 1950s: the SPD had ceased to call for nationalization and accepted the place of free enterprise in the economy. In the 1969 elections the SPD, although winning fewer votes than the CDU, improved its position sufficiently to become the dominant partner in a new coalition, with the Free Democrats. Brandt was elected chancellor by the Bundestag by a margin of two votes over the required simple majority.

The SPD 'victory' owed much to Brandt, who had succeeded in winning popularity for policies which were more pragmatic than those of his predecessors, Schumacher and Ollenhauer. His success was all the more remarkable because of the opposition to him as a result of his illegitimacy and his voluntary exile during the Nazi era.   RE

BRANDYWINE, BATTLE OF (11 Sept. 1777), engagement in the American War of Independence. At Chadds Ford on the Brandywine Creek, PA, American troops under George Washington unsuccessfully attempted to prevent Gen. Howe and superior British forces from advancing on Philadelphia.

BRANICKI, FRANCIS XAVIER (1730–1819), Polish nobleman. He joined the popular movement of the 1790s, but declared in favour of the Russians and left Warsaw in 1794. He was condemned to death in his absence, and ended his career as a general in the service of Catherine the Great.

BRANT, JOSEPH (1742–1807) (Thayendanegea), Mohawk chief, who fought with the Loyalists in the American War of Independence and became a colonel in the British army. He was a protégé of Sir William Joseph, who sent him to Eleazar Wheelock's Indian School in Lebanon, CT. After the war he helped the US Commissioners, signing treaties with the Indians. He became an Anglican and took part in missionary work, translating part of the Bible into Mohawk. In 1786 he went to England to raise funds for the first Episcopal Church in Upper Canada. The British settled him on an estate on Lake Ontario, where, until his death, he continued to help his people adjust themselves to the white man's ways. The town of Brantford, Ont., is named after him.

BRANTING, KARL HJALMAR (1860–1925), Swedish prime minister and pioneer of social democracy. He became political editor of the daily *Socialdemocraten* soon after its foundation (1885). He was prominent among the founders of the Social Democratic Labour Party in 1889 and was the only social democrat in the *riksdag* (1896–1902). In 1907 Branting became leader of the party and in March 1920 formed the first Social Democrat government of Sweden. It lasted for only six months, but he regained the premiership (1921–3, 1924–5). He also led the Swedish delegation to the League of Nations, where he was a member of the 'left wing' which advocated a greater degree of initiative for the Council. For his services to Sweden and the League, Branting was awarded the Nobel Peace Prize in 1921.

BRAOSE, WILLIAM DE (d. 1211), leading English baron of the reign of King John, on whose behalf he captured Arthur of Brittany in 1202. His rapid rise to power alarmed John, who imprisoned, and starved to death, William's wife and son. Braose died in exile.

BRASIDAS (d. 422 BC), enterprising Spartan commander in the first phase of the Peloponnesian War. He distinguished himself in the defence of Methone (431), in naval operations in north-west Greece (429, 427), and at Pylos (425). While at Corinth preparing an expedition to support Athens' discontented allies in Chalcidice, his prompt action saved Megara (424). Marching north with 1700 hoplites, he won over Acanthus and other cities, including Amphipolis, with plausible diplomacy backed by threats of force (424). After more successes in 423, he defeated Cleon outside Amphipolis, but died in action. He enhanced Spartan prestige with Athens' allies and his victories redressed the balance, making possible the peace of Nicias (421).

BRASÍLIA, federal capital of Brazil situated in the state of Goiás. Since 1789 plans to move the capital inland, and thus open the unused interior, had gone unimplemented. Brasília was built during the presidency of Juscelino Kubitschek and the government was installed there in April 1960. The city is famous for the beauty of its location and architecture.

BRASS, or Nembe, Niger Delta kingdom founded in about the 15th cent., which rose on the proceeds of internal and overseas trade. Brass fought the British monopolist Royal Niger Co. in 1895 to protect her middleman interests, but lost her sovereignty in so doing.

BRASSEY, THOMAS (1805–70), British civil engineer, whose meeting with George Stephenson (1834) led him to build railways in many countries, *eg*, Argentina, Britain, Canada, France, and India.

BRATIANU, ION I. C. (1864–1927), Rumanian politician and statesman who presided over the making of the greater Rumanian state. Bratianu was the heir to the Liberal dynasty begun by his father Ion (1821–91), who ruled the country for much of the 1870s and 1880s. Ion was educated as an engineer in French universities and worked for a short time as a state engineer when he returned to Rumania. He entered parliament in 1895, rose to cabinet post a year later, and became prime minister in 1909. Whether in or out of office, Bratianu ruled Rumania during the period 1914–27. In August 1916 he negotiated the secret alliance which took Rumania into the First World War on the Allied side. He led the Rumanian delegation to the Paris peace conference, but resigned when the conference refused to yield to his maximum territorial demands and sought to impose the minority treaty upon them. Bratianu resumed the premiership in 1922 and drafted a new constitution almost single-handed. In 1923 this centralist document was promulgated over the protests of the opposition parties. Bratianu represented the sagacity and pragmatism which has loomed large in the Rumanian political tradition.

BRAUCHITSCH, HEINRICH VON (1881–1948), commander-in-chief of the German army (1938–41). After serving in the First World War, he experimented in the 1920s with the co-ordination of aircraft and motorized troops. By 1933 he was commander of the East Prussian (1st Army) Military Area, and in 1938 was appointed commander-in-chief of the army and made a field marshal. Beck, and many of his fellow officers, tried to persuade Brauchitsch to make a stand against Hitler's adventurous foreign policy but, as was shown clearly on many occasions, Brauchitsch lacked the moral courage to act resolutely. In Aug. 1938 he refused to resign with Beck; later in the year he failed to support those plotting the 'Berlin Putsch'. On 5 Nov. 1939 he advised Hitler against attack in the west, but backed down before Hitler's fury. Adverse weather conditions prevented the offensive, but by then Brauchitsch had lost much of his remaining influence. After the failure of the assault on Moscow, which was undertaken against his advice, Brauchitsch was dismissed (Dec. 1941). At the end of the war he was to have been tried as a war criminal, but died before being brought to trial.

BRAUN, EVA (1912–45), wife of Adolf Hitler. From 1936 she lived at the Berghof as Hitler's mistress, then (April 1945) joined him in Berlin. They were married on 29 April. The next day Eva committed suicide and Hitler (it is believed) shot himself at her side.

BRAUN, WERNHER MAGNUS MAXIMILIAN VON (1912–   ). German-American rocket engineer, who directed the development of the V2 missile weapon, first used (1944) by the Germans during the Second World War. Von Braun was responsible for launching America's first satellite into orbit in 1958. Subsequently he led the Saturn rocket development for the Apollo lunar landing project and in 1970 was appointed to direct the American space exploration programme.

BRAVO, MURILLO JUAN (1803–73), Spanish statesman. He belonged to the party of 'Moderados', who were concerned to suppress any liberal rising. He was minister of finance in the government of Narváez (1848–51), whom he forced into resigning by publishing the national accounts. He succeeded Narváez as first minister (1851–2) and introduced an efficient, authoritarian, and highly unpopular regime, dissolving the Cortes and leaning on clerical support. He signed a Concordat with the papacy (1851) and resigned in Dec. 1852.

BRAY, THOMAS (1658–1730), an English clergyman, who was sent to Maryland by the Bp of London to strengthen the Anglican Church in that colony. He was the founder of the Society for Promoting Christian Knowledge (1698), and the Society for the Propagation of the Gospel (1701). He set up libraries in 30 parishes from Baltimore to Charleston and established semi-public libraries which were next in importance to the libraries of Harvard and William and Mary Colleges.

BRAZZA-SAVORGNAN, PIERRE DE (1852–1905), French explorer of Italian origin who pioneered the European penetration of the lower Congo and Gabon regions of Africa and opened the way for French colonial rule.

BRÉBEUF, JEAN DE (1593–1649), French Jesuit priest, and founder of Huron Indian missions in southern Ontario, Canada. He was author of a dictionary and grammar of the Huron language, some religious works, and the *Jesuit Relations* of 1635 and 1636. Brébeuf was martyred at the mission of Saint-Ignace by raiding Indian parties and was canonized in 1930.

BRECKINRIDGE, JOHN CABELL (1821–75), US vice-president, presidential candidate, and Confederate leader. He was a democrat from Kentucky and elected vice-president (1856). With the Democratic Party divided (1860), he became presidential candidate of the pro-slavery Southern wing, and came second to Lincoln in the electoral college, with 72 votes. A reluctant secessionist in 1861, he became a major-general in the Confederate army, and served briefly (1865) as Confederate secretary of war.

BREDA, CAPITULATION OF (1625), to the Spanish during the Thirty Years War. On 5 June, after a siege of nearly six months, the Dutch garrison surrendered to Ambrogio Spinola, the Dutch relieving force under Frederick Henry of Orange being unable to break through the Spanish outworks. On 10 Oct. 1637 Frederick Henry recaptured Breda after a siege of nearly a year.

BREDA, DECLARATION OF (1660), King Charles II's manifesto on the eve of his restoration. It was drawn up and issued on 14 April 1660 on behalf of Charles II whilst he was still in exile, and was based upon advice offered to him by Gen. Monck, who had earlier marched from Scotland upon London, and who was the person most effectively in control of the situation. Charles promised an amnesty to all except those specifically excluded by parliament; some degree of religious freedom, 'a liberty to tender consciences'; the payment of all the arrears due to Monck's soldiers, and their absorption into the forces of the Crown; and the reference of the land problem to parliament. In the event, the declaration was largely but not completely fulfilled. The Act of Indemnity passed by the Convention confirmed the royal pardon for all except 50 persons, about 30 of whom were still alive, and only 13 of whom were in fact executed. Provision was also made by the Convention for continuing the collection of the monthly assessments to pay Monck's army. The land problem was so difficult that it was bequeathed by the Convention to be solved by its successor, the principle then adopted being that all confiscations should be returned to their original owners, whereas all sales should be regarded as valid. It was the promise of 'liberty to tender consciences', however, that was most flagrantly disregarded. The so-called Clarendon Code of the Cavalier Parliament was thoroughly intolerant, whilst the attitude of Charles II himself towards Dissent was, at best, equivocal.

BREDA, TREATY OF (1667), by which the Second Anglo-Dutch War was ended. After successful Swedish mediation, the terms were signed on 31 July 1667. England gained from the Dutch their colony of New Netherlands in North America (later renamed New Jersey and New York) and in West Africa Cape Coast Castle (in present-day Ghana). However, she renounced any claim to the Dutch colonies of Pulo-Run in the East Indies and Surinam (Dutch Guiana) in South America. She recognized Acadie as French, while France returned to her St Christopher, Antigua, and Montserrat in the Windward Islands. The Dutch repeated their recognition, originally contained in the treaty of Westminster (1654), of the English claim to a salute in the Channel, although now in a more restricted area than hitherto. The English agreed to a less rigorous definition of 'contraband' when searching neutral shipping. The Dutch interpretation of the English navigation laws, whereby manufactures from the Spanish Netherlands and German lands were treated as though made in the Dutch republic, was accepted by the English. The peace was clearly a compromise. English ambitions in North America were to some extent gratified, while Dutch predominance in the East Indies was preserved. For their part, the Dutch did not push their claims as far as the English might have feared in view of the recent Medway disaster.

BREDERODE, HENRY, Count of (1531–68), Dutch Protestant nobleman, one of the original *Gueux*, and an early leader of the Netherlands revolt. As a member of the League of the Nobility, he presented the nobles' petition to Margaret of Parma (April 1566), demanding the abolition of the Inquisition and the religious Edicts of Philip II. Later that year he led the occupation of Antwerp in defiance of the Spanish authorities, but in 1567 was forced to flee to Cleves for refuge and to seek money and men for the rebellion. His unexpected death left William of Orange the sole leader of the revolt.

BREERO, GERBRAND ADRIAENSZOON (1585–1619), Dutch poet and playwright, author of *The Spanish Brabanter* (1619). He helped to make Amsterdam the centre of the literary and intellectual life of the Netherlands.

BREISACH, FALL OF (1638). Breisach was the strategic key to the Rhine, and it had been besieged by French-paid troops under Bernard of Saxe-Weimar from the middle of Aug. 1638. It capitulated on 17 Dec. after several relief attempts by the imperialists had failed, and the Habsburg stranglehold on France was broken.

BREITENFELD, BATTLES OF (1631, 1642), fought near Leipzig during the Thirty Years War. On 17 Sept. 1631 the Swedish–Saxon alliance under Gustavus II Adolphus defeated the Catholic League under Tilly. The victory opened central and southern Germany to the Swedes, and established the reputation of Gustavus Adolphus as a tactical innovator. On 2 Nov. 1642 a Swedish–French army under Torstensson defeated an imperial army under the Archduke Leopold in the second battle of Breitenfeld.

BRENDAN OF CLONFERT (d. *c.* 577), founder of the monastery of Clonfert in Ireland. Brendan is known as the Navigator because of his voyages into the Atlantic, accounts of which became one of the most popular medieval stories. It is possible that he reached Greenland and even North America.

BRENNAN, CHRISTOPHER JOHN (1870–1932), Australian poet and classical scholar, was educated at Riverview College and Sydney University. A complex and sophisticated poet, he used European themes and techniques (notably those of Mallarmé) at a time when most Australian verse was local and nationalist in flavour. Brennan's most important book was *Poems 1913* (1914).

BRENNUS, leader of a marauding army of Senonian Gauls, who sacked Rome in 390 BC after crossing the Apennines from their new home in Cisalpine Gaul and defeating the Romans at the Allia. After a six-month siege of the Capitol, Brenner accepted a ransom to raise the blockade and return home; a Roman chauvinistic tradition overlaid this withdrawal with a fictitious massacre of him and his army by Camillus.

BRENTWOOD, WILLIAM JOYNSON-HICKS, 1st Viscount (1865–1932), British politician who achieved fame in 1908 as the successful Conservative candidate who defeated Winston Churchill, the president of the board of trade, in the northwest Manchester by-election. He championed air defence before and during the First World War. In 1922 he was active in bringing down the Lloyd George coalition. In the Conservative governments that followed, his promotion was rapid. He first entered the cabinet in 1923 and was (1924–9) home secretary. As such he organized the government's reaction to the General Strike. He supported the police, and was responsible for the police raid on Arcos Ltd, the Soviet Russian trade agency in London. This led Russia to break off relations with Britain. He was strongly religious and discouraged new tendencies in art. Paintings by D. H. Lawrence were seized, and etchings of William Blake were threatened. He also took a prominent part in defeating (1927–8) the proposed new Prayer Book for the Church of England. He was responsible for the introduction of summer time and was associated with the extension (1929) of the franchise to all women over 21.

BRESLAU, CONVENTION OF (1813), provided for Russo-Prussian co-operation to drive French troops out of Germany and for an appeal to the German princes and people for support.

BRESLAU, TREATY OF (1742), between the Archduchess Maria Theresa and Frederick II, temporarily ended the hostilities between Austria and Prussia. By the spring of 1742 Frederick needed a respite in the war to rest his army and raise fresh funds. In addition, he felt the French war effort was unreliable. Maria Theresa, for her part, was under strong pressure from Britain to make peace in order to free her resources for the conflict with France. She believed that a combined British, Dutch, and Austrian invasion of France was to be launched from the Austrian Netherlands. Another defeat by Frederick's army in May 1742 finally persuaded her to come to terms which were negotiated in June at Breslau. Frederick's possession of Lower Silesia, Glatz, and most of Upper Silesia was recognized, although Maria Theresa hoped this recognition would only be temporary. The terms were, however, confirmed by the treaty of Berlin (1745).

BREST, BATTLE OF (April 1513), unsuccessful prelude to Henry VIII's invasion of France later in the year. Sir Edward Howard, lord high admiral, was killed in an assault on the French galleys defending Brittany, and his ill-equipped expedition had to return to Plymouth.

BREST EXPEDITION (1694), was intended to capture the naval arsenal and destroy the French fleet at anchor. Britain and her allies used their naval superiority to keep the coasts of northern France apprehensive of amphibious attacks and thus to divert French troops and munitions from Flanders. However, news of the expedition reached Paris, possibly being revealed by Marlborough in the Camaret Bay Letter. Thereupon Vauban was sent with a strong garrison to fortify the post. William III and his council realized that their plans had been discovered, but nevertheless decided to send the expedition, giving the commander, Lieut.-Gen. Tollemache, discretionary powers of attack. The attack was repulsed with heavy loss, including the life of Tollemache himself. The expedition, though strategically sound, was ill-prepared and badly executed, emphasizing the squandering of allied resources during the war.

BREST-LITOVSK. After the October revolution, the Bolsheviks offered an armistice to all belligerent states. On 22 Dec. 1917 they started peace negotiations with the Central Powers at Brest-Litovsk. The chief Bolshevik negotiators were Joffe and Kamenev; Austria-Hungary was represented by Czernin, the foreign secretary, and Germany by Kühlmann, the foreign secretary, and Maj.-Gen. Hoffmann.

Divisions soon emerged between and within the delegations. The German military authorities, already occupying the Baltic region, wished to secure the Eastern front before launching a major Western offensive. Hindenburg and Ludendorff wished to create a buffer zone outside Prussia, and to establish economic domination of the Ukraine to counter the Allied blockade. The Central Powers' less ambitious civilian governments desired an Eastern peace with the minimum of delay.

The Bolsheviks announced their objective as democratic peace, without annexations, on the basis of national self-determination. They hoped that a German revolution would destroy the Central Powers' negotiating position. Their main tactic was procrastination. After the Christmas recess, Trotsky, commissar for foreign affairs, joined the delegation. On 18 Jan. 1918 the 3rd Congress of Soviets endorsed his policy of resisting German domination of Poland, the Ukraine, and the Baltic, thus defeating Lenin's proposal to acquiesce in German annexations.

On 10 Feb. Trotsky astounded the Central Powers by demanding 'neither war nor peace'; though proclaiming the state of war at an end, he refused to sign a treaty. On 13 Feb. the German army, overruling the chancellor and foreign secretary, denounced their armistice with Russia and advanced into the Ukraine.

A majority of the All-Russian Central Executive considered armed resistance the only honourable course, still hoping for an international revolution. Only Lenin insisted that Russian territory, and hence the revolution, was endangered. Russia must capitulate, whatever the price, to preserve the administrative and organizational gains of the revolution. Lenin convinced his hearers. The preservation of 'socialism in one country' thus became the cornerstone of the Russian revolution. Russia accepted Germany's demands on 24 Feb., and signed peace on 3 March. Trotsky resigned from his Commissariat on 8 March.

The Brest-Litovsk treaty established German domination over Lithuania, Estonia, Livonia, Courland, Poland, and the Ukraine. Russia also ceded important regions to Turkey. Russia surrendered 34 per cent of her population, 32 per cent of her agricultural land, and the bulk of her industrial undertakings. All propaganda was to cease.

The Brest-Litovsk negotiations prompted President Wilson, who hoped to counter Bolshevik propaganda and keep Russia in the war, to propose (8 Jan. 1918) a '14 points' settlement on a basis of national self-determination. The treaty, revealing the character of German militarism, determined the Allies to impose a draconian peace on Germany.

The treaty brought Germany little advantage. Bolshevik propaganda continued, as Lenin maintained that the Communist Party itself had not signed the treaty. The Ukraine hoarded its harvest. The treaty was cancelled in Germany's armistice with the Allies in Nov. 1918. However, German troops were permitted to remain in the Baltic region during the subsequent Allied intervention against the Bolsheviks.

J. Wheeler-Bennett, *Brest-Litovsk, the Forgotten Peace* (London, 1938).

ASJ

BRETHREN OF THE COMMON LIFE, a religious sect, founded by Gerard Groote (1340–84), whose members took no vows, but lived a life of communal poverty. The sect spread fairly widely in the Netherlands and northern Germany, its most famous member being Thomas A'Kempis, author of the *Imitation of Christ.*

BRÉTIGNY, TREATY OF (1360). Following the English victory at Poitiers (1356) and the capture of the French King John II, the terms of truce were drawn up at Brétigny near Chartres. John's ransom was fixed at 3,000,000 gold crowns (£500,000) and England was given full sovereignty over Gascony, Calais, and Ponthieu.

BRETON CLUB (1789), formed originally by deputies to the French states general from Britanny. It later became the Jacobin Club.

BRETTON WOODS (New Hampshire, US), scene of a conference held in 1944 which established the International Monetary Fund and the International Bank for Reconstruction and Development. Representatives of 44 countries (the Soviet Union was a notable absentee) gathered in July to discuss the basis of post-war economic and monetary co-operation. The nationalistic and restrictive policies of the inter-war years had clearly played a part in the onset of depression and in the reduction in world trade. It was therefore agreed to form an International Monetary Fund with an initial capital of $8,800 million subscribed on a quota basis by its members, who agreed to stabilize exchange rates and confer with the fund before any major change in parity. In the event of a short-term deficit in the balance of payments, the fund was to make available facilities for short-term borrowing within set limits.

It was also decided to establish an International Bank for Reconstruction and Development with an initial capital of $10,000 million. The bank was designed to meet the problem of long-term investments, especially those connected with the reconstruction of war-devastated economies and major projects of economic development.

Many of the hopes expressed at Bretton Woods were to be shattered in the post-war period. Political division prevented the formation of a world-wide economic community and caution prevented the adoption of the imaginative policies put forward by the British economist, J. M. Keynes. None the less, the conference established institutions of major importance to international economic co-operation.

BREUGHEL, JAN (1568–1625), Flemish painter, younger son of Pieter Breughel. He settled in Antwerp and enlarged his artistic range, painting views of the Flemish countryside and peasant life. He also painted some of the landscapes that make the background for the figures of Rubens.

BREUGHEL, PIETER (c. 1529–69), Flemish painter, who was born in a village near Bruges and whose work was always influenced by his peasant origins. He was a pupil of Koek but his early engravings, with their devils and multiplicity of figures, were rather in the style of Bosch. His style changed when he moved from Antwerp to Brussels (1563), and his work was later noted for his naturalistic treatment of Flemish village life and its rural customs. He was one of the first artists to depict the common man engaged in everyday activities.

BREZHNEV, LEONIDILICH (1906–), Soviet politician; chairman of the Presidium of the Supreme Soviet (1960–4), and first secretary of the Central Committee after Khrushchev's fall in Oct. 1964. (The 23rd Party Congress in 1966 changed the title of the post to 'Secretary General'.) Brezhnev, the son of a steelworker, was born in the Ukraine and joined the Communist Party in 1931. He studied at the Dneprodzerzhinsk Metallurgical Institute, from which he graduated in 1935. During the Great Purge he advanced rapidly. In

1938, he became a departmental head under Khrushchev, as first secretary of the Central Committee of the Ukrainian Republic, and subsequently a secretary in the Dnepropetrovsk *oblast* (regional administrative unit). During the Second World War Brezhnev served as a political commissar at the front. After the war he returned to the Ukraine and in 1947 became first secretary of the Dnepropetrovsk Oblast Committee. In 1950 he was appointed first secretary of the Moldavian Central Committee and in 1952 became, briefly, a member of the Central Committee of the CPSU and a candidate member of the Presidium. After Stalin's death (1953) Brezhnev fell from favour, but Khrushchev's patronage soon restored his position. In 1954 he was sent to Kazakhstan, where he played a leading part in the Virgin Lands programme. At the time of the 20th Party Congress (1956) he was elected a member of the Central Committee and a candidate member of the Presidium, being made a full member in 1957 as a reward for his support for Khrushchev's bid for supremacy. In May 1960 Brezhnev replaced Voroshilov as chairman of the Presidium of the Supreme Soviet (*ie*, titular head of state). In July 1964 Brezhnev was replaced as head of state by Mikoyan and became second secretary in the Central Committee. On the fall of Khrushchev in Oct. 1964 Brezhnev became first secretary and together with Alexei Kosygin formed the ruling duumvirate of the Soviet Union. Whatever his part in the coup against Khrushchev, Brezhnev was the main beneficiary. It is widely believed that he was the chief advocate of the invasion of Czechoslovakia in 1968.

BRIAN BORU (d. 1014), King of Ireland, made himself master of Munster in 978, received the submission of the rulers of Leinster in 984, and began to aim at becoming supreme king of Ireland. Ruling as 'Emperor of the Irish', Brian was the first real High-King of Ireland. He failed to conciliate the Dublin Danes and was defeated and killed at Clontarf, near Dublin, by the King of Leinster aided by Vikings from throughout the British Isles. His reign witnessed the beginnings of a revival of culture and learning in Ireland which he fostered personally.

BRIAND, ARISTIDE (1862–1932), French statesman noted for his exertions for international peace and Franco-German reconciliation. Briand began his political career as a socialist, but soon moved to the right after entering parliament (1902) where he rapidly came to the fore through his powers as an orator. He was *rapporteur* of the law separating Church and state (1905), and as a minister in subsequent governments was responsible for carrying out this controversial policy in a conciliatory spirit. He became prime minister in 1909, the first of 11 periods in that office. As prime minister during the First World War (1915–17), he helped initiate the Salonika campaign.

After the war, Briand concentrated on foreign affairs, and directed French foreign policy (with one short break) from 1925 onwards. In an earlier period (1921–2) he had believed in the full enforcement of the Versailles treaty, although even then he had been criticized for lack of firmness towards Germany. Later, especially after the failure of Poincaré's occupation of the Ruhr, Briand believed that the best guarantee of peace was to bring Germany into the international community and to make concessions where she had just grievances against Versailles.

The treaty of Locarno (1925) and the admission of Germany to the League of Nations were the first fruits of this policy, whose success was based largely on Briand's personal relations with Stresemann, especially after their meeting at Thoiry (1926). There followed a series of concessions, culminating in the evacuation of the Rhineland (1930), which dismantled the safeguards against Germany given to France at Versailles. But Stresemann's death (1929), and the growing strength of national feeling in Germany, were undermining the foundations of Briand's German policy even before Hitler came to power.

Briand's wider hopes for international peace rested on the League of Nations, disarmament, the arbitration of international conflicts, and the 'outlawry of war'. He inspired the Briand–Kellogg pact (1928), by which the powers renounced the use of war as an instrument of policy. Briand also advocated a federal 'United States of Europe'.

Briand's eloquence and idealism inevitably seem somewhat hollow in the light of later events, but his policies were not necessarily unrealistic in the optimistic period before the onset of the Depression.

BRIAND, JEAN OLIVIER (1715–94), French-born Roman Catholic Bp of Quebec (1766–84). As vicar-general of Quebec, his conciliatory policies after the city's capitulation to the British won him the support of Gov. Murray, who advised the imperial authorities to approve his appointment as Bp of Quebec, and he was officially recognized by the British government as superintendent of the Roman Catholic Church of Canada. At the time of the American invasion (1775) he commanded his adherents to honour their oath of allegiance to the British Crown and resist the invaders. Although his appeal was largely ignored, it helped to keep the vast majority of the French–Canadian population neutral.

BRICKER AMENDMENT (1953), attempt by Senator John Bricker and other right-wing Republicans to amend the US constitution to require congressional ratification of all international agreements. Despite opposition from President Eisenhower, this attempt to reduce executive discretion in foreign policy only narrowly failed to pass the Senate (1954).

BRIÇONNET, GUILLAUME (d. 1514), a French financier, descended from the leading bankers of Louis XI. He became a bishop in 1493. He was the principal adviser of the simpleminded Charles VIII and was mainly responsible for the French invasion of Italy in 1494. When the French reached Rome, the terrified Pope Alexander VI made Briçonnet a cardinal and in 1497 he became Abp of Rheims. He was the first of a succession of cardinals who were the chief ministers of the kings of France.

BRIÇONNET, GUILLAUME (1470–1534), bishop of Meaux, son of Guillaume Briçonnet, Charles VIII's chief minister, and a member of a family of lawyers, merchants, and financiers, he was a leader of the humanist movement in France during the reign of Francis I. He reformed the clergy in his diocese and gathered round him a dynamic group of scholars, including Lefèvre d'Etaples, Gerard Roussel, and Guillaume Farel. He also became the friend and confessor of Margaret d'Angoulême, the king's sister. In 1525, however, the Meaux group disbanded, threatened by the authority of the *parlement* of Paris and the Sorbonne faculty of theology, the champions of religious orthodoxy. Briçonnet faced the investigations of the *parlement* for apparent unorthodoxy, while his fellow reformers fled abroad. Briçonnet, protected by the patronage of Margaret, conformed and escaped the penalties of heresy.

BRIDGER, JAMES (1804–81), US fur trader, frontiersman, and scout. He discovered Great Salt Lake (1824), and established Fort Bridger (1843) as a way-station on the Oregon Trail. Though completely illiterate, he was renowned for his unsurpassed knowledge of the West.

BRIDGES, EDWARD ETTINGDENE BRIDGES, 1st Baron (1892–1969), civil servant. After serving in the First World War, Bridges entered the home civil service and served in the treasury (1919–38). He then became secretary to the cabinet (1938–46).

BRIDGES, SIR WILLIAM THROSBY (1881–1915), Australian soldier, who served in the Boer War. He planned the Australian military college at Duntroon and was its first commandant. In 1914 he raised the first Australian Division and other troops, to whom he gave the title Australian Imperial

Force. He commanded them on Gallipoli, where he was mortally wounded.

BRIDGEWATER, FRANCIS EGERTON, 3rd Duke of (1736–1803), pioneer of British inland navigation. He owned coal mines at Worsley, and ordered the construction of canals from Worsley to Manchester (1760), which reduced the price of coal in Manchester, and later from Longford Bridge to Runcorn (1762–72), which connected Manchester and Liverpool. Both canals were constructed by Brindley.

BRIENNE, ÉTIENNE CHARLES LOMÉNIE DE (1727–94), archbishop of Toulouse, was appointed *principal ministre* with complete control over French governmental finances in May 1787. He inherited a difficult position from his free-spending predecessor, Calonne. Although he had opposed Calonne's edicts for financial reform in the Assembly of Notables, he soon saw that they were the only means of staving off complete bankruptcy. But he had no more success with the Notables and immediately dissolved them. His attempts to get the *parlements* to register the edicts led to widespread opposition by the aristocrats to protect their financial privileges. After a year of protest, Louis XVI finally dismissed Brienne and agreed to call the states general (Aug. 1788). The archbishop's methods had been applied too late to save the collapse of the regime.

BRIGANTES, largest native British tribe encountered in the Roman conquest, extending from the Peak District through most of northern England into south-west Scotland. They lived by stockbreeding rather than settled agriculture and had fifteen centres of population. Militarily powerful, but possessing precarious unity, they became a Roman client kingdom. The authority of their queen, Cartimandua, depended on Roman support and when she surrendered the native hero Caratacus (AD 51), who had fled from Wales to Brigantia in advance of the Romans, relations were ruptured between her and her consort Venutius. Consequently, in 71 there began the Roman advance into Brigantia, which was completed by Agricola.

BRIGGS PLAN, to combat communist insurgency in Malaya, launched by Lieut.-Gen. Briggs in 1950. It involved shifting about 500,000 rural squatters, mostly Chinese, into compact protected 'new villages', where government machinery could reach them.

BRIGHT, JOHN (1811–1889), British orator and Liberal statesman. He was deeply influenced by his Quaker ancestry and education, and by the Rochdale carpet mills which he helped to run. He was a leading Anti-Corn Law League orator (1841–6) and a Liberal MP (1843–89). He conducted a sustained attack on aristocratic landownership, whose worst injustices he detected in war and the game laws. He courageously denounced the Crimean War, and his peculiar provincial and religious perspective enabled him from the late 1840s to pioneer the defence of the Irish and Indian peoples against British exploitation. He helped to create the Gladstonian Liberal Party by leading several moralistic crusades which culminated in the successful campaign for household suffrage, launched in 1858.

By the 1870s, Bright and his class had fewer grievances, greater wealth, more reason to suspect working-class movements, and greater governmental experience. Bright's entry into the cabinet in 1868 symbolized the absorption of the middle class and of dissenters into government circles. His latent conservatism became increasingly apparent when he opposed republicanism, land nationalization, and feminism. As president of the board of trade (1868–70), he experienced at last the complexities involved in wielding power, and his health gave way. He was chancellor of the Duchy of Lancaster (1873–4, 1880–2), then resigned in protest against the bombardment of Alexandria, and in 1886 opposed Home Rule. Although he was a firm opponent of factory and sanitary reform, Chartism and trade unions, Bright's absence from Labour Party historiography is unjust, for he was crucially important in encouraging working men into the political community, and in preserving for them those civil liberties without which the Labour Party could never have been born.

G. M. Trevelyan, *The Life of John Bright* (London, 1913).

BHH

BRIGHT, RICHARD (1789–1858), British physician at Guy's Hospital, London. He was the first to establish the connection between dropsy and kidney diseases and his name has been given to one such disease. He illustrated both his own *Reports on Medical Cases* (1827, 1831) and travel books on Iceland and Hungary. He was among those 19th-cent. clinicians who combined the study of patients and the use of advancing scientific methods to evaluate diseases.

BRIGID OF KILDARE (d. *c.* 520), daughter of a slave woman of Leinster in Ireland, who founded the great double monastery of men and women under a bishop and an abbess at Kildare. Her cult became one of the most popular in Ireland and Britain.

BRIGID OF SWEDEN (*c.* 1302–73), patron saint of Sweden. She was the mother of several children, including St Catherine of Sweden, and a mystic and visionary. After her husband's death, she founded (1346) the contemplative Bridgettine order with double monasteries.

BRIHUEGA, BATTLE OF (1710), French victory during the War of the Spanish Succession. This defeat of Britain and her allies strengthened the British determination to make peace in spite of the war aim of 'No Peace Without Spain'.

BRILL, small port in Zeeland captured by 600 Dutch Sea Beggars under Lumey de la Marck, 1 April 1572, from which time the revolt of the Netherlands gathered a new and ultimately successful impetus.

BRINDLEY, JAMES (1716–72), British engineer, who built canals for the Duke of Bridgewater. He later constructed the Trent and Mersey Canal.

BRINKELOW, HENRY (d. 1546), English Protestant, originally a Franciscan friar. He attacked the wealth and immorality of the clergy, but *The Complaint of Roderick Mors* (1542) was directed against the even greater greed and oppressiveness of the new secular landlords. Brinkelow argued that the wealth of the monasteries should have been used for schools, hospitals, and the relief of the poor.

BRINON, FERNAND DE (1885–1947), French collaborationist under the Vichy regime. As a journalist in the 1930s, Brinon was an admirer of Hitler and a founder of the *Comité France-Allemagne*. He became the Vichy government's 'ambassador' in Paris (1940) and as a minister (1942–4) he supported a pro-German policy until the end. He was tried and executed in 1947.

BRIONI, group of Yugoslav islands (Italian before 1947) and scene of the neutralist 'summit' in July 1956. The meeting between Tito, Nasser, and Nehru at Brioni was taken as a sign of the development of Asian neutralism into a worldwide association. It was hoped that such a combination would be able to influence the great powers. But the strength of the movement, which was united by little more than small power status and anti-colonialism, proved illusory.

BRISBANE, SIR THOMAS McDOUGALL (1773–1860), Scots-born governor of New South Wales (1821–5). A distinguished military career preceded his appointment to NSW, where he took the opportunity to pursue his interest in astronomy. Brisbane implemented recommendations of the commissioner, John Bigge, for the future of the colony and also introduced major reforms himself in land, convict, and economic policy.

BRISSOT, JACQUES PIERRE (1754–93), French politician, who entered the French states general after a career as a political journalist and became leader of the Brissotin or Girondin Party. He initially concentrated on urging the emancipation of the slaves in the colonies, but from Oct. 1791 he acted as spokesman for a group of deputies who were demanding an armed crusade against Europe. He believed that war would both free the other oppressed nations of Europe, and reduce the king's influence by exposing his treasonable correspondence with the emperor. Once the war had begun (1792), power moved towards Paris and the Jacobin extremists, although Brissot and his friends dominated the Legislative Assembly and Convention. While coming to support the idea of a republic, he none the less tried to save Louis XVI's life, a move which really ensured his own execution the same year. In the struggle with Robespierre he failed to match his political realism.

BRISTOL, JOHN DIGBY, 1st Earl of (1st of 1st creation) (1580–1653), English statesman and moderate royalist. He was constantly employed (1611–24) as an ambassador by James I. In 1623 he incurred the hostility of Buckingham by revealing the truth about Prince Charles's mission to Spain. On the death of James I he was removed from the privy council and Charles I attempted to deny him his seat in the Lords (1626). Having failed, Charles prosecuted Bristol for high treason in the Star Chamber. He was sent to the Tower, but was released when parliament demanded his liberation (1628). Though he supported the Petition of Right, he was soon restored to royal favour, but took no active part in politics until the Bishops' War (1639). He was the leader of the great council at York and a commissioner to negotiate with the Scots at Ripon (1640), and he strongly advised the summoning of parliament. Though an advocate of reform, he tried to save Strafford's life. He was declared an evil councillor by the Commons (Dec. 1641) and was imprisoned in the Tower (March–April 1642), joining Charles at Oxford on his release. He was not in favour of continuing the war and retired abroad (July 1644) by order of parliament.

BRISTOL, English seaport, second city in the kingdom until the development of Liverpool and the industrial north. It has a sheltered tidal harbour at the junction of the Avon and the Frome.

There were settlements at Bristol in British and Roman times, and silver coins were struck there under Aethelred the Unready (978–1016), when slaves were exported to Ireland. At the Conquest the castle fell to the Normans, and its possession was frequently contested during the domestic struggles of the Middle Ages. Bristol was given a charter (1171), recognized as a wool staple (1353), and made a county borough (1373).

In medieval times it was an outlet for the western cloth industry, developing a flourishing commerce with Gascony and the Iberian peninsula, and it was unique among the larger English ports in that its trade was controlled by the native merchants. Later it was an important centre of the 'triangular trade' in slaves and sugar with Africa and the West Indies. John Cabot sailed from Bristol to discover the American mainland (1498), John Guy settled Newfoundland (1610), and William Penn was one of many Bristol men who helped to colonize America.

In the Civil War the town was besieged and captured by Prince Rupert (1643), but surrendered by him two years later. It was one of the few towns in the west that refused to receive Monmouth (1685) and there were riots in 1715 following the accession of George I. Rioting also occurred in opposition to a bridge toll (1793) and on the rejection of the Reform Bill by the Lords (1831).

Docks were opened (1809) and have been considerably enlarged under municipal ownership. The *Great Western*, the first transatlantic steamship, was built and launched there (1838). The principal modern industries include ship-building, cars, aircraft, tobacco, cocoa, chemicals, pottery, and glass.

Ecclesiastically, Bristol was made a separate diocese (1542), comprising parts of the sees of Salisbury, Gloucester, Worcester, and Bath and Wells. It was joined to Gloucester (1836) but again separated (1897).

The cathedral was originally a Norman abbey. Other famous buildings are the church of St Mary Redcliffe, Colston Hall, the Clifton suspension bridge, and the Theatre Royal. The university was founded in 1876.   MMR

BRISTOL RIOTS (1831) in Britain, most serious of the riots which preceded the passage of the 1832 Reform Bill. Although the 1831 general election strengthened the franchise reformers, the House of Lords rejected the second Reform Bill (8 Oct.). Rioting followed in Nottingham and Derby, but was most serious at Bristol. The riots began when Sir Charles Wetherell, the prominent opponent of reform, arrived at Bristol for judicial duties. A mob sacked the Mansion House on 30 Oct., and the authorities lost their nerve. The mob were allowed to enter the prisons and to burn the bishop's palace and several other buildings. According to official figures, 12 people were killed and 94 wounded.

By activating latent fears that a revolution of the French type could occur in England the riots helped to convince property-owners that the reform crisis must be settled quickly, and lent credibility to the Political Unions as bastions of order against anarchy. By revealing the fragility of the social structure in England the riots left memories which profoundly affected early Victorian social reformers like Charles Kingsley and Mary Carpenter.

BRISTOL, TREATY OF (1574), between England and Spain, to settle the compensation due for various acts of confiscation, since Elizabeth had seized ships carrying money to pay Spanish troops in the Netherlands (1568). Spain replied by seizing the goods of English merchants in Flanders, and trade had come to a standstill. In the treaty Spain's liabilities were agreed at £89,000 and England's at £68,000.

BRITAIN, ROMAN, province set up by the Emperor Claudius after Aulus Plautius' successful invasion (AD 43) and extended to its limits in England, Wales, and Scotland by 84. First Camulodunum (Colchester), then Londinium (London) was the capital of the unified province, but later two provinces (3rd cent.) then five provinces (4th cent.) were formed. Urban centres emerged from military settlements, eg, Deva (Chester) and Eboracum (York), and tribal administrative points, eg, Venta Silurum (Caerwent) and Calleva Atrebatum (Silchester). Roman roads radiating from London anticipated most modern trunk routes. With unprecedented peace, exploitation of resources and agriculture, prosperity grew and survived Roman withdrawal (c. 400), but the veneer of Romanization diminished.

BRITAIN, BATTLE OF (Aug.–Sept. 1940) between the German Luftwaffe and the RAF fought over Britain. As a prelude to the German invasion of Britain Göring ordered attacks first against the shipping and ports, then against the airfields and finally against the towns of Britain. Air chief marshal Dowding, however, had disposed his squadrons well and, guided by radar, the British fighters inflicted heavy losses on the Luftwaffe. On 15 Sept. the British claimed to have destroyed 185 aircraft. Although the figure was exaggerated as a result of double counting, the exaggeration had great value in maintaining morale. 'Never', said Winston Churchill, 'in the field of human conflict was so much owed by so many to so few.' Hitler and Göring had erred when on 7 Sept. they switched the attack from the airfields to London. Had the Luftwaffe continued to throw its full weight against the fighter stations, it might well have achieved the air superiority necessary to protect the invasion force.

BRITANNICUS (AD 41–55), son of the Emperor Claudius and Messalina. When Claudius married Agrippina the Younger and adopted her son, Nero, Britannicus was gradually excluded from his position as the obvious successor to Claudius. He died, probably having been poisoned, soon after Nero's accession.

BRITISH-AMERICAN LAND COMPANY, commercial development company organized in London (1832), which acquired land in the eastern townships of Quebec for the settlement of British emigrants. This alleged attempt to destroy the ethnic balance between the French and British of Lower Canada was one of the grievances of the French-Canadians against the British in the Ninety-Two Resolutions (1834).

BRITISH AND FOREIGN ANTI-SLAVERY SOCIETY (1839). Negro apprenticeship in the British colonies was ended in 1839, but while slavery survived in other countries there was little prospect of ending the slave trade. The society was formed to exert moral and religious pressure for the abolition of slavery and the slave trade in other countries, but it rejected the use of force.

BRITISH AND FOREIGN BIBLE SOCIETY (1804), founded by Thomas Charles, an evangelical who had left the Church of England and became a Calvinistic Methodist minister in Wales. His first intention was to provide Bibles in Wales. The society had the support of leaders of the Clapham Sect, and grew rapidly, distributing Bibles in many parts of the world.

BRITISH ASSOCIATION (1831), was founded largely through the influence of the Rev. W. V. Harcourt, on the model of the Deutscher Naturforscher Versammlung (1822) to provide a meeting point for scientists, with each other and with the public. The association's meetings were divided into sections from 1835. Section F (Statistics) was of contemporary importance for the exchange of information on public health and preventive medicine.

BRITISH BROADCASTING CORPORATION (BBC), organization, established (1927) by Royal Charter, which operates radio (in which it has a monopoly) and television services in Great Britain. The BBC was the successor to the British Broadcasting Company which operated from Nov. 1922 to Dec. 1926. The manager of the company and director-general of the corporation (1927–38) was J. C. W. Reith. British broadcasting owes much to Reith, who saw broadcasting as a mission to propagate 'all that was best in every department of human knowledge'. He supported the doctrine of broadcasting which was neither outright commercialism nor government controlled. The BBC's home services (1970) (two television channels and four radio programmes) are financed by licence fees. Its extensive world service is supported by grant-in-aid voted annually. Although by its charter the BBC is ultimately responsible to parliament, in practice it enjoys a wide degree of independence.

BRITISH COLUMBIA, extreme western province of Canada. Bounded in the north by the 60th parallel and in the south by the 49th, it extends from Alberta and the Rocky Mountains in the east to the Pacific Ocean and the Alaskan 'panhandle' in the west.

Although the Pacific coast was previously sighted by Spaniards, it was Capt. Cook who first landed and claimed the country for Britain (1778). Trading with the Indians in Nootka Sound, he obtained sea-otter pelts which subsequently drew an armada of trading vessels. This so incensed the Spaniards that they seized British ships in Nootka Sound (1789). War was averted by the Nootka Sound Convention

1789 and Capt. George Vancouver went ahead with the first comprehensive mapping of the coast north of San Francisco (1790).

Alexander Mackenzie reached the mouth of the Bella Coola river overland (1790), paving the way for the fur trappers and traders of the North-West Co. which, with the purchase of Fort Astoria from an American rival (1813), gained complete control of the fur trade on the north Pacific coast. Hudson's Bay Co., after amalgamation with the North-West (1821), dominated trade throughout New Caledonia (now British Columbia) and Columbia (now Oregon and Washington states). In Columbia, however, American missionaries, working among the Indians, provided centres for the American settlers, who grew rapidly in numbers and claimed the whole Pacific coast up to Alaska. Ultimately, America and Britain agreed (1846) to the boundary along the 49th parallel. Partly as a bulwark against further American expansion, Vancouver Island was made a British colony in 1849.

The discovery of gold on the Fraser river (1858) brought an influx of miners and their suppliers to the mainland of New Caledonia and, as settlement increased and the economic future of the province seemed assured, it was proclaimed a British colony under the name of British Columbia (1859). In 1866 Vancouver Island was annexed to British Columbia, with Sir James Douglas, formerly of the Hudson's Bay Co., as its first governor and Victoria its capital. In 1871, British Columbia agreed to become a province of Canada on condition that a transcontinental railway was speedily built, and in 1885 the Canadian Pacific railway was opened. The employment of orientals in mining and railway construction led to a movement to restrict immigration (1884). A head tax and federal regulations limited Chinese immigration but, because of Britain's special relations with Japan, and India's membership of the empire, immigration from these countries was dealt with by agreement with the governments concerned (1908).

The province entered Confederation in 1871, with a single-chamber legislature and full responsible government. Members of the legislature were elected on a non-party basis until Richard MacBride organized the Conservative Party on his accession to power in 1903. Conservatives and Liberals alternated in power until they formed a coalition government (1941), with the Co-operative Commonwealth Federation (CCF) constituting the main opposition. In 1952 the Social Credit Party, under the leadership of W. A. C. Bennett, came to power and has held it since, with CCF forming the main opposition and the Conservatives and Liberals forming small minorities.   WM

BRITISH COTTON GROWING ASSOCIATION (1902). In the 19th cent. Britain had been dependent on supplies of cotton from the US. With the growth of the textile industries in other countries, there were periodic shortages by the end of the century. The association was founded in 1902 to sponsor the growth of cotton within the empire. The establishment of cotton-growing in the West Indies, Egypt, and, most importantly, in the Sudan, owed much to its efforts.

BRITISH EXPEDITIONARY FORCE, THE, originally consisting of six divisions of infantry and one of cavalry, was created by the Haldane reforms of the army in 1906. In 1914 on the outbreak of the First World War its potential as an independent striking force was not realized, and it was sent to France, where, under the command of Sir John French, it played a useful but not crucial role on the left flank of the French armies (1914–15). It was rapidly expanded by dominion, territorial, and 'new army' units, and by the end of the war it consisted of well over 1 million men organized in five armies. In 1917–18, under Sir Douglas Haig, it contributed largely to the Allied victory.

After the war, a field force of five divisions was retained for imperial, rather than continental, purposes. It was hoped that the navy and the RAF would make a sufficient British contribution to any future European war by blockade and bombing. However, plans for sending two divisions to the Continent as a gesture of Allied solidarity were drawn up in March 1939, and the need to prevent the Germans obtaining air and submarine bases in Belgium soon led to greater emphasis on this commitment. When the German offensive (Operation Yellow) began, in the Second World War, in the spring of 1940 there were 13 British infantry divisions and a substantial air force in France under Lord Gort. This second BEF was involved in the French defeat and, though its equipment was lost, many of its men were evacuated from Dunkirk and other ports (1940). These men formed the nucleus of the British armies in the later part of the war.

RWD

BRITISH GUIANA LABOUR UNION, first trade union in British Guiana. Established (1919) by Hubert Critchlow, the BGLU was a founding member of the British Guiana Trades Union Council (1941).

BRITISH IN ADEN. Proposals to establish a base at Aden had been canvassed intermittently since 1799, and on 20 Jan. 1839 it was occupied by an expedition from India, ostensibly following a dispute arising out of the plunder of an Indian-owned vessel, the *Daria Dowlat*, sailing under British colours, although its seizure from the Abdali Sultan of Lahej was also influenced by the desires to establish a coaling station between Bombay and Suez and to control the activities of Muhammad Ali of Egypt in south-west Arabia.

After its occupation treaties were negotiated with neighbouring tribal chiefs to secure supplies for Aden. Following the Ottoman attempt to extend influence southwards from the Yemen in the 1870s, these treaties were replaced by new treaties of protection modelled on the 1886 Socotra treaty, designed to control the foreign affairs of the Fadhlis, Lower Aulaqis, Wahidis and Lower Haura (1888), the Subeihis (1889), the Lower Yafa'is, Haushabis and Alawis (1895), Beihan and Upper Yafa'is (1903), Upper Aulaqis (1904), and Audhalis (1914), so forming, with similar treaties, the West Aden Protectorate. Similar treaties were concluded with certain chiefs of the East Aden Protectorate, nearly 1400 of whom signed a truce (Ingram's Peace) in 1937. The protected territories retained internal self-government, subject to British advice. From 1959 most of the West Aden Protectorate was formed into the Federation of Arab Emirates of the South, which eventually merged with Aden Colony (1963) to form the Federation of South Arabia.

After 1963 Britain aimed to establish in South Arabia an independent, unitary state in alliance with Britain, which would supply assistance and retain a base in Aden Colony. This policy failed owing to the inability of local rulers to agree and to the rise of a popular opposition, supported by Republican Yemen and Egypt. The principal popular organization was the National Liberation Front (NLF, founded 1963; leader Qahtan al-Sha'bi), which, in 1966, temporarily united with the Organization for the Liberation of the Occupied South (FLOSY, founded 1965; leader Abdullah al-Asnaj) to form the Federation for the Liberation of South Yemen. The NLF later withdrew from FLOSY and the two organizations conducted separate terrorist campaigns. In Feb. 1966 Britain announced plans to withdraw in 1968. After withdrawal began in June 1967, the NLF came to control the Federation (the government of which had collapsed), the East Aden Protectorate, and, after a struggle with FLOSY, Aden Colony. The last British troops withdrew on 29 Nov. 1967 and at midnight the People's Republic of South Yemen was proclaimed, with Qahtan al-Sha'bi as first president.

MEY

BRITISH IN CENTRAL AFRICA. Britain became interested in central Africa from two directions, the west and the south. In the west, British attempts to suppress the Atlantic slave trade took the form of seeking new types of economic activity. In the lower Congo region a growing trade in palm oil, rubber,

coffee, and other commodities developed, and by the 1880s, when Britain was ousted by the Congo Independent State, its commerce was worth £2 million per annum. In the south, British interest derived from South Africa, and the expansionist ambitions of the Rhodes mining and finance empire. The British government reluctantly declared protectorates over Northern Rhodesia and Nyasaland in the 1890s.

By the 1950s there were 75,000 white settlers in Northern Rhodesia and 5000 in Nyasaland, many of British origin. The Northern Rhodesian settlers were prominent in establishing the Central African Federation (1953). But British interests in central Africa were not confined to settlers, who were expendable. British capital had developed mining in Northern Rhodesia, and was closely involved with that in Katanga and Angola. The British South Africa Co. owned all mineral rights in Northern Rhodesia, and farmed out concessions to other companies, such as the Anglo-American Corporation and Roan Selection Trust. In Katanga, Tanganyika Concessions had considerable shares in the huge Union Minière du Haut Katanga. All these companies were closely linked, in directors and capital. An estimated £300 million of British capital was invested in central Africa and Southern Rhodesia. These British interests, represented by a body of Conservative MPs, favoured the maintenance of the Central African Federation, and supported Katanga's secession under Tshombe from the Congo (1960–3). When Zambia gained independence in 1964, the BSACo's rights were abrogated, but Britain retained large financial interests in the Copper Belt.

Roger Anstey, *Britain and the Congo in the Nineteenth Century* (London, 1962).
Patrick Keatley, *The Politics of Partnership* (London, 1963).

AEA

BRITISH IN EAST AFRICA. British naval ships first called at Zanzibar in 1799, and began a close British connection with the sultan, pressing on him several anti-slave trade treaties. From the 1850s to the 1880s British explorers penetrated from the coast and from the Sudan as far as western Uganda. British missionaries and traders followed, and the Imperial British East Africa Co. began trading in, and administering, parts of the interior. When this proved unprofitable, they handed over to the British government. British Protectorates were established in Uganda (1893), and in Kenya (the East Africa Protectorate) in 1895.

By the 1900s British settlers, along with many from the Dominions, were establishing farms in what soon became exclusively the 'White Highlands' of Kenya. A few settled in western Uganda, and more in the Kilimanjaro and Southern Highland areas of Tanganyika, when Britain began to rule it as a League of Nations mandated territory after 1918. In all three territories, the numbers of colonial administrators and technical officers grew from a mere handful to several thousand. Missionaries and teachers gradually spread Christianity and western education among Africans.

Hopes of white self-government for Kenya settlers were ended in 1923; in Tanganyika and Uganda numbers were insufficient for British or other settlers to entertain this prospect. In all three territories, however, they were strongly represented in the legislative councils. After the Second World War a new influx of British settlers went to Kenya, and in the 1950s the British in Kenya numbered 45,000–50,000, compared with approximately 18,000 in Tanganyika and 11,000 in Uganda. Many stayed after independence, and with the expansion of commerce the British business community grew rapidly in the 1960s. Africanization again caused others to leave, though some British teachers and technicians remained.

BRITISH IN WEST AFRICA, from discovery to empire. The earliest recorded English voyage to the western mainland of Africa appears to have been that of John Landye (1540); for many decades after that few followed him, though of these several made their fortunes. Early in the 17th cent. Dutch maritime enterprise caused increasing English competition, and then, with the English settlement of colonies in the Caribbean and North America, the demands of the Atlantic slave trade rapidly enlarged court and commercial interest in West African ventures.

Four chief areas of contact gradually crystallized: respectively, from west to east, the estuary of the Gambia river, the seaboard of Sierra Leone, parts of the Gold Coast (modern Ghana), and the delta of the Niger river (together with the estuaries of nearby rivers, such as the Benin on the west and the Cross on the east). Especially in the last two areas, the slave trade continued throughout the 18th cent. to maintain and develop British interest, though it was not until the middle of the 19th cent. that any idea of territorial possession (apart from ground rented from African chiefs for trading stations and forts) began to make itself felt.

Throughout the 19th cent. a network of pressures led steadily from mere presence to territorial encroachment and eventual invasion. Among these pressures were a growing rivalry with the French for influence in the interior, as well as along the seaboard; a general policy of attempting to end the slave trade on land as well as by sea; and, not least, a call by British mainland traders for government protection against the hostility of African rivals, who resented British trading interference with what had always been, until now, an African monopoly. After about 1850 these pressures took shape in new expeditions, whether 'punitive' or otherwise; and these led inexorably to the building of an empire in West Africa.   BD

BRITISH INDIAN ASSOCIATION, a political body formed in Calcutta (1851), with an entirely Indian membership, to draw attention to Indian grievances. In 1853 it submitted an important memorial to the British parliament. Although chiefly a society of landed proprietors, in 1859 its members refused to join the indigo planters in their disputes with their *rayat*s and sympathized with the latter. Kristo Das Pal, editor of the *Hindu Patriot* and an influential member of the association, was in close touch with Frank Hugh O'Donnell, the Irish MP for Dungarvan, who drew attention to Indian grievances in the House of Commons. Of 49 Indians nominated to the Bengal legislature (1862–92), 35 were members of the association. Its importance declined after the establishment of the Indian National Congress (1885).

BRITISH MUSEUM (1753). The nucleus of the collection consists of the Cotton collection of manuscripts (given 1702) and the Sloane and Harleian collections (purchased 1753). These purchases, and Montagu House, Bloomsbury, to house them, were provided by Act of Parliament in 1753. The museum was opened in 1759.

BRITISH NORTH AMERICA ACTS. British North America refers to those territories in North America which remained British colonies after American independence (1783). These colonies were separate and disunited and, in the case of British-settled Upper Canada (Ontario) and French-settled Lower Canada (Quebec), often in conflict. The rebellion of 1837 affected both Canadas and resulted in Britain sending Lord Durham, as governor-general, to enquire into the causes of the rebellion. The Durham Report (1839), which recommended that the two Canadas be united and given responsible government, became the basis for the British parliament's Act of Union 1840. By this act Upper and Lower Canada were renamed Canada East and Canada West respectively, and united into the Province of Canada under one legislature in which the partners were given equal representation. However, the traditional conflict failed to abate even with the repeal of the prohibition on the use of the French language (1848). Equal representation in the legislature meant that Canada East was initially 'over-represented' and subsequently, because of its faster population growth,

'under-represented'. Each side proved intransigent to the needs and demands of the other. In 1865, at the Quebec Conference (called on the initiative of the maritime colonies of Nova Scotia, Newfoundland, New Brunswick, and Prince Edward Island), a scheme for confederation was drawn up which became the basis for the British North America Act (1867). By this act, three colonies, Nova Scotia, New Brunswick, and Canada, were united with provision for others to enter. Prince Edward Island and Newfoundland entered under this provision in 1873 and 1949 respectively. The province of Canada was divided into the provinces of Quebec (Canada West) and Ontario (Canada East). American objections to a monarchy in the new world led Westminster to reject the Canadian request to name the confederation the Kingdom of Canada and it became instead the Dominion of Canada. However, Queen Elizabeth II was proclaimed Queen of Canada in 1952. The act conferred on the new dominion a constitution similar in principle to that of Britain, with a parliamentary and cabinet government. The federal legislature consisted of an appointed Senate, and a House of Commons, whose members were elected from the provinces on the principle of representation by population. The provinces were similarly endowed. The federal government has general and overriding powers, listed in Section 91, whilst the provinces have particular and restricted powers listed in Section 92, among which are exclusive jurisdiction over civil (not criminal) law and education.

The BNA Act 1867 created modern Canada, and it embodied the principle of representation by population while giving French Canada (Quebec) important safeguards, but it failed to provide Canada with independent means of amendment. Despite numerous attempts, the Canadians have failed to agree to a formula whereby Britain could pass this power to Canada, although the second BNA Act 1949, passed by both parliaments, which gave Canada the power to amend the constitution on matters lying solely within federal jurisdiction, is a step in that direction.   WM

BRITISH NORTH BORNEO COMPANY, sovereign authority in British North Borneo (mod. Sabah, Malaysia) (1881–1946). The British government granted it in 1881 the first royal charter since the 17th cent. which conveyed sovereign rights; the example was soon followed by several African chartered companies. Its principals, led by Alfred Dent & Co. (London), had already negotiated articles on cession to the territory from the Sultans of Brunei and Sulu in 1877–8. Unlike the African chartered companies, the BNBC did not trade, but limited itself to administering its territory on the model of British Malaya.

BRITISH POSSESSIONS ACT (1846), permitted the British colonies to repeal the restrictions on their trade imposed by previous Possessions Acts. It followed protests from Canada at the loss of imperial preference entailed by the repeal of the Corn Laws (1846), and facilitated the development of free trade. It was also an important step in the growth of colonial legislative independence. The whole power of enacting tariffs was now handed over to colonial legislatures, subject to the disallowing power of the Crown.

BRITISH SOUTH AFRICA COMPANY, THE, was established by Rhodes and Beit and received a Royal Charter in 1889. Mineral rights' concession treaties made with Lobengula, Lewanika, and other African rulers became the pretext for the extension of company rule over Southern Rhodesia (1890–3) and Zambia from 1897. The company relinquished rule over Southern Rhodesia in 1923 and over the territory north of the Zambezi in 1924. It retained vast mineral rights, however, which it sold to the Southern Rhodesian government in 1933 and, after much wrangling, to Zambia in 1964. Early expectations of profits were unjustified, and it was not until 1924 that the company paid its first dividend. Subsequently, it became commercially successful and influential.

BRITISH STANDARDS INSTITUTION (founded 1901), acknowledged authority in Britain for the compilation and distribution of national standards. It represents Britain in the International Organization for Standardization (ISO), in the International Electrotechnical Commission (IEC), and in West European organizations having similar aims. Its work includes the preparation of glossaries of terms, definitions, and symbols; establishing methods of test, specifications for quality, performance, or dimensions; preferred sizes and types; and codes of practice. It is also concerned with certification and approval of products complying with standards and with the international aspects of this subject.

BRITISH UNION OF FASCISTS, union between Sir Oswald Mosley's New Party (founded in 1931 after his break with the Labour Party) and various small Fascist groups within Britain. Despairing of the existing party system and of his own success within it, Mosley founded the BUF on his return from Italy in 1932. The Fascist salute and black shirt were adopted and in 1933 a Black House was established in Chelsea. The movement gained the support of many respectable Conservatives, including Lord Rothermere. The BUF, however, almost certainly never had more than a few thousand active members. It suffered a setback in June 1934 after the notorious Olympia meeting; the brutality used by Black Shirts to silence hecklers and the party's strongly anti-Semitic line offended a large section of the community. The Public Order Act (1936) virtually killed the movement by prohibiting political uniforms and empowering the police to forbid political processions. Out of the 1769 British subjects interned in 1940, 763 had been members of the BUF. Mosley had failed to create anything approaching a mass movement. The plight of the unemployed was not such that they were willing to turn to extremism, and as there was no communist danger, or nationalist grievances, the factors upon which Fascism might have fed were absent.

BRITISH WEEKLY, nonconformist periodical edited by the Scottish free church minister W. R. Nicoll (1851–1923), who 'habitually conceived of theology and philosophy and literature as parts of an organic whole' (T. H. Darlow). The paper greatly broadened nonconformist culture and mobilized dissent behind Liberal imperialism, Lloyd George's social reforms, and the First World War.

BRITISH WEST INDIES REGIMENT, raised in the First World War. The regiment saw service in France, the Middle East, and East Africa. It was disbanded in 1926 and re-formed (1959–62) under the Federation of the West Indies. An older military unit from the region, the West India Regiment, was formed during the American War of Independence and served in the Caribbean and Africa until it was disbanded after the First World War.

BRITTANY, WAR OF SUCCESSION TO (1488–91). The death of the Duke of Brittany in 1488, leaving only a young daughter to rule the duchy, provided France with an opportunity to bring Brittany, the last independent duchy in France, under royal control. Charles VIII of France was to marry Anne of Brittany. A treaty made with the duke just before his death stated that the king's permission had to be obtained before she married. But other suitors, all with political motives, came forward, among them Maximilian, Archduke of Austria. When it was heard that Anne had married Maximilian a large French army attacked Brittany. Spain and England became allies in order to assist Maximilian, though both pursued their own interests and were not really concerned with the Breton question. By 1491 Charles's troops had overrun Brittany. Anne renounced her previous marriage and married Charles.

BRNO, TREATY OF (1364), agreement between Rudolph IV, Duke of Austria, and the Luxemburg Emperor Charles IV, by which it was agreed that if one house died out, the remaining house would inherit the lands of the other. It was part of a longstanding Luxemburg plan for a powerful state in south-eastern Europe including Bohemia, Hungary, and the Austrian lands, but eventually it led to the Habsburgs swallowing up the Luxemburg lands and enabled them in the 15th cent. to regain permanently the German kingship.

BROAD BOTTOM ADMINISTRATION in Britain, formed after George II's dismissal of his favourite minister, Carteret, on the advice of Orford. Rising taxation to pay for the army involved in the Pragmatic war and unreliable continental alliances encouraged the Pelham–Hardwicke group to demand Granville's dismissal. On 23 Nov. 1744 the king accepted Granville's resignation. The new administration, led by Henry Pelham, as first lord of the treasury, lacked the dominating personality of a Walpole or a Carteret. It included members of all the factions, such as William Stanhope, Earl of Harrington, Pitt's friends, Lord George Lyttelton and George Grenville, Sir John Hynde Cotton (a Jacobite), and the Earl of Chesterfield. Of the anti-Carteret Whigs, William Pitt alone was excluded from the new ministry by George II, who deeply resented his open hostility to England's Hanoverian responsibilities. Under this ministry with its 'broad bottom' of opinion and interest, British foreign policy lacked direction and suffered further military defeats.

The crisis of the Jacobite rebellion (1745) caused George to vent his criticism of the Pelhams, whereupon the ministry, led by Harrington, proffered their resignations. When the royal nominees, Bath and Granville, were unable to form an alternative government, the king reluctantly accepted the inclusion of Pitt and the return of the Pelhams (1746).

BROADCASTING, term originally applied in farming to the free scattering of seed, began to be employed during the first decade of the 20th cent. to describe the diffusion of 'messages' by wireless telephony, a newly developing branch of radio technology. It had been felt to be a handicap in the application of radio to telegraphy that messages from A to B could be picked up by other parties. Yet when it was realized, at first by a few pioneers, that there was a potential audience for music and news 'broadcast' by radio, the handicap was converted into an amenity. Amateur radio enthusiasts made up the first audiences, but the basic patents necessary to the operation of broadcasting stations were in the hands of business interests by 1918. The great American broadcasting boom began in 1922, when regular 'programmes' were broadcast by privately controlled stations, later linked by 'networks'. In the same year regular weekly broadcasts began in Britain, and after complex negotiations the British Broadcasting Co. was formed (Oct. 1922); it became a public corporation in 1927. By then 'broadcasting systems', some based on monopoly, others on competition, existed in many countries, and international regulation of broadcasting wavelengths, necessary to prevent 'chaos of the ether', had started in March 1925.

In all countries broadcasting depended on the same technology; its policy and organization, however, reflected differences in national incomes and levels of development (through the numbers and distribution of receiving sets) and in social and political systems (through the control of transmissions). By 1939 three main types of broadcasting patterns had evolved—those controlled by the government, as in Germany and the USSR; those operated for profit, through advertising, as in the US; and those directed, as in Britain, by independent non-profit-making public corporations.

Broadcasting became a weapon of war between 1939 and 1945, but after 1945, despite new technical advances (eg, use of very high frequencies and of transistors), it began to take second place in many countries to television. The terms 'mass communications' and 'communications complex' became current and efforts were made to measure and evaluate their social impact.   A Bri

BROADHURST, HENRY (1840–1911), British trade unionist and stonemason, whose career in his London trade union led him into politics as Liberal MP at a time when the party needed to strengthen its democratic image. Secretary of the TUC parliamentary committee from 1875, he became under-secretary to the home department in Gladstone's 1886 ministry. In later years, by clinging to the Liberal Party, he lost touch with the Labour movement.

BROADWAY, major thoroughfare in New York City running north from Battery Park, Manhattan. Between 10th and 75th Streets it cuts diagonally across the rectangular street pattern. The mid-town section around Times Square became the centre of the theatre district and popularly known as the 'Great White Way'.

BROCK, SIR ISAAC (1769–1812), entered Canada (1802) in command of the 49th Regiment, was given command of the forces in Upper Canada (1810), and in 1811 was promoted to major-general and appointed administrator of the province. Imminence of war with the US led him to secure a change in the militia act by which flank companies were formed, and to make plans for a surprise attack in the west aimed at securing the support of Tecumseh and the Indians. When war was declared (1812), Brock's strategy proved effective and he led the force that captured Detroit (Aug. 1812).

BROCKDORFF-RANTZAU, ULRICH CARL CHRISTIAN (1869–1928), Prussian aristocrat and diplomat, who was foreign minister at the time of the Versailles conference and later an exponent of German–Soviet friendship. Educated for a career in law, he entered the German diplomatic service in 1894. He was German minister in Copenhagen (1912–18). In Feb. 1919 he led the delegation which received the Allied peace terms on 7 May. He argued in vain for an amelioration of the terms and, rather than sign, resigned (21 June). In Nov. 1922 he was appointed ambassador to Moscow, a post he held until his death. Brockdorff-Rantzau believed that a revision of the peace treaty could only be achieved through collaboration with Russia. At first, he merely wanted to use the USSR to return Germany to her former position of greatness, but he soon became a proponent of an alliance with Russia for its own sake. Brockdorff-Rantzau, however, exaggerated the ability of diplomats like Chicherin, with whom he had a close personal friendship, to change the ideological content of Soviet policy. None the less, he played an important part in ending Germany's diplomatic isolation following Versailles and in evading the military provisions of the treaty by his advocacy of the policy of Rapallo.

BROCKWAY, ARCHIBALD FENNER BROCKWAY, Life Baron (1888–), British politician. Born in India, he first achieved prominence as an organizer of the No Conscription fellowship in 1917. Thereafter he turned to politics, becoming secretary of the Independent Labour Party (1922–46), the period of the break with the Labour Party (1932), and a brief 'common front' with the communists. He rejoined the Labour Party in 1946. He is associated particularly with penal reform, and overseas (especially Indian) socialist and trade union movements.

BROEDERBOND, AFRIKANER, was founded in 1918 as a cultural association. In the 1930s it became a secret ultra-nationalist and racist society. By the 1960s many leading Afrikaners had become members.

BROGLIE, CHARLES FRANÇOIS, Comte de (1719–81), French diplomat who acted in the 1750s and 1760s as head of Louis XV's *secret du roi*, while ambassador to Poland. The *secret* aimed at keeping Turkey, Poland, and Sweden in alliance with France and free from Russian control, despite the entirely different policy being pursued by the French secretaries of state.

BROGLIE, FRANÇOIS-MARIE, Duc de (1671–1745), son of Victor Maurice, Comte de Broglie and marshal of France, he was himself created marshal in 1734 and duke in 1742. He took part in many French campaigns in the German and Italian states from 1685, but was an indifferent commander-in-chief of the French army in the War of the Austrian Succession. In the Bohemian campaign of 1741–2, which was Broglie's responsibility, disaster was averted only by his second-in-command, Belle-Isle.

BROGLIE, JACQUES VICTOR ALBERT, Duc de (1821–1901), French statesman, and leader of the Orleanists after 1870. He had kept out of politics during the Second Empire, but became prominent in organizing the royalist majority in the chamber against Thiers, whose overthrow, and replacement by the royalist MacMahon he organized in 1873. He had served as ambassador to London (1871–2) and in 1873 became minister of foreign affairs and subsequently minister of the interior. The election of a republican majority (1876) undermined his position and he was dismissed in 1877. A member of a distinguished noble family, he was Whiggish in politics, aiming to unite moderate conservatives and dissociate them from clericalism.

BROKEN HILL, Australian (NSW) mining city, 253 miles (405 kms) north-east of Port Pirie (SA), where most of its silver-lead is smelted. The line of lode, about 4 miles (6 kms) long and shaped like a coat-hanger, was discovered by a German-born horseman in Sept. 1883. It produced more wealth than any other mining field in the continent, profoundly influenced the industrialization of Australia, and showed no signs of decline in 1969, its 87th year. The flotation process, employed throughout the world for separating minerals, was largely pioneered there, and by 1910 Broken Hill was 'floating' more ore than the total of all the other fields in the world.

BROMLEY, SIR THOMAS (1530–87), succeeded Nicholas Bacon as lord chancellor (1579–87). He was noted for being a skilled and trained lawyer in the post-Wolsey tradition of professional, lay chancellors.

BROMLEY, WILLIAM (1664–1732), English High Church Tory leader in the Commons, who entered parliament for Oxford University (1690), and held the seat for over 30 years. He held immense influence through his Highflyer connections, as Tory whip for the Midlands and through his friends Nottingham and Harley. In three successive sessions (1702–5) Bromley unsuccessfully introduced Occasional Conformity bills to parliament, including the attempt to 'tack' to a finance bill. He was elected speaker (1710) after two unsuccessful attempts (1705 and 1708) and later became secretary of state (1713). He was a party man, aiming to put power solely in the hands of the Tories and leading attacks on Whigs such as Walpole and the Marlboroughs. However, when St John tried to form a party of High Tories, Bromley moved towards the moderates, becoming a Hanoverian Tory. With the death of Anne, Bromley fell from office, though he maintained his influential position in the Tory Party.

BRÖMSEBRO, PEACE OF (1645), between Sweden and Denmark in the Thirty Years War. In Sept. 1643 Oxenstierna instructed Torstensson to attack Denmark without a declaration of war, and by Jan. 1644 he had overrun Jutland. On 18 Sept. 1644 Queen Christina came of age. She favoured peace, and in Nov. 1644 the Swedish government submitted the dispute to the mediation of Brandenburg. The result was the peace of Brömsebro, giving Sweden certain trading advantages over her rival.

BROOK FARM (1841–7), experiment in Utopian Socialism at West Roxbury, MA. Its members tried to build a co-operative community in which manual and intellectual labour might be united within a simple but cultivated society. The experiment was supported by transcendentalists and other intellectual leaders of the time.

BROOKE OF BEAUCHAMP COURT, FULKE GREVILLE, 1st Baron (1554–1628), English poet and politician, who served Elizabeth I as war treasurer and James I as chancellor of the exchequer. In his youth, he was one of a group of poets working closely with Philip Sidney at Penshurst Place and Wilton House, where he was associated with the reception of ideas and forms of the Italian Renaissance.

BROOKE, SIR CHARLES (1829–1917), second 'white rajah' of Sarawak (1868–1917). Born Charles Johnson, he changed his name when chosen as heir by his uncle James Brooke. He organized a stable administration of residents and district officers, allowed the missions to begin education and the Borneo Co. to lay the basis of the state's modern economy. He also negotiated the present Sarawak boundaries with Brunei and the Dutch authorities, and was granted a formal British protectorate in 1888.

BROOKE, SIR JAMES (1803–68), founder and first ruler of Sarawak, Borneo. A quixotic imperialist with a life-long admiration for Raffles, he used an inherited fortune of £30,000 to equip a private expedition in 1838, with Borneo principally in mind. In Sarawak he befriended Raja Muda Hassim, the chief minister of Brunei, who was trying to suppress an anti-Brunei revolt there. In 1840 Brooke accepted from Hassim the government of Sarawak in return for help against the rebels, though the grant was only formally approved by the sultan after some intimidation by Brooke. During 1842–5 his prestige in Borneo rose enormously through his obtaining the co-operation of the local British naval commanders to destroy the pirate strongholds of Saribas, Sekrang, and Marudu. In 1845 Britain recognized Brooke as honorary 'confidential agent' in Borneo and in 1847 he was given the governorship of Labuan, a small island off Brunei which he had persuaded Britain to annexe as a coaling station in 1846. But opinion in Britain, led at first by merchants opposed to his policy of keeping speculative commerce out of Borneo, turned against him. Later, the Aborigine Protection Society mounted a virulent campaign against his treatment of the pirates. A commission of enquiry in 1853 exonerated him of impropriety, but held that his position as Raja of Sarawak was inconsistent with the governorship of Labuan, which he had, in any case, resigned. Thereafter, Brooke's position was insecure, despite the extension of Sarawak territory to the Batang Lupar basin in 1861, because British recognition remained ambiguous until 1863, the year of his final departure from Borneo. In 1857 his regime was almost destroyed in a Chinese rebellion. Though dedicated to uplifting the Dayak population, his rudimentary administration rested mainly on the Malay Datos, who had served the earlier Brunei regime.

Steven Runciman, *The White Rajas, a History of Sarawak from 1841 to 1946* (Cambridge, 1960). AJSR

BROOKEBOROUGH, BASIL STANLAKE BROOKE, 1st Viscount (1888–), Irish politician. After serving in the British army during the First World War, he entered the parliament of Northern Ireland as a Unionist in 1929. Thereafter his rise was rapid. He was first minister of agriculture and then of commerce (1933–45), and became prime minister in 1943. He was closely associated with a rigid Unionist policy, the maintenance of a Protestant supremacy, and cool relations towards the Republic of Eire. This policy he pursued with success for 20 years until his replacement by Capt. Terence O'Neill in 1963.

BROOKS, PRESTON SMITH (1819-57), US politician. Brooks, a Democratic congressman from South Carolina (1853–57), achieved brief notoriety when he physically attacked Charles Sumner of Massachusetts in the Senate (1856) after Sumner had slandered his uncle, Senator Andrew Butler of South Carolina, as a champion of slavery.

BROOKS, VAN WYCK (1886–1963), US literary critic. After graduating from Harvard (1904), he devoted his life to an interpretation of American literary history. Before *Emerson and Others* (1927) his work was characterized by antipathy towards the Puritan tradition. His talent lay mainly in his ability to reconstruct, in anecdotal form, the literary life of the past. His best-known works include *The Ordeal of Mark Twain* (1920), and *Makers and Finders: A history of the writer in America, 1800–1915* (1936–52).

BROSSES, CHARLES DE (1709–77), French geographer, whose writings acted as an inspiration for the voyages of James Cook.

BROTHER JONATHAN, a nickname for the American people. When the British vacated Bunker Hill, they left straw effigies labelled 'Welcome Brother Jonathan'. During the American War of Independence, loyalists and British soldiers used the term to ridicule the Americans, but it was not used by the Americans themselves. After the war it was often used in New England to denote country bumpkins.

BROTHERHOOD OF THE COAST (Frères de la Costé), an international confraternity of buccaneers operating in the 1640s against the Spanish from the West Indian island of Tortuga.

BROUGHAM AND VAUX OF BROUGHAM, HENRY PETER, 1st Baron (1778–1868), English politician. He was born and educated in Edinburgh and first made his name by contributions to the *Edinburgh Review*. He came to London in 1804 and became prominent in the campaign against the slave trade, and later led a sustained opposition to the Orders in Council. He was elected MP (1810) and became a leading speaker for the opposition, successfully campaigning for the abolition of income tax. In the 1820s he gave strong support to the revived anti-slavery agitation and to the contemporary campaign to reform and ease the harshness of criminal law. He encouraged the development of popular education and took a leading part in the foundation of the London Mechanics' Institute, the Society for the Diffusion of Useful Knowledge, and University College London. When the prospect of a reform administration became imminent in the summer of 1830, Brougham was at the height of his career. Invited to stand for Yorkshire, he was elected after a speech-making tour of industrial districts, in which he declared himself in favour of household suffrage and annual parliaments. On the formation of Grey's ministry (Nov. 1830) Brougham became lord chancellor, which prevented him from expressing his form of popular radicalism in Commons debates. After 1830, though he continued to work for law reform, his prestige and influence had declined.

BROUGHTON DE GYFFORD, JOHN CAM HOBHOUSE, 1st Baron (1786–1869), British statesman aho entered radical politics in 1819 when he unsuccessfully contested Westminster, but was elected in 1820. In the 1820s he worked for the Greek Committee. He was one of Byron's closest friends and his executor, and Byron's *Memoirs* were destroyed on his orders. He was excluded from Grey's ministry (1830) but joined it in 1832-3 as secretary-at-war in which office he carried out reforms. He was a member of the Whig cabinets (1835–41, 1846–52) as president of the board of control.

BROUGHTON, WILLIAM GRANT, bishop (1788–1853), an English scholar, who went to Australia as an Anglican archdeacon (1829), becoming first—and only—Bp of Australia (1836) and Metropolitan Bp of Sydney (1847). Broughton's period saw a large increase in the number of churches, schools, and clergy, due partly to his organizing ability. New bishoprics were founded and Broughton himself presided at an episcopal conference (1850) to determine policies for a Church now virtually separated from the state. As a strong High Churchman and a Tractarian sympathizer, he made few concessions to the 'popular' position on education, social regulation, or Anglican hegemony.

BROWDER, EARL RUSSELL (1891–   ), US Communist leader during the party's most successful years (1930–45), and presidential candidate (1936, 1940). He was replaced by William Z. Foster (1945), and expelled from the party for ideological reasons in 1946.

BROWN, CHARLES BROCKDEN (1771–1810), first US novelist. His three best novels, *Wieland* (1798), *Arthur Mervyn* (1799), and *Ormond* (1799), are Gothic romances, clearly influenced by Godwin, Richardson, and Mrs Radcliffe, but their American materials and settings and their morbid neurotic intensity make them distinctive and often compelling. His last novel was *Jane Talbot* (1801).

BROWN, GEORGE (1818–80), Canadian journalist and leading Liberal. He left Scotland for New York (1838), where he established the *British Chronicle* (1842), then moved to Toronto and established the *Globe* (1844), through which he influenced the reform movement and the formation of the Liberal Party. In 1854 he joined forces with the Clear Grits, advocating elective institutions ('Representation by Population') and the acquisition of the north-west territories of the Hudson's Bay Co. He was elected to the Canadian House of Assembly (1851) and in 1864 he joined the Sandfield–MacDonald coalition ministry, pledged to achieve confederation, but resigned owing to differences with the Conservatives (1865), after attending the Charlottetown and Quebec conferences. He continued to advocate confederation and though appointed to the Senate (1873), he diverted his energies to the *Globe*.

BROWN, GEORGE (1835–1917), pioneer Pacific missionary, who migrated from Durham to New Zealand (1855), joined the Wesleyan Mission in Samoa (1860–74), and went to New Britain and New Ireland (1875). He was criticized for burning several villages with some loss of life in reprisal for the murder of a Fijian pastor and three teachers in 1878. He was appointed secretary of the mission in Sydney (1887) and founded Wesleyan missions in New Guinea and the Solomons.

BROWN, JOHN (1800–59), US abolitionist martyr. Born in Torrington, CT, he grew up in Ohio and tried his hand at various jobs for which he showed little aptitude. As early as the 1830s he was helping fugitive slaves to escape from the South and in 1850 organized, in Springfield, IL, a League of Gileadites, pledged to offer physical resistance to enforcement of the Fugitive Slave Act. He achieved notoriety at the time of the Kansas troubles by conducting guerrilla warfare against pro-slavery settlers, and by the massacre at Potawattomie Creek (1857). He had long dreamed of organizing a slave rebellion in the South, and led a band of followers against the Federal arsenal at Harper's Ferry, VA (Oct. 1859). He was subsequently tried, convicted of treason against the state of Virginia, and hanged. The song 'John Brown's Body' became one of the most popular marching songs of the Civil War.

BROWN, LANCELOT (1715–83), known as 'Capability Brown', English landscape gardener. He adopted the principles of design introduced to England by William Kent whereby parks and gardens were designed in imitation of romantic landscape painting. Formal gardens were abolished in favour of parkland sweeping up to the house, vistas were arranged, sometimes at the cost of extravagant civil engineering works, to lead the eye to picturesque ruins or temples. Examples of his work may be seen at Blenheim, Stowe, and in the original layout of Kew Gardens.

BROWN, ROBERT (1773–1858), British officer in a Scottish regiment, who became a protégé of Sir Joseph Banks, of whose collection he later became librarian and, eventually, British Museum custodian. Banks's influence secured Brown's appointment (1800) as naturalist with Matthew Flinders on *Investigator*. Brown's work on Australian plants was revealed in his *Prodromus Florae Novae Hollandiae et Insulae Van Diemen* (part 1, 1810; reprinted complete, 1960), on which rests his claim to recognition as originator of the science of plant geography.

BROWN, THOMAS STORROW (1803–88), Canadian rebel and pamphleteer and temperance advocate, who founded the *Vindicator* (1832) and commanded the insurgents at St Charles in the rebellion of 1837. He escaped to the US, but returned to Canada (1844) and investigated misappropriation of funds in government departments (1862).

BROWN v. BOARD OF EDUCATION OF TOPEKA, 347 US 483 (1954), a major civil rights decision of the US Supreme Court, overruling the 'separate but equal' doctrine of *Plessy v. Ferguson* (1896). The court was unanimous in declaring that official segregation of black and white schoolchildren violated the 'equal protection of the laws' clause of the Fourteenth Amendment to the US Constitution. In stating his opinion Chief Justice Warren avoided both legal and historical complexities, argued simply that in the 20th cent. school segregation imposed inferior status on black children and that separate educational facilities were therefore inherently unequal. The court, heavily influenced by sociological evidence, ignored historical questions of congressional intent and disregarded or reversed judicial precedents supporting school segregation.

The decision had a tremendous psychological impact on black leaders and directly influenced the activities of the civil rights movement in the next decade. It was condemned by Southern conservatives as both a violation of traditional federal–state relations and a usurpation of legislative functions by the judiciary. Some legal experts also criticized the decision as 'judicial legislation'. In a later explanatory opinion the court directed states and school districts to 'make a fair and reasonable start' and proceed 'with all deliberate speed' towards desegregation.

BROWNE, GEORGE, archbishop of Dublin (1536), assisted Henry VIII to introduce the Reformation into Ireland. He spoke in favour of the royal supremacy, procured monastic revenues for the Crown, and introduced the first English Prayer Book. On Mary's accession he was deprived of his posts.

BROWNE, ROBERT (c. 1550–1633), leader of a group of Elizabethan separatists. In 1580 he established a separatist church at Norwich. He was imprisoned 32 times because of his preaching and in 1582 was exiled to the Netherlands. He eventually accepted convention and obscurity and was made rector of Achurch, Northants (1591–1633), by Burghley, with whom his father claimed kinship.

BROWNE, SIR THOMAS (1605–82), English physician, author, and antiquarian. In *Religio Medici* (1635) he sought to reconcile scientific medicine with Church doctrine. His *Enquiries into Vulgar and Common Errors* (1646) is a plea for experimental research, and his *Urn Burial* (1658) is a history of the various modes of disposal of the dead.

BROWNE, THOMAS ALEXANDER (1826–1913), Australian writer (pseud. Rolfe Boldrewood), born in England, who emigrated with his parents in 1830. His many novels of 19th-cent. Australian life include *Robbery Under Arms* (1888), *The Miner's Right* (1890), and *A Sydneyside Saxon* (1891).

BROWNE, SIR THOMAS GORE (1807–87), NZ governor at the outbreak of the Maori Wars, was an able soldier, but without experience or abilities suited to the situation which he found when he arrived in 1855 to inaugurate responsible government. Perceiving the danger of settlers' demands for Maori land, he retained control of native affairs. Thwarted by ministers and parliament, relying too heavily on the able but devious McLean, and dubbed 'Angry Belly' by Maoris, Browne failed to halt the drift to war in Taranaki. His celebrated Waitara speech (Feb. 1860) precipitated the war he sought to avoid. Though formally approving his actions, the UK government replaced him with Grey in 1861.

BROWNING, ROBERT (1812–89) and **BROWNING, ELIZABETH** (1806–61), English poets. Robert's work included *Men and Women*, and *The Ring and the Book*. His marriage to Elizabeth (1846) rescued her from a tyrannical father and improved her health. Her own talent is best shown in *Poems* (1844) and *Sonnets from the Portuguese*. Both Brownings hold a significant place in Victorian literature.

BROWNISTS, followers of a system of church government advocated *c.* 1580 by Robert Browne. They were pioneers of free churches in England, *ie*, churches existing independently of the secular government. Consequently they underwent much persecution. Their system was later adopted by the Independents and Congregationalists.

BROWNRIGG, SIR ROBERT (1759–1833), governor of Ceylon (1812–20), who brought the whole island under British rule. After secret negotiations with certain Kandyan chiefs, who disliked the reigning house of the Kandyan kingdom, Indian by race, he sent an expedition to Kandy which met with easy success. The king was captured and sent to India (1815).

BROWNSON, ORESTES AUGUSTUS (1803–76), US theologian, philosopher, and reformer. Successively a Presbyterian, Universalist, Unitarian, and Roman Catholic, Brownson tended to reject dogma for his own liberal brand of preaching and writing. He helped to organize the Workingman's Party (1828), and formed the Society For Christian Union and Progress (1836) among the labouring men of Boston. His first book, *New Views of Christianity, Society, and the Church* (1836), condemned both Protestantism and Catholicism. He established the *Boston Quarterly Review* (1838), later *Brownson's Review*, and was closely associated with the Transcendentalists. After his conversion to Catholicism (1844), he devoted himself to uncompromising praise of that faith.

BRUCE OF MELBOURNE, STANLEY MELBOURNE BRUCE, Viscount (1883–1967), Australian prime minister. Though Melbourne-born, he was less distinctively Australian than his predecessors or his successor. Bruce, who was educated at Melbourne Grammar School and Cambridge, began by practising at the bar in England. He returned to Australia in 1917 to manage the Melbourne warehouse founded by his family, having been invalided out of a British regiment at Gallipoli. Within twelve months, Bruce reluctantly stood for the Commonwealth parliament, and in 1923 became prime minister after one year as treasurer. He retained office until he lost his seat in the elections of 1929, which brought Labor back to power. He re-entered parliament in 1931, then went to London in 1932 as Australian high commissioner until 1945. As prime minister he was responsible for the significant Commonwealth–States financial agreement (1926) and he established the Council for Scientific and Industrial Research. He attempted in the later 1920s to curb the economic irresponsibility encouraged by his own slogan 'men, money, and markets'. Bruce's pre-war and wartime services in London were recognized in Australia as well as in England and his activity in international economics won him his peerage. He acted as an elder statesman in the House of Lords, besides taking an active part in British business administration, until shortly before his death. He was the first chancellor of the Australian National University (1951–1961).

C. Edwards, *Bruce of Melbourne: man of two worlds* (London, 1965).

BRUCE, EDWARD (d. 1318), younger brother of King Robert I of Scotland, who was offered the high kingship of Ireland (1315). Edward's invasion of Ulster met with considerable success, but he was killed in battle at Farghart. This invasion permanently weakened England's hold over medieval Ireland.

BRUCE, ROBERT (1210–95), one of the chief claimants to the Scottish throne in the disputed succession, which followed the death of Alexander III. The court of 1291–2, presided over by Edward I of England, decided in favour of John Balliol, but Bruce's grandson proclaimed himself king in 1306 as Robert I.

BRUCE, SIR WILLIAM (1630–1710), Scottish architect and politician. He encouraged Gen. Monck to support the restoration of Charles II, and later became the king's surveyor of royal palaces and castles in Scotland. In this capacity he rebuilt Holyroodhouse.

BRUGES, Belgium, originally the capital of the earliest counts of Flanders. It owed its later development to economic factors. Though it had ceased to be a harbour by the 13th cent., it maintained its supremacy through its outports until the late 15th cent. as the financial and commercial centre of the Netherlands and as a meeting place of Italian, Spanish and German merchants in north-western Europe. From the 16th–19th cents it suffered a period of decline, from which it emerged only in the 20th cent., becoming once again an important trading centre, partly because of its canal (1907).

BRUGES, MATINS OF. France had conquered Flanders in 1300, but the excessive reliance of the French governor, Jacques de Châtillon, on the landed nobility and the urban patriciates alienated the populace. A group of exiles penetrated Bruges during the night of 17–18 May 1302 and several Frenchmen were killed. This was a signal for a general popular revolt of the Flemings against France.

BRUGES, TREATY OF (1521), negotiated personally between the Emperor Charles V and Henry VIII, pledging their mutual friendship and determination to crush France by a combined invasion. Despite Francis I's overtures to Henry VIII at the Field of the Cloth of Gold (1520), and English gratification at being courted by both France and the emperor, Wolsey favoured, from motives of self-interest, an alliance with the pope and Charles V. He therefore arranged the meeting between Charles and Henry which produced the treaty of Bruges (25 Aug. 1521). By this agreement Charles was to marry Henry's daughter, Mary, and a joint declaration of war on France was to follow. The agreement was confirmed by the treaty of Windsor (19 June 1522). England thus committed herself to expensive and useless campaigns in northern France while the ultimate result was the crushing defeat of France at Pavia (1525), from which the emperor alone profited.

BRUHL, COUNT HEINRICH VON (1700–64), chief minister of Frederick Augustus of Saxony and virtual ruler of both Saxony and Poland from 1738. He was noted for his extravagance.

BRULÉ, ÉTIENNE (*c.* 1592–1633), French explorer and interpreter. He left France for Quebec at the age of sixteen. In 1615 he guided Champlain to Lake Huron and supported his unsuccessful campaign against the Iroquois. He also led an expedition to Chesapeake Bay (1618–20) and was the first white man to explore the Lake Superior region (1621–3). In 1629 he piloted the British expedition under David Kirke which captured Quebec (and Champlain). Brulé lived intimately among the Hurons, was said to have outdone them in savagery, and was eventually killed and eaten by them.

BRULÉ INDIANS, sub-tribe of the Teton division of the American Dakota tribe, noted in 1804 by the explorers Lewis and Clark on both sides of the Missouri, White, and Teton rivers. Other observers described the Brulé as good hunters, generally well fed and clothed. They were buffalo hunters, wild horse trappers, and raiders of other tribes. They were nearer to the California emigrant trail than any other division of the Dakota and suffered heavily from diseases introduced by the settlers. Their chief, Makatozaza, was noted for his friendly attitude to the white man, and for his skill as a governor. Another chief, Swift Bear, was largely responsible for the treaty of 1868 between the Sioux bands and the US government. The Brulé were ultimately confined to reservations in South Dakota.

BRUMAIRE, _COUP D'ÉTAT_ (1799), brought the Directory to an end and installed Napoleon in power in France. The Directory's survival had come to depend increasingly on the support of the army. It was only a matter of time before one of the revolutionary generals took over himself. As the most successful and popular of the generals, Napoleon was in the best position to effect such a coup. The opportunity was provided by a group of politicians around Sièyes, who wanted a change of government to strengthen the executive and provide stable government. They intended to use Napoleon only as an instrument, but he saw it as an opening to personal power. On 10 Nov., after a temporary loss of nerve on his own part, his troops turned out the Legislative Councils.

BRUNEI, sultanate in northern Borneo, which gave its name to the whole island. Though a centre of Chinese trade since at least the 13th cent., its political prominence dates from the establishment of the Muslim sultanate (_c._ 1500). At its early 16th-cent. peak, it predominated over most of Borneo and the Sulu archipelago, but by the mid-17th cent. only the north-western Borneo coast remained. The Brunei Malays controlled the river mouths, but exploited rather than ruled the animistic peoples of the interior. In the 19th cent. Brunei was notoriously a prey to pirates and slave-traders, and its territory was reduced to a tiny enclave by the Brookes in Sarawak and the British North-Borneo Co. before Britain granted a protectorate (1888). Brunei's economic fortunes were dramatically reversed by the discovery of oil (1929), the revenues of which later influenced the sultan's decision against joining Malaysia (1963).

BRUNEL, ISAMBARD KINGDOM (1806–59), engineer and son of **SIR MARC ISAMBARD BRUNEL** (1769–1849), surveyor, engineer, and designer of the Thames tunnel (1825–1843), for which project I. K. Brunel was resident engineer. Both father and son were elected FRS.

I. K. Brunel designed track, stations, bridges, tunnels, and viaducts for the Great Western Railway, and also the docks at Bristol and Plymouth. Among his other achievements were Clifton suspension bridge and Paddington station. His vision of a Paddington–New York line led him to pioneer steam vessels such as the _Great Western_ (1838), the _Great Britain_ (1845), and the _Great Eastern_ (1858). His technical contribution to engineering brought developments in iron-clad ships, screw-propulsion, and steam-power. His social and economic contribution opened up internal communications in Britain, and eventually established her supremacy in commercial shipping for the rest of the 19th cent.

BRUNELLESCHI, FILIPPO (1379–1446), chief creator of the Renaissance style of architecture in Florence. He imitated the proportions of classical buildings, adapted ancient decorative patterns, and borrowed also from older Florentine romanesque buildings. Everything constructed by him was extremely reliable and his engineering was triumphantly vindicated by the construction of the great dome on the cathedral at Florence (1419–36).

BRUNI, LEONARDO (1369–1444), a leading Italian humanist, chancellor of Florence (1427–44), and a pioneer in translating from Greek into Latin. In his history of Florence he successfully adapted the models of Cicero and Livy to a modern theme, combining it with critical use of narrative and official sources. His biographies of Petrarch and Dante were unusual among the works of the early humanists in defending the use of Italian in literature and scholarship.

BRUNKEBURG, BATTLE OF (1471), resulted in the defeat near Stockholm of King Christian I of Denmark by the Swedes, led by Sten Sture, the Protector of Sweden. This ended effectively the Danish claim to the Swedish throne and destroyed Danish royal authority in Sweden.

BRUNO, archbishop of Cologne (925–65), brother and one of the best collaborators of Emperor Otto I. Chancellor of Germany from 940, he was appointed Abp of Cologne and Duke and viceroy of Lorraine, the most westerly portion of the empire. He was canonized in 1870.

BRUNO, GIORDANO (1548–1600), Italian philosopher, whose pantheistic extension of the Copernican concept of a moving universe led to his being burnt as a heretic (1600). His case aroused bitter Protestant hostility and led to Catholic mistrust of Copernicanism and later to the trial of Galileo.

BRUNSCHWIG, HIERONYMUS (_c._ 1450–1512), author of _Liber de arte distillande_, a treatise on the process of distillation, the chief branch of chemistry studied in the early 16th cent.

BRUNSFELS, OTTO (1464–1534), German botanist, who was one of the first to describe and illustrate the plants of the world then known. He was also interested in the purported medical values and domestic uses of plants.

BRUNSWICK, FERDINAND, Duke of (1735–1806), Prussian general in the Seven Years War and Revolutionary and Napoleonic Wars, who was disastrously defeated at Auerstädt (1806).

BRUNSWICK MANIFESTO (25 July 1792), issued by the Duke of Brunswick, threatened Paris with military execution by the Prussian army if the French royal family was harmed. It merely hastened the fall of the monarchy.

BRUNSWICK-LUNEBERG, German duchy created in 1235, lying between the Weser and Elbe rivers. At the death of Duke Ernest in 1546 the line split into two branches. His younger son, William, founded the modern line of Brunswick-Luneberg and from his youngest son, George, Duke of Hanover, was descended the British Hanoverian royal line.

BRUNSWICK-WOLFENBUTTEL, ducal line founded in 1546 on the death of Ernest of Brunswick and Luneberg by his elder son, Henry, Duke of Luneberg-Dauneberg. His descendants were those two dukes of Brunswick who were Prussian generals in the Napoleonic Wars. The state of Brunswick was later absorbed into the North German Confederation.

BRUSSELS, capital of modern Belgium. It originated as the chief town of the dynasty of the dukes of Brabant, who since the 12th cent. controlled the most central and war-like of the Belgian principalities. After Brabant was merged in the Burgundian state (1428) Brussels became the capital of the

Burgundian dukes, who made it into one of the most important European artistic centres. The emergence of an independent Belgium started with the revolt of Brussels against the Dutch in 1830.

BRUSSELS CONFERENCE (1876), international gathering called by Leopold II of Belgium ostensibly to discuss a code of conduct for the further exploration and colonization of Africa. Out of it under his auspices was formed the International Association for the Exploration and Civilization of Africa. Although it had branches in other countries besides Belgium, a large part of its capital came from Leopold's own fortune and it was a business run by him for commercial profit, despite its avowed objects, exploration and the suppression of slavery. The association financed expeditions by Stanley into the Congo (1879), which was exploited ruthlessly and brought under Leopold's personal control.

BRUSSELS CONFERENCE, DECLARATION OF (1874), on the rules of military warfare, dealt with the conduct of troops in enemy territory, the treatment of prisoners of war, and the procedure to be followed over armistices and truces. All the European powers took part in the conference and agreed to the terms, most of which were later embodied in the first Hague Convention.

BRUTUS, DECIMUS IUNIUS (d. 43 BC), Roman noble, an officer of Julius Caesar in Gaul and the Civil War, who joined the conspiracy to assassinate him. He defended Mutina against Antony (44), pursued him to Gaul, and was betrayed and killed.

BRUTUS, L. IUNIUS, Roman consul in 509 BC. The legendary account of how, after the suicide of Lucretia, he overthrew King Tarquinius Superbus, established Roman liberty, and executed his two sons for conspiring to restore the monarchy, has been imaginatively developed, but his historical existence need not be doubted.

BRUTUS, M. IUNIUS (c. 85–42 BC), the Roman 'tyrannicide', one of Julius Caesar's murderers. Son of Servilia, half-sister of Cato the younger, whose daughter he married, Brutus was brought up by Cato after his father's death and joined the Pompeians in the Civil War. Pardoned and favoured by Caesar after Pharsalus, he became governor of Cisalpine Gaul (46) and praetor (44), but was nevertheless a leader of the conspiracy against him. Finding it impossible to remain in Rome after Caesar's murder, he seized Macedonia and with Cassius in Syria gained control of the East, but committed suicide after he and Cassius were defeated by Antony at Philippi.

BRYAN, WILLIAM JENNINGS (1860–1925), US lawyer and journalist, orator, and political leader. He dominated the radical agrarian wing of the Democratic Party from the 1890s to the 1920s and helped to transform the party into the vehicle of reform that it became under Woodrow Wilson and Franklin Roosevelt. His career was founded on his complete identification with rural and small-town America.

Soon after moving to Nebraska (1887) he was returned as a Democratic representative to Congress (1890–4). This was a time when the growth of Populism was threatening the established party structure throughout the west and he became converted to the Populist demand for the free coinage of silver (1892). In 1893 he led the unsuccessful fight in the House of Representatives against repeal of the Sherman Silver Purchase Act. After becoming editor of the Omaha *World Herald* (1894), which was owned by silver-mining interests, he campaigned to convert the Democratic Party to 'free silver'. His success was underlined at the Democratic national convention in 1896 when, after his emotional 'Cross of Gold' speech, he was given the presidential nomination.

In the campaign that followed, Bryan's concentration on the silver issue was a handicap in the east, and when the votes were counted the 'Boy Orator of the Platte' had suffered his first major defeat. His opponent, McKinley, not only had the backing of big business, but also appealed to widespread fears of radicalism. Bryan was renominated in 1900, but his concentration on anti-imperialism and independence for the Philippines proved even less successful than free silver. The conservative wing of the party gained control in 1904, but such was Bryan's standing that he was again nominated in 1908, on a wide reform platform. By this time, the Republicans had adopted progressive policies without losing the support of business, and Bryan went down to his third presidential defeat, thus completing a record unique in American history.

In 1912, with the Republicans divided and a Democratic victory likely, Bryan played an important part in securing the nomination of Woodrow Wilson. As Wilson's first secretary of state, Bryan energetically pursued his long-standing interest in arbitration agreements, and, in the belief that they would help to preserve peace, negotiated 30 conciliation treaties. When war broke out in 1914 he was determined to maintain American neutrality, became increasingly estranged from Wilson, and resigned over the president's handling of the *Lusitania* crisis (1915).

Although remaining active in politics, his last years were largely devoted to the prohibition and anti-evolution campaigns. He appeared as counsel for the prosecution in the Scopes trial in Tennessee.   AJT

BRYANT, WILLIAM CULLEN (1794–1878), emerged as the leading US poet after the publication of *Thanatopsis* (1817). As editor of the New York *Evening Post* from 1829, he was largely responsible for elevating journalism to a respected means of influencing public opinion. He consistently opposed slavery and helped found the Republican Party (1854).

BRYCE, JAMES BRYCE, 1st Viscount (1838–1922), British historian and Liberal statesman and ambassador to Washington (1907–13). The Bryce Commission on secondary education (1894–5), of which he was chairman, paved the way for the Education Act of 1902. As an historian he is remembered for *The Holy Roman Empire* (1864), *The American Commonwealth* (1888), and for his share in the establishment of the *English Historical Review* (1886).

BRYDGES, SIR HARFORD JONES (1764–1847), British diplomat, who, as ambassador to Iran (1807–11), negotiated an Anglo-Iranian agreement which eventually became the treaty of Teheran (1814).

BRYDON, Dr (1811–73), was in the medical service of the East India Co. (1835–59). He served in the First Afghan War (1838–42) but, contrary to popular belief, he was not the sole survivor of the disastrous retreat from Kabul. In the Mutiny (1857) he was one of the beleaguered garrison at Lucknow.

BRZESC, UNION OF (1596), religious agreement between the Catholic Church in Poland and the majority of the Greek Orthodox hierarchy in Lithuania which established the Uniate Church, bearing allegiance to the papacy but retaining Orthodox ritual. It marked a further step in the process of union between those two countries started by the union of Lublin (1569), which created the multi-lingual and multi-religious commonwealth of Poland, Lithuania, Mazovia, West Prussia, Courland, and Livonia (*Rzeczpospolita*).

BU SA'ID, AL-, Muslim dynasty ruling in Muscat and Oman since the 18th cent. in succession to the Ya'rubid imams. It was founded (c. 1749) by Ahmad ibn Sa'id, who assumed the title of Imam (of the Ibadi sect), a title also borne by his son, Sa'id. Subsequent rulers were known as sayyid and by foreigners as sultan. In 1798 Sayyid Sultan ibn Ahmad (1792–1804) entered into a treaty with Britain which formed the basis of an enduring alliance between Britain and the dynasty. The greatest Al-Bu Sa'id ruler was Sa'id ibn Sultan (1806–56), who expanded the Omani empire in Africa, based upon Zanzibar. After his death, Zanzibar and Oman were divided between two branches of the dynasty. The Zanzibar branch was overthrown by revolution in 1964.

BUCARELI Y URSÚA, ANTONIO MARÍA (1717–79), Spanish general and reformer. As viceroy of New Spain (1771–9), he brought many administrative and social reforms to the colony. He is considered to have been one of Spain's most enlightened colonial administrators.

BUCCANEERS. West Indian pirates and privateers, originally multi-national Europeans who in the 17th cent. hunted wild cattle in Hispaniola. The name comes from *boucan* or dried meat. Driven from Hispaniola (*c.* 1630), they settled in Tortuga and turned to raiding Spanish ships. Buccaneers in Port Royal, Jamaica, were encouraged by the British and used against the Dutch and Spaniards. Under Henry Morgan they attacked Cuba, Venezuela, and Panama. By orders of the British (1670) and French (1684) government buccaneers were suppressed in the West Indies.

BUCER, MARTIN (1491–1551), German Protestant reformer (his real name was Cowhorn), who came to England in the reign of Edward VI and helped to give the Reformation a more radical direction. Originally a Dominican friar, he was converted by Luther and taught for 20 years at Strasbourg, where he vainly attempted to reconcile the Lutheran and Calvinist schools of thought. Placed in personal danger by his refusal to sign the compromising Augsburg Interim (1548), he came to England at Cranmer's invitation and, although he could speak no English, was made Regius Professor of Divinity at Cambridge. His writings and disputations influenced the Prayer Book of 1549, and he could not accept Christ's corporal presence at the Eucharist. In religious observance Bucer was a rigid disciplinarian and he deplored the moral and economic licence practised by many of the secular supporters of the Reformation. His *De Regno Christi*, presented to the king in 1550, proposed a system of religious and moral discipline more severe than anything advocated later by the English Puritans.

BUCHANAN, JAMES (1791–1868), US president in the years preceding the Civil War. A Pennsylvanian of Scots–Irish descent, he had a remarkably long and varied career as diplomat and Democratic politician. He was a member of the House of Representatives (1821–31), US minister to Russia (1832–3), Senator from Pennsylvania (1834–45), secretary of state in President Polk's administration (1845–9), and US minister to Britain (1853–6). An ardent expansionist, he favoured the purchase or annexation of Cuba, and, with the US ministers to Spain and France, drew up the Ostend Manifesto (1854). His presidency (1857–61) was dominated by the north–south dispute over slavery and its extension into the western territories. He supported the Supreme Court's decision in the Dred Scott case, and the pro-slavery Lecompton constitution in Kansas. In the last months of his presidency (1860–1), with his party split, and with Lincoln already elected as his successor, he denied the right of the southern states to secede, but believed he had no authority to use force against them. An unassertive man, with a limited view of presidential power, he was ill-fitted to cope with the unprecedented secession crisis.

BUCHAREST, PEACE CONGRESS OF (1772–3), failed to end the Russo-Turkish War (1768–74). Catherine the Great of Russia was eager for peace, despite her military successes, because of increasing peasant unrest at home and the danger of Swedish attack. But the Turks refused to cede Kerch and to allow the Russians free use of the Black Sea for their warships, although they were forced to concede both demands a year later at the peace of Kuchuk-Kainardji (1774).

BUCHAREST, TREATIES OF (28 May 1812). The first treaty brought the Russo-Turkish War, which had begun in 1806, to an end with the cession of Bessarabia to Russia. Although Russian troops had occupied the Danubian Provinces, Alexander I needed peace to release troops to face Napoleon's planned invasion of Russia. Under the treaty the Turks promised to grant autonomy to the Serbs, who had helped the Russian advance by their revolt, but they failed to carry out this promise.

The second treaty (6 Aug. 1913) was signed under German pressure at the end of the Second Balkan War, in which Bulgaria had suffered a humiliating defeat at the hands of her former allies against Turkey. Bulgaria was forced to acknowledge the division of Macedonia between Serbia and Greece, as well as to surrender Western Thrace and its important port of Kavalla to Greece and the southern Dobrogea to Rumania. Resentment over these losses and the great increase in Serbian power helped to push Bulgaria into the Austro-German camp at the outbreak of the First World War.

BUCHAREST TREATY (7 May 1918), concluded between Rumania and the Central Powers shortly after the peace of Brest-Litovsk. When the Bolsheviks withdrew from the war, Rumania had little option but to follow Russia out of the alliance with Britain, France, and the US. The Central Powers acquired control of Rumania's grain supplies and oil wells. Rumania ceded the Dobrogea and the edge of the Carpathians to Austria–Hungary. The Central Powers did not object to the incorporation of Bessarabia in Rumania.

BUCHEZ, PIERRE JOSEPH BENJAMIN (1796–1865), French Christian socialist and founder of the French cooperative movement, who began his political career in opposition to the restored Bourbon regime. As a member of the St-Simonist group, he tried to combine catholicism with socialist ideas, teaching that socialism was the modern embodiment of Christianity. During the revolution of 1848 he acted as president of the constituent assembly, but on Louis Napoleon's assumption of power Buchez retired from the political scene.

BUCHLAU CONVENTION (15 Sept. 1908), informal understanding reached between the Austro-Hungarian foreign minister, Aerenthal, and his Russian opposite number, Izvolsky. The contradictory accounts of what had been agreed were in a large part to cause the international crisis over the Austrian annexation of Bosnia-Herzegovina. Izvolsky seems to have agreed to the annexation in return for support for Russian policy towards the Straits. Unfortunately, he did not get a signed agreement, nor a clear understanding of how Austria should annex these provinces. Aerenthal undoubtedly deceived him into believing that Austria would not act alone and would get the agreement of the powers to their moves over Bosnia and the Straits before acting.

BUCK, SIR PETER HENRY (Te Rangi Hiroa) (1877–1951), leader of NZ's Young Maori Party. After graduating as a doctor (Otago, 1910), he was elected MP for Northern Maori (1909–1911), and became a minister (1912). He served in the First World War and in 1927 joined the Bishop Museum, Hawaii, where he remained until his death. His *Vikings of the Sunrise* argues the now conventional view that Polynesians entered the Pacific down the Micronesian chain.

BUCKINGHAM, HUMPHREY STAFFORD, 1st Duke of (1st creation) (1402–60), figure of rare integrity during the Wars of the Roses, who tried to prevent open warfare between Henry VI and Richard of York by exerting a moderating influence over the latter. Buckingham was murdered by the Yorkists after their victory at Northampton in 1460.

BUCKINGHAM, HENRY STAFFORD, 2nd Duke of (1st creation) (d. 1483). A very different man from his father,

Humphrey (d. 1460), who had stood above faction. Henry's hatred of the widow of King Edward IV of England, Elizabeth Woodville, and her relatives led him to support the usurpation of the throne by Richard III, and the disinheritance of her children. But Buckingham soon came to distrust Richard, regarding as inadequate the lavish grants that he himself had received. Moved perhaps by an ambition to secure the Crown for himself, Buckingham rebelled in Oct. 1483. He was caught and executed. Several of his supporters rallied to Henry Tudor in 1485.

BUCKINGHAM, GEORGE VILLIERS, 4th Duke of (1st of 2nd creation) (1592–1628), English statesman, court favourite of James I and Charles I. On his introduction to James I (Aug. 1614), the king took an instant liking to him and appointed him to several minor offices. After the fall of James's Scottish favourite, the Earl of Somerset (Oct. 1615), Villiers's progress was swift. Successively he became master of the horse, Viscount Villiers (1616), Earl (1617), Marquis (1618), and Duke (1623) of Buckingham, and lord high admiral (1619). The vast influence he had over the king and his aspiration to be an active statesman and administrator contributed to his own and the government's unpopularity. In 1623 he accompanied Prince Charles to Spain to negotiate the latter's marriage. The mission proved a failure, and Buckingham returned, demanding war with Spain. He advocated Charles's French marriage, and was responsible for the French and Dutch alliances. He proved a poor military organizer, and was attacked over the Cadiz fiasco in the 1625 parliament, being saved from impeachment by its dissolution. Later, in the war against France, he personally commanded a disastrous expedition to relieve La Rochelle (1627). The 1628 parliament demanded his dismissal. He was murdered at Portsmouth by Lieut. John Felton, who had served in the Cadiz and La Rochelle expeditions.

BUCKINGHAM, GEORGE GRENVILLE, 1st Marquis of (1753–1813), British politician and son of George Grenville. Under the name of Grenville he was MP for Buckinghamshire (1774–9) and lord lieutenant of Ireland (1782–3, 1787–1789). Though not condemning his father's Stamp Act, he later came to condemn British policy towards America. He played a key role in the younger Pitt's rise to power, conveying to the House of Lords George III's message of personal enmity for any peer supporting Fox's India Bill. The bill was defeated in the Lords and George dismissed the Fox–North coalition. The attempt to influence the Lords was criticized as unconstitutional and, possibly for this reason, Buckingham resigned after holding office for three days as secretary of state in Pitt's administration.

BUCKINGHAM, JAMES SILK (1786–1855), sailor, author, traveller, and temperance advocate. He established the *Calcutta Journal* (1818), which was suppressed for its criticism of British officials. He was MP for Sheffield (1832–7), and wrote voluminous pamphlets, books about his travels, and an autobiography (1855).

BUCKINGHAM AND CHANDOS, RICHARD PLANTAGE-NET CHANDOS-GRENVILLE, 2nd Duke of (1797–1861). As Marquis of Chandos he introduced the Chandos Clause into the Reform Bill in the British parliament and obtained the appointment of a select committee on agricultural distress in 1836. He was regarded as leader of the agriculturists in parliament. His bankruptcy (1847) was a *cause célèbre*, unique in the high aristocracy of the time.

BUCKINGHAM PALACE in London, on the site of Buckingham House (built in 1705), which King George III acquired in 1762. The present palace, begun by the architect John Nash in 1821, has additions by Edward Blore (1847) and Sir Aston Webb (1913). It has been the official London residence of the British sovereign for over a century.

BUCKINGHAMSHIRE, JOHN HOBART, 12th Earl of (2nd of 6th creation) (1723–93), British statesman and diplomat who was ambassador at St Petersburg (1762–5) and lord lieutenant of Ireland (1776–80). The period of his Irish office saw concessions by England. The Navigation Acts were relaxed to include Irish-built ships (1778), Garner's Relief Act (1778) allowed Roman Catholics to hold or inherit land on long leases, and the Test Act for Irish Protestant dissenters was repealed (1780).

BUCKINGHAMSHIRE, ROBERT HOBART, 14th Earl of (4th of 6th creation) (1760–1816), British statesman who was Irish chief secretary (1789–93). Though strongly anti-Catholic he was charged with piloting the Catholic Relief Act of 1793 through the Irish parliament. His hostility to the act has been held to be largely responsible for its failure to satisfy the Catholics.

BUCKLE, HENRY THOMAS (1821–62), English historian and author of the *History of Civilization in England* (1857–61). He was a free-thinker, who attempted to write scientific history, free from theological presuppositions.

BUCOVINA, a region of some 10,400 sq. kms at the extreme north of Moldavia, bordered by the Carpathians to the west, the Pruth river to the north, and the Sereth river to the east. The province was long part of Moldavia and contains its medieval capital, Suceava. In 1775 Bucovina was annexed by Austria. The population of the province was mixed, the Ruthemes predominant in the north and the Rumanians in the south, with a sizeable Jewish community centred in the capital, Czernowitz. In 1848 the Rumanians outnumbered the Ruthemes by two to one, but by 1910 the balance had shifted to three to two in favour of the Ruthemes. Nevertheless, the entire province was promised to Rumania in the secret treaty of Aug. 1916 and a congress meeting at Czernowitz (Nov. 1918) voted for union with Rumania. In June 1940 the Soviet Union demanded the cession of northern Bucovina (and Bessarabia). King Carol II's acquiescence in this demand unloosed revisionist claims in Hungary and Bulgaria and led ultimately to his abdication. Rumania recovered the lost area when it made war on the Soviet Union in 1941, but the Red Army reoccupied the territory in 1944 and the Soviet annexation of northern Bucovina was recognized in the Rumanian armistice agreement (12 Sept. 1944).

BUDA, on the right bank of the Danube, opposite Pest, became in 1541 the centre of the Ottoman *beglerbeglik* of Budin. The armies of the Habsburgs attacked it without success (1542, 1598, 1602–3, and 1684). It fell to the Austrians after a bitterly fought siege (Sept. 1686).

BUDDHA, 'The Enlightened One', term applied usually, though not exclusively, to the historical founder of Buddhism: Siddhartha Gautama. The reconstruction of his life is beset with difficulties due to differences in traditions of Buddhist sects. Moreover, the Buddha came soon to be surrounded by an aura of divine holiness. By a judicious comparison between versions a plausible reconstruction seems, however, possible. He was born *c*. 560 BC as son of Shuddhodhana, ruler of the Shakya tribe near the present border between India and Nepal. He was brought up as a prince, married and had a baby son; then, after four significant encounters, he decided to abandon worldly life to seek the ultimate truth in meditation. After years of asceticism, concentration, and complete victory over the senses he attained Full Enlightenment under a pipal tree near Gaya in present Bihar. A few weeks later the Buddha, as he was henceforward called, moved to near Benares, where, in the Deer Park of Sarnath, he set out the basic doctrines of the new religion for the first time. In Buddhist texts this event is called the 'Turning of the Wheel of Law' (the wheel, a cosmic symbol, emphasizing the universality of Buddhism). The first sermon was followed by over 40 years of uninterrupted activity during which Lord

Buddha, together with his disciples (the best known of whom is Ananda), wandered over vast parts of northern India, elaborating the new doctrine and explaining it to all kinds of different people. Some of these decided to follow the Buddha in renouncing worldly life, whereas others sought refuge in the new religion without completely breaking their mundane attachments. The former became the nucleus of the new monastic order: the Sangha. The latter constituted the Buddhist laymen (*upasaka*) who by their support provided the means of livelihood for the monks. Originally the monks stayed in caves and other natural shelters during the rainy season but regular monasteries were built in later times.

The Buddha's life after his Enlightenment was free from major conflicts except for one incident when he was attacked by a mad elephant let loose by his jealous cousin Devadatta. The fierce animal became, however, immediately placated at the sight of the undisturbed saint.

Lord Buddha's death was a calm fading away into the supreme bliss of complete extinction (*nirvana*) by the roadside near Kushinagara (mod. Kasia, Gorakhpur District, Uttar Pradesh). This event is dated *c*. 486 BC by most scholars, though Buddhists generally accept the traditional date of 544 BC.

Lord Buddha's life became the ideal of later generations, which often introduced details reflecting sectarian views. The first representations of the Buddha date back to the beginning of our era or slightly earlier. The images are invariably attempts at giving visible shape to the concept of the Perfect Being as conceived of by Buddhists. Differences in detail reflect the evolution of ideas as Buddhism spread in space and time.

A. Bareau, *Recherches sur la biographie du Buddha* (Maisonneuve, Paris, 1963).   JG de C

BUDDHA SASANA COMMISSION, unofficial body of Buddhist laymen set up in 1956 to examine the reasons for the alleged neglect of Buddhism in Ceylon under European rule. It presented its report in the Buddhist *Jayanti* year, the 2500th anniversary of the enlightenment of the Buddha. Though not favoured by the leaders of the Sangha (the general body of Buddhist clergy), the report, which condemned the neglect of the religion, was widely read and contributed in no small measure to Bandaranaike's success at the 1956 general election.

BUDDHISM, world religion founded by Lord Buddha more than 25 centuries ago. It was originally a sect developing in the context of, though in a few important respects in opposition against, the then prevalent trends in Hinduism, from which it adopted a firm belief in transmigration (*samsara*) and in the force of deeds (*karman*) in the present and past lives as determinants of the shape and quality of the next. It also recognizes the existence of numerous gods and other divine powers though (in common with many Hindus) denying them absolute bliss and immortality. It accepts caste but (again in common with many Hindus) rejects its excesses. In contrast to Hinduism, however, Buddhism denies the authority of the Vedas, for which it substitutes its own sacred scriptures, and is strongly opposed to animal sacrifice and other rites. Consequently it contests the privileged status accorded to Brahmans in Hindu society. These last features prevented its absorption into Hinduism, the ultimate fate of most heterodox sects. But perhaps the most striking aspect of Buddhism is its universality. Unlike Hinduism, inseparable from Indian social divisions such as caste, clan, and tribe, Buddhism claims to be founded on a rational analysis independent of place and time.

The essence of the new doctrine, as contained in the Four Noble Truths, enunciated by the Master in His First Sermon in the Deer Park of Sarnath near Varanasi, is that all life is of its very nature impermanent and therefore painful, even though this may not always be apparent. Analysis reveals that this sorrow is rooted in ignorance. Its elimination by full understanding of Buddhist teachings will lead to the extermination of passions which obscure reality and thus keep all living beings attached to this world of suffering and separated from the bliss of Nirvana. Monastic discipline can break the attachments and thus liberate man from suffering. This principle is further elaborated in the doctrine of Dependent Origination: a chain of 12 factors of existence, each preceding link conditioning the next. The doctrine demonstrates how, according to complex laws of causation, ignorance supplies the fuel for the incessant cycles of death and rebirth.

The monastic order founded by Lord Buddha to enable others to obtain supreme wisdom and Nirvana, the Sangha, is the most significant social innovation associated with Buddhism. It overlapped other social divisions, such as those of caste, class, and, sometimes, region. Close relations between the Sangha and society in general were the rule because, except during the rainy season, the monks usually wandered through towns and villages offering spiritual guidance in exchange for food and other necessities. The well-being of the order depended upon the support it received from the people; an important place being taken by the Buddhist laymen, who firmly believed in Buddhism but could not abandon worldly activity. Their number, from an early stage, included influential people, even kings. Such a relationship may, in individual cases, have entailed some influence of the Sangha on affairs of state but it is impossible to gauge its extent.

During the rainy season the monks required shelter. Only small numbers could live in caves and other natural shelters. The majority were lodged in monasteries, where the monks were subject to strict discipline. A large body of texts, ascribed to the Buddha but, in their present form, written down centuries later, contained detailed regulations on monastic life, including those concerning the entrance into the order of novices (*samanera*) and, later, their full ordination as monks (*bhikkhu*). Initially the order was relatively democratic with voting for offices but strong emphasis on seniority.

The absence of central authority facilitated the growth of sectarianism and rivalry between sects. The history of Buddhism is largely concerned with the development of new views and practices within the basic doctrine. Whenever innovations proved unacceptable to the dominant group they led to schisms. Buddhist councils, though aimed at the re-establishment of unity, often had the opposite effect by giving expression to latent differences. The most significant dichotomy in Buddhism, however—that between the Lesser Vehicle (*Hinayana*) and the Greater Vehicle (*Mahayana*)—was not revealed at a council. It is apparently due to differences in emphasis which gradually gathered momentum from *c*. 1st cent. AD. While *Hinayana* emphasized monastic discipline with Nirvana (originally probably complete extinction but later conceived of as a state of incomprehensible absolute bliss) as the ultimate goal, *Mahayana* developed the Bodhisattva ideal: the pious Buddhist, instead of striving after his own salvation, should swear never to deviate from the path leading to Buddhahood and practise all the virtues to perfection. He may then become a Bodhisattva (future Buddha) and, after many rebirths, a Buddha. Only a minority would, however, follow this arduous path. For the great majority the main duty was that of paying devotion to Buddhas, Bodhisattvas, and saints. This entailed emphasis on temple and image worship similar to that in Hinduism.

Though *Mahayana* probably started in Andhra Pradesh its main centres in early medieval India were Bihar and Bengal, from where it spread to Tibet and East Asia, as well as to parts of South-East Asia. Barabudur in Java and the Bayon in Angkor, Cambodia, are among its greatest monuments there. In India itself it declined after the 9th cent. and disappeared after the 12th.

Monastic Buddhism too disappeared from India but became the established religion of Ceylon in or after the 3rd cent. BC. The Buddhist order enjoyed the patronage of most Ceylonese rulers and associated itself with the Sinhalese in their struggle to maintain their own identity *vis-à-vis* the Indians from the mainland. In or about the 1st cent. AD the sacred texts on doctrine, discipline, and philosophy were written down and sanctioned as canonical (namely the *Tipitaka*, 'the Three Baskets'). The language is Pali, an offshoot of Sanskrit akin to the language of some of the Ashokan inscriptions. The most famous of the numerous Buddhist scholars who worked on the analysis of this immensely rich body of texts is Buddhaghosa (5th cent. AD). Soon afterwards we notice the beginning of the expansion of Theravada ('Lore of the Elders'), as this form of Buddhism was henceforward called, into South-East Asia. Theravada continued to flourish in Ceylon. Most Sinhalese kings made donations to the order (especially of land free from tax) but Buddhism suffered temporary setbacks during foreign occupation of the island such as that by the South Indian Cholas (1017–70) and later the Portuguese.

The importance of Buddhism for social, cultural, and economic history cannot be overrated. It mitigated caste and other divisions and provided a minimum of educational and medical facilities. Crafts and trade were stimulated in some periods, and the development of art, architecture, and painting—notably of the outstanding frescoes in Ajanta (India), Sigiriya (Ceylon), and Pagan (Burma)—owes much to its impetus. It greatly contributed to Indian philosophy, particularly metaphysics and logic, and to the literature of South and South-East Asia, where the Buddha's life and thoughts were rich sources of inspiration. It even stimulated historiography: the *Mahavamsa* and *Culavamsa* of Ceylon, the *Sasanavamsa Chronicle* of Burma, and the *Jinakalamali* and *Chamadevivamsa* of Thailand are among the most significant historical achievements.

T. W. Rhys Davids, *Buddhism, its History and Literature*, 2nd edn (London, 1926).
A. L. Batham, *The Wonder That Was India* (London, 1954).
JG de C

BUDDHISM, FAR EASTERN. Buddhism reached China, via Central Asia, by the 1st cent., flourished there until the 11th cent., and, without completely dying out in the interval, was revived again early in the 20th cent. From China it had spread by the 2nd cent. to Viet-nam, and in the 7th cent. to Japan. The Buddhism of these countries was (and is) mainly of the Mahayana ('Great Vehicle') tradition which developed in India between the 1st and 6th cents, and is characterized by a number of beliefs not found in Theravada Buddhism, notably that of salvation through devotion to Buddha, usually either the Sakyamuni Buddha or the former Buddha Amitabha. The 'Great Vehicle' also embraces certain meditational forms of Buddhism, such as that known to Westerners as *Zen*.

Buddhism became increasingly important in China from the 4th cent., and remained so under the Sui and T'ang dynasties. By the T'ang period (618–907) the Chinese, having translated many Indian Buddhist texts, were beginning to develop schools or sects of their own. Most emperors were tolerant of the religion, but from time to time persecutions occurred, notably in 573–5 and 841–5, when monasteries and shrines were destroyed and their property confiscated. Buddhism, though less richly endowed, continued to flourish under the Sung and Yuan dynasties, but under the Ming, from the 14th cent., it began to decline in importance, as Confucian orthodoxy gained a firmer hold on society. Meanwhile, in Japan, where Buddhism was introduced in the 7th cent., the 12th and 13th cents saw a considerable expansion of the religion. Many sects which are still important were founded in that period. In Viet-nam, too, the Ly and Tran periods (11th–14th cents) are regarded as the 'golden age' of Buddhism.

Since it failed to supplant Confucianism as the orthodoxy of the court, Far Eastern Buddhism developed as a religion of sects rather than as a state religion. The various sects (not all of them have flourished at all periods) follow their own

practices and concentrate on particular scriptures. Several similar sects have appeared in both China and Japan, but with independent organizations. There is no Mahayana Buddhist equivalent of the Christian papacy, largely because, unlike Christianity, Buddhism is not based on any principle of divine authority. Among the most important Buddhist sects or schools in Far Eastern history have been the *Ch'ing T'u* ('Pure Land'), the *T'ien-T'ai*, and the *Ch'an* (known in Japan as *Jodo* and *Tendai* and *Zen* respectively), and the sect founded in Japan by Nichiren. In time, elements of Buddhist belief were also incorporated into various syncretic *cults*, notably the religion of the White Lotus Sect, which developed in the early 12th cent. and was part-Buddhist, part-Taoist, placing special emphasis on an apocalyptic belief in salvation.

In the 20th cent. there has been a considerable revival of Mahayana Buddhism. In China, a number of Buddhist institutes were founded in the 1920s, and there was a movement to re-create a Chinese Sangha which might have become a state institution, but it failed. The revival was interrupted in mainland China in 1949, but still continues among overseas Chinese in South-East Asia. The revival in Japan was hindered by national emphasis on Shinto until 1945, but since that date Buddhism has been Japan's dominant religion.

K. Ch'en, *Buddhism in China, a Historical Survey* (Princetown, 1964)
Masaharu Anesaki, *History of Japanese Religion* (London, 1930).
RBS

BUDDHISM, THERAVADA, the form of that religion still practised in Ceylon, Burma, Thailand, Cambodia, and Laos; the name (Pali, *Theravada*; Sanskrit, *Sthaviravada*) means 'School of the Elders'. Buddhists of the *Mahayana* ('Greater Vehicle') refer to Theravada as the Buddhism of the *Hinayana* ('Lesser Vehicle'), but the Theravadins themselves insist that their beliefs and practices are closest to the actual teachings of the Buddha. They place special emphasis on the Sangha or monkhood, and on strict adherence to the discipline of the Pali scriptures, especially the *Vinaya Pitaka*. Pali is the language of the Theravada canon, and the classical language of all countries where this form of the religion is found. Proper ordination of monks is important, with rules laid down in the *Vinaya Pitaka*; which explains why on several occasions Buddhist kings in South-East Asia sent monks to be reordained in Ceylon in order to 'purify' the religion in their own countries. Since in Theravada countries Buddhism was, and is, the dominant orthodoxy, the Sangha was specially protected by the king and the monarchical tradition was deeply imbued with Buddhist values and ritual. The Indian King Asoka (268–231 BC) served as a model for Theravada Buddhist rulers. Conflicts between king and Sangha, though not unknown, were rare: there is no religious basis in Buddhism for a clash of authorities such as occurred frequently in medieval Christendom.

Whilst Buddhism of all kinds had died out in India by the 12th and 13th cents, Theravada Buddhism was preserved in Ceylon, which was the most important Theravada country from the 6th to 15th cents. It was there that the Pali scriptures were written down in the 6th cent.; there too that the Buddha tooth relic was preserved at Kandy. Great emphasis was placed on relics by Theravada Buddhists, and the Sinhalese style of *stupa* is now found throughout Burma, Thailand, and Cambodia. An important 'purification' of Buddhism was carried out by Parakramabahu I of Ceylon (1164–97), with the reordination of many monks by the Kalyani river. By that period, Theravada Buddhism had spread also to the Burmese kingdom of Pagan, and, (c. 1180) Burmese monks went to Ceylon to be ordained there. On their return home they established a 'Sinhalese' School which in time became orthodox. In the 13th cent. Theravada Buddhism spread to Siam, where it was practised at the court of Ram Khamheng at Sukhothai (c. 1300). In Cambodia, the first Pali inscription, possibly denoting Theravada influence, dates from 1309. In 1361 a king of Sukhothai invited a senior monk from Ceylon to reform the Sangha in his kingdom. Ceylon was still the principal Theravada centre in the 15th cent.: in 1425 a 'purification' was begun at Ayuthya by a group of Thai monks who had been ordained in Ceylon and who went on to Chieng Mai; and in 1476 a similar purification after a mission to Ceylon was initiated by Dhammaceti, King of Pegu. After 1500, however, Ceylon became subject to Portuguese and later to Dutch and British intrusions. By 1750 a Sinhalese king was sending monks to Ayuthya to be ordained, and a 'Siamese' School of Buddhism developed in Ceylon as a result. In 1802 an Amarapura School was also founded in Ceylon by monks who had been to the Burmese capital. Kings and princes continued to be concerned with the well-being of Theravada religion in the 19th cent., and above all with revision of the Pali scriptures. In Siam Prince Mongkut, abbot of a leading monastery between 1836 and 1851, sent five monks to Ceylon and on their return established a 'reformed' Sangha, the Dhammayutika, which still exists alongside the main Sangha. In 1868–71 a Buddhist Council was held by King Mindon at Mandalay and the revised canon was inscribed on marble slabs.

By the early 20th cent. all the Theravada countries except Siam had come under European rule, and their monarchies were extinguished or overshadowed. The Buddhist Sangha, as the only surviving national institution, became, from c. 1916, a focus for the development of nationalism in both Burma and Ceylon. In these countries the monks remained a powerful force after independence and Buddhism became a state religion once more. In Burma, U Nu organized a great Buddhist Council, not unlike Mindon's in 1954. A reflection of the vigour of Theravada Buddhism in the post-independence period was the celebration by all the Theravada countries of the Buddhajayanti year, 1956, the 2500th anniversary of the Buddha's enlightenment.

N. R. Ray, *Introduction to Theravada Buddhism in Burma* (Calcutta, 1946). RBS

BUDDHISM, TIBETAN, sometimes called Lamaism, from the title *Lama* used by leading Tibetan monks. Mahayana Buddhist doctrines and practices were imported progressively (7th–12th cents AD) from India and Nepal into Tibet, where they partly replaced, partly mingled with, pre-existing beliefs. By 1100 the Nyingmapa, Sakyapa, Kadampa, and Kargyüpa sects were distinguishable, each following different Indian traditions, but with essentially the same doctrines. In the absence of organizations embracing laymen, the foundations of Tibetan Buddhism are the communities of monks, and to a lesser extent nuns, which besides being religious centres may control extensive property and undertake trade and commerce. Buddhism's political influence grew steadily from c. 1100, various sects and sub-sects being associated with rival noble factions. The principle of succession of abbots through reincarnation, established by the 13th cent., became politically significant especially when Buddhist dignitaries dominated political life (1642–1959) under the Gelugpa. This sect grew out of the teachings of Tsong Khapa and spread rapidly in the 15th–17th cents under a series of energetic leaders, becoming the dominant sect by 1642. Its adherents, sometimes called 'Yellow Hats', are celibate and generally keep to a strict monastic discipline. It was especially powerful around Lhasa, where the monasteries of Ganden, Sera, and Drepung numbered thousands of monks, many of them members of aggressive fraternities of lay brethren. With the Chinese closure of monasteries since 1959, Buddhism is fast disappearing in Tibet, though the Tibetan type of Buddhism continues to exist in Bhutan, Sikkim, parts of the Indian and Nepalese Himalayas, the Buryat Mongol SSR, and among Tibetan refugees.

BUDDHIST ERA (abbreviated as BE) is used as a measure of historic time in the Theravada Buddhist countries of South-East Asia and is the official era in Thailand. It is reckoned on the basis of a traditional date of 544 BC for the death of the Buddha. Burma, where the 2500th year of Buddhism fell in AD 1956, counts years on a current basis, while Thailand, Cambodia, and Laos count full elapsed years, and celebrated BE 2500 in AD 1957.

BUDDHIST REVOLT, against the rule of Ngo Dinh Diem in South Viet-nam (1963). It began with a demonstration at Hue in May, which led to bloodshed. In June–July there were demonstrations in Saigon, and several Buddhist monks immolated themselves by fire, reviving an ancient Buddhist practice for a political end. In Aug., the government suppressed the revolt and occupied many pagodas. The subsequent overthrow of Ngo Dinh Diem was regarded as a triumph for the Buddhists, who continued to play an important part in South Viet-namese politics until 1966, when their movement was crushed, for the time being, by General Nguyen Cao Ky.

BUDE, GUILLAUME, master of requests and French political writer of the first half of the 16th cent., who supported the authority of the king, but insisted that it was limited in practice by the sovereign's responsibility to God, by the traditions inherited from his predecessors, by his moral obligation to govern in his subjects' interests, to maintain peace, and to keep his financial demands within the bounds of necessity. His chief works are *De asse et partibus ejus* (1515) and *De l'institution du prince* (1522).

BUDI UTOMO ('Noble Endeavour'), the first Indonesian nationalist organization, founded in 1908. It sought a gradual transformation of Indonesian society, in which the modern-educated members of the elite would guide the population with the aid of an enlightened colonial government. Its sponsors came from the lesser ranks of the Javanese gentry and from educated commoners, but the colonial authorities encouraged more conservative aristocrats to join it, blunting its reformist aspect. A lasting contrast thus developed between progressive 'younger' and conservative 'older' generations within the organization. Budi Utomo was too willing to co-operate with the Dutch to suit the increasingly militant Indonesian nationalists of the 1920s. It continued, however, as a small and highly respectable reformist party until 1934, when it was absorbed into the conservative nationalist Parindra.

BUENA VISTA, BATTLE OF (22–23 Feb. 1847), fought near Saltillo during the US–Mexican War. Despite unfavourable odds of three to one, Gen. Zachary Taylor, commanding 4700 troops, defeated Santa Anna and gained control of northern Mexico.

BUFFON, GEORGES-LOUIS LECLERC, Comte de (1707–1788), French naturalist and philosopher. His *Histoire naturelle* (1749) in 44 volumes was a great literary success and challenged orthodox thought in the mid-18th cent. Buffon stressed the need for empirical method in the study of the natural sciences and set the fashion for collecting specimens. He also supervised the creation of the Jardin des Plantes in Paris. His interest in geology forced him to reject the biblical time-structure of the world and in his *Époques de la Nature* he enunciated a concept of evolution.

BUGIS EXPANSION in South-East Asia. Partly by learning Portuguese and Dutch techniques, the Bugis people of south-western Celebes became noted as outstanding warriors and seamen. They were widely used as mercenaries by the English and Dutch companies, and the Javanese kings. After the Dutch conquered Makassar (1669) and ended the flourishing trade of the area, groups of enterprising Bugis gradually built up a trading network outside the reach of the monopolistic Dutch, based on centres such as Riau, Pontianak, and Pasir (Borneo). In the 18th cent. they dominated, either directly or through the Malay sultans, most of the peninsular Malay states from Kedah in the north to Riau-Johor in the south, as well as Kutei, Pasir, and Pontianak in Borneo. A Bugis dynasty was established in Atjeh (1727). The Bugis were the main opponents of the Dutch in Malacca. In the 19th cent. they became assimilated into the Malay population.

BUI QUANG CHIEU (1873–1945), founder of the Constitutionalist Party in French Cochin-China. Though a native of Ben-Tre province in South Viet-nam, he was educated in France and in 1897 entered the administrative service of the Indo-Chinese Union, in which he rose to an important position in the agricultural service. In 1917 he joined with other French-educated Cochin-Chinese to found the Constitutionalist Party, which as French citizens they were entitled to do. After an abortive attempt in 1919 to boycott Chinese goods and merchants, and to promote Viet-namese business activity, the party became increasingly opposed to French corruption in the colony and sought to promote the same civil rights as were guaranteed by the constitution in France. In 1926 the party won all ten seats in the Colonial Council of Cochin-China, elected on a narrow franchise. But thereafter its moderate views led to its being overtaken by more extreme groups demanding outright independence for Viet-nam. Bui Quang Chieu subsequently became representative of Cochin-China in the Council of France Overseas at Paris (1932–41). In 1945 he was arrested and killed by the communists, who feared that he might head a government of more moderate views than their own.

BUKHARA, Central Asian city and state on the Zarafshahan river in modern Uzbekistan (USSR). Under the Samanid dynasty (10th cent.) it became a major centre of Muslim learning. In 1220 it was conquered by the Mongols and in 1500 by the Uzbeks. In the late 18th cent. it became the centre of a new state under the Mankit dynasty, which ruled until 1920. In 1868 Bukhara came under Russian protection. In 1917 a revolutionary intellectual group, the Young Bukharans, requested Bolshevik assistance against the ruler, Sa'id Alim Khan. Bukhara was eventually captured (Sept. 1920) and the new Bukharan Republic allied with Russia. In 1924 it was incorporated into Uzbekistan.

BUKHARI, AL-, MUHAMMAD IBN ISMA'IL (810–70), famous student of the sacred traditions (*hadith*) of Islam. His most notable work, the *Sahih*, took him 16 years to compile. It is one of the most important collections of *hadith* and has been the subject of numerous learned commentaries.

BUKHARIN, NIKOLAY IVANOVICH (1888–1938), Russian journalist and politician, who was an early member of the Bolshevik Party, editor of *Pravda*, and the author of several influential theoretical works, *eg, ABC of Communism* (1922). Though he lacked the strength of character to survive the struggles of the 1920s, Lenin thought well of him, in spite of their clashes over such issues as the desirability of accepting the German peace terms in 1918, when Bukharin passionately advocated a continuation of the war. He also disputed with Lenin about the role of the state in the post-revolutionary period and advocated the impractical view that the state would wither away immediately. For a short time in 1920 he backed Trotsky against Lenin in their debate concerning the relationship of the party to the trade unions : but shortly after this he enthusiastically threw in his lot with Lenin when the latter declared the new economic policy. To this revisionist line he remained loyal throughout the 1920s. After Lenin's death he supported Stalin against Trotsky because he erroneously believed that Stalin was Lenin's political heir. When Stalin abandoned NEP in 1928 Bukharin tried in vain to mobilize party opinion against him. He courageously published a pamphlet, 'Lenin's Political Testament', in which he argued against the folly and cruelty of the collectivization of the peasants. But he was out-manœuvred by Stalin, expelled from the Politburo in 1929, and forced to recant his former views. His political career was now finished, although he was one of the authors of the 1936 Constitution. His loyalty to the party led him to admit the charges of sabotage brought against him in the show trial of 1938, after which he was shot, refusing to the end to admit the charge that he had plotted to murder Lenin in 1918, in spite of 'pressure' applied by the NKVD.   GS

BULALA, a people, said to be a branch of the Saifawa, now living around Lake Fittri in Tchad. In the 14th cent. they were able, in alliance with Arab nomads, to drive the Saifawa from Kanem into Bornu. In the 16th cent. the *mais* of Bornu reduced them to tributary status. In the 17th cent. they were driven from Kanem to Fittri by the fugitive Tunjur of Wadai. Leo Africanus's kingdom of Gaoga is usually equated with the Bulala kingdom.

BULATOVIC, MIODRAG (1930–   ), Serbian writer. Bulatovic, born in poverty in Montenegro, did not read a book until he was 16. His most important novels, *The Red Cockerel* (1962) and *A Hero on a Donkey* (1966), deal with the individual's efforts to assert his personality and integrity against the ravages of war.

BULAVIN, K. (d. 1708), Don cossack who led a revolt in 1707 against the Russian government's attempt to recapture runaway serfs in the area of the Don river. Peter the Great sent a military expedition to the area and the rising was suppressed with difficulty. Bulavin was captured in Cherkassk, where he committed suicide.

BULFINCH, CHARLES (1763–1844), US architect, much influenced by the Adam brothers in England. He adapted American colonial architecture into a neo-classical 'Federal' style. Notable among his works are the Massachusetts State House (1799) and the Old Meeting House, Lancaster, MA (1816).

BULGANIN, NIKOLAI ALEKSANDROVICH (1895–   ), Russian politician and prime minister of the USSR (1955–8), who joined the Bolshevik Party in 1917 and held a variety of state and party posts, including those of chairman of Moscow city council (1931–7), prime minister of the RSFSR (1937–1938), and chairman of the state bank (1938–41). During the Second World War he was a political officer on the western front (1941–3), a member of the state defence committee, and deputy minister for defence (1944–7). At the end of the war he was created marshal and became defence minister (1947–9, 1953–5), as well as deputy prime minister (1947–55). He was appointed to the central committee of the party in 1934 and to its Presidium in 1948.

After the death of Stalin (March 1953) he was one of the less important members of the 'collective leadership' of the Soviet Union. Following Malenkov's resignation from the premiership (Feb. 1955) he was appointed to succeed him. He became prominent in international affairs when he visited Yugoslavia and Rumania, and then Britain (Spring 1955) and attended the Geneva conference (July 1955), but his role was subordinate to that of Khrushchev. In 1957 he was one of those who unsuccessfully opposed Khrushchev in the Presidium of the CPSU. He was not immediately dismissed, but in March 1958 he surrendered the premiership to Khrushchev. He was later dismissed from his chairmanship of the state bank (Aug. 1958), and from the Presidium (Sept. 1958), and publicly denounced by Khrushchev as having belonged to the anti-party group (Nov. 1958). Thereafter he lived in obscure retirement.   WFK

BULGARIA, PEACE TREATY (1947), restored Bulgaria to the frontiers of Jan. 1941. Bulgaria retained southern Dobrogea, which had been ceded by Rumania. The frontier with Greece was confirmed but was to be demilitarized.

BULGARIAN ATROCITIES (1876). In 1875 the Serbs revolted against Turkish rule and the revolts spread to the Bulgarians in Eastern Rumelia in the spring of 1876. They were crushed by Turkish irregular troops, the bashi-bazouks, and in the process over 15,000 persons were murdered and 70 villages destroyed. Disraeli's Conservative government, following the traditional foreign policy of support for Turkey and suspicion of Russia, minimized the severity of these massacres, but in the summer of 1876 reports from foreign correspondents, notably MacGahan of the *Daily News*, began to appear. There developed an agitation, by Liberals, nonconformists, and high Anglicans, in support of the Christians under Turkish rule. Gladstone, at that time retired from the Liberal leadership, stimulated the agitation with his pamphlet, 'The Bulgarian Horrors and the Question of the East'. The Bulgarian question was settled at the Berlin Congress (1878).

BULGARIAN CRISIS (1885–8), once again brought the danger of war over the Near East. The rebellion of Turkey's autonomous province of Eastern Rumelia (Sept. 1885), and the agreement of Prince Alexander of Bulgaria to annex it at the request of the population, brought bitter opposition from the Russians. Beginning as a Russian puppet, Alexander had slipped from their control and become anti-Russian. Because of this Russian opposition, Britain and Austria-Hungary supported the annexation and refused Turkey's request for help. The issue was complicated by a Serbian attack on Bulgaria (Nov. 1885) in an attempt to get compensation, although the Serbs were rapidly defeated.

In April 1886, a compromise was worked out by the European powers, which allowed the union of Bulgaria and Eastern Rumelia in fact, if not in name. But the crisis continued through Russian determination to control the country. Bulgaria was thrown into confusion in Aug. and Sept. by the kidnapping of Alexander, by Russian sympathizers, and his abdication. None the less, the Russians still failed to exert their control and there was some danger (Nov.) that they would invade Bulgaria. Because of this the Austro-Hungarian foreign minister, Kalnócky, warned the tsar. The crisis subsided somewhat when the Russians did not invade and Bismarck advised Kalnócky that German support for Austria would not be forthcoming.

Bismarck wanted above all to avoid conflict over Bulgaria, hoping Austria and Russia could divide the Balkans peacefully into spheres of interest. In June 1887 he signed the Reinsurance Treaty with Russia, approving of her policy in Bulgaria, although surreptitiously encouraging Austrian opposition. A new Bulgarian prince, Ferdinand of Saxe-Coburg-Gotha, elected in Sept. 1887, was still unacceptable to the Russians and the crisis continued. Two months later Britain, Austria, and Italy came together in the anti-Russian Second Mediterranean Agreement (Dec.). Bismarck's publication (Feb. 1888) of the terms of the Austro-German defensive alliance of 1879 forced Russia to retreat finally from her position; she now directed her attention from the Balkans to concentrate on the Far East.

M. S. Anderson, *The Eastern Question, 1774–1923* (London, 1966).

D MCK

BULGARIAN INDEPENDENCE (1908), from Turkey, declared on 5 Oct. Since 1878 Bulgaria had been a tributary of the sultan, although this had little practical effect. Prince Ferdinand of Bulgaria took advantage of the Austrian decision to annex Bosnia-Herzegovina to announce the setting up of an independent Bulgarian kingdom. He did this two days before the annexation and the move may have been taken in agreement with the Austro-Hungarian foreign minister, Aerenthal, whom he had met in Budapest a fortnight before.

BULGARIAN NATIONAL MOVEMENT, 19th-cent. religio-cultural movement amongst western-educated Bulgarian Christians stressing Bulgarian unity against both Muslims and Greek Orthodox Christians. Later, under the leadership of G. S. Rakovskii and L. Karavelov, political demands were made, first for local autonomy within the Ottoman empire, and, after the Crimean War, for an independent state. A revolt planned by émigré Bulgarian nationalists provoked the Bulgarian atrocities (1876), but Bulgarian nationalists had little influence over the creation of a large autonomous Bulgaria at San Stefano (1878) or its subsequent division into a smaller autonomous Bulgaria and Eastern Rumelia under Ottoman rule (Congress of Berlin, 1878). Bulgarian nationalism reasserted itself in 1885 in an Eastern Rumelian revolt, its purpose being union with Bulgaria, which was achieved in 1886.

BULGARIA–YUGOSLAV PACT (24 Jan. 1937). After 1918, the outstanding issue between Bulgaria and Yugoslavia was the latter's possession of North Macedonia. German commercial links with both countries, as well as the wish to end frontier tensions, facilitated a rapprochement. Yugoslavia's distrust of France increased after King Alexander's assassination there in Oct. 1934. At the Little Entente meeting at Bratislava in Sept. 1936, Yugoslavia, on German advice, delayed acceptance of France's projected general treaty of alliance. Negotiations began with Germany and Bulgaria. Before announcing the agreement, Yugoslavia conferred with her Balkan Pact partners to allay fears of Bulgarian irredentism.

BULGARS, nomadic people which moved westward in the wake of the Huns and settled in the lands north and east of the Black Sea. Some of the Bulgars became absorbed (*c.* 560) in the Avars. Others continued to inhabit the region of the Kuban steppe. In the face of increasing pressure from the Khazars, some of these Bulgars went northward from the Kuban and established themselves in the territories around the confluence of the Kama and Volga rivers. Most of them, however, led by their khan, Asparukh, advanced into the lands along the lower Danube. In 681 the Byzantine Emperor Constantine IV was compelled to recognize the existence, in the ancient Moesia, of a new Bulgar state. The Bulgars soon became assimilated to the more numerous Slav population around them and in 864 adopted the Orthodox Christian faith. Their domination, in the time of the Tsar Symeon (893–927), extended from the Danube to the Adriatic. The Byzantine Emperor Basil II brought the Bulgar state to an end, subjugating it in a long series of campaigns during the years 986–1014.

BULHOEK, an African sub-location in the Eastern Cape, where, in May 1921, 800 police were attacked by, and then fired upon, a millenarian sect, the 'Israelites'. These, in obedience to the prophecies of their leader, Enoch Mgijima, had refused to move from common lands. One hundred and sixty-three were killed and one hundred and twenty-nine wounded.

BULL, OLE BORNEMANN (1810–80), Norwegian musician, who established the first theatre in Bergen presenting specifically Norse drama. His work contributed to the recognition by other nations of a Norwegian culture.

BULL MOOSE PARTY (1912–16), popular name of the US Progressive Party, which comprised the personal following of Theodore Roosevelt. Alienated from his Republican successor, President Taft, Roosevelt formed his own party, and stood as a presidential candidate against Taft and Woodrow Wilson in 1912. He frequently used the totemistic term 'bull moose' as a synonym for vigour and strength. The party collapsed in 1916 when Roosevelt refused renomination.

BULL RUN, BATTLES OF (1861, 1862), in the American Civil War, fought near Manassas (the Confederate name for the battles), 30 miles (48 kms) south-west of Washington. In the first major battle of the war (21 July 1861) Southern forces under Pierre Beauregard and Joseph E. Johnston sent a Northern army under Irvin McDowell, attended by

Congressmen and sightseers, fleeing back to Washington, which might have fallen if the Confederates could have followed up their success. The second battle (29–30 Aug. 1862) came after a flanking movement by Thomas J. Jackson and Robert E. Lee, and ended in the rout of Union forces under John Pope, who was subsequently relieved of his command. Lee's victory encouraged him to invade Maryland in Sept. 1862.

BULLER, CHARLES (1806–48), British philosophic Radical. He was MP for Liskeard (1832–48) and an associate of Grote, Molesworth, and Roebuck. He went to Canada as chief secretary to Lord Durham (1838) and drafted the Durham report with the aid of Gibbon Wakefield. Russell's ministry of 1846 included a few Radicals in minor posts and Buller became chief poor law commissioner in 1847. He belonged to the group of Radicals who, in contrast to the Manchester school, took a positive interest in the political development of colonies.

BULLETIN, THE, Australian weekly newspaper, founded in Sydney in 1880 by J. F. Archibald and John Haynes. Its greatest literary and political influence was achieved during the 1890s.

BULLINGER, HENRY (1504–75), leading German reformer, who carried on the Zwinglian tradition of Protestantism in Zürich after Zwingli's death (1536). Famous as a pastor and teacher rather than as a politician, he nevertheless influenced the growth of Protestantism in Poland and the course of the English Reformation through the person of Cranmer. He was a determined opponent of Anabaptism and contributed to the unity of the Swiss reformed churches by helping to produce the first Helvetic Confession (1536) and by writing the second Helvetic Confession (1566).

BULLION, precious metals of gold and silver whose discovery on a large scale in Central and South America by Spanish adventurers precipitated an international monetary crisis in the 16th–17th cents. The apparent wealth derived from its accumulation led some economic theorists, the bullionists, to over-emphasize its importance to the state.

BULNES, MANUEL (1799–1866), Chilean independence leader and president. Bulnes fought in the wars of independence. In 1839 he defeated the forces of the Peruvian–Bolivian Confederation. He was Conservative president of Chile for two terms (1841–51), and encouraged the expansion of the educational system.

BÜLOW, BERNHARD, Prinz von (1849–1929), German foreign secretary (1897) and chancellor (1900). He had little interest in domestic politics; his foreign policy increased apprehension over Germany's ultimate aims and helped create the Triple Entente. In trying to satisfy William II's colonial ambitions by blackmailing the other powers, he achieved little but hostility. In Europe he pursued a 'free-hand' policy of avoiding committment to Russia, France, and Britain and at keeping them apart. But by rejecting British alliance proposals (1898–1901), forming a continental bloc against Britain in the Boer War, and allowing the building of a German fleet, and by blustering interference in Morocco (1905–6), he merely assisted the formation and strengthening of the Anglo-French Entente. Russia was also completely alienated by Bülow's actions in the Bosnia-Herzegovina crisis (1908–9). By 1909 William II had lost confidence in him and Bülow resigned.

BUNAU-VARILLA, PHILIPPE JEAN (1860–1940), Panamanian engineer, diplomat, and Panama Canal promoter. As representative of the New Panama Canal Co. he encouraged the US to use the Panamanian route for the proposed canal. Because of Colombia's opposition to his plans he aided Panama's secession. Appointed Panamanian minister to the US (1903), he was the principal negotiator behind the Hay–Bunau–Varilla Treaty, which gave control of the Canal Zone to the US.

BUNCHE, RALPH JOHNSON (1904–), one of several US Negroes appointed to senior administrative posts by F. D. Roosevelt, and later a UN diplomat. He acted as UN mediator in Palestine (1948), director of the Trusteeship Division of the UN (1948–54), and special representative in the Congo (1960). He was awarded the Nobel Peace Prize (1950).

BUND (1897), abbreviation of General Jewish Workers' Union in Russia and Poland. It was the largest Social-Democratic organization in Russia. It broke with Lenin (1903) over autonomy within RSDLP and mass party organization, and when readmitted (1906) it sided with the Mensheviks. It was suppressed in Russia in the 1920s.

BUNDELAS, ruling clan of Bundelkhand, a tract of hilly country extending south of the Jumna river between Etawah and Allahabad into the state of Madhya Pradesh. They rose to prominence in the 14th cent. The Afghan ruler Sher Shah was killed while besieging the stronghold of Kalinjar in 1545. A Bundela raja murdered Akbar's confidant Abu'l Fazl in 1598. In the 18th cent. their territory provided a corridor for Maratha advances into the Gangetic plain.

BUNDSCHUH MOVEMENT. Name given to conspiratorial unions of peasants, with some townsmen, formed in south and west Germany in the late 15th cent., which took as their emblem the rough laced shoe of the peasant. Their programme varied from mild reforms of the peasants' position to revolutionary schemes for the complete overthrow of society, but in general they sought to improve the lot of the common man in a time of rising prices and social unrest. The movement gave rise to a series of revolts, ending in total defeat in the Peasants' War (1525–6).

BUNGA EMAS, gold and silver ornamental tree sent triennially to the court of Siam by those northern Malay states which acknowledged Siamese superiority. Difficulties frequently arose in the 19th cent. when Siam interpreted it as a recognition of sovereignty.

BUNKER HILL, BATTLE OF (17 June 1775). Sixteen hundred Americans, commanded by Col. William Prescott, had built a stronghold on a height overlooking the Charleston peninsula and Boston. The original plan had been to fortify Bunker Hill which was higher, but through some error never explained the stand was made on Breed's Hill. Gen. William Howe and 2400 British soldiers stormed the height and were twice repulsed. During the third assault the Americans' powder gave out and the British seized the hill. They lost 1000 men including 92 officers, and the Americans about 400. Although it was a defeat, the battle served to unite the colonists and inspire them to greater resistance.

BUNNAG FAMILY, the most important ministerial family of Siam from the 17th to the 19th cent. The founder of the family was an Arabo-Persian who came to Siam from the Persian Gulf in 1602 and by 1610 was a minister of state. From then onwards, with a few brief interludes, there was always at least one Bunnag among the six ministers of the Siamese kings. The family name, officially adopted only much later, derives from the given name of Chaophraya Mahasena, who was Kalahom (ie, minister of military affairs and the southern provinces, 1787–1805). His son, Chaophraya Phrakhlang (Dit Bunnag), was minister of finance and foreign affairs (1822–51) and concurrently Kalahom (1830–51), and as such was primarily responsible for negotiating the Burney treaty (1826). He was succeeded as Kalahom by his son, Chaophraya Si Suriyawong (Chuang Bunnag), who played a major role in negotiating the Bowring treaty (1855) and was the dominant figure in the politics of the Bangkok court until his death in 1883.

BUNTING, JABEZ (1779–1858), secretary of the Methodist Conference (1814) and president (1820). An able but overbearing man, he imposed order and organization on Wesleyan Methodism, but in such a way as to stimulate secession. Under his guidance Methodism became finally separated from its Anglican base.

BUNTLINE, NED (1823–86), pseudonym of Edward Zane Carroll Judson, US adventurer and writer. After a riotous youth spent on the frontier, Judson became notorious as a leader of the destructive, anti-British Astor Place Riot in New York City (1849) and as a founder of the Know Nothing Party. After Judson met W. F. Cody, he gave him the nickname of Wild Bill, encouraged him to form a 'Wild West' show which toured the US and Europe (1883), and, as Buffalo Bill, made him the hero of numerous 'dime' novels. Buntline was the author of over 400 novels and western thrillers.

BUNYAN, JOHN (1628–88), English preacher and writer. He began as a tinker and served on the parliamentary side in the Civil War (1644–6). Undergoing a religious conversion after his marriage in 1648, he became a popular nonconformist preacher. He was imprisoned in Bedford gaol (1660-1672) because of his refusal to abandon preaching when it became illegal at the Restoration. While in gaol he preached and wrote religious works, eg, *Grace Abounding to the Worst of Sinners* (1666), which describes his religious conversion. When he was released he was licensed to preach and became pastor of the nonconformist congregation at Bedford. Part I of his most famous work, *The Pilgrim's Progress* (1678, part II 1684), was written at this time. It describes in allegory life's journey through temptations to eternal salvation. His other works include *The Life and Death of Mr Badman* (1680).

BUOL-SCHAUENSTEIN, KARL FRIEDRICH, Graf (1797–1865), Austrian foreign minister, whose policies did little to prevent the defeat of the monarchy in the Italian War (1859). He was appointed (1852) after serving as ambassador in London, where he had been described as 'most coarse and insolent'. His policy of neutrality during the Crimean War gave Austria a decisive influence over its outcome, but at the same time it alienated Russia, whose military support had helped save the Austrian empire from internal collapse in 1849. This alienation proved important in 1859, when Buol, misunderstanding the weakness of Austria's position in Italy, also expected British and Prussian support against Sardinia and France. Buol was dismissed (May) just before Austria's defeats in the war.

BUONAROTTI, PHILIPPE MICHEL (1761–1837), French revolutionary conspirator, of Italian birth, who acted as a link between the conspiracy of Babeuf (1796) and such 19th-cent. revolutionaries as Blanqui. He escaped execution for his part in the Babeuf plot and lived largely in exile from France till after the July Revolution (1830). Although his main aim was absolute equality, produced by universal revolution, he also played a part in the Carbonari movements for Italian unification. In 1828 he published his *Conspiration pour l'Égalité Dite de Babeuf*, which acted as a textbook for the extreme revolutionaries, and until his death he was a prophet of the socialist and Jacobin movements against Louis Philippe.

BURAIMI, eastern Arabian oasis disputed between Saudi Arabia, Abu Dhabi, and Muscat since 1949 and involving rival US and British oil interests. After the failure of abritration, Saudi police were expelled by Muscati and Trucial Oman forces (1955), which contributed to a diplomatic breach between Britain and Saudi Arabia (1956–63).

BURBAGE, RICHARD (*c.* 1567–1619), English actor, the first to play Shakespeare's Hamlet, Lear, Othello, and Richard III. He and his brother, Cuthbert (*c.* 1566–1636), built the famous Globe theatre in Southwark.

BURCKHARDT, PROFESSOR CARL J. (1891–), Swiss historian and diplomat. As high commissioner of the League of Nations in Danzig (Feb. 1937–Sept. 1939) he sought to achieve a peaceful settlement of the status of the Free City, as well as to temper Nazi excesses. He was criticized for his failure to bring any question connected with Danzig before the League Council. Open defiance of the Nazis, however, would have deprived him of any ability to resist their more extreme policies. After Munich his influence declined. A solution proved impossible, and after the signing of the Nazi-Soviet Pact the local Nazi Gauleiter, Forster, was appointed head of state.

BURDETT, SIR FRANCIS (1770–1844), radical politician and husband of Sophia, daughter and heiress of Thomas Coutts, the banker (1793). He entered parliament in 1796 and, as a friend of Horne Tooke, became the mouthpiece of radical discontent with repression and war taxation. He was re-elected, for Westminster (1807), and remained an MP until 1837. With his great wealth he supported many radical activities and was first chairman of the Hampden Club. In the Commons he joined the opposition led by Whitbread. His most notable act was his defence in the House of John Gale Jones, an arrested radical orator. In defiance of the speaker's ruling he published his speech and was arrested and committed to the Tower. His release was the occasion of large radical demonstrations in London. In the 1830s he abandoned radicalism in favour of Tory democracy, and represented Wiltshire (1837–44).

BUREAU OF FINANCE, supervising financial body established in 1577 in each French *généralité*. Following the financial reforms of Francis I in 1543, the country was divided into 16 *généralités*, though the number had increased to 34 by the end of the *ancien régime*. In each *généralité* a collector-general was responsible for the collection of all royal revenues and he was joined by a number of treasurers. Together they composed the bureau of finance.

BURGAGE BOROUGHS in Britain, 39 pre-1832 parliamentary boroughs where the right to vote was attached exclusively to the ownership or occupation of properties of ancient tenure. The franchise conditions, other than possession or occupation, varied according to local usage. In the 17th and 18th cents many were acquired through purchase by the aristocracy. In some, residence was not possible because houses did not exist, and only title-deeds to the land were necessary, eg, Old Sarum.

BURGENLAND, PLEBISCITE in (Dec. 1921) was held in Burgenland's chief town, Sopron, Oedenburg, a German-speaking area about 3890 sq. kms, which lay until 1919 on Hungary's western frontier. Its purpose was to decide whether there should be a corridor linking Czechoslovakia and Yugoslavia which would pass through Burgenland. The Paris Peace Conference refused the request of the new states for this to be brought about and accepted Austria's suggestion to transfer it to her. Hungary organized armed resistance, but eventually, although the vote was in Hungary's favour, only the town and a small surrounding area remained outside Austria.

BURGH, SIR JOHN (1562–94), English military and naval commander, who led troops under the Earl of Leicester and

Lord Willoughby in the Netherlands and France (1585–90). He commanded Sir Walter Raleigh's ship *Roebuck*, which captured (1592) the Spanish treasure ship *Madre de Dios*.

BURGHER, in Ceylon a generic name denoting people of mixed blood, but more properly restricted to the descendants of the Dutch, who had settled in Ceylon in the 18th cent. and in many cases had married Sinhalese or Tamil women. The 'Dutch Burghers' have always remained a separate community and their home language is English. In the early 19th cent. Burghers filled almost all the clerical posts in government service and mercantile firms. Throughout the British occupation they provided many lawyers, doctors, and educationists, some of them of outstanding merit. Some, too, such as Lorenz in the mid-19th cent. and Keuneman in the 20th, were prominent in politics. Owing to their westernized way of life their value to the country was out of all proportion to their numbers. In 1953 there were about 45,000 Burghers and Eurasians, but since Ceylon became independent a number of them have emigrated to Australia and Britain.

BURGHLEY, WILLIAM CECIL, 1st Baron (1520–98), English statesman who exercised a powerful influence over Elizabeth I. Burghley, the son of a Northamptonshire gentleman who had been a courtier of Henry VIII, married the sister of Sir John Cheke and through him gained employment with Somerset. He was briefly imprisoned on Somerset's fall but was secretary of state (1550–3), discreetly attended mass under Mary, was reappointed secretary (1558–72), made Baron Burghley (1571) and lord treasurer (1572–98).

In his early years Cecil walked the tightrope delicately. He held office under Northumberland without wholly approving of his religious policy; knew of the conspiracy to put Lady Jane Grey on the throne, without actually committing himself to support it; disguised his moderate Protestantism sufficiently for Mary to employ him on diplomatic missions; and yet was in such close contact with the Princess Elizabeth that she made him her secretary within three days of her accession. He had learned finesse in a hard school, and their partnership lasted until his death. Leicester was jealous of it and the Howards resented it, but his place in Elizabeth's confidence was unique and unassailable.

Burghley is not easily associated with a particular policy. He lived at a time when any ill-considered or over-confident action might have upset an always delicate balance. He is sometimes credited with an ambition to form a Protestant confederacy, but he knew that the Spanish alliance was necessary to the cloth trade and 'a realm gaineth more by one year's peace than by ten years of war'. Whatever his own religious views, he opposed the Puritan radicals because they were a threat to unity and order. For years he advocated the execution of Mary Queen of Scots, but he understood Elizabeth's reluctance to make a martyr of her.

He realized that financial stability was the essence of sound government, though he may at times have carried this too far. His economy, which did not save him from being swindled by the naval contractors, meant that the seamen chasing the Armada were short of stores and ammunition. In the 1590s he and the queen were regarded as parsimonious and obstructive. It was in their nature to frown upon new adventures, and men felt that opportunities were being wasted. But in his sanity, competence, and ascetic patriotism Burghley stands in the great line of British administrators. He helped to preserve the statutory compromise in religion, defended the prerogative in the Commons, and controlled the complex machinery of government after Thomas Cromwell's reforms. Whereas Philip II was several times bankrupt and could only borrow at crippling rates, Elizabeth's credit was always good. On his deathbed Burghley urged the conclusion of the Spanish war, as Henry IV was making a separate peace.

Through his two marriages Burghley left sons who became the earls of Exeter and Salisbury. He built three splendid mansions, Theobalds in Hertfordshire, Cecil House in London, and Burghley House at Stamford.

B. W. Beckingsale, *Burghley, Tudor Statesman* (London, 1967).
Conyers Read, *Mr Secretary Cecil and Queen Elizabeth* (London, 1955). MMR

BURGMANN, ERNEST HENRY (1885–1967), Australian bishop and advocate of an Australian Anglican Church, led by Australians. He was a radical critic of economic injustice and ecclesiastical conservatism. Seeing Asia as the setting and Canberra as the focus of Australia's nationhood, he made the national capital his headquarters from 1946, changing the see's name (1950) from 'Goulburn' to 'Canberra and Goulburn'.

Burgmann, who was a serious student of Marx, proclaimed his belief during the economic depression that the only remedy for unemployment was employment promoted by the state. Belief in the right of free expression underlay his much-criticized, successful opposition to the 1951 Communist Party Dissolution referendum proposal.

His episcopate (1934–60) was marked by insistence on thorough pastoral work and by a highly individual, experimental leadership devoid of prelacy.

BURGOS, inland city of northern Castile, the centre of the medieval Spanish wool trade which enjoyed great prosperity in the 16th cent. It was the home of a large number of wealthy merchants, *eg*, the Salamanca and Miranda families, organized in a powerful guild with connections in Bruges, Antwerp, Rouen, Nantes, and Florence. This institution was modified in 1494 by Ferdinand into the famous *consulado* of Burgos, a guild and mercantile court, with extended powers of jurisdiction under which the wool trade could be more efficiently organized. Wool was sold to merchants at the rural fairs of Castile, then transported to Burgos, whence it was taken by mule to the port of Bilbao for export to northern Europe.

Burgos suffered in proportion to the whole Spanish economy in the 17th cent. and by 1646 its population had fallen to 3000.

During the Spanish Civil War it was the scene of the emergence of the fascist 'legions' of Dr Albinaña and had a considerable Falangist group. It fell to the military rebels (June 1936) with hardly a shot being fired. Thereafter, it became the seat of the Nationalist government. The Burgos Junta, as well as the treasury, the ministry of justice, and the ministry of labour were sited in the town.

BURGOS, LAWS OF. These 32 laws, promulgated 27 Dec. 1512, were the first Spanish attempt to establish a recognized legal code for the treatment of the Amerindians. Complaints by friars about the ill-treatment of the Indians led to debate over their legal status. In response to this Ferdinand V drew up a series of regulations and royal officials in the New World were commanded to assume the role of protectors of the Indians. Strict rules were made about hours of work, and Spaniards were ordered to supply their Indian labourers with adequate food, shelter, and instruction. The laws were inadequately enforced and complaints that the Indians were being abused and exploited continued to reach Spain, the result being a second code of laws, the famous 'New Laws' of 1542.

BURGOYNE, JOHN (1722–92), British general, best known for his surrender to the Americans at Saratoga (1777). As an MP from 1761, he was active in Indian affairs, on which he moved for a Select Committee in 1772. He led the attack on Clive in parliament in 1773, and from 1787 was one of the managers of the impeachment of Warren Hastings.

BURGUNDIANS, people who were part of the Germanic migration. They crossed the Rhine in 406 and established a kingdom around Worms. The Roman commander Aetius brought in the Huns against them in 437 and the ensuing massacre of the Burgundians probably forms the historic origin of the *Niebelungenlied*. The remnant, settled by the Romans on the Rhone, gave rise to the later province of Burgundy. The Burgundians were Arians, but it is possible that their king, Sigismund, was baptized as Catholic earlier than the Frankish king Clovis, whose sons exterminated the Burgundian dynasty in 520.

BURIDS, princes of Turkish descent ruling at Damascus (1104–54). The first of the Burid line was Tughtakin (d. 1128), the *atabeg* of Shams al-Din Dukak, the son of the Seljuk Sultan Tutush. Two factors in particular inclined the Burids towards an entente with the Crusading kingdom of Jerusalem—the exposure to Christian attack of the areas, *eg*, the Hawran, which supplied Damascus with its food, and the existence, at Mosul and Aleppo, of a powerful Muslim state under the Zangids. The ill-advised campaign of the Latins against Damascus at the time of the Second Crusade (1148) broke the entente and led to an event unfavourable for the Christians, *ie*, the Zangid occupation of Damascus in 1154.

BURKE, EDMUND (1729–97), British political theorist and Whig politician. He was born in Ireland and came to London in 1750. In 1765 he entered parliament, became secretary to Rockingham, and was political manager for the Rockinghamites in their period of opposition and attacked successive governments' American policies and demanded a reduction of Crown influence. In Rockingham's second ministry (1782) —which brought a measure of economic reform and independence for Ireland—Burke was paymaster of the forces, as he was again in the Fox–North coalition (1783). After the coalition's fall, over Fox's India Bill, Burke began his ten-year campaign against Warren Hastings.

Burke's writings nearly all take the form of pamphlets purporting to be either long letters or speeches, carefully constructed pieces of rhetoric in magnificent, persuasive prose. His political views were often exaggerated and based on a distortion of facts. But his political philosophy, which was woven round his response to political events, is of lasting importance. For example, his violent reaction against the French Revolution was linked with his detestation of the English reforming societies, which he believed shared its aims. It led him to break (1792) with Fox, his old associate, and turn to Pitt. But his *Reflections on the French Revolution* (1790), though obviously partisan, and written at a time when most Englishmen still approved events in France, elaborates an attitude towards the French and the English revolution (1689) which greatly influenced later historiography. Moreover, its criterion of judgement—looking for justification to history and to the natural organic growth of a community, and denying the existence of abstract rights and logic—has something in common with romanticism and was an important strand in later political thought.

BURKE, JOHN (1787–1848), publisher of *Burke's Peerage and Baronetage* (1826), *Burke's Extinct Peerage* (1831), *Burke's Commoners* (1833–8), later known as *Burke's Landed Gentry*. The issue of these works was continued by his son, Sir John B. Burke. They form a valuable source for research into the genealogy and history of the aristocracy.

BURKE, ROBERT O'HARA (1821–61), Australian police official and explorer. Burke, a member of the Royal Irish Mounted Constabulary, emigrated to Australia (1853) and became a Victorian police inspector. He later led the south to north crossing of the Australian continent, but the undue haste with which he conducted the expedition reduced its contribution to knowledge of the country it traversed. His decision on the return journey, against the advice of his second-in-command, William John Wills, to press on from Cooper's Creek was the direct cause of the deaths of himself

and Wills; a third member of the party, John King, survived to tell the story.

BURKE ACT (1906), supplemented the Dawes Act (1887). It entitled Indians to become US citizens after 25 years' probation and it gave the secretary of the interior greater control over lands awarded to Indians under the Dawes Act.

BURLAMACCHI, FRANCESCO (d. 1548), leader of a conspiracy in Lucca nominally against the Medici, but in general against papal acquiescence in Spanish control of Italy. Burlamacchi was executed four years after the plot was discovered.

BURLAMAQUI, JEAN JACQUES (1694–1748), Swiss jurist, who made Geneva, his native city, the model for his political ideals. Under the influence of Locke, he dispensed with the absolutism of Grotius and Pufendorf, believing that a sovereign's power rested on his ability to govern in the people's interest and that if power was abused, the people had the natural right of resistance. His ideal was a government of aristocracy, tempered by democracy and the existence of fundamental law.

With the French theorist Barbeyrac, Burlamaqui and the natural law school provided the proper intellectual climate for the development of Rousseau's theories.

BURLINGAME, ANSON (1820–70), US diplomat, best known for the so-called Burlingame Treaty concluded between the US and China (1868). As a congressman he opposed the political ideas of the southern states. He was nominated as envoy to Vienna by President Lincoln, but his outspokenness in favour of Italian unity made him *persona non grata* there and led to his appointment as minister at Peking (1861). His co-operative policy towards the Chinese resulted in his appointment as China's roving ambassador to the West. Accompanied by two Chinese officials, he left for Washington in 1868 and signed a treaty with the US on egalitarian terms. His sudden death brought to an end a tour of the European capitals. Burlingame was a visionary and an orator: his announcement that China was ready to westernize itself and to receive Christianity was premature and misleading, but his mission there was important in that it established the precedent in China of sending envoys abroad. But the provision in the Washington Treaty encouraging the immigration of Chinese labour into the US, though welcomed at first, led to bad feelings between the two countries.

BURLINGAME TREATY, agreement between the US and China (1868), negotiated on behalf of the Chinese government by Anson Burlingame (1820–70), former US minister to China (1861–7). It recognized 'the mutual advantage of the free migration and emigration of their citizens and subjects respectively from one country to the other . . .' and the US specifically disavowed 'any intention or right to intervene in the domestic administration of China. . . .'

BURMA CAMPAIGNS in the Second World War. From 8 Dec. 1941, Burma, as part of the British empire, was at war with Japan. There were three major campaigns (1942, 1944, and 1945) and minor campaigns in Arakan and northern Burma (1943).

The first major campaign began in Jan. 1942, when the Japanese entered south-eastern Burma from Siam, their main drive being directed upon Moulmein and Rangoon. After severe losses in the battle of the Sittang Bridge, the remnants of the British–Indian forces retreated northwards towards Toungoo, while the Japanese advanced to encircle Rangoon. On 7 March the Rangoon garrison was extricated northwards. By this time Chinese aid had been accepted by the British, and forces of the Chiang Kai-shek regime took over the front facing the Japanese astride the road and railway through Toungoo. The British–Indian forces established a front across the Irrawaddy valley near Prome, and after the capture of Rangoon the Japanese resumed their advance against both these fronts; the oilfields at Yenangyaung were lost about 20 April. On 30 April the railway bridge over the Irrawaddy at Ava was blown up and Mandalay was abandoned, the British–Indian forces retreating into Manipur. The Chinese retreated by the Burma Road and across the mountains into China. By 20 May 1942 the Japanese had occupied all Burma except for small areas in the far north and west.

The second major campaign began in Feb. and March 1944, the Japanese launching offensives in Arakan and Assam, intending to break into the plains of India. Making use of newly developed techniques of air supply, the British–Indian forces, although surrounded, held the 'Administrative Box' in Arakan, and Imphal and Kohima in Assam, the latter after particularly bitter fighting. The Japanese lacked both the flexibility to change their plans and an adequate supply organization, relying upon reaching India to replenish supplies. Failing in this, their offensive withered away with heavy losses not only in battle but from starvation and sickness.

The third major campaign developed in 1945 with the Allied advance into Burma, upon Mandalay. The Irrawaddy was crossed near Myimmu and Nyaungu. Mandalay was taken on 21 March. Meiktila was seized at the end of March, cutting off the Japanese forces opposite Mandalay. The advance continued down the road and railway and down the Irrawaddy upon Rangoon. Allied forces advanced in Arakan to establish air–sea bases for the air-supply of the main advance upon Rangoon. Meanwhile Chinese–American forces and the Chindits were advancing upon Myitkyina in the north to reopen the Burma Road. At the end of April the Japanese withdrew from Rangoon towards Moulmein. On 3 May Rangoon was reoccupied by a virtually unopposed amphibious operation from Arakan, a few days before the arrival of the land forces. The Japanese continued to extricate their defeated forces towards Siam. On 14 Aug. they surrendered unconditionally.

S. Woodburn Kirby, *The War against Japan*, 5 vols (London, 1957–69).   FSVD

BURMA NATIONAL ARMY, developed from the Burma Independence Army raised by Aung San to co-operate with the Japanese as they invaded Burma (1942). On 27 March 1945 it defected to the Allies and co-operated in the ejection of the Japanese. Renamed the Patriotic Burmese Forces, it was partially absorbed into the Regular Burma Army, but almost half of it continued in existence as the People's Volunteer Organization, ostensibly an ex-service organization for social work but actually Aung San's private political army.

BURMA ROAD. The Japanese invasion and blockade of China in 1937 progressively cut off China's supplies of munitions by sea. The Burma Road was constructed in 1938 to link the Burma railhead at Lashio with Kunming and Chungking, to permit introduction of supplies overland through Burma. In 1940, under pressure from the Japanese, the British, with their backs to the wall in Europe and unable to risk a second war, temporarily closed the road. The Japanese invasion of Burma in 1941 cut this lifeline, after which supplies were flown to China from India over 'the Hump'.

BURMA SOCIALIST PROGRAMME PARTY, formed on 4 July 1962. In 1963 it became state-subsidized. In 1964 all other political parties were proscribed. It is no political party in the Western sense, but an instrument of government of the kind common in totalitarian states.

BURMESE WARS.
(a) First War (1824–6). Frontier incidents, particularly in Arakan, embittered relations between Burma and British India. Burmese preparations to invade Chittagong led to war. The main British–Indian force landed at Rangoon, which fell without opposition, and there were subsidiary operations in Assam, Arakan, and Tenasserim. The Burmese general Bandula, returned from Arakan but was unable to eject the invaders from Rangoon. The British operations were strategically sound but administratively disastrous and it took nearly two years before Bandula was defeated and killed in action at Danubyu. The war was concluded by the treaty of Yandabo.

(b) Second War (1852). Barbarities in Upper Burma shocked British opinion, and frontier irritations and oppressive treatment of British traders produced a drift towards war. Attempts to extort money from two British sea captains by false accusations resulted in a British ultimatum. When this was rejected, blockade, reprisals, and sporadic shooting followed until war was declared in April 1852. British forces occupied Rangoon, Martaban, and Bassein and advanced on Prome, where the Burmese were defeated. This time operations were administratively exemplary. On the conclusion of fighting (Dec. 1852) the Burmese refused to enter into a treaty. The British annexed the old kingdom of Pegu, so joining Arakan to Tenasserim, but the Burmese refused to recognize this.

(c) Third War (1885). Once again barbarities and oppressive treatment of British traders embittered relations, but it was not until the British discovered that secret negotiations had taken place between the Burmese and the French, which might lead to the establishment of French influence in Mandalay, that war became probable. When the Burmese imposed heavy fines upon the Bombay-Burma Trading Corporation, a British company extracting timber from Upper Burma (fines which may or may not have been justifiable but which were imposed in order to withdraw the firm's concession and give it to a French company), the British delivered an ultimatum requiring that the case against the BBTC be reopened. When there was no reply the British marched on Mandalay and occupied it a fortnight later, virtually without resistance. On 1 Jan. 1886 Upper Burma was annexed and, after some hesitation, incorporated in the Indian empire.

D. G. E. Hall, *Burma* (London, 1950).
John F. Cady, *A History of Modern Burma* (New York, 1958).   FSVD

BURMI, BATTLE OF (1903), fought in northern Nigeria between a British force and the followers of Sultan Al-Tahir of Sokoto. The sultan and about 500 of his men were killed, as was the British commander.

BURNABY'S CODE. Codification by British admiral Sir William Burnaby in 1765 of the usages of the settlers on the Bay of Honduras. The Code later formed the basis of the first constitution of British Honduras.

BURNELL, ROBERT (d. 1292), the best loved servant and most trusted adviser of King Edward I of England. He served Edward before his accession to the Crown and in 1275 became Bp of Bath and Wells and chancellor of England. The great period of legal reforms in Edward's reign coincides with his chancellorship. After Burnell's death, Edward's government became much less successful.

BURNET, SIR (FRANK) MACFARLANE (1899–), Australia's leading medical scientist. His experiments in immunology led to a much clearer understanding of disease processes, graft-rejection, cancer, and the acquisition of specific immunity.

BURNET, GILBERT (1643–1715), historian and bishop of Salisbury. He was educated at Marischal College, Aberdeen, and ordained by Bp of Edinburgh (1661). As a young clergyman he criticized the Scottish bishops in a letter sent to each of them, and received a rebuke for his unsolicited advice, which may have coloured his later writings, as a Whig his torian, about Scottish affairs. He was professor of divinity at Glasgow (1669–74), then moved to London, where his writings began to be published. During this time he was introduced to the Prince of Orange, and when the prince came to England, Burnet accompanied him as royal chaplain. As a believer in the divine right of kings, Burnet was troubled by the revolt against James, and also by the joint monarchy, believing as he did that Mary was the rightful sovereign after James. In 1689 he was consecrated Bp of Salisbury, and when Bp Rose of Edinburgh went to London to plead on behalf of the Scottish Episcopal clergy, he visited Burnet, knowing him to have influence at court. But Burnet was no longer concerned with Scots affairs. When a bill was introduced into the House of Commons in 1712 seeking religious toleration in worship for the Scottish Episcopal Church, it was carried by a large majority in both houses, Burnet being among the few Whig dissentients in the Upper House. Burnet is best known for his writings, which besides political pamphlets include numerous others defending the Broad or Low Church position. He wrote a *History of the Reformation in England*, and *A History of My Own Time*, his most famous book, published posthumously (1723, 1734). This is neither a diary nor an autobiography, and was periodically rewritten to try to produce a survey of history throughout Burnet's life-span. It illustrates his Protestantism and his support of the war against Louis XIV, and also emphasizes that it is difficult to categorize Burnet entirely as a Whig, since he was friendly with Nottingham, the High Church leader, and was not in favour of the exclusion of James from the succession to the Crown.

G. Burnet, *History of My Own Time*, 6 vols (Oxford, 1833).
AW

BURNEY, FANNY (1752–1840), English novelist. Her first novel, *Evelina*, published anonymously in 1778, enjoyed enormous popularity. She was the second keeper of the robes to Queen Charlotte (1786–90), and her published diary for this period gives a valuable and perceptive account of court life, including the first period of George III's insanity (1788). She married (1793) Gen. D'Arblay, a French refugee.

BURNEY TREATY (1826) between Siam and the English East India Co. marked Siam's first accommodation to the Western presence and demands, beginning the process which ultimately would secure Siam's independence. Negotiated by Capt. Henry Burney and Chaophraya Phrakhlang (Dit Bunnag) immediately upon the conclusion of the First Anglo-Burmese War, it improved the conditions of foreign trade in Bangkok and recognized Siamese suzerainty over the states of Kedah, Trengganu, and Kelantan on the Malay peninsula. The treaty brought about changes in Siam's tax system, worked well, and strengthened the position of those in the Siamese government who were confident of their nation's ability to reform and to resist Western domination.

BURNHAM, DANIEL HUDSON (1846–1912), US architect and early civil planner. With John W. Root, he designed the Montauk Building in Chicago (1881–2), which was a precursor of the modern skyscraper. Root died (1891) during the preparatory work, and Burnham completed the designs, using a neo-classical scheme, for the World's Columbian Exposition (Chicago, 1893). After completing the Flatiron Building in New York City (1902), Burnham made comprehensive city plans for several major cities in the US and the Philippines.

BURNHAM, LINDEN FORBES SAMPSON (1923–). Guyana political leader who, with Cheddi Jagan and others, founded the People's Progressive Party. He split with Jagan and in 1957 established the People's National Congress. Burnham was leader of the opposition (1961–4), chief minister after the 1964 elections, and with independence (1966) became Guyana's first prime minister. He led the People's National Congress to victory in the elections of 1968.

BURNS, JOHN (1858–1943), pioneer of the Labour movement. By occupation he was a journeyman engineer. He joined the Social Democratic Federation in the 1880s and was arrested on Bloody Sunday (1887). In 1889 he was elected to the newly formed London County Council as a Progressive. He thus became a prominent Labour figure and, with Tom Mann, was called in by Ben Tillett to help to organize the dock strike (1889), when he led dockers' processions through the city. He was elected MP for Battersea in 1892, but did not take part in the Bradford conference of 1893, which set up the Independent Labour Party. He was, as president of the Local Government Board (1905–14), the first working man to enter the cabinet. In that office he became dominated by departmental tradition and resisted the reform of the poor law proposed by Sidney and Beatrice Webb.

BURNS, PHILP AND COMPANY, a merchandising firm founded at Townsville, Qld, in 1873 by (Sir) James Burns (1846–1923) and (Sir) Robert Philp (1851–1922). By the 1890s it had branches throughout Australia. While investing in shipping, insurance, and large-scale retailing, the firm was most noted for its pioneer trading in New Guinea and the south-west Pacific.

BURNSIDE, AMBROSE EVERETT (1824–81), US major-general, who briefly succeeded McClellan as commander of the Army of the Potomac (1862). After Fredericksburg he was replaced and transferred to Ohio. He served under Grant at Petersburg, but was accused of incompetence and resigned. He became governor of Rhode Island (1866–69) and US senator (1875–81).

BURR, AARON (1756–1836), American lawyer, soldier, and politician. After distinguished service in the War of American Independence, he became attorney-general of New York (1789–91), and US senator (1791–97). After tying with Jefferson for the presidency of the US (1800), he became vice-president, but this did not prevent his becoming involved in a plot for the secession of New England. This collapsed after he failed to secure election as governor of NY (1804). Embittered by the opposition of his rival, Hamilton, Burr killed him in a duel (July 1804). After involvement in a scheme for the creation of an independent nation in the West, he was indicted for treason, but was acquitted (1807). After some years in Europe, where he continued to plot against the US, Burr returned (1812) and resumed his law practice in New York.

BURROUGHS, WILLIAM SEWARD (1855–98), US inventor, the adding machine being his best-known invention. After several failures, he was granted a patent (1893) on a machine that recorded individual items as well as the total. The machine was marketed through the Burroughs Adding Machine Co., forerunner of the modern computer firm.

BURRUS, SEXTUS AFRANIUS (d. AD 62), Roman politician and member of Nero's government. He was a native of Vasio (Vaison) and served as a military tribune and as an imperial procurator. In 51 he was appointed prefect of the praetorian guard through the influence of Agrippina the Younger. On Claudius' death in 54, Burrus, together with the philosopher, Seneca the Younger, dominated Nero's government, exercising power in a responsible if unenterprising way. They excluded Agrippina from power and probably knew of Nero's plan to murder her. After Burrus' death, Seneca soon lost influence at court and Nero's government deteriorated.

BURSCHENSCHAFTEN, patriotic student societies in German universities. The first was founded at Jena (1815) by students who had fought in the War of Liberation against Napoleon. The societies spread to most German universities and tried to foster the spirit which had existed during the war in favour of German unity. With their nationalism they combined liberal opposition to the German regimes, which became increasingly anxious about their development. In 1817 they celebrated the Lutheran tercentenary at Wartburg with patriotic songs and speeches and the burning of reactionary books and symbols. The German princes finally decided to suppress them after the murder of the reactionary playwright, Kotzebue (1819). The resulting Carlsbad decrees included measures to suppress the societies, which then went underground, re-emerging in the revolutions of the 1830s and 1848.

BURSLEM, home of the modern pottery industry in England, where Josiah Wedgwood worked as a boy and started his pottery factory in 1759.

BURTON, SIR RICHARD FRANCIS (1821–90), British explorer, who acquired considerable knowledge of oriental languages and culture in the Indian civil service. After exploring in Arabia and Somalia, he joined John Speke to explore the East African lakes and find the source of the Nile (1857–9). At Lake Tanganyika Burton became ill, so Speke continued and later claimed he had discovered the source of the Nile to be Lake Victoria, a claim which Burton bitterly contested. Stanley afterwards showed that Speke was right, though more recently the Kagera river, supplying the lake, has been acknowledged as a source. Later, as British Consul at Fernando Po, Burton explored the Cameroon mountains and visited the King of Dahomey. His last expeditions were to Arabia and the Guinea Coast. His books included *The Lake Regions of Central Africa* (1860).

BURTON, ROBERT (1577–1640), English essayist, whose collection of essays, *The Anatomy of Melancholy* (1621), was stimulated by those of Montaigne. It remains one of the most famous books of the 17th cent., not only in its use of the English language, but also in its range of interests which covers such diverse fields of scholarship as medicine, poetry, history, geography, and classical literature.

BURUNDI (28,000 sq. kms), region on the north-eastern shores of Lake Tanganyika with 3,210,000 people, chiefly Rundi. Formerly part of the UN trust territory of Ruanda/Urundi under Belgian control, it became independent in July 1962. Since 1966 it has been a republic with a legislative assembly and senate elected by adult suffrage.

BURY ST EDMUNDS, town in Suffolk, England, which owed its origin to a Benedictine abbey founded in 1020 at the burial place of St Edmund, the last English king of East Anglia, killed by the Danes in 870. Offerings of pilgrims and gifts of numerous estates made the abbey into one of the richest English monasteries. It was perennially in conflict with its townsmen, who rebelled in vain in 1326 and 1381.

BUSBY, JAMES (1801–71), British Resident in NZ before its annexation by the British (1840). He arrived in 1833 from Sydney, but without adequate status or resources, or support from the governor of NSW, Busby's position was precarious. He promoted an abortive Maori confederation, but his 'moral' authority impressed neither settlers nor Maoris. His failure pointed the way to annexation, in which he assisted Hobson.

BUSCH, GERMÁN (1904–39), Bolivian Chaco War hero and president, he became provisional president by *coup d'état* (1937), and was elected to a full term the following year. In 1939 he dismissed congress and ruled by decree. He expropriated the property of the Standard Oil Co., but his reform programme was halted by his death.

BUSCH, JOHANN GEORG (1728–1800), German historian, economist, and mathematician. He founded the Hamburg Academy of Commerce, whose director he remained for 30 years and which attracted entrants from all over Europe.

He was said to have known all the languages of Europe, and travelled widely throughout the continent.

BUSH, VANNEVAR (1890–), US technologist and administrator, and former professor and dean of engineering at Massachusetts Institute of Technology (1923–38). He became director of the Office of Scientific Research and Development (1941–6) and organizer of the Manhattan Project to construct the first atomic bomb.

BUSHFIRES IN AUSTRALIA. Periodic combination of drought conditions, low humidity, and high winds made parts of Australia's eucalyptus forests and grasslands susceptible to devastating bushfires, recorded since the beginning of European settlement. Ninety per cent of modern outbreaks are attributed to human agency and 10 per cent to lightning, with current annual damage estimated at $A4m. and a total recorded death-roll to mid-1969 of 270. The state of Victoria suffered most. In the worst fire there, in Gippsland (Jan. 1939), 71 persons died, 1300 homes were destroyed, and damage of $A28m. caused. A fire in southern Tasmania in 1962, which reached the suburbs of Hobart, claimed 66 lives, 1350 homes, and $A50m. damage. Despite the work of 5000 volunteer brigades with a membership of 250,000 and of full-time bodies, together with an increase in study of prevention methods, no really effective means of fire control had been found by 1970. The more sophisticated measures of aerial spotting, water-bombing, and chemical dousing, as practised in North America, had not been used to any great extent.

BUSHIDO, the 'War of the Warrior', the moral code of the samurai class of feudal Japan. It was concerned basically with the relationship between lord and retainer, the emphasis being more on the latter's absolute loyalty, even unto death, and less on the lord's obligation to protect his retainer than was the case in European chivalry. As well as loyalty and military prowess, honour, simplicity, and frugality were exalted. Although the code was often breached, *bushido* produced many outstanding examples of heroic self-sacrifice which have inspired later generations of Japanese.

BUSHRANGING, the name given in Australia to highway robbery or banditry. The first bushranger, a Negro convict named John ('Black') Caesar, escaped (June 1789) from a settlement at Sydney Cove 17 months after the arrival of the first convicts. Before 1851 nearly all bushrangers were escaped convicts. During the regime of Gov. Sir Ralph Darling (1825–31) so many convicts 'took to the bush' that a 'bushranging act' gave, to 'any person whatsoever', the right to arrest, without a warrant, anyone suspected of being 'a transported felon unlawfully at large'. Most, though not all, of these early bushrangers pursued their calling on foot.

In 1852 transportation to eastern Australia ceased, but bushranging continued for the next 30 years, particularly during the 1860s, when transport from the goldfields provided rich pickings. The much-praised Ben Hall, shot dead in a police ambush in 1865, was a free-born Australian of Irish descent and convict stock, like many of the post-gold-rush brigands.

Bushranging practically expired with the legendary Ned Kelly, hanged in Melbourne in 1880. The reason it lasted so long was that most bushrangers sought to cultivate a 'Robin Hood' image. As far back as 1837 James Macarthur wrote that most Australians were 'in favour of the criminals' and the image was more readily accepted in the 1860s and 1870s because of the prevailing hostility of small settlers (to whom the Kellys belonged) to powerful pastoralist 'squatters'. The persistence of bushranging thereafter in popular tradition—though greatly exaggerated—contributed something to the 20th-cent. Australian's lack of respect for the police.

R. Ward, *The Australian Legend* (Melbourne, 1958). **RW**

BUSSY, Marquis de (1718–85), French officer of great distinction. He went to India with the expedition of La Bourdonnais (1746) which took Madras. On the death of the Nizam Muzaffar Jung (1751) while being escorted to Hyderabad by French troops, Bussy raised Salabat Jung, the first nizam's third son, to the throne, and thereafter sustained him in power through many vicissitudes for seven years. He secured the grant of the northern Sircars to maintain his troops and created the model of a European-sponsored Indian state which Clive later tried to imitate in Bengal. In 1758 he was recalled by Comte de Lally, governor of Pondicherry, to face the English in the Seven Years War. The French were defeated at Wandiwash (1760) and Bussy was taken prisoner. He returned to India in 1783 with the fleet of Admiral de Suffrein and landed at Cuddalore, but before he could make any impression peace was declared.

BUSTAMANTE, SIR ALEXANDER (1894–), Jamaican statesman. Born William Alexander Clarke, he took the name Bustamante from a Spanish mariner who adopted him at the age of 15. He did military service in Spanish Morocco, was an inspector of police in Havana, Cuba, and lived for a short time in the US. In 1932 he returned to Jamaica, where he organized the Bustamante industrial trade union and in 1943 the Jamaica Labour Party. He served as chief minister (1953–5) and as opposition leader (1955–62). After Jamaican independence (1962) he was prime minister until 1967.

BUSTAMANTE, ANASTASIO (1780–1835), Mexican general and Conservative president. He fought with the Spaniards against Hidalgo and Morelos. Later he joined the independence movement under Iturbide. His presidential terms (1830–2, 1837–41), were both cut short by revolts led by Gen. Santa Anna and the Liberals.

BUSTAMANTE Y RIVERO, JOSÉ LUIS (b. 1894), president of Peru, who was elected (1945) with the support of the powerful but illegal Aprista Party. He was overthrown by the army in 1948.

BUTE, JOHN STUART, 3rd Earl of (Scottish) (1713–92), minister of George III. Bute had been a Scottish representative peer since 1737, and by virtue of his family connections had a potentially strong position in parliament. He was a leading figure of the Leicester House group, and after the death of Frederick, Prince of Wales (1751), became tutor to his son, the future George III. On his accession, George leant upon Bute in political matters, thus exciting the suspicion and dislike of established politicians. He was made secretary of state (1761) in a ministry which included Pitt and Newcastle. Disputes occurred when Bute and the king wished to open peace negotiations with France, and Pitt wished to continue the Seven Years War. On the resignation of Pitt (1761) and Newcastle (1762), Bute became first lord of the treasury. The peace of Paris, the cider tax proposal, the especial favour Bute enjoyed with the king, and the fact that he was a Scot, combined to earn Bute great unpopularity inside and outside parliament, and led to John Wilkes's agitation against king and government. Bute resigned in 1763. His botanical interests and accomplishments were of note. He was instrumental, with Sir William Chambers, in the development of Princess Augusta's garden at Kew as a great botanical collection, when the vogue for 'natural' landscape gardening was still banishing all flowers from view.

BUTLER OF SAFFRON WALDEN, RICHARD AUSTEN BUTLER, Life Baron (1902–), British politician, instigator of the 1944 Education Act. Butler, who was born in India, entered parliament as MP for Saffron Walden (1929), was made under-secretary for the India Office (1932–7), for the ministry of labour (1937–8), and then for the foreign office in the reshuffle that followed Eden's resignation. He therefore became involved in the general opprobrium that was subsequently attached to Munich, and the fruitless search for an Anglo-German *modus vivendi* over Czechoslovakia and Poland. When Chamberlain's government collapsed in 1940, Butler continued in the foreign office.

As minister of education (1941–5), his liberal and reforming policies led to the 1944 Education Act. This measure, by the division of the secondary school system into academic ('grammar') and more largely vocational schools ('technical' and 'secondary modern'), set the pattern of British education for nearly a quarter of a century. When Butler was in opposition (1945–51), he helped, with Lord Woolton, to reshape the Conservative Party machine and under his direction the research department became the centre of the 'New Conservatism' with which Butler became closely associated.

In 1951 Butler was made chancellor of the exchequer, a position he held during the Korean War. In 1955 he became lord privy seal and leader of the House and, in 1957, home secretary. Then began his second great period of liberalizing reform. In 1962 he became deputy prime minister, but resigned from politics in 1964 to become master of Trinity College, Cambridge.

Butler occupied a central position in British politics for over 20 years. His particular brand of reforming Conservatism influenced an entire generation of Conservatives, especially the post-war generation associated with the research office. The hostility this aroused among older Conservatives, together with a suspicion of indecisiveness, perhaps cost him the premiership in 1957 and 1963. His work, nevertheless, constitutes a body of achievement with little parallel in this century.

BUTLER, BENJAMIN FRANKLIN (1818–93), notorious Union military governor of New Orleans during 1862, and radical Republican Congressman (1867–75, 1877–9), who initiated the attempt to impeach President Johnson. He was influential during Grant's administrations, became governor of Rhode Island (1882–4), and presidential candidate of the Greenback and Anti-Monopoly parties (1884).

BUTLER, JOSEPH (1692–1752), High Church bishop of Durham and one of the most prominent figures in the Anglican Church during the 18th cent. He was the son of a Presbyterian draper, was educated in a dissenting academy, Samuel Jones's at Tewkesbury, and was for ten years rector of Stanhope in Weardale, Durham. His *Analogy of Religion Natural and Revealed* (1736), the product of this tranquil period of his life, was an important refutation of deism, emphasizing the superiority of man's conscience over his reason.

BUTLER, JOSEPHINE ELIZABETH (1828–1906), feminist and social reformer, who was influenced strongly by the anti-slavery views of her father, John Grey of Dilston. She promoted women's higher education in the 1860s, reclaimed Liverpool prostitutes, and successfully led the women's campaign against the Contagious Diseases Acts (1869–86).

BUTLER, NICHOLAS MURRAY (1862–1947), US educationist, leading advocate of international co-operation for the preservation of world peace. An exponent of what subsequently came to be called 'progressive education', he was one of the founders and first president of NY Teachers College (1886–91), and also founded and edited the influential *Educational Review* (1889–1920). He was president of Columbia University (1902–45). Butler, an active Republican, became President Taft's running mate when vice-president Sherman died after his renomination by the party convention (1912). He was an ardent internationalist and became president of the Carnegie Endowment for International Peace (1925–45). In 1931 he shared the Nobel Peace Prize with Jane Addams.

BUTLER, SAMUEL (1612–80), English satirist, son of a Worcestershire farmer, and author of *Hudibras*, a three-part satire on the Puritans (1663–78). It is a mock-epic in the style of *Don Quixote*, describing the ludicrous adventures of Hudibras, a Presbyterian squire, and his page Ralpho, who is an Independent. Hudibras was modelled on Sir Samuel Luke, a Bedfordshire justice and former Cromwellian officer, whom Butler served as a clerk. Refusing to allow the Puritans any virtues, Butler wrote in scurrilous terms about their sectarian quibbles and personal greed, hypocrisy, and superstition. He also wrote some verse *Characters* in the manner of Theophrastus and a satire on the Royal Society, *The Elephant in the Moon*, in which the elephant is only a dead mouse lodged in the telescope. Although rewarded by Charles II for *Hudibras*, Butler is believed to have died in poverty.

BUTLER, SAMUEL (1835–1902), writer and artist. On leaving Cambridge University, he became a sheep farmer on the upper Rangitata, NZ (1859–64). This provided the background to his book *Erewhon* (1872), a satire upon an imaginary country. In his later works he expounded current views on evolution, classical criticism, and translation (*eg*, *The Humour of Homer*), Shakespearian sonnets, and a biography of his grandfather, Bp Samuel Butler. His autobiography, *The Way of All Flesh* (1903), influenced 20th-cent. English literature.

BUTLER, SIR SPENCER HARCOURT (1869–1938), Indian administrator. Butler served in the Oudh region of the United Provinces (1890–1907) and gained a reputation for administrative skill and political acumen that brought him a series of high offices. He was made foreign secretary in the government of India (1907), where he had contact with the princes. As the first education member of the viceroy's executive council (1910) he made an important reassessment of university education. As head of the provincial administration in Burma (1915–18, 1923–8) and the United Provinces (1918–22), he was responsible for the introduction of constitutional reforms. His last official task in India was to be chairman of the Indian States Committee (1928–9).

BUTLER, SIR WILLIAM FRANCIS (1838–1910), British soldier and author. Butler, who first served in Canada in 1867, was an *avant-courier* of the expedition to quell the Red River Rebellion and secured an interview with the rebel leader, Louis Riel. In Oct. 1870 Butler was sent to report on conditions at the Hudson's Bay Co.'s posts in the Saskatchewan country. This journey took him to the Rocky Mountains and his account of it, *The Great Lone Land*, is a classic in the literature of the north-west. Books on his other journeys followed, including one on the manners and customs of the Indians. Butler left Canada in 1873 and spent the rest of his life in other parts of the British empire, mainly Egypt and South Africa.

BUTLER COMMITTEE, or Indian States Committee (1928–1929). It was appointed in response to complaints by the princes concerning their treatment by the government of India and they hoped for some relaxation of British paramountcy. The committee accepted the princes' claim that their relationship was with the Crown and not the government of India, and it recommended that the viceroy should act personally as the Crown's agent in all future dealings with the states, but it rejected the argument that the relationship was a mere 'contractual' one. It asserted that paramountcy was absolute and that the British government had a right, and a duty, to oversee the internal affairs and the external relations of the states. The British would uphold the princes, but would also dictate the manner in which they must rule. The committee ruled out any rapid progress to all-India federation and insisted that the Chamber of Princes could have only a consultative role in the foreseeable future.

The report was regarded as a mere restatement of government doctrine by the princes and it was rejected by nationalist opinion as being a continuation of the effort to keep 'Indian India' isolated from the progressive political movements of the British provinces. It proved an insubstantial base for British policy towards the states in the rapidly changing political climate of the 1930s.

BUTRUS AL-BUSTANI (1819–83), Maronite Lebanese writer, who became converted to Protestantism, played an influential role in the Arabic literary revival, in the formation of a concept of Syrian territorial nationalism, and in the spread of western ideas in the Middle East.

BUTT, ISAAC (1813–79), founder of the Irish Home Rule Party (1874). He left the Irish parliamentary party with a hard core of about 20 followers from 1874 until he was superseded by Parnell (1878). Butt worked for Irish self-government, but strongly opposed separatism. He refused to accept the support of revolutionary movements, and dissociated himself from Biggar and from the Land League.

BUTTERFIELD OVERLAND MAIL, semi-weekly US stagecoach service between St Louis, Memphis, and San Francisco. The 25-day schedule was successfully maintained over this southern route from 1858 until the Civil War, when the overland mail was transferred to the central route along the Platte river.

BUVELOT, ABRAM LOUIS (1814–88), Swiss-born painter whose work profoundly influenced the first distinctively Australian school of Impressionist painters.

BUWAYHIDS (BUYIDS), dynasty ruling (945–1055) over western Persia and Iraq. The Buwayhid domination was the work of three brothers, Ali (Imad al-Dawla, d. 949–50), Ahmad (Mu'izz al-Dawla, d. 967), and Al-Hasan (Rukn al-Dawla, d. 976). The brothers, coming from the mountainous region of Daylam, south of the Caspian Sea, and professing the Shi'i faith, rose to prominence as condottieri soldiers. Ali established himself in Fars, Al-Hasan in the Jibal area, and Ahmad in Kirman and in Khuzistan. It was Ahmad who, in 945, took over Iraq, becoming *amir-al-umara* at Baghdad. The dynasty was at the summit of its power during the years 978–83, when Adud al-Dawla, the son of Rukn al-Dawla, held under his own control all the Buwayhid territories. Although adhering to the Shi'a, the Buwayhids did not abolish the caliphate at Baghdad, but retained it as a means to legitimize their rule in the eyes of the Sunni Muslims. The caliph still exercised certain religious and legal prerogatives. All political, military, and financial power was vested, however, in the hands of the Buwayhid amirs. After the death of Adud al-Dawla in 983 the Buwayhid regime began to decline. The economic situation, in general, became less favourable to the Buwayhids when, around the year 1000, there occurred a notable shift of trade from the Persian Gulf to the Red Sea. There was trouble, too, for the Buwayhid amirs within their armed forces. To the Daylami troops, of Shi'i allegiance, who formed the original core of their armies the Buwayhids added Turkish mamluks, of Sunni faith, in large numbers. The differences in race and religion led to violent quarrels among the Buwayhid forces. There was dissension, too, within the dynasty itself. Under the stress of these discords the Buwayhid regime broke down before the advance of the Seljuk Turks, who overran Persia and Iraq, capturing Baghdad in 1055.

VJP

BUXAR, BATTLE OF (22 Oct. 1764), fought between the forces of the East India Co., commanded by Maj. Hector Munro, and the army of the Emperor Shah Alam and the Vizier, Shuja-ad-daula of Oudh. The battle was fought on the borders of Bihar in an effort to restore Mir Kasim to the control of Bengal, from which he had been ejected in the previous year. The defeat of the Mughals finally secured to the British the control of Bengal and Bihar.

BUXTON, THOMAS FOWELL (1786–1845), brewer, philanthropist, and Liberal MP (1818–37), who led the anti-slavery crusade in parliament from 1822 to its successful outcome in 1833.

BYBLOS (mod. Jubayl, Syria), Phoenician city, the site of which has been continuously inhabited since Neolithic times. It was the chief port for the export of timber, and also exported fine linen and handled Egyptian papyrus in transit to Greece.

BYCZYNA, BATTLE OF (1588), defeat of the Austrian forces by John Zamoyski, which secured the succession of Sigismund III to the Polish throne and ended Habsburg hopes of election.

BYNG OF VIMY, JULIAN HEDWORTH GEORGE BYNG, Viscount (1862–1935), Canadian field marshal and governor-general of Canada. He saw service in the Sudan (1884), the South African War, and the First World War, in which he took command of the newly formed Canadian Corps (1916) and with them captured Vimy Ridge (1917). Byng was appointed governor-general of Canada in 1921 and towards the end of his period of office became the centre of a constitutional crisis. He refused to dissolve parliament (June 1926) when requested to do so by W. L. MacKenzie King. King thereupon resigned and Byng persuaded Meighen, the opposition leader, to form a new administration which was promptly but narrowly defeated in parliament. Byng granted Meighen's request for a dissolution and in the ensuing election King accused Byng of playing politics and reducing Canada to colonial status. It is now widely agreed that Byng acted correctly. He became a popular, reforming commissioner of police in London (1928–34)

BYNG, JOHN (1704–57), British admiral. He was sent to prevent the French from taking Minorca at the outbreak of the Seven Years War (1756), but was defeated, recalled, and sentenced to death for neglect of duty. His execution (1757) provoked Voltaire's supposition that it was 'pour encourager les autres'.

BYRD, WILLIAM (c. 1542–1623), English polyphonic composer. He was organist of Lincoln cathedral (1563–74) before joining Tallis as organist of the Chapel Royal. He composed masses for the Latin rite, services for the English liturgy, motets, anthems, madrigals, and string music.

BYRD FAMILY, citizens of Virginia.
WILLIAM BYRD (1652–1704), planter, merchant, and Indian trader, who had been born in England, came to VA and acquired land on the James river. He grew wealthy by planting tobacco and trading in rum, slaves, dry goods, and furs. He was a member of the House of Burgesses (1677–82), became a member of the Council of State, a body of wealthy men who dominated the government of the colony, and was auditor-general of VA.

WILLIAM BYRD (1674–1744), son of the above, was born in VA, educated in England, studied law, and became a member of the Royal Society. On the death of his father he returned to VA to manage the estate and later became a member of the Council of State (1709), and founded the city of Richmond. Byrd's library of 4000 volumes was the largest private library in the colonies. His *History of the Dividing Line Betwixt Virginia and North Carolina* is a classic of colonial literature, and his diary (published in 1941), is a valuable record of the domestic economy of a 17th-cent. plantation.

His son, **WILLIAM BYRD, III,** squandered his father's property and committed suicide. The family plantation,

Westover, was sold and his sons migrated to the upper Shenandoah valley. Until the 20th cent. the Byrd family played no further role in American history.

HARRY F. BYRD (1887–1966), VA politician and descendant of William Byrd, who developed in the Shenandoah valley one of the largest apple-growing regions in the world. He was a member of the VA state senate for 10 years, was governor of VA (1926–30), and of the US Senate (1933–1965), serving on the finance committee and the joint committee on reduction of non-essential expenditure, whereby he became known as 'Mr Economy' and the 'Watchdog of the Treasury'.

RICHARD E. BYRD (1888–1957), brother of the above, was a pioneer airman and Antarctic explorer. He flew the Atlantic with three companions (29 June 1927) and instituted the first official air mail service. In 1926 he made the first flight over the North Pole, and four years later was the first man to fly over the South Pole. He made four expeditions to the south polar regions and established Little America there. He wrote *Discovery* (1935) and *Alone* (1938) about his Antarctic explorations.

BYRNES, JAMES FRANCIS (1879–   ), US politician from SC. He served as congressman (1911–25), senator (1931–41), justice of the US Supreme Court (1941–2), director of the Office of Economic Stabilization (1942–3), director of war mobilization (1943–5), US secretary of state (1945–7), and governor of SC (1951–5). As a loyal Southern Democrat, he commended himself to F. D. Roosevelt because of his support for New Deal legislation. Although inexperienced in foreign affairs, he had, as secretary of state, to try to build a post-war foreign policy. At the Moscow Conference (Dec. 1945) he appeared ready to compromise with the Soviet Union and secured agreement concerning the Balkans, but under increasing domestic pressure his attitude toughened. In his retirement he became identified with southern conservatism.

BYRON, GEORGE GORDON, 6th Baron (1788–1824), English poet. He sympathized with radical causes and offered to join the Greek insurgents (1823). He landed at Missolonghi in Jan. 1824 and died there of malaria in April. In Greece, and among continental liberals generally, he became revered as a symbolic figure.

BYRON, JOHN (1723–86), British admiral. He circumnavigated the globe (1764–6) and in 1778 was sent to intercept the French fleet en route to the American colonies. He failed, however, to prevent the French occupying Grenada.

BYZANTIUM (med. Constantinople, mod. Istanbul), Greek colony founded by Megara (c. 650 BC) on the western shore of the Bosphorus, finely situated for trade and fishing. Subjected by the Persians (c. 540), it joined the abortive Ionian revolt, was liberated by Pausanias (478), and finally from his tyranny (c. 476). Because of its position on the corn route from southern Russia it was valuable to Athens. It was a lukewarm member of the Delian League, from which it seceded in 440–439 and 411–408, and of the Second Athenian Confederacy, breaking free from it in 364 and opposing Athens in the Social War (357–355). But with Athens's help it withstood a siege by Philip II of Macedon (340–339), before becoming an autonomous ally of Alexander the Great. Wooed by his successors, it maintained a precarious independence in the 3rd cent. paying tribute to barbarian neighbours. After assisting the Romans in the Macedonian (200–149) and Mithridatic Wars (90–63), it achieved its greatest prosperity as a centre of military communications in the imperial period, and in AD 330 was refounded by Constantine as his new Rome, to be known shortly afterwards as Constantinople.

CABAL, THE (1667–73), informal group of advisers to King Charles II of Britain. Its members were Thomas Clifford, Lord Arlington, the Duke of Buckingham, Lord Ashley, and the Earl of Lauderdale. Because the combination of their initials spelled the word 'Cabal', they have been regarded by many as an organized ministry which replaced that of Clarendon on his fall in 1667. This was not so. In the first three years of their greatest influence, a period marked by vicious political intrigue as they competed among themselves and with other aspiring policians for Charles II's favour, there was little to distinguish them from others in the privy council. The five were not of equal weight in the king's counsels: Arlington and Buckingham were the dominant rivals and their rivalry was a basic political factor between 1668 and 1673. Buckingham did not at any time hold a major office of state; his influence with Charles II was on a personal level. None of the five succeeded in achieving a position of pre-eminence, as did Clarendon and Danby. While their disharmony showed on the surface of politics, underneath Charles was making his own policy.

Charles II's aim was to free himself from the influence of parliament, and this, if he was to be successful, he had to do without arousing its suspicions. Consequently he chose a divided group of advisers to provide himself with camouflage. The members of the Cabal agreed on two things only: a willingness to serve the king, and dislike of the Anglican monopoly in religion.

The secret treaty of Dover (1670), intended to achieve Charles II's domestic objective of independence from parliament by means of a French alliance and subsidy, illustrates the divisions with the Cabal. Clifford supported it enthusiastically, but Arlington only grudgingly, and the other three members did not know what was involved. By 1674 Charles was no nearer his objective; in fact, he was in a worse position than in 1667, having been forced by parliament to back down over the Declaration of Indulgence (1672).

An attempt to impeach Arlington (Feb. 1674), led by Buckingham, is usually given as the terminal date of the Cabal; but the group's influence had ended by Nov. 1673, with Shaftesbury's dismissal as lord chancellor. By that time Clifford was dead, Buckingham out of favour, and Lauderdale's iron rule of Scotland was weakening when opposition intensified in the Scottish parliament. Arlington was to remain secretary of state until late 1674, and Lauderdale in charge of Scottish affairs until 1680, but Charles had decided to change his policies in mid-1673 with the appointment of Thomas Osborne (later Earl of Danby) as lord treasurer in place of Clifford. The disguised attempt at absolutism—the Cabal—had failed.

Maurice Lee, *The Cabal* (Urbana, IL, 1965).
David Ogg, *England in the Reign of Charles II* (London, 1934).   CJ

CABALLERIAS, land grants of varying size awarded to Spanish nobles (*caballeros*) during the conquest of Spain from the Moors. The term is still used as a unit of land measurement in some parts of Latin America.

CABASILAS, NICOLAUS (d. *c.* 1396), Byzantine theologian and moderate supporter of the Hesychast movement. He was the author of spiritual tracts, homilies, and letters, and initiated a dispute between the Roman and the Greek Churches over the form of the Eucharist.

CABEZA DE VACA, ALVAR NUÑEZ (1490–1551), treasurer of the expedition of Narváez from Spain to FL (1528). Of the 300 men in the expedition only four returned to Spain. After wandering in the FL swamps, the men built five small boats and set out from the vicinity of Tampa to sail to Cuba. Storms capsized four of the boats, but Cabeza and three other men landed on the TX shore near Galveston. They were captured by Indians, but escaped and made a 3000-mile (4828 kms) trek lasting six years across TX and Mexico to the Pacific. Cabeza returned to Spain in 1537 and told of his adventures in his book *Relacion y Comentarion*, the first account of travel in the present US. His reports were useful to later explorers in the New World.

CABILDO, governing council of Spanish colonial towns, consisting of 4–12 councillors (*regidores*), judges (*alcaldes ordinarios*), an ensign (*alférez*), a constable (*alguacil*), and others.

CABILDO ABIERTO, meeting of all the householders (*vecinos*) of a Spanish colonial town, called by the governor or town council (*cabildo*) in times of emergency. All *vecinos* were entitled to both speak and vote on such occasions. The *cabildo abierto* was an ineffective political device until the early 19th cent., when it played a vital role in the incipient independence movements. Buenos Aires successfully defeated the British invasion of 1807 under the guidance of its *cabildo abierto*. The early independence movements in various Spanish colonies (1810) were guided by these open assemblies, which were dominated by creoles.

CABINET IN BRITAIN, group of the most important ministers in the government which discusses and co-ordinates the business of state, initiates legislation, and takes the decisions which set the machinery of government in operation. Members are chosen by the prime minister.

The cabinet originated late in the 17th cent. through the sovereign's practice of consulting a small group of confidential advisers in preference to the privy council. Its secrecy was resented, but although it had no legal status, the king's right to consult such a body was firmly established by 1705. During the 18th cent. the cabinet was regularized in such a way as seriously to undermine the king's right to determine its composition. By the end of the 19th cent. the collective responsibility of the cabinet had virtually replaced the joint authority of the king and his ministers for carrying on the work of government. Its evolution from a deliberative to an executive council was complete.

Powerful ministers such as Walpole had been able to influence the choice of the cabinet from the beginning of the 18th cent. and already cabinets tended to include most of the important officers of state. They also tended to be too large and the modern cabinet descends from the inner or 'confidential' cabinet which met regularly by the 1730s. By the beginning of Pitt's ministry (1783) the most important ministers were automatically included in the cabinet. The first lord of the treasury, whose control over the sources of patronage made him a key figure in the management of the Commons, automatically led its deliberations. But although in practice it became increasingly difficult for the sovereign to determine either the choice of prime ministers or the appointment of other leading ministers, these were not entirely removed from the royal prerogative. Queen Victoria's refusal to allow the inclusion of Dilke in Gladstone's cabinet (1892) was the last time this prerogative was successfully exercised.

The cabinet had thus established its ascendancy over the Crown. But its authority could only be maintained through control of parliament, to which it was responsible. The ascendancy of the cabinet was secured by continuing its tradition of secrecy (regular cabinet minutes were kept only after 1916), and by presenting a united front to the Commons through the acceptance of collective cabinet responsibility, whereby the whole cabinet supports the decisions of the majority and dissenting ministers are expected to resign. This solidarity (increased after 1832 by the practice of appointing an entirely new cabinet with every change of government), combined with ministerial responsibility to parliament, is of fundamental importance to the maintenance of stable, constitutional government.

W. I. Jennings, *Cabinet Government* (Cambridge, 1936).
B. Kemp, *King and Commons, 1660–1832* (London, 1957).

SDH

CABINET COUNCIL, English constitutional body, sometimes known as the cabinet committee, which evolved in the later 17th cent. It originated in Charles II's practice of dispensing with the unwieldy privy council as the governing body and his reliance instead on the advice of a few leading councillors. During William III's reign this developed into a regular pattern of conducting government business through committees of the privy council or cabinet councils, which met regularly twice a week, usually including Sundays, to discuss matters such as naval, Irish, or trade affairs, and were presided over by the king. By the mid-1690s, however, a distinction had developed between the cabinet council and a smaller committee of that council, whose members were summoned by the king and whose business was secret. This was the origin of the 'inner cabinet', which grew in importance during Anne's reign, when the exigencies of war necessitated highly secret military and political decisions. This smaller inner or 'efficient' cabinet met informally and frequently, and its policy discussions and decisions were often unrecorded. It usually consisted of the lords president of the council, privy seal, chamberlain, chancellor, the two secretaries of state, and lords of the treasury and admiralty boards. After 1717, when George I ceased to attend cabinet meetings, there started the long, slow process by which corporate ministerial responsibility developed and also cabinet domination by one outstandingly able or 'prime minister', *eg*, Walpole and the younger Pitt.

CABINET MISSION TO INDIA, a group of three cabinet ministers sent to India (March 1946) in an effort to solve the problem of British withdrawal, which the Muslim League demand for partition had exacerbated. The mission, comprising the secretary of state for India, Lord Pethick-Lawrence, Sir Stafford Cripps, and A. V. Alexander, proposed (16 May) a constitution and suggested (16 June) the formation of an interim government representative of the main Indian parties. The constitution would have preserved an Indian unity with responsibility for defence, external affairs, and communications, all other matters devolving upon the provinces. The mission's scheme provided for the provinces to combine into groups and for a constituent assembly to meet on the basis of three such groups, 'A' comprising the Hindu majority provinces, 'B' comprising the Muslim provinces of Punjab, Sind, North-West Frontier Province, and Baluchistan, and 'C' comprising Bengal and Assam, which would also have a Muslim majority. The scheme thus attempted to give the semblance of 'Pakistan' while preserving Indian unity. Hopes that the Indian parties would accept the scheme as at least a basis for discussion were dashed by doubts about Congress's

intentions and difficulties over the appointment of Muslim members to the interim government. When the mission left India at the end of June its proposals lapsed and the deadlock remained.

CABIRA, BATTLE OF (72 BC) (near mod. Niksar, northern Turkey), the victory of the Romans under Lucullus over Mithridates VI of Pontus, which forced him to abandon his kingdom and flee to Armenia.

CABLE, GEORGE WASHINGTON (1844–1925), US author and journalist, known for his stories and novels of the Creoles of southern LA, including *Old Creole Days* (1879) and *The Grandissimes* (1880). In his essays, *The Silent South* (1885) and *The Negro Question* (1888), he attacked southern white attitudes towards Negroes.

CABOCHIENS (1413), popular revolt which broke out in Paris and was supported by John, Duke of Burgundy for his own political ends. Its causes included the extravagance of the court under the mad king, Charles VI, the demoralization caused by the struggle between the Orleanist and Burgundian factions, and the rapacity of royal officials. It was led by the butchers and skinners, its leader being the skinner, Caboche. It started in April and the Bastille was besieged and the nobility harried. In May a long and detailed *Ordonnance Cabochienne* was published which also reflected the complaints of the *parlement* and Paris University. Many of the reforms were desirable, but could not be carried out in the absence of an effective government. When the reaction came it also involved a political reorientation in Paris from Burgundian to Orleanist (Armagnac) predominance and the English invasion (1415) restored some vestige of order and unity.

CABOCLO, rural Brazilian agriculturalist and peasant, originally an Indian farmer, later a farmer of mixed Indian–European (*mestiço*) origin.

CABOT, JOHN (1450–98), native of Genoa, became a merchant in Bristol, England. King Henry VII commissioned him to sail on an expedition of discovery under the English flag. He sailed in May 1497 due west to look for the North-West Passage. In June he arrived off Cape Breton in North America, thinking he had reached north-west Asia. He returned to England and reported finding the cod-fishing grounds off the Grand Banks. The purpose of Cabot's second expedition was to reach the Spice Islands. He is thought to have reached Chesapeake Bay, but his own ship was lost off Nfld. Cabot's voyages gave England her first claims to lands in North America.

CABOT, SEBASTIAN (*c.* 1476–1557), Venetian explorer and son of John Cabot, who started as a sailor serving King Henry VII of England. In 1509, seeking a North-West Passage to Asia, he sailed with two ships past the southern point of Greenland and thence across Davis Strait. To the west he found a channel, known later as Hudson Bay. On his return to England Cabot found that his royal patron had died, so in 1512 he moved to Spain, taking service with King Ferdinand, and rising ultimately, through his skill and knowledge of navigation, to become Pilot Major of the mercantile marine. He explored unsuccessfully the river system of the Rio de la Plata for a passage to the Pacific (1526–30). He also navigated the Paraná and Paraguay rivers, established the first settlement in La Plata, and brought gold and silver back to Spain (1530). However, Cabot retained his interest in the North-West Passage project, and in 1548 he returned to England. Joining a syndicate of London merchants, he organized (1551) an expedition to Morocco, led by Thomas Wyndham. At the Duke of Northumberland's invitation he planned (1552–3) a large-scale expedition to find a North-East Passage, backed by the financial resources of a joint-stock company and led by Willoughby and Chancellor, a venture which failed in its object, but led to the establishment of commercial links between England and Russia.

CABRAL, AMILCAR (1926–), one of Africa's most original and effective political thinkers, who was born in Bafata, Portuguese Guinea, of local African and Cape Verdean parentage. Cabral, an engineer, worked on sugar plantations in Angola, where he helped to found the MPLA (Angolan nationalist movement) in Dec. 1956, three months after founding in Bissau, Portuguese Guinea, a similarly clandestine nationalist party for that colony, the Partido Africano por la Independência de Guiné e Cabo Verde (PAIGC). From Sept. 1959 he devoted himself entirely to the work of the PAIGC, whose military and political control embraced some two-thirds of Portuguese Guinea by 1969.

CABRAL, PEDRO ALVARES (c. 1460–1526), Portuguese navigator who secured Portugal's claim to Brazil and established trade relations with India. Following Vasco da Gama's discovery of a sea route to India, King Manuel I of Portugal dispatched Cabral with 13 vessels to Calicut. Sailing west rather than south, Cabral reached the Brazilian coast (22 April 1500) and laid claim to the region for Portugal. Whether he sailed to Brazil under secret orders or by virtue of a storm is a matter of unresolved controversy. Cabral then sailed east to the Cape of Good Hope, where he lost four vessels, and subsequently reached India.

CABRERA DE CORDOBA, LUIS (1550–1623), Spanish soldier and chronicler, who published (1619) a history of Philip II's reign.

CABRILLO, JUAN RODRIGUEZ DE (d. 1543), Portuguese conquistador and explorer for Spain, who took part in the conquest of the Aztecs (1521). The viceroy, Antonio de Mendoza, dispatched Cabrillo northwards along the Pacific coast in search of a route to the East Indies—the fictitious 'Strait of Anian'. In 1542 he sailed from Navidad, Mexico, in search of a route to the East Indies, and discovered San Diego Bay, being the first white man to see CA. He proceeded as far north as Drake's Bay, but died at the Santa Barbara Islands on the return journey.

CACCIA, HAROLD ANTHONY, Life Baron (1905–), British diplomat, who entered the foreign service in 1929 and spent much of the next decade in service in China and Greece. In the Second World War he was a political adviser in North Africa and Greece. He held appointments in the foreign office (1946–51), and subsequently took the embassies at Austria (1951–4) and Washington (1956–61). He was head of HM Diplomatic Service (1964–5), retiring as a period of major change began upon the amalgamation of the foreign and colonial offices. In 1965 he became provost of Eton College.

CÁCERES, ANDRES AVELINO (c. 1833–1923), provisional president of Peru (1883) and military dictator (1886–90, 1894–5). Cáceres rose to prominence as a general in the War of the Pacific and led a revolt against the Chilean-backed President Iglesias (1885–6). Cáceres attempted to reorganize the country's bureaucracy and taxation structure.

CACHIN, MARCEL (1869–1958), founding father of the French Communist Party. Originally a follower of Guesde, he was a leader of the Socialist Party before 1914. At the party's Congress of Tours (1920) Cachin successfully proposed a motion for adhesion to the Communist International, which led to the split between Communists and Socialists. Cachin directed the Communist newspaper *L'Humanité*, was the party's first senator, and was active in parliament until his death. Throughout his career he was a champion of colonial independence.

CACIQUISMO, term given to the system of electoral corruption and falsification prevalent in Spain from the 1830s until the Civil War. The word comes from the South American Indian word *cacique*, meaning chief, and in country areas, at least, *caciquismo* was based on the rule of political chiefs or bosses. The system was at its height during the Restoration period (1874–1923). Then the Conservative leader, Canovas del Castillo, used it to bring stability to Spanish politics. He made an agreement with Praxedes Sagasta, the leader of the Liberals, that they would rotate in office. Free elections would only have produced a welter of conflicting groups, so 'fixed' elections were held, to give a semblance of stable two-party government. The *caciquismo* made this possible by allowing whichever government made an election to win it. The ministry of the interior issued provincial governors with the names of the candidates who were to win, and sometimes even their approximate majorities. In the towns municipal officials dependent on the governor's favour were usually prepared to falsify the returns. Sometimes they sent the governor blank returns, so that he might fill in his own results, or the votes of dead persons might be used.

In the country the *cacique* provided the required results in return for favours from the government. In the north he was often a money-lender; in the south a landowner. The *caciques* controlled votes by undertaking to provide jobs, threats of physical harm, or foreclosing on mortgages. They usually had the police and the judiciary under their control and their power was often absolute.

The system survived several attempts to reform municipal and local government. It ceased functioning for the duration of Primo de Rivera's dictatorship and reappeared sporadically in the Second Republic. It ended with the Civil War.

CACOS, poverty-stricken Haitian farmers, historically available for the private armies of individuals or political factions. Haitian *cacos* bitterly opposed US occupation forces (1918–1919).

The term was also applied to the pro-independence faction in Central America in the early 19th cent.

CADDO INDIANS, confederacy of tribes belonging to the southern branch of the Caddoan linguistic family, first encountered by Spanish and French explorers in LA. The tribes were reduced in numbers in the 18th cent. during a conflict between the French and Spanish for territory occupied by the Caddo. After the US acquired LA, settlers pushed the Caddo from their lands, and in 1835 they moved by agreement to TX, but the laws there gave them no right to occupy land. An appeal to the US government after TX became a state secured them a tract of land (1855). In 1859 a band of white settlers threatened to massacre the Caddo, and they made a forced march to a reservation in OK, where, in 1902, they received allotments of land as individuals and were given US citizenship.

CADET CORPS, Russian institute founded in 1730 by the Empress Anna to prepare the sons of the nobility as officers for the army.

CADILLAC, ANTOINE DE LAMOTHE (1658–1730), Gascon originally named Laumet, and French colonial governor. He emigrated to Acadia (1683) and was granted a seigniory near Mount Desert (ME, US). Cadillac urged the French court and de Frontenac, governor of New France, to attack the English colonies. He was appointed governor of Michilimakinac (1694) and made a fortune from illegal traffic in furs. Being anxious to expand French trade and influence, he returned to France (1698) and obtained permission to trade on the Detroit river. Backed by the French court and the new governor, Callières, Cadillac fortified Fort Pontchartrain (now Detroit), where he settled. Because of illegal trading Cadillac was recalled (1710). He was made governor of LA, but after being accused of discouraging settlement he was dismissed (1716) and imprisoned in the Bastille (1718). From 1723 until his death he was governor of Castlesarrasin in Gascony.

CADIZ, Atlantic port of southern Spain, part of the great complex of ports situated at the mouth of the Guadalquivir river, which include Seville and Sanlucar. Cadiz became the great naval base in which the American convoys assembled in the 16th–17th cents, and as such was the object of spectacular raids by Spain's enemies, eg, Drake (1587) and Essex (1596). After c. 1680 Cadiz superseded the declining Seville as Spain's principal port and naval arsenal.

CADOGAN, WILLIAM CADOGAN, 1st Earl (1675–1726), British general who was an ardent supporter of the Protestant succession in the critical period 1713–16. He fought ably under Marlborough in the War of the Spanish Succession, at Oudenarde and Wynendael (1708), and was MP for New Woodstock (1705–16). In February 1716 Cadogan superseded Argyll as commander of the Anglo–Dutch forces occupied in crushing the Earl of Mar's Jacobite rising. His ruthlessness eliminated the remnants of Scottish opposition within two months.

CADOGAN, SIR ALEXANDER GEORGE MONTAGU (1884–1968), British diplomat. He was ambassador to China (1933–1936), then became permanent under-secretary of state for foreign affairs and was made Britain's permanent representative at the United Nations in 1946. He was chairman of the BBC (1952–7).

CADORNA, LUIGI (1850–1928), Italian general, who became chief of staff (July 1914). He achieved limited successes in the Isonzo campaigns (1915–17), but was held responsible for the Caporetto defeat and dismissed (9 Nov. 1917).

CADOUDAL, GEORGES (1771–1804), French royalist leader, who was involved in most of the peasant risings against the Revolution in Brittany and the Vendée (1793–1800). After three years' exile in England he returned to Paris (Aug. 1803) with English money to organize a plot to kidnap or kill Napoleon, but was arrested with others, including the republican generals Pichegru and Moreau, and guillotined (June 1804). Napoleon was able to use the outcry over the conspiracy to turn the Consulate into the hereditary Empire.

CAEPIO, Q. SERVILIUS, Roman consul (106 BC), whose refusal as proconsul (105) to co-operate with the consul Cn. Mallius caused the Roman defeat at Arausio, which he survived, only to be condemned and imprisoned in 95.

CAERE, earlier Agylla, an Etruscan foundation (8th cent. BC) on the site of Cerveteri, where an Etruscan necropolis survives. Recent discoveries at its port, Pyrgi, reveal a close connection with Carthage in the 6th cent. Caere refused aid to her neighbour Veii against the Roman advance in 396, and sheltered the Vestal Virgins during the Gallic sack (391). But in 353 she joined Tarquinii against Rome, but was defeated and granted a 100-year truce. Caere was the first *municipium* to be given *civitas sine suffragio* (citizenship without the vote), and by the Second Punic War had become loyal to Rome, contributing vital commodities to the Roman invasion of Africa (203).

CAESAR, *cognomen* or last name of a branch of the Roman Julian family, of which the most famous member was Julius Caesar (102–44 BC). His great-nephew and heir, Octavian, later the first emperor and known as Augustus, took the name in 44. Thereafter all emperors were known as Caesar Augustus, even when, after AD 69, they were no longer connected with the Julian family, and the title Caesar was at times conferred by emperors on sons or heirs, eg, by Antoninus Pius on Marcus Aurelius (139). Under Diocletian's 'Tetrarchy' system of government (295–324), the emperors were Augusti and their deputies Caesars.

CAGOULE, popular name for the *Comité Secret d'Action Révolutionnaire*, a French right-wing extremist organization of the 1930s which specialized in acts of violence. The assassination of the Rosselli brothers (1937) is attributed to it. The *Cagoule* was uncovered by the police in 1937 and its leaders imprisoned. During the Second World War most of the *Cagoulards* supported the Vichy regime, but some joined the Resistance. The *Cagoule's* leader, Eugène Deloncle, died in 1943.

CAHIERS DE DOLEANCES, addresses to the French Crown embodying complaints and demands, most notably on the summoning of the national assembly in 1789. Particular *cahiers*, drawn up by every electoral assembly in a constituency, were combined into one general *cahier* which was presented by the deputy at Versailles. They provide evidence of the differing grievances of the three estates, the *cahiers* of the nobility and of the clergy being chiefly concerned with the maintenance of their privileged status, while those of the third estate indicated concern with the evils of arbitrary government among the middle-class and economic distress among the poor.

CAHIERS DE HUYGENS take their name from the Congress of Huygens held by the French Socialist Party (SFIO) in 1932 to determine the conditions upon which it would participate in the formation of a government. The congress, after much internal conflict, approved a programme drawn up by Vincent Auriol which in effect ruled out any participation with the Radical-Socialist Party. The *Cahiers* demanded the reduction of military service, a capital levy, a 40-hour week, and the end of arms sales to other countries.

CAHOKIA, French settlement founded by missionaries from a seminary at Quebec (1699). It was the first stable European settlement in the Illinois country. After being occupied by British after 1763, it was seized by George Rogers Clark's American troops (1778) and passed to US sovereignty (1783).

CAHORSINS, merchants and money-dealers from Cahors in south-western France who, in the 13th cent., spread to England, elsewhere in France, the Netherlands, and southwestern Germany. Their name became synonymous with the business of money-lending secured by the pledging of valuables and other objects. Thus in the 14th cent. the chief pawnbroking establishment at Bruges in Flanders was known as Great 'Cahorse'.

CAICOS, group of small British-owned West Indian islands. In the 18th cent. they were a notorious haunt of pirates, their possession being disputed between France and Britain. The Caicos were incorporated in the British colony of the Bahamas (1770–1848), made a separate colony subordinate to the governor of Jamaica (1848–74), and formed a part of Jamaica (1874–1962). Since 1962 they have been a British colony.

CAILLAUX, JOSEPH (1863–1944), French politician of the Third Republic, whose career resembles that of many other French political figures in its progression from the Left to the Right. He belonged to an old Catholic and Conservative family and started his career in the ministry of finance. In 1898 he was elected deputy for the Sarthe, and in 1899 became minister of finance in Waldeck-Rousseau's cabinet. He also held this post in Clemenceau's cabinet of 1906, and in that of Monis in 1911, before becoming *President du Conseil* in that year.

He was a leading advocate of a progressive income tax and in 1907 piloted a tax bill through the chamber, only to have it defeated in the senate. It was, however, as an advocate of Franco-German rapprochement that he was best known. He negotiated the Franco-German treaty (1911), giving Germany part of the Congo in return for a free hand in Morocco. Caillaux symbolized (1911–14) the policy of appeasement towards Germany and after the outbreak of the First World War the policy of a compromise peace. He resigned from Doumergue's government in 1914 following the shooting of the editor of *Figaro* by Mme Caillaux. His advocacy of a compromise with the Germans, his shady acquaintances, and his talent for making bitter and lasting enemies left him open to charges of treason, and in 1920 he was accused of intelligence with the enemy and sentenced to three years' imprisonment. After the victory of *Cartel des Gauches* in 1924 he was released under an amnesty and in 1925 was appointed minister of finance in Painlevé's second ministry. His attempt to settle the question of French war debts to the US failed and he left office in Oct. 1925. Though he never again joined the cabinet, he continued to exert an important influence as president of the Senate Finance Commission, and made his peace with the Conservatives by his financial orthodoxy. He played a leading part in instigating the downfall of Blum's first cabinet in 1937.   PMK

CAIRD, SIR JAMES (1816–92), Scottish agriculturalist and politician, whose vivid surveys of British farming, notably in *The Times* (1850–1), made clear the prevalence of antiquated methods. He secured the annual compilation and publication (1866 onwards) of agricultural statistics for the UK.

CAIRO CONFERENCE (12–25 March 1921), held after the First World War between Winston Churchill (as colonial secretary) and other British experts on the Middle East, at which it was decided to establish Hashemite rulers in Transjordan and Iraq and replace the British army by RAF units in Iraq.

CAIRO CONFERENCE (Nov.–Dec. 1943) during the Second World War had two distinct phases. It preceded and followed the meeting between Stalin, Roosevelt, and Churchill at Teheran. Chiang Kai-shek conferred with Roosevelt and Churchill on their way to Teheran, where (since the Soviet Union was not at war with Japan) China was not represented. As a result of this discussion, a communiqué was issued outlining the disposition of Japanese territory after the war. The communiqué assumed an unforeseen importance subsequently when Formosa and Korea were at the centre of the Cold War in east Asia. The communiqué included the words:

'. . all the territories Japan has stolen from the Chinese, such as Manchuria, Formosa, and the Pescadores, shall be restored to the Republic of China. Japan will also be expelled from all other territories which she has taken by violence and greed. The aforesaid three great powers, mindful of the enslavement of the people of Korea, are determined that in due course Korea shall become free and independent.

At the same time, strategic discussions were held between the British and the US, which were resumed at Cairo after the Teheran conference, and an additional discussion was held with President Inonu of Turkey. In the outcome, the American plan for an amphibious attack in Burma (in concert with Chiang) was abandoned, and landing craft were brought back for use in the European theatre; but Churchill's plans for an attack in the Aegean (which in any case depended on Turkish belligerency) were over-ruled.

CAISSE DE LA DETTE PUBLIQUE, commission established (2 May 1876) to represent the interests of British bondholders after the 1875 Egyptian bankruptcy. The Caisse controlled a large part of Egyptian revenues, which were assigned to the debt, and acted as a major brake on Egyptian development until the 1904 Anglo-French agreement reduced its powers.

CAJETAN, TOMMASO DA VIO, cardinal (1469–1534), conservative general of the Dominican order. An eminent Thomist, opposed initially to humanism, he wrote his treatise on the *De Ente et Essentia* of Aquinas while teaching at Padua University (1494–7). His commentaries on the *Summa Theologica* (1507–22) remain among the classics of neo-Thomism. He defended Pope Julius II against Gallicanism at the council of Pisa and asserted that the pope alone could convene a council (1512). In August 1518 he was sent by Leo X as papal legate to the diet of Augsburg, with the special task of raising a new tax to finance a crusade against the Turks. He failed in this, but remained to interview Luther at Augsburg (Oct. 1518). He demanded an immediate retraction and future silence, but became involved in a fierce theological argument with Luther and their three meetings achieved nothing. The only outcome was the decretal *Cum Postquam* (Nov. 1518), clarifying the papal attitude to indulgences, which Cajetan requested from the curia.

CAKOBAU (THAKOMBAU) (1817–80), greatest Fijian of his time, was war chief (1837) and high chief (1853) of Mbau (Fiji). He waged numerous bloody cannibal feuds, notably against Qaraniqio of Rewa (1843–55). In a new war with heathen malcontents following his own conversion he was fortuitously rescued by King George Tupou I (Tonga) and, in gratitude, declared Fiji Christian (1855). The rapid rise of Tongan influence in the eastern islands under Ma'afu and growing European predominance having frustrated his bid for absolute power as Tui Vita, he finally agreed to unconditional British annexation (1874).

CALABAR (OLD), Efik entrepôt state in south-eastern Nigeria, founded probably in the 17th cent. Old Calabar's prosperous slave and, later, palm-oil trade attracted many European merchants, and (from 1846) the Church of Scotland Mission.

CALAIS, French channel port, originally a fishing village, enlarged by Baldwin IV, Count of Flanders (*c*. 997) and fortified by Philip, Count of Boulogne (1224). After the English victory at Crécy, the town was besieged for almost a year by a large English force under Edward III (1346–7). At its capitulation (1347) the famous incident occurred of the six burghers of Calais, whose lives were spared by the king at the personal intervention of his French queen, Eleanor. Calais, part of England's medieval empire for the next 200 years, was captured during Mary I's reign by the forces of the Duke of Guise (1558). It was retained by the French at the treaty of Cateau-Cambrésis (1559), but temporarily occupied by the Spaniards (1596–8), then restored to France by the treaty of Vervins (1598). During the 17th and 18th cents it became a refuge for French privateers from which to harry English and Dutch shipping. Napoleon encamped 6000 soldiers in the port in readiness for his invasion of England (1805). It was one of the main objectives of the German drive to the channel in May 1940, and was part of German-occupied France until its relief by the Allied forces in Sept. 1944.

CALAMITY JANE (?1852–1903), nickname of Martha Cannary Burke, a colourful US frontier character from MO, who lived most of her life in the Black Hills of SD. She has been pictured both as a Florence Nightingale and as a crude female in masculine clothing who in drinking, swearing, and lying could surpass any man. She was noted for her horsemanship and marksmanship, and was supposed to have been a scout for Custer and others.

CALAMY, EDMUND (1600–66), English Presbyterian and part-author of *Smectymnuus* (1641), a violent refutation of the divine institution of episcopacy. He was a member of the Westminster Assembly (1643) and opposed the execution of Charles I. At the Restoration he was a Presbyterian representative at the Savoy Conference. He refused a bishropric and was ejected from his living after the Act of Uniformity (1662), thus identifying himself with the cause of Nonconformity. His grandson, Edmund (1671–1732), a historian of Nonconformity, produced an account of the Nonconformists penalized under the Act of Uniformity.

CALAS, JEAN (1698–1762), French Huguenot cloth merchant of Toulouse whose judicial murder was a *cause célèbre*

in Louis XV's reign. Under the pressure of bigoted public opinion, he was accused of murdering his eldest son, Marc-Antoine (13 Oct. 1761), to prevent his conversion to Catholicism. He was condemned by the Toulouse *parlement*, and though tortured and broken on the wheel, died protesting his innocence. The Calas case was taken up by Voltaire, who brought it to the attention of the king's council. Louis XV reversed the judgement on Calas and compensated his family (9 March 1765).

CALCINATO, BATTLE OF (1706), French victory during the Italian campaign of the War of the Spanish Succession, in which the Austrians under Graf Reventlau were routed by Vendôme. Prince Eugène, who arrived soon after the battle to assume command, withdrew the Austrian army into the protection of the Alps.

CALCULUS. The system used for calculating the relations between variable quantities which provided a general method for all difficult calculations. It was not so much the discovery of one great mathematician as the synthesis of the work of several men, particularly Leibniz (1646–1716) and Newton (1642–1727). Both claimed the honour of the discovery and were involved in an ignominious squabble.

CALCUTTA, on the Hughli river in Bengal, the capital of the state of West Bengal in the Indian Union. Until it was overtaken by Bombay, Calcutta was the most populous city in India (pop. (1970) about 4 million, including Howrah and the southern suburbs). Calcutta was founded by the East India Co.'s merchant, Job Charnock (1690), after being driven from Hughli by the Mughals and at the end of the disastrous Anglo-Mughal War (1686–90). In 1696 the merchants received permission to fortify their settlement and in 1702 Calcutta became an independent presidency directly responsible to London. In 1717 Surman's embassy to Delhi obtained privileges from the Mughal court, which, despite constant disputes, formed the basis of Calcutta's prosperity for the next 40 years. In 1742 fortification of the city, now marked by the Lower Circular Road, was begun as a precaution against Maratha attack.

It was an attempt to fortify the city against the French without permission (1756) which led to the Nawab of Bengal's capture of Calcutta and the Black Hole incident. With Clive's recovery of Calcutta and the control of Bengal and Bihar from 1764 a period of great prosperity and fevered activity began. Calcutta became formally the capital of British India from 1774 and witnessed the disputes of Warren Hastings and Philip Francis and the triumphs of Wellesley. Its prosperity rested on the import of European goods, the export of indigo, saltpetre, opium, and cotton goods, and the profits of European officials and others from private trade. From 1818 Calcutta was the virtual capital of India and its chief city.

During the 19th cent. its importance was further enhanced by the development of the jute export trade and industry from the time of the Crimean War (1854–6) when the supply of Russian jute for Dundee in Scotland was cut off. It also became the outlet for the rising tea industry of Assam and the Sikkim hills. It was further enriched by the developing coalfield of Burdwan and, from the early 20th cent., the steel plant of Jamshedpur.

Calcutta has had an active intellectual life: in 1784 Sir W. Jones founded the Asiatic Society of Bengal. In the early 19th cent. began the Bengal renaissance, led by the reformer Ram Mohan Roy and encouraged by the Baptist missionary William Carey and the Presbyterian Alexander Duff. Roy founded the first modern Hindu reform movement, the Brahmo Samaj; Duff was instrumental in the founding of Calcutta University in 1857. With the Tagore family Calcutta retained its intellectual primacy into the 20th cent. Bengalis, the first Indians to take advantage of western education, spread all over India in professional capacities.

The large European commercial population created a problem in race relations. There was the Mutiny panic of 1857 and the agitation against the Ilbert bill in 1883, which was a factor in the foundation of the Indian National Congress. Calcutta's importance as a centre of the nationalist movement contributed to the transfer of the imperial capital to Delhi in 1912. Bengali leaders were prominent in the movement until they were eclipsed by Gandhi and north Indian leaders after 1920.

Imperial Gazetteer of India, vol. IX (Oxford, 1908).   TGPS

CALCUTTA, BLACK HOLE OF (20–1 June 1756), the occasion was the capture of Calcutta by the Nawab Siraj-ad-daula and the surrender of the East India Co.'s garrison headed by J. Z. Holwell. The company, though constantly bickering about trading privileges, had remained at peace with the Mughal governors since the grant of an imperial *farman* in 1716. On this occasion a headstrong young ruler was enraged by the company's failure to stop fortifying Calcutta in preparation for the expected outbreak of war in Europe. After three days' resistance, the governor and the commandant fled down the river, leaving J. Z. Holwell and a remnant of the garrison to their fate. After a further day's resistance Holwell surrendered and was placed with other survivors in the local lock-up known as the 'Black Hole', a room 18 ft × 14 ft 10 ins (5·5 × 4·25 metres) with two small windows.

Holwell later wrote an account of the incident, alleging that of 146 persons placed in the Black Hole only 23 emerged alive the next morning. Not much was made of the affair at the time, but as the years passed and Holwell's account was published it gradually became a major item in the hagiography of British Indian imperialism, being cited as evidence of British heroism and the nawab's callous cruelty. In 1915 this view was questioned by J. H. Little, who suspected Holwell's credibility as a witness and indicated discrepancies in the evidence. He suggested that the incident had been invented by Holwell in order to glorify himself. In the controversy which followed it became clear that the nawab was not implicated, since he knew nothing of the matter until the next morning. The charge, on the Indian side, was at most one of negligence. On the other hand, the claim that the incident never occurred could not be sustained in the face of other evidence besides Holwell's. A recent examination of the probabilities suggests that only about 64 entered the Black Hole and that 21 survived.

H. H. Dodwell, *Cambridge History of India*, vol. 5 (Cambridge, 1929).
Brijen K. Gupta, *Siraj-ad-daulah and the East India Company, 1756–57* (Leiden, 1962).   TGPS

CALDARA, ANTONIO (d. 1736), Italian musician, who was assistant to Johann Joseph Fux, the composer, and helped to establish the reputation of Vienna as the European centre for opera.

CALDERA RODRIGUEZ, RAFAEL (1916–), president of Venezuela (1969–) and unsuccessful COPEI (Venezuela) candidate for the presidency on three previous occasions (1947, 1958, 1963).

CALDERÓN, RODRIGO (1570–1621), Spanish adventurer, who insinuated himself into the confidence of the Duke of Lerma, Philip III's favourite, and retained considerable political power during Lerma's regime. Shirking the demands for reform from the *arbitristas*, he acquired an annual income of 200,000 ducats and the marquisate of Siete Iglesias. Arrested on trumped-up charges in Feb. 1619 after Lerma's downfall, he was publicly executed two years later on the orders of the Duke of Olivares.

CALDERÓN DE LA BARCA, PEDRO (1600–81), Spanish dramatic poet, whose works were performed at the court of Philip IV and contributed greatly to the golden age of Spanish literature. They include light comedies and religious-philosophical plays, *eg*, *Life's a Dream*, *The Prodigious Magician*, *Devotion to the Cross*.

CALDERÓN GUARDIA, RAFAEL ANGEL (1900–), president of Costa Rica (1938–9, 1940–4) and member of the National Republican Party. Exiled by a reformist revolt (1948), Calderón returned in 1958 after leading two unsuccessful attempts at invasion from Nicaragua.

CALENDAR (NEW STYLE) ACT, BRITISH (1751), replaced the Julian, old style, calendar with the more accurate Gregorian revision already adopted by most European countries. This was a measure of major importance, for Britain's dates grew more out of alignment with her neighbours' every year, inconveniencing international trade and diplomacy. Agreements had to specify both old and new style dates and these now differed by 11 days from the British new year beginning on 25 March. The reception of the act, passed in Henry Pelham's ministry, justified the fears of his brother Newcastle and provoked some of the worst riots of the 18th cent. Popular protest sprang from deep suspicion of any alteration in traditional practice and was directed in particular at the elimination of the 11 days 2–14 Sept. 1725, giving rise to the cry, 'Give us back our 11 days.'

CALENDAR (REVOLUTIONARY) IN FRANCE (1793–1805). To mark the supposed start of a new epoch for humanity, the Convention, in France, introduced a year of 12 30-day months, each containing three *decadi* or ten-day periods. Fabre d'Églantine devised its nomenclature. Year 1 began with the founding of the French republic on 22 Sept. 1792.

CALENDAR, ROMAN, ancient Roman system for fixing the beginning, length, and sub-divisions of the civil year. Originally of ten months only, the year in the Republic had 355 days, divided into 12 months and beginning, until 153 BC, on 1 March, thereafter on 1 Jan. Dates were reckoned by counting backwards from the Kalends, Nones, and Ides of each month. A 'leap' month (Mercedonius) was occasionally intercalated between 23 and 24 Feb., but by Julius Caesar's time the civil year was about three months ahead of the solar. He made the year 46 BC total 445 days, bringing the ordinary calendar up to 365 days, with an extra day between 23 and 24 Feb. every fourth year.

CALHOUN, JOHN CALDWELL (1782–1850), US statesman and defender of Southern interests. He was a South Carolinian who served in his state legislature (1808–9) and the US House of Representatives (1811–17). As chairman of the committee on foreign affairs and a 'war hawk' Republican, he vigorously supported the War of 1812. He advocated nationalist policies, including strong armed forces, internal improvements, a national bank, and a protective tariff, and was an effective secretary of war under James Monroe (1817–1825). He failed to secure presidential nomination but was elected vice-president (1824). Meanwhile, SC turned against the tariff, as providing unfair protection for Northern industry at the expense of Southern agriculture. Calhoun's policy reflected this change. He guided his state's resistance to the 'tariff of abominations' (1828), diverting demands for secession by writing anonymously the *South Carolina Exposition and Protest*, in which he enunciated the doctrine of nullification based on the concept of state sovereignty (1828). He was elected as Andrew Jackson's vice-president (1828), but quarrelled with him on personal and political grounds and resigned on election to the Senate (1832). He reluctantly condoned the SC Nullification Ordinance directed against the tariffs of 1828 and 1832, but supported Henry Clay's compromise tariff to end the crisis (1833). Realizing that states could not act individually, Calhoun began to cultivate Southern unity largely by defending slavery, which he argued was a 'positive good' (1837). A state-rights Democrat, he briefly joined the Whigs in their attacks on Jackson, but then fought their programme in Congress (1841–3). Having withdrawn from the Senate in another bid for the presidency (1843), Calhoun served as John Tyler's secretary of state (1844–5), concluding an unratified treaty for the annexation of TX before returning to the Senate (1845–50), where he opposed the Mexican War and the Wilmot Proviso (1846). He argued that federal territories were owned by the states collectively and thus citizens were entitled to federal protection of their slave property in the territories. Believing therefore that the inhabitants could not prohibit slavery, he resisted the organization of OR as a free territory (1848). At a meeting of Southern Congressmen (1849) he obtained only minority support for his *Southern Address*, which called for unity regardless of party affiliation. When CA's application for admission to statehood (1849) reopened the slave question, Calhoun resisted Clay's 'omnibus bill', which sought to resolve a number of problems related to it, but he died while the Compromise of 1850 was being debated. His major contributions to political theory, the *Disquisition on Government* and *Discourse on the Constitution and Government of the United States*, were published posthumously (1851). Being concerned to protect minority interests against domination by the majority, and particularly the South against the North, he advocated the doctrine of the 'concurrent majority', which required affirmative votes of both elements on important issues, and the creation of a dual executive. Calhoun was a brilliant theorist and ambitious politician, whose career was moulded and inhibited by concern for his state and section.

Charles M. Wiltse, *John C. Calhoun*, 3 vols (Indianapolis, 1944–51).
Gerald M. Capers, *John C. Calhoun: Opportunist* (Gainesville, FL, 1960).

CALIBAN, MR, pet name for the Duke of Marlborough used by Queen Anne of Britain during the period of her close friendship with Marlborough and his wife.

CALICUT, town of 250,000 inhabitants on the Malabar coast of India within the Kerala state. Under its ruler, known as the Zamorin, it was the chief port in south India for the spice trade with the Middle East and the interchange trade with Indonesia. It was dominated by Arab traders, who opposed the Portuguese on their arrival in 1497. Escaping the Portuguese, it fell under the dominion of Haidar Ali in the late 18th cent. and of the British in 1792. Calicut gave its name to the cloth calico.

CALIFORNIA, US state, admitted to the union in 1850 as the 31st state, and now (1970) first in population and third in size. Its name derives from that of an imaginary island in a Spanish romance by Ordonez de Montalvo (1510), but the first Spanish contact only came with the expedition of Juan Rodríguez Cabrillo to the coastlands between present-day San Diego and Santa Barbara (1542). Other Spanish explorers visited parts of the region and Drake put in at an anchorage north of San Francisco Bay during his voyage of circumnavigation (1579). Permanent settlement began during the viceroyalty of Juan de Galvez (1765–71) in order to safeguard Spanish interests from British and Russian encroachments from the north, and was stimulated by the missionary zeal of the Franciscan friar Father Junipero Serra (1713–84), which led to the foundation of a chain of missions, each roughly a day's journey apart, from San Diego (1769) to Sonoma (1823). Military presidios, or garrisons, were also established at San Diego, Santa Barbara, Monterey, and San Francisco.

After 1822 CA was a province of Mexico, and the commercial rivalry of American, British, and Russian fur-traders and whalers aroused considerable American interest in the region. Anarchic political conditions in Mexico and fears of British intervention led to US complicity in the so-called Bear Flag Revolt, designed to throw off Mexican rule. During the Mexican War (1846–8) American naval and military forces gained control of CA, which was ceded to the US by the treaty of Guadaloupe Hidalgo (1848). A few days earlier gold had been discovered at Coloma, news of which led to the gold-rush (1849). The consequent rapid increase in population demanded the institution of regular civil government in place of military occupation. A constitutional convention was held at Monterey which drafted a constitution debarring slavery (Nov. 1849). This was accepted by Congress ten months later as part of the Compromise of 1850, and CA became a state without passing through the usual territorial stage.

The continued economic progress of CA and considerations of national strategy led to completion of the transcontinental railroad link with the East (1869). Developments in agriculture and, later, the discovery of oil maintained CA's growth after the goldfields declined, while its rapid economic development since 1941 may be attributed to its strategic position and favourable climate.   WJR

CALIFORNIA TRAIL, pioneered 1841–6, an emigrant route in the US from Independence, MO, to the lower Sacramento valley of CA. Following the Oregon Trail to South Pass, and then the Humboldt river across the Great Basin, it crossed the Sierra Nevada at Truckee Pass.

CALIGULA (GAIUS CAESAR) (AD 12–41), the youngest son of Germanicus and Agrippina the Elder, who survived to succeed Tiberius after the premature deaths of his parents and brothers. Though popular while still a youth, he later quarrelled with the Senate, which he delighted in humiliating, and appears to have aimed at transforming the principate into a sacred monarchy on Hellenistic lines. He was intelligent and witty, but lacked self-control and was alleged by some critics to be insane. A military campaign in Germany instigated by him had little result, and a projected invasion of Britain was cancelled; he also planned to set up a statue of himself in the temple at Jerusalem, which increased anti-Roman feeling in Judea, but this move was interrupted by his assassination. As a whole, the effects of his rule upon the empire were slight.

CALIMALA GUILD OF FLORENCE, originally an association of importers of foreign cloth into Florence, it derived its name from the dyeing and finishing of white woollens brought from the Netherlands and northern France. By the early 14th cent. the guild included all the most important Florentine commercial and banking companies, whose members played a leading part in the government of Florence.

CALINESCU, ARMAND (1893–1939), Rumanian politician and strong man of Carol II's dictatorship. Calinescu, renegade National Peasant, joined the right-radical cabinet of Octavian Goga in 1937, but left it to become a king's man. He became prime minister in 1939 and in Sept. was murdered by the Iron Guard.

CALIPHATE. After the death of Muhammad (632), Abu Bakr was chosen to be the new head of the Islamic state, ie, to act as the Imam of the Muslims and to assume all the responsibilities which had fallen to Muhammad, except for those functions and capacities deriving from his prophetic office. It was thus that the Khalifat Rasul Allah, ie, Caliph (or successor) of the Messenger of Allah, came into being. The principle of election was operative during the time (632–61) of the first four caliphs, Abu Bakr, 'Umar I, 'Uthman, and 'Ali. Yet there were some among the Muslims who believed that the caliphate ought to descend in the line of 'Ali, the cousin of Muhammad, and of his wife, Fatima, the daughter of Muhammad. The principle of hereditary succession had much to recommend it, now that the Muslims, following the great campaigns of conquest waged after 632, had to govern a vast empire. This was indeed to triumph through the efforts of the Caliph Mu'awiya (661–80), who was able to ensure that the throne should go to his son, Yazid I. The Umayyad line of caliphs thus established was to last until 750. In that year the office of caliph passed to the House of 'Abbas which was destined to hold it until 1258. After the fall of the Abbasid caliphate, the title 'Caliph' was used by many minor potentates. A Shi'i caliphate, that of the Fatimids, flourished in North Africa from 909—it was transferred to Egypt in 969 and came to an end only in 1171. After the success of the Abbasids in 750, one Umayyad prince escaped to Spain and founded there an amirate which reached its apogee under 'Abd al-Rahman III (912–61). This monarch assumed the title of Khalifa (929), the new caliphate being destined to endure until 1031. The Mamluk Sultan of Egypt and Syria, Baybars (1260–77), invited to Cairo in 1261 a member of the 'Abbasid house and created in Egypt a pseudo-caliphate which lasted until 1517. The title of Caliph was to be revived and exploited in the Ottoman empire for political reasons during the 18th–20th cents. The emergence of the Turkish Republic after the end of the First World War led to the abolition of the Ottoman sultanate (Nov. 1922). The designation of Caliph, still allowed to the House of Osman, was abolished in March 1924.   VJP

CALIXTUS II (*reg.* 1119–24), Pope, the son of William, Count of Burgundy and Abp of Vienne (1088). He was a leading church reformer and in 1120 he negotiated with the Emperor Henry V the Concordat of Worms, which effectively ended the Investiture Contest.

CALLAGHAN, LEONARD JAMES (1912–   ), British Labour politician. Entering the civil service as a tax officer in 1929, Callaghan first achieved prominence for his work on the staff federation of the Inland Revenue. After war service in the Royal Navy, he became MP for South Cardiff in 1945. He was parliamentary secretary of the ministry of transport (1947–50) and admiralty (1950–1), and was also much involved with the European Movement. After 1951 he did much work within the Labour movement as a whole, and also established his importance within the parliamentary party. He was consultant to the police federations (1955–64), in which he was responsible for significant improvements in police working conditions.

He was chancellor of the exchequer (1964–7). For three years he strove, but without success, to correct Britain's international trading deficit through an unpopular series of deflationary measures. In the fiscal crisis of late-1967 sterling was devalued, and in consequence Callaghan resigned as a matter of honour and became home secretary in 1967 until the defeat of the Labour government in the 1970 general election.

CALLEJA DEL REY, FELIX MARIA (1750–1820), Conde de Calderón, viceroy of New Spain (1813–16) and Spanish general. He successfully put down the revolts of Padre Hidalgo (1811) and Padre Morelos (1814).

CALLES, PLUTARCO ELIAS (1877–1945), revolutionary general, president of Mexico (1924–8), and manipulator of three subsequent presidents (1928–34). Calles, who was born at Guaymas, followed Álvaro Obregón in the revolution (1911–1917). He served first as governor of Sonora (1917), then as secretary of the interior under Obregón (1920–4), before becoming president. During his administration, Obregón's programme was continued, emphasis being given to its anticlerical aspects and agrarian reform. He supported a government alliance with organized labour and the extension of rural education. Difficulties arose between Calles and the Church when he attempted to force priests to register with the state (1926). Overseas investment interests also clashed with the president, who demanded that foreign oil interests should exchange their land titles for 50-year leases. Diplomatic problems with the US were overcome only when Calles moderated his demands (1927).

His formal retirement from office (1928) was followed by six years of informal rule through co-operative figurehead presidents. Emilio Portes Gil, Pascual Ortiz Rubio, and Abelardo Rodriguez in turn carried out the increasingly conservative politics of the *jefe maximo.* But Gen. Calles could not control Lázaro Cardenas, who succeeded Rodriguez (1934), and the new president broke sharply with the policies of his former mentor. In 1936 Cardenas exiled Calles, who was becoming intrigued with fascism, but in 1941 Calles returned to Mexico and regained his position as a general.

CALLIAS, PEACE OF (449 BC), treaty said to have been made between Athens and Persia to end hostilities that had continued since the Persian invasion of 480–479. The Persians retained Greek Cyprus, but agreed to keep out of the Aegean. Thucydides' silence and the scepticism of Theopompus about the inscribed record of the terms visible in the 4th cent. has led some scholars to regard the peace as the product of 4th-cent. Athenian propaganda, but fighting did cease and there probably was at least an agreement with the western satraps.

CALLICRATES (d. 150 BC), successor of Philopoemen as general of the Achaean league in Greece (183–150 BC). He undermined the status of an independent ally achieved for the league by his predecessor by persuading the Roman Senate to support unpopular aristocratic factions in the cities against the democratic elements. On his advice the Romans after the battle of Pydna (168) deported to Rome 1000 Achaeans, including the historian Polybius, thus depriving the cities of popular leaders. His death released a flood of anti-Roman activities, which ended with Mummius' destruction of Corinth (146).

CALLIÈRES, LOUIS-HECTOR, Chevalier de (1646–1703), French soldier and colonial governor. He was appointed governor of Montreal (1684) and during his governorship he fortified the settlement and campaigned against Indian tribes and British settlements. His plan for the conquest of New York was adopted by the French government (1689), but the attack was forestalled by storms during the campaigning season. Callières helped to defeat the British, under Sir William Phipps, at Quebec (1690) and led the French to victory over the Mohawk Indians and the British at Laprairie (1693). He was appointed governor of New France (1699) and paved the way for French expansion southwards by sending Cadillac to found a settlement on the Detroit river and assisting at the conclusion of peace between the Iroquois and Indian tribes allied to the French.

CALLISTRATUS (d. c. 355 BC), Athenian orator and statesman. As an advocate of co-operation with Thebes against Sparta, he prosecuted Andocides and the envoys to Sparta, who recommended peace (391), and later became a leading diplomatic and financial adviser to the Second Athenian Confederacy, formed to ensure Greek freedom against Spartan encroachment (378–7). By 371, recognizing the expense of war, the diminished Spartan threat, and lack of Theban co-operation, he recommended peace with Sparta and after the battle of Leuctra supported an alliance with her against Thebes (370). Charged with an unknown offence, he was acquitted in 366, but condemned in his absence c. 362 and executed on his return to Athens.

CALOMARDE, FRANCISCO TADEO (1775–1842), Spanish statesman renowned for his reactionary policies. He was born in Aragon and received a legal education at Saragossa. Calomarde, a staunch supporter of Ferdinand VII (restored in 1813), held several minor posts, then became minister of justice (1823), which he remained for ten years. During this period he acquired a reputation, possibly exaggerated, as the scourge of Spanish liberals. In recognition of his support for the Portuguese absolutist pretender, Dom Miguel, he was created Marquis of Almeida. After Ferdinand VII's death (1833), Calomarde supported the Carlists in the ensuing civil war. He fled to France when the first attempts to enthrone Don Carlos failed, and died in exile at Toulouse.

CALONNE, CHARLES ALEXANDRE DE (1734–1802), French minister, whose reform plans precipitated the aristocratic revolt of 1787–8. A brilliant provincial administrator, he was appointed controller general (1783) to solve the government's financial crisis after the American War of Independence. At first, he succeeded in raising more loans by restoring confidence in the government through promoting expensive public works, but when the supply of loans ran dry (Aug. 1786) he proposed a complete administrative and tax reform, including new provincial assemblies for administration, the abolition of internal customs duties, and the taxation of the privileged nobility and clergy. He knew the *parlements* and provincial estates would not agree, so an Assembly of Notables was called (Feb. 1787), but this proved equally intractable. Failure, and his enemies at court, persuaded Louis XVI to dismiss and exile him (April 1787). After the outbreak of the Revolution he acted as financial adviser to the émigrés at Coblenz and then in England.

CALVIN, JOHN (1509–64), French-born theologian and reformer, who with Martin Luther ranks as the dominant figure in the Protestant Reformation.

A native of Noyon in Picardy, he was destined for an ecclesiastical career, but two years after his appointment to his first benefice moved to Paris (1523), where he studied theology under Mathurin Cordier, and formed friendships with scholars like Guillaume Budé. In 1528 he moved to Orléans and then to Bourges, studying Greek and law. Returning to Paris (1531), he added Hebrew to his curricula and was soon drawn into the humanist circle surrounding Jacques Lefèvre d'Etaples. He published his first work (1532), a commentary in Latin on Seneca's treatise *De Clementia*, which characteristically was concerned with the moral philosophy of stoicism. Calvin was probably converted to the Protestant faith (c. 1533), and in Nov. of that year was driven from Paris as an associate of the university's rector, Nicholas Cop, whose oration in defence of Lutheran views aroused the opposition of the French king. Calvin resigned his benefice, went first to Angoulême (1534) and then to Basle (1535), where he was welcomed by reformers like Heinrich Bullinger. There he wrote in Latin his full statement of Protestant belief, the *Institutes of the Christian Religion*, which he dedicated to Francis I. After visiting the court of Renée, Duchess of Ferrara, he was diverted to Geneva by the war between the armies of Francis I and Charles V. Here he was persuaded by the fiery evangelical Guillaume Farel to promote the reform movement, for which Calvin drew up a plan for the close moral supervision of the city. Drawn into conflict with the civil authorities (1537–8), Calvin was expelled and moved to Strasbourg, where he became pastor of the reformed church serving French refugees. He was greatly influenced by Martin Bucer's ideas of predestination and the reform of the ministry and also the need for unity in the Church. Calvin therefore attended the conferences at Frankfurt (1539), Hagenau (1540), and Worms (1540–1). Meanwhile, he published a revised edition of the *Institutes* (1539), wrote short treatises on *The Lord's Supper* and *The Form of Prayer and Manner of Ministering the Sacrament*, and married the widow of an Anabaptist, Idelette de Bure.

Recalled to Geneva (1541), he began to implement his original scheme for the creation of theocratic government embodied in his *Ecclesiastical Ordinances*. He became involved in theological controversies with the Lutherans over the nature of the Lord's Supper and with more extreme reformers like the anti-Trinitarian Michael Servetus, for whose death at the stake (1553) he was partly responsible. He was deeply concerned with the political, economic, and legal decisions of Geneva and also continued to write prolifically. With Theodore Beza he founded the academy in Geneva (1559) which became the intellectual centre of international Calvinism, teaching the reformed theology there until his death. His services to Protestantism were fundamental: he systematized its doctrine on a theocentric basis and established the organization of ecclesiastical discipline. By his writings and his zeal he created a new, vigorous brand of

Protestantism which united the scattered body of reformed opinion throughout Europe.

B. Hall, *John Calvin* (London, 1956).
F. Wendel, *Calvin, The Origins and Development of his Religious Thought*, tr. by P. Mairet (London, 1963).

MKS

CALVINISTIC METHODIST CHURCH IN WALES, founded in 1790 by Thomas Charles, following the preaching of Howell Harris and George Whitefield. From Bala he organized churches on a Presbyterian pattern in each district (1790–1), and in 1801 issued a constitution. It was penalized under the Conventicle Act and Welsh Methodists then ordained their own ministers (1811), thus separating themselves from the established Church.

CALWELL, ARTHUR AUGUSTUS (1896–), leader of the Australian Labor Party opposition in the Commonwealth parliament (1960–7), and a former public service officer. As a member of the House of Representatives from 1920, Calwell was an energetic, controversial, and sometimes illiberal minister for information (1943–9) but, as minister for immigration (1945–9), he planned and launched Australia's imaginative post-war immigration programme, which included European displaced persons, though he rigorously maintained the 'White Australia' policy. As deputy Labor leader (1951–60) and as leader, he was vigorous, often bitter, and sometimes extremely inept. A Roman Catholic, he nevertheless stood by the ALP in the schism of 1954–5, and relentlessly opposed the breakaway Democratic Labor Party.

CAMALDOLESE REFORMED ORDER restored in 1520 the strict observance of their 11th-cent. founder's rules for an order of hermits, but interpreted them in a new spirit. The parent house was at Camaldoli in Italy. Led by Paolo Giustiniani, a Venetian of noble family and a humanist, they undertook pastoral and social work, especially among the poor of southern Italy.

CAMARET BAY LETTER (1694), supposedly written by Marlborough to ingratiate himself with the Jacobite court at St Germaine. The letter allegedly gave information about the coming attack on Brest (1694). No such letter has ever been found, but the rumour of the existence was enough to discredit Marlborough.

CAMBIO, ARNOLFO DI (1240–*c*. 1302), Italian sculptor, who worked with Nicolo Pisano in Siena. His early commissions were in Rome, including possibly the statue of St Peter in St Peter's cathedral. Both the Sienese and Roman periods had important influences on his later work in Florence visible, especially, in the cathedral and the Franciscan church of Santa Croce. The Roman basilica influenced the layout of Santa Croce and the Sienese experience suggested the striped decoration of the cathedral. He was also the first to place statuary on the outside of buildings in Florence.

CAMBON, PIERRE PAUL (1843–1924), French diplomat who served in the prefectoral and colonial services and became an ambassador, mainly in London (1900–20), where he was largely responsible for negotiating and maintaining the *entente cordiale*.

His brother, Jules Martin Cambon (1845–1935), an administrator and diplomat, was ambassador in Berlin (1907–14) and sought to avert the impending war. He was head of the foreign office (1915–19) and a delegate to the Versailles peace conference.

CAMBRAI, town originally fortified by Charlemagne which protected the valley of Oise river. As part of the Spanish Netherlands from the 16th cent., it became French during Louis XIV's reign by the treaty of Nymwegen (1678). Cambrai was the centre for the manufacture of fine cottons,

from which the term 'cambric' is derived. Cambrai was used by the British army as its headquarters after the defeat of Napoleon; it was the centre of major fighting in the First World War and again damaged in the Second World War.

CAMBRAI, BATTLE OF (20 Nov. 1917), fought during the First World War. The first battle in which tanks were used en masse rather than in small numbers. The British 3rd Army, under Gen. Byng, with 324 tanks, attacked a section of the Hindenburg Line on 20 Nov. Achieving complete surprise, they made the unusually large advance of 6 kms in one day, but their inability to exploit this advantage enabled a German counter-attack to nullify most of the gains. Despite its relative failure, the battle pointed the way for the future development of armoured warfare techniques.

CAMBRAI, CONGRESS OF (Oct. 1720–April 1725), international conference held to settle outstanding differences between France, England, the Empire, and Spain after Alberoni's downfall and Spanish accession to the Quadruple Alliance. Spain had two outstanding grievances, British possession of Gibraltar, over which George I continued to prevaricate, and the Emperor Charles VI's refusal to allow the Spanish Farneses to occupy the Italian states of Parma, Piacenza, and Tuscany. Charles VI, for his part, resented George I's hostility to the Pragmatic Sanction and his own dependence on financial subsidies from the maritime powers. His establishment of the Ostend Co. to exploit the newly acquired Austrian Netherlands was opposed by British mercantile interests, and voiced by the Duke of Newcastle, who came to power as secretary of state in 1724. The Dutch and the Spaniards pressed for a review of the company's activities at the congress, and although the French diverted such discussion, Charles lost faith in his maritime allies.

By June 1724 Spain had still not recovered Gibraltar and the question was only then referred to the congress by France and England. The death of Grand Duke Cosimo III of Tuscany (1723) aggravated Spanish fears of losing the promised lands in Italy, and though Charles VI placated Philip V of Spain by granting to Don Carlos letters of investiture to Parma and Tuscany, he delayed the actual possession of those states. The humiliating return of the Infanta, Louis XV's intended wife, to Spain (Feb. 1725) finally chilled Franco-Spanish relations. Meanwhile, Spanish and Austrian disillusionment with their allies led to a secret rapprochement between the two ex-enemies, engineered by Ripperda. This diplomatic revolution (March–April 1725) so alarmed England and France that the congress broke up in confusion and the defensive alliance of Hanover split Europe into two armed camps.

CAMBRAI, LEAGUE OF (1508), alliance of almost all the European powers with ambitions in Italy against the state of Venice. Inspired by the Genoese Pope Julius II, the alliance was ostensibly a holy league against the Turk, but in reality arose from his desire to recover the Romagna towns from Venice, the bulwark of Christendom. To gain support Julius bargained away Venetian territory to France, Spain, the emperor, the Hungarians, the Swiss, and the smaller Italian states. In the face of this formidable coalition the Venetians were shattered by the French army at the battle of Agnadello (1509).

CAMBRAI, TREATY OF (Aug. 1529), between the Emperor Charles V and Francis I after the emperor's victory at Landriano (June 1529). The treaty was the culmination of imperial supremacy in Italy and the western Mediterranean. The French king again renounced his claims in Italy, while Charles gave up his to the French duchy of Burgundy. It was a shattering blow to Cardinal Wolsey for the reconciliation of the Habsburg, and Valois rulers left England isolated in Europe.

The peace was relatively short-lived. The death of the last Sforza Duke of Milan (1535) gave Francis I an opportunity to reassert French claims to that state. Charles replied to this breach of the treaty's terms by renewed hostility to France. However, the intensity of conflict in Italy abated after Cambrai and its terms were to be reflected in the peace of Cateau-Cambrésis 30 years later.

CAMBRIDGE, UNIVERSITY OF. The first evidence for the existence of a university at Cambridge was the migration there of scholars from Oxford in 1209; presumably there were already schools at Cambridge, though this is not known. Ordinances regulating student behaviour were issued by Henry III in 1231 and by 1246 a chancellor and proctors had been appointed. The university was formally recognized by the bull of John XXII in 1318. A recent discovery has established the existence of a full university with approved statutes from at least the middle of the 13th cent. onwards.

Like Oxford and medieval Paris, Cambridge is a collegiate university; the first college was Peterhouse, founded by Hugh of Balsham, Bp of Ely, in 1284; other medieval foundations include Clare (1326), Pembroke (1347), Gonville and Caius (1349), Trinity Hall (1350), Corpus Christi (1352), King's (1441), Queens' (1448), St Catharine's (1475), and Jesus (1497).

Cambridge was comparatively unimportant until the 16th cent., when the chancellorship (from 1504) of John Fisher, who brought Erasmus there, and the Reformation made it the equal of Oxford. The university generally embraced Protestantism and produced not only Tyndale and Coverdale, the founders of the English Bible, but Cranmer and Latimer, eminent victims of the Marian persecution. The influence of Abp Parker, formerly of Corpus Christi College, and that of the chancellor, William Cecil, Lord Burghley, ensured considerable support for the Elizabethan settlement and in 1570 the Puritan, Thomas Cartwright, was dismissed from the Chair of Divinity. In the same year (1570) Cambridge was given its governing code, establishing the *Caput Senatus* as the supreme body.

If the 16th cent. saw the establishment of Christ's (1505), St John's (1511), Magdalene (1542), Emmanuel (1584), and Sidney Sussex (1596), and the refoundation of Trinity (1546) and Gonville and Caius (1558), the only advance in the next half-century was the grant of parliamentary representation (abolished 1948). The appointment of Isaac Newton as professor of mathematics (1669) gave Cambridge its international reputation in that field. Though the Regius Chair of Modern History was established in 1724 no lecture was given by its holders between 1725 and 1773, and the university began an undistinguished period of its history.

Reform and growth came slowly—although Downing was founded in 1800—and not until the Cambridge University Act (1856) were the obsolete Elizabethan statutes revised. The foundation of the women's colleges, Girton (1869) and Newnham (1871), and Selwyn College (1882) points to the reinvigoration of Cambridge in the late Victorian period. The Cavendish Laboratory and the physicists who worked there, *eg*, Rutherford, the Thomsons, and the Braggs, made Cambridge a world centre for science. Churchill College, founded in 1960 as the national memorial to Sir Winston Churchill, gives recognition to that fact by allocating 70 per cent of its places to students of mathematics, engineering, and natural sciences. The university is also noticeable in the 20th cent. for a major contribution to historical studies.

The position of women students, not given full university status until 1948, has improved with the foundations of New Hall (1954) and the Lucy Cavendish Collegiate Society for graduates (1965), while post-graduate education has been stimulated by the establishment of Darwin College (1964), St Edmund's House (1965), University College (1965), and Clare Hall (1966).

The university library, which early in the 15th cent. listed 122 books, now (1970) contains about 3 million. MKS

CAMBYSES II (*reg. c.* 530–522 BC), Achaemenid King of Iran, who previously held the title of King of Babylon.

Continuing the conquests of his father, Cyrus II, he invaded Egypt, defeated the Egyptians at Pelusium, took Thebes and Memphis, and put the administration under an Egyptian official (525). Unsuccessful expeditions were sent against Ethiopia, Carthage, and the oasis of Ammon. The Greeks of Libya, Cyrene, and Barka submitted, giving him control of their wealth.

CAMDEN, CHARLES PRATT, 1st Earl (1714–94), British constitutional lawyer and Whig politician. In the Wilkes case, he deprecated the use of general warrants (declared illegal in 1766). He was appointed lord chancellor (1766), and, like his friend Chatham, favoured a conciliatory approach to the Americans. He consistently supported measures to secure and extend the liberties of the subject.

CAMDEN, WILLIAM (1551–1623), English antiquary, who travelled the country collecting material for *Britannia* (1586–1607), a valuable storehouse of facts of which a selection appeared in his *Remains Concerning Britain* (1605). He also wrote *Annals* of the reign of Elizabeth. He established a chair of ancient history at Oxford (1622). The Camden Society (in the interests of historical research) was founded (1883) in his memory.

CAMELOTS DU ROI, militant arm of the French right-wing movement known as *Action française*. The Camelots, organized in 1908, were used for violent demonstrations and street fighting in a way which anticipated the techniques of later fascist movements. They included an inner elite, the *Commissaires*. The *Camelots* were active in the 1920s, and participated in the riots of 6 Feb. 1934. They were dissolved with the parent movement in 1936.

CAMERALISM, German school of political economy of the late 17th and early 18th cents, advanced particularly by Seckendorff, Pufendorf, Becker, Hornighk, and Schroder, justifying the paternalistic bureaucratic state. The early cameralists believed that the basis of a powerful state was a healthy and prosperous people. They concentrated on the ways of strengthening the economy, so important to political and military strength, and emphasized the need for administrative efficiency in the bureaucratic machinery, state control of industry, agriculture, and social welfare. Although based on Christian assumptions, the ideas and interests of the cameralists were secular rather than spiritual and in this they reflected European development. The cameralists provided the theoretical background for the government of German rulers from Leopold I to Frederick the Great.

CAMERON, RICHARD (d. 1680), Scottish preacher and covenanting leader. After exile in the United Provinces (1678–80), he returned to Scotland, joined Donald Cargill and Thomas Douglas in the Sanquhar declaration, and took up arms against the episcopacy. He and his supporters were killed after being surprised by royalist troops at Airdsmoss.

CAMERON, SIMON (1799–1889), US politician and party organizer. After a successful business career, he helped to establish the Republican Party in PA (1854) and dominated the party organization in that state for many years. He served in the Senate for various periods (1845–9, 1857–61, 1867–77) and his political influence won him a place in President Lincoln's cabinet (1861–2). Under his control, the war department was inefficient and corrupt in the early stages of the Civil War. He served briefly as US minister to Russia (1862). He was a prime example of the American party 'boss', and remained a powerful and influential figure in the era of the 'spoilsmen' after the Civil War.

CAMEROON (476,000 sq. kms), a West African federal republic with a population (1970) of 5,200,000, chiefly of the Bamileke, Fulbe, and Bassa groups. Formerly two UN trust territories under British and French rule, Cameroon became independent in Feb. 1961. The federal president is elected by adult suffrage, as is the national Assembly.

CAMILLUS, M. FURIUS (*c.* 447–365 BC), hero of the early Roman republic whose achievement is overlaid with legend. As a soldier, he is chiefly famous for advancing the frontier northwards against the declining Etruscan cities. Following victories over Falisci and Fidenae, he led the capture of Veii in 396. Exiled for misappropriation of spoils, he was recalled to meet the Gallic threat (391); but his confrontation with Gallic armies over a 20-year period, beginning with the alleged rout of Brennus, has been exaggerated. As a political leader, his greatness lay in the patient restoration of Roman morale after the ignominious fall of the city to the Gauls.

CAMISARDS, rebellious French bands in the Cevennes mountains who rose in protest against the persecution following the revocation of the Edict of Nantes (1702). Led by Jean Cavalier, Couderc, Roland, and Ravenel, the rebels continued their sporadic atrocities until 1710, although most had been pacified by 1705 by Marshal Villars.

CAMÕES, LUIS DE (1524–80), Portuguese epic poet and author of one of the most famous heroic poems in modern literature, *Os Lusiadas* (1572), which glorified the Portuguese empire and the expeditions of Vasco da Gama. Camões travelled as a common soldier for nearly 17 years (1553–69) in Portugal's far-eastern colonies.

CAMPAIGN FOR NUCLEAR DISARMAMENT (CND), group formed early in 1958 to agitate for the unilateral abolition of nuclear weapons by Britain. Among the leaders of the movement were Bertrand Russell and Canon Collins. The movement continued until Sept. 1960, when Russell broke away from the parent body to form the Committee of 100, for 'civil disobedience against nuclear warfare'. Russell resigned from the committee in 1963, and in 1969 it expired. In the early 1960s both CND and the Committee of 100 proved to be active and popular movements, galvanizing much radical (and predominantly youthful) support for public demonstrations, the most notable being the annual Easter march from Aldermaston nuclear research establishment to London.

CAMPBELL, ROBERT (1808–94) Canadian explorer, who was born in Scotland and migrated to Canada where he managed a sheep farm for the Hudson's Bay Co. on the Red river (1832). The farm failed and he was transferred to the company post at Fort Liard, then sent westward to establish a trading post at Dease Lake (now in BC) and reached the source of the Stikine river. His most notable discoveries were in the Yukon country; they included Frances Lake and the Pelly and Lewes rivers. Campbell built the first trading posts in the Yukon and was appointed chief trader of the Athabaska district (1856) and also a chief factor (1867). He was dismissed (1871) for sending furs by an unofficial route and spent his remaining years on a ranch in Man.

CAMPBELL CASE (1924) in Britain, cause of the downfall of the first Labour government, formed in Jan. 1924. J. R. Campbell, acting editor of the Communist *Workers' Weekly*, was charged in Aug. 1924 under the Incitement to Mutiny Act for urging soldiers to disobey orders to fire upon their 'fellow workers'. The government, after first announcing their determination to press the charge, decided to drop the case on the grounds that the article referred only to industrial disputes, not to war.

Parliament was reconvened in Sept., and the attorney-general, Sir Patrick Hastings, defended his decision against the criticism of Conservative MPs. A crisis arose when the Conservatives decided to table a motion of censure. Mac-Donald's cabinet decided to treat, as matters of confidence, both the Tory motion and a Liberal demand for a select committee of enquiry. The Labour leader was subsequently much criticized for this. Part of the explanation would seem to lie in Ramsay MacDonald's exhaustion—he was both prime minister and foreign secretary; it is also suggested that the likelihood of defeat over the Anglo–Russian trade and general treaties (8 Aug. 1924) persuaded him to risk a trial of strength, both with the Conservatives and his own left-wing supporters.

The 'Campbell Case' was debated on 8 Oct. Hastings admitted that he had consulted his colleagues before deciding to drop the case, but otherwise rejected the Conservative charge that he had given in to back-bench pressure. Nevertheless, MacDonald's clumsy handling of the debate forced the opposition's hand. The Conservatives decided to support the Liberal amendment, which was carried by 364 to 198. The following day, despite King George V's reluctance, parliament was dissolved.   GD

CAMPBELL-BANNERMAN, SIR HENRY (1836–1908), British prime minister (1905–8), who encouraged social reform and achieved a settlement of the South African conflict and the formation of the Triple Entente (1907). He was a stabilizing force in British politics and led the Liberal Party through a period of internal strife. He became MP for Glasgow (1868), serving as financial secretary to the war office (1871–4, 1880–2), secretary to the admiralty (1882–4), and chief secretary to Ireland (1884–5), where he supported Home Rule. As Gladstone's secretary for war (1886, 1892–5), he obtained the resignation of the Duke of Cambridge as commander-in-chief of the army, where he had impeded all reform. Campbell-Bannerman occasioned the fall of the government on the cordite vote (1895) though the party was already in disarray. He became leader of the Liberals on the resignation of Harcourt (1898), his rival, Asquith, declining to oppose him. During the South African war he maintained a middle course, but attacked the 'barbarism' of Britain's conduct towards the Boer civilian population. Tensions within the party eased with the end of the war, and Chamberlain's tariff campaign (1903) united it in defence of Free Trade. Campbell-Bannerman adopted a policy of gradualism over Home Rule which was acceptable to most Liberals, though not to Rosebery. On the resignation of Balfour, he insisted on forming a minority government and his judgement and courage were vindicated by a landslide electoral victory (1906). His cabinet included Asquith, Haldane, Grey, Lloyd George, and Burns, men of disparate views and talents, and he obtained mastery over a lively and inexperienced Commons.

In foreign affairs he achieved the settlement by which responsible government was granted to the Transvaal and Orange Free State (1907). In response to German threats before the Algeciras conference, military conversations were held with France and later with Belgium, while the Anglo-Russian convention also drew Britain into closer association with Russia's ally, France. Campbell-Bannerman campaigned for an end to the armaments race at the unsuccessful Hague conference of 1907 and service estimates were cut, though the army was strengthened by the creation of a general staff and an expeditionary force.

Under Campbell-Bannerman's guidance, domestic reforms included the Trade Disputes and Merchant Shipping Acts (1906), and the Smallholdings and Evicted Tenants Acts (1907), together with provision for free school meals for needy children and medical inspection in elementary schools as proposed by the Labour Party. The Qualification of Women Act (1907) enabled women to serve on city and borough councils, though the militant suffragette campaign continued. Other bills on education and plural voting were defeated or greatly amended by the Lords. In reply, Campbell-Bannerman showed that the Commons would support a plan to curb the Lords' veto on legislation, thus foreshadowing the Parliament Act (1911). Ill-health forced his resignation, and Asquith succeeded him in office (1908).

J. A. Spender, *Sir Henry Campbell-Bannerman*, 2 vols. (London, 1923).   VEC

CAMPBELLS OF ARGYLL, politically one of the most important Scottish highland families from the end of the 15th cent. Although Argyll's original seat was in mid-Argyll, the family's power extended from the Isles to the Lowlands, where cadet branches had established themselves by the early 16th cent., *eg*, the Campbells of Loudon in Ayrshire. The clan Campbell grew in power and possessions in the 17th cent. as the Crown relied on special lieutenancies in Scotland such as theirs. During the civil wars Archibald, 8th Earl and 1st Marquis of Argyll, joined the Covenanters and his son Archibald, the 9th Earl, was condemned to death for leading a Whig rebellion against James Stuart (1685). In the 18th cent. the family were the chief support of the Hanoverian government in Scotland, *eg*, John Campbell, the 2nd duke, who checked the Earl of Mar's rebellion in 1715, and his brother Archibald, the 3rd duke, who supported Walpole.

CAMPERDOWN, BATTLE OF (11 Oct. 1797), re-established British naval supremacy during the French Revolutionary Wars through Admiral Duncan's defeat of the Dutch fleet.

CAMPION, EDMUND (1540–81), English Jesuit martyr, formerly a fellow at Oxford, who became reconciled to Catholicism after studying at Douai and Rome. He returned with Parsons on the Jesuit mission to England (1580), but was arrested, tortured, and executed at Tyburn. In 1886 he was beatified.

CAMPION, THOMAS (1567–1619), English poet and musician (by profession a doctor), who wrote Latin poems, court masques, a treatise on music, and five *Books of Airs* (1601–17), graceful lyrics arranged for a lute accompaniment. His *Observations of the Art of English Poesie* (1602), a plea for the use of unrhymed metres on classical models, was answered by Daniel's *Defence of Rhyme*.

CAMPO FORMIO, PEACE OF (17 Oct. 1797), signed by France and Austria after Napoleon's Italian campaign. Napoleon negotiated the peace with little reference to the Directory and imposed his own ideas of an Italian settlement. To the disgust of the French Left and English liberals, Venice was destroyed as a political entity. The city itself, Istria, and Dalmatia were given to Austria and the Ionian islands to France. The western half of Venetia was added to the Cisalpine Republic, which had been formed from Austrian Lombardy. Austria had to recognize this as well as the Ligurian Republic. She also recognized the French annexation of Belgium and in secret articles agreed to a French Rhine frontier in return for support for her own claims on Salzburg and part of Bavaria. Germany was to be reorganized at a congress to be held at Rastadt.

CAMPOMANES, PEDRO RODRIGUEZ, Conde de (1723–1803), Spanish theorist and architect of the reforms of the enlightened despot, King Charles III. A lawyer from a poor Asturian family, he wrote on social welfare and education. He was Fiscal of the Council of Castile (1762–89) and, believing firmly in the need for control and change from above, he directed a series of administrative and economic reforms. Industry and trade were improved by removing internal tariffs and attacking the guilds, while the peasants were helped by extensive land reforms. Soon after the accession of Charles IV Campomanes was dismissed with the other enlightened ministers (1791).

CAMPO-SANTO, BATTLE OF (1743), indecisive battle of the War of the Austrian Succession, fought in the papal states between the Spaniards under Gages and an Austro-Sardinian army. Gages retreated, but Charles Emmanuel refused to allow the Sardinians to pursue the enemy, as he was contemplating changing sides to join the Franco-Spanish bloc.

CAM-RANH BAY, most important of the bases established by the US in South Viet-nam in 1965. It was visited by President Johnson in 1966 and 1967.

CAMULODUNUM (Roman Colchester), originally the Trinovantian capital in Britain, occupied by the Catuvellauni (*c.* AD 5–10). The Romans founded Colonia Victricensis nearby as the intended provincial capital (49). As the imperial cult centre, it was sacked by Boudicca.

CAMUS, ALBERT (1913–60), French writer, born in Algeria of a poor family. He began life as a journalist and during the Second World War was active in the Resistance and wrote for clandestine newspapers. From 1945 his interest was in promoting some form of world government. His best-known work of this period is *La Peste* (1947). In all his works Camus rejects the easy optimism of liberal Europe, conceiving life as a struggle doomed to fail. After 1945, however, his work began to reflect some of the hopes fostered by the Liberation.

Camus lost much intellectual credit among the younger generation by his equivocal attitude over the Algerian War. He refused to condemn or support either side and appealed for a truce. In 1957 he was awarded the Nobel Prize for Literature.

CANAAN, biblical name for Phoenicia, later used to denote Palestine generally.

CANADA, DOMINION OF, established (1 July 1867) by the British North America Act. The act created a federal colony with internal self-government. The Dominion gradually evolved into a sovereign national state within the Commonwealth as British governor-generals took decisions on the advice of Canadian ministries rather than from Westminster. The ministries of Macdonald (1867–73, 1878–91) and Laurier (1896–1911) assumed greater control of external relations, but more was achieved by Sir Robert Borden through his work in the imperial war cabinet during the First World War and his insistence on Canada's signing the Versailles treaty in its own right. The imperial conference of 1926 and the Statute of Westminster (1931) gave formal recognition to the change.

CANADA COMMITTEE, British House of Commons select committee appointed to investigate and report on Canadian grievances. It recommended that the laws, customs, and religion of French Canadians be respected, that the Canadian legislatures should receive the Crown revenues in return for a Civil List, and that taxes from land speculation, the sale of Clergy Reserves, and income from the Jesuits' estates should be used for education.

CANADA CORN ACT, THE (1912). The act and its amendments instituted government supervision, through a board of grain commissioners, of the sale, storage, and transport of grain. The board was also made responsible for grain research and statistics, inspection of grain, and the adjudication of disputes within the trade.

CANADA FIRST, patriotic organization of the 1870s taking its name from the speech by W. A. Foster, 'Canada First: or, our new nationality'. The aim of the movement was to encourage the growth of national pride through the study of Canadian history and the propagation of literature and the arts. Politically it hoped to make Canada independent, or an equal partner, of Britain. The group's growth was hindered by the conflicting personalities of some of the leaders and public opposition to union with the US advocated by Goldwin Smith, leader of the Toronto branch. Canada First did not survive as an organization beyond the 1870s. However, its aims were partly realized in the Canadian literary achievements of the next decade and a growing national self-awareness.

CANADA LAND COMPANY, founded (1824) at the instigation of John Galt, the Scottish novelist, to promote settlement in Upper Canada. The company bought and contracted to settle over 2 million acres (8000 sq. kms) of Crown land in the Lake Huron area, where it founded the towns of Guelph, Galt, and Goderich.

CANADA TEMPERANCE ACT, THE (1878), passed by the Dominion House of Commons, made the regulation of the liquor trade a matter of local jurisdiction throughout Canada. The court declared in *Russell v. the Queen* (1882) that the act was constitutional and thus extended the power of federal authority in Canada.

CANADA TENURES ACT (1826), passed by the British parliament, allowed French-Canadian holders of seigniories, which were modelled on those of pre-revolutionary France, to convert their land tenure to the English freehold pattern.

CANADA TRADE ACT, THE (1822), enacted by the British parliament to regulate the distribution of customs duties between Upper and Lower Canada and to encourage the adoption of freehold land tenure.

CANADIAN COUNCIL OF AGRICULTURE, THE, organized (1909–10) to co-ordinate the activities of farming organizations throughout Canada. It issued the 'New National Policy' (1918), demanding reduced tariffs, reciprocity with the US, increased imperial preference, and nationalization of railway and telegraph companies. The council was replaced by the Canadian Chamber of Agriculture (1935).

CANADIAN INTERCONTINENTAL RAILWAY, direct 950-mile (1520 kms) railroad linking Quebec with Halifax, completed in 1874. Construction of the railway was a condition set by the Maritime Provinces for acceptance of the British North America Act (1867).

CANADIAN NATIONAL RAILWAYS COMPANY, government-owned railroad system. The National Co., started in 1917, included by 1923 all railways, apart from the Canadian Pacific. The management of the company was given to the Canadian Railway Board. Demand for nationalization of the railroads had come from farmers but it was the financial failure of the Canadian Northern and Grand Trunk railroads which led the Conservative Party to propose government ownership.

CANADIAN PACIFIC RAILWAY, first Canadian transcontinental railroad. Originally mooted in the 1840s, it did not become a serious proposition until BC joined the Dominion of Canada (1871). Sir John Macdonald, the prime minister, after failing to obtain co-operation of two competing groups, issued the Canadian Pacific Railway Co. charter (1872) to a consortium of Montreal capitalists led by Hugh Allan. L. S. Huntingdon, a Liberal MP, declared that the offer of the charter to Allan had been accompanied by a request for contributions to Conservative Party funds. The ensuing 'Pacific Scandal' brought down the government, which was replaced by the Liberals under William Lyon Mackenzie (1873), who favoured the railway but did not initiate its construction. BC threatened secession and extracted a promise of the railway from the British colonial secretary. On his return to power (1878), Macdonald chartered a new company which chose a southerly route from Lake Superior, on grounds of economy, and completed the railway in 1885. The CPR was the only railway company to escape nationalization and show a profit after the First World War.

CANADIAN-AMERICAN RECIPROCITY TREATIES, first suggested in Canada in the 1840s to boost trade in grain and lumber, then facing strong competition in the free-trade market of Britain. The issue divided Canadians; some feared and some hoped that reciprocity treaties would lead to political union with or economic dependence on the US. A treaty reciprocally abolishing tariffs on agricultural products, fish, coal, and lumber was signed in 1854; it excluded the Pacific coastal area. America cancelled this treaty in 1866.

Canadians hoped to revive it at the Washington Conference (1871), but agreement was confined to the use of waterways and fisheries. The American Senate refused to ratify another treaty in 1875, as did the Canadian parliament in 1911, this treaty concerning the abolition of tariffs on natural produce and lower rates on some manufactured articles. A reciprocal trade agreement between Canada and the US was signed in 1935 and has since been extended.

CANALS. The first important canal in modern Europe was the Canal du Midi (opened 1681), connecting the river systems of the Bay of Biscay and of the Mediterranean. Numerous river navigation systems were built in England in the late 17th and early 18th cents which used and improved existing rivers, by cuts and locks, without departing from them for their water supply. The first true canal in England, an artificial waterway not wholly dependent on a river, was the Bridgewater canal, built by Brindley for the Duke of Bridgewater and opened in 1761, which joined Manchester and Liverpool. Other canals followed, most of them similarly providing access from a coalfield to a town with industries. Widespread canal-building (1780–1800) ('canal mania') attracted extensive investment of unsuspected and relatively unused local savings. By 1790 the main framework of the English canal system had been laid out, connecting the river systems of Trent, Mersey, Severn, and Thames, and by 1830 the greater part of the network was complete. Canals were also built in Scotland, notably the Forth and Clyde (opened 1792) and the Caledonian (opened 1822), but here the geographical formation made it impossible to construct a network.

Canals were a boon to developing industry, particularly those in which bulky materials were used, by lowering the cost of transporting heavy goods, *eg*, the short Worsley canal halved the price of coal in Manchester. China clay for the potteries, ores, timber, bricks, salt, and above all coal benefited by canals, provided the industries were situated near them, and not merely in regions served by them. Canals were not, in the long run, of great importance to agriculture, and those that crossed the watersheds of southern England, where goods traffic was mainly agricultural, never made a profit. Some canals in industrial areas, whose construction had involved expensive engineering works, were also unprofitable. A weakness of the system was that canals, being built by private enterprise with no centralized control, had no common regulations, so that boats might be too long, too wide or of too deep a draught for some routes.

In the 19th cent. many of the canal companies suffered severely from competition by railways, having failed to cut their rates soon enough, or to co-ordinate their systems. Early railways, *eg*, that from Liverpool and Manchester, were often built deliberately to compete with canals, whose charges were frequently higher. Some canals reduced their rates and continued to function at a moderate profit, but they could not compete in passenger transport, nor in goods traffic for which speed was necessary. In 1845 railway companies began to buy up canals, and in some cases allowed them deliberately to deteriorate. But canals, whether owned by railways or independently, that were efficient and not unduly costly continued to function profitably into the 20th cent.

E. C. R. Hadfield, *British Canals* (London, 1959).
J. H. Clapham, *An Economic History of England*, vol. I. *The Early Railway Age* (2nd ed., Cambridge, 1930). RMM

CANARIS, WILHELM (1887–1945), German admiral, who headed German military intelligence (Abwehr) in the period of rivalry with the Nazis. Although of delicate health he joined the navy, where he had an uninterrupted career.

With the rank of admiral he was appointed chief of the Abwehr (Jan. 1935), a post to which he was suited by his linguistic gifts and organizational talents. But he was forced to defend the Abwehr against the encroachments of Heydrich's rival organization the Sicherheitsdienst (SD). He succeeded in delaying, but could not prevent, the merging of the Abwehr with the SD. He was then appointed chief of the Special Staff for War Economy and War Economic Measures (July 1944). He was arrested for complicity in the 20 July plot and executed at Flossenbürg concentration camp. Some of the plotters had been enlisted in the Abwehr, although the extent of Canaris's involvement is difficult to determine.

CANARY ISLANDS (12,130 sq. kms), known as the Fortunate Isles, an Atlantic archipelago, regarded by Ptolemy as the western edge of the habitable world. From the mid-14th cent. they were gradually settled by Castilians, who found them inhabited by the Guanches, a primitive but war-like people. The Portuguese under Henry the Navigator disputed Spanish rights to the Canaries, but Alfonso V of Portugal surrendered his claims by the treaty of Alcacovas (1479). With the capture of Palma (1490) and Teneriffe (1493) Spain's hold on the islands was permanently established. They now produce sugar, wine, and wheat, send members to the Cortes in Madrid, and have a Spanish governor.

CANDACE, Meroitic title used for royal ladies, probably queens and queen mothers. The title is used in Meroitic inscriptions and is also known from classical writers and the Bible.

CANDIA. In 1645 the Ottoman Turks entered into a new war against Venice for the possession of Crete. The Signoria directed its war effort towards two main objectives: to cut the sea communications which enabled the Ottomans to maintain their forces in Crete, and to concentrate the defence of the island in one great fortress, ie, Candia. After over-running most of Crete (1645–7), the Ottomans began to blockade and later to besiege Candia. The siege dragged on for several years until the Ottomans, after a bitter conflict, captured the fortress (1667–9). Venice then made peace, ceding Crete to the sultan.

CANISIUS, PETER, Saint (1521–97), Dutch-born Jesuit, described as the second St Boniface, who became the first provincial of the German Jesuits and the intellectual leader of the German Counter-Reformation. He entered the order at Mainz in 1543 through the influence of Loyola's companion, Pierre Favre, and his proselytizing activity began in 1549. In 1552 he moved to Vienna, after gaining a great reputation with the Emperor Ferdinand I as teacher, preacher, administrator, and writer of theological tracts. Subsequently, with imperial encouragement, he founded Jesuit university colleges at Ingolstadt, Cologne, Nymwegen, Prague, and Innsbruck, and a number of colleges for boys, through which he influenced the training of some 1100 Jesuit priests to continue his crusade against the spread of Protestantism in Germany. He also visited Poland (1558) and initiated the Catholic reformation there by sending a group of Jesuit missionaries to reconvert the people (1565).

CANNAE, BATTLE OF (Aug. 216 BC), the victory of Hannibal in the Second Punic War over four Roman legions and allied forces under Aemilius Paullus and Terentius Varro, the most significant defeat of any ancient Roman army. The site in Apulia is disputed, some scholars indicating the north bank of the Aufidus and others the south. The victory was achieved by the containment of the Roman centre to permit a pincer movement by the cavalry on both wings. The Roman losses were 35,000 (25,000 dead), the Carthaginian 5700.

CANNES CONFERENCE (Jan. 1922), convened on the initiative of Lloyd George, who wished to discuss trade problems arising from the post-war depression and, in particular, Germany's and Russia's participation in the economic restoration of Europe. The conference invited both countries to an economic conference at Genoa the following April.

The Cannes conference was, however, dominated by problems of inter-Allied policy. A month earlier, Anglo-French conversations had been held on the questions of German reparations and France's security. Lloyd George hoped that, in return for the long-awaited treaty of guarantee, France would limit her reparations claims in the coming year. The reparations schedule presented to, and accepted by, the conference adjusted the distribution of payments between the Allies and granted Germany a partial moratorium in return for increased Allied control over her internal finances. The draft treaty submitted to France by Britain offered assistance against unprovoked aggression, joint action if the status of the Rhineland were breached, and joint consultation if the armaments clauses of the Versailles treaty were infringed.

Briand, France's prime minister and foreign minister, was anxious to cement relations with Britain, but was strongly opposed by members of his cabinet, by Millerand, president of the Republic, and by Poincaré, leader of the Senate foreign affairs committee. French public opinion was incensed by newspaper photographs of Lloyd George teaching Briand golf at Cannes, this being thought to imply that he was in the hands of Britain. Briand was recalled to Paris, and shortly afterwards resigned, to be replaced by Poincaré. The security discussions were dropped. Poincaré accepted the partial moratorium, but successfully proposed stricter conditions of supervision and control over German finance.

CANNING, CHARLES JOHN CANNING, 1st Earl (1812–62), governor-general of India during the years of the Mutiny (1857) and the first viceroy. He was the son of George Canning, the prime minister, and was educated at Christ Church, Oxford, where he was the contemporary of Gladstone, Dalhousie, and Elgin. Entering parliament (1836), he became under-secretary of state for foreign affairs (1841–6) and postmaster-general (1853–5). He succeeded Dalhousie as governor-general of India (1856), inheriting a difficult situation. The military causes of the Mutiny included weaknesses in army administration and lack of military discipline. Growing centralization of authority at headquarters had deprived the commanding officers of their powers to promote, reward, or punish, and there was as yet no system of summary court-martial. The progress of the Mutiny was gradual and resulted from British incompetence in the early stages, when sterner and prompter action might have prevented its extension. But Canning was incapable of rapid decisions and mediocrity was the prevailing note on his council. He delayed in punishing the mutinous 34th Native Infantry and failed to provide for the safety of Allahabad.

Canning was a scholar who had admirable qualities in private life—whether he was a great governor-general remains a matter of dispute. He acquired the name of 'Clemency Canning' because he objected to indiscriminate reprisals after the Mutiny. By the Government of India Act (1858) he became the first viceroy on the assumption of direct government by the Crown in the place of the East India Co.

After the Mutiny Canning was faced with many problems, such as the reorganization of the Indian army, the re-establishment of Indian finances, the restoration of confidence in the minds of the Indian princes, and legislative and administrative reforms. The princes had been alarmed at Dalhousie's doctrine of lapse. Canning's policy was to grant *sanads* of adoption in the case of the failure of direct heirs. At one time he proposed to abolish his executive council and replace all his councillors by secretaries, but he was persuaded to introduce the portfolio system instead. His rules of procedure for his council facilitated the dispatch of business, and the Indian Councils Act (1861) eventually gave non-officials a voice in the making of laws. He retired in March 1862 and died three months later.

M. Maclagan, *Clemency Canning* (London, 1962).   CCD

CANNING, GEORGE (1770–1827), British foreign secretary and prime minister, whose clearly defined principles of independent action strongly influenced 19th cent. foreign policy. A firm parliamentary supporter of Pitt, he did not hold major office until Portland's ministry, when he became foreign secretary (1807) and organized the assault on Copenhagen. Quarrels with the secretary for war, Castlereagh, over the conduct of the war and a duel with him, led to the collapse of the government (1809). Canning's personal differences with the new prime minister, Spencer Perceval, and with Castlereagh, kept him out of the Tory ministries until 1816, when he became president of the board of control for India. Castlereagh's death (1822) brought him the foreign secretaryship as well as making him leader in the Commons. He developed Castlereagh's later policy to its logical conclusion and became openly hostile to interference by the great powers against European liberal or revolutionary movements, separating Britain from the congress system and clearly putting British interests before collective European ones. Although he was only able to prevent this interference on the European continent in Portugal, he did ensure the independence of Spain's American colonies. His main achievement was to separate Russia from the other powers over the question of Greek independence. Canning was more popular in the country than in parliament; and because of his bold foreign policy, his support of Catholic emancipation, and, perhaps, his association with certain liberal aspects of the government's domestic policies, when he succeeded Liverpool as prime minister (March 1827) seven Tory ministers resigned. Four Whigs accepted places in his cabinet and until his death he depended on a section of Whig support.

CANNIZZARO, STANISLAO (1826–1910), Italian organic chemist and pupil of Avogadro, whose most memorable contribution to science was the clear explanation he gave of the molecular hypothesis, leading to its general adoption.

CANNON, JOSEPH GURNEY (1836–1926), US 'Old Guard' Republican politician and speaker of the US House of Representatives (1901–11), where his abuse of power made the term 'Cannonism' a synonym for dictatorial control of the House. Born in NC, he settled in IL and in 1872 was elected to Congress, where, except for two periods (1891–3, 1913–15), he remained until 1923. As speaker he blocked progressive legislation through control of the rules committee and removal of insurgent Republicans from committee chairmanships. Resentment at his congressional dictatorship merged with the deepening rift between progressive and conservative Republicans during Taft's administration, and in 1910 a combination of Democrats and insurgent Republicans effectively reduced the speaker's control of the rules committee, but they were unable to remove Cannon until the Democrats gained control of Congress (1911).

CANNON, general name for guns too large for hand use, first known in Europe in the second quarter of the 14th cent. The earliest known illustration of a cannon occurs in a work (1327) dedicated to Edward III, the king who introduced the weapon to England. Charles VIII of France used truly mobile artillery during his Italian wars at the end of the 15th cent. and in 1544 the Emperor Charles V ordered a seven-size standardization of the calibre of all his cannon. Until the late 17th cent. the word usually denoted siege pieces.

CANNONBALL, projectile fired from a cannon, at first a rough-hewn sphere of stone, later of cast or wrought iron. Cannonballs weighed approximately from 6 to 68 lbs (2·7–31 kilos), according to the cannon's fire-power.

CANO, JUAN SEBASTIAN DEL (d. 1526), Spanish circumnavigator, who accompanied Magellan on his voyage round the world (1519–21), succeeding him as commander when the latter was killed in a conflict with Indians.

CANO, MELCHOR (1509–60), Dominican theologian of the Spanish Counter-Reformation, and the most trusted religious

adviser of Philip II. He was a student and later a professor at the college of San Gregorio in Valladolid, where he was a contemporary and rival of the future Abp of Toledo, Cardinal Carranza, to whose destruction he contributed in 1559. Believing that the tendency to personal religion was the greatest heresy of the age, he belonged to the conservative wing of his order. Distrustful of the Jesuit order, which appeared to escape the control of the Inquisition and the Crown, he supported Philip II in his attempt to extend his ecclesiastical prerogatives. Cano was a representative at the final assembly of the Council of Trent (1562–3).

CANOES in the Pacific were primitive, single-hulled, paddled dug-outs (*waka*) with semi-square (kite) sails raised in aft winds. In a 16th-cent. nautical revolution, fast, carvel-built, lateen-sailed vessels, based on a Spanish prototype, were developed in the Carolines. Similar vessels (outrigger and double) in the Tuamotu–Society Islands were apparently modelled on Mendana's and Quiros's zabras or galliots (1595–1606) and Roggeveen's wrecked *De Afrikaansche Galei* (1722). In Micronesian-influenced Samoa–Tonga–Fiji the trend was towards heavy double-hulled dug-out craft, upwards of 100 feet (30 metres) long, propelled by single massive lateens. Later navigation was thus restricted to angle-sailing (normally between fetching and broad-reaching) in relation to the trade winds; hence the end of former contacts up wind between east and west (Tonga–Tahiti–Marquesas) and between central Polynesia and New Zealand and Hawaii. The construction of such craft died out rapidly in the 19th cent.

CANOL PROJECT, joint American–Canadian venture directed by the Permanent Joint Board on Defense during the Second World War. It involved the construction of pipeline to supply the US army in western Canada and AK with oil from wells in northern Canada.

CANON LAW, code of law made by an ecclesiastical authority for the government of a Christian community. In particular, it is the code sanctioned or issued by successive popes for the ordering of government of the universal Church, which in medieval times meant all western Christendom. The law developed independently in the eastern, African, Italian, and Spanish churches. The destruction by Islam of the Syrian, African, and Spanish churches effectively reduced the number of codes to two, and the split which developed in the 8th and 9th cents between the Greek and Roman churches meant that their codes thereafter developed in different ways. In the west, Frankish, Irish, and English codes of law developed variously during the Dark Ages, though a real attempt was made under Charlemagne and his successors to develop one universal system. There was further fragmentation in the chaos of the later 9th and 10th cents but under the reforming popes of the later 11th cent. great strides were made towards achieving the ideal of a universal canon law and systematic collections of canons began to circulate widely. The appearance (c. 1142) of the *Decretum* of Gratian is a turning point in the history of canon law. Gratian was a lawyer at Bologna, the first and greatest of the medieval law schools; here Justinian's code of civil law, and especially one of its parts, the *Digest*, was the basis of study. Using the new dialectic methods introduced by Abelard, and applying the principles of codification from civil law, Gratian produced one coherent and consistent code of canon law. Gratian's *Decretum* became accepted as authoritative, and formed the basis of the *Corpus Juris Canonici*, the body of Roman canon law, which drew together the *Decretals* of Gregory IX (1234), the *Sext* of Boniface VIII (1298), and the *Clementines* of Clement V into one code, promulgated as a unit in 1582 and governing the Roman church until the major revision made in 1917.

Until 1540 Roman canon law obtained in England. But the Submission of the Clergy (1534) denied its absolute validity, and provided for its submission for Crown approval. By

1545 Henry VIII had forbidden the study of the subject at Oxford and Cambridge.

The next collection formulated (1571) did not receive royal assent, although subsequent codes (1576, 1584, 1597) did so, but only for the lifetime of Queen Elizabeth I. The position at her death was resolved by the collection of 141 canons approved by the convocations of Canterbury (1603) and York (1606), which received the royal assent, and remained to form the basis of modern canon law, together with the appropriate legislation and decisions of the church courts. Canon law is still recognized by the civil courts in England as binding on the clergy. JG

CANOVAS DEL CASTILLO, ANTONIO (1828–97), distinguished historian and right-wing statesman, who dominated the politics of Restoration Spain (1875–97). Canovas represented the interests of the landed oligarchy, which regained power on the accession of Alfonso XII, despite the supposedly constitutional monarchy and the introduction of manhood suffrage (1885). Canovas achieved a period of prolonged stability by controlling the electorate with bribery and police terror and by sharing power with Sagasta's Liberal Party, which contained many disaffected republicans. But this respite from the political turmoil of 19th-cent. Spain was not used to hasten the economic advance and modernization so urgently needed to relieve the tensions in Spanish society. Anarchism flourished in Barcelona and in 1890 Canovas was forced to reveal that his country was bankrupt. He was murdered by an anarchist.

CANTERBURY, originally the chief settlement of the Cantii. It was known as Durovernum Cantiacorum during the Roman occupation of Britain, when it grew to be as large as the present walled city. Recent excavation has shown that throughout the 5th cent. a small community lived in huts amid the ruins of Roman buildings. The medieval street plan bears no relation to the Roman, although the walls have Roman foundations. By the 6th cent. the city had become Cantwarabyrig, and the seat of the kings of Kent. King Aethelbert, the most powerful of these, became the convert and protector of Augustine, the Roman missionary and first archbishop, after his arrival at Canterbury in 597. In 1011 the city was largely destroyed by the Danes. Later, William the Conqueror built a royal castle there. Great prosperity came to the city following the murder in 1170 of Thomas à Becket in his own cathedral and the rapid spread of his cult thereafter. Until its destruction by Henry VIII, Becket's shrine was one of the most famous objects of pilgrimage in Christendom. Before the Dissolution, Canterbury possessed two great monastic houses in Christchurch (the cathedral) and St Augustine's Abbey, and also three friaries. In 1964 the university of Kent was established at Canterbury.

CANTERBURY, PROVINCE OF (NZ). Founded by the Canterbury Association (1848) as a settlement for Anglicans, Canterbury embodied 'Wakefield' principles more than previous attempts at 'systematic colonization', but soon conformed broadly to the common Australasian social pattern. The first body of colonists (1850) briefly formed a fairly concentrated settlement, but the association's agent, J. R. Godley, set aside restrictions on pastoralism. Sheep-runs spread rapidly, Canterbury becoming the leading wool province. A progressive superintendent, W. S. Moorhouse, initiated NZ's first railway (1863), the one-and-a-quarter mile (2 kms) Lyttelton Tunnel (1861–7), and provincial government buildings (1859–65). Under W. Rolleston (1868–76), Canterbury set the standard in provincial administration and by 1906 it had become the most populous South Island province.

CANTILLON, RICHARD (1680–1734), English banker in London and in Paris, where he was associated with John Law. His *Essai sur la nature du Commerce en Général* (known in his lifetime but not published until 1755), anticipated important aspects of classical economic theory.

CANTILUPE, THOMAS, Saint (d. 1282), came of baronial stock and was a graduate and lecturer in canon law at both Oxford and Paris, and was twice chancellor of Oxford (1261–1263, 1273–4). He was chancellor of England under Simon de Montfort (1264–5), became Bp of Hereford (1275), and was the last Englishman to be canonized (1320) in the Middle Ages.

CANTILUPE, WALTER (d. 1266), Bp of Worcester (1235–66) and a prominent figure in the baronial reform movement (1258–65) during the reign of King Henry III of England. He was a friend of Simon de Montfort, and remained his staunch supporter throughout the civil war (1263–5).

CANTINO CHARTS, maps indicating the known extent of the American coastline (1500–4), drawn by Alberto Cantino, the cartographer.

CANTON COMMUNE (Dec. 1927), misconceived attempt to establish a revolutionary base in south China. After the Shanghai Purge (April 1927), the Chinese Communist Party, under Comintern direction, switched from a policy of cooperation with the Kuomintang to one of insurrection against it. During the late summer and early autumn a series of abortive attacks, known as the Autumn Harvest Uprisings, were launched in southern China. Dissension among local military chiefs had created a confused situation in Canton, and a plan to seize the city to coincide with the opening of the 15th Congress of the Communist Party of the Soviet Union (13 Dec.), with the resultant propaganda coup, failed, for the attempt was launched two days earlier; and, to the consternation of Moscow, collapsed on 13 Dec. A commune was proclaimed in Canton on the day of the uprising, and sweeping social reforms were announced, but the masses did not rally to the communists, and the commune was easily crushed. There were savage reprisals: at least 5000 people were executed in the immediate aftermath. The Comintern planners, notably Heinz Neumann, had overestimated popular support, and underestimated the capacity of the local militarists. Their miscalculation sacrificed the lives of countless Chinese communists.

CANUDOS, the north-eastern Brazilian locale of a theocratic state, dedicated to the Good Jesus (*Bom Jesús*), founded by Antônio Maciel, or Antônio Conselheiro, as he was called by his followers. The cult at Canudos survived (1862–97), ending with the death of its leader, who wished to restore the monarchy to Brazil, and the extermination of its garrison by the Brazilian federal army. Canudos was the centre and fortress of the rebellion, approximately 480 kms north-west of Bahia. The great Brazilian novel, Euclides da Cunha's *Os Sertões*, a protest against the campaign of extermination, resulted from the rebellion.

CAODAISM, the name of a syncretic Viet-namese religion which was formally established in French Cochin China (now South Viet-nam) in 1926. It seeks to incorporate the three traditional Viet-namese religions of Confucianism, Buddhism, and Taoism, together with elements of Christianity. Its deepest affinities, however, are with Taoism. An important element in the religion is spirit-mediumship, practised by the method of automatic writing. Through spirit-messages the High Spirit 'Cao Dai' (identifiable with the Taoist 'Jade Emperor') gives advice and instructions to his adherents, who by now are estimated to number somewhere between 500,000 and 2 million. The religion has a priestly hierarchy, with a 'holy see' at the town of Tay-Ninh (South Viet-nam). Since its inauguration however, a number of schisms have appeared: by the 1950s there were at least ten sects, many of which were not affiliated to Tay-Ninh.

Caodaism is not only a religious movement; its leaders

have from time to time shown political aspirations, especially during the years 1941–56. During the period of Japanese expansion in South-East Asia (1941–5), the Caodaist hierarchy had hopes of receiving Japanese assistance to establish a new regime in South Viet-nam, the French authorities in Saigon imprisoning several Caodaist leaders as a result. Subsequently (1946–7) after the Japanese surrender and the return of the French, the Caodaists split. Some joined the Viet-minh (against the French); but the main body decided to co-operate with the French in return for a degree of autonomy. From 1947 until 1954 Tay-Ninh was the centre of a Caodaist province defended by its own private army. In 1954–5, after independence, a conflict developed between the South Viet-namese sects (the Caodaists and the Hoa-Hoa) and the regime of Ngo Dinh Diem, in which the former were eliminated from the political life of the country until the present time (1970). RBS

CAOPOLICAN (d. 1558), Araucanian leader who fought with Lautaro against the Spaniards in Chile. He led the Araucanians after Lautaro's death (April 1557) and until his own execution by the Spaniards.

CAPE BRETON ISLAND, large Canadian island above NS, first sighted by Jacques Cartier (1536). Because of its proximity to rich fishing waters, Cape Breton was coveted by both France and Britain. A Scottish settlement (1629) was destroyed almost immediately by the French under Charles Daniel, who compelled the Scots to build a fortification for French use. After the cession of Nfld and Acadia to Britain (1713), the French made Cape Breton and its fortress at Louisbourg a key point in their defence of Canada. The island, captured by the British (1745, 1758), was ceded by France (1763) and united to NS. Settlement by Americans loyal to King George III of Britain led to the creation of Cape Breton as a separate colony (1784). It was reunited with NS (1820). Large groups of Scottish settlers came to the island following the Highland clearances of the early 19th cent.

CAPE COAST, commercially important coastal town in Ghana, which passed into British hands in 1664. The fort subsequently built there served as the seat of British administration for the Gold Coast and for Lagos until 1876.

CAPE COLONY. Occupied by Britain (1795–1803 and 1806), the Cape Colony of South Africa was formally ceded to Britain by the Netherlands in 1814. It attained its present (provincial) boundaries by the end of the century. In 1853 the colony achieved representative government for the settlers, who secured political power in spite of some franchise concessions to non-whites; responsible government followed in 1872. The Cape was the largest in size and population of the four colonies which formed the Union of South Africa in 1910.

CAPE ST VINCENT, BATTLE OF (14 Feb. 1797), in the French Revolution war, resulted in the joint Franco-Spanish fleet being defeated by the British.

CAPE VERDE ISLANDS (4033 sq. kms) off the north Atlantic coast of Africa are ruled by Portugal through a governor and a Legislative Council elected from a single party. There are (1970) 222,000 inhabitants. A clandestine movement in the islands is part of the PAIGC (Partido por la Independência de Guiné e Capo Verde).

CAPELLEN, G. A. VAN DER, Baron (1778–1848), governor-general of the Dutch East Indies (1816–26). Born in Utrecht, he became (1816) a member of the Dutch High Commission (with Elout and Buyskes) which took over the Dutch Indonesian possessions from the temporary English administration under Raffles. Thereafter he remained in the East Indies as the new governor-general. During his administration, he faced serious problems throughout the East Indies which involved the Dutch in military action in Sumatra, Borneo, South Celebes, and in Java during the rebellion of Dipanagara (the Java War). These actions caused serious financial troubles for the administration.

CAPETIAN DYNASTY (987–1328), the line of kings who ruled France for over 300 years. The name was taken from the founder of the dynasty, Hugh Capet, who was elected king in 987. Outstanding Capetians include Philip Augustus and St Louis. The dynasty came to an end through lack of male heirs.

CAPITANIA, extensive land grant in colonial Brazil, 12 of which were made to Portuguese nobles by King John III (1532).

CAPITANT, RENÉ (1901–   ), French politician and one of the earliest followers of De Gaulle, a leading left-wing Gaullist under the Fifth Republic and minister (1943–5). He was a leader of the RPF Party, and minister of justice (1968–9). He resigned to avoid serving under De Gaulle's successor.

CAPITATION TAX, poll tax levied in France in 1695 to supplement the *taille* and theoretically not subject to exemption. Described as 'the first step taken under the *ancien régime* towards equality of taxation', it divided the nation into 22 classes or ranks to be taxed according to wealth and social standing. It was imposed in order to finance the War of the League of Augsburg. In practice, many towns compounded and the tax failed to raise as much as was expected. It was suppressed in 1698, re-established in 1701 (to provide money for the War of the Spanish Succession), and increased in 1705. By the middle of the 18th cent. it had become one of the permanent direct taxes of the *ancien régime*.

CAPITOLINE HILL, the religious centre and early citadel of ancient Rome. It was situated at the western end of the Roman forum, and was probably incorporated into the city early in the 6th cent. BC. The Capitolium, or temple of Jupiter, on its southern summit was reputedly completed by the Tarquins, and traces of its subfoundation have been unearthed dating to the Etruscan occupation of the 6th cent. The temple housed the Sibylline books, and all sacrifices of particular civic significance were offered on its altar. On the northern summit, where the citadel had been, stood a temple of Juno, whose sacred geese were said to have saved the citadel from a Gallic night-attack (391 BC).

CAPITULARY, term used for legislative ordinances issued by the Frankish King Charlemagne and his successors. Legislation was enacted very rarely by Frankish rulers until Charlemagne started to issue ordinances in 779. They were entrusted for enforcement to special royal envoys and the summaries of the instructions issued to these envoys (*capitula missorum*) originated the word capitulary.

CAPITULATIONS, term denoting agreements under which one state granted to another state rights of extra-territorial jurisdiction within its own territories, that jurisdiction to be exercised over nationals of the recipient state resident within the dominions of the grantor. The name derives from the Latin *capitulum*, a clause, whence the noun *capitulatio*. The conferment of such privileges can be traced far into the past: examples are available in the practice of Byzantium or in the relations existing in the Middle Ages between the Muslim regimes established in Syria and Egypt and the Italian republics like Genoa and Venice. Among the most typical instances are the capitulations which the Ottoman sultan, as a unilateral act of grace rather than as a bilateral obligation, allowed to France (1536), to England (1583), and to the Dutch (1612). The privileges thus conferred included protection for one's person and goods; freedom of movement, as for purposes of trade; the right to follow one's own religious faith; and the right to be judged under one's own national law in the case of disputes between the subjects of a given state. The system of capitulations was not confined to the Middle East. With the advance of European influence it came to embrace countries farther afield such as Abyssinia, Siam, China, and Japan. In the course of time the granting of capitulations led to numerous abuses, above all to the emergence of a class of protégés, *ie*, of men who, entering the service of a foreign ambassador or consul, claimed and often secured exemption from the laws of their native land. As the eastern nations became more aware, during the 19th and 20th cents, of their own sovereign status, so the capitulations assumed in their eyes the character of a badge of servitude to an alien domination. Agitation grew and was long sustained against the system, which was brought to an end mainly in the two decades following the First World War.

CAPODISTRIAS, GIOVANNI ANTONIO, Count (1776–1831), president of Greece (1827–31). Though a Greek, born in Corfu, he entered the Russian diplomatic service (1809) and was joint foreign minister with Nesselrode (1815–21), with special responsibility for relations with Turkey. He refused to join the *Philike Hetairia* (1817), but after revolution broke out in Greece (1821) he left Russia, hurt by Alexander I's refusal to give immediate aid to the rebels. He rightly regarded Russia as the main champion of Greek independence and during his presidency was distrusted by the Western powers as being too pro-Russian. In 1828 he proposed a plan to Russia to turn the Balkans into a confederation of five independent states, with Constantinople as a free city. He became increasingly unpopular in Greece because of his centralizing policy and was assassinated.

CAPONE, ALPHONSO (1895–1947), Italian-born US bootlegger and racketeer. With the beginning of prohibition (1920), Chicago, IL, became the most notorious mid-western centre for the importation, manufacture, distribution, and sale of illegal liquor, and the lucrative trade spawned violent competition between different underworld gangs. Al Capone became a supporter of the gang leader John Torrio. To avoid law enforcement officials in Chicago, Torrio and Capone established a base in Cicero, a Chicago suburb and the fifth largest town in IL. The Chicago Crime Commission later estimated that they had an annual income of $30 million from the sale of liquor and $15 million from gambling, prostitution, and drugs. When Torrio retired (1925) Capone expanded the business in the city of Chicago and consolidated his position by systematically destroying opposition gangs. During the period 1925–30 more than 500 gangsters were killed, the most sensational incident being the St Valentine's Day Massacre (Feb. 1929). The massacre was an outrageous ending to the 'roaring twenties'. Public sentiment had started to turn against the earlier romanticized view of the bootleggers, and the first nation-wide meeting (1929) of gangsters in Atlantic City, NJ, which attempted to end the violence by allocating specific districts to different gangs throughout the US, came too late. Immediately after the meeting, Capone was arrested and convicted in Philadelphia for carrying a concealed weapon. When he was released (1930), the sobering realities of the Depression had turned public sentiment against the underworld, and law enforcement bodies, lacking real evidence, conducted a highly successful publicity campaign against Capone and other criminals. Many gangsters, earlier considered 'untouchables', were convicted and Capone was arrested (Oct. 1931) for the federal crime of income tax evasion. He was heavily fined and sentenced to jail for 11 years. After his release (1939), he lived in seclusion and fear of his enemies until his death in Miami, FL.

Kenneth Allsop, *The Bootleggers* (London, 1961).
Herbert Asburg, *The Great Illusion* (Garden City, NY, 1950). FPK

CAPPADOCIA, a Persian satrapy in eastern Asia Minor between the Halys and the Euphrates, which became an independent kingdom recognized by the Seleucids in *c.* 255 BC. After 190 its kings, descended from the Persian satrap Ariarathes, became clients of Rome, though vassals of Mithridates VI of Pontus ruled at times (*c.* 115–73), and when Antony's nominee, Archelaus, died (AD 17), it became a province, and later was joined with Galatia by Vespasian and with Pontus by Trajan. By the mid-3rd cent. it was largely Christian and produced in the 4th cent. the theologians Gregory of Nazianzus, Gregory of Nyssa, and his brother, Basil of Caesarea.

CAPRIVI, GEORG (1831–99), chancellor of Germany (1890–4) after Bismarck. Being threatened by social revolution at home, he planned a policy of conciliation, but was thwarted by failure to control the Reichstag, the growing power of the SPD, and the reactionary attitude of the Kaiser. His role as federal chancellor lost credibility when he was deprived of the presidency of Prussia and failed to prevent a wholesale fragmentation of parties over the passage of an army bill (1892). Caprivi intended to safeguard Germany's interests by a more open diplomacy and on Holstein's advice did not renew the Reinsurance treaty with Russia, but sought to strengthen the Triple Alliance by a rapprochement with Britain. This policy failed. Russia turned to France, leaving Germany dangerously dependent on Austria.

Caprivi resigned in 1894 because he refused to associate himself with the growing demand for anti-revolutionary legislation in a year of increased anarchist activity, which included an attempt on his own life.

CAPTAIN GENERAL, governor of colonial Brazil (16th–17th cents) and an official in colonial Spanish America charged with the defence and, after the mid-16th cent., the government of an autonomous region.

CAPUA, principal city of southern Italy in 4th and 3rd cents BC. Earlier known as the Etruscan settlement of Volturnum, it was seized by Sabellian migrants about 445 and soon prospered as a Campanian agricultural market and manufacturing centre. When allied with Rome against the Samnites in the War of 343–2, it accepted the Roman 'citizenship without vote' in 338. Apart from a brief secession during the second Samnite War, the city remained faithful to Rome until it went over to Hannibal after the battle of Cannae (216). It surrendered to the Romans after a siege in 211, lost all political rights, but became a Roman colony in Sulla's time (82 BC).

CAPUCHINS, order of Franciscan friars, authorized by Clement VII to revert to the strict rule of St Francis (1528). Barefooted and bearded, wearing brown habits and peaked cowls, they dedicated themselves to poverty and charitable works. Their selfless example made many converts and they were an important force in the Counter-Reformation. Since 1619 they have been independent of the parent order. They still maintain about 200 missionary stations in various parts of the world.

CARABOBO, BATTLE OF (24 June 1821) secured Venezuelan independence from Spain. Simón Bolívar and José Antonio Páez shattered Spanish resistance near Valencia on the Plains of Carabobo.

CARACALLA (M. Aurelius Antoninus) (*reg.* AD 211–17), Roman Emperor who succeeded his father, Septimius Severus, and became sole ruler after the murder of Geta, his brother and colleague (212). Caracalla issued the *Constitutio Antoniniana*, by which Roman citizenship was extended to all free inhabitants of the empire, and built the baths at Rome named after him. After campaigning on the northern frontier (213) he went to the east in 214 to invade Parthia. During this campaign he modelled his behaviour upon that of his hero, Alexander the Great. He was murdered near Edessa in Syria, and succeeded by Macrinus.

CARACAS, CONFERENCE OF, an Inter-American conference, meeting for the tenth time (March 1954), voted 97 resolutions, the most publicized being the anti-communist declaration, sponsored by the US.

CARATACUS, a son of Cunobelinus (d. AD 40–1) the native ruler of south-east Britain, and chief opponent of the Roman invasion (AD 43). He and his brother, Togodumnus, abandoned their father's policy of co-operation with the Romans, who then controlled Gaul, and their expulsion of Verica, the pro-Roman ruler of the Atrebates, who fled to Rome, precipitated the Roman invasion. After early Roman victories, Caratacus led resistance in Wales and the south-west. After further Roman successes involving the capture of his family, he sought refuge with the Brigantes (51), but their queen, Cartimandua, surrendered him to the Romans, who sent him to Rome, where his days ended in honourable captivity.

CARAUSIUS (d. AD 294), Roman fleet commander at Boulogne, who declared himself emperor (287) and crossed to Britain, where he maintained independence until his assassination by Allectus. Allectus was himself defeated by the Caesar Fl. Valerius Constantius (297).

CARBERRY HILL, BATTLE OF (15 June 1567) between Mary Queen of Scots and her supporters against the united opposition of the Scottish Confederate lords led by Morton and Atholl. The queen was captured and imprisoned at Loch Leven and her husband, Bothwell, fled into exile.

CARBO, CN. PAPIRIUS (d. 82 BC), Roman politician, and as consul in 85 and 84 leader, with Cinna, of the Marian party. After Cinna's death he led the resistance to Sulla's return and was consul in 82 when, after defeat by Sulla's general Metellus Pius at Faventia, he was caught and executed by Pompey in Sicily.

CARBONARI (charcoal burners), a secret society which originated as a war-time resistance movement against the French government in Naples during the Napoleonic wars and remained active in post-war Italy against foreign domination by Austria. The *carbonari* helped to foment revolutions in Sicily and Naples (1820) and in the papal states (1830), but both were crushed by Austrian troops. More ambitiously, under the inspiration of Menotti, they planned to seize Modena as a base for a national uprising, but were foiled by the duplicity of its ruler, Francis IV. Since they represented the sectional interests of the upper classes, who resented their exclusion from power, the *carbonari* did not contribute to the mainstream of the Risorgimento, which was essentially middle class and democratic.

CARCHEMISH, ancient city on the upper Euphrates at the crossing place of a trade route from Nineveh to the Orontes valley and the Mediterranean. Its important position frequently led to its conquest by the great powers of the time, and, in 605 BC, it was the site of a battle in which Nebuchadnezzar II defeated the Egyptians and the remnant of the Assyrian army.

CARD MONEY was introduced by the *intendant* de Meulles, of New France (1685). Playing cards were used to represent sums of money to circumvent the shortage of coins. Their use became a regular monetary system, but was stopped by the French government (1717) although the system was again used between 1741 and 1763.

CARDENAS, LÁZARO (1895–1970), president of Mexico (1934–40). He gave great impetus to social reform in general, and agrarian reform in particular, after the Revolution (1911–17). Cardenas, who was born in Jiquilpan de Juarez, Michoacan, of partly Tarascan Indian origin, joined the

Revolution (1913), and rose to become brigadier-general (1924). He began his political career as provisional governor of Michoacan in 1920 (governor 1928–32). He entered the cabinet (1931) as minister of the interior, then became minister of war and marine (1933). The former president, Plutarco Elias Calles, chose Cardenas for the presidency (1933), unaware that as president he would take an independent course of action. In effect, Cardenas sought to realize the programmes suggested by the revolutionary leadership and authorized by the constitution of 1917. Cardenas's achievements were many and varied. He distributed some 40 million acres (162,000 sq. kms) of land in village communal holdings (*ejidos*). Urban labour obtained his support. Foreign oil interests were nationalized (1938), following the nationalization of most of the railroads. Rural schools were built in large numbers for the first time in Mexico. On the other hand, the trend of foreign investment showed fears abroad of both organized labour and the president.

Cardenas created the PRM (Partido de la Revolucion Mexicana) before the election of his successor (1939), to carry forward the tasks of the 'Revolutionary Family', as the leadership is often called. He formally withdrew from that party 22 years later (May 1961), charging it with having strayed from the revolutionary path. In his opinion, a new revolution was needed, closer to that of Cuba under Fidel Castro. Cardenas's influence continues, especially among youthful Mexicans and the influential political left.

CARDIFF, capital of Wales, seaport, and county town of Glamorgan, situated near the mouth of the Taff river. It was the site of a Roman fort (*c.* AD 75) and a Norman castle (*c.* 1090). Cardiff received its first charter in 1147 and by the early 14th cent. was a trading centre and port of some importance. The castle was stormed by the Welsh in Owen Glendower's revolt (1404) and on Richard III's death (1485) the seigniory escheated to Henry VII, passing in 1550 to Sir William Herbert, later Earl of Pembroke, whose father had already acquired the town's dissolved Dominican and Franciscan friaries (1538). In the English Civil War the castle passed from Royalist to Parliamentary control (1645). By the 18th cent. it had become a 'creek' port to Bristol, but an economic revival started in the 1790s with the construction of a canal (1794) and the promotion of a railway and new docks by the Marquess of Bute, to whom the castle estates had passed by marriage. The development of the modern city dates from the opening up of the South Wales coal and iron industries in the 19th cent.

CARDINALS, COLLEGE OF. By the 11th cent. the cardinal-bishops and cardinal-priests, whose original functions were purely liturgical, had begun to perform administrative duties also and were acting as the principal counsellors of the popes. They had also begun to have a corporate existence which was recognized when the Lenten Synod of 1059 vested in the college of cardinals the right of electing the pope. The college also became representative of the universal rather than the local Roman church when non-Roman and non-resident clergy were appointed members (*eg*, Henry Beaufort). The dean of the college is the Bp of Ostia, who consecrates the new pope, and the members of the college are the heads of the various offices of papal government. The number of members fluctuated in the Middle Ages and was usually less than 50, but was fixed at a maximum of 70 in 1586 by Pope Sixtus V. Pope John XXIII raised the number to 87 and his successor, Pope Paul VI, raised it again to 136 (1969).

CARDONNEL, ADAM DE (d. 1719), British MP, secretary, and close associate of the Duke of Marlborough. He was appointed secretary-at-war in 1710, but was expelled from the House of Commons in 1712, with Walpole, on the evidence of the Commission of Accounts.

CARDOZA, BENJAMIN NATHAN (1870–1938), US jurist and associate justice of the US Supreme Court. A NY lawyer, he was elected to the state supreme court (1913), and appointed to the state court of appeals (1917), becoming chief judge in 1927. He was nominated to the US Supreme Court by President Hoover (1932) and served until his death. Cardozo was an influential liberal on the Supreme Court, and applied the libertarian philosophy and sociological jurisprudence he had enunciated in his classic treatise, *The Nature of the Judicial Process* (1921).

CARDWELL OF ELLERBECK, EDWARD CARDWELL, 1st Viscount (1813–86), British statesman, who entered parliament in 1842 and held minor offices in Aberdeen's and Palmerston's governments before achieving distinction for his comprehensive programme of army reforms as secretary for war in Gladstone's government (1868–74). He expanded, modernized, and reorganized the army to meet the situation created by Prussian victories on the continent. He abolished the purchase of commissions, withdrew troops from the self-governing colonies, introduced a system of short-service enlistments, reorganized regiments on a county basis, and established the *Linked Battalion System* whereby one battalion would serve abroad while the other remained at the county depot. Flogging was abolished during peacetime, the infantry were equipped with the Martin Henry breech-loading rifle and the conflict of authority between the secretary of state for war and the commander-in-chief resolved by making the minister supreme. Cardwell accomplished these reforms despite the fierce opposition of Conservatives, Lords, and army officers, and in so doing laid the foundations of the modern British army.

CAREW, SIR GEORGE (d. 1612), English lawyer and diplomat, MP for Cornish boroughs (1584–1601), secretary to Chancellor Hatton, and envoy to Sweden and Poland (1598). Under James I he conducted negotiations for union with Scotland, and was ambassador to France (1605–9) and author of *Relation of the State of France* (printed 1749). As a master in Chancery he drew up valuable reports of Chancery cases.

CAREW, SIR PETER (1514–75), English adventurer. He served in Henry VIII's wars in France and was sent to put down the western revolt (1549), aggravating the rebels' grievances by his abrupt methods. He kept Devonshire loyal on the accession of Mary (1553), but objected to her Spanish marriage and tried unsuccessfully to raise the west in sympathy with Wyatt (1554). He was a commissioner for the treaty of Leith (1561) and later infuriated the natives during an English attempt to colonize Munster.

CAREW, THOMAS (1595–1639), English court poet and disciple of Donne and Jonson. He wrote a masque, *Coelum Britannicum* (1634), and many lyrics and amatory poems.

CAREY, WILLIAM (1761–1834), British oriental scholar and Baptist missionary. At first he was apprenticed to a shoemaker and was known in later life as the 'consecrated cobbler'. He became a Baptist in 1783 and helped to found the Baptist missionary society at Kettering. Under great difficulties he studied Greek, Latin, and Hebrew. Proceeding to India in 1793 without a licence from the directors of the East India Co., he had to seek refuge under the Danish flag at Serampore. Wellesley appointed him a teacher of languages in his college for civil servants at Fort William, and personally subscribed £800 to Carey's church at Serampore. During his 40 years in India he published, with the help of pundits, grammars in Bengali, Sanskrit, Marathi, Punjabi, Telegu, and Kanarese, compiled dictionaries in Bengali, Sanskrit, and Marathi and helped to lay the foundations of Bengali prose literature. He also drew attention to social evils such as child sacrifice and *sati* (*suttee*).

CARGILL, DONALD (?1619–81), Scottish covenanting preacher and leader of the 'Society People' or the 'Cameronians'. He was hanged with five others after publicly disavowing allegiance to King Charles II by the Sanquhar Declaration (22 June 1680).

CARGO CULTS, common phenomenon in the post-conversion period in the Pacific, which may be attributed chiefly to the failure of expected benefits from acceptance of a literate faith, Christianity. Major modern manifestations, all Melanesian—*eg*, John Frum (Tanna); Marching Rule (Malaita); Paliau (Admiralty Islands)—reflect a non-acquisitive or communal approach to property-holding, the peculiar frustrations resulting from the termination of longstanding connections with Fiji and Queensland, and the failure of missions, when tried after 1884 to provide a satisfactory alternative route to 'cargo' (goods); hence the almost complete renunciation of the church in affected communities and the formation of anti-churches. Belief in salvation from America has been inspired by the supposed status of the US Negro and the material wealth displayed by Americans in the Melanesian theatre during the Second World War. Early repressive measures by government have given place to constructive efforts to exploit the new, island-wide affiliations in the interests of political independence.

CARÍAS ANDINO, TIBURCIO (1876–), president and dictator of Honduras (1933–49). As a conservative leader and general, Carías opposed the Liberals and reformists throughout his long political career. He was an unsuccessful presidential candidate (1924), obtaining a plurality, but not an absolute majority. Negotiations (supported by the US) followed within the congress and Carías's vice-presidential choice was named president. Carías won the election of 1933 and ruled dictatorially for 16 years. The Liberals rebelled unsuccessfully on numerous occasions and Carías imposed his minister of war as president in 1949.

CARIBBEAN LABOUR CONGRESS held its first conference in Barbados (Sept. 1945) with 34 delegates representing trade unions and labour parties from 15 Caribbean colonies. The congress, divided by political and ideological differences, collapsed (1953).

CARIBOO ROAD, constructed (1862–4) to reach the goldfields of the Cariboo region of BC, Canada. The road, a remarkable engineering accomplishment, opened new lands for development and provided a route along the Fraser river for the Canadian Pacific Railway (1885).

CARICATURE, POLITICAL, used in Britain from the mid-18th cent. as a means of influencing public opinion by attacking or commending public figures and their views. Caricature as we know it originated in late 16th-cent. Italy in the studio of Agostino Caracci (1557–1602) and travelled via France to England in 1740, when the print-maker Arthur Pond published 25 caricature drawings by Italian and French masters.

The commercial success of the new genre continued throughout the century, being enhanced by the production of the coloured print, and it was swiftly taken up as a political weapon, of which an early example is the portrait of Lord Lovat on trial for his part in the Jacobite Rising (1745) by William Hogarth (1697–1764). Later, in the 1760s, George, Viscount Townshend, sponsored a series of comic portraits of his opponents with apposite titles. The career of John Wilkes was also the subject of many caricatures by Hogarth and others. In the 1780s Thomas Rowlandson (1756–1827) and the even more hard-hitting James Gillray (1757–1815) satirized the Fox–North coalition, the Younger Pitt, and the private life of the future George IV at the instigation of vaious factions. With the advent of the French Revolution caricaturists tended to react in favour of 'Church and King', though George Cruikshank (1792–1878) lampooned all parties.

The tradition also flourished in France under Napoleon I, but reached its apogee with Henri Daumier (1808–79), whose cartoons appeared in Charles Philipon's *La Caricature* and form a commentary on the rise and fall of the Third Empire. In England a change occurred with the careers of John Doyle, 'H.B.' (1797–1868), and his son Richard (1824–83), whose lithographs killed the demand for the individual coloured print and diverted the art of caricature into magazines and journals. *Punch*, the greatest of these, was founded in 1831. Although *Punch* became more restrained in approach after 1832, Queen Victoria and her family were the subject of many cartoons. Comments on domestic and international concerns were made by Sir John Tenniel (1820–1914) *eg.*, his famous drawing of Bismarck, *Dropping the Pilot* (1890). Sir Leslie Ward, 'Spy' (1851–1922), also drew a series of well-known political portraits, as did the Australian-born Phil May (1864–1903), whose work was famous for its economy of line. In the US Thomas Nast (1840–1902) was for long the scourge of the Democratic Party. In the 20th cent. the outstanding exponent of political caricature in England was Sir David Low (1891–1963), whose work appeared most influentially in the *Evening Standard* and the *Manchester Guardian* in the 1930s.

M. D. George, *English Political Caricature*, 2 vols (Oxford, 1959).　　　　　　　　　　　　　　　　　　　　　VEC

CARINTHIA, area of 3681 sq. miles (9524 sq. kms) with a population of half a million (1970), of whom 4 per cent are Slovenes; politically organized as a *Bundesland* (federal state) of Austria.

Except for the years 1809–14, when Slovene Southern Carinthia was included in Napoleon's Illyrian provinces, Carinthia formed part of the Habsburg empire (1335–1918). Thus, most of the Slovenes remained Austro-Slav even when the other minorities of the empire were advocating national liberation. Yugoslav demands for the incorporation of Southern Carinthia in the new Yugoslav state met with little local enthusiasm, as the results of the Klagenfurt Plebiscite (Oct. 1920) showed.

In the 1930s Yugoslav irredentism in Carinthia increased, largely because of Italo-Yugoslav rivalry, and Italian control over the Austrian government (1934–6) led some Yugoslavs to want Southern Carinthia as a defensive buffer against Italy. Nazi ill-treatment of Slavs during the Second World War also provoked Yugoslav claims to the area, and in 1944 Tito's Partisans tried to recover the Klagenfurt basin, but were forced to withdraw by the Anglo-American authorities in Austria.

After the war the Yugoslav government continued to demand the Slovene areas of Southern Carinthia. The Soviet decision in June 1949 to drop their support for this claim was one of many factors leading to the deterioration of Yugoslav–Soviet relations. Four years later Yugoslav fears of Russia made Tito increasingly aware of the necessity of improving relations with non-Cominform neighbours, and thus he relinquished the Yugoslav claim to Southern Carinthia.

CARINUS, M. AURELIUS (*reg.* AD 283–4), Roman Emperor, son and successor of Carus, who had left him in Gaul during the eastern campaign, on which he died. Carinus visited Rome (283), but was suppressed in Pannonia by Diocletian.

CARLETON OF CARLETON, HENRY BOYLE, 1st Baron (d. 1725), British Whig politician, and MP for various seats between 1689 and 1710, being chancellor of the exchequer (1701–8) and lord treasurer of Ireland (1704–15). He was promoted to the cabinet (1708) as secretary of state of the northern department, being replaced by St John in 1710. Carleton was a moderate Court Whig who was described as a man 'without any party violence'. He had a reputation for cool and restrained political behaviour, and, fearing the domination of the Junto, was usually prepared to place his duty to the Crown above obligations to party leaders. In 1708–9 he supported Godolphin against the Junto attack and was contemptuously labelled a 'Treasurer's Whig'. He later became lord president of the council under Walpole (1721–5).

CARLILE, RICHARD (1790–1843), British freethinking Radical journalist whose advocacy of almost every extreme cause earned him numerous prison sentences. With his publications, *eg*, his periodical *The Republican*, he battled above all for press freedom.

CARLISLE, FREDERICK HOWARD, 9th Earl of (5th of 3rd creation) (1748–1825), British politician and one of North's three commissioners who treated unsuccessfully with the Americans (1778). Though a friend of Fox, Carlisle gave general support to Pitt's administration after the outbreak of the French war in 1793.

CARLISLE, GEORGE WILLIAM FREDERICK HOWARD, 10th Earl of (6th of 3rd creation) (1802–64), British politician. As Lord Morpeth, he was chief secretary for Ireland in Melbourne's second ministry (1835–41). He piloted through the Commons three important Irish measures, relating to tithes, municipal reform, and the Poor Law.

CARLISLE PROVINCE, grant by King Charles I of Britain to the Earl of Carlisle, confirming proprietary rights over the Caribbean islands lying between 10° and 20° N latitude (1627). Settlers brought to the islands opposed Carlisle's interest and the province passed to royal control (1661).

CARLISTS, supporters of the claims of Don Carlos (1788–1855) and his heirs to the throne of Spain, who engaged in unsuccessful political opposition and open civil war against successive Spanish governments. The death of Ferdinand VII (1833) was the signal for a rebellion in favour of his brother, Don Carlos, against the regency for his daughter, Isabella, whose abdication (1868) was followed by another rebellion (1870–5). This also was suppressed, although Carlist political activity continued till Franco's advent to power. The Carlists, centred largely in the Basque provinces and Navarre, opposed liberalism and centralization with tradition, the Church, royal absolutism, and regionalism. Although Carlism had clerical and some aristocratic support, it remained largely a rural movement without any influence in the army or towns and was unable to expand effectively from its northern mountains.

CARLIST WARS (1833–9, 1870–5), fought in favour of the Spanish Carlist pretenders, included more local guerrilla activity than pitched battles. In both wars the Carlists' strength was in Navarre and the Basque provinces of the north, although even here the larger towns, including Bilbao, held out for the government in Madrid. In the first war the Carlist army, led by Zumalacárregui, had 20,000 effectives in the north and was successful there until the regular army, financed by Anglo-French loans, was brought against it in strength. An attempted march on Madrid failed (1837) and showed that Carlism had no real appeal in the rest of Spain. At the end of the first war the Carlists gained no more than the confirmation of the northern provinces' privileges, but Carlist sentiment stayed alive there till the outbreak of the second war, which followed a similar pattern to the first and led to Carlist defeat.

CARLOS MARIA DE LOS DOLORES, DON ('CHARLES VII') (1848–1909), grandson of the first Carlist pretender. In the Second Carlist War he failed to seize the Spanish throne.

CARLOS MARIA ISIDRO, DON ('CHARLES V') (1788–1855), brother of Ferdinand VII and pretender to the Spanish Crown at the time of the First Carlist War.

CARLOWITZ, PEACE OF (1699), consisting of four separate treaties, three signed in the devastated town of Carlowitz between Austria, Poland, Venice, and the defeated Turks, with whom Russia signed a truce, confirmed in 1700 at Constantinople. By the peace, which marked the first stage in

Turkish withdrawal from Europe, the Porte suffered a considerable loss of territory and prestige. Venice gained the Morea, which she had conquered in the late war, Poland won back Podolia and part of the Ukraine, and the Habsburgs received Transylvania and all Hungary except the Banat of Temesvar. Russia received Azov, although she got no access to the Black Sea. The peace also marked the last territorial expansion of Poland and the last occasion on which Poland participated in a war against the Turkish infidel. The terms of these treaties were superseded within a generation, so that in retrospect they constituted a truce in the eastern question rather than a permanent settlement.

CARLSBAD DECREES (1819), Metternich's answer to the increasing revolutionary and nationalist activity in the German states, which had culminated in the assassination of the reactionary playwright Kotzebue. After ensuring the agreement of King Frederick William III of Prussia, the Austrian chancellor persuaded representatives of nine German states to accept the decrees at Carlsbad in Aug. These suppressed the student *Burschenchaften*, installed inspectors in the universities, increased press censorship, and set up a commission at Mainz to investigate revolutionary movements. The Diet of the German Confederation ratified the decress (Sept.). Germany was turned over to counter-revolution and the liberals were imprisoned or driven underground.

CARLSTADT, ANDREAS RUDOLF BODENSTEIN VON (1480–1541), German scholar who instigated the reformation of the Church in Wittenberg (1522). The mass and religious images were abolished, and in the outbreak of violent iconoclasm which followed Carlstadt became associated with a group of extreme reformers from Zwickau. Later, he gave up his academic career for a pastoral life and joined the peasants' revolt in Franconia (1525).

CARLTON CLUB, founded (1831) as a political centre in Britain for the Tory Party in response to Whig dominance. It enabled the building up of local Tory associations to organize the registration of voters necessary to electoral success in a period of limited franchise.

CARLTON HOUSE, in London, was built in the 18th cent. and became the home of George IV, as Prince of Wales. As such it was the centre of political opposition to King George III.

CARLTON HOUSE, two Hudson's Bay Co. posts. The first (1794), on the Saskatchewan river, was removed to a site near Duck Lake, on the North Saskatchewan river, and later became a Royal Canadian Mounted Police post. It was destroyed during the North West Rebellion (1885). The other Carlton House was built (1795) on the south bank of the Upper Assiniboine river and abandoned in 1821.

CARLYLE, THOMAS (1795–1881), Scottish essayist, philosopher, and moralist, who exerted an immense influence in mid-19th-cent. Britain. After studying mathematics and law at Edinburgh University, he became a schoolmaster in Scotland. His articles in the 1820s (especially in the *Edinburgh Review* and the *London Magazine*) and his *Life of Schiller* (1825) helped to popularize German literature in England. In 1834 he settled in London and published his spiritual autobiography, *Sartor Resartus*, putting forward a romantic and anti-rationalistic philosophy. His fame began with his *French Revolution* (1837), a romantic epic story rather than a history, reminiscent of Michelet. Carlyle's influence as a social prophet was at its height in the 1840s. It was based particularly on *Chartism* (1840) and *Past and Present* (1843), and was acknowledged by Dickens, Thackeray, Kingsley, Mrs Gaskell, and many others. He coined the phrase 'condition of England question', and the concept of the 'two nations' later found in Disraeli's novels. Carlyle's public

lectures (1837–40), published as *Heroes, Hero-Worship and the Heroic in History* (1841), elaborated the theme that human progress was the achievement of great men or heroes and this theme was found again in his *Cromwell* (1845) and *Frederick the Great* (1857–65). At the end of the 19th cent., when a reaction against Carlyle set in, it was based on the potential dangers and distortions of his teaching, an approach which is itself a distortion because it ignored his relevance to, and influence on, his contemporaries.

CARMATHIANS (QARAMITA), movement of subversion and revolt arising in Lower Iraq after the servile war of the Zanj (869–83). After 899, the Qaramita established in north-east Arabia, *ie*, in Al-Ahsa and in Bahrayn, an independent regime which opposed the caliphate at Baghdad for more than 100 years. The movement was at its height under Abu Tahir Sulayman (b. Adb al-Qays al-Jannabi, 914–43). Qaramita forces cut the pilgrim routes to the Hijaz and captured Mecca (930), the Black Stone of the Ka'ba being now taken to Al-Ahsa and not restored to Mecca until 951. The Carmathians seem at first to have favoured the rise of the Fatimids, but later turned against them and did much, after 969, to thwart the extension of Fatimid control into Syria.

CARMICHAEL, STOKELY (1941–), US civil rights leader, who grew up in New York city, became active in the civil rights movement, and gained notoriety as a Black Power activist.

CARNAC, region in the Morbihan department of southern Brittany, famous for its stone alignments made up of nearly 3000 individual standing stones, or menhirs, which may be dated to the early second millennium BC. They are almost 6·4 kms long, and among the oldest surviving architectural monuments of north-western Europe. Carnac is also remarkable for the quantity and variety of megalithic tombs concentrated in and around it, some of which are decorated in an art-style with carved symbols.

CARNARVON, HENRY HOWARD MOLYNEUX HERBERT, 9th Earl of (4th of 3rd creation) (1831–1900), British statesman, who was devoted to the ideals of just imperial rule, but opposed to the advance of democracy in Britain. As colonial secretary under Lord Derby (1866–7) he introduced the British North America Act, and under Disraeli (1874–8) sponsored the abolition of slavery in the Gold Coast Protectorate (1874). His defence of native rights and encouragement of federation on the Canadian pattern in South Africa led to clashes with the Boers and the subsequent annexation of the Transvaal, of which he approved. He retired in protest against Disraeli's abandonment of neutrality in the Russo-Turkish dispute (1878). He opposed the Reform Bills of 1867 and 1884, asserting that they would increase class warfare. On the return of a Conservative government in 1885 he became lord-lieutenant of Ireland, where he favoured pacification. Following a controversial meeting with Parnell he resigned and devoted himself to supporting the Imperial Federation League.

CARNATIC, THE. The term properly refers to the area occupied by the Kanarese-speaking people or Karnatikas, which is roughly coincident with the modern Indian state of Mysore. In modern historical record, however, it has come to mean the eastern coastal strip (the Tamil country) as far as Nellore. This usage probably began with the conquest of this area by the Vijayanagar kings in the 14th cent., whose power was based on the real Carnatic.

In the 18th cent. the coastal Carnatic was a dependency of Hyderabad within the Mughal empire. Succession disputes led to a clash between the British and French East India companies. The English candidate, Muhammad Ali, succeeded largely owing to the exploits of Clive. The Mughal Carnatic remained an ally of the company, its court a centre of financial intrigue, until 1801, when Wellesley took over the state and pensioned the ruler. Nominal sovereignty ended in 1853, the title Prince of Arcot being conferred on the head of the family later.

CARNEGIE, ANDREW (1835–1919), US industrialist and philanthropist, whose career is often regarded as the prototype of the modern American success story. His family emigrated from Scotland to Allegheny, PA (1848), and he worked as a bobbin boy, messenger, and telegraph operator. Becoming private secretary to Thomas A. Scott, of the Pennsylvania Railroad (1853), and superintendent of the Pittsburgh division of the railroad (1860), Carnegie was responsible for a number of innovations, including the introduction of Pullman sleeping cars. During the American Civil War he helped to organize the Union telegraph and military transportation systems. Resigning from the railroad in 1865, he turned his attention to iron, oil, and other business interests. In 1868 he built the Union Iron Mills at Pittsburgh and in 1873, after observing the British experience, began to specialize in steel at the J. Edgar Thomson Steel Works, then the largest mill in the US. During the remainder of the 19th cent. Carnegie made his company a model for heavy industry. His success in controlling supplies of raw materials and transportation lines, his willingness to accept innovations in techniques and machinery, and his flair in choosing managers such as Henry C. Frick and Charles M. Schwab, resulted in a vast vertically integrated industrial complex. He sold his interests (1901) to a group headed by the banker J. P. Morgan for over $400 million and these became the basis of the giant US Steel Corporation. An articulate exponent of laissez-faire and champion of the American democratic system, Carnegie often contributed to reviews and magazines. His book, *Triumphant Democracy* (1886), stressed the superiority of republican over monarchical government, and the famous essay on 'Wealth' published in the *North American Review* (June 1889) set out his notions of the moral superiority of acquiring riches and the social responsibility of the wealthy. On retiring from business he put this 'gospel of wealth' into practice and distributed his fortune for the public benefit, his benefactions reflecting a philosophical commitment to self-improvement. His support to public libraries in both the US and Scotland and his many endowed trusts and institutions, particularly the Carnegie Endowment for International Peace (1910) and the Carnegie Corporation (1911), have established for him a reputation for philanthropy that has equalled his earlier renown as a steel magnate.

Burton J. Hendrick, *The Life of Andrew Carnegie*, 2 vols (New York, 1932).   MW

CARNET B (1914), a list of trade union leaders and revolutionary politicians whom the French government planned to arrest on the outbreak of war. It was feared that they would attempt to sabotage France's mobilization by a general strike. In the event, the working-class movement rallied to the cause of war, and *Carnet B* was not used.

CARNOCK, ARTHUR NICOLSON, 1st Baron (1849–1928), British diplomat, who supported the French and Russian ententes. He travelled widely in the diplomatic service in the 1870s, serving in Berlin, Peking, Constantinople, Cairo, Teheran, and Athens. He was appointed minister at Tangier (1895), experienced the tensions leading to the first Moroccan crises, and advocated a policy of agreement with France, whom he steadfastly supported against Germany at the Algeciras conference, where he secured the treaty of Algeciras. On his transfer to St Petersburg he helped to negotiate the Anglo-Russian Entente (1907). As under-secretary of state for foreign affairs in 1916 he followed Sir Edward Grey in wishing to dissipate the Russophobia of 19th-cent. British policy. After Sarajevo (1914) he was active with Grey in proposing an international conference to discuss the Serbian crisis, and then in recommending mobilization of the army and navy.

CARNOT, LAZARE HIPPOLYTE (1801–88), French educationalist and politician, who became an active St Simonian journalist and republican deputy (1839). Prominent in both educational and political reform movements, he was briefly minister of education under the Second Republic (1848). He twice refused to take a deputy's oath to Napoleon III (1850, 1857), but eventually took his seat (1864). After the fall of the empire, he was a leading republican deputy and life senator. He undertook considerable historical research, and published memoirs of his father (1861–4).

CARNOT, LAZARE NICOLAS (1753–1823), French army engineer and 'the organizer of victory' for France in the Revolutionary Wars. He was the member of the Committee of Public Safety, with general control over the conduct of the war. His genius was shown in feeding, equipping, and training the conscript army of over a million and in the strategic concepts he imposed on the revolutionary armies. He escaped the fall and execution of the other Jacobins (1794) to become one of the first Directors (1795), although his advocacy of peace led to false accusations of royalism in the *Fructidor coup* (1797) and his flight from the country. Returning under the Consulate, he acted as minister of war (1800–1) and later of the interior in the '100 Days', an action which led to his exile under the restored Bourbon, Louis XVIII.

CARNOT, MARIE FRANÇOIS SADI (1837–94), French statesman and engineer. In the war with Prussia he served under Freycinet and as Préfet of Havre. He opposed the peace treaties and retired to local government. When elected to the Chamber (1877) he served first as under-secretary (1878–80) and then as minister of public works (1880–1). After moving to finance (1885–6), he was selected as a compromise candidate for the presidency (1887), but his attempts while in office to develop national unity were cut short by his assassination in Lyons by the anarchist Caserio.

CARNOT, NICOLAS LEONARD SADI (1796–1832), French physicist and pioneer of thermodynamics. He belonged to a prominent political family, his father, Lazare, being involved in the Revolution, and his nephew becoming a president of France during the Third Republic. Carnot published in 1824 *Réflexions sur la Puissance Motrice de Feu*. This remarkable study of the efficiency of devices for turning heat into work had on the one hand important practical consequences for the design of the prime movers of the Industrial Revolution, on the other it displayed a breadth and generality that led directly to the formulation of the Second Law of Thermodynamics by Clausius and Kelvin.

CARNUNTUM (mod. Patronell), Roman legionary fortress with an associated town on the middle Danube and on an important trade route from Italy to the Baltic, which flourished (early 1st cent. AD–late 4th). Some important remains survive.

CAROL I (1839–1914), Prince (1866–81) and King (*reg.* 1881–1914) of united Rumania. Carol I was the second son of Prince Carl Anton of Hohenzollern-Sigmaringen, onetime chancellor of Prussia and head of the Catholic branch of the Prussian dynasty. Carol became a candidate for the Rumanian throne after the overthrow of Alexandru Ion Cuza and was proclaimed prince by a plebiscite on 20 April 1866. Keenly interested in the affairs of state, Carol enjoyed a strong position under the constitution promulgated upon his election. He led Rumania into the Russo-Turkish War (1877–8), from which it gained its independence at the Congress of Berlin. In March 1881 Rumania became a kingdom and Carol its first king. Carol extended his personal link with Germany to the state he ruled in 1883 by making Rumania the fourth partner to the Triple Alliance. When war broke out in 1914 Carol urged his nation to honour its alliance, but his advice was overwhelmingly rejected in the decisive Crown Council of 3 Aug. 1914. Carol's unswerving sense of duty and appetite for work distinguished his reign.

CAROL II (1893–1953), King of Rumania (*reg.* 1930–40), and eldest son of Ferdinand and Marie. A headstrong youth, he resented Ion I. C. Bratianu's hold over his father and the consequent weakness of the Crown. He married Princess Helen of Greece in 1921, but soon began an affair with Mme Elena Lupescu. In 1925 he went abroad with her, and when Ferdinand demanded his return without her, he renounced his right to the throne. Ferdinand's death in 1927 made Carol's renunciation a political issue. The National Peasant Party charged the Liberals with thwarting a reconciliation between father and son and managing the succession for political advantage. After much equivocation and intrigue, Carol returned in 1930, largely on his own initiative. Maniu's National Peasants welcomed him, but on the understanding that Mme Lupescu remained abroad. However, she took up residence at the palace and Maniu resigned. With his resignation political power began to pass to Carol. In the early years of his reign he veiled his authority behind various governments while seeking to resolve Rumania's economic problems and maintain its traditional foreign policy. About 1934, as his authoritarian inclinations emerged and conditions worsened, Carol began to rely on the right. A skilful but short-sighted politician, he steadily undermined the parties and laid the basis for a royal dictatorship, which was confirmed (1938) by the promulgation of a corporatist constitution and the formation of the Front of National Rebirth. The deterioration of the international situation proved Carol's undoing. He chose to enter the German orbit and was compelled to replace his corporatist state with a totalitarian one in which fascist elements shared power. Soviet, Hungarian, and Bulgarian annexations of Rumanian lands in 1940, in which Rumania acquiesced, destroyed Carol's fragile legitimacy. He was forced to abdicate and with his *camarilla* fled the country before the Iron Guard.

CAROLINA PROPRIETORS. English promoters obtained a patent (1629) from Charles I to land between the 31st and 36th parallels and from coast to coast. They planned to establish a colony with a feudal system of government, but the scheme failed and in the early 18th cent. North and South Carolina became Crown colonies.

CAROLINE, AMELIA ELIZABETH, Queen (1768–1821), daughter of Ferdinand, Duke of Brunswick and wife of the Prince of Wales, later George IV, whom she married in 1795. Soon after the birth of their daughter, Princess Charlotte, in the next year, they separated. The king's attempt (1820) to divorce the queen on the grounds of her misconduct was abandoned in face of violent public hostility, which added to the disrepute of the monarchy.

CAROLINE AFFAIR, Canadian–American quarrel which endangered Anglo-American relations. An Anglo-Canadian force under Capt. Andrew Drew crossed the Niagara river and seized (29 Dec. 1837) the American steamer *Caroline*, which had been ferrying supplies to Canadian rebels on Navy Island, above Niagara Falls. Those on board were captured, the ship fired and cut adrift. One American was killed and the ship sank before reaching the Falls. It was asserted, however, that the steamer was sent over the Falls with people on board. Outraged Americans demanded redress and the US government requested reparation and an apology from Britain. Disguised Americans boarded, looted, and burnt the Canadian steamer *Sir Robert Peel* on the St Lawrence river in retaliation (May 1838). Alexander McLeod a Canadian, was arrested in New York (Nov. 1840) and accused of murder and arson through the destruction of the *Caroline*. Palmerston, the British foreign secretary, threatened war if McLeod was executed, but McLeod was acquitted. No formal apology was proffered by Britain, but the ambas-

sador, Lord Ashburton, expressed his regret at British handling of the affair.

CAROLINE OF ANSBACH (1682–1737), Queen of George II of England, whom she married in 1705. Her support of Walpole and his policy of economy and peace kept him in office after her husband's accession (1727). She was a patron of learning and literature.

CAROLINE ISLANDS in the Pacific, inhabited by light-skinned Micronesians, were sighted in 1565. Spanish priests (settled 1686) were driven out in 1733. Whalers, beach-combers, and traders moved in after 1820. American Protestant missionaries (Ponape, 1852, Kusaie, 1857) were initially frustrated by epidemics but with the arrival of the printing press Christianity made rapid strides, notably at Truk (1879). In 1877 Spain, Germany, and Britain agreed to free trade. In 1885 (after a brief disagreement) a papal arbitration awarded the group to Spain, and the Marshalls to Germany, a move bitterly contested by the islanders, notably at Ponape (1890). The group later passed to Germany (1899), Japan (1914), and the US (1945), which now (1970) administers it as a UN trust territory.

CARONDELET, DON FRANCISCO LUIS HECTOR, Baron de (*c.* 1748–1807), Spanish colonial governor, born in Flanders. Carondelet entered the service of Spain and was governor of San Salvador, then of LA and west FL (1791); there he was particularly concerned to contain the spread of American influence. A fleet of Spanish gunboats was launched on the Mississippi and military posts established in territory disputed with the US. Indian tribes were incited to attack American frontiersmen and attempts were made to persuade Kentucky to leave the US. Carondelet directed the building (1794) of the canal called after him, which links New Orleans with the sea via Lake Pontchartrain. He was appointed governor in Equador (1797).

CAROTHERS, WALLACE HUME (1896–1937), US industrial chemist, who started (1928) a research programme at the firm of E. I. du Pont de Nemours on the preparation and properties of polymers, organic compounds of high molecular weight. The first major result was the discovery, with J. A. Nieuwland (1878–1936), of neoprene, the first commercially successful synthetic rubber, first marketed in 1932. Later, Carothers developed the synthetic fibre known as nylon. The Second World War stimulated the production and use of these important materials.

CARP, PETRE (1837–1918), Rumanian politician, founder of the *Junimea* (youth) society, and chief protagonist of Rumania's participation in the First World War on the side of the Triple Alliance.

CARPETBAGGERS, name applied in the US to Northerners who moved into the defeated South after the Civil War (1861–5) and played a prominent part in the political and economic reconstruction of the Southern states. The name is derogatory, implying that such men could carry all their belongings in a carpetbag, a popular form of hand luggage of the period. Carpetbaggers were often accused of corruption, extravagance, and dishonesty during their control of Southern state governments, and of economic exploitation of the defeated South. However, many of them had a genuine concern for the freed Negro, and made notable contributions to the life of their adopted states in the decade after 1865. They occupied many important posts, including several state governorships, during the period of radical reconstruction, but their influence declined in the 1870s, as the Southern white 'redeemers' regained control of the state governments.

CARPI, BATTLE OF (1701), defeat in northern Italy of the French forces of Marshal Catinat, who was outmanœuvred by Prince Eugène of Savoy and his imperialist army in the War of the Spanish Succession.

CARR, THOMAS (1839–1917), bishop of Galway, then archbishop of Melbourne (1886). A calm man of warmth and great administrative ability, most of his life was given to building churches and schools in a rapidly growing archdiocese, and to asserting the claims of Catholic education to state finance. Towards the end of his life, he fully supported his more vehement coadjutor, Abp Mannix.

CARRACK, the first type of full-rigged ship of three or four masts. It was extensively used throughout western Europe in the latter half of the 15th and first half of the 16th cent. and formed an important element in Portuguese trade with India. Without it, the long-distance voyages of discovery would have been more precarious.

CARRANZA, BARTOLOME DE, cardinal (1503–76), archbishop of Toledo (1558–76), who rose from poor *hidalgo* parentage through the Dominican order to become professor of theology at the College of San Gregorio in Valladolid. He was sent in 1545 as a Spanish delegate to the Council of Trent, where he gained a great theological reputation. He was later arrested by the Inquisition in mysterious circumstances after less than a year in his archbishopric (1559), and imprisoned for 17 years.

CARRANZA, VENUSTIANO (1859–1920), Mexican revolutionary leader who attempted to unite all factions following the murder of President Francisco I. Madero, and de facto president of Mexico after 1915 and later legal president (1917–20). Carranza, member of a wealthy landowning family, was born at Cuatro Ciénegas, Coahuila. Under the dictatorship of Gen. Porfirio Díaz, he was senator from Coahuila (1901–10). He vigorously supported Madero's revolt (1910) and became governor of Coahuila (1911). After Gen. Victoriano Huerta's murder of Madero (1913), Carranza proclaimed the 'constitutionalist revolution' with himself as 'first chief'. Huerta's overthrow (1914) was followed by open revolt led by Emiliano Zapata in the south and Pancho Villa in the north, who both refused to recognize Carranza as 'first chief'. By 1917, Carranza had secured his position as president.

The US was slow to recognize him and made demands which he could not accept; meanwhile he consolidated his popularity. Revolutionary leaders from all parts of Mexico forced the constitution of 1917 on the regime, despite Carranza's objections to its social reform provisions. When he failed to support the candidacy of Gen. Álvaro Obregón, who had brought him to power, Obregón drove Carranza from the capital. He was murdered at Tlaxcalantongo, Puebla, en route to Veracruz, thereby terminating the overt divisions within the revolutionary leadership.

CARRERA, RAFAEL (1814–65), president and dictator of Guatemala (1840–65). He led the Conservative revolt against the Central American Federation (1839), which had been dominated by Liberals. Though illiterate and of mixed (*mestizo*) peasant origins himself, Carrera was supported by the white aristocracy of Church and *hacienda*. As dictator of Guatemala, he influenced developments in other Central American states. He made war against El Salvador (1850–3, 1863) to prevent the Liberals there from coming to power. His aims were to maintain the Church in its customary political and economic position and to prevent the reunification of Central America.

CARRHAE, BATTLE OF (53 BC), Roman defeat in Mesopotamia (mod. Charran) which ended Crassus' invasion of Parthia. Crassus' unacclimatized army, deficient in cavalry, was shot to pieces by the Parthian mounted archers, although the latter were outnumbered three to one. Crassus died, and of his 44,000 men, 34,000 were killed or captured. The battle marks a turning point in military history as the first great defeat of the developed Roman legionary army. The death of Crassus, by leaving Pompey and Caesar face to face, had a profound influence on Roman politics.

CARROLL, CHARLES (1737–1832), American political leader and signatory of the Declaration of Independence. After being educated in French Jesuit colleges he returned to his estate in MD (1765). He was a patriot leader during the American Revolution and tried with Franklin and others to persuade the Canadians to join the revolutionary cause. He was a member of the Continental Congress (1776–79) and of the US Senate (1789–92). He was a staunch Federalist and said to be the wealthiest American of his time. Carroll assisted in the development of the Baltimore and Ohio Railroad and presided over its board of directors (1828).

CARROLL, SIR JAMES (1853–1926), Maori orator and politician, who was a member of the NZ Liberal ministries (1891–1912), and acting prime minister (1909, 1911). He sought to defend remaining Maori lands and to promote Maori local government.

CARROLL, JOHN, archbishop (1735–1815), first Catholic bishop in the US. He was educated in Flanders, ordained as a priest (1769), and then returned to his birthplace, MD (1774). He was an active patriot and worked for religious liberty. Carroll founded Georgetown University and was made Apb of Baltimore, seeking to free the American Catholic Church from European influence.

CARSON, EDWARD HENRY CARSON, Baron (1854–1935), Irish politician and lawyer who, as leader of the Irish Unionists (1910–21) in the House of Commons, vehemently opposed Home Rule. He was largely responsible for the creation of the Ulster Volunteer Force (1912) and brought Ireland to the brink of civil war (1914) before accepting the compromise solution of the exclusion of the Ulster counties from the Home Rule Bill.

CARSON, CHRISTOPHER ('Kit') (1809–68), one of the great US frontier heroes, and personification of the Wild West tradition. As hunter, guide, and Indian fighter in the American south-west, he was associated with John C. Fremont in CA in the 1840s, fought in the Mexican war, and on the Union side in the American Civil War, and served as a US Indian agent (1853–60, 1865–8).

CARTAGENA, Spanish settlement on the mainland of Central America. It was captured by Drake during the unofficial war between England and Spain (1586). After devastating its buildings, Drake extracted a ransom of 107,000 ducats before withdrawing. The incident helped to strengthen Philip II's conviction that an invasion of England was necessary to protect Spain's imperial might.

CARTEL DES GAUCHES, alliance of left-wing parties which was victorious in the French election of 1924. The victory led to the formation of a Radical government with socialist support under Herriot (1924–5), but this fell because of economic difficulties and the hostility of financial circles (the '*mur d'argent*'). There were further cartel governments under Painlevé, Briand, and Herriot, but a new financial crisis led to the formation of a government of national unity under the conservative Poincaré (1926).

CARTERET, SIR GEORGE (1610–80), British royalist and colonial proprietor. He was born in the island of Jersey, which he made a royalist stronghold and refuge during the Civil War. He was one of the Carolina proprietors who received a grant of land between the Hudson and Delaware rivers, which was named New Jersey in his honour. After his death it was sold to the Quakers.

CARTERET, PHILIP (1639–82), first colonial governor of NJ. His governorship was rife with controversy over quit-rents and over Dutch claims to NJ as part of New Netherlands.

CARTERET, PHILIP (d. 1796), British navigator, who, while commanding the second ship in Samuel Wallis's expedition to the southern hemisphere (1766), discovered Pitcairn Island and other small islands, one of which bears his name.

CARTESIANISM, philosophy deriving from the work of Descartes, fashionable at the turn of 17th-18th cents, by which it was maintained that all the problems of the universe could be solved by mathematical analysis. Springing from the discoveries of mathematicians such as Copernicus, Kepler, and Galileo, and translated into philosophy by Descartes, Spinoza, Bayle, Newton, and Leibniz, the new intellectual attitudes amounted to a fundamental revaluation of the world. The evolution of new aspects of mathematics— eg, logarithms, trigonometry, algebra, calculus—and the invention of precision instruments such as the balance, barometer, thermometer, microscope, air-pump, and telescope, together with the development of experiments, gave rise to a knowledge of laws governing the universe.

CARTHAGE, on the coast of Tunisia, north-west of modern Tunis, one of the most powerful and prosperous city-states of antiquity, and finally Rome's greatest enemy. Founded by Phoenicians from Tyre, probably slightly later than the traditional date of 814 BC, it was at first one of many Phoenician settlements on the coasts of northern Africa, western Sicily, Sardinia, and Spain, designed to provide anchorages for ships trading for metals in the western Mediterranean. During the 6th cent. Carthage became leader of the western Phoenicians and successfully defended her position in wars with the Greeks of Sicily during the 5th and 4th cents, acquiring meanwhile inland territory covering much of modern Tunisia.

Carthage's prosperity rested on its monopoly of sea-borne trade in precious metals from Spain and West Africa. Enormous profits enabled it to control, with a small population, a large empire through mercenary soldiers. Its system of government was oligarchic, with annually changing magistrates and a council of wealthy citizens, and many attempts to set up a 'tyranny' failed. Carthage's religion was notorious for its widespread use of human sacrifice. Its art was undistinguished and derivative from Phoenician, Egyptian, Greek, and Etruscan patterns. The long struggle with Rome, the Punic Wars, began in 264. In the first Carthage lost its naval supremacy and possessions in Sicily and, soon after its end (241), Sardinia. Hamilcar then built up a new empire in Spain from which at the start of the second war (218) Hannibal invaded Italy and nearly overwhelmed Rome. But Rome's superior resources told and this war's end (202) saw Carthage reduced to virtual dependence on Rome. A modest attempt to assert some independence ended with its destruction (146). Carthaginian civilization had considerable effect in beginning the urbanization of parts of North Africa.

It was refounded as a Roman colony by Augustus (29 BC) and rapidly grew to be the largest city in the west after Rome, becoming the administrative, economic, and cultural centre of North Africa and playing an important part in the spread of Christianity in the western Mediterranean. After falling to the Vandals in AD 439, it was reconquered by the Byzantines in 533, but was occupied by the Arabs in 698. A few remains survive.

B. H. Warmington, *Carthage*, revised ed. (London and New York, 1969).   BHW

CARTHUSIAN ORDER, semi-eremitic order, observing strict silence, founded by St Bruno in 1084 at Chartreuse (anglicized as Charterhouse) in the French Alps. Each monk lives in separate quarters, meeting the others only in chapel and chapter. The order was much respected for its intense spirituality. Although relatively undisturbed by historical events, the order was temporarily divided at the time of the Great Schism (1378–1409), and suffered persecution during both the English Reformation and the French Revolution. Anti-clericalism in France in the 20th cent. led to the order's expulsion from Chartreuse (1901–40).

CARTIER, SIR GEORGE-ÉTIENNE, Baronet (1814–73), Canadian political leader. Involvement in the Rebellion of 1837 led Cartier to be exiled in the US for a year. He was elected to the House of Assembly (1848), where his two main interests were the promotion of railways and the protection of French-Canadian rights. He became leader of the French Canadians in the Conservative Party (1857), and as a member of 'the great coalition' he won them over to the idea of the confederation of British North America (1867). Cartier helped negotiate government purchase of the Hudson's Bay Co.'s lands (1869). His reputation suffered through his involvement in the 'Pacific Scandal' shortly before his death.

CARTIER, JACQUES (1492–1557), pioneer of Canadian exploration. On being appointed 'Captain and Pilot for the King', Francis I of France, Cartier sailed from his native St Malo (1534) on a voyage of exploration along the east coast of Canada. He visited Labrador, and proceeding south to Gaspe Bay took possession of it in the name of France. He returned to France with the sons of the Indian chief Donnacona and in the following year used them as interpreters on a voyage up the St Lawrence river, when he visited villages on the sites of Quebec and Montreal. Cartier returned (1541) as the advance party of the Roberval expedition, the first French effort to colonize Canada. A fortified post was established along the St Lawrence river (near present-day Quebec), but abandoned two years later, as were attempts at colonization and further exploration during Cartier's lifetime.

CARTIER, JOHN (1733–1802), governor of Fort William in Bengal (Dec. 1769–April 1772), formed (1765–7) with Verelst the link between the second governorship of Clive and that of Warren Hastings. These years were politically uneventful, but they saw the revival of administrative abuses suppressed by Clive and a heartless disregard of the famine which swept Bengal in 1769–70, carrying off a third of the inhabitants.

CARTRIDGES, GREASED, issued to Indian sepoys when the Enfield rifle was introduced in 1856. The troops refused to use them when, it was rumoured, they were lubricated by a mixture of pigs' and cows' fat, the use of which offended their religious susceptibilities. This was skilfully used as a pretext for the 1857 Mutiny.

CARTWRIGHT, EDMUND (1743–1823), British inventor of the power loom. While rector of Goadby Marwood a chance meeting (1784) with Arkwright awakened his talent for invention and within a year he had patented a power-driven loom (1785). Further inventions followed, but material success eluded him until the government granted him a pension of £10,000 (1809).

CARTWRIGHT, JOHN (1740–1824), a leading radical, who played a prominent role in the Society for Constitutional Information and by founding the Hampden clubs helped to keep the cause of parliamentary reform alive during the Napoleonic Wars. In his pamphlet 'Take Your Choice' (1776), Cartwright outlined a programme for reform from which he never wavered. It went as far as the most advanced political opinion up to and beyond the Chartists, demanding annual parliaments, the payment of MPs, a secret ballot, and adult manhood suffrage. He was still propounding these views in the periodical *The Black Dwarf* in 1818.

CARTWRIGHT, SIR RICHARD JOHN (1835–1912), Canadian statesman, who was elected as a Conservative to the

Canadian House of Assembly (1863), but left the party over the 'Pacific Scandal' (1873). He was finance minister in the liberal Mackenzie government (1873–8) and minister of trade under Sir Wilfrid Laurier (1896). He was elevated to the senate (1904) and was government leader there from 1909.

CARTWRIGHT, THOMAS (1535–1603), English Presbyterian, lecturer, and professor at Cambridge, who was deprived (1570) of his post for opposing episcopacy and the Elizabethan settlement. He helped to prepare the *Admonition to Parliament* (1572), which involved him in theological controversy with Whitgift, and was twice imprisoned for his outspoken Puritanism.

CARUS, M. AURELIUS (*reg.* AD 282–3), Roman Emperor, who, after appointing his sons Carinus and Numerianus as Caesars, invaded Persia, where he died on a campaign, allegedly being struck by lightning. Carinus succeeded in the west, but the eastern army acclaimed Diocletian as emperor.

CARVALHO, HENRIQUE DIAS DE (1845–1909), Portuguese soldier, explorer, and first governor of Lunda District in north-eastern Angola. He travelled (1884–8) from the Atlantic coast via Malange to the court of the Muata Yamvo, hereditary ruler of the Lunda empire. The empire was afterwards partitioned between Portugal and the Congo Free State (later Belgian Congo). An account of this journey was published in Lisbon in 1895.

CARVER, GEORGE WASHINGTON (*c.* 1864–1943), US Negro educator and agricultural expert. The son of slave parents, he taught at Tuskegee Institute, AL (1896–1943), and helped the diversification of Southern agriculture by his work in developing soy beans, sweet potatoes, and other crops.

CARVER, JOHN (1576–1621), first governor of Plymouth colony. He was a London businessman, who transferred his fortune to Leyden when he became a member of the Pilgrim congregation there. As one of the leaders who arranged the financing of the *Mayflower* venture, he hired the ship and sailed with the Pilgrims. He was the leader of the group who decided to settle in New England rather than on the Hudson, and was one of the first to step ashore at Plymouth. As first governor, he was active in organizing the colony and made a treaty with the Indian, Massasoit (March 1621).

CARYSTUS, city of south-east Euboea in Greece. Sacked by the Persians in 490, it Medized in 480 and was the first city to be forced into the Delian League (*c.* 474).

CAS ROYAUX, serious crimes in France *eg, lèse-majesté,* forgery of the royal seal, sedition, private warfare, highway robbery, adultery, murder, incest, bankruptcy, sacrilege, usury, debasement of the coinage—which under the French judicial system of the *ancien régime* had to be tried by royal judges, in the first instance in the bailiwicks and on appeal by the *parlement* of Paris.

CASA DE CONTRATACIÓN, or House of Trade, the principal body charged with the organization and regulation of Spanish colonial commerce. The *Casa* was originally created by Ferdinand and Isabella to govern the Spanish Indies from Seville (1503), under the leadership of Bb Juan Rodríguez de Fonseca. Trade with the colonies was required to pass through the customs house at Seville. The *Casa* dispensed licences for all shipping in both directions, as well as for migration to the colonies. It collected duties on trade and received the precious metals accruing to the Spanish government. In trade matters the *Casa* was also a law court. It was first moved to Cadiz (1718) and finally abolished (1790).

CASA DI SAN GIORGIO, Genoese association of state creditors formed in 1407 to administer the public debt. It also acted as a bank, and in the course of the 15th cent. developed a variety of other functions, *eg,* it administered Genoese territories outside Italy, ran the salt monopoly, collected taxes and customs duties, and controlled the mint.

CASA MATA, PLAN OF, the revolt against Emperor Augustín I (Iturbide) of Mexico (Feb. 1823), headed by his Spanish confidant, Gen. José Antonio Echávarri. Gen. Santa Anna had rebelled at Veracruz in order to establish a republic and Casa Mata was an attempt by the army leadership and the masonic lodges to restore the powers of the congress, rendering the emperor powerless. After losing the support of his army officers, Iturbide resigned (March 1823) and went into voluntary exile.

CASABLANCA CONFERENCE (Jan. 1943) marked a turning point in the Second World War, although this was scarcely evident at the time. The battles of Stalingrad and Alamein had been won and American troops had landed in north-west Africa to join Montgomery's forces advancing from the east. The main participants at the conference were Churchill and Roosevelt, and their chiefs of staff (a conference with Stalin having proved impossible, as he would not leave the Soviet Union). Strategic decisions were reached with relative ease, since the immediate objective was to finish the war in North Africa, to bomb German industry, and prepare for a second front later in the year; meanwhile there was to be a general attack on the periphery of the Japanese conquests in Asia.

The conference was of major political significance, since it was here that Roosevelt announced that peace could only come 'by the total elimination of German and Japanese war power' and that this meant 'unconditional surrender by Germany, Italy, and Japan'. His declaration was later supported by Churchill and Stalin, and determined the way in which the war ended.

The conference was also important in bringing together the two French generals, De Gaulle (as leader of the Free French) and Giraud, with whom the British and Americans had worked in the invasion of the French North African territories. Their agreement made possible the setting up of a National Committee (May 1943) of which they were for a short time joint presidents.   WFK

CASALIS, EUGÈNE (1812–91), French missionary, who formed, with Thomas Arbousset, the first French Protestant mission to the Basuto people in 1833, and became the confidant of their leader and statesman, Mosheshwe I.

CASANOVA, LAURENT (1906–), French communist leader. He was responsible in the post-war years for cultural matters and the party's relations with intellectuals, but was expelled from the party in 1961. His wife, Danielle, also an active communist, died in Auschwitz (1943).

CASCO, TREATIES OF. The first treaty of Casco (1678) between the Indians and Massachusetts Bay colony made peace after fighting during King Philip's war in 1675 and arranged for an exchange of prisoners. The second treaty of Casco (1703) was an unsuccessful attempt by the governor of Massachusetts Bay colony to prevent fighting between the colonists and the Indians. The Indians promised peace, but within two months were on the warpath again.

CASELEY-HAYFORD, JOSEPH EPHRAIM (1866–1930), Ghanaian journalist, lawyer, author, and nationalist leader. He served on several government commissions and in the Gold Coast Legislative Council. Through such writings as *Gold Coast Native Institutions* (1903), *Ethiopia Unbound* (1911), *The Truth About the West African Land Question* (1913), *United West Africa* (1919), and others, he influenced the development of national consciousness. Until about 1914 he took an active part in the Gold Coast Aborigines' Rights Protection Society, a nationalist organization founded in

1897, and in 1920 founded the National Congress of British West Africa.

CASEMENT, ROGER DAVID (1864–1916), British colonial administrator and martyr for Irish independence. Born and educated in Ireland, of Protestant stock, Casement entered the British consular service and spent some 20 years travelling in Africa. In 1903, in response to popular agitation against the Congo Free State, the British government sent Casement to report on conditions there. The resultant report was a damning indictment of the conditions of near-slavery under which the rubber trade was conducted in the interior of the Congo; it was also a remarkable success for Casement. In 1905 he was transferred to South America. Five years later, as consul-general at Rio de Janeiro, he investigated similar charges against the Peruvian Amazon Co. Again, after extensive investigation in the rubber-bearing regions, he found the charges proven, but with the coming of war in Europe the matter was allowed to drop.

While in the consular service, Casement had nevertheless been a fervent propagandist for Irish independence. In 1914, now retired, he flung himself into the Irish movement. Convinced that the first World War offered a unique opportunity, he spent two years in Berlin fruitlessly negotiating for German support. In 1916 he returned to Ireland in a German submarine, but was captured on landing and in due course convicted of high treason and sentenced to death. Ironically, his mission had been to stop the uprising planned for that Easter. A strong movement for his reprieve was undermined by the discovery of his so-called 'Black Diaries', which contained details of his homosexuality. Stripped of his knighthood and other honours, Casement was hanged.

CASEROS, BATTLE OF (3 Feb. 1852). Gen. Justo José de Urquiza's army of Argentine, Brazilian, and Uruguayan troops defeated Juan Manuel Rosas's army at Monte Caseros and ended Rosas's Argentine dictatorship.

CASEY, RICHARD GARDINER CASEY, Life Baron (1890–   ), after going to Melbourne Grammar School, Melbourne University, and Cambridge (1913) and seeing military service overseas, he accepted an offer by the prime minister, S. M. Bruce, to act as the first Australian liaison officer with the British foreign office (1924–7, 1927–31). After election to the Commonwealth parliament (1931), he held the treasury and other portfolios, but resigned (1940) to become first Australian minister at Washington, DC. Later appointments as British minister of state in the Middle East, a member of the war cabinet (1942–3), and governor of Bengal (1944–6) implied Casey's withdrawal from Australian politics, but he returned to the Canberra parliament in 1949. As minister of external affairs (1951–60), he greatly strengthened Australia's relations with Asian countries by personal visits and the establishment of additional embassies and legations. On receiving a life peerage (1960) he retired from the Commonwealth parliament, but in 1965 returned to Canberra for a three-and-a-half-year term as governor-general—the first Australian to be appointed on the recommendation of a Liberal prime minister.

CASH PAYMENTS RESTRICTION (1797–1823), came about in Britain through heavy government expenditure in the French Revolutionary War. The prime minister, Pitt, was slow to expand taxation to meet the war's costs and relied heavily on borrowing. Credit had become difficult because of bad harvests and military failures, and the breakdown of peace negotiations led (Feb. 1797) to a run on the Bank of England which forced Pitt to instruct the bank to cease paying in cash. This effectively put the country on paper currency, but without any central control of the note issue and without notes being legal tender. Prices of necessities had risen and stayed high throughout the wars, reaching their peak in 1812–13. Though the government had increased the scale of taxation in the Wars, neither it nor the bank had the means to prevent over-issue of paper and the decline of the pound on the international exchange. When it was realized in 1810 that the pound had depreciated, there was a considerable demand by economists for an end to the restriction, which war policy made it impossible for the government to consider until peace came. In 1821, after a period of drastic deflation, the pound was fixed in terms of gold and in 1823 the bank resumed payments in cash.

Inflation was only one sign of economic strain in the war period, a sign which meant particular hardship for the working classes, although it may have helped the process of industrialization. After the war the monetary issue tended to divide those who feared deflation, particularly the landed interest and some small manufacturers and exporters, from the bankers and classical economists, who wished for financial orthodoxy. The increasing use of Bank of England notes during the war helped the bank in its progress to the position of a central bank.

CASIMIR III THE GREAT (1310–70), King of Poland, last Piast king of Poland (*reg.* 1333–70). By 1343 he managed to conclude peace with his most dangerous enemy, the Teutonic Order, recovering some of the territories lost by his father, Ladislas I. In 1349 he annexed eastern Galicia, with its flourishing commercial centre of Lwòw. Casimir preferred diplomacy to warfare and with the help of his nephew and designated heir, Louis the Great of Hungary, he achieved a position of considerable prestige in eastern Europe. In 1364, Casimir founded the first Polish university at Cracow, where special stress was laid on the study of Roman Law. He welcomed the economic contribution of numerous German Jews into his kingdom.

CASIMIR IV (d. 1492), King of Poland, who was elected king of Poland in 1447. Casimir's greatest achievement was to regain for Poland access to the sea by conquering eastern Pomerania from the Teutonic Order (1454–66). His eldest son became King of Bohemia in 1471 and three other sons were successive kings of Poland.

CASIMIR V, JOHN (1609–72), King of Poland, who was elected king in 1648 after the death of his brother, Vladislav IV (1595–1648), and a year after he had received a cardinal's hat (1647). He abdicated in 1668, to be succeeded by Michael Wisnowiecki. During his reign Poland faced partition by aggressive neighbours and continued to suffer from the internal strife of aristocratic factions. In 1661 Casimir warned the assembled estates of the consequences of their elective monarchy. Meanwhile, in the northern war (1655–60) Poland was attacked by Charles X of Sweden and Casimir was driven to seek refuge in Austrian Silesia. On his return he was defeated outside Warsaw by Swedish–Brandenburg forces. Only the death of Charles X saved Poland from territorial losses at the peace of Oliva (1660). In 1663 the war with Muscovy, which had first broken out in 1654, was resumed and by the treaty of Andrusovo (1667) Casimir recognized the cession of part of the Polish Ukraine, including Smolensk and Kiev.

CASKET GIRLS, name derived from the *cassettes* or boxes of clothes carried by girls imported in the 1720s by the Compagnie des Indes into Louisiana to marry French settlers. The Casket Girls were drawn from poor but virtuous inmates of Church institutions.

CASKET LETTERS, allegedly found in a silver casket after the flight of Mary Queen of Scots and Bothwell following their defeat at Carberry Hill (1567). If genuine, they prove Mary to have been Bothwell's mistress and an accomplice in the murder of her husband, Darnley (1566), but their authenticity has been contested. They were produced as evidence in a commission of enquiry held at York and later at Westminster (1568), which ended with a statement that there was no case against the Scottish lords for their rebellion, while the case against Mary was incomplete. The letters remained in the possession of the regents of Scotland until they disappeared after the execution of Gowrie (1584).

CASS, LEWIS (1782–1866), US political leader, soldier, and diplomat, a New Englander by birth, who spent most of his life in the west. He fought in the war of 1812, was governor of Michigan territory (1813–31), secretary of war under Andrew Jackson (1831–6), and minister to France (1836–42). As a senator from MI (1845–8, 1849–57), he was an ardent expansionist, a supporter of compromise between North and South, and one of the first exponents of the popular sovereignty principle that the inhabitants of US territories should themselves decide whether or not to allow slavery to exist within their borders. He was the Democratic presidential candidate in 1848, and was hurt by the defection of anti-slavery Democrats into the Free Soil Party and defeated by the Whig, Zachary Taylor. Cass was secretary of state under James Buchanan (1857–60), but resigned in protest against the president's inaction in the secession crisis.

CASSAGNAC, PAUL GRANIER DE (1843–1904), French journalist, politician, and duellist. The son of a Bonapartist publicist, he worked as a journalist on *La Nation* and *L'Indépendance*. He fought with the Zouaves in the Franco-Prussian war and was captured at Sedan (1870), but continued to advocate the Bonapartist cause with such vigour that his paper, *Le Pays*, was suspended and the Bonapartist pretender broke with him. He was elected a deputy (1876) and supported both MacMahon and Boulanger.

CASSANDER (*c.* 358–297 BC), one of the ablest of Alexander the Great's successors, ruler of Macedon from 316, and son of the regent Antipater, after whose death (319) he wrested Macedon from his nominee Polyperchon. Politically ruthless and having no legitimate title, he connected himself with the royal house by marrying Thessalonice, daughter of Philip II (315), and after removing the other claimants, *eg*, Alexander's widow, Roxane, and son, Alexander IV (310), he proclaimed himself king (306). In Macedon, he founded Cassandreia (315) and Thessalonica, and in Greece rebuilt Thebes (315), destroyed by Alexander the Great; but his unpopularity in Greece, aroused by his autocratic governors, was undiminished. After being opposed by Antigonus Monophthalmus after 315, he joined Ptolemy, Lysimachus, and Seleucus in the constant warfare in which Antigonus was eventually defeated (301).

CASSANO, BATTLE OF (Aug. 1705), indecisive battle between Prince Eugène of Savoy's imperialist forces and the French under Vendôme in the War of the Spanish Succession. The latter attacked to prevent Eugène's army crossing the Adda river to relieve Turin. The imperialists suffered heavy casualties and were unable to cross the Adda, but Eugène's morale remained unshaken.

CASSAVA (*manioc*), Brazilian root crop introduced to tropical Africa during the 16th cent. Though deficient in protein, it proved a valuable addition to food resources, being easy to plant and resistant to disease, and yielding well even in poor soil. It has long become a staple over wide areas of the African continent.

CASSELL, JOHN (1817–65), British pioneer of the popular educational press. Self-educated son of a Manchester publican, he was successively millhand, joiner, temperance lecturer (from 1836), and tea- and coffee-dealer. By the 1850s he had become an educational publisher and radical champion of a free press, launching his *Popular Educator* (1852) and founding a publishing firm (1859).

CASSIN, RENÉ (1887–   ), French jurist, awarded the Nobel Peace Prize (1968) for his work for international organizations, notably UNESCO and the European Court of Human Rights. Cassin was one of De Gaulle's closest collaborators during the Second World War.

CASSIODORUS, FLAVIUS MAGNUS AURELIUS (*c.* 485–*c.* 580), chief minister of Theodoric the Great, King of the Ostrogoths, consul (514), pupil of Boethius, and founder of the monastery of Vivarium. He was also the author of a number of works on history and theology, including the *Institutes of Divine and Secular Learning*, written for his monks at Vivarium. It had incalculable effects on the development of medieval education, and was the basis of the syllabus of study of the seven liberal arts.

CASSIUS, C., LONGINUS (d. 43 BC), the Roman 'tyrannicide', one of Julius Caesar's murderers. As Crassus' quaestor (53) he rescued the remnants of the Roman army defeated at Carrhae. Tribune in 49, he commanded a Pompeian fleet in the Civil War, but was pardoned by Caesar after Pharsalus, becoming praetor for 44. Nevertheless, he was a leader of the conspiracy against Caesar, but after his murder was unable to remain in Rome. He went to Syria and with Brutus in Macedonia gained control of the East. He committed suicide after his defeat by Antony in the first battle of Philippi.

CASSIUS DIO (*c.* AD 163–230), Roman senator from Bithynia, twice consul, and author in Greek of a history of Rome from its origins to his own day. This massive work, in 80 books, took ten years to research and a further 12 to write; and although substantial sections survive only in the summaries of Byzantine authors, it is of very great importance for the history of the first two centuries AD, and for the time of the Severi, in which Dio spent his active career, and of which he records many personal impressions.

CASSOU, JEAN (1897–   ), French intellectual active in left-wing politics, author of novels, poetry, and criticism, and director of the national museum of modern art (1946–65). Cassou had a distinguished Resistance career.

CASTBERG, JOHN (1863–1926), Norwegian lawyer and politician who founded the Radical People's Party and encouraged social reforms on the lines of those pursued in Germany and Britain. His work included the securing of accident insurance and of sickness benefits. He was concerned that the industrial revolution in Norway—coming later than that in the rest of Europe—should avoid the evils of exploitation. During the First World War Norway gained financially in 1915 through her carrying-trade, and he was able to translate this temporary prosperity into further reforms.

CASTE (ancient India), term of Portuguese origin describing the basic division of Indian society until fairly recent times and translating the two Indian concepts of *varna*: the fourfold division of the majority of Indians into brahmans (originally priests, but later also scholars and officials), kshatriyas (originally warriors, but later officials and landed nobles as well), vaishyas (free farmers, craftsmen, and traders), and shudras (bonded peasants, servants, and craftsmen, but of a lower type), as well as *jati*: caste in its more precise connotation of a social group characterized by endogamy, commensality, adherence to a common craft or trade, and, often, the possession by its members of some common institutions.

The four-fold classification is constantly emphasized in religious texts, epics, and other literature, notably lawbooks (*dharmashastra*). It is explained that these four classes have existed since the creation of mankind; their existence is, indeed, part of the order of things, just as are the different plants and animals. The apparent injustice of this system is attributed to the laws of *karman*, according to which merit and demerit in one life determine the type and quality of the next. The existence of numerous *jatis* is ascribed to unions between parents belonging to different classes. In this respect, however, a basic distinction is made depending on whether the husband or the wife belongs to the higher class. In the former case (*anuloma*) the offspring became a new *jati* of a status intermediate between those of the parents, but in the latter (*pratiloma*) the progeny were considered as being of impure castes and would by their mere presence pollute members of the 'clean' castes. Among those considered lowest in order were the Chandalas, theoretically the offspring of a shudra male and a brahman female.

Actual conditions were quite different and more complicated than the theory—meant to lay down norms rather than to give a description—would suggest. Glimpses from inscriptions and non-brahmanic (*eg*, Buddhist) texts show much more flexibility than might be expected from the theory, especially with regard to the link between caste and craft or trade. As time went by, however, the system tended to grow more rigid, with practice gradually being modelled upon theory. Precise data are, however, difficult to obtain not only on account of the immensity and variety of the Indian sub-continent, but also because we possess few sources of information other than normative texts of usually uncertain date.

The origins of caste in India are undoubtedly complex. It is assumed that the Indo-Aryans who had invaded the sub-continent by the middle of the 2nd millennium BC were already divided into classes. Subsequently, in the ever-continuing process of integration of tribes into what gradually became Hindu society, the new groups acquired a definite status by being identified as a caste. Certain guilds, especially of craftsmen, may, as a protective attitude, have confined social intercourse to their own members as far as possible, thus assuming the basic features of a caste. The same probably happened to some religious sects. Once the pattern of a caste society was established it was the vested interest of the most privileged castes to enforce the theoretical rules and strengthen the barriers between castes. Outside threats to Hindu society, first from 'Scythians', later from Muslims and Europeans, may have led to further hardening of the structure as a kind of defensive response.

The overall effect of caste has certainly been divisive but, on the other hand, the institution may sometimes have provided some social security and, while separating society into numerous mutually interdependent strata, may have promoted some mobility between members of the same caste in different areas. If so, it may well have contributed to the growth of pan-Indian values.

J. H. Hutton, *Caste in India* (Cambridge, 1946). JG dec

CASTELAR, EMILIO (1832–99), Spanish journalist and professor, also fourth and last president of the first Republic (1873). Castelar described himself as a 'possibilist' republican. Although a liberal, he found it necessary, when in power, to resort to military dictatorship to end civil war in Spain, before himself being overthrown by a military coup. In 1888 he weakened republicanism by advising his followers to support the constitutional monarchy of Alfonso XII.

As professor of history at Madrid University earlier in his career, he gave impetus to student intervention in Spanish politics by an article, 'The Gesture' (1865), exposing the futility of Isabella's apparently generous gift of part of her estates to the nation. Castelar was dismissed, but ensuing student unrest helped to bring down the government.

CASTELNAUDARY, BATTLE OF (1632), defeat of Gaston of Orléans by Schomberg. Gaston, brother of King Louis XIII and heir to the throne of France, rebelled against the influence of Richelieu. Having fled to Lorraine, he invaded France (June 1632), and allied himself with the Duke of Montmorency. After their defeat Gaston, who was pardoned, fled to Flanders, but Montmorency was executed.

CASTELO BRANCO, HUMBERTO DE ALENÇAR (1900–67), Brazilian field marshal, commander of the army, and military leader of the *coup d'état* which overthrew President João Goulart (1964). He was president-dictator of Brazil (1964–7).

CASTIGLIONE, COUNT BALDASSARE (1478–1529), Italian diplomat, connoisseur of art, and author of *Il Cortegiano* (*The Courtier*) (1513–18). Written in dialogue form, it described the artistic life of the Italian courts and depicted the courtier as the universal man of the Renaissance. Its influence in Italy, England, and France was considerable.

CASTILLA, RAMON (*c*. 1797–1867), president of Peru (1845–51, 1855–62). He supported the entry of foreign capital, abolished slavery (1856), and, with liberal support, proclaimed a new constitution (1860).

CASTILE, most highly populated, rich, and powerful kingdom in the Iberian peninsula, which became the nucleus of the Hispanic state. The union of the thrones of Castile and Aragon under Isabella and Ferdinand (1469) was a landmark in the extension of Castilian authority. During and after Isabella's reign Castile's prestige developed through its leadership of the Arab kingdom of Granada in southern Spain (1491). Although federal in character, the Spanish state was politically dominated by Castile, and the acquisition and development of the American colonies, with their vast resources of gold and silver, produced the economic hegemony of Castile.

The internal economy of the kingdom depended, in the 16th cent., upon agriculture. Although wheat was the main cereal crop, more important was sheep rearing on the pasturelands of the south, and the production of wool for export from the great markets at Burgos and Medina del Campo, dating from the 13th cent. Sheep rearing was controlled by the Mesta, a national guild of sheepowners, whose wealth enabled them to act as royal bankers for Charles V, who in return protected their interests. Seville, the port most advantageously placed for the American trade, was granted the monopoly of commerce, both export and import, and rapidly expanded in the 16th cent. into the largest city in the Iberian peninsula.

From the mid-16th cent. the Castilian economy began to decline sharply. The colonization and development of the New World sapped Castilian manpower and contributed to an inflationary situation, which, though common to all Europe, was to affect Castile the most adversely in the 17th cent. MKS

CASTILIANIZATION, a process of centralization within the Hispanic kingdoms by which the state of Castile dominated the administration and undermined the traditional federal structure. Started by Isabella of Castile (1474–1504), the process was encouraged by Philip II.

CASTILLO, RAMON S. (1871–1944), acting president of Argentina (1940–2) and president (1942–3). He favoured neutrality in the Second World War and was removed from office by a military coup (4 June 1943).

CASTILLO ARMAS, CARLOS (1914–57), president of Guatemala, first as head of a military junta, then as constitutional president (1954–7). Castillo Armas spent 1945–6 in the US, undergoing military training. After returning to Guatemala, he participated in an unsuccessful coup against the reformist government of Juan José Arévalo Bermejo. Castillo Armas was sentenced to death, but escaped from prison. With US military assistance, he launched an invasion from Honduras against the Guatemalan government of Jacobo Arbenz Guzmán (June 1954) and was formally elected president (Oct. 1954). Terrorism prevailed during his rule and on 26 July he was assassinated, allegedly by a member of his guard.

CASTLE, BARBARA ANNE (1911–), British Labour politician. She entered municipal politics as a borough councillor for St Pancras (1937) and spent much of the Second World War at the ministry of food. After being elected MP for Blackburn (1955), she quickly rose to prominence in the

Labour Party and was successively minister of overseas development, and transport (1964–8), then became secretary of state for employment and productivity (1968).

CASTORS, nickname given to the Ultramontane right wing of the Conservative Party in Que. (1883) because it founded a newspaper, *L'Étendard,* bearing a beaver (Fr. *castor*) as its emblem.

CASTRILLO, GARCIA DE HARO Y AVELLANEDA, 2nd Count of (*fl.* 17th cent.) Spanish minister, who contributed to the downfall of Olivares (1643), ruled Spain (1661–5) for Philip IV, together with the Duke of Medina de las Torres, and was chosen as one of the five members of the junta to advise the Queen Regent Mariana during Charles II's minority (1665–75).

CASTRO, CIPRIANO (*c.* 1858–1924), provisional president of Venezuela (1899–1902), president-dictator (1902–8) and the first of a line of Táchira *caudillos* who ruled 20th-cent. Venezuela.

CASTRO ALVES, ANTÔNIO DE (1847–71), Brazilian poet and social critic. His best-known work, 'O Poema dos Escravos', concerns slavery in Brazil.

CASTRO RUZ, FIDEL (1927–), Cuban guerrilla leader against Batista, the Cuban prime minister, and first communist head of state in the western hemisphere. Castro was born in Mayarí and received a law degree at Havana University (1950). His revolutionary activities as a student were followed by a futile attack on the Moncada barracks at Santiago (26 July 1953), for which he was sentenced to 15 years' imprisonment, but after an amnesty (1955) he went to the US and Mexico, where he surrounded himself with Cuban exiles. The subsequent invasion of Cuba (Dec. 1956) was planned by him, his brother Raúl, and the Argentine revolutionary Ernesto 'Che' Guevara.

Guerrilla warfare and urban unrest brought Batista's regime to an end and Castro assumed de facto power in Havana (1 Jan. 1959). He was appointed prime minister in Feb. and continued to occupy that position, leaving the presidency to others. He demonstrated his antagonism towards the US and foreign capital by drastic reforms, and by nationalizing US companies. Breaking with some of his early collaborators, he chose a marxist route for economic development and sought aid from the communist countries. After declaring himself a Marxist-Leninist (Dec. 1961), Castro asked for, and obtained, military supplies from the USSR for the defence of Cuba. These supplies were put to good use when a US-backed invasion attempt by Cuban refugees was repulsed. When the USSR began to supply Castro with offensive missiles (1962), the US demanded their withdrawal. This the USSR agreed to, despite Castro's protests.

Up to 1970 Castro continued to concentrate power and decision-making in his own hands and seemed unwilling to delegate authority. Rural labour and the militia appeared to look to him rather than to the growing party apparatus for direction and inspiration. Next in importance was his brother Raúl, considered by many to be the heir-apparent.

CAT AND MOUSE ACT (1913), introduced in Britain by the home secretary, McKenna, enabling the authorities to release on licence imprisoned suffragettes on hunger-strike.

CATALANS. The merchants and sailors from Catalonia in north-eastern Spain became important outside their country during the 13th cent. Catalan merchant galleys were used in opening up a regular sea route between the Mediterranean and north-western Europe, calling at England and Flanders frequently from at least the late 13th cent. Catalan expansion in the Mediterranean became important after 1282, when they provided the naval forces for the conquest of Sicily by the Aragonese kings, whose subjects they were. In the second

decade of the 14th cent. Catalan mercenaries founded a principality in Greece which was centred on Athens and endured for 80 years. The decline of Catalan prosperity began in the middle decades of the 15th cent. and a prolonged civil war in 1460 marked the end of the great age of Catalan expansion.

CATALONIA represents a special problem of Spanish regionalism. Both linguistically and culturally the area is an extension of southern France, and has always been more European than Castile. Its agriculture (mainly wheat and grapes) is based on the efforts of secure peasant farmers, and, unlike that of the rest of Spain, is intensive and prosperous. There also exist thriving textile and cork industries.

Separatist feeling has existed since the 17th cent., and in the 19th cent. there was a literary revival of Catalan, and the Federal Republic of 1874 revived autonomist sentiment. The manifesto of this Catalanism was the *Bases de Manresa,* drawn up in 1892. At the same time, Catalan industrialists, angered by the policy of Madrid's free trade and resenting excessive taxation, were inclined to separatism, especially after the loss of their markets in Cuba in 1898.

The upper classes formed the *Lliga Regionalista* under Francisco Cambó, which from 1901 began to achieve electoral successes. The government retaliated by encouraging left-wing demagogues like Lerroux and by employing gangsters to produce chaos sufficient to justify the suspension of constitutional guarantees. These tactics culminated in 1909 in Barcelona's Tragic Week. The shock of this, together with the granting of a measure of local government—the *Mancomunidad*—in 1911 ameliorated the situation. However, in the slump after the First World War, Catalan industrialists turned their backs on Catalanism in order to wage war on the Confederacion Nacional del Trabajo (CNT). This they did, aided by the army, with results that encouraged the growth of left-wing Catalanism as embodied in the *Esquerra,* a development strengthened by Primo de Rivera's anti-Catalan policy. Thus, Catalonia became republican in sympathy. In April 1931 Macía proclaimed its independence, but was persuaded to abandon this move in return for autonomous government, the *Generalidad.* But right-wing governments' opposition after Nov. 1933 to autonomy provoked in Oct. 1934 a declaration by Companys of a separate Catalan state. When civil war came, Catalonia fought for the Republic, but was overrun by the Nationalists in Jan. 1939.   PP

CATARGI, LASCAR (1832–99), Rumanian statesman. In a political career spanning half a century Catargi was instrumental in the formation of an independent Rumania. He aspired unsuccessfully to the throne and achieved the first period of political stability in Rumania as leader of a Conservative cabinet (1871–6).

CATEAU-CAMBRÉSIS, PEACE OF (April 1559), settlement ending the long series of Habsburg–Valois wars. The peace terms reflected the stalemate which the long dynastic struggle had produced and underlined the terms of the peace of Cambrai (1529).

Spain emerged supreme in Italy, directly controlling Sicily, Sardinia, Naples, Milan, and the coastal fortresses in Tuscany. France withdrew from Savoy and Piedmont, except for garrisons left in six cities, but retained her strength in northern Europe by recovering Calais, which the Duke of Guise had taken from Philip II's late wife, Mary Tudor, and holding the strategically important cities of Metz, Toul, and Verdun.

The peace was sealed by the dynastic marriages of Philip II of Spain with Henry II's daughter, Elizabeth of Valois, and that of Spain's Italian ally, Emmanuel Philibert of Piedmont-Savoy, with Henry's sister, Margaret.

For France the peace had a tragic consequence. At the jousting tournament held to celebrate its conclusion Henry II was mortally wounded and died soon afterwards, leaving his country to a succession of young and weak kings.

CATESBY, ROBERT (1573–1605), English conspirator and member of a wealthy Catholic family in the Midlands. He was fined for supporting Essex's rising (1601) and briefly imprisoned on the accession of James I. He was the main instigator of the Gunpowder Plot (1605) and on Fawkes's arrest fled to Holbeche, Staffs, where he was shot while resisting arrest.

CATHARISM, term derived from the Greek word for 'pure'. It has been loosely applied to a variety of medieval heretical movements having as their central feature a belief in two elements, material things (including men) created by Satan and spiritual things created by God. This dualism had an early Gnostic background and in the 4th cent. was a rival to orthodox Christianity. From the Byzantine empire Catharism reached the Balkans and penetrated into Italy and southern France in the 12th cent. Its adherents, who denied the humanity of Christ or the possibility of his incarnation, were quite distinct from the Waldensians, who also flourished in Italy and France in the 12th and 13th cents and who represented an evangelical movement accepting Catholic beliefs, though estranged from the established Church hierarchy. The Cathars were ruthlessly persecuted, their chief centres in southern France being destroyed by the Albingensian crusades (1209–29). Information about their theology largely perished with them. They had their own hierarchy of the 'perfect', who were the chosen few prepared completely to disregard bodily preoccupations.

CATHCART EXPEDITION (1741). British expedition against the Spanish colonies led by Lord Cathcart in command of 12,000 largely untrained English troops and 3000 men from the North American colonies. Cathcart died before reaching Jamaica, and was succeeded by the inexperienced Gen. Thomas Wentworth. The British troops landed near Cartagena (March 1741) but, ravaged by disease and repulsed with heavy losses by the Spanish, were forced to abandon the attack.

CATHER, WILLA SIBERT (1873–1947), US writer. Born in VA of farming stock, she grew up in NB in a mixed immigrant community only recently developed beyond frontier conditions. The publication of *April Twilights* (1903) founded her literary career. She worked for *McClure's Magazine* (1906–12), read and travelled widely, and after 1912 devoted herself to writing. In three early novels, *O Pioneers!* (1913), *The Song of the Lark* (1915), and *My Antonia* (1918), she portrayed NB frontier life, exploring the problems of change, home, and community through the interaction of strong female characters with both local society and the dominant landscape. *Death Comes for the Archbishop* (1927) and *Shadows on the Rock* (1931) reveal, in addition to a continuing preoccupation with regionalism, a strong religious concern, particularly with Roman Catholicism.

CATHERINE I (1682–1727), Empress of Russia (*reg.* 1725–7). Catherine Skavronsky, once a servant girl of Latvian peasant stock, was the second wife of the Tsar Peter I and on his death succeeded as reigning Empress of Russia, through the influence of Prince Menshikov and the Guards regiments. Sent as a prisoner to Moscow after her capture in the Great Northern War, she rose to influence through her relationship with Menshikov and became Peter's mistress (1702). He married her in Nov. 1707 and she bore him several children, including Ann of Holstein, mother of the future Tsar Peter III, and the future Empress Elizabeth. During her short reign real power lay with the Supreme Privy Council led by Menshikov. Catherine was succeeded by Peter II, grandson of Peter I by his first marriage.

CATHERINE II (1729–96), Queen of Russia (*reg.* 1762–96). During her reign Russia expanded to the Black Sea and emerged as a European power. She was born Princess of Anhalt-Zerbst and married the future Peter III (1745), whom she deposed (1762) with the support of the Guards. His death and that of the deposed Ivan VI (1764) were necessary to secure the throne, but throughout her reign Catherine relied on noble support. Her first chief minister, Panin, and three of her many favourites—Orlov, Potemkin, and Zubov—influenced politics, but Catherine ruled.

An ambitious, intelligent woman, she was sensitive to European opinion and became an excellent publicist and diplomat. Her image as a European Enlightened Autocrat, established by her correspondence with Voltaire and the Encyclopaedists, had little in common with her internal policies which expanded noble privileges and heightened serfdom.

Her *Instruction* (1767), based on Montesquieu and issued as guidance for an elected legislative commission of all classes except serfs, impressed Europe but omitted the intended law code. Local government was decentralized (1775) and a charter confirmed the nobility's freedom from obligatory state service (1785) while extending their power over serfs. Despite Catherine's declared humanitarianism, serfdom reached its height in her reign and even the serf's right to petition the throne for redress was cancelled (1767). The peasant rebellion under Pugachev (1773–4) was partly against conditions and partly a Cossack and Tatar protest against the expansion of state power southwards to the Black Sea, which was the greatest achievement of Catherine's reign.

After war with Turkey (1768–74) the treaty of Küchük Kaimarja started the Eastern Question by giving Russia ill-defined rights to protect Turkish Christians and the right of merchant ships to pass the Straits. Catherine and Potemkin had grandiose plans to conquer Constantinople and even India, but the actual gains (Crimea, 1783; Orchakov, 1792; and the port of Odessa, 1794) were impressive. Catherine joined in the three partitions of Poland (1772, 1793, 1794) and gained Courland and Lithuania. The Armed Neutrality scheme (1780) showed Russia's new power in European affairs. Catherine's wars resulted in huge expansions of territory and population, but left a legacy of debt and dissident minorities of Tatars, Poles, and Jews. Some educational advance was made, much building achieved, and a Free Economic Society and the Russian Academy founded. Catherine's own writings encouraged Russian literature, but the reign also saw the beginning, with Radishchev and Novikov, of intellectual protest which Catherine, abandoning even the theory of Enlightenment with the French Revolution, persecuted.

I. Grey, *Catherine the Great* (London, 1961).
D. Maroger (ed.), *The Memoirs of Catherine the Great* (New York, 1955).   BJW

CATHERINE OF ARAGON (1485–1536), first queen of Henry VIII, was the daughter of Ferdinand and Isabella of Spain. She married Arthur, Prince of Wales (1501), and on his death received a papal dispensation to marry his brother Henry. Their marriage took place on Henry's accession (1509) and at first was happy and successful, Catherine organizing the defence of the country against a Scottish invasion (1513) and working for the Spanish alliance which was popular with the merchant classes. But only one of their children, a daughter, Mary, survived infancy, and Henry's need of a male heir led him to seek an annulment of the marriage on the ground that the papal dispensation was invalid. Clement VII refused to grant the 'divorce', and with dignity and courage Catherine refused to plead before any other judge. Henry secretly married Anne Boleyn and his marriage to Catherine was annulled by Abp Cranmer (1533). Catherine lived in retirement, persistently asserting the legality of her marriage and her daughter's right to succeed.

CATHERINE OF BRAGANZA, Queen, (1638–1705), daughter of King John IV of Portugal. A marriage treaty and alliance with King Charles II of England was concluded in 1661. Portugal offered a dowry of 2 million *cruzados*, the strongholds of Tangier and Bombay, and free trade with the Portuguese colonies. England offered in return to defend Portugal by land and sea. The marriage proved childless and Catherine returned to Portugal in 1692.

CATHERINE DE' MEDICI (1519–89), Queen of France, daughter of Lorenzo, Duke of Urbino, was brought up in the intellectual atmosphere of the Florentine court. She married Henry, Duke of Orléans, on 28 Oct. 1533, and became queen on 31 March 1547, when her husband succeeded to the throne as Henry II. Throughout her life she loved music and pageantry. She was regent for her eldest son, the 15-year-old Francis II, who succeeded as king on 10 July 1559, and for her second son, the 10-year-old Charles IX, who succeeded on 5 Dec. 1560. She influenced royal policy for 30 years, maintaining her authority in the reign of her third son, Henry III (1574–89). As queen mother she tried to assert the sovereignty of the Crown, which her young, irresponsible, and quarrelsome sons failed to do, and to appease the warring factions of Guise, Montmorency, and Bourbon, who threatened the dissolution of the French state under the pretext of religion. To restore unity and order Catherine, an orthodox Catholic, abandoned the repressive religious policy of Henry II, and, acting upon the advice of the chancellor, L'Hôpital, instituted religious toleration, permitting the Colloquy of Poissy (July 1561) and consenting to the January Edict (1562). Infuriated by her policy, the Guise family, which represented extreme Catholicism, initiated the Wars of Religion (1562), which were to continue intermittently for the rest of Catherine's life.

After the peace of Amboise (1563) and the end of her regency, she conducted Charles IX on a royal progress through France (1564), which culminated in the Bayonne conference with her daughter, Elizabeth of Valois, Queen of Spain, and the Duke of Alva, where a Franco-Spanish plot to destroy protestantism appeared to be hatched. In the ensuing war (1567–8) Condé failed to capture the royal family, but his attempted coup alienated the queen mother, who was disillusioned by the effects of toleration. However, when the royal forces failed to suppress the Huguenots in the renewed civil wars (1568–70), Catherine and her son returned to a policy of moderation and granted limited toleration (peace of Saint-Germain, 1570). To cultivate the spirit of unity and vent her dynastic ambitions, Catherine devised a series of marriage alliances, that of another daughter, Marguerite of Valois, to the Bourbon Huguenot, Henry of Navarre, that of Charles IX to Elizabeth of Habsburg, daughter of the tolerant Emperor Maximilian, and that of her son Henry, Duke of Anjou, to Elizabeth I of England. While the Habsburg–Valois marriage took place in 1570, the Bourbon–Valois union was the occasion of the notorious massacre of St Bartholomew, when thousands of Huguenots, including their leader, Coligny, who had gathered in Paris for the wedding celebrations, were slaughtered with Catherine's connivance (23–4 Aug. 1572). By countenancing this desperate episode Catherine revived faction at home and destroyed the last hopes of an Anglo-French marriage. Her youngest son, Alençon, joined the *politique* party in support of the Huguenots, and while Anjou sought the Crown of Poland (1573–4) she and Charles IX found themselves again in Guise control. Anjou's accession as Henry III (May 1574) was secured by Catherine against the intrigues of Alençon, but the new king lacked authority and Catherine could not prevent a renewal of war (1576–7, 1584–9). Latterly she saw alliance with the Guise-dominated Catholic League as the only salvation for the monarchy. Her influence over Henry dwindled rapidly in 1588, being marked by the dismissal of eight advisers whom she had appointed, and the assassination of the Duke and Cardinal de Guise (23, 24 Dec. 1588).

N. M. Sutherland, *The French Secretaries of State in the Age of Catherine de Medici* (London, 1962).
J. E. Neale, *The Age of Catherine de Medici* (London, 1943).
                                                MKS

CATHERINE OF SIENA, Saint (1347–80), important mystic and spiritual writer, the first woman to receive the stigmata and remembered for the part she played in persuading Pope Gregory XI, whom she met in 1376, to return from Avignon to Rome, thus ending the period of the Avignonese papacy.

CATHOLIC CONFEDERACY (1642–9), name assumed by the Irish rebels after the meeting of the general assembly at Kilkenny in Oct. 1642. By their oath of association they were pledged to restore the rights of the Roman Catholic Church, maintain the prerogatives of the Crown, and defend the liberties of the nation. The confederacy was meant to be an effective union of the whole Irish nation (excepting Protestants), but this unity was never achieved. The supreme council was rivalled by a separate military organization for each province, and inter-provincial jealousies made co-operation impossible. Also personal rivalries, *eg*, between Owen Roe O'Neill and Thomas Preston, meant that there was no unified military command. The longstanding distrust between the Old English settlers and native Irish, temporarily overcome in 1642, soon reasserted itself. The Old English dominated the supreme council and were anxious for a speedy settlement with Charles I. The native Irish, having no land at stake, were ready to continue the war in support of the Catholic Church. They were supported by Rinuccini, the papal nuncio to Ireland, and a fresh rivalry emerged between lay and secular powers. The Old English were suspicious of episcopal influence. Thus a welter of rival factions grew, which, with military weakness due to lack of supplies, training, and leadership, caused the final collapse of the confederacy. In Jan. 1649 the Confederates signed a treaty with the royalists under Ormonde, which formally dissolved the confederacy.

CATHOLIC CONFEDERATION AT KILKENNY (1642–9) represented the native Irish and the Anglo-Norman (Old English) Catholics and functioned as an independent Irish parliament. Resulting from an initiative by the clergy under Abp O'Reilly of Armagh, the Irish rebels established a provincial government (May 1642) under a 'supreme council' of nine pending the meeting of a general assembly to represent the nation. On 24 Oct. 1642 the general assembly of the Confederate Catholics met at Kilkenny and assumed the powers, though not the name and form, of a parliament. They regarded themselves as a provincial assembly for self-defence and confined themselves to providing for the administration of justice, the assessment of taxes, and the organization of their military affairs. The supreme council was enlarged to 24 members, 12 of whom were to reside permanently at Kilkenny to form a central government for the management of all civil and military affairs. Local government and justice were in the hands of county and provincial councils, while each province had its own army and commander.

CATHOLIC EMANCIPATION (1829) removed from British politics the issue which had been a touchstone of liberal attitudes for two generations. The Catholic Relief Act (1829) allowed Roman Catholics to enter parliament and to hold public office except as lord chancellor or lord lieutenant of Ireland.

Pressure for Catholic emancipation rose in the late 18th cent. Ireland, with three-quarters of its population Catholic peasants, contained a vocal minority who detested religious discrimination as a degrading, harmful symptom of alien rule. By the 1793 Catholic Relief Act, Ireland's parliament enfranchised the numerous Catholic forty-shilling freeholders and removed certain civil disabilities. Catholics' admission to parliament seemed imminent, but George III's opposition, and the 1798 rebellion, caused Pitt to link emancipation with a legislative union of the two kingdoms.

Irish Catholics supported the Act of Union (1800), believing that emancipation would follow. Pitt resigned (1801) when George III prevented it. On resuming office (1804), he promised not to raise the matter again, and for some years the Catholic cause languished. Of Grattan's Relief Bills, that of 1813 was only lost on the veto question (the right of the Crown, accepted by English but not Irish Catholics, to reject papal nominations to Catholic bishoprics).

Peel's appointment as home secretary (1822), balancing that of the 'Catholic' Canning as foreign secretary, seemed to preclude major concessions, but in 1823 O'Connell, with other Irish barristers, formed the Catholic Association. Backed by the priests, it soon embraced all Ireland's Catholics. They contributed a penny a month 'Catholic rent', which by 1825 brought in £1000 a week. The association was banned, but reformed under various names.

O'Connell saw emancipation, a prominent issue in the 1826 election, as a necessary prelude to repeal of the Union and abolition of tithes. At Waterford and Louth, pro-emancipation candidates were successful. In 1828 O'Connell, although ineligible, stood at a County Clare by-election, defeating the popular Vesey Fitzgerald. Seeing that continued obduracy could lead to civil war, Wellington and Peel pushed through the Relief Bill with Whig support. George IV reluctantly assented (April 1829).

At the same time, Ireland's Catholic forty-shilling free-holders were disfranchised. A £10 per annum voting qualification was introduced and the Catholic Association dissolved. O'Connell fought and won County Clare again before being admitted to the Commons. The apostasy of Wellington and Peel threw the Tories into confusion and contributed to the formation of a Whig administration (1830). The rise of an Irish Catholic Party at Westminster proved even more significant.

D. Gwynn, *The Struggle for Catholic Emancipation* (London, 1928).   MRB

CATHOLIC LEAGUE (Thirty Years War), formed originally in 1609 by the Catholic princes in Germany under Maximilian of Bavaria to counteract Anhalt's Protestant Union. Fearing Habsburg domination of the league, Maximilian recreated it in 1617, confining it to the southern German states under his own aegis. At the outbreak of the Bohemian revolt Maximilian put the league's considerable military resources under Count Tilly at the disposal of the Emperor Ferdinand (1619), on condition that he should have complete control of the Bohemian campaign and the right to retain the lands he conquered. In 1623 the alliance between the emperor and the league was renewed as Maximilian won the pledge of the Upper Palatinate. With the rise of Wallenstein, Ferdinand's dependence on the league waned. Since imperial prestige was rapidly growing, the league was summoned to Wurzburg, where its members demanded the conclusion of peace with the Protestants. The disgrace of Wallenstein, however, recreated Ferdinand's dependence on the league's army, but in 1635, with imperial power at its height after Nordlingen, Maximilian agreed by the peace of Prague to dissolve the league and place his troops under direct imperial command.

CATHOLIC LEAGUES (1576, 1584), spontaneous revolutionary associations of nobles, priests, bourgeoisie, and artisans which sprang up throughout France to defend Catholicism against first a feeble monarchy, with its inconsistent policy towards the Huguenots, and later the prospect of a Huguenot succession.

In response to the peace of Monsieur the league was founded initially by the Catholic nobility, who took an oath to observe its strict articles of organization (1576). In the states general of Blois (1576) the league exercised their new-found authority. Fearful of its weakening effects upon royal absolutism, Henry III tried to undermine it by declaring himself its leader, instead of the Duke of Guise (1577). The league collapsed, contributing nothing to Henry's military successes against the Huguenots.

The death of the Duke of Anjou (1584), making the Huguenot leader, Henry of Navarre, the legitimate heir to Henry III, caused the reappearance of the league. In Paris the Catholic citizens organized themselves into a militant

party under a committee of 16, to be copied in the provincial towns and in rural France the nobility placed themselves under the leadership of Guise and joined forces with the Paris League, while in many towns royal officials were replaced by league officials. Guise concluded a formal treaty with Spain (1584), agreeing on joint action against Huguenot heresy and pledging the league's support for Spain's recovery of Navarre and Cambrai in return for Spanish military aid. Thus the league's activities caused great anxiety to Henry III and Catherine de Medici, who tried to pacify its members (1585) by abolishing all previous edicts favourable to the Huguenots. Navarre took up the challenge and civil war broke out again (1585–94).

By 1588 Henry III had tired of his humiliating dependence upon Guise and the league. He instigated Guise's assassination, which served to stiffen the league's hostility to the monarchy. The Sorbonne declared Henry's subjects absolved from their allegiance to him and the league recognized another Guise, the Duke of Mayenne, as the lieutenant-governor of the realm. Henry was driven from Paris and his effective authority was limited to the Loire valley until his own assassination. The dying monarch threw a final challenge to the league by recognizing Navarre as his heir on condition that he became a Catholic.

With Spanish military aid the league continued the struggle against the new king. Catholic royalists were, however, increasingly divided. Mayenne found it difficult to unite the popular and noble groups within the league and reconcile them to Philip II's clear-cut aim to place his daughter on the French throne. The conversion of Henry IV to the Catholic faith totally undermined the league's position (1593), for he alone could defend both the Catholic Church and French territorial integrity against Spain. With his re-entry into Paris the league collapsed (22 March 1594).

N. M. Sutherland, *The French Secretaries of State in the Age of Catherine de Medici* (London, 1962).   MKS

CATHOLIC MONARCHS, THE, was the joint title given to Isabella I (1451–1504), Queen of Castile (*reg.* 1474–1504), and Ferdinand II (1452–1516), King of Aragon (*reg.* 1479–1516), whose marriage in 1469 united the royal houses of Castile and Aragon and paved the way for Spain's emergence as a world power. Although both monarchs were nominally responsible only for their respective kingdoms, Castile took the upper hand in the partnership. Isabella, devoting herself to home affairs, asserted the supremacy of the Crown over the nobility by bringing the powerful military orders and their vast income under Crown control. She initiated a programme of ecclesiastic and monastic reform which made the Reformation irrelevant in Spain and established an Inquisition which was used as an instrument to harness Spain's religious aspirations to the cause of national unity. In 1492 she completed the conquest of Granada and in the same year dispatched Columbus on his voyage of discovery of America. Ferdinand, who on his wife's death became Ferdinand V of Castile, was a consummate diplomatist and devoted himself to foreign policy, preventing the French from taking over Sicily and Naples and regaining for Spain those parts of Navarre which lay south of the Pyrenees.

CATHOLIC PROGRAMME, THE, political programme of the right wing of the Canadian Conservative Party drawn up (1871) by Adolphe-Basile Routhier. It reflected the 'Ultramontane' view of Bps Bourget and Laflèche that the clergy had a responsibility to guide the choice of the electorate. The programme demanded that legislation on marriage, education, the creation of parishes and other matters of interest to the Church be framed under episcopal direction. It also asked Catholic electors to vote for candidates who supported the programme or those whose ideas were nearest to it.

CATILINE, L. SERGIUS CATILINA (*c.* 109–62 BC), Roman aristocratic revolutionary, notorious from Cicero's Catilinarian orations. Born into an impoverished and politically obscure patrician family, he was a murderous partisan of Sulla. Quaestor in 77, praetor 68, and governor of Africa 67–66, he stood for the consulship of 65 but was disbarred because of impending prosecution for misgovernment. After trial and acquittal, he again stood for 63, but was defeated by Cicero. Defeated again for the consulship of 62 he tried to salvage his pride by revolution. Being forced by Cicero to leave Rome, he joined his motley army in Etruria and fell fighting near Pistoria.

CATINAT, NICOLAS DE (1637–1712), French general who was responsible for the cruel extermination of the Waldensian Protestants in Piedmont (1685–6). As French commander in Italy during the Nine Years War he won a notable victory at Staffarde, near Pinerolo, against the Duke of Savoy (1690). With inferior forces he repulsed Victor Amadeus's attempt to break through the Alps (1692) and beat him again at the battle of Marseilles (1693), for which he was rewarded with a marshal's baton. At the opening of the War of the Spanish Succession Catinat occupied Milan but was outmanœuvred by Prince Eugène, who led the Austrians across the Alps, cutting off the French communications (1701). This displeased Louis XIV, who replaced Catinat by his favourite, Villeroy, and transferred him to the Rhine, where with half the forces of his adversary he was unable to prevent the Margrave of Baden from capturing Landau with 50,000 men (1702).

CATLIN, GEORGE (1796–1872), US painter. A self-taught artist, his portraits of DeWitt Clinton, Dolly Madison, and other notables established his reputation as a portrait painter. He travelled in the trans-Mississippi West (1829–38), and his numerous paintings, drawings, and sketches comprise an account of western landscapes and Indians.

CATO, M. PORCIUS, the elder, 'the Censor' (234–149 BC), renowned conservative and isolationist Roman politician. Born a *novus homo*, he served in Roman armies against Hannibal, in Spain (where in 196 he led four legions to subdue the Turdetani and other insurgents), and in Greece, where he routed Antiochus III at Thermopylae (191). Meanwhile, thanks to the patronage of Valerius Flaccus, he became praetor, in which office he governed Sardina (198), and consul (195). He was renowned for his anti-Hellenist attitudes, and fought a running battle with the Scipionic group and hounded Scipio Africanus into voluntary exile (184), when he was himself elected censor with Flaccus. He opposed a proposed attack on Rhodes (168), and advocated a free Macedonia after the battle of Pydna (167), to keep Rome pure from the infection of the East. Later in life, fear of Carthage became obsessive with him, and he above all persuaded an increasingly ruthless Senate to crush the resurgent African city. He was famous as an advocate and as one of the earliest Latin historians.

CATO, M. PORCIUS, the younger (95–46 BC), Roman politician, whose obstinate leadership of the opposition to Pompey and Julius Caesar, though courageous, destroyed any chance of reconciling their ambitions within the republican constitution. As tribune in 63 he supported Cicero's demand for the death penalty on the Catilinarian conspirators. In 61–60 he rejected Pompey's overtures for a political alliance and vigorously opposed the First Triumvirate and Caesar's actions in 59 and later. Eventually, being forced to accept Pompey against Caesar (52), he fought in the campaign of Pharsalus and afterwards went first to Corcyra, then to Africa, where, after Caesar's victory at Thapsus (46), he was besieged in Utica and committed suicide, thus becoming the republicans' chief martyr.

CATO STREET CONSPIRACY (1819), in Britain, a plan proposed by the radical, Arthur Thistlewood, and some accomplices to seize London, murder the cabinet, and foment a general uprising. Their failure and subsequent execution helped to reconcile the country to the Tory government's repressive measures, and to turn popular radicalism into less conspiratorial courses.

CATROUX, GEORGES (1877–1969), French general, the most distinguished military leader to join De Gaulle in 1940. Catroux had spent most of his career overseas, serving under Lyautey in Morocco, and was governor-general of Indo-China until he resigned after the Franco-German armistice (1940). Catroux commanded the Free French forces in the Syrian campaign (1941), and later negotiated the agreement between De Gaulle and Giraud (1943). After the war, he was noted for his liberal views on colonial policy, and was entrusted with various political missions.

CATS, JACOB (1577–1660), Dutch advocate and politician, who became grand pensionary of Holland. He was also famous as a poet and his work exercised considerable moral influence over the northern provinces of the Netherlands. His didactic poems included 'Marriage' (1625) and the 'Wedding Ring' (1637). His best work is probably the 'Mirror of the Old and New Time' (1632). Cats, who succeeded Adrian Pauw in 1636, was politically ineffective and so enabled the *stadtholder*, Frederick Henry, to dominate foreign policy.

CATT, CARRIE LANE CHAPMAN (1859–1947), US woman-suffrage and peace advocate. Her work as state organizer of the Iowa Woman Suffrage Association (1890–2) and president of the National American Suffrage Association (1900–1904, 1915–47) was instrumental in bringing about passage of the 19th Amendment which gave women the vote. She was a founder of the League of Women Voters (1920), which has become an important source of non-partisan voting information, and was also an organizer and member (1925–32) of the National Committee on the Cause and Cure of War which was an influential lobby working for world peace.

CATTLE KINGDOM (1865–90), name given to the open-range cattle industry of the Great Plains of the US. These semi-arid grasslands within the public domain were appropriated after the Civil War by enterprising cattlemen as grazing for their herds of semi-wild cattle. The spring round-up for branding and the autumn drive to the railheads and the northern ranges added new elements to America's cultural heritage. It is estimated that some 5·5 million head were driven north from TX (1866–85). Largescale speculation in the early 1880s encouraged overstocking, and a cycle of blizzards and drought undermined the stability of the industry. Challenges to the cattlemen came also from sheepherders, and from homesteaders, who used barbed wire to fence the open range. By 1890 the industry had been forced to readjust itself to the new conditions.

CATULLUS, C. VALERIUS (*c.* 84–*c.* 54 BC), Roman poet, born at Verona into a wealthy family of local notables. His 113 extant poems range from intimate love lyrics to mythological epics in a variety of styles and metres.

CATULUS, TREATY OF (241 BC), negotiated between the Roman consul, Lutatius Catulus, and the Carthaginian, Hamilcar, at the end of the First Punic War. Carthage agreed to evacuate Sicily and to pay 2200 talents; before ratification of the treaty, the Roman people demanded also the cession of islands between Sicily and Italy, and a further 1000 talents. Both sides agreed not to attack the other's allies, but differing interpretations of this clause emerged when Hannibal attacked Saguntum in 219 and so precipitated the Second Punic War.

CATUVELLAUNI, the most powerful tribe in south-east England at the time of the Roman conquest. Under King Cassivellaunus they disconcerted Julius Caesar's invading legionaries at the Stour (55 BC). They moved their tribal capital from Wheathampstead to Prae Wood (*c.* 20 BC) and then, contravening their treaty with Rome by incorporating Trinovantian territory, gained coastal access by occupying Camulodunum (Colchester). The death of King Cunobelinus and the hostility of his sons, Caratacus and Togodumnus, precipitated the Roman invasion of Britain (AD 43).

CAUCASUS, RUSSIAN CONQUEST. Russia's occupation of Transcaucasia after 1800 made Russian control over the intervening mountain range of the Caucasus necessary. The establishment of this control involved Russia in its greatest colonial war, in which an estimated 500,000 Russians died, mostly of disease, before the conquest was completed in 1864. The conquest falls into two parts, (a) that of the western Caucasus or Circassia (Cherkessia) in which Ottoman and, occasionally, unofficial British help was given to the tribesmen, who maintained their resistance until 1864, when, following final defeat, 300,000 emigrated to the Ottoman empire; and (b) the conquest of the eastern Caucasus (Daghestan and Chechenia), where the first attempt to crush resistance by Gen. Mikhail Yermolov (1777–1861) led to a reaction in the form of a religio-political movement called Muridism under the leadership of Shamyl (c. 1796–1871). Shamyl's principal hope of success was to link his movement with that of the Circassians by occupying the intervening Russian-controlled territory of Kabarda. After the failure of his 1846 attack on Kabarda, defeat became only a matter of time, although years of hard planning and campaigning under the viceroyalties of Count Voronzov (1782–1856) and Prince Bariatinsky (1815–79) involving the cutting down of forests, and the construction of roads and bridges, were needed before Shamyl's final defeat (which also owed something to internal tribal opposition to his ruthless rule) was achieved (1859).

CAUDILLO (CAUDILLISMO), the maximum leader under a Spanish-American political system whereby the chief of state at all levels of government exercises virtually absolute authority, enjoys the personal loyalty of his followers, and, by extension, of his people. The transition from one *caudillo* to the next is sometimes violent and the succession is seldom certain, nor is the completion of the *caudillo's* 'legitimate' term in office. *Caudillismo* stems from the social system which has prevailed in much of Latin America since independence. Society has often been seen as an extension of the *hacienda* at the state or national level. Constitutionalism and western democratic systems are normally violated by *caudillismo*.

CAUDINE FORKS, BATTLE OF (321 BC), successful ambushing of a Roman army near Caudium in Samnium during the Great Samnite War. By surrender and submitting to the yoke, the consuls Veturius Calvinus and Spurius Postumius incurred national ignominy.

CAULAINCOURT, ARMAND AUGUSTIN DE, Duke of Vicenza (1773–1827), French general, diplomat, and foreign minister, who was forced because of his aristocratic background to begin his military career in the ranks under the French Republic. His promotion was rapid and he was sent by Napoleon as ambassador to St Petersburg (1807) with the task of consolidating the Tilsit agreement. After the invasion of Russia he was appointed French foreign minister (1813) and held the same post during the Hundred Days, although Napoleon paid little attention to his advice or to the effective use of diplomacy. Tsar Alexander I's regard for Caulaincourt ensured his survival and retirement in France under the restored Bourbons.

CAULET, ETIENNE FRANÇOIS DE (1610–80), French cleric, who was one of four bishops who resisted the condemnation of Jansenism by the French clerical assembly (1660–1). The assembly instructed all clergy to sign a formulary to the effect that certain propositions condemned by the pope in 1653 were contained in the Augustinus. Bp Caulet and his colleagues claimed that the assembly had exceeded its powers,

and when the pope, at Louis XIV's request, composed a new formulary, they resisted this too. Louis tried to force a trial of the bishops by papal commissaries, but provoked greater opposition from the other bishops. After the death of Pope Alexander VII a compromise was reached. Caulet and the other three bishops signed the formulary, but with reservations (1668). Caulet later resisted Louis XIV's extension of the *régale* (1673, 1675). He was deprived of his see of Pamiers and condemned by the Abp of Toulouse, his superior. Caulet appealed to Pope Innocent XI, who supported him, but the deadlock over the *régale* continued until 1693.

CAUTIONARY TOWNS, Flushing, Brill, and Rammekens, entrusted into English hands by the Anglo-Dutch treaty of 1598 as security for the debt of £800,000 which the Dutch owed for English military assistance against Spain. The towns were returned in 1616 for a payment of £215,000.

CAVAGNARI, SIR PIERRE LOUIS NAPOLEON (1841–79), soldier and diplomat, served on the Indian north-west frontier, became deputy commissioner, Peshawar (1877–8), and resident in Kabul (July 1879), where he was murdered.

CAVAIGNAC, LOUIS EUGÈNE (1802–57), French republican general and politician, who fought successfully in Algeria and was involved at the barricades on the republican side in the revolutions of 1830 and Feb. 1848. Though appointed minister of war by the provisional government of 1848, he was determined to suppress the more extreme republicans and socialists at the first opportunity. This came in the 'June Days', when Cavaignac was given dictatorial powers. He suppressed the revolt mercilessly, executing or deporting those captured. As president of the council of ministers, he was largely in control of the country after the revolt, but in the presidential elections he lost overwhelmingly to Louis Napoleon, and retired from politics.

CAVALIER, JEAN, leader of the Camisard revolt against the persecution of the Huguenots in the Cevennes (1702–5). Though only 23 years old and a baker's assistant at the time, Cavalier helped to organize the guerrilla campaign in the mountains. Having been won over by Marshal Villars in 1704, he was made a colonel in the French army and raised troops from among the former rebels.

CAVALIER PARLIAMENT in England, or Long Parliament of the Restoration, which lasted from May 1661 until Jan. 1679, during which period it underwent a remarkable political evolution. It was composed originally of landowners and their nominees, with a small number of merchants, naval and army officers, lawyers and placemen, who were staunchly royalist during the early sessions. Later, partly through by-elections, it developed a hardy core of disgruntled and extreme Whigs. It began by passing a series of laws designed to strengthen the king's authority and establish an Anglican monopoly in Church and state. While pandering to the intolerant Anglicanism of its members, Charles II and his minister, Danby, secretly negotiated with Louis XIV for money which would minimize Charles's dependency upon the Commons' supplies. At the same time, the judicious prorogation of parliament enabled Charles to avoid an anti-French foreign policy. However, during the Popish Plot scare the Commons attacked the king's control of the army, questioned the loyalty of James, Duke of York, heir to the throne, and finally presented articles of impeachment against Danby. On 30 Dec. 1678 Charles prorogued parliament, but dissolved it ten days before it was due to reassemble.

CAVALOTTI, FELICE (1842–98), leader of the extreme left wing in Italy after 1866, and a radical republican whose patron was Garibaldi. Cavalotti, a romantic figure, earned national fame as a poet, journalist, and politician, but he was unable to provide a clear-cut policy for his party despite its importance in a period of coalition government. He never became fully reconciled to constitutional monarchy and concentrated his attack on the corrupt quality of political life. His most important contribution was to undermine the reputation of Crispi. In a 'Letter to the Honest Men of All Parties', which sold 300,000 copies, Cavalotti showed that Crispi was implicated in the bank scandal, which he was using to pillory his rival, Giolitti.

Cavalotti's funeral following a duel (his 33rd) attracted great crowds, and contributed to the current social and political unrest by sparking off violent demonstrations.

CAVE ART. Engraving, painting, and carving on the walls and ceilings of caves and shelters is the enduring achievement of the hunters of the Advanced Palaeolithic phase of pre-historic Europe (ie, until c. 10,000 BC). The geographical distribution of cave art is concentrated in France, south of the Loire and west of the Rhone (notably in the Dordogne), and in the Cantabrian mountains of Spain; there are outlying examples in southern Italy, the island of Levanzo, off Sicily, and the South Ural district of Russia. Most cave art depicts the hunting of animals, some of them being shown assailed by weapons and possibly suffering wounds, which have been variously interpreted as records of success or belief in magic. Some of the comparatively infrequent human figures appear to be concerned with ritual functions connected with success in hunting; others, and with them the representations of particular symbols, suggest an explicitly sexual interest in fertility.

CAVENDISH, LORD FREDERICK CHARLES (1836–82), British politician and chief secretary to the lord lieutenant of Ireland (1882), who was murdered in Phoenix Park, Dublin, by members of an Irish terrorist organization, the Invincibles. He had been groomed for office as Gladstone's private secretary and his murder increased abhorrence of Irish nationalism in England.

CAVENDISH, HENRY (1731–1810), English scientist, who identified the properties of hydrogen and carbon dioxide and was the first to prove that water is a compound, not an element. His most famous experiment was the determination of the density of the earth (1798), though the apparatus he used had been devised earlier by John Michell. Much of his work, however, remained unpublished, including many discoveries in electricity that anticipated those of Coulomb and Faraday. The Cavendish Laboratory at Cambridge is named after him.

CAVENDISH, JOHN (1732–96), British statesman, noted for his devotion to the cause of political freedom, who opposed the expulsion of John Wilkes from the House of Commons. He served as chancellor of the exchequer in Lord Rockingham's administrations (1765–6, 1782), but declined to serve under Shelburne after Rockingham's death and carried a resolution censuring the terms of the treaty of Versailles against the government. In 1783 he was again chancellor under Portland and in his only budget brought in a bill to raise revenue by annuities and a lottery, and a tax on quack medicines. As a supporter of Economical Reform, he encouraged the gradual abandonment of sinecures as they fell vacant and substituted salaries for fees as payment of officials. After Pitt's rise to power in 1783 Cavendish never again held office.

CAVITE MUTINY (20 Jan. 1872), attempt to seize San Felipe fort, in Cavite province of the Philippines. Led by Sergeant La Madrid, 200 of the Fort's Filipino garrison mutinied, but the mutiny was suppressed by two infantry regiments from Manila. The uprising was the immediate reaction of the Filipinos to the abolition of privileges they had enjoyed for over a century, which were withdrawn (1871–3) by Izquierdo, the reactionary governor-general. During the term (1868–71) of his predecessor, the unusually liberal Gen. de la Torre, certain Filipinos, including the secular priests M. Gomez, J. Zamora, and J. Burgos, had led a movement against the Spanish friars to secularize Philippine parishes, in keeping with a Council of Trent ruling. The two priests expressed their desire for more liberty and justice for the people of the Philippines, which the Spanish Revolution of 1868 had won for Spaniards. In these circumstances the mutiny at Cavite was magnified by the Spanish authorities in order to justify heavy penalties: three secular priests were sentenced to die by strangulation; others were given prison sentences or exiled to the Marianas. The mutiny and the executions awakened the Filipinos to the sad state of affairs in their country, whilst national feeling was reinforced by the Spanish decision to entrench the friars in their positions as parish priests, because only they could be depended upon to preserve Spanish sovereignty in the colony. The Philippine Revolution broke out in 1896, ending Spanish domination over the Philippines in 1898.

H. De la Costa, *Readings in Philippine History. Selected historical texts presented with a commentary* (Manila, 1965).
JS

CAVOUR, CAMILLO DI, Count (1810–61), Piedmontese liberal parliamentarian and, as prime minister of Piedmont-Sardinia (1852–61), architect of Italian unity and European diplomat.

As a member of D'Azeglio's ministry (1851–2) Cavour contributed to, but did not initiate, an ambitious programme of economic, religious, and military reforms, designed to modernize Piedmont and earn European respect. He became prime minister in 1852 by the doubtful device of the *connubio*, by which he attracted both the right and left centres to his policies. The creation of a consensus coalition of the centre and the virtual destruction of the two-party system, together with the gerrymandering in subsequent elections, had an unfortunate effect on Cavour's successors, who adopted as normal practice what he regarded as crisis measures.

Cavour's initial aims were almost certainly Sardinian rather than Italian in scope. He was only gradually drawn into the larger theme of Italian unity by way of the annexationist policies of Sardinia. Probably Victor Emmanuel rather than Cavour suggested the enterprising policy of sending Sardinian troops to the Crimea (1855), enabling Cavour to raise the issue of Austrian rule in Italy at the Paris Congress (1856). He received no more than vague promises of support from England and France, but after the Orsini incident (1858) French initiative led to the pact of Plombières. This secretly proposed that Cavour should provoke Austria into war. France would then send an army to assist in the annexation of Lombardy and Venetia by Piedmont and receive Nice and Savoy in return. However, Napoleon's separate peace with the Austrians at Villafranca secured only Lombardy, and Cavour resigned in frustration. But he returned to office to preside over the plebiscites, mutually agreed upon with France, which gave Nice and Savoy to France and enabled Piedmont to annex the Central Duchies.

More than a third of Italy and over half its population were now united in the new kingdom and Cavour, who profoundly distrusted the populist and republican elements in the Risorgimento, might well have been content with this had not Garibaldi reopened the issue by his invasion of the Two Sicilies. Since public opinion was overwhelmingly in support of Garibaldi, Cavour could not prevent the landing. But he forestalled the international crisis which would have been caused by Garibaldi's invasion of Rome, by sending Piedmontese troops into the papal states and persuading Garibaldi to give up his conquests to Victor Emmanuel.

At Cavour's death Rome and Venetia were still in foreign hands. Italy had been created, but not Italians. Without Cavour this achievement might have taken another generation. But his assistance cost the Risorgimento some of its richness and popular support.

D. Mack Smith, *Cavour and Garibaldi, 1860: a study in political conflict* (Cambridge, 1954).

A. J. Whyte, *The Political Life and Letters of Cavour 1848–1861* (Oxford, 1930).
SDH

CAWNPORE, city and district in Uttar Pradesh, northern India, ceded to the British in 1801. During the Mutiny (1857) a small British garrison held out for three weeks until on 26 June they capitulated on a sworn promise of protection from the notorious Nana Sahib, the leader of the mutineers. But as they were embarking on boats for Allahabad they were fired on. The women and children were imprisoned in a building known as the Bibigarh, where on 15 July over 200 were hacked to death on the Nana's orders. In the morning the dead and dying were thrown down a well in the compound. The day after the massacre Cawnpore was captured by Havelock's troops.

CAXIAS, LUIZ ALVES DE LIMA E SILVA, Duke of (1803–80), Brazilian general, minister of war, and prime minister under the empire. His military fame was acquired by suppressing revolts and as Brazilian commander in the Paraguayan War.

CAXTON, WILLIAM, (c. 1422–91), translator and first English printer, who turned to literature after long and successful career in trade, pursued for the most part in the Low Countries. In 1469 he began to translate the *Recuyell of the Histories of Troye*, but found the labour of transcribing it so daunting that he learned the art of printing, set up a press in Bruges, and published the work in 1475. He returned to England (1476) and established a press at Westminster. Here he printed the most notable works of Chaucer, Gower, and Malory, as well as a considerable number of translations, including Virgil's *Aeneid*, French prose romances, and contemporary learned works.

CAYLEY, SIR GEORGE (1773–1857), English scientist and 'Father of Aerial Navigation'. As early as 1799 he had established the basic shape of modern aircraft (fixed wings, fuselage, and tailplane with rudder and elevators). Powered human flight was impossible with the engines then available, but he experimented with models driven by rubber bands and finally with full-sized gliders, in one of which his coachman made the first manned glider flight in history, of 500 yards (575 metres) in 1853.

CAYMANS, West Indian islands discovered by Columbus (1503), who named them Tortugas. In the 18th cent. they were colonized by the British from Jamaica, with which they were closely linked. On Jamaica becoming independent (1962), the Caymans became a British colony.

CAYUGA INDIANS, N. American tribe of the Iroquoian confederacy. The Cayuga were probably an offshoot of the Seneca, and incorporated remnants of several defeated tribes, including the Huron, Delaware, and Illinois. During the American War of Independence they sided with the British, and many fled to Canada when American troops burned their village (1779). After the war, the Cayuga signed three treaties ceding their lands to NY state, and after signing the last one (1803) they dispersed to live among other tribes. Some went to Canada, others eventually to Indian Territory in OK, and some remained in NY with the Seneca.

CAYUSE WAR (1847–50), arose after the murder by Cayuse Indians of Marcus Whitman and other whites at a religious mission on the Walla Walla river, Washington. The war ended when the murderers surrendered.

CAZALÈS, EDMOND DE (1804–76), French catholic writer and historian, who strongly defended the Church and clerical education in the Constituent and Legislative Assemblies (1848–9).

CAZALÈS, JACQUES ANTOINE MARIE DE (1758–1805), a minor French *robe* nobleman from Toulouse, who became one of the leaders of the extreme right in the early phases of the French Revolution. He fought in the émigré army and tried to defend Louis XVI during his trial.

CAZALLA, AGUSTIN (1510–59), Spanish humanist chaplain of Charles V, who was associated with the heretical communities discovered at Seville and Valladolid in 1557 and 1558. After being accused of heretical 'Illuminist' tendencies he was garrotted, then burnt at the stake for heresy (1559).

CEAUSESCU, NICOLAE (1918–), secretary-general of the Rumanian Communist Party and president of Rumania. He joined the party in 1936 and before and during the Second World War spent a considerable time in prison because of his political activities. In 1944 he was secretary of the Union of Communist Youth. After the party came to power Ceausescu rose steadily through its hierarchy, becoming a candidate member of the central committee in 1945 and a full member in 1948. When the Muscovites were purged (he had mistakenly been thought to be aligned with Ana Pauker's Muscovite faction) he moved up to the secretariat of the central committee (May 1952) and in April 1954 was made a candidate member of the politburo. His elevation to the secretariat forced him to give up his post as deputy minister of the armed forces, which he had held since 1950. In Dec. 1955 he became a full member of the politburo and two years later, when Chisinevschi was purged, emerged as second-in-command to Gheorghiu-Dej. Both at home and abroad he began to take an increasingly important part in affairs, serving on numerous party and state bodies and representing the party in foreign capitals. Meanwhile, he was securing his succession by keeping a firm hand on the party organization, for which he was responsible. When Gheorghiu-Dej died in 1965, Ceausescu took his place. But his position was not as secure as it seemed, and though his denunciation of Gheorghiu-Dej and purge of Alexandru Draghici went some way towards strengthening his grip, it was only with the ousting of two senior rivals, Gheorghe Apostol and Chivu Stoica, that it became firm.

Ceausescu, who was much concerned with relations with foreign communist parties, was admirably suited in 1970 to continue the policy of national independence begun by his successor, and the utterances of his administration became even more strident in defence of Rumania's sovereignty than those of Gheorghiu-Dej. He refused to participate in the invasion of Czechoslovakia, which he condemned, and likewise refused to follow Soviet policy in the Middle East. The old conflict between Rumania and the Soviet Union—Comecon and the Warsaw Pact—remained.

Ceausescu's rehabilitation of victims of past purges and his relaxation of some of the more severe practices of Gheorghiu-Dej's draconian rule have earned him considerable respect at home and abroad.

He was the first communist leader to become host to a US president when he received Nixon in 1969. JMK

CECIL OF CHELWOOD, EDGAR ALGERNON ROBERT GASCOIGNE-CECIL, Viscount (1864–1958), British statesman and one of the chief architects of the League of Nations. As Conservative MP from 1906, he was much concerned with foreign affairs after 1914 and played a large part in drafting the covenant of the league in 1919. He was often British representative to the league, and in 1926–7 at the Geneva disarmament talks; he was also president of the League of Nations Union (1923–45). In 1934 he helped promote the Peace Ballot and three years later won the Nobel Peace Prize.

CELAYA, BATTLE OF (1915), the bloodiest engagement of the Mexican revolution, resulting in the victory of Álvaro Obregón over Pancho Villa and assuring Constitutionalist government under Venustiano Carranza.

CELESTINE V (1215–96), Pope, founder of an order (1244) of Benedictine hermits (later called Celestines) of whom he required considerable austerities. In July 1294, after a two-year electoral deadlock, the cardinals chose the aged hermit as pope, but he accepted the office unwillingly, and, proving too unworldly to rule effectively, abdicated (Dec. 1294).

CELIBACY. In the early Christian era clerical marriage was regarded as lawful and clerical celibacy was laudable but voluntary. The Trullan Synod (692) insisted that bishops should, if married, put away their wives and the law in the Greek Church is still that parochial clergy should marry but that bishops are celibate. In the west, the decree of the Council of Nicaea (325) enjoining clerical celibacy was the starting point for later legislation insisting on celibacy of priests, deacons, and subdeacons, which was reinforced by Pope Gregory I at the end of the 6th cent. In the next four cents, marriage became common among secular clergy, though monks were celibate. Complete clerical celibacy was one of the main points insisted on by the 11th-cent. reformers, especially Pope Leo IX (1049) and Nicholas II (1059). The first and second Lateran councils (1123, 1139) went further: henceforth the marriage of clergy of the rank of subdeacon or above was not only illicit but invalid, and this remained the law for the rest of the Middle Ages and in the Catholic Church until the present time, though it had become by 1970 a matter of some controversy within the Church.

CELLAMARE, ANTONIO GIUDICE, Prince of (1657–1733), Spanish ambassador to France, who, at the instigation of Alberoni, became the centre of a conspiracy against Philip of Orleans, Regent of France, which involved also the Duke and Duchess of Maine (1718). Cardinal Dubois was able to use the Cellamare plot as an excuse for French troops to invade Spain (1719), forcing Philip V to dismiss Alberoni and accede to the Quadruple Alliance.

CELLARIUS, MARTIN (1499–1564), German Protestant extremist theologian and writer, who successively embraced Lutheran, Anabaptist, and Anti-trinitarian beliefs.

CELSUS, author of a bitter but well-informed attack on Christianity, 'The True Doctrine', of which a large part survives in verbatim quotations in Origen's refutation, the *Contra Celsum* (*c.* 248). The identity of Celsus, who wrote *c.* 177–80, was uncertain to Origen. Celsus criticized Christians for abandoning their ancestral (Jewish) worship and encouraging others to do the same, and for rejecting reason for faith and appealing to the uneducated.

CELTIBERI, people comprising immigrant Celts and native Spaniards, living in central Spain, south of the Ebro, who constantly obstructed the Romanization of Spain in 2nd and 1st cents BC. After the expulsion of the Carthaginians from Spain in the Second Punic War, they joined in the widespread rising against the Romans (197 BC) which was put down by Cato. The Celtiberian Wars (181–179, 153–151, 143–133) were three of the more violent episodes in a half-century of sporadic disturbance, which culminated in the burning of Numantia by Scipio Aemilianus. Even in the 1st cent. the Celtiberi were not wholly subdued; Sertorius drew much of his strength from them (81–72), and only under Augustus were they finally pacified.

CELTS, barbarian people of the first millennium BC, whose homeland was central Europe east of the Rhine. From the 7th cent. BC, iron-using and Celtic-speaking Hallstatt cultures were established throughout central and western Europe. Their influence was felt as far west as Britain; their wealth was characterized by imports from the classical world to Burgundy and south Germany. In the first period of La Tène culture (*c.* 450–400 BC), a distinctive art-style grew up on the middle Rhine, whence Celts were trading with Greeks and Etruscans. The Celts arrived in northern Italy *c.* 400 BC, and from there went south to Rome (sacked *c.* 390), southern Italy, Greece (Delphi sacked 279), and Galatia in central Asia Minor. Archaeology, Posidonius, and early Irish literature combine to give us a picture of Celtic society as essentially tribal, with graded obligations of service that could have contributed to the feudal concept in the Middle Ages.

CENSORATE, institution of Chinese government from the T'ang period onwards, but traceable to earlier periods. The censors were responsible for inspecting the activities of officials, for bringing cases of injustice or corruption to notice, and for criticizing proposed decisions of policy or administration.

CENSORS, Roman magistrates, instituted in 443 BC, to review the rolls of citizens, cavalry, and senators, regulate public morals, and ritually purify the Roman people. The two censors were, perhaps, originally elected for the whole *lustrum* (five-year period), but in 433 their term of office was fixed at 18 months, at first at four-yearly and then, from 209, five-yearly intervals. The authority, prestige, and rarity of the office made it the summit of a republican political career. Last filled as an independent office in 22 BC, its power became a prerogative of the emperor and Domitian (AD 81–96) appointed himself censor for life.

CENSUS, periodic count of the population, within a short space of time, by enumerators (or counters). Early censuses taken in Roman times and in ancient Egypt were incomplete and probably concerned only adult males. Evidence of an early complete census comes from ancient China, where details of instructions and penalties for refusing to answer questions have survived. Censuses were used locally in medieval Europe to estimate the needs of a besieged community or the amount of tax to be charged. In 1624 Virginia was the first of the American colonies to carry out a census, only a few years after its foundation. Iceland was the first European country to carry out a reasonably complete census (1703). Other Scandinavian countries and Austria followed later in the same century.

The first country to initiate a series of censuses was the US. Every ten years since 1790 a census has been carried out. In England in the 18th cent., although some recognized the value of a census, the majority regarded it as an infringement of personal liberty. A bill in parliament to introduce a census failed in 1753, although a fairly full survey for Scotland was produced by Alexander Webster two years later.

In 1801 came the first census in Britain, requiring overseers of the poor in England and schoolmasters in Scotland to collect information. This, together with church records of baptisms, marriages, and burials, supplied a moderately satisfactory collection of statistics. Since then there has been a census every tenth year (except 1941). In 1841 the householder became responsible for compiling information, while the registration of births, marriages, and deaths became a statutory requirement (England, 1837; Scotland, 1855).

20th-cent. censuses in Britain have asked questions about the relation of those living in a household to the head of the house, their age, sex, and nationality, their occupation, their place of work or school, and the number of rooms in the house. So rapidly have events and circumstances changed that ten-year gaps in such information have seemed too great for careful planning at central and regional levels, and a sample census was introduced in 1966. This census selected at random one in every ten households. It asked 27 questions, new ones being about car-ownership, garaging, travel to work, and qualifications in higher education.

Similar developments to those in Britain have happened elsewhere. All the main European powers had inaugurated census systems by 1900. Now (1970) new techniques and standardization of terms are agreed upon at international level by a United Nations sub-commission, following up the work done by the League of Nations between the two World Wars. Accurate world-wide census has still not been achieved. Many difficulties stand in the way, the chief of which is mass illiteracy. Nevertheless, the statistics gained from censuses are of immense value in surveys of the public health, and in estimating the needs of a population.

F. A. E. Crew, *Measurements of the Public Health* (Edinburgh, 1948).

M. W. Flinn, *British Population Growth* (London, 1970).

AMCGH

CENTRAL AFRICAN FEDERATION (1953–63). Abortive attempts to establish a union between Northern and Southern Rhodesia were made by white settlers before the Second World War. After the war, Welensky and Huggins renewed such proposals, which met with the support of the British Labour government on condition that Nyasaland (Malawi) be included, and that Britain continued to be responsible for the internal affairs of the northern territories, and for the overall interests of Africans. Federation was established in 1953, despite African opposition. The British Conservative government wanted to make Central Africa multi-racial, in contrast to South Africa, and hoped that the economic benefits that were expected to accrue from federation would enable this to come about. The one lasting achievement was the Kariba dam on the Zambezi (1960), but economic benefits were unequally distributed between black and white.

The federal constitution was complex. Salisbury was the seat both of the federal and of the Southern Rhodesian governments. The first prime minister was Huggins (Lord Malvern), who was followed in 1956 by Welensky. Territorial governments remained, that in Southern Rhodesia being responsible to the mainly white electorate, those in the northern countries to the British government. The federation was probably too cumbersome to survive in the best of circumstances, but mounting African opposition, led by well-organized nationalist parties, broke into strong resistance in 1958. A commission led by Lord Monckton acknowledged in 1960 the failure of 'partnership' and recommended that each territory should have the right to secede. A special ministry under R. A. Butler was formed to 'unscramble' the federation, which was done by the end of 1963. Malawi and Zambia became independent African states, while Rhodesia (Southern) continued under the rule of its white minority.

P. Keatley, *The Politics of Partnership*. (London, 1963).
N. Sithole, *African Nationalism* (London, 1954).   AEA

CENTRAL AFRICAN REPUBLIC (617,000 sq. kms) in west central Africa with a population of 2,088,000, chiefly Madjia-Baya and Azande people. Formerly the Ubangi-Shari province of French Equatorial Africa, it became independent in 1960. The constitution was suspended in Jan. 1966 and government (1970) is by a revolutionary council.

CENTRAL AMERICAN FEDERATION, an aspiration and a political goal which has waxed and waned throughout the history of Central America. Following independence, Central America joined (1821) then withdrew from Mexico (1823). 'The United Provinces of Central America' resulted, with its capital at Guatemala City. Civil war between Liberals and Conservatives followed, with the Liberals at first victorious. Unity became associated with Liberalism, and the Conservatives, led by Rafael Carrera, fought to end the union (1837–8). Carrera won and the federation was divided into five independent states.

Since 1838 approximately 25 unsuccessful attempts have been made to restore unity. The Organization of Central American States (ODECA) was created (Oct. 1951) to further co-operation and a Central American Common Market came into being.

CENTRAL ELECTRICITY BOARD, THE, established in 1926, was a landmark in the development of public enterprise in Britain. Among the achievements of Baldwin's first administration (1924–9) was the establishment of public corporations to control economic activity in areas where private enterprise seemed inefficient or undesirable; examples were the CEB and BBC. Electricity supply had been provided by a multiplicity of small private and municipal agencies, working on different frequencies and voltages. The government decided that there should be a central body to control the generation of power, the supply in each area remaining in the hands of the previous agencies. The board, though chosen by the minister of transport, was free from all governmental and parliamentary influence in its day-to-day operations. The chief achievement of the CEB was the spread of the national grid, a process largely complete by 1939. Electricity supply was nationalized in 1948.

CENTRAL INTELLIGENCE AGENCY, US security organization created (1947) to co-ordinate intelligence operations. It is responsible to the National Security Council, and subject to minimal congressional supervision. The agency also engages in direct operations.

CENTRAL TREATY ORGANIZATION (CENTO), defensive alliance and organization for regional co-operation which is a direct successor to the Baghdad Pact, the change having occurred on Iraq's withdrawal from the pact (March 1959). The members of the organization were, in 1970, Britain, Turkey, Pakistan, and Iran; the US was an associate member and, particularly in the military sphere, played a part as important as that of the full members. The organization was established on lines similar to those of NATO, with a council which met at both ministerial and deputies' level. Its military importance was small, since the regional members each had local objectives of greater importance to themselves than defence against the Soviet Union—Pakistan its rivalry with India; Turkey the Cyprus question; and Iran opposition to Arab radicalism, while the US pursued its policies through bilateral agreements, as well as through CENTO.

On the economic side the organization's achievements were by 1970 more important. CENTO was one of the agencies through which aid has been transmitted to the regional members. A separate organization, Regional Co-operation for Development (RCD) 'parallel to but outside CENTO', was established in July 1964 to develop co-operation between its own members, Iran, Turkey, and Pakistan.

CENTRALES, the 'factories in the field' that have ground the sugar cane of Spanish America and Brazil since the 16th cent.

CENTRE PARTY (*Zentrums partei*), of the Weimar Republic in Germany, founded in 1870, as the Roman Catholic political party in the German Reichstag. Theoretically, its policy was based on Catholic teaching about the state and society, but in practice it was a defensive alliance originating in the minority position of Catholics in a united Germany. The Centre Party therefore opposed any extension of federal power. It gained strength through Bismarck's attacks on the Church during the *Kulturkampf*, holding about one-quarter of the seats in the Reichstag. It was among the few parties whose organization survived the collapse of the Wilhelmine Monarchy intact. However, on 12 Nov. 1918 it suffered the loss of its Bavarian wing which, concerned about its particularism, decided to form the Bavarian People's Party (BVP). While for ideological reasons the Centre was bound to reject the violent overthrow of the Hohenzollerns, its peculiar traditions no doubt eased the acceptance of a constitutionally established order. The most significant feature of the Centre Party was its denominational (Catholic) basis. It was not tied to a particular class, but rather cut across different social groups and attracted voters from all strata of society, almost all of whom belonged to the Catholic minority in the Reich. The first advantage of the Centre's structure was that until the end of the Weimar Republic electoral support remained fairly stable—between 15 and 17 per cent (incuding the BVP). Second, it gave the leadership a good deal of room for tactical manœuvre as long as the latent tensions between the working-class and the middle-class wings of the party were prevented from reaching the surface. It was due to this flexibility that the Centre managed to collaborate with both the SPD and the bourgeois parties and to share government responsibility in either left-wing or right-centre coalitions. However, from 1927 onwards the authoritarian conservatism of Kaas asserted itself, its progress being accelerated by the desertion of working-class voters in 1928. When the chairman of the party's Reichstag faction, Brüning, became Reich chancellor in March 1930, the idea of anti-parliamentary rule with a firm hand had been formulated into a political programme. Under the impact of the Great Depression the leadership pursued an anti-socialist policy of 'national concentration' which, if possible, was to include a 'tamed' National Socialist movement. This concept collapsed with the dismissal of Brüning in May 1932, and henceforth the Centre Party manœuvred helplessly until Jan. 1933. Kaas had no basic objections to the apparently 'moderate' dictatorship of Hitler's cabinet, provided it guaranteed Catholic cultural and religious interests. When this was promised, the Centre supported the Enabling Act and was dissolved on 5 July 1933.

DMK

CENTURION, the principal professional officer of the ancient Roman army. Each of the ten cohorts in a legion contained six centuries (nominally 100 men), commanded by centurions graded in fixed order of seniority. They were promoted from the ranks or recruited from men of equestrian status or from former members of the Praetorian Guard. Under the empire, many centurions acquired during their service sufficient capital to qualify for admission to the Equestrian Order, for which they provided an important source of recruitment.

CEORL, term signifying a free peasant in Anglo-Saxon times. Some ceorls were relatively wealthy landholders, others quite poor labourers, but they all possessed the same blood price (wergeld). It was not unknown for wealthy ceorls to become lower-rank nobles (thegns). Poor ceorls, however, might be depressed by economic circumstances into slaves.

CERESOLE, BATTLE OF (1544), in Piedmont during the Fourth Italian War. The French under Enghien defeated Spanish and Milanese troops fighting for the emperor, but had to make peace at Crespy a few months later. The French cavalry were armed with the horse-pistol (petronel), which enabled them to fire on the enemy instead of charging with the lance.

CERIGNOLA, BATTLE OF (1503), a victory for the Spanish under Cordova, which led to the capture of Naples and the end of the French occupation of southern Italy. The battle was fought in Apulia, on the Via Traiana, and Cordoba enticed the French to make a costly attack against a ditch protected by stakes and ramparts.

CERNY, JAN (1874–1957), Czechoslovak politician, who was originally an Austrian civil servant. He was twice entrusted by the Czechoslovak parliament to form a government (Sept. 1920–Sept. 1921, and March 1926–Oct. 1926), when the political parties failed to agree on the composition of a coalition government. On the first occasion Cerny gained admiration by liquidating a revolutionary movement without bloodshed.

Although he remained in government, being appointed as minister of the interior at various times, he preferred the less political post of provincial president of Moravia.

CERULARIUS MICHAEL (*reg.* 1043–58), Patriarch of Constantinople, during whose tenure of office the divergence of views between the Catholic and the Orthodox Churches became much sharpened. In 1054 Cerularius broke off relations with the legates whom Pope Leo IX had sent to Constantinople in an effort to ease the prevailing tensions and to establish an alliance between Rome and Byzantium against the threatening power of the Normans. This incident proved to be the beginning of a permanent schism.

CERVANTES SAAVEDRA, MIGUEL DE (1547–1616), Spanish writer, author of *Don Quixote.* He fought at Lepanto (1571), where he was wounded and was imprisoned in Algiers (1575–80) after being captured by Turkish pirates.

Although a prolific dramatist, he was unable to earn a living either from his plays or from humble government employment, and was more than once imprisoned for debt. *Don Quixote* (1605), a satire on the medieval romances still popular in Spain, was to some extent a wry reflection on his own failures and frustrations. Despite its wide and immediate success, the novel did little to relieve his fortunes and he died in poverty. As well as plays, Cervantes wrote *La Galatea*, a pastoral poem (1583), and some short stories, *Novelas Exemplares* (1612).

CESAIRE, AIMÉ (1913–), Martinican poet whose themes are revolt, denunciation of colonialism, and négritude, a term he introduced as 'the simple recognition of the fact of being a Negro and the acceptance of this fact and of its cultural and historical consequences'. His work has influenced black nationalists in Africa and in the Caribbean. He broke with the Communist Party (1957) and founded the *Parti Progressiste Martiniquais*, which adopted (1964) a policy of home rule for Martinique.

CESALPINO, ANDREAS (1519–1603), Italian physiologist and naturalist, who led the Averroist school of Aristotelian philosophy in 16th-cent. Italy. His scientific publications reveal the limitations of his Aristotelian concepts. His *Practice of the Art of Medicine* (1606) discussed pulmonary circulation.

CETNIKS, the royalist resistance forces in occupied Yugoslavia during the Second World War. The name *cetnik* was taken from the members of the *ceta*, Serbian bands which fought the Turks in the 19th cent. The *cetniks* were drawn primarily from the Yugoslav army and were almost exclusively Serbian. Conservative and particularist, the *cetniks* were equally hostile to communists and Croats. The first groups formed in Bosnia, where Serbs fell under severe attack from the Ustase. Although units existed in all regions, the most effective was that commanded by Col. Draza Mihailovic, which operated in central Serbia. Other units were poorly organized and badly disciplined. As the war went on, Mihailovic came to believe that victory depended more on the Allies than upon his *cetnik*s and that his principal mission was to destroy the communists. His refusal to engage the enemy, after encouragement by the Allies, led the Allied command to give their support to the rival Partisans in 1943. In 1944 the Allies abandoned Mihailovic and the *cetnik*s altogether upon learning that many of his subordinates, and perhaps he himself, had collaborated with German, Italian, and Ustase forces against the communist Partisans.

CETSHWAYO (d. 1883), last of the Zulu kings (*reg.* 1873–83), when he killed his chief rival in a civil war. His determination to retain Zulu independence and territorial integrity against the encroachments of the Transvaal and Natal, together with British schemes to confederate all the South African territories, led to the Anglo–Zulu War (1879). Although dramatically successful at the battles of Isandlwana and Rorke's Drift, Cetshwayo's armies were ultimately defeated, and the king was exiled to St Helena. In 1883 he returned to a truncated kingdom, rife with warring factions. Cetshwayo himself was forced to flee, and died at Eshowe shortly afterwards.

CEUX DE LA LIBÉRATION, French Resistance movement in the Second World War. It was the most conservative of the movements, and was said to include many former members of the *Croix de feu.* It was strongest in the Paris region. CDLL absorbed the *Vengeance* movement, and was renamed *Ceux de la Libération Victorieuse.*

CEUX DE LA RÉSISTANCE, one of the leading French Resistance movements in the Second World War. Originating in Normandy, it spread throughout northern France. Léo Hamon was its most prominent member.

CEYLON NATIONAL ASSOCIATION, founded in the 1880s by Ponnambalam Ramanathan. Its membership was drawn mostly from the English-educated elite. It was a symptom of the growing unrest in the upper and middle classes with the British bureaucracy. Its memorials to the British government had ultimately some effect in obtaining a small measure of self-government.

CEYLON NATIONAL CONGRESS, formed (1919) to press for constitutional advancement. It absorbed the Ceylon National Association and the Ceylon Reform League, the latter having arisen from the discontent with the government's mishandling of the riots in 1915. Ably drafted memoranda were sent to the British government by congress and, despite the opposition of the governor, some elected representation in the legislative council was conceded in 1921, and more in 1924. The congress at first included members of most communities, but after 1926 became almost entirely Sinhalese. Its principal leaders were James Peiris, D. B. Jayatilleke, F. R. and D. S. Senanayake, and E. W. Perera. Though modelled on the Indian Congress, it never exerted authority comparable to that of Congress. After the Donoughmore Constitution (1931) had been accepted by the Legislative Council, and several congress leaders had become ministers, its importance declined. It came to an end during the Second World War.

CHAADAEV, PYOTR YAKOVLEVICH (1793–1856), Russian thinker and philosopher, whose *First Philosophical Letter* (1836) opened the Westernizer–Slavophile debate. Chaadaev rejected Russian history and insisted that her future must be reassociated with Catholicism and western progress and could eventually surpass it.

CHABAN-DELMAS, JACQUES (1915–), a follower and confidant of De Gaulle and one of the leading figures of the Fifth Republic. Chaban-Delmas had a distinguished record in the Resistance ('Chaban' was originally a Resistance pseudonym), becoming De Gaulle's military delegate in France and reaching the rank of general in this capacity. After the war, he entered politics as a Radical, but joined the Gaullist RPF party on its foundation. He was leader of the Social Republican group of deputies which succeeded the RPF, and was a minister in the Fourth Republic governments of Mendès-France and Mollet. As minister of defence (1957–8), he is thought to have helped to prepare the way for De Gaulle's return. Under the Fifth Republic he served as president of the national assembly until his appointment as prime minister by President Pompidou (1969). Chaban-Delmas has been mayor of Bordeaux since 1947.

CHABRIAS (d. 357 BC), Athenian general, who devised new antihoplite tactics, and achieved prominence by defeating the Spartans at Aegina (388). Subsequently he assisted Evagoras, tyrant of Cypriot Salamis, in revolt from Persia, and served as a mercenary in the Egyptian revolt against Persia, until recalled to Athens at Persia's demand (380). He helped contain Spartan moves towards Attica and Boeotia (378–7) before defeating the Spartan fleet at Naxos (376) and won new members for the Second Athenian Confederacy. After Athens' alliance with Sparta he fought against Thebes (?369), survived a charge of treason (366), and secured Ceos for Athens (?363) before further mercenary service in Egypt. Recalled to fight Athens' seceding allies in the Social War, he fought in the Hellespont, and died in action at Chios.

CHACABUCO, BATTLE OF (12 Feb. 1817), important victory near Santiago, Chile, of the Argentine–Chilean independence army under José de San Martín against the royalists.

CHACO WAR (1928–35), conflict between Bolivia and Paraguay over possession of the Chaco Boreal, which resulted in the mutual exhaustion of the two nations. Foreign mediation divided the Chaco between the combatants. The war was fostered by longstanding territorial disputes over the region and by foreign oil interests desirous of developing the oil deposits believed by many to exist in the Chaco. Armed clashes began in 1928, when the Paraguayans seized a Bolivian fort. Bolivian Indians were forcibly sent to the lowlands to fight Paraguayans, who believed they were defending their homeland.

The League of Nations and the Pan-American Conference on Arbitration failed to end the conflict. A temporary truce was negotiated (April 1930), but hostilities were soon renewed (1932). The Paraguayan army controlled most of the Chaco by 1935. A truce was facilitated by the US and several Latin American states (June 1935) and the Chaco Peace Conference met to resolve the conflict. The Conference included the US, Argentina, Brazil, Chile, Peru, and Uruguay. The resulting peace treaty, signed at Buenos Aires, provided for the division of the Chaco between Paraguay (180,000 sq. kms) and Bolivia (76,800 sq. kms); the latter was assured an Atlantic outlet by way of the Paraguay river and the use of Puerto Casado in the Chaco as a free port.

The war had important effects on Bolivia. While Paraguay lost some 36,000 men, Bolivia lost 52,000. A party of the Bolivian officer corps, stunned by their experience, became committed to national regeneration and rehabilitation of the Indian. The oil companies were frustrated, since until the mid-20th cent. the Chaco failed to produce the anticipated oil.

HDS

CHADWICK, SIR EDWIN (1800–90), British pioneer of accurate social investigation, champion of expertise in government appointments, leading Benthamite administrator, and sanitary reformer. His influence over factory and poor law reform in 1833 and 1834 was partly original, and fostered the growth of centralized inspection and administration. He was a controversial secretary to the poor law board (1834–47), partly because he campaigned against providing outdoor relief to the able-bodied, and partly because his uncompromising attitude alienated the politicians.

As an administrator who detested waste and amateurism, he was impatient with democratic processes, typified, for him, by the London vestries which obstructed his pioneering public health work, a natural development from his concern with poverty in the late 1830s. His widely read *Sanitary Report* (1842) was a manifesto for the sanitary movement. Permanent commissioner on the board of health (1848–54), he then retired on a pension, and was henceforth a busy projector of reforming schemes.

He was ill-rewarded for his pioneering work, and did not receive his knighthood till 1889. His many enemies were more often wrong than he was, and he had to overcome formidable obstacles of scientific and technological ignorance. Yet his firm belief in preventive medicine and in the atmospheric rather than the germ theory of disease led him into serious errors, particularly when combating cholera.

CHAERONEA, city of western Boeotia in Greece. Founded in the Mycenean age, and overrun early by Dorian invaders, it tended later (450–350 BC) to support Theban leadership of Boeotia against its neighbour Orchomenos.

It was captured briefly by the Phocians in the Second Sacred War and was the site of Philip II of Macedon's famous victory in 338.

CHAERONEA, BATTLE OF (338 BC), Philip II of Macedon's victory over Athens, Thebes, and their allies, which gave him control of Greece. Entering Boeotia from the west, Philip found about 35,000 Greek infantry arrayed between mountains and the Cephissus river. A feigned retreat enticed the Greek left and centre to advance. Philip's cavalry, led by his son Alexander (the Great), charged through the gap. They encircled and annihilated the Theban Sacred Band on the Greek right. Thebes capitulated at once, and Athens shortly accepted terms.

CHAFFEY, GEORGE (1848–1932), Canadian-born pioneer of irrigation in CA, Ont., and Vic., Australia, in the 1880s. With the aid of his brother, William Benjamin (1856–1926), he sought to make Mildura and Renmark centres of a flourishing region in Vic. irrigated by the waters of the Murray river. The Chaffeys faced opposition in parliament and elsewhere, but were supported by, among others, the future prime minister, Alfred Deakin, who was impressed by their success in Ont. The Mildura scheme failed and the brothers were ruined, partly because of their unfortunate choice of business associates, and partly because they were caught in the depression following the land boom of 1888–90. George returned to North America, where he rehabilitated his reputation and his finances. William remained to inspire other settlers, paying off his debts, and proving the soundness of the original irrigation plan.

CHAGHATAY (d. c. 1241), son of Chingiz Khan. He fought in his father's campaigns against China (1211–16) and against the Khwarazm Shah (1219–22). From this prince the Chaghatay khanate was to take its name. He received from Chingiz Khan the territories extending from the Uyghur lands in the east to the region of Bukhara and Samarkand in the west. The khanate did not assume its definitive form until after the death of Chaghatay. The real founder was, in fact, Alughu, one of his grandsons, who won control over much of Central Asia in the years after 1259. Mubarak Shah (1266) was the first of these khans to become a Muslim. He was deposed almost at once, Buraq Khan following him on the throne. In 1282 Du'a, the son of Buraq, became Chaghatay Khan and ruled until 1306–7. Thereafter the khanate remained in the hands of the descendants of Du'a until 1370. After the death of Qazan Khan in 1347 effective power rested, however, with the Turkish begs (military chiefs), who enjoyed great influence and prestige within the state.

CHAIN or SCALES OF JUSTICE, known as the *Mizan-i Adal*, set up by the Mughal Emperor Jahangit (1605) between the Agra fort and the bank of the Jumna. The chain bore bells that could be rung by his subjects, and symbolized his concern for justice.

CHAIT SINGH, the *zamindar* (landholder) of Benares and Ghazipur, was deprived of his *zamindari* by Warren Hastings in 1781. He was a subject of Shuja-ud-daulah, the ruler of Oudh, until the accession of Asaf-ud-daulah (1775), when by the treaty of Faizabad his *zamindari* was transferred in full sovereignty to the English Co., to whom he swore an oath of fealty and promised to pay annually 23 lakhs of rupees. In 1778, during the war with the French, Hastings demanded an extra five lakhs annually while the war lasted. Chait Singh delayed his payments and refused military aid. In 1781 Hastings proceeded to Benares and placed him under arrest. This led to his rebellion and flight, after which he was removed from his *zamindari*. Hastings's treatment of Chait Singh was one of the charges brought against him at his impeachment.

CHAITANYA (1485–1533), leading figure in the *bhakti* movement of devotional religion. Chaitanya was a Brahmin of Nadia in Bengal. He became a devotee of Vishnu in his incarnation as Krishna, preaching in Orissa and in the Deccan and elsewhere. His pilgrimage to Brindaban, Krishna's traditional birthplace, revived the popularity of this holy place. He believed that through religious devotion and adoration, supported by religious songs and dances, a state of ecstasy could be achieved in which the presence of God could be directly experienced. This belief found expression in the *sankirtan* religious exercise. Chaitanya's Krishna cult of Vaishnavism had a strong following in Bengal, where it appealed to the people as distinct from the *bhadralok* or literary classes.

CHAKRAVARTIN RAJA (lit. king who turns the wheel, symbolizing the cosmos), or universal ruler which, in the Indian context, means ruler of the Indo-Pakistani sub-continent. The term apparently first emerges in Buddhist literature. The concept was important as an ideal in the mind of ambitious Indian kings. Only Asoka, however, came near to attaining this ideal. The term became devalued in later times and was then used by rulers whose real powers, unlike their ambitions, were confined to small areas.

CHAKRI DYNASTY of Thailand, founded by King Rama I (1782). Its name perpetuates his earlier title as minister of the north (*Mahatthai*): Chaophraya Chakri. It continues down to the present reign of King Phumiphon Aduldet (Rama IX).

CHALAIS CONSPIRACY (1626), one of a series of unsuccessful noble plots to overthrow Richelieu. Henri de Talleyrand, Comte de Chalais, lent his name to a plot involving Gaston d'Orléans, Condé, Soissons, the Vendôme brothers, and Mme de Chevreuse. Chalais was persuaded to reveal the plan to Richelieu, but continued to hatch another plot with Gaston d'Orléans. Chalais, betrayed by a friend and by Gaston's revelations, was made the scapegoat for the princes of the blood, and executed (Aug. 1626).

CHALCEDON, ancient Greek colony founded by Megara *c*. 675 BC in Asia Minor at the southern end of the Bosporus. Despite its important strategic position, for which both Athens and Sparta fought, the Persian Megabazus dubbed it 'the city of the blind', as its founders ignored the more favourable site on the opposite European shore, occupied later by Byzantium. It was bequeathed to Rome by Attalus III of Pergamum (133), and destroyed by Mithridates VI of Pontus in his attack on Roman Asia (88). In AD 451 the fourth general council of the Church assembled there, convened under imperial patronage, with the object of promulgating a single statement of the Christian faith; a *definitio fidea* regarding the person of Christ that reasserted the formularies of both east and west, which defined the limits of legitimate speculation.

CHALCEDON, COUNCIL OF (AD 451), important ecumenical council of bishops who met to discuss the vexed question of the nature of Christ. Rival views were the Monophysite, holding that Christ had a divine nature only; the Nestorian, which held that Christ had two natures, co-existing separately, a divine, and a human; and the Orthodox, which maintained that there were indeed two natures, but that these were indivisibly, if mysteriously, united in one Person at once human and divine. This last view gained the day, and remains the official doctrine of Greek Orthodox, Roman Catholic, and all other Christians, save Unitarians and Copts. The deliberations of the Council were conducted in a spirit of passionate intolerance; but they were certainly decisive, and marked the defeat of the attempts of the patriarchs of Alexandria to dominate the Byzantine Church.

CHALCIDIAN LEAGUE, federal association of Greek communities on the Chalcidice peninsula, founded in 432 BC by small communities seceding from the Athenian alliance and centred on Olynthus. In the great Peloponnesian War (431–404) it resisted Athenian coercion, forming the basis of support for Brasidas' campaign of liberation (424–422) and of opposition to unfavourable stipulations in the peace of Nicias (421). Little is known of the league's constitution or growth, but attempts at extending it over the whole peninsula were resented by some cities and by Amyntas III of Macedon, and the Spartans broke it up, subjecting Olynthus (382–380). It was revived after 378 and joined the Second Athenian Confederacy, but later seceded, identifying itself with Philip II of Macedon, only to be overthrown by him (349–348).

CHALCIDICE, peninsula of Macedonia comprising the promontories of Acte, Sithonia, and Pallene with their hinterland.

In antiquity it was inhabited by two main ethnic groups, the Chalcidians and the Bottiaei, closely related to the Greeks and interspersed from c. 750 BC with Greek settlers from Chalcis and Eretria, eg, at Scione, Mende, and Torone, and from Corinth at Potidaea (c. 600). The area, an important source of timber, was controlled by Athens for much of 5th cent. After 433 a powerful Chalcidian and Bottiaean nationalist movement, forming the Chalcidian League based on Olynthus, gained some success against Athens, Sparta, and Macedonia.

CHALCIS, ancient Greek city-state in Euboea, prominent in Greek expansion overseas during the 8th–6th cents BC. In the 8th cent., initially together with Eretria, Chalcis established trading settlements in both the east (eg, Poseidium in Syria) and the west (eg, Cumae in Italy); many other settlements followed in Sicily, eg, Naxos, Leontini, and Zancle. Eretria was probably defeated in the Lelantine War (c. 700) and by the 6th cent. the manufacture of pottery and arms for export flourished. Chalcis later lost ground to Athens, who severely defeated her (c. 506). She fought closely alongside Athens in the Persian Wars (480–479) and joined the Delian League (477). After an unsuccessful revolt (446), she paid tribute to Athens until 411. Later she joined the Second Athenian Confederacy (377), but, after much Macedonian and Athenian intrigue, was lost to Philip II (338), and became thereafter a key Macedonian stronghold.

CHALDAEANS, Aramaean tribe which settled in southern Babylonia (c. 10th cent. BC) and gradually extended their control over the area. In 626 they founded the last Babylonian dynasty, the Chaldaean or Neo-Babylonian kingdom, under Nabopolassar (c. 626–605). He was followed by Nebuchadnezzar II (c. 605–562), who conquered Syria and Palestine and rebuilt the city of Babylon. The dynasty ended with Nabonidus (c. 555–539), at the end of whose reign the country was conquered by the Persians.

CHALDIRAN, the Safawid regime in Persia (1499–1503), recruited most of its armed forces from among the Turcoman tribes living in Asia Minor. This process, if allowed to continue unchecked, would have undermined the dominance of the Ottomans in that area. In 1514 the Ottoman Sultan Selim I marched against the Safawid Shah Isma'il. At Chaldiran, on the road to Tabriz, the Ottomans routed the Safawids after a hard battle (24 Aug.). Chaldiran did not lead to an Ottoman conquest of Persia, but it did set a limit once and for all to the extension of Safawid influence amongst the Turcomans of Asia Minor.

CHALFONT, ALAN ARTHUR GWYNNE JONES, Life Baron (1919–) and British diplomat. After various staff and intelligence appointments in the army, he became defence correspondent of the London *Times*. In 1964 he was appointed a minister of state at the foreign office, and later given special responsibility for disarmament negotiations.

CHALMERS, ROBERT CHALMERS, Baron (1858–1938), British civil servant, oriental scholar, and governor of Ceylon (1913–16). In 1915 a religious riot broke out between Buddhists and Muslims, which was put down with undue severity, for which Chalmers was blamed. The measures employed included placing leaders, such as D. B. Jayatilleke and D. S. Senanayake, briefly under detention, which did much to stimulate the national movement in Ceylon. Chalmers later became master of Peterhouse College, Cambridge.

CHALUKYAS, name of a number of different, but related, ancient Indian dynasties dominating all or parts of the northern Deccan and Gujerat for long periods between the middle of the 6th and the end of the 12th cent. AD. The principal centres of the main branch in the earlier period were Vatapi (mod. Badami) and Aihole in northern Mysore state. A small independent kingdom had been founded there in the 6th cent. and expanded into a powerful state under Pulakeshin II (608–42), who, by ceaseless campaigning, conquered most of the northern Deccan from Gujerat in the west to Andhra Pradesh in the east. In the north, Pulakeshin's empire was separated from that of his contemporary Harsha of Kanauj by the Narmada river. A remarkable eulogy of Pulakeshin's achievements, composed in ornate Sanskrit verse, is contained in the great Aihole inscription.

This empire did not, however, remain united for long. A minor branch came in charge of Gujerat, while Andhra Pradesh was entrusted to Pulakeshin's brother Vishnuvardhana, who headed a long line of rulers: the Eastern Chalukyas or Chalukyas of Vengi (c. 624–1118, but in a somewhat subordinate alliance with the Cholas during the last of these five centuries). The main branch, also called Western Chalukyas, remained in control of the western Deccan, notably Karnataka (mod. Mysore state) until the middle of the 8th cent. During this period they were involved in intermittent warfare with the Pallavas of Coromandel. This time is of particular interest for the development of the Deccani style of art and architecture. There are numerous inscriptions in Sanskrit and Old Canarese belong to this period.

By the middle of the 8th cent. the Chalukyas were temporarily eclipsed by the Rashtrakutas (c. 753–973), but remained in a subordinate position. From 973 to the 2nd half of the 12th cent. a branch of the Chalukyas was again in control over approximately the same area as before, but now from the capital, Kalyani, about 100 miles (161 kms) northeast of Badami. The Chalukya kingdom flourished especially in the long reign of Vikramaditya VI (1075–1127). The poet Bilhana, originally from Kashmir, worked at his court and made the early career of this king the subject of an ornate Sanskrit text. The period of the Chalukyas of Kalyani is especially important for the development of Canarest literature (in which the most famous name is that of the poet Pampa). It is no less interesting for religious developments, both in Jainism and in Shivaism, where a new sect, that of the Linggayats, became influential. Adherents of this sect, in contrast to almost all other Hindus, opposed image worship as well as the caste system.

G. Yazdani (ed.), *The Early History of the Deccan*, 2 vols (London, 1960).   JG de C

CHAMBER, KING'S, one of the offices of medieval English government, from which, in a sense, all the others grew. The chamber was originally the king's private apartment and bedroom with a closet or wardrobe adjacent, and was the natural place to keep valuables. The existence of staff of the chamber can be traced back to the 10th cent., though it was not until after the Norman Conquest that the office and its staff emerge clearly. One of the officers of the chamber was the treasurer, and the first stage of development ended when the treasurer and the exchequer moved out of the royal household (c. 1130) to become the central accounting office, leaving the chamber as the king's private treasury. The next stage saw the emergence of the wardrobe, firstly as a suboffice of the chamber under Peter des Rievaux (c. 1218–32), and then as a separate office taking over most of the important functions of the chamber, especially the custody of the king's privy seal and personal finance. The chamber revived as an important office under Edward II, when it began to administer lands forfeited to the king, such as those of the Templars and of Thomas of Lancaster and his adherents. Also, as the wardrobe became increasingly an office of state under Edward I and Edward II, the chamber became increasingly once more the king's private treasury, drawing revenues from the lands it administered, but without accounting for them at the exchequer. This led to the danger of a state within a state, governed in the interests of the personal prerogative of the king, and aroused such distrust and suspicion that it was abandoned in 1356, the administration of chamber lands and most of its functions being distributed among the other offices of government. Thereafter the chamber ceased to be a really major office of government and administration until its re-emergence as a major financial office under Edward IV and especially Henry VII (after 1487).   JG

CHAMBER OF PRINCES, consultative and deliberative body consisting of rulers of Indian states (1921–47). The chamber was intended to provide the princes with an embryonic corporate identity in political affairs and a forum for the discussion of common problems. In fact, it developed little initiative or constructive influence. The viceroy was the president, but a ruling prince was elected chancellor, an office held by some of the most able of the princes, including Bikanir (1921–5), Patiala (1926–30, 1933–6), Bhopal (1931–2, 1944–7), and Nawanagar (1937–44). There were 121 members, of whom 109 were ruling princes with salutes of 11 guns or with full internal powers in their states, who sat in their own right. The other 12 members were elected to represent 127 rulers of smaller states. Although it did include many important princes, particularly those of the medium-sized states, the chamber was hampered throughout by the refusal of the rulers of several of the largest states, notably Hyderabad and Mysore, to join it.

CHAMBERLAIN, JOSEPH (1836–1914), British statesman, who supported social reform at home and imperialism abroad. He split the Liberal Party on Home Rule (1886) and the Conservative–Unionist alliance on Tariff Reform (1903).

Chamberlain retired from business with a fortune (1874), having already reorganized the Birmingham Liberal Association (1868), guided the National Education League (1869), and served as town councillor (1869–73). Under his mayoralty in Birmingham the city was remodelled and its amenities improved (1873–6). Though unsuccessful at Sheffield (1874), he became MP for Birmingham (1876).

Chamberlain strengthened radicalism within the Liberal Party by extension of the Birmingham caucus organization through the National Liberal Federation (1877), of which he was founder and first president. He served Gladstone as president of the board of trade (1880–5), supporting the reform bill of 1884 with hard-hitting speeches. He pressed for strong measures in Egypt (1882), but opposed coercion in Ireland, negotiating the Kilmainham treaty and resigning over the cabinet's rejection of his plan for limited autonomy in Ireland (1885). In the subsequent election campaign Chamberlain issued the unauthorized programme, including agricultural reform ('three acres and a cow'). Returning to office as president of the local government board, he resigned in protest against the adoption of Home Rule, which was defeated with Liberal–Unionist help (1886). Conversations on Liberal reunion failing, Chamberlain moved towards the Conservatives, exacting promises of social reform as the price of his support.

Chamberlain served Salisbury as British plenipotentiary in the discussion on Canada's fishery dispute with the US (1887–8) and colonial secretary (1895–1903). His influence was seen in the Workmen's Compensation Act (1897) and the committee on old age pensions (1896), which he had suggested in 1892. He helped to avert war with the US on the dispute between Venezuela and British Guiana (1895–7) and exerted a moderating influence in South Africa, though he was accused of complicity in the Jameson Raid (1895–6), suspicion remaining even after his exoneration by a commitee of enquiry (1897). Chamberlain negotiated unsuccessfully with Kruger at the Bloemfontein Conference (1899) and the subsequent Khaki election was fought on his policies (1900). He guided the passing of the Commonwealth of Australia Act (1900) and presided over the colonial conferences of 1897 and 1902 in which imperial preference was advocated. Opposing the maintenance of British isolation, he negotiated unsuccessfully for an Anglo-German alliance (1898–9).

Chamberlain did not oppose Balfour's succession as prime minister (1902), but resigned on the cabinet's refusal to abandon Free Trade and campaigned with the Tariff Reform League (1903) in the constituencies, with resulting support at Conservative Party conferences (1903–5). Party disunity led to Balfour's resignation and electoral defeat (1906), though Chamberlain's influence held Birmingham for the unionists and he achieved a common policy with Balfour in opposition. Though Chamberlain's health forced his retirement from active politics (1906), his influence remained in the decline of laissez-faire doctrines and British isolationism.

J. L. Garvin and J. Amery, *The Life of Joseph Chamberlain* (London, 1932).

P. Frazer, *Joseph Chamberlain: radicalism and empire, 1868–1917* (London, 1966).   VEC

CHAMBERLAIN, SIR JOSEPH AUSTEN (1863–1937), British statesman. Entering the House of Commons (1892) as a Liberal–Unionist, he held office in the Conservative administrations of Salisbury and Balfour (1895–1905), of Baldwin (1924–9), and three times in coalition governments (1915–17, 1918–21, 1931). His leadership of the Conservative Party (1921–2) ended because of party dissatisfaction with his support of Lloyd George. As Baldwin's foreign secretary (1924–9), he secured the Locarno pacts (1925). He tried through regular personal contacts at the League of Nations Council, and especially through friendship with France, to sustain European peace though aware of growing German power.

CHAMBERLAIN, NEVILLE (1869–1940), British Conservative prime minister and MP (1918–40), who attained political success despite formidable obstacles. His early career was spent as a successful Birmingham businessman, of which city he was twice mayor. He was summoned by Lloyd George during the First World War to the difficult post of director-general of national service (1916–17). He entered parliament in 1918, at the age of 50, but politically he was overshadowed until the 1930s by his half-brother, Austen. Yet his promotion was rapid, and his administrative skills striking. He was postmaster-general (1922–3), paymaster-general (1923), minister of health (1923, 1924–9, 1931), chancellor of the exchequer (1923–4, 1931–7), and ultimately prime minister (1937–40).

Chamberlain felt no doctrinaire hostility to state intervention or centralization. He could delegate, he was lucid and crisp in parliamentary exposition, and he achieved many valuable reforms in local government (1929), poor law, housing, and public health. He disliked party in-fighting, but his zeal for precision and purity of administration and his distaste for sentimentality sharpened his rejoinders to Labour Party criticism. He wanted his party to become more popular in character, and in 1931 preferred the title 'national' to that of Conservative. He greatly improved Conservative Party organization and research facilities, and was Baldwin's right-hand man after 1931. He helped to introduce Protection in 1932 as a radical remedy for unemployment, but he opposed deficit financing. After 1933 he introduced legislation to deal with the problem of special unemployment areas.

During his premiership, war and foreign affairs dominated world events. His courageous visits to Hitler during the Munich crisis (1938) conceded self-determination to the Sudeten Germans. By thus postponing war, Chamberlain won a brief popularity at home. But he had always distrusted Germany; and though trusting Hitler on this occasion, he knew that he was merely gaining time for Britain to build up her defences. With the Nazi invasion of Czechoslovakia (March 1939) Chamberlain's policy crumbled, and, though he broadened his cabinet, he was an unconvincing war leader. The British withdrawal from Norway (April 1940) caused his downfall, and Winston Churchill succeeded him. Though he remained as lord president of the council, ill-health forced him to resign in Oct. 1940.

Chamberlain's faults inevitably derived from his virtues. His efficiency sprang from a temperament which despised sentimentality, mediocrity, and public emotion. His passionate integrity and extreme industriousness led him to neglect his public image.

K. Feiling, *Life of Neville Chamberlain* (London, 1946).

BHH

CHAMBERLAYNE, EDWARD (1616–1703), English chronologist, who published *Angliae Notitiae*, or *The Present State of England* (1668).

CHAMBERLEN, PETER (d. 1631), English surgeon of French descent, who became the most celebrated accoucheur of his day. He attended the queens of James I and Charles I of England. His younger brother and nephew, both called Peter, were also surgeons, the latter being physician to Charles II.

CHAMBERS, WHITTAKER (1901–61), former member of US Communist Party who became a national figure in 1948, when he testified before the Congressional committee on un-American activities that Alger Hiss had been a communist agent.

CHAMBERS, SIR WILLIAM (1723–96), British architect, whose *Treatise of Civil Architecture* (1759) became the standard work on the correct use of the Orders. His work includes Somerset House, London, Harewood House, Yorkshire, and parts of Trinity College, Dublin. The *chinoiserie* in Kew Gardens shows that he was capable of fanciful as well as grand treatment.

CHAMBERS OF COMMERCE (and/or Manufactures) in Britain. Groups of city businessmen were organized into pressure groups at the end of the 18th cent. and in the 19th cent. for fiscal or legislative grievances. Among their particular concerns were the Corn Laws, the risk of railway monopoly, and the interests of dominant local specializations. The first chamber was started in Glasgow (1783) and the idea gradually spread to English industrial and commercial cities. Though by the late 19th cent. many of them had joined together to form an association, which increased their chances of being consulted by royal commissions, the association never had any powers over its members, and the chambers themselves were not important.

CHAMBORD, French royal palace on the Loire, begun in 1519 and built on a grand symmetrical scheme of the late Gothic style, with round towers and a central staircase, possibly derived from an idea of Leonardo da Vinci's. It was much frequented by French kings in the 16th and 17th cents, and was occupied by Stanislas Leczynski and Maurice de Saxe in the 18th cent.

CHAMBORD, HENRI DIEUDONNÉ, Comte de (1820–83), last Bourbon claimant to the throne of France. A posthumous son of the murdered Duc de Berri, he was known as the '*enfant de miracle*', and received the Château de Chambord (1821) as a national thank-offering for the birth of a legitimist claimant. Having been educated by pious and old-fashioned conservatives, he used his Chambord title in preference to that of Duc de Bordeaux when he began actively to advance his claims as pretender (1843). Charles X had abdicated in his favour (1830), but not till the death of the Duc d'Angouleme (1844) did all legitimists recognize Chambord's claim. He travelled widely in Europe before establishing himself (1848) at Frohsdorf, near Salzburg, with his wife, Marie Thérèse of Modena. He refused to negotiate with the Orléanists after 1848, and played a limited role until the 1870s. In 1873 he refused to abandon the white flag of Henry IV, and so prevented a restoration. He left no heirs, and the claim passed to the Orléans family, with whom he had become partially reconciled.

CHAMBORD, TREATY OF (1552), between Henry II of France and Maurice of Saxony in opposition to the Emperor Charles V, who after his victory at Muhlberg (1547) had enforced the Augsburg Interim (1548), an attempted religious compromise unsatisfactory to the Lutherans. Charles had also imprisoned the Landgrave of Hesse, and his policy in Germany was so much resented that Maurice, formerly his ally, changed sides. In the treaty Henry promised to aid Maurice with an army and subsidies in return for the formal possession of Metz, Toul, and Verdun, which the French had captured in 1551. At Passau (1552) Charles was forced to agree to the toleration of Lutherans, while this and other outstanding differences were referred to the imperial diet.

CHAMBRE ARDENTE, additional temporary chamber of judges in France, established in the *parlement* of Paris during Henry II's reign to deal with the problem of Protestantism.

CHAMBRE AUX DENIERS, the chief financial department of the household of the French kings from the 13th cent. The name is first recorded in 1286, but the institution itself existed much earlier. Until the early 14th cent. it may also have functioned as the chief auditing department for all the royal finances until a separate *chambre des comptes* was created for this wider purpose (*c.* 1303).

CHAMBRE DE LA MAREE, French chamber in the *parlement* of Paris whose members were delegated from the judges of one of the court's permanent chambers and whose duty was to try cases, civil and criminal, involving the traffic and sale of sea-fish. Such a commission existed because the Church's laws of abstinence made fish a valuable commodity.

CHAMBRE DE L'ARSENAL, extraordinary commission in France appointed by Richelieu in 1631 to judge certain crimes, *eg*, counterfeiting and the removal of money from the country, in which state security was involved. Its arbitrary establishment and its tendency to ignore traditional legal practices aroused the opposition of the *parlement* of Paris, but the court's remonstrances were ignored by Louis XIII, who confirmed the commission's authority.

CHAMBRE DE L'EDIT, French chamber established in the *parlement* of Paris by the Edict of Nantes (1598) to ensure impartial justice for the Huguenots. It consisted of a president and 16 judges, of whom six had to be members of the Reformed Church, and had to judge all cases in which Huguenots were involved.

CHAMBRE DES COMPTES, French court established to judge in the last instance matters relating to the king's finances. Before the end of the *ancien régime* there were 12 such courts, though the original one in Paris, which had begun as an offshoot of the *curia regis* in 1320, remained the most prestigious.

CHAMBRE DES LUTHÉRIENS, extraordinary tribunal in France which appeared in the reign of Henry II as a reaction against the spread of Protestantism and included some members of the *parlement* of Paris. Its alternative title was *Chambre de la Reine*.

CHAMBRE INTROUVABLE, first chamber of deputies of the French Restoration, so called by Louis XVIII because of its extreme royalism. The chamber, summoned on a restricted franchise in the aftermath of Waterloo, was composed of 402 deputies, of whom many were young and inexperienced, and 176 who were *ancien régime* nobles. They demanded stern reprisals against Bonapartists, favoured the White Terror, and opposed the king on the budget and other issues. This and their unpopularity with the allies led to the dissolution of the chamber (Sept. 1816).

CHAMBRE MI-PARTI, temporary chamber in France established in the *parlement* of Paris in the reign of Henry III.

CHAMBRE SAINT-LOUIS, meetings held in this chamber in France between deputies of the *parlement* of Paris, the *cour des aides,* the *grand conseil,* and the *Chambre des Comptes* in May–June 1648 and the political demands which came out of them marked the beginning of the first *Fronde.*

CHAMBRUN, RENÉ DE (1906–), French lawyer and son-in-law of Laval, whose political emissary he was on several occasions under the Vichy regime.

CHAMILLART, MICHEL I. (1652–1721), industrious but incompetent minister of Louis XIV. A councillor of the *parlement* of Paris and close friend of Saint-Simon and other peers, he was reputed to have risen to royal favour through his proficiency at billiards. Appointed controller-general of finances by Louis in 1699, he was promoted to minister of state in 1701, replacing Barbésieux as minister of war. He directed the war effort during the Spanish Succession conflict until he was dismissed in 1709 because of repeated French military failures. He was replaced by Mme de Maintenon's protégé, Voysin.

CHAMLAY, JULES LOUIS BOLE, Marquis de (1650–1719), minister and military strategist to Louis XIV, who advised the king on the conduct of his major wars. He suggested the devastation of the Palatinate in 1688.

CHAMOUN, CAMILLE (1900–), Lebanese Maronite lawyer and politician who led (with Kamal Janbalat) the opposition to President Bishara al-Khuri after 1948. As president (1952–8), his pro-Western policies and personal ambitions alienated his political rivals and provoked the 1958 Lebanese crisis.

CHAMPA, kingdom which flourished in central Viet-nam from the 4th to the 17th cents. In the early centuries of its existence, Cham hegemony extended from the present Quang-Binh province southwards to Binh-Thuan; but in the 11th cent., as a result of wars with Dai-Viet, it began to lose territory to the Viet-namese, and eventually was extinguished altogether. Thus from 854 to *c.* 1000 the capital was at Indrapura, just south of modern Da-Nang; but then it had to be moved south to Vijaya (present Binh-Dingh), where it remained until it was sacked and annexed by the Viet-namese in 1471. Thereafter, Champa included only Nha-Trang and Phan-Rang; and those areas too were annexed by the Viet-namese towards the end of the 17th cent. The culture of Champa was strongly Indianized, its religions being Hinduism and Mahayana Buddhism in its Indian form. A number of Hindu temples, dating from the 7th to the 13th cents, still survive along the Central Viet-namese coast. Marco Polo visited the country briefly on a return voyage from China in the late 13th cent., shortly after it had successfully resisted a Mongol attack.

CHAMPASAK, principality in southern Laos, founded near the ancient site of Vat Phou at the end of the 17th cent. by descendants of the royal family of Lan Xang. It controlled southern Laos and parts of north-eastern Thailand, and was brought under Thai control between 1777 and 1819, being gradually reduced by 1893 to the status of a Thai province. It was transferred to French administration in 1893 and 1904 and its ruling family, led by Prince Boun Oum, subsequently agreed to its incorporation into the kingdom of Laos.

CHAMPETIER DE RIBES, AUGUSTE (1882–1947), French lawyer and founder of the first French Christian Democrat Party (Parti Démocrate Populaire) (1924). Champetier de Ribes was interested in social questions and helped to organize the Catholic trade union movement. He was a minister under the Third Republic, and was active in the

Resistance. He was chief French prosecutor at the Nuremberg trials.

CHAMPLAIN, SAMUEL DE (*c.* 1567–1635), French explorer, born in Brouage, France, the son of a naval captain. As a young man he fought with Henry of Navarre. Between 1599 and 1601 he commanded a ship for the Spanish, visiting and making maps and sketches of the West Indies, Mexico, Cartagena, and the isthmus of Panama. Upon his return to France he was granted a pension and a title by Henry IV. He joined an expedition in 1603 under the command of François Gravé, Sieur du Pont (Pontgravé), and explored along the St Lawrence river as far as the Lachine rapids. From Indians he heard stories of large stretches of water to the west, and he returned to North America the following year, remaining until 1607; during this time he helped to found Port Royal in NS and made exploratory trips as far south as Cape Cod. He persuaded Henry IV to found a colony on the St Lawrence river, and on 3 July 1608 he laid the foundation for Quebec. He established good relations with the Hurons by using his firearms to defeat a hostile Iroquois band, and thus inadvertently committed the French to an alliance with Algonquin tribes against the Iroquois and their (later) Dutch and British allies. Backed by a charter granted in 1611 and a royal patron, Prince de Condé, Champlain continued his explorations. In 1613 he went up the Ottawa river, and two years later he explored and mapped Georgian Bay and Lakes Huron and Ontario. This marked the end of his personal explorations, although he was responsible for sending Jean Nicolet as far west as Lake Michigan and Green Bay.

Champlain remained in Canada for the rest of his life, apart from a journey to seek aid for the colony from Cardinal Richelieu (1625), and a period when the colony was occupied by a British force (1629–32). He died in Quebec.

CHANAK, scene of an Anglo–Turkish crisis in 1921. The treaty of Sèvres (1920) had set up a neutral zone between Greece and Turkey on the Asiatic side of the Straits. This was endangered by the revolt of Mustafa Kemal against the Sultan of Turkey, and the attempt of the Greeks to interfere on the sultan's side. The Greek army were defeated (Smyrna, Aug. 1922) and the Kemalist forces advanced on the Straits. The Anglo–French guarantee of the neutral zone now came into force; despite the French and Italian withdrawal of troops, Lloyd George's government decided to resist the Turkish advance. Although much outnumbered, the British general, Harington, was ordered to deliver an ultimatum to Kemal. Harington, however, judged the Turks to be too strong, and instead negotiated an armistice.

In Britain there was much criticism of Lloyd George's pro-Greek position. The Conservatives under Bonar Law took the opportunity to break the coalition with the Liberals after the famous Carlton Club meeting of October. Curzon, who remained foreign secretary, managed to extricate Britain from her difficulties at the Lausanne Conference (1922–3). The allied occupation of Constantinople was ended, and the territorial demands of the Kemalists were conceded. The British interest in the demilitarization of the Straits, and the establishment of an international commission, were provided for in the Lausanne treaty of 1923.

CHANCELLOR, RICHARD (d. 1556), English navigator, who first established trading contacts with Russia and founded the Muscovy Co. (1553–4). A sea captain with Mediterranean experience, Chancellor was briefed by the old sailor Sebastian Cabot and the geographer John Dee on the search for a north-east passage. Sailing in the *Edward Bonaventura,* together with two other ships of the Merchant Adventurers' Co. under the command of Sir Hugh Willoughby, Chancellor alone reached Archangel via the White Sea. He and some of his men travelled by sleigh through the Russian winter from Archangel to Moscow, where they were warmly greeted by Tsar Ivan IV and laid the ground for diplomatic as well as commercial exchanges. Chancellor was drowned off the Scottish coast after making a second voyage to Russia.

CHANCELLORSVILLE, BATTLE OF (2–4 May 1863), a notable Confederate victory in the American Civil War, fought on the south bank of the Rappahannock river in VA. It was the springboard for Robert E. Lee's second invasion of the North which culminated in the Battle of Gettysburg. The victory, perhaps Lee's most brilliant battle, was shadowed by the death of 'Stonewall' Jackson.

CHANCERY, COURT OF, in England. Before the Conquest and in the early Middle Ages the king's chaplain (*capellanus*) was the only cleric necessarily attached to the king's household and thus, in an age where few laymen were literate, also his secretary. As such he was entrusted with the king's seal (*cancella*) and all the king's communications both within and without the realm, except in certain financial matters, were conducted through his *cancellarius* or chancellor.

Henry II created the legal system of writs originating an action; these were in the form of royal commands and issued out of the chancery, whose business was thus greatly increased. In the 13th cent. the chancery became a separate department of state, permanently situated in London; its officers included the keeper of the rolls in chancery and the keeper of the hanaper (a financial post created in 1244) and its functions included the receiving and trying of petitions at the start of a new parliament. In 1349 Edward III transferred additional legal functions to the chancery, which assumed more the character of a court than a secretariat.

Under Henry VIII the chancellor's court, which had already begun to claim a separate jurisdiction, achieved practical independence. The chancellor, who was always a leading figure in the king's council, had legal functions to perform, such as the appointment of puisne judges, and had an efficient department to assist him. Cardinal Wolsey, an ecclesiastic with a natural flair for the administration of justice, was succeeded by the first lawyers to hold the office of chancellor, Sir Thomas More and Sir Thomas Audley; in the same reign the master of the rolls, or vice-chancellor, was commissioned to hear cases on his own, and all appointments in the chancery began to be held by laymen. The foundation of the chancellor's court was not in the existing common law, but in natural justice, or equity, and operated not by disregarding the common law, but in overriding it or supplementing it. As 'Keeper of the King's Conscience', the chancellor gave relief in cases where the common law gave no remedy, especially in the development of 'uses', the forerunners of trusts; where advantage had been gained in the courts of common law by fraud, forgery, or duress, and by remedies which the courts of common law did not give, notably specific performance and injunction. The overbold use of those remedies was the occasion of Wolsey's downfall.

From Tudor to Victorian times the chancery, under great lawyers such as Nottingham and Eldon, developed and administered a system of 'equity' principally directed towards the creation and administration of family settlements and other dealings in land. Its principles grew progressively more rigid and its procedure more complex and dilatory, and in the mid-19th cent. it stood in urgent need of reform. In 1871 it became the chancery division of the high court of justice, and its prime function in relation to the courts of common law was established by the provision that, in any court, where the rules of equity and of common law conflict, the rules of equity shall prevail. Since then, lord high chancellors have seldom sat at first instance, the work of the division being carried out by its puisne judges, and the master of the rolls has had the care of the public record office, a direct legacy of his original function, and has presided over the civil work of the court of appeal.   JRLS

CHANDA, SAHIB (d. 1752), popular name for Husain Dost Khan, son-in-law of Dost Ali, Nawab of the Carnatic (1732–1740), and admired as a general in his time. In 1740 he was captured by the Marathas and, on his release (1748), claimed the nawabship with French support. Later he was surrounded near Trichinopoly owing to Clive's action and forced to surrender (1752). His rival, Muhammad Ali, procured his execution.

CHANDELLAS, early medieval Indian dynasty of kings (c. AD 950–1310) ruling in present Bundelkhand. The first king, Dhanga, made himself independent from the Pratiharas of Kanauj and maintained himself in a natural well-protected area. Though politically hardly of prime importance, the Chandellas are famous on account of the temple group of Khajuraho, built during their reigns. These monuments may appear over-decorated at first, but they are among the most splendid examples of a school of art remarkable for its vitality and sensuality.

CHANDERNAGORE, former French settlement about 30 miles (48 kms) north of Calcutta on the Hughli river. It was permanently occupied by the French East India Co. in 1688 as an entrepôt for the Bengal trade, and developed rapidly under J. F. Dupleix (1730–41). In 1756 it was captured by Clive to prevent help being given to Siraj-ud-daula, the Nawab of Bengal. It was restored in 1764, but recaptured in 1794 on the outbreak of the French revolutionary war. It was finally restored to France in 1816, but from then on was little more than a residential French-speaking town and a convenient base for smuggling. In 1950 it was ceded by France to India, and was merged with West Bengal in 1954.

CHANDLER, ZACHARIAH (1813–79), US politician, senator from MI (1857–75), and a prominent Radical Republican, who opposed many of Lincoln's wartime policies and Andrew Johnson's reconstruction programme, and was involved in the attempt to impeach Johnson (1868). As secretary of the interior in the Grant administration (1875–7), Chandler was a leading manipulator of the 'spoils system'.

CHANDOS, JAMES BRYDGES, 1st Duke of (1673–1744), British politician, MP for Hereford (1698–1714), and officeholder. Appointed commissioner of public accounts to submit a report to parliament after the death of William III (1702), he became an admiralty councillor (1702–5) and later gained the lucrative office of paymaster of the forces. Brydges was little concerned with party principles, serving under any ministry, though was regarded by contemporaries as a Court Whig. He was implicated in the charge of peculation made against Walpole (1711) by the Tories, being defended by his friend St John. In the following year Brydges tried unsuccessfully to defend Marlborough against a similar charge. In later life he left politics and became chancellor of St Andrews University.

CHANDOS CLAUSE, in British politics, amendment by Lord Chandos to the second of the Whigs' parliamentary reform Bills (introduced June 1831), which enfranchised £50 tenants-at-will in the counties. Since the main beneficiaries were farmers with tenancies renewable annually, the clause strengthened the position of the landed aristocracy by enabling them to control more votes. It reappeared in the third Reform Bill (Dec. 1831) and formed part of the 1832 Reform Act. Though some reformers disliked it as a device for riveting aristocratic control upon county elections, other radicals welcomed any extension of the franchise.

CHANDRAGUPTA, name of several ancient Indian kings, notably (*a*) Chandragupta Maurya (c. 320–296 BC), founder of the Maurya empire after the fall of the Nanda dynasty; (*b*) Chandra Gupta I (usually thus spelt to avoid confusion with Maurya), first Gupta emperor (c. AD 320–35) who, by marriage alliance and by conquest, transformed a little kingdom in present Bihar into a large state dominating the Gangetic valley; (*c*) Chandra Gupta II (AD 376–415), also known as Vikramaditya, grandson of Gupta I, one of the most powerful Gupta emperors and patron of some of the greatest figures in ancient Indian civilization such as the poet Kalidasa.

CHANG CH'IEN, Chinese explorer and diplomat. He was sent *c.* 135 BC to secure an alliance against the Hsiung-nu being one of the first known Chinese travellers to explore Central Asia and northern India. The contacts which he made with local communities and his report on the geographical, ethnic, and economic features of areas such as Bactria and Parthia stimulated Chinese interest in Central Asia, and led to the establishment of the Silk Roads.

CHANG CHIEN (1853–1926), Chinese scholar and industrialist. Although placed first in the metropolitan examinations of 1894, he denied himself an official career, and entered industry to save China from poverty and weakness. In 1898 he founded a cotton mill in his native town, Nantung (Kiangsu). By 1910, his business had expanded to include cotton mills, transport companies, and other industries. He became the chief manager of the Han-Yeh-P'ing coal and iron company (1913), and was minister of agriculture and commerce and director-general of the National Water Conservancy Bureau under the Republican government (1913–15). He retired because Yuan Shih-k'ai denied him much of the necessary authority to implement his plans. Chang also devoted much of his energy and wealth to welfare, philanthropic, and educational work.

CHANG CHIH-TUNG (1837–1909), Chinese official and reformer, the son of a family of office-holders in Nan-p'i, Chihli. In his youth he received an excellent classical education and, in 1863, obtained the *chin-shih* degree. Subsequently, he passed the palace examination with distinction. His first official appointments (1873–7) were concerned with the civil service examination in various provinces. At the same time, he became associated with a group of relatively young officials at Peking known as the Ch'ing-liu (lit. 'pure group'), whose members regarded themselves as protectors of Confucian values. Chang's vociferous condemnation of Ch'ung-hou's agreement with Russia over the Ili Dispute and his support for the Empress Dowager (Tz'u-hsi) in 1879, when the legitimacy of her political power was questioned, resulted in a series of promotions culminating in his appointment as governor of Shansi (1882). Chang and the Ch'ing-liu group continued to serve Tz'u-hsi's interest by their bellicosity against the French in Annam and the Japanese in Korea. Chang's promotion to the governor-generalship of Kwangtung and Kwangsi in 1884 was therefore no political accident. His use of the Black Flags and his vigorous war effort saved him from disfavour after China's defeat.

The bitter experience of 1885 converted Chang to modernization. As the governor-general of Kwangtung and Kwangsi, he established an arsenal, strengthened the provincial fleet, set up a military and naval academy, and founded China's first modern mint. His proposal for the construction of a railway between Peking and Hankow (the Lu-Han line) led to his appointment as governor-general of Hunan and Hupei in 1889 for executing the project. In his capacity as the governor-general at Wuhan, Chang established the Hanyehping Coal and Iron Co., instituted schools for Western learning, as well as cotton mills, silk filatures, hemp factories, and tanneries. Many of these official-managed enterprises suffered from bad management and corruption, however, and in 1902 several of them had to be 'leased' to private merchants. In addition, Chang used German instructors to drill a modern army. His long tenure of office at Wuhan (1889–94, 1896–1907) enabled him to pose as Li Hungchang's chief rival in 'self-strengthening' and political influence.

In his effort at modernization, Chang stressed the importance of education as the basis for gradual change. On this he parted with the radicalism of the reformers of 1898. After the Boxer Rising, Chang became committed to certain institutional reforms along Western lines and contributed much to the abolition of the time-honoured examination system (1905), the development of a new school system, and the sending of students to Japan. But the changes he had helped bring about only whetted the appetite for more; his famous formula, 'Chinese learning for the essential principles, Western learning for the practical application', was soon forgotten in the revolutionary tide.   DP

CHANG HSÜEH-LIANG (1898–), Ruler of Manchuria (*reg.* 1928–31), son of Chang Tso-lin. After his father's assassination (1928), Chang threw off his self-indulgent style of living, and took over his father's satrap in Manchuria, which he defended against Japanese encroachment. He was unsuccessful, and was forced to abandon Manchuria after the Mukden Incident (1931). He remained a powerful figure in north China, and a campaigner for resistance to Japan. He played a leading role in the Sian Incident, in which Chiang Kai-shek was arrested and released only on condition that he fought Japan. Chang Hsüeh-liang was sentenced to house arrest for his part in the incident. He was released in 1961.

CHANG HSÜN (1854–1923), Chinese war-lord active in north China shortly after the 1911 Revolution. He remained loyal to the fallen dynasty, and attempted to restore the last emperor of China to the throne (1917).

CHANG KUO-T'AO (1897–), former Chinese communist leader, and only major defector from the party. Chang was a founder member of the party, and subsequently played an important role as an industrial organizer. In the early 1930s he built up a small soviet in west China, which he was forced to evacuate in 1935. He moved further west and joined Mao Tse-tung, who had just completed the first stage of the Long March. At this point Chang was militarily stronger than Mao and his superior in the party, and thus felt that he could challenge him. A serious clash developed over the direction in which the communist forces should advance. Mao eventually won, and Chang was severely criticized. He defected to the Kuomintang in 1937.

CHANG MYON (1899–1966), prime minister of South Korea (1960–1). Under the Japanese, Chang did educational work for the Catholic Church, and lived for a time in America (1919–25). After 1945 he took various posts in the provisional Korean governments. He was appointed representative at the UN (1948), and ambassador to the US (1949), holding these two key positions in South Korean diplomacy with success. But he disagreed with Syngman Rhee's political attitude in Korea, and from 1951 campaigned continuously against the autocracy of Rhee and his Liberal Party. In 1956 he was elected vice-president on a Democratic Party ticket, defeating the Liberal Party candidate, but he was unable to play any active part in government. After Rhee's overthrow in 1960, a new constitution gave power to a prime minister and cabinet responsible to parliament, and Chang was elected prime minister. The system proved ineffective, but Chang refused to resort to authoritarianism. His government was overthrown by a military coup in May 1961, and Chang was banned from politics, imprisoned for a short time for defying that ban, and spent his remaining years again in church work.

CHANG PING-LIN (1868–1936), prominent Chinese classical scholar who, because of his anti-Manchu sentiment, joined forces with the revolutionaries at the turn of the century. He attacked K'ang Yu-wei's idea of a constitutional monarchy under the Manchus and was imprisoned. He went to Japan (1906), where he became a chief editor of Sun Yat-sen's organ, *Min Pao*, and gained considerable support from Chinese students in Japan. After the revolution of 1911, he opposed Sun and advocated a more moderate political programme. His political leanings thus gravitated towards Yuan Shih-k'ai. Chang was a classicist at heart, and spent his last years as a bitter opponent of the 'New Thought' and its literary movement.

CHANG TSO-LIN (1873–1928), major Chinese war-lord, leader of the Fengtien Clique, and father of Chang Hsüehliang. He started his career as a bandit and mercenary, and eventually came to control Manchuria, one of China's richest regions. He allowed the Japanese to play a major role in the economic development of Manchuria, but was never their puppet. When, after military defeats in north China (1928), he seemed on the point of submitting to the Kuomintang, his Japanese allies became dissatisfied and assassinated him.

CHANGA, by tradition the first ruler of the Rozwi empire, which arose in the southern part of Rhodesia at the end of the 15th cent. His successors, and possibly himself, had the royal title of Changamire.

CH'ANG-AN, capital of China, principally during the Han and T'ang periods. The city was expanded by the T'ang and modelled on a strictly regular grid plan, and for long it formed China's cultural and intellectual centre, and attracted visitors from many parts of the world. Ch'ang-an is mod. Sian, in the province of Shensi.

CHANGARNIER, NICOLAS ANNE THÉODULE (1793–1877), French politician and soldier. After a wild youth he served with distinction in the army in Spain (1823) and Algeria (1829–30, 1835–43). Given control of the National Guard (1848), he played a large part in defending the Second Republic; but his conservative outlook led him into exile under Napoleon III (1851). He eventually returned to serve against Prussia, and became a royalist life senator (1875).

CHANNING, WILLIAM ELLERY (1780–1842), US theologian, writer, and minister of Federal Street church, Boston (1803–1842), who led liberal churchmen against the orthodox Congregationalism of New England. The *Baltimore Sermon* (1819) and *The Moral Argument against Calvinism* (1820) underlined the extent of his departure from traditional Trinitarianism. He founded *The Christian Register* (1821) and the American Unitarian Association (1825), and became the dominant figure in the Unitarian movement. He had a wide influence, especially on younger New England writers such as Emerson, Longfellow, Lowell, and Holmes, and in *Remarks on American Literature* (1830) urged the creation of an American style. Channing was an active social reformer and a powerful spokesman for temperance, prison reform, public education, and the anti-slavery and peace movements.

CHANSONS DE GESTE, French heroic poems written between the late 11th and early 14th cents which were distinguished from the nearly contemporary romances by being composed, not in rhymed couplets, but in units of a number of syllables linked together either by assonance or by full rhyme. Their subject-matter ranged widely over historical events, much elaborated and altered by the successive minstrels (*jongleurs*) who transmitted the stories. The heroes most represented are Charlemagne, Roland, and Oliver, and the ethos is both heroic and Christian. Love stories intrude into some of the later poems.

CHANTRY, a foundation for the purpose of celebrating mass for the souls of the founder and others. The word is derived from the French *chanter*, 'to sing', and was used in the Middle Ages specifically for the singing of masses. It began to be associated with the place—either an altar in a specially reserved chapel, or a separate building—for such a purpose, and for the priests engaged in it.

The practice of endowing a foundation to pray for the repose of one's soul after death was common after the 13th cent.—there were, for example, over 80 such foundations in Rouen cathedral. The intention, indeed, lay behind all pious foundations at the period; intercessions both for the living and for the dead was the concern of those able to make provision for it, and the practice is closely linked with the rise of the middle class. Chantry foundations often had independent financial provision, and were sometimes linked with schools, eg, Eton and Winchester.

In England the chantries themselves, though not their associated institutions, were condemned for dissolution in 1545 (although the decision was not fully implemented until 1547, after Henry VIII's death) with the object of converting their property to charitable and educational uses. Some of the proceeds were devoted to the foundation of grammar schools.

CHAO, Chinese kingdom of the Warring States period, which ended in 222 BC; also the name of a short-lived dynasty of the 4th cent. AD.

CHAO ANOU (d. 1829), King of Vientiane in Laos (*reg.* 1805–28), also known as Anouvong and as Sai Setthathirat III. After gaining control of Champasak in 1819, he attempted the reunification of Lan Xang, divided since the death of Soulignavongsa, by a rebellion against Thailand in 1826–8. Attacking to within 60 miles (96 kms) of Bangkok, he was repulsed by Thai armies which twice sacked Vientiane and led him away to captivity in Bangkok, where he died. Anou's rebellion marked the final collapse of Lao unity, the incorporation of central Laos into the Thai kingdom, and the beginning of massive population movements from central Laos into north-eastern Thailand.

CHAO K'UANG-YIN (*reg.* AD 960–76), founder and first Emperor of the Sung dynasty, with the title Sung T'ai-tsu.

CHAPLEAU, SIR ADOLPHE (1840–98), Canadian Conservative politician. He was successively solicitor-general, provincial secretary, and prime minister of Que., then was appointed federal secretary by Sir John Macdonald (1882), an office he held for ten years. He was lieutenant-governor of Que. (1892–8).

CHAPLIN, CHARLES SPENCER (1889–), London-born film actor and director, outstanding comedian of the silent film era. He performed in vaudeville as a child, and while touring in the US was engaged by the Keystone Film Co. (1913). His portrayal of the tramp in Keystone comedies won him international fame, and he was soon writing and directing his own films. He developed the tramp in various full-length feature films, eg, *The Kid* (1920), *The Gold Rush* (1925), *City Lights* (1931), and *Modern Times* (1936). In 1940 he abandoned his silent role and in *The Great Dictator* parodied Hitler. He never became a US citizen, and during the 1940s his loyalty was frequently questioned by right-wing patriotic organizations. In 1952 he was barred from re-entering the US and took up residence in Switzerland.

CHAPLIN, HENRY (1840–1923), British Conservative MP., devoted to the agricultural interest, who became a convert to imperial preference. As president of the local government board (1895–1900), he forwarded the Agricultural Rates Act (1896) and the Vaccination Act (1898). Chaplin led the opposition to the proposal for a coalition government (1915–1916).

CHAPMAN, GEORGE (*c.* 1559–1634), English poet and dramatist, and translator of Homer's *Iliad* and *Odyssey* which influenced Keats. He was the author of six tragedies and several comedies, a prolific poet and a classical scholar in the tradition of Renaissance humanism.

CHAPPE, CLAUDE (1763–1805), French inventor of the semaphore telegraph, who perfected (1791) a visual semaphore, a pivoted beam with movable arms at its ends. A line commissioned from Paris to Lille was completed in time to bring news of the recapture of Le Quesnoy.

CHAPTAL, JEAN ANTOINE, Comte de Chanteloup (1756–1832), French chemist and industrialist who acted as minister of the interior under the Consulate and introduced the metric system.

CHAPULTEPEC, ACT OF (1945), inter-American security agreement signed by all the American republics except Argentina. It provided for combined action to meet aggression. The principle of regional security arrangements which it expressed was provided for in the UN Charter and implemented by the Rio treaty (1947).

CHAPULTEPEC, BATTLE OF (12–13 Sept. 1847), final victory of the US invasion force under Gen. Winfield Scott in the conquest of Mexico City during the Mexican War (1846–8).

CHAPULTEPEC, CONFERENCE OF (Feb.–March 1945), Inter-American Conference on Problems of War and Peace which met in Mexico City. The US came to discuss hemispheric security, and the conference resolutions reflected the success of the US aims. The major agreement signed in Mexico City defined an act of aggression against any American state as an attack against all, calling for collective action in such cases. Argentina boycotted the conference.

CHARAKA, author of the oldest extant ancient Indian medical treatise, datable to the 1st–2nd cents AD. This work exposes the classical Indian doctrine of medicine with its physiology based upon the presence in the body of three types of humours and five types of winds.

CHARDIN, JEAN-BAPTISTE (1699–1779), French artist of the *ancien régime*, who scorned the artificiality of aristocratic subjects, preferring to paint domestic scenes, *eg, The Pancake-Maker* and *Lady Making Tea*. One of his pupils was Fragonard.

CHARDONNET, LOUIS MARIE HILAIRE BERNIGAUD, Count of (1839–1924). French chemist, who in 1884 patented the production of fibres from nitrocellulose, which were called rayon. In a modified, less inflammable form rayon became the first artificial fibre material in common use. Although it was only a modified cellulose, its development pointed the way towards that of a completely synthetic fibre by the American, Wallace Carothers, and others half a century later.

CHARES (d. 332 BC), Athenian general first known fighting at Phlius against Argos and Sicyon (366 BC). In the Social War he commanded the fleet against Athens' seceding allies at Chios (357). After failure there and at Embata (356) the Athenians sent him to help Artabazus, the rebelling Persian satrap, but soon recalled him after Persian threats. From 353 he held several commands against Philip II of Macedon, to whom his forces succumbed in the Greek defeat at Chaeronea (338). Escaping the demands of Alexander the Great for his extradition, he fled to Sigeum, where he died after fighting with the Persians against the Macedonians at Mytilene.

CHARETTE DE LA CONTRIE, FRANÇOIS (1763–96), Vendéan general, leader of the French royalist rebels in the 1790s. Believing that the Thermidoreans, led by Boissy d'Anglas, would be willing to restore the monarchy, he signed the pacification of La Jaunaye (Feb. 1795), which halted the rebellion in the western provinces of France; but the death of the young Louis XVII (8 June 1795) ended hopes of a constitutional monarchy. In response to the Comte de Provence, the émigrés tried to launch a counter-revolutionary offensive in Brittany, but were defeated by Hoche. Charette was taken prisoner and executed.

CHARGE OF THE LIGHT BRIGADE (25 Oct. 1854) resulted from the misinterpretation of an ambiguous order from the British commander-in-chief, Lord Raglan, to Lord Lucan, commander of the cavalry division. The light cavalry brigade (636 horses), led by Lord Cardigan, was launched without support in a frontal attack on a battery of some 30 Russian guns. The brigade, in advancing for about 2 kms across an open plain, was shot to pieces. The sole result was the loss of some 440 men and 500 horses.

CHARIOT, used in warfare in Sumer as early as the 3rd millennium BC but, with its solid wheels and traction by ox or wild ass, was too cumbersome to have any considerable importance. A revolution in warfare was produced by the advent of the light two-wheeled, horse-drawn chariot with spoked wheels in the 16th cent. BC, which appeared almost simultaneously in several areas of the Near East, including Kassite Babylonia, Mitanni, and Egypt. The practice of the new war chariot spread rapidly, and by c. 1300 it was used from China to Sweden. It was used in Mycenaen Greece from the 16th cent. and was taken into India by the Aryan invaders from c. 1500. The charioteer is the characteristic military hero of the Vedas and the *Iliad*. Chariots were most effective in open country, but their disadvantages in broken, marshy, or mountainous country led to their progressive replacement by cavalry in the great Assyrian armies of the 8th cent. onwards, although they remained a significant component of Asian armies until 3rd cent. BC. By the dawn of the Christian era, their use was virtually confined to ceremonial or sporting purposes, and the western Celts were almost the last to employ them extensively in war. The characteristic Egyptian and Indo-Aryan chariot carried a driver and warrior, and was drawn by two horses; the Hittite chariot carried three men; the Assyrian occasionally four, and was drawn by three horses. The use of shafts, in place of a pole, and yoke harness was apparently a late development, when the chariot was already declining, and the practice of attaching blades to the wheels seems to have been common only among the Persians and western Celts.

MEY

CHARITY SCHOOLS in Britain, elementary schools established in the early 18th cent. to give free instruction to children of the poor. The movement was inspired and led by the Society for the Promoting of Christian Knowledge, though the schools, maintained by public subscription or endowment, were locally controlled. They were intended to arrest 'the growth of Vice and Debauchery' by reducing the 'gross ignorance of the principles of the Christian Religion especially among the poorer sort'. Their teaching, of very variable quality, was based almost entirely on the catechism, the Bible, and *The Whole Duty of Man*, but often included long hours of simple industry, such as spinning. This curriculum was expected to fit the pupils for the duties of the station to which they were born, rather than to raise them out of it, but although the movement waned, it provided an important basis for the later growth of state education.

CHARLEMAGNE (c. 742–814), King of the Franks (*reg.* 768–814), elder son of King Pepin. His reign saw a tremendous expansion of Frankish territory and influence. He campaigned extensively (772–85) against his most intransigent enemies, the pagan Saxons, who bordered his realm to northeast. Their conquest was punctuated by numerous rebellions, that of 778 under Widukind being particularly serious, and was accompanied by savagely repressive laws and deportations. His reign saw campaigns against the Avars of the middle Danube in 791 and 802–3, ending in their extermination; the conquest and absorption of the Lombardic kingdom in 774; punitive expeditions against the Gascons and the Basques (with the disastrous battle of Roncesvalles in 778); campaigns against the Muslims in Spain (796–811) and the establishment of a Catalan march; the creation of a Breton march, and the building of coastal defences against increasingly frequent Viking raids. Conquered territory was divided into bishoprics, where a rapid if nominal conversion to Christianity took place. Charlemagne championed the Church, in whose affairs he was intensely interested, and especially the papacy, which had long sought Frankish aid against the Lombards. The papacy ultimately became dependent upon Charlemagne, and the new pope, Leo III, personally crowned Charlemagne as emperor on Christmas Day 800. His reign was firm and was characterized by the use of 'royal envoys' who conveyed his wishes to counts and bishops. Increasing use was made of personal ties, forged by grants of land, between the king and his men. Charlemagne also brought the leading intellectuals and craftsmen of Europe to his court, which must have been brilliant. This in turn fostered the growth of the so-called Carolingian renaissance which blossomed after his death. The last years of his reign were undistinguished, government grew slack, and the growth of courtly factions precipitated the break-up of his empire. With his death his personality became enshrouded in legend which helped to create an image that neither he nor his successors could match. JD

CHARLES THE BOLD, Duke of Burgundy (1433–77), became effective ruler of the Burgundian state in 1465, during the lifetime of his father, Philip the Good. At that time the dukes of Burgundy were the greatest vassals of the kings of France, and were pursuing an independent foreign policy. Charles's rule seemed promising. He pursued an efficient centralizing policy and tried to establish a system of fairer justice. He was, however, aggressive and anxious for glory and this was heightened by a personal feud with Louis XI. In 1465 Charles had the support of the malcontents of France, including Charles, Louis's younger brother, in a League of the Public Weal. Louis, by his usual tactic of bribery, bought the chief rebels. Charles obtained the upper hand again in 1468 when Louis made the mistake of being his guest at the time of one of the anti-Burgundian outbreaks which he had fomented amongst Charles's neighbours, the Liègeois. However, Louis bribed his way to freedom and the death of his disaffected brother in 1472 and his bribery of Charles's English allies in the treaty of Picquigny (1475) greatly undermined the Burgundian position. Charles's invasion of Switzerland to avenge Swiss support given to Charles's rebellious subjects in Alsace led to three defeats, in the last of which (Nancy, 1477) he was killed. Louis tried then to annex the Burgundian state but managed only to capture some of its territories, while the rest passed to the Habsburgs.

CHARLES III THE FAT (*reg.* 881–7), Carolingian Emperor, one of the sons of Louis the German. The only surviving son of Louis, he succeeded to West Francia when the only surviving heir was a minor. This reappearance of the Carolingian empire, united under one man, masked only superficially the general disintegration. The Frankish notables disregarded royal authority and Charles, partly through ill-health, proved incapable of effective government. He was deposed in 887 and died a few months later.

CHARLES IV (1316–78), Holy Roman Emperor (*reg.* 1347–1378), member of the Luxemburg family who was elected as anti-king to Louis of Bavaria. He had a strong territorial basis for his power in Bohemia, which he fostered assiduously, and compromised with the pope and his rivals in Germany to avoid trouble, although he left Italy alone. Sound government and finances, and the liberal distribution of bribes, secured order in the empire. He wrote an instructive autobiography, and was a patron of the poet Petrarch.

CHARLES V (1500–58), Holy Roman Emperor (*reg.* 1519–58), ruler of all the lands belonging to the Austrian and Burgundian Habsburgs and to the crowns of Aragon and Castile. This scattered agglomeration of territories, known to contemporaries as a 'monarchia', eventually proved to be incompatible with the essentially medieval ideal of a united Christendom under a single emperor, which Charles brought to the task of ruling it. As far as possible he ruled through members of his own family, without attempting to follow the advice of his chancellor, Gattinara, to create a single unifying administration. Although he surrendered the eastern Habsburg lands to his brother Ferdinand in 1521–2, his method generally was to retain for himself all major decisions and important patronage, with consequent delays and inefficiency and a weakening in the authority of his governors and viceroys. The cost, particularly of the almost constant wars, was supported by increasingly heavy taxation in northern Italy and the Netherlands and then in Spain, and by his German bankers; his power did not long outlast his credit, which was suspended in 1552.

Although his wars with France in Italy gave Spain complete control of the peninsula, by the peace of Cambrai (1529), which was not reversed at Cateau-Cambrésis (1559), the French continued attempts to break Habsburg encirclement by alliances with the Turks and the Protestant princes of Germany. Against the Turks in the Mediterranean, Charles's one successful raid on Tunis (1535) was neutralized by the defeat of Doria's fleet at Prevesa (1538).

Thus, frequently distracted, Charles was unable to deal with the problem of the Lutheran reformation. He gave Luther a hearing at the Diet of Worms (1521) and, when the latter refused to recant, the Diet condemned him in the Edict of Worms, confirmed at Speyer (1529). For the sake of peace, Charles attempted to reconcile the Protestants by discussions at the Diets of Augsburg (1531) and Regensburg (1541), but what little agreement was reached at these was nullified by the intransigence of the two sides at large, the Protestants having used the interval to form the League of Schmalkalden. Charles repeatedly called for a general council of the Church, hoping to resolve the differences by an Erasmian policy of moderation and reform; but when the Council of Trent met (1545) it began by defining the differences between the creeds. Charles achieved an apparently decisive victory at Mühlberg (1547), but the fragility of his position was revealed by the treachery of his ally, Maurice of Saxony. At the peace of Augsburg (1555) Charles accepted the existence of both Lutheran and Catholic churches in Germany, each territory following the religion of its prince.

Defeated, he resigned the rule of the Netherlands (1555) and Spain and Italy (1556) to his son Philip, and the Crown of the Empire to Ferdinand, thereby dividing Habsburg power into its Spanish and Austrian parts, and retired to a Spanish monastery, where he died.

K. Brandi (tr. by C. V. Wedgwood), *The Emperor Charles V* (London, 1939). HNBM

CHARLES VI (1685–1740), Holy Roman Emperor (*reg.* 1711–40), second son of Leopold I. As Archduke Charles, he was put forward as the Austrian candidate for the Spanish inheritance (1700). During the War of the Spanish Succession he went to Spain and was crowned king in Madrid (1706), but he was unable to gain Castilian support and his position depended solely on allied troops. This support was denied him on the death of his brother, Joseph I, when Charles inherited the Habsburg possessions as emperor, since the allies had no intention of rebuilding a Habsburg empire similar to that of Charles V.

By the treaty of Radstadt (1714) Charles gained Naples, Sardinia, Milan, Tuscany, and the Spanish Netherlands. He refused, however, to yield his Spanish title and in 1718 found himself at war with a revitalized Spain anxious to re-establish herself in Italy. These western provinces were especially vulnerable, since Charles was at war with Turkey, and were only saved by the intervention of the Quadruple Alliance powers, anxious to maintain the status quo.

Charles's Turkish war brought Austria immense gains in Hungary and Serbia by the treaty of Passarowitz (1718). However, at the peace of Belgrade (1739), after a disastrous war with the Turks, most of these acquisitions were lost.

Charles had married Elizabeth Christina of Brunswick-Wolfbüttel in 1708 and her failure to provide a male heir was to prove a matter of great significance. In his determination to prevent a partition of the Austrian empire, Charles prepared his Pragmatic Sanction (1713) to gain support for the succession of his daughter, Maria Theresa. For the rest of his life Charles's foreign policy was directed towards obtaining recognition of this document. By 1740 all the Habsburg dominions and most European powers had guaranteed the Pragmatic Sanction, but few honoured their guarantees after Charles's death.

Under Charles VI, Habsburg rule, especially in the newly won provinces, tended towards stagnation. Charles believed in the right of each province to maintain its historical constitution and liberties, so that government from Vienna became even more disjointed and inefficient. His economic policy was largely a failure. Austrian provinces were impoverished after years of war and a venture like the establishment of the Ostend Co., which had little chance of success, did nothing to improve the situation.

Charles VI was a conscientious ruler, but by pinning his hopes on the Pragmatic Sanction rather than rebuilding a strong Austrian state, he bequeathed to his daughter an impoverished and vulnerable inheritance.   AW

CHARLES I (1600–49), King of Britain (*reg.* 1625–49) and second son of James I. He became heir to the throne on the death of his elder brother, Henry (1612). He was created Prince of Wales (1616), and succeeded as king on 27 March 1625. Soon afterwards, he married Henrietta Maria, sister of the King of France, an earlier match with the Spanish infanta having failed, despite Charles's incognito visit to Spain (1623) with the Duke of Buckingham.

Buckingham was the dominating influence in Charles's life until 1628, and was the main cause of the rupture between Charles and his first three parliaments. The failure of the Spanish war was criticized in the 1625 parliament, which refused to vote Charles tonnage and poundage (customs duties) for more than 12 months. The second parliament (1626) was even more critical, and the Commons tried to impeach Buckingham. A war with France (1627) led Charles to impose a forced loan, which was one of the grievances listed by the third parliament (1628–9) in the Petition of Right, which Charles was forced to accept. At the end of this parliament the Commons resisted adjournment by holding the speaker in his chair and passing resolutions condemning the king's government.

The so-called 'eleven years' tyranny' of Charles's personal rule followed, in which he revived anachronistic feudal levies, *eg*, knighthood fines and fines for breaches of forest laws, which increased opposition among the gentry. To pay for the navy, Charles raised ship money, first in the ports, but later from inland counties. Widespread opposition was not quelled, even when the king won a test case against John Hampden (1637). Many people also grew restless over the growing High Church practices of Abp Laud.

The first Bishops' War with Scotland forced Charles to call a parliament (April 1640). Under the leadership of John Pym, the Short Parliament, as it came to be called, refused subsidies until grievances were discussed. Charles dissolved the parliament (5 May), but was forced to call another (Nov. 1640) by the military disasters of the second Bishops' War.

The Long Parliament was determined to curb Charles's arbitrary rule, and it destroyed his government by executing the Earl of Strafford, imprisoning Laud, and causing most of his other councillors to flee. The legislation of 1641 was seen by parliament as a return to the Elizabethan form of government, of king in parliament. In fact, it was a collection of revolutionary acts which bound the king close to parliamentary government; but it left two questions unanswered: the control of the army and the nomination of councillors. The party under Pym felt parliament had to control both, if they were to trust Charles with the government. The Irish rebellion (Oct. 1641) made the decision on the control of the army imperative. The Grand Remonstrance (Nov. 1641) was the signal for the emergence of royalist and parliamentary factions. In Jan. 1642 Charles impetuously tried to arrest five

MPs for treason, but failed. From then on the two sides drifted into civil war, the parliamentary leaders were unable to trust Charles, and Charles was unwilling to give up his prerogatives. After fruitless attempts at compromise, Charles raised his standard at Nottingham (Aug. 1642).

The war at first went well for Charles, though he could make no decisive breakthrough. Finally, the superior economic and military position of parliament proved decisive. In May 1646 Charles surrendered to the Scots at Newark, and in Jan. 1647 was handed over to parliament. Hoping to regain his power, he exploited the split between parliament and the army. In June 1647 he was seized by the army, but escaped to the Isle of Wight (Nov. 1647), where he entered into an 'engagement' with the Scots for military aid in return for establishing Presbyterianism in England for three years. The second Civil War united the army against Charles, and on 20 Jan. 1649 he was brought to trial for treason against the people of England. Charles refused to recognize the legality of the court, but he was executed.

J. P. Kenyon, *The Stuarts* (London, 1958).
C. V. Wedgwood and others, *Charles I* (London, 1949).   CJ

CHARLES II (1630–85), King of Britain (*reg.* 1660–85) and the eldest surviving son of Charles I. He spent his early years (1645–60) in exile, except for a brief visit to Scotland (1650–1), where, in exchange for accepting the Covenant, he was crowned and given military support. His defeat at Worcester ended his immediate hopes of the English throne, and he fled to France.

In 1660 he was restored by the Convention Parliament, which imposed no terms beyond acceptance of the Declaration of Breda (1660), which expressed Charles's desire for a general amnesty, liberty of conscience, and an equitable land settlement. Charles's role in the Restoration settlement was generally a passive one.

Parliament left Charles with a serious financial problem, having provided him with a totally inadequate revenue. His marriage to Catherine of Braganza (1661) left him with no legitimate children to succeed him. His brother and heir, James, Duke of York, became a Catholic (1668). Financial insolvency and the lack of a Protestant heir were the central features of Charles II's reign.

His first government (1660–7), under Edward Hyde, 1st Earl of Clarendon, provided Charles with a religious settlement, the Clarendon Code, which rejected toleration and alienated many of Charles's subjects. The king's attempts to grant tolerance by his Declarations of Indulgence (1662, 1672) were frustrated by parliament.

Debt hampered the pursuit of a vigorous foreign policy, and the Second Anglo–Dutch War (1665–6) was such a disaster that it caused the downfall of Clarendon, who had in fact opposed the war. After 1667 the king carried on his own policies under the guise of a divided group of advisers (miscalled the Cabal). In 1670 he abandoned the Triple Alliance with Sweden and Holland, and entered into the secret treaty of Dover with Louis XIV of France. In return for a French subsidy which would help to make him independent of parliament—the object of his domestic policy— Charles agreed to engage in a war with the Dutch and to declare himself a Catholic. Parliament and most of his advisers were duped with a false treaty which omitted the conversion clauses.

The Third Anglo–Dutch War (1672–4) was unpopular and parliament forced on Charles the Test Act (1673), which drove Roman Catholics, including the Duke of York, from office. The political crisis of 1674 brought the control of government into the hands of Sir Thomas Osborne (later Earl of Danby. By his pro-Anglican and anti-French policy and his financial acumen, he succeeded in maintaining an obedient pro-court party in parliament. Charles, however, maintained secret negotiations with France to which Danby was forced to become a partner. The revelation of his duplicity caused his impeachment.

The exposure also led to the Popish Plot and Exclusion crisis. A cleverly woven fiction of lies and half-truths caused general hysteria, fanned by the opposition within and without parliament led by the Earl of Shaftesbury. The Cavalier Parliament was dissolved (1679), but the two succeeding parliaments were no more amenable, and both brought forward Exclusion Bills designed to bar James from the throne. Charles refused to compromise, and eventually a royalist reaction set in, of which the climax was the discovery of the Rye House Plot (1683) to assassinate Charles and James. The Exclusionist cause collapsed in a wave of popular loyalty. Two of its leaders were executed, and Shaftesbury fled into exile.

For the rest of his reign Charles ruled without parliament. He died on 6 Feb., having professed himself a Catholic.

K. H. D. Haley, *Charles II* (London, 1966).
J. P. Kenyon, *The Stuarts* (London, 1958).   CJ

CHARLES IV (1294–1328), King of France (*reg.* 1322–8), called 'the Fair'. His rule succeeded the peaceful reign of his brother, Philip V. He intervened indecisively in Flanders against the people of Bruges, who had revolted against their new pro-French count, Louis of Nevers, but his most successful operations were against England. He waged a campaign against the weak Edward II over the disputed town of Saint-Sardos in Agenais, where the English had murdered a French official. When Edward was deposed by his wife and Roger Mortimer, France regained the disputed areas of Agenais and Bazadais. This success led to further attacks (1337), which precipitated the Hundred Years War. Charles died childless, the last Capetian king, and the Crown passed to his cousin, Philip of Valois.

CHARLES V (1337–80), King of France (*reg.* 1364–80). He was both wise and well served and carried out many excellent internal measures among them reform of the currency, reorganization of taxes, and improvements in public order. These reforms were intended primarily to enable France to renew the war against England, which was also the purpose of his diplomatic triumph in arranging the marriage of his brother, Philip of Burgundy, to the heiress of Flanders, whereby he was assured permanently of Flemish support. The encouragement given by Charles to the rebellion of the chief Gascon nobles against Edward, the Black Prince, precipitated the war (1369). Charles's commander, Bertrand du Guesclin, markedly improved the discipline of the French forces. On the English side, both the Black Prince and his father, Edward III, were past their prime, while the king's other son, John of Gaunt, proved an incompetent commander, and was distracted by his desire to gain the throne of Castile; this only had the effect of ensuring a Castilian alliance for the French. The Castilian fleet deprived the English of the command of the sea (La Rochelle, 1372) and this ensured the French conquest of most of the English possessions in France, so that by 1375 Edward III held less territory in France than he had at the beginning of the Hundred Years War (1337), and England's chief ally in France, Charles the Bad, King of Navarre, was defeated (1378). The last years of Charles V were spent in efforts to assure the continuance of the Avignon papacy despite the election of another pope at Rome. To achieve this he even contemplated peace with England.

Charles was a patron of scholars. He created a splendid library, and was partly responsible for the rebuilding of the Louvre palace.   EBF

CHARLES VI (1368–1422), King of France (*reg.* 1380–1422) was dominated by the struggles of his ambitious and rapacious relatives; by the time of his coronation they had already appropriated a large part of the treasure accumulated by his father, Charles V. Until 1388 the Duke of Burgundy was the dominant political figure, then Charles assumed power, aided by his younger brother Louis, Duke of Orléans. Together they governed France (1388–92), employing the former ministers of Charles V and introducing various reforms. But Charles suffered (1392) the first of the many bouts of insanity; the eclipsed power of the Duke of Burgundy revived, and the rest of the reign was to be dominated by the irresponsible struggle between him and the Orléanist (Armagnac) faction. The situation was complicated by the devious role played by Charles's wife, Isabella of Bavaria, first an ally of the Duke of Burgundy and then of the Duke of Orléans. John of Burgundy was responsible for the murder of Louis (1407), but the struggle was taken up by Louis's son. The rebellion of the Cabochiens (1413) gained for the Duke of Burgundy a temporary predominance in Paris. The English invasion of 1415 repaired the internal conflict only temporarily, and the bulk of the Burgundian forces was not engaged when Henry V defeated the French at Agincourt. John of Burgundy was murdered (1419) by the adherents of the heir of Charles VI, the future Charles VII. John's son, by the treaty of Troyes (1420), retaliated by agreeing to accept Henry V as heir to Charles VI, whose daughter Henry married, while the future Charles VII was left in precarious control of such parts of southern France as were not dominated by the English and their Burgundian allies. Henry V predeceased Charles VI and, on Charles's own death, Henry's infant son was proclaimed King of France.
                                                            EBF

CHARLES VII (1403–61), King of France (*reg.* 1422–61), inherited the Crown as a youth (1422) in unpropitious circumstances. Most of northern France was in the hands of the English, and the infant English king also was proclaimed King of France. Doubts were even cast on Charles's legitimacy, but his position was strengthened by the divisions in the English council, notably the quarrel between the Duke of Gloucester and Bp Beaufort which paralysed the English government, and by the repressive government of the Duke of Bedford in France. The remarkable campaigns of Joan of Arc re-established morale in France. From being king of only part of the south in 1422, Charles was crowned at Rheims (1429). However, Joan was captured by the Burgundians (1430), who sold her to the English. Her martyrdom at Rouen (1431) was not fatal to Charles's cause, which benefited from the alliance made between the Burgundians and the French (1435), ending their long feud. In the same week the English regent in France, Bedford, died. By 1453 only Calais remained to the English, and the unity of France was a reality for the first time. Charles enjoyed great prestige and established the right to tax the kingdom at will. Indirect taxation was extended and for the final campaigns against the English (1449–53) Charles had adequate financial resources, including large loans from his chief financier, Jacques Cœur. The Estates Council went into eclipse after 1439. The Pragmatic Sanction of Bourges (1438) severely restricted papal rights of taxation, provision, and appeal. A heavy hand was taken against treasonable nobles. Charles VII succeeded in placing France in an extremely favourable position for the next 100 years.

CHARLES VIII (1476–98), King of France (*reg.* 1483–98). It was his advisers who largely governed France, and they were able to take advantage of the unity built up by his father, Louis XI. Brittany presented the main problem at the beginning of the reign, as there was a danger that its sole heiress might marry an enemy of France, but Charles ended this menace by marrying her himself. On reaching his majority he was dominated by a desire to conquer Italy and use it as a base for a crusade against the Turks. He secured peace with England (1492), and abandoned the important frontier territories of Rousillon (to Ferdinand of Aragon) and Artois and Franche-Comté (to Maximilian of Burgundy) in order to have a free hand to conquer Italy. His Italian venture proved at first surprisingly successful. He secured Florence without resistance, and entered Rome and Naples (1494–5). The rest of Italy trembled at this success, and the League of Venice was formed against him. Charles was forced to retreat and was ambushed at Fornuovo in the Apennines. He managed, however, to extricate his army and reach France. The French garrisons left behind him surrendered. Charles's invasion was the beginning of 60 years of futile attempts by France to conquer Italy.

CHARLES IX (1550–74), King of France (*reg.* 1560–74), second son of Henry II and Catherine de Medici. He succeeded his elder brother, Francis II, as king (1560). During his minority the first War of Religion broke out between the Catholic Guise party and the Huguenots, during which Charles was seized by the Guise faction (1562). In 1571 he fell under the spell of the anti-Spanish policy in the Netherlands. Unable to prevent the Massacre of St Bartholomew, in which Coligny perished, and haunted by its memories, Charles died in 1574 at the age of 24.

CHARLES X (1757–1836), King of France (*reg.* 1824–30), succeeded his elder brother, Louis XVIII, as the last of the Bourbon dynasty. As Comte d'Artois, his reactionary ideas made him one of the first émigrés (1789), inciting the other European rulers to help his eldest brother, Louis XVI, to suppress the Revolution. He spent most of his exile in Britain, returning briefly to France to head the revolt in the west (1795). After the Restoration he made Louis XVIII's attempt to rule constitutionally more difficult by identifying himself with the aristocratic and clerical *Ultra*s. His attempt as king to maintain *Ultra* ministries, to ignore the chambers, and to indemnify the émigrés provoked widespread liberal opposition, culminating in the July Revolution and his deposition (1830), after he and his minister, Polignac, had threatened to change the constitution by the St Cloud Ordinances.

CHARLES THE BALD (823–77) King of the Franks (*reg.* 840–77) and Emperor (*reg.* 875–7), was the youngest son of the emperor, Louis the Pious. At Louis's death he was in control of Francia west of the Rhone, Saone, and Meuse, but he was obliged to defend his kingdom, not only against the attacks of the Vikings, but also against his elder brothers, the Emperor Lothaire and Louis the German. He and Louis forced Lothaire into the partition of Verdun (843). Charles was confirmed in the possession of his western realm, and Louis was given the German principalities; Lothaire was left with the central portion of mid-Francia. Modern France and Germany are often seen as owing their beginning to this division. Charles permitted the mass grouping of lands or countships which was the origin of the great French duchies.

CHARLES THE SIMPLE (*reg.* 893–929), King of the Franks (West), whose nickname referred to his inability to deceive, was the great-grandson of Charles the Bald. He was crowned king at Rheims in opposition to King Eudes, who was not a Carolingian, and in 897 Eudes acknowledged him as his heir. He was compelled to cede Normandy to the Viking king, Rollo (911), but he annexed the whole of Lotharingia (Lorraine). His preference for Lorraine was an element in a west Frankish revolt (922), the result of which was the acclamation as king of Robert, Count of Paris, the brother of Eudes, who was killed in battle (923); his son-in-law, Raoul of Burgundy, was then proclaimed king. Shortly afterwards Charles was captured by a supporter of Raoul and imprisoned until his death.

CHARLES I (ROBERT) (*reg.* 1309–42), King of Hungary, called Carobert, an Angevin of the royal house of Naples. He was papal candidate for the Hungarian throne after the extinction of the Arpád dynasty (1301). Though crowned King of Croatia in 1301, he had to wait eight years until his rivals were defeated before he won the Hungarian throne. One of the greatest rulers of Hungary, he made it into a formidable power. By his efficiency and ruthlessness, he curbed the power of the magnates and established a council and army beyond their control. The gold and silver mines at

Szepes made him one of the richest rulers in Europe and he maintained a brilliant court. He encouraged commerce and the development of towns. By his internal and foreign policy he laid the foundations for his son, Louis the Great, who brought Hungary to its medieval apogee.

CHARLES II, THE BAD (1332–87), King of Navarre (*reg.* 1349–87), inherited also a claim to the French throne and extensive French possessions through his mother. He gained his nickname and an evil reputation for treachery by his efforts to take advantage of Anglo–French hostilities. His alliance with England in 1355 reopened the war between France and England, and he only came to terms with France in return for wide concessions. He acquired Normandy under an agreement with the Dauphin, later Charles V, on whom he exercised a baleful influence, but he lost part of his lands after a defeat by King Charles V in 1378–9. He pursued a similar tortuous policy towards his Spanish neighbours, but he was defeated by Castile, lost more of his lands, and ended his days in poverty under Castilian domination.

CHARLES I (1839–1914), King of Rumania (*reg.* 1881–1914), minor German prince and relative of Napoleon III, who became prince of the united Rumanian principalities (1866), and declared himself king. Although exercising strong personal control, he was unable to persuade the country to join Germany in the First World War.

CHARLES I OF ANJOU (*reg.* 1265–85), King of Sicily, youngest brother of Louis IX of France, and founder of an important French state in the south of Italy which tried to dominate most of the Italian peninsula. He seized the opportunity offered when a French pope, Clement IV, invited him to oust Manfred, son of Emperor Frederick II, from the kingdom of Sicily, in an attempt to establish a dependent state in the south strong enough to support the papacy without threatening to dominate it. Once Charles had established himself by defeating and killing Manfred at Benevento (1266), he was firmly established. A counter-invasion from Germany (1267–8), led by Frederick II's grandson, Conradin, was also defeated, and its leaders were ruthlessly executed.

Charles was a brave soldier and an extremely able ruler, and at the height of his power he was one of the strongest princes in Europe. But he failed to appreciate the underlying weakness of his overcentralized system of government. His attempts to spread his influence throughout Italy made him many enemies. He was on the point of trying to conquer the Byzantine empire when his oppressive rule provoked a popular uprising in Sicily (the 'Sicilian Vespers', Easter 1282). The rebels secured the help of Peter of Aragon, husband of Manfred's daughter, and of all Charles's other enemies. He died while the war was going badly, and left a chaotic inheritance.

CHARLES II (1661–1700) (*reg.* 1665–1700), King of Spain, last monarch of the Spanish–Habsburg dynasty, was plagued by ill-health, and his diseased body symbolized Spain's own disorders. He succeeded to the throne at the age of four, the queen mother acting as regent, but there was no halt in Spain's decline, as one court intrigue followed another. Charles II's only claim to fame arose from his inability to beget heirs. Of the three claimants to the throne—Austrian, French, and Bavarian—only the last was acceptable to the great powers, who were fearful of either French or Austrian aggrandizement. The Bavarian prince's death made partition the obvious solution, but Charles, determined not to dismember Spain, signed a will naming the French candidate as successor. Austria, however, would not accept this and, after Charles's death, the War of the Spanish Succession began.

CHARLES III (1716–88), King of Naples and Sicily (*reg.* 1734–59) and King of Spain (*reg.* 1759–88) after the death of his half-brother, son of Philip V and Elizabeth Farnese, and the most successful Spanish Bourbon. Personally religious and with limited intelligence, Charles shared the enlightened despots' belief in royal absolutism, and the omnipotence of the state in all but strictly spiritual matters. While King of Naples, he supported Tannucis' efforts to subject the Church to the state, but his accession to the Spanish throne gave far more scope for his practical ideas. He was determined on Spain's economic, cultural, and political revival, and was to be largely successful.

Although he made the early mistake of depending on Italian advisers, violent riots against them in Madrid (1766) made him turn completely to native Spaniards. He assembled and supported a remarkable group of educated ministers largely from the lower nobility (Aranda, Campomanes, Floridablanca, and Jovellanos), who worked for a strong monarchy and the general welfare of the population, and were to serve as models for 19th-cent. Spanish liberals. The Jesuits were expelled (1767) and the Church became almost a department of state; some attempt was made to end the privileges of the higher nobility and provinces and to foster the growth of 'enlightened' classes. Hoping to end Spain's economic decline and put her own and colonial trade in native hands, Charles supported physiocratic reform and an enlightened agricultural policy, multiplying the volume of trade by five during his reign. In foreign policy the king held closely to the French connection because of the danger of British colonial supremacy, and he was able to keep the colonial empire intact.

CHARLES IV (1748–1819), King of Spain (*reg.* 1788–1808), was weak and incompetent, leaving control of the country to his wife's lover, Godoy, who ended the reforming period of Charles III and pursued a foreign policy largely subservient to France. In an attempt to destroy Godoy's control and subservience to France, Charles's son and heir, Ferdinand, illogically appealed to Napoleon for help. Before French help reached Madrid, Godoy was imprisoned following a military revolt and Charles was forced to abdicate. The new king and his father were then summoned by Napoleon to Bayonne, where both were persuaded to abdicate in return for a pension, the throne being given to Joseph Bonaparte.

CHARLES IX (1550–1611), regent and King of Sweden (*reg.* 1604–11), where he safeguarded the Reformation. The youngest son of Gustavus I, he helped John, his brother, to seize the crown from Eric XIV, but opposed his religious policy and that of his successor, the Catholic Sigismund of Poland. The latter appointed Charles to rule jointly with the council in his absence from Sweden, but he gained the backing of the strongly Lutheran states against the councillors, whom he distrusted, and defeated Sigismund at Stangebro (1598). After Sigismund's deposition in the next year, Charles became nominally regent for a nephew, who, on coming of age (1604), declined the throne. In an attempt to conquer Livonia, Charles was heavily defeated by the Poles at Kirkholm (1605), but Sigismund was unable to carry the war into Sweden, where Charles had much popular support. Though he personally leaned towards Calvinism, his reign confirmed the acceptance of the Augsburg Confession, made by Council and clergy at the Uppsala Meeting (1593).

CHARLES X (1622–60), King of Sweden (*reg.* 1654–60), was a soldier who brought Swedish power in the Scandinavian peninsula to its zenith. He was the son of a count of Zweibrücken, who married Catherine, the stepsister of Gustavus Adolphus. He commanded the Swedish forces in Germany (1648), and was made heir to the throne by Queen Christina (1649), who refused to marry him, but finally abdicated in his favour. As king, he tried to improve the financial situation by the Reduction, which required the nobles to restore one-quarter of their acquisitions of Crown land. He married a daughter of Frederick, Duke of Holstein-Gottorp, thus gaining useful support against Denmark, but his policy relied mainly upon the sword.

In 1655–6 he captured both Warsaw and Cracow, and forced the Elector of Brandenburg to become his vassal for Prussia and his secret partner for partitioning Poland. Polish national resistance, however, put an end to both projects. Charles achieved more durable results against the Danes, who declared war while he was in Poland. He invaded Jutland from the south, crossed both the Belts at enormous risk on the ice (Jan. 1658), and exacted the cession of Scania and other Danish territory east of the Kattegat, the Baltic island of Bornholm, and the diocese of Trondheim in Norway. Not content with these vast gains, he renewed the war (June 1658), but failed to capture Copenhagen and was checked elsewhere by Dutch, Polish, Brandenburger, and Austrian opposition. Charles then summoned the Diet to meet at Gothenburg, where he was preparing for an onslaught on Norway when he died suddenly.

CHARLES XI (1655–97), King of Sweden (*reg.* 1660–97), created an efficient absolute monarchy. The regency which governed until 1672 ended the Danish war of his father, Charles X, and allied itself with France against the Netherlands. Sweden became embroiled with Brandenburg, which inflicted a significant defeat at Fehrbellin (1675), and the youthful Charles had also to cope with a three-fold Danish invasion. But in Dec. 1676 he defeated Christian V at Lund, where both kings commanded their armies in person, and Louis XIV limited his war losses to a strip of Pomerania, surrendered to Brandenburg. Charles's marriage (1680) to the Danish king's sister, Ulrika Eleonora, inaugurated nearly two decades of peace.

Charles laid the basis of his power by a comprehensive Reduction, which confiscated all alienated Crown lands above a certain annual value and, later, many smaller estates that had been mortgaged since the outbreak of the Thirty Years War. The status of the great nobles was further diminished by degrading the council to make it a purely advisory body, while the Diet of 1682 resulted in an arrangement which left the legislative power also in the hands of the king. The Church and the law courts were among the many other institutions which Charles reorganized, and he finally consolidated his position by the *indelningsverk*, an apportionment of Crown land for the maintenance of soldiers and sailors. Thus his son (Charles XII) inherited a standing army of 38,000 men, and another 11,000 provided crews for 38 ships of the line.

CHARLES XII (1682–1718), King of Sweden (*reg.* 1697–1718), and the central figure in the Great Northern War. His father, Charles XI, schooled him in the work of a ruler long before his accession at the age of fifteen and a half. His courage and energy, which were phenomenal, were combined with intellectual gifts which might have made him a great peacetime king. But the challenge of war offered by Denmark, Russia, and Poland-Saxony filled his life. The first campaigns showed his daring, and made him famous throughout Europe, though the victory at Narva was mainly the work of his greatest general, Rehnskiöld. His own battle-honours began with Kliszow (1702), and culminated at Holowczyn (1708). The strategy, however, was always the king's, including successive bold thrusts into Denmark, Ingria, and Livonia in 1700–1, the long campaign in Poland (1702–6), and the decision to march on Russia, which led to the disaster at Poltava (1709).

Charles's five-year exile in Turkey is famous for two episodes—the *Kabalik* ('affray') in 1713, when an overwhelming force of Turks lost 40 men in storming the headquarters of their no-longer-welcome guest at Bender, and the return journey to the Baltic coast (Nov. 1714), in which Charles covered 2000 kms (1250 miles) in 14 days, mainly on horse-back. The response which the Swedes then made to his call for further levies of men and money showed the loyalty which his personality still inspired, as well as the strength of the absolutist system established by his father. The king's plan was to employ Görtz in a diplomatic offensive for detaching Russia or another of his enemies, while he used his remaining military resources to secure a springboard in southern Norway. He occupied Oslo briefly in 1716, and the siege of Fredriksten, where he was shot (Dec. 1718), was intended as the first stage in a big scheme of recovery. There is no evidence that he was murdered, though Frederick of Hesse was suspiciously prompt in securing the succession for his wife, Charles's sister. Charles had never married or named a successor.

R. M. Hatton, *Charles XII of Sweden* (London, 1968).
F. S. Bengtsson, *The Life of Charles XII* (abbrev. Eng. trans., London, 1960).   TKD

CHARLES XIII (1748–1818), King of Sweden (*reg.* 1809–18) and of Norway (*reg.* 1814–18), was regent (1792–6) for his nephew, Gustavus IV, and again, briefly, after Gustavus's abdication. He was elected king under the new constitution (June 1809), but soon became senile, and from 1810 the effective ruler was the crown prince, Bernadotte. In 1814 the peace settlement between Norway and Sweden made Charles King of Norway.

CHARLES XIV (1763–1844), King of Sweden and Norway (*reg.* 1818–44). He was born Jean Bernadotte and joined the French army at 17, rising rapidly during the Revolutionary Wars. He married Napoleon's ex-fiancée, Desirée Clary (1798), became a marshal of France (1804), and played a prominent part in the campaigns of 1805–9. In 1810 the Swedish Estates elected him as Crown Prince.

Turning against Napoleon, who had never fully trusted him, he allied himself with Russia (1812), and later with Britain and Prussia. Swedish troops under his command fought in the campaign of 1813 and then briefly against Denmark, his main object being to secure the cession of Norway. In the spring of 1814 there was some support for the idea of making him King of France, but the allies considered Norway sufficient reward for his services. After an almost bloodless invasion, the Norwegians accepted a union of Crowns. Although Bernadotte could not speak his subjects' languages, the death of Charles XIII (1818) began a long and successful reign in both Sweden and Norway. Charles XIV (John, as he was styled) preserved good relations with Russia and Britain. While increasing rapidly in population, his realms kept their constitutions in a reactionary age. Charles John was now conservative in outlook, and the Norwegian parliament was often a stumbling-block to him, *eg*, when it tried to escape payment of its debt to Denmark approved at the conference of Aix-la-Chapelle (1818–20). But his charm and adroitness staved off any serious threat to the Swedish and Norwegian bureaucracies through which he governed and he created the only stable monarchy to arise out of Napoleonic Europe.

CHARLES, Prince of Wales (1948–   ), eldest son of Queen Elizabeth II and heir to the British throne. He was educated at Gordonstoun, Scotland, Geelong Grammar School, Australia, University College of Wales at Aberystwyth, and Trinity College, Cambridge. He was invested as Prince of Wales (1969) and it was announced in 1970 that he would enter the Royal Navy.

CHARLES ALBERT, Elector of Bavaria (1697–1745), succeeded to the electorate in 1726. On the death of the Emperor Charles VI (1740), he claimed the succession to the Habsburg lands in defiance of the Pragmatic Sanction upholding Maria Theresa's right. In May 1741 he allied himself with the French by the treaty of Nymphenburg and invaded Austria and Bohemia (July 1741), and became recognized by their Estates as king. By the autumn, however, Austrian forces had driven out his troops and had themselves occupied Bavaria. In the ensuing War of the Austrian Succession there were

many changes of fortune. In Jan. 1742 Charles Albert was elected emperor as Charles VII. After Dettingen (1743) his position deteriorated so much that he negotiated the treaty of Hanau with Carteret, renouncing his claims to Maria Theresa's lands. The treaty was never implemented and shortly after re-entering his duchy, from which the Austrians had withdrawn, Charles died.

CHARLES ALBERT (1798–1849), King of Sardinia-Piedmont (*reg.* 1831–49) in the formative years of the *Risorgimento*. Because of his sympathies with the nationalist *Carbonari* he was made regent, when his relative, Victor Emmanuel I, was deposed (1821), but was exiled when the new king, Charles Felix, received Austrian help. He became king at Charles Felix's death (1831), but although wanting the Austrians to be expelled from Italy and encouraging economic progress, he was illiberal and suppressed all political activity. The Italian moderates regarded him as a potential leader, but when revolts broke out throughout Italy in 1848, the conservative constitution which he granted aimed at containing revolutionary activity. Seeing the revolutions as a chance to expel the Austrians with popular support, he declared war, but was defeated and forced to abdicate (1849).

CHARLES AUGUSTUS, Grand Duke (1757–1828), enlightened ruler of Saxe-Weimar, who on his assumption of real power (1775) reformed his small German state on paternalistic lines and made his capital the cultural centre of Germany, patronizing both Goethe and Schiller. An advocate of German unity, he consistently opposed France in the Revolutionary and Napoleonic Wars. After the Vienna Settlement Weimar was granted a constitution and became a centre of liberal activity. Although Charles Augustus was forced to accept the Carlsbad Decrees (1819), he imposed them only lightly.

CHARLES EDWARD STUART (THE YOUNG PRETENDER) (1720–88), grandson of James II, was leader of the last Jacobite rising. Although he had no French support, 'Bonnie Prince Charlie' landed in Scotland (Aug. 1745), hoping to overthrow the Hanoverian dynasty while it was involved in war with France. He received support from some of the clans and soon controlled Edinburgh (Sept.), but his invasion of England proved a fiasco, as he received no English support. After defeat at Culloden (April 1746) he escaped to France after months of hiding, but was soon expelled (1748) and spent the rest of his life as a dissolute drunkard in Italy.

CHARLES EMMANUEL I, Duke of Savoy (1562–1630), son of the pro-Spanish Duke Emmanuel Philibert, who had established rigid absolutism in Piedmont-Savoy succeeded in 1580 and is considered to be the founder of traditional, pragmatic Savoyard foreign policy. In 1588, taking advantage of the French civil wars, he attacked French-occupied Saluzzo. In 1590 he claimed the French throne on the death of the cardinal of Bourbon, but withdrew in the face of stronger candidates. When Henry IV's forces invaded Savoy in 1601, Spanish backing enabled Charles Emmanuel to conclude a reasonable peace. By the treaty of Lyons (1601) Savoy retained Saluzzo in return for giving up French-speaking territory west of the Rhone. With the French withdrawal from Italy he was free to attempt to take Geneva, albeit unsuccessfully (1602).

In the Thirty Years War Charles Emmanuel at first sided with the Elector Palatine, providing him with mercenary troops against the Habsburgs, in return for promises of support for the imperial candidature and the Bohemian Crown (1618). When neither materialized, he changed sides, allowing Spanish troops to cross Savoy into Germany. In 1624 he again reversed his alliance, joining France and Venice to close the Val Telline to the Habsburgs (1625). In 1628 he made a final incursion into power politics. While Richelieu was involved with the Huguenots, he claimed Montserrat with Spanish concurrence and invested Casale (1628). The French, however, relieved the fortress and forced him to make peace (1629).

CHARLES EMMANUEL II (*reg.* 1638–75), Duke of Savoy, tried to emulate his neighbour, Louis XIV, not only by carrying out reforms in legislation, finance, and the army, and by creating an absolutist state, but in his expansionist foreign policy. In 1672 Savoy invaded Liguria and tried to stir up a revolt in Genoa. However, the Genoese checked the Savoyard schemes and Charles Emmanuel, humiliated, withdrew with French mediation.

In his reign Savoy enjoyed an artistic revival. Under the duke's patronage the architects Amedeo di Castellamonte, Francesco Lanfranchi, and above all Guarino Guarini, enlarged and transformed his capital, Turin, with fine examples of baroque building, *eg*, the Cappella della SS Sindone and the church of San Lorenzo.

CHARLES LOUIS, Archduke (1771–1847), Austrian general of the Revolutionary and Napoleonic wars. He defeated Napoleon at Essling (1809), but was decisively beaten by him later the same year at Wagram.

CHARLES LOUIS (1617–80), Elector Palatine, son of Frederick of Bohemia and Elizabeth, daughter of King James I of England. His childhood was spent in exile with his family in the Hague. He succeeded to his father's claims to the palatinate in 1632. As one of the Protestant princes in the Thirty Years War, he raised on army with English money, only to be defeated by imperial forces at Vlotho (1638). Although dispossessed of his hereditary lands on the death of Bernard of Saxe-Weimar, he sought the Protestant leadership in Europe, but when venturing on to French soil was captured by Richelieu and imprisoned at Vincennes, while Erlach bargained away the Weimar army to the French. Remaining intransigent in his opposition to the emperor and in support of the Swedes, he received for his pains a new palatine electorate centred on Heidelberg and the Rhenish palatinate at the peace of Westphalia (1648).

CHARLES MARTEL (*c.* 688–741), illegitimate son of Pepin, the Austrasian mayor of the palace, in the Merovingian Frankish kingdom. By 1717 Charles had become mayor in Austrasia, and had subdued Neustria in 724. He conducted a long series of campaigns against Aquitaine, Bavaria, Burgundy, and especially the Saxons, and also defeated the last great invasion of Frankish territory, a large-scale Muslim raid from Spain near Poitiers in 732. The Merovingian King Theudric, who died in 737, was not replaced, although Charles did not transfer the Crown to his own dynasty. However, on his death in 741 he divided the kingdom between his two sons, Pepin and Carloman.

CHARLES RIVER BRIDGE v. WHEELING BRIDGE. II Peters 420 (1837), major US Supreme Court case involving the law of contract, in which Chief Justice Taney modified substantially the earlier doctrine of Chief Justice Marshall. The Charles River Bridge Co. sought an injunction against a Massachusetts state charter authorizing a new and potentially toll-free bridge adjacent to its own toll-bridge built under a 70-year state charter. The company argued that its charter, by implication, gave it the sole right to operate a bridge at the point in question during the specified term, and that the new charter constituted an impairment of the obligation of contracts. Taney supported a narrow construction of charter grants, arguing that no implied right could be assumed and that ambiguities must be construed in favour of the state. This controversial but pragmatic decision circumscribed but did not abandon Marshall's ruling in the Dartmouth College case (1819).

CHARLEVOIX, PIERRE-FRANÇOIS-XAVIER DE (1682–1761), French explorer and historian, born in St Quentin, France. Charlevoix entered the Jesuit order in 1698, taught in Quebec (1705–9), and was ordained in Paris in 1713. Six years later he was sent by the French regent to investigate possibilities of finding a route to the Pacific. Starting in March 1721 he travelled from Quebec through the Great Lakes and down the Mississippi river, arriving in New Orleans on 5 Jan. 1722. He returned to France, where he wrote his *Histoire et description générale de la Nouvelle France, avec le Journal historique d'un voyage fait par ordre du roi dans l'Amérique septentrionalle* (1744).

CHARLOTTENBURG, TREATY OF (1723), defensive alliance concluded in Berlin between George I of Britain and Frederick William I of Prussia. The treaty was the brainchild of Lord Townshend, who sought Prussian friendship against the Emperor Charles VI, whose promotion of the Ostend Co. aggrieved British mercantile interests. It was readily accepted by the King of Prussia, who was alarmed by the growing strength of Russia under Peter the Great. This treaty was reaffirmed two years later by the alliance of Hanover.

CHARNOCK, JOB (*c.* 1635–93), the East India Co.'s chief at Hughli in Bengal and the founder of Calcutta. After being ejected from Hughli during the Anglo–Mughal War (1686–1690), Charnock, at the third attempt, established a trading factory at Calcutta.

CHARTE AUX NORMANDS, granted by King Louis X to the barons, clergy, and people of Normandy (19 March 1315). It was the first of a series of charters conceded by him to end provincial revolts that had broken out in France against the heavy exactions of his father, Philip IV, whose death (Nov. 1314) alone had prevented an even more serious rising. Outside Normandy these charters were soon forgotten, but the Normans successfully insisted on the enforcement of the legal and fiscal concessions made to them. After 1339 the French kings had to secure Norman consent to taxes and the resultant Provincial Estates of Normandy continued to be summoned until the reign of Louis XIV.

CHARTER, THE (1814), constitution granted to France by Louis XVIII. It was drawn up hastily by Louis and his advisers to satisfy the allies and the Bonapartists. It stated that all power resided in the king, but also guaranteed the civil liberties of the revolution and parliamentary government. It consisted of six sections: civil rights, royal powers, peerage, chamber of deputies, ministers, and specific guarantees. It was later revised in a more liberal sense (1830).

CHARTER ACTS were passed in 1793, 1813, 1833, and 1853 to renew the charter of the East India Co., whose affairs were first brought under parliamentary control by North's Regulating Act (1773). The act of 1793 extended the company's charter for 20 years and continued its commercial monopoly. At this time there was little interest in Indian affairs because of the war with France and because Indian finances were in a tolerably satisfactory state. The power, conferred in 1784, on the governor-general to over-rule a majority on his council was now repeated and extended to the governors of Madras and Bombay. If the governor-general or the commander-in-chief left India for Europe he would vacate his office. In future, payment of members of the Board of Control was to be out of Indian revenues.

The act of 1813, which extended the company's charter for another 20 years, was preceded by a searching investigation into Indian affairs, Wellesley's annexationist policy having involved the company in financial difficulties. Napoleon's economic blockade led British traders to demand admission to the ports of Asia. This resulted in the general Indian trade being thrown open, but the China and tea trade were still to remain a monopoly. In future, Europeans, other than company servants, required a licence to go to India. Missionary enterprise was sanctioned. A grant was made for the encouragement of education before such a responsibility was recognized in England.

The act of 1833 was of great importance. When it was passed Bentham's views on legislation and codification were influencing the minds of law reformers. Macaulay was secretary of the Board of Control, and James Mill, a disciple of Bentham, was examiner of Indian correspondence at India House. The act was the first practical step towards the codification of the law in British India and Macaulay became the first law member of the governor-general's council for legislative purposes. The reforming spirit of the age was also embodied in other provisions of the act. It was laid down that no native of British India should be debarred by reason only of religion, place of birth, descent, or colour from holding any place, office, or employment under the company. An enquiry was to be made with the object of extinguishing slavery in the company's Indian territories as soon as practicable. The remaining monopoly, the China trade, was abolished.

The last Charter Act (1853) fixed no definite term for the continuance of the company's powers. Its chief importance was that it threw the Indian civil service open to general competition.

C. Ilbert, *The Government of India* (Oxford, 1907)   CCD

CHARTER COLONIES. In the 17th cent. the British Crown issued charters to trading companies for trade and colonization in the new lands in North America, which England controlled by right of discovery. Colonies were established by the Virginia Co. (1606, 1609, 1612), and by the Massachusetts Bay Co. (1629). The Virginia Co. had its charter amended to include Bermuda, and later (1615) sold the new colony to the Bermuda Co. Already existing colonies, such as Connecticut (1662) and Rhode Island (1663), were granted charters. The proprietary charter, or patent, granted hereditary rights to land and governing rights to an individual or group, eg, MD to Lord Baltimore and PA to William Penn. These charters were useful to England in originating settlements, but later were a hindrance in the forming of an integrated empire. Accordingly, England reduced or cancelled several charters, eg, Virginia Co., abolished (1624), Massachusetts charter, in 1684 declared forfeit and a new charter issued (1691). By the time of the American War of Independence MA, RI, and CT were the only remaining charter colonies with the two proprietary colonies—PA–DE, and MD.

CHARTER OF NOBILITY (1785). Decree of Catherine II which extended the privileges of the Russian nobility and thus heightened serfdom, although, by confirming Peter III's decree (1762) freeing the nobility from obligatory state service, it removed the theoretical justification for serfdom. The charter granted the inviolability of a noble's honour, hereditary landed and serf property, except through a trial by his peers. It exempted the nobility from personal taxation and corporal punishment and granted the right to manufacture and trade.

A system of elected provincial assemblies provided some corporate organization, but Peter I's table of ranks was retained and government service remained the normal form of ennoblement and occupation.

CHARTERED COMPANIES OF LATIN AMERICA. The colonial governments of both Spain and Portugal experimented (17th–18th cents) with private chartered monopoly companies which were given exclusive trade privileges in a specified region, in order to stem foreign incursions into their colonies. The companies were expected to defend their regions in exchange for these privileges. The Portuguese began the process with the Brazil Co. (founded 1649, abolished 1720–1), and the Maranhão Co. (1678–84), followed by others (18th cent.). The Spaniards began with the Honduras Co. (1714) and the Guipúzcoa (Caracas) Co.

(1728–80s). The latter was the largest and only profitable Spanish operation. Several other Spanish chartered companies were established, but all were financial failures.

CHARTISM. The People's Charter (1838) comprised six Points or demands for radical parliamentary reform: manhood suffrage; annual parliaments; equal electoral districts; vote by ballot; payment of members; and abolition of members' property qualifications. It looked back to 18th-cent. radicalism and was a protest against the Reform Act (1832). All six demands had been made by Maj. John Cartwright (*Take Your Choice*, 1771) and by the London Corresponding Society, the first working men's political association, formed in 1792. The only demand still unachieved is that for annual parliaments.

The charter was drawn up by six members of the London Working Men's Association, formed in 1836 on the model of the Corresponding Society, and six radical MPs. Most of the work was done by William Lovett, founder of the association, with help from the veteran radical Francis Place, and the lawyer J. A. Roebuck. The charter was drafted in the form of a parliamentary bill and presented to the Commons in 1839, 1842, and 1848, each time introduced by a petition stating social, economic, and political grievances.

Although Chartism may be seen as a social movement, arising during the depression of the second half of the 1830s and declining after 1842, with a revival during the bad harvests of 1847–8, its only agreed programme was the charter. The movement differed widely in different parts of the country. Many of its leaders were small independent craftsmen, shoe-makers, cabinet-makers, tailors, etc. The rank-and-file were engaged in small old-style occupations rather than in new large-scale industry, and many belonged to decaying trades, especially hand-loom weaving. They were distressed by high food prices, angered, especially in Yorkshire and Lancashire, by attempts to implement the new Poor Law (1834), and they complained of class legislation. By 1842, when the demagogue O'Connor had displaced the original leaders of Chartism, it was stronger in the provinces (particularly Yorkshire, Lancashire, the east Midlands, and parts of Scotland and Wales) than in London, and its central organization was weak. After 1842 improving economic conditions began to reduce Chartism's appeal and, after a short revival in 1848, it was moribund by 1850. What remained of it thereafter was really a new movement, with a defined social programme, 'the Charter and something more'. This was socialism, the programme of a small group of extremists who gained control of the National Charter Association in 1850. Their leaders were Julius Harney and, later, Ernest Jones. The new Chartism had connections with European revolutionary movements. It did not inherit the working-class support of the older Chartism, which was directed into other channels (eg, trade unions).

A. Briggs (ed.), *Chartist Studies* (London, 1959).
M. Hovell, *The Chartist Movement* (Manchester, 1918).
                                                                                                          BK

CHARTRES, cathedral city in northern France, south-west of Paris. It was the leading school in western Europe in the 11th and early 12th cent. until it was eclipsed by the rise of Paris under Abelard. Chartres became pre-eminent under Bp Fulbert (d. 1028), a pupil of Gerbert of Rheims (Pope Sylvester II), and was renowned for mathema... ...ilosophy. Among the famous masters of Cha... ...chancellors Bernard of Chartres (d. 1126) an... ...Porrée (d. *c.* 1154), Bp Ivo (d. 1126), the gre... ...the Englishman, John of Salisbury (d. 11... ...scholar of his day and himself a product of... ...cathedral, with its statuary and stained gl... ...glories of French 12th-cent. architecture.

CHARVAKA, name of the only truly ... ...ancient India, also called Lokayatika. The...

was Ajita Keshakambalin, a contemporary of Lord Buddha. Their basic tenet was that the soul is material like the body, and so also disintegrates at the time of death. They therefore deny the existence of *karma* and rebirth. Though they appear never to have had large numbers of adherents in ancient India, their views apparently exerted considerable influence, especially on texts concerning statecraft such as the *Arthashastra*.

CHASE, SALMON PORTLAND (1808–73), US anti-slavery leader, member of Lincoln's cabinet, and chief justice of the Supreme Court. A New Englander by birth, he practised law in OH, and supported the anti-slavery Liberty and Free Soil parties in the 1840s. He was senator from OH (1849–55), governor of the state (1855–9), and a founder of the Republican Party, and unsuccessfully sought the presidential nomination (1860). As secretary of the treasury (1861–4), he struggled with the problems of wartime finance and secured passage of the National Bank Act (1863). The most radically inclined member of the cabinet, and still ambitious for the presidency, he challenged Lincoln, again unsuccessfully, for the nomination in 1864. However, Lincoln appointed him chief justice (1864–73), and he presided with restraint and good sense over the impeachment proceedings against Andrew Johnson (1868).

CHASE, SAMUEL (1741–1811), American Revolutionary leader and signatory of the Declaration of Independence. He was a member of the Continental Congress. Washington appointed him to the US Supreme Court, where he made many important decisions. He was radical Federalist and his overbearing manner made him many political enemies. He was impeached (1804), but was acquitted and restored to the court (1805).

CHASTELLAIN, GEORGES (1415–74), official historian of the Burgundian dukes, he was a friend of Duke Philip the Good and his son, Charles the Rash. His integrity made his writings a reliable source for the French and Burgundian history of this period.

CHÂTEAU CLIQUE, name taken from the governor's residence in Quebec, the Château St Louis, and applied to English officials and their supporters who ruled Lower Canada (1763–1848).

CHATEAUBRIAND, FRANÇOIS RENÉ, Vicomte de (1768–1848), writer, memorialist, and statesman of the romantic era. Though coming from an old but impoverished Breton family, he frequented the court (1786) and began to publish poetry. He refused to take the oath to the Revolution, and despite his being an army officer, retired to America (1791) and then fought with the émigrés (1792). He afterwards spent several years in England, returning to France to publish his first major work, *La Génie de Christianisme* (1802). This earned him a post in the diplomatic service (1803–4), but he resigned, travelled in the east (1806), and became a critic of the empire. After being minister of state (1814), he had to wait for the office he so much desired, that of minister of foreign affairs (1824), but he was soon dismissed because his projects were too ambitious. He remained a legitimist, but devoted most of his time to his writings, particularly to his *Mémoires d'outre Tombe*.

CHATEAUBRIANT, EDICT OF (1551), heresy edict of King Henry II of France, who followed Francis I's policy of extermination of the Huguenots. The edict laid down that proceedings against suspected Protestants should be accelerated and the punishment of heretics became the responsibility of new *présidial* judges.

CHÂTEAU-GAILLARD, CASTLE OF, built (1197–8) on the ⬛⬛ of the crusading castles in the east, by Richard I of ⬛⬛⬛ at Andeli on the Seine, to act as the key point in his defence of his Norman lands. It was captured by King Philip Augustus of France (1204) after a six-months' siege because Richard's successor, King John, made no attempt to relieve it. It is regarded as the masterpiece of defensive fortresses of the period.

CHÂTEAUGUAY, BATTLE OF (26 Oct. 1813), fought on a bend of the Châteauguay river in Canada. Lieut.-Col. Charles de Salaberry and the Canadian Voltigeurs stopped the invasion of Lower Canada by Gen. Wade Hampton's US army.

CHÂTEAU-THIERRY, BATTLE OF (31 May–1 June 1918) successful Allied defence of a strategic crossing of the Marne, 144 kms from Paris, during the First World War. Gen. Foch, by using divisions of the American Expeditionary Force alongside French Colonial forces, held the German advance and dealt a severe blow to German morale.

CHATELET, French tribunal of the *prévôt* of Paris, responsible for the maintenance of law and order in the capital. Its importance lay in the fact that it was immediately subordinate to the *parlement* of Paris and that the law of Paris was applied over a wide area.

CHATFIELD COMMITTEE, appointed (1938) under the chairmanship of Lord Chatfield to report on the modernization of the Indian defence forces. It recommended (1939) the re-equipment and mechanization of the army and the expansion of the ordnance industry to make India self-sufficient in munitions. It also proposed a functional redistribution of army forces, a reduction in the number of British troops in India, together with increased Indian responsibility for external defence, and increased British financial contributions to Indian defence costs.

CHATHAM, Thames naval base, first called Gillingham Water and founded in 1550. It was ignominiously attacked by the Dutch fleet under De Ruyter in 1667.

CHATHAM, WILLIAM PITT, 1st Earl of (1708–78), British politician, grandson of Thomas 'Diamond' Pitt, and known as Pitt the Elder, to distinguish him from his equally famous political son, William Pitt the Younger. He was drawn into politics through being connected with the Temple and Grenville families, one of the most powerful groups in the land-owning oligarchy which ruled 18th-cent. England. His early years in the Commons, as MP for Old Sarum, were spent in opposition to Sir Robert Walpole and in the company of Lord Carteret and other discontented Whigs surrounding Frederick, Prince of Wales. Pitt soon displayed great talents as an orator, as well as independence of thought, and exercised popular appeal. During Carteret's government, from which he had been excluded, he attacked the system of continental alliances, favouring instead a colonial war against the French. This was one of the main policies he was to follow in government and opposition for the rest of his life.

He first attained office in 1746 as vice-treasurer of Ireland and paymaster-general of the forces, and there won a reputation for honesty and efficiency. He was excluded from the cabinet on Henry Pelham's death (1754), and, after bitterly attacking the Newcastle–Fox coalition, was dismissed from the pay office (1755). The confusion into which Newcastle's government fell on the outbreak of the Seven Years War led to Pitt forming a ministry (Nov. 1756) with the Duke of Devonshire as its nominal head. Newcastle returned to the government (June 1757) to control patronage, while Pitt, as secretary of state, was left in sole charge of the conduct of the war. His strategy was one of a national war at sea with America and India as his objectives, while subsidizing the armies of Frederick the Great in Europe. The treaty of Paris (1763) saw the vindication of these policies, but Pitt had resigned in 1761 because George III wanted to end the war. He was rewarded with a pension and a peerage. While in opposition he supported John Wilkes and the American colonists in their fight against the Stamp Act.

In July 1766 he formed an all-party ministry intended to provide a strong, coherent, and efficient administration. In this he failed, partly because in accepting an earldom his influence and talents were removed from the Commons, and partly because his health began to fail. The Duke of Grafton, left in control of the government, was unequal to the problems presented by the American crisis and the hostility of John Wilkes. In 1768 Chatham himself resigned. Once again in opposition, he continued to attack the policies of the various governments, though more intermittently as his illness grew worse. In his last years he appealed for a more generous treatment of America, but he broke with his Whig associates over their proposal to recognize the colonies' independence.

B. Williams, *The Life of William Pitt, Earl of Chatham* (London, 1913).

B. Williams, *The Whig Supremacy, 1714–1760* (London, 1962).   CJ

CHATHAM, JOHN PITT, 2nd Earl (1756–1835), was discredited (1809) when, as master of the ordnance, he was in charge of British troops in the unsuccessful Walcheren expedition.

CHATHAM ISLANDS, THE, an outlying group forming part of NZ, discovered by Broughton in the *Chatham* (1791). They then supported about 1000 so-called 'Morioris', Maoris long thought, erroneously, to be ethnically distinct. Full-blooded Morioris died out by 1934. European settlement was established by German missionaries (1842), sealers and whalers, and Canterbury sheep-farmers (1865), but the isolated fishing and farming community declined by 1960 to about 500.

CHATILLON, RENAUD DE (d. 1187), younger son of a French noble house who went to Palestine, where he acquired the principality of Antioch by marriage (1153). He ravaged Cyprus, with the object of striking at his overlord, the eastern emperor (1155), but was forced to accept Byzantine sovereignty (1158). In 1160 he was captured by Muslims and remained imprisoned for 16 years. After his release his frequent breaches of the truce with Saladin and a naval raid in the Red Sea caused a renewal of the holy war by the Muslims, ending in the great defeat of the crusaders at Hattin (1187) and the loss of Jerusalem. Renaud was captured by Saladin, and executed.

CHÂTILLON, CONGRESS OF (1814), held in Feb., led to an allied offer of peace on the basis of France's 1792 frontiers, which Napoleon I rejected.

CHATTANOOGA, BATTLES OF (23–5 Nov. 1863), a series of engagements in the American Civil War. Union forces under Grant, Sherman, and George H. Thomas broke the Confederate stranglehold over their position at Chattanooga, TN, where they had retreated after the battle of Chickamauga, Braxton Bragg's forces were driven from Missionary Ridge south into GA.

CHATTERJEE, BANKIM CANDRA (1838–94), Bengali novelist and essayist. After graduating from Calcutta University, he entered the Indian civil service and became a district magistrate in Bengal. In 1872 he started the *Bangadarshan*, a Bengali journal, which became a religious paper expounding Hindu philosophy and culture. In 1886 he published his *Krishnacharita* in which he depicted Krishna not as divine, but as the ideal man. His *Dharmatattva* (1888) was an attempt to reconcile rationalism with devotion. In *Kamalakanter Daptar* (1885) he pleads for social equality. His best-known novel was *Ananda Math* (*The Abbey of Bliss*), which depicts the Sannyasi rebellion in Bengal at the time of Warren Hastings. It contained the famous hymn 'Bande Mataram', which inspired the people to sacrifice all for their motherland. During the agitation following the partition of Bengal it became the song of the revolutionary party.

CHATTI, early German tribe living east of the Rhine in and north of the Main valley, who took part in the defeat of the Romans in the Teutoberg Forest (AD 9) and the Batavian revolt (AD 69–70). Driven from their homes by Domitian, they subsequently declined; the medieval Hessi in modern Hesse were probably their descendants.

CHAUCER, GEOFFREY (c. 1343–1400), English poet, who had a varied diplomatic and administrative career under Edward III and Richard II. He went on missions for the king, including two to Italy; these journeys gave him an opportunity for contact with literary works of great importance in his development as a poet. His earliest work was the *Book of the Duchess* (1369); his last and greatest work, the *Canterbury Tales*, remained incomplete at his death. It was once customary to divide his work into three periods (French, Italian, and English) according to the principal influences which could be detected in it; but the division is unreal, and the most mature of the Canterbury tales, for all their realistic English settings, are in their own way as dependent on French literary models as are his earliest works.

CHAUHAN or Cahumana, name of one of the Rajput dynasties in early medieval India, with branches ruling in parts of Gujerat, Rajasthan, and Punjab from the end of the 10th to the end of the 12th cent. AD. The earliest known reference is AD 756, when an inscription mentions a Chauhan chief at Broach recognizing the supremacy of the Pratiharas of Kanauj. By the end of the 10th cent. several branches became independent, notably the Chauhans of Shakambhari (Sambhar), about 60 miles (96 kms) north-east of Ajmer, Rajasthan. Though militant and engaged in intermittent warfare with their neighbours, their resistance against the Muslims, though often heroic, proved unsuccessful. The greatest ruler was Prithviraj III (c. 1179–92), whose numerous victories are described in an ornate Sanskrit text, the *Prithvirajavijaya*. In 1192 he was, however, defeated and captured by Muhammad Ghori and was later executed at the latter's court.

CHAUMONT, TREATY OF (1814), signed on 9 March by the members of the Fourth Coalition against Napoleon I. The initial failure of the allies' invasion of France was followed by mutual recriminations which endangered the coalition. Castlereagh, the British foreign secretary, hurried to the continent and persuaded Austria, Russia, and Prussia to renew their alliance with Britain against France for another 20 years. The powers were to put 150,000 men in the field each and Britain to furnish a subsidy of £5 million. The treaty formed the basis of the later Quadruple Alliance.

CHAUNCEY, CHARLES (1705–87), life-long pastor of the First Church in Boston. He opposed the doctrines of Jonathan Edwards, leader of the Great Awakening, and was the champion of liberal religion.

CHAURI CHAURA, village in Gorakhpur district in the United Provinces of India (now called Uttar Pradesh), in which 22 policemen were killed when a police station was set on fire (5 Feb. 1922) by a mob during the non-co-operation movement. As a result of this and other outbreaks Gandhi suspended (12 Feb.) the non-co-operation campaign.

CHAUTAUQUA, US educational movement founded by Lewis Miller and John Vincent, a Methodist minister, at Chautauqua, NY (1874). Originally concerned with improving Sunday schools, it expanded its activities and attempted to bring general education to the people through a national summer school, home study courses (1878), local assemblies, and travelling lecture and recital programmes (1900).

CHAUTEMPS, CAMILLE (1885–1963), French politician remembered chiefly as a 'defeatist' member of the government in 1940. Chautemps, whose father had been a minister, entered parliament as a Radical in 1919 and held office in several governments. His second term as prime minister (1933–4) was ended by the Stavisky scandal. Chautemps was a supporter of the Popular Front experiment. He was prime minister again after the fall of Blum (1937–8), and deputy prime minister under Daladier, Reynaud, and Pétain (1938–1940). He supported the request for an armistice in 1940, but resigned when Pétain assumed dictatorial powers, and spent most of the rest of his life in the US.

CHAUTH (lit. one-quarter), the term used by the Marathas for the levy of one-fourth of the revenue of a district over which they claimed rights of passage or overlordship. With it was usually associated *sardeshmukhi* or a levy of one-tenth of the revenue. This device was specially used by the Marathas in dealing with the Mughal empire. It was claimed to confer protection from other attacks or exactions, but this was rarely so in practice.

CHAUVEL, SIR HENRY GEORGE (1865–1945), Australian general, was born at Tabulam, NSW. He joined the Queensland Permanent Forces in 1896, served in the Boer War, and was adjutant-general (1911–14). In 1916 his skilful handling of the Anzac Mounted Division brought victory at Romani. He was the first Australian to become a lieutenant-general, and led the Desert Mounted Corps in the victory at Gaza and the great drive behind the Turks at Megiddo. He was inspector-general (1919–23) and CGS (1923–30).

CHAUVELIN, GERMAIN-LOUIS DE (1685–1762), French statesman descended from an old and wealthy *parlementaire* family of Grisenoy. President *à mortier* and *avocat-général* in the *parlement* of Paris, he was created Keeper of the Seals in 1727 and for the next decade was responsible for foreign affairs, working closely with Cardinal Fleury. His forthright manner contrasted with the latter's blandness and he openly undermined the Anglo-French alliance until in 1737 he was dismissed for intriguing with the Duke of Bourbon in pursuit of a belligerent policy line. Exiled first to Bourges and then to Issoire, he returned to Paris after Fleury's death (1743), but was never restored to high office.

CHAUVINISM, bellicose form of patriotism, so called after Nicolas Chauvin, an aggressive Napoleonic veteran who became the symbol of ultra-nationalism.

CHEFOO AGREEMENT (13 Sept. 1876), signed between Britain and China at Chefoo, formally closed the Margary Affair. Early in 1875, Augustus Raymond Margary, interpreter to a British exploratory expedition from Burma into Yunnan, was murdered by armed Chinese. Thomas Wade, British minister, used this as an excuse for demands over and above the redress of the immediate grievance. The agreement provided for the settlement of the Margary Affair, including the sending of a mission of apology to London, improved diplomatic relations, and the opening of four additional treaty ports and other commercial facilities.

CHEHRIN (CZEHRYN), fortress attacked unsuccessfully by the Ottoman Turks, entering into hostilities with the Russians along the lower Dnieper, during the first campaign of the war in 1677. A second attempt led to their capture of the fortress in 1678. The conflict came to an end with the peace of Radzin in 1681.

CHEKA, Russian secret police (1917–22). The full title of the organization gives a better idea of its scope—the All Russian Extraordinary Commission For Combating Counter Revolution, Sabotage and Speculation. Within a few weeks of the Revolution in Nov. 1917 Lenin decided that a secret police force similar to the Tsarist Okhrana (of which he and his fellow Bolsheviks had had considerable experience) would be necessary. He entrusted the task of its formation to the Polish Bolshevik, F. E. Dzerzhinsky, who undertook it with ruthless enthusiasm. At first the Cheka, ignoring the recent abolition of the death sentence, concentrated its attention upon the more obvious enemies of the new regime, such as the wealthy bourgeoisie. In July and Aug. 1918, however, following an attempt to murder Lenin, the Cheka unleashed a Red Terror in which thousands of victims of all classes were executed on the flimsiest evidence of counter-revolutionary activities. During the civil war the Cheka provided formations of troops which were used in desperate situations, *eg*, the mutiny at Kronstadt in 1921. They also helped to force the recalcitrant peasants to disgorge reserves of grain. The Cheka now no longer concentrated its efforts against the more obvious enemies of the party, its victims often being peasants and workers. The local Soviets and the commissars of justice complained about its high-handed actions, and Lenin, perhaps fearing the development of an organization not strictly under party rule, abolished it in 1922. Most of its functions, however, were transferred to the GPU, later the OGPU.   GS

CHEKE, SIR JOHN (1514–67), English classical scholar, who, as professor of Greek at Cambridge, introduced a new pronunciation used until quite recently. He became a Protestant and tutor to Edward VI and joined the conspiracy to give the throne to Lady Jane Grey. He was arrested abroad and returned to the Tower, where he abjured his new religion.

CHELMSFORD, FREDERICK JOHN NAPIER THESIGER, 3rd Baron (1868–1933), viceroy of India (1916–21). A law scholar and fellow of All Souls (1892–9), Chelmsford became governor of Qld (1905–9) and NSW (1909–13). He was on military service in India when he was made viceroy (1916). Later he was chairman of the University College (London) Committee (1920–32), briefly first lord of the admiralty (1924), and finally warden of All Souls (1932–3).

His viceroyalty was marked by nationalist discontent and rapid political change. In the Home Rule League movement and the Gandhian campaigns of 1919–21 he had to contend with widespread and militant political movements at a period when constitutional reforms were being discussed and inaugurated. Chelmsford initiated discussions on reforms almost as soon as he assumed office and he urged India's inclusion in the Imperial War Conference (1917). However, his contribution to reform awaits objective assessment. His role is often represented as secondary to that of the secretary of state, the ebullient E. S. Montagu, whose *Indian Diary* gave a somewhat one-sided account of the growth of reforms. In fact, the work of Chelmsford's government during the reforms discussions corrected some of the wilder tendencies of the provincial governments and probably helped to preserve the liberal intentions with which Chelmsford had begun and which Montagu certainly shared. The problem of dealing with the Home Rule and non-co-operation movements was partly that they were unknown quantities and partly that executive authority had to be delegated to local governments. Chelmsford's government looked mainly to the rallying of the moderates, and although this did not provide a long-term solution it did have some impact on the situation in the early part of 1921.

CHEMIN DES DAMES (1917, 1918), in France, road along the ridge between the valleys of the Ailette and the Aisne in Champagne, the scene of several sharp engagements in the First World War between German and Allied troops in 1917 and 1918. The name, however, usually refers to the third stage of the German spring offensive of 1918. The Chemin des Dames offensive was the last attempt of the Germans to win the war before the weight of US troops made itself felt. Its failure, after initial advances, ensured eventually Germany's defeat.

CH'EN CHIUNG-MING (1878–1933), Chinese revolutionary and Cantonese nationalist. Ch'en was one of Sun Yat-sen's chief supporters at the time of the 1911 Revolution. He had a large following among the separatist-minded Cantonese in Kwangtung, where Sun's revolutionary activities were centred. Eventually Ch'en's devotion to the Cantonese cause became stronger than his devotion to Sun, whom he expelled from Canton (1922). Ch'en himself was driven from Canton the next year, and from Kwangtung in 1926. His actions delayed the establishment of the Kuomintang's base in Canton, and turned him into its major enemy.

CH'EN LI-FU (1900–), Chinese politician, and leader, with his brother Ch'en Kuo-fu, of the conservative faction of the Kuomintang, the CC Clique. The brothers were nephews of Ch'en Ch'i-mei, a political mentor of Chiang Kai-shek. Ch'en Li-fu became very close to Chiang in the 1930s and 1940s, when his rigid conservatism and extreme anti-communism paralleled Chiang's own attitudes.

CH'EN PO-TA (1905–), Chinese communist theoretician and secretary to Mao Tse-tung. Ch'en's closeness to Mao, rather than his theoretical insights, have given his work considerable importance. During the Cultural Revolution (1966–), he played a leading role, and now (1970) holds one of the highest posts in China, as member of the Standing Committee of the Politburo of the Communist Party.

CH'EN TU-HSIU (1879–1942), founder member and first secretary of the Chinese Communist Party. Ch'en was already a distinguished academic and leading intellectual innovator when he helped to set up the Chinese Communist Party (1921). He was dean of the College of Letters at Peking University, and editor of *New Youth*. His conversion to Marxism was a byproduct of his efforts to introduce Western scientific and democratic ideas to China. He was an idealist rather than a practical man, and lacked the toughness needed to lead an emergent Communist Party. He found his authority as party secretary circumscribed by that of the Comintern advisers sent to China in 1923; he was forced to accept the Comintern scheme for co-operation with the Kuomintang, and for the formation of a block within the Kuomintang, which he himself mistrusted. Nevertheless, when this policy failed (1927), and the party which Ch'en had nurtured was smashed, he was made the scapegoat for its failure. He was dismissed from his office, and two years later expelled from the party. He became a Trotskyist, and formed his own tiny circle in Shanghai. In 1932 he was arrested by the Kuomintang and held in prison for five years. Ch'en's role in introducing Marxist ideas to China and in establishing the party has never been recognized by his successors, though it was undoubtedly crucial.

CH'EN YI (1901–), Chinese communist marshal and foreign minister. As a general, Ch'en achieved spectacular successes during the Anti-Japanese War (1937–45), and in the civil war which followed it. After the Liberation in 1949, he was made mayor of Shanghai, and undertook the formidable task of cleaning up the wickedest city in the Far East. He made considerable progress against odds which seemed almost impossible. Since 1958 he has been foreign minister. He was denounced during the Cultural Revolution as a 'capitalist element', but defended himself with great verve and customary pugnacity.

CHENG CH'ENG-KUNG (1624–62), known also as 'Koxinga', Chinese general who fought for the lost cause of a succession of southern Ming emperors against the Ch'ing dynasty. He was born of a Japanese woman in Hirado, Japan. His father, Cheng Chih-lung (1604–61), was a pirate and adventurer, who in 1628 decided to serve the Ming government. In 1645, after the establishment of the retreating Ming court at Foochow, the father presented his son to the emperor, who liked him so much that he conferred upon him the imperial sur-

name Chu. For this reason Cheng Ch'eng-kung was popularly known as *Kuo-hsing-yeh*, 'Lord of the Imperial Surname', from which the Dutch derived Koxinga. Using off-shore island bases such as Quemoy, he conducted military operations in the provinces of Fukien and Chekiang until Sept. 1659, when he was defeated. He retreated to Taiwan in 1661, ousting the Dutch in the process, and set up a civil and military government, but committed suicide the following year. For the Chinese, Cheng symbolized loyalty and, for the rest of the Ch'ing period, he was a 'patron saint' of the Chinese in Taiwan.

CHENG FENG (RECTIFICATION) CAMPAIGN (1942–4), campaign to establish orthodoxy within the Chinese Communist Party. The campaign was launched by Mao Tse-tung at a time when the party had experienced rapid growth, and a corresponding loss in discipline and organization. Its aim was partly to give a grounding in Marxist-Leninist theory to new recruits, partly to eradicate heterodox tendencies, and partly to establish the authority of Mao's embellishments of Marxism, notably the concept that Marxism could have a national form. Mao believed that the Chinese party had to develop its own variants on Marxism to suit local needs. This view was contested by a group led by Wang Ming, who believed that China had to follow unquestioningly a Moscow line. The campaign produced a disciplined party, loyal to Mao and ready to start the conquest of China.

CHENG HO (*fl.* 15th cent.), Chinese Muslim eunuch and maritime traveller, who led a series of seven expeditions (1405–33) for the Ming government comprising up to 60 ships and 28,000 men, and reaching Ceylon, Hormuz, Aden, and Mogadishu. The expeditions were probably intended to extend Chinese prestige and to examine trading prospects.

CHEN-LA, the name by which Cambodia was known to the Chinese from the 6th to the 19th cents. Envoys from Chen-la brought tribute to China on many occasions down to the 15th cent.

CHERASCO, TREATIES OF (1631) between France and the emperor and Savoy ending the War of the Mantuan Succession. In 1630 France under Richelieu had intervened in the war and had conquered Savoy. The imperialists had taken Mantua (18 July 1630), but had been unable to take Casale. The successes of Gustavus II Adolphus in Germany tied the opponents of France and she was able to make a favourable peace on 16 April 1631. By the treaties the Duke of Mantua recovered his duchy; the Duke of Savoy received a small territorial compensation; Monteferrat was evacuated, and French troops withdrew from Savoy and Piedmont; France retained Pinerolo and its approaches—the gateway to Italy—by arrangement with the Duke of Savoy, who became France's ally. The French possession of Pinerolo and most of the other terms of Cherasco were ratified by the peace of Westphalia in 1648.

CHERNOV, VIKTOR MIKHAILOVICH (1873–1952), Russian politician and theoretician of the Socialist Revolutionary Party. During the 1890s he led the Populist groups out of anarchism, violence, and despair into a closer relationship with the changing problems of 20th-cent. Russia, *eg*, urbanization. He played an important part (1902–6) in several congresses which welded the different Populist groups into the Socialist Revolutionary Party, of whose Central Committee he became a member. His contribution to this unity was two-fold: first, he persuaded his comrades to accept the existence of an industrial proletariat in Russia and the fact of its revolutionary role alongside the peasantry; second, he evolved an agrarian policy, summarized in the slogan 'the land belongs to no one and labour alone confers the right to use it'. He returned to Russia in April 1917, having been in exile abroad since 1899, and in May he joined Kerensky's Provisional government as minister of agriculture. As the leader of the largest socialist party his position should have been one of commanding strength, but was in fact one of increasing weakness, partly because his land policy forced him to prevent the peasants from seizing the land on their own account. His waning hold over the masses was shown when, in July 1917, he was saved by Trotsky from the hands of the angry crowd. He resigned from the Provisional government in Sept. 1917. He was unable to prevent the seizure of power by the Bolsheviks. As the leader of the majority party he was elected chairman of the constituent assembly, and it was characteristic of his moderation that he insisted that the demonstration against the dispersal of the assembly should be unarmed. In 1920 he emigrated and in his leisure wrote *Mes tribulations en Russie* (1921) and *The Great Russian Revolution* (1936).   GS

CHERNYSHEVSKY, NIKOLAI GAVRILOVICH (1828–89), outstanding member of the Russian radical, nihilist intelligentsia of the 1860s. He and his friend Dobrolyubov were heirs to the rationalist, utilitarian ideas of Belinsky as literary critics, and Chernyshevsky's articles in *The Contemporary* provided the moral inspiration and theoretical basis for the Russian populists and, later, influenced Lenin. Independently of Marx, he combined Hegelianism with economic materialism and developed Herzen's theory of Russia's peasant commune as a way to socialism, although without the latter's nationalist and romantic overtones. His utopian novel *What is to be Done?* advocated co-operative labour associations and feminine emancipation and became the bible of the radicals. Becoming disillusioned with the Emancipation of the serfs, he worked for social revolution, and his influence remained strong after his arrest (1862) and deportation to Siberia.

CHEROKEE INDIANS, American Indian tribe of the Iroquoian family, and one of the Five Civilized Tribes, formerly occupying the southern Allegheny region of the US. Though the Cherokees were first encountered by the Spaniard De Soto (1540), the tribe avoided conflict with European powers until the 18th cent., when they fought the Spanish (1740), the British (1759), and the Americans (1775–83). After 1796 they accepted white teachers and missionaries, established a government based on the US constitution, and adopted the white man's system of agriculture. A Cherokee alphabet, invented by Sequoya (*c.* 1820), made the tribe literate. On being forced by the American government to sell their lands (1835), they were removed, at a loss of a quarter of their number, to the Indian Territory (1838–9). Cherokees who refused to leave were fugitives until lands were set aside for them in NC (1842). In 1893 a federal commission began negotiations for the liquidation of the Cherokee nation. Tribal lands were apportioned individually to members of the tribe and the Cherokees became US citizens (1906).

CHEROKEE NATION v. GEORGIA, 5 Pet. I (1831), US Supreme Court case concerning efforts of the state of GA to gain jurisdiction over lands held by the Cherokee Indians under US treaties. The Supreme Court decided it lacked jurisdiction to hear a case brought against a state by an Indian tribe, because the tribe was not a foreign nation.

CHERUSCI, early German tribe living between the Weser and the Elbe, who, revolting under their chieftain Arminius, destroyed three Roman legions in the Teutoberg Forest (AD 9), ending Roman hopes of conquering Germany between the Rhine and the Elbe. Shortly afterwards the tribe disintegrated and disappeared from history.

CHERVENKOV, VULKO (1900–), Bulgarian communist leader, who joined the Bulgarian Communist Party in 1919 and later became secretary of the Sofia youth organization. In 1925 he fled to Moscow, escaping reprisals which followed the bombing of Sofia cathedral. After completing his studies in Moscow he entered the Agitprop section of the Comintern and became director of the Lenin School. During the Second World War he managed the Khristo Botev radio station, which broadcast to Bulgaria. He returned to Bulgaria (Sept. 1944), and although he did not gain high office at once he enjoyed considerable power and prestige because of his links with the Kremlin. When Dimitrov died in 1949 Chervenkov became deputy prime minister and in 1950 succeeded Kolarov as prime minister and became party chief. His personal dominance was greater than that of any other communist leader in Eastern Europe. His downfall began with Stalin's death and was hastened by the 20th Party Congress of the CPSU. He resigned from his party post in 1954, lost the premiership two years later, and was successively demoted until 1961, when he was dismissed from such posts as he still held.

CHERWELL, FREDERICK ALEXANDER LINDEMANN, Viscount (1886–1957), British physicist and politician, who worked on problems of aircraft design at Farnborough (1914–1918), and was professor of Experimental Philosophy (Physics) at Oxford (1919–57). He was responsible for major improvements in the position and status of the Natural Sciences at Oxford and encouraged many German scientists to move there in the 1930s. He was the inspirer and organizer of important research, rather than an active researcher himself.

In politics a Conservative, he knew and advised many leading politicians on scientific affairs, and collaborated actively with Sir Winston Churchill in pressing for better air defences, radar, and other defence preparations (1935–9). He was appointed chief scientific adviser to the prime minister by Churchill in 1940, became paymaster-general in 1942, and controlled much of the defence research of Britain throughout the Second World War. As head of the cabinet office statistical section, he was involved also with economic and strategic policy decisions and had great influence on Churchill. While continuing to supervise the expansion of the Clarendon Laboratory at Oxford, he was again paymaster-general (1951–3) and mainly responsible for the supervision of Britain's atomic research programme. It was on his initiative that a separate Atomic Energy Authority was set up in 1954.

CHESAPEAKE-*LEOPARD* INCIDENT (22 June 1807), occurred during the Napoleonic wars, when HMS *Leopard* boarded an American frigate off Hampton Roads to impress British deserters. The American captain refused the request and his ship was attacked, 3 sailors were killed, 20 wounded, and one deserter and 3 American seamen impressed. War between the US and Britain was only narrowly averted.

CHESHME, town on the western coast of Asia Minor. During the Russo-Turkish war of 1768–74 a Russian squadron defeated the Ottoman fleet near Chios, drove the Turkish ships into the harbour at Cheshme, and there set them on fire.

CHESTER, HUGH D'AVRANCHES, 2nd Earl of (1st of 2nd creation) (d. 1101), supporter of first Norman kings and possible kinsman. He was known to the Normans as the Fat and to the Welsh as the Wolf. In 1071 he created the great Anglo-Norman border palatinate of Chester. With his nephew, Robert of Rhuddlan, he achieved striking military successes against the North Welsh.

CHESTER, RANULF, 5th Earl of (2nd of 2nd creation) (d. 1153), one of the most powerful of the protagonists in the civil wars which filled the reign of King Stephen of England. Private grievances led him to attack Stephen, whom he captured at the battle of Lincoln (1141). He changed sides twice during the next decade, each time seeking more power and territory. On the whole, Ranulf played an indecisive part in the civil wars and his death (he was possibly murdered) contributed to the peaceful accession of Henry II in 1154.

CHESTERFIELD, PHILIP DORMER STANHOPE, 4th Earl of (1694–1773), English politician and writer. At first favoured by George II, he was Lord of the Bedchamber in 1727, and served as ambassador to the Hague (1728–32). But by 1733 he had come to resent Sir Robert Walpole's ministerial predominance, and joined the opposition to the Excise Bill, for which he was dismissed by the king. In opposition he contributed to *Fog's Weekly Journal* and *Common Sense*. In 1745, despite the king's protests, he was brought into the 'broad bottomed' administration by the Pelhams, as lord lieutenant of Ireland (1745–6), where his tact helped keep the peace during the 1745 Jacobite rebellion.

CHETARDIE, Marquis de la (1705–59), French ambassador at St Petersburg, who was assigned the task of undermining the Austro-Russian alliance of 1726. With the help of the Swedish ambassador and the Tsarevna Elizabeth's physician, Dr Lestocq, he engineered a palace revolution, backed by the palace guard, by which Elizabeth became ruler of Russia (Nov. 1741). However, the Austro-Russian alliance was consolidated by the Two Empresses treaty (1746).

CHEVALIER, MICHEL (1806–79), French economist and free trader, who published important studies in applied economics and was adviser to Napoleon III. He hoped that the Anglo-French commercial treaty of 1860, which he helped to negotiate, would be a step towards a more liberal French commercial policy.

CHEYENNE INDIANS, American tribe of the Algonquian family. The Cheyenne originated in MN, but were driven westward by other tribes. The explorers Lewis and Clark found them in SD (1804). Shortly after the Cheyenne made their first treaty with the US government (1825), the tribe divided, and the treaty of Ft Laramie (1851) recognized the Northern and Southern Cheyenne as distinct. After 1840, the Cheyenne joined the Arapaho, Kiowa, Kiowa Apache, and Comanche in wars against other tribes and white settlements. The southern group suffered heavily in the Chivington Massacre (1864) and in the battle of Washita (1868). The Northern Cheyenne joined Sitting Bull and were at the battle of the Little Big Horn (1876).

CHEYNE, ANDREW (d. 1865), English supercargo on the pioneer sandalwood voyage to the Isle of Pines, who later established a trading empire at Yap (Palau Is.), where he was killed, a retributive act for which the mild-mannered 'king', Abba Thule, was executed.

CH'I, Chinese kingdom of the pre-imperial age, ending 221 BC; also a dynastic title adopted by minor regimes of the Six Dynasties Period (222BC–AD 589).

CHIA-CH'ING, reign-title of Yung-yen (1760–1820), who became the 5th emperor of the Ch'ing dynasty (1796–1820) on the abdication of his father, the Ch'ien-lung emperor. The empire he inherited was in a lamentable state and although Chia-Ch'ing was conscientious, he lacked the qualities needed to reinvigorate the administration, even after the destruction of Ho-shen. The government's corruption is reflected in the length of time taken to suppress the White Lotus Rebellion (1796–1804). He combated economic problems with a policy of retrenchment which made him unpopular. His reign saw also the rejection of the Amherst Mission (1816), the second attempt by the British to improve trading conditions, and the continuation of Christian persecution.

CHIANG CH'ING (?1915–   ), fourth wife of Mao Tse-tung, whom she married in 1939 after a brief career as a film actress. Her marriage was not approved by Mao's colleagues, because it meant the dismissal of his revolutionary third wife. Chiang Ch'ing was not allowed to play a public role until the Cultural Revolution (1966), when she emerged as the 'mother' of the Red Guards, and a strident critic of most of her husband's former colleagues.

CHIANG KAI-SHEK (1887–   ), Chinese head of state and leader of the Kuomintang. Chiang, the child of an impoverished merchant family, was educated at military schools in China and Japan. He first became active in politics during the 1911 Revolution; then followed several obscure years when it is believed that he was involved in business in Shanghai. At the same time he built up useful contacts with Shanghai secret societies. In 1922 he became a full-time official in the Kuomintang's military apparatus, and within three years had emerged as the party's leading soldier; by the time the Northern Expedition started (1926) he was the most influential figure in the Kuomintang. Although he did not distinguish himself as a general, he showed a genius for political manœuvre and intrigue which resulted in his leadership at the end of the expedition (1928), but his purging of the communists and left-wingers from the Kuomintang in 1927 had turned the once revolutionary party into a reactionary one. In the early 1930s, Chiang was still obsessed with the communists, at that stage only a rump, and did his best to try to exterminate them. He was also involved in periodic wars against rebellious subordinates. All this left him little time for the real enemy, the Japanese, who were allowed to encroach on northern China with impunity. In his internal policies also Chiang became increasingly conservative; the launching of the New Life Movement (1935) was an anachronistic attempt to restore Confucian virtues. Only after his kidnapping at Sian (1936) did Chiang agree to form a united front to resist Japan, but by then it was too late to avoid full-scale war, which resulted in the Japanese taking over all China's eastern, northern, and southern provinces. Chiang retired with his government to the west, and instead of counter-attacking waited for his American allies to defeat the Japanese in the Pacific, keeping the bulk of his army on guard against the communists in readiness for civil war, which he believed inevitable. But the inactivity of the Kuomintang weakened it enormously, and when the Civil War did start (1946) the morale of the party and the army had been so seriously undermined that, even with generous American aid, the situation was lost. Chiang's reliance on men who were loyal to him rather than on men of talent vitiated the Kuomintang's war effort, since many of his supporters, though not Chiang himself, were corrupt. At the beginning of 1949 Chiang retired from the presidency and went to Formosa, taking with him the navy, the air force, and the reserves of the Bank of China. By the end of the year, the mainland of China was in communist hands. Chiang blamed its loss on Soviet aggression, but the fault really lay with the Kuomintang's inability to modernize China or to resist Japan. Chiang's own refusal to trust subordinates who were not sycophants deprived him of the services of many capable men. Since 1949 his rule has been limited to Taiwan, which, with American help, has become one of the most prosperous areas of the Far East.

H. K. Tong, *Chiang Kai-Shek, Soldier and Statesman* (London, 1937).   DCML

CHIAPPE, JEAN (1878–1940), French prefect of police (1927–34), who was dismissed after the Stavisky scandal. He had compromised his position by his right-wing political sympathies, and his dismissal was one cause of the riots of 6 Feb. 1934. He was appointed high commissioner in Syria by the Vichy regime, but died when the aircraft taking him there was shot down.

CHIAROSCURO (lit. light and dark), a term in painting to describe contrast by the use of light and shade rather than by distribution of colour. Caravaggio and Rembrandt were perhaps its greatest exponents.

CHIBCHAS. Generally considered to have been one of the higher civilizations of Pre-Colombian America, the Chibchas of the Colombian highlands were composed of five nations, each ruled by a priest-king. Their religion focused on sun and moon worship and required human sacrifices. The Chibcha were accomplished craftsmen, particularly with gold, as their jewellery attests. The legend of the gilded man was probably of Chibcha origin. The Spaniard Jiménez de Quesada conquered the Chibchas (1537–8).

CHICAGO FIRE (8–9 Oct. 1871) began in the lumber yards and engulfed an area of 3·5 sq. miles (9 sq. kms). Seventeen thousand structures were destroyed in the business district and 80,000 people rendered homeless. Within three years the city was rebuilt.

CHICAGO TREATIES (29 Aug. 1821, 26 and 27 Sept. 1833), in which the Chippewa, Ottowa, and Potawatamie Indians surrendered title to the south-western part of MI (1821), north-eastern IL, and south-eastern WI. They agreed to move west of the Mississippi (1833), leaving the area free for white settlement.

CHICAGO TRIBUNE, nationalist newspaper with a high circulation in the American Mid-west. Founded in 1847 by John L. Scripps and established as a leading newspaper during Joseph Medill's editorship (1855–99), it was controlled from 1914 until his death in 1955 by Robert R. McCormick, a conservative Republican and isolationist.

CHICHERIN, BORIS NIKOLAYEVICH (1828–1904), professor of legal history at Moscow University and the city's mayor (1881–3). His sympathies were with the west, presaging those of the Kadet party, and he wanted a constitutional monarchy and western legal reform.

CHICHERIN, GEORGII V. (d. 1936), Russian People's Commissar for Foreign Affairs (1918–30) and successor to Trotsky, who was born into an aristocratic family. After serving in the Tsarist foreign office he joined the Menshevik wing of the Russian Social Democratic Party, becoming (1907) secretary of its foreign bureau. He joined the Bolshevik Party in Jan. 1918.

Chicherin's post was a difficult one because the foreign office, or *Narkomindel*, shared the conduct of foreign relations with the Politburo, acting either directly or through the Comintern, with the secret police censoring *Narkomindel*'s dispatches.

Chicherin had to avoid Russia's total isolation among hostile capitalist powers, and to maintain the fiction that Russia's government was not responsible for Comintern attempts to foment revolution abroad. The German communist rising (1923) was an embarrassing sequel to *Narkomindel*'s Rapallo treaty with Germany (1922), especially as the Comintern had given Chicherin no notice of the attempted revolution.

When Stalin subordinated foreign affairs to a policy of strengthening socialism at home, Chicherin's position was undermined. He increasingly ceded responsibility to Litvinov and (partly on health grounds) was released from his post in 1930.

CHICHESTER, SIR ARTHUR (1563–1625), lord deputy of Ireland in James I's reign who suppressed a rebellion in Ulster (1608).

CHICHESTER, SIR FRANCIS (1901–), British airman and sailor who made the first long-distance seaplane flight (1931), and won the first Atlantic solo sailing race (1960). He sailed solo round the world (1966–7) and was knighted.

CHICHESTER, THOMAS PELHAM, 6th Earl of (2nd of 3rd creation) (1756–1826), British politician who was a Whig adherent of Lord Rockingham and a friend of Fox; he became surveyor of the ordnance (1782). He later supported the Younger Pitt's foreign policy in the French Wars and in

t

1795 became chief secretary to the lord lieutenant of Ireland, where he attempted pacification. Under Addington he became home secretary (1801) and was paymaster-general (1807–26).

CHICKAMAUGA, BATTLE OF (19–20 Sept. 1863), Confederate victory in the American Civil War. Braxton Bragg drove William S. Rosecrans's Union army back into Chattanooga, TN, but failed to achieve decisive success, partly through the heroic resistance of Union troops under George H. Thomas, 'the Rock of Chickamauga'.

CHICKASAW INDIANS, American Indian tribe of Muskhogean linguistic stock, and one of the Five Civilized Tribes. The Chickasaws were first encountered by Spanish explorers under De Soto (1540) in the northern part of the present state of MS. They supported the English against the French in the colonial wars of the 18th cent. Generally friendly to the US government, the Chickasaws signed a treaty (1786) accepting the Ohio river as their northern boundary. They ceded their lands in a series of treaties (1805–34) and were moved west to the Indian Territory. Initially they joined the Choctaw Indian tribe, but in 1855 formed their own government, modelled on the US constitution. When the Indian Territory was ended (1906), Chickasaw tribal lands were apportioned individually and the Chickasaw became US citizens.

CHIENG SAEN, in the extreme north of Thailand on the banks of the Mekong river, was the centre of a Thai state as early as the 7th cent., but was later to be superseded by Chiengrai and Chiengmai.

CHIENGMAI, on the Ping river in northern Thailand, was founded by King Mangrai in 1296 and became the centre of the kingdom of Lan Na. Constantly at war with Ayudhya, it reached its cultural and political apogee under King Tilokaraja (*reg.* 1442–87). Its conquest by Bayinnaung of Pegu in 1556 inaugurated more than three centuries of Burmese influence in the region. Thai troops brought Lan Na under Bangkok's influence in 1775, and the region was gradually incorporated within the kingdom of Thailand, following the stationing of a royal commissioner there (1875) and the imposition of centralized provincial administration early in the 20th cent.

CH'IEN-LUNG, reign-title of Hung-li (1711–99), 4th emperor of the Ch'ing dynasty (*reg.* 1736–96). He was an industrious ruler who regarded T'ang T'ai-tsung (*reg.* 627–49) as the supreme embodiment of benevolence and martial glory. Under his rule, the dynasty reached its zenith of power and the emperor was able to record ten major victories along and beyond the boundaries of the empire. He was responsible for mammoth literary compilations, the most famous being the *Ssu-k'u ch'uan-shu*, a manuscript library of the classics, history, philosophy, and belles-lettres in 36,000 volumes, which took 15,000 copyists nearly 20 years to complete. The last 15 years of his reign became increasingly corrupt as power fell into the hands of Ho-shen; and the White Lotus Rebellion (1795–1804), the largest revolt for over 100 years, marred an otherwise glorious reign. The Ch'ien-lung emperor abdicated in favour of Chia-ch'ing in 1796, so that his reign would not outlast that of his grandfather (K'ang-hsi). However, he continued to rule effectively until his death.

CHIFLEY, JOSEPH BENEDICT (1885–1951), Australian prime minister (1945–9), was probably the ablest and most widely respected trade unionist leader to be recruited to the higher ranks of the Australian Labor Party. He joined the NSW Railways in 1903 and became a union advocate and negotiator, and was an active participant in the 1917 railway strike. He campaigned politically without success until 1928, when he entered the Commonwealth parliament and became minister for defence in the Scullin government (1931). In the Labor split of that year, he lost his seat and was out of parliament until 1940, meanwhile fighting J. T. Lang for leadership of the movement in NSW. The importance of regaining and maintaining unity within the party, and his fellow workers' sufferings during the Depression, deeply impressed Chifley. Labor's return to office under Curtin in 1941 brought Chifley the treasury portfolio, to which that of post-war reconstruction was added (1942–5).

After Curtin's death Chifley led the party and the government through the problems of peace-making, extending social security reforms (begun during the war) and economic reconstruction and development, including the Snowy Mountains hydro-electric project. His electoral defeats in 1949 and in 1951 were due partly to an inevitable swing of the political pendulum, the reconstitution by R. G. Menzies of the Liberal Party, and public weariness with persistence of some wartime controls. A more important cause was Chifley's insistence on embodying his strong socialist convictions in the 1947 legislation nationalizing private banks, which the high court in 1948 and the privy council in 1949 declared unconstitutional. His popularity in political and industrial wings of the Labor movement, the personal loyalty of public servants, and the respect of parliamentary opponents, could not compensate for inability to project his personality through modern mass media.

L. F. Crisp, *Ben Chifley* (London and New York, 1961).

FA

CHIHLI CLIQUE (*c.* 1916–26), one of the war-lord cliques which contended for power in China between the death of Yuan Shih-k'ai (1916) and the establishment of the Kuomintang government (1928). The clique operated in north and central China. Wu P'ei-fu was its leader for most of its active life.

CHILD, SIR JOSIAH (1630–99), London merchant and one-time victualler to the navy who became a director of the East India Co. (1674), was four times its governor between 1681 and 1688, and a dominant figure in its counsels (1680–90). Though not governor at the time of the actual breach with the Mughals, he is generally credited with the policy of armed settlements which led to the Anglo-Mughal War (1686–90). The attempt to intimidate the Mughals having failed, the company was forced to make peace in 1690. The rest of Child's life was occupied with wrangles which led to the abeyance of the company's monopoly and eventually to the foundation in 1702 of a rival one.

CHILD, ROBERT (1613–54), leader of a faction which opposed the theocratic principles of Massachusetts Bay colony. He worked against civil and religious discrimination practised upon non-Puritans, and opposed laws based upon the Bible rather than English law. He was tried for sedition, heavily fined, and allowed to return to England.

CHILDERIC I (d. *c.* 481), King of the Salian Franks, who had been settled between the Somme and the Meuse since 428, was father of King Clovis. Childeric was an important ally of the western empire against the Visigoths, whom Clovis finally drove out of southern France. Childeric's magnificent tomb was discovered at Tournai in 1633.

CHILDERS, HUGH CULLING EARDLEY (1827–96), British and Australian statesman of Liberal principles. As a young emigrant to Australia, he forwarded the establishment of Melbourne University, and became commissioner of trade and customs in the first cabinet of Vic. After returning to England (1857), he entered politics, becoming an efficient first lord of the admiralty (1868–73). As secretary for war (1880–2) he was responsible for campaigns in the Transvaal (1881) and Egypt (1882), and reformed the army by regrouping it on a territorial basis and improving pay and conditions. As chancellor of the exchequer (1882–5) he lowered income tax, faced a deficit, and occasioned the fall of the

government by his proposal to tax beer. Childers, who preceded his friend Gladstone as supporter of Home Rule for Ireland, returned to office as home secretary (1886).

CHILDERS, ROBERT ERSKINE (1870–1922), Irish writer and propagandist for Home Rule. From 1895 to 1910 he was a clerk in the House of Commons. He served in both the Anglo-Boer War and the First World War, although in 1914 he supported the efforts of Irish gun-runners. In 1917 he joined the convention which was seeking a settlement of the Irish question, and in 1921 became a Sinn Fein deputy. By this time his views had become strongly republican and, although he took part in the Anglo-Irish treaty talks, he joined with De Valera in repudiating the treaty. In the Irish Civil War he was director of publicity for the dissident Republican forces. In Nov. 1922 he was arrested and executed for carrying arms. His best-known book, *The Riddle of the Sands* (1903), was a novel about a threatened invasion of England.

CHILEAN POPULAR FRONT, a left-wing union of Chilean political parties in the 1930s. The world Depression and the resultant Chilean distress caused the Communist, Socialist, and Radical parties to seek an alliance. This coalition took power in 1938 behind President Aguirre Cerda. After various splits and quarrels the alliance collapsed (1941), and the socialists, under Oscar Schnake and Marmaduque Grove, led an attack on the communists, the party being outlawed in 1948. Attempts to revive the Popular Front have met with some success, and the present (1970) left-wing alliance in Chile (FRAP), contains most of the groups which were in the Popular Front.

CHILEMBWE, JOHN (*c.* 1871–1915), Malawi national hero, who was educated partly in a militant black American environment. He returned to his native Malawi in 1900 to establish an independent Baptist mission, from which he launched (23 Jan. 1915) an abortive rising against colonialism, in which he was killed.

CHILESHYE, paramount chief of the Bemba (*c.* 1827–60). He pioneered the expansion of the Bemba into Bisa territory, making inroads into the Yao and Kazembe trading spheres.

CHILLIANWALLA, BATTLE OF, fought (13 Jan. 1849) about 85 miles (136 kms) north-west of Lahore during the Second Sikh War between the Sikhs, under Sher Singh, and the British, under Lord Gough. About noon on 13 Jan. Gough reached the vicinity and was preparing to camp with the intention of fighting the next day. He decided to attack the entrenched Sikh army in the face of masked batteries and through dense scrub, where his cavalry had little room to manœuvre. Desperate fighting continued until nightfall. Faulty handling of the British cavalry led to confusion. Although Sher Singh was forced to retreat, Gough lost 89 officers and more than 2300 men. These losses led to Gough being superseded by Sir Charles Napier, but before this happened Gough had destroyed the Sikh army at Gujrat.

CHILLINGWORTH, WILLIAM (1602–44), English theologian, who was converted to Rome (1630–4) after a controversy with the Jesuit Fisher, but was recovered by Abp Laud, his godfather, and in *The Religion of Protestants a Safe Way to Salvation* (1638) proclaimed scripture to be the source of religious truth. He took part in the royalist siege of Gloucester (1643) and died after being taken prisoner during the defence of Arundel castle.

CHILON, first ephor of importance in ancient Sparta (556 BC). He greatly increased the ephors' powers over the kings, and by insisting on Spartan ties with the pre-Dorian Achaeans became, together with the unwilling Anaxandridas, architect of the Peloponnesian League.

CHILTERN HUNDREDS, STEWARDSHIP OF THE, the most frequently used of the offices which enable British MPs to resign their seats. Its first use for this purpose, in 1750, was possible because the original duties of the office had lapsed and it was one of the offices under the Crown which required MPs to vacate their seats on acceptance (though with the possibility of re-election). The practice inaugurated a new category of by-elections, and, though normally regarded simply as a convenience for MPs, also gave constituents a means of forcing the resignation of members whose conduct displeased them. After 1832, therefore, the practice was sometimes considered as strengthening the democratic or radical view that MPs are the delegates of their constituents. The office has been specifically exempted from later modifications of the requirement of re-election on appointment to Crown office.

CHIMU, ancient Indian civilization of the northern Peruvian coast, noted for its urban organization and splendid pottery. The Inca conquered the Chimu (15th cent.).

CHIN, Chinese kingdom of the pre-imperial age, which split into Wei, Han, and Chao in 403 BC. In addition, there was an imperial dynasty which bore this title, *ie*, Western Chin (265–316) and Eastern Chin (317–419), and which should be distinguished from the Chin (Jürched) Dynasty.

CH'IN, Chinese kingdom of the pre-imperial age which succeeded in taking over all contemporary states and forming China's first imperial dynasty in 221 BC.

CH'IN DYNASTY (221–205 BC), earliest political authority in China able to claim the elimination of all rivals and the practice of universal rule. The Ch'in empire was formed after nearly two centuries in which the kingdom of Ch'in had adopted strong, realist measures of government, defeated its neighbours, and taken over their territories. Ch'in's methods of government have been represented as an example of injustice, oppression, and the suppression of civilized values. The statesman Li Ssu took a prominent part in establishing the Ch'in empire and in its government.

CHIN (JÜRCHED) DYNASTY (1122–1234), founded in North China by leaders of the Jürched people of the northeast. This house took over control of north China from the Sung dynasty.

CHIN HILLS, mountainous territory in north-west Burma inhabited by Chins, war-like and primitive Tibeto-Burman tribes, speaking a wide variety of languages and dialects. Under the British the Chins were indirectly administered and much recruited into Burma regiments of the Indian army. After independence the Chin Special Division was constituted with the prospect of becoming ultimately a separate state within the Union. The present (1970) government's writ scarcely runs in the Chin Hills.

CHIN PENG (b. 1922), Chinese-born leader of the Malayan Communist Party since 1948, when his predecessor Lai Teck disappeared during a political shift to the left. He led the MCP into a guerrilla war, and emerged publicly from the jungle only in Dec. 1955, during his abortive Baling talks with Malayan leaders.

CHINA MERCHANTS' STEAM NAVIGATION COMPANY, founded (1872) on the recommendation of Li Hung-chang, the task of organization and fund raising being left to two of his aides, Chu Ch'i-ang and Sheng Hsuan-huai. It was a joint government–merchant enterprise competing successfully with foreign firms in the coastal trade in China in its early years. In 1877 it bought the entire property of Russell & Co., an American firm. However, mandarin inertia, corruption, and lack of merchant support prevented it from developing into a healthy business concern, and its capital stock remained static for the most part of the 19th cent.

After 1911, it became a purely merchant enterprise, but was unable to free itself entirely from official interference. The company still operates in Taiwan (1970).

CHINCHON, DIEGO DE FERNANDEZ DE CABRERA Y BOBADILLA, Count of (?d. 1608) Castilian statesman and treasurer-general of the councils of Aragon and Italy for most of Philip II's reign. He resisted Antonio Perez's claim to be secretary of state for Mediterranean as well as northern affairs (1578) and in 1580, after Perez's disgrace (1579), was entrusted with Aragonese and Italian matters in a secretarial committee under Vazquez.

CHINDITS (a corruption from *Chinthé*, a Burmese mythical animal), forces raised by Gen. Wingate to operate within Japanese-occupied Burma in 1943 and 1944. They achieved little militarily, but raised morale by demonstrating that the Japanese were not invincible in jungle warfare.

CHINESE BRONZES. Weapons, tools, and ritual vessels of bronze were made in China from *c.* 1500 BC and are a characteristic mark of the Shang-yin civilization. Four main stages can be distinguished in the evolution of differently shaped vessels and different styles of decoration from then until *c.* 250 BC. Bronze vessels were held as treasures by the families or rulers of small communities on whom they had been bestowed and were often lodged in the ancestral shrines. Bronzes frequently bear inscriptions recording the circumstances of bestowal or manufacture.

CHINESE CLASSICS, term denoting a group of early Chinese texts which exercised a dominant influence on education, literature, scholarship, and the practice of Chinese government from the Han period until 1911. They also formed one of the major characteristics of Chinese cultural activity as this became spread in Japan, Korea, and Viet-nam. The texts were first given prominent attention by the establishment in 136 BC of five posts in the government for academicians. These were severally charged with the duty of studying five texts, *ie*, the *Shih-ching* (Classic of Songs), *Shu-ching* (Classic of Documents), *I-ching* (Classic of Changes), *Ch'un-ch'iu* (Spring and Autumn Annals), and *Li-chi* (Records of Propriety). Further texts were singled out for attention from time to time, until the list finally included 13 works; the additional books likewise had a philosophical or historical content, and in one case formed a collection of explanatory notes to literature.

The authority of these texts depended partly on their association with Confucius, who was believed to have played the major role in the production of at least some. Thus he is said to have collected popular songs (in the *Shih-ching*), or documents of leading dignitaries (in the *Shu-ching*), and to have edited the state records of Lu (in the *Ch'un-ch'iu*). The texts were intended to be used for didactic purposes so as to bring home popular suffering to governments (in the *Shih-ching*); to inculcate the moral lessons of history (in the *Shu-ching*) or the values of established social behaviour (in the *Li-chi*); or to act as a handbook for purposes of divination (in the *I-ching*). In the 11th cent. four comparatively short texts were selected from the main body as containing the essential elements of Confucian doctrine; these became known as the Four Books (*ssu shu*), *ie*, the *Lun-yü* (Analects of Confucius), the *Meng-tzu* (Sayings of Mencius), the *Ta-hsüeh* (Greater Learning), and the *Chung-yung* (Doctrine of the Mean).

An accurate and immediate knowledge of the Classics was a requirement for candidates seeking office in the civil service by way of examination. The texts therefore exercised a formative effect on the literary style of officials and formed the traditional intellectual context for decisions of policy or administration. The authority of the Classics became scriptural and could be gainsaid by a statesman, scholar, or official only at his peril. Variations occurred both in the versions of the texts themselves and in their interpretation from the Han period onwards, and from time to time imperial governments undertook to promulgate particular editions or commentaries to serve as versions that were officially accepted as orthodox.

W. de Bary, *Sources of Chinese Tradition* (New York, 1960).
ML

CHINESE COMMUNIST PARTY. The First Congress of the party was held in 1921, in a girls' school in Shanghai, and was attended by 12 delegates, one of whom was Mao Tse-tung; the first party secretary was Ch'en Tu-Hsiu. Soviet influence on the party was at first very strong, as was evidenced by the presence of two Comintern representatives at the First Congress, and it was Soviet influence which pressed the CCP into an alliance with the Kuomintang (1923), under an agreement formulated between Sun Yat-sen and Adolf Joffe, of the Comintern. For the next four years Chinese communists worked alongside and within the Kuomintang, a policy very strongly advocated from Moscow, but which many leading Chinese communists were unhappy about, including Ch'en Tu-hsiu. The communists and the Soviet advisers in China made great contributions to the success of the Kuomintang in uniting the whole of south China. But the aims of the two parties were very different—the Kuomintang standing for limited democracy while the CCP favoured much more radical programmes, and in 1927 Chiang Kai-shek struck at the communists. The Shanghai Purge (April 1927) was followed by a series of disastrous reverses for the Communist Party. Ch'en Tu-hsiu was made the scapegoat for these reverses, and was replaced as leader of the CCP by Ch'u Ch'iu-pai, who inaugurated a policy of 'Left opportunism', launching a series of unsuccessful putsches. The party was now divided, two general tendencies emerging: the party leadership still believed that the future lay in the cities, while Mao Tse-tung and others put their faith in China's peasantry. Mao was developing a strong base area (the Kiangsi Soviet), and similar projects were under way in other rural areas. Within the party leadership, a succession of unsuccessful policies was tried. Ch'u Ch'iu-pai was replaced by Li Li-san (1928), who in turn was ousted by Wang Ming and the 'returned students' (1931). Eventually it was realized that the urban situation was for the moment not revolutionary, and the party headquarters moved to Kiangsi (1933). Mao emerged as the leader of the party at the Tsunyi Conference (1935), a position he has retained ever since. Under his leadership the party has become increasingly peasant-oriented, and has developed a national style of its own. Mao has always been wary of accepting Soviet aid or advice; he has regarded the Soviet attitude to China as patronizing and unnecessarily paternalistic. After the end of the Long March (1936), the main centre of communist activities was in north-west China; the communist 'capital' was at Yenan. Here the communists gradually built up a formidable power base, rectified the party (Cheng Feng Movement), and engaged in ceaseless guerrilla warfare against the Japanese, then occupying much of China. The end of the Anti-Japanese War (1945) saw the communists in a much more powerful position than ever before; their stand against the Japanese had won them massive popular, nationalist support, which proved crucial in the Civil War (1946–9). Since 1949 the Communist Party has ruled China. Until the Cultural Revolution (1966–9) it operated as the key organ of integration and control, providing political leadership and inspiration, closely linked with the government executive.

Benjamin L. Schwartz, *Chinese Communism and the Rise of Mao* (New York, 1967).
DCML

CHINESE EASTERN RAILWAY. After China's defeat by Japan in 1895 the European powers competed to obtain exclusive privileges in 'spheres of interest', anticipating the partition of the Manchu empire. A principal area of rivalry lay in obtaining railway concessions, usually associated with mining rights and other commercial privileges. This 'scramble for China' was initiated by the Sino-Russian treaty of 3 June 1896, which provided for the construction of a railway across

northern Manchuria by the Chinese Eastern Railway Co., a subsidiary of the Russo-Chinese Bank, a thinly disguised agency of the Russian government. This line, leaving the projected Trans-Siberian railway at Chita and joining it again at Ussuriysk, would shorten the journey to Vladivostok by some 805 kms; it was widely seen as the first step in a project for the domination of Manchuria, Korea, and all north China, though the actual plans of the Russian government were vague.

Construction began in 1898, when Russia also obtained a 99-year lease of the important harbours of Port Arthur and Talienwan in the extreme south of Manchuria, and was authorized to build the South Manchurian Railway from Port Arthur, north through Mukden, to meet a branch of the CER at Changchun. The railway treaties gave Russia considerable economic privileges. In addition, she claimed rights to move troops on the railways, to station garrisons along them for their protection, and to maintain order among, and even tax, their employees. After the Boxer Rising (1900) afforded a pretext for the occupation of important towns, these claims were the basis for the establishment of an informal protectorate over all Manchuria, carrying Russian power within 161 kms of Peking, and to the frontiers of Japanese-dominated Korea.

This apparent threat to the Far Eastern status quo led to the Anglo-Japanese alliance in 1902, and in 1904–5 Japan made war on Russia, defeated her decisively, and occupied Korea. The peace treaty (treaty of Portsmouth, 5 Sept. 1905) also obliged Russia to surrender to Japan the Liao-tung Leased Territory and the SMR, thus ending her expansionist activities in the Far East.

Russia, however, retained control of the CER as a vital strategic link with Vladivostok, and she and Japan agreed to co-operate in upholding their interests in Manchuria; in 1910 they resisted an American bid to internationalize the two railways. In 1918 Chinese and Allied forces intervened to support the Tsarist administration in the railway zone against the Bolshevik authorities in Russia; when it regained control of the CER the Soviet government made it an exception to its policy of renouncing Russia's 'unequal' treaty rights in China, and defeated a Kuomintang attempt to seize it by force in 1929. However, in 1931–2 it did nothing to oppose Japan's occupation of Manchuria and the establishment of the puppet regime of Manchukuo (whose capital was appropriately sited at Changchun, the junction of the CER and the SMR) and in 1935 it sold its interest in the CER to the Japanese as part of a policy of appeasement designed to free its hands for the coming war in Europe.   PJBD

CHINESE EDUCATIONAL MISSION (1872–81), proposed and organized by Tseng Kuo-fan, Li Hung-chang, and Yung Wing. It represents China's first effort to educate its youth in Western science abroad. Four contingents of 30 pupils each were sent between 1872 and 1874 to schools in the Connecticut valley, US. Owing to conservative opposition to the pupils' increasing Americanization, the mission was abolished in 1881, when some of the pupils were still in high schools and few had completed their technical training. Among the 120 sent, some eventually became engineers, diplomats, admirals, and even prime ministers.

CHINESE EXCLUSION ACTS. US legislation to restrict Chinese immigration. Between 1852 and 1882 an average of 16,000 Chinese annually entered the US, and the Burlingame treaty (1868) was amended (1880) to allow the US to control Chinese immigration. They were excluded by act of Congress (1882, 1892, 1902) but in 1943 Congress allowed Chinese immigration under the quota system.

CHINESE GENTRY, landowning class who exercised a formative influence on the government and cultural growth of China from the Sung period onwards. The rise of the gentry accompanied (a) the growing preponderance of a bureaucracy which was appointed according to merit, at the expense of an aristocracy, which was based on birth; (b) the growing importance geographically and economically of the south at the expense of the north; and (c) the steady development of cities as cultural and commercial centres. The power of the gentry depended on a combination of wealth, which had been acquired commercially, with government office, which had been achieved by way of education and the examination system. The influence of the gentry was expressed in the leadership which they lent to cultural movements in the towns, where they lived more regularly than the landowners who had previously formed China's dominant class and where a new standard of luxurious living was being evolved to meet their demands. By the Ming period the gentry families were characterized as families of whom at least one member had successfully passed the state examinations, but had not necessarily been appointed to office; and they usually possessed some wealth in the form of land-holdings. The gentry's leadership of local communities was complementary to the exercise of administrative authority by officials; they demonstrated the ideals of Confucianism by raising funds for charitable purposes; by maintaining publicly needed amenities such as irrigation projects, canals, or dams; by supporting schools, and by having religious ceremonies performed. As cultural leaders of local communities they worked for the upkeep of morality, law, and order, thereby earning the gratitude of officials for their co-operative attitude.

Chang Chung-li, *The Chinese Gentry, Studies in their Role in Nineteenth Century Chinese Society* (Seattle, 1955).
Ho Ping-ti, *The Ladder of Success in Imperial China* (New York, 1962).   ML

CHINESE IN SOUTH AFRICA.
Over 50,000 Chinese were employed on the Witwatersrand gold mines (1904–10). Opinion in Britain, and of whites in South Africa, was critical of their employment, and they were repatriated.

CHINESE LABOUR IN LATIN AMERICA.
The exploitation of Chinese labour began (mid-19th cent.) in Peru in the guano islands and on railroad construction. Chinese labour was imported for use on the Cuban sugar plantations at the same time. Mexico received migrants, as well as many Chinese fleeing persecution in CA (late-19th cent.), who then suffered further persecution in Mexico (1910–17). Today descendants of these immigrants have prospered and are engaged in commerce.

CHINESE SYSTEM OF GOVERNMENT.
Imperial government of China was operated between 221 BC and AD 1910 under the aegis of sometimes a native house, sometimes an alien family. But despite the apparent succession of one dynasty from its predecessor, government was by no means fully effective over the whole of the sub-continent or continuously in time, and there were many and long periods when two or more governments claiming imperial authority were established simultaneously. The institutions of government were adapted or remodelled throughout 2000 years to meet the evolving needs of society, the sophistication of growing culture, and the demands of an increasingly more complex economy.

Authority for government was vested in the emperor, who claimed possession of the mandate from Heaven, and who regarded himself a steward of the human race on Heaven's behalf. Government was practised by means of a compromise between the ideal morality of the Confucians and the realistic measures deemed necessary by the Legalists. To assist the emperor, officials were appointed to posts in the civil service, thus constituting China's sole professional 'class', and attracting greater prestige than any other members of the population. The civil service included a whole hierarchy of posts and grades, ranging from those of senior statesmen to clerks in a local office. At times the officials were strong enough to eclipse the power of the emperor, which, however, could sometimes be asserted in a highly dramatic way. The tasks of government included the maintenance of civil order and security from both internal rebels and external invaders; the collection of tax, often in kind, and the distribution of staple commodities; the maintenance of a balanced economy and the exploitation of natural resources; the conscription of men to serve in the army or labour corps; and the retention of a harmonious relationship with the powers of Heaven and Earth.

The central government, which took decisions of policy, included from time to time an establishment of consultative senior statesmen, or chancellors, who bore supreme responsibility next to that of the emperor; ministers of state with specialist responsibilities for matters such as justice, tax or foreign visitors; officials of the palace and its household; and officers in command of the army. At times senior officials formed a cabinet or council which conferred to take major decisions; sometimes an emperor relied on an unofficial or private secretariat to circumvent or replace the official establishment; and there was also a censorate which was responsible for inspecting and reporting cases of corruption. Government was conducted by decree to meet particular circumstances rather than by recourse to a systematic set of legal principles. However, executive officials usually took due note of administrative precedent; of lists of decisions taken in comparable cases of the past; and of the compendious descriptions of state institutions that were compiled from the 8th cent. onwards.

Provincial government, which implemented the decisions of the central government, was similarly conducted by a variety of civil servants operating in a hierarchy of units that extended from the village to the province; and it was with local officials rather than those of the central government that individuals met the force of imperial government. In general, imperial China comprised some 1200 to 1500 prefectures (comparable with English counties) which were grouped together, eventually in 18 provinces.

R. Dawson, *The Legacy of China* (Oxford, 1964).
N. Lowse, *Imperial China* (London, 1966).   ML

CH'ING DYNASTY (1644–1911),
the last dynasty of imperial China, established by the Manchus. Constituting only 2 per cent of the population of China, the Manchus had to make use of the gentry-literati, the upper class in Chinese society, while maintaining a special status for themselves. However, the Manchus, like rulers of previous dynasties of conquest, became increasingly sinicized. The dynasty reached its apogee during the Ch'ien-lung reign (1736–96), when it began to decline rapidly, this process being hastened by Western and Japanese expansion. It gave way to the Republic in 1911.

CHINGIZ KHAN (1167–1227),
founder of the Mongol empire, was born in the Chita region of eastern Siberia. He was the son of Yesügei, a nephew of a khan of the Mongol tribe proper, which was to give its name later to all the Mongol-speaking peoples. The personal name of Chingiz Khan was Temüjin, the title under which he is best known, being accorded to him only when the princes of the Mongol tribe itself chose him to be their khan. It was now that Chingiz Khan began his career of conquest. In the ten years following 1196 he brought under his own control all the Mongol-speaking tribes of eastern Siberia, being recognized formally as their supreme lord in 1206. The reduction of the Tangut in the region of Kansu (1205–9) opened the routes towards northern China. As a result of the campaigns that Chingiz Khan waged in 1211–16 almost all the vast area north of the Yellow river came under Mongol rule, although the subjugation of these territories was not in fact to be complete until 1234. Chingiz Khan thereafter turned his attention to the western steppe lands of Central Asia. In 1218 his forces overran Semirechye and Sinkiang, bringing low the power of the Kara Khitay. Still further to the west the Mongols now came into conflict with the state of the Khwarazm Shahs. Bukhara and Samarkand yielded in 1220.

Mongol troops thrust forward into Azerbayjan, the Caucasus, and southern Russia. Balkh and also the region of Khurasan in Persia fell in 1221, during which year the Khwarazm Shah, Jalal al-Din, was driven to seek refuge in India, only to be defeated by the Mongols on the banks of the Indus. Chingiz Khan now made a slow return (1222–5) through Samarkand and the Tashkent area to the Irtish river and thence to Mongolia. He died in the district of Ch'ing Shui on the Hsi river in Kansu.

CHING-TU, the Buddhism of the 'Pure Land', which once flourished in China and is still important in Japan and Vietnam. It is a devotional form of Buddhism in which adepts follow the *Sukhavativyuha-sutra* and worship the former Buddha Amitabha (Jap., *Amida*). The school was introduced into China in the 2nd cent. and was developed by the monk Hui-Yüan (334–416). In Japan, where it is called *Jodo*, the school was introduced by Genku (1133–1212), and still has over 8000 temples. The *Shin* sect in Japan, founded by Shinran (1173–1262), and having over 20,000 temples, is also Amidist in its beliefs.

CHINGUNJAB (d. 1757), princely leader in the anti-Manchu rebellion of 1756 in Khalkha Mongolia. The continual wars between the Jungars, or West Mongols, and the Manchus in the 18th cent. imposed a heavy strain on the Mongols, who had to furnish supplies and men for the Manchu forces. The Mongols were also suffering from exploitation by Chinese traders. Chingunjab, prince of the Khotogoits in the northwest of Mongolia, took advantage of this discontent to plot a common campaign with Amursana, leader of the Jungars, against the Manchus. At his call a rising broke out in Mongolia, especially among the soldiers in the post-stations and frontier posts. However, the projected alliance was bungled; Chingunjab did nothing effective and was soon captured. He was taken to Peking and executed, and the popular uprising was brutally put down. This was the last large-scale anti-Manchu movement until the Chinese revolution of 1911.

CHINOOK INDIANS, tribe of the Chinookan family, which took its name from them. They lived on the Pacific coast near the mouth of the Columbia river, where the explorers Lewis and Clark visited them (1805). They were widely known among British and American traders, and their language formed the basis of a jargon first used in trading, and later as a medium of communication from CA to AK. An unidentified fever killed about four-fifths of the tribes of the Chinookan family in 1829, and by 1855 only about 150 Chinook remained. They later fused completely with the Chehalis, a Salishan tribe.

CHINSURA, town in Bengal about 25 miles (40 kms) north of Calcutta on the Hughli river, and close to Hughli itself, with which it is now united. The Dutch East India Co. had a factory there from the early 17th cent., which Clive captured (1759) when the company tried to interfere in Bengal affairs. It was restored to the Dutch but eventually ceded to the British (1825) in part-exchange for English possessions in Sumatra.

CHIOGGIA, WAR OF (1376–81), naval war between Venice and Genoa, the last of several wars between them, named after the scene of the main action near Venice. An amphibious blockade was broken when the Venetians trapped and starved out the besiegers in Chioggia.

CHIOS, ancient Greek island city-state in the eastern Aegean, first settled in the Ionian migrations in 10th cent. BC. Famous for poetry and wine, by the early 6th cent. it traded with Egypt, issued coinage, and had a moderate democratic constitution. It was subjected by the Persians (c. 514) and took part in the abortive Ionian Revolt (499–494). On being freed after the Persian defeat (479), it joined the Delian League. Being permitted to retain a fleet longer than any other ally, it helped Athens to subject Samos (440–439) and Mytilene (428–427), but rebelled in the second part of the great Peloponnesian War (412). After submitting to a Spartan-backed oligarchy, it supported Athens from 394 continuously until the Social War (357–355), when it seceded. It was a founder-member of the Second Athenian Confederacy. Chios was punished by Alexander the Great for assisting the Persians (332) and sacked by Mithridates VI of Pontus for loyalty to Rome (86 BC).

CHIPPENDALE, THOMAS (1718–79), English furniture maker, whose work is thought to typify the taste of his age. He was the son of a Yorkshire joiner, and began by making plain oak furniture for his father. By the middle of the century he had set up a workshop in London. Working at first on a small scale, he made his reputation by publishing a comprehensive collection of furniture designs, *The Gentleman and Cabinet-Maker's Director* (1754), which included 160 plates showing almost every type of domestic furniture, mainly in the prevailing rococo style, but also examples of neo-classical, Gothic, and Chinese styles. From *c.* 1760 he won large commissions to furnish great houses, such as Harewood House, Yorks, where he undertook the whole of the interior decoration.

CHIPPEWA INDIANS, one of the largest tribes north of Mexico, and part of the Algonquian family, ranging from the eastern shore of Lake Huron to ND. They were visited by Jesuit missionaries in the 17th cent. and their relations with the French were friendly. After they acquired firearms from white traders (*c.* 1670) they fought territorial wars with the Fox, Sioux, and Iroquois, pushing their western frontier to the Turtle Mountains in ND. The Chippewa fought with other tribes in the North-west Territory against advancing white settlements at the close of the War of 1812. Those living within the borders of the US made treaty with the government (1815) and retired to reservations where they still live (1970).

CHIPPEWA, BATTLE OF (5 July 1814), brief encounter near Niagara Falls betwen 1300 American regulars under Winfield Scott, who repulsed an attack by 1500 British troops under Gen. Riall.

CHIRICAHUA, division of the North American Apache Indians, and the most war-like. Their raids extended into NM, southern AZ, and northern Mexico. In 1872 the US government sent an envoy to make an agreement with Cochise, then their chief, to end hostilities, and many were settled on reservations, but dissidents, including the famous chief Geronimo, continued to make raids. When Geronimo surrendered (1886), he, his followers, and about 400 peaceful Chiricahua were sent to a military prison in FL. They were moved to Fort Sill, OK (1894), and released in 1914. Some returned to reservations in NM, and the rest stayed in OK.

CHIRIKOV, ALEKSEI (d. 1748), Russian sailor, who sailed with Vitus Bering on the government-sponsored Great Northern Expedition of 1733–43. He reached America at latitude 56° N, but was unable to land, although the valuable furs acquired by his crew from the Alaskan offshore islands stimulated later voyages by Siberian merchants.

CHISHOLM, CAROLINE, née Jones (1808–77), pioneer of assisted- and directed-female migration to Australia. She had an English evangelical upbringing, but married a Roman Catholic officer in the East India Co. Having accompanied him to NSW on sick leave in 1838, she remained behind after he returned to duty. Despite official discouragement and some sectarian hostility, Mrs Chisholm established an Immigrants' Home in Sydney and a free registry office for new arrivals. She placed her charges after careful investigation of local conditions and encouraged married couples to supervise young girls employed in the same district. In 1846 she went to London, where she organized a 'Family Colonization Loan Society', with a NSW section, which selected migrants and chartered vessels to transport them under humane conditions. She raised funds by writing pamphlets and getting help from others, including Charles Dickens. Her efforts to secure free land grants for her settlers conflicted with the mid-cent. land sales policy, but a grant of 4000 acres (16 sq. kms) enabled her to settle a group of 30 families.

Mrs Chisholm's main work, before the gold-rushes, reduced the ratio of males to females in Australian colonies from 2 to 1 in 1840 to 1·43 to 1 in 1850. After their return to Australia in 1854, she and her husband tried to ameliorate gold-rush conditions.

M. L. Kiddle, *Caroline Chisholm* (Melbourne, 1957).   FA

CHISHOLM TRAIL, US cattle trail from east TX through Indian Territory to the stockyards and railhead at Abilene, KS (1867). The boom period of cattle drives lasted until 1871, when Abilene lost its predominance because of the westward advance of settlement and of the railroads.

CHISHOLM v GEORGIA, 2 Dallas 419 (1793), US Supreme Court decision affirming that, under Article 3 of the constitution, the court had jurisdiction over a suit brought against a state by a citizen of another state. Immediate congressional action led to a direct curtailment of such jurisdiction by the 11th Amendment (1798).

CHIT HLAING, U (1879–1952), Burmese barrister and political leader. He was a member of the Young Men's Buddhist Association, president of the General Council of Burmese Associations, and a delegate to the Indian and Burma Round Table Conferences in London (1930–1). He was elected to, and became president of, the Legislative Council (1932), and Speaker of the House of Representatives (1937). He was a privy councillor under the Japanese, and later formed the Union of Burma League (1951).

CHITAPANKWA, paramount chief of the Bemba from about 1860 during their last major phase of expansion, when guns were being acquired through trade with the Arabs and Nyamwezi.

CHITOR, former capital of the state of Mewar, later, from the name of its new capital, known as Udaipur. Chitor is famous for its fort on a narrow hill 500 feet (153 m.) high and over 3 miles (5 kms) long. Chitor was twice taken by Muslim kings (Ala-ad-din Khilji in 1303 and Akbar in 1568). On each occasion the rite of *jauhar* or holocaust of the Rajput women of the garrison was performed.

CHITPAVAN BRAHMANS, the most powerful of the Maratha brahmans. The name is probably a corruption of Chitapolan, the original home of the caste. There is a tradition that they were of foreign extraction. Another explanation is that the name means pure in heart. The peshwa, chief minister on Sivaji's *Ashta Pradhan* (Council of Eight), was a Chitpavan, but the ministers gradually usurped the power of the Satara rajas and became heads of the Maratha confederacy forming the dynasty of the Peshwas at Poona. The seventh and last peshwa, Baji Rao II (1796–1818), fought the British but was defeated by Lord Hastings, who abolished the peshwaship. The Chitpavans remained fiercely anti-British, but availed themselves of western education and were to be found in all the professions. They also controlled the vernacular press. They were prominent in the terrorist movement and were responsible for the murder of several British officials.

CHITRAL, state on the extreme north-west frontier of West Pakistan. By the Durand Agreement (1893) the Amir of Afghanistan recognized that it was under British protection. After the siege of a British mission there in 1895, a permanent garrison was maintained to protect British interests.

CHOATE, RUFUS (1799–1859), US lawyer and politician. Choate, a member of the Whig Party, represented MA in the US House of Representatives (1831–4) and in the Senate (1841–5), where he spoke on the OR Boundary, the Tariff, and the Annexation of TX.

CHOCTAW INDIANS, American Indian tribe, the largest of the Southern Muskhogean linguistic group and one of the Five Civilized Tribes. The Choctaws were first encountered by the Spaniard De Soto (1540), along the lower Mississippi river. They became French allies in wars against other tribes. Some Choctaws supported the British, which caused an intra-tribal war lasting until the defeat of the French (1763). The Choctaws were friendly to the US government, and began ceding their lands (1801) about the time they adopted the white man's culture. By the treaty of Dancing Rabbit (1830), they ceded the last of their lands and were moved to the Indian Territory. They established a government modelled on that of the other Civilized Tribes. When the Indian Territory was liquidated (1906), the Choctaws became US citizens.

CH'OE CHE-U (1824–64), founder of the Korean religion Ch'ŏndogyo. Born in Kyŏngju, Kyŏngsang South Province, he was an eager student of the Buddhist scriptures in his youth. He gained a reputation for mastery of Taost magic after two periods of seven weeks spent in prayer, in 1856 and 1857, and was also acquainted with the primitive Christian communities in the remote parts of his province. He published the basic teachings of Tonghak, later called Ch'ŏndogyo, in 1860, and was executed for heresy and anarchism.

CH'OE CLAN, most successful of those clans which ruled Korea after the military families seized power from the literati in 1170. Ch'oe Ch'ung-hon, whose private retainers were said to outnumber the soldiers of the government, gained control in 1198; his family held power for four generations, and were largely responsible for moving the court to Kanghwa island in 1232, in an effort to avoid the Mongol invasions.

CHÖ-GYEL, religious kings of Tibet. Namri Löntsen (d. *c.* AD 627) was chosen by leaders of Tibetan clans as the first Chö-gyel (*c.* 600). His line was that of the rulers of Yarlung, the first six of whom had been supposedly lowered from and withdrawn to heaven. The successors retained a semi-divine status. His son, Srongtsen Gampo (*c.* 609–49), sponsored the introduction of Buddhism and the Tibetan alphabet, and by his expansionist policies and marriage alliances established Tibet as the dominant Central Asian power, which it remained till the mid-8th cent. The last Chö-gyel, Lang Darma (born *c.* 803), a persecutor of Buddhism, was assassinated in 842, after which the kingdom disintegrated and the descendants of the Chö-gyel moved to western Tibet.

CHOIBALSANG (1895–1952), the 'Stalin' of the Mongol revolution. He belonged to a poor family and was educated at Urga and Irkutsk. After taking a leading part in revolutionary plotting and in the partisan war of 1921, he emerged as dictator in the 1930s, his power being based on his position as minister of internal affairs from 1936 onwards. He occupied all important government posts simultaneously, and with the help of Soviet security forces had eliminated all the old revolutionaries by 1940. Under Choibalsang, an unswerving supporter of the USSR, the final destruction of the old society, and especially of the Lamaist Church, was effected.

CHOISEUL, ÉTIENNE FRANÇOIS, Duc de (1719–85), career diplomat, who was appointed French foreign minister (1758) through the influence of Mme de Pompadour, and brought control and purpose to Louis XV's foreign policy. Control of the army and navy as well as of foreign affairs made him the first effective chief minister since Fleury. He intended to reestablish French power and destroy that of Britain through an alliance with Austria and Spain. Although he was unable to stave off defeat in the Seven Years War, he put France in a position to embark on a successful war against Britain after his fall (1770), which was probably caused by the hostility of Mme du Barry.

CHOLAS, one of the most important ancient Indian dynasties, first mentioned as a tribe in the 3rd cent. BC, and controlling the east coast of the Deccan (9th–12th cents AD) and making their power felt far beyond that area during most of the 11th cent. Their original basis was the fertile Kaveri valley with Tanjore and Trichinopoly as their main centres. There they first made themselves independent from the Pallavas of Conjeevaram, who had been their overlords till the middle of the 9th cent., and expanded their power during the 10th cent. During the reigns of Rajaraja I and Rajendra Chola I they developed into a great maritime power and successfully carried out at least one devastating raid along the Straits of Malacca (1024). Most of Ceylon was occupied (1017–70). In addition, the Cholas are important for the development of Tamil literature and of art and architecture as well as for the thorough system of local government and the activities of mercantile and military guilds.

CH'ŎLCHONG (1831–63), King of Korea (*reg.* 1849–63) and member of a minor branch of the royal family, who was a farmer before he became king at the age of 18. These circumstances enabled the Andong Kim family to regain its power over the court, and their oppressive administration caused his reign to be marked by almost continuous popular revolts. One of his last acts was to authorize the execution of Ch'oe Che-u.

CHOLERA. This disease, with its high fatality rate, first spread over the world from Asia in the 1820s and 1830s, manifesting itself in Britain in 1831–2. It returned again in 1848, 1853, and 1865–6, being concentrated mainly in the poorer parts of towns, usually spreading through contaminated water supplies. The 1831 outbreak led the British government to offer financial help for the first time to local authorities, and the 1848 outbreak stimulated the passage of the Public Health Act of that year. But the relatively small impact of the disease outside working-class areas, the resistance of medical opinion to the idea that a disease could be communicated by an apparently clean water supply, and the occasional nature of the outbreaks prevented cholera from being the occasion of a sustained pressure for sanitary reform.

CHOLO, term used in the central Andes to refer to a *mestizo* (mixed parentage), an Indian or a servant.

CH'ŎNDOGYO, a Korean religion, first preached by Ch'oe Che-u under the name of *Tonghak*, in 1860. Its main slogan was 'Man and God are one', and Ch'oe preached purity in life, ranging from personal and household hygiene to the sacrifice of self-interest for the sake of the community. *Tonghak* means literally 'Easternism' and is usually explained as meaning that this religion combined Buddhism, Confucianism, and Taoism, and was opposed to 'Westernism' in general and Christianity in particular, but it may be better understood as 'Koreanism', Korea being known as 'the Eastern Kingdom'. Ch'oe's teaching originated in the realities of Korean provincial life, combining the mixture of Buddhism and Taoism as practised in local temples with the primitive Christianity practised at the time in several communities in Kyŏngsang Province. It was regarded as heresy by the state, which based its claims to legality on Neo-Confucianism, and it also had contacts with extreme nationalist groups in Japan.

As the only nation-wide organization outside the government, this religion became the vehicle for the expression of general popular discontent in the provinces, which culminated in the *Tonghak* rising of 1894. Following the failure of this revolt, the religion lost most of its adherents, and was driven underground for several years. Ch'oe Sihyŏng, its patriarch since the execution of Ch'oe Che-u in 1864, died in 1898, and his successor, Son Pyŏnghŭi, spent some time in virtual exile in Japan. In 1906 Son was able to defeat the faction led by Yi Yonggu, which advocated union between Japan and Korea. He revitalized the basic religious teaching of *Tonghak*, and reorganized it under the name of *Ch'ŏndogyo*, 'Religion of the Way of Heaven'. Son retired in 1908, and was succeeded by Pak Inho. Again this religion grew into the most effective non-governmental organization in Korea, and as such was again the vehicle for nation-wide protest, this time against the Japanese Government General, in the 'March First Movement' of 1919. The Japanese oppression which followed this seriously weakened the Ch'ŏndogyo, and was one cause of the factionalism which marks this, as much as any other, religion in Korea. There is a resulting lack of conviction in the Ch'ŏndogyo's reaction to the various crises in recent Korean history, particularly to the establishment of a communist regime in North Korea, but it continues to hold one of the leading places among the religions in Korea.

B. Weems, *Reform, Rebellion and the Heavenly Way* (Tucson, AZ, 1964).   WES

CHŎNG TASAN (1762–1836), founder of modern Korean philosophy. He was a leading proponent of *Silhak*, 'Practicalism', a school of thought which concerned itself primarily with government administration, and denied that orthodox Confucianism should hamper efficient and beneficial government. He held high office in the 1790s, and again briefly in 1818, but, as he belonged to one of the first Christian families in Korea, and refused to accept the orthodox view that all western thought was to be banned as subversive heresy, he lived most of his life in provincial exile, studying, teaching, and writing.

CHŎNGJO (1752–1800), King of Korea (*reg.* 1776–1800). His reign was the last in a 150-year period of stability, and is noted for the publication of important surveys of Korea's past, the institution of the court diary, which is the most reliable source material for Korean history up to 1910, and the founding of two royal libraries, which together contain practically all the source materials for the study of traditional Korea.

CHŌSEN, official name of Korea during the Japanese occupation (1910–45). In this period the Japanese Government General developed Korea considerably, particularly its communications and exploitation of mineral resources, but denied almost all civil rights to Koreans. Chōsen is the Japanese pronunciation of Chosŏn, the name of the Yi dynasty of Korea (1392–1910), and this Korean name itself was a resurrection of the oldest Chinese name for Korea, Ch'ao-hsien. The origin of that name is unknown. It is popularly, though incorrectly, translated 'Land of the Morning Calm'.

CHOSEN COUNCIL, body of advisers upon whom Tsar Ivan ('the Terrible') of Russia (1530–84) relied in the first half of his reign to help him make governmental decisions. The council included the Metropolitan Makary, the court chaplain Sylvester, and the chamberlain Adashev.

CHŌSHŪ, important autonomous domain (*han*) of Tokugawa Japan. In the 16th cent. its *daimyō* had opposed Ieyasu and, with other south-western *han*s, Chōshū played a leading role in the Tokugawa *bakufu*'s overthrow (1868). After the Meiji Restoration ex-samurai of Chōshū origin figured prominently in both government and army for at least half a century.

CHOSON, name of an ancient state in northern Korea with its capital at P'yong-yang; it was conquered and annexed by China in 108 BC. At a later period the name became the official title of the Yi Dynasty state from 1392, when the Yi royal house gained the throne, until the proclamation of the Han 'Empire' in 1896. The Japanese form, Chōsen, wa used to designate Korea under Japanese rule (1910–45).

CHOSROES I (reg. 531–79), Sasanian King of Iran, who came to power after the disturbances connected with the Mazdakites. He restored the king's authority by bringing the army under his control. The great aristocracy lost its power, which passed to the lower nobility and the bureaucracy, both of which owed their positions to the king. Social conditions were improved by laws which dealt with the position of noble families, which had been disrupted during the recent disturbances; by tax reforms based on surveys, the land tax becoming a fixed sum instead of an assessment which fluctuated annually, and the poll tax depending on a man's productive capacity; and by the rebuilding of villages, the repair of roads and bridges, and the clearing of canals. Fortifications were built on the frontier and nomads were settled in frontier districts to form defensive buffers. It was a period of scientific, artistic, and literary achievement. The national legends and epics were written down and translations were made of Greek and Indian works. In 540 Chosroes broke the peace with Byzantium, invaded Syria, and captured Antioch. In the east he discontinued payment of tribute to the Ephthalites and, in 565, in alliance with the western Turks, he ended the power of the Ephthalites and divided their territories with his ally. The Yemen was also conquered and annexed. The Romans, alarmed by the growing power of Iran, tried to contain it by diplomacy but failed, and the Persians invaded Mesopotamia. Chosroes died during the course of the subsequent peace negotiations.

CHOSROES II (reg. 590–628), Sasanian King of Iran, who became king on the deposition of his father, Hormidz. After being temporarily unseated by a *coup d'état*, he regained the throne with Byzantine help, given in return for the cession of most of Armenia, which however he recovered with Edessa and Caesarea (610). His Syrian troops conquered Antioch, Damascus, and Jerusalem, where 50,000 Christians were massacred (611). Egypt was invaded (616) and, at the same time, Ankara was captured and Constantinople besieged. A Byzantine counter-attack brought the Greeks to Ctesiphon and Chosroes was assassinated. He had spent lavishly on his court, but the people were burdened by taxes and heavy demands on manpower for the military campaigns.

CHOTEK, RUDOLPH CHRISTIAN, Count (1707–71), Austrian nobleman, who, as chancellor of Bohemia, helped Kaunitz and Haugwitz to reform and direct the Habsburg administration for the Empress Maria Theresa.

CHOTIN, BATTLE OF (1673), victory of John Sobieski, later King of Poland, over a large Turkish army sent to the Ukraine in support of the Cossacks.

CHOU, Chinese kingdom, founded, traditionally, in 1122 BC and brought to an end in 256 BC. In contemporary and subsequent writings, Chou has been regarded as the only kingdom to have possessed legitimate authority to rule during that period, which, however, saw the rise of a number of states and kingdoms which could effectively dispute Chou's claim. The culture, practices, and institutions ascribed to Chou were regarded during the imperial age as ideally inspired models, and some of the kings of Chou have been cited as paragons of royal behaviour. In the imperial age, Chou was sometimes adopted as a dynastic title (eg, during the Six Dynasties period).

CH'OU AN HUI (Peace Planning Society), political organization in early Republican China. The society was founded in 1915 at Yuan Shih-k'ai's prompting to promote his plan to make himself emperor.

CHOU EN-LAI (1898–), Chinese communist politician. Chou was born into an impoverished gentry family, and educated in China and Japan. He spent four years in France (1920–4), organizing Chinese workers and students there, and was a founder member of the branch of the Chinese Communist Party set up in Paris in 1921. He returned to China (1924) and worked as a political instructor at the Whampoa Military Academy. In 1926 he moved to Shanghai, then under war-lord control, where he was a clandestine labour organizer. He helped organize the liberation of the city (March 1927) and was then arrested in the Shanghai Purge (April 1927) of communists. He was released on the intervention of Pai Ch'ung-hsi, and in 1928 went to Russia, where he stayed until 1930. On returning to China he managed to disentangle himself from the disgraced Li Li-san, whom he had previously supported. For the next few years, he was closely identified with military affairs, and was one of the chief planners of the Long March, after which he became increasingly concerned with external relations; he was communist representative in negotiations following the Sian Incident (1936), and communist 'ambassador' to Chiang Kai-shek during the Anti-Japanese War. Chou's sophistication, skill in negotiation, and personable nature made him an excellent front man for the communists. After the Liberation (1949), Chou became prime minister and foreign minister in the new communist government. He played crucial roles in economic development and foreign affairs, leading China into closer co-operation with the 'Third World', and promoting gatherings such as the Bandung Conference (1955). He has travelled widely, and is the only Chinese leader known to foreigners. He is generally seen as an urbane, pragmatic figure, sometimes known rather unkindly as 'China's Mikoyan', in contrast to the romantic revolutionary Mao Tse-tung, or the ascetic Liu Shao-ch'i. During the Cultural Revolution (1966–), Chou has acted as the last bastion against chaos, and managed to water down some of the excesses of the Cultural Revolution, notably in the economic sphere.   DCML

CHOU TA-KUAN (d. c. 1346), Chinese traveller in South-East Asia during the Yüan dynasty. His *Notes on the Customs of Cambodia*, written after his visit there (1296–7), are an important source for the history of Angkor in its latest phase.

CHOU YANG (1908–), Chinese literary theorist, and chief proponent, after Mao Tse-tung, of Chinese communist cultural policy. A rigid and doctrinaire critic, Chou led the attack on creative independence, notably in the attacks on Hu Feng (1954). He himself was denounced as a 'poisonous weed' during the Cultural Revolution.

CHOUANS, bands of peasant guerrillas in revolt against the French republican government from 1793. Although the name was originally given to the rebels in Brittany and Normandy, it came to be applied also to the participants in the general revolt in the west of France against the central government's attempts to enforce conscription and its attack on the clergy. The rebels, led by royalist nobles, engaged in barbarous fighting against government troops. The revolt was suppressed in 1793, but there were further outbreaks of violence (1795, 1799) before Bonaparte succeeded in conciliating the rebels (1800).

CHOUTEAU FAMILY. René Auguste Chouteau (1749–1829), a native of New Orleans, established in 1763 a trading post at the confluence of the Missouri and Mississippi rivers which became St Louis. His half-brother, Jean Pierre Chouteau (1758–1849), an Indian trader and soldier, was a founder of the St Louis Missouri Fur Co., a pioneer company in exploring the western beaver trade. Pierre Chouteau (1789–1865), his son, a leading financier of the west, and an agent for Astor's American Fur Co., organized Pierre Chouteau, Jr. and Co (1838), which carried on trading enterprises from the Mississippi to the Rocky Mountains. A brother, Auguste

René Chouteau (1786–1838), traded for many years along the Arkansas river and served as a contact between Americans and Indians.

CHREMONIDEAN WAR (*c.* 267–262 BC), so-named after the Athenian statesman Chremonides, who brought Athens into a coalition with Ptolemy II of Egypt, Sparta, Elis, and the Achaean League against Antigonus Gonatas of Macedon. Ptolemy wanted to supplant Antigonus influence in Greece, but was strong only in ships; his admiral, Patroclus, proved unable effectively to support his allies on land, who were defeated separately. Finally, Athens capitulated to Antigonus, who imposed a garrison on the city.

CHRÉTIEN DE TROYES (*fl.* 1160–81), author of the earliest and most distinguished Arthurian romances to have survived. Much of his creative life was spent at the court of Marie de Champagne, daughter of Eleanor of Aquitaine. His most interesting works include *Lancelot* (*Le Chevalier de la Charrette*) and *Perceval* (*Le Conte du Graal*), both left unfinished. They are loose in structure, but include a wide and fascinating range of adventures.

CHRISTADELPHIANS (1848), or Thomasites, founded in the US by John Thomas (1805–71), an Englishman who related biblical prophecy to future events. His followers were grouped in local *ecclesia*, with the Bible as the basis of their beliefs, including the coming of the millennium and the conditional immortality of the body.

CHRISTCHURCH, NZ. Planned as cathedral city of Canterbury, Christchurch was named by J. R. Godley after his Oxford college. The Avon river site, settled (1843) by the Deans brothers, was chosen (1849) by Joseph Thomas, who surveyed the Adelaide-like street pattern. Reputedly 'English', Christchurch was by 1891 the largest South Island centre.

CHRISTIAN II (1481–1559), King of Denmark and Norway and the last Danish king of Sweden. After serving as viceroy in Norway, he succeeded his father, King John in 1513. He suppressed a long-continued rebellion in Sweden, but the 'Stockholm Blood Bath' (1520), in which about 80 leading Swedes were executed, nominally as heretics, resulted in the triumph of Gustavus Vasa. In Denmark and Norway Christian encouraged the rise of the middle classes. In 1523 the nobles in Jutland rebelled in favour of Christian's uncle, who became king as Frederick I, whereupon he fled to the Netherlands to get help from his brother-in-law, the Emperor Charles V. This was delayed, partly through Christian's temporary aberration to Lutheranism, but in 1531 he was enabled to reoccupy eastern Norway. A Danish expedition persuaded him to go to Copenhagen under a safe-conduct to treat with his uncle, instead of which he was imprisoned for the rest of his life.

CHRISTIAN III (1503–59), King of Denmark and Norway, where he established Lutheranism. The death of his father, Frederick I, in 1533 was followed by a civil war, in which he triumphed over the supporters of his Catholic younger brother, John, and those of the ex-king Christian II. Christian III, a zealous Protestant, made himself head of the Church, annexed its lands to the Crown, and gave it a Lutheran basis formulated by Bugenhagen of Wittenberg. The last Catholic Abp of Trondheim fled from Norway, which was in principle reduced to a provincial status, and was forced to accept Lutheranism at the behest of the Danish King and Council. Until the Diet of Speyer (1544), Christian was allied with the German Protestant princes against Charles V, but in his later years Denmark was both peaceful and prosperous.

CHRISTIAN IV (1577–1648), King of Denmark and Norway from 1588 and the most important of their 16th- and 17th-cent. rulers. He travelled up to the North Cape and paid altogether about 30 visits to Norway, where he designed new towns, fortresses, and palaces; developed industries—especially mining—commanded his forces in action by land and sea; and begot a numerous, partly illegitimate, family. His popularity was great among the middle and lower classes, both in Denmark and Norway, though he was opposed by many nobles, including eventually his own sons-in-law.

Christian IV's ambitious foreign policy ended in disaster. In 1611–13 his first war against Sweden secured the frontier of Norway from encroachment in the far north, checked the growth of Swedish territory on the Kattegat coast, and confirmed Danish possession of the Baltic island of Ösel. The power of Denmark was at its zenith. But Christian was tempted to intervene in the Thirty Years War by hopes of gaining Bremen and Verden for his younger sons, restoring his niece Elizabeth in the Palatinate, and eclipsing the growing fame of Gustavus Adolphus. The Council vainly resisted, and the result of the intervention was a crushing defeat by Tilly at Lutter-am-Barenberg (1626), after which Jutland was overrun by Wallenstein and Christian had to beg help from Gustavus. After making peace with the emperor (1629), he tried to mediate between the empire and the Swedes, although his position was weakened by lack of support from England or the Netherlands, due to their resentment at his raising of the Sound tolls. Finally, in 1643 Christian provoked an attack by the Swedes, whose army occupied Jutland, while his heroism at the naval battle of Kolberg Heath (July 1644) only postponed the destruction of his navy by the Swedes and Dutch. The king's last years were saddened by the peace of Brømsebro (1645), involving loss of territory to the Swedes in east Norway, on the west coast round Gothenburg, and in the Baltic (Gotland and Ösel).

J. A. Gade, *Christian IV, King of Denmark and Norway* (London, 1927).   TKD

CHRISTIAN V (1646–99), King of Denmark and Norway from 1670, and son of Frederick III. He added to the absolutist regime a new nobility of counts and barons created for public service, and codified the laws of Denmark and of Norway (1683, 1687). He had some early successes in a war against Sweden (1674–9), in which the people of Scania sought to rejoin Denmark, but the Swedes defeated him at Lund (Dec. 1676) and in the end restored no territory.

CHRISTIAN VI (1699–1746), King of Denmark and Norway from 1730, and the son of his predecessor, Frederick IV. He married a German princess, with whom he shared a deeply pietist outlook, and gave the Church in both his kingdoms a more serious moral tone and conducted a pacific foreign policy, forming alliances with Sweden, Britain, and (later) France.

CHRISTIAN VII (1749–1808), King of Denmark and Norway (1766), who married Caroline Matilda, younger sister of George III of Britain. He was reduced by debauchery to an imbecile condition, which enabled Struensee, the court doctor and reputedly the queen's lover, to seize power (1770). In January 1772 his authority was nominally restored, but ministers acted for him until 1784, when his son Frederick became regent.

CHRISTIAN VIII (1786–1848), King of Denmark from 1839. His cousin, Frederick VI of Denmark and Norway, sent him to Norway as viceroy (1813) and when Norway was ceded to Sweden the Norwegians chose him as king (May 1814). Opposition from the powers and from Bernadotte forced him to retire to Denmark the same autumn. As King of Denmark he proved less democratic than had been expected, and his assertion that the Danish succession law applied to Schleswig largely provoked the March 1848 insurrection in Schleswig-Holstein.

CHRISTIAN IX (1818–1906), King of Denmark from 1863. He claimed the throne through the female line, but had been accepted as heir to Schleswig-Holstein as well as Denmark by the treaty of London (1852). His accession was quickly followed by the war in which he lost the Duchies to the German powers. Later, the king supported the Conservatives in the upper house of parliament on the question of defence expenditure, opposed by the Liberal majority in the lower house, but finally Christian gave way (1901). He also played a part in dynastic politics, a son becoming George I of the Hellenes, a grandson Haakon VII of Norway, and his daughters marrying the heirs to the thrones of Britain and Russia.

CHRISTIAN X (1870–1947), King of Denmark (*reg.* 1912–47), and King of Iceland (*reg.* 1918–44), under whom Iceland became a separate kingdom until declaring itself a republic (1944).

CHRISTIAN I OF ANHALT (d. 1630), chancellor and tutor to Frederick V, Elector Palatine, upon whom he exerted considerable influence. He negotiated Frederick's marriage to Elizabeth, daughter of King James I of England. He also secured the creation of the Protestant Union after the Donauworth incident (1608), and was responsible for the election of Frederick to the Crown of Bohemia, which provoked the Thirty Years War (1618–48). Christian commanded the Bohemian army in the disastrous battle of the White Mountain (Nov. 1620). When Frederick fled from Prague on his advice, Christian made his way to Sweden, whence he tried to make his peace with the emperor, although he later secretly returned to Frederick's service (1623).

CHRISTIAN OF HALBERSTADT (1598–1626), younger brother of the Duke of Brunswick-Wolfenbuttel, who was created administrator of the secularized bishopric of Halberstadt. He entered the service of Frederick, Elector Palatine, the exiled King of Bohemia, during the Thirty Years War (1621). In 1623 Christian established himself as 'protector' of the lands of his elder brother, but in the face of Tilly's advance he abdicated from Halberstadt and retreated towards the Netherlands to rejoin Frederick, to be soundly defeated by Tilly near the frontier at the battle of Stadtlohn (6 Aug. 1623). With an army raised by Dutch subsidies in 1625 Christian re-entered the war and marched for Hesse (1626) but, worn out by disease and ill-luck, he withdrew to Wolfenbuttel, where he died.

CHRISTIAN BROTHERS, religious teaching order founded at Rheims in 1680 which, despite its loyalty to the papacy, incurred none of the opposition aroused by the Jesuits. Its members are all laymen and the brotherhood, now no longer confined to France, provides elementary, secondary, and technical education.

CHRISTIAN CIVIC LEAGUE (1528), Swiss evangelical confederation organized by Zwingli to defend Zürich and the Protestant cantons against their Catholic neighbours. It included Berne, Basle, Constance, Biel, Muhlhausen, Schaffhausen, and St Gall by 1529; Strasburg joined in 1530.

CHRISTIAN DEMOCRATIC UNION PARTY in the German Federal Republic (in association with its Bavarian wing it was called the Christian Social Union), founded under the Allied military occupation (1945) and in some respects the successor of the Centre Party of the Weimar Republic. But from its inception it was open to Protestants as well as Catholics, and the political structure of the German Federal Republic enabled it to broaden its political base still further. Its political attitude was similar to that of the British Conservative Party and its organization reflected the dominant leadership of Konrad Adenauer. It remained, in 1970, the only party to have achieved power since the establishment of the Federal Republic, so its formal structure has been of relatively small

importance. Real power rested with the leadership in the Reichstag and with the government. The CDU–CSU was outstandingly successful in each of the five federal elections which occurred from 1949.

CHRISTIAN DEMOCRATS, '*democristiani*', currently (1970) meaning adherents of Italy's largest party, *Democrazia Cristiana* (DC). From the 1890s the term commonly described members of unions or parties, *eg*, Sturzo's *Partito Popolare* (1919), inspired by Christian principles, dedicated to social reform, and antagonistic towards Marxist materialism. De Gasperi formed the *DC* (1943), and it has since governed Italy, alone or in coalition. By 1947 socialist–communist support was dropped, under strong Vatican and US pressure, and central alliances formed. Fanfani and Moro have led a slow opening to the left since 1963. Though not strictly a Catholic confessional party, the Vatican and clergy exert powerful influences on conservative party factions and voters.

CHRISTIAN MISSIONS IN CENTRAL AFRICA. In the 16th and 17th cents the attempts of the Portuguese to establish an empire in the south-east African hinterland were accompanied by Roman Catholic missionary ventures into the interior, resulting in 1561 in the martyrdom of the Jesuit Goncalo da Silveira in the northern Shona kingdom of Mwenemutapa, the penetration of the Dominicans up the Zembesi in 1577, and the baptism in 1652 of the new Mwenemutapa. By the end of the 17th cent. the decline of Portuguese power led to the virtual extinction of these Christian influences. Christianity in central Africa did not revive effectively until the mid-19th cent. Then it was advanced northwards from South Africa by Protestant missionaries, such as Robert Moffat who, in 1857, established the Matabeleland (Ndebele) mission, and his son-in-law, David Livingstone, which led to the short-lived Universities Mission to Central Africa of 1861–3. The Livingstone legacy was responsible for the entry of Scottish Presbyterian missionaries into the Lake Nyasa regions in 1875–6. In the early 1880s British and American Baptists began the process which resulted in the missionary penetration of the south-east Congo area. At the same time the Scottish Plymouth Brethren missionary Frederick Stanley Arnot and François Coillard of the Paris Evangelical Missionary Society pioneered the advance into the Barotse country; and in 1886 Arnot established a mission station at Katanga.

Thereafter, as the European partition of Africa proceeded, missionaries of many denominations entered the spheres of Christian influence which these pioneers had demarcated. By the beginning of the 20th cent. a complex pattern of sectarian rivalry had been created in central Africa, to which colonial governments often attributed such expressions of African discontent as the Chilembwe Rising in Malawi in 1915 and the millenarian outbursts in the Congo. The European missionaries in central Africa reduced the vernacular languages to writing, established schools and colleges, and, both consciously and unconsciously, stimulated African nationalism. Central African Christians, orthodox and unorthodox, now build on the foundations which they laid, and attempt to resolve in the independent African states the problems which they introduced, such as the relations between Church and state and Christianity and secularism.

C. P. Groves, *The Planting of Christianity in Africa*, 4 vols (London, 1948, 1954, 1955, and 1958). GS

CHRISTIAN SCIENCE (1879), religious denomination founded in Boston, MA, US, by Mary Baker Eddy. A development from earlier faith-healing practices, Christian Science asserts that the body of man is the manifestation of his mentality and spirit and that, consequently, bodily diseases can be prevented and cured by the realization of God. The Church has successfully established branches in many parts of the world and publishes a distinguished international newspaper, *The Christian Science Monitor*,

CHRISTIAN SOCIALISM, a mid-19th-cent. movement in England within the established Church, for greater concern with social problems. It was in part a reaction against the Oxford Movement's stress on dogma and ritualism, and the realization that the Church had lost contact with the leaders of working-class opinion. Its leaders included J. F. D. Maurice, Charles Kingsley, and Thomas Hughes, who published their views in *Politics for the People* and *Tracts for Church and People* (1854), encouraged working-class education, ran co-operative workshops, and fostered the liberal theology which appeared in *Essays and Reviews* (1860).

CHRISTINA (1626–89), Queen of Sweden from 1632 until her abdication (1654). She was the only child of Gustavus Adolphus, and on coming of age (1644) tried for a time to shake off the influence of Axel Oxenstjerna, who had been virtually regent. The queen strongly supported a policy of peace, but only Oxenstjerna could cope with the financial problems which followed the Westphalia settlement and which were accentuated by the extravagance of the court. Christina combined the imitation of French court life with a liberal cultivation of arts and sciences that attracted foreign savants such as Descartes. In 1654, however, she announced her intention to abdicate in favour of her cousin (Charles X) and immediately left Sweden, which she revisited only twice. The date of her conversion to Catholicism and the part which this played in her decision are still disputed. The ex-queen made her home in Rome, where she strongly influenced the arts, became the friend of three popes, and was particularly intimate with Cardinal Azzolino, who is the least unlikely of her many reputed lovers. At times she plotted to gain a Catholic throne, either Naples or Poland, but she died poor and forgotten.

CHRONICLES (and ANNALS) in the Middle Ages, characteristic forms of medieval historical writing in western Europe. It is not easy always to distinguish between the two forms, but the origins of their names are significant; 'annals' comes from the Latin 'year' and 'chronicle' from the Greek 'time'. Essentially, an annal consists of a series of very brief notices of events made more or less immediately by a usually anonymous contemporary; a chronicle deals with events over a much longer span of time and in much fuller detail. An annal which extends over a period of years is usually the work of a series of continuators, contemporary with the events recorded; a chronicle is usually the work of a single author and covers a span of years much longer than the author's lifetime—indeed, the universal chronicle beginning with the Creation was a common form (*eg*, Matthew Paris, *Chronica Maiora*). Lastly, the annal was essentially a product of the Dark Ages and the chronicle a product of the Middle Ages proper.

The origin of annals is to be found in the Easter tables. Because of the extreme complexity of the calculations of the date of Easter, it became customary to compile tables giving the date of Easter for as long as a century ahead, usually with additional astronomical information. Such tables were a necessity for every monastery and major church and it became common practice to write notices of events between the lines. When these notes became detached from the tables and were copied as independent texts, the annal proper was born. The chronicle is much fuller and more sophisticated and was rare in early medieval Europe, becoming more common only from the 11th cent. onwards.

CHRYSLER, WALTER PERCY (1875–1940), US automobile manufacturer. He began his career as a railroad apprentice and then worked for the American Locomotive Co. before joining the Buick Division of General Motors Corporation (1910–19). He reorganized the ailing Willys–Overland and Maxwell Motor Co. (1920–5), launched the famous Chrysler Six (1924), and turned the company into the Chrysler Corporation (1925). Introduction of the inexpensive Plymouth, and combination with the Dodge Brothers (1928), established the corporation as one of the outstanding automobile manufacturers.

CHRYSLER'S FIELD, BATTLE OF (11 Nov. 1813). A British force of 800 under Lieut.-Col. Morrison took up a position on the north bank of the St Lawrence between Sackets Harbour and Montreal and routed an attacking American force of 2000 under Gen. Boyd.

CHRYSOLORAS, MANUEL (*c.* 1350–1415), the most important of the scholars who reintroduced the knowledge of Greek and the study of Greek literature into western Europe. A chair of Greek was created for him in Florence in 1397. He introduced into Italy the superior Greek methods of commenting on classical texts and his teaching influenced profoundly the study of Latin as well as Greek classics. As a translator he encouraged the abandonment of literal translations and the substitution of a more flexible method of rendering the meaning of a text rather than the exact words. After a period at Florence, Chrysoloras taught at Milan, Pavia, and Venice. He greatly impressed Italians by his high character as well as his scholarship and most of the leading Italian humanists of the early 15th cent. were his pupils or disciples of his pupils.

CHRYSOPOLIS, BATTLE OF (AD 324), on the east side of the Bosphorus, was Constantine the Great's defeat of the eastern Emperor Licinius, by which he became sole ruler of the Roman empire.

CH'U, Chinese kingdom of the pre-imperial age. Situated in the Huai and Yangtze river areas, Ch'u comprised elements of a southern type of culture, practice, and literature that were very different from those of China's early northern civilization, represented by Chou.

CH'Ü CH'IU-PAI (1899–1935), early Chinese communist, who became leader of the Chinese Communist Party in 1927, ousting the discredited Ch'en Tu-hsiu. Ch'ü introduced a disastrous new policy of insurrections, notably the Canton Commune (Dec. 1927). He was called to Moscow after a year, and kept there until 1930. His own party denounced him as a 'Left-extremist and Left-opportunist' and he was arrested by Kuomintang authorities in 1934, and executed the following year.

CHU HSI (1130–1200), also called Chu Yüan-hui, a major Chinese philosopher who contributed more than any other individual to the system of thought known as Neo-Confucianism. A native of Fu-kien province, he passed some of the Confucian examinations and from time to time held various local and provincial offices. But most of his life was spent in reflection and writing; he wrote many commentaries on the Four Books and Five Classics, some of which were grouped into a collection now translated as *Reflections on Things at Hand* (1967).

CHU TE (1886–), Chinese communist marshal and close associate of Mao Tse-tung. As a young officer, Chu served under Ts'ai O in the revolt against Yuan Shih-k'ai (1915–16), but later degenerated into a semi-warlord figure. In 1921 he decided to reform, and went to Germany to study military science. He stayed there for four years and became a member of a branch of the Chinese Communist Party, then returned to China, served in the Kuomintang army, and was one of the leaders of the Nanch'ang Uprising (1927). He later joined Mao Tse-tung in Kiangsi and together they set up the Kiangsi Soviet. Chu subsequently held many important posts in the Red Army and People's Liberation Army.

CHU YÜAN-CHANG (1328–98), founder of the Ming dynasty. Of humble origin, he served at one time in a Buddhist monastery, later joining one of the rebel groups which arose towards the end of the Yüan dynasty. Forming his own group, he succeeded in taking Nanking, winning control of the Yangtze valley, and founding his own dynasty to replace that of the Mongols. By 1382 he had established a unified rule over China. He is sometimes referred to as the Hung-wu emperor, Hung-wu being the *nien-hao* adopted for his reign (1368–98).

CHULAVAMSA, text attributed to Chuang Chou (?369–286 BC). This highly imaginative work illustrates by parable and allegory the transient nature of human life and the misconception of the human mind. As in the *Tao-te ching*, *Tao* is seen as the only permanent reality.

CHULAVAMSA (lit. the Small Chronicle), in contrast to the *Mahavamsa*, the Great Chronicle. (These terms do not describe the lengths of the two texts, both written in Pali, but reflect upon the character of the periods with which they deal.) It records the history of Ceylon from the middle of the 4th cent. AD, where the *Mahavamsa* ends, to AD 1815, when the island lost its independence following the British occupation of the Kandyan kingdom. Four different authors can be distinguished but they all followed essentially the same principles of historical description as applied in the *Mahavamsa*. The last parts of the text, however, from the middle of the 14th cent., are historically less satisfactory than the earlier portions.

CHUNGJONG (*reg.* 1506–44), 11th ruler of the Yi Dynasty in Korea, whose reign was entirely taken up by factional struggles amongst the Confucian scholar-bureaucrats. As a result of these struggles, the officials of the censorate emerged as a power base which successive cliques, or even the king himself (as in 1537–8), could use to destroy their opponents.

CHÜN T'IEN or equal field system. This tax system, evolved in China under the Northern Wei Dynasty from 485 and based essentially on a per capita principle, was applied more universally and effectively under the Sui and T'ang dynasties, but had in fact become inoperable from *c.* 700. The system provided for the state's grant of land to able-bodied males in specified allotments of two parts; of these the larger, which was intended for cereal crops, was returned to the state at death, and the smaller, which was intended for mulberry orchards, could be retained in the family on an hereditary basis. In return, the holder was obliged to render labour service and taxation in kind (grain and textiles). The system evolved at a time before the Chinese economy depended on the universal circulation of money, and could have brought about the effective collection of tax and distribution of produce, the reduction of the large estates and groups of retainers attached to major landlords, the extensive reclamation of land, and the wider distribution of land population. Records found at Tun-huang show that the system was actually implemented at least in some areas during the T'ang period. However, it suffered from inefficient administration, and large land-holdings of certain groups, *eg*, officials and Buddhist monasteries, were retained in private hands despite the restrictions of the system.

CHURCH, BENJAMIN (1639–1718), American soldier and Indian fighter. He was born in Plymouth colony and early became acquainted with the Indians. He commanded detachments of troops in King Philip's war (Philip being an Indian chief) and taught his men Indian methods of fighting. He advocated pursuit of the enemy rather than the building of forts. At the age of 66 (1705), he led a regiment against the French in Nova Scotia.

Benjamin Church (1734–76) was a grandson of the Indian fighter. After graduating from Harvard he studied medicine in London and became a doctor in Boston. He was a member of the Continental Congress and surgeon-general to the continental army. He wrote vigorously for the patriots' cause, but, being suspected of having passed confidential information to Gen. Gage, was court-martialled, convicted of sedi-

tion, and imprisoned. Later he was allowed to leave the country for the West Indies, but his ship was lost at sea.

CHURCH ARMY, Anglican organization founded (1882) by Wilson Carlile (1847–1942) for evangelical and social work among the poor in Britain. During the two World Wars it provided numerous facilities for troops and homeless civilians.

CHURCH IN DANGER, 18th-cent. slogan in England, expressing the concern felt by High Church Anglicans at the divisive effect of nonconformity upon Church and state. The slogan was exploited by Tory politicians against their Whig rivals.

CHURCH MISSIONARY SOCIETY (1799), founded by the Clapham sect, and symptomatic of the Evangelical upsurge within the Church of England. Missionary deputations rallied support in English parishes for the work overseas and interdenominational co-operation was encouraged. The late 18th and early 19th cents found Protestantism active in founding foreign missions, the Baptist Society sending William Carey to India in 1793. The interdenominational London Missionary Society (1797), the British and Foreign Bible Society (1804), and the Methodist Missionary Society (1814) worked alongside the larger CMS and the much older (1698) Society for Promoting Christian Knowledge.

CHURCH OF ENGLAND IN NEW ZEALAND, THE. Anglican foundations in NZ were laid by the Church Missionary Society and by Bp Selwyn. In 1857 a conference in Auckland under Selwyn established 'the Church of the Province of NZ'. Seven dioceses were created: Christchurch (1856), Waiapu, Wellington, Nelson (1858), Auckland, Dunedin (1869), and Waikato (1925); a Maori Bp of Aotearoa was created in 1925.

CHURCH OF THE BRETHREN, the *Unitas Fratrum*, a sect within the Hussite movement which survived persecution to become a flourishing minority in Bohemia and Poland during and after the Reformation. It discarded pacifism under the leadership of Brother Lukas but preserved the radical elements in Hussitism, its scriptural theology, democratic government, and evangelical practice.

CHURCH ORDINANCES in Sweden (1571), drawn up by Abp Laurentius Petri, became the basis of government of the Swedish Lutheran Church. John III replaced them by a new ordinance and liturgy under Catholic influence (1575–6), but they were reaffirmed at the Meeting of Uppsala (1593), where 300 clergy conferred with the members of the council and other nobles.

CHURCHILL, LORD RANDOLPH HENRY SPENCER (1849–1895), British statesman, who advocated Tory democracy. As MP for Woodstock (from 1874) he enlivened opposition to Gladstone (1880–5) with the back-bench group known as the fourth party. Maintaining the traditions of Disraeli, Churchill pressed for social and constitutional reform, including the acceptance of the 1884 Reform Bill. He opposed coercion in Ireland, but his negotiations for its abandonment in return for electoral support from the Nationalists embarrassed his party and pushed the Liberals towards Home Rule (1885). A founder of the Primrose League (1881), Churchill became chairman of the council of the National Union of Conservative Associations, demanding more power for the constituency associations and successfully resisting opposition from Lord Salisbury (1884).

Churchill served under Salisbury as chief secretary for India (1885–6), being responsible for the annexation of Upper Burma (1886). After fighting a brilliant election campaign against Home Rule, he became chancellor of the exchequer (1886). Influenced by Chamberlain, he demanded reform at home and support for the central powers and freedom for the

Balkan peoples abroad, vindicating his views at the subsequent party conference. His budget proposals included sweeping changes in taxation and cuts in the service estimates, which had implications for foreign policy. The latter were opposed in cabinet and Churchill insisted on resigning. Support for him evaporated and increasing ill-health ended his effective career in public life He was the father of Sir Winston Churchill.

VEC

CHURCHILL, SIR WINSTON LEONARD SPENCER (1874–1965), British statesman and prime minister, historian, and painter.

After army service in Cuba, India, the Sudan, and (as a war correspondent) in the Boer War, he became Conservative MP for Oldham in 1900, and remained almost continuously in parliament until 1964. Leaving the Conservatives in 1904 over tariff reform, he held Liberal office as under-secretary for the colonies (1906–8), president of the board of trade (1908–10), home secretary (1910–11), and first lord of the admiralty (1911–15). He ensured that the fleet was ready for war in 1914, but the failure of the Dardanelles attack led to the Conservative opposition forcing his resignation (1915). After serving in the trenches Churchill returned to office (1917) in Lloyd George's coalition as minister of munitions.

In the first ten years after the First World War Churchill held variously the secretaryships of war, air, and colonies (1919–22), before returning to the Conservative Party as chancellor of the exchequer (1924–9) under Baldwin. He contributed towards a solution in Ireland (1921) and to the swift end of the general strike (1926).

The policy of appeasement, with which most politicians were identified (1929–39), made no appeal to Churchill. Out of office, he vainly drew the nation's attention to the rise of Nazism and the statistics of German rearmament.

When war came in 1939 he returned to the admiralty (1939–40), and succeeded Neville Chamberlain as prime minister in 1940. With her allies falling and her troops retreating from Dunkirk, Britain faced defeat. Churchill, through his broadcast speeches, lifted morale from its lowest abyss. Thereafter he planned relentlessly for victory. His leadership, co-operation with the US and Russia, and tireless energy accomplished this by 1945.

Yet the electorate rejected Churchill as the man to face post-war social and economic problems. Labour came to power and Churchill, as leader of the opposition (1945–51), spoke on world platforms, notably at Fulton, US, and Zürich (1946). His speeches gave strength to new supra-national bodies such as UNO, NATO, and the Council of Europe. Less enthusiastically did he witness the independence of India (1947) and the emergence of the concept of Commonwealth within the British empire.

Churchill returned to office as Conservative prime minister (1951–5) and became a knight of the garter in 1953.

His comparative obscurity from public life in the 1930s allowed the literary side of his talents to flourish. As a young man he had written on his campaigns and a life of his father, *Lord Randolph Churchill* (1906). Then had come *The World Crisis* (1923–9). Now he wrote the life of his ancestor, *Marlborough* (1933–8), and worked on his *History of the English-Speaking Peoples* (1956–8). Later he wrote *The Second World War* (1948–54), and many of his speeches and broadcasts were also published.

Churchill's honours were numerous: he received honorary citizenship of the US, of which nation his mother, Jennie Jerome, was a citizen. His literary work won him a Nobel Prize and his paintings were hung in the Royal Academy.

His death ended an era in British and world history. His state funeral was attended by the sovereign and foreign heads of states.

Randolph Churchill (and others), *Winston S. Churchill* (London 1966).

R. R. James, *Churchill: a study in failure* (London, 1970).

GMDH

CHURCHILL–STALIN CONFERENCE (Oct. 1944), during the Second World War, a meeting which took place on Churchill's initiative at a time when he was alarmed by the fluid state of affairs in the Balkans resulting from the rapid advance of the Soviet armies. Roosevelt did not participate (the presidential election was pending in the US), but sent Averell Harriman to act as observer.

Churchill and Stalin made an agreement that the Russians should exercise pre-eminent influence in Rumania, Bulgaria, and Hungary; that Britain should have a similar position in Greece; and that their influence in Yugoslavia was to be divided equally.

The US government was not committed by the arrangement, and insisted on the inclusion of a declaration on liberated territories (promising assistance in the establishment of democratic government) in the Yalta declaration. However, Stalin made no move to assist the Greek communists when British forces helped the provisional Greek government to defeat them. It has subsequently been argued that Stalin considered that he had a wider understanding with Britain and the US on the division of spheres of influence which they then disregarded when they tried, by protest and pressure, to resist the imposition of communist rule in Eastern Europe.

CHUTE, SIR TREVOR (1816–86), general Imperial commander in NZ (1865–8). After advancing through bush, Chute destroyed Maori strongholds and ended the main Taranaki campaign (1865–6). He supervised the withdrawal of Imperial troops from NZ (1867–70).

CHUTER-EDE, JAMES (1882–1965), British politician. After an early apprenticeship in public life through municipal government and local unionism, Chuter-Ede entered parliament in 1929. He was parliamentary secretary to the minister of education in Churchill's coalition government (1940–5). Thereafter, as home secretary until 1951, he initiated social reforms in Attlee's Labour administration.

CHWEZI, early kings in central and southern Uganda, probably of Hima origin, who ruled *c.* 1300–1450, and were the source of later ancestral and political cults.

CIANO, GALEAZZO (1903–44), son of fascist minister and admiral, who married Mussolini's daughter Edda, and became an influential aide to the dictator, and an unpopular intermediary with others in the government. As foreign minister (1936–43), he was instrumental in developing Italo-German relations. Realizing (summer 1939), German war aims, and Ribbentrop's despisal of himself and Italy, Ciano became violently anti-Nazi, as is seen in his *Diaries*, but lacked the determination to change Mussolini's attitudes or policies. He voted against Mussolini in the Fascist Grand Council (July 1943), for which act, under Nazi pressure, he was tried and executed at Verona.

CIBBER, COLLEY (1671–1757), English actor, poet, dramatist, theatrical manager, critic, and poet laureate (1730). Although recognized as a capable manager and competent critic, and an excellent actor in comedy parts (particularly fops), he suffered merciless and apparently undeserved ridicule from writers far greater than himself, including Pope, Johnson, and Fielding.

CIBOLA, SEVEN CITIES OF, a collection of mud and stone villages of the Zuñi Indians in western New Mexico. They were first reported by Álvar Cabeza de Vaca in 1535. Antonio de Mendoza, the Spanish viceroy of New Spain, sent a Franciscan friar, Marcos de Niza, to investigate these reports (1539) and Niza returned with stories of fabulously wealthy cities. The Spanish connected these cities with the seven mythical cities of Cibola, founded according to Spanish legend by seven bishops who fled westward in the 8th cent. to a rich land beyond the Atlantic. Francesco Vásquez de

Coronado led an expedition to find them (1540). He found no rich cities, but did explore a vast amount of previously unknown territory between Mexico and Kansas.

CICERO, M. TULLIUS (106–43 BC), Rome's greatest orator and a leading political figure in the last decades of the Republic. He was born at Arpinum, and was *quaestor* in Sicily (75), *curule aedile* (69), *praetor* (66), consul (63), holding all his offices at the minimum legal age, a unique achievement for a *novus homo* from a family unconnected with Roman politics. He won early fame by his oratory, especially in his defence of Roscius of Ameria (80), and the prosecution of Verres (70). As consul he suppressed Catiline's conspiracy. He refused an invitation to join the First Triumvirate, and because of his opposition to the Triumvirs was exiled by Clodius, ostensibly for having executed the Catilinarians without trial. On being recalled in 57, he found himself politically ineffective. In 51 he governed Cilicia, but returned to Italy on the outbreak of the Civil War. Having joined Pompey after much hesitation, he was pardoned by Julius Caesar after Pharsalus, but remained unreconciled to his policies. After Caesar's murder he re-entered public life and in defence of the Republic he violently attacked Mark Antony, who was declared an outlaw. But again Cicero was impotent when Antony joined Lepidus and Octavian in the Second Triumvirate and he was proscribed and killed. His reputation rests mainly on his voluminous correspondence, and by his oratory, poetry, and rhetorical and philosophical treatises he greatly influenced the development of Latin language and literature.

CID CAMPEADOR (d. 1099), hero of an early Castilian epic. The eulogistic title of El Cid was conferred by Arab chroniclers on Ruy Díaz de Vivar, a nobleman in the court of Alfonso VI of Castile, by whom he was exiled. He served under the Muslim King of Saragossa and later captured Valencia (1092), making it a Christian state which recognized the sovereignty of Castile.

CIDER TAX (1763), a duty of 4s a hogshead, payable by the maker, on cider made in Britain. It was part of the attempt by Bute's government to raise revenue to cope with the huge debts incurred during the Seven Years War. The tax was disliked because it gave government agents an excuse to search private houses. Coinciding with rumours that Bute and George III were plotting to subvert the constitution, it provided useful ammunition for Bute's opponents, who accused him of trying to increase government patronage and to impose a general excise. The outcry in the country, especially from the cider counties and the City of London, was thought to have hastened Bute's resignation. Rockingham abolished the tax in 1766, amid general approval.

CIENTÍFICOS, an influential group of Mexican politicians, intellectuals, and financiers who benefited most from the Porfirian dictatorship (1876–1911). The term was popularized by their enemies, who rejected their 'positivist' orientation. The *científicos* misconstrued French positivism and their outlook was more akin to social Darwinism. The dictator, Porfirio Díaz, apparently distrusted the *científicos*, but their influence—financial and political—was great during the final two decades of the regime. The leaders of the *científicos*, in order of succession, were Rosenda Pineda, Romero Rubio, and José Yves Limantour. The latter sought unsuccessfully to salvage the old regime on the eve of the revolution (1911).

CIEZA DE LEON, PEDRO DE (1518–60), Spanish conquistador, better known as a chronicler of the conquest. His two most important works were *Crónica del Perú* (published in four parts) and *Historia de la Nueva España*.

CILICIA, in antiquity the coastal region of south-east Asia Minor, especially Cilicia Pedias, the plain south-east of the Taurus mountains, important because of its position on the land route from Europe to Syria and the east. After subjection

to Assyria, it fell to Persia (547 BC) and became subject to hellenizing influences, especially at Tarsus, from the 5th cent. After being overrun by Alexander the Great (333), it was disputed by Seleucids and Ptolemies. The Roman province of Cilicia, originally constituted in 102, was extended eastwards to include Cilicia Pedias after Pompey's campaigns of 67. Cicero's letters while he was its governor (51–50) throw interesting light on Roman provincial administration.

CILICIAN GATES, the Pylae Ciliciae of the ancients, known to the Turks as Külek (Gülek) Boğazi, a celebrated pass constituting one of the few practicable roads through the Taurus mountains. The Cilician Gates have been, in terms of war and commerce throughout the centuries, a route of great importance linking Asia Minor and Syria.

CIMARRON, an African slave who ran away from his Spanish American master, a maroon. In colonial New Spain African insurrections as early as 1537 led to temporary suspensions of the importation of slaves. These *cimarrones* (lit. 'wild' Negroes) often fled to the hills and formed small kingdoms, living by agriculture and the sword. They terrorized important highways, such as that from Veracruz to Mexico City. *Cimarrones* were a constant source of insecurity throughout the colonial period in much of Spanish America. Much of the Guianas was populated by 'maroons' who had fled the surrounding countries.

CIMBRI, Germanic tribe which, after emigrating from Jutland because of its over-population, defeated the Romans under Cn. Papirius Carbo at Noreia (113 BC) and under M. Iunius Silanus on the Rhone (110), and in 105 destroyed the armies of Cn. Mallius and Q. Servilius Caepio at Arausio. They then made for Spain, returning to Gaul in 103 and attempting with the Teutones and Ambrones to invade Italy. After routing the Teutones and Ambrones at Aquae Sextiae (102), Marius with Q. Lutatius Catulus annihilated the Cimbri on the Raudine Plain near Vercellae (101).

CIMMERIANS, people of unknown origin inhabiting south Russia before the 8th cent. BC. They invaded Asia Minor in the 7th cent., ending the Phrygian kingdom. They settled in Cappadocia and Azerbayjan, and were in frequent conflict with Urartu and Assyria.

CIMON (d. 449 BC), son of Miltiades, an Athenian general and statesman noted for his hostility to Persia and friendship towards Sparta, whither he was despatched as envoy to secure co-operation against Persia (479). He played a leading role in the operations of the Delian League against Persia, expelling the disloyal Spartan regent Pausanias from Byzantium, capturing Eion, the chief Persian stronghold in Europe (?476), and destroying a new Persian fleet at Eurymedon (*c*. 467). Subsequently he worked to strengthen the league and curb attempts at revolt, eg, at Thasos (465–3). In 462 he persuaded the Athenians to send him with help to Sparta in her helot revolt, but was discredited politically, as the Spartans, suspicious of Athenian motives, dismissed his force. As a result, he was ostracized (461) and his radical democratic opponents, among them Pericles, prevailed. Their policies led to prolonged and unsuccessful hostilities with Sparta and so Cimon's return (451) facilitated a five-year truce. He then led an expedition to combat Persian resurgence in Cyprus (450) and, though he died there, a naval victory made possible the peace of Callias between Athens and Persia.

CINADON (*fl.* 4th cent. BC), disenfranchised Spartan who unsuccessfully tried to organize a rebellion of helots, *perioeci*, and others in 398 BC.

CINCAR-MARKOVIC, ALEXANDER (1889–1948), career diplomat and Yugoslav minister for foreign affairs in the Cvetkovic cabinet of 1939. Cincar-Markovic accompanied

Cvetkovic to Vienna and took part in the signing of the Tripartite Pact (25 March 1941).

CINCINNATI, SOCIETY OF THE (1783–) in the US, organization of Revolutionary War Officers founded near Fishkill, New York, to maintain wartime friendships and extend help to deserving officers and those of their families that were in need. With hereditary membership, and 14 constituent societies, one in each of the 13 original states and one in France, its main purpose now (1970) is maintenance of the Revolutionary War Museum at Anderson House in Washington, DC, together with social and educational activities.

CINCINNATUS, L. QUINCTIUS, legendary hero and idealized peasant-farmer of the early Roman Republic. Tradition records that he was called from the plough to assume the dictatorship and save the Roman army imperilled by the Aequi at Mt Algidus (458 BC); and that he again assumed the dictatorship in 439 to save the state from an imminent *coup d'état* by Sp. Maelius.

CINNA, L. CORNELIUS (d. 84 BC), Roman patrician politician, who, as consul in 87, attempted to seize Rome and secure the return of Marius after Sulla's departure for the east. He was expelled from the city and deposed from office by his colleague Octavius. He then joined forces with Marius, captured Rome, and massacred Sulla's adherents. After Marius' death he became leader of the anti-Sullan forces with Carbo and as consul in 86, 85, and 84 was virtual dictator at Rome. He took measures to relieve debt and to give the newly enfranchised Italians their rights, but was murdered by his own troops at Brundisium while preparing to oppose Sulla.

CINQ GROSSES FERMES, in France, private syndicate of financiers, who from Henry III's reign acted as tax-gatherers (*traitants*), collecting five royal impositions over a large area of central France.

CINQ MARS, HENRI D'EFFIAT, Marquis of (1620–42), son of one of Richelieu's servants, who led an unsuccessful rising (1642) to overthrow the cardinal. He was introduced to Louis XIII by Richelieu and soon became the royal favourite and master of the horse. Growing to hate Richelieu, he plotted with Bouillon and Gaston d'Orléans to negotiate a treaty with the King of Spain (March 1642), but Richelieu, informed of the plans, arrested Cinq Mars, who was executed on 12 Sept.

CINQUANTIÈME, French tax of 2 per cent on all net incomes imposed in 1725 by the Duke of Bourbon's administration; it was modified considerably in the face of opposition led by the *parlements*.

CINQUE PORTS were originally the five British ports of Hastings, Dover, Romney, Hythe, and Sandwich, to which were later added the 'ancient towns' of Rye and Winchelsea. To all but Winchelsea were attached a number of subordinate ports and towns called 'limbs'. From the time of Edward the Confessor their chief function was to provide the Crown with ships—normally 57 upon call—in return for tax exemption and other privileges. The jurisdiction of the ports was exercised by the Lord Warden, who was also Constable of Dover Castle. The joint posts remain as an appointment, largely honorary, awarded for distinguished services to the Crown. The creation of a regular navy in Tudor times made the system largely obsolete.

CINTRA, CONVENTION OF (1808), led to the French evacuation of Portugal after Junot's defeat by Wellesley (Wellington) at Vimiero in August. A British expeditionary force had been sent to Portugal because of the Spanish revolt against Napoleon. Wellesley's successor, Dalrymple, signed the convention on 30 Aug., allowing Junot to ship his 25,000 men back to France in British vessels. Not unnaturally, the convention was fiercely attacked in Britain.

CIOMPI REVOLT (1378), popular revolution in Florence, precipitated by conflicts within the ruling groups, which allowed the poorer classes to voice their demands. These included access to public offices for the bulk of the population and the right of the textile workers to organize themselves into guilds. A new government, the most democratic in the history of Florence, was set up in July 1378, but a renewal of popular violence played into the hands of the propertied classes and led to its downfall after a rule of six weeks. The revolution had not caused more than about 20 deaths and the new regime had not tried to alter Florentine society radically, but after the re-establishment of the old oligarchy in 1382, the memory of this upheaval was used to justify repressive and restrictive policies that perpetuated the exclusive rule of the propertied classes and the prohibition of all organization among the workers.

CIPRIANI, ARTHUR M. (1875–1945), West Indian labour leader. He was born in Trinidad and served with the West Indian Regiment in the First World War. Cipriani established the Trinidad Working Men's Association (later the Trinidad Labour Party), and, after 1925, was the outstanding radical on the Trinidad Legislative Council. He was responsible for the Minimum Wage Ordinance of 1935 and the Old Age Pensions Ordinance of 1939.

CIRCASSIANS (CHERKES), a general designation given to the various groups (Abkhaz, Abaza, Ubakh) which form the north-western branch of the Ibero-Caucasian peoples. Cherkes elements rose to dominance within the Mamluk sultanate of Syria and Egypt during the late 14th and 15th cents, above all from the time of Sultan Barquq (d. 1399). In the Caucasus itself the Cherkes came under the influence of the Tatar khanate of the Crimea in the 16th and 17th cents, a period which saw the slow advance of Islam, first among the eastern tribes (the Kabards) and then among the western Cherkes. Not until after 1700 did the process of conversion become marked in the mass of the people. As a response to the southward extension of Russian influence the Cherkes entered into a certain dependence on the Ottoman empire. The Russo–Turkish War of 1768–74 saw the Kabarda region along the Terek river reduced to Russian control. In 1829, at the peace of Adrianople, the Ottomans had to renounce their pretensions in the Caucasus. The Cherkes offered a stubborn resistance to the Russian authorities until 1864–5, no small number of them (especially from the western tribes) seeking a refuge in the Ottoman empire. The Cherkes, now under Soviet rule, are to be found in three administrative areas: the autonomous regions of Adighe and Karačay-Čerkes and the republic of Kabard-Balkar

CIRCLES, IMPERIAL, regional groupings of the Estates of the Holy Roman empire, set up by the Emperor Maximilian (1495) to carry out tasks which the Estates were unwilling to entrust to the emperor or which the empire could no longer fulfil. By 1512 the original six circles had increased to ten with the incorporation of the Habsburg and the electoral territories, and in 1556, by the 'executive regulation', they were charged with the maintenance of public peace and supervision of economic matters. Their effectiveness depended on the power of the presiding princes, appointed 'captains', and on the co-operation of the Estates, and, although they helped to ameliorate the effects of political fragmentation in the empire, they shared the weaknesses of the imperial Diet itself.

CIRCUS, ROMAN, Latin term for an enclosure for chariot and other racing, usually with parallel sides and semi-circular ends, *eg*, in Rome itself the Circus Maximus (the earliest), beneath the west side of the Palatine Hill, Domitian's Circus preserved in the shape of Piazza Navona, and, the best preserved, Maxentius' Circus near the Via Appia (AD 309). Racing in the circus, a highly popular entertainment, spread throughout the empire, especially in the east, where, by providing a focus for religious rivalries, it became the bane of Constantinople.

CIRTA (mod. Constantine, Algeria), virtually impregnable fortress on the Ampsaga river (mod. Rummel), capital of the kings of Numidia, and scene of a massacre of Italian merchants by Jugurtha (112 BC). Under the Roman empire it became highly prosperous and was restored and renamed by Constantine the Great.

CISNEROS, FRANCISCO JIMENEZ DE (1436–1517), Spanish Catholic reformer. After the conquest of Granada, he pressed for the mass conversion of Muslims and as Inquisitor-General extended the powers of the Inquisition. He was responsible for a vigorous programme of monastic reform. As patron of learning, he encouraged the foundation of Alcalá University (1508) and the compilation of the Polyglot Bible, which contained the Greek, Hebrew, and Latin texts.

CIS-SUTLEJ STATES, a group of mainly Sikh states, between the Sutlej and Jumna rivers, or 'this side' of the Sutlej. They were taken under British protection by the treaty of Amritsar (1809), when a limit was placed on Ranjit Singh's expansion eastward. The largest of the states was Patiala.

CISTERCIAN ORDER. Initially, the order of Cistercians or White Monks grew slowly. Robert, abbot of the Cluniac house of Molesmes, wishing to follow the Benedictine rule in greater austerity than Cluny allowed, founded the abbey of Cîteaux in the wilder parts of Burgundy in 1098, and his successor, Alberic, gave the order its distinctive white habit. But the real birth of the order came under the third abbot, the Englishman St Stephen Harding (1109–34). In 1113 the first daughter house was founded at La Ferté and this led (c. 1119) to the drawing up of the rule of the order, the *Carta Caritatis* (rule of charity).

The *Carta* insists that each house subsist on the produce of its monks' manual labour; finds time for this labour by severely restricting the elaborate liturgy favoured by Cluny; sets out the basic plan to which all Cistercian houses were to be built; ordains that the churches were to be austere in style and plainly furnished; and sets out the life of the monks. They were to observe silence and live on a strict diet; physical comforts were shunned and, except for the Infirmary, only one room had a fire. Discipline was in the hands of the general chapter of the order, which was to meet annually (later biennially) at Cîteaux.

The real expansion of the order began with the arrival at Cîteaux in 1113 of Bernard of Clairvaux, who was himself responsible for founding 65 houses, including Clairvaux (1115) and Rievaulx in England (1136). By the time of Bernard's death (1153) there were more than 300 houses in Europe and by the time of the Reformation 742 (including 53 in England and Wales and 246 in France). Although Cistercian houses were generally of very good repute, the order suffered badly from the Great Schism which, by making it impossible for houses recognizing the Roman pontiff to attend general chapters, led to a loosening of the ties of discipline.

CITIES, GROWTH OF. Although in 1500 only five cities—Paris, Naples, Venice, Milan, and Constantinople—had a population of about 100,000 inhabitants or more, by 1600 the number of such cities had risen to 12, including London, Lisbon, Rome, Amsterdam, Palermo, Seville, and Antwerp. Paris and Naples doubled their population in the 16th cent., and that of Constantinople probably increased four-fold. Urban growth occurring in Italy and on the Atlantic coasts undoubtedly stimulated the economic boom of the 16th cent. However, the rising population proved too great a burden for the underdeveloped European economy, and, coupled with the effects of war, famine, and disease, led in the 17th cent.

to social dislocation within Europe's towns, which was only partially relieved when the techniques of the modern Industrial Revolution achieved an increase in production.

CITRINE, WALTER McLENNAN CITRINE, 1st Baron (1887–19), British trade union leader who became associated with the trade union movement in the Merseyside area, and by 1920 had become the assistant general secretary of the Electrical Trades Union. In 1926 he became general secretary of the TUC, and for 20 years presided over momentous developments in the union movement. The effect of the abortive general strike of 1926 and the repressive 1927 trade union legislation had had a serious effect on the movement, and membership declined steeply.

Citrine, working closely with Ernest Bevin, worked for a moderate and co-operative policy in which the TUC could exert the influence it was recognized to possess, *eg*, the nomination of representatives to statutory advisory boards in various industries. In the Labour Party, too, Citrine and Bevin exerted much influence on the union's behalf. In 1931 they opposed MacDonald over deflationary measures, and the formation of the National government. Nevertheless, Citrine helped to lead the moderate wing of the parliamentary party in the next years. In the late 1930s Citrine supported Bevin's stand for a firm front against fascism; as the situation deteriorated he threw the movement behind plans for air-raid precautions and national mobilization. After the outbreak of the Second World War, he helped to draw up plans for national and regional production boards, and the policies of co-operation with the employers were successfully developed through the war.

In 1946 he resigned from the TUC. As chairman of the Central Electricity Authority (1947–57), he presided over nationalization from 1948, during a time when the rationalization of the previously unco-ordinated supply and distribution system was a major concern. After 1957 he remained active in various consultative positions in the industry.

CITROËN, motor manufacturing firm founded by André Citroën (1878–1935), who made his name in the First World War by creating a giant munitions factory in Paris. After the war this became a motor works, which produced its first car in 1919. Citroën was a pioneer of mass-production methods in France—and also of spectacular publicity techniques, including the promotion of motorized expeditions in Asia and Africa. The firm went bankrupt shortly before Citroën's death, and was bought by the Michelin company. It has retained its autonomy and its position as one of France's largest industrial enterprises.

CIVIL CONSTITUTION OF THE CLERGY, THE, approved by the French National Assembly on 12 July 1790, was a comprehensive scheme for the future organization of the French Church. It has a good claim to be the single measure which, more than any other, divided Frenchmen during the Revolution. Before it, in 1789, tithe had been abolished and Church lands taken over by the state. One consequence of this had been the assumption of the responsibility of the maintenance of the clergy by the state and the regulation of this was one part of the civil constitution. But it was much more comprehensive than merely this: it entirely reorganized diocesan boundaries, relating them to a new system of local government; it provided for the election by the laity of bishops and parish clergy; and disciplinary measures were provided to combat the dangers of absenteeism and distraction by secular affairs. In all this there was much that was welcomed by many clergy, much that was tolerable even to those who were not enthusiastic, and much that could be represented as a continuation of the logical development of principles which had always been thought part of the heritage of the Gallican Church. It was not, in the end, practical details, but a quite fundamental matter of principle that divided men: had the state, in fact, powers to legislate for the Church in the way that the civil constitution implied? If it had, then other and more dangerous changes might also be made by a parliamentary body including Protestants, Jews, and atheists: such powers the kings of France had not claimed. The issue came to a head in the oath laid down in article XXI of the document. It prescribed civic loyalty and the upholding of the constitution, which, of course, implied a possible conflict with loyalty to the pope. In Nov., the taking of this oath was made obligatory for all clergy who wished to retain their livings. In March 1791, after the purging of the parishes and dioceses had already begun, the pope himself belatedly condemned the civil constitution. But schism had already occurred, when the first bishops of the 'Constitutional' church (that is, the church of oath-takers) were consecrated by three bishops (of whom one was Talleyrand). This opened one of the great ideological divisions of the Revolution; henceforward, those who regarded themselves as loyal members of the Church of Rome were forced to be anti-patriotic and disloyal to the Revolution if they wished to avoid schism. Similarly, loyal patriots were driven into hostility to a Church whose ministers they now felt authorized to persecute as the spreaders of sedition and discord. In the aftermath, the whole structure of French life was convulsed, civil war was enflamed by religious feeling, and thousands of clergy were to be driven into exile before the Consulate finally healed the quarrel with Rome.

A. Aulard, *Christianity and the French Revolution* (transl., London, 1927).

A. Latreille, *L'Église catholique et la Révolution française.* (Paris, 1946).   JMR

CIVIL DISOBEDIENCE MOVEMENT (1930–4), major Congress campaign, led by Gandhi, to secure India's independence. The Lahore Congress (1928) threatened civil disobedience (*satyagraha*), by means of deliberate breaches of the law, if Dominion Status were not granted within one year. Lord Irwin's promise of eventual dominion status (Oct. 1929) was rejected and the Calcutta Congress (Dec. 1929) resolved to launch the movement to gain 'complete independence' forthwith. 'Independence Day' celebrations were held (26 Jan.) and Gandhi issued an eleven-point ultimatum for the 'substance of independence'.

The first phase began with Gandhi's defiance of the salt laws (March–April 1930) and ended with the Delhi Pact (March 1931). The salt march from Sabarmati ashram to the sea at Dandi (12 March–6 April) was a brilliant dramatization of the Congress cause. When Gandhi made salt illegally a nation-wide violation of the salt monopoly followed. This, together with other acts of disobedience, led to large-scale arrests. Gandhi sought to give the movement a fresh impetus by announcing a 'raid' on the government salt works at Dharsana (May 1930). Hitherto the government had avoided arresting him for fear of a popular outburst, but now they took him into custody. Disturbances spread quickly, particularly in Bombay presidency, where, in Scholapur city, martial law was imposed. T. B. Sapru and M. R. Jayakar attempted a settlement (July–Aug. 1930), but the government would not accept the conditions imposed by the Congress. The campaign continued and in the United Provinces Jawaharlal Nehru tried to link peasant grievances, exacerbated by the Depression, with civil disobedience. In March 1931 Gandhi took advantage of the goodwill generated by the first Round Table Conference to conclude the Delhi Pact, which secured the release of political prisoners in return for the discontinuance of civil disobedience and Congress participation in the second Conference. This agreement was ratified by the Congress at Karachi (March 1931) and Gandhi was appointed sole delegate to the Conference.

The ensuing period (April–Dec. 1931) was marked by mutual charges of breaches of the pact, by Congress attempts to mount local campaigns, and by the hardening of government attitudes during Lord Willingdon's viceroyalty (from April 1931). By Dec., when Gandhi returned frustrated from London, strong ordinances had been introduced, especially in the North-West Frontier Province and in the United Provinces, where attempts were still being made to mount a 'no-rent' campaign. Gandhi protested, but Willingdon refused to parley unless civil disobedience was abandoned. The Congress response was to recommence (4 Jan. 1932) civil disobedience, but the government moved swiftly and checked the impetus of the movement by arresting the leaders and outlawing the entire Congress organization. There was, none the less, a substantial popular response and by April 1932 there were 32,000 detainees. The movement declined, although a total of 66,000 arrests were made during the year. In Sept. Gandhi himself became more concerned to prevent the creation of separate electorates for untouchables and his anti-untouchability campaign tended to obscure the object of civil disobedience. His fast for self-purification (May 1933) marked the effective end of the movement and two months later he discontinued mass civil disobedience. He himself was imprisoned for individual *satyagraha* (Aug. 1933), but the abandonment of all forms of civil disobedience by mid-1934 was a formality in the face of dwindling support and growing Congress interest in other activities.

Although they showed themselves capable of withstanding the attacks launched in this campaign, the British governments in India were forced overall to recognize the strength and political pre-eminence of the Congress. Civil disobedience greatly expanded support for Congress, so that imperial governments could contain nationalist challenges only by increasingly autocratic and unacceptable methods.

D. G. Tendulkar, *Mahatma: Life of Mohandas Karamchand Gandhi*, vol. 3, 1930–4 (Bombay, 1952).

S. Gopal, *The Viceroyalty of Lord Irwin, 1926–1931* (London, 1957).   PDR

CIVIL ESTABLISHMENT ACT (1782) in Britain, sponsored by Burke, abolished about £70,000 worth of sinecures in an attempt to curb royal influence by economical reform. But the act was important chiefly as an improvement in public finance.

CIVIL LAW. The amalgam of custom, case law, law of Republican Rome, and imperial edicts which made up the law of the later Roman empire was made into a coherent and modernized system by the Emperor Justinian. In 529 he published the *Codex Justinianus*, revised in 534, containing all the imperial edicts and constitutions; in 533 the *Digest* or *Pandects* added republican and early imperial law and the *Institutes*, private law; later additions and changes were made by the publication of new constitutions called *Novellae* or *Novels*. These altogether form the *Corpus Juris Civilis*, the standard body of Roman or civil law.

The process by which this code of law was received in western Europe is obscure, but manuscripts of it had been available in Italy since the 6th cent. and the *Corpus* was being studied at Pavia early in the 11th cent. and later in the century at the great law school of Bologna, where Irnerius had founded the school of Glossators. Thereafter Roman civil law became the foundation of several civil codes (especially of France and Italy) and as early as *c.* 1142 the publication of Gratian's *Decretals* began the codification of Roman canon law on the model of and according to the principles of civil law.

CIVIL LIST ACT (1831) stated the principle that the British monarch's personal income should cover only his personal expenses, leaving government expenses to be met entirely from revenue granted and controlled by parliament. The small items remaining in William IV's civil list which were not strictly personal disappeared in Victoria's reign, finally separating the monarch's income and expenditure from those of the government. This ended the process begun in 1698, when in the first Civil List Act parliament relieved the king of the cost of the army and navy in peacetime, leaving the civil list to cover all other ordinary expenses of government.

The main steps in the complementary process of making the monarch dependent entirely on parliament for his ordinary income were the surrender of the feudal dues (1660), and of the hereditary revenue—the main sources in 1760 and the remainder (except for the duchies of Cornwall and Lancaster) in 1820, 1830, and 1837. In return, the monarch received an annual grant, at first in the form of taxes and later directly from the Consolidated Fund. The grant is fixed at the beginning of each reign.

CIVIL ORDINANCE (1667), or Code Louis, one of the great French legal ordinances of Louis XIV's reign relating to the reform of civil procedure.

CIVIL REGISTRATION ACT (1836) in Britain by which registrars were appointed in each poor law union to record births, marriages, and deaths. It was passed by Russell, previous attempts by himself and Peel having been frustrated by the Church of England, whose ministers had hitherto (from 1695–6) partly performed this duty. The act enabled nonconformists to enter into civil marriages, so dispensing with publication of banns in church, and resulted in the acceptance of divorce as a civil action, for which a special court was established (1856). It also led to the accumulation of accurate statistics necessary to reforms in public health, housing, etc., and to the better enforcement of regulations dealing with the employment and schooling of children. The requirement of a medical certificate of cause of death assisted detection of crime. From 1871 the local government board had charge of registration.

CIVIL RIGHTS ACTS, US legislation seeking to protect civil rights from individual and government infringement. Until the end of the Civil War, determination of civil rights was left almost entirely in the hands of state governments. After the Civil War, steps were taken to provide federal guarantees of racial equality with the passage of the 14th and 15th Amendments. Between 1866 and 1875 Congress also enacted five major civil rights and reconstruction bills, but by 1910 these had been so modified by further statutes, or had been so narrowly construed—in some cases even declared unconstitutional by the US Supreme Court—that they had little or no effect.

Between 1910 and the Second World War the federal government assumed a very limited role in the protection of the exercise of civil rights by Negroes and other ethnic and racial minorities, but this role changed after 1945 to one laying greater stress on active involvement. This change was initiated by the courts and the executive branch of the federal government. Not until 1957 did Congress enact new civil rights legislation, and both the Civil Rights Act of 1957 and 1960 were confined principally to voting rights. The 1957 act did, however, create a US Civil Rights Commission and a Civil Rights Division of the Justice Department, while the 1960 act provided penalties against the use of mob action to obstruct court orders.

In response to increased Negro discontent, as expressed by demonstrations, and the demands of numerous church, union, and civil liberties groups, President Kennedy sought to obtain a comprehensive new civil rights law, but Congress did not act until after his assassination. The 1964 Civil Rights Act guaranteed access to public accommodations for Negroes, strengthened voting rights, outlawed job discrimination, and sought to use direct sanctions to prevent discrimination in programmes receiving federal government funds by threatening to withhold such funds.

In 1965 new voting rights legislation was passed in response to increased civil rights demonstrations against voting discrimination in the South. The act provided for direct federal action to enable Negroes to register and vote. In 1966 and 1967 Congress rejected further civil rights legislation, but in 1968, following the murder of the Negro civil rights leader Martin Luther King, a new bill was passed. The major provision of the 1968 act sought to ban racial discrimination in the sale and renting of houses, and was the first federal open-housing legislation for over a century. The act also included anti-riot provisions, with penalties for specified riot activities.

The effect of the spate of federal civil rights legislation in the 1960s has been mixed. Lack of firm implementation in the face of violations has meant that, although significant changes have taken place as a result of the legislation, genuine compliance has been limited.

Revolution in Civil Rights, Congressional Quarterly Inc. (Washington, DC, 1968).   JDL

CIVIL RIGHTS CASES, 109 US 3 (1883), five cases considered together, in which the US Supreme Court held void the 1875 Civil Rights Act in so far as it denied proprietors of hotels, restaurants, places of amusement, and public conveyances the right to refuse accommodations to a person on account of his race, colour, or previous condition of servitude. The decision made it clear that the prohibitions of racial discrimination in the 'equal protection' and 'due process' clauses of the Fourteenth Amendment to the US Constitution were confined to state action and could not protect Negroes against discrimination by individuals. The implication of the decision was that the system of 'white supremacy' was generally beyond the control of the federal government.

CIVIL SERVICE COMMISSION (Britain), created by order-in-council (May 1855), resulted from Palmerston's adoption of an important reform proposed by the 1854 Northcote–Trevelyan Report. It led by degrees to the abolition of patronage (which has been called 'a more fundamental political revolution than the reform of parliament') and to an increasingly efficient and unified cohesive public service.

At least a dozen offices set tests before 1855, to establish their clerks' competence in elementary skills. The three commissioners' own earliest examinations (1855–60) only tested the basic qualifications of departmental nominees. Recruitment remained a departmental matter, usually based on political patronage. Competition arose only if departmental nominations exceeded the number of vacancies. The 1859 Superannuation Act required newly appointed civil servants to hold the commissioners' certificate in order to qualify for a pension. Regular, if limited, competition appeared after 1860, and another order-in-council (June 1870) brought full open competition to the Home Civil Service. The commission now had stronger control over entry, subject to agreement with the treasury and with individual departments.

Arguments for and against open competition (operative in the Indian civil service since 1853) had been cogently stated at the commission's inception. Gladstone, who sponsored the 1854 report, and Utilitarians like Chadwick and J. S. Mill, were strong supporters of competition. Whigs and Radicals had long demanded administrative reform to promote economical, efficient government. The tragic effects of inefficient administration during the Crimean War added point to their strictures. Sir Charles Trevelyan, part-author of the report, believed with Gladstone that open competition would strengthen 'our aristocratical institutions'. Jowett welcomed the impetus that open competition could give to university reform. The report had recommended that 19–25 candidates for 'superior situations' should take examinations of a literary character. The public service should try to attract the best men from the universities.

Queen Victoria feared examinations would not test personal qualities and practical abilities. Graham thought that parliamentary government might not work without the lever of jobbery. Other statesmen concurred. Even some committed reformers felt the 1854 report had denigrated the existing service, improved as it had been by Pitt, Peel, and Gladstone himself.

Edward Romilly, one of the original commissioners, saw promotion by merit as more crucial than open recruitment. He also stressed the anomaly of 'a democratic Civil Service, side by side with an aristocratic Legislature'. In the event extension of the franchise (1867) preceded open competition by three years.

W. J. M. Mackenzie and J. W. Grove, *Central Administration in Britain* (London, 1957).   MRB

CIVIL WAR, THE ENGLISH (1642–9), between royalists and parliamentarians. The constitutional and religious conflict between Charles I and the Long Parliament became civil war when Charles raised his standard at Nottingham on 22 Aug. 1642. He marched on London, confronting the parliamentary army under the Earl of Essex in the drawn battle of Edgehill, after which Charles occupied Oxford, which remained his headquarters until 1646. Essex, with the help of the trained bands of London, stopped the king's advance at Turnham Green and forced him to withdraw to Oxford.

In 1643 the strategy of the war revolved around the royalists' intended three-pronged attack on the capital, with Charles's route from Oxford barred by Essex; the Earl of Newcastle from Yorkshire confronted by Lord Fairfax and his son, Sir Thomas, based on Hull; and Sir Ralph Hopton from the south-west faced by Sir William Waller in Gloucestershire. The parliamentary defeats of Adwalton Moor, Lansdown, and Roundway Down left most of the north and west (except for Gloucester, relieved by the march of Essex from London in early Sept.) controlled by the royalists. The drawn battle of Newbury ended the inconclusive second year of the war with only East Anglia, with the army of the Eastern Association under the Earl of Manchester, firmly adhering to parliament.

On 25 Sept. 1643 the whole strategic, political, and religious concept of the war changed with the alliance of parliament with the Scots by the Solemn League and Covenant, by which Presbyterianism was to be established in England. In Jan. 1644 the Scots invaded England and joined the Fairfaxes in besieging York. Prince Rupert marched to its relief and the two armies fought at Marston Moor. Though the battle ended in a massive defeat for the royalists, parliament failed to follow up its victory. Meanwhile, in the west, Essex had committed the strategic blunder of marching into Cornwall, where most of his army was lost at Lostwithiel. He escaped and joined Manchester and Waller, who were defeated at the second battle of Newbury. Oliver Cromwell, Manchester's second in command, became disgusted by the lack of professionalism and willingness to follow up victories amongst the parliamentary commanders. He therefore charged Manchester—the worst offender—before the Commons for his 'backwardness to all action'. The result was the Self-Denying Ordinance (April 1645), which barred all peers and MPs from army commands, and the New Model Army (Feb. 1645)—an instrument forged for total victory—which was to be commanded by Sir Thomas Fairfax. Despite the Self-Denying Ordinance, Fairfax made Cromwell head of the cavalry.

In Jan. 1645 Charles I had rejected the stiff Anglo–Scottish peace offer of the treaty of Uxbridge. The sack of Leicester by the royalists determined Fairfax upon a battle. Naseby proved the decisive victory for parliament. At Langport, Fairfax defeated the south-western royalists, while the Scots cleared northern England. In June 1646 Oxford itself fell to parliament. Charles fled to the Scots at Newark, but was handed over to parliament when the Scots left England (Jan. 1647). This ended the first Civil War.

The whole of 1647 was occupied with the attempt by parliament and the army to negotiate a treaty with the king. Charles, using the dissension between moderates and extremists and the split between parliament and the army, played off each side against the other. He escaped from custody to the Isle of Wight and his Engagement with the Scots (26 Dec. 1647), by which he promised to introduce Presbyterianism into England, united the various factions in England.

The second Civil War started with risings in Pembroke (March 1648), put down by Cromwell, and in Kent and Essex, suppressed by Fairfax. On 8 July the Scots, under the Duke of Hamilton, invaded England, only to be defeated by Cromwell in the three-day battle of Preston. The trial and execution of Charles I followed (Jan. 1649) and ended the Civil War.

C. V. Wedgwood, *The King's War, 1641–1647* (London, 1958).
Austin Woolrych, *Battles of the English Civil War* (London, 1961).   CJ

CIVIL WARS, ROMAN, the wars which destroyed the Roman Republic, beginning with Sulla's march on Rome (88 BC). On his withdrawal to Asia, Marius and his partisans captured the city, but Sulla invaded Italy and defeated the Marian forces (84–82). Civil war again broke out with Julius Caesar's invasion of Italy. He defeated the Pompeian forces in Italy and Spain (49), at Pharsalus (48), Thapsus (46), and Munda (45). After Caesar's murder there was almost continuous civil war between the Triumvirs and Brutus and Cassius (43–42), Octavian and L. Antonius (41), Octavian and Sextus Pompey (40–36), and Octavian and Antony, who was finally defeated at Actium (31).

CIVIL WORKS ADMINISTRATION, emergency US work relief programme during the winter 1933–4. Under its administrator, Harry L. Hopkins, the CWA created over 4 million jobs and spent more than $900 million before it was disbanded.

CIVILIAN CONSERVATION CORPS, organization established by US Congress (31 March 1933) to provide work relief during the first phase of the New Deal. The Corps was authorized to establish camps for up to 250,000 men between the ages of 18 and 25 and employed over 2 million men on conservation projects between 1933 and 1941.

CIVILIS, GAIUS JULIUS, leader of a revolt of the Batavi against Rome in AD 69–70. A tribal chieftain commanding levies in Roman service, he first led his men ostensibly in support of Vespasian against the Rhine legions who backed Vitellius, but later with the help of Germans from beyond the Rhine fought for independence, being joined also by some Gallic tribes and forming a so-called 'Empire of the Gauls'. The Roman position on the Rhine disintegrated and was only restored by fresh legions brought in by Petilius Cerealis. Civilis surrendered, but his fate is unknown.

CIVITATE, BATTLE OF (1053), the defeat and capture of Pope Leo IX by a Norman Sicilian army. The pope was held until he signed an agreement with the Normans. The battle was part of the Norman struggle for papal recognition of their possessions in southern Italy, gained six years later by the treaty of Melfi.

CIVITATES FOEDERATAE, states, especially in Italy, allied to Rome by individual treaties which could be on terms of equality or inequality. In the latter case they were sometimes bound 'to respect and observe the power and majesty of Rome'. The terms of the treaties varied, but the *civitates foederatae* retained in theory at least the internal rights of sovereign states, paid no tribute, but had to supply troops to Rome when required. They disappeared in Italy when the whole peninsula gained Roman citizenship, but continued in the provinces as a small, specially favoured class of community, which under the empire declined in privilege, *eg*, losing exemption from taxation.

CLAIBORNE, WILLIAM (1587–1677), leader in Virginia colony. Arriving there in 1621, he served as surveyor, secretary of state, and a member of the council. He and Lord Baltimore disputed the ownership of land in neighbouring Maryland. He stirred up opposition to the Catholics in Maryland, incited an insurrection, and drove out Gov. Calvert.

CLAIBORNE, WILLIAM CHARLES COLES (1775–1817), governor of Louisiana. He was born in Virginia, became a lawyer, and moved to Tennessee (1796), where he helped to frame the state constitution. Claiborne served in Congress and President Jefferson appointed him governor of the Mississippi Territory. In 1803 he became governor of the newly acquired territory of Louisiana. His lack of knowledge of the language and customs of the French made his position difficult, but his honesty, diligence, and tact helped him to improve as a territorial executive. During the War of 1812 his efforts to defend Louisiana were not popular and his tactics were held in contempt by Gen. Jackson. He was exonerated from blame, however, and was elected a US senator, but died before he could serve.

CLAIM OF RIGHT (1689), declaration (11 April) by the Scottish Convention, meeting at Edinburgh under Hamilton's presidency, that James VII had tried to alter the constitution from 'a legal, limited monarchy to an absolute despotic power'. The claim incorporated a resolution that William and Mary be declared King and Queen of Scotland.

CLAIRAC, SYNOD OF (1560), Huguenot assembly which divided the French province of Guyenne into seven *colloques* or communities. Each had its own colonel, usually the local nobleman, who was appointed to organize a regional body of armed retainers to defend the Protestants against the Catholic population. By 1562 the reorganization of religious communities into military groups was also established in Languedoc, Provence, and Dauphiné.

CLANRICKARD, EARLS OF, Anglo–Irish aristocratic house descended from Richard de Burgh (d. 1243). The 4th earl, Richard (d. 1635), married the daughter of Sir Francis Walsingham and loyally served Elizabeth I against the Irish–Spanish forces (1597). He was appointed governor of Connought and was an Irish privy councillor. His son, Ulick, 5th earl, accompanied Charles I against the Scots (1640). Governor of the town and county of Galway, he was nominated chief commissioner by Charles I to negotiate with the Irish Confederates at Meath (March 1643). He was appointed commander of the English army in Connaught (1644), was granted the title of marquis (1645), and became a privy councillor of both England and Ireland. He tried to negotiate peace between Charles I and the Confederates (1646) and in 1650 was appointed deputy to the absent Duke of Ormonde, viceroy of Charles II's government in Ireland. After his surrender of Galway and the conclusion of terms with the English parliamentary forces (1652), he was distrusted by many Irish royalists. He withdrew to his estates in Kent, where he died (1657). His cousin, Richard, eldest son of his uncle, William de Burgh, became the 6th earl.

CLANS, social system which remained effective particularly in the Scottish highlands as late as the mid-18th cent. The longstanding personal and political rivalry of the clans and the poverty of the highland economy, based on cattle rearing, made for endemic lawlessness. The Act for disarming the Highland Clans (1716) remained a dead letter until it was brought into effect by Duncan Forbes and Gen. Wade (1725). Road construction in the highlands also helped to end political isolation (1726–37). Despite the loyalty of Argyll's Campbells to the Hanoverians, most of the clans led by the Macdonalds rallied to Prince Charles Edward Stuart in the 1745 rebellion, but were severely repressed by Cumberland after Culloden (1746). Three parliamentary acts of 1747 effectively crushed the clan system. The bearing of arms and the wearing of kilts and tartans were forbidden, and the powers of the clan chieftains to hold law courts independently of Crown justice and to claim military service as a condition of tenancy, were abolished in return for compensation totalling £152,000. The raising of loyal highland regiments by Pitt during the Seven Years War is usually taken as an indication of the British government's success in eradicating the clan system.

CLAPHAM SECT, leading group of Evangelicals, mainly within the Anglican Church, living at Clapham, then a favourite suburban village, where John Venn was rector (1792–1813). They included William Wilberforce; the banker Henry Thornton; the Cambridge theologian and mathematician Isaac Milner; Zachary Macaulay, father of the historian, who edited their journal *The Christian Observer* (1802–16); James Stephen; and Granville Sharp. They sponsored a lobby of MPs known as 'The Saints', and despite their conservative outlook co-operated at times with radicals over reforms such as the improvement of education and of prisons. Their energy met success in securing the abolition of the slave trade (1807) and slavery (1833). Other members not living in Clapham included the philanthropist Hannah More. In some respects they were the Christian forerunners of humanitarian propaganda groups such as the Fabians.

CLARE, JOHN FITZGIBBON, 1st Earl of (Irish) (1749–1802), lord chancellor of Ireland (1789–1802), who opposed concessions to the Catholic majority, and strongly supported the Act of Union as a guarantee of the Protestant ascendancy.

CLARE, Saint (1194–1253), foundress of the Poor Clares who received the Franciscan habit from St Francis himself in 1212, and may be regarded as the foundress of all the orders of Franciscan nuns, as Francis is of all the orders of Franciscan friars.

CLARENCE, GEORGE, 3rd Duke of (1449–78), younger brother of Edward IV. He betrayed Edward in 1469 when he joined the Earl of Warwick, his father-in-law, in a rebellion in favour of the deposed King Henry VI, but rejoined Edward in April 1471 just before Warwick's defeat at Barnet. By 1477 his ambitions led to a breach between himself and the king, who had him arrested and executed for treason.

CLARENDON, EDWARD HYDE, 1st Earl of (1st of 1st creation) (1609–74), English lawyer, politician, and principal minister of King Charles II, who entered the House of Commons as a member of the Short Parliament (1640). During the first session of the Long Parliament he proved himself an opponent of Charles I's 11-year 'tyranny' (1629–40), favouring the remedial legislation which was enacted and the impeachment of Strafford. During the second session, however, he veered in a royalist direction, and when Charles I fled to York after having failed to arrest the five members, Hyde joined him. His moderation may well have helped to rally support for the king on the eve of the first Civil War. He was appointed to the council of the Prince of Wales, the future Charles II, thus establishing a formal association which was to last until 1667. At the time of Charles I's execution (1649) he was not in England but on the continent, where he remained in the service of the new king throughout the interregnum, eventually becoming lord chancellor (1658). On the eve of the Restoration (1660) he performed one of his most important tasks by phrasing the Declaration of Breda in terms acceptable to all. Until 1667 he was at the height of his power, presiding over the destinies of a constitutional monarchy not unlike that which he had advocated in 1641. By this time he was the father-in-law of the future James II. None the less, policy and legislation did not always reflect his particular opinion, eg, the term 'Clarendon Code' is a misnomer. Nor was the Second Anglo–Dutch War of his making, yet he was made the scapegoat for his country's ensuing misfortunes. The king dismissed him, he was impeached and withdrew to France, where he died at Rouen. In exile he wrote his *Life* and completed *The True Historical Narrative of the Rebellion and Civil Wars in England*, which he had begun more than 20 years before. Neither was published in his lifetime.

B. H. G. Wormald, *Clarendon 1640–60: Politics, history, religion* (Cambridge, 1951).   BM

CLARENDON, HENRY HYDE, 2nd Earl of (2nd of 1st creation) (1638–1709), English politician, who entered the Cavalier parliament in 1661. Upon James II's accession to the throne (1685), he was appointed lord privy seal, and later lord lieutenant of Ireland, but was dismissed in 1687. At the time of the 1688 revolution, he tried to reconcile his loyalty to the Church of England with his loyalty to the monarchy, and not until after his son, Lord Cornbury, had gone over to the side of William of Orange, did he himself make a similar decision. Even then, as one of a group of about 50 peers and bishops, he urged James to summon a free parliament. He did not favour making William and Mary joint rulers and refused to swear allegiance to them. Consequently he was unable to play an active role in politics after 1688. He was associated with various Jacobite intrigues, and spent two very brief spells in the Tower of London (1689, 1691).

CLARENDON, GEORGE WILLIAM FREDERICK VILLIERS, 8th Earl of (4th of 2nd creation) (1800–70), British statesman, diplomat, and foreign secretary (1853–8, 1865–6, 1868–70). After varied diplomatic experience, he became envoy-extraordinary to Madrid (1833–9), where he mediated in the civil war and negotiated the Quadruple Alliance (1834). On succeeding to the peerage (1838), Clarendon became a privy councillor and lord privy seal (1838–41). A supporter of Corn Law repeal, he was appointed president of the board of trade (1846) and lord lieutenant of Ireland (1847–52). Clarendon was canvassed for the premiership (1852) and became foreign secretary under Aberdeen (1853). He participated in negotiations before the Crimean War (1853) and represented Britain at the peace conference at Paris (1856). His refusal to join Derby or Russell and his support for Palmerston showed his political influence (1855). Clarendon served as chairman of the commission on the nine public schools (1861) and chancellor of the duchy of Lancaster (1864), resuming the post of foreign secretary under Russell and Gladstone, under whom he negotiated the *Alabama* settlement.

CLARIS, PAU (1586–1641), Catalan clerical leader who started the revolt of Catalonia (1640–68). In Jan. 1641 he announced the independence of the province from the Spanish Crown and its allegiance to France, as a result of which the French sent assistance for the defence of Barcelona. Claris died soon after the victory of Montjuich (1641), after which the Catalan movement split into factions.

CLARK (JAMES BEAU)CHAMP (1850–1921), US lawyer and politician, born in Kentucky. He practised law in Kansas, served in the Missouri legislature (1889–91), and (apart from the term 1895–7) was a Democratic congressman from Missouri (1893–1921). On becoming Democratic minority leader in the US House of Representatives (1907) he led a revolt against the Speaker, Joseph Cannon, (1910) whose successor he became (1911–19). He was the leading contender for the Democratic presidential nomination in 1912, but was eclipsed when William Jennings Bryan transferred his support to Woodrow Wilson. Clark opposed the Selective Service Act (1917), was again Democratic minority leader (1919–21), lost his bid for re-election to the house (1920), and died before his unexpired term was complete.

CLARK, MARK WAYNE (1896–) US general, who was commander of the II Corps (1942), and 5th Army (1943–4), and became Allied commander in Italy (1944–5) and US High Commissioner in Austria (1945–7). He succeeded MacArthur as US commander-in-chief in the Far East and UN supreme commander in Korea (1952–3). In 1953 Clark became president of the Citadel Military College, SC.

CLARKE, SIR ANDREW (1824–1902), British lieutenant-general, governor of the Straits Settlements (1873–5). He initiated British intervention in the peninsular Malay states by negotiating on his own authority the 'Pangkor Engagement' with Perak.

CLARKE, JOHN (1609–76) arrived in Boston from England in 1637. His liberal sympathies led him to go to Rhode Island (1639), where he was a Baptist minister and physician. He acted as colonial agent for Rhode Island in England and secured the liberal charter of 1663 from Charles II.

CLARKE, WILLIAM BRANWHITE (1798–1878), English clergyman, known as 'the father of Australian geology'. He was educated at Cambridge and migrated to Sydney in 1839. His writings and geological expeditions did much to develop Australian mining.

CLARKSON, THOMAS (1760–1846), British social reformer who publicized the horrors of the slave trade (abolished by Great Britain in 1807) and sought its international suppression. Later, he campaigned against slavery itself within the British empire.

CLASSES, ACT OF (1649), in Scotland, excluded all except sincere covenanters from all offices or military commands. It was repealed in 1650, after the defeat of Dunbar had destroyed the extreme Presbyterians' stranglehold on Scottish politics.

CLASSICAL ECONOMISTS, the name given to certain early 19th-cent. theorists (notably James Mill, Ricardo, and McCulloch) whose description of the basic elements of economic thought was fundamental in the 19th cent. and is still of importance. They tended to accept the idea, associated in France with the physiocrats, that political economy should be treated as a logical and scientific system, based on laws of universal validity, and they introduced the 'classical' divisions of economic theory: production, distribution, exchange, and consumption. Adam Smith's *Wealth of Nations* (1776) stands as the first analysis of the workings of the economic system as a whole. Believing that nature, left to itself, produced good results, he taught that wealth is promoted by free competition and division of labour. David Ricardo, in his *Principles of Political Economy and Taxation* (1817), took Smith's analysis further, concluding that legislative interference was harmful, emphasising the benefits of laissez-faire, and omitting Smith's qualifications. Ricardo's work is the most notable achievement of the classical school, and all later economists, whatever their views, took it as a point of departure and derived from it a lesson in systematic thought.

The classical economists made a fundamental contribution to the progress of economic thought, and had an undoubted influence on legislative policy, particularly in the spheres of native industry and of commerce.

CLASSICISM, the adoption in the arts of rigid aesthetic principles derived from ancient examples. The term refers partly to the conscious imitation of the artists and writers of Greece and Rome which flourished, for instance, during the early Italian Renaissance and in the neo-classicism of the 18th cent. In a broader sense classicism means the observance of fixed rules of composition, and thus involves the foundation of academies, or gatherings of licensed experts, to ensure that this occurs. Corneille's tragedy *Le Cid* (1636), though successful on the stage, was criticized by the French *Académie* for its neglect of the dramatic unities, and Ben Jonson complained that Shakespeare 'lacked art'. Classicism stands for a formal, intellectual approach that condemns romantic excess, but since no art can exist without feeling, the distinction may not be very significant.

CLAUDE, GEORGES (1870–1960), French technologist, who was responsible for several innovations of major industrial importance. In 1902 he perfected a process for liquefying air in quantity. During the First World War he produced liquid chlorine for use as a poison gas. Claude demonstrated in 1910 that electrical discharges through inert gases could produce light. Later, 'neon lights' became widely used as advertising signs, it being possible to bend their gas-filled tubes into any shape required.

CLAUDEL, PAUL (1868–1955), French Catholic writer, best known for his plays. He served in the French diplomatic service, his posts including that of ambassador at Washington (1927–33). He retired in 1935. His early service in the east inspired some of his writings.

CLAUDIAN (Claudius Claudianus), last of the great classical Latin poets. Born a Greek speaker, probably at Alexandria, he arrived at Rome (AD 394), and under the patronage of Stilicho became a notary and a senator, but nothing is known of him after 404. His works are an important historical source, but on topics like the guardianship of Honorius and Arcadius, the causes of Gildo's rebellion, Stilicho's relations with Alaric, and the personalities of Eutropius and Rufinus, he conveys Stilicho's propaganda.

CLAUDIUS (10 BC–AD 54), Roman Emperor (*reg.* AD 41–54) and younger brother of Germanicus. He had lived mostly on the fringes of the imperial court, being excluded from important posts by a physical disability and devoting himself to the study and writing of history. But when the praetorian guards were sacking the palace after Caligula's assassination, they found Claudius in hiding, hailed him as emperor, and forced the Senate to proclaim him. Showing an unexpected and wide-ranging concern for the imperial government, he gave Roman citizenship widely to properly qualified provincials, introduced some Gauls into the Senate, and made use of Greeks in the equestrian order. He increased centralized control over the imperial administration through the use of former imperial slaves, a development highly unpopular with the Senate. In foreign policy he resumed Caligula's plan for the conquest of Britain, but rejected the idea of expansion elsewhere. His reign was rocked by scandals involving his third and fourth wives, Messalina and Agrippina the younger, the latter being interested in power for herself and her son, Nero. Claudius' death was generally attributed to poison administered at Agrippina's instigation.

CLAUDIUS, M. AURELIUS VALERIUS (GOTHICUS) (*reg.* AD 268–70), Roman Emperor, who was acclaimed after the murder of Gallienus, and initiated the work of military restoration continued by his successors, especially Aurelian (270–5) and Probus (276–82), earning him the title 'Gothicus' after his Gothic victories.

CLAUSEWITZ, KARL VON (1780–1831), Prussian general, whose concept of 'total war' and the primacy of military factors influenced a century of German military thought. He served as a Prussian officer in both the Revolutionary and Napoleonic Wars, being taken prisoner at Jena. On his release, he first co-operated with Scharnhorst and Gneisenau in the Prussian military reforms and then served in the Russian army as an officer (1812–14). His influence came from his directorship of the Berlin Military Academy (1818–1830) and his posthumous work, *Vom Kriege* (1832).

CLAY, HENRY (1777–1852), US political leader. Clay, 'the great compromiser', with his contemporaries Daniel Webster and John C. Calhoun, dominated congressional politics for 40 years, but, like them, never became president. He was born in Virginia and spent most of his life in Kentucky. After brief periods in the US senate (1806–7, 1809–10), he was elected to the House of Representatives (1810) and immediately chosen as Speaker, in which post he wielded great influence (1811–14, 1815–20, 1823–5). He was one of the leading 'War Hawks' before the war of 1812, and a member of the US delegation which negotiated the treaty of Ghent (1814). He was also a spokesman for western interests, a champion of the cause of the newly independent Latin-American republics, and one of the architects of the Missouri compromise (1820), as well as an advocate of an 'American system' of economic development, based on the protective tariff and federal internal improvements. In the presidential election of 1824, he came fourth, and when the election was decided by the House of Representatives he gave crucial support to John Quincy Adams rather than to his fellow-westerner, Andrew Jackson, who had received the largest number of electoral college votes. Clay then became secretary of state (1825–9), thus incurring allegations of a corrupt bargain with Adams. As a senator from Kentucky (1831–42, 1849–52), he was a dominant figure in the National Republican and, later, Whig parties. He promoted the compromise tariff (1833) which helped to end the nullification crisis. In the election of 1832 he was heavily defeated by Jackson, and his third major bid for the presidency (1844) ended in defeat by James K. Polk. A border-state man and a slave-owner, Clay had misgivings about slavery, but profoundly disliked the abolitionists. For the third time he played a major part in settling a sectional crisis between North and South when he laid the foundations of the compromise of 1850.

Though renowned for his charm, eloquence, political skill, and devotion to the Union, Clay was frustrated in his presidential ambitions for 30 years. One of the first western politicians to emerge on the national stage, he was overtaken by the newer frontier spirit of the Jacksonians; his conception of an American system of national development was increasingly out of step with the rising democratic and entrepreneurial spirit of the times; his ambivalent attitude towards the slavery issue suited his role as compromiser, but hampered his presidential aspirations.

C. Eaton, *Henry Clay and the Art of American Politics* (Boston, 1957). PJP

CLAY, LUCIUS DUBIGNON (1897–), US general, army engineer, and staff officer, who became deputy to Gen. Eisenhower (1945). He was appointed commander-in-chief, European Command, and governor of the US Zone in Germany (1947), and retired in 1949, but returned as President Kennedy's personal representative during the Berlin crisis (1961–2).

CLAYTON ANTI-TRUST ACT (1914), US legislation designed to remedy the defects of the Sherman Act (1890). The act, a part of Woodrow Wilson's 'New Freedom' programme, listed and banned a number of unfair trade practices tending 'substantially' either to lessen competition or to create monopoly. Interlocking directorates were condemned and prohibited. 'Labor, agricultural, or horticultural organizations instituted for the purposes of mutual help' were guaranteed freedom to carry out their 'legitimate objects'. Strikes and picketing were legalized and injunctions prohibited in labour disputes, 'unless necessary to prevent irreparable damage to property'. The Act is sometimes called the 'Magna Carta of American Labor', but legal loopholes were quickly found to nullify many of the safeguards apparently given to organized labour.

CLAYTON–BULWER TREATY (1850), agreement between the US and Britain, providing joint Anglo–American guarantees of the neutrality and security of any isthmian canal constructed in Central America. The two powers also agreed not to occupy, fortify, or colonize any part of Central America. The treaty was superseded by the Hay–Pauncefote treaty (1901).

CLEAR GRIT PARTY, a radical wing of the Reform Party of Canada West. Its name is attributed to David Christie, an opponent of the Baldwin–Lafontaine ministry of 1848, who appealed (1849) for members who were 'all sand and no dirt, clear grit all the way'. The name was popularized in the

Toronto Globe by George Brown, with whom the Clear Grits subsequently joined forces (1855) to form the nucleus of the Liberal Party in Ontario. The term 'Grit' became a colloquialism for Liberal.

CLEAVER, LEROY ELDRIDGE (1935–), US militant 'black power' leader, a disciple of Malcolm X, minister of information of the Black Panther Party (1967), and presidential candidate of the Peace and Freedom Party (1968).

CLEISTHENES OF ATHENS, son of the Alcmeonid Megacles and grandson of Cleisthenes of Sicyon, one of the architects of Athenian democracy. He was archon under Hippias (525 BC), and later joined other Alcmeonids in exile (514) and encouraged Hippias' expulsion by Cleomenes I (510). Outdone in subsequent aristocratic faction by Isagoras, Cleisthenes won popular support by proposing radical constitutional reforms (508). These were eventually effected despite Spartan opposition (507–500). In Attica and Athens itself local resident groups (*demes*) replaced kinship groups (*phratries*) and cult groups as the basic units of political identity. Local government became the responsibility of the *demes* and Athenian citizenship henceforward depended upon enrolment in the *deme* registers. Ten new artificial Attic tribes were so constituted from the *demes* as to make Attica a close-knit political unit with parts looking to the centre, Athens, rather than to local leaders of clans and local cults. In central government Cleisthenes restricted the power of the Areopagus and the archons by confirming the right of the Athenian citizen body (*ecclesia*) to elect and control the archons, by reconstituting Solon's second council as a popular Council of Five Hundred (*boule*) chosen by lot from representatives of the *demes* and, perhaps, by introducing ostracism. Nothing certain is known of Cleisthenes after 507.

CLEISTHENES OF SICYON, famous Tyrant of the ancient Greek city-state of Sicyon, c. 600–570 BC. At home he supported non-Dorians against Dorians, calling the three Dorian tribes Pigmen, Assmen, and Swinemen, and his own non-Dorian tribe *Archelaoi* (Rulers). Abroad he opposed Argos, attempting to remove all Argive traces from Sicyonian cult and festivals. After being initially opposed by Delphi, he successfully led the First Sacred War against Crisa (c. 590), reorganized the Pythian festival at Delphi, introduced a similar festival at Sicyon, built a treasury at Delphi, and subsequently had Delphi's support. Suitors from all over Greece competed on a famous occasion (c. 570) for his daughter Agariste, who eventually married the Alcmeonid Megacles.

CLEMENCEAU, GEORGES (1841–1929), French statesman, who held the nation together during the last stages of the First World War and negotiated the treaty of Versailles. A man of tremendous will power, passion, and intransigence, he was one of the most feared and controversial politicians of the Third Republic. The son of a republican doctor in the Vendée, he himself studied medicine in Paris, became associated with the opposition to the empire (1862), and visited America before starting to practice, (1869). He served ably as mayor of Montmartre and deputy (1870), but resigned when the Commune began. His real political apprenticeship was as municipal councillor for Clignancourt (1871–6).

His national political career began with his election as a radical to the Chamber (1876), where he soon made himself feared for his love of conflict, his epigrams, and his ability to wreck ministries. He broke with Gambetta when the latter accepted the new constitution and later turned against Boulanger, whom he had originally sponsored (1888). He failed to obtain office, however, because of his personality and because he was accused both of being an English agent and of being involved in the Panama scandal. He was not re-elected (1893) and only returned to public life during the Dreyfus affair. He became senator for the Var (1902) and a

radical leader, heading the longest ministry of the Third Republic (1906–9). Yet he did not achieve many of his desired reforms and was brought down over his failure to expand the navy. After 1914 he became a trenchant critic of the inefficient way in which the war was run, and was eventually called to be prime minister and minister of war (1917). He ran the war effort on almost dictatorial lines and inspired the army and the population to resist the final German onslaughts and to assume the offensive. He played a large part in negotiating the treaty of Versailles (1919), but his popularity was undermined by his failure to secure all the demands of the right and he was not chosen as president (1920). He retired and spent his last years travelling and writing.

G. Bruun, *Clemenceau* (Cambridge, MA, 1943).
J. H. Jackson, *Clemenceau and the Third Republic* (London, 1946).   CHC

CLEMENS, SAMUEL LANGHORNE ('MARK TWAIN') (1835–1910), US writer, born in Missouri. He was apprenticed as a printer (1847) and later trained as a Mississippi steamboat pilot. When the river boats stopped operating during the Civil War, he served briefly as a Confederate volunteer, then spent the rest of the war wandering through Nevada frontier country writing for various newspapers under the pseudonym 'Mark Twain', and lecturing. He became immediately famous with his version of an old folk tale, 'The Celebrated Frog of Calaveras County' (1865), and after further lecturing visited the Mediterranean and the Holy Land. His early life inspired *The Adventures of Tom Sawyer* (1876), a succession of humorous incidents worked into a contrived plot and designed for young readers; *Life on the Mississippi* (1883), based on his experiences as a river pilot; and *The Adventures of Huckleberry Finn* (1884), which has demanded close critical study and compares in stature with Melville's *Moby Dick*. His other major works include *The Innocents Abroad* (1869); *Roughing It* (1872); *A Connecticut Yankee in King Arthur's Court* (1889); and *The Tragedy of Pudd'nhead Wilson* (1894). Twain's reputation had quickly become international and he rivalled Dickens and Kipling as the highest-paid author of the century. As his use of fingerprinting in *Pudd'nhead Wilson* illustrated, he had an enthusiasm for new inventions and ideas which, together with publishing the books of others, led him into a number of financially disastrous ventures. He was proud of and yet distrusted America, and increasing pessimism is revealed in his essay 'What is Man?' (1906) and *The Mysterious Stranger* (posthumously published, 1910). Twain enjoyed a long prolific life as a writer and is still considered to be one of the greatest 19th-cent. satirists.

William Dean Howells, *My Mark Twain, reminiscences and criticisms* (New York, 1910).
A. B. Paine, *Mark Twain: a Biography: the personal and literary life of Samuel Langhorne Clemens*, 3 vols (New York, 1912).   AW

CLEMENT IV (*reg.* 1265–8), Pope, French lawyer who took orders after his wife's death and became in rapid succession Bp of Le Puy (1257), Abp of Narbonne (1259), cardinal (1261), and pope. He supported Charles of Anjou's claim to the throne of Sicily, and was the patron of Roger Bacon.

CLEMENT V (1264–1314), Pope (*reg.* 1305–14), a Frenchman and first pope of the Avignonese papacy and Abp of Bordeaux. He was elected in order to end the quarrel between the papacy and Philip IV of France, for whom Clement packed the college of cardinals with Frenchmen and suppressed the Templars. His *Clementines* are an important addition to canon law.

CLEMENT VII (1342–94), Pope (*reg.* 1378–94), son of a Duke of Savoy. As Cardinal Robert of Geneva he was principally responsible for the election of Urban VI at Rome in April

1378, but on Urban showing himself to be extremely autocratic, Robert himself accepted election (1378) and has been regarded as an anti-pope. His princely origin greatly strengthened his position and he returned to Avignon, where several previous 14th-cent. popes had resided, thus precipitating the Great Schism between the followers of the rival popes at Rome and Avignon.

CLEMENT VII (1478–1534), Pope (*reg.* 1523–34). As a Medici Clement tried unsuccessfully to promote the interests of his family in Florence as well as the protection of the papal states. After the French defeat at Pavia (1525), he joined with France, Milan, and Florence in a holy alliance to expel the Spanish-Imperialist armies from Italy. This led to the occupation and sack of Rome (1527) and after further French defeats Clement had to crown Charles V at Rome and recognize his possession of Naples. In Germany Clement demanded the enforcement of the Edict of Worms against Luther and his heresies, but Charles and the German princes recommended him first to summon a general council to reform the doctrine and discipline of the Church. In England he was faced with Henry VIII's request for the annulment of his marriage to Catherine of Aragon, which Charles, as Catherine's nephew, forbade him to grant. So Henry went his own way and withdrew England from the Roman communion.

CLEMENT VIII (1536–1605), Pope (*reg.* 1592–1605), a patron of learning, who appointed Bellarmine and Baronius among his cardinals and issued a new edition of the Vulgate. He also added Ferrara to the papal states. When Henry IV renounced Protestantism, Clement solemnly received him into the Church, but he deplored the Edict of Nantes (1598) as 'the most cursed edict I could imagine . . . whereby liberty of conscience is granted to everyone, which is the worst thing in the world'.

CLEMENT IX (1600–69), Pope (*reg.* 1667–9), a pacific and respected pope whose death was mourned even by Louis XIV. He temporarily reconciled the Jansenists in France; by recognizing the independence of Portugal he restored order to the Church there; and in good faith he helped to bring France and Spain to the treaty of Aix-la-Chapelle. He failed to persuade Europe to help Venice against the Turks.

CLEMENT X (1590–1676), Pope (*reg.* 1670–6), began the great struggle with Louis XIV over rights to the revenues of vacant dioceses and abbeys. His efforts to preserve the peace of Europe and to mobilize Russian and Polish resistance to the Turks were respected but unsuccessful. He erected the see of Quebec and canonized Rose of Lima, the first saint of the New World.

CLEMENT XI (1649–1721), Pope, who maintained the religious authority of the papacy during his reign (1700–21), but suffered political humiliation, especially in the treaty of Utrecht. In the bull *Unigenitus* (1713), at the request of Louis XIV, he condemned the Jansenist propositions contained in Quesnel's popular *Réflections morales*, but with only temporary effect. Appealed to by the Jesuit missionaries of China in their quarrel with the Dominicans over Chinese rites, he decided against the Jesuit adaptation of Christian rites to Confucian customs, with the result that western preaching was forbidden in China and the opportunity of converting the most important scholar class was lost. In the struggle over the Spanish succession he was forced to recognize first the French and then, when the papal states were invaded by Austrians, the Austrian candidate. At Utrecht, Parma and Piacenza were given to Philip V of Spain, and Sardinia and Sicily to the Duke of Savoy, without regard for papal overlordship of these territories, and a struggle over vacant benefices and immunities in Sicily soon followed.,

CLEMENT XII (*reg.* 1730–40), Pope, restored papal finances, but was unable to resist continuing encroachments of temporal powers on papal authority. Rights of investiture were granted to the Bourbons in Naples and Sicily, papal suzerainty over Parma and Piacenza ceased, and papal territories in Italy were invaded and plundered by Spanish and Austrian armies.

CLEMENT XIII (1693–1769), Pope (*reg.* 1758–69), powerless defender of the Jesuits against the Catholic sovereigns, who were determined to extinguish the society. France, Spain, and Portugal each suppressed or expelled the Jesuits during his pontificate, and by diplomatic and military pressure on the pope sought their total extinction, a defeat from which death released this pope but not his successor, Clement XIV.

CLEMENT XIV (1705–74), Pope (*reg.* 1769–74), conceded to the temporal sovereigns the *de jure* suppression of the Society of Jesus, by the Brief *Dominus ac Redemptor* (1773). This was perhaps the greatest single defeat of the papacy in a century marked by a succession of surrenders to temporal rulers, for whom the Jesuits represented the quintessence of papal ultramontanism. The diplomatic campaign against the society, already intense before the death of Clement XIII, played havoc with the conclave in which Clement XIV was elected, and it was suggested that agreement to dissolve the Jesuits was a condition of election, but the pope was still able to prevaricate for several years by promising to call a general council. After the occupation of Avignon and Benevento, upon the advice of members of the curia bribed by Spain, and with the avowed intention of maintaining peace with the sovereigns for the sake of war against irreligion, the pope finally surrendered.

CLEMENT OF ALEXANDRIA (*c.* AD 150–215), Christian Platonist who sought to reconcile Christianity with the Greek tradition. He was converted in adult life and became head of the Catechetical School in Alexandria, but left the city during the persecution of Severus in 202 and died in Asia Minor. His chief works are the *Protrepticus*, An Exhortation to the Greeks; the *Paedagogus*, on Christian life and manners; and the *Stromateis* or Miscellaneous Studies. His type of Christianity emphasized knowledge rather than faith, but he was a loyal Churchman and may have been ordained presbyter.

CLEMENTIS, VLADIMIR (1902–52), Czechoslovakian politician who was born at Tisovec, Slovakia; elected a communist deputy in 1935, then spent the Second World War in London as a member of the exile Legislative Council. He was appointed an under-secretary of state on his return to Czechoslovakia, then foreign minister (1948). He was dismissed (1950) and arrested (1951) in the last of the Stalinist purges. Together with Slansky he was condemned and executed (1952).

CLEOMBROTUS (*reg.* 380–371 BC), Spartan King, brother of Agesipolis, whose rivalry with Agesilaus he continued, though without his liberal attitude. He was killed while leading the Spartan army, that was defeated by the Thebans at Leuctra.

CLEOMENES I (*reg. c.* 520–490 BC), son of Anaxandridas, Spartan Agiad King. He refused Samian (*c.* 516), Scythian (*c.* 513), and Ionian (499) appeals for help against Persia and attempted instead to strengthen Sparta's control of the Peloponnese and extend it to central Greece. His diplomatic and military efforts to secure Athens, where he first expelled Hippias (510) and then tried to prevent Cleisthenes' reforms (508) and restore Hippias (*c.* 503), were opposed by Corinth and the Eurypontid King Demaratus. Later, his victory at Sepeia (*c.* 494) rendered Argos harmless in the Persian Wars and his intervention prevented Aegina supporting the Persian invasion of 490. He also had Demaratus removed, but was himself soon exiled. After intrigues with the Arcadians, he was recalled and arrested. Herodotus' story of his final madness and suicide is not improbable.

CLEOMENES III (*c.* 260–219 BC) Spartan King from 235, social reformer, who, influenced by his wife, Agiatis, Agis IV's widow, planned to use social reform to strengthen Sparta for renewed imperialism. After victories over the Achaean League, Cleomenes felt strong enough to carry his reforms at Sparta (227). Like Agis, taking 'Lycurgus' constitution' as his slogan, he cancelled debts, redistributed land, and enlarged the citizen body. But time was against Cleomenes and the Achaean war preoccupied him, particularly when Aratus' appeal to Antigonus Doson brought the Macedonian army into Peloponnese (224). Defeated at Sellasia (222), he fled to Egypt, whose king, Ptolemy III, had financed him. Ptolemy IV, however, no lover of lost causes or their dangerous exponents, imprisoned Cleomenes, who committed suicide after failing to escape.

CLEON (d. 422 BC), Athenian democratic politician, prominent in the great Peloponnesian War after Pericles' death (429) and unremittingly hostile to Sparta. His forceful manner and status as a tannery proprietor rather than landed gentleman made him the butt of Aristophanes. Following the revolt of Mytilene, his proposal to execute or enslave the whole population was only just frustrated (427). After the naval victory at Pylos (425), he opposed Spartan peace overtures and in his first military command captured the Spartans on Sphacteria. His role in the unsuccessful attack on Boeotia (424) is unknown, but after the year's truce (423–422), he was defeated by Brasidas outside Amphipolis. The deaths in action of both commanders cleared the way for the peace of Nicias (421).

CLEOPATRA (69–30 BC), Queen of Egypt, the last of the Ptolemaic dynasty. On becoming joint ruler with her brother (51), she was expelled by his guardians, but won the support of Julius Caesar, who restored her. She was probably in Rome at the time of Caesar's murder. On returning to Egypt, she met Mark Antony in Cilicia (41), and married him in 37. Her aim to restore the Ptolemaic empire was assisted by additions of territory from Mark Antony by the Donations of Alexandria (34). In Octavian's propaganda against Antony, she was a god-send to him, though she supported Antony in the civil war. She was present at the battle of Actium (31), and committed suicide a few days after Octavian's capture of Alexandria.

CLEOPHON (d. 404 BC), Athenian politician prominent in the last stage of the great Peloponnesian War. He derived his wealth from a lyre-making business, not from the traditional aristocratic landownership, and was dubbed 'the lyre-maker' by Aristophanes. Being optimistic of Athenian victory, he vehemently opposed Spartan overtures in 410 and 406 and even after the defeat at Aegospotami (405) tried to prevent negotiations, but was condemned to death by the *Boule*.

CLERGY RESERVES, a requirement of the British Constitutional Act (1791) that one-seventh of the land granted to settlers in Canada be allocated to the support of the Protestant clergy. In 1854 the reserves were secularized and handed over to Canadian municipalities.

CLERICAL DISQUALIFICATION ACT (1801), in Britain, disqualified Anglican clergy and ministers of the Church of Scotland from membership of the House of Commons. It replaced a common-law disqualification, and was occasioned by the agitation caused in the Commons by Horne Tooke, MP, an ordained Anglican.

CLERICAL SUBSCRIPTION ACT (1865) in Britain allowed the clergy of the Church of England at ordination to assent to the Thirty-nine Articles in general rather than to affirm support for each in detail. In part a reaction to the Oxford Movement, it indicated modernization and reform of the Church in face of disunity and disbelief.

CLERK-MAXWELL, JAMES (1831–79), Scottish physicist and principal founder of the electromagnetic theory of light and the dynamical theory of gases. His work on light was based on that of Faraday, the theory being developed in its early stages in terms of a highly complex model of 'aether vortices'. The complete theory, one of the monuments of classical physics, appeared in essentially the form in which it is still taught in his 'Treatise on Electricity and Magnetism' (1873).

Maxwell's development of the dynamical theory of gases applied the theory of probability to the motions and collisions of the individual molecules. He was able to deduce the equations that describe the bulk properties of the gas. This statistical mechanics forged the quantitative link between the macroscopic phenomena that were the chief preoccupation of 19th-cent. physics and the submicroscopic world that was increasingly to dominate the 20th cent.

CLERMONT, COUNCIL OF (Nov. 1095), council of the Church at which Pope Urban II proclaimed the First Crusade, to bring aid to the Eastern Christians and to free the Holy Places. The truce of God was proclaimed, the possessions of crusaders guaranteed, and remission of sins promised to them.

CLERUCHY (Greek *Klēroukhia*), term used for settlements abroad of Athenian citizens who did not form a separate city-state or colony, but remained part of the Athenian people. Established on land taken from defeated enemies (*eg*, Chalcis, 506 BC) or subjected allies in the Delian League (*eg*, Naxos, Andros 449, Chalcis 446, Mytilene 427) or in places of strategic importance (*eg*, the Chersonese, *c.* 451), they acted as garrisons, providing support for Athens' friends and relief from over-population at home. They were deeply resented as a feature of 5th-cent. Athenian imperialism and were prohibited in the charter of the Second Athenian Confederacy (377). Their reappearance after 365 (*eg*, Potidaea) increased the Athenians' unpopularity, which produced the Social War (357–355).

CLEVE-JULICH, important but fragmentary state on the lower Rhine, consisting of the territories of Julich, Cleves, Berg, Mark, and Ravensburg. It was divided by the treaty of Xanten (1614) between the Calvinist John Sigismund, of Brandenburg-Prussia, who received Cleves, Mark, and Ravensburg, and the Catholic Wolfgang William of Neuburg, who gained Julich and Berg. The dispute which broke out in 1609 almost developed into a full-scale religious war in Germany.

CLEVELAND, STEPHEN GROVER (1837–1908), the only Democratic president of the US between Buchanan (1857–1861) and Wilson (1913–21), and the only president to serve two non-consecutive terms (1885–9, 1893–7). He was a moderate reformer, whose devotion to honest and economic government was outstanding in an age dominated by political spoilsmen, but he was unable to remove the causes of agrarian and labour unrest which came to a head during his second term.

He was born in Caldwell, NJ, and settled in Buffalo, NY (1855). After serving as assistant district attorney (1863–6) and sheriff (1870–3) of Erie County, he was elected mayor of Buffalo (1881) and his political fortunes began to rise. He attracted wide recognition by his veto on extravagant and corrupt appropriations and on being elected governor of NY (1882) came into conflict with the Tammany Democrats because of his honesty. He was elected president in 1884 after a campaign dominated by personal vilification on both sides, having been supported by the Mugwumps, a group of insurgent Republicans who left their party in protest at Blaine's nomination. In office he disappointed the Mugwumps over civil service reform, but, helped by an increasing government surplus, he regained their confidence by appealing for downward tariff revision, and campaigned largely on the tariff issue

(1888). Despite his gaining a plurality of the popular vote, his bid for re-election was unsuccessful.

Cleveland's marriage in 1886 led him to devote less time to politics, but Democratic successes in 1890, coupled with the threat of agrarian radicalism, lured him back into the arena. His second term began with a major financial panic, and was dominated by unemployment, labour strife, and agrarian discontent. He secured the repeal of the Sherman Silver Purchase Act (1893) and refused to countenance any move off the gold standard, a policy which split the party and ended his hopes of tariff reform. In 1894 he alienated both labour supporters and states rights advocates by sending federal troops to Chicago to end the Pullman strike. In 1896, when the silver Democrats gained control and nominated William Jennings Bryan as the party's presidential candidate, Cleveland and his supporters organized an independent National Democratic party which, together with fear of radicalism, helped to bring about the election of the Republican McKinley. To the end of his life, despite his sharing of Bryan's opposition to imperialism, Cleveland remained an inveterate opponent of the Bryan wing of the Democratic Party.

A. Nevins, *Grover Cleveland: a Study in Courage* (New York, 1933).
AJT

CLIFF DWELLINGS, habitations found in the arid plateau country of the American south-west, where natural recesses and shallow caverns have been weathered in the cliffs. Primitive tribes which settled this region before the Spanish explorations used these recesses for living, storage, burial, hiding, and defence. Where rock formations permitted, recesses were often excavated for greater space. Such dwellings are called cavate houses. Archaeologists also distinguish the cliff-house proper, which was built of masonry. The date of their first occupancy is not established, but there is evidence that the dwellings were lived in after the Spanish arrived (1540). The Hopi have a well-authenticated tradition that some of their clans deserted their villages for cliff dwellings during an epidemic in the 18th cent.

CLIFFORD OF CHUDLEIGH, THOMAS CLIFFORD, 1st Baron (1630–71), English MP during the Restoration, and member of Charles II's administration which replaced that of Clarendon (1667), known from the initials of its members (Clifford, Arlington, Buckingham, Ashley, and Lauderdale), as the Cabal. With Arlington, Clifford had formed a group in the Commons which described themselves as 'the king's friends', and during the Dutch War (1665–7) his career advanced swiftly, with Arlington's help. He became commissioner for the care of sick prisoners of war, served with the fleet, and later as an ambassador extraordinary to Denmark. In 1667 he was appointed to the commission of the treasury. Probably a Catholic, and the most francophile of the king's ministers, he disliked the conclusion of the Dutch War in 1669, and was the king's confidant in the intrigues with France that lead to the secret treaty of Dover, the full nature of which was not known to the Cabal as a whole. He encouraged Charles to override constitutional limitations and advised the Stop of the Exchequer of 1672. In the same year he was made lord high treasurer. The Declaration of Indulgence (1672), which he supported, raised fears of popery and with the passage of the Test Act (1673) Clifford was obliged to resign.

CLIFFORD, SIR HUGH (1866–1941), British colonial administrator and author. After 20 years in the civil service in Malaya he became colonial secretary of Ceylon (1907). In 1912 he was appointed colonial governor of the Gold Coast and after that of Nigeria. He returned to Ceylon as governor (1925), but disliked the constitutional structure. After writing a critical report on it (the ultimate result of which was the Donoughmore Commission) he was at his own request transferred to Malaya.

CLINTON, DE WITT (1769–1828), US senator (1802–3), mayor of New York city (1803–15), and governor (1817–21, 1825–8). A devoted public servant, seeking to develop the economic and social life of his state, he avoided national party affiliations, but became Madison's rival in the 1812 presidential election.

CLINTON, GEORGE (1739–1812), American soldier and politician. As governor of New York (1777–95, 1801–4) Clinton opposed ratification of the Federal Constitution of 1787 in a series of letters signed 'Cato' advocating the cause of state sovereignty, which Hamilton answered under the pseuodonym 'Caesar'. As vice-president of the US (1805–12) Clinton used his casting vote in the Senate against the re-chartering of the Bank of the US (1811).

CLIPPER SHIPS, long, narrow, three-masted sailing vessels that brought American marine design to its zenith in the 1840s and 1850s. Built more for speed than capacity, Isaac McKim's design in 1832 was perfected by Donald McKay and others in the US and was copied by ship-builders in Britain. McKay's *Flying Cloud* established a record of 89 days for the voyage from New York to San Francisco in 1851. Designed for the tea and opium trade from China and the gold-rush trade to California and Australia, American interest was curtailed by the slump of 1854, the Civil War, and the coming of the steamship, but British shippers continued to use clipper ships like the *Cutty Sark* for many years.

CLIVE OF PLASSEY, ROBERT CLIVE, 1st Baron (Irish) (1725–1774), British Indian soldier and statesman. In 1746 he was sent to Madras as a 'writer' of the East India Co. After two attempts at suicide he was given military employment in 1748 and proved a brilliant guerrilla leader. In 1751 he seized Arcot, the capital of the Carnatic, and held it for 50 days against a superior force under Chanda Sahib. He returned to England in 1753 with a modest fortune. After an unsuccessful attempt to enter parliament, he returned to south India (1755) as governor of Fort St David, capturing the pirate stronghold of Gheria near Bombay on the way. The troops, intended for the purpose of dislodging the French from the Deccan, were soon sent to recover Calcutta, with Clive in command of 900 Europeans and 1500 Indians. By a series of deft political and military moves Clive recovered Calcutta (Jan. 1757), won the battle or cannonade of Plassey in June, overthrew the Nawab of Bengal, and seized the French post of Chandernagar. He then installed a new nawab, intending to turn Bengal into a 'sponsored' state with British control and Indian management, as De Bussy had done in Hyderabad. This was the policy he pursued during his first governorship (1756–60), sustaining the nawab from plots within and attacks from without the state. He secured the Northern Sircars from the French (1758) and Chinsura from the Dutch (1759).

This policy failed because of Clive's internal measures. He secured virtual free trade for the company's merchants as well as for the company itself and accepted such large presents for himself and others that the floodgates of corruption were opened in a state lacking the means to control it; he received £234,000 in cash and an estate worth £30,000 a year. For his services he received a peerage.

Three years later the company was at war with a new nawab, threatened with a Mughal attack, and unable to produce the promised profits. In 1765 Clive returned, as governor and commander-in-chief of Bengal, to restore the situation. He found the Mughal emperor already defeated at Buxar and made a settlement (1765). Oudh was restored to Shuja-ad-daula, Allahabad to the emperor with an annual tribute, in return for which he conferred the *diwani* or revenue-collecting power for Bengal and Bihar on the company. This power was exercised through a deputy nawab, who was also the Nawab of Bengal's deputy for judicial affairs. Thus Bengal passed under British control with Indian management and became virtually a British province.

This was Clive's system of Dual Government. There remained the reform of the company's service. Clive suspended the Calcutta council, suppressed a 'white mutiny' of the company's military officers, prohibited private trade (providing in its place salaries by means of a 'Society of Trade'), and the taking of large presents. These measures were only partly successful, but they stopped ten years of corruption which had nearly ruined Bengal.

Clive returned to England (1767) to face an embittered opposition from within and without the company. This culminated in a parliamentary attack in 1772, when, after many strictures and a vigorous defence, it was declared that 'he had rendered great and meritorious services to his country'. But the strain upon him was too great, and he died by his own hand.

To Clive must be attributed the acquisition of Bengal, the measures which led to the years of plunder, and the reforms which presaged ordered administration.

A. M. Davies, *Clive of Plassey* (London, 1939).
H. H. Dodwell, *Dupleix and Clive* (London, 1920).   TGPS

CLIVEDEN, seat of the Astor family, near Maidenhead, England. It was Lady Astor's house-parties there in the 1930s that created the image of the 'Cliveden set', of which Geoffrey Dawson (editor of *The Times*), J. L. Garvin, Lord Lothian, and other prominent pro-Germans were notable members. Their critics, as far removed as Eden and the communist polemicist Claud Cockburn, made much in the late 1930s of the supposed influence of the 'set' in shaping the policy of 'appeasement'.

CLODIUS ALBINUS, D. (d. AD 197), Roman governor of Britain, who rebelled against Didius Julianus (193), proclaiming himself emperor, and was for a time recognized by Julianus' supplanter, Septimius Severus. In 196, however, Albinus crossed to Gaul, and in the ensuing civil war was defeated by Severus near Lyons, and committed suicide.

CLODIUS, P., PULCHER (d. 52 BC), Roman patrician politician and mob-leader. He fomented a mutiny among Lucullus' troops in Asia (68), appeared as a collusive prosecutor of Catiline (64), and caused a political crisis by profaning the feminine rites of the Bona Dea, celebrated in the house of Julius Caesar, whose wife was Clodius' mistress (62). He was tried in 61 for sacrilege but secured acquittal by bribery, although Cicero disproved his plea of alibi. In revenge, he won Caesar's support, had himself adopted into a Plebeian family, obtained the tribunate, and exiled Cicero (58). After gaining control of Rome with his factions, he attacked Pompey, but, losing Caesar's support, was out-fought by rival factions under Milo and Sestius. Though Cicero was restored (57), Clodius remained a menace to public order until he was murdered by Milo near Bovillae.

CLONTIBRET, BATTLE OF (1595), defeat of an English force in Ireland under Sir Henry Bagenal by his brother-in-law, Hugh O'Neil, later Earl of Tyrone, in the Tyrone War or War of the Northern Confederacy.

CLOSURE, procedural rule of the British House of Commons (established 1882), by which a debate can be terminated by a majority decision. This had been done in 1881 by Speaker Brand, on his own authority, to end a debate on the introduction of Protection of Person and Property Bill (Ireland), which Irish members' obstructionist tactics had prolonged for 41½ hours.

CLOVE, introduced and developed in Zanzibar and Pemba on the orders of Seyyid Said, Sultan of Zanzibar (1806–56).

CLOVIS (?465–511), King of the Franks (*reg.* 481–511), son of Childeric I and the greatest of the early Merovingian kings. Between 486 and 496 he made himself master in Gaul by defeating Syagrius, the last representative of Roman rule in northern Gaul, the Thuringians, and, finally, the Alemanni and Visigoths. After his marriage to Clotilda, a Catholic Christian princess, he was himself baptized as an orthodox Catholic. This act immeasurably strengthened Frankish rule in Gaul by winning more support from the Gallo-Roman population and even that of the Byzantine emperor Anastasius at the height of the Arian controversy.

CLUB JEAN MOULIN, the best-known of the 'clubs' which are a feature of contemporary French politics. The discussion and promotion of reformist policies is their main function. The Club Jean Moulin, founded in 1958, draws its membership chiefly from intellectuals and civil servants, and seeks reforms of a modernizing, 'technocratic' character. Its ideas are liberal rather than socialist, but it has been allied politically with the Socialist Party, and helped promote the abortive presidential candidacy of Defferre (1963–5).

CLUBS, REVOLUTIONARY (1789), were formed by the deputies to the French states general for political discussion, and soon came to act as extra-parliamentary pressure groups. The Jacobin and Cordelier clubs were the most influential, but by 1791 there were numerous other clubs throughout Paris, which catered for the *sans-culottes* as well as the bourgeois politicians. Their influence on the regular insurrections was very important. The Jacobin club soon surpassed all others in significance and established a system of corresponding clubs throughout France, which reached more than 5000 in 1793 and were used to establish Jacobin authority over the whole country.

CLUNE, PATRICK JOSEPH (1864–1935), first Roman Catholic Abp of Perth, WA (1913–35), was born and ordained in Ireland. After service in the diocese of Goulburn, NSW, he returned home, joined the Redemptorists, moved with them to WA in 1899, and was appointed Bp of Perth in 1911. His warm personality and missionary zeal won admiration from Western Australians of all creeds. He supported conscription in 1916 and, while visiting Ireland and England in 1921, aided negotiations culminating in the Anglo–Irish treaty.

CLUNY, town in Burgundy, famous for the monastic order founded by the Benedictine monks of its abbey. The foundation of the abbey as a reformed house by William the Pious, Duke of Aquitaine, in 910 saw the first real attempt at the closer organization of the Benedictine order. Cluny itself was increasingly approached to reform other monasteries and gradually a succession of able abbots built up a network of client monasteries in every country in western Europe. The Cluniac order was distinguished by strict discipline and by exacting liturgical services. Its monks were usually nobles and the order prided itself on the eminence of its princely patrons and the large number of former Cluniacs among bishops and even popes.

CLYDE OF CLYDESDALE, COLIN CAMPBELL (né McIver), Baron (1792–1863), British soldier who served in many parts of the world and was raised to the peerage for his part in suppressing the Indian Mutiny. He fought in the Peninsular War, the China War (1842), and in India, where he commanded a brigade in the Second Sikh War (1848–9). After further active service on the North-West Frontier he returned to England in 1853. In the Crimean War he commanded the Highland Brigade that formed 'the thin red line'. During the Indian Mutiny he served as commander-in-chief. He relieved Lucknow (Nov. 1857) and later recovered Cawnpore. He suppressed the risings in Oudh and Rohilkhand, pursued the Rani of Jhansi, who was killed in action, and captured Tantia Topi.

CLYNES, JOHN ROBERT (1869–1949), British politician, trade union leader, and pioneer of the Labour movement. His aim was to establish the Labour Party as an independent Socialist political party, and he was a founder-member of the Independent Labour Party (ILP).

His conviction that Labour could only function properly when free of alliances kept him out of the first Coalition government of 1916; but with the deterioration of the military situation in the First World War he joined the second Coalition, and eventually became minister of food. After the war, while continuing to be active in trade union affairs, he became chairman of the Parliamentary Labour Party. In the first Labour government (1924) the party leadership fell largely on Clynes's shoulders because of MacDonald's pre-occupation with foreign affairs. In the industrial tension of these years he opposed the extremists, who advocated a general strike as a means of bringing about a socialist society in Britain.

In 1929 Labour returned to office, and Clynes became home secretary. In 1931 the Labour government collapsed, MacDonald having decided unilaterally upon a National government. Clynes was invited to lead the Labour opposition but, at his own suggestion, Arthur Henderson was nominated instead. In that year, he lost his seat in the National government landslide. He returned to parliament in 1935, but took no further part in government.

CNIDUS, BATTLE OF, (Aug. 394 BC) fought off Cnidus, north of Rhodes, the decisive victory in the Corinthian War of the Persian fleet under the Athenian Conon over the Spartans, which deprived them of the maritime empire inherited after the defeat of Athens (404).

CNOSSOS, most important centre of Minoan civilization in Crete. Its huge palace, famous for its sophisticated construction, drainage, and frescoes, was excavated from 1900 onwards by Sir Arthur Evans and others. It was begun *c.* 2000 BC, rebuilt after an earthquake, *c.* 1700, temporarily damaged by another earthquake, *c.* 1575, probably further damaged by the massive eruption of Thera, *c.* 1460, and subsequently occupied by a succession of belligerent Mycenaeans from mainland Greece (*c.* 1450–1100). Sometime, either early (*c.* 1380) or late (*c.* 1150), in the period of Mycenaean occupation, the palace was mysteriously destroyed. After the Dorians entered Crete (11th cent.) Cnossos retained only local importance as the rival of Gortyn.

CNUT (*c.* 995–1035), King of Denmark (*reg.* 1013–35), King of England (*reg.* 1017–35). Cnut, son of King Swein of Denmark, was acknowledged in 1016 as ruler of the Danes in England by Edmund, King of Wessex. Cnut succeeded to Wessex in 1017 when Edmund died. Though a young Viking warrior, he showed himself to be a statesman. In England he retained traditional law, but he exacted permanent taxation in the form of *Heregeld*, an army tax, to maintain his large army of mercenary housecarles and his fleet. In 1027 he visited Rome and gained trading concessions for English merchants. Cnut was deeply involved in Baltic politics, and for a time he ruled Norway. After his death England and Denmark drifted apart, following a contest for the succession between his sons, Harold and Harthacnut.

CNUT IV (*c.* 1040–86), King of Denmark and grandnephew of Cnut the Great. As king (*reg.* 1080–6) he tried to create a fixed system of taxation for state and church purposes, but heavy burdens caused his subjects to rebel. Having previously raided York Minster (1075), Cnut was preparing a large-scale invasion of England when his people slew him before the altar in Odense. The Church had him canonized, with little popular approval, in 1101.

COAL MINES ACT (1919) in Britain, granted miners a seven-hour day, as recommended by the Coal Industry Commission set up under Sir John Sankey in 1919. The Sankey Commission also considered the question of nationalization

of mines, but their majority report in favour of this was rejected by Lloyd George's government.

COAL MINES ACT (1930) in Britain, one of the major acts of the Labour government (1929–31). It attempted to restore the seven-hour day, but compromised on 7½ hours. The coal-owners were offered district production quotas with guaranteed minimum prices. Schemes of amalgamation were also to be encouraged by a Coal Mines Reorganization Commission, but this proved unsuccessful.

COALBROOKDALE, ironworks in Shropshire, England, close to the Severn river, where between 1709 and 1717 Abraham Darby first successfully smelted iron, using coke as a fuel instead of charcoal, and thus made possible the great expansion of iron-smelting later in the 18th cent.

COATES, JOSEPH GORDON (1878–1943), NZ statesman and administrator, who was elected as 'freehold' Independent Liberal in 1911 and joined the Reform Party in 1912. He was promoted (1919) to Massey's post-war ministry, and as minister of public works (1920–6) and railways (1923–8) showed exceptional vigour and initiative. In 1925, Coates became prime minister, following a spectacular newspaper campaign in his favour. After being defeated in 1928, he reorganized the Reform Party, but was compelled by party notables to join G. W. Forbes in a coalition (1931). In an unpopular 'depression' government, Coates stood out as a constructive planner, but a hated figure. After 1935 he was cast aside as leader, but defied his party (National) by remaining in Fraser's war cabinet, again with administrative success, until his death. Forthright but unstable, more at ease with civil servants than politicians, Coates never fulfilled his great promise as a leader.

COBB, HOWELL (1815–68), US politician from Georgia, and a key figure in the secessionist movement (1860–1). He belonged to the southern planter class, and was a Democratic congressman (1843–51, 1855–7). After a bitter struggle (1849) he was elected speaker of the House. Being at that time an opponent of extreme southern sectionalism, he refused to sign John C. Calhoun's 'Southern Address' (1849), supported the compromise of 1850, and joined Georgia Whigs in successful campaigns on behalf of the compromise and the Union (1850, 1851). Cobb was governor of Georgia (1851–3) and secretary of the treasury in Buchanan's administration (1857–60). After Lincoln's election (1860), he advocated immediate secession, and became chairman of the Montgomery convention which established the Southern Confederacy (Feb. 1861), but his earlier Unionist sympathies ruled him out as a possible president of the Confederacy. Throughout the Civil War he served in the Confederate army.

COBB, TYRUS RAYMOND (1886–1961), US baseball player. Known as the 'Georgia Peach'. For 12 seasons he led the American League in batting.

COBBETT, WILLIAM (1763–1835), British radical leader, tribune of the transition from rural to industrial England. The son of a small farmer-innkeeper in Farnham, Surrey, he was self-taught and served in the army in Canada (1784–91), until he was court-martialled for trying to expose a scandal in quarter-mastering. After this first experience of the wide-spread corruption in society, which he called 'The Thing', he went to France, tired of the Revolution, and emigrated to the US (1793–1800), where he discovered his true vocation as a journalist and political pamphleteer with his patriotic anti-French and pro-Federalist writings and his attacks on Tom Paine. After being heavily fined for libel, he fled to London. He declined invitations to write for Pitt's government and began his weekly *Political Register* (1802), denouncing faulty government finance, worthless paper money, and the locusts of fund holders and money-lenders devouring the land. He called London 'the great Wen'. As a sincere champion of the agricultural and, later, the industrial workers, he urged large-scale reform of parliament. His reports of current parliamentary debates (begun in 1804) were sold to Hansard (1812). After two years in Newgate gaol for attacking the army's flogging of freeborn Englishmen he produced his cheaper *Register*, called by his opponents 'Cobbett's Twopenny Trash', selling 40,000 copies weekly. He denounced the evils of the post-war slump and preached controlled agitation for objectives later adopted by the Chartists. In exile in the US (1817–19), after the Tories' suspension of *habeas corpus*, he wrote his *Grammar of the English Language*, combining grammatical rules with apt political examples. After returning home with the bones of his former opponent, Tom Paine, he threw himself into ebullient writing and agitation, championing Queen Caroline, fighting three libel actions, denouncing the Six Acts, and supporting Catholic Emancipation, though he quarrelled with O'Connell. His famous accounts of his journeys on horseback, *Rural Rides*, begun in 1821 and published in book form 1830, stand out as the best record of a lost England, combining vivid detail, fascinating digressions, and bold generalizations. These, together with his *Sermons* (1822) and *Advice to Young Men* (1829), show him as the pattern John Bull of the age, mixing robust wisdom, egotism, and satire with which to bombard his many enemies, ranging from Wilberforce to Malthus. He conducted his own campaign (1830–2) for the Reform Bill and secured acquittal from charges of inciting the agricultural labourers to violence in 1831. In 1832 he became MP for Oldham, but was too old an individualist to lead any organized group in parliament, though he made an excellent speech on factory reform (1833) and vehemently opposed the unneighbourly New Poor Law (1834).

In some ways a Tory, Cobbett wished to return to what he saw as the Golden Age of the yeomen of England before monopolists, usurers, 'Spinning-Jenny Baronets', railways, and effeminate habits like tea-drinking, ruined English society. His independent spirit and pugnacity in attacking injustice, corruption, and abuses made him a courageous and colourful radical. His own favourite work was his *Poor Man's Friend* (1826), 'a Defence of the Rights of those who do the Work and fight the Battles'.

G. D. H. Cole, *The Life of William Cobbett* (London, 1947).
W. Baring Pemberton, *William Cobbett* (London, 1949).

JRA

COBDEN, RICHARD (1804–65), British politician. He was born of Anglican yeoman stock and, though poorly educated, became the most intelligent ideologist of the early Victorian industrial middle class. He started a calico-printing business in Lancashire (1831). His activities in Manchester local politics prepared him for his greatest achievement—the successful attack on the corn laws through the Anti-Corn Law League (1839–46). His energy, fertility in campaigning ideas, and tactical shrewdness converted both the country and the prime minister, Sir Robert Peel. He sat as a radical MP from 1841 till his death, except for a brief interval (1857–9).

Unfortunately, his supporters did not share his internationalist and educational enthusiasms, and the rest of his career was beset with disappointment. On slavery, public education, and peace, the dissenters were incurably sectarian. Working men, whom Cobden always refused to flatter, flocked into the Chartist and trade union movements, whose class-consciousness he detested. The manufacturing middle classes realized that trade was more compatible with war and aristocracy than Cobden supposed, and therefore ran after aristocratic titles and classical culture, and prostrated themselves before Cobden's chauvinist *bête noire*, Lord Palmerston. But the Cobden–Chevalier treaty (1860) with France constituted a great personal triumph against aristocratic diplomacy. Cobden, though not indifferent to public health and factory reform legislation, was an ardent advocate of self-help, though the incompetence and corruption of the state and the formidable achievements of voluntary action made his outlook popular. His ideal seems to have been some form of local self-government, resting on cultivated and self-directed citizens peacefully tilling their smallholdings. He was unduly optimistic in assuming that foreign countries would level their protective barriers to enable Britain to remain the workshop of the world, but his charming, modest, and humane letters frequently show his amazement at John Bull's crudities and cruelties overseas.

Yet the fact that Cobden remained a political outsider throughout his lifetime distorted his political insight. He was much misunderstood, and misunderstood others, and he underestimated the competence, disinterestedness, and popularity of aristocratic government. His suspicions of it led him to reject offers of office (1847, 1859) and he refused to enter 'society' or to attend ministerial dinners. Though experience of office would have enabled him to grow intellectually, it would have damaged the reputation for consistency on which his political influence rested and also might have exposed his administrative incompetence.

J. Morley, *Life of Richard Cobden* (London, 1879).
I. Bowen, *Cobden* (London, 1935).   BHH

COBDEN CLUB, founded in London (1866) to campaign as a pressure group for Richard Cobden's political and economic principles—free trade, peace, and parliamentary reform. It had an annual dinner, first addressed by Gladstone in praise of Cobden, and paid for books, pamphlets, and meetings. Its members actively opposed Joseph Chamberlain in the Tariff Reform struggle.

COBHAM, RICHARD TEMPLE, 1st Viscount (1675–1740), British soldier and politician who served under Marlborough throughout his campaigns. In 1719 he commanded the expedition to Vigo. He was dismissed from his regiment in 1733 when he opposed Sir Robert Walpole's excise scheme. With Lyttelton and Grenville he formed the independent Whig faction known as 'the boy patriots'. He was granted the rank of field marshal (1742) and joined the coalition on Walpole's fall the same year. He was a life-long opponent of the subordination of English interests to Hanover.

COCCEJI, SAMUEL VON (1679–1755), Prussian chief justice. Early in his career, Cocceji, an ardent reformer, published a modernized version of the East Prussian code of law and some minor reforms in criminal procedure, but was hampered by Frederick William I's contempt for lawyers. Under Frederick II Cocceji aimed at establishing a single centralized judicial system with uniform procedure and one code of law for all Prussia's territories, the first two aims being fulfilled by 1751. He was unable to complete the legal code or to abolish administrative justice, which was jealously controlled by the provincial chambers, but he influenced later Prussian legal codification.

COCHIN-CHINA, name applied by Europeans to different parts of Viet-nam in different periods. Originally 'Cochin' was a corruption, by the Portuguese, of Kiao-Chi, and was used by them in the 16th cent. to indicate Tongking; 'China' was added to distinguish it from Cochin in India. In the 17th and 18th cents the name was applied to the Nguyen principality of central Viet-nam, which by 1770 had expanded its territory southwards to include the lower Mekong area conquered from Cambodia. Between 1860 and 1867 the French annexed this latter area, calling it henceforth 'French Cochinchina'; thereafter the name was applied exclusively to the southernmost part of Viet-nam. From 1946 to 1949 there existed, under French control, an 'autonomous state' of Cochin-China, but it was eventually absorbed into the Associated State of Viet-nam.

COCHISE (*c.* 1820–74), Chiricahua Apache Indian chief. Cochise and Mangas Coloradas, with their Apache bands, harassed Arizona settlements and fought US cavalry and California state militia (1862–71). Cochise surrendered (1871), then escaped, and with 800 men remained free until the summer of 1872. He persuaded his followers to settle on the Chiricahua Reservation in Arizona, where he died.

COCKAYNE, WILLIAM (d. 1626), alderman of the city of London, who attempted to undermine the Merchant Adventurers' privileges by promoting a project to dress and dye English cloth before export. It had been supported by James I, who granted the patent to Cockayne and his associates in return for promises of £300,000 per annum as the royal share of increased profits from exported finished cloth. The scheme collapsed (1614) because the new company was unable to match the skill of Dutch dyers and the cloth trade was dislocated by Dutch reprisals, eg, the prohibition of the import of dyed and finished cloth.

COCKCROFT, SIR JOHN (DOUGLAS) (1897–1967), British physicist and pioneer of atomic physics. Cockcroft worked in the Cavendish Laboratories, Cambridge, as a member of Lord Rutherford's research team. There, in 1932, he and E. T. S. Walton succeeded in splitting the atom. He became director of the Atomic Energy Research Establishment at Harwell (1946–58) and thereafter master of Churchill College, Cambridge (1958–67).

COCK-FIGHTING, favourite pastime in the ancient world, probably introduced into Britain by the Romans. Although condemned by the Puritans, it continued to be popular, especially during the Regency, until its legal abolition in 1849. All towns at one time had their cockpits and the sport attracted much gambling. It is still surreptitiously practised in parts of northern England.

COCKPIT, THE, residence in Whitehall, London, of Anne Stuart, later Queen Anne, and Prince George of Denmark. Given to them by Charles II after their marriage in 1683, it remained their home until Anne came to the throne (1702). It gained importance in William III's reign as a rival court and meeting place for important personages.

COCKPIT MEETING, eve-of-session meeting of British MPs who were thought to be favourable to the government, to hear the King's Speech read. Such meetings were probably held during most of the 18th cent.

COCONUT OIL in the Pacific, used after 1840 in the making of soap and candles, rapidly became the chief source of local income (in kind). In the 1870s the economy turned to copra (dried coconut meat), employing Gilbertese plantation labour. This precipitated a new land scramble and the final carving up of Pacific islands among colonial powers

CODDINGTON, WILLIAM (1601–78), American colonist and governor. His liberal religious views led him to Rhode Island (1638). He helped to found the city of Newport in Rhode Island and was its first governor. He attempted unsuccessfully to keep his colony of Rhode Island separate from Roger Williams's colony of Providence Plantations. Coddington later became a Quaker.

CODE HENRI (1811), corpus of laws promulgated by King Henri I (Cristophe), Negro sovereign of northern Haiti (1811–20). The code consisted of some 133 articles and shows Cristophe's authoritarian views. Exasperated by the decline in productivity after the Haitian wars of independence, he came to believe that permissive liberty had made the peasantry slothful. His solution was to curtail their freedom and force them back to intensive agricultural labour. The Code's aim was to reduce the peasantry to renewed serfdom by tying them to the soil and obliging them to perform assigned tasks involving hard labour.

CODE MICHAU, French royal ordinance of 1629, consisting of 461 articles, covering a wide number of subjects, eg, justice, military reorganization, the universities, parlements, and hospitals. The code was the work of Michel de Marillac, the keeper of the seals under Louis XIII (1626–30) and a protégé of Richelieu.

CODE NAPOLÉON (1804), name given from 1807 to the Civil Code imposed on all France by Napoleon as First Consul, and introduced into those areas of Europe directly controlled by him and his family. The Revolution had swept away the vestiges of feudalism, privilege, and the jumble of local legal codes, but had put nothing concrete in their place. Although the code was pushed through by Napoleon, it was not his own work. It retained the principle of equality, except for women, but reverted to a more reactionary view of civil relations and property.

CODE NOIR, issued by Louis XIV (1685), ordered the expulsion of the Jews from French colonies, the banning of all but Catholic religious practices in French colonies, and established the framework for the government of French slave societies. The overseers of slaves were to be Catholics and Christian slaves had the right to sacraments and to burial in consecrated ground. Slave marriages were to have the consent of the master, but were not to be enforced by him. The code detailed minimum standards for slaves in terms of clothing and food, and laid down rules about marriages between Europeans and slaves, and the position of their children. It prescribed heavy penalties, including death, for certain offences by slaves. Slaves could appeal to officials in cases of neglect and maltreatment by their masters. The code was superseded by the Code Napoléon (1805).

CODE OF CIVIL LAW. Codifications of Roman Law and collections of commentaries upon it were made from time to time from the 2nd cent. AD onwards. The most comprehensive and authoritative of these was ordered by Justinian, who set up a commission of jurists under Tribonian, which produced a code of civil law (corpus juris civilis). The commission collected in summary form all law then in force and added to it a wide range of precedents and interpretative commentary. The compilation, in three parts, the Code of Justinian, the Digest or Pandects, and the Institutes, appeared with some revisions between 529 and 534 AD. The Code was a collection of imperial enactments of general validity, the Digest a series of abstracts from famous jurists, and the Institutes a compact textbook for the use of law students. These works represented the unquestioned legal authority of the empire. They contained the sole valid statement of the law, were the only source of authentic reference in the courts, and comprised the single body of authorized material for study in the law schools. They became the foundation for the revival of the use and study of the Roman law in western Europe from the 11th cent. onwards.

CODE SAVARY (1673), one of the great French ordinances of Louis XIV's reign initiated by Colbert, establishing a code of commercial procedure.

CODEX, FREDERICIAN (1794), the culmination of the work in the reign of Frederick the Great of the Prussian jurists, Cocceji and Suarez, which covered civil, criminal, and administrative law and remained in force in Prussia until 1900. Although it recognized the equality of the individual, freedom of conscience, and the sanctity of property, the Codex also confirmed the hierarchical structure of Prussian society and the subjection of the serfs.

CODREANU, CORNELIU ZELEA (1899–1938), founder and leader of the Legion of the Archangel Michael, Rumania's most important fascist organization. Codreanu completed his military training just as the First World War ended, then joined the Guard of the National Conscience, a group of strike-breakers and street-fighters engaged in harassing left-wing radicals in Moldavia. His efforts to transform the guard into a political party—the National Christian Socialist Party—failed and instead he entered Jassy University. There he studied in the law faculty, then dominated by A. C. Cuza. Although Codreanu was expelled from the university for his political activities, Cuza's faculty awarded him a degree. Together with Cuza he formed the League of National Christian Defence (LANC) in 1923 and the next year set up the Brotherhood of the Cross, a nationalist youth movement. The prefect of Jassy sought to shackle his activities, so Codreanu shot him. During his trial for murder, at which Codreanu won considerable notoriety, the charge was dropped. But Codreanu's violent methods disturbed Cuza and caused dissension within LANC. In 1927 the movement split and in June Codreanu founded the Legion of the Archangel Michael. The Iron Guard, the militant political arm of the legion, was established in 1930. Three times the legion was dissolved by decree (1931, 1932, 1933), but its members continued to participate in elections as members of the All for the Fatherland Party. In 1937 Codreanu made an electoral pact with the National Peasant Party and at the polls the legion emerged as the third strongest party. King Carol II quarrelled with Codreanu and called a Cuza–Goga coalition to power. In 1938 Codreanu reached an accord with Goga and agreed to give up electoral politics. But Carol II asserted his authority and set out to crush the legion. Codreanu was arrested in March 1938 and sentenced to ten years' imprisonment for conspiracy against the state. In Nov. he and other convicted legionnaires were shot by prison officers.

CODRINGTON, CHRISTOPHER, the younger (1668–1710), English colonial administrator. He distinguished himself against the French in Flanders during the reign of William III, and succeeded his father as governor of the Leeward Islands (1699). Reforms which he introduced were resented by the great plantation owners, *eg*, an increase in the number of small settlers, and the rigorous application of laws restricting planters' trade to British ships plying between Britain and the West Indies. He also carried out an intensive revision of the law courts in the Leeward Islands. When war broke out with France (1701), Codrington advocated an immediate attack on Martinique, but the essential naval force arrived too late: accordingly, the attack was diverted to Guadeloupe, where much booty was taken, though permanent control by British troops proved impossible. Codrington bequeathed a library to All Souls College, Oxford, which placed it next in rank to the Bodleian. In Barbados, where he lived (1704–10), he left two sugar plantations to the Society for the Propagation of the Gospel, which used the funds to found Codrington College for training clergy to do missionary work in the West Indies.

CODRUS, descendant of Nestor of Pylos and legendary King of Athens in the 12th cent. BC, whose self-sacrifice saved Athens from the Heracleidae and whose sons subsequently led the Ionian migration. The legend owes much to 5th-cent. Athenian imperial propaganda.

CODY, WILLIAM F. (1846–1917), US buffalo hunter, known as 'Buffalo Bill', who worked on behalf of railroad construction camps on the American prairies. He was also an army scout during the Civil and Sioux Wars, and proprietor of a famous Wild West show.

COEN, JAN PIETERSZOON (1587–1629), founder of Dutch power in the Indonesian archipelago. In March 1619 Coen became the fourth governor-general of the Dutch East India Co. In the following May he led a military force which defeated the indigenous residents of Djakarta, and the Dutch fort there was made the company's headquarters with the name of Batavia. Coen is also remembered as the initiator of the brutal policy of extirpation in the Molucca islands, in the east of the archipelago, introduced in order to protect the Dutch spice monopoly by wiping out the recalcitrant population, who were to be replaced by Dutch colonists. In 1623 Coen returned to the Netherlands, but in 1624 was again appointed governor-general. He took up his post only in 1627 after managing to return to Batavia despite British attempts to prevent his departure from Holland. During his second administration Batavia was twice besieged unsuccessfully by Javanese forces under Sultan Agung. Coen died during the second siege.

CŒUR, JACQUES (*c*. 1395–1456), French merchant of the 15th cent., whose enterprises and agents covered much of France and western Europe. His loans contributed greatly to the French reconquest of Normandy in 1449–50, but he was suddenly imprisoned and ruined (1451) by Charles VII, who perhaps did this in order to avoid repaying royal debts due to Cœur, who died in exile.

COFFEE HOUSES were important in London as centres of social and cultural life (*c*. 1660–1800). Coffee, drinking chocolate, and liquors were sold to patrons, who gathered to gossip, play cards, and hear and read the latest news. Some were centres of business (Jonathans) or insurance (Lloyd's) where merchants and stock-jobbers gathered. Others were meeting places for political factions of Whigs and Tories (St James's), for literary men such as Addison and Steele (Will's), for wits and artists (Bedford), for scholars, antiquarians, and members of the learned professions. There were over 3000 coffee houses in London by 1700, but they declined with the growth of private clubs, of which White's (1736) was the first.

COFRADÍA, or confraternity, a voluntary association of members enlisted from a village or craft in Latin America and Spain. The institution arrived in America with the Spaniards and was sanctioned by the Church in the colonial period as a socio-religious organization useful for maintaining hospitals and institutions of public assistance. Indians were also organized in *cofradías*. These religious, philanthropic guilds multiplied in the 17th and 18th cents and members were frequently required to serve the village priest personally. The *cofradía* was guided by its chaplain and elected officers who celebrated the feast day of its patron saint with pomp and ceremony. Each craft guild was also organized as a *cofradía*.

COG, large single-masted ship, first used in the Baltic and the North Sea. It developed during the course of the 12th–13th cent. and was in general use in the Atlantic trade by the mid-14th cent. It had stern- and fore-castles and a square-ended stern. It was the first type of ship to be fitted with a stern-rudder rather than a steering-oar. Some of its features were combined with the Mediterranean types of shipping to produce the superior carracks of the 15th cent.

COGHLAN, SIR CHARLES PATRICK JOHN (1863–1927), first prime minister (1923) of Southern Rhodesia, where he had practised as a solicitor.

COGHLAN, SIR TIMOTHY AUGUSTINE (1856–1920), Sydney-born statistician and economic historian, who became the first head of the NSW government department of statistics in 1886. He was agent-general for NSW in London (1905–26). He wrote *Labour and Industry in Australia from the first Settlement in 1788 to the Establishment of the Commonwealth in 1901* (1918).

COGNAC, TREATY OF (1526), created a league of France, the papacy under Pope Clement VII, Venice, and Florence (May 1526). The treaty repudiated the agreement made by Francis I while still a prisoner in Madrid (Jan. 1526). The French king turned to the Italian states for support, anticipating a renewed struggle with Charles V in Italy. Ostensibly to promote peace by preserving the balance of power in Italy, the league of Cognac presented a challenge to imperial preponderance. Charles responded by invading Italy (1527) and sacking Rome.

COGNIOT, GEORGES (1901–), a leader of the French Communist Party, and its chief expert on educational questions. He was a founder of the review *La Pensée*. Cogniot first entered parliament in 1936, and has been a senator since 1959.

COHEN, FRANCIS LYON (1863–1934), rabbi of the Sydney Great Synagogue, the mother congregation of Australian Jewry (1905–34), was chairman of its ecclesiastical court (Beth Din). He founded the Jewish Lads' Brigade in London, was first Jewish chaplain in the British army, and, later, chief Hebrew chaplain in Australia. He was an authority on synagogal music, and author of *The Voice of Prayer and Praise*.

COHENS v. VIRGINIA, 6 Wheaton 264 (1821), US Supreme Court case in which Chief Justice Marshall reaffirmed the court's right to consider cases on appeal from state courts. The Cohens were convicted by a VA court of selling lottery tickets in violation of state law. They appealed to the Supreme Court, claiming the protection of an act of Congress authorizing a lottery for the District of Columbia. Marshall, while upholding the state court's decision, asserted the Supreme Court's power to review state court decisions.

CO-HONG, group of 13 Chinese mercantile firms in Canton licensed in 1720 to trade with foreign merchants. They had a semi-official status and were responsible for the payment of taxes and fees and for seeing that the foreign merchants abided by the restrictive regulations imposed by the Chinese government. Despite the many abuses of the system, the *Co-Hong* merchants coped well with the situation and had the full confidence of the foreign traders. But the abolition of the British East India Co. in 1833 created many legal, diplomatic, and commercial problems which the *Co-Hong* were ill-equipped to handle. These problems finally led to the Opium War, after which the *Co-Hong* were abolished.

COHORT, unit of the ancient Roman army. Originally it denoted the infantry formation of its allied contingents, and was first used as a legionary unit, consisting of three maniples, by Scipio Africanus in Spain (210–206 BC). After Marius' reforms (104–101 BC) the cohort became the regular tactical unit of the legion, which consisted of ten cohorts, each divided into six centuries. The cohorts of the auxiliary troops consisted of 500 or 1000 men and the Praetorian Guard, the *Vigiles*, and the urban troops were organized into cohorts of 1000.

COILLARD, FRANÇOIS (1834–1904), French Protestant missionary in Lesotho (Basutoland) (1857) and from 1884 in Bulozi (Barotseland, now western part of Zambia), where he became adviser to the Lozi king, Lewanika.

COIMBRA, ancient university town of Portugal and centre of the budding Portuguese Renaissance in the late 15th cent. Under the humanist Cataldo Parisio, formerly of Padua, it became the stronghold of Catholic theology of the Counter-Reformation. The Jesuits established a missionary training school in Coimbra, which became associated with the order. From the 17th cent. Coimbra gradually sank in intellectual status, until it was reformed by Pombal in the 1770s.

COINAGE, DEBASEMENT OF THE, reducing the mineral content of currency by the addition of alloy, brings short-term advantages to the government, which can increase the output of coins without using more precious metal; but by the operation of Gresham's law, that 'bad money drives out good', it ultimately defeats its object by causing prices to rise. Henry VIII debased the coinage to finance his French war

(1544) and made an immediate profit, but further debasements until 1551 led to the hoarding of 'good' money, drove up prices, and so far reduced foreign and domestic confidence in English currency that Northumberland had to restore its original value. Mary and Elizabeth followed him and by 1560 confidence had been largely recovered. The 'lightening' of the currency is still punishable by heavy terms of imprisonment.

COINAGE, GREEK, first struck in electrum by Ionian cities *c.* 620 BC in imitation of earlier Lydian regal issues. Aegina, Corinth, and Athens (*c.* 550) followed with silver coins bearing the city's patron deity (*eg*, Athena at Athens) and/or peculiar emblem (*eg*, Aegina's turtle). In the 6th cent. mints sprang up throughout Greece, with important exceptions, *eg*, Sparta. In the 5th cent. Athenian coins were dominant and Athens tried unsuccessfully to close down allied mints. In Sicily, Syracuse minted coins of great artistic quality. In the 4th cent. Persian darics encouraged the issue of gold coins, *eg*, by Macedon. In the Hellenistic kingdoms bronze and copper were increasingly used and the ruler's head first appeared on coins.

COINAGE, ROMAN, first struck in silver *c.* 269 BC after the remarkably long survival of rough bronze bars as the medium of exchange. The silver *denarius* became standard 169 BC; bronze coins were also minted, but gold rarely. Early designs were religious or national in character, but historical references occurred increasingly in the 1st cent. BC. Julius Caesar was the first living Roman to be portrayed on coins. Later, coinage was controlled by the emperors, being used extensively as a medium of propaganda. Roman coinage replaced other currencies in the west during the 1st cent. AD, and in the east during the 3rd. Catastrophic depreciation of silver coinage occurred in the 3rd cent., but Constantine the Great created a stable gold coinage (72 *solidi* to the pound of gold), which remained the standard for centuries.

COINAGE ACT (1792), US legislation establishing a decimal, bimetallic currency. As the 15–1 ratio of silver to gold undervalued gold, and the weight of the silver dollar exceeded that of the Spanish dollar still in circulation, the new national system failed.

'COIN'S FINANCIAL SCHOOL' (1894) US propaganda pamphlet by William Hope Harvey (1851–1936), supporting bimetallism, in which the suave financial genius, 'Coin', was shown lecturing to businessmen and journalists on gold monometallism as the main cause of the 1893 depression. It was widely circulated in cheap editions and prepared the way for Bryan's 1896 'free silver' presidential campaign.

COKE, SIR EDWARD (1552–1634), English lawyer and parliamentarian. He entered public life under Lord Burghley and was successively solicitor-general (1592), speaker of the Commons (1593), and attorney-general (1594). As attorney-general he championed the Crown and its prerogative courts, and brutally conducted the great treason trials of the Earls of Essex and Southampton (1601), Sir Walter Raleigh (1603), and the Gunpowder plotters (1605). In 1606 he became chief justice of the court of common pleas and began to defend the common law against the king's prerogative, a position he maintained after his elevation to the office of chief justice of the king's bench and to the privy council (1613). Collision with James I was inevitable, and in 1616 he was dismissed. He worked his way back into public life and the privy council by marrying his daughter to Buckingham's brother. He was a leading member of the opposition in the 1620 Commons, opposing Prince Charles's proposed Spanish marriage and helping to draw up charges against his former rival, Francis Bacon. He was imprisoned for nine months (1621) after defending the liberties of parliament, but his views triumphed in the Petition of Right (1628), in which he moulded ancient precedents into a charter of liberty limiting the royal prerogative.

COKE, THOMAS (1747–1814), British Anglican clergyman, who joined the Methodists, twice becoming president of the English Methodist conference. He visited the US on many occasions and had the title 'bishop' conferred on him by the American Methodist Conference (1787). He wrote a *History of the West Indies* (1808–11) and was part-author of a life of John Wesley.

COLBERT, JEAN-BAPTISTE, Marquis de Seignelay (1619–83), principal minister of Louis XIV (1661–83), whose protectionist economic programme in France made him the most famous exponent of mercantilism in Europe.

Born at Rheims, the son of a wealthy master-draper, Colbert became a secretary in the ministry of war under Le Tellier (*c.* 1640), and entered the service of Mazarin (1651), rising to become his chief assistant and business manager, a position which enabled him to purchase the barony of Seignelay (1657). After Mazarin's death (1661) Colbert encouraged Louis XIV to order Fouquet's arrest and to abolish the office of *surintendant*; instead, a new council of finance was established, in which Colbert sat as *intendant des finances*. On 1 Jan. 1664 he became director-general of buildings, arts, academies, and manufactures, and in 1669 controller-general of finances and secretary of state. However, he was effectively Louis's chief financial adviser from Sept. 1661 and as such initiated a rigorous policy of protection and regulation designed to establish France's economic hegemony in Europe.

Colbert aimed at centralization and economy in financial administration, and his work resulted in the creation of a more disciplined bureaucracy in France. He tried to raise the standards of office-holding (1665) and instituted an enquiry into the usurpation of noble status. Royal *intendants* were forced to send detailed reports to Paris of provincial administration. To rationalize the tax structure he began the unification of internal customs duties through the *cinq grosses fermes* (1664). He dealt harshly with the *rentiers* to reduce the funded debt. He carried through a debt conversion (1661–4) and in 1665 established a fixed interest rate of 5 per cent, although the outbreak of the Dutch war (1672) forced him to raise new loans and to resort to sale of offices.

An important element in his protectionism was the tariff system. After infant industries had been established with the help of foreign artisans, he reversed his freer tariff policy of 1664 to one of almost total prohibition of imports (1667). Meanwhile, since industrial self-sufficiency was considered vital for a healthy balance of payments he not only encouraged private industrial ventures, but stimulated the *manufactures royales* with subsidies and monopolies (1663–73). Industry was regulated through a hierarchy of *intendants*, inspectors, and magistrates (1669) and a strengthened guild system (1673), administering some 200 ordinances introduced by Colbert. Although he gave encouragement to certain agricultural activities, *eg*, horse-breeding and forestry, arable farming and vine cultivation were sacrificed by the 1664 and 1667 tariff arrangements to the needs of manufacturing industries.

Internal commerce was stimulated by the construction of roads and canals, *eg*, the Canal du Midi (1666–81), and overseas trade by an ambitious colonizing programme in India, West Africa, and the Americas. The American and African trade was entrusted to the Co. of the West (1664) and the French East India Co. was founded (1664). Demobilized soldiers were granted farmland in Canada and provided with tools, seed, stock, and wives. Colbert ordered the rebuilding of the merchant marine to sustain this overseas empire. Great arsenals were built at Rochefort and Toulon, naval enlistment was organized (1669, 1673), and the fleet was increased by 1672 to the size of the combined British and Dutch fleets.

His interests were not confined to the economic sphere. Colbert undertook the last great codification of the civil and criminal codes in the *ancien régime* (1667–9, 1670). He sought to enhance Louis XIV's image of majesty through government patronage of science and the arts. He initiated a public building programme in Paris, established academies of architecture (1671) and music (1672), and created the French Academy of Sciences (1666), persuading Louis to finance the first modern scientific expedition to Cayenne (1672).

Colbert amassed a personal fortune and was as much a nepotist as his ministerial predecessors: his son, Seignelay, and his nephews, Torcy and Desmaretz, all succeeding to high office. Many of his schemes ended in failure or created hardship, yet his indefatigable energy and devotion to royal authority made him the ideal servant for the ambitious Louis XIV.

G. Mongrédien, *Colbert 1619–1683* Paris, 1963).   MKS

COLBERT, WILLIAM (*c.* 1755–*c.* 1820), Chickasaw war chief, who aided the US in the American War of Independence. After the war he led the Chickasaw in Gen. Arthur St Clair's army in assaults against tribes in the Ohio river valley. He served for nine months in the US army during the War of 1812 and after leaving the army led his warriors against hostile Creeks. As the head of a Chickasaw delegation to Washington, DC (1816), he was styled a general. He was one of the many half-breed sons of James Colbert (*c.* 1730–83), a Scot who came to the Chickasaw nation about 1750 and fought for the British in the American War of Independence.

COLBERTISM, protectionist economic policy, mercantilist in outlook, initiated in France by Louis XIV's minister, Colbert, in the later 17th cent. By taxing imports heavily and instituting paternalistic regulations for French industry, it was hoped to stimulate the economy and make it self-sufficient. When carried to extremes by Colbert's successors, the system provoked retaliatory policies in England and the Dutch Republic, France's chief trading rivals.

COLBY, BAINBRIDGE (1869–1950), US lawyer and politician. Originally a Republican, then a Progressive (1912), Colby became a Wilsonian Democrat when Theodore Roosevelt rejected the Progressive presidential nomination in 1916. As Wilson's last secretary of state (1920–1), he sought to protect US interests in the settlements that followed negotiation of the treaty of Versailles.

COLCHESTER, CHARLES ABBOT, 1st Baron (1757–1829), British politician and speaker of the House of Commons (1802–16). Generally regarded as an outstandingly able and impartial speaker, he became a close associate of Addington and was prominent as chairman of the finance committee of 1797. In 1800 he moved for a committee on the care of public records, and in the same year introduced the first Census Act. He was Irish secretary for a few months in 1801. In 1805, after the Commons had divided 216–216 on Whitbread's resolutions attacking Melville, Pitt's closest associate, it fell to Abbot, as speaker, to give a casting vote. He gave it, in a scene of the greatest tension, against Melville, thereby widening the rift between Pitt and Addington. In 1810 he issued the warrant committing Sir Francis Burdett to the Tower, the legality of which was challenged by Burdett.

COLD HARBOR, BATTLE OF (3 June 1864), engagement during the American Civil War. Grant's Union army, pressing southwards after the Wilderness and Spotsylvania campaigns, was repulsed by Lee at Cold Harbor, six miles (9 kms) north-east of Richmond, the Confederate capital. Union losses were severe, numbering over 12,000 during the battle and preceding skirmishes.

COLD WAR, the relationship between the Soviet Union and its satellites and the 'Western powers'—principally the US—in the period following the Second World War, characterized by continuous tension between them, aggressive actions with limited objectives which were not allowed to grow into major conflict, and extreme difficulty in the attainment of diplomatic agreements, in spite of a continuous succession of conferences.

The Cold War is generally dated from 1947, with the rejection of the Marshall Plan by the Soviet Union (June) and the breakdown of the London Conference on Germany (Dec.) to the death of Stalin (March 1953). It was most intense at the time of the Czech *coup d'état* (Feb. 1948), the Berlin blockade (June 1948–May 1949), and the Korean war (June 1950–July 1953). The Berlin blockade can be seen as the most typical contest in the Cold War: it began when the Soviet Union cut all communication between Berlin and the west after prolonged negotiations between the four powers occupying Germany had failed to produce agreement; it involved the use of coercive force in the imposition of the blockade—but the western powers decided to supply Berlin by air rather than try to break the blockade, and their flights over the Soviet zone were not opposed by Soviet forces; the conflict did not extend beyond Berlin; the opening move in negotiations which brought the blockade to an end was not made through normal diplomatic channels but in a comment by Stalin to an American journalist.

While there is general agreement in dating the most intense period of the Cold War, there is great diversity among historians in identifying its origins. The Truman doctrine (March 1947), the succession of Truman to the American presidency (April 1945), and the Yalta conference (Feb. 1945) have all been seen as starting points, while other writers have traced the origins of the Cold War to the Russian revolution of 1917 and the Allied intervention which followed it. Similarly, the Cold War can be seen as continuing until the present time. In addition, the phrase is sometimes used to refer to other chronic states of tension, *eg*, between the Arab states and Israel, or between rival camps within the Arab world, or between India and Pakistan.

Historians of the Cold War have generally taken the view that it owed its origins to the expansionism of the Soviet Union supported by communist parties under Stalinist direction throughout the world—expansionism to which the western powers reacted by the policy of containment, including the formation of NATO and the mobilizing of United Nations forces in Korea. However, this view has been challenged by a 'revisionist' school [including D. F. Fleming in *The Cold War and Its Origins* (1961); David Horowitz in *The Free World Colossus* (1965)], which attributes the Cold War variously to the failure of the US to uphold a division of the world into spheres of influence and to aggressive actions on its part.

Wilfrid Knapp, *A History of War and Peace 1939–65* (London, 1967).
Walter Lippmann, *The Cold War* (New York, 1947).

WFK

COLDEN, CADWALLADER (1688–1776), English public servant and man of learning. After graduating from Edinburgh University and studying medicine in London, Colden became a doctor and merchant in Philadelphia. He moved to New York (1720) and served as surveyor-general, and lieutenant governor (1761–76). He was a man of great versatility of mind, being interested in history, mathematics, botany, medicine, and philosophy. He corresponded with Linnaeus, Benjamin Franklin, and Samuel Johnson. He classified the flora of New York according to Linnaeus's system, wrote a treatise on stereotyping, and many medical treatises, *eg*, on yellow fever, throat distemper, and cancer.

COLDSTREAM GUARDS, the second regiment of foot guards and, next to the Royal Scots, the oldest regiment in the British army. They were formed for Gen. Monk in Scotland (1650) and took their name from their halt at the Border village of Coldstream before marching into England to accomplish the Stuart Restoration. Their motto is *Nulli Secundus*. The regiment served with distinction in many campaigns, notably at Namur (1695), Gibraltar (1704–5), Oudenarde and Malplaquet (1608–9), Dettingen (1743), the Peninsula and Waterloo (1808–15), the Crimea (1854–6), and on several fronts during the two World Wars.

COLE, GEORGE DOUGLAS HOWARD (1889–1959), British economic and social historian and a prominent figure in the Socialist movement. Cole, a pacifist in the First World War, developed his interests in Socialism while an undergraduate. From the early 1920s on, he worked on economics and the history of working-class movements, publishing over 50 volumes in these fields (many jointly with his wife, Margaret). At first a supporter of Guild Socialism, he later turned to the Fabian Movement. In the Second World War he made an important contribution to social policy through his organization of Nuffield College's Social Reconstruction Survey.

COLEBROOKE–CAMERON COMMISSION (1832), royal commission sent out to Ceylon by Britain to investigate financial and other conditions in its Asian colonies. Maj. Colebrooke arrived in 1829 and Mr Cameron in 1830, the latter to study judicial conditions. Their report is a landmark in the island's constitutional, administrative, and judicial development. Colebrooke recommended that the separate administration of the former Kandyan kingdom should be ended, and the whole island brought under a unified administration; that an Executive and a Legislative Council should be established, the latter to include both European and Ceylonese unofficial members; that compulsory service (*rajakariya*) on public works should be done away with; and that government monopolies, particularly of trading in cinnamon, should be abolished. His financial proposals, especially the reduction in the number and in the salaries of civil servants, were less satisfactory, and had unfortunate effects on the service for some years. Cameron recommended a large-scale reform of the judicial system by setting up a supreme court, unifying all other courts, bringing in *habeas corpus*, and retaining the jury system, which had been earlier introduced. Both commissioners advocated the opening of higher posts in the administrative and judicial services to Ceylonese, but this was not really acted upon for many years.

Despite objections from the governor, whose autocratic powers would be modified by the adoption of these recommendations, they were practically all accepted by the British government. The Executive Council consisted entirely of officials. The Legislative Council had an official majority, but was reinforced by three European and three Ceylonese, a Sinhalese, a Tamil, and a Muslim, unofficial members. After 15 years the Legislative Council was given the right to scrutinize expenditure and taxation. This constitution subsisted practically unaltered until the early 19th cent. and became the model for Crown colony government elsewhere in the British empire.

G. C. Mendis, *The Colebrooke–Cameron Papers* (London, 1956).

SAP

COLENSO, WILLIAM (1811–99), missionary printer and authority on the Maori language and people. He set up a press at Paihia, Bay of Islands, NZ, where he produced numerous religious works in Maori (1835–42) and printed Hobson's first proclamations and the treaty of Waitangi (1840).

COLET, JOHN (*c*. 1467–1519), English humanist, friend of More and Erasmus, and founder of St Paul's School (1506). He was a son of a lord mayor of London, and was educated at Oxford, whence he returned after studying in Europe. His lectures at Oxford on the New Testament made a deep impression. He was dean of St Paul's (1505–19) and used his father's fortune to endow a school where 153 pupils (a number chosen from the miraculous draught of fishes, John 21) should be taught 'a good Christian life and manners'. The grammarian Lily was the first high-master. Although Colet was conservative in his doctrinal views and looked to the Church to reform itself through its own institutions, he stressed the literal as opposed to the allegorical sense of the gospels and epistles, and his spirit of free enquiry was characteristic of 'the New Learning'.

COLIGNY, GASPARD DE CHATILLON, Count of (1519–72), French noble of the house of Montmorency, admiral of France, and leader of the Huguenots in the civil wars after Condé's death (1569). He was also one of the first Frenchmen to attempt to found an overseas empire, by financing expeditions to Canada, Brazil, and Florida to establish Huguenot settlements.

Although a convert to Protestanism, Coligny remained a fervent royalist, and sought only religious freedom for the reformed churches in France. Under his leadership the Huguenots came to dominate the towns and provinces of south and western France, and victory in the third civil war (1568–70) gave them the right to exercise their religion in these areas and to garrison four towns (1570). In 1570, Coligny returned to court and in the king's council pressed for a united French attack on the Netherlands to support the Dutch rebels against Spain. Despite Charles IX's favour Coligny was unable to dominate the queen mother, who plotted unsuccessfully to have him murdered. In the revived mood of religious bitterness of 1572 Catherine de Medici persuaded her son Charles to crush the Huguenot leaders. In the ensuing purge, known as the Massacre of St Bartholomew (23 Aug. 1572) Coligny was murdered on the orders of the Duke de Guise.

COLLECTIVE SECURITY. After 1919 it was widely felt that the pre-1914 alliances had been chiefly responsible for the outbreak of the First World War, and that a system of collective security should be designed to contain acts of aggression as breaches of the peace. Alliances in defence of the national interest would thus be rendered unnecessary. Resistance to aggression would follow from an inclusive system to maintain international order even when immediate national interests were not affected.

The League of Nations enjoined responsibility for collective security on all its members and France, in pursuit of its own security, championed the ideal after the lapse of the proposed Anglo–American guarantee of her frontiers. The 1923 Draft Treaty of Mutual Assistance and the 1924 Geneva Protocol represented the most serious attempts to provide formal machinery for the fulfilment of league members' obligations. But they were never ratified because of the difficulty of defining aggression, and because of the British objection to a degree of military preparedness which they thought inimical to peace (and which cut across Commonwealth obligations). Collective security was closely linked to disarmament, which was seen by some as itself contributing to security (the British view) and by others as a further development once security had been achieved (as the French thought).

The idea of collective security and the use of economic sanctions to contain aggression without the use of force won considerable popularity, especially in Britain. But the Manchurian crisis of 1931 revealed the weaknesses of the league system. In 1935 the British government found itself pressed by public opinion (and the small powers of the league) into a policy of sanctions against Italy which, being incomplete and lacking the full support of France, was bound to fail. Subsequently the term 'collective security' has been used to refer to the system of security which the UN sought to establish, and has been extended to cover what are in fact old-style alliances such as NATO.   ASJ

COLLECTOR, official responsible for the collection of the revenues in British India. In 1772 Warren Hastings was faced with the stupendous task of taking over the revenue administration and English collectors were appointed, but in the next year they were replaced by Indians. In 1781 the English collectors were reappointed to the various districts, but were not placed in complete charge of the revenue collections until 1786. In 1793 Cornwallis separated the revenue and judicial functions, thus depriving the collector of his magisterial powers. Cornwallis's policy was reversed between 1821 and the arrival of Bentinck as governor-general, and not, as is

often supposed, after Bentinck's arrival. From 1886 onwards the Indian National Congress passed frequent resolutions deploring this union of the executive and judicial functions. The chief objections to separation, unassailable as an abstract principle, were those of cost.

COLLÈGE DE FRANCE, founded in 1530 by Francis I with the advice of Guillaume Budé and formerly called the *Collège royale*. It was based on humanistic principles, with an emphasis on Greek and Latin literature. Although opposed at first by the Sorbonne, the college was united with the university in 1772.

COLLEGIA, Roman associations, of private persons forming a club or guild, or of public officials forming a college of magistrates or priests. Private *collegia* consisted of men of the same craft or trade, of young men for sport and recreation, or of ex-servicemen. Freedom of association was allowed, provided that the aims and actions of the members were legal, until 1st cent. BC, when *collegia* became used for political activities. Many were suppressed in 64 and again by Julius Caesar. Under Augustus each *collegium* had to be approved by the Senate and the emperor. Subsequent imperial policy towards *collegia* varied, but they aroused little suspicion after AD 100.

COLLEGIATE SYSTEM, type of educational organization, originating with the medieval universities, *eg,* Paris and Oxford, in the 13th cent., which has continued as an element in western European education to the present day (1970). The earliest colleges were hospices endowed by some benefactor for poor scholars who studied under university masters and gave educational guidance to the junior students living with them in hired residences. Gradually the endowed houses became recognized as legal corporations or colleges. The tutorial system, an essential ingredient of college life, developed strongly in Oxford and later in Cambridge, but declined in Paris, where the powerful influence of the university swamped the autonomy of the colleges.

Following the development of colleges at the universities, the system started also among the secular clergy in England. New collegiate churches, with their own schools, were established from the mid-13th cent. until the Reformation. Unlike the university college, where education was the prime aim, the principal purpose of the collegiate church was preparation for religious services. A landmark in the development of the collegiate system came in 1382 when the foundation deeds were drawn up for William of Wykeham's 'Saint Marie College of Winchester'. Not only was Winchester larger than earlier colleges, its main purpose was the education of the boys as a preparation for further study at the twin foundation of New College, Oxford, rather than their religious training. It was the model for another important foundation, that of Eton College (1440), from which scholars progressed to King's College, Cambridge.

The Renaissance influence of humanism gave a new impetus to the collegiate system from the late 15th cent. Colleges such as the school at Deventer founded by the Brethren of the Common Life added the element of character-development to the established function of academic instruction in Latin grammar and rhetoric. Moreover, with the coming of the Reformation religious indoctrination gave new strength to the moral training inspired by revived interest in Greek studies. Both the Protestant foundation of John Sturm at Strasbourg (1538) and the large numbers of colleges for boys established by the Jesuit order from the later 16th cent. emphasized moral education.

The collegiate system was later revived by British educationists, who applied it, not only in 19th-cent. university colleges, but in the founding of public schools, theological colleges, and teachers' training colleges. At Rugby, Thomas Arnold emphasized the concept of 'Godliness and good learning' which became the pattern for the public schools.

The future prime minister, W. E. Gladstone, was similarly

influenced in founding Trinity College, Glenalmond (1847), a unique combination of public school and theological college in Scotland, while Bp Samuel Wilberforce founded a theological college at Cuddesdon (1854) and a training college for schoolmasters at Culham (1852) within his diocese of Oxford. Examples of collegiate education, such as these, became particularly widespread in 19th- and 20th-cent. Britain. Nevertheless, a trend against the collegiate system, particularly in the attitude of those *in statu pupillari*, had become apparent by 1970.

W. Boyd, *The History of Western Education* (London, 1964).

MKS

COLLETT, JOHN (1758–1810), Norwegian farmer of English origins who introduced into Norway the improved farming methods of agriculture being practised in England.

COLLIER, JEREMY (1650–1726), non-juring divine who made a celebrated attack on the stage in his *Short View of the Immorality and Prophaneness of the English Stage* (1698).

COLLIER, JOHN (1884–1968), educator, author, and US Commissioner of Indian Affairs (1933–45). His main purpose was to increase the (American) Indians' self-sufficiency and to allow them self-government, and his policies transformed the US governmental attitude towards the Indian. He made changes in the Indian education system and re-emphasized tribal life. Collier created an interest in Indian art, music, folklore, and customs. He later became professor of Sociology and Anthropology at City College, NY.

COLLIER, PHILIP (1874–1948), Labor prime minister of Western Australia (1924–30, 1933–6), who migrated from Victoria to the WA goldfields in 1904, and sat in the state legislature (1905–48). His first term of office saw great agricultural expansion. A solitary but effective leader, he held his party together during the world-wide economic Depression which split the Labor movement in most parts of Australia, and he successfully damped down a strong movement for secession from the Australian Commonwealth, which had been quickened by the distress suffered by primary producers in WA in the early 1930s.

COLLINGS, JESSE (1831–1920), British politician and Birmingham associate of Joseph Chamberlain. He advocated 'three acres and a cow', founded the Agricultural Reform Movement, and carried the Allotments Act (1887) and the Smallholdings Act (1892). He left the Liberal government over Home Rule (1886) and served under Lord Salisbury (1895–1902).

COLLINGWOOD OF COLDBORNE AND HETHPOOLE, CUTHBERT COLLINGWOOD, Baron (1750–1810), British admiral. Collingwood, who was at sea for 45 years with scarcely a break, fought in the American War of Independence and in the Revolutionary and Napoleonic wars, assuming command at Trafalgar upon Nelson's death (1805).

COLLINS, DAVID (1756–1810), Australian colonial administrator, was born in London and joined the army at 14. He was deputy judge-advocate in NSW from its foundation (1788) to 1797, and his *Account* of the colony is excellent. In 1803 Collins founded Hobart Town, and stayed there as lieutenant-governor until his death.

COLLINS, SIR JOHN AUGUSTINE (1899–), Australian vice-admiral, was born at Deloraine, Tas., and served in the Royal Australian Navy in both World Wars, achieving distinction for his sinking of the Italian cruiser *Bartolomeo Colleoni* in 1940. He was the first Australian to become chief of the naval staff (1947–55) and was high commissioner to New Zealand (1956–62).

COLLINS, MICHAEL (1890–1922), leader of the Irish struggle for independence. He had become interested in the Republican movement while working in London, and took part in the Dublin rising of Easter 1916. After a brief period of detention, Collins threw himself into Sinn Fein politics, being elected member of the Dail in the 1918 general election.

In 1919 the Dail met and declared for Irish independence and a republic; Collins took charge of home affairs and, later, finance. His major work in the ensuing 'Troubles', the struggle with the British government, was, however, his organization of the Irish Republican Army. In three years, as he built an intelligence network of unprecedented efficiency, and directed the guerrilla attacks on the British authorities, he laid the foundation of eventual victory.

A truce was concluded in July 1921. Collins played an important part in the negotiations with Lloyd George's government that followed, and strongly supported the peace treaty signed by both parties in Dec. But the treaty, which provided for Irish partition, was violently attacked by De Valera and others. Although both sides tried to patch up the schism in the ensuing general election, large-scale fighting broke out in the IRA. Collins, as chief of staff, led the fight against De Valera's republicans; in 1922 he succeeded Arthur Griffiths as head of state. The war continued until 1923, when the resistance to the treaty was crushed. Collins, however, did not live to see his work reach fruition; in Aug. 1922, while advancing on Munster, he was ambushed and shot by republican forces.

COLOGNE. In the Middle Ages, the largest German city, having been, under the Romans, an important trade centre. It owed its importance to its position as a transit port for trade on the Rhine, as a river-crossing point, and as a key place in the political conflicts between the Holy Roman empire and France. It drew added importance from its status as the seat of an archbishop who, after 1180, was also duke of a large principality of Westphalia. It was very wealthy and Cologne measure became a standard for the silver coinage of the whole empire. Its university, founded in 1388, was a centre of Catholic orthodoxy, whose authorities played a leading part in the condemnation of Luther. During the Second World War most of the city was destroyed by bombing.

COLOMAN (1070–1116), King of Hungary, Hungarian Kálmán, the illegitimate son of King Geza I. He was intended by his uncle, Laszlo I, for the Church, but fled abroad. On Laszlo's death (1095) he returned and seized the throne from his younger half-brother, Almus. Coloman proved one of the greatest kings of the Arpád dynasty, instituting major legislative and administrative reforms. He completed the conquest of Croatia (1106) and became its king in personal union with Hungary and made conquests in Dalmatia.

COLOMBIAN NATIONAL FRONT, a political compromise by which power alternated for 13 years (1957–70) between the dominant Liberal and Conservative parties. After years of civil war and the dictatorship of Gustavo Rojas Pinilla, the two leading parties agreed to stop fighting and let the nation return to representative democracy. By 1970 two Liberals and one Conservative had held power, but opposition to the coalition was growing from right and left.

COLOMBO PLAN for Co-operative Economic Development in South and South-East Asia sprang from the initiative of the Australian government at a meeting of Commonwealth ministers in Colombo (Jan. 1950). The original plan was devised to last for six years and was based on development programmes for the underdeveloped Commonwealth countries of the area. However, it was immediately widened beyond the Commonwealth. The US and Japan joined Britain, Australia, Canada, and New Zealand as major donor countries. The other members were (1970) Afghanistan, Bhutan,

Burma, Cambodia, Ceylon, India, Indonesia, Iran, Republic of Korea, Laos, Malaysia, Republic of Maldives, Nepal, Pakistan, Philippines, Singapore, Thailand, and the Republic of Viet-nam.

The directing body of the Colombo Plan is a Consultative Committee which meets annually. Formal organization is, however, relatively unimportant, and the success of the plan is attributable rather to continuous consultation (in which the World Bank and the UN agencies participate, when appropriate) and in the records which are kept under the aegis of the Council for Technical Co-operation. By 1969 the total cumulative flow of aid was US $27,495 million, of which US $1200 million was devoted to technical co-operation.

COLONIA DO SACRAMENTO, fortified colony founded by Portuguese from Rio de Janeiro on the eastern banks of the Rio de la Plata estuary (1680), and repeatedly destroyed by the Spaniards, creoles, and Indians of Buenos Aires. Each time the Spanish and Portuguese were at war in Europe, the Spanish colonists attempted to seize the town. With the restoration of peace, the attackers were invariably compelled to retire. A Spanish settlement was finally established in the Banda Oriental (1729) at Montevideo. Two treaties between Spain and Portugal (1751, 1777) established boundaries favourable to Spain in the Banda Oriental.

COLONIAL CHURCH UNION, society founded in Jamaica (Jan. 1832) to defend by constitutional means the interests of the colony, to oppose the Anti-slavery Society, and to uphold the established Church. The union was declared illegal (1832) after the members destroyed nonconformist chapels.

COLONIAL CONFERENCES began in Queen Victoria's jubilee year (1887) as a means of fostering unity within the British empire. Their discussions were centred mainly on defence, economic development, and problems created by the growth of self-government in the colonies. They survived until the creation of the modern commonwealth by the Statute of Westminster (1931).

Colonial conferences were first officially suggested in 1869, when the Royal Colonial Society addressed a circular to the colonial office and interested colonial governments advocating a meeting of representatives in London. The idea was supported by the Imperial Federation League (1884), but the first conference did not discuss federation, concentrating on problems of defence and communication and laying down no rules for membership or formal organization. At the subsequent Ottawa conference (1894) a declaration in favour of preferential trade within the empire foundered on British adherence to Free Trade.

Chamberlain transformed the conference system at the London meeting of 1897 by negotiating a constitution under which the self-governing colonies were to be represented by their prime ministers, though decisions were not binding on any member. Imperial federation, defence, and tariff reform were all discussed. The help accorded to Britain by the colonies during the South African war led to feelings of independence and at the 1902 conference they resisted more stringent organization for government and defence. Demands for imperial preference were supported by Chamberlain in the interests of imperial unity, but his campaign split the Conservative–Unionist alliance (1905). In the same year, a proposal for a permanent commission with advisory powers was resisted by Canada. After 1907, the conference became known as the 'Imperial Conference'. Its meetings, which were to take place at four-yearly intervals, were to be attended by the British prime minister and the colonial secretary, and the prime ministers of self-governing dominions and some of the colonies, provided that voting was by countries and not by heads. In 1911 the small number of members showed the internal consolidation of the empire and the approach of war resulted in the creation of a committee of imperial defence.

The contribution of the empire to Allied victory resulted in British acquiescence in their greater influence on policy (1917). At the Versailles conference (1918) the effective autonomy of the self-governing dominions in foreign policy was manifest. Though statistical, entomological, and customs conferences were held (1920–1) and the imperial defence committee was revived (1923), the League of Nations constituted a more important forum for discussion than the colonial conference. Also, in 1923 hopes of attaining imperial preference faded when Baldwin, though converted to protection of industry, would not impose duties on food imports. At the 1926 conference Canada raised the constitutional issue of relations between Britain and the dominions, forcing acknowledgement of equality of status under the unifying force of allegiance to the Crown which was expressed in the Statute of Westminster.

R. Jebb, *The Imperial Conference*, 2 vols (London, 1911).

VEC

COLONIAL DEVELOPMENT CORPORATION, established (1948) under the Overseas Resources Development acts, for the purpose of assisting British colonial territories in the development of their economies. Its name was changed to Commonwealth Development Corporation (1963) to cover all countries which had achieved independence since 1948, as well as existing colonies. The corporation assumed responsibility for nearly 100 projects, *eg*, agriculture, factories, housing, electricity, and transport. Private enterprise, working in conjunction with the territories involved, organized such undertakings, being allowed extensive borrowing powers from Britain.

COLONIAL DEVELOPMENT FUND, established by the Colonial Development Act of 1929, for financing economic development in the colonies with a grant or loan in underdeveloped territories, *eg*, the West Indies. The fund was increased by an amending act of 1940.

COLONIAL LAND EMIGRATION BOARD (1840–78), set up, for the British empire, following a select committee (1836), to regulate and support settlement in colonial territories. The ensuing Waste Lands Act (1842) fixed a minimum price for land, half of which accrued to the emigration board. The board had most effect in Australia and New Zealand, but declined with growing colonial autonomy.

COLONIAL LAWS CONFIRMATION ACT (1863) in Britain regulated the constitutional relationship between the acts of the imperial and colonial parliaments, so that dominion laws were invalid if they conflicted with those passed at Westminster, though the former could not be impugned unless they were repugnant to an imperial act which was expressly intended to apply to the colony in question. With the growth of colonial autonomy difficulty arose and an act had to be passed to confirm acts of the New South Wales, Queensland, and Western Australian assemblies, the legality of which were disputed (1901). The dubious status of colonial law was resolved by the Statute of Westminster (1931), which repealed the act of 1863.

COLONIAL LAWS VALIDITY ACT (1865) in Britain clarified the position in regard to the validity of acts passed by colonial legislatures. Colonial laws were stated to be valid unless they were repugnant to an imperial statute applying to the colony concerned. The imposition of a single test of validity abolished two obsolescent tests—repugnancy to the English common law, and repugnancy to instructions issued to a governor—and so enlarged the scope of colonial legislation. The act is, like the Declaration Act, an assertion of parliament's imperial sovereignty. It was the major legal landmark in imperial relations until the Statute of Westminster (1931), which abolished the test of repugnancy imposed in 1865.

COLONIAL OFFICE in Britain. English colonies were the responsibility, at various times, of a committee of the privy council, a council for trade, and a board of trade and plantations. In 1801 one of the secretaries of state was given executive authority for war and for colonies, the office of colonial secretary itself being separately established in 1854.

Throughout the 19th cent. its numerous occupants regarded it as a political stepping-stone, though superior in status to presidencies of the various boards (eg, trade). Often it was the permanent under-secretaries who contributed more to colonial policy, eg, James Stephen (1836–47). Joseph Chamberlain enhanced the importance of the secretaryship (1895–1903) and by 1907 the office had assumed considerable significance, with dominion, colonial, and protectorate responsibility. In 1925 the dominions office was separated from the colonial, an idea first mooted in 1910. (Both colonies and dominions are distinguished throughout from the affairs of India.)

After the Second World War the dominions office gave way to the commonwealth relations office (1947). Between 1946 and 1970 the peoples for whom the colonial office was responsible shrank from 65 million to 4 million. The commonwealth relations office, absorbing the new emergent self-governing territories, was itself absorbed into the foreign office in 1968.   GMDH

COLONIAL OFFICE GOVERNMENT, in the British empire, a pattern of colonial rule also known as the crown colony system.

COLONIAL POLICY, BRITISH, IN NORTH AMERICA (1607–1775). The British government demonstrated no consistent policy towards her American colonies until after the peace of Paris (1763). Officially, Britain's economic policy was mercantilism, and colonies existed for the benefit of the mother country. In reality, however, the colonies operated under a system of 'salutary neglect' with only ineffective controls from abroad. The first Navigation Act (1651) forbade colonial intercourse with foreign countries and insisted on the use of English or English colonial ships as carriers of colonial goods. This was not strictly enforced, and after the Restoration (1660), new attempts at control were made. The Navigation Act (1660), Staple Act (1663), and Plantations Duties Act (1673) restated the 1651 Navigation Act and in addition specified certain colonial goods which were not to be exported to foreign countries, taxed the shipping of these goods from one colony to another, and ruled that all colonial imports had to be shipped from English ports. These regulations were circumvented or openly defied. A coherent colonial economic policy was not instituted until after the Seven Years War, when Britain found herself with a sizeable war debt. Parliament passed various acts, including the Stamp Act (1765) and the American Import Duties Act (1767), which integrated colonial taxation into the structure of a mercantilist empire. These taxes, and measures to enforce them, led to colonial resistance and revolution. Nor did Britain have a consistent policy for colonial government; crown colonies, charter colonies, and proprietary colonies existed side by side. James II tried to consolidate the colonies by instituting vice-royalties, but these were opposed by the colonists and were abolished in 1689. The British government favoured crown colonies, and by 1775 only Pennsylvania, Rhode Island, and Connecticut did not have royal governors. Lands obtained from the French (1763) were under crown authority and after 1774 ruled from Quebec. The northern reaches of Canada were governed by the Hudson's Bay Co. (1670–1870). In practice, the colonies were left to govern themselves through colonial legislatures, the only stipulation being that the colonies obey the laws of parliament and remain loyal to the Crown. Differences between the powers of parliament and Crown and colonial legislatures (1763–75) helped lead to the revolt of the American colonies.

J. H. Rose *et al.* (eds), *The Cambridge History of the British Empire*, vol. 1, *The Old Empire from the Beginnings to 1783* (Cambridge, 1960).   ERS

COLONIZATION, GREEK. The Greek city-state's normal solution for over-population, most frequent in 8th–6th cents BC, following the greater stability of the 9th cent. and increased trading abroad. From *c.* 750 Chalcidians and Eretrians colonized Chalcidice and, closely followed by Corinthians, Megarians, and Achaeans, led settlers to southern Italy and Sicily, *eg*, Cumae and Syracuse. In the 7th cent. settlers in Sicily moved westwards, *eg*, Himera, while Aegean islanders attempted the hostile Thracian coast, *eg*, Thasos. By 600 Spanish silver had encouraged Phocaeans to found Massilia, but settlements in Corsica and Spain later failed under Phoenician pressure (*c.* 535, battle of Alalia). Corinth meanwhile (*c.* 600) settled north-western Greece and beyond, *eg*, Apollonia, and established Potidaea. Thera sent her starving to Cyrene (*c.* 630) and Megarians and Milesians colonized the Black Sea, *eg*, Sinope, and its approaches, *eg*, Byzantium (*c.* 650–600). Athens was first active in the 6th cent. in the Thracian Chersonese and Sigeum (*c.* 540). Ties between mother-city and colony were usually cultural and commercial rather than political. Sea-borne trade flourished and trading centres established at Poseidium (before 750) and Naucratis (*c.* 620) increased Greek awareness of developed alien civilizations. Coinage, mercenaries, hoplites, tyranny, orientalizing art, monumental stone sculpture and architecture, lyric poetry, and the beginnings of philosophy, all resulted directly or indirectly from the impulse of the colonial movement.

COLONIZATION, ROMAN. Settlement abroad of citizens and allies which, following the Etruscans' example, the Romans used widely in their conquest of Italy to defend existing possessions or new conquests, and to secure lines of communication. Initially, they founded such settlements in concert with members of the Latin League. Towns like Signia, Velitrae, and Norba received mixed contingents to defend Latium against the surrounding hill-peoples (hence the term 'Latin colony'). When Rome achieved predominance over the Latin League, these Latin colonies officially remained allies on equal terms with Rome, enjoying mutual trading and marriage rights with her, but not with each other. A second type of foundation, called Roman colonies and consisting only of citizens and their families, was established from the late 4th cent. onwards. Initially planted at strategic points on the Italian coast (*eg*, Antium, Tarracona, etc.), they were complemented in the 2nd cent. by a few established inland, but Roman colonies numbered only 27 by 177 BC, whereas there were more than 40 Latin colonies. Caius Gracchus was the first to develop colonization systematically for overspill and for commercial development, planting Neptunia and Minervia in southern Italy and proposing Junonia on the site of Carthage (123–122); by 100 BC settlements had spread to many overseas territories. Sulla founded ten colonies to accommodate his 120,000 discharged troops in Italy; Julius Caesar extended this plan by settling 100,000 veterans in 20 colonies abroad. Augustus, too, founded more than 30 colonies in Italy and abroad to house his discharged troops— an example followed by later emperors.

COLONNA, powerful Roman aristocratic family which rose to prominence in the 11th cent. and provided a number of cardinals and Roman officials. Members of the family, outlawed by Boniface VIII, helped to arrange his capture at Anagni (1303), which caused his death. They aided the Emperor Louis of Bavaria in capturing Rome (1328). A Colonna pope, Martin V, ended the Great Schism in 1417.

COLORADO, 38th member state of the US, admitted 1876. Spain formally claimed possession of the Colorado region in 1706, but failed to establish permanent settlements and the indigenous Indian population was left free from white exploitation. Eastern Colorado passed to the US by the Louisiana Purchase (1803), and the expeditions of Z. M Pike (1806), S. H. Long (1820), and J. C. Fremont (1842–53) kept American interest in the region alive. However, unfavourable reports deterred settlement, apart from that of a scattered population of trappers and a number of military posts. The US acquired title to the whole of Colorado as a result of the Mexican War (1846–8). Originally included in the Territory of New Mexico (1850), Colorado became a separate Territory (1861). The Pike's Peak gold-rush (1859) led to the proliferation of settlement, and after the Civil War the remaining Indian tribes were brought under control, mining operations expanded, and agriculture developed.

COLORADO PARTY in Paraguay, founded by Gen. Bernardino Caballero (1874), dominated Paraguayan politics until 1904, when it lost control to the popular Liberal Party.

COLORADO PARTY in Uruguay, the liberal party of Uruguay since the 1830s, when civil war began between *blancos* (conservatives) and *colorados*, led by José Fructuoso Rivera, the first president of Uruguay. The *colorados* revolted (1836–8) and captured the government from the *blancos*. They, however, rallied with Argentinian support and a lengthy civil war followed (1840–51). The *colorados* controlled Montevideo and with the weakening of the Argentine effort (1851) *colorados* and *blancos* united briefly (1851–3). Then Brazilian interference provoked the *colorados* to seize the reins of government again. The Brazilians favoured the *blancos* repeatedly until 1864, when both Argentines and Brazilians supported the *colorados* and thereby precipitated the Paraguayan War (1864–70). After the war, *colorado* rule was firmly established for nearly a century (1870–1959). The party was reformed by José Batlle y Ordóñez early in the 20th cent. and became committed to welfare state ideas.

COLOSSEUM, medieval and modern name of the Amphitheatrum Flavianum in Rome, begun by Vespasian and completed by Titus in AD 80. It was used for gladiatorial and wild beast shows and could accommodate some 50,000 spectators. Despite extensive damage, it remains the most impressive single monument of Roman building.

COLOURED PEOPLE OF SOUTH AFRICA, the result of intercourse between various racial groups from the earliest days of white settlement at the Cape. Despite social and criminal sanctions, racial intermixture continues; coloureds now number about 2 millions. A majority are skilled and semi-skilled urban-dwellers. Culturally, they are predominantly Afrikaans-speaking and members of the Dutch Reformed Church. Some 6 per cent, the Cape Malays, are Muslims.

In the 18th and 19th cents the coloured were hunters, traders, and explorers, who took Western products and ideas beyond the white frontier. In the British Cape Colony, they had political and legal equality, but in the remaining territories were always discriminated against. After the unification of South Africa, discrimination spread to the Cape. After 1948 they were disenfranchised in both national and local Cape elections.

COLT, SIR HENRY (1579–1635), English trader, who wrote one of the first accounts of conditions in the West Indies (1631–2). He founded a settlement in Trinidad which was destroyed by the Spanish (1633).

COLT, SAMUEL (1814–62), US inventor of the revolving-breech firearm (the 'six-shooter'), which he patented (1835–6) and became standard equipment in the US army. His first major commercial success was a government contract for pistols at the outbreak of the Mexican War in 1846. Colt's business became the world's largest private armoury, a feature of which was its automated production methods.

COLUMBA, Saint (521–97), member of the Northern Irish dynasty of U Neil, who founded the monasteries of Derry, Durrow, and Kells in Ireland and in 563 founded the church and monastery on the island of Iona, which became one of the most influential Christian centres in Scotland. He made several journeys to convert Brude mac Maelchon, King of the Picts, who lived near Inverness.

COLUMBIA, DISTRICT OF, an area coterminous with the city of Washington, capital of the US and seat of the federal government. Situated on the Potomac river, a few miles from George Washington's estate at Mount Vernon, the District originally comprised a ten square mile (2·6 sq. kms) cession of territory from Maryland and Virginia, but the Virginia portion remained undeveloped and was retroceded (1846). Designed by Maj. Pierre-Charles L'Enfant under the direction of President Washington, the new capital was not established until the inauguration of Jefferson (1801). In 1814 the Capitol, White House, and other official buildings were destroyed by British troops. As the seat of the federal government the District falls under the sole jurisdiction of Congress. Although not represented in Congress, its inhabitants have been able to vote in presidential elections since ratification of the 23rd Amendment (1961). The District's estimated population in 1970 exceeded 800,000, of whom the overwhelming majority were Negroes.

COLUMBUS, CHRISTOPHER (*c.* 1451–1506), Genoese navigator-explorer, who in the service of Spain became the first modern European to reach America. Though Asians and north Europeans probably reached America long before 1492, Columbus is usually cited as the 'discoverer'. He was probably born in Genoa, went to sea early in life, and moved to Lisbon (1477), where, under the influence of Portuguese navigators, he took up chart-making.

The accepted idea that the earth was round suggested to Columbus that Asia might best be reached by sailing west, though he greatly underestimated the distances involved. After a number of setbacks, he convinced the Spanish court of the wisdom of his cause and was granted a contract (*capitulación*) (17 April 1492), that granted him the governorship of all lands that he might discover, as well as the title of Admiral of the Ocean Sea. Columbus and the Pinzón brothers set sail on 3 Aug. 1492 and sighted land in the Bahama islands on 12 Oct.

Columbus's first voyage was limited to skirting the coasts of Cuba and Haiti, which he believed to be off the coast of China. On a second voyage he landed at the Leeward Islands, St Christopher, Puerto Rico, and Jamaica. His third voyage took him to Trinidad and to the mouth of the Orinoco river in modern Venezuela (1 Aug. 1498).

Columbus's achievements were recognized by the monarchy, but the Crown eventually revoked his original offices, rights, and titles. His government in the colonies came under attack and he was sent to Spain in chains. The Crown released him, but relieved him of his most important contractual rights. He then embarked on a fourth voyage, during which he landed at Honduras, Costa Rica, and Panama (1502).

In his later years Columbus made numerous attempts to revive his perquisites for his son Diego. He died with his honour secure and moderately wealthy, never ceased believing that he had reached Asia. His heirs subsequently accepted a land settlement in Central America as a resolution of their claims against the crown.   HDS

COLUMBUS, DIEGO (*c.* 1484–1526), elder son of Christopher Columbus, who became governor of Hispaniola (1509) and, though he lost power to an *audencia* (high court) (1511), retained his office until 1526.

COMANCHE INDIANS, plains tribe of Shoshonean stock. The Comanche were at war for two centuries with the Spaniards of Mexico, from whom they got horses which they introduced to other tribes. Their raids against settlements in Texas prompted the organization of the Texas Rangers. The Comanche were also famous as raiders of emigrant wagon trains. They signed their first peace treaty with the US in

1835. Several efforts were made to confine them to reservations before they signed the Medicine Lodge treaty (1867), under which they agreed to live on a reservation in Oklahoma. They did not settle on their assigned lands until after the last outbreak of the southern plains tribes (1874–5).

COMBINATION ACTS in Britain. Until 1824 combined action in restraint of trade was illegal under English common law: in addition, numerous statutes had been passed against it. The acts usually referred to by historians were the last of these, those of 1799 and 1800, which created no new offence, but which were intended to make the law easier to enforce by summary procedure and lighter sentences. They were passed in the general nervousness of the 1790s about radical disturbances.

In practice, prosecutions continued to be made under the older laws. Technically, employers who combined to raise prices or lower wages could also be prosecuted. 'Masters', Adam Smith had written, 'are always and everywhere in a sort of tacit but constant and uniform combination', but action against them was rare. The laws of combination and of criminal conspiracy made open trade unions impossible, but many acknowledged combinations of workers continued to exist and influence wages and conditions of work. Unionism also disguised itself in friendly societies. Undoubtedly, the laws handicapped incipient trade unionism, but not so much as did the continued existence of a large pool of labour.

Combination was made legal in 1824 through the efforts of Francis Place and Joseph Hume. This repeal of the whole body of combination laws was followed by an outbreak of strikes, and in 1825 parliament reimposed the common law of conspiracy which it had repealed in 1824. It remained legally possible to organize trade unions, but not for them to use effective pressure on employers.

COMBINED CHIEFS OF STAFF COMMITTEE was established (1941), during the Second World War, at the 'Arcadia' conference in Washington. The British and US chiefs of staff were given authority over the entire 'strategic conduct of the war' and were responsible, through their meetings, for preserving continuity in the different major war-conferences. The committee was wound up at the end of the war. It had served as a pattern for the integration of staffs established under NATO and, at the same time, contributed to the Anglo–American 'special relationship'.

COMBINES INVESTIGATION ACT (1923), Canadian antitrust act empowering a registrar to investigate alleged combinations in restraint of trade and to take criminal proceedings against any combinations so found. A 1910 act made it an offence only to continue in combination.

COMENIUS (Jan Amos Komensky) (1592–1670), educational reformer, philosopher, theologian, and last bishop of the Moravian Church. He was born in Moravia, but with thousands of other Protestants left the kingdom of Bohemia when the emperor Ferdinand II imposed a Catholic, absolutist rule, following the defeat of the Protestant nobility at the battle of the White Mountain (1620). For the rest of his life Comenius wandered Europe as an exile, unable to return because of the Thirty Years War and then because of the anti-Protestant settlement of the peace of Westphalia.

He was educated at Heidelberg University and ordained a priest, but finding himself in charge of a school as well as a church, he set about rethinking the whole educational process. The basis of his work is the perception of the intelligibility of all created things and of the consequent necessity to unify all human knowledge, both sacred and profane. He called this 'pansophia', and expected that its dissemination by universal education would ultimately bring about a permanent political peace, if first of all a religious peace could be established by uniting all Christian churches on the basis of Protestantism. His optimistic view of man is central to his philosophy, and it was set out at the beginning of *Didactica Magna* (the Great Didactic) written 1627–32, in the form of a proposition: 'Man is so situated among visible creatures as to be (i) a rational creature (ii) the lord of all creatures (iii) a creature who is the image and joy of his Creator.'

Although his visions of universal books, universal schools, a universal college, and a universal language were not put into practice, his more immediate and practical work in that direction had revolutionary effects, particularly in the teaching of languages. In *The Gate of Languages Unlocked* (1631) and *The Visible World in Pictures* (1658), he showed how language was best taught through real things and concrete situations, the second of these two books using pictures to teach words and phrases. In the place of traditional education, which he attacked in the satirical *Labyrinth of the World* (1631), he envisaged a system so far ahead of its time that it has only recently become educational orthodoxy. Up to the age of six, a child's education depended entirely on the earliest experiences of life in the whole home environment. From six to twelve all children, in complete equality of sex and class, should learn about the visible and tangible world and their immediate environment in the Vernacular School, and even after passing to the Latin School (12 to 18) they should continue learning by experience and observation rather than by authority. Latin should become the language of natural philosophy in school, not an arsenal of pagan literature. Science, far from being incompatible with religion, would only lead to a greater understanding of God's nature.

Comenius visited England, Sweden, Poland, Hungary, and the Netherlands, and although his efforts to set up a pansophic school came to nothing, he inspired the Royal Societies of London and Berlin, and left his influence throughout Europe.

E Beres *et al.*, *Comenius. The Teacher of Nations* (Cambridge, 1942). HMBM

COMESTOR, PETER (*c.* 1100–*c.* 1180), dean of Troyes cathedral (1145–*c.* 1165) and chancellor of Paris (1164–8, 1178–80), where he taught theology and was one of the most famous teachers. 150 of his sermons survive and he was the author of several commentaries on the Bible and on the *Sentences* of Peter Lombard.

COMINFORM (Communist Information Bureau), established in Oct. 1947 'to organize the exchange of experience' and 'where necessary to co-ordinate the activities of the communist parties on the basis of mutual agreement'. Its members were Bulgaria, Czechoslovakia, Poland, Rumania, Yugoslavia and the Soviet Union—all (except at this time the Czech party) were ruling parties together with the largest communist parties in Western Europe, namely those of France and Italy.

The original purpose of the Cominform appears to have been to help the Soviet Union to tighten the control that it was establishing over the countries of Eastern Europe, whether in accordance with Stalinist practice in Russia or because of the increasing momentum of the Cold War. It published a journal, the main purpose of which was to transmit directives to the members.

Soon after the establishment of the Cominform the Soviet Union entered into political conflict with Yugoslavia, Tito having refused to bend to the requirements of the Soviet government. A formal breach occurred with the expulsion of Yugoslavia from the Cominform (June 1948), whose importance thereafter declined. When Khrushchev sought a reconciliation with Tito, the latter made it a condition of the renewal of friendly relations that the Cominform should be dissolved, and the dissolution was anounced (April 1956) on the grounds that the organization had 'exhausted its functions'. WFK

COMINTERN, Communist International or Third International, proclaimed (March 1919) at a Moscow meeting, convened by Lenin, of left-wing European socialists. At the end of 1920 important sections split from the French and German socialist parties to affiliate themselves to the Comintern. This sealed the international socialist movement's division between the Comintern and the Second, or Socialist International, whose member parties refused to accept Bolshevik discipline.

At first, all Comintern sections were equally represented on its Executive Committee. Although Zinoviev, a Russian, was its first president, the Russian representatives were not formally predominant until the expected revolution outside Russia failed to materialize. Foreign communists lost control over their own parties to Comintern central office agents. Their policies, streamlined, followed both Russian revolutionary strategies and the dictates of Russia's conventional diplomatic dealings. They also followed the vagaries of Soviet internal politics. After Lenin's death (Jan. 1924), Stalin's controversy with Trotsky dominated Comintern affairs. The failure of the German revolutionary attempt of 1923, which Trotsky had encouraged, was the pretext for the first of the Executive Council's many large-scale purges of the foreign sections.

Capitalist governments considered Soviet diplomacy merely a cover for Comintern agitation, as was the case in Germany in 1923. Russia's foreign ministry was subject to party control; Russian embassies housed many Comintern central office agents. However, Stalin permitted the Comintern to serve only Russian interests. As in China, foreign communists were often forced to abandon revolutionary policies. The European communists' inability to act autonomously was tragically displayed in the early 1930s. Stalin's equation of social democracy with 'social fascism' cut the German communists off from political alliances against the rising Nazi Party.

The Comintern's dissolution, announced (15 May 1943) in Moscow, was probably designed to mollify Stalin's allies while war separated Russia from many European revolutionary and resistance movements.　　　　　　　ASJ

COMITÉ DES FORGES, trade association of the French iron and steel industry, founded in 1864. It exercised considerable political influence (1919–39), controlling the newspaper *Le Temps*, and became a popular symbol of the intervention of big business in politics. Previously it had concentrated on questions of price and tariff protection. It was dissolved in 1940, but later reconstituted as the Chambre syndicale de la Sidérurgie française.

COMITÉ FRANCE-ALLEMAGNE, propaganda organization established in France in the 1930s by the Nazi sympathizer Fernand de Brinon. It concentrated on influencing political, business, and intellectual circles, and contributed to the growth of the mood of 'appeasement'.

COMITES (comrades), a Latin word used by the Romans especially for groups of young nobles accompanying provincial governors, and later the emperor when travelling abroad. In the 4th cent. governors of military areas were known as *comites* (later counts), and smaller districts were under *duces* ('leaders', later dukes).

COMITIA CENTURIATA, most important of the political assemblies in early republican Rome, its composition being based on the classification, ascribed to King Servius (6th cent. BC), of five propertied grades, sub-divided into centuries. It took over many functions of the *comitia curiata*. Its duties were to approve or reject proposals of war, to elect the higher magistrates (consuls, *praetors*, censors), to hear appeals on capital charges, and to pass laws proposed by magistrates, though this legislative function passed almost completely to the *comitia tributa* and the *concilium plebis* after 287 BC. Until *c.* 220 the timocratic basis of its organization gave the first class an effective majority; after that date the centuries were more equitably divided between the classes. Under Julius Caesar, Augustus, and Tiberius it lost successively its control over war and peace, its legislative role, and its electoral powers, and by the 3rd cent. AD had faded away.

COMITIA CURIATA, earliest form of Roman public assembly, with military, political, and religious functions. Its composition was based on 30 *curiae* or groups of kin. It conferred the king's powers, ratified declarations of war and exercised legal functions. After the foundation of the *comitia centuriata*, it survived only for the ritual conferment of *imperium* on the magistrates elected by the *comitia centuriata*.

COMITIA TRIBUTA, Roman popular assembly convened by tribes (30 by the classification ascribed to King Servius and 35 after 241 BC). After its establishment, probably in the 5th cent. BC, it appropriated many functions of the *comitia centuriata*. The geographical basis of the tribes, and their fewer number as against the 193 centuries, made the *comitia tributa* both easier to administer and more democratic. It elected *curule aediles* and *quaestors*, heard appeals against fines, nominated priests and members of religious colleges, and passed laws proposed by magistrates. Under the empire it survived as a picturesque institution till the 3rd cent.

COMMAGENE, in northern Syria between the Taurus and the Euphrates, part of the Seleucid empire, which became an independent kingdom in 162 BC when its governor revolted. Made a client-state of the Roman empire by Pompey (64), it was annexed by Tiberius (AD 17), but was restored to client status by Caligula (38), whose nominee reigned, with one interruption, until 74, when he was deposed by Vespasian for alleged pro-Parthian sympathies. The kingdom was then finally annexed and incorporated into the Roman province Syria.

COMMEDIA DELL' ARTE, improvised drama by professional actors, originated in Italy, where it was invented by a favourite actor of Pope Leo X (1513–21). The stock characters, Clown, Harlequin, Columbine, and Pantaloon, wore masks and developed the entertainment by filling in the bare outlines drawn by the dramatist. Other characters were added from traditional sources, such as the braggart soldier, the unworldly pedant, and the hopeful young lovers. This sort of drama was popular until about 1700, when it was replaced by the scripted and more regular comedy of Goldoni. Italian companies performed at several European courts. In England the ad-lib. performances of clowns like Tarleton and Kempe had obvious affinities with the Commedia dell' Arte, but the native drama had taken too strong a root for the visiting companies to be more than a passing fashion that lingered on in the harlequinade.

COMMINES, PHILIP DE (d. 1511), French historian, and adviser and diplomat in the court of King Louis XI of France. He began his career in the court of Charles the Bold of Burgundy, but defected to Louis in 1472. It is from his narratives that our picture of Louis XI is largely drawn.

COMMISSARIAT GENERAL DU PLAN in France, established in 1946 as a central body for economic planning. Although directly responsible to the prime minister, the commissariat remained, relatively independent of the rise and fall of political fortunes (a fact of major importance in the 'crisis and compromise' of the Fourth French Republic). It remained responsible in 1970 for periodically drawing up plans for the French economy, which were then approved by the government and parliament. Its early success made it a model for planning elsewhere, although it was not easy to emulate the close understanding between the main centres of economic power, in the public and private sector, on which the commissariat's work depended.

COMMISSION ON ECONOMIC DEPRESSION (1622), in Britain, permanent body established to overlook trade in general and textiles in particular during the economic depression of the 1620s. It resulted from an expert committee of investigation established by the privy council on 10 April 1622, which produced a report on 22 June after consultations with local opinion from the 25 textile counties. The commission, meetings of which began in Nov. 1622, consisted of over 50 members, with a broad representation of economic interests and geographical areas. Their wide terms of reference covered most areas of contemporary commercial and industrial policy. The commission was the principal administrative move to counteract the depression. It took over most of the executive matters concerning cloth trade and general economic life from the privy council. While its appointment was of great institutional significance (it was a precursor of the board of trade) it did not lead to a radical change in policy. The commission was renewed in 1625.

COMMITTEE ON AGRICULTURE in Britain, formed in 1966 as an offshoot of the government's National Economic Development Council. It began to function in 1967, and concentrated on the industry's manpower problems and on economizing in imports.

COMMITTEES OF CORRESPONDENCE (1772–5), organizations of radicals in colonial America, founded by Samuel Adams (1772) to keep Massachusetts radicals in contact with each other. The Virginia House of Burgesses issued a successful call for inter-colonial committees of correspondence (1773). The committees led the movement for the First Continental Congress (1774). Local branches worked with the Continental Association to boycott British goods and to organize extra-legal provincial congresses, from which delegates were chosen for the Second Continental Congress (1775).

COMMITTEE OF THE COUNCIL, in England, name given to the inner group of ministers chosen by the king from the privy council in the late 17th cent. to give advice on government. In the early 18th cent. the term was applied to selected ministers chosen for the same purpose from the cabinet council.

COMMITTEE OF 1826 DECEMBER 6. Secret Russian committee, chaired by Kochubey and including Speransky, established by Nicholas I to examine undecided reform projects of Alexander I. It submitted proposals (1830) regarding central and provincial government and the rights of the estates. Working on conservative and autocratic lines, it merely amended the existing structure.

COMMITTEE TO DEFEND AMERICA BY AIDING THE ALLIES, US pressure group organized (May 1940) to encourage popular support for President F. D. Roosevelt's foreign policy. Under its chairman, William Allen White (1868–1944), a highly respected newspaper editor from Emporia, KS, and a Republican, the committee reflected the president's view that American security rested on British victory in the war in Europe and insisted that the role of the US should be all-out assistance to Britain short of active intervention in the war. The committee was influential in securing acceptance of the Destroyer Deal (Sept. 1940) and the Lend-Lease Act (March 1941). As the international situation continued to deteriorate members of the committee moved, like the president himself, towards the belief that the US would have to intervene militarily. White resigned over this issue in Jan. 1941.

COMMITTEE OF GENERAL DEFENCE, the *grand comité*, created (1 Jan. 1793) at Brissot's suggestion. It included three representatives of each of the French revolutionary Convention's committees. It was intended to exercise surveillance over the ministries, and was superseded in April by the Committee of Public Safety.

COMMITTEE OF GENERAL SECURITY, set up by the Convention (1792–5), exercised important police functions before, during, and after the Terror. It controlled the *représentats en mission* and national agents, who supervised the ideological struggle and revolutionary administration in the provinces. Rivalry with the encroaching Committee of Public Safety encouraged the Thermidorian reaction.

COMMITTEE OF IMPERIAL DEFENCE, in Britain, an advisory cabinet committee, established in Dec. 1902, responsible for the supervision of foreign and imperial defence strategies. The need for the co-ordination of imperial defence policies had been recognized in the Colonial Defence Committee (1878–9), reconstituted by the Salisbury government in 1885. This brought together the chiefs of staff, with representatives of the treasury and colonial office. Salisbury's attempt to strengthen this co-ordination resulted in the cabinet committee of defence (1895), though, owing to admiralty obstruction, this did not include representatives of the forces. Balfour, who replaced Salisbury in 1902 took the view that the Boer War showed the need for a more effective central direction of defence.

By 1904, largely as a result of the Esher report on war office organization, the CID had assumed its final shape. The prime minister was to be the only permanent member; the rest of the committee were to be drawn, as occasion demanded, from senior cabinet ministers and the chiefs of staff. Even more radical was the creation of a permanent secretariat, at first under Sir George Clarke, to keep minutes of the proceedings and to collate information.

By the time war broke out in 1914 the CID had become of paramount importance; working through many sub-committees, it controlled all aspects of inter-departmental policy and strategy. When, in 1916, it was temporarily superseded by Lloyd George's war cabinet, its procedures and secretariat were absorbed by the new body. In 1919, when it was reformed, there were two developments in defence policy. One was the creation of a joint chiefs of staff committee, the other the use of the CID secretary, Lord Hankey, to head the new cabinet secretariat.

Lord Ismay, who succeeded Hankey in 1938, transformed the committee into an important part of the war cabinet in the following year. The CID was then formally suspended. In 1946 it was replaced by a cabinet defence committee, the minister of defence being charged with the supervision of the chiefs of staff.

COMMITTEE OF PUBLIC ACCOUNTS, in Britain, select committee of the House of Commons, set up annually since 1861. It is assisted by the comptroller and auditor-general in its task of ensuring that public money is spent as parliament has directed.

COMMITTEE ON PUBLIC INFORMATION, US agency established (April 1917) to win public support for the war against Germany. In addition to its work of propaganda, the committee, under the chairmanship of the Progressive Western journalist George Creel, persuaded the press to accept voluntary censorship in the interests of national security.

COMMITTEE OF PUBLIC SAFETY (1793), set up by the French Convention (April) to conduct internal and foreign policy. It gave France an effective executive, which soon fell into the hands of Robespierre and the Jacobins (July), who used the committee ruthlessly and dictatorially to suppress their internal enemies through the Terror and to achieve victory in the war. The members of the Committee were never in complete agreement and this contributed to the fall of Robespierre (July 1794), after which the committee was reduced by the convention to one of several government committees.

COMMITTEE OF THE SIXTEEN, by which the revolutionary Holy or Catholic League in Paris governed the city during the civil war (1585–94). It consisted of bourgeois representatives of the 16 administrative regions of the city, bitterly opposed to the Parisian aristocracy. The Duke of Mayenne, leader of the league, tried to curb the committee by arresting several of its members, but succeeded only in infuriating the popular elements in the league, whom the committee represented. It finally collapsed with Henry of Navarre's conversion to Catholicism and his return to Paris (March 1594).

COMMITTEE OF UNION AND PROGRESS (1889), revolutionary political group founded in Istanbul, although not known as CUP until 1895. The CUP was based in Paris (1895–1908) under the leadership of Ahmed Riza. After 1908 it became the dominant force in Ottoman politics, first as a secret society and, after 1909, as a fissiparous political party, supporting strong centralizing policies. It was ousted from power (1912), but was restored by a coup, led by Enver Pasha (Jan. 1913). From 1913 until its dissolution (Oct. 1918) the CUP, under the domination of the triumvirate, Enver, Talat, and Jamal Pashas, ruled the Ottoman empire, all other political parties being suppressed.

COMMITTEES OF SAFETY (1774–5), usual title of American committees established by the Colonial Association of the First Continental Congress to enforce local boycotts of British goods.

COMMITTUS legal privilege under the *ancien régime* of certain French royal officials and ecclesiastical dignitaries, originally members of the king's feudal household, to be tried in the first instance before the *parlement* of Paris, if involved in civil or criminal proceedings.

COMMODUS, M. AURELIUS (*reg.* AD 180–92), Roman Emperor, son, and successor of Marcus Aurelius. He immediately terminated the wars upon which Marcus had been engaged and returned to Rome, where he spent most of his reign, despite the military difficulties which beset the provinces. Being prodigal with gifts and entertainments, Commodus was liked by the people of Rome, but his unpopularity with the upper class made him the object of many plots, the last of which (192) was successful. His reign was marred by famine and plague in Rome and the empire, and was succeeded by a period of political disorder until the accession of Septimius Severus (193).

COMMON LAW, in England, term originally used of the body of law which, after the Norman Conquest, became common to the whole kingdom, as opposed to the customary laws applied in particular places, chiefly merchant towns. The lawyer Blackstone applied the term to the law common to Saxons, Mercians, and Danes before the Conquest, but there is no evidence of any such codification.

After the Norman Conquest the King's Court established jurisdiction over the local courts and, especially by its monopoly of trial by jury and by the writ of *Quo Warranto* (first used in the reign of Edward I), superseded them. From the King's Court derived the Courts of Exchequer, Common Pleas, and King's Bench, which shared the distinctive features of writs to initiate actions, trial by jury, and judges who were laymen trained at the secular Inns of Court. The combination of a well-organized legal profession from which alone judges were recruited settled procedure with some, though limited, flexibility, and written records of cases to establish precedent enabled the Courts of Common Law to become an effective force in the development of the law as well as its administration. In particular the courts were able to resist the attempt by the Stuart kings to govern by decree.

In its second sense the term is used of the system of law developed by these three Courts of Common Law, first, as distinguished from 'equity', the system of law developed in the Court of Chancery; and secondly to distinguish judicial systems deriving from the English system, such as those of Australia and the US, from those deriving from other systems of law and particularly the Roman, or Civil Law. In

this sense the term includes statute law; these two sources of law interact, for statute amplifies, codifies, and sometimes reverses the decision of the courts and further decisions interpret the statutes.

The term is also used to distinguish secular law from ecclesiastical or 'Canon' law, and to distinguish law deriving from judicial precedent from law embodied in Statute or Statutory Instrument.   JRLS

COMMON PEACE, term used by later Greek historians (*eg*, Diodorus Siculus) and in some contemporary documents to describe a series of international peace treaties concluded or proposed in the 4th cent. BC, applicable to all homeland Greek states on the basis of universal independence. These terms, devised originally by Sparta to win Persian support in the Corinthian War (392), were first imposed in the King's Peace (387). They were exploited by Sparta to break up hostile federations (*eg*, Theban-led Boeotia, Chalcidian League) and by Athens and Thebes to defeat Spartan aggrandizement after 378, but were renewed in the treaties of 375–4, 371, and 362–1, before Philip II of Macedon used them (338–7) with an international peace-keeping council (the so-called League of Corinth), as the basis of his settlement of Greece, which remained as an example to Alexander the Great and his successors in dealing with Greek states they controlled or wooed.

COMMON PLEAS, Court of, in England, was established as a separate part of the King's Court in 1178, having five judges who were to remain at Westminster and not follow the king. No distinct jurisdiction was allocated to it, but it came to concentrate on 'common pleas', or actions between subjects as opposed to 'pleas of the Crown'. Magna Carta determined that common pleas should not follow the Crown, and the fixed place for their hearing was before this court at Westminster. The court's records are the plea rolls, extant from 1194, and the 'feet of fines' from 1195, and its first chief justice was appointed in 1272. The court's principal concern was with real property actions and the older personal writs of debt, detinue, covenant, and account. The procedure in these was cumbersome and expensive and the adequacy of their remedies did not outlast the Middle Ages; thereafter the court declined as the Court of King's Bench progressed. In 1875 the court became the Common Pleas Division of the newly created High Court of Justice, but was later merged with the King's Bench Division.

COMMONS SUPPLICATION AGAINST THE ORDINARIES (1532), in England, comprehensive attack by the Reformation parliament on clerical legislation for its independence of royal control, on clerical jurisdiction for its cost and unpredictability, and on a number of misdemeanours committed by ecclesiastical officials. It showed the current anti-clerical temper of the laity, particularly the gentry. As a result of the Supplication, the clergy surrendered their legislative independence. The Ordinaries were the judges in the ecclesiastical courts, *ie*, bishops or their deputies.

COMMONWEALTH, THE (1649–53, 1659–60), term often applied to the whole period of the English republic (1649–1660), but more specifically to the period when the republic was not ruled by a lord protector. Charles I was executed on 30 Jan. 1649, but monarchy was not abolished until 17 March, and it was not until 19 May that England was declared to be 'a Commonwealth or Free-State'. On 13 Feb., however, the executive functions of the monarchy had been invested in a council of state of 40 members, 31 of them MPs. The supreme legislative and executive authority of the Commonwealth resided in the one remaining estate of parliament (the Lords having been abolished on 19 March). The speaker of the Commons was the first in dignity in England, and the House was unhampered by any checks except what might be self-imposed by the knowledge that its authority finally rested on the army. The Commons, however, was only a fragment—about one-tenth—of the body elected in 1640, and the remaining MPs (the Rump), purged several times by the army, were practically confined to those who approved of the king's death. They represented a very small section of the nation and were not wholly acceptable to the army. Though the Rump and the army were mutually dependent, parliament made little effort, despite pressure from the council of officers, to implement the programme of social and legal reforms which the army had been advocating since 1647; and on the question of religion the Rump was particularly dilatory and tried to continue tithes, though the army demanded their abolition. The army wanted the Rump to dissolve itself and to institute elections for a new parliament, but the Rump was not anxious to do this. Army pressure produced reforms grudgingly granted, but these were insufficient to satisfy the army or the public, with whom the Rump became very unpopular.

Oliver Cromwell, the lord-general of the Commonwealth's forces, restrained the army from interfering, until his hand was forced; he realized that the Rump for all its faults represented the only surviving legal and constitutional authority in England. In April 1653 the Rump produced a bill which made the tenure of sitting members perpetual, and a proposal to dismiss Cromwell from his command. On 20 April 1653 Cromwell ejected the members. For three months England was ruled by a military dictatorship consisting of the council of officers and Cromwell, who was the only remaining constitutionally appointed authority. The council's solution for ruling, a nominated assembly of the godly (later known as Barebone's Parliament), was established on 4 July 1653 and assumed responsibility for the government of the Commonwealth. This experiment failed and the moderate members resigned their authority in Cromwell's favour (12 Dec. 1653). Within a week, the Commonwealth ended with Cromwell's acceptance of the Instrument of Government, which established the Protectorate.

The Commonwealth was in effect re-established on 7 May 1659, when the army recalled the Rump, though Richard Cromwell technically remained protector until his resignation to the Rump on 25 May. The members of the Rump learnt nothing from their six-year adjournment and friction with the army continued. The result was again the expulsion of the Rump by the army (Oct. 1659), this time under John Lambert. Events, however, were moving out of control of the English army officers and into the hands of Monck and his Scottish army. Monck declared in favour of the Rump, and on 26 Dec. 1659 it was hastily recalled by Lambert and Charles Fleetwood. Monck, on his arrival in London (Feb. 1660), soon realized the perversity of the Rump and its inability to prevent the anarchy which threatened to break out. On 21 Feb. therefore, Monck readmitted the excluded members of the Long Parliament and the way to the Restoration lay open. On 16 March the Long Parliament dissolved itself and effectually ended the Commonwealth, Charles II being declared king on 8 May 1660.

G. Davies, *The Early Stuarts* (London, 1927).
I. Roots, *The Great Rebellion* (London, 1966).   CJ

COMMONWEALTH, THE BRITISH EMPIRE AND. In the 15th cent. technical advances made it possible for the known world, in the European concept of things, to be carried beyond the Iberian peninsula to the Americas and India. A decaying feudalism stimulated the economic forces behind such activity, while medieval christendom reflected an age of faith that encouraged missionary endeavour.

England at first contributed nothing to such enterprises; only gradually was the challenge to Spanish and Portuguese imperialism taken up. In the 16th cent. there was a progression of thought in men who allied seamanship with business acumen and political understanding, the Elizabethan sailors making possible a British Empire. Hawkins saw the immediate need to establish a profitable economy on the Spanish Main; Drake linked this with the 'prestige' role of military

and Protestant defiance of the Spaniard; and Raleigh envisaged the settlements in the New World which would give a permanent claim to an empire.

By the 17th cent. English emigrants, separatist in outlook, had made their homes in North America or the West Indies. In the east, the agents of the English East India Co. were traders rather than colonists. Those who worked for the company hoped to return to England wealthy.

No worthwhile philosophy yet belonged to this 17th-cent. pattern of empire. The economic historian labels it 'mercantilist'. The tight nexus of mother-country and daughter colonies—or trading posts—was something 'self-sufficient'. It was an economy which relied as little as possible on neighbours and claimed the dependent territories as subservient. This was reflected in the West Indies, where the British created a powerful sugar-interest. In the 18th cent. the mercantilism of Britain and her European rivals led to wars over colonial territory and trading concessions. In both west and east the conflict was basically Anglo–French, with the Dutch, Spanish, and Portuguese playing subsidiary roles.

Within the British American colonies there had grown a sophistication about which those 'at home' knew little. Despite economic depression and balance-of-trade deficits, colonial society had reached a level of material comfort and of political maturity. To men like John Adams revolution had been 'in the minds and hearts of the people from the beginning'. Colonial self-government and economic freedom were the ambitions of an independent people. Britain, in facing her first exercise in imperial relations, refused to yield equality.

While the newly fledged 'Americans' found their philosophers of independence, *eg*, Thomas Jefferson, others in Britain were rethinking the role of empire. Adam Smith, in his *Inquiry into the Nature and Causes of the Wealth of Nations*, attacked the system of mercantilism, and sought to 'free' trade rather than 'protect' it. In so arguing he contributed to the changed economic interpretation of empire. Edmund Burke, who had sympathized with the American colonies, became involved in Indian affairs, as the first great moralist of empire. His concern was with dependent people and the tyranny of government. He was a liberal—but no democrat. From Burke came the doctrine that empire was a trust and a responsibility. This was to be the philosophy of the 19th cent.

Both Smith and Burke influenced the policies of William Pitt the Younger. His legislation upon the newly acquired Canada and on India provided a scheme of administration for those territories for half a century, and his ad hoc acceptance of Botany Bay as a convict settlement led to the growth of the Australian colonies.

Australia, together with Canada and New Zealand (after 1840), represented what came to be called the white dominions. They may be regarded as an uncomplicated aspect of empire. While the integration of convicts and free settlers, the discord of Anglo–French interests, and the conflicts with the Maoris all posed their own particular problems, these territories had a placid relationship with Britain. Each progressed towards self-government. The outstanding example of contemporary thinking in this direction occurred in the Durham Report of 1839, which inspired the doctrine of responsible government. The political significance of this document may be matched, constitutionally, by the Colonial Laws Validity Act (1865).

Meanwhile, in 19th-cent. India, Bentinck and Dalhousie and the Lawrences sought to establish good government, to reform and to cultivate. They had an instinct for administration and a great sense of mission.

Less altruistic motives were also evident in this period of imperial history. Britain, along with other European nations, was caught up in the 'scramble for Africa'. In 1870 a tenth of that continent was in the possession of Europe; at the end, a tenth remained independent. Economic attraction in terms of investment in technical and trading enterprises explains much of this process of imperial expansion. White nations were caught in the web of the 'prestige' rivalries which dominated their relationships up to 1914. Less distinctly, a similar pattern of events was taking shape in the Far East.

In South Africa, where the Cape had been the starting-point of British interest, the philosophies that divided Boer and Briton culminated in a war (1899–1902) which in the long run settled nothing. South Africa's departure from the Commonwealth in 1961 was the ultimate step for the descendants of those who had made the Great Trek.

The 19th-cent. empire did not lack men with a vision of the future. Lord Macaulay envisaged the day when colonial peoples would demand for themselves the control of their own institutions. Lord Rosebery, in a speech at Adelaide (1887), anticipated a Commonwealth of Nations. The constitutional lawyers took up the phrase in the Statute of Westminster in 1931. In 1947 began the chain of events from which the contemporary Commonwealth takes its origin. India and Pakistan led the way for the colonies of the old empire to become the multi-racial partners in Commonwealth in an association of nations occupying nearly a quarter of the land space of the world. Diversity in colour, class, and creed is the essence of this union. Its existence as a focus for world peace, racial tolerance, and as a source of mutual technological and economic help enables it, even under stress, to make a contribution towards the unification of all peoples.

Lord Elton, *Imperial Commonwealth* (London, 1945).
T. Soper, *Evolving Commonwealth* (London, 1965).

GMDH

COMMONWEALTH OF AUSTRALIA, CONSTITUTION OF THE, was enacted by the UK parliament (1900). Its terms had been adopted by an elected constitutional convention in Australia (1897–8) and thereafter approved at referenda held in the various states after the enactment, but before its proclamation. The constitution provided for a new commonwealth entity, invested with legislative, executive, and judicial powers. Its bicameral legislature comprised the House of Representatives, reflecting population distribution, and the Senate, formed by equal representation of the states. The commonwealth parliament was invested with enumerated and specific powers, among them defence, taxation (with customs and excise taxation exclusively vested in the Commonwealth), the regulation of inter-state and overseas trade, external affairs, and the power to legislate for conciliation and arbitration in inter-state industrial disputes. The state constitutions and powers were preserved, except where these were affected by specific provisions of the commonwealth constitution. There were areas of concurrent legislative power, in which the grants of power to the Commonwealth parliament did not *ipso facto* withdraw power from the state legislatures. In such cases, where conflict or repugnancy occurred in the exercise of powers, it was provided that the commonwealth exercise of power should prevail.

The constitution provided for an executive government of the commonwealth and specifically declared for a parliamentary executive by prescribing that ministers must be or become members of one of the two houses of the commonwealth parliament. Provision was also made for a federal judiciary, the most important element of which was the High Court of Australia, to which was assigned the important role of interpreting the constitution; but it was also given a very wide jurisdiction as a general court of appeal from the state as well as from lower federal courts. Unlike the US constitution, the commonwealth constitution did not contain a comprehensive body of 'bill-of-rights' provisions: there were one or two, but they assumed comparatively little importance in Australian constitutional history and its interpretation. Undoubtedly, the most important limitation upon the powers of commonwealth and states alike was that imposed by section 92, providing that trade, commerce, and intercourse among the states shall be free. This broad provision, as interpreted in many cases, proved a potent restraint upon the exercise of legislative and governmental powers.

The process of amending the constitution, involving sub-

D W H—N

mission of amendment proposals to popular referenda, became a formidable obstacle to constitutional change: a few substantive amendments of importance were adopted, but most proposals failed, the constitution remaining in form very much as originally enacted. The role of the high court as a constitutional court was of major importance, its interpretations in various respects giving the constitution an adaptability to meet conditions unanticipated by the founding fathers.

Time brought a substantial increase in central power, partly as the result of war and its aftermath, when judicial interpretations of the commonwealth defence power were very broad, and partly because the commonwealth was able to establish a controlling fiscal position. Wide interpretations of the power to make grants to the states on terms and conditions specified by the commonwealth also gave the central authority power to influence areas (*eg*, education) where no power was originally seen as residing with the commonwealth. One of the major frustrations of the states became the disparity between sources of constitutional authority and responsibility, and the availability of financial resources. One of the more hopeful developments was the emergence of co-operative federalism—of states, and in some cases groups of states, working together and with the commonwealth to achieve common policies.

W. A. Wynes, *Legislative, Executive and Judicial Powers in the Commonwealth of Australia* (Sydney, 1962).
R. Else-Mitchell (ed.), *Essays on the Australian Constitution* (Sydney, 1961).

LC

COMMONWEALTH SUGAR AGREEMENT ACT (1951), British law designed to permit long-term planning of sugar production and marketing in the British Commonwealth. By 1970 the act had guaranteed a degree of economic stability for Commonwealth countries dependent on sugar prices. For Britain sugar paid for in sterling saved foreign currency.

COMMUNAL AWARD, scheme announced by the British prime minister, Ramsay MacDonald (16 Aug. 1932), following the failure of the delegates at the first and second Round Table Conferences (1930–1) to agree on a formula. It provided for the representation of the various Indian communities in the new constitution. The award gave separate electorates to Muslims in all provinces and to Sikhs, Europeans, Anglo–Indians, Indian Christians, and Depressed Classes where their numbers warranted it. These provisions were to be reviewed after ten years and a provision that Depressed Classes voters were to have a vote in the general constituencies as well as their separate electorates was to be reviewed after 20 years. Although the British government refused to enter into further negotiations itself regarding these provisions, it would accept modifications agreed by Indians themselves. Consequently the provisions for Depressed Classes seats were revised in the light of the Poona Pact (25 Sept. 1932), which gave the Depressed Classes increased representation, but through reserved seats rather than separate electorates. There was also a further supplementary award by the secretary of state, Sir Samuel Hoare (24 Dec. 1932), which assured the Muslims of one-third of the seats in the federal legislature, although the overall composition of the federal chambers had to be postponed until agreement on federation was reached. The award gave the Muslims all that they had expected in terms of representation, but Hindu opinion was generally hostile. The Congress, claiming to represent all communities, refused either to accept or reject the award and pressed for a constituent assembly representative of Indian opinion in order to devise a national solution to the problem.

COMMUNERO REVOLT (1520–1), serious outbreak of popular discontent in the towns of Castile against the steady undermining of their financial independence by the Crown, inspired in particular by the demand for money to finance

Charles V's journey to Germany to be crowned emperor. From early in the 16th cent. the towns resented the growing control of the Crown over their deputies in the *cortes* of Castile, and the imposition of the *corregidores* to supervise town administration added to their resentment. During the regency of Cardinal Jimenes (1516–19), relations between the towns and the Crown deteriorated, with the prospect of a ruler whose interests lay outside Spain. At the *cortes* of Curunna and Santiago (1520) only strong pressure ensured the voting of the required supplies. As Charles left Spanish shores, the citizens of Toledo and Valladolid repudiated their deputies to the *cortes* and set up a revolutionary junta. In many towns the people joined together in communes, appointed their own officials, and claimed to be acting for the true kingdom. Throughout the winter of 1520–1 the revolutionary elements in the towns seized control of the *comuneros*, causing alarm to the once-sympathetic urban nobility. The latter defected to the royalists, headed by the governor, Adrian of Utrecht, and the *communero* forces were defeated at the battle of Villalar (23 April 1521). The collapse of the movement gave the Crown complete authority over the towns and *cortes* of Castile.

COMMUNIST MANIFESTO (1848), most important political pamphlet of the 19th cent. and the classic exposition of Marxixm. Written by Marx and Engels in London (1847) in the growing discontent which led to the revolutions of 1848, its influence on the outbreak and course of these risings was slight. Its influence lay in the later 19th cent. and the foundation of the national communist parties and international communist movement. The pamphlet, published originally in German (1848) and then translated into English (1850), adopted a scientific approach to history, which was seen exclusively in terms of a class struggle: real historical change occurs only when one class overthrows its oppressor. Drawing up a programme for political action, Marx and Engels called for the overthrow of the existing bourgeois capitalist system in western Europe, claiming that its downfall was inevitable, and the substitution of a collectivist system, directed by the dictatorship of the proletariat, and the elimination of class.

COMMUNIST PARTY OF ALBANIA, smallest ruling communist party in the world. The origins of communism in Albania reach back to the followers of Fan Noli, the exiled leader. Several of his associates found their way to Moscow by way of Vienna and Paris and there formed a National Revolutionary Committee. Sejfulla Maleshova, Noli's secretary, and Lazar Fundo were the most important of these early communists. Maleshova was purged from the central committee in 1948 and Fundo was killed in 1944 after deserting the party for the nationalists. It was a Geg tribesman, Ali Kelmendi, who organized the first cells in Albania. But he was forced to flee the country in 1936. As a result of his activities, four cells or discussion groups were established, the most significant being run by Enver Hoxha and Koci Xoxe. These discussion groups were welded into a political party by the Yugoslavs. In 1941 Miladin Popovic and Dusan Mugosa were sent to Albania by Tito to organize the communist resistance there in anticipation of the future union of the two countries. Between 1941 and 1948 the Albanian party was an extension of the Yugoslav. The party was founded on 8 Nov. 1941. In the spring of 1943 the communist resistance initiated the formation of the National Liberation Movement and later the National Liberation Council. Enver Hoxha was made secretary general of the party at this time. When Albanian communists announced that the future of Kosmet would be decided by a plebiscite, Tito suppressed what he regarded as a nationalist deviation. In May 1944 the National Liberation Council proclaimed itself the national government and in Nov. forcibly seized power. The years before the Soviet–Yugoslav split were marked by efforts towards closer association between Yugoslavia and Albania, initiated by the Yugoslavs and furthered

by Xoxe in the Albanian leadership. The split in 1948 freed Albania from Yugoslav domination and secured Hoxha's supremacy in the party. Later efforts at a Soviet–Yugoslav rapprochement threatened both Albanian independence and Hoxha's position. Both were saved by the Hungarian events of 1956, but by 1959 the problem had reappeared. Hoxha, afraid of being forced into an unnatural relationship with Yugoslavia by the Kremlin, aligned his party with the Chinese, exploiting the Sino-Soviet rift to assure Albania's position. The Albanian party broke with the CPSU in Nov. 1961 and since then has been the strident champion of Chinese-style communism and Albanian nationalism in the Balkans.   JMK

COMMUNIST PARTY IN AUSTRALIA, developed out of the Australian Socialist Party (1920). With adherents of International Workers of the World attempting 'to bring about a socialist Australia', the CPA was established in Dec. 1921. Membership grew to 2100 in 1932 and the party controlled the 'Unemployment Workers' Movement'. Though declared illegal (15 June 1940), the prohibition was lifted after Germany's invasion of USSR and party membership rose to approximately 22,500 by 1944. CPA influence in the trade union movement also grew rapidly, its leaders seeking to divert trade union funds and affiliations from the Australian Labor party to their own. Early post-war strike activities by the CPA provoked a strong reaction from the Chifley Labor government. Its successor, the Menzies coalition government attempted, in 1950, to debar communists from holding office in trade unions and the public service, but the high court declared these moves invalid and a referendum on a proposal to amend the constitution was rejected in three states by a small overall majority. The CPA's fortunes in the 1950s and 1960s reflected the ferment and diversity in world communism. Revelations about Stalin, repression in Hungary and Czechoslovakia, and the Sino-Soviet conflict caused a party split, the pro-Chinese membership forming a rival faction. With party membership in decline, communist leaders were searching to adapt their philosophy to Australian conditions.

COMMUNIST PARTY DISSOLUTION ACT, THE (1950), in Australia, was introduced by the Menzies–Fadden Liberal–Country Party government which came into office (Dec. 1949) pledged to suppress communism. The bill dissolving the Communist Party and excluding its members from public and trade union office contained many illiberal features which provoked strong opposition inside and outside parliament, which was not confined to ALP ranks. The bill, considerably amended in the light of this criticism, was passed, but was declared unconstitutional by the high court (March 1951). A referendum on a constitutional amendment to make possible the valid re-enactment of the defeated measure was rejected.

COMMUNIST PARTY OF GERMANY, Kommunistiche Partei Deutschlands (KPD), established at a Congress of the Spartakus League in Berlin, 30 Dec. 1918–1 Jan. 1919. The Spartakists were led by Rosa Luxemburg and Karl Liebknecht; also present were the International Communists of Germany (IKD) and four Russian Bolsheviks, headed by Radek. The new party favoured giving all power in Germany to the workers' and soldiers' councils which had appeared in the Nov. Revolution, and decided to boycott parliamentary elections. On 5 Jan. 1919 the KPD became involved in an attempt to overthrow the government in Berlin. Although Rosa Luxemburg opposed this enterprise, she could not desert her followers. The subsequent conflict, known as the Spartakus rising, was violently repressed. On 15 Jan. government troops murdered her and Liebknecht.

Paul Levi assumed the party leadership and won many Independent Social Democrats over to the KPD. He resigned in 1921, having clashed with the Comintern over Italian socialist policies. Although the KPD joined the Comintern in 1919, Rosa Luxemburg had not wanted to submit to

Lenin's dictates. Radek, the Comintern's expert on Germany, regarded her followers with suspicion, and persistently interfered with KPD affairs. In Oct. 1923 the KPD attempted to launch a full-scale revolution, but was prevented by the army. Although the Comintern leadership and radical KPD groups were responsible for this failure, the party's leader, Heinrich Brandler, was blamed and was forced to resign.

The KPD subsequently became an obedient Comintern servant. Its leader, Ernst Thälmann, possessed physical courage, but limited intellect. It gained working-class support during the 1920s, especially among the young, profiting from the inability of the Social Democrats (SPD) to inspire working-class youth. The KPD also attracted the unemployed, the Depression providing an opportunity for expansion. In 1930 it became the third largest Reichstag party, with 77 seats. By Nov. 1932 it had 100 seats, having polled over 5 million votes. Unlike the Nazi Party, its fortunes were still rising in the autumn of 1932.

Although the KPD stressed its opposition to Fascism, its main target of abuse was the more moderate SPD, which it rightly saw as its main rival for working-class support. When Hitler took power the KPD expected his rule to be a short prelude to the final crisis in Germany's capitalist system. The Nazis acted quickly to repress the communists, who suffered severely at their hands. In 1944 Thälmann was murdered in Buchenwald. Some communists did, however, maintain underground cells in Germany, which probably accounted for the most active resistance to Hitler before July 1944. Many KPD functionaries fled abroad; some took refuge in Russia and died during Stalin's purges. Those surviving included Walter Ulbricht and Wilhelm Pieck.

On 1 May 1945 Ulbricht's group returned to Germany's Soviet-controlled zone to build a political movement there. On 11 June a KPD manifesto declared it did not want to force a Soviet system on Germany, and called for a democratic, anti-fascist republic. In April 1946 the Soviet Zone KPD merged with the SPD to form the Socialist Unity Party (SED) under the leadership of Ulbricht, Pieck, and Otto Grotewohl. The KPD continued to exist in Western Germany, with poor support, winning no seats in the 1953 Bundestag elections. On 17 Aug. 1956 the German Constitutional Court ruled the KPD an illegal organization. In Sept. 1968 a new communist party, the DKP, was established there.

W. T. Angress, *Still-born Resolution: the Communist bid for power in Germany, 1921–1923* (Princeton, 1963).

R. Fischer, *Stalin and German Communism* (Cambridge, MA, 1948). AJN

COMMUNIST PARTY IN GREECE emerged as a result of dissensions and schisms in the socialist movement after the First World War. It appeared as a distinct group in 1918, but only called itself 'communist' in 1920. During the 1920s it had little success; its recruits were mainly radical students, professional men, discontented Macedonian tobacco workers, and refugees from Asia Minor. In 1926 ten of its candidates were elected to parliament, eight of them from Macedonia. After the 1936 elections the communists, who with 15 seats, held the balance in parliament, called for a popular front government. Negotiations were begun with the major parties and a deal was made with the Liberals by which the communists agreed to support a Liberal government on the promise that reforms would be introduced. However, a non-party government was formed and this understanding was dropped. A strike revealed the extent of communist power and gave Metaxas a premise on which to demand emergency powers. Until the Second World War the party was forced underground by the repressive measures of Metaxas's dictatorship, but after the war broke out the underground provided the basis for a resistance movement. The National Liberation Front (EAM) and National Popular Liberation Army (ELAS) were established under communist direction, both to resist the German occupation and initiate a communist revolution. As the strongest and best-equpped of the various resistance movements, it was able to cripple its opponents while ostensibly fighting the occupation forces. By the end of the war the communist resistance units presented a severe threat to the established order in Greece. In Dec. 1944 they precipitated a civil war in which they were defeated only by the intervention of a British military mission. A truce was reached in Feb. 1945, but a second insurrection began after the return of Nikos Zachariades, the communist leader, from Dachau. It had, however, little chance of success; the implementation of the Truman doctrine, Tito's closure of the frontier, and widespread opposition in Greece gave the so-called Democratic army not much hope of victory. The government outlawed the party in 1947 and in a major campaign (1948–9) captured the revolutionary stronghold at Mt Grammos in Aug. 1949. The memory of the civil war and the communist threat has ever since been a major and often decisive force in Greek politics. Although the party remained (1970) outlawed in Greece, many Greeks turned to communism to express their opposition to the conservative and authoritarian parties which had ruled since the civil war.

JMK

COMMUNIST PARTY OF HUNGARY, known as the Hungarian Socialist Workers' Party (Magyar Szocialista Munkáspárt—MSZMP), formerly the Hungarian Communist Party (1918–48) and Hungarian Workers' Party (after the absorption of the Social-Democrats in 1948). The Hungarian Communist Party was founded on 21 Nov. 1918, on the initiative of Hungarian prisoners of war in Russia, with Béla Kun as its leader. Just four months later the party found itself in power in Hungary, where it proclaimed a Soviet Republic which lasted 133 days. Under the Regency which followed, the Hungarian Communist Party was illegal and remained so until 1945; in the interval, rent by internal quarrels, penetrated and suppressed by the Hungarian police, and its émigré leadership decimated in the Russian purges, the party was of no importance. On being reorganized after the Second World War, the party gained 17 per cent of the votes at the 1946 elections, as against 57 per cent for the Small-holders' Party; but by 1948, relying on Soviet support and using what the party leader, Mátyas Rákosi, called 'salami tactics', it had eliminated the Small-holders and split and absorbed the Social-Democrats. In 1949 the Soviet–Yugoslav dispute was made the occasion for the purge and execution of Rákosi's chief rivals in the party, notably those who had spent the war years in Hungary rather than in the USSR. After Stalin's death, Imre Nagy, the prime minister, introduced some economic relaxation—the beginning of a process which, interacting with events elsewhere in the Soviet bloc, led in 1956 to the revolt against Soviet domination and repression by Soviet troops. Under the impact of the revolt the Communist Party virtually disintegrated. A new party, which claimed to be untainted with the crimes of its predecessor, was therefore announced on 1 Nov. 1956: the Hungarian Socialist Workers' Party (MSZMP). Whereas the old party had 800,000 members, the new one was much smaller, numbering 100,000 in Jan. 1957, a figure that rose to 400,000, and later to 580,000 (1966). Its composition was correspondingly more elite and less proletarian. Under its new first secretary, János Kádár, the party first suppressed the remaining supporters of the 1956 revolt, and then aimed with some success at reaching a *modus vivendi* with the Hungarian people. Internationally, both within the world communist movement and outside it, the MSZMP has been loyal to the Soviet Party, though there were signs of hesitancy in its support of the Soviet invasion of Czechoslovakia in 1968. RKK

COMMUNIST PARTY OF INDIA. Communist activities started in the early 1920s, but only began to be effective with trade union and Workers' and Peasants' Party agitation (1927–9), which was conducted with the advice of British communists. These developments were interrupted by the Meerut conspiracy case (1929–34), when almost the entire leadership was arraigned. It was not until the leaders were released and a provisional central committee was established under P. C. Joshi that a firmly based communist party appeared. In the later 1930s the party infiltrated the Congress and Congress Socialist Party organizations to operate a united front. On the outbreak of war many communist leaders were arrested, but after the German attack upon the Soviet Union the communists were eager to help efforts to wage the 'people's war' and the party was made legal (1943). The war enabled the party to consolidate its position within the trade unions, in peasant associations (*kisan sabhas*) and among students. Membership, which had been about 150 in the mid-1930s and had risen to about 5000 by 1943, exceeded 50,000 in 1946.

Following independence there was a sharp reappraisal of the party's strategy. P. C. Joshi was replaced (1948) by B. T. Ranadive, who instituted adventurist attacks upon the government with a view to armed insurrection. He, in turn, was replaced (1950) by Rajeshwar Rao, who was to bring the CPI into line with the lessons of the communist victory in China. On the eve of the first general elections Ajoy Ghosh became general secretary, and during his ascendancy (1951–1962) the party's strategy changed from insurrectionary to constitutional communism. Under his direction, but not without left-wing criticism, the party gained electoral victory in Kerala (1957) and became the largest opposition party in the Lok Sabha. After Ghosh's death (1962) the cleavages within the party deepened and led to the holding of rival party congresses (1964) by the left, led by E. M. S. Namboodiripad and the Bengali party leaders, and the right led by S. A. Dange, a veteran communist from the early 1920s. This split widened through the later 1960s, linked as it was increasingly with a growing Sino-Soviet cleavage.

COMMUNIST PARTY IN INDONESIA, Partai Komunis Indonesia (PKI), oldest communist party in non-Russian Asia. It was established in May 1920 from the Indies Social Democratic Association (ISDV), which had been founded in 1914 and whose members formed a bloc within the first Indonesian mass movement, *Sarekat Islam*. After a bitter fight for control, the communists were expelled from the *Sarekat Islam* in 1923, but took with them the bulk of its followers. Their popularity rested on their radical opposition to Dutch rule, and as their opportunities for legal activity diminished, they decided to stake all on rebellion. In 1926 and early 1927 communist-led revolts took place in West Java and West Sumatra; thereafter the movement, crushed, was dormant until the outbreak of the Indonesian revolution.

In Nov. 1945 the party re-emerged under the unorthodox leadership of Mohammad Jusuf. In 1946 it was purged by leaders returning from abroad, and it adopted a course of self-effacement, supporting the republican government in its negotiations with the Dutch. At the beginning of 1948 it reversed this course after the replacement of the left-wing government of Amir Sjarifuddin by a non-parliamentary, conservative cabinet under Vice-President Muhammad Hatta. It allied itself with major left-wing organizations in the People's Democratic Front (FDR) coalition. Its rapidly worsening relations with the government culminated in the Madiun Affair of Sept. 1948; in this clash the communist forces were defeated, but the PKI resumed legal activity in 1950, after the end of the revolution.

In Jan. 1951 party control was seized by D. N. Aidit and other young leaders, who wished to see it pursue a more clearly national line. Under their command the party rapidly gained support. The elections of 1955 showed it to be Indonesia's fourth largest party, and its rapid advance in the 1957 elections threatened to bring it into first place. None the less, its leaders decided it could not afford to oppose the replacement of the parliamentary system by Guided Democracy, and they concentrated on making themselves indispensable to Sukarno under the new system. Between 1963 and 1965 it advanced rapidly in visible popularity and in Sukarno's sympathy. It claimed to be the largest communist

party not in power, with 3 million members. The PKI attempted to play a mediating role in the Sino–Soviet dispute, but leaned increasingly to Peking's side.

In spite of the communists' public prominence, they were unable to gain positions in the bureaucracy or army, and they had few positions in formal government, so that they remained outside the country's power structure; neither did they possess arms of their own. Mounting social and economic pressures in 1965 led to extreme tensions; with General Suharto's seizure of power following the defeat of the Sept. 30 Movement, the army sought to destroy the PKI and encouraged the massacre of its adherents. Regrouping underground, party leaders denounced the Aidit policy of legalism and called for guerrilla struggle based on agrarian revolution.

COMMUNIST PARTY IN ITALY, Partito Comunista Italiano (PCI), founded (1921) by socialists, under Bordiga and Gramsci, unconditionally accepting Lenin's 21 conditions for membership of the Third International. After a split in its membership, it waited for the liberal–fascist–socialist struggle to destroy capitalism. With the arrest of Gramsci and other leaders, and a ban on the party (1926), it went underground, maintained anti-fascist cells, and played a major role in the wartime partisan struggle in northern Italy. Under Togliatti's leadership, and Moscow's orders, the PCI joined the early coalitions (1944–7) and rejected immediate revolution. It has become the largest western communist party, and the second largest party in Italy, with support in all social groups. Though out of national government, it has remained active in local council coalitions. Maoists have weakened its authoritarian leadership by attacking reformism in the 'national path to socialism', but new moderates want more co-operation with socialists and left-wing Catholics for active social reform, through local 'dialogues'.

COMMUNIST PARTY IN NEW ZEALAND, formed in 1921, was refused affiliation with Labour, but has had occasional footholds in militant unions, notably in 1951. Its highest share of votes in a general election was 0·3 per cent (1949).

COMMUNIST PARTY OF POLAND, known as the Polish United Workers' Party (Polska Zjednoczona Partia Robotnicza—PZPR), formed in 1948, when the left-wing fraction of the Polish socialists was absorbed by the Polish Workers' Party (PPR), the name then used by the Polish communists. Earlier names of the party had been the Communist Workers' Party of Poland (KPRP), 1918–25, and Communist Party of Poland (KPP), 1925–38. The original Communist Workers' Party had been founded in 1918 by the fusion of two left-wing socialist parties, and had joined the Comintern in 1919, by which time it had something over 6000 members. During the next two decades the party was illegal, though some communists, acting through front organizations, were elected to the Seym. There were frequent changes of leadership, imposed by Moscow in response to the demands of Russian, as much as Polish, intra-party struggles. These culminated in the dissolution of the party and the murder of most of its leaders on Stalin's orders at the height of the Russian purges in 1938. The KPP has since been officially cleared of the charges of police penetration then brought against it, but Stalin's precise motives for this action, which left an indelible mark on Polish communism, remain a matter of speculation.

After the German attack on the USSR, two organizations—a Union of Polish Patriots on Soviet soil and a Polish Workers' Party (PPR) in occupied Poland—were founded under communist control. In 1944 these jointly formed the Committee of National Liberation under Soviet protection in Lublin. Through this organization, which declared itself the provisional government of Poland at the end of 1944, the PPR made its way to power. A recruitment drive increased membership from about 20,000 at the end of the war to 250,000 by Dec. 1945. Elections were postponed until 1947, by which time the PPR could ensure itself of 80 per cent of the votes for a 'democratic bloc' under its own control. Its main adversary, the Polish Peasant Party, was intimidated and its leaders driven abroad. The left-wing socialists were then absorbed, leaving a spurious coalition which has ruled Poland ever since. But the Polish United Workers' Party (as it now became) was split between the 'Muscovite' and 'native' factions—the Muscovites who had spent the pre-war and war years in the Soviet Union and the natives who had been in Poland. Gomulka, the leader of the native faction and the main proponent of a 'Polish way to socialism', was forced out of office and put under house arrest, and from 1948 till the death of Stalin the Muscovites prevailed. In Oct. 1956 Gomulka's dramatic return to power marked a new victory for the native faction, and a peak of popularity which the party had never achieved before or has reached since. Subsequently, with Krushchev in power in the USSR, new factions were formed, notably the so-called 'Partisans', who represented a challenge to the leadership on the basis of nationalism, anti-semitism, and repressive domestic policies. In the international communist movement, the PZPR at one time tried to mediate between the Soviet and Chinese parties, but subsequently became a loyal supporter of the CPSU, maintaining its support even on the invasion of Czechoslovakia in 1968.

M. K. Dziewanowski, *The Communist Party of Poland* (Harvard, 1969).   RKK

COMMUNIST PARTY IN RUMANIA grew out of the socialist movement. A delegation sent to Moscow by the Socialist Party in 1920 affiliated the party with the Third International. The bulk of the party, however, opposed affiliation and the party became divided. In 1921 the dissident group, dubbing themselves socialist-communists, held a congress, but it was broken up by the police before a new party could be firmly established. During the next year a central committee was elected and party statutes were drafted.

The history of Rumanian communism has traditionally been marked by conflict between its national and foreign elements. From the beginning, the party was an instrument of Soviet foreign policy wielded by the Comintern, which interfered regularly in the party's affairs, and imposed its own programme on the party. The party's lack of success in the inter-war years can largely be ascribed to the Comintern's interference in its affairs. Considerable instability was caused by frequent changes in leadership, which in 1932 involved the replacement of Rumanians with men of other nationality, constant criticism of the party's deviationist tendencies, and perpetual changes in tactics. The party's programme, following the Comintern's nationality policy, called for the virtual dismemberment of the Rumanian state. It is not surprising that with these handicaps Rumanian communism was both the weakest and most unpopular in East Europe. One event, however, stood out in the party's history: in 1933 the railway workers at Grivita struck. They were led by communists, one of whom was Gheorghe Gheorghiu-Dej, whose reputation as a courageous radical had survived 12 years' imprisonment. At the outbreak of the Second World War the party was divided. Imprisoned in Rumania, and supported by a handful of intellectuals who had avoided prison, were the working-class communists who had gathered round Gheorghiu-Dej. In the Soviet Union were the former leaders of the party linked to the Comintern bureaucracy and led by Ana Pauker. The division between the 'home' communists and the Muscovites dominated the early years of communism in Rumania after the war.   JMK

COMMUNIST PARTY OF SOUTH AFRICA, originated in 1915 in the International Socialist League. After its legal suppression (1950), its members found their sphere of action in the rising industrial towns of South Africa. Many members continued to campaign against apartheid and its consequences, especially in the trade union field, until all legal forms of protest became effectively impossible (1962); some then went underground, others into exile.

COMMUNIST PARTY OF SPAIN (Partido Comunista de España—PCE), founded 7 Nov. 1921. The party was banned by Primo de Rivera in 1923 and suffered repeated changes of leadership at the hands of the Comintern in the 1920s, during which period it remained numerically and politically weak and unable to compete with anarchist and socialist forces in the Spanish labour movement. With the proclamation of the republic in 1931, the PCE, which numbered no more than 800 members, was restored to legality. In the following year it held a congress at Seville. In the uneasy political atmosphere of the first years of the republic membership grew quickly, reaching perhaps 10,000 in 1934, mostly in and around Madrid. In Oct. 1934 the Asturias rebellion temporarily united all left-wing forces in the area, and when Popular Front tactics were adopted in 1935 they were carried further in Spain than anywhere else. In the elections of Feb. 1936 Popular Front candidates won 256 seats in the Cortes, of which 14 went to communists. A Popular Front government was formed and in Sept. 1936, after the Civil War had begun, it was joined by two communists—against the inclination of the PCE Central Committee, but in obedience to Comintern instructions. Although Comintern policy served Soviet interests rather than those of the PCE, the latter nevertheless gained much power and influence by participation in government, where they could claim credit for Soviet arms supplies. Communists were also prominent in the army commands. Much of their power was used against other left-wing organizations, particularly anarchists, and, when the purges in Moscow got under way, against Trotskyists and others. Unlike these groups, the communists, acting on Comintern instructions, eliminated measures of social revolution from their immediate programme. However, although Stalin did not want a victory for the nationalists, he feared that a communist Spain would drive the Western powers into alliance with Hitler and Mussolini. Furthermore, he was not ready to risk a major war for the sake of a republican victory. The PCE was thus deprived of any chance of achieving full power. Before the nationalist victory, the PCE claimed as many as 300,000 members; after the fall of the republic it was banned, and has remained so ever since. Its leaders went into exile in France (from which, however, the PCE was banned in 1950), in various communist countries, and in Latin America.   RKK

COMMUNIST PARTY OF THE SOVIET UNION (CPSU), was officially born, under the title of the Russian Social Democratic Labour Party, in Minsk in 1898. Under Lenin's leadership it took on several of its leading characteristics at the Brussels–London Congress in 1903. He insisted that all party members should be activists, that they should accept without question the decisions of the leadership, and that they should be prepared to seize power by revolutionary rather than democratic means. Lenin's faction of the RSDLP (known until 1918 as the Bolsheviks) seized power in 1917; it then consisted of about 80,000 members. By 1939 it had 2,306,973; by 1947 this figure had increased to 6,300,000, and by 1961 to 9,716,005. During this period a party of revolutionaries had changed itself into the driving force behind every aspect of Soviet economic and political life. 'The guiding principle of the organizational structure of the Party' is defined in the party rules as 'Democratic Centralism'. This concept embraces two apparently contradictory ideas: first, 'the election of all party executives from bottom to top', and second, 'the absolutely binding character of the decisions of higher bodies upon lower bodies'. In practice, the latter idea is dominant. Democratic forms are preserved for the election of all party bodies from the Presidium (known until 1952 as the Politburo) at the top, through the Republic, provincial, town, and district committees to the party cells at the bottom. But in effect democratic forms are merely used to confirm decisions already made.

The key to this vast organization is the Secretariat, which took shape under Stalin in the early 1920s: control of this group enabled him to pack the interlocking committees of the party and thus to insure a majority obedient to his will. The Secretariat is concerned with the selection and appointment of the full-time party bureaucrats, the *apparatchiki*: this is the ruling elite of the Soviet Union. Its exact size is never revealed, but it is estimated to be about a thirty-fifth of the total party membership. The Secretariat moves these key professionals either into party organizations or into leading posts in industry or agriculture. Outside this group other party members have jobs in factories, universities, or government administration and are supposed to act as yeast upon the dough of the non-party personnel. The ideal or dedicated communist is the willing instrument of the decisions of his superiors. The difficulty is to select persons who are sufficiently dynamic to do responsible jobs, yet sufficiently docile to obey orders. Criticism and self-criticism are encouraged so long as the object is the slackness of individuals rather than the main lines of party policy. Candidates are admitted to the party only after careful scrutiny by the basic party cells. Since the 1930s the tendency has been to recruit educated, technical, and professional members rather than proletarians. The CPSU is a unique instrument for the total control of all aspects of national life. No other political party outside the communist world has aspired to the same universality of control. GS

COMMUNITY, FRENCH, abortive attempt, through the Gaullist constitution in 1958, to replace the French Union of the Fourth French Republic. It recognized the 'autonomy' of member states, which 'administer themselves and manage their own affairs democratically and freely'. The institutions of the community were to be an Executive Council, a Senate, and a Court of Arbitration. The idea of the community was accepted by some member states (who, indeed, sought a more integrated organization), and electoral colleges throughout the community elected De Gaulle to the presidency (1959). But a majority of the French colonies in Africa sought complete independence, with the result that the community never came into existence, although France retained its ties with these colonies through bilateral treaties and aid agreements.

COMONFORT, IGNACIO (1812–63), Mexican liberal politician, provisional president (1855–7) and president (1857–8). His willingness to compromise alienated him from both the liberals and conservatives. Comonfort was born in Puebla of creole parentage. He was active in the liberal movement against the Santa Anna dictatorship, gathering arms in the US and organizing exiles for the cause. He actively supported the Plan of Ayutla (1855) and with the fall of Santa Anna became minister of war in the government of Gen. Juan Alvarez. When Alvarez resigned, Comonfort became provisional president. He was elected president under the liberal constitution of 1857. His conciliatory attitude in the dispute over the constitution's liberal provisions could not save his government from the military reaction which followed. Comonfort had accepted the *Ley Lerdo* (June 1856) in hopes of conciliating both factions, but the attack on corporate land holdings drove the ecclesiastical conservatives to war. Comonfort fled to the US when Mexico City fell to the conservatives (1858). He returned to fight the French (1861–3) and was killed in action.

COMORO ISLANDS (2236 sq. kms; 650 sq. miles) off the western coast of Madagascar, with 245,000 inhabitants of mixed Malagasy–Arab–African origin. The islands are part of the French Republic under a high commissioner, with one senator in Paris.

COMPAGNIE DES HABITANTS, first French fur-trading organization, formed at Quebec (1645) and given a monopoly of trade in New France. The company was unprofitable and ceased to exist when New France became a crown colony (1663).

COMPAGNIES D'ORDONNANCE, the name given to the cavalry and mounted infantry units established, in the face of considerable opposition, in France (1445–6) during a truce in the Hundred Years War. King Charles VII and the constable, Arthur de Richemont, had long planned a series of reforms to provide France with effective armed forces and to regularize the relationship between the state and the bands of mercenaries (*routiers*) who ravaged the countryside while not at war. The best mercenary commanders and *routiers* were placed under permanent contract by the Crown and billeted in towns, and a system of taxation was instituted for their maintenance. When the war against England was resumed (1449), they contributed to French successes and helped keep internal order in the royal dominions, becoming the core of a permanent royal army.

COMPANY OF THE NORTH (1682–1713) formed by French-Canadian merchants to trade in furs in Hudson Bay. The company built Fort Bourbon on the Hayes river, and despite keen competition from Hudson's Bay Co. it survived until 1713, when under the treaty of Utrecht all French claims to Hudson Bay were surrendered.

COMPASS. Early documentary evidence establishes use of the compass by the Chinese *c.* 1100 and by western European mariners in 1187. It may have been known to both of them long before its earliest recorded use. There are numerous references to a needle compass from the 13th cent. onwards, although it appears to have been used for checking wind direction in heavy weather rather than for precise navigation.

COMPETITION WALLAH, a derisory term applied to those who entered the Indian civil service by competitive examination after 1856. It was an English–Hindustani hybrid, probably invented by Haileybury members of the service who had gained admission by private interest, family connection, or as a reward for political support. The name was quickly taken up in India, but its use in England was due in no small part to Sir G. O. Trevelyan's *The Competition Wallah* (London, 1864), purporting to be letters written by a competition wallah, to which title Trevelyan had no real claim.

COMPIÈGNE, TREATY OF (1624), agreement of friendship signed on 10 June 1624 between France and the United Provinces. This diplomatic move, instigated by Richelieu, encouraged the anti-Habsburg forces to rally in the Thirty Years War. Later in June, England joined the Franco–Dutch bloc against Spain and the empire, and were followed in July by Sweden, Denmark, Savoy, and Venice, and in Oct. by Brandenburg.

COMPIÈGNE, TREATY OF (1635), negotiated between Richelieu for France and Oxenstierna for Sweden, and signed on 30 April 1635. Sweden, repudiating the agreement made between France and the Heilbronn League in Nov. 1634, extracted more favourable terms from Richelieu. The French agreed to recognize Sweden as an equal ally, to grant the Swedes Worms, Mainz, and Benfield, to promise not to make peace without them, and to declare war on Spain. In return, Sweden recognized the French right to the left bank of the Rhine from Breisach to Strasbourg.

COMPLETE SUFFRAGE UNION. In England in April and Dec. 1842 radical provincial manufacturers and nonconformists conferred with Chartist working men in two Birmingham conferences chaired by the Quaker Joseph Surge. The middle-class supporters swallowed the Chartist programme, but their fear of violence and distaste for O'Connor prevented them from adopting the Chartist name, and the movement therefore collapsed.

COMPOSICIONES, procedure used in colonial Spanish America to obtain royal approval for a previous unauthorized seizure of lands. The forced gathering of the Indians into communities (*congregación*) and the seizure of lands for which the Indians lacked a formal title (*denuncia*) were common occurrences. Since all empty lands (*tierras baldías*) theoretically pertained to the Crown, it was necessary to regularize the results of a questionable process, for which reason the Crown periodically provided for legalization of 'suspicious' titles by the payment of fees to the royal treasury. This led to other greater usurpations and became an important source of Crown revenue.

COMPREHENSION, in England, 18th-cent. movement, supported by certain Whig bishops, *eg,* Abp Wake, for the reunion of the Church of England with the Trinitarian Dissenters and even of the Anglican and other European Protestant churches, a project which indicated a decline in doctrinal bitterness.

COMPROMISE OF 1850, a series of measures passed by the US Congress at a time of mounting crisis between North and South. Controversy centred around the extension of slavery into the territories acquired from Mexico (1848), which included California. The final compromise, initiated by Henry Clay and helped through Congress after months of debate by Stephen A. Douglas, provided for the admission of California as a non-slave state. Embracing the principle of popular sovereignty, by which the inhabitants of a territory should decide their own institutions, Congress created the territories of Utah and New Mexico with no restrictions on slavery. The Texas boundary was settled, a much stricter fugitive slave law passed, and the slave trade abolished in the District of Columbia. The compromise, condemned by Northern anti-slavery men and Southern 'fire-eaters', secured considerable support for a time from moderate opinion, but the reduction of tension between North and South did not endure for long.

COMPTON, HENRY (1632–1713), bishop of London, son of the Earl of Northampton. A soldier before entering the Church, he became Bp of Oxford (1674) and London (1675). He was suspended for opposing the Catholic policy of James II and was one of the seven signatories of the invitation to William of Orange, supporting his accession by marching into Oxford as colonel of a volunteer regiment. He crowned William and Mary (1689) and acted as primate during the suspension of Sancroft as a non-juror. He spoke in favour of the Toleration Act (1689), but, being disappointed in his hope of succeeding Sancroft at Canterbury, withdrew from public life and occupied himself with the care of his diocese and missionary work in North America.

COMPULSORY CHURCH RATE, ABOLITION OF (1868), in England, ended the levying of a rate on all denominations for the upkeep of Anglican parish churches. The rate had roused little hostility before the 19th cent., but dissenters began to refuse payment for the upkeep of churches they did not attend. Abolition was first proposed in 1834, the revenue to be replaced from the land tax, and again in 1837, when it was suggested that better management of church lands and additional pew rents could raise an adequate sum. Both suggestions were defeated by the bishops, who resented the suggested dependence on government funds, or the loss of revenue to which they were legally entitled. But the real issue was hostility to the Whig reformers and dislike of their alliance with the dissenters to promote religious freedom. They feared that reform of parliament might be a prelude to reform of the established Church. By 1868 the exaggerated fear of anti-clericalism from without had, as a result of the Oxford Movement, given way to fear of popery from within. Gladstone's abolition of the rate ended what had degenerated to a source of petty local disputes.

COMPURGATION. In Germanic society a man accused at law had to defend himself on oath with the aid of compurgators or oath-helpers, each of whom swore that he was innocent. The number of compurgators required was determined by the seriousness of the accusation.

COMSTOCK LODE, deposit of silver and gold, located in Mt Davidson, NV, the richest single source of bullion in the US, producing ore worth $500 million between 1859 and 1879. It led to the founding of Virginia City, the development of the NV mining industry, and stimulated the growth of San Francisco.

CONANT, JAMES BRYANT (1893–), US chemist, educationalist, and diplomat. After a long career at Harvard (1916–53), including 30 years as its president, Conant became US High Commissioner to Germany (1953–5) and ambassador (1955–7). In *The American High School Today* (1959) and other writings sponsored by the Carnegie Corporation he revitalized educational thinking in the US.

CONCENTRATION CAMPS were set up in Germany shortly after Hitler became chancellor. Hindenburg's presidential decree (28 Feb. 1933), suspending civil liberties in the wake of the Reichstag fire, provided for Schutzhaft—protective custody—for those considered dangerous to the state. About 50 camps were set up in 1933, mainly under Sturm Abteilung (SA) control; however, the Sicherheitsdienst (SS) controlled the camp at Dachau, already distinguished for its brutal regime. In June 1934 the SA was suppressed and the concentration camp system was controlled by the SS, under Theodor Eike. Some small camps were closed and larger ones constructed. Sachsenhausen replaced the camp at Oranienburg; Ravensbrueck was set up for women. The Prussian decree of 10 Feb. 1936 handed the system over to the Gestapo, at the same time freeing the Gestapo from all control by administrative tribunal. Shortly after the Anschluss with Austria, Himmler and Heydrich set up an SS concentration camp at Mauthausen near Linz. Concentration camps already existed in Austria, set up for the detention of Nazis and socialists by the corporatist 'Fatherland Front' regime of Dollfuss and his successor, Schuschnigg.

Before 1939, treatment of political prisoners in concentration camps was extremely harsh, with summary capital punishment a feature of camp discipline. Only after the outbreak of war, however, did the camps also become centres for slave labour, medical experiments, and the extermination of the Jews.

CONCESSION COMPANIES IN FRENCH EQUATORIAL AFRICA. The territories of the Moyen Congo, Gabon, Oubangui-Chari, and Tchad were constituted into the Federation of French Equatorial Africa in 1910. Before then, the French had run their colonies in central Africa through a commissioner, later a commissioner-general, stationed at Brazzaville, with an administrator for each of the other territories. At the same time, the French government, after dismissing De Brazza, the first commissioner and commissioner-general of the Congo in 1898, decided to exploit the economic potentialities of Equatorial Africa and develop it through commercial firms. The inspiration to do this came from the examples of Britain with her chartered company administrations, and of Belgium with the concessionary companies in the Congo. The first concessions were granted to two private companies by Théophile Delcassé between 1893 and 1894, but the floodgate was opened to concessionary companies only in 1898.

In return for the payment of fixed sums and 15 per cent of their annual profits to the state, Equatorial Africa was divided up into areas apportioned to companies which exercised almost sovereign powers. The companies were granted exclusive rights over all agricultural, forest, and industrial exploitation for 30 years; after that they were to have outright ownership of whatever land they had developed and of forests in which they had regularly collected rubber. They were to build roads and maintain order in their areas.

But having got their concessions, the companies brutally misused their immense political powers. To maximize their profits, they imposed forced labour (corvées), and organized punitive expeditions which destroyed farms and houses and cost the lives of women and children as well as men. By 1905 the horrors perpetrated by the companies were being widely publicized in the French press. Public outcry forced the French government to introduce some reforms in 1906, and the system was wound up in 1930.

S. H. Roberts, *History of French Colonial Policy* (London, 1929).
Virginia Thompson and Richard Adloff, *The Emerging States of French Equatorial Africa* (London, 1960).   BOO

CONCIERGERIE, medieval Parisian gaol, now part of the Palais de Justice, in which offenders arrested within its confines were imprisoned. Its chief officer, the *concierge*, was nominated by the *parlement* of Paris. The two round towers of the Conciergerie which guard the entrance date from the 13th cent.

CONCILIAR MOVEMENT, attempt in Europe early in the 15th cent. to establish a form of ecumenical government to which even the papacy would be subject. The movement was initially a reaction to the Great Schism (1378–1415). In 1409, in an attempt to end the Schism, the cardinals of both parties summoned a council to meet at Pisa. This decreed the deposition of the rival popes and proceeded to elect a third pope. To add greater scandal and confusion, the second Pisan pope, John XXIII, was a former freebooter. In calling for a second council to meet at Constance in 1414, Sigismund of Bohemia, the future emperor, gave stimulus to ideas current in the universities. The bishops and theologians constituting the Council of Constance (1414–18) were essentially conservative reformers. They saw the teachings of Wycliffe and Hus as threatening an established order made vulnerable by the vagaries of papal autocracy. In 1415 Hus was burnt by the council after coming to Constance under promise of Sigismund's safe-conduct. In the same year the Schism was ended by the effective removal of the three popes. The next task was to establish the doctrine of conciliar supremacy. It was held that a General Council was superior to the pope, that the 'five nations' into which the council was divided should participate in papal elections, and—by the edict *Frequens* (1417)—that councils should meet at fixed intervals. This attempt to give a type of parliamentary government to the Church failed, not only because of national divisions but because the ending of the Schism allowed the papacy to recover much of its former power and authority. The crisis came during the Council of Basle (1431–9). In 1439 the council decreed the deposition of Eugenius IV and elected as pope one of its own number. The move was ineffectual and, deprived of secular support, the council dissolved itself in 1449. The advocates of the conciliar reform of the Church had correctly diagnosed the dangers which shattered it only a century later, but they lacked the power to carry their ideas into effect.   BP

CONCILIATION, BOARD OF, first labour–management board in Canada. Founded (1900) for the boot and shoe industry of Quebec under the direction of Abp L. N. Bégin, the board served as a model for the Canadian Industrial Disputes Investigation Act (1907).

CONCILIUM PLEBIS, Roman assembly of citizens from non-patrician families formed as a sectional pressure-group. It assembled by tribes under plebeian magistrates and was probably legalized in 471 BC. It elected the plebeian tribunes and aediles, had judicial powers later arrogated by the *comitia tributa*, and passed *plebiscita* which in time attained the force of laws. The date when these became legally binding is variously given in the sources as 445, 339, and 287. The earlier dates probably represent stages towards absolute legality, attained by the Hortensian Laws in 287.

CONCINI, CONCINO (d. 1617), Italian adventurer who came to France with Marie de Medici. He married the queen's favourite maid, Leonora Galigai (1600), and after the death of Henry IV (1610) rose to power and became a royal minister during Marie de Medici's regency. Concini was hated by the princes of the blood, *eg*, Condé, Bouillon, and Soissons, as a foreign upstart who had usurped their rightful role as royal advisers, and to try to reduce his influence they demanded the summoning of the estates general (1614). Concini was killed by order of the young King Louis XIII (24 April 1617), who is reputed to have claimed, on hearing of the Italian's death, 'I am king now'. Leonora was beheaded shortly after as a sorceress.

CONCORD COACH, most famous make of stagecoach in 19th-cent. US. Built in Concord, NH, it revolutionized Western travel after adoption by the Butterfield Overland Mail (1858). The reinforced chassis, suspended on leather thoroughbraces, rode on broad iron-tyred wheels set wide apart.

CONCORDAT (1753), brought papal recognition of Ferdinand VI of Spain's right to make church appointments and led to the virtual independence of the Spanish Church from Rome.

CONCORDAT (1801), agreement between Napoleon, as First Consul of France, and Pope Pius VII, which was an attempt to solve the differences that had arisen between successive French governments and the papacy since the Revolution. Napoleon used the Concordat to conciliate the Catholic peasantry and at the same time to bring security to those who had bought church lands. The agreement recognized Catholicism as the 'religion of the majority of Frenchmen', and provided for government nomination of bishops and payment of clergy.

CONCORDAT (1821). The bull *Salute Animarum* settled diocesan arrangements in Prussia, but a satisfactory working relationship between the Catholic Church and the state was not established until 1829–30, when Frederick William III agreed to pay ecclesiastical stipends. The Church regained considerable authority over its members.

CONCORDAT, GERMAN (1933), concluded with the Vatican. The German negotiator was the former chancellor, Von Papen. Before Hitler's accession to power in 1933, the Catholic hierarchy in many German dioceses had prohibited the faithful from joining the Nazi Party. In June the German Bishops' Council at Fulda had deprecated racial discrimination. However, a council at Fulda in March had removed prohibitions against joining the party, and the hierarchy was concerned to preserve its institutions by coexisting with the new regime.

The Concordat confirmed Concordats previously concluded with Bavaria, Prussia, and Baden. It guaranteed Church property, the freedom of public worship, and such privileges as the secrecy of the confessional in a court of law. Of great importance to the hierarchy was its guarantee of the existence of Catholic schools and cultural associations, and of a list of 'protected organizations' which were to be agreed upon later. The appointment of bishops and archbishops was to be subject to the approval of a district governor. Bishops had to swear allegiance to the Reich and to their provincial state. Political activity was forbidden to monks and priests.

State protection of Catholic associations did not preclude their subsequently being forbidden the insignia, sporting activities, and group excursions vital to youth organizations. Catholic trade unions were unable to function outside the framework imposed on all workers by the Third Reich. The Church's right, granted in Article 32, to public instruction in moral doctrine and dogma, was precarious. Nazi policies on race and genetics, *eg*, on sterilization, resulted in many priests being tried, and censorship of the Catholic press became general. The Concordat was pregnant with conflicts between Church and state such as it had been designed to eliminate. ASJ

CONDILLAC, ÉTIENNE BONNOT DE (1715–80), philosopher and economist of the French enlightenment. His theory of knowledge is a development of Locke's empiricism, tending to eliminate from the cognitive process all activity not relating to sensation, thus offering a contribution to later scientific psychology. His principal philosophical writings are *Essai sur l'origine des connoissances* (1749), *Traité des sensations* (1754), and *Traité de logique* (1780). In *Le commerce et le gouvernement considérés relativement l'un à l'autre* (1776), which investigates the problem of subjective value, Condillac applied his philosophical theories in an economic context.

CONDOMINIUM AGREEMENT, Anglo-Egyptian agreements (Jan. and July 1899) which established the status of the Sudan as a separate state under joint British and Egyptian sovereignty, reserving effective power to the British-appointed governor-general.

CONDORCET, ANTOINE NICOLAS DE (1743–94). French philosopher and moderate revolutionary statesman. His apologia *Esquisse d'un tableau historique des progrès de l'esprit humaine* affirmed the supremacy of reason and the ultimate perfectibility of humanity. Condorcet, a mathematician and protégé of Turgot, admired the Americans' republican constitution and advocated racial, religious, and sexual equality. He envisaged a system of universal state education comprising an autonomous, pyramidal structure and a curriculum biased towards scientific and practical subjects. The Convention found this idea insufficiently egalitarian and shelved it. Condorcet's Brissotin sympathies and liberal outlook caused his imprisonment and suicide.

CONDOTTIERI, leaders of mercenary armies available for hire during the troubles in Italy from the 13th to the 15th cents. The *condottieri* enjoyed great political prominence because of Italy's military weakness, resulting from political fragmentation and the inability of the businessmen who ran Italian city-states to lead armies effectively. The first *condottieri* were mostly German and French, but after the superiority of trained armies over the Italian citizen militias became obvious, Italian *condottieri* appeared in the late 14th cent. The aim of the *condottieri* was not only money, but land and noble status, and they were usually undisciplined and preyed on the countryside. They were ruined by the introduction of organized foreign armies into Italy at the end of the 15th cent. The most successful *condottieri* were the Sforzas, who rose from minor origins to become dukes of Milan.

'CONDUCT OF THE ALLIES' (1711), political pamphlet written by Jonathan Swift which had an immense effect on public opinion. By criticizing the war effort of Britain's continental allies during the War of the Spanish Succession and vilifying the Whig leaders, Swift succeeded in gaining public support for the Tory peace policy.

CONESTAGA INDIANS, Iroquoian tribe formerly living in the eastern US. The Conestaga, driven from their lands along the Susquehana river by the Iroquois Confederacy (1675), settled in Maryland. After conflicts with Maryland and Virginia colonists they returned to their ancient town of Conestaga, where the remaining 20 members of the tribe were massacred by a Pennsylvania mob (1763).

CONESTOGA WAGON, canvas-covered, broad-wheeled wagon developed by German immigrants in south-eastern Pennsylvania and used extensively in the US (1750–1850). It

was designed for the inadequate road system of late colonial America and was an important means of transport between the eastern seaboard and the interior. The western prairie schooner was a developed form of the Conestoga wagon.

CONEY ISLAND, New York city day-resort on Long Island. Its name is probably derived from the Dutch, *Konijn Eilandt*, meaning Rabbit Island. Its first hotel was built in 1829, and later in the 19th cent. it became popular for its prize fighting, horse-racing and amusement park. It is estimated to attract over 40 million visitors a year.

CONFEDERACIÓN ESPAÑOLA DE LAS DERECHAS AUTÓNOMAS in Spain, founded in 1933 to rally Spanish Catholics against the new republic's anti-clericalism. Its motto was 'Religion, Nation, Family, Order, Work, and Property'. Wealthy agrarian groups, such as Acción Castellana and Derecha Regional Valenciana, were its main supporters. Nevertheless, its founder, Angel Herrera, a socially conscious priest, hoped to make it a social Catholic party. Herrera soon surrendered the political leadership to Jose Maria Gil Robles, who organized a campaign for the revision of the republic's laic constitution. The movement, which was joined by like-minded right-wing groups, became, in Feb. 1933, CEDA, a 'defensive agglomeration' to protect the spiritual and material interests of Catholics by legal means.

In the Nov. 1933 elections CEDA won 115 seats, and although the most powerful party on the Cortes it lacked a clear majority. Two years of government instability followed, largely because CEDA was excluded from power by the president, Alcala Zamora, who distrusted Gil Robles. Yet CEDA proved its respect for legality by not using its strength to disrupt government.

The test came in Oct. 1934 when CEDA joined in a coalition government with Lerroux's Radicals. In power, it dropped its social Christian ideals. The party's wealthy backers prevented agricultural reforms and demanded the execution of Socialists involved in the Asturian rising which broke out on CEDA's assumption of power. As minister of war, Gil Robles promoted anti-Republicans and purged left-wingers.

In Nov. 1935 the coalition fell. At elections in the following Feb. CEDA won only 88 seats. Faced with the Popular Front's victory many Cedistas joined the Falange and became involved in the preparations for a military rising. Gil Robles instructed all members to act according to their consciences, as individuals, and not to involve the party. After 1936 Gil Robles was in exile and in the chaos of war the party was dissolved. PP

CONFEDERACIÓN NACIONAL DEL TRABAJO (CNT), in Spain, founded in 1911 to unite scattered anarchist federations which had adopted syndicalism. The CNT was strongest among the workers of Barcelona and the landless labourers of Andalusia, but as each local unit was independent, coordinated risings and strikes were impossible.

During the First World War the CNT grew stronger and in 1919 it faced its first trial of strength. Employers hired gunmen to terrorize unionists and the anarchists retaliated in kind. A strike in the Canadiense electric plant in Barcelona was the start of five years of bloody conflict, during which a wave of strikes swept the south. Peace was restored by Primo de Rivera and the CNT was forced underground; in 1927 its militant wing formed the Féderación Anarquitta Iberica (FAI).

Under the Second Republic, the CNT was split between militants and more moderate unionists. The moderate *Treintistas*, the followers of the 30 who had signed an anti-FAI manifesto, were expelled. This division of the movement handed it over to the revolutionary infantilism of the FAI, which declared war on the bourgeois republic. Henceforth, the CNT squandered its strength in ill-timed risings and strikes, which achieved little except to arouse right-wing disgust with the republic. The CNT's abstention from the election of Nov. 1933 facilitated a right-wing victory.

The anarchists, while staying apart from the Popular Front, nevertheless voted for it in Feb. 1936. In May, the Congress of Zaragoza reunited the FAI and the *Treintistas*, although the policy of isolated lightning action was maintained. CNT members opposed the military rising in July and took over Barcelona. Factories, shops, hotels, and public transport, as well as farms in Valencia and Aragon, and villages in Andalusia were all collectivized. The CNT even entered the *Generalitat* and the central government. However, the needs of wartime, combined with communist pressure, gradually forced the abandonment of collectives and egalitarian militias. After joining with the Partido Obrero de Unificación Marxista (POUM) in a final battle against the communists, the CNT's rank-and-file fought in Barcelona in May 1937. Thereafter, with their ideals aborted, members of the CNT became infected with defeatism.

CONFEDERATE STATES OF AMERICA, the 11 southern states of the US which unsuccessfully sought independence (1861–5). While the North, which was hostile to slavery, was industrializing itself, many southern states, dependent on agriculture and slave labour, felt themselves by 1860 to be increasingly isolated within the Union. The South, fearing political, social, and economic domination by the North, relied increasingly on a 'strict construction' of the Constitution and claimed the right to secede if its interests were continually ignored. The election of Abraham Lincoln to the presidency was seen as a direct threat to slavery and provoked the secession of SC (Dec. 1860). GA, FL, AL, MS, and LA also left the Union (Jan.–Feb. 1861) and delegates from these six states met at Montgomery, AL, and established the Confederate States of America. A provisional constitution was drafted and Jefferson Davis elected president (Feb. 1861).

Lincoln's call for troops at the outbreak of the Civil War prompted VA, NC, TN, and AR to join the Confederacy (April–May) and ineffectual secessionist governments in KY and MO were also recognized. Richmond, VA, became the Confederate permanent capital in June and a constitution modelled on the US Constitution, but explicitly recognizing state sovereignty, though not the right to secede, came into effect in Feb. 1862. Slavery was explicitly protected and the general welfare clause of the US Constitution, which the Confederates believed had led to the expansion of federal powers, was omitted. Protected tariffs, and bounties and appropriations for internal improvements, were prohibited in deference to agrarian interests. With a population of 9 million, including 3,500,000 slaves, and very limited industrial resources, the Confederacy was seriously handicapped in fighting against the North, but while Lincoln had to achieve total victory to restore the Union, the South needed only to fight defensively. The Confederacy, which had several brilliant generals, notably Robert E. Lee, fought well and at times seemed likely to be successful in preserving its independence. Its civil policies, however, were less effective. Though it was ingenious in improvising war material, its inadequate financial resources and unsound fiscal policies led to rampant inflation. It failed to obtain French and British recognition, in spite of attempting coercion by withholding cotton from the world market, and was only moderately successful in bringing supplies through the Federal blockade The exemptions permitted under the Conscription Act (1862) created friction, especially in mountain areas hostile to slavery and unsympathetic to secession. The political situation eventually became critical. Successful prosecution of the war required a vigorous central government, but the South had seceded partly to protect local autonomy. Many states were unco-operative, being fearful of slave rebellions and more concerned with their own narrow interests than with the long-term interests of the Confederacy. President Davis offered vigorous leadership, but his political insensitivity failed to resolve tensions between the executive and legislature. The Confederacy, exhausted and divided by invading Federal armies, disintegrated after Lee's surrender at Appomattox (9 April 1865).

E. Merton Coulter, *The Confederate States of America, 1861–1865* (Baton Rouge, 1950).
Clement Eaton, *A History of the Southern Confederacy* (New York, 1956).

CONFÉDÉRATION FRANÇAISE DES TRAVAILLEURS CHRÉTIENS in France, founded in 1919 to group together some 800 local unions of Christian workers. It was inspired by the Christian progressive ideas of Marc Sangier and by the principles expressed in Pope Leo XIII's encyclical, *Rerum novarum*. The CFTC, while seeking to promote the interests of Christian workers, refused to acknowledge the class struggle and was usually much less militant than the Confédération générale du travail (CGT) or the Confédération générale du travail unitaire (CGTU). It accepted capitalism and demanded only that employers should develop a sense of social responsibility.

The wartime Resistance opened many new political vistas to French Catholics and after 1945 the CFTC emerged as a dynamic force in the French labour movement. It revealed itself as less conservative and on certain occasions more militant than either of the other union organizations. In 1964 a new organization, the Confédération française démocratique du travail (CFDT) was formed. A minority had remained (1970) in the CFTC to try to maintain a Christian-inspired unionism.

CONFÉDÉRATION GÉNÉRALE D'AGRICULTURE in France, was established in 1944 in an attempt to organize the peasantry and attach it to the Socialist Party. Pierre Tanguy-Prigent, the socialist minister of agriculture (1944–7), who was the driving force behind it, intended that it should be the principal agent of rural modernization. The CGA was organized into four federations: agricultural technicians; Catholic farm labourers; non-Catholic farm labourers; and, most important of all, owners and tenants, who were organized in the Fédération nationale des syndicats d'exploitants agricoles (FNSEA). With the renewed respectability of conservatism after 1947, FNSEA established itself as the most powerful agricultural organization. In 1946 the CGA had 30 seats in the Economic Council, but in 1951 this number was reduced to three; 15 were allocated to FNSEA, and 12 to other affiliated organizations. Thereafter, the CGA still remained in existence but by 1970 had lost its importance.

CONFÉDÉRATION GÉNÉRALE DU TRAVAIL (CGT) in France, formed in 1895, was a triumph of the revolutionary syndicalists over those who wished to subordinate the labour movement to political parties. In its early years the Confédération consisted of a secretariat which co-ordinated somewhat loosely the actions of the constituent unions. Partly because of its weakness, the CGT had little to gain from parliamentary action. The doctrine of the general strike was the result of the labour movement's weakness and the influence of revolutionary syndicalism. The Charter of Amiens, adopted by the CGT in 1906, forbade any alliances with political parties and defined the general strike as the ultimate weapon for the liberation of the workers.

Under the leadership of Victor Griffuelhes and Leon Jouhaux, the CGT called a series of strikes, the failure of which blunted its revolutionary enthusiasm. After 1910, while continuing to pay lip service to the general strike, it settled down to the task of organizing the French working class. In 1914, repudiating all its previous decisions, the CGT gave its complete support to the French war effort. But as the war continued, opposition to it within the CGT increased. Disagreements were concealed until 1920, but the failure of the strikes in that year provoked a split between the revolutionaries, who had in mind the success of the Russian Revolution, and the reformists, led by Jouhaux. The revolutionaries hived off to form a new organization, the CGT *Unitaire*

(CGTU), leaving the CGT to spend the 1920s in recovering its losses. Gradually, however, it was pushed out of the centres of influence which it had established during the war. Then in the 1930s fascism led to the reunification of the two bodies (Feb. 1936) and a tremendous increase in membership. Although the Confédération refused to join Blum's government, it adhered to the programme of the Popular Front. Its pre-eminence in the French labour movement was implicitly recognized in the Matigon Agreements of June 1936, although after Blum's defeat there was a drastic decline in both its influence and membership. The CGT was divided over the Nazi–Soviet Pact and in Aug. 1940 it was dissolved by the Vichy government. Its role in the Resistance enabled it to emerge at the Liberation as a revitalized organization comprising 7 million workers. It was, however, controlled by the communists and its constant resort to strikes, called for political reasons, provoked another split in Dec. 1947, when the non-communist element formed the CGT *Force Ouvrière*. After 1948 the CGT itself maintained a fairly firm link with the Communist Party, and though still the largest French labour organization, its influence (1970) was by no means commensurate with its size.   PMK

CONFEDERATION OF MEXICAN WORKERS (CTM), founded in 1936, under Vicente Lombardo Toledano, was a federation of industrial trade unions, with considerable influence in the administration of President Lázaro Cárdenas. The CTM headed the labour sector of the official party following the reorganization of the latter. It succeeded the CROM (Confederación Regional de Obreros Mexicanos) as the officially sanctioned labour confederation. Under the guidance of Lombardo Toledano, the organization experimented with union control of the means of production, but was forced to desist from this when President Cárdenas found that the railroads ceased to operate.

CONFEDERATION OF THE RHINE (1806–14), set up by Napoleon under his protection on the dissolution of the Holy Roman empire. The 16 (later 18) German member states, which included Mecklenburg, Baden, Bavaria, and Saxony, were nominally independent, but French military control was strict. The extent to which French administrative, political, and social reforms were introduced depended, however, on the individual rulers. The confederation contributed loyally to the French war effort, but by the autumn of 1813 individual members were leaving it. Although the confederation was not officially dissolved until 1814, it had disintegrated the year before.

CONFEDERATION RIOTS (1876), occurred in Barbados over proposals for federation of the Windward Islands, including Barbados. Whites, organized in the Barbados Defence Association, believed the federation would destroy their political domination, and Negroes that federation would result in an increase in wages and the distribution of land. The disturbances, in which eight people were killed, lasted for a month, in spite of the arrival of troop reinforcements from British Guiana and Jamaica. The Barbados governor, John Pope-Henessey, was transferred to Hong Kong (1876) and the proposals for federation were abandoned.

CONFEDERAZIONE GENERALE DEL LAVORO (CGL), started (1906) as a non-aligned union federation in Italy, but is normally associated with Partito Socialista Italiano. In June 1914 the CGL called a general strike, its objectives being anti-militarist, anti-capitalist, and anti-police; this brought north-central Italy towards revolution, some republics being declared, eg, Ancona. The reformist leaders rejected the calls for revolution during the workers' seizure of the factories (1920), but thereafter failed to produce clear policies or control the militant unionists, who forced the July 1922 general strike, which drove many non-unionists to support fascist strikebreakers. After harassment the CGL was dissolved (1927), leaving an ineffectual fascist federation. An

all-party Confederazione Generale Italiana del Lavoro (CGIL) re-emerged (1944), but during the late 1940s increasing communist domination led Catholic, social democrat, and republican members to form their own federations.

CONFEDERAZIONE ITALIANA DEL LAVORO (CIL), a Catholic union federation (1918–26), largely recruited from the agricultural sector. Its objective was to turn labourers into co-managers and co-proprietors. Both militant socialists and fascists fought bitterly against its organizations, especially in Emilia-Romagna (1920–2). Until its dissolution it resisted fascist and Catholic Action pressure to link itself with fascist unions. The contemporary equivalent is the Confederazione Italiana dei Sindacati Lavoratori (CISL, 1950–), loosely associated with Christian Democrat factions.

CONFERENCE, IMPERIAL (1911), a meeting of the prime ministers of the dominions in the British empire, much of which was held in secret, and at which, for the first time, the foreign secretary was present to explain the urgency of the international situation. The New Zealand prime minister proposed the creation of an imperial parliament of defence to control foreign policy as well as naval and military affairs, but received no support. At this conference, Britain promised to consult the dominions over matters of foreign policy which concerned them.

CONFESSIO BELGICA (1561), written by Guido de Brés and based on the Gallican Confession of 1559, conciliated the Flemings by rejecting Anabaptism and, when accepted by the Synod of Antwerp (1556), led to the adoption of Calvinism in the Netherlands. Its basic principles were reaffirmed at the Synod of Dort (1618–19).

CONFESSIO BOHEMICA (1575) sought common ground to unite the Protestant groups of Bohemia against Rudolph II and the Counter-Reformation. It was drawn up by the Lutherans and two Hussite sects, the Utraquists and the congregationalist Church of the Brethren.

CONFESSIO GALLICANA (1559), formulary drafted by Calvin and accepted by a national synod of French Protestants at Paris. It contained the central dogmas of Calvinism and, with some modifications, was ratified at the Synod of La Rochelle (1571).

CONFESSIO HAFNIENSIS (1530), statement of Danish Protestant doctrines prepared for an expected disputation at a national diet to discuss the religious controversy. It demanded reforms based on the principle that scripture is the law of God.

CONFESSIO HELVETICA (1536), formulary of Swiss Protestantism, drawn up at Basle by Bullinger and Myconius. It combined Lutheran and Zwinglian elements and was accepted by the Protestant cantons, but rejected by Strasburg and Constance. A second declaration prepared by Bullinger (1564), after Frederick III, Elector Palatine, had been converted to Calvinism, was generally accepted in Switzerland and by Calvinist churches elsewhere.

CONFESSIO PENTAPOLITANA (1549), statement of Lutheran belief accepted in synod at Mediasch by representatives of five cities in Upper Hungary, where Lutheranism flourished among German immigrants. It was similar to the Twelve Articles of Erdöd (1545), which themselves were based on the Augsburg Confession (1530).

CONFESSIO SCOTIANA (1560), Protestant formulary drafted by Knox and approved by the Scottish parliament after the expulsion of the French. Calvinist in tone, it rejected transubstantiation and asserted the doctrines of election and justification by faith. Although civil magistrates were to be regarded as God's deputies, salvation could not be attained outside the Kirk.

CONFESSION OF FAITH (1647), the standard exposition of English and Scottish Presbyterianism, prepared by the Westminster Assembly (1643–52) and ratified by the Long Parliament in 1648. It affirmed the dogma of predestined election and declared a presbytery to be 'agreeable to the word of God'. It has been adopted by all English-speaking Calvinist churches and, with some modifications, by the Baptists and Welsh Methodists. With certain additions introduced in 1874, it is still the formula to which candidates for the Scottish ministry must give general assent.

CONFINDUSTRIA (Confederazione Generale dell' Industria Italiana), emerged (1910) from a league of Piedmontese industrialists formed to expand the common front in bargaining with unions. It was reconstituted in 1920. It opposed workers' councils and backed fascism. In 1923 it was recognized as the sole industrialists' organization and in 1925 was allowed a seat on the Fascist Grand Council. *Confindustria* was influential in the formulation of the government's protectionist policies, but remained free of government infiltrators. After being reformed in 1944, it backed the Christian Democrat Party, but switched (1954) to the Liberals to fight increasing government economic interference. It later lost campaigns against nationalization and enforced investment in southern Italy.

CONFIRMATION OF THE CHARTERS (Oct.–Nov. 1297), in England. The confirmation of Magna Carta and the Forest Charter, together with new concessions, notably the need for consent to taxes was made by King Edward I in 1297. Edward needed the support of the opposition to avert a Scottish attack at the time, but later obtained papal release from his oath (1305).

'CONFRONTATION', policy of harassment pursued by Indonesia towards Malaysia from 1963 to 1966. Plans for the formation of Malaysia were objected to by Indonesian leaders on the grounds that changes envisaged would represent a neo-colonist effort to preserve British influence. They saw the Brunei revolt (Dec. 1962) as evidence of a national liberation movement in the territories assigned to Malaysia. Indonesian politicians also asserted that Britain ought not to dispose unilaterally of territory on Indonesia's border, and army leaders declared that the Chinese would dominate Malaysia and pose a threat to Indonesia's Borneo territory. In addition, there were internal reasons for a foreign campaign: the army needed to justify its continuing prominence in national affairs after the end of the regional rebellions and the West Irian dispute; the communists needed an issue that would divert the military from attacking them; and President Sukarno wanted a campaign that would arouse popular sentiment, yet prevent internal conflict. At the beginning of 1963 Indonesia proclaimed its 'confrontation' of the Malaysia project, and in spite of efforts at compromise, culminating in the 'Maphilindo' conference, the formation of Malaysia (Sept. 1963) intensified Indonesian hostility.

Indonesia pursued 'confrontation' with tactics similar to those employed in the West Irian dispute. It embarked on a campaign of military harassment, to which it gave maximum publicity, but its calculations rested on persuading the British by bluff and diplomacy that Malaysia was not worth defending. A mood of nationalist fervour was aroused, and for the first time many Indonesians began to see their country as the major power in South-East Asia. The British embassy in Djakarta was burnt and British enterprises were seized. Large military forces were concentrated in Kalimantan (Indonesian Borneo) and northern Sumatra, and raids were carried out across the border and the Straits of Malacca. By 1965, however, this policy was being questioned by politically powerful elements, particularly in the army. The campaign

was very expensive, and Indonesia's finances were in a critical state. It was evident that there was no popular Malaysian sympathy for Indonesia's position. Communist power was growing and had Sukarno's increasingly visible encouragement, so that Indonesian anti-communists felt it urgent to concentrate army efforts on dealing with that threat. Even before the coup in Oct. 1965 that broke Sukarno's power, army officers had entered into secret negotiations with Malaysia to end the crisis. As soon as Gen. Suharto obtained effective power, he attempted to relax the 'confrontation' policy, although some officers—notably Gen. A. H. Nasution —urged its continuation. During 1966 the 'confrontation' forces were dismantled and Indonesia began instead to emphasize the need for South-East Asian co-operation and the close ethnic and cultural bond between its people and the Malays. RTM

CONFUCIANISM, values and ideals envisaged for a properly governed state and well-balanced society in traditional China. Traced or attributed to the personal teachings of Confucius and Mencius, these have undergone considerable changes in 2000 years, as they have been adapted by Chinese and alien dynasties to meet changing political, social, and economic needs. Although Chinese imperial governments have nearly always claimed to follow Confucianism, in its cult and practice the state has included ideas taken from other philosophies that are often in marked contrast with the rules for ethics and statecraft advocated originally by Confucius and his disciples. State Confucianism has at times embraced a belief in the active interference in human affairs by Heaven, the establishment of shrines for the veneration of the master, and institutions of state devised to preserve social hierarchies and the maintenance of government. A radical reassessment from the 12th cent. onwards resulted in the incorporation of new ideas, and the emergence of Neo-Confucianism.

CONFUCIUS, or K'ung Ch'iu (551–479 BC), native of Lu, one of the states of East China. A comparative failure in practical affairs during his lifetime, Confucius thereafter exercised more influence on Chinese culture than any other single person. Various texts are ascribed to his editorship, but his main contributions were made as a teacher, and the ideas that he expressed subsequently moulded much of Chinese literature and thought. Seeing the need to establish law and order in the confused political and social circumstances of his time, he stressed the value of morality and the need to practise human kindness. He believed that acknowledged forms of behaviour and the observance of prescribed rites formed an indispensable instrument with which to improve individual character and to inculcate social responsibilities. While not seeking to make contact with divine or supernatural powers, he respected the power of Heaven as a dispenser of a natural order that implied moral considerations. He believed that the rulers of man should be people endowed with broad vision and ideals, and that such qualities depend on character and training and are not the result of circumstances of birth or social status.

CONGIARIA, Roman term for gifts in cash or kind to the voters by candidates for office, and by generals to their soldiers. In imperial times only the emperors could give *congiaria*, which they generally did to celebrate some happy event.

CONGO (BRAZZAVILLE) (342,000 sq. kms), a republic in central west Africa with 4 million inhabitants chiefly of the Kongo, Bateke, and Sangha groups. Formerly a part of French Equatorial Africa, it became independent in Aug. 1960 and revised the constitution in 1963 to establish a president and legislature elected by adult suffrage.

CONGO (KINSHASA) (2,345,409 sq. kms), a republic in central Africa, formerly the Belgian Congo, with a population of 15,449,000, including Luba, Kongo, and Lunda people among many others. It became independent in 1960, but intermittent civil war continued until 1967. The new constitution (June 1967) provided for a president and legislature elected by adult suffrage.

CONGO FREE STATE (1885–1908), territory of some 2,590,000 sq. kms, and formerly 'free' in the sense of tariffs on export–import trade. Colonized on the personal initiative of King Leopold of the Belgians, with the active support of H. M. Stanley, it employed a multi-national collection of colonial pioneers. The king's declared aim was to abolish the slave trade, but his own regime of economic development became even more oppressive than the Arab exploitation it replaced. The accumulating evidence of administrative abuses eventually forced Leopold to hand the territory over to the Belgian government as the Belgian Congo.

CONGREGACIONES, Indian towns of Spanish America during the colonial period. The Spanish policy of concentrating the Indians in villages located near Spanish towns or close to the mines and large *haciendas* had an obvious economic explanation. Beginning in the mid-16th cent. and continuing through the colonial era, the system facilitated the acquisition of labour by the non-Indian sector of colonial society. It also simplified the collection of royal revenues and the fulfilment of Indian obligations to Church and state. The policy was also intended to contribute to the Christianization of the natives. There were two types of *congrega*s in America: the civil congregations, administered by the state, and the religious congregations, administered by the Church.

CONGREGATIONALISM, separatist religious movement which evolved in England in the 16th cent. While Puritans, in general, accepted the Elizabethan Church settlement despite their protests, Congregationalists did not. Their aim was the expression of the true church as a community of people living and worshipping independently of church organization and discipline; and under the influence of Robert Browne they became numerous. The related factors of religious persecution and emigration took them to the Netherlands and America. By the 17th cent. English Congregationalists had, under the guise of Independents, become involved in the politics of the Civil Wars. By the 19th cent. English Congregationalism and Independency found a common basis of agreement in the Congregational Union of England and Wales (1831).

CONGRESS, LIBRARY OF, US library founded (1800) to provide for the needs of Congress that has become, in effect, the national library of the US. The Legislative Reference Service continues to function exclusively for Congress, but all other departments serve general scholarly and public needs. The library is mainly supported by congressional appropriations and is a library of deposit under the copyright system. With over 55 million items, it is probably the largest library in the world.

CONGRESS, 15th, of the Soviet Union Communist Party, took place in 1927, and was remarkable for the victory of the Stalinist centre over the Left Opposition, led by Trotsky. Although Trotsky had been expelled from the Politburo in 1926, his hopes were raised by the disastrous failures of Stalin's policy in 1927—such as the defeat of the Chinese Communist Party and the suspension of diplomatic relations by Britain. In a document presented to the Politburo, known as the 'Platform of the 83', Trotsky blamed the Stalinist leadership for these disasters. He realized that he had no chance of getting a fair hearing in a Politburo and Central Committee now dominated by Stalin's nominees, so he decided to commit the ultimate 'sin' of a party member— an appeal to the opinion of the masses against the party. But the OGPU (Secret Police) was ready for him and his underground printing press was seized.

On 7 Nov. 1927, the tenth anniversary of the revolution, Trotsky and his allies tried without effect to address crowds in Moscow and Leningrad. Immediately afterwards they were expelled from the Central Committee and the party. In this atmosphere the congress met and the well-drilled Stalinists drowned the voices of those Trotskyites who tried to speak. Only Kamenev got a hearing. He pointed out that the expulsion of the Left Oppositionists meant that opposition had now become synonymous with treachery.

During this congress Stalin gave the first hints that New Economic Policy was to be abandoned. He announced that the middle peasants were to be encouraged to disgorge some of the grain which they grew but refused to deliver to the towns. The Central Committee was ordered to prepare a five-year plan for the development of industry.   GS

CONGRESS, 16th, of the Soviet Union Communist Party, took place in 1930, and was officially known as 'the Congress of the Broad Offensive along the whole Front'. This was the first congress at which no opposition was recorded, delegates having been cowed by Stalin's action in recently purging some 116,000 members of the party.

The congress met at a time when the collectivization of agriculture had produced a crisis, and Stalin told the delegates that the kulak had not yet been beaten and would continue to show 'savage resistance'.

Important changes in the organization of the Secretariat were announced by Kaganovitch. The Five-Year Plan had made great demands upon the *Orgraspred* section of the Secretariat because more party members were urgently needed for work in industry and agriculture. To assist *Orgraspred* in its assignment of jobs it had been divided into two parts, the assignment department being sub-divided into sections dealing with heavy industry, transport, agriculture, etc. Reorganization of the party at the lower levels made some 30,000 party members available for the industrial front. At this congress the leaders of the Right Opposition made an abject avowal of their previous 'errors'. Rykov, Bukharin, and Tomsky were re-elected to the Central Committee, but not to the Politburo. Tomsky's fall was followed by stern words to the trade union movement: it was made clear that its function was merely to represent the state's interest to the worker.

According to unsupported rumours, the unanimous front shown at the congress concealed violent disagreements. The composition of the new Politburo suggested that Stalin may not have had his way altogether, since several of its members were shortly afterwards purged.   GS

CONGRESS, 18th, of the Soviet Union Communist Party, took place in 1939, and was summoned immediately after the end of the Great Purges. Its composition reveals how heavily Stalin's hand had fallen on the party. Of the 1996 delegates at the last congress, 1108 had been arrested; of the rest only 59 were re-elected to the 18th Congress. Of the 71 members of the Central Committee elected at the last congress, 55 failed to reappear in 1939; Stalin had remodelled the party by virtually eliminating the Old Bolsheviks. The congress was immediately followed by the promotion of four Stalinists to the Politburo: Zhdanov and Khrushchev became full members, Beria and Shvernik candidate members. There was little debate at this congress and much fulsome adulation of the leader. One delegate said: 'At that moment I saw our beloved father Stalin and I lost consciousness.' Yezhov had just been dismissed and, upon orders from above, delegates fell over each other to denounce the excesses committed during the Purges. Stalin announced that 'we shall have no further need of resorting to the method of mass purges. Nevertheless the Purge of 1933–6 was unavoidable...' Stalin made a long speech explaining why the state was not withering away: predictably, the reason was that the USSR was still encircled by capitalist enemies. Zhdanov announced that the party's control over industrial enterprises would be decentralized. Stalin hinted at the possibility of better relations with Germany. The delegates were informed that congress would meet every three years: in fact, the next congress was not summoned until 1952. GS

CONGRESS, 19th, of the Soviet Union Communist Party, took place in 1952. It was called after a lapse of 13 years since the 18th in March 1939, in spite of the provision in the party rules that a congress should meet every three years. Stalin was nearly 73, and did not take a leading part in the congress; but the discussion was dominated by the ideas which he had just published under the title 'Economic Problems of Socialism', and the proceedings were punctuated by the customary eulogies and standing ovations for the leader. The question of Stalin's successor was obviously in the minds of the delegates, and it was noted that the main report of the Central Committee to the congress was made by Malenkov, while Khrushchev reported on changes in the party rules.

The congress made important changes in the leading organs of the party—although these later proved to be of greater significance for immediate political than for long-term organizational reasons. A newly created Presidium replaced the Politburo and the Orgburo. (Malenkov was a member of the latter, but not the former.) With 25 members and 11 candidate members, the new Presidium was as large as the two bodies it replaced, and (as was revealed after Stalin's death) a small secret Bureau was established at the same time. The arrangement was interpreted as serving to bring fresh blood into the leadership of the party before the removal, by Stalin, of the older members of the Politburo. At the same time, the Central Committee was enlarged to include 236 members, twice the size it had been in 1939.

The congress, together with Stalin's essay, appeared to indicate important changes of policy. Emphasis was placed on conflict among the capitalist countries rather than between them and the Soviet Union, and this was interpreted as presaging a more flexible foreign policy in contrast to the intransigence of the preceding five years. Such a change in foreign policy did in fact occur in the succeeding years, but Stalin's death (1953) meant that it was the work of his successors, and left open the question of his own intentions had he lived longer.

CONGRESS, 20th, of the Soviet Union Communist Party, took place in 1956. It was the first congress of the CPSU after the death of Stalin (March 1953) and marked a major turning point as a result of the secret speech made by Khrushchev on the night of 24–25 Feb. Khrushchev denounced the 'Stalin cult', which, he said, 'became at a certain specific stage the source of a whole series of exceedingly serious and grave perversions of Party principles, of Party democracy, of revolutionary legality'. Stalin was condemned for a range of offences, from his rudeness to his wife to the purges of the 1930s (starting, Khrushchev suggested, with police complicity in the murder of Kirov), and incompetence in the conduct of the war.

Khrushchev also spoke (consistently with the reconciliation with Yugoslavia in June 1955) of the possible 'different roads to socialism' and this theme was stressed by major speakers at the congress. It was stated that there could be different ways of achieving power and different ways in which this power could be used for the establishment of socialism—which could even be by parliamentary means. Khrushchev also argued that it was possible to 'coexist' with the imperialist powers. He denied that war was inevitable, and said that there were now social and political forces—in the new states of Africa and Asia, and in the 'workers' movement'—sufficiently strong to prevent the imperialists fighting a new war, which because of nuclear weapons would be destructive of communist and capitalist states alike.

The denunciation of Stalin was accompanied by the rehabilitation of some of those who had been purged and liquidated under his rule (although this did not extend to Trotsky and his followers, any more than the denunciation was

allowed to touch Khrushchev's colleagues, in spite of their complicity in Stalinist rule). The speech was of major importance in contributing to the risings which followed in Poland (where Gomulka, rehabilitated by Khrushchev, assumed the leadership) and Hungary (Oct. 1956). WFK

CONGRESS, 21st, of the Soviet Union Communist Party, took place in 1959. The major themes developed at the congress were a continuation of those enunciated by Krushchev at the 20th Congress, including the possibility of a detente with the West, in conditions where war was no longer 'fatalistically inevitable' and where the 'capitalist encirclement' of the USSR (an important element in Stalinist doctrine) had ended. The prospect for internal development was equally hopeful: the USSR was moving from the socialist to the communist stage of development, which would be achieved when there was economic abundance for all and would be accompanied by the withering away of the state— a gradual reduction of the police and the administrative functions of the state (but not of the party) which, Khrushchev asserted, had already begun.

The congress was important in Khrushchev's drive to re-establish his dominance over the party following the challenge to his leadership in 1957. It also formed part of the dispute with China, which laid claim to greater achievements in revolutionary development (by the 'great leap forward') and rebutted Khrushchev's thesis of the possibility of detente with the West.

CONGRESS, 22nd, of the Soviet Union Communist Party, took place in 1961. The congress was marked by a further attack by Khrushchev on his defeated rivals, notably Kaganovich, Malenkov, and Molotov. Their opposition to him in 1957 was linked to the 'crimes' of the Stalin period, and in the course of the congress Stalin's remains were removed from the Lenin mausoleum. It was also marked by a further stage in the Sino-Soviet dispute, particularly in the attack on the Albanian leaders (Hoxha and Shehu), and the identification of the Chinese as their supporters.

CONGRESS, 23rd, of the Soviet Union Communist Party, took place in 1966. It was the first congress to be held after the fall of Khrushchev (Oct. 1964) and was marked by a moderate rehabilitation of the Stalinist period and restrained denunciation of Khrushchev. It had been preceded by the arrest of the writers Sinyavsky and Daniel (Feb. 1966) and clearly represented a swing to conservatism, which included the abandonment of Khrushchev's optimistic views of the economic development of the Soviet Union and detente with the West. The dominant note of the new leadership was the cautious pursuit of a middle path between 'revisionism' and 'dogmatism'.

CONGRESS OF COMINTERN, 1st (March 1919). The idea of founding a new organization to unite those left-wing socialists in various countries who were indignant with the leaders of the Second International for the support of their respective governments in 1914, had been contemplated by Lenin, Trotsky, and others since the outbreak of the First World War. The Bolshevik Revolution in Russia, the founding of several communist parties, including that of the German in 1918, and above all the apparently imminent revival of the Second International at the Berne Conference of Feb. 1919, created conditions which made it possible, and indeed in Bolshevik eyes imperative, to found the Third International (Communist International, or Comintern). In Jan. 1919, therefore, the Russian Communist Party invited some 39 parties and groups of left-wing socialists to a conference in Moscow. Fifty-one 'delegates' claiming to represent organizations in 30 countries attended. However, most of them were émigrés already living in Russia; only four came from abroad; of these, only two had specific mandates from their parties; and one of these mandates was to oppose, as premature, the foundation of the Communist International at what was plainly an unrepresentative gathering. There was thus some doubt at first whether the Comintern would be founded at this juncture; but a speech from the Austrian delegate changed the mood of the conference, and the Third (Communist) International was proclaimed on 4 March. The congress set up an executive committee of seven, of which the Russian party was one, but decided that pending the arrival of more non-Russian representatives the Russians should assume the burden of the work. This gave the Russians a dominant role in the Comintern from the beginning. Grigori Zinoviev (1883–1936) became chairman of the executive committee. The congress also issued a number of documents, including a *Platform*, *Theses on Bourgeois Democracy and Proletarian Dictatorship*, and a *Manifesto*, which were drafted by Bukharin, Lenin, and Trotsky respectively. The keynote of these documents was a warning against the deceptions of 'bourgeois democracy' and the historic socialist parties; and the importance of the First Congress lay more in the challenge thus issued than in any organizational or political achievement of the new International.   RKK

CONGRESS OF COMINTERN, 2nd (July–Aug. 1920), attended by 169 voting delegates, was chiefly noteworthy for two documents. These were the '21 Conditions' for entry into the Comintern and the *Theses on the National and Colonial Question*. By the summer of 1920 the Bolshevik leaders had grounds for optimism: the Civil War in Russia had been won; a number of important European parties had asked for affiliation to the Comintern; moreover, when the congress opened, Soviet armies were driving the Poles back towards Warsaw at high speed. At the close of the congress, Zinoviev prophesied that its successor would be a world congress of Soviet Republics. This self-confidence led the Russian leaders to proclaim the transformation of the Comintern from a 'propaganda association' into a 'fighting organ of the international proletariat'. The Comintern was to become 'a single Communist Party with branches in different countries'. The enforcement of centralized control and organization from Moscow begins at the 2nd Congress. With this aim the Russians imposed the so-called '21 Conditions' of entry to the Comintern. These required each member party to revise its programme and submit it for confirmation to the executive committee; to adopt the name of 'Communist Party'; to accept all Comintern decisions; to expel 'opportunist leaders' (some of whom were specifically named); and to engage in illegal as well as legal activities. The effect of these conditions on European socialism was to split the 'centre' socialist parties, notably in Germany, France, and Italy, into communist parties owing allegiance to Moscow, and socialist parties which ultimately rejoined the Labour and Socialist International.

The other important product of the 2nd Congress was Lenin's *Theses on the National and Colonial Question*. The idea of an alliance between the proletariat of the advanced capitalist countries and nationalist movements in 'oppressed' or colonial Asian countries, already advocated in earlier works by Lenin and others, and tentatively put into practice by Soviet dealings with such countries as Afghanistan, Persia, and Turkey in 1919–20, here received full ideological elaboration. The congress accepted both Lenin's *Theses*, which argued for wholehearted, if temporary, support of bourgeois anti-imperialist movements in backward countries, and those of the Indian communist, M. N. Roy, which laid more emphasis on proletarian revolution in such areas. But Lenin's *Theses* were remembered while Roy's were forgotten, and the Comintern was henceforth involved in a number of ambivalent and sometimes disastrous relationships with nationalist movements, *eg*, the Kuomintang in China.   RKK

CONGRESS OF COMINTERN, 3rd (June–July 1921), attended by 291 voting delegates, was marked by a recognition that the tide of revolution in Europe was receding. Specifically, the congress was much preoccupied with the failure of the so-called 'March Action' in Germany, in which Comintern representatives had been directly involved in an attempt at revolution. In consequence, the congress resolution censured the German Communist Party for failing to emphasize the defensive character of the struggle at the present juncture. The principal slogan which emerged from the congress was 'To the Masses!'—which was to be understood as an injunction to organization and propaganda activities rather than violent attempts at revolution. It also foreshadowed the adoption six months later of the policy of 'United Front' with Social-Democrats, which remained the official Comintern line until 1928. Whereas a year earlier the emphasis had been on doctrinal purity, the 3rd Congress now urged all parties to increase their membership. Just as in the Soviet Union economic difficulties had forced the Soviet leaders to the compromises of NEP, so in the Comintern the failure of revolution abroad drove them to a more cautious long-term policy. This did not mean a deal with the socialist leaders; indeed, the 3rd Congress expelled the Italian Socialist Party from the Comintern, but member parties were enjoined to adapt their slogans and tactics to a realistic assessment of the situation.   RKK

CONGRESS OF COMINTERN, 5th (June–July 1924), attended by 324 voting delegates, was the first Comintern Congress held after the death of Lenin. It was dominated by the struggle for power in the Russian Communist Party, the failure of the German Revolution in 1923, and the de jure recognition of the Soviet Union by the British Labour government. The general analysis of the world situation presented at the congress confirmed the retreat from revolutionary optimism which had been sounded at the 3rd Congress, but introduced a note of cautious ambiguity. According to Zinoviev, the revolution in Europe might either ripen in two, three, or four years, or it might do so slowly over a longer period. These ambiguities nevertheless allowed the dominant faction in the Russian party to appear as champions of the left. Zinoviev, now in alliance with Stalin and Kamenev against Trotsky, found scapegoats for the German failure in Brandler and Radek, and used Trotsky's association with them to brand him as a right-wing element; and the Labour victory in Britain was similarly used as an argument in favour of a swing to the left. The chief slogan which emerged from the congress was the need for 'Bolshevization' of communist parties outside Russia: more even than hitherto they were required to accept the lessons of Soviet experience, and specifically to become mass parties, monolithic, manœuvrable, and engaged in the subversion of bourgeois armies. But Bolshevization was also a key word in the Russian intra-party struggle, for Trotsky's Bolshevism could be questioned because of his late entry into the Bolshevik Party. By Bolshevization, the Russian triumvirate carried the struggle against Trotsky into the Comintern, and the campaign against 'Trotskyists' in foreign communist parties originated in the 5th Congress. The congress issued a uniform demand for obedience to Comintern directives, and for Bolshevization; but the specific situations of various parties required detailed interpretation of the general line, and the congress dealt in some detail with the affairs of the British, French, German, Czechoslovak, and eight other parties. It also adopted Statutes based on the principle of 'democratic centralism'.   RKK

CONGRESS OF COMINTERN, 7th (July–Aug. 1935), attended by 371 voting delegates, summoned after an interval of seven years since the previous congress marked the proclamation of 'Popular Front' tactics in the international communist movement. With some little delay, Hitler's seizure of power in Germany had led Stalin to revise the line of Soviet foreign policy: no longer could this be based on a covert understanding with Germany, opposition to the Versailles treaty, and a boycott of the League of Nations. By joining the league in 1934, the Soviet Union began a new relationship with the entente powers. In the Comintern context this entailed a new attitude towards Social-Democracy. As late as Feb. 1934, at the 17th Congress of the CPSU, the view that Social-Democrats were 'social-fascists' was still maintained, but during 1934 a change occurred. This was precipitated by the events of Feb. 1934 in France, when the appearance of right-wing extremists on the streets led to a move towards socialist–communist unity; and on Moscow's prompting the French communists signed a formal pact with the socialists in July 1934. United Front proposals soon followed from communist parties elsewhere. In Spain, communists and socialists co-operated in the Asturias revolt of Oct. 1934. In May 1935 the Franco-Soviet Pact was signed, and there was informal co-operation at the Paris municipal election between communist, socialist, and even radical candidates. The scene for a change of line at the 7th Congress was thus set before it met. The congress was dominated by the Bulgarian, Georgi Dimitrov, an anti-fascist, who was elected secretary-general of the Comintern. The report on the work of the executive committee since the previous congress was, however, presented by the German, Wilhelm Pieck, who attacked Social-Democratic leaders, and blamed communist parties for a 'mechanical' interpretation of the resolutions of the 6th Congress and for a narrow sectarian approach. Pieck called not only for a united front with social-democrats, but also a 'broad people's front' (ie, one including non-socialists) against fascism. The need for a broader domestic appeal led to a revival of professions of patriotism—a process already beginning in Russia itself at the time, and now countenanced by communist leaders such as Thorez, Earl Browder, and Dimitrov himself at the congress. The Comintern was now firmly harnessed to the objectives of Soviet foreign policy, which were to gain allies in the West: the Popular Front policy, which did not remove the achievement of a communist revolution from the ultimate agenda, but postponed it indefinitely and meanwhile allowed communist parties to seek a measure of national integration, was intended to serve this end.

Franz Borkenau, *World Communism* (Michigan, 1962).
T. Brannthal, *History of the International (1914–1943)* (London, 1967).
RKK

CONGRESS OF INDUSTRIAL ORGANIZATIONS, American labour organization established (Nov. 1938) in Pittsburgh, PA. The failure of the Executive Committee of the American Federation of Labor to pursue the aggressive policy of promoting industrial unionism demanded by an overwhelming vote of the federations's 1934 convention led a number of unions under the leadership of John L. Lewis and the United Mine Workers of America to organize the Committee for Industrial Organization (9 Nov. 1935). Suspended from the AF of L, the committee nevertheless continued its plan for organizing on an industrial basis. The steel industry was planned as the first objective, but industrial organization spread so rapidly in the automobile industry that the first major battles were fought at the General Motors Corporation plant in Flint, MI (31 Oct. 1936). After spectacular strikes, in which the sit-down technique was used to full advantage, the CIO automobile union was recognized as the bargaining agency for its members in General Motors and Chrysler plants (1937). The Ford Motor Co. only recognized the CIO Automobile Union after a bitter struggle (1941).

The major steel companies signed contracts with the CIO (1937), but the independent producers ('Little Steel') refused recognition and a strike against these companies led to the Memorial Day Massacre (31 May 1937) and the first important defeat for the CIO. The independent steel producers finally agreed to recognition (1939) and industrial unionism then spread rapidly. By 1940, membership had reached 4,000,000. The breakaway of the CIO had revitalized the American labour movement and by making use of New Deal legislation favourable to union organization brought effective organization to US mass industries for the first time.

In Nov. 1938 the Committee for Industrial Organization

had changed its name to the Congress of Industrial Organizations, adopted a constitution, and elected as president John L. Lewis. Lewis resigned (1940), after political quarrels resulting from Franklin D. Roosevelt's bid for a third term, and was succeeded by Philip Murray. Murray followed an aggressive policy, and helped to organize a Political Action Committee that supported sympathetic Congressional candidates and endorsed Roosevelt in 1944. Post-war strikes and the passage of the Taft–Hartley Act (1947) slowed down the membership drive and the CIO turned to the internal problem of communist domination of some of its constituent unions. Eleven such unions were expelled (1949–50).

With the death of Murray (1952), Walter Reuther became president and began to seek a merger with the AF of L. Although the CIO's industrial unions and the AF of L's craft unions still had differences, they now felt that their methods and objectives were basically the same and that a merger would be mutually beneficial. The two groups joined in Dec. 1955 and became the AFL–CIO.

Philip Taft, *Organized Labor in American History* (New York, 1964).
Walter Galenson, *The CIO Challenge to the AFL* (Cambridge, MA, 1960).
DHP

CONGRESS OF RACIAL EQUALITY (CORE), militant US civil rights organization, founded in 1942, largely on the initiative of James Farmer. The organization's commitment to non-violent direct action drew its inspiration from Gandhi and reflected a disillusionment with the legalistic approach of the major civil rights organization, the National Association for the Advancement of Colored People. CORE directed its major efforts against public segregation, and in 1958 organized the first successful Negro boycott, against a St Louis bread manufacturer. In 1961 it sponsored bi-racial Freedom Rides in the Deep South to challenge segregation in inter-state transportation. In 1966 James Farmer was succeeded as national director by Floyd B. McKissick, and CORE subsequently became part of the militant Black Power movement.

CONGRESS OF THE UNITED STATES, legislative body established by Article I of the constitution. It is a bicameral institution, with a lower chamber, the House of Representatives, composed of members chosen biennially from districts apportioned on the basis of population, and an upper chamber, the Senate, composed of elected members, two from each state, for six-year terms, with one-third chosen every second year. These basic structural features resulted from a compromise between the conflicting interests of the large states and the small states at the Constitutional Convention (1787), although it may be doubted whether, contrary to the expectations of the framers, such conflicts have ever again proved to be of primary political importance.

Among the more important congressional powers specified by the constitution are the powers to lay and collect taxes, to borrow money, to regulate inter-state and foreign commerce, to create and support the armed forces, and, most generally, to 'make all laws which shall be necessary and proper' in executing these and other functions. Revenue bills must originate in the House of Representatives, although the Senate may amend them, and the Senate is allocated the power to give 'advice and consent' to the making of treaties and to confirm presidential nominations for executive and judicial positions. Legislation passed by Congress must be approved by the president; in the event of an executive veto a bill may still become law if it is passed again by a two-thirds vote of each house. In sum, the Congress created by the authors of the constitution was a representative, national law-making body with substantial powers designed to give it the strength necessary to 'check and balance' the executive branch.

Two major changes in the politics and functions of Congress have occurred. Internally the Senate has grown in prestige and influence at the expense of the House. This is probably due in part to the special role guaranteed by the constitution in the area of foreign policy and executive appointments. Other factors contributing to this development may be the larger and hence less parochial constituencies represented by senators, and the longer terms of office which they enjoy.

The other major change in Congress's position as a whole has been in its relation with the president and the executive branch. Throughout most of the 19th cent. the Congress tended to be the dominant power in the partnership. The peak of congressional power was reached in the last quarter of the 19th cent., when the president lost virtually all control over executive appointments and made almost no effort to influence policy. The result was aptly described by Woodrow Wilson as 'congressional government'. However, the emergence of the US as a world power, coupled with the growing complexity of a modern economy, has brought about a shift in the constitutional balance of power, so that policy initiative clearly lies with the executive branch, while the still considerable power of Congress is exercised in response to presidential proposals, and in oversight of legislative implementations by the administration.

Woodrow Wilson, *Congressional Government* (Boston, MA, 1885).
Bertram Gross, *The Legislative Struggle* (New York, 1953)
JPY

CONGRESS SYSTEM (1815–25), was devised as a means of settling differences between the European powers, but became a means for the suppression of revolution. Russia, Britain, Austria, and Prussia agreed (Nov. 1815) to maintain the Vienna Settlement by force and to meet in periodic conferences. An amicable congress was held at Aix-la-Chapelle (1818), which admitted France to this European concert, but differences emerged as revolution swept southern Europe and Germany (1819–20). Austria and Russia wanted to use the congress system to suppress these revolts, but Castlereagh, and then Canning, the British foreign ministers, insisted that it was 'never intended as a union . . . for the superintendance of the internal affairs of other states'. When a congress met at Troppau (1820), and then at Laibach (1821), to discuss measures to suppress the Italian revolts, Britain sent only an observer. At a further congress at Verona (1822) Britain formally withdrew from the congress system because of demands from the other powers for intervention in Spain and Greece. The system finally collapsed on the death of Tsar Alexander I (1825) and the accession of the less internationally minded Nicholas I.

CONGREVE, WILLIAM (1670–1729), English dramatist, brought up and educated in Ireland, who came to London in 1691, where his friends included Steele, Pope, and the Duchess of Marlborough. His plays, of which *The Way of the World* is the best known, deal wittily with the manners of society.

CONKLING, ROSCOE (1829–88), US politician, New York political 'boss', and one of the outstanding Republican 'stalwarts' of the 'gilded age'. He served in the US House of Representatives (1859–63, 1865–7) and the Senate (1867–81). Although a man of some oratorical skill and elegant style, he wielded his greatest influence, especially during the presidency of Ulysses S. Grant (1869–77), through his control of the NY state Republican machine and skilful manipulation of the spoils system.

CONNALLY–FULBRIGHT RESOLUTION (1943), US congressional resolution of support for a post-war organization to keep the peace. Sponsored in the House of Representatives by William J. Fulbright and in the Senate by Tom C. Connally, it paved the way for US membership of the United Nations.

CONNECTICUT, English colony in North America. The first European explorations in Connecticut were made by the Dutch (1614), who established a settlement on the Connecticut river (1633) at the site of Hartford. In the same year, members of the Plymouth Co. founded a trading post on the river, near present-day Windsor, and John Oldham (1600–1636), of the Massachusetts Bay Colony, explored the Connecticut river valley. His account of fertile lands led about 800 settlers from the colony into Connecticut, where they founded Windsor, Wetherfield, and Hartford (1635–6). Under the chief promoters of the colony, Thomas Hooker (c. 1586–1647), Roger Ludlow (c. 1590–1665), and John Haynes (d. 1654), representatives of the three towns drew up the Fundamental Orders of Connecticut, the first constitution written in America. It copied the practices of Massachusetts, but omitted a religious test for citizenship and limited the prerogative of the governor. The Congregational Church was established and not until 1791 was free incorporation allowed to small sects. Puritans from England formed a colony at Saybrook (1635) and a Puritan 'Bible commonwealth' was founded at New Haven (1638). Saybrook was sold (1644) and New Haven was joined to Connecticut by royal charter (1662). Connecticut's charter allowed self-government. Efforts by Sir Edmond Andros to seize the charter (1687) failed, though he dissolved the Connecticut government (1687–9). The Connecticut legislature supported colonial opposition to British acts and during the War of American Independence raised troops and supplies for the Continental army. The colony became a state (1776) in the US and the charter of 1662 was adopted as its state constitution.

L. S. Mills, *The Story of Connecticut*, 5th ed. (West Ridge, NH, 1958). RCR

CONNECTICUT COMPROMISE (1787), name given to proposals offered at the Philadelphia Convention to break a deadlock over principles of representation in the new US constitution. The large states wanted representation in the federal legislature proportionate to population. The small states insisted on equal representation by state. The compromise suggested a bicameral legislature with equal representation in the upper house, but proportionate representation in the lower. Although originating from Connecticut delegates, the name of the compromise is misleading because delegates from other states helped to draft its final, amended form.

CONON (d. 392 BC), Athenian general, first known in the great Peloponnesian War in command at Naupactus (414). He was active in the Aegean from 407 as commander at Samos and he replaced Alcibiades, then in exile after Lysander's victory at Notium (407). He survived the furore after Arginusae (406), involving the condemnation of eight colleagues, and was the only general to escape the defeat at Aegospotami (405), by fleeing to Cyprus. After Athens' surrender to Sparta he accepted mercenary command from Pharnabazus, the Persian satrap, and annihilated the Spartan fleet at Cnidus (394) in the Corinthian War. Using Persian resources he helped to reconstruct the Athenian fleet and Long Walls, until Spartan diplomacy caused his arrest by the Persians; he escaped but died soon after.

CONQUISTADORS, general term for the Spaniards who participated in the conquest of America (1492–1550s).

CONRAD II (reg. 1024–39), the first Salian Emperor. He based his power on the support of the lesser nobility, whose right of inheritance to their fiefs he was the first to recognize. He brought the monarchy to a position of great strength by recovering Crown lands and rights to build up a territorial and financial basis for his power. He accumulated great wealth and made extensive conquests in the east, destroying the power of the recently created Polish monarchy. He also established firm government in Italy and incorporated Burgundy in the empire on the death of the last native king. His reign inaugurated a period of order and prosperity which was ruined only by the long minority after the death of his son, Henry III, in 1056.

CONRAD OF MONTFERRAT (1146–92), went (for the second time) to Constantinople (1187) and thence to Palestine, where he defended Tyre against the Muslims under Saladin and had also a prominent role in the siege of Acre (1189–91). He married Isabella, the sister of Queen Sybil, heiress to the Kingdom of Jerusalem and wife of Guy de Lusignan. By so doing Conrad became heir to the kingdom after Guy de Lusignan and, in addition, Lord of Tyre, Sidon, and Beirut. He met his death at the hands of the Assassins.

CONRADIN OF HOHENSTAUFEN (1252–68), grandson of the Emperor Frederick II and last male Hohenstaufen. He spent his brief life trying, against good advice, to vindicate claims to the Neapolitan Crown against Charles of Anjou. His invasion of Italy in 1267 as a tool of the anti-Angevin party ended in defeat at Tagliacozzo (1268).

CONSALVI, ERCOLE (1757–1824), Roman cardinal, who became Pius VII's secretary of state (1800). He helped to negotiate the French and Italian (1803) Concordats, resisting the Organic Articles' Gallican implications and Napoleon's attacks on papal temporalities. Consalvi resigned (1806) as opposition became futile, but resumed office in 1814 and represented the papacy at the Congress of Vienna. Although unable to maintain many Napoleonic innovations, he modified some of Rome's administrative abuses. Consalvi remained outside the Congress System, refused an Austrian alliance and advised co-operation with the new South American republics, but he generally supported legitimacy, distrusting liberal movements.

CONSCRIPTION for the armed forces was introduced in Britain considerably later than in any other major European country. France had had conscription since the French Wars, Germany since 1870. The international tension of the 1900s, however, revived the issue, and the argument persisted until the First World War. Much of the opposition had been led by the Quakers and on the outbreak of war found expression in the No Conscription Fellowship. There was also opposition on strategic grounds, from those who resented Britain's resources being committed to a European land war. In Parliament this opposition was expressed strongly by the Labour Party, and also, though less forcibly, by the Liberals. Nevertheless, the pressures towards conscription mounted through 1914–16, although the voluntary enlistment campaign had originally been very successful. With the deterioration of the situation on the Western Front, Kitchener demanded 70 divisions: 35 seemed the most that would be likely to be raised by voluntary means. The government therefore bowed to the inevitable, although as a political concession the Military Service Act (1916) at first exempted married men; later these too were included. There remained three major grounds for exemption; ill-health; the importance of an applicant's civil occupation; and 'conscientious objection'.

According to one estimate, some 16,000 genuine conscientious objectors registered between 1916 and 1918. Local tribunals, appointed by borough and district councils, were set up, with powers to grant 'total' or 'qualified' exemption. Appeal tribunals were also established; nevertheless, large numbers of conscientious objectors were conscripted, though many disobeyed orders in order to avoid service. A virtual amnesty was granted them by the Home Office Scheme, by which some 4000 were discharged from active service in the war.

Conscription ended with the war, but in 1939 it was re-enacted in the Military Training Act (May 1939). When the Second World War broke out (Sept. 1939) conscription was in full force. Most of those exempted were workers in 'reserved' occupations. The objectors were dealt with much as before; some 70,000 applied for exemption, and most of them were directed to non-combatant services, such as the Home Guard, or coal mining. By the National Service Act (1941), women were also conscripted, both into priority civilian occupations and the armed forces. The employment of labour in essential war industries was also regulated by the government; this was termed 'Industrial Conscription'.

Conscription continued through a 'call-up' of 18 months (1948) or two years (1950). The last 'call-up' took place in 1960.

D. Prasad and T. Smythe, *Conscription* (London, 1968).

GD

CONSCRIPTION, FRENCH, caused the raising of national conscript armies by the other European powers in the 19th and 20th cents. The Committee of Public Safety introduced the first *levée en masse* and the concept of the nation at war (1793) and the Directory perpetuated them (1799). Conscription produced armies of over a million men and gave the Revolutionary governments and Napoleon immediate numerical advantage over the other European states, which were consequently forced to follow suit.

CONSCRIPTION REFERENDA (1916–17). Australian politics were bedevilled for half a century by the consequences of the decision of the Labor prime minister, W. M. Hughes, on returning from England in 1916, to use compulsion to increase the contribution made overseas by the voluntarily recruited Australian Imperial Force. Hughes, lacking sufficient support from within his own party, sought a mandate by referendum. The result (28 Oct. 1916) was a NO majority: increased at a second referendum (20 Dec. 1917). Conscription campaigns split the Labor Party, divided the nation, impaired the war effort, and left a legacy of suspicion of military involvement overseas in the Labor Party, which retarded the emergence of rationally based foreign and defence policies. Labor did not regain office until 1929; sectarian feeling was increased by the opposition to conscription of Abp Mannix; ALP policy in opposition during the 1920s and early 1930s was largely isolationist and even compulsory training for home defence was abandoned by the Scullin Labor government in 1929. When Labor returned to office under Curtin late in 1941, critical wartime conditions induced the party to accept increasing military commitments, including the use of conscripted troops not only on the mainland and in New Guinea, but also, under the 1943 amendment of the Defence Act, in other parts of the southwest Pacific. This extension was unsuccessfully opposed in caucus by Arthur Calwell, who later, as Labor leader (1960–7), revived the old policy to oppose the Menzies government's 1964 introduction of conscription by ballot and its application thereafter to Viet-nam.

R. Forward and B. Reece (eds.), *Conscription in Australia* (Queensland, 1968).

FA

CONSEIL DE FINANCES ET DIRECTION, section of the royal council in France which shared responsibility with the *Conseil d'État et Finances* for financial affairs from the reign of Louis XIII. Its particular concern was with financial issues arising out of disputes between public and private interests.

CONSEIL DE MARINE, one of the seven government councils in France collectively known as the *Polysynodie*, established in 1715 by the Regent of France, Philip of Orléans. It survived until 1722.

CONSEIL D'EN HAUT, most important of the councils of Louis XIV of France, which was presided over by the king in person. The great issues of state were discussed there under conditions of the utmost secrecy, no written record being kept. Diplomatic correspondence was read and the replies agreed upon. Normally only five or six officials attended and they were given the title of ministers of state. The secretaries of state for foreign affairs, war and the navy, and the controller-general of finance, were usually included, but there were no *ex-officio* members, the king deciding who would attend each session. The council normally met three times a week.

CONSEIL DES AFFAIRES, section of the royal council in France, under Francis I, which was primarily concerned with international politics and with great matters of state. It may be identified with the *conseil secret* of his predecessors and the *conseil d'en haut* of the Bourbons.

CONSEIL DES DÉPÊCHES, section of the royal council in France, inaugurated in 1630, to control the interior administration of the kingdom and oversee the relations between the king and the clergy, the towns and the *pays d'état*. It also exercised a judicial capacity and was used to withdraw controversial cases from the *parlement's* jurisdiction and quash controversial decrees issued by the sovereign courts.

CONSEIL DES FINANCES, section of the king's council in France which made intermittent appearances during the 16th cent., its chief task coming at the end of the century with the urgent need to balance the royal budget.

CONSEIL DES PARTIES, judicial section of the king's council which appeared in France towards the end of the 16th cent. It was primarily concerned with matters which could not readily be settled by the sovereign courts or which had caused unsatisfactory verdicts to be given at that level.

CONSEIL D'ÉTAT, phrase used under the *ancien régime* in France to describe the king's council as a whole, as well as that section of the council which dealt with administrative matters, partly fiscal and partly judicial, within the kingdom.

The phrase was also used to describe a body created by the Constitution of the Year VIII which became one of the most effective organs of Napoleonic government. Its 29 members, often under Napoleon's presidency, drafted legislation, advised on legal and administrative matters, and supervised the work of the various ministries.

CONSEIL D'ETAT ET FINANCES, section of the royal council which existed under the *ancien régime* in France from the reign of Louis XIII and was responsible for those day-to-day financial affairs in which no great decisions of principle were involved.

CONSEIL DU ROI, one of the titles by which the king's council was known in early 16th-cent. France, though by the end of the century it had given way to the phrase *conseil d'état*.

CONSEIL ÉTROIT, one the titles by which the king's council was known in early 16th-cent. France, though by the end of the century it had given way to the phrase *conseil d'état*.

CONSEIL NATIONAL DE LA RÉSISTANCE set up in 1943 to co-ordinate the activities of the French Resistance. It was composed of representatives of the Resistance movements, of political parties, and of trade unions. De Gaulle's emissary, Jean Moulin, was its first chairman; when Moulin was captured, Bidault took over. The CNR's powers of action were limited, but it was able to set up local liberation committees and to impose some unity on the various clandestine forces. Its most important achievement was perhaps the 'Resistance Charter', a programme of social reforms which formed the basis of post-war legislation. When De Gaulle's provisional government was established after the Liberation, the CNR soon disappeared, although there were attempts to continue it as an independent authority.

CONSEIL PRIVÉ one of the titles by which the king's council was known in early 16th-cent. France. It later became an alternative title for the *conseil des parties*.

CONSEIL SECRET, section of the royal council in France which became the *conseil des affaires* in the reign of Francis I.

CONSELHEIRO, ANTONIO (1828–97), spiritual leader of Bahia, Brazil, who headed an unsuccessful rebellion against the national government (1897). The Counsellor, whose real name was Antônio Vicente Mendes Maciel, led a fanatical group in an attempt to establish a separate theocratic state in the interior of Bahia. The Brazilian government used federal troops to end the rebellion, which proved costly to both sides. Conselheiro died in battle and the separatist community of Canudos was virtually exterminated. This episode was the most famous of a series of similar messianic phenomena in Brazil. Euclides de Cunha immortalized the rebellion in his classic *Os sertões (The Backlands)*.

CONSENSUS MUTUUS (1570), agreement concluded at Sandormierz by the various Protestant groups in Poland— Calvinist, Lutheran, and Polish Bohemian Brethren—providing for occasional synods and based on a vague eucharistic formula acceptable to all three sects. However, the *Consensus* proved ineffective in the defence of Polish Protestantism against the Counter-Reformation.

CONSENSUS TIGURINUS (1549), theological agreement of the Zwinglian churches of Zürich and Geneva by which the Reformed Church in Switzerland presented a common front.

CONSERVATION MOVEMENT IN THE UNITED STATES, attempt to restrain traditional profligate use of natural resources. Abundance had given rise to the belief that resources were inexhaustible, and delayed the realization that material progress was defiling the land and undermining future prosperity. By the mid-19th cent., however, attitudes were beginning to change. George Perkins Marsh, in *Man and Nature* (1864), emphasized man's role in changing the face of the earth. John Wesley Powell, in a *Report on the Lands of the Arid Regions of the US* (1879), directed attention to the nature and problems of the western lands, and John Muir aroused public interest in preserving the Grand Canyon and the Sierras. Federal action was, however, impeded by western congressmen unwilling to revise the land disposal system. When the cost of the exploitive agriculture of 19th-cent. America was finally estimated, it was found that 100 million acres (55,000 sq. kms) had been irreparably destroyed by erosion and 200 million acres (110,000 sq. kms) rendered almost useless.

Large-scale land, timber, and mineral frauds finally aroused public agitation for conservation. Yellowstone National Park was established in 1872, the first forest reserve was designated in 1891, and Theodore Roosevelt's presidency showed a firm commitment to the principles of conservation. The Newlands Reclamation Act (1902) created the Bureau of Reclamation, and Gifford Pinchot finally succeeded in forming the Forest Service (1905) and established multiple-use concepts of forest management. Roosevelt set aside further vast forest reserves (1907) and appointed an Inland Waterways Commission to study flood conditions on the lower Mississippi river. This commission recommended a comprehensive plan for the development and utilization of water resources. Roosevelt called a national conservation conference, the White House Conference of Governors (1908), which led to the establishment of several state departments of conservation. A National Conservation Commission, headed by Gifford Pinchot, began a preliminary inventory of natural resources, and Roosevelt evolved the concept of 'stewardship' of the public domain.

During the First World War the conservation movement lost momentum, although Congress authorized the establishment of the National Parks Service in 1916. During the 1920s and early 1930s the deterioration of resources was emphasized by the increasing prevalence of droughts and dust-storms, and conservation changed from a crusade to a scientific study of an economic problem. Under President F. D. Roosevelt's New Deal the federal government undertook wide-ranging conservation programmes, beginning with the Civilian Conservation Corps (1933). The Taylor Grazing Act (1934) and establishment of the Soil Conservation Service (1935) underlined preoccupation with problems of erosion, and the Tennessee Valley Authority demonstrated on the regional level how desolated lands could be rehabilitated. By 1960 various agencies had managed to slow down the exhaustion of America's natural resources and by 1970 public awareness of the dangers of pollution had made conservation a dominant political issue.

S. P. Hays, *The Gospel of Efficiency: the progressive conservation movement, 1890–1920* (Cambridge, MA, 1959).
Ruben Parson, *Conserving American Resources* (Englewood Cliffs, NJ, 1956).   AB

CONSERVATIVE PARTY, IN CANADA, originally the Liberal–Conservative Party founded (1854) by John A. Macdonald from a coalition of the Robert Baldwin Liberals, high Tories, Conservatives of Upper Canada, and the *bleus* of Lower Canada. Its foundation was largely a reaction to the radical policies of the extreme wing of the Reform Party, and the platform with which the Conservatives won power in 1854 advocated secularization of the Clergy Reserves, abolition of seigniorial tenure, and an elective legislature. In general, the party favoured the British connection, federal rights as opposed to provincial rights, and, later on, protection. The Conservatives remained in power until 1862 and were returned again in 1864, when, out of the deadlocked legislature, emerged the Great Coalition of Conservatives and Liberals which achieved confederation (1867). Macdonald became the first prime minister of the Dominion and, to retain Liberal support, he made a genuine attempt to form a non-partisan government. Most Liberals opposed this policy and Macdonald won the election of 1872 on a conservative platform. Discredited by the Pacific Scandal, however, Macdonald resigned (1873). The Conservative answer to the depression and the Liberal advocacy of free-trade was the National Policy, which aimed to put 'Canada First' by using protective tariffs to stimulate east–west trade within Canada at the expense of the north–south, US–Canadian trade; though this secured their return to office (1878), their influence in Quebec waned because of dissension among Quebec Conservatives and the execution of Louis Riel (1885). Nevertheless, the Conservatives won the next three general elections (1882, 1887, 1891). With Macdonald's death (1891) the party divided into factions and was defeated in 1896 and again, even more severely, in 1900. Under Richard Borden's leadership, the Conservatives attacked the Liberal government's 1911 reciprocity agreement with the US, and before the end of the year Borden was prime minister. The party truce which the Liberal leader, Wilfred Laurier, proclaimed (1914) was ended by him (1917) when Borden decided to introduce conscription. Some Liberals, however, supported conscription and with these Borden formed the Unionist Party, which won a massive majority (1917). When Borden resigned (1920) and Arthur Meighen took over, the Unionists held a convention at which, to retain Liberal support, they renamed the party National Liberal and Conservative. They were heavily defeated (1921) and their recovery (1925) still left them seven seats short of an overall majority, so the Liberals hung on to office to find themselves not only losing control of the House, but also being refused a dissolution in June 1926 by Lord Byng, the governor-general. At Byng's request Meighen formed a government which, when defeated in the House, was granted a dissolution and roundly defeated in the ensuing election (1927). The Conservatives, led by R. B. Bennett, returned to power (1930), but were defeated (1935), and though the party was renamed Progres-

sive Conservative (1943), it was not until 1957 that, under John Diefenbaker's leadership, they regained office with a small majority that was considerably augmented in an election the following year. Economic problems led to a reaction against the Conservatives and following the election of 1962 they ruled a coalition. Since an election in 1963, the Conservative Party has been in opposition.

John R. Williams, *Conservative Party of Canada: 1920–1949* Durham, Ont., 1956).   WM

CONSERVATIVE PARTY, IN BRITAIN, emerged under the leadership of Robert Peel after the failure of the Tories to respond to the growing pressure for administrative and institutional change which culminated in the Whig Reform Bill of 1832. However, the bill did not introduce a long period of Whig hegemony, for despite Tory hostility to reform, the parties had much in common. Both were aristocratic in outlook, suspicious of democracy, and desirous that property should remain the chief title to political power. Where they differed was in their interpretation of events. The Whigs believed that some political innovation was necessary to improve and preserve the existing order. The Tories suspected that any major change would threaten the fabric of society. Peel and the 'responsible' Conservatives, by creating a party more responsive to change, were able to remain as contenders for power in an age demanding Benthamite reforms. In his Tamworth Manifesto (1835) Peel accepted the Reform Bill and promised to redress abuses and grievances without infringing established rights. F. R. Bonham was appointed election manager (1832) and created a unique apparatus for mobilizing Conservative provincial opinion through local associations and official registration. The Conservatives thus eroded Whig power and formed their first majority government in 1841. But it proved impossible to reconcile the conflict between the landed interest and the demand for free trade. The party split over repeal of the Corn Laws (1846). The Peelites, who had supported repeal, eventually formed a coalition with the Whigs to form the Liberal Party. The remaining Conservatives, led by Derby and Disraeli, prevented the disintegration of conservatism (1846–67) before it re-emerged as an effective political force.

Disraeli had championed protection in 1846 on grounds of expediency rather than principle. He retained this flexibility, and after Gladstone's conversion to parliamentary reform outwitted the Liberals by passing his own Reform Bill (1867), justifying the extension of the electorate by an appeal to the natural alliance between aristocracy and people. Both parties now sought to woo the electorate with programmes of reform. So Disraeli, to give conservatism a distinct identity, reinforced his programme of Tory democracy with support for the established Church and approval of the pursuit of empire.

After Disraeli's death Conservative unity was threatened by Randolph Churchill's radicalism. Lord Salisbury tried to consolidate his Conservative government by outbidding Gladstone for Irish support (1885). He lost the initiative to the Liberals when Gladstone's conversion to Home Rule was revealed. But Home Rule split the Liberals, and the Liberal Unionists, including Chamberlain's radicals, joined what now became the Conservative and Unionist Party. The Conservatives were unable to absorb the new radical element. Chamberlain's conversion to imperial preference caused the disintegration of A. J. Balfour's cabinet and the landslide Liberal victory of 1906. But although they began the new century in disarray, the Conservatives and not the Liberals were to provide the long-term alternative to socialism. In 1911 Balfour was succeeded as leader by Andrew Bonar Law, and the party's organization was strengthened by the appointment of a chairman. But the conflict in the party between the protectionists and their opponents was not to be so easily resolved. In 1915, however, the party entered Asquith's coalition government, and remained there until 1922. Discontent with Lloyd George, and opposition to the Irish treaty, then brought about the famous Carlton Club meeting which led to a Conservative election victory. In 1923 Bonar Law resigned and was succeeded by Baldwin. After the Labour interregnum of 1924, the 'Baldwin Age' began in earnest. At home the emphasis on tranquillity survived the 1926 General Strike. Under Neville Chamberlain there was much social reform, and Conservative industrial policy even extended to a pragmatic view of nationalization. The device of the 'public corporation' began with broadcasting and electricity generation (1926), and extended to the airways, leading in 1940 to the creation of the British Overseas Airways Corporation (BOAC). Abroad, the 1925–9 ministry concentrated on a search for Franco-German amity on the European continent. Protectionism was accepted, at the Ottawa Conference (1931), and the party endorsed the idea of imperial prefence.

In 1929 Labour formed a minority government, but this was replaced by a coalition in 1931, in which Baldwin asserted his power. In 1935 the Conservatives won a landslide victory at the polls; Baldwin presided for another two years, being replaced by Chamberlain in 1937. The great crisis was now in foreign policy. In 1933–4 a programme of rearmament had been begun, but little result was visible when the crisis broke. The policy of 'appeasement' followed by Baldwin and Chamberlain reached its climax in the Munich Conference of 1938. Chamberlain had been a popular prime minister, but was superseded soon after the outbreak of the Second World War. Churchill's Coalition government (1940–5) was characterized by radicalism at home, and proved successful in conducting the war. When, however, the Coalition broke up, Churchill was swept out of office.

In the 25 years thereafter, the Conservatives governed from 1951 to 1964; the prime ministers were, successively, Winston Churchill (1951–5), Anthony Eden (1955–7), Harold Macmillan (1957–63), and Sir Alec Douglas-Home (1963–4). The foundations had been laid in the pioneering work of Lord Woolton and R. A. Butler at the Conservative Central Office in the years in opposition. Thus, in power, Conservative rule was characterized by the acceptance of the 'Welfare State' with few exceptions. Abroad, the US Alliance, the support of anti-Soviet alliances (NATO, SEATO) continued, and decolonization was extended to Africa. Under Churchill and (more successfully) Macmillan, there were repeated diplomatic initiatives designed to secure a detente with the USSR. In 1962 the emphasis turned to Europe, in part a mark of the success of the colonial and Soviet policies.

In 1965 Sir Alec Douglas-Home resigned as party leader and was succeeded by Edward Heath. Heath became Conservative prime minister in the general election of 1970.

G. Kitson Clark, *Peel and the Conservative Party* (London, 1929).
R. T. MacKenzie, *British Political Parties* (London, 1963).
SDH
GD

CONSILIUM PRINCIPIS, the private council of the Roman emperors, who followed the Roman tradition, which insisted that all holders of power should seek advice before taking decisions. Members of the *consilium*, mostly senators, were called *amici*—friends of the emperor. There was no fixed number, emperors choosing whom they thought most suitable, military, diplomatic, and judicial experience counting for much. The judicial element increased in importance under Hadrian and his successors, sometimes meeting separately. The council had no official place in the constitution, but its members could provide continuity of policy on a change of ruler. As the Senate declined in importance, emperors took all important decisions in the council. Its functions were absorbed in Constantine's new organ of government, the *consistorium*.

CONSILIUM PRINCIPIS (1787), in Britain ended the system of holding public money in separate funds by having the customs and excise paid into a single fund. It was part of Pitt's rationalization of public finance, which also abolished the practice of using separate ledgers for each increase in duty.

CONSOLS (1751), the stock created by the consolidation of part of the national debt, certain 3 per cent annuities, the earliest dating from 1731. The amount of stock was at first less than the 3 per cent Reduced stock created after Pelham's conversion (1749), but by the end of the 18th cent. Consols had become by far the most important element in the national debt.

CONSTABLE, title of the French commander-in-chief, the highest military office under the Crown until the 17th cent. Usually held by a great noble, the office carried considerable privileges and had its own court of law, the *connétablie*. The constable also sat in the king's council. After the death of Lesdiguières in Sept. 1626 Richelieu ordered the abolition of the office with that of admiral, depriving the nobility of a post of great political significance.

CONSTANCE OF SICILY (d. 1198), Empress, daughter of King Roger II of Sicily, who married Frederick Barbarossa's son, the future Holy Roman Emperor Henry VI, in 1185. The death of the childless King William II in 1189 made Constance his heiress. The potential threat of a union of the empire and Sicily was instantly recognized by the papacy, which faced the danger of encirclement. She acted as regent for Henry after his victory over his Norman rival, King Tancred, though there is suspicion that she was implicated in a national Sicilian conspiracy against Henry. For a brief period after her husband's death she ruled Sicily for her minor son, the future Emperor Frederick II, and on her death she left him under papal guardianship.

CONSTANCE, PEACE OF (25 June 1183), concluded more than 20 years of warfare between the Emperor Frederick Barbarossa and the Lombard cities which had been supported by Pope Alexander III. The cities of the Lombard League agreed to recognize the emperor as their supreme overlord, but their right to govern themselves was safeguarded. The peace marked the end of the attempts of German kings to exploit effectively the wealth of the Lombard cities.

CONSTANS, FL. JULIUS (d. AD 350), Roman Emperor who, as son and joint successor of Constantine the Great, ruled Illyricum, Italy, and Africa (337–40). He then defeated an invasion by his brother, Constantine II, and took over the entire west, governing successfully until his defeat by the pretender Magnentius (350).

CONSTANT DE MAGALHÃES, BENJAMIN (1838–91), sometimes referred to as Botelho de Magalhães, more often simply as Benjamin Constant. He was the most influential Brazilian teacher of positivist doctrines, as well as a leader of the republican revolution which overthrew the empire of Pedro II (Nov. 1889). Constant exerted his influence as a teacher in the military academy, where the officers who would lead the early republic were educated. He was a noted liberal and a republican, as well as an abolitionist.

CONSTANT DE REBECQUE, HENRI BENJAMIN (1767–1830), novelist, political writer, and politician. He went with Mme de Stael to Paris (1794), where he supported the Directory and, for a time after Brumaire, the Consulate. In 1802 he was expelled from the tribunate and left France. His meetings with Goethe and Schiller helped to transmit their literary influence into France. Although an opponent of Napoleon, Constant supplied a liberal constitution for the empire after Napoleon's escape from Elba. After the Restoration he became a deputy (1819), campaigned for press freedom, edited liberal political reviews, and welcomed the

July monarchy. His psychological novel *Adolphe*, based on the rupture of his relationship with Mme de Stael, remains a literary landmark.

CONSTANTINE OF MARAVAL IN TRINIDAD AND OF NELSON, LEARIE NICHOLAS, Life Baron (1901–), West Indian leader, born in Trinidad. Constantine became first a solicitor's clerk, then a civil servant, and later a clerk in an oil company. As a cricketer he won recognition as one of the world's greatest all-rounders, playing for Nelson in the Lancashire League (1929–40) and for the West Indies Test sides. During the Second World War he was a welfare officer in the ministry of labour. He was called to the Trinidad bar (1954) and became minister of works and transport (1956). He returned to Britain as high commissioner of Trinidad and Tobago (1962–4). He practised law in Britain, was appointed a member of the newly formed Race Relations Board (1966), and became the first Negro peer (1969).

CONSTANTINE I (1868–1923), King of Greece (*reg.* 1913–1917, 1920–2). As commander of the Greek armies in the Graeco-Turkish war (1897) Constantine was blamed for a humiliating defeat which nearly cost his father the throne. His policy of favouritism as commander-in-chief led to the formation of the anti-dynastic Military League which successfully campaigned for his dismissal in 1909. Constantine took the throne when his father was murdered on 18 March 1913. During the First World War he clashed with Venizelos over Greece's policy, the king favouring the Central Powers, his minister the Allies. In March 1915 Constantine, together with Metaxas, forced Venizelos to resign over Greek participation in the Dardanelles campaign. After Venizelos had won an electoral victory in June, Constantine continued to frustrate him and again he resigned (Oct. 1915) as Allied forces landed at Salonika. Constantine drove Venizelos's supporters from the Chamber and obstructed the Allied army at Salonika, prompting Venizelos to form a provisional government in Oct. 1916 which had Allied recognition. In June, 1917, in the face of an Allied ultimatum, Constantine withdrew without formally abdicating. When Alexander died in 1920 the choice again fell between Constantine and Venizelos. Constantine won an overwhelming victory in the plebiscite of 5 Dec. 1920 and returned to Greece on the 19th. He identified himself with the war in Asia Minor and when the Greek armies were beaten, a revolutionary committee centred in the army demanded his abdication. Constantine abdicated (27 Sept. 1922) and retired to Sicily.

CONSTANTINE II, FL. IULIUS (*reg.* AD 337–40), Roman Emperor, son and joint successor of Constantine the Great, and ruler of Britain, Gaul, and Spain until 340, when he attacked his brother and colleague, Constans, and was defeated and killed at Aquileia.

CONSTANTINE II (d. 952), King of Scotland (*reg.* 900–43), imposed Scottish custom on the Pictish Church. In 927 he acknowledged Athelstan, King of Wessex, as overlord, but later organized the great coalition with the Scandinavians against Athelstan, which was defeated at Brunanburh in 937. He became a monk at St Andrew's in 943.

CONSTANTINE VII PORPHYROGENITUS (905–59), Byzantine Emperor (*reg.* 913–59), son of Leo VI the Wise. He had no real share, however, in the government of the empire until after the exile of his father-in-law, the Emperor Romanus Lecapenus, in 944. Constantine VII, a patron of literature and art, wrote the *De Thematibus* (a geographical account of the empire), the *De Administrando Imperio* (a handbook on the government of the empire, written for his son, Romanus II), the *De Cerimoniis* (a work on the customs and ceremonial of the Byzantine court), and also a life of his grandfather, Basil I, extant now as book V of the chronicle known as *Theophanes Continuatus*. His works are also a valuable source of information about eastern and central Europe.

CONSTANTINE XI PALAEOLOGUS (1404–53), last Byzantine Emperor, who was governor of the Despotate of the Morea. He was proclaimed emperor at Mistra in 1449, after the death of John VIII. Constantine XI, defending Constantinople against the Ottoman Turks under Sultan Muhammad II, died in the fighting which led to the fall of the great fortress on 29 May 1453.

CONSTANTINE THE GREAT (Fl. Valerius Constantinus) (*reg.* AD 306–37), the first Christian Emperor of Rome. Having been passed over for the succession by Diocletian and Maximian, Constantine joined his father, Constantius, in Britain, and was acclaimed emperor at York by the army after Constantius' death (306). After overcoming his rivals in a series of complex dynastic struggles (306–12), he won recognition from the eastern emperor Licinius, whom, after some years of uneasy peace, he defeated at Chrysopolis (324), to become sole emperor. In secular policy, Constantine continued Diocletian's reorganization of the administration and army and achieved lasting financial stability by introducing a new gold unit of currency, the *solidus*. His foundation of Constantinople as the 'New Rome' (330) made this city the second in the empire, and illustrates the increasing importance in it of the eastern provinces. Constantine's conversion to Christianity preceded his victory over the usurper Maxentius at the battle of the Milvian Bridge (312), which he fought under the emblems of his new faith. He agreed with Licinius (313) to suspend the persecutions of the Christians begun by Diocletian, and extended toleration to all recognized religions. Despite some ambiguities in public expressions of his faith, and despite of his postponing his baptism until he was on his death-bed, his personal sincerity is clear. He was actively interested in ecclesiastical affairs, notably in promoting the councils of Arles (314) and Nicaea (325), and he extended privileges to Christian clergy, founded churches (*eg,* at St Peter's shrine at Rome) and provided them with generous donations of property and plate. After executing Crispus, his son by his first marriage, and his second wife, Fausta, in 326, he promoted her sons, Constantine, Constans, and Constantius, as Caesars, and was succeeded by them.

A. H. M. Jones, *Constantine and the Conversion of Europe* (London, 1948). JFM

CONSTANTINE NIKOLAYEVICH, Grand Duke (1827–92), Russian statesman and liberal-minded brother of Alexander II. He was chairman (1857) of the Main Committee of Peasant Affairs which prepared the Emancipation decree, and viceroy to Poland (1862). As head of the navy and president of the Council of State he supported reforms and was dismissed on Alexander III's accession.

CONSTANTINE PAVLOVICH, Grand Duke (1779–1831), Russian soldier and brother of Alexander I. As commander-in-chief of the Polish army, he governed Poland (1814–31) and the Polish rebellion (1830–1) was partly against his rule.

CONSTANTINOPLE, ancient Byzantium, already a flourishing city in the 6th cent. BC, commended itself to Emperor Constantine the Great as the site of the New Rome in the East by its superb strategic location, its network of fine natural harbours, and its commercial possibilites. It was begun in AD 324 and virtually completed by 330. Increasingly after Constantine's time the city became identified with a new Roman–Christian civilization that owed much also to the language and traditions of Greece. From an early date the see of Constantinople rivalled that of Antioch and of Rome itself, although, placed as he was firmly under the interested supervision of the emperor, the patriarch could never command the supremacy of the Roman pope. In essentials, Constantinople *was* the Byzantine empire—always the heart of Byzantine culture, political institutions, and military power. The historical and emotional link with the First Rome remained a matter of pride and a stimulus to its citizens, who to the last age of Byzantium called themselves Romans. Alternately through the centuries dominating vast provinces or standing as a lonely if crowded bastion confronting the desolation of alien conquests, Constantinople retained a unique civic prestige. Persians, Slavs, Arabs, Latins (who conquered the city in the 13th cent.), and Turks successively hurled their power against it. Finally, the empire, reduced to the bounds of the imperial city itself, fell to the attack of Sultan Muhammad II. Its last emperor, Constantine XI Palaeologus, perished on the walls in the defence of his capital in 1453. Though the fall of Constantinople may seem inevitable, granted the relative strengths of Turk and Byzantine at the time, the end was hastened by the rivalries of powerful Western states such as Genoa and Venice and the sullen reluctance of the Greeks to rally to the support of a dynasty which, in the great schism between Catholic and Orthodox, pope and patriarch, had chosen to try to heal relations and had acknowledged papal primacy in return for vague assurances of assistance. The divisions of Christendom helped to ensure the collapse of its Eastern realm.

CONSTANTINOPLE AGREEMENT, exchange of notes between Russia, Britain, and France (March–April 1915) recognizing Russian claims to Constantinople, the Straits and adjacent areas, British predominance in the Iranian neutral zone, and providing for British and French compensation elsewhere in Ottoman territories. The agreement, precipitated by the Dardanelles campaign, paved the way for the partition of the Ottoman empire.

CONSTANTINOPLE CONFERENCE (Dec. 1876). Ambassadorial conference after the Serbian declaration of war on Turkey and the Bulgarian atrocities, which agreed on proposals for Turkish reform and the status and boundaries of Bulgaria. War with Russia followed Turkey's rejection of these.

CONSTANTINOPLE, SIEGES OF. The Muslims attacked Constantinople for the first time in 669. Their second assault, in 674–80, was more sustained, but also unsuccessful. Most of the fighting occurred between the Byzantine and the Muslim fleets, the latter operating from a base (for land and naval forces alike) on the peninsula of Cyzicus. The Muslims besieged Constantinople for the third time in 717–18, abandoning the campaign at last before the bitter resistance of the Byzantines and their allies, the Bulgars, but also on account of the losses arising from the rigours of a severe winter. In 1204 the Latins of the Fourth Crusade captured Constantinople—an event which ended the greatness of Byzantium and led to the establishing of the brief-lived Latin Empire of Constantinople (1204–61). The great fortress was destined to survive, after 1261, as the centre of a declining Byzantine regime until 1453. In that year, on 29 May, the Ottoman Turks took Constantinople by assault, thus bringing to an end the Byzantine state.

CONSTANTINOPLE, TREATY OF (1700), between Russia and the Ottoman empire. Russia gained Azov and a stretch of coastline on the Sea of Azov, including the new naval base of Taganrog, but failed to gain Kerch and an outlet to the Black Sea. The treaty followed the breakdown of an anti-Turkish coalition when Austria, Poland, and Venice deserted Russia at the treaty of Carlowitz (1699). From this, Peter concluded that Russia was not only too weak to fight Turkey alone, but too weak to force her attentions on the rest of Europe as yet. With the breakdown of the coalition against the Turks, Peter turned his back on his new acquisitions and altered his whole foreign policy, switching his sphere of activity to the Baltic and an anti-Swedish coalition.

CONSTANTIUS II, FL. IULIUS (*reg.* AD 337–61), Roman Emperor succeeded his father, Constantine the Great, as eastern emperor, becoming sole legitimate ruler after the deaths of his brothers Constantine II and Constans. After defeating the pretender Magnentius (353), he installed Julian as Caesar in Gaul (355), and after visiting Rome (357) returned to the east. Challenged by Julian (360), Constantius prepared for war, but died prematurely and was succeeded by him. More distinguished for his success in domestic than in foreign wars, Constantius gained notoriety for his attempts to impose Arian heterodoxy upon the western Church, and for his interest in theological debate.

CONSTANTIUS, FL. VALERIUS (d. AD 306), later nicknamed 'Chlorus', father of Constantine the Great who, as deputy Roman Emperor or Caesar (293–305) under Diocletian and Maximian, suppressed the British rebellion of Allectus (297) and conducted wars in the west. Appointed joint emperor (Augustus) with Galerius in 305, he died at York and his son was acclaimed by the army.

CONSTITUENT ASSEMBLY (18–19 Jan. 1919), in Russia. Ever since the time of Alexander Herzen, Russian radicals had demanded a democratic assembly; so it was natural that one of the Provisional Government's first actions in March 1917 was to promise to summon such an assembly after the war, and later Kerensky announced that elections would be held on 25 Nov. Until they seized power, the Bolsheviks had supported the convening of the assembly. The elections took place in free conditions in most of the constituencies and 27·8 million votes were cast. Of these the Bolsheviks received 9·8 million; the Socialist Revolutionaries 17 million; the Mensheviks 1·4 million; the Kadets 2 million; and various non-Russian parties 7·6 million between them. Of the 707 deputies elected 175 were Bolsheviks, 40 Left Socialist Revolutionaries, 370 Socialist Revolutionaries, 16 Mensheviks, 17 Kadets, and 86 representatives of various national parties. This result, unfavourable to the Bolsheviks, was contemptuously described by Lenin as the product of 'bourgeois democracy'. When the deputies met, the Bolsheviks demanded that the assembly should recognize the decrees already passed by the Congress of Soviets; this motion was rejected by 237–136 votes, upon which the Bolshevik and Left SR delegates walked out. The Chairman, V. M. Chernov, attempted to keep order in spite of interruptions by Red Guards, who at length closed the session early in the morning of 19 Jan., complaining that they were tired. No further session was allowed and little commotion was caused by the dissolution of the only assembly in Russian history elected according to Western ideas of legality.   GS

CONSTITUTIO ANTONINIANA, enactment of the Emperor Caracalla (AD 212–17), by which all inhabitants of the empire, with certain exceptions, became Roman citizens. The purpose of this apparently liberal enactment is not known for certain, but was probably to increase revenue.

CONSTITUTION OF CADIZ (1812) provided a model for subsequent Spanish and Italian liberal constitutions. It was drawn up in the last stage of the war against Napoleon by the liberal majority in the Spanish Cortes. Proclaiming the sovereignty of the nation and equality of all citizens, the constitution severely limited the royal veto and power of appointing ministers and put legislative power in the hands of a single chamber, elected indirectly by universal suffrage. The conservative majority in Spain never recognized it and Ferdinand VII denounced it on his return from France (1814). The constitution was temporarily reinstituted by the liberal revolutionaries of 1820, and both the Neapolitan (1820) and Piedmontese revolutions declared in favour of it.

CONSTITUTION OF 1791, which was proclaimed by Louis XVI of France on 28 Sept., lasted a year, disappearing with the fall of the monarchy (1792), but was to act as a model for the 19th cent. liberals. It was the work of the middle-class constitutional monarchists, and severely limited the king's executive power by giving him only a four-year 'suspensive' veto on legislation. His ministers were responsible to a single-chamber Legislative Assembly, which initiated legislation and controlled finance, and was elected indirectly by tax-paying 'active' citizens. The constitution embodied most of the legislation passed since 1789 and also provided for an extensive reorganization of the administration and judiciary.

CONSTITUTION OF THE UNITED STATES, drafted by the Philadelphia Convention (1787) and ratified by the states (1788–91), came into effect in 1789 and has subsequently been amended 25 times. It established a tripartite federal government, consisting of an executive, a legislature, and a supreme court, and separated powers among the three branches of the national government while at the same time constructing a system of checks and balances in order to prevent the dominance of any one branch over the others. The constitution also established the principle of divided sovereignty by making the federal and state governments supreme within their respective spheres of competence. Whereas the Articles of Confederation had operated on the states, the new constitution operated directly on the people and gave the national government powers that it had previously lacked, including the power to tax, regulate commerce, and establish a federal court system. Article I of the constitution delineated the powers of, and limitations on, Congress, which was to have a senate comprising two members from each state and a house of representatives apportioned according to population. A separate executive, the presidency, was established by Article II, while Article III authorized Congress to establish a federal court system. Article IV required states to give 'full faith and credit' to the acts and judicial decisions of other states, guaranteed their republican institutions, and provided for the admission of new states. Under Article V amendments to the constitution could be made by a vote of two-thirds of both houses of Congress and approval by three-quarters of the states, or by a constitutional convention and later approval by the states. Article VI declared the constitution, and laws and treaties made under it, to be the supreme law of the land, and required federal and state officials to uphold it. The constitution left certain issues unresolved, and debate developed over whether the document was subject to 'strict' or 'loose' construction. It has largely developed through interpretation and undergone little formal change, although amendments have been made at various times for specific purposes. The first ten amendments comprise the Bill of Rights (1791), the tenth reserving to the states or to the people those powers not granted to the federal government, and amendments 11 and 12 made technical changes in the scope of the judicial power and presidential election procedures. Slavery was abolished and attempts made to protect Negro rights by the 13th (1865), 14th (1868), and 15th (1870) amendments. The 16th and 17th (1913) authorized a federal income tax and the direct election of US senators. The 18th amendment imposed Prohibition (1919), but was repealed by the 21st (1933). Women were enfranchised by the 19th amendment (1920). The 20th (1933) altered the dates of presidential and congressional terms of office and the 22nd (1951) restricted the president's period of office to two elected terms. Residents of the District of Columbia were given a presidential vote by the 23rd amendment (1961). The 24th prohibited payment of a poll tax as a requirement for the franchise (1964), and the 25th determined presidential succession in the case of the president's death, sickness, or disability (1967).

Alfred H. Kelly and Winfred A. Harbison, *The American Constitution: Its origins and development* (3rd ed., New York, 1963).
Edward S. Corwin, *The Constitution and What it Means Today* (Princeton, NJ, 1958).

CONSTITUTION, USS, American 44-gun frigate designed by Joshua Humphreys and built in Boston (1797). She was used as a US flagship during the naval war with France (1798) and the war with Tripoli (1804), and became famous during the war of 1812, notably through engagements against HMS *Guerière* and HMS *Java*. Affectionately known as 'Old Ironsides', she is laid up in Boston.

CONSTITUTIONAL ACT (1791), British law dividing Quebec into the provinces of Upper and Lower Canada, each with a governor, an executive council, and a legislative council, all appointed by the Crown, and a legislative assembly elected by the populace. Existing seigniories were unaffected, but future land grants were required to be made freehold, and one-seventh of the grant was to be set aside for clergy reserves. The measure was passed by William Pitt's administration.

CONSTITUTIONAL CONFERENCE (1910), in Britain abortive attempt (June–Nov. 1910) to reach agreement between government and opposition on the procedure for dealing with clashes between the House of Lords and the House of Commons. Its failure led the Liberal government to produce its own proposals, which were eventually passed as the Parliament Act (1911). The Lords' own proposals for reform, before and after the conference, were ignored.

CONSTITUTIONAL DEMOCRATIC PARTY (*KADETS***),** Russian political party of left-wing liberals led by P. Milyukov. It was founded in 1905 from P. B. Struve's Union of Liberation and left-wing *zemstvo* men under I. Petrunkevich and V. A. Maklakov. The right wing of the *zemstvo* movement became Octobrists. The *Kadet* programme (1905–6) demanded constitutional monarchy, four-fold suffrage, and a compensated expropriation of landowners' land for the peasantry. The party dominated the First Duma (1906) with 179 seats, but refused to co-operate with the government, demanded a revision of the Fundamental Law to establish parliamentary democracy, and was prominent in the Vyborg manifesto. It was renamed the Party of the People's Liberty, and in later Dumas its numbers decreased. It entered the Progressive Block (1915) and dominated the Provisional Government (March–July 1917).

CONSTITUTIONAL DEVELOPMENTS IN NEW ZEALAND. Crown colony government was set up in 1840 by briefly including NZ in NSW territory. NZ and UK agitation led to a complicated Act (1846) granting representative institutions, but Grey obtained suspension of this. Though his own councils were boycotted by settlers, the 1852 Constitution Act (the basis of NZ's parliamentary government) was primarily of his devising. Six provincial councils met in 1853, and a General Assembly of two chambers in 1854, responsible government being granted after a 'mixed' executive had failed. Though the assembly had overriding powers, a quasi-federal system operated, especially in land policy, until the provinces declined and were abolished (1876). Control over native policy, at first withheld, was, with some reservations, exercised by the General Assembly from 1863. Some degree of 'double government' continued until the withdrawal of British troops (1870), when full internal self-government was virtually operating. The growing party system eliminated the governor's remaining powers by the 1890s, after which period NZ had almost as much internal and external independence as her political leaders desired. This view persisted after the Statute of Westminster (1931) conceded legal autonomy, adoption by NZ (1947) being tied to internal politics and the abolition of the ineffectual Legislative Council (1950). Agitation for a written constitution to fill the gap was partly answered by the Electoral Act (1956), whose 'entrenched' clauses depended on party agreement, and by the creation of an Ombudsman (1962). The House of Representatives from 1902 numbered 80 seats (4 Maoris included) and became a unicameral legislature in 1951. In 1969 the number of seats was increased to 84.

CONSTITUTIONAL INFORMATION, SOCIETY FOR PROMOTING, in Britain, was founded in 1780 to spread propaganda for the radical reform of parliament, and remained active until *c.* 1794. It published and reprinted many tracts to prove that the demand for parliamentary reform was based on the principles and practice of the past. In its last few years the society encouraged the formation of working-class corresponding societies on the model of the London Corresponding Society.

CONSTITUTIONS, NAPOLEONIC, mixed authoritarianism with a form of democracy. The Consulate (1800) had three consuls as its strong executive. The most important was the first consul, who appointed ministers, civic and military heads, and the Council of State. His power to initiate laws effectively limited the legislative powers of the Senate, Tribunate, and Legislative Body. Elections were conducted on the basis of official lists, although the Consulate was ratified by a popular plebiscite, as was the empire (1804), which merely substituted a hereditary emperor for the first consul.

CONSUBSTANTIATION, term given to the Lutheran belief that at the eucharist Christ's body and blood are really present 'in, with, and under' the sacrament of bread and wine, although the substance of these remains unchanged. In their meeting in 1529 Luther refused to compromise with Zwingli, who denied a physical real presence, and the doctrine kept both reformers apart.

CONSUL, the highest ordinary magistrate of Republican Rome. According to Roman tradition, at the republic's foundation (509 BC) two annually elected consuls replaced the king and inherited his power. Despite various limitations a consul, by virtue of his *imperium*, could do anything not forbidden by law or the veto of his colleague or of a plebeian tribune. They commanded the army, convened, presided over, and transacted business with the Senate and popular assemblies, and gave their names to the year. The senior ex-consuls effectively ran the state and in the late republic tenure of the consulship conferred nobility. Under the empire there were regularly several pairs of consuls a year, each holding office for two to four months. After Diocletian and Constantine the consulship lost all power, although its glamour remained.

CONSULADOS, the merchants' guilds of Spain, which were extended to Spanish America during the colonial period and survived into the 19th cent. The *consulados*, which developed in the principal ports and cities of the colonies, monopolized wholesale and, to some degree, retail commerce, regulated commerce through its function as a tribunal, and generally saw to the welfare of the richest Spanish merchants in the colonies. The power of the *consulados* in colonial affairs was considerable. In early 19th-cent. New Spain, for example, the *consulado* at Mexico City succeeded on at least two occasions in removing and selecting viceroys.

CONSULATE (1799), system of government erected in France by Napoleon Bonaparte after his *coup d'état*. He transformed it into the empire (1804) without any fundamental change in its institutions.

CONTAINMENT, initially the policy adopted by the US and its allies in response to Soviet expansion at the end of the Second World War. Its clearest formulation was given by George Kennan in a paper of Jan. 1947 (published under the pseudonym 'X' in *Foreign Affairs* (July 1947), as 'The Sources of Soviet Conduct'). Kennan argued that Soviet diplomacy was 'at once easier and more difficult to deal with than the diplomacy of individual aggressive leaders like Napoleon and Hitler'—easier since the Soviet Union would more readily yield tactically when confronted with determined resistance, more difficult because it was undeterred by a single defeat. He therefore advised that:

the main element of any United States policy toward the Soviet Union must be that of a long-term, patient but firm and vigilant containment of Russian expansive tendencies.

Western policy, in its refusal to make further concessions to the Soviet Union in the reconstruction of its own strength through NATO, the rearmament of Germany, and resistance in Korea can be seen as following the policy outlined by Kennan, who was placed at the head of a newly established Policy Planning Staff in the state department (May 1947). While the policy of containment meant resistance to communist demands it also implied the rejection of any attempt to force the communists out of positions they had already won. To this extent it was similar to the pursuit of spheres of interest, with the difference that in the short run it was accompanied, not by the detente which could be expected from such a division, but by the tension of the Cold War.

Kennan expected that the effect of containment on the Soviet Union would be to produce a 'mellowing' of its system of government and would lead eventually to the possibility of negotiation between the US and Soviet Russia. He therefore reproached his own government for not taking advantage of the opportunities opened up, in his view, by the death of Stalin and the disintegration of the communist monolith. But Kennan was no more than the clear exponent of a policy which governments put into effect. Following the success of the communists in China and the threat of the spread of communist rule in South-East Asia, the policy of containment was extended round the world; but while it can be seen as producing stability in Europe and a successful, limited operation in Korea, it led to the involvement of the US in prolonged war in Viet-nam.

G. F. Kennan, *American Diplomacy 1900–1950* (London, 1953).

G. F. Kennan, *Memoirs* (London, 1968). WFK

CONTARINI, GASPAR, Cardinal (1483–1542), Venetian aristocrat and diplomat, who was a great liberal Catholic reformer of the Reformation period.

In 1511 he experienced a personal crisis which made him place great emphasis upon justification by faith in the Augustinian tradition. At this time he was pressed by his fellow Venetians, Paolo Giustiniani and Vincenzo Quirini, to join them as hermit-monks of the Camaldolese order, but after much heart-searching he rejected the cloistered life. In 1516 he published his treatise, *De immortalitate Animae*, and in the decade 1517–27 he became associated with the members of the Oratory of Divine Love in Rome. Though a layman, he was raised to the cardinalate by Pope Paul III, who named him as one of the papal commissioners appointed to study Church reform (1536). In March 1537 he and his colleagues presented their report, the *Consilium de Emendanda Ecclesia*, which condemned the scandalous state of monasticism and the financial abuses within the Church, laying much of the blame upon the papacy, but Paul III did little to act upon their recommendations.

He was charitable in his attitude to Lutheran heresy and sincerely hoped for reunion with moderate Protestants, although he had published a book entitled *A Confutation of the Articles or Questions of Luther* (1530). He was sent as papal legate to the Diet of Regensburg (1541), which achieved some agreement with Melanchthon on free will and original sin, and a compromise formula on justification by faith, which Contarini elaborated in his *Epistola de Justificatione*. However, no compromise was possible on the question of transubstantiation and the Colloquy of Regensburg was denounced by both Caraffa and Luther. To the former, Contarini's theological interpretations smacked of heresy, and weary with failure, he returned to Rome. His death in the following year marked a turning point in the history of 16th-cent. religion. Hopes of reconciliation declined sharply as, under Caraffa's leadership, the Catholic Church moved away from spontaneous internal reform towards counter-revolutionary measures.

A. G. Dickens, *The Counter Reformation* (London, 1968).

MKS

CONTINENTAL ARMY, the army serving under the revolutionary government during the American War of Independence. The army was created (15 June 1775) by the Second Continental Congress from colonial militia besieging Boston, MA.

CONTINENTAL ASSOCIATION (1774), an agreement among American colonial delegates of the First Continental Congress to boycott British imports, encourage home manufactures, discontinue the slave trade, and threaten to halt colonial exports. Local elected committees were responsible for enforcement of the agreement.

CONTINENTAL CONGRESSES, American colonial and national governments. The First Continental Congress (Sept.–Oct. 1774) represented by delegates from 12 colonies, was called by members of the Virginia House of Burgesses. Meeting in Philadelphia, the congress issued a Declaration of Rights and Grievances which condemned the 'Intolerable Acts' of the British parliament. The congress formed the Continental Association to bring economic pressure on British merchants and shippers. It called for a Second Continental Congress, which met in May 1775. The new congress assumed control over military forces and served as the revolutionary government until July 1776, when it became the national government of the US. The Continental Congress was given a constitutional basis under the Articles of Confederation (1 March 1781). A new government under the American Constitution replaced the Continental Congress (4 March 1789).

CONTINENTAL SYSTEM, form of economic warfare intended by Napoleon I to destroy British economic power after Trafalgar had ended his hopes of invasion. The Berlin Decree (1806) prohibited all European trade with Britain and her colonies and was soon accepted by the other European powers. Britain responded by Orders in Council, requiring all neutral shipping to pass through British ports on their way to the continent, which Napoleon tried to prevent by the Fontainebleau and Milan Decrees (1807). The struggle over neutral shipping involved Britain in war with the United States (1812). Britain, seriously hit by the economic blockade, suffered from a commercial and industrial slump, unemployment, and food shortage, especially in 1811; but disaster was avoided by large-scale smuggling and new commercial outlets in South America. Napoleon, on the other hand, found the system increasingly difficult to maintain. The benefits to French industry were temporary, because of shortage of raw materials, and were matched by the harm to French agriculture. The rest of Europe suffered more than France, and Napoleon's attempts to impose the system contributed to his disastrous intervention in the Peninsula (1808) and Russia (1812). By 1813 the system had collapsed.

CONTINUISM (*CONTINUISMO*), tendency common throughout Latin America during the national period for presidents to continue in office beyond the time limits established by constitutions.

CONTRABAND, illegal traffic in goods, which embraces smuggling of all kinds, but more particularly refers to the shipping of materials and provisions in time of war. Belligerent nations claim the right to seize articles of war bound for enemy countries, but the difficulty of definition has often led to interference with the legitimate trade of neutrals. Britain's insistence on a right of search provoked the Armed Neutrality of the North (1780 and 1801) and caused a war with America in 1812. International conferences to determine the exact nature of contraband have failed to reach a satisfactory agreement and in wartime each participant tends to make its own rules.

CONTRABAND IN LATIN AMERICA, recurrent feature of Latin American commerce and society since the early colonial period. Smuggling first came to prominence in the 16th cent. Spain and Portugal's restrictions on foreign trade, coupled with their inability to supply the colonies with the goods which they desired, resulted in smuggling between colonials and the ships of Holland, England, and France. Smugglers were particularly active in the Caribbean and in the River Plate, where rich Creoles and even Spanish government officials were involved. Curaçao, Tortuga, and Jamaica were the main Caribbean bases and Colonia do Sacramento was the main port for the River Plate. Restrictive commercial legislation makes contraband across national frontiers a common feature of Latin America today.

CONTRACT, IDEA OF. Although the idea of a covenant between God and man and a contract between the king and his feudal vassals had been present in medieval thought, the Protestant reformation gave a new impetus to the theory of contract. This concept undermined the authority of princes whose power had grown considerably from the mid-15th cent. Calvinist theory stressed the idea of two contracts, one between God and the people and the other among the people at the foundation of the state. The most famous Huguenot tract, the *Vindiciae Contra Tyrannos* (1579), claimed that the second contract was between the king and his people and argued in favour of the right of resistance to a tyrannical ruler, an argument which supported Huguenot action in the French civil wars, the radicalism of John Knox, and the English Puritans of the 17th cent. The idea of contract continued in the constitutionalism of later English political theorists, *eg*, John Locke, for whom there was but one contract, that between monarch and people, and it survived into the 19th cent. with liberal theorists, *eg*, John Stuart Mill.

CONTRARIANTS, name given to the supporters of Thomas, Earl of Lancaster, in 1321–2, when he took arms against his cousin, King Edward II of England, leading to their defeat at the battle of Boroughbridge (1322) and Thomas's execution. The Contrariants included Humphrey Bohun, Earl of Hereford, and Roger Mortimer.

CONTRERAS REBELLION, unsuccessful movement initiated in 16th-cent. Nicaragua by the Contreras brothers to separate that colony from Spain.

CONVENTICLE ACTS (1664, 1670), part of the Clarendon Code, aimed at suppressing meetings of nonconformist sects. Attempted risings in Durham and Yorkshire (1663) were the excuse for the first act, which imposed penalties for attendance at non-Anglican forms of worship. Assemblies of five or more persons over 16 years of age for the purpose of religion were punishable by a fine of £5 for a first offence, and transportation to a plantation other than Virginia or New England for a third offence. Though the act was nominally in force until 1669, it was little used. The 1670 act fined persons £20 for permitting conventicles to be held in their homes. Constables were empowered to break into premises in search of conventicles. This act was followed by an intensive campaign against the sects (May 1670–April 1671) in which the militia was used and summary justice was dispensed at quarter sessions. None the less, the law was often applied unevenly: in towns where large communities of Dissenters existed, offences were often ignored, while the imprisonment of John Bunyan for 12 years testifies to its possible severity.

CONVENTION, FRENCH (1792–5). Elected by universal suffrage (Sept. 1792) after the collapse of the monarchy and 1791 constitution, the assembly proclaimed a republic, executed the king (Jan. 1793), and established committees to rule France. Despite the power of these committees, and intimidation from the *sans-culottes*, the convention remained the final authority and decided the outcome of the political struggle between the Jacobins and Girondins and the overthrow of Robespierre. The destruction of the Jacobin dictatorship and suppression of the Paris mob by the army brought control back to the convention, which established the Directory and dissolved itself in Oct. 1795.

CONVENTION PARLIAMENT (1660) of England, an unconstitutionally summoned assembly designed to effect the restoration of Charles II. The Long Parliament finally dissolved itself on 16 March 1660 and a general election was held without the king's writ. The convention met on 25 April, and conditional upon the terms of the Declaration of Breda, proclaimed Charles II king on 8 May. On 1 June the convention declared itself a parliament, and before its dissolution (6 Dec. 1660) settled three outstanding problems: (*a*) it passed an Act of Indemnity which pardoned all except 50 named individuals; (*b*) it settled the land question by restoring all royal and Church lands, but not generally privately owned land; (*c*) it made a financial settlement upon the king of an estimated £1,200,000 per annum from taxation and hereditary revenues. The constitutional settlement was left to the next parliament (1661), which confirmed the legislation of the convention.

CONVENTION PARLIAMENT (1689–90) in England, an unconstitutionally summoned assembly designed to effect a settlement of the interregnum caused by the flight of James II. Following James's departure from England, William of Orange called for a general election (29 Dec. 1688) on the advice of an assembly consisting of MPs of Charles II's parliaments and the rulers of the City of London. The convention, summoned without the king's writ, met on 22 Jan. 1689, settled the Crown jointly on William and his wife, and drew up a Declaration of Rights, which was accepted by William III and Mary II on 13 Feb. On that day the convention declared itself a parliament, and was not dissolved until Feb. 1690. Like the 1660 convention, its enactments were ratified by the second parliament of the reign.

CONVENTION PEOPLE'S PARTY, founded (1949) by Kwame Nkrumah and others. Under Nkrumah's leadership it dominated Ghanaian politics and government (1952–66). Socialism at home, and Pan-Africanism abroad inspired its political programme.

CONVOCATION, the assembly of the clergy of the Church of England, consisting of upper and lower houses for each of the provinces of Canterbury and York. Convocation now sits simultaneously with the sessions of parliament. A representative synod was first summoned by Abp Langton (1225), and by the time of Edward I Convocation had established some degree of legislative independence, including the right to assess the taxes to be raised from the clergy. But Henry VIII forced Convocation to acknowledge the royal supremacy, to agree to a revision of canon law, and to submit all future laws for royal approval (1530–2). In 1664 the clergy surrendered their right to tax themselves, and after the Bangorian controversy (1717), Convocation was suspended and did not meet again until 1852.

CONVOY, in its maritime sense an assembly of non-combatant vessels sailing under naval protection, the latter varying from armed merchant vessels to elaborate combinations of escort screens, aircraft, and rescue ships. Convoys were used increasingly in the period of European overseas expansion in the 16th, 17th, and 18th cents. During the Napoleonic Wars, groups of several hundred vessels were not uncommon.

In the 20th cent. the revival of the convoy system effectively defeated German efforts in both World Wars to destroy Allied sea communications. The shipping losses following the German declaration of unrestricted submarine warfare (Feb. 1917) threatened to undermine the entire Allied war effort and the introduction of convoys on a large scale (April–May 1917) was due to the personal initiative of Lloyd George in overriding a conservative Admiralty. In fact, the practical difficulties prophesied by the latter were soon overcome and only 1 per cent of all vessels sailing in convoy were lost. The submarine threat was countered and a further step was taken towards a fully controlled war effort.

In the Second World War convoys were employed from the beginning on the major shipping routes. However, the initial shortage of escort vessels, especially in the Atlantic, and the skilful direction of the German submarine campaign from 1941 by Admiral Doenitz resulted in heavy losses and it was not until March 1943 that a turning point was reached. This was brought about by American shipbuilding resources and the development of new weapons, but also by supplementing the conventional close escort with independent hunting groups and, above all, with increasingly effective air support. Allied losses steadily declined and the way was now open for the great convoys of war material necessary for the invasion of Europe. The survival of Malta and the transport of 4 million tons of equipment to Russia were further proof of the inestimable value of the convoy system.

COOK, ARTHUR JAMES (1885–1931), British trade union leader, foremost figure in the General Strike of 1926. From 1905 Cook distinguished himself in Syndicalist and Pacifist causes. After the First World War he became leader of the National Miners' Federation and foreseeing an attempt, following negotiations in 1924, to cut miners' wages because of industrial depression, he worked to build up an alliance with road, railway, and engineering workers that would resist this. This culminated in the General Strike of May 1926. Despite Cook's public truculence, the TUC support for the strike crumbled before the government's obvious determination. Cook appeared to be moving towards communism after the collapse of the strike, but his views moderated before his death.

COOK, JAMES (1728–79) British naval captain and explorer, first made his mark as surveyor of the St Lawrence river. As commander of the 1768–71 expedition to Tahiti for the transit of Venus, he charted NZ with remarkable accuracy, skirted eastern Australia from Botany Bay northwards, and, after a perilous encounter with the Great Barrier Reef, threaded Torres Strait. Ever careful of his crew, he conquered scurvy, though he lost 34 men at Batavia from malaria (1770). In 1772–5 he discovered or rediscovered every major island group in the south Pacific except Fiji and the lost Solomon Islands, probed Antarctica to 71° 10′ S, and finally ended any lingering beliefs in Quiros's southern continent. In 1777–8, in quest of a north-west passage, he discovered Hawaii, where he was initiated as votary or ceremonial chief of the god Lono, and explored the North American coast from Nootka to Alaska. On a return visit to Hawaii (1779), prolonged by damage in a squall, he provoked suspicion while in pursuit of 'stolen' property, and was killed, a victim of over-confidence, at the height of his powers. He was an ethnographer and navigator-cartographer who ended the age of reconnaissance in the Pacific and opened the way for British settlement in eastern Australia.

COOK, SIR JOSEPH (1860–1947), Staffordshire pit-boy who became one of Australia's lesser statesmen, having migrated to NSW in 1885. He was self-educated and never developed an original or enquiring mind. Though he entered the colonial legislature in 1891 as a Labor member, he accepted office in 1894 with a party which, in Commonwealth politics after 1901, came to represent conservative interests. A loyal colleague of G. H. Reid, whom he succeeded as party leader in 1908, Cook thereafter opposed Labor bitterly. In 1913 he became prime minister in an unproductive government, notable chiefly for invoking the double dissolution provision in the Commonwealth Constitution, but losing the resultant election of Sept. 1914. In opposition until the coalition following Hughes's Labor defection over conscription, Cook's main achievements were his commitment of Australia to war in 1914 and his prominent part in the two anti-Labor fusions of 1909 and 1917. He served with Hughes at the Paris peace conference and, on retiring from politics, as Australian high commissioner in London (1921–7).

COOK, THOMAS (1808–92), self-educated English Baptist, temperance reformer, and publisher, who in the 1840s pioneered railway excursions and later founded the famous travel agency.

COOK ISLANDS, in the Pacific, discovered by Cook (1777), Bligh (1789), the *Bounty* mutineers (1790), and Goodenough (Rarotonga, 1814). Aitutaki was the first island to accept Christianity (1822). In the 1840s and 1850s literacy spread rapidly. The new native theocracy and its police became all-powerful. Depopulation and disillusion led in the 1860s to a brief, violent reaction and residual addiction to alcohol. Fear of France provoked an unsuccessful request, on Rarotongan terms, for British protection (1864–6). Eventually the islanders reluctantly agreed (1888) to accept a protectorate under a NZ resident, F. J. Moss. They were annexed to New Zealand (1901) and accorded internal self-government in 1965.

COOKE, JAY (1821–1905), US banker and financier. His bank, Jay Cooke and Co. (1861–73), so encouraged the sale of Federal bonds that he was called 'the financier of the Civil War'. Railroad speculations wrecked his financial empire in Sept. 1873, but later he retrieved his personal fortunes through mining speculations.

COOLIDGE, JOHN CALVIN (1872–1933), US president, who held office during the boom period of the mid-1920s. He appeared to have reached the peak of a 20-year career in MA Republican politics with his election as governor in 1918, but his statement during the Boston Police Strike, 'There is no right to strike against the public safety by anybody, anywhere, any time', struck a popular chord which carried him to the vice-presidency in 1920. He became president on Harding's death (1923), and secured re-election in 1924 with the slogan, 'Keep cool with Coolidge'. A dour, puritanical Vermonter, he restored public confidence after the scandals of the Harding administration, while in his belief in laissez-faire and his simple trust in business leadership he mirrored the complacency of the era. His surprising decision not to seek re-election in 1928 spared him the upheavals of the Depression.

COOMARASWAMY, ANANDA (1877–1947), son of Sir Muttu Coomaraswamy, the Tamil member of the Legislative Council of Ceylon in the late 19th cent., and of an English mother. He was educated in England, but returned to Ceylon in 1906 and did much to promote social reforms and education in the island, and especially to revive interest in the ancient art, culture, and philosophy not only of Ceylon, but also of India, where he lived for some time, and on which he wrote such authoritative books as *Medieval Sinhalese Art* and *The Arts and Crafts of India and Ceylon*. The last 30 years of his life were spent in the Museum of Fine Arts, Boston, US, as keeper of the section on Indian, Persian, and Muhammadan art.

COOMBS, HERBERT COLE (1906–   Australian central banker. After working in the Commonwealth Bank and the Commonwealth Treasury in the late 1930s, he became director-general of J. B. Chifley's department of post-war reconstruction, and then governor of the Commonwealth Bank of Australia (1949). Under him—as head of the Reserve Bank after the banking reorganization of 1960—central banking in Australia gradually evolved a more co-operative relationship with the trading banks, and considerable indirect influence was exercised over fringe banking institu-

tions. As foundation chairman of the Australian Elizabethan theatre trust (1954–68) he helped to channel governmental and business aid to the performing arts. He became (1968) chairman of two new Commonwealth bodies: the Australian council for the arts and the Australian council of Aboriginal affairs.

COOPER, JAMES FENIMORE (1789–1851), first major US novelist, born in NJ. In *The Spy* (1821) he discovered the formula for success that he was to use throughout his prolific career. Within three years his popularity, both at home and abroad, was second only to Sir Walter Scott's. Author of a wide range of novels, from sea-stories like *The Water-Witch* (1830) to the satire *The Monikins* (1835), and the social and political comment of *Satanstoe* (1845), *The Chainbearer* (1845), and *The Redskins* (1846), he is still primarily remembered for the Leather-Stocking Tales, *The Pioneers* (1823), *The Last of the Mohicans* (1826), and *The Deerslayer* (1841). In Natty Bumppo ('Leatherstocking'), an unsophisticated trapper unequalled in the skills of the forest, Cooper created the first truly American literary hero.

COOPER, PETER (1791–1883) US manufacturer, inventor, and philanthropist. He made a fortune from glue, built the first steam locomotive in America (1830), pioneered the use of iron for building, and founded Cooper Union in New York, a free institution for the advancement of science. He was an energetic reformer and presidential candidate of the Greenback Party (1876).

COOPER, THOMAS (1805–92), Chartist leader and Christian lecturer. A journalist and former Wesleyan local preacher, he became an extremist Chartist leader at Leicester (1840) and began editing Chartist periodicals. After imprisonment (1843–5), he became an atheist lecturer, but did not participate in the Chartist activities of 1848. He later became an itinerant Christian lecturer, and joined the Baptists (1859). In 1872 he published his rather puritanical but moving autobiography. In this he defended his political extremism of the 1840s, which he felt was justified by the local economic distress.

CO-OPERATIVE COMMONWEALTH FEDERATION, THE, a Canadian socialist party, the result of an alliance between farming and labour interests and a university-based League for Social Instruction. The 'Commonwealth Party', headed by J. S. Woodsworth, was formed (1932) by members of the league and independent MPs of socialist sympathies. They joined with members of the Western Labour Conference to produce the Co-operative Commonwealth Federation at Calgary (Aug. 1932). The party's *Regina Manifesto* (1933) demanded encouragement of co-operatives, price stabilization, greater security for farmers, increased public ownership of natural resources and communications, a national health service, unemployment insurance, and the treatment of unemployment as a national emergency. The party's greatest electoral successes were in 1945; thereafter its popular support declined. It formed the provincial government in Saskatchewan (1944–64) and joined the wartime coalition in Manitoba. The CCF merged with the Labour Party (1960) to form the New Democratic Party.

CO-OPERATIVE MOVEMENT (1844). The opening of a co-operative store in Toad Lane, Rochdale, Lancs, by the 28 founder-members of the Rochdale Society of Equitable Pioneers, marked the beginning of the modern British co-operative movement. Shareholders contributed a minimum stake of £1, receiving 5 per cent interest on it. Members who paid a shilling entrance fee also received a dividend upon purchases, which initially were limited to such basic necessities as oatmeal, butter, flour, sugar, and candles.

Many of the Pioneers, who included a number of distressed weavers, were imbued with Owenite ideals, expecting moral as well as material benefits to accrue from co-operation. Their widely copied 'Rochdale principles' included democratic control (one vote per member, however large his holding), open membership, no religious or political discrimination, the sale of only pure goods, and use of true weights and measures, and the education of members. They succeeded where earlier ventures had failed, partly because of their sound trading practices, including cash sales, generous depreciation allowances, and the limited interest paid on shares. Their primary aim, unlike that of the Chartists, was immediately attractive, promising an end to retailers' profiteering and the thraldom of credit and truck. Wider schemes, for the provision of members' houses and for producers' co-operatives, remained inoperative—perhaps fortunately, in view of the experiences of Robert Owen and of the Christian Socialists.

The Industrial and Provident Societies Act (1852) gave co-operative societies the rights of friendly societies, and in 1862 they gained the right of limited liability.

The English Co-operative Wholesale Society (1863) provided a central buying agency for co-operative retailers. It distributed dividends to member societies in relation to purchases, and later proceeded from wholesale buying to the direct manufacture of goods.

CO-OPERATIVE MOVEMENT IN INDIA, first suggested by Frederick Nicholson, a Madras civilian, as a means of combating rural indebtedness. As a result of Curzon's investigations, the first Co-operative Societies Act was passed in 1904, which provided for the starting of rural and urban credit societies. Another act in 1912 widened the range of societies to include other than agricultural credit societies. The Maclagan report (1915) resulted in the overhauling of the whole system. Under the Government of India Act (1919) it became a provincial transferred subject. Agricultural Credit Societies, central financing agencies, and provincial banks were established, but the movement did not make the progress that was expected. Except in the Punjab, Bombay, and Madras it reached only a small part of the rural population. In the long run its dependence on government initiative was a radical defect and it cannot be said to have undermined the predominant position of the money-lender.

COORNAERT, DIRK VOLKERTSZOON (1522–90), Dutch remonstrant theologian, who challenged the accepted Calvinist doctrine of predestination and converted Jacob Hermandszoon, the minister who replaced him in Amsterdam, to his theological views, thus instigating the Arminian movement.

COOTE, SIR EYRE (1726–83), British general in India. He went there in 1754 and took part in Clive's Plassey campaign (1757). In the Seven Years War he defeated the French general Lally at Wandiwash (Jan. 1760), and took Pondicherry, the French headquarters, (1761), after nearly a year's siege. His greatest feat was the checking of Haidar Ali, the Mysore chief's victorious onslaught on Madras in a series of actions (1780–82).

COPAL TRADE, based on the important export centre of mainland opposite Zanzibar. In the 17th cent. copal was used by the Portuguese for caulking ships; in the 19th cent. for varnish for carriages in Europe.

COPE, SIR ANTHONY (c. 1548–1614), English Puritan and MP for Banbury (1586–1604), who introduced a bill for the withdrawal of the prayer book in favour of a Puritan book of discipline (1587). Its prohibition led to Peter Wentworth's assertion of parliamentary privilege, and he and Cope were both imprisoned.

COPE, SIR JOHN (d. 1760), commander-in-chief in Scotland at the outbreak of the 1745 rebellion, was routed in ten minutes at Prestonpans, although he was personally exonerated from blame by a court of enquiry. In 1742 he had commanded an English force sent to the assistance of Maria Theresa.

COPENHAGEN, originally a small fishing village, owed its growth to its important strategic position, its fine harbour, and the patronage of the bishops of Roskilde. The city played an important part in the Wars of the Hanseatic League, passed to the Danish Crown in 1417, and became the royal residence in 1445. From the late 16th cent. it was an important shipbuilding centre and naval base.

COPENHAGEN, BATTLES OF (1801, 1807), were measures by Britain which prevented Denmark's neutrality from being of assistance to Napoleon. Hyde Parker's naval attack (2 April 1801), with Nelson commanding the smaller vessels, was heavily resisted, but was successful and Crown Prince Frederick agreed to a truce, abandoning the Armed Neutrality. In Sept. 1807, after the Danes had rejected Canning's demand for custody of their fleet to prevent its seizure by Napoleon, the city was besieged by a combined naval and military force under Gambier and Wellesley. After a three-night bombardment, the Danes surrendered 17 ships of the line and all naval stores.

COPENHAGEN, PEACE OF (1660), established the modern Scandinavian frontiers. Sweden restored the diocese of Trondheim to Norway and Bornholm to Denmark, but retained Scania and other Norwegian or Danish territory conquered on its western borders since 1643.

COPERNICUS, NICOLAS (1473–1543), Polish-born astronomer, who first put forward the hypothesis that the sun was the centre of the universe, around which the earth and the planets revolved. After studying at Cracow University, Copernicus moved to Italy and went to the universities of Padua, Bologna, and Ferrara, becoming a typical product of the Italian Renaissance. He then moved to Frauenburg, a small town in East Prussia, where he spent the next 30 years as a canon of the cathedral, while pursuing his own studies in astronomy. His approach was essentially mathematical, but his methods were traditional and his attitude conservative. As early as 1512 he evolved a revolutionary heliocentric theory, which clashed with the Aristotelian–Ptolemaic system accepted by the Church, according to which the sun revolved around the earth. He was unable to prove his idea mathematically, a task which fell to Galileo and Newton, and his work *De Revolutionibus Orbium Coelestium* was not published until 1543, the year of his death. However, Copernicus was championed by the mathematician Johann Kepler and later by Galileo, who was tried by the Inquisition for his advocacy of the astronomer's ideas (1633).

COPLAND, AARON (1900–), US composer, of Russian-Jewish descent, whose adaptation of jazz and folk themes within a classical structure has helped to create an American national music. Among his compositions are the ballets *Billy the Kid* (1938), *Rodeo* (1942), and *Appalachian Spring* (1944), and the *Third Symphony* (1946).

COPLAND, SIR DOUGLAS (1894–), Australian economist and diplomat, who moved from his native NZ to Australia, where he became professor of economics at Tasmania University (1920–4) and of commerce at Melbourne (1924–1945). He officially advised governments during the 1930s Depression and was Commonwealth prices commissioner during the Second World War. Two short periods in the diplomatic service—as Australia's minister to China and as high commissioner to Canada—were divided by service (1948–53) as first vice-chancellor of the Australian National University.

COPPER MINING IN AFRICA probably began with the advent of the Iron Age. In Western Africa copper was a fairly scarce commodity mined either in very small deposits or in remote sites on the Sahara fringe. The great African deposits of the Congo and Zambia copper belt were in production by the 8th cent. AD. Copper wire, cross-shaped ingots, and personal ornaments were exported over increasing distances, probably as far as the Atlantic coast and the northern Congo.

COPPERHEADS, US political term derived from the name of an American snake. It was used, mainly by Republicans, to describe those northern Democrats, particularly in the middle west, whose opposition to the Civil War (1861–5) and advocacy of a compromise peace incurred allegations of disloyalty.

COPYHOLD ACT (1894) in Britain. Most copyhold had been destroyed in the English enclosure movement, and much of what was left had been got rid of by agreement in the 19th cent., but there remained vestiges of it which could, by the survival of incidents such as heriots, create hardship. This act consolidated, under the supervision of the Board of Agriculture, the acts passed since 1841 enabling either tenant or landlord to insist on enfranchisement. The tenure was finally abolished in 1925.

COPYHOLDERS, tenants holding land at the will of the lord of the manor in return for dues or services fixed by manorial custom, the tenure being proved by a copy of the court roll. Statutes of 1852 and 1858 gave compulsory powers for the conversion of copyhold into freehold, and all copyhold was finally abolished by the Law of Property Act (1922).

COQUILLE, GUY (1523–1603), French jurist, who sought to unify customary law into a single code. After settling in Nevers, he wrote his famous *Commentaire sur la coutume de Nivernois* and a history of Nevers (1595). He also upheld royal authority and Gallican principles during the critical period of the French civil wars.

CORAL SEA, BATTLE OF (7–8 May 1942), naval engagement between US and Japanese forces in the Second World War fought entirely by carrier-based aircraft. Both sides sustained considerable losses, but the Japanese abandoned their design of effecting a landing at Port Moresby in south-eastern New Guinea that would have threatened eastern Australia.

CORBULO, GNAEUS DOMITIUS (d. AD 67), Roman general, whom Nero in 54 put in command during a war against Parthia over control of Armenia. A strict disciplinarian but a cautious commander, Corbulo sought to settle the conflict by diplomacy and the manœuvre of overwhelming forces rather than pitched battles, and reached a mutually satisfactory agreement in 63, but he attracted Nero's mistrust, which was perhaps justified, and was ordered to commit suicide.

CORCYRA, ancient Greek island city-state (mod. Corfu), originally a colonial settlement from Corinth (*c.* 730 BC). Occupying an important position on the sea-route to Italy and Sicily, it defied Corinthian attempts to retain control and became powerful in its own right. Though courted by the homeland Greeks before the Persian invasion of 480, the Corcyreans never committed their substantial fleet, and it was chiefly to prevent it falling to potential enemies that the Athenians helped them in a quarrel with Corinth in 433, the first of the incidents leading to the great Peloponnesian War. Weakened by internal strife, Corcyra played little part in this war. A member of the Second Athenian Confederacy (375–358), it later joined the coalition against Philip II of Macedon, but became subject to him in 338. In the struggles of Alexander the Great's successors, Cassander was prevented from capturing the island by Agathocles of Syracuse (*c.* 300), who gave it to Pyrrhus of Epirus. Later it was saved from the Illyrians by the first Roman expedition east of the Adriatic (229) and passed under Roman control.

CORDELIER CLUB (1790), the most extreme of the Parisian revolutionary clubs, founded by Danton and later dominated by Marat and Hébert.

CORDOBA, Umayyad capital of Andalus, situated in southern Spain on the plains of the Guadalquivir. It was a rich and populous centre of contemporary urban civilization and reached its apogee under the caliphate during the 10th cent., when its Great Mosque was completed. Later it lost power and prestige to other Andalusian cities, such as Seville, whose economic strength could better justify their size. In 1236 Cordoba fell to Castile.

CORDOBA, GONZALO DE (1453–1515), known as the Great Captain, established a reputation as a military leader during the Catholic Monarchs' campaign against Granada. During Spain's successful campaigns against Charles VIII of France in Italy (1495–7, 1501–4), he reformed the structure and strategy of the Spanish army, in particular by developing the infantry, and laid the foundations for Spanish military successes in the 16th and 17th cents.

CORDOBA, TREATY OF (24 Aug. 1821), signed by Agustín Iturbide and Spain's viceroy, Juan O'Donujú, at Cordoba, New Spain, acknowledging the separation of Mexico from Spanish hegemony, but calling for a member of the Bourbon family to govern the Mexican empire. O'Donojú recognized the strength of the independence movement and sought, without authorization, to save the Crown for Spain while granting the colony independence. Neither the Crown nor the parliament (Cortes) would accept the legality of the act. Iturbide used the treaty to obtain the peaceful surrender of Mexico City.

CORDUBA (mod. Cordoba), Roman city in Spain. It was founded in 152 BC and apparently received colonial status in 45 BC, becoming one of the richest cities in Roman Spain. It was the birthplace of Seneca and Lucan.

CORFU, one of the Ionian Islands, known in classical times as Corcyra. Its history in the Middle Ages was varied, and included possession by Robert Guiscard, Duke of Apulia (1081), and by the Venetians (1401). It became French (1797), British (1815), and was finally annexed to Greece (1863). During the First World War it provided a base for Serbian troops. In 1923 the Italians occupied it during the Corfu Incident.

CORFU INCIDENT. On 27 Aug. 1923 Gen. Tellini and three other Italians were murdered in Greece. The victims were members of a commission appointed by the Conference of Ambassadors to delimit the Graeco–Albanian frontier. Mussolini sent an ultimatum to the Greek government, demanding an enquiry and an indemnity of 50 million lire. On 31 Aug., after Greece had replied with only a partial acceptance of Mussolini's terms, Italy bombarded and occupied Corfu. On 1 Sept. the Conference of Ambassadors delivered a protest note to Greece on the subject of the murders. In replying the Greek government agreed in advance to submit to any decision which the ambassadors might reach after an enquiry. However, on 1 Sept. Greece had also sent a note to the Council of the League of Nations, calling its attention to the Italian ultimatum. There was thus some confusion as to which international body was competent to discuss the incident.

The league's supporters, particularly Sir Robert Cecil and the representatives of the smaller states, felt that the league should condemn Italy's act of aggression. Mussolini, however, threatened Italy's resignation from the league if the council took any action, and France, embroiled in her occupation of the Ruhr, was reluctant to antagonize him. A compromise was reached whereby an informal council meeting transmitted its recommendations to the ambassadors. In consequence the murder of Tellini remained the point at issue, and the bombardment of Corfu was not discussed. Although an Inter-Allied Commission of Inquiry failed to establish the responsibility for the crime, Mussolini made it clear that he would not evacuate Corfu until he had received satisfaction. He withdrew on 27 Sept. after the Conference of ambassadors decided that Greece should pay the 50 million lire indemnity.

CORINTH, ancient Greek city-state, important because of its position by the isthmus joining the Peloponnese to the northern mainland. A Mycenean centre occupied by Dorian Greeks *c.* 1100 BC, it became prosperous under the Bacchiad aristocracy (*c.* 750–*c.* 650) and the tyrannies of Cypselus and Periander (*c.* 650–586), through overseas trade and colonization, *eg*, at Syracuse (733), Corcyra (*c.* 730), Potidaea (*c.* 600), Corinthian pottery dominating the markets (*c.* 750–*c.* 550). The Corinthians became allies of Sparta, but, though the Athenians were emerging as commercial rivals, they prevented Cleomenes I of Sparta from attacking Athens (506) and supported it against Aegina. However, after fighting with Athens and the other Greeks against the Persian invasion of 480–479, they became increasingly alarmed by Athenian ambitions and were closely involved in launching both Peloponnesian Wars against them (459, 433–431), leading the opposition to the compromise peace of Nicias (421) and pressing for Athens' destruction in 404. Neglected by the triumphant Spartans, they joined Argos, Thebes, and Athens against them in the Corinthian War (395), but at the King's Peace an incipient union with Argos was dissolved and Corinth returned to the Spartan alliance, remaining loyal even after the Spartan defeat at Leuctra (371). Corinth joined Athens against Philip II of Macedon (343–342) and after his victory at Chaeronea (338) was garrisoned. The maintenance of the garrison remained thereafter a cardinal point of Macedonian policy in Greece. Liberated eventually by Aratus of Sicyon (243), Corinth was returned to Antigonus Doson (224), but freed from Philip V by the Romans (196), who later destroyed it after the massacre of an embassy (146). After being refounded as a Roman colony by Julius Caesar, it recovered its prosperity, attested by substantial ruins, before falling to the Goths (AD 521).   TTBR

CORINTH, BATTLE OF (3–4 Oct. 1862), engagement in the American Civil War in which Union forces under William S. Rosecrans repulsed Van Dorn's Confederate force. Corinth, in northern Mississippi, was an important communications centre, occupied by the Union army four months earlier.

CORINTH, LEAGUE OF, name commonly given to the settlement imposed on Greece by Philip II of Macedon after his victory at Chaeronea (338 BC). The league was properly not a federal structure, but a peace treaty (Common Peace) backed by an international peace-keeping council, with Philip's own interests guaranteed and himself as its chief executive (*hegemon*). The council voted to support him, and later Alexander the Great, in invading Asia, sentenced Thebes for Alexander (335), and referred to him the fate of Sparta (331). After being dissolved by Antipater following the Laminian War, its restoration was proclaimed by Polyperchon (319) and briefly effected by Demetrius Poliorcetes (302) in attempts to organize Greek support. It was revived by Antigonus Doson and Philip V (224–200).

CORINTHIAN WAR (395–387 BC), fought by the Spartans and their allies against two former allies, Thebes and Corinth, backed by Athens, which they had decisively defeated in 404, and by their old enemy Argos, and initially, by the Persians, whom they had been fighting in Asia since 400. After Lysander's defeat and death at Haliartus, the Spartans were victorious at Nemea (early summer 394) and Coronea, where Agesilaus' return from Asia was challenged. But despite vigorous operations round Corinth (393–390) the Spartan forces could not use their tactical superiority. The

Persian fleet, victorious at Cnidus, broke their Aegean empire and helped the Athenians to rebuild their walls and construct a fleet. Spartan attempts to win over Persia (392) and make peace in Greece (391) failed, but Athenian expansion in the Aegean and assistance to Evagoras of Cyprus induced Artaxerxes II to support the Spartan Antalcidas in a naval campaign and to impose the King's Peace in Sparta's favour.

CORIOLANUS (*fl.* 5th cent. BC), Cn. Marcius, traditionally regarded as a noble Roman, who won his name at the capture of Volscian Corioli. Impeached for attacking popular sovereignty, he joined the Volsci as their general, marched on Rome (489 BC), and was deterred only by his mother, Veturia, and his wife, Volumnia. The absence of his name from the Roman *Fasti* makes the story of desertion dubious; he may have been a 5th-cent. Volscian whose forays against Rome have been developed into a romantic legend.

CORK, RICHARD BOYLE, 2nd Earl of (Irish) (1st of 2nd creation) (1566–1643), Irish statesman who went to Ireland in 1588, but made little political headway until employed by the Earl of Essex (1598). He was sent to England to report the condition of Ireland (1602). In 1604 he bought 12,000 acres near Cork, Waterford, and Tipperary for £1000 from Sir Walter Raleigh. This was the basis of his tremendous fortune. By prodigious improvements, *eg*, the introduction of English settlers and industries, and an enormous building programme, he established his position as the leading English settler. He became a privy councillor of Ireland (1612), one of the lord justices of Ireland (1629), and lord high treasurer (1631). Royal favour ended with the appointment of Thomas Wentworth as lord deputy (1633), but Cork struggled to maintain his position, and his skilful and persistent opposition led to Wentworth's impeachment. He was the centre of resistance to the Irish rebellion in Munster (1641), which consumed much of his wealth.

CORN LAWS in England. These were instituted in the late 17th cent. as part of a policy of encouraging grain production. They forbade corn export when the home price was high, but encouraged it by a bounty when the price was low. In years of low price there was a duty on import. The system was extended to Scotland after the Act of Union. Whether as a result of it or not, grain prices were relatively stable and low in the first half of the 18th cent. and enough land was kept under grain for Britain to be frequently a corn exporter. During the war period (1793–1815) Britain ceased to export grain and found difficulty in importing it. Grain prices rose very high, and rents followed. At the end of the wars, when importation again became feasible, the country was bearing a heavy load in taxation and poor rates, and the system of landed settlement meant that many estates had charges laid on them in the expectation of continuing high rents. Both landowners and farmers were unwilling to face adjustment to lower prices and lower rents. The Corn Law of 1815 was a concession to them: the import of wheat was forbidden when the home price was below 80 shillings a quarter, and similar price levels were fixed for the import of other grains. Since Britain had ceased to be a corn exporter the legislation was now aimed at protecting the landed interest and not at maintaining even prices. Under it sharp fluctuations of price took place. In an unsuccessful attempt to reduce these the Corn Laws were changed in 1828, allowing imports below the 80-shilling price on a sliding scale of duty.

Already by 1815 there was a strong movement of opinion among political economists in favour of free trade, and progressively after 1815 import duties were lowered or removed, leaving corn as the only important commodity with high duties. Manufacturers in particular objected to the corn duty, regarding it as a tax on labour for the benefit of a sectional interest and arguing that other countries could not be expected to import British manufactured goods if Britain seemed unwilling to buy their grain. The result of the conflict of interests was that the Corn Laws became the centre of considerable political debate, especially after the founding of the Anti-Corn Law League (1838), which was devoted to putting pressure on parliament for the law's repeal. Peel, prime minister after 1841, gradually became convinced that the Corn Laws raised prices for the consumer and were unnecessary for the producer, and in the crisis of 1846 over the Irish potato famine announced their gradual repeal. In 1849 this major exception to the policy of low duties was abolished, except for a small constant duty of one shilling a quarter. Corn prices for the next two decades were, on average, slightly lower than before repeal, a fact which suggests that some of the arguments against the Corn Laws were well founded.

D. G. Barnes, *A History of the English Corn Laws from 1660 to 1846* (London, 1930).

S. G. Checkland, *The Rise of Industrial Society in England, 1815–1885* (London, 1964). RMM

CORN LAWS, ROMAN, measures to provide state-subsidized corn to the inhabitants of Rome, first introduced by Gaius Gracchus (123 BC). Despite the drain on the treasury and their temporary abolition by Sulla (88), the price was cheapened until Clodius made corn a free distribution (58). Julius Caesar reduced the number of recipients by 170,000 (46) and Augustus, who wished to abolish the dole, reduced it to 200,000 and later established a permanent food commissioner. Although a demagogic device, these laws concerned a serious social problem—the existence at Rome of a large free proletariat unemployable in a non-industrial society which relied heavily on slave labour.

CORNEILLE, PIERRE (1606–84), French dramatist, who was admired by Richelieu for his early comedies. He turned to tragedy in *Médée* (1635), and *Le Cid*, which was criticized by the Académie for its imperfect observance of the canons of classical drama. Corneille's later tragedies, notably *Horace, Cinna,* and *Polyeucte*, were strictly classical in structure, and *Le Menteur* (1643) has been called the best French comedy before Molière. Although his powers declined after the failure of *Pertharite* (1652) and Racine superseded him in popular favour, Corneille is among the supreme exponents of heroic drama. The intensity and passion of his style matched the grandeur of his theme, which was to display the human soul as master of circumstance.

CORNISH RISING (1549) in England, was in opposition to the new prayer book, which in replacing Latin by the vernacular seemed to the rebels to turn the services into 'a Christmas game'. They demanded the Mass, the Six Articles, and the restoration of the monasteries. The Protector Somerset acted hesitantly, but the rising was savagely crushed by the local gentry with the help of foreign mercenaries.

CORNPLANTER (c. 1732–1836), American Indian chief, who signed several treaties ceding Indian lands to the US government. This made him unpopular with his tribe but he later presented the grievances of his people to the president, George Washington. The state of Pennsylvania gave him a land grant in recognition of his services to the whites.

CORNWALL, PIERS DE GAVESTON, 4th Earl of (3rd creation) (d. 1312), son of a Béarnais knight, and from childhood the companion and friend of King Edward II of England. His greed and waspish wit aroused the resentment and fear of the baronage. He was twice exiled (1306 and 1308), and was treacherously killed (while under safe conduct) by the Earl of Warwick, one of the Lords Ordainer.

CORNWALLIS, CHARLES CORNWALLIS, 1st Marquis (1738–1805), governor-general of India and lord-lieutenant of Ireland. After leaving Eton, he was commissioned in the Grenadier Guards (1756) and became a major-general in 1775. He served in the American War of Independence but

was forced to capitulate at Yorktown (1781). He became governor-general of India and commander-in-chief (1786–1793). His policy towards the Indian states was one of non-intervention, with two important exceptions. He found non-intervention impossible in the case of Oudh because it was an important buffer state on the borders of Bengal. He was also compelled to go to war (1790) with Tipu Sultan of Mysore, who made an unprovoked attack on a British ally, the Raja of Travancore. Tipu was defeated and by the treaty of Seringapatam (1792) forced to surrender half of his dominions.

In 1793, against the advice of Sir John Shore, his ablest revenue official, Cornwallis made a permanent settlement of the land revenues of Bengal. Not only was the revenue demand from the *zamindars* (landholders) fixed in perpetuity but the *zamindars* were declared to be the hereditary proprietors of their holdings. This was a grave error, as the same advantages could have been obtained by a long temporary settlement. The permanent settlement was also made without a survey or a detailed valuation of the lands. Cornwallis sought to protect the *raiyats* by issuing instructions prohibiting the *zamindars* from levying *abwabs* (extra cesses), and by ordering that *pattas* (rent-rolls) should be issued to each *raiyat*. Unfortunately, these orders were not enforced. Cornwallis also attempted to reform the administration of justice. One fatal defect in these measures was his distrust of Indians, for he relied entirely on Europeans. He also separated the revenue and judicial functions by vesting the collection of the revenues and the administration of justice in separate officers, thus making the collectors purely fiscal agents. This arrangement proved unworkable and expensive. Another serious defect was the difficulty in bringing the new laws to the notice of an illiterate peasantry. The courts were too few to cope with the cases brought before them and accused persons were confined to prison for long periods pending trial. Cornwallis also reorganized the Indian Civil service by forbidding the collectors from engaging in private trade and by substantially increasing their salaries, thus reducing corruption. In this respect Cornwallis was more powerful than his predecessors, who had to placate powerful interests in England.

He was viceroy of Ireland (1798–1801), where he suppressed the 1798 rebellion. In 1805 he was once more appointed governor-general of India, where he again attempted a policy of non-intervention, but he died at Ghazipur in October of the same year.

W. S. Seton-Karr, *The Marquess of Cornwallis* (Oxford, 1890).

A. Aspinall, *Cornwallis in Bengal* (Manchester, 1931). CCD

CORONADO Y VALDES, FRANCISCO VASQUEZ DE (1510–54), Spanish explorer and conquistador in North America. He explored the region which was to become the south-western US (1535–42), in hopes of discovering a rich Indian civilization, similar to that of Mexico. Coronado arrived in Mexico (1535) and left for the north (1539), authorized by the viceroy, Antonio de Mendoza, to search for the legendary Quivira and Cibola. Coronado traced the Colorado and Río Grande rivers, explored Arizona, New Mexico, Texas, Oklahoma, and Kansas (1540–2) before returning to Mexico.

CORONADO EXPEDITION (1540), undertaken by Francisco Vasquez de Coronado (1510–54), governor of Nueva Galicia in Mexico, in search of the seven cities of Cibola, reported to be fabulously wealthy. Travelling through Arizona and New Mexico, he found Indian pueblos, but no gold or silver. A second expedition to find Quivira took him into the Texas panhandle, Oklahoma, and Kansas. He found no mineral wealth here either, but brought back an idea of the vastness of the American continent and opened the great south-west to Spanish colonization. The men of his expeditions were the first white men to see the pueblos of New Mexico and the Great Plains.

CORONEA, BATTLES OF, in western Boeotia, Greece, some 32 kms west of Thebes. The first ended in the defeat in the First Peloponnesian War (447 BC) by the Boeotians of an Athenian force under Tolmides returning from capturing Chaeronea, which began the eclipse of Athenian power in central Greece; Tolmides was killed and the Athenians agreed to leave Boeotia free. The second ended in victory over the Thebans and allies of the Spartan king Agesilaus returning from Asia at the beginning of the Corinthian War (394 BC), which enabled him to reach the Peloponnese.

CORONER, this office, doubtfully of Anglo-Saxon origin, was regularized in England (1194) when the King's Justices were directed to ensure the appointment in each county of three knights and one clerk to keep the records of the Court as 'custodians of the pleas of the crown' (custodes placitorum coronae); Magna Carta (1215) coroners were directed not to try cases. By the reign of Edward I, the coroner had acquired the special duty of holding inquests on treasure trove and on violent and unnatural deaths and sudden deaths of unknown cause.

Today (1970), all high court judges have coroners' powers throughout England, and coroners with local jurisdiction are appointed by county and certain borough councils. The Divisional Court of the Queen's Bench Division of the High Court has general jurisdiction over coroners' courts.

The coroner sits with a jury and directs them on the relevant law, the facts being for the jury to find. If the jury finds any person guilty of murder or other crime the coroner must bind over all witnesses at the inquest to give evidence at the trial.

CORPORATION ACT (1661), in England, excluded from municipal government all dissenters from the Church of England. The act imposed five obligations on all officials within the franchise of a corporation: (1) the oath of allegiance; (2) the oath of supremacy; (3) the taking of the sacrament according to the practice of the Church of England; (4) an oath of non-resistance; and (5) a declaration against the validity of the Solemn League and Covenant.

The Crown succeeded in purging several boroughs (1661–1664) with the help of local commissions composed of the lords lieutenant and gentry. As a consequence, the gentry came to dominate the municipal corporations, as mayors or recorders. However, difficulty was experienced in obtaining suitable replacements for the men ejected. The government often brought pressure to bear on corporations, forcing them to remodel their charters by threatening forfeiture for some technical offence or by the threat of issuing writs of quo warranto.

The act formed part of the so-called 'Clarendon Code', which legislated for a policy of intolerance.

CORPORATION BOROUGHS, in Britain, unreformed parliamentary constituencies in which the MPs were chosen by the mayor and corporation.

CORPUS EVANGELICORUM, organization of the Protestant members of the Diet of the Holy Roman empire, set up in 1653 under the presidency of the Elector of Saxony. The name is also attached to the league which was planned by Gustavus Adolphus of Sweden after his victorious advance into Germany (1631–2).

CORREGIDOR, BATTLE OF (10 April–6 May 1942), unsuccessful attempt by US forces under Gen. Jonathan M. Wainwright to maintain a position in the Philippines after the Japanese capture of Manila.

CORREGIDORES, system of Spanish royal officials revived in the late 15th cent., to supervise the administration of the towns on behalf of the Crown. The cortes of Toledo agreed to the appointment of a corregidor in 1480 and by 1500 the duties and rights of this official over all the municipalities were clearly defined. His authority aroused hostility in many towns and caused a breakdown in the traditional alliance between the cities and the Crown in Castile, producing the revolt of the communeros (1520–1). The system of corregidores was however extended to the administration of Spain's overseas empire.

CORRUPT PRACTICES ACTS (1854, 1883), in Britain, aimed to check electoral corruption by precise definition and by scrutiny of expenses. The statutory disfranchisement of St Albans for corruption led to a general act (1852) enabling the House of Commons to appoint commissioners to visit boroughs and examine witnesses on oath. The 1854 Act contained definitions of corrupt practices and provided for the appointment of auditors to examine candidates' election expenses. These acts had some effect, but the 1883 Act provided the first really effective check on corruption by fixing, for every constituency, the maximum amount which candidates and their agents could spend on an election.

CORSICA, island in the Mediterranean of 8740 sq. kms. After forming part of the Roman empire, it fell into Vandal hands (AD 469). In subsequent centuries it was controlled by the Byzantines, the Saracens, the Genoese, and, ultimately, the French (1768). The island was the birthplace and childhood home of Napoleon Bonaparte and retained henceforth its association with France, of which it forms (1970) a département.

CORT, HENRY (1740–1800), English iron-master, who was largely responsible for the expansion of the industry in the reign of George III. He developed (1783–4) the puddling and rolling processes by which bars of malleable iron of improved quality were produced at speed, so lessening the need for imports.

CORTENUOVA, BATTLE OF (1237), defeat of the army of the Lombard League by Frederick II. It was one of the few medieval battles won by intelligent tactics. Unable to draw the Lombards into open battle, the emperor pretended to withdraw his army to winter in Cremona. The confederate army broke up and marched home and was attacked by the imperial cavalry, which had marched on to its flank. Taken by surprise, the Lombards were defeated. Frederick subsequently squandered the victory by insisting on unconditional surrender. The league, instead of wavering and breaking up, resolved on stiffer resistance.

CORTÉS, HERNAN (1485–1547), Spanish conquistador and explorer, and commander of the force which conquered the Aztec confederacy. He was born at Medellín and migrated to Hispaniola (1504). Cortés, who accompanied Diego Velásquez to Cuba (1511), gained the confidence of the governor of Cuba, who then chose him to head an expedition to the coast of Yucatan and Mexico. Cortés later flouted Velásquez's authority and took the expedition to Mexico on his own (Feb. 1519).

That the conquest succeeded was due to Spanish alliances with subject tribes and Spanish possession of firearms and horses. After having assured the loyalty of the Spaniards by burning his fleet at Veracruz, thereby preventing retreat, Cortés allied himself with the Tlaxcalans. The Spaniards entered Tenochtitlán, the Aztec capital (Nov. 1519), and took the hesitant Moctezuma as hostage. A second Spanish expedition arrived at Veracruz, under Pánfilo de Narvaez, and succumbed to a surprise attack by Cortés, who had left Pedro de Alvarado in charge at Tenochtitlán. In Cortés's absence the Aztecs revolted and the returning commander was forced to undertake a disastrous retreat from the city (30 June 1520). At Tlaxcala the Spaniards and their allies embarked upon a second conquest of Tenochtitlán. After a lengthy siege and aided by hunger and disease, the Spaniards seized and destroyed the city (Aug. 1521).

Cortés governed Mexico briefly (1521–6) and distributed

encomienda (rights to Indian labour) to his followers, on his own initiative. He sent two expeditions to Central America (1523–4) and he himself journeyed to Honduras (1524–6) to assure the expeditionaries' loyalty. During the march he ordered the heir to the Aztec throne (Cuauhtémoc) to be hanged for conspiracy. Cortés returned to Spain (1528), having been removed from the governorship. He returned to New Spain as captain general (1530), ruled his vast estates in central Mexico, and discovered lower California (1536).

CORTES, traditional hispanic representative institution which evolved eventually into the parliament of the 19th cent., in which the estates of nobility, clergy, and towns were represented and which embodied the regional prerogatives or *fueros* of the various kingdoms.

In Castile by the late 15th cent., the cortes was totally dependent on the Crown, which controlled its composition and right of representation. The estates could petition the monarchs, but had no legislative powers, except the right to oppose the revocation of an existing, valid law (1387). Again, although a law of 1307 provided for the cortes' consent to extraordinary taxation, the exemption of the nobility and clergy from taxation limited the effectiveness of its fiscal powers.

The cortes of Aragon had more genuine privileges. There was a general cortes of the kingdom of Aragon and its dependents, which met in Monzon, and a separate one for the component provinces, of Aragon itself, Catalonia, and Valencia. Represented by the four estates of nobles, gentry, clergy, and towns, whose rights to attend were independent of royal summons, the cortes of Aragon also enjoyed rights of procedure, taxation, and legislation, the latter won in 1283, which constituted a restraint upon royal absolutism. Even between sessions of the cortes its powers were invested in a committee of estates (*diputacio*) to supervise the observance of laws and the administration of revenue. In Aragon the cortes also had powers over the office of *Justicia*, which provided a further limitation upon royal sovereignty.

The cortes of Catalonia and Valencia were similarly independent, consisting of the traditional three instead of four chambers.

The Portuguese also had a similar cortes which continued to function even after Philip II's annexation of that country (1580).

CORUNNA, BATTLE OF (1809), fought during the Peninsular War. French troops under Soult defeated and killed the British commander, Sir John Moore, but were unable to prevent the British embarking and leaving Spain.

CORVEE, obligation to provide public labour for a certain number of days each year which Frenchmen of the third estate owed to the Crown under the *ancien régime*. In addition, there was the seigneurial *corvée*, a similar labour service owed by tenants to their lords.

COSMAS (*fl. c.* 550), Byzantine merchant, called the 'traveller to India'. His *Christian Topography*, written (*c.* 550) to prove that the earth was flat, includes a valuable account of his voyages to north-east Africa and much information about Persia and India and about Christians in those countries.

COSSACKS, were originally runaway peasants from the estates of Muscovy and Lithuania. They became an identifiable social group in the 15th cent., when they settled in the wild steppelands forming the frontier between those states and the Tatar lands. They lived by hiring their labour on a piecework basis and undertook any enterprise, *eg*, fighting, scouting, and trading. In the 16th cent. the Cossacks established themselves in the river basins of the Dnieper, around the Zaporog Fastness, the Don, the Iaik (later the Ural), and the Terek. Here they evolved their own form of democratic government under the *hetman* or *ataman*. Being trained as riders from childhood, they were outstanding horsemen and

natural rebels. From the turn of the 15th–16th cents Cossack detachments entered the service of the grand dukes of Moscow and Lithuania, and became the first of the 'service Cossacks', whose distant successors harassed Napoleon's retreating army in 1812. However, as serfdom increased in the 16th cent. the number of free Don and Dnieper Cossacks increased and formed a natural source of opposition to the central government in Muscovy. Under their leader, Zarutsky, they were active in the Time of Troubles in support of the false Dmitri (1607–8), before pushing the election of Michael Romanov (1613). A turning point in their history came with the treaty of Pereyaslavl (1654), when Bogdan Khmelnitski offered Tsar Alexis sovereignty over Little Russia (Ukraine) and the homage of the Cossacks, in return for confirming their freedom to elect their own *hetman*, conduct their own diplomacy, and administer their own lands. Yet dissatisfaction with the Muscovite government led to repeated Cossack alliances with Muscovy's enemies, *eg*, Poland, Sweden, and Turkey, and sweeping revolts, *eg*, the rebellion of Stenka Razin (1667–71), of Bulavin (1707), and of Mazeppa, the *hetman* of the Dnieper Cossacks (1709). Their last great rising as a free race occurred in 1773–4, when the Cossack Pugachev, posing as Peter IV, won widespread support east of the Volga and the Urals against Catherine II. The empress retaliated by razing the Zaporog Fastness and extending serfdom to the Ukraine. Though their own free form of government was destroyed, the tradition of independence survived and led the Cossacks to side against the communists in the civil war of 1917–18.

P. Longworth, *The Cossacks* (London, 1969).   MKS

COSSIJURA CASE (1779), resulted from the claim of the Supreme Court (India) to exercise jurisdiction over the whole Indian population of Bengal, Bihar, and Orissa. Warren Hastings and the Supreme Council successfully contended that *zamindars* were only subject to the court's jurisdiction if they were servants of the East India Co.

COSTA, JOAQUIN (1846–1911), Spanish historian and patriot, and the outstanding figure in the radical regeneration of intellectual life in Spain in the period of disillusionment following the loss of Cuba to America (1898). Costa's political influence was limited. He wanted to replace the existing system with an interim presidential regime which was to make the Spanish people fit for democratic government and to enact a 'programme of realizations', modernizing industry and agriculture. However, the National League of Producers established under his presidency (1899) soon came to reflect middle-class prejudices and Costa himself was unable to work with any of the political parties. More important than his impracticable policies was the long-term influence of his diagnosis of Spanish backwardness. He concluded that the Spanish people 'lacked the aptitudes for modern life', giving rise to a tradition of pessimism about Spain which became more fashionable than constructive criticism in the early 20th cent.

COSTE-FLORET PAUL (1911–   ), French politician of the MRP (Christian Democrat) Party. He entered parliament after a career in the Resistance, and sat until 1967. As minister for the colonies (1947–9, 1950) he was responsible for the conduct of the Indo-China War.

COSTER, SAMUEL (1579–1665), Dutch dramatist, physician, and founder of the Netherlands Academy. He also ran a theatre and performed the plays of his rival dramatists, *eg*, Vondel. He was a member of the *Muiderkring* (Muiden circle), a famous literary group formed by a fellow dramatist, Pieter Corneliszoon Hooft, governor of Muiden.

COT, PIERRE (1895–   ), French lawyer and left-wing politician, who began his political career as a Radical, and was minister of air in several governments of the 1930s. After the Second World War he sat in parliament as a Progressive, allying himself with the Communist Party and supporting a neutralist foreign policy.

COTONOU, capital of Dahomey, major West African port since the 18th cent. Taken over by the French in 1890 after their conquest of the country, it served as an administrative headquarters during the colonial period.

COTTON, SIR ARTHUR THOMAS (1803–99), irrigational engineer in Madras. He fought in the First Burmese War (1824–6) and was mentioned in despatches. He constructed irrigational works on the Cauvery, Coleroon, Godavari, and Krishna rivers. He did a great deal in mitigating famines.

COTTON, SIR HENRY JOHN STEDMAN (1845–1915), entered the Bengal civil service (1867) and was Commissioner of Assam (1896–1902) and president of the Indian National Congress (1904). He was the author of *New India* (1885) and *Indian and Home Memories* (1911). He became a Liberal member of parliament after retirement and head of the so-called Indian group.

COTTON, JOHN (1584–1652), American clergyman and author. Born in England and educated at Cambridge, Cotton was ordained in 1610. His advanced Puritan views forced him to flee to the Massachusetts Bay colony in America (1633), where he became a religious and political leader. He opposed religious liberals such as Mrs Anne Hutchinson and Roger Williams. Cotton wrote catechisms, church music, commentaries on prayer, and several works on the theory and methods of Congregationalism in New England, of which *The Way of the Churches of Christ in New England* (1645) was the best known.

COTTON FAMINE (1862–5) was caused in Britain by the blockade of the South during the Civil War. It revealed how closely the industry of Lancashire was tied to the short-staple cotton of the US. The resulting unemployment and hardship, particularly in areas specializing in the coarser grades of cloth, also showed how little the working class had benefited by the prosperity of the industry in the past. Unemployment would have been even worse if the British manufacturers had not been overstocked at the start of the war. While the linen and worsted industries gained from the difficulties of their rival—cotton—the cotton manufacturers in England made strenuous efforts at reinvestment and modernization, which partly account for the boom of the 1870s. In Scotland, on the other hand, the cotton famine marked a decisive point in the run-down of the industry.

COTTON INDUSTRY was the original 'take-off' sector of the Industrial Revolution in Britain. In the early 18th cent. the cotton industry had been small and backward, producing a poor quality cloth. Mechanized spinning techniques came into wide use after 1750, and in the 1780s growth was exceptionally rapid. Cotton-spinning became the first large-scale factory-based industry, concentrated mainly in Lancashire and south-west Scotland. This very fast development was based on a cheap, easily transportable raw material in the New World, a fibre strong enough for crude mechanization, an expanding market both at home and overseas, and the advantages of a new industry in the absence of restrictive regulation. It continued to grow throughout the period of the Napoleonic wars, in spite of export difficulties created by the Continental system, and by 1815 provided 40 per cent of Britain's exports. Weaving followed spinning into mechanized production in the 1830s, but the change-over on this side was slower.

The cotton industry was labour-intensive and needed relatively little capital. For this reason it has frequently been an important element in the industrial revolution in other countries. In spite of this competition, the industry in Britain developed markets outside Europe and continued to be a major exporter until 1914.

COTY, FRANÇOIS (1874–1934), French perfume magnate who used his wealth to promote right-wing political causes. He built up a press empire which included *Le Figaro*, and founded the *Solidarité française* movement which participated in the right-wing demonstrations of 6 Feb. 1934. Other movements subsidized by him included the *Croix de Feu*.

COTY, RENÉ (1882–1962), president of France (1954–9). His support was a crucial factor in De Gaulle's return to power (1958). Coty, who had previously tried to remedy the weaknesses of the Fourth Republic by supporting constitutional reform, chose De Gaulle as prime minister to end the crisis caused by the Algerian rebellion, and later resigned office in De Gaulle's favour. Before his election as president, Coty was a conservative politician.

COUCY, DECLARATION OF (16 July 1535), issued by Francis I, offering an amnesty to Protestant fugitives who abjured their faith within six months. Despite this moderate step Francis later returned to a policy of religious repression in France.

COUDENHOVE-KALERGI, RICHARD N., Count (1894–   ), founder and publicist of the Pan-European Union. He was well suited to the role of cosmopolitan propagandist, having an Austrian-Greek father, a Japanese mother, and, after the First World War, Czech nationality. He published his book *Paneuropa* in 1923. The first Paneuropa Congress met at Vienna in Oct. 1926. Coudenhove-Kalergi thought the League of Nations unworkable, and wished the European states, while remaining independent, to have joint economic, foreign, and military policies. He thought that a united Europe was alone capable of defeating Bolshevism and solving the problems of disarmament and national minorities.

The movement's headquarters were in Vienna until 1934. Its first members were chiefly Germans and Austrians who thought its programme promised the benefits of the Austro-German Anschluss prohibited by the Versailles treaty. The movement criticized the treaty on other counts, including reparations and the loss of German colonies, demanding equal political rights for Germany among European nations. Realizing that Paneuropa must fail if it were to be identified with the sabotage of Versailles, Coudenhove-Kalergi approached French politicians through Beneš, Czechoslovakia's foreign minister. His ideas appealed to Herriot, and to Briand, who accepted the honorary presidency of the Pan-European Union (1927). Paneuropa reached the peak of its influence on international politics in Sept. 1929, when Briand proposed a scheme of European union to the league. But Briand's proposals, being set within the framework of the league, disappointed Coudenhove-Kalergi. He blamed British apathy and Commonwealth concerns for weakening French championship of his cause. He had never included Britain integrally in his scheme, because of her extra-European interests, and failed to realize how much French policy depended on Britain. Briand's death in 1932, and Hitler's assumption of power in 1933, were decisive setbacks for the Pan-European Union, which concentrated increasingly on economic programmes. In 1947 Coudenhove-Kalergi sponsored a European Parliamentary Union.

COUGHLIN, CHARLES EDWARD (1891–   ), US Roman Catholic priest and broadcaster. After he became pastor of the Shrine of the Little Flower, Royal Oak, MI, in 1926 he began his popular radio addresses. He vehemently attacked international bankers and the Hoover administration, accusing them of responsibility for the Depression, and supported the presidential candidacy of F. D. Roosevelt (1932). But, growing disenchanted with New Deal measures, Coughlin established the National Union for Social Justice (1934) and organized the presidential campaign of William Lemke and the Union Party (1936). Despite the disapproval of his ecclesiastical superiors, Coughlin was virulently anti-communist, anti-Semitic, and demagogic. His weekly newspaper, *Social Justice* (1936–42), ceased publication when Coughlin became involved in charges of sedition and he abandoned his political activities.

COULOMB, CHARLES AUGUSTIN DE (1736–1806), French physicist and military engineer, who served for many years in the West Indies before returning to France in 1779. His early work was in mechanics, but his fame was founded in the field of electricity and magnetism. He established the laws of attraction and repulsion of electric charges and of magnets, fundamental to the understanding of this field.

COULONDRE, ROBERT (1885–1959), French diplomat. As ambassador in Moscow (1936–8) and Berlin (1938–9) he was hostile to 'appeasement' and tried to bring about a Franco–Soviet alliance against Hitler.

COUNCIL OF THE ARMY (1647–8) in England, general body consisting of the higher officers and two officers and two privates from each regiment. This officer-dominated assembly, established early in June, had been forced on the higher officers by the election of agitators by the rank and file. It was designed to counteract the influence of agitators, whose frustration can be seen in the Putney debates (Oct.–Nov. 1647), and whose influence proved more potent outside the council. Though the council met as late as Jan. 1648, it effectually ended when the agitators were ordered back to their regiments after Putney.

COUNCIL OF BLOOD, known also as the Council of Troubles, was a tribunal of seven members, three of whom were Spaniards, set up in Brussels in 1567 on Philip II's instructions. Its president was the new governor of the Netherlands, the Duke of Alva, and its purpose was to extirpate heresy and political opposition. Two of its early victims were the Counts of Egmont and Hoorn.

COUNCIL OF CONSCIENCE, French royal council of the *ancien régime* which dealt with ecclesiastical matters, *eg*, the granting of benefices.

COUNCIL OF EUROPE, established in May 1949 as the result of the movement for European unity which culminated in the Hague Congress (May 1948). The formal decision to establish the council was taken by the Consultative Council of the Western Union (Oct. 1948), whose members (Britain, France, Belgium, Holland, and Luxemburg) were joined by Denmark, Ireland, Italy, Norway, and Sweden as original signatories of the constitution. Subsequently eight other countries joined, namely Greece and Turkey (Aug. 1949), Iceland (March 1950), German Federal Republic (May 1951), Austria (April 1956), Cyprus (April 1961), Switzerland (May 1963), and Malta (May 1965). Greece withdrew from the council when it became obvious that a majority of the members would vote for its expulsion on the grounds of the violation of human rights (Dec. 1969).

The constitution of the council provides for a Committee of Ministers and a Consultative Assembly. The powers of the Assembly were at first strictly limited (it was not allowed to discuss defence or to determine its own agenda) as a result of British opposition to the creation of any supranational European institutions. The constitution was soon revised (1951) to allow a wider initiative to the Assembly, but by this time the federalists in the European movement had turned their attention to the European Coal and Steel Community and the European Defence Community as the nucleus of a European federal union.

The council has thus served to develop the concept of European unity without forming (as some of its original protagonists hoped) the basis for a European government. The Consultative Assembly consists of 147 members, chosen by their own parliaments, or appointed; they are normally members of their own parliaments, although they need not be and there have been a few exceptions to the general practice. Proposals by the British government to make the council a linking organ to bring together the institutions of the 'Six' with the OEEC or the European members of NATO have not been accepted; at the same time, the pressure for a directly elected European parliament has been focused on the Assembly of the 'Six', which bears that name.

The council has a number of practical achievements to its credit. Of these the most important is the acceptance of a European Convention for the Protection of Human Rights (Nov. 1950). It has developed a procedure known as the Partial Agreement (1960) which enables a number of member states to develop close co-operation, using the secretariat and consultative facilities of the council without the necessity of involving all members. Partly through this procedure, and also through means of the committees of the council, a number of wider-ranging agreements and conventions have been accepted, covering aspects of local government, education and social and public health activities.　　　WFK

COUNCIL OF INDIA, a body formed (1858) to advise the newly appointed Secretary of State for India. It consisted of 15 members, not less than nine of whom were to be persons who had served in British India for at least ten years, and who had not left India more than ten years before their appointment. They were appointed, like English judges, to serve only as long as they conducted themselves properly (*se bene din pesserint*). They met once a week, five members forming a quorum. Each member received an annual salary of £1200 and the service was pensionable. The secretary of state presided over the council and exercised a casting vote. His salary of £5000 a year and the expenses of his office were charged to Indian revenues. The council was chiefly of an advisory nature and the secretary of state could override it, except in matters concerning expenditure and loans, the distribution of patronage, and other matters mentioned in the act. He took responsibility for all despatches to India, and dissenting minutes were not forwarded to India unless he thought it advisable, nor was he required to consult the council on urgent or secret matters, such as war and peace, or negotiations with Indian states or foreign powers.

In 1869 the term of office for members was reduced to ten years and the secretary of state was empowered to fill all vacancies. The number of members was reduced to ten in 1889. In 1907 members had to be persons who had not left India for longer than five years and their term of office was reduced to seven years. Morley appointed two Indians as members of his council, Sayyid Husain Bilgrami and Krishna Gupta. In 1917 Austen Chamberlain appointed a third Indian. The act of 1919 reduced the number of members to eight and their term of office to five years.

After 1858 the powers of the secretary of state grew, both at the expense of the council and of the viceroy. Experts of all types served on the council, from the Indian civil service, the army, commerce, and banking. Because of their Indian experience and qualifications they were more expert than the purely commercially minded directors of the East India Co.

The abolition of the council was proposed by the Crewe committee in 1919, but the proposal was not introduced into the Government of India Act of that year. The Indian National Congress regularly passed resolutions demanding its abolition because they considered it to be an unduly conservative influence. Since all proceedings of the council were confidential, the Congress did not sufficiently appreciate the care it had taken of Indian revenues. The council ceased to exist under the Act of 1935.

Malcolm C. C. Seton, *The India Office* (London, 1926).
R. J. Moore, *Sir Charles Wood's Indian Policy, 1853–66* (Manchester, 1966).　　　CCD

COUNCIL OF THE INDIES (*Real y Supremo Consejo de las Indias*), the principal governing body, after the Crown, of the Spanish colonies in America. It was founded by Charles V (1 Aug. 1524) to assume the highest political and judicial position in the colonial administration. The council possessed broader authority than the House of Trade, since it legislated in the king's name and was the highest court of appeals for colonial matters. Theoretically, the council approved all significant policies put into effect in the colonies. Its power was somewhat diminished by distance, however, and its authority was finally limited by a royal decree (1790), which reduced it to an advisory body.

COUNCIL OF JAMAICA, established 1661, was appointed by the governor, and was the upper house of the Jamaican legislature. It advised the governor when sitting as an executive body, and with him was the highest court of appeal. It disappeared when crown colony government was established in Jamaica (1866).

COUNCIL, KING'S in England (the origin of the privy council), was distinct from the great council (*magnum concilium*) which had descended from the Anglo-Saxon witanagemot and is the ancestor of the House of Lords. It emerged early in the 13th cent. and consisted of those people whom the king kept near him to advise him on day-to-day affairs of government; these were largely of the baronial class, but included great officers of state, *eg*, the chancellor, and the treasurer, with clerks who were responsible for administering the government of the realm. It was the resentment of the barons at the king's dependence on these administrators and on their influence in the council which led to baronial opposition to the monarchy in the later 13th and early 14th cents.

Thus by the mid-14th cent. these baronial magnates, assisted by their clients and nominees in the Commons, had virtually taken over the royal council, and it was the achievement of Henry VII, following some tentative moves by the Yorkists, to rebuild a genuinely professional council consisting of men of the monarch's personal choosing, even though some of them might still be holders of hereditary titles. An inner ring of active and trusted ministers exercised an initiative in justice and administration that made it the mainspring of the Tudor machine. Cardinal Wolsey temporarily concentrated its powers within himself, but, with bureaucratic tidiness, Thomas Cromwell established it as a formal institution: a privy council of 19 members, with a clerk, minutes, agenda, and recognized responsibilities. Its gradual enlargement to over 40 members under Edward VI and Mary indicated the Crown's progressive loss of control but Elizabeth I and her minister, Burghley, reduced it again to an effective body, sometimes of no more than 12 in number, which governed England for 45 years. The accession of the Stuarts in 1603 saw once more a fatal enlargement, with a consequent confusion of loyalty and purpose, and an even more fatal attachment to objects contrary to the interests of an emergent and politically conscious House of Commons. When the Long Parliament abolished conciliar offshoots, such as the Courts of Star Chamber and of High Commission, and the Grand Remonstrance proposed the appointment only of ministers whom parliament 'may have cause to confide in' (1641), the modern idea of ministerial responsibility to parliament was about to supersede the ancient idea of a royal council as a body of officials personally attendant and dependent upon the king.
                                                                                                    JC
                                                                                                    MMR

COUNCIL FOR MUTUAL ECONOMIC ASSISTANCE (COMECON or CMEA) in Russia, established at a conference held in Moscow (Jan. 1949) attended by representatives of Bulgaria, Czechoslovakia, Hungary, Poland, Rumania, and the Soviet Union—all founder members. Albania was admitted in Feb. but left in 1961 as a result of the stand it took in the Sino–Soviet dispute. Other members to be admitted were the German Democratic Republic (Oct. 1950) and the Mongolian People's Republic (June 1962).

Comecon had limited practical significance during Stalin's life. Its foundation was a riposte to the organization of Western Europe under the Marshall Plan, and it was a useful instrument for the economic blockade of Yugoslavia after the Soviet–Yugoslav split (1948). But co-operation between sovereign states did not fit the Stalinist system, and the more important relationships were bilateral, between the Soviet Union and each of its satellites.

With Khrushchev's succession to the leadership, COMECON was given greater importance. Once again the competition of the West, by its establishment of the European Economic Community, provided an incentive, and more importantly COMECON appeared of value in permitting the greater degree of co-operation, rather than coercion, that Khrushchev tried to establish in Eastern Europe. Congresses of COMECON were now held regularly. A Charter was drafted in Dec. 1959 (effective, April 1960) and some 23 permanent commissions were established. Yugoslavia was admitted to partial membership in Sept. 1964 (effectively from April 1965).

As a result, COMECON has succeeded in co-ordinating economic development within the Soviet bloc and expanding trade between member countries. An International Investment Bank was established (May 1970) with a capital to the value of 1,000,000,000 roubles, of which 30 per cent is in convertible currency. Rumania did not join the bank, having always opposed the intrusion of COMECON into its national sovereignty and objecting that the bank made provision for majority rather than for unanimous decisions.

The success of COMECON by 1970 had been achieved under certain important constraints. It was necessarily a more bureaucratic organization than EEC, since it lacked the free trade element of the latter; and it worked in currencies convertible within the bloc but not outside it, at a time when its members sought to increase their exports in convertible currencies.
                                                                                                    WFK

COUNCIL FOR NEW ENGLAND, English land and trading company. James I granted to the Plymouth branch of the Virginia Co., under the leadership of Sir Ferdinando Gorges, lands along the North American coast between 40° and 48° latitude with monopoly trading and governing rights (1620). The council brought over the Pilgrims (1620) and gave them a clear land title (1629). Though the council fostered a few other settlements, its territories were limited by a royal grant of Nova Scotia to Sir William Alexander (1621) and to the Massachusetts Bay Co. (1629). The council surrendered its charter (1635) and the Gorges family were granted Maine.

COUNCIL OF THE NORTH, in England, originally a judicial and administrative body dependent on the personal presence of a prince or magnate. It was reorganized by Thomas Cromwell after the Pilgrimage of Grace (1537). It was then controlled from London and manned by permanent officials, and although unable to prevent the rising of the Northern Earls (1569), it was largely successful in maintaining order in the north and in enabling the policies of the Crown to take effect. Under the presidency of Strafford (1628–32) the northern magnates learned the meaning of 'thorough', and, along with other prerogative courts, the council was abolished by the Long Parliament (1641).

COUNCIL OF STATE in England, keystone of the administration established by the Instrument of Government (1653). It controlled the executive power with, and was designed as a check upon, the lord protector, and contained between 13 and 21 members. Councillors were appointed for life and 15 were nominated in the Instrument. To fill vacancies parliament was to name six persons, of whom the council would select two, the final choice being left to the protector. In most things the protector had to consult the council and act by its advice. It could, and did, meet in his absence, and he was not always involved in or even aware of its deliberations. It was reorganized and renamed the privy council by the Humble Petition and Advice (1657). With the Restoration (1660) it disappeared as a machinery of government.

COUNCIL OF WALES originated in the medieval councils set up to administer the Prince of Wales' estates in the Principality. Edward IV appointed a larger body (1473) with powers to repress disorder in Wales and the border counties, and a similar council set up by Henry VIII for his son Arthur continued to function after Arthur's death (1502). This council was reorganized on a statutory basis by Thomas Cromwell (1534). It lost its criminal jurisdiction in 1641 and was abolished as a civil court in 1689.

COUNCIL OF THE WEST, in England, set up by royal commission to maintain order in Devon and Cornwall after a minor insurrection in 1537. It was unpopular with the gentry and disappeared about 1543.

COUNCILLOR OF STATE, member of the French *Conseil d'État*, which under Louis XIV consisted of heads of the chief departments. Louis permitted no single minister to have the eminence previously enjoyed by Richelieu or Mazarin, but preferred a balance of interests, as between the Le Telliers and Colbert. The council had judicial functions in administrative law and in modern times it was a body of permanent civil servants with important advisory powers.

COUNT (MEDIEVAL), title of a Roman office (Latin *comes*) in both the civil and military hierarchies. In the Frankish state it was used under the Carolingian dynasty to denote the chief deputy of a king in a district (county), who administered the royal property, led the military levies, and presided over the judicial court. By the 9th cent. all the counts of the Carolingian state were also the feudal vassals of the king. When that state disintegrated in the later 9th cent. counts became autonomous potentates, appropriating the royal properties under their administration. In France their 10th-cent. successors became rulers of virtually independent principalities, but in Germany counts remained royal officials for a much longer time, evolving into autonomous rulers only in the 13th cent. In England the Latin title of count (*comes*) was used after the Norman conquest as an equivalent of the English earl. It denoted a high nobiliary dignity, but after the 12th cent. it ceased to have any important connections with an office.

COUNTER REFORMATION, movement for reform in the Roman Catholic Church and a response by the Church to the Protestant Reformation of the 16th cent., which also contributed to European political conflicts until the mid-17th cent.

Spontaneous regeneration of religious life was the source of both Protestant and Catholic reform movements. Humanist scholars such as Erasmus rejected medieval scholasticism and criticized ecclesiastical abuses. In Spain, Cardinal Ximenes (d. 1517) began the reform of religious houses, established Alcala University as a centre of humanist studies, and financed the Polyglot Bible in which parallel texts were printed in Latin, Hebrew, and Greek. In Italy Giberti, Bp of Verona, worked ceaselessly to rejuvenate parochial life. Pietistic movements among clergy and laity established new or reformed Orders to restore spiritual discipline and undertake social work, *eg*, the Camaldolese, Capuchins, and Observant Franciscans, Theatines, Barnabites, and Oratorians, and among laymen, the Oratory of Divine Love. The Society of Jesus, founded for the propagation, and later defence, of the faith, was likewise a spontaneous creation.

Demands for reform of many of the abuses which provoked the early Protestants, from men who had shared in these movements—Contarini, Caraffa, Giberti, and others—had little influence on the popes until 1534, and attention shifted to a General Council, which Emperor Charles V also wanted. Pope Paul III (1534–47) appointed reformers as cardinals, and set up a commission on reform which reported on nepotism, non-residence, misuse of papal powers, inadequacy of clerical education, and the corruption of Rome and the curia itself (1537). It had no positive result, but after the failure in 1541 of the attempted reconciliation with the Lutherans, Paul began the offensive by establishing the Roman Inquisition to purge Italy of heresy, and summoning the council.

The Council of Trent (1545–63) fixed the doctrinal differences between Catholic and Protestant, on justification, authority, and the nature of the sacraments. Catholicism was more clearly but more narrowly defined than before. A vast body of legislation was enacted to restore discipline. The order that had the most lasting effect was that there should be a seminary in every diocese for training priests. The council affirmed, and the popes consolidated, the primacy of the papacy within the Church.

Caraffa, as Pope Paul IV (1555–9), expanded the Inquisition, and issued the first Index of prohibited books, but this severity was tempered by Pius IV (1559–66). Thereafter the Counter Reformation was directed by reforming popes as a political as well as a spiritual offensive. Pius V supported the Spanish war in the Netherlands, Gregory XII the French Catholic League, and Sixtus V (1585–95) was active throughout Europe. The main outlines of the territorial division between Catholic and Protestant Europe were fixed at Westphalia (1648).

A. G. Dickens, *The Counter Reformation* (London, 1968).

HNBM

COUNTRY PARTY in England, loose political definition of those MPs who were critical of Crown policies and the political establishment from the middle of Charles II's reign into the 18th cent. It described that substantial number of MPs, mostly country gentlemen subsisting on incomes derived from their landed estates, who were disinterested in the attractions of place or pension but were concerned for careful and just government.

The term was originally applied to the supporters of the Test Act (1673), who thwarted the application of Charles II's declaration of indulgence (1672), and was widely used to describe the followers of Shaftesbury, who exploited national hysteria over the Popish Plot (1678) to rally support for his exclusionist policy. In the 1679 elections Shaftesbury's sympathizers won many seats and in the years of reaction which followed were frequently abused as 'Whigs'. After the 1689 revolution vindicated many of the Whig principles and William III came to depend on an increasingly Whig administration, it was left to others to champion the anti-establishment cause. These others included the new country party of Harley, who disliked the exercise of the prerogative by a Calvinist foreigner and the policies of the Whig Junto. Many of them were Tories but disliked the label 'Tory', with its factional implications. As the terms 'Whig' and 'Tory' came into acceptable use in Anne's reign the tradition of disinterested opposition still survived, cutting across those party divisions, and the concept, if not the term 'country party', lingered throughout the 18th cent. until the emergence of the 19th-cent. party system.

COUNTRY PARTY, THE AUSTRALIAN, emerged as an independent parliamentary force in WA in 1914, and became nation-wide with the establishment of the Australian Country Party in Jan. 1920. CP candidates nominated in all states in 1922 won the balance of power in the House of Representatives of the Commonwealth parliament. For 32 of the next 48 years the CP joined Nationalist, United Australia, or Liberal parties in Commonwealth coalition governments, its members usually holding important ministerial posts. CP leaders, such as Earle Page, Arthur Fadden, and John McEwen, vigorously pursued farmers' interests and each served for short terms as prime minister. In the states, the party also participated in coalition governments, normally in partnership with the Liberal Party, but governing in its own right in Victoria (1950–2). In the 1960s, drift of population to the cities threatened the electoral strength of the party; in reaction, it re-expressed its objectives to embrace 'all Australians and the advancement of Australia'.

COUNTRY PARTY, THE NEW ZEALAND, formed in Auckland in 1922, became essentially a regional party of Auckland's hard-pressed small dairy farmers, who were discontented with the Reform Party. Two seats were won from Reform between 1928 and 1938, but by the Second World War the party was in eclipse.

COUP D'ÉTAT (2 Dec. 1851), military operation by which Louis Napoleon overthrew the Second Republic and paved the way for a return of the Empire. The decision to stage a coup was taken late in Aug. 1851, after months of conflict between the president and the Assembly, but action was postponed because St Arnaud, the general called in to stage the coup, thought it unwise to act while the Assembly was not sitting, as deputies might lead resistance in the provinces. In Nov. St Arnaud was made minister of war, money was raised by Louis Napoleon's mistress and others, reliable officers were appointed to command both the army and the National Guard, and Maupas was appointed to the prefecture of police. The Assembly, when it reconvened, was uneasy and Changarnier and others may have considered staging a coup of their own. That which took place was planned for 2 Dec. and at 11 p.m. on the previous evening the conspirators were called from a reception at the Élysée to receive their orders. At dawn, posters appeared all over the city, the police arrested some 70 leading personalities, and the army occupied key positions. Though there was little reaction to the dissolution of the Assembly, a state of siege was declared and a plebiscite was to be held on the subject of new institutions. Some deputies tried to meet, but were dispersed. Workers gathered in the Faubourg St Antoine and a resistance committee was set up by Victor Hugo and others. But the only real resistance came on 3 Dec., when Baudin, a deputy, was killed in a barricade. The next day some 70 barricades were stormed and 600 rebels and bystanders killed. There were disturbances in some large towns and in 32 departments in the south a state of siege had to be declared. Special commissions tried several thousand people, 5000 being put under police surveillance, 1000 sent before regular courts, 2800 interned, and 1550 deported. Although this was not on the scale of 1848 and did not prevent the declaration of the Empire, it gave it a bad reputation and denied the new regime the popular support it desired.   CHC

COUPON ELECTION, THE (1918), in Britain, held by Lloyd George after the Armistice of 1918 which ended the First World War. The idea of continuing the wartime Coalition government had been widely canvassed, especially in the Northcliffe press. The Conservatives under Bonar Law were willing to carry on; the Labour Party, after much debate, withdrew. Since Asquith still commanded loyalty from a large section of the Liberals, this left Lloyd George very much in Bonar Law's hands. It was therefore decided that the majority of new candidates for the Coalition should be Conservatives: of these there were some 400, and there were 150 Liberals. Endorsement of candidates (the 'coupon') or their rejection was made dependent on the way they had voted in the 'Maurice Debate' in the Commons in May 1918, in which Asquith's motion for a select committee of enquiry into Haig's conduct of the war as British commander-in-chief had been defeated: the names of those who had supported the motion were not endorsed.

The campaign has been described as a violent whipping-up of emotions over German reparations, although it seems likely this view is much exaggerated. Nevertheless, the famous 'Hang the Kaiser' slogan commanded much support, as did demands for reparations. Lloyd George had not intended to seek such a mandate; the reason for this emotional outcry was probably the campaign in the *Daily Mail*, *The Times*, and other newspapers. The bogy of 'Bolshevism' was also much exploited.

The result of the election, the first in which women voted, was a victory for the Coalition, which secured 484 seats, 338 being Conservative and 136 Liberals. Labour gained 59 seats, but lost many of its most distinguished leaders; Asquith's Liberals won 26 seats. The Sinn Fein party won 73, but its members did not take their seats.

The three most important consequences of the election were the evidence it gave of Conservative strength, the effectual end of the Liberals as a governing party, and the strength it gave to the supporters of a Peace Settlement. This was what Lloyd George had helped to stir up, and thus had to control in the 1919 Versailles talks.

COUR DES AIDES, French sovereign court, based on Paris and instituted by the estates general in 1355 to supervise the payment of subsidies voted to the Crown in that year. Taken over by the Crown, it became a royal court of appeal from lesser administrative tribunals for cases involving taxes, *eg,* the *taille,* the *gabelle,* and the *aides.*

COUR DES MONNAIES, special French court of the *ancien régime* situated in Paris to deal with offences committed by the employees of the 30 royal mints, *eg,* counterfeiting or devaluation of the currency. A second court was established in Lyons in 1704, but was abolished in 1771.

COURCELLES DANIEL DE RÉMY, Sieur de (1626–98), French soldier appointed governor of New France (1665–1672). He ravaged Mohawk territory (1666) and concluded peace with the Iroquois Indians (1667). After organizing the first Canadian militia unit, he left Canada (1672) and became commander of Toulon.

COUREURS DES BOIS, unlicensed traders under the French regime in Canada who plied their trade from Indian villages (*c.* 1660). The *coureurs des bois* played an important role in exploration and in the development of fur trading.

COURLAND, DUCHY OF, a German Baltic province which came under Polish suzerainty in 1561. In 1710 the duke married Peter the Great's niece, later the Empress Anne, and the duchy became a minor satellite of Russia, becoming incorporated into that empire in 1795.

COURNOT, ANTOINE AUGUSTIN (1807–77), French economist, notable for his rigorous use of mathematical techniques. His *Recherches sur les principes mathématiques de la théorie des richesses* (1838) investigates exchange value, regarded as one of the sources of wealth in an economic sense, and analyses monopoly and duopoly.

COURT, CHARLES WILLIAM MICHAEL (1911–   ), English-born accountant, was a member of the Legislative Assembly of WA from 1953. As minister for industrial development and the north-west from 1959, he was primarily responsible for attracting investors to develop WA's very large iron ore resources and for persuading the Australian Commonwealth government to help finance the Ord River scheme, Australia's biggest attempt at irrigated tropical agriculture.

COURT OF CLAIMS in Britain considers applications to perform services at coronations. It originated in the court of the Lord High Steward. John of Gaunt presided over a court which heard petitions claiming a right to function at the coronation of Richard II. The work is now done by a court of claims appointed at each accession.

COURT OF POLICY, organ of government established in the 17th cent. by the Dutch West India Co. to control Essequibo, Demerara, and Berbice. It was originally composed of company officials, but settlers' representatives were gradually introduced into the court. Under British domination (1803) the system was maintained until 1891, when the Court of Policy became the elected legislature of British Guiana.

COURT PARTY in England, term denoting those MPs and peers who consistently supported the king and his ministers in parliament during the second half of Charles II's reign and in the 18th cent. The origin of the definition was to be found in the royalist group of MPs who were consolidated by the staunch Anglican parliamentarian Thomas Osborne, Earl of Danby after the disintegration of the Cabal (1672–3). From the time of the Exclusion crisis (1679) the court party were nicknamed 'Tories' by their political enemies, Shaftesbury's country party. However, after the 1689 revolution and William III's growing dependence on the Whigs the term 'court party' cut across Whig and Tory divisions. The powers of the Crown remained considerable, not least in the growing system of royal patronage to dispense titles, pensions, and places in both Church and state, and royal influence in parliament was upheld by those MPs and lords collectively referred to as the court party, who believed that the king's administration should always be supported as a matter of principle and whose loyalty was assured by the benefits of placeholding, *eg*, in the Commons there were always about 60 MPs of the court party sitting as members for the 30 treasury boroughs. These court peers and MPs fulfilled the role of the modern civil servant, and whether they were labelled Whig or Tory on other grounds, they were invariably men of moderate political views, *eg*, the court Tories Thomas Herbert, Earl of Pembroke and Sir Charles Hedges, and the court Whigs Henry Boyle and the Dukes of Devonshire, Shrewsbury, and Somerset.

COURTEAN, SIR WILLIAM (1572–1636), English colonial trader. Courtean, a partner in his family's trading company, formed a syndicate to create a plantation in Barbados (1625) and a settlement was established at Jamestown. The syndicate was backed by the Earl of Montgomery and Barbados was included in the Montgomery Province (1628). It was also included in the royal grant to the Earl of Carlisle (1627). In the subsequent dispute Carlisle's claims were validated (1629) and Courtean lost all his investments.

THE COURTIER (*Il cortegiano*) (1528), by Baldessare Castiglione, an Italian diplomat, consisted of dialogues between ladies and gentlemen at the court of Urbino, presenting the Renaissance ideal of courtly behaviour in the arts, politics, love, and war. It was translated by Sir Thomas Hoby (1561) and had a considerable influence on contemporary literature.

COURTNEY OF PENWITH, LEONARD HENRY COURTNEY, 1st Baron (1832–1918), British journalist and politician. He was professor of political economy at University College, London (1872–5), a Liberal MP (1875–1900), and held minor office in Gladstone's 1880 administration. He resigned (1884) when the cabinet rejected proportional representation. A Liberal Unionist from 1886, he was politically isolated in the 1890s by his distaste for imperial expansion and became a national figure when he opposed the Boer War. A courageous but sensitive politician, his non-party cast of mind embroiled him with the party caucus, and made him seem faddish to professionals like Chamberlain and Gladstone. He is an interesting example of a Liberal whose contempt for state aid to paupers lent attractions to an electoral system which would protect the propertied minority from the tyranny of an unpropertied majority. He often expressed concern before 1914 about Grey's diplomacy, and became unpopular during the First World War for advocating negotiation with Germany.

COURTRAI, BATTLE OF (11 July 1302), this notable defeat of French chivalry by the townsmen and peasants of Flanders was the outcome of the unwarranted aggression of Philip the Fair, King of France, against Flanders, which he had conquered in 1300. The oppressive French administration,

backed by the Flemish nobles and richer burghers, provoked a popular uprising. The Flemish forces at the battle consisted almost entirely of infantry, but they surprised and massacred the huge French army. The victory encouraged the Flemings to resist the French for three more years and the resultant peace in 1305 recognized the independence of Flanders.

COURTS-MARTIAL, for trying disciplinary offences in the British armed forces, inherited the jurisdiction of the old court of chivalry, the *curia militaris*, under the presidency of the earl marshal. With the decline of feudalism, military and naval law were increasingly developed by the articles of war evolved by commanders at sea and in the field, and courts-martial in their modern form first appeared in England under Charles I. The Crown issued ordinances for the setting up of these courts, and one of the grievances in the Petition of Right (1628) was that civilians had been brought within the reach of martial law. The administration of military law received statutory sanction in the Mutiny Act (1689), which through fear of a permanent standing army had to be renewed annually. This lasted until the Army Discipline Act (1879) and the Army Act (1881), which itself was renewed annually until 1955. Naval discipline had similarly evolved from royal commissions and the articles of war, under the general authority of the admiralty, but in practice its administration depended on the variable discretion of individual commanders. The Naval Discipline Act (1866) introduced a more uniform procedure, with each court required to have five officers of prescribed rank. The code of the RAF was largely based on military law, and in 1955 three complementary acts established a common code of discipline and procedure for all three services. The right of appeal from courts-martial had been granted earlier (1951).

COUSIN, VICTOR (1792–1867), French educationist and philosopher. Though of a poor working-class family, he was well educated, and was one of the first entry to the École Normale (1810–12). He then became deputy to the professor of Greek in the school and later to Royer-Collard in the Sorbonne (1815), where he became one of the Doctrinaires. He travelled in Germany, discovering Kantian and Hegelian philosophy, and his lectures and writings became very popular. After 1830 he was elected to the *Académie*, advised the government on educational reform (1833), obtained a peerage and a chair in the Sorbonne, and became both a councillor of state and minister of education. His philosophy became almost the official philosophy of the regime. He opposed the 1848 revolution and the 1851 *coup d'état* and afterwards devoted himself to historical studies.

COUSINS, FRANK (1904–), British trade union leader and politician, who, having been active in the trade union movement since the late 1930s, became in 1956 the general secretary of the Transport and General Workers' Union. His activities in the Council for Scientific and Industrial Research in the early 1960s led to his secondment from the Union to the Labour government (1964–6), where he was made minister of technology. In July 1966 he resigned this office, but continued to work in governmental bodies such as the National Economic Development Council. In 1968 he was appointed chairman of the Community Relations Commission, and in 1969 he joined the National Freight Corporation.

COUTRAS, BATTLE OF (20 Oct. 1587), victory of the Protestant forces of Henry of Navarre against the royalist army of Henry III of France during the French civil wars.

COUVE DE MURVILLE, MAURICE (1907–), French diplomat who became foreign minister and later prime minister under the Fifth Republic. He entered the *inspection des finances* in 1930, and occupied various posts in the ministry of finance until his dismissal by the Vichy regime (1943), when he joined De Gaulle at Algiers. He represented

De Gaulle's government in Italy (1944–5), and his post-war career was in the foreign ministry. He was ambassador in Cairo, Washington (1955–6), and Bonn (1956–8), before becoming De Gaulle's foreign minister, in which post (1958–68) he identified himself completely with De Gaulle's ideas. He was briefly finance minister and prime minister (1968–9) but resigned on the election of President Pompidou.

COVENANT, SOLEMN LEAGUE AND (1643), agreement of the English parliament with the Scots, who were to give military aid in the Civil War against the king, in return for which a Presbyterian form of Church government would be imposed uniformly on the kingdoms of England and Ireland, and preserved in Scotland. The Scots had been pressing for such an alliance since the conclusion of the Bishops' Wars in 1641, but parliament was reluctant at that stage to pay the price of uniformity with the presbyterian Church in Scotland. Parliament's unwillingness to commit itself continued when the royalist members withdrew, but after the early defeats of its forces in the north and west it passed an ordinance establishing the Westminster Assembly to confer on the liturgy, discipline, and government of the Church of England, the preamble to this ordinance pledging parliament to the abolition of episcopacy. A committee of both Houses then sent Sir Henry Vane (the younger) to seek help in Scotland, the result of his mission being the Solemn League and Covenant, signed on 17 Aug.

Besides 'the reformation of religion in . . . England and Ireland in doctrine, worship, discipline, and government', the signatories agreed to 'endeavour to bring the churches of God in the three kingdoms to the nearest conjunction and uniformity in religion, confessing of faith, form of church government, directory for worship, and catechising'. For parliament, however, it remained primarily a political alliance for military purposes, the two main obstacles to its religious programme being the strength of the Independents and the desire of parliament not to relinquish the authority of state over Church established in the 16th cent. By 1645, when an ordinance for the election of elders was issued, and the Directory of Worship was substituted for the Prayer Book, real power was slipping to the army, which was dominated by Independents. The military results of the agreement were decisive in 1644. The royalist position in the north of England collapsed when the Scottish army crossed the border, and following the defeat at Marston Moor, parliament dominated the north.

The Scots, dissatisfied with the progress of the religious programme, tried to interest the king in it, after he had taken refuge with them in 1646. He refused their conditions then, but made a secret agreement in 1648, which gave him a Scottish army, but not the disciplined army of the Covenant, and it was beaten at Preston. Oliver Cromwell's Union of England and Scotland, imposed by military means in 1654, realized none of the hopes of the Covenanters.

In the end the Solemn League and Covenant had served only the limited military purposes of parliament before the creation of the New Model Army.

G. Donaldson, *Scotland. James V to James VII* (Edinburgh and London, 1965).   HNBM

COVENANT IN ULSTER (1642), imposed when Gen. Munro was sent with seven Lowland regiments to suppress the Catholic rebellion in Ireland. The Scottish covenant of 1638 was made a test of Protestant loyalty in Ulster, and the chaplains in Munro's army organized the first Irish presbytery.

COVENTRY AIR ATTACK (1940–1), in the Second World War, one of the most notable examples of German *blitzkreig* bombing of Britain. Coventry was one of several cities, including London and Liverpool, selected for night bombing in 1940–1, and to a lesser degree later on. The destruction of houses in Coventry was exceptionally heavy. Nevertheless,

the raids were not a strategic success and their effect on war production was unimportant, and many of the factories recovered from the effects of the raids in less than a week. In the heaviest raid of all (14 Nov. 1940) the Gothic cathedral was destroyed. The new one, built in the 1960s, attracted wide interest in the Christian world and symbolized a spirit of reconciliation among the nations who had warred against each other.

COVERDALE, MILES (1488–1568), English translator of the Bible, was an Austin friar at Cambridge, but on his conversion went to Europe (c. 1528) and may have assisted Tyndale in his translation of the Pentateuch. With encouragement from Thomas Cranmer and Thomas Cromwell, he published at Zürich his own version, based on Latin and German texts (1535) which he dedicated to Henry VIII. It was the first complete English translation. Coverdale next supervised a new version (1538–9), based on Matthew's Bible and other sources, and this, with a preface by Cranmer, was the Great Bible of which a copy was to be placed in every English church. He left England on the fall of Cromwell (1540), but returned in 1548 and the impression made by his preaching to the western insurgents led to his appointment as Bp of Exeter (1551). He was deprived under Mary and with other exiles worked on the Geneva Bible (1557–60). Wearing a black gown instead of the traditional robes, he assisted at the consecration of Abp Parker (1559), and although too extreme in his views to resume his bishopric, he was given a London rectory.

COVILHAM, PERO DE (*c.* 1487–*c.* 1521), Portuguese explorer sent by King John II to India in 1487. He transmitted the news that the sea route round Africa to India was practicable, which probably influenced the subsequent decision to send Vasco da Gama's expedition. From India Covilham travelled (*c.* 1493) to Abyssinia, where he was found by other Portuguese led by Alvares in 1520. The latter brought to Portugal valuable information about Abyssinia derived from Covilham.

COWBOYS, hired manpower of the open-range cattle industry of the Great Plains of the US. They were by necessity expert horsemen, and both their accoutrements and their techniques emphasized the continuing Spanish–Mexican tradition in the cattle industry. They declined rapidly in numbers after 1885, having made a distinctive contribution to the legend of the West.

COWELL, DR JOHN (1554–1611), English lawyer and Regius Professor of Civil Law at Cambridge, published *The Interpreter* (1607), a dictionary of legal terms. His assertion that the king 'is above the law by his sovereign power' offended the common lawyers and in 1610 the book was condemned by the Commons for its absolutist doctrines.

COWEN, JOSEPH (1829–1900), prominent British radical, and champion of liberal movements in Europe. He was proprietor and editor of the important provincial newspaper the *Newcastle Daily Chronicle* from 1859, and MP for Newcastle (1873–86).

COWLEY, ABRAHAM (1618–67), English poet and essayist, a royalist exiled to France with Charles II (1644–54). He was a versatile poet much influenced by Jonson and Donne. He served as cipher secretary to Henrietta Maria while in France, for which he was rewarded with a land grant at the Restoration. After his return to England (1654), he was imprisoned by Oliver Cromwell as a spy, but in 1657 in apparent submission to the regime he was studying medicine and botany at Oxford. He was one of the first members of the Royal Society, to which he addressed an ode elevating scientific reason above received authority, but to the end of his life he was regarded as the leader of the literary world.

COWPENS, BATTLE OF (17 Jan. 1781), US victory over British and Loyalist troops in SC during the American Revolution. Although brilliantly executed, the action failed to halt Cornwallis's march northwards.

COWPER, WILLIAM COWPER, 1st Earl (d. 1723), British lawyer and moderate Whig office-holder. Though he led the Whigs in the House of Commons for a time, Cowper was free from party prejudices, was never identified with the Junto, and was friendly with many leading Tories. Created lord keeper (1705) and lord chancellor (1707–10), he served ably and efficiently, refusing bribes and treating Tory and Whig lawyers with equal fairness. In 1706 he was appointed by Queen Anne as a leading English commissioner to negotiate for the Union with Scotland. His resignation (1710) was opposed by the Queen and Harley, but Cowper insisted on joining the Whigs in opposition. On the death of Anne, Cowper represented the Whig opposition, meeting with Bolingbroke to arrange the Hanoverian succession. On George I's accession Cowper again became chancellor and held office until his death.

COWRY CURRENCY in Africa. The small cowry, *Cypraea moneta*, of the Maldive Islands, was used as small-change currency in Bengal and Mali in the 14th cent. and had reached the Guinea coast by the early 16th cent. Cowries were carried to North Africa via the Red Sea and Mediterranean, then taken overland on the caravan routes between North Africa and the Niger Bend. Later, the Portuguese, Dutch, and English brought them by sea to trading stations on the West African coast. In the 18th and 19th cents the larger cowry of East Africa, *Cypraea annulus*, was also used, but not accepted everywhere. Given the wide use of cowries as trading currency in Africa, there were good profits to be made in supplying the shells, but exchange rates varied considerably.

COX, JAMES MIDDLETON (1870–1957), US newspaper proprietor and politician. Congressman from OH (1909–13), and then governor (1913–15, 1917–21). He was the unsuccessful Democratic presidential candidate in 1920, and remained an influence within the party. He was vice-chairman of the US delegation to the World Monetary and Economic Conference (1933).

COX, SIR PERCY (1864–1937), Indian political official, who served as Resident in the Persian Gulf (1904–13). As chief political officer with the Mesopotamian expeditionary force (1914–17), he was largely responsible for the decision to advance to Baghdad; as acting ambassador in Iran (1918–20) for the Agreement; and as high commissioner in Iraq (1920–3) for the establishment of Faisal as ruler.

COX, RICHARD (1500–81), English Protestant divine, who supported the second Edwardian Prayer Book against the Calvinist ideals of John Knox while a Marian exile in Frankfurt. Returning to England on Elizabeth's accession (1558), he was elevated to the bishopric of Ely, though as a married clergyman he met with the queen's disapproval and failed to succeed Parker in the see of Canterbury (1575).

COXEY'S ARMY, name given to US groups of unemployed who 'marched' from Massillon, OH, to Washington, DC, in April 1894. Joseph Sechler Coxey (1854–1951), a wealthy former Greenbacker, had been advocating an issue of paper money to be used for hiring unemployed to build roads and other public works to end the depression. The march was organized as a 'petition in boots' to put the idea to Congress, but was given fantastic revivalist trappings by the IA radical Carl Browne, self-styled reincarnated 'Cerebellum of Christ' who named the movement the 'Commonweal of Christ'. Coxey and Browne were arrested and jailed. The eccentricities of Browne and other weirdly garbed, ideological nonconformists and misfits who joined the march made 'Coxey's army' a synonym for work-shy tramps and spongers. Other 'industrial armies', however, followed Coxey to Washington, and the movement was symptomatic of the unrest which followed the panic of 1893.

CRACOW, ancient capital of Poland, situated on the upper Vistula in the province of Galicia. The city was a bishopric and the seat of the first university of Poland (founded 1364), whose most illustrious pupil, Nicolas Copernicus (1473–1543), studied there when it was the intellectual centre of the country. From the mid-12th cent. the principality of Cracow was inherited by the eldest son of the ruling dynasty, and it was here that Polish kings were crowned and buried. In 1655 Cracow was overrun by Charles Gustavus of Sweden, and in 1702 by Charles XII. Although superseded in size and population by Warsaw, it played an important part in the national revival after the first Partition of Poland (1773). It was in Cracow that Kosciuszko declared his intention of ousting the Russian invaders (1794) and the great rising of that year started in the city, which was captured by the Prussians shortly afterwards. In the third Partition (1795) Cracow was assigned to Austria. After the latter's defeat by Prince Joseph Poniatowski in the Napoleonic War (1809) Cracow, together with Austria's other acquisitions of 1795, was ceded to the Grand Duchy of Warsaw. In the Vienna settlement (1815) it became a free and independent city republic under Austria's protection. The Polish insurrection of 1846 freed Cracow from foreign occupation, but the republic was suppressed by Metternich's forces, which were aided by the disaffected Polish peasantry, and despite English and French protests, it was annexed by Austria, remaining within the Austro-Hungarian empire until the end of the First World War. During this period Cracow was again the focus of intellectual life and in 1872 the Cracow Academy of Sciences and Arts was founded. In 1919 the city was restored to a reconstructed Poland, but in 1939, after Poland's surrender to Nazi Germany, it became the capital of the government-general. The Germans interned in concentration camps almost all Poland's intellectuals, including the professors of Cracow's ancient university, the bulwark of Polish civilization for over five centuries.

O. Halecki, *A History of Poland* (London, 1942). **MKS**

CRACOW INSURRECTION (Feb. 1846) broke out in the free city in support of the Polish gentry's revolt in Austrian Galicia. Polish nationalists, hoping for a rising throughout Russian and Prussian Poland as well, set up a national government and proclaimed a Polish republic in the city. Russian troops rapidly occupied Cracow (March), while Austria suppressed the Galician revolt by force and in some cases by inciting the serfs against their landlords. To prevent further trouble from the city, Austria annexed it with Russian and Prussian consent.

CRAFT GUILDS (MEDIEVAL). In most medieval towns craftsmen were organized into guilds grouping together all artisans engaged in the same occupation. The governing group of a guild consisted of fully trained masters, who employed apprentices undergoing professional training. In between these two groups came the journeymen, who, through lack of sufficient experience or of financial means, were unable to qualify as masters, though they hoped to do so at some future date. Initially these craft guilds were often subordinated to the merchant oligarchies who ruled most medieval towns until the later 13th cent. This was one of the most important causes of popular revolts that occurred in many European towns between c. 1250 and 1400. Where such revolts proved successful, a new type of municipal government was set up in which the main craft guilds were adequately represented. But in some of the most important medieval towns, such as Florence or Venice, an exceptionally wealthy and powerful merchant class never allowed this to happen for long. In Florence many craftsmen were excluded altogether from any guild, as was the case with the majority of the humbler employees of the two leading guilds of cloth makers and cloth finishers (*calimala*).

CRAFTSMAN, THE, English newspaper, started in Dec. 1726, by Nicholas Amhurst, who ran it for ten years. Bolingbroke and Pulteney were frequent contributors, making virulent attacks on Walpole's policies. The paper played a large part in his withdrawal of the excise scheme (1733).

CRAGGS, JAMES, the younger (1686–1721), Whig politician and office-holder who served in Spain as Stanhope's secretary during the War of the Spanish Succession. Thereafter his political fortunes were closely connected with those of Stanhope. He became secretary at war (1717) and later secretary of state for the south (1718–21).

CRAIG, SIR JAMES HENRY (1748–1812), British general and governor-in-chief of Canada (1807–11). He served throughout the War of American Independence, subsequently serving in Ireland, Africa, India, England, and the Mediterannean area. As governor-general of Canada, he distrusted the French Canadians in the Assembly of Lower Canada. He closed *Le Canadien* (1810) and imprisoned its founder, Pierre Bédard.

CRANBROOK, GATHORNE GATHORNE-HARDY, 1st Earl of (1841–1906), British Conservative minister. As secretary for war (1874–8), he firmly supported Disraeli's foreign policy, preparing for war with Russia in the Eastern crisis. At the India office (1878–80), he backed Lord Lytton's forward policy which led to the Afghan war and massacre of the British legation at Kabul (1879). Cranbrook, who sympathized with Lord Salisbury, supported the Anglican voluntary schools as Lord President of the Council (1886–92).

CRANE, STEPHEN (1871–1900), US writer, variously described as a realist and as a naturalist. He was born in Newark, NJ, and went as an aspiring writer to New York, where he worked intermittently for newspapers and accumulated material for his first novel, *Maggie: A Girl of the Streets* (1893), which was partly responsible for his later reputation for depravity. His *The Red Badge of Courage* (1895) was a study of the mind of an unseasoned soldier during battle, though it was written before Crane had seen warfare, his knowledge of which was derived from reading Tolstoy and *Battles and Leaders of the Civil War*. Later he became a war correspondent during the Graeco-Turkish and Spanish-American wars. He published two volumes of poetry the first of which, *The Black Riders* (1895), shows the influence of Emily Dickinson.

CRANMER, THOMAS (1489–1556), archbishop of Canterbury, compiler of the liturgies of the Church of England, who supported the royal supremacy and the breach with Rome (1534), wrote a preface to the vernacular Bible placed in every English church (1539), issued the first English prayer books and the Forty-two Articles (1549–52), and was martyred in the Catholic reaction under Mary.

As a Cambridge don Cranmer put forward the opinion that Henry VIII's marriage to Catherine of Aragon, being void by the law of God, might be annulled by an English court without reference to the pope. Henry sent him to consult the universities of Europe, and at Nuremberg he married a niece of the Lutheran Osiander, in breach of canon law.

In 1533 Henry made him Abp of Canterbury, a post he tried to avoid, since he was neither an administrator nor a politician. He was a scholar, unworldly, temperate and unambitious, but he was valuable to Henry because his studies had convinced him of the justice and legality of the royal supremacy. The subject might differ, might even demur, but the godly prince must be obeyed. So Cranmer formally freed

Henry of Catherine (just as over the years he was to release him from three more of his queens) and declared him married to Anne Boleyn. He assented to the measures which separated England from Rome and to the policy of establishing uniformity of belief by royal decree, although he was personally opposed to the dissolution of the monasteries (believing that they should be preserved as cathedral schools) and to the reactionary Six Articles (1539), which compelled him to send his wife overseas. His compliance, high-principled even when it was most casuistical, endeared him to Henry, who three times defended him against accusations of heresy.

Except in the matter of clerical marriage, Cranmer was slow to adopt distinctively Protestant opinions. But he believed that the Bible should be distributed in English, and in the last few years of Henry's reign he translated the litany, decided that faith was sufficient for salvation, and began to have doubts about the Mass.

Change was rapid after Henry's death, but the first prayer book (1549) was still mainly traditional, although it had certain Lutheran characteristics and modified the ritual of services that were now in English. It was not until after its publication that, under the influence of Swiss reformers who had invaded the country, Cranmer finally reached the position of denying transubstantiation and a corporal presence. The second prayer book (1552), which made the Eucharist a commemorative rite in the Zwinglian style, and the Forty-two Articles a formulary of English Protestant belief, was a compromise between Swiss and German doctrine, Catholic only where the old views were uncontroversial.

For giving his sanction to the attempt to keep Mary from the throne (1553), Cranmer was deprived and arrested for treason, but the government had a higher use for him. He was brought to trial as a heretic in the hope that by recanting he would persuade others to follow his example. Cranmer was torn between his spiritual convictions and his belief in the authority of the civil power. After much agony of soul he cheated the government of their expected triumph by withdrawing his earlier recantation and dying bravely at the stake. But his true memorial is in his English liturgies, the fruit of his long hours of study, whose tranquil strength has comforted even non-believers.

A. F. Pollard, *Thomas Cranmer and the English Reformation* (London, 1905).
J. Ridley, *Thomas Cranmer* (London, 1962).   MMR

CRASHAW, RICHARD (1612–49), English poet, son of a Puritan rector, and a High Anglican. While a fellow of Peterhouse, Cambridge (1637–43), he was converted to Catholicism (1645), and died at the Cathedral of the Holy House of Loreto in Italy. His poetry, mainly devotional, made much use of erotic metaphor. He published *Steps to the Temple* (1646) and *Carmen Deo Nostro* (1652).

CRASSUS, M. LICINIUS (*c.* 112–53 BC), Roman politician, noted for his wealth. He first became prominent fighting for Sulla against the Marians (83–82), and enriched himself in the Sullan proscriptions. As praetor he crushed Spartacus' revolt (72), but joined with Pompey to use their armies to obtain the consulship of 70, for which Pompey was not qualified, and to overthrow Sulla's constitution. Between 66 and 63 he tried to establish a position to counter the prestige that Pompey was winning by his campaigns against the pirates and Mithridates VI of Pontus and became very influential in the Senate. Julius Caesar joined him in several unsuccessful schemes, including support for Catiline as consular candidate (though not as conspirator), and in 60 Crassus joined him and Pompey in the First Triumvirate. Despite differences with Pompey, he renewed the compact at the conference of Luca (56), was again consul with him (55) and received the province of Syria to govern for five years. His invasion of Parthia (54) ended disastrously at Carrhae (53) and he was captured and killed.

CRATHORNE, THOMAS LIONEL DUGDALE, 1st Baron (1897–), British Conservative politician who entered politics in 1929, was appointed secretary of state for the colonies in 1931, and took part in much of the crisis then developing over India and the Middle East. After a brief period as secretary of state for air (1935), he became parliamentary private secretary to Baldwin (1935–7). During the Second World War he played an important part in the Conservative Party plans for post-war organization. He was minister of agriculture (1951–4).

CRAWFORD, WILLIAM HARRIS (1772–1834), US politician and one of the first powerful political organizers in American history. He was successively senator from Georgia (1807–13), US minister to France (1813–15), secretary of war (1815–16) and secretary of the treasury (1817–25).

CRAWFURD, JOHN (1783–1868), British scholar-diplomat in south-east Asia. Crawfurd made his name as Resident at the court of Jogjakarta during the British occupation of Java (1811–16). Thereafter he became the second Resident of Singapore (1823–6), and led two important missions, to Thailand and Viet-nam (1821) and to Burma (1826–7). Though he failed to open these countries to British trade and influence, he was a keen observer. His writings included the journals of his two diplomatic missions (pub. 1828 and 1829 respectively): a *History* (1820) and a *Descriptive Dictionary* (1856) of the Malay Archipelago, and a *Malay Grammar* (1852).

CRAZY HORSE (1844–77) (Ta Sunka Witko), Sioux Indian chief, whose band of about 600 Minneconjou Sioux and Cheyenne met other Sioux on the Powder river and joined Sitting Bull on the Little Big Horn river. Crazy Horse led the assault on Gen. George Custer's US cavalry (25 June 1876). In the following year he surrendered with 2000 followers and was placed on the Pine Ridge Reservation, where he was suspected of stirring up the Indians. Crazy Horse was killed in a struggle with a reservation guard.

CRÉCY, BATTLE OF (26 Aug. 1346), first major land battle of the Hundred Years War, fought in Picardy near the Somme. The superiority of the English longbow over the French feudal army ensured a crushing defeat of the French and gave King Edward III of England the freedom to undertake the siege of Calais. It was the first European battle in which cannon were used.

CREDIT MOBILIER SCANDAL (1872), US scandal involving prominent politicians and business leaders, exposed by a Senate investigating committee after allegations made in the press during the American presidential election campaign. Credit Mobilier of America was organized (1867) by the promoters of the Union Pacific Railroad to arrange construction contracts to their financial advantage. To stave off congressional investigations one of the leading promoters, Oakes Ames, a MA Representative in Congress, offered Credit Mobilier stock to fellow congressmen on such favourable terms as to be tantamount to open bribery. As a result of the enquiry Ames and another congressman were censured. Others implicated included the retiring and incoming vice-presidents, Schuyler Colfax and Henry Wilson, and a future president, James Garfield. The episode besmirched Congress with a reputation for financial corruption that had already tainted the executive branch of the federal government during the Grant administration.

CREE INDIANS, Algonquian tribe which formerly ranged over a large area of western Canada. The Crees were first encountered by French traders and missionaries early in the 17th cent. The French employed them as guides and hunters in the fur trade. After 1667, when the English made contact with them through the Hudson's Bay Co., the two European powers competed for Cree support. An alliance with the Assiniboin, acquisition of rifles, and the impetus of the fur trade led them to expand their territory from their original habitat, which extended from the James Bay to the Saskatchewan river. Smallpox epidemics (1786, 1838) reduced their numbers to an estimated one-eighth of the former population. They were eventually confined to reservations in Manitoba.

CREEK INDIANS, confederacy of tribes of Muskhogean stock, whose tribal homeland was formerly the present American states of Alabama and Georgia. De Soto's army discovered them in 1540, and treated them badly. Thereafter the Creeks were hostile to the Spanish. The Creeks were allies of the English in the Apalachee Wars (1703–8), and sold large portions of their lands to them. They rebelled against the Americans (1813–14), but were defeated. The Seminole War (1835–43) subdued the southern tribes of the confederacy, and most of the Creek people were removed to Indian Territory (1836–40).

CREEK INDIAN WAR (1813–14), the result of an Indian uprising on the US south-western frontier during the war of 1812. Andrew Jackson defeated the Creeks at Horseshoe Bend (27 March 1814), and by the treaty of Fort Jackson two-thirds of the Creek lands were ceded to the US.

CREFELD, BATTLE OF (23 June 1758), in which a Hanoverian army under the Prussian general Ferdinand of Brunswick defeated the French under Clermont during the Seven Years War.

CRÉMIEUX, ISAAC MOISE (known as **ADOLPHE**) (1796–1880), French liberal statesman and jurist and a leading member of the Jewish community in Paris, who made his reputation by defending rebels against the July Monarchy. He secured election to the Chamber (1842), persuaded Louis Philippe to flee (1848), and was responsible for judicial affairs in the Provisional Government. After opposing the *coup d'état*, he resumed his legal practice and his campaign for religious toleration. He was elected to the Legislature (1869) and the Government of National Defence, again being responsible for judicial affairs (1871). His action in giving Algerian Jews civic liberties was unpopular, but obtained him election for Algiers (1872) and later a Life Senatorship (1876).

CREMONA, BATTLES OF (AD 69), important in Roman history in the 'Year of the Four Emperors'. Cremona, a Roman colony on the Po, which was strategically important in the defence of Italy against attack from the north, fell in the spring of 69 after a march from Germany over the Alps by Vitellius' army in revolt against the Emperor Otho, whose defensive measures were dilatory. Otho's army was defeated a few miles from the city and he committed suicide. Later the same year Cremona became vital to Vitellius' troops as an army in support of Vespasian advanced from Illyria. They reached it before the attackers, but were defeated outside the city, which was sacked.

CREOLES, American-born whites, as distinguished in Latin America from the Spanish or Portuguese-born residents. *Criollos*, as the term is rendered in Spanish, or *crioulos* in Portuguese, were relegated to a secondary political and social position during the colonial era because of the greed of the Europeans, the caution of the timorous monarchs who chose colonial officials, and the fear of possible racial mixture which might have tainted the creole's lineage. Antagonism between creole and European grew in intensity before the era of independence, contributing to the creole-dominated rebellions of the early 19th cent. The term creole is also used in the West Indies.

CRESAP'S WAR (1774) occurred after most of the family of John Logan (Tah-gah-jute), a Cayuga Indian sachem, had been murdered by whites at Yellow Creek in southern Ohio

(30 April 1774). The events of this war were a phase of Lord Dunmore's War and ended with a white victory at Point Pleasant, WV (10 Oct. 1774).

CRESPY, PEACE OF (1544), settlement made between Francis I and the Emperor Charles V in an effort to restore Catholic unity in Europe. Francis agreed to help Charles against the Porte, formally the ally of France, and to support him against the Protestants should they refuse to accept the decisions of the council that was to meet at Trent. In return, a marriage was to be arranged between Francis's second son and a Habsburg princess and Charles agreed to cede to them either Milan or the Netherlands. However, when the Duke of Orléans died shortly afterwards (1545), Charles was persuaded that there was no need to renew his territorial offer to France and the terms of the peace ceased to be effective.

CRESWELL, SIR WILLIAM ROOKE (1852–1933), Australian admiral, who entered the South Australian naval service in 1885 and was an early and persistent advocate of an Australian navy, which he did more than any other man to establish. He became first director of Australian naval forces (1905), and was first naval member of the Naval Board (1911–19).

CRETAN QUESTION. After her own achievement of independence (1833), Greece demanded the cession of Crete, whose revolt had been suppressed in 1825. In 1866 Cretan revolutionaries, supported by Greek volunteers, demanded union with Greece. Turkish suppression of this revolt resulted in an unsuccessful European intervention (Paris Conference 1869) to prevent war between Greece and the Turks. In 1897 Greece was defeated and again intervened in support of a Cretan revolt, but European powers forced the Turks to concede autonomy to Crete (1897). In 1905 the Cretan Assembly declared union with Greece, although this was not recognized by the Great Powers until 1913.

CRETE, BATTLE OF (1941). After the evacuation of Greece the British high command landed 27,000 troops on Crete to hold the refuelling base at Suda Bay for the Royal Navy. On 20 May the Germans launched an air-borne assault and, despite British control of the seas, secured the Suda Bay airstrip. German reinforcements poured in both by glider and troop transport, isolating British units defending minor positions. By 2 June organized resistance ceased and the evacuation was begun. After struggling across the mountains and sheltering in caves to avoid air attack, some 16,500 men were taken off Crete to Alexandria. Altogether 15,000 men were lost during the fighting and the evacuation.

CRÈVECŒUR, MICHEL-GUILLAUME JEAN DE (1735–1813), Franco-American author. Though born in France, he studied in England and emigrated to Canada (*c.* 1754), where he explored and mapped along the Great Lakes and the Ohio river. He moved to New York (1759), where he became a farmer (1769–80), then to France (1780–3), returning to the US as a French consul and a contributor to American newspapers. Crèvecœur's *Letters from an American Farmer* (1782) achieved international fame through their descriptions of American rural life and their analyses of 'the American, this new man'. Crèvecœur claimed to have introduced alfalfa into America and the potato into Normandy.

CREWE, ROBERT OFFLEY ASHBURTON CREWE-MILNES, 1st Marquis of (1858–1945), British diplomat and politician, who first entered politics in 1883, as assistant private secretary to Lord Granville, the foreign secretary. In Gladstone's last ministry he was appointed viceroy of Ireland. In 1895 Rosebery's Liberal government collapsed, and Crewe resigned office.

His increasing stature in the Liberal Party in the House of Lords culminated in his appointment to the leadership; he was already a prominent member of Campbell-Bannerman's cabinet. Asquith appointed him colonial secretary, in which capacity he took over responsibility for the negotiations of the union of South Africa. He was secretary of state for India (1910–15), and during this period he supervised the transfer of British rule from Calcutta to Delhi; he also took part in the abortive constitutional conference of 1910. In 1916 Crewe resigned with Asquith, and this effectively marked the end of his career in political office. In 1917 he became chairman of the London County Council. He was British ambassador to France (1922–8). Thereafter he returned to politics, leading the Independent Liberals in the Lords.

CREWE'S ACT (1782), in Britain, disfranchising revenue officials (of whom most were employees of the Customs and Excise Boards) was the most extreme of the economical reform acts of the Rockingham Whigs, aimed to reduce government influence over elections. Revenue officers were the only placemen to be deprived of the right to vote as well as the right to sit in parliament. The act contributed little, in practice, to the general decline of government influence in the late 18th cent. It was repealed in 1874, in response to a petition from the Association of Customs and Excise officers.

CRICHEL DOWN (1950–4) in Britain, political scandal which raised issues of ministers' responsibilities for their civil servants' actions, and of redress for maladministration. Crichel Down had been requisitioned by the ministry of agriculture in 1937. In 1952 the former owner attempted to repurchase the land, but was constantly thwarted by ministry officials. There was eventually a public enquiry, which exonerated the officials concerned from allegations of corruption, but severely criticized them for inefficiency and partiality. In consequence, the minister of agriculture, Sir Thomas Dugdale, resigned office.

CRICKET. English monks played a form of cricket in the Middle Ages, and the game is mentioned in 14th-cent. wardrobe accounts. In the 17th cent. Sunday cricketers were fined, Oliver Cromwell proscribed the game in Ireland, and John Churchill, future Duke of Marlborough, played it at St Paul's School, London.

Cricket was firmly established in England in the 18th cent. The Laws were published (1744), the Marylebone Cricket Club (MCC) founded in London (1787), and the game became associated both with the aristocracy and with the village green.

In the 19th cent. the Duke of Wellington required cricket grounds to be an adjunct to military barracks (1841) and the game was furthered at the universities and public schools. The career of Dr W. G. Grace (1848–1915) typified the identification of the new professional and business middle-classes with cricket, while the growth of industry and communications led to factory and works teams, Sheffield being one of the early centres.

Matches between English and Australian cricketers (including Aborigines) led to the first 'Test' match at Melbourne in 1877. Subsequently these international contests were extended to South Africa, New Zealand, the West Indies, India, and Pakistan. At a lower level the game flourished in Canada, Ceylon, Fiji, Hong Kong, Kenya, and Malaysia.

The connection between cricket and the British Commonwealth was a factor in the ending of cricketing relations with the former Commonwealth territory of South Africa in 1970 because of the latter's apartheid policy.

Although English military and naval forces introduced cricket into Europe in the 18th and 19th cents it has only continued to be played in Holland and Denmark. There is a slight following in the US, Argentine, and Israel.

No game has produced a greater response from artists, poets, and men of letters, while some distinguished players have later held high office in Church and state throughout the Commonwealth.

H. S. Altham and E. W. Swanton, *A History of Cricket* (London, 1926, 1962).
E. W. Swanton, *The World of Cricket* (London, 1966).

GMDH

'CRIME OF 1873', popular cry adopted in the US particularly after 1876 by advocates of bimetallism. The Currency Act (1873) demonetizing silver coincided with increased production in the western states and resulted in a marked decline in the price of silver bullion. 'Silverites' alleged that demonetization was a conspiracy of Anglo-American financiers to bring about the adoption of the gold standard by the US. This notion of an insidious plot, and persistent Anglophobia, perpetuated the issue in American political controversy until after the 1896 presidential election. In fact, silver dollars had not been in circulation for many years and the 1873 act was a respectable attempt to establish a sound monetary system.

CRIMEAN WAR (1854–6), paved the way for the reorganization of central Europe, as well as for the propping up of Turkey after Russia's defeat. Russo-French quarrels over the Holy Places in Palestine (1852–3) and attempts by Tsar Nicholas to bully Turkey into a form of protectorate, led the Aberdeen government in Britain to believe that Russia intended the destruction of Turkey and of Britain's position in the Mediterranean. Napoleon III welcomed the opportunity of war with Russia as a way of winning domestic support and rearranging the map of Europe. Britain and France declared war on 27 March 1854, although the motive for war—the Russian occupation of the Danubian Provinces—was removed through Austrian pressure. The western powers landed troops in the Crimea (Sept.) and the object of the war soon became little more than the capture of Sevastopol. Elderly commanders and ill-equipped troops on both sides made for indecisive action and atrocious conditions, which were somewhat alleviated by Florence Nightingale's nurses and the force of public opinion in Britain. Russian attempts to relieve Sevastopol were repulsed at Balaclava and Inkerman (1854) and the port was eventually taken (Sept. 1855). As the new Russian Tsar, Alexander II, wanted peace and the allies had no further attainable objectives, peace was made at Paris (1856).

CRIMINAL JUSTICE ACT (1948) in Britain, comprehensive measure for legal liberalization undertaken by Chuter-Ede, home secretary in Attlee's government; among its provisions was the abolition of corporal punishment. During the bill's passage through parliament a proposal to suspend capital punishment was passed by the Commons in a free vote; this was against the advice of the home secretary, who argued that public opinion was not ready for it. The Lords reversed this vote, and the ensuing crisis was resolved only by a promise by the government of a further enquiry into the possibility of limiting the death penalty.

CRIMINAL JUSTICE ACT (1961) in Britain, legislative measure of legal reform, chiefly concerned with young offenders. The act extended the work of the Criminal Justice Act (1948), especially in the replacement of short prison sentences by the use of detention centres. The extension of compulsory after-care for all prisoners, and improvements in the administration of approved schools, were among the act's other provisions.

CRIMINAL LAW REFORM (1826–9) in Britain, undertaken by Sir Robert Peel as home secretary, who aimed to reduce the existing law to certainty and to remove, where possible, the death penalty. Partly inspired by Bentham's criticism of the law, a campaign in the House of Commons against the frequency of death sentences, albeit often commuted, was conducted by Samuel Romilly and James Mackintosh. By 1823 Peel was converted and a new code was prepared by the legal writer, Anthony Hammond (1758–1838).

Reforms in procedure (1826–7) included rules to be observed by justices regarding bail, a cause of complaint being the length of time which the accused might spend in prison awaiting trial with no redress if acquitted. The right of trial by jury was ensured to those who might be too ignorant to claim it, and a plea of not guilty was to be entered in case of refusal to plead. Punishment for non-capital felonies was defined, so that sentences could run successively if more than one offence was involved. Judges were enabled to punish more heavily for second and subsequent offences and this, together with the greater willingness of juries to convict, over 100 offences being made exempted from the death penalty, gave the law more deterrent effect.

In 1827 the law relating to larceny was reformed and the death penalty retained only for stealing from the person with violence, burglary, house-breaking, and sacrilege, but not for stealing from a shop or warehouse. Another statute (1827) categorized malicious damage to property, so that the death penalty was invoked against attacks on churches, etc.; transportation was the penalty for machine-breaking, and fines and short sentences were prescribed for vandalism of trees, fences, etc. The statute of 1828 dealt with offences against the person and 57 statutes dealing with murder and being an accessory to murder were repealed. In future, non-felonious homicide was not punishable.

Peel's reforms led to further revisions of the legal code in 1841, 1861, 1878–9, and 1916. From 1832 house-breaking, horse and sheep stealing, and coining false money ceased to be capital offences. After 1838 no one was hanged except for murder or attempted murder (up to 1961). Transportation ceased and was replaced in 1841 by penal servitude. In 1837 the pillory was abolished.

L. Radzinowicz, *A History of Criminal Law and its Administration from 1750*, 3 vols (London, 1948–56).   VEC

CRIMINAL ORDINANCE (1670), one of the great French ordinances of Louis XIV's reign, incorporating the last major revision of criminal procedure during the *ancien régime*. The ordinance confirmed the severity of criminal law inherited from the Middle Ages, and particularly of the 'extraordinary procedure', by strengthening the hand of the prosecution. The secrecy of proceedings, the use of torture, and the barbarity of punishments continued, although by the mid-18th cent. their validity was seriously questioned by the writings of Montesquieu, Voltaire, and Beccaria.

CRIPPS MISSION (22 March–12 April 1942), visit to India of Sir Stafford Cripps, a member of the British government, in an attempt to bring Indian political leaders into the war effort. Congress had not participated in the provincial governments after Oct. 1939 and attempts by the viceroy, Lord Linlithgow, to regain their co-operation, notably in Aug. 1940, had failed. Japan's entry into the war and its advance in south-east Asia, which culminated in the fall of Singapore (7 March 1942), forced the British government to make a further attempt to bring Indian nationalist forces to support the war effort. Churchill, the British prime minister, announced (11 March) that the cabinet had agreed on its Indian policy and that Cripps would go out to secure India's acceptance of it. The draft declaration that Cripps took with him promised the concession of full self-government to a new Indian Union, including the provinces and the states, immediately after the war. It provided that an elected constituent assembly would draw up the constitution for the Union, thus conceding one of Congress's major demands, but it also allowed for the non-accession of any province, thus reassuring the Muslim League of the possibility of 'Pakistan'. Cripps discussed the declaration with officials and Indian nationalist leaders and sought the full and effective participation of the latter in the war effort and the government of the day.

Congress, whose acceptance was crucial, rejected it (10 April) on the grounds that only an immediate transfer to a national government with full powers would be sufficient to bring the Indian people wholeheartedly into the war, especially in view of the refusal to give an Indian defence member an effective role in the conduct of the war. It also expressed disquiet about non-accession provisions and states' representation on the constituent assembly. The Muslim League rejection was largely on the grounds that non-accession was not a clear enough recognition of Pakistan. Had Cripps been allowed to negotiate fully, these objections need not have been insuperable but he was not given the power to make any advance on the declaration, although he went as far as possible to meet the Congress on the defence member's responsibility.   PDR

CRIPPS, SIR RICHARD STAFFORD (1889–1952), British lawyer and politician, began his career as a brilliant advocate, specializing in commercial cases. His only public interest at first was in the reunion of the Christian Churches. In 1930 he became solicitor-general in the Labour government and entered parliament in Jan. 1931.

He refused to join the National government in August. 1931, and was among the tiny group of Labour members who survived the ensuing general election. Being a former minister he took his place on the Opposition front bench along with Attlee as the two principal deputies of George Lansbury, the leader of the Labour Party. Cripps moved left with the zeal of a convert. He assisted in the foundation of the Socialist League, of which he became the outstanding figure. In 1935, at the time of the Abyssinian crisis, he opposed sanctions on the grounds that the League of Nations was a capitalist institution. He advocated a Popular Front of the Socialist League, the Independent Labour Party, and the Communist Party. The official Labour Party opposed this, and in 1937 the Socialist League was dissolved. He continued to advocate united action against Fascism, and in 1939 was expelled from the Labour Party for doing so.

During the early days of the Second World War he sought to promote a government of national unity under the leadership of Lord Halifax. In May 1940 Churchill sent him as ambassador to Moscow. He was soon disillusioned with the Soviet Union. When Hitler attacked Russia, he was convinced that Soviet Russia would be defeated within a few weeks. He returned to England early in 1942, resolutely hostile to Soviet policy; the public however still regarded him as a leader of the Left, and as such he was made Leader of the House of Commons, in which post his intolerant rigidity soon made him a failure. His mission to India failed for the same reason and by Oct. 1942 his usefulness was exhausted: he left the war cabinet, but became an efficient minister of aircraft production.

He was an outstanding figure in the post-war Labour government, first as president of the board of trade and then as chancellor of the exchequer. He followed a policy of deflation, economy, and rationing, characterized by critics as 'strength through misery', and his puritanical outlook largely contributed to the ultimate failure of the Labour government. In politics he was always the trained lawyer, switching from one brief to another without thought of consistency. He was first on the extreme Left, then on the extreme Right. His character was 'saintly', and he had all the arrogance which often goes with this.

G. D. H. Cole, *History of the Labour Party from 1914* (London, 1948).
Colin Cooke, *The Life of Richard Stafford Cripps* (London, 1957).   AJPT

CRISPI, FRANCESCO (1819–1901), Italian prime minister (1887–91, 1893–6), whose practical achievements in reforming Italy were overshadowed by his colonial adventures and short-sighted foreign policy. Crispi had sailed with Garibaldi in 1860 and was passionately concerned with the preservation of a united Italy, but he failed to create a party of principle and governed in an arbitrary manner ill-suited to the growth of parliamentary democracy. His foreign policy involved Italy, through the Italo-German military convention (1888), in expensive commitments to Bismarck's system. Crispi initially strengthened Italy's international standing by the

Second Mediterranean Agreement with Britain (1887), but when he returned to office in 1893 the British were unwilling to renew it. His expansionist policy in Africa led to Italy's humiliating defeat at Adowa (1896) and he fomented a tariff war with France which Italy could ill afford. Nevertheless, his popularity was such that it took a major political scandal, the crisis in Africa, and near anarchy in parts of Italy, to unseat him.

CRISTERO **REVOLT**, terrorist movement in Mexico (1927–30), instigated and directed by militant Catholics in response to the anti-clerical policies of the Plutaco Elias Calles regime. The name *cristero* was derived from their battle cry '*Cristo Rey*' (Christ the King). The government overcame the challenge by force, after the bombing of trains and the murder of government officials and rural school teachers. As the movement spread through Jalisco and the west-central states—the principal farming regions—the government intensified its anti-clerical campaign. The clergy responded by withholding mass, but failed to alter the government's attitude.

CRISTOPHE, HENRI (1767–1820), Negro general in the Haitian wars of independence, and King of northern Haiti (*reg.* 1811–20). He was born a slave in Grenada, and joined the Haitian independence movement under the leadership of Toussaint L'Ouverture. Later, he served briefly with the French under Gen. Leclerc, but deserted to the revolutionary armies. He fought with Jean-Jacques Dessalines in the wars of 1803–4, and succeeded him as ruler after his assassination in 1806. Although proclaimed King Henri I, ruler of all Haiti (1811), Cristophe was never able to assert his authority in the mulatto-dominated south, where Pétion resisted his attempts to do so. In his northern kingdom he sought to restore the war-torn agricultural economy by forced labour, and to increase literacy by a rapid increase in educational programmes. His rule was authoritarian, but efficient. The fortress of La Ferrière is considered to be his greatest achievement. Threatened by revolt and partially crippled by a stroke, Cristophe forestalled his enemies by committing suicide with a silver bullet.

CRITCHLOW, HUBERT N. (1884–1958), West Indian trade union pioneer who organized a strike in 1905 which temporarily paralysed the industrial life of British Guiana. He formed the first trade union in the Caribbean (1919), the British Guiana Labour Union, and was prominent in the establishment of the British Guiana and West Indies Labour Congress (1926). Thereafter Critchlow was a leading figure in labour politics in the Caribbean for 30 years.

CRITIAS (*c.* 460–403 BC), anti-democratic Athenian politician associated with Socrates. He was prominent in establishing the oligarchic 'Thirty Tyrants' and eliminated the moderate Theramenes (403), but perished in the democratic restoration.

CRITICAL PERIOD, THE, term applied to the period of US history when the Articles of Confederation were in effect (1781–9). John Fiske, in *The Critical Period of American History* (1888), argued that during these years the Union was disintegrating and implied that the principal reason was the weakness of the central government. More recent historians have considered that the period was generally one of recovery from war and expansion, being critical only in that major decisions were taken about the course of US development. Barriers hindering inter-state trade were being lowered by the states, several of which, since Congress lacked the funds, were assuming responsibility for retiring the Revolutionary War debt. By 1787 the economy was recovering from the post-war slump. The greatest triumphs of the Critical Period were the Land Ordinance (1785) and North-west Ordinance (1787), which established the basis for western development. Difficulties remained, however. Congress depended on erratic state appropriations, US prestige abroad was low, and British troops remained in the US 'north-west forts' in defiance of the peace treaty. The demands of a small group of nationalists, notably Alexander Hamilton, Robert Morris, and James Madison, for a stronger central government attracted wider support, especially after Shays' Rebellion (1786). The Mount Vernon Conference (1785) and Annapolis Convention (1786) led to the Philadelphia Convention (1787), which, instead of amending the Articles of Confederation, drafted a new constitution that came into operation in 1789.

CRITTENDEN COMPROMISE (1860–1), an eleventh-hour attempt, initiated by Senator John J. Crittenden, of Kentucky, to heal the breach between North and South in the US. Crittenden proposed a series of constitutional amendments to define and protect the position of slavery in the US. They provided for the re-establishment of the 36° 30′ Missouri Compromise line in the territories, with protection of slavery south of the line, and no interference with slavery where it already existed. The proposals were eventually rejected, largely through the opposition of the Republicans, including the president-elect, Abraham Lincoln, who feared that the South would attempt to acquire further slave territory in Mexico or the Caribbean, south of the compromise line.

CROATIA, area of 56,540 sq. kms with a population of 4,148,222 (1961) which, since 1946, has been politically organized as one of six republics of Federal Yugoslavia with Zagreb as its capital.

Croatia's history differs considerably from Serbia's: her early adoption (10th cent.) of Roman Catholicism and the Latin alphabet led to her dependence upon Catholic countries, especially Austria and Hungary, for survival during the Turkish invasions, and to her sharing their assumptions of superiority over eastern peoples. Although Croatia increasingly resented domination by Hungary (which began in 1102) and shared in the general growth of national consciousness of the 19th cent. (rebelling against Hungarian rule in 1848, and increasingly discontented after the compromise of 1868), before 1914 she did not envisage union with independent Serbia, which she still regarded as inferior. The war revolutionized the situation, so that in July 1917 Croatian and Serbian representatives signed the Pact of Corfu, which proclaimed the future Serbo-Croat-Slovene kingdom, founded in Oct. 1918. Neither country was prepared for the sacrifices entailed by union. The Serbians treated Croatia as part of Greater Serbia, ignoring the promised federal constitution, and thus converting Croatian feelings into open hostility.

The instability of Stephen Radic, the Croatian peasant leader, gave the Serbians an excuse to bypass Croatian demands, and after he was assassinated (June 1928) a royal dictatorship, from which the Croatians believed they would benefit, averted a crisis. But nothing was done, and, in Oct. 1934, a Croatian terrorist assassinated the king.

Despite Croatian dissatisfaction, a common Yugoslav fear of Italy preserved the kingdom. Macek (Radic's successor) strove to reach agreement with Paul, the prince regent, which was finally signed in Aug. 1939: under it Macek became deputy prime minister and a degree of federalism was promised. But for most Croatians it lacked validity, being merely a personal document between the two men and unrepresentative of the predominantly Serbian government's intentions.

War aroused extremism, for when the Germans invaded (April 1941) some Croatian troops turned against Serbians rather than Germans. A Fascist puppet state—Greater Croatia—was established under Pavelic, the former terrorist (Ustase) leader, who embarked upon a campaign of ruthless extermination of Serbians. However, the Croatian communist leader Josip Broz (Tito), who had built up a force originally composed mainly of Croats and Slovenes, pledged in Nov. 1943 that post-war Yugoslavia would be a genuinely federal state: now recruitment increased—Croatians and Serbians joining to make it a unified and effective liberation force.

Post-war Croatia never showed the same hostility to the Serbs and Croatian separatism became unthinkable; but some grievances remained. The Roman Catholic Church's hostility to the new regime, which abated somewhat after 1960, largely represented Croatian feelings (although Slovenes are Catholics too), while Zagreb complained that she had to make a disproportionate economic sacrifice in subsidizing the poorer regions of Yugoslavia.   MN

CROCE, BENEDETTO (1866–1954), Italian philosopher, historian, art theorist, and critic, who explicated the theories of Hegel, Marx, Sorel, Vico, etc. He championed the lay culture of south Italy and was a dominating influence on widely differing intellectuals in modern Italy. As Giolitti's education minister (1920–1), and as a senator, he welcomed the fascist movement, whose power he underestimated, for making Italians politically conscious. He despised its vulgarity and materialism rather than its violent authoritarianism, and used his review, *La Critica*, for veiled intellectual anti-fascism.

CROCKETT, DAVID (1786–1836), US frontiersman and picturesque politician from Tennessee. He served as a scout under Andrew Jackson in the Creek War (1813–14) and was elected to his state legislature (1821, 1823). He was twice a congressman (1827–31, 1833–5), but lost a bid for re-election, joined the Texas revolutionaries, and was killed at the Alamo.

CROESUS (*reg. c.* 560–*c.* 547 BC), last King of Lydia, who was deposed and perhaps killed by Cyrus II of Persia in *c.* 547 BC. He introduced coins in gold and silver alloy, of new sizes and design, which were copied by the Greeks and Persians.

CROGHAN, GEORGE M. (d. 1782), American frontiersman, born in Ireland. Croghan migrated to the American frontier (1741), where he learned several Indian languages and established trading posts in the Ohio river valley. He served as an Indian agent and a soldier during the French and Indian War (1754–63) and opened the Illinois country for British traders (1764). Croghan acquired vast land holdings in NY and PA. He was accused falsely of being a loyalist during the American War of Independence, his lands were confiscated, and he died in poverty.

CROISSY, CHARLES COLBERT, Marquis de (1625–96), French diplomat, secretary of state and foreign minister under Louis XIV and the brother of J. B. Colbert. Though often obstinate and opinionated and with a narrowly legalistic mind, he none the less served Louis conscientiously.

CROIX DE FEU, largest of the French right-wing 'leagues' in the 1930s. Founded in 1928 as an ex-servicemen's organization, the *Croix de Feu* developed as a political movement under the leadership of Col. De La Rocque, and grew rapidly after its participation in the demonstrations of 6 Feb. 1934. It was dissolved by the government in 1936, but reorganized as a political party, the *Parti social français*. Though it had over 2,000,000 adherents, it had no chance to display its strength in an election. Some of its members joined the Resistance in the Second World War.

CROKER, JAMES WILSON (1780–1857), British politician and writer, famous for his severity as a reviewer. As an associate of Arthur Wellesley, he became MP (1807) and secretary for the admiralty (1810–30), where he resisted the pressures of the future William IV as lord high admiral, and encouraged science and exploration. He opposed the Reform Act of 1832 and refused a seat in the reformed house, but remained a close associate of Peel until the repeal of the Corn Laws (1832–46). Croker was the editor and chief political writer of the *Quarterly Review* (1831–54), edited Boswell's *Life of Johnson* (1831) and Lord Hervey's memoirs (1848).

His *Correspondence and Diaries* (1884) are an important source of information for his time.

CROKER, RICHARD (1841–1922), Irish-born US political boss. He succeeded 'Honest John' Kelly as leader of the Tammany Hall organization in New York City established by Tweed (1886). Findings by the Lexow Commission (1894) of corruption in city government hastened his retirement from politics (1902).

CROLY, HERBERT DAVID (1869–1930), US author, editor, and political philosopher, who became prominent after publication of *The Promise of American Life* (1909). His advocacy of the determined use of governmental authority to achieve social goals is generally believed to have given an impetus to the Progressive movement and to have strongly influenced the character of Theodore Roosevelt's New Nationalism. In 1914 Croly founded the liberal weekly periodical *New Republic*. It was erroneously believed to reflect the ideas of Woodrow Wilson, and was very influential during the years up to 1919, when denunciation of the Versailles treaty terms as a 'punic peace of annihilation' halved its circulation. Croly demanded in his *Progressive Democracy* (1914) that democratic institutions should be constantly revised to meet changing conditions.

CROMER, EVELYN BARING, 1st Earl of (1841–1917), British consul-general in Egypt (1883–1907). After military and Indian service, Baring acquired experience of Egyptian finances as British member of the Caisse de la Dette (1877–1880). As consul-general he established an autocratic governmental system, gradually extending the practice of control by British advisers over Egyptian ministers and making no concessions to Egyptian nationalism. He had considerable success in reducing the burden of debt and taxation in Egypt, but failed to provide any real solution to the main economic and political problems, preferring to hold down the level of public investment. His period of office also saw the conquest of the Sudan (1898).

CROMPTON, SAMUEL (1753–1827), British inventor, whose 'spinning-mule' (1779) combined the principles of Arkwright's and Hargreaves's machines. Its distinctive feature, the spindle-carriage, produced yarn suitable for the manufacture of fine muslins, previously chiefly imported from India.

CROMWELL, OLIVER (1599–1658), parliamentary general in the English Civil War and lord protector of England, Scotland, and Ireland (1653–8). He first became prominent in national politics in the early months of the Long Parliament. In 1642 he served on parliamentary military committees, and his prompt action secured Cambridgeshire for parliament. The Civil War revealed Cromwell's military genius. He fought at Edgehill in 1642, where he learned the importance of cavalry. In the next two years he served in the army of the Eastern Association, becoming second in command to the Earl of Manchester in 1644, and created his own regiment of horse, the Ironsides. He also was a member of the Committee of Both Kingdoms, the body responsible for the direction of the war after parliament's alliance with the Scots in 1643. At Marston Moor, Cromwell's cavalry was decisive in parliament's victory. However, he became angered that Manchester's 'backwardness' was nullifying such victories. The result of Cromwell's charge in the Commons against his superior officer was the establishment of the New Model Army, of which Cromwell was eventually appointed second in command.

The end of the first Civil War saw the return of Cromwell to active politics. He was prepared to come to an understanding with Charles I, provided the army was fairly treated and liberty to tender consciences was guaranteed. He was opposed by the Presbyterians in the Commons, and he threw in his lot with the army. With Ireton, he drew up the Heads of the Proposals (July 1647) to be offered to the king. While Charles intrigued with the army and parliament, the Levellers bid for control of the army and a wider suffrage in politics. Cromwell and Ireton, searching for unity and compromise, debated with the army agitators at Putney (Oct.–Nov. 1647). Their failure led to the suppression of two mutinous regiments by Cromwell.

Charles I's Engagement with the Scots (Dec. 1647), which precipitated the second Civil War, turned Cromwell against the king. He put down a rising in Pembrokeshire and then destroyed the Scottish army at Preston and Warrington (17–19 Aug. 1648). While supervising the siege of Pontefract (Nov.) he became convinced of the necessity of Charles's trial and execution. In the succeeding Commonwealth Cromwell was chosen as first chairman of the council of state.

In mid 1649 he was appointed lord lieutenant of Ireland, with the task of suppressing the rebellion, in which he partially succeeded with the capture of Drogheda and Wexford. In May 1650 he was recalled to England to command, as captain-general, the army intended for a march to Scotland. At the battles of Dunbar (3 Sept. 1650) and Worcester (3 Sept. 1651) he destroyed Charles II's immediate hopes of recovering his throne. Cromwell became dissatisfied with the government of the Rump, which he came to view as a self-perpetuating oligarchy antagonistic to the army. He expelled it (20 April 1653), and after experimenting with a nominated assembly (Barebone's Parliament), he accepted the Protectorate established by the Instrument of Government (16 Dec. 1653) drawn up by the army's leaders. As lord protector Cromwell pursued a very active foreign policy, capturing Jamaica, and winning victories at sea and in Flanders against Spain (1655–8) which established England's prestige abroad. At home Cromwell was mainly unsuccessful. He did achieve a measure of toleration in religion, but failed to establish his rule upon consent rather than force. The experiment of government through 11 major-generals (1655–1657) reveals the protector's ultimate dependence on force, though he reverted to a civil and more traditional form of government in 1657. The culmination of this was the offer of the Crown to Cromwell by his second parliament. After much hesitation and pressure from the army, he refused the offer (May 1657), but accepted the amended Humble Petition and Advice, which established a quasimonarchical government. Though Cromwell was forced to dissolve his second parliament because of the factious opposition of republicans (4 Feb. 1658), the last few months of his rule saw the Protectorate established on a broader basis. He had striven earnestly for the welfare of the Commonwealth; his death made its collapse certain.

C. H. Firth, *Oliver Cromwell and the Rule of the Puritans in England* (London, 1900).
Austin Woolrych, *Oliver Cromwell* (London, 1964).   CJ

CROMWELL, RICHARD (1626–1712), son of Oliver Cromwell and lord protector of England (3 Sept. 1658–25 May 1659). Nominated by his father as his successor, he proved unable to control the army, which rebelled and forced him to dissolve his parliament, which was hostile to the army (22 April 1659). Placed in an untenable position, he resigned to the restored Rump, and passed into private life and exile (1660–80).

CROP ROTATION. In medieval conditions of agriculture land could seldom be cultivated continuously, because as a rule it could not be adequately fertilized. Hence the growing of crops had to be interrupted by periods when it lay fallow. In the Mediterranean countries the need for accumulating sufficient moisture in the soil provided an additional reason for leaving land fallow every few years, except where continuous irrigation was possible. In Europe north of the Alps the two-field system was the rule in the early Middle Ages, with half the arable land being under crops each year, while the other half lay fallow. It was also known that if different types of crops are grown in succession it is possible to cultivate a piece of land for at least two successive years, followed by a year when it lies fallow, but for various practical reasons such three-course rotation was at first seldom practised. The earliest evidence of it comes from northern France *c.* 800, but it did not become widely applied in northern Europe until the 13th cent., producing then a three-field system. Under this one part of the arable land would each year be under crops sown in the autumn, a second part would be cultivated with crops sown in the spring, while the remainder would lie fallow. More elaborate types of rotation using special plants that actually enriched the soil (*eg,* plants contributing nitrogen compounds) were used in some places in the later Middle Ages, especially in some parts of the Netherlands, but did not become common until the 17th and 18th cents.

CROPREDY BRIDGE, BATTLE OF (6 June 1645), royalist victory in the English Civil War when Charles I checked the Roundheads under Sir William Waller, whose army thereupon mutinied.

CROQUANTS, peasant rebels whose sufferings in the devastation produced by the French civil wars and the crushing taxes levied by the Church, Crown, and feudal lords, led to their revolt (1594–5) and suppression in battle by a league of nobles (1595). The *croquant* movement was only one of several unsuccessful peasant outbursts under the *ancien régime.*

CROSBY, BRASS (1725–93), British MP (1768–74) and lord mayor of London (1770). The Commons sent him to the Tower for releasing from custody a printer who had refused their summons to attend at the bar.

CROSBY, JAMES (1806–80), immigration agent-general for British Guiana (1858–80). Crosby advocated the rights of Indian immigrants to proper working conditions and adequate protection from the law. He aroused enmity among plantation owners and his work was restricted by the colonial governor, Sir Francis Hinks.

CROSLAND, CHARLES ANTHONY RAVEN (1918–), British Labour politician. After service in the Second World War, and being a lecturer in economics at Oxford, he was elected to parliament (1950), but lost the seat in 1955. In the Labour governments of 1964–70 he was associated with the development of economic policy, as minister of state for economic affairs (1964–5), president of the board of trade (1967–9), and secretary of state for government and regional planning (1969–70). He was also secretary of state for education and science (1965–7).

CROSS OF BROUGHTON-IN-FURNESS, RICHARD ASSHETON CROSS, 1st Viscount (1823–1914), British Tory politician, who was home secretary (1874–80). His measures for trade union reform, slum clearance, and factory regulation were among the notable achievements of Disraeli's second ministry. He gave substance to ideas of 'Tory Democracy' while at the same time representing in his own person the increasing alignment of the mid-Victorian provincial middle class behind the Tory Party.

'CROSS OF GOLD' SPEECH (1896), US political speech by William Jennings Bryan at the Democratic Party presidential nominating convention. His emotional appeal, 'You shall not press down upon the brow of labor this crown of thorns, you shall not crucify mankind upon a cross of gold' was attractive to many elements within the party, including eastern working men and western advocates of free coinage of silver, and won him the nomination.

CROSSMAN, RICHARD HOWARD STAFFORD (1907–), British politician and journalist. After being a tutor of New College, Oxford (1930–7), he was assistant editor of the *New Statesman* (1938–55). During the Second World War he was an assistant director of psychological warfare. Elected Labour MP for Coventry East in 1945, he joined the parliamentary left, being critical of the government's foreign policy. With Michael Foot and Ian Mikardo he produced the pamphlet 'Keep Left' (1947), a plea for a more radical socialist policy. As a member of the Anglo-American Commission on Palestine he was a supporter of the Zionist case. While Labour was in opposition he took up a more central position within the party. He was minister of housing and local government (1964–6), leader of the House of Commons (1966–8), and secretary of state for social services from 1968 until the Conservative victory in the general election (1970), when he assumed the editorship of the *New Statesman.*

CROSS-STAFF, nautical instrument invented in the 16th cent. to measure latitude in relation to the altitude of the stars. It replaced the astrolabe and was itself improved by the back-staff.

CROSTHWAITE, SIR CHARLES (1835–1915), chief commissioner of British Burma (1887–90) and lieutenant-governor of North-Western Province and Oudh (1892–5). He was the author of *The Pacification of Burma* (1912).

CROTON, Greek city in southern Italy, founded *c.* 710 BC by Achaeans from the Peloponnese. It was at its most prosperous *c.* 500, after destroying Sybaris (*c.* 510), and was the adoptive home of the Samian Pythagoras (*c.* 530) and was famous for its doctors and athletes.

CROW INDIANS, an American Siouan tribe which broke from the parent Hidatsa group residing on the Missouri river and migrated to the Rocky Mountains, where they lived a nomadic and war-like existence until they became confined to reservations. They also acted as middlemen in trade between various Indian groups. Lewis and Clark found them on the Bighorn river (1804) and other expeditions found them in Wyoming and Montana. The Crow accepted reservations lands in south-eastern Montana (1868), where they still live.

CROWN COLONY SYSTEM, in the British empire, a pattern of colonial rule adopted in the early 19th cent. by which power was concentrated in the hands of a governor and an executive council. Later, legislative councils were added to assist the governor in making laws, though he could still veto laws which were against colonial office policy. The system was developed with the encouragement of Lord Liverpool after the Napoleonic Wars. It solved the problem of newly acquired territories where the representative system of government adopted in the first empire would have resulted in a non-British majority or one opposed to the philanthropic and other policies of the British government, *eg,* in the Cape or in the former French possession of Trinidad, where slavery flourished. After 1880 the new legislative councils in India and Africa led to progress towards self-government and the crown colony system declined. Its major limitation was its failure to gain popular support, and in the 20th cent. its paternalism was subject to increasing criticism from those who sought greater popular participation in government, particularly the native populations. In the years after the Second World War the crown colony system was mostly superseded by the development of independent states out of Britain's former colonies.

CROWN POINT, promontory on the west shore of Lake Champlain, US. Forts were erected there by New York colonists (1690), the French (1730), and the British (1760). Crown Point was captured by Vermont militia (1775) in the American War of Independence.

CROWTHER, SAMUEL AJAYI, bishop (*c.* 1806–91), Yoruba slave who became a pioneer missionary in Nigeria. He was sold to the Portuguese (1821), but was recaptured by a British anti-slave trade squadron off Lagos and taken to Freetown, where he was educated.

He accompanied the 1841 expedition through which British commercial and missionary influence sought to penetrate the interior of Nigeria. When that failed, Crowther and others encouraged freed Yoruba slaves from Freetown to return to the Yoruba country, whence missionaries followed them. Crowther was ordained in 1843, and with Townsend and Gollmer established the Anglican Mission at Badagri, south-western Nigeria, a few months after Freeman established the Methodist mission there. They were followed by Scottish Presbyterians at Calabar and American Baptists, who came to Yoruba country in 1851. Crowther played an important part in establishing Christianity in Yoruba country, the building of schools, and working out a written form of the Yoruba language, into which he translated the Bible and other works.

He accompanied Niger expeditions (1854, 1857) and from then on led an all-African team of missionaries that established Anglican Missions at Aboh and Onitsha among the Igbo, at Lokoja, and Egga among the Igalla and riverain Nupe, and at Brass, Bonny, and Kalabri among the Niger Delta peoples. He had little evangelical success at Lokoja or Egga, but helped to open the Niger to European trade. His best mission fields were at Onitsha, Bonny, and Brass.

Meanwhile, from 1875 onwards, Sir George Goldie began to unite all British firms on the Niger, bought off the French, hounded the African traders from the river, and eventually secured a charter from the British government, giving him political power to protect his economic monopoly. Goldie saw in the African leadership of Crowther a threat to the new white Colonial rule he was creating. This troubled the last years of Crowther's life, but could not obscure his achievements as a religious leader.

J. F. Ade Ajayi, *Christian Missions in Nigeria*, 1841–91 (London, 1965).   JFAA

CROY, GUILLAUME DE, Sieur de Chievres (1458–1521), imperial statesman and French-speaking nobleman from Hainault in the Burgundian Netherlands, who became the protagonist of peace between France and the Habsburgs as the best solution for Burgundian prosperity and of the emperor's multiple problems. He wanted to confine relations with England to matters of commerce rather than to rely on a political alliance with France's traditional enemy. In this way he hoped to retain the European status quo. As head of the *conseil privé* in the Burgundian lands, Croy governed the Netherlands for both Philip the Fair and his son Charles, becoming their confidential adviser. In 1501 he negotiated the treaty of Lyons with Louis XII and arranged for Philip to cross through France to Spain, a journey which involved his triumphal entry into Paris. During Charles's minority (1506–15) Croy, as first chamberlain, was in a position to influence the boy ruler. He led the opposition to the anti-French lobby of Margaret of Austria and accepted a balance of power in Italy by confirming French control of Milan, conquered by French arms at Marignano (1515). After Croy's death imperial policy altered under the influence of Gattinara.

CROZAT, ANTOINE, MARQUIS DU CHATEL (1685–1738), French financier, who was successively receiver-general of the clergy and treasurer of the Estates of Languedoc. On 14 Sept. 1712 Louis XIV granted him monopoly of trade and government in Louisiana for 15 years, and Crozat can be regarded as the founder of the colony. After spending 1,250,000 livres, but achieving disappointing profits, he returned the colony to the Crown (1717), and the grant was transferred to John Law's Compagnie de l'Occident (1718). Crozat's daughter, Anne-Marie, was a famous wit, and his son, Joseph-Antoine, devoted his life and fortune to the arts.

CRUIKSHANK, GEORGE (1792–1878), English caricaturist, who reached the peak of his powers in the 1830s and who illustrated works by Dickens, Harrison Ainsworth, and others. He gained great notoriety with his series of temperance cartoons, *The Bottle* (1847) and *The Drunkard's Children* (1848), which diverted him—much to Ruskin's disgust—into producing many temperance drawings in later life.

CRUSADE, CHILDREN'S (1212), a wave of religious hysteria in north-eastern France, the Netherlands, and the Rhineland (1211–12) which caused large numbers of children to gather and march across Europe under obscure leaders, with the expressed aim of liberating the Holy Land. Several thousand travelled in three groups to Marseilles and into Italy, where they appear to have dispersed. Many died on the way and it was later reported that European merchants had sold many others into slavery in Egypt and Algeria.

CRUSADE, THE FIRST (1095–9). The immediate causes of the first crusade were the capture of Jerusalem by Malek Shah and rising Seljuk power. The Eastern emperor, Alexius, appealed frequently to the pope for his help in obtaining Western recruits for his armies to resist the threat of Turkish conquest. Pope Urban II's appeal for a crusade at the council of Clermont (1095) met with an immediate response. Several spontaneous popular movements, the People's Crusade, preceded the official crusade, but ended in disaster. Four distinct feudal armies under mainly Norman and French leaders took part in the organized campaign. The main aim of the participants, apart from their religious motives, was the acquisition of land. The crusaders' defeats of the Turks in Asia Minor enabled the Byzantines to reconquer areas lost there. After the march across Asia Minor, Baldwin of Boulogne left the main army and took the county of Edessa, the first Latin state in the East. Antioch was besieged and after its fall (1098) Bohemond of Taranto, appointed commander-in-chief for the battle against a relieving army, became its prince. In July 1099 Jerusalem was captured and became the centre of the third Latin state under Godfrey of Bouillon, Duke of Lower Lorraine. The crusade ended with the destruction of an Egyptian army, whose aim had been to recover Jerusalem, at Ascalon (Aug. 1099).

CRUSADE, THE SECOND (1147–9). In 1144 the Latin county of Edessa fell to Zengi, ruler of Mosul. This led to the preaching of a new crusade. French and German expeditions under Louis VII and Conrad III respectively took part, but both were severely mauled by the Turks in Asia Minor after trouble with the unco-operative Byzantines, and a joint attack on Damascus, a state friendly to the Latins, was abandoned after a four-day siege. This tarnished the lustre of the crusading movement and discouraged western Europeans from sending further help to the Latin states in Syria and Palestine.

CRUSADE, THE THIRD (1189–92) proclaimed by Gregory VIII (1187) after the capture of Jerusalem by Saladin. The Emperor Frederick Barbarossa took the cross (1188), but died while crossing Asia Minor (1190), and only a small part of his force reached the Holy Land. The main armies, under King Richard I of England and Philip Augustus of France, arrived in 1191 and the crusade centred on the reduction of Acre, which had been under siege by King Guy of Jerusalem since 1189. Both kings soon became anxious to return home. The early departure of Philip and the machinations of Prince John, Richard's younger brother, made Richard's return to England urgent. After the fall of Acre (July 1191) and the crusaders' victory at Arsuf (Sept. 1191), negotiations with Saladin began. Thus the crusaders won brilliant victories but lost the war, retaining, by a treaty of 1192, only the coastal cities as far as Jaffa and a right of access for pilgrims to the Holy Places.

CRUSADE, THE FOURTH (1202–4). The accession of Pope Innocent III produced a new crusading movement. A mixed force under Boniface of Montferrat assembled and arrangements were made for Venetian ships to transport them to Egypt. As they were unable to pay the costs, they agreed to help the Venetians, under Doge Enrico Dandolo, to capture Zara, a Hungarian town in Dalmatia. After its capture, under the influence of the anti-Byzantine doge and Montferrat, the crusade was diverted to Constantinople to restore the deposed Emperor Isaac Angelus, whose son Alexius fled to the West (1201) to seek help. He promised men and money for a later attack on Egypt and the submission of the Greek Church to Rome. It is impossible to say whether the diversion was planned from the beginning. Alexius and his father were restored, but were unpopular and were overthrown by their Byzantine enemies. The crusaders then took and devastated Constantinople (Feb. 1204), setting up a Latin emperor, Baldwin of Flanders, and a Latin patriarch. The Venetians acquired important possessions and rights in the city, Greece, and the Aegean and there was a distribution of fiefs among the crusaders. The crusade ruined the Eastern empire and made the schism between the Churches unbridgeable. The new Latin empire of Romania lasted until 1261.

CRUZ, OSWALDO (1872–1917), a Brazilian physician, whose efforts resulted in the elimination of yellow fever in Rio de Janeiro (1903–9).

CRUZADA, direct contribution levied on the Spanish laity as a crusade subsidy, granted by the pope to Isabella and Ferdinand for the war on the Moorish province of Granada. It continued to provide revenue for the Spanish Crown even after the conquest (1491), and by Charles V's reign was regarded as a permanent and regular source. It was renewed by the papacy at intervals throughout the 16th cent.

CTESIPHON, Parthian city, near modern Baghdad, originally built by Mithridates 1 (171–138 BC) as a military camp, facing Seleucia on the Tigris. It became the capital of the Parthian and later Sasanian empires of Iran. The ruins include a great Sasanian hall which has the widest singlespan vault of unreinforced brickwork in the world.

CUARTELAZO, military *coup d'état,* theoretically of barrack origin. The term is derived from the Spanish *cuartel* (barracks), and is in common use as a political term in Latin America.

CUAUHTÉMOC (*c.* 1495–1525), also known as Guatemotzín, the last Aztec king and defender of Tenochtitlán during its siege and destruction by the Spaniards (1521). He was the nephew and son-in-law of Moctezuma II and inherited his position after the death of Cuitlahuac, Moctezuma's successor. Cuauhtémoc attempted to escape from Tenochtitlán, but was captured and held as a hostage by Cortés for four years, then executed. Cuauhtémoc tends to be seen today as a defender of Mexico against the foreign invader.

CUBAN REVOLUTION, movement led by the Cuban revolutionaries Fidel Castro, his brother Raúl, and the Argentinian Ernesto 'Ché' Guevara. They came to power by overthrowing the regime of President Batista, and establishing a government of communistic tendencies in Cuba.

While in exile in Mexico Castro organized his movement and named it the '26th of July Movement', so called because of an unsuccessful attack on a Cuban army barracks on that date. The revolutionaries sailed from Mexico to Cuba aboard the yacht *Granma,* and encountered heavy attacks from Batista's army. The leaders began a guerrilla war in the mountains of the Sierra Maestra in Oriente Province, and gradually increased their numbers and popular support.

In 1958, after three years of fighting, the Batista regime collapsed and Castro assumed power (1 Jan. 1959), amid manifestations of popular enthusiasm.

Cuba then underwent a rapid political, social, and economic revolution towards communism. Foreign sugar holdings were expropriated, most of the island's major businesses soon passed into government hands, and farms were collectivized. At first the Castro government sought to lessen Cuba's dependence on the foreign exchange earned by sugar, and proposed rapid diversification of the economy, but after an alarming slump the government was forced to return to the old policy of emphasizing sugar production. Attempts were made to increase literacy, improve rural housing, and extend health services throughout the countryside. Relations between Cuba and the US steadily worsened, while Cuban ties with the USSR and China increased.

In 1961 Cuba began to import large quantities of arms from the Soviet Union. When the US government became aware the following year that these arms included missiles capable of reaching major population centres in North and South America, it demanded that the Soviet Union remove them. After a tense period of waiting the Soviet prime minister, Nikita Khruschev, agreed to do so. At the same time he repeated his promise to defend Cuba against attack.

By 1966 the Cuban economy had achieved the planning and organizational apparatus of a communist state, but Castro, through his mass popularity, especially with the young, had gained a decision-making position which defied control by either the apparatus or foreign powers. Though the numerous exiles in Miami and elsewhere continued to hope that the Castro regime would be overthrown, it appeared to be stronger than ever by the tenth anniversary of the revolution.   HDS

CÚCUTA, CONGRESS OF (1821), constituent assembly representing Venezuela and New Granada, summoned by Simón Bolívar to meet at Cúcuta, near the border of the two countries. The peoples of the two areas were inadequately represented, partly through their own apathy and partly because of the creoles' determination to exclude mixed elements from the management of affairs. In addition, members of the congress were partly independent of Bolívar's control. The congress appropriated to itself the title of 'Majesty' and, while Bolívar was engaged in military campaigns, produced a constitution (1821) for Gran Colombia. Bolívar was dissatisfied with its terms, especially with the provisions for an executive and the fact that the upper house was not to be hereditary. He accepted the congress's offer of the presidency, however, and acknowledged the legality of the constitution. After the congress Bolívar returned to the army to lead the struggle against the Spanish forces and Francisco de Paula Santander accepted the vice-presidency and political control of Gran Colombia. The Venezuelans were basically opposed to the Bolivarian union approved at Cúcuta and to government from Bogotá, as provided by the congress.

CUGNOT, NICHOLAS JOSEPH (1728–1804), French military engineer and pioneer of steam traction, who invented a steam-propelled gun carriage, the prototype of which carried four passengers at several miles per hour in 1770, 11 years before George Stephenson was born.

CUIUS REGIO, EIUS RELIGIO, theory that states should determine the religion of all their inhabitants, was supported not only by rulers for their own purposes, but also by religious groups looking for a prince to adopt or tolerate their views. It was accepted to a limited degree at the peace of Augsburg (1555), which allowed rulers to be Catholic or Lutheran, but not Zwinglian or Calvinist, and was a fundamental principle of the peace of Westphalia (1648).

CULLODEN, BATTLE OF (1746), the last battle to take place on British soil, four miles east of Inverness. 5000 Jacobites, mainly from the Highland clans, and commanded by Prince Charles Edward Stuart, the Young Pretender, and Lord George Murray, met a government force of 9000 commanded by William Augustus, Duke of Cumberland. Rival Highland clans also fought each other, Campbells fighting alongside the government forces, while their ancient enemies, the MacDonalds, Camerons, and Stewarts, fought for the Jacobites.

The Jacobite forces, tired and dispirited after an abortive night attack, fighting on a battlefield that favoured the government forces, and suffering heavy casualties from Cumberland's artillery, were completely destroyed, while the Hanoverian army suffered slight loss. The remains of the Jacobite army dispersed into the Highlands, bringing the Rebellion of 1745 to an end. Indeed, Culloden ended the Jacobite menace for all time. The '45 Rebellion had proved that loyalty to the Hanoverians was deeply rooted, while in Scotland only some of the Highland clans were staunchly Jacobite.

After the battle, Cumberland's army carried out the task of subjugating the Highlands and ending all Jacobite inclinations. In a campaign of terror which earned Cumberland the nickname 'Butcher', the Highlands paid for their loyalty to the Stuarts. Culloden completely changed the way of life of the Highland clans. By two statutes of 1747 the chiefs' jurisdiction was abolished and money rents were substituted for military service. The clan was no longer a family with the chief as the father; rather the relationship became one of landlord–tenant.

CULPEPPER'S REBELLION (1677–9), an early American uprising. John Culpepper led North Carolina settlers in an attempt to overthrow the rule of the colony's Proprietors. Culpepper, though chosen as governor, was removed by the Proprietors, but never punished.

CULTURAL REVOLUTION, major political movement in China, launched in 1966. The Great Proletarian Cultural Revolution, which involved a degree of upheaval and confusion unprecedented even by the Great Leap Forward, was launched in 1966 as an attack on all forms of bureaucracy and privilege in China. Those under attack constituted practically the whole of China's managerial, party, and educational elite; the army stood on one side during the early stages of the revolution. Mao Tse-tung assumed direct leadership of the Revolution, aided by his 'close-comrade in arms', Lin Piao, and by his wife, Chiang Ch'ing. Since the party was under attack, and found difficulty in fulfilling its usual leadership role in a political movement, Mao was forced to turn elsewhere for his shock troops, and found them in the Red Guards, a very loose organization of China's youth. Mao's aim was to restore China's lost revolutionary purity, and to abolish the new class of privileged people associated with the party. In this he may have been partly successful; the party was purged from top to bottom, most of China's ruling elite, including the president of China, Liu Shao-ch'i, were removed from office, and thousands of old practices swept away. But all this was done at the cost of great disruption; all educational institutions were closed, communications dislocated for long periods, and urban areas in particular subjected to frequent eruptions of strife. Finally, in 1968 the army, which had remained on the sidelines, stepped in to restore order, putting China under much tighter military control than Mao can have desired. Chou En-lai, one of the few top leaders to survive the revolution, was apparently successful in preventing too much interference with China's industrial sector.   DCML

CULTURE SYSTEM, Dutch colonial policy in Java from 1830 to the late 19th century. The *Culture-stelsel* (cultivation system) was a system of forced agricultural deliveries levied on the indigenous population instead of land-rent, the produce being sold by the government at a profit. The system, directed by the Dutch governor-general, used the traditional tax-collecting administration staffed by indigenous officials.

CUMAE, oldest Greek city in Italy, founded on the Campanian coast by Chalcidians and others from Ischia (*c.* 750 BC) and an important intermediary between the East, Greece, and Etruria. In return for metals, especially tin, the Cumaeans introduced Greek orientalized pots and eastern metalwork, which profoundly influenced Etruscan art, and the Euboean version of the Phoenician alphabet, later adopted for Latin. In the 6th cent. under Aristodemus (*c.* 524–492) Cumae resisted Etruscan attacks by land and later (474), with Syracusan aid, won a great naval victory. The city, subsequently conquered by the Sabelli (*c.* 425), came under Roman control in the 4th cent. Although eclipsed later by Puteoli, Cumae remained famous for her Sibyl, whose oracular cave still exists.

CUMAE, BATTLE OF (474 BC), naval victory in which the Cumaeans, supported by Hieron of Syracuse, defeated the Etruscans and temporarily restored Greek control of the Etruscan seas.

CUMAN (KIPCHAK), name of a Turkish people established on the Volga (c. 1030). In 1228–38 the Kipchaks offered a stubborn resistance to the Mongols. Thereafter, remnants of this people settled in the Hungarian and Balkan lands. The last dynasties of medieval Bulgaria were of Cuman descent. Kipchak Turks also constituted the main element amongst the Mamluks of Syria and Egypt during the 13th and 14th cents.

CUMBERLAND, WILLIAM AUGUSTUS, Duke of (1721–65), British general and commander-in-chief (1745–57), the second son of George II. He was created duke in 1726. He fought alongside his father at Dettingen (1743), where he was wounded, and commanded the British forces that opposed the Jacobite Rebellion (1745). His brutal subjugation of the Highlands, after crushing the Jacobites at Culloden (1746), earned him the name of 'Butcher'. During the War of the Austrian Succession he was defeated in Flanders by Saxe at Fontenoy (1745) and Lauffeld (1747). During the Seven Years War he commanded the allied army defending Hanover, and after being defeated at Hastenbeck, signed the Convention of Klosterzeven (1757), by which 40,000 English soldiers were disarmed, after which he retired in disgrace. He showed no special qualifications as a commander, his military reputation resting on his handling of the troops at Culloden.

CUMBERLAND, GEORGE CLIFFORD, 3rd Earl of (1558–1605), English mathematician, navigator, and privateer. His first voyage to the New World explored the Plata river (1586), but made little profit. He fought against the Spanish Armada (1588) and led several expeditions in the 1590s, attacking Portuguese and Spanish shipping off the Azores with considerable success, for which he was knighted. He led the last great privateering expedition of the 16th cent., capturing the Spanish port of San Juan (1598). In his last years he was lord lieutenant of Cumberland.

CUMBERLAND GAP, major break in the Appalachian mountains of the US on the borders of KY, TN, and VA. Discovered by Thomas Walker (1750), and exploited by Daniel Boone (1760s–1770s), it became an important gateway on the Wilderness Road, a major route of westward migration to the 'blue-grass' country of Kentucky. It was the scene of conflict between Union and Confederate armies during the American Civil War.

CUMBERLAND ROAD, first federally financed national road in the US. The first section, running west from Cumberland, MD, was opened in 1811. By 1838, it had reached Vandalia, IL. Also called the National Road, it was a major artery of commerce and migration between the eastern seaboard and the Ohio and Upper Mississippi valleys.

CUM NIMIS ABSURDUM (1555), papal bull of Paul IV proclaiming that the Jews should be separated from Christian peoples. They were therefore condemned to live in urban ghettoes and could neither employ Christian servants nor own property or land.

CUM OCCASIONE (1653), papal bull condemning the five controversial propositions allegedly contained in the *Augustinus*. The Jansenists circumvented the bull's effects by replying that, although the censure was legitimate, the propositions were not in fact in Bp Jansen's book.

CUNAXA, BATTLE OF, in Babylonia (401 BC) between the Persian king, Artaxerxes II, and his brother, Cyrus the Younger, who, with an army that included 13,000 Greek mercenaries, had marched from Asia Minor to dispute the throne. Cyrus was killed, but the Greeks' easy defeat of the Persians' left and the subsequent fighting retreat of the Ten Thousand reaffirmed the superiority of Greek hoplites over Asiatic infantry, which gained them wide employment in the Persian empire and inspiring some Greeks with notions of Asian conquest.

CUNEDDA, chief of the Votadini tribe in north-east Britain, migrated early in the 5th cent. to North Wales, where he began the expulsion of the Irish (Scots) and founded the kingdom of Gwynedd. His sons are said to have given their names to other regions and kingdoms in Wales.

CUNEIFORM WRITING, system by which wedge-shaped signs were cut with a stylus in wet clay. The system, originally logographic in pre-Sumerian times, was developed by the Sumerians by the addition of phonograms. It was later adapted to Akkadian, Hittite, Hurrian, Elamite, and Urartian, and was used until the first millennium BC. It was deciphered in the first half of the 19th cent., largely through the efforts of Sir Henry Rawlinson, Edward Hincks, and Jules Oppert.

CUNHA, EUCLIDES DA (1866–1909), Brazilian novelist and social critic, author of *Os sertões* (*The Backlands*) (1902), a sociological account of the rebellion headed by Antonio Conselheiro (1897).

CUNLIFFE REPORT (1919), in Britain, by the Committee on Currency and Foreign Exchange after the War, was a major step towards the re-establishment of the Gold Standard after the First World War. 'Nothing can contribute more to the speedy recovery from the effects of the war . . . than the re-establishment of the currency upon a sound basis', the committee said in its first interim report (Aug. 1918), by which was meant the pound freely convertible into gold.

The committee's final report was presented in 1919: it argued for the restoration of the Gold Standard, with sterling valued at its pre-war level. The committee's recommendations were gradually implemented during the next seven years, the Gold Standard being restored in 1925. The policy advocated by the committee also tended to be highly deflationary at home. Criticism of its recommendations came from Keynes, who argued that the pound was over-valued if related to its pre-war parity to the dollar; but his view was over-ruled by most of the economic experts of the mid-1920s.

CUNLIFFE, WALTER CUNLIFFE, 1st Baron (1855–1920), English banker who founded (1890), with his brother, a merchant banking business in London. In 1895 he became a director of the Bank of England, and was later governor (1913–18). He played a prominent part in the evolution of war-financing policies, and was important in the negotiations for financial aid from the US. in 1917.

CUNNINGHAM, SIR ALEXANDER (1814–93), British soldier and archaeologist. He joined the Bengal Engineers (1833), became ADC to Lord Auckland (1836–40), served in First and Second Sikh Wars, and helped to delimit the boundary between Ladakh and Chinese Tibet (1846–7). In 1854 he was appointed executive engineer in Gwalior, where he explored the Buddhist monuments of Central India and published *The Bhilsa Topes*. During the Mutiny he was chief engineer in Burma, and later in the North-West Provinces. He retired from the army (1861) as a major-general and was archaeological surveyor to the government of India until the department was abolished (1866). He then went to England, where he published his *Ancient Geography of India*. In 1870 he returned to India as director general of archaeology, resigning in 1885, after 52 years' service in India.

CUNNINGHAM, JOSEPH DAVEY (1812–51), official of the East India Co. employed in its military and political service on the Sikh frontier. He was present at Aliwal and Sobraon in the First Sikh War. Because of his pro-Sikh proclivities he was removed from the Punjab to Bhopal, where he wrote his famous *History of the Sikhs* (1849).

CUONG-DE (1871–1951), Viet-namese prince, who (1905–1951) was pretender to the throne. He was the candidate of a group of anti-French nationalists, led initially by Phan Boi Chau, who smuggled him out of the country to Japan in 1905. He spent the greater part of his life in Japan, and was not allowed to return home even during Japanese control of Indo-China (1941–5).

CURAÇAO, largest island of the Netherlands Antilles. It was discovered by Alonso de Ojeda (1499) and settled by the Spanish. Johannes van Welbeck, of the Dutch West India Co., occupied and fortified the island (1634), which became the base for a rich entrepôt trade in the 18th cent. The colony was ruled by officials of the Dutch West India Co. Britain held Curaçao during the Napoleonic wars, but returned it to the Netherlands (1815). Control of the colony was vested in the Dutch Crown, which ruled the colony through a governor. The economic decline of Curaçao ended when Royal Dutch Shell established a large refinery (1918). Curaçao was linked with Surinam as a fully autonomous part of the kingdom of the Netherlands in 1954.

CURIE, PIERRE (1859–1906), French scientist, discoverer with his wife, Marie (1867–1934), of radium, for which they received the Nobel Prize for chemistry (1903). In physics he established that the magnetic properties of substances change at certain temperatures (Curie Point). Marie Curie isolated radium and polonium and laid the foundation of later research in nuclear physics and chemistry. She published her *Traité de Radioactivité* in 1910 and was the first person to receive the Nobel Prize twice (1903, 1911).

CURIO, C. SCRIBONIUS (d. 49 BC), Roman politician, son of the consul of 76 and husband of Fulvia, later the wife of Mark Antony. He revealed the mysterious plot of Vettius and others to assassinate Pompey (59) and subsequently opposed Julius Caesar until, bought over in his tribunate (50), he consistently frustrated attempts to recall him from Gaul, proposing that both Caesar and Pompey should disband their armies. He carried Caesar's ultimatum to the consuls (late Dec. 50) and fled from Rome with Antony to Caesar at Ravenna (Jan. 49). Having captured Sicily for Caesar (April 49), he crossed to Africa with his army, but was defeated and killed by Juba of Mauretania.

CURIUS DENTATUS, Marius, representative of the emergent plebeian nobility at Rome and consul in 290 BC, famous as conqueror of the Gallic Senones in 284 and for ending Pyrrhus' Italian ambitions at Beneventum in 275.

CURLEW MOUNTAINS, BATTLE OF (1599), defeat of Sir Conyers Clifford, president of Connaught, by the Irish rebels under O'Rourke. The Earl of Essex planned to attack the Earl of Tyrone in Ulster and sent Clifford to create a diversion. The infantry tried to force a passage in the Curlew Mountains, leaving the horses and baggage behind. Though they held their ground against the Irish, they ran out of ammunition and Clifford and 121 men were killed.

CURLEY, JAMES MICHAEL (1874–1958), US politician and Democratic political leader in Boston, MA. Curley used the local 'machine' to become congressman (1911–14, 1943–6), mayor of Boston (1914–18, 1922–6, 1930–4, 1946–50) and governor of the state (1935–7). He was imprisoned by federal authorities for fraud (1947), but his sentence was commuted by President Truman. He tried but failed (1949) to get re-elected to Congress.

CURRAGH MUTINY in Ireland, one of the most notable Unionist demonstrations against the Irish nationalist movement. This movement had become very vigorous in the 1890s, and after the 1910 general election was in a pivotal position because the Liberal government had only two seats more than the Conservative opposition. Asquith's government promised to bring in a Home Rule Bill in return for the Nationalists' support in its struggle with the Lords, and in 1912 such a bill was introduced. The Conservatives and Unionists, led by Sir Edward Carson, and with the sanction of Bonar Law, threatened armed resistance in their determination to keep at least Ulster out of an Irish Free State. Cavalry officers stationed at the Curragh, near Dublin, showed their sympathy with the Unionists in March 1914 by announcing that they would resign if called upon to coerce Ulster. The only immediate result of the mutiny, much as it shook the Liberal government, was the supersession of the war minister by Asquith. Concern over the deteriorating situation in Northern Ireland diminished rapidly on the outbreak of the First World War.

CURRENCY ACT (1764), British law extending the Currency Act of 1751, applicable to the New England colonies, and to all North American colonies. The acts outlawed colonial issues of paper money and generated colonial opposition to British rule.

CURRENCY LADS in New South Wales, native-born white Australians, the majority of convict stock. The name, popular between 1815 and 1851, derived from their being, like the early makeshift colonial currency, 'locally made' as distinct from sterling coinage (or people) 'made' in Britain.

CURRIE, SIR ARTHUR (1875–1933) Canadian soldier, who rose from the ranks to become commander of the Vancouver Highland Battalion (1914). He succeeded Sir Julian Byng as commander of the Canadian Corps (1917) and in 1920 became principal of McGill University.

CURRIE, SIR FREDERICK (1799–1875), official of the revenue and judicial departments of the East India Co. (1820–53). He was foreign secretary in 1842 and drew up the peace treaty after the First Sikh War. He was director of the EIC (1854) and last chairman of the company. He became a member of the Council of India in 1858.

CURRIER AND IVES, US lithographers whose voluminous production left a record of American life in the 19th cent. Nathaniel Currier (1813–88) founded the firm in New York (1834) and took James Merrit Ives (1824–95) as partner in 1857. Their prints, although often sentimental, are of high technical quality and eagerly sought for by collectors.

CURTIN, JOHN JOSEPH (1865–1945), Australian Labor journalist and prime minister (1941–5), son of a police constable. After a difficult youth, Curtin left Victoria to become editor of the *Westralian Worker*. He rebuilt the

divided Labor Party in WA, was elected to the Commonwealth House of Representatives for Fremantle (1928), but lost his seat during the Depression. After being re-elected in 1934, he defeated F. M. Forde by one vote (1935) for leadership of the Parliamentary Labor Party, which he reunified and led back into Commonwealth office a few months before Pearl Harbor.

Though Curtin's supporters were at first uncertain of his stability, he proved a skilled and reliable tactician as well as a brilliant speaker. Criticized at times for being 'all things to all men', he not only held a divided party together by quiet persuasion, but also retained the votes of two Independents essential for the maintenance of his difficult wartime administration, until the 1943 elections gave Labor a large majority. Impatient with party members who wanted to proceed with social legislation when all Australia's resources were needed for protection from Japanese invasion, he nevertheless co-operated with his friend and successor, J. B. Chifley, in planning post-war reconstruction and promoting social security measures (1942–4).

The many paradoxes of Curtin's career indicate his frequent changes of mind and his attempts to approach objectively all issues within the Australian Labor movement. Thus, though he opposed compulsory military training before the First World War, during which he was a pacifist, as prime minister in the Second he became the trusted associate of Australian and American military advisers and himself extended conscription to the south-west Pacific area. In the 1930s Curtin urged that Australia's best defence was in the air; as prime minister he not only shaped the change in Labor's defence attitudes, but was also responsible for greatly strengthening the wartime RAAF.   LR

CURTIUS, JULIUS (1877–1948), German lawyer and politician of the Weimar Republic, who represented the German People's Party (DVP) in several coalition governments. He was minister of economic affairs (1926–9) and in 1929 succeeded Stresemann as foreign minister. In both capacities he helped to negotiate the Young Plan on reparations. His principal achievement as foreign minister was to negotiate the Allied evacuation of the Rhineland zone, which had been occupied since 1918.

The extreme nationalist groups and parties fiercely opposed Curtius's attempts to accommodate Allied demands on Germany. Their political pressure became more effective with the electoral successes of the right in Sept. 1930, and with the deepening of the European economic crisis in 1931. In Dec. 1930 Curtius suggested to Britain, unsuccessfully, a moratorium on reparations payments. In the following spring he began negotiations for a customs union with Austria. He hoped the initiative would impress the German right, but the project backfired. France and Britain objected to not having been told in advance of a plan which might infringe the 1919 peace settlement. Austria, on the verge of financial collapse, was amenable to their pressure. Curtius further exasperated the Allies by refusing to drop the project, but drew the nationalists' fire for agreeing to submit it to the Hague International Court. After Austria's public renunciation of the project in Sept. 1931, the German National People's Party demanded the Cabinet's resignation, especially that of Curtius, and Chancellor Brüning reformed the government without him. By 1932 Curtius, recognized as the leader of the DVP left, was expelled from its Reichstag group. After leaving political life he resumed his profession as a lawyer.   ASJ

CURZON OF KEDLESTON, GEORGE NATHANIEL CURZON, Marquis of (1859–1925), British Conservative statesman. As viceroy of India (1898–1905) Curzon undertook financial and administrative reforms, and advocated a forward policy in Tibet, Afghanistan, and the Persian Gulf. He did much to preserve and restore India's art and architectural treasures. In the First World War he opposed withdrawal from ⌐ poli and demanded conscription. In Dec. 191

Lloyd George's war cabinet, with responsibility for the country's routine administration. As foreign secretary (1919–1924) Curzon's greatest achievement was the Lausanne settlement with Turkey (1923). He deprecated France's occupation of the Ruhr, and tried unavailingly to mediate between France and Germany. Curzon effectively discouraged Poincaré's efforts to foster Rhineland separatism, and began the moves leading to the establishment of the Dawes committee on reparations. He confidently expected to succeed Bonar Law as prime minister (May 1923); but failed to do so, as much through personality factors as through his being a peer.

CURZON LINE, running from Grodno in the north, through Bialystock to Brest-Litovsk in central Poland, was originally proposed by the supreme council as an armistice line between Russia and Poland in the former congress kingdom; it did not then apply to southern Poland (formerly Austrian Galicia), as that territory's future had not yet been decided. The next year it gained its name when Lord Curzon, British foreign secretary, strongly recommended it as a frontier at a time when Russia had almost overrun Warsaw.

Russia accepted the line, as it corresponded to her maximum ethnical claim. Poland always opposed it: her rulers, who were extremely nationalistic, wanted the restoration of the 1772 frontier, far to the east; they were also deeply suspicious of Russia and felt that more Polish territory would give greater security against her. The British could not understand such feelings, believing that a smaller 'national' Poland, without the minority conflicts which greater territory would entail, would be stronger. Against British advice, at Riga in April 1921, the Poles incorporated 103,600 sq. kms of territory east of the Curzon Line, plus the whole of eastern Galicia, to which they never granted the autonomy the allies requested. These events left a legacy of mutual distrust: the British suspected that the Poles were expansionist by nature; the Poles that the British would conciliate Bolshevik Russia rather than admit their claims for a viable, independent Poland. Poland's suspicions (in different circumstances) proved justified 20 years later: when, after the Nazi-Soviet Pact, Russia claimed Polish territory up to the Curzon Line (now including Galicia, to which Russia had no ethnical right), Britain, allied to Poland, condemned her. After Russia joined the Allied side in June 1941, it soon became clear to Churchill that Stalin would not withdraw to the Riga frontier, but, in order to preserve Allied unity, he attempted to reassure the Polish government in London. Yet he was aware that he could not oppose Stalin, for Soviet power was vital to the Allies, and he feared that the attempt to block his way in Poland might induce Stalin to make a separate peace with Hitler.

At Teheran, in Nov. 1943, Stalin was left in no doubt of Churchill's and Roosevelt's acquiescence, although the latter afterwards tried to save Lvov and the Galician oilfields for Poland. Russia was to acquire 46 per cent of pre-war Polish territory. While Churchill attempted unsuccessfully to persuade the London Poles to accept the Curzon Line, promising compensation elsewhere, Stalin took the first steps to establish a puppet government in Poland which would agree to it. Later Churchill claimed that the stubbornness of the London Poles had jeopardized Polish independence, maintaining that Stalin's only original aim had been to gain a secure frontier. But the view that Stalin would ever have agreed to a non-communist Poland is open to serious doubt.

The Curzon Line was formally acknowledged as the frontier at Yalta (Feb. 1945), Poland securing German territory as compensation. MN

CUSA (CUES, CUSANUS), NICHOLAS OF (1401–56), German cardinal, theologian, mathematician, astronomer, statesman, and reformer, who came to prominence at the Council of Basle. His work on ecclesiastical law (*De Concordantia Catholica*) is the clearest expression of the conciliar movement. He was a leading adviser of three popes, con-

stantly used on diplomatic and legatine missions (especially to Constantinople in 1438 and as legate to Germany 1450–2).

CUSHING, CALEB (1800–79), US lawyer, politician, and statesman, born in Newburyport, MA. He graduated from Harvard (1817), practised law, contributed to the *North American Review*, and entered politics as a supporter of John Quincy Adams. After being elected a member of the state legislature (1833–4) and a Whig congressman (1835–43), he transferred his allegiance to the Democrats. As commissioner to China (1843–44), he negotiated a commercial treaty that opened Chinese ports to US trade. On being again elected to the MA legislature (1845–6), he became an exponent of western expansion and raised a regiment that served in the Mexican War (1846–8). Having failed as a candidate for the governorship of MA (1847, 1848), he served again in the state legislature (1850), became mayor of Newburyport (1851–2), and associate justice of the state supreme court (1852). He was a spokesman for 'manifest destiny' and US attorney-general in Franklin Pierce's administration (1853–7). As permanent chairman of the Democratic presidential convention (1860) he tried to bring about a compromise over the secession issue and when this failed, became a Republican and legal adviser to Abraham Lincoln. Cushing was one of the chief US negotiators in the dispute with Britain over the *Alabama* claims (1871–2). He was unsuccessfully nominated by President Grant as chief justice of the US Supreme Court (1873), and served as minister to Spain (1873–7). An accomplished linguist, lawyer, scholar, and lecturer, his intellectual approach adversely affected his political career, but gave distinction to his other activities.

CUSTER, GEORGE ARMSTRONG (1839–76), US cavalry officer, whose 'last stand' is one of the most dramatic and controversial episodes in American frontier history. He served throughout the Civil War with the Army of the Potomac, became a brigadier-general (1863) at the age of 23, and made a reputation as a dashing cavalry leader. During later service in the west an expedition under his command confirmed reports of gold in the Black Hills, SD (1875). In the second Sioux War he and his force of 264 men were wiped out in an encounter, precipitated partly by Custer's own recklessness, with 2500 Sioux warriors under chiefs Sitting Bull and Crazy Horse, at the Little Big Horn in MT (25 June 1876).

CUSTOMARY LAW is that law which is neither made nor written, but grows and develops through usage and passage of time. In England, customary law is the essential feature of and basis of the common law and was the only kind of law known in Anglo-Saxon times. It was essentially vague and undefined and the 'laws' of the Anglo-Saxon kings, Aethelbert of Kent, Alfred of Wessex, and Cnut were not new or made laws, but statements of the customs of the realm as they existed in their time. These customs differed from kingdom to kingdom (*eg*, Kent, Wessex, Mercia) and, depending as they did on the length of human memory, from one period to another. With the unification of England in the 11th cent. one unified system of customary law gradually emerged as the common law of the kingdom.

CUSTOZZA, BATTLES OF (1848, 1866), two Austrian victories over the Italians in northern Italy. On 24 July 1848 Radetzky crushed a Piedmontese army, forcing King Charles Albert to sue for peace. The young kingdom of Italy, as an ally of Prussia, was defeated in the same place by the Austrian Archduke Albert on 24 June 1866.

CUTHBERT, Saint (d. 687), became prior, then in 684, Bp, of Lindisfarne, and acquired a legendary reputation for sanctity as a hermit on Farne Island. His allegedly uncorrupted body was treasured by the monks of Lindisfarne and subsequently preserved at Durham.

CUTLER, MANASSEH (1742–1823), US clergyman and land speculator. He was born in Connecticut and graduated from Yale University (1765) and became a pastor in Massachusetts (1771). He served as a military chaplain, practised as a physician, engaged in scientific research, chiefly of a botanical nature, and opened a school. Cutler was a founder of the Ohio Land Co. (1786) and as the company's lobbyist obtained from the Continental Congress a grant of 1½ million acres in the Ohio river valley at a price of 8 cents an acre (1787). Cutler served in the US Congress (1800–4).

CUZA, A. C. (1857–1946), inspiration and ideologue of nationalist and anti-Semitic politics in modern Rumania. Cuza held the chair of political economy at Jassy University, where his lectures were marked by conservative nationalism, xenophobia, and anti-Semitism. With the historian Nicolae Iorga, he founded the National Democratic Party (1906) in which Ion Zelea Codreanu, father of the future Iron Guard leader, was a militant participant. Before the First World War Cuza used the swastika as a political symbol. At Jassy he taught Corneliu Codreanu and together they founded the League of National Christian Defence in 1923. Cuza was more a moderate than Codreanu and relations between the two soured. In 1927 the party divided. Cuza went on with the National Christian Party and sat in the cabinet of Octavian Goga in 1937. When the Iron Guard came to power the influence of Cuza and his followers diminished severely.

CUZCO, ancient Incan capital in the southern highlands of modern Peru, where there is an impressive array of Incan ruins and Spanish colonial edifices, mainly religious. Its cathedral, in Renaissance style, was built of granite blocks removed from Incan buildings. Cuzco was founded by Manco Capac, the earliest Inca monarch (11th cent.), as his capital. After its capture by the Spaniards, and the civil strife which followed, the city lost approximately 90 per cent of its pre-conquest population. With the creation of the viceregal capital at Lima, Cuzco declined in importance.

CVETKOVIC, DRAGISA (1893–1968), prime minister of Yugoslavia (1939–41). He conducted negotiations with the Croats which led to the conclusion of the Sporazum (25 Aug. 1939). Attempts to loosen Yugoslavia's bonds with the Axis by establishing a neutral bloc with Bulgaria, Greece, and Turkey having failed, Cvetkovic was summoned to Vienna, where he signed the Tripartite Pact (25 March 1941). Yugoslavia's adherence to the pact prompted the army coup of 27 March which ended both Cvetkovic's government and Prince Paul's regency.

CYAXARES (c. 653–584 BC), Median King (reg. 625–584) who liberated his people from Scythian suzerainty and imposed his overlordship on the Mannai and Persians. Allied to Babylon, he attacked Assyria, destroying Nineveh in 612. Urartu was probably conquered at the same time.

CYLON (fl. 7th cent. BC), Athenian son-in-law of the Megarian Tyrant Theagenes, the first to aim at tyranny at Athens (c. 632 BC). His failure and sacrilegious murder by Megacles resulted in the first banishment of the Alcmeonidae and the legislation of Draco (c. 621).

CYNICS, Greek philosophical school, whose members followed Diogenes of Sinope (c. 400–325 BC) in rejecting material values and cultivating asceticism for peace and contentment. The school declined after the 3rd cent. BC, but revived under Stoic influence in the 1st cent. AD.

CYNOSCEPHALAE, BATTLE OF (197 BC), decisive engagement in the Second Macedonian War (197 BC), in which the Roman Quinctius Flamininus defeated Philip V in Thessaly, affirming the superiority of Roman legion over Macedonian phalanx.

CYPRESS HILLS, MASSACRE OF (1873), the shooting by Americans of 80 Assiniboine Indians accused of stealing horses. Such lawlessness in the Cypress Hills (southern Alberta and Saskatchewan) by Montana traders led to the formation of the North-West Mounted Police (1873).

CYPRIAN (c. AD 200–58), bishop of Carthage and the first great teacher of ecclesiology, ie, the doctrine of the Church and Ministry. Originally a pagan rhetorician, he was converted to Christianity (c. 246). His episcopate was troubled by pestilence, by the persecutions of Decius and Valerian, and by controversies concerning those who had apostatized and the rebaptism of heretics, but he steered a middle course between strictness and laxity, carrying the North African Church with him. His works on the Church, Ministry, and Sacraments are of theological importance and his letters enjoyed great popularity in their day. He was martyred during the persecution of Valerian, being the first African bishop so to die for his faith.

CYPRUS, KINGDOM OF, a province of the Byzantine empire, taken in 1184 by the great-nephew of Emperor Manuel I, Isaac Ducas, who allied himself with Saladin and styled himself king. In May 1191 Cyprus was captured by King Richard I of England, on the way to Palestine. He sold it to the Templars and in 1192 caused them to sell it to the ex-King of Jerusalem, Guy of Lusignan. The Lusignans, whose possession was confirmed in 1197 by the Emperor Henry VI, held the kingdom until 1489, establishing a feudal monarchy with barons and colonists attracted to the rich island from Palestine. The commercial importance of Cyprus made it a major centre for Spanish, French, and Italian merchants. It became a source of men and money, a base for later crusading activities, and the headquarters of the Templars until their suppression early in the 14th cent. The population remained largely Greek and there was constant friction until the 16th cent. over attempts by the Lusignans to suppress the Greek Church. Cyprus became Venetian in 1489 and was captured by the Turks in 1571.

CYPRUS CONVENTION (4 June 1878), agreement reluctantly conceded by the Ottomans, providing for British occupation of Cyprus as a base for the defence of Ottoman Asia against Russia and the protection of the routes to India and as part of a project for the reform of the Ottoman empire.

CYPRUS DISPUTE gathered momentum in the 1950s as the result of a movement among the Greek Cypriot population for union with Greece (Enosis). The movement was under the leadership of Abp Makarios and was supported by a guerrilla and terrorist organization (EOKA). The movement originated in the 19th cent., when Cyprus was under Turkish rule, but it was ignored by the great powers when Cyprus was taken over by Britain in trust for the Sultan (1878). In the inter-war years the movement used constitutional methods to oppose British rule, though there were occasional disturbances, which were suppressed by British troops (1931). The British government, which had ruled Cyprus as a crown colony since the outbreak of the First World War, introduced constitutional and economic reforms on a limited scale without thereby removing the causes of unrest.

The Second World War and the Italian invasion of Greece brought about an alliance between the Greek Cypriots and the British (19,000 Cypriots are said to have been under arms in Oct. 1941), but in Cyprus, as elsewhere, the war contributed to the growth of nationalism. With the end of the war the British government proposed further constitutional reforms, but these stopped short of the demands for Enosis.

There were two major obstacles to the smooth process of decolonization which the British government had pursued in Asia. The first was that Cyprus had come to play an increasingly important part in British defence policy as a partial substitute for the base in Palestine, surrendered at the end of the Mandate (May 1948) and for the base in Egypt, from which British troops had withdrawn in 1954. Britain's commitments had in the meantime been increased by the Baghdad Pact (1955). The second obstacle was that the nationalist movement's demand for union with Greece was bitterly opposed by the Turkish population of Cyprus, which constituted some 18 per cent of the total.

Meanwhile the strength of the Enosis movement increased, benefiting from the skilled leadership of Abp Makarios (who, in the Orthodox Church, disposed of a well-articulated political organization) and from disorders created by EOKA and the consequent domestic pressure on the British government to end coercion. The Greek government now espoused the Enosis cause, and in 1954 referred the Cyprus question to the United Nations. A tripartite conference (1955) between the British, Greek, and Turkish governments failed to produce results and Abp Makarios, together with the Bp of Kyrenia, was deported to the Seychelles (March 1956). A few months later (Oct. 1956) the limited strategic value of Cyprus (where there was no harbour of adequate size) was revealed by the Suez expedition. In the following year the first breaks in the deadlock appeared. The UN accepted an Indian resolution calling for a negotiated settlement (Feb. 1957) and the EOKA leader, Gen. Grivas, expressed his readiness to suspend operations if Makarios were released. The British government, after receiving assurances from Makarios based on the UN resolution, agreed to his release (March 1957).

None the less, it took a further two years for the two Cypriot communities and the three governments (British, Greek, and Turkish) to reach a settlement. The London agreements (Feb. 1959) provided for Cyprus to become an independent republic (it later joined the Commonwealth) with a Greek Cypriot president, a Turkish Cypriot vice-president, and a communal structure in the proportion of 70 per cent Greek to 30 per cent Turkish, to be maintained in all fields of government. Britain, Turkey, and Greece entered into a treaty of Guarantee with Cyprus, under which British sovereignty was limited to the area of its base in Cyprus. In addition, a treaty of Alliance between the Republic of Cyprus, Greece, and Turkey provided for common defence and a tripartite headquarters in Cyprus, staffed by Greek and Turkish contingents.

The settlement showed considerable ingenuity, but depended ultimately on goodwill which, after the strife of the previous decade, no longer existed. The Greek Cypriots were in a position of dominance, enhanced by Makarios being the president; on the other hand the Turkish government was in a far stronger military position than that of Greece to safeguard the interests of its compatriots on the island. Fresh disturbances in 1964 led to the Cyprus question being referred once more to the UN. A Security Council resolution (March 1964) established a UN force (which included British troops) in Cyprus and its mandate was still being renewed at intervals in 1970. It succeeded in interposing itself between the two sides in the dispute and thus maintaining peace, although this stopped short of the degree of co-operation between the communities which the London agreements assumed.

The Cyprus dispute was of importance within NATO. To a limited extent the good offices of NATO contributed to a settlement, but more important were the tensions created within the alliance (and within CENTO), since both Greece and Turkey would have wished for the support of the major powers when it was in the latter's interests to remain neutral between the two.   WFK

CYPSELUS (*fl.* 7th cent.), son of the non-Dorian Aetion, popular champion and first tyrant of Corinth *c.* 650–620 BC. Cypselus was favoured by Delphi and overthrew the hated Bacchiads with non-Dorian and hoplite support.

CYRANKIEWICZ, JÓZEF (1911–), Polish communist politician. Before the Second World War Cyrankiewicz was a member of the Polish Socialist Party (PPS) and secretary of the party's district workers' committee in Cracow (1935–9). During the September campaign (1939), he, then being in the army, was captured by the Germans, but managed to escape and returned to Cracow, where he joined the underground socialist movement. As editor of *Wolność*, an underground newspaper, he wrote many articles attacking the Soviet Union. In 1941 he was arrested by the Germans and imprisoned in Auschwitz, where he went over to the communists.

After the war he returned to Poland and together with Bierut split the socialists and reorganized the PPS, giving it a pro-communist orientation. He was general secretary of this new party (Dec. 1945–Dec. 1948). His aim during this period was to unite the PPS with the Communist Polish Workers' Party (PPR), and after a drastic purge the Polish United Workers' Party (PZPR) was created (Dec. 1948). In the PZPR Cyrankiewicz was a member of the Central Committee, the Politburo, and the organization section, and later became a secretary of the party. He was prime minister of Poland (Feb. 1947–Nov. 1952), deputy prime minister (Nov. 1952–March 1954), and again prime minister (March 1954).

Cyrankiewicz's capacity for political survival is remarkable. It is not clear how far this has been due to crude opportunism and how far it results from political skill. Although extremists in the party were said to mistrust him as a moderate, he fully associated himself with the anti-Zionist campaign of 1968.

CYRANO DE BERGERAC, SAVINIEN (1619–55), French writer and soldier who fought at Mouzon and Arras. He has been immortalized in Edmond Rostand's play, *Cyrano de Bergerac* (1895).

CYRENE, an ancient Greek city in Libya founded (*c.* 630 BC) from Thera by 'Battus' (Libyan, 'king'), was a centre of Greek influence on the North African coast between Carthage and Egypt. Rich in corn and silphium and strengthened by further Greek settlers (*c.* 570), it prospered under the Battiads, but from *c.* 525 was subject to the Persians. In 332 it was won by Alexander and subsequently became subject to the Ptolemies, from whom it passed in the 1st cent. BC to Rome. Its large Jewish colony caused much unrest under Trajan (*c.* AD 115) and its prosperity declined. Recent excavations have revealed outstanding examples of Greek art and architecture.

CYRIL, Saint (*c.* 827–69), worked (*c.* 860) with his brother Methodius for the conversion of the Khazars in the lands north-east of the Black Sea. From 863 the two brothers began to labour among the Slavs, translating the scriptures into the language known later as Old Church Slavonic and devising for that purpose an alphabet based on Greek characters which, as the Cyrillic alphabet, is still in use amongst the Slav peoples. Cyril, with Methodius, soon became recognized as a saint of the Greek Orthodox Church—a status also accorded to the brothers within the Roman Catholic Church since 1880.

CYRIL (*reg.* 412–44), patriarch of Alexandria. In an age of intense religious controversy Cyril posed as a champion of Orthodoxy against the alleged heresy of Nestorius, patriarch of Constantinople. The third ecumenical council, held in Ephesus, pronounced against Nestorius under the influence of Cyril, who sought the support of the pope, Celestine, by sending him tendentious reports of Nestorian statements. Cyril also drew up a series of anti-Nestorian 'anathemas', which in effect claimed for the see of Alexandria a primacy over that of Constantinople. Meanwhile Cyril's cause was advanced by the use of mob terrorism against the Nestorians. Cyril's contribution to the Nestorian controversy is important in that he implied the supremacy of the pope in such issues over the authority both of the patriarch of Constantinople and the Byzantine emperor. It ended after Cyril's death with the defeat of the ambitions of Alexandrian patriarchs at the Council of Chalcedon (451), but the outlawed Nestorian Church has persisted in Asia ever since.

CYRUS II (*reg. c.* 559–530 BC) (the Great), Persian Emperor. From his modest beginnings as king of part of Anshan he built the Achaemenid empire of Iran, the greatest empire the world had then seen. He first united the two parts of Anshan and established his capital at Pasargadae, where he built a palace and temples. He rebelled against his overlord, King Astyges of Media, defeated him (*c.* 549), and took Media and the Median lands of Urartu, Assyria, and eastern Asia Minor, and made Ecbatana the capital of the growing empire. He then moved against Lydia, which had seized some Median territory during the war with Astyges, and captured King Croesus (*c.* 547), while another army conquered the Ionian cities. Cyrus now turned to Babylon, which was restive under its king, Nabonidus. In 539 Babylon was captured and the Babylonian vassals in Syria submitted. The Jews exiled in Babylon were allowed to return to Judah. Although the conquered lands were formed into satrapies, Cyrus did not introduce great changes. Indigenous institutions were left untouched, the native gods honoured, and subject peoples treated generously. In each area he tried to show himself as the legitimate ruler, rather than as a conqueror. In the east he seems to have conquered Bactria, Arachosia, and Sogdia as well as to have taken over lands which had previously owed allegiance to Media. The nomads on the frontier were a continual threat to the empire and it was while fighting one of these tribes, the Massagetai, that Cyrus was killed.

CYRUS THE YOUNGER (d. 401 BC), son of King Darius II of Persia, and important in Greek history during and after the closing years of the great Peloponnesian War. Superseding the ineffective Tissaphernes and Pharnabazus as satrap of western Asia Minor in 407, he quickly implemented Darius' agreement with the Spartans, in co-operation with their admiral, Lysander, who in 405 destroyed the Athenian fleet at Aegospotami and ended the war. After Darius' death, Cyrus decided to challenge his brother, Artaxerxes II Mnemon, for the throne. With Sparta's support, he raised 13,000 Greek mercenaries and marched to Babylonia, but was killed in battle at Cunaxa, leaving his Greeks, the 'Ten Thousand', to make their famous retreat to the Black Sea.

CYZICUS, Greek colony founded from Miletus on an island off the southern shore of the Propontis (Sea of Marmora), probably *c.* 675 BC, possibly *c.* 750. Later it became a trade centre, its prosperity being due partly to fishery, hence the tunny-fish on its famous gold coins. After subjection to Persia, it joined the Delian League, but in the 4th cent., like all Asiatic Greek states, it reverted to Persia until it was liberated by the Macedonians (336). An independent ally of Pergamum, it joined the Romans in the Second Macedonian War (200), retaining their favour, especially after resisting siege in the Third Mithridatic War (74), until unrest led to loss of privileges (20 BC and AD 25).

CYZICUS, BATTLES OF (*a*), the defeat (410 BC) in the great Peloponnesian War of 60 Peloponnesian ships under Mindarus, the Athenians being under Alcibiades. The victory restored Athenian naval supremacy after the intervention of Persia and the revolts of allies in 413–412 and was followed by a Spartan offer of peace, which was rejected by the democracy restored at Athens; (*b*), in the Third Mithridatic War the victory (74 BC) of the Romans under Lucullus over Mithridates VI of Pontus, withdrawing from an unsuccessful siege of Cyzicus. It ended Mithridates' last attempt to expel the Romans from Asia.

CZARTORYSKI, ADAM, Prince (1770–1861), Polish statesman and adviser to Alexander I. He was made to enter Russian government service in exchange for the return of his estates, confiscated after the third partition, and was befriended by Alexander and became a member of the Unofficial Committee (1801–3) and foreign minister (1804–6). In the Instructions to Novosiltsov (1804) and his *Essay in Diplomacy* (1827) he proposed a Concert of Europe to guarantee peace and national independence under an Anglo-Russian aegis. He resigned over war with France and devoted himself to his post as curator of the new Polish university at Vilna (1804–24). Czartoryski's aim of a united autonomous Poland under Russia was largely met (1815) and he drafted the Polish constitution and sat on the Council of State. Nevertheless, he joined the rebellion against Russian rule as president of the Provisional (later National) government (1830–1), and died an exile in Paris.

CZARTORYSKI FAMILY, one of Poland's wealthiest and most powerful families in 18th–19th cent., descended from the Lithuanian princely house. After Prince Augustus Alexander Czartoryski's marriage in 1731 to a Sieniawska, Poland's richest heiress, the family was rivalled only by the Potockis. Since neither family was strong enough to dominate the other, they both conducted independent foreign policies and collaborated with foreign powers to interfere in the internal politics of Poland, whose elective monarchy invited such intervention. In the 1730s the Czartoryskis looked to France to support their candidate for the throne, Stanislas Leszczynski, but after 1736, with the latter's defeat in the War of the Polish Succession, they championed internal reform and cultivated Habsburg and Russian friendship to counterbalance the Franco-Prussian leanings of the Potockis. From 1756 Prince Michael Frederick (1695–1775), grand chancellor of Lithuania, also cultivated Sir Charles Hanbury Williams, the English ambassador at St Petersburg. In the later 18th cent. Prince Adam Casimir (1731–1823), son of Augustus Alexander and cousin of Stanislas Poniatowski, the puppet king of Poland, supported the Patriot Party's plans for internal reform. His son was Prince Adam George (1770–1861).

CZECH LEGIONS were made up of Czechs and Slovaks who, from 1916, were encouraged by Czechoslovak leaders-in-exile to desert the Austro-Hungarian armies for those of the Entente, and thus aid the diplomatic campaign for the recognition of a Czechoslovak state.

The most significant legion, in this respect, was one of 50,000 which, after the treaty of Brest-Litovsk (1918), remained the only force in Soviet Russia still at war with Germany. The British wished to intervene in Russia to maintain the Eastern Front, and the presence there of a friendly army gave them an excuse to do so. The French, weak on the Western Front, were impressed by the strength of the Legionaries, who fought their way across Siberia, gaining control of the Trans-Siberian Railway and Vladivostok, and wanted them as part of the Allied army, then under French command. The American public followed the exploits of the Legion with great sympathy, and with the British, persuaded their president to support a full-scale intervention in Russia to rescue them. Beneš and Masaryk skilfully capitalized on all these desires, and gained from the Americans and British recognition as allies, and from the French definite pledges of support in their territorial demands.

In the new Czechoslovak state, the importance played by the Legionaries in its foundation was recognized by the government. They received great privileges especially from land redistribution, to the detriment and resentment of many peasants.

CZECHOSLOVAK–POLISH AGREEMENT (23 April 1925), comprised a treaty of arbitration for all except territorial disputes, a liquidation convention to settle border and minority questions, and a technical convention to allow the transit of war material to Poland via Czechoslovakia if Poland should suffer unprovoked aggression. No political pact was signed. The agreement was encouraged by France who, being allied to both parties, desired a united front in discussions with Germany at Locarno. Poland, fearing that her frontiers would be discussed, hoped for closer relations with Czechoslovakia, who, however, took no steps to concert action with Poland after this agreement.

DABLON, CLAUDE (1619–97), French Jesuit missionary in Canada (1655), where he explored north of Lake St John (1661), founded the missions of Sault Ste Marie (1668) and Michilimackinac (1670), and became superior of the Jesuit missions in Canada (1670). He edited the Jesuit *Relation* (1671–2), in which appears his account of Marquette's Mississippi explorations.

DACCA, since 1947 the capital of East Pakistan, is 150 miles (240 kms) from Calcutta on the Burhi Ganga river, formerly the main channel of the Padma (1970 pop. about 600,000). Dacca was famous for its cottons and muslins, but with the French wars and import of British cotton goods the industry collapsed and between 1800 and 1830 the population fell from 200,000 to 57,000. In the later 19th cent. the revival of the weaving industry and a new jute industry restored prosperity.

In 1608 the Mughal governor made Dacca the capital of all Bengal, being a convenient base for his operations against the Ahoms of Assam. In 1704 the capital was moved to Murshidabad, but Dacca remained important as a provincial and commercial centre. It was the capital of the short-lived British province of Eastern Bengal and Assam (1905–12).

DACIA, Roman province north of the Danube, covering much of modern Rumania. It was formed when the Dacians, who were akin to the Thracians and under Decebalus posed a formidable threat to the Roman Danube frontier, were conquered by Trajan in two campaigns (AD 101–2, 105–6). Numerous colonists were introduced from the western provinces to exploit Dacia's mineral and agricultural wealth, but the Carpathian mountains, which formed its northern boundary, proved insufficient protection against semi-nomadic invaders, and Aurelian (AD 270–5) evacuated the region, settling many inhabitants south of the Danube in a new province of Dacia. It is claimed that enough remained behind to form the origin of the Rumanian nation.

DACKE, NILS (d. 1543), leader of a peasant revolt in Smaland against King Gustavus I of Sweden. Its causes included increased taxation, religious innovations, and restrictions on exportation through Denmark. The movement had support from the king's Catholic opponents in Germany, and in 1542 the king was obliged to make a compromise with Dacke, but in the following year Gustavus mustered a considerable force and killed him.

DACOITY, gang-robbery, a crime of frequent occurrence all over India. In 1772 Warren Hastings decreed that every convicted dacoit should be executed in his own village, his family made slaves of the state, and the village fined. Orders were issued in 1782 that *zamindars* (landholders) should be answerable for robberies committed within their limits, but these were ineffective, as the *zamindars* were in league with the dacoits and the ordinary peasant dared not complain. In 1839 a special *thagi* and dacoity department was instituted. Acts were passed (1843, 1851) but by terrorism and false witnesses the dacoits managed to evade punishment. In 1852 there were at least 35 gangs operating near Calcutta. Dacoity later revived (1905–16), the proceeds from it being used by

the *bhadralok* in Bengal to finance terrorism. Progress in eradicating this evil remains slow (1970).

DAENDELS, HERMAN (1762–1818), governor-general of the Dutch East Indies (1808–11) during the Napoleonic administration of Holland. He had the reputation of being a dictatorial administrator and was responsible for a broad range of changes in the administration of the colonies, from defence and justice to the selling of land to private individuals.

DAFYDD AP GWILYM (*fl.* 1340–70), Welsh poet of the Middle Ages. The acceptance and bardic use of the 'cywydd' metre, subsequently one of the most popular of Welsh metres, is largely due to him. His poetry, written in a new, simpler style, showed a personal response to nature and an ability to absorb foreign influences.

DAFYDD AP LLYWELYN (d. 1246), Prince of Gwynedd and son of Llywelyn I. His rule was challenged by his half-brother, Gruffydd, and King Henry III of England also began to destroy Llywelyn's position in Wales. Gruffydd died in 1244 and in the next year Dafydd defeated Henry III; after Llywelyn's death his territories and allegiances disintegrated.

DAGOHOY, FRANCISCO (*fl.* 18th cent.), first leader of a protracted Philippine revolt (1744–1829) in Bohol, one of the Visayan islands in the southern Philippines. Bohol had a long history of uprisings, including the Tambolt revolt (1621–2). In 1744 Dagohoy rallied 3000 followers there to defy Spanish rule. By the time the revolt was suppressed (1829) they numbered 20,000. The immediate cause of the revolt was the refusal of a Jesuit parish priest to bury Dagohoy's brother, who had been killed in a duel. The rebels repulsed all Hispano–Filipino expeditions dispatched against them, and continued to threaten Spanish sovereignty over Bohol even after Raon, the governor-general (1765–70), had granted them an amnesty and withdrawn government troops from most of the area. Dagohoy's followers submitted to Spanish colonial rule in 1829.

DAGUERRE, LOUIS JACQUES MANDÉ (1759–1851), French inventor, who between 1826 and 1839 evolved a method of photography by mercury vapour development of silver iodide exposed on a copper plate (the 'daguerrotype'), in the early stages in association with Joseph Niépce (1765–1833). Although subsequently improved, photography remained a tool of the chemical technician until 50 years later, when George Eastman (1854–1932) introduced the techniques which made it a universal hobby.

DAHL, JOHN CHRISTIAN CLAUSEN (1788–1857), Norwegian landscape painter who founded Norway's national gallery.

DAHL, MICHAEL (1656–1743), Swedish portrait painter who enjoyed considerable prestige in England, where he painted George II.

DAHLBERG, ERIK (1625–1703), Swedish count, the 'Vauban of Sweden', who played a part (exaggerated in his *Diary*) in Charles X's famous advance across the ice against Copenhagen (1658). He was Sweden's greatest fortress-builder and as governor-general of Livonia withstood Augustus of Saxony's attack on Riga (1700).

DAHLERUS, BIRGER (1898–), Swedish businessman and friend of Göring, who was involved in last-minute attempts to negotiate between Britain and Germany and so to avert the Second World War. In Aug. 1939, he brought about a weekend meeting in Schleswig-Holstein between Göring, a group of English businessmen, and some German military figures: the occasion was acknowledged only unofficially by the British foreign minister, Lord Halifax. In late August, as Hitler's demands on Poland became more menacing, Göring sent Dahlerus on constant flights to London to explain Hitler's successive desiderata to Halifax and the prime minister Neville Chamberlain, and to report their unofficial replies.

DAHOMEY (112,000 sq. kms), west African republic, formerly a province of French West Africa. It became independent in 1960 and from 1965 was ruled by an army council. The population of 2,306,800 (1970) includes Fon, Bariba, and Yoruba people.

DAIL EIREANN (the Assembly of Ireland), parliament of the Irish republic, first established in 1919, the Irish republicans elected in the 1918 'Coupon election' having proclaimed an Irish state. Although the Dail acted to present Ireland's claim to independence at the Versailles peace conference, it was not recognized by the British government, and was proscribed in Sept. 1919. In 1920 the British held elections in Ireland for the two separate parliaments which had been set up under the Government of Ireland Act. The overwhelmingly nationalist and republican vote of the southern 26 counties doomed the act; but although the Irish MPs refused to participate in the parliament, it was they who constituted the second Dail.

This emerged from its underground operations in Aug. 1921, when a truce had been concluded with the British. The Anglo-Irish treaty, negotiated by De Valera and others, was presented to the Dail at the end of the year. Its ratification, by 64 votes to 57, was opposed by De Valera himself, and in Jan. 1922 Griffith replaced him as prime minister. The result was a Republican insurrection by the IRA (Irish Republican Army), which recognized only the republican minority in the Dail. Despite the Civil War, the Dail went ahead with the proclamation of the Irish Free State; in Sept. 1922 a senate was nominated by the chamber of deputies, in accordance with the constitution which was ratified by both countries in Dec.

In 1936 the senate was abolished, but in 1937 was reconstituted under a new constitution, but with reduced powers.
GD

DAILY EXPRESS, British ½d newspaper founded (1900) by C. Arthur Gibson. It was acquired by a syndicate headed by its editor, R. D. Blumenthal (1912), and then by Lord Beaverbrook, a supporter of imperial preference (1922). In the 1930s its circulation rose owing to lively journalism and a free gifts campaign.

DAILY MAIL, British newspaper, founded (1896) as a ½d daily by Alfred and Harold Harmsworth. Its vigorous journalism, use of the short paragraph, and other typographical innovations led to a circulation of 2 million by the mid-20th cent.

DAILY NEWS, British newspaper founded (1846) under the editorship of Charles Dickens. It championed Liberal causes, the Italians' struggle for independence, and the Bulgarians and Armenians against the Turks. It absorbed the *Morning Leader*, acquired *The Star* (1909) and *Westminster Gazette* (1928), and was amalgamated with the *Daily Chronicle* to form the *News Chronicle* (1930) which became extinct in 1960.

DAIMYŌ (lit. 'great name'), a term denoting the feudal lords who emerged in 14th- and 15th-cent. Japan and who, by the 16th cent., had gained control of almost the whole country. During the intense warfare of the 16th cent. almost all the older *daimyō* families (*shugo daimyōs*) were overthrown by lesser lords who had built up their power from local bases, but most of these *sengoku daimyōs* were themselves overthrown by ambitious vassals (*shokuhō daimyōs*) who had developed more effective methods of organization. After 1600 many *daimyōs* were dispossessed and their lands given to vassals and relatives of the Tokugawa family, known respectively as *fudai* and *shimpan daimyōs*. A third of Japan, however, remained under more than 100 independent (*tozama*), *daimyōs*, whose historical role did not end until the establishment of central control by the modernizing Meiji government (1869–71).

DAI-VIET, name by which Viet-nam was known from the 11th to 18th cents, under the dynasties of Ly, Tran, and Le. The kingdom had to defend its separate existence against Chinese attacks in 1075–7 and 1282–8. Chinese rule was reimposed in 1407, but Dai-Viet recovered its independence in 1427. The kingdom initially included only the area of the present North Viet-nam, but during the 14th and 15th cents its territory was expanded to include a large part of the kingdom of Champa, which formerly existed in central Viet-nam.

DAI-VIET PARTY, Viet-namese nationalist group founded in 1943, with Japanese encouragement. It still plays (1970) some part in the politics of South Viet-nam, although split into a number of factions.

DAKIN, WILLIAM JOHN (1883–1950), foundation professor of biology at Western Australia University (1913–20), after research experience in Britain and Europe. He was Australia's wartime technical director of camouflage. Dakin's special interests were marine biology, oceanography, and experimental zoology.

DAKOTA INDIANS, largest division of the Sioux family, originally occupying an area in what are now the American states of WI, MN, and MI. The Dakota were driven westward by the Chippewa, against whose French firearms they pitted their arrows. During the American War of Independence and the War of 1812 the Dakota supported the British. They signed a peace treaty with the US (1815) and another treaty (1851) established territorial boundaries for the tribe. The Dakota rose against the whites in MN (1862) but were subdued, and in 1867 sent to a reservation in SD. Discovery of gold on Indian land in the Black Hills caused an Indian uprising in which the Dakota took part. Their last conflict with the whites was during the Ghost Dance movement (1890–1891). The tribe is now (1970) located on several reservations in ND, SD, MT, and NB.

DALADIER, ÉDOUARD (1884–), French statesman who was prime minister in the years immediately before the Second World War. His name is linked with the policy of 'appeasement'. He was active in Radical politics before 1914, and entered parliament in 1919 after war service, soon becoming a leading figure in the Radical Party. Daladier first held office in 1924. He was a minister in several governments, and prime minister for the first time in 1933. His reappointment in 1934 provoked the right-wing demonstrations of 6 Feb., in the face of which he resigned.

At this time, Daladier was known especially as a defence expert. He wanted France to have a strong army, but thought modern equipment more important than a large army, and he opposed the extension of military service from one to two years (1935).

Daladier was a strong supporter of Radical participation in the Popular Front alliance, and became minister of war in Blum's government (1936). He retained this post until he became prime minister (1938), and was responsible for the beginning of French rearmament to meet the German threat. He opposed the social reforms of the Popular Front—especially the 40-hour week—when he thought that they threatened the pace of rearmament, and his own government, with Reynaud as finance minister, applied a rigorous austerity programme.

Daladier signed the Munich agreement for France, and must bear the final responsibility for French diplomacy in these years. It seems clear, however, that he saw appeasement as a way of gaining time for rearmament, and did not share the defeatist attitude of some of his ministers. On the outbreak of war, he took over the direction of foreign affairs from Bonnet.

As the war progressed, Daladier's leadership was increasingly felt to lack vigour, and, when it appeared that he had lost the confidence of parliament, in March 1940 he resigned in favour of Reynaud. After France's defeat he was imprisoned by the Vichy regime, and accused at the 'Riom trial' (1942) of neglecting France's interests when in office. He defended himself vigorously, the trial was suspended, and Daladier was deported to Germany.

Daladier's reputation as the 'man of Munich' did not prevent his return to parliament under the Fourth Republic. He did not hold office, but was a prominent figure in the Radical Party, where he backed the left-wing tendencies of Mendès-France. He retired from politics after the return of De Gaulle, which he had opposed.

D. W. Brogan, *The Development of Modern France 1870–1939*) (London, 1940). RDA

DALAI LAMA, title of the chief abbot of the Gelugpa sect of Tibetan Buddhism and, after 1642, head of state in Tibet. The Mongol title 'Dalai' (meaning 'ocean') was conferred on Sonam Gyamtsho in 1578 by the Mongol ruler Altan Khan and applied retrospectively to his two predecessors, who thus became the 1st and 2nd Dalai Lamas. Succeeding Dalai Lamas, regarded as successive reincarnations of the *bodhisattva* Avalokiteshvara, have been selected as young children. During their minority, rule is exercised by regents. The 5th Dalai Lama was an outstanding national leader, as was the 13th. The 6th was a rake and poet. Of the 7th–12th only the 8th played any part in politics, and all died at early ages. The 14th headed the Tibetan administration in exile from 1959.

DALAI LAMA, 5th (1617–80), Ngawang Lopsang Gyamtsho, emerged as effective temporal and spiritual ruler of Tibet after the Mongol/Gelugpa faction defeated the King of Tsang and his Karma Kargyüpa allies (1642). Under nominal Mongol patronage, his firm, centralized rule of the whole country enabled him to regularize the administration and revenue collection, check local political abuses, and end factional and inter-sect warfare. The main interruptions to peace were three small campaigns against Bhutan. The lama encouraged the foundation of monasteries and the literary and religious arts, and wrote several historical and doctrinal works.

DALAI LAMA, 13th (1875–1933), Thupten Gyamtsho, fled to China in 1904 and to India in 1910, in the face of the British and then the Chinese incursions into Tibet. After returning in 1913 he assumed autocratic power within the traditional sphere of the Dalai Lamas, but his attempts to introduce Western educational, military, and economic methods, and to establish secure relations with other countries, were strongly opposed by the monks.

DALHOUSIE, GEORGE RAMSAY, 9th Earl of (Scottish) (1770–1838), British soldier and colonial governor, who fought throughout the Napoleonic Wars. He was appointed lieutenant-governor of NS (1816) and governor-in-chief in Canada (1819–20), where he antagonized the French-Canadian majority, who refused him a civil list. He declined to accept Papineau as Speaker and dissolved the Assembly (1827). He was recalled (1828) and made commander-in-chief in the East Indies (1829–32).

DALHOUSIE OF DALHOUSIE CASTLE AND THE PUNJAB, JAMES ANDREW BROUN-RAMSAY, Marquis of (1812–60), British statesman, who succeeded Gladstone as president of the board of trade (1845). In Jan. 1848 he became governor-general of India in succession to Hardinge. He was responsible for the extension of the British frontiers, the consolidation of British possessions, and major internal reorganization. As a stage in the growth of British power in India his administration is comparable only to those of Wellesley and the Marquis of Hastings. Six months after his arrival he became involved in a war with the Sikhs and, after a stern struggle, the Punjab was annexed to British India (1849). This advance, by making the political and geographical frontiers roughly conterminous, strengthened the British position on the north-west frontier and brought closer relations with the Amir of Kabul. In 1852 a long series of acts of oppression against British merchants by the Burmese forced Dalhousie to declare war. After a successful campaign he limited his annexations to Pegu (Lower Burma), which gave the British control of the Burmese coastline and enabled them to develop the port of Rangoon. In accordance with the doctrine of lapse he annexed any tributary or dependent Hindu state whose ruler had died without a natural successor or without having previously adopted an heir with the sanction of the British paramount power. He thus annexed Satara (1848), Jaitpur and Sambalpur (1849) Jhansi (1853), and Nagpur (1854). The annexation of Oudh (1856) was not in accordance with this doctrine but because of chronic misgovernment.

He introduced railways, the electric telegraph, and an efficient postal system. The first railway from Bombay to Thana was opened in 1853 and one from Calcutta to Ranigang in 1854. He also created a department of public works, and built roads, canals, and irrigation works. He secured to converts from Hinduism their rights as citizens, sanctioned the remarriage of Hindu widows, suppressed *sati* in the native states, and introduced special measures to combat dacoity. He placed the gaols under proper inspection, abolished the practice of branding convicts, and made efforts to prevent the crime of *meriah* (human sacrifice). He encouraged the culture of tea, protected forests and preserved ancient monuments. He also helped to lay the foundations of India's educational system.

Dalhousie has been blamed for weakening the European army in India and thus encouraging Indians to revolt in 1857. Recent research has proved the falsity of this charge for Dalhousie's protests against the reduction in army strength had been pigeon-holed by the Home government in London. Eight years of unremitting attention to duty ruined his health and on 29 Feb. 1856 he handed over the government to Canning. He must be regarded as one of the greatest proconsuls the British ever sent to India.

W. Lee-Warner, *The Life of the Marquis of Dalhousie*, 2 vols (London, 1904). CCD

DALIP SINGH (1837–93), son and successor of Maharaja Ranjit Singh. During his minority the Sikhs were defeated and the Punjab annexed to British India (1849). Dalip was granted a pension. He turned Christian and became an English landowner in Norfolk, but in 1886 re-embraced Sikhism.

DALJUNKER, THE (d. 1528), name given to an unidentified leader of a revolt against Gustavus I of Sweden, who pretended to be the son of Sten Sture the Younger. The revolt began in 1527 among the independent peasantry of Dalarne and received help from the anti-Danish party in Norway, but was eventually crushed by Gustavus. The leader escaped to Norway and thence to Rostock, where he was executed at the king's request.

DALLAS, ALEXANDER JAMES (1759–1817), US secretary of the treasury under President Madison (1814–16). Born in the West Indies, he emigrated to the US (1783) and pursued a legal career in PA. During his period in office he initiated proposals for the Second Bank of the US (1816–36).

DALMATIA, region of Yugoslavia, approximately 371 kms long but only 72 kms wide at its broadest, which comprises the central stretch of the Yugoslav littoral and a fringe of islands on the Adriatic; its population is predominantly Croatian and since the Second World War the whole area has been included in Croatia within Federal Yugoslavia.

Dalmatia's history differs from the rest of Croatia's in two important respects: first, Dalmatian ties were with Italians rather than Hungarians, Venice dominating Dalmatia from 1420 to 1797, and the Italian minority being granted exceptional privileges over the Slavs under Austrian rule (1815–1918). Second, it had attained a greater degree of independence, *eg*, Dubrovnik (Ragusa) having been self-governing for some 450 years before 1809. With the growth of national consciousness these two factors predisposed Dalmatian intellectuals to grow resentful of Italians and proud of Dalmatia's past. Realizing that an independent Dalmatia would not be viable, they thus played a prominent part in the Yugoslav movement, and during the First World War the most important members of the Yugoslav Committee were Dalmatian Croats. At the same time, Italian nationalists wanted to recover their Dalmatian possessions, and in 1915, in the secret treaty of London, they were granted North Dalmatia and islands off the South Dalmatian coast as their price for joining the entente. At the peace conference, President Wilson refused the Italian claims to Dalmatia as contradictory to the principle of 'self-determination', but was unable to suggest an alternative settlement. The Yugoslavs and Italians eventually reached an agreement at Rapallo (Oct. 1920), the latter renouncing all of Dalmatia except Zadar (Zara) and four small islands, and being compensated with a large part of Istria and a favourable compromise over Fiume (which Italy annexed later). But although Italy also gained far-reaching concessions over the treatment of the Italian minority in Dalmatia, nationalists, and, later, fascists, continued propaganda and terrorism in order to undermine the settlement, using Zadar as their base. Meanwhile, the Croats and Slovenes of Dalmatia harassed the Italian minority, claiming the forced Italianization of their compatriots in Istria as their justification.

Such activities served to keep Dalmatia apart from the internal Serb–Croat conflict which weakened Yugoslavia between the two world wars, and to reinforce their belief in the Yugoslav ideal. This proved important during the Second World War. After Yugoslavia's defeat in April 1941, the Germans allowed the Italians, who again claimed Dalmatia, to take a portion of the coast from Zadar to Split with zones in the south, while the rest of the region was absorbed in the puppet state of Croatia. Following the collapse of Fascist Italy in the autumn of 1943, the Croatian leader, Pavelic, tried to take back the Italian areas, but he was defeated, largely because the Dalmatian population enthusiastically supported and aided Tito's Partisan forces, who promised a united, federalized Yugoslavia.   MDN

DALNASPIDAL, BATTLE OF (July 1654), defeat of a royalist insurrection in Scotland under the Earl of Glencairn against the Cromwellian regime of George Monck. The insurrection failed through lack of Dutch support and divided leadership.

DALRYMPLE, ALEXANDER (1737–1808), Scottish colonial theorist, who served with the East India Co. from 1752, becoming its hydrographer in 1779 and hydrographer to the admiralty (1795–1808). His account (1769) of European voyages to the South Pacific, incorporating recently discovered Spanish material, revived interest in a Great South Land. Through temperamental difficulties he lost the chance of leading James Cook's 1768–71 voyage and consistently attacked Cook's achievements thereafter.

DALTON, JOHN (1766–1844), British chemist, who advanced in 1803 a fundamental scientific theory that the atoms of different elements were distinguished by differences in their weights. Since then, scientific thought has been profoundly influenced by Dalton's atomic theory.

DAMAD FERID PASHA (1853–1923), Ottoman statesman, and leader of the Liberal Party (1911). As grand vizier (1919–20) his policy of co-operation with the Allies was defeated by nationalist opposition.

DAMASCUS PROTOCOL (1915). Syrian nationalist statement laid down conditions for Arab co-operation with Britain against the Ottoman empire, set out the frontiers of the prospective independent Arab area, and offered economic concessions to Britain.

DAMASIAS, Athenian archon in 582 BC, whose illegal retention of office until 580 and replacement by a board drawn equally from *eupatridae* (hereditary aristocrats) and non-*eupatridae* illustrates the aristocratic discord following Solon's reforms (594).

DAMASKINOS, DEMETRIOS PAPANDREOU (1890–1949), archbishop of Athens and regent of Greece. After serving in the army, Damaskinos took orders in 1917 and became metropolitan of Corinth in 1922. He became Abp of Athens and primate of all Greece in 1938, but was soon deposed by Metaxas and exiled to Salamis. Although recalled by the Axis occupation authorities in 1941, Damaskinos became an outspoken opponent of the Nazis. In 1944 he was arrested for his part in the National Organization of Christian Solidarity (EOCKA). Damaskinos was appointed regent at the behest of the British on 31 Dec. 1944 in an effort to allay the issue of the monarchy while the battle for Athens was at its height. He was prime minister briefly in 1945 before resigning the regency in 1946.

DAMBADENIYA, capital of the principal Sinhalese kingdom of Ceylon (*c.* AD 1232–80), situated about 10 miles (16 kms) south-west of Kurunegala. Most of this period encompassed the reign of Parakramabahu II (1236–70), a scholar-king who brought most of the island under his control.

DAMBIGANTSAN (d. 1922), known also as Ja Lama, a lama and war-lord in western Mongolia. Dambigantsan was a Russian subject from Astrakhan who appeared for the first time in Mongolia in the 1890s, claiming to be a reincarnation of Amursana, leader of the Jungars in the 18th cent. By the time of the revolution of 1911 his prestige had enabled him to collect a small army, and he played a leading part in the capture of the city of Khobdo from the Chinese in 1912. He lived as a princeling in western Mongolia until he was arrested and deported by the Russians in 1914. In 1918 he reappeared, and set himself up as an independent prince in a fortress on the borders of Sinkiang. The revolutionary government distrusted his intentions. A group of ministers and officials was executed in Sept. 1922 on charges which included that of counter-revolutionary plotting with Dambigantsan, who was soon afterwards murdered.

DAMEL, title of the Wolof rulers of Cayor, Senegal. When *damel* Lat Dior (1871–82) accepted Islam, many Wolof followed his example.

DAMIAN, PETER, Saint (d. 1072), born at Ravenna, he joined a quasi-eremitical order of monks (1035) of which he became prior, reforming its rule to accord with that of St Benedict. He was an ardent but moderate supporter of the Hildebrandine (Gregorian) reform movement. He mediated in the dispute between the Emperor Henry IV with his wife and that of the Bp of Macon with abbot Hugh of Cluny (1063). In 1057 he was created cardinal. He was a prolific writer and a great number of his letters, sermons, and philosophic works survive.

DAMIETTA, CRUSADE OF (1218–21), Fifth Crusade, was diverted from inactivity in Palestine to Egypt, then the centre of Muslim power and a base for the reconquest of Jerusalem. The town of Damietta was besieged by a disunited army of mixed nationalities under the weak leadership of King John of Jerusalem. In spite of inventive siege methods, the town held out and, under the influence of Pelagius, the papal legate, offers of terms by the Muslims, including the cession of Jerusalem, were rejected. Damietta eventually fell, but an advance against Cairo ended in heavy losses and the capture of the whole crusading army. Damietta was surrendered and the country evacuated. The crusade, in which imperial troops took part, embittered relations between the pope and the Emperor Frederick II, who was blamed for the disaster.

DAMMARTIN, RENAUD DE, Count of Boulogne (d. c. 1227), one of the most powerful lords in northern France, from which he was exiled. He became a leading organizer of the anti-French coalition between King John of England and the Emperor Otto, which was defeated at Bouvines (1214), and remained a captive of the French kings until his suicide.

DAMMAZEDI (reg. 1472–92), King of Pegu. Having been a monk, and favoured by Queen Shinsawbu, he left the order and in 1475 sent a religious mission to Ceylon which led to a Buddhist revival in Burma.

DAMPIER, WILLIAM (1651–1715), English buccaneer, author, thrice circumnavigator of the globe (1673–91, 1699–1701, 1704–10), and the first Englishman to land in Australia. He sailed to Nfld and Java before joining the royal navy in 1672, later deserting to become a planter in Jamaica. After a year he joined the English logwood cutters of the Caribbean and thence drifted into privateering. He took part in the looting of the Panama Isthmus and the capture of Porto Bello (1679) and in 1686 he crossed the Pacific and explored the East Indies, visiting the Philippines, Indo-China, the Dutch East Indies, the Nicobar Islands, and Australia. He returned to England in 1691 and wrote his *New Voyage Round the World* (1697), which provided Defoe and Swift with material for *Robinson Crusoe* and *Gulliver's Travels* respectively. In 1699 Dampier commanded a royal ship, the *Roebuck*, which explored the western coast of Australia and discovered New Britain Island and what came to be called Dampier Strait. During the War of the Spanish Succession he became pilot to the privateer Captain Woodes Rogers, who rescued Alexander Selkirk from Juan Fernandez island and captured the Manila treasure ship off CA (1709). In this way he again became associated with Defoe's *Robinson Crusoe*.
MKS

DAMRONG RAJANUBHAB, Prince (1826–1943), Thailand's foremost scholar and civil administrator, the 57th child of King Rama IV (Mongkut). Founder and first director of the education ministry (1884–92), his administrative skills caught the attention of King Rama V, who made him minister of the interior (1892). He created the system of centralized provincial administration which persists to the present day. After retiring as minister (1915), he devoted the rest of his life to literary and historical scholarship—after 1932 from exile in Penang—his most notable works being *Thai rop phama* (*Thai Wars with the Burmese*) and *Nithan borannakhadi* (*Tales of the Past*).

DANA, CHARLES ANDERSON (1819–97), US newspaper editor. Born in NH and educated at Harvard, he was for five years a leading member of the utopian socialist community at Brook Farm. He joined the *New York Herald Tribune* (1849–62), served in the war department (1862–5), and in 1868 became principal owner and editor of the *New York Sun*.

DWH P

DANA, RICHARD HENRY (Jr) (1815–82), US lawyer and author. *Two Years Before the Mast* (1840), an account of a voyage made as a common sailor, brought him immediate fame. His concern with their conditions at sea stimulated him to write *The Seaman's Friend* (1841), which became a standard manual of maritime law.

DANCE, GEORGE (1700–68), British architect and surveyor to the City of London, whose public buildings included the Mansion House (1739). His son, George Dance (1741–1825), also an architect and surveyor to the City of London, designed the (rebuilt) Newgate Prison and the facade of the Guildhall.

DANDOLO, ENRICO (d. 1205), Doge of Venice, a member of an old-established noble family, who was blinded earlier in life in a war against the Byzantine empire. As leader of the extreme anti-Byzantine party he helped (1202–3) to engineer the deflection of the fourth crusade from its original Muslim objectives to an expedition against Constantinople. The Byzantine capital was captured by the Crusaders (1204), and Venice acquired all the desired maritime bases as its share of the spoils.

DANELAW, area of Scandinavian settlement in East Anglia, the eastern Midlands, and northern England. The Danelaw, even after its subjection in the 10th cent. to the kings of Wessex, retained very largely its own administrative, social, and legal peculiarities.

DANEV, STOYAN (1858–1940), Bulgarian politician and jurist, who became prime minister of Bulgaria (1901–3) and later foreign minister (1913). Best known for his strong pro-Russian sentiments, Danev lost favour when Russia refused to support Bulgarian ambitions in Macedonia.

DANEVIRKE, earthworks and wall, 16 kms long, built (c. 807–1182) to protect Hedeby and the Danish frontier in Jutland. The line was defended against the Prussians (1848–1850), and after some modernization was contested briefly during the Prussian–Austrian invasion of Feb. 1864.

DANGEAU, PHILIPPE DE COURCILLON, Marquis de (1638–1720), French soldier, courtier, and author of the *Journal de la cour de Louis XIV* (1684–1720). He served under Turenne in Flanders (1657) and was later aide-de-camp to Louis XIV (1672). As an envoy extraordinary, he arranged the marriage of James, Duke of York (later James II of England), to Mary of Modena.

DANIEL, METROPOLITAN OF MOSCOW (d. 1547), a Riazanian by birth, he became a close friend of Grand Duke Vasili III, succeeded Joseph as abbot of Volokolamsk monastery (1515) and was ordained metropolitan of Moscow in 1522. In this post he gave full support to the grand ducal authority and imposed Josephism firmly upon Church and state. He chose and ordained Makary as Abp of Novgorod (1526) and consented to Vasili's divorce and second marriage to Helen Glinsky (1526), with whom he served as regent for the child Ivan IV (1533).

DANIEL OF MOSCOW (d. c. 1264). The permanent line of Moscow princes starts from Daniel, the youngest son of Alexander Nevsky. Nevsky, at his death, left the office of Grand Prince vacant (the Grand Prince being recognized by the Tatars as responsible for the collection and delivery of tribute). By regular order of seniority the office passed to Nevsky's younger brothers, Yaroslavl of Tver and Basil of Kostroma and thence to the succeeding generation. Moscow at this time was a minor principality, and Daniel shared the Grand Princedom with Tver, alternating according to the whims of the khan.

DANIELS, JOSEPHUS (1862–1948), US journalist and public servant, editor of the North Carolina *News and Observer* and Democratic presidential campaign publicity manager (1908, 1912). He was secretary of the navy (1913–21) and US ambassador to Mexico (1933–42), experiences which he described in *The Wilson Era* (1944–6) and *Shirt-Sleeve Diplomat* (1947).

DANILEVSKY, NIKOLAI YAKOVLEVICH (1822–85), Slav anti-Darwinian Russian biologist, whose *Russia and Europe* (1869), advocating a Russian-led Slav federation in south-east Europe, became the handbook of militant Pan-Slavism. He developed a cyclical theory of history in which the Slav civilization was hostile to, and destined to succeed, the European.

DANISH CONSTITUTION. In 1849 absolutism (dating from 1660) was replaced by limited monarchy, and the consultative provincial Estates of 1831 by a bicameral legislature. All male householders received the vote at 30 years of age, electing the lower house in single-member constituencies from candidates over 25, the upper house indirectly in county-size constituencies from candidates over 40. After the war against Austria and Prussia (1864), the upper house was modified under a more conservative constitution (1866): one-fifth had to be Crown nominees and two-fifths were elected on a high property qualification. But in 1901 the ministry became responsible to the lower house, and the 1915 constitution restored a more democratic upper house and extended the vote to women.

DANISH EAST INDIA COMPANY, first established in 1616, set up its headquarters at Tranquebar in south India in 1620 and later extended its operations to Masulipatam and Bengal. At first activities were chiefly concerned with the carrying trade to Indonesia; later tea was brought from China and smuggled into England, until the UK Commutation Act (1784) made this unprofitable. In 1755 Serampur on the Hughli was settled. The Danish settlements, twice occupied by the British during the French wars, were sold to the British East India Co. in 1845. The settlements were important in affording a base for Christian missionaries at a time when they were not allowed on British territory, and a Danish mission was established in Tranquebar. From 1799 Serampur became the headquarters of the Baptists William Carey, Joshua Marshman, and William Ward.

DANISH WEST INDIA COMPANY, founded in 1625, occupied St Thomas (1671) and bought St Croix (1733), and developed a flourishing slave trade on the Guinea Coast. It was taken over by the state in 1754.

DANISHMENDS, Turkish house ruling in central Asia Minor during the 11th–14th cents. The Danishmends rose to prominence in the confusion following the death of the Seljuk prince Sulayman ibn Kutlumish, in 1085. Their forces came into conflict with the Latins of the First Crusade. After 1142 dynastic discord weakened the Danishmend regime. The end came in 1178, when the Danishmend territories became absorbed into the Seljuk Sultanate of Rum.

DANNOURA, BATTLE OF (1184), fought in the Shimonoseki straits and won by Minamoto Yoshitsune. It ended one of the most notable wars in Japanese history, the struggle between the Minamoto and the Taira.

DANQUAH, JOSEPH BOAKYE (1895–1965). Ghanaian scholar, lawyer, and politician, who founded and led the United Gold Coast Convention (1947). He opposed Nkrumah's rule in Ghana and died in political detention.

DANTE, ALIGHIERI (?1265–1321), Italian vernacular poet and political theorist. He belonged to a prosperous Florentine family and entered politics, his wife, Gemma Donati, coming from the family which provided the leader of the White faction of the Guelf party. When the Whites were

exiled in 1302 Dante's life was saved by his absence from Florence, but he spent the rest of his life in political exile. He had already written his *Vita Nuova* (*c.* 1293), in which he recollects with great precision, in prose and poetry, the development of his love for Beatrice Portinari. Though influenced by Provençal troubadours, it was a new departure in love poetry in its attempt at total recollection of emotions. In exile, Dante travelled widely in Italy and achieved considerable fame in his own lifetime.

It is uncertain when he began the *Divine Comedy*, though he ascribed it to a vision in 1300 He completed its final part only a few months before he died. With great emotion and bitter irony Dante consigns to Hell, Purgatory, and Heaven the great personalities of antiquity and his own day. He acknowledges his different debts to Virgil and to Beatrice by making them his guides: Virgil through Hell and Purgatory, and Beatrice through Heaven. He was unusual in having a scholastic education, uncommon in Italy, and there is a possibility that he studied at Paris University. Already in the Middle Ages he was the most widely read of Italian writers and through him the Tuscan dialect became the standard literary Italian.

DANTON, GEORGES JACQUES (1759–94), French politician, who played a vital role in the overthrow of the monarchy and in defending France against foreign invasion. A large venal mob-orator, he dominated Paris in the summer of 1792 and was probably directly responsible for the attack on the Tuileries (Aug.). As minister of justice immediately afterwards, he devoted his energies to preparing France for invasion. Although wanting to mediate between the Jacobins and Girondins, the latters' attacks on his financial probity made them support the Mountain and the execution of Louis XVI (Jan. 1793). He introduced the constitution of June 1793. He first proclaimed the doctrine of natural frontiers, and controlled the Committee of Public Safety from its inception in April, but failed to achieve a military victory and was ousted by Robespierre (July). Although he later returned to active politics, hoping to stop the Terror and the war, he lost the political struggle to the Jacobins and was guillotined.

DANUBE, major European river rising in the Swiss Alps and flowing through the south German states, Austria, and Hungary, into the Black Sea. Its broad basin was settled by the Slavs and the Magyars and from the Middle Ages provided the main overland trade route between the Holy Roman empire and Constantinople. From the mid-14th to the late-17th cents the eastern half of the Danube was controlled by the Ottoman Turks.

DANUBIAN PACT (7 Jan. 1935), publicly proposed by Mussolini and Laval. It was to be established between Germany, Austria, Hungary, Italy, Czechoslovakia, and Yugoslavia, open to accession of France, Poland, and Rumania; and envisaged a guarantee of Austrian independence, non-intervention in the internal affairs of each signatory state by the others, non-aggression and consultation in emergencies. However, the primary Franco-Italian aim was to protect Austria from German aggression.

This result was unlikely to be realized through the pact. Neither Austria nor Yugoslavia was keen to join an anti-German combination. Czechoslovakia and Hungary regarded each other as principal enemy, the former refusing Hungarian rearmament, a condition Hungary sought to impose for her acceptance of the pact. Moreover, the Little Entente announced their determination to intervene in Hungary or Austria in the event of a Habsburg Restoration, thus contravening a fundamental clause of the pact.

The great powers did not strive energetically to avoid failure. When Hitler, predictably, showed no interest in it, Britain sought peace through conciliation of, rather than in barriers against, Germany. Neither France nor Italy risked losing the allegiance of its respective allies, Czechoslovakia and Hungary, by pressing them too hard to make concessions, and neither abandoned provocative designs elsewhere. France cultivated a Russian alliance, and Italy pursued a 'forward' Abyssinian policy. The negotiations were dropped in Aug. 1935.

DANZIG, Baltic port at the mouth of the Vistula river. Seized from Poland by the Order of the Teutonic Knights in 1308, it was restored to the Poles by the peace of Torun (or Thorn) in 1466. By the later Middle Ages Danzig's population was largely German and the town had become an important trading centre within the Hanseatic League. It remained under the Polish Crown until the Second Partition of Poland (1793), when it was incorporated into Prussia. Captured by the French under Marshal Lefebvre during the Napoleonic Wars (1807), the town was declared a free republican state by the peace of Tilsit (7 July 1807). It was restored to Prussia in 1815 and remained German until the First World War. Despite President Wilson's 14 points (8 Jan. 1918), which included the need to create an independent Polish state with 'a free and secure access to the sea', and the protracted discussions at the Paris peace conference about Danzig's future, it became a free city in which Poland had special rights, but under the guardianship of the League of Nations (1919).

There was continual friction between Danzig's population and the Polish state and its representatives. In consequence, Poland began in 1924 to construct an alternative corridor port at Gdynia. By 1938 this took two-thirds of Poland's maritime trade and it seemed that Danzig was being deliberately ruined. In 1930 the Nazis gained seats in Danzig's *Volkstag* and in 1931 the Polish commissioner-general resigned. However, Nazi electoral successes were relatively smaller than those in Germany. While Hitler attained power in the Reich, the league's presence in Danzig prevented a Nazi coup there.

Danzig's relations with Poland began to improve after the 1934 German–Polish agreement. In 1936 Poland, accepting German guarantees of her interests, supported Germany's efforts to oust the league from Danzig. In Sept. the league withdrew its commissioner, accepting the Polish–German settlement in Jan. 1937. This enabled Danzig's Nazis to suppress political opposition.

After Munich (1938), Germany demanded that Poland should return Danzig and grant Germany extra-territorial routes across the corridor. Poland, considering this to be a prelude to further territorial demands, and to a provocative alliance against Russia, refused, being encouraged by Britain to do so (March 1939). Britain urged Polish–German negotiations until 29 Aug., when Germany's demand for negotiations amounted to an ultimatum. Poland rejected the demand, and was invaded.

After the Second World War Danzig was assigned to Poland, became the capital of the Polish central province of Pomerania, and its German population was expelled.

C. M. Kimmich, *The Free City: Danzig and German foreign policy, 1919–34* (New Haven and London, 1968)   ASJ

DAR AL-HARB (the Abode of War), expression used by Muslims to denote all the lands which stood outside the Dar al-Islam and which could be regarded therefore as subject to *jihad, ie,* to war on behalf of the Muslim faith.

DAR AL-ISLAM (the Abode of Islam), expression denoting the lands united in allegiance to the faith and law of Islam. The Muslims refer sometimes to such territories, taken together, as dārunā, *ie,* 'our land'.

DARA SHEKOH, Prince (1616–59), eldest son of the Mughal Emperor Shah Jahan and Mumtaz Mahal. On Shah Jahan's illness in 1657, he administered the empire, but was defeated by his younger brother, Aurangzeb, at Samugarh, south of Agra, in 1658, and eventually executed. He was known for his

liberal religious views and attempts to promote understanding between Islam and Brahminism.

DARBY FAMILY, English iron manufacturers Abraham Darby I (1677–1717) set up the Baptist Mills Brass Works at Bristol. He believed that cast iron might be substituted for brass in sole manufacturers and experimented with moulds of sand. In 1708 he took out a patent for 'a new way of casting iron pots and other iron-bellied ware in sand only, without loam or clay', with the result that he was able to supply the home market with a variety of goods formerly imported from abroad and which were cheaper and intended for use by the poorer classes. He next invested his capital in an old furnace at Coalbrookdale, Shropshire (1709). It was here that he successfully smelted iron ore with coke, a process which freed the iron industry from dependence on timber for charcoal supplies. It also meant that larger blast furnaces, previously restricted by the inadequacy of charcoal to a maximum of 35 ft, could be used.

His son, Abraham Darby II (1711–63), was, in 1743, probably the first man to use the Newcomen steam engine, with which a more effective blast could be driven into the furnace. He continued and improved Coalbrookdale after his father's death, fully implementing his father's innovations and firmly linking the iron and coal industries.

Darby II's son, Abraham Darby III (1750–91), again improved and perfected the coking process by more careful selection of coal suitable for coking and by increasing the strength of the blast necessary to dissipate sulphurous fumes that would otherwise produce metal too brittle for working. He built the first iron bridge, across the Severn at Coalbrookdale (1779).

DARDANELLES CAMPAIGN (1915–16), Allied campaign aimed at the seizure of Constantinople and the Straits, and the withdrawal of the Ottomans from the war in order to open the Black Sea route to Russia and establish Allied predominance in the Balkans. The failure of a naval attack (18 March 1915) was followed by a series of landings under Sir Ian Hamilton at Gallipoli (Helles and Saba Tepe, the latter better known as Anzac, from the bloody baptism of Australian and NZ troops, 25 April) and Suvla Bay (6 Aug.). No penetration was achieved, despite heavy casualties, and the stalemate was ended by the Allied evacuation of Suvla and Anzac (18 Dec.) and Helles (8 Jan. 1916). Winston Churchill, one of the earliest advocates of the Dardanelles strategy, opposed evacuation and resigned from the British government.

DARE, VIRGINIA (b. 1587), first English child born in North America. She died with Sir Walter Raleigh's ill-fated colony on Roanoke Island, NC.

DARFUR, 'homeland of the Fur', large western province of the Sudan Republic, bordering on the Chad Republic, and distinguished by its topography and its history. The first includes the massif of Jebel Marra, rising to 10,073 ft (3070 metres) from grassland plains, with smaller hills immediately to the north. Its peoples have long been the outcome of mixing with their neighbours, together with 'aboriginal' peoples whose origins remain obscure; nomadic Arabs began to immigrate late in the 16th cent. and with them came Islam. Before that Darfur, always a 'passage zone' between the Middle Nile valley and the Lake Chad region, was probably under the influence of the Christian Nubian kingdom of Makuria. Its political history begins with semi-legendary peoples in remote antiquity, continues with a people called the Tunjur, certainly historical but of whom little is securely known, and emerges factually with the Keira or Fur dynasty. This began with Suleyman Solong early in the 17th cent. and ended with Ali Dinar (*reg.* 1890–1916), after whose reign Darfur was incorporated in the Anglo-Egyptian Condominium. Some of these kings built impressive brick mosques and dwellings, and for long dominated the important east–west trade route through Darfur, as well as the 'Forty-Day Road' to the Nile near Dongola.

DARIUS I (*reg. c.* 522–486 BC), Achaemenid King of Iran, member of a minor branch of the ruling family, who seized the throne after murdering Bardiya, who had proclaimed himself king shortly before the death of Cambyses (*c.* 522). There was immediate widespread revolt among the subject peoples, who hoped for independence, and among the satraps, who did not recognize Darius as king. To celebrate his victory over the rebels (*c.* 521), Darius had the Behistan Inscription cut and in each new palace he built he commemorated the loyalty of Cambyses' bodyguard, the Ten Thousand Immortals, who had helped him to crush the revolt. Aiming at a firmly controlled but contented state, he divided the empire into 20 satrapies, each governed by a trusted official, usually a Persian, but the subject peoples were allowed to retain their own languages, institutions, religions, and customs. A carefully supervised network of roads was created, linking the various centres to facilitate administration. A new system of land tax, calculated on average yield, was adopted, and a legal code, based probably on Hammurabi's, was drawn up and distributed to the main provincial centres. Various measures were introduced which encouraged trade. Weights and measures were standardized, as were the new coins. The improved roads helped the caravan trade and a canal through the Isthmus of Suez was planned and may actually have been built. Darius was a prodigious builder, being especially noted for the palaces and other buildings at Susa and at Persepolis, which he planned and started. He increased the extent of the empire by conquering parts of West India and the Indus valley (before 513) and sent a fleet down the Indus to survey a route to Egypt. A huge campaign was launched against the Scythians of south Russia (*c.* 510), perhaps to cut off supplies of timber and wheat to Greece or to facilitate control of the frontier nomads, but the Scythians adopted a scorched-earth policy and Darius had to turn back. He did, however, conquer East Thrace and the Getae and Macedonia became a vassal state. While the Greek states were disunited, he conquered the coastal districts and suppressed a revolt of the Ionian Greeks, eventually destroying Miletus and deporting its inhabitants to Susa (497). When a similar fate befell the inhabitants of Eretria, the Greeks united and defeated the Persians at Marathon (490). Egypt rebelled and Darius died before either the Greek or Egyptian campaign was finished.

A. T. Ormstead, *History of the Persian Empire* (Chicago, 1948). JKG

DARIUS II (*reg. c.* 423–404 BC), Achaemenid King of Iran during a period of growing stability, when financial payments tended to replace feudal military obligations and gold was increasingly used diplomatically, especially in the Greek wars in which Athens was defeated (*c.* 404).

DARIUS III (*reg. c.* 336–330 BC), last Achaemenid King of Iran, who, having tried unsuccessfully to negotiate with Alexander the Great, whose ability he underestimated, was defeated in battles at Issus (333) and Gau Gamela (331). He was subsequently assassinated by a Persian.

DARK, ELEANOR (1901–), Australian author of several novels on life in Sydney during the 1930s, but mainly noted for a trilogy, *The Timeless Land* (1941), *Storm of Time* (1949), and *No Barrier* (1953). Set during the foundation years of NSW, these show considerable insight into the problems of white–Aboriginal contact.

DARLAN, FRANÇOIS (1881–1942), French admiral, and controversial figure in the Vichy regime. Darlan was commander of the French navy at the outbreak of the Second World War, and became minister of marine in Pétain's government (1940). In 1941 Pétain chose him as head of government and as his own successor, but in 1942 replaced him by Laval.

Darlan, although undoubtedly a patriot, went further than most Vichy leaders in his willingness to collaborate with, militarily, Germany and his ambiguous policies and enigmatic character have made him the subject of controversy. He was in Algiers at the time of the Allied landings in North Africa (1942), and, with the secret approval of Pétain, agreed to co-operate with the Allies, becoming head of the French forces in North Africa. He was later assassinated.

DARLING, SIR CHARLES HENRY (1809–70), governor of Vic., Australia (1863–6), who was born in NS. He held various public offices in London and the West Indies, becoming lieutenant-governor of Cape Colony (1851) and governor of Nfld (1855–7) and then of Jamaica, Honduras, and the Bay Islands, from which appointment he moved to Vict. There he suffered from the prevailing uncertainty as to the governor's role in the early days of responsible government. Involved in controversies between the lower and upper houses of the Victorian parliament, he had the doubtful distinction of being the only colonial governor of the period recalled for alleged partisanship in local conflicts.

DARLING, SIR RALPH (1775–1858), British general, governor of NSW (1825–31), who had a distinguished military career during and after the Napoleonic wars, culminating in military government of Mauritius (1819–23). This experience enabled him to effect valuable administrative and financial reforms in Sydney, but scarcely fitted him for the delicate task of managing executive–legislative council relationships, under the original 1823 and amended 1828 Judicature Act, in a community moving from penal settlement to free colony. Darling also lacked the imaginative insight to grapple successfully with the major problem of land ownership and occupation in an era of pastoral expansion. Hostility to his handling of the case of Sudds and Thompson, friction with Chief Justice Forbes over his attempt to control the Sydney press, and failure of his 1829 plan to confine squatters to the 'nineteen counties', within 150 miles (241 kms) of Sydney, all contributed to the non-renewal of his six-year term of office. Contemporary critics, before and after his return to England, tended to ignore Darling's administrative efficiency and his encouragement of exploration and expansion of settlement, the fruits of which are clearly marked on modern maps of Australia.

DARNAND, JOSEPH (1897–1945), French politician, who was head of the *Milice*, a French political police which collaborated with the Germans under the Vichy regime. A war hero and a man with a taste for violence, Darnand had been involved in various right-wing movements in the 1930s. The *Milice* was created in 1943, and Darnand later became a minister with authority over all police forces. The *Milice* committed many atrocities, and Darnand was tried and executed after the Second World War.

DARROW, CLARENCE SEWARD (1857–1938), US lawyer and an early defender of the rights of organized labour. He helped to secure amnesty for the Chicago 'anarchists' convicted after the Haymarket riot (1886). An opponent of capital punishment, he defended some 50 people on charges of first-degree murder, and only one was executed.

DARTMOUTH, GEORGE LEGGE, 1st Baron (new creation) (1648–91), British sailor and courtier. Though a Protestant, Legge was a close friend of King James II and owed much of his advancement to him. Legge's military career included service in the Second Dutch War (as a sailor as well as a soldier) and in Africa, where as admiral of the fleet and governor he supervised the evacuation of Tangier (1683). In 1688 he was given command of James's channel fleet, but was out-manoeuvred in action and failed to prevent the invasion of England by William of Orange. James II ordered

Dartmouth to conduct the queen and her son to France, but he refused to do so. He took an oath of allegiance to William III and Mary II, but was nevertheless relieved of his command. In 1691 he was accused of conspiring to aid a French invasion and was sent to prison, where he died.

DARTMOUTH, WILLIAM LEGGE, 1st Earl of (1672–1750), British courtier and office-holder. A moderate Tory, Legge owed his advancement to his friendship with Harley and the confidence of Queen Anne. He was a member of the board of trade (1702–10) but had an undistinguished administrative record. However, in 1710 he was the first Tory to be brought by Queen Anne into Godolphin's discredited ministry, replacing Sunderland as secretary of state for the southern department. In this capacity he signed preliminary articles for peace (1711). In 1713, in the face of High Tory agitation, Dartmouth was forced to resign, becoming instead lord privy seal (1713–14). On the death of Queen Anne he, as a Hanoverian Tory, was named as a regent until the arrival in England of George I. He then retired from public life.

DARTMOUTH, WILLIAM LEGGE, 2nd Earl of (1731–1801), British statesman, who held office as president of the board of trade (1765–6), secretary of state for the colonies (1772–5), and lord privy seal (1775–82). He was an opponent of compromise with the American colonists, and rejected the Olive Branch Petition (1775).

DARTMOUTH COLLEGE v WOODWARD, 4 Wheaton 518 (1819), US Supreme Court case, significant as an important early opinion by Chief Justice Marshall on the contract clause of the US Constitution. The Case arose following attempts by the NH legislature to alter a 1769 charter granted to the trustees of Dartmouth College. The state judiciary upheld the actions of the state legislature in passing laws designed to place control of the college under a board of supervisors appointed by the governor, and the trustees of the college appealed the case to the US Supreme Court.

By a 5–1 vote the US Supreme Court decided that the NH laws in question were unconstitutional as an impairment of the obligation of contract. Marshall claimed that Dartmouth College was a private institution whose charter of incorporation was a contract protected by the constitution from legislative infringement.

DARUL ISLAM REVOLT, religious rebellion against the Republic of Indonesia, led by S. M. Kartosuwirjo, head of the West Java branch of the Masjumi party. Disturbed by concessions to the Dutch, requiring Indonesian revolutionary forces to abandon West Java, and desirous of seeing Indonesia become an Islamic rather than a secular state, Kartosuwirjo recruited guerrilla forces in West Java and on 7 Aug. 1949 proclaimed the Islamic State of Indonesia, with himself as Imam. He was supported by religious conservatives and disaffected Muslim irregular troops. The movement's greatest strength lay in upland West Java, where its members became the spokesmen for peasant interests and economic grievances. As the post-revolutionary Indonesian capital was located in western Java, the rebellion posed a considerable security threat, but though it severely drained the state's finances and energy, it was never able to shake the central government. In 1957 the Darul Islam forces were at the height of their strength, with some 13,000 men, but soon afterwards the army broke their hold on the countryside and with the capture of Kartosuwirjo in 1962 the revolt was brought to an end.

DARWIN, CHARLES ROBERT (1809–82), British naturalist whose *Origin of Species* (1859) established the fact of evolution and provided the explanation by the mechanism of natural selection, which did away with all ideas of design. Evolution had been adumbrated by his grandfather, Erasmus Darwin, and by J. B. de Lamarck, but with insufficient evidence and unacceptable explanations of its cause. Darwin's

conclusions were arrived at as a result of his observations when serving as naturalist in HMS *Beagle* on a voyage (1831–6) to South America, the Galapagos Islands, Australasia, South Africa, St Helena, etc. His solution of the problem was independently put forward by Alfred Russel Wallace, and the first publication (1858) was a joint one by both. *The Descent of Man* (1871) applied his conclusions to human evolution, with the help of sexual selection; his *Expression of the Emotions in Man and Animals* (1872) was a pioneer investigation in animal psychology; his *Cross- and Self-Fertilization in the Vegetable Kingdom* (1876) provided the first experimental evidence of hybrid vigour (and of the reason for the existence of two sexes); and his *Power of Movement in Plants* (1880) was the start of the science of growth hormones in plants.

DARWIN, ERASMUS (1731–1802), British physician and natural scientist, whose *Zoonomia* (1794–6) anticipated the ideas of his grandson, Charles Darwin. He also wrote on religious and educational topics and was a member of the Birmingham Lunar Society.

DAS, CHITTARANJAN (1870–1925), Indian National Congress leader of Bengal, known as *Deshbandhu* ('friend of the country'). His effective entry into political life was in 1917, when, in a presidential address to the Bengal provincial Congress, he called for the building of a nationalist base in Bengal; thereafter he became dominant in the Bengal Congress (1919–25). Although at first opposed to non-co-operation, preferring a policy of legislative obstruction, he turned the movement to his own advantage in Bengal after Gandhi agreed (Dec. 1920) that he should have a free hand there. He organized volunteers (Nov.–Dec. 1921) and expanded the base of Congress. The effectiveness of his activities drew younger men, such as Subash Chandra Bose, to him and ensured him of enthusiastic supporters. He also made his mark at the national level. He was elected president of the Ahmedabad Congress (1921), but resigned from it to help form the Swaraj Party which contested the 1923 elections in furtherance of its policy of 'non-co-operating from within'. Das also gained a reputation for his skill as a negotiator, *eg*, his pacts with Gandhi and with the Bengal Muslims (1924). At the time of his death he was in touch with the British secretary of state, through the Bengal government, in an effort to find an agreed basis for Indian political advance.

DAS, SARAT CHANDRA (1849–1917), Indian explorer and Tibetan scholar, who learned Tibetan in Darjeeling, where he was a schoolmaster and whence he travelled with a lama to Lhasa (1879, 1881). He later travelled to Sikkim (1884) and Peking (1885) and published several books about his journeys. He was Tibetan translator to the government of Bengal (1881–1904) and published a *Tibetan–English Dictionary* (1902).

DASHKOVA, Princess (1743–1810), friend of Catherine II of Russia, whose *Memoirs* are a basic source of information about the empress's accession and court life. She was director of the Academy of Sciences, a member of the Free Economic Society and founder of the Russian Academy (1783).

DASSAULT, MARCEL (1892–   ), French aircraft manufacturer and a political follower of De Gaulle. He has been active as an aeronautical designer since the First World War, though the present Dassault company, whose success is based on its military aircraft, was founded only after the Second World War. Dassault's business interests are wide-ranging, and include a publishing empire. He has sat as a Gaullist deputy in both the Fourth and the Fifth Republics.

DASSEL, RAINALD VON (d. 1167), archbishop of Cologne and chancellor of the empire under Frederick I. He advocated an ambitious imperial policy in Italy, where he established the emperor's authority in the north.

DASTAK, word meaning in general 'passport' or 'permit', used to describe documents carried by the East India Co's servants in northern India exempting the company's trade from all permits and dues. In 1757 Robert Clive obtained from the nawab, Mir Jafar, free passes for the company's servants' private trade as well. As Indian merchants paid upwards of 40 per cent in duties of all kinds, this placed them at a great disadvantage. In 1762 the governor, Vansittart, agreed that European merchants should pay 9 per cent *ad valorem*. The Calcutta Council reduced this to $2\frac{1}{2}$ per cent, whereupon nawab Mir Kasim abolished the duties altogether. This led to war, his defeat in 1763, and Clive's second governorship. The matter was settled in 1772 by Warren Hastings, who imposed duties of $2\frac{1}{2}$ per cent on both Indian and European merchants. At the same time, all except five main customs stations were abolished.

DATO, Malay title for non-royal aristocracy. In the pre-Spanish Philippines it indicated the head of a kinship group (*barangay*).

DATTA, MICHAEL (Madhusudan Datta) (1824–73), Christian convert and Bengali poet who broke away from the old literary restrictions by using blank verse. He wrote the *Virangana Kavya* and the *Meghnad-vadh*, the greatest epic in Bengali.

DA'UD PASHA (1767–1851), last of the Georgian Mamluk pashas in Baghdad, whose attempt to establish an independent power in Iraq broke down owing to his failure to secure British assistance, and to plague, floods in Baghdad, and Ottoman determination to recover the area.

DAUGHTERS OF THE AMERICAN REVOLUTION, US women's organization founded in 1890 to promote patriotic ideals. Membership is restricted to descendants of persons who furthered the cause of American independence during the Revolution.

DAUGHTERS OF THE CONFEDERACY, THE UNITED, US women's society (founded 1894). Its members, descended from those who served the Southern cause in the Civil War, preserve the traditions of the Confederate States of America.

DAULATABAD or DEOGIRI, ruined fortress city standing on and around a conical rock which rises 600 ft (183 metres) from the plain near the city of Aurangabad in Maharashtra state, India. Deogiri was the capital of the pre-Muslim Yadava dynasty. It was captured by the Khilji sultans of Delhi, and in 1339 Sultan Muhammad Tughluq moved his capital from Delhi to Deogiri, giving it the name of Daulatabad. The removal, however, was a failure and the city later became part of the Bahmani kingdom.

DAUMIER, HONORÉ (1808–79), French artist, famous chiefly for his satirical lithographs. His work for Charles Philipon in the periodicals *La Caricature* and *La Charivari* forms a biting commentary on government and society.

DAUN, LEOPOLD JOSEPH MARIA, Count (1705–66), Imperial field-marshal, who came from an Austrian military family. He fought against Frederick II of Prussia in the Seven Years War (1756–63), defeating him at Kolin (1757) and Hochkirch (1758), and took Dresden (1758). Daun was himself defeated at Torgau (1760).

DAUPHIN, title given to the eldest son of the reigning monarch in France.

DAURA, in northern Nigeria, was traditionally the oldest of the Hausa states, and represented the other six in dealings with Bornu. In the 19th cent. it was partitioned between a Fulani and two Hausa dynasties. The original ruling family was restored in 1912.

DAVENANT, CHARLES (1656–1714), British political economist. He was an MP, commissioner of excise, and secretary to the commission that settled the Union with Scotland. His numerous pamphlets were mercantilist in tone, but in 'An Essay on the East India Trade' (1701) he argued in favour of buying in the cheapest market, which would reduce costs, promote trade, and, by stimulating competition, encourage the invention of labour-saving machinery.

DAVENANT, SIR WILLIAM (1608–68), English poet laureate (1638) and dramatist, being the author of *The Wits* (1633) and other plays. He was an active royalist and served during the Civil War at the siege of Gloucester (1643). His *Siege of Rhodes* (1656) was the first English opera libretto. He staged elaborate productions at the Duke's Theatre, London, and collaborated with Dryden in an adaptation of *The Tempest* (1667). He also wrote a long epic, *Gondibert*, and several lyrics.

DAVENPORT, JOHN (1597–1670), English-born nonconformist clergyman, who emigrated to the New Haven, CT, colony (1638) and became leading protagonist of liberalizing tendencies in New England Calvinism. Davenport protected the English regicides Edward Whalley and William Goffe (1661).

DAVID (*c.* 1000–961 BC), Hebrew King, once the favourite, and later the enemy, of King Saul. On Saul's death, David seized control of the southern part of the kingdom (Judah), gradually subdued the north (Israel), and conquered Jerusalem, making it the capital and religious centre of the state. He defeated the Philistines, taking Gath and Ashdod, and conquered Moab, Ammon, Damascus, and Edom. His later years seem to have been occupied mainly with troubles arising from quarrels and rivalry within his own family. He was succeeded by his son, Solomon.

DAVID I (*c.* 1085–1153), King of Scotland (*reg.* 1124–53), most Normanized of all the sons of Malcolm III and Margaret, who began the systematic introduction of feudalism into Cumbria. He developed a royal household on Norman lines and introduced new monastic orders into Scotland. The defeat of Angus, Lord of Moray, a descendant of Macbeth, in 1130 made David master of Moray. David supported his niece, the Empress Matilda, in England against King Stephen and took advantage of the anarchy to ravage and annex temporarily the northern English shires. He is regarded as one of the greatest of the Scottish kings.

DAVID II (1324–71), King of Scotland (*reg.* 1329–71), son of Robert. He married Joan, sister of Edward III, in 1328, and succeeded his father in 1329. He was in exile in France (1333–41) after the battle of Halidon Hill and imprisoned by the English after his defeat at Neville's Cross (1346–57), but was ransomed under the treaty of Berwick. He died childless and was succeeded by the first of the Stewarts, Robert II.

DAVID, Saint (d. *c.* 589), patron saint of Wales. That David was a historical figure of the 6th cent. is certain, but his *Life* contains much legendary material. David seems to have been one of the leaders of an ascetic, evangelical movement in the Celtic church, active mainly in south-western Wales, where most of the churches dedicated to him are to be found. His shrine is at St David's, Pembrokeshire. He was canonized early in the 12th cent.

DAVID, JACQUES LOUIS (1748–1825), chief painter of the French Revolution, Consulate, and First Empire, who established the neo-classical style of painting in France. His paintings of revolutionary heroes, such as the dead Marat and Napoleon, dignified the new regime and he was exiled on its collapse (1816).

DAVID, SIR TANNATT WILLIAM EDGEWORTH (1858–1934), Australian geologist and Antarctic explorer. He joined the NSW Geological Survey (1882) and his exploration of the Hunter Valley Permian coal-measures opened up the South Maitland coalfield. As professor of geology at Sydney University (1891–1926) he worked on glacial phenomena in Australia and on the formation of coral atolls at Funafuti, Ellis Islands. After Antarctic exploration with Shackleton and Mawson, he was chief geologist to the British armies on the western front. Primarily a field geologist, David was a great correlator; using scattered state records, he produced a geological map of the whole continent. He wrote *The Geology of the Commonwealth of Australia* (1950).

DAVIDOVIC, LJUBOMIR (1863–1940), Serbian and Yugoslav political leader, who was a school-teacher and university professor before entering politics. Within the Serbian Radical Party he led a dissident faction, the 'Young' or 'Independent' Radicals. Before the First World War, however, he served in several Radical governments as minister of education, a post he held in the wartime coalition. After the war he joined his 'Young' Radicals to the Habsburg (precani) Serbs of Pribicevic, forming the Democratic Party, of which he became the leader. From the 1920 elections the Democrats emerged as the second party in the assembly. The party supported the constitution of 1921, but a year later Davidovic grew disenchanted with Serb hegemony in the new state. The party fared badly in the 1923 elections and soon split. Pribicevic led the Independent Democrats into alliance with the Radicals, and Davidovic took the Democrats into the opposition bloc with the Croats and formed a short-lived government (July 1924). This group suffered heavily in the 1925 elections and was overshadowed by the Serb and Croat parties.

DAVIES, SIR JOHN (1570–1626), English statesman and poet, who went to Ireland, where he became first attorney-general and then speaker of the Irish parliament (1613). He published *Discovery of the true causes why Ireland has never been subdued* (1612).

DAVIS, HENRY WINTER (1817–65), US politician. As a 'Know Nothing' congressman from MD (1855–61) he broke the deadlock in the House of Representatives in 1860 by supporting the Republican nominee for speaker. As a Republican congressman (1863–5) he was a leading opponent of presidential plans for reconstruction of the South, and he co-sponsored the Wade–Davis bill (1864).

DAVIS, JEFFERSON (1808–89), US politician and first and only president of the Confederate States of America. He was born in KY and taken to MS during his childhood. After graduating from the US Military Academy at West Point and several years of soldiering (1828–35), he became a planter at Brierfield, MS, growing increasingly attached to the Southern social system. As a benevolent master, he resented outside interference in the South and advocated state rights as a defence against abolitionist attacks on slavery. He was a Democratic congressman (1845–6), but resigned to serve in the Mexican War, and his belief in his own military abilities was heightened when he achieved distinction at the battle of Buena Vista (1847). As a US senator (1847–51) he approved the annexation of Mexican lands in 1848, but resisted the organization of OR as a territory without slavery (1849) and the admission of CA as a free state (1850). He resigned from the Senate to run (unsuccessfully) for the governorship of MS, being relatively moderate on the secession issue (1851). While serving as Franklin Pierce's secretary of war (1853–7) Davis advocated selection of a southern route for the transcontinental railroad and initiated the Gadsden Purchase (1853). Returning to the Senate (1857–61), he countered Stephen A. Douglas's 'popular sovereignty' doctrine by arguing that neither Congress nor the inhabitants could interfere with slavery in the territories. Davis, reluctant to secede, withdrew with his state, and, although hoping for high military command, accepted the provisional presidency of the Confederacy (Feb. 1861). Later he was elected to a full six-year term. He was probably the best available candidate for the office, and although handicapped by constant neuralgia, worked hard, doing much to sustain the Confederacy in face of the inherent weakness of the South in comparison with the North. He had also to contend with vitriolic criticism of his leadership and the unco-operativeness of many Southern politicians, especially state governors. Some of his difficulties were of his own making: he was politically insensitive, a poor administrator, and an inefficient chairman. As commander-in-chief, he appreciated that Southern strategy should be largely defensive, but over-estimated his own military ability, and devoted too much attention to his army's affairs to the detriment of his civil responsibilities. The appointment of Robert E. Lee as general-in-chief was delayed until Jan. 1865, and loyalty to subordinates sometimes led Davis to retain incompetent generals, such as Braxton Bragg. Being a strict constructionist, he was, unlike Abraham Lincoln, unwilling to extend governmental powers in time of emergency. Even in the closing months of the war he refused to accept any terms which rejected Confederate independence. As the Confederacy disintegrated he left the capital, Richmond (April 1865), stopped briefly at Danville, VA, and Charlotte, NC, then was captured at Irwinville, GA (10 May 1865). For two years he was imprisoned at Fortress Monroe and though indicted for treason, was never brought to trial. He defended his policies in his *Rise and Fall of the Confederate Government* (1881).

Hudson Strode, *Jefferson Davis* (New York, 1955–64).

DAVIS (or DAVYS), JOHN (c. 1550–1605), Arctic explorer and Elizabethan sea-captain. He went to sea as a boy and in 1585, 1586, and 1587 made voyages to the north-east coast of America and explored the shores of Davis Strait, Cumberland Sound, and Baffin Bay in search of the North-West Passage. He also fought against the Spanish Armada (1588). In his later years he made several expeditions to the South Seas, and is the reputed discoverer of the Falkland Islands. He was killed near Singapore by Japanese pirates.

DAVIS, JOHN (*d.* 1622), English scientific navigator and seaman, who continued Frobisher's work, seeking a north-west passage between Greenland and the North American archipelago (1585–7, 1591). He later took service with the Dutch to learn the Cape route to the East and was chief pilot for the first East India Co. expedition (1601). He also converted the backstaff, which he described in his *Seaman's Secrets* (1549), into the improved quadrant.

DAVIS, JOHN WILLIAM (1873–1955), US lawyer and politician, who served as solicitor-general of the US (1913–1918), and ambassador to Britain (1918–21). His nomination as presidential candidate on the 103rd ballot at the Democratic national convention (1924) was made in an attempt to reconcile the differences between the urban and rural wings of the party, but in the election Davis was heavily defeated by Calvin Coolidge.

DAVIS, NORMAN HEZEKIAH (1878–1944), US businessman, public servant, and diplomat. Born in TN, he made a fortune through banking and sugar enterprises in Cuba, became an adviser to the US treasury (1917–19), assistant secretary of the treasury (1919–20), and under-secretary of state (1920–1). He served as US delegate to the International Economic Conference at Geneva (1927), the Geneva Disarmament Conference (1932–4), the London Economic Conference (1933), the London Naval Conference (1935), and the Brussels Conference on the Far East (1937). In 1938 he was appointed chairman of the American Red Cross. Davis was one of President F. D. Roosevelt's leading advisers on problems of foreign policy.

DAVIS, STUART (1894–1964), US painter who, fascinated by abstract art, experimented with shape and colour and was a leader of American 'modernism'. In the 'Eggbeater' series (1927–8) he painted nothing but an eggbeater, an electric fan, and a rubber glove, reducing them to abstract relationships. His work helped to inspire the Pop Art movement of the 1960s.

DAVISON, WILLIAM (? 1541–1608), English diplomat and secretary of state under Elizabeth I, by whom he was sent to negotiate with William of Orange (1577). He was later made the scapegoat for Mary Queen of Scots' execution, being fined and imprisoned in the Tower for forwarding the warrant of execution (1587), although in fact he had acted strictly in accordance with Queen Elizabeth's wishes.

DAVISON, WILLIAM SOLTAU (1846–1924), pioneer of NZ's refrigerated trade. He established (with James Little) the Corriedale sheep-breed (1874), organized the first shipment of frozen meat (1882), and planned the first scientific dairy factory in NZ (1881–2).

DAVITT, MICHAEL (1846–1906), Irish nationalist and agrarian agitator, who was imprisoned (1870–7) for his part in Fenian outrages. In 1879 Davitt secured 'the new departure', whereby John Devoy, representing American Fenian extremists, supported Parnell's agitation for political and agrarian reform. Parnell's presidency of Davitt's Land League (founded Oct. 1879) powerfully augmented his backing in Ireland. The two leaders disagreed over tactics, eg, Davitt's 'No Rent' manifesto, and over ultimate aims, for Davitt wanted land nationalization and an industrial, secular, and independent Ireland. He denounced the Phoenix Park murders and exposed the Pigott forgeries, but repudiated Parnell's parliamentary leadership (Nov. 1890).

DAVY, SIR HUMPHRY (1778–1829), British chemist and president of the Royal Society (1820). At the age of 22 he became a lecturer at the Royal Institute, where the wide range of his lectures attracted distinguished audiences. He discovered the physiological action of nitrous oxide (1800) and the composition of the alkalis (1807). His investigations into mine explosions, led him to invent the safety lamp (1815).

DAWES, CHARLES GATES (1865–1951), Chicago banker and vice-president of the US (1924–8). During the First World War he was outspoken as purchasing agent for Gen. Pershing's expeditionary force. He was the first director of the budget bureau (1921–3), and became chairman of the committee on German reparations that produced the Dawes plan (1924). As Republican vice-presidential candidate in 1924 his international reputation and vigorous campaigning were exploited to the full to secure the election of Calvin Coolidge. He later served as ambassador to Britain (1929–32) and president of the Reconstruction Finance Corporation (1932). He was awarded the Nobel Peace Prize (1925).

DAWES ACT (1887) (Severalty Act), in the US, authorized the president to divide the lands of any Indian tribe, giving 160 acres to the heads of families and lesser amounts to bachelors, women, and children. The land was to be held in trust by the government for 25 years. All those receiving grants were to become citizens and the remaining reservation lands were to be sold by the government, the profits being deposited in an educational trust fund. It was hoped that this act would hasten Indian assimilation, but the policy failed and the Indians lost 90 million acres (364,100 sq. kms). The Indian Reorganization Act (1934) overthrew the basic premise of the earlier act, marking a return to a policy of respect for the Indians' cultural traditions.

DAWES PLAN (1924). After France's invasion of the Ruhr in 1923, following Germany's default in her reparations payments, it was felt, especially in Britain and America, that reparations should be treated more as an economic than as a political issue. A sub-commission of the Reparations Commission was appointed at the end of 1923, with the American general Charles G. Dawes as chairman. Its report on reparations was presented on 9 April 1924.

The Dawes Commission considered reparations problems since 1919 and those arising from the Ruhr invasion. The latter included currency inflation and the customs division between occupied and unoccupied zones. The former included estimating Germany's capacity for payment, and devising guarantees other than the threat of military sanctions.

To stabilize the new Rentenmark, the Dawes plan proposed that there should be an 800 million goldmark foreign loan to establish a central gold reserve. The bank of issue was to be reorganized to bring it partly under foreign control. To prevent Germany's reparations payments' causing her currency to depreciate, she was to deposit goldmarks to the reparation agent's account in a designated German bank. The agent would arrange the transfer of funds to foreign creditors.

The payments were to increase in five years from 1000 million goldmark to 2500 million, and to be raised partly from German industrial debentures and state railway bonds —a concession to France's demand for 'productive guarantees'. The government was to transfer railway administration to a corporation partly controlled by creditors. However, French control over railways in the occupied region was to end; the Dawes plan was based on the assumption of Germany's fiscal and economic unity. The total reparations debt was not fixed.

The London Accord on the Dawes plan was signed on 30 Aug. 1924 after a conference in which Germany participated. In Oct. the necessary loan was floated. The largest subscription was American.   ASJ

DAWN, English-language daily newspaper founded (1938) by M. A. Jinnah in Delhi to give expression to Muslim League interests. In 1947 the paper was moved to Karachi, where it continued publication in English and added Urdu and Gujarati editions.

DAWSON, SIMON JAMES (1820–1902), Canadian civil engineer and politician, who emigrated from Scotland. He was appointed (1857) by the Canadian government to explore the country from Lake Superior westward to the Saskatchewan river, and his report was among the first to draw attention to the possibilities of the north-west as a home for settlers. In 1868 he was employed to open communications with the Red River country, and the Dawson Road, completed by troops of the Red River Expedition (1870), was used by immigrants until 1876. Dawson was a Conservative member of the Ont. legislature (1875–8) and of the Canadian House of Commons (1878–91).

DAWUD IBN ASKIA MUHAMMAD I (d. 1583), sixth *askia* of Songhay (*reg.* 1549–83). Like his father, a strong supporter of Islam, he campaigned against the non-Muslim Mossi and Gurma and encouraged Islamic scholarship.

DAY, THOMAS (1748–89), British philanthropist. His concern with moral and social welfare found practical expression in extensive farming conducted on philanthropic principles. He wrote poems attacking the American War of Independence and his book, *The History of Sandford and Merton* (1783–9), is an adaptation of Rousseau's *Émile* to English conditions.

DAY OF DUPES, climax (10–11 Nov. 1630) of the French crisis in which Marie de Medici, the Queen Mother, tried to overthrow Richelieu while her son, Louis XIII, was ill. However, Louis disregarded her and was reconciled with Richelieu, who later ordered reprisals on his aristocratic enemies. Marie de Medici played no further part in government.

DAYANANDA SARASWATI. Swami (1824–83), founder of the Arya Samaj, a religious movement which played an important part in the awakening of Indian national consciousness. He was born of an orthodox Brahman family, but came to believe that the Hinduism of his time contained accretions that were contrary to the spirit of the Vedas. He offended orthodox Brahmans by his condemnation of later Hindu commentators and philosophical systems. He denounced polytheism and the use of images, the caste system, and child marriage. His claims for the infallibility of the Vedas were carried to absurd limits; he even argued that they contained the germ of modern science. His most important literary work was the *Satyartha Prakash*.

DAYLAM, geographical expression denoting the highlands of Gilan, south of the Caspian Sea, and the adjacent territories. The local population, perhaps of pre-Iranian stock, had a notable role as mercenaries in the time of the Sasanid state in Persia. The Daylamis long maintained their independence against the Muslims. After an Alid prince, Yahya b. Abdallah, had taken refuge amongst them in 791 the Shi'i faith made progress in Daylam. Under the House of Buya the Daylami warriors won for themselves control over much of Persia, Iraq, and the neighbouring areas. Baghdad fell to them in 946. The Buyid domination lasted until the rise of the Seljuk Turks, who entered Baghdad in 1055.

DE HAERETICO COMBURENDO (1401), English statute authorizing the burning of heretics, passed on the petition of clergy and Commons to check the spread of Lollardy. It was later used by Henry VIII to crush opposition to his formulation of doctrine, was repealed by the Duke of Somerset (1547), but revived by Mary I to give statutory authority to her persecution of Protestants.

DE JURE BELLI ET PACIS (1625), major work of Hugo Grotius written in exile, in which he tried to base the security and peace of international society upon law and a social contract between states.

DE REVOLUTIONIBUS ORBIUM COELESTIUM (1543), major work of Nicholas Copernicus, in which his heliocentric theories of the universe were expounded as a mathematical hypothesis. It was dedicated to Pope Paul III.

DEAD SEA SCROLLS, collection of Hebrew and Aramaic works discovered (1947–56) in caves in the neighbourhood of Qumran, at the north-west end of the Dead Sea. About one-quarter are biblical manuscripts which have thrown new light on the history of the Old Testament text; they originally belonged to the library of a strict Jewish monastic community which lived at Qumran in two periods between the 2nd cent. BC and AD 68. The community, possibly Essenes, regarded itself as the true Israel involved in a cosmic struggle against the forces of evil. Its organization revealed in its Rule, the Manual of Discipline, presents certain parallels with that of the early Christian Church as portrayed in the Acts of the Apostles.

DEÁK, FERENCZ (1803–76), chief Hungarian architect of the *Ausgleich* with the Habsburg monarchy, who supported the first stages of the 1848 revolution, but refused to follow Kossuth in his more extreme demands and the declaration of independence. In the late 1850s and early 1860s Deák emerged as the leader of Hungarian opposition to Austrian centralism and of demands for a measure of autonomy on the basis of the 1848 constitution. His determination and tactical skill were largely responsible for achieving the peaceful settlement of the *Ausgleich*, although he refused to become a member of the first Hungarian government (1867).

DEAKIN, ALFRED (1856–1919), second prime minister of the Commonwealth of Australia and dominant influence in successive parliaments of its first decade. He was born in Melbourne of English parents, and though he qualified as a barrister, his main youthful occupation was journalism with the radical newspaper, *The Age*. Entering colonial politics in 1879 as an advanced Liberal, he rose rapidly to ministerial office in Vic. in 1883. As joint leader of a coalition government (1886–90), he pioneered irrigation schemes to assist agriculture. At the London colonial conference of 1887 he made a strong impression as an Australian nationalist. He was an outstanding figure through all the phases of the federal movement after 1889: a member of the federal conventions of 1891 and 1897–8, leader of the movement in Vic., and conciliator behind the scenes. On inaguration of the Commonwealth he became attorney-general (1901–3) and was prime minister in 1903–4, 1905–8, and 1909–10. He retired from parliament in 1913. His politics had included factory legislation, industrial arbitration, the 'new protection' (an attempt to link tariff protection with legal enforcement of fair wages), and the foundation of an independent Australian navy.

Though a champion of imperial ties, political and economic, Deakin consistently asserted the claims of the self-governing dominions to have a voice in imperial decisions affecting them. In domestic affairs he saw himself as a national rather than a party leader; indeed, until the Labor victory of 1910 no single party had a majority in the Commonwealth parliament. Alliances were inevitable and there were seven governments between 1901 and 1910. At various times Deakin was much criticized for his willingness to act with former opponents, notably in 1909, when he formed an anti-Labor 'fusion' of Protectionists with former Free Traders.

A man of great charm and wide culture, whose oratorical gifts enlivened the proceedings of colonial and national parliaments, Deakin had fervent admirers and bitter critics. In private he was an incessant student and writer, with a strongly philosophical and religious bent. His *Federal Story* (1963) contains personal memoirs of the federal movement in Australia.

W. L. F. Murdoch, *Alfred Deakin: a sketch* (London, 1923). J. A. La Nauze, *Alfred Deakin: a biography* (Melbourne, 1965).   JALaN

DEAN, RURAL, English equivalent of the continental archpriest. Each archdeaconry was divided into a number of deaneries, each consisting of a group of parishes presided over by one of the local clergy, the rural dean. The office was in existence by 1150 and remains (1970) in the Church of England.

DEANE, SILAS (1737–89), American lawyer and diplomat. He was a leader of the revolutionary movement and a delegate to the First and Second Continental Congresses (1774, 1775), was sent as a commissioner to France (1776), and helped negotiate the treaties of 1778. Recalled after charges of financial peculation, he became disillusioned with the American cause, returned to Europe, and advised reconciliation with Britain.

DÉAT, MARCEL (1894–1955), French intellectual and politician who moved from socialism to admiration of Nazism. He formed a 'neo-socialist' party with authoritarian tendencies when expelled from the Socialist Party (1933), and opposed French entry into the Second World War. He was a leading collaborator during the German occupation of France, and as minister of labour (1944) organized the deportation of French workers to Germany. After the War he fled to Italy, where he lived clandestinely until his death.

DEATH DUTIES IN BRITAIN, payable as graduated estate duty upon real and personal property, were levied from 1894. Reformers thought this flexible tax on capital could make the rich pay a fairer contribution towards the nation's expenses and help to redistribute wealth. Others thought it discouraged public and personal thrift and struck unfairly at the landowning interest. Britain, like other European countries, had earlier levied legacy and succession duties upon personal and real property respectively, graduated according to the beneficiary's degree of relationship with the testator. Sir William Harcourt's budget (1894) imposed death duties (payable, as probate already was, before bequests were distributed) on the total net value of estates of over £5000. In his 'People's Budget' (1909), Lloyd George increased the scales on estates valued at £5000–£1 million, for political as well as fiscal reasons. Death duties have remained (1970) as a considerable source of revenue to the exchequer.

DEBOW, JAMES DUNWOODY BROWNSON (1820–67), US editor, statistician, and spokesman for the South. After serving as editor of the *Southern Quarterly Review* (1844–6), he moved to New Orleans, where he founded the monthly *Commercial Review of the South and Southwest* (1846), later *DeBow's Review*, which acquired considerable influence and the largest circulation of any magazine in the South. Always an advocate of southern economic development, including industrial expansion and a transcontinental railroad, he defended slavery and eventually supported secession. He was superintendent of the US census of 1850 and wrote a *Statistical View of the United States* (1854), which incorporated important suggestions for the improvement of the census. During the Civil War he was the Confederate government's chief agent for the purchase and sale of cotton.

DEBRAY, RÉGIS (1941–), French author and sympathizer with the Cuban revolution. His book on Latin America, *Revolution in the Revolution?* (1967), attracted wide attention. After visiting the guerrillas of Ché Guevara in Bolivia, Debray was arrested by the government and sentenced to 30 years' imprisonment (1967).

DEBRÉ, MICHEL (1912–) French politician and disciple of De Gaulle, who chose him as first prime minister of the Fifth Republic. Debré had a legal training, and was a civil servant before the Second World War. He served in the 1939–40 campaign and was later active in the Resistance, being a leader of the *Ceux de la Résistance* group. At the Liberation he became a *commissaire de la République* (regional administrator), then joined the political staff of De Gaulle, being especially associated with administrative reform and German affairs.

Originally a Radical in politics, Debré joined De Gaulle's RPF movement, and entered the senate in 1948. He became known as the Fourth Republic's most vigorous parliamentary critic, and published books and articles attacking the weaknesses of the constitution and advocating a strong executive. On De Gaulle's return to power (1958), Debré became minister of justice, and was responsible for drafting the new constitution, whose detailed provisions were based on his own theories.

When De Gaulle became president, Debré was appointed prime minister (1959), and he served De Gaulle loyally until his resignation in 1962, despite his lack of sympathy with the evolution of the president's Algerian policy. Debré later returned to office as minister of finance (1966–8), of foreign affairs (1968–9), and of defence (1969). He remained (1970) a leading exponent and interpreter of Gaullist ideas.   RDA

DEBS, EUGENE VICTOR (1855–1926), US socialist leader, born in Terre Haute, IN. As a youth he worked in the railroad shops and became a locomotive fireman. Through taking an early interest in union activities, he was elected editor of the *Locomotive Fireman's Magazine* (1880–93). Being convinced that craft unionism was a mistake, he helped to found the industrially based American Railway Union (1893). Its organizing activities led to the Pullman Strike (1894), during which Debs was arrested and imprisoned for six months. On being converted to socialism he organized the Social Democratic Party of America (1897), and stood as the Socialist Party candidate for the US presidency five times between 1900 and 1920. He was editor of the socialist weekly, *Appeal to Reason*. During the First World War he was arrested for violation of the Espionage Act and was again imprisoned (1918). After his release (1921), he remained America's most respected advocate of socialism and industrial unionism.

DEBT PEONAGE, system introduced in Spanish America in the 16th cent. which provided labour services for the plantations (*haciendas*) to offset the labour shortages created by population decline and the inadequacy of existing systems of labour rotation. The system, which still exists (1970) in many regions of Latin America, operates as follows: the *hacendado* (landowner) advances food and other necessities to a labourer, who is then obliged to work off the debt. In practice the labourer can never achieve this, since repeated advances are inevitably required. Debt peonage solved the agricultural requirements of the Spanish colonial population and served to speed racial mixture (*mestizaje*) and cultural assimilation.

DECATUR, STEPHEN (1779–1820), US naval officer, who fought against the Barbary pirates (1803–5) and held command during the War of 1812. He was instrumental in concluding a treaty with Algiers (1815) which ended the payment of tribute. He is credited with originating the phrase 'our country, right or wrong'.

DECAZES, ELIE, Duke of (1780–1860), French liberal prime minister in the early years of the Restoration of the monarchy. He was the son of an advocate and himself practised as a lawyer until he became secretary to Napoleon's mother. He refused to take the oath to Napoleon during the Hundred Days, and was made prefect of police (1815) by Louis XVIII, with whom he formed a close personal relationship. He supported the White Terror at first, but later, as minister of police, urged a reconciliation with the liberals. He managed the elections for some years and eventually became prime minister himself (1819), only to fall from grace because his policy had given too much encouragement to the liberals, and was blamed for the assassination of the Duc de Berri (1820). He founded a famous industrial dynasty based on coal and iron.

DECCAN, English form of the Sanskrit word *Dakshina*, meaning south, applied in its widest sense to India south of Vindhyas and the Narbada river between the eastern and western Ghats. Historians restrict it to the plateau south of the Narbada and north of the Krishna and Tungabhadra, or the area roughly covered by the modern states of Madhya Pradesh, Bombay, and Andhra Pradesh. Because of its distance from Delhi and its geographical isolation, the Deccan had a separate history from that of northern India until the intrusion of the European nations and the development of communications under British rule. It formed part of the Maurya empire in the 4th cent. BC and Asoka's empire (3rd cent.) extended as far south as Nellore, in the neighbourhood of which are the rock edicts of Maski, Kopbal, and Siddapura. After the decline of Mauryan power the Andhras ruled over central India for five centuries until *c.* AD. 250.

Ptolemy refers to their ruler as the king of Paithan (Pratishthana) and it is mainly to the Andhra kingdom that the account of eastern trade in the Periplus refers. Later dynasties were the Gangas, Vakatakas, and Kadambas. The Gupta emperors of northern India failed to overthrow the Vakatakas. Similarly, Harsha, the great Hindu emperor (*reg.* 606–47), failed to penetrate the Deccan, which was then strongly protected by the Chalukyan King, Pulakesin II, whose northern frontier was the Narbada river. Throughout the 9th cent. the Rashtrakutas of the Deccan successfully resisted the Gurjara-Prathiharas of Kanauj. While the Muslim invaders were consolidating their power in Hindustan in the 13th cent., the Deccan was weakened by internecine struggles, being divided between three rival dynasties, the Yadavas, with Deogir as their capital, the Hoysalas of Mysore, and the Kakatiyas, who ruled Warangal.

Towards the end of the 13th cent. Muslim forces from the north began to cross the Narbada. There was a fundamental difference between Khilji and Tughluq policy in the Deccan. Khilji policy was not one of occupation whereas the Tughluqs, like the Mughals under Aurangzeb, aimed at permanent conquest, which was difficult because of the backwardness of communications. The Deccan formed part of the extensive empire of Muhammad bin Tughluq (*reg.* 1325–51) until a Muslim governor rebelled and founded the Bahmani kingdom (1347). In the 15th cent. this kingdom broke up into five Muslim sultanates which, by the reign of Aurangzeb (1659–1707), had been incorporated in the Mughal empire. Mughal rule in the Deccan was challenged by the Marathas under Sivaji (1627–80). His successors were puppets who, as titular heads of the Maratha confederacy, came into conflict with the rising British power. It was not until 1818 at the end of the final Maratha war that the British became the paramount power and established their rule over the Deccan. *Cambridge History of India*, 6 vols (Cambridge, 1922–32).

C. Collin Davies, *An Historical Atlas of the Indian Peninsula* (Madras, 1965).   CCD

DECCAN EDUCATION SOCIETY, founded at Bombay (1884) by M. G. Ranade. Young men educated by the Society had to devote their lives to the service of their country and were required to serve for at least 20 years on a nominal salary. Gopal Krishna Gokhale was trained there.

DECCAN RIOTS, (1875) in India occurred because of moneylenders' widespread expropriation of peasant proprietors, who became tenants at will subject to rack-renting. The Deccan Riots Commission (1875) emphasized the improvidence of the peasants and their failure to realize the consequences of their extravagant borrowing. The Deccan Agriculturists' Relief Act (1879) afforded the peasants protection similar to that provided for bankrupt debtors and exempted their immovable property from liability to sale in execution of decrees. It allowed the courts to modify contracts in favour of the peasants so as to reduce an oppressive rate of interest and prevent the sale of land not specifically pledged. Creditors had to publish accounts and grant receipts. The results of this legislation were disappointing, as the act was largely evaded or ignored. It also increased litigation and the difficulty of borrowing.

DECEBALUS (d. AD 106), King of the Dacians and opponent of Rome, who united his scattered people for the first time for a century, conquered neighbouring tribes, and in 85–6 attacked the Roman province of Moesia with some success, admitting no more than formal subordination to Rome after a counter-invasion. Attacked by Trajan allegedly for a breach of treaty, he submitted to stiffer terms while still preserving some independence (102), but in 105–6 Trajan decided to annex all Dacia; Decebalus' capital, Sarmizegetusa, was taken and he committed suicide. Trajan's column in Rome depicts the campaigns.

DECELEA, in Attica, north-east of Athens, was fortified (413 BC) by the Spartans in the second part of the great Peloponnesian War. The Athenian countryside, hitherto subjected only to brief summer invasions, was thus rendered unusable, 20,000 Athenian slaves were encouraged to desert, and Athens was put virtually under siege.

DECEMBRISTS, members of secret societies involved in the insurrection of Dec. 1825 against the Russian monarchy. Although they were aristocratic army officers, their revolutionary plans had more in common with the ideals of the 19th-cent. intelligentsia than with an 18th-cent. palace coup. Being influenced by the French Revolution and the Revolu-

tionary and Napoleonic Wars, they opposed the government with organizations modelled on freemasonry and contemporary Italian and Greek secret societies.

The Union of Salvation (1816) and the Union of Welfare (1818) together aimed to achieve representative government, abolition of serfdom, and a scheme of social welfare. The movement split after 1820 into two separate societies. The Northern Society (1822) re-established the Union of Welfare and, led by Princes Obolensky and Trubetskoy and N. Muraviev, advocated a constitutional monarchy. Muraviev's constitution was based on that of the US and proposed a bicameral legislature with elected officials, the franchise related to a property qualification, and freedom of speech, conscience, and association. Serfs were to be freed, but noble estates preserved and the empire reorganized on a federal system.

The Southern Society (1821), under its leader, P. Pestel, was more radical. Pestel's 'Law of the Russian People' (Russkaia Pravda) abolished all noble privileges, including serfdom, and established a two-fold system of landownership, half private and half a national pool for the needy. Pestel, a firm republican, aimed to establish an elected unicameral assembly under a council of state. Government was to be strongly centralized, not federal, and national minorities, except Poland, Russified. A smaller Society of United Slavs was incorporated into the Southern Society.

The rising was fixed for 1826, but no agreement on details was reached. Pestel wanted a revolutionary dictatorship and the execution of the emperor. The 'dictator' of the Northern Society, Trubetskoy, envisaged a provisional government which would call a constituent assembly. Muraviev hoped that Alexander himself would agree to the reforms.

Alexander's death (1 Dec. 1825) took the Decembrists by surprise, but the Northern Society tried to prevent regiments in the capital swearing allegiance to Nicholas I. Not only were the leaders of the revolt hostile to mob participation, they had little army support and were disorganized and badly led. The revolt itself and a rising in the south (Jan. 1826) were easily suppressed. An investigating commission sentenced six leaders to execution and over 100 to Siberia, creating a legend of martyrdom to be fostered later by Herzen.

A. Mazour, *The First Russian Revolution* (California, 1937). M. Zetlin, *The Decembrists* (New York, 1958).   BJW

DECEMVIRATE, commission of ten patricians appointed at Rome (451 BC) to reconstruct the legal basis of Roman citizenship; their codification, completed by a succeeding patrician-plebeian decemvirate, became the Twelve Tables, the basis of Roman and much European law. The commission dominated by Appius Claudius, was compelled to resign in 449, under pressure from both patricians and plebeians aspiring to the suspended elective magistracies.

DECENTRALIZATION IN MALAYA, major constitutional issue between the two World Wars. It involved a series of proposals by Governors Guillemard (1919–27) and Clementi (1930–3), designed to keep faith with Britain's treaty obligations to the four Federated Malay States, and at the same time attract the Unfederated States into a looser union, by returning to the states some of the powers and symbols assumed since 1896 by the British-officered federal bureaucracy. The schemes were opposed by European and Chinese commercial interests, and little was achieved except the transfer of education, health, agriculture, and public works to the states in the 1930s.

DECET, final papal bull of excommunication pronounced on Martin Luther (3 Jan. 1521).

DECIMAL SYSTEM, using the number 10 as a group unit or base, was widely adopted in Europe after the French Revolution, providing a rational, convenient system of weights, measures, and monetary units. The US first used decimal coinage, based on dollars and cents (1786). In France, many pre-revolutionary *cahiers* demanded a uniform system of weights and measures to foster internal trade. The metric system, devised in 1791–2, was decimal and based on natural measurements. The Convention introduced decimalized money (1793), halving the new franc's value (1795) to accord approximately with the old livre. The Consulate completed the undertaking. The system was introduced into various parts of the British Commonwealth in the 1960s and gradually implemented into British coinage by 1970. It was fully introduced into Britain in 1971.

DECIUS, C. MESSIUS QUINTUS TRAIANUS (*reg.* AD 249–251), Roman Emperor, who was raised to the throne in Pannonia after defeating the pretender Pacatianus, and overcame the Emperor Philip at Verona (249). Inspired by a sense of traditionalism, he ordered a general persecution of Christians which was widely enforced. In 250 he returned to the north for a Gothic war, during which, after some success, he was defeated and killed.

DECLARATION OF LONDON (1909), international convention permitting the free transit of all goods, except contraband, in time of war. The convention, which was never ratified by Britain and the US, followed a disagreement between them at the Hague Conference (1907). It was an unrealistic attempt to reduce the intensity of the naval race. Nevertheless, President Wilson, intent on maintaining strict neutrality, suggested in 1914 that the rules of 1909 be adopted by the belligerents. Britain refused to agree and went ahead with a blockade designed to suppress all commerce with the central powers, relying on sympathetic public opinion in America to prevent retaliation.

DECLARATION OF RIGHTS (1689) was issued by the English Convention Parliament to solve the constitutional crisis following the flight of King James II. Its clauses, which laid down the conditions on which the Crown was to be offered to William of Orange and his wife, Mary, were later incorporated in the Bill of Rights.

DECLARATION OF RIGHTS AND GRIEVANCES (1774), American colonial protest. The declaration was issued by the first continental congress. It listed the rights of British colonial subjects, including the right of colonial self-taxation, and argued that recent laws of the British parliament, the 'Intolerable Acts', were violations of these rights. The American Declaration of Independence (1776) was, in part, modelled on the Declaration of Rights and Grievances.

DECLARATION OF SAINT-OURS (7 May 1837), statement made by Canadians opposing British colonial policy and supporting Louis-Joseph Papineau. The declaration marked the beginning of the Canadian Rebellion of 1837.

DECLARATION OF THE ARMY (1647), in England, by which the army intervened in the negotiations between King Charles I and the Long Parliament on the plea that it was more representative of the nation than the parliamentary leaders. It was issued by the council of the army on 14 June at St Albans and demanded that parliament expel MPs hostile to the army, arrange its own dissolution, and provide for regular succeeding parliaments. On 26 June, under pressure from the army, 11 of the Commons leaders withdrew, but parliament made no further attempt to comply with the declaration, and at the end of July the 11 returned.

DECLARATION ON GENERAL SECURITY (1943), signed by the US, the Soviet Union, Britain, and China, at the foreign ministers' conference in Moscow (Oct. 1943)—the Chinese signature being that of the ambassador to Moscow. Paragraph 4 of the declaration included the words: 'they recognize the necessity of establishing at the earliest practicable date a general international organization'. The declaration was thus the first step in the founding of the UN. The inclusion of China among the signatories was attributable to US diplomacy.

DECLARATORY ACT (1719) gave the English parliament the right to legislate for Ireland and denied the Irish House of Lords any appellate jurisdiction over the Irish courts.

DECLARATORY ACT (1766), asserting the sovereignty of the British parliament over the American colonies, was passed immediately after the repeal of the Stamp Act (1765). Thus the principle of parliament's competence to legislate for the colonies was maintained, although the immediate practical aspect of it was withdrawn.

DECURIONES, Latin term for town-councillors of Roman colonies and *municipia*, self-governing boroughs, in the Roman empire. They effectively controlled the public affairs of their cities, but their responsibility for collecting taxes due from the community became in the 3rd cent. AD an intolerable burden, ruinous to the city life, turning a sought-after privilege into an unavoidable inherited duty.

DEDMAN, JOHN JOHNSTONE (1896–), Scottish-born Australian farmer, soldier and politician, who was a Labor member of the Commonwelth parliament (1940–9). He was a minister with various portfolios—war organization (1941–5), post-war reconstruction (1945–9), defence (1946–9), and scientific and industrial research (1941–9). Dedman made solid contributions to the planning of Australia's war and post-war economic and defence policies.

DEE, JOHN (1527–1608), English mathematician and polymath. He seems to have combined the characteristics of scientist and alchemist, astronomer and astrologer. He was a fellow of St John's College, Cambridge (1545), and one of the original fellows of Henry VIII's foundation, Trinity College (1546). He went to Louvain (1548), where he became a friend of the Dutch cartographer Mercator. On the death of Mary I (1558), he was taken into Queen Elizabeth's service as her astrologer. His *Preface to Euclid* (1570) was a popular exposition of all the basic assumptions of number, harmony, and proportion in the Renaissance tradition. His attempt to recreate a classical theatre in London probably contributed to the form of the Globe theatre.

DEERE, JOHN (1804–86), US manufacturer responsible for the development of the steel plough in the 1830s and 1840s. Steel ploughs, unlike their cast-iron predecessors, were suitable for farming the tough prairie soils of the Mid-west and by 1857 Deere was producing 10,000 ploughs annually at his plant in Moline, IL.

DEERFIELD MASSACRE (Feb. 1704), committed by a French-led party of Caughnawaga Mohawk and Abnaki Indians during Queen Anne's War. About 300 people lived in Deerfield, MA, 50 of whom were killed and 110 taken prisoner.

DEFENCE OF INDIA ACT (1915). Modelled on the Defence of the Realm Act (1914) in Britain, the act was introduced to give Indian governments powers to exclude, confine, and intern individuals, to create new offences, to establish special tribunal procedures to deal with revolutionary crime, and to control the press for the duration of the war and for six months thereafter. Some 1800 persons were interned under the Act's provisions and its special powers were extensively used in Punjab (1915) and Bengal (1916–17). It was to replace the act and preserve its wide powers that the 'Rowlatt Bills' were introduced (1919).

DEFENCE OF THE REALM ACT (1914) in Britain, legislative measure which became the basis of restrictive wartime legislation. Censorship of newspapers, much of it covert, was initiated by the act, which was continuously strengthened throughout the First World War, and gave the government extensive powers of intervention in, *eg*, the regulation of manufacturers' profits and workers' wages. The negotiations between the British prime minister, Lloyd George, and Ulster Unionists in 1916 involved much discussion of whether the DORA could be continued in Ireland after Home Rule, but this idea was rejected. In the Emergency Powers Act (1920) Lloyd George's government, faced with the prospect of a miners' strike spreading through sympathetic action, institutionalized many of DORA's provisions.

DEFENDER OF THE FAITH (*Fidei Defensor*), title borne by English sovereigns since 1521, conferred by Pope Leo X after the publication of Henry VIII's *Defence of the Seven Sacraments* in reply to Luther's attack. *Fid. Def.*, later abbreviated to *F.D.*, has appeared on British coins ever since.

DEFENESTRATION OF PRAGUE (23 May 1618), explosive incident which preceded the Bohemian revolt against the Catholic King-elect, Ferdinand. After his election to the throne (1617), Ferdinand took steps to crush Bohemian Protestantism. Protestant opposition came to a head at a meeting of nobles, gentry, and burghers held in Prague on 21 May 1618. The Protestant leader, Count Thurn, demanded the setting up of a Protestant provisional government and death for two Catholic members of the Bohemian estates, Jaroslav Martinitz and William Slavata, who had been appointed deputy-governors of Prague by the Emperor Matthias. Trapped in the castle of Hradschin by a determined crowd of Protestant deputies and the Prague mob, the two deputy-governors were flung out of an open window, and only a pile of dung beneath saved their lives. Their defenestration was followed by the setting up of the Bohemian directorate and the offer of the Bohemian Crown to Frederick of the Palatinate.

DEFFERRE, GASTON (1910–   ), leader of those within the French Socialist Party who sought (1970) an alliance with the Centre rather than with the Communists. After Resistance activity, Defferre entered politics under the Fourth Republic, and was several times a minister. He was responsible for an important law of 1956 which prepared the way for the independence of France's colonies. He has been mayor of Marseilles since 1953.

A campaign proposing Defferre as centre-left candidate for the presidency in 1965 was abortive, but he was the Socialist candidate in the 1969 presidential election.

DEFICIENCY LAWS, in the British West Indies. Fearful of the shortage of free men, British West Indian legislatures passed laws in the late 17th cent. requiring planters to employ more white servants. Planters preferred slave labour and found paying the fines cheaper than complying with the laws.

DEHEUBARTH, one of the four major kingdoms of medieval Wales. Being the south-western kingdom, it was open to the east and bounded by areas of Norman power and consequently Norman influence, but this waned after 1070. In 1075 Rhys ap Tewdwr succeeded to the throne and under his supremacy Deheubarth enjoyed a measure of stability and he was allowed to retain his possessions in return for an annual render to the king. After his death in 1093, the kingdom once again fell under Norman control.

DEHRA DUN ACADEMY, the Indian Military Academy, established (1932) to train officers for the Indian army. Previously (1922–31) cadets had been sent to Sandhurst. The intake for the new academy was 60 from British India and 20 from the states and the first graduates passed out in 1935. In 1949 a joint services wing was added to provide facilities for naval and air force officers also until the completion of the National Defence Academy at Khadakvasala near Poona (1955). Dehra Dun served after that time as the centre for fourth-year training for officer cadets of the Indian army, following their three years at the National Defence Academy.

DEIOTARUS (d. 40 BC), King of Galatia, who took Pompey's side in the Roman Civil War, was pardoned by Caesar, but was later accused of trying to murder him. Cicero defended him and Caesar's death interrupted the case. He then supported Brutus and Cassius until he surrendered to Antony after Philippi (42).

DEISM, belief in the existence of an eternal god governing the world, but not in the rest of Christian theology. First popularized by English free-thinkers of the late 17th and early 18th cents, *eg*, Shaftesbury, Locke, Bolingbroke, Deism spread to France, where its most eminent exponent was Voltaire.

DEKKER, THOMAS (*c.* 1570–*c.* 1632), English dramatist and pamphleteer, a valuable source for life in Elizabethan London, as in his comedy *The Shoemaker's Holiday* (1603) and the pamphlets 'The Wonderful Year', about the plague of 1603, 'The Seven Deadly Sins of London' (1606), and 'The Gull's Horn-Book' (1609), a satire on the gallants. Most of his work for the theatre was written in collaboration with other playwrights.

DELAMER OF DUNHAM MASSEY, GEORGE BOOTH, 1st Baron (1622–84), English MP who supported the parliamentarians in the Civil War but later, during the Protectorate of Cromwell, was associated in attempts to restore Charles II. He was defeated at Nantwich in 1659, but on the restoration was ennobled by the king.

DELANE, JOHN THADDEUS (1817–79), British journalist, who was editor of *The Times* (1841–77). His public spirit and shrewd judgement raised *The Times* to a position of great power and influence throughout the world.

DELAWARE, English colony in North America. Delaware Bay was discovered by the Dutch navigator Henry Hudson (1609) and named after the governor of VA, Lord De La Warr (1577–1618). Following Dutch explorations (1615–16) and an unsuccessful attempt at settlement by the Dutch West India Co. (1631), a combined Dutch–Swedish expedition under Peter Minuit (1580–1638) founded (1638) Fort Christina (present-day Wilmington). Control of the area passed to the New Sweden Co. and settlements of Dutch, Swedes, and Finns were made on both banks of the Delaware Bay. The Dutch West India Co. seized the Swedish holdings (1655) and sold them to the city of Amsterdam. The British occupied the colony (1664–73) and in the treaty of Westminster (1674) it passed to England. DE was granted to the Duke of York, who conveyed it to William Penn (1682) and it became part of PA. DE was granted a deputy governor (1691), a separate legislature (1704), and an Executive Council (1710), but remained under the governor of PA until 1776. A boundary dispute with MD was settled as part of the Mason and Dixon line agreement (1767). DE became a state in the US in 1776.

DELAWARE, CROSSING OF THE (26 Dec. 1776), event during the American Revolution. By ferrying troops across the ice-filled Delaware river in small boats, Gen. George Washington was able to make a surprise attack on British soldiers, largely Hessian mercenaries, stationed at Trenton, NJ.

DELAWARE INDIANS, confederacy of American Algonquian tribes, formerly occupying the basin of the Delaware river. They made their first treaty with William Penn (1682). The

Iroquois asserted control (c. 1720), and forbade the Delaware to declare war or sell lands, a situation which lasted until the beginning of the French and Indian War (1754). Pushed westward into OH by expanding settlements, the Delaware, until the treaty of Fort Greenville (1795), attempted to resist the advancing whites. Most of the tribe were placed on a reservation in KS (1830s) and were later (1867) transferred to the Indian Territory in present-day OK.

DELBRÜCK, RUDOLF VON (1817–1903), Prussian minister who was largely responsible for drafting the 1871 constitution of the German empire. He played an important part in the extension of the Zollverein (1849–67), was president of the North German Confederation (1867–71), and headed the administration of the imperial chancellery (1871). In 1870 he formulated the agreements with the South German states which preceded their entry into the German empire. He retired (1876) because of disagreement with Bismarck's mperial policy.

DELCASSÉ, THÉOPHILE (1852–1923), French diplomat and statesman, originally a journalist, who was drawn into politics by Gambetta and after serving in local government was elected to the Chamber as a radical (1889). An able and well-informed speaker, he soon secured office, first as under-secretary (1893) and then as minister for the colonies (1894–5), in which capacity he presided over renewed colonial development, particularly in Madagascar. His main achievement, however, was his long tenure of the ministry of foreign affairs (1898–1905), during which he fostered the *entente cordiale* (1904). After his fall, resulting from the Tangier crisis, he temporarily retired from politics, but returned (1908) to serve not only as minister for both the navy (1911–13) and foreign affairs (1914–15), but also as ambassador to Russia (1913–14).

DÉLÉGATION DES GAUCHES, steering committee in the French parliament formed by the left-wing parties after their victory in the 1902 election. It gave the majority a cohesion which was rare in French politics and made possible the anti-clerical legislation of Combes's government (1902–5). The real significance of the Délégation des gauches was the membership of Jaurès, and the support given to the government by his socialist group. Jaurès's policy was strongly criticized by other socialists, and his withdrawal in 1905 put an end to the Délégation.

DELFT, small town near the Hague in the Dutch-speaking province of Holland which rose to eminence in the mid-17th cent. as the centre for the manufacture of blue and white earthenware coated with a tin glaze. This Delftware was copied by English and German potters and, despite the competition of imported Chinese and German hard-paste porcelain, dominated the European market until the wide-spread use of English cream wares in the late 18th cent. William the Silent was assassinated in Delft (1584).

DELHI, capital city of modern India since 1911 (1970 pop. about 2,500,000). The word Delhi is a corruption of the Muslim form Dehli and the Hindu form (always used by Sir Charles Metcalfe) Dilli. Its mythical foundation was by a Raja Dhilu before Alexander's invasion, and it is traditionally the site of the Pandava city of Indraprastha described in the epic *Mahābhārata*. There are remains of the Gupta period (4th cent. AD) but the first known historic city was that built by the Tomar Rajput Anang Pal (c. AD 1050). About a century later the Chauhan chief Prithvi Raj built a city on what is now known as the Qutab site. On his defeat in 1192 by the Muslim Turks, Delhi became the capital of their north Indian empire (1193–1398). In 1398 the Tughluq dynasty was overwhelmed by Taimur, who sacked the city. Until 1562 it was successively the site of a local Sayyid dynasty and of the large, loosely knit Afghan monarchy of the Lodis. During the sultanate Ala-ad-din Khilji and

Muhammad Tughluq enlarged the Qutab city, while, in the 14th cent., Firoz Shah built a new fortress palace by the Jumna river bank, now known as Firoz Shah's *kotla* or fort. It is adorned with an Asoka pillar.

Delhi was the centre of the Mughal dynasty from 1526, when Babur took it, until 1803, when the British occupied it after defeating the Marathas. The second Mughal emperor, Homayun, began the citadel known as the *Purana Qila* or old fort, which Sher Shah the Afghan, his supplanter in 1540, completed, so that it was the new Delhi of its day. Akbar preferred Agra as a residence, and Jahangir Lahore. It was Shah Jahan who returned, founding what is now the old walled city under the name of Shahjahanabad. The palace or Red Fort was completed in 1648, and the Jama Masjid and the walls by 1650. These, with Homayun's and Safdar Jung's tombs to the south, are the chief monuments of Mughal Delhi.

In 1739 Delhi was sacked and its inhabitants massacred by Nadir Shah the Persian. Between 1750 and 1761 it was the scene of civil war between Mughal officers and of alternate occupation by Marathas and Afghans. From then till 1803 it was the centre of a limited state dominated at first by Afghans and, after an interval of revival, by the Marathas under Sindhia.

Delhi under the British was at first administered by Sir Charles Metcalfe, who discovered and praised the autonomous village system of the Delhi territory and did much to secure its recognition in the land settlements of northern India. In 1857 Delhi was seized by mutinous troops from Mirat, who restored the aged Emperor Bahadur Shah for a four-month reign until the city was retaken by British troops. Bahadur Shah was exiled and the city suffered harsh reprisals. On recovering, it became a prosperous provincial city and commercial centre. At King George V's durbar (1911) it was declared the capital of India. The latest New Delhi was inaugurated with the opening of the Viceroy's House in 1930. As the capital of independent India it experienced grave riots precipitated by the arrival of Sikh and Hindu refugees from the Punjab, and later by the trauma of Gandhi's assassination. Since independence the city has grown to about five times its previous size.

Sir H. Sharp, *Delhi, its Monuments and History* (London, 1928). TGPS

DELHI PACT (5 March 1931), sometimes called the Gandhi–Irwin pact, an agreement between Lord Irwin (afterwards Lord Halifax), the viceroy of India, and Gandhi, which brought to an end the first phase of the civil disobedience campaign. The pact was concluded after long negotiations between the two men, but satisfied the followers of neither, though at Gandhi's insistence the Congress ratified it at its Karachi session (30 March 1931). Many British officials and politicians felt that Irwin had given too much to the Congress and had made their own position more difficult. However, Irwin felt that for little cost he had gained a truce in the civil disobedience campaign and the acquiescence of Congress in the constitution-making process of the Round Table Conference. While he had agreed to lift the ordinances promulgated against civil disobedience, to release political prisoners, to remit some fines and punitive police charges, and to allow peaceful picketing and the local manufacture and sale of salt, he had parried Gandhi's major demand for an enquiry into Congress allegations against the police and secured the lifting of the boycott of British goods, particularly cloth. For his part, Gandhi saw advantages in this clear acknowledgement of the Congress as a mediator for the Indian people's demands.

DELIAN LEAGUE, alliance of Greek city-states in and around the Aegean, formed under Athenian leadership in the winter of 478–477 BC to continue the war against Persia, so called because initially meetings of the allies were held at Delos and the League's treasury kept there. The Spartans' reluctance after 479 to undertake the liberation and protection of the Asiatic Greeks and the tyrannical methods of their commander, Pausanias, induced the Ionian cities to approach the Athenians, who readily responded. Oaths of eternal loyalty were exchanged between Athens and the individual cities and a system of annual contributions in ships and men or in money was established, Aristides the Athenian being chosen by the allies to assess their liabilities. The league's fleets achieved successes against the Persians, especially in Thrace, capturing Eion, and in southern Asia Minor, defeating them decisively at the Eurymedon river (c. 467). But the denial of the allies' right to secede (eg, Naxos, c. 468), their readiness to pay money instead of maintaining their own ships, and Athenian control of the meetings at Delos (where each ally had one vote) all contributed to increasing Athens predominance. In 463 the Athenians crushed a leading ally, Thasos, and in 459 began the First Peloponnesian War in Greece. Failure against the Persians in Egypt (459–454) caused the transfer of the treasury from Delos to Athens and widespread unrest (eg, at Erythrae, Miletus), leading to tighter control through garrisons, cleruchies, and political interference, while further repression followed the reimposition of financial contributions after the peace of Callias with Persia (449). When Samos rebelled and was subdued (440–439), the league was beyond doubt an Athenian empire, to be broken up only in the last stages of the great Peloponnesian War (412–405).

DELISLE, JOSEPH (1688–1768), French scholar who was appointed astronomer to Peter the Great of Russia, and became one of the first members of the St Petersburg Academy. He published *Mémoires pour servir à l'histoire de l'astronomie* (1738).

DELIUM, BATTLE OF (424 BC), in the great Peloponnesian War was a victory of the Boeotians under the Theban Pagondas over the Athenians returning from fortifying Delium in eastern Boeotia, and counterbalanced Athenian successes in 425. Pagondas' tactical innovations foreshadowed the later developments of Epaminondas.

DE LÔME LETTER (1898), private letter written by the Spanish minister in the US, Dupuy de Lôme, in which he made undiplomatic remarks about President William McKinley. Publication of the letter in the New York *Journal* (9 Feb. 1898) led to De Lôme's resignation and stimulated a nationalistic reaction in the US that contributed to the later declaration of war against Spain.

DELOS, small island in the Aegean Sea, in antiquity sacred to Apollo, and the religious centre of the Ionian Greeks. As such, it was chosen as the meeting-place and treasury of the Delian League, the alliance formed by Athens in 478–477 BC to continue the war with Persia. Thereafter it was controlled by Athens until 322, apart from a brief period of freedom (404–c. 377). It was later developed by the Romans as a free port after the Third Macedonian War (171–168) to punish Rhodes for lukewarm loyalty, but was sacked in the First Mithridatic War (87) and never recovered.

DELPHI, home of Apollo's famous oracle on Mt Parnassus, Greece. Having been a religious centre since the 2nd millennium BC, it gained political importance in the 8th cent. from association with the early colonial movement. In the 7th–6th cents, as the centre of the Amphictyonic League and most important oracle in Greece, it had considerable influence in Greek city-state affairs. Many cities built treasuries there and important foreigners, eg, Croesus of Lydia, sent dedications. Of uncertain loyalty in the Persian War (480), the oracle, despite Athenian attempts to control it (Second Sacred War, c. 447), supported Sparta in the great Peloponnesian War (431–405). After despoliation in the Third Sacred War (355–346), Delphi was controlled by Philip II and later (c. 300) by the Aetolian League. Subsequently of

little political and decreasing religious importance, the oracle was finally closed by Theodosius in AD 390.

DELYANNIS, THEODOR (1826–1905), Greek minister who, under pressure of popular feeling, ordered general mobilization against the Turks in 1897, starting the Greco-Turkish War. He represented Greece at the Congress of Berlin (1878), and was twice prime minister (1890–2, 1895–7).

DEMADES (d. 319 BC), Athenian orator and statesman, who was instrumental in the conciliation of the Macedonians Philip II (338) and Alexander the Great (335) and in the fall of the anti-Macedonian Demosthenes and Hyperides (322). Later, however, he was executed in Macedon for intrigue as an envoy.

DEMAK, first Islamic Javanese kingdom in succession to the 'Hindu' kingdom of Madjapahit, which is traditionally said to have fallen in 1478. Javanese legends claim that the first ruler of Demak, Raden Patah (Senapati Djimbun), was descended from the last King of Madjapahit. The kingdom was centred on Demak in north-central Java and probably lasted to the mid-1540s. Its history is adumbrated in semi-historical tales of dubious reliability. The mosque at Demak is believed to be the oldest of Java. In the second decade of the 16th cent. power passed to the Central Javanese kingdom of Padjang, and then to Mataram.

DEMARATUS (*reg. c.* 510–491 BC), Spartan Eurypontid King, who quarrelled with his colleague Cleomenes I over the invasion of Attica (506) and Aegina (491), and was removed through Cleomenes' intrigues. He fled to Persia and returned with Xerxes' unsuccessful expedition (480).

DEME, group of local residents in ancient Athens and Attica. After close geographical definition by Cleisthenes (508 BC), the demes, numbering about 170, constituted the basic unit of the Athenian democratic constitution.

DEMERARA, area in north-eastern South America along the Demerara river, settled by the Dutch in the 17th cent. and ruled by the Dutch West India Co. until it passed to Britain (1814). Demerara, Essequibo, and Berbice were combined (1831) to form British Guiana, later (1966) Guyana.

DEMERTZIS, CONSTANTINE (1876–1936), Greek jurist and politician, who was the last parliamentary prime minister before 1946. Demertzis was educated at Athens and Munich and became professor of law at Athens in 1900. He was a parliamentary deputy (1910–36) and twice minister of the navy (1913–14, 1917). In 1924 he founded the Progressive (Union) Party and in 1926 challenged Pangalos for the presidency, only to withdraw on the eve of the election. Demertzis was made prime minister in Nov. 1935 by King George and, with Liberal support, held the position until the general election of Jan. 1936, dying in office (April 1936). Without consulting the party leaders, King George called Metaxas to power.

DEMESNE, ANCIENT. An estate in England was regarded as ancient demesne if it could be shown that it once belonged to the Crown, usually by reference to Domesday Book. From the 13th cent. villeins of such an estate were, in law, royal villeins and could appeal to the king against their lord—a useful device in the restriction of feudal privilege.

DEMETRIAS, Greek fortress in Thessaly, founded (c. 293 BC) by Demetrius Poliorcetes. Strategically and commercially important, it was called by Philip V a 'fetter of Greece' and was held by Macedon until 196. Though freed by Rome, it joined Antiochus III of Syria (192), was restored to Macedon after his defeat, and freed again in 167, but its prosperity declined with Macedon's collapse.

DEMETRIUS OF PHALERUM (b. *c.* 350 BC), pupil of Theophrastus and peripatetic philosopher, famous in Athenian politics and for his rhetoric and scholarship. For his distinction Cassander of Macedon appointed him governor of Athens (317), a position he held for ten years until Demetrius Poliorcetes restored the democracy. He then took refuge with Ptolemy I in Alexandria, where he was influential in establishing the Museum, of which he became librarian, but he died in disgrace under Ptolemy II.

DEMETRIUS OF PHAROS (d. 214 BC), Greek pirate chief who, after accepting Roman protection in 229 BC, seceded to Antigonus Doson of Macedon and gained Illyria. A Roman expedition in 219 caused him to flee to Macedon, where he helped to persuade Philip V to embark on the First Macedonian War with Rome.

DEMETRIUS POLIOCETES (336–283 BC), 'the Besieger', son of Antigonus Monophthalmus, in whose plan to reunite Alexander's empire he was an energetic but unstable aide. After being defeated at Gaza (312), he gained many places by the use of Antigonus' fleet, including Athens (307) and Cyprus (306), though his siege of Rhodes failed (305). After the victory at Ipsus (301) of Antigonus' rivals, Cassander and Seleucus, Demetrius retained only his sea-power, but when Cassander died (297) he exploited the dynastic chaos in Macedon and became king (294). Still dreaming of re-uniting Alexander's empire, he lost the loyalty of war-weary Macedon to Lysimachus and Pyrrhus (288). In desperation he invaded Asia with a small army (287), but was captured by Seleucus (285).

DEMIDOV, NIKITA (1656–1725), Russian ironmaster and founder of a dynasty of industrialists. His workshops at Tula provided muskets for Peter I's army from 1686, and in 1702 he leased the Neviansk ironworks, near St Petersburg, from the Crown in return for guaranteeing to supply munitions for the Russian forces in the Great Northern War. By 1725 he also owned five iron and copper foundries around Ekaterinburg. Ennobled by Peter in 1720 for his services, Catherine I conferred the right of hereditary nobility upon his family in 1725.

DEMISE OF THE CROWN ACT (1901) provided that the British monarch's death should not affect the tenure of office of ministers of the Crown. Earlier important steps in the process of dissociating the government of the country from the king's person had made judges' tenure of office (1760) and parliament's duration (1867) independent of the monarch's life.

DÉMOCRATES POPULAIRES or PDP, the first true Christian Democrat party in France, founded in 1924 by Champetier de Ribes. It was a new phenomenon in French politics, combining Catholicism with firm republicanism and support for social reform. The party was never large, and its strength was limited to certain Catholic areas, but it was able to play a significant part in politics because of its central position in the parliamentary spectrum. After the Second World War the PDP was absorbed with other groups into the new MRP Party.

DEMOCRATIC ACTION PARTY in Venezuela. *AD*, or *Acción Democrática*, was founded (1936) to bring an end to rule by dictatorship in Venezuela. *AD*, which attempted to acquire the presidency by ballot (1940) and bullet (1945), succeeded in placing Rómulo Betancourt in the presidency (1945–8). He was succeeded by Rómulo Gallegos, who was soon removed by a military coup. Under the dictatorship of Pérez Jiménez (1952–8) all parties were banned and the constitution enacted by *AD* (1947) was ignored. The revolt of 1958 restored *AD* to its former position and Betancourt was elected president (1959–64). He was succeeded by Raúl Leoni (1964–9). Factionalism steadily weakened *AD* until

the party lost its dominant position and the presidency to the Social Christian Party (1969).

DEMOCRATIC LABOR PARTY in Australia, founded (1955) as the Australian Labor Party (anti-communist), following a split within the party. Most of its members and supporters are Roman Catholics. Organized in each state, it contests both Commonwealth and state elections, and has averaged approx. 7·5 per cent of the national vote in elections since its formation. In the senate elections of 1967 when, because of proportional representation it increased its senators from two to four, it achieved 9·7 per cent of the national vote.

DLP policies on domestic issues differ little from those of the ALP, but in defence and foreign affairs DLP spokesmen claim that ALP policies are open to influence by members of the Communist Party, because of ALP organizational links with the trade union movement, and that an Australian Labor government would bring insecurity to the South-East Asian region and advantage to communist powers.

In 1967 the DLP claimed 18,300 financial members, but in elections for the Commonwealth House of Representatives (preferential voting for single-member electorates), the party has been unable to gain representation, whereas the Australian Country Party, with supporters concentrated in country areas, polled approximately 8·5 per cent of the national vote at the 1969 elections and won 20 seats.

The DLP's ability to direct up to 80 per cent of its candidates' preferences to non-ALP candidates nevertheless helped appreciably to ensure a Canberra Liberal–Country Party coalition government (1955–69) and affected state political results, notably in Vic.

DEMOCRATIC PARTY (GERMAN) (DEUTSCHE DEMO-KRATISCHE PARTEI) (DDP), founded 20 Nov. 1918. The DDP combined elements of the Progressive and National Liberal parties of the Wilhelmine Reich. The long list of prominent founder members (A. Einstein, H. Preuss, W. Rathenau, H. Schacht, Th. Wolff) shows that it was a party of the left-liberal intelligentsia and those sections of the industrial bourgeoisie which viewed the collapse of the old Reich as an opportunity for a fresh start. The first programmatic pronouncements accepted the Revolution and professed firm allegiance to the Republic. The DDP also showed a genuine willingness to effect basic reforms of the political, social, and economic structure. Despite the party's later opposition to the ratification of the Versailles treaty, the leaders were prepared to break with the power politics of the empire, and refused to incorporate former annexationists, most prominent among them G. Stresemann, who subsequently founded the DVP. The original idea of offering a democratic rallying point for the bourgeoisie, however, never made such headway. The DDP remained a party of individualists, torn between its right wing (aiming at closer co-operation with the DVP) and its left wing (advocating an alliance with the SPD). It has been called the 'Weimar' party *par excellence*, its own fate reflected in the fate of the Republic as a whole: in the 1919 elections for the National Assembly the DDP polled 18·6 per cent, gaining 74 seats and becoming the strongest middle-class party. Less than 18 months later its share was 8·3 per cent, with a consequent loss of 45 seats. By 1924 the figure was around 6 per cent, declining further to 4·8 per cent (25 seats) in the 1928 elections. Ideological factors and the general right-wing shift of the German bourgeoisie apart, the DDP's unwavering support for the numerous coalition governments and the latter's unpopular policies no doubt contributed to the gradual erosion of its former strength. By the time the Brüning cabinet was formed the party's position had grown so weak that a merger with other organizations became a question of survival. Negotiations ensued with the *Volksnationale Reichsvereinigung* and A. Mahraun's *Jungdeutscher Orden*, which led to the founding of the *Deutsche Staatspartei* at the end of July 1930. This combination managed to capture 3·8 per cent of the votes (20 seats) in the Sept. elections, but it was a precarious alliance. On 7 Oct. Mahraun and his adherents dropped out, and were followed a little later by the *Volksnationale Reichsvereinigung*. Thenceforth the decline of the DDP was irresistible, leaving it with two seats (1 per cent) in the elections of Nov. 1932. But the *Staatspartei* never abandoned its support for the Republic, which the majority of the population did not love, nor cease to voice its opposition to National Socialism. The five DDP candidates who succeeded in the elections of March 1933 voted for the Enabling Act, after which the party's dissolution was merely a matter of time.   VRB

DEMOCRATIC PARTY

DEMOCRATIC PARTY in the US, major political party claiming direct descent from Jefferson's Democratic-Republicans and coherent organization at least from the period of Jackson's presidency (1829–37). The name Democratic Party was officially adopted at a national party convention in Baltimore (1840).

Although generally dominant in national politics until 1860, a party split over the slavery issue, and the emergence of the Republican Party in the 1850s, resulted in Democratic defeat in the presidential election of 1860. Its identification with the Confederacy during the American Civil War, and consequent accusations of treason against the party, completed its eclipse. Republican control of the Union government during the war years continued throughout the post-war period of reconstruction. The consolidation of traditional southern support led to near victories for the Democratic Party in the presidential elections of 1876 and 1880, and it regained the presidency with the election of Cleveland (1884). However, this, together with Cleveland's second election in 1892, was its only presidential success between 1856 and 1912. By 1896 the national party was dominated by southerners and western agrarian radicals, allowing the Republicans to return to power as the party of business, representing employer and employee alike. The result was a series of divisive Democratic national conventions and decisive presidential election defeats. Only a serious Republican split in 1912 between the rival followings of W. H. Taft and Theodore Roosevelt opened the way for Democratic victory, and in the candidacy of Woodrow Wilson the party sought to shed its image of rural radicalism and southern conservatism.

However, although during Wilson's first term as president (1913–17) a generation of young Democrats emerged who were devoted to his brand of progressivism, the party remained fragmented and Wilson was re-elected only by a narrow majority. In 1920 his ill-health and abdication of party leadership led to the choice of a compromise candidate and electoral defeat. In 1924 inherent antagonisms between 'Wets' and 'Drys' over Prohibition, between Protestants and Catholics, and rural and urban groups, produced a deadlock at the party convention, another compromise candidate, and crushing defeat. By 1928 urban northern elements began to dominate the party and the convention nominated Alfred E. Smith, of NY, the first Catholic presidential candidate. Despite a split in the Democratic 'Solid South', he improved the Democratic share of the total vote, especially among immigrant groups in large urban centres. Internal factionalism declined, and farmers and organized labour became increasingly disenchanted with Republican policies.

The stock market crash (1929) and the ensuing Depression provided the final impetus for a dramatic realignment of party support. The 1932 nomination and election of Franklin D. Roosevelt heralded not merely a period of Democratic dominance of national politics, but a major political revolution. Controlling the presidency, and dominating Congress for the next 20 years, the party established itself as the normal majority party, a pattern broken only temporarily by the 'personal' presidential victories of Dwight D. Eisenhower (1952, 1956). Election victories in 1960 and 1964 by a Catholic (J. F. Kennedy) and a Southerner (L. B. Johnson) obscured the fragility of the coalition. The defection of the South, allied with liberal opposition to increased involvement in the Viet-nam War, allowed the Republicans to recapture the presidency (1968) and forced Democratic leaders to make a major reappraisal of the party's goals for the 1970s.

R. Goldman, *The Democratic Party in American Politics* (London & New York, 1966).
W. E. Binkley, *American Political Parties—their natural history* (New York, 1962).   JDL

DEMOCRATIC REPUBLICANS, early US political party, known as Republicans by its members, Democrats by its enemies, and also as Republican Democrats or Jeffersonian Republicans. The later Democratic Party claimed that its origins lay in this group. Divisions over ratification of the constitution (1787–8) gave way to national harmony with the inauguration of President Washington (1789). However, opposition to Alexander Hamilton's financial programme (1790–2) stimulated the emergence of the embryonic Republican Party, led by James Madison, with the secretary of state, Thomas Jefferson, initially in the background. The Republicans were generally more liberal and sensitive to popular interests than were the Federalists. Though they were often less aristocratic than their opponents, and included artisans and small farmers, their strength lay principally in rural areas, especially in NY and VA. They defended agrarian interests, accepting commerce only in a subordinate role, particularly condemned the growth of paper wealth, symbolized by Hamilton's Bank of the United States, and argued in favour of 'strict construction' of the constitution and local responsibility in government. The party was sympathetic towards the French Revolution and received support from the many Democratic Republican clubs which it had stimulated (*c.* 1793). It opposed the Federalists' policy of neutrality during the ensuing European wars, though Jefferson became embarrassed by the activities of the French minister, Edmond Genet (1793). The Republicans rapidly organized themselves at all local and national levels, the debate over Jay's treaty indicating that the party was well established by 1795. In the first presidential election fought on party lines (1796), Jefferson, the Republican presidential candidate, was by a quirk of the constitution (later corrected by the Twelfth Amendment) elected vice-president. Exploiting the difficulties of John Adams's administration, with the unpopular Alien and Sedition Acts producing a Republican response in the Kentucky and Virginia Resolutions (1798), the party was victorious in the elections of 1800. It won both Houses of Congress for the first time, but its presidential and vice-presidential candidates, Jefferson and Aaron Burr, each received 73 votes in the electoral college compared with Adams's 65. In accordance with the constitution, the election therefore went to the House of Representatives, which selected Jefferson (1801). Thereafter, in successive elections the Republicans consolidated their control of national politics until it became virtually a one-party system. During this period, which included the Era of Good Feelings, Republican attitudes changed to permit a more vigorous use of federal powers. But harmony was short-lived, and in the 1820s the party split into factions. Some, who became known as Democrats, supported Andrew Jackson, but others, the National Republicans, supported John Quincy Adams and later became Whigs.

Noble E. Cunningham Jr, *The Jeffersonian Republicans* (Chapel Hill, NC, 1957).
Noble E. Cunningham Jr, *The Jeffersonian Republicans in Power* (Chapel Hill, NC, 1963).

DEMOCRITUS (b. *c.* 460 BC), Greek philosopher from Abdera, who, in opposition to Heraclitus and Parmenides, developed Leucippus' atomic theory, explaining natural change and causation by supposing that all things consisted of indestructible particles, similar in quality but variable in size, shape, and combination. His works, surviving only in fragments, covered a wide field. In ethics he anticipated

Epicurus' ideas of happiness achieved by moderating one's desires.

DEMOSTHENES (d. 413 BC), Athenian general in the great Peloponnesian War, first prominent in the offensives associated with Cleon's dominance (427–424). After failure in Aetolia, he defeated the Spartans' allies in north-west Greece at Olpae (426). He was responsible for the fortification of Pylos in Messenia and for capturing the Spartan garrison on nearby Sphacteria (425), and took Nisaea in a surprise attack, but was prevented by Brasidas' arrival from winning Megara itself. His role in the attack on Boeotia ended in a fiasco (424). Nevertheless, he remained politically active and in 413 was joint commander of an expedition sent to relieve Nicias outside Syracuse. A night attack under his command was unsuccessful and having failed to persuade Nicias to withdraw until it was too late, he was executed when the expeditionary force was destroyed.

DEMOSTHENES (384–322 BC), Athenian statesman and Greek orator, a determined opponent of Macedonian domination, and a man so virulent, especially in attacking Philip II, that 'Philippic' became an accepted word for political invective. He was a master of the prepared oration, was trained under Isaeus, and began by prosecuting his guardians for misappropriating his estate. Politically he was an admirer of Callistratus and gained experience by assisting public prosecutions, *eg*, against Androtion (355), and himself prosecuted Leptines (354). Demosthenes concentrated on public finance and diplomacy, advocating active policies for Athens as the traditional champion of Greek liberty. Bowing to necessity, he helped to arrange the peace of Philocrates with Philip (346), but later charged his co-envoy Aeschines with treachery, though his charges were not upheld (343). Their political enmity endured until Aeschines' defeat and exile (330). Being implacably opposed to reconciliation with Philip, Demosthenes organized a coalition against him. Though it was defeated at Chaeronea (338), he survived extradition demands by Philip and Alexander the Great and exercised masterly caution in biding time for a resurgence. When Alexander's treasurer, Harpalus, fled to Athens (324) Demosthenes probably received some of his money for political purposes and went into exile, being unable to defend himself against charges of embezzlement. After Alexander's death (323) he organized opposition to Macedon in the Lamian War and returned to Athens, but after Antipater's victory and dispatch of a Macedonian garrison, he anticipated execution by committing suicide.

W. Jaeger, *Demosthenes* (Cambridge, 1938).   DJM

DEMUTH, CHARLES (1883–1935), US painter, whose water-colours showed a fascination for the circus, theatre, and vaudeville. As an illustrator of James, Zola, and other novelists he displayed sensitivity, cynicism, and exquisite style. He was attracted by Cubism, and in works like 'My Egypt' (1927) used semi-abstract geometrical techniques to portray the industrial technology of his age.

DENAIN, BATTLE OF (1712), fought in northern France during the War of the Spanish Succession. Villars and the French army revived French fortunes by defeating Albemarle.

DENIKIN, ANTON IVANOVICH (1872–1947), White Russian soldier and 'Supreme Ruler' of the White armies, who took part in Kornilov's attempted coup (Sept. 1917), and was afterwards imprisoned, but escaped to join the volunteer army formed by Alexseyev in the Caucasus. In April 1918 Kornilov was killed and Denikin took command of the volunteers and skilfully led the remnant on a 700-mile (1126 kms) march to Novocherkassk. He refused to accept any help from the Germans, his policy being one of pure nationalism; it mattered not to him whether a republic or a monarchy prevailed. His Great Russian chauvinism made it

hard for him to co-operate with the lesser nationalities (*eg*, the Don Cossacks). In 1918 he broke through to the Black Sea port of Novorossiisk, whence he received British supplies. In May 1919 he started a triple attack on Moscow. His advance was rapid and in Oct. he reached Orel, only 250 miles (402 kms) from Moscow. But on 20 Oct. the Red Army counter-attacked and drove him back. His retreat was as rapid as his advance, his supply lines being greatly over-extended and ravaged by Reds and independent partisans, especially those of Makhno, for peasants resented Denikin's attempt to restore the landlords. The remnant of his force was evacuated by the British in March 1920 and Denikin handed over command to Wrangel. Denikin was honourable but limited: one of his worst errors was to fail to curb the cruel excesses of his subordinate, Mai-Maevsky. In exile he lived in Belgium, France, and the US. He wrote *The Russian Turmoil* (1922) abd *The White Army* (1924).

DENISON, SIR WILLIAM THOMAS (1803–71), British colonial administrator. As chief executive in Van Diemen's Land (1846–54), NSW (1854–61), and Madras (1861–6, including two months as acting governor-general of India in 1863), his outstanding characteristics were political conservatism, administrative ability, and interest in public works.

DENMARK, INVASION OF (1940). The German invasion of Denmark on 9 April 1940 was an essential part of her invasion of Norway, aimed to safeguard her sea and air communications and to provide air bases for operations further north. Denmark's military strength was such that opposition was hopeless and all resistance ceased within 24 hours on the orders of the king and the government. The Danes accepted general German supervision of their affairs, but retained their own government.

DENNIS v US, 341 US 494 (1951), US Supreme Court case in which the conviction of members of the American Communist Party was upheld. Chief Justice Vinson developed the 'gravity of evil' test, substantially modifying earlier court doctrine in similar cases and implicitly accepting the constitutionality of the Smith Act (1940).

DENONVILLE, JACQUES-RENÉ DE BRISAY, Marquis de (1642–1710), French soldier and governor. After 30 years of military service, he was appointed governor of New France (1685), where he supported expansion of the fur trade and recovered trading posts seized by the Hudson's Bay Co.

DENTZ, FERNAND (1881–1945), French soldier and the Vichy regime's commander in Syria. He fought the British and Free French troops which landed in 1941 until he was forced to surrender. After the war he was condemned to death for aiding the Germans but the penalty was commuted, and he died in prison.

DENYS, NICOLAS (1598–1688), French merchant, who brought settlers to Acadia, NS (1633), and established fishing and fur-trading enterprises there. His treatise 'The Description and Natural History of the Coasts of North America' (1672) is the principal scource of information on 17th-cent. Indians and fisheries in Acadia.

DEOBAND, town in the Saharanpur district of the Indian state of Uttar Pradesh. It owes its name to the presence of a sacred grove (*Devi ban*) where there is a temple to Devi. Its theological college, founded in 1867, is, after the Aznar of Cairo, the most important academy in the Muslim world, and the library has a large collection of Arabic, Persian, and Urdu manuscripts. Theologically, the college is rigidly orthodox and opposed to all innovation, defending polygamy and opposing compulsory education for Muslim girls. Its students come from all parts of India and the Islamic world. In the past they participated in various revolutionary movements such as the *Ghadr* (rebellion) of 1915, and despite their orthodoxy were supporters of Congress nationalism. They also believed in Pan-Islamism and during the First World War entered into secret relations with Turkey.

DEPEW, CHAUNCEY MITCHELL (1834–1928), US lawyer, railroad executive, and politician. He served as a Republican state legislator (1862–3), secretary of state for NY (1863–5), and in 1866 refused nomination as the first US minister to Japan to become chief legal and political negotiator for Cornelius Vanderbilt's railroad interests. He later became president of the New York Central Railroad (1885–99) and US senator (1899–1911).

DEPOPULATION in Pacific Islands, 18th–19th-cent. phenomenon variously attributed to syphilis, endemic yaws, firearms, wet European clothes, psychological damage by missionaries, etc., but resulting in fact from bacillary and virus diseases against which islanders had no immunity. Radical changes followed in the population structure of all major island groups, notably the Marquesas. In Barotonga (1823 pop. 8000) 4000 died of mumps, measles, influenza, or tuberculosis (1827–45) and another 1800 during the next nine years. Measles epidemics in the New Hebrides (1860–1) and Fiji (1875) carried off one-third of the population in a few weeks. Epidemic malaria exacerbated the process in Melanesia, destroying the population of Aneityum and Erromanga, whereas Tanna, Tongoa, and Aoba (New Hebrides)—all comparatively malaria-free, but exposed to regular contact with the outside world—recovered rapidly.

DEPRETIS, AGOSTINO (1813–87), Italian politician and leader of the moderate left in Italy, who was continuously in office as prime minister or minister of the interior, from 1876 until his death. His sensible and moderate rule gave Italy the chance to consolidate her unity. His success was based on the avoidance of radical reform and the introduction of a system of political manipulation, reminiscent of Cavour's *connubio*, known as *trasformismo*. Opponents of the liberal centre were invited to co-operate, and to abandon controversy in favour of liberal progress. Depretis wanted to avoid conflict in foreign policy also, but Italy's dangerous isolation caused him, reluctantly, to join the Triple Alliance with Austria and Germany (1882). His foreign minister, Robilant, re-negotiated the alliance in Italy's favour and buttressed it with the Mediterranean agreement with Britain (1887).

DEPTFORD, English royal dockyard on the Thames, established in the 16th cent. by Henry VIII for the construction and repair of the navy. With Woolwich, it came to rival Portsmouth.

DERBY, EDWARD SMITH-STANLEY, 23rd Earl of (14th of 3rd creation) (1799–1869), British prime minister. As a Whig MP (1822), Stanley supported Catholic emancipation and the 1832 Reform Act. As chief secretary for Ireland (1830–3), he sponsored the act (1831) which created a national system of Irish education, and as colonial secretary (1833–4) he achieved the abolition of slavery in the British empire (1833), but resigned both from the ministry and his party in protest against the appropriation of ecclesiastical revenue for secular purposes. After a period of independence, Stanley became colonial secretary in Peel's Conservative administration (1841–6) and assumed the leadership of the protectionist majority after the repeal of the Corn Laws, of which he disapproved. He subsequently persuaded the Conservatives to abandon Protection, and though without a majority in the Commons he formed administrations in 1852, 1858, and 1866–8. He saw the passing of the 1867 Reform Act before ill health led him to resign the premiership in favour of his associate, Disraeli.

DERBY, EDWARD HENRY STANLEY, 24th earl of (15th of 3rd creation) (1826–93), British politician, who succeeded his father in 1869. He sat as an MP (1848–69) and held office in his father's three Conservative administrations (1852, 1858–9, 1866–8). As foreign secretary (1866–8) and, again, under Disraeli (1874–8), he strove to avert the Franco-Prussian war (1870), sought reforms in Turkey, and opposed the acquisition of Cyprus (1878). Leaving the government in 1878, he joined the Liberals (1880), under whom he held office as colonial secretary (1882–5), finally finding political satisfaction as leader of the Liberal–Unionist group in the House of Lords (1886–91). For nearly 50 years he was actively concerned with most of the main political questions of the day, *eg*, university education in England and Scotland, relations with the Boers, the Suez Canal, and Britain's role in India.

DERBY HOUSE COMMITTEE (1648), body in England responsible for the direction of the second Civil War. In Jan. 1648 parliament, on perceiving that Charles I had reached agreement with the Scots (the Engagement of 26 Dec. 1648), dissolved the Committee of Both Kingdoms and substituted its English representatives, generally known from their place of meeting as the Derby House Committee.

DERBY PETITION in England (1659), list of grievances and demands drawn up and submitted to parliament by the military force which had dispersed Booth's rising in favour of the restoration of Charles II. It was circulated among other forces, except Monck's in Scotland, but was rejected by parliament on 23 Sept. John Lambert, the commander of the force, who apparently had not connived in the petition, supported a second petition calling for a new government. Parliament expelled him from his seat in the Commons, but he forcibly dissolved the parliament (15 Oct.).

DEREBEY ('valley lord'), Turkish name for certain families (*khanedan*) which, during the 18th–19th cents, established autonomous regimes in various districts of Asia Minor. Among the more important of these families were the descendants of Ali Pasha of Janik, influential in the region of Trebizond; the Chapan-Oghlu at Bozok, Kayseri, Amasya, Ankara, and Nigde; and the Qara Osman-Oghlu, who dominated the sanjaks of Sarukhan and Aydin. The derebeys were at the height of their influence in the period following the Russo-Turkish war of 1768–74. Sultan Mahmud II (1808–39) made an end of most of these families, restoring the control of the central regime through the appointment of officials sent out from Istanbul.

DERMOT MAC MURROUGH (1134–71), King of Leinster, was politically overshadowed by the power of Rory, the King of Connaught. In his attempt to overthrow Rory, he employed Norman mercenaries and by this means initiated the Norman conquest of Ireland.

DEROULÈDE, PAUL (1846–1914), French chauvinistic poet and politician, who volunteered for the army in the war against Germany (1870), was captured, escaped, and fought against the Paris commune (1871). He started to publish patriotic and military verse (1872) and went on to found the *Ligue des patriotes* (1882), which claimed 300,000 members and supported Boulanger. He was a deputy (1889) for the Bonapartist district of Charente, but resigned after one of many duels (1893). As a rabid anti-Dreyfusard, anti-German, and anti-republican, he helped to bring down Brisson's government, tried to stage a coup during President Faure's funeral (1899), and as a result was exiled for ten years. Although he was allowed to return (1905), he was unable to obtain re-election and died before the war he had so long desired broke out.

DEROZIO, HENRY LOUIS VIVIAN (1809–31), teacher, journalist, and poet, of Portuguese and Indian extraction, son of a Calcutta merchant. He was educated at Drummond's School, Dharmtala, the headmaster of which was a free-thinker of some repute. Derozio was extremely precocious and at the age of 18 became a teacher of philosophy at the Hindu College, Calcutta, where he exerted an immense influence over the students and created a group of free-thinkers known as Young Bengal. Long before any idea of Indian nationalism had been formulated, Derozio, David Hare, and other reformers attacked the caste system. He established a newspaper, the *East Indian*. His attacks on Hinduism were resented by the orthodox, who accused him of propagating atheism and in 1831 he was forced to resign, later dying of cholera.

DERWENTWATER, JAMES RADCLIFFE, 3rd Earl of (1689–1716), impoverished northern earl and leader of the English Jacobite forces in the 1715 Rebellion. He was captured at Preston and was one of the few rebels to be executed.

DESAIX DE VEYGOUX, LOUIS (1768–1800), reputedly the best French general during the French revolutionary wars. He served in the Rhine campaign (1794) and was later made commander of the expeditionary force to Egypt, where he captured Alexandria and defeated the Mamluks at the Pyramids (July 1798), after which all upper Egypt was conquered. While returning to France he was taken prisoner by the English, was later released, and returned to Toulon (May 1800). He joined the French at Marengo, contributing greatly to victory against the Austrians by the brilliant way in which he led his division back to Napoleon's depleted army.

DESCAMISADOS (lit. 'the shirtless ones'), in Argentina, the indigent 20th-cent. urban followers of the Argentine dictator Juan Perón and his wife, Eva.

DESCARTES, RENÉ (1596–1650), first outstanding modern philosopher and one of the world's greatest pure mathematicians, known for his natural philosophy and his contribution to the invention of co-ordinate geometry.

Born in Touraine, France, the son of a councillor in the *parlement* of Brittany, in his early life he served as a soldier in the Thirty Years War under Maurice of Nassau and the Duke of Bavaria, and travelled widely. He lived in Amsterdam for 20 years (1629–49), and died five months after moving to Sweden at the request of Queen Christina.

Abandoning the assumptions of medieval scholasticism, Descartes applied the mathematical approach of deductive reasoning to philosophy: to the discovery of truth, to the existence of God, and to the mechanism of the universe. His most famous dictum, 'I think, therefore I am', was the central theme of his *Discours de la méthode* (1636), in which his philosophy was expounded. In *Principes de la philosophie* (1644) he developed his mechanistic concepts of the physical universe.

Cartesian science was based on the axiom that all natural phenomena could be reduced to the motion of matter. By importing the idea of motion into geometry he prepared the way for the calculus, which was based on the curves and graphs of co-ordinate geometry.

Descartes's whirlpool theories of gravitation were later refuted by Newton, and the conflict between the Cartesian and Newtonian systems continued until the mid-18th cent. His views were opposed, too, by the Jesuits, as mechanistic and materialist, and his works were later placed on the Index (1663). However, his thought profoundly influenced 17th-cent. philosophy and his great contribution to dynamics was to make it the primary science of his age.

DESCHANEL, PAUL (1856–1922), president of France, elected in 1920 (in preference to Clemenceau) after a distinguished political and literary career; illness forced him to retire.

DESEADA, West Indian island discovered by Columbus (1493) and, since 1814, a French possession.

DESHIMA, specially constructed island in Nagasaki harbour, where the Dutch traders who, alone among Europeans, were permitted to enter Japan between 1639 and 1854 were kept under strict surveillance.

DESIDERIUS (*reg.* 757–74), King of the Lombards. His quarrel with the papacy brought him into direct conflict with Charlemagne, who invaded Lombardy and captured Desiderius at Pavia in 774.

DESMOND, Earls of, kinsmen of the Fitzgeralds of Kildare, owned estates in Kerry and Munster and in the 16th cent. used their influence to harass the English government. Their rivals, the Butlers of Ormonde, supported the Lancastrians, but the Desmonds were Yorkist, and Maurice, the 9th earl (d. 1520), assisted Warbeck at the siege of Waterford. James, the 10th earl (d. 1529), allied himself with Spain against Henry VIII, but James, the 14th earl (d. 1558), after a period of opposition, submitted to the Tudors and was made lord treasurer. He attempted to pacify Munster, but his son Gerald, the 15th earl (d. 1583), resisted Elizabeth's attempted centralization, quarrelled with the Ormondes and terrorized the south by his lawlessness. With his cousin Fitzmaurice, he openly rebelled (1579) and after being defeated in battle was outlawed and became a fugitive in his native hills. He was betrayed and murdered at Glanaginty. Munster was devastated by the English, the earl's estates were confiscated and the earldom extinguished, his son James being imprisoned in the Tower for 16 years. James Fitzthomas, known as the Sugan Earl, assumed the title (1598) and waged war in Munster for three years, but was captured and died in the Tower (1608).

DESMOND REVOLT (1569–73), led by James Fitzmaurice Fitzgerald when his cousin, the 15th Earl of Desmond, was imprisoned by the lord deputy, Sir Henry Sidney, for persistent lawlessness. When Sidney appointed a president in Munster to break the power of the Desmonds and other local chiefs, Fitzmaurice raised the whole province in revolt. He captured Kilmallock, but failed to raise help in Spain and on his return was compelled to submit. Humphrey Gilbert, the explorer, was knighted for his assistance in suppressing the rebellion. Fitzmaurice went abroad to renew his efforts to get foreign help and in 1579 he landed at Smerwick with a small force provided by Pope Gregory XIII. He was killed in Tipperary and the rebels, now augmented by a contingent from Spain, were butchered and scattered.

DESMOULINS, LUCIE SIMPLICE CAMILLE (1760–94), French revolutionary journalist and editor of *Le Vieux Cordelier*. He was an associate of Danton, with whom he was tried and executed.

DESPENSERS, THE (*fl.* 13th–14th cent.), English nobles. Hugh the elder was a leading baron of Edward I's reign and the only one who stood with Edward II and Piers Gaveston in 1308, which won him the confidence of Edward II, whose most trusted adviser he became after Gaveston's death in 1312. Hugh the younger, his son, married Edward's cousin, Eleanor de Clare, sister and co-heiress of Gilbert, Earl of Gloucester. He was, until *c.* 1318, a supporter of Thomas of Lancaster, but joined the king's party because of dissension with other barons over his share of the Clare inheritance. Thereafter father and son used their ascendancy over the king to further their greed and ambition. They received large grants of land and honours, including the earldom of Winchester, granted to the father. The hatred and fear of them felt by Queen Isabella and most of the barons was complete: they were attacked by Lancastrian armies in 1321 and were largely responsible for the defeat and death of Lancaster in 1322. They were also the chief target of attack by Isabella and Mortimer when they invaded England in 1326; Hugh the elder was captured and beheaded at Bristol and his son, captured in Wales, was tried and executed as a traitor at Hereford.

DESSALINES, JEAN-JACQUES (1758–1806), Haitian Emperor, of African ancestry, who fought beside Toussaint Louverture in the independence movement and ruled as Jacques I (1804–6). He was born a slave at Grande Rivière, joined the revolt against the French (1791), and linked up with Toussaint (1797). He shared the black's animosity towards the mulatto and, following the victory, ordered the execution of about 10,000 mulattos. Dessalines was subdued by Leclerc's invasion (1802), but helped by disease, he managed to defeat and expel the remaining French (1803). He formally declared Haiti independent (1 Jan. 1804), naming himself as governor-general. With the elevation of Napoleon, Dessalines too declared himself emperor. He ruled by force of arms and his policies and practices caused alarm among the remaining French residents and mulatto farmers. The British gained commercial advantage over the French during his regime. A mulatto-inspired revolt ended his rule, Dessalines being killed in an ambush while leading his army to engage the rebels.

DESSAU, BATTLE OF THE BRIDGE OF (25 April 1626), fought on the Elbe, was a victory for the imperialist forces under Wallenstein against the Protestants led by Ernst von Mansfeld in the Thirty Years War. Mansfeld's forces were decimated by the imperial artillery and retreated into Brandenburg, cut off from their ally, Christian of Denmark.

DESTOUR PARTY in Tunisia, was founded (1920) as a means of campaigning for the restoration of Tunisian sovereignty against French colonial rule. After declining early in the 1930s, it was displaced in 1934 by the Néo-Destour (New Constitution) Party; this rejuvenated nationalist organization, headed by Habib Bourghiba, led Tunisia to independence in 1956.

DESTROYER BASES DEAL (2 Sept. 1940), Anglo-American agreement by which certain over-age American weapons were exchanged for leaseholds on British North American bases. Britain obtained 50 obsolete destroyers and 250,000 rifles, the US received bases in Nfld, Bermuda, the Bahamas, Jamaica, St-Lucia, Antigua, Trinidad, and British Guiana on a 99-year lease. The agreement was effected by an exchange of notes between the British ambassador in Washington and the US secretary of state and, although of questionable constitutionality, met with general American approval. It represented a further breach in American neutrality, and was welcomed in Britain as a sign of increasing US commitment to the Allied cause.

DETTINGEN, BATTLE OF (1743), fought in Bavaria during the War of the Austrian Succession. The 'Pragmatic Army', a mixed force of English, Hanoverians, and Austrians, defeated the French on the Main river. It was the last battle in which an English king (George II), led his troops.

DEULINO, TRUCE OF (1618), armistice at the end of the Russo-Polish war (1610–18) by which the Tsar Michael Romanov ceded to Poland the Smolensk and Seversk lands which had been taken from Muscovy during the Time of Troubles (1605–13).

DEUTSCHSOZIALE ARBEITER PARTEI (DAP) was formed in Munich in Jan. 1919 under the leadership of Anton Drexler and Karl Harrer. The total membership was then only 40. In Sept. Hitler joined the party and at the start of 1920 was placed in charge of propaganda. For the first meeting under his control on Feb. 24 he attracted an audience of almost 2000 and used the occasion to announce the party's new name, the National Socialist German Workers' Party. This corresponded to Drexler's original aim, to create a party both nationalist and working class in character.

DEVANAGARI, modern name of the script used in most of northern India (excluding Bengal) for writing Sanskrit and Hindi from about the 10th cent. AD, it having gradually evolved from earlier Brahmi script. It is written from left to right in bold letters apparently hanging down from a solid line. There are about 50 simple letters and some complicated ligatures.

DEVARAJA, Khmer (Cambodian) cult of the Angkor period, practised from the 9th to 12th cents. The *devaraja*, a sort of protective deity, resided in a royal *linga* kept in the capital. The cult was closely related to worship of the Hindu god Siva.

DEVAWONGSE VAROPRAKAR, Prince (1858–1923), foreign minister of Thailand (1885–1923), the 42nd child of King Rama IV (Mongkut). He founded and institutionalized the modern foreign ministry at a time when Thailand's survival as an independent state was in doubt. Through the Paknam Incident (1893) and treaties with France and Britain up to 1909, Thailand's survival and sovereignty were his unflagging concerns; and although he did not live to see the abolition of extra-territoriality in treaties of 1925–6, the policies by which this was effected were primarily his.

DEVIL'S ISLAND, once notorious as a French penal settlement. It lies in the Îles du Salut group, part of French Guiana, about 48 kms off the northern coast of South America. The French Jewish officer Alfred Dreyfus was imprisoned there (1894–9).

DEVOLUTION, WAR OF (1667–8), was started by Louis XIV in May 1667 when a French army of 50,000 men under Turenne invaded the Spanish Netherlands to give effectual authority to the law of devolution. This law, peculiar to Brabant and Hainault, gave females the right to inherit property before males of a second marriage. Louis therefore claimed the Netherlands on behalf of his wife, Maria Theresa, daughter of Philip IV of Spain by the latter's first wife, Elizabeth of Bourbon, challenging the right of the child-monarch Charles II, who had succeeded on his father's death in 1665. The Spanish governor of the Netherlands, Castel Rodrigo, was unable to prevent the French from seizing a line of fortresses, including Lille, and from overrunning Flanders (1667). Alarmed by these successes, the Dutch joined their recent enemy, England, in an alliance (Jan. 1668), to which Sweden acceded (May 1668) to form the Triple Alliance.

Meanwhile, in Feb. 1668, a French army of 15,000 men led by Condé swept into Franche-Comté and occupied it in less than three weeks. At the same time, Louis signed a secret treaty with the Emperor Leopold I, whereby in the event of Charles II's death the Spanish empire was to be divided between the Habsburgs and the Bourbons. This prospect persuaded Louis to bring the War of Devolution to a swift close. He signed the treaty of Aix-la-Chapelle (2 May 1668), restoring Franche-Comté to Spain and retaining the frontier fortresses.

DEVON COMMISSION, appointed by the British prime minister, Sir Robert Peel (1843), to investigate Irish landlord–tenant relations. It recommended that outgoing tenants should be compensated for improvements. Peel's bill to effect this was later withdrawn.

DEVONPORT, HUDSON EWBANKE KEARLEY, 1st Viscount (1865–1934), British businessman and politician, who, after a successful career in retailing, entered parliament as a Liberal in 1892. In 1905 he became parliamentary secretary to the president of the board of trade. In 1909 he gave up his political career in order to become chairman of the new Port of London Authority, from which he retired in 1925. In the First World War he was appointed food controller in Lloyd George's coalition ministry. He pioneered a scheme of voluntary food rationing, and had prepared a system of compulsory rationing when ill-health brought about his retirement.

DEVONSHIRE, WILLIAM CAVENDISH, 4th Duke of (1720–64), British Whig politician, who was lord-lieutenant of Ireland (1754–5), and first lord of the treasury (Nov. 1756–May 1757). On the outbreak of the Seven Years War (1756), the public called for Pitt's appointment as prime minister, but his refusal to serve with Newcastle, and George II's antipathy towards him, produced an impasse. Devonshire, who was popular although ineffectual, was recalled from Ireland and made nominal head of what was virtually Pitt's administration. This face-saving arrangement ended when Pitt and Newcastle were reconciled and formed a new administration.

DEVONSHIRE, SPENCER COMPTON CAVENDISH, 8th Duke of (1833–1908), British politician. As Marquis of Hartington, he increasingly lost sympathy with Gladstonian Liberalism, particularly disliking Gladstone's Irish policies, his lack of interest in imperial matters, and the 1884 Reform Act. In 1884 Hartington supported the sending of Gen. Gordon to the Sudan and shared in the criticism of the government when Gordon was murdered. Hartington spoke powerfully against the first Irish Home Rule Bill (1886). He became president of the Liberal Unionists and from 1895 held office under Salisbury and Balfour in Conservative and Unionist administrations. He resigned (Oct. 1903) when most Unionists seemed to favour tariff reform. He refused the premiership three times: in 1880, when Queen Victoria would have preferred him to Gladstone, and in 1886 and 1887, when Salisbury contemplated Conservative–Liberal Unionist coalitions.

DEVONSHIRE, CHARLES BLOUNT, 1st Earl of (1st creation) (1563–1606), Elizabethan commander and lord deputy of Ireland, who suppressed Tyrone's rebellion (1594–1603) after the return and disgrace of Essex. Blount's success was due to his intelligent approach to the problems of guerrilla warfare. He fought winter campaigns to deprive Tyrone's forces of the opportunity to sow the grain and rear the cattle which they needed for food. While his deputy, Sir George Carew, reconquered Munster, Blount subdued Ulster and Connaught. He defeated a Spanish force under De Aguila, besieged in Kinsale, and an Irish force under O'Donnell and Tyrone which came to relieve them (1602). Finally, Tyrone surrendered to Blount (1603).

DÉVÔTS, orthodox, ultramontane Catholic group in the French court during the 17th–18th cents, favoured by Anne of Austria, Maria Theresa, and Maria Leczsynska. The *dévôts*, who were opposed to Gallicanism, Jansenism, and the *parlement* of Paris, usually associated themselves with Jesuit attitudes, and owed their original inspiration to Pierre de Bérulle (1575–1629) and St Vincent de Paul (1580–1660). They opposed those ministers who proposed reforms in the *ancien régime*, such as Machault, who introduced the *vingtième* in 1749, and the physiocrat Turgot.

DEVSHIRME, Ottoman name for the tribute of children levied at intervals from the Christian populations subject to the sultan, and above all from the Slav races in the Balkan lands under Turkish rule. The institution was established perhaps in the reign of Bayezid I (1389–1403), lapsed in the troubled years following the battle of Ankara in 1402, and was revived in the time of Murad II (1421–51). Most of the recruits thus obtained for the service of the sultan went into the corps of Janissaries or into other corps belonging to the central regime. The best endowed amongst them entered the palace schools and, after a long training, were sent out to hold high office in the administration of the empire. The application of the *devshirme* became more and more irregular during the late 16th and 17th cents, the last-known attempt to raise the tribute being made in 1705.

DEW, THOMAS RODERICK (1802–46), US economist and president of William and Mary College, VA (1836–46). His *Review of the Debate in the Virginia Legislature of 1831 and 1832* (1832), republished in *The Proslavery Argument* (1852), was a major contribution to the development of the proslavery argument in the South.

DEW LINE, system of 50 integrated radar stations across AK and northern Canada, jointly established by the US and Canada (1954–7). Later extended to the Aleutian Islands and Greenland (1959–61), this Distant Early Warning Line was designed to protect North America from surprise aircraft attack from the north.

DEWAR, SIR JAMES (1842–1923), Scottish physicist and chemist, who was a pioneer of low-temperature studies. In 1872 he invented the vacuum (Dewar) flask, which was adapted for domestic use and as such is better known as a Thermos flask. In addition to his fundamental work, Dewar was involved in explosive research and in 1891 together with Sir Frederick Augustus Abel (1827–1902) developed the first smokeless powder, cordite, to replace gunpowder.

DEWEY, GEORGE (1837–1917), US naval officer. As commander of the Asiatic squadron in 1898 he defeated the Spanish fleet at Manila and secured the Philippines.

DEWEY, JOHN (1859–1952), US philosopher, educationalist, and critic who became deeply influenced by Hegelianism and, after completing a doctorate on Kantian psychology, taught at Michigan University (1884–94), and was then appointed chairman of the department of philosophy, psychology, and education at Chicago University. In 1904 he moved to Columbia University in NY, where he remained until his retirement (1930). He lectured widely both in the US and abroad, and visited China, Japan (1919–21), and Russia (1928). In 1896 he founded the Dewey School in Chicago, as a practical laboratory for testing his educational and psychological theories. He helped to found the American Association of University Professors (1915) and the American Civil Liberties Union (1920), headed the commission to Mexico (1937) that investigated charges made in Moscow against Leon Trotsky, attacked on grounds of academic freedom the refusal to allow Bertrand Russell to teach at City College, New York (1941), and through numerous articles in periodicals like the *New Republic* reached a wide audience as a champion of liberalism.

Dewey was a prolific if not entirely elegant writer. His major works include *The School and Society* (1900), *Studies in Logical Theory* (1903), *The Child and the Curriculum* (1902), *Democracy and Education* (1916), *Reconstruction in Philosophy* (1920), *Experience and Nature* (1925), *Art as Experience* (1934), and *Freedom and Culture* (1939). From his early preoccupation with philosophical idealism Dewey moved towards the acceptance of experience as the central issue and necessary preoccupation of philosophy, stressed an empirical approach, and is identified with pragmatism. Most influential perhaps in his philosophy of education, Dewey emphasized 'learning by doing' and stressed the importance of creating a flexible environment in which the child may develop his own experience and hence, as he has naturally a curious intellect, stimulate his intellectual imagination. For Dewey the school, as a microcosm of society at large, was therefore the most important medium for strengthening democratic institutions and processes.

Sidney Hook, *John Dewey: an intellectual portrait* (New York 1939).
Richard J. Bernstein, *John Dewey* (New York, 1966).   DKA

DEWEY, MELVIL (1851–1931), US librarian who founded the first library school in the US (1887) and was director of the New York State Library (1888–1905). He evolved the Dewey Decimal System for classifying books (1876), which has become the international standard.

DEWEY, THOMAS EDMUND (1902–   ), US politician. As district attorney of New York City during the 1930s he prosecuted several notorious racketeers. He was an effective governor of New York (1942–54), and twice Republican presidential candidate (1944, 1948), his defeat by Truman (1948) being one of the most sensational events in American political history.

DEZA, PEDRO DE (1520–1600), Spanish lawyer and president of the *audencia* of Granada, who was responsible for the enforcement of the Pragmatic of 1566–7 suppressing Morisco customs, against the advice of the captain-general, the Count of Tendilla. Deza's action resulted in the rising of the Alpujarras (1568–70).

DEZHNEV, SEMYON (*fl.* 1648–9), Cossack explorer who sailed around the north-eastern tip of Asia from the Kolyma estuary in the Arctic Ocean to the Anadyr river (1648–9), thus passing through the straits later called after Vitus Bering.

DHARMA, basic ancient Indian concept, impossible to translate but roughly corresponding to 'cosmic order', of which human law forms an important constituent part. Human law thus acquires superhuman authority with human effort limited to the interpretation, elaboration, and application of the sacred principles. It is, above all, the duty of the king to maintain dharma and thus to keep society in harmony with these hallowed principles. It is this duty that bestows upon him the right to mete out punishment if dharma is infringed or even to interfere in the affairs of a neighbouring state in the case of presumed violation of dharma. Wars of conquest were sometimes justified as efforts to restore dharma. Emphasis on dharma therefore by no means excluded the use of force, but probably mitigated its effects by eliminating the worst practices. As there existed several traditions of sacred law, as laid down in different *dharmashastra*s and other texts, there was always a certain flexibility in the application of law and clear evidence for at least limited adaptation of the principles to a changing society.

DHARMAPALA, DON JUAN, King of Kotte, Ceylon (*reg.* 1551–97), the principal of the three Sinhalese kingdoms during the 16th cent. These were frequently at odds with each other and the Portuguese took advantage of the dissensions to increase their influence. Dharmapala was converted to Christianity (1557) and in 1565 abandoned his capital city. He thereby lost his power over his subjects, and became a puppet king in the hands of the Portuguese, who induced him to bequeath his kingdom to the King of Portugal (1580). After his death they claimed and exercised sovereignty over the kingdom of Kotte, which included some of the lands on which cinnamon grew. This spice was a major inducement to the Portuguese to gain territory in the island.

DHARMASHASTRA, ancient Indian lawbooks or, more precisely semi-sacred Sanskrit texts on dharma, including law and social order, religion and cosmology. The earliest and most authoritative text of this type is the *Manava Dharmashastra*, which, though based on older traditions, was written in the beginning of the Christian era or slightly earlier.

DHARMAT, BATTLE OF (15 April 1658), fought 14 miles (23 kms) from Ujjain, between Prince Aurangzeb and the Mughal imperial army of Raja Jaswant Singh sent to intercept him. Unknown to Jaswant, Aurangzeb had been joined by the army of his younger brother, Murad, which gave him a decisive advantage. This battle led to the fall of Dara and the imprisonment of Shah Jahan.

DHARMAWANGSA TEGUH, King of ancient Java (*reg.* c. 991–1016), who ruled in the Brantas delta, and probably married into the lineage of Sindok. He launched a raid against Sri Vijaya in southern Sumatra and apparently succeeded in occupying part of the country for some two years. This invasion led, however, to retaliation by Sri Vijaya, resulting in the destruction of the East Javanese capital (1016). In the cultural field his name is associated with the oldest extant dated Old Javanese texts (apart from inscriptions), *ie*, paraphrases of part of the Indian epic, the *Mahabharata*.

DHAT AL-SAWARI (655), the 'Battle of the Masts'. The Umayyad governor of Syria, Mu'awiya, having begun a series of naval expeditions against the Byzantines, occupying Cyprus (649) and Rhodes (654), the Byzantines, under the Emperor Constans II, made a counter-offensive at sea, only to meet with disaster off the Lycian coast.

DHIMMA, 'compact' through which the Muslims assured to members of other revealed religions the right to follow their own faith on condition of their acknowledging the domination of Islam. The subjects of the caliph who received such a compact were known as *ahl al-dhimma* (people with a compact) or *dhimmi*s, *eg*, the Christians, the Jews, and the Zoroastrians. The *dhimmi*s paid to the Muslim government a poll-tax (*jizya*), and also suffered other disabilities, but remained in effect autonomous under their own religious law.

DHU'L-QADR, Turcoman house which for almost 200 years (1337–1522) dominated the region of Mar'ash-Malatya, first as clients of the Mamluk sultanate in Egypt and Syria, then of the Ottoman empire. In 1515 the Ottomans crushed the forces of Dhu'l-Qadr and in 1522 made an end of the regime, transforming its territories into an Ottoman *beglerbeglik* with its centre at Mar'ash.

DIAMOND MINING in Africa. Diamonds were discovered in South Africa in 1867 near the junction of the Orange and Vaal rivers, and were rapidly exploited. Cecil Rhodes consolidated the diamond-mining companies at Kimberley into the monopolistic De Beers Co. (1889). De Beers also controls the vast alluvial diamond deposits of the lower seaboard of South-West Africa, since the Second World War a 'restricted area' under South African government order. Several other African countries also have valuable diamond deposits, notably Angola, Congo (Kinshasa), and Sierra Leone. Africa produces (1970) more than 97 per cent of the world's diamonds annually.

DIAS, BARTHOLOMEW (d. 1500), Portuguese seaman who, blown off course on a voyage of exploration, discovered the Cape of Good Hope. Originally called the Cape of Storms by Dias, the Cape was rechristened by the King of Portugal because its discovery indicated the existence of a sea passage to the Indian Ocean.

DIAZ, ARMANDO (1861–1928), Italian general who, in the First World War, replaced Cadorna as chief of staff (Nov. 1917), and was credited with Italy's subsequent recovery and victories. As senator (1918), he supported the fascist movement and was its first war minister (1922–4).

DÍAZ, JOSÉ DE LA CRUZ PORFIRIO (1830–1915), Mexican general, supporter of the liberals until 1868, leader of the revolts of La Noria (1872) and Tuxtepec (1876), provisional President of Mexico (1876–7), and president-dictator (1877–1880, 1884–1911). The period of his activities is known in Mexico as the 'Porfiriato', so great was his influence. Díaz was a *mestizo* from Oaxaca, who rose in the liberal army during the war with the French (1861–7) and captured the capital for President Juárez. He aspired to the presidency himself and openly opposed Juárez's successor, Sebastián Lerdo de Tejada. Twice he rebelled against Lerdo, on the second occasion (1876) successfully, under the banner of 'no re-election'.

As provisional president and then president, Porfirio inherited the pattern and practices of earlier days: he ignored constitutional limits, interfered in state and local elections, and manipulated the courts even more successfully than had his predecessors. He avoided revolt by constantly shifting his military commanders and by effectively using *jefes politicos* throughout the nation to manipulate local politics. He controlled labour, preventing unionization and brutally suppressing strikes. Mexican courts applied a dual standard of law with government approval, favouring foreigners; this made Mexico a prime investment area for foreign capital, particularly from the US and Britain. The Social Darwinism of the age created a new upper class, composed of foreign migrants and creole families who were served by the *mestizo* majority. Díaz's government was dominated by a creole elite—the *cientificos*, who discussed positivism and played a leading role in the financial affairs of the nation.

The plight of the masses was difficult: prices rose and wages lagged, landownership narrowed and scarce food-producing acreage was acquired through fraudulent means by *hacendados* (landowners), who often used such land for commercial crops. Anarcho-syndicalist activities spread and liberal clubs were formed after 1900, threatening the dictatorship. Finally, popular unrest outstripped even the political protest of liberals and the resulting revolution drove Díaz into exile (May 1911).   HDS

DÍAZ DE SOLIS, JUAN (1470–1516), Spanish navigator, explorer, and chief pilot of Spain. He traced the Atlantic coast of South America and explored the estuary of the Plate river.

DÍAZ DEL CASTILLO, BERNAL (1492–1584), Spanish conquistador and chronicler, best known for his *True History of the Conquest of New Spain*, an eye-witness account of the Spanish destruction of the Aztec confederacy, which he wrote in Guatemala (c. 1568). Díaz had served as a soldier with Cortés in Mexico and while admiring him, felt that the 'official' accounts (such as Francisco de Gómara's *History of the Indies and Conquest of Mexico*) did not give enough credit to those who, like himself, served the commander. Díaz's work was edited (1904–5) by Genaro García.

DÍAZ ORDAZ, GUSTAVO (1911–), president of Mexico (1964–70), and leader of the PRI (*Partido de la Revolución Institucional*). He encouraged both industrialization and private ownership of land.

DICASTERIA, judicial panels in ancient Athens responsible for all except trivial cases. In the 5th cent. BC, 6000 citizen volunteers were enrolled annually, drawn in proportion to population from demes and tribes. Assigned by lot to ten sections (*dicasteria*) they formed juries, of uneven numbers from 201 upward, for trying allotted cases, for which they received subsistence payments. Under a presiding official, they heard cases presented directly by the parties, supporters, and witnesses, acting as judge and jury of law and fact. Bound by written law, but not by case law and precedents, without retiring, they gave verdicts reflecting public opinion—a central democratic principle.

DICKENS, CHARLES (1812–70), English novelist and journalist, whose childhood experience of poverty and family debt, and his knowledge of London, influenced his writing. In numerous novels, *eg*, *Oliver Twist* (1837), *Nicholas Nickleby* (1838), and *Hard Times* (1854) he portrayed conditions of living among the poor and defenceless in the new urban society of the Industrial Revolution. The wide popularity of his books, many of them serialized in the periodicals *Household Words* and *All the Year Round*, which he edited, was enhanced by Dickens's public readings (1858–70). These, originally for charity, and later for personal profit, drew immense audiences in Britain and the US, besides compensating Dickens for unfulfilled theatrical ambitions. He made a major contribution to the exposure of 19th-cent. social evils and their redress by parliamentary legislation.

DICKINSON, EMILY ELIZABETH (1830–86), US poet, born and educated in Amherst, MA. She wrote in secret and after her death over 1,700 short lyrics were discovered. The publication of *The Poems of Emily Dickinson* (1955) made a reliable text available. Characterized by intelligence, wit, precision, and a complete refusal to accept dogma in any form, her work stands as a memorial to a unique poetic sensibility. Generally regarded as America's best woman poet, she rivals Walt Whitman as the greatest American poet before the 20th cent.

DICKINSON, JOHN (1732–1808), American statesman, born in MD. After studying law in London, Dickinson returned to America and opened a law practice in Philadelphia (1757). He entered politics (1760) and represented PA at the Stamp Act Congress (1765). He opposed resistance to the Crown, but helped to write the Congress's resolution. Dickinson expressed his conservative views in *Letters from a Farmer in Pennsylvania to the Inhabitants of the British Colonies* (1768). He served in the Continental Congress (1774–6, 1779) and voted against the Declaration of Independence (1776). Dickinson was a delegate to the Constitutional Convention (1787) and was influential in securing the adoption of the constitution.

DICTATION TEST, THE, in Australia a device taken from Natal, at Joseph Chamberlain's suggestion, was used in Australia to restrict immigration (chiefly of Asians) without specifically naming their country of origin or colour of skin. The Immigration Restriction Act (1901) made entry conditional on a successful test in a European language. Amended in 1905 (to meet Japanese susceptibilities) to 'any prescribed language', the requirement maintained the so-called White Australia policy until, under the Migration Act (1958), it was abandoned in favour of a simple ministerial discretion to admit or exclude—a prelude to significant easing of administrative procedures by which selected Asians with special qualifications were admitted to permanent residence from the later 1960s.

DICTATOR, ROMAN, extraordinary magistrate of ancient Republican Rome, nominated in exceptional military or civil crises by one or both of the consuls, the choice being ratified by the Senate. The dictator appointed his subordinate *Magister Equitum* and held office with power superior to all other magistrates for six months or until the completion of his particular task, whichever was the shorter. Dictators were also appointed for certain religious rites and occasionally to hold the elections. The dictatorship fell into disuse after the Second Punic War. Sulla and Julius Caesar revived it as the basis of autocracy, but it was abolished in 44 BC after Caesar's death.

DIDEROT, DENIS (1713–84), French writer and critic, whose *Encyclopédie* (1751–72), which he edited with d'Alembert, collected and disseminated the rational and anti-clerical ideas of the French Enlightenment. His advocacy of enlightened despotism and his defence of the First Partition of Poland brought him a pension from Catherine II of Russia in his last years.

DIDIUS JULIANUS (*reg.* March–June AD 193), Roman Emperor, was raised to the throne after the murder of Pertinax, but was soon defeated and killed by Septimius Severus. The story that he won the empire by public auction from the praetorian guard is an elaboration of the fact that he won its support by offering a large donative.

DIEFENBAKER, JOHN (1895–), Canadian lawyer and statesman who entered parliament in 1940. He was elected leader of the Progressive Conservative Party (1956) and became prime minister in June 1957, when his party defeated the Liberals for the first time since 1935. His Baptist farming upbringing in Ont. recalled the pioneer spirit of the Prairies and gave him an evangelical style. A supporter of the Commonwealth, he encouraged a more buoyant feeling of national pride in a period when there was concern over Canada's increasing dependence on the US. Despite a recession in the US and a return of unemployment, he gained a huge majority in the 1958 elections, winning every province except Nfld. His majority was reduced in 1962 and the Liberals regained power in 1963.

DIEN-BIEN-PHU, BATTLE OF (March–May 1954), decisive conflict in the Indo-China War. The French established a fortress at Dien-Bien-Phu, which by March 1954 was defended by 12 battalions, occupying eight strong points on a plateau near the Laos–Tongking border. The French, hoping for a pitched battle, misjudged the strength of the forces the Viet-minh were able to mass in this area, as well as their artillery capacity. The Viet-minh began to surround the fortress before the end of 1953, and by March 1954 were strong enough to attack and take two of the eight positions. After nearly two months of continuous fighting, the last position fell to them on the 8 May; the same day, the Geneva Conference began to discuss Indo-China, and to negotiate an armistice, which was eventually signed on the 20 July.

DIENG (old Javanese, *Dihyang*—Mountain of the Gods), volcanic plateau some 6000 ft (1828 metres) above sea level in Central Java about 50 miles (80 kms) south south-west of Semarang. The plateau contains the remains of several large groups of small temples datable to the 7th–8th cents. Numerous images of badly weathered sandstone, all associated with Shiwaitic worship, were discovered there. The plateau is unsuitable for normal cultivation and was apparently mainly inhabited by priests, monks, and ascetics, many of whom acted as teachers. It was abandoned before the 10th cent.

DIEPPE RAID (19 Aug. 1942), Allied combined-operations attack during the Second World War. The raid, which involved mainly Canadian troops, produced little tangible success for the Allies, who suffered over 3000 casualties out of a force of 5000 men. The Germans made great propagandist use of the failure, emphasizing the blow to Russian hopes of an Allied Second Front. The operation was heavily criticized in the Dominions, although French-Canadian support for the war was momentarily stimulated by the gallantry shown in the assault; surviving French-Canadian heroes were employed for propaganda by the Canadian government, but this led to resentment. Although the Germans were able to improve their defences, the Allied experience gained at Dieppe undoubtedly contributed to the success of the Normandy landings (1944).

DIESEL, RUDOLF (1858–1913), German engineer, who developed (1890–8) the internal combustion engine (Diesel engine), in which the fuel is ignited by the heat produced by the compression of the fuel–air mixture to a high pressure. Because of its size and weight this engine has proved to be most suitable for heavy-transport vehicles. Heavy oil is used as the fuel and the engines are remarkably economic to operate. From the end of the First World War oil has gradually replaced coal as the fuel used in ships and locomotives.

DIESKAU, JEAN-HERMAN, Baron de (1701–67), French-born soldier who was commander in Canada at the beginning of the Seven Years War. He was defeated (1755) near Lake George, NY.

DIET, IMPERIAL, ABOLITION OF (1806), dissolved the Holy Roman empire of the German nation, although merely con-

firming an established fact. The power of the emperor and of the Diet, as well as the unity of the empire, had been destroyed by the religious split and the increasing independent power of the German princes since the Reformation. The Diet had long since ceased to legislate, and although the princes, imperial knights, and free cities were all represented it had become no more than a repository for law cases. The rise of Prussia in the 18th cent. effectively ruined the occasional plans for strengthening the position of the emperor and the role of the Diet. It was the Revolutionary Wars and the Napoleonic Wars which finally destroyed the empire. French desire for a Rhine frontier and pressure for German satellites to match those in Italy and the Netherlands led first to a territorial reorganization of Germany at the expense of the petty states (1802). After the crushing defeat of Austria at Austerlitz (1805), nothing stood in Napoleon's way and on 6 Aug. 1806 the Holy Roman empire was dissolved and its institutions abolished, most of the German states having already joined a French-controlled Confederation of the Rhine.

DIETRICH, SEPP (1892–), German soldier, whose career began as leader of Hitler's personal bodyguard. In 1934 he directed executions in the Stadelheim prison, where Roehm met his death in Hitler's purge of the SA. Dietrich fought as colonel-general with the 1st SS Armoured Corps in Russia. In 1944 he commanded the 6th SS Panzer Army which, together with the 5th, took the main brunt of the Ardennes offensive, known as the 'Battle of the Bulge'. In 1946 a US tribunal at Dachau sentenced him to 25 years' imprisonment for complicity in the murder of at least 71 American prisoners in Dec. 1944. He was released after ten years and brought to Munich in 1957, where, on 14 May, he was sentenced to 18 months' imprisonment for his part in the 1934 purges. His sentence and that of Michael Lippert, one of Roehm's killers, was the first punishment given to any Nazi executioners of the 'night of the long knives'.

DIEZMO, church tithe of 10 per cent collected by the colonial governments of Spanish and Portuguese America (*dizimo* in Portuguese). It was mainly used for expanding and maintaining religious buildings in America.

DIGBY, SIR KENELM (1603–65), English courtier, diplomat, naval commander, philosopher, scientist, and writer. Digby, whose father was executed for his part in the Gunpowder Plot, was brought up as a Roman Catholic. A member of King Charles I's household, he served Queen Henrietta Maria in exile. He returned to England (1654) and negotiated with Oliver Cromwell for Catholic toleration.

DILKE, SIR CHARLES WENTWORTH, 2nd Baronet (1843–1911), British radical politician, whose political career was shattered when he was cited as co-respondent in a divorce case (1886). In the 1870s Dilke attracted attention by his oratory, his republicanism, and his close association with Joseph Chamberlain. As under-secretary for foreign affairs (1880–2), and president of the Local Government Board (1882–5) with a seat in the cabinet, he proved an impressive administrator, steering the 1885 Redistribution Bill through the Commons. He combined radicalism, including support of Chamberlain's Unauthorized Programme of 1885, with an informed interest in imperial and military affairs.

DIME NOVELS, cheap paperback fiction selling at ten cents a copy that had great vogue in the US between 1860 and 1910. Launched by Beadle and Adams in New York, with Ann S. Stephens's *Malaeska: the Indian Wife of the White Hunter*, they were typically outdoor adventure stories in which virtue was always ultimately triumphant. Prentiss Ingraham and Edward Z. C. Judson ('Ned Buntline') were among the most popular writers of this school. Dime novels were widely imitated and formed the models for five-cent boys' fiction such as the *Deadwood Dick* series of Edward L. Wheeler and the *Frank Merriwell* stories of W. G. Patten ('Burt L. Standish').

DIMITRI DONSKOY (*reg.* 1359–89), Grand Prince of Moscow. His surname was derived from the Don river, in the region of which he led the Russian forces to their first victory over the Tatars since the subjugation of Russia to the Tatar yoke in the middle of the 13th cent. This Russian victory, the battle of Kulikovo (1380), did not mean the end of Tatar rule, but it showed that the Tatars were not invincible.

DIMITRIEVIC, DRAGUTIN, alias **APIS** (1876–1917), Serbian founder and leader of the Black Hand, a secret terrorist society whose aim was the union of all Serbs. Dimitrievic played a key role in the conspiracy that resulted in the murder of Prince Alexander Obrenovic in 1903. He founded the Black Hand in 1911, which he headed while serving as chief of the intelligence section of the Serbian general staff. Dimitrievic probably knew of the Sarajevo plot. He was executed after being tried at Salonika for an alleged attempt against the life of Prince-regent Alexander in June 1917.

DIMITROV, GEORGI (1882–1949), Bulgarian communist politician, who played a major part in the international communist movement between the two World Wars. From the age of 20 he helped to organize the left wing of the Bulgarian Socialist Party. He was both militant and extremist, being as opposed to any concessions to reformism as he was to war and militarism.

After the First World War he was imprisoned briefly (1918), then went abroad and became a member of the Executive Committee of the Comintern. He returned to organize communist risings in Bulgaria (Sept. 1923). After escaping capture he was sentenced to death *in absentia*. He achieved international fame by his own defence of charges, brought by the Nazi government of Germany, of instigating the Reichstag fire (Feb. 1934). He succeeded in making his defence an indictment of the newly established Nazi regime and, together with his three communist colleagues, was acquitted.

He then went to the Soviet Union and took Russian citizenship, became secretary-general of the executive committee of the Comintern, and a deputy to the supreme Soviet of the USSR. During the Second World War he directed communist resistance in Bulgaria, returning there (Nov. 1945) to take Bulgarian citizenship again and to become prime minister. He was thus in power in Bulgaria at a time when Stalin was imposing his rule, through leaders of his own creation, on the satellites of eastern Europe. Dimitrov, who had close relations with Tito and favoured the creation of a Balkan federation (which would be to some extent independent of Moscow), may have fallen victim to Stalin's purge as a result; but he became ill and died in the Soviet Union.

DIN ILLAHI, cult developed by the Mughal Emperor Akbar under the influence of the intellectualist brothers, Abu'l Fazl and Faizi. Akbar began to entertain doubts about Islam *c.* 1575. For some years religious discussions were carried on in the *Ibadat Khana* with representatives of Islam, Hinduism, Jainism, Zoroastrianism, and Christianity. The spokesmen for the last were provided by the Jesuit mission of Father Aquaviva from Goa. The defeat of an orthodox reaction headed by Akbar's brother, Muhammad Hakim (1580–1), enabled Akbar to develop his cult undisturbed. It adopted the prohibition of beef from Hinduism, reverence for life from Jainism, and reverence for light as a divine principle from Zoroastrianism. The cult centred round the person of the emperor, who received a semi-divine status. A religious society rather than a new religion, it was confined to the court circle and disappeared after Akbar's death. But its long-term effect was to magnify the person of the emperor, endowing him with a general religious sanctity in a way not known in Muslim India before.

DINAR, name of a Muslim gold coin, first minted in 691 in imitation of the gold solidus of the Byzantine Emperor Heraclius. The degree of fineness of this coin was maintained at a high level (often 98 per cent over much of the Muslim world until the fall of the Abbasid caliphate in 1258.

DINGANE (*reg.* 1828–38), King of the Zulus, succeeded his brother Shaka, whom he assassinated. To avert the threat to his kingdom from white settlers, he attacked the 'Voortrekkers' arriving in Natal in 1837. In 1838 he was himself vanquished by Boers and dissident Zulus under another brother, Mpande, and fled to Swaziland, where he was killed.

DINGISWAYO (d. 1818), chief of the Mthethwa people, who built up one of the most important corporate kingdoms in South-East Africa at the beginning of the 19th cent. He introduced many new ideas, especially in military organization, which were taken further by his protégé, Shaka, founder of the Zulu empire. Dingiswayo fostered trade with Delagoa Bay and had a reputation for magnanimity and enlightenment. He was killed by his rival, Zwide of the Ndwandwe people.

DINGLEY TARIFF (1897), US legislation named after its sponsor, Nelson Dingley of ME, that raised duties on imported goods to the highest level to date. The act, which established a complex rate structure that set tariffs at an average of 57 per cent, was designed to protect American industry and agriculture rather than to provide revenue.

DINH TIEN HOANG (Dinh Do Linh), (*reg.* 968–79), King of Viet-nam during a crucial phase of its establishment of independence against Sung China.

DINSHAWAY INCIDENT (June 1906), disturbance between British soldiers and Egyptian villagers at Dinshaway village. The incident led to harsh deterrent sentences on the villagers and provoked the first major demonstration of Egyptian hostility to British control of Egypt.

DIO CHRYSOSTOM (AD 40–120) of Prusa, Bithynia, author of 78 orations representative of the Second Sophistic and an important source for social conditions and educated opinion in the early Roman empire. Restored after exile by the Emperor Nerva, he addressed his *On Kingship* to Trajan.

DIOCLES (*fl.* 5th cent BC), general and politician at Syracuse. He is said to have opposed mercy to the defeated Athenians in 413. Later he led a democratic revolution which banished Hermocrates (409) and, after Diocles' own exile (407), led to Dionysius I seizing power (405).

DIOCLETIAN (C. Aurelius Diocletianus) (*reg.* AD 284–305), Roman Emperor, founder of the late imperial system of government. He was acclaimed emperor by the eastern army after the death of Carus and chose Maximian as colleague for the west (286). The principle of collegiality was further extended by the promotion in 293 of Galerius and Constantius as Caesars, respectively under Diocletian and Maximian, to produce the system known as the 'Tetrarchy', or college of four emperors. Diocletian's other reforms are obscure in detail, although certain tendencies are clear: the division of the provinces into smaller units; the development of a mobile field army alongside the standing army of the frontiers; and the separation of military and civil power. Diocletian did much to achieve financial stability by reforming the currency, a process modified and completed by Constantine the Great. He attempted, without much success, to control the maximum price of commodities, and introduced new methods of taxation. Many of these developments were already implicit in the 3rd cent., so that in some respects Diocletian appears as a stabilizing rather than an innovatory influence. He was by temperament not a 'reformer' but profoundly conservative, persecuting Manichees (from 297) and Christians (from 303) in an attempt to re-establish traditional Roman virtues. In 305, after restoring stability and military ascendancy to the empire, Diocletian and Maximiam retired and were succeeded by Galerius and Constantius, with Maximinus and Severus as Caesars under them. The strict 'Tetrarchic' system was soon abandoned; but the principle of collegiality and territorial division of the empire was retained, and was the foundation of the political stability of the 4th cent.

A. H. M. Jones, *The Later Roman Empire*, vol. 1 (Oxford, 1964). JFM

DIODORUS SICULUS (*fl.* 1st cent. BC), Greek historian from Agyrium, who compiled a World History in 40 books from the mythological period to Julius Caesar's Gallic War, beginning with an account of the antiquities of the Mediterranean World. Books 1–5 and 11–20 are fully preserved with considerable fragments of most others. Though valuable for periods not otherwise well covered by the sources, Diodorus is clumsy in fitting material into a rigid chronographic scheme and uncritical in following just one authority for particular periods and regions.

DION of Syracuse (d. 354 BC), uncle of the tyrant Dionysius II, whom he sought to influence by introducing Plato as his tutor. Honourably exiled by Dionysius in 366, he eventually seized power (357). His attempt to fight off a counter-attack by Dionysius (355) led to his being suspected of aiming at tyranny and he was murdered.

DIONYSIUS I (428–367 BC), tyrant of Syracuse (*reg.* 405–367), outstanding figure in the history of ancient Greek Sicily. Elected sole general with absolute powers to combat the Carthaginian invasion, he made peace and secured his own position with a mercenary bodyguard, rigorously suppressing opposition. In later wars with the Carthaginians (398–392, 383–378, 368–367) he survived a siege of Syracuse (397–396) and achieved notable successes, *eg*, in storming Motya (398) and in the battle of Cabala (383), but these years brought ruin to nearly every Greek city in Sicily; some he destroyed himself, *eg*, Naxos and Catana. He also extended his empire to southern Italy, destroying Rhegium (387). Though allied with Sparta, who helped him in 396, and ultimately with Athens, he was unpopular in the homeland. The orator Lysias provoked an angry demonstration against him at an Olympic festival and later tradition saw him as the worst of tyrants.

DIONYSIUS II (*reg.* 367–343 BC), tyrant of Syracuse and son of Dionysius I. More liberal than his father, he was induced to accept Plato as tutor, but quarrelled with his uncle, Dion, who seized power (357). Dionysius fought back and after Dion's murder (354) and the failure of two further tyrants, drove out a third, Nysaeus (347), before being himself besieged in the citadel (344). When Timoleon arrived to liberate Syracuse, Dionysius made an agreement with him, and in 343 retired to Corinth.

DIOSCORIDES PEDANIUS (*fl.* 1st cent. BC), Greek physician, whose *De Materia Medica* was the leading text on pharmacology for 1500 years. The medical properties of some 600 plants are described.

DIPANAGARA (d. 1855), Javanese rebel leader of the Java War (1825–30), earlier known as Pangeran Antawirja. He was a son of Sultan Hamengkubuwana III of Jogjakarta and was probably born in the 1780s (while Hamengkubuwana I still reigned). Pangeran Dipanagara was not only a highly placed Javanese aristocrat, but also an Islamic mystic, with a feeling of enmity towards the infidel Dutch. After his expectation of becoming Sultan of Jogjakarta was frustrated, and following an incident provoked by the Dutch resident, Smissaert, he rebelled against the Dutch, thus causing the Java War. He now assembled his own court, and took the title of sultan. The rebellion found support among both high and low Javanese of Jogjakarta, many of whom rankled under abuses inherent in the Dutch system of indirect and imperfect control of the Central Javanese principalities. The Sultanate of Jogjakarta fell almost entirely into the hands of Dipanagara's troops, who slaughtered both Chinese and Europeans. Alibasa Sentot Prawiradirdja and Kjai Madja functioned respectively as military and religious leaders under Dipanagara. The rebel troops fought a guerrilla campaign against the forces of the Dutch and the Javanese rulers. Losses by attrition were high. In 1829 Sentot went over to the Dutch and Kjai Madja was captured. Finally, in 1830 Dipanagara was induced by Gen. de Kock, the lieutenant-governor-general, to attend a truce discussion in Magelang, where the Dutch arrested him on 28 March 1830. He was exiled to Menado, where he died. During his exile, he wrote *Babad Dipanagara*, a history of Java, which included an account of his own part in it.

DIPLOMATIC REVOLUTION (1756) changed the alliances between Austria and Britain and between Prussia and France, which had held together with difficulty during the War of the Austrian Succession (1740–8), into a new alignment during the Seven Years War (1756–63) of Austria, France, and Russia against Prussia and Britain. In signing the first treaty of Versailles with France (May 1756), the Austrian chancellor, Kaunitz, recognized that the new rivalry with Prussia in Germany had made his country's centuries-old rivalry with France an anachronism. Prussia and Britain had come together a few months before (Jan. 1756). Throughout these changes the rivalry between Britain and France remained and they stayed opposed to each other until 1815.

DIRAC, PAUL ADRIEN MAURICE (1902–), British physicist who was cofounder of modern quantum mechanics. He produced, in 1926, a Cambridge Ph.D. thesis containing essentially the whole formal theory of modern quantum mechanics (which governs the properties of all matter on the submicroscopic scale), surely one of the most remarkable theses ever. He went on to relate this work to relativity, to predict the existence of 'antimatter' (subsequently discovered) and to many other fundamental researches. He was appointed Lucasian Professor of Mathematics at Cambridge in 1932 and shared the 1933 Nobel Prize for physics with Erwin Schrödinger.

DIRECT ACTION DAY (16 Aug. 1946). The Council of the All-India Muslim League called (29 July) for 'direct action' by Muslims in retaliation for an alleged British breach of faith over the formation of the Interim Government, and to force the government to recognize the Muslim League as the sole body representative of Muslims. Jinnah envisaged a day for protest and the mobilization of support, but was unable to control his followers and the result was four days of communal riots, the worst of which became known as 'the Great Calcutta Killing'.

DIRECTORY, FRENCH (1795–9), made up of men who had overthrown the Jacobins. It ruled France by a series of coups against the left and the right until it was itself overthrown by Napoleon.

DIRECTORY, THE, Presbyterian substitute for the English Book of Common Prayer, was imposed by an ordinance of 1644. During the protectorate, under pressure from the Independents, its use was made optional according to the parishioners' wishes, but the Anglican liturgy continued to be proscribed until 1660.

DIRHAM, Arabic name for a weight (*cf.* Greek drachma) and for a silver coin current in the lands of Islam down to the time of Mongol domination. The earliest examples are imitations of the late Sasanid drachma. From *c.* 1000, dirhams of base silver (*eg*, of the Buyid amirs and the Khwarazm shahs) and even of copper (*eg*, of the Zangids and the Ayyubids) exist.

DIRIGISME, French term for state intervention in the direction of the economy. It refers to state action within a basically free-enterprise economy rather than to socialist planning. Dirigisme was much discussed in the 1930s, but became an established practice only after the Second World War.

DIRKSEN, EVERETT MCKINLEY (1896–1969), US politician, a Republican congressman from IL (1932–50), and US senator (1950–69). His flamboyant oratory and frequent appeals to patriotic emotions disguised an acute political sensibility. His position as Senate minority leader (1959–69) made him an influential figure in congressional and Republican national politics (1960–8).

DISARMAMENT CONFERENCE (1927 in Europe). The final protocol of the Locarno pact expressed the signatories' desire to work for general disarmament. In Dec. 1925 the League of Nations council appointed a preparatory commission for a disarmament conference to take place by the end of 1927. By then, however, although the preparatory commission had been attended by two important non-league members, Russia and America, it had reached only its fourth session, and the general conference seemed a remote prospect.

The commission's first meeting in Geneva (May 1926) was itself subject to delay. Russia was reluctant to deliberate in Switzerland because of the murder of its delegate to the 1923 Lausanne conference. Russo–Swiss differences were not resolved before 1927. The commission's discussions in 1926 mainly high-lighted the conflicting opinions of the delegations. France was more preoccupied than Britain by problems of security. There were disagreements as to the definition and limitation of 'war potential' in its many forms, such as trained reserve forces and heavy industrial equipment. The commission's report in April 1927 presented rival proposals side by side.

In Nov. 1927 Litvinov, Russia's assistant commissar of foreign affair, attended the commission's fourth session. His presence was due less to the settlement of the Swiss quarrel than to Russia's realization that its recent policies in Europe and Asia had been unsuccessful. A genuine fear of anti-Bolshevik hostilities prompted Litvinov's mission to Geneva. He chose to demonstrate Russia's will to peace by denouncing the capitalist states as inevitably prone to war, and presented a 14-point draft convention for total abolition of land, naval, and air forces. Since this sweeping approach was thought to contribute little to the commission's labours, discussion of it was postponed until 1928.   ASJ

DISAVA, an official of the ancient kingdoms of Ceylon, directly subordinate to the *adigars* (ministers), who was responsible for the administration of a sizeable district. He was remunerated, in the semi-feudal conditions of the time, by a grant of certain rights over the land and people of his district. The Portuguese and Dutch retained this form of administration, though their *disava*s were usually Europeans.

DISCIPLES OF CHRIST, North American Protestant denomination officially called the Christian Churches. Founded in Lexington, KY (1832), by fusion between the 'Christians', followers of Barton W. Stone (1772–1844), and the 'Disciples', led by Thomas Campbell (1763–1854), and his son, Alexander (1788–1866), they became an important sect on the American frontier. The Disciples have (1970) more than 6000 congregations in the US and Canada, a membership of almost 2 million, and stress an interdenominational approach to Christian unity.

DISCIPLINE, BOOKS OF (1560, 1578). The first book was drawn up by John Knox and others for the establishment of the Reformed Church in Scotland and its endowment out of the wealth of the Catholic Church. The book outlined doctrinal proposals and a financial scheme for paying ministers and encouraging education and poor relief. Many Scots nobles and landowners, who had acquired property and wealth from the deposed Church, were reluctant to part with either to endow the Reformed one. Thus the plan failed. The second book, mainly the work of Andrew Melville, emphasized the role of presbyterian government in the structure of Church organization. Though the book itself never received civil recognition, presbyterianism was ultimately established in Scotland (1690) after a century of alternating supremacy and episcopacy.

DISCOURS DE LA MÉTHODE (*Discourse on Method*) (1636), major work of the French philosopher René Descartes, written while he was living in Amsterdam. In it he propounded the axiom that existence depended on rational thought, ('I think, therefore I am'), and that through the application of reason the mechanism of the universe as well as the certainty of God and of man's soul could be proved.

DISCOURSE OF THE COMMON WEAL (1549), literary monument of the reforming Commonwealth Party in England, which may have been written by John Hales. It was in the form of a dialogue between a knight, a merchant, a husbandman, and a doctor, and offered the first serious appraisal of the economic revolution of the 16th cent.

DISESTABLISHMENT (IRISH CHURCH) ACT (1869) severed the legal connection between Church and state in Ireland after 1870, thereby removing a longstanding Roman Catholic and, to a lesser extent, Presbyterian grievance. The measure, passed by Gladstone's Liberal administration, evoked bitter criticism from English and Irish Anglican churchmen, but the Lords were reluctant to use their veto against it after the 1868 Liberal landslide. Responsible and considerate compensation arrangements, accounting for about £16 million, sugared the pill of disendowment. The remainder of the Church's wealth, about £13 million, was devoted to relieving poverty, encouraging agriculture and fisheries, and endowing higher education.

DISESTABLISHMENT (WELSH CHURCH) ACT (1914). This measure, which had been British Liberal policy since 1891, was introduced by Asquith's Liberal government (April 1912) and three times rejected by the Lords. Many Anglicans feared it would be the first step towards a similar measure for England. The law did not become operative, because of the First World War, until 1920.

DISNEY, WALTER (1901–66), US film cartoonist and producer. The creator of Mickey Mouse and Donald Duck, he pioneered animated feature films with *Snow White and the Seven Dwarfs* (1937), made impressive nature documentaries such as *The Living Desert* (1953), and in popular family entertainments like *Mary Poppins* (1965) combined cartoon fantasy with realism. Disneyland, an amusement park in CA, divided into Adventureland, Frontierland, Fantasyland, and Tomorrowland, embodies the mixture of imagination and reported reality that characterizes his work.

DISPENSATION, the relaxation of a law in a particular case by a competent authority which was a special feature of canon law in the Middle Ages. All orders of the ecclesiastical hierarchy had the power to dispense, though this was graded from the universal power of the pope to the very restricted power of a parish priest.

DISPENSING POWER in England, used under the Great Seal, enabled the monarch to dispense in particular cases with the requirements of statutes and to pardon offences. This power had never been denied, but after the *Godden v. Hales* case (1686) it was used so often by James II that, as exercised under his rule, it was declared illegal in the Bill of Rights (1689).

DISSENTERS in England, general term for religious groups outside the established churches. They included three broad groups, the Catholic dissenters or recusants, and unitarian and trinitarian nonconformists. All were equally persecuted by the laws up to and including Charles II's reign. The trinitarians were granted the right to build conventicles and to worship freely by the Toleration Act (1689), from which the unitarians were excluded. The Occasional Conformity Act (1711) and the Schism Act (1714) were the last Stuart blows against Protestant nonconformists, and their repeal in 1718 left the Test and Corporation Acts as the main penal restrictions until 1829. Catholic dissenters were further penalized by the revolution settlement, and by the acts of George I's reign, which compelled them to register their names and estates and to pay a double land tax. Although Catholics were granted no toleration before Savile's Act of 1778, the laws against them were seldom rigidly enforced after the 1720s.

DISSOLUTION OF PARLIAMENT, in Britain, a royal prerogative, raises important constitutional problems because parliament has a maximum but not a fixed duration. The royal prerogative has never been restricted in law except by statutes prescribing a maximum duration for each parliament: three years by the 1694 Triennial Act, seven years by the Septennial Act (1716), five years by the Parliament Act (1911). George III's dissolution, in March 1784, of the parliament that met in 1780 infringed the post-1716 convention that parliament should normally last for nearly its permitted life of seven years, in order to save Pitt from resignation though he was several times defeated in the Commons. This posed the problem clearly. The king's ministers needed the confidence of the Commons; if they lost it, the proper course was surely that they should 'yield to parliament', in Burke's phrase, and resign, not that parliament should yield to them and be dissolved. Premature dissolutions in the early 19th cent. were less successful, and that of June 1841 resulted in a decisive electoral defeat for Melbourne's government. After 1841 Victoria held to the view (expressed by Fox in 1784 and Peel in 1841) that ministers defeated in the Commons should resign and not ask for a dissolution, which she defined as a royal prerogative to be used sparingly and only if there was 'a certainty of success'. She believed that the 1841 electoral defeat was tantamount to a defeat for her, and never afterwards so openly associated herself personally with the electoral fortunes of any particular minister.

After 1867, when general elections came to be the determinant and also the immediate prelude of changes of ministry, Burke's answer to the problem posed in 1784 became unacceptable. It came to be thought, generally though not universally, that if a government was defeated in the Commons there ought to be a general election—either at once, under the auspices of the defeated government, or after its resignation under the auspices of the new government. Preference between these two alternatives often depended simply on circumstances. For example, in June 1885, Gladstone resigned after defeat in the Commons and Salisbury, who succeeded, was granted a dissolution (Nov.), while in June 1886, after defeat on Home Rule in the Commons, Gladstone was granted a dissolution and resigned after defeat at the polls in July. Although this shift of emphasis raised the question of whether the prerogative of dissolution had passed from monarch to prime minister, it can reasonably be maintained that this had not happened by the 1920s and perhaps still has not. No monarch has refused a prime minister's request since 1858, when Victoria refused Derby, but refusal has been considered since then (eg, 1910, 1924) and Asquith in 1923 thought that these were certainly circumstances in which the monarch constitutionally could and should refuse. The question was debated in Canada in 1926—when Lord Byng, the governor-general, refused a dissolution to Mackenzie King and subsequently granted one to his successor, Arthur Meighen—and in South Africa in 1939.

C. S. Emden, *The People and the Constitution* (Oxford, 1933).

E. A. Forsey, *The Royal Power of Dissolution of Parliament in the British Commonwealth* (Toronto, 1943).   JK

DIVINE, FATHER (c. 1875–1965), US Negro religious leader. Born in GA, he moved to Harlem, changed his name from George Baker, and became the leader of a religious cult, the Peace Mission Movement, in which he was regarded as the incarnation of God. The movement emphasized communal living and flourished particularly during the Depression of the 1930s.

DIVINE LOVE, ORATORY OF, Catholic order of clerks regular, formed in Rome (1516) to stimulate reform in the Church by personal example of piety and discipline. From this order sprang the Theatines, founded (1524) by two of its members, Caraffa (the future Paul IV) and Cajetan. After the sack of Rome (1527) the Theatines moved to Venice.

DIVINE RIGHT OF KINGS, belief that kings, as God's deputies on earth, are owed unquestioning obedience and cannot be restricted by man-made law, was asserted in an exaggerated form by the Stuart kings in Britain and was a chief cause of their difficulties.

The theory took shape in the Middle Ages in opposition to the papal claim to universal obedience. Marsiglio of Padua, Dante, and William of Ockham were among those who maintained that the secular power of princes was also ordained by God: Jesus would render unto Caesar the things that were Caesar's. As the centrifugal forces of feudalism were gradually overcome by territorialism and centralization, kings found it intolerable that the spiritual estate should exercise its own law and justice and give wealth and allegiance to a foreigner overseas.

In this conflict Divine Right had the effect of making obedience to the king a religious duty. Aided by the stirrings of nationalism, kings asserted authority over all men who lived within their boundaries, and during the Reformation they claimed that the divine institution of the secular power entitled them to control the clergy and establish whatever religion they chose. They also needed to be strong enough to discipline those who disagreed, and Luther and Calvin both upheld the sacred rights of the civil magistrate. On a more balanced level, Shakespeare acknowledged the divinity that supported kingship, and his histories proclaim from end to end the importance of unity, the subject's duty to the commonwealth, and the destructive wickedness of rebellion.

In England the Stuart kings failed to profit from this valuable instrument of power politics and the failure of James II merely emphasized the passing of the concept. Although a vestige of Divine Right was preserved in the obliging fiction that he had abdicated, its chief expression was in non-juring toasts to the king 'over the water'. In Scotland its dying struggles were fiercer, but it perished in the severities that followed Culloden.

In France Bossuet wrote a quasi-religious justification of the absolutism of Louis XIV. But there too it perished in the Revolution (1789) and its attempted revival by the Bourbons after 1815 was an anachronistic, short-lived folly.

J. N. Figgis, *The Divine Right of Kings* (Cambridge, 1914).   MMR

DIWAN, word meaning a collection of poems; a register; an office or department of state. As a Muslim administrative institution the *diwan* appeared in the reign of the Caliph Umar I (634–44), ie, the *diwan al-jund* (of the army). Thereafter, other government *diwan*s came into being and similar *diwan*s existed at the level of the provincial administration. Much later in the Ottoman empire, the *diwan* was the high council of state. Under the Indian Mughals the *diwan* was the chief financial officer of a province or state as a whole, charged specially with collecting revenues. The title was retained by the English East India Co. for a subordinate revenue official.

DIWANI OF BENGAL. The word *diwani* applies to the functions of the office or court of *diwan*, which under the Mughals came to be identified with revenue matters. The *diwani* power was therefore the authority to raise and regulate the revenue of the individual provinces and of the whole empire. It was matched with the *nizamat*, or the judicial and magisterial power. Formerly kept separate, these powers were united in the person of the nawab of 18th-cent. Bengal, thus making him virtually independent. Clive's settlement in 1765 consisted in obtaining the grant of the *diwani* direct from Shah Alam and administering it through a nominated deputy nawab, Muhammad Reza Khan. The nawab of Bengal thus had no control of the revenue and was politically powerless. In 1772 Warren Hastings went a step further when he caused the East India Co. 'to stand forth as *diwan*', ie, to undertake the revenue collection in Bengal directly through its own agents.

DIX, DOROTHEA LYNDE (1802–87), US reformer, whose campaign for better conditions in prisons and asylums began in MA (1843) and was then carried to the other states and to Europe. She was superintendent of female nurses during the Civil War.

DIXIE, colloquial designation of the American South, particularly of the 11 states that formed the Confederacy during the Civil War (1861–5). Its origins are obscure, but may stem from the French word Dix that had been printed on ten-dollar bills in LA. The song 'Dixie' composed by Daniel D. Emmett (1859), became a popular Confederate marching song.

DIXIECRAT PARTY in US, state rights party organized by breakaway southern Democrats in the 1948 presidential campaign. The party's main aim was to secure President Truman's defeat and so show the Democratic Party that it could not afford to ignore southern opposition to Negro civil rights. Its strength was concentrated in the Deep South, whence it drew both its presidential candidate, senator J. Strom Thurmond, of SC, and its vice-presidential nominee, Gov. Fielding L. Wright, of MS. The Upper South remained loyal to the Democratic Party, and the Dixiecrats carried only LA, MS, AL, and SC, the four states in which they controlled the regular Democratic organization.

DIXIÈME, French tax of 10 per cent on all gross incomes imposed by Louis XIV on all classes in 1710 to help finance the War of the Spanish Succession. It was opposed by the aristocracy as a threat to their financial privileges and was suppressed in 1717. It was revived by Fleury in 1733 and reimposed in 1741 and 1746, again as a wartime emergency measure.

DIXON, SIR OWEN (1886–), the greatest constitutional lawyer to sit on an Australian bench. An outstanding member of the Victorian bar, he was high court justice (1929–52), Australian minister in Washington (1942–4) and chief justice of the high court of Australia (1952–64). His approach to matters arising under the Australian constitution was conditioned by a strong sense of the continuity and authority of the law and an enduring habit of studying each contemporary statute against the circumstances prior to its enactment. He saw himself not as an innovator, free to give expression to his own sociological ideas, but as an interpreter, going back constantly to the terms and substance of the constitution itself.

Dixon was no legal pedant. The constitution to him was not just another statute to be examined and expounded but the basic instrument of government. It was to be interpreted broadly and with that degree of flexibility which is inevitable if a constitution is to retain its applicability to change and changing circumstances; but the constitution must remain the master document. 'It may be that the Court is thought to be excessively legalistic,' he said on acceding to the chief justiceship: 'I should be sorry to think that it is anything else.'

Leading members of Dixon's profession in Britain, the US, and Australia deemed his qualities unsurpassed by those of any judicial lawyer in the English-speaking world. His reputation elsewhere was attested by his selection in 1950 as United Nations mediator in the Kashmir dispute.   RGM

DJILAS, MILOVAN (1911–), Yugoslav communist leader, whose campaign for democratic and humanistic communism led to his disgrace and imprisonment. In 1937 Tito, the new Communist Party chief, discussed with him means of organizing communist activity in Belgrade University. Djilas became a member of the central committee (1933) and of the politburo (1934). During the Second World War he commanded the Partisan units in Montenegro and rose to the rank of general. In April–May 1944 he headed the Yugoslav military mission to the Soviet Union. After the war he entered the government as minister without portfolio, became speaker of the chamber of deputies, and then vice-president of Yugoslavia. In 1945 he visited Moscow and participated in the formation of the Cominform in 1947, yet in 1948–9 he played a key role in the talks that led to Yugoslavia's split with the Soviet Union.

In 1950 Djilas published a series of articles in which he argued that party and administration must be separated and that the totalitarian character of the party must be changed. Minor reforms were undertaken, but by 1953 Djilas found himself virtually alone in urging further changes. He wrote another series of articles in Nov. 1953–Jan. 1954, calling for a withering away of the party, complete freedom of thought and expression, the abolition of totalitarian discipline, and an end to 'careerism'. These articles met with disapproval among his colleagues in the leadership. In Jan. 1954 Djilas published 'Anatomy of a Moral', a bitter, personal attack on the manners and morals of the ruling class, for which he was dismissed from his various positions of responsibility, and in April 1954 he resigned from the party altogether. In Dec. 1954 he gave the *New York Times* an interview in which he stressed the need for an opposition party in Yugoslavia. After being secretly tried he was put on three years' probation, which ended in 1956, when he told the *New York Times* that his manuscripts were rejected on political grounds, attacked Soviet leaders while Tito was in Moscow, and criticized his ambiguous attitude over the rebellion in Hungary. As a result, he was sentenced to seven years' imprisonment. In 1957 *The New Class*, a harsh critique of communism, marking his transition from communist to social democrat, appeared in the West. Although conditionally released in 1961, he was again imprisoned in 1962 for publishing *Conversations with Stalin*, an account of his experiences as a Yugoslav representative at Moscow. After his release in 1965 Djilas continued to write, combining journalism with fiction, autiobiography, and history.   JMK

DJOSER (*reg. c.* 2700 BC), first Egyptian King of the 3rd dynasty, who is chiefly remembered for building the Step Pyramid at Sakkara, near Memphis.

DLUGOSZ, JOHN (1415–80), medieval Polish historian. As a royal official he had access to all the Polish chronicles and numerous archives. Diplomatic missions to Italy acquainted him with humanist historiography. His critical history of Poland until his own time is an invaluable source of historical information.

DMITRI I (d. 1606), the false Tsar, Russian pretender who claimed to be Dmitri, the half-brother of Fyodor I, who was assassinated in 1591. Supported by the mass of the peasants and by the Cossacks, he led a revolt against Boris Godunov, becoming tsar after the latter's death (1605). His association with Catholicism and with Poland—he married Maria Mniszchowna, daughter of a rich Polish landowner, amid great pomp—made him unpopular with the *boyars* and he was assassinated in his Moscow palace within three weeks of his marriage (1606).

DMITRI II (d. 1610), the false Tsar, Russian pretender, probably the son of a Ukrainian priest, who claimed to be the Tsar Dmitri I. Supported by the Cossacks and some of the *boyars*, *eg*, Prince Trubetskoy, he started a revolt against Tsar Vasily Shuisky (1607) and defeated his army at Tushino (1608). The civil war was prolonged by the intervention of Sigismund III of Poland on Dmitri's side (1610) and ended when Shuisky was deposed and replaced by Sigismund's son, Vladislav. Dmitri was killed by a friend of the Tatar Khan of Kasimov, whom he himself had murdered (Dec. 1610).

DMITRI (*fl.* 1611–13), the false, one Sidorka, Russian pretender who claimed to be the son of Dmitri I and Maria Mniszchowna when he appeared in Pskov (1611). His claim was not considered by the *Zemsky Sobor* in 1613.

DNIEPER RIVER, rising to the west of Moscow, this vast waterway flows south about 1610 kms to the north-west shores of the Black Sea. The steppe lands of its southern basin were settled successively by Scythians, Sarmatians, Goths, Khazars, Kievans, Mongols, and Zaporozhie Cossacks. Though the principal artery for Russian trade in the Kievan state (9th–10th cents) and during the Muscovite period frequently the dividing line between Russia and Poland (*eg*, 1667), the southern basin and mouth of the Dnieper were not brought under Russian control until 1774.

DOBELL, SIR WILLIAM (1899–1970), Australian portrait and genre painter, represented in all major Australian collections. He studied in Sydney and later at the Slade, London.

DOBROGEA, region of some 23,000 sq. kms lying between the Danube and the Black Sea. Since the Congress of Berlin (1878) the Dobrogea has been a subject of contest between Bulgaria and Rumania. At that time the Ottoman empire was forced to give up the entire region, the northern Dobrogea going to Rumania and the southern to Bulgaria. Rumania annexed the southern Dobrogea by the treaty of Bucharest (1913), which followed the Balkan Wars. Rumania's possession of the entire Dobrogea was reaffirmed by the treaty of Neuilly (1919). By the treaty of Craiova (23 Aug. 1940) Rumania returned the southern Dobrogea to Bulgaria under Axis pressure. An exchange of populations accompanying this treaty sent 62,000 Bulgarians to Bulgaria from the north and 110,000 Rumanians to Rumania from the south. This settlement and the population exchange was confirmed by treaty after the Second World War. The population of the Dobrogea is mixed; the north is predominantly Rumanian, the south Bulgarian. However, a large Turkish minority in the south has caused strained relations between Bulgaria and Turkey since the Second World War.

DOCTRINAIRES, ideological pressure group in restoration France which advocated a liberal monarchy. Its members derived from the *idéologues* of the empire and the pupils of Royer-Collard, and believed in enunciating rational political principles as a guide to action. They supported Decazes and hoped to use royal power to check the reactionary chamber (1817). With the rise of the Ultras they fell from prominence, but bequeathed the idea of '*la juste milieu*' to French politics. The group included Barante, De Broglie, Cousin, Guijot, Jordan, Mounier, De Serre, Rémusat, and Villemain.

DOCTRINE OF LAPSE, implemented by the British governor-general in India, Lord Dalhousie, in the 19th cent. It enabled him to annex Hindu states on the default of natural successors or where an heir had not been legally adopted with the sanction of the paramount power. Although previously seldom exercised, this was a well-established Hindu doctrine, not one invented by Dalhousie. He was also acting in accordance with instructions from the Court of Directors of the East India Co. in London, which had laid down (1834) that the right to adopt should be granted only as a special mark of approbation, and he restricted it to dependent states. The states accordingly annexed (1848–54) were Satara, Jaitpur, Sambalpur, Jhansi, and Nagpur. After the Mutiny (1857) this policy, which had alarmed the Indian princes, was reversed by the issue of *sanads* of adoption, but these states remained part of British India.

DODDRIDGE, PHILIP (1702–51), British nonconformist divine, whose dissenting academy in Northampton during the mid-18th cent. was noted for its progressive curriculum.

DODGE–LEAVENWORTH EXPEDITION (1834), organized at Fort Gibson, AR, US, by Gen. Henry Leavenworth and led by Col. Henry Dodge. It was sent to the south-west to promote peace with the Wichita, Comanche, and Kiowa Indians. As a result, the first treaty with the Indians of the Great Plains was made on the North Fork of the Red River in OK (24 Aug. 1835).

DOENITZ, KARL (1891–), German sailor, a leading member of the German High Command during the Second World War, and, for a brief period, Hitler's successor. Having played an important part in the reorganization of the German U-boat fleet in the 1930s (in violation of the Versailles treaty), he was one of the foremost experts on submarine warfare. Hitler's ultimate conversion to its possibilities is reflected in Doenitz's replacement of Admiral Raeder as commander-in-chief of the German navy in Jan. 1943, though this occurred too late to affect Germany's worsening situation in the Atlantic. Hitler's growing bitterness towards the army and the Luftwaffe, both of which he blamed for Germany's defeat, was probably one of the reasons that he chose Doenitz as his successor in April 1945. Another was Doenitz's loyalty to him throughout the war: Doenitz subsequently confessed that like many senior officers he felt unable to assert his will and judgement against Hitler. The achievements of Doenitz's short-lived government in Flensburg—he himself acted as reich president, minister of war, and supreme commander of the armed forces, Goebbels being chancellor—were limited. The NSDAP was dissolved, Himmler was dismissed from all his posts, and a fruitless attempt was made to reach a separate peace agreement with the Western Powers. Nothing then remained but to accept unconditional surrender (4–8 May 1945). On 23 May Doenitz and his government were arrested and in 1946 Doenitz himself was sentenced to ten years' imprisonment as a war criminal.

DOGGER BANK, BATTLE OF (5 Aug. 1781), indecisive and savage naval action between the Dutch and British during the American War of Independence.

DOGGER BANK, BATTLE OF (1915), battle-cruiser action in the North Sea during the First World War between a British squadron commanded by Admiral Beatty and a German force under Admiral Hipper. The Germans, with three battle-cruisers and a heavy cruiser, made a sortie towards the Dogger Bank, but were intercepted by Beatty with five battle-cruisers. The Germans turned for home and a high-speed stern chase ensued. The *Blücher*, a heavy cruiser in the rear of the German line, was crippled, but a British error in not engaging the *Derfflinger*, despite their numerical superiority, enabled the Germans to concentrate their fire on the *Lion*, Beatty's flagship at the head of the line. Beatty lost tactical control of the action when the *Lion* was forced to draw out of the line; his senior subordinate, misunderstanding his intentions, directed the fire of the remainder of the squadron on the already sinking *Blücher* and permitted the rest of the German force to escape. The action reveals many of the deficiencies of the Royal Navy at the time: the lack of initiative among subordinate commanders, inadequate ship-to-ship communications in battle conditions, and a weakness in the design of the battle-cruisers' armour, which gave inadequate protection to the ammunition hoists between the main magazine and the gun turrets.

DOGGER BANK INCIDENT (22 Oct. 1904). The Russian Baltic fleet, en route to fight Japan, fired on Hull trawlers in the North Sea, mistaking them for Japanese torpedo-boats. International arbitration and Russian acceptance of claims for compensation eased tension and Anglo-Russian relations were not worsened.

DŌKYŌ (d. 772), ambitious Japanese monk who gained the favour of the Empress Shōtoku and became chancellor (764). At a time when Buddhism was making great strides, Dōkyō represented a threat to the power of the nobility. His plan to succeed Shōtoku was thwarted when, upon her death (770), he was banished.

DOLCI, DANILO (1924–), Italian practitioner and theoretician of non-violent social, apolitical protest called 'the Gandhi of Sicily'. He moved from Milan to the Sicilian village of Trappeto (1952) to campaign against Sicily's poverty and neglect. His books (eg, *To Feed the Hungry*, *Waste*) publicized conditions. His demonstrations, 'work-ins', and major fasts in the 1950s exerted pressure for building dams (Iato, Bruca), for adequate use of government grants and relief after the (1968) earthquake. His Centres, eg, the Borgo at Trappeto (1968), financed and staffed by Italians and foreigners, provide health facilities, education, and discussion on self-help for poor Sicilians. He was awarded the Viareggio Prize (1957), Lenin Peace Prize (1958), but was facing (1970) virulent opposition from many officials, clergy, and the Mafia, incurring imprisonment, long trials, and fines.

DOLGORUKY FAMILY, aristocratic Russian dynasty which produced military commanders, eg, Prince Yuri Dolgoruky, who was killed in the Bulavin rising (1707), and ambassadors, eg, Prince Jacob Dolgoruky, who served in France from 1687. Prince Alexis and his brother, Vasili, enjoyed considerable political influence after the death of Peter the Great. Supporting the claim of Peter's grandson and namesake, to whom he was deputy tutor, Alexis undermined the favourite Menshikov on the death of Catherine I (1727) and betrothed his daughter, Catherine, to the young Tsar Peter II. After Peter's death from smallpox on the day fixed for his wedding (Jan. 1730), Prince Alexis failed to engineer his daughter's succession and lost power when the supreme privy council put forward Peter I's niece, Anna. In the reaction that followed the family suffered banishment and deprivation of rank and property, four members being executed as late as 1739.

DOLLAR DIPLOMACY, term often applied by critics of US diplomacy to policies seemingly motivated by economic imperialism. It was first used descriptively of Philander C. Knox's attempts to increase US overseas trade during the presidency of William H. Taft (1909–13).

DOLLARD'S EXPEDITION (1660), designed to defend the fur trade of New France from the Iroquois Indians. Led from Montreal by Adam Dollard des Ormeaux (1635–60), the expedition was wiped out at the Long Sault on the Ottawa river after a heroic stand. French Canadian nationalists in the 19th cent. argued that Dollard des Ormeaux and his men sacrificed themselves to save New France.

DOLLFUSS, ENGELBERT (1892–1934), Austrian politician and chancellor (1932–4), whose political career began in Lower Austria, where he organized a Peasants' League and helped to create a provincial chamber of agriculture, later a model for other provinces. In 1931 he entered the cabinet of he Christian Socialist, Dr Ender, as minister of agriculture.

He became chancellor and foreign minister in 1932, in a coalition government possessing a majority of only one in the national assembly. His coalition contained Christian Socialists, conservative nationalists, and members of the Peasants' League and of the fascist *Heimwehr*. The latter's links with Italy antagonized other government parties, straining the coalition. The government was opposed by the extreme right, particularly the Austrian Nazi Party, which became more active and subversive after Hitler attained power in Germany in Jan. 1933. In the autumn of 1932 Dollfuss's difficulties with the National Assembly led him to dispense with parliamentary consultation and govern by emergency decree. On 19 March 1933—legislative business having reached an impasse—Dollfuss dissolved the Assembly and proclaimed government by decree while a new constitution was prepared.

The political divisions that rendered parliamentary government impossible doomed Dollfuss's dictatorship, known as the 'Fatherland Front', from the start. He wished Austria to be neither dominated by Italian fascism nor absorbed in *Anschluss* with Nazi Germany. However, he isolated himself by refusing the support of the largest party, the Social Democrats, while accepting that of the next largest party, the Christian Socialists, who were dividing into moderate and extreme nationalist wings. Reluctantly, Dollfuss opted for the support of the *Heimwehr* and Mussolini. On 19 June 1933 his government banned all Nazi activity. Later that summer Mussolini urged Dollfuss to outflank the Austrian Nazis on the right by crushing the Social Democrats.

In Feb. 1934, after Dollfuss's pressures on the socialists had provoked armed resistance, civil war broke out. Its suppression was followed on 1 May by the proclamation of a new corporatist constitution containing references to the Papal Encyclical, *Quadragesimo Anno*. The *Heimwehr* leader, Starhemberg, became vice-chancellor. However, although Dollfuss had suppressed the socialist opposition, the Nazis maintained their agitation against his dictatorship. In an attempted coup on 25 July 1934 a Nazi group invaded the Chancellery and murdered Dollfuss. ASJ

DOLLIER DE CASSON, FRANÇOIS (1636–1701, vicar-general of New France (1678–1701) and probable author of *Histoire du Montreal*. He was a French cavalry officer, who entered the Sulpician Order and went to Montreal (1666), where he established missions and encouraged public improvements.

DÖLINGER JOHANN JOSEPH IGNAZ VON (1799–1890), Bavarian professor and ecclesiastical historian. In his early works he attacked Protestantism and the Enlightenment, but later he turned against ultramontanism. He refused to recognize papal infallibility and was excommunicated (1871). He supported, without formally joining, the Old Catholics.

DOLONNOR, CONVENTION OF (1691), the political act by which Khalkha Mongolia was incorporated into the Manchu empire. The Khalkha khans and the Jebtsundamba Khutuktu were forced by their defeats by the west Mongol ruler Galdan to accept the overlordship of the Manchu empire. In 1911, when the Manchus fell, the Mongols claimed that this personal relationship was dissolved, and that nothing bound them to China.

DOMAGK, GERHARD (1895–1964), German biochemist, who in 1932 established that a dye, prontosil red, could control streptococcal infections. It was shown later that the antibacterial action was due to only part of the molecule, the sulphonamide group. This discovery led to the development of a range of sulphonamide drugs effective in the treatment of several highly pathogenic infections, including some varieties of pneumonia. Domagk was awarded the 1939 Nobel Prize for medicine and physiology.

DOMBO, *changamire* (king), of the Rozwi (Shona) empire, founded *c.* 1500 in the southern half of what afterwards became Rhodesia.

DOMBROWSKI, JAN HENRYK (1755–1818), Polish soldier and patriot. He was one of Kosciusko's lieutenants in the rising against the partitioning powers of Austria, Prussia, and Russia (1794). Because of the French Republic's sympathy for the cause of Polish unity, he agreed to raise Polish legions to defend France's sister Cisalpine Republic in northern Italy (1797). His Polish troops fought there until the conclusion of the peace of Lunéville (1801). Napoleon, when he moved into eastern Europe (1806), authorized Dombrowski to organize a revolt in Poland. Although Dombrowski led Polish troops in Napoleon's Russian and German campaigns (1812–13), Tsar Alexander I made him a senator in the kingdom of Poland reconstituted under Russia in 1815.

DOME OF THE ROCK. Jerusalem fell to the forces of the Caliph Umar I in 638. Within the temple area at Jerusalem the Muslims built a primitive mosque (Al-Aqsa). In 691 the Umayyad Caliph Abd al-Malik began the construction, on this site, of the famous mosque now known as the Dome of the Rock.

DOMESDAY BOOK (*c.* 1086). At the Christmas court of 1085, King William I of England ordered a survey of the land, as it had been held on the day that Edward the Confessor had died, by what terms it was held, by whom, and its value. Commissions of enquiry sent into the shires were to record the number of cattle and sheep, the amount of woodland, the amount of land under the plough, the names of the landowners and their peasants, the number of slaves. Only some of this information was incorporated in the surviving Domesday Book, but it is one of the most remarkable documents of the Middle Ages and a tribute to the power and efficiency of William's government. It must have played a considerable part in the efficient collection of revenue.

DOMESTIC INDUSTRY, in Britain, chiefly involved the spinning and weaving of textiles in the home. The wife would fleece and spin the wool from the sheep her husband reared. But the Middle Ages were already familiar with the semi-capitalist clothiers, known as 'putters-out', who supplied the yarn to the cottager and paid him for the finished product. The final and more technical processes, like fulling and dyeing, were carried out by the supplier, but in almost every cottage the women and children would be busy teasing, carding, and spinning, while the husband wove the cloth on his hand-loom. There were many regional variations, and capitalist organization was more highly developed in some areas than in others, but by the 16th cent. the domestic system was almost universal, not only for wool but for cotton, worsteds, draperies, linen, and silks.

For the cottager the system had many advantages. He was not just a wage-earner, because he had his patch of land and his animals, and spinning and weaving gave supplementary employment when work in the fields was impossible. He may even have had the better of the deal, since he could work when he felt like it, and it was difficult for the clothier to be certain that the cloth returned to him represented all the raw material that had been put out.

The system was destroyed by the Industrial Revolution in the second half of the 18th cent. Early inventions like the flying shuttle and the spinning jenny did not disturb it because they could still be used in the home and they speeded output, but the application of power concentrated industry into the areas where water or steam was available. At the same time enclosures and the invention of improved but expensive agricultural methods made it harder for the labourers to earn a living from the land. He had to make the choice between struggling to exist in agriculture or going off to the factories to become a wage-earner. He no longer had the one to supplement the other.

Nevertheless, hand-loom weaving continued as an occupation for some time after the introduction of machinery, because at first machines could not cope with the more elaborate techniques of fancy weaving, and because hand-loom weavers provided the manufacturers with spare capacity in boom times.

Again, the speed of the change should not be exaggerated because many clothiers were reluctant at first to invest in expensive building and machinery. Many preferred the system they knew, and in some areas it survived well into the 19th cent. Nor were textiles the only domestic industry. Almost until the First World War labourers were still working in their homes at boot-making, leather, tailoring, dressmaking, and similar crafts.

Domestic industry in Britain was revived by the introduction of the Selective Employment Tax (1966), which imposed a tax on employees in so-called 'service' industries. Some firms engaged in upholstery, interior decoration, and similar crafts thereupon dismissed all their staff, but re-engaged them on a contract basis, 'putting-out' materials in the old-fashioned way and collecting the finished products which their former workers, now nominally self-employed, had manufactured in their homes.   MMR

DOMESTIKOS, GREAT, supreme officer in command of the land forces of the Byzantine empire. This office came into being under the emperors of the House of Comnenus (1081–1185) and continued in existence under the succeeding dynasties. If the emperor were present in the field, the Great Domestikos became the general acting at his side.

DOMETT, ALFRED (1811–87), prime minister of New Zealand (1862–3), who failed to control both his Maori-phobe, land-speculating colleagues and the governor, Sir George Grey. He published 'Ranolf and Amohia, an epic poem (1872).

DOMINGO, CHARLES (*c.* 1875–*c.* 1930), pioneer Nyasaland nationalist. He broke away from the Livingstonia Mission (1907), established his own churches, and issued literature critical of colonialism.

DOMINIC, Saint (*c.* 1170–1221), founder of the Dominican order. He was born in Old Castile and became canon (*c.*1196) and sub-prior (1201) of Osma. Dominic accompanied Diego, bp of Osma, on royal embassies (1203, 1205–6) which took them to the Languedoc, where he first came into contact with the Albigensians, whom he determined to reconcile to the Church. In 1206 Dominic and Diego joined a Cistercian mission and until 1217 Dominic worked in the Languedoc, founding (1206) a convent for women converts from Albigensianism at Prouille, which became his base. In 1208 the murder of Peter of Castelnau, one of his former Cistercian companions, led to the calling of the Albigensian crusade, which ran completely counter to Dominic's work. He had sought to convert the heretics while the crusaders set out to destroy them. He believed that the best weapon against error and heresy was not force of arms but argument and example. He used his knowledge of logic and theology to destroy the arguments and doctrines of the Albigensians and countered complaints of the wealth of the Church by going barefoot and becoming penniless. Unlike his contemporary, St Francis (whom he almost certainly met in Rome in 1215), Dominic always intended to found an order characterized by its mendicant poverty, learning, and mission of preaching. In 1215 he went to Rome to seek papal recognition of his order and bulls of foundation were granted by Honorius III in 1216 and 1217. In the next few years Dominic founded houses all over western Europe, particularly in university cities, *eg*, Paris, Bologna, and Oxford and in 1221 presided over the first general chapter of the order at Bologna. He was canonized in 1234.   JG

DOMINICA, West Indian island, discovered by Columbus (1493), and granted to the Earl of Carlisle (1627). The native

Carib Indians, however, prevented the British from occupying it. It was made a Carib preserve (1748), but was de facto a French settlement from the mid-17th cent. It was captured by the British in 1761 and ceded to them in 1763 but was later subjected to French attacks (1795) and seizure (1778–83, 1805). It was governed from Antigua (1833–71), part of Leeward Islands Colony (1871–1939), until its transfer to the Windward Islands (1940–60), and was given internal self-government (1960), becoming an associate state of Britain (1967).

DOMINICAN ORDER. Order of Preachers (OP), commonly called Dominicans, after its founder, or Blackfriars, after the colour of its habit, was founded to combat heresy by preaching to the people. As a mendicant order it owned no property and has always been associated with places of learning, *eg*, Paris (1217), Bologna (1218), and Oxford (1221) and with scholars (*eg*, Albert the Great and Thomas Aquinas). It was because of its particular purpose and learned character that the order was especially connected with the Inquisition. There are three branches of the order. The first is that of the friars and lay-brothers, the second of contemplative nuns, and the third of associated laymen, called 'Tertiaries'. The rule is based upon that of the Augustinian order, which Dominic had followed as a canon of Osma, and was confirmed when the order was recognized by Pope Honorius III in 1216 and 1217. The order spread rapidly—by 1277 there were nearly 400 houses —and quickly became a dominant factor in the intellectual life of the 13th cent. In the 14th cent. and afterwards, despite missionary work in Africa, India, and even China, the order began to decline in numbers and influence. Its concern with orthodoxy led to its adopting a persecuting attitude, distorting the spirit of St Dominic, and to a narrow obscurantism.

DOMINION PARTY, in Southern Rhodesia, a pre-Second World War white Rhodesian party, revitalized by Winston Field (1956–7) in opposition to any extension of African political rights. It fused with the Rhodesian Front in 1962.

DOMINION STATUS DECLARATION (31 Oct. 1929), an avowal by Lord Irwin, viceroy of India, supported by the British government, that Britain's ultimate purpose was to create an Indian dominion. Irwin hoped thereby to meet the Congress ultimatum of Dec. 1928 which threatened civil disobedience if India were not granted dominion status within one year. Irwin also declared that following the publication of the Simon Commission's report, a conference of British government, British Indian, and Indian states' representatives would be held to discuss the reform of the Indian constitution. Reaction in India was generally favourable, Indian Liberals and Muslims accepting the declaration readily. Militant Congress opinion was suspicious, but moderate congressmen and supporters of Gandhi were not prepared to reject out of hand an opportunity to get the substance of their demands. However, general support was soon dissipated by widespread British opposition in press and parliament to the declaration, and by Irwin's patent inability to confirm that the conference would be concerned with framing a dominion-status constitution. A meeting between Irwin and Indian leaders (23 Dec.) made it clear that Congress was deeply suspicious of Britain's sincerity, though Liberal and Muslim opinion remained favourable. Congress went on (31 Dec.) to commit itself to the attainment of complete independence, to the boycott of the Round Table Conference, and to a new civil disobedience campaign.

DOMITIAN (AD 51–96), Roman Emperor (*reg.* 81–96), younger son of Vespasian. In 83 the powerful Chatti were overcome in Germany and a substantial defensive system was built between the upper Rhine and Danube. Attacks along various parts of the Danube by the Dacians, Marcomanni, Qadi, and Sarmatians were resisted, and in Britain Agricola advanced the Roman frontier into Scotland. Domi-

tian, a responsible ruler, particularly in matters of finance and in the administration of the provinces, quarrelled with the Senate because of the autocratic tendency of his government and his hard and unforgiving personality. Mutual hostility, exacerbated by an unsuccessful revolt of the governor of Upper Germany in 88 and the discovery of other plots, led to his assassination.

DOMITIUS AHENOBARBUS, L. (d. 48 BC), Roman politician and consul (54), whose opposition to Julius Caesar precipitated the Conference of Luca. In the Civil War he surrendered Corfinium to Caesar (49) and was freed, but joined Pompey and was killed at Pharsalus.

DON GRATUIT, financial subsidy voted by the French clergy in the assemblies of bishops and abbots for the benefit of the French Crown. In theory, the tax was a voluntary and exceptional gift, since legally the king could not tax the clergy of ancient France, but from the mid-16th cent. it became a regulated subsidy. The amount varied according to the king's needs, but the sum tended to increase from the early 16th cent. as constant warfare imposed a strain upon the royal finances.

DON PACIFICO INCIDENT (1850) occurred when Lord Palmerston, British foreign secretary, ordered a blockade of the Greek coast to enforce compensation for damage to property in an Athenian riot for Don Pacifico, who claimed British nationality. This unilateral action offended Russia and France, fellow guarantors of Greek Independence, but Palmerston vindicated his actions in parliament.

DON QUIXOTE DE LA MANCHA (1605, second part 1615), satirical novel by Cervantes, parodying the popular romances of chivalry, in imitation of *Amadis de Gaul*, which he thought were undermining the Spanish national character. But the story, of a self-appointed knight engaging ogres that sprang from his own imagination, deepened into a criticism of life which immediately captured the European mind. There were six editions in 1605, and the first of many translations was an English version by Thomas Shelton (1612).

DON RIVER, rising south of Moscow in the Central Russian uplands and flowing southwards to the Sea of Azov through the great steppelands which formed the home of the semi-independent Don Cossacks from the 15th cent. until their gradual assimilation into Russia from the early 18th cent. The Grand Duke Dimitri of Muscovy, victor over the Mongols at Kulikovo (1380), took his name from the river (Dimitri Donskoy). As a waterway for Russian trade with the Black Sea area, the Don was limited by the possession of Azov, at its mouth, by the Crimean Tatars, and by the fact that the Sea of Azov is frozen from Nov. to March. Despite the temporary capture of Azov in 1696 and again in 1739, it was not until the late 18th cent. that the mouth of the Don fell into Russian hands. The foundation of the fortress of Rostov (1761), the reunion of Azov with Russia by the treaty of Kuchuk-Kainardji (1774), and the acquisition of the Crimea (1783) were landmarks in this process.

DONATÁRIO, recipient and colonizer of one of the 12 *capitanias* or grants into which John III of Portugal divided the Brazilian colony (1532).

DONATELLO (DONATO BARDI) (*c.* 1386–1466), Florentine artist and sculptor, who worked mostly in marble and bronze. In the 1440s he spent several years in Padua, where he produced the St Anthony altar and the equestrian statue of the Venetian general, Gattamelata.

DONATI, CORSO *c.* 1255–1309), member of an old Florentine family and a professional *podesta* (a high judicial and military office, held in Italian cities for limited periods by non-citizen foreigners). As leader of the anti-papal Black

Party, supported by Dante, he was driven out of Florence in 1302 and was killed while attempting to recover power for his faction.

DONATUS (d. *c.* AD 355), a Christian leader of the puritanical Donatist movement in North Africa, first heard of between AD 306 and 310. A great orator, he was remembered as a reformer 'who purged the Church of Carthage from error'. He ruled the Donatist Church for 42 years.

DONAUWÖRTH, BATTLE OF (1714), fought in Bavaria during the War of the Spanish Succession. Troops led by Marlborough and Prince Lewis of Baden stormed strong Bavarian defensive positions on the Schellenburg hill overlooking Donauwörth.

DONGAN CHARTER, city charters granted by Gov. Thomas Dongan to New York City and Albany (1686) and later to other towns in NY. The charters established boundaries and city governments.

DONG-KINH NGHIA-THUC, Viet-namese nationalist movement which flourished in Hanoi and Saigon (1906–8). Its name means 'Tokyo School', and its principal aim was to encourage young Viet-namese to study in Japan, the one Asian country which had mastered the techniques of the West. The movement was eventually discovered by the French, and suppressed. In 1909 the Japanese government agreed with France not to take any more Viet-namese students. Among the nationalists associated with the movement were Phan Boi Chau and Phan Chau Trinh.

DONG-SON CULTURE, important bronze-using culture associated with an archaeological site at Dong-Son (Thanh-Hoa province, North Viet-nam), and characterized by a special type of bronze drum. It flourished in the period immediately prior to Chinese annexation of the area, 1st cent. BC.

DONNE, JOHN (1573–1631), English poet and divine. His wit and learning endeared him to James I, on whose repeated persuasions he eventually took orders (1615) and became a royal chaplain, preacher at Lincoln's Inn, and, in 1621, dean of St Paul's. His involved but sublimely moving sermons reminded Izaak Walton of 'an angel from a cloud'. There has been a 20th-cent. revival of interest in his poetry, little of which was published in his lifetime. Donne was the greatest of the 'Metaphysicals', poets difficult to approach because of their witty conceits, metrical irregularities, and far-fetched imagery, much of it derived from natural philosophy. Even in the erotic verse of his younger days Donne decorated the language of sensuality with images taken from his theological and scientific studies, so that it seemed that he could scarcely think of love, whether secular or divine, except in terms of mortality and decay. But the power of his best work is irresistible, as in 'The Ecstasie', the 'Epithalamium' for Princess Elizabeth, the song 'Go, and catch a falling star' or the sonnet 'Death, be not proud'.

DONNELLY, IGNATIUS (1831–1901), US political reformer, journalist, and author who served as lieutenant-governor of MN (1859–63), as a Republican congressman (1863–69), and in the state senate (1873–8). As editor of the *Anti-Monopolist* (1874–9), he became a spokesman for reform politics and helped to organize the Granger Movement. He was a founder of the Populist Party, a key figure in drawing up the Omaha Platform (1892), and editor of the Populist journal, *The Representative* (1894–1901). He stood as the party's vice-presidential candidate in 1900. He wrote *Atlantis* (1882), *Caesar's Column* (1891), and *The American People's Money* (1895).

DONNER PARTY, in US, a group of emigrants from Central IL who left Independence, MO, in the spring of 1846. Organized by Jacob and George Donner, and bound for CA, they followed the California Trail to Fort Bridger, where 87 left the main party and took the Hastings Cutoff route across the Great Salt Lake Desert. Though considerably delayed by rugged terrain and internal dissension, this group finally seached the foothills of the Sierra Nevada too late in the reason for easy passage of the mountains. Despite the approach of winter they decided to continue into the High Sierras, but were soon snowbound at Truckee Lake by early winter storms. Rescue parties reached them in mid-Feb. 1847, but many had by then died of starvation or exposure. Some of the 47 who survived are believed to have resorted to cannibalism.

DONOUGHMORE COMMISSION (1927). Although a modicum of self-government was extended to Ceylon (1908–1924), it failed to satisfy the aspirations of the National Congress leaders. The 1924 constitution did not work well and in 1927 the British government sent out a commission headed by the Earl of Donoughmore, the other members being Sir Matthew Natham, a former colonial administrator, Sir Geoffrey Butler, a Conservative MP, and Drummond Shiels, a Labour MP. In their report they criticized the 1924 constitution on the grounds that it gave the Ceylonese legislative councillors 'power without responsibility', and they made far-reaching proposals for constitutional advance, nearly all of which were adopted by the British government. The most important were the abolition of communal representation, which had figured in all the earlier constitutions, and the extension of the franchise to all adults. Instead of the Legislative and Executive Councils, a State Council of 58 was instituted. Of its members 50 were territorially elected and eight nominated by the governor. The constituencies were so delimited as to ensure some representation for the Tamil and Muslim minorities. The eight nominated members were to represent interests inadequately covered, such as those of European business and planting, and smaller minority communities. In addition there were three 'officers of state'—the chief secretary and the financial and legal secretaries. These could sit but not vote in the State Council.

The 58 members were divided into seven 'executive committees', each with control of a group of government departments. However, the foreign affairs, defence, public, finance, and law departments remained in the control of the appropriate officers of state. A public services commission was established to handle appointments and promotions. The members of each executive committee elected one of their number as chairman, and the seven chairmen so elected formed the board of ministers, together with the three officers of state (who again had no vote). The board was responsible for the annual budget and for general financial matters. As time went on it tended to become more and more like a cabinet, deciding matters of policy. The chief secretary was chairman of the board and the vice-chairman was one of the Ceylonese ministers, the first being Sir Baron Jayatilleke.

The reasons given by the commissioners for this novel constitution were the keen interest taken in administration rather than in legislation by Ceylonese councillors, and the opportunity it gave them to become acquainted with administrative methods and details, as a preparation for a further advance in self-government.

The proposed constitution was not acceptable to Congress leaders, who wanted more internal self-government on the Westminster model, and did not approve of full adult suffrage. But after pressure from the British government the Legislative Council gave its approval by a very narrow majority.

The constitution, which took effect from 1931, lasted for 16 years. Ceylonese leaders continued to press for full internal self-government, but the Second World War held up further constitutional advance.

Ceylon: Report of the Special Commission on the Constitution, Cmd. 3131 (1928).

S. Namasivayam, *The Legislatures of Ceylon, 1928–48* (London, 1951). **SAP**

DONOUGHMORE COMMITTEE (1932) in Britain considered ministers' powers. Agitation for an enquiry had followed Lord Chief Justice Hewart's attack on delegated legislation three years before, in which he criticized the growing use of statutory instruments by government departments. The committee reported in favour of delegated legislation; in cases of great administrative complexity, or great urgency (such as the Defence of the Realm Act), such legislation was clearly more effective than relying upon Acts of Parliament. The committee did, however, recommend that the various methods by which instruments were laid before the two Houses of Parliament should be rationalized; in particular, it suggested the establishment of a small standing committee of parliament to examine such legislative instruments. Most of the proposals of the committee were implemented in the Statutory Instruments Act of 1946.

The committee also reported on administrative adjudication. It rejected proposals for the setting up of separate administrative courts, but again decided that the system was insufficiently safeguarded against abuses. Here it recommended that the tribunals should not deal with purely judicial decisions, that they should where possible act instead of ministers, and that the findings of the tribunal inspectors should be publicized. This part of the committee's report was not acted upon, and the question was reconsidered by the Franks Committee in 1955. GD

DOOLITTLE, JAMES HAROLD, lieutenant-general (1896–19), US aviator. He was the first man to fly across the North American continent in under 24 hours (1922), held a number of speed records, and was also an accomplished aircraft engineer and inventor. On 18 April 1942 he led the first US air attack on Tokyo with planes from the carrier USS *Hornet*.

DOOMSMEN. According to the legal customs of the early medieval Germanic peoples, legal disputes should be settled before a court attended by all the free men of a district, who knew the custom and would award an appropriate procedure for trial. In practice, a group of notables (doomsmen) usually acted for this purpose because of their personal importance or their special knowledge of local customs. In order to prevent the highest local officials, the counts, from exerting undue influence over justice, Charlemagne introduced in each county groups of permanent doomsmen (*scabini*). They were appointed for life by royal envoys who periodically visited each district. In England the activities of groups of doomsmen may form one of the origins of the jury.

DORCHESTER, GUY CARLETON, 1st Baron (1724–1808), British soldier, who began his military career in America as quartermaster to the expeditionary force which attacked Quebec (1759). As lieutenant-governor of Quebec from 1766 and governor from 1768, he opposed wholesale anglicanization and had much to do with the content of the Quebec Act of 1774. Carleton was almost captured by American forces at Montreal on 11 Nov. 1775, but he escaped by canoe and later, during the American War of Independence, defeated an American force at Quebec. He resigned the governorship (1778) after a quarrel with the British secretary of state. He was appointed commander-in-chief of British forces in North America (1782) and directed the evacuation of New York. As Lord Dorchester he was made governor-in-chief of British North America (1786), a rank he retained when he was made governor of Lower Canada following the division of Quebec by the Constitutional Act of 1791.

DORCHESTER COMPANY, group of English merchants who obtained a licence (1622) to establish a settlement of fishermen on the New England coast. When the company failed, it was replaced by the New England Co. (1628), the forerunner of the Massachusetts Bay Co. (1629).

DORGÈRES, HENRI (1897–), French politician and right-wing demagogue, who sought to exploit French peasant discontent in the 1930s. The movement reached its peak with the formation of a 'Peasant Front' in 1935, but collapsed soon afterwards. It had included ('greenshirt') fascist activists. Dorgères reappeared as a right-wing deputy (1956–8), and was briefly associated with Poujade.

DORIA, ANDREA (1466–1560), Genoese admiral, who joined the French when his native city was sacked by the imperialists (1522). When the French gave commercial favours to the rival port of Savona, he changed sides and recovered Genoa for Charles V, governing it as an independent republic until his death. He maintained constant warfare against Turkish corsairs in the Mediterranean.

DORIANS, Greek ethnic group originally settled, from *c.* 2000 BC, in northern Greece, who at the collapse of Mycenaean civilization (12th cent. BC) moved southwards and occupied all the Peloponnese except Achaea and Arcadia, later (10th cent.) crossing into Crete, Melos, Thera, and eastwards to Rhodes and the adjacent Asiatic coast. At Sparta and in Crete they preserved in the 6th–4th cents much of their original tribal constitution and customs by remaining separate from their subjects. Elsewhere, especially during the revolutionary period of the 7th–6th cents, they merged with the original non-Dorian inhabitants, *eg*, at Corinth (*c.* 650), Sicyon (*c.* 600), and Argos (*c.* 490). Ethnic pride, however, still continued in 5th-cent. inter-state rivalry, particularly between the predominantly Ionian Athenian empire and the predominantly Dorian Peloponnesian League.

DORIEUS (d. *c.* 510 BC), son of the Spartan King Anaxandridas, who after unsuccessfully contesting the succession of his half-brother, Cleomenes, was frustrated by strong Phoenician opposition in colonial enterprises in Libya (*c.* 514 BC) and in western Sicily, where he was killed.

DORION, SIR ANTOINE-AIMÉ (1818–91), French-Canadian lawyer and politician, who helped to found the *Institut Canadien* and the *Rouges* party. As a member of short-lived ministries (1858, 1863–4), he supported federal union but opposed the British North American Confederation (1867). He later laid aside his objections and became minister of justice in Mackenzie's government (1873).

DORIOT, JACQUES (1898–1945), French politician and leader of the *Parti populaire française*, one of the largest and most extreme of French right-wing parties of the 1930s. Doriot, a worker by origin, had been a leading communist deputy, but was expelled from the Communist Party for advocating co-operation with the socialists (1934). Thenceforth anti-communism was of great significance in his political career.

The PPF was declining by the time of the Second World War, but with France's defeat Doriot became a leading collaborationist. He organized the legion of French anti-Bolshevik volunteers and himself fought on the Russian front. In 1944 he fled to Germany and formed a 'liberation committee' with Hitler's support.

DORJIEFF (*fl.* 20th cent.), Russian Buriat and Buddhist from Siberia. When Lord Curzon became viceroy of India (1899) Dorjieff had been settled for 20 years in Tibet. Here he had won the confidence of the Dalai Lama, whose tutor he had been. In 1900 and 1901 he visited Russia and was received in audience by the tsar, at a time when the Dalai Lama refused to correspond with the viceroy. The ostensible object of these visits was to collect subscriptions from Russian Buddhists for Buddhist temples. Curzon refused to accept Russian assurances that these visits had no political significance and his fears of the growth of Russian influence in Tibet led to the Younghusband expedition (1904). Dorjieff was again received by the tsar (1906) and in 1913 he took 15 Tibetan boys to be educated in Russia. He is said to have negotiated the treaty of Urga (1913) between Tibet and Mongolia.

DORMAN SMITH, SIR REGINALD (1899–), English diplomat and governor of Burma (1941–6). During the period of Japanese occupation of Burma, his government was located in Simla. When he re-established civil administration (1945), Aung San, the national leader, and his Anti-Fascist People's Freedom League, demanded a controlling share in the government. Dorman Smith rejected this as incompatible with the British policy of rehabilitating Burma before transferring responsibility to the Burmese. Whereupon the AFPFL formed a determined opposition. Later the question arose whether to prosecute Aung San for the murder of a British-appointed headman in 1942. Prosecution was recommended by Dorman Smith and his advisers, but opposed by the military authorities. The British government first gave and then withdrew their sanction to prosecute.

DOROGOBUZH, BATTLE OF (1500), victory by Ivan III, Grand Duke of Muscovy over Grand Duke Alexander and the knights of the Lithuanian Order, from whom he recovered the lands of the Upper Oka and Chernigov (1503).

DORSET, THOMAS SACKVILLE, 4th Earl of (1st of 3rd creation) (1536–1608), English politician, poet, and dramatist, who served on diplomatic missions (1571, 1587, 1589, 1598). He was chancellor of Oxford (1591) and lord high treasurer from 1599 until his death. He is best remembered, however, as the editor of the collection *A Mirror for Magistrates* (1563) and for the earliest English drama in blank verse, *The Tragedy of Gorboduc* (1561).

DORT, SYNOD OF (1618–19), general council of most of the reformed Churches, at which the Calvinist, or Gomarist, majority condemned the Arminian beliefs that Christ died for all men and that grace is resistible and may be lost. The synod reflected the political dispute in Holland between the Arminian republicans and the predominantly Calvinist nobility and clergy. The central issue was whether or not God had condemned most of his children before they were born. The synod decided, with scriptural reference, that he had, that the cause of election is the pure grace of God, which grace is irresistible and cannot be forfeited, and that Christ died to save only the elect.

DORTICÓS TORRADO, OSVALDO (1919–), president of Cuba, following the resignation of Manuel Urrutia (July 1959). He headed the revolutionary underground in Cienfuegos (1957–8) and served as minister of laws in Fidel Castro's regime.

DORYLEUM, BATTLE OF (30 June 1079), between a crusading army and the Seljuk Turkish ruler Kili Arslan, was fought in Anatolia on a major crossing point of the roads between Constantinople and the Holy Land. The crusaders, who won, temporarily destroyed Turkish power in the area, opened the way to the Holy Land, and enabled the Byzantines to reconquer Asia Minor.

DOST MUHAMMAD (c. 1798–1863), Barakzay noble and one of the leaders of the revolt which ended Sadozay rule in Afghanistan. He became ruler of Kabul (1826), amir (1834), and gradually extended his power over the rest of the territories now forming the kingdom of Afghanistan (Kandahar 1855, Afghan Turkestan 1850–9, Herat 1863). He thus deserves to be called the founder of that kingdom.

DOSTOEVSKY, FEDOR MIKHAILOVICH (1821–81), Russian novelist, journalist, and thinker. After being arrested as a member of the Petrashevsky circle (1849) he suffered mock execution, was condemned to forced labour, and spent ten years in Siberia. He made his name as a novelist in the 1860s and 1870s with *Memoirs from the House of the Dead, Crime and Punishment, The Idiot,* and *The Brothers Karamazov*. Repudiating his earlier revolutionary interests, he evolved his own brand of slavophilism, Orthodox Christianity, and mystical populism, and was associated with the *Pochvenniki* or Men of the Soil group. *The Devils* (1871), the material for which was culled from newspaper accounts of the Nechaev trial, satirized the revolutionary terrorists, and the *Diary of a Writer* (1876), serialized throughout the Balkan crisis, was Pan-Slavist and chauvinistic in tone.

DOUAI, town in the southern Netherlands, where Cardinal William Allen founded (1568) an English college to train missionary priests for the restoration of Catholicism in England. Douai provided the pattern for the English College at Rome, founded in 1579.

DOUAI BIBLE, work of scholars at the English College in Douai, Flanders. Translation of the New Testament was completed in 1582 and of the Old in 1609. It provided the English version of the Bible used by Roman Catholics after the Reformation.

DOUGHTY, THOMAS (d. 1578), English scientist and sailor, who was a fellow-officer of Drake's in the expedition of 1577 and captain of one of his ships. After the expedition had been halted at Port Julian, to the north of the Straits of Magellan, Doughty and some of his crew mutinied and after an improvised court-martial he was hanged on board the *Golden Hind,* possibly from a gibbet used by Magellan for his own mutineers 60 years before.

DOUGLAS, GAVIN (c. 1475–1522), Scottish Renaissance poet. His *Palice of Honour* (1501) and *King Hart* are still in the medieval allegorical tradition.

DOUGLAS, STEPHEN ARNOLD (1813–61), US senator and Democratic Party leader, who was one of the key figures in American politics in the pre-Civil War years. Born in VT, he settled in IL as a young man and soon became active in state politics. As a congressman (1843–7) and senator (1847–61), he became a spokesman for the 'Young America' movement which emphasized nationalism and expansion in reaction to sectional politics. He helped to devise and secure congressional approval of the compromise of 1850, and was the unsuccessful Young America candidate for the Democratic presidential nomination in 1852. He sponsored the Kansas–Nebraska Act (1854), which settled the KS and NB territories according to the principle of popular sovereignty—that is, a decision by the local inhabitants on the question of slavery in their territories. But this measure, designed to promote sectional harmony, only provoked further trouble in 'Bleeding Kansas' itself, and throughout the nation. It also led to Douglas himself being accused of political expediency and economic self-interest because of his connection with the promotion of railroads in the area. His denunciation of the Lecompton's pro-slavery constitution for KS (1857–8) as a perversion of popular sovereignty alienated him from Buchanan's administration and from southern Democrats. He was re-elected to the Senate (1858) after a campaign which involved him in a series of widely reported debates with his Republican opponent, Abraham Lincoln, in which he enunciated the 'Freeport Doctrine'. This failed to satisfy either his northern or southern critics. Long ambitious for the presidency, he was the leading contender at the Democratic Party's Charleston convention (1860), but a southern walk-out denied him the requisite two-thirds majority. When the convention reassembled at Baltimore, Douglas was nominated, but the Southern Democrats, meeting separately, chose a rival candidate, John C. Breckinridge. In the election itself, Douglas came a poor fourth in the electoral college, but second to Lincoln in the popular vote. In the secession crisis, he still sought a sectional compromise, but once war had broken out, actively supported Lincoln in defence of the Union. A powerful orator, and a resourceful, bold, and ambitious politician, Douglas, known to his contemporaries as the 'Little Giant', has been variously judged by historians as the statesmanlike champion of sectional compromise or as a political opportunist who failed to grasp the full moral and emotional implications of the slavery issue.

Gerald M. Capers, *Stephen A. Douglas: defender of the Union* (Boston, 1959).   PJP

DOUGLAS FAMILY, Scottish warrior family, founded by a follower of Robert Bruce. The earldom of Douglas was created in 1358 and the second earl was the hero of the Scottish victory over the English at Otterburn (1388). By 1400 the family controlled south-western Scotland and owned much property elsewhere. The Douglases fell in the reign of James II of Scotland, the last earl being attainted in 1455.

DOUGLASS, FREDERICK (?1817–95), US Negro anti-slavery leader and the most famous ex-slave in the US in the years before emancipation. Born Frederick Augustus Washington Bailey, son of a white father and a slave mother, he escaped from slavery in MD (1838) and took the name Douglass. He became a prominent lecturer and fund-raiser for the anti-slavery movement, and finally bought his freedom after a visit to Britain (1845–7). As the founder of the abolitionist weekly *North Star* at Rochester, NY (1847–64), he supported John Brown's raid on Harper's Ferry (1859), helped to raise Negro regiments during the Civil War, and was received at the White House by President Lincoln. His autobiography, *Narrative of the Life of Frederick Douglass*, was first published in 1845 and appeared later in extended versions.

DOUKHOBOR (Russ. *Doukhobortsi*, 'Spirit Wrestlers'), a Russian mystical sect with 18th-cent. origins, whose members considered the invisible assembly of all righteous men to be the true Church. Their fanatical separatism and pacifism led to their persecution in Russia and, assisted by Count Tolstoy, about 7000 emigrated (1898). They established communes in Canada, where some settled peacefully. In the 1950s and 1960s, in support of supposed grievances, the Doukhobors in western Canada demonstrated by removing all their clothing in public gatherings, burning property, and attaching time-bombs to railway bridges, causing $20 million damage.

DOUMER, PAUL (1857–1932), president of France (elected 1931). His previous political career included a constructive period as governor-general of Indo-China (1896–1902). He was assassinated by a Russian émigré.

DOUMERGUE, GASTON (1863–1937), French politician and president of France. He entered parliament in 1893, and served as a minister under the anti-clerical Combes and under Clemenceau. He was prime minister (1913–14), but resigned after scandals arose involving Caillaux and other ministers. As president (1924–31) he was generally popular and his recall as head of a national coalition government after the right-wing demonstrations of 6 Feb. 1934 was intended to restore national unity and confidence. But his plans for constitutional reform, which aimed at strengthening the executive, aroused the distrust of the Radicals, and Doumergue resigned when they withdrew their support from his government in Nov. 1934.

DOUWES DEKKER, EDUARD (1820–97), Dutch author of *Max Havelaar* (1860), the most famous literary protest against colonial rule in the Dutch East Indies, which was a fictionalized account of his colonial experience, under the pseudonym 'Multatuli'. He served as an Indies government official, but was ousted for his strong defence of native interests. His work, ignored at first, was much used by advocates of the Ethical Policy and later attacks on the colonial system.

DOVER, one of the principal gateways to England from Roman times onwards. By the late 11th cent. it ranked among the principal towns of England. After the Norman conquest a splendid castle was built. Dover was the most important of the original Cinque Ports.

DOWDESWELL, WILLIAM (1721–75), English politician, MP for Tewkesbury (1747–54) and Worcester (1761–75), and chancellor of the exchequer under Rockingham (1765). He refused an offer of the board of trade from Chatham (1766) and became leader of the Rockingham group in the Commons and director of its strategy. In 1767 he carried a motion reducing the land tax from 4s to 3s. This deprived the exchequer of £500,000 per annum and encouraged Townshend in his decision to raise money from the American colonies. Dowdeswell, with Fox and Burke, was a leading advocate of the American cause, favouring moderation and pointing out the dangers of armed conflict.

DOWDING, HUGH CASWALL TREMENHEERE DOWDING, 1st Baron (1882–1970), British airman, who was commander-in-chief of Fighter Command during the Battle of Britain. He joined the army in 1900, and was seconded to the Royal Flying Corps (now Royal Air Force) in 1914. In 1930 he was appointed to the Air Council and became concerned with the evolution of new fighters, notably the Hurricane and the Spitfire, and with the early work on radar. In 1936, when Britain's air defence was divided into Bomber, Fighter, and Coastal Commands, Dowding became, and remained until Nov. 1940, commander-in-chief, Fighter Command. His main tasks were to show the fighter's ability to intercept and destroy the bomber, which many thought invincible, and to prepare Fighter Command to meet the increasing challenge of the Luftwaffe. Following the introduction of the new fighters and the establishing of a chain of early-warning radar stations, Dowding created a central control system to link the two, based on his headquarters near Stanmore, Middx. The Germans' invasion in Europe in 1940 brought their bombers within easy range of Britain, but at the same time Fighter Command's strength was drastically reduced by units being sent to France to support the Allied forces. Dowding ran the risk of Churchill's displeasure by vehemently opposing this movement, and subsequent events fully justified his stand. Hardly had Fighter Command finished providing cover for the evacuation from Dunkirk than the Battle of Britain began. Dowding was at the centre of a struggle crucial for the nation's survival, and revealed his skill as a strategist and tactician, as well as his concern for the men under his command. There has been a conflict of opinion, both at the time and subsequently, about his views on the best size of tactical unit for defensive fighter operations: Dowding and Air Marshal Park, commander of 11 Group, based on south-east England and which bore the brunt of the Luftwaffe's attack, favoured the squadron; Air Marshal Leigh-Mallory, in command of 12 Group, based in the Midlands and East Anglia, supported the larger wing formation. At the height of his success Dowding was relieved of his command in a manner that has since been criticized, and was placed on the retired list (1941).

DOWLAND, JOHN (1563–1626), English lutenist and composer, court lutenist to Christian IV of Denmark (1598–1606), and from 1612 a court musician in England. His three *Books of Songs or Airs* for lute accompaniment (1597–1903) were among the many collections of accompanied solo songs printed during the great age of English native music. He also wrote *Lachrymae* for Anne of Denmark, *Pilgrim's Solace*, and a treatise on lute-playing.

DOWNING, ANDREW JACKSON (1815–52), US architect and landscape gardener. In *Cottage Residences* (1842) he expounded his theories of rural 'decorated' architecture, and his *Treatise on the Theory and Practice of Landscape Gardening* (1841) and *The Fruits and Trees of America* (1845) were widely influential. He was engaged (1851) to design the grounds for the White House, the Capitol, and the Smithsonian Institution in Washington, DC.

DOWNING, SIR GEORGE (1623–84), English soldier and politician, who advanced with equal facility under Cromwell's protectorate and Charles II's Restoration, and was reputed to be the richest man in England. Downing Street, the official residence of the prime minister and chancellor of the exchequer in London, is named after him.

DOWNS, BATTLE OF THE (1639), sea battle in the Thirty Years War between France and Spain, in which the Dutch, as allies of France, destroyed the Spanish fleet and its treasure. This defeat prevented relief reaching the Spanish in the Netherlands, effectively destroyed the Spanish navy, and aggravated Spanish financial weakness.

DOWNSHIRE, WILLS HILL, 1st Marquis of (Irish) and 2nd Viscount Hillsborough (1718–93), British statesman who was secretary of state for the colonies (1768–72) and thus played a part in the events leading to the American Revolution. He supported a hard line against the colonists, ordering Gage to send a regiment to Boston when the Massachusetts Assembly invited the colonists to resist imperial taxes. He piloted resolutions condemning the assembly through the House of Lords, and resigned when the cabinet decided to drop indirect colonial taxes except that on tea.

DRACO (*fl.* 7th cent. BC), quasi-legendary figure held to be responsible for the first codification of law at Athens (*c.* 631 BC). Only his homicide laws, perhaps the first serious attempt to transfer the responsibility for punishment of murder from the family to the community, survived—considerably modified—in 5th-cent. Athens.

DRAFT RIOTS, NEW YORK CITY (13–16 July 1863), the most serious of the protests against conscription during the American Civil War. Mob violence, much of it directed against Negroes, led to the loss of several hundred lives and considerable destruction of property before troops restored order.

DRAFT TREATY OF MUTUAL ASSISTANCE (1923) in Europe. The League of Nations council entrusted to a temporary mixed commission the preparation of a general disarmament plan according to article 8 of the league covenant. It soon became apparent that the disarmament principle, warmly espoused by British public opinion and the Labour government, was closely allied in France to the question of security against aggression. In 1922 the commission laid before the 3rd assembly a proposed treaty, for which the British representative, Sir Robert Cecil, was chiefly responsible, attempting to reconcile these two positions. Each signatory, if it had reduced armaments according to a general plan, would be entitled to immediate support against aggression from any other signatories in the same continent. The assembly empowered the commission to prepare a formal draft treaty on this basis, taking note of suggestions from member governments.

The draft treaty of mutual assistance was submitted by the Czech Foreign Minister, Beneš to the 4th assembly in 1923. It empowered the council to designate an aggressor, decree economic sanctions, and determine the military contributions of the signatory powers. Groups of signatories could also, with the council's approval, conclude special mutual assistance agreements which would not require the council's designation of an aggressor—a proposal containing the seeds of the future Locarno Pact. The 4th assembly did not accept these proposals; only France wholeheartedly supported the draft treaty. Its fate was sealed by British objections to the linking of disarmament proposals with proposals for armed action, and to accepting a military commitment without close definition of the circumstances requiring it. This impasse encouraged Britain and France to give closer attention to the problem of defining aggression.

ASJ

DRAGE, THEODORE SWAINE (*fl.* 18th cent.), English sailor and author of *An Account of a voyage for the discovery of a Northwest Passage . . . 1746 and 1747 . . .* which described the Arctic expedition of William Moor. Drage is probably also the 'Charles Swain' who made two similar abortive expeditions in the ship *Argo*.

DRAGO DOCTRINE (1902), formulated by the Argentine foreign minister, Luis María Drago, stated that the use of armed force to collect public debts among nations should be prohibited.

DRAGONNADES, in the 17th cent., compulsory billeting of soldiers on French Protestants to enforce their conversion. This followed earlier severe measures when Huguenots were excluded from professional careers and their churches and schools were closed; they were forbidden to emigrate, and many who resisted were sent to the galleys. *Dragonnades* were instituted by Marillac, *intendant* of Poitou, and under the personal supervision of Louvois were considerably extended after a rising in the Cévennes in 1683. Thousands of conversions were claimed as a result of these brutal methods, but many Huguenots had emigrated secretly before the formal repeal of the Edict of Nantes (1685).

DRAIN THEORY, economic argument used by Indians against British rule in India. Certain payments, termed the 'Home Charges', had to be made in England out of Indian revenues. They increased rapidly, from about £5 million in 1860 to about £30 million in 1930, which gave rise to the accusation that India's connection with England had involved an annual drain of capital from India for which no adequate return was received. However, loans were raised in England because it was difficult to raise capital in India, while the construction of railways and irrigation works was of immense value to India. Certainly, interest was payable in England on account of pensions, furlough pay of officers, and the expenses of the India Office, but for these India received naval protection, military security, and a highly trained civil service and public works department. It may, of course, be argued that India paid too heavily for these.

DRAKE, EDWIN LAURENTINE (1819–80), US engineer, who carried out the first drilling operations at Oil Creek, near Titusville. His strike in Aug. 1859, although only small, nevertheless may be considered to have been the beginning of the modern petroleum industry.

DRAKE, SIR FRANCIS (1540–95), Elizabethan seaman and MP, renowned for his Caribbean exploits against the Spaniards, his circumnavigation of the globe, and his defence of England against the Spanish Armada.

Of west country parentage, staunchly Protestant, Drake was brought up in the dockyard town of Chatham, where his father was chaplain, and learnt his seamanship in the Channel. His first voyage to the Caribbean was in 1566, and he sailed there again in 1567 with Hawkins, commanding the *Judith*, an unsuccessful expedition culminating in the treacherous attack at San Juan de Uloa (1568). Drake visited the Caribbean yet again in 1571 and 1572, and with 70 men he attacked Nombre de Dios, looted Spanish ships the length of the Main, and ambushed a treasure train on the isthmus of Panama, seizing £40,000 worth of silver (1572).

Drake's exploits did not always please Elizabeth's ministers, who periodically tried to heal the breach in Anglo

Spanish relations before the outbreak of war (1585). Little is known of his activities in the years 1572–6, but in 1577 he was chosen to command an expedition to the Moluccas, financed partly by the queen. Despite difficulties with the crew, Drake reached the Pacific, but lost two ships in bad weather, and with only the *Golden Hind* raided the western coast of South America (1578–9), capturing the *Cacafuego* with its cargo of silver. Continuing northwards along the coast of CA, which he named New Albion, and failing to find a northern passage to the Atlantic, he turned sharply westwards and reached the Moluccas in 1579. Here he made a treaty with the Sultan of Ternate and bought three tons of cloves. Continuing homewards via the Cape of Good Hope and the west coast of Africa, he reached Plymouth in Sept. 1580, his ship laden with bullion and spices. He was knighted there in April 1581.

In 1586 Drake embarked on another Caribbean expedition and in April 1587 he attacked the Spanish naval base of Cadiz, destroyed 30 ships, captured the fort and harbour of Sagres, and replenished his fleet in the Azores, returning home with the cargo of a captured Spanish carrack. Drake's attacks delayed the departure of the Armada. Appointed vice-admiral, he wanted to destroy the Spanish fleet in its own waters but contrary winds kept him in Plymouth. He played a prominent part in the pursuit of the Armada up the Channel and in the battle off Gravelines. With the dispersal of the Armada, Drake led the counter-offensive against Spain—the Portuguese expedition of 1589. The English took Corunna and made an ill-conceived attack on Lisbon, failing to capture a permanent base in the Azores. In 1595 he and Hawkins sailed for the last time to the Caribbean, both of them dying on the voyage.

It was his conviction that the new world should not be a Catholic monopoly that determined Drake's anti-Spanish attitudes, at a time when the equation between religious and political loyalty was firmly accepted.

J. A. Williamson, *The Age of Drake* (London, 1946).
K. Andrews, *Drake's Voyages* (London, 1967).   MKS

DRASKOVIC, MILORAD (1873–1921), minister of the interior in the provisional government of Yugoslavia (1920–1) and architect of its repressive policies. Early in 1921 Draskovic retired after an attempt on his life. A second attempt on 21 July was successful. A Bosnian communist was charged with his murder, which was taken as an occasion for outlawing the Communist Party in Yugoslavia.

DRAVIDA MUNNETRA KHAZAGAM, the 'Dravidian Progressive Federation', political party in Madras state, based on an appeal to Tamil 'nationalism' and to low caste interests. It was formed in 1949 by C. N. Annadurai (1908–69) as a breakaway from the Dravida Khazagam, which E. V. Ramaswamy Naicker (1879–) had organized (1944) from the once-influential Justice Party, the party of the Madras 'non-Brahmins'. Initially, the DMK was more socialist than Naicker's party and it represented a rejection of his autocratic control, but it had the same basic aim as the DK: the formation of Dravidisthan, a federation of the four linguistic areas of south India as a separate 'Dravidian' nation. The DK dropped this demand in 1956 and called instead for Tamilnad, a separate Tamil-speaking state. The DMK has ceased to espouse a policy of secession as it has increased its political power in Madras. In 1967 its overwhelming victory in the general elections in Madras enabled it to form a government.

DRAVIDIANS, from Sanskrit *Dravida*, a term which linguists and historians apply to the population of South India (about 120 million Indians), comprising the speakers of Telugu (Andhra Pradesh), Kanarese (Mysore), Tamil (Madras), and Malayalam (Kerala). There are also important Tamil minorities outside India, notably in Ceylon and Malaya. From the early cents AD the Dravidians contributed an increasingly important part to the political and cultural life of the Indo-Pakistani sub-continent.

DRAYTON, MICHAEL (1563–1631), Elizabethan poet, whose patriotic poem-chronicles include *Agincourt* and whose best sonnets perhaps equal Shakespeare's, *eg*, 'Since there's no help, come let us kiss and part'.

DREADNOUGHT, class of all-big-gun battleship pioneered (1906) by Britain to counter the growing naval strength of Germany. However, its introduction inadvertently threatened Britain's naval supremacy, for with ten big guns instead of four it could out-gun any number of conventional ships and thus rendered all existing battleships obsolete. The advantage of British superiority in old ships was therefore lost and a more urgent and expensive phase of the naval race followed.

DREBBEL, CORNELIUS (1572–1634), Dutch physician and inventor, who discovered cochineal as an aid to the dyeing industry, and made improvements in the telescope. He is said to have experimented with a submarine boat in the Thames river.

DRED SCOTT v SANDFORD, 19 Howard 393 (1857), US Supreme Court case of significance in the constitutional dispute over the legal status of slavery in the US territories before the Civil War. Dred Scott, a Negro slave, was taken by his master to the free state of IL and to the Wisconsin Territory, which was free soil under the Missouri Compromise (1820), and later returned to MO. In 1846 Scott brought suit in the MO state courts for his freedom. Though obtaining a favourable decision in the lower courts, the MO supreme court rejected his plea (1852) on the grounds that the laws of IL and of free territory had no status in MO and could not affect his slave status after his return. Scott was then transferred to John San(d)ford of NY, thus allowing him to bring a new suit (1853) in the federal courts on the contention that he was a MO citizen and the suit involved citizens of different states. Sandford argued that the court had no jurisdiction because Scott was a Negro and so not a MO citizen, and demanded that the court dismiss the case for want of jurisdiction. The US circuit court for MO considered the case, thereby implying that Scott might be a citizen, but declared against him and Scott appealed on a writ of error to the US Supreme Court.

The Supreme Court heard arguments on the case at the height of the controversy following the Kansas–Nebraska Act (1854). Most of the justices wished to dismiss the case for lack of jurisdiction, having a clear and recent precedent in *Strader v. Graham* (1850), thus allowing them to avoid discussion of the status of slavery in the territories. This attempt was thwarted by two anti-slavery justices, Mclean and Curtis.

The significance of the controversy surrounding the case is reflected in the fact that all nine justices wrote separate opinions, seven majority and two minority. No two reasoned precisely alike, but six justices joined with Chief Justice Taney in the final judgment.

Taney affirmed that Scott could not sue because he was neither a citizen of a state nor a US citizen, but a Negro and a slave. Negroes were not US citizens within the meaning of the constitution, only Congress being able to confer federal citizenship and define its privileges. As to Scott's status as a slave, Taney argued that the federal government had no general sovereignty over the territories and Congress could not prohibit slavery there, because the right to hold slaves was a local property right, and so concluded that the Missouri Compromise was void. Scott's residence on free soil had not made him a free man because slavery had not lawfully been excluded from the Wisconsin Territory. Six justices concurred with Taney's view that Scott was a slave, though giving different reasons. Justices Curtis and Mclean dissented both on the status of Scott and the constitutionality of the Missouri Compromise.

V. S. Hopkins, *Dred Scott's Case* (New York, 1951).

JDL

DREIKAISERBUND (THREE EMPERORS' LEAGUE) (1873, 1881, 1884), attempt by Bismarck to ensure security for Germany by maintaining close relations with Russia and preventing an Austro–Russian conflict in the Balkans. After personal meetings (1872) between the three rulers (William I of Germany, Francis Joseph of Austria, and Alexander II of Russia), an Austro–Russian agreement providing for consultation in case of attack was signed (June 1873). In Oct. Germany also became a party to the agreement. Because of continuing friction between his partners over the Balkans, Bismarck tried to achieve his aim with a more formal alliance (18 June 1881), which provided for the neutrality of two of the powers if a third were attacked. It was renewed (1884) and then allowed to lapse (1887).

DREISER, THEODORE HERMAN ALBERT (1871–1945), US author and journalist. He projected his own desire for success into Cowperwood, hero of *The Financier* (1912), *The Titan* (1914), and *The Stoic* (1947). His novels deal with the hypnotic allure of the big city and the compulsive crispness of the banknote. His characterization and relentless amassing of detail counteract the vulgarity of his prose. His most influential novel was *An American Tragedy* (1925).

DREPANA (mod. Trapani), Carthaginian port in northwestern Sicily and scene of the Romans' only defeat at sea in the First Punic War, when in 249 BC Claudius Pulcher lost 93 of his 123 ships.

DRESDEN, ancient capital of Saxony, situated on the Elbe river, and centre of the German hard-paste porcelain industry. From the reign of Augustus the Strong (1694–1733) until the later 19th cent. the royal factory at Meissen, 17 kms outside Dresden, and later several other factories nearby, produced the *chinoiseries* and porcelain figures associated with the town's name. The development of railways in the 19th cent. renewed its importance. Much of Dresden was destroyed in bombing attacks (1945) during the Second World War.

DRESDEN, BATTLE OF (26–7 Aug. 1813), Napoleon's last victory, in which he defeated an Austro–Russian army. He was unable, however, to avoid defeat himself some months later at Leipzig in Germany.

DRESDEN, TREATY OF (1745), between Prussia, Saxony, and Austria, ended the Second Silesian War. The gains of the Breslau settlement (1742), ie, Silesia (except Teschen), Troppau-Jägerndorf, and Glatz, were confirmed as belonging to Prussia. Maria Theresa of Austria was forced to agree to the cession of these territories because of the threat that British subsidies would be cut off if she did not; because of the Prussian invasion of Saxony; because of the failure to make a separate peace with France; and because of the worsening position in Italy. Frederick II of Prussia was eager to make peace in order to consolidate his gains. However, the Dresden settlement was not a lasting one. It did not make Frederick II's tenure of Silesia secure, as it left Maria Theresa embittered and strong enough to contemplate a war to recover her lost territories.

DRESDEN CONFERENCE (1850–1) of German princes, convened to discuss the reform of the German Confederation. They decided to revert to the 1815 constitution.

DREUX, BATTLE OF (19 Dec. 1562), victory of the French royalist forces, led by the Duc de Guise, over the Huguenots in the first French religious war. The Protestant leader Saint-André was killed and Condé captured. The battle left Guise supreme in the Council of Charles IX.

DREW, DANIEL (1797–1879), US stock manipulator. As cattle dealer during the Civil War, he gave his cattle salt so that they drank heavily and thus increased their weight before being sold. This practice of 'stock watering' was applied to the Erie Railroad after Drew, together with Fisk and Gould, gained control from Vanderbilt (1866–8). The railroad was ruined because they artificially enlarged the common stock of the company.

DREXEL, ANTHONY JOSEPH (1826–93), US banker and philanthropist. His Philadelphia firm, Drexel and Co., expanded after the Civil War and in 1871 combined with J. P. Morgan, of New York. The New Wall Street firm of Drexel, Morgan and Co., became the most powerful investment banking house in the US.

DREYFUS AFFAIR (1894–1906), a case which became a military and legal *cause célèbre* in France, resulting in violent public discussion. Alfred Dreyfus, a brilliant officer, became a scapegoat when it was found that a French officer was passing information to the German military attaché in Paris. Dreyfus, who was Jewish, unpopular, and an outsider, was convicted on forged evidence communicated to the judges behind the back of Dreyfus's lawyer. Dreyfus was sentenced to detention for life and sent to Devil's Island (1895). The matter was reopened in 1896 by an intelligence officer called Picquart, who discovered that leakages were continuing and traced them to an infantry officer called Esterhazy. In an attempt to hush the matter up the army transferred Picquart to Tunisia, but the matter was eventually brought before parliament and Esterhazy was formally denounced. But once more the army succeeded in clouding the issue and Esterhazy was acquitted. The army's triumph was short-lived however. Émile Zola, by publishing an open letter accusing the military authorities of persecuting Dreyfus, forced them to sue him, thereby bringing the matter before the civil courts (1898). Zola lost the case, but now the truth began to emerge and Henri, the man responsible for the forgeries, committed suicide. Amid mounting conflict between the Right—who wished to defend the army at all costs because of the international situation—and the Left—who felt that justice must prevail—the case was taken to the court of appeal, which ordered a new court-martial. This sat at Rennes (1899) and the army, by playing on its special position in society, secured Dreyfus's conviction, but with a verdict of extenuating circumstances. President Loubet gave Dreyfus a free pardon and Waldeck-Rousseau's government succeeded in curbing the incipient violence of the anti-Dreyfusards. Eventually the case was reopened, the decisions of both courts-martial quashed (1904), and Dreyfus and Picquart both reinstated. But the bitterness which had arisen over the affair lingered on and played a large part in the separation of Church and state (1905).

D. Johnson, *France and the Dreyfus Affair* (London, 1966).
R. Kedward, *The Dreyfus Affair, Catalyst for Tensions in French Society* (London, 1965). CHC

DROGHEDA, seaport in Leinster, Ireland, where Oliver Cromwell conducted a systematic massacre of the royalist garrison after it had refused to yield to mercy (Sept. 1649). This was Cromwell's first action after his arrival in Ireland and, like his whole campaign there, it was intended to bring peace quickly. In its consequences it embittered Anglo–Irish relations.

DROUYN DE LHUYS, EDOUARD (1805–81), French foreign minister of the Second Empire, a diplomat, and a protégé of Guizot. He was elected deputy for Melun (1842) and was also returned to the Constituent assembly (1848). He served as foreign minister in 1848–9 and under the empire (1851),

1852–5, 1862–6). He was used by Louis Napoleon to give his early diplomacy a reassuring appearance, and was discarded for his handling of the Roman and Crimean questions. He was recalled (1862) to balance Thouval's anti-Austrian policy, but was finally dismissed for the vigour with which he pursued claims for compenstion in Germany at the time of Sadowa (1866).

DRUIDS, Celtic religious leaders who combined native and Mediterranean religious and intellectual traditions, especially in pre-Roman Gaul, Britain, and later Ireland. Their culture embodied belief in the soul's immortality, and their inherited technique of oral instruction was instrumental in educating ruling and noble classes. Their political gatherings, transcending tribal boundaries, handled justice and inter-tribal disputes. Their influence and certain objectionable practices, *eg*, human sacrifice, aroused conflict with the Romans and made Druidism the force of nationalist resistance to Roman advance, but it was eventually submerged by the spread of Roman civilization.

DRUMCLOG, BATTLE OF (1679). During the second rising of the Scottish Covenanters against the repressive policy of King Charles II's secretary of state, Lauderdale, a Covenanter force led by John Balfour defeated at Drumclog in Lanarkshire the army of Viscount Dundee, which was marching to put down the rebellion.

DRUMMING, AFRICAN. From the evidence of rock gongs found in Nigeria and elsewhere, this was a neolithic art. The introduction of iron tools, however, probably boosted the making of wooden slit-drums and wooden drums with skin membranes. African drumming consists of three principal modes—for signals, speech, and dance—serving the purposes of ritual, communication, and entertainment. Among some central and West African peoples drumming is used to establish contact with the ancestors and the spirit world, to induce possession, conduct possession dances, or to mark the stages of ritual performance.

The speech and signal modes of drumming have been wrongly compared with the Morse code. In fact, African talking drums imitate the speech of the community that uses them and thus their range of comprehension is limited. The acoustic range of a single drum is, in any case, only 5–10 miles (8–16 kms). Tone factors in many African languages have greatly facilitated drum speech. Thus the drums reproduce the high and low tones, rhythm, pauses, and punctuation of speech. Talking drums often come in pairs reproducing a high and a low tone; in slit-drums two lips produce differently pitched notes. In west Africa single skin-membrane drums are made to talk by devices that alter the tautness of the drum face to reproduce high and low tones.

Drum language comprises set poetic pieces, phrases, and texts known to both drummer and public. There are texts suitable for invoking spirits, for praise appellations, greetings, warnings, emergency calls and announcements, and texts of proverbs. Talking drum texts can also be a useful source of oral historical information.

J. F. Carrington, *Talking Drums of Africa* (London, 1949).
J. H. Nketia, *Drumming in Akan Communities of Ghana* (Edinburgh, 1964).   EJA

DRUMMOND, WILLIAM, OF HAWTHORNDEN (1589–1649), Scottish poet, historian, and inventor, whose verses had an elegiac melancholy, conspicuous in his 'Sonnets' (1616), 'Flowers of Zion' (1623), and 'The Cypress Grove', a prose meditation on death. He wrote a *History of Scotland 1423–1542* (published 1655) and in his later years produced pamphlets supporting the royalist and episcopalian party against the Scottish covenanters. Drummond also patented 16 mechanical inventions which included ideas for machine-guns and tanks. Notes he made during a visit from Ben Jonson were published as *Conversations* (1842).

DRURY, ERNEST CHARLES (1878–1968), Canadian farmers' leader, prime minister of Ont. (1910–23), and a pioneer member of the United Farmers of Ontario (1914), whom he led to success in the provincial elections of 1919. He formed a coalition government under the title of the People's Party, but it was stigmatized as being a 'class' party and was defeated by the Ontario Conservatives (1923). Drury's ministry marked the high tide of rural discontent in Ontario.

DRUSUS, NERO CLAUDIUS (38–9 BC), Roman general, younger brother of the Emperor Tiberius, and son of Livia Drusilla, who later married Augustus. He subdued the Rhaeti and the Vindelici with Tiberius (15) and was appointed imperial governor of the Three Gauls, which he organized (13). In 12 he invaded Germany, advancing to the Elbe in three campaigns, but died after falling from his horse. As part of Augustus' dynastic plans he married Antonia, daughter of Augustus' sister Octavia, and Mark Antony, their son being the future Emperor Claudius.

DRUZES (DURUZ), Syrian people professing a faith derived from Isma'ilism. The Druzes, who now call themselves Muwahhidun (unitarians), live in various parts of Syria and the Lebanon, and number some 200,000. The Druze faith came into being during the reign of the Fatimid Caliph al-Hakim (996–1021), whom some of the Isma'ilis regarded as a divine figure, and sought to organize a public following. One of these adherents, Al-Darazi, gave his name to the movement; another bestowed on the cult of Al-Hakim its definitive form in the years after 1017. The Druze religion survived the disappearance of the caliph in 1021 and found a refuge in the mountain fastnesses of north-western Syria.

DRYSDALE, SIR GEORGE RUSSELL (1912–), Australian painter, one of the first to record the Australian 'outback' and its people. After studying in Melbourne, London, and Paris, he settled in Sydney, (1940) and began his characteristic paintings of outback landscapes and genre scenes.

DUAL CONTROL, name given to the system adopted in Egypt (1876–9, 1880–2) by which two European controllers supervised Egyptian state revenue and expenditure, following the inability of the Egyptian government to pay interest on its public debt.

DUAL SYSTEM of Bengal, was set up by Lord Clive, under the treaty of Allahabad with Shah Alam (1765). By this treaty Shah Alam transferred the *diwani* (the revenue-collecting power) from the Nawab of Bengal to the East India Co. and the nawab retained the *nizamat* (the judicial and magisterial power). Both the company and the nawab were in theory the subordinate agents of the Mughal emperor, and were jointly responsible for the government of Bengal. This was the meaning of the term 'dual system'. In practice, the company wielded decisive power, since it collected the revenue which paid the army. But it had no responsibility for administration or justice, and sought to bridge this gap by appointing an officer who was deputy both to the company, for the *diwani*, and to the nawab of Bengal, for the *nizamat*. But this scheme did not work smoothly because the company's officers would submit to no authority but their own.

DUANE, WILLIAM (1760–1835), American journalist, born in New York. As editor of the Philadelphia *Aurora* (1798–1822), an important Jeffersonian organ, Duane was tried under the Seditions Act (1799), and although he was acquitted the charges against him were not dropped until Jefferson was elected president.

DUBCEK, ALEXANDER (1921–), Czech communist politician, who became first secretary (Jan. 1968) at the height of the movement for reform which led to the invasion of Czechoslovakia by Soviet forces and his subsequent dismissal. He joined the Communist Party in 1938 and at the end of the Second World War (1944) was identified with the Slovak resistance (the Slovak National Uprising) in the Tatra mountains. After the war he became a communist party official and was appointed to regional office, then (1962) became a member of the Presidium and secretary of the party's Slovak branch. He came to power as the result of an inner party dispute in which he had criticized President Novotny for the slowness with which economic reforms were proceeding and for his not giving adequate attention to the problems of Slovakia. Dubcek's aim was to liberalize the economy and to widen the area of discussion within the communist party, without departing from the external policy of the Warsaw pact or giving cause for Soviet intervention. When Soviet forces invaded the country (21 Aug. 1968) he at first retained his office, but later resigned (April 1969), was progressively demoted, and finally suspended from party membership. He was appointed ambassador to Turkey (Dec. 1969), dismissed six months later, and expelled from the party (June 1970).

DUBE (John Langalibalele) (1871–1946), African politican and epitome of the 'new independent African' in Natal at the turn of the century. He founded the first Zulu-controlled school based on the ideas of Booker T. Washington, as well as the Zulu–English newspaper, *Ilanga lase Natal*. He was president of the African National Congress (1913–17), and prominent in Natal African politics.

DU BELLAY, JOACHIM, French lyric poet (1522–60) and a leading member, with Ronsard, of the group of poets known as the *Pléiade*, which sought to create, through imitation of the ancients and Italians, French poetry which could rival these models. He wrote *Défense et Illustration de la Langue Française* (1550), a milestone in the history of French literature.

DU BELLAY, PIERRE (*fl.* 16th cent.), first theorist in France to expound fully the theory of the divine right of kings. Bellay, who studied law at Toulouse University, published *De L'Autorité du Roi* (1587), in which he maintained that authority was created and conferred by God and that, as his lieutenant, the king could only be responsible to God. Such a view helped to establish the power of Henry IV and to end the Wars of Religion in France.

DUBINSKY, DAVID (1892–), Polish-born US labour leader, who was a member of the American Federation of Labor's Executive Council (1934–6), resigning to join John L. Lewis in the Committee for Industrial Organizations. On returning to the AF of L (1945), he again served on the council and held his place after the merger with the CIO (1955). Dubinsky was a believer in developing labour union political action and was a founder of the American Labor Party (1936), the Liberal Party (1944), and the Americans for Democratic Action (1947). Under Dubinsky's leadership the International Ladies Garment Workers Union pioneered welfare unionism.

DUBLIN, Irish city which owes its foundation to an important Norse settlement of the early 9th cent. Intermittent Norse supremacy ended with the Anglo–Norman invasion of 1170 and thereafter the city became a trading colony of Bristol and was granted a charter in 1172. Throughout the Middle Ages Dublin was the effective capital of the Pale. It was held for the king at the outbreak of the Civil War, but surrendered to the parliamentary forces in 1647 to prevent itself from falling into Irish hands. The city was the meeting place of the Irish parliament until its abolition with the Act of Union of 1800 and it was later the scene of violent disturbances during the Irish struggle for independence, notably the Easter Rising of 1916, until it became the capital of the Irish Free State in 1921.

Dublin has some fine Georgian architecture and its maternity hospital, the Rotunda (founded 1745), is famous. It is the seat of two universities, Trinity College and University College, the latter is part of the National University of Ireland. It also has two archiepiscopal sees, Catholic and Anglican.

DUBOIS, GUILLAUME, cardinal (1656–1723), French statesman who rose to power during the regency of Philip of Orléans (1715–23). Originally tutor to Orléans, he became his chief adviser on matters of foreign policy and was the architect of the English alliance. In 1716 Dubois went to Hanover to discuss with Stanhope an Anglo–French alliance which in accordance with the treaty of Utrecht, would guarantee the exclusion of Philip V from the French succession. Dubois' real aim was the recognition of Philip of Orléans as heir to the young and sickly Louis XV. An Anglo–French treaty was concluded late in 1716, which, with the accession of the Dutch in Jan. 1717, became the Triple Alliance.

Dubois continued to direct French policy during the Alberoni crisis and used the Cellamare conspiracy as an excuse for declaring war on Philip V and to send French troops to occupy northern Spain (1719). Thus Dubois forced the dismissal of Alberoni and Philip V's renunciation of the French succession (1720). Orléans' right of succession was recognized and Louis XV was betrothed to a Spanish infanta. Dubois was rewarded first with the archbishropric of Cambrai (1720) and then with a cardinal's hat (1721), before becoming *premier ministre* (1722).

DUBOIS, PIERRE (*c.* 1250–*c.* 1321). French thinker, who was notable for his polemical writings, inspired by the quarrel between Boniface VIII and the French Crown, in which he advocated the complete withdrawal of the papacy from secular affairs, including the government of the papal states. There is no evidence that his ideas had any influence on the French government.

DUBOIS, WILLIAM EDWARD BURGHARDT (1868–1963), US Negro spokesman, historian, writer, and teacher. DuBois and other black intellectuals rejected Booker T. Washington's 'gradualism' and advocated education of the 'talented tenth' of the black race. He was a founder of the Niagara Movement (1905), and the National Association for the Advancement of Colored People (1909), and became editor of its official publication, *Crisis* (1910–32).

DuBois organized the Pan-African Congress (1919) and was a staunch advocate of African nationalism at the Versailles peace talks after the First World War. After the Second World War he became vice-chairman of the Council on African Affairs (1949–54). His work for improvement of the Negro's position in the US continued, but disillusionment with the US led him to Ghana, of which he became a citizen. He was working on an Encyclopedia Africana when he died. His numerous publications include *The Suppression of the African Slave-Trade* (1896, *Black Reconstruction* (1935), and *In Battle for Peace* (1952).

DUCASSE, JEAN-BAPTISTE (1646–1715), French admiral and colonial administrator, who went to sea for the Senegal Co. He was in the West Indies as a slaver (1680), turned to privateering, and in 1691 was made French governor of Santa Domingo. During the War of the League of Augsburg, he organized an invasion of Jamaica (1694) and took part in the capture of Cartagena (1697). As governor he ended buccaneering. He also directed attacks against Spanish ports in the War of the Spanish Succession.

DUCCIO (DI BUONINSEGNA) (d. 1319), early Sienese painter. His work combines a strong Byzantine influence with great richness of colour, especially red. His greatest works are the Ancona altarpiece for Siena cathedral (1311) and the Siena Majesta (1315).

DUCETIUS (d. 440 BC), hellenized Sicel chieftain, who led the only significant national movement against the Sicilian Greek colonies. After some successes against inland centres he was defeated and exiled by the Syracusans (450), but returned with Greek settlers to found Cale Acte on the north coast.

DUCHIES, GERMAN, political units which grew out of the German tribes in the 9th and 10th cents. The military title of 'duke' was given by the Carolingians to counts entrusted with the defence of frontiers especially menaced. These dukes gradually extended their power and established hereditary dynasties. The most important 10th-cent. German duchies were Saxony, Swabia, Bavaria, Franconia, and Lotharingia, though later new duchies without clearly recognized separate tribal identities, such as Carinthia, were established. The duchies were centres of regionalism and it was the policy of the Ottoman emperors to fill the posts with their own men or to take the duchies under their own direct rule. They were not stable units, most having been split up among the rising principalities by the end of the 12th cent.

DUCLOS, JACQUES (1896–   ), French communist politician, who was drafted into the army in 1915, wounded at Verdun, and taken prisoner in 1917. His experience of the horror and futility of the First World War convinced him of the need for a radical new alternative to the existing society. This conviction was translated into an unshakeable loyalty to the French Communist Party (PCF) and he became in 1920 a militant in the Association républicain des Anciens Combattants (ARAC) and in 1932 its vice-president. He progressed rapidly within the party, becoming a member of the central committee in 1926 and a member of the political bureau in 1931. In that year he was also appointed secretary of the party.

Much of his work for the party was as a parliamentarian. He was elected deputy for the Seine in 1926 and, with the exception of the years 1932–6 remained a deputy until 1958, when he was elected a senator. In the Chamber his main interests were pensions and foreign policy.

After his refusal to disavow the Nazi-Soviet Pact in 1939 he fled to Switzerland. He returned to France during the Second World War and reorganized the propaganda services of the party while directing the clandestine activity of the PCF. In the Fourth Republic his prominence as leader of the PCF parliamentary group and his arrest at the demonstration against Gen. Ridgway in 1952 made him one of the best-known political figures in France. He was nominated by the PCF as their candidate in the presidential election of 1969 and polled 21·5 per cent of the votes.   PMK

DUCS ET PAIRS, category of French nobility who took precedence over all the aristocracy after the royal family and the princes of the blood. Originally consisting of only six clerical and six lay nobles, it had increased greatly in numbers by the 18th cent. As peers they had the right to attend the full sessions of the *parlement* of Paris.

DUDLEY, SIR EDMUND (1462–1510), English lawyer and statesman, associated with Sir Richard Empson in the ruthless exaction of taxes and penalties allegedly owing to the Crown under Henry VII. Being lawyers, they were adept at producing obsolete statutes and customs to support their demands. In an immediate bid for popularity Henry VIII executed them both on charges of treason.

DUDLEY, THOMAS (1576–1653), MA governor who emigrated from England in 1630. He was governor of the Massachusetts Bay Colony four times and deputy governor thirteen times. He signed the charter for Harvard College (1650).

DUE PROCESS CLAUSES, legal restrictions on the US and state governments set out in the Fifth and Fourteenth Amendments to the US constitution, and in state constitutions. Deriving originally from English common law restraints on arbitrary executive actions depriving persons of life, liberty, and property without due process of law, these restrictions have been expanded in the US to cover all departments of government. They include both procedural protections for individuals and substantive limitations on legislation affecting property rights. In the US such clauses have become a guarantee of constitutional limitations on governmental authority, with the courts defining the degree and extent of such limitations.

DUEL, JUDICIAL, or trial by battle, is to be distinguished from the judicial appeal, which it much resembled. The judicial appeal was a criminal action and the judicial duel a civil action; in neither case was the Crown an interested party. The duel was a form of trial introduced into England by the Normans; it was essentially feudal in character and could be used only in disputes over ownership of land and between two Frenchmen or Normans. The battle was fought not by the disputants themselves but by champions who were originally witnesses for and tenants of the two parties but, by the 12th cent. hired professionals were invariably employed. The decline of the judicial duel as a form of legal action began with the introduction of the Grand Assize (*c.* 1179), which offered a defendant the option of electing for the issue to be settled by a jury of 12 knights. This process gradually replaced trial by battle.

DUELLING, fighting between two armed persons, originating with the Teutonic tribes who, having no system of jurisprudence, settled disputes by an appeal to arms, relying upon their gods to grant victory to the combatant whose cause was just. It was condemned by the Church and, like other primitive forms of trial by ordeal, was gradually superseded by the development of legal processes. Duelling persisted, however, as a knightly accomplishment and a means of settling private quarrels, vindicating one's honour and avenging personal affronts. It was particularly fashionable in France, where as many as 4000 people were said to have died in this way during the reign of Henry IV; in 1626 Richelieu abolished the practice on pain of confiscation, banishment, or death. Duelling spread from France into England, and the younger Pitt, Canning, Castlereagh, and Wellington were among the eminent men who thus hazarded their safety. It was not formally abolished in England until 1818. In Germany it survived among the military classes until 1939.

DUFAURE, JULES ARMAND STANISLAUS (1798–1881), French politician and member of a republican family. He became a leading liberal lawyer under the Restoration, and was elected to the chamber (1834), where he was an active and vociferous deputy; he was minister of public works (1839–40). He reluctantly accepted the Second Republic and was a conservative minister of the interior (1848, 1849–1851). On being dismissed before the *coup d'état* (1851), he returned to the bar and only secured re-election to the legislature after the fall of the empire (1871), when he twice served as minister of justice (1871–2, 1875–6). He later became a life senator (1876), a member of the Académie (1863), and prime minister under MacMahon (1876). He was dismissed on *Seize Mai*, but returned to preside over the persecution of the Right (1877–9).

DUFF, ALEXANDER (1806–78), Scottish Presbyterian missionary and educationist in Calcutta (1830–63). He started an English school which developed into the Duff College. Besides converting Indians to Christianity, he taught them European literature and science. He played an important part in the establishment of universities in India, and was closely connected with Calcutta University, developing its examination system and emphasizing the physical sciences. He was editor of the *Calcutta Review* (1845–9), and Moderator of the general assembly of the Free Church (1851, 1873). After leaving India he became professor of evangelistic theology at the Free Church College, Edinburgh.

DUFFERIN AND AVA, FREDERICK TEMPLE HAMILTON TEMPLE-BLACKWOOD, 1st Marquis of (1826–1902), British statesman. First known as an author, through his *Letters from High Altitudes* (1857), Dufferin was sent to Syria by Palmerston (1860) after the massacre of Christians. Having been secretary of state for India (1864–6) and for war (1866), he was made chancellor of the duchy of Lancaster by Gladstone (1868). As governor-general of Canada (1872–1878), he fostered the construction of the Canadian Pacific Railway. Dufferin served as ambassador to Russia (1879–81) and Turkey (1881) and was sent to Cairo to settle affairs after Arabi Pasha's rebellion (1882–3). As viceroy of India (1884–8), he settled Anglo-Russian conflicts over Afghanistan and helped secure the annexation of Burma (1885). After resigning as viceroy (1888) he became ambassador at Rome (1889–91) and at Paris (1891–6).

DUFFY, SIR CHARLES GAVAN (1816–1903), Australian politician and one-time associate of the Irish politicians Daniel O'Connell and John Dillon. Duffy came to Vic. in 1856, at the beginning of colonial responsible government, with a considerable reputation as an Irish radical and a British MP (1852–5). He was to found one of the few Australian families which maintained a record of distinguished public service over several generations.

As a member of the first Legislative Assembly of Vic. he held ministerial office in 1857 and 1858 and, as minister for lands (1861–3), carried legislation to break up 'squatter' estates and encourage free selection by farmers. As prime minister (1871–2) he was insufficiently protectionist to command support from David Syme and the *Age* and, though he later became Speaker (1877–9), withdrew from Vic. politics and left Australia. In his advocacy of federation, Duffy was ahead of Australian opinion of his day.

The eldest of Duffy's sons, John Gavan (1844–1917), held ministerial office in Vic. His second son, Sir Frank Gavan Duffy (1852–1936), sat on the bench of the high court of Australia, becoming chief justice. The third son, Charles Gavan (1855–1932), was a senior public servant in Vic. and in the Commonwealth until 1920. Sir Frank's son, Charles Gavan (1882–1961), was a judge of the supreme court of Vic. (1933–61).

DU GUESCLIN, BERTRAND (d. 1379), Breton in the military service of Charles V, King of France. On the eve of Charles's coronation he defeated the king's chief internal enemy, the King of Navarre. Twice when Du Guesclin was captured Charles paid huge ransoms for his recovery. Du Guesclin was responsible for the chief victories over the English, overrunning Ponthieu in 1370. In 1372 Charles made him Constable of France. His enemies tried to turn Charles against him and his position was ambivalent, since his direct overlord, the Duke of Brittany, was pro-English. To free himself of suspicion he launched a campaign against the mercenary armies (companies) overrunning France, in the course of which he died.

DUILLIUS, GAIUS, (*fl.* 3rd cent. BC), Roman consul (260 BC), who took command of the new navy and defeated the Carthaginians off Mylae (north-east Sicily) by using the *corvus* or boarding-plank.

DUKE, title of a Roman military office (Latin *dux*), it was used in the Frankish state under the Carolingian dynasty to denote holders of high commands on dangerous frontiers, who controlled several counties. When the Carolingian state disintegrated in the later 9th cent. the successors of these dukes became the most important of a growing number of autonomous potentates who were creating virtually independent principalities for themselves. In Germany this process of disintegration was arrested for a time in the 10th cent. but after the 12th cent. here too dukes became the most important of the independent territorial princes. In England the title of duke first appeared in 1337, when it was conferred on Edward, the Black Prince, as the highest nobiliary distinction. Until the 16th cent. it was bestowed almost always only on men of royal descent. Others received dukedoms in England in the 17th and 18th cents, but the title again became virtually a royal monopoly after the dukedom of Wellington was given to Arthur Wellesley (1814).

DUKE, JAMES BUCHANAN (1856–1925), US tobacco magnate. His American Tobacco Co. (1890) controlled the cigarette industry, and by 1900 had a monopoly of all tobacco products except cigars. Capitalized at $502,000,000, it was dissolved by the US Supreme Court (1911), as an illegal combination in restraint of trade.

DUKES, JOSEPH (1811–61), half-breed interpreter for missionaries to the Choctaw Indians of North America. He helped to prepare a Choctaw grammar and dictionary, and a translation of the Old Testament.

DULANEY, DANIEL (1722–97), American pamphleteer. Son of Daniel Dulaney (1685–1753), and a prominent MD politician and judge. He opposed the Stamp Act (1765) and the British principle of colonial 'virtual representation' in parliament.

DULHUT, DANIEL GRESOLON (1639–1710), French-born fur trader, who explored the northern shores of Lake Superior and the headwaters of the Mississippi river.

DULL KNIFE (*c.* 1836–79) (Tah-me-la-pash-me), chief of a band of Northern Cheyenne Indians of North America. He first came to public notice as a signatory of the treaty of Fort Laramie (10 May 1868). His band and other Cheyenne joined Sitting Bull in the battle of the Little Big Horn (1876). Dull Knife surrendered and was moved to Oklahoma Territory, whence he escaped (1878), but he was recaptured. He was killed in another attempt to escape.

DULLES, ALLEN WELSH (1893–1969), US diplomat and international lawyer. He was educated at Princeton, and after working in the foreign service (1916–26) he entered the family law practice in New York. While with the Office of Strategic Services in Switzerland during the Second World War he was in charge of secret negotiations which led to the Nazis' surrender in northern Italy. In the post-war years he and his brother, John Foster Dulles, acted as foreign affairs advisers to Thomas Dewey. Being an expert on intelligence operations, he was appointed (1951) deputy director of the Central Intelligence Agency, and later became its director (1953–61). During his directorship the CIA was active in both intelligence and covert operations. He retired soon after the Bay of Pigs invasion of Cuba (1961).

DULLES, JOHN FOSTER (1888–1959), US lawyer, diplomat, statesman, and secretary of state (1953–9). The son of a Presbyterian minister, the nephew of Robert Lansing and grandson of John W. Foster, both former secretaries of state, he came from a family active in public service. He was educated at Princeton (1904–8), the Sorbonne (1908–9), and at George Washington University Law School (1909–11), entering the law firm of Sullivan and Cromwell (1911), where he specialized in international financial litigation. He accompanied his grandfather to the Second Hague Peace Conference (1907), was a member of the American delegation at the Versailles Peace Conference, drafting the treaty clauses on war reparations (1919), and frequently assisted at international monetary conferences during the 1920s and 1930s. Disturbed by the worsening situation in Europe, he published *War, Peace and Change* (1939), which sought, in the Wilsonian tradition, to align American foreign policy with

Christian principles. During the Second World War Dulles was chairman of the Commission for a Just and Durable Peace, established by the Federal Council of Churches, and as a prominent Republican advocated bipartisanship in US foreign policy. He served four successive Democratic secretaries of state as special consultant (1944–52), broken by a brief interlude as interim senator from New York (1949–50). He helped to draft the United Nations Charter at the San Francisco Conference (1945) and served as acting chairman of the American delegation at the UN (1948–9). His greatest achievement during these years was the negotiation and conclusion of the Japanese Peace Treaty for the Truman administration (1950–1).

Dulles stated his foreign policy views in *War or Peace* (1950) and his career culminated in appointment as President Eisenhower's secretary of state (1953). Although he worked closely with Eisenhower, Dulles's forceful personality made a considerable impact on the conduct of US foreign policy. His record in office is controversial. He has been accused of insensitivity, of domineering behaviour towards the Western allies, particularly during the Suez crisis (1956), and of over-reacting to Soviet pressure. His preoccupation with holding Soviet expansionism in Europe led him to neglect Latin America, and, failing to understand the meaning of neutralism, regarded the uncommitted nations as immoral. The zealous rhetoric of terms such as 'liberation' and 'massive retaliation' sometimes carried him beyond the realities of American power. However, his shrewd exposition of American strength (labelled 'brinkmanship') allowed him to preserve the free status of West Berlin and retain the islands of Quemoy and Matsu for the Chinese Nationalists against Chinese Communist harassment. He firmly supported the movement towards European unity and strengthened the web of international alliances designed to contain Communism, cementing West Germany within NATO and establishing the South-East Asia Treaty Organization (1954). He was hard-working and undertook a heavy burden of personal diplomacy in addition to routine administration.

R. H. Ferrell and S. F. Bemis (eds), *The American Secretaries of State and their Diplomacy*, vol. XVII, L. L. Gerson, 'John Foster Dulles' (New York, 1967).

R. Goold-Adams, *The Time of Power: a reappraisal of John Foster Dulles* (London, 1962). ICP

DUMA (1906–17), the Russian parliament established during the 1905 revolution. Nicholas II having agreed to the election of a national assembly in Feb. 1905, Bulygin made proposals (pub. in Aug.) for a consultative assembly on a limited franchise with large peasant representation. After Witte became head of the government, the tsar accepted his advice and issued the manifesto of Oct. 17–30, which gave a constitutional guarantee of civil liberties and freedom of speech, conscience, and association. The franchise was to be broadened to include urban workers, legislation could be introduced by the Duma, and all laws would have to be approved by it.

Before the Duma met in May 1906, however, the Oct. manifesto had been modified, especially by the Fundamental Laws of April 1906. The Duma was to have two chambers: the Council of State, the upper chamber, and the State Duma, the lower chamber; the Duma was to have only limited control of the budget and—most important—ministers, although they could be questioned, remained individually responsible to the tsar and not the Duma. The tsar could veto the Duma's decisions, dissolve it, and pass laws under article 87 of the Fundamental Laws when it was not sitting. Election was to be through class colleges and indirect.

The First Duma, dominated by Kadets, had strong national minority representation and was firmly oppositional. It attacked the Fundamental Laws and demanded expropriationary land reform, making co-operation with the government impossible and in July the assembly was dis-

solved. Some members, who fled to Vyborg in Finland and called for passive resistance, were arrested and disfranchised. The Second Duma (March 1907) saw an increase in both government supporters and social democrats and a decrease in Kadet influence, and within four months, after refusing to sanction Stolypin's land reforms, it was dissolved.

A change in the electoral law, severely restricting the franchise, made the Third and Fourth Dumas (1907–12, 1912–17) conservative bodies which managed to enact some useful legislation. In 1915 a Progressive Block within the Duma demanded a government responsible to the assembly and, although the Duma had supported the government in 1914 over the war, by the time the monarchy fell it was basically hostile to Nicholas. A committee of the Duma formed a Provisional Government in March 1917.

A. Levin, *The Second Duma* (New York, 1940).

J. Walkin, *The Rise of Democracy in Pre-Revolutionary Russia* (London, 1963). BJW

DUMBARTON OAKS CONFERENCE (1944), major conference in the elaboration of plans for the United Nations Organization. The conference (named after the house in Washington, DC, where it was held) was in two parts: representatives of Britain, the US, and Russia met first; the Soviet delegates were then replaced by the Chinese, since the Soviet Union, which was not at war with Japan, would not attend a conference at which the Chinese were present. The latter half of the conference added nothing of major significance to the discussions.

Agreement was easily reached on the outline of the proposed organization, with its General Assembly, a Security Council consisting primarily of the great powers, a Secretariat, and an International Court of Justice. On Churchill's insistence France was included as a permanent member of the Security Council.

Differences arose over the membership of the organization: the US proposal included six Latin American republics, while the Soviet Union insisted that membership should be confined to countries at war with Germany and proposed that all 16 republics of the USSR should be given separate membership. On this point no agreement was reached. The second most important difference was over the use of the veto in the Security Council: the British proposal that the veto should not be used by a party to the dispute was not accepted by the Soviet or American delegates. A compromise was proposed—a complete veto over decisions concerning enforcement action, and a veto which a party to the dispute could not use in decisions over the investigation of disputes.

These and other questions of detail were taken up again at Yalta and at San Francisco. WFK

DUMMER, JEREMIAH (c. 1679–1739), American colonial agent, born in Boston. Dummer emigrated to England, where he practised law. He was colonial agent for MA (1710–21) and CT (1712–30) and helped to found Yale University (1701).

DUMMYING and **PEACOCKING**, terms used in Australian colonies during the long struggle of farmers to unlock land held by pastoralist 'squatters'. Legislation of the 1860s in NSW and Vic. particularly, linked with the names of John Robertson and Charles Gavan Duffy respectively, sought to achieve this by 'free selection before survey' but was often evaded. Squatters used 'dummies' to acquire land for them on favourable terms; ostensible settlers 'picked the eyes' out of a pastoral run by selecting vital areas, usually around waterholes.

DUMONT, ÉTIENNE (1759–1829), Swiss cleric, who was secretary to the English philosopher Bentham and to the French politician Mirabeau. When democratic ideas were proscribed at Geneva he left for St Petersburg (1783), where he became minister of the French Reformed Church. From Russia he went to England (1785) and assisted Bentham in preparing his works for publication, which he translated into French. During most of the Revolutionary period he was in France, where he edited the *Courrier de Provence* for Mirabeau, and from time to time visited England. In 1809 Alexander I made him a member of the commission charged with codifying Russian law. He returned to Geneva in 1814, renounced his clerical status, and was elected to the Representative Council, for which he drafted rules of procedure, based on English practice. He set up a model prison and drafted a projected penal code on Utilitarian lines.

DUMONT, GABRIEL (1838–1906), Canadian politician and Louis Riel's adjutant-general in the Canadian North-West Rebellion (1885). He was president of the St Laurent 'provisional government' (1873) and one of the deputation which invited Riel to lead the Métis rebellion in the Saskatchewan valley (1884).

DUMONT D'URVILLE, JULES-SÉBASTIEN-CÉSAR (1790–1842), French explorer who led two Pacific expeditions (1826–9, 1837–40), the latter on Louis Philippe's suggestion, taking in Antarctica (Adélie Land). Both were prodigious voyages, rich in scientific observation, and brought a fitting end to the great age of Pacific discovery.

DU MOULIN, CHARLES (1500–66), French lawyer in the *parlement* of Paris, whose *Premier Commentaire sur La Coutume de Paris* (1539) enquired into the origin of customary law with a view to its codification and revision. He was an ardent royalist, and his *Traité de l'Origine . . . du Royaume et Monarchie de François* (1561) upheld royal authority over the discipline and government of the Church.

DUMOURIEZ, CHARLES DU PÉRIER (1739–1823), French soldier and diplomat of the *ancien régime*, who won the Revolution's first military victories. He was appointed foreign minister because of his contacts with the Girondist leaders (1792), and was largely responsible for the war against Austria and Prussia. After the desertion of Lafayette, he took command of the army, winning the battles of Valmy and Jemappes (1792). But in 1793 he deserted to the enemy after his invasion of Holland had failed and his troops refused to march on Paris to restore the power of the monarchy, which he had secretly supported throughout

DUNBAR, WILLIAM (*c.* 1460–1520), Scottish court poet. He enjoyed the favour of James IV of Scotland and assisted the king in his negotiations to marry Margaret Tudor, whom Dunbar welcomed to Scotland with his poem. 'The Thrissil and the Rois'.

DUNBAR, BATTLE OF (1650), victory of Oliver Cromwell over the army of Charles II's Scottish allies, on the coast east of Edinburgh, which made it possible for Cromwell to besiege the city. Cromwell had previously failed to break the Scots' commanding position, and had withdrawn to Dunbar. The Scottish leaders retired to Stirling.

DUNCOMBE, THOMAS SLINGSBY (1796–1861), British politician, from 1834 a courageous and popular radical MP for Finsbury. He defended the Chartists in parliament in 1840 and presented their petition in 1842.

DUNDEE, JOHN GRAHAM OF CLAVERHOUSE, 1st Viscount (Scottish) (1649–89), served as a volunteer in the French and Dutch armies before being given a captaincy in the Duke of York's regiment to enforce the Clarendon Code against the Scottish covenanters (1677). He was defeated by a small covenanting force at Drumclog (1679), but gained his revenge in assisting Monmouth's victory at Bothwell Brig (1679) and afterwards repressed the rebels with some severity. He was made a viscount (1688) for supporting James II against William III. On being allowed to return to Scotland after James's flight, he raised 3000 men from the clans of Lochaber and was killed while fighting a government army in the pass of Killiecrankie.

DUNDONALD, THOMAS ALEXANDER COCHRANE, 10th Earl of (Scottish) (1775–1860), British admiral and MP. After service in the Revolutionary Wars and Napoleonic War, he faced charges involving financial malpractice, as a result of which he was fined, imprisoned, and expelled from parliament. He subsequently sought naval employment by serving the Chilean, Peruvian, and Brazilian independence efforts. As commander of the Chilean navy (1818) he drove the Spanish squadron from the Pacific coast of South America. He transported the Argentine-Chilean force which was to liberate Peru and terrorized the Spanish-held ports. Abandoning the Peruvian effort before its termination, he offered his services to Brazil and as commander of the Brazilian navy secured the Brazilian ports against Portuguese reactionary movements in the north-east (1823). He then moved on to command the Greek navy before being reinstated in the British navy (1832), in which he became commander-in-chief on the North American and West India station. Dundonald had some talent as an inventor, and welcomed the application of steam power and the screw propeller to shipping.

DUNEDIN, capital of Otago, NZ, founded in 1848, was surveyed as 'New Edinburgh', and became a staunch 'Free Church' town. The gold rushes of the 1860s expanded Dunedin without altering its character. It became NZ's chief commercial centre and largest city (1864), but had fallen to fourth place by 1906. Its 19th-cent. 'Victorian-Scottish' atmosphere persisted into the 20th cent.

DUNES, BATTLE OF THE (1658), defeat of a Spanish relieving force which attacked Anglo-French troops under Turenne while they were besieging Spanish-held Dunkirk, during the last year of the long Franco-Spanish wars of the 17th cent. The inability of the Spanish to bring up their artillery through the dunes east of Dunkirk contributed to their defeat, and Dunkirk was taken ten days later. In the treaty of the Pyrenees (1659) England received Dunkirk, which it sold to France in 1662.

DUNGAN HILL, BATTLE OF (1647), fought near Trim in the Irish Rebellion. The parliamentary forces under Michael Jones forced a battle with the Irish Confederacy army under Thomas Preston. Preston tried to cut off Jones's communications with Dublin, but Jones's superior cavalry decided the issue and Preston's army was almost exterminated. It was the first of a series of disasters for the Confederacy.

DUNGENESS, NAVAL BATTLE OF (1652), in which a Dutch fleet under Van Tromp outnumbered and defeated the English under Blake during the first Anglo-Dutch War.

DUNKIRK, free Channel port and fortified base belonging to the Spanish Netherlands until its capture by Cromwell's forces during the Franco-Spanish hostilities (1648–59). It was sold to France by Charles II of England (1662), and became the refuge for French privateers, *eg*, Jean Bart, who harried English shipping during the War of the League of Augsburg and the War of the Spanish Succession. The peace of Utrecht (1713) stipulated that the naval base was to be razed, but this was disregarded and Dunkirk continued to be an important French base.

During the Second World War Dunkirk was the scene of the retreat of the British Expeditionary Force from France (1940) after Germany had broken through and reached the coast. Some 336,000 men were rescued in an improvised operation by vessels of all descriptions from Britain. Immediately after the evacuation, France surrendered.

DUNKIRK TREATY (March 1947), Anglo-French treaty of alliance by which the two signatories pledged themselves to give mutual support in the event of renewed German aggression, and to take common action should Germany default on economic obligations. The treaty was of symbolic rather than practical importance, and was surpassed by the Brussels treaty (1948).

DUNLOP, JOHN BOYD (1840–1921). British veterinary surgeon, who in 1888 patented the pneumatic bicycle tyre after experimenting for a year with air tubes to reduce shock from the wheels of his son's bicycle. With W. H. Du Cross he later formed a company to exploit the tyre, which developed into the Dunlop Rubber Co.

DUNNE, FINLEY PETER (1867–1936), US journalist and humorist, famous for his 'Mr Dooley' sketches, the kindly satiric comments of a mythical Chicago Irish saloon-keeper. These first appeared in the Chicago *Evening Post* and attracted a wide readership both in the US and in Britain during the Spanish American War (1898).

DUNNINGS' RESOLUTION (6 April 1780) deplored the increase in the influence of the British Crown and called for its diminution. The Commons passed the resolution (by 233 to 215), but attempts to implement it did not succeed until Rockingham's administration (March 1782).

DUNRAVEN AND MOUNT-EARL, WINDHAM THOMAS WYNDHAM-QUINN, 4th Earl of (Irish) (1841–1926), Anglo-Irish statesman of independent outlook who inaugurated the commission into sweated labour (1888–90). He supported moderation in Ireland and persuaded fellow landowners to accept Wyndham's Land Act (1903). He was president of the Irish Reform Committee and was nominated to the first senate of the Irish Free State (1921).

DUNS SCOTUS, JOHN (c. 1265–1308), one of the most important and influential philosophers and theologians of the Middle Ages. He was probably born at Duns, Scotland, and entered the Franciscan order (c. 1280). He graduated at Oxford before being ordained in 1291 and at some time lectured at Cambridge. At various times he studied and taught at Paris and died while lecturing at Cologne. He was known as *doctor subtilis*, his thought being deep and subtle rather than original. He was regarded as the archetypal product of scholasticism, so much so that in the Renaissance reaction against medieval philosophy 'duns' became a synonym for stupidity. His thought was essentially conservative and he abandoned the Aristotelianism of Aquinas. Much of what he wrote is notoriously difficult to understand, partly because at his early death his works were left in an incomplete state, and also because his pupils arranged and altered his works, ascribing to him many things that he did not actually write. The Scotist school founded by him was influential from the mid-14th cent. and dominated Franciscan thought, to which he is what Aquinas is to Dominican thought.

DUNSTAN (909–88), archbishop of Canterbury (959–88), a West Saxon closely related to the royal family and a pioneer of Benedictine monastic reform. He was abbot of Glastonbury in 943, treasurer to King Edred (946–55), and became archbishop on the accession of Edgar in Wessex. He used his influence to ensure that reforming monks rose to high office in the Church and he contributed to a revival of the monastic ideal.

DUNSTERFORCE, force commanded by Maj.-Gen. L. C. Dunsterville (the original of Kipling's Stalky), employed in Trans-Caucasia (1918) to prevent the Central Powers' penetration after Russia's withdrawal from the First World War. The use of the force in Baku (Aug.–Sept.) led to communist accusations of British intervention.

DUPERREY, LOUIS-ISIDORE (1786–1849), French explorer. In a scientific expedition (1822–4) he studied terrestrial magnetism and surface currents in the south Pacific and undertook the pioneer survey of the Gilbert and Caroline islands.

DUPETIT-THOUARS, ALBERT AUBERT (1793–1864), French commander who was sent on a peaceful mission and annexed (ostensibly in Catholic interests) the Marquesas (1842) and Tahiti (1843).

DUPIN, ANDRÉ MARIE known as 'the elder' (1783–1865), French jurist and politician, of Breton origin. He became a lawyer (1800), and defended Ney and other political offenders during the Restoration. Having established himself as a liberal, he was elected to the Chamber (1827). He served as administrator of the Orléans estates and after the 1830 Revolution, in which he participated, he became an adviser to the king. He was minister without portfolio (1830) and thereafter president of the chamber (1832–7) and eventually a leader of the middle party, which oscillated between government and dynastic opposition. At one stage he joined Thiers, Guizot, and Barrot with the aim of overthrowing Molé (1838). He never obtained ministerial rank, as he had hoped to do, and was ridiculed for his ambition and rustic character. He was prominent during the 1848 Revolution, became president of the Legislative Assembly, and accepted Napoleon III.

DUPLEIX, JOSEPH FRANÇOIS, Marquis de (1697–1764), governor of French India, whose aim was to acquire territorial possessions as a basis for both trade and empire. He was jealous of La Bourdonnais's capture of Madras and engaged in a sordid squabble over the town's fate. When La Bourdonnais withdrew to repair his fleet, Dupleix plundered and set it on fire (1746). He repelled the attack on the French factory at Pondicherry by Boscawen (July 1748). After the treaty of Aix-la-Chapelle (1748) Dupleix tried to exploit local Indian politics to France's advantage in the Carnatic and the Deccan. He was appointed deputy over the provinces of southern India by Muzaffar Jang, and on the latter's assassination the French recognized Salabat Jang as his successor, Dupleix gaining Arcot, Trichinopoly, and Madura free of tribute (1751). Over-optimistic about the financial resources of the French East India Co. and inclined to underestimate the English, he was recalled (1754) by a French ministry which failed to appreciate his contribution in India.

DUPLESSIS, MAURICE LE NOBLET (1890–1959), Canadian politician. He was elected to the House of Assembly (1927) and became leader of the Quebec wing of the Conservative Party (1933). With Paul Gouin he formed the Union Nationale and adopted the social reform programme of L'Action Libérale Nationale (1935). He forced the Liberal provincial prime minister, L.-A. Taschereau, to resign through the exposure of administrative scandals. As prime minister of Quebec (1936–9), Duplessis abandoned his previous policies and supported large corporations with such measures as the anti-communist 'Padlock Law' (1937). In 1939 he called an election on an anti-conscription platform and was defeated. He was re-elected as prime minister in 1944, and dominated Quebec politics until his death. He used provincial police to suppress strikes and he opposed federal social legislation as an infringement of provincial autonomy.

DU PLESSIS-MORNAY, PHILIPPE (1549–1623), French Huguenot statesman and writer. After escaping the Massacre of St Bartholomew's Eve, he fled to England (Aug. 1572), but returned in 1576 to join Henry of Navarre, becoming his counsellor on foreign affairs. He was instrumental in reconciling Henry III to the idea of Navarre's succession and in the passing of the Edict of Nantes (1598), but was dismissed by Henry IV for his intolerance.

DU PONT FAMILY, wealthy US industrial dynasty. Its members are descended from the distinguished Frenchman Pierre Samuel du Pont (1739–1817), who emigrated to America during the French Revolution (1799). His son, Eleuthère Irénée du Pont, who had worked under the chemist Lavoisier, established a gunpowder mill beside the Brandywine Creek near Wilmington, DE (1802). Irénée became first president (1802–34) of E. I. du Pont de Nemours and Co., the family manufacturing concern. Producing a superior gunpowder, largely the work of Lammot du Pont (1831–84), the company monopolized supplies of smokeless explosives to the US government. It was prosecuted under the Sherman Anti-Trust Act, but although it was forced to create two new, independent companies it remained sole supplier of smokeless gunpowder (1907–11). Consolidated by T. Coleman du Pont, company president (1902–15), it grew and diversified during the First World War, becoming the largest US chemical producer, and investing large sums in General Motors. Pierre Samuel du Pont (1870–1954) presided over General Motors (1920–3) and while president of E. I. du Pont (1915–19) initiated a policy of fundamental scientific research which reaped such rewards as the development of nylon by W. H. Carothers. Pierre and his brothers, Lammot and Irénée, were investigated by the Nye Committee (1934), which sought to apportion blame among munitions manufacturers for American involvement in the First World War. The company expanded rapidly during the Second World War, increasing its investments in related industrial and commercial fields and secretly manufacturing plutonium for the Manhattan Project. It was obliged, when prosecuted under the Clayton Act, to divest itself of its 23 per cent shareholding in General Motors (1963). Since 1939, the company has been the subject of 39 anti-trust suits.

The family has remained closely knit and can command an estimated capital of $7·5 billion (as of 1969), chiefly invested in E.I. du Pont de Nemours and General Motors stock and the family holding company, Christiana Securities. The largest of the family's 18 foundations, Winterthur and Longwood, are both former du Pont estates and have assets of over $122 million.

W. H. A. Carr, *The Du Ponts of Delaware* (New York, 1964).
F. Lundberg, *The Rich and the Super Rich* (London, 1969).
                                                                                                            ICP

DUPONT DE L'EURE, JACQUES CHARLES (1767–1855), French liberal politician and minister, who, before the Revolution, was a lawyer. He sat in the Council of Five Hundred (1798–9) and in 1800 became a judge in Normandy. After being elected to the legislative body (1814–15) he emerged as a liberal, and sat in the Chamber (1817–48). During a brief period as a minister (1830), he earned the reputation of being an austere and blunt liberal, and was therefore selected as president of the Provisional Government (1848), but he made little impact and thereafter retired from politics.

DUPONT DE NEMOURS, PIERRE SAMUEL (1739–1817), French economist and propagandist of physiocratic theories. He held administrative office under Vergennes and under Turgot. As a member of the states general, he proposed the decree confiscating ecclesiastical revenues (June 1790).

DUPRAT, ANTOINE, cardinal (1463–1535), archbishop of Sens and French statesman. He was chancellor and leading minister under Francis I and also forced the Concordat of Bologna upon the *parlement* and the Sorbonne (1515). After becoming a priest and then an archbishop (1516), he aspired unsuccessfully to the papacy. In 1524 he opposed the Duke of Bourbon and provoked him into rebellion. He presided over the Council of Sens (1528), which vigorously pronounced on the authority of the Church and strengthened parish discipline. In 1533 Duprat directed a commission of enquiry into the orthodoxy of Theodore Beza and Gerard Roussel, which resulted in the former's banishment from Paris.

DUPUIS, JEAN (1829–1912), French merchant and adventurer in China and Viet-nam. He first arrived in China in 1860 as an observer with the Anglo-French expedition to Peking, and shortly afterwards began trading in arms at Hankow; he also learnt Chinese and entered into the spirit of Chinese society. After meeting Francis Garnier at Hankow in 1868, Dupuis went to Yunnan, where in 1869 he negotiated an arms deal with the provincial authorities, then fighting a Muslim revolt. After supplying them with arms, in 1871, he obtained another contract, and then explored Southern Yunnan to confirm the navigability of the Red River route via Tongking. In 1872 he went to Paris and persuaded the French government to support a trading expedition to Yunnan via Tongking. Dupuis reached Tongking by this route in 1873, but clashed with the Viet-namese on his way back, which led the French at Saigon to dispatch a small force to Hanoi, later the same year. The force's early success was not maintained, and following the death of its leader, Francis Garnier, it was withdrawn. Dupuis continued to press the idea of trade with China through Tongking, but it was not till 1881 that the French finally decided to occupy the area in force.

DUQUESNE, ABRAHAM (1610–88), French Protestant sailor, who, as a young man, fought successfully against the Spaniards in the Caribbean. After being promoted to lieutenant-general of marine by Colbert (1667), he defeated the Dutch and Spanish fleet off Messina, when De Ruyter, the Dutch admiral, was killed (1676). Duquesne achieved naval supremacy for France in the Mediterranean and bombarded Algiers (1682, 1683), but was expelled from France after the revocation of the Edict of Nantes (1685).

DURACK FAMILY in northern Australia. Two brothers emigrated from Co. Clare to Goulburn, NSW, after the Irish famine of 1846. Patrick Durack (1834–98) founded a chain of cattle stations in the newly opened 'Channel country' of western Queensland during the 1860s, and in 1883–5 sent three parties 2000 miles (3200 kms) overland with cattle to stock new country in the Kimberley district of WA—one of the major feats of Australian droving. By 1890 most of the family was established there, holding over 3 million acres until 1950. Among the original overlanders were Patrick's cousins, John (1849–86), Patrick Mantinea (1851–1933), and Michael (1854–1936). Michael Patrick Durack (1865–1950), Patrick's eldest son, sat in the WA legislature for Kimberley (1917–24), and chaired a royal commission on the meat industry (1928). His son, Kimberley Michael Durack (1917–68), was an early advocate of tropical agriculture in northern Australia, and pioneered rice-growing in the Kimberleys.

DURAND, ASHER BROWN (1796–1886), US engraver of historical scenes, portraits, and bank-notes. He was a founder of the Hudson River School of landscape painting, his 'Kindred Spirits' (1849) illustrates his preoccupation with romantic realism.

DURAND LINE, delimited (1893) to show the respective spheres of influence of the Amir of Afghanistan and the government of India over the frontier tribes. It possessed no strategic value and was not an ethnic line; nor was it a tripartite agreement, for the tribesmen were not consulted.

DURÃO, JOSÉ DE SANTA RITA (1721–84), Brazilian poet, renowned for his epic poem 'O Caramurú' (1781) about the adventures of Diego Alvares among the Tupí Indians of Bahia.

DURBAWA, dynasty of Katsina, northern Nigeria, term applied (1970) both to the original inhabitants and to the ruling group conquered by Kumayo, grandson of the Hausa culture-hero Bayajida. The Durbawa rulers are said to have alternated with the newcomers. Later, when a new dynasty, the Wangarawa, appeared, they continued as kingmakers. They retain much of their influence in the court of Maradi in Niger.

DÜRER, ALBRECHT (1471–1528), German painter and engraver, probably the inventor of etching and coloured woodcuts. Although he travelled widely, his style continued to be essentially Germanic. Dürer was Lutheran in sympathy, and a pictorial moralist, susceptible to the traditional superstitions of his race and time, but anxious also to expose and end them. Although his designs and drawings were richly elaborate, nothing was included for merely decorative effect. Dürer's best-known works include the murals at the city hall in Nuremberg, portraits of Maximilian I, Raphael and Erasmus, engravings of *Adam and Eve, The Knight, Death and the Devil* and *The Prodigal Son*, woodcuts of the Apocalypse and the Passion, and paintings of *The Adoration of the Magi, The Feast of the Rosary* and *The Crucifixion*.

DURGA DAS, son of Askaran, the minister of Raja Jaswant Singh of Jodphur or Marwar. In 1679 he organized the escape of Jaswant's infant son Ajit from the Emperor Aurangzeb in Delhi and eventually secured Ajit's recognition as raja (1708). He also supported the cause of Prince Akbar against Aurangzeb in 1681 until he left for Persia (1687).

DURGAVATI, RANI (d. 1564), princess of the Chandel dynasty of Mahoba, married to the Gond Raja of Garha-Katanga. She governed the state for her son from 1549, and was noted for her military prowess and good government. She was killed in battle by the Mughal general, Asaf Khan I.

DURHAM, JOHN GEORGE LAMBTON, 1st Earl of (1792–1840), British radical statesman whose *Report on the Affairs of British North America* (1839) reshaped British colonial policy. Lambton, who was elected Whig MP for Co. Durham (1811), and became Lord Grey's son-in-law (1816), held more advanced opinions than his parliamentary leaders. He denounced Liverpool's ministry for their part in the Peterloo affair, championed Queen Caroline, and introduced a Commons motion (April 1821) demanding household suffrage, equal electoral districts, and triennial parliaments. His opposition to Catholic Emancipation caused a breach with Brougham, whose malice pursued him thereafter.

Durham, who became lord privy seal in Grey's cabinet (Nov. 1830), supervised the drafting of the Reform Bill (regretting the ballot's omission), selected Lord John Russell to introduce it in the Commons, and kept non-parliamentary Radicals like Place and the political unions' leaders in touch with cabinet intentions. After the Reform Bill's passage, Durham was sent to Russia. On his return, he resigned over Stanley's Irish policies. Durham's vanity and arrogance made him 'an impossible colleague' in cabinet. Out of office, he remained a brilliant individualist, too self-seeking and erratic to found a stable, fruitful radical group or to aspire to the party leadership which his undoubted talents might otherwise have brought him.

Melbourne shared the general ministerial distrust of Durham, but in 1838 dispatched him to investigate the situation created by the 1837 Canadian rebellions and suggest remedies. Ill-health, continuing disorders, and parliamentary controversy over his *ultra vires* Bermuda Ordinance dogged Durham's abbreviated five months' mission. None the less, materially helped by his Utilitarian secretary, Charles Buller, by Gibbon Wakefield, and others, he produced his striking, positive report.

Durham seemed paradoxical. 'Radical Jack' derived an immense fortune from coal-mining royalties and accepted an earldom (1833). He supported Belgian nationalism; yet his hope of submerging the French-Canadian identity by a legislative union of the two Canadas (1840) and intensive English immigration into Canada, struck even Melbourne as illiberal and impracticable. His concept of responsible government was not new, but it disconcerted the cabinet.

Durham died before it was implemented in Canada by his son-in-law Elgin and before its much wider application, *eg,* to Australia and New Zealand (1855).

Chester New, *Lord Durham* (London, 1929). MRB

DURHAM REPORT (1839), report on Canada prepared by Lord Durham, who was sent to Canada to investigate the causes of the 1837 rebellion and propose changes in Canadian institutions. His report covered Canadian land grants, religion, immigration, local government, legal systems, hospitals, and finances. Its most important recommendations favoured the union of Upper and Lower Canada and the establishment of responsible (cabinet) provincial government. The Canadians would have internal self-government, the Crown concerning itself with the Canadian constitution, foreign relations, trade with foreign nations, and public lands. The union of Upper and Lower Canada was provided for in the Act of Union (1840) and responsible government was accepted in Nova Scotia and Canada in 1848. The Durham Report became the basis for local self-government in all British North American possessions.

DURRANI, western Afghan tribal group which has provided the ruling families of Afghanistan since the 18th cent. Their name, originally Abdali, was changed by Ahmad Shah (1747).

DURRUTI, BUENAVENTURA (1896–1936), Spanish anarchist, who typified the anarchist movement's amalgam of violence and idealism. He was a railway worker from Leon, and made his mark in 1917 by organizing sabotage on the railways. With his friend, Francisco Ascaso, he was exiled to France, and on returning to Spain in 1923 they assassinated the Abp of Zaragoza. In Paris, in 1924, they attempted unsuccessfully to kill Alfonso XIII. Durruti was imprisoned, but was amnestied by the Republican government in 1931 and became a prominent extremist in the Federation Anarchista Iberica (FAI). After the Llobregat rising of Jan. 1932, he and Ascaso were imprisoned in Spanish Guinea, from whence they managed to organize various crimes of violence, including the stealing of evidence from the judges who were trying anarchists accused in connection with the Zaragoza rising of March 1934.

During the civil war Durruti was one of the FAI's representatives on the Anti-Fascist Militia Committee which ruled Catalonia. He formed a column of militants and set out from Barcelona to recapture Zaragoza. On the way, he tried to force anarchist collectivism on the villages of the Aragon front by mass terrorism. In Nov. 1936 he took his column to help in the defence of Madrid, but his men refused to fight. On 21 Nov. he was shot by an unknown assailant.

DUSSINDALE, BATTLE OF (27 Aug. 1549), defeat of Robert Ket's Norfolk rebels by John Dudley, Earl of Warwick. The economic policy of the Protector Somerset had caused widespread agrarian discontent and rioting. By his victory, achieved mainly with German mercenaries, Warwick gained in popularity at Somerset's expense.

DUTCH IN SOUTH AFRICA. The Dutch first rounded the Cape of Good Hope in 1595, nearly a century after Da Gama. In 1652 a Dutch East India Co. expedition under Van Riebeeck occupied the Cape as a refreshment station. This small settlement soon came into conflict with the indigenous San and Khoikhoi (Bushmen and 'Hottentots') and many of its servants left for the hinterland, where they became cattle ranchers, and referred to themselves as 'trek boers'. British invasion in 1795 brought Dutch company rule to an end. The brief Batavian Republic (1803–6) introduced revolutionary social and economic reforms, but these had no lasting effects, owing to the republic's short existence.

DUTCH IN WEST AFRICA. The Dutch began trading with west Africa in the last decade of the 16th cent. and quickly outstripped their European rivals, building their first forts at Mouree (1612) and Gorée (1617). In 1621 the Dutch West India Co. was founded, with a monopoly of all Dutch trade in the region. It managed to drive the Portuguese from the Gold Coast, but after 1650 found the profits from its gold trade consumed by unsuccessful enterprises in Angola and Brazil. After drastic reorganization (1674), the company concentrated upon the slave trade with the West Indies and after 1734, when it lost its monopolistic position, was joined by smaller Dutch companies. In 1795 the company's trading posts were taken over by the Netherlands government, which handed them to the British in 1872. The Dutch played an important part in introducing firearms and the system of 'trust' or credit trading in the region.

DUTCH PATRIOTS (1787), movement which tried to seize control of the Dutch Republic through a 'democratic' revolution. From the late 1770s many of the substantial merchants and manufacturers of Amsterdam and Rotterdam were engaged through the Patriot movement in a struggle aimed at William V. They hoped to abolish the privileges of the urban oligarchs and the power of the *stadtholder*. Through their pressure the republic entered the American War of Independence on the side of the Americans and French, despite the sympathy of William V for Britain; France in consequence looked on the Patriots as a means of exerting influence within the Netherlands. By 1787 pressure from the Patriots' societies and clubs had become sufficient to persuade the estates of Holland, the largest province in the republic, to suspend the *stadtholder*, who appealed for English and Prussian help. Prussian troops entered the country the same year and restored William's authority with little opposition. France had been unable to help because of her financial position, while the lower classes in the towns had supported the *stadtholder*, and the peasantry had remained passive. The revolutions in France and the Austrian Netherlands in 1789 had little effect on the Patriots, who were too cautious to move again, although they did begin to reopen their clubs. There was also no real support for the first French invasion (1793), but at the second (1795) the Patriots rose, seized control with French help, and established the Batavian Republic.

DUTCH REFORMED CHURCHES in southern Africa. Most of the Afrikaans-speaking people, and 30 per cent of the coloured people, of South Africa belong to one or other of the three branches of Dutch Calvinism in that country: the Nederduits Gereformeerde Kerk, the oldest and largest; and the Gereformeerde Kerk, and the Nederduits Hervormde Kerk, both of which split from the parent body for doctrinal reasons in the 19th cent. and now operate mainly in the Transvaal.

Calvinism in this region derives from the beliefs of Dutch and German settlers of 1652 and from a form of Protestantism revitalized by French Huguenot arrivals in 1688–9. During the first half of the 19th cent. the Dutch Reformed Church lacked the means of training its ministers locally and was unable to obtain recruits from the Netherlands. Six Presbyterian ministers, led by Andrew Murray, were therefore sent by the British government from Scotland. Their impact on Church doctrine and practice, especially in education, was marked; their descendants continue to play leading parts in Afrikaner life.

Aspects of this Calvinism, such as predestination and the community of the elect, formed a basis for white racism which developed in the early years of confrontation at the Cape between settlers and indigenous peoples. In the 20th cent. there has been a relationship, often close but never well defined, between the Reformed Churches and Afrikaner nationalist parties and elitist groups such as the Broederbond. On the other hand, some Calvinist ministers have been among the few Afrikaners to question the doctrine of apartheid on moral and theological grounds.

Although the Dutch Reformed Church has done little missionary work in South Africa (except among the coloured community, organized in separate churches), it has done so in some other parts of the continent, notably Malawi.   AEA

DUTRA, EURICO GASPAR (1885–), Brazilian general, minister of war in the government of Getulio Vargas, and president of Brazil (1946–51). He was supported by a conservative coalition known as the Social Democratic Party.

DUTT, ROMESH CHANDRA (1848–1909), Indian official, author, and politician. He entered the Indian civil service in 1869 and eventually became commissioner of a division (1894). After his retirement he presided over the Indian National Congress at Lucknow (1899) and became chief minister of the state of Baroda. For a time he was lecturer in Indian history at University College, London. He also served on the royal commission on Indian decentralization (1907). His *Economic History of British India* (1901–3) followed in the footsteps of Digby and stressed the economic exploitation of India. In 1900 he published, as a series of open letters to Lord Curzon, a book on *Famines in India,* in which he attributed the prosperity of Bengal to the Permanent Settlement. Curzon, in his reply, the *Land Revenue Policy of the Indian Government* (1902), had no difficulty in proving that Dutt's facts were wrong.

DU VAIR, GUILLAUME (1556–1621), French cleric, philosopher, and a magistrate in the *parlement* of Paris during and after the French Civil Wars of Religion, noted for his promotion of Christian Stoicism in his work, the *Holy Philosophy* (1600). He became keeper of the seals under Henry IV.

DUVALIER, FRANÇOIS (1907–), Haitian ethnologist, physician, and president of Haiti. After a distinguished career as a country doctor in the anti-yaws campaign, Duvalier entered national politics in the 1950s. He emerged as a prominent figure in the confused situation following the overthrow of Paul Magloire, and was elected president for a six-year term in 1957. His government quickly became noted for its repressive nature. It showed anti-elite tendencies, and claimed to represent the African and rural rather than the European and urban part of Haiti's heritage. Voodoo, for example, has generally escaped persecution, but the Christian churches have not enjoyed government favour.

After four years of office Duvalier called irregular legislative elections and claimed that the success of his candidates meant that he had been re-elected for a second six-year term. In April 1964, after rumours that he intended to declare himself emperor, it was announced that he was to become president for life.

There were several attempts (1964–70) to invade Haiti by exile groups, but all met with failure. Severe repression by the notorious Tontons Macoutes prevented internal unrest and Duvalier continued (1970) to control the island republic as a private fiefdom.

DUY-TAN PLOT (May 1916), attempt by Viet-namese nationalists to take control of Hue. The young emperor, whose reign-title was Duy-Tan, was smuggled from the palace; and this move coincided with plans for an uprising in two provinces of Central Viet-nam. But the French discovered the plot, recaptured the emperor, and executed the leaders involved.

DVARAVATI, ancient kingdom of central Thailand, founded in the 5th or 6th cent. Its Mon population practised Buddhism of the Theravada School. Its chief archaeological remains are at Phra Pathom and Lopburi. Dvaravati was absorbed by the Khmer empire in the 9th cent.

DVORYANSTVO, Russian nobility of service originally called *pomeshchiki* who, from the reign of Ivan IV (1533–84), superseded the old hereditary *boyar* class. Ivan IV rewarded men for service to the state, particularly in the military field, but granted the lands on conditional service tenure (*pomestie*), even forcing the *boyar*s to exchange their allodial estates (*votchina*) for service tenure. A law of 1556 systematized the amount of military service owed by the *dvoryanstvo*.

Despite the anarchy of the Time of Troubles the *boyar*s were unable to revive their unconditional hereditary rights. The abolition in 1682 of the *mestnichestvo* (strict order of precedence among the nobility) enabled Peter the Great (1672–1725) to work from the principle that there was only one class of nobles and that its right of hereditary tenure depended on the obligation to serve the state in a military or civil capacity. Peter's edict of 1722 laid down the system of life service and a table of ranks for the *dvoryanstvo*. However, during the reigns of Peter's ineffectual successors his system was gradually undermined. In 1730 compulsory service in the navy, which had long been unpopular, was abolished, and from 1736 service was reduced from life to 25 years. Finally, under Peter III, obligatory service was abolished altogether (1762), although the privileges of hereditary possession and the exploitation of serfdom, formerly the rewards of service, increased under his successors.

DYNAMITE was invented in 1866 by Alfred Bernhard Nobel. Nitroglycerin, too sensitive to shock to be used alone as an explosive, was found by Nobel to be absorbed readily in an infusorial earth known as kieselguhr or diatomite. In this form it can be safely handled and detonated.

DYNASTICISM, major factor in European international politics throughout the early modern period (late 15th–18th cents). It was stimulated by the concept of divine right and was deliberately pursued by, in particular, the houses of Habsburg, Valois, and Bourbon. Thus dynasticism resulted in the creation of the vast empire of Charles V and the rivalry of the great dynasties. It ceased to dominate political action when the concept of *realpolitik* developed.

DYSON, JEREMIAH (1722–76), British official who was a clerk of the House of Commons (1748–62) and later an MP (1762–74). He was an expert in Commons procedure and an administrative reformer, abolishing the sale of offices in the clerks' department.

DYULA, Nanding term (trader), originally applied to clans with specialized trading functions—particularly in gold—and their symbiotic clerical lineages, and later extended to Soninke traders in the Niger Bend. In Arabic and Hausa sources they are called Wangara, probably after a district of ancient Mali.

The search for gold led Dyula south to Begho (Brong region of Ghana) and they were already at Elmina when the Portuguese arrived (1482). In the 15th cent. they were influential in the Islamization of some Hausa dynasties and may have founded the 'Wangara' dynasty of Katsina, *c*. 1450. In the 18th and 19th cents they established petty states around their trade posts at Kong and Odienne (Ivory Coast).

DZERZKINSKY, FELIKS EDMUNDOVICH (1877–1926), head of the Russian secret police (1918–26). In 1906 he was elected to the central committee of the Russian Social Democratic Party. Later he was exiled to Siberia, but in 1917 he appeared in Petrograd, joined the Bolshevik Party, and played an important part in preparations for the November Revolution. He attended the meeting (Oct. 23) of the central committee of the Bolshevik Party, where he voted with Lenin and the majority for insurrection. At this meeting he put forward a motion which led to the creation of the Politburo. During the uprising, he was responsible for the capture of the postal and telegraph headquarters in Petrograd. In Dec. 1918 Lenin appointed him head of the Cheka, or secret police, and he remained in this post until his death. He was for a time alleged to belong to the Left Communist group, but by the end of the revolution he clearly belonged to the Stalinist faction, and was named in Lenin's will as one of Stalin's adherents.

Until Lenin's death Dzerzkinsky had been loyal to him, though they disagreed about the correct Bolshevik line with regard to nationalism, Dzerzkinsky arguing against the revolutionary possibilities of national self-determination.

In 1921 he became commissar of transport, and in 1924 chairman of the supreme council of the national economy, which caused him to delegate much of his work in the OGPU (the successor to the Cheka) to his subordinate, Menzhinsky. Dzerzkinsky was also chairman of the central committee's sub-committee on party discipline. He regarded it as a duty that members should inform on comrades who were attached to anti-party factions. He thus enjoys the melancholy distinction of having first played a leading role in exterminating the enemies of Bolshevism and then turning the weapon used for its destruction against Stalin's party enemies. GS

EADRED (*reg.* 946–55), King of Wessex, son of Edward the Elder. Eadred's reign is distinguished by the support he gave the monastic reformers and by the final subjugation of the Northumbrian Danes in 954, which ended Northumbrian independence.

EADS, JAMES BUCHANAN (1820–87), US engineer, and an expert on all Mississippi river matters. He constructed a number of steam-propelled, armour-plated gunboats for use by Union forces on the western rivers during the American Civil War. He designed the great St Louis Bridge (1874), and was the first to make extensive use of steel. His reputation as a consultant engineer was world-wide.

EALDORMAN, originally the ruler of a folk-group for Anglo-Saxons kings. The *ealdorman* subsequently became the ruler of a shire or group of shires and presided at the shire-court. He governed with vice-regal powers. The office disappeared in the 11th cent.

EAM (National Liberation Front), communist-dominated popular front movement of the Greek resistance. EAM was formed at Athens on 27 Sept. 1941. Although controlled by the Greek Communist Party (KKE), EAM included socialist, agrarian, and republican elements and spawned a number of subsidiary organizations to discharge specific functions, among them EPON (United All-Greece Youth Organization), EA (National Mutual Aid), and EEAM (Workers' National Liberation Front), and ELAS (National Popular Liberation Army), which was the most important, being the military arm of EAM formed in Dec. 1942. Estimates of the personnel of EAM and its subordinate units range between 500,000 and 2 million, though it is acknowledged to have been the largest and most effective of the resistance movements. In liberated territories EAM set up a hierarchical administrative system based on the village and governed by a central committee composed of regional delegates representing the political and functional components of the EAM network. On 10 March 1944 EAM established the Political Committee of the National Liberation (PEEA), which was charged with securing EAM a place in the government and administering the liberated territory. And in April 1944 an assembly, the National Council, was elected. By mid-1944 EAM had developed a nearly complete state apparatus. When the government-in-exile returned to Greece in the van of British forces the major problem was to disarm the resistance forces, chiefly EAM, in order to transfer power to the legal but impotent government. The failure to resolve the problem of disarmament led to the battle of Athens in Dec. 1944, in which British forces were hard pressed to defeat ELAS. When the fighting ended a military agreement was reached (Jan. 1945) and a political agreement concluded at Varkiza on 12 Feb. 1945, by which KKE and EAM achieved legal status. In March 1946 EAM boycotted the elections, which brought victory to the right. Later that year KKE, using the network established by EAM during the war, opened the second civil war in Greece.   JMK

EARLY, JUBAL ANDERSON (1816–94), US Confederate general and divisional (later corps) commander under Lee during the American Civil War. His independent command in the Shenendoah valley ended with defeat at Waynesboro (March 1865). After the war, he returned to his law practice in VA.

EARLY ENGLISH STYLE. The first period (*c.* 1175–*c.* 1300) of the Gothic style of architecture in England has been known since the time of Thomas Rickman (*c.* 1819) as 'Early English'. Its characteristics are tall, narrow lancet windows, pillars composed of groups of slender shafts round a central shaft (often as, *eg*, at Salisbury, composed of contrasting stones), decoration in arches and windows restricted to trefoil (three-leaf) and quatrefoil (four-leaf) piercing and cusps and, on capitals and bosses, to foliation (*eg*, the leaves of Southwell). Vaulting is simple transverse and diagonal ribbing. Above all there is the replacement of the single-centred, semi-circular Romanesque arch by the double-centred pointed Gothic arch. The introduction of the pointed arch was one of the most profound and fundamental developments in the history of architecture. Its basic advantage was that by making the 'thrust' more vertical and less horizontal it enabled buildings to be made high and wider with larger window space and thinner walls, so that buildings were not only physically lighter but brighter and airier. The pointed arch also solved a number of basic problems of vaulting such as crossing of transepts and naves of different widths. The first real introduction of the new style—which originated in the Île de France—was in the choir of Canterbury Cathedral, rebuilt between 1174 and 1185, and in the choir and lesser transepts of Lincoln Cathedral (1190–1200). The first building completely in the Early English style was Salisbury Cathedral (1220–58: west front, 1258–65; chapter house, 1263–84). Westminster Abbey, begun in 1245, is largely in this style, but was not completed until the late 14th cent. Other notable examples of Early English are the west fronts of Wells, Peterborough, and Ripon Cathedrals, Southwark (St Mary Overy) Cathedral, Southwell Minster, York Minster, and the choirs of Fountains and Rievaulx Abbeys, now both in ruins.

EARTHQUAKES IN NEW ZEALAND. Lying roughly on the Pacific Ocean rim, NZ shares in moderate degree its proneness to seismic disturbance. Sixteen earthquakes of magnitude 7+ have occurred since European settlement began, the heaviest being in Wellington in 1855. The most destructive, in Hawke's Bay (1931), claimed 255 lives, mostly in Napier.

EAST ANGLIA was the Anglo-Saxon kingdom of eastern England. It seems, to judge from the Sutton Hoo burial ship, which was found within its boundaries, to have had affinities with Sweden. The kingdom was subject to repeated Mercian attacks and its history in the 8th cent. is very obscure. The names of the rulers of the first half of the 9th cent. are known only from coins. In 870 Edmund, the last native king, was slain by the Danes and until 917 East Anglia was in Danish hands. By the late 10th cent. she was developing as a great earldom, dependent on Wessex. She was consequently influenced by the West Saxon monastic revival, though Norfolk and Suffolk escaped division into shires on the West Saxon model.

EAST INDIA ASSOCIATION, London society founded (1866) to promote the welfare of the inhabitants of India. The man mainly instrumental in its foundation was Dadabhai Naoroji, who delivered the first lecture on 'England's Duties to India'. The association provided a forum for the free discussion of

Indian problems. Its lectures and discussions were published in its journal, which is a mine of information for the student. The council of the association made representations to the India office, the colonial office, and parliament on questions such as the import duties on cotton and the grievances of Indians domiciled in South Africa. Indian and British were brought together at social functions, and a warm welcome was given to distinguished Indians, the delegates to the round Table Conference, and Indian representatives at the Imperial Conference.

EAST INDIA COMPANY, THE, was incorporated by royal charter on 31 Dec. 1600 as 'the Governor and Company of Merchants of London trading into the East Indies'. It was given a monopoly of trade with the east and its object was to take a share in the spice trade, the obstacle of Spain having been removed by the defeat of the Spanish armada. Until 1612 trade was carried on by a separate subscription for each voyage and distribution at its conclusion. From 1612 the method of temporary joint stocks was employed, while from 1657 a permanent joint stock was raised.

The first obstacle encountered was the presence of the Portuguese in India and the second of the Dutch in Indonesia. Though fellow Protestants, the Dutch were also monopolists. After the 'massacre of Amboina' (1623) they virtually excluded the English from the Indonesian spice trade, who consequently fell back on India. Here Portuguese opposition was overcome (1612) and trading privileges obtained from the Mughals by Sir Thomas Roe (1618). During the 17th cent. the three main settlements of Madras, Calcutta, and Bombay were established, the latter being a cession from the Portuguese Crown (1662) on the occasion of Charles II's marriage. The company brought mainly textiles, saltpetre, and indigo from India. It tried to sell broadcloth and make up for bullion by the profits of the carrying trade.

The company's first period ended when profits under the later Stuarts aroused envy and the formation of a rival company, the English Co. Trading to the East Indies, with which it merged to form the United Co. in 1708. At the same time the attempt to found an independent dominion broke down with the failure of the Mughal War (1686–90). Until its involvement in French hostilities from 1742 the company continued its peaceful trading from fortified factories within the Mughal empire, except in the case of Bombay.

The French wars led the company into Indian politics and the virtual control of Bengal from 1757. Its failure to control its own servants led to grave abuses in India and the appearance of opulent retired officials in England known as nabobs. In 1772 threatened bankruptcy led to state intervention in the form of the Regulating Act (1773), which was increased by Pitt's India Act of 1784. A dual authority of the state through the Board of Control and the company was set up and lasted till 1858. Inquests were held every 20 years at each renewal of the charter. The company gradually lost its political power and commercially became more and more dependent on the tea and opium trade with China. In 1813 it lost its trade monopoly with India and in 1833 that with China. From then onwards it was a virtual managing agency for the British government, which had declared all its territories British in 1813. In 1853 the old patronage system of nominating its servants in India was abandoned in favour of competitive examination. After the Indian Mutiny the company was deprived of its ruling powers (1858) and it finally expired when its last charter lapsed (1873).

Sir W. Foster, *John Company* (London, 1926).   TGPS

EAST INDIA HOUSE, London headquarters of the East India Co., situated in Leadenhall Street (1638–1858) in the city of London. The work of the house was divided among committees, of which the Committee of Correspondence was the most important. From 1784 all important political business was conducted by a secret committee consisting of the chairman, the deputy chairman, and one other member, who corresponded with the Government-appointed Board of Control in Whitehall.

EASTER ISLAND, south-eastern Pacific island, settled by Polynesians around the 4th cent. 17th-cent. Marquesan immigrants introduced the sweet potato, a pseudo-script, and megalithic monuments, possibly commemorating Mendana's Spaniards. Early accounts (Roggeveen, 1722; Gonzalez, 1770; Cook, 1774) describe a numerous, peaceful people. Whalers (from 1805) brought disease and strife. Peruvian recruiters (1859–62) seized 1000 islanders, of whom only 15 returned, with smallpox, which carried off thousands more. A Picpus mission (1863) withdrew after the arrival (1870) of a French trader, Doutroux-Bornier. In the ensuing conflict many islanders were shot and hundreds deported to Tahiti. In 1877 Doutroux was murdered, at which time only sick islanders remained. The island was annexed by Chile (1888), fenced, and leased as a sheep run until 1934; subsequently its population began to increase.

EASTER RISING (April 1916) in Ireland, armed revolt, mostly in Dublin, against British rule in Ireland and to achieve Ireland's independence as a republic. The Act to give Ireland Home Rule (devolution, but not independence), had been passed in 1914, but suspended because of the First World War. Most of the Irish Volunteers, led by John Redmond, campaigning for Home Rule, went off to fight for the Allies, leaving a small group, led by Eoin MacNeill, who refused to do so. These were infiltrated by a still smaller group, the Irish Republican Brotherhood, led by the veteran Tom Clarke, who, with the poet Patrick Pearse and the revolutionary socialist James Connolly, planned an armed uprising.

The rising went badly. An attempt shortly before to land Sir Roger Casement with a consignment of German arms resulted in the capture of both; and on Easter Sunday (April 23), the day planned for the rising, MacNeill, having discovered Clarke's plan, ordered the cancellation of all Volunteer action. The rising was thus confined to 1200 insurgents, who proclaimed the Irish Republic from Dublin's General Post Office on Easter Monday.

Militarily, the rebellion was easily crushed; the last rebel strongholds surrendered after six days. Of the leaders 15 were court-martialled and executed and hundreds of their supporters imprisoned or deported. These measures succeeded, where the rising itself had failed, in swinging Irish opinion from support for Redmond and Home Rule to the Republicans and Sinn Fein (We Ourselves). On Easter Monday the rebels were booed in the streets; by 1917 the ex-deportees were popular heroes, and the executed men martyrs. Owing largely to the aftermath of the rising, the Irish Party was annihilated by Sinn Fein in the 1918 General Election; three years of sporadic fighting led to the Irish–British treaty of 1921 which set up the independent Irish Free State.   ISM

EASTERN ASSOCIATION, united forces of the eastern counties of England in the Civil War under the leadership of the Earl of Manchester. Formed by parliament in 1643 for their defence against the royal army, its cavalry was incorporated into the New Model Army under Oliver Cromwell (1645).

EASTERN LOCARNO. Germany's withdrawal from the League of Nations and the Disarmament Conference in 1933, and her subsequent pact with Poland, led to Franco-Russian initiatives for the conclusion of an Eastern security pact in 1934. Russia wished to include her Baltic allies in a pact to block Germany's eastward expansion. France was more concerned to secure a German guarantee for her Little Entente allies, analogous to the guarantees which Germany had given in the west in the Locarno Pact (1925).

In June 1934 France submitted to Britain the proposals elaborated with Russia. A treaty of Regional Assistance was to be concluded between Germany, Russia, the Baltic states, Poland, and Czechoslovakia. The obligation of assistance to any signatory under attack was to be adopted by France only towards Russia. Russia would assume the Locarno obligations towards France alone. The proposals were amended in consultations with Britain, to make Franco-Russian obligations operate in favour as well as against Germany. The whole scheme was throughout made conditional upon Russia's admission to the league.

On 10 Sept. a German note rejected the proposal, stressing Germany's preference for bilateral over multilateral pacts, and refusing to join any security arrangements not granting Germany equality of armaments. This was followed by a note from Poland, who refused to join any pact not including Germany. The recent German–Polish Pact was the decisive influence in Poland's rejection of this Eastern Locarno. Poland also, however, objected to guaranteeing the frontiers of her neighbours, Czechoslovakia and Lithuania.

The failure of this initiative did not hold back Russia's entry into the league. It led to the further pursuit of a Franco-Soviet understanding, which both parties claimed had the wider Eastern pact as its ultimate objective.

EASTLAND COMPANY, founded in England in 1579 to trade with the Baltic seaboard in naval stores in exchange for coarse cloth and salt. The company profited from the decline of the Hanseatic League and flourished in Elizabeth I's reign. It continued until the Restoration, when foreign competition and shortage of English tonnage led to its eclipse after 1673.

EASTMAN, GEORGE (1854–1932), US inventor and philanthropist, who in 1884 patented the first photographic film, in which the chemical emulsion was coated on to a flexible backing. Four years later he marketed the first Kodak 'box' camera. His mass production methods helped to make photography a universal hobby and the Eastman Kodak Co. (founded 1892) rapidly achieved a dominant position in the industry. Among the institutions which benefited from his generous benefactions were Rochester University, Massachusetts Institute of Technology, the Tuskegee and Hampton Institutes, and Oxford University.

EATON, PEGGY (Margaret L. O'Neale) (1796–1879), wife of the secretary of war, John H. Eaton, and the central figure in US political controversy during Andrew Jackson's first administration (1829–33). She was ostracized by Washington society, including John C. Calhoun, because of rumours concerning her early life. Her reputation was defended by Jackson and Van Buren and the affair contributed to the political rift between Jackson and Calhoun.

EATON, THEOPHILUS (1590–1658), American colonizer. After working as a merchant and diplomat in England and Denmark, Eaton became one of the patentees of the Massachusetts Bay Co. and emigrated to North America (1637), where he founded the colony of New Haven (1638) and with John Davenport organized its government. He was elected governor of the colony annually for 19 years.

EBERT, FRIEDRICH (1871–1925), German politician, chairman of the council of peoples' deputies and first president of the Weimar Republic. He settled in Bremen in 1891, where he organized the local trade union movement and campaigned for the Social Democrat Party (SPD). He was elected to the Bremen party executive, and in 1900 the Bremen and Hastedt Trade Union Cartel appointed him labour secretary. He was a delegate to SPD party congresses and was elected (Sept. 1905) secretary of the Berlin central organization, where he helped to streamline the party machine. In the theoretical dispute over Revisionism he assumed a centrist position, urging the party to get on with the practical nonrevolutionary side of its programme. He was elected to succeed Bebel as party chairman in Sept. 1913, and being concerned to avoid a party schism, acted as mediator between radicals and revisionists.

Although he supported the 1914 *Burgfriede*, the truce between social classes, he opposed the Reich government's expansionist aims, which threatened to split the nation as well as the SPD. But when, in March 1916, it became clear that the left wing was bent on division, he let them found the Independent Socialist Party (USPD). By now Ebert held the three key positions of party chairman, chairman of the party committee, and (jointly with P. Scheidemann) of the Reichstag faction. After the split he commanded a more homogeneous organization which he could lead into co-operation with the Centre Party and the Progressives. He helped to prepare the 1917 Peace Resolution, joining the strike movement of Jan. 1918 only to bring it to an early end.

When military defeat became certain, he considered Kaiser William II's abdication inevitable, but favoured the preservation of the monarchy. With revolution spreading throughout Germany, Prince Max von Baden, the Reich chancellor, saw in Ebert and his party the last resort for defence of the established order and, on 9 Nov. 1918, handed government responsibility over to him. Ebert concluded a pact with the army to prevent a Bolshevik revolution and the next day put himself at the head of the war-weary masses and, by forming a coalition with the USPD, established the revolutionary Council of People's Deputies. His primary objective was to postpone all basic changes in the political, social, and economic structure until after the National Assembly had been elected, and in the meantime to ensure the re-establishment of law and order. He thereby considerably helped the conservative forces to overcome their paralysis, while bitterly antagonizing the USPD and all forces on his left.

On 11 Jan. 1919 Ebert was elected president of the Weimar Republic, which office he held until his death. He did much to stabilize the republic and to preserve national unity.

C. E. Schorske, *German Social Democracy, 1905–1917* (Cambridge, MA, 1955).   VRB

EBRO, THE BATTLE OF THE (July 1938), on the Ebro river in Spain. Spanish Republican leaders decided in July 1938 on a spectacular military action in the hope of stemming the inexorable erosion of Republican territory by Nationalist successes. The prime minister, Negrin, also hoped that a renewed effort might heal divisions in the Republican camp. An offensive over a broad front was precluded by lack of men and materials, so an assault across the Ebro river was chosen in order to strike at the Nationalists' communications, and because hill fighting would nullify their material superiority and encourage the hope of restoring contact with the rest of Republican Spain. The conflict began at a bend in the river between Fayon and Cherta. Within a week 50,000 Republican troops had occupied the area. But it was a rash venture and, like previous Republican offensives, its initial success was soon turned to defeat by the arrival of Nationalist reinforcements. Nevertheless, Negrin's prestige was raised and at first there was consternation in the Nationalists' camp.

Later, the main battle took place at the town of Gandesa, with heavy losses on both sides. Franco rushed in reinforcements and the Nationalists opened the dams on the Pyreneean tributaries of the Ebro, whose flood waters washed away the Republican pontoons, but by 1 Aug. the advance had been contained. The Republican troops suffered a fierce artillery bombardment and attacks from Nationalist bombers. However, they clung on doggedly for three months, concentrating devastating machine-gun fire on Nationalist infantry attacks.

Despite a government crisis in Barcelona, the Nationalists, under Generals Valino and Yague, advanced only a few miles in their slow and relentless struggle. Franco was determined on victory and at the end of Oct. some 30,000 fresh troops, with new German equipment, pushed forward against the exhausted, badly equipped Republicans, and by 14 Nov. had cleared the last village in the salient captured in July.

The Republicans left behind many dead and much valuable equipment. It was the most gruelling battle of the whole Spanish Civil War and both sides suffered heavy casualties. But the Nationalists' victory was decisive. Franco pushed northwards against the shattered Republican forces and on 15 Jan. 1939 the Nationalists entered Tarragona; on the 22nd Barcelona fell. The Ebro offensive was thus the last despairing effort of Republican Spain.

EBROIN (d. *c.* 680), one of the most powerful Frankish mayors of the palace who were the official heads of the royal Frankish court and who exercised the effective power under a succession of weak and young Merovingian kings. Ebroin's chief centre was in the western Frankish kingdom of Neustria, which he dominated from *c.* 664 to the death of King Clotaire III in 673. After being temporarily expelled, he achieved control of the eastern kingdom of Austrasia and regained power in Neustria, where he ruled as mayor until his murder. His fall paved the way for the emergence of the Carolingian family from Austrasia as the sole mayors of the palace in all the Frankish territories.

ECBATANA (Iran), capital city of Media and Achaemenid Iran, on the site of modern Hamadan.

ECCLES, SIR JOHN CAREW (1903–), Australian neurophysiologist, who was director of the Kanematsu Institute, Sydney (1937–43), and professor of physiology at the Australian National University (1951–66). His best-known achievement was the disclosure of basic communication-mechanisms between nerve cells by microelectrode techniques.

ECCLES, MARRINER STODDARD (1890–), US banker who developed large-scale financial interests in UT and adjoining states. He was an assistant to the secretary of the US Treasury (1934), joined the Federal Reserve Board (1934), and eventually became chairman of the board of governors (1936–48). Believing that fiscal management of the economy was essential to the restoration of prosperity, he helped to formulate the Banking Act (1935), which strengthened the Federal Reserve and gave it power to control the money market.

ECCLESIA, ancient Greek assembly of citizens. Of little political importance at Athens until Solon defined its powers (594 BC), the *ecclesia* first moved towards effective sovereignty after Cleisthenes' reforms (508). Temporary aristocratic reaction was halted by Ephialtes (462) and from *c.* 450 the *ecclesia*, comprising all Athenian males over 18 of citizen birth on both sides (perhaps about 30,000), in conjunction with its council (*boule*), enjoyed total sovereignty. Meeting regularly 40 times a year on the Pnyx (average attendance perhaps around 5000) it decided all state business by a show of hands. Any citizen could speak to motions introduced by the *boule*. Its later instability produced an unsuccessful revolutionary attempt to restrict its membership to 5000 (411) and a subsequent codification of agreed rules of procedure (410–400). Payment was first introduced for attendance in the 4th cent.

ECCLESIASTICAL CENSUS (1851) in England. Though there have been several surveys of English religious behaviour, notably those by the *British Weekly* (1886) and the *Daily News* (1903), the only official religious census was taken in 1851. Despite its statistical inadequacies, it is invaluable to historians. It made a powerful contemporary impact by revealing the relative strength of nonconformity in relation to Anglicanism, but also the relative weakness of religious observance in relation to religious apathy.

ECCLESIASTICAL COMMISSIONERS (1835–1948), body in England appointed by the Tory prime minister, Sir Robert Peel, to implement Whig proposals for managing the finances of the Church of England. It had power to redress the balance between wealthy sees and poor parishes, and to purchase land. It represented the first major change in the Church since the Reformation, adapting it to the demands of the Industrial Revolution: 7000 churches were restored and 1700 built (1840–76), vitalizing anglican religious life in Victorian England. Its membership included the archbishops and diocesan bishops, the lord chancellor, chancellor of the exchequer, and a secretary of state. In 1948 (with Queen Anne's Bounty) it was fused into the Church Commissioners to manage the revenues, estates, trusteeship, and legal structure of the Church of England.

ECCLESIASTICAL RESERVATION, important proviso modifying the effect of the principle of *cuius regio eius religio* in the peace of Augsburg (1555). It laid down that no ruling prelate of any rank should retain his lands if converted to Protestantism, a rule which was ignored by the Calvinists in the later 16th cent.

ECCLESIASTICAL TITLES ACT (1851), in Britain, prohibited the assumption of ecclesiastical titles already held within the Church of England. It was intended to counter Pope Pius IX's plan to establish a diocesan hierarchy in England. The Catholic Church simply used other names for the new sees, *eg*, Cardinal Wiseman became Abp of Westminster. Gladstone, who had opposed the measure, repealed it in 1871.

ECHEVERRIA, ESTEBAN (1805–51), prominent Argentine socialist, poet, and anti-Rosas literary figure. He injected Romanticism into Argentine literature and later wrote on socialism.

ECK, JOHANN VON (1486–1543), Catholic theologian, orator, and professor at Ingolstadt, who took a leading part in the refutation of Protestantism for a quarter of a century. He successfully debated the themes of grace and free will with Carlstadt and Luther in the Leipzig disputation (July 1519). He again clashed with Luther at the Diet of Worms (1521) and debated with Oecolampadius at Basle (1526). He drew up 404 articles as a basis for discussion with the Protestants at Augsburg and contributed to the Confutation of Melanchthon's Confession (1530). In 1537 he produced a version of the Bible and took part in a conference at Speyer-Hagenau (1540) between Protestants and Catholics. At the Diet of Regensburg (1541) Eck was again spokesman for the Catholic viewpoint, but his rudeness and uncompromising attitude contributed to the failure of the conference to reach any agreement.

ECKEREN, BATTLE OF (29 July 1703), French victory over the Dutch in Flanders during the War of the Spanish Succession. The Dutch, under Gen. Opdam, were surprised by the enemy, and their defeat put an end to Marlborough's plans for a surprise attack on Antwerp.

ECKHART, MEISTER (*c.* 1260–*c.* 1328), one of the most influential European mystics of the Middle Ages. He was a German Dominican, a lecturer at Paris (1302–3, 1311–13) and provincial of his order in Saxony (1303–11). His teachings were condemned by the Church in a qualified manner (1329). His influence on later mysticism was deep, but its importance has been perverted and exaggerated by those who tried to make him an ancestor of the Nazi theories of Aryan racialism.

ECNOMUS, CAPE, BATTLE OF (256 BC), naval victory off southern Sicily of the Romans under Regulus and Manlius Vulso over the Carthaginians, which opened Africa to invasion.

ÉCOLE LIBRE DES SCIENCES POLITIQUES, school of political science founded at Paris by Émile Boutmy (1871). It enjoyed great success, and under the Third Republic a high proportion of France's senior civil servants and diplomats were recruited from its graduates. It was a private school, and its conservative and Catholic tendencies caused concern to the Left. After the Second World War it was taken over by the state and renamed the Institut d'Études Politiques.

ÉCOLE NATIONALE D'ADMINISTRATION, French school for training professional administrators, from which the higher ranks of the French civil service are generally recruited. It was set up after the Second World War to make access to the civil service more democratic and to counter the exclusive influence of the conservative École Libre des Sciences Politiques. It has been admired and imitated in other countries, but sometimes criticized in French for its elitist spirit.

ÉCOLE SOCIALE POPULAIRE, Canadian lay organization formed in 1911 under Jesuit direction to study papal teaching in industrial society. Strongly anti-capitalistic, it also encouraged French-Canadian nationalism during its most active period (1921–44). Its most important pronouncement, *Le programme de restauration sociale* (1933), called for the adoption of a corporate state.

ECONOMIC CO-OPERATION ADMINISTRATION (1948–1951), US agency established by the Economic Co-operation Act (1948) to administer the European Recovery Program. In 1951 its functions were transferred to the Mutual Security Agency.

ECONOMIC DEPRESSIONS IN AUSTRALIA (1841–4, 1892–4, 1929–34). Each reflected world trends through falling export prices and decreased investment. The depression of the 1840s arose from over-extension of the pastoral industry; recovery was slow until the gold discoveries of 1851. The depression of the 1890s, caused by falling wool prices and the breaking of the land boom in eastern Australia, was prolonged by drought but partly offset by a gold-mining boom in WA and Qld. Coming after a period of excessive public borrowing and a world slump, the Depression of the 1930s was the worst, bringing up to 30 per cent unemployment; recovery was incomplete until the Second World War. The two latter depressions gave rise to some significant Australian literature and stimulated nationalist and radical politics, especially in the Labor movement. From the mid-1930s the Australian economy became more diversified; its urban industries were increasingly rationalized, and all parties, on Labor's initiative, accepted planned development, social security, and full employment as national objectives. Subsequent recessions were minor (unemployment never exceeding 2½ per cent) and increasingly unrelated to overseas trends.

ECONOMIST, THE, weekly journal founded (1843) in England at the height of the Corn Law agitation, with the full support of the Anti-Corn Law League, 'to discuss financial questions in their wider social and commercial aspect'. It has survived as a standard weekly, its coverage now extending to the full range of international and domestic affairs.

ECQUEN, EDICT OF (1559), heresy law of Henry II, declaring war on French Protestantism and ushering in a bitter period of religious relations in France which were only modified after the accession of Henry IV in 1589.

EDDA (POETIC), also Elder Edda, a collection of 29 mythical and heroic poems in several distinct rhythmical alliterative measures preserved in a 13th cent. Icelandic manuscript, but of varied dates and places of origin. Similar poems in other Icelandic sources are also called Eddaic.

EDDA (PROSE), written (*c.* 1220) by Snorri Sturluson, consists of a valuable though rationalized summary of Scandin-

avian myths and explanations of the diction and metre of scaldic poetry, *ie*, Norse syllabic poetry on contemporary subjects.

EDDÉ, ÉMILE (1886–1949), Lebanese Maronite lawyer and politician, noted for his support of French influence. He was president of the Lebanon (1936–41) and organized the National Bloc.

EDDY, MARY BAKER (1821–1910), US founder of the practice of Christian Science. Already a practitioner of mental healing, she formulated the principles of Christian Science in 1866, established a spiritual healing practice at Lynn, MA (1870), and five years later published *Science and Health with Key to the Scriptures* (1875), which enunciated the basic tenets of Christian Science. The Christian Scientists' Association (1876) was chartered as The Church of Christ Scientist in 1879. Two years later Mrs Eddy obtained a charter for the Massachusetts Metaphysical College (1881), founded to train Christian Scientist practitioners. The First Church of Christ Scientist, the mother church of the organization, was established in Boston in 1892. In 1883 Mrs Eddy started publishing the *Journal of Christian Science. The Christian Science Monitor*, a daily newspaper with an international circulation, was founded in 1908.

EDEN, SIR FREDERICK MORTON (1766–1809), English writer, whose *The State of the Poor* (1797) is still a valuable source of social history. It was an enquiry into the income and household economy of the working classes, particularly agricultural labourers, and into the working of the English Poor Law. The study was made in response to the high grain prices of 1794–5, and represents both the social conscience of the upper classes and the rising demand for accurate information on social and economic matters.

EDES (National Democratic Greek League), leading non-communist resistance movement during the Second World War. EDES, formed in 1942, was led by Gen. Napoleon Zervas. EDES did not match the strength of EAM and without British support would have collapsed. EDES was confined to a small area in Epirus and numbered only 12,000 effectives. During the fighting between ELAS and the British, the EDES forces were dispersed in four days by their ELAS rivals. They were disarmed under the Varkiza Agreement of Feb. 1945.

EDESSA (mod. Urfa, south-eastern Turkey), capital of ancient Osrhoene, named by its founder, Seleucus I, after the first Macedonian capital. It was important in Rome's wars with Parthia and was captured by Lucius Verus (AD 165), becoming a Roman colony and the seat of a bishopric. In 639 it fell to the Arabs. During the first crusade it was acquired in 1098 by Baldwin of Boulogne, brother of Godfrey de Bouillon, who in 1099 became the first head of the Latin kingdom of Jerusalem. Edessa became the capital of a county of that name. It was the most easterly of the Latin states, always the most vulnerable of them, and in 1144 it fell to Zengi, ruler of Mosul, who ended the disunity in the Muslim world which had permitted Edessa's survival. Its fall led to the second crusade, but the crusaders failed to recapture it.

EDGAR (*reg.* 959–75), King of England and son of Edmund I, King of Wessex. He was a powerful ruler whose fleet is said to have patrolled the British Isles annually. Edgar gave support to Dunstan and the monastic reformers. In recognition of his supremacy in Britain he is said to have been rowed by seven kings on the Dee at Chester.

EDGEHILL, BATTLE OF (1642), fought in Warwickshire in the English Civil War. Charles I, having raised his standard at Nottingham in Aug. 1642, decided to march on London to quell the rebellion. On 23 Oct. his army encountered a parliamentary army of similar size—10,000 infantry and 2500 cavalry—under Robert Devereux, 3rd Earl of Essex, in the first battle of the Civil War. Prince Rupert of the Palatinate, nephew of the king, led a cavalry charge which routed the two flanks of the parliamentary army. In carrying his pursuit too far, he left the royalist infantry exposed, and they were severely beaten by a parliamentary attack which captured the royal cannon. Rupert returned in time to prevent a rout, and both sides withdrew, leaving 4000 dead upon the field. Essex returned to Warwick, leaving the way to London open, but Charles failed to take the opportunity and occupied Banbury and Oxford, making the latter his headquarters.

EDINBURGH, PHILIP, 6th Duke of (1st of 4th creation) (1921–), husband of Queen Elizabeth II of Britain, and a descendant of Queen Victoria. He was formerly Prince Philip of Greece, and was educated at Gordonstoun School, Scotland. He served in the Royal Navy, has undertaken many visits abroad and identified himself with scientific, environmental, industrial, and sporting aspects of the British Commonwealth.

EDINBURGH, TREATY OF (1560), expelled the French from Scotland and effectively ended their centuries-old interference in the country as a means of embarrassing the English. In Scotland John Knox had inspired a Protestant revolt (1559) that grew fat on the loot of churches and abbeys and against which the French prepared a punitive expedition. Queen Elizabeth I's response was to send Admiral Winter to the Forth (1560) with instructions to 'impeach' the French in any way he could, short of provoking a declaration of war, and an army under Lord Grey de Wilton joined the army of the Lords of the Congregation in the siege of Leith. After this show of force Elizabeth sent William Cecil to Scotland to try to end the dispute by negotiation. The Tumult of Amboise (March 1560) foreshadowed the coming civil war in France, and sapped the French will and capacity to continue the struggle in Scotland. Discussions for peace had opened even before the capitulation of Leith, and the treaty was signed in July.

Elizabeth was unsuccessful in her demands for the restoration of Calais and a substantial indemnity for the expenses of the English intervention, but the treaty satisfied her real interests. The French were to leave the country and destroy their fortifications at Leith, Dunbar, and Eyemouth; England and France were to agree to a policy of non-intervention in Scotland, where government was to be carried on by a committee of 12, seven nominated by Mary Queen of Scots, five by the Scottish lords; and Mary and her husband, Francis II of France, by ceasing to wear the arms of England and Ireland, would surrender Mary's claim to the English throne.

For the first time an English army had been welcomed in Scotland and had left it in peace, and the two countries would henceforth be bound by a common interest in the survival of Protestantism. Now that she had gained her immediate ends Elizabeth refused to pay pensions to the Scottish lords for being of the same mind as herself. Nor would she marry the Earl of Arran, whose claim to the Scottish throne would have involved her in an embarrassing diplomatic tangle.

J. B. Black, *The Reign of Elizabeth* (Oxford, 1936).
G. Donaldson, *Scotland. James V to James VII* (Edinburgh and London, 1965).   MMR

EDISON, THOMAS ALVA (1847–1931), US inventor. He patented 1100 inventions, many of these during his most productive years (1876–84), which revolutionized man's way of life. By the age of 23 he was the proprietor of his own business, which effectively was the first industrial research organization. Edison improved the telephone, developed a few years earlier by A. G. Bell, and made it practicable. His most original invention was the gramophone (phonograph), in 1877, and probably his most significant the incandescent electric lamp, which he perfected in 1879. Edison developed an electric generating system to make the electric light practical and constructed the first central power station in 1881. A decade later he made the first commercial motion pictures and later worked effectively in other fields.

EDMUND (841–70), King of East Anglia (*reg.* 856–70), was defeated and killed by the Danes. He was the last native East Anglian king and was soon regarded as a saint and martyr. His cult at Bury St Edmunds became one of the most popular in England.

EDO, the pre-1868 name of Tokyo, prosperous village which, by 1457, had become a minor castle town. It experienced a meteoric development after 1590, when Ieyasu made it his headquarters. As the seat of government during the Tokugawa or Edo period (1603–1868), it expanded to become perhaps the most populous city in the world in the 18th cent., with an estimated 1 million inhabitants.

EDOM, Semitic kingdom, south-west of the Dead Sea, established *c.* 1200 BC. Despite periodic conquest by Judah it maintained its prosperity until *c.* 800 BC. It was a vigorous community, engaged in agriculture, mining, metallurgy, pottery, commerce, and building.

EDUCATION ACTS (1646, 1696) in Scotland, legislative measures passed by the Scottish parliament to improve parochial education. The 1646 act provided for the founding of a school and the appointment of a schoolmaster in every Scottish parish, the heritors being responsible for providing a school-house and for raising a tax to maintain the buildings and pay the master's stipend. The 1696 *Act for settling schools* confirmed and reinforced the existing legislation after the disorders of the Civil War and Restoration period.

EDUCATION ACTS (1870–1902) in England, legislation in which the community assumed responsibility for providing elementary and secondary education. Forster's Education Act (1870) was the greatest landmark in the history of English education. Progress had been slow since the first government grant to church and chapel schools (1833), little being taught beyond the 'three Rs'. Robert Lowe's system of paying teachers by pupils' examination results had a drearily mechanical effect in the 1860s. The demand for a national system grew rapidly, England being far behind other industrial countries. Better education would mean better workers and better soldiers. The North had beaten the South in the American Civil War (1861–5), the Prussians defeated the Austrian empire (1866). The Second Reform Act (1867), giving the vote to workmen in towns, made their schooling an urgent problem.

W. E. Forster (1818–86), Quaker vice-president of the privy council's committee for education in Gladstone's ministry (1868–74), carried the far-reaching measure aimed at ending the rivalry between Church and Chapel which had handicapped education by a compromise, creating enough schools open to state inspection but allowing religious freedom. Denominational schools were left untouched and their grants increased in areas where they were working well. Elsewhere schools for children under 13 were to be built by locally elected school boards empowered to levy rates and provide teachers. The Cowper–Temple Clause made religious instruction in the board schools 'undenominational'.

After this decisive step Sandon's (1876) and Mundella's (1880) Acts made school compulsory for children under 10 and it was made free in 1891. England still lagged behind Germany and industrial competitors in the quality of its secondary education, which was being developed partly by county councils and boroughs under the Technical Instruction Act and partly by the school boards under the Elementary Education Act.

In 1902 the Conservative prime minister, Balfour, carried the Education Act which scrapped the school boards and simplified the complicated administrative muddle by setting up local education authorities, which were committees of the county councils and county borough (large town) councils. The new LEAs controlled not only the old board schools, but also the voluntary schools, whose managers, in return for providing the buildings, were to retain the right of appointing teachers, while the current expenses of these schools were met by the local rates. Public money was thus first made available to ensure minimum standards of payment for teachers and of education for all children. Balfour's act, supervised by a distinguished civil servant, Sir Robert Morant, led to the building of large numbers of grammar schools by LEAs and accelerated the expansion of secondary education. It also gave new life to the older endowed grammar schools by enabling them to be aided from the rates, though it disappointed nonconformists in 'single school areas', who had hoped for an end to the church school monopoly. Balfour and Morant resourcefully fought this opposition, centred in Wales under Lloyd George and Dr John Clifford's 'revolt', and accomplished for English secondary education what Forster had achieved for elementary schools.

H. C. Barnard, *A Short History of English Education 1760–1944* (London, 1947).

S. J. Curtis and M. E. A. Boultwood, *Introductory History of English Education since 1800* (London, 1960).   JRA

EDUCATION ACT (1918) in Britain, legislative measure which was mainly the work of H. A. L. Fisher, Lloyd George's president of the board of education. It was part of a series of measures designed to repair the damage caused to education by the First World War—the premature employment of children in 'war work', the shortage of teachers, and a general shortage of facilities. The act's main provisions were: the universal raising of the school-leaving age to 14 (local authorities being permitted to raise it to 15); the establishment of 'continuation schools' for school-leavers of 14–16, with a compulsory attendance of one day a week; abolition of all fees in public elementary schools; and that the board of education would subsidize local education authorities by at least 50 per cent. Moreover, Fisher provided for increased and standardized teachers' salaries with pensions, and set up the University Grants Committee to subsidize university education.

Many of these provisions were attacked in the Geddes economy proposals of 1922. The 'continuation schools' were nearly all scrapped and teachers' salary increases were cut. However, Fisher's Act had decisive consequences—more children in schools, increased literacy, and a quantitative leap in spending on education. But the extension of the state's responsibilities made spending on public education more subject to the vagaries of public finance. This resulted in the failure to raise the school-leaving age to 15, which in turn affected the proposal in 1926 to provide three years' secondary education for all—hence the 'break at eleven' between primary and secondary school. In general, the act provided more efficient mass education without lessening educational inequality.   RH

EDUCATION ACT (1944) in Britain, legislative measure which was the first major piece of social reconstruction to meet the conditions which would follow the Second World War. It was the work of R. A. Butler, minister of education.

The principles of the act were set out in a 1943 White Paper, *Educational Reconstruction*: first, it was 'as important to achieve diversity as . . . to ensure equality of educational opportunity'; second, education should be carried out in discrete stages; and third, all children should enjoy secondary education 'of equal standing', though not of the same type. The act therefore prescribed the raising of the school-leaving age to 15 (achieved in 1947) and then to 16 (projected in 1970, but not achieved); free secondary education for all children at local authority schools with government subsidy; three separate types of secondary school—grammar, technical, and modern, with an examination at 11 years to determine where each child should go. There was one further important provision, introduced after long debate on the role of religion in schools: all schools for all ages subsidized by the state were forced to begin the day with some form of collective undenominational worship.

EDUCATION COMMISSION (1858–61) in England, set up under the Duke of Newcastle to enquire into the state of popular education. It found that one child in 20 was attending a school of guaranteed efficiency, rejected free, compulsory education and advocated the system of payment of teachers by the examination results of their scholars. Its findings paved the way for the Education Act of 1870 introduced by W. E. Forster.

EDUCATION, HIGHER, IN AUSTRALIA. From the mid-19th cent. until the First World War Australian institutions of higher education were mainly reflections of British university practice. Scottish academic influence was strong in the first two Australian universities, Sydney (1850) and Melbourne (1853), and in Adelaide (1874), though the traditions of Oxford, Cambridge, and Trinity College Dublin were followed by some early professors and copied in affiliated residential colleges. In the remaining pre-war universities the 'modern' or civic, 'red-brick' English universities' influence became increasingly evident. It was not, however, until after the Second World War that the Australian pattern changed appreciably, with the entry of the government into an educational field previously left to the states. Not until the 1960s, moreover, did this expansion extend to institutes of technology or 'colleges of advanced education'.

All the pre-Second World War universities were primarily undergraduate, teaching bodies. Most universities had residential colleges on the campus, usually denominationally financed and controlled. Direct Commonwealth finance was negligible. It was given to state universities during the Second World War, primarily for scientific training and for other aids to the national war effort.

The action of the Labor government in securing the passage through the Commonwealth parliament (1946) of legislation establishing the Australian National University for post-graduate research and study at Canberra broke new ground in Australian higher education. The annual running cost to the Commonwealth amounted to approximately $\frac{1}{10}$th of the total income of all the state universities for both undergraduate and graduate work but the act was received with mixed feelings in existing universities. Dissatisfaction at the higher salaries and better conditions at the ANU strengthened fears that badly needed funds for research would be denied to existing state institutions. These feelings, gradually lessened by useful co-ordinating practices adopted by some ANU research schools, largely disappeared when the Menzies government brought the Commonwealth more actively into the field after the Keith Murray *Report of the Committee on Australian Universities* (Canberra, 1957)—a landmark in the history of Australian higher education.

The following decade saw marked progress in uniformly higher salaries, improved research, and other equipment including libraries, accelerated building programmes, and increased graduate and undergraduate scholarships. All universities became increasingly concerned with honours and graduate students; enrolments for higher degrees rose from 1120 in 1956 to 8124 in 1967.

In the later 1960s there was some academic expression of concern that increase in bureaucratic and treasury influence, exercised through the Commonwealth Universities' Commission, threatened the traditional independence which Australian universities had largely inherited from British, including Scottish, academic practice. Significant post-war progress was nevertheless made in all branches of higher education.

During 1946–67 ten new state universities and university colleges were established, making 17 in all: seven in NSW, three in Vic., two in Qld, two in SA, one in each of WA and Tas. and one in Papua–New Guinea. Two additional metropolitan universities were also foreshadowed for the first half of the 1970s, in Qld. and WA.

Student numbers at all universities rose from 4200 in 1914 to 12,000 in 1948 and 107,000 (approx. 68,000 full time) in 1969—estimated to increase to 127,000 by 1972. Some 40,000 students were enrolled in 1969 at colleges of advanced education (1972 est. 70,000). There were 595 graduate and 3700 undergraduate enrolments at the ANU in 1969 and 5429 overseas students (predominantly Asians) at all Australian universities in 1968.

D. S. Macmillan, *Australian Universities* (Sydney, 1968). FA

EDUCATION, HIGHER, IN BRITAIN. University education began in England in the 12th cent. with the movement to Oxford of scholars from the continent. Gradually, there grew up colleges, of which University (1249), Balliol (1263), Merton (1264), and Exeter (1314) were among the first. By the 13th cent. Cambridge was developing similarly, its earliest foundation being Peterhouse (1284) and its greatest medieval college being King's (1441).

While Oxford and Cambridge remained for centuries the only English universities, four were established in Scotland: St Andrews (1411), Glasgow (1451), Aberdeen (1494), and Edinburgh (1583). In both countries university education flourished under the cultural influence of the Renaissance. In Scotland this persisted into the 18th cent., especially in philosophy and medicine.

Oxford and Cambridge, however, fell victims to the torpor of the 18th cent. The academic fortunes of both were restored in the 19th cent. at a time when the Industrial Revolution and the growth of professional classes dictated new requirements in education. In consequence of this, London University (1836) grew up as an institution recognizing the claims of all classes and creeds, and of both sexes. Students were offered a wide range of faculties and external examination became possible. Other institutions, principally in the commercial north, followed and advanced to university status in the two decades before 1914, eg, Birmingham (1900), Liverpool (1903), Leeds (1904), Manchester (1904), and Sheffield (1905). It was a characteristic which spread elsewhere in the country during the 20th cent., eg, Reading (1926), Nottingham (1948). The 1960s saw a spectacular growth of universities in England, 16 receiving their charter, including Sussex (1961), Keele (1962), Lancaster (1964), and Warwick (1965). Scotland, whose ancient universities had met the nation's needs for centuries, shared in the expansion, four new ones being founded, two of them in existing university cities—Strathclyde in Glasgow (1964) and Heriot-Watt in Edinburgh (1966).

University education in Ireland was primarily centred on the Queen's University of Belfast (1908) and Ulster (1965) in Northern Ireland, and on the University of Dublin, Trinity College (1591), and the National University of Ireland (Dublin) (1908) in the Republic. In Wales collegiate institutions in different parts of the province were incorporated in the University of Wales (1893) while St David's, Lampeter (1827), gave its own degrees.

The phrase 'higher education' is a contemporary usage. Until the 19th cent. the universities were its sole repository. Thereafter there grew up various institutions for students seeking a vocational training for a wide range of occupations for which a degree was not necessarily a requisite. By the mid-20th cent. many entrants into occupations as varied as estate-management and engineering were acquiring degrees in a wide variety of ways. The universities themselves widened their courses and there existed, by 1970, several different methods of graduating. The Colleges of Education, formerly teachers' training colleges, awarded, through their

local university, a degree to a proportion of their students; polytechnics—of which the first four were established in 1969—grew out of technical colleges and undertook degree work; the council for national academic awards assumed, in 1964, the power to give degrees while, in 1970, the Open University set out to undertake undergraduate teaching through the use of television and radio.

By 1970 the extent of Britain's student population, following full-time or 'sandwich' courses in higher education, posed new issues of both a social and economic nature.

W. R. Niblett, *Higher Education: demand and response* (London, 1969).

Sir Sidney Caine, *British Universities: purpose and prospect* (London, 1969). GMDH

EDUCATION, HIGHER, IN FRANCE. As French education in the 18th cent. lay primarily in the hands of the Church, the anti-Church measures taken by Revolutionary governments after 1789 resulted in the closing down of almost all educational establishments, including universities. The need for the state to take over the task of educational provision was recognized, and national schemes of education were put forward by such men as Talleyrand and Condorcet. Despite coherent plans, little was in fact achieved during the Revolution, except in the field of higher education. Here the need for qualified personnel was recognized as immediate. In some cases *ancien régime* institutions were preserved, eg, the Collège de France (founded in 1530 by Francis I); in others, old institutions were combined and given a new sense of purpose, eg, the École Polytechnique, which replaced two previously existing engineering schools; and, finally, many new *Grandes Écoles* were opened to provide the doctors, teachers, officers, engineers, and other experts required by the new regime. Some of the institutions only survived a few months, but more were created during the 19th cent.

It was Napoleon who created a unified system of state education, but the system he created was to serve his personal form of centralized government rather than the well-being of the 'peuple'. In 1806 the Université Impériale, later to become the Université de France, was founded as the body charged 'exclusively' with education in France. In 1808 its hierarchical organization was specified: the country was divided up into *académies*, each under a *recteur*. The whole was supervised by a *Grand Maître*, helped by a council. Higher education was to be dispensed not only by the *Grandes Écoles*, but by faculties, essentially those of law, medicine, letters, and science. The faculties were independent of each other and their task was to prepare students for the degrees the state alone was permitted to grant. The *baccalauréat* examination, also established in 1806, helped to guarantee the academic standards of pupils leaving the *lycées* (set up in 1802).

The highly organized structure of the Université remained more or less unchanged until the last quarter of the century. In 1875 the right to open an institute of higher education was granted to any Frenchman over the age of 25. This law, primarily beneficial to the Catholic Church, was however much circumscribed when, in 1880, the state reaffirmed that it alone had the right to grant degrees. During the period 1885–93 the individual faculties were given a better-defined constitution, financial powers, legal status, and some measure of corporative organization. These moves led in 1896, by the combination of faculties, to the creation of 15 universities, one in each *académie*. The faculty remained, however, the basic element within the university.

The 20th cent. witnessed the foundation of new institutions (both new universities and specialized research institutes), the introduction of new disciplines, and the restructuring of courses; for instance, the creation of the *année propédeutique* (preparatory year) in 1948. However, despite the problems caused by the *explosion scolaire* the distinctive features of French higher education—the highly centralized system and the existence, side by side, of *Grandes Écoles* and universities—remains unchanged.

H. C. Barnard, *Education and the French Revolution* (Cambridge, 1969).

Antoine Prost, *L' Enseignement in France 1800–1967* (Paris, 1968).   MRH

EDUCATION, HIGHER, IN GERMANY. At the beginning of the 18th cent. German universities were in a state of decadence. Teaching methods and content had become stultified, student discipline was lax and rioting frequent. General standards were low and there was considerable overlap in the teaching of schools and universities.

In Prussia, in particular, a climate was gradually created in which reform became possible. Prussian rulers not only set out to curb the influence of the Church in the sphere of education, but saw the value of universities which could produce civil servants of high calibre. After many attempts to strengthen matriculation requirements, a turning point was reached with the establishment in 1787 of the *Oberschulkollegium*, a permanent central administrative body to supervise university entrance. The *Abiturientenexamen* was introduced in 1788.

German defeats in the Napoleonic wars stimulated the search for a national identity. As Friedrich Wilhelm III expressed it, there was a feeling that 'the State must replace in intellectual strength what it has lost in physical'. Thus the establishment of a new university at Berlin (1810) was more than an additional foundation, for it was based on a complete rethinking of a university's role and organization. The man primarily responsible for the pioneering ideas was Wilhelm von Humboldt, and to him are attributed many of those fundamental characteristics which have distinguished German universities: the non-involvement of the university in vocational training, the dual task of professors to teach and to conduct research, the freedom of professors to choose what they taught, and the freedom of students to study for as long as and where they pleased. The pursuit of learning for its own sake led to a high degree of scholarship being attained in the 19th cent., though, as a result, the academic world became unduly sheltered from political involvement.

The detachment of the universities from vocational aims along with their immersion in Classical culture stimulated the establishment of a parallel, but more practically oriented, educational system. The *Realschule* developed alongside the Classical *Gymnasium* and, at university level, *Technische Hochschulen* were set up and provided facilities for advanced scientific studies.

The whole scope of higher education continued to expand at the beginning of the 20th cent. When numerical increases seemed likely to destroy university efficiency, plans for reform were aired. However, the advent of Nazi government not only put an end to both expansion and progressive trends, but also gave rise to the denigration of higher studies as a worth-while pursuit.

After the war, Germany returned to a pre-Nazi pattern of education. But pre-1930 institutions often proved inadequate to cope with post-war conditions, and the rapid numerical increase in the student body submitted the traditional universities to destructive pressures. Reform was seen as necessary, but was hard to effect. The difficulties of introducing reform in a country where education was the concern of the individual *Land* began to be overcome by the establishment of various national bodies which set out to co-ordinate policy and planning. These included the *Konferenz der Kultusminister* (1948), the *Westdeutsche Rektorenkonferenz* (1949), and the *Wissenschaftsrat* (1957). Some new universities have been founded, but modernization has not come quickly in a country where traditions are jealously guarded.

Friedrich Paulsen, *Geschichte des gelehrten Unterrichts auf den deutschen Schulen und Universitäten*, 2 vols (Berlin, 1965).

H. Schelsky, *Einsamkeit und Freiheit. Idee und Gestalt der deutschen Universität und ihrer Reformen* (Reinbek bei Hamburg, 1963).   MRH

EDUCATION LEAGUE in Britain, pressure group centred in Birmingham to champion the nonconformists against the retention of the church schools by Forster's Education Act (1870). Its organization of grass-roots opinion attracted Joseph Chamberlain, who, with Schnadhorst, adapted its methods in forming the National Liberal Federation (1877), the origin of the modern party machine.

EDWARD I (1239–1307), King of England (*reg.* 1272–1307), son of Henry III. Edward was a warrior and an efficient ruler: intelligent, brave, and devout, but also deceitful, cruel, and arrogant. It was in the troublous times of his father's reign that he first emerged as a politically important figure. For a time he was a follower of De Montfort, but became reconciled with his father and emerged as a royalist leader. Though captured at Lewes (1264), he was the victor of Evesham (1265), which ensured victory for the king. From 1265 Edward was the effective ruler of the country, succeeding to the throne in 1272. Two features distinguished Edward's rule of England—his legal reforms and his use of parliament as an instrument of government. Under Edward, English law was intelligently reviewed. He used parliament chiefly to grant him money, and he set the pattern of future parliaments. But he was not the deliberate creator of parliament and his arbitrary rule in the French war (1294–8) led to a crisis. He was compelled to confirm the charters and admit the principle of consent to taxation in 1297, but later gained papal release from his promises. Probably it is as a great warrior that Edward would wish to be remembered. In two campaigns against Llewelyn, Prince of Wales, in 1277 and 1282, he conquered Wales. Massive castles like Conway, Caernarvon, and Beaumaris were built to keep the Welsh in subjection.

Edward failed in Scotland. Invited by the Scots to arbitrate in a disputed succession, he chose John Balliol as king (1292) and obtained recognition as overlord of Scotland. His treatment of Balliol led the Scots to rebel. In 1296 Edward superficially conquered Scotland, but again the Scots rose. At Falkirk in 1298 Edward quelled them but the emergence of Robert Bruce meant that Edward had lost his chance to conquer Scotland. He died on yet another Scottish campaign in 1307.   DBe

EDWARD II (1284–1327), King of England (*reg.* 1307–27), eldest surviving son of Edward I. He was born at Caernarvon and created the first English Prince of Wales (1301). His reign was troubled and tragic. His cousin, the powerful Thomas, Earl of Lancaster, the chief of the Lords Ordainers, led an armed rising which culminated in the murder of Edward's friend, Piers Gaveston, in 1312. Thomas was later defeated at Boroughbridge, and executed (1322). In 1314 the defeat at Bannockburn ended English hopes of conquering Scotland and laid northern England open to invasion and devastation for years after. Edward's domestic life was equally troubled. His wife, Isabella, resented the influence of the Despensers over Edward and a series of personal humiliations at their hands led her, while in France (1325–6), to take Roger Mortimer as her lover and to lead a group of exiles in an invasion of England (Jan. 1327) in favour of their son Edward III. Edward was imprisoned at Berkeley Castle and murdered (?1327). He inherited a number of major problems from his father but failures of his reign were due to his own lack of sense and ability.

EDWARD III (1312–77), King of England (*reg.* 1327–77), son of Edward II and Isabella of France. He was placed on the throne after his father's deposition by his mother and her lover, Roger Mortimer, who, to consolidate their position, arranged his marriage to Philippa, daughter of the Count of Hainault. The birth of their first child, Edward of Woodstock, the Black Prince, in 1330, encouraged the young king to overthrow Mortimer and assume personal power (Oct. 1330). Edward was physically impressive, a considerable knight and warrior, and of much more ability than his father.

The greater part of his reign was successful. The humiliation of Bannockburn was avenged by the victories of Haildon Hill (1333) and Neville's Cross (1346), where David II of Scotland was captured. The war with France, begun in 1337, brought greater triumphs to English arms than ever before at Sluys (1340), Crécy (1346), Calais (1346-7), and Poitiers (1356), where the capture of the French king led to the treaty of Brétigny (1360), the climax of Edward's reign, by which he gained absolute sovereignty over Aquitaine, Calais, and Ponthieu. Thereafter his fortunes declined and he himself deteriorated physically and mentally. The victories over the Scots and French proved more dazzling than conclusive and new military ventures went awry. Queen Philippa died in 1369 and Edward sank into an early senility, comforted by a sordid relationship with the mercenary Alice Perrers. Internally England was entering a period of unrest, aggravated by the premature death (July 1376) of the Black Prince and the prospect of a child, Richard of Bordeaux, succeeding to the throne, which he did as Richard II.

EDWARD IV (1442-83), King of England (*reg.* 1461-83), eldest son of Richard, Duke of York. Upon his father's death in 1460, Edward succeeded him as Yorkist claimant to the throne. His reign began in the following year, after London had opened its gates to him and he had defeated the Lancastrians at Towton. In 1470, having quarrelled with his most powerful ally, Warwick 'the Kingmaker', Edward had briefly to flee the country, but upon his return in 1471 he finally broke the power of Warwick and the Lancastrians at Barnet and Tewkesbury. The rest of Edward's reign was mostly peaceable, and witnessed the growing influence and prosperity of the commercial middle class. The king himself engaged with great profit in the wool trade, and he also patronized Caxton, the country's first printer. Edward could act with energy and shrewdness in a crisis, but was otherwise indolent. He angered Warwick by impulsively and secretly marrying Elizabeth Woodville, a young Lancastrian widow—a step which ultimately secured the destruction of his sons.

EDWARD V (1470-?1483), King of England (*reg.* April-June 1483), elder son of Edward IV. His uncle, Richard, Duke of Gloucester, lodged Edward and his younger brother Richard in the Tower of London and then usurped the throne, alleging that they were illegitimate. The two princes were not seen alive after Oct. 1483. Two skeletons discovered under a staircase in the Tower in 1674 and re-examined in 1933 were of boys of their age and bore signs of strangulation.

EDWARD VI (1537-53), King of England (*reg.* 1547-53), only legitimate son of Henry VIII, his mother, Jane Seymour, dying shortly after his birth. His short and disorderly reign saw the adoption of Protestantism in England.

Edward's tutors were of Protestant sympathy and they saw to it that besides the academic and courtly accomplishments of the age, he received a thorough grounding in theology. He took to his studies with remarkable precocity and came to the throne with the intellectual equipment of a Protestant zealot.

In his will Henry VIII decreed that Edward should succeed in preference to either of his two elder sisters. He also nominated a council to govern during Edward's minority, but effective power passed to Edward's uncle, the Duke of Somerset, who established himself as Protector. Edward was too young to have any personal influence on the events of his reign, but he welcomed the outriders of continental Protestantism who invaded the country, and his own convictions were reflected in measures which took England further away from Rome. The pace of these doctrinal and administrative changes quickened when Northumberland replaced Somerset as regent, and it is difficult to say how far the religious revolution might have gone if Edward had not been tubercular. As he neared death, he was easily persuaded by Northumberland to agree to the attempt to keep Mary from the throne, because he was genuinely distressed at the prospect of a Catholic reaction.

Edward did not marry. Plans were made to betroth him to the infant Mary Queen of Scots (1542-7), but these collapsed when Henry and Somerset tried to execute them by force. He was later (1551) pledged to a daughter of Henry II of France, although it is hard to imagine him in the arms of a Catholic bride.

His *Journal*, in which he recorded events both great and small, shows an acute grasp of political and economic issues, and there is no doubt of his intelligence. His business was to be a king, and he conscientiously versed himself in his responsibilities. These jottings also show him to have been bigoted, priggish, and strangely devoid of human sympathy, whether for fallen politicians or misguided rebels. Nor did he have any understanding of people whose religious opinions differed from his own. At the same time, they are the comments of a child who was deliberately sheltered by self-interested ministers from contact with people and events. Their fault is immaturity and inexperience.

The several grammar-schools founded in Edward's name have given him some fame as a patron of learning. These schools were simply established from that small part of the charitable and educational endowments of guilds and chantries that was not misappropriated for private use.

H. W. Chapman, *The Last Tudor King* (London, 1958).
W. K. Jordan, *Edward VI: the young king* (London, 1968).
MMR

EDWARD VII (1841-1910), King of Britain (*reg.* 1901-10), eldest son and second child of Queen Victoria. He was educated by tutors, following a rigorous timetable devised for the future ruler by the Prince Consort. In 1863 he married Princess Alexandra (1844-1925), daughter of King Christian IX of Denmark. He soon became the leader of a rich, sophisticated society and unrivalled arbiter of fashion, his promiscuity and fondness for gambling being common knowledge. He had great charm, but his self-indulgence brought frequent complaints from the queen about his frivolity and had far-reaching effects on social life. Edward was a vital witness for the prosecution in the Tranby Croft Case (1891), in which Sir William Gordon-Cumming was accused of cheating at cards, though to some observers it looked as though the monarchy was on trial. In many ways 'Bertie' wore down conventions he disliked, weakening strict Sunday observance by giving Sunday dinner parties at Marlborough House, and encouraging the 'weekend'. Whether yacht racing at Cowes, horse racing at Ascot, or deer stalking in Scotland, his activities gave vicarious enjoyment to many, but his mother, alarmed by his indiscretions, refused to give him experience of a sovereign's duties. It was not until 1892 that he was allowed to see copies of the prime minister's reports on cabinet meetings. Although a novice in the practice of monarchy when he became king, he was balanced by his forcefulness, boyish zest, a sense of occasion, and tact. His tastes were thoroughly English, despite his slight German accent, and he had some feeling for the instincts of his subjects.

As king he determined to enjoy power and influence while ensuring that his successor (George V) received the sympathetic and understanding training he had been denied. He relished travel and ceremonies. His usual programme consisted of Biarritz in the spring, seeing French ministers, more royal visits and calls in May, based on his yacht in the Mediterranean, then an August cure at Marienbad Spa, meeting more royalty or statesmen en route. His influence on British foreign policy has been greatly exaggerated, especially by German writers, who saw his visits to Paris and contact with the Russians, together with his difficult relations with the Kaiser, as a part of a deliberate policy to encircle Germany with the Entente powers.

His frequent absences abroad prevented regular meetings with his ministers. The personal influence and power of the monarchy in the constitution declined during his reign, though he added the idea of impartiality between parties to the Victorian conception of constitutional monarchy, and he still played an important part in the House of Lords crisis (1909–11). He informed the prime minister, Asquith, that he would not consent to the creation of new peers to pass the Parliament Bill until after a second general election in 1910, but he died before it was held. The nation was stunned by the death of a popular king who gave his name to the decade.

Sir Sidney Lee, *King Edward VII* (London, 1925–7).
Sir Philip Magnus, *Edward VII* (London, 1964).   JRA

EDWARD VIII (1894–19), King of Britain (*reg.* 1936), eldest son of George V, who became king in Jan. 1936. As Prince of Wales, following his investiture in 1911, he had been immensely popular, having served in the army during the First World War, made extensive tours of the British empire and the US, and shown an interest in social questions, particularly the condition of the unemployed. For some years he had been attached to Mrs Wallis Simpson, of Baltimore, US. However, through voluntary press censorship this remained unknown to the mass of the British people. In Oct. 1936 Mrs Simpson divorced her husband. This provoked a crisis between the king, who considered his intention to marry her as a private matter, and his ministers, who foresaw public disapproval of a divorcée as queen. Baldwin, the prime minister, tried repeatedly to persuade the king to abandon Mrs Simpson, and reported to him the Dominions' rejection of the king's proposal for a morganatic marriage. At the beginning of Dec. the king's problem had become a matter of public knowledge. Opinion in all classes was sharply divided, but was mostly critical of the king. Against the weight of the government and the major parties, the churches, and the Dominions, the king could only claim ill-assorted political support, which included that of Churchill, Beaverbrook and Rothermere. On 10 Dec. the king abdicated. The crisis was dissipated by a speech by Baldwin and a dignified broadcast from Edward, created Duke of Windsor by his brother, the new king, George VI. Apart from serving during the Second World War as governor of the Bahamas, the Duke lived privately.

EDWARD THE CONFESSOR (*reg.* 1042–66), King of England, son of Aethelred II by Emma of Normandy. Edward spent his early life in exile in Normandy. When he succeeded to the throne of England he married the daughter of Godwin, Earl of Wessex. The extent to which Edward sought to build up a French party in England has been exaggerated. He abandoned the army tax (heregeld) and reduced the size of the fleet and this may have weakened Anglo-Saxon military strength in 1066. In his later years he built Westminster Abbey and gained a reputation for chastity and piety. Though William, Duke of Normandy, his cousin, visited him in 1051, it is not certain that he ever promised William the throne of England. On his deathbed he was said to have nominated Harold, son of Godwin, as his heir. He was canonized in 1161.

EDWARD THE MARTYR (*reg.* 975–8), King of England, son of Edgar, whose reign witnessed a reaction against the monastic reform movement of the reign of Edgar. Edward was murdered and was later venerated as a saint.

EDWARD THE ELDER (*reg.* 899–924), King of Wessex and son of King Alfred. He maintained a determined offensive against the Vikings in eastern and midland England by the building of *burh*s (forts) and the systematic capture of Danish army bases. In 920 his overlordship was acknowledged by the Danes and by the rulers of north Britain.

EDWARD OF WOODSTOCK, THE BLACK PRINCE (1330–1376), eldest son of King Edward III of England. He was a popular figure and a considerable general, who led a wing of the English army at Crécy (1346), captured the French king at Poitiers (1356), and won the battle of Najera (1367)

in Castile. His reputation was tarnished by the merciless sack of Limoges in 1370. His son became Richard II.

EDWARD PRINCE OF WALES (1453–71), only child of King Henry VI of England and Margaret of Anjou. His birth removed Richard of York's chance of inheriting the Crown and thereby contributed to the outbreak of the Wars of the Roses. The Yorkists subsequently claimed that Edward was the son of Margaret by an English noble. Edward died mysteriously after the defeat of the Lancastrians at Tewkesbury.

EDWARDES, SIR HERBERT (1819–68), English soldier and administrator on the north-west frontier of India. He fought in both Sikh wars and later held important appointments at Hazara and Peshawar. His treaty with Dost Muhammad of Afghanistan in 1855 secured Afghan neutrality during the Indian Mutiny.

EDWARDS, JONATHAN (1703–58), American philosopher and theologian, whose writings fused a stern Calvinism with evangelical revivalism and made a major impact on American religious thought. He was a Presbyterian minister in New York and a tutor at Yale University before joining his grandfather in the Congregational church of Northampton, MA (1725). He preached that man could be saved only if he experienced spiritual uplift from God. His sermons led directly to the Northampton revival (1734–5) and indirectly to the Great Awakening (1740–2). Edwards, a strict Calvinist, argued that Arminianism would have a degenerate effect on Congregationalism and believed that church membership should be open only to those who had had a religious experience. This brought him into conflict with his congregation and he was dismissed (1750). He then became a minister and an Indian missionary at Stockbridge, CT (1751–7). He was appointed (1757) president of the College of New Jersey (Princeton).

EDWIN (583–633), King of Northumbria (*reg.* 617–633), first northern ruler to establish himself as overlord (or *bretwalda*) of all the English kingdoms, except Kent, and the first Christian ruler of the north. His death in battle at the hands of the Welsh caused a temporary collapse of Christianity in Northumbria.

EFATE, in the New Hebrides, island discovered by Cook (1774) which drew casual sandalwooders (1842) and early Samoan teachers (1845). In the 1860s hundreds of Efatese died of measles or malaria, and others migrated to Fiji or Queensland. When the first resident Presbyterian missionary arrived (1865) the Efatese (mixed Polynesian, Melanesian, originally about 12,000) had almost disappeared. British settlers were later brought out, mainly by Higginson's French company, and in 1886 the French flag was briefly raised in defiance of the 1878 Anglo-French agreement. The French element finally concentrated at Vila, the eventual seat of government (1907).

EGBERT (*reg.* 802–39), King of Wessex, whose reign saw the end of the greatness of Mercia when Egbert won the battle of Ellendun (825) and received the submission of the Northumbrians (829).

EGEDE, HANS (1686–1758), Norwegian missionary, the 'apostle of Greenland'. He led a mission to the Eskimos of the west coast of Greenland (1721–36) and converted many. He also began a New Testament translation, and organized trade with Copenhagen.

EGER (German: *Erlau*), old Hungarian town some 110 kms north-east of Buda. The Ottoman Turks made an unsuccessful attack on Eger in 1552. It fell to them, however, in 1596 after a siege of three weeks, becoming thereafter the centre of an

Ottoman *beglerbeglik*. The Habsburg forces recovered control of Eger in 1687 during the long war of 1683–99.

EGGLESTON, SIR FREDERIC WILLIAM (1875–1954), Australian lawyer, politician, publicist, and social critic. Legal work with the first AIF led to his membership of the Australian delegation at the peace conference. In post-war Victorian politics (1920–7), Eggleston held various posts and was state attorney-general and assistant treasurer. After six years in private practice he became active in bodies concerned with pacific relations and international affairs. He was the first chairman of the Commonwealth Grants Commission (1933–40). In the Second World War he was Australian ambassador to China (1941–4), and the US (1944–6). Eggleston's varied teaching and consultative services (1946–1954) brought increasing respect for his intellectual approach to local and international politics.

EGMONT, LAMORAL, Count of (1522–68), Flemish nobleman who, with the Prince of Orange and Count Hoorn, led the first revolt in the Netherlands against Philip II's ecclesiastical reforms. He helped to form a league of the discontented nobility against Cardinal Granvelle, president of the council of state, under whom the reorganization of ecclesiastical provinces had taken place (1561). Egmont, Orange, and Hoorn sent a request to Philip II to abandon his Edict and contributed to Granvelle's recall (1564). On Philip's decision to implement the decisions of the Council of Trent in the Netherlands, Egmont went to Spain to dissuade the king from such action (1565). He remained loyal to the Spanish monarchy, wavering in his support of the League of Nobles in the face of the wave of iconoclasm (1566–7). However, 18 days after the Duke of Alva's arrival (9 Sept. 1567) in the Netherlands, Egmont and Hoorn were arrested as rebels, and on 5 June 1568 were executed.

EGMONT, JOHN PERCEVAL, 1st Earl of (Irish) (1683–1748), Whig philanthropist, politican, and author of a famous private diary recording political and religious events in George II's reign. He was a patron of John Wesley and George Whitfield.

EGMONT, JOHN PERCEVAL, 2nd Earl of (Irish) (1711–1770), British Whig politician and member of the opposition group surrounding Frederick, Prince of Wales. He was first lord of the admiralty (1763–6). Like his more eminent father, Egmont kept a political diary.

EGYPT, BRITISH OCCUPATION OF (1882). Following the 1875 Egyptian financial difficulties, British and French influence became predominant in the Egyptian government. In 1882 their influence was challenged by an army-controlled nationalist government and Britain decided to intervene, largely to safeguard the Suez Canal. Alexandria was bombarded (July) and the Egyptian army defeated at Tel-el-Kebir by Gen. Wolseley (13 Sept. 1882).

EGYPT, HELLENISTIC, kingdom established after Alexander the Great's death by his general, Ptolemy, and ruled by his descendants until the Roman annexation (30 BC). In the 3rd cent. BC Egypt offered attractive opportunities to Greeks, who flocked to the new cities of Alexandria and Ptolemais, and reclaimed land in the Fayûm. Being chiefly interested in exploiting Egypt's natural resources, the Ptolemies organized a complex system of economic regulation and taxation, run mainly by Greeks. The official language was Greek and the mercenary army was non-Egyptian. From *c.* 217 native dissatisfaction caused frequent rebellions, which resulted in concessions to them and improved the position of Egyptians, who were thereafter recruited to military and government service, while the Egyptian temples regained much of their pre-Ptolemaic power. Thus complete Greek control was comparatively short-lived, and Greek culture and institutions found few willing native converts.

EGYPT, ROMAN, annexed by Octavian (30 BC), who forbade senators to enter and put it under an equestrian prefect with equestrian assistants, otherwise, retaining the Ptolemaic bureaucracy. As one of the great granaries of the empire, it had in Alexandria, with its mixed population of Egyptians, Greeks, and Jews, the largest city in the eastern provinces and a centre of manufacture and trade. Christianity appeared from *c.* 200 and gradually became dominant; after the Council of Chalcedon (451) a Coptic-speaking monophysite church separated from the established orthodoxy. Diocletian (284–305) had split civil and military administration, but Justinian reunited them (538) under four governors of equal rank. Torn by faction, Egypt was eventually overrun by Persians (616) and Arabs (640).

EGYPTIAN COTTON. The introduction into Egypt early in the 19th cent. of new varieties of long-staple cotton, to be grown as a summer export crop on irrigated land, eventually revolutionized the Egyptian economy. Cotton became the principal Egyptian foreign exchange-earner and made Egyptian prosperity wholly dependent upon world cotton prices.

EGYPTIAN DYNASTIES. Manetho divided ancient Egyptian history into 30 royal dynasties and this division has been largely retained by historians, although the dynasties themselves can be grouped into distinct periods, and it seems that certain so-called dynasties must include various nobles ruling in different areas in Egypt. The Thinite period (*c.* 3100–2700 BC), dynasties I and II, brought the first unification of the country. The Old Kingdom (*c.* 2700–2200) comprised dynasty III (*c.* 2700–2620), when Djoser's pyramid was built; dynasty IV (*c.* 2620–2480), which saw the construction of the great pyramids of Giza; dynasty V (*c.* 2480–2340) (pyramids at Abusir and the first Pyramid Texts); and dynasty VI (*c.* 2340–2200), when there were signs of government disintegration. The First Intermediate Period, which followed the Old Kingdom, covered the VIIth and VIIIth dynasties, while the period of the IXth and Xth dynasties is known as the Herakleopolitan period. The Middle Kingdom (*c.* 2134–1786) was formed by the XIth dynasty (*c.* 2134–1991), which united the country once more, and the XIIth dynasty (1991–1786). The Second Intermediate Period (*c.* 1786–1575), which followed the Middle Kingdom, is an obscure and apparently disorderly time and includes the Hyksos Period. The New Kingdom, which comprises the rule of the XVIIIth (*c.* 1575–1309), XIXth (*c.* 1309–1194), and XXth dynasties (*c.* 1184–1087), is the great period of imperial conquest and impressive building and includes the Amarna period. The XXIst dynasty comprised two families, one ruling from Tanis, the other being the High Priests of Amen. A period of Libyan rule followed (*c.* 945–715) and makes up the XXIInd–XXIVth dynasties. The Ethiopian Period XXVth dynasty (*c.* 715–656) saw the conquest of Egypt by the Assyrians. During the Saite Period (XXVIth dynasty, *c.* 668–525) which followed, Egypt was reunited and there was an artistic renaissance. The country was under Persian rule for the period of the XXVIIth–XXXth dynasties (525–343) and a later chronologer added a XXXIst dynasty of three Persian kings (343–332) to Manetho's list. In 332, the conquest of Egypt by Alexander the Great ended Persian rule. There is still considerable controversy concerning Egyptian chronology, which depends upon inscriptions, certain documents, especially the Turin Canon, certain astronomical phenomena, and correspondence with events in western Asia which can be dated. In this way certain fixed points can be established and the regnal periods used for intermediate dates. In this dictionary the system followed by Sir Alan Gardiner (*Egypt of the Pharaohs*, 1961) has normally been adopted.

Cambridge Ancient History (revd. ed.), vol. 1 (Cambridge, 1920).　　　　　　　　　　　　　　　　JKG

EGYPTIAN EXPEDITION (1798), French expedition under Napoleon, which left Toulon (May 1798), defeated Mamluk rulers of Egypt (battle of the Pyramids, 21 July), and eventually surrendered to Anglo-Ottoman forces (July–Aug. 1801). After being defeated at Acre, Bonaparte returned to France (Aug. 1799). Because of the resulting European strategic interest in the area, the expedition became an important landmark in the history of the Middle East.

EGYPTIAN NATIONALISM, political attitude characterized by a belief in Egypt as the primary object of political loyalty. Until the 19th cent. there was no Egyptian nationalism. Since the Persian conquest Egypt had been governed by a series of rulers from outside; the Egyptian fellahin were excluded from political life. Although the ruling group remained Turkish under the Muhammad Ali dynasty, Egyptians were, for the first time, admitted to the army and to government service, and through education became exposed to Western ideas. The writer Al-Tahtawi first expressed an interest in pre-Islamic Egypt and a territorial patriotism. By the 1870s this feeling was widespread and, through a combination of financial and economic difficulties, became directed against foreign influence in government. A nationalist party was formed (1878) and the army mutiny of Arabi Pasha took on a nationalist colouring especially in the speeches and writings of Abdulla al-Nadim (1844–96), expressing hostility to foreigners, Turco-Circassian as well as European. Temporarily eclipsed or confined to salons by the British occupation, Egyptian nationalism regrouped itself in the 1890s around the Khedive Abbas Hilmi in his opposition to British control. Three political parties were founded (1907) in the political upsurge which followed the Dinshaway incident. Still nationalists were divided in their objectives. The supporters of Abbas Hilmi looked to the restoration of Khedivial authority; others hoped for a constitutional regime. Some, like Mustafa Kamil, stressed the reassertion of Ottoman links; others, including the followers of Muhammad Abduh, were preoccupied by Pan-Islamic interests. Nationalism was still a movement of the educated elite alone. After the First World War, however, Egyptian nationalism lost its Ottomanist elements and became a mass movement under the leadership of Sa'd Zaghlul and the Wafd Party. Independence was achieved (1922), established on a formal basis (1936) and British troops finally left (1955). After a long struggle the Muhammad Ali dynasty met defeat in 1952. Still the ultimate directions of Egyptian nationalism were unsettled and different elements stressed the relative importance of unity with the Sudan, other Arab countries, other Muslim countries and links with the Mediterranean world, as well as emphasis on the development of Egypt alone.

P. J. Vatikiotis, *The Modern History of Egypt* (London, 1969). MEY

EGYPTIAN RELIGION. Ancient Egyptians worshipped a vast number of gods, originally local deities, some of whom became regional or national gods, *eg*, Horus became the national god who was believed to be incarnate in the king. Some came to preside over certain crafts, *eg*, Ptah of Memphis became patron of artists. There were also great nature gods like Re, the sun-god. The earthly manifestations attributed to the gods were frequently animals, originally a wooden statue of the animal; later all animals of a species in which a god would reveal himself became sacred. Some animals, *eg*, bulls, were considered sacred in their own right. The wooden statue of the patron god was housed in a temple and other temples were provided for visiting deities. The Egyptians believed in an after-life similar to life on earth (providing the deceased was supplied with the necessary means of existence *eg*, food, by the living), and a soul which depended for its existence on the preservation of the body. This led to the custom of mummification. The ancient Egyptians appear to have had a sense of contact with their gods and to have believed that the gods cared for them, and after 1300 BC the idea of a god who would punish, but also forgive, emerged.

D W H—R

EGYPTIAN REVOLUTION (1952), political movement which replaced the government of the Muhammad Ali dynasty by that of a group of army officers who subsequently carried through important social and economic changes. After the Second World War Egyptian governments became increasingly incapable of solving the political, economic, or financial problems which confronted Egypt. The Wafd Party, which had previously represented a radical alternative with substantial popular support, was now regarded as corrupt and incompetent. Mass support passed to extremist parties like the Muslim Brotherhood and the Socialist Democratic (Young Egypt) Party, which precipitated a clash with British forces in the Canal Zone (Jan. 1952), the burning of Cairo (26 Jan.), and the breakdown of law and order. Government now depended on the army, within which was a group of so-called Free Officers, largely recruited from among those who had entered the army in the big expansion after 1936 and were hostile to the Faruq regime, partly because of the disasters of the 1948 Palestine War. These officers seized power (23 July 1952) under the leadership of Col. Gamal Abdul Nasser, although Gen. Muhammad Naguib, a senior officer, was chosen as figurehead. King Faruq was deposed and in June 1953 the dynasty abolished, Egypt becoming a republic with Naguib as president. He, however, was arrested in Nov. 1954 and replaced by Nasser, who became president in June 1956. The revolution began as a political movement designed to break the power of the Muhammad Ali family and its great landlord supporters (1959–61) and gradually sought to set up a system of rigid state-socialism as the only way to deal with Egyptian problems. Because of its challenge to the existing political, economic, and social order the Egyptian revolution had profound repercussions throughout the Middle East. MEY

EHELAPOLA (d. 1828), first adigar in the last years of the Kandyan kingdom in Ceylon. In 1814 he intrigued unsuccessfully with the British against the king, Sri Vikrama Rajasinha, and afterwards fled to Colombo. His family were cruelly put to death. In 1818 Ehelapola was suspected of supporting rebellion against British rule, and exiled to Mauritius.

EHRENBURG, ILLYA GRIGORIEVICH (1891–1967), Russian journalist and novelist. In 1908 he was imprisoned because of his activities in the Bolshevik Party and later lived in Paris. During the First World War he worked as a labourer and wrote articles for the Russian press. In 1917 he returned home and met Pasternak, Mayakovsky, and Mandelstam. Following his arrest on suspicion of his being a White agent, he went back to Paris. Although he lived in the West he remained sympathetic towards the Soviet regime, as is shown in *The Fall of Paris*, in which the decadent French bourgeois is shown in opposition to the vigorous French communist. During the Second World War he returned to the Soviet Union and played an important part in maintaining national morale. Afterwards he travelled in the West as a sort of cultural ambassador. After Stalin's death he published the work by which he is best known outside the Soviet Union, *The Thaw* (1954), in which he attacked some aspects of Stalinism. Towards the end of his life he seemed to lose the knack of pleasing his master. In 1963 Khruschev is said to have stigmatized him as 'a purveyor of the mouldy idea of absolute freedom'. His autobiography, *Men, Years, Life*, was published in England in 1966.

EHRLICH, PAUL (1854–1915), German bacteriologist, who was the founder of chemotherapy, by which chemical treatment of a disease was sought by scientific investigation. Previous chemical cures had been accidental. Ehrlich's most notable discoveries were the compounds trypan red and salvarsan, which are used in the treatment of trypanosomiasis and syphilis respectively. Despite the hopes then of chemical cures for all infectious diseases, the more common smaller bacteria remained resistant until Domagk's discoveries 25 years later.

EIGHTY YEARS WAR (1568–1648), name given by the Dutch to the long struggle of certain provinces of the Netherlands for independence from the Spanish Crown. Beginning with the bloody regime of the Duke of Alva (1568), which provoked a general revolt led by the native aristocracy, after the Perpetual Edict (1577) which reconciled the southern, predominantly Catholic, provinces to Spain, the war changed in character. It developed into an anti-Spanish religious–political struggle of the northern provinces led by Holland and Zeeland. Welded into the Union of Utrecht and inspired by Calvinism, the Dutch were periodically supported by the French and English governments.

The final boundary between the Spanish Netherlands and the United Provinces was decided by the military fortunes of first Parma, and later Spinola, on the one hand and Maurice, Prince of Orange, on the other. By the early 17th cent. the struggle had reached a stalemate, which gave rise to the Twelve Years Truce with Spain (1609). Renewed war was certain in 1621, but before then the Bohemian crisis initiated the bitter European struggle known as the Thirty Years War. Self-interest impelled the Dutch to support Frederick, Elector Palatine, nephew of Maurice, against the Habsburgs (1620). Only the intervention of Sweden and France on the Protestant side and Habsburg involvement in Germany saved the Dutch. Finally, by the peace of Munster (30 Jan. 1648) the war between Spain and the United Provinces was brought to an end, the Dutch gaining political independence and the economic advantage of the closure of the Scheldt river.

EIJKMAN, CHRISTIAAN (1858–1930), Dutch physician, who in 1896 demonstrated that disease could be caused by the absence from the diet of some essential components that need to be present only in trace quantities. Although Eijkman misinterpreted his results, later research, particularly that of Sir F. G. Hopkins (1861–1947), suggested the correct explanation and the missing trace components were then called vitamins. When the significance of his results was fully realized, Eijkman shared the 1929 Nobel Prize for medicine and physiology with Hopkins.

EIKON BASILIKE, or *The Portraiture of His Sacred Majesty in His Solitudes and Sufferings*, book venerating the memory of King Charles I of England which appeared in many editions and languages in 1649 and aroused widespread horror at the significance of the king's execution. The reputed author is Dr John Gauden (1605–62), Bp of Worcester.

EIKONOKLASTES, written by John Milton, and published in England, to counteract the impact of the *Eikon Basilike*. It failed, however, to destroy the growing cult of Charles I's martyrdom.

'EIN FESTE BURG' is described as the great battle hymn of the Reformation. Its words and music were written by Martin Luther. It was based on the Vulgate version of the 46th psalm which, translated, begins, 'Our God is a refuge'.

EINAUDI, LUIGI (1874–1961), Italian Republic's first nationally elected president (1948–55). He was an influential liberal economist, and as a lecturer, journalist, editor of *La Reforma Sociale* (1900–25), and *Rivista di storia economica* (1936–43), and a senator (1919–   ), he tried to direct industrialists away from fascism after its early liberal economic policies ended (1923). As minister of the budget (1947–8) he curbed inflation by strict credit controls and high interest rates. As president he actively backed the 1954 Trieste settlement, but abstained from domestic party politics.

EINSTEIN, ALBERT (1879–1955), German physicist. In 1919 he became famous after his theory of General Relativity had been confirmed by stellar photographs of a solar eclipse taken on an expedition sponsored by the British Royal Astronomical Society. Since 1914, Einstein had been director of Theoretical Physics at the Kaiser Wilhelm Institut, Berlin. In 1933, in view of the Nazi menace, he accepted a post at the Institute for Advanced Study at Princeton, which he retained until 1945, having become a US citizen in 1940.

In 1905 he had published three papers on almost wholly distinct branches of physics—restricted relativity, Brownian movement, and the quantization of the photo-electric effect, for the last of which he was awarded the Nobel Prize for Physics in 1921.

The aim of the Restricted (Special) Theory of Relativity (*Elektrodynamik bewegter Korper*) was to remove fundamental discrepancies emerging from the attempt to base the new theories of electricity (Maxwell–Hertz field, and emerging electronic theories) on classical (Newtonian) mechanics. The most awkward anomaly had been the demonstration (1887) by Michelson and Morley that the velocity of light was unaffected by the motion of the body emitting it. Though Einstein must have known of this, no single anomaly stirred his imagination so much as the radical critique by Ernst Mach of the classical interpretation of the *measurement* of distance, time, and force. The significance of light is limited to its being the fastest-known medium of information regarding distant objects. By taking the 'absolute' constancy of the velocity of light *in vacuo* as a *postulate* Einstein created a system in which physical laws are unaffected by the (uniform) relative motion of the 'observer'. An inescapable consequence of this is, however, that events recorded as simultaneous by one observer might be regarded as successive by another elsewhere; and the question as to which was the 'correct' estimate was shown to be meaningless. The term 'observer' was an unfortunate choice, since it opened the door to accusations of 'idealism'—irrelevant, since the 'observer' need not be a sentient being. In this theory there also occurred the fateful equation

$$E = mc^2$$

the latent expression of nuclear power. When, in 1939, the potentialities of atomic fission were recognized it was Enstein who, urged by other leading physicists, wrote to President Roosevelt, emphasizing the need for immediate investigation of its possible application to weapons of destruction.

In the General Theory (completed only in 1916) the restriction 'uniform' is removed, making possible the inclusion of accelerated (eg, gravitational) motions. An approach to this problem had already been made by the mathematician Henri Poincaré; the merging of the 'space' and 'time' of the Restricted Theory into a four-dimensional (geometrical) continuum had been effected by Einstein's former teacher, Hermann Minkowski. But Einstein denied that 'physics had been reduced to geometry'; rather, *Euclidean* geometry was the consequence of an implicit *physical* assumption shown to be no longer valid on the cosmical scale.

The significance of Einstein's theory of the photo-electric effect (the release of electrons from a metal surface irradiated by light) is that the previously accepted distinction between 'waves' of light and electronic 'particles' could no longer be maintained. Though his own theory of the Brownian movement implies that our knowledge of the world expressed in even the classical laws of physics is inescapably statistical in character, Einstein maintained that the later Uncertainty Principle of Werner Heisenberg, though operationally effective, could not form the basis of our knowledge of the 'physically real' (*physikalisch-Realen*).

Though suffering for his Jewish racial origin, Einstein himself was a 'deeply religious agnostic', refusing to accept the alleged breakdown of causality, Conscious of the universal pressure of evil, he did what he could for the persecuted and worked strenuously for world peace. His chief solace was his violin.

A. Einstein, *The Meaning of Relativity* (London, 1956).
C. Seelig, *Albert Einstein, a Documentary Biography* (London, 1956).   WW

EISENHOWER, DWIGHT DAVID (1890–1969), US soldier and statesman and 34th president (1953–61). Born in TX and raised in Abilene, KS, he attended the US Military Academy (1911–15) and graduated with distinction from the Army Command and General Staff School at Fort Leavenworth (1926). He became assistant first to the secretary of war (1929) and then to Gen. Douglas MacArthur, chief of staff, whom he accompanied to the Philippines as military adviser (1935–9). Returning to the US at the outbreak of the Second World War with the rank of lieutenant-colonel, he attracted the attention of Gen. George C. Marshall, then chief of staff, and was appointed chief of operations for the army. He planned the reorganization of US forces in Europe and as Allied commander-in-chief, North Africa, directed the successful desert campaigns and the invasion of Italy (1942–3). In Dec. 1943 he was made supreme commander of the Allied Expeditionary Force in Western Europe and was responsible for the D-Day assault upon Normandy (6 June 1944) and the conclusion of hostilities on the western front. After governing the US occupation zone in Germany (1945), he returned to Washington as chief of staff (1945–8), being promoted to the rank of five-star general (1946). On retiring from the army, he became president of Columbia University (1948–50), but returned to military service as supreme commander of NATO forces in Europe (1951–2).

As the Republican Party's nominee for the presidency (1952), Eisenhower was elected by a large majority over his Democratic opponent, Adlai Stevenson. His re-election by nearly 10 million votes (1956), the biggest popular majority up to that time, was an indication of his personal popularity. He was no party politician and failed to establish 'Modern Republicanism', was persistently opposed by the Republican right-wing, and after 1954 had to deal with a Democratic majority in Congress. Despite such unfavourable political conditions and his own economic conservatism, Eisenhower's domestic legislation was moderately liberal and included the extension of social security benefits. He has been criticized for not taking a stronger stand against McCarthyism and for his lukewarm support of civil rights, but his behaviour reflected his conception of the presidential role in domestic affairs as one of leadership by persuasion. He believed in orderly administration, established a White House staff under Sherman Adams, and regularly consulted the cabinet. Taking a bolder lead in foreign affairs, he firmly supported mutual security programmes to combat communism and yet sought a clearer understanding with the Soviet Union. His popularity waned at home during his second term of office, largely because of the economic recession (1957–8) and doubts about his health. On leaving office (1961), he retired to his farm at Gettysburg, PA, recounting his early years in *At Ease: stories I tell to friends* (1968) and his presidency in *Mandate for Change* (1963) and *Waging Peace* (1965). He recalled his wartime experiences in *Crusade in Europe* (1948).

R. J. Donovan, *Eisenhower: the inside story* (New York, 1956).
E. J. Hughes, *The Ordeal of Power, a political memoir of the Eisenhower years* (New York, 1963). ICP

EISENHOWER DOCTRINE, principle of US foreign policy contained in a Congressional Joint Resolution on the Middle East (9 March 1957), stimulated by fears of communist subversion and aggression in that area. The resolution empowered the president to give economic and military aid and armed support to any independent Middle Eastern government requesting such assistance.

EISENSTEIN, SERGEI (1898–1948), Russian film-maker, whose first film, *The Strike*, was followed by *The Battleship Potemkin* (1924), *October* (1927–8), and *The General Line* (1926–9). His most influential contribution to the cinema was the technique of 'montage', the use of sharp images in violent succession to generate ideas in the spectator. To this purpose he broke the rules of story-telling and characterization to produce 'a purely intellectual film freed from traditional limitations, achieving direct forms for ideas, systems and concepts without any need for transitions or paraphrases'.

EISNER, KURT (1867–1919), German journalist and Social Democrat politician, who became the first Republican prime minister of Bavaria. In 1897 he was sentenced to nine months imprisonment for lese-majesty for a satirical attack on William II. In 1898 he became an editor of *Vorwärts*, the organ of the German Social Democratic Party (SPD), but resigned in 1905 with other members of the editorial board as the result of conflicts with more radical party members. He left Prussia, whose authoritarian character he greatly disliked, and went to Bavaria, where, after a spell as editor of the *Frankischer Tagespost* in Nuremberg, he went to Munich and became a political, literary, and theatre correspondent for the Social Democratic press.

During the period preceding the First World War he was highly critical of Germany's diplomacy and in 1906 published an attack on William II's Moroccan policy, called *Sultan des Weltkrieges*. When the war broke out in 1914 he at first accepted the official view that Russia was to blame, but in 1915 had become convinced of Germany's responsibility. His opposition to the war alienated him from the SPD and in 1917 he joined the Independent Social Democratic Party (USPD). He was not, however, regarded with particular favour by the more radical revolutionaries in Germany. In Jan. 1918 he was imprisoned for helping to organize a series of anti-war strikes in Munich. He was released in Oct. 1918 in order to campaign for a by-election to the German Reichstag, and he and his small group of Independent Socialist followers organized a demonstration which, on the night of 7–8 Nov. 1918, overthrew the Wittelsbach monarchy. Eisner proclaimed a Republic based on the authority of workers' and soldiers' councils. While not rejecting parliamentary democracy, he hoped that the councils would act as a liberating factor in an authoritarian society. He was greatly concerned about international relations and tried to establish private contacts with President Wilson through the Bavarian Legation in Berne. He wanted Germany to purge her war-guilt by removing all those in any way responsible for imperial policies. He was therefore critical of Ebert's government in Berlin, which he considered to be compromised by association with the old regime. He aroused great hostility in official circles by publishing, on 24 Nov., extracts from Bavarian documents proving Germany's complicity in Austrian aggression against Serbia in July 1914. Eisner's government in Bavaria did not have wide popular support and on 12 Jan. 1919 his party was decisively beaten in an election for the Bavarian parliament. Despite speculation that he might use the workers' and soldiers' councils to maintain his authority against the will of the electorate, he was prepared to resign at the opening session of parliament on 21 Feb., but on his way to the session he was mortally wounded by a counter-revolutionary officer, Count Arco-Valley.

Alan Mitchell, *Revolution in Bavaria: the Eisner regime and the Soviet Republic* (Princeton, 1965). AJN

EJIDO, policy of Mexican agrarian reform during its formative years (1917–40), whereby land which had been absorbed by private estates (*latifundia*) was returned to villages for communal use and declared to be inalienable. The term derives from the Spanish, meaning 'the way out'. In Spain it referred to village common lands. The Spaniards used the term to refer to the lands pertaining to Indian villages in America. The 19th-cent. liberal attack on communal (corporate) holdings was reversed by the Mexican constitution of 1917 (Art. 27), which called for the restoration of *ejidos*. Since 1940 the trend has been not to create new *ejidos*, but to provide private grants.

EKATHOTSAROT (*reg.* 1605–10), King of Thailand, recognized by his elder brother, King Naresuan (*reg.* 1590–1605), as 'second king' and co-equal. His own reign was peaceful and uneventful.

ELAGABALUS (M. Aurelius Antoninus) (*reg.* AD 218–22), Roman Emperor, was proclaimed in an uprising against Macrinus while serving as boy priest of the god Elagabal at Emesa in Syria, his birthplace. He went to Rome in 219, and promoted there his native cult, importing the sacred stone of Elagabal and installing it with great pomp. His rumoured immoralities and his religious innovations made him notorious. He raised popular entertainers to the highest state offices and, without any firm achievements to his credit, was murdered during a mutiny at Rome, being replaced by his cousin, Alexander Severus (222–35). The sacred stone was returned to Emesa.

ELAM, ancient country or state, with its capital at Susa, in the mountains bordering eastern Mesopotamia. Little is known about the country or its people. There was already a dynasty ruling in Elam in the early 3rd millennium BC and from that time onwards the history of Elam reveals a continuous struggle with the Mesopotamian states, the Elamites periodically invading the plains and being invaded. Sargon of Akkad (*c.* 2334–2279) twice invaded Elam, but Elam revived, attacked Babylonia, and destroyed Ur (*c.* 2006). Perhaps the 13th cent. BC was Elam's greatest period, when a new dynasty founded towns, repaired existing ones, built temples, and revived Elamite language, art, and architecture. King Shutruk-Nahhunte (*reg. c* 1207–1171) invaded Babylonia, as a result of which the Elamite empire was extended from Kirkuk to the Persian Gulf, only to be destroyed by Nebuchadnezzar I (*reg. c.* 1124–1103), after which Elam disappeared from history for three centuries. Consequently the settlement of Persian and Aramaean tribes and constant trouble with Assyria led to its decline, and Elam's independence was finally ended when Ashurbanipal of Assyria attacked and devastated the country (*c.* 639). Elam was greatly influenced throughout its history by Mesopotamia. Many of the surviving documents were written in Akkadian and the Elamites adapted cuneiform writing to Elamite. In turn, Elamite culture spread eastwards, far into the Iranian plateau. Women seem to have had an important place in Elamite society and many statues of a mother-goddess have been found. The political system was peculiar in that the succession passed from brother to brother.

ELARA (*c.* 205–161 BC), Tamil Ruler of Ceylon who, unlike other Tamil rulers of the island, is praised for his love of justice in the Ceylonese chronicles. Though a Hindu, he was kindly disposed towards the Buddhists, whose cause was, already by that time, identified with the interests of the Sinhalese majority. In *c.* 161 BC Elara was killed by his main Sinhalese adversary, Dutthagamani.

ELAS (National Popular Liberation Army), formed in Dec. 1942, military arm of EAM, the communist-dominated Greek resistance movement. Some, who have minimized its military achievements, claim that its chief aim was the elimination of rival resistance organizations. Nevertheless, ELAS survived severe German attacks in the autumn of 1943 and took the offensive in Jan. 1944. By the time the Germans withdrew two-thirds of Greece was held by ELAS and ruled by EAM. At their peak ELAS forces numbered some 50,000. The refusal of ELAS to disarm according to the terms offered by the government and Allied representatives led to the battle of Athens (Dec. 1944–Jan. 1945). After bitter fighting between ELAS and British forces ELAS withdrew, defeated. An armistice was signed on 11 Jan. 1945 and the Varkiza Agreement followed in Feb. Under this settlement ELAS was bound to disarm within two weeks. But when civil war broke out the next year ELAS units and arms were used by the communist forces.

ELBA (1814–15), Mediterranean island which served as Napoleon's first place of exile before the 'Hundred Days'.

ELDON, JOHN SCOTT, 1st Earl of (1751–1838), British lawyer and Tory politician, who resisted every notable reform during his political career. As solicitor-general, he drafted the Regency Bill (1788). While attorney-general, he introduced repressive legislation, *eg*, suspension of *habeas corpus* (1794). Eldon's conservatism equalled his political tenacity (he was lord chancellor 1801–6 and 1807–28). He opposed the slave trade's abolition, penal reform, repeal of the test, and corporation acts, Catholic emancipation, and the first Reform Act, but warmly welcomed Sidmouth's Six Acts (1819). Although he was accused of dilatoriness, Eldon's judicial decisions were sound and subtly reasoned.

EL DORADO, mythical region which led numerous Spanish conquistadores to search for the place in Central Colombia where a native monarch was said to have bathed annually covered with gold dust.

ELEANOR OF AQUITAINE (*c.* 1122–1204), a woman of strong self-will, intelligent, beautiful, cultivated, and imperious, who played a dominant role in the affairs of England and France for many years. As the eldest daughter of William X, Duke of Aquitaine, she inherited that vast duchy and the county of Poitou a few weeks before her marriage (1137) to Louis VII of France. Their relationship was not happy; there was a suspicion of adultery on her part and no male child of the marriage, which was dissolved (1152) to their mutual satisfaction on grounds of consanguinity. Eleanor immediately married a man some 15 years her junior, the Duke of Anjou, who became King Henry II of England in 1154. Although they had a number of children, including the future Kings Richard I and John, the marriage was not happy. Eleanor aided her elder sons in rebellion against their father in 1173, for which she was placed under arrest for the rest of Henry's life. Eleanor was very active in Richard's interests both before and after his accession in 1189. She was virtually his regent during his prolonged absences from England and was responsible for his leniency to John on his return from captivity in 1194. She was also largely responsible for his accession on Richard's death in 1199. She was a great patroness of poets and troubadours and introduced the chivalric courts of love to England.

ELECTORAL COLLEGE, GERMAN, group of prominent German princes who successfully established the convention that their votes alone could elect a German king. A large body of princes participated in the election of 1198, but by that of 1257 a college of seven monopolized the right. The *Sachsenspiegel* of the early 13th cent. described a college of six, the three Rhenish archbishops, Mainz, Trier, and Cologne, and the imperial steward, marshal, and chamberlain, the countpalatine of the Rhine, the Duke of Saxony, and the margrave of Brandenburg. In addition, the King of Bohemia, as imperial cup-bearer, came to enjoy the right during the 13th cent. The 'Golden Bull' of Emperor Charles IV (1356) permanently established this body of electors, assuring to its secular members the indivisibility of their electorates.

ELEPHANTA, island outside the harbour of Bombay, famous for eight cave temples dedicated to the worship of Shiva. The caves were excavated during the rule of the Rashtrakutas (8th cent. AD). Cave I, the largest, contains a 20-ft three-faced Shiva image, one of the most beautiful examples of the Deccani style of this period.

ELEUSIS, Greek city in Attica, home of the famous Mysteries of Demeter. Though originally independent, it was effectively united with Athens perhaps first by Peisistratus (*c.* 540 BC), who built the first hall of initiation (*telesterion*), enlarged and rebuilt by Pericles (*c.* 440). Initiation, open to all Greeks, slave and free, was encouraged in the late 5th cent. by imperial Athens. The ceremony retained its fascination during the Roman empire and Roman initiates included Augustus, Hadrian, and Marcus Aurelius. In AD 306 the sanctuary was destroyed by Alaric.

ELGIN MARBLES (1815), collection of antique Greek sculptures removed from Athens by the 7th Earl of Elgin, bought for the nation (1816), and placed in the British Museum. Contemporaries debated their aesthetic value and the propriety of their acquisition.

EL GRECO (1541–1614), otherwise Domenikos Theotokopoulos, Spanish painter of the counter-Reformation period, though born a Greek. He came from Crete and was trained as a painter in Italy, but moved to Spain. At Toledo he developed a strikingly original style to which both his Greek–Byzantine and Italian experience contributed. His pictures reflect the mystical element of the religious life of counter-Reformation Spain.

ELHUYAR, FAUSTO DE (1755–1833), Spanish scientist, who taught at the school of mines, Mexico City, and concerned himself with the improvement of silver processing in New Spain.

ELIOT, SIR CHARLES NORTON EDGECUMBE (1862–1931), British colonial official who held several diplomatic posts, and was then commissioner and consul-general of the East Africa Protectorate (Kenya) and Zanzibar (1900). He was largely responsible for encouraging British settlers to farm in Kenya, and for reserving the 'White Highlands' for them.

ELIOT, CHARLES WILLIAM (1834–1926), US educationalist, who became professor of chemistry at the Massachusetts Institute of Technology (1865) and president of Harvard (1869–1909). During his period of office the numbers at Harvard grew from about 1000 students and a teaching faculty of 60 to 4000 students and a faculty of 600. The subjects offered were greatly extended, a graduate school established, and the professional schools of divinity, medicine, and law reformed. The 'elective system' was devised to give students full opportunity to pursue their academic interests freely, and Eliot encouraged athletics. His support for the admission of female students led ultimately to the foundation of Radcliffe College (1894). After his retirement he edited the 'five foot' shelf of Harvard Classics, which he claimed would provide any man with a true and full liberal education.

ELIOT, GEORGE, pseudonym of **MARY ANNE EVANS** (1819–80), English journalist and novelist. A strict evangelical upbringing, a study of the Tractarian controversy within the Church of England, friendships with the rational philosophers Herbert Spencer and G. H. Lewes, and the rejection of Christian doctrine all influenced her novels, which were marked by their didactic approach, characterization, and sense of humour. They include *Adam Bede* (1859), *The Mill on the Floss* (1860), and *Middlemarch* (1871–2).

ELIOT, SIR JOHN (1592–1632), English parliamentarian in the conflicts between Charles I and the Commons. He was the son of a wealthy west-country landowner, and as MP for his native borough of St Germans, Cornwall, in the Addled Parliament first sat in the Commons (1614). He was knighted through the influence of his patron, George Villiers, Marquis of Buckingham (1618), and in 1622 was appointed vice-admiral of Devon.

In 1624, as MP for Newport, Cornwall, he won a reputation as an orator. Though he praised Buckingham and the king, he condemned the government's taxes and defended the Commons' right to freedom of speech.

Gradually (1624–6) Eliot and Buckingham became alienated. Eliot was involved in a quarrel with Sir James Bagg, vice-admiral of Cornwall, who had greater influence with Buckingham. Eliot was also angered at the failure of the Cadiz expedition organized by Buckingham.

In 1626, again as MP for St Germans, he attacked the government and Buckingham became one of the managers of his impeachment. On 11 May he was sent to the Tower on Charles I's orders, but was released a few days later. After a commission of enquiry he was suspended from his vice-admiralty. He was again imprisoned (June 1627–Jan. 1628) for refusing to contribute to the king's forced loan.

In 1628 he returned to parliament as MP for Newport, Cornwall, and was recognized as the leader of the parliamentary opposition to the court. He fiercely defended the liberty of the subject, claimed that the rights of parliament were being violated, again attacked Buckingham, and was foremost in forcing the Petition of Right on the king.

In the 1629 parliament, with Buckingham dead, Eliot made a direct assault upon the king's government. He drew up three resolutions condemning its religious policy and the illegal levying of customs duties. These extreme resolutions were passed, despite the king having ordered the adjournment of parliament, the speaker being forcibly held in his chair. By 1629 Eliot, for most of his life a moderate churchman, had developed pronounced Puritan views. He and eight others were arrested, and he was fined £2000 and ordered by the court of King's Bench to be detained at the king's pleasure in the Tower, unless he admitted his offence and gave security for good behaviour. This Eliot refused to do, claiming parliamentary privilege for his actions. While in the Tower he wrote a number of books, but his confinement undermined his health. Charles, who never forgave him for his attacks on Buckingham, refused him permission to leave the Tower. He died a martyr to the parliamentary cause on 28 Nov. 1632. In Dec. 1667 the House of Lords reversed the judgment of the court of King's Bench on Eliot.

H. Hulme, *The Life of John Eliot* (London, 1957).   CJ

ELIOT, JOHN (1604–90), American missionary, who emigrated from England to MA (1631). He moved from Boston to Roxbury, where he was a teacher at the church for 60 years. He became interested in the Indians, began preaching to them (1646), and translated the Bible into an Algonquian language (1661–3). He also organized the first of 14 independent Christian Indian communities (1651). His evangelizing among the Indians was successful until Puritan retaliation during King Philip's War (1675–6) destroyed most of the villages. Eliot selflessly tried to protect the Indians, but those who survived became so distrustful of the whites that the remaining few Christian villages disappeared.

ELIS, ancient Greek state in the north-west Peloponnese, an early ally of Sparta and at times organizer of the Olympic Games. Its claims to small independent neighbours brought trouble with Sparta (421–418), which led to military coercion in 399, and, after Sparta's decline, with the Arcadian League (369–362).

ELIZABETH I (1533–1603), Queen of England (*reg.* 1558–1603), second daughter of Henry VIII by his second wife, Anne Boleyn. She succeeded her sister Mary I and proved to be the most politically gifted of the Tudor dynasty. Her reign was notable for the settlement of the Church of England (1559); for her tactful and on the whole successful handling of the maturing parliamentary system; for the first efficient statutory attempts to solve the major social problems of vagrancy and poverty arising from economic change; for the maritime exploits of Hawkins, Drake, and Raleigh; and for the artistic achievements of Marlowe, Spenser, Shakespeare, Tallis, Dowland, Gibbons, and Byrd.

In foreign policy Elizabeth steered a tenuous course between friendship and enmity towards the two major Catholic powers, France and Spain. She concluded a successful peace with the former (treaty of Edinburgh, 1560) and preserved the alliance which she inherited with Spain until economic rivalry dictated assistance to the Netherlands and political hostility (Anglo–Spanish War, 1585–1604). The threat from Scotland ceased effectively with the end of Franco–Scottish relations (1560) and with the imprisonment of Mary Stuart (1568–87), for although Elizabeth refused to recognize Mary's son James as the lawful heir to the English throne, it was tacitly accepted that he would unite the two Crowns after her death.

The circumstances of her birth suggested that Elizabeth was unlikely to favour the restored Catholic Church. Yet she deplored the tenets of Calvinism, and the religious settlement of 1559 followed a judicious *via media* calculated to reconcile the majority of her subjects. However, the challenge of papal excommunication and Jesuit missionaries forced her to approve anti-Catholic legislation, though the threatening Puritan wing of the Anglican Church had also to be repressed.

Elizabeth was intelligent, strong-willed, courageous, and astute, but she was served by men who in different ways were no less able than herself, *eg*, the Cecils, Walsingham, Sidney, and Abp Parker. Although given to favourites, *eg*, Leicester and Essex, she did not allow them to undermine the nation's interests. Despite growing parliamentary truculence on matters of religion, finance, and the royal prerogative, she retained the affection and respect of the nation until her death.

J. E. Neale, *Queen Elizabeth* (London, 1934).   MKS

ELIZABETH II (1926–   ), Queen of Britain (*reg.* 1952–   ), and head of the Commonwealth, daughter of King George VI. In 1947 she married her third cousin, Philip Mountbatten, son of Prince Andrew of Greece; they have four children, Charles, Prince of Wales (1948–   ), Anne (1950–   ), Andrew (1960–   ), and Edward (1964–   ). On 6 Feb 1952, while touring Kenya, she became queen. Her coronation in June 1953 produced some talk of a new Elizabethan age, partly in reaction to the austerity of the post-Second World War years. By 1970 the pattern of the reign has been set by the assiduous performance of her duties, which included numerous visits throughout the Commonwealth. Towards the end of the 1960s she and her family sought a closer identification with the people than had been the traditional practice of the British royal house. In this, the queen was particularly aided by her husband and by her eldest son, who was educated at Gordonstoun School, Scotland, and Trinity College, Cambridge.

ELIZABETH OF BOHEMIA (1596–1662), second child of James I of England and his wife, Anne of Denmark. She became wife of Frederick V, Elector Palatine, whose election as King of Bohemia began the Thirty Years War (1618). The marriage (1613) was brought about in order to strengthen the Union of German Protestant states against the Catholic counter-Reformation, by alliance with the most important Protestant country in Europe, but in fact neither Frederick and Elizabeth nor the Protestant states received any material aid from England when the Bohemian Protestant forces were crushed at the battle of the White Mountain (1620). Frederick and Elizabeth found refuge with Frederick's uncle, Maurice of Nassau, and after Frederick's death in 1632 Elizabeth remained there in deepening poverty until her return to England in 1661 at the invitation of her former servant and friend, Lord Craven. Of Elizabeth's 13 children, her second son, Frederick Louis, was restored to the palatinate in 1648, her third son, Rupert, commanded the royalist cavalry during the English Civil War, and her youngest daughter, Sophia, who married Ernest Augustus of Brunswick and Luneberg, became a candidate for the English throne under the Act of Settlement (1701). King George I of Britain was Elizabeth's grandson.

ELIZABETH PETROVNA (1709–62), Empress of Russia *reg.* (1741–62), youngest daughter of Peter I by his second wife, Catherine Skavronsky. She seized power, with the support of the Guards regiments, in a palace revolution that overthrew the infant Ivan VI and his mother, the Regent Anne of Brunswick-Luneburg.

In the cultural sphere her reign marked the progress of French influence. French fashions were introduced and the Academy of Fine Arts was founded (1757) in imitation of the Paris Academy. The first Russian university was established at Moscow (1755), and the Imperial theatre, built at St Petersburg (1756), was the model for other permanent theatres there and in Moscow. An attempt was made to codify the laws by a legislative commission established in 1761 and an edict was passed abolishing the death penalty, although it continued to be invoked for political offences.

Politically her reign saw the return of conservative, old Russian traditions after a decade of German influence under the Empress Anna (1730–40). Ruling with the help of several favourites, *eg*, Counts Shuvalov and Bestuzhev-Ryumin, the pro-Austrian chancellor (1744–58), she adhered firmly to an anti-Prussian foreign policy despite the fact that the heir-apparent, Peter, Duke of Holstein, and his wife, Sophia of Anhalt-Zerbst (later Catherine II), were strongly pro-Prussian. Under Elizabeth Russian armies entered the Seven Years War on the side of Austria and Britain, defeating the Prussians at Gross-Jagersgorf (1757), Zorndorf (1758), and Kunersdorf (1759). Only Elizabeth's death, as a childless spinster, on 5 Jan. 1762 saved Prussia from total disaster.

ELIZABETH OF YORK (1465–1503), Queen of King Henry VII of England and daughter of Edward IV by his second wife, Elizabeth Woodville. She was the Yorkist claimant when the Lancastrian Henry seized the throne, and he married her (1486) after parliament had acknowledged his title in his own right. Her four children who outgrew infancy were Arthur, Henry VIII, Margaret, Queen of Scotland, and Mary, Queen of France.

ELKIN, ADOLPHUS PETER (1891–   ), Australian anthropologist, who was professor of anthropology at Sydney University (1933–56). Elkin influenced anthropological development in Australia and welfare policies for indigenous Australian and New Guinea peoples. He specialized in Australian aboriginal social organization, kinship, and totemism. His *Australian Aborgines: how to understand them* (1936) is a classic.

ELKINS ACT (1903), US legislation designed to eliminate the system of rebates on railroads. The act provided for the prosecution of railroad corporations as well as their officials for giving or receiving rebates, and made any deviation from published rates a misdemeanour.

ELLENBOROUGH, EDWARD LAW, 1st Baron (1750–1818), lord chief justice of England (1802–18) and author of Ellenborough's Act (1803), which created ten new capital offences. He opposed criminal law reform and Catholic emancipation.

ELLICE ISLANDS in the Pacific were originally settled from Samoa and the Gilberts. In the 1850s (on traders' advice) many islanders abandoned their religion. In 1861 Manihikian castaways introduced Christianity. Peruvian ships (1863–4) removed most of the inhabitants of Nukulaelae and Funafuti. The rest were converted on the arrival of the *John Williams* (London Missionary Society). The group was eventually amalgamated with the Gilberts as a British protectorate (1892).

ELLIOTT, EBENEZER (1781–1849), English poet, who wrote the 'Corn Law Rhymes' (1833–5) and whose ideals were 'Free Trade, Universal Peace, Freedom in Religion and Education for All'. He was an active propagandist against the Corn Laws and was also an early Chartist. He wrote vivid descriptions of life among the poor, as well as popular hymns, but in the clash of priorities between the Anti-Corn Law League and Chartism his sympathies lay with the league.

ELLIS, HENRY HAVELOCK (1859–1939), British psychologist concerned with the analysis of human sexuality. His numerous books include *Man and Woman* (1894), the seven-volume *Studies in the Psychology of Sex* (1897–1928), *The Task of Social Hygiene* (1912), and *On Life and Sex* (1922–1931). Through varied studies (which included the first major treatment of homosexuality) Ellis came to view love as the basis of human relations and campaigned against sexual puritanism and ignorance.

ELLIS, WELBORE (1713–1802), British politician, who was secretary at war (1763–5), treasurer of the navy (1765–82), and secretary of state for the American colonies (1782).

ELLIS ISLAND, principal point of entry for millions of European immigrants to the US (1892–1943). It is situated in Upper New York Bay and at its peak period during the first decade of the 20th cent. it received as many as 15,000 arrivals a day.

ELLORA (Elura), archaeological site near Aurangabad, Maharashtra, India, famous for 34 cave temples and two rock-cut temples dating from the 5th to the 8th cents AD. They belong to the Hindu, Buddhist, and Jain religions. The Kailasanath rock temple, excavated in the reign of the Rashtrakuta king, Krishna I (AD 758–73), is one of the finest achievements of Indian art.

ELLSWORTH, OLIVER (1745–1807), US lawyer and politician, educated at both Yale and Princeton. He rose rapidly in the legal profession and became prominent in politics during the American Revolution. He represented CT in six successive annual terms in the Continental Congress (1777–1783), serving on several committees concerned with the conduct of the war against Britain. As one of the 'Founding Fathers' at the Philadelphia Constitutional Convention (1787), he was co-author of the 'Connecticut Compromise' on the question of representation in the federal legislature. As a US senator from CT (1789–96) he was a leading supporter of Hamilton's economic programme and the chief designer of the Federal Judiciary Bill (1789). As chief justice of the US Supreme Court (1796–1800), he was sent by John Adams as one of the commissioners to settle the 'quasi-war' with France (1799). The strain of prolonged voyages in the depth of winter permanently impaired his health, which, together with widespread blame for the failure to obtain better terms from Napoleon, led to his premature retirement from public life (1800).

ELMINA (São Jorge da Mina), stone fortress on the Ghana coast, built by the Portuguese in 1482 as a centre for their gold trade. After capture by the Dutch in 1637 it became the African headquarters of the West India Co. The Dutch ceded it to Britain in 1872.

EL PARDO, CONVENTION OF (Jan. 1739), agreement between the British prime minister, Sir Robert Walpole, and the Spanish ambassador in England, purporting to settle Anglo–Spanish differences in the Caribbean. Illicit English trading with Spanish America had led to brutal reprisals by Spanish coastguards and the episode of Capt. Jenkins (March 1738) had imposed fresh strains on Anglo–Spanish relations. Walpole therefore negotiated an agreement by which Spain was to pay £95,000, representing the excess of Spanish over English depredations. The South Sea Co., however, refused to recognize the convention because it contained no guarantee of a renewal of the *asiento*, nor of their rights of navigation; and as popular opposition mounted and rumours of a Franco-Spanish pact, grew, Newcastle sent Admiral Haddock to patrol Spanish waters. When war broke out in Oct. 1739 the convention ceased and the promised compensation was not paid.

ELPHINSTONE, MOUNTSTUART (1779–1859), British colonial servant in the political service of the East India Co. and historian. He belonged to a remarkable group of able and liberal-minded Indian civilians whom the company's service produced in the early 19th cent., eg, John Malcolm, Thomas Munro, and Charles Metcalfe. Such men were not only practical administrators but serious students of Indian history, customs, languages, and institutions. The growth of their influence prevented the extension of the Bengal permanent settlement to other parts of India and led to the fall from power of those officials who belonged to what had been termed the 'Cornwallis caste'.

Elphinstone went to India in 1795, becoming (1801) assistant to the resident at the court of Baji Rajo II, the last peshwa and titular head of the Maratha confederacy. He became resident in the Maratha state of Nagpur (1804–8). Then French intrigues in Persia so alarmed Minto that he dispatched Malcolm to the court of the shah at Teheran, Metcalfe to Ranjit Singh in Lahore, and Elphinstone to the camp of the Afghan amir at Peshawar (1809). Although Elphinstone negotiated a friendly alliance with the amir it proved of little use because, before it was ratified, Shah Shuja became a refugee from his kingdom. One important result was Elphinstone's book, *An account of the Kingdom of Caubul and its Dependencies* (1815). In 1810 he was appointed resident at Poona. He took a firm line with the Peshwa Baji Rao II and compelled him to surrender his minister, Trimbakji Danglia, who had been privy to the murder of an envoy from the Gaekwar of Baroda. In 1817 he practically dictated a treaty to the peshwa, but the latter's word could not be trusted, for in Nov. of that year he attacked the British forces at Kirki, but was defeated.

Elphinstone was governor of Bombay (1819–27). He maintained the legal system under which minor cases were tried in the villages by the local *panchayat*s and encouraged the teaching of English and developed popular education in Bombay. Elphinstone College was founded in his honour. After he retired from India he twice refused the office of governor-general of India. Besides his history of Afghanistan, he wrote a *History of India* (1841), on the Hindu and Muslim periods down to 1761, and *The Rise of the British Power in the East* (1858).

T. E. Colebrooke, *Life of Mountstuart Elphinstone*, 2 vols (London, 1884).
K. A. Ballhatchet, *Social Policy and Social Change in Western India, 1817–1830* (London, 1957).   CCD

ELPHINSTONE, WILLIAM, bishop (1431–1514), chancellor of Scotland under James III and ambassador to France under James IV. He introduced the printing-press to Scotland, and, while Bp of Aberdeen, founded the university and the first chair of medicine in Scotland.

EL SUPREMO (1766–1840), title given to José Gaspar Rodríguez de Francia, dictator of Paraguay (1814–40).

ELTHAM, ORDINANCE OF (1526) in England, planned survey of the complete reform of the royal household and council of Henry VIII, drawn up by Wolsey. Much of it was not implemented, partly because the changes it envisaged would have undermined Wolsey's supremacy in government and partly because of Henry's lack of political ambition at that period. Thomas Cromwell used the reforms of the council outlined in the ordinance to establish the privy council of 19 leading counsellors (1534–6).

ÉLUS, financial representatives of the French Crown in the *élections* (financial administrative units) under the *ancien* *régime*. Like the bailiffs in the bailiwicks, the *élus* had limited powers to try cases arising out of financial impositions. They were usually local men whose families were known in their *élections* and were directly subordinate to the *généraux des finances* in the *généralités*. Their office represented the top echelon of the third estate, although they themselves enjoyed exemption from the personal *taille* and by the mid-17th cent. were regarded as men of some prestige for whom further ascent up the social ladder was likely.

ELYOT, SIR THOMAS (*c*. 1495–1546), English diplomat and scholar, in whose work, *The Governour* (1531), were expounded the ideals of 16th-cent. gentlemen.

ÉLYSÉE AGREEMENT (8 March 1949), a letter written by President Auriol of France to Bao Dai, recognizing the internal independence and territorial integrity of Viet-nam, and thus establishing the Associated State of Viet-nam.

EMANCIPATION OF SERFS in Austria (1781). Most peasants in the Habsburg lands were serfs when Maria Theresa became empress in 1740. She freed those on Crown lands and undertook widespread reforms elsewhere, ending the nobility's exemption from taxation, forbidding the lords to acquire peasant land, granting the peasant the right of appeal against the lord and free legal aid in this, limiting boon services to two days a week, not exceeding ten hours in summer and eight in winter, and dividing the common pasture among the peasants who had enjoyed customary grazing rights. Such divided pasture land became virtually inalienable.

In 1781 the Emperor Joseph II proclaimed the abolition of personal serfdom throughout the empire, giving the peasant the right to marry, to take up a profession, and to move where he wished within the empire, and abolishing fines in the manorial court. The peasant's right of inheritance, and the right to pawn, mortgage, sell, or exchange land were also protected. The Urbarium of 1789, commuting all dues and services, including noon work, to a money rent, was strongly opposed, especially in Hungary on constitutional grounds, and was repealed immediately after the emperor's death four months later.

By 1848, the lords were finding the limited hours of boon work inconvenient and supported commutation. The revolutionary diets of both Vienna and Budapest demanded the commutation of boon work, and this was subsequently granted by the restored imperial government.

The laws protecting peasant rights and the gradual emancipation of the serfs in Austria, preceded throughout by enquiry into the special conditions of each province, protected the peasants, though not the farm labourers, from exploitation by big landlords in the transition from medieval to modern farming. The laws did, however, delay the introduction of labour-saving machinery.

E. Murr Link, *The Emancipation of the Austrian peasantry, 1740–1798* (New York, 1949).   DMK

EMANCIPATION OF SERFS in Russia (1861), most important of Alexander II's reforms. Defeat in the Crimean War, fear of peasant revolts, and humanitarian principles were immediate causes. Economic necessity was hardly argued at the time.

In a speech to the Moscow nobility (1856) Alexander referred to the advisability of abolishing serfdom from above before it abolished itself from below, and a secret committee was established. Divided between conservatives, *eg*, Orlov and Panin, and reformers, *eg*, Rostovstsev and Lanskoy, it made little progress until the Grand Duke Constantine, who, together with the Grand Duchess Elena Pavlovna, exercised a liberal influence on the tsar, was made chairman (Aug. 1857). The rescript to Nazimov laid down the principle that serfs should be freed with sufficient land to enable them

to meet their obligations to the nobility and the state. Provincial committees showed that most nobles opposed the reform, but a vocal minority hoped also for representative government, and Slavophile influence was one reason for the retention of the commune. Early in 1858 the secret committee became the Main Committee for Peasant Affairs and an editing committee under Rostovstsev and D. A. Milyutin was established to draft the act.

The decree of 19 Feb.–3 March 1861 granted personal freedom, although all obligations were to continue for two years. Then there was a period of temporary obligation during which money and labour dues were still to continue and the landowners and peasants were to reach a settlement. No time limit was set for this period, which was abolished in 1881. All serfs except household serfs, who were freed without land, had to accept an allotment and pay for it over 49 years as redemption payments to the state. Government bonds were used to refund the nobility. The amount of land given to the peasants varied according to area and type of soil. The government established a maximum and minimum norm and the average plot per person was 36,000 sq metres, although some serfs took 'beggars' allotments'.

The statute dealt with groups of families and communes, not individuals. The traditional commune received official administrative standing as a village community (*sel'skoe obshchestvo*), although the boundaries of old and new often did not coincide. The commune was responsible collectively for taxation, redemption payments, and land organization. Bondage to the commune (which made the growth of a proletariat difficult), repartitional tenure, and strip farming continued into the 20th cent. and hampered agriculture. Land shortage, financial burdens, and loss of wood, pasture, and stream rights were opposed by the intelligentsia and caused immediate peasant outbreaks, *eg*, at Bezdna. State peasants were freed on better terms in 1866.

J. Blum, *Lord and Peasant in Russia from c. 9 to c. 19* (Princeton, 1961).
G. T. Robinson, *Rural Russia under the Old Regime* (New York, 1932).   BJW

EMANCIPATION PROCLAMATION, military order issued by President Abraham Lincoln (1 Jan. 1863), proclaiming the emancipation of all slaves in those regions still under Confederate control in the American Civil War. Such action had been promised in Lincoln's preliminary proclamation of 22 Sept. 1862. The proclamation did not apply to the four border slave states remaining in the Union or to designated areas of the Confederacy already occupied. It therefore became effective only gradually as Union armies advanced. Yet the document also amounted to a national commitment, fulfilled in 1865 when slavery was abolished by the 13th Amendment in the Constitution.

EMANCIPISTS, Australian, term originally confined to official use and to convicts pardoned by the governor, but later used generally and applied to all ex-convicts. In convict times in NSW (1788–1840) emancipists were usually ostracized socially by respectable people who had arrived free. These latter were often termed 'exclusionists' or 'exclusives'.

EMBARGO POLICY OF THE US (1807–9), attempted by President Thomas Jefferson to maintain US neutrality in the Napoleonic Wars. An act of Congress (22 Dec. 1807) virtually prohibited all maritime trade with foreign nations, supplementary laws extended the ban to land commerce, closed certain other loopholes, and authorized severe methods of enforcement. The embargo, enacted at Jefferson's urgent request, was a bold experiment in economic coercion as an alternative to war. Its purpose was to compel respect from European belligerents for the maritime rights of a neutral US. With Britain pressing its blockade against France, and Napoleon tightening his 'continental system', the orders in council and imperial decrees had become so sweeping that an

American ship could scarcely satisfy the requirements of one power without risking seizure by the other. The embargo was expected to weigh more heavily on the British, whose naval superiority posed the greater threat to US commerce and produced the larger number of rankling incidents.

Northern mercantile interests, having found their swollen wartime trade exceedingly profitable, in spite of increasing hazards, were bitterly opposed to the legislation and, in many cases, determined to resist it. Being federalist for the most part, they regarded the embargo as maliciously partisan both at home and abroad. Evasion of various kinds and outright smuggling became not only common but respectable. The government responded to the problem of enforcement with energy and considerable success, but its policy measures provoked charges of tyranny and awakened echoes of colonial resistance to British authority before the American Revolution. Although the amount of illegal trade is unknown, the embargo apparently reduced exports by about 75 per cent and imports by about 50 per cent. Given enough time, the coercive purpose of the policy might have been at least partially achieved, but the immediate effects proved far more distressing to the US than to Britain or France. The prostration of commerce and the depression of agriculture were but slightly offset by the stimulus given to manufacturing. Federalism recovered some of its lost political appeal, and Jefferson's second presidential term closed on a muted note of defeat.

Clinging tenaciously to his experiment, Jefferson nevertheless had to accept repeal of the embargo just before leaving office in 1809. Congress replaced it with the Non-intercourse Act, which forbade only direct trade with the two major belligerents and was even more difficult to enforce. Later, under 'Macon's Bill No. 2' (1810), the administration of James Madison gullibly authorized the resumption of commerce with France. From that point, the US drifted steadily towards its declaration of war against Britain in 1812.

DEF

EMERGENCY DECREES in Germany. Under the Weimar Republic's constitution, two ways were open to the executive to obtain dictatorial powers in times of crisis. Emergency legislation could be enacted, if and when the Reichstag and Reichstat (Parliament, and Council of Regional Governments) granted an Enabling Act. If, however, the government failed to obtain the two-thirds majority required for such an act, or lacked a simple majority to get legislation passed, legislative rights could be assumed under Art. 48. Para. II of this article provided that the Reich president could, if public safety and order were seriously disturbed or threatened, 'take the measures necessary for the restoration of public safety and order', including the suspension of certain basic rights. Under Para. III the Reichstag had the power to demand the revocation of these measures. But the president could nevertheless assert himself by dissolving parliament and using the Reich government as his executive agent. In connection with Arts 25 and 53, Art. 48 therefore offered an instrument for protracted dictatorial rule, which was employed for the first time in the summer of 1930. For when in June 1930 the Reichstag refused to approve the budget which Chancellor Brüning had submitted, President Hindenburg invoked Art. 48 and the bill was reissued as an emergency decree. A majority of the deputies then demanded that this decree be nullified under Para. III, whereupon Brüning, on 18 July 1930, dissolved the Reichstag. The government was thus independent of parliament and ruled with the help of decrees, signed by Hindenburg. If Brüning ever hoped to regain a parliamentary majority to end 'presidential government', he was soon disappointed. The outcome of the elections of Sept. 1930 forced him to continue to govern by emergency decree. What prevented his measures from being constantly challenged by a negative majority in the Reichstag, was the 'toleration' of the SPD. Whereas Brüning could thus still count on the tacit support of a parliamentary majority, his successors deliberately turned the Weimar Republic

gradually into an authoritarian regime based on the presidential powers of Art. 48. This development reached a climax when, on 28 Feb. 1933, Hitler persuaded Hindenburg to sign two decrees which put the essentials of the constitution out of action and paved the way for a National Socialist dictatorship.

E. Eyck, *A History of the Weimar Republic* (New York, 1967).
F. M. Watkins, *The Failure of Constitutional Emergency Power under the German Republic* (Cambridge, MA, 1939).

VRB

EMERGENCY POWERS in the French constitution. The constitution of the Fifth Republic was the first to make specific provision for an emergency situation, though previous constitutions had allowed the temporary delegation of legislative powers to the executive. Under Art. 16 of the 1958 constitution, the president may take measures on his own initiative in a grave emergency. The president is sole judge of the emergency, and opponents of the Gaullist regime have strongly criticized this article as open to abuse. Art. 16 was used in 1961 after the military rebellion in Algeria.

EMERGENCY POWERS ACTS (1920, 1939, 1940) in Britain. The two most notable occasions on which an Emergency Powers Act has been passed were when a threat of concerted industrial action was made in Lloyd George's ministry (1920), and on the outbreak of the Second World War.

The Emergency Powers Act (1920) in effect resurrected the powers granted to the government under the Defence of the Realm Act (1914). Faced with the threat of industrial action, especially from the Triple Entente of manual workers, the act was threatened or used by the Coalition (1920), the first Labour government (1924), and the Conservatives in the General Strike (1926). Under its provisions, the government could appropriate any powers it wished through Orders in Council; these then had to have parliamentary approval, though this proved no obstacle. In 1926 the government thus possessed the right to commandeer most sources of food, transport, and power, and had also sweeping and arbitrary rights of censorship, search, and arrest.

Emergency Powers Acts were also passed in Aug. 1939 and May 1940. Neither of them was innovatory in extent; originally both were demonstrations of national determination rather than significant administrative measures. They granted to the government much the same discretionary powers as the 1914 and 1920 measures.

EMERSON, RALPH WALDO (1803–82), US Transcendentalist, poet, and man of letters. He was born in Boston, the son of a Unitarian minister, and brought up in the New England tradition. After his father died (1811), an aunt, Mary Moody Emerson, became Emerson's spiritual mentor, teaching him far more than orthodox theology. At Harvard (1817–21) his eclecticism increased but, despite his growing independence of mind, he returned, after a brief period of teaching, to the Divinity School. He was made pastor of the Second Church of Boston (1829). He resigned his pastorate (1832) because the principles of Unitarianism conflicted too strongly with his own beliefs. He toured Europe (1832–3), where he met Carlyle, Wordsworth, and Coleridge, and returned to Boston full of transcendental theories, and spiritually emancipated. 'Henceforth', he wrote in his journal, 'I design not to utter any speech, poem, or book that is not entirely and peculiarly my own work.' He settled in Concord, MA, where he emerged as the central figure of the group known as the Transcendentalists, and edited its magazine, *The Dial* (1842–1844). He was a powerful orator and began lyceum lecturing, and also formulated the ideas later incorporated in his writings. *Nature* (1836), a collection of essays based on his lectures, advocated the individual's potential divinity. 'The American Scholar' (1837), an energetic plea for cultural emancipation from Europe, was hailed by Oliver Wendell

Holmes as America's 'Intellectual Declaration of Independence'. Emerson's 'Divinity School Address' of the following year advocated intuitive religious experience, and was even more sensationally received. Two collections of *Essays* (1841, 1844) established his reputation both nationally and abroad. The successful lecture series of 1845 was published as *Representative Men* (1850). Emerson also published two volumes of poetry, 'Poems' (1847), and 'May Day and Other Poems' (1867).

Although it has become fashionable to discredit him for his optimism, his naivety, and his inconsistency, Emerson is nevertheless one of the giants of American letters. Emersonianism dominated nearly half a century of US literary thought, and was a major influence on Hawthorne, Melville, Thoreau, Whitman, and Emily Dickinson. His poetry, affirmative, didactic, and meditative, explores the use of the symbol, and demonstrates his belief that a poem's content should determine its form. With Poe (whose work he detested), Emerson was largely responsible for freeing American poetry from the borrowed conventions of Europe.

E. W. Emerson (ed.), *The Complete Works of Ralph Waldo Emerson*, 12 vols (Boston, 1903).

R. L. Rusk, *The Life of Ralph Waldo Emerson* (New York, 1949). EFAL

EMIGRATION from Britain in the 19th cent. The causes were largely spontaneous, *eg*, the departure of individuals and families under the pressure of economic need, of which the most conspicuous example is the movement of over a quarter of a million from Ireland to North America in 1847. The government did little more than attempt to regulate the conditions of transport in the series of Passenger Acts from 1803, and until the mid-1820s opposed the departure of skilled workers. In the 1820s various parliamentary committees encouraged Poor Law authorities to 'shovel out paupers' to the US and the colonies. In the 1830s parliament came under the influence of the work of Edward Gibbon Wakefield, who wished to encourage a type of settlement more beneficial to the receiving community, by attracting capital and useful labour. He proposed to have grants of colonial land stopped, and sales made instead, the proceeds of which would be used to pay for the transport of selected settlers. The Board of Colonial Land and Emigration Commissioners (1840–72) was set up to pursue this policy, and did so as far as was practicable, but with decreasing effectiveness because the colonies, as they achieved a measure of self-government, withdrew from its operations. Though only three or four hundred thousand people went out under its auspices, in contrast to some 7 million who left independently in this period, the board played an important part in determining the nature of settlement in southern Australia and New Zealand. RMM

EMIGRATION FROM IRELAND. Since at least the middle of the 18th cent. there had been seasonal migration from Ireland, when Irish labourers came over to England for the harvest. In the middle of the 19th cent., especially after the famine (1847), permanent immigration on a massive scale took place. At the census of 1861 there were over 600,000 persons of Irish birth in England alone. The immigrants were numerous in Lancashire and Cheshire, in Glasgow, Dundee, and in South Wales. They found employment particularly in the rapidly expanding textile industries and in railway construction. The sudden influx of large numbers of very poor Irish presented problems to Roman Catholicism in England and Scotland.

ÉMIGRÉS (1789), aristocrats who left France at the beginning of the Revolution, who were later joined by priests and others. They were led by Louis XVI's brothers and their constant aim was to induce the European rulers to intervene against the Revolution. Although their direct responsibility for the outbreak of war (1792) was small, they did much to produce an atmosphere of suspicion between the Revolutionaries and Europe. Until the Bourbon Restoration (1814), those who had not made their peace with the Revolutionary or Napoleonic governments moved from one European court to another, depending on which would offer them asylum.

EMILIA, Emilia-Romagna region, dominated by Bologna and the Po river, the scene of Italy's most bitter social and political conflict, connected especially with chronic rural unemployment. From the late 19th cent. onwards local unions, socialist and syndicalist, of landless labourers (*Braccianti*) developed power over the labour market, terrorizing landowners and sharecroppers, and created 'red baronies' of political power. The general strike and 'Red Week' (June 1914) produced local republics and waves of violence before the army restored order. Post-war land seizures and strikes drove landowners, sharecroppers, and businessmen to react, turning (1920) to the embryo fascist movement and providing its squads with transport, money, and men. Their successes, replacing 'red' bosses and councils with new groups, deflected the national character of fascism away from its syndicalist origins. Old scores were settled in bitter partisan fighting (1943–5). After 1946 moderate communist and socialist coalitions were strong in local government.

EMMET, ROBERT (1778–1803), Irish nationalist hero, whose ill-judged Dublin uprising (1803) ended in his capture and death.

EMPEROR WORSHIP, ROMAN, of living or dead rulers, was foreign to the Roman Republic, though some generals received divine honours in the east after Roman conquests. Julius Caesar was the first Roman so honoured in Rome itself in his lifetime, and after his death was declared a god (*divus*). Augustus allowed provincials to celebrate his cult in association with Roma (personification of Rome), and in Rome and Italy the Genius Augusti was honoured, but he rejected direct worship of himself by official bodies. He, too, was deified after his death, as were later emperors who were approved by their contemporaries. A few rulers, *eg*, Caligula and Domitian, moved towards a claim to direct worship, but usually the impulse, rather more than an expression of loyalty, but less than true worship, came from below. In the 3rd cent. some emperors were identified with specific gods, *eg*, Diocletian with Jupiter. The earliest Christian emperors were formally deified, but the official cult soon faded away.

EMPIRE, THE FIRST BRITISH, territories acquired before the loss of America (1783) and administered under 'the old colonial system'. These territories were mainly in North America, the West Indies, and India. The first attempt to establish a settlement in America resulted from Gilbert's unsuccessful voyage to Nfld (1583), and there were failures in VA before a plantation was established there in 1606. The *Mayflower* pilgrims (1620) colonized New England, and with the exception of GA (1732), all 13 American colonies were established in the 17th cent. In Canada, Britain's possession of Nfld, NS, and the Hudson's Bay territory was confirmed at Utrecht (1713) and Que. and Ont. were acquired from France in the Seven Years War (1756–63).

During the 17th cent. the English also settled some of the smaller Caribbean islands, neglected by countries that had arrived there earlier; among them were Barbados, St Christopher, the Bahamas, and Bermuda. Jamaica was seized from Spain (1655). The East India Co. was formed (1600) to secure trading rights in an area mainly occupied by the Dutch and Portuguese, but after the massacre of English merchants at Amboyna (1623) the company began to be more interested in establishing trading factories on the Indian mainland, Surat (1612), Madras (1639), Bombay (1668), and Calcutta (1696). In the 18th cent. the company vied with the French in trying to secure political and commercial privileges from the native princes, the struggle ending in a British victory in the Seven Years War. In West Africa the British occupied Senegal as a depot for the slave trade.

Although considerations of national power were not ignored, the purpose of these settlements was primarily trade and the development of a mercantile marine. The colonies were therefore subjected to an economic policy designed to further the interests of the mother country. Their role was to supply commodities that could not be grown at home and to provide a market for British manufactures. A series of Navigation Acts ensured that this trade should be carried only in British ships or ships of the colonies immediately concerned. Certain 'enumerated' products, such as sugar, tobacco, dyes, cotton, molasses, and rice, were to be sent only to Britain or, on payment of duty, to other colonies, and in theory colonies trading with other European powers or their dependencies could only do so by way of Britain.

In practice the rigours of the system were partly relieved by smuggling, and the authorities were well aware of it. Until aggravated by other issues, these Acts of Trade were not a major cause of the American revolt, because the colonies recognized the advantages to themselves. Britain provided a guaranteed market, steady prices, and preferential rates for colonial produce and for colonial manufactures that were not in competition with her own. This encouraged certain industries, eg, timber and shipbuilding, and gave sugar and tobacco planters an incentive to organize their estates efficiently. Britain even gave up the cultivation of home-grown tobacco to assist colonial trade.

To some extent the old colonial system was discredited by the success of the American revolt, but it was also becoming fashionable to question the value of the mercantilist principles on which it had depended. Free competition might be more profitable than tariffs and a protected market. At the same time, the impeachment of Warren Hastings (1788) was a sign that the British were beginning to have second thoughts about the nature and purposes of empire. The new spirit that gradually evolved after 1783 was moral and political as well as economic.

The Cambridge History of the British Empire (Cambridge, 1929 sq.).
J. A. Williamson, *A Short History of British Expansion*, vol. 1, *The Old Colonial Empire* (London, 1930).　MMR

EMPIRE IN THE WEST, DISAPPEARANCE OF (476). The year 476 is accepted as the conventional date for the end of the Roman empire in the West, when the Herulian leader Odoacer formally deposed the young Emperor Romulus Augustulus, mockingly nicknamed 'Augustulus' (little Augustus) and retired him to a monastery. The deposition of Romulus was intimated by Odoacer to the Eastern Emperor, Zeno, as signifying the end of a separate imperial administration in the West, not as ending the empire as such.

EMPRESS OF INDIA, title assumed by Queen Victoria in 1877. Disraeli assured the House of Commons that the new title would only be employed in India as *Kaisar-i-Hind*. In 1893 the words 'Ind. Imp.' were engraved on the British coinage.

EMPSON, SIR RICHARD (d. 1510), English lawyer and minister of Henry VII, associated with Edmund Dudley in the rigorous and extortionate administration of Crown revenues. His career survived the change of dynasty in 1485, and in 1494 he became the only member of Henry VII's council not of gentry family. He was chancellor of the Duchy of Lancaster in 1504, and, through a committee of the Council, dealt with a wide variety of cases in which the king's prerogative was enforced and debts collected. This made him very unpopular, and after Henry's death he was charged with treason and executed.

EMS, PUNCTUATION OF (25 Aug. 1786), document drawn up at a meeting of the German ecclesiastical princes, who supported the Emperor Joseph II in his quarrel with Pope Pius VI. It amounted almost to a declaration of independence from the papacy, although its provisions were never seriously applied.

EMS TELEGRAM (1870), dispatch from King William I of Prussia to Bismarck, reporting the French chargé d'affaires' request that William I should promise never to support the candidature of any Hohenzollern for the Spanish throne. Bismarck released to the press a truncated version extremely insulting to the French, who then declared war on Prussia.

EN, early Sumerian name for the priestly ruler of a city. In later periods the secular duties were taken over by a governor called 'ensi'.

ENABLING ACTS (1923–1933) in Germany. Under the Weimar Republic's constitution, the Reichstag (Parliament and Council of Regional Governments) could, with a two-thirds majority and for a limited period, surrender legislative powers to the Reich government, if in times of crisis swift executive action was required. Thus, at the height of the Inflation of 1923, Stresemann's cabinet was given dictatorial powers to prevent the complete collapse of the economy. The Enabling Act (13 Oct). was restricted to financial and economic matters and expired prematurely when, on 2 Nov. 1923 the Social Democratic Party (SPD) withdrew its support in protest against the overthrow of the Thuringian Popular Front government by the army. Another act with similar powers was passed on 8 Dec. 1923 to enable the Marx government to take measures for the stabilization of the republic. Whereas the idea of this emergency provision of the Weimar constitution was to restore normal parliamentary processes, Hitler, when he came to power in Jan. 1933, was quick to realize the potential of an enabling act for the establishment of a permanent dictatorship. On 23 March 1933 he introduced a bill demanding full legislative authority for a period of four years. Furthermore he asked for his powers to be extended to include the control of civil rights, which enjoyed the special protection of the constitution, a proposal that went beyond the scope of previous enabling acts. Moreover, Reichstag and Reichsrat were to abandon their rights to participate in the ratification of international treaties. The bill merely guaranteed the powers of the Reich president, as well as the existence of both Reichstag and Reichsrat, and contained promises with regard to the inviolability of the Churches and the judiciary. While the Reichsrat, following the *Gleichschaltung* (co-ordination) of the regional governments, posed less of a problem, the approval of the Reichstag was uncertain. Under the constitution, two-thirds of the deputies had to be present, and fearing that the opposition might obstruct the bill by staying away from the final vote, Frick introduced a last-minute change of the by-laws: absentees without an excuse were not to be counted. The stipulation was unnecessary: out of the 538 deputies present, 444 voted for the Enabling Act, thus securing the end of parliamentary government in inter-war Germany.　VRB

ENCISO, MARTIN FERNANDEZ DE (c. 1470–1528), Spanish lawyer and geographer, who settled in Santo Domingo (1500), worked at colonization, and wrote the first Spanish relation of the New World, *Suma de geografía* (1519).

ENCLOSURE ACTS in Britain, feature of agrarian development principally from the 16th cent. to the 19th cent. Enclosure of open fields and grazings could take place in Scotland and much of Ireland at the will of the landowner, for there was no real tenant right. In England it could be done by agreement or by private act of parliament, the latter being the preferred method after 1760. This method was expensive and sometimes lengthy, but gave long-term certainty, finalized agreements for the extinction of tithe, and protected the legal rights of copyholders and small freeholders. In 1774 for their further protection parliament insisted that notice of an enclosure scheme should be posted at the parish church for three successive Sundays, and in 1801 the Enclosure Consolidation Act (often called the General Enclosure Act) simplified the procedure by instituting a common form for Enclosure Bills.

Enclosure Acts became very frequent during the French Wars (1793–1815), when high grain prices encouraged investment in improved farming, and when peace came most of England had been enclosed either in the period before parliamentary enclosure or under the acts. Enclosure was necessary for improved farming on the heavier soils which needed draining, and on all soils it was a help in segregation and breeding of stock, for the creation of large farm units, and for any cropping system that interfered with the common timetable and plan of land use of the open fields. It must therefore be considered an important element in the increased grain production of Britain after 1750. Since it was the first step to intensive farming on a non-mechanized system, it did not usually lead to depopulation of rural areas, though the new large farms involved the reduction of many farmers to the status of labourers. Though careful of legal rights, Enclosure Acts have often been criticized, probably with some justice, on the grounds that they enabled prescriptive or usurped claims for the use of common lands to be ignored by small occupiers or cottagers, and that the new, capitalized farming, which they made possible, was incompatible with the continuance of numerous small holdings. It is therefore probable that parliamentary enclosure completed the long-term movement to large units of landownership.

J. D. Chambers and C. E. Mingay, *The Agricultural Revolution, 1750–1880* (London, 1966).
T. S. Ashton, *An Economic History of England: the Eighteenth Century* (London, 1955). RMM

ENCLOSURES, process by which common land, waste land, and arable strips found in many of the medieval village communities of western Europe were formed into compact, enclosed areas under a single proprietor.

In England enclosing began in the early 13th cent. and enclosure for large-scale pasture farming and better husbandry by peasants and bigger proprietors became commonplace during the 15th cent., in the aftermath of the Black Death. The first great phase of English enclosure, however, occurred in the first half of the 16th cent., when, to satisfy the market for wool and to meet the challenge of inflation and the economic demands of a growing population, wealthier proprietors evicted tenant farmers or purchased their lands to engross several farms, creating pasture for sheep or sometimes for rearing cattle. Although the evils of 16th-cent. enclosures were perhaps exaggerated by contemporary preachers and pamphleteers, who misled posterity into overestimating the extent of the transformation, none the less the social consequences of enclosure were important in Tudor life and politics. However, after the decline of the Netherlands wool and cloth market in the mid-16th cent. enclosure for sheep pasture gave way to that for arable farming.

Although the pace and pattern of the movement varied across the country, at the end of the 17th cent. half the cultivable land in England was still unenclosed, and in these areas, chiefly lying in a central wedge from Dorset to Yorkshire, agriculture remained wastefully unproductive. The 18th-cent. rise in population provided a new stimulus to economic farming, particularly for cereals and meat production, and enclosure of the open fields for more productive mixed farming went ahead rapidly between 1760 and 1830. Enclosure was carried out by agreement ratified first in chancery and then by private act of parliament until the General Enclosure Act of 1801 facilitated the process. Enclosures thus reached a peak early in the 19th cent. during the struggle for national survival.

The enclosure movement was not confined to England. In the states of western Germany landlords hit by the 15th-cent. agrarian crisis tried to retrieve their position by enclosing common land and changing from arable farming to pasture. The Peasants' War (1525) in south-west Germany was prompted partly by resentment against enclosure of common fields. In the 16th–17th cent. in eastern Europe, the peasants were unable to prevent the creation of vast arable estates (*gutsherrschaft*). Most cultivable land in Spain was organized in open pasturelands owing to the entrenched position of the *mesta* or guild of sheep-owners and the enormous demand for merino wool in the 15th–16th cent. It was not until the 17th cent., after the decline of the Netherlands market, that Spanish proprietors began to enclose for wheat growing.

France had scarcely experienced any change from arable cultivation to pasture comparable with the Tudor enclosure movement because of the damaging effects of the Hundred Years and Civil Wars. The peasantry clung to their small plots for subsistence farming, while the great landowners lived on rents extracted from tenant farmers. Despite the enlightened propaganda of the Physiocrats and the royal edict of 1767 establishing a procedure for the enclosure of common land, and although enclosure had always been permitted by customary law in Normandy, the continuation of the *vaine pature* or common grazing rights in most of France precluded a wholesale enclosure movement during the *ancien régime*. As Lefebvre observed, the failure of the French to effect an agrarian revolution contributed to the social and political revolution of 1789.

J. Thirsk (ed.), *Agrarian History of England & Wales, 1500–1640*, vol. 4 (Cambridge, 1967). MKS

ENCOMIENDA SYSTEM, distribution of American Indians' labour services, and sometimes the Indians and their land, among the Spanish settlers of 15th- and 16th-cent. Spanish America. The practice was transferred from Spain as a means of satisfying the demands of conquistadores and early colonizers. The institution persisted as long as it solved the labour requirements of both farm and mine for the white colonists. Royal objections were raised to the *encomienda* almost from the outset because it threatened to create a colonial nobility sufficiently powerful to escape Crown control. Also, as labourers became scarce after the radical population decline of the early colonial period, the Crown was forced to compete with the colonists for labour services.

As introduced into the West Indies, the *encomienda* consisted ideally of a grant of the Indians in a village to a Spaniard who was to care for their welfare and christianization. In practice, the system resulted in great hardships for the natives, since the Spaniards exacted the maximum amount of work from the Indians, in spite of the illness and economic dislocation which followed the conquest. Hernán Cortés introduced the *encomienda* into New Spain (1522) and *encomiendas* were granted in Peru as well (1530s). *Encomenderos* (grantees) on the mainland insisted upon the hereditary character of their contracts, but the Crown increasingly resisted these petitions. This was partly because of a moral crusade against the institution conducted by the Dominican Order and Friar Bartolomé de las Casas. To the consternation of the *encomenderos*, the Crown decreed the New Laws (1542), which sought to eliminate *encomienda*. Rebellion threatened in New Spain and actually occurred in Peru, forcing the Crown to rescind the decree. The definitive royal order abolishing the system was slow in coming (1720), but by the mid-18th cent. the *encomienda* had virtually ended throughout the empire. The substitution of debt peonate and other devices as a means of securing a permanent labour force had been more commonly used in most regions since the mid-16th cent. HDS

ENCYCLOPAEDIA BRITANNICA, first published in Scotland (1768–71) as a three-volume dictionary of arts and sciences, edited by William Smellie. The scope of the second edition (10 vols, 1778–83) was enlarged to include history biography, and geography. Since 1929 it has been published in the US. The 1970 edition contained 24 vols.

ENCYCLOPÉDIE, work of reference, arranged alphabetically, published in France in 17 large folio volumes (1751–72), and taking its form from Ephraim Chambers's *Cyclopedia* (2 vols, 1728). Its editors (Diderot and d'Alembert), and its contributors (who included Voltaire, Condorcet, Montesquieu, Rousseau, and Helvetius) made it the most notable product of the French enlightenment. Their general philosophical approach was empirical, propounding a rational explanation of the universe, a secular morality, and freedom of thought and expression. Because their criticism of the monarchy and the Church was, on the whole, not explicit, and because Malesherbes was tolerant, the *Encyclopédie* was published in full, although publication was twice temporarily suspended.

ENDICOTT, JOHN (*c.* 1589–1665), governor of MA, who held various colony posts before being governor (1655). He was strict in his beliefs, and deported non-Puritans from the colony, being particularly harsh towards the Quakers.

ENGELS, FRIEDRICH (1820–95), German political writer and Marx's disciple and collaborator in the creation of Marxist socialism. He was the son of a Rhenish textile manufacturer. Engels came into contact with the factory system and the industrial proletariat through working in Manchester for his family's firm (1842–4). His experiences there induced him to write the *Condition of the Working Class in England* (1845). He was active on the continent in the revolutionary movements leading to 1848 and took part in a minor rising in Baden (1849). He collaborated with Marx in writing *The Communist Manifesto* (1848) and from 1850 to 1870 worked in the family business in Manchester, from which he provided Marx with both subsidies and a constant supply of economic data. After 1870 he engaged entirely in political activity, acting with Marx as a co-ordinator of the European socialist movements.

ENGHIEN, LOUIS DE BOURBON-CONDÉ, Duc d' (1772–1804), close relative of the exiled Bourbons, who was kidnapped, brought to France and executed on a false charge of conspiracy.

ENGLER, ADOLPH (1844–1930), German botanist, whose 20-volume *Die natürlichen Plantzenfamilien* (1887–99) provided a means of identifying, by keys and illustrations, all known genera of plants from algae to the most advanced seedbearing species.

ENGLISH COMPANY TRADING TO THE EAST INDIES, set up by parliament (1698), as a rival to the East India Co. in consequence of an association of interlopers petitioning for a charter and offering a loan of £2 million at 8 per cent to the government. This move was caused by the prevailing jealousy of the old company's monopoly and prosperity, and the odium it incurred after the 1688 Revolution owing to its close connection with James II and the Tories. But the income from the loan proved insufficient to provide the necessary capital and the old company difficult to dislodge from its eastern stations. In 1702 the 'old' and 'new' companies agreed to unite and this was achieved in 1709, following Godolphin's award of 1708. The reformed company took the name of 'The United Company of Merchants of England Trading to the East Indies'. It was generally known as the United Co.

ENGLISH PALE, derived from the Latin, *palus*, a stake, usually applied to that area or enclave of Ireland which, from Henry II's expedition of 1171–2, was directly subject to the English authorities in Dublin, though the actual term was not used until the late 14th cent. The area varied according to the strength of the occupying English, but until Henry VIII's reign broadly comprised the counties of Meath, Louth, Dublin, and Kildare, and it continued to exist until the subjugation of the entire country under Elizabeth I.

There was also an English Pale around Calais, stretching from Gravelines to Wissant and inland during the period of English occupation (1347–1558).

ENGLISH-SPEAKING SOUTH AFRICANS who, together with the Afrikaners, form the dominating white community in South Africa, first arrived with the British annexation of the Cape in 1806. Despite steady immigration—notably to the Eastern Cape (1820), Natal (after 1843), and to the diamond and gold mines at Kimberley and the Witwatersrand—English-speakers have always been outnumbered by Afrikaners, except in a few, mainly urban, areas. The two white groups remain divided socially and culturally. In racial attitudes there is little to distinguish the two, though their overseas contacts and different traditions probably dispose English-speakers to a more pragmatic and flexible policy.

Until 1910 English-speakers dominated politics in both the Cape and Natal, but after the Union they only held power as part of groupings founded by both white communities. After 1948 they were excluded from all political power, despite their continued industrial and commercial strength, until recently far greater than that of the Afrikaners.

ENLIGHTENED DESPOTISM. In the second half of the 18th cent. most of the European rulers, influenced by the French and German Enlightenment and imitating the successful methods practised by Frederick the Great of Prussia, tried to increase their personal power at the expense of the traditional institutions of Church, aristocracy, and estates. In some cases (Joseph II of Austria, Grand Duke Leopold of Tuscany, and Gustavus III of Sweden), this increase in monarchical power went hand in hand with reforms aimed at improving the general welfare of the population. Inevitably these reforms, which extended civil equality to the emerging middle class and ended serfdom, often produced demands for more representative government which were incompatible with the maintenance of royal despotism. The most successful enlightened despots were those in the smaller states (Tuscany, Baden, Saxe-Weimar), who did not have to divert their resources to competing in the international states system, and the rulers of Prussia and Russia. Both Frederick II and Catherine II, while abolishing torture and religious intolerance and destroying the political power of the nobility, ensured a stable government through the support of the aristocracy, who were allowed to keep their economic and social privileges. Although many of the despots' reforms had anticipated those of the French Revolution, its outbreak produced a reaction and an end to the experiment of enlightened despotism.

ENLIGHTENMENT, philosophical movement of the late 17th and 18th cents, which embraced the greater part of Europe and most aspects of human life. Its immediate origins were in England and arose from the ideas and methods of both Locke and Newton, Their rational approach to society, science, and religion served as a model for a large group of European thinkers, largely French, embracing Voltaire and Montesquieu, the Encylopaedists, and Helvétius, Beccaria, and Rousseau. All of them shared the basic belief that man was a rational being, able to work out his own salvation without the intercession of the Church or tradition. Inevitably, the main objects of their attacks were the Roman Catholic Church and the abuses of absolutism and feudalism. Most of these *philosophes*, however, believed that the way to end these abuses and to ensure the good life was through the power of an absolute ruler—an 'enlightened despot'—rather than through constitutional government. In Germany Herder, Goethe, and Schiller were all products of a native but related *Aufklärung*, although their immediate impact was far less than that of the Cameralists, who admired the efficient Prussian administrative machine and believed that human happiness could be achieved through enlightened administration.

Although the influence of these French and German *philosophes* on the outbreak of the French Revolution and the work of the Enlightened Despots is debatable, they certainly created an anti-clerical and rationalist climate of opinion among the educated European middle class and aristocracy. It would be difficult to explain the expulsion of the Jesuits, the general spread of free-trade measures, which the French Physiocrats advocated, religious toleration, the abolition of torture, and a more rational approach to justice and education without admitting their influence.   DMCK

ENNIUS, QUINTUS (239–169 BC), Greek Calabrian, brought to Rome by Cato. Under the patronage of Fulvius Nobilior and Scipio Africanus, Ennius gained fame as the founder of Hellenized Latin poetry in several genres. His *Annals*, a verse-history of the Romans, attained in later ages almost the status of holy writ.

ENNOBLING by French kings. From the late 13th cent. the French kings insisted on their sole right to ennoble men who were nobles by birth, to the exclusion of claims by various French dukes and counts to do likewise. Men usually paid the king for ennoblement and from the reign of Philip IV (1285–1314) onwards this became one of the regular sources of royal revenue. Ennoblements were not frequent before 1461, the beneficiaries usually being outstanding royal officials or rich financiers and merchants. The firm recognition of the exemption of nobles from taxation after 1438 increased the value of the dignity. Many important men sought illegally to pass for nobles without formal ennoblement and litigation over liability to taxes brought more precise definition of what constituted noble status and how it could be lost (*eg*, through *derogeance*, the exercise of non-noble occupations). Louis XI (1461–83), who was unique among the French kings in disliking the nobility, was eager to ennoble on a larger scale than any of his predecessors, thus making the nobility less of a closed caste. He ennobled many who claimed noble status illegally and permitted the citizens of many important towns freely to acquire non-noble land, which often formed the first step towards ennoblement. In his reign for the first time over 1000 men became nobles and his successors, for financial considerations, increased ennoblements ever faster. In 1789 the overwhelming majority of the French nobles descended in the male line from men who had been ennobled only after 1500.   EBF

ENRAGÉS (1793), most extreme French political group to emerge from the Parisian *sans-culottes*, whose main demand was for economic controls on the price of food. Their leaders, including Jacques Roux, were executed by the Jacobins.

ENSENADA, ZENO SOMODEVILLA, Marquis de la (1702–1781), Spanish statesman, noted for his economic reforms in the reign of Ferdinand VI. His early experience was in naval matters, as mayor of Cartagena (1730), and conqueror of Naples (1733). He was recalled to Spain from Italy by Philip V on the death of Campillo (1743) to become minister of finance, war, marine, and the Indies. He improved the naval base at Cadiz and the arsenals at Cartagena and Caracca, increased the fleet, reformed the customs service (1749), built new roads, and introduced a new single tax (1749). He also drew up a number of reports and schemes, *eg*, a unified code of law, which were not implemented before his downfall in 1754.

ENTAIL LAW OF PETER I (1714), Russian edict on inheritance, establishing the principle of sole succession and the indivisibility of immovable property, in place of the former practice of land division. In effect the law created a new system of land tenure, of indivisible, hereditary, and obligatory ownership. Unpopular with the landed nobility, it was abolished in 1731.

ENTERPRISE OF ENGLAND, translation of name given by the Spaniards to Philip II's attempt to invade England (1588) with his armada.

ENTRADA, or 'entry', in colonial Spanish America, a military expedition into previously unexplored or unconquered areas. By extension the term was sometimes applied to the conversion of Indians to Christianity by military means. In colonial Brazil the term referred to the exploratory movements into the interior, often sponsored by the colonial administration of the colony.

ENTREPÔT TRADE, process of distribution of goods from one country or town to another, carried on by middlemen, factors, or brokers, who provided the capital and transport needed. In the ancient world Athens had been the great emporium or market-place for this trade. In later centuries it was superseded by other cities, *eg*, Marseilles, Venice, Antwerp, and, in modern times, Amsterdam and London. From the late 16th–mid-18th cents the entrepôt trade was particularly associated with the Dutch, whose commercial supremacy was based upon this economic activity. Dutch traders and shippers, who had already superseded the Hanseatic League in handling the east–west trade between the Baltic and Biscay countries, enlarged their sphere of activity to the Portuguese and Spanish empires, their own possessions in the Americas and in the Far East, and the important markets of the Mediterranean and the Levant. During the 18th cent. the Dutch were overtaken by the British, who established their maritime supremacy over the Dutch, French, and Spaniards, and who held the lead in the entrepôt trade throughout the 19th cent.

ENVER PASHA (1881–1922), Ottoman army officer who played an important role in the 1908 Young Turk Revolution and later led the Jan. 1913 coup which established a military dictatorship in the Ottoman empire. As minister of war he was principally responsible for the Ottomans joining the Central Powers in 1914. He fled to Germany (1918) and in 1921 went to Turkestan to lead an anti-Soviet movement.

ENZEIM, BATTLE OF (1674). During Louis XIV's Dutch War his commander-in-chief, Turenne, devastated the Palatinate in the summer of 1674, but on his withdrawal across the Rhine into Alsace he was followed by imperial forces under Count Montecuccoli, who came up to challenge him at Enzheim, 12 kms from Strasbourg. Montecuccoli was joined by the Elector of Brandenburg, whereupon Turenne broke off the engagement.

ENZIO (*c.* 1225–72), son of the Emperor Frederick II. As his father's legate-general in Italy he fought against the Guelphs. The Bolognese captured him in 1249 and imprisoned him until his death, thus depriving the Hohenstaufen party of a potential leader after Frederick's death in 1250.

EOKA (National Organization of Cypriot Combatants), terrorist organization championing the union of Cyprus with Greece. EOKA, founded in April 1955 by George Grivas, was secretly encouraged, though publicly disavowed, by Abp Makarios. Its first attacks were against unpatriotic Greek Cypriots, but it soon turned its attention on the Turkish inhabitants of the island and, in 1956, the British authorities.

EON, CHARLES DE BEAUMONT D, (1728–1810), French royal equerry and unofficial representative of Louis XV in Britain. While a secretary in the French embassy the Chevalier d'Eon was chosen by De Broglie to further the royal plot to foment a war of revenge against Britain. He quarrelled with his ambassador and threatened to reveal the invasion plans to the English ministers. After avoiding attempts by French royal agents to kidnap him, he brought a successful lawsuit against his ambassador in the English courts and in 1766 was able to extract a pension of 12,000 livres per annum from Louis XV in exchange for incriminating diplomatic documents.

During his residence in England doubts arose concerning his sex, and at a trial in July 1777 he was declared to be a female, though this was disproved after his death.

EPAMINONDAS of Thebes (d. 363 BC), general and statesman in Thebes' brief period of primacy in Greece (371–362), which ended with his death. He was a leader of the exiles who freed Thebes from Spartan control (Dec. 379), and joined Pelopidas in developing Theban military power. At the peace conference at Sparta (371) he defended Theban leadership of Boeotia against Spartan charges and three weeks later led the Thebans to victory over the Spartans at Leuctra. During the winter of 370–369 he commanded an expedition which permanently crippled the Spartans' leadership of the Peloponnese by invading their homeland and liberating Messene. Though opposed by other less liberal Theban leaders, he led two further expeditions, neither as successful as the first, into the Peloponnese (summer 369 and 367), but a third seemed about to restore Theban influence to its peak when Epaminondas died at Mantinea.

EPHESUS, most important Ionian Greek city in Asia Minor, founded c. 1000 BC. Though initially overshadowed commercially and intellectually by Miletus, Ephesus nevertheless began under Lydian control and with Croesus' help the colossal marble temple of Artemis (c. 550). It was the birthplace of the philosopher Heracleitus (c. 500). After two centuries of alternating domination and 'liberation' by Persians, Athenians, and Spartans, it was finally 'liberated' from Persia by Alexander the Great (334). The importance of Ephesus as a commercial centre increased under Lysimachus, who replanned and enlarged it (296), and the Attalids (189–133). After its transfer to Rome (133) it became both the wealthiest city in the province of Asia and the home of one of the earliest Christian communities.

EPHIALTES (d. 461 BC), Athenian statesman, who worked with Pericles to strengthen democratic institutions against the aristocratic Areopagus Council. After stripping it of political power (462) he was murdered, possibly by political opponents.

EPHORS, five magistrates of ancient Sparta, appointed annually from the whole citizen body in the *apella* by acclamation. Instituted c. 700 BC as a popular check on the kings, the ephors first gained strength after Chilon (c. 550). However, despite their extensive powers, including the presidency of the *gerousia* and the *apella*, first audience with foreign ambassadors, considerable control over the kings, and absolute power over lesser magistrates and the secret police (*krypteia*), their brief tenure prevented the office becoming a vehicle for consistent policies or a source of lasting power for any individual. Most ephors known to us are little more than names. The office survived the revolutionary period c. 200 and lasted at least into the 2nd cent. AD.

EPHORUS, Greek historian of the 4th cent. BC and pupil of Isocrates from Aeolian Cyme. His comprehensive history from the Dorian invasions to 340 in 30 books, widely used by Diodorus Siculus (1st cent. BC), survives only in quotations by other writers.

EPHTHALITES, nomadic people of uncertain origin, known to the Byzantines as 'White Huns' because, although associated with the Huns, they had white skins and a different physical appearance. They apparently moved from the area north of the Tien Shan mountains, south-westwards into Bactria early in the 5th cent., establishing their capital near Herat. They caused almost continual disturbances on the Sasanian frontier for 150 years and attacked India (c. 465), overthrew the declining Gupta empire, and formed a short-lived empire in northern India (c. 500–30). Their power in

Bactria was finally destroyed by a combined attack from the Sasanian Chosroes I (531–79) and the Turks (c. 565).

ÉPICES, originally gifts of oriental spices given by a French litigant to the judge of a case in which he was involved. They were commuted into a compulsory monetary fee payable on a fixed scale according to ordinance. The fees, paid into a common salary fund, were then distributed to all members of the court by the *receveur des épices*, a practice which survived until the Revolution (1789).

EPICTETUS (c. AD 50–130), moral teacher of Nicopolis, Epirus, who had been born a slave in Phrygia. Combining stoic and cynic attitudes he wrote nothing, but his pupil Flavius Arrianus took down and published his *Manual* and *Discourses*. Distrusting systematic thought, he called for moral effort and a life of helpfulness and simple self-sufficiency, speaking with religious emotion of the divine providence whose decrees a wise man will learn to accept. He thus exemplifies the religious features of pagan philosophy which were to facilitate the success of Christianity.

EPICURUS (341–270 BC), Athenian philosopher, the first to admit women to his school, which he conducted at Athens after 306 in his house and garden. The community's simple life was decried by opponents, who distorted Epicurus' doctrine that pleasure was the highest good—though by 'pleasure' he meant merely 'freedom from trouble'. His writings filled 300 rolls, but only three short 'letters' and some ethical aphorisms survive. Epicurus held that sense-perception was the only basis of knowledge; his *Physics*, whereby he sought to free men from fear of death and the gods, propounded a version of Democritus' atomism. Among Epicurus' later followers was Lucretius, whose *De rerum natura* expounds Epicurean thought.

EPIDAURUS, ancient Dorian Greek city-state in northeastern Peloponnese. It was subject periodically to pressure from neighbouring Argos and threats from Athens across the Saronic Gulf and kept close contacts with Corinth. From the 6th cent. BC it was a loyal ally of Sparta in the Peloponnesian League, notably after the peace of Nicias (421) in the great Peloponnesian War, and after the Spartan defeat at Leuctra in 371. Its territory included the sanctuary of Asclepius, god of healing, a pan-hellenic centre of pilgrimage, of which extensive ruins survive, including a magnificent 4th-cent. BC theatre.

EPIRUS, mountainous area of north-west Greece, remote from the classical city-states, and not united politically until Alexander the Molossian (king 342–330 BC) formed a federal state. Epirus' brightest period was under Pyrrhus (king 297–272), who consolidated it and even seized some Macedonian territory. But he was over-active and his Italian expedition and constant struggle with Macedon left Epirus weakened. On becoming a republic (c. 232) it was immediately confronted with Roman expansion. Largely unenthusiastic about Rome, it remained effectively neutral in the First Macedonian War, only reluctantly joined Rome in the Second, and after sympathizing with Perseus in the Third, was sacked and 150,000 captives were taken. Roman colonies were subsequently founded at Nicopolis (30 BC) and Buthrotum, and roads built.

EPISCOPIUS, SIMON (1583–1643), Dutch Remonstrant minister and professor of theology at Leyden University, where he had formerly been a student under Gomarus and Arminius. Condemned by the Synod of Dort (1618–19) and forced into exile, he returned to Holland in 1626, when the persecution of Remonstrants declined, and became professor of theology in the Remonstrant seminary (1634–43).

EQUAL FRANCHISE ACT (1928) in Britain, legislative measure designed to end various anomalies of the 1918

Franchise Act, especially over the voting qualifications for women. Under the 1918 Act men over 21 were entitled to vote after six months' residence in a constituency. Women over 30 were enfranchised on the same basis as for the local government vote, *ie*, occupancy by the voter (or her husband) of premises of at least £5 annual value. There was much opposition to the bill, based, as in 1918, on the fears that women voters would outnumber men by some 2 million. The 'flapper vote', however, was finally admitted; the voting age for women became 21, and the qualifications for men and women became three months' residence. The act retained the plural voting system under which the business and university franchises granted a second vote to some half a million. About 5 million were enfranchised by the 1928 Act.

EQUAL RIGHTS ASSOCIATION, Canadian anti-Catholic organization, founded (1889) by Clarke Wallace, Dalton Macarthy, and William E. O'Brien. It favoured imperial federation and abolition of the use of the French language in schools and courts. The association declined in the 1890s.

EQUATORIAL GUINEA (28,051 sq. kms) in west Africa, formerly Rio Muni and Fernando Po, became independent in Oct. 1968. The Bubi and Fang are the main groups in the population of 310,500. A president and national assembly are elected by adult suffrage.

EQUIANO, OLAUDAH (*c.* 1745–?), Ibo who was taken from Africa as a slave to VA. Later he went to England, where he purchased his freedom (1766) and took an active part in the anti-slavery movement. He published his autobiography in 1789.

EQUITES (Latin 'horsemen'), originally the Roman cavalry organized in the 18 centuries of *equites* in the Comitia Centuriata. Since these centuries comprised the wealthiest citizens, the term came also to be applied loosely to the non-senatorial members of the Roman upper class and in the later 1st cent. BC was extended to include the notables of Italian towns, financiers, businessmen, etc. Augustus, drawing on certain partial Republican precedents, organized the class into a regular order of society comparable with the senatorial. Entry was open at the emperor's pleasure to any freeborn citizen of good character and a census of 400,000 sesterces. By creating specifically equestrian posts, the most important being the Prefectures of the Praetorian Guard and of Egypt, Augustus began the development of an equestrian career structure which was further extended by Hadrian until in the 3rd cent. AD *equites* displaced senators from many provincial and military commands. After the reconstruction of Diocletian and Constantine the *equites* survived only as a social order.

EQUIVALENT, THE, French indirect tax of the *ancien régime*, levied from 1444 on meat, fish, and wine in the province of Languedoc.

'ERA OF GOOD FEELINGS', phrase originated in the US (1817) by the *Columbian Centinel*, a Boston newspaper, and since commonly to designate the two presidential terms of James Monroe (1817–1825). The occasion that inspired the phrase was Monroe's visit to Boston during a tour of the north-east undertaken soon after he became president. The cordiality of his reception in this federalist stronghold seemed to signify an abatement of the bitter sectional animosities that had been aroused by Jefferson's Embargo and the War of 1812. One aspect of a national euphoria that set in after the treaty of Ghent in 1815—the spirit of sectional and political reconciliation—was also promoted by the neo-federalist policies of the Jeffersonian Republicans, such as enactment of a protective tariff and creation of a second Bank of the United States. Monroe's re-election in 1820 with

only one dissenting electoral vote provided a gloss of national consensus.

Yet the 'Era of Good Feelings' may have been wholly an illusion. At best, it was a brief interlude that ended with the financial panic of 1819 and the simultaneous renewal of sectional hostilities in the Missouri controversy. The election of 1820 confirmed the death of federalism as a national party, but political conflict merely shifted into other channels, and triumphant republicanism did not long withstand the internal pressure of personal, factional, and sectional rivalries. Thus, Monroe's second term was actually a period of political disintegration and increasingly bad feelings. His administration is remembered best for its conduct of foreign relations under secretary of state John Quincy Adams. The principal achievements in this realm were the Rush–Bagot agreement with Britain (1818), the acquisition of FL from Spain (1819), and the enunciation of the Monroe Doctrine (1823).

George Dangerfield, *The Awakening of American Nationalism, 1818–1828* (New York, 1965). DEF

ERASMUS, DESIDERIUS (1466–1536), Dutch scholar, moralist, and satirist. He studied at Paris University (1495), paid several visits to England (1499–1517), and went to Louvain. After 1521 he spent most of the rest of his life at Basle, where he worked for a printer and bookseller. His principal works were *Adagia* (1500), a popular collection of classical and patristic sayings; *Manual of a Christian Soldier* (1504), a theological treatise; *Praise of a Folly* (1509), a satire on monks, lawyers, philosophers, and obscurantism in general; *De Copia Verborum et Rerum* (1511), a textbook on rhetoric; the New Testament in Greek (1516); an edition of Jerome (1516), the first of several editions of patristic works; *Colloquies* (1518), on the vices of the clergy; and *Discourse on Free Will* (1526), a criticism of Lutheran doctrine.

On his first visit to England Erasmus met Grocyn, Linacre, and More and studied at Oxford under Colet. In his longest stay (1509–14), he taught Greek and divinity at Cambridge, and was given a rectory and a pension, but he did not get the substantial preferment for which he had hoped and so resumed his continental travels.

His influence was wide because he was able to articulate the dissatisfaction which most educated men felt with the follies, impostures, and superstitions of the Church. He directed his remarkable talent for ridicule also against merchants, lawyers, statesmen, and the sterilities of scholastic controversy, but his principal target was clerical ignorance and corruption. His shafts were delivered with so much wit and learning that at first even the pope and his cardinals were willing to enjoy the joke. But his Greek text of the New Testament corrected the Vulgate in important points affecting the authority of the priesthood, and with the spread of Lutheranism his writings were regarded as dangerously heretical and were condemned by the Inquisition and the Sorbonne.

But Erasmus was not a reformer—he was much too concerned with his health and his material comforts to have a crusader's temperament. His purpose was only to goad the Church by ridicule into correcting its abuses and renouncing the logic-chopping of its professional theologians. He and Luther were mutually antipathetic, and his balanced, comprehensive mind was able to perceive the dangers in some of Luther's teachings, particularly his dogma about the enslavement of the human will.

Erasmus died a Catholic, but despite himself his humanism and devotion to the principles of 'the new learning' had helped to prepare the ground for the growth of ideas he mistrusted and disliked; and it was a renewal of faith, not the artillery of scholarship and wit, that ultimately persuaded the Church to reform itself.

M. M. Phillips, *Erasmus and the Northern Renaissance* (London, 1949).

J. Huizinga, *Erasmus of Rotterdam* (English edition, London, 1950). **MMR**

ERASTUS, THOMAS (1524–83), Swiss physician and theologian, who gave his name to erastianism, the belief that the state should direct and determine the affairs of the Church. This tradition was inherited from the monarchies of late medieval Europe but it received a great impetus from the 16th-cent. Reformation.

ERATOSTHENES (*c.* 275–194 BC), successor to Apollonius as head of the Alexandrian library and a poet and polymath, who wrote on mythology, literary criticism, chronology, mathematics, geography, and philosophy. He had wide influence on many later writers.

ERCILLA Y ZUÑIGA, ALONSO DE (1533–94), Spanish soldier, who, while fighting the Araucanian Indians in Chile, wrote *La Araucana*, the greatest epic poem of the Latin American colonial period.

ERCKER, LAZARUS (d. 1593), superintendent of the mines in the Holy Roman empire and author of a notable work on metallurgy, the *Treatise on Ores and Assaying* (1574).

ERETRIA, Greek city in Euboea and partner of Chalcis (*c.* 750 BC) in leading Greek traders eastwards to Poseidium and westwards to Cumae. Hostilities with Chalcis over the Lelantine plain (*c.* 750–700) led to Eretria's exclusion from the West and its subsequent decline. In the 6th cent. the city co-operated with the Peisistratids (*c.* 550) and helped Athens defeat Chalcis (*c.* 506). In 499 only Eretria joined Athens in supporting the Ionian revolt and for this was destroyed by the Persians in 490. Thenceforward the city followed Chalcis' lead in relations with Athens until it became subjected to Macedonia and eventually Rome.

ERFURT CONFERENCE (1808), second meeting between Napoleon and Alexander I of Russia, both of whom had failed to carry out agreements reached since Tilsit (1807). However, Napoleon's growing preoccupation with Spain made him anxious to compromise. Alexander's admiration for Napoleon was waning. Napoleon had no intention of allowing Russia free reign to her ambitions in Turkey, and Russia was unwilling to bully Austria, who now appeared as a useful buffer between herself and France. However, it suited both powers to reach some temporary understanding and they renewed the treaty of Tilsit, leaving France free to concentrate on Spain and Russia to complete her conquest of Finland.

ERFURT UNIVERSITY was renowned in the 15th cent. for its school of law. Luther was a student there (1501–5) before he entered the Erfurt house of Austin friars.

ERGAMENES (*reg. c.* 220–200 BC), Kushite king mentioned by Diodorus Siculus, probably to be identified with the known Meroitic King Arqamani. His rule marked a period of prosperity for Kush, and he joined with Ptolemy IV in building temples at Dakka and Philae, indicating that relations with Egypt were unusually friendly. Diodorus relates that Ergamenes killed the priests of Amun, presumably at Napata, to forestall his own ritual murder by them—a practice alleged by Diodorus to have been common in Kush when the king's vigour began to fail.

ERHARD, LUDWIG (1897–), German economist and politician, who directed the West German economy at the time of its recovery after the Second World War and succeeded Adenauer as chancellor. After serving in the First World War he embarked on a career of economic research and eventually became director of the Institut für Wirtschaftsbeobachtung, an institute attached to the Nuremberg *Handelschochschule* (1928–42). His refusal to join the Nazi Party obliged him to leave the institute, and he became head of the Institut für Industrieforschung (1943–5).

At the end of the Second World War, as a 'technocrat' without political affiliations, he was chosen by the US occupation authorities to reorganize the economy of the Fürth Nuremberg region, then became economics minister of the Bavarian *Land* government (Oct. 1945). After the amalgamation of the British and American zones of occupation he was made president of the Advisory Committee on Currency and Credit, the body responsible for planning currency reform, and then (Feb. 1948) appointed director of the department of economics created by the Frankfurt Charter. He joined the Christian Democratic Union (CDU) and was elected to the first Bundestag. By this time Germany's economic recovery had established his reputation and he was appointed by Adenauer to be minister of economics, a position he retained in Adenauer's four governments. His economic policy, known as *Soziale Markwirtschaft*, implying a free-market economy, was supported by the introduction of a substantial measure of social welfare. It owed much of its success to factors outside Erhard's control—currency reform, which undervalued the Germany mark, and assistance under the Marshall plan—but his understanding of the needs and possibilities of the German economy amply justified Adenauer's confidence in him.

When Erhard himself became chancellor (1963), he continued Adenauer's policies while practising a different style of government which, being less personal, was more acceptable to the Bundestag. His party maintained its majority in the elections to the Bundestag (Sept. 1965), but thereafter he found it increasingly difficult to hold together the coalition with the more right-wing Free Democrats. He resigned in Nov. 1966 and was succeeded by Kiesinger.

ERIC, Duke of Södermanland (1282–1318), representative figure in the feudal nobility of Scandinavia, and a younger son of Magnus I of Sweden. He held a compact territory within all three Scandinavian countries. In 1312 he married Ingeborg, heiress to the throne of Norway. He died a prisoner of his elder brother, King Birger.

ERIC XIV (1533–77), King of Sweden (*reg.* 1560–8), eldest son and successor of Gustavus I, whose will provided dukedoms for Eric's half-brothers, a fact which fed the new king's fears of treason. He imprisoned John, Duke of Finland (1562–7), and put to death the Stures and other nobles, in one case assisting with his own hand. His lack of success in the Seven Years War of the North and his choice of queen and low-born ministers helped John to overthrow him. He died in prison, perhaps poisoned on John's orders.

ERIC BLOODAXE (d. 954) succeeded his father, Harold Fairhair, as King of Norway, but was later expelled. He then established himself (947) King of York. In 954 he was betrayed by Oswulf, the English lord of Bamburgh, and killed at Stanmoor. He was a pagan and the last of the Scandinavian kings of York.

ERIC HAKONARSON (d. *c.* 1023), a confederate in the overthrow of Olaf Tryggvason in 1000 and subsequently regent of western Norway for Danish kings. He supported his wife's brother Cnut in his invasion of England in 1015 and was rewarded with Northumbria, having meanwhile lost Norway to Olaf Haraldsson.

ERIC THE RED (*fl.* 10th cent.), Norse explorer, who was outlawed successively from Norway and Iceland for manslaughter. He rediscovered and named Greenland, which he explored for three years. In 985 or 986 he brought several hundred Icelandic settlers to Eystribyggd (modern Julianehåb district). His farm and his Christian wife's church have been excavated.

ERICCSON, JOHN (1803–89). Swedish-American engineer and inventor, who in 1836 patented the screw propeller to replace the cumbersome paddle-wheel then used as the propulsive device for steamships. In 1861 he built the ironclad warship *Monitor*. Its victory for the North during the American Civil War at Hampton Roads on 9 March 1862 marked the end of the supremacy of wooden naval vessels.

ERIDU (Abu Shahrain), sacred city of Sumeria dating from the 3rd millennium BC, discovered near Ur (AD 1946–9).

ERIE CANAL, US waterway from Albany to Buffalo, opened in 1825. Settlers across the Appalachians wanted a cheaper and more reliable means of communication with the eastern seaboard, and DeWitt Clinton, of New York, envisaged a waterway from the Hudson to the Great Lakes through the Mohawk Gap. He continued to be its major supporter during many years of frustration and delay, when it was known derisively as Clinton's Ditch. The NY State Legislature authorized the canal's construction in 1817 and it was completed eight years later, being 363 miles (590 kms) long and with 83 locks. It cost over $7 million, was one of the greatest engineering undertakings of its time, and established New York city as the gateway for Western trade. The lowering of freight rates, raising of land values, and stimulation of urban growth along its route encouraged a national canal mania. The relative importance of the canal declined through railroad competition after 1850.

ERIE INDIANS, large Iroquoian tribe found in the 17th cent. around Lake Erie. In 1654 they fought the last of several wars with the Iroquois confederacy, in which most of them were either destroyed, dispersed, or led into captivity.

ERIK (d. *c.* 1160), King of West Gothland (or, according to his son and successor, of all Sweden, of which he became patron saint). He was killed in a civil war. Legend associates him with a crusade to Finland.

ERNEST, Archduke of Austria (1553–95), brother of the Emperor Rudolph II. He was appointed governor of the Netherlands by his cousin, Philip II, on the death of Parma (1592), to strengthen the links between the German and Spanish Habsburgs. He arrived in the southern Netherlands in 1594 and proposed a peaceful reconciliation with the northern provinces, inviting the states general at the Hague to join in negotiations. The states, led by Oldenbarnevelt, rejected his proposal, while the southern provinces voiced to him their bitter grievances, the results of a generation of war and the prospect of renewed fighting with France.

ERSKINE, THOMAS ERSKINE, 1st Baron (1750–1823), British lawyer and politician of radical sympathies. After successfully defending Lord George Gordon (1781), he sat as an MP (1783–4, 1790–1806), speaking in major debates as an ardent Foxite and opponent of Pitt, *eg*, against Pitt's India bill (1784) and the Seditious Meetings bill (1795). He defended Thomas Paine (1792) and others prosecuted by the government, and as lord chancellor (1806–7) presided at the trial of Lord Melville. He supported the abolition of slavery, free trade in corn, opposed the Six Acts (1819–20), and Greek independence, and was an improving farmer.

ERSKINE, ALEXANDER (*fl.* 17th cent.), Scottish soldier of fortune who served as one of Sweden's military commanders during the Thirty Years War (1618–48). He administered the town of Erfurt as official resident and spoke for the Swedes at the Münster negotiations (1646–7).

ERYX (mod. Erice), mountain (750 metres high) in northwest Sicily near Drepana (Trapani) and the town at its top, important in antiquity in the Carthaginians' wars with the Greek colonies and with Rome as a stronghold guarding their harbours at Motya and Lilybaeum. Twice it was briefly captured by Dionysius I of Syracuse (398–397 and 368–367 BC). It fell to the Romans (249), but Hamilcar Barca partially re-

covered it from 244 to 241, when the Carthaginians evacuated Sicily under the treaty of Catulus.

ERZBERGER, MATTHIAS (1875–1921), German politician and signatory of the armistice of 1918. His early life was spent in journalism (he was on the staff of the *Deutsches Volksblatt*), in trade union organization, and in scholarly writing. In 1903 he was elected to the Reichstag as a member of the Centre Party, and gained prominence in 1906 by attacking Germany's policy of colonial administration. In the years leading up to the First World War he was a leading advocate of military and naval armament; at the same time his Catholic interests led him to support the cause of the Poles under German rule.

During the war he travelled abroad on various diplomatic missions. In 1917, following the March revolution in Russia, he worked to bring about a negotiated peace and was a leading supporter of the Peace Revolution adopted by the Reichstag (19 July 1917). He joined the government of Prince Max of Baden (Oct. 1918) and led the delegation which signed the armistice. Thereafter he took a leading part in securing the ratification of the Versailles treaty. He was minister of finance (June 1919–March 1920) and was responsible for radical tax reforms, but the hostility of the nationalists drew him into a damaging lawsuit which led to his resignation. On 26 Aug. 1921 he was murdered by extreme nationalists.

ERZERUM TREATY (1847) between Iran and the Ottoman empire, made under Russo–British advice to establish a firm frontier. Actual delimitation was the subject of later surveys.

ESARHADDON (*reg.* 681–669 BC), King of Assyria who came to the throne after defeating his brothers, who had previously murdered his father, Sennacherib. In the north and north-east he had to face Scythian and Cimmerian invaders and, although he had some success, by the end of his reign at least two provinces were lost. A revolt in Sidon was crushed and, in 671, in order to end Egyptian intrigue in Syria, Esarhaddon invaded Egypt, defeated the Egyptian army, and took Memphis. He died on the way to Egypt to deal with revolt there (669).

ESCALANTE–DOMÍNGUEZ EXPEDITION (29 July 1776–3 Jan. 1777), Spanish expedition led by Fray Silvestre Vélez de Escalante and Fray Francisco Atanacio Domínguez from the Zuñi mission in Santa Fé. The purpose of the expedition was both to find a better route between Santa Fé and the settlement at Monterey, CA, and to open new areas for Franciscan evangelizing among the Indians. The expedition failed to reach Monterey, but exploration of the Rocky Mountains and Great Salt Lake basin extended Spain's territorial claims in North America.

ESCHEATOR, officer of the Crown in medieval England responsible for lands which escheated (*ie*, reverted) to the Crown through failure of heirs or as a penalty for felony. There were two escheators until the reign of Edward II, one with jurisdiction over England south of the Trent, the other with jurisdiction to the north of it. Thereafter they were appointed for each county.

ESCOCESES AND YORKINOS, two principal masonic groups involved in a series of political and revolutionary struggles in Mexico (1825–8). The Scottish rite (*escocés*) harboured monarchists, centralist republicans, Spaniards, and members of prominent families generally, headed by Gen. Nicolás Bravo. The Yorkist rite (*yorkino*) attracted federalist republicans and persons of obscure origin, both creole and *mestizo* (mixed), led by Gen. Vicente Guerrero. The latter group was vigorously anti-Spanish. The *escoceses* rebelled (Dec. 1827) when the forced expulsion of Spaniards began, but were defeated and their leaders were exiled. The *yorkinos* then divided into two factions—one favouring and the other opposing Vicente Guerrero.

ESCORIAL, THE, royal residence of the kings of Spain, built (1563–84) by Philip II. It was begun two years after the translation of the Spanish court to its permanent home in Madrid, the site being chosen in the Guadarama Hills to afford Philip some private life at a convenient distance from the court. It was designed by Juan Battista de Toledo and Juan de Herrera to achieve 'simplicity of form, severity in the whole, nobility without arrogance, majesty without ostentation'. Philip II brought to it the treasures of a vast empire: tapestries from the Netherlands, Milanese silver-work, woods from the New World, marble from the Sierra Nevada, and from Venice paintings by Titian and Tintoretto.

ESCORIAL, TREATY OF THE (1733), Franco–Spanish alliance, aimed against Austria and Britain, and usually known as the First Family Compact, since it was concluded between the two Bourbon powers. In return for abandoning the Austrian rapprochement sought by Ripperda in 1725, Elizabeth Farnese of Spain secured from the French minister, Fleury, a guarantee that the Italian duchies of Parma and Tuscany and any other territories conquered from Austria should devolve upon her eldest son, Don Carlos.

ESCOVEDO, JUAN DE (d. 1578), Spanish official and secretary to Don John of Austria, who was murdered on Philip II's orders and at the instigation of Antonio Perez for alleged treason (1 March 1578). In reality he was the scapegoat for Don John's unpopularity with Philip and for Perez's guilty fears that his intrigues against the king might be revealed.

ESIGIE (*c.* 1516–*c.* 1550), Ruler of Benin, who is believed to have been baptized and educated by Portuguese missionaries as a child. He fought a number of successful expansionist wars, the most important being those against Idah and Udo. The art of brass-casting made significant progress in his reign.

ESKIMO, group of American aborigines, forming part of the Eskimauan linguistic group, formerly occupying nearly all the coasts and islands of Arctic America from eastern Greenland and the northern end of Nfld to the western-most Aleutian Islands. They are the only aborigines who had contact with Europeans before Columbus (1492), for Greenland was occupied by Norsemen during the 10th and 11th cents. Later European navigators encountered the Eskimo along the eastern coasts, and the Russians discovered and annexed the western part of their domain. They number (1970) approximately 50,000, living mainly in Greenland, Canada, and AK. A few live in the Soviet Union.

ESNAMBUC, PIERRE BELAIN, SIEUR D' (1585–1637), French naval officer and a pioneer of Caribbean colonization. After trading with St Christopher (St Kitts), Esnambuc persuaded wealthy patrons, including Cardinal Richelieu, to sponsor the Compagnie de Saint Christophe (1626) and send several hundred settlers to the island (1627). Esnambuc and Sir Thomas Warner, leader of St Christopher's English settlers, massacred the island's Indians and afterwards agreed to partition the island and preserve peace in the event of war between France and England.

ESPARTERO, BALDEROMO (1793–1897), Spain's first military dictator, who ousted Maria Cristina to become Isabella's regent (1840–3). His career illustrated the extent to which the 1812 constitution failed to coincide with the realities of Spanish politics, for he emerged as a champion of the constitution, through the prestige he gained in ending the civil war with the Carlists, but once in power he failed to see the need for a solid political base for his rule and relied on increasingly heavy-handed military methods. Espartero provoked a further civil war (1842) by suppressing the rights

that he himself had secured for the Basques. After Barcelona had been bombarded into submission, the army turned against him and forced him into exile. He returned as joint ruler of Spain during the brief biennium (1854–6).

ESPEJO, FRANCISCO JAVIER EUGENIO (1747–96), liberal intellectual and journalist of colonial Quito and Bogotá, founder of numerous cultural societies in New Granada and outspoken critic of Spanish colonial policies and institutions.

ESPERANTO CONFERENCE (1906), first of many international conferences to popularize the use of Esperanto, an international language devised by Dr L. Zamenhof, a Pole, at the end of the 19th cent. It represented the desire of many Europeans for fuller international understanding to counter the aggressive nationalism of their age.

ESPINOSA, DIEGO DE (1502–72), Spanish cardinal, Inquisitor-general, and president of the council of Castile under Philip II. In 1566 he drew up an edict imposing severe restrictions upon the Moriscos which provoked a serious revolt (1568–70). He may have been a party to Philip's connivance in the murder of the mentally and physically abnormal heir, Don Carlos (1568).

ESPIRITU SANTO, island in the New Hebrides, thought by Quiros to be part of the lost 'continent' (1606), was identified by Cook (1774). Whalers (1810) and sandalwooders (Big Bay, 1860) were followed there by labour recruiters in the 1870s and many Melanesian villagers migrated to Fiji and Qd. Later, Presbyterian missionaries had much success, but in fostering coastal settlement they contributed to drastic depopulation of the interior. In 1902 Australian ex-servicemen were settled on mission lands as a counter to French expansion and possible annexation, thus paving the way for the Anglo–French Condominium (1907).

ESQUERRA, THE, in Spain, became the most important Catalan separatist party, at the expense of the conservative *Lliga* of Cambó, when after 1917 the Catalan upper classes began to ally themselves with the Madrid government against revolutionary workers. Under the leadership of Col. Francisco Macía, the Esquerra emerged as a union of left-wing Catalanist groups, consisting largely of small businessmen and the lower middle classes of the towns and the countryside. The party grew in strength during the Dictatorship because Primo de Rivera's anti-Catalanism encouraged separatist sentiment, and also because Macía became a national hero by hatching plots against Primo from behind the French border.

In April 1931 the Esquerra won the municipal elections. Macía consequently intended to declare an independent Catalan Republic, but a deputation from Madrid persuaded him to await parliamentary sanction. However, in 1933 he died and was replaced by Luis Companys, a lawyer who had once helped anarchists and now had close ties with the peasantry. Despite losses in the Nov. 1933 elections, the Esquerra won the elections to the *Generalitat*, the Catalan parliament.

There was soon conflict with the right-wing government. In Catalonia, as in the rest of Spain, landlords were raising rents and evicting tenants. Companys, who was dependent on the small wine-growing peasantry, the *Rabassaires*, passed the *Ley de Cultivos* which protected their tenures. Though the conservative landowners managed to get the government to annul the law, Companys disregarded the annulment. At the same time, he was involved in a struggle for power within the Esquerra. The *Estat Catalá*, the youthful extremist wing, led by José Dencas, advocated total separatism, and rather than see the party split, Companys declared Catalonia a separate state within the Spanish Federal Republic. At the same time, revolutionary strikes were starting in Asturias and the Basque country (Oct. 1934). Companys's revolution was suppressed within a few hours.

Companys reappeared at the head of the Esquerra after the Popular Front elections. Following the outbreak of civil war, the party was submerged in the political chaos of Barcelona. Officially it continued to share the government with the anarchists and socialists, but effectively much of its rank-and-file went over to the communists.   PP

ESSAYS AND REVIEWS (1860), collection of essays by seven Anglican churchmen (six of them clergymen) including Benjamin Jowett, Mark Pattison, and Frederick Temple, later Abp of Canterbury. It was denounced by Bp Wilberforce of Oxford and condemned by convocation as heterodox for its advanced biblical criticism.

ESSENES, Jewish ascetic sect, the 'pious ones', practising a type of piety akin to that of the Pharisees. It is not mentioned in the Bible, but is referred to by other Jewish and pagan writers. The sect, which originated in the 2nd cent. BC, numbered around 4000 at the beginning of the Christian era and came to an end in the 2nd cent. AD. Its members lived a highly organized life in monastic settlements in Palestine, having forms of worship and teaching which may owe something to non-Jewish sources. Candidates for membership served a three-year novitiate during which they took oaths of obedience and secrecy. There is no certain evidence that John the Baptist or Jesus belonged to the sect.

ESSEQUIBO, province of Guyana along the Essequibo river, settled by Dutch and English (1604), and later granted to the Dutch West India Co. (1621). Essequibo became British (1814) and part of British Guiana (1831).

ESSEX, GEOFFREY DE MANDEVILLE, 1st Earl of (1st of 1st creation) (d. 1144), English soldier who, in the civil wars between King Stephen and Matilda, twice changed sides, each time achieving greater territorial concessions. As a grandson of a former keeper of the Tower of London under William I (*reg.* 1066–87), he secured the custody of this key fortress and used his control over it to create a virtually autonomous principality for himself in Essex, Hertfordshire, and Middlesex. The Londoners became 'his mortal enemies' (in the words of a contemporary text) and their revolt against Geoffrey in 1141 prevented the crowning of Matilda (whom Geoffrey was then supporting) as queen of England. This proved a decisive turning point in the decline of Matilda's fortunes. When, after 1142, Stephen became strong enough to break the earl's power, Geoffrey turned brigand and terrorized the Fen Country until he was killed by Stephen's forces. His career is illustrative of the ambitious and savage character of an unchecked feudal baronage.

ESSEX, THOMAS CROMWELL, 16th Earl of (6th creation) (1485–1540), English politician of humble birth who became in turn a mercenary, a money-lender, and a merchant, before entering the service of Wolsey (*c.*1514). He also became an MP (1523) and studied law, and he suggested and carried through parliament the measures which brought the Church under royal supremacy. He was appointed king's secretary (1534) and as vicar-general (1535), superintended the dissolution of the monasteries. As part of a scheme to engage England in a Protestant alliance, he arranged the marriage of Henry VIII to Anne of Cleves (1540). Though given an earldom in 1540, he was executed in the same year for treason.

When the dispute between the pope and Henry VIII began over the annulment of his first marriage, Henry did not intend a constitutional revolution. It was Cromwell who suggested that he might solve his difficulties by becoming head of the Church. The idea of royal supremacy was not in itself new, but Cromwell saw how it could be established. By using statute as the instrument to declare and enforce it, he created the sovereign national state where the will of parliament is supreme.

The removal of the pope's authority left an administrative and legislative vacuum which Cromwell filled by creating courts and officials to take over the organization of the Church as a department of state. In a few years of immense industry and purposeful administration he created a modern bureaucratic machine that was no longer exclusively dependent on the energies of the royal household. He reorganized the privy council as an efficient working unit, made the secretary the principal executive officer, established six courts for the collection and administration of revenue, and sent out staffs of permanent officials to man the provincial councils that supervised the outlying districts. These reforms, sometimes sanctioned by statute, created a permanent structure of government. Cromwell also found time to pass the first modern poor law (1536), mitigated the hardships caused by enclosure, and attempted to establish London in place of Antwerp as an international woolmart.

The genuineness of his religious convictions has been questioned. His mind was essentially practical and secular, and his instinctive radicalism made him sympathetic to men who favoured doctrinal change. He wanted the Bible to be available in English, and issued injunctions (1536, 1538) to enforce compliance with the Ten Articles and condemned 'superstitious practices'. In 1539 the fear of a Franco–Spanish alliance led him into more positive action. He negotiated with the Lutherans and persuaded Henry into marriage with the daughter of the Protestant Duke of Cleves. The lady was uncouth and unattractive, and by the time she arrived in England the international situation had changed again. Saddled with a wife and a policy both of which he found distasteful, Henry listened to the aristocratic faction which had long hated Cromwell as an upstart and a heretic. Ironically, it was Cromwell's own instrument, an omnicompetent parliament, that brought him to the block. He was not tried in court of law, nor allowed to speak in his own defence. He was simply condemned by an act of attainder that declared him guilty of heresy and treason.

A. G. Dickens, *Thomas Cromwell and the English Reformation* (London, 1959).
G. R. Elton, *The Tudor Revolution in Government* (Cambridge, 1953).   MMR

ESSEX, ROBERT DEVEREUX, 19th Earl of (2nd of 8th creation) (1566–1601), English soldier, courtier, and royal favourite who took part in the battle of Zutphen (1586) and the attack on Corunna (1589), and commanded the English expedition sent to assist Henry of Navarre's Protestant forces in the siege of Rouen (1591). During 1595 he established a kind of intelligence network in foreign countries and in 1595 commanded jointly with Howard of Effingham the English attack on Cadiz which resulted in the destruction of a fleet of Spanish merchant ships and the sack of the town. He wanted to hold Cadiz with a permanent garrison but was persuaded that such a strategy would displease Queen Elizabeth I. Adverse winds having prevented another attack on Spanish ports, he set out with a fleet for the Azores to intercept the Spanish treasure fleet (1597). He was given the post of earl marshal, though the Islands Voyage was a failure (1597). His political enemies were now multiplying. He alienated Raleigh, Blount, and Burghley, rejecting the latter's peace policy in favour of the vigorous prosecution of the war against Spain (1598). Finally Elizabeth I appointed him lord lieutenant and governor-general of Ireland (1599). After prevarication he invaded Ulster too late and concluded a truce with Tyrone (1599). Returning to London without royal authorization (Sept. 1599) he was imprisoned for a year until tried before a private commission for desertion and other charges. He was then deprived of his offices and confined to Essex House but rashly plotted with dissident elements to secure the dismissal of Elizabeth's ministers. His attempt to raise the citizens of London having failed, he was tried at Westminster Hall and sentenced to death. HNBM

ESSEX, ROBERT DEVEREUX, 20th Earl of (3rd of 8th creation) (1591–1646), English parliamentary commander in the Civil War, who was given command of a national army which parliament was raising to support the militia. He was the first commander-in-chief of parliamentary forces because of his personal and territorial influence. Despite his reputation for dilatoriness he checked both Charles I's army at Edgehill (Oct. 1642) and Prince Rupert's attack on London at Turnham Green (Nov. 1642), and in the following year, by swift marching, relieved the siege of Gloucester and then intercepted the king's advance on London at Newbury. In 1644, however, he was forced to abandon his forces in Cornwall, and in 1645 resigned his commission in anticipation of the Self-Denying Ordinance.

ESSEX AFFAIR (1804–5), Anglo–American diplomatic and legal dispute during the Napoleonic wars, arising from the British capture of the American vessel *Essex*. In its attempt to destroy neutral trade between France and the French West Indies, the British government had applied the 'Rule of 1756', which provided that a belligerent could not open to neutrals trade with its colonies that was banned to them in time of peace. American ships had evaded the rule by carrying cargoes from the West Indies first to a US port and then on to France. The British decision in the *Essex* case reversed earlier recognition of such 'broken voyages', declared that they would henceforth be regarded as 'continuous', and resulted in a considerable increase in British seizures of American ships.

ESTE FAMILY, DUKES OF FERRARA, ancient Italian family dating from the 10th cent., whose 15th-cent. dukes, Lionel, Borso, and Ercole I, were keen patrons of humanism. The Este court at Ferrara became a centre of the new learning through the scholarship of Guarino Veronese (1370–1460) and Ludovico Ariosto (1474–1533) and was famous for its performances of fashionable Latin plays. In 1528 Duke Ercole II married Renée of France, also a keen humanist and a sympathizer with the Protestant reform movement. In 1537 the court was visited by Calvin at Renée's invitation, who afterwards continued to correspond with him and to defend persecuted Protestants, (*eg*, Fanini); while, under the court's protection, Protestant literature was published and distributed. Her son, Duke Alphonso II, a devout Catholic, forced his mother to return to France (1559) and allied himself with the papacy. On Alfonso's death (1598) without issue the duchy was annexed by Pope Clement VIII. The line of his younger brother Cesare d'Este continued to rule in Modena.

ESTERHAZY, MARIE CHARLES FERDINAND WALSIN, Comte (1847–1919), French officer, for whose sale of military information to Germany (1894) another officer, Capt. Dreyfus, was blamed, though eventually Esterhazy himself was cashiered.

ESTIENNE, ROBERT (1503–59), humanist scholar, author of a Latin–French dictionary (1538) and a famous edition of the Bible (1540).

ESTIGARRIBIA, JOSE FELIX (1888–1940), commander of the Paraguayan army during the Chaco War (1932–5), Liberal Party leader, and president of Paraguay (1939–40).

ESTIME, DUMARSAIS (1900–53), president of Haiti (1946–1950), reformer and friend of the black man as opposed to the *mulatto*. Estimé sought to terminate the Haitian caste system whereby the *mulattoes* had enjoyed supremacy over the blacks.

ESTRADA CABRERA, MANUEL (1857–1924), president-dictator of Guatemala (1898–1920). Though elections were held as prescribed in the constitution, their outcome was never in doubt. Foreign, and particularly US, capital entered Guatemala under government protection. The banana industry spread rapidly and sugar production boomed. Both products were exported and profits were absorbed by foreign corporations and the landed elite. The Indians were hampered by a shortage of land. Estrada Cabrera was overthrown by Carlos Herrera y Luna.

ESTRADA PALMA, TOMAS (1835–1908), revolutionary leader of the Cuban Ten Years War (1868–78) and first president of Cuba (1902–6).

ESTREES, LOUIS CHARLES CESAR, LE TELLIER, D', Marquis de Courtanvaux, Count (1697–1771), French marshal, and member of an eminent military family, who fought in the War of the Austrian Succession and the Seven Years War. He helped to decide the battle of Fontenoy in favour of France (11 May 1745) and defeated the Duke of Cumberland at Hastenback (26 July 1757). Shortly afterwards he was relieved of his command through the influence of his enemy, Paris-Duverney, but was created minister of state (July 1758).

ESTREMADURA, Spanish province bordering on Portugal. Before the Civil War, its estates were usually large *latifundios*, belonging to absentee landlords, badly cultivated and often used for stock-breeding. The peasantry, either landless labourers, *braceros*, or owners of teams of plough mules (*yunteros*), lived in great poverty. The landlords could always keep them in order by letting some land go out of cultivation. In any case, some soil was so poor that it could only support a crop once every 12 years. In 1930 over 80 per cent of the population of Estremadura was earning an average of one peseta per day. The consequent revolutionary sentiments of the peasantry were kept from legitimate expression by the strength of *caciquismo*.

The harshness of conditions was sharply revealed in Jan. 1932. A small isolated village, Castilblanco, was the scene of a strike meeting. The Civil Guard, which tried to prevent it were fallen upon by the villagers, beaten to death, and mutilated. This was a primitive act of collective revenge against oppressive conditions. The Republican agrarian act (1932) brought a measure of relief to Estremadura, but it was short-lived. When the right wing came to power in Nov. 1933 those peasants who had been settled on untilled land were evicted.

In the Feb. 1936 elections Estremadura voted for the Popular Front in defiance of the *caciques*. Tired of awaiting formal reform, the peasants began a spontaneous revolutionary *reparto* or division of estates. After a few violent clashes with the Civil Guard, the government hastily recognized the seizures. Most of Estremadura fell to the rebels in July 1936. Badajoz held out until Aug. when it was taken by foreign legionnaires and the town's left wing massacred. PP

ETCETERA OATH (1640), included in the canons promulgated by the convocation of the Church of England, which required all men in holy orders and all men with degrees from Oxford or Cambridge University to swear by Nov. 1640 that they would uphold the established government of the Church by 'archbishops, bishops, deans, and archdeacons, etc'. It united the various opponents of the government and the Church, who considered it illegal, as convocation had continued sitting after the dissolution of parliament (May 1640). The oath was greeted by a stubborn refusal to enforce it and it was suspended (Oct. 1640) until the next convocation met.

ETHICAL POLICY in the Dutch East Indies, attempt by the Netherlands government to improve the social and economic condition of the Indonesian people and to prepare them for taking a share in governing the colony. The speech from the throne of 1901, stressing the depressed condition of the Javanese peasantry, marked its inauguration as official government policy. The next two decades saw the rapid extension of government services and authority to the village level, the expansion of education, and the beginning of political organization and representation. Conservatives, especially among the Dutch colonial civil servants and planters, attacked the policy on the grounds that it falsely assumed a congruence of interests between the Netherlands and the Indonesians. As Indonesian political activity grew rapidly more radical, their arguments gained increasing weight. Political disorders (1918–19) were followed by increased government repression, reducing the independence movement to a revolutionary core. After communist-led rebellions (1926–7) the few remaining ethically minded politicians declared that that policy could be applied only to economic and social questions, not to political matters.

ETHIOPIA, conversion to Christianity of (c. 330). When Meropius, a Christian merchant from Tyre, was shipwrecked off the coast of the Aksumite empire two Syrian brothers in his service, Frumentius and Aedesius, were saved. They gained influence with the emperor of the day, Frumentius becoming his secretary and Aedesius his cup-bearer. On the death of the emperor, Frumentius became tutor to his son, who was probably Ezana, and converted him to the Christian faith, the court following his example. Frumentius was later appointed by Patriarch Athanasius of Alexandria as Bp of Ethiopia. Churches and monasteries were established with close ties with Coptic Egypt.

ETHIOPIA, invasion and liberation of (1935, 1941). Though Ethiopia and Italy had signed a 20-year treaty of Friendship and Arbitration in 1928, the Italian dictator, Mussolini, decided in 1932 to embark on an aggressive policy in East Africa. His pretext came with the Walwal incident (Dec. 1934), when an Anglo–Ethiopian boundary commission encountered Italian troops at Walwal on the Ethiopian side of the frontier with Italian Somaliland. After an armed clash the Ethiopians retreated, but the Italians demanded that Ethiopia should pay compensation and recognize the area as Italian. Emperor Haile Selassie refused these demands, and submitted the dispute first to direct arbitration in accordance with the 1928 treaty, and later to the League of Nations. The Italians, requiring time to complete their military preparations in Eritrea, directed their efforts to delaying a league solution. Talks dragged on until Oct. 1935, when Mussolini's army attacked. The League of Nations condemned Italy and introduced limited sanctions, omitting, however, the crucial ban on oil which would have brought the invading army to a halt. The Italians, who possessed heavy superiority of weapons and used poison gas, occupied Gondar and Harar in April 1936 and in May Addis Ababa, the emperor having left for Europe a few days earlier.

Though Ethiopian patriots continued their resistance in many areas, Italy's conquest was recognized by most countries. But Mussolini's declaration of war on Britain and France in June 1940, and the consequent threat to British territories in the area, led to a British offensive against Italian East Africa. The Emperor was flown to the Sudan to join in the liberation of his country, and returned to Addis Ababa in triumph on 5 May, five years to the day after its occupation by Italian troops. Though there were at times considerable difficulties between the restored Ethiopian government and its liberators, the country soon regained its full sovereignty which was recognized in a succession of Anglo–Ethiopian agreements. The former Italian colony of Eritrea was later federated with Ethiopia under the Ethiopian Crown by a United Nations decision (1952), and completely united as an integral part of Ethiopia in 1962.

A. J. Barker, *The Civilising Mission: the Italo–Ethiopian war 1935–6* (London, 1968).
L. Mosley, *Haile Selassie* (London, 1964). RP

ETHIOPIA, reunification of. The 16th-cent. invasion of Ahmad Gragn and subsequent civil wars had left Ethiopia dismembered. In the second half of the 19th cent. Emperor Tewodros attempted in vain to unite the country however, Subsequently his successor, Yohannes IV, brought the

Christian highlands largely under his control. Later Menelik II, the ruler of Shoa, succeeded to the imperial throne, and after obtaining large quantities of firearms occupied the 'lost provinces' to the south. He thus gained control, eg, of Kaffa and Jimma in 1882, Harar in 1887, and Ogaden in 1891; by the end of the century he had reunited the entire empire, except Eritrea, which was reincorporated after the Second World War. Ethiopia in 1970 had become a territory of 1,221,900 sq. kms, ruled by an emperor and with an elected Chamber of Deputies and a nominated senate. The population (1970), consisting chiefly of the Amhara and Galla groups, numbers 22,997,000.

ETHIOPIAN PERIOD in Egypt (c. 730–663 BC), that in which Egypt was ruled by Nubian kings, after its invasion by the Nubian ruler Pianki, who advanced as far north as Memphis (c. 730), and his brother, Shabako, who completed the conquest (c. 711). The latter king and his successors came into conflict with the Assyrians, who invaded the country in 670, 667, and 663, and drove the last Ethiopian ruler, Tanuatanum, back to Nubia.

ETHIOPIANISM, religio-political movement among Africans in southern and central Africa. It was so-called because, in the Authorized Version of the Bible, black men are referred to as 'Ethiopians'. African Christians, restive under white tutelage and indignant at segregation in churches, took as their slogan the 'Ethiopian' liberatory verse 31 of Psalm 68 and in 1872 began in South Africa to establish their own churches, free from white control. The movement spread northwards into central Africa. The defeat of the Italians at Adowa in 1896 by the Emperor Menelik of Ethiopia stimulated racial pride amongst the movement's adherents and added to the fear of southern and central African whites that 'Ethiopianism' was a threat to their privileged positions.

From 1897 some of these independent African Christian groups became affiliated with black American churches. This created the largely unjustifiable fear among whites in southern and central Africa that Negroes from the US were attempting to subvert their governments, particularly at the time of the 1906 Zulu Rebellion in Natal; the 1915 Chilembwe Rising in Malawi; the clash between the South African police and Mgijima's 'Israelites' at Bulhoek in 1921; and in the 1920s with Marcus Garvey's Universal Negro Improvement Association. Furthermore, the chiliastic Watch Tower (Kitawala) movement in central Africa was often identified by whites with African political militancy, especially in Malawi in 1908 and in Zambia, up to at least the Copperbelt disturbances of 1935.

By the 1930s, however, political militancy was disappearing from the independent African churches in southern and central Africa. 'Ethiopian'-style churches were tending to be replaced by a wide and heterodox variety of messianic, millenarian, and witch-finding movements, often led by African prophets claiming divine revelations. Although these movements sometimes clashed with established political authority, they were fundamentally otherworldly in orientation. In South Africa many of these groups, unlike the original Ethiopianism, which tended to be inter-tribal in its appeal, were restricted to particular ethnic groups. This often had the effect of bolstering the emerging system of apartheid in South Africa. Proliferation accelerated during the 20th cent.: by 1960 there were then 2000 sects in South Africa, many being separated from already independent black churches.

G. Shepperson and T. Price, *Independent African* (Edinburgh, 1968).
B. G. M. Sundkler, *Bantu Prophets in South Africa* (London, 1961). GS

ETRUSCANS, ancient people first known in Italy about 700 BC, who were influential in the development of Rome. Modern Etruscologists mostly declare a moratorium in the debate on their origins, preferring to concentrate on their culture in Italy; earlier scholars are divided between those who believe with Herodotus that they emigrated from Lydia *c.* 1200, and those who support the view of Dionysius of Halicarnassus that they were autochthonous. By 700 they were a powerful people with a flourishing urban civilization centred round the rich mineral deposits of Tuscany, and extending into Umbria and Latium. The federation of 12 cities, its composition varying at different eras, met yearly for religious and political purposes, but gradually the cities tended towards greater individualism. In the 7th and 6th cents they dominated the peninsula in the face of Greek attempts to exploit the same sources of wealth. Rome became an Etruscan city about 600, providing lines of communication through Latium into Campania, where Capua was earlier an Etruscan foundation. This expansion was their undoing. Harassed by Gallic settlers on the Po, and defeated on land and at sea by the Greeks at Cumae (524) and Himera (480), their power declined and in the 4th cent. they were gradually absorbed into Rome's growing empire. The riddle of their language (probably non-Indo-European) remains unsolved. Their material culture was especially notable for architectural and engineering skills and the tomb-paintings found at Tarquinia, Cerveteri and elsewhere reveal a spiritual depth reflected also in their religious observances, from which many Roman practices were derived.

EUBULUS (405–330 BC), Athenian politician expert in finance. His cautious foreign and financial policy and preservation of the Theoric Fund for subsidizing festival seats irked Demosthenes, yet he was not a pacifist, for, although he extricated Athens from the Social War (355), opposed intervention to help foreign democracies, and avoided provoking Philip II of Macedon, he supported military resistance to his southward penetration at Thermopylae (352) and, after Olynthus fell (348), tried to rally the Greeks. In 346, however, he and others, recognizing Athens' weakness, brought about the peace of Philocrates.

EUCLID (*fl. c.* 300 BC), Alexandrian mathematician, whose book *Elements* provides the basis of much modern geometry and numerical theory. He also wrote on astronomy and music.

EUDES II (d. 1037), Count of Blois and Champagne, one of the most powerful and undisciplined vassals of 11th-cent. France who sought to extend his own lands. He rebelled against King Henry I and, at the same time, was at war with the emperor over Burgundy. His defeat led to the union of Burgundy with the empire and saved the Capetian King of France from being dethroned.

EUDES (*reg.* 888–98), King of France, famous for the defence of Paris against the Vikings in 888 and proclaimed king in place of the useless Carolingian, Charles the Fat. Eudes was the first Capetian king and after his death a Carolingian recovered the Crown.

EUGÈNE OF SAVOY, Prince (1663–1736), imperialist statesman, diplomat, and soldier, who served in the Austrian army against the Turks at the siege of Vienna (1683), the capture of Buda (1686), and the siege of Belgrade (1688). In 1689 he was sent to Italy to effect co-operation between his cousin, the Duke of Savoy, and Italian and Spanish troops, but, defeated at Staffarda (1690) and hampered by the desertion of Savoy, was forced to retreat. By then, however, his military reputation was such that Louis XIV tried unsuccessfully to procure his services by bribery. Eugène again fought the Turks, winning the decisive battle of Zenta (1697) and negotiating the extremely favourable peace of Carlowitz (1699).

At the beginning of the War of the Spanish Succession Eugène served in Italy, forcing Catinat from prepared defensive positions, defeating and capturing his successor, Villeroy, in a surprise raid, and pinning down the forces of Vendôme. Recalled to Vienna (1704), he was rewarded with the post of president of the council of war and for a short time served against the Hungarian insurgents.

In 1704 Eugène went to Bavaria, where he began his long military association and friendship with the Duke of Marlborough. Together they destroyed a French army at Blenheim (1704) and forced the French out of Bavaria. Returning to Italy, Eugène relieved Turin (1706) and forced La Feuillard out of Italy. The following year he advanced on Toulon. Though he failed to capture the city, he diverted large concentrations of French troops from the Flanders battlefields. He served (1708–13) in Flanders alongside Marlborough, playing a leading role at Oudenarde (1708), the siege of Lille (1708), Malplaquet (1709), and the allied defeat at Denain (1712).

After the treaty of Utrecht (1713) the empire continued alone in the war, with Eugène defending the Rhine frontier against the combined might of France and Spain. The task proved too much for imperial resources and Eugène negotiated the treaty of Radstadt (1714) with France on behalf of the emperor.

Eugène again turned against the Turks, defeating them at Peterwarden (1716) and Belgrade (1717). His last campaign was on the Rhine (1733). In his later years Eugène reformed the Austrian army and played an important part as an adviser to the Emperor Charles VI. He was also a celebrated art collector.

N. Henderson, *Prince Eugen of Savoy* (London, 1964).   AW

EUGÉNIE DE MONTIJO DE GUZMAN (1826–1920), Empress of France and daughter of a Spanish grandee. She married Napoleon III (1853), by whom she had one son (1856), and maintained a brilliant court. Through her influence on her husband she was largely to blame for France's disastrous foreign policy of 1870.

EUGENIUS, FL. (d. AD 394), Roman rhetorician, who was installed as emperor by the general Arbogastes at Lyons (392). Having invaded Italy, he established his court at Milan and under him a pagan revival was conducted at Rome by Nicomachus Flavianus; but his rebellion was crushed by Theodosius at the battle of the Frigidus river (Sept. 394), and Eugenius executed.

EUGENIUS III (*reg.* 1145–53), Pope, Italian Cistercian, and friend of St Bernard of Clairvaux, who was unexpectedly elected pope, the first Cistercian to be chosen. He gave Bernard the task of preaching the Second Crusade (1145–6). Being a peacemaker, he worked for better relations with the emperors and opened discussions with the Byzantine clergy to heal the schism between the Greek and Roman Churches.

EUGENIUS IV, Pope (*c.* 1383–1447), nephew of Pope Gregory XII, who abdicated at the council of Constance (1415) and by whom he was made a cardinal (1408). His pontificate (1431–47) is notable for the council of Basle, to whose conciliarism he was opposed. He convoked the rival council of Ferrara-Florence (1438–9), whose apparent success in healing the schism between the Greek and Roman Churches won him praise and led to the withdrawal of general support for Basle. He proclaimed a crusade which ended with the disastrous defeat at Varna (1444).

EUGENIUS (*c.* 1130–*c.* 1202), chief minister of the last Norman kings of Sicily (1189–94) and a scholar at the Sicilian court. He translated into Latin with equal facility works from Arabic and Greek, including important mathematical and scientific treatises. He was also probably the author of histories of the Sicilian kingdom.

EULER, LEONARD (1707–83), Swiss mathematician and physicist in the Newtonian tradition, who was appointed professor at St Petersburg (1730) and Berlin (1741), returning to the former city in 1766. He published numerous treatises and papers, including *Lettres à une Princesse d'Allemagne* (1768–72), and assisted naval progress by his work on fluid resistance and floating bodies.

EUMENES II (197–159 BC), Attalid King of Pergamum, who continued his predecessor Attalus I's pro-Roman policy. He helped to prevent compromise between Rome and Antiochus III, and his support in the subsequent war won him vast tracts of territory at the settlement of Apamea (188). After precipitating the Third Macedonian War by making accusations at Rome against Perseus (172), his loyalty wavered during Rome's early reverses and he was subsequently discredited there.

EUMENES OF CARDIA (*c.* 362–316 BC), secretary to Philip II of Macedon, and chief secretary, archivist, and close friend of Alexander the Great, after whose death he remained important. As a secret negotiator at Babylon (323) Eumenes supported Perdiccas (who made him satrap of Cappadocia), and fought for him until Perdiccas' death (320). Thereafter, by keeping his Macedonian troops loyal by claiming to represent the Macedonian Royal House, he fought with Antigonus Monophthalmus for control of Asia in Asia Minor, Mesopotamia, and Iran, where he was killed at Gabiene.

EUNUCHS in China. Known from earliest times, eunuchs served at the imperial courts in a variety of capacities, such as supervisors of the palace services or attendants on imperial consorts and princesses. Being closely attached to the palaces, eunuchs had a more ready and informal access to the emperor than officials serving in the government, whose audiences, reports, and contacts were usually restricted by attention to protocol. Being able to perform intimate services for their masters, eunuchs could ingratiate themselves into positions of favour and could exercise considerable influence or pressure on the conduct of affairs. This was done either through appointment to the senior offices of state or by acting as members of a private secretariat or staff which would prepare documents for the emperor and arrange for the implementation of his orders. Eunuch power arose conspicuously during the Eastern Han, the T'ang, and the Ming periods, but there were occasions when, as a group, the eunuchs fell as victims to their rivals, suffering oppression and elimination from the court. Being usually antagonistic to the officials of the civil service, the eunuchs have been denigrated in the standard histories and described as masters of intrigue or oppression, while the virtues of those eunuchs, whose services may have saved a dynastic house from ruin, have often been left unrecorded.

EUPATRIDAE, general term for noble families in ancient Greece, *ie,* 'men of good fathers', at Athens, especially the inner circle of noble families who monopolized the archonship and the Areopagus until Solon's timocratic redefinition of eligibility for office.

EUPHRATES EXPEDITION (1835–7), under the command of a British officer, Col. F. R. Chesney, to investigate the possibilities of steam navigation on the Tigris and Euphrates for purposes of communication with India.

EUREKA STOCKADE, THE (1854), minor rebellion which acquired legendary proportions in Australian history, named after the Eureka lead mines on the Ballarat (Vic.) goldfields. The stockade, constructed by diggers on 30 Nov., and commanded by an Irishman, Peter Lalor, was overrun on 3 Dec. by 400 armed police and troops. About 30 of the 150 defenders were killed; the rest (never more than 1000, or one-tenth of the Ballarat diggers) drifted back to their claims.

Like most Australian miners, the Ballarat diggers were unrepresented in their colony's legislative council. They wanted land reform and, with yields falling, objected to miners' licence fees. Grievances were heightened by rigorous enforcement of the Victorian licensing system and arduous working conditions peculiar to Ballarat's deep-lead mining. The diggers' suspicions of administrative corruption and their hostility to police engaged in licence hunts were increased by a murder. Their resentment rose after a number of arrests on 30 Nov. but violence might have been avoided had the resident commissioner, Robert Rede, been less determined to assert his authority.

Subsequently, the stockade's significance was exaggerated by nationalists, radicals, trade unionists, Irish Catholics, and communists. Each sought nobility and elements of their own creeds in the rebels' cause and helped to propagate the view that the Eureka incident launched Australian democracy—pointing, in particular, to the Chartist programme, which the diggers endorsed. There is, however, little evidence that miners were interested in democratic experiments. Primarily, they wanted costs reduced, a policy of land reform, and an alternative livelihood. Democratic reforms in eastern Australia were accelerated by the rebellion, though there had been influential champions and public support for such reforms earlier. Nevertheless, there were few diggers in the parliaments of the later 1850s and early 1860s. The rebellion's effect was most marked in the goldfields: miners were given more say in local administration and the licence system was abolished. The Victorian government had, however, been preparing these reforms before the Eureka rebellion.

G. Serle, *The Golden Age* (Melbourne, 1963).
G. Blainey, *The Rush That Never Ended* (Melbourne, 1969).
JAM

EURIPIDES (*c.* 480–406 BC), youngest of the three great Athenian tragedians, author of 80–90 plays, of which 19 survive, 5 having won first prizes. Euripides, who was perhaps influenced by the philosophers Anaxagoras and Socrates, questioned traditional values and beliefs concerning the gods' moral influence. Consequently he found life in Athens uncomfortable and ended his days in Thessaly and Macedon. He was noted for developing the prologue and for his characters' startling apothegms, also for the fine lyrical interludes with which he tended to replace the traditional type of choral ode and for introducing a *deus ex machina*. He high-lighted human, as opposed to divine, tragedy, especially in *Medea* and *Hippolytus*, and so became popular with Roman and later European dramatists.

EUROPEAN ADVISORY COMMISSION (1943), established by the foreign ministers' conference with British, US, and Russian membership, meeting in London. It was to consider specific questions relating to the terms of surrender at the end of the Second World War which might arise between the Allies, and make recommendations for common action. In practice its range of action was severely limited. In the event, the conclusion of the war and the occupation of Germany created issues of major political importance which the Allies were not prepared to leave to an advisory commission, so that much of its preparatory work was ignored or over-ruled.

EUROPEAN ATOMIC ENERGY COMMUNITY (Euratom), most specialized of the three European communities established under treaty (March 1957; effective 1 Jan. 1958) signed between France, the German Federal Republic, Italy, Belgium, Holland, and Luxemburg. The institutions of the Community were similar to those of the already existing Coal and Steel Community, consisting of a Commission, a Council of Ministers, an Assembly, and a Court of Justice. The last two were merged into common institutions with their counterparts in the Coal and Steel Community and the Economic Community to form a European Parliament and a Court of Justice (1958). The Commission was later absorbed (1967) into a single European Commission.

In contrast to the other two communities, which were concerned with existing industries, Euratom's task was to develop nuclear energy for peaceful uses. It promoted research primarily through its Joint Research Centre (which has establishments at Ispra in Italy, Geel in Belgium, Karlsruhe in Germany, and Petten in the Netherlands), but also through research contracts with undertakings in member countries. It also sought to contribute to the peaceful development of the peaceful uses of atomic energy by creating a common market in equipment and materials, by an insurance convention against damages arising from atomic energy, and by the protection of health and security. At the same time, its work was still in 1970 hindered by the inseparability of peaceful from military aspects of nuclear research and the consequent sensitivity of the French government in particular.

Euratom signed collaboration agreements with the US (1958), Britain (1959), Canada (1959), Brazil (1961), and Argentina (1962).

W. F. Knapp, *Unity and Nationalism in Europe since 1945* (Oxford, 1969).

M. Camps, *Britain and the European Community* (Oxford, 1964).   WFK

EUROPEAN COAL AND STEEL COMMUNITY,

first of the Western European organizations to be established with a degree of supranational authority. It emanated from a proposal made by the French foreign minister (the 'Schuman plan'; 9 May 1950) that a single authority should be created to control the coal and steel production of France and Germany, 'within the framework of an organization open to the participation of other countries of Europe' and 'as a first step in the federation of Europe'.

The French proposal was accepted by West Germany, Italy, Belgium, Holland, and Luxemburg, who together signed and ratified (1952) the treaty setting up the Community. The treaty provided for the creation of a High Authority of which the distinctive feature was its supranational quality, as expressed in the words:

The members of the High Authority shall exercise their functions in complete independence, in the general interest of the Community . . . They will abstain from all conduct incompatible with the supranational character of their functions.

The High Authority, consisting of eight members appointed by national governments and a ninth co-opted by them, was given the power of initiative. It was checked by a Council of Ministers, consisting of one representative from each member country, and was ultimately responsible to an Assembly (which was in practice consultative, since its only power was to dismiss the High Authority as a whole by a vote of censure). A Consultative Committee representing producers, workers, dealers, and consumers was also established. In addition, a Court was instituted to hear appeals from industrial concerns and governments.

Euratom and the European Economic Community were established (1958) with similar institutions and the Assemblies and Courts of the three communities were merged into a European Parliament and a Court of Justice respectively. The other institutions were merged by treaty (signed 1965; effective 1 July 1967) setting up a single European Commission (which absorbed the High Authority), and a single Council of Ministers.

The work of the Community was in the first place to establish a common market in coal and steel. Initially, this proceeded without difficulty. All barriers to trade were eliminated and a common external tariff established. The completion of the common market (1958) was however preceded by the beginning of a major crisis in the coal industry, which suffered from structural defects consequent on the competition from oil. To meet the crisis the Community had no choice but to allow national governments to take extensive measures for the running down of their own coal industries, including the elimination of uneconomic mines. At the same time, the social policies of the Community, particularly in making provision for the transfer of miners, were developed.

The British government did not enter the negotiations for the establishment of the Community because of the commitment to a supranational policy which they called for. Subsequently, an agreement of association was signed with Britain (1955) and a Consulation agreement signed with Switzerland (1956).

W. F. Knapp, *Unity and Nationalism in Europe since 1945* (Oxford, 1969)

H. Kohn, *Nationalism: its history and meaning* (Princeton, 1965).   WFK

EUROPEAN DEFENCE COMMUNITY,

abortive attempt (Sept. 1950) to establish a European defence force which resulted from American pressure to rearm Germany. The proposal for German rearmament sprang from alarm caused by the Korean War and was made when Ernest Bevin and Robert Schuman met Dean Acheson in New York before the NATO Council meeting. It was linked to America's readiness to strengthen her forces in Europe and to provide an American Supreme Commander.

The French government would not agree to the creation of a German army and proposed instead that German troops should serve in small multi-national units. This plan, the Pleven plan, was modified and enlarged into the proposed Defence Community, modelled on the Coal and Steel Community which was already under discussion. The British government, which had already declined to join the Schuman plan, accepted German rearmament, but would not join EDC, and this attitude persisted when the Conservatives replaced the Labour government (Oct. 1951).

The British refusal to join contributed to the reluctance of the French National Assembly to agree to the Community, even when the treaty establishing it had been signed by all six members of the Coal and Steel Community (including France) and ratified by all except Italy (whose abstention was for purely procedural reasons) and France. There were however indigenous reasons which would probably have persisted even if Britain had gone further than the guarantees which it offered (as to the retention of troops on the continent and commitment to EDC if it were attacked) and actually joined as a full member. Above all, French opinion was alarmed at the prospect of German rearmament, and in large part opposed to the abandonment of French sovereignty over the armed forces.

The ratification of the treaty by the French parliament was thus repeatedly postponed. In an attempt to break the deadlock, Pierre Mendès-France negotiated a compromise which he hoped would be acceptable to the Assembly and to the other signatories to the treaty. But his proposals were unacceptable to the latter, while in the National Assembly a vote (on which the government abstained) was carried, rejecting the EDC Treaty by 319 to 264 (30 Aug. 1954)

W. F. Knapp, *Unity and Nationalism in Europe since 1945* (Oxford, 1969).

Z. Brzezinski, *The Soviet Bloc: unity and conflict* (New York, 1960).   WFK

EUROPEAN ECONOMIC COMMUNITY,

established by the treaty of Rome (signed March 1957; effective 1 Jan. 1958), provided for the progressive establishment of a common market, including agriculture (where a special controlling regime would be developed), with free movement for labour, services, and capital and with provision for the association of the overseas territories of the members. The Community represented the second stage in the movement towards European union between the six countries which were members of the European Coal and Steel Community (ECSC). Negotiations to this end were begun, after the collapse of the European Defence Community (EDC), at the Messina conference (June 1955). The British government took part in the conference and sent a representative to meetings of the inter-governmental committee which it established, but did not accept the principles of supranationality and soon withdrew from the negotiations (Nov. 1955).

The treaty of Rome established institutions of the Community along the lines of ECSC. In place of the High Authority it set up a Commission, and it provided for a Council of Ministers, an Assembly, and a Court. The Assembly and the Court were merged with those of ECSC and Euratom (1958) to create a European Parliament and a Court of Justice respectively. The Commission and the Council of Ministers were similarly merged by treaty (signed 1965; effective 1 July 1967). The European Commission thus created is larger than any one of its predecessors, having 14 members, but its membership was reduced to nine in 1970.

The scope of the Community covers the whole economy of the six members, in contrast to the limited areas of coal and steel and atomic energy, which are the province of the other two communities. The powers given to the Commission were in consequence different from those of the High Authority, lacking its uncompromising claim to supra-nationality. Instead the treaty laid down in detail the stages by which the common market was to be achieved by an ir-reversible process (so that members would adhere to its pro-visions without the fear that their fellow members would abandon the enterprise) and the Commission was entrusted with the task of making detailed arrangements and acting as supervisor in the implementation of the treaty.

The Community achieved unexpected success in the establishment of a common market (ie, a free trade area with a common external tariff) in industrial goods—it was complete by 1 July 1968, two years earlier than the shortest period foreseen in the treaty. The formation of a common agricul-tural policy proved more difficult. The main lines of the policy, formulated in 1960, were based on common prices, a single fund for price supports (the Agricultural Guidance and Guarantee Fund), and import levies to help finance this fund. But the proposal for an agricultural fund increased the financial resources under the control of the Community and was therefore unwelcome to De Gaulle's government in France. Moreover, they were under discussion at the time when, under the treaty, qualified majority voting on some decisions would replace the unanimity hitherto required in the Council of Ministers—a further extension of supranation-ality which was equally unacceptable to France. These fac-tors produced the community's gravest crisis when France withdrew its representatives (July 1965). Discussions were resumed (Jan. 1966) and a compromise reached which per-mitted the development of the common agricultural policy, but effectively halted any further move towards supranation-ality.

Meanwhile the community had undertaken the measures provided for in the treaty to extend economic integration beyond the establishment of a common market in the strict sense. These include the setting up of a European Investment Bank and a European Social Fund (to facilitate the mobility of labour). The free movement of capital was established by a directive of the Council of Ministers (May 1960) and progress was made towards a common policy towards trans-port, cartels, and the turnover tax.

The treaty of Rome was accompanied by a Convention on the Association of Overseas Territories of the members; soon after its expiry a second convention, the Yaoundé Convention, was signed (July 1963; effective 1 June 1964) between EEC and associated African states and Madagascar. It has freed trade between the signatories, with safeguards for the developing countries, and provided for aid through a European Development Fund, as well as the Investment Bank. Nigeria signed a separate agreement (July 1966) under the terms of the Yaoundé Convention, but the civil war pre-vented its becoming effective.

Agreements of Association were signed between EEC and Greece (July 1961) and Turkey (Sept. 1963). They provided for a liberalization of trade, including the increase of the common market's quotas on imports, and development loans to the associate members. Trade agreements were signed with Israel (July 1964) and Lebanon (May 1965).

The applications which Britain made for full membership

of EEC (Aug. 1961 and May 1967) gave rise to major questions of policy for Britain, the Commonwealth, and the Community. Britain's application was accompanied by others from its European Free Trade Association partners and from Ireland. Denmark twice applied for full membership at the same times as Britain. Austria, Sweden, and Switzerland, as neutral countries, applied for forms of associate membership (Dec. 1961) and Sweden applied for full membership (July 1967). Norway applied twice for full membership (May 1962 and July 1967); Ireland applied for full membership (Aug. 1961) and again at the same time as Britain's second applica-tion (May 1967). Portugal applied for some form of member-ship (June 1962) and Israel applied for associate membership in Oct. 1966. After 1970, a change of government in Britain and the retirement and subsequent death of De Gaulle in France, led to new and careful negotiations with Britain and other countries being admitted to membership in 1973.

W. F. Knapp, *Unity and Nationalism in Europe since 1945* (Oxford, 1969).
I. Walter, *The European Common Market* (New York, 1967).
                                                              WFK

EUROPEAN FREE TRADE ASSOCIATION (EFTA), estab-
lished in May 1960 under a treaty signed (Dec. 1959–Jan. 1960) between Austria, Britain, Denmark, Norway, Portugal Sweden, and Switzerland. The association, which has a per-manent secretariat in Geneva, has applied the Convention (initialled Nov.–Dec. 1959) which provides for a progressive reduction of tariffs on industrial goods produced with the association. All tariffs and quotas on trade in industrial goods were abolished by the end of 1966, except for some excep-tions under special arrangements.

EFTA owed its origin to the independent policy which the British government pursued at the time of the formation of the European Economic Community. The British objective was to establish a free trade area in the whole of Western Europe (ie, among the Organization for European Economic Co-operation (OEEC) countries, into which the EEC would fit as a single economic unit. The plan was defeated, largely by French opposition, and EFTA emerged as a result. In contrast to the EEC treaty the EFTA convention does not establish a common external tariff, nor does it cover agricul-tural products, although the association has in practice facilitated agreements between members in respect of trade in agricultural and marine products.

Finland became associated with EFTA under an agree-ment (March 1961) which included special provisions to avoid conflict with its trade treaty with the Soviet Union.

EUROPEAN LAUNCHER DEVELOPMENT ORGANIZATION
(ELDO), established under convention (signed April 1962; effective March 1964) with membership comprising Australia, Belgium, Britain, France, German Federal Republic, Italy, and the Netherlands. The organization was established to develop an earth satellite launcher for 'various purposes' and since 1966 has been primarily concerned with a synchronous telecommunications satellite. Its work was slowed down in 1970 by disagreements about the sharing of costs, in which Britain's disagreement with the other members had nearly led to British withdrawal from the organization in 1966.

EUROPEAN ORGANIZATION FOR NUCLEAR RESEARCH
(CERN or Conseil Européen pour la Recherche nucléaire). European Council for Nuclear Research was set up under the auspices of the United Nations Educational, Scientific, and Cultural Organization (UNESCO) in May 1952 by agree-ment between Denmark, France, German Federal Republic, Greece, Italy, the Netherlands, Sweden, Switzerland, and Yugoslavia; Norway and Belgium became signatories later. A full convention establishing the council as an international organization was signed by the same countries, and by Britain (July 1953). The organization constructed a major laboratory for experimental research in the physics of high-energy

particles at Meyrin near Geneva, and supervised the organization and financing of experiments by scientists from member countries.

An agreement was signed in June 1960 for the exchange of scientists with the Soviet Union. Yugoslavia withdrew from full membership in 1963, while Poland and Turkey assumed observer-status.

EUROPEAN POLITICAL COMMUNITY, abortive proposal to integrate the European Coal and Steel Community (ECSC) and the European Defence Community (EDC) into an embryonic federal government of Europe, with a popularly elected European parliament, which was framed in a treaty (March 1953) which collapsed with its rejection by the French National Assembly of EDC in 1954.

EUROPEAN RECOVERY PROGRAM (1948–51), US foreign aid programme designed to repair Europe's war-ravaged economy and generally known as the Marshall Plan. First proposed by secretary of state George C. Marshall on 5 June 1947, after preliminary work by the under-secretary of state Dean Acheson, the details of the programme were worked out by the European Committee for European Economic Co-operation and implemented by the US with the Economic Co-operation Act of 1948 and subsequent legislation. The Economic Co-operation Administration funnelled over $13,000 million to the Organization for European Economic Co-operation to finance reconstruction projects in Austria, Belgium, Britain, Denmark, Eire, France, Greece, Iceland, Italy, Luxemburg, the Netherlands, Norway, Portugal, Sweden, Trieste, Turkey, West Germany, and Yugoslavia. Marshall Aid quickly stimulated European recovery, strengthened democratic institutions, and helped to check the spread of communism. Scheduled to end in June 1952, the programme became part of the larger US foreign aid effort when ECA was replaced in Oct. 1951 by the Mutual Security Agency.

EUROPEAN SPACE RESEARCH ORGANIZATION (ESRO) resulted from a conference convened by Conseil Européen pour la Recherche nucléaire (CERN) (Nov.–Dec. 1960) and the signing of a Convention (June 1962; effective 1964). Its members are Belgium, Britain, Denmark, France, German Federal Republic, Italy, the Netherlands, Spain, Sweden, and Switzerland—Austria and Norway being observers. It had in 1970 a programme of space research for which it established installations for research, launching, and tracking.

EURYBIADES, Spartan commander of the Greek fleet which fought at Artemisium and Salamis against the Persian invasion (480 BC). Though belittled by pro-Athenian sources, he kept the fleet together and supported Themistocles' strategy at the critical moments.

EURYMEDON RIVER, BATTLE OF (c. 467 BC), victory by land and sea on the southern coast of Asia Minor of the Athenian and Delian League's fleet under Cimon, which defeated a Persian armada apparently planning to re-enter the Aegean. The Persians lost 200 ships, but retained control of much of Cyprus.

EURYPONTIDS, junior of the two Spartan royal houses. After Cleomenes I and Pausanias had brought the senior Agiads into disrepute, the Eurypontid kings of the 5th and 4th cents BC (especially Archidamus II and III, Agis II and III and Agesilaus) eclipsed their Agiad counterparts.

EUSEBIUS OF CAESAREA (c. AD 260–339), bishop and 'Father of Church History'. His *Ecclesiastical History* is our chief source for the history of the Christian Church down to c. 300. Later editions continued its history down to 325, ending with the final victory over Licinius. Although poor in style, it is valuable in that Eusebius quotes works by many earlier authors, some now lost. He also wrote a *Life of Con-*

stantine based on hellenistic theories of divine kingship. As a leader of the moderates in the Arian controversy he appears to have been on trial for orthodoxy at the Council of Nicaea in 325—and certainly never gave Athanasius his full support.

EVAGORAS (d. 374 BC), Greek captain of fortune, who seized Cypriot Salamis from the Phoenicians and by 399 ruled the rest of the island. Acknowledging at first the suzerainty of the Persian king, Artaxerxes II, he enabled the Athenian Conon, fled to him after defeat at Aegospotami (404), to become commander of the Persian fleet which entered the Aegean and defeated the Spartans off Cnidus (395). Evagoras, who was admired by Isocrates, was publicly honoured by the Athenians (393) and, when Artaxerxes threatened to overthrow him (389), they sent help. Artaxerxes replied by helping Sparta to impose the King's Peace on Athens and its allies, but Evagoras fought on, supported by the rebel King Achoris of Egypt. After being defeated in 381, he recognized Artaxerxes' authority and remained King of Salamis until his death.

EVANDER, mythological Arcadian émigré who, as peace-loving king of Pallanteum on the future site of Rome, welcomed Aeneas, eg, in Virgil's *Aenid*, Book 8.

EVANGELICAL ALLIANCE (1846), association of English churches and individual Christians of different denominations holding Evangelical views, founded in London, 'to . . . concentrate the strength of an enlightened Protestantism against the encroachments of Popery and Puseyism, and to promote the interests of a dogmatic Christianity'. The leaders, who included Sumner, the Abp of Canterbury, and Lord Shaftesbury, aimed at spiritual union rather than unified organization of Evangelical Anglicans and Dissenters. They attacked the Oxford Movement at the time of the Gorham Case (1849) and the Catholic Church in their 'papal aggression', which resulted in the abortive Ecclesiastical Titles Act (1851). The alliance spread over the world, though disputes over slavery prevented the American branch from joining until 1867. In Germany the alliance was encouraged by Frederick William IV, and its work was continued by the *Evangelische Bund* (1886), whose influence was strong up to 1914. The alliance supported the cause of oppressed Protestant minorities in Ireland, the Turkish empire, Russia, and Sweden and campaigned for toleration. Its influence lessened in the 20th cent., though it established the universal week of prayer observed each Jan. and became the World Evangelical Missionary Alliance (1958).

EVANGELICAL UNION (1843) in Scotland, breakaway group of Christians formed during the split in the Church of Scotland. The union, led by the Rev. James Morison, who had been suspended by his presbytery in Kilmarnock for his anti-Calvinistic views, and three other ministers, was often referred to as the 'Morisonians'. It was soon joined by other Scottish Congregationalists in a loosely organized association of independent churches which eventually merged in the Congregational Union of Scotland (1897).

EVANGELICALISM, name given to the beliefs of a Low Church group within the Church of England, prominent from the mid-18th cent. The Evangelicals shared many of the Methodists' aims. Both wished to revive personal faith and moral earnestness, put total reliance on the evidence of the Scriptures, vehemently opposed Roman Catholicism, and emphasized the doctrine of Justification by Faith. Evangelicals disapproved of Wesley's ordination of ministers. They attacked the worldliness and wealth of the Church, the links between parson and squire, the pluralism and abuses of the day and propagated their convictions through best-selling works of devotion like Venn's *Complete Duty of Man* and Milner's *History of the Church of Christ*. They wrote hymns, hitherto not much used in services, eg, John Newton's 'How sweet the name of Jesus sounds', and William Cowper's 'God moves in a mysterious way'.

The movement owed much to the leadership of outstanding individuals and groups such as the Clapham Sect. One of its centres was Cambridge, where Charles Simeon, vicar of Holy Trinity (1783–1836), exerted a powerful influence, aiming by constant prayer and sacrificial giving, at a general reformation of morals and the salvation of souls.

Evangelicals believed in missionary action at home and abroad and were the pioneers of Sunday Schools. They founded the Church Missionary Society (1797) and the British and Foreign Bible Society (1804). Their most famous attack was on the slave trade, against which a small group, 'the Saints', campaigned vigorously. Granville Sharp won Somersett's case (1772), making slavery illegal in England. They joined the Quakers in launching the Abolition Committee (1787) and won over Pitt's friend, William Wilberforce, a brilliant society figure who had experienced a sudden religious conversion, giving up social pleasures, cards, and gambling. Intensely Tory, like many Evangelicals, the supporter of every repressive measure against the Radicals, and an opponent of trades unions, factory reform, and Corn Law repeal, he was utterly sincere in his championship of the slaves, living to see the Evangelical triumph of their emancipation (1833).

Many of the implications of Victorianism began, not with Queen Victoria and Prince Albert, but with Wilberforce and his friends, who founded the Society for the Suppression of Vice and set their seal on the British Sunday. The work of the Evangelicals went forward in the 19th cent. through leaders like Lord Shaftesbury (1801–85) and his friends, with their crowded services at Exeter Hall and through pastors like W. W. Champneys, the rector of St Mary's, Whitechapel. Evangelicalism was the dominant form of religion motivating both Churchmen and non-conformists such as Spurgeon, and in its broadest aspects permeating the opinions even of High Churchmen like Gladstone, the moral approach of agnostic scientists like T. H. Huxley, and the imperialism of Kipling. Evangelicalism, like its rivals in the Oxford Movement, remained a potent force within the Church.

G. Kitson Clark, *The Making of Victorian England* (London, 1962).

E. M. Forster, *Marianne Thornton 1797–1887* (London, 1956).   JRA

EVANS, GEORGE WILLIAM (1780–1852), Australian explorer and the first European to follow (1813) Gregory Blaxland through the Blue Mountains and to cross the divide further west of Sydney, NSW, to and along the Macquarie river. He combined public surveying with private farming in NSW, prior to intermittent service in the Van Diemen's Land survey office from 1812. Though his duties in the island were at first interrupted frequently for field exploration on the mainland, *eg*, to the Macquarie in 1813 and the Lachlan in 1815, he played an influential part in Tasmanian land survey and allocation.

EVANS, OLIVER (1755–1819), American inventor of many wool-carding and flour-milling machines. His most important invention was the high-pressure steam engine.

EVELYN, JOHN (1620–1706), English lawyer, man of letters, and landscape gardener. Although firmly Anglican in religion and royalist in political sympathy he kept out of the English Civil War. After the Restoration (1660) he was appointed to serve on various commissions dealing with the improvement of London, and in the Dutch wars served on the commission for sick and wounded prisoners, with individual responsibility for Kent and Sussex; he was helped in this by Pepys. Although he was appointed a commissioner of the Privy Seal in 1685, he lost his sympathy with the Stuarts in James II's reign and approved of the Revolution of 1688.

Evelyn was one of the founder members of the Royal Society (1661–2), and a friend of Locke, Newton, and Wren,

whom he met regularly. At the request of the admiralty, and with the support of the Royal Society, he wrote a study of forest trees and the propagation of timber, *Sylva, a Discourse of Forest Trees* (1664), which was a landmark in the evolution of modern forestry techniques. He is chiefly remembered for his private *Diary*, first published in 1818, which describes his travels, acquaintances, and a wide range of events and experiences over a period of half a century.

EVERETT, EDWARD (1794–1865), US scholar, Whig politician, and orator from MA. He served as a US congressman (1825–35) and senator (1853–4), was governor of MA (1836–9), US minister to Britain (1841–5), president of Harvard University (1846–9), secretary of state (1852–3), and vice-presidential candidate of the Constitutional Union Party (1860).

EVERSLEY OF HECKFIELD, CHARLES SHAW-LEFEVRE, Viscount (1794–1888), British politician and a skilful Speaker of the House of Commons (1839–57), interested in procedural reforms. His three re-elections (1841, 1847, 1852) established the convention that the Speaker shall not change with changes of government or general elections.

EVESHAM, BATTLE OF (4 Aug. 1265). Simon de Montfort's brief rule of England (1264–5) was brought to an end by the battle of Evesham. There, hemmed in by a loop in the Avon river, Simon and many of his followers were killed by the royalist forces led by Henry III's son, Edward, and Earl Gilbert of Gloucester.

EVIAN AGREEMENTS (1962) followed months of negotiation between the French government and the Provisional government of the Algerian Republic. They provided for a referendum on self-determination for the people of Algeria (held 1 July 1962) and laid down the terms for Algeria's independence. Algeria guaranteed French interests, including the rights acquired by individuals and organizations, and France undertook to provide Algeria with technical, cultural, and financial assistance. The development of the subsoil (primarily oil) in the south was to be undertaken under Franco–Algerian co-operation; French troops were to be withdrawn, but France was to keep the naval base of Mers-el-Kébir and the air base of Bou-Sfer for 15 years, in addition to other military areas in the Sahara which were required for rocket and nuclear testing. The French government announced that it would evacuate the base of Mers-el-Kébir (Oct. 1967).

EWE people, numbering about 1 million, inhabit the trans-Volta region of south-east Ghana and south-west Togo. They are related in culture and language to the Aja-Yoruba speaking peoples, constituting with them an important focus for European trade and, in the 19th cent., for missionary activities. Missionaries reduced the Ewe language to writing and established schools, thus giving the Ewe people a headstart in Western education over their neighbours and so laying the foundation of a pan-Ewe nationalist movement. This arose as a reaction against the previous segmentary political situation which made the Ewe a regular battleground for their more powerful neighbours, being shaped by the changing political frontiers and divisions of the colonial period: first between the British Gold Coast and German Togo in 1899; then, after a period of unification under British occupation (1914–19), between the Gold Coast, British Togo, and French Togo. This movement later had to contend with other nationalist forces seeking to prevent the fragmentation of the Republic of Togo and of the modern Ghana, which has incorporated the Ewe of the Gold Coast and British Togo.

EWES, SIR SIMONDS D' (1602–50), English Puritan antiquary and diarist, who published *Harangue concerning the antiquity of Cambridge* (1642) and compiled his *Diary* and the *Journals of the parliaments of Elizabeth*.

EWLIYA CHELEBI (1611–*c.* 1684), author of the famous Seyahat-name ('Travels'), a record of the numerous journeys that he made in the Ottoman empire and the adjacent lands (*c.* 1640–76.)

EWUARE, effective founder of Benin city and the Edo kingdom, reigned for some 30 years in the mid-15th cent. He was responsible for transforming an existing agglomeration of lineage settlements into a city in which a great ditch and rampart enclosed an extensive palace and a large number of wards inhabited by guilds that served the court. He reorganized the palace chiefs and servants into three bodies for the service of his person, his wardrobe, and his harem. Those chiefs living in the city were also brought together in an association which participated with those of the palace in governing the kingdom. Several important rituals and customs introduced by Ewuare emphasized the supernatural attributes of his kingship. Economic support for this elaborate court and city came in the form of tribute from dependent territories which Ewuare greatly enlarged by his military campaigns.

EX ILLA DIE, papal bull (1715) condemning as idolatrous the religious rites of the Chinese with whom Christian missionaries came into contact.

EX OMNIBUS, papal bull pronounced in 1756 by Benedict XIV to calm the Jansenist opposition to *Unigenitus* centred on the *parlement* of Paris. The bull refrained from describing *Unigenitus* as a rule of faith and withheld approval of the policy of refusing sacraments which had led to hysterical scenes at St Médard.

EXAMINATION SYSTEM in China. The origins of this system can be traced to the early part of the imperial period, at least, and systematic forms of written examinations were practised from the 6th cent. until 1905, as a means of recruiting the best qualified men for the civil service. Tests included examination in the Chinese classics and in the composition of prose and poetry. Candidates faced a complex series of examinations both to win a place in the service and at later stages during their careers. The system was sometimes subject to abuse for political purposes, but at times admitted men of humble origins to government.

EXAMINER, THE, British Tory weekly periodical started by Henry St John (later Viscount Bolingbroke) in the autumn of 1710. The editorship was soon taken over by Jonathan Swift, who wrote the numbers from 2 Nov. 1710 to 14 June 1711. In all, about 40 numbers were published. It engaged in controversies with two of the other papers of the day—Steel's *Guardian* and Addison's *Whig Examiner* and achieved unprecedented success with its policy of defending ministerial actions while expressing the general weariness with the War of the Spanish Succession.

EXARCH, title accorded in the Byzantine empire at first to high dignitaries ecclesiastical and civil, but later to officers commanding the armed forces on land and on sea (*cf.* Lat. *dux*). The title assumed even more amplitude with the emergence, in 584, of the Exarchate of Ravenna and, in 591, of the Exarchate of Africa—these two officials being in fact vice-gerents of the emperor at Constantinople endowed with full control—civil, military, and judicial—over the territories assigned to their care. The title continued to be used in the ecclesiastical sphere, *eg,* the head of the Orthodox Church in Bulgaria had the rank of an exarch until his office was raised to the status of a Patriarchate in 1953.

EXCHANGE, BILLS OF. Because transport of precious metals and coins was always risky in the Middle Ages, Italian merchants developed in the 13th cent. a network of credit transactions, which was used also by merchants of all the other western European countries. A traveller setting out for a foreign destination purchased at home letters of credit payable by the foreign agents or correspondents of the banker who had issued these documents. As payment would be made abroad in a foreign currency, such 'letters of payment' came to be known as bills of exchange. The making of profit on an exchange transaction was never condemned as illicit by the medieval Church. The selling of bills of exchange became a common device for disguising loans that otherwise could be censured as usurious and this contributed to their enormous circulation among merchants in the late Middle Ages. They were negotiable. The growth of business negotiations in the 13th cent. led to other financial developments such as the system of double-entry book-keeping to reveal error and malpractice. This system, originating possibly at Florence in the 13th or early 14th cents, was first used by Italians, and by the end of the Middle Ages it was recommended by the standard Italian manuals for businessmen.

EXCHEQUER, COURT OF, in England. The financial work of the *curia regis* was initially carried out by the king and his principal officers of state forming the exchequer of account (upper exchequer); the lower exchequer, or exchequer of receipt, was an office for the receipt and payment of money. The term exchequer derived from the chequered cloth used for the counting of coins.

The work of the exchequer of account included the determination of debts due to and from the king, and was thus in part judicial. As the procedure was formalized, the justiciar generally presided (this office was abolished in 1234) with the chancellor, the treasurer, and (from *c.* 1240) the chancellor of the exchequer; other specialists, co-opted later, were known as the barons of the exchequer (*barones scaccarii*). Finally, the judicial functions were exercised by the barons alone, the office of chief baron being created in 1312. After 1579, when all other barons were required to be lawyers, one was always a financial expert whose duty was to advise the others on the practice of the exchequer (*cursus scaccarii*); the office was later named that of cursitor baron.

The court of exchequer was forbidden to hear cases which could be heard by the courts of king's bench or common pleas, but extended its jurisdiction by a legal fiction, the writ of *quo minus*: this presupposed that the plaintiff owed a debt to the king which he was unable to discharge because the defendant would not pay to him his claim in the action.

In theory the court's decisions were merely departmental, so that the court was not subject to review by the court of king's bench on writ of error. It was abolished by the Judicature Act (1873).   JRLS

EXCHEQUER, NORMAN. The abacus or chequered board, from which the exchequer took its name, was known in England in the reign of William Rufus, but the term 'barons of the Exchequer' appears first in a document of 1110, witnessed by Roger of Salisbury, who was the king's principal administrator. The exchequer is generally associated with his name, for he was justiciar (though this office had not yet developed fully) and the justiciar presided over the exchequer to receive, twice a year, the annual accounts of sheriffs which were entered on the Pipe Rolls, an important series of financial records surviving continuously from the reign of Henry II to the early 19th cent. In the 1170s the treasurer Richard, son of Nigel, wrote the *Dialogue of the Exchequer*, which describes in detail the working of this institution.

EXCISE, indirect tax on commodities levied within a country, which can be placed on articles of home production as well as on imports. In a partially industrialized economy the collection of such taxes inevitably involves intrusion, and this fact and the wide range of articles that can be subjected to it account for its unpopularity in the 18th cent. This unpopularity was partly justified by the economic effects of particular taxes. Excise on the glass industry was a block to development and experiment; on salt it was a handicap to fisheries and to the chemical industry; on malt it placed a heavy burden on the incomes of the poorer people.

The Commissioners of Excise in Britain were one of the most efficient branches of the 18th-cent. machinery of taxation. By the middle of the century excise was a major element in the country's revenue. In the early 19th cent. the list of commodities subject to it was reduced, but it retained its general importance, particularly in the period when there was no income tax. The main sources of excise revenue in the 19th and 20th cents have been alcohol and tobacco.

EXCISE BILL (1733) in Britain was introduced by Sir Robert Walpole to raise more revenue, since the excise duty proved to be a more lucrative alternative to customs duties. Walpole proposed to extend the bonded warehouse scheme, by which imported goods were subject to an excise duty when taken out of storage for sale to retailers. In 1723 he had applied this scheme to tea, coffee, cocoa, and chocolate and had successfully curbed smuggling, producing an increased revenue from a lower rate of duty. By his 1733 plan to extend the excise to wine and tobacco he hoped to produce sufficient revenue to abolish the land tax. His political opponents, *eg*, Pulteney and Bolingbroke, played on popular hatred of the officious exciseman and possible loss of individual liberty. After the Commons second reading Walpole withdrew his bill in the face of the hostility shown towards it.

EXCOMMUNICATION, process which cut a member of the Catholic Church off from all benefits given by that membership. It was the ultimate ecclesiastical sanction in medieval times and could be used very effectively (*eg*, against the Emperor Henry IV in 1076–7 and King John of England in 1209–13) but lost its efficacy through abuse in later times.

EXODUS, movement of a Hebrew tribe out of Egypt, probably *c.* 1260 BC. Led by Moses, they crossed Sinai and made their way to Kadesh.

EXPERIMENTAL METHOD, hall-mark of empirical research, which is the basis of all modern science. It was generally neglected by medieval thinkers, whose methods, based on Aristotelian concepts, were deductive and were upheld by Descartes and the cartesian school. Experimental or inductive method was pioneered in Europe by Bacon, Harvey, and above all Newton in the 17th cent.

EXPLANATION, ACT OF (1665), passed by the Irish parliament to solve the difficulties created by the land settlement of 1661 following the Restoration. The act effectively transferred disputed lands to the Protestants, who owned about two-thirds of the cultivable land in Ireland after 1665 and created a legacy of bitterness among the dispossessed Catholics.

EXPLORATION, in Australia. Exploration was confined to the Sydney area (1788–1813) and to unsuccessful attempts to cross the Blue Mountains. Their crossing in 1813 allowed George William Evans to discover the Macquarie (1813) and Lachlan (1815) rivers, which John Oxley followed downstream (1817–18) to 'impenetrable' swamps which, he thought, bordered an inland sea.

The problem of the destination of the inland rivers was accentuated by the discovery of rivers, including the Murray, between Lake George and Port Phillip, by Hamilton Hume and William Hovell in 1824, and by Allan Cunningham between Bathurst and the Darling Downs (1823–7). During drought in 1828–9 Charles Sturt penetrated the Macquarie marshes to the Darling and in 1829–30 followed the Murrumbidgee to the Murray and that river to the sea. The fact that all the interior rivers of the south-east joined the Murray became clear following Sir Thomas Mitchell's work in the headwaters of the Darling in 1831–2, along the Bogan and Darling (1835), and on the Lachlan and Murray (1836).

Meanwhile, working from Adelaide, Edward John Eyre explored the Lake Torrens area (1839–40) and in 1840–1 journeyed through the desert on the shores of the Great Australian Bight to Albany and Perth, and Charles Sturt discovered the Stony Desert and Cooper's Creek in the north-east of South Australia (1844–6).

By the end of the decade most of eastern Australia had been explored by expeditions or by settlers fanning out from their tracks with sheep and cattle, and attention was turned to the centre and west. In 1859 the South Australian government offered a reward for the first south–north crossing. This stimulated several expeditions, the most notable of which were those led by John McDouall Stuart and by Robert Burke.

The final phase of heroic exploration followed the completion of the Adelaide–Darwin telegraph line in 1872 with journeys crossing the deserts between the west coast and the telegraph line. The first was made by John Forrest, who had already travelled from Perth to Port Augusta in 1870 and between Geraldton and Oodnadatta in 1874. Two were made by Ernest Giles in 1875 and 1876, and one by Peter Warburton in 1873. The north-west was explored by Forrest in 1879.

By the 1880s most of the major geographical features of the continent were known, but its exploration was not complete. Subsequent major expeditions were few but survey and mapping, particularly in the less populous parts of the country, still proceeded in the second half of the 20th cent.

TMP

EXPORT BOUNTIES in Europe were part of the system of encouragement to particular industries, often for political rather than economic reasons, to which the name 'mercantilism' has been given. The system included rebates, drawbacks, and bounties on certain imports, as well as the general framework of control by the Navigation and Staple Acts. Though Adam Smith described any trade which needed a bounty as 'necessarily a losing trade', two of these bounties appear to have been of economic importance. The success of the linen industry in Scotland seems to have been closely geared to the bounty put on exports in 1742, and the bounty on corn exports, part of the complicated structure of the Corn Laws, was related to the prices in the home market and appears to have encouraged production and so helped to even out price fluctuations so long as Britain's population had not outrun her agricultural resources. Export bounties disappeared with the coming of Free Trade in the 19th cent.

EXPORT-IMPORT BANK, US government agency, created to stimulate overseas trade. Established as a banking corporation by President F. D. Roosevelt (1934) to advance credits to facilitate trade with the Soviet Union and later Cuba, its lending functions were steadily widened and increased. In 1945 it became an independent agency of the federal government.

EXSURGE DOMINE, Bull of June 1520 in which Pope Leo X condemned 41 errors of Martin Luther, giving him two months to recant and threatening excommunication if he did not do so. Much of the Bull was written by Johann Eck, professor of theology at Ingolstadt and Luther's adversary at the Leipzig Disputations of 1519. It ordered that Luther's books should be burnt, and a copy of the Bull was publicly burnt by Luther himself at Wittenberg in Dec. 1520, together with books of canon law. On 3 Jan. 1521 Luther's excommunication was made absolute by the Bull *Decet*.

EXTRAORDINARY PROCEDURE, form of criminal trial used in France under the *ancien régime*. It was characterized by secret proceedings and the use of judicial torture as a means of obtaining proof of guilt. Torture to extract a confession was abolished in 1780 and torture as a preliminary to execution to extract accomplices' names in 1788.

EXTRA-TERRITORIALITY, legal system under which foreigners in China, Japan, and Siam were subject to the laws of their own countries. First formulated in the treaty of Wanghia (1844) between China and the US, it was soon extended to nationals of all powers having treaty relations with China. In practice, Chinese Christian converts and residents of foreign concessions in treaty ports also benefited from the system. In China, extra-territoriality was formally abolished in 1943, but effectively not until 1949, owing to the presence of large numbers of GIs under American jurisdiction after the Second World War. In Japan, extra-territorial jurisdiction was first established by the Ansei treaties of 1858. It stimulated the introduction of Western-style legal codes, which helped to persuade the Western powers, in 1899, to accept Japanese jurisdiction over their nationals. Extra-territoriality in Siam was first introduced by the Anglo–Siamese (Bowring) treaty of 1855, and then extended to other powers. It was brought to an end by treaties with the US in 1920, and the European powers in 1924–5.

EYLAU, BATTLE OF (8 Feb. 1807), fought in East Prussia. Although costly in men, it failed to give Napoleon the decisive victory he wanted over the Russians.

EYRE, EDWARD JOHN (1815–1901), British colonial governor. Eyre migrated to Australia, where he became famous as an explorer. He was a magistrate and protector of Aborigines (1836); lieutenant-governor of New Zealand (1846); lieutenant-governor of St Vincent (1854); acting-governor of the Leeward Islands (1860–1); lieutenant-governor of Jamaica, (1862) and governor (1864). He resented criticism of constituted authority, and clashed frequently with the Jamaican Assembly which he dissolved in 1863 when it began investigating frauds and irregularities involving high government officials. However, a newly elected assembly renewed their attack on Eyre's administration. Eyre's most persistent critic was George William Gordon, a coloured member of the assembly and a religious nonconformist. When the Morant Bay Rebellion occurred (1865) Eyre rid himself of Gordon by arresting him. Gordon was court-martialed, condemned, and executed. Many excesses were committed in suppressing the rebellion and Britain appointed a Commission of Inquiry. While commending Eyre for acting swiftly, the commissioners found that his punishments had been excessive and he was recalled. The Jamaica Committee, among whose members were John Stuart Mill, T. S. Huxley, Sir Thomas Buxton, and Herbert Spencer, collected evidence which led to Eyre being charged with murder. The Grand Jury (1869) finding no true bill, he did not stand trial. Among Eyre's supporters, were Carlyle, Charles Kingsley, Tennyson, and Ruskin.

Sidney Olivier, *The Myth of Governor Eyre* (London, 1933).
Bernard Semmel, *The Governor Eyre Controversy* (London, 1962).   RH

EYSTEIN (AUGUSTINE) (d. 1188), Norwegian archbishop and supporter of the Hildebrandine papacy. Appointed to the see of Nidaros (Trondheim) in 1157, he secured great privileges for the Church from King Magnus V, whose claims he established through a succession law, but Magnus's rival, King Sverre, drove him into exile in England (1180–3).

EZANA (*fl.* 4th cent.), ruler of the Aksumite empire, knowledge of his exploits being recorded in stone inscriptions at Aksum, one in Sabaean, Geez, and Greek, and the others in Geez alone. Each tells of a different expedition: to Begemder, where he settled people on the land; two different areas along the Red Sea coast, where he punished wrong-doers; the mountains of Semien, where he issued laws; and Meroitic Kush, where he destroyed the temples and cotton plantations of his enemies. Towards the end of his reign he was converted to Christianity. He issued many coins, at first as a pagan with the sun and moon, but later with the Cross, and so is thought to have been the first Christian ruler of Aksum.

EZRA (*c.* 460 BC), leader of the Jews in Babylon. He returned to Jerusalem (*c.* 458) and reorganized religion on the principles of obedience to God, exclusion of foreign elements and worship through the synagogue, the scriptures, and the revised Torah.

FABIANISM in Britain, policy of the Fabian Society, a small group of socialists founded in London (1884), named after Fabius Cunctator, the Roman general who defeated stronger forces by elusive delaying tactics, avoiding a pitched battle. Early members included Sydney and Beatrice Webb, George Bernard Shaw, Annie Besant, Graham Wallas, and Edward Pease. Believing in permeation, not Marxist revolution, middle-class intellectual Fabians at first aimed to achieve municipal socialism and the collectivist state by influencing Liberal and Conservative politicians. They assisted in the birth of the Labour Representation Committee and affiliated with the Labour Party. They published *Fabian Essays in Socialism* (1889) and used the results of their Bureau's research into economic and social problems to educate the public through pamphlets, lectures, and summer schools. Later, they extended their approach to foreign and colonial affairs (1940s). *New Fabian Essays* (ed. R. H. S. Crossman, 1952) outlined fresh paths to socialism since much of early Fabian policy had been effected in the welfare state policy of 20th-cent. governments.

FABIUS MAXIMUS CUNCTATOR, Quintus, the 'delayer' (d. 203 BC), Roman general and politician in the Second Punic War. He was a high aristocrat and ex-consul who was appointed dictator after the Trasimene disaster (217), and pursued a strategy of cautious non-engagement with Hannibal. After the reversal of this strategy by the consuls at Cannae (216), he reimposed it as consul for successive years (215–214) and as senior pro-magistrate. The strategy was recognized as having saved Rome, but, though Fabius took some part in recovering lost allies (*eg*, Tarentum, 209), his mentality was too defensive for the second phase of the war, in which Rome moved to the offensive, and he strenuously, but unavailingly, opposed Scipio Africanus' plan to invade Africa (205).

FABRICIUS, HIERONYMOUS OF AQUAPENDENTE (1537–1619), Italian physician, embryologist and anatomist, who taught Harvey at Padua in his early studies in connection with the circulation of the blood.

FABRY, JEAN (1876–1968), French journalist and conservative politician. In the 1930s he was one of those who warned of Germany's aggressive intentions and called for a modernized French army. He was briefly minister of war (1935–6).

FACTA, LUIGI (1861–1930), Italian politician and prime minister who served various cabinets (1902–21). Forming his own government (March 1922), he underestimated the fascist threat and failed to curb political violence. Having allowed the fascists to gather for the 'March on Rome', he belatedly asked King Victor Emmanuel to sanction resistance and a state of seige in Rome. But his indecisiveness encouraged the king to decline this military confrontation (28 Oct. 1922) and Mussolini emerged to power as head of a coalition.

FACTORY LEGISLATION in Britain. The first regulation of child labour in factories was the elder Peel's Health and Morals of Apprentices Act (1802), which limited hours of work to 12 per day. This and the act of 1819, which banned children under nine from cotton mills and limited the hours of those under 16 to 12 per day, were ineffectively enforced because no means of inspection was provided for. Althorp's act of 1833, prompted by Ashley and introduced by Grey's government, ensured the appointment of paid inspectors. It banned the employment of children under nine in textile factories, limiting the hours of children from 9 to 13 to nine, with two hours' schooling and no more than 48 hours per week, and those of young persons from 13 to 18 to 12 hours per day and 69 per week. The compulsory registration of births (1836) enabled the provisions to be enforced. Meanwhile, adult male workers who were excluded from protective legislation by the prevailing belief in the free negotiation of contracts between employer and workman saw that their hours could be limited by those of women and children and campaigned for a Ten Hours Bill. They were supported by humanitarians of all parties, including the Tories Sadler and Oastler and the radicals Hobhouse and Fielden. Agitation led to a parliamentary committee appointed by Peel's government to examine the working of the 1833 act. The resulting Factory Act (1844) limited female labour in textile factories to 12 hours per day, and though children were allowed to work at eight, instead of nine, their hours were cut to 6½ and the provision was extended to silk mills. Finally, an act in 1847 was passed with the design of ensuring a 10-hour day in textile factories for all workers by imposing this limit on the hours worked by women and young persons (13–18). It was introduced by Fielden, in Ashley's absence from parliament, and passed under Russell's administration with Tory protectionist support. The intention of the act was frustrated by mill-owners, who worked a relay system during a 15-hour day, and Ashley was forced to accept a 10½-hour day with a 1½-hour break for meals in return for the mills remaining open only for 12 hours (1850). This lost him support from operatives whose employers had not worked the relay system, but it secured the establishment of a normal working day for all textile workers without loss of production.

After the success of the Ten Hours Campaign (1847–50), existing provisions were extended to calico printing (1855) and, with Palmerston's help, to bleaching and dyeing (1860) and lace manufacture (1861). Hours and conditions in the potteries and the match industry were limited, and Disraeli's act extended the ten hours and other provisions to all factories and workshops of a certain size (1867).

J. T. Ward, *The Factory Movement 1830–55* (London, 1962).
VEC

FACUNDO, novel by Domingo Faustino Sarmiento, Argentine writer and statesman, about the struggle between 'civilization and barbarism' on the Argentine Pampas. It was published in 1845 and is a fictionalized account of the life of the rural *caudillo* Facundo Quiroga. Using Facundo as a vehicle, Sarmiento describes the Argentine countryside and the ruthlessness of its local bosses.

FADDEN, SIR ARTHUR WILLIAM (1895–), Australian politician and member of the Canberra House of Representatives (1936–58). He became a cabinet minister in 1940, leader of the Country Party later that year, and was prime minister for six weeks after the resignation of R. G. Menzies (Aug. 1941). He became deputy prime minister and treasurer in Menzies' Liberal–Country Party coalition government (1949–58) and maintained a vigorous control of central banking geared to the expanding post-war economy. Fadden did much to strengthen the coalition by his loyalty, sound judgement, and cordial relations with members of all parties.

FAHRENHEIT, GABRIEL DANIEL (1686–1736), German physicist, whose graduated mercury scale (*c*. 1714) advanced thermometry as an aid to physics and chemistry. He came to live in England and made metereological instruments for the Royal Society.

FA-HSIEN, also spelt Fa-hien (*fl.* 4th cent.), Chinese Buddhist monk from Shansi, who in AD 399 left China for India and Ceylon to visit Buddhist holy places, to converse with other monks, and, especially, to copy Buddhist texts. His account is interesting for the light it throws upon social, particularly religious, conditions in Central Asia and the Gangetic valley during the early Gupta period. It is no less interesting for the lively description of the return voyage, when, after surviving a severe storm, Fa-hsien spent five months in Java before returning to China in 414.

FAIDHERBE, LOUIS-LÉON-CÉSAR (1818–80), French soldier and colonial administrator, who served in Algeria (1842), Guadeloupe (1848–9), Senegal (1852 and 1863, with an interlude in France), and in the Franco–Prussian War, after which he became a senator of the Third Republic. His principal overseas campaigns were in Soudan, where he led French troops against Al-Hajj Omar.

FAIR DEAL in US, term applied to the domestic legislative programme of President Harry S. Truman (1945–53). Modelled on Theodore Roosevelt's Square Deal, and F. D. Roosevelt's New Deal, it was used by the president in his annual message to Congress (1949) to describe the reform programme embracing civil rights and fair employment practices legislation, and federal aid to education, public housing, and public health.

FAIR EMPLOYMENT PRACTICES COMMITTEE in US, committee established (1941) by executive order of President F. D. Roosevelt to prevent racial discrimination in war industries. The attempt (1946) to establish a permanent committee failed, but a number of state laws, city ordinances, and federal regulations embody FEPC policies.

FAIR LABOR STANDARDS ACT (1938) in US, first permanent legislation establishing maximum working hours and minimum wages for industries engaged in inter-state commerce. The standard 40 cents an hour for a 40-hour week was raised by later acts.

FAIRFAX, JOHN (1804–77), Englishman, who emigrated to Australia in 1838 and became a newspaper owner and politician in NSW. In 1841, with Charles Kemp, he bought *The Sydney Herald*, and later became its sole owner. He was also a member of the NSW legislative council. Fairfax built up *The Sydney Morning Herald* into one of the most respected influential newspapers in the country. It is (1970) Australia's oldest surviving newspaper.

FAIRFAX OF CAMERON, Thomas Fairfax, 3rd Baron (Scottish) (1612–71), English parliamentary military commander in the Civil War. In 1643 he captured Wakefield, but after being routed by the royalist forces of the Marquis of Newcastle at Adwalton Moor in June was unable to prevent the royalists from assuming control of all the Yorkshire clothing towns. However, he kept command of Hull and from there harassed the northern wing of the king's attempted triple advance on London in 1643. His position in the north was completely transformed by the Solemn League and Covenant, which gave parliament Scottish military aid, and when the Earl of Leven's army crossed the border in Jan. 1644 Fairfax emerged from Hull, overwhelmed the royalist forces trying to protect Newcastle's

rear while he was trying to stop Leven, and then with Leven besieged Newcastle at York. Joined there by the army of the Eastern Association under Cromwell and Manchester, and attacked at Marston Moor by Prince Rupert, he took part in the first decisive victory over the royalists, and in 1645 was given command of the New Model Army. In the next year he beat the king at Naseby, and took control of the west of England. In 1650 he was relieved of his command because his refusal to swear allegiance to the republic, or show approval for the execution of the king, undermined parliament's confidence in him, thus, at the age of 38, relinquishing the most powerful position in the country to Cromwell. In 1660 at the restoration of the monarchy he resumed his place in parliament.

FAIRFAX, THOMAS (1693–1781), owner of the Northern Neck of VA, US. George Washington worked for him as a surveyor and estate manager.

FAIRS in medieval Europe. Fairs were centres of periodic meetings between merchants of different regions. They catered for types of trade which could not be transacted profitably throughout the year, though large activity might be stimulated during a limited period. The most important medieval business centres, such as Venice, never developed fairs because a high level of business activity was maintained there all the time. Some fairs were specialized, *eg*, the great English wool and cloth fair at Boston, and the wine fair at Winchester. The most important international fairs, though starting as specialized meetings, developed into occasions for the exchange of most varied goods. The most famous example of this type of evolution is provided by the Fairs of Champagne. Starting in the 12th cent. as a specialized cloth fair, they developed first of all into a meeting place between the Italians and the men of northern France and Flanders and later on came to attract merchants from every part of western Europe. The Champagne Fairs developed into a cycle of six fairs held at fairly equal intervals in the course of each year. The existence of a cycle of fairs was one of the features of the other leading international fairs in the later middle ages, *eg*, at Geneva and Lyons in the 15th cent.

FAIZI, SHAIKH (1547–95), son of Shaikh Mubarak of Nagor and elder brother of Abu'l Fazl, confidant of the Mughal emperor Akbar. He and his brother influenced Akbar in a liberal and heterodox direction. He was a voluminous poet in Persian and a translator of Hindu works.

FAKHR AL-DIN II (1572–1635), of the Druze house of Ma'n, who made himself the master of the Lebanon (1591–1613). The Ottoman Turks, viewing his power with suspicion, now moved against him. Fakhr al-Din spent the next five years as an exile in Tuscany, a state with which he had been in contact since 1608. Returning to the Lebanon in 1618, he soon regained control of the territories that he had held before his exile. He was at the height of his fame between 1623 and 1631 but his regime rested more on the weakness of the Ottoman government than on his own strength. With the emergence in 1632 of Sultan Murad IV as the effective master of the empire, the end of Fakhr al-Din's career was in sight. His power crumbled rapidly (1633–4). Defeated in the field, he was captured, brought to Istanbul, and executed.

FALANGE, mass party in Nationalist Spain, which originated from a movement founded by Primo de Rivera in 1933. He had hoped for an authoritarian rebirth of Spain within the concept of a nationalist ideology which would embrace the working classes. The appeal of the Falange was at first limited to students and intellectuals and its support was meagre. In 1934 it became amalgamated with another small national-syndicalist movement, the *Juntas de Ofensiva Nacional Sindicalista*, led by Ramiro Ledesma Ramos and Onesimo Redondo Ortega. This movement, influenced by

Nazism, aimed at violent revolutionary nationalism, its slogan being 'Arise, Spain, One, Great and Free!'

The Falange was ignored by the workers, but it increased its support in the university towns of Seville, Valladolid, and Madrid. Politically, its only effect was seen in the involvement of Falangists in street warfare with the left. Rich monarchists were interested in the movement, in which they saw a means of attacking the Republic, but Primo rejected both monarchism, which was discredited, and violence. However, after the victory of the Popular Front, the Falange was flooded by right-wing volunteers, who had had enough of moderation.

The Falange took part in the rising of July 1936, and since its ideology gave coherence to the Nationalist war effort, it received further support from disgruntled individuals who wished to serve the movement in a civilian capacity. The Nationalists needed a political doctrine under which to mobilize these elements and to provide a viable framework for government, and in April 1937 the Falange was forcibly joined to the Carlists. All that remained was a national cult of Primo and a mild state corporativism. The Falange became an ossified, faction-ridden bureaucracy, forming merely part of the balance of forces in Franco's Spain.

FALIER, MARINO, Doge of Venice (1354–5), member of an old noble family, long trained for government in many civil and military posts. After his election (1354), he conspired to restore the personal power of the doge, which had long passed to an oligarchic Council of Ten, and was executed after less than a year in the office. All subsequent doges were inaugurated on the spot of his execution.

FALKIRK, BATTLES OF (1298, 1746). The Scots, who had thrown off English rule in 1297 by their victory at Stirling, were defeated at Falkirk in 1298 by the English cavalry and Welsh archers. This started a gradual reconquest of Scotland by King Edward I, who was briefly in control of the country (1304–5), but lost it again through the rising of Robert Bruce in 1305. In 1746 Falkirk was the scene of the victory of Prince Charles Edward during the Jacobite rebellion in Scotland, preventing an English force under Gen. Hawley from marching to relieve the rebel siege of Stirling. Despite this victory Prince Charles was unable to take Stirling and after subsequently being defeated at Culloden he fled the country.

FALKLAND ISLANDS, British possession in the South Atlantic Ocean. Discovery of the islands has been attributed to Esteban Gomez, a member of Magellan's expedition round the world (1520) and to the English navigator John Davis (1592). Until the 19th cent. they were known by the Spanish name Malvinas. The first permanent settlement (1764) was French. In the following year a British colony was established on West Falkland. Spain purchased the islands from France (1766) and at first raised objections to the British colony, but later (1771) recognized British claims to a part of West Falkland. Three years later the British settlers abandoned the colony, the Spaniards also abandoning the islands in 1811. In 1820 settlers from the United Provinces of La Plata (later Argentina) attempted unsuccessfully to establish a colony. Reviving the old claim, Britain established the colony of the Falkland Islands (1833), named after a treasurer of the Royal Navy, Viscount Falkland. Argentina still claims both the main islands and several of the Falkland Island Dependencies. Chile claims most of the Dependencies. Both these republics maintain naval outposts in the islands but neither has pursued its claim by force. Most of the islanders are of British descent and acknowledge British nationality. The colony is governed (1970) by a resident British governor assisted by an elected legislature and an Executive Council.

FALKLAND ISLANDS, BATTLE OF (1914), first major British naval success of the First World War. On receipt of the news of Cradock's defeat at Coronel, the admiralty dispatched Admiral Sturdee with the battle-cruisers *Invincible* and *Inflexible* to the South Atlantic to search out the German squadron. On 8 Dec. the British vessels were coaling in Port Stanley in the Falkland Islands when Spee appeared to destroy the wireless station there. In the subsequent engagement the Germans were overwhelmed and four of Spee's five ships were sunk. The battle eliminated the only significant German naval force outside European waters.

FALL, ALBERT BACON (1861–1944), US lawyer and politician. He was a senator (1912–21) and secretary of the interior (1921–3). Later, he was deeply involved in the scandals of President Harding's administration, was convicted (1929), and imprisoned (1931–2).

FALL LINE, junction of the coast plain of the eastern US with the Piedmont plateau of the Appalachian mountain system. On the rivers of the Atlantic and Gulf coasts, from NJ to AL, waterfalls and rapids established the heads of navigation. In the early 18th cent. the Fall Line marked the inner limit of settlement in the Middle and Southern Colonies. As population pressure and soil exhaustion in the Tidewater lands of the Coast Plain encouraged settlers to push on to the Piedmont, the Fall Line became a line of social and economic demarcation. It also provided water-power for processing goods at the trans-shipment points, and thereby stimulated early urban and industrial growth. A series of Fall Line cities developed, from Trenton, NJ, to Montgomery, AL.

FALLEN TIMBERS, BATTLE OF (20 Aug. 1794), fought near Fort Miami in northern OH. Gen. Anthony Wayne's attack was successful and the US was able to dictate the treaty of Greenville to the defeated Indians (1795). The power of the north-western Indians was broken and new territory was open to American expansion.

FALLOUX, FRÉDÉRIC ALFRED PIERRE, Comte de (1811–86), French Catholic politician and minister and son of a bourgeois ennobled by the Restoration. He was elected to the Orleanist Chamber (1846) and although a legitimist he rallied to the Second Republic. Elected to the Constituent Assembly (1848), he encouraged its conservatism and has been blamed for the closure of the Ateliers Nationaux and thus for the 'June Days'. He served as minister of education (1848–9), drafting the law which bears his name, but refused to accept the coup and retired to farming and writing, being elected to the *Académie* (1856). As royalist elder statesman, he supported MacMahon and liberal Catholicism against the more intransigent schools of thought.

FAMILY ALLOWANCES in Britain, principle conceded in the Unemployed Workers Dependants' (Temporary Provisions) Act (1921), although there had been provision made for the dependants of those demobilized in 1919. The scales of payment were 25p (5s) for the wife and 5 p (1s) for each of the children of the unemployed. There was much pressure during the inter-war years for a system of comprehensive family allowances, eg, from Seebohm Rowntree, who surveyed poverty in York in 1935–6, as he had also done at the turn of the century. There was also much pressure from those worried by the fall in the birth-rate which characterized the 1930s. The payment of allowances remained tied to unemployment insurance or national assistance, however; the latter proved particularly objectionable through the use of the 'means-test'. Family Allowances were finally provided for in 1945.

FAMILY COMPACT in Canada, term applied to a small ultra-conservative group in Upper Canada. In the 1830s reformers seeking responsible government claimed that the compact used its power for control of land and the aggrandizement of the Church of England. Resentment against the compact contributed to the Rebellion of 1837.

FAMILY COMPACTS, alliances concluded in the 18th cent. between the Bourbon rulers of France and Spain, which reversed the diplomatic trend of the 16th–17th cents by which the two countries, ruled respectively by Bourbon and Habsburg kings, were constant rivals. The first family compact, between Louis XV of France and Philip V of Spain, was the treaty of the Escorial (Nov. 1733), which marked the effective end of the Anglo–French friendship that had stabilized European diplomacy since 1717. It was prompted by Elizabeth Farnese's Italian ambitions. Franco–Spanish co-operation in the ensuing War of the Polish Succession ensured the possession of Lorraine for Louis XV's father-in-law, Stanislas Lesczynski, and its ultimate reversion to France, while Don Carlos, the eldest son of Philip V and Elizabeth Farnese, conditionally acquired Naples and Sicily. The second compact, the treaty of Fontainebleau (Oct. 1743), committed Spain against Austria in the War of the Austrian Succession (1740–8), after which Don Philip, the younger son, received Parma and Piacenza. The third compact (Aug. 1761), between Charles III of Spain and Louis XV of France, was caused by colonial rather than European considerations. Spain was worried in case Britain's victories over France in the Seven Years War might lead to her complete colonial supremacy. Charles therefore promised to enter the war within eight months if peace had not been made, and Louis agreed not to make peace till Spanish grievances had been rectified by Britain. Spain duly entered the war and participated in the treaty of Paris (1763).

FAMINE IN EUROPE, recurrent feature of European society due to the failure of harvests and frequent while agriculture remained at subsistence level. Famine caused demographic stagnation or decline and was often followed by attacks of the plague, eg, the Andalusian dearth of 1595 was followed by the great plague of 1596–1600. Since the 17th cent. Europe has been free of the extreme consequences of famine, although the two World Wars of the 20th cent. brought Germany close to famine conditions.

FAMINE IN INDIA, periodic calamity caused chiefly by a failure of the monsoon. It is impossible to compare ancient and medieval famines with those of modern times because of the absence of statistics before the British period. No well-organized system of relief was possible before the development of communications in the second half of the 19th cent. The East India Co. displayed little capacity for dealing with famines. During that of 1770 in Lower Bengal a third of the population is said to have died, but no reliance can be placed on these figures. Between 1770 and 1858 India suffered from 12 famines and four periods of severe scarcity. During the 1792 famine relief works were first opened by the Madras government. After the Crown took over in 1858 it was recognized that famine relief was the responsibility of the state. During the famine of 1860–1 in the North-Western Provinces and Rajputana some 33,000,000 units were relieved (a unit is the technical term for one person relieved for one day). This was also the first occasion when a famine formed the subject of a special enquiry. The famine of 1865–7 affected a population of 47½ millions in Madras and Bengal. Government food supplies came too late to check the heavy mortality, but when relief did come it was marked by a profusion hitherto unexampled. The Famine Commission of 1867 laid the foundations of a more humane policy and enunciated the principle of saving life. The Rajputana famine of 1868–70 was caused by a failure of the rains and aggravated by poor communications. Cholera broke out and the autumn harvest of 1869 was destroyed by swarms of locusts. In the Bihar famine of 1873–4 village inspection, the basis of modern famine relief organization, was carried out for the first time. The idea of famine insurance originated

with Sir John Strachey, who, in 1874, realized that famines were periodic calamities against which it was essential to make financial provision. During the Southern Indian famine of 1876–8 the government made the mistake of relying on private traders for the importation of food. For a time the reduced or Temple ration (named after Sir Richard Temple) was adopted, but was soon abandoned as insufficient. The Famine Commission of 1878–80 laid down the principle that it was the paramount duty of the state to afford relief and recommended that a definite procedure should be embodied in a famine code to be carried out by the local governments. This policy was first tested in the famine of 1896–7 and the principle confirmed by a commission in 1898. The mortality during the famine of 1899–1900 was appalling despite the enormous expenditure on relief. The commission of 1901 placed special emphasis on the importance of moral strategy, for moral depression led to physical deterioration. A serious famine took place in Bengal in 1943, largely because of wartime administrative dislocations. Since independence famine conditions due to regional shortages have been relieved by the emergency provision of supplies from abroad. The Bihar famine of 1967 again revealed to the world the disastrous consequences of the failure of the monsoons for a peasantry among whom hunger is endemic.

A. Loveday, *The History and Economics of Indian Famines* (London, 1914).
B. M. Bhatia, *Famines in India, 1860–1945* (London, 1963).   CCD

FAN NOLI, STYLIAN (1882–), leader of the Albanian national movement and prime minister of Albania. Fan Noli was educated at Greek schools and, after some years in Athens, went to Egypt to teach in a Greek gymnasium. Later, in Boston, US, he founded the Albanian Autocephalous Orthodox Church (1908) and graduated from Harvard University (1912). In 1920 he returned to Albania at the head of the Albanian–American association *Vatra*, for which he was the spokesman in the national assembly. Fan Noli's group joined the Popular Party, forming its reformist faction. He was minister of foreign affairs in the Popular government of 1921, but resigned in 1922 over Zogu's policy towards Yugoslavia. That same year Fan Noli left Zogu to ride out a tribal rebellion alone, from which he emerged prime minister. Fan Noli's faction quit the party to form an opposition bloc which ousted Zogu in 1924. On 17 June 1924 Fan Noli formed a cabinet and announced a 19-point reform programme. But in Dec. Zogu returned from exile in Yugoslavia, leading a military force which drove Fan Noli from office. Fan Noli fled to Italy and was outlawed. He eventually returned to the US and resumed his role as a church leader in Boston. In 1950 Fan Noli accepted an invitation from the communist regime to adhere to the reconstructed church on behalf of the American organization.

FANFANI, AMINTORE (1908–), Italian prime minister (1954, 1958–9, 1960–3), president of UN Assembly (1965), and foreign minister (1965–8). As a noted economic historian he joined the Christian Democrat Party (DC), and served as labour and agriculture minister in De Gasperi's cabinets (1947–53). A leader of the intellectual left of the party, he sought as general secretary (1954–9) to prepare DC to share power with democratic left parties, and to make party organization independent of clerical domination. His fourth cabinet (1962–3), with the social democrats, introduced national economic planning, nationalized electricity, and produced limited educational reforms. Fanfani sought to free policies from excessive Vatican or US influence, but involvement in Viet-nam mediation (1965) led to his temporary resignation. Conservative hostility within the DC limited his power, but he became president of the Senate (1968).

FANJUL GOÑI, JOAQUÍN (1880–1936), Spanish soldier and politician, who made his military reputation in Morocco. He was never sympathetic to the Republic and entered politics in order to fight it legally. He became a deputy to the Cortes in the conservative Agrarian Party of Martínez de Velasco, which was allied to Gil Robles's CEDA. During the early years of the Republic he displayed his right-wing bias by attacks on Azaña's army reforms and the separatist tendencies of the Catalans, whom he branded as traitors.

When Gil Robles became minister of war in May 1935 he appointed Fanjul as his under-secretary. In this position, he assisted in the promotion of anti-Republican officers. On at least two occasions, notably after the fall of the CEDA–Radical coalition (Nov. 1935), he offered to stage a coup on behalf of Gil Robles, but these offers were refused.

In 1936 Fanjul became involved in the preparations for a military rising. His task was to capture the centre of Madrid from the stronghold of the Montaña military barracks. On 18 July he declared for the nationalist rebellion, but the barracks were soon surrounded by hostile armed workers. After heavy firing, the barracks fell. He was saved from mob violence by being captured and taken to prison. He was court-martialled, found guilty of treason, and shot.   PP

FANON, FRANTZ (1925–61), Martinican writer and psychiatrist, who associated himself with the Algerian Front of Liberation and the cause of African independence. His writing influenced French-speaking African intellectuals. His *Les Damnés de la Terre* (*The Wretched of the Earth*) indicts colonial rule.

FANTE people in southern Ghana, West Africa, branch of the Akan people, whose development in this region long precedes the earliest European contacts of the 15th cent. During the 16th cent. and later they played an important role, as middlemen (like the Nzima to their west and the Ga to their east along the same seaboard of the 'Gold Coast'), between Europeans in trading forts at places such as Elmina and Cape Coast (Cabo Corso) and the Akan states of the inland country, notably Denkyira and then Asante (Ashanti).

During the 18th cent. the Fante tended to turn to the Europeans, notably the British, as allies against the Asante, who claimed the Fante as their tributaries. With the extension of British coastal influence this tendency increased. In 1844 a number of Fante and other chiefs signed an agreement which became known—and was locally famous—as 'the Bond'. This had the effect of maintaining Fante traditional institutions while admitting Fante acceptance of British overlordship. Later again it had the effect of enabling a number of Fante leaders to acquire modern education and to operate within the colonial framework while, at the same time, pressing for constitutional reform to African advantage. In 1970 the Fante were an integral part of the Republic of Ghana.

FARABI, AL-, ABU NASR MUHAMMAD (the Alfarabius or Avennasar of the Latins) (*fl.* 10th cent.), Muslim philosopher, of Turkish origin who based his philosophical ideas on Aristotle's, as revealed in the Greek commentaries deriving from the late Hellenistic world, and was the author of works on logic, metaphysics, ethics, and politics.

FARADAY, MICHAEL (1791–1867), British scientist, who started his career in 1813 at the Royal Institution as assistant to Sir Humphry Davy. His scientific genius was soon evident and he is considered to be the greatest physical scientist of the 19th cent. His outstanding achievement was the construction of a complete descriptive theory of electricity, including the electro-magnetic theory of light. He discovered electromagnetic induction and invented the transformer and the dynamo. His investigation and theory of electrolytic dissociation of solutions and his discovery of benzene were significant contributions in the field of chemistry.

FARAIDHI MOVEMENT, religious sect founded in eastern Bengal by Haji Shariatullah on his return (1802) from a 20-year stay in the Hijaz and Mecca. Though probably not a Wahabi, Shariatullah conveyed much the same message to the Muslims of rural Bengal, which was to purify their faith of non-Muslim accretions, both Hindu and animist. He considered that Muslims under the British lived in *dar-ul-harb*, or a land of war, and that the Id and Friday prayers could not properly be held. His son, known as 'Dhadu Miyan', organized the sect efficiently on community lines and also organized an agrarian movement against Hindu landlords which was suppressed by the British. The sect later became preoccupied largely with questions of Islamic law.

FARAS, (known also as Pachoras), in the northern Sudan, seat of the bishop and of the *Eparch* (civil ruler) of Nobatia. As the centre of Christianity in this area from the mid-6th cent., Faras contained many churches, and a fine cathedral, decorated with a remarkable series of frescoes which owe much to Byzantine influence. It was an important centre during much of the Sudan's early history and has remains of Pharaonic, Meroitic, and post-Christian occupation.

FARGE, YVES (1899–1953), French Resistance leader and founder of the *Franc-Tireur*, the military arm of the resistance group known as 'Front National', organized and dominated by the Communist Party. After the Second World War he was a leader of the 'fellow-travelling' peace movement. As minister of food (1946) he acted vigorously against black marketeers.

FARINACCI, ROBERTO (1892–1945), Italian politician and secretary of the Fascist Party (1925–6), responsible for the violent suppression of opposition organizations and individuals. He helped to found the Fascist Movement (1919), ejected the socialist local government of Milan (Aug. 1922), and established himself as Mussolini's leading radical and violent supporter. Maintaining a critical, independent viewpoint in his Cremona newspaper, he encouraged anti-clerical, anti-semitic, and pro-German policies. He was shot by partisans.

FARINI, LUIGI CARLO (1812–66), minister of Pius IX (1847) and prime minister of Italy (1862–3). As a neo-Guelph, Farini sought to unite Italy in a papal confederation, but when the pope's short-lived flirtation with liberalism ended he turned reluctantly to Piedmontese leadership. He headed the provisional government of Modena, Parma, and Bologna which successfully asked for annexation to Piedmont in 1860. Despite his earlier opinion that some Italian states feared Piedmont as much as Austria, he joined the Italian government, but became one of the leading advocates of decentralization.

FARLEY, JAMES ALOYSIUS (1888–), US political manager and businessman. On election as Democratic chairman of Rockland County (1918) he moved into state politics and worked closely with Gov. Alfred E. Smith. In 1924 he became associated with F. D. Roosevelt, whose successful gubernatorial campaigns (1928, 1930) he helped to manage. With a well-organized New York Democratic Party behind him, he began to work for Roosevelt's presidential nomination. A masterly political organizer, he created support throughout the country and Roosevelt's success in 1932 was a tribute to his efforts. He became chairman of the Democratic National Committee (1932–40), then postmaster general of the US in Roosevelt's cabinet (1933–40), and he organized the successful 1936 campaign. He resigned in 1940 because he opposed Roosevelt's breaking of tradition by standing for a third term and thus thwarting his own presidential aspirations. He allowed himself to be nominated at the Democratic national convention, and after Roosevelt's victory he effectively retired from national politics, and became chairman of the Coca-Cola Export Corporation.

FARMER–LABOR PARTY, US political party formed (1920) by representatives of labour unions and radical farmers and labourers in the Mid-west and North-west. It advocated nationalization of public utilities, establishment of government banks, farm-relief measures, and labour reforms. In 1924, its members, making little headway at the national level, supported La Follette's Progressive Party The Farmer–Labor Party of MN, a direct offshoot from the Non-partisan League (1915–20), successfully returned Floyd B. Olson as governor of MN (1930, 1932, 1934) and elected a number of congressmen who supported President Roosevelt's New Deal.

FARMERS' ALLIANCES, US agricultural organizations in the 1880s and 1890s. The Northern or North-western Alliance, founded in 1880, was organized in the farming states of KS, NB, ND, SD, and MN. The Southern Alliance, originating around 1874, but not growing in strength until the late 1880s, was supported by farmers in LA, AR, and TX and spread into other southern states. Both organizations aimed at improving agricultural conditions by broadly similar programmes of curbing the power of railroad companies and trusts, lowering interest rates, and easing mortgage payments. Both organizations were active in local politics. However, sectional economic differences between the two impeded efforts at amalgamation and the Southern Alliance carefully avoided third party political action since this might have split the white solidarity of the South. As a political force, the alliances were fading by the early 1890s, but they had provided an important link between the Grange and the Populists.

FARMERS' UNION, in NZ. Regional grievances of struggling dairy farmers in the 'Roadless North' led to the formation of the NZFU in Kaitaia (1899). More general fears of radical land and taxation proposals lay behind the formation of a colonial union (1902), with a political programme. The NZFU, allied with the Reform party, helped to end Liberal power in 1912 and to smash the 1913 waterfront strike. In the 1920s membership grew among mortgage-burdened farmers, but the NZFU was divided in its attitude towards financial remedies, especially rural credit. A more united, less directly political body, Federated Farmers of NZ, was formed in 1945.

FARNBOROUGH, THOMAS ERSKINE MAY, Baron (1815–1886), a clerk of the British House of Commons (1871–86) and author of *Treatise on the Law, Privileges, Proceedings and Usages of Parliament* (1844), which was periodically revised, often by later clerks, and was also used in 1970 in all Commonwealth parliaments.

FARNESE, name of an Italian family who were dukes of Parma. Pietro Luigi (c. 1490–1547), son of Pope Paul I, established the duchy of Parma and Piacenza (1545). His son, Ottavio (c. 1520–85), was the husband of Margaret, daughter of the Emperor Charles V, and became governor of the Netherlands, After eight years of confusion and war with Siena, following his father's assassination, Ottavio recovered his duchy in 1555. His son, Alexander (1546–92), was the general who recovered the southern provinces of the Netherlands for the Spanish Crown (1578–9). The male line died out with the death of Antonio Farnese (1679–1731), but the family had deteriorated both mentally and physically before the end of the 17th cent.

FARNESE, ALEXANDER (1520–89), cardinal, grandson of Pope Paul III, who elevated him to the college of cardinals (1535). He was a prominent papal diplomat and legate to the imperial and French courts. Known above all as the most influential patron of artists and scholars in 16th-cent. Rome, he helped the Catholic Church to bridge the cultural worlds of the Renaissance and the Counter-Reformation and was responsible for the survival of humanist values in the post-

tridentine period. He was also protector and patron of the Jesuit order.

FARNESE, ELIZABETH (1692–1766), Queen of Spain and second wife of Philip V. She dominated Spanish political life and helped to rejuvenate the Spanish empire. Philip having had children by an earlier marriage, Elizabeth realized that her sons were unlikely to rule Spain and she determined on an ambitious foreign policy to gain territories for them. She was attracted by the Italian possessions of the Farnese family, then under Austrian domination, and so decided to push Spain into a war with Austria. Her hopes were dashed when Spain was confronted by the powers of the Quadruple Alliance, which were anxious to preserve European security. However, her overriding ambition was finally gratified when the problem of the Polish Succession enabled her son Don Carlos to establish himself on the throne of Naples (1733–5), while Don Philip gained Parma and Piacenza after the War of the Austrian Succession (1748). The death of Philip V (1746) finally removed Elizabeth from the centre of political life.

FARRAGUT, DAVID GLASGOW (1801–70), first US admiral (1866). Entering the US navy as a midshipman in 1810, he rose, during the American Civil War, to command the Union fleet which captured New Orleans (1862), established Federal control of the Mississippi river, and overcame Confederate defences at Mobile Bay (Aug. 1864).

FARRER, WILLIAM JAMES (1845–1906), Australian farmer who contributed to primary production expansion by successful wheat cross-breeding. He also worked on a drought-resistant strain of wheat especially adapted to the drier areas of Australia.

FARUQ (1920–65), King of Egypt (*reg.* 1937–52). Although a skilful politician, Faruq was crushed between British influence, radical nationalism, and the economic and social problems of Egypt.

FARUQI DYNASTY ruled the small Indian state of Khandesh in the Tapti valley. It was founded by Malik Ahmad (c. 1382), who took the surname Faruqi because he claimed descent from the second Caliph, Umar-al-Faruq, or the Discriminator. For some time he and his successors were content with the title of khan, from which circumstance the principality came to be known as Khandesh, the country of the Khan. Malik Ahmad's son Nasir founded Burhanpur (1400) and captured the Hindu stronghold Asirgarh. The dynasty was extinguished by the Mughals when Asirgarh surrendered to the Emperor Akbar (1601).

FASCES, 'bundle' of rods and an axe carried by the attendants of the higher magistrates in ancient Rome to symbolize their power of scourging and beheading.

FASCIST GRAND COUNCIL (Gran Consiglio del Fascismo), founded by Mussolini (Dec. 1922) as the chief advisory body of the regime, combining ministers, under-secretaries, leaders of the party, the militia, and the unions. Initially it was consulted on most state matters of importance, and influenced party organization. Despite reductions in membership (1928–9) it proved cumbersome, and uncongenial to Mussolini, who increasingly disregarded it. It did not meet from Dec. 1939 until the extraordinary session 24–25 July 1943, when Grandi's no-confidence motion against Mussolini was carried 19–7, giving the king the excuse to dismiss Mussolini.

FASCIST MOVEMENT in Italy, derived from the *Fasci Italiani del combattimento* by Mussolini on 23 March 1919, in Milan. *Fascio* (pl. *fasci*), meaning 'bundle', 'group', was included in the title of previous political bodies. Ideas and attitudes behind the movement varied, and fascism defies precise definition. From *c.* 1925, when Mussolini finally established himself as an indispensable leader, the movement's history is that of Mussolini and his fluctuating policies. Until then others, *eg*, De Ambris, Farinacci, Grandi, Marinetti, and Gentile, considerably influenced the movement's theory and practice. Its early supporters were mainly ex-servicemen, ardent nationalists, and some violent adherents of Marinetti's 'Futurist' movement. The first programme, drafted by De Ambris, supported syndicalist principles. The Milan *fasci* failed in the 1919 elections, but *fasci* were formed in other cities, opposing the dominant political parties. Landowners, sharecroppers, small businessmen, etc. of Emilia, resisting 'red' union intimidation and strikes, joined *fasci* and gave them financial support. This agrarian fascism changed the movement's character. Anti-socialist, anti-syndicalist violence grew, and new bosses (*ras*), *eg*, Grandi, Balbo, and Farinacci, challenged Mussolini's leadership. Giolitti chose the *fasci* for his National Bloc (1921 elections), and the resulting 35 seats gave the fascists power and respectability. Anti-party principles were discarded, and the movement became the *Partito Nazionale Fascista* (Nov. 1921), with a full party organization. Strike-breaking activities by the squads won support from some liberal politicians, ministers, army, police, and industrial leaders. Anti-monarchist and anti-clerical attitudes were modified. Facta's weak government was intimidated and the situation culminated in the assembly of squads around Rome—'the March'. King Victor Emmanuel refused Facta's belated request for him to impose martial law, and allowed Mussolini to form a coalition (28 Oct. 1922). Fascists were united in their nationalism, their desire for 'action', their opposition to international Marxism, to old 'liberal' parliamentarianism, and to individualism. Disagreements over positive policies were reflected in two years of indecision. After Matteotti's murder (1924) Mussolini emerged as the only possible national leader, but he had to accept militant, anti-socialist authoritarianism from Farinacci and others. Syndicalist elements partly persisted in 'corporate state' theories, widely publicized as fascist economic-social doctrine, though even the paper structure was not completed till 1939. Party membership in the 1930s became a convenience for employment. The movement's enthusiasts were most united over the Ethiopian conquest (1935), most divided over racialist and pro-Nazi policies (1938–).

Nostalgic fascists and new adherents form the present Italian Social Movement (MSI), whose brief entry into a coalition (1960) led to violent protests.

H. Finer, *Mussolini's Italy* (London, 1935, 2nd ed. New York, 1965).

F. Chabod, *A History of Italian Fascism* (London, 1963).

CFB

FASHODA INCIDENT (1898), climax of the colonial dispute between France and Britain over Egypt. Joint Anglo–French interests in Egypt had been superseded by a British protectorate and by 1898 both powers were anxious to consolidate their African interests in the Sudan. Britain dreamt of a continuous territory from the Cape to Cairo; France longed to extend her influence from Dakar to Aden. Sudan was the missing link in both projects and a race to Fashoda took place. The French arrived first, and were followed by a numerically superior British force, bringing the two countries to the brink of war. The French, realizing the importance of British friendship in the event of German hostility, backed down, thus opening the way for a settlement. The incident improved relations between the two powers and was a prelude to the entente cordiale (1904). It also indicated that colonial disputes were not decisive in the alignment of powers in 1914.

FASILADAS (*reg.* 1632–67), Emperor of Ethiopia. On ascending the throne he abandoned the pro-Roman Catholic policy of his father, Susneyos, and expelled the Portuguese Jesuits from the country (1633). He later made agreements with the pashas of Massawa and Suakin on the coast to prevent more Roman Catholics from entering the area. Anxious to develop contacts with the East, he tried to negotiate treaties with the Sultan of Turkey, the Grand Mogul, the Imam of the Yemen, and the King of Adel. He founded the city of Gondar (1636) and built there the first of several fine castles.

FASTI CONSULARES, lists of Roman consuls from the foundation of the Republic (509 BC), the best-known and most complete surviving example being the *Fasti Capitolini* set up by Augustus in the forum at Rome and continued to AD 13.

FATH ALI SHAH (1771–1834), second ruler (1797–1834) of the Qajar dynasty of Iran. During his reign Iran suffered major defeats at the hands of Russia, allied itself with Britain, and began a programme of army reform. Fath Ali was survived by 57 sons and 46 daughters.

FATHPUR-SIKRI, royal palace and city 26 miles (41·8 kms) from Agra, India, built by the Emperor Akbar, and the chief royal residence (1569–85). In addition to the exquisite palace buildings, still almost intact, Fathpur-Sikri is notable for the Buland Darwaza, or great gateway, the largest of its kind in India, which gives access to the noble mosque and exquisite tomb of Salim Shah Chishti.

FATIMIDS, name denoting the line of Shi'i imams descended from Ali, the cousin and son-in-law of the Prophet Muhammad, through his wife, Fatima, the daughter of Muhammad. Isma'ili propaganda on behalf of these imams—under the guidance of an able architect of revolution, Abu Abdallah al-Shi'i—won much success among the Berbers of North Africa and brought about the emergence there, in 909, of a Fatimid caliphate opposed to the Abbasid caliphate long established at Baghdad. In 969 the Fatimids took control of Egypt. Their subsequent efforts to bring Syria under their rule met with only a limited success in the course of the 10th and 11th cents. During the long reign of the Caliph Al-Mustansir (1036–94) the Fatimid regime began to decline. The years 1060–73 were a 'time of troubles' for Egypt, with famine in the land for six years and violent conflict between the ethnic groups composing the armed forces of the Fatimid state (Turks, Sudanese, Maghariba). The price paid for relief from these ills was the establishment of a militarized regime in Egypt—a regime which was the creation (1073–7) of the Armenian soldier Badr al-Jamali (d. 1094). His efforts and the work of his son and successor as vizier, Al-Afdal (d. 1121), gave to the Fatimid caliphate almost another 100 years of life, though as a 'secular' state rather than as the embodiment of a vast movement of religious opposition. A decisive split occurred in 1094 between the more moderate (Musta'lian) and the more extreme (Nizari) elements amongst the Isma'ilis and the last caliphs had little influence on the conduct of affairs, power resting in the hands of the generals. Egypt itself was now a prize, the acquisition of which was the main objective of the Muslims under the Zangid master of Mosul, Aleppo, and Damascus, Nur al-Din, and of the Crusaders in Palestine, notably under the King of Jerusalem, Amalric II. In 1168–9, after two earlier but unsuccessful attempts in 1163 and 1167, Shirkuh, the general of Nur al-Din, seized control of Egypt. His death (1169) left his nephew, Salah al-Din (Saladin), in command of affairs at Cairo. Saladin brought the Fatimid caliphate to an end in 1171.

VJP

FAUBUS, ORVAL EUGENE (1910–), US politician and early leader of Southern resistance to school desegregation. As governor of AR (1955–67), he called out the national guard to prevent Negro students entering Little Rock High School (1957).

FAUJDAR, executive head of a Mughal district, responsible for law and order and with criminal jurisdiction. Under the British in Bengal the term continued in use and meant the head of the district police. It was also used for a commander of troops (lit. *fauj*, army or troop; *dar*, holder).

FAUJDARI ADALAT, court of the *faujdar*, which had magisterial and criminal jurisdiction. In Warren Hastings's organization of Bengal, each district was provided with a *faujdari adalat* for criminal cases and a *diwani adalat* for civil cases, the British collector presiding over each. There were corresponding appeal courts in Calcutta.

FAULKNER, WILLIAM (1897–1962), US novelist whose work includes *The Sound and the Fury* (1929), *As I lay Dying* (1930), and the trilogy, *The Hamlet* (1940), *The Town* (1957), and *The Mansion* (1959). Faulkner's concern was with the problems of the South, and his work was uncompromisingly moral in its approach and universal in its significance.

FAUPEL, WILLIAM (1873–1945), German soldier and diplomat, who was Hitler's first ambassador to the Nationalist government in Spain during the Civil War. As a *Freikorps* commander he was prominent in the suppression of the 1919 Spartacus uprising, and of the Ruhr disturbances following the 1920 Kapp *putsch*. He later became ambassador to the Spanish Nationalist government, but was disliked by Franco and other Nationalist leaders because he was anti-religious and because he and his entourage encouraged the more radical members of the Falange. During the Civil War he advocated heavy German military commitment under his own direction, but this was unpopular with his own war and foreign ministries, who undermined his position and forced his retirement in Aug. 1937. In 1945, as the Russians entered Berlin, he committed suicide.

FAURE, EDGAR (1908–   ), French politician. He was unusual in holding high office under both Fourth and Fifth Republics. He entered parliament in 1946 as a Radical, and was frequently a minister. He was prime minister in 1952 and again in 1955–6, when he took the decisions which led to the independence of Morocco. Under the Fifth Republic he served as minister of agriculture (1966–8) and education (1968–9), introducing in the latter post some controversial reforms intended to liberalize higher education.

FAURE, FRANÇOIS FÉLIX (1841–99), French politician and sixth president of the Third Republic. He rose from humble origins to be a deputy (1881), and a minister (1882). He was elected president in 1895 and identified himself with the proposed Franco–Russian alliance.

FAURE, PAUL (1878–1960), French politician and leader of the pacifist wing of the French Socialist Party, which supported the Vichy regime. He had been secretary-general of the Socialist Party and a close colleague of Blum until their paths diverged at the time of the Munich agreement. Faure was a member of the Vichy National Council (1941).

FAUSTIN I (1785–1867), Emperor of Haiti (*reg.* 1851–9), who rose to the presidency of Haiti as the puppet of interested groups in the Haitian senate, but he soon crushed his mentors and all other opposition and in 1851 declared himself emperor. His regime was marked by black nationalism, a return to Voodoo, attempts to reincorporate the breakaway Dominican Republic by means of invasion, and skilful negotiations with the three great powers, US, Britain, and France, which were attempting to exert pressure on Haiti. He was eventually overthrown by a revolt led by one of his own generals, Nicolas Fabre Geffrard, and fled to exile in Jamaica (1859). Geffrard ended the empire and himself became president of the restored republic.

FAVORITE SON, US political term to describe a presidential candidate with little or no support outside his own state. The nomination of such a candidate is often a local gesture of

respect, but it can have serious political implications if support for the candidate is switched to another at a crucial stage in the party convention.

FAVRE, JULES GABRIEL CLAUDE (1809–80), French politician, regarded as the epitome of republicanism. Though trained as a lawyer, he became a journalist, held minor office in the Provisional government, and was elected to the Constituent Assembly (1848). There he turned against the radicals, but later tried to oppose the *coup d'état*. After returning to the bar, he became one of the first republicans in the imperial legislature (1857) and went on to become vice-president of the Government of National Defence (1871). His handling of the armistice and the peace treaty at the end of the Franco–Prussian War (1871) discredited him and his only other political role was as a life senator.

FAWCETT, HENRY (1833–84), British Liberal statesman, and, though blind from 1858, an MP from 1865 till his death. Fawcett was a radical intellectual whose hostility to compromise made him troublesome to Gladstone as Liberal Party leader. He championed feminism, resisted encroachments on public parks, and used his knowledge of Indian finance to defend the unrepresented native population against exploitation. As a reforming postmaster-general (1880–4), he benefited both staff and public.

FAWCETT, DAME MILLICENT (1847–1929), British feminist, who had influence among the political parties through her husband's career as an economist and politician and her own Liberal-Unionist activities. She was an ideal president of the moderate and constitutional National Union of Women's Suffrage Societies (1897–1918). Unfortunately her feminism sprang from her libertarianism, and this, together with her views on political economy, which she expounded in a textbook (1870), led her to oppose many reforms more important to women than the vote, *eg*, family allowances, compulsory and free education, and special legislation to protect women at work.

FAWKES, GUY (1570–1606), English conspirator, who became a Roman Catholic and served with Spanish forces in the Netherlands. He was involved in the final stages of the Gunpowder Plot (1605) directed against James I and parliament, being arrested in the cellars of the parliament buildings. Under torture, he revealed the names of other conspirators and was subsequently executed.

FAYSAL I (1883–1933), King of Iraq (*reg.* 1921–33), third son of Sharif Husayn of Mecca. He was northern military commander in the Arab Revolt (1916–18), and, after his entry into Damascus (Oct. 1918), leader of the Arab nationalist cause in Syria. He subsequently failed to obtain British support against France or to reach agreement with France. On 24 July 1920 his Syrian forces were defeated by French troops under Gen. Gouraud at Maysalun, and Syria passed under French rule. Faysal then became a candidate for the throne of Iraq and, after receiving public approval in a referendum (July 1921), was enthroned. As an able, efficient, and realistic ruler, he guided Iraq rapidly to independence by a careful balancing of nationalist and British forces.

FAYSAL II (1935–58), King of Iraq (*reg.* 1939–58) in succession to his father, Ghazi I. The regency formed during his minority was terminated (2 May 1953), but the former regent, Abd al-Ilah, continued to exercise a predominant influence. In Feb. 1958 Faysal was nominated head of the projected Arab Federation of Iraq and Jordan.

FAYSAL (1905–   ), King of Saudi Arabia (*reg.* 1964–   ) in succession to his deposed brother Sa'ud (1953–64). His early attempt, as prime minister (1958–60), to restore financial order and modernize Saudi government was frustrated by the opposition of Sa'ud, but he became prime minister again

(1962 and 1963), and achieved supreme power (March 1964), becoming king in Nov. As king he continued the policy of internal modernization, combined with a foreign policy which accentuated Islamic unity and traditions in the face of the revolutionary Arab nationalism represented by Egypt.

FAZENDA, Portuguese–Brazilian variant of the large, undercapitalized landed estate (Sp. *hacienda*), which has dominated Latin American land-tenure patterns for centuries.

FAZL-I-HUSAIN, MIAN, SIR (1877–1936), political leader of Punjab Muslims, who took part in both Congress and Muslim League activities in the Punjab and also established a strong political base as secretary of Islamia College (1906–1918). He was president of the Punjab provincial Conference (1916) and representative of Punjab University on the provincial Legislative Council (1917–20). He saw the reforms of 1919 as offering important advantages to the Muslim community in the Punjab because they would give it a majority in the Legislative Council. He therefore opposed the non-co-operation boycott of the legislatures, and was elected to the Punjab council. Thereafter, he served in a succession of high executive offices in the Punjab government and in the government of India. He was minister of education in Punjab (1921–5), revenue member, Punjab (1926–30), education member in the government of India (1925, 1929, 1930–5) and minister of education in Punjab (1936). He acquired control over Muslim political developments in Punjab, both by his personal influence and through the Punjab National Unionist Party. He organized the Unionist Party (1921) on the basis of the Muslim legislators, but with the addition of Hindu and Sikh landholders in the legislature who were attracted to the policy of protecting agrarian interests. He was a strong advocate of separate Muslim electorates and intervened vigorously and successfully to prevent his co-religionists from surrendering them during negotiations with the Hindus (1930–1).

FAZL-UL-HUQ, ABUL KASEM (1873–1962), Bengali Muslim leader, chief minister of Bengal (1937–43), and governor of East Pakistan (1956–8), formerly a lawyer, teacher, and journalist in Barisal and Calcutta (1896–1906). Huq's connection with Nawab Salimullah of Dacca brought him appointment in the service of the new province of Eastern Bengal and Assam (1906–12), where he rose to be deputy-registrar of co-operative societies. The reunification of Bengal (1912) ended this official career but opened the way to political leadership of the Muslim community. As secretary (1913–16) and then president (1916–21) of the provincial Muslim League he helped to draw the League and Congress closer together and supported the Lucknow Pact (1916). He presided over the All-India Muslim League session (1918) and was a general secretary of the Congress (1918–19). He attended all three Round Table Conferences (1930–2), was an elected member of the Bengal legislature (1913–35), and a minister briefly in 1924. His most important activities were concerned with the political organization of rural interest groups. He helped to found the Nikhil Banga Praja Samiti or 'All-Bengal Tenants' Association' (1929) and from among its more radical members he formed the Krishak Praja Party KPP in 1936. This 'Cultivators' and Tenants' Party' did not secure a majority of Muslim seats in the 1937 elections, but Huq was able to take the lead in a basically Muslim coalition ministry which took the KPP label. Huq remained chief minister until 1943 although he broke with the Muslim League (1941) and had to reconstruct his ministry with the aid of Hindus. In Pakistan he served first as advocate-general of East Pakistan (1948–54) and then briefly as chief minister of East Pakistan and as a minister in the central government before becoming governor of East Pakistan (1956–8).

FEALTY, OATH OF, one of the two essential features, besides homage, of a ceremony by which in medieval feudal society men became military vassals of their superiors. In origin it represented, perhaps, a Christian element in what was initially a purely secular relationship.

FEATHERS PETITION (1772), to the House of Commons, drawn up at the Feathers Tavern in the Strand, for relief from the requirements of subscription to the Thirty-Nine Articles of the Church of England. Of its 250 signatories, 200 were clergymen. The motion to receive it was rejected by 217 to 71. Shortly afterwards, an approach to the bishops also failed, though some clearly sympathized. Supporters of the movement included both those who wished to see the Articles of the Book of Common Prayer revised and those who objected to formal subscription of any kind, believing that, as Protestants, they had the right to interpret Scripture for themselves. After the petition's failure some of those who had doctrinal objections left the Church: the first Unitarian Church was opened in Sept. 1773. Those who remained continued to press for relief and revision until the French Revolution took away all chance of success.

FEBRERISTA PARTY, Paraguayan political movement, originally composed of the followers of President Rafael Franco, who came to power by a *coup d'état* in Feb. 1936, hence the name of the party. The Febreristas have repeatedly tried to overthrow various Paraguayan dictators, such as Higinio Morínigo (1940–8) and Alfredo Stroessner (1954–). As a result, most prominent Febreristas live in exile. The party is classified as a left-of-centre social democratic party, and belongs to the Socialist International.

FEDERACÍON ANARCHISTA IBERICA (FAI), founded in Valencia in 1927 and represented the response of purist militant anarchists to the increasing reformism of the Confederación Nacional de Trabajo. The extremists of the movement sought the ideals of Bakunin and a total opposition to the state. The FAI was to be an elite secret society which would infiltrate the CNT with militants. In Sept. 1931 the FAI gained control of Solidaridad Obrera, the anarchist newspaper, and also expelled the moderates from the CNT as traitors. In Jan. 1932 the FAI took control of the national committee of the CNT. The effect of this was to divide the anarchist movement and to place the direction of its efforts into the hands of extremists. The FAI advocated wild-cat strikes, armed insurrection, and heroic gestures which merely fragmented effort and intensified the climate of violence.

After the Casas Viejas massacre of anarchists by Civil Guards, the FAI increased its influence and its conviction that nothing was to be gained from the Republic was hardened. Thus, the militants supported the 'Don't Vote' campaign in the Nov. 1933 elections, which assisted the victory of the right and they stayed out of the Popular Front in Feb. 1936.

When the Civil War started, the FAI entered enthusiastically into the creation of militias and the collectivization of agriculture and industry. However, the anarchist militants soon fell foul of the communists' determination to organize the war effort. On the Aragon front, they were starved of weapons and in May 1937 they joined the POUM in a despairing battle against the communists in Barcelona. Peace was restored and FAI members continued to fight heroically for the Republic, but towards the end of the war they became affected by defeatism. PP

FEDERAL ART PROJECT (1935–9), US programme under the New Deal's Works Progress Administration to provide work for unemployed artists. Under the direction of Holger Cahill, thousands of projects were sponsored, the art of mural painting being revived in the decoration of post-offices, schools, and other public buildings, and a record of American folk art compiled. Although much of FAP's work was mediocre 'imaginative realism', it also encouraged artists like Ben Shahn and Stuart Davis.

FEDERAL BUREAU OF INVESTIGATION, chief police and investigative agency of the US Department of Justice. It was originally established at President Theodore Roosevelt's request as the Bureau of Investigation (1908), and over the years Congress has given the FBI powers to deal with various 'federal crimes', mainly dealing with inter-state travel, such as white slavery, national motor vehicle theft, kidnapping, national bank robberies, narcotics offences, sabotage, conspiracy, and treason.

When attorney-general Harlan F. Stone reorganized the bureau (1924), John Edgar Hoover was appointed director. Under his supervision, the FBI expanded its activities during the early 1930s into the area of crime detection by establishing a national clearing house for criminal data and an FBI laboratory.

By a presidential directive of 6 Sept. 1939, the FBI, rather than the military, became responsible for protecting the internal security of the nation. With the passage of legislation requiring security clearances for many state, federal, and military employees after the Second World War, the operations of the FBI became even more widespread. The Bureau, which has nearly 6000 agents, who are all qualified accountants or graduates of law schools, has established a high reputation for both probity and efficiency.

FEDERAL COMMUNICATIONS COMMISSION in US, federal agency established (1934) to regulate inter-state and overseas telephone, telegraph, cable, radio, and television communications. Its seven members, appointed by the president but confirmed by the US Senate, hold office for seven-year terms, are authorized to fix rates, grant licences, and exercise general supervisory functions.

FEDERAL DEPOSIT INSURANCE CORPORATION in US, government agency established (1933) by the Glass–Steagall Act (1935) to insure bank deposits of up to \$15,000. Managed by the comptroller of the currency and two other directors appointed by the president, with the advice and consent of the Senate, the FDIC also exercises general supervision over banking practices.

FEDERAL EMERGENCY RELIEF ADMINISTRATION in US, programme (1933–5) under the New Deal through which federal funds for relief of the unemployed were channelled directly to the states. With an initial appropriation of \$500 million, the FERA, under its director, Harry Hopkins, assigned half its funds to the states on the basis of \$1 of federal aid for each \$3 spent by local agencies for relief, and the rest was used to finance construction and other work relief projects.

FEDERAL HOUSING ADMINISTRATION in US, government agency established (1934) during the New Deal to insure private institutional loans for housing improvements. The act also increased the borrowing power of the Home Owners Loan Corporation. In 1965 FHA became part of the Department of Housing and Urban Development.

FEDERAL LABOUR PARTY, loose alliance of West Indian political parties during the federation period (1958–62). The FLP, opposed by the Democratic Labour Party, won the election of 1958.

FEDERAL MOVEMENT in Australia. First moves towards Australian federation occurred during the mid-19th-cent. transition to responsible self-government, when Earl Grey in London and Deas Thomson, Wentworth, and Duffy in the colonies stressed the need for a federal legislature. With public opinion as yet unready for such proposals, the new constitutional arrangements confirmed the division of Australia into six separate colonies, each increasingly jealous and mistrustful of its neighbours, particularly over tariffs. Matters of common concern were dealt with, rather unsatisfactorily, by occasional inter-colonial conferences, until a Federal

Council was established (1855), mainly to voice Australian objections to the activities of France and Germany in the Pacific region.

Limited powers and patchy support rendered the council ineffective. A new initiative by Henry Parkes led to the 1891 National Convention, which framed a federal constitution, mainly the work of Samuel Griffith, but a severe depression accompanied by industrial turmoil temporarily interrupted progress towards federation. The depression nevertheless emphasized the need for economic integration, while the steady growth of distinctively 'Australian' attitudes and values also fostered a more sympathetic climate of opinion. The leadership of such men as Edmund Barton, Alfred Deakin, and Charles Kingston, backed by enthusiastic federation leagues, culminated in a popularly elected convention which met three times in 1897–8 and drafted another constitution which was then referred to the electors.

At first the affirmative vote in NSW fell short of the required total, but in 1899, after a few amendments had been made, all states except WA voted for federation in 1900. The new constitution, conferring important specified powers on a bicameral federal legislature, was enacted by the Imperial Parliament with only minor alterations, and the Commonwealth of Australia was inaugurated on 1 Jan. 1901.

BK de G

FEDERAL RESERVE SYSTEM in US, national banking system established by the Federal Reserve Act (1913), as part of President Wilson's national monetary and banking reform programme. The country was divided into 12 districts, each with its regional reserve bank, and 24 branch banks were established in other key financial centres all responsible to a national board of seven governors, appointed by the president with the advice and consent of the senate. Some 6000 private banks, with both national and state charters, holding more than 80 per cent of the nation's banking assets, belong to the system. Working through their district federal reserve banks, which act as bankers' banks, member banks are able to clear and collect cheques, discount loans and securities, and transfer funds. In return, the member banks deposit approximately 6 per cent of their capital, as a reserve, with the nearest federal reserve bank. At the national level, the board of governors establish discount and interest rates for the system, which in effect guarantees their acceptance as national rates, sets reserve requirements for its members, acts as fiscal agents for the treasury department and other federal agencies, issues and discounts US loans and bonds, establishes guidelines for margin buying of real estate and securities, and issues approximately 85 per cent of the nation's currency as federal reserve notes.

FEDERAL THEATRE PROJECT in US, programme (1935–9) under the New Deal's Works Progress Administration to provide work for unemployed actors, directors, and technicians. Directed by Hallie Flanagan, it produced over 1200 plays for audiences that exceeded 30 million, experimented with new forms of theatre, and sent touring companies into areas previously outside theatre circuits.

FEDERAL TRADE COMMISSION in US, independent administrative agency of the government established (1915) as an integral part of President Wilson's trust regulation programme. The FTC, as a quasi-judicial body, is empowered to investigate and issue 'cease and desist orders' in cases of infraction of the US anti-monopoly and fair practice legislation. In recent years it has increasingly turned from business regulation to consumer protection. The five members of the commission are all appointed by the president, with the advice and consent of the US Senate, for seven-year terms.

FEDERAL WRITERS PROJECT in US, programme (1935–41) under the New Deal's Works Progress Administration for the relief of unemployed writers. Under the direction of Henry Alsberg, the project sponsored about 1000 publications, including the 150–volume *Life in America* series and the famous *American Guide Series* that provided an authoritative state and regional coverage for the first time. In 1939 the states were required to contribute 25 per cent of the cost of FWP, and in 1941 it was entirely transferred to state sponsorship.

FEDERALISM, originally the unwritten constitutional expression of the strong local feelings, institutions, and laws which were a legacy of medieval Europe. Remaining side by side with the growing authoritarianism of princes from the 15th cent. onwards, federalism was in many states a real force, limiting the power of the Crown, *eg*, Spain, the Netherlands, and the German states of the Holy Roman empire. From the 18th cent. onwards federalism became a formal type of constitutional government, answering the political needs of larger states, where total centralization of government would have been impossible. The US provided the first major example (1776) and Canada (1867) and Australia (1900) followed. In the 20th cent. federation was a device used with varying degrees of success by colonial territories in the British empire and Commonwealth, *eg*, federation, as a step towards independence, failed in the West Indies, and its members became unitary independent states.

FEDERALIST, THE, analysis of the principles and conduct of US government, originating mainly in a series of newspaper articles intended to promote ratification of the American Constitution in New York (1787–8). Of 76 published anonymously over the signature 'Publius' before the state ratifying convention, Alexander Hamilton wrote 42, John Jay, his first collaborator, wrote five on foreign policy, and James Madison of VA wrote 26. Hamilton and Madison collaborated in writing three others and Hamilton added a further nine, all of which were published in book form after the convention (1788). *The Federalist*, extensively reprinted in New York city, was much less frequently published in other parts of the state and elsewhere, although several articles were used effectively at the VA ratifying convention. Though long and erudite, it had little immediate influence as propaganda, but in later years was regarded as a brilliant commentary on American government and an authoritative source often cited by the US Supreme Court as evidence of the nature of the constitution and the intentions of its framers. Hamilton and Madison sought in *The Federalist* to defend the concept of a federal system of government by showing that it could operate at several levels and that the central government should act directly on the people rather than through the states. They condemned the Articles of Confederation, but the Papers demonstrate that Hamilton advocated a stronger central government than did Madison. They contended that in an effective federal system power should be divided between the federal and state governments, each being supreme within its own sphere of authority, and each having powers adequate to its functions. Both authors advocated the separation of legislative, executive, and judicial powers, with which Hamilton associated the doctrine of judicial review. Analysing the nature of political society, Hamilton argued in Paper IX that the chief division was between rich and poor; but in the much more influential Paper X Madison postulated a multi-factional system of politics which could be regulated and exploited by a federal government which controlled an extensive territory.

Jacob E. Cooke (ed.), *The Federalist* (Middletown, CT, 1961).
Benjamin Fletcher Wright (ed.), *The Federalist* (Cambridge, MA, 1961).

FEDERALISTS, early US political group, and, later, party. During the debate over ratification of the constitution (1787–1788), those who supported ratification appropriated the term 'Federalist', although in some ways it was more suited to their opponents, the Antifederalists. The Federalists in-cluded many leading members of the Philadelphia Convention (1787), such as James Madison, Alexander Hamilton, James Wilson, and George Washington, and were well organized throughout the country. They controlled many newspapers and, unlike their opponents, offered a positive remedy for the nation's ills. Sometimes ruthless and occasionally brilliant, as in *The Federalist* papers, published to promote ratification in New York, their triumph was the product of political manœuvring rather than widespread popular support. After 1789 party development took a different course. The first Congress was non-partisan and President Washington always regarded himself as a national leader, but party divisions, stimulated by Alexander Hamilton's financial programme, were already apparent by 1792 and crystallized during the struggle over ratification of Jay's treaty (1795). Some of those, like James Madison, who had supported the constitution became Democratic Republicans; others, together with some of the Antifederalists, began to form a Federalist party. They supported Hamilton, favoured strong national government and were concerned to protect property rights. Being conservative, prosperous, and suspicious of the advancing tide of democracy, they believed that the upper classes had the responsibility and right to rule in the interest of the entire nation. Fearful of the harmful influence of the French Revolution, they were often Anglophile and favoured neutrality during the Revolutionary Wars. Their major support came from commercial centres and large-scale farming areas on the eastern seaboard and they were particularly strong in MA and SC. The Federalist John Adams won the first presidential election to be decided on party lines (1796), but because of a provision in the constitution that was later changed by the 12th Amendment Thomas Jefferson, a Republican, became vice-president. The party was weakened by internecine strife, and this, together with the passage of the unpopular Alien and Sedition Acts at the instigation of extreme Federalists, enabled the Republicans to win the presidency and both houses of Congress in the elections of 1800. The Federalists, unwilling to adjust themselves to new circumstances and unable to regain national power, unsuccessfully nominated presidential candidates until 1816, and the party continued to be influential in several states, particularly in New England. Its disintegration was accelerated by involvement in the Hartford Convention's threat of secession (1814), but its concepts of 'federalism' and the nature of property rights continued to find expression in the opinions of the US Supreme Court under Chief Justice John Marshall.

William Nisbet Chambers, *Political Parties in a New Nation* (New York, 1963).
John C. Miller, *The Federalist Era* (New York, 1960).

FEDERATED MALAY STATES (1896–1941), administrative federation of the four peninsula Malay states (Perak, Selangor, Negri Sembilan, and Pahang) which had, in 1895, accepted a British Resident whose advice must be followed. It was composed of a British Resident-General in Kuala Lumpur, a unified administration, and from 1909 also an appointed Federal Council. While promoting a rationalized economy and administration, the federation arrangement insulated from these modern developments the traditional Malay elite of the respective states. Despite attempts to preserve the fiction of Malay sovereignty, and after 1920 to promote administrative 'decentralization', there remained no inducement for the five Malay sultanates which accepted British advisers in the 20th cent. to join the federation. These 'Unfederated' states preserved a more distinctly Malay character and population.

FEDERATION OF LABOUR in NZ, formed in 1911, opposed both the Liberal arbitration system and moderate Labour, adopting an IWW-based 'class-struggle' platform. Defeat in the 1912–13 strikes, followed by restrictive labour laws and wartime regulations, broke the federation. Its militant successor, the Alliance of Labour (1919), was reconciled to the Labour Party and to arbitration by Depression in the early 1930s. The first Labour government introduced 'compulsory unionism', and helped to initiate the formation of a new NZFOL (1937) to control swiftly growing unions. In the industrial disputes of 1949–51 the federation opposed the militant unions and their TUC, but thereafter straddled labour groups with more success.

FEDERATION OF MALAYA (1948–63), constitutional structure replacing the post-war Malayan Union, which had foundered on Malay opposition. Like its predecessor it brought together the Federated and Unfederated Malay States and the Straits Settlements except Singapore, but it won Malay acceptance by tighter conditions for non-Malay citizenship and the elimination of terminology implying a loss of sovereignty by the Sultans. A British High Commissioner in Kuala Lumpur headed the Federal Government, which moved steadily towards independence after 1952 despite the continuing emergency created by communist insurgents. From independence (1957) until the formation of Malaysia (1963), the country continued to use this title, although citizenship was again broadened and the elective Yang di-pertuan Agong became head of state.

FÉDÉRATION NATIONALE DES SYNDICATS D'EXPLOIT-ANTS AGRICOLES, principal farmers' organization in France and a major political pressure group. The FNSEA was founded in 1946 as a subsidiary of the Confédération générale de l'agriculture, but soon became more important than the parent body. It has tended to be dominated by the large-scale farmers of northern France rather than the smaller peasants, and under the Fourth Republic had close links with conservative deputies. The FNSEA has concentrated its attention on obtaining government price support for agriculture, but a younger element in the leadership was advocating (1970) structural reform and greater militancy.

FÉDÉRATION RÉPUBLICAINE, French conservative party founded (1903) and led by Louis Marin. Catholic and nationalist, and supporting the interests of big business, it was the most conservative of the democratic parties. It was at the height of its influence between the First and Second World Wars, and did not survive into the Fourth Republic.

FEDERMANN, NICOLAS (c. 1501–43), German explorer in Venezuela and Colombia, as an agent of the banking house of Welser. The Welsers were creditors of the Habsburg Emperor Charles V, and had obtained concessions in Venezuela.

FEHMGERICHTE, 'hooded courts', in the Middle Ages (also called 'free courts'), presided over by masked judges. Originally they were instruments of local self-government and were common in many parts of Germany and Switzerland during the anarchy of the Investiture Contest and imperial interregna from the late 11th cent. onwards. They exercised a rough and ready jurisdiction to keep order, operating in the emperor's name but outside his control, and perpetrating many outrages. Some courts still operated as late as the 16th cent.

FEHRBELLIN, BATTLE OF (1675), defeat of the Swedish forces of Charles XI by Frederick William, Elector of Brandenburg, north-west of Berlin. The Swedes had taken the opportunity to invade Brandenburg while the elector was fighting on the Rhine against the French. The elector's return was rapid, and the victory at Fehrbellin was followed by the invasion of Swedish Pomerania and the seizure of Stettin and Stralsund.

FEHRENBACH, KONSTANTIN (1852–1926), German Centre Party politician, last president of the Wilhelmine Reichstag (1918), and president of the new National Assembly at Weimar (1919). In June 1920 he became chancellor, heading the first cabinet of the Weimar Republic, which did not include the Social Democrat Party. His government's attempts to reach accommodation with Britain and France on the reparations question at the Spa and London conferences met with fierce nationalist opposition. He resigned in June 1921. In 1923 he became chairman of the Centre group in the Reichstag.

FEIJÓ, DIOGO ANTÔNIO (1784–1843), priest, politician, and regent of Brazil (1835–7) during the minority of Pedro II. His rigidity alienated all sectors of the population and caused civil strife which finally forced his resignation.

FEITORIA, word used to describe Portuguese trading posts during the early years of overseas expansion in the 15th and 16th cents. The largest were in the East Indies and Brazil.

FÉNELON, FRANÇOIS DE SALIGNAC DE LA MOTHE (1651–1715), archbishop of Cambrai and writer on social and political subjects, regarded as a precursor of the 18th-cent. *philosophes.* He represents the transition in Louis XIV's reign from creative, imaginative writers to those who used literature to criticize royal arbitrariness and French involvement in costly foreign wars. His political treatise, *Télémaque,* was written for the Duke of Burgundy, Louis XIV's eldest grandson, to whom he was appointed tutor (1689), and was published in the Dutch republic in 1699. This was a guide to government in which he praised rulers who avoided wars and excessive luxury.

Fénelon also anticipated the concepts of the Enlightenment. He was an idealist and an optimist, believing in the idea of progress. His study of history, which was to him a science for discovering the truth, taught him that society was constantly evolving. He believed that education was an important element in the creation of a better society and expounded in his *Traité de l'éducation des filles* (1687) an idea to be found later in Rousseau's *Émile*—that a sound education depended on the fulfilment of a child's natural abilities rather than on the acquisition of knowledge.

Fénelon scorned Augustine, the inspiration of the Jansenists, and saw God as a reasonable supreme being who created a world governed by rational laws, a concept which was translated from Christian into deistic philosophy by some of the *philosophes.* He was a prolific writer and his works include *Dialogue des morts, Manuel de piété, Fables,* and *Lettre sur les occupations de l'Académie.*

FENG KUO-CHANG (1859–1919), war-lord in early Republican China. Feng made his career as a subordinate of Yuan Shih-k'ai, but abandoned him in 1915. He was briefly president of China (1917–18).

FENG TAO (882–954), Chinese official. Living in the unstable conditions of the end of the T'ang dynasty (618–906) and the Five Dynasties (906–59), Feng Tao served several successive and rival courts. Being anxious to support the claim of the later T'ang dynasty (923–35) to be a responsible government capable of promulgating traditional Confucian ideas, Feng Tao arranged for an accepted version of the Classical texts to be engraved as a permanent record. These were actually made on wooden blocks, and as a byproduct of the project the blocks were used for printing copies of the Confucian works. As a statesman serving one of China's most short-lived dynasties, Feng Tao contributed immeasurably to the development of block-printing and left China a precedent whereby the state sponsored large-scale printing projects in the interests of scholarship.

FENG YÜ-HSIANG (1882–1948), Chinese war-lord, often known as the 'Christian General'. He differed from most war-lords in that he was not attached to one particular region of China, but roved about, dominating one area after another. Feng was a reformist by nature, and was attracted first to Christianity and then to a form of socialism. From 1926 he was associated with the Kuomintang, but soon rebelled against Chiang Kai-shek's leadership (1929). He was defeated and stripped of power, though he retained nominal posts within the Kuomintang. He died in a mysterious accident aboard a Russian ship, as he was returning to China, supposedly to work for the communists.

FENGTIEN CLIQUE (active *c.* 1920–8), war-lords' clique in Republican China. Under its leader, Chang Hsüeh-liang, the clique dominated Manchuria and made periodic forays into China proper.

FENIAN RAIDS, abortive attempts by Irish-American members of the Fenian Brotherhood to conquer Canada. The Fenians, formed in New York (1859), crossed from the US (1866), and unsuccessfully attacked border towns in NB, Canada East (Que.), and Canada West (Ont.). Another raid (1870) was dispersed when an American marshal arrested the Fenian leader, 'General' John O'Neill. The invasion led many Canadians to favour the Confederation movement. Canadian demands for payments resulting from Fenian depredations were rejected by the US. Because of confusion over national status of such Americans, the US and Britain agreed (1870) to mutual rights of naturalization.

FENIANISM, Irish–American movement, taking its name from the Fianna, legendary Irish warriors, whose members were bound by oath to the establishment of an independent Irish Republic. It was founded in the US (1858) by John Mahoney and other Irish emigrants with an Irish wing, the Irish Republican Brotherhood. The end of the American Civil War (1865) increased recruitment of fenian agents in Ireland. In spite of widespread arrests and the suspension of *habeas corpus* in Ireland (1866) outrages spread to England (1867). The fenian movement split between those supporting revolt in Canada (1866–71) and Ireland respectively. The Irish peasantry did not respond, partly owing to opposition from the Roman Catholic Church, but fenians were active in obstructionist tactics in the Commons after 1875 and in the founding of the Irish Land League (1879), encouraging Gladstone to undertake land reform and Church disestablishment in Ireland.

FENNO, JOHN (1751–98), American publisher and journalist. His *Gazette of the United States*, published in New York (1789) and Philadelphia (1790), was the organ of Alexander Hamilton and the Federalists in partisan disputes with Jeffersonian Republicans during Washington's presidency.

FERDINAND I (1793–1875), Emperor of Austria (*reg.* 1835–48), who became emperor so that the hereditary principle should not be broken, although he was a mentally sub-normal. There was no official regency for him, but control of the state was in the hands of his uncle, Archduke Ludwig, and of Metternich and Kolowrat. Their quarrels eventually paralysed the government. To restore the monarchy's prestige during the 1848 revolution, Ferdinand was forced by his family to abdicate in favour of his nephew, Francis Joseph.

FERDINAND I (1503–64), Emperor (*reg.* 1558–64), member of the Habsburg family, grandson of Maximilian I and younger brother of Charles V, who made over to him (1521–2) the rule of the family's eastern lands and secured his election as King of the Romans in 1531, so that he, rather than Charles's son Philip, should inherit the empire in 1558.

The eastern lands comprised Austria, Carinthia, Styria, Carniola, and the Tyrol, together with the duchy of Württemberg, and to these Ferdinand added—by his marriage to the daughter of the King of Bohemia and Hungary (1521)—claims to both these kingdoms, which he realized when his brother-in-law, Louis, died in the battle of Mohacs (1526). Ferdinand's interests were thus centred on the defence of Habsburg possessions in eastern Europe, and he was the effective founder of the Habsburg Austrian empire, which lasted until the First World War.

The attention which he gave to securing his inheritance in Hungary and Bohemia and to preserving his political position in the empire obliged him to give less than wholehearted support to Charles in the struggle with the Protestant League of Schmalkalden. Ferdinand did help Charles in the war against the League, which resulted in its defeat in 1547, but when Charles's late ally, Maurice of Saxony, turned against him in 1552, Ferdinand remained neutral, partly because he felt that he had not received adequate support himself in his wars with the Turks in Hungary. For the sake of support against the Turks he was content to allow the spread of reforming practices in his territories, according to the terms of the peace of Augsburg (1555), and even tried to persuade the pope to sanction communion in both kinds and clerical marriage.

The struggle for Hungary swayed to and fro, Ferdinand's election to the crown by a minority of the nobility in 1526 being purchased at the cost of acceptance of the elective principle; his control of the kingdom was contested by John Zapolyai, Duke of Transylvania, with the support of Soleiman the Magnificent. The Turks threatened Austrian lands in 1529, 1532, and 1541, on the first occasion besieging Vienna itself. On the death of Zapolyai in 1540 Ferdinand's right to succeed in Hungary was partially recognized, though two-thirds of the country remained in Turkish hands.

In Bohemia after 1547 he was able to achieve a more thorough control and the Habsburg right of inheritance was recognized. His attempt to create a general Diet for all his dominions made little progress and at his death he divided them among his three sons.

Hajo Holborn, *A History of Modern Germany. The Reformation* (London, 1965).   HNBM

FERDINAND II (1578–1637), Emperor (*reg.* 1619–37). He was adopted as heir to the Habsburg dominions by the childless Emperor Mathias and became the defender of imperial, Habsburg, and Catholic interests during the Thirty Years War. He was in fact the eldest son of the Archduke Charles of Lower Austria and was educated by the Jesuits and imbued with the ideals of absolutist rule and of obedience to the Church of Rome. He imposed his ideals ruthlessly in the duchy from 1596, and set about the same policy when he was accepted as king in Bohemia and Hungary (1617, 1618). It was ill-matched to the religious and constitutional liberties which the Estates of these lands had extracted from his predecessors, Rudolph and Mathias, and in Bohemia it was met by rebellion of the Protestant nobles. They defenestrated two of the seven Catholic governors at Hradcin Castle in Prague, which amounted to a declaration of war between Habsburg king and Bohemian Estates.

In Ferdinand's place the Bohemians now elected as king the Protestant Elector Palatine, Frederick V (Aug. 1619), but they were unable to prevent Ferdinand's unanimous election as emperor. Ferdinand arranged for the occupation of the Palatinate by Spanish troops sent from the Netherlands, made an alliance with the Elector of Saxony by offering him Lusatia, and, with the assistance of Maximilian of Bavaria and the Catholic League, won a crushing victory over the Bohemians at the battle of the White Mountain (1620). There was now no obstacle to the subjugation of Bohemia and the execution of the leaders of the revolt, and the confiscation of their estates in favour of loyal Bohemian or Austrian nobility was followed by the reduction of liberties of towns and nobility and the transference of the central chancery from Prague to Vienna, in the 'renewed constitution' of 1627. Toleration for any church but that of Rome was withdrawn, thousands of Protestants emigrated, and the Czech kingdom effectively lost its individual character, becoming an hereditary Habsburg possession.

In Germany, as a whole, imperial arms were so successful that in 1629 Ferdinand felt strong enough to attempt at one blow a reassertion of imperial sovereignty and the restoration of the Catholic Church to its territorial position of 1552, by issuing without consultation with the Diet or the Estates his famous Edict of Restitution. The result was to alienate both Catholic and Protestant princes and to make possible the incursions of Swedish forces under Gustavus Adolphus (1630–2), which undid the earlier achievements of the Catholic League. At the same time, his decision to uphold a Spanish claim to the Mantuan succession led to the re-establishment of French power south of the Alps. Ferdinand recalled to his aid the adventurer Wallenstein, but dismissed him again in 1634 and agreed to his assassination when he feared that he was conspiring to bring about an independent solution of Germany's problems.

The emperor's authority was restored in the peace of Prague (1635), but the Edict of Restitution was repealed for 40 years. In 1637 Ferdinand secured the election of his son Ferdinand III as his successor in the empire.

C. V. Wedgwood, *The Thirty Years War* (London, 1957).

HNBM

FERDINAND III (1608–57), Emperor (*reg.* 1637–57), eldest son of Ferdinand II. He was also King of Hungary from 1626 and King of Bohemia from 1627. Unlike his father, whose Catholic orthodoxy and absolutist ambitions had contributed to the Thirty Years War in Germany, he was prepared to sacrifice unity in the Church and the integrity of the empire for the sake of maintaining his hold on the hereditary Crown lands of the house of Austria.

In 1634 he assisted in the overthrow of Wallenstein and succeeded him as nominal commander of the imperial armies, recovered Regensburg and Donauwörth, and defeated the Swedes at Nordlingen, thereby regaining control of the whole of south Germany. This gave him the advantage in negotiations for the peace of Prague (1635), which temporarily prolonged the ascendancy of imperial authority over the princes of Germany. But this ascendancy was lost with the active participation of France against Spain from 1635, and the recovery of Sweden, so that at the peace of Westphalia the Estates were granted full sovereignty and Protestants were admitted to the remaining imperial institutions on a basis of equality with Catholics. From this date the imperial interests of the Habsburgs were those of their house, not those of the Holy Roman empire, despite the formal survival of the latter until 1806. The territorial concessions, made by the emperor in 1648 to the Swedes, the north Germans, and the French, were the first tangible evidence of this change.

To gain the election of his eldest son, Ferdinand IV, as King of Hungary in 1647, he conceded toleration to the Protestants of Hungary, and on the death of Ferdinand IV his second son, Leopold I, was elected King of Hungary in 1655 and of Bohemia in 1656.

FERDINAND III (1769–1824), Grand Duke, younger brother of the Emperor Francis II. He became ruler of Tuscany (1790) but was deposed by the French (1799), then restored by the allies (1814), and ruled progressively until his death.

FERDINAND I (d. 1416), King of Aragon (*reg.* 1412–16), who acted as regent during the minority of his nephew John II of Castile, when he captured the town of Antequera from the Moors. On the death of Martin I of Aragon, Aragon demonstrated its political maturity by resolving the disputed succession to the throne in Ferdinand's favour (1412) on legal grounds.

FERDINAND II (1452–1516), King of Aragon (*reg.* 1479–1516) and, by his marriage to Isabella of Castile, joint founder of the kingdom of Spain. His line, a junior branch of the Castilian royal house of Trastamara, had occupied the throne of Aragon since 1412, but it was only the persistence of Ferdinand's father, John II, and the preference of the 18-year-old Isabella which brought about the marriage of

heir and heiress in 1469. The purely dynastic union of the crowns was not accomplished until 1479, when Ferdinand inherited Aragon and, after five years of civil war and diplomacy, secured Isabella's succession to Castile.

The relationship of Crown and subject in Aragon was fundamentally contractual, each of the three peninsular provinces—Catalonia, Aragon, Valencia—having a constitutional tradition firmly defended by Cortes, or estates, and the Mediterranean possessions of the Crown (Sardinia and Sicily) remained semi-autonomous provinces ruled by viceroys. Ferdinand ended disorders in Catalonia by restoring constitutional government and by an agrarian reform which effectively emancipated the peasants from the power of their lords. The mercantile character of the kingdom of Aragon, and its now declining prosperity, contrasted with the aristocratic, crusading, and pastoral character of the much larger kingdom of Castile which did not complete the conquest of Granada until 1492, and was in that year on the threshold of a great American empire. Castile was in anarchy in 1479 and Ferdinand's methods of restoring order were very different from those applied in Aragon. The immensely wealthy Church was deprived of its fortresses and armies, and Ferdinand claimed for himself the grand-mastership of the three great military orders. He extended royal control over benefices, imposed royal jurisdiction over Church estates, and controlled the Inquisition, set up in Castile in 1478. Royal justice was likewise brought to the municipalities, which were drawn together into a single brotherhood under royal supervision, and in each of which a royal official, the *corregidor*, was installed. The nobility were excluded from the Council of Castile and deprived of usurped revenues. Administration of all the possessions of the Catholic kings was by three councils, for Castile, for Aragon with the Italian possessions, and for the Indies, the last of these regulating trade and settlement in the Americas for the exclusive benefit of Castilians.

The outcome of Ferdinand's foreign policy in two directions was unforeseen and incalculable. By checking Castilian advance in North Africa, after the conquest of Granada, he made possible the eventual formation of a Muslim Algerian state which contested control of the sea, and by his marriage alliances with England and the Habsburgs, intended to contain French power, he brought about the inheritance of Charles V, a Burgundian and a Habsburg, and from 1519 Holy Roman emperor.

J. H. Elliott, *Imperial Spain 1469–1716* (London, 1963).
H. Mariejol, tr. by B. Keene, *The Spain of Ferdinand and Isabella* (Rutgers, 1961).   HNBM

FERDINAND I (1861–1948), King of Bulgaria (*reg.* 1908–18) until his enforced abdication (1918) after Bulgaria's defeat in the First World War. He had previously ruled Bulgaria, as a prince, from 1887 before declaring himself king.

FERDINAND I (d. 1065), King of Castile (*reg.* 1035–65), dominant Christian monarch in the Iberian peninsula, who annexed the kingdoms of León and Galicia and part of Navarre to Castile. He was favoured by dissension in Muslim Spain and used his power to conquer the northern part of the Muslim kingdom of Toledo.

FERDINAND III (1199–1252), King of Castile (*reg.* 1217–52), secured the permanent union of the kingdoms of Castile and León. By initiating a movement towards greater uniformity in the laws of Castile he paved the way for the work of his son, Alfonso X. He brought extensive areas of Andalusia under Christian control and because of his crusading fervour and piety was canonized in 1671.

FERDINAND (1865–1927), King of Rumania (*reg.* 1914–27), nephew of Carol I. Ferdinand had little political experience prior to his accession and the Crown's power, which had been considerable, diminished during his reign. In Aug. 1916

Ferdinand presided over the Crown Council which decided Rumania's intervention in the First World War on the side of the Allies. In April 1917, when Rumania's armies were defeated and riven by rebellion, Ferdinand made a dramatic appeal to the troops, promising them land and votes. He was crowned king of the Greater Rumanian state at Alba Iulia on 15 Oct. 1922 in a ceremony boycotted by the opposition parties in protest against the Liberal government's failure to implement promised reforms.

FERDINAND VI (1713–59), King of Spain (*reg.* 1746–59), second son of Philip V and his first wife, Marie-Louise of Savoy, who succeeded his father in 1746. He was himself a political nonentity and the political and economic regeneration of Spain, which had started under Philip V, was maintained by his ministers, *eg*, Carvajal and Ensenada. Ferdinand encouraged the foundation of the Academy of Fine Arts (1752) and the first botanical gardens and astronomical observatory in Spain.

At the outset of his reign Spain was involved in the War of the Austrian Succession. Ferdinand, however, was inclined towards peace, and after concluding the treaty of Aix-la-Chapelle (1748) he steered a neutral course, influenced by his pro-British, Portuguese wife, Barbara of Braganza, whom he had married in 1728. In 1752 he joined with Charles Emmanuel of Sardinia and Maria Theresa of Austria in a guarantee of each other's possessions, and a concordat with Rome improved Spanish relations with the papacy. He was succeeded by his half-brother, Charles, King of Naples and Sicily.

FERDINAND VII (1784–1833), King of Spain (*reg.* 1808, 1814–33), was an absolutist by nature but was prepared occasionally to pose as an enlightened monarch. After deposing his father, Charles IV, by a military conspiracy (1808), he was forced to abdicate by Napoleon and surrender his rights to Joseph Bonaparte. On being restored by the allies (1814), he immediately suppressed the liberals and their constitution of 1812. He based his rule on the support of the peasantry and the Church, but was forced by a liberal revolution (1820) to restore the constitution. The intervention of French troops (1823) helped him reassert his absolute power, but he failed to regain control of the breakaway South American colonies. Before his death he tried to frustrate the claims of his brother, Don Carlos, by revoking (1830) the Salic Law to ensure the accession of his daughter, Isabella.

FERDINAND I (1751–1825), King of the Two Sicilies (*reg.* 1815–25). He had ruled Naples and Sicily under a regency since the accession of his father, Charles III, to the Spanish throne (1759). Until 1777 the government was dominated by the enlightened Tanucci, and Ferdinand did not turn to reaction until the outbreak of the French Revolution, when he became the worst of the Italian absolutists. He was deposed temporarily by the French in 1798 and again in 1806, when he fled from Naples to Sicily. Restored to his throne by the Allies (1815), he ruled despotically, depending on Austrian support and calling in Austrian troops to suppress the revolution of 1820.

FERDINAND II (1810–59), 'King Bomba', whose reactionary rule as King of the Two Sicilies was condemned by Gladstone as 'the negation of God erected into a system of government'. He pursued a fiercely anti-liberal policy from soon after his accession (1830). Revolutions in Palermo and Naples made him in 1848 grant a constitution—the first Italian ruler to do so—but he soon regained control and absolute power by the use of Swiss mercenaries (1849).

FERDINAND, the Cardinal-Infant (1609–41), brother of Philip IV and Anne of Austria, who was appointed governor of the Low Countries for the Spanish Crown (1632–41). In 1634 he led a large Spanish army from Italy to join up with his cousin, Ferdinand of Hungary. The two Habsburg princes, with superior forces, defeated the Protestant army of Horn and Bernard of Saxe-Weimar at the battle of Nordlingen, a landmark in the Thirty Years War (1634). The Cardinal-Infant then proceeded to the Netherlands where his ability and charm won him favour with the Flemish. He led the Spanish armies in a series of successful actions against the French (1636), capturing La Capelle, Le Catelet, and the fortress of Corbie, and devastating the country between the Somme and the Oise, but the loss of Breisach (1638) and the revolt of Portugal (1640) left him without reinforcements or money.

FERDINAND MARIA (1636–79), Elector of Bavaria (*reg.* 1651–79), successor to Maximilian I, he emulated Louis XIV's system of absolutism. He called the Diet for the last time in 1669 and ruled without the estates but with an active privy council and the bureaucratic machinery of the *rent-meister*, officials akin to the French *intendants*, who supervised local government, agriculture, trade, industry, and police matters. He introduced new taxes and granted monopolies, from which increased revenue he maintained a standing army and patronized the arts.

FERMANAGH, most south-westerly of the six counties of Northern Ireland. It is predominantly Catholic but includes a number of Protestant towns and villages. In the Irish treaty negotiations of 1921, the British prime minister, Lloyd George, simultaneously persuaded Southern Irish negotiators that Catholic areas of the border counties would be able to vote themselves into the new Free State, and Northern Irish Unionists that the Six Counties of the north would be kept intact. When it emerged that this had happened, the South felt itself tricked; though in practice changing border counties such as Fermanagh into Unionist (Protestant) and Free State (Catholic) would have been impossible.

FERGUSON, ADAM (1723–1816), Scottish philosopher and historian, who taught moral philosophy at Edinburgh University. He wrote *Principles of Moral and Political Science* (1792).

FERGUSON, GEORGE EKEM (d. 1897), surveyor, explorer, and administrator in the Gold Coast. During his civil service career there he proved a distinguished political agent and treaty-maker for the British, helping to bring the Northern Territories under British rule. He was killed accompanying Henderson's expedition to Wa.

FERGUSON, GEORGE HOWARD (1870–1946), Canadian politician. As prime minister of Ontario (1923–31), he fought two elections on the issue of liquor control, gaining an overwhelming victory in 1929. He successfully advocated federal consultation with the provinces.

FERMAT, PIERRE DE (1601–65), French mathematician, who discovered methods for finding the maximum and minimum values of curves and for drawing tangents to them (1638). He demonstrated that refraction towards the perpendicular occurs when the velocity of light in the second medium is less than in the first.

FERMI, ENRICO (1901–54). Italian-American nuclear physicist, who was awarded the 1938 Nobel Physics Prize for his work on neutron bombardment. Following Hahn's discovery of uranium fission later that year, Fermi and others considered that the neutrons emitted as a result of fission could propagate a nuclear chain reaction, which in turn would produce enormous amounts of energy in a fractiton of a second. In 1941–2 Fermi directed the construction of a structure in Chicago in which such a chain reaction could take place. This reactor became operational on 2 Dec. 1942 and was the forerunner of all nuclear weapons and nuclear power plants,

FERNAN GONZALEZ (d. 970) united a number of Castilian counties and established Castile as an independent and hereditary state which later became the kingdom of Castile. He is the subject of a 13th-cent. Castilian epic poem.

FERNÁNDEZ, JUAN (*c.* 1535–1602), Spanish maritime explorer whose voyages off the Pacific coast of South America in the latter half of the 16th cent. led to the discovery (1563) of the islands named after him.

FERNÁNDEZ DE CÓRDOBA, LUÍS (1798–1840), with his brother Fernándo typified the new race of soldier-politicians who dominated Spanish politics in the reign of Isabella (1833–68). His prestige derived from his role in the civil war against the carlists in northern Spain (1833–40) and he coined the phrase 'the languid war' to describe the stalemate against the carlist guerrillas. The army had emerged as the main defender of the liberal constitution, but when the radical politicians of Seville asked Luís to head a local revolution (1838) he agreed, allegedly to contain the uprising. But he had underground connections with southern radicals and may have aspired to found and lead a liberal union government.

FERNÁNDEZ DE LIZARDI, JOSÉ JOAQUÍN (1776–1827), Mexican colonial writer and pamphleteer, whose *Itching Parrot* (1830) is considered the first true novel produced in the New World. His political opinions were anti-monarchical and contributed to the independence of the colonies.

FERNANDO PO (or Poo), small island off the coast of the Niger delta in the Bight of Biafra, named after its first European discoverer, Fernão do Po, who reached it *c.* 1469. Its Bubi inhabitants (immigrants from the adjoining equatorial mainland) repulsed attempts at European settlement, but the island was none the less claimed as part of Portugal's African domains. In 1778 the Luso-Spanish treaty of Pardo awarded the island to Spain, together with its still smaller southern neighbour, Annobón, but there was little or no effective administration until 1920. In 1968 the island was given its political independence, together with Annobón and the adjoining equatorial enclave of Rio Muni. A census taken in 1960 gave the island's population as 62,612.

FEROZESHAH, BATTLE OF (21–2 Dec. 1845), fiercely contested struggle during the First Sikh War, in which the Sikhs were defeated. The British drove them from their entrenchments at the village of Ferozeshah, about 12 miles (19 kms) from the Sutlej.

FERRARA, FRANCESCO (1810–1900), Italian economist and advocate of the principles of laissez-faire. His chief contribution to economic theory was the concept of reproduction cost—an attempt to analyse the various comparisons which guide individuals when making economic choices.

FERRARA, town in Emilia (north-eastern Italy), south of the Po river. It was ruled (1208–1597) by the family of Este, who in the 15th cent. created a brilliant court that made it famous as one of the scholarly and artistic centres of Italy. In 1429 Guarino of Verona established an Italian humanist school and a university. Its artists, notably Pisanello and Ercole de Roberti, made a distinguished contribution to Renaissance painting.

FERRY, JULES FRANÇOIS CAMILLE (1832–93), French politician and prime minister, who was one of the architects of both the modern state education system and the colonial empire. As administrator of Paris (1870), he was accused of causing famine and resigned when the Commune broke out (1871). He later served as envoy to Greece (1872–3) and as a deputy, becoming a leading Opportunist. As minister of education (1879) he introduced universal, free, secular education. As prime minister (1880–1, 1883–5), he was

responsible for great colonial expansion, but this was unpopular and led to his fall (1885). He failed to secure reelection, entered the Senate (1891), and was eventually assassinated.

FERSEN, HANS AXEL, Count von (1755–1810), Swedish soldier and counter-revolutionary leader. He entered the French military service and fought at Yorktown, but is best known because of his friendship with Marie Antoinette. He organized the royal flight to Varennes, returned to Paris in disguise (1792), and worked for the Bourbon cause in Brussels. In Sweden he supported the Gustavian dynasty and the claim of Prince Gustavus after his father, Gustavus IV, abdicated (1809). When the rival claimant to the throne died suddenly (1810), Fersen was unjustly suspected of his murder, and at his funeral procession in the streets of Stockholm was lynched by the mob.

FESSENDEN, REGINALD AUBREY (1866–1932), Canadian-born radio engineer. After working for Thomas A. Edison and the Westinghouse Electrical Manufacturing Co. he founded the National Electrical Signalling Co. (1902), developed the continuous-wave system of wireless transmission and the heterodyne, and was one of the first broadcasters of music and the spoken word.

FESSENDEN, WILLIAM PITT (1806–69), US Republican senator from ME (1855–64, 1865–9), and Abraham Lincoln's secretary of the treasury (1864–5). A moderate supporter of radical reconstruction after the Civil War, he was an influential chairman of the Congressional Joint Committee on Reconstruction. He cast one of the crucial votes against impeachment of Andrew Johnson (1868).

FÊTE DE LA FÉDÉRATION (1790), held in Paris on 14 July by armed representatives of the provincial revolutionary clubs to celebrate the fall of the Bastille. It remains (1970) a French national holiday.

FÊTES NATIONALES (1792) in France, whose celebration by the rival Parisian revolutionary clubs became an excuse for increasing lawlessness.

FEUDALISM denotes the medieval system of land leasing in return for an obligation of military service. Another essential ingredient was an oath of fealty to the lord from whom the land was held, and indirectly to the king, who was the ultimate overlord of all. It was by this military service that monarchs were able to raise armies in times of crisis. This was essential in a time when taxation was sporadic and taxes difficult to collect. If the direct overlord of a tenant happened to be the king, then the tenant was known as a tenant-in-chief. Whether held in chief or not, the unit of land was known as a fief or fee. Feudalism probably came into being because in the chaotic sub-Roman period men took oaths of allegiance to powerful men, theoretically surrendering final ownership of their land as surety for their loyalty in return for the protection which the magnate gave them. A recognizable form of feudalism certainly existed in Charlemagne's time in western Europe and prototypes have been found in eastern civilizations. In the west, feudalism has been regarded as having been most efficiently organized by the Normans, both in their kingdom of southern Italy and in England. The system broke down some time in the 15th cent.; the decimation of the aristocracy in the civil wars of that period led to impossible confusions of loyalties and an enormous number of tenants fell into the spheres of influence of disproportionately few magnates, making the system unworkable. The more frequent minting of money also led to the substitution of payment to many soldiers who previously would have been given a portion of land.

FEUILLANTS, moderate deputies in the French Constituent and Legislative Assemblies, who tried unsuccessfully to give

France a constitutional monarchy. Because of their disgust at a petition to the assembly demanding the king's dethronement, the moderate members of the Jacobin Club left the club and formed their own Feuillant Club (July 1791). Under the leadership of Barnave, Bailly, and Lafayette, the Feuillants hoped to bring the king and nation together on the basis of the constitution of 1791. Although they dominated the ministries from the summer of 1791, their position was basically weak. The king had no intention of working through them, while the Legislative Assembly soon came to be dominated by Brissot and his friends, who demanded war with Austria and Prussia. By March 1792 war was inevitable and the Feuillant ministry and party collapsed.

FEZ, city of northern Morocco on the Wadi Sebou, founded *c.* 800 by the first Idrisids, to supersede classical Volubilis (Walila). It was developed by Andalusian immigrants and was the main urban centre between the coast and the Middle Atlas, at a commercially and strategically important point in the Taza gap. Its political potential was fully realized from the time of the Marinids (13th–15th cents), when it superseded Marrakesh as capital of Morocco, remaining so with some interruption under the Sa'dians (16th–17th cents). In modern times it has been eclipsed by Rabat and Casablanca.

FEZ, brimless headgear of north African origin. Its compulsory adoption (1828–9), in place of the turban, in the Ottoman empire became a symbol of the first period of modernization, just as its abolition (1925) in favour of the hat became a symbol of Kemalist secularization.

FEZZAN (classical Phazania), southernmost of the three provinces of the modern kingdom of Libya. An area of oases, it was settled in neolithic times; Herodotus first mentions the inhabitants, the Garamantes, who developed trans-Saharan trade and later (1st–2nd cents) clashed with the Romans. It was raided by the Muslim commander Uqba ibn Nafi (666), but not Islamized until after Zamila replaced Jermo as capital under the Banu Khattab dynasty (918).

In the 13th cent. Fezzan fell first to the Turkoman adventurer Al-Ghuzzi, then to the Saifuwa of Kanem, allied to the Hafsids of Tunis. The new capital, Trughen, attracted many immigrants from the south. In the 16th cent. the Awlad Muhammad founded Murzuq, a new capital. The Turks and their successors in Tripoli claimed suzerainty over Fezzan from 1577, but accepted tribute. The Karamanlis of Tripoli occupied the area from 1811–31, and the Awlad Sliman Arabs from 1831–42. The Italians temporarily occupied it (1914), but were unable to establish themselves there until 1929. The Fezzan is now (1970) part of independent Libya.

FICHTE, JOHANN GOTTLIEB (1762–1814), German philosopher and first rector of Berlin University, famous for his *Addresses to the German Nation* (1807–8) delivered in Berlin during the French occupation.

FICINO, MARSILIO (1433–99), Florentine churchman and canon of Florence Cathedral, who embarked in 1462 on the task of translating from Greek into Latin all the known works of Plato. This task he had completed by 1469, and for the first time western Europe became familiar with Plato's thoughts. Subsequently Ficino translated the most important neo-platonist philosopher, Plotinus (1492). In his commentaries on Plato, Plotinus, and various other neo-platonist writers, and in his main philosophical work, the *Platonic Theology* (1482), Ficino attempted a reconciliation of Christian and neo-platonist teaching, which profoundly influenced Christian thinkers of the late 15th and 16th cents.

FICQUELMONT, KARL LUDWIG, Graf von (1777–1857), Austrian diplomat of the Metternich era. After serving in the Austrian army during most of the campaigns against France, he entered the diplomatic service and was ambassador at Stockholm, Florence, Naples, and finally St Petersburg (1829–39), where he was a pillar of Metternich's diplomatic system. He later served in the foreign office, where he was his closest collaborator. Although a staunch conservative, he was made foreign minister and briefly Minister President when revolution broke out (1848) in Austria.

FIDALGO (Sp. equiv., *hidalgo*), the Portuguese–Brazilian term for a nobleman under the monarchy.

FIDAYAN-I ISLAM, extremist religio-political Iranian terrorist group founded (*c.* 1943) by Sayyid Mujtaba Mirlawhi (Nawab-i Safawi). The group was responsible for several political murders, including that of Gen. Razmara (1951). It was partially suppressed (1955), and several of the leaders, including the founder, were executed.

FIEF denoted the endowment of a military vassal in the Frankish society. The word probably derived from the Germanic name for cattle (*Vieh* in modern German). It became synonymous in later medieval usage with an area of land held by a feudal tenant enabling him to perform the military service expected of him by his overlord. Such an endowment could, however, take the form of an annual pension paid by the overlord and such money fiefs were increasingly in use from 12th cent. onwards.

FIELD, CYRUS WEST (1819–92), American businessman, who was solely responsible for initiating, organizing, and financing the laying of the first Atlantic telegraph cable in 1866, the project taking 13 years to complete. Technical expertise was provided by the American oceanographer Matthew Fontaine Maury and the Scottish physicist William Thomson (later Lord Kelvin).

FIELD, STEPHEN JOHNSON (1816–99), US jurist. He was elected to the CA state legislature (1850), helped to reorganize the state judicial code, and drafted mining legislation that became a model in the west. Having been a judge on the state supreme court (1857–9) and chief justice (1857–63), he was appointed in 1863 to the US Supreme Court and served one of the longest terms in the court's history (1863–97). Field, a strict constructionist of the US constitution, believed that the privileges or immunities and the due process clauses of the 14th Amendment protected private property rights, and his dissenting opinions in the *Slaughterhouse Cases* (16 Wallace 36, 1873), *Munn v. Illinois* (94 US 113, 1877), and other cases later came to be accepted by the majority on the court.

FIELD OF THE CLOTH OF GOLD, scene of a diplomatic meeting in 1520 between Henry VIII of England and Francis I of France. The place was between Guisnes and Ardres, near Calais, the name denoting the chivalric splendour of the occasion. The meeting was part of Wolsey's attempt to ensure a favourable position for England in the approaching Habsburg–Valois duel. It had no positive result because a French alliance was unpopular in England, and Wolsey became committed to the imperial cause in the following year.

FIELDEN, JOHN (1784–1849), British politician and cotton manufacturer in Todmorden, Yorks, whose first political activities were opposition to paper money and the support of parliamentary reform. After the success of the Great Reform Bill he became, with Cobbett, MP for Oldham (1832–47), and opposed the Whigs' New Poor Law, preventing the introduction of the Birth, Marriages, and Deaths Act (1836) into Todmorden and delaying the building of a workhouse there. His influence was widespread in the North as champion of the Ten-Hour Day, ostensibly for ensuring shorter hours for women and children; in practice for the men. He joined Attwood and the Chartists of 'Moral force' views, presenting the first and second petitions (1839, 1842) to the House of Commons. He voted consistently on radical lines in parliament and achieved his greatest success with his sponsorship of the Factory Act (1817) securing a 10-hour day or 58-hour week.

FIELDING, HENRY (1707–54), English novelist, journalist, and dramatist. After struggling to make a living as a playwright and managing the Little Theatre in Haymarket, he conducted a literary campaign against Sir Robert Walpole until he was silenced by the Licensing Act of 1737. Walpole became the target of his second novel *Jonathan Wild* (1743). His other novels included *Joseph Andrews* (1742), *Tom Jones* (1749), and *Amelia* (1751). Between 1739 and 1741 he wrote the periodical *The Champion*. His writing did not prevent him from also following a legal career. He was called to the bar in 1740 and from 1748 was a JP for Middlesex and Westminster.

FIELDING, WILLIAM STEVENS (1848–1929), Canadian journalist, politician, and prime minister of NS (1886–96). He was Canadian finance minister in the Liberal ministries under Sir Wilfred Laurier (1896–1911) and Mackenzie King (1921–5). Under Laurier he negotiated a series of commercial treaties culminating in an agreement with the US (1911) which precipitated the Liberals' defeat.

FIENNES, CELIA (1662–1741), English author of a journal of extensive travels in England (1685–1703), first published in the 19th cent. as *The Journeys*. She was a nonconformist and a Whig and her journal is interesting as an eye-witness account of domestic events of the period.

FIESCHI CONSPIRACY (1547), unsuccessful plot hatched by the Fieschi family in Genoa against the pro-Spanish Doria family.

FIFTEEN, THE (1715), rebellion of Jacobite supporters in Scotland and England to resore the Stuarts, in the person of James Edward, the Old Pretender, to the throne. The rising began in Scotland, where the Earl of Mar, a minister whom George I had dismissed, retaliated by raising the Jacobite standard at Braemar. Much of Scotland rallied to Mar and eventually his force far outnumbered that of Argyll, who commanded the government forces. However, risings elsewhere failed and the Duke of Ormonde was unable to land to support English Jacobites.

Mar did, however, detach a force of Highlanders, led by Mackintosh of Borlum, to contact the lowland Jacobite lords Kenmure and Nithsdale. A smaller force of English Jacobites, led by Thomas Forster, Lord Derwentwater, and Lord Widdrington, joined them after failing to raise the border counties, and this combined army, after aimlessly wandering about the borders, marched south in the hope of raising Lancashire. At Preston the Jacobites were surrounded and capitulated (13 Nov. 1715). On the same day Mar's army met the government forces at the battle of Sheriffmuir. This battle, though indecisive, ended Mar's activities. In Dec. the Old Pretender arrived from France, but by then government troops in Scotland had been reinforced and the Jacobite forces began to melt away. In Feb., Mar and the Old Pretender sailed for France, leaving their forces to face Cadogan's government troops. By April 1716 the rising had been suppressed in England and Scotland. Of the captured Jacobites Derwentwater and Kenmure were executed, and many were forced into exile for fear of their lives. Of the other Jacobite prisoners many were released by the Act of Grace (1717).

The Fifteen showed how few Englishmen were willing to take up arms for the Stuarts. Thenceforth the government realized that a Jacobite restoration could only be brought about by force of foreign arms, and so began a series of

alliances guaranteeing the Protestant Succession in England as laid down by parliament.

C. Petrie, *The Stuart Pretenders: a history of the Jacobite Movement, 1688–1807* (New York, 1933).

FIFTH COLUMN in Spain. In 1936 Gen. Mola was asked how he would capture Madrid. He said that four columns of his troops would march from without, but that he was relying on his 'Fifth Column' of secret nationalist supporters within. He had good reason for his assertion, knowing that 45 per cent of Madrid's population had voted for the right in the Feb. 1936 elections and that many people who had voted for the left would have been alienated by revolutionary excesses. In fact, most Republican towns had their 'Fifth Column', made up of Falangists and other right-wing supporters who had been trapped in the loyalist zone. The majority waited for a Nationalist victory in order to show their true colours, like many of the middle class who took refuge in the foreign embassies in Madrid. However, an active minority indulged in sabotage and sniping. In April 1937 a Falangist plan for a rising in Madrid was discovered. In Aug. 1937 an actual rising of the 'Fifth Column' took place in Santander.

The phrase passed into general usage during the Second World War to denote a hidden enemy, assisting orthodox forces by sabotage and disruption.

FIFTH MONARCHY MEN, extreme Puritan sect at the time of the English Civil War. They believed that the last of the five universal monarchies foretold by Daniel was at hand, when Christ would reign on earth with his saints for 1000 years. The Second Coming would take place in 1656 and would end the Roman monarchy (represented by the pope), which had itself succeeded the Assyrian, Persian, and Greek monarchies.

The sect at first supported Cromwell and hoped that Barebone's Parliament would herald the rule of the godly. The establishment of the protectorate dashed these hopes and turned the monarchy men against Cromwell. The violence of their agitation led to the arrest of their leaders, *eg*, Maj.-Gens Thomas Harrison and Robert Overton, Christopher Feake, and John Rogers. In April 1657 an attempted armed rising led by Thomas Venner was easily suppressed, as was a second rising led by him in Jan. 1661, after which he was executed. Soon after the Restoration the sect died out.

'FIFTY-FOUR FORTY OR FIGHT', slogan of US expansionists in 1844, who demanded the whole of the OR territory up to the 54° 40′ line of latitude, including parts of what is now BC and AK. Since 1818, the area between the 42nd parallel and 54° 40′ had been ruled jointly by the US and Britain. Although President Polk and his party had campaigned on an expansionist platform in 1844, he accepted British proposals (1846) for a boundary along the 49th parallel, despite protests from the champions of '54° 40′ or fight'.

FIGUERAS, ESTANISLAO (1819–82), leader of the minority federal republican party in Spain and first president (1873–4) of the first Spanish republic Figueras failed to give the decisive lead needed to endear the republic to an unenthusiastic people. By posing as a neutral arbiter and leaving the task of instituting federalism to the constituent Cortes he gave the radicals time to organize opposition. His more forceful successor, Pi y Margall, had to suppress the ensuing coup.

FIGUERES FERRER, JOSÉ (PEPE) (1906–), Costa Rican rancher, leader of the reformist National Liberation Party, and an outspoken enemy of Latin American communists and dictators.

FIJI ISLANDS in the Pacific were discovered by Tasman (1642) and Bligh (1789). Early sandalwooders at Mbua Bay (1804–15), bicho-do-mar and shell traders and later white settlers at Levuka added fuel to local conflicts. In the 1840s and 1850s the group was convulsed by bitter cannibal feuds, notably between Mbau and Rewa (Vita Levu), culminating in Cakobau's victory over heathen dissidents, the conversion of Fiji to Christianity (1855), and, eventually, unconditional British annexation (1874). The new regime under Sir A. H. Gordon began badly, with both a measles epidemic causing 30,000–40,000 deaths (Feb.–March 1875) and a revolt of heathen mountain tribes, but soon won confidence. The Fijians were confirmed in their customs and lands, the 12 leading provincial chiefs (*roko*) being given wide powers. Indian coolies were recruited by Europeans for casual and plantation work, but this well-meant measure, designed to preserve Fijian culture, was vitiated by inadequate provision for Indian repatriation. European agitation for annexation to New Zealand (1900) contributed to the establishment (1904) of a legislative council with ten official and eight elected (including two Fijian) members, Indians being excluded until 1916. Adult suffrage and representation of each race by four members was introduced in 1963 pending a suitable accommodation between the numerically equal Fijians and Indians. Fiji achieved independence on 10 Oct. 1970.

FILARET (d. 1633), patriarch of All Russia and father of Michael Romanov, founder of the Romanov dynasty. On the death of Ivan IV his claim to the throne was upheld by some of the *boyars* (1584), for which he was forced by the regent, Boris Godunov, to become a monk and take the name of Filaret before being sent into exile (1601). His wife was also forced into a convent under the ecclesiastical name of Martha. After Godunov's death, Filaret was appointed metropolitan of Rostov (1605), but was ousted from the patriarchate by the elderly Hermagen. During the Time of Troubles he was seized by the Cossack supporters of the second false Dmitri and taken to Tushino to be made patriarch (1608). After the abdication of the Tsar Shuisky, he was sent as envoy to Poland with Prince Golitsin to conclude a treaty by which the heir to the Polish throne, Vladislav, should become Tsar of Russia (1610). At Smolensk they were arrested for refusing to accept Sigismund III, Vladislav's father, as tsar instead, and imprisoned in Marienburg (1611–18). During his imprisonment Filaret's son Michael was elected tsar by the Zemsky Sobor (1613) and after being released from Poland he was made patriarch and granted the title of Great Sovereign (1619). For the next 14 years he ruled Russia jointly with his son, over whom he exercised considerable influence. Although he tried with little success to reform the administration and the finances, both of which had suffered in the Time of Troubles, he was an inherently conservative figure and he retained the confidence of the *boyar* class until his death.

FILARET, Metropolitan (1782–1867), rector of St Petersburg Spiritual Academy and metropolitan of Moscow (1821). He supervised the translation of the Bible into modern Russian, wrote a catechism, and drafted the Emancipation proclamation.

FILIBUSTER, procedure used in the US Congress to prolong debate and prevent a vote being taken. Originally common in both houses of Congress, by 1900 the filibuster was rendered virtually impossible in the House of Representatives by new rules restricting its practice. Senate Rule 22 allows for the possibility of unlimited debate, thus making it possible for a determined minority to seek to 'talk out' any bill they oppose. It is possible but difficult to end debate by applying the cloture rule, since this requires the affirmative vote of two-thirds of the senators present 48 hours after a cloture petition has been filed by 16 senators. Most senators are reluctant to use this device to curb debate, and attempts to make it easier to end a filibuster, *eg*, by allowing it to be terminated by a simple majority vote, have not been successful.

FILIPESCU, NICOLAE (1861–1916), Rumanian politician and partisan of the entente during the First World War. In

the summer of 1915 he led an interventionist faction out of the Conservative Party and into alliance with Take Ionescu's Conservative Democratic Party.

FILLMORE, MILLARD (1800–74), 13th US president (1850–3). He became a Whig while serving as a US congressman (1833–5). After being re-elected (1837–43) he became vice-president (1848), and succeeded to the presidency on Zachary Taylor's death, but was not renominated (1852). He was unsuccessful presidential candidate of the Know-Nothing Party (1856).

FILMER, SIR ROBERT (1588–1653), English political writer of the time of Charles I, who defended the authority of the king in his book *Patriarcha, or the Natural Power of Kings*. This described the origin of government as an enlargement of the microcosm of the family. It was circulated privately among Royalists during the Civil War, but was not printed until 1680, when the Tories revived the idea and John Locke attacked it.

FINCA, Spanish term for a rural property. In Latin America the exact meaning has varied historically and from region to region.

FINCH OF FORDWICH, JOHN FINCH, Baron (1584–1660), Lord Chief Justice of England and a pillar of Charles I's judicial system during his years of personal rule (1629–40). He was appointed lord keeper of the seals in 1640. In 1641 he was impeached, but escaped to the Hague, to return at the Restoration (1660).

FINIAN OF CLONARD (?–549), founder of the monastery of Clonard (*c.* 520) and a distinguished teacher. He established Clonard as one of the principal centres of learning in Ireland. An early Penitential (system of penance) ascribed to Finian is still extant.

FINKENSTEIN TREATY (4 May 1807), Franco–Iranian agreement by which France promised military advice and equipment and her help in inducing Russia to evacuate Georgia in return for Iranian co-operation with a possible French invasion of India.

FINLAND (1809). Transfer of Finland from Swedish to Russian sovereignty resulted from the Franco-Russian agreements at Tilsit for enforcing the Continental System on Sweden. Anticipating British naval support for the Swedes, the Russians began to invade Finland in Feb. 1808. The surrender of Sveaborg, the 'Gibraltar of the North', by defeatists in May outweighed some Finnish victories which followed. In the autumn the troops were withdrawn to Sweden, where they surrendered in the same month (March 1809) as the Finnish Diet met to negotiate a constitution under Alexander.

FINLAND, DUCHY OF, appanage provided by Gustavus I of Sweden in 1556 for his second son, John. John's separate rule, based on Turku (Swedish Åbo), lasted only seven years, but as King of Sweden he granted Finland the appellation of 'Grand Duchy'. Subsequently, a court of appeal (1623) and a university (1640), were established, both at Turku.

FINLAND, TREATY OF (1940), ended the first phase of the Finnish–Soviet war which had begun when the Soviet Union attacked Finland (Nov. 1939). The Soviet Union acquired the whole Karelian isthmus with the city of Viipuri (Viborg), the fourth largest industrial city, and other areas west of Lake Ladoga (amounting in all to one-tenth of Finland's territory). The Soviet Union also acquired the use of a naval base at Hango.

FINLAND, TREATY OF (1947), one of the peace treaties signed with the former German satellites (Finland having declared war on Russia in June 1941) to recover territory lost by the treaty of 1940, as a result of which Britain declared war on Finland (Dec. 1941). The frontier with the Soviet Union under the 1940 treaty was confirmed; the Soviet Union renounced its right to the naval base at Hango and obtained instead the lease of the Porkalla-Udd area.

FINLAY, CARLOS JUAN (1833–1915), Cuban physician noted for his pioneering research on the relationship between the mosquito and yellow fever.

FINNEY, CHARLES GRANDISON (1792–1875), US evangelist preacher and educator, who launched (1825) the Great Revival which swept through the northern states. Finney's preaching emphasized 'disinterested benevolence'. This attracted well-educated and socially conscious followers to his cause, some of whom, *eg*, Theodore Dwight Weld, became prominent in the anti-slavery movement. Finney later became associated with Oberlin College, then a newly established co-educational institution in OH, which he served as president (1851–66).

FINNISH CONSTITUTION OF 1809, home-rule system respected for nearly a century by the Emperors of Russia as grand dukes of Finland. The representatives of Finland in the Swedish Estates were summoned to the Diet of Borgå (March 1809), six months before the cession of the country by the Swedish Crown; at which time it was to the interest of the emperor to placate the Finns by promising to maintain the form of government set up (1772, 1789) by Gustavus III. The Diet did not meet again until 1863, and the country was ruled by its aristocracy through an executive called the Senate. But no attempt was made to introduce Russian institutions until the independence of the Finnish army was attacked in 1898. The subsequent policy of Russification led to the suspension of the constitution in 1903.

FIRDAWSI (*c*. 940–*c*. 1020), author of the Persian epic, the 'Shahnama' or 'Book of Kings'. His famous poem, written perhaps *c*. 980–*c*. 1010, embraces both heroic legends and also historical data from the time of the Sasanid regime in Persia.

FIRE INSURANCE, in Britain. The popular belief that the Great Fire of London (1666) was the origin or cause of this practice is incorrect, but this fire certainly gave it a strong stimulus. Fire insurance companies in the 18th cent. gave an encouragement to building in relatively non-inflammable materials, and started fire brigades for the use of their members, institutions which later became available for all and were supported by public funds.

FIRELOCK, gun-lock (or a musket furnished with such a lock, or a soldier armed with such a weapon), in which sparks were produced by friction or percussion to ignite the priming. In the 17th cent. it was also called a flintlock.

FIRESIDE CHATS in US, frequent and informal addresses to the American people over the radio by President F. D. Roosevelt. From the first fireside chat on 12 March 1933, Roosevelt exploited the wireless as a medium of disseminating information and propaganda throughout his terms of office. The talks were one of the most effective ways of taking the nation into his confidence, sustaining morale, explaining policies, and consolidating political support.

FIRISHTA, MUHAMMAD KASIM (*c*. 1570–*c*. 1620), son of an immigrant to India from Turkestan who settled at the court of Ahmadnagar. After his father's death he settled at Bijapur and wrote his general history, the *Tarikh-i Firishta*, called by himself *Gulshan-i Ibrahimi* at the request of Sultan Ibrahim II of that state. It formed a basis for Elphinstone's *History of India,*

FIRST ESTATE, French social order of the clergy, whose representatives were traditionally of first importance in the estates-general. Though varying considerably in wealth, the first estate shared the enormous prestige of the spiritual calling and the tangible privileges of tax concessions. Although the Crown raised taxes from the clergy, *eg*, the *don gratuit* and the *décime*, they were exempt from more onerous impositions, *eg*, the *taille*, *aides*, *gabelle*, and *corvée*. They were also protected by the Church's judicial authority, exercised through the *officialités* (ecclesiastical courts).

FIRST FRUITS AND TENTHS, COURT OF, in England, set up in 1540 to enforce payment by the clergy of the first year's income from a benefice and in each year thereafter of a tithe or 10 per cent tax. These dues, originally paid to the pope, had been annexed to the Crown (1534). The court was merged with the Exchequer in 1554, and in 1703 the dues were assigned to Queen Anne's Bounty for the augmentation of poorer livings.

FIRST LORD OF THE TREASURY in England, office of state which became identified with the function of prime minister during the 18th cent. Although until the 19th cent. all ministers appointed by the Crown were theoretically equal, in practice the lord treasurer had become predominant as early as the reign of Anne, when Robert Harley, 1st Earl of Oxford, had been described as 'prime minister'. This ascendancy was maintained by the first lords after 1714 chiefly because the office gave its holder the duty of appointing revenue officers, a far larger field of Crown patronage than belonged to any other minister. Distribution of places of profit under the Crown to members of parliament, their friends and supporters was the principal method of providing a ministry with enough support in the House of Commons to carry on the king's government, and its effectiveness was little affected by the Place Acts which excluded revenue officers from the Commons. In addition to his influence through patronage, the first lord could also manage the Commons in person when he was himself a member, or through his deputy, the chancellor of the exchequer, an office normally held by himself unless he was in the Lords. All the stable and lengthy ministries of the 18th cent. were led by first lords of the treasury who sat in the Commons. The only occasions when ministries were led by secretaries of state, who had more immediate control over government at home and policy abroad, were those when the first lord was not in the Commons and foreign policy was especially important, *eg*, 1718–21 and 1757–61.

As the practice of framing policy and advising the king through a small inner ring of ministers, a 'cabinet council', was gradually accepted as legitimate during the 18th cent., so the first lord's influence was consolidated, while the king's freedom to choose his ministers was correspondingly diminished. By the mid-19th cent. the Crown had effectively lost the freedom to choose the first lord, the decisive influence having passed to the electorate and to the political parties, while the title 'Prime Minister' was accepted in recognition of established practice.

Betty Kemp, *King and Commons* (London, 1957).
E. N. Williams, *The Eighteenth-Century Constitution, 1688–1815* (London, 1960).   HNBM

FIRST PRESIDENT, senior legal officer appointed by French kings, effective head of the *parlement*, who presided over the court's plenary sessions and on all ceremonial occasions when the chancellor was absent. The first president of the *parlement* of Paris in particular was a leading public figure and from the 16th cent. a permanent member of the king's council, with extensive social as well as judicial duties.

FIRST WORLD WAR, known at the time as 'the Great War' or 'the European War', later as the First World War.
  (*a*) *Outbreak.*   On 28 June 1914 Archduke Franz

Ferdinand was assassinated at Sarajevo by a Bosnian Serb. On 23 July Austria–Hungary presented an ultimatum to Serbia and, when this was not accepted, declared war against her on 28 July. Germany declared war on Russia on 1 Aug., when the Russians refused to demobilize, and against France on 3 Aug. Britain declared war against Germany on 4 Aug., when the Germans failed to promise to respect Belgian neutrality. Austria–Hungary declared war on Russia on 6 Aug. Britain and France declared war on Austria-Hungary on 12 Aug.

(b) *1914*. The French offensive in Lorraine was a catastrophic failure. The Germans advanced through Belgium and were halted at the battle of the Marne on 7–9 Sept. After the first battle of Ypres in Oct. the line of trenches was stabilized on the western front. Russian armies invaded East Prussia and were defeated at the battle of Tannenberg on 25 Aug. In the autumn the Russians were victorious over the Austrians in Galicia. Turkey entered the war against the Entente Powers at the end of Oct. The Turkish winter campaign in the Caucasus against Russia ended with great Turkish losses. At sea, there was no great fleet engagement. A British squadron was destroyed by the Germans off the coast of Chile at Coronel on 1 Nov., and the German squadron was in its turn destroyed at the battle of the Falkland Islands on 8 Dec.

(c) *1915*. Deadlock persisted on the western front throughout the year, despite British and French attempts to break it. At the second battle of Ypres in April the Germans first used poison gas. The British planned to force the Dardanelles and take Constantinople. When naval action alone proved ineffective, British troops landed on the Gallipoli peninsula on 25 April. Superior Turkish forces pinned them to the coast. Further landings, especially at Suvla Bay in Aug., were equally unsuccessful. These failures led to the fall of the British Liberal government and its replacement by the first Coalition in May. Britain and France induced Italy to enter the war by lavish promises of territory in the secret treaty of London (26 April), and Italy declared war, though only against Austria-Hungary, on 22 May. The result was disappointing. Italian forces could make no headway on the mountainous frontier and fought 11 battles of the Isonzo without any success. Meanwhile the Germans stood on the defensive in the west and moved the bulk of their forces to the eastern front. There they broke through the Russian lines at Gorlice in May. The Russians retreated for hundreds of miles and abandoned most of Poland. The front was not stabilized until Sept., but Russia remained in the war despite German approaches for a compromise peace. Bulgaria joined the Central Powers in Nov., and Serbia was overrun. At the end of the year the British forces withdrew from Gallipoli, virtually without loss. The idea of a way round against Germany was henceforth discredited.

(d) *1916*. The Germans attacked Verdun with the intention of bleeding the French armies to death. Neither the attack nor the defence had any strategic purpose. Verdun was an operation of mutual slaughter. In Mesopotamia British forces were compelled to surrender at Kut-el-Amara on 29 April, whereupon new forces were diverted to avenge the defeat. On 31 May the only great naval engagement of the war was fought at Jutland. The Germans inflicted the heavier losses, but withdrew when faced by the British Grand Fleet. On 1 July the British army in France launched an offensive on the Somme, which produced heavy casualties and nothing else. Rumania entered the war against the Central Powers in Aug. Her territory was overrun towards the end of the year. The record of failure produced a fresh upheaval in Britain, where Lloyd George succeeded Asquith as prime minister on 6 Dec.

(e) *1917*. The Germans began unrestricted submarine warfare on 1 Feb. This nearly brought Britain to defeat until convoys were instituted, at Lloyd George's insistence, on 26 March. In answer to the German submarine campaign,

the US declared war against Germany on 1 April. This brought financial and economic aid to the entente, but no military aid until the following year. A French offensive on the Aisne in April was a failure and caused widespread mutinies in the French army. On 31 July the British opened an offensive in Flanders, sometimes known as the battle of Passchendaele. This too was a useless slaughter, redeemed only by the first tank victory at Cambrai in Nov. Russia ceased to be an effective combatant after the revolutions of March and Nov. On 24 Oct., German and Austro-Hungarian armies won a great victory over the Italians at Caporetto.

(f) *1918*. The year opened badly for the entente. Russia made a separate peace in March. On 21 March the Germans broke through the British lines and maintained a series of offensives against the British and French until 17 July. Foch became supreme commander of the Allied forces. On 8 Aug. the British began an Allied offensive, which was thereafter maintained until the end of the war. Meanwhile, a British army entered Damascus. British and French forces advanced into the Balkans from Salonika. Bulgaria concluded an armistice on 29 Sept. The Germans sought an armistice and peace terms from President Wilson. They accepted the Fourteen Points, without understanding what this involved. Turkey surrendered to a British admiral on 30 Oct. The Austro-Hungarian high command signed an armistice with Italy on 3 Nov., and the Austrian empire broke up. Revolution broke out in Germany. William II fled to Holland, where he abdicated. A German republic was proclaimed. German delegates sought an armistice from Foch. This came into force at 11 a.m. on 11 Nov. Germany abandoned all her conquests, and Allied forces occupied the Rhineland. The victory of the entente was, or seemed to be, complete. The war to end war was over. Democracy and self-determination had triumphed. Such, at any rate, was the theory of the moment.

C. R. M. F. Cruttwell, *A History of the Great War* (Oxford, 1936).

A. J. P. Taylor, *The First World War: an illustrated history* (London, 1963).   AJPT

FISCAL AUTONOMY CONVENTION, the name commonly given to the recommendation of the Joint Select Committee on the Government of India Bill (1919) that, in order to reassure India, it should be decreed that the British secretary of state would not interfere with fiscal policies agreed by the government of India and the Indian legislature, except to safeguard arrangements within the empire as a whole. The government of India was to deal specifically with tariffs for India's benefit. The fiscal commission which followed (1921) recommended the establishment of a Tariff board (1923) and a general policy of Protection.

FISCHER, EMIL (1852–1919), German chemist who made significant contributions to the chemistry of sugars and proteins, and in 1902 was awarded the Nobel Prize for Chemistry.

FISCHER, RUTH (née Eisler) (1895–   ), German politician and journalist, who became a member of the Politbureau of the Kommunistische Partei Deutschlands (KPD) and of the Presidium and the Executive of the Communist International in 1924–5 and held a seat in the Reichstag (1924–8). Belonging to the 'left' wing of the KPD, she was expelled from the party for 'left deviationism' in 1926. After 1945 she engaged in research into the history of the communist movement and published several books, dealing particularly with the influence of Stalin and the Comintern on KPD policies.

FISCHER VON ERLACH, JOHANN BERNHARD (1656–1723), Austrian-born architect and representative of the Northern Baroque style. From 1686 he worked in Vienna and Graz as a medallist, sculptor, designer, and architect, and in 1696 designed the palace of Schonbrunn for King Joseph I of Hungary. As architect to the king he received commissions in Salzburg and for the Prince-Abp of Salzburg, Count Thun-Hohenstein, he built the Dreifaltigkeitskirche and Seminary and the Collegienkirche (1694). In 1705 he began his *Entwurf einer historischen Architektur*, a monumental series of engravings.

FISCUS, Latin term used most frequently of the financial administration of the Roman empire. Originally meaning a wicker basket in which coin was kept, *fiscus* also meant the treasuries of each province of the empire, and separate taxation departments at Rome. But above all it referred to the emperors' private wealth (*patrimonium*) and then by extension to the imperial finances as a whole, as the *patrimonium* increased in importance through constant enlargement by bequests, intestacies, fines, confiscated property, and even some public revenues. Thus a substantial body of fiscal officials, mostly skilled slaves and freedmen, grew up and by the 2nd cent. AD the old official treasury of the Roman state (*aerarium*) was superseded.

FISH, HAMILTON (1808–93), US lawyer, politician, and secretary of state. He became lieutenant-governor (1847–8) and governor of NY (1849–51) and served one term as US senator (1851–7). With the disintegration of the Whigs he joined the Republican Party and served as federal commissioner for the relief of prisoners during the Civil War. He reluctantly became secretary of state under President Grant (1869–77), and his refinement and disinterestedness stood in marked contrast to the general quality of public life during the Gilded Age. His clear-headed and able conduct of foreign affairs was a valuable counterpoise to Grant's impetuousness. Fish's major achievement was the negotiation of the Washington treaty (1871), by which various disputes with Britain, including that over the *Alabama* claims, were settled by arbitration.

FISHER, JOHN ARBUTHNOT FISHER, 1st Baron (1841–1920), British admiral, who revolutionized training, tactics, and strategy to counter the German threat. Though trained under sail with a midshipman's experience of the Crimean War, he was always far-sighted about new developments such as the torpedo, submarines, and oil-burning. As second sea lord (1902) he reformed the education of naval officers through Osborne to the Royal Naval College, Dartmouth. As first sea lord (1904–1910) he drastically changed policy, together with the Earl of Cawdor, first lord of the admiralty. He redistributed the fleet, drawing the major forces much closer to Europe, based at Malta, Gibraltar, and the home ports, and promoted the construction of the *Dreadnought*, the first all-big-gun battleship together with the Invincible class of battle cruiser. The *Dreadnought* accelerated the race with Germany and the widening of the Kiel Canal, completed 1914, and gave the British fleet a comfortable margin of strength.

A genius, with drive, determination, and a flair for publicity, he made enemies easily, retired after a clash with Lord Beresford (1910), was brought back by Churchill as first sea lord (1914), but resigned in opposition to the diversion of ships to Gallipoli (1915).

FISHER, JOHN, Saint (1459–1535), bishop of Rochester, who with Sir Thomas More refused to take the oath to uphold the first Succession Act in the reign of Henry VIII because he rejected the royal supremacy over the Church. Because of his refusal he was executed. He had a European reputation for learning and holiness and was made a cardinal by Pope Paul III while in prison. He was canonized in 1936.

FISHER, ANDREW (1862–1928), Australian politician and first Australian Labor prime minister with a parliamentary majority. Emigrating to the Gympie (Qld) coalfield in 1884, he was elected to the colonial legislative assembly in 1893. In the Commonwealth House of Representatives (1901–15), he disagreed with his predecessor as leader, J. C. Watson, and his successor, W. M. Hughes, on the Boer War issue, supported Watson's parliamentary alliance with Deakinite Liberals for common social legislative objectives, but was opposed to granting them electoral immunity.

Having succeeded Watson in 1907, Fisher's minority Labor government of 1908–9 introduced such bipartisan projects as compulsory military training and the establishment of the Royal Australian Navy. After ten months in opposition, his majority in both houses (1910–13) made possible basic Labor legislation establishing the Commonwealth Bank, ending private Note Issues, and imposing Commonwealth land taxation. Though defeated in May 1913, he was returned to power in the Sept. 1914 election, during which he pledged support for Britain in the First World War, honouring his promise by dispatching the voluntarily recruited Australian Imperial Force overseas.

Fisher's resignation in 1915 to become high commissioner in London was a decisive event. He refused to follow Hughes in seeking to impose conscription for overseas service in 1916 and 1917 and on his return to Australia in 1921 he urged an alliance with the Country Party against Hughes, then Nationalist prime minister.

Fisher, a calm and constructive thinker, opposed racism, worked for women's enhanced status and increased Commonwealth powers, and supported the League of Nations. His consistent policies and conciliatory manner maintained the unity of the Labor Party, which Hughes wrecked within a year.   KEB

FISK, JAMES (1834–72), US speculator, who amassed a fortune trading in cotton and Confederate bonds during the Civil War, but soon lost it. He recouped his losses by joining forces with Daniel Drew and Jay Gould, with whom he manipulated Erie Railroad Stock in the 1860s and attempted to corner the gold market (1869).

FISKE, JOHN (1842–1901), born Edmund Fisk Green, US philosopher and historian and the first important American exponent of the evolutionary theories of Herbert Spencer and Charles Darwin. He lectured with enormous popular success on American history, and wrote numerous books on both philosophical and historical themes, mostly works of synthesis and popularization rather than products of original research or precise scholarship. His books include *The Outlines of Cosmic Philosophy* (1874), *Excursions of an Evolutionist* (1884), *The American Revolution* (1891), and *The Critical Period of American History, 1783–89* (1888), in which he stressed the weakness and instability of the US under the Articles of Confederation and the necessity of strengthening the national government.

FITCH, JOHN (1743–98), American inventor, born in Hartford, CT. Fitch established a metal-crafts business in Trenton, NJ, which was destroyed during the American War of Independence. He surveyed land in Kentucky, where he was captured by Indians and imprisoned by the British (1782–3). After surveying in the North-west Territory (1783–5), he moved to Bucks County, PA. He launched his first large steamboat at Philadelphia (22 Aug. 1787) and obtained a patent from the US government for his invention (26 Aug. 1791). Throughout his career financial difficulties plagued him, and he was unable to make his invention commercially practicable (1807).

FITCHETT, WILLIAM HENRY (1841–1928), Australian Methodist minister. In 1882 Fitchett founded Methodist Ladies' College, Melbourne, and was its principal until his death. Educator, journalist, preacher, and ecclesiastical statesman, he successfully advocated the union of the various Methodist denominations and became the first president-general of the Methodist Church of Australasia (1904–7).

FITZGERALDS, EARLS OF KILDARE AND DESMOND, a family descended from Gerald of Windsor, castellan of Pembroke early in the 12th cent., whose descendants went to

Ireland in the reign of Henry II (1154–89). Maurice Fitzgerald was justiciar of Ireland between 1233 and 1245 and henceforward the office was frequently held by a Fitzgerald. The eldest branch of the family was given the earldom of Kildare in 1316 and a younger branch the earldom of Desmond in 1329. The family attained its greatest importance in the second half of the 15th cent. The Yorkist victory in England in 1461 led to the eclipse of the Butlers, the chief Lancastrian family in Ireland, and left the earls of Kildare, their chief Yorkist rivals, in undisputed power. Their importance was effectively ended by Henry VIII.

FITZGERALD, FRANCIS SCOTT KEY (1896–1940), US author. His first novel, *This Side of Paradise* (1920), an immediate success, was a semi-autobiographical reflection of Princeton life and a revaluation of the Jazz Age. There followed two volumes of short stories, *Flappers and Philosophers* (1920) and *Tales of the Jazz Age* (1922), and another novel, *The Beautiful and Damned* (1922). In 1925 came Fitzgerald's most important work, a portrait of the post-First World War era, *The Great Gatsby*. This was followed by *Tender is the Night* (1934), and the autobiographical *The Crack-Up* (published posthumously, 1945). His last (unfinished) novel, *The Last Tycoon* (1941), depicts the Hollywood motion picture industry observed at close range. Throughout his writing there is an underlying concern about his times which made him the laureate of the 'Lost Generation' of young people who came to maturity during and just after the First World War.

FITZGERALD, JAMES EDWARD (1818–96), NZ politician who was elected superintendent of Canterbury (1853) and advocated liberal policies in religion and education. In the first general assembly (1854), he led demands for responsible government, and considered himself 'prime minister' in the abortive 'mixed' executive formed by Wynyard. He founded the Christchurch *Press* (1861) to oppose Moorhouse's Lyttelton tunnel and to advocate 'prudent' finances. Though a skilled orator and an enlightened advocate of Maori rights, he proved incapable of sustained leadership.

FITZHUGH, GEORGE (1806–81), Virginian lawyer and journalist, the most influential apologist for Negro slavery in the pre-Civil War American South. He contributed to many newspapers and periodicals, including *DeBow's Review*, and wrote two important books, *Sociology for the South: the failure of free society* (1854) and *Cannibals All! or, Slaves without Masters* (1857). He vigorously denounced laissez-faire capitalism as practised in the North, and contrasted the oppressed wage-slaves of the North unfavourably with the Negro slaves of the South, 'the happiest and, in some sense, freest people in the world'. Slavery, he argued, was the normal basis of civilized society, and socialism was only 'the new fashionable name for slavery'.

FITZNIGEL (FITZNEAL), RICHARD (d. 1198), bishop, member of the great le Poer family of administrators and officials. His father, Nigel, was Bp of Ely (1120–69), and his father's uncle, Roger le Poer, Bp of Salisbury, chancellor, and justiciar. Nigel purchased the treasurership for his son (*c.* 1159) and Richard held the post until 1196. He became Bp of London in 1189. He was a man of whom all contemporaries spoke very highly and was one of the greatest of all medieval officials. He was the author (*c.* 1176–8) of the *Dialogus de Scaccario* (*Dialogue of the Exchequer*), an invaluable and unique account of the workings of that great office of state in its initial period.

FITZRALPH, RICHARD (*c.* 1295–1360), archbishop, an Irishman who studied at Oxford and Paris, was chancellor of Oxford (1332–4), and Abp of Armagh (1346–60). He is chiefly important as the author of *De Pauperie Salvatoris* (*On the Poverty of the Saviour*), a theological work which

profoundly influenced the views of John Wycliffe on dominion and grace.

FITZROY, SIR CHARLES AUGUSTUS (1796–1859), governor of NSW (1846–55) in succession to Sir George Gipps. He had the combined advantages of aristocratic connections, previous colonial experience at the Cape of Good Hope, and service as lieutenant-governor of PEI (1837) and of the Leeward Islands (1841). With devolution of governmental power to Vic, Van Diemen's Land, and SA, FitzRoy's increased status as governor-general gave him supervisory authority which extended even to WA.

FITZROY, ROBERT (1805–65), governor of NZ in a time of crisis (1843–5): Maoris were restive, settlers fearful, and finances chaotic. As a supporter of missionaries he was disposed to protect Maoris against European encroachment and upheld Ngati Toa chiefs over the Wairau affray (1843). He also whittled down NZ Co. land claims, thereby conciliating Maoris and infuriating settlers. To sustain his virtually bankrupt government, FitzRoy was forced into unsuccessful expedients. NZ Co. supporters engineered his recall (1845), but FitzRoy's despised 'weakness' may have been the means of avoiding racial war in the infant British colony.

FITZWILLIAM OF NORBOROUGH, WILLIAM WENTWORTH-FITZWILLIAM, 2nd Earl (1748–1833), British politician, who supported Pitt from July 1794. His appointment as Ireland's lord-lieutenant (Dec. 1794) ensured the support of the Portland group for Pitt's ministry. It led Irish reformers to expect sweeping changes in policy and personnel. Despite Pitt's instructions, Fitzwilliam dismissed Beresford, a powerful 'pro-English' conservative, and other officials. His inopportune efforts to persuade the English cabinet to take up Grattan's Relief Bill led to his hasty recall (March 1795), and to consequent disillusionment among Irish Catholics and reformers.

FIUME, until 1919 a Hungarian port, with a mixed Croat and Italian population. After the First World War its possession was disputed between Italy and Yugoslavia. At the Paris Peace conference Italy's demand for Fiume, which had not been included in the territories promised her in the secret London treaty of 1915, was rejected. In Sept. 1919 the Italian poet D'Annunzio invaded Fiume with a force of demobilized soldiers and blackshirted volunteers. He maintained the semblance of a corporate state there until Nov. 1920, when Italy and Yugoslavia concluded the treaty of Rapallo. Under its terms the Italian government renounced most of its claims on Dalmatia, and undertook to expel D'Annunzio from Fiume, henceforth to become a free city. D'Annunzio was duly expelled, but nationalist opinion in Italy, strengthened by Mussolini's assumption of power in Oct. 1922, continued to claim Fiume. Mussolini did not immediately repudiate the treaty of Rapallo, but in Sept. 1923, while Yugoslavia was preoccupied with internal Serbo-Croat dissensions, Italy incorporated Fiume. Yugoslavia accepted the de facto occupation, in return for the recognition of her sovereignty over Port Baros, in the pact of Rome (or 'Adriatic pact') of 27 Jan. 1924. Further conventions relating to Fiume were signed at Nettuno in July 1925. Yugoslavia refused to ratify these until the autumn of 1928, when internal difficulties again reduced her resistance to Italian pressures.

FIVE CIVILIZED TRIBES, term applied to the Cherokee, Chickasaw, Choctaw, Creek, and Seminole tribes of North American Indians, because they adopted many elements of the dominant culture after the European conquest of America. Their governments were formulated according to the provisions of the US constitution.

FIVE DYNASTIES, period between the formal end of the T'ang dynasty (906) and the reunification of China under the

Sung dynasty (960). During the interval, the government of China was divided between some ten successive kingdoms in the south (907–78) and five, mostly alien, dynasties in the north (907–59).

FIVE FORKS, BATTLE OF (1 April 1865), south-west of Petersburg, VA, last significant engagement of the American Civil War and a victory for Union forces under Philip H. Sheridan. It led to Robert E. Lee's evacuation of Petersburg and Richmond, and his surrender at Appomattox.

FIVE KNIGHTS' CASE (1627) in England, decision of the king's bench as a result of which men imprisoned for refusing to contribute to Charles I's forced loans were not eligible for bail. (It is sometimes known as Darnel's Case, despite Darnel's withdrawal at an early stage.) The 1626 parliament had been dissolved without voting any supplies for the Spanish War, and Charles decided to levy a forced loan, which, despite opposition, proved successful. Five knights, imprisoned for refusing to contribute, applied for a writ of *habeas corpus* in order to bring their case before the king's bench. The writ was granted, but the return to the writ stated that they were imprisoned by special command of the king. At this point Darnel withdrew, but the other four contended that they should be released on bail, having been committed without just cause being shown. The judges ignored the opportunity to discuss whether forced loans and imprisonment without cause shown were legal, or whether the subject had a right to 'due process of law'. The bench adhered to the precedent of Sir Edward Coke's Case (1623), in which Lord Chief Justice Hobart held that in cases of doubt (and in the Five Knights' Case precedents, as well as statutes, were by no means clear) the verdict must always be for the king in the king's courts. Though the knights were released in 1628, the Commons were not placated. Two articles of the Petition of Right (1628) condemned non-parliamentary taxation and imprisonment without cause being shown.

FIVE-MILE ACT (1665), in Britain, the fourth and last statute of the Clarendon Code, attempted to stamp out Puritanism in the next generation by forbidding ministers to teach in a school or come within 5 miles (8 kms) of a corporate town where they had once held office, unless they took an oath not to subvert the Church and constitution. The act was passed partly as a consequence of the brave and selfless work of Puritan clergy in London during the plague, the government fearing that they might have won converts thereby.

FLACCUS, M. FULVIUS (d. 121 BC), Roman politician, who, as consul (125), was the first to propose enfranchising Rome's Italian allies. On being forced to withdraw the proposal, he later took the lesser office of tribune (122) to support a similar fruitless effort by Caius Gracchus, with whom he was killed.

FLAGLER, HENRY MORRISON (1830–1913), US businessman, who, after making a fortune through the grain commission business, then turned to salt manufacturing in MI. In this he lost his fortune and then, joining forces with J. D. Rockefeller (1865), became active in the management of Standard Oil Co. In the 1890s Flagler promoted the development of FL real estate, railroads, and hotels, helping to turn the state into a luxurious resort area.

FLAHERTY, ROBERT (1884–1951), American author and film-maker. In 1920 he made the documentary film *Nanook of the North* about the Eskimos. In his films of other isolated societies, *Man of Aran* (1934), *Elephant Boy* (1937), *The Land* (1941), and *Louisiana Story* (1948), he tried to show the interaction of man and nature. Flaherty is considered the pioneer of the documentary film.

FLAMINIA, VIA, great road from Rome to Ariminum (Rimini), begun in the censorship of Flaminius (220 BC).

FLAMINIUS, GAIUS (d. 217 BC), known chiefly as the Roman general whose rashness precipitated the disaster at Lake Trasimene in the Second Punic War (217). He was nevertheless a distinguished plebeian, anti-senatorial politician. In 232 as tribune he carried through an agrarian law in the *concilium plebis* without consulting the Senate, and in 223 as consul he ignored a senatorial instruction to return to Rome, and secured a triumph for his campaign against the Insubres. As censor (220) he began the Via Flaminia to Ariminum. His election as consul in 217 reflected popular irritation with the handling of the war, but the Trasimene debacle encouraged supporters of the Senate to denigrate his memory.

FLAMINIUS, T. QUINCTIUS (d. 174 BC), philhellenic Roman leader who, as consul in 198 BC, took over the conduct of the Second Macedonian War against Philip V. By diplomacy or force he detached Philip's Greek allies, and the decisive battle of Cynoscephalae (197) compelled Philip to evacuate Greece. His famous declaration of the freedom of Greece at Corinth (196) was followed by the liberation of Argos from Nabis of Sparta. The relatively generous terms to Philip, which alienated Aetolia, and the evacuation of Roman forces from Greece (194), on which he insisted despite the threat of Antiochus III of Syria, show that Rome had at this stage no imperial aspirations in the east.

FLAMSTEED, JOHN (1646–1719), English astronomer royal at Greenwich observatory, who remapped the fixed stars and observed the motion of the moon. He considerably reduced the degree of error in astronomical measurement.

FLANDERS, most westerly part of Belgium. In the late 9th cent. it became an autonomous state under an able dynasty of counts who successfully organized its defence against Viking attacks. Its coastline attracted a large population and a chain of important harbours had developed by *c.* 1200. Bruges, the principal port of medieval Flanders, became one of the leading commercial and financial centres of Europe. Ghent and other towns became seats of one of the leading European woollen industries. Flanders was at the height of its prosperity in the 13th cent., when it became one of the most densely populated areas of Europe. A series of internal conflicts in the Flemish towns provoking wars between Flanders and its suzerains, the kings of France, undermined the prosperity of the county in the 14th cent. After 1384 Flanders was merely one province of a rapidly expanding Burgundian state, whose dukes regarded it as the most turbulent of their possessions and tended to neglect its special needs. A period of particularly destructive civil wars between the people of Flanders and the dukes in 1477–92 culminated in the supplanting of Bruges by the Brabantine harbour of Antwerp while the Flemish industry was partly eclipsed by other European competitors.

Flanders was often the battleground of major wars from the 16th cent. onwards, suffering terrible devastation in the First World War.

FLANDERS GALLEYS. Regular voyages of merchant galleys from the Mediterranean to Flanders were started by the Genoese (*c.* 1298). The Venetians followed suit from *c.* 1314–1315, and Catalan galleys from Barcelona started coming at about that time. Florentine voyages began after Florence acquired convenient harbours in 1421. These fleets brought chiefly spices, silks, chemicals for the textile industry, sugar and fruit, and carried away Flemish and Brabantine cloth. From the late 14th cent. voyages to Flanders were usually combined with visits to England to fetch wool, tin, and English cloth.

FLANDIN, PIERRE-ÉTIENNE (1889–1958), French politician and one of the supporters of 'appeasement' in the 1930s. He was a leading conservative and a minister in many governments. As prime minister in 1934–5 he favoured friendship with Italy, and he was foreign minister at the time of the Rhineland crisis (1936). He did not hold office after 1936, but supported the Munich agreement. He later gave his backing to the Vichy regime, and was foreign minister—in effect, head of the government—for a few months in 1940–1 until he proved too anti-German for Pétain. Flandin's undoubted patriotism and integrity have exempted him from the condemnation accorded to most ministers of Vichy.

FLEET PRISON, London gaol of 12th-cent. origin, used to house victims of religious persecution and of the star chamber in the 16th–17th cents and later debtors and persons convicted of contempt of the courts of chancery, exchequer, and common pleas. It was also the scene of clandestine marriages from the early 17th cent. until the Marriage Act (1753). It was abolished in 1842.

FLEET SYSTEM (*FLOTA* SYSTEM), Spanish colonial use of the maritime convoy. The output of New World gold and silver mines was constantly threatened by other European nations and by pirates while being taken over the Atlantic to Spain. Consequently the Spaniards instituted a system in the mid-16th cent. whereby merchant ships were obliged to sail in convoy, usually protected by warships. Two fleets sailed annually. The *galeones* traded with Cartagena and Porto Bello, thus serving South America. The *flota* sailed to the Caribbean islands and Veracruz. Early the year following their arrival the two fleets met in Havana and sailed back to Spain together. Great fairs in Porto Bello, Cartagena, Jalapa, and Havana heralded the arrival or departure of these fleets. Although the system was generally a success, in that losses to foreign enemies were surprisingly low, it fell into disuse in the late 18th cent.

FLEETWOOD, CHARLES (d. 1692), English parliamentary general during the civil wars. He was the son-in-law of Oliver Cromwell and commander of the army in Ireland, which country he subdued in 1652. After Cromwell's death he was the most prominent military leader and the power behind Richard Cromwell, but was out-manœuvred by Monck (1659–60). Excepted from the amnesty in 1660, he escaped and died in obscurity.

FLEMING, SIR ALEXANDER (1881–1955), Scottish bacteriologist, who in 1928 discovered an anti-bacterial substance, which he called penicillin. It was not until 15 years later that it was isolated by Howard Walter Florey (later Lord Florey) and Ernst Boris Chain. Military requirements during the Second World War stimulated investigations of its chemical structure and methods of quantity production. Penicillin was the first and is still among the most commonly used of the antibiotics. Fleming, Florey, and Chain jointly shared the 1945 Nobel Prize for medicine and physiology.

FLEMING, SIR SANDFORD (1827–1915), Scottish-born surveyor and engineer, who emigrated to Canada. He helped to found the Royal Canadian Institute (1849) and became chief engineer of the Inter-continental Railway (1863) and of the Canadian Pacific Railway (1871), which he had long advocated.

FLETCHER, ANDREW, of Saltoun (1655–1716), Scottish writer. He opposed Lauderdale's anti-Presbyterian policies in Scotland (1678), joined Monmouth's rebellion (1685), and was restored to his Scottish estates after aiding the accession of William III. He supported the unfortunate Darien scheme (1695) and the Act of Security (1703), which asserted the right of the Scots to choose their own successor after Anne's death. He wrote speeches and pamphlets in opposition to Scottish union with England (1707) and published works on agriculture and free trade.

FLETCHER, JOHN (1579–1625), English dramatist, who collaborated with Beaumont, Massinger, and other playwrights (possibly including Shakespeare) in *Henry VIII,* *The Two Noble Kinsmen,* and the lost *Cardenio.* He also wrote some 15 plays on his own. He had a graceful, limpid style and chiefly wrote tragi-comedies plotted with great dramatic effect.

FLETCHER v. PECK, 6 Cranch 87 (1810), US Supreme Court case involving the obligations of contracts clause of the US constitution. In 1795 the GA legislature sold 35 million acres (133,500 sq. kms) along the Yazoo river to four land companies for only $500,000. During the next session of the legislature this sale was rescinded. The status of the Yazoo lands became a matter of both congressional and legal debate, and in 1810 the Supreme Court invalidated the rescinding act of the GA legislature, declaring that the obligations of contracts clause of the constitution applied to public grants as well as to private contracts. This was the first occasion in which the US Supreme Court held a state law void because it conflicted with a provision of the US constitution.

FLEURUS, town in Hainault, Belgium. In 1622, during the Thirty Years War, the Lutheran army of the court of Brunswick defeated the Spaniards; in 1690 the French army of Louis XIV beat Waldeck's army of the Grand Alliance; and in 1794 the Austrians were defeated by the French in the Revolutionary Wars.

FLEURY, ANDRÉ HERCULE DE, cardinal (1653–1743), bishop of Fréjus and tutor to the young King Louis XV, who became first minister in fact, if not in name, at the age of 73 (1726) and successfully governed France until his death. He helped to restore French greatness after the humiliations of Louis XIV's last years and the economic disasters of the Regency.

Fleury came to power after three years of vacillating government under the Duke of Bourbon, who finally tried to oust Fleury from the king's presence, but was instead exiled from court. Louis turned to his elderly, trusted mentor, who picked an able and industrious team of ministers to help him govern the state. During Fleury's regime the Chancellor, d'Aguesseau, continued the important work of legal codification; Orry, the controller-general, concentrated on financial reform; Maurepas strove to build up the French navy; and first Chauvelin and then Amelot de Chaillou managed foreign policy under the cardinal's direction.

The keynote of Fleury's domestic and foreign policies was stability. Despite the criticisms of economic writers (*eg,* Saint-Pierre and d'Argenson), he favoured the protectionism of Colbert and concentrated on economy of expenditure and the creation of national solvency. Under him the currency was stabilized and French overseas trade encouraged. Being an opponent of free discussion and divisive movements in Church and state, he suppressed the *club de l'entresol* (1731), damped down the Jansenist movement, and curbed the authority of the *parlement* of Paris, the chief supporter of that movement.

Stable government was also promoted by a peaceful foreign policy, although his pacifism masked the skilful diplomacy with which he manœuvred the tangled European political scene to French advantage. At first he maintained the Anglo-French alliance of 1717, which prevented the creation of a hostile coalition, but gradually he negotiated alliances with neighbouring powers against the traditional Habsburg enemy, *eg,* treaties with Charles Albert of Bavaria, promising French support for his imperial candidature (1727), with Spain (1733), and with Prussia (1739). While fostering English neutrality by his apparent moderation in the conflict over the Polish succession, he used his support for Stanislas Lesczynski, Louis XV's father-in-law, to gain the reversion of Lorraine for France (treaty of Vienna, 1735–8), a diplomatic coup which bore fruit in 1766 and gave France her last permanent territorial advance on her eastern border. With her prestige restored, France was invited to mediate between the Turkish and Holy Roman empires (treaty of Belgrade, 1739).

Anxious to avoid involvement in a new struggle with Austria, from which France could gain little, Fleury attempted to restrict hostilities, but his authority was increasingly undermined by the war party, led by Marshal de Belleisle (1741–3). After the cardinal's death Louis reverted to his predecessor's system of personal government, while France was soon drawn into the profitless war of the Austrian Succession which Fleury had tried to avoid.

A. M. Wilson, *French Foreign Policy during the Administration of Fleury* (London, 1936). MKS

FLINDERS, MATTHEW (1774–1814), English navigator and explorer of Australia's coasts, who joined the navy in 1789, and served under Bligh on his Tahiti–West Indies voyage (1791–3). In 1795 he sailed with Gov. John Hunter in *Reliance* for Sydney, NSW, where with George Bass he made two voyages in open boats to explore Botany Bay and George's River, and the coast further south. His observations (1798) in the Furneaux Islands, and Bass's esperiences during a whaleboat voyage to Western Port, convinced him that a strait lay between the mainland and Van Diemen's Land, and as commander of the sloop *Norfolk* he sailed with Bass through the strait and circumnavigated Van Diemen's Land. In 1799, again in *Norfolk*, he explored part of the coast discovered by Cook between Port Jackson and Hervey's Bay.

In England in 1801 Flinders was ordered to explore the unknown south coast of Australia and the imperfectly known north and north-east coasts discovered by the Dutch and Cook. In HMS *Investigator* he sighted Cape Leeuwin in Dec., then charted the south coast eastwards to Port Phillip, discovering Spencer's and St Vincent's gulfs. He later (July 1802–March 1803) charted part of the east coast northwards from Hervey's Bay and the whole of the Gulf of Carpentaria. He returned to Sydney, circumnavigating the continent, then sailed for England. At Mauritius he was arrested as a spy and was held captive until 1809.

On his return to England he prepared for publication his charts and *A Voyage to Terra Australis . . .* (1814) and conducted experiments on the effect of iron on ships' compasses, which resulted in 'Flinders bars' being placed in binnacles. Beside his valuable contributions to knowledge of Australia's coasts, and to the science of navigation, Flinders introduced several innovations to the drawing of hydrographic charts.

E. Scott, *The Life of Captain Matthew Flinders R.N.* (Sydney, 1914).
K. A. Austin, *The Voyage of the Investigator* (Adelaide, 1964). TMP

FLINTLOCK, small arm widely used in the 17th–19th cents. The musket or rifle was fired when a flint hit and ignited a small charge of gunpowder placed in a pan and this charge in turn ignited a larger charge in the barrel, so expelling the bullet.

FLODDEN, BATTLE OF (1513), victory of the English over an invading Scots army near the Tweed river. The Scots, in alliance with the French, hoped to take advantage of the absence of both Henry VIII and Wolsey campaigning with imperial forces on the Continent, and led by King James IV himself marched in force to take up a strong position on Flodden Ridge. Finding himself unexpectedly attacked by an English army led by the Earl of Surrey, who had marched round behind the Scots, James panicked, descended from his safe ground, and was killed, together with 13 earls and three bishops. His heir was a baby, the regent was Henry's sister Margaret, and the government a council of feuding nobles. The battle was a disaster for the Scots.

FLOOD, HENRY (1732–91), Irish politician, who sought Ireland's legislative and commercial independence. The demands of him and his colleagues included *habeas corpus*, judges' security of tenure, a Septennial Act, a national militia, and few placemen, but Flood himself opposed Catholic emancipation and severance of English ties. As the leader of the Volunteers, he helped to secure the repeal of most British restrictions on Ireland's commerce (1779–80) and on her legislative freedom (1782). He fruitlessly demanded parliamentary reform, and, more successfully, British reaffirmation of Ireland's legislative independence. He was a British MP in the last years of his life.

FLORA (FIORE), JOACHIM OF (*c.* 1130– *c.*1201), Cistercian mystic and abbot of Carozzo in Italy, who founded the abbey of Fiore in Calabria (1196). His writings on the Trinity were taken up by the spiritual Franciscans, who became known alternatively as Joachimites. He influenced some late medieval Italian heretics.

FLORENCE OF WORCESTER (d. 1118), name of an English monk to whom an important Worcester chronicle is attributed. It may have been written by a younger Worcester monk, John. It is a version of the Anglo-Saxon Chronicle, but with much additional material relating to the West Midlands.

FLORENCE, chief city of Tuscany, originated in a Roman colony founded in *c.* 81 BC. It first became important in the 12th cent. as the leading military power of its region. It developed an important textile industry and, by siding in the 13th cent. with the papacy, it secured papal support throughout Europe for its merchants and bankers. In the second half of the 13th cent. Florentine bankers became the leading European financiers and one of these, the banking family of the Medici, ultimately became, after 1434, the virtual rulers of Florence.

Florence's main churches and civic buildings date from the late 13th cent. and in Dante (d. 1321) it produced the greatest of all medieval poets. In the next generation Petrarch and Boccaccio were early pioneers of Italian humanism and the establishment of a chair of Greek at Florence University in 1397 was of decisive importance in introducing Greek studies into Italy. In the first half of the 15th cent. Florence was the most influential centre of Italian humanism and the first important buildings in the Renaissance style were built there, the most notable feature of which was the great dome of Florence Cathedral, constructed by Brunelleschi (1418–1434). Under Cosimo de Medici (d. 1464) and his grandson Lorenzo (d. 1492) Florence came to be generally recognized as the artistic and intellectual centre of Italy. The Italian wars, starting in 1494, were a period of economic decline and in the 16th cent. Florence's leadership in scholarship and the arts passed elsewhere, especially to Venice and Rome. Florence was the capital of united Italy (1865–70).

FLORENCE, THE COUNCIL OF, continuation of the council inaugurated at Ferrara in April 1438 and transferred to Florence in Jan. 1439. The council brought about a formal union of the Roman Catholic Church with the Greek Orthodox Church (July 1439, through the Bull *Laetentur Coeli*, establishing unity of faith and equality of rite); with the Armenian Church (Nov. 1439, a rapprochement lasting till 1475), with the Copts (Feb. 1442), with some of the Syrian Christians (Sept. 1444), and with the Chaldeans and the Maronites of Cyprus (Aug. 1445). The Greek Orthodox delegates accepted the union mainly in order to secure assistance against the Ottoman Turks. After their return to Constantinople and when it was clear that effective aid would not be forthcoming, the Byzantines rejected the union. The Council of Florence was also notable for its definition of doctrine (eg, of Purgatory) and for its assertion of papal primacy.

FLORES, JUAN JOSÉ (1800–64), general in the Latin American wars of independence, and twice president of Ecuador. He was born in Venezuela, served with distinction under Bolívar, and is noted for his victory at Tarqui (1829). When Ecuador broke away from Gran Colombia (1830),

Flores became the first president of the new state. He reached a compromise on the presidential succession with his rival, Vicente Rocafuerte, and returned to the presidency for a second term (1839–45), but this period was characterized by dictatorial government and he was overthrown. Evidence of his negotiations with Spain as part of his efforts to regain power has diminished his historical reputation.

FLORES MAGÓN, RICARDO (1873–1922), Mexican pamphleteer and revolutionary and a bitter opponent of Porfirio Díaz, because of whom he and his brother Jesús were exiled to the US. His anarcho-syndicalist views led to his imprisonment by US authorities.

FLORIDA, Spanish colony in North America. The Spaniard Juan Ponce de Leon discovered and named Florida (1513). Further Spanish explorations were made by Diego Minuelo (1516), Juan Ponce de Leon (1521), Panfilo de Narvaez (1528), Hernando de Soto (1539–40), and Tristan de Luna (1559–1561). Jean Ribault and René de Laudonnière led a group of French Huguenots into Florida (1562). They were attacked by Spaniards under Pedro Menéndez de Avilés, and the colony destroyed (1565). Menéndez established the settlement of St Augustine, the oldest city in the US. As English power in North America expanded, conflict with Spain over Florida was inevitable. Gov. Moore of South Carolina devastated Spanish missions in the Apalache country after failing to capture St Augustine (1702). The establishment of the English colony of Georgia (1732) led to intermittent conflict with the Spaniards in Florida (1739–48). At the peace of Paris (1763) Spain ceded Florida to England. During the American War of Independence Spain captured West Florida, and later (1783) England ceded East Florida to her. Spain then found herself in conflict with the US. On President Madison's order America assumed rule over West Florida (1810), an area between the Pearl river and Lake Pontchartrain. When Gen. Andrew Jackson entered Florida while chasing Indians (1818), Spain realized her inability to govern her colony successfully and ratified the Adams–Oñis treaty (1821), ceding it to the US. Jackson was appointed provisional governor. Florida became a territory (1822) with William DuVal as her first governor. Her growth was impeded by the Seminole War (1835–42), but in 1845 Florida became a state.

R. W. Patrick, *Florida under Five Flags* (Gainsville, 1955).
ERS

FLORIDABLANCA, JOSÉ MONINO Y REDONDO, Count of (1728–1808), Spanish statesman. After serving as Spanish ambassador to Pope Clement XIV, he was appointed chief minister to Charles III (1777). He was a reformer and reorganized government administration, built canals, and established agricultural societies. He was reluctant to join France and America in war against Britain (1778). After being dismissed by Charles IV (1792) and imprisoned in his castle at Pampeluna, he was rescued in the Spanish uprising of 1808 and made president of the national junta.

FLOTE, PIERRE (d. 1302), French lawyer of humble origin who became, under Philip IV, the first lay chancellor of France. He was one of several legists and propagandists who elevated the power of the French king and denigrated the papacy during Philip's quarrel with Pope Boniface VIII. He fell in battle at Courtrai against the rebel Flemings.

FLUSHING, seaport situated on the island of Walcheren, in the Dutch-speaking province of Zeeland and the second town to fall to the Dutch Sea Beggars (1572). It played a crucial part in the early years of the Dutch War of Independence from Spain (1568–1648).

FLUYT, flyboat, type of Dutch merchant ship, the greatest innovation in marine technology of 16th–17th cents. It had a broad bottom, round stern, and narrow deck, and being cheap both to build and to operate was extensively used in the Baltic and Mediterranean Seas and for local trading in the Dutch East Indies, giving the Dutch maritime trading supremacy.

FLYNN, JOHN (1880–1951), Presbyterian minister and founder of the Australian Inland Mission and the Royal Flying Doctor Service of Australia, established in 1912 to provide religious, medical, and social services to isolated settlers in an area of 2 million sq. miles (5,200,000 sq. kms). The service was the first of its kind in the world. As 'Flynn of the Inland' he became an Australian legend.

FOCH, FERDINAND (1851–1929), French marshal, appointed supreme allied commander after the German offensive of 1918, and thus the organizer of Germany's defeat. Before the First World War, Foch was a leading military theorist, and head of the French staff college. He held various commands on the western front, was Pétain's chief of staff in 1917, and was himself responsible for developing the idea of a unified allied command.

As the government's military adviser in the peace talks, Foch's insistence on French control of the Rhineland brought him into conflict with the Allies and with Clemenceau.

FOIX, GASTON DE (1489–1512), Duke of Nemours, brother of Germaine de Foix, Queen of Aragon, and French commander in Italy (1511–12) during the reign of his uncle, Louis XII. He raised the siege of Ravenna and took Brescia (Feb. 1512) before being killed during the French victory over the Spaniards at Ravenna (11 April).

FOIX, GERMAINE DE (1488–1538), niece of Louis XII of France, who became the second wife of Ferdinand of Aragon as a result of the treaty of Blois (1505), and as part of Ferdinand's diplomatic manœuvre to acquire a male heir to rival the Habsburg candidature for the Spanish Crown. Germaine bore a son in 1509 but the baby's immediate death removed the threat that the Spanish union might be dissolved. Ferdinand used Germaine's claims to the succession of Navarre to occupy that province and incorporate it into Aragon (1512).

FOKKER, ANTHONY HERMAN GERARD (1890–1939), Dutch-born German aircraft designer and manufacturer, who became involved with the development of military aircraft, many of which bore his name. His most important invention was that of an interrupter mechanism which permitted a machine gun positioned in the nose of an aircraft to be fired between the propeller blades; this led to major changes in the tactics of aerial combat. After the First World War he returned to Holland, but later emigrated to the US, where he devoted his talents to the production of civil aircraft.

FOKSHANI, village in Moldavia, south of the Sereth river. Here (18 July 1788) the Russian general Suvorov defeated the Ottoman forces under the command of Kemankesh Mustafa Pasha.

FOLK HIGH SCHOOLS, distinctive Scandinavian contribution to adult education. They originated in North Schleswig (1844) under the influence of the religious leader N. F. S. Grundtvig. The courses are residential and intended to suit the rural community, usually with young men attending in winter; women in summer. Instruction is based upon 'the living word', ie, informal lectures with a strongly national, democratic, and ethical content.

FONDS DE DÉVELOPPEMENT ÉCONOMIQUE ET SOCIAL, part of the machinery of French economic planning. The FDES, which replaced the Fonds de Modernisation et d'Equipement in 1955, is the fund through which state investment in the nationalized industries and in regional development, etc., is channelled.

FONSECA, HERMES DA (1865–1923), Brazilian army marshal and president (1910–14). He became a hero of the conservatives because of his authoritarian and elitist views. His presidential term was dictatorial and repressive, and was troubled by an economic depression. He and his ministers proved to be incapable of resolving the prolonged crisis caused by a fall in the price of coffee and rubber on the world market.

FONSECA, MANOEL DEODORO DA (1827–92), Brazilian general and president (1889–91). His military career included service in the war against Paraguay, and he became a leader of the army opposition to Pedro II. He was head of the first provisional republican government (1889–91), and was elected president in 1891, but was overthrown that same year for attempting to govern without the help of congress. He helped to formulate the first republican constitution of Brazil (1891).

FONTAINEBLEAU, French royal palace situated about 48 kms south of Paris, probably founded by Robert the Good at the end of the 10th cent. and rebuilt by Louis VII in 1169. It was constantly enlarged by French kings and has architectural features of many styles. After Louis XIV commissioned the building of Versailles, Fontainebleau was occupied by Mme de Montespan, and in Louis XV's reign Mme du Barry lived there. Pope Pius VII was imprisoned in the palace for two years by Napoleon.

FONTAINEBLEAU CONFERENCE (July–Sept. 1946), between the French government and representatives of the Viet-minh. The Viet-minh, having established a provisional government in Hanoi in Aug. 1945, sought a greater measure of independence than the French were prepared to grant, and refused to countenance any separation between Cochin-China and the rest of Viet-nam. On this issue the conference broke down, and a *modus vivendi* between Ho Chi-minh and the French failed to avert the Indo-China War, which broke out in Dec. 1946.

FONTAINEBLEAU DECREE (18 Oct. 1807), issued by Napoleon I as part of his Continental System. It ordered the seizure and burning of all English goods in France.

FONTAINEBLEAU, EDICTS OF (1540, 1685). By the 1540 edict Francis I of France entrusted the suppression of the Huguenots to the lay judges of the *parlements*. The 1685 edict effectively revoked the Edict of Nantes (1598) by ordering the destruction of all Protestant churches in France and the proscription of both public and private worship. All ministers were to leave France within 15 days, and recent concessions to Huguenots, *eg*, tax exemption for new converts, were ended. Liberty of conscience remained, in theory, but in practice Protestantism was almost crushed and some 200,000 Huguenots emigrated to other European countries.

FONTAINEBLEAU, PEACE OF (1679), settlement between Sweden, the Dutch Republic, and Denmark mediated by Louis XIV at the end of the Scanian War (1675–9). The status quo was restored, but the Swedes felt bitter because the commercial advantages granted to the Dutch in 1659 were not repealed through the influence of their French ally.

FONTAINEBLEAU, TREATY OF (1785), settlement under French auspices between the Emperor Joseph II and the Dutch arising from the Habsburg scheme to open the Scheldt river to Austrian shipping in contravention of the treaty of Munster (1648).

Hostilities between the Austrians and the Dutch were threatened when the latter rejected Habsburg pressure to withdraw from the barrier towns and give up their monopoly of Scheldt trade. The Dutch appealed to France for moral support, while Joseph intimated that concessions over the Scheldt would be made in return for French agreement to the exchange of the Austrian Netherlands for Bavaria. France, however, fearing a threat to the balance of power in Germany, demanded Prussian consent, forcing Joseph to drop the exchange scheme.

Negotiations in Paris concerning the Scheldt culminated in the Fontainebleau treaty (8 Nov. 1785). Austria received territory in Brabant and Limburg, complete control of the Scheldt above Sanftingen, and ten million florins in return for surrendering claims to Maastricht. However, the Scheldt remained closed—a diplomatic defeat for Joseph II.

FONTENELLE, BERNARD LE BOVIER DE (1657–1757), French philosopher, and nephew of Corneille, whose literary career spanned three-quarters of a century. He combined scholarship with elegance of style and was one of the first popularizers of science. As a convinced Cartesian throughout his life he championed the claims of the moderns in the philosophical battle with the ancients in his *Digression sur les anciens et les modernes* (1688). Fontenelle was elected permanent secretary of the Academy of Sciences in 1697 and wrote its history (1666–99). His other published works include *Dialogue des Morts* (1683), *Histoire des oracles* (1686), *Entretiens sur la Pluralité des Mondes* (1686), a treatise in which he expounded the Cartesian concept of the universe, *Poésies Pastorelles* (1688), and *Eloges des Académiciens* (1708–1719).

FONTENOY, BATTLE OF (1745), French defeat of an Anglo-Hanoverian army led by the Duke of Cumberland near Hainault during the War of the Austrian Succession. The victory prevented the British from raising the siege of Tournai.

FOOCHOW NAVY YARD, founded by Tso Tsung-t'ang in 1866 in an effort to strengthen China against Western threats; it was the only full-scale navy yard in imperial China. In its first years it was staffed by a number of Europeans (mostly French), the majority of whom were dispensed with in 1874; but standards of Foochow products were far behind those of Europe. During the Sino-French War (1884–5) both the Foochow squadron and the navy yard suffered heavy damage. Up till 1907, 40 boats were constructed; thereafter, for financial reasons, the navy yard was used chiefly for repair. Its most significant achievement was the training of naval personnel and skilled labour.

FOOD AND AGRICULTURE ORGANIZATION, established at Quebec in 1945 by members of the wartime alliance, which then became one of the specialized agencies of the UN. Its purposes were to raise levels of nutrition and improve the production and distribution of food. It had in 1970 113 member-governments, including Poland and Rumania but not the Soviet Union or other members of the Soviet bloc.

FOOT, MICHAEL (1913–   ) British politician, who began his career as a Liberal, but became a left-wing socialist in the 1930s. He founded (1937) *Tribune*, an independent left weekly 'born out of the agony of the Spanish Civil War'. In 1940 he was co-author of *Guilty Men*, an indictment of the so-called appeasers. As a Labour MP (1945–55) he became a close associate of Aneurin Bevan; on Bevan's death in 1960 he took over his old seat at Ebbw Vale and began his biography. Despite his abilities as writer, orator, and parliamentary tactician, he never sought a position comparable to Bevan's on the Labour left, although he challenged Callaghan in 1967 for the treasurership of the Labour Party. Following the Labour defeat in 1970, he became 'shadow' minister of power.

FOOTBALL, ASSOCIATION, has existed since the earliest times. It was played in China under the Han dynasty, in

Japan, and ancient Greece, and was brought to Britain by the Roman legionaries. In the Middle Ages it was a tumultuous scramble conducted without laws or boundaries, sometimes between whole villages, and even horsemen would join in. But apart from its inherent disorders, the game was unpopular with authority because it seduced healthy men from the practice of archery, necessary for national defence, and a typical prohibition in 1349 bracketed football with skittles, quoits, and fives as 'foolish games which are of no use'.

The English Puritans disliked it too, because it was considered frivolous and was played on Sundays, and it only achieved respectability with the grammarians' liking for manly and disciplined exercise. They established it in the *curriculum vitae* of universities and schools. This led in time to a demand for codification, since no competitive fixtures could be arranged while everyone played by different rules. The 'Cambridge Rules' (1848), produced by old boys from the schools, have acquired the Mosaic aura of a code that embraced 'the true principles of the game with the greatest simplicity', but at first they were in conflict with rival schemes that favoured handling, as practised at Rugby, and also holding, tripping, and hacking. At the founding of the Football Association (1863) the Cambridge formula was adopted, and hacking and handling clubs like Blackheath seceded to form the Rugby Union (1871). Standardization encouraged the formation of new clubs, although regional variations still existed, and Eton, Harrow, and Winchester persevered with their own arrangements for more than a century.

Football meanwhile was also growing in the narrow streets of the cities and mining villages of the Industrial Revolution, where conditions remarkably resembled the cloisters and stony playgrounds where the sons of the rich were acquiring similar footwork and control. The two streams of development merged when young clergymen from the schools went to city parishes and formed sports and social clubs. Aston Villa, Barnsley, Wolverhampton Wanderers, and Southampton are among the many clubs to have originated as offshoots of church and chapel. The FA Cup, launched in 1871, was early monopolized by teams drawn from the professional classes, but when unknown Darwen held the Old Etonians to two draws (1879), the balance of power was shifting towards the working-class clubs in the provinces. Professionalism was legalized (1885) and three years later the Football League was founded with 12 clubs, all from Lancashire and the Midlands. By 1958 there were 92 clubs playing in four divisions.

England first met Scotland in 1870, and with the game rapidly spreading overseas, the Fédération Internationale de Football Association (FIFA) was set up to organize it on an international basis (1904). The World Cup was inaugurated in 1930 and the European Cup in 1955.

G. Green, *Soccer: the world game* (London, 1953).
P. M. Young, *A History of British Football* (London, 1968)
MMR

FOOTBALL, RUGBY, traditionally began at Rugby School, England, when William Webb Ellis, dissatisfied with the local rules, picked up the ball and ran with it (1823). Clubs and schools that preferred the handling game withdrew when the Football Association was formed (1863) and founded the Rugby Union (1871). The four British countries soon organized an international tournament, to which France was later admitted, and the game was enthusiastically adopted in many parts of the British empire and Commonwealth. The New Zealand 'All Blacks' and South African 'Springboks' established themselves as the most powerful teams in the world. The Rugby Union game is limited tactically by the rule that players may not interfere when in front of the man in possession, so that the ball mostly moves backwards or has to be kicked out of play. Distinctive Gaelic, American, and Australian rules have been devised in an attempt to make the game more varied and fluent. There was also an important secession in England with the formation of the Rugby League (1875), Northern Union (1895), now the Rugby League (1922). This is a professional organization, whereas rugby is strictly amateur, and with 13 a side instead of 15, there is less scrummaging and the game is more open. It is mainly played in the north of England, but there is a following in France, Australia, and New Zealand.

FORAL, in colonial Brazil, the contract between the Portuguese monarchs and the recipients of captaincies (*donatários*), to regulate their conduct and their treatment of the colonial population.

FORBES, ALEXANDER (1817–75), bishop, writer, and scholar, who was an East India Co. clerk before being ordained. As Bp of Brechin (1847–75) he sought to establish Tractarian principles in the Scottish Episcopal Church, established a cathedral at Dundee, and was noted for his constant visiting of slums during cholera epidemics.

FORBES, DUNCAN, of Culloden (1685–1747), Scottish highland laird and lawyer, who supported the Anglo-Scottish union. He helped to recapture Inverness (1715) from the highland supporters of the Earl of Mar, thus contributing to the failure of the 1715 Jacobite rebellion in Scotland. He supported the pro-Hanoverian administration of the Duke of Argyll and the Earl of Islay, being lord advocate (1725–37) and lord president of the court of session (1737–1747). During this period he carried out sweeping reforms. In the early stages of the 1745 rebellion he succeeded in preserving the loyalty of the Inverness clans towards the British government. However, during the 1746 Jacobite retreat, Prince Charles took Inverness and forced its governor, Loudoun, and Forbes to flee into the highlands, where they wandered as fugitives. After the battle of Culloden (1746) and the end of the Jacobite rebellion he protested against Cumberland's inhumanity towards the Scots.

FORBES, SIR FRANCIS (1784–1841), first chief justice of NSW (1824–36) under the Judicature Act (1823). His position was in some respects anomalous since, as a member of Gov. Brisbane's legislative council, he was involved in political as well as judicial activities and also had the constitutional right and duty to certify that any measure submitted by the governor to the council was not inconsistent with English law.

Forbes's good relations with Brisbane extended into the early part of Sir Ralph Darling's governorship, but they became estranged by Darling's attempt to control the press and over other matters where his 'exclusivist' views conflicted with Forbes's 'emancipist' sympathies. When Bourke became governor (1831) relations improved and even in times of tension the chief justice's critics recognized the quality of his judicial work; he retired in 1836 through ill-health.

FORBES, GEORGE WILLIAM (1869–1947), New Zealand politician and prime minister (1930–5). Forbes was, from 1908, Liberal 'leasehold' backbencher, and rose to leadership of his declining party in 1925. He stepped down for Sir Joseph George Ward, but unexpected electoral advance (1928) and Ward's death (1930) made him prime minister with conditional Labour support. In the deepening Depression, Forbes introduced deflationary measures, breaking with Labour, and virtually forcing the Reform Party into coalition under his continued leadership (1931). Forbes became the symbol of orthodox, unpopular policies, and his 'National' government was heavily defeated in 1935.

FORCE OUVRIÈRE, French trade union movement, formally independent, but in fact closely allied with the Socialist Party. It was formed after a breakaway from the communist-dominated CGT in 1947, and has remained strongly anti-communist. Force ouvrière, which recruits many members among white-collar workers and civil servants, has tended to be the least militant of France's three major trade-union organizations.

FORCED LOANS, financial expedient used periodically from the 15th–18th cents to increase the royal revenues of European monarchs, hard-pressed by the growing cost of administration and war and by the effects of inflation. Such loans produced occasional outbursts of opposition, *eg,* the Frondes in France (1648–9) and the parliamentary Petition of Right (1628) in England.

FORCES FRANÇAISES DE L'INTÉRIEUR, name given early in 1944 to the military forces of the French Resistance. The various clandestine groups which already existed were combined and put under the command of Gen. Koenig. The FFI came into action when the Allies landed in Normandy, and made an important contribution to the liberation of France by acts of sabotage, by guerrilla warfare in mountainous areas, and by acting in support of the regular forces. The liberation of Paris was also under their direction. After the liberation, the FFI were disbanded or absorbed into the regular army.

FORD, HENRY (1863–1947), US automobile industrialist and philanthropist, who built his first 'horseless carriage' in 1896. After making his first racing car, the '999', Ford organized the Ford Motor Co. (1903), which in 1908 produced the first Model T, a dependable, light, sturdy and inexpensive automobile. By 1913, the company had branch plants in 31 American and 14 foreign cities. To meet the steadily increasing demand for cars, mass production methods, including continuous assembly lines, were instituted in 1912. By 1914 Ford's Highland Park plant was turning out over 1200 cars a day. In that same year Ford also introduced the novel $5 minimum wage for an eight-hour day and a profit-sharing plan for his employees. During the First World War the company produced a wide range of equipment for the US government, including gun carriages and Liberty motors for aircraft. Although it survived the 1920–1 post-war crisis, the Ford Co. failed to cater for the changing car market, which was demanding style and speed as well as economy. Its refusal to alter the Model T Ford lost it dominance of the car market under increased competition from other automobile firms, notably General Motors. It achieved a significant recovery, however, with the introduction of the Model A (1927). Although Henry Ford's son, Edsel B. Ford, had assumed the presidency of the Ford Motor Co. in 1919, Henry remained the dominating figure and upon Edsel's death (1943), resumed the presidency and served until he died. Henry Ford also engaged in other diverse activities. During the First World War he was an ardent pacifist, and in 1915 chartered the *Oscar II,* the 'Peace Ship', which took a group of idealists to Scandinavia to try to stop the war by neutral mediation. In 1918 he was an unsuccessful candidate for the US Senate. During the 1920s he engaged in anti-Semitism and in the 1930s took a strong stand against organized labour. In the Second World War he was once again a pacifist. Before his death, he placed most of his estate in the Ford Foundation, which became the richest philanthropic institution of its type in the world.

Allan Nevins and Frank E. Hill, *Ford: the times, the man, the company* (New York, 1954).
Allan Nevins and Frank E. Hill, *Ford: expansion and challenge, 1915–33* (New York, 1957).
Allan Nevins and Frank E. Hill, *Ford, decline and rebirth, 1933–1962* (New York, 1963)   MW

FORD, JOHN (1895–), US film director, mainly identified with 'Westerns' that embodied a blend of legend and realism, as in such films as *Stagecoach* (1939), *My Darling Clementine* (1949), and *The Man Who Shot Liberty Valence* (1962). Among his best-known films was *The Grapes of Wrath* (1940).

FORD OF THE BISCUITS (Aug. 1594), opening engagement of the Tyrone War. Near Enniskillen, Ireland, a small English force was defeated by Hugh O'Donnell and Cormac MacBaron, brother of Hugh O'Neil, later Earl of Tyrone.

FORDE, FRANCIS MICHAEL (1890–), Australian Labor politician, and prime minister for one week (1945). He was a Commonwealth MP (1922–46), minister for customs under Scullin (1929–32), minister for the army (1941–6), and deputy prime minister (1941–5) under Curtin, who had defeated him for the party leadership by one vote in 1935. He was again passed over for Chifley on Curtin's death and became high commissioner in Canada (1946–53). Forde sat also in the Queensland State parliament (1917–22, 1955–7).

FORDNEY–McCUMBER TARIFF (1922) in US, legislation raising the average tariff rates to 38·24 per cent. The act aimed to protect both 'new' industries developed during the First World War and farmers hit by declining prices. It encouraged the growth of monopolies, helped to prevent the payment of European war debts, and provoked tariff reprisals.

FOREIGN LEGION, French military unit for foreigners founded in 1831. Athough stationed in Algeria, it fought in many colonial campaigns elsewhere, and in both World Wars. The legion fought in the Indo–China War of 1947–54, and enhanced its reputation as a tough, elite force. It was involved in the war in Algeria and in the military interventions in politics which the war caused. The legion became based in France after the French withdrawal from Algeria in 1962.

FOREST, JOHN WILLIAM DE (1826–1906), US writer. His first book was a *History of the Indians of Connecticut* (1851). He travelled widely in Europe and the Near East, wrote several travelogues and novels, and returned to the US (1861) to fight in the American Civil War. After the war he commanded a district of the Freedman's Bureau and served until 1868. His novels, particularly *Miss Ravenel's Conversion from Secession to Loyalty* (1867) and *Kate Beaumont* (1872), are early realistic works displaying an acute eye for social detail as well as perceptive characterization.

FOREST, LEE DE (1873–1961), US inventor. Among his most important inventions was the audion tube (1906), which paved the way for the development of broadcasting. He also helped to develop sound films, television, and radio-therapy.

FOREST CANTONS, three cantons, Uri, Schwyz, and Unterwalden, around Lake Lucerne in central Switzerland which were the original core of the Swiss Confederation. They occupied an important position on a major land and water route to the south, approaching the St Gotthard pass. They were either direct Habsburg possessions or subject to Habsburg jurisdiction. The treaty of mutual help signed between them in Aug. 1291 is the first extant record of the beginnings of the Swiss Confederation, which began as a union to resist Habsburg expansion.

FOREST CHARTER. Forest laws in England were introduced by William the Conqueror and extended by Henry I and Henry II. These laws created vast game reserves over which there was a royal monopoly and in which the inhabitants were subject to extremely harsh restrictions of rights and liberties, culminating in the Assize of Woodstock (1184) which set up for the forests a separate court system parallel to the shire courts. The first mitigation of the forest laws were the clauses (44, 47, and 48) of the 1215 version of Magna Carta. These clauses were in 1217 expanded into a separate Charter of the Forest. This removed the heaviest burdens of the forest laws; reduced the area subject to forest laws to that which existed before 1154; and abolished death and mutilation as punishment for breaches of forest law, substituting instead fines, imprisonment, and banishment. The charter also abolished the separate forest jurisdiction. Although substantial part of the country remained under the irksome restrictions of the forest laws, their grossest and most despotic features were removed. The charter marks the beginning of the decline of the forest laws, finally abolished in the 17th cent., though leaving their legacy in later game laws.

FORGOTTEN MAN, THE, sociological concept that became a political slogan in the US during the 1930s. In a radio address of 7 April 1932 during his campaign for the Democratic presidential nomination, Gov. F. D. Roosevelt of New York referred to 'the forgotten man at the bottom of the economic pyramid' and the phrase came to characterize the New Deal's concern for the under-privileged.

FORMULA OF CONCORD (1580), definitive statement of Lutheran theology published in German at Dresden and revised in a Latin edition published at Leipzig in 1584, which restored a broad unity after the bitter controversies between the Gnesiolutherans and the Philippists. It was signed by the Lutheran princes, nobles, and representatives of the cities, and though attacked by a few German Lutherans and by the Calvinists, it remained the basis of the Lutheran churches in the empire and eventually in Scandinavia.

FORNUOVO, BATTLE OF (July 1495), fought between the retreating French forces of Charles VIII and those, mostly Italian, of the League of Venice. Though the French were outnumbered and weary after a long retreat through Italy, the king distinguished himself in the battle and the result was indecisive.

FOROS (Sp. approx. equiv. *fueros*), in colonial Brazil special rights and privileges granted by the Crown to individuals or corporate entities, such as towns or guilds, in return for past or future favours or services. *Foros* included exemption from specific taxes, titles of nobility, and grants of Indian labour and servitude.

FORREST, OF BUNBURY, JOHN FORREST, Baron (1847–1918), Australian explorer and statesman, and son of a Scottish migrant miller. Entering the survey department of WA in 1865, he became its first locally born surveyor-general (1883). He and his brother Alexander Forrest (1849–1901) twice traversed the desert between Western and South Australia (1870, 1874) and opened much new pastoral country. Forrest was WA's first prime minister under responsible government (1890–1901) at a time of expansion following gold discoveries, and he enthusiastically developed the colony's natural resources, using his control of parliament for vigorous legislation, which included large-scale public works, the creation of an industrial arbitration system, and votes for women.

He supported WA's entry into the federated Australian Commonwealth, after some hesitation and against considerable local opposition, after bargaining successfully for special tariff arrangements and a transcontinental railway (completed in 1917). He entered the first Commonwealth cabinet as a protectionist and held various portfolios in most non-Labour cabinets between 1901 and 1918, becoming acting prime minister in 1907. He was an active administrator in both Commonwealth and colonial fields, laying the foundations of Australia's defence system and in his later years giving good service as treasurer. He died en route to London to take his seat in the House of Lords.

FORREST, GEORGE (1873–1932), British botanist and plant collector, who explored in north-west China, Yunnan, and Tibet from 1905 onwards. His collections included hundreds of species, many of them new to science. Some of these are now common garden plants in temperate climates.

FORREST, NATHAN BEDFORD (1821–77), US planter and confederate soldier who, without formal education or military training, became a brilliant cavalry commander in the western theatre of the American Civil War. After returning to Memphis, TN (1865), he became Grand Wizard of the Ku-Klux-Klan, which he disbanded in 1869.

FORRESTAL, JAMES (1892–1949), US businessman who held cabinet office during the Roosevelt and Truman administrations. He was a personal assistant to President Roosevelt (1940), became under-secretary of the navy (1940–4), and supervised the navy's wartime mobilization and expansion. In 1944 he was promoted to secretary. He was a believer in the inevitability of conflict with Russia and a firm advocate of military preparedness. He became secretary of the newly unified department of defence (1947–9).

FORSTER, WILLIAM EDWARD (1818–86), British statesman, with whose name the 1870 Education Act is associated. As vice-president of the council (1868–74) Forster inaugurated a national system of education by directing debates on the Endowed Schools Act (1869) and the Education Act (1870). He found a compromise between voluntary and secular education, but failed (1873) to achieve compulsory elementary education for all. As a parliamentary reformer, he fought for wider franchise (1867, 1884), and piloted the Ballot Act (1872) through the House of Commons. On Gladstone's resignation (1875) the Whig faction supported him for leadership of the Liberal Party, but he gave way to Lord Hartington because of hostility from Chamberlain and others antagonized by his educational policy. As chief secretary for Ireland (1880–2) Forster reluctantly brought in a Coercion Act (1881), but resigned in protest against the Kilmainham treaty. He later opposed Home Rule and supported Imperial Federation. He was the son-in-law of Thomas Arnold and brother-in-law of Matthew Arnold, both 19th-cent. educationists.

FORT ASTORIA, fur-trading post founded in 1810 near the mouth of the Columbia river by John Jacob Astor's Pacific Fur Co. and a group of dissidents from the rival North West Co. During the War of 1812 it was seized by the North West Co. but was returned to Astor in the treaty of Ghent, though run by the Hudson's Bay Co. until they transferred their operations to Fort Vancouver in 1825.

FORT BEAUSÉJOUR, established by the French (1751) in Arcadia, part of which later became New Brunswick. It was renamed Fort Cumberland after its capture by the British (1755). It was abandoned after the War of 1812.

FORT CHAMBLY, or Fort St Louis, Canada, erected by Capt. Pierre de Chambly (1665) as one of a series built on the Richelieu river by the French. The fort was captured by the British (1760) and the Americans (1775).

FORT CHURCHILL, built (1718) on Hudson Bay as a centre for the fur trade. It was rebuilt (1732) by the Hudson's Bay Co. and named Fort Prince of Wales.

FORT CONDE, on the Gulf of Mexico, was originally the French fort of Louis de la Mobile (1711). It was renamed Fort Conde (1720) by order of the Company of the Indies, Under British rule (1763) it was renamed Fort Charlotte).

FORT CUMBERLAND, Canada, originally Fort Beauséjour, built at the head of Cumberland Bay by the French (1751) and captured by the British (1755), who renamed it Fort Cumberland. There was also a Fort Cumberland in Sask., which was the first inland post of the Hudson's Bay Co. (1774), and a Fort Cumberland in MD, built by colonial and British troops (1754–5).

FORT DOUGLAS, Canadian post, built in 1812 and the administrative centre of the Red River settlement (Man.) until 1836. After the Seven Oaks Massacre (1816) it was held by the North West Co. until Lord Selkirk sent a detachment to regain it (1817).

FORT DUQUESNE, built by the French (1754) and captured by the British (1758), was on the strategic site of what is now Pittsburgh.

FORT EDWARD, built (1755) in NY by Gen. Phineas Lyman to control the portage between Lake George and the Hudson river and to defend NY from French attacks. The British occupied the fort on their march to Saratoga during the American War of Independence (1777).

FORT ERIE, Canadian post seized by US forces (3 July 1814) and abandoned (5 Nov. 1814) after a siege by a British force under Gen. Sir Gordon Drummond. Fort Erie was also seized by Irish-American Fenians (31 May 1866), who withdrew when Canadian reinforcements arrived.

FORT ESPÉRANCE, Canadian post built (1787) for the North West Co. on the Qu'Appelle river, near the Assiniboine. It was moved near the Hudson's Bay Co.'s Fort Qu'Appelle in 1814 when the Métis, led by Cuthbert Grant, looted on their way to the Seven Oaks Massacre (1816).

FORT GARRY, built (1817–22) on the site of the old Fort Gibraltar. It was owned and operated by the Hudson's Bay Co. and named after Nicholas Garry, a deputy governor of the company. The present city of Winnipeg, Man. is on the site of the fort.

FORT GEORGE, military post on the Niagara river, Ont. During the War of 1812 it was captured by the Americans (1813), reoccupied seven months later, and garrisoned by the British until 1845.

FORT GIBRALTAR, built (1809–10) as a fur-trading post by the North West Co. on the junction of the Red and Assiniboine rivers. It was seized by the Hudson's Bay Co. (1816) and destroyed. Fort Garry was later built on its site.

FORT GOOD HOPE, first European settlement in the Connecticut valley of America. Founded by the Dutch (1633), it was seized by English settlers (1653).

FORT HAMILTON, built (1791) on the Miami river, north of Cincinnati, OH, US, by Gen. Arthur St Clair as a part of his unsuccessful campaign against the Indians of the Northwest Territory. It was the first in a line of forts between Fort Washington (Cincinnati) and the Maumee valley. The town of Hamilton was established here by Israel Ludlow (1795).

FORT HARE UNIVERSITY COLLEGE, founded (1916) in the Eastern Cape, as a multi-racial college. In 1959 entry was restricted to the Xhosa people. Many African political leaders were educated there.

FORT HENRY, built on the site of Wheeling, US (1774), and named (1776) after Patrick Henry. The fort was attacked by Indians (10 Sept. 1782) in the last battle of the War of American Independence. Fort Henry was also the name of a Confederate post on the Tennessee river captured by Gen. U. S. Grant (6 Feb. 1862) in the American Civil War.

FORT JESUS, built by the Portuguese in 1593, was lost in 1631 to the Mazrui leaders of Mombasa. In 1632 it was recovered and taken by Omani Arabs after a siege of two years and nine months (1696–8). In the 18th–19th cents it was used as barracks for Omani and Baluchi soldiers, and in 1958 was restored as national monument and museum.

FORT, MAUREPAS, located on Biloxi Bay, the first French settlement in LA. It was founded by Iberville in 1699.

FORT MIMS, MASSACRE OF (30 Aug. 1813), occurred on the lower Alabama river of the US, when a band of about 1,000 Upper Creeks attacked a makeshift fort in which the 'progressive' branch of the Upper Creeks had sought shelter. A number of whites were also killed and the attack provided cause for an American campaign against the Indians.

FORT NIAGARA, originally established by the French (1726) on the east bank of the Niagara river. It was captured by the British (1759) and although within the area ceded to the US (1783) was not actually surrendered until 1796 (Jay's treaty).

FORT ORLEANS, built (1723) in western MO, US, in an attempt to win the trade of western Indians and to undercut Spanish influence. Outbreaks of hostilities by the Natchez and Fox Indians east of the Mississippi forced the French to abandon the fort and their plans for a trading empire on the Great Plains.

FORT OSWEGO, North American post built by the British (1727). Owing to its important position on Lake Ontario it was contested by the French and British. Pontiac signed a peace treaty with Britain there (1766).

FORT ST DAVID, near Cuddalore on the east Indian coast, about 100 miles (161 kms) south of Madras. Originally built by a Hindu, it was sold by the Marathas to the East India Co. in 1690. Its territory was fixed by a 'random shott of a great gun', the villages thus included being called 'cannonball villages'. It withstood a French attack in 1746 after the fall of Madras. In 1756 Clive became its governor with reversion of Madras. In 1758 it was taken by the French general Lally, but abandoned when Pondicherry was attacked, and taken again by De Bussy (1782), but restored (1785). With the establishment of British supremacy in south India it was abandoned and later lay in ruins.

FORT ST GEORGE, the citadel of Madras. The East India Co. settlement at Masulipatam on the east Indian coast was moved to Madras in 1639 on account both of the unfriendliness of the kings of Golkonda and its distance from the weaving centres from which the company obtained its goods. Permission to build a fort was given by the Raja of Chandragiri, who ruled the remnant of the Vijayanagar empire. Madras passed successively under the suzerainty of Golkonda and the Mughals. It became the company's headquarters from 1641. Though sometimes threatened, it was not captured until 1746, when the French, under La Bourdonnais, seized it. On its restoration to the company (1748) the fort was practically rebuilt and this enabled Lord Pigot to resist another French attack under Lally (1758–9). It was threatened by Haidar Ali (1769, 1780) and afterwards largely rebuilt, to become the centre of the British South Indian administration.

FORT ST JOSEPH, military post and mission near present Niles, MI, US, founded by the French (c. 1700) and transferred to the British (1763). During Pontiac's Rebellion, the British garrison was massacred by Pottawattamie Indians (1763). The fort was seized by Spanish forces (1781) and passed to American control under the treaty of Paris (1783).

FORT SEVERN, fur-trading post, originally called Fort Churchill, built by the Hudson's Bay Co. (1685), near the mouth of the Severn river, Canada. In 1690 it was evacuated and burnt. The French built Fort Phélipeaux on the ruins (1699). The Hudson's Bay Co. returned to the site and built Fort Severn (1756).

FORT SUMTER, in the US, fortified island at the mouth of Charleston harbour, SC, and scene of the opening engagement of the American Civil War (12–13 April 1861). When the Union commander, Maj. Robert Anderson, refused to surrender to SC forces, the fort was bombarded and taken.

FORT TICONDEROGA, originally known as Fort Carrillon, was built by the French (1755) on a strategic promontory at the southern end of Lake Champlain. During the French and Indian War it was successfully defended by Montcalm (1758) against a superior force led by Abercrombie, but was later (1759) captured from the French by Amherst, when the British gave it the Indian name Ticonderoga. After being taken by American forces (1775) under the joint command of Benedict Arnold and Ethan Allen, the fort's heavy artillery was transported to Boston, where it played a vital role in forcing the British evacuation. The fort was surrendered to the British without a fight (1777) by Arthur St Clair. Fort Ticonderoga was ceded by Britain to the US (1783), since when it has been restored as a museum.

FORT VICTORIA, originally a Canadian fur-trading post and fort of the Hudson's Bay Co., now Victoria, capital of BC.

FORT WAYNE, TREATY OF (1809), US agreement with Indians of the North-west Territory by which 2½ million acres (10,100 sq. kms) of the present state of Indiana was purchased for $7000 in cash and a $1750 annuity. The Indian leader, Tecumseh, protested against the treaty and fostered a revolt in an attempt to regain the lost lands.

FORT WELLINGTON, British military post built at the outbreak of the War of 1812 at Prescott, Ont., as a main defence between Kingston and Montreal. It remained garrisoned until 1826.

FORT WILLIAM, headquarters of the Canadian North West Co. (1805), named after William McGillivray, director of the company. With the completion of the Canadian Pacific Railway (1882) it became a port for shipping grain brought from the western part of Canada.

FORT WILLIAM, the citadel of Calcutta. The first fort was built (1696–1702) with the Nawab of Bengal's permission, for security reasons, and named after King William III of Britain. In 1707 it became the centre of a separate presidency. In 1756 the fort was taken by Siraj-ud-daulah, Nawab of Bengal, and was the scene of the incident of the Black Hole. On the recovery of Calcutta the old fort was demolished and replaced by the present one on a site further south, with an unobstructed field of fire. The clearing of the surrounding jungle provided the site for the present *maidan*. The new fort was completed in 1773.

FORTESCUE, SIR JOHN (d. *c.* 1478), chief justice of England (1442–60). His treatises, written during exile in France (1461–71), though unoriginal in thought, have to be used for lack of better evidence, as a major source for the study of the 15th-cent. constitution and law.

FORTIFICATIONS. In the Dark Ages progress in the development of military architecture was almost entirely confined to the Byzantine empire, but from the 10th cent. onwards there was a rapid development in western Europe. With the growth of feudalism in France there was a spread of private fortresses, whilst the elaborate Viking ring-works of Trelleborg and Fyrkat in Denmark show that there were developments in Scandinavia as well. From the 10th to the latter half of the 12th cent. the normal castle type was either a free-standing stone tower (keep or donjon) with an appended courtyard (bailey) defended by an earthwork or palisade, or a timber or stone tower on an artificial mound (motte) with or without a bailey. The keep was either a rectangular, circular, or shell structure and normally housed the castellan's private apartments, while the bailey housed the garrison, stabling, and stores. From the latter half of the 12th cent.

the use of elaborate siege techniques, and to a lesser extent experience in building powerful fortresses in the Levant, saw the increasing use of a multiplicity of defence works. The keep is often dispensed with and replaced by an elaborately defended gatehouse, whilst the castle conforms to a 'concentric' type of plan with a series of baileys defended by towers providing enfilading fire along the walls. The apogee of medieval techniques of fortification was reached in the powerful fortresses founded by Edward I in Wales. Town defences were similarly improved. It is impossible to generalize about medieval fortifications since they vary so much in type. Simple ring-works with a timber gate-tower sufficed in many cases until the early 13th cent., whilst mottes were still built as late as the 1270s. In mountainous countries the castle merely consisted of a single tower perched on an inaccessible crag. From the latter half of the 14th cent. there is a sharp break between military and domestic architecture. The development of artillery made castles obsolete, although some castles and town defences, *eg*, Southampton, sport early gun-ports. From then on really effective fortification almost entirely becomes a state prerogative.

                                                                    JD

FORTUNATE ISLANDS (or Isles of the Blest), mentioned by Hesiod, Pindar, Plutarch, and Ptolemy. Greek mythology endowed these islands with perpetual summer and a population of immortals, and places them in the western ocean. They may thus be compared with Homer's island of the Phaeacians, Plato's Atlantis, the Welsh Avalon, the Cornish Lyonnesse, etc., and have been associated by some with Madeira and the Canary Islands.

'FORTY ACRES AND A MULE', phrase prevalent among US Negroes in the South (1865). It expressed their hope that the Freedmen's Bureau would, out of confiscated plantation lands, provide each Negro family with a small farm.

FORTY MARTYRS, used with reference to 40 Christian soldiers martyred at Sebaste (*c.* 320). In 1961 the same term was applied to 40 men and women who were executed by King Henry VIII of England, and who formed the remnant of a list of some 350 martyrs of the English Reformation proposed for canonization by Cardinal Manning in 1874.

FORTY SHILLING FREEHOLDER in England, category of small landowners who qualified for the right to exercise parliamentary franchise in the English counties from 1430 onwards. Their significance disappeared in the 19th-cent. political reform measures.

FORTY TWO ARTICLES (1553) in England, formulary of faith drawn up for the Church of England by Abp Cranmer and a committee of six, including John Knox, in the last phase of the Edwardian Reformation, to supplement the Protestant Prayer Book of 1552. The Articles form the basis of the Thirty Nine Articles, which were issued in 1563 and form the creed of the modern Church of England.

Several of the Forty Two Articles were borrowed directly from the Augsburg Confession. Many of them were specifically directed against the Anabaptists and a few exclusively against the Catholics, *eg*, Roman primacy and the doctrines of purgatory and transubstantiation were rejected. Article 17 on predestination is Pauline and Augustinian but not Calvinist. Indeed, the general tenor is a compromise between the Lutheran and Zwinglian creeds.

FORTY-NINERS, name given to those who trekked west to the CA goldfields of the US (1849). After President Polk's enthusiastic report to Congress (5 Dec. 1848) of the discovery of gold in the Sacramento valley, an estimated 80,000 gold seekers went to CA during 1849. Perhaps 25,000 travelled by sea via Cape Horn or Panama and probably

55,000 by land, mostly along the Central Overland Route through South Pass.

FORTY-SEVEN *RŌNINS*, heroes of a famous episode in Japanese history (1701–3). The story of their loyalty has been re-enacted on stage and screen on countless occasions. Led by Oishi Yoshio (Kuranosuke), these 47 *samurai* accepted humiliation in the cause of avenging their lord after he had been ordered to commit *harakiri* for wounding a *bakufu* official who had insulted him. Then, when they had surprised and killed their lord's enemy, they gave themselves up. The question of their punishment created great difficulties for the *bakufu*, which needed to preserve its authority, but at the same time wished to encourage such older values. Eventually it was decided that the 47 *rōnin*s should commit *harakiri*. They all complied and, together with their ex-*daimyō*, were buried in the Sengakuji temple.

FOSCARI, FRANCESCO, Doge of Venice (1423–57), leader of the war party favouring an unprecedented policy of unlimited Venetian expansion on the mainland. In 1425 he brought about alliance with Florence, beginning 30 years of intermittent warfare against Milan, as his predecessor had forecast. He gave Venice a territorial state, but left it hated and distrusted by all other Italian powers. Eventually accusations of corruption against his son and of general war-weariness led to his deposition.

FOSDICK, HARRY EMERSON (1878–), US Baptist minister and theologian, professor of practical theology at Union Theological Seminary, New York (1915–46), and first pastor of Riverside Church (1930–46). He used both the pulpit and the radio to project his concern for individual and social problems and was widely influential. Among his numerous books are *Christianity and Progress* (1922) and an autobiography, *The Living of These Days* (1956).

FOSTER, STEPHEN COLLINS (1826–64), US songwriter, whose ditties, mostly written for Negro minstrels, enjoyed enormous popularity throughout the US and Britain. They include 'The Old Folks at Home' (1851) and 'My Old Kentucky Home' (1853).

FOSTER, WILLIAM ZEBULON (1881–1961), US communist leader, who joined the Socialist Party in 1900, affiliated it with the syndicalist IWW, and helped to organize the steel strike of 1919. Following the establishment of the US Communist Party (1919), he ran three times as its presidential candidate, (1924, 1928, 1932), but was then ousted from the party leadership by Earl Browder. Foster was again national Communist Party leader (1945–8).

FOUAGES, French direct taxes using houses as units of assessment (from *feu allumant*—fireplace), it being assumed that each house comprised one family. Occasional taxes assessed in this way were imposed under Philip IV after 1294. They became a regular annual tax only under Charles V (1364–80), when they were subject to periodic reassessments. From the reign of his son, Charles VI, they were based on a fixed assessment. Each province was henceforth allotted a fixed quota, roughly equivalent to its economic means (*eg*, Languedoc paid one-tenth of the total of each direct tax). These provincial quotas were redistributed among individual localities in a similar fixed manner. *Fouages* were thus transformed into a *taille*, which became an annually levied royal tax from the 1430s onwards.

FOUCAULT, NICHOLAS-JOSEPH (1643–1721), French financier, who was successively *avocat-général* and *maître des requêtes* in the *grand conseil*, and *intendant* of the *généralités* of Montauban, Pau, Poitou, and Caen. He was a sound administrator, a patron of letters, and encouraged public works. He was made a councillor of state by Louis XIV.

FOUCHÉ, JOSEPH, Duc d'Otranto (1759–1820), French politician, who was largely responsible for Napoleon's peaceful control of France. Despite his early years in the Church, Fouché developed into both a Jacobin and an atheist (1793). He won notoriety by his use of terror in suppressing the revolt in Lyons, but was denounced by Robespierre because of his atheism. One of the leaders of the *Thermidor coup d'état*, Fouché became minister of police under the Directory (1799). Having helped Napoleon to power, he continued in this post till his dismissal (1810). Although an effective police chief, he soon lost confidence in Napoleon's capacity to survive. Like Talleyrand, he played a devious game at the time of Napoleon's abdication and the Hundred Days. Although he retained the confidence of Louis XVIII, he was too suspect for the majority of royalists and retired to Prague (1816).

FOUCHET PLAN, proposals suggested by De Gaulle after the Second World War for a confederate Europe of States. The plan was put to the European parliament by Christian Fouchet, French minister of education, but did not win enough support, no doubt because it seemed to undercut the supranational structure of the European communities and to establish a French hegemony. The plan was abandoned in 1962, but in an attenuated form it inspired the Franco–German treaty (1963).

FOUL RAID, THE (1417), unsuccessful attempt by the Scots, led by the Duke of Albany and the Earl of Douglas, to capture Roxburgh and Berwick, profiting from the absence of King Henry V in France.

FOUNDLING HOSPITAL in London, established in 1745 by the philanthropist Capt. Thomas Coram (1668–1751) to care for abandoned children. It benefited from the generosity of many leading artists, *eg*, Handel and Hogarth.

FOUQUET, NICOLAS, Vicomte de Melun et de Vaux (1615–80), French politician, protégé of Mazarin, and superintendent of finances during the early part of Louis XIV's reign (1653–61). Fouquet was noted for his ambition, corruption, and the confused state in which he left French finances. He had acquired a fortune during Mazarin's ministry, symbolized by his magnificent château at Vaux-le-Vicomte, designed by Le Vau and decorated by Le Brun in the baroque style, which provided a model for Versailles. His manipulation of the revenue system endeared him to the tax farmers and tax collectors, who acquired some 50 million livres while he was in office. After his arrest on the king's orders in 1661, his successor, Colbert, found that the expected revenue for 1662 and part of 1663 had already been spent in advance. Fouquet was sentenced (1664) to life-long detention at Pignerol.

FOUQUIER-TINVILLE, ANTOINE QUENTIN (1746–95), French public prosecutor before the Revolutionary Tribunal during the Terror. He was himself executed after the fall of the Jacobins.

FOUR DAYS' BATTLE, THE (June 1666), naval engagement in the Anglo–Dutch Wars between a British fleet of 60 ships under the Duke of Albemarle and a Dutch fleet of 90 under Van Tromp and De Ruyter. The action lasted four days, and despite late reinforcements from Prince Rupert Albemarle lost 20 ships and suffered heavy casualties.

FOUR FREEDOMS, THE, in US. Declaration by President F. D. Roosevelt of US of objectives in a message to Congress (6 Jan. 1941), advocating support of the Lend Lease bill during the Second World War. He listed freedom of speech and expression, freedom of worship, freedom from want, and freedom from fear as the essential human freedoms for which all men should strive.

FOUR HUNDRED, REVOLUTION OF (411 BC), temporary overthrow of democracy in Athens during the great Peloponnesian War, following defeat in Sicily and widespread rebellion among Athens' allies aided by Sparta and Persia. Dissatisfaction with the conduct of the war was already manifest, when Alcibiades promised Persian help if oligarchy were established; a constitutional commission was set up and the *graphê paranomon* suspended. Persuaded by a mixture of terrorism and patriotic calls to duty, the assembly (*ecclesia*) suspended itself and replaced the council of 500 (*boule*) with the Four Hundred. With Alcibiades' pledge unfulfilled and the fleet at Samos unsympathetic, the oligarchs failed to produce the promised list of 5000 enfranchised citizens and were compromised by violence, by negotiations with Sparta, and by losing Euboea. The moderate Theramenes broke with the extremists and democracy re-emerged in two stages in 411 and 410.

FOUR POINTS, document drafted during the Crimean War by France and Austria, without Britain, in July 1854, which stated that peace between Russia and Turkey depended on the replacement of the Russian protectorate over the Principalities by a European guarantee; freedom of navigation on the Danube; the revision of the Straits convention (1841) in the interests of the balance of power in Europe; and a five-power guarantee of religious freedom for the Christian subjects of Turkey in place of a Russian one. Russia in fact withdrew from the Principalities in Aug. 1854, and had conceded the 4th Point, in principle, in Aug. 1853. The four Points, and above all the interpretation of the third, dominated the diplomacy of the war. More closely defined, they formed the basis of the treaty of Paris (1856).

FOURAH BAY COLLEGE, first seat of a Western type of university education in black Africa. Established in 1827 by the Church Missionary Society as Fourah Bay Institution with four students, including Samuel Ajayi Crowther (later bishop), it was essentially a clergy-producing institution, until 1876, when it became affiliated to Durham University. From that date to the end of the Second World War, and in spite of vicissitudes, Fourah Bay College supplied graduates to the Church, the civil service, and secondary grammar schools throughout former British West Africa. Unaided by the Sierra Leone government until 1949, the institution concentrated on the Humanities until 1928, when science was introduced, but began to grow markedly in the 1950s, becoming a university college by Royal Charter in 1960. By 1965 the student population had grown to 600 and in 1967 Fourah Bay became a university.

FOURIER, CHARLES (1772–1837), French philosopher, economist, and utopian socialist. He proposed to eliminate class conflicts by abolishing the central government and organizing production through small self-sufficient communities—'phalanstères'—where land, buildings, natural resources, and machines were held in common.

FOURQUEVAUX, RAYMOND DE (1508–74), French military analyst, whose *Instructions sur le Faict de la Guerre* (1548) was widely read and throws considerable light on military techniques of the 16th cent. His book was written largely for the guidance of the legions which made up the regular infantry corps. He revealed the weakness of employing mercenaries, *eg*, at Pavia, and forecast the static nature of siege warfare. He warned of the wastefulness of giving the arquebus to unskilled soldiers, but underestimated the use of artillery.

FOURTEEN POINTS, THE, US President Woodrow Wilson's statement of the principles that should underlie the peace settlement at the end of the First World War. Presented in a message to Congress (8 Jan. 1918), they included 'open covenants openly arrived at', freedom of navigation on the high seas, the lowering of tariff barriers and the reduction of armaments, application of the principle of national self-determination to both European and colonial settlements, and the establishment of a general association of nations to guarantee the political independence and territorial integrity of all states. In subsequent speeches Wilson expanded and clarified his 14 points to a total of 23, and they aroused tremendous enthusiasm throughout the world. The 'fourteen points' were accepted by Germany as the basis for an armistice, but the reservations of the Allied powers and their insistence on reparations meant that negotiations at the Paris Peace Conference differed radically from Wilson's expectations, and the treaty of Versailles that emerged embodied traditional policies rather than the new order of Wilson's hopes.

FOURTH PARTY in Britain originated in the attempt by four friends, A. J. Balfour, Lord Randolph Churchill, J. E. Gorst, and Sir H. D. Wolff, to embarrass Gladstone's second administration during the Bradlaugh dispute of 1880. The 'Fourth Party' eventually became a campaign against the unimaginative Tory leadership of Northcote and the 'Old Gang' in the House of Commons. The four members displayed an irresponsibility which lightened the atmosphere but lowered the tone of politics. In 1883–4 Churchill courageously mobilized the party's provincial machine in an attempt to secure 'Tory Democracy', *ie*, to extend middle-class influence in a predominantly aristocratic party. When Churchill became chancellor of the exchequer in 1886 it became clear that his brand of Tory Democracy had nothing new to offer as a benefit to Tory working men.

FOX, CHARLES JAMES (1749–1806), British statesman, orator, and champion of civil and religious liberties. Elected MP for Midhurst at 19, Fox soon held minor offices, but by 1774 was in opposition, attacking North's American policies. He supported the petitioning movement for parliamentary reform (1779–80) and in parliament, with his friend Burke and the other supporters of Rockingham, demanded economical reforms. Fox, who after 1780 represented the 'popular' constituency of Westminster, believed in a constitution where 'monarchy, aristocracy, and democracy were mutually blended and united'.

As foreign secretary in Rockingham's ministry (1782), Fox clashed with Shelburne over the American peace negotiations, resigning when Shelburne became prime minister after Rockingham's death. Fox had, however, helped to establish Grattan's parliament, believing that in Ireland, as in America, and, later, in France, government should be founded on popular consent. The Fox–North coalition (1783), formed after Shelburne's fall, was widely regarded as an unnatural, frivolously opportunist arrangement. George III, who found Fox repulsive on political, moral, and personal grounds, used the outcry over his India Bill to destroy the ministry and install Pitt in office (Dec. 1783). At the March 1784 election, over 100 of Fox's 'Martyrs' were unseated, and Pitt's ascendancy began.

Fox's opposition to the ministry was brilliant but unavailing. His support of the Prince of Wales's Regency claims (1788–9) again made him seem factious and inconsistent. With Burke and Sheridan, he promoted the unsuccessful impeachment of Warren Hastings; but the outbreak of the French Revolution, which delighted Fox, later caused a breach between him and both Burke and the Portland Whigs. Fox's Libel Act (1792), a liberalizing measure, allowed juries to bring in general verdicts in libel cases. After 1793 Fox incurred unpopularity by opposing the French war and Pitt's repressive domestic measures, and in 1797 he and his followers virtually withdrew from parliament for several years. George III vetoed Fox's return to office (1804), but he joined Grenville's 'ministry of all the talents' (1806). The slave trade was abolished, but Fox was unable to conclude an honourable peace with Napoleon or to carry Catholic emancipation.

Fox's 'negligent grandeur' made him a faulty tactician,

insensitive to public opinion and lacking in single-mindedness. His three spells at the foreign office lasted less than a year altogether. Yet his lucid parliamentary exposition helped to transmute faction into party, and 19th-cent. Whigs were imbued with his principles. His warmth, courage, and eloquence in noble causes captivated his contemporaries.

J. L. Hammond, *Charles James Fox, a political study* (London, 1903).
MRB

FOX, GEORGE (1624–91), English religious leader of the Puritan revolution and founder of the Quaker movement. At first scarcely distinguishable from the mass of self-appointed prophets, known as 'Seekers', who emerged in the religious ferment of the Civil War period, he matured as a religious leader and organizer. He gave to the movement a stability which ensured its survival to the present day.

Finding it impossible to get spiritual nourishment from orthodox Anglican worship Fox gave up attending church (1646) and began to read the Bible in the fields and orchards round his home. By 1647 he was an evangelist and quickly attracted a following among the Seekers, calling themselves the Friends of Truth.

Like the Anabaptists, the Friends abhorred external forms of religion, recognized no higher obedience than to the 'inner light' and refused to recognize the authority of magistrate or minister. They thus constituted a collective protest against the presbyterian system which some sought to impose in England, but their attempted union with the Baptists broke down when the Friends baulked at baptism with water.

Obedience to the inner spirit naturally gave scope for the development of individual eccentricities, such as Fox's refusal to take off his hat to anyone and his interruption of church services as the spirit moved him, and although he never went to the extremes of some enthusiasts and fanatics, such as James Naylor, or indulged in body-shaking manifestations of the agitation of the spirit, he was several times involved in public brawls. The nickname 'Quaker' was coined by a magistrate in 1650 after one such brawl. Under the influence of his wife, Margaret, Fox developed the political and organizational sense which gave the movement its enduring character. The Quakers' registration of births, marriages, and deaths anticipated the national system by a century and a half.

George Fox, *A Journal*, ed. J. L. Nickalls (London, 1952).
HNBM

FOX, SIR WILLIAM (1812–93), NZ politician and four times prime minister of NZ, but more noted as an opposition leader. He emigrated from England in 1842 and became principal agent of the NZ Co. following William Wakefield's death. Both in England and NZ, he took part in the campaign for a constitution for the colony. A pronounced provincialist, he initiated the 'compact of 1856', giving the provinces greater revenue. In opposition a powerful advocate of conciliatory policies towards the Maoris, in office (thrice in the early 1860s) he accepted responsibility from Britain for native affairs. Fox failed to promote his views, yielding as prime minister to stronger colleagues who advocated confiscation of Maori lands (1863), thereby increasing Maori resistance. His 1869–72 ministry covered a watershed in NZ history: the wars died away and Vogel's development policies were started. Fox only supervised these changes, and did not hold office after 1873, quitting politics in 1881. Turning his attention to social issues, particularly prohibition, he helped to found the prohibitionist NZ Alliance (1886). He was commissioner on west coast Maori lands (1880–4).

FOX, WILLIAM JOHNSON (1786–1864), British Unitarian preacher, journalist, and politician, whose chapel at South Place became from 1824 an important centre of radicalism and free religious enquiry for London intellectuals and nonconformists. He was prominent Anti-Corn Law League orator and radical MP for Oldham (1847–63).

FOX INDIANS, American tribe, first discovered by French explorers along Lake Winnebago and the Fox river in WI. They were the only Algonquian tribe to wage war on the French, who aided their enemies, the Chippewa. The Fox were nearly annihilated in a battle with the Chippewa (*c.* 1780) and the remnant incorporated with the Sauk Indians. With the Sauk, they signed the first of a series of treaties ceding their lands (1804). Under Chief Black Hawk the Sauk and Fox attempted to regain lands in WI and IL, but were defeated by the US army and state militia forces (1832). The Sauk and Fox signed a treaty with the US government (1842) and took up lands in KS (1845). After being transferred to the Indian Territory (1869), they were given land allotments when that Territory was liquidated (1906).

FOXE (or FOX), LUKE (1586–1635), 'North-West Fox', English navigator sent to find the North-west Passage (1631). He met Thomas James on a similar mission and together they charted parts of the western coast of Hudson Bay. Then he partially explored Foxe Channel.

FRANCE IN NORTH AFRICA. French military and political presence in the Maghrib began on 14 June 1830, when a French expeditionary force of 37,000 landed at Algiers and imposed on Dey Husain an act of capitulation signed on 5 July. Later, Algerian resistance to French occupation of the country, associated especially with the Amir Abd al-Kader, lasted sporadically for the next four decades, but was substantially quenched by the beginning of the Third French Republic, whose governments treated Algeria even more emphatically as a 'colony for settlement' than the Second Empire had done.

Extension of French control to Tunisia began in 1881, when two military expeditions overran the country without opposition, Bey Muhammad al-Sadiq accepting capitulation on 12 May of that year. With the collapse of the Sharifian empire of Morocco some 20 years later, French direct control took shape in 1908–9 after France had secured, in 1904, British and Italian acceptance of her claimed preponderance in Morocco. A French protectorate was formally established in 1912, Spain retaining her zone of occupation in the north and Tangier acquiring by international agreement an 'open regime' formally confirmed in 1923. French occupation was from the first marked by the strongly imperialist zeal and effectiveness of Marshal Lyautey, who put down successive risings and printed French influence deeply into the administrative life of the country. Morocco and Tunisia regained their political independence in 1956, and Algeria in 1962.

FRANCE, UNIVERSITY OF, operative from 1808, was a hierarchical organization, under close imperial control, which directed all French secondary education. Its five faculties (theology, law, medicine, science, literature) functioned through Academies—one to every appeal court area.

FRANC-FIEF (tax of). Acquisition of noble land by non-nobles was prohibited in France by King Louis IX. But it was impossible to enforce this prohibition effectively and under his successor, Philip III, the practice developed of carrying out periodic enquiries into its breaches. By the late 15th cent. it was customary to hold such enquiries every 30 years and to exact from the non-noble holders of noble land fines levied according to a fixed tariff (the tax of franc-fief). These enquiries provided one of the occasions for investigating unjustified claims to noble status. This was one of the reasons why, under Louis XI, the citizens of several important towns sought and gained exemptions from this tax, as did some privileged provinces, *eg*, Normandy.

FRANCHET D'ESPEREY, LOUIS (1856–1942), French marshal of the First World War. He held various commands on the western front, but his main independent achievement was the offensive launched from Salonica which led to the capitulation of Bulgaria (1918).

FRANCIA, JOSÉ GASPAR RODRÍGUEZ DE ('El Supremo') (1766–1840), dictator of Paraguay (1814–40). He was a leader of the independence movement in Asunción and assumed dictatorial powers for life soon after the expulsion of the Spaniards. His regime was based on repression and on the supervision of all facets of daily life. He was noted for his anti-clericalism, and during his long regime the Roman Catholic Church was excluded from the country. He feared rivalry and as a result members of the upper classes suffered, many being executed. Francia also dreaded foreign interference and under his rule the land-locked Paraguayan nation found itself cut off from the outside world. Few foreigners were allowed to visit the country and those who were admitted were mostly technicians hired to start industries which would make the nation more self-sufficient. For the same reason Francia fostered the growing of agricultural staples and the development of cottage industries.

He believed that the Indian and *mestizo* majorities of Paraguay were not ready for self-government or a democratic system, and should be ruled accordingly until in the distant future they reached political maturity.

FRANCIABIGIO (FRANCESCO DI CHRISTOFANO) (1482–1525), Italian painter who settled in Florence, and specialized in portraiture. His works included 'The Bath of Bathsheba' (1523) and a series of frescoes on which he worked in conjunction with Andrea del Sarto.

FRANCIS, Duke of Brittany (1435–88), succeeded his uncle, Arthur III, in 1458. He wanted to preserve Breton unity against French threats, and to achieve this joined the League of the Public Weal against Louis XI. Subsequently, in 1467, he invaded Normandy on behalf of Louis' brother, Charles, who had been dispossessed. He then made an alliance with Edward IV of England but in 1468 they were forced to sign a treaty with Louis at Ancenis. Seven years later he and Edward again attempted to defy Louis, but were brought to terms. Throughout his reign, Francis had internal quarrels with his nobility. His daughter Anne was betrothed to the elder son of Edward IV—one of the Princes in the Tower—in 1481, but no marriage took place. Instead, she succeeded her father and married two French kings in succession, Charles VIII and Louis XII, linking Brittany and France, while preserving Breton traditions.

FRANCIS I (1708–65), Emperor (*reg.* 1745–65), Francis Stephen, Duke of Lorraine and Bar and great-nephew of Louis XIV of France, who married Maria Theresa, daughter of the Emperor Charles VI (12 Feb. 1736). He was the father of the Emperors Joseph II and Leopold II and Queen Marie Antoinette of France. After Austria's defeat in the War of the Polish Succession his duchy of Lorraine was relinquished to Stanislas Lesczynski and he received the grand duchy of Tuscany instead (1738). Francis was elected emperor after the death of Charles Albert, who had been the anti-Austrian candidate in 1740.

FRANCIS II (1768–1835), last Holy Roman Emperor of Germany (1792) and, as Francis I, first Austrian Emperor (1804). His accession (1792) marked not only the beginning of Austria's long struggle against Revolutionary and Napoleonic France, but also the end of the enlightened policies in Austria of his father, Leopold II, and uncle, Joseph II. Presided over by an unimaginative , although not philistine, bureaucratic emperor, Austria became a police state and remained so throughout his reign. After repeated military defeats by France he took the title of Emperor of Austria (1804), emulating Napoleon and trying to bind his diverse territories together. He knew the Holy Roman empire was finished and there was little regret when he was forced to relinquish his imperial title (1806). From 1809 Austrian foreign policy was in Metternich's hands and his advice led to the marriage of Francis's daughter, Marie Louise, to Napoleon (1810). Although Metternich was supported in imposing his system on Europe after 1815, Francis maintained his own reactionary domestic policy.

FRANCIS JOSEPH (1830–1916), Austrian Emperor and King of Hungary (*reg.* 1848–1916), who kept the Habsburg monarchy alive for nearly 70 years, but failed to prevent its final collapse. He was made emperor by the Austrian generals, who put down the revolutionary and nationalist movements and who had forced his uncle Ferdinand to abdicate. His main purpose was to see the dynasty survive by any expedient. His faith in the value of dynastic monarchy was not shaken by a succession of domestic tragedies—the suicide of his son (1889), the murder of his wife (1898), and the morganatic marriage of his nephew and heir (1900). His first years as emperor saw the expulsion of Austrian influence from Italy (1859) and Germany (1866), which made him determined to renounce foreign adventures abroad and to depend on the alliance with Germany (1879) to provide external security, although he was prepared for expansion in the Balkans—a cause of the First World War (1914).

After twenty years of absolute and centralizing government, after the suppression of the 1848–9 revolutions, he was forced to make the *Ausgleich* with the Hungarians and become king of a semi-independent Hungary (1867). Although the Hungarian problem was largely solved, the rest of Francis Joseph's life was spent facing the demands of the other nationalities within the monarchy, especially the Czechs and South Slavs, for autonomy, as well as increasing pressure from all quarters for democratization. A series of liberal ministries from the German middle class was accepted reluctantly by the emperor in Austria (1867–79), but the real power still lay with his military and aristocratic advisers. In 1879 he dismissed the liberals, preferring to depend on his conservative friend Taaffe who, as prime minister, ruled through a coalition of conservative Catholics, Poles, and Czechs, who were given minor concessions. Although dropping Taaffe (1893) for suggesting the introduction of universal suffrage, Francis Joseph adopted it (1906) after struggling with a series of stop-gap ministries, which had been unable to placate the Czechs or deal with the growth of the mass parties of the Christian Socialists and Social Democrats. Two years after his death Austrian defeat in the First World War provided a partial solution to the problems he had faced unsuccessfully.

C. A. Macartney, *The Habsburg Empire, 1790–1918* (London 1968).   DMCK

FRANCIS I (1494–1547), King of France (*reg.* 1515–47). He was Count of Angoulême and Duke of Valois, and married Claude, daughter of Louis XII. He succeeded to the throne on the latter's death. Francis was the model of the chivalrous knight and sportsman who relied on his powerful personality rather than on the attributes of an administrator in the continuing process of establishing royal absolutism.

The dominant feature of his reign was his rivalry with the Emperor Charles V. Although Italy was the primary area of dispute, the possession of Burgundy, Flanders, Artois, Alsace, Lorraine, and Navarre were also sources of friction. The rivalry led to a series of wars (1521–6, 1528–9, 1536–8, 1542–4) interspersed with uneasy truces, eg, Nice (1538), ineffective meetings, eg, Aigues Mortes (1538), and temporary agreements, eg, Noyon (1516), Madrid (1526), and Cambrai (1529). In 1515 the 21-year-old king met with brilliant success in his first Italian campaign, defeating the Swiss mercenaries at Marignano (14 Sept. 1515) and gaining recognition of French control of northern Italy (treaty of

Cambrai, 1517). In 1519 Francis offered himself as the anti-Habsburg candidate for the imperial election, but after Charles V's assumption of the imperial title he sought an understanding with Henry VIII at the Field of the Cloth of Gold (June 1520). His early victory over Charles was counter-balanced by the defeats of the 1520s, at Bicocca (1522), Pavia (1525), where he was captured (later to be imprisoned in Madrid), and finally at Landriano (1529). His modest successes in this period, eg, the recapture of Milan (1524), were only achieved with the help of Venice, Florence, and the papacy. Despite the renunciation of his Italian claims in the treaty of Cambrai (1529), Francis continued to nurse ambitions there and embarked on an invasion of Savoy and Piedmont in 1537, but his hopes of Italian domination were never fulfilled.

His enmity towards Charles V raised Protestant hopes that he would defend the reformers against the secular leader of Catholicism, and both Zwingli and Calvin dedicated their major works to him. However, the anti-Catholic placards of 1534 turned him against the Reformation and he remained an orthodox Catholic, although his sister, Margaret of Angoulême, patronized eminent Protestants. Yet Francis was also an ardent Gallican, prepared to use the papacy as a tool to defend the French churches, and in the Concordat of Bologna (1516) he extracted from Leo X an agreement granting him a remarkable degree of control over them, including the power to nominate some 620 officers in cathedrals and monasteries, to be confirmed by papal appointment. During the pontificate of Clement VII he seemed prepared to lead France into schism and to back the Turks against a Habsburg–papal coalition (1525), but he also posed as the protector of Rome against Charles V and tried to undermine the emperor's attempts to reach agreement with the German Protestant princes.

His ambitious foreign policy strained the royal finances and a series of administrative reforms were initiated, eg, a new central treasury (1523) and 16 financial and administrative divisions (*généralités*) with a collector-general over each (1543) were established. To swell the exchequer's resources Francis introduced state investments (*rentes*) and under him the sale of office, eg, in the *parlements*, increased rapidly. He recognized the separate identity of the court of criminal justice (*Tournelle*) and founded two new chambers of *enquêtes* in the Paris *parlement* (1522, 1543). By holding frequent *lits de justice* he effectively controlled that institution's activities, although it regained some authority during the time of his imprisonment in Madrid (1525–6).

R. J. Knecht, *Francis I and Absolute Monarchy* (Historical Association Pamphlet, London, 1969).

MKS

FRANCIS II (1543–60), King of France (*reg.* 1559–60), eldest son of Henry II and Catherine de Medici. He married (1558) Mary Stuart, Queen of Scotland. After his father's sudden death in 1559 he succeeded to the French throne. His accession was followed by the rise to power of Mary's uncles, the Duc de Guise and the cardinal of Lorraine, whose repressive anti-Huguenot policy he endorsed. Faced with Protestant plots, eg, the conspiracy of Amboise (March 1560), he condoned Guise's arrest of the aristocratic Huguenot leader, Condé (Oct. 1560), but died on 5 Dec., leaving the throne of France to his nine-year-old brother, Charles IX.

FRANCIS OF ASSISI, Saint (*c.* 1181–1226), founder of the Franciscan order. Francesco di Bernardone was born at Assisi of a wealthy merchant family. His religious conversion owed much to his famous meeting with a leper and with the belief that he had heard a voice from the Cross in the church of St Damiano in Assisi (1205–6). Francis evolved the ideal of the perfect imitation of Christ and the literal following of his precepts, living in complete poverty, owning nothing, and having no permanent home. This bold ideal and his strong and attractive personality attracted many followers and

Francis was forced to face the problem of having to establish an organized order. This he found distressing and it was with reluctance that he drew up the rule (now lost) in 1209 and gained papal approval of the foundation of the order in 1209, but he refused to be its head. He went on the Damietta Crusade (1219–20) and at Christmas 1223 performed at Greccio the crib ceremony which was the beginning of the popularity of that devotion.

The continued popularity of Francis lies in the simplicity and beauty of his ideals and character and in his love for all the creatures of God, but the ideal was essentially mystical and individual.

FRANCIS, SIR PHILIP (1740–1818), British politician. After various clerical appointments in government offices (1756–72) which brought him into touch with leading personalities, he became a member of the council to the governor-general of India (Warren Hastings). Francis's violent antipathy to Hastings weakened his authority in India and after his return to England he was prominent in the events leading to Hastings's impeachment. As an MP, after 1784, Francis at first confined himself to Indian affairs, but later identified himself in all important issues with the Foxite opposition. He is one of the possible authors of the *Letters of Junius*.

FRANCISCAN ORDER, also Greyfriars, has since 1525 consisted of the Friars Minor and Capuchins, to which, since 1897, has been added the Conventuals. All three communities originated in the divisions of the order in the Middle Ages. Its medieval history was very troubled. St Francis had not, unlike his contemporary St Dominic, wished to found an order. But it was only the need to provide for those who had joined him, that he unwillingly drew up a rule emphasizing the three principles of poverty, preaching, and penance. This rule was given oral approval by Innocent III in April 1209, which marks the official foundation of the order, but the rule was too vague and insufficient and, as the order grew, revision became necessary—already in 1221 over 3000 friars had attended the general chapter meeting. During Francis's absence in Egypt (1219–20) changes were made of which he could not approve, and at his request Cardinal Hugolinus, later Gregory IX, and Brother Elias of Cordona (vicar-general 1221–7 and 1232–9) drew up a revised rule which was given papal approval in 1223. The order was still subject to dissension because the rule was open to differing interpretations and this problem continued to trouble the order, leading eventually to the separate communities existing today. More fundamental even was the problem of reconciling the ideal of poverty with the necessity of owning property. The order was riven on this issue. One group, the Community, was prepared to accept the solution of Pope Innocent IV of 1245, which vested ownership of Franciscan property in the Holy See. The other, the *Zelanti* (later called the Spirituals), stood for absolute poverty and claimed this as the practice of Christ and his disciples. The bull *Cum Inter Nonnullos* of 1323 declared this belief heretical and most of the Spirituals, led by the general of the order, Michael of Cesena, went into schism, seeking the protection of the Emperor Louis the Bavarian.

JG

FRANCISME, French fascist movement founded in 1934 by Marcel Bucard. Its members wore blue shirts. The movement was never very significant, but it was taken up and subsidized by the Germans after 1940.

FRANCK, SEBASTIEN (1499–1542), radical religious reformer of the 16th cent., who advocated a return to the primitive Christian Church to recover the spirit of the apostles. He called the Bible 'the paper pope', and rejected the significance attached to it by Protestant scholars and reformers. He also advocated religious toleration and freedom of conscience.

FRANCO, RAFAEL (1896–), Paraguayan army colonel and president, hero of the Chaco War against Bolivia. Franco returned from the war as a reformist leader of those who were disgusted with the status quo. Backed by a coalition of war veterans and university students, he seized power on 17 Feb., 1936 and founded the Febrerista Party. His programme of land redistribution, encouragement of labour unions, and social welfare measures soon alienated groups among the elite, and his government was overthrown after being in power some 18 months. Since then the Febreristas have lived in exile.

FRANCO BAHAMONDE, FRANCISCO (1892–), Spanish soldier, politician, and dictator, who became in quick succession the army's youngest captain, major, colonel, and general. He was an excellent organizer, interested in military history and strategy, and showed concern for the welfare of his men. His right-wing sympathies led him to take part in the suppression of the revolutionary strikes of 1917. In 1925 he led the landing of Alhucemas Bay which ended the Moroccan wars. By 1926, he was a brigadier-general and head of the Foreign Legion.

The social peace of Primo de Rivera's rule convinced him of the benefits of dictatorship. While director of the Spanish military academy, he came to believe that Spain's greatest enemy was communism. However, under the Republic, he behaved circumspectly and avoided Sanjurjo's plot (1932). Nevertheless, he was disturbed by Azaña's army reforms, Catalan separatism, and growing social disorder. In 1934 he organized the repression of the Asturian rising, for which he was hailed by the upper and middle classes as the saviour of Spain. In May 1935 Gil Robles appointed him chief of staff, in which capacity his reforms and his elimination of left-wing officers increased his popularity with the army.

In 1936 the Popular Front government posted him to the Canary Islands. He was increasingly concerned about a communist take-over, yet he still avoided complicity in right-wing plots. When he joined the conspiracy is not clear, but on the day of the rising he flew from the Canaries to Morocco. At first, he shared command of the Nationalist forces with Mola and Queipo. But his command of the African army and the fact that it was he who had managed to arrange for the German and Italian aid which had made the rising possible led to his being made commander-in-chief and Head of State.

Thereafter, Franco directed both the strategy of the Civil War and the politics of Nationalist Spain. Though never actually risking his own reputation in the field, he planned the offensives which ultimately brought victory to the insurgents. He organized the rebel zone and later Spain itself under the guidance of his brother-in-law, Serrano Suñer. The Falange and the Carlists were merged to create the state party. Franco ruled as a fascist dictator. He skilfully avoided joining Hitler and Mussolini in the Second World War. After the war he remained in power through his ability to divide and rule the political forces of Spain and because of a general fear of further bloodshed. In 1970 only his advanced age offered any indication that his long period of rule was drawing to an end.

L. E. Snellgrove, *Franco and the Spanish Civil War* (London, 1965).
J. W. D. Trythall, *Franco* (London, 1970).   PP

FRANCO-AMERICAN ALLIANCE (1778), treaty by which France recognized US independence and the two countries agreed to support each other in the event of an Anglo–French war. Each side agreed not to make a separate peace, nor one that failed to acknowledge American independence. France, anxious to avenge the humiliating treaty of Paris (1763), had secretly responded to early American requests for supplies and subsidies as a means of weakening Britain (1775). She remained nominally neutral until the crucial American success at Saratoga (1777). She then acceded to US requests for both an alliance and a commercial treaty. In spite of difficulties during the peace negotiations in Paris (1782–3),

the alliance remained in force until it was suspended by the US during the Franco–American 'Quasi-War' (1798), and annulled by the Convention of 1800.

FRANCO-BELGIAN AGREEMENT (7 Sept. 1920) provided for joint measures during the occupation of the Rhineland by the victors in the First World War, and for consultation between both countries' general staffs in the event of aggression, or threat of aggression, by Germany. The agreement followed the lapse of the proposed Anglo–American guarantee of French security. It contributed to a settlement of Franco–Belgian disagreement over the economic future of Luxembourg.

FRANCO-CZECH ALLIANCE (25 Jan. 1924) provided for concerted action in such matters as the prevention of a German–Austrian *Anschluss*, and of either a Habsburg or a Hohenzollern restoration. Policies in east and central Europe would be co-ordinated and disputes would be submitted to arbitration. Secret letters were exchanged shortly afterwards on details of co-operation between general staffs, and a French military attaché was appointed in Prague. The failure of France's Ruhr policy, and of League of Nations security discussions, helped to consolidate the alliance. In Berlin and London rumours of large-scale military agreements were current; however, Beneš, the Czechoslovak foreign minister, avoided such entanglements.

FRANCO-CZECH TREATY (16 Oct. 1925), treaty of mutual guarantee, signed at Locarno, was simultaneous with and identical to the Franco–Polish treaty. Armed assistance against Germany depended upon either party's being the victim of unprovoked aggression and invoking Article 16 of the League of Nations covenant. If the League Council could not unanimously define an aggressor, assistance would be rendered under Article 15, section 7, of the covenant. The treaty referred to German aggression in the context of a breach of the Locarno pact of 1925. Simultaneously with the signing of the pact, Germany had concluded an arbitration treaty with Czechoslovakia, which did not guarantee Czechoslovakia's frontiers.

FRANCO-GALLIA (1573), political treatise of François Hotman (1524–90), in which he stressed that power sprang from the people, who were represented by the estates general and who thus provided a fundamental restraint upon the French monarchy.

FRANCO-GERMAN TREATY OF CO-OPERATION (1963), provided for co-operation between France and the German Federal Republic by means of regular meetings of the heads of state, foreign and defence ministers, and chiefs of staff of the two countries, and the establishment in each country of an inter-ministerial commission responsible for questions of co-operation. The two governments undertook to 'consult each other before taking any major decision on all questions of foreign policy'.

The treaty was of major political importance. It cemented the close alliance which had been established between France and Germany under the personal leadership of De Gaulle and Adenauer immediately after the French government had vetoed Britain's entry into the European Economic Community. It was based on De Gaulle's concept of a Europe of nation-states linked together by consultation between their governments, under the leadership of France. The consultation for which the treaty provided had, by 1970, duly taken place, but not on the scale which it had suggested, so that its practical importance was less than its political significance, particularly at the time of its signature.

FRANÇOIS, JEAN (*fl.* 18th cent.), slave, born in Haiti, who became a leader of the slaves who rebelled there in 1791. He was defeated by the French planters, but accepted Spanish settlers' aid. He was later ousted by his subordinate, Toussaint-Louverture.

FRANÇOIS-PONCET, ANDRÉ (1887–   ), French ambassador to Germany (1931–8) and Italy (1938–40). He established close contacts with the Nazi leaders, and, while warning of the danger presented by Hitler, worked for Franco–German rapprochement and supported the Munich agreement. After the war he was high commissioner and ambassador in West Germany (1949–55).

FRANCO-ITALIAN ARMISTICE (24 June 1940), signed during the Second World War 14 days after Italy's entry into the war with France. Italian troops remained in possession of the minimal gains which they had made and an area 50 kms from these lines was to be demilitarized. The Armistice provided for similar demilitarization along the Libyan border with Tunisia, and for demilitarization of naval ports in North Africa during the war with Britain.

FRANCO-JAPANESE TREATY (1907) guaranteed the integrity of China and the status quo in the far east, contained a 'most favoured nation' clause, and provided for co-operation for security in areas of mutual interest. It strengthened Japan's alliance with Britain (1905), with which both Russia (1907) and France (1904) were associated.

FRANCO-LEBANESE TREATY (Nov. 1936), negotiated on a similar basis to the Franco–Syrian treaty and not ratified largely because of the development of French policy towards Syria.

FRANCO-POLISH ALLIANCE (Feb. 1921) consisted of a political alliance and a secret military convention. Both were to become operative after the signing of economic agreements; these were delayed until 6 Feb. 1922. The political alliance was an engagement to act in concert on questions of international policy, and in cases of unprovoked aggression against either or both parties; and to consult together before concluding agreements connected with east and central Europe. In the military convention, mutual aid was promised if either party suffered aggression from territory dependent on Germany (this provision covered Upper Silesia), and each party promised to prepare to help the other whenever the German situation appeared to threaten war, as in the case of a German mobilization. The parties would also be prepared for common action in execution of the Versailles treaty. In case of a Russo–Polish war, France was to check Germany on land or sea and to help Poland by keeping open her lines of communication; a pledge which might require French intervention in Danzig or Pomerania. The convention also stipulated the size of the Polish army and arranged for co-operation between the two general staffs. An annex provided for a 400 million franc loan for arming the Polish forces. Poland was to purchase war material exclusively in France.

The alliance was facilitated by joint Franco–Polish fears of German claims on Upper Silesia. It followed the Polish victory over the Bolsheviks at Warsaw, which had proved the Polish forces superior to the White Russian forces supported by France. Throughout the negotiations for the alliance, France avoided any official recognition of Poland's new eastern frontiers.   ASJ

FRANCO-POLISH TREATY (16 Oct. 1925), treaty of mutual guarantee, signed at Locarno, was simultaneous with and identical to the Franco–Czech treaty. This reduced French military commitments accepted towards Poland in 1921. Armed assistance against Germany now depended on either party's being the victim of unprovoked aggression and invoking Article 16 of the League of Nations covenant. If the League Council could not unanimously define an aggressor, assistance would be rendered under Article 15, section 7, of the covenant. The treaty referred to German aggression in

the context of a breach of the Locarno pact of 1925. These agreements fell far short of Poland's original hopes. She concluded only an arbitration treaty with Germany, which Stresemann refused to allow France to guarantee. It contained no guarantee for Poland's frontiers. France's new security agreements with her eastern allies were not enshrined in the Locarno pact itself.

FRANCO-PRUSSIAN WAR (1870–1), won by Prussia, who was thereby able to create a unified German empire. The immediate cause of the war was the Hohenzollern candidature, exacerbated by the Ems telegram. The ultimate causes lay in Napoleon III's ambitions and the change in the balance of power in Europe caused by the creation of the North German Confederation. Both sides used railways to assist mobilization, but the Germans were more speedy and efficient. Moltke had recently reformed the Prussian army, which had superior artillery and an outstanding general staff. Lebœuf had begun the reform of the French army, which had superior rifles and the *mitrailleuse*. The war was almost over within three months with the French surrenders at Sedan and Metz, but Paris held out under siege for three and a half months, while in eastern France Garibaldi fought with volunteers and Bourbaki formed a new French army. The war was ended by the Frankfurt treaty.

FRANCO-RUSSIAN ALLIANCE (1891–4), military alliance negotiated after William II's refusal to renew the Reinsurance Treaty on Bismark's dismissal. The Balkan crisis (1885–6), economic friction over protectionist tariffs, and the closure of the Berlin bank to Russian securities had strained Russo–German relations. Fear that England would join the Triple Alliance made Russia look for another ally, and French loans had been available from 1888. Increasing reliance on these loans was to keep the alliance in being until 1917.

The visit of a French squadron to Kronstadt (1891) led to a military convention in 1892 (ratified Dec.–Jan. 1893–4) which provided for all available military aid if one power were attacked by Germany alone or with an ally, and for mobilization if the Triple Alliance mobilized.

FRANCO-SPANISH TREATY (1935), commercial convention with a secret provision that Spain would buy war material from France to the value of 20 million francs. In July 1936 the Spanish Republic wished to acquire French pilots and aircraft and the French prime minister, Blum, agreed that these should be made available under this secret provision. The French cabinet, divided over intervention in the Spanish Civil War, achieved a compromise by issuing an official refusal of the arms request while in fact permitting private shipments of arms.

FRANCO-SWISS ALLIANCE (1777), general treaty of alliance prompted by Swiss concern over possible Austrian aggression after the 1st Partition of Poland (1772). The Franco–Austrian alliance, of which Louis XV's marriage to Marie Antoinette was a symbol, further alarmed the cantons. Fear therefore united the 13 cantons in their negotiations with France (1776–7) and on 28 May the treaty was signed, establishing peace with France and Swiss neutrality for 50 years. France was to have the right to levy 6000 Swiss recruits for her armies, promising in return to examine the privileges of Swiss residents in France. Only the turbulent canton of Geneva, and Neuchatel, a Prussian dependency, were excluded from the terms.

FRANCO-SYRIAN TREATY (1936), Franco-Syrian agreement providing for the end of the French mandate and Syrian independence, negotiated in response to renewed nationalist agitation and strikes in Syria by the more sympathetic Popular Front government in France. It conceded the incorporation of the Jebel Druze and Lataqiya areas in the Syrian state, and paved the way for the reintroduction of responsible internal self-government. In the latter part of 1937, however,

Franco–Syrian relations deteriorated, France refused to ratify the treaty, and in 1939 the constitution was suspended.

FRANCO-YUGOSLAV TREATY (1926–7) marked Yugoslavia's growing estrangement from Mussolini, which was chiefly due to the increase of Italian influence in Albania. France and Yugoslavia agreed to the pacific settlement of all disputes between them, and to the joint consideration of any possible threats to the order established by treaties which both parties had signed. This latter provision indicated the fears of treaty revision roused by Italy's friendship treaty with Hungary in April 1927.

FRANC-SALÉ, concession of exemption from the *gabelle* or salt tax under the French *ancien régime*. It was widely granted by the Crown to members of the first and second estates, royal counsellors and secretaries, and magistrates of the sovereign courts.

FRANCS-ARCHERS. After the truce of 1444 in the Hundred Years War, attempts were made in France to establish a permanent reservoir of archers as part of the sweeping military reforms organized by Arthur de Richemont. Each group of 50 peasant households was required to provide one archer or crossbowman, with equipment if necessary, who was exempt from taxation. All men were also required to take part in regular archery training. The 'free archers' were not very successful, as the peasants taken from their homes without experience were not soldiers. They ceased to be of military importance in the late 15th cent.

FRANK, HANS (1900–46), German lawyer and politician, who at the age of 26 was a member of the Nazi Party's court set up to enforce discipline among members. Subsequently he became leader of the party's legal division. After the Nazis assumed office in 1933, he was successively Bavarian minister of justice, Reichsminister without portfolio, and reich minister of justice. He was also president of the Academy of Law and of the German Bar Association. On 12 Oct. 1939 he was appointed governor-general of Poland, whence he provided food, supplies, and forced labour for the Germans in the Second World War. He also presided over the liquidation of the intelligentsia and the Jews. His 42-volume journal of these proceedings was produced as evidence at the Nuremberg trials, where he was sentenced to death.

FRANKENHAUSEN, BATTLE OF (1525), defeat of Thomas Munzer and the rebellious peasantry of Franconia on 15 May by the forces of the German nobility led by the evangelical Philip of Hesse. The rebels were surrounded and routed by the artillery, Munzer being captured in hiding in Frankenhausen shortly afterwards and executed.

FRANKFORT PROPOSALS (8 Nov. 1813), made to Napoleon—but rejected by him—during the French Wars, offering France her natural frontiers as a basis for peace.

FRANKFURT, major imperial free city on an important trade route between northern Germany, France, and northern Italy, which enjoyed rapid growth in the course of the 14th cent. It was the site of one of the most important trade fairs in the empire and after the late 15th cent. became one of the greatest European publishing centres, especially for the distribution of German Protestant works. After 1356 it was the scene of the election of the Holy Roman emperors. It continued to grow in importance after the Thirty Years War. In the 19th and 20th cents it became an industrial and cultural centre in western Europe.

FRANKFURT, DIET AND INTERIM OF (1539), meeting held between the Protestant members of the Schmalkaldic League and the imperial plenipotentiary, John of Weza, Abp of Lund, the Diet being called at the instigation of the Emperor Charles V, who feared a general Protestant alliance which would undermine his plans for a Turkish crusade. On 19 April

1539 Lund reached agreement with the Protestants, the terms of which were embodied in the Frankfurt Interim. The Protestants were promised security from attack for 15 months from 1 May, and it was agreed to hold exploratory talks with a view to finding an acceptable doctrinal agreement, while the likelihood of religious war, implicit in the truce of Nice and the League of Nuremberg, receded.

FRANKFURT, LEAGUE OF (1741), anti-Habsburg coalition of the German electoral princes, formed through the pressure of the Marshal de Belleisle at the Diet of Frankfurt. It was pledged to defend the Bavarian claim to the imperial crown, successfully fulfilled in 1742. The league was joined by Frederick II of Brandenburg-Prussia in 1744.

FRANKFURT ASSEMBLY (1848–9) failed to unite Germany on a liberal basis. After the German states and Austria were swept by liberal revolutions, one of the aims of which was a united Germany, a *Nationalversammlung* was elected by varying degrees of direct universal suffrage. When the assembly met (May 1848) it was made up almost entirely of professional men, whose contact with the rural and urban masses was slight and often hostile. Although it elected an Imperial Regent, the Archduke John, and a provisional government, they lacked real power, since control of the military remained with the princes who had been forced to make temporary concessions. In making war on Denmark over Schleswig-Holstein and suppressing a left-wing revolt in Frankfurt itself (Sept.) the assembly had to depend on Prussian troops. The deputies were sharply divided over what kind of Germany they wanted, especially over its frontiers, and whether Austria and its non-German lands and Prussian Poland should be included. By early 1849 there was no hope of bringing Austria in, so that a liberal constitution for the rest of Germany was drawn up and the hereditary imperial crown was offered to Frederick William IV of Prussia (March). He rejected it, as an 'imaginary little crown baked from mud and clay'. The princes had regained their authority within their own states by then and the assembly collapsed, the rump being dispersed by force (June).

FRANKFURT TREATY (1871), signed by France and Prussia at the end of the Franco–Prussian war. France ceded Alsace and Lorraine (without Belfort, but including the fortress of Metz) to the new German empire, and agreed to pay a war indemnity of 5 milliard francs. North-east France was to remain under German occupation until this was paid (1873). Alsace and Lorraine had been French for over a century and the cession was opposed by the majority of the population. It caused ill-feeling in France, making friendship between France and Germany impossible until the territory became French again in 1919.

FRANKFURTER, FELIX (1882–1965), US jurist, lawyer, and writer. He was born in Vienna and taken to the US at an early age. During the First World War he acted as chairman of the War Labor Policies Board. A staunch liberal, he helped to found the American Civil Liberties Union (1920). He was an adviser of President F. D. Roosevelt during the 1930s, and was appointed associate justice of the US Supreme Court (1939), where he served with distinction until his retirement (1962). He was a Harvard Law School professor (1914–39).

His major contribution as a jurist was his staunch defence of judicial self-restraint. This often led to his upholding legislation of which he personally disapproved. Equally, though an articulate advocate of civil liberties, he was against over-ruling other branches of government, thus involving the court unnecessarily in 'political' questions best left to congressional or state action.

FRANKING, ABOLITION OF (1839), in Britain. From the start of a public postal service in the mid-17th cent., MPs and certain officials enjoyed the privilege of sending and receiving letters and packets (and, after 1764, newspapers) free of postage duty. The loss of revenue increased rapidly in the 18th cent., as the volume of mail handled by the Post Office increased, and attempts to limit the privilege and prevent its abuse (eg, enquiries of 1715 and 1734, acts of 1764, 1784, 1795) were ineffective. The solution, to abolish franking, was suggested by the Post Office in the late 18th cent., but political objections were not overcome until the proposals of the Wallace committee (including penny postage) were adopted in 1839.

FRANKLIN, BENJAMIN (1706–90), American scientist, writer, and statesman. Born in Boston and apprenticed as a printer, he migrated to Philadelphia to make his fortune (1723). After visiting England (1724–6) he set up his own business, published the *Pennsylvania Gazette* and the popular *Poor Richard's Almanack* (1732–57), a compendium of useful information and dicta. He helped to found the American Philosophical Society (1743), was a prolific inventor and experimenter, and being fascinated by electricity, demonstrated his theory of the electrical nature of lightning by flying a kite during a thunderstorm (1752). He was also active in politics and served as clerk to the PA assembly (1736–51), assemblyman (1751–4, 1762–4), deputy postmaster at Philadelphia, and deputy postmaster-general for the colonies (1753–74). He proposed a plan for colonial union at the Albany Congress (1754) and acted as agent for the PA assembly in London (1757–61). Returning there (1764–75) and acting for GA, NJ, and MA as well as PA, he attempted to reconcile the colonies and Britain. Having first opposed the Stamp Act, he played a major part in its repeal, misleadingly asserting that the colonists distinguished between internal and external taxes (1766). Ambivalent in his attitude towards Britain, he constantly expressed the colonial view during the deteriorating imperial crisis. While rejecting the authority of parliament over the colonies he none the less continued to seek a compromise, though with diminishing hope, until he left for America (March 1775). On being elected to the second Continental Congress, Franklin submitted a draft plan of union (July 1775). He served on the corresponding, or foreign affairs, committee, led a delegation to Quebec, which sought to associate Canada with the colonial rebellion (1776), and sat on the committee which drafted the Declaration of Independence. He was also a member of the PA constitutional convention (1776). His greatest contribution to the cause of American independence was in the diplomatic field. Arriving in Paris (Dec. 1776), he enjoyed a personal triumph as the embodiment of Enlightenment simplicity. With semi-official assistance he obtained supplies, and by exploiting news of the American victory at Saratoga and British overtures towards reconciliation, secured the Franco–American Alliance (1778). Franklin was a peace commissioner with John Adams and John Jay (1781–3), and at a crucial stage of the negotiations he ignored his instructions to work with the French and obtained an agreement with Britain. In the treaty of Paris (1783) Britain acknowledged US independence. On returning home (1785), Franklin served as president of the executive council of PA (1785–8). He was a delegate to the PA Convention (1787), giving it the prestige of his attendance although, because of advancing years, he took little active part in proceedings.

A pragmatist in his personal life, politics, and diplomacy, Franklin had a brilliant, wide-ranging, and supple mind. He was the first American to establish a world-wide reputation for himself and is considered second only to Washington for the contribution he made to the Revolution.

Carl Van Doren, *Benjamin Franklin* (New York, 1938).
Esmond Wright, *Benjamin Franklin and American Independence* (London, 1966).

FRANKLIN (STELLA MARIA SARAH), MILES (1879–1954), Australian novelist, who lived in US and Britain (1905–27).

Like nearly all her fiction, her major work, *All That Swagger* (1936), dealt with the pioneering history of Australia.

FRANKLIN EXPEDITION, commanded by Sir John Franklin (1786–1847), set off in 1845 to search for the North-west Passage. The expedition was never seen again. Several others were sent to search for it, but not until 1859, after an expedition financed by Lady Franklin and led by Capt. F. L. McClintock, was the story of the Franklin expedition pieced together. Evidently Franklin's ship had been trapped for two years in the pack-ice near King William Land. Franklin himself died in 1847 and his surviving crew, after abandoning ship, perished as well.

FRANKLIN-BOUILLON AGREEMENT, signed (20 Oct. 1921) by M. Franklin-Bouillon for France and Yusuf Kemal Bey for the Turkish Nationalists, by which France agreed to evacuate Cilicia and other territory on the northern Syrian border, while retaining Alexandretta. The agreement marked the end of French attempts to resist the Kemalists and uphold the Sèvres settlement.

FRANKS, people of Germanic origin whose existence is first recorded in the 3rd cent., when they lived east of the Lower Rhine as far south as Mainz. They were divided into three branches, the Salians, the Ripuarians, and the Hessians. They took an active part in the mid-3rd-cent. invasions of Gaul, but by the late 4th and early 5th cent. many were given federate status and extensively settled within the borders of the Roman empire in Gaul and in the lands east of the Rhine. The Salian Franks co-operated with Rome, especially under Childeric I, while some of the Ripuarian and Hessian Franks fought with Roman troops against the Huns. Under Clovis the Salians became masters of Gaul and established a lasting Frankish kingdom, which, under the Carolingians, brought about the submission of most of the Germanic peoples.

FRANZ FERDINAND, Archduke (1863–1914), heir to the throne of the Austro-Hungarian monarchy, assassinated at Sarajevo in 1914. His death plunged Europe into the First World War. He favoured the conversion of the Dual Monarchy into a federation of Austrians, Magyars, and Slavs.

FRANZESI BROTHERS (Albizo and Musciatto) (d. 1307), heads of a Florentine firm of bankers to King Philip IV of France between 1289 and 1307. Nicknamed *Biche et Mouche* by the French, they replaced the Templars as Philip's treasurers in 1295–6. They both contributed to the financing of the war against England (1294–8). They also provided the money and headquarters for the attack on Pope Boniface VIII at Anagni.

FRASER, PETER (1884–1950), NZ politician and Labour prime minister. He took a leading part in Federation of Labour strike-action and conferences (1912–3) and in the formation of the Labour Party (1916). He was gaoled for opposing conscription and later entered parliament (1918). As an opposition critic, Fraser did much to attune Labour policies to a suspicious electorate. He became a minister of education and health in 1935, and prime minister in 1940. In directing NZ's war effort and her overseas strategy, Fraser showed firmness and courage. At San Francisco (1945), he achieved prominence as an advocate of collective security, restricted veto, and trusteeship in the UN Charter.

FRASER, SIMON (1776–1862), Canadian fur trader and explorer, who joined the North West Co. and became a partner in 1801. He established the first permanent trading posts on the western slopes of BC. In 1808 he led the first party down the turbulent Fraser river from Fort George to the Straits of Georgia. He served the company until he was arrested in 1816 for complicity in a massacre of 20 settlers. He was acquitted and later became a farmer and mill owner in Cornwall, near Montreal.

FRASER RIVER GOLD RUSH. The discovery in 1858 of gold along the Thompson and Fraser rivers in western Canada brought an influx of prospectors, mostly from the US. The boom period lasted until 1867, although profitable mining operations went on into the 1870s. The increase of population in the Fraser river area led to the creation of the province of BC.

FRASSATI, ALFREDO (1868–1961), Italian lawyer, Giolittian liberal journalist, and ambassador to Germany (1920–2). His Turin newspaper *La Stampa* was the only liberal paper to maintain a clear stand against fascism until it was taken over by the government (1926).

FRAUSTADT, BATTLE OF (13 Feb. 1706), in the Great Northern War, Charles XII of Sweden's decisive defeat on 13 Feb. 1706 of the Saxons under Johann Matthias von der Schulenburg, resulting in the collapse of Augustus II's attempt to link up with the Russian forces under Gen. Ogilvie.

FRÉCHETTE, LOUIS HONORÉ (1839–1908), French-Canadian poet who migrated to the US (1865), where he founded and edited *L'Observateur* and *Amérique*. He returned to Canada (1871) and sat in the House of Commons as a Liberal (1874–8). In 1889 he was appointed clerk of the Legislative Council of Quebec. Fréchette is recognized as the leading French-Canadian poet of the 19th cent. His work *Les Fleurs Boréales* (1879) won him the Prix Montyon of the French Academy. His poetry is in the epic style, praising liberty and the great events of Canadian history.

FREDERICK II (*reg.* 1230–46), Duke of Austria and Styria, called 'the Quarrelsome'. In 1237 the Emperor Frederick II occupied Austria. Duke Frederick briefly won back his lands, but his death in battle against the Hungarians led to the reannexation of Austria by the emperor.

FREDERICK III, Elector of Saxony (1463–1525), a leading German prince of the Holy Roman empire in the early 16th cent., known for his patronage of Martin Luther. The elder son of Ernest and grandson of Frederick the Good, he belonged to the Ernestine branch of the Saxon house, which was later deprived of the electoral title in favour of the younger, Albertine branch. Frederick succeeded his father in 1486. Moderate and honest, if inflexible in his attitudes, he repeatedly declined the Emperor Maximilian's offers in return for his electoral vote and rejected the overtures of Francis I and Pope Leo X to stand against the Archduke Charles in the imperial election of 1519. Although influenced by his humanist chancellor, George Spalatin, his Catholic faith was traditionalist and he was a keen collector of religious relics, having some 17,000 in his Church of All Saints, Wittenberg. Yet he became the most prominent supporter of Luther among the German princes, partly in his opposition to Charles V and partly because of the Augustinian's association with Wittenberg University, which Frederick had founded in 1502 to eclipse the prestige of the Albertine family. He insisted that Luther be given a papal hearing in Germany rather than in Rome (1520) and promoted the confrontation with the emperor at Worms (1521). He was succeeded by his brother, John the Constant, in 1525.

FREDERICK I (1122–90), Emperor (*reg.* 1152–90), called Barbarossa, who succeeded his uncle, Conrad III, to the German throne. He inherited an empire in which the feudalization of society was already well advanced and royal authority much weakened. In 1168 he took possession of Swabia and Goslar and began to construct a belt of territory across Germany as the necessary prerequisite of any attempt to restore the power of the Crown. He had an ambition to make his Swabian lands the basis of his power. To this was added the imperial county of Burgundy by his marriage to its heiress. He had a vision of a strong royal state embracing Swabia, Switzerland, and northern Italy, controlling the Alpine passes, as a base for his enterprises in Germany and Italy. Frederick has been credited with a concerted design to restore the strong united empire of Otto the Great. His reign saw a great propaganda offensive in support of this ideal, organized by the chancellor, Rainald von Dassel, which placed special emphasis on the sanctity of the empire as the paramount state in Europe. Dassel used Roman Law in defence of the imperial position and consciously looked back to Charlemagne and Otto the Great for examples. The title 'Holy Roman emperor' was first used systematically under Frederick. The main enemies of his schemes were the German nobility and the north Italian communes. Frederick tried to preserve the balance among the German princes to win them as allies against the lesser nobility. He was ready to recognize the wide rights of the princes if they would acknowledge him as their feudal overlord. His attempts to employ north Italian resources, to which he believed he had a right, brought him into conflict with the Lombard League, in particular with Milan. Although Frederick eventually imposed direct imperial government in central Italy, he was unable to subordinate the communes permanently. The marriage of his heir, the future Emperor Henry VI, to the heiress of Sicily paved the way for Henry's annexation of southern Italy in 1194 which, but for his sudden death in 1197, might have left the Hohenstaufen predominant in Italy, encircling the papacy. Papal obsession with this threat led eventually to the extinction of the whole Hohenstaufen family. Frederick's power was at its greatest after the fall of Henry the Lion of Bavaria-Saxony in 1180 and the division of his lands. His achievements incommoded too many people and his enemies were already gathering before his death. He was unable to achieve recognition of the hereditary kingship in Germany and his achievements lacked permanence. Time has added greatly to his reputation and in the 16th cent. a legend arose that he was asleep on the Kyffhaüser mountain waiting to restore the empire to its old glory.

P. Munz, *Frederick Barbarossa: a study in medieval politics* (London, 1969).   MH

FREDERICK II (1194–1250), Emperor (*reg.* 1211–50), son of the Emperor Henry VI and Constance of Sicily, he was brought up in southern Italy. Initially he regarded Germany as merely a source of men and money and his representatives in the country were expected to placate the German notables. Like his grandfather, Frederick Barbarossa, he planned in later years a strong state controlling the Alps and he managed in 1246 to acquire Austria. His southern Italian state was his most favoured possession, where he chiefly lived. There, building on the foundations laid by his Norman predecessors, he tried to create an efficient centralized despotism. Papal opposition finally ruined his plans, as Pope Gregory IX regarded Frederick as a deadly menace and instigated trouble in both Italy and Germany. Gregory's successor, Innocent IV, fled to France, whence he could safely organize Frederick's downfall. In Germany anti-kings were raised by the pope in 1246–7 and in Italy Frederick was involved in almost incessant warfare from 1237 until his premature death. He left the reputation of being the ablest ruler of his time, but his failures were due partly to his suspiciousness, cruelty, and selfishness. He was a poet and scientist with a sceptical and curious mind and the centre of a brilliant court. He founded Naples University.

FREDERICK III (1415–93), Emperor (*reg.* 1440–93), a weak and indolent ruler whose importance consists in the marriages he arranged for his children which ultimately gave his family control over the Burgundian state and the kingdoms of

Bohemia and Hungary, thus laying the foundations of the European power of the Habsburgs.

FREDERICK III (1831–88), German Emperor (*reg.* 1888), married to Princess Victoria of England. He died three months after his accession. As crown prince he had sought a more liberal approach to home affairs and had clashed with Bismarck, who feared his accession and the influence of his feminist and liberal consort. He fought in the battles of Sadowa and Sedan, and suggested the use of force if necessary to bring unwilling German princes into the German empire.

FREDERICK V (1596–1632), King of Bohemia (*reg.* 1619–20), who succeeded his father, Frederick IV, in 1610 as Elector Palatine, and was later known as 'the Winter King' after his election to the Crown of Bohemia, which precipitated the Thirty Years War (1618–48). In 1613 this Calvinist prince married Elizabeth, daughter of James I of England. In 1619 he was offered the Crown by the Protestant Bohemian nobility in defiance of the Habsburg king, Ferdinand, who had been elected in June 1617. For a year Frederick and his family lived in Prague, but were driven out by Tilly and the army of the Catholic League at the battle of the White Hill (Nov. 1620). After being proscribed and deposed by the Emperor Ferdinand and driven from his native Palatinate by the Spanish army, he sought refuge in the Netherlands. He visited several European courts, soliciting military and financial aid (1620–2), but was forced to conclude an armistice with Ferdinand in 1624. In his quest to recover the Palatinate, he was given military assistance by his wife's uncle, Christian of Denmark (1625), and later by Gustavus Adolphus of Sweden (1629).

FREDERICK I (1471–1533), King of Denmark (*reg.* 1523–33) and of Norway (*reg.* 1525–33). During the reigns of his elder brother, John, and his nephew, Christian II, he ruled a part of Schleswig-Holstein based on Gottorp. The nobles of Jutland offered him the Danish Crown, whereupon Christian II fled, and Denmark's choice was later accepted by Norway. Frederick tolerated Lutheranism, but skilfully avoided provoking an attack by Charles V on Denmark or Schleswig-Holstein.

FREDERICK II (1534–88), King of Denmark and Norway (*reg.* 1559–88), whose reign was marked by the Seven Years War of the North. He was the son of Christian III. More interested in war than politics, he joined his uncles, who were Dukes of Holstein, in conquering the ancient peasant-republic of Ditmarsh, between the Elbe and the Eider (1559). In 1563 he began the long war against his maternal cousin, Eric XIV of Sweden, which the Swedish fleet held its own against those of Denmark and Lübeck, but the main Danish army was victorious under Rantzau at Axtorna (1565) and the Swedes at the peace of Stettin (1570) had to pay ransom for the lost fortress of Älvsborg. In his later years Frederick was the popular king of a strong state and a prosperous people, who delegated much business to his ministers.

FREDERICK III (1609–70), King of Denmark and Norway (*reg.* 1648–70) and the founder of the absolute monarchy. Unlike his father, Christian IV, Frederick thought deeply and never acted on impulse. In 1657 he tried to take advantage of the Polish–Swedish war to get the better of Sweden, but was heavily defeated and lost much territory at the peace of Copenhagen (1660). The successful resistance of that city to the Swedish siege, however, gave the king a new opportunity. Like earlier Danish sovereigns, he had secured his election to the throne by granting a charter of privileges to the nobility. The enthusiasm generated among the citizens by dangers surmounted in common with the king now enabled him to replace the charter by a pragmatic sanction, in which each estate of his subjects accepted him as 'absolute sovereign lord' (1661). Four years later absolutism was

defined in the *Lex Regia*, which was published after his death and remained valid until 1849.

FREDERICK IV (1671–1730), King of Denmark and Norway (*reg.* 1699–1730), and a participant in the Great Northern War. When he succeeded his father, Christian V, he had no political experience, but he challenged the still more youthful Charles XII of Sweden by attacking the Swedish satellite, Holstein-Gottorp, whose defences Charles was strengthening. Frederick was quickly defeated and made peace at Travendal (1700). Nine years later he re-entered the war, overrunning much Swedish territory in Germany and the Holstein-Gottorp lands in Schleswig, which became his by the treaty of Frederiksborg in 1720.

FREDERICK V (1723–66), King of Denmark and Norway (*reg.* 1746–66), married Louisa, the daughter of the British king, George II. He brought J. H. E. Bernstorff into office and pursued a peaceful policy.

FREDERICK VI (1768–1839), King of Denmark (*reg.* 1808–1839) and the last Danish King of Norway (*reg.* 1808–14). He seized power by resolute action from the councillors governing in the name of his imbecile father, Christian VII (1784), and supported the liberal measures of A. P. Bernstorff and other ministers. His influence on foreign affairs was less fortunate, for he was partly responsible both for the hasty surrender to the British Admiral, Nelson, in 1801, and for the failure to compromise with Britain, which led to the loss of Norway by the treaty of Kiel in 1814. In 1831 he established consultative Estates for the Danish islands, Jutland, Schleswig, and Holstein.

FREDERICK VII (1808–63), King of Denmark (*reg.* 1848–63), last direct male heir of the Oldenburg dynasty, who began his reign by granting a liberal constitution. On his accession he rejected his ministers' proposal for partitioning Schleswig. Later, looking to Sweden–Norway for support, he approved the November constitution (1863) for unifying Denmark and Schleswig, which came into force just after his death.

FREDERICK VIII (1843–1912), King of Denmark (*reg.* 1906–1912). Like his father, Christian IX, he favoured the Conservative policy of strong defences for Copenhagen, but his outlook was more strictly that of a constitutional sovereign.

FREDERICK I (1657–1713), King of Prussia (*reg.* 1701–13). He succeeded his father, 'the Great Elector', in 1688 as Elector Frederick III and, constantly overshadowed by his memory, he joined the anti-French coalition and was ultimately rewarded for his loyalty to the emperor with a royal title. In the Turkish campaigns (1691–7) Frederick served Leopold with distinction at the battles of Salenkamen, Belgrade, and Zenta. His prime aim was not to be outclassed by his rival electors, Frederick Augustus of Saxony, who had acquired the Polish Crown, and George Louis of Hanover, who was heir, after his mother, to the English throne. Although the duchy of Prussia was situated outside the empire, Frederick, as Elector of Brandenburg, wanted imperial approval. In 1700, with the War of the Spanish Succession looming as Charles II's health increasingly failed he renewed the Prussian alliance with Leopold, promising to supply 8000 men for the war's duration in return for a subsidy of 100,000 thalers and recognition of his royal dignity. On 18 Jan. 1701 Frederick crowned himself King of Prussia at Konigsberg.

His love of pomp and grandeur moved him to emulate Louis XIV. He commissioned the building of a fine new palace in Berlin, fostered the arts with the founding of the Academy of Arts (1696), and the economy with the Academy of Sciences. He also founded a new university at Halle (1694) and patronized Leibnitz and the sculptor Schluter.

FREDERICK II (FREDERICK THE GREAT) (1712–86), King of Prussia (*reg.* 1740–86), enlightened despot and creator of

Prussia as a great power. His father, Frederick William I, forced him to renounce intellectual pursuits for the parade ground and cabinet office, but left him a highly organized, efficient military state, whose essentials Frederick hardly changed and which provided the basis for 19th-cent. Prussia. Under him the purpose of the state, of himself as king, and of his subjects, was to maintain the army and Prussia's position among the great powers. Necessary to his system was state service by the nobility (*Junkers*), who were appeased by tax privileges and control of their serfs. The whole was controlled by an initiative-stifling royal despotism, which was, however, tempered by an enlightened attitude, which gave it the admiration of the *philosophes* and aspiring enlightened despots. The king, who was intellectual, patronized Voltaire, founded an academy, enforced religious toleration, and abolished torture.

Frederick's fame rests largely on his genius as a military commander, the greatest between Marlborough and Napoleon. This was demonstrated in his naked seizure of Silesia from Austria and his defence of it (1740–5), and then in his struggle in the Seven Years War (1756–63) to prevent Austria regaining the province in alliance with Russia and France. By his own superhuman efforts and the fortunate death of the Empress Elizabeth, Prussia beat off the great coalition. After 1763 he was determined never to have to face another war and at the same time to prevent any disturbance in the balance of power to Prussia's detriment. An alliance with Russia (1764) was essential to this largely diplomatic policy, which culminated successfully in the peaceful First Partition of Poland (1772) with Austria and Russia. In his last years he successfully resisted the attempts of Austria to expand into Bavaria, first with Saxon help in the War of the Bavarian Succession (1778–9), and then with most of the German princes in the *Fürstenbund* (1785).

D. B. Horn, *Frederick the Great and the Rise of Prussia* (London, 1964).   DMCK

FREDERICK I (1676–1751), King of Sweden (*reg.* 1720–51). He was Landgrave of Hesse-Cassel, married Charles XII's sister, Ulrika Eleonora (1715), and helped her to become queen in 1718. She was induced to abdicate in his favour, so that Sweden might have a ruler wholly amenable, as he was, to the new constitution.

FREDERICK, Prince of Wales (1707–51), eldest son of King George II of Britain and the first Hanoverian prince to identify himself with English interests and lead the opposition politicians, both Tories (*eg*, Bolingbroke) and the discontented Whigs (*eg*, Cobham, Lyttelton, Carteret, Pulteney, and Pitt) against the supremacy of Walpole. In 1736 he quarrelled with his parents over the question of a higher allowance after his marriage to Augusta of Saxe-Gotha. Frederick set up a rival establishment to the royal court at Leicester House, where he patronized the literary figures of the day, as well as his political friends. After Walpole's resignation, he was reconciled with his father and accepted an additional £50,000 allowance, but in his last few years he attracted the support of opposition nonentities, *eg* the 2nd Lord Egmont.

FREDERICK HENRY, Count of Nassau, Prince of Orange (1584–1647), soldier and statesman, youngest son of William the Silent, *stadtholder* of five provinces of the Netherlands and successor (1625) to his brother Maurice as Captain-General and Admiral-General by the states general. As a young man he commanded the troops of the states general to bring about the surrender of Utrecht (1610), but his reputation was established in the later stages of the Dutch War of Independence when he captured the Brabant fortress of Hertogenbosch (1629) and retook Breda (1637). In the 1640s he clashed with the regents of Holland, whose suspicions were aroused by his desire to pursue the war against Spain rather than to negotiate; by fears that his pro-French sym-

pathies would lead the Netherlands into subordination to France (a nearer and more powerful threat than Spain itself); and by the dynastic ambitions which made him contemplate intervention in the English Civil War on the royalist side. The conflict was resolved by his death and peace was concluded between the states general and Spain at Münster (1648).

FREDERICK WILLIAM I, Elector of Brandenburg (1620–88), who succeeded his father, the Elector George William, in 1640. He was known as 'the Great Elector'. His long reign marked a turning point in the development of Brandenburg-Prussia.

At the age of 20 he inherited scattered territories which had been violated by both Catholic and Protestant armies in the Thirty Years War, and was faced in 1648 by major political and economic problems. Although he was rewarded with three bishoprics and East Pomerania by the peace of Westphalia for Brandenburg's contribution to the Protestant cause, it was 1653 before the Swedes could be evacuated from his Pomeranian lands. By intervening in the Northern War (1655–60), first on the Swedish side and then on Poland's, he won the recognition of both states on his sovereign possession of Prussia (treaty of Oliva).

Meanwhile, Frederick William reorganized the administration of his heterogeneous lands. He forced the *Landtage*, nobility, and towns to subordinate their local interests to the good of the Hohenzollern state. He created central institutions to organize the army, which numbered 30,000 men before his death (*Generalkriegs Kommissariat*), and the finances needed to sustain it (*Amtskammer*), as well as the royal officials who manned the new bureaucracy. These reforms laid the basis of the Prussian state.

His economic policy was much influenced by the protectionism of Colbert. The construction of the Oder–Spree canal stimulated the growth of Berlin and diverted trade from Saxon and Swedish control. He laid the foundations of 19th-cent. German colonialism by his project for an East India company, an expedition to the Gold Coast, the foundation of Grossfriedrichsburg, and the creation of an African company (1682). He bought Dutch ships to protect his merchantmen, but the burden on his small state proved too great and his colonial schemes were abandoned by his successors.

In the later years of his reign Frederick William was drawn into the anti-French coalition (1686), having failed to acquire Stettin by his alliance with Louis XIV (1679–85). His economic programme benefited from the influx of French Huguenots invited by the Edict of Potsdam (1685). He died as Brandenburg prepared to enter the War of the League of Augsburg.

F. Schevill, *The Great Elector* (Chicago, 1947).   MKS

FREDERICK WILLIAM I (1688–1740), King of Prussia (*reg.* 1713–40), member of the Hohenzollern family, and son of Frederick III, Elector of Brandenburg, who from 1701 took the title of King of Prussia, and whom he succeeded. The cumulative efforts of the three kings, Frederick I, Frederick William I, and Frederick II, welded the composite 'territories' which they possessed in the 17th cent. into a powerful modern state by the end of the 18th cent., Frederick William's contribution to the process being the development of a centralized bureaucracy and the large army which was to be the basis of modern Prussia.

The title of king belonged strictly to East Prussia, which lay outside the Holy Roman empire, but inside the empire Frederick William was variously Elector of Brandenburg, Duke of Pomerania, Magdeburg, and Cleve, Count of Ravensburg and Mark, and Prince of Halberstadt and Minden. To the problem of the economic backwardness of these lands, most of which lay between the middle Elbe and the Baltic coast of Pomerania, was added the particularism of the Estates and the corporations within them, whose strenuously defended liberties had been steadily consolidated since the Middle Ages. To the king his office was a sacred trust, and his single objective the increase of its power on an authoritarian basis.

Frederick I had already laid the foundations for his successor by making himself financially independent of the Estates and establishing a standing army. Frederick William, who habitually wore military uniform and thought of himself as an officer, doubled the size of the army to 80,000 in peacetime and militarized the nobility by demanding from their sons service in the army, checking and recording their activities in the *Table of Vassals*. Despite initial hostility and the severe discipline, such service came to be regarded as an honour. In 1733 he introduced a cantonal system of recruitment to maintain particular regiments, and by 1740 had amassed, by financial and administrative reforms, a war chest of 8 million thalers.

Constantly at work in his office at Potsdam, except when drilling his favourite regiment of grenadiers for relaxation, he worked to increase his revenues and to undermine the autonomy of Estates and corporations, setting up centrally appointed local commissaries and rural commissioners for town and country respectively, who were responsible in each province to the War Commissary. Their first task was the collection of the revised and improved taxes, the 'Contribution' in the country and the 'Excise' in the towns. Town councils were abolished and guilds brought under state supervision. The entire administration was regulated by a 'General Directory' from 1723, and ministers were kept subordinate to the king's will.

To improve the economy of his territories Frederick William tried to raise the peasantry from their condition of near-serfdom, and promoted internal colonization, especially in East Prussia, where he re-established agriculture after the plague of 1709, and he promoted the woollen industry by mercantilist protection.

It was left to Frederick II to apply these resources in an aggressive foreign policy.

R. A. Dorwart, *The Administrative Reforms of Frederick William I of Prussia* (Cambridge, MA, 1953).   HNBM

FREDERICK WILLIAM III (1770–1840), King of Prussia (*reg.* 1797–1840), supported the reforms of Hardenberg and Stein, as well as the military reorganization of Scharnhorst and Gneisenau. He was too nervous of Austria to join the second or third coalition, but was finally goaded into war over Hanover and was defeated at Jena. After the disasters of 1812 he joined Russia against Napoleon, and after 1815, he supported the Holy Alliance and Metternich and the forces of conservatism. He took no part in the creation of the Zollverein.

FREDERICK WILLIAM IV (1795–1861), King of Prussia (*reg.* 1840–61). His wish to return to a medieval paternalism and a rejuvenation of the estates was mistaken by the liberals as sympathy for their ideas, especially as he spoke proudly of 'the German nation'. After initial compromises with the Berlin revolution (March 1848) he soon took measures to destroy it, and also rejected the Frankfurt assembly's offer of the imperial crown (April 1849). Although keeping a restricted constitution afterwards, he followed the Austrian lead in the German confederation and in counter-revolutionary policies until he was incapacitated by a stroke (1858), when his brother William became regent.

FREDERICKSBORG, TREATY OF (1720), concluded between Sweden and the coalition of states—Hanover, Prussia, Saxony, and Denmark—ranged against her in the Great Northern War. Sweden was forced to cede Bremen and Verden to Hanover, Stettin and part of Pomerania to Prussia, the Gottorp share of Schleswig and the rights of free passage through the Sound to Denmark, and the recognition of Augustus of Saxony's right to the Polish Crown. Peace

with Russia, the only power not included in the treaties of Stockholm and Fredericksborg (1719–20), followed in 1721.

FREDERICKSBURG, BATTLE OF (13 Dec. 1862), engagement during the American Civil War. Union troops, commanded by Gen. Burnside, crossed the Rappahannock river, fought their way through Fredericksburg, VA, and unsuccessfully attacked Lee's smaller Confederate force which was well entrenched on hills overlooking the town. Union losses of 12,600 were twice those of the Confederacy.

FREE CHURCH FEDERATION (1892), formed in Britain after the Manchester congress of Free Churches to watch over nonconformist interests in civil and religious affairs. The federation was a loose alliance of local Free Church councils and its national assembly dealt with a wide range of political and theological subjects. Its leaders included the Methodist minister Hugh Price Hughes and the Baptist John Clifford, who stiffened Welsh resistance to Balfour's Education Act (1902) and the continuing monopoly of Anglican Church schools in certain areas. The federation joined with the Federal Council of Evangelical Free Churches to form the Free Church Federal Council (1940) and worked with the ecumenical movement which developed after the Second World War.

FREE CHURCH OF SCOTLAND (1843) formed 18 May at the 'Disruption' when 474 ministers and supporters withdrew from the General Assembly of the established Church of Scotland and set up a rival General Assembly. The new Free Church took a third of the ministers and more than a third of the laity with them, led by the Rev. Thomas Chalmers, the first Moderator, an able leader and organizer, who financed the church by every member's weekly subscription on Wesleyan lines. The Disruption came through the presbyteries' demands for a voice in matters of patronage to a benefice after a long series of clashes between the General Assembly and the civil courts. The conflict between Church and state in Scotland meant little to the English, but Chalmers's secession was felt to be a victory for liberalism and radicalism and a blow to Peel's Conservative government. The Free Church joined with the limited Presbyterians to form the United Free Church of Scotland (1900). The schism with the Scottish Established Church was healed in 1929.

FREE DEMOCRATIC PARTY of the German Federal Republic, won 11·9 per cent of the votes to the Bundestag (1965). Its importance sometimes outweighed its electoral strength as a result of the delicate parliamentary balance which emerged from the Bundestag elections of 1953 and 1961. Its policies were those of political and economic liberalism—including freedom of any form of state control of the economy—and its electoral appeal was primarily to the Protestant and free-thinking middle classes, especially in business.

The party was seriously weakened after 1966, having provoked the government crisis which led to Erhard's resignation (Nov. 1966) and the formation of a CPU–SPD coalition. It lost two of its outstanding leaders in 1967, with the death of Thomas Dehler and the resignation of Erich Mende. One of its leaders in 1970 was Ralf Dahrendorf.

FREE PORT ACT (1766) in Britain, opened certain British West Indian ports to foreign vessels. The act, proposed by Edmund Burke, marked a change in the mercantilist Navigation Acts.

FREE PORT SYSTEM. A free port is an area of a port which is outside its customs system. Its existence, provided it is big enough, not only makes re-export simpler but also encourages imports, since an importer need not tie up money in paying duties until the marketing of the goods is arranged for. In some cases simple processing takes place in the free port area. Free ports were sometimes created by governments to develop new areas of foreign trade, as the British did in the West Indies in the 18th cent., or were old, independent cities gradually undergoing closer incorporation in a state, such as the Hanseatic cities in 19th-cent. Germany. Britain did not have free ports at home in the mercantilist period, and there was little advantage they could give in the free trade period.

'FREE SILVER', slogan adopted in US after 1873 by western mining and farming interests demanding a bimetallic currency and the 'free and unlimited coinage of silver'. They attributed the severe economic crisis of the 1870s to the 'Crime of 1873' —the dropping of the silver dollar from the coinage list, and urged the re-establishment of silver at the 16 to 1 ratio with gold that had been prescribed in the Coinage Act of 1837. This, like the 15 to 1 ratio of the 1792 Currency Act, had over-valued silver, with the result that the silver dollar had never gone into general circulation. The discovery of large silver deposits in the West, economic depression, and ignorance of monetary theory led to renewed popular demand for the silver dollar which was reinforced by sentimental attachment to it as the poor man's coin. The 16 to 1 ratio came to be regarded as sacrosanct. Pressure from silver mining interests led to the passage of the Bland–Allison Act (1878) and the Sherman Silver Purchase Act (1890), which in effect gave subsidies to the industry. The financial panic of 1893 evoked agitation from 'sound money' interests that forced repeal of the Sherman Act, but the controversy over 'free silver' remained a major issue in Bryan's presidential campaigns (1896, 1900, 1908). The catastrophic slump of 1929, which saw the silver dollar price falling to 18 cents, led to a last upsurge of 'free silver' in 1933, when more than a third of the Senate voted in favour of bimetallism in the traditional 16 to 1 ratio. Devaluation of the gold dollar in the following year (1934) brought the value of the silver dollar up to 27 cents, but from that time the issue was dead.

Allied as it was with agrarian and working-class discontent, the campaign for free silver had much wider significance than an academic controversy over monetary theories. 'Sound money' protagonists from big business were blamed for the original 'Crime of 1873', and the 'gold bugs' for repealing the Sherman Act. The whole movement in consequence assumed the appearance of a crusade for social and economic justice, which was high-lighted by Bryan's 'Cross of Gold' oratory and the defection of leading western Republicans, such as Senator Teller of CO, to the Democratic Party.   WJR

FREE SOIL PARTY, short-lived US political party founded on opposition to the further extension of slavery. The party comprised a mixture of 'Barnburner' Democrats from New York, anti-slavery 'conscience' Whigs, and survivors of the earlier Liberty Party. In the presidential election of 1848 the Free Soil ticket of Martin Van Buren and Charles Francis Adams polled nearly 300,000 votes and helped to swing the election to the Whigs. In 1852 the vote for the Free Soil presidential candidate, John P. Hale, dropped by almost half. As the party disintegrated most of its members moved into the new Republican Party, of which it was the immediate precursor.

FREE TRADE, in Britain. The main theoretical exponent of Free Trade was Adam Smith in *The Wealth of Nations* (1776), where he argued against government restrictions and controls on trade and industry on the ground that the individual knew his own interest best and that the wealth of a nation was the wealth of its individuals. He was able to support his argument with instances of the ineffectiveness of government control, and on its general tendency to reduce trade and raise prices. He was writing in the period now called mercantilist when trade was subject to prohibitions, high duties, bounties, and other regulations and incentives designed to maintain a high level of skilled employment in Britain. It was impossible to deny assent to much of Smith's argument, and the century after his publication saw the gradual adoption of Free Trade in Britain. The chief ministers associated with this were Pitt the younger, Huskisson, Peel, and Gladstone. Pitt was intellectually convinced of Smith's argument, but in practice the main motives for reduced customs duties in his ministry were either the prospects of an increased level of legal trade which would bring in a similar revenue, as in the case of the duties on tea, or specific advantages obtainable by agreement from other countries, as in the Eden treaty with France. In Peel's ministries the obstacles to lowering duties were the opposition of specific interests—for instance, the landed interest; to competition from overseas; and the problem of finding alternative revenue. By reintroducing income tax in 1842, Peel was able to bring down many duties and rationalize the system of control. Gladstone completed the policy by lowering the duties on sugar and timber (which were intended to encourage colonial production) and on manufactured goods, and the main steps in this process were his budgets of 1853 and 1860 and the Cobden treaty of 1860. The stages in this programme were handicapped by the dislike of the Liberals for income tax, which they regarded as an inquisitorial system of taxation.

After 1860, Britain was basically a Free Trade country, though small duties remained on many articles for revenue purposes. So long as she was the only advanced industrialized country the system suited her interest well, for her industries had no competitors, and the general expansion of world trade, encouraged both by this policy and by the strength of sterling, favoured her exports. Free Trade also gave practical help to the growing political independence of Britain's colonies, since trade had been the main sphere of Westminster's intervention in their affairs. From the 1870s onwards arguments could be raised against the system. British agriculture suffered heavily from the competition of American wheat, and the newly industrialized Germany and US protected their home markets from Britain by tariffs, while they freely sent goods to her. In the early 20th cent. there was some feeling that agriculture and industries connected with defence should be protected in case of war. Joseph Chamberlain wished to give the empire a more formal structure and common economic interest by a system of imperial preference, which would have meant duties on foreign produce, but his attempt to drive the Conservative Party in this direction led to its conspicuous failure in the 1906 election and showed the strength of the sentiment for Free Trade. To many it had become not just an argument of economic expediency but a basic principle of political thought, and was associated with laissez-faire and the general idea of a limited sphere of action for the state. Britain remained a Free Trade nation, except for some duties imposed in the First World War on luxuries, until 1932, when she turned instead to imperial preference and organized bilateral trade agreements.

C. P. Kindleberger, *International Economics* (London, 1955). N. McCord, *Free Trade* (London, 1970).   RMM

FREE WILL, DOCTRINE OF, theological concept that man can choose to co-operate with God in the process of his own salvation and that his eternal life is not predestined. The doctrine was one of the controversial issues of the Reformation, both among Protestant reformers and between them and the Catholic Church.

FREEDMAN, DAVID ISAAC (1874–1939), Rabbi of the Hebrew Congregation, Perth, WA (1897–1939), and founder of Perth Hebrew School, was an AIF chaplain on Gallipoli and in France. He became a member of the senate of the University of Western Australia (1932–9).

FREEDMEN'S BUREAU, agency established (1865) to help former Negro slaves at the end of the American Civil War. Its life and powers were extended by Congress (1866) despite a veto from President Andrew Johnson. A mixed civilian-military organization, chronically short of funds and relying greatly on voluntary help, the bureau aimed to avoid a 'welfare' approach, but rather to protect the Negro in his new-found freedom while educating him to stand on his own feet, especially by exercising the vote. Many southerners alleged that the bureau was corrupt and acted as a political machine to mobilize the Negro vote for the Republican Party, but it achieved a good deal in face of severe difficulties before its operations were wound up (1872).

FREEDOM RIDERS, US civil rights group who protested against racial segregation in transportation (1961). White and Negro members of the Congress of Racial Equality sought by the non-violent action of riding on buses to test the extent to which racial segregation still existed in certain Southern states. At Birmingham, Anniston, and Montgomery, AL, the riders met with violence from mobs. As a result of these disorders the Inter-state Commerce Commission outlawed segregation in all inter-state trains, buses, and terminals. When freedom riders sought to test these desegregation orders in MS they were attacked. Despite the legality of their actions, over 300 freedom riders were arrested and prosecuted in Jackson, MS, for trying to use the inter-state bus terminal on a desegregated basis. This short-lived non-violent form of protest did, however, help to eliminate the systematic segregation of Negroes in inter-state transportation.

FREEMAN, MRS, name used in private correspondence by Queen Anne to her close friend, Sarah Churchill, Duchess of Marlborough. The pseudonym was used to emphasize their friendship and overcome the gulf between their ranks.

FREEMAN BOROUGHS in England, unreformed parliamentary constituencies in which all freemen had the vote. Since the methods of qualifying as a freeman varied, manipulation of their numbers, either by restriction or by swamping, according to the size of the borough, was a well-known method of influencing elections.

FREEMASONRY, fraternity originally based on medieval craft associations among stonemasons which during the 17th and 18th cents developed into a speculative system of deistic character open to men in all walks of life, inculcating a lofty morality and engaging in charitable works. Although the medieval origins are obscure, it appears that the 'lodges' where stonemasons worked and lived together developed regulations and secret means of identification in order to distinguish workers qualified by apprenticeship from interlopers, a need peculiar to their craft since they were mobile and entirely dependent on wages. Their interests must have broadened beyond those of their craft alone, for during the 17th cent. gentlemen began to join existing lodges as non-operative masons. This probably happened first in Scotland, where the first known non-operative mason, John Boswell, laird of Auchinleck, joined the Edinburgh lodge in 1600; but by 1686 it seems that the custom of admitting men into the 'Society of Free-masons' had spready over the whole of Britain. The masons' emphasis on brotherhood and peace contributed to a rapid growth in numbers and a multiplication of lodges, on a world-wide scale, during the 18th cent. Lodges were founded, *eg*, in India (1730), Jamaica (1742), North America (1730), Spain (1728), Italy (1763), and Russia (1771). The first Grand Lodge was formed in London in 1717 and its authority was gradually extended over other English lodges during the century, and although a rival Grand Lodge was later set up the two formed the United Grand Lodge of England in 1813. Organization under Grand Lodges was similar in Scotland and Ireland, but in the US Grand Lodges in each state remained autonomous, the only general body, the Masonic Service Association, being merely advisory. Since the early 18th cent. the highest officials of the movement in England were markedly aristocratic, but it has also brought together people of widely different social rank.

Freemasonry was condemned by the papacy in 1738 and 1751 on the grounds that it was a deistic or pagan religion, but this did not prevent its rapid growth in Catholic Europe among rulers, nobles, intellectuals, and even clerics. At times masons were suspected of revolutionary political activity. The movement was suppressed by the National Socialists in Germany, but restored in 1949 and is proscribed in communist countries.   HNBM

FREEPORT DOCTRINE in US, enunciated by Stephen A. Douglas in debate with Abraham Lincoln at Freeport, IL (1858). Confronted by Lincoln with the apparent contradiction between his doctrine of popular sovereignty regarding slavery in the US territories, and the Supreme Court's Dred Scott decision (1857) upholding the legal status of slavery in the territories, Douglas argued that a territory could still exclude slavery by refusing to pass the local legislation necessary to protect it. The Freeport Doctrine cost him much southern support in his bid for the presidency (1860).

FREI MONTALVA, EDUARDO (1911–), president of Chile (1964–70), and first president elected by Christian Democrats in Latin America. His party has been described as moderate reformist.

FREIBOURG, ETERNAL PEACE OF (1516), agreement between Francis I and Cardinal Schinner, Abp of Sion, on behalf of the Swiss whom he had just led to destruction at the battle of Marignano (1515). The Swiss were to surrender Domodossola, which controlled the Simplon Pass, although they retained the Ticino valley, the great part of Lake Lugano, and the Locarno end of Lake Maggiore, roughly the modern boundary between Switzerland and Italy. The Swiss also became the pensioned mercenaries of France.

FREIBURG, BATTLE OF (1713), imperial reverse at the end of the War of the Spanish Succession, resulting in the French capture of the fortress of Freiburg, after a three-month siege, from the Austrian commander, Von Harsch. The French victory, followed by the treaties of Radstadt and Utrecht, increased the resentment of the German princes in the empire, especially the Elector of Hanover (later George I, King of Britain), towards the English Tories.

FREIKORPS (Free Corps) in Germany, counter-revolutionary volunteer units formed in 1918. The dissolution of the German imperial army after the collapse of the monarchy in Nov. 1918 left the new government without a military force to restore law and order or to defend Germany's frontiers. Fearing that the German Revolution might develop along Russian lines and that the Reich might fall apart, Ebert agreed to the drafting of volunteers to form the *Freikorps*. The first units were established in Dec. 1918 and immediately began to suppress the left-wing revolutionary movement. Detachments of the corps put down the Spartacus uprising of Jan. 1919 and were also used to put an end (1919) to the Bavarian Soviet Republic. Other units were employed in the so-called *Grenzshutz Ost* (Eastern frontier defence), mainly against Poland. Most members of the corps were uprooted young soldiers of middle-class background who, having survived the First World War, found it difficult to adjust themselves to civilian life. Many of them developed a ruthless mercenary mentality and were attracted by the promise of adventure and rewards. In so far as they held specific political views, they were violently nationalistic, anti-Semitic, and anti-communist. The most radical among them fought in the Baltic states against the Red Army (*Baltikumer*) until, on the Allies' insistence, they were disbanded. They then returned to Germany full of resentment against the Weimar Republic, which they believed had betrayed them. In 1919, with the removal of the internal and foreign threat, most of the corps was disbanded, but many of its members were absorbed into the *Reichswehr*, the state armed forces. Others, when faced with dismissal, began to consider the destruction of the Weimar 'system'. This was attempted by Ehrhardt and

Lüttwitz in an unsuccessful *coup d'état* which became known as the Kapp *putsch* (1920). Its collapse brought the *Freikorp's* existence to an end, except for its brief revival during the war in Upper Silesia (1921), but many of its members continued to be active in the innumerable paramilitary and right-wing organizations which contributed to the downfall of the Weimar Republic.

FREIRE SERRANO, RAMÓN (1787–1851), leader in the Chilean wars of independence and president of Chile. He succeeded O'Higgins as dictator and expelled the remaining Spaniards from the island of Chiloe (1826). Both his presidential terms ended with *coups d'état*, and his overthrow.

FREISING, OTTO OF (?1114–58), bishop. After studying in Paris, where he came into contact with the teaching of Peter Abelard, he was created Bp of Freising. He was the author of a history of the world and also of the more famous *Gesta Friderici*, a history of the early years of the reign of his relative, Emperor Frederick I.

FRELINGHUYSEN, FREDERICK THEODORE (1817–85), US politician and statesman, who helped to found the Republican Party in NJ. He was an influential US senator (1866–9, 1871–1877) and served on the commission which decided the disputed presidential election of 1876. As secretary of state (1881–5), he unaggressively but actively promoted US interests in Latin America and the Pacific.

FRÉMONT, JOHN CHARLES (1813–91), US explorer, soldier, and presidential candidate. His spectacular exploits as 'Pathfinder' in the American west stand in sharp contrast to his unhappy political and military career. He made three major expeditions of scientific importance through the Rockies and the Pacific coast region (1842–6) which stimulated interest in the west and heightened enthusiasm for westward expansion. His third expedition involved him in the US conquest of CA and he was associated with the short-lived Bear Flag Republic (1846). He became governor of CA (1847), but the following year was court-martialled and found guilty of mutiny. President Polk remitted the sentence and Fremont became senator from CA (1850–1). The first presidential candidate of the Republican Party (1856), he was defeated by James Buchanan. In the Civil War he commanded the Department of the West (1861), but was removed shortly after issuing a controversial proclamation confiscating the property of southern sympathizers in MO and freeing their slaves. He served without distinction in the eastern theatre (1862) and was the presidential candidate of the abortive 'Radical Democracy' movement (1864).

FRENCH ACADEMY, first of the many academies established in 17th-cent. France to encourage intellectual and artistic activity. It originated with the gatherings of men of letters at the home of Valentin Conrart (1603–75) in 1634, and received official recognition with the publication of letters-patent (Jan. 1635) on Richelieu's initiative. Its principal task was to define the French language by drawing up a grammar, works on rhetoric and poetry, and a dictionary, which was started in 1639 and first published in 1694. From 1643–72 the academy was housed in the Hôtel Séguier and later at the Louvre. It became one of the formative influences of French literature, and contributed to the supremacy of the French language in 18th-cent. European society and culture. In 1793 the academy was dissolved and reconstituted two years later as the third class of the *Institut National*. Napoleon promoted it to the second class, and in 1816 the academy was finally re-established under its old name.

FRENCH AND INDIAN WAR (1754–63), conflict between Britain and France in North America. The French and English colonists had long been rivals in the attempt to control western lands, and the French had established a series of forts along the Ohio river valley. Some of these forts intruded into lands claimed by the colony of Virginia and granted to the Ohio Land Co. Gov. Robert Dinwiddie, of Virginia, sent George Washington and Christopher Gist to warn the French to leave the Ohio lands. The French refused, and when Washington returned with colonial troops he was defeated at Great Meadows, PA (1754). A British and colonial force under Gen. Edward Braddock attempted to seize Fort Duquesne and were defeated by French and Indians (9 July 1755). The outbreak of the Seven Years War (1756) in Europe led France and Britain to extend hostilities in North America. After French victories in NY at Fort Oswego (1756) and Fort William Henry (1757), British forces seized Louisbourg, Cape Breton (1758), and Fort Frontenac on Lake Ontario (1758). The French abandoned Fort Duquesne (1758) and in the battles of Ticonderoga and Crown Point (1759) were driven out of NY by British and colonial troops led by Gen. Jeffrey Amherst. In a battle on the Plains of Abraham the British general, James Wolfe, defeated the Marquis de Montcalm (3 Sept. 1759) and Quebec fell. The next year (7 Sept.) Montreal fell, and French Canada was in British hands. It was formally surrendered in the treaty of Paris (1763).

FRENCH EAST INDIA COMPANY. From the 16th cent. stray French vessels found their way to India and the east and a station was set up in Madagascar. From the beginning of the 17th cent. interest quickened, and the land route was explored, notably by the traveller Tavernier. The first attempt to set up a French trading company was made by Henry IV of France (1604–9). On Colbert's inspiration the Compagnie des Indes Orientales was formed in 1664, Louis XIV backing it with an interest-free loan of 3 million livres. It had 21 directors, a 50-year trading monopoly east of the Cape of Good Hope, and a mandate for colonization. Dutch opposition and French apathy hindered development until the site of Pondicherry was obtained from the Bijapur general, Sher Khan, in 1673. Here François Martin founded a French settlement (1674) which, with the French factory at Surat, began to flourish. In 1690 Chandernagar in Bengal was established. But the European wars of the French affected their prospects. Pondicherry was taken by the Dutch (1693), but restored in 1699. It was then fortified, and revived until Martin's death (1706), by which time it had become a prosperous town of 40,000 inhabitants. The War of the Spanish Succession again affected the company and its trading privileges were leased to merchants in St Malo (1708–20).

In 1723, after the crash of Jean Law's enterprises in which the French company was involved, it was reconstituted as 'the Perpetual Company of the Indies' and began a new career. It took possession of Mauritius (1721) and, for the spice trade, Mahé, which was fortified (1724), and acquired Karikal on the Coromandel coast (1739). Trade prospered under Lenoir and Benoist Dumas in Pondicherry and Dupleix in Chandernagar. The company benefited by the ability of its servants, the pacific policy of Cardinal Fleury, and its own concentration on trade rather than politics, so that by 1740 its sales were half those of the British company.

The outbreak of the War of the Austrian Succession (1740) and the arrival of Dupleix in Pondicherry (1742) changed this situation. War was forced on the company, and at its conclusion Dupleix preferred politics to trade, believing that dominion was a prerequisite of profits. This experiment ended with the recall of Dupleix and the capture of Pondicherry by the British (1761) during the Seven Years War. Thereafter Pondicherry was an open town, to be occupied by the British whenever war broke out with France. In 1769 the company was suspended after criticism of its finances by the physiocrat, Morellet. In 1785 it was re-established on a purely commercial monopolistic basis.

A. Martineau, *Dupleix et l'Inde Française*, 4 vols (Paris, 1920–8).
S. P. Sen, *The French in India, first establishment and struggle* (Calcutta, 1947).   TGPS

FRENCH GUIANA, French possession between Surinam and Brazil. The original French settlement in Guiana was made at Cayenne island (1604). During 17th-cent. struggles the French emerged triumphant over English and Dutch competitors, but not until the 18th cent. did the French expand to the mainland. British and Portuguese interlopers, seizing control (1808), were expelled (1816). Sugar plantations, once prosperous, declined after the abolition of slavery (1849). To revive economic activity the country was declared a penal settlement (1852). Convicts serving eight or more years had to remain permanently. But despite 50,000 convicts being released up to the abolition of penal status (1946), little development occurred. Ruled originally by trading companies, Guiana came under the French state (1672) and in 1946 was made a *département* of metropolitan France.

FRENCH IN MADAGASCAR. The French occupied a fort in south-eastern Madagascar (1642–74) and claimed an undefined sovereignty over the island. During the 19th cent. Europeans became increasingly involved with the expanding inland Merina kingdom. In 1820 the London Missionary Society started work in Merina. Malagasy Christians were persecuted, and in 1845 Britain and France intervened unsuccessfully on their behalf. Later in the century the two powers were at odds over Madagascar.

Britain was satisfied with informal relations with an independent and, by the 1860s, Christian Merina, but France pressed claims of sovereignty. In 1883 French marines invaded Merina; two years later the kingdom was forced to become a French protectorate. Malagasy resistance to French rule was prolonged. In 1896 General Gallieni deposed the Merina monarch and made the island a colony. His system of 'pacification' followed by paternal authoritarian rule became a model for other parts of the French empire.

The French imposed their culture and their kind of administration over the Malagasy, and a number of Frenchmen became settlers, owning plantations. The superficial calm of the inter-war years was disturbed in 1942, when British forces occupied Madagascar to prevent its pro-Vichy government handing over bases to Japan. A violent nationalist uprising broke out in 1947, triggered off by the mismanagement of the Rice Board, rice being one of the island's staple crops. Ten years after the suppression of this revolt, Madagascar became an autonomous republic within the French Community (1958). It achieved complete independence as the Malagasy Republic in 1960.

H. Deschamps, *Histoire de Madagascar* (Paris, 1960).
O. Mannoni, *Prospero and Caliban* (London, 1956).   AEA

FRENCH IN SOUTH AFRICA. 200 French Huguenots settled at the Cape of Good Hope (1688–9), and introduced winemaking. Individual Frenchmen contributed during the 18th cent. to the distinctive 'Cape Dutch' architecture.

FRENCH IN WEST AFRICA, French penetration of this area began with the settlement of a French party at St Louis-du-Sénégal in 1637. Later on other settlements were added, notably at Gorée Island, Rufisque, and Joal. In the 18th and early 19th cents the French had to struggle with the British for the possession of these settlements, the British seizing control of the territories on several occasions until 1817, when they finally handed them over to the French.

From their earliest settlement, the French concentrated on commerce and made little attempt to expand territorially until the mid-19th cent. Their main commercial interests centred around the gum trade and the distribution of French manufactures. From 1817 attempts were made to develop for export to France crops like cotton and groundnut, but the results were not encouraging. By about 1850, moreover, commercial activities were proving a disappointment. Attempts to maximize profits from the gum trade led to the desire to cut down the role and share of African middlemen, and led to wars in the 1830s and in 1854.

This disappointment with plantations and commerce motivated a political reorganization of French coastal settlements and a decision to expand French influence into the Western Sudan, regarded as a vast commercial hinterland that should be tapped for the benefit of the settlements. The first forceful attempt to translate this policy into reality came during the governorship of Louis Faidherbe, beginning in 1854 and lasting with a short break till 1865. But a major obstacle to the French was the emergent Tukulor empire, led by Al-Hajj 'Umar b. Sa'id Tall; French expansion was checked after a series of wars against the Tukulor between 1855 and 1860. Thereafter the French embarked on diplomatic missions to promote their commercial and political influence, the first of such missions being sent to the ruler of the Segu empire. Led by Mage, the mission remained at Segu from 1864 to 1866. An abortive attempt was made to renew diplomatic contact in 1874 by Gov. Valière. Interested chambers of commerce sent out a mission led by Paul Soleiller in 1878, but by this time colonial enthusiasts among the military and civilian groups had assumed the direction of French expansion.

A railway scheme to link the Niger with the Senegal was conceived and approved in 1879, and in the 1880s attempts were made to execute the project. New military expeditions were undertaken to penetrate the Western Sudan. By 1889 these expeditions had assumed the character of wars of conquest. Under Lieut.-Col. (later Gen.) Louis Archinard the Tukulor empire was conquered between 1890 and Jan. 1894; the campaign against the Wasulu state of Samori Turé, which had begun in 1883, continued until the latter was defeated in 1898. Other expeditions fought against the Mossi and states in the present areas of Chad and Niger republics. All these wars resulted in the establishment of French West Africa.

The territories were administered by the military between 1890 and 1894. In 1894 a civilian governor was appointed for the Sudan. In 1895 the areas were constituted into a Federation of French West Africa with headquarters at Dakar, Senegal. A governor-general based at Dakar exercised overall federal control, while a Lieutenant-Governor exercised control over each of the component territories. This remained the framework of French colonial administration in West Africa until the post-Second World War period, when developments led to the emergence of separate independent states in place of the Federation.   BOO

FRENCH MUSKETEERS, two companies of musketeers, the first known as the grey musketeers and the second as the black musketeers, after the colour of their horses, were the elite of the king's household troops. The grey company originated in 1622, when they succeeded the king's carabineers. The black musketeers originated as Cardinal Mazarin's guard, but in 1664 were reorganized by Louis XIV on the same lines as the first company. All the musketeers were noblemen and four of them always led official royal processions. The two companies were suppressed in 1775 by Saint-Germain.

FRENCH REFERENDUM (1945), coincided with the first elections in France after the Second World War and opened the way to the establishment of the Fourth Republic. The Third Republic had, for practical purposes, been brought to an end (10 July 1940) by a vote of the National Assembly giving full powers to Pétain; but it had never been formally abrogated. De Gaulle's government, with Allied recognition, controlled France after the liberation, but had no constitutional foundation. The referendum (21 Oct. 1945) offered a choice of a return to the constitution of the Third Republic (when the newly elected assembly would become a Chamber of Deputies under that constitution) or a new constitution, when the assembly would be a Constituent Assembly. The vote, 18½ million to 700,000, was overwhelmingly in favour of a new constitution.

FRENCH REFERENDUM (1946). Two referenda were held to establish the constitution of the Fourth Republic. The constitution proposed at the first referendum (5 May 1946) had the support of the socialists and communists; it made provision for a single-chamber government. It was rejected in the referendum by 10½ million to 9½ million votes.

A revised proposal, which included provision for the Council of the Republic as a second chamber, was put to the electorate (13 Oct. 1946) and accepted by 9 million to 8 million votes (some 8½ million abstaining).

FRENCH REFERENDUM (1958) established the Fifth Republic, following De Gaulle's assumption of power in France (May 1958). The constitution established a stronger executive power than had existed under either the Third or the Fourth Republics. The referendum (28 Sept. 1958) was preceded by a massive campaign by the government to secure the largest possible participation and the largest possible majority. In metropolitan France the referendum proved a success: some 85 per cent of the electorate voted, 18 million voting *Yes* against 4½ million voting *No* (representing a decline for the communists, the principal opponents of the constitution).

The referendum was held throughout the French empire, since the constitution of the Fifth Republic introduced important changes in the government of the overseas territories and established the French Community. The government of Guinea opposed the constitution and it was rejected by popular vote in that country—in effect a vote for independence, which was followed by the severance of all French aid. In the other overseas territories there were large majorities in favour.

In Algeria Muslims and Europeans voted on an equal basis for the first time and Muslim women were given the vote. The Algerian rebel leadership advocated abstention from the vote, but the French army was successful in bringing voters to the polls. Of those who voted 96 per cent voted *Yes*.

FRENCH REFERENDUM (1962) changed the election of the president from indirect to direct election. De Gaulle's use of the referendum to effect this change was vigorously attacked by the opposition and described as unconstitutional; the government was forced to resign by an adverse vote in the assembly. None the less, the referendum was successful: 13 million voted *Yes*, nearly 8 million voted *No*. As a result the president ceased to be elected by an electoral college drawn from local governments and henceforth was elected directly (De Gaulle was re-elected Dec. 1965). After the referendum De Gaulle dissolved the assembly and the Gaullists won a sweeping victory in the ensuing parliamentary elections.

FRENCH REFERENDUM (1962). At the conclusion of the Algerian war the question of the independence of Algeria in accordance with the Evian agreements was submitted to referendum (8 April 1962). In the whole electorate (including overseas territories) 17·9 million voted *Yes*, 1·8 million voted *No*.

FRENCH REFERENDUM (1969) led to De Gaulle's resignation from the presidency of the republic. The electorate was invited to approve of constitutional reforms which would change the composition and functions of the Senate, and establish regional councils of government. The reforms were set out in a complicated document, longer than the constitution itself. Their importance was overshadowed by De Gaulle's campaign for them and his insistence that the referendum would be a vote of confidence in himself. The result of the referendum (27 April 1969) was: nearly 11 million for the reform, 12 million against. Immediately afterwards De Gaulle announced his decision to resign.

FRENCH REVOLUTION (1789), name given to the events of the summer and autumn of that year which brought to an end the ancien régime and opened a series of changes and upheavals lasting until the *coup d'état* of 18 Brumaire. Increasingly, a shortage of money had made the king's ministers search for new sources of revenue in the years before 1789. Such attempts usually foundered in conflicts with vested interests; in the end it was decided to summon the states general, in order to obtain something like national agreement on reform. The meeting of this body (5 May) is the conventional date for the start of the Revolution. The states general soon transformed itself into the National Assembly, which was in the next two years to fundamentally remould French institutions and French life. Its more radically inclined members were able to push forward their colleagues in changes more sweeping than those at first envisaged because of the danger of popular violence if reform were delayed. In 1789 a grave economic crisis was causing distress immediately to most Frenchmen through high food prices and shortages which amounted in some areas to famine. During the summer there were outbreaks of violence in the countryside, where manor-houses and the archives of great estates (where rent-rolls were kept) were attacked. After April Paris itself was in a continual ferment, which came to a climax with the attack of 14 July on the Bastille. After this, neither the king's advisers nor the assembly (even if it had wished to) could resist the current of reform. The major revolutionary landmarks of the next few months were the almost complete abolition of feudal rights and privileges, the most important of which, it was intended, should be redeemed by payments over a number of years by those formerly owning the dues (4–12 Aug.); the drawing up first of a Declaration of the Rights of Man, and then of a new constitution, founding a limited monarchy with a one-chamber elected legislature (Aug. 1789–July 1790); the abolition of nobility (June 1790), of the old provincial divisions (Dec. 1789), and of the *parlements*; the confiscation of the estates of the Church (Nov. 1789); and a reorganization of the relations of Church and state under the Civil Constitution of the Clergy. This huge work of reconstruction was accompanied by a gradual dying-down of the popular passions aroused by hard times in 1789. Nevertheless, suspicions justifiably remained widespread that opponents of the Revolution were numerous both in the royal entourage and in the assembly. After 14 July the next important popular insurrection which helped decisively to keep the Revolution moving forward occurred on 5–6 Oct., and brought about the removal of the royal family and the assembly to Paris from Versailles. In the capital both were much more exposed to popular pressures, yet these in fact decreased somewhat over the next two years as better economic conditions were re-established and the assembly pressed forward steadily with its work. Popular pressure only began to revive in 1791, after the flight to Varennes. Shortly after this, in Sept. 1791, the Constituent Assembly (so-called because its main task had been to make a constitution) dissolved itself, and the next phase of the Revolution began with the election of its successor, the Legislative Assembly. Much of what had been done since 1789 was to be swept aside in the next few years, but in this first phase of the Revolution the foundations of modern France were laid, and the ideals of Liberty, Equality, and Fraternity were first enshrined in a public document. Europe and the world were to copy both; in this sense the 'first' French Revolution was also the birth of modern European liberalism.

J. M. Thompson, *The French Revolution* (Oxford, 1943).
A. Aulard, *A Political History of the French Revolution* (tr. London, 1910).   JMR

FRENCH REVOLUTION (1830), popular movement which overthrew the Bourbons and led to the establishment of the July Monarchy. The Bourbons seemed well entrenched, but there was a growing liberal movement and considerable agitation because of economic depression, and when the regime was faced with a crisis of its own making, these forces found expression.

When Polignac was made prime minister (1829) to strengthen the conservatism of the regime the opposition was encouraged to resist and won a clear victory in the elections of 1830. The government decided to fight and drafted five ordinances. These suspended the liberty of the press, reduced the number of electors and voters, dissolved the new Chamber before it met, called for new elections under the revised franchise in Sept., and appointed Ultras to key offices. The government believed its security arrangements were adequate, although neither the Minister of War nor the governor of Paris were informed, and when the Ordinances were published at 10 a.m. on 26 July, King Charles was hunting. The politicians were taken by surprise, although some journalists did protest and the populace and some of the middle classes newly deprived of the vote did demonstrate. Marmont brought troops in on the afternoon of the 26 July, but met with little resistance and the troops returned to their barracks.

However, overnight the secret societies and others raised barricades all over Paris, and on 28 July when Marmont sent three columns to disperse the rebels his troops were attacked on all sides and were forced to retreat, exhausted and dispirited, on the Tuileries. On the following day, weakened by desertions and pressed by the rebels, they retreated in disorder, by which time some 1800 insurgents and 200 soldiers had died. Meanwhile, the liberal politicians, led by Lafitte, began to take over authority, and since Charles refused to make sufficient concessions they turned towards an Orleanist solution. By 30 July placards in support of the Duke of Orléans went up and he was proclaimed king, much against the wishes of the insurgents, on the following day. Charles continued to resist until the Parisian forces marched on Rambouillet on 3 Aug. The revolution brought little structural change in France and was not simply a middle-class movement. Posing as many problems as it solved, it was in some ways a prelude to 1848.

G. Bertier de Sauvigny, *The Bourbon Restoration* (New York, 1967).   CHC

FRENCH REVOLUTION (1848), popular movement which swept the July Monarchy from power, but failed to establish the social democratic republic of which many of its supporters dreamed. It was largely a revolution by accident, in which a clash between the government and the liberal opposition, over a banquet in Paris to press for parliamentary reform, escalated into revolution. The government came to a tacit agreement with the leaders of the opposition to ban the banquet but still allow speeches to be made, but other reformers organized a procession. The government sought to prevent this, but crowds gathered none the less on the morning of 22 Feb. The government called out the army, but there was no firing and the troops returned to their barracks at about 1 a.m. The following day they reoccupied their positions, reinforced by the unreliable National Guard. The continuing agitation and the attitude of the guard led the king to dismiss Guizot at about 4.30 p.m. on the 23 Feb., but this merely encouraged the demonstrators, and when firing broke out—for some unknown reason—killing 50 people, barricades went up. The government was helpless, as neither Molé nor Thiers could form a government and Bugeaud's attempt to suppress the rising during the night failed. On the morning of the 24th, Louis capitulated, first agreeing to dissolve the Chamber, then to abdicate and finally to leave Paris altogether.

The crowd then invaded the Chamber, swept aside the young heir, and forced Lamartine and the opposition politicians to declare a republic and establish a provisional government, which included two socialist representatives. The fall of the monarchy caused a tremendous feeling of euphoria and emancipation, but before long the government found itself in conflict with the more radical movement, grudgingly agreeing to the ten-hour day, the National Workshops, and the Luxembourg Commission. The conservative financial

and diplomatic policies which circumstances forced on the government were unpopular, as the mass demonstration on 11 March showed. A further demonstration on 16 April had to be put down by the National Guard, and when the elections in May produced a very conservative assembly the scene was set for a final confrontation. On 15 May the radicals tried to establish an insurrectionary government and finally they rose in open rebellion when the assembly tried to close the National Workshops. They were crushed after several days of bitter street fighting in June, and though the Republic continued in being most of its dynamic was gone.

G. Duveau, *The Making of a Revolution* (London and New York, 1967).   CHC

FRENCH REVOLUTIONARY WARS began in 1792 with French declarations of war on the Habsburg ruler of Austria (20 April) and on Prussia and Sardinia (8 and 18 July). This started a struggle which lasted on and off until 1815, merging into the Napoleonic Wars. The war between 1792 and 1797 is usually called the War of the First Coalition; that which began in 1798 and was still going on when Bonaparte took power in the War of the Second Coalition. The cycle of wars opened with high French hopes, soon dashed by the steady advance of the Austrians and Prussians into northern France. The battle of Valmy in Sept. 1792 ended the advance and the French took the offensive on the Rhine, in the Netherlands, and in Savoy. The annexation of Savoy, a temporary occupation of Frankfurt, and the conquest of Brussels and the Austrian Netherlands followed. In Feb. 1793, confident of their strength, the French declared war also on Britain and Holland and, later, Spain (1 Feb. and 7 March). Almost at once, a series of defeats followed which encouraged the émigré royalists. A civil war which broke out in the summer brought on the most serious crisis of the Revolution. The adoption of the system of extraordinary government called the Terror followed; among other steps it brought conscription and the reorganization of the army. Largely thanks to this and to the divisions of her opponents, France survived and began to win victories again in the autumn. By June 1794 the French again held Belgium; during the following winter they invaded Holland and in 1795 set up the Batavian Republic there. In April 1795 Prussia made peace, Spain followed in July, and in December the Austrians made an armistice. The coalition was breaking up. 1796 brought new French offensives: that in Germany failed after initial successes; that in Italy was very successful, though its commander, Bonaparte, disregarded his orders by negotiating preliminaries of peace. The terms were modified at Campo Formio, which left France in effect at war only with England. An expedition to Egypt under Bonaparte now seemed for a variety of reasons the most attractive course for France. It sailed in May 1798, but was marooned in Egypt by the British victory at the Nile (1 Aug.). As the French had already once more antagonized their neighbours by making revolutionary changes in Italy and Switzerland after Campo Formio, the attack on Egypt, which was Turkish, and the seizure of Malta en route by the expedition (by which the tsar was antagonized) led to the crystallizing of the Second Coalition in Dec. Austria, Russia, Naples, Portugal, and Turkey now joined Britain. By the end of 1799 the Russians had withdrawn, and an Anglo–Russian campaign to free Holland had been a failure. Nevertheless, almost all of Italy had been cleared of the French and the French armies had been pushed back across the Rhine. This was the situation confronting Bonaparte on his return from Egypt in October.

G. Lefebvre, *The French Revolution*, 2 vols—tr. (London, 1962, 1964).
R. W. Phipps, *The Armies of the First French Republic* (Oxford, 1926).   JMR

FRENCH, SECOND REPUBLIC (1848–52), political regime established by the February Revolution and overthrown by Louis Napoleon. The republic's inauguration as a result of popular pressure, and somewhat against the wishes of the liberal politicians, symbolized a lack of general support—one of the republic's gravest weaknesses. This was shown by the elections of April 1848, which, despite the efforts of Ledru-Rollin and his commissioners, produced only 80 radical republicans and 38 socialists, against 500 moderates, 200 Orleanists, and 100 legitimists. Not surprisingly, the assembly soon fell out with the Paris popular movement and crushed it after bitter fighting (23–8 June). Many believed with Lamartine that 'the republic was dead', but the assembly was too divided to reject it, and proceeded to draft a republican constitution.

The constitution provided for a directly elected president and a single-chamber legislature, but the hopes of the Constituent Assembly were shattered at the presidential election (Nov.), when Louis Napoleon won 5·4 million votes and Cavaignac and the other candidates only 1·9 million. At first Louis Napoleon was a passive president, leaving government to an Orleanist ministry under Barrot, but in the spring of 1849 he was active in sending a French expeditionary force to suppress the Roman Republic. The first regular elections of the Second Republic produced another very conservative majority and also a large radical minority, the moderates of 1848 being decisively rejected. The conservatives were frightened by their situation, especially as Ledru-Rollin attempted another rising in June, but they were soon at loggerheads with the president, who liked to pose as a radical. There was conflict over Louis Napoleon's choice of ministers, his demands for a larger allowance, and especially his desire to see the constitution revised so as to allow him to stand for re-election. The assembly debated this in June, but failed to give it the necessary two-thirds majority, and both sides began to think of resolving the stalemate by force. The president acted first, dissolving the assembly and remodelling the constitution on the lines of the Consulate (1851). Thereafter the republic existed, in name only, until the declaration of the empire (1852). It led a troubled and undistinguished existence, but saw the introduction of universal suffrage and the passing of the *loi Falloux*.

J. Plamenatz, *The Revolutionary Movement in France, 1815– 1871* (London, 1952).   CHC

FRENCH TERRITORY OF THE AFFARS AND ISSAS
(23,000 sq. kms) in north-eastern Africa is still ruled as part of the French Republic and returns one deputy to the National Assembly in Paris. The population of 90,000 is composed of Somali and Affar people.

FRENCH UNION (UNION FRANÇAISE),
political framework of France and its possessions overseas, created by the constitution of 1946. It included, besides metropolitan France, a number of overseas departments which were integral parts of France, and a growing number of 'Associated States' with varying degrees of independence. The Union gave place to the Communauté Française in 1958.

FRENEAU, PHILIP MORIN
(1752–1832), American poet, sailor, pamphleteer, and journalist. Anti-British satires such as 'The British Prison Ship' (1781) earned him the sobriquet 'poet of the American Revolution'. Between periods as a sea captain, he edited the influential *National Gazette* under Jefferson's patronage (1791–3) and other newspapers in NY and NJ. His later poetic style foreshadowed that of the American Romantics.

FRERE, SIR HENRY BARTLE EDWARD
(1815–84), British colonial servant in the Indian Civil Service (1834–67) and an administrator in South Africa. He was Resident of Satara (1846) and Chief Commissioner of Sind (1850–9), where he kept the peace during the Indian Mutiny. He was a member of the governor-general's Supreme Council (1859–62) and governor of Bombay (1862–7), where he introduced many educational reforms. He supported the proposal to occupy

Quetta and criticized the Punjab system of punitive expeditions. He was member of the Council of India (1867–77). In 1872 he was sent to Zanzibar to negotiate a treaty for the suppression of the slave-trade. In 1877 he was appointed governor of Cape Colony and first Commissioner of South Africa, with instructions to ensure peace. He became involved in the Kaffir War (1878) and the Zulu War (1879) and was recalled in 1880.

FREYBERG, BERNARD CYRIL FREYBERG,
1st Baron (1889–1953), NZ soldier and governor-general. He won the VC in the First World War and led the Second NZ Division in the Middle East and Mediterranean in the Second World War. He served as governor-general (1946–52).

FREYCINET, CHARLES LOUIS DE SAULCES DE
(1828– 1923), French engineer and politician. His career as a mining engineer ended when Gambetta appointed him as head of the military department at Tours during the Franco-Prussian War. As minister of works (1877) he fostered the development of canals and railways. He held office through most of the years 1876–99, being (always for short periods) four times prime minister and three times minister of war. He resigned because of the Panama scandal (1893).

FREYCINET, LOUISE CLAUDE DE SULCES DE
(1779– 1842), French explorer and cartographer, whose expedition to the Pacific (1817–20) to study terrestrial magnetism revived French interest in Oceania.

FREYRE, GILBERTO DE MELLO
(1900–), Brazilian social scientist. His best-known work is *The Masters and the Slaves* (1946), a study of colonial and plantation Brazil.

FRIARS
(Lat. *frater*, brother), used of the members of a particular type of monastic order. These were mendicant, *ie*, owned no property and lived by begging or on gifts in kind. They are also distinguished from the older orders such as the Benedictines and Cistercians in that, unlike them, the friars were members of their order rather than of a particular house of the order; and in that work of the friars—usually preaching—entailed their spending a great deal of time outside the cloister.

The 13th cent. was the great age of the friars and orders proliferated to such an extent that a decree of the Council of Lyons (1274) tried to limit them to four only—the Dominicans, Franciscans, Carmelites, and Augustinian or Austin Friars—though the Servites (founded 1256), Friars of the Sack (1251), and the order of the Holy Cross, or Crutched Friars (1248) survived.

FRICK, HENRY CLAY
(1849–1919), US industrialist and philanthropist, who was active in forming the giant US Steel Corporation (1901), of which he became a director. Being an adamant anti-union man, his policies contributed to the Homestead Strike (1892). The Frick Museum in New York City houses the art collection that he left to the public.

FRICK, WILHELM
(1877–1946), German lawyer and National Socialist politician. He met Hitler in the early 1920s while serving with the Munich police administration and subsequently rose to high office in the Nazi movement. He was elected (1924) to the Reichstag and became minister of the interior and education in Thuringia in Jan. 1930, but was forced to resign 15 months later because of his blatant nazification policies. He entered Hitler's cabinet on 30 Jan. 1933 as Reich minister of the interior and in this capacity had a major share in the *Gleichschaltung* as well as the drafting of the racial laws. In later years his influence declined. He acted as Reich Protector for Bohemia and Moravia (1943– 1945) and was sentenced to death at the Nuremberg trials.

FRIEDLAND, BATTLE OF
(1807), fought by Alexander I of Russia to save Königsberg, home of the Prussian monarchy,

from the French. Napoleon, by using a massed artillery attack for the first time, shattered the Russian army and pursued it to the frontier. The ensuing armistice led to a secret alliance between France and Russia in the treaty of Tilsit.

FRIEDLINGEN, BATTLE OF (1702), defeat of the German imperialist troops of the Margrave of Baden by a numerically inferior French force under Villars in the War of the Spanish Succession (14 Oct. 1702).

FRIENDLY SOCIETIES ACT (1829) in Britain, marks the beginning of the transfer of regulation of friendly societies from local to central government. It required the rules of the societies to be certified at Quarter Sessions and passed as sound by the justices. Annual balance sheets had to be published and a quinquennial statistical return transmitted to the central government. This information eventually made possible the establishment of sounder finance for the societies.

FRIENDS OF THE PEOPLE (1792) in Britain, society for the reform of parliament founded by Grey, Erskine, Sheridan, and other prominent members of the opposition to the younger Pitt. The Friends represented the more cautious, aristocratic element in the 18th-cent. reform movement, basing their claims on the 1688 settlement rather than on the popular radicalism of Thomas Paine. An important achievement was their report on 'The State of the Representation' (1793), documenting the shortcomings of an electoral system in which 71 peers and the treasury returned 170 MPs. The society sponsored Grey's unsuccessful motion for parliamentary reform (1793), but refused to take part in a convention of reform deputies (1794).

FRIESLAND, one of the seven northern sea-girt provinces of the Dutch Republic, where cattle-breeding was a principal industry. The *stadtholder* was traditionally a member of the Nassau branch of the Orange family.

FRIHETSTIDEN in Sweden, period of constitutional government which began with Charles XII's death (1718) and ended with Gustavus III's *coup d'état* (1772), when political power lay in the hands of the four estates of the realm. It was variously interpreted as an era of crippling internal division or a democratic interlude.

FRISIANS, inhabitants of the coastal areas from the mouth of the Rhine to Schleswig since Roman times. Some mixing of populations probably occurred in this area in the 5th and 6th cents, with Anglo-Saxon settlement in Frisia, and the Frisians themselves played some part in the Germanic settlement of East Anglia. By 600 Frisia Magna had been formed with Frisian expansion to the south, which brought them into direct conflict with the Franks. By 734 Charles Martel had defeated them and dissolved Frisia Magna. Their conversion to Christianity absorbed much of the energy of 8th-cent. Anglo-Saxon missionaries until their permanent conquest and conversion by Charlemagne. A seafaring people, they played an important part in trading activities with the Rhine, Meuse, and northern France.

FRITSCH, WERNER FREIHERR VON (1880–1939), German soldier, who was Hitler's commander-in-chief (1934–8). He was antipathetic to National Socialism and complied reluctantly with Hitler's plans to expand the army's numbers and equipment, and tried to dissuade him from reoccupying the Rhineland. After the SA's elimination in 1934, he clashed with Heydrich and Himmler, who wanted the SS to control all the armed forces. In 1938 Himmler, to prevent Fritsch's succeeding the deposed defence minister, Blomberg, fabricated charges of homosexuality against him. Hitler announced Fritsch's resignation on 4 Feb. 1938, with other changes which consolidated his control of the armed forces. On 18 March a military court of honour, whose proceedings

received no publicity, cleared Fritsch. He died during the conquest of Poland.

FROBISHER, SIR MARTIN (?1535–94), English seaman and explorer who tried to find a North-west Passage to China and the Indies, and was prominent in the action of the English fleet against the Spanish Armada (1588). His three voyages in search of the North-West Passage were sponsored by merchants of the city of London, but on the first (1576) he found only the deep inlet, now named Frobisher Bay, and some rock which he mistakenly thought to be gold ore. The third voyage, to plant a colony, was also unsuccessful. In 1585 he sailed with Drake to the West Indies.

FROISSART (1337–1410), French chronicler of medieval chivalry. His chronicles, which are of great literary merit were intended primarily as a record of the chivalry of the aristocracy rather than as an account of events in general. Froissart, who was born in Hainault, became secretary to Philippa of Hainault, wife of Edward III, King of England. When she died, Froissart joined the entourage of the Duke of Brabant. Here, as well as writing verse, he began his chronicles. The first volume was finished by 1371 and covered events in England (1325–69); a second edition extended this to 1377. A third volume covered events in Spain.

FRONDA, term coined to identify the aristocratic groups in Chile (1850–90) which struggled, usually by peaceful means, against executive absolutism, and in favour of more parliamentary yet elite government.

FRONDES, THE, complex series of civil disturbances in France during the regency of Anne of Austria and the ministry of the unpopular Cardinal Mazarin, prompted by a mixture of economic hardship and widespread disaffection with the government's extension and abuse of traditional powers. Falling into two main episodes (1648–9, 1650–3) and deriving its name from a contemporary Paris street urchins' game, the *Frondes* constituted the most serious revolt against the central government during the *ancien régime*.

The first or *parlementaire* Fronde began on 15 Jan. 1648 with the *lit de justice* held to register certain arbitrary financial measures which pin-pointed the bankrupt social and economic policies of Mazarin. As an additional expedient the government declined to renew the right to hereditary possession of office in certain law courts, whose enraged members sought the assistance of the Paris *parlement* (30 April 1648). In the face of this united opposition the queen mother and the cardinal-minister released some arrested magistrates and offered to restore the right of hereditary office (21 June 1648), but the *parlement*, together with the other sovereign courts, demanded further reforms, making imprisonment without trial illegal, abolishing the office of *intendant* in all but border regions, reducing direct taxation and prohibiting new taxes except by registered edicts (July 1648). Further, a member of the *parlement* of Paris, one Broussel, demanded embezzlement proceedings against the tax-farmers (4 Aug. 1648), while the *parlement* declared illegal all existing financial edicts not registered by it. The government reacted by arresting Broussel and another *parlementaire*, Blancmesnil (26 Aug. 1648), which provoked serious riots in Paris (The Days of the Barricades, 26–8 Aug. 1648). Anne of Austria ordered their release to placate the crowds, and the court, with the young Louis XIV, left the capital (13 Sept. 1648). While the *parlement* took defensive measures, Mazarin weakened and a conference between royal and *parlementaire* representatives (25 Sept.–4 Oct. 1648) resulted in important royal concessions, incorporated in a declaration of 24 Oct. In Jan. 1649, when the court retired from Paris, Mazarin prepared to repudiate his concessions. Royal troops under Condé encircled the capital, while rioting mobs supported the *parlement*, but renewed threats of a Spanish invasion and an unsuccessful royal siege brought the two sides to terms, embodied in the treaty of Reuil (1 April 1649), confirming the royal declarations of May–July and Oct. 1648.

Several nobles, *eg*, Conti, the Duke and Duchess of Longueville, Beaufort, Elbœuf, Bouillon, and Rochefoucauld, had supported the *parlementaire* cause, and after the court's return to Paris (Aug. 1649) the uneasy alliance between Mazarin and the ambitious Condé gradually broke down, leading to the *Fronde* of the princes. The *frondeur* nobles, led by Coadjutor Gondi (later Cardinal de Retz), did not resist Mazarin's order for Condé's imprisonment, with that of Conti and Longueville (Jan. 1650), but the Princess of Condé raised provincial revolts, *eg*, in Bordeaux, which capitulated before royal troops (Oct. 1650). Mazarin's position was still insecure, and Retz's plots and serious disturbances forced him to leave Paris for Brühl (6 Feb. 1651). Condé returned triumphantly to the city, but his arrogance alienated his allies so he departed to raise a rebellion in Guyenne. The declaration of Louis XIV's majority (7 Sept. 1651) undermined the legality of the prince's opposition, hitherto made in the king's name. Mazarin returned to France (Dec. 1651), but the rival armies, under Condé and Turenne, manœuvred across France (April–June 1652) until Condé's forces were hemmed in under the Porte Saint-Antoine (Paris). Under the divided *frondeur* princes Paris remained in chaos, *eg*, the massacre of deputies in the Hôtel de Ville (4 July 1652). Mazarin again retired (Aug. 1652), but Louis XIV re-entered Paris unopposed (11 Oct. 1652), while Mazarin followed later (6 Feb. 1653). Condé had joined the Spaniards, and, as royal authority was reasserted, the remnants of aristocratic opposition in Bordeaux collapsed (July–Aug. 1653).

P. R. Doolin, *The Fronde* (Cambridge, MA, 1935).
E. H. Kossmann, *La Fronde* (Leyden, 1954).   MKS

FRONDIZI, ARTURO (1908–   ), candidate of the Intransigent Radical Party who won the Argentine presidential elections of 1958 with Peronist support. In spite of complicated manœuvres to satisfy the army, his permissiveness to the Peronist movement brought his overthrow (1962), and the military took power.

FRONT PALACE INCIDENT, crisis in Thailand in 1875 which delayed the country's modernization. It grew out of strained relations between King Rama V and his *uparaja*, Prince Wichaichan. The latter was named heir-apparent in 1868, without the young king's concurrence; as reforms strengthened the king's position, Wichaichan feared for his survival. A privy council speech attacking his prerogatives provoked the gathering of his troops and then, fearing royal countermeasures, his flight to the British Consulate (1 Jan. 1875). French and British pressures, including a demand for partition of the kingdom, mounted against the king. Concessions to conservative factions gained their support for the Crown, and the crisis was resolved with British mediation in Feb., Wichaichan returning to the Front Palace and further reforms temporarily halted.

FRONTENAC, LOUIS DE BUADE, Comte de (1622–98), French nobleman, godson of Louis XIII and twice governor of New France (1672–82, 1689–98). Before coming to Canada Frontenac served with the French army during the Thirty Years War and as a soldier of fortune with the Venetians against the Turks (1669). As governor of New France Frontenac encouraged and aided the expeditions of La Salle and Marquette and Jolliet. He developed the western fur trade and built Fort Cataracqui (later Fort Frontenac) to control the outlet of Lake Ontario. He arrested the governor of Montréal for illegal trading with the Indians (1674), disputed the powers of the *intendant* (1678–9), and quarrelled with the Bp of Quebec over the latter's liquor trade with the Indians (1675). Frontenac was relieved of his duties (1682), but returned (1689) to lead successful campaigns against the Iroquois (1689–98). He was also engaged in successfully defending Quebec against a British invading force led by William Phipps (1690).

FRONTIER, IN AMERICAN HISTORY, the land on the outer edge of the settled areas of the US from 1607 to 1890. Defined by the US Bureau of the Census as an area containing not less than two nor more than six inhabitants to the square mile (2·6 sq. kms), the frontier was in fact a plurality of lines and was constantly changing. Geographically the settlement moved in westward ripples up to the Mississippi river. First came the colonial frontier (1607–1763), in which the frontier was the area between the Appalachian Mountains and the Atlantic Ocean. From 1763 to 1812 pioneers pushed west of the Appalachian Mountains into the OH River valley. The purchase of LA (1803) and the end of British claims in the North-west Territory (1815) opened up the MS Valley frontier and the line of settlement steadily advanced to the Mississippi river. As this latest area became populated, pioneers moved to the Far West and opened a new frontier in CA and OR (1825–48), avoiding the 'Great American Desert', until the close of the American Civil War. The last stage of geographical frontier development was the settling of the area between the Rocky Mountains and the Mississippi river, which lasted until 1890, when the US Bureau of the Census announced the end of a continuous geographic frontier in the US.

With the disappearance of the physical frontier, an episode which covered almost 300 years of American history came to an end, but the experience provided by this large area of relatively unoccupied and fertile land on the edge of advancing settlement played an important part in shaping the character of the people who had settled it. The question of just how important this influence was arose in 1893, when Frederick Jackson Turner (1861–1932), of Wisconsin University, presented a paper entitled 'The Significance of the Frontier in American History'. Turner rejected the old 'germ theory' of history, which stated that American institutions were a direct result of the European past and suggested instead that the frontier process had played an important role in shaping Americans and their institutions and that this frontier experience accounted for the differences between Americans and Europeans. Turner viewed the fostering of democracy and individualism as the most significant contribution to the constant rebirth of civilization as the frontier moved westward. Turner's sweeping statements on the role of the frontier in America have been severally challenged and on many points refuted, but his hypothesis opened an entirely new approach to the study of American history and he must be considered as the seminal figure in any study of the American frontier.

F. J. Turner, *Frontier in American History* (New York, 1920).
R. A. Billington, *Westward Expansion: a history of the American frontier* (New York, 1949).   DHP

FRONTIERS, NATURAL, doctrine of, proclaimed by Danton in 1793. He declared the Rhine, the Atlantic, the Mediterranean, the Pyrenees, and the Alps to be the natural frontiers of France. Of these, the Rhine and the Alps were highly debatable and the claim to the Rhine frontier strategically disastrous, for it encouraged the French invasion of Belgium which threatened the balance of power and contributed to Britain's declaration of war on France (1793). This extension of the revolutionary wars in the pursuit of national interest conflicted with the avowed idealism of the republican armies and Danton's own sponsorship of the Decrees of Fraternity.

FROST, JOHN (1784–1877), Welsh radical, Chartist, and mayor of Newport in 1836. He was never a national figure in the Chartist movement, but he gained notoriety by leading the one serious Chartist attempt at insurrection, at Newport on 4 Nov. 1839. He was transported for life, but returned in 1856 after being granted a free pardon.

FROST, ROBERT LEE (1874–1963), US poet, identified with rural New England. The publication of *A Boy's Will* (1913) and *North of Boston* (1914) established his reputation. His most memorable work is contained in *North of Boston, Mountain Interval,* and *New Hampshire.* Working within a strong regional tradition that embraces Emerson and Emily Dickinson, the simple, conversational, and often humorous tone of his poetry obscures his serious, sometimes pessimistic vision.

FRY, ELIZABETH (1780–1845), British social reformer and Quaker. After visits to Newgate, she championed reform of women prisoners' treatment and conditions (1813–18) and became a European authority on prison reform.

FU'AD, AHMAD (1868–1936), Ruler of Egypt (*reg.* 1917–36; Sultan 1917, King 1922). Fu'ad's rule spanned the difficult period following the 1922 British declaration of Egyptian independence when a struggle for power between the Crown and the Wafd party ensued, with Britain retaining substantial influence. Fu'ad was a great intellectual patron and an able but unpopular politician.

FUAD PASHA, MEHMED (1815–69), Ottoman statesman of the Tanzimat period, who served several times as foreign minister and Grand Vizier and was chiefly responsible for the reorganization of provincial administration.

FUDAI, Japanese word meaning 'successive generations' or 'hereditary', used mainly to describe the numerous Tokugawa vassals who were raised to *daimyō* status after 1600. Though individually less powerful than some independent *tozama daimyōs,* as a group the *fudai daimyōs* acquired great influence over *bakufu* policy.

FUENTERRABIA, BATTLE OF (1638), French victory at the siege of the town of Fuenterrabia in Guipuzcoa during the Franco-Spanish War (1635–59). The Catalans refused to support Olivares's war effort by sending military aid.

FUENTES, PEDRO ENRIQUEZ DE AZEVEDO, Count of (d. 1610), Spanish general and brother-in-law of Alva who was sent by Phillip II to the Netherlands to take over from Parma as the effective ruler (1592), although the official governor was the Archduke Ernest. Fuentes dismissed Parma's Italian and native Flemish councillors, replacing them by Spaniards. After Ernest's premature death in 1595 he took over the government on behalf of the Spanish Crown.

FUERO JUZGO, Castilian title of the *Liber Judiciorum* (c. 654), a compilation of Visigothic law. Translated into Castilian in the 13th cent., it was regarded by Spanish monarchs as the ultimate law of the land in their attempt to impose legal uniformity. It tended to conflict with the jealously guarded *fueros* (municipal rights based on common law), which were granted in large numbers to encourage the settlement of areas reconquered from the Moors.

FUEROS, term used in Spanish and Spanish American history to denote the special privileges and charters awarded by the monarchy to individuals or corporate groups in return for favours or services. Beneficiaries included the Church, towns, guilds of artisans, and certain types of landowners. One of the most socially disruptive *fueros* was the right given to certain groups, such as the clergy, to try their own members in their own courts. Charges of favouritism and jurisdictional overlapping resulted. Revocation of *fueros* in the 19th cent. caused resentment among previously favoured groups. *Fueros* were an important ingredient of Spanish medieval, corporate society.

FUGGER FAMILY, greatest money-lenders of the 16th cent. and the principal financial support of the Habsburgs until c. 1560. Of the two branches of the family of Hans Fugger (d. 1409), an Augsburg weaver who founded their business, that of his son Andreas made at first the most rapid progress by financial business in Antwerp and Venice, as well as in Augsburg. The other branch, known as the Fuggers of the Lily, descended from Hans's other son, Jakob I, whose trading business continued to expand steadily but modestly under his sons, Ulrich (1441–1510) and Georg (1453–1506). It was Jakob II (1459–1525), known as 'the Rich', who made them the greatest financial house of their day in Europe.

Jakob II took into partnership his nephews, establishing the principle that male heirs and descendants should leave their property in common in the business. Under his management the family extended their transactions from the textile trades to spice, then to financial dealings with the Roman curia, and, in 1482, to mining. Their interest in Tyrolean silver was greatly extended when Jakob II made the first loan to the Habsburg family, to Sigismund of Tyrol, on the security of the Tyrolean silver and copper mines in 1487. In 1492 and 1494, aiming at a monopoly in silver and copper, they extended their Tyrolean interests by alliance with Johannes Thurzo and established processing plants for the ores in Carinthia and Thuringia, and leased mines in Hungary.

Heavy lending to the Habsburgs began with Emperor Maximilian, who pledged two counties to the Fuggers in 1507 for a loan of 50,000 florins. But their greatest service was the advance of over half a million florins to help secure the election of Charles V as Holy Roman emperor in 1519. From then on they were drawn into a symbiotic relationship with Charles and Spanish interests, acquiring from him in 1525 the revenues belonging to the Spanish military Orders, including the mercury of Almaden and the silver of Guadalcanal. Jakob II had so extended the business at his death that the accounts of 1527 showed an increase of profits since 1511 of 927 per cent, amounting to 1,824,411 florins, but although his successor, Anton (1493–1560), saw a dramatic expansion of business, it consisted to an increasing extent of loans to the Habsburgs which were only slowly, if ever, repaid, and which could only be raised by further borrowing at high rates of interest. The reason was the vast increase of Habsburg expenses in wars against the German protestants, the Netherlands rebels, the Turks, and the French. After the financial crisis of 1560 the Fuggers began to shed their commercial interests.

R. Ehrenberg (tr. by H. Lucas), *Capital and Finance in the Age of the Renaissance* (New York, 1963).   HMBM

FUGITIVE SLAVE ACTS (1793, 1850), US legislation providing for the return of runaway slaves to their masters. The federal act of 1793 embodied the general provisions of earlier colonial statutes, but was increasingly ignored in the northern states, and the number of slaves escaping by the 'Underground Railroad' was a mounting cause of anxiety to the South. Up to 50,000 fugitives may have left the southern states between 1830 and 1860. The compromise of 1850 included a new Fugitive Slave Act which established higher penalties and a much more rigorous system of enforcement. Throughout the 1850s, attempts in the North to rescue fugitive slaves inflamed sectional animosities, and several northern states passed personal liberty laws to counteract the federal measure.

FUJIWARA PERIOD, the three centuries (c. 858–1160) of Japanese history when the central government was dominated by the Fujiwara. The family first rose to great prominence when Nakatomi Kamatari was given the name of Fujiwara in recognition of his role in the Taika *coup d'état* (645), but it was not until 858, when Fujiwara Yoshifusa became the first regent not of imperial blood, that the Fujiwara were able to control the throne. The key to their power was their marriage policy, by means of which almost every emperor for two centuries had a Fujiwara mother and could be easily manipulated. Considerable political ability, monopoly of government office, especially the position of regent, and extensive estate ownership, however, also contributed to their extraordinary success. Although Fujiwara dominance became so great that their family council rather than the grand council of state was the seat of decision-making, the Fujiwara leaders were content to possess real power and never attempted to become emperors themselves. They did however marry their women into the imperial clan. Fujiwara, Michinaga (966–1027), head of the family at the time of its greatest power, had four emperors as sons-in-law, two as nephews, and three as grandsons. They thus set a pattern of indirect rule which was followed in succeeding centuries and helps to account for the survival till the present day of the imperial line. In the mid-11th cent. the growth of provincial disorder and rivalry between the different branches of the family undermined Fujiwara power, and the accession in 1068 of an able emperor without a Fujiwara mother broke their grip on government. They continued, however, to fill most of the higher offices until 1160, when the Taira family rose to control the throne.

FUKUZAWA YUKICHI (1834–1901), Japanese thinker, publicist, and educationalist. More than any other individual, he introduced the West to Japan during the latter's formative stages of modernization. His autobiography, translated into English in 1930, tells a fascinating story of his early study of Dutch and English, his visits to America and Europe, and the enormous success of his works of popularization, particularly *Seiyō Jijō* (*Western Conditions*), which sold 150,000 copies almost immediately. Fukuzawa's interests ranged widely, from history, politics, and economics to morality and marriage. Though active in journalism, he always refused to enter the government, preferring to maintain an independent position. He had an enormous influence on Japanese thinking, much of it through Keiō University, which he founded.

FULBE (sing. **PULO**), also called Fulani, Fellata, Peul, etc., an essentially pastoral people now widely dispersed over the savannah lands of West Africa from the Gambia to the Cameroons, with important settlements in the Nilotic Sudan. Scholars have been fascinated by their origins. Their own legends claim descent from a union of the Arab conqueror of North Africa, Uqba ibn Nafi (d. ?682) and an African woman, but this probably reflects later intermarriage between some Fulbe clans and Arab – Berber elements. Linguistically, they are purely African. Their language—Fulfulde—for long unclassified, has now been shown to belong to the West Atlantic group together with Wolof and Serer.

They emerge from the realm of myth in the 11th cent., when groups migrated from southern Mauretania into Futa Toro. There, some clans adopted Islam and fanned out, generally eastwards, over the next three centuries. By the 15th cent. some had settled in Masina, which then became a new dispersion centre. In the mid-15th cent. they appear in Hausaland and Bornu as itinerant scholars. Muslim Fulbe tended to intermarry and sedentarize, particularly in Futa Jalon (Guinea), Masina, and Hausaland. Many of the pastoralists (*bororoje*) never adopted Islam and tenaciously preserve their old beliefs and customs.

In the 18th and 19th cents settled Fulbe produced a number of reformist scholars who embarked on *jihad*s and set up states: Karamoko Alfa (d. 1751) in Futa Jalon, Abd al-Qadir (d. 1806) in Futa Toro, Uthman ibn Fudi (d. 1817) in Hausaland, and Ahmad Lobbo (d. 1844) in Masina. The greatest of these, that of Uthman ibn Fudi, based on Sokoto, lasted for a century until the British occupation of Hausaland (1903). Many Fulbe then emigrated eastwards, attempting to reach Mecca, but settled along the Blue Nile at Sennar and elsewhere.

J. S. Trimingham, *A History of Islam in West Africa* (Oxford, 1962).
D. Stenning, *Savannah Nomads* (London, 1959). JOH

FULBRIGHT, JAMES WILLIAM (1905–), US lawyer, academic, and politician, whose career has been dominated by an interest in foreign affairs. As a congressman from AR he successfully sponsored a resolution favouring post-war international co-operation (1943); as a US senator (1945) he promoted the Fulbright programme of educational exchange; and as chairman of the Senate Foreign Relations Committee (1959–) he supported economic rather than military foreign aid and advocated disbursement on a multilateral basis through international organizations. In 1965 he opposed US military intervention in the Dominican Republic and became the major senatorial opponent of the Viet-nam war. In *Old Myths and New Realities* (1964) and *The Arrogance of Power* (1966) he articulated dissent from administration policies and concern about the expansion of presidential power in making overseas commitments for the US.

FULFILMENT in Germany, policy of carrying out the obligations of the 1919 Versailles treaty after the First World War. The policy was controversial because all shades of German opinion considered as grossly unjust both the treaty's terms and the conditions of blockade in which it was dictated. The Weimar National Assembly's decision to sign the treaty was always opposed by the right, who considered that Germany would never have reached this point of submission had she not been weakened by the 1918–19 socialist revolution. The conflicting policies of 'fulfilment' and 'resistance' constantly exacerbated Germany's political divisions. The treaty's reparation clauses were a frequent cause of dissension because the amount to be paid was unspecified and subject to negotiations and investigations between Germany and the Allies. Post-war economic upheavals and the crisis after 1929 made it impossible ever to reach a definitive settlement. Other treaty terms raising the 'fulfilment' issue included German disarmament, the plebiscitary division of Upper Silesia (1921), and the military occupation of the Rhineland zone for 15 years after the peace.

The first Weimar government openly and specifically committed to 'fulfilment' was that of Wirth and Rathenau, based on the Centre Party, which took office in 1921 to accept the London ultimatum containing the Allies' first statement of the reparations bill. 'Fulfilment's' most notable supporter was Stresemann, head of the right-wing *Deutsche Volkspartei*. He was chiefly responsible for the Rhineland's evacuation, and the disbandment of the Inter-Allied Military Control Commission, as well as reparation negotiations. The Centre, the Social Democrats, and the moderate wing of Stresemann's party all favoured 'fulfilment', but with significant reservations and nuances. The earliest reparations negotiators considered Allied demands quite unrealistic. They hoped to gain goodwill by complying with short-term schemes of payment, and subsequently to convince the Allies that their original expectations were unreasonable. Stresemann always desired to redraw the 1921 frontier with Poland, and never disarmed Germany as the treaty required. His policy of accommodation was designed to win Allied confidence and the relaxation of arms control; and to regain an international position, symbolized by Germany's admission to the League of Nations, from which treaty modifications could be demanded and obtained.

Opposition to 'fulfilment' was more fundamentally dishonest. Its proponents never considered the military defiance of the Allies. In 1923 'passive resistance' to France's occupation of the Ruhr could not save Germany from disastrous inflation and near disintegration, and had to be abandoned. However, the 'resistance' policy was maintained in right-wing—and especially Nazi—slogans. The proponents of 'fulfilment' never received credit for the early evacuation of the Rhineland (1929–30), and the negotiation of a reparations moratorium in 1932, and were harried in their progress to these ends through to the collapse of the Weimar Republic in 1933. ASJ

FULK (1092–1143), King of Jerusalem (*reg.* 1131–43), succeeded his father as Count of Anjou in 1109. In 1129 he married Mélisande, the daughter of Baldwin II, King of Jerusalem. To meet the rising power of Zangi, the Muslim Atabeg of Mosul, he maintained a close entente with the Burid amirs of Damascus. He also built the great fortress of Karak, south of the Dead Sea, thus securing an important point of vantage, which overlooked the routes uniting Syria and Egypt.

FULLER, SIR BAMPFYLDE (1854–1935), British colonial administrator and first lieutenant-governor of the province of Eastern Bengal and Assam, created in 1905. He entered the Indian civil service in 1875 and was employed on land revenue settlement work in the Central Province. He was successively agricultural adviser (1896–7) to the Egyptian government, secretary to the government of India in the revenue and agricultural department (1901–2), and Chief Commissioner of Assam (1902–5). As lieutenant-governor of Eastern Bengal and Assam (1905–6), he issued circulars forbidding student political agitation and appealed to Lord Minto to have two schools disaffiliated from Calcutta University. Because he failed to get government support he resigned. He published *Studies in Indian Life and Sentiment* (1910).

FULLER, MELVILLE WESTON (1833–1910), US lawyer and jurist, who was active in Democratic politics until his appointment as chief justice of the US Supreme Court (1888). As a jurist he favoured a strict construction of the constitution and was a staunch defender of private interests against social legislation.

FULLER, THOMAS (1608–61), English Anglican divine, ardent royalist, and 17th-cent. historian, whose book *The Church History of Britain* (1655) is the earliest general work on English ecclesiastical history. He also published *History of the Holy War* (1640) and *Worthies of England* (1662).

FULLING MILL. Fulling was an essential process in the production of the more expensive varieties of medieval woollen cloth. At first it was carried out entirely by human labour and formed the most exhausting of all the processes of the textile industry, requiring large numbers of unskilled, miserable workers. Human labour could be replaced by revolving wooden hammers propelled by water power and such fulling mills appear in French records from the 11th cent. onwards. The spread of the fulling mills in England in the 13th cent. encouraged the movement of the woollen industry into hilly regions with fast-flowing streams. The use of fulling mills led to the concentration of textile manufacture in south-western England and promoted its introduction into Lancashire and western Yorkshire.

FULTON, ROBERT (1765–1815), US pioneer in steam navigation, who spent 20 years (1786–1905) in Europe studying painting, engineering, and experimenting with mines, torpedoes, and submarines. Supported financially by Robert R. Livingston, he built several steamboats, notably the *Clarmont*, which successfully made the round trip from New York to Albany in 1807.

FULTON SPEECH, address delivered by Winston S. Churchill at Westminster College, Fulton, MO (1946), in which he warned that an 'iron curtain' had descended across Eastern Europe. Being suspicious of Soviet intentions, he proposed the creation of an international military force under the United Nations and stressed the existence of a 'special relationship' between Britain and the US.

FU-NAN, name given by Chinese sources to an ancient kingdom which flourished in Lower Cambodia, and sent tribute to China, from the 3rd to the 6th cents. Its culture, strongly influenced by Hindu India, is known especially from a series of excavations conducted at Oc-Eo, a site in the Mekong delta area, which was the kingdom's principal port. The extent of the area controlled by the King of Fu-Nan is still a matter of uncertainty. Its decline corresponds to the rise of the kingdom which the Chinese called Chen-La.

FUNDAMENTAL LAWS IN FRANCE, unwritten constitutional principles upon which the French state was based from the 9th cent. to the Revolution (1789). These tenets provided the basis for the French monarchy, requiring that the Crown rest with a Catholic monarch whose claim derived from his being the eldest male relative in the direct line of descent. It was further understood that the Crown was indivisible, inalienable, and sovereign. From time to time disputes arose over the precise interpretation of these traditional principles, *eg*, the *parlements* at various periods claimed that the free registration of edicts was a fundamental law of the land, but the Crown denied this and asserted that unequivocal and universal obedience to the king had always been an essential tenet.

FUNDAMENTAL ORDERS OF CONNECTICUT (1639–62), basic CT law, and first written constitution in North America.

FUNDIKIRA (*fl.* 19th cent.), Chief of Unyanyembe, greatest of the chieftancies among the Nyamwezi of Tanzania during the middle years of the 19th cent. A favourable relationship with coastal traders who had set up a settlement in Unyanyembe assisted Fundikira to enhance the power and expand the influence of the chieftaincy. One of his daughters married Muhammad bin Juma, to whom she bore a remarkable son, Tippu Tip. During Fundikira's lifetime relations between the Nyamwezi and the Arab traders remained amicable, though tensions appeared after his death in 1858.

FUNJ, formerly a nomadic cattle people of unknown origin, although Ethiopia, the Bulala and Shilluk regions have been suggested. They arrived on the Upper Blue Nile *c.* 1500, and founded the sultanate of Sennar *c.* 1504. Expanding northward, they clashed with southward-moving Arabs under the Abdullah tribe, who had recently overthrown Alodia, the last Christian kingdom of Nubia. At Arbaji the Funj were victorious and their sultan became supreme with the Abdullab Shaykh as manjilak or viceroy. The court quickly accepted Islam and the sultans encouraged scholarship.

The Funj kingdom reached its greatest extent in the late 16th cent., when Kordofan and the Shilluk lands were made tributary, while the 3rd Cataract of the Nile formed its northern boundary. A war was fought with Ethiopia in 1618–19, and another in 1744, when the Funj were victorious. Decline set in during the late 17th cent., when revolts disrupted trade. In 1720 the throne passed from the direct line to Nul, a nephew of the previous ruler; Nul and his son Badi IV stemmed the decline for a while, but the latter was deposed by Muhammad Abu Likaylik, viceroy of Kordofan, who became vizier and de facto ruler of Sennar. His descendants, the Hamaj viziers, remained in power until 1821, when an invading Turko-Egyptian army put an end to the sultanate. Throughout the period of Funj power the area formed an important centre of trade, commercial links being maintained with Bornu, Egypt, Ethiopia, and India.

FUNK, WALTHER (d. 1960). German journalist and politician, who was Hitler's second minister of economics. During the 1920s he was editor-in-chief of an important financial newspaper, the *Berliner Börsen-Zeitung*; he resigned in 1931 to work as a contact man between the Nazi Party and the world of industry and business. Under Wagener, head of the party's economic policy department, Funk ran an economic press and information service through which he supported Hitler's repudiation of the anti-capitalist views of some notable National Socialists such as Feder. He **succeeded** Schacht in two capacities, as minister of economics (1937) and as president of the Reichsbank (1939). In the latter position he dealt in valuables such as gold from the dentures of Jews killed in concentration camps. As Funk's appointments were made at a time when Hitler's plans were tending to a war economy, he was unable to exercise much independent influence on German economic development.

FUR TRADE in North America, first large-scale frontier enterprise in North America and a major factor in exploration and settlement. From the early days of settlement the skins of beavers and deer found a ready market in Europe. French explorers discovered that American Indians were eager to trade pelts for knives and other products of industrial Europe. The fur trade in New England was started by the Pilgrims (1620), and was to remain the mainstay of the New England economy for over 50 years. Settlers in all areas of North America exchanged weapons, utensils, tools, clothing, ornaments, tobacco, and liquor for furs. This profitable trade was the cause of serious rivalry between all the nations which established colonies in the New World. Sweden and the Netherlands fought for control of the trade in what is now NY. The English fought with the Dutch, the French, and the Spanish, and the US were to quarrel with Spain, Britain, Russia, and Mexico over various aspects of the fur trade.

The Hudson's Bay Co., founded in England (1670) to exploit the Hudson Bay area, held supremacy over the north and west Canadian trade until 1869. Other companies were formed, the North-West Co. (1787), the American Fur Co. (1808), the Missouri Fur Co. (1809), and the Rocky Mountain Fur Co. (1821), to exploit other areas and the trade became highly organized. Trading posts were established and traders and trappers operated from the posts under the auspices of large corporations.

The advance of settlement after American Independence doomed the fur trade in the eastern US, but traders were already moving westward across the Mississippi river. Settlement soon followed them and once again the fur trade moved westward. The trade remained of importance to sparsely settled parts of North America but the traders, by opening up areas for settlement, consistently brought about their own demise. Changing fashions also lessened the European demand for beaver pelts, deerskins, and buffalo hides and the trade, which had produced the first American capitalists, guides, trail-blazers, and picturesque characters such as the *coureurs de bois*, and the mountain men, was of little importance to a settled and rapidly industrializing society.

P. C. Phillips, *The Fur Trade*, 2 vols (Norman, OK, 1961).
DHP

FUR TRADE in Russia developed in the Novgorod period (10th–11th cents) as the result of a European demand for such luxurious furs as fox, beaver, squirrel, etc. The traders of Novgorod hunted first in the basins of the north Dvina and Mezen rivers, but later penetrated north-eastwards into the tayga region of the Pechora basin and to the Urals and beyond. By 1600 the main hunting ground had become the Ob–Irtysh basins of Siberia, sable being the most coveted fur. The explorers levied tributes on the natives in the form of furs and then moved the pelts from local *ostrogs* or forts by river and portage to the collecting centres of northern Russia, whence they were transported to Archangel for export or to Moscow, the central fur mart. The fur trade increased rapidly from the time of the first contact with English traders in 1553 until the end of the 17th cent., when demand outstripped supply, and the trappers moved eastwards to the Asian coast in search of new grounds. By 1725 St Petersburg had replaced Archangel as the main port for the European market and Yakutsk was the principal collecting centre. Furs were still the chief export commodity of Russia at the end of Peter I's reign, but as competition from North America affected the West European market and

supplies had to be transported across the vast Asian land mass, the trade steadily contracted.

FURIO CERIOL, FADRIQUE (1527–92), Valencian humanist and political theorist, who proposed that the Aragonese federalist traditions of empire should be instituted throughout the scattered Spanish possessions (1559) and accompanied Requesens as Spanish governor to the Netherlands (1573) to try to implement them.

***FÜRSTENBUND* (LEAGUE OF THE PRINCES)** (July 1785), agreement signed in Berlin by Prussia, Saxony, and Hanover, and then joined by most of the German states. The league checked the forward policy of the Emperor and Austrian ruler, Joseph II. He had hoped to exchange the Austrian Netherlands (Belgium) for Bavaria and had secured the agreement of the Bavarian ruler, Charles Theodore. Posing as the defender of the status quo and the constitution of the Holy Roman Empire, Frederick the Great created the league to prevent any increase in Austrian power in Germany. Its members agreed secretly to resist Austrian annexation of Bavaria, but this was unnecessary because the formation of the *Fürstenbund* was sufficient to make Joseph drop his plan.

FÜSSEN, TREATY OF (1745), peace concluded between the Archduchess Maria Theresa of Austria and the Elector of Bavaria, Maximilian Joseph, restoring the status quo existing before the War of the Austrian Succession. The elector renounced his claim to the imperial crown, but his rights to Bavaria were recognized.

FUSTAT, garrison town which the Arabs, perhaps in 643, established in Egypt after their conquest of that land in 639–42. It was located on the east bank of the Nile, close to the Greco-Coptic town of Babalyun. Its remains are to be found in the quarter of the present Cairo known as Old Cairo.

FUSTEL DE COULANGES, NUMA DENIS (1830–99), French historian, who aimed at scientific objectivity and stressed the unreliability of secondary sources. He was a professor at Strasbourg (1860) and the Sorbonne (1878) and also instructed the Empress Eugénie. His works include *La Cité Antique* (1864) and *Histoire des Institutions Politiques de l'Ancienne France* (1892).

FUTA JALON, extensive hilly area of central Guinea. It assumed historical importance in the 18th cent. when Fulbe groups which had migrated from both Masina and southern Mauretania in the late 17th cent. united to proclaim a *jihad* against the non-Muslim populations of the area. A complex series of wars and internal struggles took place under the leadership first of Karamoko Alfa (d. 1751) and then Ibrahim Sory (d. *c.* 1784). A theocratic Muslim state was established (1776) under Ibrahim, who took the title *almamy*, and though it was beset with internal quarrels was not destroyed until the French occupation (1896–7).

FUTA TORO, hilly region on the south bank of the Senegal river. In this area in the 10th–11th cents existed the state of Takrur, whose rulers adopted Islam before the Almoravid movement and later assisted Yahya ibn Umar against the Godala. Later the name Takrur was applied to any or all West African Muslim lands. Futa Toro was a major dispersion point for the Fulbe from about the 14th cent. Later, Fulbe settled there, rallied to a *jihad* under the *almamy* Abd al-Qadir, and an unstable theocratic state was established (1776). When the 54th *almamy* died (1890), Futa Toro became part of French Senegal.

FUTUWWA, term commonly used to denote various urban movements and organizations in the medieval Middle East. Often characterized by strong mystical or radical associations, they were of fundamental importance in social organization and frequently played a significant political role.

FUZULI, MUHAMMAD b. SULAYMAN (*c.* 1480–1556), born in Iraq (perhaps at Karbala) and of the Shi'i faith, was one of the greatest of Ottoman poets.

FYODOR I IVANOVICH (1557–98), Tsar of Moscow (*reg.* 1584–98), last of the Rurik dynasty, who succeeded his father, Ivan IV, and though pious, was a bigoted weakling. His reign was dominated by his brother-in-law, the *boyar* regent, Boris Godunov, who was blamed for the assassination of the tsar's half-brother and heir, Dmitri (1591).

FYODOR II ALEKSEVICH (1657–82), Tsar of Moscow (*reg.* 1676–82), insignificant son and heir by his first marriage of the Tsar Alexis Romanov, whom he succeeded. His reign was notable for the abolition of the *mestnichestvo* (system of noble precedence).

FYRD, Anglo-Saxon local army, recruited from the shires and led by the *ealdormen* of the shires. It seems to have been composed mainly of thegns, though with some peasant ceorls, who served for two months in the year. The *fyrd* was preserved by the Norman kings.

FYSH, SIR PHILLIP OAKLEY (1835–1919), Australian politician and a merchant in Tas. after 1859. He was twice colonial prime minister, a prominent federalist, and a minister in early Commonwealth governments (1901–4).

GABBARD, BATTLE OFF THE (2 June 1653), fought in the first Anglo-Dutch War, east of Harwich. Tromp, with 98 men-of-war, engaged an English fleet of 100 men-of-war under Lawson and Monck. The English fleet was superior in size and weight of guns, and the calm sea favoured them. After the first day's fighting the Dutch ran short of powder, and on the second day Blake reinforced the English with 13 new ships. The English captured 20 Dutch ships and Tromp retreated. As a result, the Dutch coast was blockaded.

GABELLE, salt tax in France, one of the main indirect taxes of the *ancien régime* first introduced by the French Crown in the 14th cent. and collected in the administrative areas known as *greniers* throughout the *pays de grandes gabelles, ie,* most of northern and central France. The *gabelle* was not uniformly enforced. Certain towns, *eg,* Paris and Arles, certain provinces, *eg,* Flanders, Artois, Béarn, Hainault, Navarre, and Brittany, and the two estates of clergy and nobility all enjoyed exemption. Francis I tried to make it a universal tax throughout France but submitted to the resistance of the people of Languedoc, Provence, and Dauphiné, the *pays de petites gabelles,* where salt was widely produced. However, elsewhere the *gabelle* was harshly enforced and became one of the most hated taxes of the *ancien régime,* encouraging widespread smuggling, which in turn incurred the rigorous imposition of the penal laws.

GABINIUS, A. (d. 47 BC), Roman soldier and politician. He proposed the law giving Pompey supreme command against the pirates (67), as consul (58) supported Clodius in banishing Cicero, and governed Syria (57–54). After being prosecuted he was exiled, but was recalled by Caesar (49) and died fighting in Illyricum.

GABON (267,000 sq. kms), formerly a province of French Equatorial Africa. It became a republic in 1960 and its constitution (1967) provided for a president, council of ministers, and national assembly of 47 members elected by adult suffrage. The Fang form the largest group in a population of 630,000.

GABOR, BETHLEN (d. 1629), Calvinist prince of Transylvania from 1613, a brilliant soldier and skilful diplomat, whose reign was remarkable for his form of enlightened despotism and his ambitious foreign policy. He developed Transylvania's mines and industrial resources, controlled its foreign trade, and patronized the arts and education. He intervened in the Thirty Years War against the Emperor Ferdinand (1619) and was offered the Crown of Hungary by the Protestant nobility (1620). In Dec. 1621 he signed the treaty of Nicholsburg with Ferdinand, thereby gaining the emperor's guarantee of religious freedom for his subjects and the recognition of his titles of Prince of Transylvania and Hungary. War between Bethlen and the imperialists was renewed in 1624 and again in 1626–9. By the time of his death his position was being undermined as a result of Jesuit missionary activity among the Hungarian nobility.

GACETA DE BUENOS AIRES, newspaper founded *c.* 1810 in Buenos Aires during the struggles for independence. It was used by Mariano Moreno and other independence leaders to make their new opinions known to the public.

GACHUPÍN, Spanish colonial term of disrespect, of uncertain origin, applied in New Spain to people of Spanish rather than colonial birth. The term is still (1970) in use in Mexico.

GADES (Cadiz), probably the earliest Phoenician foundation in the western Mediterranean, dating from at least 850 BC. It remained in Carthaginian hands till the Second Punic War, after which Spain became a Roman province. It was granted Roman citizenship by Julius Caesar in 49 BC.

GADSDEN, CHRISTOPHER (1724–1805), American politician, who served in the SC assembly (1757–87). He supported the colonial agitation against Britain and was prominent in the Stamp Act Congress (1765). Gadsden was a delegate to the first and second Continental Congresses (1774–5) and commanded forces from SC in the American War of Independence (1776–8). After returning to SC (1778), Gadsden led the successful struggle for separation of Church and state. In 1788 he was a delegate to the SC ratification convention and voted in favour of ratifying the new constitution.

GADSDEN PURCHASE, area of approximately 45,000 sq. miles (110,650 sq. kms) along the Gila river in southwestern NM and southern AZ bought by the US from Mexico in 1853–4 for $10 million. The treaty of purchase, negotiated by James Gadsden, resolved a boundary dispute and certain other issues that had arisen after the US–Mexican War of 1846–8. Its original terms embraced somewhat larger amounts of land and money. The reductions were made in the US Senate, where the treaty met strong opposition from anti-slavery elements. The transferred area, which was largely desert, was valued primarily because it included a practicable southern route for a transcontinental railroad.

GAEKWAR, Maratha ruler of Baroda state in India until its merger with the state of Saurashtra, and subsequently Gujarat, after Indian independence (1947). The family fortunes were founded by Damaji Gaekwar (d. 1725) and emerged as a state through the efforts of his son Pilaji (d. 1732), whose son Damaji continued the process of its consolidation until his death (1768). From the fall of Mughal Ahmadabad (1753) the province of Gujarat was divided between the peshwa and the gaekwar. The gaekwars were thenceforward involved in disputes between rival heirs and with other Maratha chiefs, which from 1772 led them into relations with the East India Co. The gaekwar served the interests of both himself and his state by entering into a subsidiary alliance with the company (1805) and by supporting the British during the last Maratha War (1817–18). The then gaekwar was deposed in 1875 after an attempt to poison the resident, Col. Phayre. His successor, Sayaji Rao, who lived until 1938, made Baroda into a model state.

GAFENCU, GRIGORE (1892–1957), Rumanian minister of foreign affairs and ambassador to Moscow. Gafencu was a well-known journalist and a member of the National Peasant Party. He served as minister of foreign affairs (Dec. 1938–June 1940) during Carol II's royal dictatorship and negotiated the Anglo-French guarantee to Rumania in 1939. In June 1940 he became Rumania's first ambassador to the Soviet

Union. He wrote *The Last Days of Europe* (1947) and *Prelude to the Russian Campaign* (1945), recounting the beginnings of the Second World War.

GAG RULE in US Congress, series of rules against the reception of anti-slavery petitions adopted by the House of Representatives from 1836 to 1844. The Senate followed the same policy without a formal rule. Opponents of the rule, led by John Quincy Adams, denounced it as a violation of constitutional rights and eventually won their long fight to repeal it.

GAGE, THOMAS (1721–87), British general and last royal governor of MA. After serving in Scotland (1745) and Flanders (1747–8), he was sent to North America (1754), where he later succeeded Sir Jeffrey Amherst as commander-in-chief, British forces in North America (1763–75). As governor of MA (1774), his action in sending troops to secure stores at Concord led to the first engagement of the American War of Independence at Lexington (18 April 1775).

GAGERN, WILHELM HEINRICH (1799–1880), president of the Frankfurt Assembly in 1848, and son of a liberal member of the Dutch *Bundestag*. As a student he was a member of the *Burschenschaft* and in 1820 entered the service of Hesse-Darmstadt, but was dismissed 1833 because of his liberal views. He sought a united Germany under Prussia, but without the exclusion of Austria.

GAHADAVALA DYNASTY, royal dynasty in medieval India, founded after the invasions of Mahmud of Ghazni (*c.* AD 1090 or a few years earlier) in Kanauj, Upper Pradesh. The greatest king was Govindachandra (1114–54), who dominated present Upper Pradesh and part of Bihar. His reign was followed by decline, and the dynasty disappeared during the Muslim conquest at the end of the 12th cent.

GAILLARD, FÉLIX (1919–70), French Radical politician and prime minister (1957–8). His government, like all others at the time, failed to overcome the Algerian problem, and its fall in May 1958 began the crisis which ended the Fourth Republic.

GAINSBOROUGH, THOMAS (1727–88), English painter of portraits and landscapes. His patrons and sitters included George III, the Prince of Wales, and other leaders of society. He was a founder member of the Royal Academy, but quarrelled with it in 1784.

GAITÁN, JORGE ELIÉCER (1903–48), Colombian radical politician and strike organizer. He lost the presidential elections of 1946 because of a split in his Liberal Party. His assassination in Bogotá caused widespread rioting during the ninth Pan American Conference.

GAITSKELL, HUGH TODD NAYLOR (1906–63), British Labour politician. As a young man, he supported the general strike (1926) and while tutoring unemployed Nottinghamshire miners saw poverty at first hand. Before the Second World War he advised the Labour Party on financial questions and during the war was a senior civil servant in economic departments, working with a Labour minister, Hugh Dalton. He entered parliament in 1945 and became (1947) minister of fuel and power, with responsibility for organizing the nationalized mines, gas, and electricity industries and administering controls. In 1949 he did much to persuade his colleagues of the need to devalue the pound. He was appointed (Feb. 1950) minister of economic affairs, understudying Sir Stafford Cripps, whom he succeeded as chancellor of the exchequer in Oct. At the treasury he dealt with such international problems as the Colombo Plan and the European Payments Union. His one budget, dominated by rearmament during the Korean War, imposed charges on National Health teeth and spectacles, which led Aneurin Bevan and Harold Wilson to resign from the government.

In opposition (1951–63), he was a critic of Conservative budgets, and of Labour's left wing, notably in his Stalybridge speech of 1952, which earned him trade union support. This enabled him to defeat Bevan for the post of party treasurer in 1953 and 1954. In Dec. 1955 the Parliamentary Labour Party, seeking a leader young enough to serve for 20 years, gave him 157 votes to 70 for Bevan and 40 for Herbert Morrison. The Labour left disliked his pro-US outlook and his style of opposition, which appreciated governmental problems as if he were in office himself; but they welcomed his vehement opposition to the Suez expedition (1956) and his choice of Bevan as shadow foreign secretary. Labour's political energies were temporarily directed to detailed and moderate policy-making instead of internal strife, and the party's severe election defeat in 1959 thus came as a great disappointment.

Gaitskell then advised the party to amend the commitment to total public ownership in Clause 4 of its constitution, but had to retreat when the party's trade union centre joined his old left-wing opponents. His position was further shaken in 1960 when several major trade unions (and consequently, by a narrow margin, the Labour Party Conference) endorsed a demand for Britain's unilateral nuclear disarmament. Gaitskell undertook to 'fight and fight again' to reverse this decision, and was challenged for the leadership by Wilson, whom he defeated by 166 votes to 81. By also defeating the unilateralists at the 1961 conference he established his ascendancy in the party and his reputation in the country. In 1962 he denounced immigration controls, and foreshadowed Labour's opposition to Britain entering the Common Market. But for his death in 1963 he would have become Labour prime minister following the party's general election success in the following year.   PMW

GAIUS, Roman jurist of the 2nd cent. AD, and a teacher rather than a practising lawyer, whose books were the most widely used legal textbooks in the 4th and 5th cents. His most famous work, the *Institutes*, formed the basis of Justinian's *Institutes* and exerted a profound influence on the civil law of later Europe.

GAJAH MADA, Javanese statesman (*c.* 1318–64), who started his career as a captain of the life guard of King Jayanagara of Majapahit (1309–21) and gradually climbed to the post of prime minister of the empire (from 1329). A brave but ruthless soldier and a cunning diplomat, he succeeded in establishing Javanese supremacy all over Indonesia and southern Malaya. Though this pan-Indonesian empire lasted less than a century, it seems that Gajah Mada's efforts were an important factor in the shaping of Indonesian unity.

GALAWDEWOS (*reg.* 1540–59), Emperor of Ethiopia, who was responsible for the defeat of the Muslim conqueror Ahmad Gragn.

GALBA, SERVIUS SULPICIUS (*c.* 3 BC–AD 69), Roman emperor (*reg.* 68–9), and member of an old patrician family, who, when governor of Hispania Tarraconensis, joined Vindex's revolt against Nero (68) and was proclaimed his successor. He was killed when the praetorian guard mutinied in favour of Otho.

GALEN (*c.* AD 129–99), Greek physician from Pergamum, who settled at Rome and was a friend of Emperor Marcus Aurelius. Besides over 100 extant medical texts he wrote works, mainly lost, on philosophy, language, and literature.

GALERIUS, VALERIUS MAXIMIANUS (*reg.* 305–11), Roman Emperor, who as deputy (Caesar) under Diocletian undertook campaigns against Persia (297–8) and ruled Illyricum until Diocletian's retirement (305), when he became emperor (Augustus) of the east. He continued the Christian persecution begun by Diocletian, but suspended it in 311, shortly before his death. He was succeeded in the east by his Caesar, Licinius (311–24).

GALIANI, FERDINANDO ABBÉ (1728–87), Neapolitan economist and public servant. He was for a time ambassador at Paris and a critic of physiocratic theories.

GALICIA, until the end of the First World War a province of the Habsburg empire. The western half of the province was predominantly Polish, and was absorbed by the newly independent Polish state. Eastern Galicia was predominantly Ruthenian and was disputed between Polish and Ukrainian forces until early 1919, when it was occupied by Poland. In June 1919, as part of their campaign against the Bolsheviks, the Allies authorized Poland to strengthen her eastern frontiers by setting up a civil administration in eastern Galicia, but they maintained reservations regarding the incorporation of a non-Polish population. In Nov. 1919 Poland rejected the Allies' suggestion of a 25-year mandate in eastern Galicia, and also their proposal of the 'Curzon line', a Russo-Polish frontier, because this assigned eastern Galicia and the Ukraine to Russia. Russia renounced all claims on Galicia in the treaty of Riga, signed with Poland in March 1921. In Feb. 1923, after Polish objections had frustrated all attempts by the League of Nations and the Allied Supreme Council to secure a statute of autonomy, eastern Galicia was awarded to Poland. The area witnessed a resurgence of Ukrainian nationalism in the 1930s.

GALICIA, BATTLES OF (1914), fought between Austrian and Russian forces at the beginning of the First World War. Austrian troops under Conrad von Hotzendorff were at first successful in northern Galicia, but almost simultaneously the Russians under Gen. Ivanov attacked in the south and overran the province. Their success, however, was short-lived: German forces were moved southwards to assist their Austrian allies and by the end of the year the front had been stabilized, though for the rest of the war the Germans were compelled to commit troops badly needed elsewhere to supporting the Austrians.

GALILEI, GALILEO (1564–1642), Italian philosopher, astronomer, and empirical scientist. He invented the thermometer (1597) and in 1609 constructed his own telescope with which he observed the validity of Copernicus's laws. He discovered the law of the vibrations of the pendulum (1583) and disproved Aristotle's erroneous belief that heavy bodies fall more rapidly than light ones in a vacuum (1638), thus anticipating Newton's laws of motion.

He was professor at Padua University (1592–1610), the leading scientific school in Europe, lecturing there on both mathematics and astronomy, and studying mechanics and engineering. His first publication (1606) described a measuring tool for military purposes which he invented in his university workshop. After 1610 Galileo's relations with the Aristotelians in Padua became increasingly strained, so he lived mainly in Florence, working there under the patronage of the Duke of Tuscany. In 1616 he came into conflict with the Church, when the Copernican system, which he upheld, was condemned by the Inquisition. However, in his magnum opus, *The Two Principal World Systems* (1625–9), he undermined the whole Aristotelian system. In 1633 he was censured by the Inquisition for his Copernican beliefs, though his timely recantation averted his being burnt at the stake, and after a brief imprisonment he was given a light penance.
MKS

GALÍNDEZ, JESÚS DE (1915–56), Dominican lawyer, writer, and enemy of the Dominican dictator, Rafael L. Trujillo. Galíndez was exiled first from Franco's Spain and then from the Dominican Republic. On 12 March 1956 he was abducted in New York, and it has been claimed that he

was flown to the Dominican Republic and murdered on Trujillo's orders.

GALLACHER, WILLIAM (1881–1965), British engineer and communist politician. During the First World War he was prominent in engineers' strikes against the introduction of unskilled labour which gave Glasgow's 'Red Clydeside' the spurious appearance of a centre of revolutionary shop-floor agitation. He became a leading member of the British Communist Party, having been dramatically converted from syndicalism to rigid communism after visiting Lenin in 1920. He became MP for West Fife in 1935, when the Labour vote was split because of a dispute in the miners' union, and held the seat until 1950.

GALLAS, MATTHIAS, Count (1589–1647), Imperialist field-marshal in the Thirty Years War, who replaced Wallenstein in 1634. He took part in the Swedish defeat at Nordlingen (1634) and invaded Lorraine (1635) and Franche-Comté.

GALLATIN, ABRAHAM ALFONSE ALBERT (1761–1849), US statesman and financier, born in Geneva, Switzerland, who emigrated to America (1780) and settled in western Pennsylvania (1784). He was a member of the Harrisburg meeting to discuss the US constitution (1788), and of the Pennsylvania constitutional convention (1789–90) and served in the state legislature (1790–2). Though elected US senator (1793) he was ousted on a technicality by the Federalists (1794). As a Democratic Republican congressman (1795–1801), he became minority leader and was instrumental in establishing the House Ways and Means Committee. His record as secretary of the treasury (1801–14) under Thomas Jefferson and James Madison was brilliant. Wishing to exploit America's natural resources and stimulate national growth without resorting to heavy taxation, he promoted international improvements and encouraged industry, commerce, and western expansion. His financial policy comprised stringent economy, retirement of the national debt from income, reduction of taxation, and appropriation of moneys for specific rather than general purposes. Only the deteriorating international position after 1807, culminating in the War of 1812, prevented fulfilment of these objectives. Senate attacks on his execution of the Embargo Policy, increased internal taxation during the war, and controversy over banking policy led to his resignation. Thereafter he served on a diplomatic mission to Russia (1813), as a peace commissioner at Ghent (1814), and then as minister to France (1816–23) and to Britain (1826–7). He continued to exercise considerable financial influence as president of the National Bank of New York (1831–9), and as the author of pamphlets on currency and tariff matters.

GALLEGOS, RÓMULO (1884–1969), Venezuelan novelist and president (Feb.–Nov. 1948), who was overthrown by a military junta. Author of many works, his best-known novel is *Doña Bárbara* (1929).

GALLEON, Mediterranean sailing vessel derived from the galley and adapted to sailing in oceanic waters by 15th-cent. explorers. The term was also applied to that part of the Spanish fleets which sailed annually from Seville to Cartagena and the isthmus of Panama.

GALLIC WAR, Julius Caesar's campaigns in Gaul (58–51BC) which enabled him to build up an army strong enough to dominate the Roman world. He first defeated the migrating Helvetii and the Germanic Suebi under Ariovistus (58). Having wintered his army outside the Roman province, he overran northern France and Belgium (57) and subdued the Veneti on the Atlantic coast (56). Believing Gaul pacified, he crossed the Rhine into Germany and twice invaded Britain (55–54). The tribes of Gaul rose under Vercingetorix (53), but were defeated in the siege of Alesia (52) which finally broke Gallic resistance.

GALLICAN ARTICLES (1682) in France, four celebrated propositions containing Gallican principles, drawn up by an assembly of the French clergy, convened by Louis XIV, and opened by Bp Bossuet (9 Nov. 1681), as a result of the king's quarrel with Pope Innocent XI over the right of *régale*. The articles were later incorporated into an edict (March 1682) and registered by the *parlement* of Paris as a law of the state. They stipulated that the king was not subject to the pope in temporal matters, nor could he be excommunicated or his subjects freed from their obligatory obedience to him; that the pope's authority was not superior to that of a general council of the Church; that in matters of faith the pope's decisions required the Church's approval; and that the customs and rules of the Gallican Church were to remain inviolate.

In 1693 Louis made a compromise settlement with Innocent XII, in which he promised that the Gallican articles would no longer be enforced, although the *parlement* considered this agreement invalid.

GALLICANISM, French doctrine which emphasized the king's authority or that of the French bishops over the French Church in ecclesiastical matters and correspondingly played down the power of the papacy as exemplified in *Unam Sanctam*. Gallicanism developed at the close of the 13th cent. with the struggle between Philip the Fair and Pope Boniface VIII, and flourished in the aftermath of the Great Schism, when, representing conciliar opposition to papal sovereignty, it found expression in the Pragmatic Sanction of Bourges (1438). The movement defended the customs of the French Church, the decisions of its own councils, and deprived the papacy of its jurisdiction over major benefices and the financial dues formerly exacted at and after the conferment of those benefices. It derived support from many of the clergy and from members of the *parlement* of Paris, as well as from the Crown, the defender of the established liberties of the French Church. Some monarchs, *eg*, Louis XI and Francis I, repudiated extreme Gallicanism, and the growth of ultramontane theories during the French religious wars threatened traditional Gallicanism until Henry IV restored royal authority. The doctrine was forcibly restated in Pierre Pithou's *Les Libertés de l'Église Gallicane* (1594) and much later in the Gallican Articles (1682). However, many clergy and *parlementaires* regarded the papal bull *Unigenitus* (1713) as a combined attack by Louis XIV and the pope on the Gallican liberties and it provoked some 40 years of religious and political controversy in France.

The destruction of the monarchy and Church of the *ancien régime* (1792–3) did not put an end to the Gallican movement in its broadest sense. Napoleon's Organic Articles (1802) established the complete control of the French Church by the state and initiated a new form of Gallicanism, which remained after the restoration of the monarchy (1815) and represented the overriding authority of the French bishops over the lower clergy. In the later 19th cent. the ultramontane movement, led by Louis Veuillot, aroused the Gallican spirit of liberal Catholics, but with the success of ultramontanism (1870) and the growth of anti-clericalism, associated with republicanism, Gallicanism ceased to be of significance, except in the vague sense of hostility on the part of Catholic Frenchmen to the excessive interference of Rome.   MKS

GALLIENI, JOSEPH-SIMON (1849–1916), posthumous Marshal of France, with Faidherbe and Lyautey, one of the great military builders of the French empire in Africa. During the 1880s he completed Faidherbe's work of conquest in Senegal and westward into the Sudanese grasslands; during the late 1890s he carried through the full installation of French colonial rule in Madagascar; in between, he served with distinction in Indo-China (Tonkin). During the First World War, he fought the battle of the Ourq and opened the battle of the Marne, which saved Paris from German occupation.

GALLIENUS, P. LICINIUS EGNATIUS (d. AD 268), Roman Emperor, first with his father, Valerian (253–60), and, after Valerian's capture by the Persians, sole emperor (260–8). His reign was marred by provincial dissidence, in Gaul under Postumus and his successors, and in Syria under Odaenathus and Zenobia of Palmyra. Despite this political uncertainty, the court of Gallienus became a noted cultural centre, including among it associates the philosopher Plotinus. Gallienus was assassinated by his own officers and succeeded by Claudius Gothicus.

GALLIPOLI (1915), operation during the First World War. Largely at the instigation of Winston Churchill, the first lord of the admiralty, British forces were dispatched to the Dardanelles early in 1915 with the triple objective of inflicting a defeat on Turkey, relieving pressure on Russia, and strengthening the Balkan front against the Central Powers. Furthermore, there was considerable support for the proposal that the British should exploit their maritime supremacy by outflanking the already deadlocked trenches on the Western Front. Naval attempts in Feb. and March to force the Dardanelles in order to reach Constantinople failed, and were followed by an amphibious landing on the Gallipoli peninsula on 15 April. Despite any contemporary experience of combined operations, indifferent leadership, and a lack of proper planning, Gen. Sir Ian Hamilton's forces landed on the southern tip of the peninsula at Cape Helles and at Anzac Cove. The Turkish defenders were thrown into confusion, but the Allied troops failed to exploit the situation and to occupy the heights which commanded the Dardanelles. Their bridgeheads were ultimately contained, largely through the exertions of Mustafa Kemal, then a junior officer. Static trench warfare set in, and despite the arrival of substantial reinforcements and also an attempt in Aug. to outflank the Turks by landing at Suvla Bay, the situation remained unchanged. Heavy casualties and disease so debilitated the Allied army that in Nov. Kitchener decided to order a withdrawal, which was carried out in Dec. and Jan. with considerable skill and no loss of life.

The strategic concept of the operation, though still debated, is now generally held to have been imaginative, though its tactical handling left much to be desired. Admiral Fisher, the first sea lord, resigned in the course of the operation, and Churchill lost office when the coalition government was formed in May. The failure of the operation strengthened the hand of the 'Westerners', who argued that the war could be won only on the Western Front, and deterred the British high command from further amphibious operations of this nature for the rest of the war. On the Turkish side, Kemal's brilliant rallying of the defenders started him on the path which led to his achieving political power after the war.
                                                                        NRB

GALLISPANS, term used to describe the French and Spanish Bourbon forces which combined to invade and occupy Italy during the War of the Austrian Succession. The reinforcement of Charles Emmanuel of Savoy by 30,000 Austrian troops checked the Gallispans, who withdrew from northern Italy (1746–7).

GALLOIS, PIERRE (1911–   ), French strategist and advocate of the independent French nuclear deterrent. He was an air force general and became an executive of the Dassault aircraft company.

GALLOWAY, JOSEPH (1731–1803), American politician and British loyalist, who served in the PA assembly for almost 20 years (1756–76). He joined Benjamin Franklin (1764–5) in petitioning George III to end the Penn proprietary in PA. On his return to the assembly he became speaker, a post he held until 1775. Galloway was a moderate in the conflict between colonies and parliament. He was a delegate to the first Continental Congress (1774), where his Plan of Union, advocating a continental legislature with authority to deal with colonial affairs, was narrowly defeated. Galloway refused to attend the second Continental Congress and during the American War of Independence he became Sir William Howe's civil administrator in Philadelphia. At the end of the war his estates were confiscated and never returned. After 1778 he lived in England on a government pension.

GALLUP, GEORGE HORACE (1901–), US public opinion analyst. While simultaneously acting as director of research for an advertising agency (1932–47), he pioneered techniques of radio audience measurement and market research for newspapers and magazines. He was founder of the American Institute of Public Opinion at Princeton, NJ (1935), and his successful prediction of the 1936 presidential election result contrasted with the wildly inaccurate forecast of the *Literary Digest* poll, and established his reputation as America's leading public opinion analyst. His research organization has maintained its leading position in the US, and extended its activities throughout the western world.

GALON REBELLION, in Burma, so named after the *galon,* a fabulous bird said to be capable of destroying the snake or the foreigner. It broke out in Tharrawaddy at the end of 1930. The leader, Saya San, gathered several thousand supporters and set up a stronghold in the forests. Though he was captured in Aug. 1931, the rebellion was not finally put down until March 1932. The rebellion had little to do with emergent nationalism, nor was it predominantly due to economic causes, though there was a background of agrarian discontent. It was a rising such as is common in Burmese history, to overthrow the government and usurp the throne. Leaders and led acted in naive ignorance and gross superstition, relying for success on magic and charms.

GALT, SIR ALEXANDER TILLOCH (1817–93), Canadian politician, who entered the House of Assembly of the province of Canada (1849). He resigned (1850) because of excessive pressure from land and railway interests with which he was connected. On re-election (1853), he worked with the liberal French-Canadian 'Rouge' Party. In 1856 Galt called for the grouping of Canada East and West into a federal union. He joined the Conservative Cartier–Macdonald ministry (1858) after acceptance of the condition that all Britain's North American colonies should be united. He was a delegate to the Charlottetown, Quebec, and London conferences and was a member of the coalition ministry (1864–7) which secured confederation. He served as Dominion minister of finance (1867), British representative on the Halifax Fishery Commission (1875), chief negotiator for trade agreements with France and Spain (1878–9), and Canada's first high commissioner in London (1880–3). His father, John Galt (1779–1839), emigrated from Scotland to Canada, where he served on a commission that reported that Britain should compensate Upper Canada for losses sustained during the War of 1812 (1820). In 1824 Galt acquired the Huron Tract in Upper Canada.

GALVEZ, DON JUAN DE (1746–86), Spanish soldier and colonial governor who was appointed governor of Louisiana (1776). As a result of his successful campaign in the American War of Independence Spain obtained both the Floridas and control of the mouth of the Mississippi in the 1783 settlement. Galvez was then appointed captain-general of Louisiana and the Floridas and succeeded his father as viceroy of New Spain (1785).

GÁLVEZ, JOSÉ DE, MARQUÉS DE LA SONORA (1729–86), Spanish colonial administrator and reformer. He was sent to New Spain as an inspector general by Charles III and quickly showed his reformist zeal. The viceroy was dis-

missed, the petty bureaucracy overhauled, tax farming abolished, and silver mines more uniformly regulated. Gálvez encouraged the settlement and garrisoning of the Spanish borderlands, especially California. His reform proposals were summed up in his famous report to the king (1771).

GALWAY, HENRY DE MASSUE, Earl of (Irish) (1648–1720), Huguenot soldier and diplomat, who served under the British sovereigns William III and Queen Anne. He was born near Paris, the son of the Marquis de Ruvigny, and served under Turenne. As a diplomat he conducted secret negotiations between Louis XIV and Charles II of England (1678). After the persecution of the Huguenots, he went into exile (1690) and entered the service of William III, for whom he worked in Ireland (1690–2), Flanders (1692–7), and Spain and Portugal (1702–8). He fought at the battles of Aughrim (1691) and Neerwinden (1693), and commanded the forces defeated by France at Almanza (1707). He was Lord Justice of Ireland (1697–1701), created Earl of Galway, and received a grant of Irish estates. He returned to Ireland in 1715 as one of the lord justices during the Jacobite insurrection.

GAMA, VASCO DA (*c.* 1469–1524), Portuguese navigator, the first to establish trading links with the Far East. Drawing on the experience of Bartholomew Dias's voyage to India via the Cape of Good Hope, he sailed from Lisbon (July 1497) with four ships, rounded the Cape, and landed at several outposts along the East African coast. With the help of Ibu Majid, a Muslim pilot whom he picked up at Malindi, he crossed the Indian Ocean and reached Calicut on the Malibar coast (1498). After a voyage lasting two years, da Gama returned home with a cargo of pepper and cinnamon, exchanged with unwilling Indian traders. He sailed again, as admiral of the Indies (1502) with 14 ships and bombarded Calicut before defeating a fleet of the Malibar Arabs.

GAMARRA, AGUSTÍN (1785–1841), Peruvian army general and president, who seized the presidency of Peru (1829), and ruled for four years. After supporting the Chileans in their war against the Peruvian–Bolivian Confederation he again became president (1839). His dictatorial rule ended with his death at the battle of Ingaví in Bolivia.

GAMBETTA, LÉON (1838–82), French republican leader and statesman, who was largely responsible for French resistance to Prussia after the collapse of the empire. He first made a political reputation for himself when he defended Delescluze (1868) and was elected to the Legislature on the basis of this and his radical Belleville programme (1869). In 1870 he called for the overthrow of the empire and on 4 Sept. he led the crowd to the Hôtel de Ville, where the republic was proclaimed. As minister of the interior in the government of national defence, he was flown by balloon to Tours, where he became war minister as well, and organized the volunteer armies that were able to resist the Prussians for six months. He opposed both the capitulation and the treaty of Frankfurt, but resisted his friends' demands that he should use his dictatorial powers to set up a new regime. On being re-elected he led the Union Républicain, a group of extreme radicals, but the group split when he decided to drop some of his demands and accept the institutions of 1875. He led the resistance to MacMahon after the *Seize Mai* (1877), stumping the country in the republican cause, but his popularity and influence frightened many people, and although he decided not to stand for the presidency after MacMahon's resignation (1878), he was excluded from office for some years. Gambetta served, however, as president of the budgetary commission (1876–9) and of the Chamber (1879–91) and was eventually called upon to form a ministry (1881). His hopes of enlisting all leading republicans in a strong government fell through and he formed a purely opportunist government. His hopes of revising the constitution so as to reduce the powers of the senate and consolidate the parties were rejected by a frightened assembly and his ministry ended after three months. Ill and worried by domestic troubles, he died soon afterwards. His loss was one that France could ill afford, for he was one of the few men who might have overcome the failings of the political system.

J. P. T. Bury, *Gambetta and the National Defence* (London, 1936).   CHC

GAMBIA, 3862 sq. miles (10,000 sq. kms), in West Africa, became an independent member state within the British Commonwealth in 1965. A House of Representatives is elected by adult suffrage, and the prime minister and cabinet hold executive power. The population of 315,400 (1970) includes Manding, Wolof, and Fulbe.

GAME LAWS. Rights in game in Britain, which in general belonged to landowners of moderately sized estates, were not, by common law, absolute property in the wild animals, and therefore had to be defended against infringement by civil, not criminal, law. For this reason landowners had to use their own efforts, including traps and gamekeepers, to apprehend poachers. The early 19th cent. was a period of increasing enthusiasm for, and commercialization of, 'sport', and at the same time of expanding demand for game birds for the dinner tables of the urban middle classes, and this clash of interest led to poaching for financial gain, often resulting in serious affrays between poachers and keepers. The trend of legislation up to mid-century was for game laws and penalties to be clarified and stiffened by statute, though in 1861 man-traps and spring guns were made illegal. The machinery by which these laws were enforced had a strong element of class bias, for it involved prosecution of labourers by landowners in courts where the magistrate was usually a landowner. Penalties were modified in the latter part of the century, but the class bias remained. The game laws caused bad relations between landowner and tenant farmer, until in the agricultural depression of the last quarter of the century they were modified to give tenants a limited share in game rights over the land they occupied.

GAMELIN, MAURICE GUSTAVE (1872–1958), French general. As commander-in-chief, he bore immediate responsibility for France's military collapse in 1940. As defence chief-of-staff, he had drawn up France's war plans, and on the outbreak of war became commander of all the allied forces in France. After the German breakthrough he was dismissed and replaced by Weygand. The Vichy regime arrested him and arraigned him with Daladier and Blum at the 'Riom trial' (1942). He was later deported to Germany.

GAMIO, MANUEL (1883–1960), Mexican scholar and archaeologist, best known for his work on pre-Columbian Mexico.

GAMMER GURTON'S NEEDLE, early English comedy, of uncertain authorship, published 1575, but first acted *c.* 1566.

GAMONAL (GAMONALISMO), term used to describe the owner of a large estate in Ecuador, Peru, or Bolivia, and hence a system, *gamonalismo,* in which the local landowner dominates political, social, and economic life to the detriment of the Indians.

GANAPATI FESTIVALS, held in honour of the Hindu god Ganesha or Ganapati, the eldest son of Siva and leader of his *ganas* (attendants). He is worshipped in the form of a clay figure of a fat human body with an elephant's head, riding on a rat. In modern practice, especially at his festival from Aug. to Sept., he is looked upon as the remover of difficulties, the god of wisdom, and the guardian of the public ways. His image stands in the houses of well-to-do Hindus and in temples dedicated to Siva. He is venerated more in the south of India, especially in Travancore. His worshippers

never set out on a journey without invoking his protection. He is particularly interested in literary and educational activities and is the patron of grammarians. Manuscripts and printed books often begin with the auspicious formula 'Reverence to Lord Ganesha'. In the 1890s Tilak used the 'natural opportunities' that Ganapati festivals provided for the spread of national feeling among the Hindu masses. They contributed not only to anti-British feeling, but also to communal animosities.

GANDAMAK, TREATY OF (26 May 1879), between the British and Amir Yakub Khan. Kurram, Sibi, and Pishin were assigned to the British, who were also to control the Khyber and Michni passes. The British were to control Afghan foreign relations. The treaty was abrogated in Sept. 1879 by the massacre of Cavagnari at Kabul.

GANDHARA, ancient Indian name for an area, not precisely defined, in east Afghanistan and West Pakistan (roughly corresponding to 'Bactria'), notably modern Peshawar, Kabul, and Bamiyan, where Indian culture came into contact with Greek, Iranian, and Central Asian influences. Gandhara art (which probably belongs to early centuries AD), often less correctly styled Indo-Greek, is of Buddhist Indian inspiration, but shows strongly the influence of Greek sculpture.

GANDHI, MRS INDIRA (1917–), prime minister of India, and the daughter of Jawaharlal Nehru. She attended schools in various parts of India and in Switzerland and went on to Somerville College, Oxford. Her political career centred on the Indian National Congress, which she joined in 1938, having already helped her father with electioneering (1937) and in other activities. She was detained during the Quit India movement (1942). During the period of her father's prime ministership (1946–64) she acted as his hostess and companion. Until 1964 she worked in the Congress organization, but not in parliament, being a member of the working committee (1955), president of the party (1959–60), and a member of the central parliamentary board (1962). As president of Congress she had to deal with the problem of the division of Bombay into the linguistic states of Gujarat and Maharashtra, and the attack on the communist government in Kerala. Mrs Gandhi's parliamentary career began when she became minister for information in Lal Bahadur Shastri's cabinet (June 1964) and in Aug. 1964 she was nominated to the Rajya Sabha. Five months later, following Shastri's death, she became prime minister (1965) and she was confirmed in this position following the general elections (1967), when she was elected to the Lok Sabha.

GANDHI, MOHANDAS KARAMCHAND (1869–1948), Indian nationalist leader and social reformer, the major exponent of non-violence in the 20th cent., known as *Mahatma* or 'great soul'. Born of an urban professional family in the small western India state of Porbandar, he qualified as a barrister (1891), but from 1894 his legal practice was overshadowed by his political and social reform activities in South Africa and India.

Ghandi was involved in three main areas of activity. The first was in South Africa, where he campaigned against the disfranchisement of Indians in Natal (1894–6) and against attempts to humiliate, restrict, and if possible exclude, Indians from the Transvaal and other parts of the new Union (1908–14). His Natal Indian Congress succeeded only in delaying the Natal government's designs. In the second campaign the use of passive resistance (*satyagraha*) finally produced (1914) relief from some of the more onerous restrictions and the end of general Indian migration to South Africa.

Gandhi's second and pre-eminent concern was the Indian independence movement. He had published a tract on Indian political reform, *Hind Swaraj,* in 1909 but for some years after his return to India (1915) he involved himself in localized campaigns for peasants' and workers' rights. From 1919 he held the centre of the Indian political stage in a series of major confrontations with the British power: *satyagraha* against the Rowlatt Acts (1919), non-co-operation (1920–2), civil disobedience (1930–4), individual *satyagraha* against the war (1940–1) and 'Quit India' (1942). He was central to the development of the Indian National Congress, although he was only once president (1924), and on several occasions refused to identify himself at all with it.

Gandhi's third major concern was his 'constructive work' for social and economic change. He worked particularly for the welfare of the untouchables, whom he called *harijan*s or 'people of god', for the creation of village self-sufficiency and a new spirit of self-reliance within Indian society, which he symbolized by hand-spinning, and for the creation of communal harmony between Hindus and Muslims. He campaigned for the right of untouchables to enter temples, for the regular hand-spinning of cotton and the wearing of only hand-spun and hand-woven '*khaddar*' cloth, and he sought to prevent communal violence as, for instance, during the pre-partition riots (1946–7). Ironically, it was anger at what some fanatics chose to see as his concessions to Muslims, culminating in partition, which led to his assassination in Delhi by a Hindu (30 Jan. 1948).

In each area of activity Gandhi applied *satyagraha* or non-violent resistance to what was 'unjust' or 'untruthful'. Each campaign began with an ultimatum defining the issues. It moved through demonstrations to non-co-operation, which involved the boycott of the institutions and activities controlled by the opponents and the simultaneous creation of *satyagraha* institutions to replace them, and then on to civil disobedience, or the refusal to obey laws that were held to be 'unjust'. Though Indian independence was not the direct product of such campaigns, *satyagraha* brought the masses into the nationalist movement without precipitating a major violent confrontation with authority. *Satyagraha* developed a sustaining confidence in the righteousness of the nationalist course and led British governments to question the moral basis of imperial rule.

The spiritual content that Gandhi gave to political action explains his ascendancy partly, but not entirely. No mystic misplaced in politics, he was a skilful organizer, a gifted political communicator, a shrewd bargainer, and an exacting administrator. He founded and ran the Natal Indian Congress and was largely responsible for the reconstitution of the Congress (1920) that enabled it to become a mass movement. The Sabarmati, Wardha, and Sevagram ashrams in India and the Pheonix and Tolstoy farms in South Africa were exemplars of his organizational methods and ethical codes. His skill as a communicator is revealed by his use of newspapers—*Indian Opinion* in South Africa, *Young India*, *Navajivan* and later *Harijan* in India—and by his intuitive grasp of the symbols and language to which mass audiences would respond. He reached a wider audience than any earlier Indian politician.

In economic and social policy he was a conservative. He espoused a paternalistic doctrine of 'trusteeship' for landlords and employers and appealed for 'changes of heart' rather than the restructuring of society. As sectional interests seemed likely to weaken the nationalist movement this made sense politically.

Gandhi was not wholly successful in any of his objectives, but his influence, especially between the two world wars, was such that no politician, British or Indian, could afford to ignore him. He was a major force in the politicization of Indian society, he secured recognition for the *harijan*s, and his insistence on non-violence had an impact on the struggles of oppressed groups throughout the world, in his own lifetime and afterwards.

M. K. Gandhi, *An Autobiography, or The Story of My Experiments with Truth* (Ahmedabad, 1927).
B. R. Nanda, *Mahatma Gandhi. A biography* (London, 1958).
PDR

GANESH, RAJA, of Bhaduria (d. 1414), Hindu chief who dominated Bengal from the time of his defeat of Saif-ad-din Hamza (1404) until his death. His son Jadu was converted to Islam and ruled as Jalal-ad-din Muhammad Shah (1414–31). During this period Bengal was under constant threat from the Sultan of Jaunpur.

GANGA DYNASTY, name of two important, apparently unrelated, ancient Indian dynasties, one centred in present Mysore (*c.* 350–1050), the other in Orissa (*c.* 496–1434). Of the latter, the foremost ruler was Anantavarman Codaganga (1076–1146), famous for his campaigns and especially his foundation of the great Jagannath Puri temple, still one of the major sites of pilgrimage.

GANGES (Sansk., *Ganga*), one of the world's greatest and holiest rivers, descending from the Himalaya into the plain at Hardwar, whence it flows through Punjab, Upper Pradesh and Bihar to Bengal, where it develops into a broad delta. For most Hindus the water of the Ganges is believed to be endowed with purifying qualities. One of the holiest places is Prayaga (Allahabad), its confluence with the Yamuna.

GAO, town on the eastern Niger Bend in modern Mali, known in Arabic sources as Kawkaw. Founded before 874 as a caravan terminus, it become capital of the Askia dynasty of Songhay in the 16th cent.

GAOL DELIVERY in England, procedure which makes it impossible for prisoners to be kept indefinitely in gaol without a hearing. Judges on circuit are directed by royal commission to 'deliver' the town gaols, *ie*, to bring before the assize every prisoner so committed. The practice is at least as old as Magna Carta (1215), and was in regular use by the 15th cent.

GAPON, GEORGII APOLLONOVICH (1870–1906), Russian priest, who founded the Association of Russian Factory Workers in St Petersburg (1903) with police protection, and who led the procession on Bloody Sunday, 1905. He was murdered by Socialist-Revolutionaries.

GARAMANTES, tribes first mentioned by Herodotus as inhabiting the Fezzan region of Libya in the 5th cent. BC; their capital, Garama, was situated near the modern town of Djerma. In 21 BC Cornelius Balbus, pro-consul of Africa, campaigned against them and in AD 70 they laid waste the region of Leptis Magna in Tripolitania. The Romans sent two expeditions into their territory during the 1st cent. AD, one of which apparently reached the Sudan.

GARAUDY, ROGER (1913–), French communist philosopher, for many years a leader of the French Communist Party, and its principal ideologist. He fell into disfavour when he criticized the Soviet occupation of Czechoslovakia (1968), and called for a democratic transformation of the French party. In 1970 he was expelled from the central committee.

GARAY, JUAN DE (1541–84), Spanish governor of Paraguay, credited with the second founding of the city of Buenos Aires (1580).

GARBORG, ARNE (1851–1924), Norwegian novelist and poet who wrote primarily in the *landsmaal*, the form which preserved the Old Norse dialects. Much of his work was satirical of his times, *eg*, *Tired Men* (1891), or concerned with religious issues, *eg*, *The Teacher* (1896). His verse included 'Mountain Trolls' (1895).

GARCIA, CARLOS POLESTICO (1896–), president of the Philippines (1957–61), and a poet and orator who entered politics in 1925, when he became representative of the third district of Bohol in the Philippine legislature (1925–31). He served as governor of Bohol (1931–40), was elected senator in 1940, and joined the resistance movement in Bohol during the Japanese occupation of the Philippines (1941–5). After the war he resumed his seat and remained a senator until he became vice-president (1953), which office he held concurrently with that of secretary of foreign affairs in the president's cabinet. In 1957 he succeeded to the presidency, after the death of President Magsaysay. One of his administration's guidelines was 'the Filipino First' policy, not only in regard to the country's domestic affairs, but also in her foreign relations. He called for austerity at home and promoted closer relations with neighbouring Asian nations. In 1961 he was defeated by D. Macapagal in his bid for re-election.

GARCIA CALDERON, FRANCISCO (1883–1953), Peruvian diplomat and scholar, and son of the president of the same name. He is known for his analytical essays on the Latin American scene.

GARCIA MORENO, GABRIEL (1821–75), president of Ecuador and an extreme conservative who believed that the only unifying force in the new Latin American nations was the Roman Catholic Church. His concordat with the Vatican became the basis of his regime, and he attempted to turn Ecuador into a theocratic state by giving the Church total supervision of education and publication. He corrected fiscal abuses, attacked corruption in government, and encouraged railroad building, notably that between Quito and Guayaquil. He was constantly opposed by Liberals.

GARDANE MISSION, sent by France (1807) to Iran under Gen. Antoine Gardane to carry out the treaty of Finkenstein. This became impossible after the Tilsit agreement and the mission retired (1809).

GARDAR SVAVARSSON (*fl. c.* 860), Swedish sailor and reputed discoverer of Iceland. Driven there by chance, he wintered on the north coast, circumnavigated the island, and named it Gardarsholm.

'GARDEN SUBURB' in Britain, nickname given to a group of advisers, outside the government, who assisted Lloyd George during and after the First World War. This unofficial staff, based in St James's Park, London, could be compared to a US president's use of experts outside Congress. It aroused hostility among politicians and in government departments on the ground that many of their functions were being usurped, *eg*, in the handling of League of Nations matters. The arrangement was also criticized as being unconstitutional.

GARDENING, LANDSCAPE, was perfected in 18th-cent. England. The aim was to compose an idealized natural landscape to link a nobleman's mansion, perhaps Palladian in style, with its surroundings. England's countryside became the raw material for essays in the style of artists like Claude and Poussin. Bright flowerbeds were superfluous and the great landscape gardeners, *eg*, William Kent, 'Capability' Brown, and Humphrey Repton made their effects with grass, water, trees, and shrubs, using temples, arches, obelisks, bridges, and lakes to complete or punctuate a view. Their compositions, as at Stowe, combine informality with an innate rhythm, and commemorate the wealth, discernment, and preoccupations of the 18th-cent. landowners.

GARDINER, STEPHEN (*c.* 1483–1555), bishop of Winchester and lord chancellor, supported royal supremacy in the Church of England (*De Vera Obedientia*, 1535), but remained Catholic on doctrinal issues and was one of the leaders of the reaction under Mary I. Gardiner, an authority on civil and canon law, was employed in the negotiations for Henry VIII's 'divorce', and was made Bp of Winchester (1531) and royal secretary (1531–4). With Norfolk, he led the conservative reaction against the innovating policies of Thomas Cromwell and Cranmer, and after Cromwell's fall (1540) Henry made use of his diplomatic skill, sending him on missions to Charles V. But Henry mistrusted his rigid Catholicism and excluded him from the regency council set up for Edward VI's minority. Gardiner believed in the Real Presence at the Eucharist and was critical of many renderings in English translations of the Bible. Under Edward he was deprived of his bishopric (1551) and spent most of the reign in prison, but Mary restored him and made him chancellor (1553). Although he disliked her proposed marriage to Philip II, he obediently complied with her wishes and performed the ceremony in Winchester Cathedral (1554). His responsibility for the subsequent persecution is hard to determine and has perhaps been exaggerated by Foxe and other Protestant apologists. There were only three burnings in his diocese, and these occurred after his death. His severity to Princess Elizabeth, who was statutorily declared illegitimate, has also been criticized, but as a Catholic he could not have wished her to be Mary's successor.

J. A. Muller, *Stephen Gardiner and the Tudor Reaction* (London, 1926). MMR

GARFIELD, JAMES ABRAM (1831–81), US president, personification of the log-cabin-to-White-House legend, and the second American president to be assassinated. During the Civil War he became a major-general in the Union army (1861–3). He was a Republican congressman from OH (1863–80), but was a more prominent and influential figure inside Congress than outside. The Republican Party convention chose him on the 36th ballot as its compromise candidate for the presidency (1880), and in the election itself he narrowly defeated Winfield S. Hancock, with a majority of only 7000 in a vote of 9 million. He was shot by Charles Guiteau, an unsuccessful office-seeker (2 July), and died (19 Sept.) without having had time to show whether as president he would have achieved more distinction than he achieved during the earlier part of his career.

GARIBALDI, GUISEPPE (1807–82), Italian general of the Risorgimento, prototype of the 19th-cent. nationalist hero, a great leader of irregular forces, a representative of the grass-roots, socialist-republican elements to be found in the movement for Italian unification. He was born in Nice, the son of a sea captain. His defence of the Roman Republic (1849) and the victory of his 1000 redshirted irregulars against the Neapolitan troops in Naples and Sicily (1860) made him a legend in his lifetime. Garibaldi had a touching faith in the efficacy of direct action. After being implicated in an unsuccessful insurrection of the Young Italy movement in Genoa (1834) he fled, eventually, to Rio de Janeiro. For the next 12 years, first at sea and then inland, he fought for the emergent republics of South America. Here he adopted the style of dress of the Argentine slaughter-houses, and in the rough democracy of the Pampas learned his trade as a guerrilla leader.

With the outbreak of the 1848 European revolutions, Garibaldi returned to Italy and, although Charles Albert had already been defeated, took on the Austrians in a private war in Lombardy. His subsequent defence of the Roman Republic and the daring of his forced march to San Marino furnished the first real martyrs for the cult of a United Italy. The success of his irregular tactics in the War of Liberation (1859) emphasized the inadequacy of the Sardinian army. By defeating the kingdoms of Naples and Sicily (1860) he encouraged Cavour to pursue a more forceful policy than he had originally intended.

In later life, in voluntary exile on the island of Caprera, Garibaldi seemed to symbolize the failed potential of the Risorgimento. The defeats at Lissa and Novara (1866) were not redeemed by his own attempts to take Rome, ending disastrously at Aspromonte (1862) and Mentana (1867). Despite these setbacks Garibaldi became an object of veneration in his old age, his picture often replacing that of

Christ or the Pope in the cabins of Italian peasants. Lincoln offered him a command in the Civil War. In 1864 he visited London where his appearance provoked scenes of such enthusiasm among the working class that the government thought it advisable to cancel a projected tour by him to the provinces. Even so, his visit helped to revive the cause of parliamentary reform in England. He fought his last battles from a litter, for Republican France against Bismarck's Prussia (1870).

Garibaldi's politics were confused, his egalitarianism conflicting with his tendency to style himself dictator on finding himself in command of conquered territory, and his deference to monarchy ill-befitting his avowed republicanism. Yet his consistent passion was to make war against oppressors wherever he might find them. His reputation and his role in the Risorgimento were at the time—and subsequently have often been—played down by a jealous establishment.

D. Mack Smith, *Garibaldi* (Cambridge, 1957).
C. Hibbert, *Garibaldi and his Enemies* (London, 1965). SH

GARIGLIANO, BATTLE OF (27 Dec. 1503), defeat of Louis XII's French forces in Naples by the Spaniards, led by Gonzalo de Cordoba (1453–1515). After their earlier defeat at Cerignalo (April 1503) the French had withdrawn to Gaeta, delaying their drive on Naples until mid-winter. Cordoba's surprise attack at the Garigliano river forced the French to retreat in disorder to Gaeta, which capitulated on 1. Jan 1504, yielding the whole kingdom of Naples to Ferdinand of Spain.

GARLAND, HANNIBAL HAMLIN (1860–1940), US writer, remembered for his realistic accounts of the bleakness of late 19th-cent. prairie life in such books as *A Son of the Middle Border* (1917). He gave early encouragement to Stephen Crane and other naturalistic writers.

GARNER, JOHN NANCE (1868–1967), US politician, who served in the TX state legislature (1898–1902) and the US Congress (1903–33). He was speaker of the US House of Representatives (1931–3) and had some support within the Democratic Party for the presidential nomination (1932). As F. D. Roosevelt's vice-president (1933–41), he exerted considerable influence on Capitol Hill.

GARNIER, CLEMENT JOSEPH (1813–81), French economist, founder and secretary of the Société d'Économie politique, and organizer of the Association pour la liberté des Échanges (1846) and of the Congrès de la Paix (1849).

GARNIER, FRANCIS (1839–73), French naval officer and explorer. The son of a French army officer, he entered the navy in 1856 and in 1860 was a member of the Anglo-French expedition to China. After spending some time in Cochin-China, he wrote in 1864, a pamphlet in defence of colonial expansion. In 1866–8 he joined Doudart de Lagree in an exploration of the Mekong river, believing it would prove to be a gateway to China. Although he finally reached Chinese soil, it was clear that the river was not navigable for trade, and he turned his attention to the Red river route through Tongking. Having met Jean Dupuis in China, he was authorized by the French commander in Saigon to lead a small force to Hanoi in 1873, to support Dupuis's attempt to trade with Yunnan via the Red river. Garnier's force captured the citadel at Hanoi in Nov. 1873, but in December he was killed in a sortie against an attack by the Chinese 'Black Flags'. The French withdrew the force in 1874.

GARNIER-PAGES, LOUIS ANTOINE (1803–78), French republican leader of the Orleanist period, who was elected to the assembly in 1842. He became a member of the provisional government (1848), being first mayor of Paris and then minister of finances. His conservative fiscal measures made him unpopular with the radicals, but earned him election both to the Constituent and the Executive Commission. After the *coup d'état* he failed to get back into parliament until 1864, and played only a minor role in the government of National Defence (1871).

GARRAN, SIR ROBERT RANDOLPH (1867–1957), Australian public servant and first secretary of the attorney-general's department of the Commonwealth of Australia and its solicitor-general (1917–31). He was the confidant of prime ministers as different in character as Deakin and Hughes, and as a young Sydney barrister was secretary to the drafting committee of the 1897–8 federal convention. His autobiography, *Prosper the Commonwealth* (1958), revealed the wealth of his political and administrative experience.

GARRISON, WILLIAM LLOYD (1805–79), US abolitionist, who became editor of the *Genius of Universal Emancipation* (1829–30). The vehemence of his editorials resulted (1830) in his being imprisoned for libel. Convinced that the aim of the movement should be the immediate and unconditional abolition of slavery, he broke with the American Colonization Society and in 1831 established his own periodical, the *Liberator* (Boston, 1831–65), which became the mouthpiece of the movement's radical wing.

In 1833, after visiting England, where he studied British abolitionist methods, Garrison, with Arthur and Lewis Tappan, launched the American Anti-Slavery Society. However, his extremism and habit of linking anti-slavery with other causes aroused the suspicion and, ultimately, the opposition of many of his colleagues. In particular, they objected to his injection of the women's rights issue into the movement, his outspoken attacks on the churches and the constitution, and his refusal to countenance political action. Nevertheless, he enjoyed the support of a band of followers, mostly in his native New England, who in 1840 took over the ailing American Anti-Slavery Society and elected Garrison president. Later in the same year, when he and a group of followers attended the World Anti-Slavery Convention in London, a parallel schism occurred within the British movement.

Although Garrison was a difficult man to work with and may, by dividing it, have weakened the movement, he was an outstanding propagandist and played an important part in drawing attention to the moral dilemmas implicit in slavery. The outbreak of the Civil War in 1861 placed him in a difficult position since he had, since 1842, been arguing for the separation of North and South. Aware that this would place him on the side of the Confederacy, he changed his stand and for the duration of the war supported the Unionist cause. With the passage of the 13th Amendment in 1865 he effectively retired from public life.

W. P. and F. J. Garrison, *William Lloyd Garrison 1805–1879*, 4 vols (New York, 1885–89).
John L. Thomas, *The Liberator: William Lloyd Garrison* (Boston, 1963). HRT

GARTER, ORDER OF, premier English order of chivalry inaugurated in 1348. The story of Edward III and the Countess of Salisbury's garter is now generally accepted as the origin of its title. The order was restricted to 26 brother knights and still meets at Windsor.

GARVEY, MARCUS MOZIAH (1887–1940), Jamaican black nationalist leader and journalist who was struck by the helpless position of his fellow black men and helped establish the Universal Negro Improvement Association (1914). He moved to New York city in 1916. His publications, *Negro World* (1918–33), and *Negro Times* (1922–4), espousing a programme of Negro pride, unity, and action, were widely read throughout the black world. Garvey, more than any other leader, articulated the secret thoughts of the Negro masses.

GARVIN, JAMES LOUIS (1868–1947), British journalist and writer, who in 1899 became a leader-writer on the *Daily Telegraph*. In 1908 Northcliffe appointed him editor and manager of the languishing *Sunday Observer*, and within two years it became a thriving journal, vigorous in the Conservative cause. Garvin's outspoken and clear-sighted opinions made the paper a force to be reckoned with. He encouraged the House of Lords to throw out Lloyd George's budget, advocated a reconstruction of the second chamber, supported a strong policy in the First World War, and urged post-war international economic co-operation through the League of Nations. In 1931 he was a firm supporter of the coalition; he also believed Britain's strength rested in her air defences and general rearmament. To some extent, however, he supported appeasement (1935–8), believing that British protests to Italy over Abyssinia would be useless, and opposed commitments which would drag her into a war against Germany. After Munich, however, he felt that no further concessions should be made to Hitler.

In 1942 he and W. W. Astor, as, respectively, editor and proprietor, disagreed over Garvin's functions. Garvin also made statements about Churchill and Beaverbrook which were contrary to Astor's known views. In Feb. 1942 therefore his 34 years of editorship ended. For the rest of his life he wrote for the *Sunday Express* and the *Daily Telegraph*.

His work changed the pattern of Sunday journalism by creating a high-quality newspaper that showed a strong interest in the arts. Garvin was editor of the 14th edition (1929) of the *Encyclopaedia Britannica* and author of, among other works, the *Life of Joseph Chamberlain*.

GARY, ELBERT HENRY (1846–1927), US lawyer, financier, and industrialist. He became president of the Federal Steel Co. (1898) and, together with J. P. Morgan, organized the US Steel Corporation (1901), of which he was chairman (1903–27). His opposition to labour unions was partly responsible for the steel strike of 1919, but he was a firm believer in company welfare programmes and founded the steel town of Gary, IN.

GASCOIGNE, THOMAS (1403–58), chancellor of Oxford University, theologian, and preacher, who was vigorously hostile to the Wycliffite tradition. His principal work is his *Dictionarium Theologicum* (1434–57), which although mainly moral and theological is in part autobiographical and throws light on the Church and university in his day.

GASKELL, ELIZABETH (1810–65), English novelist, whose early books, *eg*, *Mary Barton* and *North and South*, contain striking scenes of northern working-class life. Her most famous novel, *Cranford*, based on her experiences in Knutsford, Cheshire, was followed by a controversial biography of Charlotte Brontë.

GASPARRI, PIETRO, cardinal (1852–1934), Italian ecclesiastic and diplomat. After a career as lecturer in, and codifier of, canon law, he became papal secretary of state (1914–30). In the First World War he dedicated himself to mediation and peace negotiations. He later negotiated with Nitti and Mussolini for a Vatican–Italy settlement, eventually signing the Lateran Agreements (1929).

GASPERI, ALCIDE DE (1871–1954), Italian politician and prime minister (1945–53). He was born in Austrian Trentino, became a newspaper editor and entered the Reichsrat in 1911, where he advocated social reforms and autonomy for his fellow Italian-speakers of the province of Trentino. After Trentino's annexation by Italy (1919), he joined Sturzo's *Partito Popolare*, and eventually became its parliamentary leader (1921–6). He rejected the idea of a socialist alliance, fearing violent anti-clericalism, and in order to avert civil war sanctioned participation in Mussolini's coalition (1922). Having failed to modify fascist policies, he became openly anti-fascist. He was consequently imprisoned (1927–8), but

was released because of illness and royal pressure. He became first a cataloguer then secretary (1939–43) of the Vatican library. Besides writing veiled anti-fascist articles, he made plans for post-fascist government and revival of the *Popolare* party, which he brought into being under the name of Christian Democracy (DC). As foreign minister (1944–5), he sought to modify Allied demands in treaty negotiations. These—and especially Churchill's—he often found hostile and uncomprehending.

Chosen as prime minister (Dec. 1945) by Prince Umberto, De Gasperi headed eight consecutive administrations. As the architect of post-war Italian reconstruction he secured foreign loans and Marshall Aid, enforced credit controls, etc., to limit inflation, backed limited land redistribution and industrial reforms, and curbed communist vendettas against fascists. The communists and socialists having opposed the Marshall Plan (1947), he was forced to rely on the smaller, centre parties for coalitions. His view of the DC as a 'centre party looking towards the left' was opposed by conservative factions, backed by the Vatican and many clerics, and he failed to rid the party organization of their controlling influence. He avoided their, and US, pressure to ban communist and socialist parties and to ally himself with monarchists and old fascists. He was a leading promoter of European unity plans, and of the Coal and Steel community. His law to change the electoral system (1953) was criticized as being 'fraudulent' and lost him supporters and thus power.

Elisa A. Carrillo, *Alcide De Gasperi, the long apprenticeship* (Notre Dame, IN, 1965).
Giuseppe Mammarella, *Italy after Fascism, A Political History 1943–1965* (rev. ed., Notre Dame, IN, 1966).

GASTEIN, CONVENTION OF (1865), agreement between Prussia and Austria that the duchies of Schleswig and Holstein, awarded to them jointly by the Vienna treaty (1864), should be separately administered—Schleswig by Prussia and Holstein by Austria. The arrangement ended in the Austro-Prussian War (1866).

GATES, SIR THOMAS (1585–1621), English soldier and colonizer, who served with the armies of the states general of Holland (1604–8). He was one of the grantees of the Virginia Co. and took 500 immigrants to settle in Jamestown (1609). His own ship was wrecked in the Bermudas and he did not reach Jamestown until 1610. The account of his nine-month shipwreck, published in 1625, allegedly formed the material for Shakespeare's *The Tempest*. Gates was governor of the Jamestown colony (1611–14).

GATLING, RICHARD JORDAN (1818–1903), US inventor of farm tools and machinery, and of the Gatling gun (1862), a rapid-fire, revolving-barrel machine gun that was adopted by the US army in 1866.

GATSI RUSERE (*fl.* 17th cent.). Ruler of the Mwenemutapa empire in Central Africa. He resisted several Portuguese attempts to size control of his mines.

GATTINARA, MERCURINO, cardinal (1465–1530), Grand Chancellor to the Emperor Charles V in succession to Jean Sauvage, Erasmian humanist, and cosmopolitan diplomat. A Piedmontese by birth, he had a concept of Charles's imperial role which transcended the interests of individual states. 'God has set you on the path towards a world monarchy', he told the youthful ruler in 1519. Gattinara generally accompanied Charles on his travels, advising him on foreign policy. While Charles was in Spain (1522–9) Gattinara remained with him as principal adviser and in this period carried out much-needed changes which established the structure of Spanish government for the rest of the 16th cent., *eg*, he reformed the council of Castile, reorganized the government of Navarre, and founded the councils governing finance and the Indies.

GAUCHO, the 'cowboy' of the Argentine and Uruguayan pampas. Once, collectively, a serious political force, known for daring and toughness, the gaucho is now (1970) a figure of nostalgia and folklore.

GAUDA (lit., 'the sugar-cane country'), ancient name of either the whole or part of present Bengal. In the latter case it applies, in an imprecise manner, to western Bengal (eastern Bengal is then denoted by Vanga). Later, in the form Gaur, the name is used as a synonym of Lakhnauti, capital of the Sena kingdom, founded by Laksmanasena in the 11th cent.

GAUGAMELA (or Arbela), **BATTLE OF** (Oct. 331 BC), Alexander the Great's second and decisive victory over the Persian imperial army. As he advanced on Babylon, Darius III deployed a vast army, including 40,000 cavalry and 200 scythe-chariots, but only about 16,000 effective heavy infantry, on the eastern bank of the Tigris near Nineveh. By advancing obliquely, so that his best troops on his right were first engaged, Alexander offset the Persian advantage in numbers, broke their centre, and put Darius to flight. He then overran Babylonia and soon afterwards the Persian homeland.

GAUHATI, capital of the ancient kingdom of Kamarupa. Under Muslim rule it became the Muslim headquarters in Lower Assam, and after the Muslims' expulsion (1681) the residence of the Ahom governors. In 1786 it was the capital of the Ahom king. After the British conquest, Shillong took its place as capital.

GAUL, ROMAN, at first an area roughly corresponding to Provence, annexed between 125 and 121 BC and extended to the whole of modern France and to the Rhine by Julius Caesar's conquests (58–50 BC). Under the empire, the provincial divisions and capitals were Narbonensis (Narbo, Narbonne), Aquitania (Burdigala, Bordeaux), Lugdunensis (Lugdunum, Lyons), and Belgica (Augusta Trevirorum, Trier). Narbonensis was rapidly Romanized and even in the 1st cent. AD resembled Italy rather than a province. Elsewhere there were few Roman settlers and the impact of Roman civilization on Celtic society and culture was much slower, the Gallic language surviving in some parts until the 5th cent. The wealth of Gallic agriculture was considerable, and craft industries, especially pottery, expanded enormously under Roman rule. Gaul was always exposed to German attacks which finally, early in the 5th cent., broke the defensive system on the Rhine.

GAULLE, CHARLES DE (1890–1970), French soldier and statesman. He was the symbol and leader of the French Resistance during the Second World War, and again guided France's destinies after his recall to power in 1958. Before 1940, De Gaulle's name was known only to military experts. He was one of those who saw the importance of tanks in modern warfare, and his book *Vers l'armée de métier* (1934), which called for a mechanized striking force, had brought him into conflict with the French military establishment. The 1940 campaign, in which he saw action as a tank commander, showed the relevance of his ideas, and he was promoted general and given a junior post in Reynaud's government just before France's collapse.

Repudiating the idea of an armistice, De Gaulle left for London, and in a broadcast speech (18 June 1940) he called on France to continue the struggle. He was supported by the British government, and became leader of the exiled Free French forces. His authority was also accepted by a number of French colonies, and by the Resistance within France when it developed.

De Gaulle's relations with Britain and her allies were often strained, not least after the landings in North Africa (1942), when the Americans preferred to work with Giraud. But by the end of 1943 De Gaulle had out-manœuvred Giraud, and was unchallenged head of the National Liberation Committee, which became the Provisional Government when France was liberated (1944). As head of government, he introduced important social reforms and established France's status as a great power in the post-war political settlements. But he found working with parliament and political parties frustrating, and resigned (1946).

De Gaulle declared his hostility to the institutions of the Fourth Republic, and especially to the parties. But his attempt to regain power through the Rassemblement du peuple français movement was unsuccessful, and he retired from public life in 1955. His followers continued to work for his return, and their chance came with the Algerian rebellion of 13 May 1958. De Gaulle was turned to as the only man who could impose his will on all parties and prevent civil war, and the crisis ended when he became prime minister. He was given power to remodel the constitution to his taste, and became president of the new Fifth Republic in 1959.

De Gaulle ended the Algerian war by accepting France's defeat (1962), but this solution was not reached easily, and he had to cope with risings of the French Algerians (1960, 1961) and extremist violence at home.

His abiding interest was in foreign affairs, and he sought to make France strong and give her an independent role in world affairs, an aspect of which involved insisting on British exclusion from the European Common Market. His domestic policies, however, were more conservative, and although he was re-elected in 1965, opposition and frustration were increasing. The regime was shaken by strikes and student riots in 1968, and in 1969 De Gaulle resigned after the defeat of a referendum which had incorporated some of his ideas for greater political 'participation'.

C. de Gaulle, *War Memoirs*, 3 vols (London, 1955–60).
A. Werth, *De Gaulle, a political biography*, new ed. (London, 1967). RDA

GAULLIST MOVEMENT, in France, under the Fourth Republic. Gaullism as a mass movement was short-lived, although De Gaulle retained an important following throughout the period when he was out of office. The Rassemblement du peuple français, launched by him in 1947, reached the height of its popularity in 1947–8, when its appeal was to those who feared communism. Some have detected fascist tendencies in the authoritarianism of the movement.

The RPF won many seats in the 1951 election, but was dissolved by De Gaulle in 1953 after internal dissensions and electoral losses. Most of the deputies wanted to take part in parliamentary politics, but De Gaulle was hostile to this, seeing the RPF as a national movement rather than a political party.

After 1953 Gaullist deputies sat as Social Republicans until the end of the Fourth Republic, and their leaders accepted office in various governments. The party lost heavily in the 1956 election. With the establishment of the Fifth Republic in 1958, Gaullism was channelled into the UNR.

GAULTIER, Abbé (d. 1720), French priest who, while chaplain to the imperial ambassador in London during Queen Anne's reign, acted as an unofficial agent for the secret peace negotiations between Torcy, the French foreign minister, the Jacobites Jersey and Berwick, and the Tory administration (1710–11).

GAUSS, CARL FRIEDRICH (1777–1855), outstanding German mathematician and astronomer who discovered the method of least squares and, with William Webber, the electro-magnetic telegraph.

GAVELKIND ACT (1704), one of the Irish penal laws of Queen Anne's reign, by which on the death of a Catholic landowner his estates were to be divided among all his sons, unless the eldest conformed to the Church of Ireland within one year or on coming of age, in which case he inherited the whole estate. The act effectively reduced the number of

Roman Catholic landowners, some of whom conformed to save the family from economic impoverishment. The term 'gavelkind' (Old English, *gafol*, rent or payment, and *gecynd*, kind or nature) was derived from an old Kentish form of land tenure.

GAWLER, GEORGE (1795–1869), second governor of South Australia, where he was influential in the surveying and opening up of country districts so as to end speculation in city blocks by settlers around Adelaide. By 1841, when he returned to England, 6000 settlers had left Adelaide for surveyed country sections, 16,000 acres (65 sq. kms) had been enclosed, half was under cultivation, and 7000 cattle and 250,000 sheep were at pasture.

Gawler not only exceeded his powers but failed to recognize the realities of his position *vis-à-vis* the authorities in London and became the scapegoat of the colonial office, which was eager to end costly colonial experiments. He also suffered from the efficiency of his successor, George Grey, with whom he had quarrelled on the latter's arrival in Adelaide. Grey's reports to the colonial office did not reveal that he had profited by Gawler's earlier efforts. This comparative lack of recognition and of adequate offers of future employment induced Gawler to resume the military career he had earlier abandoned. After his retirement in 1850 he devoted himself to literary, religious, and philanthropic activities.

GAY, JOHN (1685–1732), English poet and dramatist. He was secretary to the Duchess of Monmouth (1712–14), and held minor public offices under the patronage of various nobles. He was a friend of Pope and Swift, and is best known for *The Beggar's Opera* (1728).

GAZA, town in southern Palestine, about 40 miles (64 kms) south-west of Tel Aviv. In 1917 the British and the Ottoman armies fought three battles near Gaza, the Turks withdrawing after the British break-through at Beersheba. At the end of the First World War Gaza was included in the British mandate for Palestine. The town was assigned to Egypt under the terms of the Israeli-Egyptian armistice concluded in 1949. Presently (1970) it is under the military occupation of Israel.

GAZA, Empire of (*c.* 1831–95), founded by Soshangane in south Mozambique, as a Zulu kingdom resulting from the Shakan wars. At its height it extended from the Zambesi to the Limpopo and even reduced the Portuguese to tributaries. It collapsed through internal weaknesses and Portuguese military attack.

GDYNIA, Polish Baltic port. Difficulties in ensuring the supply of military equipment through Danzig during the Polish-Soviet War in 1920 convinced the Poles that they could not rely on the Free City as their only outlet on the Baltic. It was therefore decided to build up a seaport at the small fishing village of Gdynia. By 1939 the town comprised a large modern harbour with a population of 120,000. After the Polish defeat it was incorporated into the Reich, and was substantially damaged during the Second World War. Since 1945 it has been developed in conjunction with Gdansk (Danzig) and Sopot, and by 1970 the population was 160,000.

GEDDES, AUCKLAND CAMPBELL GEDDES, 1st Baron (1879–1954), British doctor, politician, and diplomat, whose varied career included professorships of anatomy at McGill and Edinburgh Universities, service in the Anglo-Boer and First World Wars, and the principalship of McGill University. He was director of recruiting (1917–19) to the war office, with responsibility for organizing national service during the First World War. Subsequently he became president of the board of trade (1919). He was ambassador to the US (1920–4).

GEDDES, JENNY (*fl.* 17th cent.), popularly supposed to have been the woman who, on Sunday, 23 July 1637, started a riot at St Giles's Cathedral, Edinburgh, by throwing a stool at David Lindsay, Bp of Edinburgh, in protest against an attempt to read Abp Laud's service-book. The service-book, although associated with Laud's name, was largely the work of Scottish bishops.

GEDDES AXE in Britain, name given to the programme of public economy resulting from the report in Feb. 1922 of the committee on government expenditure. Under the chairmanship of Sir Eric Campbell Geddes (1875–1937) the 'axe' led to drastic cuts in army, navy, education, and teachers' salaries, public health expenditure and the abolition of five government departments including the ministries of transport and labour.

GEDI, Arab-African town near Malindi, Kenya. Although occupied from 12th cent., its existing buildings, mosques, houses, and tombs belong to the 15th cent. They were abandoned early in the 17th cent. The town has been maintained as a national monument since 1948.

GEER, DE, FAMILY. Flemish family originating in Liège, but resident in Dordrecht, Holland, from the 1590s, where its most eminent member, Louis de Geer (1587–1652), was educated. His father was a banker and his two sisters married local merchants. In 1615 De Geer moved to Amsterdam, where he set up as an armaments dealer, financier, and general merchant. When, in 1617, Willem de Besche drew his attention to the possibilities of economic development in Sweden, he made his first contact with Gustavus Adolphus. In 1618, with a number of Amsterdam merchants, he stood surety for the payment of a large loan made by the states general to the King of Sweden. In 1627 he and De Besche were given the monopoly of arms production in Sweden and after the latter's death (1629) De Geer was the dominant figure in Swedish economic life. After taking Swedish citizenship, partly to obtain exemption from the Sound tolls, he was made joint factor for the monopolies of the salt trade and the copper industry in Sweden (1628). However, his interests were not confined to these commodities. His name was associated also with brass production, textile manufacturing, rope and sulphur factories, saw-mills, tin-mining, shipbuilding, wholesale and retail stores, banking, and above all the mining and smelting of iron ore. In the war between Sweden and Denmark (1644) he fitted out a fleet of 30 ships, costing nearly $1\frac{1}{2}$ million guilders, on behalf of the Swedish government and was rewarded for his services to the Swedish monarchy with the titles of Lord of Osterby and Finsprang. Louis de Geer's descendants remained in Sweden and included the natural scientist Charles de Geer (1720–78), whose work on insects (1752–78) made him second only to Réaumur.

GE'EZ, classical and liturgical language of Ethiopia. It is a Semitic language written in its own script, and the parent of Amharic and other modern Ethiopian tongues.

GEFFRARD, NICOLAS FABRE (1806–79), Haitian general and president. As head of the army under Emperor Faustin Soulouque, he led a rebellion against him in 1858. Geffrard then became president of the restored republic (1859–67). He sought to assure Haiti's international position and won recognition from the Holy See and the US. He was overthrown in 1867 and went into exile in Jamaica.

GEHEIMER RAT, imperial privy council created by the Emperor Ferdinand I in the mid-16th cent. to help to centralize the government of his many territories. During Leopold I's reign (1658–1705) the privy council became purely honorary because of the creation of the Geheime Konferenz, a small inner council of four or five members.

GELA, ancient Greek colony on the southern coast of Sicily, founded by Rhodians and Cretans *c.* 680 BC. Rich in agricultural land and famous for horse-breeding, it founded Acragas 67 kms to the north-west (580) and reached its zenith under the tyrant Hippocrates (*c*. 498–*c*. 491), who established an empire in eastern Sicily, but declined after Hippocrates' successor,Gelon, seized power in Syracuse, and transferred half its population thither. In 424 a pan-Sicilian peace conference at Gela settled differences to prevent Athenian intervention and Gela later supported Syracuse against Athens (415–413), but was abandoned to the Carthaginians in 405. Surviving walls date from the 4th cent., when Gela was refounded, only to be destroyed in 282.

GELASIUS (d. 496), Pope (*reg*. 492–6). He was the first pope explicitly to claim that the papacy was independent both of the state and of Church councils in matters of faith. Gelasius developed the doctrine of the 'Two Powers' (*sacerdotium et imperium*), of which the former, since it provided the instrument under God whereby souls were saved eternally, was superior to the latter.

GELDERLAND, Dutch-speaking province of the Netherlands, which included the towns of Arnhem and Nymwegen and became one of the seven component states of the Dutch Republic (1648).

GELON (d. 478 BC), Tyrant of Syracuse and leader of the Greek army which defeated the Carthaginian invasion of Sicily in 480. After usurping power at Gela when the tyrant Hippocrates died (*c*. 491), he allied himself with Theron, Tyrant of Acragas, and then seized Syracuse with the help of exiled aristocrats. Through strengthening Syracuse by transfers of population from Gela and other subject cities, his power became such that he was called on—in vain—to help to defend the homeland against Xerxes (481). In 480 he raised some 55,000 men to relieve Theron, who was being besieged in Himera by the Carthaginians. His victory ended the Carthaginian threat for 70 years and was celebrated with a notable offering at Delphi.

GEMBLOUX, BATTLE OF (Jan. 1578), victory of Don John of Austria, Spanish governor-general of the Netherlands, over the forces of the rebellious estates. Marching from Luxembourg north-westwards into Brabant, Don John routed the rebels near Namur. Many of the latter's officers were absent in Brussels and the Catholic Walloons, already hostile to the Prince of Orange, put up little resistance to the Spaniards.

GEMINI SPACE PROJECT (1965–7) in US, programme of ten orbital flights by two-man space vehicles, designed to give astronauts training in rendezvous and docking procedures in preparation for the Apollo moon programme. The series included Edward White's first US 'space walk' (Gemini 4, June 1965).

GEMMA, FRISIUS RAINER (1508–55), Louvain astronomer, who accepted the Copernican heliostatic concept of the universe in the early 16th cent. He published *Methodus Arithmeticae* (1540) and *De Principiis Astronomice* (1547). Gemma suggested improvements in the theory and practice of navigation and one of his best-known pupils was Mercator, the mathematician and cartographer.

GENERAL ACT (1928) for the Peaceful Settlement of International Disputes, the last attempt within the League of Nations to create a comprehensive system of international arbitration. It was compiled from a series of model treaties devised by the Committee of Arbitration and Security which was set up in preparation for the 1927 Disarmament Conference. The act proposed several alternative methods of settling disputes: the Permanent Court of International Justice for legal disputes, and Conciliation Commissions and Arbitral Tribunals for different stages of non-justiciable disputes. Signatures could be attached to the act as a whole or to particular chapters. The act was not an instrument for making arbitration universal and compulsory, but was a convention which came into force between any states accepting any part of it. France was the first great power to ratify her signature of the act in June 1930, on the understanding that the Arbitral Tribunals would respect established treaty rights. Britain adhered to the act in March 1931 on the understanding that Commonwealth disputes remained unaffected, and that disputes might still be submitted to the exclusive arbitration of the League Council. The act itself placed such subjects as domestic state jurisdiction outside its own scope. By 1931, 18 league members adhered to the act. These included Italy, but not Germany, which objected to it as an instrument for preserving the Versailles settlement.

GENERAL AGREEMENT ON TARIFFS AND TRADE (GATT), multilateral trade agreement (Oct. 1947) which resulted in the establishment of a secretariat and the organization of regular meetings of the 75 members and 12 associated members. The agreement provided a substitute for a proposed International Trade Organization which was devised in parallel with the World Bank and the International Monetary Fund but which, although signed, was never ratified.

Members of GATT undertake to observe certain rules in the control of their trade (*eg*, quantitative restrictions are allowed only under certain specified conditions). In addition, conferences, held at irregular but frequent intervals, have led to substantial reductions in tariff barriers.

GATT is one of the specialized agencies of the UN—an independent organization which functions in co-operation with the Economic and Social Council.

GENERAL CONFEDERATION OF LABOUR (CGT) (Argentina), used by Juan Perón to organize his support among the Argentinian working class. Since Perón's fall from power (1955) the CGT has been seriously divided. A large pro-Perón faction remained, while others have supported various political parties. In 1969 the CGT emerged as a leader in the struggle against military government and called several large strikes.

GENERAL COUNCIL OF BURMESE ASSOCIATIONS, developed in 1921 out of the Young Men's Buddhist Association and became the chief nationalist political organization in Burma. On the introduction of political reforms in 1922 the GCBA split over policy regarding the new constitution. One section, the 21 Party, co-operated. The rest of the GCBA boycotted the reforms. By 1929 the GCBA had split again into at least four groups. By 1936, after separation from India, under the leadership of U Ba Pe, it was one, probably the least influential, of three parties. It did not revive after the Japanese invasion.

GENERAL WARRANTS in Britain, were those by which the secretary of state ordered the arrest of unspecified persons and search of their property. Their issue was common in the 17th cent. and secured statutory authority in the Licensing Act (1662) and continued after its lapse (1695).

The attacks upon George III's government by John Wilkes in No. 45 of the *North Briton* led to five legal cases in which general warrants were contested, beginning when Wilkes, claiming privilege as an MP, successfully challenged the issue of a warrant against himself, secured his discharge from custody (1763), and ultimately obtained damages from the officials who issued it. In this case, and in three others, the question of the legality of general warrants was only indirectly at issue. But in the case of *Entick v. Carrington* (1765) Lord Chief Justice Camden finally ruled that general warrants were illegal. In 1766 the House of Commons, straying into the judicial field, resolved that general warrants were illegal.

GÉNÉRALITÉS, areas of France instituted by the Crown as units of financial administration, usually coinciding geographically with the provinces. By Louis XIV's reign (1643–1715) there were 23 *généralités*, each under the supervision of a *receveur-général*, who collected all royal revenues, ordinary and extraordinary, from the *élections* under his control.

GENERALKRIEGSKOMMISSARIAT, administrative body headed by von Platen and introduced in Brandenburg-Prussia by Frederick William, the Great Elector, during the Northern War of 1655–60 to organize the military machinery of the state. Although originally its officials were concerned only with handling military supplies, accommodation, and negotiations between the civil and military authorities, by the end of the 17th cent. they had also acquired tax-collecting and then general financial and police powers throughout the Hohenzollern lands. In 1723 the Generalkriegskommissariat became part of the General Directory.

GENESEE COUNTRY, famous sector of the NY frontier in the US. This fertile, lavishly advertised land was the scene of one of the earliest land rushes (1790–1800). Large-scale rural improvements to consolidate and accelerate development proved uneconomic and were soon abandoned.

GENÊT, EDMOND CHARLES (1763–1834), French diplomat. As Girondin representative to the US, his rash conduct provoked a Franco-American crisis (1793). Demanding fulfilment of what he insisted were American obligations under the Franco-American treaty (1778), he used the US as a base for French privateering and planned to conquer FL and reconquer Canada and LA, thus infringing President Washington's neutrality policy. Though warmly received at first by Jefferson and the Francophile Democratic Republicans, he antagonized the Federalists. His threat to appeal for support directly to the people prompted the US government to demand his recall. Fearing prosecution by the new Jacobin regime in France, he settled in NY, married (1794) a daughter of Gov. George Clinton, and later became a US citizen.

GENEVA, capital of the Swiss canton of Geneva, on either side of the Rhone, centre of Calvinism, seat of the League of Nations, and an important centre of European civilization. The town mentioned by Caesar was part of the Roman empire and later became incorporated into the kingdom of the Franks (534). It grew to power and prosperity in medieval times as a trade centre and the seat of a bishop. It was also the site of a major European fair in the early 15th cent., but its commercial importance declined after 1461 because of the competition of the Lyons fairs. Calvin established his theocracy there (1541–64), and Geneva acquired its cosmopolitan character as a breeding-ground for radical Protestantism and a refuge for the persecuted of all nations. It was annexed by the French revolutionary republic (1798), but recovered its independence (1815) and joined the Swiss Confederation. The Geneva Convention (1864) laid the foundations of the International Red Cross, which still has its headquarters there, and after the First World War it was chosen as the administrative centre of the League of Nations. The Geneva Protocol (1924) attempted to find a basis for the settlement of international disputes, disarmament conferences were held there in 1927 and 1932, and an international conference met there in 1954 to discuss the unification of Korea and the problem of Indo-China.

GENEVA AGREEMENT ON LAOS (1962). The 1954 Geneva agreement on Laos were followed by continuing sporadic warfare, which came to a crisis with a *coup d'état* by Prince Souvanna Phouma, supported by the Pathet Lao and a counter-coup by Gen. Phoumi Nosavan (1960). With the advent of Kennedy's administration (ready to change US support to the neutralist Souvanna Phouma), Britain and the USSR (as co-chairmen) were able to reconvene the Geneva conference, strengthened by members of the International Control Commission plus Thailand, Burma, and the US

(14 states in all). The conference, meeting in Geneva, reached agreement (Nov.–Dec. 1961) and efforts were then made to effect a cease-fire in Laos. When this was done, and a government formed under Souvanna Phouma, the conference was reconvened (July 1962) and agreed on a declaration of neutrality for Laos, guaranteed by the conference powers, who undertook not to use or threaten force, or interfere in the internal affairs of Laos, or attach conditions to aid. Should these conditions appear threatened, the powers agreed to consult with each other on the necessary measures to be taken to restore peace. The settlement was fragile, and broke down as a result of the continuance of the war in Viet-nam.

GENEVA AGREEMENTS (1954), series of agreements reached on the final night (20–21 July) of the Geneva conference, which brought to an end the war in which France was engaged in Indo-China. The agreements were based on armistice agreements for Laos, Cambodia, and Viet-nam. The Cambodian armistice provided for the withdrawal of foreign troops and the integration of the local insurgents into the political life of the country. The Laotian armistice gave the Pathet Lao (pro-Viet-minh) the choice of demobilizing or regrouping in a designated area (in the provinces of Phongsaly and Samneua) while the French High Command was allowed to retain 1500 officers to serve with the Laotian army. With this qualification all foreign forces were to be withdrawn and an election was provided for in 1955. The Vietnam armistice drew a partition line along the 17th parallel. The implication of the rest of the text was that this should be a temporary division, since elections were provided for, to be held in the whole country not later than July 1956. Meanwhile no fresh troops or equipment were to be introduced, or military bases established, or military alliances signed. A tripartite commission, provided by Canada, Poland, and India, was set up to supervise the carrying out of each of these armistice agreements.

In addition to the armistice agreements the conference drew up a 'Final Declaration on Viet-nam' (21 July 1954). The declaration 'took note' of the various armistice provisions. It particularly emphasized, with regard to Viet-nam, that 'the military demarcation line should not be interpreted as constituting a political or territorial boundary', but that 'the cessation of hostilities creates the necessary basis for the achievement in the near future of a political settlement in Viet-nam'. It also reiterated that 'elections shall be held in July 1956'.

Neither South Viet-nam nor the US signed the final declaration. Both made declarations of their own. The US declared that it would refrain from the threat or use of force to disturb the agreements. With regard to free elections, it reiterated an earlier declaration, to the effect that 'In the case of nations now divided against their will, we shall continue to seek to achieve unity through free elections, supervised by the United Nations, to ensure that they are conducted freely'. The US declaration continued:

With respect to the statement made by the representative of the State of Vietnam, the United States reiterates its traditional position that peoples are entitled to determine their own future and that it will not join in an arrangement which would hinder this. Nothing in the declaration just made is intended to or does indicate any departure from this traditional position.   WK

GENEVA BIBLE, complete English translation (1557–60) made chiefly by Marian exiles in Geneva, under the supervision of William Whittingham, Calvin's brother-in-law. It was also known as the Breeches Bible because in some editions 'breeches' appeared instead of 'aprons' in Genesis 3 : 7. It was a scholarly revision of the Great Bible (1539), but became popular because of its handy format, clear Roman type, supplementary maps and tables, and the innovation of numbering the verses. James I found it 'savouring too much of dangerous conceits', and therefore encouraged the Authorized Version (1611).

GENEVA CONFERENCE (April–June 1954), conference arranged initially to settle Korea following the armistice (July 1953). Its scope was then widened to include Indo-China, and China was brought into the conference (the US making clear that this did not imply recognition of the communist government).

As a result two parallel conferences were held. The Korea conference, in which the 16 UN members who sent troops to Korea participated (except South Africa, which declined the invitation) together with North and South Korea, China, and the USSR. This conference failed to reach agreement. The Indo-China conference was between the US, Britain, France, China, the USSR, Laos, Cambodia, South Viet-nam and North Viet-nam. The great powers were all represented by foreign ministers, but John Foster Dulles was replaced by Gen. Bedell Smith for the US after the first week of the conference, and before discussion of Indo-China began.

The conference continued against a background of military crisis in Indo-China, including the fall of Dien Bien Phu (7 May). It gathered momentum after Mendès-France succeeded to the premiership in France (17 June) and finally produced an armistice in Indo-China and a joint declaration which together form the Geneva Agreements.

GENEVA CONFERENCE (July 1955), first summit conference since that held at Potsdam (July–Aug. 1945). It was conducted in an atmosphere of detente generated by the signing of the Austrian treaty (May 1955) and proposals on disarmament made by the Soviet Union in the same month. The conference was attended by the heads of government of the four powers occupying Germany (Eisenhower, Bulganin, Eden, and Edgar Faure), with their foreign ministers and advisers (including, among the Russians, Khrushchev).

The conference was concerned with questions of European security, Germany, and disarmament. It issued a communiqué, but achieved little of substantial importance. The problem of Germany was glossed over in the formula of the communiqué, which ran:

> The Heads of Government have agreed that the settlement of the German question and the reunification of Germany by means of free elections shall be carried out in conformity with the national interests of the German people and the interests of European security.

The Soviet plan for disarmament, although it corresponded closely to previous Anglo–French proposals, was not taken up by the US government. Eisenhower responded with a counter-plan for the aerial survey of armaments.

In spite of the lack of substantial progress the conference appeared to offer hopes for a diminution of tension. But fresh anxiety was generated by the Soviet sale of arms to Egypt (Sept. 1955), and although diplomatic relations were established between the German Federal Republic and the Soviet Union, no progress was made on German reunification. (Indeed, the Soviet Union adopted a new policy of advocating a peace treaty which would recognize the government of the German Democratic Republic.) The hopes of a thaw in international relations thus diminished during the following months, and were shattered by Soviet intervention to suppress the Hungarian revolution (Oct. 1956).   WFK

GENEVA CONVENTION, series of four international agreements finally signed as a group in Aug. 1949 by 59 governments, including the Vatican, for the protection of war victims. The oldest stems from the 1864 Conference called by the Swiss federal council at Geneva, which laid down rules for the care of sick and wounded, and this was intimately connected with the development of the Red Cross; both drew their inspiration and impetus from the widely publicized medical neglect that had accompanied the Crimean and Italian Wars. This agreement was extended to cover naval warfare at the Hague Conference in 1907, and further provisions—the second clause—were added by 1949 to allow for the increased ferocity of 'total' war. The third was based on the 1929 Geneva Convention concerning the treatment of prisoners of war, again an attempt to tackle problems recently raised, this time during the First World War. Similarly the treatment of non-combatants during the years 1939–45 produced a code of regulations in 1949 that was included in the fourth of the agreements. All, of course, lack any effective sanction in terms of power politics and must rest solely on the varying humanitarian standards of the different combatant states. Events in Eastern Europe and in the Far East, and subsequently in Korea and South-East Asia, demonstrated how flexibly these standards could be interpreted.

GENEVA PROTOCOL (Oct. 1924) for the Pacific Settlement of International Disputes, was presented to the fifth Assembly of the League of Nations. It originated in a joint resolution of the British prime minister, MacDonald, and the French prime minister, Herriot, on the need to preserve peace through a combination of arbitration, security, and disarmament systems. The protocol attempted to reconcile France's desire for security with Britain's desire for the easing of international tensions. Its signatories were to submit all justiciable disputes to the Permanent Court of International Justice; non-justiciable disputes were to be submitted to the League Council or to an arbitral committee formed by the council, or by agreement between the disputants. Any state refusing to submit to arbitration, or to carry out an arbitral award, would be designated an aggressor. The victim of aggression was to receive immediate assistance from the other signatories. The protocol was to come into force only after a disarmament conference, planned for June 1925, had laid down a disarmament plan for the signatories.

The protocol, unanimously approved by the assembly, was signed on 2 Oct. by ten powers, including France, Czechoslovakia, Poland, and Yugoslavia. A month later MacDonald's Labour government was replaced by a Conservative government under Baldwin, which was strongly opposed to the principle of compulsory arbitration, and to accepting security obligations, especially in eastern Europe. The prospect of the commonwealth navy's being employed to interrupt commerce between the US and an aggressor constituted another objection. Britain's rejection of the protocol was announced to the league by Austen Chamberlain in March 1925 and in effect the project collapsed.   ASJ

GENEVA, TIME OF TROUBLES IN, a reign of terror, similar to that in France, lasting from 1794 until Geneva's annexation by the French. It was inspired by radical resentment of the narrow, oligarchic system of government.

GENKŪ, also known as Hōnen (1133–1212), founder of the *Jōdo* (Pure Land) sect of Buddhism. He was the first priest in Japan to address himself to a wide public. In a time of political upheaval his teaching, with its emphasis on salvation through faith in Amida Buddha, won many adherents, though Genkū himself was persecuted by the established sects.

GENNADIUS II (*fl.* 15th cent.), patriarch of Constantinople (1454–56, 1463, 1464–5). At the Council of Florence in 1439 he supported the union of the Roman and Greek Churches, but from 1444 opposed that union. Sultan Mehemmed II, having conquered Constantinople in 1453, approved the elevation of Gennadius to the patriarchate. Gennadius was the author of pastoral and ascetic works, of apologetics against Islam, and of commentaries on Aquinas and Aristotle.

GENOA, chief harbour of Liguria, owed its early importance to being in the late 6th cent. the Byzantine capital of north-western Italy. By the 11th cent. the Genoese ranked among the chief Italian traders in the western Mediterranean and the First Crusade (1096–9) opened up for them the Levant and the Byzantine empire. Thenceforward they rivalled the

Venetians as the leading maritime traders of southern Europe. In the late 13th cent. the Genoese were pioneers in creating a regular sea route from Italy to north-western Europe and in the 14th and 15th cents they played a major part in developing the trade and shipping of Spain and Portugal. Despite its wealth, Genoa did not become in the later Middle Ages an important artistic and intellectual centre. Politically it was a divided city-state, where rival groups of nobles and financiers were much more powerful than the city government. Its important silk industry led to the growth of a discontented proletariat of workers who staged a desperate revolt (1506–7). These internal divisions ended in the emergence (1529) of a dictatorship of the Doria family, who made Genoa virtually into a Spanish dependency.

GENOA CONFERENCE (10 April–19 May 1922). At the Cannes conference (Jan. 1922) Lloyd George proposed to invite Russia to an economic conference at Genoa to discuss post-war reconstruction and the claims of Russia's pre-war creditors. Briand, as prime minister of France, agreed, but he was subsequently replaced by Poincaré, who refused to lead the French delegation. At Boulogne in Feb. he persuaded Lloyd George not to discuss at the conference established treaties, or Allied action over Germany's failure to maintain reparations payments.

The conference thus began inauspiciously for Germany, whose delegation, under the chancellor, Wirth, and the foreign minister, Rathenau, had hoped to include reparations in a general economic discussion, and even to have the annual payments reduced. The German delegation soon became nervous lest France's and Britain's public and private negotiations with Russia should lead to a settlement at Germany's expense; and in case the Bolsheviks might be persuaded to repay Tsarist debts if these should be included in a concerted attempt to extract reparations from Germany. On 16 April, Easter Sunday—when there was a break in the conference—the Germans and Russians met outside Genoa at Rapallo and concluded a treaty, under the terms of which full diplomatic relations were to be resumed, and mutual reparations claims were effectively renounced.

The Rapallo treaty caused uproar at Genoa. A military alliance was universally suspected. However, Rapallo was concluded chiefly for diplomatic impact. A measure of German–Soviet military agreement already existed, of which Wirth and Rathenau disapproved. They had resisted Chicherin's demand for a treaty before the conference, but were persuaded by him at Genoa that the western rapprochement they sought was impossible. Poincaré's intransigence over reparations was now increased, while Russia refused responsibility for Tsarist debts. The conference continued for another month, but Rapallo had destroyed its slim chances of success.

GENOA, SIEGE OF (1747), followed the rising of the Genoese against occupying Austrian forces, during the Austro-Sardinian invasion of Provence (1747). News of the revolt caused the Austrians to withdraw hastily from French soil into Piedmont and besiege the city. The Gallispan commanders, Belleisle and La Mina, tried unsuccessfully to relieve Genoa, but their pressure forced the Austro-Sardinian forces to raise the siege, and peace preliminaries followed shortly afterwards (April 1748).

GENRŌ, small group of Japanese elder statesmen who because of their services to the Meiji state became, in the 1890s, the highest advisers to the emperor. The most important members of this select but extra-constitutional body were Itō Hirobumi and Yamagata Aritomo. The latter dominated it for a decade and a half until his death in 1922 and was the real power behind the throne. The chief function of the *genrō* was the selection of the prime minister, but they also expected to be consulted by the cabinet on important policy matters. After 1924, when only Saionji Kimmochi remained, the influence of this typical indirect Japanese institution declined. It was partly replaced later by a still more **informal** group of ex-prime ministers known as *jūshin*.

GENROKU PERIOD, the three decades centring upon the Genroku era (1688–1704), when, after half a century of peace and prosperity, Japanese urban culture, supported by the newly acquired wealth of the merchants of Osaka and Edo, reached its highest point. Outstanding dramatists such as Chikamatsu produced masterpieces for the new theatrical forms of *Kabuki* and *Jōruri*, Saikaku and others gave the novel new life with their vivid satirical portrayals of urban society, and wood-block prints acquired great popularity, while at another level amusement quarters became a significant feature of city life.

GENSERIC (*c.* 390–477), King of the Vandals, who conquered Africa (429–39), after traversing Spain. Genseric succeeded in defeating great armadas sent against him by the military chiefs of both Italy and Byzantium, and in 455 invaded Italy and occupied Rome for 14 days while sacking it. Alone among the barbarian invaders of the empire, the Vandals under Genseric became a great naval power, basing themselves on Carthage. Genseric's name inspired a terror second only to that inspired by Attila. He was an Arian and actively persecuted Catholics, and his warrior subjects gained notoriety as the desecrators of shrines both Catholic and pagan, and as the destroyers of monuments of Graeco-Roman civilization.

GENSHIN (942–1017), Japanese Buddhist monk of the Tendai sect. His *Ōjō Yōshū* ('Essentials of Salvation') was the first Japanese exposition of the idea of salvation by *nembutsu* (calling on the Buddha's name).

GENTILE, GIOVANNI (1875–1944), Sicilian philosopher, early colleague of Croce, and fascist minister. He developed a form of Idealism, and embraced fascism as its fulfilment. Mussolini did not always like his theorizing, and helped to rewrite Gentile's draft for the 'Fascismo' article (1932) in *Enciclopedia Italiana*. As minister of education (1922–4), Gentile established a uniform state examination system, and guaranteed private education, so paving the way for an accord with the Vatican. He was murdered by anti-fascists.

GENTLEMAN'S AGREEMENT (1907–8), voluntary understandings between Japan and the US for a reduction in Japanese emigration following racial tension in CA.

GENTLEMAN'S MAGAZINE in Britain, founded in 1731, as a monthly miscellany of poems and literary criticism, notes on inventions and discoveries, extracts from provincial newspapers, and, in its early years, accounts of important parliamentary debates. The *Magazine* lost its distinctive character in 1868, and ceased publication in 1907.

GENTRY in England, name given to a characteristic sector of feudal society, the middling and lesser landowners either equipped with or ambitious for knightly rank. In England, the exclusive attachment of noble rank to the parliamentary peerage placed the gentry socially with the influential elements among the commons (merchants, burgesses of towns), though the effect was to infuse the upper-class associations of the gentry into a wider sector of politically influential people: that is, commoners were in a sense approximated to the aristocracy at a time when political action was the preserve of that aristocracy. From the 14th cent., the English Crown's control of the realm depended on the co-operation of local men of gentry rank, holding office as JPs, ad hoc commissioners, and knights of the shire in parliament. The wealth and support of the gentry made possible the disruptive politics of noble factions in the 15th cent. In the 16th cent., the Crown reasserted its control over this essential layer of society, but at the expense of satisfying many of its pressing needs. Population increase, inflation, and a highly fluid land market (themselves linked phenomena) provided both pressure on landed resources and the means to solve the problem. It was the gentry—the middling sort of land-owner—who benefited most from the redistribution of Church land which followed in the wake of the Reformation, and from the buoyant market for agricultural produce. In the course of the century, the gentry completed their take-over of the House of Commons and became the socially dominant element: in the England of Elizabeth I, a country without dukes (after 1572) or marquises, it was the knight and not the lord who set the tone. The political consequences showed themselves under the early Stuarts when the clash of interests concentrated on the House of Commons rather than the House of Lords or the king's council, as in the past. The gentry's great age came to an end with the Civil War, itself a war within that particular sector of society, and with the change in economic climate that marked the later 17th cent. Concentration of land in fewer hands and aristocratic ascendancy returned with the Restoration, and the characteristic stage for the gentry's assertion of power once more contracted from the nation to the locality. Nevertheless, the continued existence of large numbers of independent gentlemen representing anti-court and anti-commercial interests in parliament helped to give the localities some say at the centre and to remind the government of its need for support among the often hard-pressed lesser landowners of the realm. The age of the gentry gradually came to an end as urbanization and industrialization destroyed a way of life characterized by a rural existence and landed wealth.   GRE

GENTZ, FRIEDRICH (1764–1832), Austrian journalist and Metternich's secretary at the Congress of Vienna (1815). He translated Burke's *Reflections on the Revolution in France* (1793) and in 1802 left the Prussian civil service for that of Austria. At the Congress of Vienna he managed the *Bureau de Protocol*, the business centre of the congress, and drafted the final treaty. As Metternich was president of the Committee of Eight, Gentz styled himself first secretary to the congress.

GEOFFREY I MARTEL (d. 1060), Count of Anjou, vassal of the French Crown and the founder of the power of the house of Anjou. Though formerly an enemy of Henry I, in his later years he helped Henry to check the ambitions of William of Normandy but by the time of his death William had defeated Anjou.

GEOFFREY OF ANJOU (d. 1151), heir to the counties of Anjou and Maine. In 1128 he married Matilda, widow of the Emperor Henry V and daughter of Henry I of England. His life was spent in the struggle to secure for his wife her inheritance in England and Normandy, disputed by Stephen of Blois, and to settle internal strife in Anjou. Three years after his death his son became King of England as Henry II.

GEOFFREY OF MONMOUTH (d. 1155), was of Norman upbringing and possibly Breton extraction. He was Bp of St Asaph (1152–5) and author of *Historia Regum Britanniae* (*c.* 1136–8), which purported to give the history of the Britons from their Trojan origins up to the Saxon conquest and, as such, was generally accepted as authentic until the 15th cent. It influenced most subsequent histories and also some aspects of the Arthurian legend. It is, however, a wholly imaginary account, though it uses some traditional material.

GEOMETRIC POTTERY, Greek pottery of the period *c.* 1050–750 BC, known in particular from the Ceramicus cemetery at Athens. The typical Protogeometric style (10th cent.), developed partly from preceding sub-Myce-naean styles and partly through the fresh inspiration and new techniques of Dorian and related north Greek intruders, showed economical use of straight and wavy lines and concentric circles. In the full Geometric period (9th–8th cents) meanders, zigzags, swastikas, and angular representations of men and animals were crowded on to the surface, and some pots serving as gravestones were over five feet high. Although recent excavations at Argos and elsewhere make it seem unlikely that Athens produced the earliest Protogeometric pottery, Athenian vases of 800–750 remain the most impressive examples of the Geometric style.

GEORGE, Duke of Saxony (1500–39), member of the younger, Albertine line of the house of Wettin. He was one of the leading Catholic princes who supported the emperor in the Reformation period. He enforced the Edict of Worms (1521) in his lands and crushed the Peasants' Revolt, led by Thomas Munzer, at the battle of Frankenhausen (1525). In 1538 he joined the Habsburg-inspired League of Nuremburg, formed to withstand the Schmalkaldic League, which was led by his rival cousins of the Ernestine branch of the Wettin family.

Known originally as 'the bearded' from the 1530s, the duke was called 'the rich' as a result of the ducal proceeds of the prosperous Saxon mining industry. During his long reign he curbed the power of the nobility and estates and protected the rights of the peasantry. After his death Saxony devolved upon successive Protestant princes.

GEORGE OF PODERBRADY (*reg.* 1458–71), King of Bohemia, Czech noble and military leader of the Hussites. He was one of several nobles who with the breakdown of central government after 1419 enriched themselves from Church land and increased their power. In 1448 he adopted the title 'governor' of the realm on behalf of the minor king Ladislas Postumus and, after defeating his rivals, was himself elected king. He was the candidate of the moderate Hussite gentry and was accepted only hesitantly by the orthodox Catholics. As a symbol of continued national independence after the Hussite wars, he became for many Czechs a national hero.

GEORGE I (1660–1727), King of Britain (*reg.* 1714–27). He was the eldest son of Ernest Augustus, Elector of Hanover from 1692, and of Sophia, grand-daughter of James I of England. He was himself Elector of Hanover (1698–1727). His mother became the heir of Queen Anne through the Act of Settlement (1701). George developed strong links with the Whig Party, and their control of the council facilitated his succession (his mother having died on 8 June and Queen Anne on 1 Aug. 1714). He formed a predominantly Whig ministry, which won the general election—made necessary by the king's succession—with a considerable majority. George's position was never seriously threatened by the Jacobite rebellion of 1715 and the attempts of 1719 and 1722. None the less, he was unpopular, and he disliked England and visited Hanover as often as possible. Contrary to popular opinion, however, he was a very diligent king, possessing shrewd judgement in foreign affairs and a very considerable knowledge of European diplomacy. Socially he preferred a withdrawn life with his friends and mistresses, the Duchess of Kendal and the Countess of Darlington.

George gave up attending cabinet meetings, not because he could not speak English, but in order to avoid meeting the Prince of Wales, with whom his relations were usually strained. The king saw his ministers privately, and they communicated in French. In 1717 a violent quarrel with his son coincided with a split in the Whig party between Townshend and Walpole on the one hand, and Stanhope and Sunderland on the other, the latter supporting the king's pro-Hanoverian foreign policy. George himself was far more active in British politics than he has generally been given credit for. In 1718 he played a part in diplomatic negotiations leading to the Quadruple Alliance, and he insisted on keeping personal control of the army.

His ministers, Sunderland and Stanhope, were often checked by Walpole and Townshend and were defeated over the Peerage Bill (1719). After Walpole and Townshend had joined the ministry, George came to accept them personally, particularly after they had salvaged the ministry and the king from the South Sea Bubble disaster (1720).

B. Williams, *The Whig Supremacy* (Oxford, 1939).
J. H. Plumb, *The First Four Georges* (London, 1956).   CJ

GEORGE II (1683–1760), King of Britain (*reg.* 1727–60), son of George I and Sophia Dorothea of Celle, who came to England as Prince of Wales when his father succeeded to the Crown in 1714. The court of the Prince of Wales and his wife, Caroline of Ansbach, at Leicester House soon became the natural focus for discontented Whig politicians. George I's mistrust of his son degenerated into an open quarrel in 1717 when the prince ordered his followers in the House of Commons to withdraw their support from the ministry. In this division of son against father lay the origins of the concept of His Majesty's Opposition.

On George II's accession as king in 1727 a change of ministry was generally expected, and he entrusted the direction of affairs to Spencer Compton. But the king's intention was frustrated by that minister's complacent tolerance of Sir Robert Walpole's continued influence over patronage through his favour with Queen Caroline. Until Caroline's death in 1737 this relationship made possible the smooth working of a constitution in which power and responsibility were still evenly divided between king and parliament, and George believed the choice of ministers was his both in theory and in practice. After Walpole's fall, however, criticism of Carteret's conduct of the war with Spain forced the king to dismiss him, and in 1746 the resignation of Pelham's ministry, because of the king's refusal to admit Pitt to office, showed the impossibility of forming an alternative administration without parliamentary support. Thereafter George tended to leave the main direction of affairs to his reinstated principal ministers—Pelham until 1754, then Pelham's brother Newcastle, whose shared ministry with William Pitt during the first years of the Seven Years War was one of the most successful of the 18th cent.

Although George regularly visited Hanover, which he preferred to England, perhaps because of the despotic simplicity of his role there, his possession of the Electorate was an advantage rather than otherwise, for it gave him a more intimate understanding of European affairs. He was the last English king to lead his army in battle, at Dettingen (1743).

With the death of his eldest son, Frederick, in 1751, the succession passed to Frederick's son, George, who succeeded his grandfather in 1760.

J. H. Plumb, *The First Four Georges* (London, 1956).
                                                               HNBM

GEORGE III (1738–1820), King of Britain (*reg.* 1760–1820), one of the longest reigns of modern times. He was the son of Frederick, Prince of Wales and inherited from his father a violent dislike of his grandfather, George II. On his accession he set to work to reverse George II's policies, suspecting him of subordinating English to Hanoverian interests. He therefore opposed the continuation of the Seven Years War. Believing that George II had allowed power to pass into the hands of ministers, George III made a determined attempt to reassert his constitutional rights, especially his right to choose ministers. These attitudes, particularly when he was young and inexperienced, and when the issues were of national importance, provoked tension and ministerial instability. This was particularly so in the years 1760–70, before the king found a suitable minister in North, and again between the fall of North (1782) and the appointment of the Younger Pitt (Dec. 1783). Similar conditions were present after Pitt's resignation (1801). Many of George III's disputes with ministers were over two issues, concerning which he felt he had a moral duty: he would not give up the American colonies and he would not undermine the Protestant religion by accepting Catholic emancipation.

His faults were those of over-conscientiousness. He was scrupulous in the exercise of patronage, courageous, and devoted to the interests of his country. He married Charlotte of Mecklenburg-Strelitz (1761), to whom he was faithful. They brought up their large family in a restricted fashion against which many of them later reacted. George III, the first modern monarch to live much at Windsor, paid great attention to the agricultural improvement of the Great Park. He had several bouts of insanity, in 1765, 1788–9, and 1801, and from 1811 was permanently insane. At other times his efficiency was undamaged, though the fear of provoking further attacks discouraged ministers from proposing measures he did not like. Recently medical research has suggested that he suffered not from insanity, but from porphyria, a disease of the metabolism. Towards the end of his life he was genuinely popular and regarded during the French wars as a symbol of British virtue.

Richard Pares, *King George III and the Politicians* (Oxford, 1953).   LMB

GEORGE IV (1762–1830), King of Britain (*reg.* 1820–30), eldest son of George III, and Prince Regent (1811–20). After a restricted upbringing he became a friend of Charles James Fox. At the time of the Regency Bill (1788) Fox and his supporters hoped that he would support them if he became regent. He was still a supporter of the Whigs in 1811, but after some hesitation recognized the need to keep the existing Tory ministry in power. The Opposition thereafter espoused the cause of his separated wife, Caroline, and their only daughter, Charlotte. On his accession George attempted to divorce Caroline, but abandoned the idea because of popular protests. She died in 1821.

As a monarch George IV was temperamentally difficult, but, unlike his father and his brother William IV, he avoided head-on collision with his ministers. He disliked George Canning and disapproved of Catholic emancipation, but accepted both with a bad grace. He was self-indulgent, morally reprehensible, and a spendthrift, but he was also a notable patron of the arts. He bought many paintings for the royal collections and commissioned from Sir Thomas Lawrence the portraits of allied sovereigns from the Waterloo Chamber at Windsor. His most notable building projects were Regent Street and Regent's Park (planned 1812–13), the rebuilding of the Brighton Pavilion (begun 1815), all of which were designed by John Nash, and the enlargement of Windsor Castle by Wyatville (begun 1824).   LMB

GEORGE V (1865–1936), King of Britain (*reg.* 1910–36), who succeeded his father, Edward VII. He spent his earlier life in the navy and only came closer in succession to the throne when his elder brother, the Duke of Clarence, died in 1892. George subsequently married his brother's fiancée, Mary of Teck. This stolid, unimaginative, obsessively punctilious but loyal and high-principled country squire, who loved horse-racing and read his Bible daily, displayed his family's worst and best traits. These accorded with the country's needs, and his popularity during the Silver Jubilee (1935) reveals his achievement in developing a new role for monarchy in a democratic and increasingly socialist age. Though he opposed extreme Prussophobia during the First World War, he helped to identify his family more closely with his country by his peculiarly English temperament and by adopting the family name of 'Windsor' in 1917. He came to symbolize stability in a rapidly changing society—not that he recognized the changes, as his traditionalism and imperialism show. But by moderating party strife over Ireland before 1914 and by encouraging the formation of a national government during the 1931 slump, he displayed under Lord Stamfordham's guidance all the virtues of the constitutional monarch. His annual Christmas broadcasts from 1932 enabled him to appear as a father-figure to an increasingly insecure nation, but his own sons found his paternalism somewhat daunting.   BHH

GEORGE VI (1895–1952), King of Britain (*reg.* 1936–52), second son of George V and Queen Mary. Having no real expectation of the throne, he had a naval training at Dartmouth and served as an air cadet at Cranwell. He served in the Grand Fleet at the battle of Jutland in 1916. Three years later he spent a short time at Trinity College, Cambridge. He was created Duke of York in 1920 and increasingly took on public duties, showing particular interest in the human problems of industry. He accepted the presidency of the Boys' Welfare Association and helped to initiate the summer camps for public school and working-class boys. In 1926 he played tennis at Wimbledon.

In 1936 on the abdication of his brother, Edward VIII, George VI ascended the throne. With the outbreak of the Second World War he continued to live at Buckingham Palace during the air raids, visited all the main war fronts, and, despite a speech impediment, made numerous broadcasts. In 1947 he and his family toured South Africa. His last important public appearance was at the opening of the Festival of Britain in 1951. In Feb. 1952 he died suddenly and was succeeded by his elder daughter as Queen Elizabeth II. Throughout his reign he owed much to the support of his wife, Elizabeth, whom he had married in 1923.

GEORGE I (1845–1913), King of Greece (*reg.* 1863–1913). He was a member of the Danish royal family, and ascended the throne at the age of 17, as the only candidate acceptable to the various powers concerned with the fate of Greece. Despite the severe strain imposed on the popularity of the monarchy during the Cretan crisis, his tact and restraint enabled him to sustain the role of constitutional monarch for half a century. Following the Cretan uprising against the Turks in 1896, the king supported the unsuccessful war with Turkey. Greece was only saved from defeat by the intervention of the powers. The monarchy was involved in further national humiliation when the government felt unable to support Crete's renewed declaration of unity with Greece (1909). But the popularity of the king revived after the constitutional crisis which brought Venizelos to power. He was assassinated in 1913.

GEORGE, Prince of Denmark (1653–1708), Lutheran husband of Queen Anne of Britain, and the son of Frederick III and brother of Christian V of Denmark. He earned the reputation before his marriage of being a competent if unimaginative soldier. He married Princess Anne in 1683, and though the marriage was unpopular politically it proved one of great domestic happiness. Though unable to express himself idiomatically in English after 20 years' residence, he was a kind, devoted husband and father. They produced 17 children, none of whom survived their parents. In 1689 George was created Earl of Kendal and Duke of Cumberland, and though he held the office of lord high admiral (1702–8), he was not active in politics. His main interest was horticulture.

GEORGE, HENRY (1839–97), US economist, journalist, and reformer. His pamphlet on 'Our Land and Land Policy' (1871) set forth the fundamentals of the single-tax philosophy which he elaborated in *Progress and Poverty* (1879). Regarding speculation in land as the cause of human poverty, George proposed the device of a land tax which would wipe out all unearned income or speculation and establish economic equality for all classes. His other works include *The Irish Land Question* (1881), *Social Problems* (1883), and *Protection or Free Trade* (1886). In 1886 he ran unsuccessfully for mayor of New York, organized Land and Labour clubs throughout the country to propagate his ideas, and again ran for mayor (1897), but died five days before the election. George, an important figure in American economic thought, influenced the movement for tax reform and the Progressive reform movement of the early 20th cent.

GEORGE-BROWN, GEORGE ALFRED, Life Baron (1914–), British Labour politician, who entered parliament as MP for Belper in 1945. He occupied a number of posts—

in the ministry of labour, the exchequer, and the ministry of agriculture (1945–51). During the years when his party was in opposition (1951–64) he rose to become one of its chief figures and a challenger for the leadership. He became secretary of state for economic affairs in 1964, with chief responsibility for the Labour Party's 'National Plan', which postulated a 4 per cent growth rate in national production, chiefly through voluntary methods. He was foreign secretary (1966–8) and entered the Lords after the defeat of his party in the 1970 general election, in which he lost his own seat.

GEORGIA, British colony in North America, first visited by the Spaniard Hernando De Soto (1540). It was claimed by England and became part of the grant to the Lords Proprietors of Carolina (1663). Georgia, regarded as the southernmost buffer against Spanish encroachment from Florida and French from Louisiana, was granted a royal charter by George II as an independent colony (1732). Under its charter the colony was to be governed by 20 trustees until, after 21 years, the colony would be directly administered by the Crown. The founders and first rulers of the colony were wealthy philanthropists, among them James Oglethorpe and Lord Percival. Their aim was to establish a refuge for the poor of England and persecuted European minorities, such as German, Piedmontese, and Swiss Protestants, and Portuguese Jews. The rule of the trustees was benevolent paternalism: rum, slaves, and self-government being prohibited. To prevent the accumulation of landed property into few hands, land-holding was restricted to 50 acres (20 hectares) per person. In 1733, 130 immigrants had settled in the new colony but by 1760 the population numbered only 6000. Restrictions on land-holding and slaves were removed when Georgia came under direct Crown rule (1752) and adapted to the plantation economy of neighbouring southern colonies. During the American War of Independence Georgia had a strong loyalist group, partly because of the popularity of the royal governor, James Wright, partly because of the need for imperial protection from Indians. However, British power in Georgia was ended with the taking of Savannah by the Continental army (1778). Georgia was the first of the southern states to ratify the constitution (1788).

J. C. Bonner, *The Georgia Story* (Oklahoma City, 1958).

RSU

GEORGIA, RUSSIAN ANNEXATION. In 1783 Russia followed her earlier contacts with the Georgian princes by establishing a Russian protectorate (treaty of Georgiersk), but she made no effort to make this a reality until after the death of Irakli of Georgia (1798). An agreement signed in 1800 was interpreted by Paul I as annexation and this was confirmed by Alexander in 1801. The annexation of Georgia opened the way for Russia's conquest of the Caucasus and Transcaucasia.

GEORGIAN DEMOCRATIC REPUBLIC, proclaimed (26 May 1918) after the dissolution of the Transcaucasian republic. Dominated by Mensheviks and led by Noi Jordania, it was hostile to the Russian Bolsheviks and sought first German, and later Allied, protection. The USSR recognized its independence (May 1920), invaded it in Feb.–May 1921, and forced Georgia to submit at the peace of Kutais (18 March 1921).

GEORGIANA, unsuccessful American colony in the MS valley (1763), fostered by Phineas Lyman, of CT. Eventually Lyman induced some New England families to settle near Natchez, MS (1774).

GEORGIEV, KIMON (1882–1964), Bulgarian political leader who was associated with Damian Velchev in the coup of 9 June 1923. In 1930 he formed Zveno, a group of reformers and the civilian counterpart to Velchev's Military League. Together these groups seized power in a second coup on 19 May 1934. Georgiev headed the authoritarian regime which liquidated IMRO, implemented social and economic reforms, restored diplomatic relations with the Soviet Union, and sought a rapprochement with Yugoslavia. But, in 1935, Boris succeeded in splitting the government and forced Georgiev to resign. Georgiev remained at the head of Zveno and in 1942 took the group into the Fatherland Front. After the Fatherland Front seized power on 8 Sept. 1944, Georgiev became prime minister of the new government. Although in 1946 Zveno crumbled under communist pressure and Velchev left the cabinet, Georgiev kept his position. Replaced as prime minister by Dimitrov in Nov. 1946, Georgiev continued to hold a place in the government until 1959.

GERALD OF WALES (1146–1223), archdeacon of Brecon and a prolific writer whose works on Ireland and Wales are useful source material.

GERALDINE LEAGUE (1536–40), union of the old English and Irish lords formed after the imprisonment of Thomas, Lord Offaly, in the Tower of London (1535) and inspired by Lady Eleanor Fitzgerald, aunt of Gerald, the last of the Geraldines of Kildare, to protect her young nephew. The league, which included Desmond and the MacCarthys of the south, Brian O'Connor of Offaly of central Ireland, and Conn O'Neill of the north, threatened the government of the Pale. Despite O'Neill's defeat at Bellahoe (1539), Gerald escaped to Florence (1541), where he grew up at court.

GERARD, JOHN (1545–1612), English botanist and barber-surgeon, whose *Herball* (1597) is the first large work of descriptive botany in English. He was superintendent of the famous gardens of Lord Burghley and became 'Herbarist' to King James of England.

GERARD, JOHN (1564–1637), English Jesuit missionary, who established several active Catholic centres in English gentry houses, especially in East Anglia (1588–94) and the south Midlands (1597–1606). He was imprisoned for three years (1594–7), and finally escaped to Europe (1606), where he lived in various English colleges. He was the spiritual director of the English College in Rome (1627–37).

GERINDO (Gerakan Rakjat, Indonesia, 'Indonesian People's Movement'), left-wing nationalist party in the Dutch East Indies, formed in 1937. It absorbed groups that had refused to work with the colonial government, but itself assumed a co-operative position. Its leaders were influenced partly by Popular Front concepts in Europe, but also by the failure of non-co-operation to achieve results. The new orientation found equally small response from the conservative colonial regime, however, and in 1939 Gerindo merged with Parindra to form the GAPI ('Indonesian Political League'), which took a less co-operative stance.

GERMAN CATHOLIC CHURCH (1844), national breakaway religious movement founded in Silesia and which spread in 1845 to West Prussia. The German Catholic Church attacked the Church hierarchy, the primacy of the pope, and the outward signs of Catholic piety, such as fasting and the worship of saints and images, and recognized the Bible as the only source of belief. It was forbidden in Austria and Bavaria, but tolerated in Prussia. After 1847 its numbers began to fall from a maximum of about 60,000 members, and the German Catholics became merged into the Free Church movement.

GERMAN COAST, area along the Mississippi river north of New Orleans, settled by Germans brought to LA by John Law's Co. of the West (1717–31).

GERMAN CONFEDERATION (1815), created by the Congress of Vienna to replace the Holy Roman empire. It was superseded (1867) by the North German Confederation, which consisted of 35 sovereign states and four free cities. It was governed by the Bundestag (Federal Diet), an assembly of representatives from the individual states, which retained full sovereignty over their own affairs. The Austrian representative presided over the Bundestag, and any action taken required unanimity.

The federal constitution of 8 June 1815, article 19, provided for the regulation of inter-state commerce and navigation between states, to be discussed at the first meeting of the Bundestag at Frankfurt. This discussion never took place, though the matter was raised in 1819. Because of the territorial fragmentation, especially in the centre of the confederation, each state had to make bilateral arrangements with its neighbours about tolls, customs, roads, and rivers, and these led to the formation of three customs unions by 1828 and to the creation of the Zollverein in 1834.

Austria dominated the confederation until 1858. Metternich's policy of repression of liberalism was adopted by the Bundestag and implemented in all states after a conference at Carlsbad in 1819. Austria's grip was temporarily relaxed during the revolutions of 1848, which made possible the Frankfurt parliament and attempts to form a union of purely German states, but Prussia's prestige in the confederation was adversely affected by the Malmö armistice, and in the Hesse crisis Austria was able to reassert her mastery.

The German Confederation did not satisfy the aspirations of the growing liberal and nationalist movement among the middle class, but was perhaps the best that could be achieved in the circumstances of 1815. Many rulers of German states had substantial possessions outside the confederation: Austria had vast Magyar, Slav, and Italian territories, East Prussia and Prussia's Polish territories were outside the confederation, Hanover was ruled by the King of Britain, Holstein by the King of Denmark, and Luxemburg by the King of the Netherlands. The creation of a strong central power would have proved unacceptable to all these rulers, who would have had to relinquish some of their sovereignty. In addition, the demand for liberal institutions came only from a minority. The concept of a national democratic state was too new and too revolutionary, being suited only to a land with better communications and more real unity. Unity was achieved, under Prussia, only after considerable economic and commercial development and several successful wars.

R. O. Flenley, *Modern German History* (London, 1953).
J. Passant, *A Short History of Germany, 1815–1945* (Cambridge, 1959).   DMK

GERMAN EMPIRE (1871–1918), created during the Franco–Prussian War to succeed the North German Confederation. The constitution was based on that of the confederation, which was enlarged to include Bavaria, Baden, Württemberg, and Hesse-Darmstadt. Each of the 26 states in the empire retained its own constitution, collected federal and state taxes, and administered federal and state law and justice. The federal constitution provided for a Bundesrat, in which each state was represented in accordance with an agreed quota, and a Reichstag, elected by universal male suffrage. There was only one federal minister, the chancellor, appointed by the emperor. The emperor and his government were responsible for foreign affairs and the navy, and in time of war the emperor commanded the army. The minting of coinage, and in some cases postal services, were state responsibilities.

GERMAN LIBERTIES, phrase much used in the 16th cent. to describe the theory of the constitutional rights of the individual German rulers in the Holy Roman empire.

GERMANIAS, urban bands or Christian brotherhoods formed from among the armed artisans of Valencia and Mallorca, which turned into a violently radical social movement, hostile to both the Crown and the aristocracy, under the leadership first of Juan Llorenz and then of Vicenç Peris (1519–22). The Germanias were suppressed by the viceroy

Mendoza outside the city of Valencia, and Peris was captured and executed (1522).

GERMANICUS (15 BC–AD 19), son of Drusus Germanicus, from whom he inherited his name. He was adopted by his uncle, the Emperor Tiberius, in AD 4 on the orders of Augustus, whose grand-daughter Agrippina the Elder he married in AD 5. His numerous children included the Emperor Caligula. He led campaigns into Germany in AD 14–16 with limited results, before being entrusted with a special commission in the eastern provinces, where he died in mysterious circumstances. His popularity, perhaps not wholly deserved, was enhanced by the general dislike for Tiberius.

GERMAN–POLISH NON-AGGRESSION PACT (26 Jan. 1934). Both parties renounced the use of force to settle their differences for the next ten years. The agreement between these traditionally hostile countries astonished Poland's other allies and was certainly not popular in Germany. Neither party believed it to represent more than a 'breathing space' in foreign policy. Poland had felt her security threatened by Hitler's withdrawal from the League of Nations in Oct. 1933. Before Germany's diplomatic overtures to Poland, Hitler stirred up German–Polish tensions in Danzig, but such pressure was hardly necessary to convince Poland of the necessity of the pact. The Polish foreign minister, Col. Beck, appointed in 1932, was convinced that the existing alliance with France was of no practical military use to Poland, and that France was chiefly concerned with Danubian security. Hitler himself intended the pact to free him for action in the Danubian region. However, he used the pact, his first diplomatic initiative after leaving the league, as propaganda to demonstrate his peaceful intentions in Europe. When the Anglo–Polish alliance was concluded in 1939 he described it as a unilateral infringement of the German–Polish Pact, and declared it automatically annulled.

GERMANS in East Africa. Germany was a late-comer to African colonial enterprise, as elsewhere. The German imperial government under Bismarck and his successors was urged along by the same mingled pressures of nationalist and commercial ambition as were Britain or France. For East Africa the outstanding pace-maker was Karl Peters, a political adventurer who concluded treaties with many chiefs in the East African interior during the 1880s. When partitioning on paper in Europe gave way to invasion on the ground, the large territories which became in the 20th cent. the republics of Tanzania, Rwanda, and Burundi fell under the control of the German East Africa Co. (*Deutsch Ost-Afrika Gesellschaft*), and this, in turn, following the Abushiri rebellion along the Mrima coast of Tanzania, was displaced in 1891 by direct administration through German government officials. Further resistance was encountered inland, notably among the Hehe under Mkwawa.

By 1898 the Germans had imposed by force a colonial structure whose economic support was assured by cash-cropping and plantations, while railways were built from Tanga to Moshi and from Dar es Salaam to Kigoma. In 1905 the Maji Maji rebellion was precipitated by cash-cropping hardships in the Rufiji area. It was put down with difficulty, and was followed by a period of improved administration under Albrecht Freiherr von Rechenberg. When the First World War broke out the German colonial army was led by Gen. Paul von Vorbeck, but was eventually overwhelmed by British-led forces. The eastern areas of German administration were awarded to Britain under a League of Nations mandate, and Rwanda and Burundi similarly to the Belgians. The most durable legacy of German rule was linguistic rather than administrative, for it led, if indirectly, to a greatly enhanced spread of Swahili throughout the interior.

GERMANS in South-West Africa. Protestant missionary endeavour was the beginning of German involvement in South-West Africa in the 1840s. Bantu and Khoikhoi resistance to missionary and trading activities failed to persuade the British or Cape governments to intervene, except for the occupation of Walvis Bay in 1878, but provided the opportunity for Bismarck to send the merchant Lüderitz to proclaim German protection in 1883–4. Under private company control German rule steadily extended inland, and from 1891 the German government took over the administration. Much land was expropriated from the Herero, Nama, and other non-white groups, cattle was confiscated, and German law replaced traditional law.

Resentment to German expropriation grew, but the whites were able to play off one group against another. In 1904 the Herero sank their differences and rose against the Germans. Until the arrival of reinforcements the Germans were reduced to holding the main centres and supply routes; when they had sufficient troops, their commander, Gen. von Trotha, crushed the rebellion. When most of the fighting was over in the Herero north, the Nama in the south rebelled, and fighting continued until 1907. The Herero–Nama revolts led to some of the most merciless repression in the history of colonial Africa.

Before the First World War, South-West Africa briefly became profitable to the German colonists and government, but in 1914 white South African forces invaded the colony. In 1919 it was mandated to South Africa as a 'C-type' mandate. Although many Germans were repatriated, some remained, and these were joined by fresh German settlers in the inter-war years. By 1960 Germans were just less than one-quarter (17,000) of the whites. As South-West Africa became politically more integrated with South Africa, the Germans identified themselves with the Afrikaner nationalists, while retaining a distinctive identity. They are opposed (1970) to United Nations trusteeship in any form.

Ruth First, *South West Africa* (London, 1963).
Ronald Segal and Ruth First (eds.), *South West Africa: travesty of trust* (London, 1967).   AEA

GERMANS in West Africa (Togo and Kamerun). The territories designated vaguely as Togo and Kamerun were taken under German imperial protection in 1884, and gradually occupied by force against much African resistance. They were delimited by bargaining with Britain and France. While Kamerun fell under the same noxious concession-company system as neighbouring French Equatorial Africa, Togo largely escaped this blight.

At the outset of the First World War small British and French forces invaded Togo and forced the Germans to capitulate after a three-week campaign; the territory was then divided between the French and British empires as two mandates of the League of Nations. German defence in Kamerun was more successful and determined, one of its objects being to retain Allied troops otherwise likely to be committed to the Western Front in France. It was not until Feb. 1916 that the end came; the Allies had been obliged to commit some 10,000 French, 8000 British, and 600 Belgian troops. Kamerun was partitioned in 1918 as two League of Nations mandates, the larger part going to France.

GERMAN–SLOVAK TREATY (23 March 1939) followed Hitler's invasion of Bohemia-Moravia, and crowned his policy of destroying the Czechoslovak state. The treaty described Slovakia as independent under Reich protection; Germany was entitled to maintain troops in Slovakia, and later received transit rights for an attack on Poland. German and Slovak foreign policies and military forces were to be co-ordinated and Germany was given a free hand in Slovak economic development.

In Nov. 1938 Slovakia and Ruthenia had received autonomy within the Czechoslovak state. However, soon after the Munich Agreement, Slovak leaders had received Göring's assurance of support in any attempt to achieve independence and close relations with the Reich. German pressure on

Slovak separatists to declare independence increased during the early spring of 1939, when political tensions between the Czechoslovak government and the Slovaks seemed likely to disrupt the state. On 13 March Hitler threatened separatist leaders with absorption by Hungary if they did not immediately secede from Czechoslovakia. On 14 March the Slovak Diet proclaimed independence in terms drafted in Berlin.

Germany invaded Czechoslovakia on 15 March on the pretext of the ill-treatment of the state's remaining German citizens. The parties to the Munich Agreement had guaranteed Czechoslovakia's frontiers; on 15 March the British prime minister, Neville Chamberlain, stated that Britain's guarantee was nullified by Slovakia's secession.   ASJ

GERMAN–SOVIET TREATY (6 May 1921), in which Germany recognized the Soviet government de jure, and agreed to expel White Russian organizations from Berlin. Provision was made for a future economic organization. Both countries sought this rapprochement to counterbalance their unsatisfactory relations with the western powers. Germany had just failed to negotiate a reparations settlement at the London Conference of March 1921, and at the same time, Soviet Russia, in the treaty of Riga, concluded a disadvantageous peace with Poland. Both countries feared a prospective Franco–Polish alliance.

The provision for an economic agreement was in keeping with Lenin's new policy of inviting the trade and investment of capitalist powers. The case of Germany, however, was of special significance. Even before the conclusion of the treaty, co-operation had been arranged between the general staffs of the German and Soviet armies and in the autumn of 1921 negotiations began for the construction of Junker aeroplanes in Russia. Soviet Russia hoped, with German assistance, to reorganize the Red army after its defeat by Poland. Germany wished to use Russian facilities to evade the Versailles treaty's restrictions on German rearmament.

GERMAN–SOVIET TREATY (24 April 1926), a renewal of the 1922 Rapallo treaty. At a period when German foreign policy, under Stresemann's leadership, was moving towards a rapprochement with the west and with the League of Nations, Soviet Russia felt it particularly important to consolidate existing German–Soviet agreements. In particular, Russia feared that German membership of the league might eventually involve her, under Article 16 of the covenant, in military sanctions against Russia. For many months Stresemann refused to sign an agreement prior to Germany's admission to the league. However, the slow progress of his application for membership weakened his resistance to Russia's appeals.

The treaty preserved the Rapallo basis for German–Soviet relations. Each party abstained from economic or financial boycotts of the other; Germany was to be neutral in the event of an attack on Russia. A protocol was appended on the subject of Germany and the league. It stated that Germany's application for membership would not affect German–Soviet relations, and that, once admittted, Germany would combat any anti-Soviet tendencies within the league.

GERMANTOWN, BATTLE OF (4 Oct. 1777), engagement during the American War of Independence. Gen. George Washington's four-pronged attack upon Gen. Howe's troops stationed at Germantown, near Philadelphia, failed because of poor co-ordination and confusion caused by fog. British losses of 535 were half those of Washington's army, which retired to winter at Valley Forge.

GERMAN–TURKISH ALLIANCE (2 Aug. 1914). By a secret agreement Turkey promised to enter the war as an ally of the Central Powers if Russia intervened in the Austro–Serbian conflict. Should Greece enter on the side of the entente, Turkey would receive the Aegean Islands. Britain's naval mission in Turkey was subsequently dismissed. On 27 Sept.

the Straits were closed to foreign shipping. On 11 Oct. Turkey promised to enter the war in return for a German loan. A Turkish squadron under German command attacked Russia's Black Sea coast on 28 Oct. By 5 Nov., Britain, France, and Russia had declared war on the Turkish empire.

GERÖ, ERNÖ (1898–), Russian official who was sent (1932) by the Comintern to aid the struggling Spanish Communist Party. He appeared intermittently throughout the Second Republic and later during the Civil War under a variety of aliases, eg, Singer, Pedro, and Gueré. During the war he was responsible for the guidance of the Communist Party in Catalonia, taking part in the vicious elimination of anarchist and Trotskyist forces from Republican power. He remained a Stalinist adherent after the Second World War and rose to importance in Stalin's settlement of Eastern Europe. He ultimately became deputy prime minister in Hungary, acting as Khrushchev's agent during the 1956 rising.

GERONIMO (1829–1909), leader of the Chiricahua Apache Indians, who opposed US Indian policies. Geronimo and his band of 36 men, pursued by 5000 US troops, made raids (1884–6) over south-western US and northern Mexico. His surrender ended armed Indian resistance in the US. Geronimo was imprisoned in FL and AL before being transferred to Fort Sill, OK, where he became a stock-raiser and a visiting celebrity at world fairs and presidential inaugurations.

GERRY, ELBRIDGE (1744–1814), US politician, who was a signatory of the Declaration of Independence and was active during the Revolution and at the Philadelphia Convention (1787), initially supporting, but later opposed to, the establishment of a strong central government. A congressman (1789–93), member of the XYZ mission (1797–8), governor of MA (1810–12), and vice-president of the US (1813–14), his manipulation of state political boundaries for political advantage gave rise to the term 'gerrymandering'.

GERSHWIN, GEORGE (1898–1937), US composer, mainly of musical comedies, eg, George White's *Scandals* (1920–4), *Lady be Good* (1924), *Funny Face* (1927), *Strike up the Band* (1927), and *Show Girl* (1929). Starting with *Rhapsody in Blue* for piano and jazz orchestra (1924), he composed a number of symphonic works, including the *Piano Concerto in F* (1925), *An American in Paris* (1928), and the Negro folk-opera, *Porgy and Bess*. He attempted to merge American popular music with the music of the concert hall and opera house (1935) and his symphonic works induced a number of composers to experiment with the new jazz idiom.

GERSON, JEAN (1363–1429), French poet, humanist, and theologian, and an architect of the conciliar movement. He was chancellor of Paris from 1395 and was occupied with the problems of the Great Schism, and when his attempts to reconcile the opposing claimants failed (1403), he turned to the conciliar theory. He led the French delegation to the council of Constance and, although he welcomed the election of Martin V (1417), he continued to believe in the superiority of council over pope. He was also deeply involved in the internecine strife of the Armagnacs and Burgundians in France, again seeking reconciliation of the factions.

GERTRUYDENBERG, PEACE NEGOTIATIONS OF (1710), between France and the United Provinces. Dutch envoys negotiated for the allies, England and Austria. The negotiations failed when Louis XIV refused to accept the controversial 37th article of the peace preliminaries, which stated that Louis XIV should compel his grandson to leave Spain.

GESSLER, OTTO (1875–1955), German politician, who represented the DDP in the Reichstag until 1924 and was defence minister (1920–8). His main problem was to assert himself as the political superior of Hans von Seeckt, the powerful chief of army command, who pursued his own policy of secret rearmament. In the circumstances Gessler frequently found himself in the embarrassing position of having to cover up illegal activities, until in 1926 he seized an opportunity to have Seeckt dismissed.

GESTAPO (contraction of *Geheimes Staatspolizei*), *ie*, Secret State Police, the political police system of Nazi Germany. The Gestapo originated in 1933 as a result of two independent take-overs of the then existing political police by the new Nazi regime; first, in Prussia, where Göring organized the Gestapa (*Geheimes Staatspolizeiamt: State Secret Police Office*); and second, in Bavaria, where Himmler gained control of a reorganized political police system, using the authority this gave him to assume by degrees similar powers throughout Germany. By the end of 1934 he was in de facto command of the political police in all the German states, including Prussia, where he and Heydrich had managed to deprive Göring of any real authority over the Gestapa. Until 1936 a covert struggle for power took place between officials of the interior ministry, who wanted to maintain supervisory authority over the system, and Himmler and his henchmen, who were increasingly assimilating the personnel and structure of the system into the *Schutzstaffel* (SS). The two Gestapo laws of Feb. and June 1936 confirmed the interior ministry's nominal authority over the Gestapo, but in effect endowed Himmler with power over the entire police and security system under the title of *Reichsführer-SS und Chef der Deutschen Polizei*. The Feb. law also absolved the Gestapo from any review of its actions by administrative courts, *ie*, withdrew its members from the sanctions of the rule of law. Heydrich was given command of the security police, *ie*, the combined Gestapo and criminal police. These he eventually (1939) transformed into the *Reichssicherheitshauptamt*, of which department IV was entrusted with the Gestapo's main responsibilities. The system was thus detached entirely from its original pre-1933 connection with the interior administration, and became in effect an independent system attached to Himmler personally.

The efficacy of the Gestapo depended to a large degree on its legislatively sanctioned freedom from administrative control, a freedom which left the Gestapo officers themselves the task of defining political offences without fear of external interference or reprimand. Thus the Gestapo was able to function as an uncontrolled extension of the ordinary police system, arresting where no legal offence had been committed, rearresting the acquitted or newly released, etc. In 1940 the justice ministry bowed to Gestapo pressure and agreed that acquitted persons or released prisoners suspected of political offences should be automatically handed over to the Gestapo, which meant, in effect, the probability that they would be sent to a concentration camp. Given these extensive powers both within Germany and in the areas occupied during the Second World War, the contribution of the Gestapo towards the maintenance of the Nazi terror was incalculable.

H. Krausnick, H. Buchheim, M. Broszat, and H.-A. Jacobsen, *Anatomy of the SS State* (London, 1968).

GETA, P. SEPTIMIUS (*reg.* AD 209–12), Roman Emperor, younger son of Septimius Severus, and, with the title Augustus, colleague of his father from 209, and from 211 of his brother Caracalla. Hostility between the brothers soon led to the murder of Geta and sole rule of Caracalla (212–17).

GETTYSBURG ADDRESS (19 Nov. 1863), speech delivered by Abraham Lincoln at the dedication of a US national cemetery on the battlefield at Gettysburg, PA. Following Edward Everett's now forgotten two-hour oration, Lincoln spoke only briefly. His address, widely criticized at the time as inadequate, or even insulting to the occasion, is now a classic of American eloquence. Expounding in less than 300 words the theme of the Civil War as a testing-ground for democracy, it ends with the famous definition of democracy as 'government of the people, by the people, for the people'.

GETTYSBURG, BATTLE OF (1–3 July 1863), major engagement in the American Civil War. After the victory at Chancellorsville of the Confederate Army of Northern Virginia under General Robert E. Lee, the army advanced into the rich farmlands of southern PA to replenish its supply of food and threaten Washington, DC, from the north. It encountered the forward divisions of the Army of the Potomac north of Gettysburg, forcing them to retreat through the town (1 July). South of Gettysburg, Lee deployed his 70,000 troops along Seminary Ridge, confronting Gen. George G. Meade's 83,000 men positioned along the parallel Cemetery Ridge. Confederate assaults upon each end of the Union line were eventually repulsed (2 July), and Pickett's frontal attack on the centre was thrown back with heavy losses (3 July). Lee lost 20,000 men and retired across the Potomac. Meade, having lost 23,000, failed to pursue the Confederate army, and, although the defeat at Gettysburg was a severe blow to the Southern cause, total disaster was thereby averted.

GEVAERTS, JOHAN CASPAR (1583–1666), jurist, philologist, poet, and secretary of Antwerp (1621–62). He was a leading figure in the vigorous cultural life of the southern Catholic provinces of the Spanish Netherlands in the first half of the 17th cent.

GEZO (d. 1858), King of Dahomey, West Africa (*reg.* 1818–58). Gezo ruled for 40 years, having overthrown his predecessor, Adandozen, by an intrigue supported by a notorious local slave-trader, Francisco da Souza, a naturalized Portuguese. His reign was a period of increased unification, imperialist expansion, and, at times, enlightened reform. He liberated Dahomey from the tribute-paying yoke of the Oyo (Yoruba) empire, embarked on territorial expansion with a reinforced standing army (giving particular attention to its corps of women soldiers or 'Amazons'), and held off or overawed the Ashanti, Mahi, and Yoruba, whose combined forces he defeated on the plains of Pawea. But he failed to realize his vision of conquest over Yorubaland and Nupe, his army suffering one rebuff after another at the hands of the Egba of southern Yorubaland.

Although only partly successful as an imperialist, he succeeded in upholding the integrity of Dahomey, especially in his diplomacy with Europeans, notably the British and the French, who had to respect the authority of his coastal officials. Gezo, fearful that missionary work would undermine his own authority, refused to allow any missionaries except in the coastal area inhabited by foreigners. He refused to sign any of the so-called slave trade treaties, partly to safeguard Dahomey's trading sovereignty and partly because he believed that the slave trade was indispensable to his country's prosperity. Yet he realized that the slave trade could not last, and from 1836 began to encourage the export of palm oil. He also humanized Dahomian laws relating to slavery.

GHADAMES (classical Cydamus), oasis town 483 kms south-west of Tripoli, occupied by the Romans and an episcopal see under the Byzantines. It was an early centre of Ibadi Islam (8th–10th cents) and an important link in trans-Saharan trade.

GHADR CONSPIRACY, an attempt by the revolutionary or Ghadr party to bring about a military mutiny and popular uprising in India (1914–15) while Britain was involved in the First World War. The Ghadr organization was developed among Indian migrant workers on the west coast of the US by leaders who had been involved in revolutionary activities, particularly in Delhi and Punjab. Lala Har Dayal, the most important leader, organized a number of smaller associations into the Hindi Association of the Pacific Coast (June 1913) and founded a weekly newspaper, *Ghadr* (Nov. 1913), before being forced to flee to Europe (April 1914). With the outbreak of war, plans were made for members of the Ghadr organization to return to India to prepare for the rising and several thousands did so late in 1914. The government of

India armed itself with the Ingress into India Ordinance (5 Sept. 1914) to deal with them. None the less, Ghadr workers did link up with revolutionary networks in Punjab, the United Provinces, and Rajputana. Between Dec. 1914 and Feb. 1915 dacoities and attacks on government treasuries and police stations were carried out, seditious literature was circulated, attempts were made to persuade troops to mutiny and to sabotage the railways, and arsenals were established. The outbreak was planned for 19 Feb. 1915, but police uncovered the conspiracy and it collapsed as the provincial governments used their special tribunal procedures under the Defence of India Act (1915) to impose severe sentences on those guilty of violence and to intern several thousands of others.

GHANA (91,843 sq. miles—240,000 sq. kms), formerly the British Crown Colony of the Gold Coast in West Africa. The name chosen (Ghana) had belonged to the old medieval state. The Akan, Ewe, and Ga are the purest groups in a population of 8,143,000. The country became independent in 1957, and a republic in 1960. It was under military rule (1966–9) before returning to civilian democracy under a new constitution.

GHANA, MEDIEVAL, name given to a state in the savannah lands of what is now the Republic of Mali. Ghana was, in fact, the honorific of its Soninke rulers, who also bore the titles *tunka* and *magha*. The state was centred on an area called Wagadu.

Little is known of Ghana's early history. The origins of the state are said to go back to before the 'emigration' (*hijra*) of the Prophet Muhammad (AD 622). It acquired fame in the Islamic world from the late 8th cent. as a source of gold. Though no goldfields lay in its actual territory, Ghana obtained supplies from further south and exported it northwards along the Awdaghust–Sijilmasa route. Awdaghast was controlled by Lamtuna Berbers, but was overrun by Ghana in 990. In *c.* 1054 the Lamtuna-dominated Almoravids retook the town and soon gained control of the Ghana capital (*c.* 1076–7), whose location is not known. The ruler fled (probably to Mema), but regained his capital later in the century (post 1087), when the Almoravid movement, by then established in Morocco, declined in the southern Sahara. It was perhaps the brief Almoravid occupation of Ghana which gave rise to the later story of Ghana's original ruling dynasty being 'white'.

Our only contemporary information about Ghana comes from the Andalusian geographer Al-Bakri writing in 1067–8, though he did not visit the state personally. His account of the royal capital reveals that the ruler was a divine king with a rich and elaborate court ceremonial. Succession passed to the king's sister's son, as among Berber chieftaincies. When the ruler died, food, beverages, utensils, and servants were buried with him, recalling Pharaonic rites, which some writers believe to have diffused into West Africa through Meroe.

In Al-Bakri's day the rulers were not Muslims, though they employed Muslim advisers and a separate town for the Muslim merchants existed near the royal capital. The ruler's residence doubtless moved many times in the course of Ghana's history. One site at Kumbi Salih ('the mound of Salih') has been partially excavated, revealing uncemented stone buildings, including a mosque, suggesting it was a merchants' town (or perhaps the Almoravids' site), rather than a royal capital.

Though the Almoravids did not utterly ruin Ghana, as is often thought, the state slowly declined from that time. It was first overcome by the Soso people and by the mid-14th cent. had been incorporated into the rising Mali empire. The name of Ghana was revived in the 20th cent.

S. J. Trimingham, *A History of Islam in West Africa* (Oxford, 1962).

E. W. Bovill, *The Golden Trade of the Moors* (London, 1958).

JOH

GHASSAN, division of the Arab tribe of Al-Azd, migrated from the Yemen and settled (*c.* 490) along the Byzantine frontier in Syria, above all in the region of Jabiya. Having accepted the Christian (Monophysite) faith, the Ghassanids received from Byzantium annual subsidies (*annonae foederaticae*) and in return sent their forces, at need, to assist the Byzantines in time of war. The Ghassanid state, attaining the height of its fame in the reign of Al-Harith b. Jabala (529–69), served the Byzantines as a safeguard against the Sasanids and their client regime of Al-Hira in Iraq; and also as a means towards the defence, against the desert tribes, of the spice routes running northward from the Yemen to Syria. The Sasanid invasion of Syria (613–14) did much to weaken the Ghassanid state; the tide of Arab conquest following the death of the Prophet Muhammad soon brought it to an end after the battle of the Yarmuk (636).

GHAT, oasis in south-west Tripoli at an important commercial crossroads where Arab, Berber, and Hausa merchants meet. It was the first base of many European travellers to West Africa in the 19th cent.

GHATGHAT, best-known Ikhwan colony in Arabia, established from a nucleus of Ataiba Bedouin in Dhurma district. The colony won a reputation for fanatical savagery before its destruction (1929).

GHAZALI, AL- (1058–1111), Muslim theologian, jurist, philosopher, and mystic, born at Tus, not far from Mashhad in north-east Persia. He became a professor (1091) at Baghdad, in the Nizamiyya, *ie*, the celebrated *madrasa* founded by the Seljuk vizier, Nizam al-Mulk. In 1095, Al-Ghazali abandoned his career as a professor and devoted himself to philosophical studies, *eg*, of the Neoplatonism of Al-Farabi and Ibn Sina, and to spiritual exercises and meditation. In 1106, he became a teacher once more, this time at Naysabur in Persia, but soon retired again, to Tus, where he died. He is generally regarded as a figure of central importance in the development of Muslim thought, his main efforts being directed towards combating the arid scholasticism which prevailed at the time and reasserting the importance of personal or mystical contact with God. His greatest work was the Ihye Ulum al-Din, 'The Revival of the Religious Sciences', which is offered to the pious Muslim as a guide to all aspects of the religious life.

GHAZAN KHAN (1271–1304), Mongol Il-Khan Ruler (*reg.* 1295–1304) over Persia, eldest son of the Il-Khan Arghun. Ghazan was brought up as a Buddhist, but later became a Muslim, Islam becoming now the state religion of the Mongol regime. In 1299–1300 Ghazan Khan took Aleppo and Damascus, defeating the Mamluks of Syria and Egypt near Hims. This success was brief-lived, for in 1303 the Mamluks routed the Mongol forces at Shahqab, near Damascus. Ghazan Khan gave careful attention to the finances and the administration of the Mongol state.

GHAZI, one who makes *ghaza*, *ie*, a raid, especially as part of a *jihad* or war on behalf of the Muslim faith. Ghaza was carried out from Transoxania against the heathen peoples of the steppe in Central Asia; also along the Syro-Mesopotamian frontier against the Byzantines. The spirit of ghaza constituted the dynamic force behind the expansion of the Ottoman state in the 14th–15th cents to include most of the Christian lands in south-eastern Europe.

GHAZI I (1912–39), King of Iraq (*reg.* 1933–9) in succession to his father, Faysal I. Under his weak control Iraqi politics became increasingly unstable and dominated by the army from 1937, while his hostility to Britain won him nationalist popularity.

GHAZI-AD-DIN IMAD-UL-MULK (1737–*c.* 1800) was a grandson of the first Nizam-ul-mulk of Hyderabad, Asaf Jah.

In 1752, on his father's death, he became Amir-ul-Umra. Turning against his benefactor, he became Vizier of the Mughal empire in 1754. He was responsible for the murder of the emperors Ahmad Shah and Alamgir II and for calling in the Marathas to oust the Afghans. After the Marathas' defeat at Panipat he disappeared into obscurity.

GHAZNAWIDS, dynasty of Turkish origin, ruling from Ghazna over eastern Persia, Afghanistan, and much of northern India. The founder of the line was Sebuktegin (977–97), a soldier who had risen to prominence within the Samanid state. Mahmud of Ghazna (998–1030) brought under his own control the Punjab, with parts of Sind and also of the territories along the Ganges. He also took over the former Samanid lands as far as the Oxus river. The rise of the Seljuks led in 1040 to the crushing defeat of the Ghaznawid Mas'ud I (1030–40) on the steppe of Dandanaqan. Although the Seljuk Turks now overran Persia, the Ghaznawids managed, during the reign of Mawdud (1041–8), to retain their hold on the territories of Ghazna, Ghur, and on the Indian lands. Ibrahim (1059–99), reaching agreement with the Seljuks, was able to strengthen the Ghaznawid domination in the Punjab and the adjacent areas. After the death of Mas'ud III (1099–1115) internal discord weakened the Ghaznawid regime. It eventually crumbled and disappeared in 1187 before the rising power of the Ghurids.

GHEE HIN, largest Chinese secret society (*hui*) in 19th-cent. Malaysia and Indonesia. Originally an offshoot of the Hung League, or *T'ien-T-Hui*, in China, the *Ghee Hin* played a more open role in the 'frontier' conditions of South-East Asia, where it often provided the only authority structure recognized by Chinese immigrants. It attempted to control Chinese life in Malaya, Riau, and East Sumatra through the migrant traffic, brothels, opium and gambling dens, and protection rackets, but was increasingly challenged from the 1830s by other *hui*s which arose to champion language groups other than the Cantonese of *Ghee Hin*. Violence between the *Ghee Hin* and its rivals culminated in the riots of Singapore (1854) and Penang (1867), and in the 'Larut Wars' (1861–2, 1872–4) over Perak tin. Straits Settlements' government attempts to control the *hui*s first by compulsory registration (1869) and then by legal suppression (1890), reduced them to criminal gangs by the turn of the century.

GHENT, Belgian city at the confluence of the two most important rivers of Flanders, the Scheldt and the Lys. It first developed as a riverine harbour in the 9th cent. The town grew outside the castle of the counts of Flanders and by the early 12th cent. it was the foremost centre of the Flemish textile industry, whose products became renowned throughout medieval Europe. It was at the height of its prosperity in the 13th cent. Despite the partial decline of the industry after 1300, Ghent remained one of the largest European towns; its population totalled some 60,000 around 1350. A more serious decline set in after a series of disastrous civil wars in the second half of the 15th cent. In the next century it had a history of popular dictatorships which challenged the power and wealth of the native nobility, backed by first imperial and later Spanish and Austrian governments, *eg*, 1539–40, 1576–7. By 1790 it was a part of the republic of the United Belgian States and it was later within the union of Belgium and Holland (1815–30). After the 1830 revolt Ghent was incorporated into the independent kingdom of Belgium, and the Industrial Revolution enabled it to achieve a position of importance not only in its historic role as a textile centre, but in chemicals and engineering.

GHENT, PACIFICATION OF (1576), agreement engineered by William of Orange, the states general, and the delegates of the Estates of Holland and Zeeland to unite together to expel the Spaniards from the Netherlands and to settle the religious differences of the 17 provinces on a regional basis, providing religious toleration for Calvinists and Catholics alike.

GHENT, TREATY OF (1814), the 'Peace of Christmas Eve', which formally ended the war of 1812 between the US and Britain. The treaty made no mention of the maritime issues that were partly the cause of the war, and it left the disputed US–Canadian border to the decision of boundary commissions. Andrew Jackson's dramatic victory over the British at the battle of New Orleans (8 Jan. 1815) was won after the treaty was signed but before news of it had crossed the Atlantic.

GHIBELLINES AND GUELFS, opposing factions in Italian internal conflicts in the 13th and 14th cents. The terms were derived from two rival German dynasties. The Ghibellines were the supporters of the German emperors of the Hohenstaufen family, one of whose chief castles was Weiblingen. The Guelfs took their name from the Welf dynasty. They were anti-imperialists and adherents of the papacy. After the destruction of the Hohenstaufen state in Italy in 1266, the divisions that had given rise to these terms ceased to have any meaning, but the terms persisted as the names of local factions that fought for power in every part of northern and central Italy. Down to the 15th cent. the ruling group at Florence was known as 'the Guelf party'.

GHOSE, LALMOHAN (1849–1909), Bengali barrister and statesman, who opposed the lowering of the age limit for the ICS examination (1877), and protested against Lytton's policy and Curzon's partition of Bengal. He was the first Indian to seek election to the British parliament. He remained loyal to the British connection.

GHOSE, RASHBEHARI (1845–1921), Bengali lawyer, politician, and philanthropist who opposed Curzon's partition of Bengal and protested against his Calcutta Convocation speech. He was president of the Indian National Congress at Surat (1907) when the moderates and extremists clashed. He gave munificent endowments to Calcutta University.

GHOSH, AUROBINDO (1872–1950), Bengali nationalist leader and religious teacher. He taught in Baroda and wrote some political articles which attracted attention, but he was not fully involved in politics until the partition of Bengal (1905), when he returned to Calcutta (Aug. 1906) to become principal of the National College. He was prominent in the *swadeshi* movement and became de facto editor of *bande Mataram*. His articles in *Bande Mataram* greatly increased the Hindu nationalist ideological fervour of the Bengali movement. He was tried for sedition (1908) and acquitted. He was an acknowledged leader of the 'extremist' group within the Bengal Congress and played an important part in the break-up of the Surat Congress session (1907). He started a new journal, *Karmayogin*, but in 1910 he left Bengal to escape the government's attentions and went into retirement in Pondicherry. There he turned from politics to the study of *vedanta* and the writing of works of spiritual guidance, the most famous of which was *The Life Divine* (1914–16).

GHURIDS, dynasty originating in Ghur, a region located in what is now central Afghanistan. Ghur—into which Islam had made little penetration before the rise of the Ghaznawids —acted in effect as a buffer zone between the Seljuk and the Ghaznawid lands. The Ghurid chieftains of the Shansab line began to extend their influence in the time of Ala al-Din (1149–61). The decline of the Ghaznawid and Seljuk regimes left the field clear for the Shansabi chieftains, of whom there were two main branches, one in Ghur and another at Ghazna. Under Shams al-Din Muhammad of Ghur (1163–1203) and Shihab al-Din Muhammad of Ghazna (1173–1206) the Ghurid power was at its apogee. Dynastic discords, ethnic rivalries amongst the armed forces (Ghurs, Afghans, Turks), and the rise of the Khwarazm Shahs led to the collapse of the Ghurid domination after 1215. The Ghurids, under the guidance of Shihab al-Din Muhammad and of his lieutenant, Qutb al-Din Aybak, had taken Multan (1175), Peshawar (1179), and Lahore (1186), bringing to an end the Ghaznawid state in India. It was on this Ghurid foundation that Shams al-Din Iletmish (1211–36) was to establish now the Delhi sultanate in India.

GI, colloquial synonym for a private soldier in the US army, originally used in the Second World War as a book-keeping contraction of the term 'government issue'.

GI BILL OF RIGHTS, US legislation giving economic and educational assistance to military veterans. The Servicemen's Readjustment Act (1944), Veterans' Readjustment Act (1952), and the Readjustment Benefits Act (1966) extended comparable benefits to all veterans of recent wars, and included home and farm loans, job counselling and placement services, and one month of educational assistance for each month of active service up to a maximum of 36 months.

GIACOBBI, PAUL (1896–1951), French politician, who entered politics as a radical, but served as a minister under De Gaulle (1944–6) after working in the Resistance. He helped to found the Gaullist RPF Party (1947), but later resigned when membership became incompatible with his radical allegiance.

GIA-LONG (NGUYEN ANH) (1762–1820), reign-title of the first Emperor of the Nguyen dynasty of Viet-nam (reg. 1802–20). As Nguyen Anh, last survivor of the Nguyen clan which had ruled at Hue since the 17th cent., he fled to the far south with his uncle in 1775, after Hue had fallen to the Trinh. His uncle was killed in 1777, and Nguyen Anh fled to an island off the coast. After further conclusive fighting, he retired to Bangkok in 1784. In 1788–9 he recovered control of Saigon and established his capital there for the next 12 years. Meanwhile he had accepted the help of Bp Pigneau de Behaine, and allowed his son to go to Paris. A Franco-Viet-namese treaty was signed at Versailles in Nov. 1787, but no effective French help was forthcoming; even before the Revolution broke out, it could not be afforded. Nguyen Anh did, nevertheless, receive the support of a number of French mercenaries, who helped him to build up a strong army and navy. In a series of campaigns from 1799 to 1802, he conquered the rest of the country, uniting the territory that is now Viet-nam for the first time in its history. As emperor, he built a new capital at Hue, and established a new administrative framework. He was not deeply Confucian in outlook, and was tolerant towards Christianity.

GIBBON, EDWARD (1734–94), British scholar, politician, and author, whose *Decline and Fall of the Roman Empire* (1776–87) brought him an international reputation as an historian, although there was disapproval of the sceptical and anti-clerical tone of the work. Gibbon was MP for Liskeard (1774–80) and Lymington (1781–2). He began by voting independently, but in the critical years 1779–82 he became a steady supporter of North. He held office as commissioner of trade and plantations (1780–2).

GIBBONS, GRINLING (1648–1721), English sculptor and woodcarver, the principal artist of the Anglo-Netherland school of carving and the most famous of the craftsmen associated with Sir Christopher Wren. During the 1670s he worked at Windsor Castle and later at the royal palaces of Kensington, Whitehall, and Hampton Court.

GIBBONS, ORLANDO (1583–1625), English musician, who was organist at Westminster Abbey and composer of church music, madrigals, and music for strings.

GIBBONS v. OGDEN, 9 Wheaton I (1824), US Supreme Court case defining congressional authority to regulate inter-state commerce. The steamboat pioneers Fulton and Livingston had received from the NY state legislature an exclusive right to navigate its waters by steamboat (1805). Ogden was licensed by them to engage in navigation across the Hudson River between NY and NJ. Gibbons competed with him under a federal licence granted under the terms of a congressional act regulating coastal trade. A suit brought by Ogden to restrain Gibbons from engaging in such inter-state navigation was sustained by the NY courts, and Gibbons appealed to the US Supreme Court.

Chief Justice Marshall's decision gave a broad definition to the term 'commerce' and to the regulatory power of Congress. He held that the state law in question violated the federal legislation, but did not assert that federal power over inter-state commerce was exclusive.

GIBBS, JAMES (1682–1754), English architect, whose most famous buildings are St Martin's-in-the-Fields, London (1722–6), the Senate House, Cambridge (1722–30), and the Radcliffe Library, Oxford (1737–49).

GIBERTI, GIAN MATTEO (1495–1543), bishop of Verona (1524–43), secretary and adviser to Pope Clement VII, and subsequently the most prominent of the reforming bishops within the Catholic Church before the Counter-Reformation. A member of the Oratory of Divine Love in Rome (1517) he aspired to the contemplative life, but was drawn into service in the papal curia, where he supported the policy of a French alliance to liberate Italy from the Spanish. After the disasters leading to the sack of Rome by the Spanish imperial troops he returned to his diocese (1528). There he became a model bishop, working ceaselessly to regenerate the life of his parishes, which he saw as congregational brotherhoods centred upon the Mass. He founded the Confraternity of the Blessed Sacrament, and issued regulations against ignorant benefice holders and non-residency, some of which were eventually incorporated into the decrees of the Council of Trent.

GIBLIN, LYNDHURST FALKINER (1872–1951), Australian politician and economist. As a young man he mined in AK and the Solomon Islands and grew fruit in his native Tas. He was Tas.'s government statistician (1920–8) and research professor of economics at Melbourne University (1929–40). Through his membership of Commonwealth agencies he influenced Australia's monetary and fiscal policies.

GIBRALTAR, SIEGE OF (1779–83), occurred when a combined Franco-Spanish force, equipped with powerful floating batteries, tried to penetrate the English defences. The garrison, commanded by Gen. Elliot, was successfully reinforced several times by British ships running the gauntlet of the blockade, enabling Britain to retain Gibraltar at the end of the American War of Independence (1783).

GIBSON, EDMUND (1669–1748), English theologian and classical scholar, who was successively Bp of Lincoln (1716) and London (1723), and acted as chief ecclesiastical adviser to the government until his quarrel with Walpole over the Quaker relief bill (1736), which he opposed.

GIDDINGS, JOSHUA REED (1795–1864), US politician and abolitionist. A congressman from OH (1838–59), he joined John Quincy Adams in the fight against the 'gag rule' applied to anti-slavery petitions in the House of Representatives (1838–44) and as one of the first anti-slavery spokesmen in Congress he supported the Free Soil Party (1848) and later joined the Republican Party.

GIEDYMIN OF LITHUANIA (d. 1341), real founder of Lithuanian power. He ruled (1315–41) a principality based on Vilna in the pagan heartland of Lithuania, and inaugurated the policy of defence against the Teutonic Order in the west, in alliance with Poland, while organizing Lithuanian expansion into White Russia and Ukraine, which reached its culmination under his son Olgierd.

GIEREK, EDWARD (1913–), Polish communist politician. Following the death of his father, who was a miner, he emigrated with his mother to France, where at the age of 13 he too became a miner. He was active in trade union affairs, joined the French Communist Party (1931), and was expelled from France for his part in a miners' strike in 1934. He returned to Poland, but in 1937 moved to Belgium, where he again worked as a miner and became a member of the Belgian Communist Party and, in the Second World War, of the resistance movement. He remained in Belgium until 1948, then returned to Poland, where he soon achieved prominence in the communist Polish United Workers' Party (PZPR). He became a secretary of the provinces committee of the PZPR (1949) and later (1954) a member of the party's central committee and politbureau (1956). In 1957 he became first secretary of the PZPR provincial committee in Silesia.

In Dec. 1970 he became first secretary of the PZPR and allied himself with the nationalist group, headed by Gen. Moczar, which ousted Wladyslaw Gomulka after riots in Northern Poland which followed an ill-conceived economic reform.

GIERS, NICOLAI KARLOVICH (1820–95), Russian politician and foreign minister (1882–95). He had a cautious and moderating influence on Alexander III and more control over policy than is often realized. Although he supported expansion in Central Asia he opposed Pan-Slavism and sought agreement with Germany. He negotiated the renewal of the Dreikaiserbund (1881) and, although this collapsed during the Balkan crisis (1885–6), he hoped that the Reinsurance treaty (1887) would be a preliminary to its reestablishment. British hostility and fear of Russian isolation caused him to negotiate the Franco-Russian alliance (1891–3), but this was ratified only when his repeated attempts to renew Russo-German relations failed.

GIL ROBLES Y QUINONES, JOSE MARIA (1898–), Spanish lawyer and politician, who entered politics through his work with Angel Herrera's social-Catholic newspaper. In 1931 he was involved in the founding of Acción Nacional, an organization for rallying Catholics against Republican anti-clericalism. When Herrera moved out of politics, Gil Robles took over the leadership of the movement. He was elected to the Cortes as deputy for Salamanca, and in 1931 organized a campaign for the revision of the constitution. He hoped to create a moderate Christian Democratic Party and adopted the notion of *accidentalism*, ie, that forms of government are accidental. He therefore followed a line of legal political activity within the Republic. This alienated him from the monarchists, whom he expelled from the movement in Jan. 1933. After this schism, he organized moderate right-wing forces into the Confederacíon de Derechas Autonomous (CEDA). He was instrumental in the creation of the electoral union of the right, which won CEDA 115 seats in the Nov. 1933 elections. Politically, Gil Robles was trapped between a sincere desire to make CEDA a moderate social-Catholic party and the fear of alienating his wealthy conservative backers and extremist followers. He pleased the right by advocating the execution of the socialist leaders of the Asturian rising. In May 1935, having been made minister for war, he purged the army of Republican officers and promoted right-wingers, such as Franco and Fanjul. Yet when the CEDA–Radical coalition fell in Nov. 1935, Gil Robles refused Fanjul's offer to put troops on to the streets.

He was criticized for his failure to seize power, and remained relatively moderate during the Feb. 1936 elections. Though he talked increasingly of the need to avoid civil war, he instructed party members to act according to their con-

sciences regarding a military rising. He was in France when the army rose, and remained in exile until 1957, refusing to be tainted with bloodshed. In 1968 he published his memoirs.

GILBERT, SIR HUMPHREY (*c.* 1537–83), English soldier, MP, explorer, and elder half-brother of Sir Walter Raleigh. He entered the service of Elizabeth I while still a boy, was wounded at the siege of Le Havre in 1563, and went to Ireland to serve under Sir Henry Sidney (1566). In 1572 he commanded the 'volunteers' who went to the Netherlands to help the rebels against the Spanish government, ostensibly against the queen's instructions but secretly with her approval, one of his main tasks being to keep the French out of the port of Flushing.

While he was in Ireland he had been working out plans for colonization, and for a voyage to China and the Indies by a north-west passage, and he wrote a *Discourse to Prove a Passage by the North West to Cathay and India* (1576). His first expedition, launched at great cost to himself, was abandoned in 1578, but in that year he obtained from the queen a patent giving him a monopoly for six years of colonization in lands 'not already subject to a Christian prince'. His expedition sailed in 1583 and was the first serious attempt to colonize North America. It was intended to set up a colony in Nfld, chosen because the Banks fisheries were already well known. At St John's in 1583 Gilbert proclaimed himself governor under the queen, issued leases of foreshore land, and made a rough code of laws. Nfld thus became the first English possession in the New World. Sailing on to establish a settlement between Cape Breton and Cape Hatteras he ran into bad weather and sank with his ship. His bearing and behaviour when last sighted have been rendered immortal in Edward Hare's account in Hakluyt's *Voyages*.

D. B. Quinn, *The Voyages and Colonial Enterprises of Sir Humphrey Gilbert* (London, 1940).   HNBM

GILBERT, WILLIAM (1540–1603), English physician to Elizabeth I, who studied elementary electricity and gravitation, evolving a theory of attractive forces expounded in his *De Magnete* (1600). His London house was the meeting place for scientists like himself, who believed in experimental method.

GILBERT DE LA PORRÉE (*c.* 1075–1154), French scholar, who, next to Peter Abelard, was the leading exponent of the teaching of logic and dialectic which was transforming the schools of 12th-cent. France. As chancellor of Chartres (1126–36), he was master at one of the most important of these schools and became Bp of Poitiers in 1142. Like Abelard, he was attacked by St Bernard, who tried unsuccessfully to obtain condemnation of his views on the Trinity.

GILBERT ISLANDS in the Pacific, discovered by Gilbert and Marshall (1788), were notoriously savage. In the 1850s local traders exercised a moderating influence, but the first missionary (Hiram Bingham) in 1857 had little success. In 1863–4 Peruvian slavers and Fiji-Samoa recruiters provoked renewed violence. Finally (1868–9), Tarawa and Abaiang rejected ancient cults and autocracy in favour of literacy and many people joined the various missions. In 1892 (with German encouragement) Britain reluctantly assumed a protectorate.

GILBERT'S ACT (1782) in Britain, general act empowering parishes to form unions for the management of the poor. This carefully drafted act was a major piece of legislation between the Elizabethan Poor Law (1601) and the Poor Law Amendment Act (1834). Under it the unpaid parish overseers were to be superseded by paid guardians, and workhouses were to be provided only for the aged, the sick, and those unable to work. This discrimination implied that the able-bodied unemployed must be given outdoor relief, a principle attacked in 1834. By 1834, 67 unions, of 924 parishes, had been established, mostly in rural areas.

GILBERT'S PATENT, royal charter granted to Sir Humphrey Gilbert by Queen Elizabeth I of England for colonizing and governing Nfld (1578). This led to the settlement of the first English colony in North America, at St John's, Nfld.

GILDED AGE, term derived in the US from the title of a novel by Mark Twain and Charles Dudley Warner (1873), used to describe the post-Civil War decade (1865–75), or more generally the later 19th cent. The reference is to the rapidly expanding commercial and industrial enterprise, the widespread corruption in political and business life, the ruthless pursuit of wealth, and the predominantly materialist values which marked the period. Its characteristic figures were Jim Fisk, Jay Gould, Commodore Vanderbilt, Roscoe Conkling, and William Tweed.

GILES OF ROME (Aegidius Colonna) (*fl.* 13th cent.), member of the influential Colonna family and an Austin Friar, who was tutor to the future Philip IV of France. His *De Ecclesiastica Potestate* (1301) is the extreme statement of the papalist doctrine and a defence of Boniface VIII's *Unam Sanctam.*

GILGAMESH (*c.* 2675 BC), semi-legendary king of Uruk and most popular hero of ancient Mesopotamia. His exploits are recounted in the 'Gilgamesh Epic', a long poem from the 2nd millennium BC.

GILLETT, KING CAMP (1855–1932), US inventor of the safety razor (1895) and founder (1901) of the Gillette Razor Co.

GILLRAY, JAMES (1757–1815), English caricaturist, author of biting satires against George III and his court. He became conservative after the French Revolution and ridiculed the pretensions of Napoleon in face of the freedom-loving John Bull.

GILROY, SIR NORMAN THOMAS (1896–), cardinal, Australian prelate. His appointment as Abp of Sydney (1940) and cardinal (1946) marked a new phase in a hitherto Irish-dominated Church, his episcopal policy being strongly Roman-oriented within Church affairs, but in secular matters largely pragmatic. His outlook conflicted in the late 1950s with that of Abp Mannix and the Movement. Secular recognition of his stature came with a knighthood in 1969.

GIN ACT (1751), in Britain, measure taken to control the spread of drunkenness in the early 18th cent. Gin, unlike imported French brandy, was cheap, and by 1733 there were about 7000 gin shops in London alone. Acts in 1729 and 1733, which attempted to restrict this increase by imposing high excise duties on gin and heavy charges for retailers' licences, were widely evaded, and an attempt to impose stricter control by reducing the cost of licences was no more successful. A public outcry, stimulated by Henry Fielding, and by Hogarth's 'Gin Lane', led to effective legislation. The 1751 act gave the magistrates power to enter gaols, workhouses, and houses of correction and search them for illegally introduced spirits.

GINGEE, rock fortress about 80 miles (128 kms) south-west of Madras, probably first constructed by the Vijayanagar kings. It fell to the Muslims (1638) and to Sivaji the Maratha by strategem in 1677. It was taken by the Mughals (1698) after a siege from 1690. It was occupied by the French (1750–61), and thereafter lost its importance.

GINGERBREAD GOTHIC, American architectural style popular during the 1870s. Although modelled upon English High Victorian, it was highly eclectic, much given to turret-ing, gabling, and the extensive use of cast-iron and carved-wood ornamentation.

GIOBERTI, VICENZO (1801–52), Italian writer and politician and representative of the neo-Guelf school of thought, whose desire to unite Italy in a confederation under the pope inspired moderate, middle-class Italians to espouse the nationalist cause. Gioberti's anxiety to distract attention from Mazzini's revolutionary plans led him to emphasize Italy's historic role rather than that of liberal or social progress. In his pamphlet, 'On the Moral and Civil Primacy of the Italians' (1843), he claimed that Italy was capable of resuming the leadership of the civilized world. His influence was profound. Pius IX was initially attracted to his ideas and proposed the formation of a customs union as a first step towards unity. But during the revolutions of 1848 the pope withdrew his support. Gioberti himself, after a brief period as prime minister of Piedmont (1848), was antagonized by the growing anti-clericalism of the Risorgimento and abandoned his hopes for Italy.

GIOLITTI, GIOVANNI (1842–1928), Italian politician, who was five times prime minister. He dominated Italian politics (1903–14), giving his country a decade of unprecedented stability. But after the First World War he underestimated the menace of fascism and strengthened Mussolini by including him in his national bloc (1920).

Giolitti was the first prime minister not to have played an active role in the Risorgimento, and the first who was willing to bring the mass of the Italian people into the constitution. He enforced strict state neutrality in labour disputes and introduced near universal male suffrage. However, he did not believe that Italy was ready for true democratic government. He based his majority on a system of parliamentary management known as *Giolittismo*, enabling his opponents to accuse him of paving the way for fascism. But by lowering the political temperature Giolitti made possible the rapid expansion of the economy and a wide range of social and administrative reforms.

In his brief post-war ministry (1920–1) Giolitti made a brave attempt to restore normalcy. But he was unable to contain fascism as he had anarchism and gravely underestimated the growth of violence on the right.

GIOTTO (1266–1327), Tuscan painter who introduced basic innovations in perspective and figure drawings. His greatest work (1304–13) is in the Arena Chapel in Padua. He also executed several commissions for Robert of Naples. In 1334 he became the official master of public buildings in Florence and in this capacity began the construction of the cathedral bell tower (1334–7).

GIPPS, SIR GEORGE (1791–1847), Australian military engineer and governor of NSW (1838–46). Gipps's appreciation of the consequences of the conflict between the pastoralists' and farmers' interests in NSW was sound and his proposals were reasonable, but he did not allow for the increasing tempo of colonial development. His failure to solve the controversies over land policy obscured his handling of Aborigine–white relations and his encouragement of inland exploration.

GIRAL Y PEREIRA, JOSÉ (1880–1962), Spanish politician, who was a member of Azaña's *Acción Republicana*, and minister of the marine in Casares Quiroga's cabinet of May 1936. He was one of the few popular front ministers to take the threat of a military rising seriously, having loyal telegraph officers posted at Madrid headquarters and in naval vessels, and he arranged for naval manœuvres to be held beyond the danger zones of Morocco and the Canaries. When some naval officers rebelled, he dismissed them and had arms distributed; consequently he was regarded by some as the assassin of the officers concerned.

On 19 July 1936, he was made the prime minister and

immediately took the crucial step of arming the workers. His failure to win help from France or Britain, together with the Nationalists' growing successes, led to a widespread demand for a more left-wing leadership and on 4 Sept. Giral resigned. For the rest of the Civil War, he concerned himself with the problem of exchanging prisoners. He was foreign minister in Negrin's cabinet (1937–8) and minister without portfolio thereafter. At the end of the war he went into exile.

GIRARD, STEPHEN (1750–1831), French-born American merchant, financier, banker, and philanthropist. He settled in Philadelphia (1776) and made a fortune in commerce, banking, and insurance. A strong supporter of the First and Second Banks of the US (1791–1811, 1816–36), he helped to finance the War of 1812 when the First Bank's charter was not renewed. He endowed Girard College in Philadelphia as a school for poor white orphan boys.

GIRAUD, HENRI (1879–1949), French general, who was a political rival of De Gaulle for a short period after the liberation of French North Africa in 1942. Giraud was backed by the Americans, but his conservative ideas had little appeal in Resistance circles. De Gaulle and Giraud became joint presidents of the Comité français de Libération nationale (1943), but Giraud abandoned this political role after a few months.

GIRAY, Tatar dynasty which ruled over the Crimea in the 15th–18th cents. The Giray Khans consolidated their hold over the Crimea during the strife which brought about the decline of the Golden Horde. After 1419 their position was in fact more or less secure. In 1475 the Ottoman Turks expelled the Genoese from the Crimea, seized Kaffa, and installed as khan their own nominee, Mengli Giray (d. 1514). After the Russian occupation of the lower Volga basin, ie, of Kazan in 1552 and of Astrakhan in 1554, the Tatar khans of the Crimea came into a closer dependence on the Ottoman sultan, seeking thus to safeguard themselves against Russian pressure from the north. At the peace of Küchük Kaimarja in 1774 the Ottomans had to accept the formal independence of th· Tatar khanate. On 21 July 1783 Russia annexed the Crimea, thus bringing the Giray line to an end. The Ottomans, at the peace of Jassy (1792), had to give official recognition to the fait accompli of 1783.

GIRÓN, FRANCISCO HERNÁNDEZ (1505–54), Spanish soldier and rebel. After helping to suppress the revolt in Peru (1548), against Gonzalo Pizarro, Girón himself led a revolt against the Crown (Cuzco, 1553), but was defeated and executed the following year.

GIRONDINS, loosely defined group of deputies in the French Legislative Assembly and Convention who received this name because some of those said to belong to the group were deputies from the Department of the Gironde. It was these few to whom the name was first applied. Among the outstanding members of the larger group were Brissot, Roland, Clavière, Barbaroux, Vergniaud, Guadet, and Gensonné. They were also sometimes called 'Brissotins' and came to be identified as 'Girondins' only because they were attacked as such by the 'Mountain'—the name given to the extremist wing in the Convention. Earlier, in the Legislative Assembly, the division between the two groups of deputies was not as great as it later became. Brissot and his friends were ardent advocates of the war with Austria and a Girondin ministry (whose main figures were Roland and Dumouriez) actually declared war. After lack of success in the field, this ministry fell. The Brissotins then pressed forward both with open attacks on the monarchy and with secret manœuvres for a return to office. The fall of the monarchy ended this and Roland and his friends became members of the provisional government which followed. It was now that the name 'Girondin' came to be used. Robespierre had already attacked the group over their war policy. He now inflamed the Moun-

tain against them in the Convention. The Girondins took an unpopular and anti-Parisian line in stressing the need to reassert the influence of the provinces against that of Paris and its extremist Commune. They were suspected of wishing to prevent the trial of the king. In the early months of 1793 the Convention was persuaded by the Girondins to take steps against popular radicals and journalists (notably by impeaching Marat) and this further excited popular feeling against them. The Commune and Jacobin Club, which the Girondins had now abandoned, organized a popular insurrection (31 May–2 June) which forced the Convention to order the arrest of 29 Girondin deputies and two ministers. The outbreak of civil war during the next month and the assassination of Marat led to further arrests. The Girondins were now believed to be fomenting civil war, and, indeed, some of them encouraged this belief by escaping to the provinces to seek help from the federalist revolt. On 31 Oct. 21 of them were executed and others subsequently. Later, they were identified with a much larger group as the party of moderation and the interests of the well-to-do in the Convention, but this is an oversimplification. They were never a very cohesive group and certainly not a party in any modern sense. They owed much of their apparent unity to the accusatory propaganda of their enemies and their ideological or social homogeneity is the creation of later historians.

M. J. Sydenham, *The Girondins* (London, 1961).
E. Ellery, *Brissot de Warville* (Cambridge, MA, 1915).

JMR

GISCARD D'ESTAING, VALÉRY (1926–), French politician, who was one of the first graduates of the then newly formed *École nationale d'administration*. He joined the ministry of finance (1949) and in 1954 became an *Inspecteur des Finances*. He was elected deputy for Puy-de-Dome in 1956 and re-elected in Clermont in 1958. He became (1959) secretary of state for finances in Debré's cabinet and was minister of finance in both his and Pompidou's cabinets (1962–6). He left the government in 1966 after the appointment of Debré as a 'super-minister' of the economy. Giscard and his parliamentary group, the Independent Republicans, represented thereafter the traditional right wing of the Gaullist majority. They remained loyal to De Gaulle while maintaining their independence with regard to certain Gaullist policies. In 1969 Giscard returned to the finance ministry in Chaban-Delmas's cabinet.

GISLEBERT OF MONS (*c.* 1150–1225), chancellor of Count Baldwin V of Hainault. By promptly notifying his master in 1191 of the death of Count Philip of Flanders on a crusade, he forestalled the seizure of Flanders by King Philip Augustus of France, allowing Baldwin to occupy Flanders as the rightful heir. His *History of Hainault* (1068–1195) is an important historical source.

GIST, CHRISTOPHER (*c.* 1706–59), American frontiersman, employed by the Ohio Co. (1750) to explore the OH and KY country. He acted as scout to George Washington on the expeditions to the French forts in the OH valley (1753–4) and to Gen. Braddock's expedition against Fort Duquesne (1755). The following year Gist was appointed Indian agent to the Cherokee country.

GIULIETTI, GIUSEPPE (1894–), Italian merchant navy officer and syndicalist leader of Genoese seamen's union, which assisted D'Annunzio's occupation of Fiume (1919). Giulietti's plans to extend the revolt to Rome failed. Mussolini gave false promises, dissolved the union (1924), and put Giulietti under restrictions.

GIUNTA, FRANCESCO (1887–), Italian politician from Dalmatia, one of the earliest organizers, in Trieste, of fascist *squadrismo* which seized Fiume (March 1922). Giunta was secretary of the Fascist Party (1923–4), and his career was hampered by opposition to Mussolini's conciliatory policy towards Yugoslavia.

GIUSTINIANI FAMILY, leading Venetian family in the 15th and 16th cents, which included Agostino (1470–1536), the orientalist and author of the first polyglot psalter; Sebastiano, the diplomat, who was Venetian ambassador in England during Henry VIII's reign; and Paolo (d. 1528), cofounder of the reformed Camaldolese order of monks.

GIZUR ISLEIFSSON, bishop (*fl.* 1081–1118), who promoted peace in Iceland. He gave his family estate at Skalaholt to be an episcopal see, established a second bishopric, enforced the payment of tithes, provided poor relief, and initiated the writing down of civil laws.

GLADDEN, WASHINGTON (1836–1918), US religious leader and social reformer, whose *Who Wrote the Bible?* (1891) helped to popularize 'modern' biblical criticism and the study of comparative religions. As Moderator of the National Council of Congregational Churches (1904–7) Gladden vainly opposed acceptance of 'the tainted money' offered to the Congregational Church's Foreign Mission Board by the Standard Oil Co. He countered social and economic doctrines of the survival of the fittest by advocacy of arbitration in industrial disputes and the ideal of social co-operation.

GLADSTONE, HERBERT GLADSTONE, Viscount (1854–1930), British politician and youngest son of William Ewart Gladstone. He was Liberal MP for Leeds (1880–1910), held a succession of minor offices in his father's ministries (1881–5, 1886) and ill-advisedly disclosed to the press his father's conversion to Home Rule for Ireland (Dec. 1885), which aroused great opposition and suspicion. As under home secretary (1892–4) and commissioner of works (1894–5), he was a competent administrator, and as chief Liberal whip (1899–1906) had the difficult task of keeping together a party divided over the Boer War, in which he supported Campbell-Bannerman's lead. He was responsible, as home secretary (1905–10), for 22 measures, including Workmen's Compensation and the Children's Charter, in which he was particularly interested. He was created governor-general of the new Union of South Africa (1910–14) and returned to head the War Refugees Association (1914–19). A champion of his father and of Asquith, he was often involved in controversy, feeling that the old Liberal Party had been betrayed by younger men and strangled by Lloyd George's coalition of 1916.

GLADSTONE, JACK (d. 1823), Negro slave in British Guiana. Gladstone planned a slave uprising to seize the capital and hold the whites to ransom until the governor proclaimed abolition of slavery. The rebellion was suppressed (1823) and large numbers, including Gladstone, were executed.

GLADSTONE, WILLIAM EWART (1809–98), British politician and prime minister. He was born in Liverpool, the son of a wealthy merchant, his ancestry and parentage being wholly Scottish, and was educated at Eton and Oxford. Sacrificing his first inclination to enter holy orders, he chose a career in politics as a deep Christian vocation. Originally a Canningite, he opposed the Reform Bill and entered the House of Commons as Tory MP for the pocket borough of Newark (1832). He represented Oxford University as a Peelite (1847–65), then South Lancashire (1865–8), Greenwich (1868–80), and Midlothian (1880–95) as a Liberal. He was a great admirer of Peel, who appointed him vice-president of the board of trade (1841). He was a convinced Free Trader and supported the repeal of the Corn Laws, afterwards making his reputation as a chancellor of the exchequer in Aberdeen's Coalition government (1852–5) and Palmerston's cabinet (1859–65). His Budgets completed Peel's progress

towards Free Trade and after 1846 made him much sought after in both Tory and Whig ministries.

His decision to join Palmerston (1859), partly out of sympathy for his pro-Italian policy and partly from rivalry with Disraeli, was a vital step towards Gladstone's leadership of the Liberal Party (1866). Urging 'Peace, Retrenchment and Reform', his first Liberal government (1868–74), following the impetus of the 1867 Reform Bill, enacted a series of long-delayed improvements in education, the army, and the legal system, and sought to solve the Irish problem by disestablishing the Church and by a first Land Act. Secret ballot was introduced, the civil service opened to competitive examination, and trade unions legalized. Though defeated in 1874, Gladstone, as the 'People's William', swept back into power (1880), after his Midlothian campaigns denouncing Disraeli's expensive foreign policy as immoral. His second ministry (1880–5), though carrying the Third Reform Bill, equalizing constituencies, and giving land reform to Ireland, was much less successful. His Home Rule Bill (1886) offended both Whigs and radicals and so split the Liberal Party for 20 years, except for the brief interludes of his fourth ministry (1892–4) and Rosebery's (1894–5). He ended his career by criticizing naval rearmament expenditure and prophesying reform of the House of Lords. He was an indefatigable scholar and his books included *The Church in its Relation with the State* (1838), *Studies in Homer* (1858), and *The Impregnable Rock of Holy Scriptures* (1890). His pamphlet on the Bulgarian massacres (1876) achieved great sales and affected British attitudes on the Eastern Question.

Gladstone was the creator, inspiration, and giant of the middle-class Liberal Party. Intellectually he was a dogmatic Churchman, spiritually a man with a restless evangelical, often radical, conscience. He kept together his mixed Whig and bourgeois supporters by his compelling faith, stamina, and magnificent oratory. His political duel with Disraeli raised the dramatic interest of parliament. His absorption with Ireland led him to neglect consultation with colleagues and led to his split with Chamberlain, whose succession to the leadership he feared could result in a 'Socialist' programme and the disestablishment of the Anglican Church. He was ahead of his time in fostering national self-determination for oppressed peoples like the Irish and the Bulgarians and won a world-wide reputation for his passionate belief in the individual.

J. L. Hammond and M. R. D. Foot, *Gladstone and Liberalism* (London, 1952).
P. Magnus, *Gladstone* (London, 1954).   JRA

GLANVILLE, RANULPH (d. 1190), English lawyer, and chief justiciar of England (1180). It is not certain that he actually wrote the treatise associated with his name, *De Legibus et Consuetudinibus Regni Anglie* (*On the laws and customs of the realm of England*), which is one of the major documents in the history of English law. He was removed from office on the accession of Richard I.

GLASGOW, ELLEN ANDERSON GHOLSON (1874–1945), US novelist, born in VA of an aristocratic Southern family. She was the first writer to attempt an accurate portrayal of the character of the South. In a long series of novels, beginning with *The Voice of the People* (1900), she expressed her rejection of the sentimental, popularized Southern myth. The conflict between inherited tradition and immediate experience, a major theme in her work, is epitomized by her autobiography, *The Woman Within* (1954).

GLASGOW RIOTS (1725), outbreak of violence prompted by Walpole's attempt to impose a tax of 6d a bushel on malt throughout Britain (1724). The Scots, having enjoyed unofficial freedom from the malt tax since 1713, resented this, and despite Walpole's reduction of the tax to 3d in Scotland Gen. Wade and his soldiers had to be called in to quell the mobs.

GLASSMAKING (MEDIEVAL). In late Roman times glassmaking was a centralized industry based on the Rhone and the Rhine valleys, more especially the latter. With the breakdown of the empire the industry suffered accordingly, and came to consist of small glassworks situated in the countryside. Relatively simple shapes were made, but elaborate 'clawbeakers' were also produced from *c.* 500. Plain glass was often produced locally in the medieval period. The Low Countries and northern France exported glassware, but there was no important centre to rival Venice, where a glass industry had been established by the 10th cent. The Venetian glassmakers, based from 1291 on the island of Murano, became famous, especially for the production of fine, enamelled glassware from the second half of the 15th cent. Venice's great export trade was however based on clear, colourless glass.

GLASS–STEAGALL BANKING ACT (1933) in US, legislation, named after its sponsors, Senator Carter Glass of VA and Representative Henry Steagall of AL, that separated commercial from investment banking and established the Federal Deposit Insurance Corporation.

GLASTONBURY, reputed site of a pre-Saxon monastic settlement in south-west England, which became (*c.* 678) the site of St Mary's abbey. The abbey gradually increased in importance in late Saxon times and became the burial place of three kings, Edmund, Edgar, and Edmund Ironside. The abbey was intimately connected with the legend of St Joseph of Arimathea and with King Arthur.

GLAUBER, JOHANN RUDOLPH (1604–70), German chemist, who understood certain types of chemical reaction and first described the preparation of spirit of salt (*sal mirabile*), sodium sulphate, and perhaps chlorine.

GLAUCIA, CN. SERVILIUS (d. 100 BC), Roman demagogue, and with Saturninus, a leader of the disturbances of 100 BC. He hoped to become consul for 99, but was killed in the riots that followed the murder of his rival, Memmius.

GLEICHSCHALTUNG (lit. 'co-ordination') in Germany, term for the process by which all political and social organization was subordinated to official control under the Nazi regime. The term, which originally came from the vocabulary of electrical engineering, was first used in this special sense in March 1933, to characterize a new law (the *Gleichschaltungsgesetz*) which introduced NSDAP majorities into the government of each federal state. *Gleichschaltung* was subsequently commonly applied to the reorganization of a great variety of local and national organizations, *eg*, trade unions were taken over entirely by the NSBO, youth clubs by the Hitler Youth, professional associations by their Nazi-run equivalents, and so on down to the trivial level of clubs and groups. The intention of the policy was deliberately to deprive people of any means of social gathering or expression outside the Nazi Party, and thus to reduce individuals to separate atoms fused only through the party. The term was used indiscriminately in the early years of the Third Reich, and fell out of favour before the Second World War.

GLEIWITZ INCIDENT (1939), ostensible Polish attack on Germany, faked by the SS at the outbreak of the Second World War. Gleiwitz was a German radio station near the Polish frontier, and was 'attacked' on 31 Aug. 1939 by SS men wearing Polish army uniforms and using Polish weapons. The purpose of the incident, staged on Hitler's orders and planned earlier in the month, was to brand Poland the aggressor in the coming conflict, thus providing an excuse for the German invasion on 1 Sept., and also absolving France and Britain from their treaty obligation to defend Poland against aggression. Two similar attacks on frontier posts at Hochlinden and Pitschen were staged at the same time.

GLEN GREY ACT (1894), claimed to be a 'Native Bill for Africa', was intended to solve the problems of rural overcrowding in the Glen Grey district of the Ciskei and to force the black man to work for the white in South Africa. It provided for the allocation of allotments of four morgen each (about eight acres) to Africans on quit-rent tenure, to be inherited by primogeniture. In practice, it did little to relieve rural congestion, the labour tax which formed part of the act being repealed in 1903. Although Africans owning land under the Glen Grey system were not eligible for the property-based Cape franchise, the act provided for the election of local and district councils. These formed the basis for the limited local self-government granted to the Transkei (1963).

GLENSHIEL, BATTLE OF (11 June 1719), defeat of a small number of Jacobite highlanders and Spaniards in a skirmish at Glenshiel in Scotland by Gen. Wightman's troops. Thus ended an international plot inspired by Alberoni, the Spanish minister, and Charles XII of Sweden.

GLOBE, cartographical instrument advocated and used increasingly as a navigational aid during the 16th cent., enabling a loxodromic course to be plotted. One of the first globe-makers was the mathematician Mercator.

GLORIOUS FIRST OF JUNE, BATTLE OF (1794), victory off Ushant won during the Revolutionary Wars by a British fleet of 25 ships under Admiral Lord Howe over a convoy of French grain ships under Villaret. Despite the capture of six escorting battleships and the sinking of the *Vengeur* by the British, the French reached Brest safely, after defying the allied blockade.

GLORIOUS REVOLUTION (1688–9) in Britain, the dethronement of James II after an invasion and a military coup, followed by a revolutionary political and constitutional settlement. James II had succeeded peaceably to the throne (1685) despite the anti-Catholic fervour displayed during the Exclusion Crisis. However, many Protestant fears reappeared when James tried to institute a Catholic autocracy by establishing a standing army and by infiltrating Catholics into prominent military and governmental positions, etc. The birth of a son to James (June 1688) seemed to promise permanency for the regime. But it also inspired a group of four Whigs and three Tories—none of whom could claim to represent more than themselves—to invite William of Orange, James's nephew and son-in-law, who had been working since the early 1680s to safeguard his English interests, to assume power. The invitation was the excuse needed to mount an invasion. Declaring himself in Oct. 1688 for 'a free and lawful Parliament', William landed at Torbay, Devon, on 5 Nov. After some delay, despite belated concessions by James, influential members of the peerage, gentry, and army deserted to William, and James fled to France. On 11 Dec. a group of peers called on William to procure a free parliament, and for the next few weeks these peers controlled civil affairs while William looked after military matters. On 23 Dec. he called a meeting of the MPs of Charles II's parliaments and the lord mayor, aldermen, and 50 common councillors of the City of London, to advise him. As a result, William was asked to take over the conduct of affairs until a convention could be elected.

The convention met on 22 Jan. 1689 and proceeded after much heated debate to a constitutional settlement, which, though illogical (as it had to be to gain the support of both Whigs and Tories), was the real heart of the Revolution. The convention declared that James had 'abdicated the government' (though in fact he had merely deserted it) and that the throne was thereby 'vacant', though this was not possible in an hereditary monarchy. In effect, on this occasion the throne became elective and was offered jointly to William and his wife, Mary, for William refused to be his 'wife's gentleman usher' and threatened to return to Holland if he were not offered the Crown. The executive power was vested in William alone, who was to remain king in the event of his wife's death. The idea of a regency for James or his son was rejected. William and Mary accepted the throne on 13 Feb. and the interregnum came to an end. They also accepted the Declaration of Rights, which barred all Roman Catholics and those married to Catholics from the throne. Thus both Whigs and Tories became exclusionists.

The Declaration, though full of vague phrases, also removed specific grievances, eg, the suspending and dispensing powers, the Ecclesiastical Commission, the standing army in peacetime, and extra-parliamentary taxation, while it also guaranteed freedom of elections to parliament, freedom of speech within parliament, and frequent parliaments. Thus a parliamentary monarchy was established with parliament as the final arbiter of the constitution.

William also issued writs for a Scottish Convention to be summoned and this body invited William and Mary to accept the Scottish Crown on 11 April 1689. The invitation arrived at Whitehall on 11 May 1689 and William and Mary accepted the same day. At the same time it issued the Claim of Right, a document similar to the English Declaration of Rights. In Ireland, Tyrconnel, the lord deputy, declared against William and a bloody struggle began to enforce the Revolution in that country too.

The Revolution marked Britain out from most of Europe, where political development was towards absolutism and centralization by the abolition of representative assemblies.

M. Ashley, *The Glorious Revolution* (London, 1966).
D. Ogg, *England in the Reign of James II and William III* (Oxford, 1955).   CJ

GLOSSATORS. Gloss is a commentary on a word or phrase of a text such as the Bible or civil or canon law. The gloss was originally written in the margin or between the lines of the text itself, but rapidly developed in the 12th cent. into a separate work dealing as much with the interpretation as with the elucidation of the text. The term 'glossator' was invented in the 12th cent., and although it can be applied to anyone making a gloss it was applied particularly and usually to the school of jurists at Bologna founded by Irnerius (c. 1088) and which included Azo, Accursius, and Hugolinus, the future Pope Gregory IX.

GLOUCESTER, THOMAS OF WOODSTOCK, 1st Duke of (1st of 1st creation) (1355–97), youngest son of King Edward III of England. He was one of the Lords Appellant against his nephew Richard II in 1386–8. They deposed Richard for a few days at the end of 1387, but Thomas quarrelled about the succession with his cousin, Henry (the future Henry IV), and they had to restore Richard, while executing some of the king's closest friends. In 1397 Richard suddenly arrested some of the leading Appellants and Gloucester died in prison at Calais, probably having been murdered.

GLOUCESTER, HUMPHREY, 2nd Duke of (1st of 2nd creation) (1390–1447), youngest brother of King Henry V of England and regent for his infant nephew, Henry VI (1422–1429). His powers as regent were restricted because of the opposition of his cousin, Henry Beaufort, Bp of Winchester, and the other lords of the king's council. He was very popular in England, especially with the Londoners, who, in 1429, staged a riot against Beaufort. His popularity waned with his marriage to Jacqueline of Holland, which angered her neighbour, the Duke of Burgundy, and put in jeopardy the Anglo-Burgundian alliance, thus endangering the English position in France. He was one of the earliest patrons of humanism in England and books from his extensive collection contributed to the formation of the Bodleian Library in Oxford.

GLOUCESTER, WILLIAM, Duke of (1689–1700), the only child of Anne Stuart (later Queen Anne) to survive infancy, thus providing the sole Tory hope of a Stuart succession, other than through the Catholic line. After his death from smallpox the succession was transferred to the Hanoverians. The dukedom was 'declared' by King William III, not created by patent.

GLOUCESTER, ROBERT, 1st Earl of (d. 1147), illegitimate son of King Henry I of England. In 1127 he did homage to his half-sister, Matilda, and, except for a brief period, was her best general in the civil war against Stephen of Blois. As such, in an exchange of prisoners in 1141, he was exchanged for King Stephen. His death had no lasting effect, as Matilda's son, Henry, was in 1154 able to secure the succession on Stephen's death. Robert was a patron of scholars, including William of Malmesbury and Geoffrey of Monmouth.

GLOUCESTER, GILBERT DE CLARE, 6th Earl of (1243–95), the most powerful of the Marcher lords, who was badly treated by King Henry III and, by joining Simon de Montfort in 1263, helped to assure his victory in the civil war of that year. His defection from Montfort in 1265 ensured the latter's defeat and death at Evesham. Gilbert continued to play an independent part and compelled the royalists to end the civil war in 1266 by a compromise peace avoiding a wholesale proscription of the rebels. He played a leading part in defeating the Welsh under Edward I, who, however, always distrusted him and finally humbled him by temporary imprisonment (1291) and repeated seizures of his Welsh lordships (1291, 1295).

GLUBB PASHA, SIR JOHN BAGOT GLUBB (1897–), British soldier, who was commander of the Arab Legion (1939–56). After serving in France in the First World War, he was posted in 1920 to Iraq, but resigned his commission in 1926 and became an administrative inspector for the Iraq government. He moved to the Transjordan in 1930, joined the Arab Legion, and two years later took command of the Desert area (Colonial Service), and in 1939 of the Arab Legion as a whole. He was largely responsible for the conversion of the wild if spirited Bedouin troops into a disciplined force with a modern outlook, the elite of the Jordanian army; it is no coincidence that it was they who put up the stiffest resistance to the Israeli forces in the 1967 War. The source of Glubb's success lay in his genuine feeling for the country and his admiration for its people, allied to a conviction that their future lay with the West. It was thus impossible for him to remain outside politics, and although he retained command of the Arab Legion under the pro-British King Abdullah, he was dismissed by King Husayn in 1956 when public opinion had swung against Britain. He wrote several books on aspects of Middle Eastern history and culture, and on his own career.

GMELIN, JOHANN GEORG (1709–55), German botanist and chemist, who became a founder member of the St Petersburg Academy of Sciences at the invitation of Peter the Great. He published *Flora Siberica* (1747–70) and many memoirs, including *Travels in Siberia* (1751–2).

GNEISENAU, AUGUST WILHELM ANTON (1760–1831), Prussian field marshal, responsible with Scharnhorst for reorganizing the Prussian army after Jena (1806). He served as a mercenary with the British during the American War of Independence and observed with interest the uncircumscribed warfare of a nation in arms. In 1786 he entered the Prussian army as an officer, but retired in 1808 when Stein was dismissed. He returned to Berlin when the war with France was renewed and served as chief of staff under Blücher at the battles of Leipzig and Waterloo. He retired again in 1816 but returned in 1831 to conduct operations during the Polish revolt.

GNESIOLUTHERANS, school of Lutheran Protestants centred on Jena University in the duchy of Prussia and led by the scholar Flacius Illyricus. They were involved in a theological controversy with Melanchthon and the 'Philippists' on the issues of free will and salvation, which came to a head in the disputation of Altenburg (1568).

GNOSTICS, name given to members of a complex religious movement which became significant in the 2nd cent. AD, although originating earlier in oriental religious circles. Within Christianity the Gnostics appeared at first within the Church, but by the end of the 2nd cent. AD had mostly formed separate sects. They emphasized Knowledge, which they claimed to derive from a secret tradition. Gnostic systems range from genuine philosophical speculation to luxuriant amalgams of mythology and magic with a veneer of Christianity. Characteristic of their teaching was the distinction between the Demiurge or Creator-God and the Unknowable Divine Being. Modern forms of Theosophy often resemble Gnostic teaching.

GOA, port about 360 kms south of Bombay on the west coast of India, and capital of Portuguese India until its occupation by the Indian army in Dec. 1961. It is now administered by the central government. With its attached territory it had an area of about 3500 sq. kms and a population (1961 census) of nearly 600,000. Its fine harbour at Marmagao makes it a desirable acquisition and its fate is now in dispute between the states of Maharashtra and Mysore.

Occupied since ancient times, and long possessed by the Kadambas of Banavasi, it was taken in 1312 by Malik Kafur, the general of the Khilji sultan of Delhi, Ala-ad-din. In 1370 it was lost to the Hindu empire of Vijayanagar for a century, then recovered by Mahmud Gawan, the Bahamani minister, then lost again to the Adil Shahs of Bijapur. It was coveted for its harbour and as a convenient port of entry for the horse traffic from the Middle East, the horse being necessary for war and south India unfavourable for breeding.

Goa was captured in 1510 by Affonso d'Albuquerque, who made it the capital of the Portuguese empire in the east. The Muslim garrison was killed and their wives were married to the Portuguese soldiers; thus began the modern Goanese or Luso-Indian race. By this means Albuquerque hoped to provide a permanent resident garrison and save the exiguous supply of Portuguese manpower. No large conquests were made on the mainland, the Portuguese efforts being concentrated on controlling the trade of the eastern seas and especially the spice trade from Indonesia, Ceylon, and the Malabar coast. For a time, in the absence of European competition, they achieved great success. During the 16th cent. Goa became one of the most famous cities of Asia, being known as Goa dourada or golden Goa. It was adorned with churches, thronged with gambling *fidalgos* and slaves, and was a centre of luxury and corruption. The bases of the Goa system were military prowess, inter-marriage, slavery, and intolerance. The first bishop arrived in 1538, Hindu temples were destroyed (1540), and the Inquisition introduced (1560). In 1542, St Francis Xavier arrived and, in contrast to overall Portuguese policy, extended evangelism to the Hindu-controlled areas of south India. The bravery of the Portuguese preserved their dominion, but their reputation for cruelty and intolerance prevented further progress.

Portuguese power declined with the arrival of the Dutch and the English early in the 17th cent. and the rise of the Marathas later. Goa was blockaded by the Dutch in 1603 and 1635 and threatened by the Marathas in 1703 and 1741. Old Goa was evacuated for the more salubrious Panjim or new Goa, at the mouth of the river. In the 19th cent. Goa retained a façade of dignified decay, and owed any continuing importance to being the headquarters of the Roman Catholic Church in India.

F. C. Danvers, *History of the Portuguese in India*, 2 vols (London, 1894). TGPS

GOBELINS, French tapestry works, one of the *manufactures royales* established in Paris by Colbert under the direction of the painter Le Brun, who was appointed in 1663. The *Gobelins* manufactured furniture as well as tapestries and still continues to do so.

GOBIR, one of the seven 'true' Hausa states. Its last sultan, Yunfa, was defeated by Uthman ibn Fudi at Alkalawa (1808).

GO-DAIGO (1288–1339), Japanese Emperor (*reg.* 1318–39). His plotting helped to overthrow the Kamakura *bakufu* (1333), but in his attempt to restore the power of the throne (Kemmu Restoration) he underestimated the great feudal lords and ended his life in exile.

GODED LLOPIS, MANUEL (1882–1936), Spanish soldier, who throughout his career was politically orientated. In 1923 he helped Primo de Rivera to seize power. Later, discontented with Primo's treatment of the army, he became involved in the abortive Andalusian rising (1929). In the confused interregnum between the Dictatorship and the Republic, Goded was considered for ministerial office in the Melquíades Álvarez government of Feb. 1931.

At the beginning of the Republic Goded was inspector-general of the army, but his sympathies were with the right. He was in touch with the plotters of the Sanjurjo coup of Aug. 1932 and when it failed he was arrested. He returned to prominence in Oct. 1934, when he was made joint chief-of-staff with Franco in order to suppress the Asturian rising. In 1935 he was appointed director of the air force.

In March 1936, in order to keep him out of trouble, the Popular Front government appointed him to the command of the Balearic Islands. Nevertheless, he was one of the major figures in the preparations for the Nationalist rising, his desire being for a regime which would guarantee public order and respect for the army. His task was to be the capture of Barcelona and he was then to march on Madrid. On 18 July he took Palma de Majorca and on the 19th flew to Barcelona. But his forces were outnumbered by the local Civil Guards and army garrison which remained loyal, and by the anarchist workers. His headquarters were shelled and he surrendered on the evening of the same day. He was court-martialled at the beginning of Aug. and shot. PP

GODEFFROY, J. C. & Sohn (Hamburg) built up extensive German trading Pacific interests (1843–55). In 1857 the firm set up its island headquarters at Apia (Samoa), where it quickly became preponderant. In 1865–9 it took in the Carolines and later the Gilberts and New Guinea, but collapsed in 1879.

GODESBERG. On 22 Sept. 1938 Neville Chamberlain, British prime minister, and Adolf Hitler, German führer, held their second meeting here during the Czech crisis. Chamberlain brought the agreement of Britain, France, and Czechoslovakia that German forces should occupy the German-speaking areas of Czechoslovakia on 1 Oct. Hitler rejected this as inadequate and demanded the immediate occupation of the Sudetenland. His ostensible motive was that Germans were being massacred—an excuse without foundation. His real motive seems to have been a hope that Polish and Hungarian demands would cause Czechoslovakia to disintegrate entirely. Chamberlain, pushed on by the British cabinet, rejected Hitler's demand and returned to London empty-handed. War now appeared inevitable.

GODFRED (*fl.* 9th cent.), King of Denmark, who vigorously opposed Charlemagne's northern expansion by a show of strength and diplomacy and ravaged and reduced the emperor's Slavonic allies. He developed the mart of Hedeby and originated the Danevirke, a defensive earthworks across south Jutland.

GODFREY, Duke of Lorraine, Marquis of Tuscany (1044–1069). After frequent rebellions against the seizure of part of his duchy by Emperor Henry III, Godfrey was exiled. He married Beatrice, widowed Marchioness of Tuscany, and the rulers of Tuscany were thenceforth the mainstays of the papal reformists in Rome, who were striving to achieve independence from the German emperors. Godfrey's stepdaughter, Matilda of Tuscany, married his son, harboured Pope Gregory VII, and forced Emperor Henry IV to humiliate himself before her castle at Canossa.

GODFREY OF BOUILLON, Duke of Lower Lorraine (*c.* 1060–1100), leader in the First Crusade who sold or mortgaged many of his lands to finance a large army for the expedition. He played a prominent part in the campaign and in 1099 after the capture of Jerusalem was elected advocate of the Holy Sepulchre and leader of the war against the Muslims. His subsequent victories helped to cement the crusaders' hold on Palestine.

GODFREY, SIR EDMUND BERRY (1621–78), English magistrate involved in the Popish Plot. In Sept. 1678 Titus Oates and two others placed before him 'evidence' of a Roman Catholic plot to murder Charles II and place James, Duke of York, on the throne. On 12 Oct. Godfrey failed to return home and his body was discovered five days later. Miles Prance, who later admitted to perjury, alleged that he was present at the murder and three men were hanged on his testimony (1679).

GODKIN, EDWIN LAWRENCE (1831–1902), Irish-American lawyer, journalist, and editor. His experiences in the Crimea as war correspondent of the London *Daily News* (1853–5), made him a life-long opponent of war. He went to America (1856), where a tour of the Southern states resulted in his identification with the anti-slavery cause. On the outbreak of the Civil War he was critical of what he regarded as the pro-Southern sympathies of the British government at the time of the *Trent* crisis. In 1865 he founded the *Nation*, which he avowed would not be 'the organ of any party, sect, or body', and his uncompromising rectitude quickly made it America's most important review. In 1881 he sold the *Nation* to the financial magnate and reformer Henry Villard, who made it the weekly edition of his *New York Evening Post*, of which Godkin became first associate and then (1883) chief editor. Godkin broke with the Republican Party over the presidential candidature of James G. Blaine (1884) and was associated with the independent 'Mugwump' reform group. After his retirement (1899) he returned to England.

GODLEY, JOHN ROBERT (1814–61), Anglo-Irish squire and co-founder of Canterbury, NZ, who joined E. G. Wakefield in founding the Canterbury Association (1848) to promote a settlement for Anglicans in NZ. While in the colony (1850–2) he reduced extravagant preparations to receive the colonists, advocated responsible government, administered the settlement, and admitted Australian pastoralists in defiance of the association's policy.

GODO (lit. 'Goth'), a Spanish word used by Latin Americans during the colonial period to designate Spaniards from the mother country.

GODOY, MANUEL (1767–1851), Spanish diplomat and the power behind the throne of Spain between 1792 and 1808. He sought to maintain his position by treating with France, but instead achieved the destruction of the Spanish fleet and the introduction of French troops into Spain. Godoy's power was virtually absolute, though his humble birth and mildly liberal outlook were bitterly resented. To counter hostility at court he made peace with France (1795), earning the title of 'Prince of Peace'. Napoleon, by playing on Godoy's ambitions in Portugal, twice gained Spanish naval aid. The Spanish navy was defeated off Cape St Vincent (1797) and destroyed off Cape Trafalgar (1805). Nevertheless, Godoy continued his flirtation with France, and in the treaty of Fontainebleau (1807) gave Murat's army access to Spain.

Napoleon's implication in Spanish politics was costly, for after the overthrow and imprisonment of Godoy during the Tumult of Aranjuez (1808), the Bourbons abdicated and popular fury in Spain turned against France.

GODUNOV, BORIS (1552–1605), Russian *boyar* of Tatar origin, brother-in-law to Tsar Fyodor I, who rose to power under the *oprichnina* in Ivan IV's reign (1533–84), became regent and effective ruler of Russia after the death of Nikita Romanov (1586–98), and finally was elected tsar by the *zemsky sobor*, and with the support of the Patriarch Job, in succession to Fyodor (1598).

Both as regent and as tsar Boris showed ability and tried to guard the interests of Muscovy. He maintained the principles of Ivan's foreign policy, recapturing from Sweden the old Russian cities of Ivangorod and Yam on the Gulf of Finland. He established fortified towns at Kursk, Voronezh, and Byelgorod to defend Muscovy from the Crimean khanate. He elevated Job to the position of Metropolitan of Moscow and later prevailed upon the Patriarch Jeremy to create for him the Patriarchate of Moscow (1589). As a supporter of westernization, he was interested in education and sent a number of Russian youths to study in western Europe.

Boris's guilt over the deaths of Fyodor's direct heirs, his infant daughter and his half-brother Dmitri (1591), is not proven. He became increasingly unpopular, however, not only with the peasantry, whose freedom was restricted in favour of the gentry (1597), but also with the *boyars*, in whose eyes he lacked the prestige of the hereditary dynasty. He dealt ruthlessly with the latter, imprisoning the Shuiskys and deporting or executing the Romanovs (1601). But he was unable to ameliorate the effects of three consecutive bad harvests (1601–3), with the consequent disasters of starvation, depopulation, and lawlessness. In his last year he faced the challenge of a pretender, the false Dmitri, who invaded Muscovy (Oct. 1604), with the support of Poles, Cossacks, and peasants.

On Boris's sudden death he was succeeded by his young son Fyodor, who shortly afterwards was deposed and murdered by *boyars* supporting the Pretender Dmitri (1 June 1605).

GODWIN, MARY WOLLSTONECRAFT (1759–97), English writer and advocate of women's emancipation and education in *A Vindication of the Rights of Women* (1792). Although in revolt against the servitude of domesticity, she made a happy marriage in 1796 to William Godwin (1756–1836), the writer and publisher, whose *Enquiry Concerning Political Justice* (1793) questioned the basis of government and morality, especially with regard to property. He narrowly escaped prosecution with other radicals (1794).

GOEBBELS, JOSEPH PAUL (1897–1945), German politician and propaganda minister in the Third Reich. After being rejected for military service (1917), he studied German literature at Heidelberg University (1923) and for a time hoped to achieve a literary career. During these years he acquired an anti-bourgeois philosophy, and might have become attracted to socialism but for his passionate nationalism. He was not politically active until 1924, when he became secretary to a nationalist politician and began to be drawn into Nazi politics in Berlin. Despite his later claims to founder membership, he did not join the NSDAP until 1925, when he started to work for the party in the *Gau* Rheinland-Nord and became Gregor Strasser's secretary. His diary of this period records his early contacts with Hitler and his growing admiration for him, as well as his own intermittently savage and theatrical approach to life.

In 1926 he was appointed provisional *Gauleiter* in Berlin, and plunged into propaganda activity in this stronghold of working-class socialism. When the NSDAP was banned in Prussia (1927) he founded the weekly *Der Angriff* as his own propaganda vehicle, and having broken with the Strasser wing of the party he used his paper to attack their radical programme and strengthen his own and Hitler's position in the North German party. In May 1928 he was elected to the Reichstag and in Nov. Hitler appointed him propaganda chief in place of Gregor Strasser.

In March 1933 he was made head of the new 'ministry of public enlightenment and propaganda', staffed mainly with officials from the party's own propaganda machine. The ministry was one of the central links between the apparatus of party and state and gave Goebbels a strong position in the Nazi hierarchy. The '*ProMi*' was theoretically in charge of all propaganda at home and abroad, a brief which covered a diverse range of activities, including active propaganda through all media, the control of the creative arts, the maintenance of ideological orthodoxy, etc. Inevitably Goebbels's authority was contested by other leaders with overlapping responsibilities, *eg*, Rosenberg, Dietrich, and Amman; and although he undoubtedly had the widest-ranging authority in the massive propaganda apparatus, he at times had difficulty in maintaining his position against outside contenders.

Although untypical of the Nazi leadership, in that he possessed a genuine and occasionally incisive intelligence, Goebbels and his machine spoke with the authentic voice of Nazism, and his cynical propaganda aptly reflected the Nazi style of government. With an entirely unscrupulous certainty he was able to excuse the barbarities of the *Kristallnacht* (1938), or whip the German people into a ferocious affirmation of total war (1944), and generally organize a continuous barrage of lies and half-truths which deprived the population of any rational criteria of judgement.

Goebbels maintained a close relationship with Hitler until the collapse of the Third Reich. In 1944 he was appointed plenipotentiary for total war, and in the last days of April 1945 Hitler designated him as his successor as chancellor. But Hitler's defeat was that of Goebbels too, and like his leader he committed suicide on 1 May 1945, having attempted unsuccessfully to negotiate an armistice with the Russians.

E. K. Bramstedt, *Goebbels and National Socialist Propaganda* (Michigan, 1965).

R. Manvell and H. Fraenkel, *Doctor Goebbels* (London, 1960).
AJC

GOEBEN–BRESLAU INCIDENT (Aug. 1914), admission by the Turks of two German warships, the *Goeben* and the *Breslau*, to the Dardanelles. Their subsequent nominal sale to Turkey gave Germany control of the Turkish fleet. By attacking Russia's Black Sea ports (Oct. 1914), the Turks entered the First World War on the side of the Central Powers.

GOERDELER, CARL FRIEDRICH (1884–1945), German politician, who was one of the leading figures in the anti-Nazi resistance after 1936. In 1931 he was appointed price commissioner by Brüning under the emergency economic programme, but later (1932) refused the offer of a ministry from Papen. At first sympathetic to the aims of Nazism, and convinced that Hitler's fanaticism would be amenable to rational persuasion, Goerdeler co-operated with the regime after 1933. But he resigned (1936) as mayor of Leipzig in protest against the removal of a bust of Mendelssohn from its place of honour in the *Gewandhaus*. Freed from his official obligations to the regime, Goerdeler soon established for himself a leading place inside the non-communist opposition movement, becoming in effect its civilian leader and taking over the direction of policy. Under his guidance detailed plans for the take-over by the resistance were drawn up, as well as long-term programmes of economic, social, and political reconstruction. Goerdeler was to have been chancellor of the new government, and selected many of its members-designate. Although he opposed the assassination of Hitler as a poor tactical move, he was involved in preparations for the July 1944 coup. A warrant for his arrest was issued some days earlier, but he was not caught until Aug. 1944. In Jan. 1945 he was executed.

GOERTZ, GEORG HEINRICH, Baron von Schlitz (1668–1719), Swedish politician and principal minister in Holstein-Gottorp (1709) and of Charles XII in Sweden (1715), where his economic planning sustained the war effort at the cost of heavy inflation. He helped Charles to play off Russia against Denmark and the Jacobites against George I of England. At Charles's death he failed to secure the succession for the young Duke of Holstein-Gottorp, and the new regime had him executed on trumped-up charges.

GOES, HUGH VAN DER (*c*. 1440–82), Flemish painter who was a master of the guild of painters at Ghent from 1467 and dean of the guild in 1474. His work is in the tradition of the van Eyck brothers, but his portraits are less idealized.

GOETHE, JOHANN WOLFGANG (1749–1832), German poet, writer, and dramatist of the Enlightenment, and author of *Faust*. He was the friend and counsellor of Prince Karl August of Weimar, worked in his service (1776–86), and headed the ministry appointed under the constitution of 1816. He disapproved of the prince's reforms, *eg*, election by ballot and freedom of the press.

GOGA, OCTAVIAN (1881–1938), Rumanian poet, who turned to nationalist and anti-Semitic politics in the 1930s. Goga, born in Transylvania and educated in Budapest and Berlin, left Austria-Hungary for Rumania in 1914 and was an active interventionist during the First World War. His anti-Semitic inclinations prompted him to break with the National Party of Transylvania and eventually he fused his dissident faction with Cuza's National Christian Party. After the 1937 elections Goga had a brief spell as prime minister (Dec. 1937–Feb. 1938), heading a government which introduced anti-Semitic measures under the guise of 'romanization'. He was seeking to strengthen his position through an accord with the Iron Guard when he was dismissed.

GOGOL, NIKOLAI VASILYEVICH (1809–52), Russian writer, traditionally but misleadingly regarded as the founder of Russian realism. His satires on Russian provincial life and bureaucracy, *The Government Inspector* (1836) and *Dead Souls* (1842), criticized neither autocracy nor serfdom. His *Selected Passages from Correspondence with Friends*, revealing him as a conservative and religious mystic, was attacked by Belinsky.

GOICOECHEA COSCULLUELA, ANTONIO (1876–1953), Spanish politician, who began his career as a follower of the regenerationist politician Don Antonio Maura. As a deputy in the Cortes and through the public agitation of the Young Maurist movement, he advocated the Maurist line of austere liberal conservatism within the monarchy after a clean-up of the political system of the Restoration. During this period he wrote *Maurismo y Democracia Conservadora* and collaborated with Maura's son, Gabriel, in the Maurist manifesto of 1923, 'Afirmación Maurista'. Thus, in line with other Mauristas, he stood aside from Primo de Rivera's dictatorship. However, the approach of the republic found him moving to the right. He collaborated in the foundation of the *Unión Monárquica Nacional*, an organization formed by ex-ministers of Primo to create a school of 'modern counter-revolutionary thought' and to provide the ideological basis for a restoration of the monarchy. In May 1931 he was involved in the establishment of the *Círculo Monárquico*. At the same time, he led the monarchist opposition to the republic, joining *Acción Popular*, the precursor of Confederacíon de Derechas Autonomas (CEDA). At the end of 1932 he and the other extreme monarchists were expelled for their violent attitudes, and in March 1933 he founded *Renovación Española*, an organization to which he imparted a tone of clerical conservatism until it was modernized by Calvo Sotelo. Goicoechea's political activities were largely confined to attacks on the moderate policies of Gil Robles and diatribes against the left, and included demands for the execution of those responsible for the Asturian rising of 1934. In March of that year he went to Rome with Carlist leaders to see Mussolini and Marshal Balbo and secure aid for a prospective rising. The rising, which started on 18 July 1936, found him conveniently in Burgos, from whence he was sent by Gen. Mola to convince Mussolini of the tie between Franco and the monarchists who had visited him earlier. After the Civil War he became president of the Bank of Spain.   PP

GOKOMERE CULTURE, earliest Iron Age phase in Rhodesia. Its distinctive pottery styles date from the 4th cent. AD, and are found at the lowest levels of Zimbabwe.

GOLAB SINGH (d. 1857), Dogra in the service of Ranjit Singh, became the first Maharaja of Kashmir (1846–57). Hardinge's dispatches expose his treachery to the Sikhs. At the end of the first Sikh War the British sold him Kashmir for 75 lakhs of rupees.

GOLD COAST, name originally given by European traders to the seaboard of modern Ghana, mainly because there they could buy relatively large amounts of gold brought from the Akan forest country to the north. By 1800 Europeans had 42 forts and trading stations on this coast. British influence became predominant in the 19th cent., and in 1874 Britain proclaimed the Gold Coast Colony, with a frontier about 50 miles (80 kms) inland, to which they annexed, by invasion, the Ashanti empire in 1902. Thereafter the region, extending about 150 miles (240 kms) further north, was constituted as the Northern Territories, thus completing the political entity of the Gold Coast under British rule. The territory became independent under the name of Ghana in 1957.

GOLD COAST LAND BILL (1897) represented the second attempt by the British colonial government to control the exploitation of forest and mineral resources in the colony. The bill was designed to give the British Crown administrative rights over Gold Coast lands. Public lands, the so-called 'waste lands', were to be administered in the public interest, thus African rights of ownership would be undermined. The bill aroused so much opposition that it was withdrawn in 1898. A direct consequence of the bill was the formation of the Gold Coast Aborigines' Rights Protection Society, an organization of educated Africans and traditional rulers, who fought the bill and later fostered nationalist objectives.

GOLD MINING in Africa. Africa has been a source of gold for several thousands of years. The Nilotic Sudan supplied not only pharaonic Egypt with gold, but West Africa, the classical Mediterranean world and medieval Europe, and across the Sahara, the Rhodesian region, India, and the Islamic countries from the 10th cent. This was either alluvial or shallow-mined gold. Gold was discovered on the Witwatersrand in the Transvaal in 1885–6. Rapidly a huge extractive industry developed which completely changed the economic status of South Africa. The hamlet of Johannesburg, at the centre of the goldfield, became the largest city in the country (1967 population 1,300,000). Large-scale mining began in the neighbouring Free State after the Second World War.

The pattern of South African industry, already outlined by the Kimberley diamond mines, became ingrained on the Rand. The amount of gold per ton of rock was so small that vast quantities of ore had to be brought to the surface. The profit margins of the gold-mining companies, most of which were financed with British capital, were not considered to be great. Consequently large numbers of very low-paid African migrant workers were employed, supervised by a few highly

paid whites. Subsequent mechanization has no more than dented the colour bar, which is enforced by legislation.

Mechanization has enabled the gold-mining companies to work extremely low-grade ores, and to push the level of mining down to 12,000 ft (3650 metres) below the surface. Although other mining and secondary industries have broadened South Africa's economic basis, gold still accounts for half of its export revenue. Uranium is now extracted from the gold-mining waste materials. South Africa produces three-fifths of the world's gold. Gold is also mined in Ghana and in Congo (Kinshasa).

D. H. Houghton, *The South African Economy* (Cape Town, 1964).
L. Katzen, *Gold Mining and the South African Economy* (London, 1965).   AEA

GOLD MINING in Australia and New Zealand. The first Australian gold rush began in May 1851, following E. H. Hargraves's discovery of gold about 150 miles (240 kms) west of Sydney. Gold fever so dislocated the NSW economy that the government tried to restrain the rush by imposing a tax of 30s a month on all gold seekers. Richer goldfields, including the famous Ballarat field, were found in July and August in the adjacent colony of Vic., and by the end of 1851 the hinterlands of Melbourne and Sydney embraced widespread goldfields that surpassed the sheeplands as Australia's main export industry. The value of gold output was £1,300,000 in 1851, nearly £13 million in 1853 and again in 1856, after which it declined steadily for three decades. In 1858 possibly some 150,000 gold miners, including about 35,000 Chinese, were digging. Vic. was celebrated for its large nuggets or lumps of alluvial gold: the Welcome Stranger nugget, found in 1869 a few inches below the soil at Dunolly, contained 2284 fine ounces, valued then at £9534.

The first decade of gold enabled Melbourne to outstrip Sydney as Australia's largest city and Vic. to outstrip NSW as the most populous colony. Gold stimulated massive immigration, democratic reforms in politics, and a trend from a big-man's to a small-man's economy: in Australia the golden 1850s was possibly the most malleable decade of the 19th cent.

In the 1860s new goldfields were found far from the inland streams of south-eastern Australia. Gabriel Read, an Australian, found rich gold at Otago in NZ's South Island in 1861, provoking a rush of gold-seekers across the Tasman Sea; NZ's gold output reached a peak of £2,800,000 worth in 1866, declined rapidly, and then revived strongly in the 1890s with the innovation of bucket-dredging, a technique in which NZ engineers led the world.

In Australia a series of rushes began to leap-frog round the continent, moving in an anti-clockwise direction from Gympie (1867) in southern Qld to Charters Towers (1871) and the Palmer (1873) in tropical Qld, Pine Creek in the NT (1873), the Kimberleys in the north-west of the continent (1886), and the hot, arid WA fields of Coolgardie (1892) and Kalgoorlie (1893). By then hard-rock mining by large companies was the vogue, and Kalgoorlie's lodes quickly became the continent's main gold source. In 1898 WA passed Vic. as the main gold-producing colony and remained the leader, but its aggregate output (68 million fine ounces to 1968) had yet to overtake Vic.'s. The peak year of gold production in WA and in Australia was 1903—the last year in which Australia mined more gold than any other country.

G. Blainey, *The Rush That Never Ended: a history of Australian mining* (Melbourne, 1969).   GB

GOLD TRADE in Africa began in Antiquity, and was for centuries the most important aspect of Africa's external trade, gold being not only a highly valued commodity but also the most acceptable means of exchange. It was thus a stimulus to other forms of trade.

There were three important regional centres of the trade. The first was the Kush (Meroe)–Egypt area. Gold production was initiated in Kush perhaps as early as *c.* 2000 BC and reached a peak *c.* 1580–1320. Although it declined thereafter, it rose again in the Napatan kingdom (*c.* 751–538) and survived into the Meroitic kingdom (*c.* 538 BC–*c.* AD 350). Trade in gold between Egypt and Kush was promoted by the Ptolemies (323–30 BC) and continued when Egypt passed under Roman rule (30 BC–AD 642).

The second centre was West Africa, whose gold was constantly sought by North African traders. The most important goldfields were four: Bambuk, Buré, Lobi, and Ashanti, the first three being in the Wangara country, the region bounded by the Senegal, Niger, Falemé, and Tinkisso rivers. As reference to it by Herodotus (5th cent. BC) suggests, north-bound trade in West African gold began quite early, through North African traders, this gold passing to Europe and the Middle East. In these areas, the gold was so much valued that their kings and princes organized many but fruitless expeditions to discover its source. Eventually, European mariners on the Guinea Coast were rewarded by indirect contact with Ashanti gold mines from which they began to have regular supply during the 16th cent. This source became more important than the declining supply from Wangara. Today, Ashanti is next to South Africa as the most important source of Africa's gold trade with the outside world.

The third centre was the Rozwi area in modern Rhodesia. Long before the pre-eminence of Ashanti gold, the Rozwi rulers of the Shona kingdoms organized a state-controlled trade in gold which they exchanged for Asian and European cloths, beads, liquor, and firearms. As European and Asian traders were generally unable to win access to the gold mines, trade was done at fairs established at several points in the interior.

The impact of the trade on politico-economic affairs within and outside Africa was great. In Africa it generally encouraged the growth of large political systems because of the type of protection needed to safeguard gold mines and trade routes. Outside Africa, the major effect was monetary. Before the discovery of the mines of the Americas, countries in Europe and Asia depended largely on African gold to mint their coins, and to finance their trade and wars.

E. W. Bovill, *The Golden Trade of the Moors* (Oxford, 1958). R. Gray and D. Birmingham (eds.), *Pre-Colonial African Trade: essays on trade in Central and Eastern Africa before 1900* (Oxford, 1970).

AA

GOLDBERG, ARTHUR J. (1908–), US lawyer, jurist, and public servant, who was appointed secretary of labor (1961) and then an associate justice of the US Supreme Court (1962) by President Kennedy. He resigned from the court to become US ambassador to the United Nations (1965–8).

GOLDEN BULL (GERMAN), constitution negotiated between Charles IV and the German princes in 1356. It was intended to stabilize the constitutional position in the empire and laid down the procedure for the election and coronation of the emperor. It was the first written constitution of the empire and codified its federative character, implicitly recognizing the greater princes and the special position of the seven imperial electors.

GOLDEN BULL (HUNGARIAN), charter of liberties granted (1222) to the Hungarian nobles after a rising against King Andrew II. All nobles were to be equal, the rights of the noble council were recognized, and important offices were reserved for natives. Infringement by the monarch would justify rebellion.

GOLDEN FLEECE, ORDER OF THE, Christian order of chivalry, the highest honour of the Burgundian court, founded by Philip the Good in 1430. Its symbol was the Golden Fleece of the Argonauts. Membership was restricted to princes of the blood and the highest nobility of the Burgundian lands, though in time these came to include the whole Habsburg inheritance in the 16th cent.

GOLDEN HIND, vessel in which the English sailor Sir Francis Drake circumnavigated the world in 1577–80. She was formerly the *Pelican*, but was renamed during the voyage. She was a vessel of 120 tons and carried 18 guns. Another, much smaller, vessel of the same name was Humphrey Gilbert's flagship on a voyage to Nfld in 1583.

GOLDEN HORDE (*cf.* Russ., Zolotaya Ordu—whence the Modern Turkish Altun Ordu), the name given to the Mongol state over which ruled (1256–1502) the descendants of Batu (the Batu'ids), a grandson of Chingiz Khan. Batu (d. 1256) overran much of southern Russia and the adjacent territories in the great Mongol campaigns (1236–41). The centre of the regime which he created was at Old (later at New) Saray on the lower Volga. Berke Khan (1257–67) entered into conflict with Hulagu, the Mongol prince who founded the Il-Khan regime (1255–1335) in Persia, for control of the Caucasus area and, in order to strengthen his position, established an entente with the Mamluk Sultan of Egypt and Syria, Baybars (1260–77). Berke was the first of the Mongol princes to be converted to Islam. The Muslim faith was slow, however, to penetrate among the Golden Horde. Its triumph was not assured until the vigorous reign of Özbeg Khan (1313–41). After the death of Berdibeg Khan in 1359 dynastic dissension and unsuccessful warfare, *eg*, the defeat suffered in battle against the Russians at Kulikovo Pole in 1380, did much to weaken the Altun Ordu. Tukhtamish strove to restore the power of the Horde, but had to meet the ruthless challenge of Timur Beg, the great conqueror from Samarkand, who overcame him in 1391 and again in 1395. An able prince, Edigü, was able to halt the decline of the Golden Horde (1399–1419). After his death independent khanates began to emerge at Kazan, Astrakhan, and in the Crimea. The last remnant of the Altun Ordu maintained a precarious existence, amid conflicting pressures from the Poles, the Lithuanians, amid the Russians, until 1502.

GOLDIE, SIR GEORGE (1846–1925), British colonial servant, who went in the late 1860s to Egypt and the Sudan. While in the Sudan, he collected information about the Niger river from Mecca-bound Hausa pilgrims and began to develop the idea of British imperial expansion from the Niger to the Nile.

He came to the Niger area in 1875 to rescue the small trading firm of Holland Jacques from financial crisis. He saw that the crisis was caused by cut-throat competition among the European traders and persuaded many of the companies to amalgamate. The result was the formation (1879) of the United African Co. Goldie also secured a royal charter (1886) which gave the company (renamed Royal Niger Co.) monopoly of trade and much-needed political control on the Niger. Through the activities of the company, the Niger area eventually became part of the British empire.

After the revocation (1900) of the company's charter, Goldie made an unsuccessful attempt to repeat the Niger achievement on the Yangtze Kiang in China.

GOLDMAN, EMMA (1869–1940), Lithuanian anarchist, orator, journalist, and author, known as 'Red Emma'. She lived in Prussia and Russia before emigrating to Rochester, New York, US (1885). She married Jacob Kershner (1887) and by 1889 was deeply involved in radical activities with the anarchists Johann Most and Alexander Berkman, for aiding whom in planning to assault Henry Clay Frick (23 June 1892) she was imprisoned (1893). After her release she continued to support radical causes. She was founder and editor of the anarchist monthly *Mother Earth* (1906–17), and was again sent to prison in 1917 for anti-constitutional activity and then deported (1919). She was the author of numerous pamphlets and books, among them *My Disillusionment in Russia* (1923) and *Living My Life* (1931).

GOLDONI, CARLO (1707–93), Venetian dramatist, described as the Molière of Italy, whose plays reflected the age in which he lived and established him as the founder of the Italian school of comedy. As a young man he left home to join a troop of comedians, but returned to study medicine and philosophy at Rimini and civil law and theology at Padua (1732). After becoming a barrister he travelled in Italy before settling in Venice (1748–60). He later went to Paris, where he wrote *Le Bourru Bienfaisant* (1771) and published his memoirs, said by Gibbon to be as amusing as his comedies. He wrote many libretti, dramas, and tragedies, *eg*, *Belisarius* (1734), and above all comedies, *eg*, the *Rusteghi*, his works running to 44 volumes in the Venetian edition (1788).

GOLDSMITH, OLIVER (1730–74), Irish writer and physician. After an early struggle, in both capacities, he met Samuel Johnson (1761), who helped him to publish *The Vicar of Wakefield* (1762). Some historical work was followed by the comedy *She Stoops to Conquer*, produced at Covent Garden in 1773. Goldsmith's poetry included *The Deserted Village* (1770), in which he deplored the destruction of villages in the south of England in favour of large estates.

GOLDWATER, BARRY MORRIS (1909–   ), US politician, Republican senator from AZ (1952–64), and a well-known spokesman for conservatism. He was the surprise choice for the Republican Party presidential nomination (1964). After suffering a heavy defeat, he played little part in national politics until after his re-election to the US Senate (1968).

GOLIARDIC POETRY, the poetry of the wandering scholars of the 12th and 13th cents, also called Goliards. The name is of uncertain origin; perhaps from the old French 'gaillard' (robust, gay). The principal collection of Goliardic poetry is in the 13th-cent. manuscript known as the *Carmina Burana* (after the Bavarian monastery of Benediktbeuern, where it was discovered in 1847). This is a collection of verse, tender and gay, ribald and satiric, sacred and profane, mostly in Latin, and contains the work of at least one major poet, the anonymous Archpoet, arguably the greatest, and certainly the most intense, post-classical Latin poet.

GOLITSIN, ALEXANDER NIKOLAYEVICH, Prince (1773–1844), Russian politician and friend and spiritual adviser to Alexander I. He was chief procurator of the Holy Synod (1802), and in charge of non-Orthodox communities. He was tolerant of Protestants and freemasons, was president of the Russian Bible Society, and he helped to form Alexander's mystical brand of Christianity. As minister of education (1816) and head of the new ministry of spiritual affairs and public education (1817–24) he established a conservative and religious-based educational policy and enforced strict censorship, forbidding all press discussion of government policies. After being dismissed on Arakcheyev's insistence (1824), he returned as a member of Nicholas I's Secret Committee (1826).

GOLITSIN, DMITRI MIKHAILOVICH, Prince (1655–1737), Russian nobleman and leading member of the supreme privy council of Russia, whose family, with the Dolgorukys, dominated the short reign of Peter II (1727–30). He drew up a series of conditions limiting imperial autocracy at the accession of Anna, Duchess of Courland (1730), but in the pro-German reaction which followed, he was imprisoned in the Schlüsselburg fortress.

GOLITSIN, VASILI VASILEVICH, Prince (1643–1714), Russian nobleman, a favourite of the regent Sophia and a convinced believer in the need to westernize Russia. He also held advanced ideas on the need for reform in many spheres of Russian life—educational, military, technical, and social. As successor to Ordin-Nashchokin in the department of foreign affairs, he favoured a close understanding with Poland (which was achieved by the Moscow treaty of 1686) and a combined Christian attack upon Turkey. He com-

manded the Russian army in both unsuccessful campaigns against the Khanate of Crimea (1687, 1689) and concurred in Russia's abandonment of her claims to the Amur valley (treaty of Nerschinsk 1689). After these failures and the deposition of Sophia he was exiled to Arctic Russia.

GOLKONDA, fortress and ruined city 5 miles (8 kms) west of the present city of Hyderabad, used by the nizams as a state prison. It is also the name of one of the five successor states of the Bahmani empire. Its founder was Sultan Quli, the Bahmani governor (*reg.* 1512–43), founder of the Qutb Shahi dynasty. The state, which spread over the eastern part of the Deccan and later into the coastal Carnatic, was overthrown by the Mughal Emperor Aurangzeb (1587). In 1589 Golkonda was abandoned as a capital in favour of the new city of Hyderabad on a more healthy site. In English literature Golkonda became synonymous with diamonds and gold which were found in parts of the state.

GOLOVIN, FYODOR, Count (d. 1706), Russian field marshal, diplomat, and chief minister of Peter the Great (1699–1706). He served in the ministry of foreign affairs, accompanying Lefort on the Grand Embassy which toured the courts of western Europe to negotiate an anti-Turkish coalition (1697–1698), and was Lefort's successor as admiral-general (1698). His first great diplomatic achievement was the conclusion of peace with the Porte (1700), and he was the first Russian to be rewarded for service with the title of Count (1698).

GOLPE DE ESTADO (or *golpe*), the Spanish equivalent of *coup d'état*. In Latin America the politics of the *golpe* is generally held to mean a change of faces and slogans, but not a change in policy.

GOMAR, FRANCIS (1563–1641), Flemish Calvinist theologian who studied at Oxford (*c.* 1583) and became professor of theology at Leyden (1594), where he opposed the doctrines of Arminius, who held the second chair there. He withdrew to Middleburg (1611) and later contributed to the condemnation of Arminianism at the Synod of Dort (1619).

GÓMEZ, JUAN VICENTE (1856–1935), president of Venezuela (1908–35). Gómez began his career in the army and first achieved prominence as a follower of Cipriano Castro. While Castro was abroad he seized power (1908). His long rule was dictatorial, and accompanied by bogus electoral procedures and 'rubber-stamp' congresses. Gómez's absolute control of the army enabled him to dominate politics. He achieved a great reputation abroad. He paid off Venezuela's foreign debt, and opened the growing oil industry to foreign investment. His severe repression of all opposition led to the formation of various clandestine groups which had become by 1970 the leading Venezuelan political parties.

GÓMEZ, LAUREANO (1889–1965), Colombian conservative president, who identified himself with corporate fascism in the 1930s. A leader of the right wing of the Colombian Conservative Party, he benefited from a split among the Liberals to win the presidential elections of 1950. He was overthrown (1953) by Gen. Rojas Pinilla, and led right-wing opposition groups until his death.

GÓMEZ, MÁXIMO (1836–1905), Dominican-born leader in the Cuban struggle for independence against Spain. He went to Cuba in 1865, participated in several uprisings, and suffered imprisonment and exile. Gómez later led the revolt of 1895, which culminated (1899) in US military intervention and the defeat of the Spanish occupation forces. He received assurances from the US of eventual independence for Cuba, and helped in the election (1901) of Estrada Palma, first president of the Cuban republic.

GOMEZ, MOISES DA COSTA (1907–66), Netherlands Antilles politician, who was founder-president of the People's National Party in Curaçao (1944), represented the Antilles

D W H—X

at The Hague (1947–8), and served as president of the Antilles governing council (1949, 1951–4).

GÓMEZ FARIAS, VALENTÍN (1781–1858), Mexican physician and Liberal Party leader. He was Santa Anna's vice-president in 1833, but was then removed from office and exiled. During the war against the US the Liberals, or *puros*, returned to power, and Gómez Farias was installed as acting president (1846–7). After again being exiled, he was allowed to return in 1857 to see the triumph of the new Liberal constitution of which he had been one of the principal architects. He was noted for his anti-clericalism and his belief in mass education.

GOMPERS, SAMUEL (1850–1924), US labour leader. Born in Spitalfields, London, he emigrated to New York city (1863), where he continued his apprenticeship as a cigar maker. He joined the Cigarmakers' Union and, after leading a reorganization drive (1877), became president of the New York branch. Gompers attended lectures at Cooper's Union, but received most of his education in the factory, where workers took it in turn to read aloud. After reorganization of the union, which increased the role and power of its national leaders, the Cigarmakers' Union became a model for others. When the American Federation of Labor (1886) was formed, Gompers was elected president and except for the year 1895 remained in office until his death.

Gompers was a strong supporter of craft unions and waged a continuous battle with advocates of industrial unions. Under his leadership the AF of L became the major labour organization in the US. He felt that labour should not play a role in politics and that capitalism could not be displaced. Under his presidency the AF of L was usually politically neutral. His basic aims and those of the AF of L were purely economic—higher wages, shorter hours, and better working conditions for craft union members. Gompers distrusted intellectual reformers, particularly socialists, feeling they would divert the federation from its economic goals. Rejecting political action, he believed that labour's aim could be better realized by persuasion and by the threat of economic action. He encouraged binding trade agreements and opposed all but essential strike activity.

As the strength of the AF of L grew, Gompers became a public figure. During the First World War he was appointed to the Council of National Defense, formed a War Committee on Labor, and was a member of the commission on International Labor Legislation at the peace conference. He dominated the American labour movement until his death and did more than any other individual to shape the conservative nature of its development.

B. Mandel, *Samuel Gompers: a Biography* (Yellow Springs, OH, 1963).
Samuel Gompers, *Seventy Years of Life and Labor* (New York, 1925).   DHP

GOMULKA, WLADYSLAW (1905–   ), Polish communist leader. In 1926 Gomulka became a member of the Communist Party of Poland (KPP) and was active in trade union affairs. He went to prison for two years in 1932 for his part in a textile strike in Lodz. After his release he spent two years in the Soviet Union, then returned to Poland and became a union organizer in Silesia. For his activities there he was sentenced in 1936 to seven years' imprisonment. He was thus in Poland during Stalin's purge and dissolution of the KPP in Russia.

After Poland's defeat (1939) he moved to Russian-occupied Poland, and after the German invasion of the Soviet Union organized resistance groups in Krosno and Rzeszow. In the summer of 1942 he was appointed secretary of the Warsaw Committee of the Communist Polish Workers' Party (formed in Jan. 1942) and later (Nov. 1943) became its general secretary. In Jan. 1945 he became first deputy prime minister in the provisional government established by the Lublin Committee, and then minister for the regained territories in the communist-dominated 'Government of National Unity' (June 1945). During this period his main achievements were to destroy, by a combination of terror and duplicity, the influence of the Peasant Party, and to settle millions of Poles in the territories taken from Germany. His concept of 'the Polish Road to Socialism' made him increasingly suspect to the more orthodox communists led by Bierut, who accepted willingly the leading role of the Soviet Union. In Jan. 1949 Gomulka lost his ministerial posts and in Nov. was dismissed from the party central committee. He was arrested in July 1951, but was not put on trial. The death of Stalin and the breakdown of the Stalinist system brought him back to prominence. In Sept. 1955 he was released from prison and in April 1956 officially rehabilitated.

In the difficult situation following the Poznan riots of June 1956 he emerged as the only man who could contain the growing political unrest. Although the Russians tried to prevent his taking power, the Polish party's first secretary, Edward Ochab, proved willing to yield to him, and in Oct. 1956 Gomulka became first secretary of the party, a post he has held to Dec. 1970.

The high hopes raised in Poland by his return to power were largely unfulfilled. It is true that he ended collectivization and established a rather uneasy *modus vivendi* with the Catholic Church. He also ended close Soviet control of Polish political life. However, he came to see 'revisionism' as the main danger in Poland, and as a result the intellectual freedoms achieved in 1956 were whittled away. It was above all his fear of 'revisionism' which made him one of the strongest proponents of armed intervention in Czechoslovakia in the summer of 1968. His hostility to economic experimentation and Poland's unsatisfactory economic progress led to a feeling that the country was stagnating. As a result, he came under attack from a younger and more nationalistic group within the party. With Russian support, he was able at first to fight off this challenge, but in Dec. 1970 was faced with widespread rioting in northern Poland, the result of a crassly implemented economic reform which involved substantial rises in the price of food. This unrest was exploited by Gomulka's opponents to remove him from power, and in Dec. he was replaced as leader of the party by Edward Gierek.

GONCOURT, EDMOND LOUIS ANTOINE HUOT DE (1822–1896), French author and critic, who collaborated with his younger brother, **JULES ALFRED HUOT DE GONCOURT** (1830–70), in writing journals, novels, and histories. As critics they wrote mostly about French and Japanese art in the 18th cent. Their *Journal* (1887–96), the most famous of their collaborations, gives an intimate picture of the intellectual life of Paris. After Jules's death Edmond continued to write novels and founded the Académie Goncourt.

GONDAR, city in north-western Ethiopia, founded by Fasiladas in 1636. It was the capital until the 1860s and is the site of notable castles.

GONDOMAR, DIEGO SARMIENTO DE ACUNA, Count of (1567–1626), Spanish ambassador in England during James I's reign, who played on the king's fears of war with Spain to prevent him from leading the union of Protestant princes. He also persuaded James of the efficacy of a marriage between Charles, Prince of Wales, and a Spanish infanta. Dazzled by promises of a dowry of £600,000, James tried to satisfy Gondomar by ordering the execution of Raleigh (1618) and by releasing a hundred Catholic priests, imprisoned under the recusancy laws. Gondomar rejoiced at the growing breach between James and parliament on matters of foreign policy, but the collapse of the marriage scheme and the signing of an Anglo-Dutch alliance (1624) ended his influence.

GONJA, state located strategically on the northern border of the central Guinea forest. Its towns were important exchange-centres for articles in the trans-Saharan trade system. Gonja, founded in the 16th or 17th cent. by a migrant group of Mande-speaking people, expanded across the confluence of the Black and White Volta rivers and straddled the trade routes to Hausa states in the east, Mossi states in the north, Mande country in the west, and Ashanti in the south.

Gonja was for long attacked, though unsuccessfully, by its neighbours, who wished to secure control of the trade routes. In the mid-18th cent. Ashanti succeeded in overcoming it and for a long time (c. 1744–1874) made tributary its eastern and western parts. With the British conquest of Ashanti, Gonja had some years of uneasy independence before (1901) it came under the colonial government of the Gold Coast. It now (1970) forms part of modern Ghana.

GONZAGO, FERRANTE (1506–57), Duke of Mantua and Montferrat, Knight of the Golden Fleece, and Charles V's viceroy in Naples and Sicily (1535–46). He organized the defence of the imperial possessions in the Mediterranean against Moorish raids and was appointed commander-in-chief of the imperial army in 1543, leading the Luxembourg campaign (1544) and sharing with Granvelle the delicate negotiations leading to the peace of Créspy with France. In 1546 he was appointed governor and captain-general of the newly acquired duchy of Milan for Prince Philip but was later recalled (1554) at the insistence of the Milanese senate.

GONZALEZ, FELIPE (?1701–92), Spanish commander, who rediscovered and annexed Roggeveen's *Paasch* (Easter Island).

GONZÁLEZ PRADA, MANUEL (1848–1918), Peruvian intellectual and writer whose attacks on the failures of Peruvian society laid the basis for the reform movements of today. The APRA party claimed him as its spiritual forerunner.

GONZÁLEZ VIDELA, GABRIEL (1898–), president of Chile (1946–52). He was elected with the support of the Chilean Popular Front but turned against the communists and outlawed them in 1948. His term was disturbed by economic difficulties and revolts.

GOOD, WILLIAM CHARLES (1879–), Canadian politician and farmers' leader, who led the movement to merge the Grange and Farmer's Association (1907) out of which the United Farmers of Ontario was formed (1913). He entered the House of Commons as a member of the Progressive Party (1921), with the radical wing of which he sided, and in 1924 he helped to split the party by joining the revolt of the 'Ginger Group'.

GOOD NEIGHBOR POLICY in US, name given by President F. D. Roosevelt in his first inaugural address (4 March 1933) to the foreign policy of the New Deal. Later it was particularly applied to Latin American policy, and embraced the concepts of equal partnership, mutual assistance, and joint hemispheric defence between the US and Latin American nations. US renunciation of the right of armed intervention in Latin America, made at the Montevideo Pan-American Conference (Dec. 1933), was one of the first practical expressions of the new attitude, although it had been foreshadowed in the policies of the Hoover administration.

GOOD PARLIAMENT (April–July 1376). This English parliament is a landmark in parliamentary history, being the longest that had yet sat, the first in which there was certainly a speaker of the House of Commons (Sir Peter de la Mare), the first in which there is any account of the debates in the House, the first in which the process of impeachment was used, and one of the first in which the Commons took an independent line and initiative against the government, openly opposing John of Gaunt, then virtual ruler of the country, and his policies.

GOODNIGHT-LOVING TRAIL, US cattle trail running from central TX up the Pecos valley to CO (1866). After 1870, it was extended to Denver and Cheyenne. The cattle were either slaughtered for local consumption in the mining camps or used to stock the newly opened ranges of CO and WY.

GOODWIN'S CASE (1604) in England, case of parliamentary privilege which produced a clash between James I and the Commons after the court of chancery's intervention to declare void the election of an outlaw, Sir Francis Goodwin, in Buckinghamshire. It resulted in the Commons winning the right to be the judges of parliamentary returns.

GOODYEAR, CHARLES (1800–60), US inventor and discoverer of rubber vulcanization. Through accidentally dropping a mixture of rubber and sulphur on a hot stove, he found the resulting substance to be tough and pliable. In 1844 he patented the process thus discovered, but spent the rest of his life in litigation on the one hand and unsuccessful promotion of his process on the other.

GOONETILLEKE, SIR OLIVER (1892–), Sinhalese governor-general of Ceylon, who entered the Ceylon government service in 1921. He was appointed auditor-general (1931), civil defence commissioner (1942) (a wartime post which he filled with conspicuous ability), and, in 1945, financial secretary, the first Sinhalese to hold such a post. He played an important and successful part in the negotiations with the colonial office for the island's independence, after which he headed three ministries and became Ceylon's first high commissioner in London. His skill as a negotiator was outstanding. He was governor-general (1954–62) and was instrumental in quelling serious inter-communal riots (1958).

GORCHAKOV, ALEXANDER MIKHAILOVICH, Prince (1798–1883), Russian foreign minister (1856–82) and chancellor (1867). As ambassador to Vienna during the Crimean War, he achieved his ambition to cancel the Black Sea clauses of the treaty of Paris at a conference in London (1871). He justified Russian expansion into Central Asia in the 1860s in terms of historical necessity, although how far he controlled the policy is unclear.

Although often on bad terms with Bismarck he tried to maintain the Dreikaiserbund during the Near-Eastern crisis of 1875–8 and worked for a settlement in Russia's interests without disturbing the European balance of power. Being hostile to Pan-Slavism, he opposed the Russo-Turkish War (1877–8) when he lost his influence over the tsar to Ignatiev.

GORDIANUS I–III (*reg.* AD 238–44), Roman Emperors. Gordianus I, acclaimed as emperor in North Africa (238), chose his son, Gordianus II, as his colleague, but they were quickly overthrown by Capellianus, Maximinus's governor of Numidia. Gordianus III, grandson of Gordianus I, was made emperor by the Senate after the murder of Maximinus (late 238) and reigned without distinction until his assassination during a campaign against Persia (244). The reigns of the Gordians mark the opening of a phase of political disorder in the Roman empire which lasted until the accession of Diocletian (284).

GORDON, CHARLES GEORGE (1833–85), British general. After a varied military career, including the command of a defence force for Shanghai against the Taiping, which earned him the nickname 'Chinese' Gordon, he became governor of Egypt's Equatorial province in succession to Sir Samuel Baker. After successfully extending the borders of the province to Lake Albert and suppressing the slave trade, he returned to England in 1879. In 1883, a *jihad* was proclaimed by a Sudanese leader, Muhammad Ahmed, and 10,000 soldiers under a British officer, Hicks Pasha, were annihilated. The British government sent Gordon to evacuate the Egyptian forces in the Sudan. Gordon was cut off by

Mahdist forces, and the relief column, under Sir Garnet Wolseley, arrived at Khartoum two days too late to save him from being murdered.

GORDON, GEORGE WILLIAM (?1820–65), Jamaican leader, and son of a Scottish planter and a Jamaican slave. He was elected to the Jamaica Assembly (1844, 1863) and became a champion of the poor and an outspoken critic of Gov. Eyre. When the Morant Bay Rebellion (1865) occurred, which was led by his election agent Paul Bogle, Gordon was in Kingston. Eyre arrested him, sent him to Morant Bay, where, at a court-martial lasting 20 minutes, he was sentenced and then executed. In 1960 the new Jamaican parliament building was named Gordon House.

GORDON, PATRICK (1635–99), general, Scottish soldier of fortune, initially a Catholic and royalist, who left Scotland to be educated abroad and fought variously as a mercenary for the empire, Sweden, Poland, and Russia. He fought for Russia in the Crimean campaign (1687), and for his services was promoted to the rank of general, and he helped to suppress the revolt of the *streltsy* against his close friend, the young Tsar Peter I (1698).

GORDON FAMILY, Scottish feudal highland clan, whose leader acquired the title of Earl of Huntly in the 15th cent. The 4th earl (1524–62) was the victor of Haddon Rigg, and the 6th earl (1576–1636) took part in Roman Catholic intrigues during James VI's reign. George Gordon, 1st Duke of Gordon (1643–1716), was a Catholic and supported James II and the Old Pretender, but the family's power was weakened after the 1745 rebellion by the abolition of heritable jurisdictions.

GORDON RIOTS (1780), instigated by Lord George Gordon, in England, a manifestation of anti-Catholic feeling that degenerated into a general attack on property in the city of London (2–9 June). The riots followed the presentation to parliament of a petition against Catholic influence after the relief bill of 1779, and ill-feeling was increased by North's trade concessions to the Irish. After indecision by the magistrates, order was restored by troops and backed by a royal proclamation. Though the ringleaders were punished, Gordon himself was acquitted of high treason. Influential classes were alarmed by the disorders, and support for North's government grew, being confirmed at the ensuing peaceful election.

GORDON WALKER, PATRICK (1907–   ), British politician and writer who entered parliament in 1945 as a Labour MP, becoming secretary of state for commonwealth relations (1950–1). He was appointed foreign secretary in the 1964 Labour government despite his defeat in the general election, but he resigned after a second defeat in a by-election in Jan. 1965. He returned to parliament in 1966 as MP for Leyton and was briefly minister without portfolio (1967) and secretary of state for education and science (1967–8).

GORE, CHARLES (1853–1932), English bishop theologian, whose essay in *Lux Mundi* (1889) helped to reconcile Anglicans to the findings of biblical criticism, and whose involvement in semi-socialist movements helped to prevent a clash between the established Church and the emergent Labour Party.

GORE, FRANCIS (1769–1852), British army officer and colonial administrator. His two administrations (1806–11 and 1815–17) as lieutenant-governor of Upper Canada, were characterized by conflicts between himself and the reform leaders Robert Thorpe and C. B. Wyatt, and with land speculators.

GORÉE, tiny island off Cape Verde, much used as a slaving base from the 16th to the 19th cents, and headquarters of 19th-cent. French commercial activities in the *Rivières du Sud*. As a *commune de pleine exercise*, Dakar was at first administered as part of Gorée.

GOREMYKIN, IVAN LOGGINOVICH (1839–1917), Russian politician. As minister of the interior and (1890s) president of the Council of Ministers (1906; 1914–16) he proved to be an unpopular and ineffectual bureaucrat. He prorogued the Fourth Duma after the formation of the Progressive Block (1915).

GÖRGEI, ARTHUR (1818–1916), commander-in-chief of the Hungarian army (1848–9) and minister of war in Kossuth's short-lived republic. Görgei's military successes forced the counter-revolutionary army of Windischgratz to evacuate Hungary, but in a major miscalculation he paused to lay siege to Buda instead of pursuing the Austrians to Vienna. This gave Austria the chance to revitalize her army, which was joined by the Russians in a successful reinvasion of Hungary. Kossuth resigned and Görgei surrendered to Russia at Vilagos. This marked the end of the attempt to establish a Magyar republic independent of Austria and the beginning of an abortive effort by the Habsburgs to integrate Hungary more successfully into their empire.

GORGES, SIR FERDINANDO (1566–1647), English colonizer who took part in the siege of Rouen (1591) and was appointed military governor of Plymouth (1600). Gorges was the leading organizer of the Plymouth Co. (1606), whose aim was to establish settlements along the New England coast. After the dissolution of the company (1619), Gorges became one of the founders of the Council for New England (1620) which was empowered to give large grants of land for settlement. From these grants came the Plymouth Colony (1621) and the Massachusetts Bay Co. (1628). The New England colonists continually defied the authority of the council and its charter was returned to the Crown (1635). Gorges, after litigation, became lord proprietor of Maine (1639), but lacking funds was unable to colonize the area, the title to the land being sold to Massachusetts by Gorges's grandson (1677).

GORGIAS (*c.* 485–375 BC), Greek sophist and orator from Leontini in Sicily. As a philosopher he denied absolute certainty in knowledge or its communication, and as a rhetorician developed a highly antithetical and symmetrical style which influenced orators and prose writers.

GORHAM JUDGEMENT (1850). Bp Phillpotts, of Exeter, refused to institute the Rev. George Gorham to the living of Brampford Speke (1848) on doctrinal grounds. The (ecclesiastical) court of arches supported Phillpotts's action, but the judicial committee of the privy council found (1850) that Gorham's rejection of baptismal regeneration was not contrary to Anglican doctrine. The decision offended High Churchmen, produced over 90 pamphlets, affected relations between Church and state, and led to the revival of convocation (1852) after a lapse of 135 years. Eventually, Abp Sumner of Canterbury, an evangelical, instituted Gorham.

GÖRING, HERMANN (1893–1946), German airman and politician, who served in the First World War as a pilot in the famous Richthofen squadron, and acquired a reputation as an air ace and war hero. After the war he worked briefly in Sweden, and on his return to Germany became one of Hitler's earliest associates in the NSDAP. After the Munich putsch (1923), he spent four years in exile in Italy and Sweden, and did not re-establish close contact with Hitler until the latter offered him a safe seat in the 1928 Reichstag elections. In the years before the NSDAP came to power Göring made himself useful to Hitler by fostering the party's contacts with industrialists and politicians of other parties, a task for which his undeniably attractive personality made him particularly suitable. He was also regarded as a moderate and restraining influence within the NSDAP, in contrast to political radicals like Goebbels, and both before and after 1933 he had the support of many conservative nationalists, who believed him capable of safeguarding their interests.

In 1933 he was made prime minister and interior minister of Prussia, two extremely important posts which gave him command of the largest sector of Germany's internal administration, and hence an initially decisive role in the new government. While the real authority of the Reich interior ministry, under Frick, was severely limited by Germany's federal constitution, it was in Prussia that the earliest remodelling of the civil service and police forces (ie, the key positions in the struggle for domestic control) took place. To begin with, Göring proved surprisingly forceful and effective in his use of his power, though this derived as much from the brutality of the methods he permitted as from his own political acumen. His assumption of the machinery of power in Prussia provided a model which was applied elsewhere in Germany but his personal ambitions suffered a setback after 1934, when he lost full control of the police to Himmler. However, he remained a highly important figure in the Nazi hierarchy at least until 1941. In the years after 1933 he acquired a large number of official posts, some genuinely influential, such as that of head of the air ministry (1933) and the chairmanship of the four-year rearmament plan (1936), and others which were merely nominal or decorative, such as Reich Forest and Hunting Master, and eventually *Reichsmarschall* (1940). His passion for titles and for the uniforms which went with them was the subject of much ribald humour, though he was probably the only Nazi leader of whom it could be said that he was genuinely popular among ordinary people.

His creation of the German air force was his most solid achievement, from the German point of view, but inasmuch as the *Luftwaffe* played a vital role in Hitler's military plans, its ultimate failure to maintain air mastery in the Second World War rebounded greatly to Göring's discredit and helped to destroy his prestige with Hitler. Towards the end of the war his status as Hitler's designated successor was increasingly under attack, especially from Bormann, who eventually helped in his downfall. In April 1945 Göring proposed the opening of armistice negotiations with the western Allies, a move which led to his arrest on Hitler's orders for treason and defeatism. He was tried at Nuremberg and sentenced to death, but escaped the gallows by committing suicide.

J. C. Fest, *The Face of the Third Reich* (London, 1970).

AJC

GORIZIA, BATTLE OF (1916), sixth in a series of 12 Italian actions against Austrian forces on the Isonzo river in the First World War. On Gen. Cadorna's instructions 22 divisions crossed the Isonzo river and captured the town of Gorizia in a battle fought between 6 and 17 Aug., but failed to exploit their gains. They suffered heavy losses at the hands of the greatly outnumbered Austrians, whose resources had been dangerously stretched by the need to meet Brusilov's offensive on the Russian front. The battle illustrated the bankruptcy of Italian strategic thinking in the war.

GORKIC, MILAN (*c.* 1890–*c.* 1937), Yugoslav communist leader and Comintern official. His father, a Ukrainian from eastern Galicia, was in the Habsburg civil service at Sarajevo when his son was born. Gorkic went to a commercial school in Sarajevo, was active in communist youth groups in 1918, and was a founder-member of the Yugoslav Communist Party. When the party was driven underground in 1921, Gorkic left Yugoslavia and entered the service of the Comintern. During the years 1922–37 he was based in Moscow, but maintained a link with Yugoslavia through Vienna. After a period of factional strife and purges, Gorkic became leader of the Yugoslav party, but soon found himself at odds with underground groups in Yugoslavia. The leadership was divided over the policy to be adopted in the 1935 elections,

Gorkic instructing the party to vote for the united opposition, and Tito urging it to run its own candidates. The Comintern shuffled the central committee, retaining Gorkic as secretary-general but naming Tito as organizing secretary. Tito distrusted Gorkic, whom he accused of submitting false reports, conniving with bourgeois elements, and obstructing the party's work. In the summer of 1937 Gorkic was summoned to Moscow and dismissed from his posts. Tito succeeded him as party leader.

GORKY, MAKSIM (pseud. of **ALEKSEI MAKSIMOVICH PESHKOV** 1868–1936), Russian writer. His autobiography describes his youth, spent in wandering, poverty-stricken, through southern Russia. He started writing in 1892 and achieved recognition with short stories and his play *The Lower Depths*. His early novels, *eg, Mother*, were written to expose the evils of capitalism. He supported the Bolsheviks after the 1905 revolution, but was associated more with the ideas of Bogdanov than with those of Lenin. During 1917 he headed an independent, left-wing group named after its newspaper, *New Life*, and he opposed Lenin's seizure of power. He joined the Bolsheviks during the Revolution, when his influence with Lenin and Stalin protected many intellectuals. He lived in Italy in the 1920s, but returned to Russia and headed the new Writers' Union (1932), and was associated with the promulgation of Socialist Realism.

GORLICE, BATTLE OF (1915), preliminary encounter in the highly successful Austro-German offensive in Galicia in the First World War. Austrian and German forces launched an attack on a thinly defended 45 kms front between Gorlice and Tarnow on 2 May. The Russian Third and Eighth Armies were forced into precipitate retreat, abandoning Galicia and most of Poland, including Warsaw, and suffering catastrophic losses. This was one of the most spectacularly successful military campaigns of the war, though it failed to destroy the Russians.

GORM THE OLD (*fl.* 10th cent.), Danish king, possibly belonging to a Danish family settled in southern Norway. Gorm ended a Swedish occupation of south Jutland, overcame other kings in the area, and established his seat at Jellinge, where there are famous earthworks, as well as memorial stones to him and his wife.

GORST, SIR JOHN ELDON (1835–1916), British politician. As a young man he lived and worked (1860–3) as a schoolmaster, newspaper editor, magistrate, and commissioner among restive Waikato Maoris, for whom he advocated more and better European government. But Maori supporters in dissent forced him to leave. Gorst recorded his impressions in *The Maori King* (1864). Later, as a Conservative MP in Britain, he held office in Salisbury's first two administrations, as solicitor-general (1885) and under-secretary for India (1886). He was one of the most active members of Lord Randolph Churchill's 'Fourth Party'. He was the last vice-president of the privy council committee on education (1895–1902), leaving the Conservative Party over tariff reform. His son, **SIR (JOHN) ELDON GORST** (1861–1911), became consul-general in Egypt (1907–11) after working as an administrator under Lord Cromer. He attempted, unsuccessfully, to reduce Egyptian opposition to British rule by liberalization, by alliance with Abbas Hilmi, and by coercion.

GORT, JOHN STANDISH SURTEES PRENDERGAST VEREKER, Viscount (1886–1946), British soldier, who was commander-in-chief of the British Expeditionary Force to France (1939–40). He was chief of the imperial general staff (1937–9) and on the outbreak of the Second World War he was appointed to command the British Expeditionary Force. The German break-through on the Meuse in May 1940 exposed his flank and led to his decision to retreat to Dunkirk, an operation which his masterly handling prevented from becoming a rout. He was an outstanding and resourceful governor of the beleaguered island of Malta (1942–4).

GORTON, JOHN GREY (1911–), Australian politician and Liberal prime minister (1968–), who was a Vic. senator in the Commonwealth parliament (1949–68) when he obtained a lower house seat following his succession to Harold Holt as party leader.

GORTON, SAMUEL (1592–1677), American clergyman, born in Manchester, England, whence he fled from religious persecution to New England (1637). His teaching led to his banishment from Boston and Plymouth, MA (1638), and he founded the settlement of Shawomet on Narragansett Bay, RI (1639). But he was taken back to MA (1644), imprisoned, and then exiled to England. He returned to the settlement at Shawomet (1648), which he renamed Warwick, after his English protector, the Earl of Warwick. The Gortonite sect, founded upon his Antinomian teaching, lasted as a distinct group for several decades after his death.

GÖRTZ, GEORG HEINRICH (1668–1719), Swedish politician and minister of Charles XII, who conducted important financial and diplomatic operations (1715–18) for Charles and became his chief confidant. He might have gained the succession for Charles Frederick of Holstein-Gottorp, but on the death of Charles XII he was executed on a trumped-up charge as a scapegoat for the king's shortcomings.

GO-SANJŌ (1034–73), Japanese Emperor (*reg.* 1068–72) who broke the Fujiwara control over government. After ruling for four years he inaugurated the practice of *insei* (cloister government), whereby an emperor escaped from the heavy demands of state ceremonial by abdicating in favour of a young son, but continued to direct affairs of state, generally from a monastery. His early death, however, frustrated Go-Sanjō's hope of dealing with the tax-immune estates which were steadily encroaching upon the public domain.

GOSCHEN, GEORGE JOACHIM GOSCHEN, 1st Viscount (1831–1907), British Liberal, and later Unionist, statesman, the son of a German merchant in London. Goschen made a reputation in banking with his *Theory of the Foreign Exchanges* (1861). He won rapid promotion to the Liberal cabinet (1866, 1868–74) and at the Poor Law Board carried useful reforms, foreshadowing the Local Government Act (1888). He opposed the radicals in the Liberal Party over parliamentary reform, lost his seat through opposing Gladstone over Home Rule, and joined Salisbury's Unionist government on Randolph Churchill's resignation as chancellor of the exchequer (1887–92). He carried out a very successful large-scale national debt conversion. He was a keen Free Trader in the Unionist Tariff Reform split (1903–6).

GOSLAR, royal town in the Harz region of Germany, near important silver mines, a vital source of imperial revenue, developed in the 11th cent. by Henry II and Henry VII, who envisaged Goslar as the permanent capital of the Salian empire. It was the key to a network of fortresses through which these emperors sought to cement their power in Thuringia and control the duchy of Saxony.

GOSNOLD, BARTHOLOMEW (1572–1607), English navigator and sailor. As captain of the *God Speed*, he was second in command of the expedition which carried the first settlers to Jamestown, VA (1607).

GOTAR (GEATAS, GOTHI), whose relationship to the Goths is uncertain, were southern neighbours of the Swedes in the Scandinavian peninsula. In the 6th cent. they were independent, but they were then defeated in a sea-borne raid on the Franks, and came to be dominated by the Swedes, though they retained certain distinctive institutions.

GOTHIC, style of architecture which developed from Romanesque during the early 12th cent., and which had become general throughout Europe by the mid-13th cent. A Gothic building seemed to be a whole differentiated into parts; a Romanesque building gave the impression of various portions added one to another. The style is characterized by the use of the pointed arch (perhaps an eastern influence) together with the introduction of ribs to Romanesque groin vaults, transforming them into ribbed vaults. The precise date at which the pointed arch first appeared in Europe is a matter of controversy: it was certainly an original feature of the arcades of the church at Cluny, begun in 1088, whose transepts were finished by 1100. Pointed arches on a grand scale formed part of the design of Autun Cathedral (1120–1132); and at St Denis in Paris (built 1137–44) they were linked with a cross-rib vault. A Gothic style of architecture can be said to have existed from then onwards.

Early Gothic first appeared in England in the choir at Canterbury (1174). But the style was already subject to a national style, first seen at Wells (*c.* 1180), with the horizontal fusion of the bays instead of the French vertical fusion. Soon after 1200 there was a fully fledged Gothic architecture, marked particularly by the appearance of windows with the bar-tracery already in existence throughout much of Europe. This classic Gothic style continued throughout the 13th cent., producing splendid perfected forms of cathedral, palace, and to a lesser extent castle, embellished with sculpture and painting. Thereafter there was a move towards national Gothic styles, England having taken the lead in this direction a century before.

During the 16th cent. Gothic architecture gave way to the increasing influence of the Renaissance, but never completely lost its hold. It still survived in the enlargement of existing Gothic buildings in the 17th cent., found some enthusiasm for its claims in the 18th-cent. romantic movement, and enjoyed a major European revival, which spread to the US in the 19th cent. In England the revival found expression in domestic architecture (Victorian middle-class housing) and places of education, from universities to elementary schools, as well as in churches. In the US a fine example is the Protestant cathedral at Washington, DC.   JD

GOTLAND, island off the east coast of Sweden, and the traditional homeland of the Goths before their migrations. By 900 the island was a Swedish possession. The Gotlanders, with a trading house at Novgorod on Lake Ilmen, served as commercial intermediaries between Russia and western Europe in the Middle Ages.

GOTTWALD, KLEMENT (1896–1953), Czech politician who established communist rule in Czechoslovakia and served in the Austro-Hungarian army (1915–18), then deserted and joined the Czechoslovak army. After demobilization he worked in a factory, became shop steward and a member of the Social Democratic Party.

He joined the Communist Party on its formation (1921), was elected to the central committee (1925), and then elected secretary general (1929–53). He was also elected to the Czechoslovak parliament (1929). As a communist leader he organized demonstrations of miners and peasants and contingents to fight in the Spanish Civil War. In parliament he denounced the Munich (1938) agreement. Thereafter he left for Moscow, where he spent the Second World War directing propaganda to Czechoslovakia.

He returned to Czechoslovakia at the end of the war and joined the provisional Kosice government under Beneš. After the elections (1946) in which the communists, who were the largest party, polled 37 per cent of the votes, he became prime minister of a coalition government. He accepted the Marshall offer but, under Russian pressure, reversed his decision.

He led the *coup d'état* (Feb. 1948) which led to the establishment of a communist government in Czechoslovakia and succeeded Beneš to the presidency (June 1948). Thereafter the Czech state was constructed on a Stalinist model, including the purge of old communists in 1952, among them Slansky, who, with Gottwald, was a founder member of the party. Gottwald's last act of state was attendance at Stalin's funeral: he died a few days after returning from Moscow.

WFK

GOUGH OF GOOJERAT AND OF LIMERICK, HUGH GOUGH, 1st Viscount (1779–1869), British field marshal. While commander-in-chief in India he won the battles of Mudki, Ferozeshah, and Sobraon in the First Sikh War (1845–6), and the battles of Chillianwala and Gujrat in the Second Sikh War (1848–9).

GOUIN, FÉLIX (1884–), French socialist politician who became prime minister on the resignation of De Gaulle (1946). Gouin, a leading figure in the pre-war Socialist Party, joined De Gaulle in London and was his party's representative there.

GOUIN, PAUL NERÉE (1898–), Canadian political leader. In 1934 he broke with the Liberal Party, believing that its policy of the rapid industrialization of Quebec would destroy the traditional culture of the province. He became leader of a new party, L'Action Libérale Nationale, and in 1935, with the conservative nationalist Maurice Duplessis, formed the Union Nationale. Gouin later left the party (1942) and played a leading role in the unsuccessful Bloc Populaire. He was appointed cultural adviser to the Quebec Executive Council (1946), where he stressed the need for the preservation of French-Canadian culture.

GOULART, JOÃO BELCHIOR (1918–), Brazilian president and labour leader. Having been vice-president under Janio Quadros, he succeeded him when he resigned in 1960. He was disliked by the Brazilian military chiefs and his friendly relations with Cuba and his pro-Labour policies led to his overthrow in 1964.

GOULBURN, HENRY (1784–1856), British politician, who was MP for Cambridge University (1831–56), and held a succession of ministerial appointments. He was Irish chief secretary (1821–7), and as a follower of Peel and Wellington became chancellor of the exchequer in 1830, when he introduced the budget permitting 'free trade in beer', *ie*, the unrestricted opening of beer-shops. He was home secretary in Peel's first ministry (1834–5), and again chancellor of the exchequer in Peel's second ministry (1841–6), though Peel introduced the famous budget of 1842 in person. Goulburn was a capable administrator and a close personal friend of Peel.

GOULD, JAY (1836–92), US financier and speculator, whose operations became infamous when, with James Fisk and Daniel Drew, he took over management of the Erie Railroad and later tried to corner the gold market (1869). In the 1870s and 1880s he gained control over many trans-MS railroads. He also owned the *New York World* (1879–83) and controlled the New York elevated railroads and the Western Union Telegraph Co.

GOUVEIA, sobriquet of **MANUEL ANTÓNIO DE SOUZE,** Portuguese adventurer, who conquered for himself, in the lower Zambezi valley, a state which subsequently facilitated the imposition of colonial rule by Portugal in 19th cent. With an army more effective than any the Mozambique government could raise, he conquered most of the *prazos* or estates held by Portuguese-speaking families in the region south of Sena, resisted African invasions of the valley estates, and established a treaty with the kings of Manyika in 1873.

GOUVERNEUR, French royal official commissioned by the king to act as his representative within a province of the country. Usually a great nobleman, his duties were originally military, though after the 16th cent. they became more general. In the same period, however, the office became in practice the hereditary possession of certain great aristocratic houses, *eg*, the Guise in Burgundy and Champagne and the Condé in Picardy, who acted independently and in defiance of the Crown during the civil wars of religion. Henry IV (1589–1610) therefore curtailed the powers of the gouverneur by appointing a lieutenant to keep a watch on his activities, while allowing him to retain his prime function of commanding the royal army. Richelieu went further and dismissed a number of gouverneurs, and from Louis XIV's reign the position became increasingly honorary, tenure of office being restricted to three years.

GOVERNMENT OF BURMA ACT (1935) in Britain, made provision for the government of Burma after its separation from India on 1 April 1937, and operated until Burma became independent (4 Jan. 1948).

Except when acting 'in his discretion' or exercising his 'individual judgement' (see below), the governor was required to act on the advice of ministers who commanded a majority in the Legislature. A real measure of self-government was conferred.

The Legislature was expanded from 103, of whom 80 were elected, to a bicameral Legislature consisting of a Senate of 36, half elected by proportional representation of the lower chamber and half nominated by the governor 'in his discretion', and of a House of Representatives of 132 elected members, 91 from general constituencies, the rest from communal, university, commercial, and labour constituencies. The Burmese always held 72 per cent of the seats in the House of Representatives, and the ministers were almost exclusively Burmese. The franchise was wide. All males over 18 who paid taxes, complied with certain property qualifications, or were military pensioners, were included, and all females over 21 able to pass an easy literacy test. The hill areas inhabited by the minority races remained outside the constitution and continued to be indirectly administered through the local chiefs.

When the governor exercised functions 'in his discretion' his ministers were not entitled to place advice before him, provision being made for the appointment of official counsellors to advise him. When the governor exercised his 'individual judgement' his ministers were entitled to lay advice before him, but the governor was in specified circumstances required to disregard this. The more important areas in which the governor was required to act 'in his discretion' were foreign affairs, defence, monetary policy, currency, coinage, and the administration of the hill areas. He was required to 'exercise his individual judgement', not in respect of specific functions of government, but in respect of any acts which affected certain special responsibilities laid upon him. These were, broadly speaking, the preservation of peace and tranquillity; the safeguarding of financial stability and the credit of the government; the prevention of discrimination against minorities, public servants, or British subjects, or against goods of United Kingdom or Indian origin; and making sure that his discretionary functions were not prejudiced.

F. S. V. Donnison, *Public Administration in Burma* (London, 1953).

FSVD

GOVERNMENT OF INDIA ACT (1858) in Britain, passed on the assumption of direct government by the Crown after the Mutiny. Government by the Board of Control and the East India Co. came to an end, the board being replaced by a secretary of state for India, assisted by the Council of India. The act required statements of the moral and material progress of India, and of Indian revenue and expenditure, to be submitted annually to parliament. The secretary of state could over-rule his council in all matters except those that required expenditure from the Indian revenues. However, the secretary of state was a member of the cabinet, and it was never intended that the council should be able to resist the cabinet by stopping supplies. It was an advisory, not a controlling, body.

Under the act, the initiative in all important questions rested with the secretary of state. The government of India required sanction for its intended policies, though there were cases of de facto vice-regal supremacy and of friction. The intention of the framers of the act to provide a 'mixed government' of Indian affairs, shared between the Crown, parliament, and the Council of India, was not realized, and power was in fact concentrated in the hands of the secretary of state.

The assumption of direct government by the Crown was the occasion for a royal proclamation, intended to make the new constitution acceptable to the princes and peoples of India. The Crown promised that in future neither race nor religion should debar Indians from employment in the government of the country. The Indian princes were assured that treaties and engagements with them would be scrupulously maintained.

C. Ilbert, *The Government of India* (Oxford, 1907).
R. J. Moore, *Sir Charles Wood's Indian Policy, 1853–66* (Manchester, 1966).					CCD

GOVERNMENT OF INDIA ACT (1935), last major constitution fashioned by the British for India before independence. The act (4 Aug. 1935), the product of lengthy enquiries (1928–34), fell short of Indian demands, but was nevertheless strongly, though unsuccessfully, opposed by some Conservatives. It made some changes in the position of the secretary of state and his advisers in London, and it separated Burma from India. But its main concerns were (*a*) the formation of a federation of British Indian provinces and princely states, and (*b*) the provision of provincial autonomy in British India.

The act envisaged a bicameral federal legislature, with clearly demarcated lists of federal and provincial-state subjects. The states were to be given 40 per cent of the seats in the upper house (Council of State) and 33⅓ per cent of the seats in the Federal Assembly, the princes having the right to decide how the states' representatives should be selected. Only a few of the most important states were to be represented individually, the rest being grouped to provide representatives. The provisions for the federation were not to become effective until states containing half of the total states' population and representing a total of half of the states' seats had acceded to it. The British Indian provinces were to be represented in both houses in proportion to their population, in the Council of State by direct election and in the Federal Assembly by indirect election through the provincial legislatures. Muslims were to have one-third of the British Indian representation in both houses. The government of India was to be dyarchic in form—Defence, External Affairs, Tribal Areas, and Ecclesiastical Affairs being reserved for executive councillors appointed by the viceroy, all other matters being handled by a council of ministers chosen by the viceroy from among the elected members of the federal legislature. The viceroy would retain his reserve powers, even to the extent of over-ruling a minister. This federal section of the act never, in fact, came into force. By the outbreak of the Second World War insufficient princes had acceded and the scheme was suspended (18 Oct. 1939). The central government and legislature continued to be based on the provisions of the 1919 constitution until 1947. However, the new Federal Court, the Reserve Bank, and the Railway and Public Service authorities provided for in the act were all established.

On the provincial side, the act was fully implemented. Sind and Orissa were made into separate provinces, each having, like the other governors' provinces, a fully elected legislative assembly. The total provincial assembly electorate was about 35 million, as compared with about 7 million under the 1919 act. There was popular control of the provincial executive government by a ministry responsible to the majority party in the legislative assembly. Though the governor retained his reserve powers, effective control was passed to the ministry. Several provinces—Bombay, Bengal, Madras, the United Provinces, Bihar, and Assam—were also given small legislative councils, elected on a much higher franchise and containing some nominated and official members, to act as a second chamber.

Neither Congress nor the Muslim League found the federation proposals acceptable and Indian opinion generally saw the reservation of defence and external affairs as the means of depriving Indians of effective power at the centre. The Liberals wanted to give the act a trial, but Congress demanded the creation of a constituent assembly to frame a truly national constitution. Still, the first elections to the new provincial legislatures (Feb. 1937) were contested by the Congress, the Muslim League, and other parties, and popular ministries remained in office until the war.

M. Gwyer and A. Appadorai, *Speeches and documents on the Indian constitution 1921–47*, 2 vols (London and Bombay, 1957).
R. Coupland, *The Indian Problem, 1833–1935* (Oxford, 1942).					PDR

GOVERNMENT OF IRELAND ACT (1920) in Britain sought to solve the intractable problem of Ulster under Home Rule. Civil war in 1914 over the Ulster Protestants' refusal to accept the proposal to give Ireland Home Rule had been prevented only by the outbreak of the First World War. During the war, the situation worsened, because of the supersession of the Home Rulers by Sinn Fein, which demanded total independence; after the war, the Sinn Fein 'parliament' —Dail Eireann—was outlawed by the British in Sept. 1919, and the Black-and-Tan guerrilla war ensued. Thus the 1914 Home Rule Act could not be brought into operation, and another attempt was made to reconcile the interests of Sinn Fein and the Unionists. One result was the Government of Ireland Act (1920), which was the first formal acknowledgement by the British government of the existence of the Ulster problem. It proposed the election of parliaments for Southern and Northern Ireland, which was defined, 'for the purposes of this Act', as comprising the counties of Antrim, Armagh, Down, Fermanagh, Londonderry, and Tyrone, and the boroughs of Belfast and Londonderry. A Council of Ireland linking the two was to be formed 'with a view to the eventual establishment of a Parliament for the whole of Ireland'. The parliament of Southern Ireland never came into being, the elections being boycotted by Sinn Fein, so that the paradoxical result of the act was to set up the Northern Ireland parliament against the wishes of the Unionists, who desired integral union with Britain. The act remains the authority behind the present-day Northern Ireland parliament at Stormont. The boundaries of Northern Ireland, thus casually defined in 1920, have never since been changed, and so Northern Ireland in 1970 still incorporated a large Catholic minority in the western counties and in Belfast.					IM

GOVERNOR-GENERAL OF INDIA, statutory head of the government of India under British rule. The term was employed in acts of parliament and in acts of the Indian legislature, in the warrant of appointment of the governor-general and in the notification of the appointment in the *London Gazette*. The title of Viceroy and Governor-General was used in warrants of precedence and in the statutes of the knightly orders. It was only in so far as the governor-general was regarded as the representative of his sovereign that he was referred to as viceroy. A proposal was made at the Round Table Conference (1930–2) to sever the office of governor-general from that of viceroy, but the Joint Committee declined this proposal. The 1935 act simply enabled the offices to be held separately, and in practice they continued to be held together.

As a rule, only men with considerable experience of politics were appointed to the office. After Cornwallis, more than two-thirds of the governors-general were members of either the House of Commons or the House of Lords. Many were cabinet ministers or had held important offices at home or abroad. It seems to have been a well-recognized principle that no ex-viceroy should become a secretary of state for India. Neither was it considered advisable, except in the case of Ripon, that a secretary of state should proceed to India as viceroy. In the East India Co. periods, Minto and Ellenborough had also held the office of president of the board of control. This usually led to friction. Neither did the promotion of an Indian civil servant prove very successful. The appointment of a member of the royal family worked successfully in other parts of the British empire, but it did not occur in India until the end of British rule.

The Regulating Act of 1773 appointed Warren Hastings as the first governor-general and named four councillors who were to hold office for five years. Unfortunately Warren Hastings was hampered by a hostile majority on his council. In 1786 Cornwallis refused to proceed to India unless given the power to over-rule his council. By the act of 1833 the governor-general and council of Bengal became the governor-general and council of India. In 1853 a separate lieutenant-governor was appointed for Bengal. The title of Viceroy first occurs in Queen Victoria's proclamation of 1858, but it had no statutory sanction and owed its origin to usage and convention.

G. N. Curzon, *British Government in India*, 2 vols (London, 1925).
A. B. Rudra, *The Viceroy and Governor-General of India* (London, 1940).   CCD

GOWER, JOHN (d. 1408), English poet and author of the *Confessio Amantis* (1390), a collection of tales mostly illustrating the seven deadly sins. He also wrote important works in Latin and French. His *Vox Clamantis* reviews the abuses found at all levels of 14th-cent. society and begins with a vivid allegorical account of the Peasants' Revolt of 1381.

GOWRIE CONSPIRACY (1600), one of history's unsolved mysteries, allegedly an attempt by the Ruthvens, of the earldom of Gowrie, to murder James VI of Scotland at their castle in Perth. It ended in the massacre of the Ruthvens by the king's retainers, and it has been suggested that the matter was contrived by James himself to rid himself of a treacherous and insubordinate family. The 1st Earl of Gowrie had been executed (1584) after an earlier attempt to keep James in custody.

GRABSKI, WLADYSLAW (1874–1938), Polish politician and economist, who was a National Democratic Deputy in the first three Russian Dumas. After the outbreak of the First World War he became president of the Central Citizens' Committee, formed to aid the Russian war effort. In independent Poland he was minister of finance (Dec. 1919–Nov. 1920) and twice prime minister (June–July 1920; Dec. 1923–Nov. 1925). This last ministry was the longest, lasting between the achievement of independence and Pilsudski's coup in May 1926, and it did much to put the country's finances on a sound footing. After the coup Grabski withdrew from active politics.

GRAÇA, ARANHA, JOSÉ PEREIRA DE (1868–1931), Brazilian writer and intellectual, whose most famous work is the novel *Canaan* (1902), which compares European culture with that of his native land.

GRACCHUS, GAIUS SEMPRONIUS (d. 121 BC), Roman aristocratic revolutionary, and younger brother of Tiberius Gracchus, on whose land commission he served, and a thorough-going opponent of the Senate. As plebeian tribune in 123 he proposed an extensive series of measures, including the sale of corn at a subsidized price, the foundation of colonies, the transference of the court on provincial maladministration from the Senate to the commercial class, and the farming of the taxes of the province of Asia, aimed at securing the support of the common people and the wealthy non-senatorials against the Senate. After being re-elected tribune for 122, he went to Carthage early in the year to supervise the foundation of his colony of Junonia. In his absence he was outbid by his fellow tribune, M. Livius Drusus, and his proposal to enfranchise Rome's Italian allies lost him popular support and he failed to secure re-election for 121. His enemies began to repeal his legislation and a riot followed, in which Gracchus, M. Fulvius Flaccus, and 3000 supporters were killed by a force under the consul L. Opimius.

GRACCHUS, TIBERIUS SEMPRONIUS (1) (*fl.* 2nd cent. BC), Roman noble, prominent in war and politics, consul in 177 BC, father of the famous Gracchi brothers, Tiberius and Gaius. He was a skilful orator, and became ambassador for the Scipios in Macedon (190). As tribune he supported them against Cato (187). He showed unusual moderation in concluding the long war with the Celtiberians in Spain (179).

GRACCHUS, TIBERIUS SEMPRONIUS (2) (*c.* 163–133 BC), Roman aristocratic reformer, grandson, by his mother, of Scipio Africanus, whose tribunate (133) began the erosion of the Senate's authority. He proposed, with the support of a powerful noble faction, to reverse the drift of citizens to Rome by resuming public land held in excess of the legal limit and distributing it to the poor, but was violently opposed by the other senators. Defying tradition, he took the bill direct to the *concilium plebis* without the Senate's approval and after deposing his colleague Octavius, who tried to veto it, had it passed. He also proposed to distribute to the people the legacy of Attalus III of Pergamum. After taking the unprecedented step of standing for re-election to safeguard himself and his law, he was murdered by a senatorial mob.

GRACE, WILLIAM GILBERT (1848–1915), English physician and cricketer. In a long playing career he was mainly responsible for establishing cricket as a national game, attracting players, supporters, and press-coverage.

GRACES, THE (1627), concessions relating to land and religion offered by Lord Falkland to Irish Roman Catholic peers and bishops, *eg*, 60-year-old land titles were to be valid against Crown claims, and Catholics could practise at the bar on a simple oath of allegiance. In return, the recusants paid £120,000 over three years, but although Charles I promised that a parliament would be called to confirm the graces, they were never in fact legalized.

GRAFF, LAURENS DE (d. 1704), French corsair, who plundered English and Dutch slavers off Africa. Later he was enlisted by the French to attack the Spanish in the West Indies. He was so successful that the French, fearing diplomatic repercussions, bought him off and enlisted him (1684) as a naval officer. He served against the English and helped to found the colony of Louisiana.

GRAFTON, AUGUSTUS HENRY FITZROY, 3rd Duke of (1735–1811), British politician. He was secretary of state in Rockingham's ministry (1765–6) and his resignation ensured its fall. He then took office as first lord of the treasury (1766–1770) with his ally, the Earl of Chatham. After the latter's illness in 1767 the ministry bore Grafton's name. Although he supported Wilkes against Lord Bute (1763), he agreed to his expulsion from the House of Commons (1768) and subsequent elections and re-elections made the administration appear tyrannical and ridiculous. Although Grafton favoured moderation towards the American colonists, he antagonized them by allowing his ministers to impose duties on their imports. Attacked by Junius for his pleasure-seeking private life, and faced with Chatham's recovery and opposition (1769),

Grafton resigned. As lord privy seal (1771–5) he argued for reconciliation with the colonists and then resigned, resuming the same office under Rockingham (1782–3). Later, becoming a convert to Unitarianism, he wrote various religious works, and his memoirs.

GRAHAM, SIR JAMES ROBERT GEORGE (1792–1861), British Conservative politician, who was an effective administrator and close associate of Peel. He had been a Canningite in the 1820s, but joined Grey's ministry in 1830 as first lord of the admiralty. In this post he began a thorough reform of naval administration. He left the Whigs, with Stanley and others, on the question of Irish Church reform (1834), and returned to the Conservatives as Peel's home secretary (1841–6). He was responsible for public order during the Chartist disturbances. After the fall of the ministry he refused to enter Russell's government. He joined Aberdeen's coalition in 1852 as first lord of the admiralty, and retained his post for a short time under Palmerston, but resigned with Gladstone and Sidney Herbert (1855).

GRAHAM, PATRICK (d. 1478), archbishop, Bp of Brechin and then of St Andrews. The pope raised St Andrews into an archiepiscopal and metropolitan see for Scotland, Orkney and the Isles. Graham had secured this—and himself as first archbishop—without sufficient consultation with James III. Ultimately, Graham's enemies persuaded the king to have Graham deposed (1478).

GRAHAM, THOMAS (1805–69), British scientist, whose main work was concerned with the molecular diffusion of gases. His Law of Diffusion expresses the relationship between the rate of diffusion of a gas and its density. In 1854 he was appointed Master of the Mint.

GRAMONT, ANTOINE, Duc de (1604–78), French peer and diplomat of an ancient and illustrious family of Navarre, who served with distinction in the French army in the Thirty Years War, being made a marshal in 1641. He fought at the defence of Mantua (1630), in Germany (1635), Flanders and Alsace (1637–9), and Piedmont (1638–41). After being present at Philippsburg (1644) he was taken prisoner by the Imperialists at Nördlingen (1645) but was released and took part in the siege of Lérida (1647). Gramont was sent by Louis XIV as ambassador extraordinary to the Diet of Frankfurt (1657–8) and in 1660 to conclude the Spanish marriage treaty between Louis and Maria Theresa. He was created duke and peer of France (1663) and as late as 1667 accompanied Louis XIV on the military campaign in Flanders. His son, Antoine Charles (1645–1720), was appointed ambassador to Spain (1704).

GRAMONT, ANTOINE ALFRED AGENOR, Duc de (1819–1880), French diplomat, the son of an émigré, who was partly responsible for the outbreak of the Franco-Prussian War. He held no public office until Louis Napoleon came to power, when he served as envoy in Kassel (1851), Stuttgart (1852), and Turin (1853). He served as ambassador to Rome (1857) and Vienna (1861), and in 1870 was suggested by the empress to Ollivier as a possible minister of foreign affairs. He was responsible both for requiring William I to promise never to revive the Hohenzollern candidature in Spain and for advocating war against Prussia after the Ems telegram.

GRAMPOUND, Cornish borough, disfranchised for corruption by a bill of Lord John Russell's (1821). Its two seats were given to the largest English county, Yorkshire, which, like the smallest, had only two representatives in the House of Commons.

GRAMSCI, ANTONIO (1891–1937), Italian communist intellectual. Though a poor Sardinian, crippled from childhood, he won a scholarship to Turin University (1911), and there became involved in working-class politics, developed marxist theories, founded a journal, *Ordine Nuovo* (1919), whose offices became a rallying point for workers and intellectuals, and developed workshop committees. He helped to found the Communist Party (1921), became its secretary and a deputy in 1924, when he belatedly attempted to form a popular front against fascism. He was imprisoned (1926) and convicted (1928) for subversion of the state. He died a week after his release. His prison notebooks and letters, adapting marxist interpretations to all aspects of Italian history and culture, and advocating communism with a human face, have been widely influential in and out of the party, though embarrassing to 'hardliners'.

GRAN (Hungarian, Esztergom), fortress situated about 40 kms north-west of Budapest, on the right bank of the Danube. It was once the capital of the Arpád kings. Gran fell to the Ottoman Turks in 1543, becoming thereafter one of the main bulwarks of their domination in Hungary. The Christians took the fortress in 1595, lost it to the Turks in 1605, and reconquered it in 1683.

GRAN COLOMBIA, post-independence federation roughly comprising the present-day republics of Venezuela, Panama, Colombia, and Ecuador. The new state was set up by the Congress of Angostura (1819) before the end of the struggle for independence. Simón Bolívar became the first president, but was only partly successful in holding the federation together. The various regions disliked his centralizing tendencies, and the wartime leaders struggled for personal power. In 1830, with the secession of Venezuela and Ecuador, the federation collapsed.

Co-operation between Ecuador, Colombia, and Venezuela showed signs of reviving in 1970 and there was a significant attempt to combine the merchant fleets of these states under the name *Flota Gran Colombia*.

GRANADA, city of southern Spain. Under the Nasrids (1238–1492), it was the last Muslim state in Spain.

GRANADA, TREATY OF (1500), signed between Louis XII of France and Ferdinand of Aragon, by which they agreed to conquer and partition the kingdom of Naples. After the surrender of King Federigo III the co-signatories quarrelled and the French were ejected by the Spaniards from the northern half of Naples (1504).

GRAND ALLIANCE (1805) of Britain, Austria, Russia, and Prussia. It was the third coalition formed by the Younger Pitt as a means of attacking France by land and was swiftly ended by Napoleon's defeat of Austria and Russia at Ulm and Austerlitz (1805), which was followed by Prussia's repudiation of her allies.

GRAND ARMY OF THE REPUBLIC, US organization of veterans of the Union armies during the Civil War. Founded in 1866, it had over 400,000 members at its peak, and its last member died in 1956. In the later 19th cent. it was enormously powerful as a pressure group and propaganda organization, usually being closely allied with the Republican Party. It enjoyed great success in securing the passage of legislation, particularly pension bills, favouring its members.

GRAND CANAL OF CHINA. On two occasions a Chinese government has unified existing canals into a single system, to facilitate the transport of supplies from productive areas to the capital city. These projects were undertaken by (a) the Sui government, c. 600, to link the lower Yangtze area with Ch'ang-an; and (b) the Yüan government, c. 1300, to link the south with Peking. The second project involved highly skilled engineering work, so as to bring the canal directly across the Yellow river and to raise it over the hills of the Shantung peninsula. Maintenance of the systems has often been problematical.

GRAND CONSEIL, French royal court of the *ancien régime,* like its rival, the *parlement* of Paris, an off-shoot of the royal council. It was established in 1497 with vague and ill-defined competence. Its judgements were enforceable over the whole of France and it heard cases involving bishoprics and other ecclesiastical benefices, cases evoked from the *parlements* by the king, disputes between the *parlements* and the *présidiaux,* and cases forwarded to it by the *conseil des parties* (or royal supreme court of appeal). There was no further appeal from its decisions. From the reign of Louis XIV up till the Revolution it met twice a week, alternately at the Louvre and at Versailles.

'GRAND DESIGN', the, comprehensive scheme for the re-organization of the European states system into a federation with a common army directed against the infidel Turks, attributed by the Duke of Sully in his memoirs to Henry IV of France.

GRAND MAITRE, French royal official, head of the king's household, whose office survived to the Revolution (1789). His duties included the official declaration of the death of a monarch and of the succession of his heir.

GRAND NATIONAL CONSOLIDATED TRADE UNION (1834) in England, inspired by Robert Owen. It aimed at a co-operative organization of workers in their various crafts and industries to exchange products on the basis of labour value, and thereby control the nation's economy and exercise political power, from which the artisan and working classes had been excluded by the Reform Act of 1832. The union's half-million supporters held local and sectional strikes, which failed and resulted in the break-up of the GNCTU and the imposition of harsh penalties against the Tolpuddle martyrs and others.

GRAND PENSIONARY, chief legal officer of the states of Holland. The office assumed great importance during the periods in the 17th and 18th cents when the house of Orange was in political eclipse. Eminent incumbents included Jacob Cats (1577–1660), Johan de Witt (1625–72), and Anthony Heinsius (1641–1720).

GRAND PRÉ, MASSACRE OF (1747), ambush of British soldiers by French and Indians at the village of Grand Pré, NS.

GRAND REMONSTRANCE (1641), manifesto to the English nation by the opposition parliamentary leaders, which proved a turning point in the pre-Civil War constitutional struggle between Charles I and the Long Parliament. After a six-week recess parliament reassembled on 20 Oct. 1641 in an atmo-sphere of crisis over Charles's Scottish visit. On 1 Nov. news of the Irish rebellion reached London and the control of the forces which would have to be raised to suppress it became the leading political question. Charles had begun to gather a party in the Commons. It consisted of 'constitutional royalists', such as Edward Hyde, Lord Falkland, and John Culpeper, who were opposed to Pym's methods and aims. They supported the king in his intention to defend the Church of England. Pym and the opposition, conscious that the king was gaining ground, realized that they must appeal over his head to the people. It was decided to bring in the Grand Remonstrance, which had been in preparation in committee since Nov. 1640. It consisted largely of a history of the grievances of Charles I's reign and a list of the achieve-ments of the Long Parliament, and was cleverly designed to woo all MPs, scarcely any of whom could object to what had happened up to the summer of 1641. It also tried to smooth over the Church question by calling for a general synod of divines drawn from England and other Protestant countries in Europe. Though no reference was made to the control of the militia, another radical demand—that the king should employ only ministers approved by parliament, which could

also request their dismissal—was included. The 'constitu-tional royalists' strongly opposed the Remonstrance in one of the longest and fiercest debates in this parliament, and it finally passed by only 11 votes (159 to 148) on 22 Nov. Even more fiercely contested was a motion that the Remonstrance should be printed, and swords were drawn in the House. Bloodshed was only prevented by the calming influence of John Hampden.

The Remonstrance, together with a petition, was presented to the king on 1 Dec., and a little later achieved its real object as a manifesto by being circulated in print. On 23 Dec. Charles indignantly rejected the Remonstrance, but it had achieved one positive objective by helping to return a pro-opposition majority in the elections to the City of London's common council. The city from then on stood firmly behind Pym and his associates.

The Remonstrance was the major stimulus to a realignment of parties: the Court-and-Country split during the first year of the Long Parliament developed into the royalist and parliamentary split of the Civil War.

G. Davies, *The Early Stuarts* (London, 1937).
I. Roots, *The Great Rebellion* (London, 1966).   CJ

GRAND TOUR, THE, journey, often lasting several years, from Britain through continental Europe to the cities of Italy. It was undertaken mainly in the 17th and 18th cents to complete the education of gentlemen. As Dr Johnson remarked, 'the man who has not been to Italy is always conscious of an inferiority from his not having seen what it is expected a man should see'.

Interest in Italy as the home of Renaissance learning and culture, beginning with English humanists such as Colet and Tunstall, who visited Italian universities, grew rapidly in the 16th cent. Sir Philip Sidney's diplomatic training was based on a tour (1572–5) which included Poland, Hungary, France, Germany, the Low Countries, and Italy. By the 18th cent. British tourists' earlier mistrust of foreigners, and especi-ally of their Catholic religion, had given way to an avid and often indiscriminate emulation of continental manners, fashion, and artistic taste. With the proliferation of travellers' handbooks, such as *The Gentleman's Pocket Companion for Travelling in Foreign Parts* (1722), itineraries became stereotyped, Paris, Milan, Florence, Rome, and above all Venice, being the usual destinations. Although the ex-perience was probably wasted on youths too immature to appreciate it, despite the efforts of their companion-tutors, the Grand Tour became so popular that it necessarily brought to British life and culture a cosmopolitan influence: it was a culture restricted to the upper class of society, but one that shared common sources between one country and another.   HNBN

GRAND TRUNK ROAD runs for more than 1500 miles (2415 kms) from Calcutta to Peshawar. It was designed primarily as a military thoroughfare. It was begun by Ben-tinck in 1839, but little progress was made until the time of Dalhousie. By 1855 it had reached Karnal, 75 miles (120 kms) north of Delhi.

GRANDE MADEMOISELLE, LA, ANNE MARIE LOUISE D'ORLÉANS, Duchess of Montpensier (1627–93), daughter of Gaston d'Orléans, brother of Louis XIII of France, a princess of the blood and political enemy of Richelieu. Her theatrical command of anti-royalist troops in Orléans during the Fronde (1652) led to her disgrace and temporary banish-ment from court (1653). Although her name was variously linked with her cousins, Louis XIV and Monsieur, a Portu-guese Infante, and the Duke of Lorraine, her romantic attachment to a Gascon gentleman, later the Duke of Lauzun, surprised the French court in 1670. After their secret mar-riage in 1671 Lauzun was imprisoned for ten years (1671–81).

GRANDE PEUR (1789), the 'great fear' which swept through most of France in the last weeks of July, reducing large parts of the country to anarchy. The continuing food crisis and the excitement caused by the revolutionary events at Versailles led to universal rumours of a royalist and aristocratic plot to unleash bands of brigands on the respectable people of France. The townsmen and peasants were equally affected. In the towns weapons were seized, civic militias formed, and municipal governments taken over to protect the citizens. The equally frightened peasantry formed armed bands and attacked the local manor houses, using the opportunity to burn the records listing their feudal dues. The crumbling royal government made little attempt to suppress these rural jacqueries, and largely because of this anarchy in the countryside the Constituent Assembly abolished all feudal obligations on the night of 4 Aug.

GRANDEES, highest rank of the Spanish nobility. In the hierarchy fixed by Charles V in the 16th cent. the top échelon consisted of 25 *Grandes de España*, though the number had increased to 32 by 1600. They were privileged to be addressed by the king as *primos* or cousins.

GRANDFATHER CLAUSE in US, name given to provision in post-Civil War suffrage laws of several Southern US states, exempting from educational tests and property qualifications persons who had voted, or whose progenitors had voted, before 1867. Such provisions were declared unconstitutional by the US Supreme Court (1915) as violations of the purposes and intent of the 15th Amendment.

GRANDFONTAINE, HECTOR ANDIGNÉ DE (1627–96), French soldier and governor of Acadia (1670–3), who rebuilt the area after the British occupation (1654–70). He served in expeditions against the Dutch in the West Indies (1675–7).

GRANDI, DINO, Count (1895–), Italian fascist minister and diplomat, whose motion of no confidence in Mussolini, put to the Fascist Grand Council (24–25 July 1943), led to the king's dismissal of Mussolini. He was a founder of Unione Italiana di Lavoro (1914), the syndicalist and interventionist trade union organization, and made himself a political leader in Bologna and fascist squad leader. Though he preferred D'Annunzio to Mussolini, he helped plan the 'March on Rome'. As under-secretary (1925–9) and minister (1929–32) for foreign affairs, he gave Italian policy a moderate, diplomatic veneer, and his pro-western attitude was continued when he became ambassador in London. His direct negotiations with Chamberlain for a Mediterranean agreement precipitated Eden's resignation (1938). He opposed links with Germany and Italy's entry into the Second World War. In consequence he left Italy, living for a time in Brazil.

GRANDMASTER OF ARTILLERY, French title given to the head of the artillery, who was responsible for all appointments and promotions, for the three centuries from Louis XI's reign to 1755. In 1599 Sully was entrusted with this important post by Henry IV, and later it was held by Schomberg (1575–1632). Until the reforms of Le Tellier and Louvois the artillery was not part of the standing army, but was simply a body of civilian technicians hired by the grandmaster during wartime in the Crown's name. From Louis XIV's reign a regiment of artillery existed with the grandmaster as its colonel. In the 18th cent. the position declined in importance and on the death of the Prince of Dombes (1755) the post disappeared and the artillery came under the direct control of the French Crown.

GRANDS JOURS, French provincial assizes of an ad hoc nature, composed of magistrates of the *parlement* of Paris, which usually sat during the summer vacation to dispense royal justice in a period of lawlessness or rebellion, eg, at Troyes in Champagne during the Wars of Religion (1583) and at Clermont after the civil wars of the Fronde (1665).

GRANGE, THE (National Grange of the Patrons of Husbandry), an organization of US farmers founded (1867) by Oliver Hudson Kelley. Originally conceived as a social and educational association, the movement quickly became political. It was at its most powerful in the early 1870s, when it was influential in persuading IL, IA, WI, and MN to pass legislation regulating the rates charged by railroads and warehouse companies. It declined in size and importance after 1877 and reverted to its primary role as a farmers' social club, although it has never abandoned its activities as a lobby for the agricultural interests.

GRANGER LAWS in US, legislation enacted by the four mid-western states of IL, IA, WI, and MN (1869–74) in an attempt to regulate rates charged by railroads and warehouse companies. Maximum freight and passenger rates were established, but the laws were challenged in the state and federal courts. In a series of cases in the US Supreme Court, notably *Munn v. Illinois* and *Peik v. Chicago and North-western Railway* (1877), the right of states to pass such laws was upheld. In *Wabash, St Louis and Pacific Railroad v. Illinois* (1886), the court modified the earlier rulings and restricted state action to inter-state traffic.

GRANICUS, RIVER, BATTLE OF (334 BC), Alexander the Great's first victory in Asia, on the southern side of the Hellespont (Dardanelles) over the army of Persia's western satraps, attempting to stop the invasion. The battle, won by a bold frontal cavalry attack across the river, opened Asia Minor to conquest.

GRANT, CHARLES (1746–1823), Scottish colonial servant in the service of the East India Co. (1768–90), and supporter of Christian missionary enterprise. In 1781 he was appointed commercial resident at Malda, where he made a fortune. He is known for his tract 'Observations on the State of Society among the Asiatic Subjects of Great Britain, particularly with respect to Morals' (1792). He defended the company's monopoly of trade, favoured missionary enterprise, and was opposed to any extension of the British empire. It is difficult to reconcile his evangelical humanitarianism with his condemnation of Lord Hastings's extirpation of the Pindari pest. He was chairman of the court of directors (1805, 1809, 1815).

GRANT, SIR JOHN PETER (1807–93), British colonial administrator. He entered the Bengal civil service (1828) and rose to be lieutenant-governor of Bengal (1859–62). He was appointed governor of Jamaica (1866–74), assuming office soon after the assembly's surrender of the constitution consequent upon the Morant Bay uprising (1865) and the recall of Edward John Eyre. Grant thus had the responsibility of operating the new Crown Colony system. As in Bengal, he reorganized and improved the revenue and judicial, educational, and police administration. He also disestablished the Church of England in Jamaica, and moved the Jamaican capital to Kingston (1872).

GRANT, MADISON (1865–1937), US naturalist and lawyer, whose belief in Nordic superiority, expressed in *The Passing of the Great Race* (1916), led him to oppose further, largely Latin, immigration into the US. He became vice-president of the Immigration Restriction League (1922) and helped to frame the Johnson (Quota) Act (1924).

GRANT, ULYSSES SIMPSON (1822–85), Union general in the American Civil War and 18th president of the US (1869–77). He was a regular army officer who rose to prominence during the Civil War. In the western theatre, he won notable victories at Fort Henry and Fort Donelson (Feb. 1862), acquiring at the latter the nickname 'Unconditional Surrender Grant'. At Shiloh (April 1862), his leadership was less distinguished, though the likelihood of his defeat was eventually turned into victory. In July 1863 he captured the key position of Vicksburg on the Mississippi, after a campaign that was a model of resourcefulness, boldness, and persistence. After a further success at Chattanooga (Nov. 1863), Lincoln made him commander-in-chief of all the Union armies (1864), and his relentless pressure and sustained aggression in VA (1864–5) led ultimately to Robert E. Lee's surrender at Appomattox. He became a full general, the first since George Washington, in 1866. On being elected president (1868, 1872) as a Republican he accepted the radical reconstruction programme, but his administration ran into difficulties in the South, and was also confronted with serious economic problems following the panic of 1873. His presidency was marred by widespread corruption and numerous scandals involving his friends and members of the administration.

His *Personal Memoirs* (2 vols, 1885–6) have a spare, straightforward style and a lucidity and a modesty which have made them a military classic. Grant's career is marked by sharp contrasts between the personal problems of his early years, the political naïveté, bad judgement, and feeble leadership of his presidential years, and his superb record in the Civil War. His strategic insight, his determination, flexibility, and resourcefulness mark him as one of the great commanders of modern times.

Bruce Catton, *U. S. Grant and the American Military Tradition* (Boston, 1954).   PJP

GRANVELLE, ANTOINE PERRENOT, Lord of (1517–86), Imperial diplomat, adviser to Charles V and Philip II, and effective governor of the Netherlands (1559–64) under Margaret of Parma on the eve of the Dutch Revolt. Born in Besançon in Burgundian Franche-Comté, he began his career as secretary to Charles V in the Netherlands and was consecrated Bp of Arras in 1543. He helped to negotiate the marriage of Philip II of Spain to Mary Tudor (1554), and the peace of Cateau-Cambrésis (1558–9). In 1559 he was made president of the Netherlands' Council of State, becoming the chief instrument of Philip's policy. Under the ecclesiastical reform of the Netherlands, by which Philip II hoped to eliminate foreign authority and crush heresy, Granvelle profited greatly, becoming Abp of Mechlin and Primate of the Netherlands (1560). He later became a cardinal (1561). He was instrumental in defending the reorganization of the bishoprics and was the object of local discontent centred on the league of nobles under the Prince of Orange and the Count of Egmont. Under pressure from this group Philip eventually recalled Granvelle (1564).

He then served Philip in Italy and negotiated the Holy League (1571). He was viceroy of Naples (1571–5) before being moved to the embassy at Rome, where he acted as counsellor. In March 1579 Philip summoned him to Spain and made him president of the Council of Italy. His first task was to organize the subjection of the kingdom of Portugal, which he successfully accomplished. After 1584 Granvelle pressed Philip to take vigorous action against Henry III of France and Elizabeth I of England, but by this time the king had tired of him and Granvelle was excluded from the royal junta in the closing three years of his life.   MKS

GRANVILLE, JOHN CARTERET, 2nd Earl (1st creation) (1690–1763), English politician, who directed foreign policy during the early years of the War of the Austrian Succession. He succeeded his father as Baron Carteret at the age of five, took his seat in the Lords in 1711, and soon identified himself with the supporters of the Protestant Succession. As a protégé of Stanhope, he was appointed ambassador to Sweden (1719) and showed diplomatic skill by gaining access to the Baltic for British commerce and by contributing to the negotiations which ended the Great Northern War (1721). Shortly after his return to England, he became secretary of state for the southern department (1721), and following the deaths of Stanhope (1721) and of Sunderland (1722) tried to form a party of his own to oust his rivals, Walpole and Townshend. The struggle continued until April 1724, when Walpole arranged for Carteret's dismissal from the secretaryship and promoted him to the lord lieutenancy of Ireland, thereby

removing him from London. Hoping to regain preferment, Carteret retained the lieutenancy until 1730, when, realizing that Walpole would never employ him, he joined the opposition, becoming one of the government's most violent critics.

After Walpole's resignation he was appointed secretary of state for the northern department (1742) and for nearly three years followed an energetic foreign policy, recognizing France as Britain's real enemy and pursuing every means to isolate her. He renewed pressure on Maria Theresa to buy off Frederick of Prussia in return for a promise of British subsidies and troops, and achieved this objective by the treaty of Breslau (1742). He effected a policy of active intervention in the war by sending a British contingent to the Netherlands, and later he accompanied George II to the continent when the contingent joined the Hanoverians and Austrians in Germany. The king's victory at Dettingen (1743) seemed to vindicate Carteret's policy and he successfully negotiated the treaty of Worms (1743) between Maria Theresa and Charles Emmanuel of Savoy. However, he was ultimately thwarted by the ambitions of Frederick II, the lack of a great commander on the British side, and the jealousy of his cabinet colleagues, who resented his high-handedness. In Oct. 1744 Carteret succeeded to the title of Earl Granville upon the death of his mother, who had been created Countess Granville in her own right (1715). By this time his system of continental alliances had crumbled, and faced with the hostility of the Pelham–Hardwicke faction, he offered his resignation to George II (23 Nov. 1744).

Yet in 1746 he was again close to power when he encouraged George to refuse to let William Pitt join Pelham's administration. Shortly after, when the government resigned, he was appointed secretary of state for both departments (Feb. 1746), but his failure to form a new ministry with his friend Bath forced him to resign within two days and the subsequent return of the Pelhams ended his real influence. Though he accepted the lord presidency of the council (1751), which he held until his death, Carteret never again assumed the centre of the political stage.

N. W. B. Pemberton, *Carteret, the Brilliant Failure of the Eighteenth Century* (London, 1936).
B. Williams, *Carteret and Newcastle* (London, 1943).   AW

GRANVILLE, GEORGE LEVESON-GOWER, 5th Earl (2nd of 2nd creation) (1815–91), English Liberal politician, Gladstone's closest political confidant, and foreign secretary. Granville was Whig MP for Morpeth and Lichfield (1836–1846) until he succeeded to the peerage. After minor posts under Lord John Russell, including responsibility for the promotion of the Great Exhibition (1851), he succeeded Lord Palmerston briefly as foreign secretary (1851). He served Lord Aberdeen's coalition as president of the council (1852–4) and chancellor of the duchy of Lancaster (1854–5), then took office under Palmerston, again as president of the council (1855–65). He led the Liberal Party in the House of Lords for over 30 years (1855–91), with one short break (1865–8).

His high standing with Queen Victoria made him an invaluable ally and go-between for Gladstone, whom he served as colonial secretary (1868–70, 1886) and foreign secretary (1870–4, 1880–5). Lord Clarendon's death (July 1870) brought him suddenly to the foreign office to face the crisis of the Franco-Prussian War. In a rare disagreement with Gladstone, he successfully gained cabinet support to prevent the prime minister from protesting officially at the annexation of Alsace-Lorraine. As a convinced neutral he refused Huers's pleas for intervention on the French side and rejected Prussian representations against Britain supplying France with war stores. He countered the Russian cancellation of the Black Sea clauses of the treaty of Paris, opposing unilateral denunciation on the grounds that it would destroy the essence of all treaties between powers. He called the London Conference (1871) and secured the principle that any future denunciation of treaties would require the consent of all signatory powers, though he had to accept the unpalatable fact of Russian ships entering the Black Sea. He warmly supported the Alabama Arbitration with the US (1872). On Gladstone's first retirement Granville became official leader of the Liberal Party (1875). His criticisms of Disraeli's Near Eastern policy were much less vigorous than Gladstone's. His opposition to the Royal Titles Act upset the queen (1876), but she correctly invited him to form a government (1880). He had no hesitation in giving way to Gladstone, who emerged from retirement, but was much less active and successful at the foreign office (1880–5) when Bismarck was effectively the arbiter of European diplomacy. When the Liberals split over Home Rule, Granville was one of the few Whig lords to stand loyally by Gladstone and to rally the shattered remnants of the party in the period of recriminations that followed. As chancellor of the University of London (1856–91) he reversed his earlier decision against the admission of women to examinations and degrees and presided over the university's expansion.

Lacking Gladstone's moral driving force and intellectual power, Granville brought to the leadership of the Liberals great natural gifts of personality as a negotiator and intermediary between the queen and Gladstone, Gladstone and the Whig aristocracy. From the trust between two very dissimilar men sprang the harmony, such as it was, of the first two Liberal governments.

Edmond Fitzmaurice, *Life of Lord Granville, 1815–91* (London, 1905).
                                                    JRA

GRAPHÊ PARANOMON, legal procedure in democratic Athens from *c.* 460 BC, whereby a citizen who considered that a motion had been proposed or passed in the council (*boule*) or assembly (*ecclesia*) contravening constitutional law or procedure could accordingly bring a charge against the proposer. On a successful action, the proposal was withdrawn or its passage annulled, and the defendant was liable to severe penalty for one year from the proposal. The procedure was an invaluable constitutional safeguard, but was frequently abused in political warfare.

GRASLIN, JEAN LOUIS (1727–90), French economist, who investigated the problem of the incidence of taxation.

GRATIAN (*fl.* 12th cent.), author of the compilation known as the *Decretum*, the most important of the early collections on Roman canon law. Except that he was a Benedictine monk of the house of St Felix at Bologna, almost nothing is known about him.

GRATIANUS, FL. (*reg.* AD 375–83), Roman Emperor, son and successor of Valentinian I as western emperor. More distinguished for his piety and literary learning than for his generalship, Gratian took measures against heresy, and in 382, inspired by Ambrose of Milan, against Roman paganism. In 378, after the battle of Hadrianople, he summoned Theodosius I to become eastern emperor, but was himself overthrown by the usurper Maximus (383).

GRATTAN, HENRY (1746–1820), Irish lawyer and politician, who campaigned for legislative independence for Ireland. This was secured in the Declaratory Act (1782), with which he was moderately satisfied. He later opposed the Act of Union (1800). As an MP at Westminster he attacked parliamentary corruption, supported the government in the French Wars (1793–1815), and fought for Catholic emancipation.

GRATTAN'S PARLIAMENT refers to the period (1782–1800) when Ireland's parliament enjoyed legislative independence. The 'constitution of 1782', hailed by Irish patriots as a final settlement, eventually proved unequal to the strains imposed upon it, and was replaced (1801) by union with Britain.

In 1783 Irish demands for annual parliamentary sessions were granted. Although Pitt's 1785 free trade proposals were defeated, Ireland's economy improved slightly, if superficially. Foster's protectionist policies encouraged tillage and the export of grain. Ireland was admitted (1793) to the East India trade. On the religious question, Catholics shed certain social and professional disabilities (1792), and they were allowed to vote in parliamentary and municipal elections on equal terms with Protestants and to sit on juries (1793). But Grattan's efforts to secure Catholics' admission to parliament, and Flood's for parliamentary reform, failed. Administrative reforms (1794) encouraged patriots to demand further concessions, but jobbery still flourished. Lord Fitzwilliam (lord lieutenant, Dec. 1794–March 1795), by encouraging Catholics to expect early relief, precipitated a state of crisis and caused Ireland's more intransigent Protestants to consider union with Britain as a hedge against a 'Papist democracy'.

The 1782 settlement failed, partly because Ireland's parliament did not control the executive. Irish Whigs' Regency Bill manœuvres (they hoped a Foxite lord lieutenant would instal them in office) showed their realization of these constitutional limitations. Moreover, a Protestant, landowning parliament was unlikely to resolve Ireland's chronic, fundamental problem of agrarian poverty, or to end its own order's political and religious privileges.

Pitt's attempt to prod Ireland's government into cautious reform foundered after 1789. Wolfe Tone's United Irishmen began (1791) in Belfast and Dublin as a radical movement for religious equality and political reform, but after 1795 aimed to set up an Irish republic with French help. The events of 1796–8, threatening Ireland with French invasion and revolutionary, sectarian and agrarian conflicts, drove many propertied Irishmen to side with conservative extremists like Clare. While moderates like Grattan and Foster resisted union, others, including Castlereagh, agreed with Pitt and the lord lieutenant Cornwallis, that union linked with Catholic emancipation and free trade would both ensure Britain's safety and conciliate Ireland's Catholics and commercial classes. Castlereagh, as chief secretary (1799), undertook the lavish deployment of cash and argument needed to steer through the Act of Union which ended Grattan's parliament.

J. C. Beckett, *The Making of Modern Ireland, 1603–1923* (London, 1966).
                                                    MRB

GRAU SAN MARTÍN, RAMÓN (1889–1969), Cuban physician and president who became provisional president (1933) after the overthrow of the dictator, Gerardo Machado. Fulgencio Batista ousted him the following year, but he won the presidential elections of 1944 as leader of the 'Authentics'. His administration was noted for its corruption, although some claimed that Grau San Martín himself was not involved in it.

GRAVELINES, BATTLE OF (1588), decisive defeat of the Spanish Armada by the English fleet, east of Calais. Fireships had broken the formation of the Armada on the night of 28–29 July, off Calais, and for the first time it was possible to bring English guns close enough to damage Spanish hulls. Although the Armada re-formed afterwards, it had lost four important vessels and had been prevented from taking on supplies from Parma.

GRAVELOTTE, BATTLE OF (1870), in the Franco-Prussian War, led the French marshal, Bazaine, to withdraw to Metz. Marshal MacMahon, coming to relieve him with 82,000 men, was defeated at Sedan. Bazaine had to surrender two months later. At Gravelotte German losses were 12,000; those of the French 2100.

GRAVINA, GIOVANNI VINCENZO (1664–1718), Neopolitan scholar and natural law jurist, who published *Origines Juris Civilis* (1701–13) and was a precursor of the ideas of Giambattista Vico.

GRAVITATION, LAW OF, springing from the ideas of Kepler and advanced by the studies of Borelli and Hooke, was first calculated by Isaac Newton in 1666 and fully expounded mathematically in his *Philosophiae Naturalis Principia Mathematica.*

GRAY, ASA (1810–88), US botanist. He was professor of natural history at Harvard (1842–88) and author of more than 350 books and papers, including the *Manual of the Botany of the Northern United States* (1848) and *Synoptical Flora of North America* (1878–84). His many textbooks, such as *How Plants Behave* (1872) and *Elements of Botany* (1836, 1887), did much to popularize the subject. A leading advocate in the US of Darwin's evolutionary theories, he was at the same time an independent theorist whom Darwin appreciated as one of his most perceptive critics.

GRAY, THOMAS (1716–71), English poet, author of 'Elegy Written in a Country Churchyard' (1750). He was the friend of Horace Walpole and the Duke of Grafton, by whose influence he became the first professor of modern history at Cambridge University (1768).

GREAT AMERICAN DESERT, early 19th-cent. designation of the Great Plains of the US, east of the Rocky Mountains. The term was first used by Zebulon Pike (1810), who believed that the semi-arid grasslands were uninhabitable by sedentary farmers. This belief, confirmed by Stephen Long (1823) and other travellers, delayed settlement of the region until the 'myth' was finally disproved by technological developments later in the century.

GREAT AND LITTLE BELTS, channels which separate Zealand from Fünen and Fünen from Denmark's mainland province of Jutland. Their existence protected Copenhagen against armies advancing from the continent, and encouraged the growth of Danish naval power.

GREAT AWAKENING, religious revival which swept the American colonies during the 1730s and 1740s. Jonathan Edwards, of New England, and George Whitefield, of England, were outstanding preachers associated with this spontaneous movement. They preached the necessity of salvation by conversion rather than good works, basing their message on the depravity of all mankind. Although causing a split among Congregationalists and multiplying denominations, the Great Awakening made for more democratic control of the churches and aided in the establishment of numerous schools and colleges.

GREAT COALITION in Canada. Coalition of conservatives formed in 1864 and led by John Macdonald and George-Étienne Cartier, who guided Canada to confederation in 1867.

GREAT CONTRACT, THE, in England, measure of financial reform proposed in 1610, by which parliament should vote James I and his successors an annual sum of £200,000 as compensation for renouncing the royal right to levy feudal exactions, including purveyance. The protracted negotiations eventually broke down owing to religious disputes over the parliamentary petition of July 1610. Feudal dues remained until they were abolished by a parliamentary ordinance of 1643 and by a confirmatory statute at the Restoration (1660).

GREAT DEPRESSION, phrase attached by some economic historians to the period 1873–96, in the western world, though even at the time businessmen were aware that it was an incorrect description. It was in general a time of falling prices, and for business in some countries, notably Britain, of reduced profits. It also saw an adjustment, sometimes painful, of European agriculture to competition from the New World. But there is little evidence in any statistical series that it was a period marked out from others for the world as a whole. German and American industry tended to be depressed in the 1870s, and French between 1880 and 1896, but none of these suffered right through. On the other hand, from 1870 onwards, or perhaps earlier, there was a marked decline in the rate of British economic growth. Since Britain was still pre-eminent in world trade, and the growth rate of other countries was not accelerating, there is reason to see a decline in the growth of demand in the world.

The fall of prices has been considered by some writers as a continuation of a general 19th-cent. trend, but the evidence for this is not decisive. However, it was sharp enough in this period for it to be a prosperous period for the working class in Britain. Money wages did not change much in any one occupation, but they were worth much more and there was also a change to better-paid occupations. There seems to have been more unemployment during these years than during the 20 years on either side, but not enough to prevent this being a time of relatively high standards of living. It was also one of heavy investment in social provision. Contemporary complaints of agricultural depression were overdrawn, for though cereal farming suffered, livestock farming did well.

The fall of prices seems to have been the result of the interaction of several factors, which included the increase in the world's supply of gold, the failure of the economy to work at full stretch, and the ending of inflationary expenditure in the European wars of the previous decades. It discouraged businessmen, and by keeping them short of the profits that they used for reinvestment was probably of long-term significance in Britain. The special problems of re-equipping well-established industries, the lack of technical and scientific education, the tendency of new capital to go either abroad or into social development combined in an atmosphere of discouragement to prevent new investment. The result was that the lessened rate of economic growth was perpetuated. The terms of trade show that Britain's exports were sustaining their prices better than those of other countries, a significant indicator of her relative decline in competitiveness. If the word 'depression' is removed from this period as inaccurate, it should be remembered that the years after 1870 saw a change of long-term importance in the disappearance of Britain's industrial lead over other countries.

S. B. Saul, *The Myth of the Great Depression* (London, 1969).
David S. Landes, *The Unbound Prometheus* (Cambridge, 1970).   RMM

GREAT DEPRESSION IN US, name commonly given to the economic collapse in 1929 and the consequent economic and social tensions of the 1930s. With the collapse of prices on the New York stock exchange (1929) the long period of general prosperity since the middle 1890s came to an abrupt end. There had been warnings of serious weaknesses in the economy before the market collapse destroyed business and investors' confidence. The international economic system had not properly recovered from problems arising from the First World War, American farmers were relatively impoverished throughout the 1920s, labour productivity was outpacing wages, the US tax system aggravated the maldistribution of income, and Republican philosophy throughout the decade inhibited the use of federal restraints on business and financial institutions. Business investment was declining well before the speculative boom on the exchange broke (Sept.–Oct. 1929). On 'Black Thursday'—24 Oct. 1929—almost 13 million shares were traded in a rapidly declining market, and a peak of nearly 16,500,000 was reached on 29 Oct. All economic indices started on a downward spiral, over 3000 banks collapsed during 1929–31, and in 1932–3 unemployment reached between 12 and 14 million. Ramifications of the Depression in the US affected most countries in the world and contributed to global economic disturbances. President Hoover, although committed to traditional beliefs of individualism and self-help, moved in the direction of federal controls and assistance, but not until the launching of the New Deal by his successor, F. D. Roosevelt, did the government attempt to mobilize resources in a concerted attack on the Depression. A considerable measure of economic and social recovery occurred during the 1930s, but widely diffused prosperity did not return until after the outbreak of the Second World War.

GREAT EAST ASIA CO-PROSPERITY SPHERE, concept widely propagated by Japan after 1941, presenting her as the liberator of east and south-east Asia from colonial control. It had some genuine roots in earlier Japanese pan-Asianism and was highly effective as a home-front slogan, but in practice it cloaked Japan's exploitation of the raw materials of territories occupied by Japanese armies. Only in 1943 were the political implications of the concept taken more seriously. Then, with defeat approaching, independence was granted to Burma and the Philippines, and at a large-scale conference in Tokyo (Nov. 1943) a Joint Declaration of the East Asiatic Nations (Pacific Charter), couched in idealistic language, was issued. In the following year independence was promised to Indonesia. Though much of this was superficial, Japanese propaganda and the break in colonial rule contributed a good deal to independence aspirations after the Second World War.

GREAT EXHIBITION OF THE WORKS OF INDUSTRY OF ALL NATIONS, in England, the first international exhibition (1851), held in Hyde Park, London. The exhibition epitomized the mid-Victorian triumph of free trade, self-help, internationalism, and the belief in progress. It grew out of a plan of the Royal Society of Arts for an international exhibition in 1851. The society had held national exhibitions annually from 1847, promoted by Albert, Prince Consort (president from 1843) and Sir Henry Cole (a member of the society from 1846). A Royal Commission was established (Jan. 1850), with Albert as chairman and Cole as a member of its executive committee, and together they worked indefatigably. At first there was a good deal of opposition, both in parliament and in the press, but in the winter of 1850 enthusiasm mounted, *The Times* changed its attitude from one of criticism to one of support, and thousands of working men throughout the country formed clubs for the purpose of visiting the exhibition, which attracted more than 6 million visitors. It was housed in a building christened by *Punch* the 'Crystal Palace' and designed by Joseph Paxton, who imaginatively exploited the architectural possibilities of glass and cast-iron construction. It was taken down in the summer of 1852, rebuilt at Sydenham, and destroyed by fire in 1936.

In 1852 the commissioners were appointed as a permanent body to use the surplus funds of the exhibition for the promotion of science and art, and their application to industry. On land which they bought in South Kensington there now stands a group of museums and colleges (including the Victoria and Albert Museum and Imperial College), all of which in some way—often by the gift of land—were helped by the commissioners.

GREAT HARRY, THE, popular name for *Henry Grâce à Dieu,* the first double-decked warship in the English navy. She was a three-master of about 1000 tons, carrying 72 guns and a crew of 700. Built in 1512 and named after Henry VIII, she was rebuilt in 1536, and was accidentally burned at Woolwich in 1553.

GREAT LEAP FORWARD (started 1958), massive political upheaval designed to bring China up to the level of advanced countries. The Leap, like the Cultural Revolution, owed much of its inspiration to Mao Tse-tung's revolutionary romanticism. Mao believed that economic and political miracles could be achieved by mobilizing the latent talents of the Chinese people. The Leap was launched as a war against backwardness and ignorance. Old customs were swept away; the commune system of agricultural organization was introduced in a matter of weeks, with the intention of improving farming techniques and tightening rural organization. At the same time, economic diversification was stressed, and production of steel and pig-iron in 'back-yard furnaces' was promoted. The mass mobilization Mao had

envisaged was achieved, but at a cost in disruption which had not been foreseen. There was considerable opposition from the established bureaucracy and from 'pragmatic' sections of the party. Eventually the Leap was toned down and China's disturbed economy allowed to readjust itself by a return to more conventional policies. Several years of acute shortages in the early 1960s were blamed in part on the excesses of the Leap.

GREAT MIGRATION (1629–40), movement of approximately 60,000 people from England to the New World. During the later years of the reign of King Charles I the demands of the Church of England, under Abp Laud, to conform led many Puritans, for religious and political reasons, to leave England. Several companies, among them the Massachusetts Bay Co., were organized by Puritans for the purposes of migration. Although Puritan discontent was the basic cause, depression in agriculture and the cloth trade caused many non-Puritans to join the migration. After the assembly of the Long Parliament (1640) the migration from England slowed down considerably.

GREAT NORTHERN WAR, THE (1700–21), precipitated the decline of Sweden and assisted the rise of Russia. In its first phase Denmark, Saxony–Poland, and Russia were incited by the Livonian patriot, Patkul, to attack Charles XII of Sweden, who replied by landing near Copenhagen with British and Dutch naval support and driving the Danes out of the war (treaty of Travendal). He completed the turning of the tables by a crushing defeat of the Russians at Narva in Ingria (Nov. 1700), and the next year expelled the Saxons from Livonia and occupied Courland. In 1702 Charles moved into Poland, seized Warsaw, and won a great victory at Kliszow, but it took him four years to complete the conquest and force the Elector of Saxony to vacate the throne for his nominee, Stanislaus Lesczynski (peace of Altranstädt). Charles's stay in Saxony (1706–7) marked the zenith of his power, when he was courted by both sides in the Spanish Succession war.

The second phase of the war opened in the autumn of 1707, when Charles decided to ignore the plight of his Baltic possessions, overrun by the Russians while he campaigned in Poland, and march on Moscow. In the following July he won his last major victory, at Holowczyn, but the Russian 'scorched earth' policy and the delay in the arrival of reinforcements and supplies from Livonia persuaded him to turn south at the then Russo-Polish frontier, to link up with the rebel Cossack, Mazeppa, and tap the food resources of the Ukraine. Few Cossacks joined him, only half the reinforcements got through from Livonia, and an exceptionally severe winter played havoc with Charles's army. In June 1709 the remaining 25,000 Swedes were overwhelmed by twice their number of Russians, with a great superiority of artillery at Poltava, from which Charles (put out of action by a wound before the battle) escaped to Turkey.

Charles XII stayed in Turkey for five years. In 1711 he induced the Turks to take up arms, but Peter quickly met their demands at the peace of the Pruth. The Russians consolidated their position in the Baltic provinces and overran Finland. The situation in Poland was reversed. The Danes re-entered the war, and although defeated in Scania, occupied Bremen and Verden and the Holstein-Gottorp territories.

The last phase of the long conflict began with Charles's return to the north in Nov. 1714. He failed to save Stralsund, whence he crossed the Baltic the following winter to Sweden. Prussia and Hanover had now joined his enemies, but Charles had hopes of breaking the ring. He raised new armies, with which he might have regained lost ground, and was negotiating with Russia when he fell at Frederiksten. Sweden then tried to make peace with her other enemies at Russia's expense (treaties of Stockholm and Frederiksborg), but received no effective help, which forced her to accept the treaty of Nystad (Aug. 1721). By the cession of Livonia,

Estonia, Ingria, and part of Finland she acknowledged her displacement as a great power.

R. M. Hatton, *Charles XII of Sweden* (London, 1968).
F. S. Bengtsson, *The Life of Charles XII* (abbr. English trans., London, 1960).   TKD

GREAT REVIVAL (1797–1805), revival movement in the western part of the US. A movement of religious renewal, influenced by Anabaptist theology and based on a strongly emotional appeal typified by large camp meetings often ending in near hysteria. James McGready, a Presbyterian minister, was the leading light of this upsurge, which began in KY and swept the West, but Methodist and Baptist ministers played important roles as well. The Great Revival accelerated the tendency in American Protestantism towards an optimistic and simplified theology, the employment of itinerate ministers, and the use of the revival as a basic method of religious propaganda.

GREAT TREK. In 1836–7 Boer farmers reacted against British policies towards Africans beyond the frontier, and towards non-whites in the colony, by trekking to the lands beyond the Cape. Led by Retief, Uys, Pretorius, and others, the 'Voortrekkers' rapidly gave the map of South Africa its modern appearance. The Great Trek ensured that most of the interior would be in Afrikaner hands. British attempts to control the trekkers exacerbated feelings between the two white groups, and culminated in the Boer war; but even defeat could not reverse the dominant racial position won for their people by the 'Voortrekkers'.

GREAT WALL OF CHINA, general term applied to a number of unified defence lines built by the Chinese in an east-to-west direction, and stretching from the Yellow Sea to Kansu province or beyond. Before the imperial period the Chinese kingdoms put up earthworks as defence lines against each other. After the unification of 221 BC the newly created Ch'in empire had these lines unified as a single system and maintained with static garrison forces. In the Han period the walls were extended to the west and acted not only as a defence against the Hsiung-nu, but also as a means of preventing the escape of deserters from China and as a safe means of conduct for Chinese envoys and trading caravans. In times of dynastic weakness or take-over by alien dynasties the walls fell into disrepair, and the most successful attempts to rebuild them were those of the T'ang and Ming governments. The situation of the walls, their size, and the material of which they were constructed have been subject to variation.

GREATER LEBANON. The realization, after 1861, that Mount Lebanon alone could not form a viable state led to the advocacy by certain Maronites of its enlargement by the inclusion of the predominantly Muslim areas of the Biqa and the coastal plain to form a Greater Lebanon. After the First World War Maronites pressed for the creation of such a state under French mandate, and (31 Aug. 1920) it was formally proclaimed and, despite early Muslim opposition, developed into the Lebanese republic (1926) which achieved independence in 1943).

GRECHKO, ANDREI ANTONOVICH (1903–   ), Russian soldier and politician, who joined the Red army in 1919 and the Communist Party in 1928. He served in the Finnish War, and rose from the post of divisional commander to that of army commander (1945) on the southern front. As a supporter of Khrushchev and an advocate of Soviet conventional military superiority over the West, he was well fitted to command the Russian troops in Germany (1953–7) and crushed the East German revolt of 1953. He became commander-in-chief of the Soviet Land Forces (1957–60), but survived Khrushchev's fall and remained in command of the Warsaw pact forces (1960–7). He took a prominent part in the coercion of Czechoslovakia (1968–9) and remained, in 1970, defence minister for the Soviet.

GRECO-TURKISH WAR (1897), caused by one of the many Cretan insurrections against Turkish rule. On the occasion of this revolt, the Greek prime minister, Delyannis, sent an expeditionary force to help the insurgents and ordered general mobilization against the Turks. The Turkish army defeated the Greeks within a month, and Greece had to cede some territory and pay an indemnity. Under pressure from the great powers, Crete became autonomous under Turkish suzerainty. Crete was joined to Greece in 1912.

GREECE, *COUP D'ÉTAT* IN (1967). Army units, headed by Brig. Stylianos Pattakos and Col. George Papadopoulos, seized power in Athens on 21 April. The coup arose out of King Constantine's dismissal of George Papandhreou's government over the question of military appointments in May 1965. Stephen Stephanopoulos deserted Papandhreou's Centre Union to form a cabinet which, despite a lingering crisis over Cyprus and a succession of strikes, ruled for nearly 18 months, primarily because of widespread reluctance to face another general election. The Stephanopoulos government fell in Dec. 1966 and was succeeded by a service government charged with holding elections in May 1967. The *Aspida* affair (1967) deeply embittered relations between Papandhreou's Centre Union and the National Radical Union of Panayiotis Kanellopoulos. When the service government was compelled to resign because of the deadlock between the principal parties, Constantine passed over Papandhreou and called Kanellopoulos to office. The election campaign was marked by violence in Athens and Salonika and Centre Union plans for a mass rally at Salonika encouraged the army to act. Apart from their ostensible motive of preserving public order, the officers were above all concerned to deny Papandhreou power. Soon after the coup an authoritarian regime was established which suppressed further political activity.

GREEK FIRE, major weapon used by the Byzantine navy, consisting basically of highly combustible chemical substances. Greek fire, which seems to have been of different kinds, was used chiefly with ballistic weapons such as hand-grenades, which were thrown from the deck of one ship against the sides or over the bulwarks of another at close quarters, and in containers hurled through the air by catapult. Greek fire ignited on impact and could wreak great havoc among the timbers of crowded galleys whose interiors were open to the wind. The Byzantines tried to maintain the secret of its manufacture, but from time to time stocks of material fell into enemy hands. The Arabs appear to have used Greek fire around the 11th cent. Its use made Byzantium formidable at sea and in close inshore bombardments for some centuries after AD 650. Finally it was superseded by gunpowder.

GREEK WAR OF INDEPENDENCE, revolt against Ottoman authority beginning in the Morea (1821) and spreading to other Greek islands. Unable to suppress the rising, despite the assistance of Greek rebel divisions, the Ottoman government requested Muhammad Ali of Egypt to send troops to the Morea (1824). Russia threatened to help the Greeks and, in an effort to prevent war, Canning allied Britain with Russia. After being joined by France (1827) the powers sought to blockade Ottoman forces in the Morea. At Navarino (20 Oct.) the Ottoman and Egyptian fleets were annihilated, and Ottoman impotence completed by the Russo-Turkish war (1828–9). Greece became autonomous (protocol to treaty of Adrianople, 1829) and, after the murder of President Capodistras (1831), an enlarged independent Greek kingdom was established (1832) under Otto of Bavaria.

GREELEY, HORACE (1811–72), US newspaper editor, reformer, and presidential candidate. He established the *New York Tribune* (1841), made it the most influential and widely circulated newspaper in the northern states and espoused many reformist causes, including anti-slavery, women's rights, temperance, the homestead law, and the Fourier brand of utopian socialism. Greeley was a founder of the Republican Party in the 1850s and pursued an erratic but generally Radical course during the Civil War. He was a severe critic of the corrupt politics of the 'Gilded Age' and he became the presidential candidate of the Liberal Republicans, and also, ironically, of the Democrats (1872), but lost heavily to Ulysses S. Grant. His writings include an autobiography, *Recollections of a Busy Life* (1868), and *An Overland Journey from New York to San Francisco* (1860), but he is now most widely remembered as the author of the admonition 'Go west, young man'.

GREEN, THOMAS HILL (1836–82), English philosopher, who fostered the 'positive' concept of liberty within the mid-Victorian Liberal Party. His *Liberal Legislation and Freedom of Contract* (1881) advocated state intervention in education, factory hours, landownership, and drinking habits. His philosophy had great practical implications, for it denied the existence of any antithesis between the Church and the world, stressed the moral life at the expense of specific theological belief, and greatly attracted mid-Victorian evangelicals, whose religious faith was crumbling. His social outlook was moulded by the puritan ideals of the 17th cent. He made no critique of capitalism, but he believed that reform could be secured by mobilizing essentially religious emotions in the governing classes, rather than by stirring up proletarian anger. He therefore helped to inspire the settlement movement in the East End of London, and himself participated in local government.

GREEN, WILLIAM (1873–1952), US politician and labour leader, who started work in the OH coal mines at the age of 16, and two years later became secretary of the Progressive Miners Union. He held various offices in the OH sub-district of the United Mine Workers and served as a Democratic senator in the OH state legislature (1911–15). He became a vice-president of the American Federation of Labor (1913–1924), and then president (1924–52). Green was cautious in organization and strongly favoured craft unionism, which led to a bitter dispute with John L. Lewis when the CIO was formed. He was instrumental in expelling the rebels from the AFL, but became reconciled with Lewis and worked hard for reunification of the two organizations.

GREEN RIBBON CLUB, most famous club in Restoration London frequented by the supporters of Lord Shaftesbury at the time of the Exclusion controversy in the 17th cent.

GREENBACK MOVEMENT, US group in the 1870s that demanded that the 'fiat paper' issued to finance the Civil War, and popularly known as 'greenbacks', be given complete legal tender status and be issued freely. This inflationary demand received its strongest support from debtor farmers and working men in the Mid-west. Farmers and some elements of labour, disappointed in the Grange's currency policies, combined to form an Independent National Party (1874), commonly referred to as the Greenback Party. Calling for the repeal of the Resumption Act (1875) and the enactment of greenback plans for a national currency, the party received only 81,000 votes in 1876. Two years later, however (1878), a new Greenback Labor Party polled over 1 million votes and elected 14 congressmen. This year saw the peak of the political phase of the Greenback movement, and though it continued to 1888 it had little success. The movement is important as the first agrarian attempt to act politically on a national scale and because the key inflationary demand was later taken over by the Populists in the form of 'free silver'.

GREENE, NATHANAEL (1742–86), American general during the War of Independence, who fought throughout the campaigns of 1776–7, and wintered with his troops at Valley Forge (1777–8). As quartermaster-general (1778) he established an efficient supply system that helped the army to survive the winters of 1778–9 and 1779–80. After attacks on

his integrity from within Congress (1780) he resigned and returned to field command. On succeeding Gen. Horatio Gates in command of the Southern department (1780), Greene adopted a highly successful mobile strategy that led to the capture of all British posts in the South, including Charleston, by Dec. 1782.

GREENLAND, discovered in 982 by Eric the Red, who led settlers there from Iceland and named the island. The southwest coast eventually sustained a population of some 3000 fishermen and dairy-farmers, with their own bishop (1112) and independent republic. In 1261 the sovereignty of Norway, to which the diocese was attached, was accepted in order to secure a regular trade connection. But when the Norwegian state declined, its ships ceased to visit Greenland, the latest known voyage being in 1410. The extinction of the colony may also have been hastened by a worsening of the climate, the effects of inbreeding, and the pressure of the Eskimos moving south.

Frobisher landed on the west coast (1578), Hudson sighted the uninhabited east coast (1607), and 17th-cent. Dutch whalers traded occasionally with the Eskimos. Colonization was restarted in 1721 by a clergyman from northern Norway, Hans Egede, who, finding the original colonists to be extinct, began the conversion of the Eskimos and developed trade with Bergen and Copenhagen under the direction of the Dano-Norwegian monarchy. In 1776 the Royal Greenland Trading Co. was set up, which had exclusive powers of government until 1908 and a commercial monopoly until 1951. The 'Greenlander' or Eskimo–Danish population, which numbered 6000 at the first census (1805), grew very slowly, and the east coast was seldom visited except by explorers, such as Nansen, who made the first crossing of the inland ice (1888).

The status of Greenland was clarified in 1933, when the International Court endorsed Denmark's claim to the sovereignty of the entire island, which had been challenged by the settlement of Norwegian hunters on the uncolonized east coast. But although the development of cryolite mining and cod fisheries had made the country less poor, it first became of international importance in the Second World War, when a temporary American protectorate was established (1941). The Germans were expelled from secret meteorological stations, and the first air-strip was constructed at the modern air base of Thule. In 1953 the island was constituted an integral part of the Danish kingdom, with parliamentary representatives and wide powers of local self-government, but its defence continued to rest upon an American–Danish agreement made within the framework of NATO.

K. Bure (ed.), *Greenland* (English trans., 3rd edn, Copenhagen, 1961).
V. Stefansson, *Greenland* (New York, 1942).   TKD

GREENLAND FISHERIES, whale fisheries, sustained by a bounty. The purpose of the bounty was partly to offset competition with the Dutch for oil for soap-boiling and for whalebone, partly the desire to train seamen. The fisheries did well in time of peace and were the special concern of east-coast ports, particularly, in the early 19th cent., those of Scotland.

GREENOUGH, HORATIO (1805–52), US sculptor. His neoclassical marble statue of George Washington, commissioned for the rotunda of the US Capitol (1833), aroused public derision, but, as the first professional American sculptor, he exerted considerable influence. He expounded his theories of art in *Aesthetics in Washington* (1851).

GREENSHIELDS CASE (1711) in Britain, asserted the jurisdiction of the House of Lords as the final appeal court for the whole of the British Isles. Greenshields appealed to the Lords after his conviction by Scottish magistrates. The Scots were outraged to find that the Lords' jurisdiction had been implicitly conceded by the treaty of Union (1707). Anger increased when the Lords reversed the Greenshields decision.

GREENVILLE, TREATY OF (1795), agreement between the US and 12 Indian tribes on the north-west frontier following the victories of the US general, Anthony Wayne. It established a line of demarcation between Indian lands and areas open to white colonization that encouraged the frontier of settlement to move into western OH and southern IN, effectively removed British influence east of the Wabash, and reduced the incidence of Indian attacks.

GREENWICH OBSERVATORY, London, founded in 1675 for the purpose of improving navigation. The building was designed by Sir Christopher Wren, who had been professor of astronomy at Oxford. The prime meridian mark, from which all countries have reckoned longitude since 1884, runs through the observatory. In 1948 all its astronomical work was transferred to Herstmonceux in Sussex and the observatory was renamed Flamsteed House after the first astronomer royal, Sir John Flamsteed (1646–1719).

GREENWICH, TREATY OF (1543), forced upon the Scots by King Henry VIII of England after their defeat at Solway Moss (Nov. 1542) and the death of King James V of Scotland. Having engineered the rise to power of the Earl of Arran instead of Cardinal Beaton, and the creation of a pro-English party, Henry sent his ambassador, Sir Ralph Sadler, to negotiate the treaty. He wanted the recognition of his right of feudal overlordship of Scotland, the betrothal of Mary Stuart to Edward, Prince of Wales, her upbringing in England, and the garrisoning of Scottish fortresses by English troops. The appearance of a French expedition off Aberdeen coincided with the signing of the treaty (1 July 1543), which did not provide for the garrisons and permitted Mary to remain in Scotland until the age of ten. Scottish patriotism was aroused, however, and Beaton persuaded Arran to renew the war with England and to revive the Franco-Scottish alliance. Mary's subsequent escape to France and her betrothal to the Dauphin Francis (1548) nullified the treaty and set back English intentions in Scotland.

GREGORY I (c. 540–604), Pope, called the Great and canonized immediately after his death. Born of a patrician family, he was a prefect of Rome before he became a monk and converted his family house on the Coelian Hill into the monastery of St Andrew. He was chosen pope in 590. His immediate problem was the danger to Rome from the Lombards. The emperor refused to aid the city, which was in his dominion, and it was Gregory who defended it (c. 592–8), winning the trust of the people, who looked to him and not to the emperor for protection, with the result that Gregory and his papal successors became, de facto, the civil rulers of Rome. His relations with the emperor and the eastern patriarchates mark an important stage in the growth of papal authority. He dared to rebuke the Emperor Maurice for his failure to protect Italy from the Lombards; he intervened in the affairs of the patriarchate of Constantinople; and he made explicit and meaningful the claims of the bishops of Rome to universal jurisdiction over the Church. He initiated the mission of St Augustine of Canterbury to convert the Anglo-Saxons (596–7), an event of enormous consequence for western civilization, which also, by being the first missionary effort initiated by the papacy, greatly reinforced its universal authority.

By writing a life of St Benedict and adopting his rule at St Andrew's, Gregory began the great expansion of the Benedictine order. The liturgy, especially that of the mass, still bears his stamp and he initiated a new movement in church music (though not that known as the Gregorian chant). Above all he was a major theologian, his main works being the scriptural *Homilies*, the *Moralia*, an exposition of the *Book of Job*, the *Dialogues* (the second book of which is devoted entirely to St Benedict), and the *Pastoral Care*, which became for the rest of the Middle Ages the standard handbook for bishops and priests. Gregory's influence on every later western theologian was constant and direct.   JG

GREGORY II (669–731), Pope (*reg.* 715–31), whose pontificate marked the first major alienation of the papacy from Byzantium and the Greek Church, largely over the iconoclasm of the Emperor Leo III. Gregory showed increased papal interest in ecclesiastical affairs in France and England, especially in the encouragement he gave to St Boniface and the Anglo-Saxon missionaries in Germany.

GREGORY VI (*fl.* 11th cent.), Pope (*reg.* 1045–6), whose high character made him despair of the corrupt state of the papacy. He bribed the unworthy Benedict IX to resign and had himself elected as pope. When the simoniac nature of his election became known he was deposed by the Emperor Henry III and went into exile in Germany, accompanied by a young relative, Hildebrand, who became Pope Gregory VII.

GREGORY VII (c. 1020–85), Pope, was wholly dedicated to the Hildebrandine (or Gregorian) movement for Church reform which bears his name. He is one of the greatest of popes and was the first whose authority in ecclesiastical as well as spiritual matters was incontrovertible and all-pervading. He also transformed the Roman curia from a diocesan organization into the office of ecclesiastical government for all Western Christendom. Gregory was a monk in Rome before accompanying Gregory VI to Germany in 1046. He returned to Rome in 1049 with Leo IX, who made him papal treasurer. He rapidly rose to leadership in the reform movement and was instrumental in the elections of Nicholas II in 1056 and of Alexander II in 1061, and was himself elected pope in 1073. He immediately launched a programme of reform in the Lenten synods of 1074 and 1075, aiming at the abolition of simony, clerical celibacy, and independence from secular control for the higher clergy, thus initiating the investiture contest and the imperial–papal struggle. Hitherto the papacy had been dependent on the emperors; Gregory sought to make it independent of and co-equal with the empire. The *sacerdotium* (priesthood) was to balance the *regnum* (temporal authority). This policy threatened imperial authority in three vital areas. First, from the time of Charlemagne, emperors had been used to acting as protectors of the papacy, with consequent interests and rights in papal elections. Second, the programme threatened imperial authority, particularly in its Italian dominions. Third, the emperors had made bishops and abbots into feudal magnates and to lose control of the higher clergy was to lose control of the greater part of their secular power. Gregory and the young Emperor Henry IV clashed, particularly on the question of appointment of the Abp of Milan. Gregory forbade lay investiture; Henry declared Gregory deposed, and Gregory excommunicated Henry, thus forcing him to make the celebrated submission at Canossa (Jan. 1077). The struggle continued and culminated in Henry's attack on Rome, Gregory being saved only by the intervention of the Sicilian Normans, who carried him off into virtual captivity at Salerno, where he died.   JG

GREGORY IX (c. 1148–1241), Pope, nephew of Innocent III, who raised him to the cardinalate (1198) and made him Bp of Osia (1200). He was part author of the rule of the Franciscan order. His pontificate (*reg.* 1227–41) was marked by a vast increase in the exploitation of the Church's resources to finance the struggle with the Emperor Frederick II, including a major extension of the practice of papal provisions. Gregory was also responsible for the addition of the *Decretals* to canon law.

GREGORY X (*reg.* 1271–6), Pope, elected to the papal throne, which had been vacant for three years, while he was on a crusade. He played a decisive part in ending the Great Interregnum in Germany, and procured the imperial election of Rudolph of Habsburg (1273), who in return ceded to the papacy all the imperial claims in central Italy. Gregory's pontificate is marked by the calling of the council of Lyons (1274) to reform the Church and to attempt to unify the Greek and Roman Churches.

GREGORY XI (*reg.* 1371–8), Pope, nephew of Pope Clement VI, who made him a cardinal in 1348. He was determined to return the papacy to Rome from Avignon and despite many difficulties and opposition from his cardinals, he eventually did so (1377).

GREGORY XIII (1502–85), Pope, was elected in 1572 and as a zealous opponent of Protestantism expressed his approval of the massacre of St Bartholomew (1572). He sent Campion and other Jesuit missionary priests to England in 1580 and substituted the Gregorian for the Julian calendar by a bull of 24 Feb. 1582, although neither the Orthodox eastern countries nor the Protestant states of northern Europe would accept it.

GREGORY XIV (1534–91), Pope, ardent supporter of the Catholic League in France. He excommunicated King Henry IV of France during his short pontificate (1590–1).

GREGORY XV (*reg.* 1621–3), Pope, who helped the Catholic interest in the early years of the Thirty Years War by sending Cardinal Charles Caraffa to supervise the return of Bohemia to the Church after the battle of the White Mountain, and by supporting the granting of the Palatinate to Maximilian of Bavaria, thus increasing the Catholic majority in the imperial electorate college. To direct the work of the missions overseas he founded the Sacred Congregation for the Spreading of the Faith, while in Europe he supported the Jesuits, canonizing both St Ignatius Loyola and St Francis Xavier. He also laid down new rules for papal elections.

GREGORY XVI (1765–1846), Pope, who was elected in 1831 at a time when the papacy, by virtue of its temporal possessions in central Italy and its spiritual authority throughout Europe, was inescapably involved in the nationalist and liberal conflicts of the age. Gregory did little to improve the corrupt and inefficient government of Rome and before his election had publicly expressed his disapproval of the revolutions in Belgium and Poland. By calling on Austria to crush rebellion in Bologna (1831) he gave moral support to Metternich's system, but undermined the belief that the papal states were a necessary adjunct to papal independence, for by this time his rule depended on foreign arms.

Gregory's most decisive stand was against the liberal Catholic movement in France. He responded to Lammenais's appeal for support with the bull *Mirari Vos* (1832), condemning the attempt to ally the Church with revolutionary liberalism, which he consistently opposed as the greatest evil of his time.

GREGORY OF NAZIANZUS, Saint (AD 329–89), one of the Cappadocian Church fathers, who became Bp of Sasima (372) and, soon after the death of the Arian Emperor Valens, Bp of Constantinople (380–1), but was forced to resign. Many of his writings survive and include sermons, letters, and a long autobiographical poem.

GREGORY, SIR WILLIAM (1817–92), British colonial servant and governor of Ceylon (1872–6), who did much to restore the island's ancient monuments, to improve the port of Colombo, and to start municipal local government.

GREGORY FAMILY in Australia. Sir Augustus Charles Gregory (1819–1905) was the second of five surveyor brothers, two of whom contributed much to land exploration in the north-east and the north-west of Australia. Augustus joined the government survey office in Perth (1841) and, in 1846, with his two brothers, Francis Thomas (1821–88) and Henry Churchman (1823–1903), made the first of two expeditions north of Perth. Coal was found on the Irwin river and, in 1848, good pastoral country along the Murchison. Augustus explored the Northern Territory in 1855–6 and in 1858 central Australia, while seeking the trail of Ludwig Leichhardt. In 1859 Augustus became surveyor-general in Qld and transferred his interests from exploration to geology and politics in that colony, where he was joined in 1862 by Francis, who also entered Qld politics. In the interim Francis had made expeditions (1858–61) in the north-west which revealed good pastoral prospects some 1000 miles (1610 kms) north of Perth.

GREMIOS, or guilds of artisans, were of importance in the structure of medieval Spanish and colonial Latin American society.

GRENADA, one of the West Indian Windward Islands, was discovered by Columbus (1498). It was the first European colony and was financed by London merchants (1609). The settlement was soon abandoned, owing to its being harassed by the Carib Indians. Grenada was included in the Earl of Carlisle's grant (1627), but the merchants backing him considered the Caribs too formidable to justify investment. The French Compagnie des Îles d'Amérique (incorporated 1635) sold the rights to Grenada to the Sieur du Parquet (1650). Having exterminated the Caribs, he sold Grenada (1657) to Count de Cerrillac, who in turn sold it to a new French company (1664) and ten years later the island was annexed to France. Grenada was conquered (1762) and formally ceded to Britain by the treaty of Paris (1763). During the American War of Independence France recovered the island, which was restored to Britain by the treaty of Versailles (1783). In 1795–6 Julien Fedor, a coloured planter, supported by many slaves, led an uprising against British rule. Sir Ralph Abercromby, helped by loyal slaves and Spanish soldiers from Trinidad, crushed the rebellion (1796). In 1876 the Grenada Assembly surrendered their constitution, accepting in lieu a Crown Colony system. Grenada continued to share a governor with the other Windward Islands until 1959. The franchise was expanded in 1951. In that year, following widespread riots, a new trade union and political leader, Eric Gairy, emerged. His Grenada United Labour Party now forms the government. The island was a member of the West Indian Federation (1958–62) and became a State in Association with Britain (1967).   RH

GRENADA, BATTLE OF (6 July 1779), fought off the island of Grenada. The British fleet, under Admiral John Byron, was defeated by a French fleet commanded by the Count d'Estaing, and Grenada surrendered to the French.

GRENADIER GUARDS, regiment of foot guards formed in England at the time of the Restoration (1660). Originally the first, their primacy was contested by the Coldstreams' motto ('Nulli Secundus'). They acquired the title Grenadier by their defeat of Napoleon I's grenadier guards at Waterloo (1815).

GRENADINES, string of about 100 islands and islets, 53 miles (85 kms) long, between St Vincent and Grenada in the eastern Caribbean. The Grenadines are administered from St Vincent and Grenada and have been British possessions since the 17th cent.

GRENFELL, SIR WILFRED THOMASON (1865–1940), Canadian doctor, evangelist, and missionary. He was appointed medical officer of the mission to deep-sea fishermen in the North Atlantic (1886) and in this capacity journeyed to Labrador and Nld (1892), to attempt to found a mission among the fishing communities there. He returned to Labrador (1893) as missionary superintendent. He initiated social and economic reforms and founded hospitals, agricultural centres, and the first Labrador co-operative (1905).

GRENVILLE OF WOTTON-UNDER-BERNEWOOD, WILLIAM WYNDHAM GRENVILLE, Baron (1759–1834), British politician who was the leader of a powerful political group and of the House of Lords. As foreign secretary (1791–1801) he strongly supported Pitt's proposals for Catholic Emancipation, and resigned with him when George III rejected them (1801). He remained in opposition on the formation of Pitt's second ministry, refusing to take office without Fox, and became first lord of the treasury in the ministry of all the talents (1806–7). On the fall of this ministry, again on the Catholic question, he went into prolonged opposition, but returned to support Liverpool's ministry in 1819, being in favour of the Six Acts.

GRENVILLE, GEORGE (1712–70), British politician. As first lord of the treasury (1763–5) he was responsible for introducing the Stamp Act (1765) and for initiating proceedings against John Wilkes (1763). He held minor offices in the 1770s, but tended to be overshadowed by his elder brother, Lord Temple, and his brother-in-law, Pitt. He became secretary of state for the northern department (1762). As the Earl of Bute lost popularity, so Grenville sought the king's favour, and on Bute's resignation became first lord of the treasury. His short administration was dogged by the political disturbances of the Wilkes affair, and by the problem of reducing post-war taxation. Grenville was noted for his assiduous and careful handling of public business.

GRENVILLE, SIR RICHARD (1542–91), English sailor, who was involved in various colonial ventures, particularly with his cousin, Sir Walter Raleigh, in local affairs in his native Cornwall, and in organizing the military defence of western England (1587–8). In 1591, as captain of the *Revenge*, he was sent to intercept a Spanish treasure fleet. North of Flores in the Azores Grenville was delayed and cut off by the Spanish. He tried to fight his way out, but after a 15-hour engagement the *Revenge*, with her 190 men, was captured. Grenville, mortally wounded, died a few days later. His exploit is commemorated in Tennyson's poem 'The Revenge'.

GRESHAM, THOMAS (1519–79), English merchant, royal financial agent, and founder of the Royal Exchange. He was the principal architect of the English Crown's high credit in the money market of the Netherlands. In 1552 he was appointed financial agent of the English Crown in Antwerp, where he handled business dealings with such punctiliousness that by 1566 he had obtained substantial Flemish loans and repaid most of them. This was possible because he had an unrivalled knowledge of the Antwerp bourse. He saw the dangers of dependence on foreign merchants and recommended that the Crown should make itself independent of them by using its own subjects. He worked for the improvement of the English trade balance and for the value of sterling by the destruction of the trade of the German Hanse towns and by the coinage reform of 1560, and in 1566–8 he built the Royal Exchange as a convenient meeting place for English merchants. He conducted an extensive news service for the English government in the Netherlands and acted as ambassador both to the Netherlands and to the Duchess of Parma. By his will in 1579 he established Gresham College, for over a century the scientific centre of England and the first home of the Royal Society.

GRÉVY, FRANÇOIS PAUL JULES (1807–91), French politician and third president of the Third Republic, who served in the Provisional government and the Constituent Assembly. After the *coup d'état* he returned to the bar, but eventually secured election (1868) and later presided over the new Chambers (1871–3, 1876–7). He was elected president in succession to MacMahon (1877), and was re-elected (1885), but was forced to resign when compromised by his son-in-law's sale of political honours (1887).

GREY, CHARLES GREY, 2nd Earl (1764–1845), British Whig politician and prime minister who secured the passage of the Reform Bill (1832). He was an associate of Fox in the Whig opposition of the 1790s. He was quick-witted and a brilliant speaker. His political views combined a strong belief in a hereditary aristocracy, support of parliamentary reform, and a stout defence of popular liberties. He introduced his first reform bill in 1797 at a time when parliament was united behind Pitt in its fear of Jacobinism. It was rejected by 256 to 291 votes and Grey and the Foxites thereupon retired from parliament. He acted with W. W. Grenville during the Younger Pitt's second ministry and in the ministry of all the talents was successively first lord of the admiralty and foreign secretary.

After Grenville's retirement he was undoubted leader of the Whigs, but he refused to exert himself and spent much of his time on his estate in Northumberland, thus contributing largely to the weakness of opposition in the 1820s. He refused office under Canning (1827). With the Tory disintegration of 1830 his conduct changed completely. He came to London, formed, in alliance with the remaining Canningites, an effective opposition to Wellington, and headed the reform ministry of 1830. He led his party through the prolonged Reform Bill crisis with skill and persistence. The Tories criticized him for appealing to popular feeling while at the same time giving too many government appointments to his relations. In 1834 a disagreement with Althorp on Irish policy prompted him to retire permanently.

G. M. Trevelyan, *Lord Grey of the Reform Bill* (London, 1920).   LMB

GREY OF FALLODON, EDWARD, Viscount (1862–1933), British statesman and Liberal foreign secretary (1905–16), his being the longest continuous tenure of that office in history. He imbibed the Whig–Liberal tradition from his family, being collaterally related to Earl Grey of the Great Reform Bill. He became MP for Berwick and later (1885–1916) under-secretary for foreign affairs (1892–5). In a party divided over the Boer War and Irish Home Rule, he was a Liberal Imperialist. He distrusted the official leader, Sir Henry Campbell-Bannerman, but was persuaded by his colleagues, Asquith and Haldane, to accept the foreign office under him.

He continued the Conservative policy of Lansdowne in the first Moroccan Crisis (1905–6), upholding the Anglo-French entente, and encouraging the belief, though he could give no guarantees, that Britain would aid France if Germany attacked her. He authorized military conversations (1906–14) between the French and British general staffs on practical co-operation should they ever find themselves at war with Germany. This vital decision was withheld from the cabinet until 1912 with the consent of the prime minister, partly to avoid Radical ministers' criticisms.

Being sincerely peace-loving, he was determined not to tie the government's hands irretrievably with entangling commitments, and he warned Germany of the consequences of aggression and tried to keep a life-line to Europe through ententes with France and Russia (1907). Though out of sympathy with more demagogic Liberals like Lloyd George on domestic issues, he had Lloyd George's support in the second Moroccan Crisis (1911) against a truculent Germany. Naval talks (1912) aimed at concentrating the British navy in home waters and the French in the Mediterranean deepened the mutual moral obligations of both governments. Though making overtures of appeasement to Germany, Grey refused to commit Britain to unconditional neutrality, stressing, to the disbelief of the German authorities, that Britain would fight if France were attacked without provocation. He hastened to end the first Balkan War by the London Conference of Powers, though he was unable to prevent the second War (1913).

The assassination of Archduke Francis Ferdinand at Sarajevo led Grey immediately to advocate negotiations to ensure peace, but Germany's invasion of Belgium brought from him a declaration that Britain had a clear obligation to help Belgium and France. His moderation and skill helped to convince a deeply-divided cabinet of the necessity of entering the war (1914), and he also brought Italy into the war through the secret treaty of London (1915). By emphasizing the need for careful handling of America's sensitive opinion about the blockade, he helped to bring the US in on to the Allies' side (1917). He left office partly through failing eyesight when Lloyd George succeeded Asquith as war leader (1916). As a champion of the League of Nations he failed in a special mission to Washington to urge membership (1919).

G. M. Trevelyan, *Grey of Fallodon* (London, 1937).
E. Grey, *Twenty-Five Years, 1892–1916* (London, 1925).
JRA

GREY, SIR GEORGE (1799–1882), British Whig politician, under-secretary for the colonies under Melbourne (1834), judge-advocate general (1839–41), and chancellor of the duchy of Lancaster (1841). As home secretary in Russell's administration (1846–52), he carried the Convict Discipline Bill, substituting penal servitude at home for transportation, and supported coercive measures in Ireland. He served Lord Aberdeen as secretary for the colonies, the first to hold this newly created office, and under Palmerston he was home secretary (1855–8), chancellor of the duchy of Lancaster (1859–61), and home secretary (1861–6).

GREY, SIR GEORGE (1812–98), British colonial governor, whose experience of peasant distress in Ireland (1830–6) interested him in colonization. As governor of South Australia, he rescued the colony from virtual bankruptcy (1841–5), though his own exaggeration of this achievement obscured the contributions made by his predecessor, George Gawler (1795–1869).

Grey's transfer to NZ (1845) brought him even greater challenges: powerful Maori chiefs openly defied British government, and settlers chafed at slow land purchase from Maoris. Grey managed, however, to defeat or pacify dissident tribes and bought great areas of land in advance of settlement needs. Settlers denounced his 'despotism', although the creation of a constitution for NZ (1852) was primarily his work.

In 1854 Grey became governor of the Cape, but his declining powers of judgement and increasing arrogance hampered the solution of various South African problems, *eg*, Bantu uprisings, the mingling of European frontier settlements and tribal communities, and the union of British and Boer colonies.

The outbreak of the Maori Wars (1860–1) led to Grey's return to NZ (1861), in the hope that he might wield his old influence with Maori chiefs. But he quarrelled frequently with his ministers and generals, and though he contrived to postpone British troop withdrawals he was abruptly recalled (1868).

Returning once more to NZ (1870), Grey entered on a long career (1874–94) in colonial politics. As prime minister (1877–9) he revealed his defects as a party leader and administrator. More influential was his high-flown, often bitter, oratory from cross-bench and city platforms advocating his own version of liberalism.

J. Rutherford, *Sir George Grey* (London, 1961). WJG

GREY, LADY JANE (1537–54), de facto queen of England for nine days. She was the daughter of Henry Grey, Marquis of Dorset (later Duke of Suffolk), and Frances Brandon, daughter of Princess Mary (sister of Henry VIII) by her second marriage, to Charles Brandon, Duke of Suffolk. Lady Jane was made the ward of Thomas, Lord Seymour, who promised to marry her to Edward VI, but Seymour was executed for treason, and in 1553 Jane married Lord Guilford Dudley, fourth son of the Duke of Northumberland. The duke then persuaded Edward VI to make a new settlement of the succession to the Crown in favour of Jane and her male heirs. Edward died on 6 July 1553 and on 10 July Jane was proclaimed queen. Mary, the eldest daughter of Henry VIII, gathered supporters in East Anglia, while Northumberland's army deserted him. On 19 July Mary was proclaimed queen by the council in London. Jane was committed to the Tower and on 14 Nov. was tried for treason. She pleaded guilty and was condemned to death. Because of her father's involvement in Wyatt's rebellion, the sentence was not remitted and Jane and her husband were executed on 12 Feb. 1554.

GREY DE WILTON, WILLIAM GREY, 13th Lord (?1509–1562), English soldier, who held commands in France under Henry VIII and was leader of the English Army which defeated the Scots at Pinkie (1547). He was imprisoned (1551) as a friend of the fallen Protector Somerset, and was implicated in placing Lady Jane Grey on the throne (1553).

GRIFFENFELD, Count (1635–99), Danish statesman and supporter of absolutism. By name Peder Schumacher, he was a tradesman's son, who was ennobled by Christian V, to whom he delivered on his accession in 1670 the Lex Regia, which he had compiled as secretary for the king's father. As chief minister he tried to build up Denmark's resources by peaceful diplomacy, but the outbreak of war against Sweden caused him to be unjustly condemned (1676) and sentenced to life imprisonment for treason.

GRIFFITH, ARTHUR (1872–1922), Irish politician and founder of Sinn Fein. His original conception of Sinn Fein, outlined especially in his book *The Resurrection of Hungary* (1904), was not at all what it later became. He hoped that passive resistance to, and civil disobedience of, British institutions in Ireland would force Britain to concede a 'Dual monarchy' (as in Austria-Hungary), whereby the Irish would conduct their own institutions under the Crown. This non-militarist, intellectual, and ineffectual movement came to be dominated, especially after 1914, by the militant conspirators of the Irish Republican Brotherhood under Tom Clarke, whose plan of armed revolt culminated in the Easter Rising (1916). It was the bloody suppression of the Rising, which made the new Sinn Fein an important party, which wrested the Irish vote from the old Irish Party. Griffith, because of his prestige, became vice-president of the Sinn Fein parliament—Dail Eireann—from 1919. 1920 and 1921 were taken up with the failure of attempts by the British government to defeat the Dail administration. When treaty negotiations were opened in Oct. 1921, Griffith and Michael Collins were the chief Irish negotiators. The treaty to which they agreed, which set up a Boundary Commission to delineate the boundaries of Northern Ireland and provided the South with the status of a 'Free State' in the Commonwealth, was rejected by President de Valera, though accepted by a majority of the Dail. In 1922 civil war broke out, and within a year of the treaty both its Irish authors were dead—Collins having been shot in an ambush. In 1923 the civil war ended with the Free State's advocates victorious over the Republicans. IM

GRIFFITH, DAVID LEWELYN WARK (1880–1948), US film director, who pioneered devices such as the close-up, flash-back, and fade-out. His *The Birth of a Nation* (1915), based on Thomas Nixon's novel *The Clansman*, was a story of the American Civil War and Reconstruction told from the white Southerner's point of view. It led to Griffith being accused of racial prejudice. Technically, however, it was a landmark in the history of the film industry. Thereafter, Griffith was a prolific film maker until 1931.

GRIFFITH, SIR SAMUEL WALKER (1845–1920), Australian politician and first chief justice of the High Court of Australia (1903). He entered Queensland politics in 1871 and was twice prime minister. As vice-president of the Federal Constitutional Convention of 1891, he played a leading part in drafting the Commonwealth Constitution Bill adopted by the convention. He became chief justice of the Supreme Court of Queensland and the Queensland criminal code owes much to his influence. His approach to the interpretation of the Commonwealth constitution was opposed to expansive notions of central power.

GRIFFON, the first sailing ship on the Great Lakes. It was built by Robert La Salle on the Niagara and launched on Lake Erie (7 Aug. 1679).

GRIGG, JOHN (1828–1901), NZ farmer, whose achievements in drainage, cultivation, and stock breeding promoted intensive farming and encouraged NZ's economy at the end of the 19th cent. He helped to initiate Canterbury refrigeration (1881).

GRIJALVA, JUAN DE (*c.* 1489–1527), Spanish conquistador. His exploration of the northern coast of Yucatan and parts of Veracruz laid the groundwork for the conquests of Hernan Cortés in 1519.

GRIMALDI, JERONIMO, Marquis de (*fl.* 18th cent.), Spanish statesman and ambassador to England in the closing stages of the Seven Years War. In Jan. 1761 he was sent to Versailles to negotiate a defensive alliance between France and Spain, which resulted in the Family Compact (Aug. 1761) and Spain's entry into the war (1762). Grimaldi continued as minister for foreign affairs until 1776, when he was replaced by Floridablanca. During this time another conflict with England arose, over Spain's claims to the Falkland Islands (1770). Only Choiseul's downfall and Louis XV's refusal to honour the Franco-Spanish alliance prevented war.

GRIMKE, SARAH MOORE (1792–1873), US abolitionist and advocate of women's rights, who was born in Charleston, SC. She was the daughter of a slave-holding SC judge, but became convinced of the barbarous nature of slavery and dissatisfied with the restraints placed on women in the South. With her sister, Angelina (1805–79), she migrated to Philadelphia, where they were accepted into the Society of Friends. During the early 1830s both were drawn into the emerging anti-slavery movement and became accomplished lecturers. The storm of protest aroused by their public appearances persuaded them of the need to promote women's rights, in which cause both became prominent. Angelina married the abolitionist, Theodore Dwight Weld, in 1838.

GRIMM, FRIEDRICH MELCHIOR, DE, Baron (1723–1807), German literary critic, whose correspondence with Diderot (1753–82), published in 1812–13, propagated the influence of the French philosophers among the European nobility and monarchs. He valued the friendship of Catherine II of Russia, to whom he wrote fulsome letters.

GRIMMELSHAUSEN, H. J. C. VON (1618–76), German writer whose *Simplicius Simplicissimus* (1669) was a vivid adventure novel of the Thirty Years War.

GRIMOND, JOSEPH (1913–), British politician, who entered parliament in 1950 for Orkney and Shetland, a seat he still held in 1970. He succeeded Clement Davies as leader of the Liberal Party in 1956 and for the next 11 years he injected a more radical spirit into the party and inspired his followers with his clarity of thought. In 1970 he was elected president of the Scottish Liberal Party, in which capacity he campaigned for greater devolution of power away from London to Scotland, Wales, and Northern Ireland. His extra-parliamentary offices included that of Director of Personnel, UNRRA European Office, and secretary of the Scottish National Trust. He published *The Liberal Future* (1959) and *The Liberal Challenge* (1963). He was succeeded as leader of the party by Jeremy Thorpe in 1967.

GRINDAL, EDMUND, archbishop (?1519–83), rose under the patronage of Nicholas Ridley, becoming Bp of London (1559), Abp of York (1570) and of Canterbury (1576). His Puritan sympathies caused conflict with Elizabeth I, with whom he quarrelled over 'prophesyings' and he was suspended from the exercise of his functions (1577).

GRINNELL EXPEDITIONS, two American Arctic expeditions sent to find evidence about the missing explorer Sir John Franklin. They were named after Henry Grinnell, an American shipping magnate who provided the ships. The first expedition (1850–1) was commanded by the US navy; the second (1853–5) was privately financed and attempted unsuccessfully to reach the North Pole.

GRIOTS, court chroniclers in the Western Sudan, who preserved the oral histories of their communities. They sometimes exercised influence on rulers by recalling traditions in such a way as to remind them of their duty to hand down a record of heroic and noble actions.

GRIQUA, name given to a group of mixed racial origin living along the Orange river (South Africa), some of whom had originally belonged to the Grigriqua (or Chariguriqua) people. In the 19th cent. they controlled the drifts across the Orange river and the disputed diamond fields on the Vaal–Hartz confluence, which gave them political significance. They are now (1970) merged in the Cape Coloured population.

GRISONS, Protestants who inhabited a strategic area adjacent to the Swiss confederation, dominating the Catholic-held valley of the Valtelline, which lies along the upper Adda. Thus the Grisons held the key to Spanish communications between their possessions in northern Italy and the Netherlands and therefore played an important part in Bourbon-Habsburg rivalry in the 17th cent.

GRITO DE YPIRANGA, or 'cry of Ypiranga' (1822), defiance of Portuguese authority and proclamation of Brazil's independence by Pedro, Regent of Brazil, on the banks of Ypiranga river. He thus became Pedro I of the new nation.

GRIVAS, GEORGE THEODOROU (1898–), Cypriot founder and leader of EOKA. Grivas was born on Cyprus and entered the Greek army. He commanded a division in the Albanian campaign (1940–1) and during the occupation he led an extreme royalist organization, 'X', and after the liberation fought the communists. Grivas met Abp Makarios in 1951 and, after an appeal for *enosis* at the United Nations failed, persuaded him (1954) to sanction the use of force. Taking the name of a legendary hero, Dighenis Akritas, Grivas formed EOKA, which announced its existence with bombs on 1 April 1955. He was outlawed by the British authorities and a price of £10,000 was placed on his head. Grivas left Cyprus in Feb. 1959 after the settlement and was welcomed as a national hero in Greece. He vainly sought to form a party, the Movement of National Regeneration, which would reverse the settlement and achieve *enosis*. In June 1964 Grivas returned to Cyprus to head the Cypriot national guard when the Greek government feared that Makarios was flirting with the communists and planning independence without *enosis*. After surviving an attempt by Makarios to oust him in 1966, Grivas tried to exploit Graeco-Turkish tension in the autumn of 1967, but overplayed his hand and was recalled to Athens.

GROENER, EDUARD WILHELM (1887–1939), German soldier and politician, who belonged to a group of officers of middle-class background who succeeded in rising to the exclusive General Staff through the technical services. In 1914 he was put in charge of railways and of supplies for the army. Later, he held the key post of *Chef des Kriegs-amts* and initiated the total mobilization of Germany's production in the First World War. On 29 Oct. 1918 he succeeded Ludendorff as first quartermaster-general and became the mouthpiece of his superior, Field Marshal von Hindenburg, in the army's attempt to survive the monarchy's collapse and to defeat the Revolution. He told Wilhelm II that the army could no longer be used to defend the monarchy, and on 10 Nov. concluded the famous pact against Bolshevism with Friedrich Ebert, the Social Democratic head of the new government. Groener resigned on 30 Sept. 1919; the army, however, maintained its autonomous political position. Although he was not attached to any particular party, Groener served in the Reich cabinet as minister of transport (1920–3), then became defence minister (1928). He continued the tradition of publicly proclaiming the army's political neutrality while exerting considerable pressure behind the scenes. One of the problems that beset him after 1930 was the rise of the Nazis and of paramilitary organizations and the challenge which they presented to the authority of the armed forces. To distract the SA and other paramilitary associations from street-fighting, a national office for youth training, the *Reichskuratorium für Jugendertuchtigung*, was founded, and Groener put in charge of a second ministry. the ministry of the interior, to supervise the plan's execution, But by spring 1932 he was caught between two fires: whereas the defence ministry, under Schleicher's influence, continued to regard the *Kuratorium* as a means of solving the problem of Nazi–SA radicalism, Groener's ministerial colleagues in the Länder urged him to ban Nazi paramilitarism. When in April 1932 he at length banned the SA, Schleicher, his 'cardinal in politics', turned against him and engineered his fall from power (May 1932).

GROL, MILAN (1876–1952), Serbian journalist and politician, was a founder member of the Serbian Democratic Party which opposed Alexander's royal dictatorship. He held a seat in the government of Gen. Simovic, formed after the coup of 27 March 1941, and was a member of the Yugoslav government-in-exile during the Second World War. In 1945 he joined the provisional government as deputy prime minister, but, with Milos Trifunovic, resigned before the elections of Aug. 1945.

GROMYKO, ANDREY ANDREEVICH (1909–), Russian diplomat who represented his country in many of the most important contacts which the USSR had with the west after 1945. He became head of the department of American countries in the commissariat of foreign affairs (1939–43), and was counsellor and then ambassador (1943–6) at the Soviet embassy in Washington. He headed the USSR delegation to the Dumbarton Oaks conference, attended the Yalta, Potsdam, and San Francisco conferences, was USSR delegate on the Security Council (1946–8), a member of the USSR delegation to the Geneva Conferences (1954, 1955), accompanied Khrushchev and Bulganin to Britain (1956), and was present at the Khrushchev–Kennedy meeting in Vienna (1961). He visited Italy and was received by Pope Paul VI in 1966.

GRONCHI, GIOVANNI (1887–), Italian president (1955–62), who actively encouraged political moves to the left, and a more independent, 'neo-Atlantist' foreign policy. He had dedicated himself (1910) to trade unionism and had helped to form the *Partito Popolare* (1919). During the Second World War he became a resistance leader. He later joined the Christian Democrats, and was a trade expert in war and post-war cabinets, and president of the Chamber (1948–55).

GRONINGEN, most northerly of the seven northern provinces of the Spanish Netherlands, whose Dutch-speaking people joined the United Provinces in the War of Independence (1568–1648).

GROOM, SIR LITTLETON ERNEST (1876–1936), Australian Commonwealth politician, who served in all non-Labor cabinets (1905–26) and as speaker (1926–9), when his refusal to vote in committee caused the fall of Bruce's government. He was associated with early Commonwealth social legislation and with the building of the national capital, Canberra.

GROOTE, GERARD (1340–84), Dutch religious reformer, who was born and died at Deventer in the Netherlands. His disciples banded themselves together as the Brethren of the Common Life, one of whom was Thomas A'Kempis, author of the *Imitation of Christ*, long attributed to Groote himself.

GROS VENTRES, name given by the French to two distinct groups of American Indians: the Atsina and the Hidatsa. The Atsina, a detached group of Arapaho, were reduced in numbers by disease and war with the Sioux and Blackfeet. They now (1970) live with the Assiniboin on the Fort Belknap Reservation, MT. The Hidatsa, a Siouan tribe, found by Lewis and Clark in ND (1804), were greatly reduced by the smallpox epidemic of 1837. They settled on a reservation at Fort Berthold in ND.

GROSEILLIERS, MEDARD COUART, SIEUR DES (1618–96), French explorer, who came to Quebec (1641) and in the service of the Jesuits travelled among the western Indians for five years. He travelled extensively around the Great Lakes (1654–60), opening the western fur trade. He voyaged to Hudson's Bay (1668) on behalf of merchants who formed the nucleus of the Hudson's Bay Co. On reaching the bay he built Charles Fort and returned (1669) to England with valuable furs. The Hudson's Bay Co. was chartered (1670) and Groseilliers was sent to establish a trading post on the Nelson river. In 1682 he established Fort Bourbon on behalf of the French Compagnie du Nord.

GROSSETESTE, ROBERT, bishop (1168–1253), English scholar and medieval scientist. He studied and lectured at Oxford and Paris and was the first chancellor (*c.* 1214–15) of Oxford University. He also lectured at the Franciscan house at Oxford (*c.* 1232–5), which he made a centre of learning, greatly influencing the Oxford Franciscans, especially Roger Bacon. He became Bp of Lincoln (1235), where through a thorough reform of his vast diocese, he raised the moral standards and level of literacy of his clergy and left a reputation for zeal and sanctity. He was a proficient early Greek scholar and translated several works into Latin. He was also one of the earliest Aristotelians, and wrote commentaries on several of Aristotle's philosophical and scientific works, as well as commentaries on the epistles and gospels. Above all, he was the first of the Oxford school of scientists. His work on physics and optics was to be profoundly and deeply influential for centuries to come, and mark him as one of the most original scientific minds since antiquity.

GROTE, GEORGE (1794–1871), British politician and historian, who during the 1820s held meetings to discuss utilitarian doctrine. He emerged as a radical, with his *Essentials of Parliamentary Reform* (1831), and was elected MP for the City of London. He regularly introduced bills or resolutions in favour of the ballot. After 1841 he worked on his *History of Greece* (1846–56) and later on philosophy.

GROTEWOHL, OTTO (1894–1964), German politician who led the Social Democratic Party of East Germany into alliance with the communists and became prime minister of Eastern Germany. He joined the Social Democratic Party in 1912 and, after serving in the First World War, became the youngest member of the Brunswick *landtag* (1920). He was elected to the Reichstag (1925) but, after the Nazis took power, led an obscure and hazardous life as a salesman, and was twice detained on charges of anti-Nazi activity. After the Second World War he reorganized the Social Democratic Party and led the section of the party which fused with the Communist Party to form the Socialist Unity Party (1946), of which he was co-chairman with Pieck. He was appointed prime minister of the German Democratic Republic, but played a subordinate role to Walter Ulbricht, who became president.

GROTIUS, HUGO (1583–1645), Dutch philosopher and jurist, who was the first exponent of international law. A native of Delft, he became pensionary of Rotterdam (1613) and a whole-hearted supporter of Oldenbarnevelt's religious policy. He was arrested as an Arminian on the orders of Maurice of Nassau (28 Aug. 1618), sentenced to life imprisonment (May 1619), and escaped from Loevestein to Antwerp (1621), where he lived in exile and produced his great work, *De Jure Belli ac Pacis* (1625). In this he tried to base the security of international politics upon a rational, universal law, arising from social instinct. His *Mare Liberum* (1609) defended the freedom of the high seas against the Spaniards and the Portuguese, a concept which only came to be generally accepted in the 18th cent. In 1632 Grotius moved to Hamburg, and in 1635 went to Paris as Swedish ambassador at Oxenstierna's request. He was much influenced in his pursuit of international understanding by the horrors of the Thirty Years War.

GROUP AREAS ACT (1950) in South Africa aimed at separating racial groups from one another and from whites in urban areas. Under the act, certain areas can be proclaimed in which only members of one racial group may live, work, and own property. After government valuation any land can be expropriated by administrative action. The act led to the removal of Africans from the few remaining areas where they had freehold rights, while the coloured and Indian communities were especially hard-hit, having had to move from homes and businesses they had built up over generations. Relatively few whites were expropriated.

GROUP SETTLEMENT IN WESTERN AUSTRALIA, special variant of the closer land settlement and assisted migration schemes adopted by Australian Commonwealth and state governments after the First World War, with the aid of the British parliament's Empire Settlement Act (1922). The scheme aimed to open up the heavily timbered south-west corner of the state and to end its dependence on dairy produce from eastern Australia. Inadequate preparation, imperfect supervision, under-capitalization, and some injudicious selection of settlers for the groups made the scheme a costly failure, accentuated by the world-wide economic depression. Most 'groupies' left their holdings, but a dairy industry was eventually established with rather more than 1000 families, at a cost of some £10 million. A group scheme for NSW was abandoned and some 800 group settlers who entered Vic. between 1923 and 1927 dwindled to 50 established farmers, at a cost to that state of £5 million.

GROZA, PETRU (1884–1958), Rumanian leader of the Ploughmen's Front and prominent political figure in the People's Republic. Groza, a Transylvanian, was trained as a lawyer at Budapest, Berlin, and Leipzig universities. After the First World War he became a prosperous landowner and industrialist. In 1933 he founded the Ploughmen's Front, a radical peasant movement centred in western Transylvania around Deva. Groza worked closely with the communists in the 1930s, resisting fascism in Rumania. After 1944 the Ploughmen's Front became the rural arm of the National Democratic Front, a coalition dominated by the communists. After the fall of Radescu's government (March 1945), Groza headed a cabinet formed of the National Democratic Front parties. He was replaced as prime minister by Gheorghiu-Dej in June 1952, and served as president of the presidium of the Grand National Assembly until his death.

GROZKA, fortress south-east of Belgrade, known to the Turks as Hisarcik. Here (22 July 1739) the Ottomans encountered the Imperialists under Marshal Wallis in a battle which ended with the retreat of the Christian forces to Belgrade.

GRUMBKOW, JOACHIM ERNST VON (*fl.* 17th cent.), general, Pomeranian nobleman and soldier, who in 1679 became the head of the Generalkriegskommissariat in Brandenburg-Prussia. Under his leadership the functions of the office were greatly increased to cover all economic matters as well as those of the minister of war and chief of the general staff.

GRUPO DE OFICIALES UNIDOS (GOU), or Group of United Officers, a society of fascist and nationalist Argentinian army officers who seized power in 1943. From this group emerged the dictator Juan Domingo Perón.

GRZESINSKI, ALBERT KARL WILHELM (1879–1947), German politician and trade union leader before 1914, and chairman of the Kassel Soldiers' and Workers' Council (1918–19). Later, as Prussian minister of the interior (1926–1930) and as police president of Berlin (1925–6, 1930–2) he became well known as a pragmatic politician who used his official powers with considerable determination in the defence of the Weimar republic against its anti-democratic enemies. After 1933 he emigrated to Switzerland.

GUADALAJARA, BATTLE OF (March 1937). Spanish Nationalists, anxious to capture Madrid and win a quick victory in the Civil War, decided on an attack from the north-east directed on Guadalajara, 64 kms from Madrid. 50,000 troops were gathered—30,000 Italians under Generals Roatta and Mancini and 20,000 legionaries, Moors, and Carlist *Requetés* under Gen. Moscardó, the hero of the Alcázar. They had 250 tanks, 180 pieces of heavy artillery, and 70 planes and were well supplied with trucks. It was the best-equipped and most heavily armed force yet to go into action in the war.

On 8 March Italian troops broke through. They moved rapidly southwards, but over-extended their lines of communication. While Republican reinforcements moved up, the Italians were caught in a heavy and prolonged storm. The planes that were covering them were trapped on their makeshift landing strips. The Republican air force, under Hidalgo de Cisneros, risked operations from the Barajas aerodrome north of Madrid and their pilots strafed and bombed the stranded Italian columns. The weather also prevented the supporting attack of Gen. Orgaz from Jarama.

Republican troops, including International Brigades, were massing under the Communists, Lister and El Campesino, and the Anarchist, Cipriano Mera. Italians of the Garibaldi Battalion organized a propaganda campaign, exhorting their fascist compatriots by loudspeaker not to kill fellow workers. This eroded their already flagging morale. Between 12 and 17 March Lister counter-attacked with Russian tanks. The Italians held on shakily until the 18th, when they were routed at Brihuega by Republicans under Lister and Cipriano Mera.

Militarily only a small defensive victory, Guadalajara was in terms of morale a huge Republican triumph. Mussolini had banked on victory and his forces had been defeated by the improvised Republican army and anti-fascist Italian volunteers.   PP

GUADALCANAL, BATTLE OF (12–15 Nov. 1942), naval engagement during the Second World War between US and Japanese forces off Guadalcanal in the Solomon Islands of the western Pacific. Heavy losses were sustained by both sides, but the battle confirmed US naval supremacy, stopped the Japanese from landing large troop reinforcements, and facilitated the final US conquest of the island in Feb. 1943.

GUADARRAMA, BATTLE OF THE (July 1936), first real conflict of the Spanish Civil War, divided itself in effect into two separate battles which took place at two passes in the ridge of mountains to the north of Madrid, Alto de León to the north-west and Somosierra to the north-east.

On 19 July Gen. Mola sent a force of 1000 regular troops— Carlists and Falangists—to capture Guadalajara. Finding it already in the hands of left-wing militia, they withdrew to Somosierra. On 21 July a mixed force of regulars and Falangists under Col. Serrador left Valladolid, heading for Madrid via the Alto de León. They found the pass occupied by a large force of militia under Col. Castillo.

Alto de León fell on 22 July after a savage engagement. Working-class militia under Capt. Galán met Col. García Escámez at Somosierra. After an equally bitter encounter Somosierra fell to the Nationalists. In each battle, the sides had enjoyed equal air power which they used to bomb each other's lines. However, the Republicans suffered greater casualties because of the Nationalists' superior artillery. The battle made it clear that both the siege of Madrid and the war were going to be protracted and fiercely fought.

GUADALUPE, VIRGIN OF, patroness of Mexico and especially of its Indians. In 1531 an Indian, Juan Diego, claimed to have seen a vision of the Virgin, with Indian features. A shrine was built on the spot, which in pre-conquest times had been associated with the worship of Tonantzín, the earth mother goddess of central Mexico. The cult of the Virgin of Guadalupe became associated with the Indian rather than the Spanish part of Mexico's heritage, and became a symbol of insurgence during the wars of independence.

GUADALUPE HIDALGO, TREATY OF (1848), US–Mexican peace treaty that ended the war of 1846–8. Negotiated, after his formal recall, by Nicholas P. Trist, emissary of the US president, James K. Polk, the treaty established the boundaries of the US and Mexico along the lines of the Rio Grande and Gila rivers. Mexico thereby renounced its claim to TX and ceded the provinces of NM and upper CA. In return, the US made a payment of $15 million and assumed the claims of its citizens against Mexico.

GUADELOUPE, French West Indian island, discovered by Columbus (1493). The Spaniards never settled there, but abandoned it entirely after a Carib massacre of visiting priests (1603). It was occupied in 1635 by the French Compagnie des Îles d'Amérique. Upon the company's failure (1648), Houel bought the proprietary rights, and later (1654) sugar production methods were improved. Guadeloupe became state property (1674). Though British attacks were repelled (1666, 1691, 1703), in 1759–60 Britain captured the island, but under the treaty of Paris (1763) it was returned to France. In 1794 Britain again captured Guadeloupe, but lost it to Victor Hugues's revolutionary army in the same year. A slave revolt caused the governor to take refuge in British Dominica (1801), but French troops regained control (1802). Again the island fell to Britain (1810), but was restored by the treaty of Paris (1814). In 1946 Guadeloupe became an 'Overseas Department' of France.

GUAM, largest and most populous of the Mariana Islands in the western Pacific ocean. The island, an unincorporated territory of the US since the Spanish–American War (1898), with a total area of 209 sq. miles (541 sq. kms) has a combined military and civilian population of more than 100,000. Since the end of the Second World War the island has played an increasingly important role as a strategic defence post for the US navy and air force.

GUANO, Spanish term for accumulations of the faecal matter of seabirds. Great quantities of guano have accumu-

lated on the islands off the Peruvian coast. In the 19th cent. its value as agricultural fertilizer was realized abroad, and Peru began to export it in bulk. The result was a boom in Peru in the 1860s and 1870s. The deposits began to be worked out and the collapse of the boom caused a depression. Guano is still quarried on the Peruvian islands for local use, but artificial chemical fertilizers have destroyed the value of guano as an export.

GUARANI INDIANS, South American group of tribes belonging to the Tupi–Guarani family. These tribes occupied large sections of southern Brazil, Uruguay, Paraguay, and north-eastern Argentina before the arrival of Europeans. The most famous contact between Guaranis and Europeans was in the Jesuit missions along the Paraná and Uruguay rivers. In the 17th and 18th cents these missions were largely destroyed by slavers from São Paulo, but Guarani language and culture have remained a vital part of the national, and especially rural, culture of modern Paraguay.

GUARNERIUS FAMILY in Italy, important violin-makers of the 17th and 18th cents. Andrea Guarnerius (c. 1626–98) was a fellow pupil under Amati with Stradivarius. The instruments of Giuseppe Antonio Guarnerius (1687–1745) are considered second only to those of Stradivarius.

GUASTALLA, BATTLE OF (1734), fought between the imperialists under the Prince of Wurtemberg and the French under Marshal de Coligny during the War of the Polish Succession. Each side lost about 4000 men. The imperialists were defeated and Wurtemberg killed.

GUATEMALAN REVOLUTION, frustrated attempt at radical change (1944–54) in the Central American republic of Guatemala. In 1944 dictator Jorge Ubico was overthrown and a liberal coalition seized power soon after. Following elections, Juan José Arévalo Bermejo became president. He was a socialist reformer and promoted legislation designed to incorporate the Indians of the nation into national life.

As the end of Arévalo's term approached one of the leading presidential candidates, Col. Arana, was murdered under mysterious circumstances, and another army officer, Jacobo Arbenz Guzmán, won the presidency.

Under Arbenz the Guatemalan Revolution accelerated its pace. In 1952 an extensive land reform and redistribution programme was initiated. Many large estates were confiscated and redistributed to the peasantry and railroads were nationalized. Opposition parties became extremely hostile to Arbenz, accusing him of allowing communists to infiltrate his government and take over the Confederation of Labour which alarmed the US government.

Right-wing groups, led by Col. Carlos Castillo Armas, began to assemble in neighbouring Honduras. His invasion of Guatemala (June 1954) received military support from the US, and the invaders took power. Castillo Armas quickly began to reverse some of the measures enacted by the two previous regimes. He also encouraged the return of large foreign investment. These policies were halted by his assassination on 26 July 1957. Since his death Guatemalan politics have been dominated by right-wing fears that the popular Arévalo will return to win an election or lead a revolution, and by left-wing guerrilla activities against the regimes in power. Guatemala in 1970 was a good example of a frustrated social revolution. MJM

GUAYAQUIL CONFERENCE (July 1822), held in Guayaquil, Ecuador, between Simón Bolívar and José de San Martín, leaders of the armies of independence in South America. The purpose of the conference was to arrange co-operation between the two armies, but Bolívar and San Martín failed to agree on the methods to be used for the liberation of Peru. San Martín left Guayaquil, and soon abandoned Peru for Chile, leaving the field clear for Bolívar.

GUDEA (*c.* 2100 BC), Ensi of Lagash, who also controlled other Sumerian cities. He built many temples and left numerous inscriptions describing his activities.

GUELDERS, province which grew up astride the Rhine and the Meuse in the north-west of the Holy Roman empire after the collapse of the Carolingian state. After steady territorial expansion it was raised to a duchy by Emperor Louis IV, a relative of the ruling count. The male line died out in 1371, after which there was a dispute over succession and the duchy eventually passed to Jülich, and in 1473 to Burgundy.

GÜEMES, MARTÍN (1785–1821), Argentinian regional dictator from the north, who was placed in power by influential families and later murdered, possibly by the same groups. Güemes's wild gaucho armies played an important role in the early independence struggles against Spain.

GUERIN (d. 1223), bishop of Senlis, one of the chief political advisers of King Philip Augustus of France. It was his tactical arrangement of French knights at the battle of Bouvines (1214) which led to the defeat of the coalition forces of the Holy Roman empire, England, Flanders, and Boulogne.

GUERNICA, small town in the Basque province of Vizcaya, 30 kms from Bilbao. Traditionally, the town and its famous oak tree have been sanctified by Basques as symbols of their independence. From the early Middle Ages, representative assemblies of all Basque males over the age of 21 met under the Tree of Guernica. There, too, came representatives of the king to swear to respect Basque rights and an executive council elected to rule the three Basque provinces every two years.

The town is celebrated as the scene of a German bombing attack during the Spanish Civil War. On 26 April 1937, a market day, waves of planes dropped incendiary bombs and high explosives for three hours, and people fleeing from the town centre were machine-gunned from the air, many casualties being caused. The town was completely destroyed, though the oak tree and the Basque parliament were undamaged. The raid was a calculated experiment in terror, since Guernica was of little military value. Field Marshal Göring said that it was a test-run for the Luftwaffe, to observe the effects of saturation bombing. The attack was commemorated by Picasso in his painting *Guernica.*

GUERRERO, VICENTE (1782–1831), Mexican leader in the wars of independence and republican politician. After the defeat of his leader, Morelos, Guerrero led a guerrilla movement against the Spanish authorities, and then reached an agreement with Iturbide (1821), a compromise proposal for Mexican independence called the Plan of Iguala. In 1829 he was chosen president, but was quickly overthrown by former supporters, among them Santa Anna and Bustamante. After his fall he was executed on Bustamante's orders. His tenure of office, though brief, saw the abolition of slavery, and the first attempt since independence to expel Spanish individuals from Mexico.

GUERRILLAS in Spain, partisan fighting force of some 30,000 men which, in the absence of an effective Spanish regular army, played an important part in the Peninsular War. The activities of the guerrillas, in small bands, or organized groups of up to 8000, tied down large numbers of French troops. They reoccupied areas evacuated by the French and often seized valuable military information. Two of the better-organized groups played an effective strategic role in Wellington's victory at Salamanca (1812). Without their constant pressure on the French, Wellington could not have operated so successfully with a small army. However, the guerrillas romanticized the cult of the individual and established a tradition of independent violent action which, exploited by both right- and left-wing extremists in the 19th cent., contributed to Spain's political instability.

GUEST, SIR JOSIAH JOHN (1785–1852), Welsh MP and industrialist, who owned an ironworks at Dowlais. He pioneered many technical advances, *eg*, the use of coke instead of coal for smelting.

GUEVARA, ERNESTO ('CHE') (1928–67), Argentine physician, writer, and guerrilla leader, who played a prominent part in the Cuban Revolution. Guevara joined Fidel Castro in Mexico, where Castro was planning his campaign against Batista, and accompanied him to Cuba, where he became one of the guerrilla leaders. His mastery of guerrilla warfare is shown in his book of that name.

After Castro seized power Guevara occupied important positions in banking and economics in the new regime. But feeling that his allegiance to revolution demanded his presence elsewhere, Guevara secretly left Cuba. After brief visits to the Congo and Argentina, he began a guerrilla campaign in Bolivia. During a skirmish with US trained counter-insurgency forces he was wounded, captured, and then shot.

GUGGENHEIM, DANIEL (1856–1930), US industrialist and philanthropist, who controlled the American Smelting and Refining Co. (1901–19), which held a virtual monopoly of copper production in the US, and a dominant position in world production of copper, tin, rubber, diamonds, and nitrates. The Daniel and Florence Guggenheim Foundation was established in 1924.

GUGGISBERG, SIR GORDON FREDERICK (1869–1930), British colonial administrator and governor of the Gold Coast Colony (1919–27). Under his energetic administration Achimota school was founded, Takoradi harbour constructed, and the Accra–Kumasi railway line completed.

GUIANA, swampy region of South America, situated between Spanish Venezuela and Portuguese Brazil. It was the object of a colonizing project planned by Raleigh and was settled in the 17th cent. by the Dutch and the French. The original English Guiana company was destroyed by the Spaniards in the 1630s, but in 1815 French Guiana became British by the treaty of Vienna.

GUICCIARDINI, FRANCESCO (1483–1540), Florentine Renaissance soldier, statesman, and historian. He was ambassador to Ferdinand of Aragon (1511) and, through the patronage of the Medici Pope Leo X, governor of both Modena (1516) and Reggio (1517). He was later lieutenant-general of the papal armies and president of the Romagna (1524). In 1526 he became Clement VII's principal adviser and for the last decade of his life he remained in Florence as the adviser of the Medici rulers, Alessandro and Cosimo. Guicciardini's main works, written in Italian, were his *History of Florence,* begun in 1508, and his *History of Italy,* which he started in 1536 and which was published in 1561. In this he analysed the disasters which resulted from the French invasion of 1494, showing a strong critical insight, but idealizing the Florence of Lorenzo the Magnificent.

'GUIDED DEMOCRACY', Indonesian governmental style from the collapse of parliamentary democracy in the late 1950s to the overthrow of President Sukarno in 1965. In Feb. 1957 Sukarno announced a 'Concept' by which the foundering parliamentary system would be replaced, and the next 18 months saw furious debate over the implementation of his plan. The new system was officially inaugurated in July 1959 with the readoption of the 1945 constitution, which provided for a strong executive government. In 1960 the Masjumi and Socialist parties were dissolved and parliament was 're-tooled'. The communists were at first divided over whether to support the system, as they had been strongly advancing through elections, but they soon realized that they could not afford to oppose it if they wished to remain legal, and they therefore made themselves into a mainstay of

Sukarno's support. Army leaders were at first active in encouraging the new system, under which they enjoyed a greatly enhanced role; but as Sukarno's personal command grew and his favours seemed increasingly granted to the left, military enthusiasm waned. From 1963 to 1965 the communists improved their position, and Sukarno pressed for government based on the principle of NASAKOM (union of Nationalist, Religious, and Communist elements), as the realization of Guided Democracy. After the coup of Oct. 1965 the expression 'Guided Democracy' was replaced by that of the 'New Order'.

GUILD MERCHANT. Organizations comprising all the more important merchants of a town began to appear in official records in northern Europe in the 11th cent. Frequently their first recorded collective action was the financing of the construction of the city walls. Such guilds became common during the 12th and 13th cents. Working craftsmen were usually excluded from merchant guilds and in many towns members of these guilds held all the municipal offices and were the main employers of labour. In some of the most important mercantile centres, such as medieval London, no single merchant guild existed, because the numerous merchants who were active there were divided between rival groups, equally numerous, of a more specialized sort, such as vintners, mercers, grocers, and drapers.

GUILDHALL, seat of the lord mayor and corporation of the City of London. Its medieval site in Aldermanbury was changed to the present site when the 15th-cent. hall was built (c. 1411–40), with its library endowed by Richard Whittington (d. 1423). After its destruction in the Great Fire (1666), the hall was rebuilt in Charles II's reign. It was severely damaged during the Second World War, but was later restored.

GUILFORD, FREDERICK NORTH, 4th Earl of (2nd of 3rd creation) (1732–92), who was known as Lord North throughout his career. He was British prime minister and first lord of the treasury (1770–82) and secretary of state in the short-lived Fox–North coalition (1783). North established the first stable administration in the reign of King George III. He regulated the affairs of the East India Co., consolidated the nation's finances, and, by setting up the Committee for Examining the Public Accounts (1780), laid the basis for Pitt's reforms. Yet after 1774 he was increasingly reviled by his contemporaries and despised by his fellow politicians, for his was the administration which failed to prevent the drift into war with the American colonies or to prosecute the war with vigour. His critics took no account of the fact that on neither side of the Atlantic was a peaceful solution to the American problem acceptable to public opinion. Moreover, without the immediate application of vast financial resources, which the taxpayer was unwilling to provide, there was little likelihood of defeating the colonists. North himself was well aware of his inadequacy as a war minister and would willingly have resigned, if there had been an acceptable alternative.

Before 1774 England seemed set for another era of Walpolian calm and good government. North was a man of tact and good sense, secure in the king's confidence, and competent in his handling of the Commons. No great issues emerged to unite the opposition, and the business community welcomed his policy of financial retrenchment. But his Regulating Act (1773) for India, although full of good administrative intentions, inadvertently sparked off the Boston Tea Party and his closure of the port of Boston played into the hands of the colonial extremists. The ensuing conflict was not of North's making, but his failure to control his cabinet, his insistence on waging the war as economically as possible, and continued plans for conciliation meant that the war effort lacked credibility.

He also had to cope with Grattan and Flood's Volunteer Movement in Ireland and the Petitioning Movement for parliamentary reform at home. In these, as in all other issues, his instinct was to delay and conciliate, an unambitious policy, acceptable to most English gentlemen, but hardly adequate to resolve great conflicts overseas.   SH

GUILFORD, FREDERICK NORTH, 7th Earl of (5th of 3rd creation) (1760–1827), first British governor of Ceylon (1796–1805). His chief secretary, for a short time, was Hugh Cleghorn, who arranged the secret transfer of the De Meuron regiment, in the employ of the Dutch in Colombo, to the British, thereby rendering easier the capture of Colombo (1795). North was eager to take over the kingdom of Kandy, but the expedition he sent (1803) was mismanaged, and failed miserably. He established a civil service and was reasonably successful in organizing the transition from Dutch rule, though he fell out with the chief justice and the officer commanding the British troops. He succeeded his elder brother as Earl of Guilford in 1817.

GUILLAUME IX, Duke of Aquitaine (1086–1126), powerful, independent, and rebellious vassal of the King of France. He tolerated no interference within his duchy, where he controlled even the Church. But he deserves to be remembered rather as a man of culture. He is the first named troubadour and was a composer of verse in the Provençal language. Eleanor, the future Queen of France and England, was his grand-daughter.

GUILLOTINE, instrument for judicial execution introduced in France during the French Revolution and named after Joseph Guillotine, a member of the Constituent Assembly, who was responsible for the law approving its introduction. Earlier forms of this method of decapitation—by a descending knife fitted into a vertical frame—had been employed throughout Europe.

The word also describes a British parliamentary procedural device, first used in 1887, by which the House of Commons allots certain fixed periods of time, in advance of debate, to various stages of a bill.

GUINEA—probably from Ghanaw, the name used in North Africa from the 12th cent. for the land of Ghana. European traders picked up various forms of the word (eg, Gunuia and Ginyia) and in the 15th cent. applied it as Guiné to the region beyond the Senegal. By the 17th cent. it was customary to speak of Upper Guinea (Senegal to Sierra Leone) and Lower Guinea (Sierra Leone to Cameroons).

GUINEA COMPANY, formed in 1588 at the request of Don Antonio, the claimant to the Portuguese throne recognized by Elizabeth as King of Portugal. It was given a monopoly of trade for ten years on the Guinea coast between Senegal and Gambia. It was formed by London and west country merchants, who agreed to pay 5 per cent of their profits and a quarter of their prizes to Don Antonio, who was to use the money to pay off his debts in England.

GUINEA, REPUBLIC OF (254,800 sq. kms), in West Africa, was, until 1958, the French colony of Guinea. A president and legislative assembly are elected by adult suffrage from one political party. Fulbe, Mande, and Kissi groups predominate in a population of 3,420,000.

GUINEA-BISSAU (36,125 sq. kms), generally so called, its capital being Bissau, so as to distinguish from the independent Republic of Guinea this West African 'overseas territory' or colony of Portugal. Its population of about 800,000 includes Balante, Mandinka, Peul, and other groups, and about 3000 Portuguese. In 1968 a nationalist movement, using guerrilla methods, won control of about two-thirds of its rural areas.

GUISCARD, ROBERT (d. 1085), member of the Norman Hauteville family and a ruthless noble adventurer who fought his way to power as the leader of Norman expansion in southern Italy in the 11th cent. In 1072 he and his brother began the conquest of Sicily and subsequently extended their operations to the mainland. Their encroachments into papal territory led to a breach with the pope, who had hitherto recognized Guiscard's possessions, but the Normans were always able to profit from the papacy's need for armed help against more dangerous enemies, in particular the German emperor. After destroying Byzantine power in Italy, Robert launched an attack on Byzantine possessions in Greece (1081), but was robbed of success by constant trouble at home with his relatives and with the nobility. His direct descendants ruled in southern Italy until 1125, when his lands were annexed by his nephew, Roger II of Sicily, who created the unified Norman kingdom of Sicily.

GUISE, FRANCIS, Duc de (1519–63), fought in the service of Francis I and of Henry II during the Franco-Habsburg conflict of the mid-16th cent. The victor of several battles in the period 1542–5, he later acquired a great military reputation as the defender of Metz against the forces of Charles V (1552–3) and the conqueror of Calais (8 Jan. 1558), which had been an English possession for 200 years. By his marriage to Anne d'Este, grand-daughter of Louis XII (1547), and that of his niece, Mary Stuart, to the Dauphin Francis, Francis acquired political prestige also, which he used to effect when Francis II succeeded to the French throne in 1559. A patron of the Jesuit order, he promoted the persecution of the Huguenots (1559). In 1561 he united with his former rival Montmorency and the marshal St André to form a triumvirate to defend French Catholicism. By his repudiation of the January Edict (1562) and his instigation of the massacre of Vassy (1 March 1562) he led France into civil war. Defying royal orders, he occupied Paris at the head of an armed band of over 2000 men (March 1562) and with his colleagues assumed control of the king and government. While leading the siege of Orléans, the Protestant headquarters, Guise was murdered by a Protestant fanatic.

GUISE, HENRY, Duc de (1550–88), son of Duke Francis and nephew of the cardinal of Lorraine, inherited the role of champion of the orthodox Catholic party in a France torn by religious and civil war. He avenged his father's death in 1563 by instigating the murder of the Protestant leader, Coligny, and the massacre of St Bartholomew (Aug. 1572). After 1575 he was known as 'le Balafré' (Scarface) from a wound received in battle. In 1576 he established the Holy League, forcing Henry III to summon the Estates-General to Blois before the king engineered its dissolution (1577), Guise revived the league in 1584 after the death of the Duc d'Alençon opened up the prospect of the succession of the Huguenot, Henry of Navarre. He had extensive support in Paris and the northern and eastern provinces, and the promise of help from Spain (treaty of Joinville 1584). By forcing Henry III to revive Huguenot persecution (treaty of Nemours 1585), he precipitated the War of the Three Henries, a struggle for the French succession between himself, the king, and Navarre. Guise achieved considerable success, *eg*, at the battle of Auneau (1587), and in defiance of royal orders he entered Paris triumphantly (9 May 1588) while Henry III left the capital a humiliated man. Henry submitted to the Holy League's demands by the Edict of Union (1588), appointing Guise lieutenant-general of the realm, but smarted for revenge. On 23 Dec. 1588 Guise was murdered on Henry's orders in the royal antechamber at Blois.

GUISE, CHARLES, cardinal of Lorraine (1524–74), younger brother of Duke Francis of Guise, with whom he led the Catholic party in France, and uncle of Mary Queen of Scots. He was a member of the *conseil privé* in Henry II's reign and Abp of Rheims. He controlled financial and governmental matters and was an able politician and skilful and cunning diplomat, *eg*, he took part in the negotiations leading to the peace of Cateau-Cambrésis (1558–9) and led the French

contingent at the Council of Trent (1562–3). After the failure of the Colloquy of Poissy (Oct. 1561), which he helped to conduct, he withdrew from court. The murder of his brother during the first civil war (1563) was a bitter blow and enabled Catherine de Medici to reassert her authority over the king and government. The cardinal's influence revived in 1568, when he persuaded Charles IX to dismiss the moderate chancellor L'Hôpital, and France was plunged again into religious strife.

GUISE FAMILY, ducal house of Lorraine, and through their relationship with the royal houses of Stuart and Valois the most influential family in 16th-cent. France. The first representative of this great feudal family to hold the ducal title was Claude, Count of Aumale and Marquis of Mayenne and Elbeuf (1496–1550), who accompanied Francis I to Italy and was wounded at Marignano. His son Francis and grandson Henry were the leaders of the Catholic party during the French civil wars and the latter's concern for the defence of French orthodoxy and the success of the Counter-Reformation led him to establish the Holy League against Henry III. With the accession of the Huguenot, Henry of Navarre, to the French throne the power of the Guise family waned. Charles of Guise (1571–1640) recognized Henry IV in 1594. On the death of the last Duke, Francis Joseph (1670–5), the family estates accrued to Mary of Lorraine, Mademoiselle de Guise, the spinster daughter of Duke Charles (1615–88) and on her death the line ended.

GUITEAU, CHARLES JULIUS (*c.* 1840–82), US lawyer and disappointed office-seeker, who shot President James A. Garfield at a Washington, DC, railroad station (2 July 1881). Garfield subsequently died (19 Sept.) and Guiteau was executed.

GUIZOT, FRANÇOIS PIERRE GUILLIAUME (1787–1874), French politician, prime minister, and historian, who was overthrown by the February revolution (1848). He was born in Nîmes, but because his father, a Protestant lawyer, was executed for participation in the federalist troubles, he spent most of his youth in Geneva, the Calvinist atmosphere of which left a marked impression upon him. Later, as professor of history at the Sorbonne (1812), he became associated with the intellectual opposition to Napoleon, which led to his becoming secretary-general of the ministry of the interior (1814) in the first restoration. During the Hundred Days he went to Ghent to plead with Louis XVIII for the adoption of a liberal policy after the defeat of Napoleon and was rewarded with a post in the ministry of justice and a place in the Conseil d'État (1815). He made a name for himself as one of the Doctrinaires and by his polemical lectures and political writings, in which he emerged as a staunch defender of the charter. He was ejected from his posts (1820–1) by the Ultras. In the next few years he devoted himself mainly to historical work, to editing English and French records, and to journalism. In 1830 he achieved a long-held ambition to become a deputy, when he was returned for Lisieux. His boldness and ability as a speaker led to his becoming prominent in opposition.

He accepted the revolution of 1830 and was made minister of the interior, in which capacity he purged the administration of legitimists. As minister of public instruction (1832–9) he was responsible for basic legislation on primary education and teacher-training (1833). During the 1830s he continued his historical work, founding the Société de l'Histoire de France, reviving the Académie des Sciences Morales et Politiques (1836), and securing election to the Académie Française itself (1832). On the fall of Thiers he was recalled to be minister of foreign affairs under Marshal Soult (1840), whom he dominated and eventually replaced as prime minister (1847). He worked very closely with Louis Philippe, whose conservatism he shared, refusing to embark on aggressive foreign ventures or to reform the political system, which was notorious because of his cynical manipulation of the elections. His rule was also closely associated with the economic interests of the *Notables* and helped to stimulate the revolution of 1848. He was dismissed in Feb. by Louis Philippe and spent some time in exile in England (1848–9). On his return to France he continued his historical, religious, and personal writings and remained a royalist. His achievement has been variously estimated, but he was in many ways an austere and high-minded man.

D. Johnson, *Guizot, Aspects of French History 1787–1874* (London and Toronto, 1963).   CHC

GUJARS, pastoral people found in great numbers from the Indus to the Ganges and from Hazara to Gujarat. Their origin is controversial, but they are probably, like many Rajput clans and Jats, descended from the Hunas or allied hordes who invaded India during the 5th and 6th cents AD.

GUJRAT, BATTLE OF (21 Feb. 1849), decisive victory over the Sikhs, known as 'the battle of the guns'. British losses were 96 killed and 700 wounded. Sikh losses were enormous. A relentless pursuit made the battle completely decisive. It was followed by the annexation of the Punjab.

GULF OF TONGKING INCIDENT (1964), turning point in the 'escalation' of the Viet-nam War. In Aug. 1964 two American destroyers were allegedly attacked by North Viet-namese craft in the Gulf of Tongking, and fired back. President Johnson responded by persuading the US Congress to pass a resolution giving him powers to take whatever action was considered necessary to deal with the situation in Viet-nam, and on that basis sent ground forces to South Viet-nam in 1965, without any declaration of war. The validity of the resolution, and even the official version of the incident itself, were challenged by the president's opponents in Congress in 1968, and subsequently there was a move to repeal the resolution.

GULISTAN TREATY (24 Oct. 1813). Russo-Iranian agreement, negotiated with British assistance, by which Iran ceded to Russia, Georgia, Baku, Derbend, Shirvan, and Karabagh.

GUNAWARDENA, PHILIP (1901–), Sinhalese politician, who became a Trotskyist and one of the founders of the Lanka Sama Samaj Party. In 1936 he was elected to the state council, and became an active trade union leader. He was elected in 1947 to the first house of representatives. In 1956 he led his section of the LSSP into a coalition with Bandaranaike's party and was appointed minister of agriculture and food, but he left the government in 1959. He failed to agree with the other Marxist groups and in 1965, somewhat surprisingly, joined Dudley Senanayake's national government as minister of industry and fisheries.

GUNDULF (?1024–1108), bishop of Rochester from 1077, he came with Lanfranc from Bec to England and rebuilt Rochester Cathedral. Gundulf was the only bishop to support Abp Anselm in his quarrel with William II and was responsible for administering the see of Canterbury during its vacancy (1089).

GUNGUNYANA (*reg.* 1885–95), King of the Gaza empire, who attempted to ward off increased European pressure by playing off one power against another and stockpiling firearms. He was eventually defeated by the Portuguese in 1895.

GUNPOWDER, oldest and most famous of all explosives. Its origin is unknown, but the names of Roger Bacon and Berthold Schwarz are associated with its development in the 13th cent. Its use as a propellant in the 14th cent. was the first effective use of chemical energy in imparting motion to missiles. The ingredients of gunpowder are saltpetre (potassium nitrate) about 75 per cent, charcoal 15 per cent, and sulphur 10 per cent. Not until the end of the 15th cent. was effective control of the firing of gunpowder achieved. From that time, until the middle of the 19th cent., it was the only known explosive of any practical value, and European wars revealed fresh techniques in the use of cannon and guns.

GUNPOWDER PLOT in England (5 Nov. 1606), conspiracy to blow up the English parliament and King James I. The chief conspirator, Robert Catesby, a Roman Catholic, was angered by the king's failure to grant greater toleration to Catholics. His principal accomplices were his cousin, Thomas Winter, his friends, Thomas Percy and John Wright, and Guy Fawkes. The necessity to prepare for the aftermath, if the plot succeeded, caused Catesby to draw in others, one of whom, Francis Tresham, wrote to his brother-in-law, Lord Monteagle, warning him enigmatically to stay away from parliament. This led directly to the discovery of gunpowder in a cellar beneath the parliament buildings, whence it had been carried by the conspirators from an adjoining house. All the conspirators were caught and executed, except Tresham, who died in prison.

GÜNS, small fortress near the Hungarian frontier, some 96 kms south-east of Vienna. Here in Aug. 1532, for more than three weeks and with few troops, Niklas Jurisić resisted the Ottoman Turks for so long that the sultan abandoned an assault on Vienna which he had intended to make that year.

GÜNTHER, JOHANN (1487–1574), German humanist and anatomist, who taught medicine at Paris and made observations on the action of the heart and arteries. He wrote *Anatomical Institutions according to Galen*, which was revised by his pupil, Andreas Vesalius (1538).

GUPTA DYNASTY, one of the greatest ancient Indian dynasties (*c.* AD 320–550). After the disintegration of the Kushan empire (*c.* AD 200), a number of kingdoms and republics arose in northern India. One of these, situated in west Bengal or east Bihar, developed into an important state in the beginning of the 4th cent. when its third ruler, Chandra Gupta I (*c.* 320–35), joined, by matrimony, his inherited domains with those of the Licchavis, a republican tribe in north Bihar. By conquest he added other areas to this state, which gave him control of the eastern part of the Gangetic valley. On this firm foundation his successor, Samudra Gupta (*c.* 335–75), built a vast empire by incessant campaigns all over the Indo-Pakistani sub-continent. These conquests did not, however, result in the foundation of a great closely knit state. Only the nucleus, roughly corresponding to the area inherited by Samudra Gupta, was directly administered, whereas most of the conquests were brought into various degrees of dependence. Gupta control in the outlying areas, such as north-west and southern India, was nominal rather than real, but, even so, undoubtedly contributed to the intensification of relations with the Gangetic valley. The next king, Chandra Gupta II (375–415), added Malwa, which had long been under control of Indianized kings of Scythian origin, to the empire. His successor, Kumara Gupta (415–55), at least maintained the empire intact. Under Skanda Gupta (455–67), an invasion of the Central Asian Huns was successfully repulsed, but after his death a slow decline, due to ever-present fissiparous tendencies rather than external pressures, set in, and led finally to a new Hun invasion under Toramana (*c.* 500). The Huns occupied vast parts of northern India for some 30 years. Although they were at last decisively defeated the Guptas never re-established their pristine power and only lingered on some time as a local Bengal dynasty.

The Gupta period is generally considered a Golden Age of India. The sources give us the impression of a well-ordered, relatively prosperous society in which impressive achievements in art and literature set standards for later generations. Sanskrit, which had earlier been confined to the religious sphere and associated fields, now became the official language and the principal medium for literature and high-class social intercourse, at least in northern India. It is also in this period that we notice the first clear evidence of Indian cultural influence in South-East Asia.

R. K. Mookerji, *The Gupta Empire* (Bombay, 1947). JG de C

GURKHAS, term loosely applied to any inhabitant of Nepal, but originally restricted to the royal family of the small kingdom of Gurkha and their followers, the Khas, Magars, Gurungs, and Thakurs. Gurkha raids into British India led to war in 1814. After a stubborn resistance, the Gurkha were forced to accept the terms of the treaty of Segauli (1816). The inhabitants of Nepal have marked Mongolian features. In order of social precedence they may be divided into Brahmans, Thakurs, Chetris, Gurungs, Magars, Newars, Limbus, Rais, Sunwars, Murmis, and Tharus. The lingua-franca is khas-khura, an Indo-Aryan dialect. Until 1947 they were enlisted in the Gurkha battalions of the Indian army and fought with great gallantry on the north-west frontier, in France, Mesopotamia, Burma, Africa, and Italy. Recently the strength of the British brigade of Gurkhas has been greatly reduced.

GURNEY, JOSEPH JOHN (1788–1847), British banker and philanthropist, who was a prison visitor, often with his sister Elizabeth Fry, and prominent in the anti-slavery struggle. He was probably the most influential evangelical Quaker from 1825 until his death.

GÜRSEL, CEMAL (1895–1966), Turkish soldier who led the anti-Menderes military coup (27 May 1960) and became acting chief of state (1960–1) and president (1961–6).

GÜRTNER, FRANZ (1881–1941), German politician, who was minister of justice in the Nazi government (1932–41). He was a member of the German Nationalist Party (DNVP) and had actively aided right-wing extremism as Bavarian justice minister (1923–32) and had helped Hitler in the aftermath of the Munich putsch. Like some of his colleagues, *eg*, Neurath and Krosigk, Gürtner held extreme nationalist-conservative rather than National Socialist views, and did his best to restrain the anarchic tendencies of the regime in the legal sphere. His tenure of the justice ministry prevented the appointment of Nazi jurists like Frank, Freisler, or Thierack, his eventual successor.

GUSTAVUS I (1496–1560), King of Sweden (*reg.* 1523–60), founder of modern Sweden and of the Vasa dynasty. He belonged to a gentry family connected with the Stures, and his father perished in the Stockholm Blood Bath. The next year (1521) he began a revolt among the peasantry, in two years of constant campaigning ousted the Danes, and was then elected king by the Diet. His reign was marked by many rebellions (which he subdued by eloquence as well as main force), the hostility of nobles ensconced in the council of state, and financial troubles. But Gustavus enriched the Crown by confiscating the Church lands (1527) and by 1554 had made the country Lutheran; in the same year the monarchy was declared hereditary in his family. Fear of Denmark necessitated a cautious foreign policy, but Gustavus freed Sweden from the dominance of Lübeck—which had helped him to the throne—and endowed it with a navy and the beginnings of a standing army.

GUSTAVUS II ADOLPHUS (1594–1632), King of Sweden (*reg.* 1611–32), creator of a great power and Protestant champion. He was declared of age on the death of his father, Charles IX, and accepted Axel Oxenstierna as his principal adviser. Together they improved the administration, organizing the government departments as 'colleges', giving the council more definite duties, fixing the procedure of the Diet, and stratifying its foremost element, the House of Nobles. At the same time, the iron and copper industries were developed, with the help of foreign capitalists, new trading companies formed, and encouragement given to education. Yet this many-sided king left his deepest imprint on the art of war. His army was based primarily upon the regiments that were raised and maintained on a regional basis throughout Sweden, though the infantry was supplemented by many mercenaries. It was strictly disciplined, united by religious feeling, and distinctively dressed. Above all, it was mobile, having light artillery, cavalry who were taught to charge effectively, and a main body of infantry that deployed itself into a line only three deep and kept up rapid fire from muskets of a novel lightness.

In 1617 Gustavus concluded his father's war against Russia by a treaty which excluded her from the Baltic coastline. He next fought Sigismund of Poland, captured Riga, secured Livonia by a great victory at Wallhof, and finally (1629) gained possession of the Prussian ports. He was now ready to face the imperial forces, whose advance across Germany threatened not only Sweden's territorial gains, but the religion of which he was a devout and dutiful champion. At Breitenfeld (Sept. 1631) he saved the Protestant cause in a battle which, in Oxenstierna's view, opened the way to a complete overthrow of the empire by a march on Vienna. Instead, Gustavus wintered at Mainz, and the following year pursued the defeated Tilly across the Danube and the Lech to Ingolstadt, where he died of his wounds. But Wallenstein, with a fresh imperialist army, reoccupied Bohemia and ravaged the lands of Gustavus's ally, the Elector of Saxony. A conquered Saxony would bar Gustavus's way back to Sweden, therefore he joined battle at Lützen, near Leipzig (Nov. 1632), where his troops gained the field at great cost, but he was killed heading a counter-charge.

M. Roberts, *Gustavus Adolphus: a history of Sweden, 1611–1632*, 2 vols (London, 1953, 1958).
N. Ahnlund, *Gustavus Adolphus the Great* (English trans., New York, 1940).   TKD

GUSTAVUS III (1746–92), King of Sweden (*reg.* 1771–92), where his version of enlightened despotism created the brilliant 'Gustavian era'. On succeeding his father, he destroyed the rule of the parties by a bloodless military coup. The four estates were required to surrender most of their powers and could only meet when summoned by the Crown. This happened rarely. In the first phase of his reign the king introduced administrative and economic reforms, granted freedom of religion and the press, and established a splendid and highly cultivated court life. Like his uncle, Frederick the Great, he practised the arts (especially as a playwright), and he founded the National Theatre, Opera, and Academy. His attack on Russia (1788) gave rise to an aristocratic conspiracy in Finland—the League of Anjala—but when Denmark entered the war against him, the patriotism of the other three estates enabled him to force the Act of Union and Security upon the nobles. By this measure the ancient Council of State was abolished and the independence of the estates further reduced, while the nobility forfeited nearly all its privileges. The Russian war having ended with a Swedish naval victory at Svensksund (1790), Gustavus tried to draw Catherine of Russia into his plans for supporting Louis XVI against the French Revolution. But in March 1792 an army officer, who had many aristocratic accomplices, wounded him fatally at a masked ball.

GUSTAVUS IV (1778–1837), King of Sweden (*reg.* 1792–1809). On coming of age (1796) he pursued a mainly reactionary and often unskilful policy. He joined, unsuccessfully, in the Third Coalition against Napoleon, quarrelled with Sir John Moore (who was sent to Gothenburg to help him), and failed to organize the defence of Finland against the Russians. In 1809 a military conspiracy, with civil support, obliged him to abdicate. He died in poverty in Switzerland.

GUSTAVUS V (1858–1950), King of Sweden (*reg.* 1907–50), married a princess of Baden descended from the older royal house of Vasa. His long reign was marked by the triumph of social democracy in Sweden. But in Feb. 1914 the king installed in office a ministry opposed by the lower house of parliament. He showed his pro-German tendencies in both World Wars.

GUTENBERG, JOHANN (?1395–1468), German inventor of printing from movable type. Pages had been printed earlier from a single block, but this method was laboriously slow. Gutenberg conceived that a series of stamps representing individual letters could be assembled to form a block and subsequently reused to form another. By this time the required components for printing (paper, ink, and type) and techniques for their manufacture were available. Gutenberg moulded these into an invention of fundamental historical importance. His *Letters of Indulgence* (1454) was partly printed, and his Bible of 1455 was the first book wholly printed with movable copper type.

GUTHRUM (d. 890), who led part of a Danish army (875), with two other kings, from Mercia to Cambridge. In 877–8 he launched an attack on Alfred, King of Wessex. Though he drove Alfred into hiding at Athelney, Alfred successfully regrouped his forces and defeated Guthrum at Edington. Guthrum came to terms with Alfred at Wedmore, accepted Christianity, and withdrew to Suffolk. Thereafter he and Alfred waged sporadic war against each other, but agreed on a formal partition of territory in 886 after Alfred had recaptured London.

GUTI, people of whom little is known, who attacked Akkad from *c.* 2250 BC onwards and ruled that country (*c.* 2200–2120), probably occupying only places of strategic importance.

GUTSHERRSCHAFT, system by which the free peasantry of the European plains east of the Elbe were by the 16th cent. reduced and replaced by the large, quasi-independent *latifundia* or estates of a powerful nobility who had broad judicial powers, both civil and criminal, over those living on their lands.

GUY, Count of Flanders (*c.* 1232–1305), loyal vassal of the kings of France until constant interference by Philip IV in the internal affairs of the county in 1294 finally drove him into resistance. He sought English help, but Edward I, himself at war with France, failed to prevent a defeat of the Flemings in 1297 and the complete French conquest of Flanders in 1300, after which Guy was imprisoned in Paris. A popular Flemish rising in 1302 restored to power Guy's son, Robert, whom Philip IV had to recognize as the new count in 1305.

GUYANA, in northern South America, formerly British Guiana, is bounded by the Amakura and Mururuma rivers in the west and the Courantyne river in the east, and faces claims from Venezuela and Surinam to about one half of her territory. Columbus reached the Orinoco river (1498), and other Spanish explorers (1517, 1584) preceded Raleigh in his search for El Dorado (1595), but they established no settlements east of the Orinoco. Dutch attempts to establish trading settlements on the Essequibo and Pomeroon rivers were destroyed by the Spaniards (1594). Dutch traders again appeared (*c.* 1600) and Dutch and English settled together on the Essequibo river in 1604. In 1613 James I granted proprietary rights over all lands between the Amazon and the Essequibo to Robert Harcourt, but that year a new Dutch settlement, financed partly by the Anglo-Dutch Courteens, was established on the Essequibo, with a fort at Kyk-over-all. Essequibo was granted to the Dutch West India Co. (1621), with similar rights over Berbice three years later. The English destroyed Dutch Essequibo and Pomeroon river settlements and the Dutch destroyed the English Surinam

colony (1667). When peace was restored, Dutch colonization was extended. Their Demerara river settlements, becoming a separate colony (1774), were reunited with Essequibo (1784). These colonies, after capitulating to Britain (1781), were soon restored. Captured again (1796), they were restored once more (1802), seized finally (1803), and formally ceded (1814). The three colonies were united to form British Guiana (1831). In 1928 the representative constitution was replaced by Crown Colony government. The legislature's composition was altered (1943) to provide for an elected majority, and (1945) a broadened franchise. Modified responsible government based on adult suffrage was conceded (1952) and Dr Cheddi Jagan's Peoples Progressive Party won the 1953 elections. Four months later the British government suspended the constitution. Constitutional government having been restored, the PPP won in 1957 and again in 1961, when internal self-government was introduced. An all-party delegation negotiated for independence in London (1961, 1962). Jagan's opponents, led by Linden Forbes Burnham, combined to defeat him (1964). Independence was granted (1966) and Guyana became a republic in 1970.

Raymond T. Smith, *British Guiana* (London, 1962). RH

GUYENNE, COLLEGE DE, famous humanist institution, was refounded in 1534 and associated with the Calvinist teachers Mathurin, Cordier, and George Buchanan. It aimed at combining a grammar school course, a full arts curriculum, and a sound moral training.

GUYON, JEANNE MARIE BOUVIER DE LA MOTTE, Madame de (1648–1717), French mystic, advocate of Quietism, and friend and protégée of Fénelon. In 1687 she published her *Short Method of Prayer*, which was condemned by the pope two years later. After the conference of Issay (1694–5) she was again condemned in 34 articles drawn up by Bossuet, Noailles, and Tronson, and signed by Fénelon, but she escaped to a convent, to be interned later at Vincennes for repeating her heresies (Dec. 1695). Bossuet then proceeded to crush Quietism, but was challenged by Fénelon, who appealed to the pope. In 1699 the latter declared 23 of Mme de Guyon's propositions erroneous, but refrained from calling them 'heretical'. She was released from prison about 1702.

GUY'S HOSPITAL in London, founded and endowed at Southwark with the bequest of the merchant Thomas Guy (1644–1724) on the profits of £180,428, which he made on South Sea stock, although during his lifetime he had a reputation for parsimony. Guy's was the first of the five great London teaching hospitals founded early in the 18th cent.

GÜYÜK (*reg.* 1246–8), third of the Mongol Great Khans in succession to his father Ogedei (*reg.* 1227–41) after a period of regency (1241–6) under his mother, Töregene. During his brief reign the disputes between the descendants of Chingiz Khan became more acute and Güyük died while preparing to march against his cousin, Batu.

GUZMÁN BLANCO, ANTONIO (1829–99), Venezuelan diplomat and president, who seized power in 1870. He was an able administrator and emphasized the importance of improving communications, public education, and economic growth through exports. By constitutional juggling he succeeded in putting the election of presidents in the hands of a small federal council which he controlled. Thus he was able, until 1888, to govern either through puppets or by himself. His extravagance while abroad eventually alienated his followers, and one of his puppets, Juan Paúl, turned against him (1889). Guzmán remained in exile in Europe and died there.

GWANDU, town in north-western Nigeria. When Uthman ibn Fudi divided the administration of his new state between his son Muhammad Bello and his brother Abdullah, the latter was put in charge of the western provinces and set up headquarters at Gwandu. His domains included western Kebbi and areas up the Niger to Say, parts of Gurma and Borgu and the emirates of Nupe (Bida) and Ilorin. Under Abdullah's successors Gwandu lost control of the western areas and after 1850 only Nupe and Ilorin remained viable emirates.

GWYER, SIR MAURICE LINFORD (1878–1952), British colonial administrator and first Chief Justice of India. He held legal appointments with a number of British government departments (1912–37), ending as first parliamentary counsel to the treasury (1934–7). His contact with India began with his membership of the Federal States inquiry committee (financial) (1932), which investigated the financial relations of the states with the future federation. While at the treasury he helped to draft the Government of India Bill (1935), which established a federal court for India as a whole. Gwyer became the first president of the court and the first Chief Justice of India (1937–43). He became vice-chancellor of Delhi University (1938–50) and from that position played an important advisory role in the drafting of the constitution of independent India (1950).

GWYN, NELL (1650–87), English actress and mistress of King Charles II of England, who bore the king two sons. She achieved some success on the stage and created two roles in Dryden's *Indian Emperor* and *Tyrannic Love*.

GWYNEDD, kingdom of north Wales, consisting anciently of north-west Wales beyond the Conway river, but later including also land east of the Conway. The kingdom formed a compact area with natural boundaries and a largely mountainous terrain, which made conquest difficult. It was less open to foreign influence than the other Welsh kingdoms and the idea of Welsh unity stems from the policies of the princes of Gwynedd. The first Norman attacks came from Chester, and under Robert of Rhuddlan the coastal regions as far as Bangor and Caernarvon were occupied by 1081. Gruffydd ap Cynan's efforts in 1094 regained a part of the lost lands, and his son, Owain Gwynedd, succeeded in extending his boundaries and in creating a stable state, able to withstand the attacks of Henry II. Gwynedd reached her full flowering in the 13th cent. in the reigns of Llywelyn I and Llywelyn II.

GYLIPPUS (*fl.* 5th cent. BC), Spartan general, who organized the successful defence of Syracuse against an Athenian expedition in the great Peloponnesian War (414–413 BC). Taking advantage of Athenian slackness in guarding the sea-routes to Sicily and in blockading Syracuse, he reached there in summer 414, restored Syracusan morale, and gradually gained supremacy by land and sea, so that in Sept. 413 the Athenian force was destroyed only two months after the arrival of substantial reinforcements. Gylippus prevented a massacre of Athenian prisoners, but failed to save their generals, Nicias and Demosthenes. He was subsequently condemned for corruption.

GYLLENBORG, CARL (1679–1746), Swedish chancellor from 1739, who was largely responsible for the unsuccessful war organized by the Hat Party against Russia. In Jan. 1717, while ambassador to Britain, he had been arrested for propaganda reasons on a charge of Jacobite conspiracy.

GYLLENSTIERNA, JOHAN (1635–80), treasurer of Sweden (1667) and later the foremost adviser of Charles XI. He strongly supported the Reduction, or reclaiming of Crown land from the nobles, and also helped the king to weaken the council. In foreign affairs he opposed the French alliance, negotiated the peace of Lund, and favoured the king's marriage to a Danish princess.

H

HAAST, SIR JULIUS VON (1822–87), German-born geologist and explorer in NZ, whose work included notable stratigraphic surveys and the history of the Moa and Southern Alps exploration.

HABE (sing. *Kado*), Fulfulde term for non-Fulbe peoples, often equated with 'pagans'. It was most commonly applied to the Hausa in pre-*jihad* days.

HABER, FRITZ (1868–1934), German chemist. His process for the manufacture of ammonia from gaseous nitrogen and hydrogen is of great importance to the fertilizer and explosive industries. He was awarded the Nobel Prize for chemistry in 1918.

HABIBULLAH (1872–1919), Ruler of Afghanistan (*reg.* 1901–1919) in succession to his father, Abd al-Rahman, whose policies of internal centralization and external neutrality in subordination to Britain he maintained, despite strong nationalist and German pressure in the First World War.

HABSBURG FAMILY, dominant ruling house of modern European history. Originating with Goutram, Count of Habsburg, the family established itself in Austria under Rudolph I (1218–91) and gained the imperial title (1273). By establishing the rule of primogeniture early, the Habsburgs won pre-eminence among the German princes, which it maintained until the late 14th cent. The division of the dynasty into two lines, followed by the growth of family strife and the rising power of neighbouring princes, weakened the authority of the Habsburgs, although Albrecht of Habsburg and Frederick III were both elected to the imperial title in 1438 and 1440 respectively. In fact, from Albrecht's brief reign (1438–9) until 1806, the title of Holy Roman emperor was vested, with one exception, in the Habsburgs. Habsburg fortunes began to revive in the reign of Frederick's successor, the Emperor Maximilian (1493–1519). The marriage between Maximilian and Mary, daughter of Charles the Bold of Burgundy (1477) redirected Habsburg interests towards western Europe and gave the family primacy among German princes.

Meanwhile, the succession in 1516 of Maximilian's eldest grandson, Charles, ruler of the Netherlands since 1506, to the throne of Spain, brought to the family vast new possessions in Europe and the Americas. The problems inherent in the government of an empire which stretched from the Caribbean to the Danube proved too great for the Emperor Charles V. On his retirement in 1556, the Habsburg inheritance was divided, his son Philip II assuming the Crown of Spain and its territories in the Netherlands, Italy, and the Americas and later the kingdom of Portugal, while his brother, Ferdinand I, King of Bohemia and Hungary, acquired the Austrian lands and was elected to the imperial title. Even so, the revolts of the Netherlands (1568) and of Portugal (1640), the Turkish threat and the challenge of Protestantism, imposed a continuous strain on the Habsburgs during the 16th and 17th cents.

After 1648 the alliance of the Spanish and Austrian branches of the family was no longer the powerful combination that it had been. The Spanish side went into a marked physical and mental decline from excessive intermarriage, culminating in the degenerate Charles II who died in 1700. The Austrian Habsburgs retained their leadership of central Europe, as yet unchallenged by the Romanovs or the Hohenzollerns, but in western Europe the ascendancy of the French Bourbons under Louis XIV was unquestioned. Bourbon–Habsburg rivalry continued throughout the 18th cent., but the succession of a Bourbon, Philip V, to the Spanish throne (1700) altered the balance. The Austrian Habsburgs were compensated with territory in Italy, and while their rivals expanded overseas they looked increasingly to eastern Europe, where the decline of the Ottoman Turks absorbed their energies. The decline of the Austrian Habsburgs was slow. The Napoleonic empire deprived them of their imperial German title and confined Habsburg authority to the Austrian empire alone. A brief restoration (1815–66) followed, particularly during the administration of Metternich, but in the face of the Italian Risorgimento and the rise of Prussia, the main concern of the Emperor Francis Joseph was to preserve his power in Austria-Hungary. The assassination of the Archduke Francis Ferdinand at Sarajevo (1914), precipitated the First World War. At the end of this war Austria-Hungary disintegrated and the Habsburg family's political hegemony ended.

A. Wandruszka, *The House of Habsburg* (English trans., London, 1964).   MKS

HACHA, EMIL (1872–1945), president of Czechoslovakia (1938–45), who began his career as a lawyer and worked as legal adviser to the land committee in Bohemia, and in a similar capacity in Vienna at the Austrian court of administration (1916–18). During the inter-war years he served at the Hague permanent court of international justice, and as president of the senate supreme administrative court in Prague. After Munich (1938) he seemed valuable as a figurehead and symbol of the Czechs' willingness to appease Hitler. The hyphen was introduced into the name of the state of Czecho-Slovakia to indicate the increased autonomy of Slovakia and Ruthenia; Hacha effectively had power over the Czech portion of Bohemia and Moravia only. Here the constitution was amended to give him authoritarian powers. This policy of trying to appease Germany by domestic concessions collapsed in March 1939, when Hacha took action against the semi-Nazi government of Slovakia, and attempted to crush the Hlinka Guard, the equivalent of the SS. Hitler used this as an excuse to intervene. Hacha was summoned to Berlin and, after being threatened with the bombing of Prague, signed away Czech independence. From then on he was forced to collaborate, still as president of the so-called Protectorate of Bohemia and Moravia. He became head of the new single party in Czech political life, Narodni Sourucentsvi, an imitation of the Nazi Party, and remained in office throughout the Second World War.

HACIENDA, term for the great *latifundium* type of rural estate which has dominated Spanish and Latin American land tenure systems at least since the 16th cent. The hacienda owner, or *hacendado*, is typically portrayed as a kind of feudal lord, controlling the lives of his labourers or peons, who in Latin America are often Indians. In the 19th cent. some of the Latin American nations were, and even in 1970 still are, governed by ad hoc alliances of *hacendados*. While they produce some market crops, one of their main purposes has been self-sufficiency. As a result, many remain inefficient in their use of land, which is only partly utilized.

HACKETT, SIR JOHN WINTHROP (1848–1916), Western Australian politician, who became part-proprietor from 1883, and editor from 1887, of the *West Australian* (Perth). He was a member of the WA Legislative Council (1890–1916) and a founder and first chancellor of the state's 'free' university (1912–16). His son, Sir John Winthrop Hackett (1910–), was deputy chief of the British army's general staff (1964–6), commander-in-chief of the British Army of the Rhine (1966–1968), and principal of King's College, London University (1968–).

HADDON RIG, BATTLE OF (1542), defeat of an English force that raided Teviotdale after King Henry VIII's failure to persuade James V to expel the French and popish faction led by Cardinal Beaton. A second expedition under Norfolk also retired ignominiously, but the Scottish counter-attack was routed at Solway Moss (1542).

HADFIELD, OCTAVIUS (1814–1904), bishop, English Anglican missionary in NZ, who acquired a profound knowledge of Maori language and customs, and became greatly trusted as peacemaker in tribal disputes. Hadfield, despite European opposition, defended Maori claims in the Taranaki dispute (1859–60). He was Primate of NZ (1890–3).

HADITH, *ie,* 'traditions' recording the utterances and actions of the Prophet Muhammad and representing for the Muslims an authoritative guide to conduct. The corpus of accepted hadith served as an instrument of great value, enabling the Muslims, as the masters of a great and complex empire, to adjust themselves to new circumstances and needs which had not existed in the lifetime of the Prophet and had not therefore received mention in the Koran.

HADRIAN, PUBLIUS AELIUS (AD 76–138), Roman Emperor (*reg.* 117–38). His family, like that of his relation Trajan, came from Italica in Spain. After becoming Trajan's ward in 85 and later serving on his imperial council and in important provincial commands, he was in a position in 117 to succeed, though not formally designated by Trajan. Hadrian reversed Trajan's expansionist policy in the east, making peace with Parthia, but he retained Dacia and at the same time systematized imperial defences in Upper Germany (earth and timber palisade) and Britain (Hadrian's Wall). Unlike most emperors, he spent much of his reign in tours of inspection in the provinces. The administration was enlarged by the creation of new posts and a more regular career structure, and the importance of the emperor as source of law was manifested by the regular inclusion of jurists in his council. Hadrian's restless activity, enquiring mind, and love of Greek culture, made him enemies among Roman traditionalists, but he did much to further imperial unity.

HADRIAN VI (1459–1523), Pope, last non-Italian pope. He attempted to reform the papal court and the notorious abuses of the Church as a whole, but was overwhelmed by the hostility of those whose corruption he denounced. Born in Utrecht, the son of a shipwright, he was educated at Louvain, and appointed tutor to the future Emperor Charles V. He went to Castile in 1515, received the bishopric of Tortosa in 1519, and became inquisitor general of the Spanish peninsula. He was a reforming associate of Cardinal Ximenes, but aroused the resentment of Castilians when entrusted with political responsibilities as Regent for Charles V, mainly because of his Flemish nationality. As pope (1522–3) his denunciations of the curia as the fountainhead of corruption were regarded as aiding Protestant propaganda and his own incorruptibility and austerity only increased his unpopularity. He tried, but failed, to organize political action against Luther and military action against the Turks, who captured Rhodes.

HADRIANOPLE, BATTLE OF (Aug. AD 378), turning point in the decline of the Roman empire. After the Emperor Valens' acceptance of the Visigoths into the Roman empire (376), relations between them and the Romans deteriorated, and a series of engagements culminated in the battle of Hadrianople (mod. Edirne, in European Turkey), in which the Roman army was destroyed and Valens killed. The defeat compelled Valens' successor, Theodosius I (379–95), to admit the Goths into Roman military service as integral tribal units under their own kings; he thus inaugurated an era of foreign policy which led to the sack of Rome by Alaric (410) and the settlement of the Visigoths in Aquitaine (418).

HADRIAN'S WALL, Roman frontier in Britain, constructed of stone from AD 122, following the Emperor Hadrian's visit and extending for 80 Roman miles on the Tyne–Solway isthmus. The complex eventually included mile-castles, two turrets to each mile interval, 15 forts, a ditch to the north, an earthwork (*vallum*), and a military way on the south. To the east it was protected by an estuary fort at South Shields and on the west by a 35-mile chain of coastal fortifications. Superseded by the Antonine Wall (*c.* 140–58) and then in commission with it until *c.* 184–5, the Hadrianic frontier otherwise endured until it was abandoned late in the 4th cent. It suffered temporary occupation and destruction by hostile forces after desertion or treachery in 197, 296, and 368, but never fell to a contested frontal assault.

HADZIACZ, TREATY OF (1658), agreement between the Poles and the Cossacks, by which Poland promised an extension of the Polish–Lithuanian Union of Lublin (1569) to the Ukraine. The palatinates of Bratslav, Kiev, and Chernigov were to be included in the Polish state as a 'Grand Duchy of Ruthenia', the Orthodox were to have the same rights as other Christians, and Cossack representatives were to sit in the Polish senate. The Cossacks were to nominate candidates for hetman and were promised their own administration and currency.

HAFIZ (*c.* 1325/6–*c.* 1390) of Shiraz, famous Persian poet, held to be the supreme master of the *ghazal* form. His poems —about such themes as love, human and mystical, the impermanence of all mortal things—reveal him as a superb craftsman, well versed in Arabic and in Persian literature and learning.

HAFIZ RAHMAT KHAN (*c.* 1710–74), Rohilla chief and uncle of Ali Muhammad Khan of Rohilkhand. When Ali Muhammad died (1749) he left six sons, but the real power remained in the hands of a group of Rohilla *sardar*s the most important of whom was Hafiz Rahmat Khan. Hafiz is used in the sense of guardian and not as a man who knew the Koran by heart. When the Marathas threatened Rohilkhand (1771), the Rohillas were helped by Shuja-ud-daulah of Oudh, but later refused to abide by their pecuniary engagements. At the Conference of Benares (1773) Warren Hastings, in return for 40 lakhs of rupees, agreed to help the ruler of Oudh to expel the Rohillas. In April 1774 the Rohillas were defeated and Hafiz was slain. Hastings's chief object was to provide Oudh with an easily defensible frontier because it was a buffer state to Bengal.

HAFSIDS, dynasty governing the eastern Maghrib in 13th–16th cents from capitals at Tunis, Bougie, and Constantine. Appointed as Almohad viceroys to restore order in Ifriqiyya (1207), they seceded under Abu Zakariya (*reg.* 1229–49) and claimed the caliphate under Mustansir (*reg.* 1249–77). After extinction in Morocco, the Almohad community survived as the military and administrative nucleus of the Hafsid state, and withstood a long period of instability (1277–1370), which ended in Moroccan invasions (*reg.* 1347–58). Under Abu Faris (*reg.* 1394–1434) and Uthman (*reg.* 1438–88), Hafsid hegemony reached as far west as Tlemcen. Such persistence shows repeatedly the strength of a regional political community which proved able to attract significantly powerful nomad peoples within its administrative scope.

This community was itself an aspect of a regional society whose cohesion was expressed in Islamic forms such as Sufism, and through the spread of vernacular Arabic. Economically, trade with Europe increased, involving the Hafsid rulers with Sicily, Aragon, and the Italian cities. While the local market had been previously dominated by urban manufactures, the emphasis in Hafsid production was on wool and leather. Particular benefit perhaps accrued in the 15th cent. from commercial difficulties in the Levant, and it may be that the dynasty's fortunes were linked with changes in Mediterranean trade. From the late 15th cent. this aspect of the economy fell into the hands of the corsairs, whose enterprise superseded that of the Italians in the region. Politically, the Hafsids collapsed through acquiescence in Spanish conquests along the coast (1505–11), and then, with Ottoman support, the corsairs won control, capturing Tunis (1534). Restored by Charles V (1535), the Hafsids lingered in the city until its final fall to the Ottomans (1574).

HAGANAH, illegal Jewish defence organization in Palestine, established (1920) in place of Ha-Shomer (1909–20), and considerably expanded (1936–9). It founded military commando units (Palmach) (1941) and was absorbed into Israel's defence force (1948). Haganah defended Jewish settlements, organized illegal immigration, and formed the mainstay of the Israeli forces (1947–8).

HAGENAU, TREATY OF (1505), confirmed French possession of Milan as agreed in the treaty of Blois (Sept. 1504) and provided for an act of homage by Cardinal d'Amboise (on behalf of Louis XII) to the Emperor Maximilian, which took place at Hagenau in April 1505.

HAGUE, ASSOCIATION OF THE (1681), between William of Orange and Sweden, though it was hoped that other powers would accede. Brought about by the *réunions* of Louis XIV, in particular his demands against Luxembourg, the association aimed at maintaining the territorial situation created by the treaty of Nymwegen (1678).

HAGUE, CONFERENCE OF THE (1691), where King William III of England asserted his leadership of the allies in the League of Augsburg. The conference was attended by numerous German princes and representatives of the emperor and Spain. The allied leaders laid plans for the coming campaign, agreeing to put 220,000 men in the field against France.

HAGUE, CONVENTION OF THE (1659), between England, France, and the United Provinces, signed on 11 May, in which they agreed jointly to mediate between Sweden and Denmark to bring about a settlement based on the treaty of Roskilde (1658). The mediators found that neither party desired peace, and the war was ended only by the death of Charles X of Sweden (1660).

HAGUE, TREATY OF THE (1596), agreement between King Henry IV of France, Queen Elizabeth I of England, and the United Provinces to destroy the Spanish empire of Philip II. An Anglo-Dutch fleet destroyed the Indies convoy in Cadiz harbour, cutting Spanish communications with the Americas, but the alliance collapsed when Henry IV made a separate peace with Spain (treaty of Vervins, 1598).

HAGUE, TREATY OF THE (1668), between the Netherlands and England. The French invasion of the Spanish Netherlands disturbed the English parliament and, despite Charles II's pro-French policy, a treaty was signed on 23 Jan. with the United Provinces, according to which the two powers were to mediate between the belligerents. Shortly afterwards they were joined by Sweden and the Triple Alliance was formed.

HAGUE, TREATY OF THE (1720), between Spain and the Quadruple Alliance powers, restored Spain's conquests to Austria, while Emperor Charles VI renounced his claim to the Spanish succession and recognised the succession of the Spaniard, Don Carlos to Tuscany, Parma, and Piacenza. Austria also exchanged Sardinia for Sicily with Savoy.

HAGUE, TREATY OF THE (1725), negotiated to provide a counterbalance to the alliance of Spain and the emperor by the treaty of Vienna (1725). Signed initially by Britain, France, and Prussia, it mutually guaranteed their possessions against the designs attributed to the Vienna allies and promised in vague terms to resist any attacks on Gibraltar and Minorca, the encroachments of the Ostend Co., and the persecution of Protestants in the empire, while Frederick William of Prussia was bribed with a guarantee of his succession to Julich and Berg. Though Prussia speedily deserted the alliance to rejoin the emperor, the United Provinces, Denmark, and Sweden acceded to the treaty of Hanover.

HAGUE TREATY (16 May 1795), signed between France and the new Batavian republic. The first anti-French coalition fell apart with the withdrawal of Austria (1794) and Prussia (1795). The latter's defection exposed Britain's ally, the Batavian republic, to French attack and forced the Dutch to come to terms with France. Under the treaty, the republic was to support the French army in northern Europe.

HAGUE PEACE CONFERENCES (1899, 1907), tentative moves towards internationalism at a time of rising European tension. The first was at the suggestion of Russia, who could not afford to compete in the arms race. The second was prompted by President Roosevelt. The conference of 1899 was attended with scepticism by the powers other than Russia and did nothing to limit the arms race. Its declaration prohibiting the use of gas was ignored in 1915. Nevertheless, it provided machinery for international commissions of enquiry into disputes between nations, successfully used by Britain and Russia in the Dogger Bank incident (1904), and established a permanent court of arbitration which was used 14 times before 1914 and has survived and grown in usefulness.

The 1907 conference appeared more impressive, since 44 states attended, including representatives from South America, but its declaration against the arms race was ineffective and its decision to reconvene eight years later was prevented by war.

HAHN, OTTO (1879–1968), German physical chemist, who in 1938 discovered that uranium atoms when bombarded with neutrons could break into two, with an accompanying release of energy. Hahn's results were published early in 1939 by his collaborator, Lise Meitner (1878–1968). However, before this Bohr brought the news of uranium fission to the US, where its military implications were realized, particularly by Szilard. For his discovery of fission Hahn received the Nobel Chemistry Prize (1944).

HAI SAN, a predominantly Hakka Chinese secret society (*hui*) in Malaya, which engaged in a fierce struggle with the rival *Ghee Hin* for control of the Larut tin-fields (1861–74).

HAIDAR ALI KHAN (*c.* 1722–82), Muslim military adventurer, who rose to power in Mysore. After entering the army of the Hindu raja, he secured the favour of the chief minister and eventually usurped all power, keeping the raja as a puppet. The raja, however, was found to be intriguing with the Marathas, so he was strangled on Haidar's orders. The turning point in Haidar's career was the capture of Bednur (1763), by which he gained enormous wealth. After this, he struck coins in his own name. He fought two wars with the

British: the first (1767–9) ended in favour of Haidar, who practically dictated terms under the walls of Madras; after the second (1780–4) there was a mutual restoration of conquests under the treaty of Bangalore (1784).

HAIG, DOUGLAS HAIG, 1st Earl (1861–1928), British commander-in-chief on the western front (1915–19), a resolute professional soldier of orthodox views, accepting as inevitable the use of mass armies and trench warfare. After succeeding Sir John French following the Allied defeat at Loos, he launched a major attack, the battle of the Somme (1916), which cost 500,000 British casualties, though the Germans also suffered heavily. The prime minister, Lloyd George, opposed him for slaughter without victory, but he skilfully retained his command with the king's support. He withstood a heavy defeat in the German spring offensive (1918). 'With our backs to the wall and believing in the justice of our cause each one of us must fight to the end.' His counter-attack penetrated the Hindenburg Line. After the war parliament voted him £100,000. His popularity was unmatched and as president of the British Legion (1921–8) he worked for disabled soldiers through his Poppy Day appeals.

HAILE SELASSIE I (1892–), Emperor of Ethiopia (*reg.* 1930–) and son of Ras Makonnen, Emperor Menelik's governor of Harar. He was christened as Tafari Makonnen, and became regent and heir to the throne of Ethiopia in 1916. He was one of the founders of modern Ethiopia and resisted the Italian invasion (1935), addressed the League of Nations (1936), and, after five years' exile in Britain, returned to his capital in 1941. Since 1963 he has taken a leading part in the work of the Organization of African Unity.

HAILEY, WILLIAM MALCOLM, 1st Baron (1872–1969), British Colonial administrator. Until 1908 he served in the Punjab as colonization officer in the newly-established Jhelum Canal Colony (1901–7). He was chief commissioner (1912–18) of the newly created Delhi territory, where he was responsible for the initial stages of the development of New Delhi. In 1919 he joined the viceroy's executive council, first as finance, then as home member. He was governor successively of two of the most important provinces of British India—Punjab (1924–8) and the United Provinces (1928–34). The latter appointment was broken twice (1930–1931, 1933–4) by his secondment to the India Office in London as adviser on constitutional reforms. In handling difficult political situations, such as the Gurdwara agitation in Punjab (1924–5) and the Hourent campaigns in the United Provinces (1930–2), he was firm and effective. However, his suspicions of Congress' intentions made it difficult for him to deal with nationalist politicians except as agitators and led him to look to the strengthening of conservative Indian elements as the foundation for political stability, even when he recognized the failure of such groups to act effectively in economic or social terms.

He later studied African affairs and was director of the African Research Survey (1935–8), from which came the monumental volume, *An African Survey* (1938). In 1940 he led an allied economic mission to the Belgian Congo which secured support for the Allied war effort. He visited Africa regularly after the Second World War and produced a second major study in his work on native authorities in the High Commission territories (1951) and a second edition of his *African Survey* (1957).

HAILEYBURY COLLEGE, in England, originated in proposals sent (1804) to the Court of Directors of the East India Co. from their factory in Canton that young men destined for the Indian civil service should have two or three years' training in England before being sent abroad, which should not be before they had reached the age of 19. In 1813 an act of parliament prohibited the directors from sending any person to India as a writer unless he had resided at the college for four terms. This was modified in 1826, as there were

not enough young men to fill the vacancies, and the directors were empowered to appoint men who had not been to Haileybury, provided they passed a qualifying examination. In 1837 the maximum age for entrance to the college became 21, and 23 the maximum age for appointment as a writer. In the last Charter Act (1853) the directors lost their privilege of nominating and appointing persons as students of the college, and appointment to the Indian civil service was thrown open to competition. In 1854 a committee under Lord Macaulay recommended the selection of candidates for the Indian civil service by competitive examination and the closure of the college at Haileybury (1887). Subsequently, a boys' public school was established at Haileybury.

HAILLON, BERNARD DE GIRARD, SIEUR DU (1535–1610), French historian, whose works include *De l'Estat et succès des affaires de France* (1570) and *Histoire Générale des Rois de France* (1576), which analyses the constitutional position of the king and institutions.

HAILSHAM OF ST MARYLEBONE, QUINTIN McGAREL HOGG, Life Baron (1907–), British lawyer and politician who entered parliament as member for Oxford in the 'appeasement' by-election of 1938. After service in the Second World War and office in the 'caretaker' government of 1945, he served continuously in Conservative administrations (1956–64) as, variously, first lord of the admiralty, minister of education, lord president of the council, and lord privy seal. He was chairman of the party (1957–9) and its leader in the House of Lords (1960–3). In 1950 he succeeded his father as the second Viscount Hailsham, disclaiming the title in 1963 in his bid for the Conservative Party leadership. While not becoming prime minister, he returned to the Commons (1963–70), holding office (1964) under Douglas-Home. When the Conservative Party returned to power in 1970 he became lord chancellor, being created a life peer for the purpose. His renunciation of a peerage and acceptance of a different creation was, in 1970, a unique instance of its kind.

HAINAULT, important state in the centre of medieval Belgium, between the rivers Scheldt and Meuse; its capital was the impregnable castle of Mons. Early in the 10th cent. its earliest rulers were dukes of Lotharingia, one branch of their descendants ruling subsequently in Hainault, while another created the duchy of Brabant further to the north-east. Throughout the Middle Ages Hainault remained a largely agrarian district, dominated by a war-like nobility, and was annexed (1428–33) to the Burgundian state.

HAIPHONG INCIDENT (Nov. 1946), turning point in the growth of tension between the French army and the Viet-minh, which led to the Indo-China War (1946–54). The Viet-minh still held Hanoi, and the French sought to prevent them importing arms through Haiphong. Following the Viet-namese seizure of a French boarding-party on an arms-carrying junk, the French demanded that the Viet-minh hand over control of the port. Their ultimatum being ignored, the cruiser *Suffren* opened fire and at least 6000 Viet-namese were killed.

HAITIAN REVOLUTION, prolonged struggle (1790–1804), which freed the predominantly Negro western part of the island of Hispaniola from French colonial rule.

In the 18th cent. the sugar-producing colony of St Domingue became France's richest overseas possession. Its economy was based on plantations worked by slaves, and by 1800 over 90 per cent of the population of half a million was Negro.

When the ideas of the French Revolution reached French Hispaniola, the Negro freedmen assumed that its slogans applied to them, but their first revolt was suppressed with great brutality. In the following year, 1791, the slaves rose, and whites were massacred. After several years of fighting,

Toussaint L'Ouverture emerged as the rebel leader. An able diplomat, he attempted to retain ties with France while, at the same time, running St Domingue independently. His skill was further tested by British and Spanish invasions of the island. He defeated the Spanish forces and occupied the eastern part of Hispaniola, and arranged with the British for the transfer to his forces of Port-au-Prince, which the British had occupied for five years (1793–8).

Napoleon's refusal to recognize Toussaint's compromise led to the sending of a French expedition. Toussaint was defeated in 1802, captured, and sent to prison in France. But the French triumph was illusory. The continuing opposition of the rebels, a British blockade, and an outbreak of yellow fever broke the morale of the expeditionary force, and the survivors departed. On 1 Jan. 1804 Jean-Jacques Dessalines, Toussaint's successor, proclaimed the independence of the former French colony, and named this western part of the island Haiti, a word of Arawak origin.

The Haitian struggle for independence had wide repercussions in Latin America: if a small slave colony could defeat Napoleonic France then the liquidation of the enfeebled Spanish regime clearly seemed attainable.   MJM

HAJJAJ, AL-, B. YUSUF (c. 661–714), of the Banu Thaqif, at Al-Ta'if, won the favour of Umayyad Caliph, Abd al-Malik. He besieged and took Mecca in 692, thus ending the long and dangerous opposition, to the Umayyad house, of Ibn al-Zubayr. Sent to Iraq (694), he restored order among the troops of Kufa and Basra, enabling the great soldier Muhallab ibn Abi Sufra to take in hand the war in Persia against the extreme Kharijis (Azarika), whose resistance was broken in the campaigns of 696–7. Al-Hajjaj, now also in command of Khurasan and Sijistan in eastern Persia, had next to meet the rebellion of Abd al-Rahman ibn al-Ash'ath, which was crushed in 701. In 702 Al-Hajjaj founded Wasit, a garrison town for Syrian troops which would curb the restless armies of Kufa and Basra. Under the Caliph al-Walid I (reg. 705–15) Al-Hajjaj organized the campaigns of conquest in Transoxania.

HAKEWILL, GEORGE (1578–1649), English theologian, who published *Apologie or Declaration of the Power and Providence of God* in 1627 and in the 17th-cent. controversy between Ancients and Moderns was one of the first Englishmen publicly to take the Modern side.

HAKIM, -AL, BI-AMR ALLAH (985–?1021), the sixth Fatimid Caliph, came to the throne in 996 on the death of his father, Al-Aziz. The first years of his reign saw him under the dominance of the eunuch Barjawan, whom he had executed in 1000. Al-Hakim was responsible for policies anti-Christian in character (perhaps as a reaction against the liberal attitude of Al-Aziz). He also tended to stress the religious basis of the Fatimid regime, building at Cairo (1004) a 'House of Wisdom' for the training of Isma'ili missionaries. Some adherents of the Isma'ili faith held Al-Hakim to be a figure of divine character and sought to win a public following for this belief. Out of this movement arose the Druze religion, which was to find a refuge in the Lebanon. Al-Hakim, a monarch ill-famed for his capricious, cruel, and eccentric conduct, disappeared in obscure circumstances in 1021.

HAKLUYT, RICHARD, the elder (*fl.* 1580), English lawyer who, as economic adviser to the Muscovy Co., was interested in industrial techniques, markets, and plantation as a means of utilizing 'the offals of our people'. It was through him that his younger cousin, also called Richard, discovered his love of overseas adventure.

HAKLUYT, RICHARD, the younger (c. 1552–1616), English geographer and archdeacon of Westminster, who acquired an interest in exploration from his cousin and when chaplain to the Paris embassy (1583–8) was angered by foreigners' taunts that the English had achieved little in the way of trade and discovery. He vindicated his countrymen in *Principal Navigations, Voyages and Discoveries of the English Nation* (1589, enlarged 1598–1600), a record of the voyages of Cabot, Willoughby, Hawkins, Drake, and others. Hakluyt had earlier written *Divers Voyages Touching the Discovery of America* (1582) to popularize Gilbert's projected settlement. *Discourse of the Western Planning* (1584) was designed to assist Raleigh in a similar colonizing scheme. Hakluyt was personally involved in the South Virginian Co., and his work, written in vigorous Elizabethan prose, was a valuable stimulus to English maritime enterprise.

HAKON, SIGURDARSON (d. c. 995), King of Norway (reg. c. 970–c. 995). With the help of the Danish king, Harold Bluetooth, he displaced the fanatically Christian Harald Greycloak as king of western Norway and restored the pagan religion. He aided the Danes in 974 against Emperor Otto II of Germany, but later quarrelled with Harold of Denmark and defeated a Danish invading fleet in the celebrated battle of Hjorungavag. His prestige declined in his later years and he was overthrown by Olaf Tryggvesson.

HAKON THE GOOD (d. c. 960), King of Norway (reg. c. 935), and son of King Harald Fairhair. He was brought up as a Christian in England by King Athelstan. He dethroned his unpopular brother, Eric Bloodaxe, in Norway and adopted the pagan religion of most of his subjects. He is reputed to have undertaken important political and legal reorganization. He was dethroned by the sons of Eric Bloodaxe.

HALAF, site in Syria overlooking the Khabur river, which has given its name to a period of proto-history in the 5th millennium BC. On the site was a village with neolithic tools, but also a cobbled street, mud bricks, stamp seals, terracotta figures, and pottery.

HALBERSTADT, tiny principality within the Holy Roman empire, situated between the Weser and the Elbe. It became a secularized bishopric of the Lutheran Church in 1564 and was acquired by Brandenburg Prussia in 1648.

HALDANE, RICHARD BURDON HALDANE, Viscount (1856–1928), British politician and philosopher, who served as a Liberal MP, secretary of state for war (1905–12), and lord chancellor (1912–15, 1923–4). His second period of office as lord chancellor was in the first Labour government. Before holding political office he had rationalized the law of real property. He was a personal friend and legal colleague of Asquith, under whose premiership he went to Germany in 1912 in an unsuccessful bid to halt the naval race. Despite a liking for Germany and an understanding of German philosophy, he had no illusions about the possibility of impending war, for which he had earlier prepared the British army by a series of reforms. Towards the end of his life he published three philosophical treatises, in which field he had been Gifford lecturer at St Andrews University.

HALDANE, JAMES ALEXANDER (1768–1851), Scottish preacher, who conducted evangelical tours of Scotland after the pattern of George Whitefield in England. In 1799 he left the Church of Scotland to become the first minister of the Congregational Church in Scotland.

His brother, Robert Haldane (1764–1842), worked with him and wrote *The Authority and Inspiration of the Scriptures* (1824).

HALDANE, ARMY REFORMS (1905–12) in Britain, important extension of Cardwell's reforms. Under Haldane, a general staff for the army was organized, an expeditionary force of seven divisions created, the old established yeomanry and volunteers formed into the Territorial Army, and officers' training corps established in public schools. The army was made ready for the possibility of a major war.

HALDIMAND, SIR FREDERICK (1718–91), British soldier and colonial governor who fought in several European armies and by 1756 was on service with the British army in North America, where he served with distinction in the Seven Years War and the American War of Independence. He was appointed governor and commander-in-chief of Canada (1778–84). He began the first effective settlement of Upper Canada.

HALE, NATHAN (1784–1863), US journalist. He edited the *Boston Weekly Messenger* (1811–14), and then the influential *Boston Daily Advertiser* which, under his guidance (1814–54), was successively Federalist, Whig, and Republican, becoming especially prominent for its anti-slavery opposition to the Missouri Compromise Bill (1820) and the Kansas–Nebraska Act (1854).

HALEBID, name of a locality and archaeological site in present Mysore, India, famous especially for the Hoysaleshvara temple, founded by the Hoysalas in the middle or latter half of the 12th cent. The temple is remarkable for its elaborate and refined sculpture rather than for its architecture.

HALES, SIR EDWARD (d. 1695), English Catholic army officer, who did not qualify under the Test Act but held his command by royal dispensation under the Great Seal. In a collusive case at Rochester assizes (1686), brought by Hales's servant, Godden, Hales was acquitted and the legality of the dispensing power was affirmed.

HALES, JOHN (d. 1571), English clerk at the courts of Henry VIII, Edward VI, and Elizabeth I, and politician who served on the Duke of Somerset's commission on enclosures. He probably came nearer than any of his contemporaries to understanding the basic causes of economic distress in the 16th cent.

HALES, JOHN (1584–1658), English theologian, whose works were published as *Golden Remains* in 1659. Though a royalist, he was also a moderate man, anticipating religious toleration and latitudinarianism.

HALFDENE (d. 882), brother of Ivar, and leader of the Danish Great Army in 865, which captured York in 866–7. After being defeated by the West Saxons at Ashdown in 871, Halfdene withdrew into the Midlands. In 873–4 he partitioned Mercia and later became King of York, sharing out the lands of Yorkshire among his followers.

HALF-KING (Scruniyatha) (c. 1700–54), Seneca Indian chief, who accompanied George Washington on his 1753 and 1754 expeditions into the west.

Also the name of a Huron chief (Petawontakas) (c. 1750–c. 1820) of Sandusky, OH, who helped the British during the American War of Independence. He saved the Moravians of Lichtenau from hostile Indians (1777).

HALF-WAY COVENANT, doctrinal revision of Massachusetts (US) Congregationalism approved by the Church Synod (1662). The Covenant admitted to Church membership the children of baptized members, thus breaking down the distinction between them and the 'elect'. A further lowering of Church membership bars followed, broadening the franchise of the Massachusetts colony.

HALHEAD, NATHANIEL BRASSEY (1751–1830), English orientalist in the service of the East India Co. and MP (1790–5). He published *A Code of Gentoo Law* (1776) and a Bengali grammar (1778).

HALIARTUS, BATTLE OF (395 BC), defeat by the Thebans of a Spartan force which invaded Boeotia at the beginning of the Corinthian War. Its commander, Lysander, who was killed, had attacked Haliartus without waiting for the arrival of a supporting force under King Pausanias, who was subsequently impeached and exiled.

HALICARNASSUS, ancient Greek city in Caria, of mixed population, founded in the 10th cent. BC by Dorians, and ruled in early 5th cent. by Artemisia I, who supported Xerxes. It was the birthplace of Herodotus. Later (c. 360), it became the residence of the Carian dynast, Mausolus, whose tomb, the Mausoleum, made Halicarnassus famous.

HALIFAX, CHARLES MONTAGUE, 3rd Earl of (1st of 2nd creation) (1661–1715), English politician, financial genius, and a prominent and unpopular member of the Whig Junto. Appointed a lord of the treasury (1692), he rapidly introduced radical methods of financing the war with France (1689–97) by public loans, which culminated in the founding of the Bank of England (1694). In 1694 he became chancellor of the exchequer and carried through a scheme of national recoinage. His success gained him the post of first lord of the treasury (1697) from William III. Montague became undisputed leader of the Commons with the departure of Russell and Wharton (fellow members of the Junto) to the Lords. He resigned in 1699 after William, who detested Montague, had withdrawn his confidence. He was created Baron Halifax (1700), and an attempted impeachment of him and the other Junto members for complicity in the Partition treaties failed (1701). Under Queen Anne, Halifax strongly favoured the Hanoverian succession, and won the confidence of the Elector. When the Elector became king, as George I, he appointed Montague first lord of the treasury and created him Earl of Halifax (1714).

HALIFAX, GEORGE MONTAGUE–DUNK, 5th Earl of (2nd of 3rd creation) (1716–71), British politician. At first a follower of the Prince of Wales, he made his peace with the Pelham ministry (1744), and, with one short interval, was head of the board of trade (1748–61). There he pursued mercantile interests, becoming known as the 'Father of the Colonies' and giving his name to Halifax, NS (1749). He was secretary of state under Bute (1762) and Grenville (1763–5) and in this office he signed the general warrant against John Wilkes, who was examined at Halifax's home and then discharged. In retaliation Wilkes took legal action, establishing the illegality of general warrants and obtaining damages against Halifax. Halifax later served under North, as lord privy seal (1770) and secretary of state (1771).

HALIFAX, EDWARD FREDERICK LINDLEY WOOD, 6th Earl of (1st of 4th creation) (1881–1959), British politician, diplomat, and foreign secretary at the time of Munich (1938). He entered parliament as Conservative MP for Ripon in 1910. In the 1920s he was successively parliamentary under-secretary for the colonies, president of the board of education, and minister of agriculture. He was Viceroy of India (1926–31) during a difficult period in which he carried out negotiations with Gandhi. On his return to Britain other ministerial positions followed: education, war, privy seal, presidency of the council, and leadership of the House of Lords.

In 1937 he extricated Baldwin's government from the embarrassment caused by the Hoare–Laval plan for Abyssinia by placing the bulk of the blame on the foreign secretary, Sir Samuel Hoare.

The most important period of his career was as foreign secretary in Neville Chamberlain's government, an office he showed some reluctance to accept, anticipating the unpopularity it might entail. However, giving Chamberlain general support on appeasement with Germany, he assured Hitler of a settlement in his favour with regard to Austria and Czechoslovakia. After Munich Halifax and Chamberlain believed that Mussolini could be used as a moderating influence on Hitler. As late as Aug. 1939 Halifax threw away the possibility of a Soviet alliance, preferring to put his hopes on a conference with Mussolini. The declaration of the

Second World War automatically brought the appeasement ministers into disfavour, though Halifax was often excluded from criticism. In May 1940 quite a substantial body of opinion, including that of some Labour MPs, was in favour of Halifax as Chamberlain's successor rather than Churchill. He continued in office under Churchill, serving in his war cabinet and as British ambassador to Washington until 1946.

In his long political career he was often at the centre of events of international significance and his opinions carried considerable weight. His publications included *The Great Opportunity*, *Indian Problems*, and *Fullness of Days*.   MEB

HALIFAX, GEORGE SAVILE, 1st Marquis of (1633–95), English politician, nicknamed 'the Trimmer', who entered parliament after the Restoration (1660), In 1673 he manifested his consistent toleration by opposing the Test Act. For a while he joined Shaftesbury in opposition to King Charles II and was appointed a member of Temple's privy council (1679), but at the height of the exclusion crisis he parted company with Shaftesbury and was more instrumental than anyone else in securing the rejection of the second Exclusion Bill. In 1681 he was present at an interview between Charles II and William of Orange and thus renewed an acquaintance with William, which he had probably made in 1672. Under James II he was for a few months president of the council (1685). He made known his views on James II's Declaration of Indulgence in his *Letter to a Dissenter*, in which he advised scepticism towards the king's supposed religious toleration. He corresponded intermittently with William of Orange, but when Dykveld visited England (1687), Halifax's message to him lacked imperative. Nor was he one of those who invited William to England (1688). In fact, he was readmitted to the council by James, and was able to assure the king that he had done nothing to bring William over. Probably Halifax believed James might retain his throne even at this late hour, if only he would summon a free parliament and dismiss Roman Catholics from posts for which they were not legally qualified. James authorized Halifax and two other peers to meet William, who insisted that the king should dismiss the unqualified Roman Catholics. By the time Halifax reported back, however, James had already decided to flee the country. Halifax then presided over the body of peers which requested William to assume the provisional government of the country, and also presided over the early sessions of the Lords in the Convention parliament. He opposed a regency in favour of the scheme of a joint monarchy, and it was he who offered the Crown to William and Mary conjointly. Once again (1689), he was appointed lord privy seal, but resigned in 1690, after which he played little active part in politics. His writings include *The Character of a Trimmer*, written in the 1680s, a classic argument for moderation in politics.

H. C. Foxcroft, *A Character of the Trimmer* (Cambridge, 1946).   BM

HALIFAX OF MONK BRETTON, CHARLES WOOD, 1st Viscount (1800–85), British politician who was chancellor of the exchequer (1846) before becoming president of the Board of Control for Indian Affairs (1852–5) when he was responsible for a despatch setting down principles for education in India. He later became first lord of the admiralty and lord privy seal (1870–4).

HALL, CHARLES MARTIN (1863–1914), US scientist. The cheap production of aluminium was made possible by his discovery in 1886 that a solution of aluminium oxide in a molten mixture of cryolite (sodium aluminium fluoride) behaved as an electrolyte, and, when electrolysed, the pure metal could be isolated.

HALL, SIR JOHN (1824–1907), NZ politician and prime minister, who defended squatters' interests in the Canterbury Provincial Council and in the General Assembly, of which he

was a member (with two intervals) in 1855–93. He held strong views on military self-reliance for NZ, and joined Stafford's ministry (1866–9) and later led the opposition to Grey's administration (1877–9). Hall's own ministry (1879–1882) restored colonial finances through lessened borrowing and retrenchment. Ill-health and quarrelling among his colleagues, especially over the Parihaka crisis (1881–2), led to his resignation. Thereafter, though refusing office, Hall wielded great influence as an elder conservative statesman. Long the leading advocate of women's suffrage, he achieved success (though in opposition) in 1893.

HALLÉ, SIR CHARLES (1819–95), German-born pianist and conductor who founded and conducted the Hallé orchestra in Manchester, England (1857). His orchestra, and his own piano recitals, offered a cultural compensation to many for the starkness of the new industrialism of the north of England. He became first principal of the Royal College of Music at Manchester (1893).

HALLECK, HENRY WAGER (1815–72), US soldier and lawyer, who served in CA during the Mexican War (1846–8), and became a prominent mining and international lawyer in San Francisco. He later held command in the MS valley, but his only active campaign, at Corinth (April 1862), was undistinguished. As general-in-chief (1862–4) and chief-of-staff to U. S. Grant (1864–5) in Washington his preoccupation with detail obscured his grasp of strategy.

HALLER, ALBRECHT VON (1708–77), Swiss scholar, naturalist, poet, and physician. His *Elementa Physiologiae Humani Corporis*, published in 1757–66, has given him the reputation of being the father of modern physiology.

HALLEY, EDMUND (1656–1742), English astronomer and mathematician, who in 1682 observed the comet which is named after him. In 1678 he became friendly with Newton, whose *Principia* he published at his own expense. By applying Newton's laws of motion he correctly predicted the return of the comet of 1682 in 1758. He had already (1676) visited St Helena to catalogue the stars of the southern hemisphere and in 1698 began sea voyaging for scientific purposes. In 1701 he surveyed the tides of the English channel for the admiralty. His talent for imposing order on great bodies of data, shown in his Breslau Table of Mortality, resulted in the first systematic application of graphical methods to show physical features on maps. He made the first meteorological chart and the first magnetic chart. Many of his papers were published in the *Philosophical Transactions* of the Royal Society.

HALL-JONES, SIR WILLIAM (1851–1936), NZ politician, who was in Seddon's ministry (1895–1906) and took office as stop-gap prime minister on the latter's death. He was NZ high commissioner in London (1908–12).

HALLSTATT CULTURE, typical early Iron-Age phase of continental Europe, named after a large cemetery in Upper Austria. The culture is characterized technologically by a major use of iron by aristocratic and Celtic-speaking communities, and commercially by contacts with Etruscans and western Greeks. Local variants of Hallstatt culture are seen as far west as Spain and Britain, where iron-using Hallstatt immigrants arrived *c.* 550 BC. The site of Hallstatt itself is also remarkable for its salt mine, which underlines the contemporary economic importance of this commodity, *eg*, as a preservative of meat.

HALS, FRANZ (*c.* 1580–1666), Dutch portrait painter, noted for his vivacious handling of oil and the lively characterization of his sitters. Hals spent his life in Haarlem, where he painted numerous single portraits, *eg*, the *Laughing Cavalier*, and several group portraits of guilds and charitable organizations.

HALSBURY, HARDINGE STANLEY GIFFARD, 1st Earl of (1823–1921), British Conservative lawyer, lord high chancellor of Britain (1885, 1886–92, 1895–1905), and leader of the Lords' Die-Hard resistance to the passing of the Liberals' Parliament Act (1911) in the constitutional crisis. He edited *The Laws of England* (1907–19).

HALSE, SIR REGINALD CHARLES (1881–1962), archbishop, left an East London curacy to become Warden of the Bush Brotherhood of St Barnabas, north Qld (1913), Bp of Riverina (1925–43), and Abp of Brisbane (1943–62). As Warden, he founded All Souls' School, Charters Towers, combining public school traditions with bush informality. Halse, a pioneer of the ecumenical movement in Australia, personally fostered closer relations with Roman Catholic and Protestant Churches.

HALSEY, WILLIAM FREDERICK (1882–1959), US admiral, who, in the Second World War, commanded units of the US Pacific Fleet and fought in the Marshall and Gilbert and the Solomon Islands campaigns (1942–4). He was commander of the US Third Fleet (1944–5) during the Philippine Islands campaign.

HALSTEAD, MURAT (1829–1908), US journalist and author. A reporter, then editor, and finally proprietor, of the *Cincinnati Commercial* (1853–84), who gained much attention through his reports of the party conventions of 1856 and 1860, of the American Civil War, and of the Franco-Prussian War.

HAMAGUCHI, OSACHI (1870–1931), Japanese prime minister (1929–31). As acting navy minister (1930), he forced through the London Naval Treaty against intense opposition, but his victory proved short-lived. His supporters in the navy were forced to retire and Hamaguchi himself received from a would-be assassin a wound which caused his retirement and death the following year.

HAMAITÁ, SIEGE OF, decisive event of the War of the Triple Alliance (1864–70). After a siege of several months, the Paraguayan fortress of Hamaitá was forced to surrender to the forces of Argentina, Brazil, and Uruguay on 25 July 1868, thus exposing the Paraguayan capital of Asunción.

HAMALLISM, offshoot of the Tijaniyya Muslim fraternity, founded at Nioro (Mali) in 1925 by the visionary Sheikh Hamallah, who preached a deviant Islam with strong Mahdist overtones among the Moors and Soninke of the Sahel area. Reaction against him led to disorders in Nioro (1925), Kaede (1930), and Nema (1940). He was accused of anti-French activities and was exiled to France (1940), where he died (1942), as new Hamallist centres emerged in Songhay, Mossi, and Hausa territories.
Hamallism reduced ritual prayer to two bows, the confession of faith to its first proposition, and changed prayer orientation from Mecca to Nioro, but emphasized slaves' rights and women's inheritance rights.

HAMBURG, CONVENTION OF (1638), renewed the Franco–Swedish alliance in the Thirty Years War. Fearing that the Swedes would not renew their treaty of alliance on its expiry, Richelieu sent an ambassador to Hamburg to win over Adler Salvius, plenipotentiary of the chancellor, Oxenstierna, and prevented Sweden from concluding peace with the emperor.

HAMBURG, PEACE OF (14 Feb. 1536), moderate agreement between the restored patrician council of Lübeck and Christian III of Denmark after the city's squadrons had surrendered to the combined fleets of Denmark, Norway, Sweden, and Prussia. Lübeck abandoned the Danish city-states of Copenhagen and Malmo, her allies in the social and political revolt of 1533–5, and her imperialist aspirations were over.

HAMDALLAY ('Praise of God'), town on the Niger, south of Mopti, founded by Ahmad Lobbo as capital of his theocratic state (1815).

HAMDANIDS, Arab family which belonged to the tribe of Taghlib and which gave rise to two dynasties, one at Mosul, the other at Aleppo. By 935–6 Al-Hasan b. Abdallah Abu'l-Hayja (d. 969), better knowh as Nasir al-Dawla, had established himself, at Mosul, as the master of Al-Jazira. In 942 he became, for a short while, *amīr al-umarā* at Baghdad. Thereafter he had to withstand the continuing pressure of the Buyids, who took Baghdad in 946. Nasir al-Dawla was deposed at Mosul in 967. With the eviction of his son, Abu Taghlib, from Mosul in 978 the Mosul emirate came to an end. The brother of Nasir al-Dawla, 'Ali (d. 967), was to become—under the title Sayf al-Dawla—the most renowned of the Hamdanids. He won control of Aleppo in 944–6. His main concern was to defend the Muslim frontier in northern Syria and in Al-Jazira against the Byzantine offensive from Asia Minor. During the years 947–62 he met with considerable success, but was less fortunate thereafter. The emirate of Aleppo became an object of contention between the Byzantines in the north and the Fatimids in the south. It survived, indeed, for some decades, but only as a protectorate of Byzantium. The Hamdanid line at Aleppo ended in 1003–4.

HAMENGKUBUWANA (or Mangkubuwana), official name of the Sultans of Jogjakarta, Central Java. Hamengkubuwana I (*reg.* 1755–92) is remembered as a powerful ruler, the founder of the Jogjakarta sultanate. As a young prince he rebelled against his brother, Susuhunan Pakubuwana II, of Surakarta (*reg.* 1726–49). In 1755, the Dutch engineered an end to the rebellion by the treaty of Gijanti, dividing the kingdom into the sultanate of Jogjakarta, ruled by Sultan Hamengkubuwana I, and the kingdom of Surakarta, then ruled by Pakubuwana III (*reg.* 1749–88).
Hamengkubuwana II (Sultan Sepuh) was Sultan of Jogjakarta (*reg.* 1792–1812, 1826–8). His career was marked by troubles with the Europeans and within his own family, and he was twice deposed. In 1826 the Dutch brought him back from exile to become sultan for a third time, in an unsuccessful attempt to wean support from the rebel Dipanagara. Hamengkubuwana II died in 1828.
Hamengkubuwana III (Sultan Radja) ruled during the first deposition of his father (1810–11) and again from 1812 until his death in 1814. He was succeeded by his son, Hamengkubuwana IV (Sultan Seda Pesijar, *reg.* 1814–22). Hamengkubuwana V (Sultan Menol) governed from 1822 until the restoration of his great-grandfather, Sultan Sepuh, in 1826, and again from 1828 to 1855. The succession of rulers of Jogjakarta thereafter has been regular and all have borne the title Hamengkubuwana.

HAMENGKU BUWONO IX (1912–   ), Sultan of Jogjakarta, a princely state in Central Java. Almost alone of the Indonesian 'feudal' rulers, he supported the revolution of 1945–9, inviting republican leaders to make Jogjakarta their headquarters. He served as minister of defence in early post-revolutionary cabinets and was close to army leaders as well as to the Indonesian Socialist Party (PSI). Inactive for most of the Guided Democracy period, he became a principal figure in Suharto's 'New Order' regime, having ministerial charge over economic affairs.

HAMILCAR BARCA (d. 229 BC), Carthaginian leader and father of Hannibal, whom he nurtured in hatred of Rome. Appointed general in Sicily (247), he maintained his army intact until the end of the First Punic War, when a realistic surrender was dictated by Roman naval mastery (241). After securing the final subjugation of a dangerous rising of mercenaries in 238, he crossed to Spain, where by diplomacy and war he built up in nine years the formidable province of economic and military strength in the south and along the eastern seaboard which formed the base for Hannibal's attack on Italy. He was drowned while attempting to escape after an unsuccessful attack on Helike. The suggestion in the sources that he had popular support but opposition from political leaders at Carthage is, in view of his successes, improbable.

HAMILTON, JAMES HAMILTON, 4th Duke of (Scottish) (1658–1712), Jacobite Tory, whose claim to a seat in the House of Lords by virtue of his British title of Duke of Brandon was rejected by the Whig majority (20 Dec. 1711). This became a test case over Scottish rights to hold British peerages with hereditary seats in the Lords, and its rejection aroused considerable ill-feeling against the Union among the Scots nobility. In 1712 Hamilton was nominated ambassador to France, but did not take up the appointment, being killed on the eve of his departure by Lord Mohun's second after a duel in which he had killed the Whig peer.

HAMILTON, ALEXANDER (1755–1804), American politician and statesman, born in Nevis, British West Indies. He went to New York in 1772, wrote pamphlets defending the patriot cause (1774–5) and served as George Washington's military secretary (1777–81). He married into the influential Schuyler family of New York (1780), served in Congress (1781–3), and established a law practice in New York. He had long advocated the establishment of a strong central government, and persuaded the Annapolis Convention (1786) to call for a constitutional convention to revise the Articles of Confederation. His influence at the ensuing Philadelphia Convention (1787) was reduced by his obvious elitism, his demands for extreme centralization at the expense of the states, and the disagreement of the other New York delegates, who neutralized his vote, but as part-author of the *Federalist Papers* he contributed to New York's ratification of the constitution (1788). Following a second term in Congress (1788–9), Hamilton became Washington's secretary of the treasury (1789–95), visualizing himself as 'prime minister', though conceding his need for the president's support. After enunciating his programme in a series of *Reports* on Manufactures, Public Credit, a National Bank, and the establishment of a Mint (1790–1), he did much to establish a viable federal government, especially by attracting support from commercial and financial interests. His policy of funding the national debt met relatively little opposition, but his proposal that the federal government should assume responsibility for state debts incurred during the Revolution aroused bitter hostility. Critics declared that it would alter the balance between the states and the federal government, and several states argued that they had already retired much of their own debt and should not be required to assist in redeeming the debts of others. Hamilton vigorously asserted the constitutionality of the first Bank of the United States by arguing that the federal government enjoyed 'implied powers' under the constitution. His excise duty on spirits provoked the Whiskey Rebellion (1794), and he exploited the suppression of this insurrection to demonstrate the effectiveness of the federal government. He also recommended protective tariffs to encourage industrial expansion. Being active in most areas of government, including foreign policy, he contributed towards the formulation of Washington's neutrality policy (1793) and the conclusion of Jay's treaty (1794). He helped to precipitate party divisions and emerged as a leader of the Federalists but conspired against President Adams, whom he mistrusted, and contributed to his defeat in 1800. After a tie in the electoral college between Thomas Jefferson and Aaron Burr, Hamilton recommended the House of Representatives to elect Jefferson rather than Burr, whom he also mistrusted (1800) and later frustrated Burr's gubernatorial ambitions in New York (1804). He was killed in a duel with Burr. Hamilton's desire for a powerful, dominant central

government was unrealistic, as was his undue reliance on the political support of the commercial classes, but his economic and governmental theories were to have considerable influence on the later development of the US.

John C. Miller, *Alexander Hamilton: portrait in paradox* (New York, 1959).
Broadus Mitchell, *Alexander Hamilton*, 2 vols (New York, 1957–62).

HAMILTON, ALEXANDER OF REDHOUSE (d. 1732), Scottish merchant and author, who travelled widely in Europe, North Africa, and the Far East (1688–1723). His experiences were recounted in his *New Account of the East Indies* (1727).

HAMILTON, SIR IAN STANDISH MONTEITH (1853–1947), British soldier, who commanded the Gallipoli operation of 1915 in the First World War. He had served in various campaigns in the late 19th cent., in the Anglo-Boer War, and was official British observer with the Japanese armies in the Russo-Japanese War (1904–5). In 1915 he was chosen by Kitchener to command the forces to attack the Gallipoli peninsula, but he lacked the flair and drive to overcome the immense difficulties posed by the operation and was relieved of his command in Oct. 1915.

HAMLIN, HANNIBAL (1809–91), US congressman (1843–7) and senator (1848–61, 1869–81) from ME, and Abraham Lincoln's vice-president (1861–5). He was originally a Democrat, but his anti-slavery views led him to join the Republican Party (1856). An inconspicuous vice-president, sympathetic to the radical wing of the party, he was replaced as Lincoln's running-mate in the election of 1864 by Andrew Johnson.

HAMMARSKJÖLD, DAG HJALMAR AGNE CARL (1905–61), Swedish civil servant and politician who became the second secretary-general of the UN. He was appointed permanent under-secretary in the ministry of finance (1936) then placed in charge of international economic and financial affairs in the foreign ministry (1947). He was given a cabinet post (1951) as minister of state, with responsibilities for foreign affairs.

He was appointed secretary-general of the UN in succession to Trygve Lie (March 1953), after an interval of five months due to the political crisis surrounding the office. He greatly enhanced the status of the office, interpreting the Charter as giving to the secretary-general a definite political responsibility. He was an active diplomat ready to exert the UN's authority wherever it was possible to do so. His success earned him the respect of members of the UN, and his authority was enhanced by the freedom they were willing to accord him to seek settlements in the broad framework of resolutions they agreed. His role was particularly important in the Middle East crisis (1956).

In 1960, the grant of independence to the Belgian Congo was followed by internal conflict and great power rivalry which proved a hazardous trap for the UN. Hammarskjöld incurred the hostility of the Soviet Union, which urged his replacement by a troika of representatives, one communist, one 'western', and one neutral. In the middle of this crisis and while flying to the Congo he was killed in an air crash at Ndola, Zambia. He was posthumously awarded the Nobel Peace Prize.

HAMMER v. DAGENHART, 247 US 251 (1918), US Supreme Court case invalidating by a 5–4 majority the Child Labor Act (1916). Justice Day asserted that the statute, which made it a misdemeanour for any manufacturer to bring in by ship inter-state commerce products of establishments employing children under 14, was not a regulation of commerce but an outright prohibition. He distinguished this from other regulations accepted by the court by claiming that the products of child labour were in themselves harmless, and that as the act was intended to regulate child labour, not protect commerce, it violated the 10th Amendment and invaded the reserved powers of the states.

This revival of the 'dual federalist' position was attacked by Justice Holmes, in a dissenting opinion, as being influenced more by social philosophy than constitutional precedent, and an impossible limitation of national governmental police powers.

HAMMURABI (c. 1792–1750 BC), sixth King of the first dynasty of Babylon and one of the outstanding figures of ancient history. He conquered the surrounding states up to the frontiers of Assyria, which was attacked but never subdued. He fortified towns, built temples, and particularly encouraged the worship of the god Marduk, who replaced the older Sumerian gods. Being interested in the welfare of his subjects, he encouraged the development of agriculture and the digging of canals and drew up a code of laws which influenced subsequent legislation in the area. Hammurabi's reign seems to have been a period of literary achievement and later texts refer to it as a golden age of Mesopotamian history.

HAMMURABI, CODE OF LAWS, collection of existing laws and traditions, dealing with certain aspects of life, drawn up by Hammurabi, King of Babylon, and found at Susa in 1901. It closely resembled earlier codes, notably those from Isin and Eshnunna.

HAM-NGHI (1872–1947), last independent emperor of Vietnam (reg. 1884–8). In July 1885, following the capture of Hué by the French, and the failure of a Viet-namese coup against them, the young emperor fled from his palace and became the focus of an opposition movement. In 1888 he was captured by the French, and spent the rest of his life in exile at Algiers.

HAMPDEN OF GLYNDE, HENRY BOUVERIE WILLIAM BRAND, 1st Viscount (1814–92), speaker of the House of Commons (1872–84). Brand had to contend with rising parliamentary disorder, from Samuel Plimsoll, the Bradlaugh case (Brand's handling of which has been criticized), and Irish obstruction, which culminated in the debate on W. E. Forster's motion for leave to introduce a coercion bill. The debate lasted for 41 hours from 31 Jan. to 2 Feb. 1881, and Brand ultimately closed it on his own initiative. This move was of doubtful constitutional legality, there being at that time no way of bringing debates to an end.

HAMPDEN, JOHN (1594–1643), English parliamentary leader and a cousin of Oliver Cromwell. He first sat in parliament in 1621 and became a popular figure and an astute debater. As a close friend of Sir John Eliot, he was involved in Buckingham's impeachment and refused to pay the forced loan imposed by Charles I (1627). He became involved in that group of future parliamentary leaders—Lords Saye and Brook and John Pym—who in the 1630s were prominent in advocating colonial ventures for the settlement of Puritans in the New World.

Hampden is famous for the test case centred round his refusal to pay the £1 ship money for his property in Buckinghamshire (1637), in which he was represented by another opposition leader, Oliver St John. Though he lost his case, the narrow majority of judges in favour of the king (7–5) gave Hampden a moral victory. The yield of ship money subsequently declined and was eventually declared illegal.

In the Long Parliament he was prominent as Pym's principal lieutenant and was one of the managers of Strafford's impeachment. In the summer of 1641 he followed Charles to Scotland as a member of the parliamentary committee sent to observe the king. On his return he took a leading part in the debates on the Grand Remonstrance, and was one of the five members Charles tried to arrest for treason (Jan. 1642).

Just before Civil War broke out Hampden was appointed to the committee of safety and made a deputy lord lieutenant of Buckinghamshire, where he arrested the royalist lord lieutenant. He raised a foot regiment in his home county, and served as its colonel at the battles of Edgehill and Brentford. In the winter of 1642–3 he was strongly opposed to peace negotiations.

In June 1643 he was serving with the army of the Earl of Essex around Oxford, when he was mortally wounded in a skirmish with Prince Rupert's cavalry at Chalgrove Field.

Lord Nugent, *Some Memorials of John Hampden, his Party, and his Times* (London, 1832).   CJ

HAMPDEN, RENN DICKSON (1793–1868), English bishop and Broad Church leader, who conflicted with the Tractarians who tried to prevent his appointment as Regius professor of divinity at Oxford (1836). In 1847 Lord John Russell offered him the bishopric of Hereford, to which he succeeded despite violent High Church opposition, 13 bishops protesting against the government's choice, which was upheld by the Evangelical Sumner, Abp of Canterbury.

HAMPDEN CLUBS in England, local societies for encouraging parliamentary reform. They were at their peak in 1816–17. Although the first Hampden Club, formed in London (1811) with Sir Francis Burdett as chairman, seems to have been an aristocratic body, later clubs had a working-class membership. Most of them were in the industrial towns and villages of the Midlands and the north and the subscription was 1d a week. They did not federate, possibly because of the legislation of the 1790s against corresponding societies. They represent a stage in the development of popular radicalism, but had no immediate effect on legislation.

HAMPTON, WADE (1818–1902), South Carolinian planter and Confederate general, who commanded Gen. Lee's cavalry corps at the end of the American Civil War (1864–5). A Democrat and an opponent of Radical Reconstruction, he served his state as governor (1876–80) and US senator (1878–91).

HAMPTON COURT in England, palatial residence in the Gothic tradition begun in 1515 for Cardinal Wolsey, but given by him to Henry VIII in 1529, after which it remained a royal palace. Henry added considerably to it, building the Great Hall with its hammerbeam roof (1533), and it was further enlarged by William and Mary and by Queen Anne.

HAMPTON COURT CONFERENCE (1604), between representatives of the English bishops and the Puritans, held at Hampton Court Palace under the chairmanship of James I. The requests embodied in the Puritans' Millenary Petition were considered and agreement was reached on three matters—specified reforms in church services, the provision of a preaching ministry, and the reduction of pluralism. Disagreement occurred over the question of Church discipline. James feared that the Puritans were aiming at a Scottish presbyterian system which would be incompatible with the monarchy and would lead to the abolition of the episcopacy. One constructive result was the royal authorization of a new translation of the Bible, the Authorized Version, which was completed in 1611.

HAMPTON COURT TREATY (1562), agreement, unfavourable to France, negotiated between the English under Elizabeth I and the French Huguenot nobles, Condé and Coligny. It guaranteed the restoration of Calais to England in return for Le Havre, 100,000 *écus*, and 6000 men.

HAMPTON INSTITUTE in US, agricultural, industrial, and teacher-training school founded (1868) for Negroes in VA. Under its first principal, Samuel Chapman Armstrong (1839–93), Hampton rapidly became one of the most successful and well-endowed Negro colleges. Armstrong's educational and social views were to influence directly many early

Tuskegee Institute teachers, notably, Booker T. Washington, who were trained at Hampton. Anticipating Washington's famous 'Atlanta Compromise' by more than 25 years, Armstrong stressed the need for Negro thrift, self-help, development of character, and mastery of basic mechanical and industrial skills. He also urged Negroes to remain in the South with their 'best friends', the Southern whites. From 1897 Hampton held annual conferences to discuss schemes such as building and loan associations and co-operative insurance ventures which would promote Negro advancement.

HAMPTON ROADS CONFERENCE (3 Feb. 1865), abortive attempt to negotiate peace between North and South in the closing stages of the American Civil War. Abraham Lincoln and William H. Seward represented the Union government, and Alexander H. Stephens led the Confederate delegation, at a meeting on the Union warship *River Queen*, anchored in Hampton Roads off the VA coast. Stephens insisted on recognition of Southern independence, while Lincoln reiterated the basic peace conditions of reunion and the abolition of slavery. Negotiations broke down, and the war dragged on for two more months.

HAMSUN, KNUT (1859–1952), Norwegian author who early revolted against the materialism and industrialism of his times, and emerged as a romantic in his prose and verse works. His admiration of German philosophers, *eg*, Nietzsche, and of German romantic ideals led him to support that nation in both world wars, despite the occupation of Norway in 1940.

HAN, Chinese kingdom of the Warring states period, ending in 205 BC, to be distinguished from the Han dynasty.

HAN, term which first appears in Chinese sources of the 1st cent. AD, indicating tribes which inhabited southern Korea. By the 3rd cent. these formed three major groups, of which Ma-han, by far the largest, comprised those in the southwest of the peninsula, while the smaller groups, Pyon-han and Chin-han, occupied the south and south-east respectively. The Han tribes seem to have been mainly agriculturalists and fisherfolk, connected with similar groups inhabiting western Kyūshū. In the 4th cent. AD the state of Paekche emerged in the area of Ma-han, while the Pyon-han tribes came under the control of the Mimana protectorate, and those in Chin-han coalesced to form the kingdom of Silla. The term 'Han' thus lost its specific application, and was subsequently used merely as a general term for Korea. It was revived as the title of the Korean 'Empire', proclaimed in 1896 and terminated by the Japanese annexation in 1910. Today it forms part of the official title of the Republic of Korea.

HAN, Japanese political units of the 17th–19th cents. Numbering about 280, they varied greatly in size, the largest (such as Kaga and Satsuma) being about a hundred times larger than the smallest. Each *han* was ruled by a *daimyō*, who was permitted considerable autonomy by the Tokugawa *bakufu*. Their abolition (1871) marked an important stage in the Meiji government's modernization programme.

HAN DYNASTY, more correctly the Western or Former Han (202 BC–AD 8) and the Eastern or Later Han (AD 25–220). The first Chinese dynasty to last more than two decades, Han has been subsequently respected as a model of imperial government which was conducted according to orthodox principles and with marked success. Although the authority of Han was neither as widespread nor as continuous as has been generally maintained by Chinese historians, the achievements of the dynasty have had a marked effect on the practice of government and the growth of Chinese culture. The institutions of central, provincial, and local government were consolidated, to the exclusion of pretenders to power; the prestige of the civil service was established,

together with the recognition that officials should be adequately educated men who would eventually rise to be statesmen of the highest responsibilities. Service to the state was rewarded by marks of status, material gifts, or legal privileges. Officials registered and counted the population, whose male members were liable to regular service in the army and labour corps. Learning was promoted, the lessons of the Classical texts promulgated, and various forms of literature developed. Attempts were made to substantiate the emperor's claim to rule by virtue of Heaven's mandate, with attention to state cults, religious ceremonies, and service to occult forces. In an age of some material extravagance, the government attempted with some success the effective collection of tax in kind, the institution of state monopolies, control of the coinage, and the diffusion of new techniques of agriculture. Open always to the danger of incursion from Central Asia, Han achieved considerable, but sporadic and short-lived, success at repelling the Hsiung-nu. The penetration of envoys and government-sponsored caravans into Central Asia was accompanied by the extension of communications and defence lines at whose sites the garrison forces practised professional military standards; at the same time Han was able to extend the empire in Korea, the south and the south-west, and contacts were made with the Japanese islands. Technological improvements included advanced iron-workings and the invention of paper; progress in mathematics resulted in revisions of the calendar and the production of sundials and a seismograph. Buddhism was introduced, probably from the beginning of the Christian era, and Taoist religious practices were evolved from the 2nd century AD onwards. Dynastic weakness, which ended in the fall of the Han house, was exemplified in rivalries and intrigues in the palace and among the emperor's establishment of consorts, leading to succession problems and bitter jealousies.

M. Loewe, *Everyday Life in Early Imperial China* (London, 1968). ML

HAN LEARNING, developed in 17th-cent. China, was based on the study of Confucian texts of the Later Han period, which the scholars of Han Learning claimed were more ancient and authentic than the Classics recovered in the Former Han. It was a reaction against the eclectic and metaphysical traits of Neo-Confucian orthodoxy. Towards the end of the 19th cent., Han Learning became the tool of reformers like K'ang Yu-wei.

HAN YÜ (768–824), Chinese official and author, who had a somewhat unsuccessful official career which left him embittered and highly critical of the weaknesses of contemporary government. He believed that China's ills derived from a failure to practise the ancient virtues; and as one of the first writers to call for a return to the true Confucian ideals he is sometimes described as the earliest protagonist of Neo-Confucianism. Deploring the taste for elaborate and somewhat artificial prose styles that had been engendered during the Six Dynasties Period, he called for a return to writing in the simple styles that marked prose of the Chou and Han periods. His essays were deliberately written as examples of such didactic works and were for long accepted as literary models. Han Yü believed that the foreign faith of Buddhism had weakened China, and the strength of his protests cost him acceptance at court and success in office. While some of his best-known essays are directed against an excessive faith in Buddhism, some carry a pointed political lesson, being clothed in allegory or satire.

HANAU NEGOTIATIONS (1743), conducted between Carteret, the English foreign minister, and Prince William of Hesse during the War of the Austrian Succession over the proposed restoration of Bavaria to the elector-emperor, in return for the abandonment of his French alliance. The negotiations came to nothing, however, for neither the British ministry nor Maria Theresa, Britain's ally, would accept the terms.

HANBURY-WILLIAMS, SIR CHARLES (1708–59), English diplomat, who first served as envoy at Dresden and later as ambassador to Russia during the negotiations leading to the Convention of St Petersburg (1755).

HANCOCK, JOHN (1737–93), US politician and MA merchant who supported the Sons of Liberty and became a popular figure when his sloop *Liberty* was seized by the British for smuggling (1768). The subsequent legal case became a symbol of opposition to British customs laws. Entering politics as a supporter of Samuel Adams, he served as president of the MA Provincial Congress (1774–5). He was the richest New Englander to support the Revolution, president of the second continental congress (1775–7), and first to sign the Declaration of Independence (1776). He was annoyed at not being appointed commander-in-chief and resigned the presidency, although he continued to sit in congress until 1780. He was elected governor of MA (1780), but resigned in 1785 shortly before Shays's rebellion, to avoid difficulties. He was again elected president of congress (1785–6) and was re-elected governor of MA (1787). As president of the state ratifying convention, he was at first silent over approval of the US constitution, but was persuaded to endorse it by Federalist promises of support for further re-election, and hints that he might become US president if VA failed to ratify (1788).

HANCOCK, SIR WILLIAM KEITH (1898–), Australian historian and the first Australian fellow of All Souls, Oxford (1923). He held chairs of history in Adelaide, Birmingham, Oxford, London, and Canberra (1926–65). His major works, include *Australia* (1930), *Survey of British Commonwealth Affairs* (1937, 1940, 1942), *Smuts*, and (ed.) *History of the Second World War* (1949).

HANCOCK, WINFIELD SCOTT (1824–86), US soldier. He was a West Point graduate, and fought in the Mexican War and on the Union side in the American Civil War, distinguishing himself at Chancellorsville and Gettysburg. His moderation in command of Southern military districts after the war led to his nomination as the Democratic Party's presidential candidate in 1880, but he was defeated by his Republican opponent, James Garfield.

HAND, LEARNED (1872–1961), US jurist. He was admitted to the New York bar (1897) and became a US district judge (1909–24). He stood unsuccessfully (1913) as a Progressive for election as chief judge of the New York Court of Appeals and achieved distinction as a US circuit court judge (1924–51). In 1950 he upheld the conviction of 11 communists under the 1940 Smith Act, reinterpreting the 'clear and present danger' test regarding freedom of speech as one of ascertaining the 'gravity of evil' of the doctrines preached, a test accepted by the US Supreme Court in *Dennis v. United States* (1951).

HANDBOOK OF A CHRISTIAN SOLDIER (1503), or the *Enchiridion Militis Christiani*, early work of exhortation to piety by Erasmus.

HANDEL, GEORGE FREDERICK (1685–1759), German-born composer, *kapellmeister* to the Elector George of Hanover (1710–12). He settled permanently in England and became a naturalized citizen (1726). A prolific musician, he wrote over 30 operas in the Italian style and some 20 oratorios, of which the *Messiah*, written in 23 days in 1741, remains the best-known. In addition, Handel wrote harpsichord suites, organ concertos, anthems, and other sacred music, the *Water Music* and *Fireworks Music*.

HAN-FEI-TZU, test attributed to the philosopher Han Fei (280–33 BC). He studied under Hsün Ch'ing and was put to death while serving on a diplomatic mission to Ch'in. The book includes essays on the principles and practice of statecraft, anecdotes designed to illustrate the needs of government, and some interpretation of Taoist texts. The political chapters form a synthesis of various Legalist views of government.

HANG TUAH (*fl.* 15th cent.), popular hero of ancient Malaya, admiral (*laksamana*) of the sultanate of Malacca during the reigns of Mansur Shah (1459–77) and Alauddin Riayat Shah (1477–88). He was also a contemporary of the prime minister, Tun Perak, and is, together with the latter, closely associated with the expansion of Malacca. His fame soon became legendary and was extolled in the later Malay text *Hikayat Hang Tuah*.

HANGÖ, BATTLE OF (1714), Russia's first naval victory over the hitherto invincible Swedish fleet in the Baltic, and the last major European sea battle in which galleys were used.

HAN'GUL SCRIPT, formerly known as Onmun, is the only truly alphabetic script to emerge in the Far East. Han'gul (lit. 'Korean letters') was developed by King Sejong of the Yi dynasty and promulgated by royal decree in 1446. It has been described as 'perhaps the most scientific system of writing in general use in any country', but until the 20th cent. it was not used for serious literary composition, for which the Chinese script was preferred.

HANIWA, rings of earthenware figures representing warriors, horses, houses, etc., found on the great mounds of the ancient tomb (*kofun*) period in Japan (3rd–7th cents).

HANKEY, MAURICE PASCAL HANKEY, 1st Baron (1877–1963), British official, and politician. After an early career in the Royal Marine Artillery and in Naval Intelligence, he was seconded as Naval assistant secretary to the committee of imperial defence in 1908. He became its secretary in 1912, and continued to exert considerable influence on British strategy from that position until 1938. He was also secretary of the war council (1914–16), of the war cabinet (1916–19), and of the general imperial conferences of the 1920s. As secretary of the peacetime cabinet (1919–38), and clerk to the privy council (1923–38), he was responsible for the development of the cabinet secretariat. He was created a baron and privy councillor in 1938, on his retirement.

He was brought back from retirement on the outbreak of the Second World War to become a member of Chamberlain's war cabinet, as minister without portfolio (1939–40).

He later wrote and spoke against the government's policy of Unconditional Surrender, and against the trials of war criminals by the victors. After the Second World War he wrote his memoirs of the war council in the First World War.

HAN-LIN ACADEMY, educational institution established under the T'ang dynasty. By the Ch'ing period it had become the most highly respected college of learning in China, whose members were selected after keen competition and later occupied influential places in the government.

HANMER, SIR THOMAS (1677–1746), British politician and speaker of the House of Commons. He was an able Tory politician whose wealth enabled him to preserve his role as an independent country gentleman, turning down at least four offers to join Harley's ministry (1710–13). Fearing the implications of Harley's pro-French policy (1713), Hanmer moved away and with Lord Anglesey shared the leadership of the Hanoverian or Whimsical Tories (1714). He was elected speaker (1714), and held office through the accession of George I until he was replaced by a Whig (1716). He then joined the High Tory opposition and attached himself to the Prince of Wales (1717) in the hope of aiding a Tory revival. Accepting failure, he gradually disappeared from politics, retiring altogether in 1727.

HANNA, MARCUS ALONZO (1837–1904), US industrialist and Republican political manager, who built up an industrial empire in oil, coal, iron, and other industries. His political rise typified the close connection between industry and politics of the period. In 1880 he acted as fund-raiser for Garfield, among fellow businessmen in Cleveland. By 1890 he controlled the Republican Party in OH and managed William McKinley's campaign for the governorship (1891). In 1896 his organization and financial support secured McKinley the presidential nomination, and in the ensuing election his business contacts provided a steady flow of money to help to defeat the Democratic and Populist candidate, William Jennings Bryan. Hanna refused a place in McKinley's cabinet and became US senator from OH (1897–1904). In 1900 he again successfully managed McKinley's election, but his influence over the party was ended abruptly by Theodore Roosevelt's accession to the presidency following McKinley's assassination (1901).

HANNIBAL (247–183 BC), Carthaginian statesman and general, son of Hamilcar Barca, who developed Spain as a personal empire, ostensibly to enable Carthage to pay reparations to Rome after the first Punic War, in fact to develop it as a source of manpower and a springboard for the invasion of Italy by land. Hannibal was proclaimed general by his army in 221 and precipitated the second Punic War by the capture of Saguntom. In 218 he marched from Carthagena, over the Pyrenees, through Gaul, across the Rhone, over the Alps, and descended into Italy with a small army and 37 elephants. At the Trebia, Lake Trasimene, and Cannae, he routed the Roman armies, the last victory being one of the most complete of all time; he drew up his line so that the Romans should attack it in its centre, then withdrew this centre so that his line became V-shaped and U-shaped, and the arms of the U closed in on the Romans from both sides and annihilated them. Hannibal's object was to shatter the confederacy of states allied to Rome. Having no siege-train, very small numbers, and no fleet to stop the supplying of Rome from Ostia, it was never his intention to storm the city, but to shatter Rome's armies by mobile warfare and to show her allies that she was unable to protect them. After Cannae, Capua sided with many other towns in southern Italy. But Hannibal was not supported from Carthage, which threw away reinforcements on subsidiary fronts. Without any base in Italy, Hannibal's army became weaker and Rome's stronger. Capua was lost, and all hope of breaking the Roman confederacy ruined. In 203 Hannibal was recalled to Africa, where at Zama in 202 Scipio destroyed the Carthaginian army. Hannibal restored order in the stricken state of Carthage, and it showed signs of such prosperity that the Romans called for the surrender of his person in 195. He escaped and joined Antiochus III, but the Tyrian fleet which Hannibal raised was prevented by the Rhodians from coming to Antiochus' support, with the result that the Romans were able to cross to Asia Minor and destroy Antiochus' army at Magnesia in 189. Hannibal escaped again, but was able to continue the fight against Rome by supporting Prusias of Bithynia. His presence was betrayed and he took poison to avoid falling into Roman hands.   G de B

HANNO (*fl.* 5th cent. BC), Carthaginian merchant-explorer of the Magnoid family, who led a naval expedition down the west coast of Africa (*c.* 450 BC) to establish Carthaginian control of the area's gold trade. A Greek version of what was said to be his report survives, but is difficult to interpret. He may have reached Cameroon, but the most southerly place where archaeological evidence of Carthaginian West African trade has been produced is Mogador.

Also the name of a Carthaginian leader (*fl.* 4th cent. BC), sometimes called 'the Great', who, after a naval victory over Dionysius I of Syracuse (367 BC), was for some two decades the wealthiest citizen and leading statesman of Carthage.

Between 350 and 340 he tried unsuccessfully to make himself sole ruler.

HANOTOUX, GABRIEL (1853–1944), French archivist in the ministry of foreign affairs, who became a deputy (1886) and minister of foreign affairs at the time of the Russian Alliance (1894–8), after which he devoted himself to historical research.

HANOVER, HOUSE OF, founded by William, second son of Ernest, Duke of Brunswick-Lüneberg (d. 1592) of the family of Guelph, whose last son, George, was Duke of Hanover and died in 1641. His son, Ernest Augustus, married Sophia, grand-daughter of James I of England, and was created Elector of Hanover in 1692. Their son, George Louis, united the territories of the family of Lüneberg and Hanover and acquired Bremen and Verden in 1716, two years after he had succeeded to the British throne (1714). The Hanoverians maintained the Crown of Britain and the electorate of Hanover until 1837, George I being succeeded by his son, George II, and his great-grandson, George III. With the death of William IV in 1837 the English Hanoverian line died out, although the Guelphs retained Hanover. The throne passed to Ernest Augustus, Duke of Cumberland, in accordance with Salic law, which forbade the accession of a woman (*ie,* Queen Victoria). Ernest I's son, George V (*reg.* 1851–66), was the last King of Hanover.

HANOVER, German state lying mostly across the northern plain between the rivers Elbe and Weser, it played an insignificant part in European affairs, being noted only for its supply of mercenary troops and its membership of the electoral college of the Holy Roman empire (1692) until the succession of the elector, George Louis, to the British throne (1714). Hanover was a kingdom from 1814 until its annexation by Prussia in 1866.

HANSA, somewhat loose association of north German merchants, which developed into an alliance of towns in the mid-14th cent., including at its zenith over 150 coastal and inland towns. Its membership covered the whole north from the eastern Baltic to the Netherlands, from Thuringia to Sweden. In origin the league was purely commercial, its prime aim being the protection of its members' commerce, but it grew, almost by default, into a power capable of waging successful wars on its neighbours. Its effective existence may be dated from the defeat of Denmark by Lübeck and its associates in 1227. The Hansa's early wealth and expansion were based on the Baltic trade in Russian products, but its commercial activities spread rapidly and at its height it was the chief intermediary between the Baltic region and the countries of the Atlantic seaboard. It was the greatest of the temporary leagues of towns which developed in Germany in the 14th cent., held together by common commercial interests. It became increasingly ineffective when divergent economic needs of the different groups of Hanseatic towns began to break it up and went into a decline in the later 15th cent. in the face of growing English and Dutch competition and the resentment of rising national states against the Hansa's monopoly. There was constant friction with Denmark. Political developments in Germany, particularly the rise of the princes, proved inimical to the Hansa and the strong central power, which elsewhere fostered competition against the league, was lacking. By the 17th cent. only Hamburg, Bremen, and Lübeck had been able to retain their status of independent city-states. Its most lasting achievement was the part played in the foundation of towns in the eastern Baltic and the encouragement of German colonization there.   M He

HANYEHPING COAL AND IRON COMPANY LIMITED, biggest industrial enterprise in Ch'ing China, the name being adopted in 1908 for the industrial complex comprising the Hanyang ironworks, the Tayeh mines (iron-ore), and the

P'inghsiang coal mines. The Hanyang ironworks, established by Chang Chih-tung (governor-general of Hupei and Hunan) with modern machinery from Europe, began operating in 1894. It was located, for political reasons, across the river from Chang's yamen in Hankow. The Tayeh mines, some 100 kms south of Hanyang, also began production in the same year. Shortage of funds and coal led to prolonged stoppages and forced Chang to transfer management to Sheng Hsuan-huai and to invite private investment. The problem of coal supplies was partly solved by the opening of the P'inghsiang mines (Kiangsi province) some 600 kms away and 150 kms from means of water transportation. The uncertainty and cost of fuel, together with lack of capital, forced Hanyehping to exchange Tayeh ore for Japanese coal and coke on unfavourable terms, and, from 1904, to depend increasingly on Japanese loans. Corruption and bad management and planning compounded Hanyehping's difficulties. The reorganization of the company in 1908 as a private enterprise brought little improvement, except in opening the road to further Japanese influence, which transformed the company essentially into a supplier of ore and pig-iron for Japanese heavy industry at prices prejudicial to Chinese interests. Bound by these arrangements, Hanyehping was unable to exploit the boom in raw materials during the First World War. The collapse of the pig-iron market after the war caused the closure of the Hanyang ironworks in 1922, and the Tayeh mines in 1925. The P'inghsiang coal mines continued to operate, but on a much-reduced scale. The Republican government nationalized what was left of Hanyehping in 1937 and in 1938, in the face of Japanese invasion, moved the equipment to Chungking. After 1949, the Communist government has developed a major iron and steel industry at Tayeh, using Tayeh ore and P'inghsiang coke.

HAR DAYAL, LALA (1884–1939), Indian revolutionary. Following a brilliant college career in Delhi and Lahore, Har Dayal went to Oxford on a state scholarship (1905), but he resigned it from nationalist convictions, repudiating the support of an imperialist government. He was associated with Krishnavarma and India House (1907–8) and on a visit to India in this period passed on his revolutionary ideas in Lahore. His own revolutionary activities fell into two phases, in the US, and in Europe. After arriving in the US (1911) he worked as a lecturer and then (1913–14) rejuvenated the political associations among the migrant Indian workers on the west coast, combining them in the 'Hindi Association of the Pacific Coast', and starting a newspaper, *Ghadr* (Nov. 1913). In 1914 the US government arrested him for interfering in domestic politics, but he broke his bail and went to Europe, first to Geneva and then to Germany. He worked with other Indian émigré revolutionaries in Berlin (1915–18), using German funds to organize risings in India and in the army. After the First World War he moved to Stockholm, where he taught Indian languages, and gradually moved away from his revolutionary ideas.

HARA, KEI (TAKASHI) (1856–1921), Japanese politician, who played a major role in the development of political parties in Japan. As effective political director of the Seiyūkai, the majority party, he reached a compromise with the prime minister, Katsura, whereby the latter not only accepted certain Seiyūkai policies but also recommended Saionji, the Seiyūkai president, as his successor in 1906. As home minister in Saionji's cabinets (1906–8, 1911–12) Hara strengthened the party by appointing Seiyūkai supporters to key bureaucratic positions and by directing government economic projects to areas which returned Seiyūkai members to the Diet. Eventually, recognition of his obvious responsibility and his cultivation of Yamagata Aritomo led the *genrō* to recommend him as prime minister (1918). His cabinet, the first led by a commoner, though conservative at home, was memorable for its acceptance of a foreign policy based on international co-operation. After Hara's assassination by

a young fanatic (1921), the Seiyūkai swiftly lost the cohesion he had given to it.

HARAKIRI, also known as *seppuku*, the practice of ritual disembowelment which began in 12th-cent. Japan, and came to form part of the samurai code of honour. Though most commonly a means of avoiding capture or disgrace, it was also an honourable form of execution. Ideally, the samurai performing *harakiri* would, with great ceremony, slit his stomach, while another samurai would decapitate him with a single stroke as he fell forward.

HARALD (*c*. 1015–66), King of Norway (*reg*. 1046–66), nicknamed 'Hardrada' (hard ruler), who consolidated the royal power and was a strong ruler, as well as a poet and a patron of poets. He tried to conquer England in 1066, but was defeated and killed at Stamford Bridge by Harold Godwinson. This Norwegian invasion made it possible for William of Normandy to land unopposed in southern England and may have been of crucial importance in paving the way for the Norman conquest of England in 1066.

HARALD GREYCLOAK (d. *c*. 970), King of Norway and leader of the sons of Eric Bloodaxe, King of York (d. 954), who after several attempts defeated their uncle, Hakon the Good, King of Norway. Harald replaced Hakon as king but he alienated his subjects by his militant Christianity and was overthrown by a coalition of enemies, led by King Harald Bluetooth of Denmark and jarl Hakon Sigurdarson, who became King of Norway.

HARALD HAIRFAIR (*c*. 860–*c*. 940), King of Norway and traditional founder of the Norwegian kingdom. Having inherited a group of provinces in eastern Norway, he allied himself with the Earl of Lade (near Trondheim) and defeated his main opponents at the battle of Hafrsfiord (*c*. 900). By establishing stronger government he stimulated the existing movement of Vikings from Norway into other lands.

HARAR, important commercial city in eastern Ethiopia. It was once an independent state ruled by its own emirs, and was incorporated into Ethiopia by Emperor Menelik in 1887.

HARCOURT, HENRI, Marquis de Beuvron, Duc d' (1654–1718), French diplomat and marshal of France (1706), who was sent to Spain by Louis XIV to engineer the succession of a French prince to the Spanish throne (1697–1700). He became the first French ambassador to Philip V. He was also one of Louis's closest confidants in the War of the Spanish Succession and in its closing stages commanded the army in Flanders and the Rhine.

HARCOURT, SIMON HARCOURT, 1st Viscount (1st creation) (1661–1727), British lawyer and politician, who entered parliament as MP for Abingdon in 1690. As solicitor-general (1702–7), he played a major part in drafting the Act of Union (1707) with Scotland. After being attorney-general (1707–8) and defending Dr Sacheverell (1710), he became lord chancellor (1713–14). As a Tory he fell from power on the accession of George I, but he had never been identified with Jacobitism. Thus he acted as a regent during George's various absences in Hanover and served as a privy councillor.

HARCOURT, EDWARD VERNON, archbishop (1757–1847), friend of British royalty from George III to Victoria. After working hard in episcopates at Carlisle and York, he inherited (1830), the family estate of Nuneham Park, Oxfordshire, where he carried out extensive additions. He was the grandfather of Sir William Harcourt, MP.

HARCOURT, ROBERT (?1574–1631), English adventurer, who founded a colony on the Wiapoco (Oyapoc) river, bordering modern Brazil (1609). James I granted him proprietary rights over all lands between the Amazon and

Essequibo rivers (1613). His colony failed (1614), and he returned to England. Harcourt and Roger North were granted a new patent for a company for the plantation of Guiana (1627), but it was insufficiently financed and the venture was abandoned (1631).

HARCOURT, SIR WILLIAM GEORGE GRANVILLE VENABLES VERNON (1827–1904), British politician, Liberal MP from 1868, home secretary (1880–5), chancellor of the exchequer (1886, 1892–5), and Liberal leader in the House of Commons (1894–8). His aristocratic birth, legal training, debating skill, and wit made him an influential parliamentarian, and he was a successful home secretary, though too absorbed in party in-fighting and disinterested in ideas at a time when the Liberal Party sorely needed them. He abandoned his libertarian opposition to temperance legislation as soon as his party seemed likely to profit by temperance support, and his budget's introduction of a single graduated estate duty (1894) stemmed from political calculation rather than radical conviction. In opposing ritualism and in cultivating parliamentary procedure, his traditionalism was undisguised. Many felt that as Gladstone's second-in-command he should have become Liberal leader in 1894, but he would have been even more temperamentally unsuitable than was Rosebery in the past. In the last months of his life he inherited the family estate of Nuneham Park, Oxfordshire, and faced the implications of his own estate-duty budget.

HARDENBERG, KARL AUGUSTE (1750–1822), Prussian minister associated with the reforms of Stein, and Prussian representative, with von Humboldt, at the Congress of Vienna. Hardenberg, a Hanoverian, entered Prussian service in 1791, was dismissed twice at Napoleon's insistence (1806, 1807), and was chief minister (1810–22). He drafted the edict emancipating the serfs, ended status regulations for professions and land-ownership and guild restrictions on trade. These reforms, together with the work of Stein, made Prussia the most efficient state in the German Confederation. At the Congress of Vienna, Hardenberg supported Metternich and Castlereagh in opposing the cession of Poland to Russia, for which Prussia was to be rewarded with Saxony. Frederick William III gave way before the tsar's anger and Prussia did not receive Saxony.

HARDIE, JAMES KEIR (1856–1915), Scottish politician. In childhood he was a miner, but was dismissed as an agitator (1878). He then worked as a journalist and as a miners' leader, becoming secretary of the Scottish Miners' Federation (1886). He was the first chairman of the Scottish Labour Party (1888) and twice chairman of the Independent Labour Party itself (1893–1900, 1913–15). He was independent Labour MP for West Ham (South) (1892–5), and Labour Party MP for Merthyr Tydfil (1900–15). He opposed both the Boer War and the First World War, and constantly campaigned against unemployment and for international socialism. After the general election of 1906, he was recognized as leader of the Parliamentary Labour Party. He was an excellent speaker and a man of honour and integrity, who did much for the British political labour movement.

HARDING, STEPHEN, Saint (d. 1134), Anglo-Saxon monk of Sherborne in Dorset, who joined St Robert of Molesmes, with whom he founded Cîteaux in 1098. He was elected its third abbot in 1109. It is now doubted that he actually wrote the rule of the Cistercian order, the *Carta Caritatis*, but it is certain that he had a profound influence on the rule and on the evolution of the Cistercian ideal.

HARDING, WARREN GAMALIEL (1865–1923), US president, formerly a smalltown newspaper proprietor from OH. Harding's only apparent qualifications for office were his oratory and his commanding presence. His political career as state senator (1900–4), lieutenant-governor (1904–6), and US senator (1914–21) was unspectacular, but in 1920 the Republican Party Convention was dead-locked and he was chosen as presidential candidate by a small gathering of party managers in the celebrated 'smoke-filled room'. Capitalizing on the national desire for domestic stability, Harding pledged a return to 'normalcy', and overwhelmingly defeated the Democratic candidate, James M. Cox. He was a conservative Republican and his administration inaugurated a period of business domination of government, and also saw the end of any hope of the US entering the League of Nations. His major failing was his reliance on the 'Ohio gang', led by the attorney-general, Harry M. Daugherty, who exploited their official positions for private gain. Harding died before the revelation of scandals such as those of 'Elk Hills' and the 'Teapot Dome'.

HARDINGE OF PENSHURST, CHARLES HARDINGE, 1st Baron (1858–1944), British diplomat and viceroy of India (1910–16). Hardinge joined the foreign office in 1880 and was permanent under-secretary both before and after his period as viceroy (1906–10, 1916–20). His early diplomatic experience was gained particularly in the Middle East and the Balkans, at Constantinople (1881–4), at Sofia (1887–9, 1890–1), and at Bucharest (1892–3). He went to Paris as head of chancery (1893–6) and was secretary successively at Teheran (1896–7) and St Petersburg (1898–1903). From 1903, when he returned as assistant secretary of state, began a close association with Edward VII, which was the basis of his influence and his reputation in European diplomacy. He accompanied the king on the tour of western European capitals, during which the Anglo-French agreement (May 1904) was signed, and returned to St Petersburg as ambassador. In 1906 he became permanent under-secretary at the foreign office. As such, he became one of the most important of the king's advisers and his essential link with foreign statesmen. This was a factor in his appointment as viceroy in preference to Lord Kitchener.

Until the First World War, Hardinge's policies helped to restore Indian confidence in the possibility of political advancement. His repartition of Bengal (1911), which produced a reunited Bengali-speaking province, a separate Assam, and a new province of Bihar and Orissa, was a disappointment to Muslims, who were little appeased by the decision to transfer the imperial capital from Calcutta to Delhi. However, it did mollify the Congress, which was encouraged by his exposition in the official despatch of a policy of gradually devolving imperial powers upon self-governing provinces.

Hardinge sought to increase government expenditure for social welfare, education, and public works, to improve relations with Afghanistan, and to take a firm stand on the treatment of Indians settled in South Africa. He supported the creation of an executive council for the lieutenant-governor of the United Provinces and he saw the need for consideration to be given ultimately to questions of constitutional reforms. However, the First World War upset his plans for social and educational improvement and led to the major failures of his administration: a series of disastrous military expeditions, notably the Mesopotamian campaign, which ended ingloriously in the surrender of British and Indian troops at Kut-el-Amara (1916). Hardinge and the secretary of state, Austen Chamberlain, were both censured for the administrative deficiencies that these failures revealed. This was a disappointing conclusion to his viceroyalty, during which he had made a genuine effort to come to terms with Indian political forces.

Hardinge served as chairman of the royal commission on the rebellion in Ireland (1916). He was reinstated as permanent under-secretary at the foreign office (1916–20) until his appointment as ambassador in Paris (1920–2).

Hardinge of Penshurst, *Old Diplomacy* (London, 1947); *My Indian Years* (London, 1948).
R. J. Moore, *Liberalism and Indian Politics, 1872–1922* (London, 1966).
PDR

HARDINGE OF LAHORE AND KINGS NEWTON, HENRY HARDINGE, 1st Viscount (1785–1856), British soldier, politician and governor-general of India. Entering the army in 1799, he served in the Peninsular War and the Waterloo campaign (1815). He entered parliament in 1820 and was secretary of war in Wellington's ministry and later under Peel. He was governor-general of India (1844–8), after the recall of Ellenborough. In the First Sikh War he served as second-in-command under Gough, when the Sikhs were defeated at Sobraon (1846). It was he who sold Kashmir to Gulab Singh. He also took steps for suppressing *sati* and infanticide in the Indian states and the practice of human sacrifice in Orissa. He succeeded Wellington as commander-in-chief of the British army (1852) and was made a field marshal (1855).

HARDOUIN, JEAN, Père (1646–1729), French Jesuit scholar who defended Catholic orthodoxy by stressing tradition. He edited Pliny's *Natural History* (1685) and published *Chronologie expliquée par les Medailles* (1693).

HARDWICKE, PHILIP YORKE, 1st Earl of (1690–1764), British Whig statesman. He was solicitor-general (1720–4), attorney-general (1724–33), chief justice of the king's bench (1733–7), and lord chancellor (1737–56). As lord high steward for the trials of the Earls of Kilmarnock and Cromartie and of Lord Balmerino (1746) and Lord Lovat (1747), he was concerned with the settlement of Scotland after the 1745 rebellion. He argued for a uniform law for the whole united kingdom and the abolition of heritable jurisdictions in Scotland. As chancellor he continued the work of harmonizing the relations between equity and common law and can be regarded as the founder of modern equity. His name is associated with the reform of the marriage law (1753), enacting the legal solemnization of marriage by clergy of the established Church of England.

HARDY, THOMAS (1752–1832), English radical. He was a London shoemaker and founder of the London Corresponding Society (1792). With other leaders of the society, he was prosecuted for high treason in 1794, but was acquitted. After his trial he dropped out of politics.

HARDY, THOMAS (1840–1928), English novelist, short-story writer, and poet, whose use of 'Wessex' as a topographical and social basis for his writing allowed him to draw, with considerable licence, on the part of Dorset where he lived. Many of his novels originally appeared in serialized form and often combined irony, imagination, and descriptiveness with an examination of social conventions. His works include *Under the Greenwood Tree* (1872), *Far From the Madding Crowd* (1874), *Wessex Tales* (1888), *Tess of the D'Urbervilles* (1891), *Jude the Obscure* (1896), and *The Dynasts* (1904–6–8).

HARE, DAVID (1775–1842), English philanthropist and pioneer of English education in Bengal. A watchmaker by trade, he arrived in Calcutta in 1800. Hare was chiefly responsible for the opening of the Hindu College in Calcutta (1817), the Calcutta School Society (1818), and the Calcutta Society for Bengali Female Schools (1820).

HARE, FRANCIS, bishop (1671–1740), English theologian and scholar, chaplain-general to the Duke of Marlborough and later Bp of St Asaph and of Chichester. He wrote the satire *Difficulties and Discouragements which attend the study of the Scriptures* (1714) and *Psalmorum Liber metrice divisus* (1736).

HARGRAVE, LAWRENCE (1850–1915), Australian inventor, who did experimental work in the 1880s and 1890s in plans for heavier-than-air flying machines. His inventions included a rotary engine (1889).

HARGRAVES, EDWARD HAMMOND (1816–91), Australian prospector, who discovered gold about 140 miles (225 kms) west of Sydney in 1851 and so initiated the great Australian gold rushes. His discovery was aided by his experience as an unsuccessful digger in CA and his knowledge of earlier Australian gold finds.

HARGREAVES, JAMES (d. 1778), English weaver from Blackburn, Lancashire, and inventor of the Spinning Jenny (1765), by which one operator could spin seven threads simultaneously. Although the threads tended to break easily, the jenny speeded up the spinning process of the textile industry and by the mid-1780s some 20,000 were in use in England.

HARIPUNJAYA, city on the site of present-day Lamphun in northern Thailand, the centre of a Mon Kingdom founded from Lavo (Lopburi) in the 7th cent. It was an early centre for the diffusion of Theravada Buddhism, and was for long at war with the Khmer empire, until it came under Thai control towards the end of the 13th cent. Its history is well known as the subject of Pali chronicles composed at Chiengmai in the 15th and 16th cents, notably *Cāmadevīvamsa* and *Jinakālamālī*.

HARLAN, JOHN MARSHALL (1833–1911), US jurist and politician, born in KY, of which he became adjutant-general (1851). He was also judge of Franklin County (1858). He fought on the Union side for the first two years of the Civil War (1861–3), then became attorney-general for KY (1863–7). He was unsuccessful candidate for governor (1871, 1875), and in 1877 was appointed by President Hayes to the US Supreme Court.
Being a former slave-holder, who had opposed the 13th Amendment, he sought at first to use the court to protect vested interests, but later emerged as a strong liberal nationalist. A notable dissenter on the court, he opposed a narrow interpretation of the commerce clause in the sugar-trust cases (1895), and the striking down of the federal income tax (1895), and bitterly attacked the 'separate but equal' doctrine of *Plessy v. Ferguson* (1896). In *Champion v. Ames* (1903) his majority opinion emphasized the plenary power of Congress in the field of inter-state commerce.

HARLAW, BATTLE OF (1411), fought near Aberdeen, in which Alexander Stewart, Earl of Mar, defeated Donald, Lord of the Isles. The latter, a Celt, sought to dominate Scotland in the west and north. Mar's victory strengthened the weak authority of the regent, Albany, during King James I of Scotland's minority and ended all Celtic threats to the Scottish throne.

HARLAY, ACHILLE I DE (1536–1619), French magistrate, and a distinguished first president of the *parlement* of Paris, who courageously opposed the Duc de Guise and the Holy League (1586) in Paris. With a number of other magistrates he was later arrested (1588) by the city authorities, but subsequently became president of the royalist *parlement* sitting at Tours (1589). Harlay built the Place Dauphiné at the western end of the *cité* and was a governor of the Hôtel-Dieu, Paris's chief hospital.

HARLAY, FRANÇOIS DE CHAMPVALLON, archbishop of Paris (1625–95), leading French cleric, courtier, scholar, and politician in the middle years of Louis XIV's reign. He was consecrated archbishop in 1671 and was one of Louis's chief advisers on religious matters from 1679, when French Gallicanism was at its height. He contributed to the movement against the Jansenists by evicting the pupils from Port-Royal (1679) and forbidding the reception of novices there. Under his direction, three clerical assemblies were held in 1680–2 which were denounced by Pope Innocent XI in 1682 on the eve of the publication of the Gallican Articles (19 March 1682).

HARLEM, congested Negro district of Upper Manhattan, New York. It was originally a Dutch settlement (1658) and remained a rural community until the mid-19th cent., but by 1880 had become a fashionable residential district. Its composition then changed rapidly, as recent immigrants moved in. By 1930 a massive Negro migration from the South had established its predominantly black character, which has been maintained despite an influx of Puerto Ricans since 1940.

HARMAR'S EXPEDITION (1790), an attempt to subdue the Indians in the Ohio river valley, led by Gen. Josiah Harmar. The expedition attempted to surprise the Indians, but was ambushed and lost 183 men near the Maumee river, OH.

HARMOST, ancient Greek term for the foreign governor of a city, especially in the Spartan empire between 411 and 371 BC.

HARNEY, GEORGE JULIAN (1817–97), British Chartist leader, who made his way into the movement through his agitation against the newspaper tax and the New Poor Law. His early quarrels with the milder reformers of the London Working Men's Association in the late 1830s foreshadowed the failure of the Chartist movement. He represented the French and European revolutionary approach to democratic reform in England after 1848.

HARO, DON LUIS DE (1598–1661), Spanish statesman and nephew of Olivares, favourite and principal minister of Philip IV of Spain, from the downfall of the Condé Duque until his own death (1643–61). His main concern was to bring peace to a defeated country facing bankruptcy. Although peace negotiations were started at Münster and Osnabrück (1644), Spain's military condition continued to deteriorate and economic collapse came in 1647. Meanwhile, in 1640 the Catalan revolt had broken out, but Haro ultimately exploited internal rivalries in Catalonia to suppress the revolt (Oct. 1652). After the Spanish defeat at the battle of the Dunes (1658), Haro entered into peace negotiations with Mazarin. The result was the treaty of the Pyrenees (Nov. 1659), which gave France considerable trading advantages and territorial gains, which were sealed by the marriage of Louis XIV to the Infanta Maria Theresa.

HAROLD II (?1022–66), King of England, who reigned for only one year (1066). He was the son of Godwin, and succeeded his father as Earl of Wessex in 1053. As the brother-in-law of Edward the Confessor, he acted as the king's right-hand man, and was acclaimed king on Edward's death (1066). Edward was said to have named Harold his heir on his deathbed, but Harold had difficulty uniting the country behind him and he was opposed by rival claimants, Harold Hardrada, King of Norway, and William, Duke of Normandy. Hardrada allied himself with Tostig, Harold's brother, but both were defeated and killed by Harold at Stamford Bridge, Yorks, on 25 Sept. After a dramatic march south, Harold was himself slain in battle with William at Hastings on Oct. 14.

HARPALUS (c. 355–323 BC), Macedonian noble, Alexander the Great's paymaster (335–333), and, after a mysterious flight to Greece, his treasurer at Babylon (331–324), until justly fearing his return from India he fled to Athens with 700 talents and thence, escaping custody, to Crete, where he died. An enquiry showing 350 talents as missing caused Demosthenes' disgrace at Athens.

HARPERS FERRY, Virginia, small US town at the confluence of the Potomac and Shenandoah rivers. On 16 Oct. 1859 John Brown seized the US arsenal as the prelude to an attempt to raise a slave insurrection in the South. Although quickly suppressed by a force of US Marines, commanded by Col. Robert E. Lee, the raid intensified Southern fears and inflamed sectional antagonisms. Harpers Ferry, occupy-ing a strategic position at the end of the Shenandoah valley, was the scene of several minor engagements during the American Civil War.

HARPER'S MONTHLY MAGAZINE (founded 1850), US literary and political magazine, called *Harper's New Monthly Magazine* until 1900, and, since 1925, *Harper's Magazine*. It published work by outstanding contemporary writers of fiction on both sides of the Atlantic, including Dickens, Trollope, Melville, and Henry James, and illustrations by artists such as Winslow Homer. After 1900 it acquired a more political and social emphasis.

HARPER'S WEEKLY (1857–1916), US illustrated literary and political magazine. Specializing in illustration, it provided a comprehensive pictorial history of its times and featured the political cartoons of Thomas Nast. The magazine also published in serial form the work of such authors as Dickens, Wilkie Collins, and Henry James.

HARRIMAN, EDWARD HENRY (1848–1909), US businessman, who, after making a fortune on the stock exchange, developed extensive railroad interests and by 1900 controlled over 20,000 miles (32,200 kms) of track, including the Illinois Central and the Union Pacific. His unsuccessful struggle with J. J. Hill for control of the Northern Pacific led to the stock market panic of 1901, their joint venture, the Northern Securities Co., being declared unconstitutional by the Supreme Court (1904), but Harriman continued to extend his activities until his methods were condemned by the Interstate Commerce Commission (1907).

HARRIMAN, WILLIAM AVERELL (1891–), US financier and diplomat, and son of the railroad magnate E. H. Harriman. He pursued an active business career before entering government service during the New Deal. As US ambassador to the Soviet Union (1943–6) he was among the first US officials to give warning of Russian expansionism. He was given numerous foreign assignments by presidents F. D. Roosevelt and Truman and was an influential foreign policy adviser in the mid- and late 1940s. He served as secretary of commerce (1946–8), and director of the Mutual Security Agency (1951–3). In 1952 he unsuccessfully sought the Democratic presidential nomination; later he became governor of New York (1955–8). When the Democratic Party returned to power in 1961, his diplomatic experience was again used by presidents Kennedy and Johnson, and culminated in the leadership of the US delegation to the Viet-nam peace talks in Paris (1968).

HARRINGTON, WILLIAM STANHOPE, 1st Earl of (1690–1756), English diplomat and politician, who was appointed special envoy in Madrid (1717–18) and Turin (1718–19) and ambassador to Spain (1719–27), where his service culminated in the negotiations of the treaty of Seville (1729). He became secretary of state for the northern department (1730) and worked closely with Sir Robert Walpole. His support for George II's Hanoverian interests kept him continuously in office for 20 years, as secretary of state (1730–41, 1744–6), lord president of the council (1741–4), and lord lieutenant of Ireland (1746–50).

HARRINGTON, JAMES (1611–77), English political philosopher. Though devoted to a republican government, he won the friendship of Charles I, whose execution he deplored. His ideas failed to gain Cromwell's approval, and his best-known work, *Oceana* (1656), was confiscated while it was being printed. Only after the intervention of Cromwell's favourite daughter, Elizabeth Claypole, was it published. There were some Harringtonians in Richard Cromwell's parliament, and his ideas were discussed in the Commons. On the fall of the protectorate he worked to get his republican schemes adopted. In 1659 he established the Rota Club as a forum for the discussion of political ideas. His persistent republicanism after the Restoration led to his imprisonment (1661), from which he was released because of ill-health.

Harrington regarded politics as a science, and believed political power followed economic power, and that the structure of a legislature should fit the structure of society. In *Oceana* a Utopian state was established by Olphaus Megaletor (a pseudonym for Oliver Cromwell), who retired when a republican constitution had been established. The written constitution embodied a bicameral legislature, rotation in office, the use of secret ballots, and provision for the indirect election of a president. Harrington's ideas influenced the Founding Fathers of America.   CJ

HARRINGTON, SIR JOHN (1561–1612), English writer and courtier, who was chosen to accompany the Earl of Essex on his expedition to Ireland (1598), and served as commander of the horse under the Earl of Southampton. He was knighted by Essex in Ireland. On the death of Abp Loftus of Dublin (1605) he applied for, but did not obtain, the chancellorship of Ireland. He took a major part in the education of Prince Henry and died in the same year as his pupil. He translated Ariosto's *Orlando Furioso* (published in folio, 1591) and wrote as a preface to it, *An Apologie of Poetrie*, an essay in criticism.

HARRIOT, THOMAS (1560–1621), English mathematician, who carried further the algebraic work of François Viete and was closely connected with the Elizabethan explorers, *eg*, he accompanied Raleigh on his first expedition to Virginia, describing it in *A Brief and True Report of the New-Found Land of Virginia* (1588).

HARRIS, SIR ARTHUR TRAVERS (1892–   ), British airman, who began his career in the Rhodesian Regiment in 1914 and saw service in German West Africa before being commissioned in the Royal Flying Corps and fighting in the European theatre in the First World War. Between the wars he held a variety of RAF posts in India, Iraq, and at home before taking command of a bomber group in 1937, from which he was transferred (1938) to become air officer commanding Palestine and Transjordan. He was deputy chief of air staff (1940–1), and after leading a delegation to the US was appointed commander-in-chief of Bomber Command in 1942, a post he held until after the end of the Second World War. He was a powerful advocate of the efficacy of independent strategic bombing as a means of bringing about victory, over-estimating the results to be achieved from it, and by his forceful arguments obtaining for Bomber Command aircraft and equipment which might have been allocated more profitably to other operational duties more closely related to the requirements of the army and the navy. From 1942, when he launched the first of the '1000 bomber' raids, he adopted a policy of indiscriminate 'area bombing', directed against the morale of the civilian population, as well as the industrial targets of the larger German cities. This policy has been criticized both on moral grounds and because it failed to arrest German industrial expansion until mid-1944; his critics argue that more emphasis should have been placed on the earlier development of precision-bombing techniques which could have been employed against carefully selected targets within the German industrial system, such as was done in the closing months of the war.   NRB

HARRIS, HOWEL (1714–73), Welsh founder of Welsh Calvinistic Methodism. He began preaching *c.* 1735 and was three times refused ordination by the Bp of St Davids on the ground of his 'enthusiasm'. By 1739 Harris had founded about 30 Methodist groups in South Wales. He was a follower of the Calvinist Whitefield rather than of Wesley, and could, unlike Wesley, preach in Welsh-speaking districts. He founded a religious community at Trevecka, his native village (1752).

HARRIS, JOEL CHANDLER (1848–1908), US writer. He spent his life in GA, and, through a gentle old Negro char-acter—Uncle Remus—told memorable stories of Br'er Fox and Br'er Rabbit with simple folk humour and in authentic dialect.

HARRIS, TOWNSEND (1804–78), US merchant and diplomat, whose trading ventures in the Far East led to his appointment as the first American consul-general to Japan (1855–9) and minister (1859–60). He negotiated a treaty (1858) which secured for American nationals full freedom to reside, trade, and promote missionary activities in Japan. Earlier, in New York city, he had been instrumental in founding the Free Academy (1847), which became the College of the City of New York.

HARRISON, BENJAMIN (1833–1901), lawyer, soldier, politician, and 23rd president of the US. He was the grandson of President William Henry Harrison. As colonel of the 70th Indiana Infantry, he fought in Sherman's Atlanta campaign, and left the army at the end of the Civil War with the rank of brigadier-general. He was defeated in the Indiana gubernatorial campaign (1876), helped to secure James Garfield's presidential nomination (1880), served as a US senator (1881–7), and chaired the important Senate committee on territories. At the confused Republican presidential convention at Chicago (1888) he was nominated as the most 'available' candidate, and then decisively defeated President Cleveland in the Electoral College, though lacking a majority of the popular votes. As president, he supported American expansion in the Pacific, but was only a lukewarm supporter of the McKinley Tariff and the Sherman Silver Act demanded by business interests. His moderation alienated both the reform groups and the party bosses, whose intrigues to supplant him contributed to his defeat by Cleveland in his bid for re-election (1892).

HARRISON, FRANCIS BURTON (1873–1957), US politician and governor-general of the Philippines (1913–21), who held the office twice as long as any of his predecessors. He broadened the extent of Filipino participation in the government, following the original American intention of Filipinizing the civil service, expressed in President McKinley's instructions to the first Philippine Commission. He also offered a retirement plan to Americans in the service, and in 1913 issued a regulation prohibiting government officials from engaging in private business. Upon the termination of his governorship in 1921, there were some 30 bureaus and offices under Filipino direction, compared with only one in 1913. Under the Jones Act (1916) Filipinos were given full control of the two chambers of the legislature. Besides giving Filipinos a majority in his cabinet, Harrison created in 1918 an extra-constitutional body, the Council of State, composed of the president of the Senate, the speaker of the House of Representatives, and the secretaries of the executive departments; he also created a Board of Control staffed by Filipinos, to advise him on the economic development of the Philippines.

Francis Burton Harrison, *The Cornerstone of Philippine Independence* (New York, 1922).   JS

HARRISON, JOHN (1693–1776), English horologist, inventor of the marine chronometer and the grid pendulum, whose length does not change with temperature. In 1714 the British government, concerned with the problem of naval navigation, offered a prize of £20,000 for an accurate method of determining longitude at sea, which involves a precise knowledge of the time of day, pendulum clocks, even in gimbals, being upset by a ship's motion. Harrison worked on the problem from 1728 onwards and perfected a series of clocks, culminating in his 'Number 4 Marine Chronometer', which though no larger than a large watch, was very accurate. After rigorous testing of his invention, Harrison was awarded £5000 in 1763; he had great difficulty in obtaining the balance of the prize money, but finally did so in 1773.

HARRISON, THOMAS (1616–60), English parliamentary general and leader of the Fifth Monarchy men. Originally an apprentice to an attorney, he enlisted in the life guard of the Earl of Essex in 1642. By 1647 he had risen to be colonel of a cavalry regiment, having served at Naseby with distinction and in Ireland. He was elected to the Long Parliament as MP for Wendover (1646), and as a Fifth Monarchist he proved an extremist in politics, demanding the prosecution of Charles I as 'a man of blood' at the army debates (1647). In Dec. 1648 he commanded the guard that brought Charles to London for trial. As a member of the council of state (20 Feb. 1651) he pressed Cromwell to dissolve the Rump and to institute the rule of the saints by establishing a nominated parliament of 70 members. Harrison soon lost faith in Cromwell's compromise solution—Barebone's Parliament. He refused to acknowledge the protectorate and lost his commission (Dec. 1653), thereafter suffering imprisonment several times. He was tried and executed at the Restoration (1660) for his part in the king's trial.

HARRISON, WILLIAM HENRY (1773–1841), US president, whose death one month after his inauguration made him the first president to die in office, and his presidency the shortest there has been. He was secretary of the North-west Territory (1798), territorial delegate to Congress (1799), and governor of Indiana territory (1800–12). He defeated the Indians under Tecumseh at Tippecanoe (1811) and, in the war of 1812, safeguarded the north-west by a victory on Canadian soil at the battle of the Thames (1813). A congressman (1816–19) and senator (1825–8) from OH, he emerged from obscurity to become one of the unsuccessful Whig candidates in the election of 1836. After gaining the nomination over Henry Clay in 1840, he was elected president after the extraordinary 'log cabin and hard cider' campaign, which greatly increased popular participation in the election. Harrison's political success, following that of Andrew Jackson, seemed to demonstrate the attraction of military heroes as presidential candidates.

HARROWBY, DUDLEY RYDER, 1st Earl of (1762–1847), British Tory statesman and close follower of the Younger Pitt. He was vice-president of the board of trade (1791–1801) and treasurer of the navy (1800–1). In Pitt's second ministry he was foreign secretary (1804) and chancellor of the exchequer (1805), and served in successive Tory administrations (1809–27), notably as lord president of the council (1812–27). He resigned and virtually retired on the formation of Goderich's administration (1827). Harrowby was a liberal Tory, who favoured the repeal of the Test and Corporation Acts, and in the Reform Bill crisis (1831–2) took a leading part in trying to persuade Tory peers to drop their opposition to the bill.

HARRYING OF THE NORTH. In 1069 the leaders of the English resistance to William the Conqueror allied themselves with a Danish fleet and sacked York. William thereupon advanced north, but his enemies melted away. He then embarked on a systematic devastation of the area which came to be described as the Harrying of the North: not a village was left inhabited between York and Durham. Even contemporary opinion was outraged by the scale of destruction, but it brought to an end resistance in Northumbria.

HARSHACARITA, earliest extant example of an ancient Indian historical biography. It deals, in ornate Sanskrit prose, with the early life, accession, and first months of the reign of King Harshavardhana of Kanauj (*c.* AD 606–47). Its author, the Brahman Bana (or Banabhatta), was a contemporary of the king and lived at his court. The purely historical content of the text, though by no means negligible, is less important for the modern historian than the manner in which Bana recreates the 'atmosphere' at the court, giving also detailed descriptions of religious ceremonies and battles.

HARSHAVARDHANA (or HARSHA) (*reg. c.* 606–47), Indian King. The basis of Harsha's power was the union of the old Vardhana kingdom of Thanesvar (Punjab) with the Maukhari kingdom of Kanauj (Uttar Pradesh). To the former he succeeded on the death of his elder brother, to the latter on that of his brother-in-law, Grahavarman, both of whom were killed after an invasion by a Bengal army under Shashanka. Subsequently, mainly as a response to earlier attacks rather than an urge for conquest, he expanded his authority still further till it comprised most of northern India from Malwa to the Gulf of Bengal. As this empire was not, however, based on centralized administration but depended largely on the loyalty of vassals, it fell apart after Harsha's death. During his reign imperial splendour, recalling that of the Gupta empire, was revived. It stimulated cultural activity and made Kanauj the most important north Indian centre for the centuries that follow. Harsha is a fascinating figure, better known to us than most ancient Indian kings owing to the existence of a literary biography of his early reign (the *Harshacarita*) and an account by the Chinese pilgrim Hsuantsang.

HARSIOTEF (*reg. c.* 404–368 BC), King of Kush. Miniature iron tools found in his tomb are, except for one spearhead of Taharqa, the earliest iron objects known in the Sudan.

HART, SIR BASIL HENRY LIDDELL (1895–1970), British military theorist and historian, who was invalided from the army with the rank of captain in 1924 as the result of wounds received during the First World War. In 1920 he had been responsible for the rewriting of the official infantry training manual in the light of the experiences of the war. He was (1925–35) the military correspondent of the *Daily Telegraph*, and of *The Times* (1935–9), positions from which he led a tireless campaign for the modernization and mechanization of the British army. He was a powerful advocate of the strategy of the 'indirect approach' and of the technique of warfare later known as *blitzkrieg*, the tactical combination of tank, aircraft, and mechanized infantry operating according to the 'expanding torrent' principle to achieve deep strategic penetration without losing the momentum of the offensive. For many years his views were heeded abroad (especially in Germany) more than in Britain, where successive chiefs of the Imperial General Staff were unwilling or unable, because of financial restrictions, to introduce more than token mechanization of the army. In 1937 Liddell Hart was appointed personal adviser to the new secretary of state for war, Leslie Hore-Belisha, with particular responsibility for reorganizing and mechanizing the army, but he found the pace too slow and resigned the following year to pursue his own campaign outside the war office. The best testimony of his perception lies in the successes achieved in the Second World War by those commanders who were his closest disciples, notably Guderian and Rommel. He continued to write on military matters after the war and established himself as unquestionably the greatest British military thinker of the 20th cent.
                                                                    NRB

HART, SIR ROBERT (1835–1911), Irishman who first went to China in 1854 as student-interpreter in the Superintendency of Trade, Hong Kong, and subsequently joined the consular service. In 1863 he became the inspector general of the Imperial Maritime Customs, a post he held for over 40 years. Under him, the Customs developed into an honest and efficient institution. His co-operative attitude towards the Chinese enabled him to act as a buying and hiring agent for the Ch'ing government in its efforts at modernization, and as an adviser on foreign affairs, particularly during the negotiations after the Sino-French War (1884). The Burlingame Mission, the T'ung Wen Kuan, and the introduction of a postal system in China, owed much to Hart's inspiration and effort.

HARTE, FRANCIS BRET(T) (1836–1902), US writer. He was born in New York, but moved to CA (1854), where he edited and contributed to local magazines. His reputation grew steadily after publication of the verse anthology *Outcroppings* (1865). He was editor of the *Overland Monthly* (1865–71), and his writing during this period brought national fame. His folk stories, including 'The Luck of Roaring Camp', 'The Outcasts of Poker Flat', and his famous comic ballad in dialect, *Plain Language from Truthful James*, popularized a 'local-colour' genre that, despite its sentimental portraits of gamblers, miners, and prostitutes, marked the beginnings of a movement towards realism.

HARTFORD CONVENTION (1814–15), meeting at Hartford, CT, US, of New England Federalists opposed to the Republican administration, and particularly to the war of 1812. The delegates, most of them chosen by state legislatures, shunned extreme proposals involving secession, but adopted a number of resolutions, including a series of proposed constitutional amendments designed to limit the power of the federal government in such matters as the imposition of trade embargoes and declarations of war. The arrival in Washington of a delegation from the convention coincided with news of the treaty of Ghent and Andrew Jackson's victory at New Orleans. The convention was dissolved, but both New England and the Federalists were tainted with a legacy of ridicule, distrust, and allegations of disloyalty.

HARTFORD, TREATY OF (1786), agreement between the American states of NY and MA to decide the ownership of western lands claimed by both. A line was drawn south from Sodus Bay to the Pennsylvania border: NY retained the territory east of the line and MA the lands west of it.

HARTLEY, DAVID (1705–57), English philosopher. Though he was a believing Christian, his writings were rationalistic in tendency. He explained mental phenomena in terms of minute nervous vibrations, and argued that pleasures and pains were derived from associations, and could be educated. Hartley thus provided one of the intellectual bases of Benthamism.

His son, David Hartley (1732–1813), MP, supported the Marquis of Rockingham's party. Because of his friendship with Benjamin Franklin, he was sent to Paris to sign the definitive treaty giving independence to the US (Sept. 1783).

HARTOG, DIRK or DIRCK (1580–1621), Dutch commander of *Eendracht*, was the first European to land on the west coast of Australia, en route from the Netherlands to Java, in 1616.

HARUN AL-RASHID (*reg.* 786–809), 5th Abbasid Caliph. His reign was to be regarded later as a golden age in the annals of the Muslim empire. Much of the splendour surrounding this caliph was due to the able administration—until their fall in 803—of the viziers of the house of Barmak. Harun al-Rashid sought to ensure the partition of the empire among his sons after his own death. The measures that he took to achieve this end led to grave internal dissension during the years 809–18.

HARVESTER JUDGEMENT, THE (1907), landmark in Australian history, given by Mr Justice H. B. Higgins as president of the Commonwealth Court of Conciliation and Arbitration. It established the essentials for a minimum wage standard which might be regarded as 'fair and reasonable', and so laid the foundation for subsequent decisions regarding the Australian basic wage. The judgement led, however, to a high court challenge on the validity of the Excise Act, 1906, within the meaning of which Higgins had refused to give Hugh Victor McKay a certificate that the conditions of work and wages at his Sunshine harvester works were 'fair and reasonable'. The majority decision of the high court, in *The Commonwealth v. McKay* (1908), 6 C. L. R., 41, that the act was unconstitutional, upset the policy of the 'New Protection'

being applied by the liberal-radical Alfred Deakin with the support of the Australian Labor Party.

HARVEY, GEORGE BRINTON McCLELLAN (1864–1928), US editor, publisher, and an influential figure in American politics. He began his career as a newspaper reporter and editor (1879–93), and made a fortune in the electric street railway business in association with William C. Whitney of New York and became owner and editor of the *North American Review* (1899–1926). He was also president of the publishing house of Harper and Brothers (1900–13) and editor of *Harper's Review* (1901–13). Though an early supporter of Woodrow Wilson, he disagreed with his foreign policy. He supported Hughes in the presidential election of 1916, and Harding in 1920, and founded *Harvey's Weekly* (1918–21) as a vehicle for attacks on the treaty of Versailles and the League of Nations. He served as US ambassador to Britain (1921–3).

HARVEY, WILLIAM (1578–1657), English physiologist and embryologist. He discovered the systemic circulation of the blood, expounded in his treatise *On the Motion of the Heart* (1628). Though not a great innovator, he gave a new interpretation to familiar data drawn from common experience. He studied at Cambridge and Padua, where he was taught by Fabricius. He wrote *On the Generation of Animals* (1651).

HARZBURG FRONT in Germany, formed in 1931 to unite the so-called 'National Opposition' against the Weimar republic and take joint action in the impending presidential elections. Although earlier efforts of this kind, *eg*, the front against the Young Plan of 1929, had brought no lasting success, a number of DNVP and *Stahlhelm* leaders, in the summer of 1931, canvassed the idea of holding a mass rally at Bad Harzburg. Hitler, whose presence was considered indispensable, agreed to participate, with his followers. But he could not be persuaded to accept the other anti-Republicans present as equal partners. Not only did the *Führer* arrive late, but he also refused to salute the *Stahlhelm* contingents during a public march-past, arguing that they were not subordinate to him. The ensuing quarrel almost led to Hitler's departure. Although this and the cancellation of his speech were avoided, the Harzburg demonstration against the republic showed that this attempt at unifying the Right was no more successful than the previous ones. Hitler's continued claim to outright leadership, in fact, soon resulted in the Front's collapse when the 'National Opposition' put up two candidates (Hitler and Duesterberg) for the 1932 presidential elections. The Front was re-established in 1933. But as Hitler had not given up his absolutist claims in the meantime, it did not take him long to inflict another (and final) defeat on his allies, who persistently overestimated their own power and underestimated the dynamism of the National Socialist movement.

HASA, AL- (LAHSA), name of a wide region in northeastern Arabia, involved in the movement of the Carmathians during the 10th–11th cents. It was to rest, later, under Ottoman rule in the 16th–18th cents and, from 1793, under the domination of the Wahhabis. The troops of Muhammad Ali held the area in 1819–25. In 1872 the Turks occupied Al-Hasa once more, but lost it to the forces of Abd al-Aziz b. Sa'ud in 1913. The main town in Al-Hasa is now (1970) Hufuf, the population of the oasis region amounting to some 200,000.

HASAN, AL-, ALIBIN (*fl.* 13th cent.), Sultan of Kilwa, who was the first of the Shirazi dynasty of Kilwa and Mafia (Tanzania). He minted copper coinage and introduced the practice of building in stone with lime mortar.

HASAN-I SABBAH (d. 1124) was born at Qumm in Persia. He became converted to the Isma'ili faith (1071–2) and studied in Egypt for three years. In 1090 he seized the fortress of Alamut in Daylam. Here he became the most important figure amongst the Nizari Isma'ilis who broke with the Fatimid caliphate in 1094. From Alamut went forth the fida'is, who earned for their sect, among the Christians, the name of Assassins.

HASDRUBAL (1) (*fl.* 3rd cent. BC), Carthaginian general and son-in-law of Hamilcar Barca. As governor of Spain between 229 and 221 BC, he stabilized the Carthaginian presence in the east by the foundation of New Carthage and ensured a peaceful advance along the coast to the Ebro by negotiating the Ebro treaty with Rome (?226–225).

HASDRUBAL (2) (d. 207 BC), Carthaginian general, left by his brother Hannibal in command of Spain south of the Ebro during the invasion of Italy in the Second Punic War. The correct Roman strategy of diverting forces to Spain when Italy was threatened blocked his early attempts to reinforce his brother. After a brief recall to Africa to quell native risings, he achieved his supreme success in engaging separately and massacring the two Roman armies commanded by the brothers Scipio (211 BC). Though defeated at Baecula by the younger Scipio (Africanus) in 208, he skilfully evaded pursuit and crossed the Pyrenees and then the Alps (early 207), but was crushed and killed by Claudius Nero and Livius Macatus at the Metaurus river.

HASHEMITE, ancient Meccan family descended from the Prophet via Ali and Hasan. The term is used, particularly, in connection with the family of Sharif Husayn (1852–1931), King of the Hijaz (*reg.* 1916–24), who had four sons, Ali (1879–1935), who succeeded Husayn as King of the Hijaz (*reg.* 1924–5); Abdullah (1880–1951), Amir of Transjordan (1921–46) and King of Jordan (*reg.* 1946–51); Faysal (1883–1933), first King of Iraq (*reg.* 1921–33); and Zayd (1898–1970). Ali's son, Abd al-Ilah (1913–58), was Regent of Iraq and heir presumptive. Faysal's son, Ghazi (1912–39) (*reg.* 1933–9), married Aliyah, daughter of Ali, and their eldest son was Faysal II of Iraq (*reg.* 1935–58). Abdullah was succeeded by his eldest son, Talal (*reg.* 1950–1), although his second son, Na'if, acted as Regent before the accession of Talal's son, Husayn (1935–), as King of Jordan. Through their participation in the Arab Revolt the Hashemites achieved an eminence in the Arab nationalist movement which they confirmed by their subsequent establishment as rulers of the Hijaz, Iraq, and Transjordan. Their long dispute with the Saudis, however, divided the Arab world, while their association with Britain and their own conservative regimes offended radical Arab opinion. The Hashemites became noted proponents of the idea of Fertile Crescent Union, which brought them into opposition to Egypt, while Abdullah's pursuance of his ambitions in Palestine in 1948 won the Hashemites the reputation of betrayers of the Arab cause. The Hashemite regime in the Hijaz fell in 1925 and in Iraq in 1958.

HASLUCK, SIR PAUL (1905–), Western Australian politician and historian, who joined the Australian department of external affairs during the Second World War and served at the United Nations (1945–7). He was the author of the official war history volume, *The Government and the People* (Canberra, 1952), was elected to the Commonwealth parliament (1949), and became minister for territories (1951–1963), for defence (1963–4), and for external affairs (1964–9). Hasluck vigorously promoted the economic and political development of Papua–New Guinea, but was sometimes criticized for inflexibility in his foreign policy. He was narrowly defeated by John Gorton for leadership of the Liberal Party and the prime ministership in 1968, following the death of Sir Robert Menzies's successor, Harold Holt. He resigned from parliament in the following year to become governor-general of Australia.

HASSELL, ULRICH VON (1881–1944), German diplomat and member of the anti-Nazi resistance, who held a variety of foreign posts before being appointed ambassador to Rome in 1932. He was at first hopeful of establishing European security on the basis of the Four Power Pact (signed in 1933, but never ratified). He was deeply opposed to the Anti-Comintern Pact (1937) and this led to his dismissal from the foreign service. He then joined an industrial enterprise, using its activities as a cloak for his opposition work. He belonged to Germany's 'old elite' of strictly upright and highly conservative civil servants and academics and the diaries he kept from 1938 until shortly before his death are a witness to the motives which inspired the conservative opposition to Hitler. He worked closely with Beck and Goerdeler in preparing the July 1944 coup, and helped to draft (1940) the first programme of action to be adopted by the provisional government, in which he was to have been foreign minister. He was arrested shortly after the failure of the plot, and tried and executed in Sept. 1944.

HASSUNA, site, 22 miles (35 kms) south of Mosul, which has given its name to a period of proto-history. First excavated (AD 1943–4) by Seton Lloyd and Fuad Safar, it has since revealed relics from the 6th millennium BC.

HASTENBACK, BATTLE OF (1757), defeat of an Anglo-Hanoverian army of 50,000 men under the Duke of Cumberland by a French force of 80,000 led by Marshal d'Estrées during the Seven Years War. Cumberland, forced to leave Hanover, exposed by his retreat from the Weser to the Elbe, submitted shortly afterwards to the Convention of Kloster-Seven.

HASTINGS CUTOFF, Western US emigrant route offering a short cut on the California Trail. Pioneered in 1846, it left the main trail at Fort Bridger, crossed the Wasatch Range and the Great Salt Lake Desert to the Humboldt river. Although shorter, its rough and arid terrain presented almost insuperable difficulties.

HASTINGS, FRANCIS RAWDON-HASTINGS, Earl of Moira, 1st Marquis of (1754–1826), British soldier, politician, and governor-general of India, who served in the American War of Independence and in the early expeditions against France (1793–5). He was governor-general of India and commander-in-chief (1813–23). His first task in India was to deal with the Gurkhas of Nepal, who were continually raiding across an ill-defined frontier into British territory. He was forced to declare war (1814–16), which was prolonged for two reasons—the incompetence of the British officers, who were not used to mountain warfare, and the stubborn resistance of the Gurkhas. By the treaty of Segauli (1816) the Gurkhas ceded Garhwal and Kumaun, together with most of the Tarai; they also agreed to withdraw from Sikkim and accept a British resident at Katmandu.

The war postponed the punishment of the Pindaris, bands of robbers who were ravaging the country. They were also attached to the Maratha armies as irregular cavalry. From all quarters appeals for protection were made to the East India Co. The non-intervention policy pursued after the departure of Wellesley, in 1805, allowed the Pindaris to plunder the country with impunity. This was a consequence of the company's policy of repression of disorder within its borders and of unconcern beyond them. Hastings took command of the Pindari War (1817–18) and the Pindaris were wiped out by a British force of about 120,000 men and 300 guns, the largest force the British had been able to command in India up to that date. The Pindari War developed into a war against the Marathas, except that neither the Sindhia of Gwalior nor the Gaikwar of Baroda opposed the English. The military power of the Maratha states was shattered, the peshwa was deposed and forced to reside as a pensioner at Bithur, near Cawnpore. With the suppression of the Pindaris, the defeat of the Marathas and the inclusion of the Rajput and other states within the pale of British protection, the British became the paramount power in India.

M. S. Mehta, *Lord Hastings and the Indian States* (Bombay, 1930).   CCD

HASTINGS, SIR PATRICK GARDINER (1880–1952), British lawyer, renowned for his skill in cross-examination. As attorney-general in the minority Labour government of 1924, he initiated a prosecution against the editor of the *Daily Worker* on a charge of sedition. It later became clear that the charge could not be sustained and it was withdrawn. The incident was seized upon by the combined Conservative and Liberal opposition to defeat the government, which fell on the acceptance by the House of Commons of a motion to appoint a select committee to enquire into the affair.

HASTINGS, LORD WILLIAM (d. 1483), close confidant of the future King Edward IV of England, who subsequently encouraged Hastings to build up a large body of military followers. During the Civil War in 1471 Hastings was one of the first to rally to Edward after the king's return from exile, and he commanded one wing of the Yorkist army on the occasion of its decisive victories at Barnet and Tewkesbury. He was henceforth Edward's lord chamberlain, but after the king's death he refused to compromise with Edward's brother, Richard of Gloucester. Richard decided that he could not usurp the Crown without first eliminating Hastings and at a session of the council Richard suddenly accused him of treachery and had him summarily executed.

HASTINGS, WARREN (1732–1818), British official and first governor-general of the British possessions in India. In October 1750 he arrived in India as a writer in the service of the East India Company. By 1761 he had risen to the position of member of the Bengal Council. He returned to England in 1764 without having made a fortune, and then went back to India in 1768 as member of the Madras Council. While at Madras he does not seem to have been implicated in the pecuniary scandals known as the Nabob of Arcot's debts, by which English officials lent money to the ruler of the Carnatic at extortionate rates of interest. In April 1772 he became president of the Bengal Council and, under North's Regulating Act of 1773, he was appointed the first governor-general of British India (1773).

His policy was to consolidate the British possessions in Bengal. His relations with the neighbouring state of Oudh were aimed at strengthening an important buffer state upon whose security the safety of Bengal depended. Although handicapped by a hostile majority on his council, led by Philip Francis, he defeated all enemies and saved the British empire in India. After Pitt's India Act (1784), Hastings, feeling he had lost the support of the ministry in England, resigned his position and returned to England in 1785.

He was the real founder of British rule in India for it was upon his internal administration and re-organization, especially his land revenue policy, his judicial experiments, and his respect for Indian customs and culture that later governors-general built. His policy towards the buffer state of Oudh involved him in questionable transactions such as the Rohilla war, the spoliation of the begams of Oudh, and the coercion of Chait Singh of Benares, for which and other supported crimes he was impeached. His impeachment began in 1788 and lasted until 1795, when the House of Lords declared him not guilty on all charges. His country gave him no honours except membership of the privy council.

G. R. Gleig, *Memoirs of the Life of Warren Hastings*, 3 vols. (London, 1841)
Keith Feiling, *Warren Hastings* (London, 1954).   CCD

HASTINGS, BATTLE OF (14 Oct. 1066). After a night march, Harold II, King of England, came unexpectedly upon William, Duke of Normandy, and his invading army and was obliged to take up a defensive position on a hill near Hastings, with insufficient men and in some measure of disarray. The English were defeated by the Normans, using cavalry attack, feigned flight and archery, and King Harold was killed with his younger brothers. The battle was the last occasion on which a foreign invader successfully set foot on English soil.

HATCH ACT (1887), in US, legislation, known after its sponsor, Representative William H. Hatch of MO, making federal funds available to the states for the establishment of agricultural research stations.

HATCH ACT (1939), in US, legislation, named after Senator Carl A. Hatch of NM, prohibiting federal employees from active participation in national politics. The act stemmed from allegations of improper activity in the 1938 elections by Works Progress Administration workers in KY, MD, and TN. An amendment to the act (1940) limited political campaign expenditure.

HATS AND CAPS, two Swedish political parties in the 'Age of Freedom'. The names originated at the Diet elections of 1738, when the opponents of Horn's government called themselves 'Hats', suggesting soldiers in uniform, and the other side 'Caps', suggesting old men in nightcaps. In 1738 the Hats secured control of the council, and although three of the four estates of the Diet had a Cap majority in 1742, the Hats retained power until 1765, the more moderate Caps being alienated from their party by its dependence upon Russia.

HATSELL, JOHN (1743–1820), British authority on parliamentary law and procedure. He was chief clerk of the Commons (1768–97), and wrote *A Collection of Cases of Privilege of Parliament to 1628* (1776), and *Precedents of Proceedings in the House of Commons* (1781).

HATSHEPSUT (*reg. c.* 1490–1468 BC), Egyptian Queen of the XVIIIth dynasty. As the widow of Thotmes II, she became regent to the young Thotmes III, but soon proclaimed herself king and had herself portrayed as a man in contemporary paintings, etc. Her reign was a prosperous period and one of extensive building activities. On her death Thotmes III resumed power and had her name erased from many buildings.

HATTA, MUHAMMAD (1902–), former vice-president of Indonesia. Hatta, a Minangkabau from West Sumatra, Dutch-educated and a radical nationalist, was arrested by the colonial authorities in 1934. On his release by the invading Japanese in 1942 he joined Sukarno as principal nationalist spokesman. With the proclamation of the republic in 1945 he became vice president, and he also served as prime minister from 1948 to 1950. The Sukarno–Hatta duumvirate was seen by many Indonesians as a symbol of governmental balance. Yet Hatta's dry, didactic personality contrasted with Sukarno's exuberance. His political sympathies for the non-Javanese, the Western-minded, and the stricter Muslims also clashed with Sukarno's views. As Sukarno gained ascendancy their relations became increasingly strained, and in 1956 Hatta resigned.

HATT-I HUMAYUN (18 Feb. 1856) (Imperial Edict), second of the two great Ottoman Tanzimat reforming edicts restating principles of reform and equality.

HATT-I SHARIF OF GULHANE (3 Nov. 1839) (Noble Edict of the Rose Chamber), first of the two great reforming edicts of the Ottoman Tanzimat, which enunciated principles of justice and equality for all citizens and foreshadowed legal, financial, and administrative reforms.

HATTIANS, the inhabitants of Hatti (Anatolia) before the Hittites (*i.e*, before *c.* 2000 BC). No written documents relating to them have been found.

HATTON, SIR CHRISTOPHER (1540–91), English politician and lord chancellor (1587–91). He served on committees concerned with Mary Queen of Scots' imprisonment and trial and strongly urged her execution. He was chancellor of Oxford University and a patron of Elizabethan letters and the theatre.

HATTUSILIS III (*reg. c.* 1289–1265 BC), Hittite King during a period of comparative peace and apparent prosperity. Following an attack by tribesmen, he had the capital, Hattusas (mod. Boghazkoy), rebuilt and the archives recopied. Many religious and administrative decrees were issued and a peace treaty was made with Egypt.

HAUGE, HANS NIELSEN (1771–1824), Norwegian businessman and lay preacher of peasant origins whose insistence upon the importance of a personal salvation had parallels with the thought and activity of John Wesley in Britain. Hauge travelled widely all over Norway, establishing meeting-places, encouraging elementary education, and distributing evangelical literature. At the same time, he was a successful businessman in Bergen, and encouraged farming settlements in remote parts of Norway.

His missionary work was mainly confined to the years 1796–1804, and was bitterly opposed by the Norwegian government and clergy. He was imprisoned (1804–11) and subsequently heavily fined. His 'crime' was that of giving encouragement to the peasants and breaking the Conventicle Ordinance (1741) which demanded orthodoxy in the Lutheran Church. Haugeanism still (1970) survives in Norway, especially on the west coast.

HAUGWITZ, CHRISTIAN (1752–1832), Prussian diplomat and protagonist of neutrality in the Napoleonic wars. With Hardenberg, he was responsible for Prussian foreign affairs (1792–1806), Haugwitz following a pro-French and Hardenberg a pro-Russian policy. At the end of 1805 Haugwitz received from Napoleon the offer of Hanover in exchange for the use of Prussian troops, but before the treaty could be ratified by the king, Haugwitz learnt that Napoleon had secretly offered George III the return of Hanover. Haugwitz persuaded the Prussian king to mobilize his army against Napoleon without waiting for allies, and this resulted in overwhelming defeat at Jena.

HAUGWITZ, WILHELM LUDWIG, Count von (1702–65), Austrian nobleman, who served as chancellor and finance minister to the Empress Maria Theresa. His first service was the reorganization of the government of that part of Silesia retained by the Habsburgs. He then produced a comprehensive plan to strengthen Austria, taking into account the Silesian loss. He calculated the need for a standing army of 108,000 men with an annual revenue of 14 million *gulden* to maintain it. The 5 million *gulden* additional to the regular contribution voted by the estates was to be raised from taxation of property, including that of the nobility. Despite opposition from vested interests, Haugwitz carried through these important reforms (1748). Such changes, however, necessitated administrative streamlining and in 1749 he was appointed president of the newly united chanceries of Bohemia and Austria (*Directorium in Publicis et Cameralibus*), through which he implemented further internal reforms.

HAUHAUISM (or Pai Marire), early NZ Maori millennial movement, founded in 1862 by Te Ua, a Taranaki 'prophet', who believed that Maoris were a lost tribe of Israel, to be redeemed by expelling Europeans. Immunity for Hauhau warriors from gunfire was to be gained by chants and raising the right hand. Brief, costly experience discredited Hauhauism, but it influenced Te Kooti and Ratana, later millennial leaders.

HAULTAIN, SIR FREDERICK WILLIAM GORDON (1857–1942), English-born Canadian lawyer and politician and prime minister of the North-west Territories of Canada (1897–1905). As leader of the Provincial Rights Party (1905–1912), he played a major role in the campaign to win provincial status for the North-west Territories. He was instrumental in the formation of the province of Saskatchewan and was its chief justice (1912–37), as well as a founder of Saskatchewan University (1907).

HAUSA, people and states, Negro and mainly Muslim people living in northern Nigeria and Niger. The Hausa language, a member of the Afro-Asiatic group, was the lingua franca of many of the commercial centres of West Africa and the Sahara. Originally inhabiting the Air Massif, they were driven south by increasing desiccation. Groups imposed themselves upon the aboriginal inhabitants, who lived in open settlements, and established walled towns under warrior chiefs. A cycle of legends associates the seven true or *bokwai* states—Daura, Katsina, Kano, Zaria, Biram, Rano, and Gobir with Abu Yazid or Bayajidda. There were also seven *banza* or illegitimate states, which included Zamfara, Kebbi, and Jukun. Ibn Battuta (*fl.* 1340) first mentioned Gobir, while Al-Maqrizi (d. 1442) mentioned Afuno, the Kanuri name for Hausa. In the 16th cent. Leo Africanus recorded the existence of Zaria, Kano, Katsina, Zamfara, and Gobir; at that time they were under the influence of Songhay, being before and after this period under the influence of Bornu. At the beginning of the 19th cent. they were incorporated in the Sokoto caliphate.

HAUSSMAN, GEORGES EUGÈNE, Baron (1809–91), French financier and civil servant, who became prefect of the Seine and was chosen by Napoleon III to undertake a large-scale rebuilding of Paris. He did much to create modern Paris, but was dismissed because of his authoritarian and corrupt methods. He later became a deputy for Corsica (1877–81).

HAUTEVILLE FAMILY, Norman family whose leading members established themselves by conquest as rulers of Sicily and southern Italy in the 11th cent. In the 1030s several Norman mercenaries entered southern Italy, displaced the Lombard, Byzantine, and Saracen rulers, and broke the power of the nascent communes. They were brigands, but militarily skilled and had great organizing ability. Among them were sons of Tancred d'Hauteville—William, Robert Guiscard, and Roger. Having been brought to Italy initially to support a Lombard revolt against the Byzantines, they turned against their employers and displaced them. In 1042 William proclaimed himself Count of Apulia. In 1072 Robert and Roger undertook the conquest of Sicily, which became the centre of their power and where they established an organized and wealthy state. Roger I (1061–1101) became Count of Sicily, his son Roger II (1101–54) united Sicily and Apulia, and in 1130 was crowned King of Sicily. Thereafter, the family reigned until 1194 and the last of the line, Constance, married the Emperor Henry VI, who achieved a union of Sicily and the Holy Roman empire. The Hauteville state was seen as a threat by the Holy Roman empire, the eastern empire, and the papacy, but they were able to preserve it by playing off one against the other. They were also regarded by the papacy as an ally against the German emperor. By the treaty of Malfi (1059) Nicholas II recognized their possessions as papal fiefs.

HAVANA, great Spanish Caribbean base, pivot of the convoy system in the 16th and 17th cents and capital of Cuba. Sacked by Jacques Sores in 1555, it was heavily fortified in the 1560s by Menendez and resisted enemy attack until it was captured for Britain in 1762 by Sir George Pocock and Lord Albemarle. It was restored to Spain by the treaty of Paris (1763) and remained Spanish until 1898.

HAVANA CONFERENCE (1928), sixth Pan-American conference, marked by Latin American hostility to the US because of its interventions in the Caribbean and Central America.

HAVANA CONFERENCE (1940), meeting of representatives of the American nations to consider problems raised by the Second World War. A solidarity pact was agreed upon and the 'No Transfer' principle was reaffirmed, whereby colonies in the Americas might not be transferred from one non-American power to another.

HAVELOCK, SIR HENRY (1795–1857), British general, the whole of whose career, except for a few months' active service in Persia (1857), was spent in India. He is chiefly remembered for his part in the First Afghan War, the First Sikh War, and the Indian mutiny, in the course of which he effected the relief of Cawnpore after the massacre of its European population, and then of Lucknow. Havelock, besides showing great ability as a field commander, had the unusual advantage of being fluent in both Hindustani and Persian. He was a man of great personal courage and deep religious convictions, with which he imbued many who served under him.

HAWAII, 50th state of the US, admitted in 1959, and consisting of a group of islands in the Pacific over 2000 miles (3200 kms) west of San Francisco. Called the Sandwich Islands by their English discoverer, Capt. James Cook, they came under American influence through the activities of missionaries and traders after 1820. HI's strategic location and its role as a major sugar producer attracted the interest of US expansionists after 1850; it was annexed in 1898 and made a territory of the US by the Organic Act (1900). It is an important strategic and communications centre and the site of the naval base of Pearl Harbor. Military expenditure sustained the economy, which was otherwise based on sugar, pineapples (after 1903), and tourism. HI's insular character, and its mixed population of Polynesian, Oriental, and American origins, distinguished it from the other states of the Union.

HAWKE, SIR EDWARD (1705–87), English admiral, who first distinguished himself as captain of the *Berwick* in the battle off Toulon (9 Feb. 1744) and later defeated the French off Finisterre (1747). He destroyed the French fleet at Quiberon Bay (20 Nov. 1759) in the Seven Years War. He was first lord of the admiralty (1766–71).

HAWKE, ROBERT JAMES LEE (1929–   ), Australian trade unionist who became president of the Australian Council of Trade Unions in 1969. His election as ACTU president ushered in a period of vigorous, aggressive trade union leadership. He was regarded in 1970 by many as a future leader of the political wing of the Australian Labor movement.

HAWKINS, SIR JOHN (1532–95), Elizabethan sea captain and founder of the English slave trade. He was a son of William Hawkins, a Plymouth merchant, whom he accompanied on his African voyages, and organized and led three large-scale voyages to the Caribbean via the Canaries and the West African coast with slaves and textiles, for which he received hides and sugar (1562–7). His hopes for a permanent, peaceful trade were, however, shattered by his next venture, when his five ships were treacherously attacked by Spanish officials at San Juan d'Ulloa (1568). Yet, out of the profits of his trading Hawkins built a formidable private fleet at Plymouth and in 1577 was appointed treasurer of the Navy Board. Here he carried out valuable reforms, *eg*, the introduction of the gun-deck, which contributed to the Spanish defeat in the Armada battles, in which he fought as a rear-admiral (1588). In the Anglo-Spanish war he was unable to convince Elizabeth's government of the strategic value of a continuous blockade of the Spanish treasure fleets. In 1594 he sailed with Drake on an expedition to Puerto Rico, but died at sea (21 Nov. 1595).

HAWKINS, SIR RICHARD (*c.* 1560–1622), English sailor. He served under his father, Sir John Hawkins, and sailed on an expedition to South America (June 1593), intending to cross the Pacific and explore Japan and China before forming an East Indian trading company. He pillaged the coast of Chile (May 1594), but after a three-day naval encounter was captured by the Spaniards (22 June 1594) and condemned to death at Lima. He was pardoned, however, sent to Spain, and eventually released.

HAWKSMOOR, NICHOLAS (1661–1736), English architect and pupil of Sir Christopher Wren, whom he assisted in many projects. From 1699 he also co-operated with Sir John Vanbrugh, notably at Castle Howard. Later he completed Blenheim Palace, which Vanbrugh had begun. From 1707 Hawksmoor branched out on his own. After 1712 he built six London churches, each distinctive yet all sharing a common vigour of style.

HAWLEY, HENRY (d. 1677), English colonial administrator. Being employed by the Earl of Carlisle, he arrested the governor of Barbados, appointed by the earl's rivals, the Courteens, when Carlisle's proprietary claim to the colony was established (1629). He himself was appointed governor (1630), but became involved in intrigues by the Earl of Warwick, who contested Carlisle's claim. Despite the planters' resistance to Carlisle's attempts to depose him, Hawley was arrested (1640). He was cleared by a privy council enquiry, and allowed to settle in Barbados. He joined Lord Willoughby's royalist faction before surrendering the island to parliament's representatives (1652).

HAWLEY–SMOOT TARIFF (1930), in US, legislation which raised average duties to 41·57 per cent, the highest level to date. It was designed partly to protect farmers growing staple crops, and was seized upon as an opportunity to obtain more concessions for industry. When all the trading and log-rolling had finished, the bill provided for about 75 increases on farm products and 925 on manufactured goods. Despite strenuous protests by professional economists, President Hoover signed the tariff, which created much hostility abroad and within two years some 25 countries had imposed retaliatory tariffs.

HAWTHORNE, NATHANIEL (1804–64), US writer, whose tales of New England appeared anonymously or pseudonymously in a number of magazines, especially *The Boston Token*. He compiled *Peter Parley's Universal History* (1837) and wrote a number of books for children. His *Mosses from an Old Manse* (1846) included two of his best stories, 'Rappacini's Daughter' and 'Young Goodman Brown', and a satire on Transcendentalism, 'The Celestial Railroad'. Instant recognition came to him with *The Scarlet Letter* (1850), a romance, set in the Salem of his ancestors, in which he explored the effect of adultery on the moral relationships of four characters and on the community to which they belonged, at the same time expounding his attitude to the New England Puritan heritage. This success was followed by *The House of the Seven Gables* (1851), and *The Blithedale Romance* (1852). A campaign biography, *The Life of Franklin Pierce* (1852), earned him the US consulship in Liverpool (1853). His European experiences are embodied in another romance, *The Marble Faun* (1860) (published in England as *Transformation*), and *Our Old Home* (1863), a collection of essays about England.

HAY, JOHN MILTON (1838–1905), US journalist, diplomat, historian, poet, and novelist. He served as assistant private secretary to President Lincoln (1860–4), assistant adjutant-general (1864–5), and then held minor diplomatic posts in Paris, Vienna, and Madrid. On returning to the US (1870) he joined the New York *Tribune* (1870–5). He served as assistant secretary of state under President Hayes (1879–81), and as President McKinley's ambassador to Britain (1897–8). As US secretary of state under McKinley and Theodore

Roosevelt, Hay supported annexation of the Philippines and the Open Door policy in China. He concluded the Hay–Pauncefote treaty with Britain (1900–1) and treaties with Colombia and Panama, paving the way for the Panama Canal. With John G. Nicolay he wrote a famous account of Lincoln's career, *Abraham Lincoln: a history* (10 vols, 1890), and edited *Abraham Lincoln: complete works* (2 vols, 1894). He also published *Pike County Ballads* (1871), and *The Breadwinners* (1884), a satirical novel attacking labour unions.

HAYA DE LA TORRE, VICTOR RAÚL (1895–   ), Peruvian writer and politician, who was exiled to Mexico, where he founded (1924) the American Popular Revolutionary Alliance (APRA), a radical party dedicated to social change in Indo-America. Over the years the party has become Peruvian rather than hemispheric.

After the fall of the dictator Leguía, Haya returned to Peru and stood as a presidential candidate. Sánchez Cerro was fraudulently proclaimed the winner of the election (1931), and Haya was imprisoned, but escaped and went into hiding.

In the 1945 elections Haya changed his tactics and gave his support to an establishment candidate, José Bustamante, after whose victory APRA was able to participate in policy making. Bustamante was overthrown, however (1948), by Manuel Odría, APRA was again driven underground, and Haya was forced to seek asylum in the Colombian embassy, where he remained for several years.

In 1956 Haya gave his electoral support to the winner of the election, Manuel Prado y Ugarteche, and his party played a large part in the Prado government. In the presidential election of 1962 Haya led in the polls, but failed to achieve the necessary one-third of the total vote. Before a president could be chosen by the congress under the provisions of the constitution, the military seized power and annulled the elections. They then called new elections (1963) and Haya was narrowly defeated by Fernando Belaunde Terry. Since then APRA has been an opposition party. Young radicals complain that Haya and the other APRA leaders have become conservative and point to his co-operation with right-wing groups, such as the followers of Odría.   MJM

HAYAM WURUK (*reg.* 1350–89), also called Rajasanagara, King of Majapahit, Java. During his reign, Majapahit was at the height of its power and controlled the entire Indonesian archipelago and southern Malaya. Hayam Wuruk's fame is reflected in Javanese literature, notably in the Nagaraker-tagama (1365), as well as in numerous religious monuments built in his reign, such as Chandi Panataran near Blitar, East Java.

HAYASHI, RAZAN (1583–1657), Japanese Confucianist. As an adviser of Ieyasu, he played an important part in the establishment of the Tokugawa political and ethical system.

HAY–BUNAU–VARILLA TREATY (1903), between the US and Panama, providing for the building of a canal across the isthmus of Panama. The US was given the 'use, occupation and control' of a canal zone, and Panama received monetary compensation of $10 million, plus an annual rental of $250,000.

HAYES, RUTHERFORD BIRCHARD (1822–93), 19th president of the US (1877–81). He served in the Union army during the Civil War and entered politics, as a moderate Republican, serving in the US House of Representatives (1865–7), and for three terms as governor of Ohio (1868–72, 1876–7). He carried through prison and charity reforms and promoted a 'sound money' campaign which attracted national attention. In 1876 he won the Republican presidential nomination, and although his Democratic opponent in the election, Samuel Tilden, secured a larger popular vote, Hayes was judged by a special Electoral Commission to have won by one electoral vote (185–184). As president, amid rumours that the election had been decided by a bargain with the

South, he ended Reconstruction by withdrawing the remaining Federal troops from the South. He was conservative on issues of finance and labour (the Bland–Allison Silver Coinage Act (1878) was passed over his veto) and he called out Federal troops to suppress the 1877 railroad strike. He alienated the 'stalwarts' in his own party by attacking the spoils system, and supported civil service reform. Faced with considerable political opposition, he fulfilled his nomination pledge by refusing to stand for a second term.

HAYMARKET RIOT (4 May 1886) in US, clash between police and labour union sympathizers in Chicago, IL. The riot occurred after a bomb was thrown at police trying to break up a street meeting. Seven police were killed and 68 wounded. The resultant conviction of eight anarchists caused widespread controversy and a general setback to the US labour union movement.

HAYNAU, JULIUS (1786–1853), Austrian general, who succeeded Windischgrätz as military governor of Hungary. He was born in Cassel and entered the Austrian army as a lieutenant (1801). His advancement was slowed by his disrespect for orders on humanitarian grounds. In Italy (1848) he became hated for his imposition of harsh financial penalties on cities which attacked Austrian soldiers in breach of truce agreements. Helped by the Croats under Jallačič and Russian troops (1849), he defeated the Hungarian rebels and punished them ruthlessly.

HAYNE, ROBERT YOUNG (1791–1839), US lawyer and politician, elected to the SC state legislature (1814). He later served in the US Senate (1823–32), and in a famous debate with Daniel Webster (19–27 Jan. 1830) advanced the doctrines of state sovereignty and nullification. After resigning from the Senate to become governor of SC (1832–4), he played a major part in the nullification crisis over the tariff of 1832.

HAYNES, JOHN (1594–1654), American colonial politician. As governor of MA (1635), he banished Roger Williams from the colony. He moved to CT (1637) and became that colony's first governor (1639), a position in which he served during alternate years until his death.

HAY–PAUNCEFOTE TREATIES (1900, 1901), agreements between the US and Britain named after the American secretary of state and the British ambassador in Washington, concerning the proposed isthmian canal linking the Caribbean with the Pacific Ocean. The first treaty modified the Clayton–Bulwer treaty (1850) to allow American control of the canal, but prohibited its fortification. The second treaty a year later specifically abrogated the 1850 agreement and Britain tacitly admitted the US right of fortification, but stipulated free access to the canal by ships of all nations at reasonable and equitable rates.

HAYWOOD, WILLIAM DUDLEY (Big Bill) (1869–1928), US labour leader. He was born in Salt Lake City, UT, and began work as a miner at the age of nine. In the mines and, later, as a cowboy and a homesteader, Haywood saw the conditions of unorganized, unskilled workers at first hand. He joined the Western Federation of Miners (1896) and served on its executive board until 1907, when he was dismissed because of his radical activities. He was one of the founders and best-known leaders of the Industrial Workers of the World and served as their secretary-treasurer (1916–18). His trial and acquittal (1907) for complicity in the murder of F. R. Steunenberg, governor of ID, made him a popular hero and the epitome of the American image of the vigorous and violent western frontier. He used his popularity to spread ideas of industrial unionism during a tour of the large US cities (1907–8).

During the First World War he was convicted under the Federal Espionage Act (1917). While out on bail from

Leavenworth Penitentiary, he fled to the Soviet Union (1920). In Russia he became leader of the American Kuzbas Colony in Siberia. He died in Moscow.

Haywood wrote numerous pamphlets and articles for the IWW, and his autobiography, *Bill Haywood's Book* (1929), was published posthumously, but it was as a speaker that he most forcefully expressed his ambitions for the world's unskilled and unorganized labourers. He accepted violence as a necessary phase of labour's struggle and advocated militant direct action, with his message of the need for 'One Big Union' to bring about a new social order. He spoke for the mass of working men and his activities helped to lay the foundation for industrial unionism in the US.

W. D. Haywood, *Bill Haywood's Book* (New York, 1929). P. Renshaw, *The Wobblies* (London, 1968).   DHP

HEADS OF THE PROPOSALS (1647), draft constitution and proposals for reform drawn up in England by the council of the army, guided by John Lambert and Henry Ireton, which were informally handed to Charles I on 23 July, and published on 1 Aug. They differed from parliament's peace proposals in their leniency to royalists and their demand for religious toleration. The proposals embodied biennial parliaments, control of the king by a council of state, supervision by parliament of the militia and of the appointment of officers of state for ten years, and reform of the electoral system and of the law. The proposals were eventually implemented, with some changes in the Instrument of Government (1653).

HEALEY, DENIS WINSTON (1917–), British politician who entered parliament in 1952. As secretary of state for defence in Wilson's Labour government (1964–70) he was responsible for streamlining the defence ministries, cutting the defence budget, and arranging for the withdrawal of British troops from Aden, the Persian Gulf, and South-East Asia.

HEALY, TIMOTHY (1855–1931), Irish politician, who entered politicis as secretary to Parnell in 1879 and became an MP in 1881. However, in 1890 Parnell's involvement in the O'Shea divorce case caused Healey to become his most bitter opponent. Within the anti-Parnellite faction of the Irish party, Healy became an antagonist of John Dillon, who wished to preserve the 'machine' politics of Parnell's day and a firm alliance with the Liberals. Healy had no taste for a centralized, disciplined party machine, and thought, especially after his expulsion from the Irish party in 1900, that tactical alliances might be made with sympathizers in either of the two English parties. Readmitted to the Irish party in 1908, he managed to avoid the indignity of being involved in its collapse between 1916 and 1918 by declaring himself sympathetic to Sinn Fein in 1917 and resigning his seat in favour of them in 1918. In becoming governor-general of the Irish Free State (1922–8), he was the only Irish politician of the pre-Sinn Fein era to receive recognition from the new regime.

HEARN, WILLIAM EDWARD (1826–88), Australian political economist, whose book *Plutology* (1863) was possibly the first to apply Darwin's evolutionary theory to political economy.

HEARST, WILLIAM RANDOLPH (1863–1951), US newspaper magnate, who acquired the ailing New York *Journal* in 1895 and increased its circulation through a combination of sensationalism and fabrication. He expanded his activities throughout the US and by the 1920s had created the largest newspaper, magazine, and radio empire in the world. He was influential in Democratic politics and served as a radical congressman from NY (1903–7). He was an unsuccessful candidate for the mayoralty of New York (1905, 1909), for the governorship (1906), and was a perennial aspirant for the Democratic presidential nomination. He made a major contribution to American politics in 1932 when he helped to swing Garner's supporters to Franklin Roosevelt, ances that Roosevelt was not an internationalist. became disillusioned with the New Deal and ported Landon. His newspapers increasingly conservatism, his intense isolationism, and his hatred of communism.

HEATH, EDWARD GEORGE (1916–), British politicia. and Conservative prime minister of Britain. After the Second World War he entered the civil service, then left to be news editor of the *Church Times* and later an executive trainee in business. He won Bexley (1950) by 133 votes, became a junior whip and eventually government chief whip (1955–9) when he distinguished himself by his handling of the party during the Suez crisis and its aftermath. He was appointed minister of labour (1959–60) then lord privy seal with special responsibilities for Europe (1960–3). He conducted the abortive negotiations for British entry to the Common Market with skill and tenacity. He was then appointed to the board of trade, where he piloted legislation on resale price maintenance against considerable opposition within the party. He became the first Conservative leader (1965) to be elected under the new procedure adopted after Macmillan's retirement, winning in the ballot against Maudling and Powell. Despite the evidence of public opinion polls against both Heath as a leader and against the Conservative Party, he led the Conservatives to victory in the general election of June 1970. At the end of 1970 Heath's administration was deeply committed to securing British entry into the European Common Market.

HEATH, NICHOLAS (*c.* 1501–78), English theologian, who was Bp of Rochester (1539), and of Worcester (1543), and Abp of York (1555). As a learned and moderate scholar he was sent by Henry VIII on an unsuccessful mission to negotiate doctrinal agreement with the Lutheran Schmalkaldic League (1535). Under Edward VI he upheld transubstantiation in the Prayer-Book discussions, rejected the Ordinal of 1550, and was deprived of his see. As Mary's Abp of York he treated heretics mercifully. He was briefly lord chancellor (1556).

Though Elizabeth I hoped this nationally minded bishop would support an inclusive religious settlement, he opposed the Supremacy Act (1559), arguing that parliament could not grant spiritual authority and Scripture forbade women to exercise it. After again being deprived of his see he lived quietly for the rest of his life.

HEATH PATENT (1629), proprietary grant by King Charles I of England to Sir Robert Heath, his attorney-general, to the region south of Virginia, to be known as Carolina. Heath failed to found a colony and the region was later assigned to eight proprietors (1663), who brought in colonists.

HEATHCOAT, JOHN (1783–1861), British inventor and MP, who patented a machine for making lace. His factory was destroyed by the Luddites (1816), but he re-established his business in Devon, making lace-manufacture an important industry in the county in the 19th and 20th cents.

HEAVENLY REASON SOCIETY (T'ien-li-chiao), a religious sect believing in the messianic role of the future Buddha Maitreya, related to the White Lotus religion. It prospered in the last years of the 18th cent. and the first years of the 19th in the provinces of Honan, Chihli, and Shantung, having among its adherents Bannermen, officials, and eunuchs. Its members rose in rebellion in 1813 and surged into the palace compounds at Peking, but the movement was quickly suppressed. It survived, however, under various names in north China, and the Boxer Rising can be traced to this sect.

HÉBERT, JACQUES (1757–94), French Revolutionary journalist and leader of the Hébertists, who largely represented the political and economic aspirations of the *sans-culottes*. He was a member of the Cordeliers Club and editor (1790) of *Le Père Duchesne*, which surpassed even Marat's *Ami du Peuple* in its advocacy of extremism. Hébert's real power, however, lay in the Paris Commune, which he began to dominate after the overthrow of the monarchy (1792). Largely through his influence, backed by the pressure of the *sans-culottes* and the sympathy of some members of the Committee of Public Safety, the Jacobin government pushed through the *Maximum* (Sept. 1793) to satisfy the *sans-culottes'* economic grievances. The Hébertists also began a violent de-christianizing campaign, mounting attacks on churches. Realizing the danger which they posed to his control, Robespierre struck first, and in March 1794 Hébert and his followers were executed.

HEBRANG, ANDRIJA (1899–1949), Yugoslav communist leader, who was purged after siding with the Soviet Union against Tito in 1948. Hebrang was a Croatian trade unionist, who became head of the party organization in Croatia before the Second World War. During the war he organized the Partisans in Croatia and was captured by the Ustase in 1942, but was later exchanged for Ustase prisoners. After the war, he became minister of industry, president of the planning commission, and a member of the presidium of the Yugoslav and Croatian constituent assemblies. In 1946 he clashed with Tito over the first Five Year Plan, arguing in favour of gradual rather than rapid industrialization. He was dismissed from several of his posts in April 1946, but continued his opposition in alliance with Sreten Zujovic. The Soviet Union began to support their opposition in 1947 and Zujovic advocated a conciliatory policy towards the Kremlin in the central committee on 13 April 1948. An investigation of the conduct of both Hebrang and Zujovic was ordered, and they were expelled from the party and imprisoned. Hebrang was accused of collaborating with the Ustase during the war and conspiring with the Soviets in 1948. He died in prison.

HEBREWS, Semitic nomads who came from Mesopotamia (*c.* 1850 BC) and, after a period spent in Palestine and Egypt, established themselves in settled agricultural communities in Palestine, divided into 12 tribes, and were led in times of trouble by chiefs called 'judges'. During the reign (*c.* 1020–922 BC) of Saul, David, and Solomon, they controlled all of Palestine and part of Syria. After 922 the kingdom was divided into two—Judah in the south and Israel in the north. From the 8th cent. the Hebrews came under the control of a succession of great powers. Their most outstanding characteristic was the strength of their religious consciousness, which has survived to the present day.

HECTEMOROI, 'sixth-parters', a class of peasants in pre-Solonian Attica (*c.* 600 BC) obliged to pay an overlord one-sixth of their annual crop. When Solon removed this obligation (594), the *hectemoroi* became small, independent farmers.

HECTOR, SIR JAMES (1837–1907), NZ geologist and scientific leader. After explorations in Otago, he was appointed founding director of the NZ Geological Survey (1864) and of the Colonial Museum, and manager of the NZ Institute (1867).

HEDGES, SIR CHARLES (d. 1714), British lawyer and politician. After losing a disputed election case (1700) Hedges entered parliament in 1701. A Tory by inclination, he owed his appointment as secretary of state (1702) to Rochester's influence. He broke away from the High Tories, however, and pursued an undistinguished career, following the court line on all important issues. Though forced out of office by the Whigs (1706), court favour assured him the compensation of a pension and two legal offices. He continued to support the court until 1712, when his Hanoverian sympathies aligned him with the Whimsicals, a group of backbench Hanoverian Tories.

HEGEL, GEORG WILHELM FRIEDRICH (1770–1831), German philosopher and professor at Heidelberg University. He was an idealist, author of the dialectical method, and protagonist of the community above the individual. He greatly influenced the development of both nationalism and Marxism.

HEIAN PERIOD, era (*c.* 794–1185) when Heian (previous name for Kyoto) was the centre of political, social, and cultural life in Japan. The city, built on Chinese lines by Emperor Kammu (*reg.* 785–94), became the setting for a unique civilization. With the imperial government functioning smoothly under Fujiwara control, the court and aristocracy were assured of a comfortable existence and were able to patronize the arts. Poetry, both Chinese and Japanese, achieved for the first time the great popularity which it has continued to possess, while important advances occurred in architecture, painting, and historiography. The most remarkable feature of the period, however, was the prose written by court ladies, who took the lead in developing both the novel and the literary diary or notebook. Their works show not only how sensitive to aesthetic values the aristocratic leaders of metropolitan society had become, and how refined and meticulous they were in their appreciation of beauty and their taste in dress, but also how permissive in their moral standards. Another notable feature of the period was the growth of Buddhism after the introduction of two broader sects, Tendai and Shingon, in the 9th cent. The continental contacts of Buddhists contributed greatly to the rapid rise in the level of civilization in the early Heian period, notably through the adaptation of Chinese characters to meet the requirements of the Japanese language, which previously lacked any written form. During the 9th cent., however, Chinese influence diminished. After 838 official court missions to China ceased, partly owing to the disorders there and the dangers of the voyage, but mainly because the Japanese, having assimilated an enormous amount in the preceding two centuries, felt ready to develop their own style of civilization. This change of attitude coincided with the modification of Chinese-style governmental institutions and the erosion of the state land system, which in the long term was to transfer political power from the capital to the rising warrior families in the provinces. By the late 11th cent. Heian was being frequently troubled by uncontrollable disputes over land rights between monasteries, and long before the establishment of a feudal government in Kamakura (1185) metropolitan society had lost its self-confidence and vitality.

Ivan Morris, *The World of the Shining Prince* (London, 1964).   RLS

HEIDELBERG CATECHISM (1563), confession of the Calvinist faith jointly drafted by Philippist Lutherans and Calvinists and promulgated by the Count Palatine, Frederick III. It was widely adopted as a standard Calvinist formulary in the later 16th cent.

HEIDELBERG SCHOOL, group of Australian painters working in the Heidelberg, Box Hill, and Eaglemont areas of Vic. (*c.* 1885–90). Their record of landscape in constantly changing light marked the beginning of Australian impressionism. Tom Roberts, Arthur Streeton, Fred McCubbin, Charles Conder, and Walter Withers were its leaders.

HEILBRONN, LEAGUE OF, union of Protestant German princes organized initially by chancellor Oxenstierna of Sweden (1633), in which France and Sweden had equal rights of protectorship over the German states. After the meeting of member-states at Frankfurt-on-the-Main (1634), France, with her greater financial resources, gradually assumed leadership. In Nov. 1634 Richelieu negotiated the treaty of Paris with Bernard of Saxe-Weimar and those states which had not yet been overrun in the Catholic advance after Nördlingen.

HEILIGERLEE, BATTLE OF (1538), defeat of Charles of Egmont, Duke of Gelderland, the ally of Francis I of France, by the imperialist forces during the renewed Franco-Habsburg hostilities of 1535–8, as a result of which Egmont surrendered Groningen.

HEIMWEHR (lit. Home Defence) in Austria, paramilitary fascist organization formed after the First World War as a coalition of regional groups. In Styria, Carinthia, and Burgenland the Heimwehr was founded to combat frontier incursions by Yugoslavs and Hungarians. In the Tyrol and Salzburg it arose more as the right-wing Christian Social Party's response to the militant socialism of Vienna, and developed links with right-wing groups in Bavaria.

In 1927 Seipel's government recruited Heimwehr units to help the police and the army to suppress the Social Democrats' general strike. In Nov. 1928 the movement became united under Steidle and Pfriemer to pledge resistance to any attempted 'Red Dictatorship'. In 1929 Seipel was replaced by Schober, who was unwilling to encourage the Heimwehr's activities, and the movement began to seek foreign support.

Despite his early Bavarian connections, Steidle, being a Catholic, disliked the growing influence of Nazism. In 1930 he visited Mussolini in Italy, and afterwards persuaded the Heimwehr to adopt a fascist programme. In Sept. 1930 Starhemberg, equally eager for support from Italy, replaced Steidle as leader. As the Christian Social leaders began to find difficulty in maintaining a parliamentary majority, and came under increasing pressure from Nazis and extreme nationalists, they made overtures to the Heimwehr. The Heimwehr leader, Fey, became head of National Security in Dollfuss's first government (1932). After the civil war of 1934 which suppressed the socialists, Starhemberg became vice-chancellor and retained this post in Schuschnigg's government which followed the Nazis' attempted coup in June 1934.

The Heimwehr's fortunes then began to wane. Mussolini developed closer links with Hitler, and ceased to act as Austria's protector and the Heimwehr's patron. He urged Schuschnigg to conciliate Hitler by concessions to the Nazis and restrictions on the Heimwehr. In May 1936 the government dismissed Starhemberg and banned demonstrations. In Oct. the government, in one of many measures which led gradually to *Anschluss* with Nazi Germany, dissolved the Heimwehr and all independent paramilitary organizations.

ASJ

HEINES, EDMUND (1897–1934), German politician, who was SA leader and NSDAP Reichstag deputy (1930–4). Thanks to his connections with Ernst Röhm, the SA's chief of staff, he rose to the rank of *Obergruppenführer* (chief group leader) in charge of the Breslau district. He was one of the 'toughs' in Hitler's revolutionary private army, and it was no accident that he was among the first to be liquidated when the *Führer* decided to emasculate the SA in the Night of the Long Knives on 30 June 1934.

HEINKEL, ERNST HEINRICH (1888–1958), German aircraft designer and industrialist, who began by specializing in marine aircraft during the First World War and continued in the 1930s with the He 115, the main German aircraft involved in the battle of the Atlantic. He also built the Luftwaffe's only long-range strategic bomber, the He 177 Griffin, used in Russia; and (1939) the world's first turbo-jet, the S 3. He also produced the He 111 medium bomber, which began life as a civilian transport, but was converted into a multi-purpose bomber, used in the Second World War in Poland, France, over Britain, and on the Eastern Front.

HEINSIUS, ANTONIE (1641–1720), Dutch diplomat and statesman. Born in Delft and trained as a lawyer, Heinsius became pensionary of Delft (1679). Though originally a staunch Loevesteiner, he became a supporter of William of Orange after a mission to France (1683), when he realized

that William was right to fear Louis XIV's policy of aggrandizement. On the death of Fagel (1689), Heinsius became Grand Pensionary of Holland. The Dual Monarchy of England and the Netherlands (1688–1702) meant that William III was forced to delegate more and more to Heinsius and the two became associates rather than servant and master. On William's death the Stadtholdership was allowed to lapse, leaving Heinsius in control. A good deal of tact was required to conciliate the separate provinces. His friendship with Marlborough contributed to the smooth running of the War of the Spanish Succession and Heinsius was also closely involved in the peace negotiations.

HEINZE, SIR BERNARD THOMAS (1894–), Australian conductor who became director of the NSW Conservatorium (1956–66) and musical adviser to the Australian Broadcasting Commission in its formative years. He was the originator of Australia's system of subsidized symphony orchestras and series of schools and youth concerts.

HEKE, HONE (c. 1810–50), NZ Maori chief, who signed the treaty of Waitangi (1840), but came to resent British authority, however weak. Four times (1844–5) he cut down its chief symbol, the flagstaff at Kororareka, but surrendered to Sir George Grey after defeat at Ruapekapeka (1846).

HELFFERICH, KARL (1872–1924), German civil servant, banker, and politician, who was vice-chancellor and state secretary (minister) of the interior (1916–17). After the First World War he became a prominent rightwing politician and from 1920 Reichstag deputy of the DNVP. His radical anti-Republican agitation helped to poison the political atmosphere of Weimar Germany.

HELIAEA, name of both the judicial assembly of Athenian citizens over 30 years old and its meeting-place. Appeal to the *heliaea* from the archons' decisions was first introduced by Solon (594 BC). Possibly Cleisthenes (508) first defined it as 6000 citizens chosen by lot from the demes, and increased its powers. But not until the introduction of Ephialtes' reforms (462) were the archons' duties confined to preliminary enquiries and did the *heliaea* become the supreme Athenian court. This realization of the ideal of direct popular justice necessitated in practice the *heliaea*'s division into several *dicasteria*, each representing the whole, and the introduction of pay for jurymen (c. 450).

HELIGOLAND, island at the mouth of the Elbe. In the late Middle Ages it was part of the duchy of Schleswig, passing to Denmark in the 18th cent. and being seized, for strategic and economic reasons, by Britain in the French Wars against Napoleon. Britain retained the island at the conclusion of war (1815). The question of its ownership was raised by Bismarck in 1884 and, after negotiations, Britain ceded Heligoland to Germany (1890). This had significance in the construction of the Kiel Canal and in both World Wars.

HELIGOLAND, BATTLE OF (28 Aug. 1914), first sea-battle in the First World War. It was a successful attempt to achieve quick moral ascendancy over the German fleet and was planned as a trap to destroy enemy squadrons patrolling the Heligoland Bight. Mist and poor co-ordination almost wrecked the plan, but enough German light cruisers were lured under the guns of Beatty's battle-cruisers to justify risking them so close to the German bases. Three German cruisers and one destroyer were sunk. Kaiser William II's predisposition to keep his fleet in port was confirmed by this evidence of the British navy's boldness and striking power.

HELIOPOLIS, ancient Egyptian city (now a northern suburb of Cairo) and centre for the worship of the god Re.

HELLENISTIC MONARCHY, kingship as practised by the Macedonian successors of Alexander the Great. The chief features common to the hellenistic monarchies were use of the Greek language, rule over peoples of different races, centralized government, dynastic succession, and sometimes the cult of the dead (or even the living) monarch. The main hellenistic monarchies were the Antigonids (based on Macedonia), the Attalids (Pergamum), the Ptolemies (Egypt), and the Seleucids (Syria and Mesopotamia).

HELMED, BATTLE OF (1501), defeat near Dorpat of the German troops of the Livonian Order, the allies of Alexander, grand prince of Lithuania, by the army of Ivan III of Muscovy.

HELOTS ('captives'), Greeks in Laconia subjected, c. 1000–750 BC, by the Dorians, together with the Messenians enslaved after the First Messenian War (c. 715). Though in time they out-numbered the full Spartan citizens, they had no political rights and their hostile presence dominated all aspects of Spartan life at home and policy abroad. In the 5th cent. the helots spent ten critical years in revolt (c. 460) and fear of a second uprising after the Athenian occupation of Pylos (425) explains Sparta's acceptance of the peace of Nicias (421). From c. 420 liberated helots (*neodamodeis*) appear increasingly in the Spartan army and a more liberal Spartan attitude might account for the loyalty of Laconian helots after the Messenians were freed (369).

HELPER, HINTON ROWAN (1829–1909), US businessman, author, and publicist, born in NC. He was a champion of non-slave-holding white southerners and argued in his book *The Impending Crisis* (1857) that economic development in the South was retarded, and the region impoverished, by the deleterious effects of slavery on free labour. Helper was, however, extremely unsympathetic towards the Negro and his prejudices are clearly revealed in later writings, such as *Nojoque* (1867) and *Negroes in Negroland* (1868). While US consul in Buenos Aires (1861–6), he was intrigued by the economic potential of Latin America and urged the construction of a railroad from Hudson's Bay to the Straits of Magellan.

HELPMANN, SIR ROBERT MURRAY (1909–   ), Australian ballet dancer, choreographer, actor, and theatrical director. He played Shakespearean parts at the Old Vic and Stratford-on-Avon, and directed Old Vic productions. He was co-artistic director with Peggy van Praagh of the Australian Ballet from 1965, and planned and directed the 1970 Adelaide Festival of the Arts.

HELVETIAN REPUBLIC (1798), French satellite state formed from the Swiss cantons. The ideas of the French Revolution were introduced by middle-class radicals and parliamentary government was put into practice on the basis of the French constitution of the Year III. Through the pressure of local 'patriots', eg, Laharpe and Ochs, universal suffrage was established. The independence of the republic was recognized by the French government in 1801 by the treaty of Lunéville. However, after some social and political reform had been achieved, the unitary constitution was abolished in 1803. The cantons were reorganized and French control over the Alpine passes was established.

HELVETII, Celtic tribe that inhabited western Switzerland in the 1st cent. BC. Their mass migration gave Julius Caesar a pretext for beginning his conquest of Gaul (58). After being defeated by him, they were incorporated by Augustus in the province of Gallia Belgica, and by Tiberius in that of Germania Superior.

HELVETIUS, CLAUDE ADRIAN (1715–71), French philosopher of the Enlightenment and friend of Voltaire. He believed that utilitarianism was the basis of law and morals. His influence on Bentham was profound and he did much to promote utilitarian thinking in Europe. In 1758 he published *De L'Esprit*, one of the most famous works of the Enlightenment, in which he propounded the principle of sensational psychology—that 'everything in man can be reduced to sensation'. The welfare of the state thus depended on the kind of education received by its citizens.

With Diderot, Voltaire, and D'Holbach, Helvetius attacked current religious teaching and the Jesuit order in particular, accusing the Church of intolerance and cruelty, and so exposing himself to the censure of the clergy, the Sorbonne, and Pope Clement XIII.

HEMACHANDRA (c. 1088–1172), Jain monk and scholar, associated with the court of the Chaulukyas of Gujarat, India. He was an encyclopedist and collected enormous amounts of data, sifted them and recorded them in the form of dictionaries. He also wrote ornate Sanskrit texts. Some of his works are important for the historian as they describe the early part of the reign of the Chaulukyas as well as earlier periods of history, especially those associated with Jainism.

HEMINGWAY, ERNEST MILLER (1899–1961), US author and journalist. His first job was with the Kansas City *Star* as a reporter. Later he became a foreign correspondent for the Toronto *Star*, and was sent to Paris (1922), where he became friends with Ezra Pound and Gertrude Stein. In 1923 he went to Spain, a country whose atmosphere was to influence much of his work. In the same year *Three Stories and Ten Poems* was published in Paris, and in 1924 *In Our Time*, in which appeared the first of a line of heroes based largely on himself—men alone in a violent, naturalistic world with which through sport, camaraderie, or alcohol they try to come to terms. His other works include *Torrents of Spring* (1926), a parody of Anderson's *Dark Laughter*, *The Sun Also Rises* (1926—published in England as *Fiesta*), and *A Farewell to Arms* (1929), a novel based on his wartime experiences. During the next ten years he wrote a number of short stories, among the best known being *The Snows of Kilimanjaro* (1936). He also wrote a study of bull-fighting, *Death in the Afternoon* (1932), and *The Green Hill of Africa* (1935), an account of big-game hunting. *For Whom the Bell Tolls* (1940), a story of the Spanish Civil War, is his longest and most ambitious novel. *Across the River and Into the Trees* (1950) showed a degeneration into self-parody, but he regained his old force in *The Old Man and the Sea*. In 1954 he was awarded the Nobel Prize for literature. An autobiographical essay, *A Moveable Feast*, was published in 1964. Hemingway committed suicide in ID.

HENDAYE, French town on the Spanish frontier, scene of Hitler's only meeting with Franco (1940). Hitler sought to bring Spain into the war to secure his position in the Mediterranean and North Africa, and promised to help in the capture of Gibraltar. Franco, anxious to avoid any involvement in the war, countered by making impossible territorial claims. Further negotiations on the same lines were abandoned when Hitler turned his attention to the Russian campaign.

HENDERSON, ALEXANDER (1583–1646), Scottish Presbyterian minister and preacher, who was involved in the theological controversy over episcopacy with Charles I.

HENDERSON, ARTHUR (1863–1935), British Labour politician, whose early political career forms the best illustration of the origins of the Labour Party in Methodism rather than Marxism. He was brought up in Newcastle-on-Tyne, where he became an iron-founder, a trade-union official, a city councillor, and a Wesleyan lay preacher. Although a Liberal agent, he nevertheless entered parliament as an independent Labour member in 1903, convinced that the Liberals were unprepared to accept working-class candidates and that an independent Labour party was needed to oppose the Taff Vale judgement, which exposed trade unions to damages for strikes involving their members. When the Labour Party was formed in 1906, Henderson became chief whip, and, in 1911, party secretary, a post he held till 1934.

In 1915 he was chairman on the union side of the negotiations in which the skilled unions accepted 'dilution' of labour. He joined the cabinet in May 1915, and Lloyd George's five-man war cabinet in Dec. 1916, as minister with responsibility for labour matters. His position was attacked by pacifists during the First World War, and by industrial militants who regarded him as having betrayed their interests; but the majority of the Labour Party stayed with him before and after Aug. 1917, when he resigned from the war cabinet because of its refusal to let him participate in a proposed international peace conference in Stockholm. During the next two years he moved Labour to the left; he produced both a Memorandum on war aims calling for a negotiated peace, and the new Labour Party constitution whose Clause 4 envisaged nationalization and 'popular control' of industry.

In the first Labour government of 1924 Henderson was home secretary, but his governmental talent lay in foreign affairs; his role as foreign secretary in the 1929–31 Labour government was generally applauded, his most solid achievements being the resumption of trading relations with Russia and his agreement to commit Britain to submit international disputes to the League of Nations. After 1931 Henderson's party was out of power, and abroad the rise of Hitler and Mussolini dwarfed French intransigence in making disarmament impossible to achieve. This led to the decline of the League's prestige.

When Ramsay MacDonald formed his national government in Aug. 1931 Henderson refused to support him, and became (though for only a year) leader of the Labour opposition, decimated by the 1931 election. The party's ability to overcome the 1931 disaster was perhaps Henderson's chief legacy. He had been the first Labour minister to reach high office and show Labour as a governmental party; had reorganized the party to admit individual members; and had expanded its electoral organization. By 1929 it was sufficiently well established as one of the two main parties to avoid being ruined by the 1931 débâcle.

G. D. H. Cole, *History of the Labour Party from 1914* (London, 1948).

M. A. Hamilton, *Arthur Henderson* (London, 1968). ISM

HENDERSON, SIR NEVILLE MEYRICK (1882–1942), British diplomat who entered the diplomatic service in 1905, interspersing spells in the foreign office with tours of duty to St Petersburg, Tokyo, Rome, Nish, Paris, Constantinople, and Cairo. In 1929 he headed the mission in Belgrade, where he became a close friend of King Alexander. This was followed in 1935 by his mission to Buenos Aires.

In 1937 came his famous Berlin assignment. He became increasingly critical of French efforts to contain Germany and he felt his mission to be the easing of tension between Britain and Nazi Germany. In 1937 and 1938 he attended Hitler's Nuremberg rallies as a sign of friendship. Even the Austrian annexation saw him still favourable to Hitler and he fully supported the Munich agreement. Germany's invasion of Czechoslovakia finally disillusioned Henderson and throughout the summer of 1939 he tried to dissuade Hitler from invading Poland. With the outbreak of the Second World War in September he returned to Britain, weak in health, and resigned his office. In 1940 he published *Failure of a Mission*, the account of his period in Berlin.

HENLEIN, KONRAD (1898–1945), German politician, who was leader of the Nazi Sudeten Germans in the 1930s. He became leader of the Sudeten German Home Front (1923–1933) and then of the Sudeten German Party, building on the grievances of the 3½ million Germans left, mostly in Bohemia, inside the new state of Czechoslovakia. The party became avowedly Nazi and raised funds to rebuild Hitler's own organization after the Munich putsch. From 1933 it grew rapidly, encouraged by the success of Nazism in Germany and by the economic slump in Czechoslovakia. The aims of both

Henlein and his rank and file are unclear. They ranged from absorption into Germany to autonomy within the Czech state; and Henlein himself probably intended to use Hitler as much as Hitler used him—he was never simply a Nazi puppet. Particularly after 1936, when Henlein controlled the largest single party in the country, he probably hoped to manipulate German support to strengthen his own domestic position, and only raised his demands step by step, precipitating internal and then international crisis, as the situation, and pressure from his own extremists, forced him closer to Hitler. He was under close German intelligence surveillance at least down to July 1938, suspected especially by Himmler and Goebbels of plotting a separate deal with Prague, and he demanded *Anschluss*, or incorporation with Germany, as late as 15 Sept. By then his boats had been burnt by an abortive Sudeten uprising, he had been forced to escape to Germany, and the initiative lay with Hitler and Chamberlain. After Munich he became local party boss, or *Gauleiter*, of Sudetenland, and in March 1939 civil commissioner for Bohemia. In 1945 he was captured by the Allies and committed suicide.

HENNELL, SAMUEL (1800–80), British political officer in the Persian Gulf (1826–54), who was chiefly responsible for the establishment of British predominance, the Trucial system, and the suppression of the slave trade.

HENNEPIN, JEAN-LOUIS (1640–1705), Belgian missionary, explorer, and writer. After being sent to Canada by the Recollet Order (1675), he became chaplain to Robert la Salle (1678) and accompanied him on his expedition in search of the Mississippi (1679), of which he wrote an account, *Déscriptions de la Louisiane* (1683). After La Salle's death (1687), however, Hennepin brought out a revised account, *Nouvelle découverte d'un très grand pay situé dans l'Amérique* (1697), in which he claimed fraudulently to have explored the Mississippi to its mouth before La Salle. He incurred the disfavour of his order and spent his last years in obscurity.

HENNERSDORF, BATTLE OF (24 Nov. 1745), defeat on the Saxon–Silesian border of an Austrian army of Prince Charles of Lorraine by Frederick II of Prussia during the War of the Austrian Succession. Charles was forced to retreat into Bohemia and the imperial attack on Berlin collapsed.

HENRICIAN ARTICLES (1572), document by which Henry of Anjou, the elected King of Poland, gave complete recognition of the political liberties of the *szlachta* (Polish landowning nobility). In particular, the clause *de non praestanda obedientia* granted the *szlachta* the right of rebellion should the king repudiate his obligations. Together with the *Pacta Conventa* and the religious agreement, known as the Warsaw Confederation, the articles gravely undermined the authority of the electoral monarchy, and when Henry hastily left Poland to succeed his late brother Charles IX as King of France, he bequeathed a state in which sovereignty lay with the landowning nobility.

HENRIETTA MARIA (1609–69), Queen consort of Charles I and youngest daughter of Henry IV of France. As a girl of 15, with no knowledge of English, she married Charles in 1625. She had little influence on English politics until the calling of the Long Parliament. She assumed that a military coup would overthrow the parliamentary opposition. Her encouragement of the younger, impulsive courtiers, in the so-called 'army plots', only served to strengthen the opposition to her husband. In 1642 she left for the Netherlands to buy arms, returning in 1643. She finally left England in 1644. Her attempts to convert her youngest son, the Duke of Gloucester, to Roman Catholicism alienated her from Charles II.

HENRÍQUEZ GONZÁLEZ, CAMILO (1769–1825), Chilean priest, rebel, and writer. Under the pen-name of Quirino Lemachez he wrote in favour of Chilean independence, and attacked slavery. After independence he became a leader of the Chilean Liberal Party.

HENRY II (*reg.* 1002–24), German King and Emperor, cousin of Otto III (*reg.* 1013–24) and a man preoccupied mainly with the Church, which he used as an instrument of his authority. He was canonized in the 12th cent.

HENRY III (1017–56), son of Conrad II, King of the Germans, Duke of Bavaria and Duke of Swabia, and finally Emperor (*reg.* 1039–56). He encouraged the spread of culture and established a regime of increasing internal peace and order, so that his reign saw imperial power at a high point. He cemented his power in Italy by alliance with the Church and reformed the papacy in 1046 by replacing local Italian politicians with a succession of distinguished German prelates. His death was followed by disastrous chaos in the empire.

HENRY IV (1050–1106), Emperor (*reg.* 1056–1106). He was a minor when he succeeded his father, Henry III, and a period of disorder ensued. Henry later appreciated the need to restore the resources of the German Crown. He developed the use of 'ministeriales' (royal serfs) in local administration and continued his father's attempts to make Goslar, among the silver mines of the Harz mountains in Saxony, the centre of a new royal domain. An ambitious programme for the recovery of royal rights provoked widespread aristocratic reaction. In 1073 a Saxon revolt, together with unrest elsewhere, led to the election two years later of a rival king, Rudolf of Swabia. Henry won a crushing victory over the Saxons at the village of Unstrutt, but at this juncture he quarrelled with Pope Gregory VII over the investiture of bishops. Henry was excommunicated in 1076 and escaped from threatened deposition only by humiliating himself before Gregory at Cannossa. Nevertheless, in 1080 Gregory declared his support for Rudolf. Henry declared Gregory deposed, and the death of Rudolf in battle during the same year greatly strengthened his position. Henry marched on Rome and had his own pope crowned as Clement III in 1084. The next year the Normans of southern Italy came to the aid of Gregory and Henry was forced to withdraw. In Germany the prolonged civil wars undermined the power of the monarchy and greatly strengthened the various dukes and counts. The future division of Germany among semi-autonomous principalities can in part be traced to Henry's reign.

HENRY V (1081–1125), Emperor (*reg.* 1106–25), last Salian emperor. Under him the princes greatly increased their power and his reign saw the rise of important new dynasties. The Concordat of Worms with the papacy (1122) ended the Investiture Contest, leaving effective royal power over the Church largely intact.

HENRY VI (1165–97), Emperor (*reg.* 1190–7), son of Frederick Barbarossa. He inherited the empire at the height of its power and had wide-ranging ambitions. In 1184 he married Constance, heiress to the kingdom of Sicily, and in 1194 conquered this southern Italian kingdom. He is credited with plans for the establishment of an hereditary monarchy in Germany and he menaced the papacy with territorial encirclement. He died when on the point of attempting conquest of the Byzantine empire.

HENRY VII (?1269–1313), Emperor (*reg.* 1308–13), elected as anti-Habsburg candidate through the great influence of his brother Baldwin, Abp of Trier. He concentrated at first on Bohemia, which he won for his son John, and established the power of the Luxemburg dynasty there. He was one of the last emperors to attempt to make a reality of the nominal subjection of Italy to the imperial throne and aroused great expectations when he entered that country, but he died three years later.

HENRY II OF TRASTAMARA (1333–79), King of Castile (*reg.* 1369–79), illegitimate half-brother of Peter I of Castile, whom he assassinated in order to satisfy his ambition for power. He became king by compromising himself with the conservative nobility, who temporarily increased their hold over the Castilian Crown. He resisted an attempt by his English rival, John of Gaunt, to secure the Crown of Castile.

HENRY I (1068–1135), King of England (*reg.* 1100–35), the youngest son of William the Conqueror. Henry was hunting in the New Forest when his brother, King William Rufus, was killed (2 Aug. 1100). Henry at once seized the royal treasure at Winchester and was crowned king three days later. He issued a Coronation Charter in which he swore to discontinue the royal abuses of feudal custom. Concessions were necessary because of support for the succession of Robert of Normandy as King of England by a section of the Anglo-Norman nobility. The rebellion in favour of Robert misfired in 1101. Henry embarked on the systematic conquest of Normandy, which he completed by capturing Robert at the battle of Tinchebrai (1106).

Henry's reign was one of ordered government, by contrast with that of his successor, Stephen, but it was also harsh and oppressive. His power rested on men who owed their fortunes to him, and who worked under the general direction of Roger of Salisbury at Winchester. Roger was in a vice-regal position, and he elaborated a judicial and fiscal administrative system which took its origins in developments before Henry's accession. The exchequer at Westminster, with which Roger was closely associated, and the activities of royal itinerant justices, in the shire courts, developed in Henry's reign. There was heavy taxation and a rigorous repression of crime, in which innocent men often suffered with the guilty. Henry married Matilda, daughter of Queen Margaret of Scotland, in 1100, thereby uniting the Norman and the old Saxon dynasties. He arranged that his only surviving daughter, Matilda, wife of Count Geoffrey of Anjou, should succeed him, but this idea was unpopular among his barons and after Henry's death Matilda's rights were successfully challenged by his nephew, Stephen, throughout whose reign civil wars were waged against Matilda.
DPK

HENRY II (1133–89), King of England (*reg.* 1154–89), son of Geoffrey, Count of Anjou, and the Empress Matilda, daughter of Henry I. He was invested with the duchy of Normandy (conquered by his father) in 1150, succeeded Geoffrey as Count of Anjou, Maine, and Touraine in 1151, and, by his marriage to Eleanor of Aquitaine in 1152, added the county of Poitou and the great duchy of Aquitaine to his possessions. His invasion of England and the death of Stephen's son, Eustace, in 1153 led to an agreement by which he was recognized as Stephen's heir to the throne of England, to which he succeeded in 1154. Henry faced the problem of maintaining his possessions in France against the determined attacks of the French kings and, in the early years of his reign, the problem of re-establishing strong royal authority in England. This he succeeded in doing with the assistance of Thomas Becket, his chancellor (1154–62), though his attempt to re-establish the control over the English Church enjoyed by the Norman kings led to the tragic quarrel with Becket. His later years were made unhappy by the disloyalty and selfishness of his sons, especially Henry (d. 1183), Geoffrey (d. 1186), and Richard, who, encouraged by their mother and by Philip Augustus of France, rose in open rebellion (1173–4). Henry died while attempting to combat a further rebellion by Richard in alliance with the French. Nevertheless, Henry managed to preserve his possessions largely intact. His reign is of major importance for the constitutional and legal developments which took place in it; eg, the use of assizes, the organization of the legal system, the formulation of the common law, and the development in the offices of administration, especially the justiciarship, exchequer, and chancellorship.
JG

HENRY III (1207–72), King of England (*reg.* 1216–72), who succeeded his father, John, at the age of nine. The country, ravaged by civil war for the first year of his reign, was ruled on his behalf by a council. Although Henry was declared of age in 1227, it was not until 1232 that he assumed personal power. He married Eleanor of Savoy in 1236. The middle years of his reign (1234–58) were marked by the loss of Poitou (formally acknowledged with the loss of Normandy, Maine, and Touraine by the treaty of Paris in 1259), an increasing burden of taxation, stagnation, and ineffectiveness of government, and deteriorating relations with his barons. A scheme, the 'Sicilian Enterprise', by which his younger son, Edmund of Lancaster, was to become King of Sicily in return for Henry's payments of the papal debts, drove the exasperated baronage into open defiance. The Provisions of Oxford (1258) effectively put the government of the country in the hands of a commission of barons. The question was put to Louis IX of France, who found for his fellow-monarch by the Mise of Amiens (1264). The barons, led by Simon de Montfort, Earl of Leicester, took up arms. From the capture of Henry at the battle of Lewes in 1264 to Simon's defeat and death at the battle of Evesham in the following year, Simon ruled the country. After Evesham the government was in the hands of the Lord Edward, Henry's elder son, even though Edward was absent on a crusade from 1270. On Henry's death in 1272 Edward succeeded automatically, being the first English king to do so. The only positive achievement that can be attributed to Henry himself was the building of the present Westminster Abbey.

HENRY IV (1367–1413), King of England (*reg.* 1399–1413), son of John of Gaunt, Duke of Lancaster. In 1398 he was exiled by his cousin, Richard II, following a quarrel with the Duke of Norfolk. When, upon the death of Gaunt in 1399, Richard seized the Lancaster estates, Henry returned from exile and was joined by many of the leading barons. Bereft of support, Richard was deposed in favour of Henry and was murdered in prison shortly afterwards. Henry's uneasy reign was marked by a number of rebellions. In 1400 the Welsh rose under Owen Glendower and, despite repeated attempts to put them down, resisted with varying success for eight years. The Percies of Northumberland, who the year before had defeated the Scots on Henry's behalf, in 1403 raised a rebel army in the north, but were defeated by the king and his son, Prince Henry, at Shrewsbury. By 1408 Henry had mastered the threat of insurrection, but had to face mounting opposition in parliament.

HENRY V (1387–1422), King of England (*reg.* 1413–22). Henry of Monmouth was the eldest son of Henry IV. Determined by means of a popular foreign policy to consolidate the precarious hold of his family upon the throne, he reopened the war with France and won a triumphant victory at Agincourt (1415). His later systematic invasion of France resulted in the treaty of Troyes (1420), by which Charles VI gave Henry his daughter Catherine in marriage, and acknowledged him—to the exclusion of the Dauphin—as heir to the French throne. In August 1422, two months before he would have succeeded his father-in-law as King of France, Henry died. Contemporaries and posterity have seen Henry as an ideal hero king, but he was bigoted in his religious opinions (he vigorously persecuted the Lollards) and in war was a ruthless realist.

HENRY VI (1421–71), King of England (*reg.* 1422–61), son of Henry V and Catherine of France. Before he was a year old he had succeeded his father as King of England, and also his maternal grandfather as King of France. He was subsequently crowned at Westminster (1429) and Paris (1431). During Henry's long minority, his uncles, the Dukes of Gloucester and Bedford, assumed the government of England and of the English possessions in France. After the death of Bedford in 1435, the English fought a losing war to hold their conquests and by 1453 only Calais remained to them. The situation at home deteriorated. With unemployable soldiers returning from France, the peasantry restive (Jack Cade's rebellion erupted in 1450), and the feudal magnates uncontrolled, the House of York challenged the claims of the Lancastrians and plunged England into the Wars of the Roses. Henry became no more than an object in the hands of masterful persons, including Margaret of Anjou, his queen. Following Edward IV's assumption of power and the Crown in 1461, Henry was for some years a refugee in Scotland and a fugitive in the North before being captured and committed to the Tower. Briefly restored by Warwick 'the Kingmaker' in 1470–1, he was put to death immediately after the destruction of the last Lancastrian army at Tewkesbury, an action in which his only son was slain. Henry was the founder of Eton and of King's College, Cambridge.

HENRY VII (1457–1509), King of England (*reg.* 1485–1509), and first of the Tudors, was born in Wales, son of Edmund Tudor, Earl of Richmond, and Margaret Beaufort, a descendant of John of Gaunt. After the death of Henry VI (1471) he was the principal Lancastrian claimant to the throne, which he obtained by an invasion from France and the defeat and death of Richard III at Bosworth (1485). Henry had his hereditary claim formally acknowledged by parliament and united the rival families by his marriage to Elizabeth of York (1486). He weakened the nobility by fines and confiscations in the revived Court of Star Chamber, gained foreign recognition by diplomatic treaties and alliances, and by maintaining order and encouraging commercial prosperity (he made important trading agreements with Flanders) he won the support of a country exhausted by civil war. The overthrow of two pretenders, Simnel and Warbeck, finally established his dynasty, and in his later years he was able to extend the powers of the Crown. He centralized the administrative machinery, strengthened the royal household courts in the provinces, gave new authority to justices of the peace in the countryside and achieved financial independence for the monarchy by severe taxation and the full enforcement of its legal rights. By maintaining a lavish court he emphasized the formal difference between king and subject. Interested in the arts, Henry was a patron of the New Learning and he built the Henry VII Chapel in Westminster Abbey. He also encouraged trade and exploration by supporting the enterprises of the Cabots. The marriage of his daughter, Margaret, to James IV of Scotland brought about the eventual union of the two thrones, and the marriage of his son, Henry VIII, to Catherine of Aragon, following her earlier marriage to his elder son, Arthur, led to the separation from Rome (1534).

MMR

HENRY VIII (1491–1547), King of England (*reg.* 1509–47), younger son of Henry VII. Earnestly cultivating the image of the Renaissance prince, he brought to his court native and foreign scholars. He also sought to prove himself as a warrior, reviving the claim to England's heritage in France, but these ventures (1511–29) gained only one hollow victory (the Spurs, 1513), wasted his father's legacy, and deprived him of bargaining power when he needed a favour from the pope.

On his accession he had married Catherine of Aragon, widow of his brother Arthur, a papal dispensation having relaxed the canonical prohibition. When the marriage failed to provide a male heir, he applied (1527–9) to have it annulled as invalid, but for political reasons the pope delayed a decision and eventually refused.

Probably at Thomas Cromwell's suggestion, Henry solved his problem by dismantling the whole structure of papal authority in England. He claimed to be resuming to the Crown the ancient *imperium* usurped by the bishops of Rome, and after having his marriage annulled in a native court from which he had forbidden any appeal (1533), he declared himself Supreme Head of the Church (1534). These actions were confirmed by statute, and there was little resistance, since papal authority was already undermined by its own acknowledged abuses, the rooted anti-clericalism of the people, and the spread of Lutheran ideas.

In doctrine Henry tried to keep the Church orthodox and Catholic, but his policies were inconsistent and ultimately he was unable to resist the pressure for change. The fall of his fifth queen, Catherine Howard (1542), established the victory of Abp Cranmer and the Protestant party in the struggle for supremacy at court. Edward VI, the heir, was brought up by Protestant tutors, and die-hard Catholics were excluded from the council that was to govern during his minority. Henry's rejection of papal jurisdiction was followed in the next reign by the rejection of Catholic beliefs.

J. Scarisbrick, *Henry VIII* (London, 1968).   MMR

HENRY I (*reg.* 1031–60), King of France, the third successive king of the Capetian house. During his reign this dynasty came nearest to being dispossessed by their rebellious vassals and he was forced to cede Burgundy to his younger brother, Robert. Henry's successor, Philip, though of mediocre ability, was left a secure inheritance.

HENRY II (1519–59), King of France (*reg.* 1547–59), eldest son of Francis I and Claude, daughter of Louis XII. He married Catherine de Medici in 1533 and succeeded his father on 31 March 1547. As a child, he was held as a hostage in Madrid with his younger brother after Francis's defeat at the battle of Pavia (1525). He was ransomed at the peace of Cambrai (1529). In many respects Henry continued the policies of his father, *eg*, under him the process of growing absolutism continued, through the use of the *grand conseil* and the establishment of the *chambre ardente* (1547–50), to deprive the *parlement* of Paris of jurisdiction over cases of heresy. At the end of his reign he launched a determined attack on French Protestantism (Edict of Ecouen, 1559) to vindicate his Catholic orthodoxy. By the treaty of Chambord (1552) with the German Protestant princes, he prolonged Franco-Habsburg rivalry, providing as the price of his assistance, subsidies and an army of 35,000 men which marched into Lorraine and occupied the bishoprics of Metz, Toul, and Verdun. However, by 1557 both France and Spain were tiring of war. Despite France's capture of Calais from the English (1558), counterbalancing her defeat at St Quentin (1557), France, like Spain, faced national bankruptcy and economic stagnation. Henry therefore acceded to the peace of Cateau-Cambrésis (April 1559), relinquishing long-standing French claims in Italy and retaining the bishoprics. A lover of hunting and martial pursuits, Henry was mortally wounded at a joust held to celebrate the peace and died a few days later, leaving his 15-year-old son, Francis II, to succeed him (10 July 1559).

HENRY III (1551–89) King of France (*reg.* 1574–89), last king of the house of Valois and third son of Henry II and Catherine de Medici, who succeeded his brother, Charles IX, in 1574. As the youthful Duke of Anjou he had led the royal forces which defeated the Huguenot armies at Jarnac and Montcontour (1569), thus acquiring an unjustified military reputation. Jealous of the influence of the Huguenot leader Coligny with Charles IX, he helped to engineer the massacre on St Bartholomew's Eve (24 Aug. 1572). In 1573 he was elected King of Poland, where he made extensive concessions to the Polish nobility in the Henrician Articles and the *pacta conventa*, but Charles IX's death necessitated his return to France (1574). Although Henry made some effort to govern France forcefully, he became increasingly effeminate, irresponsible, and self-indulgent. After his acceptance of the humiliating terms of the peace of Monsieur (1576), the mass of French Catholics despaired of his effete conduct of affairs and formed themselves into a Catholic or Holy League, under Guise leadership. It was dissolved in 1577, but in 1584 was revived, since Henry considered accepting the sovereignty of the Low Countries offered to him by the rebellious Dutch. Henry submitted to the league's demands for the suppression

of Protestantism, accepted the treaty of Nemours, and declined the Dutch offer (1585). His action initiated the War of the Three Henries, the final phase of the civil wars. Henry III sought to maintain the central government against the growing strength of the Duc de Guise and the Catholic League on the one hand, and on the other, the Protestant Henry of Navarre, heir to the French throne since the death of the Duke of Alençon (1584). Royal prestige reached its nadir on the Day of the Barricades (May 1588) and Henry III sought revenge on the triumphant Henry of Guise. Encouraged by the failure of the Spanish Armada, he ordered the assassination of the Guise brothers (Dec. 1688), and united himself with Navarre to destroy the League. Seven months later he was assassinated, leaving the throne to Henry of Navarre (1 Aug. 1589).

J. E. Neale, *The Age of Catherine de Medici* London, 1963).
                                                            MKS

HENRY IV (1553–1610), King of France (*reg.* 1589–1610), son of Anthony of Bourbon and the Calvinist, Jeanne d'Albret, was King of Navarre from 1572. He founded the Bourbon dynasty of French kings and was a dynamic ruler. He was brought up in his native Béarn, and on 18 Aug. 1572 was married to Marguerite of Valois, sister of the French king, Charles IX. The wedding provided the occasion for the massacre of St Bartholomew, when hundreds of Huguenots, gathered in Paris for the festivities, were killed at the instigation of the Duke of Anjou and the Guise family (24 Aug. 1572). During the troubled reign of Henry III (1574–89) Henry assumed the leadership of the Huguenots and became a bitter rival of Henry, Duc de Guise, for political influence. Their conflict was intensified after the death of the Duke of Anjou (Alençon) in 1584, when Henry was recognized by Henry III and Catherine de Medici as heir-apparent to the French throne. Many Frenchmen refused to consider a Protestant succession, and backed by the Catholic League and Philip II of Spain, the Guise family supported the claims of Henry's elderly uncle, the cardinal of Bourbon. Under pressure from the Guises, Henry III revoked religious toleration of the Huguenots and repudiated Henry's rights to the throne. Papal excommunication (Sept. 1585) finally provoked Henry to join in the War of the Three Henries, the final phase of the religio-civil wars (1585–9). Henry appealed to French national feeling, Protestant and Catholic, in the struggle against the enfeebled royal administration and the pro-Spanish house of Guise, who dominated the King. After his victory at Coutras (1587) and the Guises' assassination (1588), he agreed to assist Henry III in suppressing the Catholic League's forces (April 1589), and while besieging Paris he received the dying king's recognition (1 Aug. 1589).

Navarre, now Henry IV, faced with direct Spanish intervention, concentrated on defeating the armies of Farnese and the Duke of Mayenne, whose league forces he crushed at Arques (1589) and Ivry (1590). From 1593, encouraged by Henry's conversion to Catholicism, the suffering peasantry rejected the league and looked to him to restore law, order, and prosperity. Henry's entry into Paris (March 1594), the collapse of the League, and the surrender of Mayenne (Jan. 1596), enabled him to plan the expulsion of the Spaniards, on whom he had declared war (1595). His position was strengthened by English subsidies (May 1596) and Clement VIII's absolution from excommunication (1596). By 1598 Henry was able to take two vital steps to restore peace. On 30 April he signed the Edict of Nantes to promote 'union, concord, and tranquillity' between his Huguenot and Catholic subjects, the former's civil and religious rights being guaranteed. On 2 May he concluded the treaty of Vervins with Spain, whereby France's territorial integrity was assured.

Henry then concentrated on the political and economic recovery of France. With the help of able servants, *eg*, Barthélemy de Laffemas and Maximilien de Béthune, Duke of Sully, the Crown finances were overhauled and radical improvements were made to roads, bridges, canals, fortifications and the navy.

Henry's second marriage, to Marie de Medici of Tuscany (1601), was made with the aim of maintaining French influence in northern Italy, a strategic area in the Franco-Spanish balance of power. Despite the territorial settlement of 1601 with Charles Emmanuel of Savoy, Franco-Spanish tension remained, and open conflict over the succession to Cleves-Jülich and Berg in the Rhine valley was only averted by Henry's death.

He was a talented soldier, with a forceful personality and a gift for statesmanship, and his assassination by a fanatic, on 14 May 1610, deprived France of one of her greatest kings.   MKS

HENRY (1512–80), King of Portugal (*reg.* 1578–80), cardinal, and the last legitimate ruler of the house of Aviz, succeeded to the throne on the death of his great-nephew, Sebastian, at the battle of Alcazar-quivir. He reigned for only 18 months and left a council of regents, who were overthrown by Philip II of Spain.

HENRY, Prince (d. 1241), most powerful Polish prince of his time, who succeeded his father as Duke of Lower Silesia (Breslau) and of Cracow (1238). He resisted the first Mongol invasion of Poland (1241) and was killed at the disaster of Liegnitz. His principality disintegrated and Poland entered upon a period of extreme disunity.

HENRY, Prince of Prussia (1726–1802), brother of Frederick the Great, and one of the best Prussian generals during the Seven Years War.

HENRY OF ALMAINE (d. 1271), son of Richard of Cornwall King of Germany, and nephew of King Henry III of England. He played an active, if inconstant, role in the conflicts between Henry III and the barons (1258–65). At one point he was Simon de Montfort's leading supporter, but at Lewes in 1264 he fought, together with his father, against Montfort and they were captured. Simon's son Guy murdered Henry, who was his cousin, in a sudden attack, while Henry was returning through Italy from a crusade. The motives for his murder, which figures in Dante's *Divine Comedy*, remain inexplicable and it was probably unpremeditated.

HENRY ARISTIPPUS (d. 1162), chief minister of King William I of Sicily and the only 12th-cent translator of the works of Plato from Greek into Latin. By the time of his sudden arrest and execution (for reasons unknown) by orders of his royal master in 1162, Henry had completed his translation of two dialogues, the Meno and the Phaedo. The remaining Platonic dialogues were not translated until the late 15th cent.

HENRY OF BLOIS (*c.* 1090–1171), son of the Count of Blois, youngest brother of King Stephen of England, and a monk of Cluny, was made abbot of Glastonbury (1126), which benefice he retained with the bishopric of Winchester, received in 1129. He was also papal legate (1143–6). An exemplary abbot, an able administrator, an early humanist, and a great builder, he was one of the major figures of his brother's reign and tried, with some success, to mediate in the quarrel between Henry II and Becket.

HENRY OF FLANDERS (*reg.* 1206–16), Latin Emperor of Constantinople, and younger son of Baldwin, Count of Flanders and Hainault (d. 1195), had been prominent at the siege of Constantinople in 1204. After his brother, Baldwin I of Constantinople, had fallen into the hands of the Bulgars in 1205, Henry became regent of the Latin empire, and when it became known that Baldwin was dead he succeeded to the throne. Henry proved to be a capable and vigorous monarch, most of his reign being spent in efforts to enlarge the Latin empire at the expense of the Bulgars and of the Byzantines at Nikaea and in Epirus.

HENRY THE FOWLER (876–936), King of Germany (*reg.* 919–36), and Duke of Saxony, was the nominee of his predecessor, Conrad I. His accession meant an approximately three-fold increase in the royal estates and material resources of the German Crown. He began the extension of the empire eastwards against the Slavs, and his fortification of urban centres and development of a cavalry force of ministeriales (unfree serfs) were important military developments and prepared the way for the successful repulsion of the Hungarian invasions by Otto I.

HENRY OF HUNTINGDON (?1084–*c.* 1155), archdeacon of Huntingdon. He wrote a *History of the English*, which ends in 1154 and is a valuable historical source for his times. It was first printed in 1596.

HENRY, JOSEPH (1797–1878), US physicist, famous for his studies of electromagnetic induction, who in 1831 published details of an electric motor. Faraday's discovery of the generator resulted in the use of electricity in appliances worked by Henry's motor.

HENRY THE LION, Duke of Saxony (d. 1195), member of the Welf family, given Saxony, Bavaria, and wide lands east of the Elbe by his cousin Emperor Frederick I. He indulged in grandiose state-building activities in his lands and acted as an independent prince, undertaking wide conquests in the Slav lands. He founded the towns of Schwerin, Hanover, Munich, and Brunswick, his capital. In 1176 he refused to send military aid to the emperor in Italy and, in 1180, was banned from the empire and stripped of his possessions. He was reconciled with the Emperor Henry VI and regained Brunswick and Lüneburg, the core of Welf dominions.

HENRY THE NAVIGATOR, Prince of Portugal (1394–1460), responsible for the early stages of Portuguese exploration of the west coast of Africa. He was the first to put exploration on a scientific basis by establishing a naval observatory at Sagres in southern Portugal, where experts correlated knowledge about Africa, in the light of which Henry organized expeditions. His motives were complex. He was moved by the crusading spirit, seeking the legendary Christian king, Prester John, who would help him to crush the infidel. But he also sought to wrest trans-Saharan trade from Muslim hands and envisaged the eventual discovery of a sea route round Africa and Portuguese domination of trade between India and Europe. At his death, Portuguese explorers had reached at least Sierra Leone, and although their progress at first seemed slow the expertise which they acquired made possible the rapid growth of a Portuguese colonial empire.

HENRY, PATRICK (1736–99), American statesman and lawyer, born in Virginia. He was elected (1765) to the Virginia House of Burgesses where he condemned the British Stamp Act (1765) as a menace to individual liberties and a denial of the right of parliament to levy internal taxes on the colonies. He represented the radical wing in the first Continental Congress (1774) and his 'Give me liberty or give me death' speech led the Virginia legislature to form self-defence forces (1775). During the American War of Independence Henry served in the Second Continental Congress (1775) and as a colonel of the Virginia militia (1775–6). He helped to draft the state constitution of Virginia and was elected first governor of the state (1776–9), in which capacity he sent George Rogers Clark to seize British posts in the Illinois country. He was elected again as governor (1784–6), and as a delegate to the Virginia ratifying convention, he unsuccessfully opposed the adoption of the US constitution (1788). He declined posts as senator (1794), secretary of state (1795), and chief justice of the US Supreme Court (1795).   DJF

HENSON, HERBERT HENSLEY, bishop (1863–1947), English Broad Churchman whose controversial views on the Virgin Birth and the miracles led to a crisis when he was nominated to the see of Hereford (1917). As Bp of Durham (1920–39), he took a prominent part in the struggle for the revised Prayer Book (1927–8), the rejection of which by parliament caused him to become a champion of the disestablishment of the Church of England.

HENSON, JOSIAH (1789–1883), born a slave at Port Tobacco, MD, rose to be overseer of his master's Kentucky plantation and was ordained in the Methodist Episcopal Church (1828). He became one of the founders of the Dawn Institute at Dresden, Ont., a co-operative settlement for fugitive slaves. His autobiography, *The Life of Josiah Henson* (1849), brought him to the attention of the American abolitionist Harriet Beecher Stowe, who used him as her model for Uncle Tom in *Uncle Tom's Cabin*.

HENTY FAMILY, THE, played a remarkable part in the pioneering of three Australian colonies. In 1829 Thomas Henty (1775–1839), an English banker, sent three of his sons, James (1800–82), John (1813–68), and Stephen (1811–72) to the Swan river settlement. Two years later, James and John moved to Van Diemen's Land and in 1832 were joined by their father, their brothers Charles (1807–64) and William (1808–81), and other members of the family. From Launceston, Edward explored the south-eastern coast of the mainland and, in 1834, founded the first permanent settlement in Vic. at the old whaling station on Portland bay. There, two years later, the NSW explorer, Maj. Mitchell, found the Henty family well established, though with uncertain title to their holdings, owing to the government's changing policy on land tenure. When Gov. Gipps laid out a township at Portland in 1840, he sold land over the heads of the Hentys, whose claims were not met until 1846–9, and then in part only. By that time Thomas Henty had died and the sons were scattered throughout Tas. and Vic. Edward's name is linked with Portland, though the main pioneering work in this district was done by Stephen. Edward sat in Vic.'s legislative assembly and James in its legislative council. Of those members of the family who remained in Tas., Charles became a member of the house of assembly (1856–62) and William a colonial minister.

HEPBURN, MITCHELL (1896–1953), Canadian politician and prime minister of Ont. (1934–42). He was a Liberal MP (1926–34) and leader of his party. After 1934 he devoted himself purely to provincial politics. He led the Liberal party to a landslide victory in Ont. (1934) and became prime minister of the province. His career was marked by antagonism towards the federal government, both Conservative and Liberal, and by a feud with Liberal prime minister, Mackenzie King. Hepburn opposed foreign investment in Canadian industry and frequently attacked American and Que. 'power interests' and 'foreign industrial unionism'. He resigned the Ont. premiership (1942) to lead the opposition in the provincial legislature.

HEPBURN ACT (1906), US legislation designed to strengthen the Interstate Commerce Commission. The commission was authorized to establish the maximum rates to be charged by railroads. Business interests succeeded in having an amendment attached which provided for a judicial review of rates prescribed by the commission, but the burden of proof was placed on the carriers.

HERACLEIDAE, legendary leaders of the so-called Dorian invasion of the Argolid, Messenia, and Laconia *c.* 1120 BC, supposedly descendants of Heracles, who had been expelled from Argos *c.* 1250. Later Dorians used this legend to justify their earlier conquests and to claim racial affinity with the conquered.

HERACLITUS (*fl.* 500 BC), Greek philosopher from Ephesus, who denied the existence of one elemental substance, stating that all things are in a state of flux subject to the influences of 'fire' and the opposite tensions of 'harmony' and 'strife'.

HERACLIUS (d. 641), Byzantine Emperor (*reg.* 610–41). He was governor of Africa and became emperor on the assassination of the usurper Phocas, whom he overthrew. Heraclius assumed control of a ruined empire—three-quarters of which lay under the domination of Persians, Slavs, and Avars—an empty treasury, and a despairing populace. Within 12 years he had created a firm base of power in Constantinople, while the Persians continued to ravish imperial lands, capturing Damascus and Jerusalem. The Byzantine people, driven to desperation and supported by the treasures of the cathedral and abbey churches, formed a new army and fleet. Inspired by religious zeal, they fought six campaigns under Heraclius in successive years, and not only delivered Constantinople from Slavic siege, but defeated the Persian power under Chosroes. Heraclius planted the Roman banners further east than Roman armies had ever penetrated before and in 626 brought to a close 26 years of war between the Byzantine and Persian empires. But the exhaustion of both states facilitated the Arab conquests which began in the following decade. Heraclius died while the Arabs were overrunning most of the Asiatic provinces of Byzantium.

HERAT CRISES (1832–63), series of diplomatic incidents deriving from Iranian attempts to seize the valley of Herat, long disputed by Afghanistan and Iran. Following the failure of Abbas Mirza's attack on Herat in 1832, a renewed attempt was made by his son Muhammad Shah (1837) with supposed Russian support. Fearing the establishment of hostile influence on the British–Indian borders, Britain seized the Iranian port of Kharg in the Persian Gulf (1838) and launched the First Afghan War. Iran raised the siege and withdrew from Ghuriyan in the western Herat valley in 1841. A further Herat incident took place (1853) and in 1856 the Iranian capture of Herat precipitated the 1856 Anglo-Persian War. Iran gave way, but her activities had brought about an Anglo-Afghan alliance (1855, 1857) and Dost Muhammad of Kabul annexed Herat (1863).

HERBERT OF CHERBURY, Edward Herbert, 1st Baron (1583–1648), English philosopher and diplomat, elder brother of George Herbert, was given an Irish peerage (1624) after an eventful career as soldier and statesman. His *De Veritate* (1624) anticipated the metaphysics of the Cambridge Platonists and propounded a 'natural religion' identifiable with Deism. He also wrote poems, an autobiography, a life of Henry VIII, and a vindication of Buckingham's conduct at the Ile de Rhé.

HERBERT OF LEA, SIDNEY HERBERT, 1st Baron (1810–61), British Conservative politician. He was a member of the Peelite group after 1846 and became secretary-at-war in the Aberdeen Coalition (1852–5) during the Crimean War. He sent Florence Nightingale to work in the hospital at Scutari and strongly supported her. He was attacked for his part in the mismanagement of the war, but exonerated by the Roebuck committee of enquiry. After 1856 he led the movement for medical reform in the army. He returned as secretary-at-war in Palmerston's ministry of 1859 and supported the volunteer movement.

HERBERT, GEORGE (1593–1633), English metaphysical poet, Anglican clergyman, and brother of Edward, Lord Herbert of Cherbury. He wrote *The Temple*, *Sacred Poems* (1633) and *A Priest to the Temple, or the Country Parson* (1652).

HERBERT, SIR ROBERT GEORGE WYNDHAM (1831–1905), English colonial official, who became a member of the legislative council of Qld and its first prime minister (1860–5). He returned to England (1867) and was permanent under-secretary of state for the colonies (1871–92) in the period of imperial expansion.

HERCULANEUM, ancient city about 8 kms east of Naples, destroyed, with Pompeii, in the great eruption of Mt Vesuvius (AD 79), and, like Pompeii, preserved under volcanic ash which here hardened, rendering excavation difficult and crushing some structures, but preserving objects more completely, so that the city was a storehouse of artistic treasures and of information about living conditions in the 1st cent. AD. It was possibly a Greek foundation, though it could have derived its Greek character from its neighbours. It became allied with Rome in the Second Samnite War (326–304 BC), but in the Social War it joined the rebel allies and was reduced (89).

In the 18th cent. the Herculaneum Discoveries were a major archaeological find. Excavations, at Herculaneum, were carried out for more than 40 years (1738–80). They produced a collection of great scientific and artistic value.

HERCYNIAN FOREST, Roman name for the vast area of forest and mountain stretching from the middle Rhine to the Carpathians. It had a reputation for mystery and for being the haunt of wild animals of unknown species.

HEREFORD, HUMPHREY DE BOHUN, 7th Earl of (3rd of 3rd creation) (c. 1249–98), important Marcher lord, who had apparently caused no trouble to King Edward I of England before 1291, when he was tried, imprisoned, and fined together with his neighbour, the Earl of Gloucester, for breaking the king's prohibition against private war. In 1297 Hereford emerged as a leader of baronial opposition to Edward.

HERESY. In medieval western Christendom heresy was merely what had been declared unorthodox by the pope or by provincial or diocesan synods, presided over by bishops. A number of the greatest and most original medieval thinkers and spiritual leaders, including St Thomas Aquinas and St Francis of Assisi, were at one time or another suspected of heresy or even locally condemned. Many medieval heretics were singled out for condemnation for political rather than religious reasons. The Inquisition, from the 13th cent. onwards, was largely responsible for the policy of punishing heresy, while—in England—the law *De Haeretico Comburendo* (1401) gave statutory authority to the punishment of heretics until its repeal in the 16th cent.

HEREWARD (*fl.* 11th cent.), Lincolnshire thegn, popularly known as Hereward the Wake, disinherited by the Normans, who supported the Danish invasion of eastern England in 1070. When the Danes departed Hereward withdrew to the Isle of Ely, where he was besieged by William the Conqueror (1071). He escaped and then vanished from history, but has become the subject of romance and legend ever since.

HERGT, OSCAR (1869–1967), German judge, civil servant, and politician, who was Prussian minister of finance (1917–18). After the Revolution he joined the DNVP and served as its chairman until 1926. He was vice-chancellor and minister of justice in the fourth cabinet of Wilhelm Marx (1927–8). Although conservative in outlook, he did not leave the DNVP when Hugenberg took over, and remained a Reichstag deputy until 1933, when he retired.

HERKIMER, NICHOLAS (1728–77), American militia general. While leading troops to relieve Americans besieged at Fort Stanwix, NY, Herkimer was ambushed and killed, but his action delayed British troops on the way to join Gen. Burgoyne and contributed to his defeat at Saratoga (1777).

HERMOCRATES (d. 407 BC), Syracusan leader in the great Peloponnesian War, who rallied opposition to the Athenians before and during their great expedition to Sicily (415–413), and persuaded the Sicilian Greeks to make peace (424) and reject Athenian intervention. He was quick to see the danger in 415 and became one of three generals with full powers, directing the defence of Syracuse early in 414 and later co-operating with the Spartan, Gylippus, in the defeat and destruction of the Athenians (413). Between 412 and 409 he led a Syracusan squadron in the war against Athens in the Aegean, but was declared exiled after a democratic revolution. Returning to Sicily (winter 408–407), he harassed the Carthaginians, and was killed trying to re-enter Syracuse.

HERNDON, WILLIAM HENRY (1818–91), US lawyer, friend, and law partner of Abraham Lincoln. With Jesse H. Weik he wrote *Herndon's Lincoln: the true story of a great life* (3 vols, 1889), a vivid, controversial, influential, but not always reliable collection of reminiscences, mainly of Lincoln's earlier life in IL.

HEROD AGRIPPA I (d. AD 44), son of Aristobulus and Bernice, a 'timeserver' who was rewarded by the Emperor Caligula with the tetrarchies of Philip and Antipas and later the Roman province of Judaea, including Samaria. From AD 41–4 he ruled with the title 'king' over a reunited Palestine and his reign was the Indian summer of Judaism, approved even by the Pharisees. In high favour both at Jerusalem and Rome, he seemed unassailable, although Claudius' refusal to let him refortify his capital showed his insecurity. Josephus and the New Testament substantially agree that after parading himself at Caesarea as a little Caesar, he was smitten by disease and died in agony. Jews and Christians saw his end as a punishment for his heathenism.

HEROD AGRIPPA II (*reg.* 1st cent. AD), King of Chalcis, and son of Herod Agrippa I, who became ruler of Chalcis in the Lebanon in AD 50, but lived mainly in Rome. In AD 60 he tried to persuade the Palestinian Jews not to revolt.

HEROD ANTIPAS (*reg.* 4 BC–AD 39), Ruler of Galilee and Peraea and son of Herod the Great. By nature cunning, rather than strong, he married Herodias, his brother's wife, for whose daughter, Salome, he executed John the Baptist to reward her for her dancing.

HEROD THE GREAT (*fl.* 1st cent. BC), King of the Jews appointed by the Romans in 40 BC, who ruled Palestine (37–4 BC). A man of extraordinary force and political discernment, he owed his success largely to his own powers. Enjoying the life-long favour of Augustus and Agrippa, he made life and property in Palestine safe from every foe, though tyrannical himself, and so kept peace in a country that was hard to rule. He had, however, a brutal streak, shown in the murder of his wife, Mariamne, and his children. Amphitheatres and other magnificent buildings testify to his sympathies with Hellenism, but he also rebuilt the Jewish Temple with great splendour. Jesus Christ was born during his reign.

HERODIAN (*c.* AD 180–250), minor Roman official from Syria, and author of a Greek history in eight books covering the period from the death of Marcus Aurelius (180) to the accession of Gordian III (238).

HERODOTUS (*fl.* 5th cent. BC), earliest Greek historian whose works are fully preserved. Born *c.* 480 BC at Halicarnassus, he travelled widely, visiting Mesopotamia, the Black Sea, and Egypt, and continued the Ionian tradition of geographical and ethnological research. He also collected stories of the Lydian, Persian, and Egyptian past and in Greece itself such oral tradition as there was of the past of Athens, Sparta, etc. He developed, probably at Athens, a particular interest in the Persian Wars (480–479) and shortly before his death (*c.* 425) wrote a monumental account of the origins and course of the conflict between Greece and the East, culminating in Xerxes' expedition.

HERRENHAUSEN, electoral palace of the house of Hanover, where the Electress Sophia, grand-daughter of James I of England, kept up a brilliant court in the opening years of the 18th cent.

HERRENKLUB in Germany, popular name for the Deutscher Klub, a social and political club, founded in 1924. As a successor to the Juni-Klub, many of whose members it eventually absorbed, the Herrenklub was headed jointly by Heinrich Freiherr von Gleichen Russwurm and Count Hans Bode von Alvensleben. In attitude it was right-wing nationalist, monarchist, anti-democratic, romantic-conservative, and its regular weekly meetings were a gathering place for the aristocracy, heavy industry, and high finance. Although membership never much exceeded 5000 and although the club's journal, *Der Ring*, had a limited circulation of about 1000, the Herrenklub nevertheless had considerable influence on the intellectual life of the German right. The cabinet of Franz von Papen, a member and sponsor of the club and chancellor in 1932, was called by some the 'Herrenklub cabinet'. In 1933 the club was put under the surveillance of Himmler and its members gradually dispersed. It was dissolved in 1944.

HERRERA, JUAN DE (1530–97), Spanish architect, who helped to build the cathedral of Valladolid and the Escorial palace (1563–84), using an austere classical style.

HERRICK, ROBERT (1591–1674), English clergyman and poet who accompanied Buckingham as chaplain on his expedition to the Ile de Ré (1627). He was the incumbent of Dean Prior, Devon (1629–47), was ejected because of his royalist sympathies, but was restored in 1662. His *Hesperides* and *His Noble Numbers* (1648) contain about 1400 poems.

HERRIES, JOHN CHARLES (1778–1855), British Tory politician, who came from a banking family and, although never an effective speaker, was second only to Gladstone in the 19th cent. as a financial administrator. He held minor office under the Younger Pitt, was commissary-in-chief of the army (1811–16), auditor of the civil list (1816), and financial secretary to the treasury (1823–7). In the 1820s he was concerned with the consolidation of the English and Irish revenue, with customs consolidation, and with the reform of government accounting, investigated by the finance committee of 1828, of which he was a member. He was chancellor of the exchequer in Goderich's ministry (1827–8) and secretary-at-war in Peel's first ministry (1834–5).

HERRING, SIR EDMUND FRANCIS (1892–), Australian soldier and judge, who commanded 1 Australian Corps in New Guinea (1942–4). He was chief justice of Vic. (1944–64) and in 1945 became lieutenant-governor of Vic.

HERRING, vital commodity in Catholic Europe, where abstinence laws frequently forbade meat-eating. Herring was one of the main catches of Hanseatic seamen fishing in the Baltic Sea, but in the 15th cent. the appearance of large shoals in the North Sea caused salted or cured herring to become one of the principal exports of the Dutch.

HERRIOT, ÉDOUARD (1872–1957), French politician and leader of the Radical Party. Like many men of his generation, he first became active in politics as a result of the Dreyfus affair. He entered the senate in 1912, and in 1919 was elected as a deputy and as president of the Radical Party.

Herriot's first term as prime minister (1924–5) followed the election victory of the *Cartel des Gauches*, and was notable for its foreign policy initiatives. His government reversed Poincaré's policy by withdrawing French troops from the Ruhr, recognized the Soviet Union, and championed the cause of disarmament and collective security. Economic crisis at home caused its fall, and Herriot was never to hold power as effectively again, although he was prime minister briefly in 1926 and 1932 and a minister in several other governments.

In 1940 Herriot was president of the Chamber, and the constitutional importance of this office gave him a significant role in the events which ended the Third Republic. After the Second World War, he was criticized for not opposing Pétain more actively at that time. But he had been hostile to the Vichy regime, and had been arrested in 1942. After the Allied landings in 1944, Laval sought to persuade him to co-operate in his plan for the recall of the old parliament, but he refused. He was then deported to Germany.

During the constitutional debates of 1945–6 Herriot unsuccessfully defended the discredited institutions of the Third Republic. He returned to parliament, and became president of the National Assembly (1947–54). He was also active as president and elder statesman of the Radical Party, and in his last years he sought to use his prestige to heal the dissensions caused in the party by the policies of Mendès-France.

F. de Tarr, *The French Radical Party from Herriot to Mendès-France* (London, 1961).   RDA

HERSCHELL COMMITTEE, appointed in 1892 to report on the currency problem of British India, caused by the decline in the gold value of the rupee. The recommendations of the committee were accepted by the government of India and Indian mints were closed to the free coinage of silver and gold.

HERTER, CHRISTIAN ARCHIBALD (1895–1966), US diplomat and politician. After diplomatic service during the First World War he was assistant to Herbert Hoover (1919–24). Becoming a Boston journalist and editor, he was elected to the MA state legislature (1931–43) and the US Congress (1943–53). He was governor of MA (1953–7), under-secretary of state (1957–9), and secretary (1959–60).

HERTZOG, JAMES BARRY MUNNICK (1866–1942), South African statesman, who formed the Nationalist Party in 1913 and became prime minister in 1924. He held power until 1939, during which time he played a major role in securing Afrikaner cultural equality within South Africa and dominion autonomy in the Commonwealth. By Africans he is remembered chiefly for his role in drafting the Natives Land Act (1913) and for the removal of Cape Africans from the common roll (1936).

HERVEY, LORD JOHN (1696–1743), English Whig politician and poet. He was a supporter of Sir Robert Walpole and was lord privy seal (1740–2). He was 'Sporus' of Pope's satires and wrote *Memoirs of the Reign of George II*.

HERZEBERG, EWALD FRIEDRICH (1725–95), Prussian statesman, who concluded the peace of Hubertusburg (1763), which established Prussia as a great power.

HERZEGOVINA RISING (1875), revolt of a Christian peasantry against economic exploitation by Muslim Turkish landlords which began the Near Eastern crisis (1875–8). Having been influenced by Serb propaganda they hoped for Serbian and Austrian aid.

HERZEN, ALEXANDER IVANOVICH (1812–70), Russian publicist and revolutionary thinker. As a schoolboy, Herzen, illegitimate son of a nobleman, dedicated his life to the ideals of the Decembrists. He was educated at Moscow University and, with his life-long friend Ogaryov, formed one of the first circles in the 1830s to study Hegel and Schelling. As a leader of the Westernizers in the debates of the 1840s he became increasingly influenced by Saint-Simon and

Proudhon and after he arrived in Europe (1847) he became a socialist. Disillusioned with western liberalism by the revolutions of 1848, and sceptical of revolutionary prospects, he settled in London (1852) and established a Russian free press in exile to promote social change in Russia. His journals, and especially *The Bell* (Kolokol), which were smuggled into Russia, had enormous influence on the Russian scene in the early years of Alexander II's reign.

Herzen at first welcomed the new tsar as a reformer but, disillusioned by the terms of the Emancipation, he publicized his own ideas, which combined Slavophile praise of the peasant commune and belief in Russian distinctiveness with western socialist and anarchist thought. His belief that Russia could by-pass the capitalist stage and move directly to socialism through the peasant commune made him a founder of populism, coining, in *The Bell* (1861), its most famous slogans—'Land and Liberty' and 'Going to the People'. However, he quarrelled not only with the liberals of the 1840s, when he rejected parliamentary democracy, but also with Chernyshevsky and the new radicals of the 1860s, whom he found too extreme. Being primarily concerned with individual liberty, his socialism was ethical and romantic and he remained a gentry revolutionary, uninterested in economics and hostile to Marx and dictatorial revolutionary organizations. His championship of Polish independence (1863) lost his support in Russia, although he remained important in the exile movement. His memoirs, *My Past and Thoughts*, deserve to be regarded as one of the great works of 19th-cent. Russian literature.

E. H. Carr, *The Romantic Exiles* (London, 1933).
M. Malia, *Alexander Herzen and the Birth of Russian Socialism* (Harvard, 1961).   BJW

HERZL, THEODORE (1860–1904), Austrian Jewish writer. Herzl, once an assimilationist, became, after the Dreyfus case, the founder of modern Zionism, advocating in *Der Judenstaat* (1896) a Jewish state in Palestine, and establishing the World Zionist Organization (1897).

HESELRIGE, SIR ARTHUR (d. 1661), English politician. As MP for Leicestershire in 1640 he was closely associated with the attainder of Strafford and the 'root-and-branch' and militia bills, and as a result was one of the five members whom Charles I tried to arrest and impeach for treason (Jan. 1642). He took an active part in the civil wars, fighting at Edgehill (1642), and as second-in-command to Waller at Landsdowne (1643) and Cheriton (1644). On becoming leader of the Independents in parliament, he sided with the army against the Presbyterians (1647) and remained in parliament after Pride's Purge (1648). He was appointed governor of Newcastle, which he held against the royalists (1648), before accompanying Cromwell to Scotland (1648, 1650). A councillor of state under the Commonwealth, he became an enemy of Cromwell after being expelled with the other members of the Rump (20 April 1653). Foiled in his hopes of undermining the protectorate, he was elected to Richard Cromwell's parliament (1659), though he remained a bitter critic of his government. He took a prominent part in the restoration of the Rump and the Commonwealth (April–May 1659) and the summoning of Monck to London. Only the latter's intervention saved his life at the Restoration and he died in the Tower (Jan. 1661).

HESIOD (*fl.* 8th cent. BC), ancient Greek peasant poet of Ascra in Boeotia. His two poetic handbooks, the agricultural *Works and Days* and the theological *Theogony*, constitute important evidence on contemporary Greece.

HESSE CRISIS (1850) brought Austria and Prussia to the brink of war. The crisis was caused by the Elector of Hesse-Cassel, who rescinded the reforms of 1848–9, recalled his exiled minister Hassenpflug, and dissolved the Landtag. As a result, officials refused duty and army officers resigned en masse. The elector appealed to the Federal Diet, and Austrian and Bavarian troops were sent in. Prussia had already occupied Cassel and Fulda, where Prussian military roads (*Etappenstrassen*) crossed the duchy which divided the two parts of Prussia. After a minor clash, Prussia gave way, Radowitz resigned, and agreement was reached in the Convention of Olmütz.

HESSIANS, 30,000 German mercenaries hired by the British during the American War of Independence. They were recruited from Hesse Cassel and Hesse Darmstadt and took part in almost all the campaigns of the war. Many remained in America thereafter.

HESYCHASM (Gk, ἡσηχία—divine quietude), a movement influential within the Greek Orthodox Church during the 14th–15th cents. It involved the use of techniques mystical and ascetic in character, the reward of their application being an awareness of a light believed to be the pure essence of God and to be identical with the light manifest to the disciples of Christ on Mt Tabor. Hesychasm found a vigorous opponent in Barlaam of Seminara and an able advocate in Palamas. A synod was held at Constantinople in 1341 to determine the nature of the illumination vouchsafed to the adepts of Hesychasm. In 1351 the doctrine of the uncreated nature of the light seen on Mt Tabor became established as an article of faith for the Greek Orthodox Church. The Hesychast movement attained a considerable political importance during the two centuries of its efflorescence.

HETHERINGTON, HENRY (1792–1849). English radical and London compositor. He was a freethinker and supporter of mechanics' institutes. His *Poor Man's Guardian* (1831–5) gave him the leadership of the working-class campaign against newspaper taxes. Hetherington's distaste for the prevailing competitive economic system led him into the Chartist movement, but Feargus O'Connor's personality and methods frightened him out of it.

HEUREAUX, ULISES (1844–99), Negro president of the Dominican republic. He controlled Dominican politics for almost 20 years. His first presidential term (1882–3) was reformist, but his second (1887–99) became repressive and authoritarian. Because of foreign pressure, or because of his own greed—opinions vary—he was forced to accept foreign loans which put the nation's finances under severe strain. Heureaux was finally assassinated.

HEUSS, THEODOR (1884–1963), German politician and writer, who was first president of the Federal Republic (1949–59). He exemplified the attempt to find a synthesis between intellectualism and politics, as he embraced an ethical and political liberalism rooted primarily in profound humanity.

An indelible mark was left on him by his early association with Friedrich Naumann, the preacher and politician who tried to integrate nationalism, monarchism, socialism, liberalism, democracy, and Christian ethics into a viable social and political philosophy. With Naumann as his mentor, Heuss began his public life in journalism, as sub-editor (1905–12) of Naumann's journal *Die Hilfe*, chief editor (1912–18) of the *Neckar-Zeitung* in Heilbronn, and as a contributor to numerous other publications. He followed Naumann into the German Democratic Party (DDP) in 1918, and finally in 1924, after numerous frustrations in his political career, gained election to the Reichstag as deputy for Württemberg. Apart from his work as parliamentarian (1924–8, 1930–2, 1932–3) in the Weimar republic, he was active as a lecturer and dean at the German Academy (*Hochschule*) for Politics (1920–33), as a municipal politician in Berlin (1920, 1929–30), as an administrator of several cultural organizations (Artisans' League), and as a journalist. He wrote the first full-length analysis of Hitler and National Socialism, *Hitlers Weg* (1932). He was forced out of political life and teaching within months, and worked again for *Die Hilfe*, contributed to the *Frankfurter Zeitung*, and wrote biographies of Naumann, Hans Poelzig, Anton Dohrn, Justus von Liebig, and Robert Bosch.

After the Second World War, having served as minister for cultural affairs in Baden-Württemberg (1945–6), as chairman of the Free Democratic Party (1946–9), as his party's representative on the parliamentary council which framed the constitution, and as professor of modern history at Stuttgart University, he was elected president of the Federal Republic in 1949 and re-elected, almost unanimously, in 1954. Considering that his functions were largely representational and non-political in the party sense, he brought style, dignity, and culture to the presidency and successfully stamped the office with a completely civilian character. The respect which he won at home and abroad contributed greatly to the moral recovery of West Germany after Hitler. He spoke repeatedly, for example, of the 'collective shame' rather than the 'collective guilt' of the Germans.
ME

HEWART, GORDON HEWART, 1st Viscount (1870–1943), British lawyer and politician, who started his career as a journalist, reporting parliamentary affairs for the *Manchester Guardian* and the *Morning Leader*. In 1913 he entered parliament as Liberal member for Leicester and three years later he was appointed solicitor-general. In 1918 he became a privy councillor, in 1919 attorney-general, and in 1922 lord chief justice. He was generally held to be a brilliant advocate and as a law officer of the Crown was most effective, his conduct of criminal proceedings being regarded as a model. In politics he looked askance at the growth of bureaucracy and delegated legislation. In 1929 his book, *The New Despotism*, offered a reappraisal of the fundamentals of the British constitution.

HEWITT, ABRAM STEVENS (1822–1903), US ironmaster, politician and philanthropist. He went into partnership with Edward Cooper (1824–1905) as an iron-founder and together they pioneered the production of wrought-iron building beams, supplied arms to the Union forces during the American Civil War, and experimented with new metallurgical processes and production techniques (1870). Hewitt was chairman of the Democratic National Committee (1876) and served in the US House of Representatives (1875–9, 1881–6). As mayor of New York city (1887–8), he pursued reform policies and sponsored numerous urban improvements.

HEYDRICH, REINHARD (1904–42), German chief of the Nazi security forces and deputy protector of Bohemia and Moravia (1941–2). Heydrich allegedly had Jewish antecedents, but compensated for this possibility with his ideally Aryan appearance and his fanatical anti-Semitism. He joined the SS in 1930 and began to create a security and intelligence department within it, and in 1933 became the head of the official SD (*Sicherheitsdienst* or security service). He worked closely with Himmler in centralizing police powers throughout Germany, and in April 1934 was made head of the Prussian secret police, the forerunner of the Gestapo. In 1936, when Himmler's takeover of police control was complete, Heydrich became leader of the criminal police, and by 1939 had integrated his various SS and civil agencies into a single security and intelligence organization, the *Reichssicherheitshauptamt* (RSHA). Although officially Himmler's subordinate, Heydrich began to build the RSHA into a semi-independent system. He took over the control of Czechoslovakia in 1941. In June 1942 he was murdered by Czech patriots, a deed for which the Germans exacted terrible retribution at Lidice.

HEYN, PIETER (d. 1629), Dutch admiral. In 1628 he captured two richly laden Spanish galleons and later that year, with a fleet of 31 ships, captured or destroyed the entire Spanish treasure fleet on the north coast of Cuba. This loss, estimated at over 4 million ducats, was the greatest ever suffered by the Spaniards in the West Indies. The Dutch followed this victory with raids on Spanish settlements and shipping, thereby greatly reducing Spain's prestige and establishing the Dutch as a major 17th-cent. power.

HIAWATHA, title of an hereditary chieftainship in the American Mohawk Indian tribe, second on the roll of federal chieftainships of the Iroquois federation. The first man to bear the title was a noted reformer, statesman, and legislator, one of the founders of the League of the Iroquois. He was probably at the height of his power *c.* 1570. Although presumed to be a Mohawk, he began his reform work among the Onondaga, who were unreceptive. The Oneida assented to the idea of a league, and the Mohawk, Cayuga, Seneca, and ultimately the Onondaga joined. Because he had won over the Onondaga chief, Hiawatha was presumed to have magical powers, and he became the centre of a cycle of legends. Henry Wadsworth Longfellow confused Hiawatha with a Chippewa Indian deity, and the poet's character bears no resemblance to Hiawatha the reformer.

HICKS PASHA (William Hicks) (1830–83), former British officer in the Indian army, who led an Egyptian force against Mahdist forces in Kordofan. Hicks's troops were annihilated at Shaykan, south of Al-Obaid, on 5 Nov. 1883. Egyptian control of the Sudan finished thereafter.

HICKY, JAMES AUGUSTUS, editor of the *Bengal Gazette*, the first newspaper in India. Little is known of his early life. He was imprisoned at Calcutta in 1776 for debt. His *Gazette* appeared in 1780 but was suppressed by Warren Hastings because of its scurrilous attacks on government officials.

HIDALGO Y COSTILLA, MIGUEL (1753–1811), Mexican priest and leader in the struggle for independence against Spain. On 16 Sept. 1810, in the village of Dolores, where he was priest, a plot by Hidalgo against the Spanish authorities culminated in the 'Grito de Dolores', or 'Cry of Dolores', the proclamation of his revolt against Spanish rule. A huge, undisciplined army, consisting mostly of Indians, rallied to his cause and advanced on Mexico City. Their attack on the capital failed, and the racial composition and radicalism of the army alarmed the Creole, or Mexican-born, Spanish class, though Hidalgo's army often appeared to be more radical than Hidalgo himself.

He was heavily defeated at Guadalajara (1811), and shortly afterwards was captured while fleeing north. After a trial in which he tried to explain his motives, he was unfrocked and shot. The anniversary of the 'Grito de Dolores' is now Mexico's national day of independence.

HIDALGOS, lesser nobility in Spain, a class which varied widely in wealth and ancestry, distinguished by the coveted prefix of *Don* and the possession of coats of arms. The *hidalgos* shared with the grandees many privileges, including exemption from payment of royal taxes. Many were involved in trade and royal administration, especially as *regidores* in municipal government. Others played a leading part in the conquest of South America and the West Indies, *eg*, Cortés. This numerous class did not constitute a closed caste, for from the end of the 15th cent. patents of nobility were bestowed on lawyers, soldiers, and clerics who had served the Crown well, and they thus entered the ranks of the *hidalgos*. Their numbers increased in the 16th cent. as the sale of office crept in from the 1520s to augment the funds of the hard-pressed Spanish treasury.

HIDE, regarded originally *ie*, the Middle Ages, as the amount of land needed to feed one family for a year. The hide seems to have been roughly equivalent to 120 acres (0·48 sq. km), but in the course of the Anglo-Saxon period it became much more a fiscal unit than a land measurement. Early lists of the

Anglo-Saxon tribes indicate their relative importance by the number of hides occupied by each.

HIDETADA

HIDETADA (1579–1632), second Tokugawa *shōgun* (*reg.* 1605–23). He actually controlled policy in Japan from 1616, when his father, Ieyasu, died, to 1633, having made his son, Iemitsu, *shōgun* nine years before his own death. He consolidated the Tokugawa system and intensified the persecution of Christianity.

HIDEYOSHI

HIDEYOSHI (1536–98), second of the great unifiers of Japan in the 16th cent, and considered by some to be the most outstanding individual in Japanese history. He was almost certainly Japan's greatest general. His origins are obscure. He was born in a village in Owari province, and took advantage of the prevalent turmoil to enter the service of Oda Nobunaga in the 1550s. His ability soon led to promotion and contributed greatly to Nobunaga's success. When the latter was murdered (1582), Hideyoshi was campaigning against Mōri, a powerful *daimyō* of south-west Japan, but within a month he had liquidated Nobunaga's murderer and he soon established himself as the latter's principal successor. The substantial share of Nobunaga's territory allotted to him by agreement was rapidly increased by military success against Hideyoshi's fellow generals, and he followed this by securing the co-operation of Tokugawa Ieyasu, Nobunaga's ally, after some indecisive fighting. By a series of brilliant campaigns he then brought the remaining two-thirds of Japan under his suzerainty. With his ambition apparently still unsatisfied, and with the additional aim of diverting the forces of the *daimyō*s, whose combined strength was much greater than his own, he launched an invasion of Korea (1590), but this insufficiently planned project ended in an agreed withdrawal after Hideyoshi's death (1598).

Hideyoshi's internal policy was marked by largely successful efforts to separate samurai from peasantry, to assess the real value of all cultivated land, and generally to re-establish order and stability. He himself built a great castle at Osaka and enjoyed unchallenged power, living in great pomp. Though he did not seek to become *shōgun*, he did secure high court rank, and was awarded by the emperor the surname of Toyotomi, having previously used such names as Kinoshita, Hashiba, Taira, and Fujiwara. He was not, however, able to establish an enduring system of government, and after his death his family suffered the same fate which he had meted out to Nobunaga's heirs.

G. B. Sansom, *A History of Japan, 1334–1615* (London, 1961)
RLS

HIERO I

HIERO I (*reg.* 478–467 BC), Tyrant of Syracuse, brother and successor of Gelon, whose alliance with Theron of Acragas he maintained. He extended Syracusan power in north-eastern Sicily, destroying Naxos and Catana and founding Aetna for his son Deinomenes to rule, and in Italy supported Cumae against the Etruscans, whom he defeated off Cumae in 474. He was a patron of the lyric poets, Pindar and Bacchylides, who both celebrated his victory in the chariot-race at Delphi (470), and his rule enhanced Syracuse's prestige and prosperity, but favoured the upper class. His brother and successor, Thrasybulus, was quickly deposed by popular revolution.

HIERO II

HIERO II (*reg.* 269–?216 BC), King of Syracuse, was elected king by popular acclaim after defeating the Mamertines, a band of Italian mercenaries who had fought for Syracuse against Carthage, but on discharge had treacherously seized Messana in 288. He organized the revenues of his kingdom on a new system (*lex Hieronica*), which was later adopted by the Romans. When Rome allied herself to the Mamertines of Messana (264), Hiero allied himself with Carthage, but made peace with Rome in 263 and remained a model ally for half a century. His ready assistance in the Sicilian operations of the First Punic War, rewarded by immunity from taxation,

was repeated in 218; but on his death the policy was reversed by his youthful successor Hieronymus.

HIEROGLYPHS

HIEROGLYPHS, ancient Egyptian system of writing, developed from simple ideograms into a script of 24 letters, using single-consonant word signs to represent a consonant sign, with ideograms, phonograms, and pictures added to clarify the meaning. An abbreviated script, hieratic, was developed for use on papyrus, wood, etc. as distinct from stone and later the demotic script was developed by further abbreviation and joining of letters. The ability to read hieroglyphs was lost by *c.* 500 and was not regained until the deciphering of the Rosetta Stone (1822).

HIGGINS, HENRY BOURNES

HIGGINS, HENRY BOURNES (1851–1929), Australian legalist, best known for his presidency of the Commonwealth Court of Conciliation and Arbitration (1906–22). He became leader of Victoria's Equity Bar, a Vic. MP (1894), and a member of the judiciary committee of the 1897–8 federal convention. Higgins was elected to the first Commonwealth parliament (1901) and in 1904 became attorney-general. After elevation to the high court bench and presidency of the arbitration court in 1906, he won recognition for his 'basic wage' definition in the Harvester case of 1907 and its subsequent application to other cases.

Higgins's contributions to high court judgments tended to reverse the earlier trend of that court's decisions and favoured increased Commonwealth powers.

HIGGINSON, FRANCIS

HIGGINSON, FRANCIS (1586–1630), American clergyman. He was ordained in the Church of England (1614), but became a nonconformist and settled at Salem in the Massachusetts Bay colony (1629). He wrote *New Englands Plantation, A Short and True Description of the Commodities and Discommodities of That Country* (1630) and drew up a confession of faith and covenant for the church in Massachusetts.

HIGGINSON, JOHN

HIGGINSON, JOHN (1839–1904), Anglo-Irishman brought up in Melbourne, who settled in Noumes, New Caledonia (1859), and, with Rothschild capital, founded the French nickel company (1876). Having become a naturalized Frenchman, he pursued a vigorous campaign of land acquisition and colonization in the New Hebrides, at the expense of British interests, as a basis for French annexation before the Anglo-French condominium (1907).

HIGH COMMISSION, COURT OF

HIGH COMMISSION, COURT OF, in England, instrument whereby the Crown exercised control and discipline over the Church of England. The Act of Supremacy (1534) made Henry VIII 'Supreme Head' of the Church of England, with all the necessary powers of ecclesiastical visitation. The first general commission was issued by Edward VI (1549). The Crown's ecclesiastical powers were confirmed by another Act of Supremacy (1559), which also authorized the Crown to nominate persons to act on its behalf in 'spiritual or ecclesiastical jurisdiction'. Until 1565, however, the authority of the commission was regarded as temporary, to enforce the laws of the Reformation settlement. The delegation of work from the privy council enabled the commission to develop the permanent form of a prerogative court. The term 'high commission' had appeared by 1570, and the title 'court' by about 1580. The institutionalization of the court enabled the Crown to face the growing opposition of Catholics and Puritans. In the 1570s local commissions were set up under the parent body in London. Membership of the court fluctuated between 24 (1549) and 108 (1633); the hard core consisted of a small group of canon lawyers, joined by bishops as occasion demanded.

In the 17th cent. opposition grew, mainly from Puritans who objected to the court's authority in religion, and from the common-law lawyers and judges who were jealous of its legal privileges and status. Under James I the common-law judges were encouraged by the support of the parliamentary opponents of the royal prerogative. Despite Cawdrey's case

(1591), which had accepted that the Crown's ecclesiastical jurisdiction rested on its own inherent rights, the judges began to insist that the commission's jurisdiction was based on statutory and not prerogative right. Abortive bills to abolish the court were brought into the parliaments of 1607 and 1609–10.

Since the legal opposition to the commission merged with the general political opposition to the Crown, the court did not survive the legislation of 1641. With other prerogative courts it was abolished, with the stipulation that no similar court should be revived. Unlike the other ecclesiastical courts, it was not restored at the Restoration. In 1686 James II did establish a similar court which did not survive the Revolution and which was condemned in the Bill of Rights (1689) as 'illegal and pernicious'.

R. G. Usher, *The Rise and Fall of the High Commission* (Oxford, 1913).   CJ

HIGH FURNACE. Until the late Middle Ages the processing of iron ore was carried out in low furnaces, fit for use only during a short time. It was impossible to achieve in them the high temperatures needed to melt the ore. By doubling or even trebling the size of the furnaces, constructing them more elaborately, and employing powerful water-driven bellows, some unknown German or Spanish inventors devised a more permanent type of high furnace in which the melting of the ore could take place. The molten iron thus produced could either be subjected to further refining in special forges or could be poured into moulds of desired shape to produce cast-iron objects. The earliest known cast-iron goods date from the second half of the 14th cent. The introduction of high furnaces considerably increased the total iron production in Europe, especially after *c.* 1450.

HIGINBOTHAM, GEORGE (1826–92), Australian judge, who studied law and practised journalism in London before migrating to Melbourne (1854), where he became editor of the *Argus* (1856–9), entered the Victorian Legislative Assembly as an independent liberal (1861), and was eventually appointed attorney-general (1863–8). In 1880 he was elevated to the Supreme Court bench and in 1886 became chief justice of Vic., and was responsible for the consolidation of the statute law of Vic. (1888–90).

In Sir Charles Dilke's view Higinbotham was 'the most considerable man in the colony'.

HIJAZ, AL-, region of western Arabia which was the birthplace of Islam. As the land where the Prophet Muhammad lived and where Allah is believed to have bestowed on him, at Mecca and Medina, a new religious message for mankind, the Hijaz is sacred to the Muslims. The name 'Al-Hijaz' means, perhaps, 'barrier', *ie*, the mountain ranges separating the lowlands of the Tihama along the coast of the Red Sea from the inland plateau of the Najd. During the years 1916–24 Al-Hijaz was the name given to the regime established in this area under Al-Husayn b. Ali. The Hijaz, after 1925, was a part of Saudi Arabia.

HIJAZ RAILWAY, light railway from Damascus to Medina, built (1900–8) to facilitate pilgrim traffic and Ottoman control of Arabia and to enhance the prestige of Abdülhamid II in the Muslim world, although its main effect was to develop the port of Haifa. It was heavily damaged during the Arab Revolt and was never repaired.

HIJRA (latinized as 'Hegira'), an expression denoting the going out of the Prophet Muhammad from Mecca to Medina in the year 622. Muhammad, finding the situation at Mecca increasingly difficult, had entered into negotiation with the Arabs at Medina, who sought an arbiter to end the discords prevalent in their town. Almost all the adherents of the Prophet now left Mecca in small groups. These Muslims were to become known as the Muhajirun (the emigrants).

Muhammad himself, with his cousin Ali and with Abu Bakr, was the last to set out for Medina. He is said to have reached Quba' in the oasis of Medina on 24 Sept. 622. Muslim dates are reckoned according to the era of the Hijra (*anno Hegirae*) an era which begins not at the moment when the Prophet reached Medina, but on the first day of the lunar year during which that event occurred, *ie* on 16 July 622.

HIJRAT MOVEMENT (1920), an emigration of Indian Muslims to Afghanistan against the terms of the peace treaty being imposed upon Turkey, which seemed to jeopardize the position of the Caliph of Islam. At its peak (Aug. 1920) the movement involved about 18,000 Muslims from Sind and the North-West Frontier Province, but it ended in disaster when the Afghan government turned the *muhajarin* ('pilgrims') away and they had to struggle back to their former homes. Many died on the way, and of those who got back many were destitute.

HILDEBERT OF LAVARDIN (or **LE MANS**) (1056–1133), Bp of Tours, who was recognized by his contemporaries as a master of classical Latin and one of the major medieval Latin poets.

HILFERDING, RUDOLF (1877–1941), German politician and doctor, who found his real vocation as a Marxist intellectual, living in Vienna and (after 1906) in Berlin. His two early major theoretical works were a defence of Marx's economic doctrine against the damaging criticism of Böhm-Bawerk (1902) and *Finance Capital* (1910), each of them among the most significant works of creative Marxist theory in that generation. In 1906 he entered the full-time service of the German Social Democratic Party, and from 1907 was foreign editor of the party's principal newspaper, *Vorwärts*. During the First World War he followed the party's left wing into a new party, the Independent Social Democratic Party, and served (1918–22) as editor-in-chief of that party's Berlin paper, *Freiheit*. In these years he came into his own as a politician, ending as a member of the party's central committee. He stood on the right wing of his party and readily found a home in the reunited Socialist Party after 1922. He served as finance minister in Stresemann's crisis government of 1923, and again in 1928–9 in Müller's government. He was a capable minister, but in each case his streak of socialist stubbornness resulted in a forced resignation in critical circumstances. In between times he was editor of the party's theoretical journal, with the task of trying to modernize Marxist theory to fit the case of a socialist party which was the main support of a bourgeois republic. After 1933 he continued to serve the party in exile in Czechoslovakia and France, until the Vichy government turned him over to the Germans in 1941. His death followed almost at once in the Gestapo prison in Paris.

HILL OF HAWKESTONE AND OF HARDWICKE, ROLAND HILL, 1st Viscount (1772–1842), British general who fought in the Peninsula and in south-western France (1808–14) and commanded one of the two corps into which the British army was divided at Waterloo.

HILL, AMBROSE POWELL (1825–65), Confederate general during the American Civil War, formerly a West Point graduate (1847) and a respected division and corps commander. He served with the Army of Northern Virginia, opened the battle of Gettysburg (1863), and was killed while defending Petersburg.

HILL, JAMES JEROME (1838–1916), US railroad builder, born in Ont. He established himself in St Paul, MN (1856), in the freight forwarding business and then in railroads. Having bought the bankrupt St Paul and Pacific Railroad (1878), he created from it the Great Northern Railroad through the American North-west, the only transcontinental railroad built without federal subsidy or land grant. It was of great importance in helping to open the North-west to settlement. Hill was successful in his struggle with Harriman for control of the Northern Pacific Railroad, but their joint holding company, the Northern Securities Co., was dissolved by the US Supreme Court (1904) because it violated the Sherman Act. As president of the Great Northern (1882–1907) and chairman (1907–12), Hill's reputation as an efficient and innovative railroad operator was unsurpassed.

HILL, OCTAVIA (1838–1912), British reformer of housing management. She held that it was possible to provide working-class housing of a reasonable standard which would give a 5 per cent return on capital outlay. She was also one of the three founders of the National Trust (1895).

HILL, ROWLAND (1795–1879), British postal reformer. Hill was highly inventive, being interested in rotary printing and steam propulsion, and ran an experimental school where the children participated in administration through committees. He became interested in postal reform c. 1826 and the introduction of the Penny Post (1839) may chiefly be attributed to his efforts. In the 1830s he was employed as secretary to the South Australian Colonizing Society, but on the publication of his pamphlet, 'Post Office Reform' (1837), he was appointed by the Whigs to supervise the introduction of the Penny Post at the treasury (1839). Peel did not renew his appointment (1842), but on the Whigs' return in 1846, he was made secretary to the post-master-general, a post which he retained till 1864.

HILLARY, SIR EDMUND PERCIVAL (1919–   ), NZ explorer, who gained extensive NZ and Himalayan experience before joining Hunt's Everest expedition (1953). With Sherpa Tensing, he made the first ascent to the summit, on 29 May. In 1956–8 he led the NZ Antarctic expedition, making the first motorized land journey to the South Pole.

HILLMAN, SIDNEY (1887–1946), US labour leader, born in Lithuania. Hillman emigrated to the US (1907), where he became engaged in union activity and negotiated an agreement with the firm of Hart, Schaffner and Marx (1910), which became the basis for an 'impartial chairman' plan soon adopted by other industries. He became the first president of the Amalgamated Clothing Workers of America (1914). He was a strong advocate of industrial unions, and left the American Federation of Labor (1935) to become a vice-president of the Congress of Industrial Organizations (1935–40). Hillman believed that organized labour should involve itself in politics and was a founder and the first chairman of the New York State American Labor Party (1936).

HILLYARD, NICHOLAS (1547–1619), English miniaturist, whose works combined the medieval skill of illumination with the new technique of portraiture and raised English painting in this field to the same level as that elsewhere in contemporary Europe.

HIMERA, ancient Greek colony in Sicily (c. 32 kms south-east of Palermo), founded from Zancle (Messana) c. 650 BC, probably to exploit trading opportunities further west. The importation of Spanish silver enabled it to become one of the earliest western colonies to coin. It was saved from a Carthaginian siege by Gelon's famous victory (480), and resisted an Athenian attack (415), but was destroyed in the second great Carthaginian invasion (408), and never rebuilt.

HIMILCO (fl. 5th cent. BC), Carthaginian merchant-explorer, contemporary, perhaps brother, of Hanno (1), the explorer of the West African coast. He led a naval expedition from Gades (Cadiz) up the Atlantic coast of Spain, Portugal, and France as far as Britanny (c. 450 BC), aiming to establish Carthaginian control of the trade in tin along the route which extended as far as Britain. No certain archaeological evidence of this Carthaginian activity has yet been identified.

HIMMLER, HEINRICH (1900–45), German politician and leader of the Nazi Schutzstaffel (SS) (1929–45), who joined the NSDAP in 1923. He became a deputy Gauleiter in Bavaria (1925) and rose rapidly in the party hierarchy to become deputy propaganda officer (1928) and leader of the 300-man strong SS (1929). By 1933 he had built the SS into a powerful organization numbering 50,000 men, and ensured himself a permanent place in the circle of Hitler's most intimate colleagues. Within three years of the Nazi takeover, he had officially secured the personal control of all Germany's police forces (1936). Under his leadership the civil police system was closely integrated with the SS, creating an unparalleled instrument of terror and political dominion. With his authority securely anchored in this immense and hydra-like system, Himmler was probably the most powerful man in the Nazi state. He collected a variety of other official posts, becoming interior minister in Aug. 1943, and holding a military command during the war.

The full extent of his power defies brief description. He was a fanatical anti-Semite and proponent of the most outrageous absurdities of the Nazi racial ethos; his inhumanly methodical mind organized the implementation of these theories down to the last horrific detail, and he was ultimately responsible for the worst barbarities of Nazism inside and outside Germany. Although one of Hitler's most adoring sycophants, his devotion wavered towards the end of the Second World War when, at Schellenberg's prompting, he planned a futile scheme to replace Hitler and conclude his own peace with the Allies. He committed suicide immediately after being arrested by the Allies in May 1945.

HINCKS, SIR FRANCIS (1807–85), Canadian statesman and prime minister of United Canada (1851–4), who was born in Ireland and emigrated to Toronto (1832), where he became a banker, journalist, and inspector-general of Canada (1842–1843, 1848–54). His government (Hincks–Morin coalition) promoted railway construction and negotiated a reciprocity treaty (1854) with the US. He resigned in 1854 and was appointed governor of Barbados and the Windward Islands (1855) and governor of British Guiana (1862). He served as Canadian finance minister (1869–73).

HINCMAR (c. 806–82), archbishop of Rheims and leading figure in the later stages of the Carolingian renaissance. His De Ordine Palatii is an idealized description of the royal court in the days of Charlemagne and his polemical writings against papal claims to supremacy over provincial churches were often quoted in subsequent ecclesiastical controversies. He appears to be the first writer to quote, though disparagingly, the False Decretals which became an important element in the later collections of texts on Canon Law.

HINDENBURG, PAUL VON (1847–1934), German general and president of Germany. In the First World War he commanded the German army in its victories at Tannenberg and the Masurian lakes, and took overall command in 1916. He recommended the abdication of Kaiser William II at the end of the war and retired after the signature of the treaty of Versailles. Von Tirpitz persuaded him to become the right-wing presidential candidate in 1925 after the death of Ebert and the indecisive first presidential vote. He was elected president and ruled constitutionally in support of Stresemann, losing thereby the support of the extreme right wing. After 1930, no party or politician could obtain a majority in the Reichstag, and Hindenburg was obliged to resort to government by decree in support of Brüning. Eventually he tried to rule though a non-party government under von Papen, who persuaded him in Jan. 1933 to appoint Hitler as chancellor of a right-wing coalition. On Hindenburg's death, Hitler combined the offices of president and chancellor and became dictator of Germany.

HINDENBURG LINE, Allies' name for the formidable defensive position called *Siegfried Stellung* by the Germans, who built it behind their front between Lens and Rheims in early 1917 in the First World War. Ludendorff's withdrawal to it in March dislocated the Allies' spring offensive and enabled the Germans to devote their main effort in 1917 to defeating Russia. In Ludendorff's last great offensive in spring 1918 the Germans advanced beyond the Hindenburg position, but Haig's counter-attack at Amiens drove them back to it in the summer. On 29 Sept. the British attacked the strongest part of the line, between St Quentin and Cambrai, and by 5 Oct. had broken through to open country. On 3 Oct., already shaken by the surrenders of Bulgaria and Turkey and Austria's impending collapse, Ludendorff advised his government to seek peace.

HINDI, group of dialects, ultimately derived from Sanskrit, which developed in northern India from *c.* AD 1000 on the analytic instead of the previous synthetic principle. They extended from the borders of Bihar to the Sutlej river, having an eastern and western division. Hindi is related to Bengali, Bihari, Rajasthani, and Marathi, etc. In time it took a literary form in religious poetry. Its greatest poet was Tulsi Das (1532–1624), whose version of the *Ramayana* became the virtual Bible of north Indian Hindus. Hindi prose began early in the 19th cent. with translations from Sanskrit. Its use by government for local purposes furthered this process, so that Hindi became both standardized and a flexible language capable of expressing abstract ideas. The Congress declared it the national language in 1922. It was declared the national language of India in 1965, after partnership with English from 1950, a decision that caused language riots in southern India.

HINDMARSH, SIR JOHN (1785–1869), British sailor and first governor of South Australia (1836–8). His autocratic manner made for difficulties and contributed to successful local pressure for his recall. Hindmarsh's subsequent career, as governor of Heligoland (1840–56), was equally undistinguished.

HINDU COLLEGE, also known as the Vidyalaya, was established at Calcutta in 1817. It was the first secular college devoted to English education and its origin was the work of private individuals, Indian and English, the most important of whom were David Hare, Raja Ram Mohan Roy, and Sir Hyde East, the chief justice of the Supreme Court. It was financed from voluntary subscriptions. Ram Mohan Roy was excluded from the committee because of the opposition of influential and orthodox Hindus. The students of the college came under the influence of the ultra-radical sceptic Derozio, who founded the Young Bengal movement. They revolted against the existing social and religious structure of Hinduism and their excesses so alarmed orthodox Hindus that Derozio was dismissed. After 1823 the college received government help and, in 1854, it was taken over by the government and became the Presidency College of Calcutta.

HINDU MAHASABHA, an Indian political and social organization concerned with advancing Hindu nationalism and Hindu communal interests. The initial moves came in the Punjab (1907–10) and there was intermittent activity in the following decade. Specifically, Hindu nationalists claimed that Congress, though a predominantly Hindu party, would endanger the Hindu community by its concern for Hindu–Muslim unity. Within the organization there was always a division of opinion between those who sought the maintenance of orthodoxy (*sanatanists*) and those who looked to social reforms (*sangathan*) as the means of achieving Hindu unity. The *sangathan* movement and campaigns for the reconversion of Hindus who had become Muslims (*shuddhi*) were the basis of the party's expansion (1925–7) under Madan Mohan Malaviya and Lala Lajpat Rai. They encouraged the formation of provincial sabhas, but kept the national body linked with Congress. Following them, leaders such as Dr B. S. Moonje and Bhai Parmanand drew away from Congress. The Mahasabha denounced the Communal Award (1932) because it was strongly committed to joint electorates, which it saw as the basis of Hindu majority rule. A complete break with Congress occurred when V. D. Savarkar became president (1937) and set the Mahasabha on a course of uncompromising hostility to both Congress and the Muslim League. From this time, also, connections with the *Rashtriya Swayamsevak Sangh* (RSS), the National Volunteer force designed to protect Hindus, were strengthened. The imprisonment of Congress leaders during the war and the league's campaign for partition gave the Mahasabha a chance to extend its influence but it did not capitalize on this, even when the able S. P. Mookerjee became working president (1943).

The assassination of Gandhi, in which the Mahasabha and RSS seemed to be implicated, forced the suspension of political activities (Feb.–Dec. 1948). The party was then weakened by the withdrawal of S. P. Mookerjee (1948) and the detention of leaders after the Bengal riots (1950). Mahasabha electoral support declined steadily from 1952 as the Jana Sangh increasingly pre-empted Hindu nationalist and anti-Pakistan themes.

HINDUISM, predominant religion of India from the first half of the 1st millennium BC, during which, by gradual evolution, it developed from Vedic religion. Hinduism is, however, a more comprehensive concept than religion in its usual meaning, as it includes basic principles of social order, cosmology, and law. In addition, it comprises a wide spectrum of religious attitudes from quasi-atheism to absolute devotion, or from almost pedantic ritualism to the pursuance of mystical experience.

In theory, all forms of Hinduism recognize the supreme authority of the Veda, but often allow great freedom in the selection and subsequent interpretation of particular texts in this vast body of sacred literature. In practice, however, some later texts, *eg*, the Epics, Puranas, and lawbooks, receive stronger emphasis.

The fundamental doctrine of Hinduism, lying at the basis of almost all ideas, beliefs, and practices, is the theory of *karma*, according to which the morally qualified deed constitutes an indelible force producing a well-defined effect, comparable to that of a force in physics. It works, however, with retardation and normally becomes effective after death, when the total of such deeds performed by an individual determines the shape and quality of his next life. Consequently, the different features of living beings and the different courses that their lives may take are explicable as consequences of different acts in former lives. Such a theory may provide a rational explanation and justification of apparent social inequities such as, in India, those based on caste. Although the belief in transmigration may well be older than the karma theory, the two are inextricably connected in classical Hinduism, in that karma provides the fuel that keeps the cycle of transmigration (*samsara*) moving.

Another basic feature of Hinduism is the antithesis of purity and pollution. Both concepts are relative and apply no less to that which is spiritual than to that which is physical. Certain ablutions, notably those with sacred water, such as that of the Ganges, have purifying qualities that may counteract the effects of karma. Many rituals aim at restoring purity after acts and contacts that may involve pollution. Sin, including sinful thoughts or desires, is often described in terms of pollution to be counteracted by pure acts and thoughts. The antithesis of purity and pollution also pervades the caste system, as the status of each individual caste with reference to another is partly determined by whether or not contact leads to any degree of pollution.

Other aspects of Hinduism are closely connected with these principal doctrines. Of these none is more important than the emphasis on non-violence (*ahimsa*). As transmigration implies the possibility of humans being reborn as animals it follows that, in principle, killing of animals is no less sinful than that of human beings. In practice, however, there are vast differences in the application of this principle, depending on the period, region, and social class, caste, or sect. The prohibition of the killing of animals applies more strictly to some animals than to others. It is particularly strict in the case of cows. In some of the most profound expressions of Hindu thought the cow symbolizes the forbearance from evil and the bestowal of boons without the expectation of any reward.

Hindu views of society emphasize the ultimate relationship between beings whose inequalities they try to explain. They thus aim at providing a rational analysis of society. Hindu society, in addition to recognizing the divisions common to most societies, is distinguished by its *varnashrama* system, by which people are classified by caste (*varna*) and stages of life (the four *ashrama*s: pupil, householder, forest-dweller, and mendicant-wanderer). In principle, every being occupies his correct place and functions in accordance with his inherited karma. Within these limitations he has a certain freedom to act in agreement or in conflict with the sacred law (*dharma*). While the members of the Brahman (priestly) class are particularly competent in setting out the details of dharma by interpreting the scriptures, it is the duty of the *kshatriyas* (members of the warrior class), in particular the king, to enforce the rules of dharma, and ensure the smooth functioning of society. The power of the king, however great it may have seemed, was therefore limited to the executive field, at least in theory. One of his particular duties was that of maintaining or, if necessary, restoring the caste system.

As karma is easily produced but difficult to destroy, it inevitably accumulates, with the result that society deteriorates as time goes by. The Hindu view of history is therefore that of a continuous degeneration of society till it completely disintegrates. After a cosmic period of chaos, a new world is created which is initially nearly perfect. Soon, however, karma will start to accumulate, slow decline sets in and the same sequence finally repeats itself. The implications of this theory are not only a tendency to glorify the remote past, but also a cyclic view of history.

An important aspect of Hinduism which, more than its theoretical foundations, gives Hinduism its distinctive character is the existence of numerous ceremonies, festivals, pilgrimages, cults, and religious orders. Some of the ceremonies are transition rites performed at such times as birth and name-giving of children, investment with the sacred cord (only for the 'twice-born' castes), marriage, and death. Others belong to certain times of the day, month, or year. A few are common to more or less all Hindus, but most are limited to certain castes, regions, or sects. One of the most striking features of Hinduism is that of each group having its own set of rules and values: a 'law of its own' (*svadharma*). Some the the best-known ceremonies are those associated with kingship, notably the royal coronation and the horse sacrifice. Some of them are elaborate and require the presence of numerous Brahmans; others, such as domestic rites, are very simple. There are also numerous Hindu festivals, most of which have, however, clear regional or sectarian features. Sectarian features are even more pronounced in pilgrimages drawing Hindus from many parts of India to a particular site. One of the best-known is the annual pilgrimage to Jagannath Puri in Orissa, where an image of Jagannath, a form of Vishnu, is carried in a chariot thronged by many hundreds of devotees. One of the most striking principles of Hinduism connected with *svadharma* is the freedom of the individual to choose his own 'road' (*marga*) towards final deliverance from suffering.

True Hinduism is limited to India or to large settlements of Indians outside India, such as in northern Ceylon. Certain aspects of Hinduism, however, were adopted by ruling circles in ancient South-East Asia, but were affected by strong local influences. This was noticeable in Shivaism in ancient Java and Cambodia, in Hindu ideals of state and kingship, and in Hindu art and architecture. From the 13th cent., however,

these influences were gradually superseded by those associated with Islam and Theravada Buddhism.

The quest for wisdom both by solitary meditation and, more frequently, by listening at the feet of a teacher is more pronounced in Hinduism than in most other religions. Ritual of widely different types has always played an important part. Perhaps most characteristic are typical forms of worship (*puja*) and devotion (*bhakti*), involving praying, chanting of hymns, burning of incense, and offerings—mainly of food, flowers, lamps, etc.

On these foundations great religious and philosophical movements developed. The doctrinal flexibility of Hinduism favoured the rise of very divergent systems, most of which could remain within the fold of Hinduism; only a few, such as materialism (Charvaka), and especially Buddhism, proved irreconcilable with the Hindu order of society, and all but disappeared from India. The Hindu sects are usually classified as belonging to either Vaishnavism (Vishnuism) or Shaivism (Shivaism), but some, such as Jainism, fall outside this division. Vaishnavism, centring around the worship of Vishnu and his different incarnations, such as Krishna, is prevalant in northern India, whereas Shaivism, involving the worship of Shiva and associated deities, predominates in the south.

A. L. Basham, *The Wonder That Was India* (London, 1954). R. C. Zachner, *Hinduism* (London, 1962).   JG de C

HINDUSTAN, Persian word meaning the country of the Hindus. It was generally applied to India north of the Vindhyas, in contradistinction to the Deccan and the extreme south. During the 18th cent. and later the term was loosely used to include the whole of India.

HINKLER, HERBERT JOHN LOUIS (1892–1933), Australian aviator. He was a member of the RFC in the First World War and became one of the group of Australians who competed with distinction in inter-war aviation races and competitions. He made a record-breaking solo flight from Britain to Australia (1928) and non-stop flights from New York to Jamaica and across the South Atlantic (1931).

HIPPARCHUS (*fl.* 6th cent. BC), son of Peisistratus and brother of the tyrant Hippias, whose murder (*c.* 514 BC) by Harmodius and Aristogeiton, though (according to Thucydides) sexually and not politically motivated, undermined Hippias' confidence and made him more oppressive.

HIPPARCHUS OF NICEA (*c.* 190–126 BC), Greek astronomer, the first known systematic user of trigonometry in astronomy. Though supporting a geocentric system, he improved instruments and catalogued more than 850 stars. He discovered the Precession of the Equinoxes.

HIPPEIS, ancient Greek 'horsemen', *ie*, members of the social class of the landed aristocracy, precisely defined at Athens by Solon (594 BC) in terms of annual income (over 300 measures)—to the political detriment of the previous aristocratic establishment.

HIPPIAS (*reg.* 527–510 BC), Tyrant of Athens, and son of Peisistratus. He probably first introduced the national Athenian coinage, showing Athena and her owl, and optimistically began a massive temple to Olympian Zeus. His initially conciliatory policy towards important noble families, especially the Alcmeonidae and the Philaidae, broke down after the murder of Hipparchus (514). After Alcmeonid attempts to remove him failed (513), he was finally expelled by Cleomenes I (510). He took refuge in Persia and, after Cleomenes' unsuccessful attempt to reinstate him *c.* 503, he guided the Persian fleet to Marathon (490). After the Athenian victory there nothing more is heard of him.

HIPPO (mod. Bône), Phoenician and Roman town on the Algerian coast. Hippo, a Phoenician foundation of unknown date, became a residence of Numidian kings after 201 BC and hence was known to the Romans as Hippo Regius. It was a Roman *municipium* under Augustus and subsequently a colony and an important outlet for agricultural products from the interior, but is chiefly famous as the see of St Augustine (AD 396–430). Substantial remains survive.

HIPPOCRATES (b. *c.* 460 BC), Greek physician from Cos, who founded a medical school where serious scientific observation and diagnosis prevailed in ethical conditions enshrined in the 'Hippocratic Oath'. He also studied ethnography and environment.

HIPPODAMUS OF MILETUS (*fl.* 5th cent. BC), Greek architect, chiefly connected with town-planning, eg, at Piraeus (replanned *c.* 445) and Thurii (founded 443), and especially with the 'grid' street-pattern, used by his predecessors in rebuilding Miletus after 479.

HIRA, AL-, capital of the Lakhmids, located to the southeast of the present Najaf in Iraq. This Arab state attained the summit of its splendour in the time of Mundhir III (*reg.* 505–54). It was for the Sassanids of Persia a fortress protecting Iraq against the Byzantines and against the nomads of the desert; also a caravan centre on the main route leading from Persia into Arabia. Al-Hira, after 602, was under direct Sassanid control. It surrendered to the Muslims in 633, had soon to yield in importance to the Muslim garrison town of Kufa, and at last dwindled into nothingness.

HIROHITO (1901–), Emperor of Japan (*reg.* 1926–). He acceded to the throne after five years as acting regent. During his reign Japan has experienced numerous changes, but his responsibility for them has been slight. Although until 1945 the emperor theoretically embodied sovereignty and was regarded with awe by most of the nation, as heir to a long tradition of maintaining political stability and unity by separating real power from the symbol of authority, he was brought up to rely entirely on his advisers. To assert a different view of his own would have been unthinkable, and, had it happened, would have endangered his position. Only in Aug. 1945, when the government was divided and the nation's fate depended on Hirohito throwing the prestige of the imperial institution on the side of peace, did he act independently. After the war the abolition of the throne was advocated by some Americans and Japanese, but eventually more conservative views prevailed, although the emperor's nominal powers were drastically reduced by the 1946 constitution. Since then Hirohito has devoted more of his time to studying marine biology. His conduct as emperor has helped to restore some of the institution's lost respect, though it no longer figures prominently in Japanese life.

HIROSHIMA, DESTRUCTION OF (6 Aug. 1945), the first wartime use of a nuclear weapon. Much of this large garrison town was annihilated, and the official estimate of 78,150 dead and 306,545 total casualties is generally considered much too low. The dropping of this atom bomb by a US air force plane followed the threat of 'prompt and utter destruction' in the Potsdam Declaration (26 July). Its political effectiveness remains a matter of dispute. The Japanese people who for nine months had experienced frequent incendiary bomb raids, some as destructive of life as at Hiroshima, were told only that a new bomb had been used, while their government, as the US government was aware, had already decided to seek peace, though not without conditions. Moreover, the declaration of war by Russia (8 Aug.), with its threat of communist control over part of Japan, appears to have been at least as important in the decision of Japan's leaders to accept unconditional surrender. On the other hand, the destruction of Hiroshima, and, three days later, Nagasaki, undoubtedly strengthened the emperor's determination to end the war.

HIROTA, KOKI (1878–1948), Japanese politician, foreign minister (1933–6), and prime minister (1936–7) who was condemned to death as a war criminal by the Tokyo tribunal.

HISHAM (691–743), son of Abd al-Malik, became, in 724, the 10th Caliph of the Umayyad line. His reign (724–43) saw, in 730–1, the repulse of the Khazars, who had thrust southward into Armenia and Azerbayjan. In 737, at Kharistan, west of Balkh, the Arabs drove back the Turkish tribes pressing forward from the adjacent steppe lands. The forces of Hisham also carried out numerous raids into Byzantine Asia Minor, but at last met with a severe reverse at the battle of Akroinon (740). In the Maghrib a great revolt of the Berber tribes broke out in 740–1. It was crushed at Al-Asnam, not far from Qairawan, in 742. Hisham, a pious Muslim, but tolerant towards the Christians, was a wise administrator, exercising a careful control over the finances of the Arab empire.

HISN AL-AKRAD (Fortress of the Kurds), Syrian castle, known in Europe as Crac des Chevaliers. It is situated on the southern edge of the Jabal Ansariyya, about 60 kms north-west of Hims, at a height of some 750 metres. Hisn al-Akrad commanded the route leading from the coastal plain of Tripoli to the plain of Hims. The site came into the hands of the Knights of St John in 1142. The great castle was at the height of its importance in the first decades after 1200. It fell at last to Baybars, the Mamluk Sultan of Egypt and Syria, in April 1271. Hisn al-Akrad is a magnificent example of a great crusading fortress.

HISPANIOLA, Caribbean island, originally peopled by the Arawaks and settled by the Spaniards early in the 16th cent. and later the seat of the republics of Haiti and Santo Domingo. It became a centre for sugar production, for which African slaves were imported by Portuguese traders. By the treaty of Ryswick (1697) France acquired half of Hispaniola from Spain. The eastern half, known as Santo Domingo, and secured by the French in 1795, was the scene of Toussaint l'Ouverture's revolt and became an independent republic in 1801. Though restored to Spain in 1815, it broke away in 1865.

HISS, ALGER (1904–), former US State Department official, and central figure in controversial political trial in the 1940s. Hiss first entered government service in 1933, joined the State Department (1936), and later participated in the wartime conferences at Dumbarton Oaks, Yalta, and San Francisco. On leaving the State Department in 1946 he became president of the Carnegie Endowment for International Peace (1947). In 1948, Whittaker Chambers, a witness before a session of the US House of Representatives Committee on Un-American Activities, accused Hiss of having been a member of an underground communist organization in Washington. Hiss maintained his innocence and sued Chambers for libel, but was indicted for perjury by a New York grand jury. Though the jury failed to agree (July 1949) Hiss was found guilty by a second jury and sentenced to five years' imprisonment (1950). The case revealed a widespread and emotional fear of communism and gave prominence to Richard Nixon, then a junior member of the Un-American Activities Committee.

HISTIAEUS (d. 493 BC), Tyrant of Miletus (*reg. c.* 520–*c.* 515), important but enigmatic figure in Persian relations with the Greeks, especially in the Ionian Revolt (499–494). As a vassal of Darius I, he supported him on his Scythian expedition (516), but, his loyalty becoming suspect, was subsequently removed from Miletus to Darius' court. He is said to have encouraged the Ionian Revolt and was sent by Darius to mediate, but was frustrated by the satrap Artaphrenes, who favoured repression. Being rejected by the Greeks, Histiaeus took to piracy at Byzantium, but was eventually captured in the Aegean and killed by Artaphrenes.

HISTORIA AUGUSTA, collection of biographies of Roman emperors from Hadrian (117–38) to Carus and Carinus (282–4). Though purporting to have been written by six authors in the time of Diocletian and Constantine (284–337), the work is now generally believed to be by a single author writing at the end of the 4th cent.; the reasons for his deception are unknown. The work is of considerable value for the light it sheds on the 2nd and early 3rd cents, but after dealing with the reign of Caracalla (212–17) it degenerates to romance and fiction.

HISTORICAL SCHOOL OF ECONOMICS, group of European thinkers who, in the second half of the 19th cent., criticized the methods of the classical school, and wished to substitute for their abstract and deductive reasoning an approach based on historical investigation, inductive reasoning, and observation of facts. One result of their criticism, both in Germany and in England, was to awaken interest in the study of economic history.

HITLER, ADOLF (1889–1945), German chancellor and leader of the Nationalsozialistische Deutsche Arbeiter Partei (NSDAP), who was born in Braunau as an Austrian citizen and retained this nationality until 1932. He left school at the age of 16, with a poor academic record, and went to Vienna. There he made several unsuccessful attempts to become an art student (1907–8), after which he remained in the city scraping a living from casual employment, and living in doss-houses. On his own admission, these barren and hopeless years were the formative period for him, when his patterns of thought, his passions and hatreds were determined for life. On the outbreak of the First World War in 1914, he volunteered for the Bavarian army, though he had evaded Austrian military service since 1910. He served on the Western Front and won the Iron Cross, but remained a corporal.

Germany's defeat in 1918, the abortive revolution of 1918–1919, and the establishment of the republic were desperate shocks for Hitler, whose significance he spent his life trying to repudiate. The 'stab-in-the-back' myth became one of the most potent weapons in his political armoury, offering as it did a convenient rationalization of Germany's otherwise apparently inexplicable defeat. It absolved all but a clique of allegedly left-wing politicians, bourgeois, or Jewish—the so-called 'November criminals'—from any responsibility for the evils that ensued. Indeed, this thread of complaint against injured innocence and unpunished wrong-doers was characteristic of Hitler's style both as a person and as a politician.

Hitler worked for the army's political department in Munich after the war, organizing counter-revolutionary propaganda during 1919 and establishing a liaison with potentially useful right-wing groups. It was in this way that he came into contact with Drexler's German Workers' Party in Sept. 1919, a tiny nationalist and anti-Semitic group which was to form the nucleus of his own NSDAP. By 1921 Hitler had won control of the party, and given it a new name, a programme, a leadership, and a propaganda machine. He worked tirelessly to promote the party among the welter of similar political splinter-groups, until in Nov. 1923 the disastrous fiasco of the Munich putsch put a temporary stop to his activities. He spent just over a year in prison, where he wrote the first part of his autobiography and political testament, *Mein Kampf*.

After his release in Dec. 1924 Hitler was faced with the problem of recovering control over the remnants of the dispersed NSDAP, a process that lasted until about 1928, when he managed to impose his authority over opposition elements within the party. Until the Depression and the elections of 1930, the NSDAP's prospects were gloomy, but the economic crisis and the immense social disruption it caused gave Hitler a platform and an audience. He offered Germany an apparently viable alternative to the increasingly intractable Weimar 'system'; in the sense that the NSDAP

proposed to effect radical changes in the constitution, and used highly unconventional political weapons, Hitler's programme could be called revolutionary, though both the theory and the practice of the promised revolution remained extremely casual. In 1930, under his skilful leadership, the NSDAP became the second largest party in the Reichstag and the most powerful forum for right-wing extremism; its strong electoral position was strengthened less publicly by a network of arrangements with industrialists and conservatives which Hitler devised. With his sights firmly set on political power, he resisted all temptations to join a coalition government, but waited until Jan. 1933, when he was able to take control of Germany on his own terms.

His first years in office were devoted to securing the power base of the regime within Germany, and it was not until 1936 that he began to claim an equal freedom of action abroad. This year was marked by the remilitarization of the Rhineland and the inception of the four-year rearmament plan. Although it is true that Hitler played his foreign policy by ear and was never averse to repudiating his own programme in the interests of expediency, it is nevertheless quite clear that he was determined to achieve a fundamental revision of the Versailles treaty; this was not acceptable to the rest of Europe and was therefore bound to result sooner or later in a war for which Germany would bear the responsibility. When the Second World War did break out in Sept. 1939, Hitler had prepared Germany both diplomatically, by virtue of the Italian and Soviet pacts, and militarily, with the result that at first the German armies achieved astounding successes with Hitler's chosen tactic of the *blitzkrieg*. However, it was his own error of judgement which lost him the chance of destroying the Allied troops at Dunkirk in June 1940, and this blind confidence in his own strategic and tactical abilities led to the grosser errors which threw Germany into war with Russia and then thwarted all hopes of redeeming the situation. In the last catastrophic phase of the war the pathological traits in Hitler's character apparently came into their own. By the end his phenomenal capacity for self-delusion had isolated him totally from the realities of Germany's position and his own calamitous contributions to her downfall. In an appropriately melodramatic apotheosis of his own life and that of his monstrous creation, Hitler killed himself on the eve of Germany's defeat (30 April 1945), calling at the same time for the annihilation of the country which, he claimed, had failed him by its own weakness—a judgement in which he was alone.

A. Bullock, *Hitler: a study in tyranny* (London, 1962).
H. R. Trevor-Roper (ed.), *Hitler's Table Talk* (London, 1953).   AJC

HITLER YOUTH (*Hitlerjugend*) in Germany, Nazi organization for boys aged 14 to 21. The forerunner of the Hitler Youth, the National Socialist Youth League, was founded in 1922, but disappeared when the NSDAP was dissolved a year later. After the refounding of the party (1925) two organizations took the league's place, and the name Hitler Youth was first applied to one of these by Julius Streicher in 1926. In 1929 the youth arm of the party was reorganized and formally given this name. Separate organizations were founded to cover young people in universities and factories, but after 1931, when Baldur von Schirach was appointed leader of the Hitler Youth, a certain amount of consolidation and centralization took place.

In June 1933 Schirach was given the title of national youth leader, and in 1936 membership of the Hitler Youth was made compulsory for all those eligible. The main purposes of the organization were to assimilate young people into the Nazi state, to provide paramilitary training and ideological indoctrination, and to act as a school for future Nazi leaders. In 1939 its members were all automatically conscripted into the armed forces, where they provided ancillary services such as fire-watching, and towards the end of the Second World War fighting units were raised among them. A parallel organization existed for girls, the *Bund Deutscher Mädel* (League of German Maidens), and one called the *Jungvolk* for children aged 8 to 14.

HITTIN (HATTIN), village to the west of Tiberias in Galilee. Here, in 1187, was fought the famous battle between the Muslims under Salah al-Din, *ie*, Saladin, and the Latins under Guy de Lusignan, which led to the ruin of the kingdom of Jerusalem.

HITTITES, people who moved into Asia Minor (*c.* 2000 BC) and were named after the land of Hatti (Anatolia), in which they settled. They spoke an Indo-European language and appear at first to have formed a ruling class over the indigenous population. Originally they seem to have been organized in about ten principalities, which were later united under Labarnas (*reg.* 1680–1650) and Hattusilis I (*reg. c.* 1650–1620), the latter making Hattusas (mod. Boghazkoy) the capital of the kingdom. A period of expansion in Syria and Mesopotamia followed, but the Hittites' gains were soon lost amid domestic anarchy. In *c.* 1380 a new king, Suppiluliumas, ended the power of the great enemy, Mitanni, and conquered Syria and Arzawa in western Asia Minor, thus founding what is usually called the Hittite empire to distinguish it from the preceding Hittite old kingdom. From then until *c.* 1240 the Hittites were a major power in the eastern Mediterranean, largely because of their military skill, especially their development of the light, horse-drawn chariot. Under Arnuwandas III (*reg. c.* 1235–1215) the empire began to break up. It was attacked by Assyria and in *c.* 1200 new invaders moved into the area and the Mushki replaced the Hittites as the dominant people in Asia Minor. Some of the Hittites probably moved at this time, or perhaps earlier, into Syria and their culture survived there in what are called the Neo-Hittite kingdoms. The early Hittite kings were in direct control of their territories, being supreme commanders of the army, high priests, chief judicial and diplomatic authorities, and delegating authority in the provinces only to members of the royal family. It seems likely that as the empire grew more independent governors were appointed to the provinces, though important centres like Carchemish were still reserved for royal princes. On the periphery of the empire were a number of kingdoms which were drawn into the Hittite sphere as protectorates ruled by native, vassal kings. Within Anatolia itself the isolated communities retained many local rights and were ruled by local councils. The people were mainly employed in agriculture, growing vines, olives, barley, and emmer-wheat, and keeping cattle and goats. Copper and silver were mined and there was considerable iron-smelting and some iron-working. Most of the separate communities of Hatti retained their old local religions, but a state religion, based on Hattian and Hurrian ideas, was developed. It was centred at Arinna, near Hattusas, with the Sun-goddess and her husband, the Weather-god, as the principal deities. There was a large number of festivals, at many of which the king, as high priest, was expected to preside. The text of a legal code found at Boghazkoy shows Hittite law to have been comparatively advanced, especially in its treatment of offenders. Only a few crimes were capital offences and the emphasis in punishment was on reparation rather than on retribution. The study of the Hittites has gradually moved from the area of Palestine and Syria, which was originally believed to be their centre, northwards to Anatolia, where Hugo Winckler started excavations at Boghazkoy (1906) and found it to be the Hittite capital, Hattusas. Since then there has been more intense excavation and study of texts, particularly by American and German scholars.

O. R. Gurney, *The Hittites* (London, 1966).   JKG

HITTITE–EGYPTIAN TREATY (*c.* 1284 BC), famous offensive-defensive alliance between the Hittite King Hattusilis III and Rameses II of Egypt, by which each ruler undertook to ensure the legitimate succession on the death of the other.

HLINKA, ANDREJ (1868–1938), Slovak priest and leader of Slovak autonomist groups in Czechoslovakia, whose career of dissent began under the Austro-Hungarian empire and culminated in imprisonment (1906) for inciting Slovaks against the Hungarian authorities. He later believed his aims could be achieved by partnership with the Czechs, but the anti-Semitic, anti-democratic, and clericalist character of his followers was too extreme for the uneasy entente to survive. Throughout the 1930s he represented a disruptive element that could be played upon by outside powers, principally Germany. He died a few weeks before the disintegration which he had encouraged began at Munich (1938).

HLUTDAW, Executive Council of the King of Burma, consisting of four or five ministers holding office at his pleasure.

HO CHI MINH (1890–1969), founder and first president of the Democratic Republic of Viet-nam. Originally called Nguyen Tat Thanh, he subsequently took numerous pseudonyms, notably that of Nguyen Ai Quoc ('Nguyen the Patriot'), by which he was known between 1919 and *c.* 1932; he took the name of Ho Chi Minh in 1942. He was the son of a minor scholar-official, born in Nghe-An province (Central Viet-nam), and was educated both in Chinese and French, but did not take up an official career himself. About 1911 he left home and remained in exile until 1941. After a period of wandering, he settled in Paris about 1916, where he met Phan Chau Trinh and other nationalists, and wrote articles for an anti-colonialist newspaper, *Le Paria*. In 1919 he tried unsuccessfully to submit a demand for Viet-namese civil rights to the Versailles Peace Conference. The next year he was among the founding members of the French Communist Party, and in 1923 went to Moscow as a delegate to the *Krestintern* (Peasant International) Conference. After studying in Moscow he was appointed to the Comintern mission of Mickhail Borodin at Canton, where he arrived in 1925. He soon formed a 'Viet-namese Revolutionary Youth Association' and recruited followers inside Viet-nam. In 1927 he had to flee Canton owing to Chiang Kai-shek's anti-communist policies, and for the next few years his whereabouts are uncertain. In 1930–1 he was in Hong Kong, where he founded the Indochinese Communist Party and organized the Nghe-An revolt. In 1931, he was arrested by the British and imprisoned. On his release he once again disappeared, but by 1938 he was once again in south China, renewing contact with communist leaders in Viet-nam. In 1941 some of the latter, notably Vo Nguyen Giap and Phan Van Dong, joined with him in forming the Viet-minh and creating a base area in northern Tongking. But on returning to China in 1942 he was imprisoned for a time, and did not reappear in Tongking till 1943, having in the meantime adopted the name Ho Chi Minh. In Aug. 1945, following the Japanese surrender, he and his followers seized control of Hanoi and set up a provisional government, and on 2 Sept. Ho read the Declaration of Independence from which the Democratic Republic of Viet-nam dates its foundation. He was its leading spirit, and in due course its president, from then until his death. In 1946 he took part in abortive negotiations at Fontainebleau between the Viet-minh and the French, and after the latter forced the provisional government to withdraw from Hanoi in Dec. 1946 he led it throughout its years in the jungle. In 1954, after the battle of Dien-Bien-Phu and the Geneva Agreement, Ho established his government once more in Hanoi, and remained at its head for the rest of his life. His prominence was due in large part to his great political skill, but also in part to the fact that he was 15 years older than the next in age among the Viet-minh leaders, Pham Van Dong.

Jean Lacouture, *Ho Chi Minh* (London, 1968).   RBS

HO LUNG (1896–), Chinese communist marshal, who started his career as a bandit, and eventually joined the Kuomintang army. His unit played a major role in the Nanch'ang Uprising (1927). He joined the Communist Party soon afterwards, and held many key military posts. He was disgraced during the Cultural Revolution.

HO QUY LY (d. 1407), founder of the short-lived Ho dynasty in Viet-nam (1400–7). A native of Thanh-Hoa, then a frontier region of Dai-Viet, he rose to prominence as a general during the 1370s, when the country was involved in a major war with Champa. The Chams sacked the Viet-namese capital on three occasions, but in the 1380s Dai-Viet recovered its strength under the leadership of Ho Quy Ly. By 1400 he was strong enough to overthrow the Tran dynasty and place his own son on the throne. However, a Tran prince appealed to China, and in 1407 the Ho dynasty was overthrown by an invading Chinese army. For the next 20 years Dai-Viet was under Ming rule, until the Chinese were driven out by Le Loi.

HO YING-CH'IN (1890–), Chinese general and close associate of Chiang Kai-shek. Ho, a mediocre commander, made his career through devoted service to Chiang. His name is associated with appeasement of Japan, through the Ho–Umetsu Agreement (1935), which gave Japan vast concessions in north China.

HOA HOA SECT, political-religious group in South Viet-nam, founded in 1939. Its beliefs have some features in common with those of the Taiping rebels in China in the mid-19th cent., though their puritanism is Buddhist, not Christian. The founder of the sect, Huynh Phu So, was a native of Chau-Doc province, who spent part of his youth in a remote temple and then returned home to preach a new doctrine. During the years 1941–5 the Hoa-Hoa adepts were pro-Japanese. After the Japanese defeat in 1945, they co-operated with the Viet-minh, but the alliance between them broke down when Huynh Phu So was murdered by communists in 1947. From then until 1954, the Hoa-Hoa sect collaborated with the French and, like the Caodaists, was allowed its own private army. In 1955 the sect was driven from the political scene by Ngo Dinh Diem; but it had (1970) half a million adherents in the western provinces of South Viet-nam.

HOADLEY, BENJAMIN (1676–1761), English bishop, who by 1709 had entered the political arena as leader of the Low Church divines and came into conflict with Atterbury and other High Churchmen. The Tory ascendency (1710) prevented him from receiving preferment. With the Hanoverian accession, however, Hoadley became Bp of Bangor (1715). Attempting to justify the king's favour, he produced a treatise and a sermon regarding the divine authority of king and Church. High Churchmen retaliated against this attack on Church authority and the *Bangorian Controversy* was only halted by royal prorogation of convocation (1717). Hoadley was transferred from Bangor in 1721 and became successively Bp of Hereford (1721), of Salisbury (1723), and of Winchester (1734).

HOAR, GEORGE FRISBIE (1826–1904), US lawyer and politician. In 1852 he was elected to the state House of Representatives and served a term in the state Senate (1857). As a Republican congressman from MA (1869–77) and US senator (1877–1904), Hoar advocated civil service reform, helped to formulate policy on Civil War claims, was a member of the congressional electoral commission which resolved the disputed presidential election of 1876, and helped to draft the Sherman Anti-trust Act (1890). He opposed President McKinley's expansionist foreign policy and the virulent nativism of the American Protective Association.

HOARE–LAVAL PLAN (Dec. 1935), for ending Italo-Abyssinian hostilities through substantial concessions to Italy. Informal Anglo-French discussions on possible frontier adjustments and territorial exchanges in Abyssinia had preceded the outbreak of the war in Oct. 1935. The League of Nations, while condemning Mussolini's aggression, and

decreeing economic sanctions, still hoped for a compromise settlement and approved the resumption of these discussions in Paris at the end of Oct.

An impasse was reached by Dec., with Britain unwilling to make the concessions to Italy proposed by Laval, the French prime minister. Laval, undoubtedly in close touch with Mussolini, was determined not to alienate him now that Hitler's repudiation of existing treaties threatened France's security. He would not support any measure likely to provoke war with Mussolini, and refused French naval co-operation with Britain in Mediterranean defence.

Meanwhile, pro-league opinion called for a stand against the aggressor. An oil embargo, which Laval strongly opposed, seemed imminent. The British foreign minister, Hoare, visited Paris en route for Switzerland, and with his permanent under-secretary, Lord Vansittart, attended discussions with Laval on 7–8 Dec. 1935.

The agreement reached between Hoare and Laval was approved in London on 9 Dec. Italy received a zone of exclusive economic interest, and territory including most of the recently conquered Tigre province. Abyssinia received a sea outlet. The remnants of Abyssinian sovereignty would be assured by the league, which would also supervise Italy's economic activities. The plan was leaked prematurely in the French opposition press. English public opinion was outraged by this appeasement of aggression. By 18 Dec. the British government had rejected the plan. Hoare resigned and was replaced by Eden. The plan was less severe on Abyssinia than Italy's subsequent victory; it is doubtful, however, whether Mussolini would have found it acceptable.   ASJ

HOBBEMA, MEINDERT (1638–1709), Dutch 'natural painter', who specialized in landscapes, was inspired by Rubens, and was a pupil and friend of Jacob van Ruisdael. His masterpiece, *The Avenue*, has had a profound effect on British landscape painting, *eg*, that of the Norwich school.

HOBBES, THOMAS (1588–1679), English political philosopher. He was educated at Oxford, and became tutor to William Cavendish, later 2nd Earl of Devonshire, with whose family he spent most of his life. In the 1620s he was an intimate friend of Francis Bacon, some of whose essays he translated into Latin, and of Ben Jonson. He travelled on the continent and met Galileo, Gassendi, Descartes, and Mersenne, the French mathematician. In 1640 he wrote *The Elements of Law, Nature and Politics*, which embodied his basic doctrine that social peace required the existence of absolute and undivided sovereignty. By this he antagonized both sides in the English constitutional struggle between Crown and parliament and went to live in Paris (1640–51), where he was tutor in mathematics to the future Charles II (1646). His masterpiece, *Leviathan, or the Matter, Form, and Power of a Commonwealth, Ecclesiastical and Civil* (1651), brought Hobbes great disfavour on political and religious grounds, particularly among the royalists, who wrongly regarded it as designed to induce Cromwell to take the Crown. Consequently Hobbes returned to England (1652) and submitted to the council of state. In the 1650s he was involved with John Bramhall, Bp of Londonderry, in a heated controversy over free will, and in the 1660s with Seth Ward and John Wallis over mathematics and physical enquiry. He was given a pension by Charles II (1660), but was attacked by the Church party at court for his supposed atheism, and as a consequence was refused permission to publish his later political works, *eg*, *Behemoth, the History of the Causes of the Civil Wars of England* (written *c.* 1668; unauthorized publication, 1679). In his later years he wrote extensively on history, geometry, politics, and philosophy.
                                                                                                                CJ

HOBEREAUX, rural gentry in pre-revolutionary France, who enjoyed aristocratic exemption from the *taille*, the *corvée*, and other financial and judicial privileges, but in wealth were often indistinguishable from the *roturier* class or tenant farmers.

HOBSON, WILLIAM (1793–1842), British sailor and first resident governor of NZ. After visiting NZ in HMS *Rattle-snake* (1837), Hobson presented a report, recommending that Britain should set up trading 'factories' in the islands. On returning to NZ in 1840, Hobson negotiated the treaty of Waitangi (6 Feb.) as the first step to Britain acquiring sovereignty. Fears of French action led him to conclude negotiations by proclaiming British sovereignty over the whole of NZ (21 May). In May 1841 he became governor of NZ, following its administrative separation from NSW.

HOCHSCHILD, MAURICIO (1886–), with Patiño and Aramayo formed the triumvirate, known in Bolivia as *la rosca*, or 'the screw', which controlled Bolivian tin mining. The three companies which they formed were nationalized by the Bolivian revolutionary government in 1952.

HÖCHST, BATTLE OF (1622), technical victory of the imperialist army under Tilly and the Spaniards under Cordoba at the bridgehead of Höchst on the Main in the Thirty Years War. Christian of Anhalt's Protestant forces lost 2000 men and most of their baggage in crossing the river, but his prime objectives of saving his booty and joining up with Mansfeldt and Frederick, Elector Palatine, were achieved.

HOCHSTÄDEN, CONRAD VON, archbishop of Cologne (1238–61), organizer and leader of the papal party in Germany during the reign of Frederick II. In 1248 he crowned William of Holland as German king, but later successively gave his support instead to Ottokar of Bohemia and Richard of Cornwall. He symbolized the great power of the ecclesiastical electors after the death of Frederick II.

HOCHSTADT, FIRST BATTLE OF (25 Sept. 1703), victory of the French under Marshal Villars over Styrum and the imperial army at Hochstadt in Bavaria, in the War of the Spanish Succession, in which 4000 Austrians were killed and the same number taken prisoner.

HOCHSTETTER FAMILY, German house of merchants and financiers who handled the distribution throughout Europe of the Portuguese monopoly in pepper and spices from the East Indies in the early 16th cent. Before this, in 1486, they opened a branch of their company in Antwerp, but later the flow of American silver challenged their control of the German silver and Tyrolean copper markets.

HODGSON, BRIAN HOUGHTON (1800–94), English colonial servant in the political service of the East India Co. He was assistant commissioner in Kumaon (1818–20) and spent over 20 years at Katmandu in Nepal (1820–44), first as assistant resident and then as resident. He kept Nepal quiet during the First Afghan War (1838–42), but was removed from Nepal by Ellenborough because they differed over the policy to be adopted. Sir Henry Lawrence was appointed in his place and Hodgson was offered a subordinate post as sub-assistant commissioner at Simla. Hodgson resigned, and for 13 years he lived the life of a scholar and recluse in Darjeeling. He made extensive researches into the philology, ethnology, and zoology of Nepal, which earned for him an international reputation. He persuaded the government of Nepal to allow Gurkhas to be recruited for the Indian army.

HOE, RICHARD MARCH (1812–86), US inventor of the rotary printing press (1846) which substantially increased the speed of printing. Later improvements by William Bullock (1813–67) and by Hoe further enhanced the speed by printing on a continuous roll of paper instead of on single sheets.

HOESCH, LEOPOLD VON (1881–1936), German diplomat. When, during the Ruhr invasion of 1923, the German ambassador to France was recalled, Hoesch, as *chargé-d'affaires* in the embassy in Paris, impressed Poincaré so much that the latter requested his appointment as ambassador. In this position (1924–32) he proved a zealous supporter of Stresemann and Briand's policy of Franco-German rapprochement. He was ambassador in London (1932–6) and did not follow the appeal of the German ambassador in Washington, Von Prittwitz, to resign when Hitler came into office in 1933. He is considered by many to have been the most talented of the German professional diplomats of the inter-war period.

HOETZSCH, OTTO (1876–1946), German historian and politician who was professor of East European history in Berlin and Reichstag deputy and foreign policy expert of the German National People's Party. Belonging to the moderate wing of this party, his political ideal was, in his own words, the 'Tory democracy of Disraeli'. He resigned from the party in 1929 because of its swing towards extremism under the leadership of Hugenberg, and was a co-founder in July 1930 of the politically inconsequential Conservative People's Party.

HOFFA, JAMES RIDDLE (1913–), US labour leader, and president (1957) of the International Brotherhood of Teamsters. When the AFL–CIO expelled the Teamsters (1957), Hoffa welcomed the break, believing that his union had the power to break the AFL–CIO and replace it as the dominant force in American labour. Although imprisoned (1964) for attempting to suborn a jury, he remained (1970) a powerful force in the Teamsters Union.

HOFMAN, MELCHIOR (d. 1543), Swiss Anabaptist leader. After his conversion to Protestantism and his conflict with Zwingli (1523) he travelled to Wittenberg, the Baltic, northern Germany, and the Low Countries, hounded from city to city because of his fanatical missionary activities. In 1533 he returned to Strasbourg, to be immediately imprisoned by the authorities for heresy, and died there ten years later. His place as leader of the Netherlands Anabaptists was taken by Jan Matthys.

HOFMEYR, JAN HENDRIK (1845–1909), Cape journalist, closely connected from 1884 with the Afrikaner Bond party. He exercised a moderating influence upon the racism of many of his supporters.

HOFMEYER, JAN HENDRIK (1894–1948), South African politician. After an academic career he entered politics in 1924, becoming a minister in the Hertzog–Smuts coalition of 1933. He remained in the government despite his protesting publicly against the Natives Representation Act (1936), which deprived the Cape Africans of their franchise. In an increasingly racist situation he strove to retain some measure of liberalism. During the Second World War and until the defeat of the United Party in 1948, he was Smuts's deputy as prime minister.

HOGARTH, WILLIAM (1697–1754), English painter and engraver, best known for his satirical works and his depiction of popular life. Hogarth began his career by engraving arms and shop bills and then designing plates for booksellers. In 1729 he began a series of paintings which brought his work to the public's attention. *A Harlot's Progress*, a series of related pictures, emphasized his satirical talents and the engraved versions (1734), were extremely popular. Two more successes in a similar vein followed, *A Rake's Progress* (1733) and *Marriage-à-la-Mode* (1745).

Hogarth painted a number of excellent portraits, including those of Lovat, Hoadley, Wilkes, and himself. He also tried his hand at historical painting, but in this field was less successful. Nor did he succeed in the world of literature, his

Analysis of Beauty (1753) showing him to have little flair as a critic.

His contemporaries rated him highly as an engraver, but today his paintings are considered his finest achievement.

HOGG, QUINTIN (1845–1903), British philanthropist and educationalist, who founded the Regent Street Polytechnic, London (1882). Hogg, a prosperous sugar merchant, showed a life-long interest in the welfare of poor boys. He founded a ragged school in Charing Cross (1864–5), but with the passing of the Education Act (1870) the need for such schools was largely superseded. He then developed technical education and recreation in the Youths' Christian Institute (1878), which moved to Regent Street in 1882. The Polytechnic opened with 2000 members, whose numbers rose to 6800 in the first year. As well as technical education, Hogg organized holidays, savings banks, and debating societies. The Polytechnic was largely subsidized, in its early years, out of his own pocket.

HOHENFRIEDBERG, BATTLE OF (1745), defeat of the Austro-Saxon Imperial forces, 85,000 strong, by the Prussian army of 65,000 under Frederick the Great in the War of the Austrian Succession. The imperial commander, Prince Charles of Lorraine, withdrew into Bohemia, but Frederick was unable to exploit this personal triumph and force Austria to recognize the cession of Silesia.

HOHENLOHE, PHILIP, Count of (1550–1606), German son-in-law of William of Orange and commander of the army of the Closer Union of Utrecht (1579), who lacked the organizing ability and self-discipline to defeat Parma's Spanish troops during the Dutch Revolt.

HOHENLOHE-LANGENBURG, Prince Victor of (Count Gleichen) (1833–91), nephew of Queen Victoria, who served in the British navy, and was recommended for the Victoria Cross in the Crimean War. He later became a sculptor, being responsible for the statue of King Alfred the Great at Wantage, and exhibited in the Royal Academy.

HOHENLOHE-SCHILLINGSFÜRST, Prince Chlodwig (1819–1902), German chancellor and Prussian minister-president (1894–1900) and uncle of William II. As Bavarian minister-president and foreign minister, he had favoured closer union with Prussia, and after 1870 carried out the economic union of the South German states with Prussia and reorganized their troops on the Prussian pattern. He was governor of Alsace-Lorraine (1885–94), but was no more successful than his predecessor, Manteuffel. On Caprivi's resignation, he became German chancellor and his appointment marked the end of the 'New Course' policy. Despite his ability, he had little influence, as the emperor preferred to act as his own chancellor and foreign minister. His son published his *Denkwürdigkeiten* (1907), to the fury of the emperor. They remain an important source for German history in this period.

HOHENSTAUFEN FAMILY, dynasty of medieval German emperors, named after the castle of Staufen built by Frederick of Büren (1075), whose son married the daughter of Emperor Henry IV. They replaced an enemy of Henry as dukes of Swabia. This duchy remained thereafter the centre of the family's power. The first Hohenstaufen emperor, Conrad III (*reg.* 1138–52), inherited the Salian lands after that imperial dynasty died out. He inherited a much weakened position: the royal lands in Germany were no longer strong enough to support a forward royal policy and many princes had won considerable independence. Conrad was succeeded by Frederick I, his nephew, first of a succession of outstandingly intelligent and masterful emperors. The Italian ambitions of the family brought them into conflict with the papacy, which led to the eventual extermination of the whole house. To counter papal claims, the Hohenstaufen emperors over-emphasized the sacra nature of their own office. This brought them into collision with the theory of the papacy of Innocent III, who claimed the right to make or unmake emperors at will. In addition to this clash of ideas was the real fear of the papacy of encirclement by Hohenstaufen possessions in northern and southern Italy and the alliance of the imperialists with anti-papal forces in Rome. Emperor Frederick II (d. 1250) was treated as Antichrist by popes, whose overriding aim became the extirpation of the whole family. In alliance with the French, they were able to achieve this, and by 1254, had destroyed Hohenstaufen rule in Germany. The last male of the line, Conradin, was executed in Naples in 1268.

HOHENZOLLERN CANDIDATURE (1870), cause of friction between France and Prussia that led to the Franco-Prussian War. The Spaniards having deposed Queen Isabella in 1868, Leopold of Hohenzollern-Sigmaringen, a Catholic married to a Portuguese princess, was offered her throne. Reluctantly, after nine months and under pressure from Bismarck, Leopold accepted the offer and informed William I of Prussia. News of the candidature leaked out before the Cortes had met for the election, and France, fearing encirclement by Hohenzollern power, pressed William I to make Leopold withdraw, and to say that the candidature would not be renewed. William obtained the withdrawal, and said the renunciation had his entire and unreserved approval. His report of the negotiations to Bismarck is known as the Ems telegram.

HOHENZOLLERN FAMILY, German house existing from the 9th cent., which became the royal dynasty of Prussia and imperial Germany. Frederick VIII of Hohenzollern, Burgrave of Nurnberg, purchased the margravate of Brandenburg and was rewarded by the Emperor Sigismund for his services in the march with the title of Elector of Brandenburg (1415). John Sigismund, 9th elector by his marriage in 1608 to Anne of Prussia, acquired claims to the duchies of Prussia and Cleves-Jülich. These territories were inherited by his son, the elector, George William, in 1614, thus giving the Hohenzollerns a foothold on the Rhine. Ruthlessly opportunist in their exploitation of the weaknesses of neighbouring rulers, the Hohenzollerns became the leading German Protestant house after the ruin of the palatinate in the Thirty Years War (1618–48). With the acquisition of East Pomerania, Magdeburg, Minden, and Halberstadt (1648) and the suzerainty of East Prussia (1657) under the Great Elector, and West Pomerania in 1721, the Hohenzollern territories stretched across Europe from the Dutch to the Polish frontiers. The process of welding these scattered possessions into a compact kingdom became the family's purpose from King Frederick William I's reign (1713–40) and they pursued it with vigour and resourcefulness. The enforcement of a unified, centralized administration and the creation of a well-disciplined native army were fundamental to the growth of the Prussian state, which by the end of Frederick II's reign included the large provinces of Silesia and West Prussia. The rivalry between the Habsburgs and the Hohenzollerns which developed from the seizure of Silesia in 1740 was temporarily stilled during the Napoleonic domination of Germany. Prussia's defeat at Jena (1806) was followed by a remarkable revival in the reign of Frederick William III (1797–1840). The resettlement of Germany (1815) revived Austro-Prussian rivalry, however, but under Bismarck the Hohenzollern kings of Prussia united Germany, assumed the imperial title, and acquired overseas colonial possessions which they held until the defeat of Hohenzollern militarism in the First World War and the flight of William II (9 Nov. 1918).   MKS

HŌJŌ REGENCY, means through which the Hōjō family dominated government in Japan during most of the Kamakura period (1185–1334). Although of Taira descent, the regency had given Minamoto Yoritomo valuable support, and Masako, the forceful daughter of Hōjō Tokimasa, was Yoritomo's widow. After Yoritomo's death (1199) Tokimasa became the first of a line of Hōjō regents (*shikken*), while the position of *shōgun* became titular only. The foundation of Hōjō domination of the *bakufu* lay in family solidarity and the ability of successive family heads for nearly a century. Their main achievements were the formulation of the first important code of feudal law, the Jōei Shikimoku (1232), and the defence of Japan against Mongol invasions (1274, 1281). The earlier Hōjō regents were patrons of Zen Buddhism and their exercise of power was characterized by justice and frugality, but the lesser ability of later regents was a factor in the decline of the Kamakura regime.

HOLBACH, PAUL THYRY HENRY, Baron von (1723–89), German-born philosopher of the Enlightenment, whose radical materialist ideas were complementary to the philosophy of Helvetius. He is known for his *Christianisme Devoilé* (1767), *Esprit du Clergé* (1770), in which he launched an atheistic attack on the Christian Church, and *Le Système de la Nature* (1770).

HOLBEIN, HANS, the Younger (1497–1543), German portrait painter, who came to England in 1526 with an introduction from Erasmus to Sir Thomas More. He became court painter to Henry VIII, as well as his designer, decorator, and goldsmith. Among his most famous portraits are those of Henry VIII and Erasmus.

HOLBERG, LUDVIG (1684–1754), Danish writer and the founder of Danish literature, though Norwegian by birth. Holberg became a professor at Copenhagen, where he wrote comedies, histories, and other works, which established Danish as a cultural language.

HOLINSHED, RALPH (d. *c*. 1580), English historian-chronicler, who published *Chronicles of England, Scotland and Ireland*, written by himself and others (1577).

HOLKAR, family name of the Maratha rulers of Indore in central India (1728–1948). The dynasty's founder was Malhar Rao, a peasant born in the village of Hol, hence the surname Holkar. After joining the Maratha cavalry he attracted the notice of the peshwa, who granted him large assignments of land. After the third battle of Panipat (1761) the power of the low-born generals increased at the expense of the Brahman peshwas of Poona. Malhar Rao died in 1765 and his widow, Ahalya Bai, ruled over his territories for 30 years. Sir John Malcolm praises her just rule. Jaswant Rao I (*reg*. 1798–1811) defeated Col. William Monson in 1804, but was soon defeated by Lord Lake. Malhar Rao II (*reg*. 1811–34) accepted British protection under the treaty of Mandasor (1818). Indore was merged (1948) into the Indian state of Madhya Pradesh.

HOLLADAY, BEN (1819–87), US (Kansas) trader, who supplied the US army in the West during the Mexican War (1846–8), purchased the Russell, Majors, and Waddell freight lines (1862), and established the Holladay Overland Stage Co. After selling out to Wells Fargo (1866), he developed shipping interests and unsuccessfully sought to build the Oregon Central Railroad.

HOLLAND OF FOXLEY, HENRY FOX, 1st Baron (1705–74), British Whig politician, who was a supporter of Sir Robert Walpole and a member of the administrations of Pelham, Newcastle, and Bute. He specialized in obtaining majorities in the Commons, of which he persuaded Newcastle to make him leader in 1755, and, by gross bribery and intimidation, helped to obtain a large majority in favour of the peace of Paris (1763). He made a fortune out of his position as paymaster-general.

HOLLAND, HENRY RICHARD VASSAL FOX, 3rd Baron (1773–1840), British politician. On entering the House of Lords (1796), he represented the views of C. J. Fox, whose nephew he was, and the liberal ideas of the Foxite-Whigs. He held office in the Ministry of all the Talents (1806) and again in the Whig governments of the 1830s. His home, Holland House, London, was a centre for both Whig politicians and men of letters (*eg*, Sheridan, Macaulay, and Dickens). Holland himself translated Spanish and Italian works and wrote *Memoirs of the Whig Party* (ed., by his son, 1852).

HOLLAND, HENRY EDMOND (1868–1933), NZ politician and leader of the Labour Party in opposition (1919–33). He took a leading part in the strikes and labour conferences of 1912–13, and in the formation of the NZ Labour Party (1916). In 1919 he entered parliament and was elected leader of the PLP, his aim being to convert the electorate to socialism, and to unite political and industrial labour. Though Labour moderated its policies to electoral advantage, Holland's austere and unbending manner prevented his exercising a popular appeal.

HOLLAND, SIR SIDNEY GEORGE (1893–1961), NZ politician and prime minister (1949–57). He was elected to parliament in 1935, and became leader of the opposition in 1940, his choice marking a break with the National Party's 'depression' leadership. His criticism of the Labour government's economic restrictions gained increasing support, especially after 1945, and in 1949 he led the National Party to victory. However, his winning slogan, 'Make the pound go further', contrasted with continuing inflation. Holland, anticipating dangerous political trends with his tough and shrewd handling of the 1951 strike, gained electoral approval for his actions.

HOLLAND AND ZEELAND, COUNTY OF, area to the west of the Zuider Zee which first appeared as a recognizably separate county under the house of Vlardingen in the last quarter of the 11th cent. It expanded steadily at the cost of the Frisians and the Bp of Utrecht and by the early 14th cent. its long rivalry with Flanders for possession of Zeeland ended in success. The election of Count William as king of the Romans (1247) enabled him to increase his possessions and the Great Interregnum virtually ended imperial control in the area. The appearance of the Zuider Zee through the encroachment of the sea separated the West Frisians from their fellows and their conquest was complete by 1289. Towns developed later than in Flanders, but their growth was rapid in the late 13th cent. This growth was actively encouraged by Count Floris V, who made himself unpopular with the nobility, by whom he was murdered (1296). The early growth of estates and class rivalry led to the long factional strife of the Hooks and Cods. On the extinction of the native line of counts (1299), Holland passed to the counts of Hainault and eventually, on the death of William IV (1345), to the Wittelsbachs. Having freed itself from the control of the empire, Holland came increasingly under pressure from the rising power of Burgundy. In 1428 Jacqueline of Bavaria was forced to recognize Philip of Burgundy as her heir and in 1433 the county passed to his rule. During the Burgundian period it experienced rapid commercial growth, largely at the cost of the German Hansards, and it eventually became the most important province of the Dutch republic.

HOLLAND, INVASION OF (1940). The German invasion of Holland in the Second World War was simultaneous with, and an integral part of, those of Belgium and France. The Dutch had long relied on their neutrality for their defence, even to the extent of refusing to discuss joint plans with Britain, France, and Belgium, and their army comprised only ten divisions. Their defensive system consisted of two lines, an outer one based on geographical features, notably the Yssel and Meuse rivers and the Peel Marshes, and an inner one, the Vesting Holland, protecting Rotterdam, The Hague, and Amsterdam. The German attack opened on 10 May with extensive airborne landings by 4000 paratroopers in the rear of the Dutch defences; these troops, reinforced by troops brought in by air, captured airfields near Rotterdam and The Hague, and key bridges at Moerdyk, Dordrecht, and Rotterdam. This brilliantly conceived tactic and the new technique of *blitzkrieg* employed by the advancing ground troops threw the Dutch defenders into hopeless confusion, and by 13 May the main German force, under Gen. von Kückler, had advanced to the outskirts of Rotterdam. On the following day negotiations for the surrender of the city were under way when aircraft of the Luftwaffe carried out a devastating bombing raid on the city in which nearly 1000 civilians were killed. It now seems likely that this attack was the result of a breakdown of signal communications between the air forces and the ground, but it was the first occasion of the mass bombing of civilians in the Second World War, and its effect was magnified by German propaganda which claimed that 130,000 casualties had been inflicted. The Dutch army, commanded by Gen. Winkelman, surrendered on 15 May, Queen Wilhelmina and the bullion reserves having been evacuated to Britain two days before.   NRB

HOLLES OF IFIELD, DENZIL HOLLES, 1st Baron (1599–1680), English politician and MP for Dorchester, who attacked the royal right to adjourn parliament (1629) and was one of the five members whom Charles I tried to arrest for treason in Jan. 1642. With the others, he took refuge in the city of London and a week later returned triumphantly to Westminster. He was one of the commissioners who negotiated with the king in 1646 and demanded the dissolution of the army (1647). He went abroad in 1648 to escape the purge of parliament and returned to England after the civil wars. He was employed by Charles II to negotiate the peace of Breda (1667). His memoirs of the civil wars were published posthumously (1699).

HOLLYWOOD, district in Los Angeles, CA, that was for about 40 years from 1913 the production centre of the US film industry. The Nestor Co. was the first to be established in Hollywood, and others followed, attracted by the climate, nearby scenery for outside locations, cheap labour, and local business support. Hollywood became synonymous with the star system and lavish productions.

HOLMAN, WILLIAM ARTHUR (1871–1934), Australian politician and a founder of the Labor Party in NSW, who was born in London. Having migrated to Australia in 1888, he became a member of the colonial legislature in 1898. While retaining his seat in the state parliament (1906–20), he was successively NSW attorney-general (1910–13) and prime minister (1913–20) and established several state-owned enterprises without winning the full confidence of the industrial labour movement. In 1916 he supported conscription and left the party, but retained the premiership in what became a Nationalist government. After practising successfully at the bar, he was elected to the Commonwealth parliament in 1930.

HOLMES, OLIVER WENDELL jr (1841–1935), US lawyer, jurist, and scholar. He graduated from Harvard Law School (1866), practised in Boston, returned to the Law School as professor (1882), became an associate justice of the MA Supreme Court (1883) and chief justice (1899–1902). He was appointed associate justice of the US Supreme Court by Theodore Roosevelt (1902), and served until he was 90. A notable dissenter, with a clear view of the court's role, he was essentially a sceptical conservative who refused to use the court to prevent social experimentation or the free expression of ideas. He opposed the Sherman Anti-trust Act (1890), yet his enunciation of the 'stream of commerce' doctrine in *Swift v. US* (1905) later became a basic concept justifying the expansion of the federal commerce power. In various dissenting opinions he attacked attempts by a majority of the court to limit state and national legislation on matters of social welfare. As a result, he became a strong supporter of judicial self-restraint, sustaining the right of law-makers except where there were specific constitutional prohibitions.

In *Schenck v. US* (1919), while denying the absolute right of free speech, he developed the 'clear and present danger' doctrine which later became a principal judicial guideline in cases involving the First Amendment of the constitution, and opposed any attempt to restrict the 'free trade in ideas'. He also opposed early attempts at 'wire-tapping', and supported those claiming the right of peaceful picketing. His opposition to the notion of the common law as a fundamental all-pervasive set of principles is emphasized in his writings, which include *The Common Law* (1881) and *Collected Legal Papers* (1920).

M. DeWolfe Howe (ed.), *Holmes–Pollock Letters* (Cambridge, MA, 1941).
M. DeWolfe Howe (ed.), *Holmes–Laski Letters* (Cambridge, MA, 1953).   JDL

HOLMES, SIR ROBERT (1622–92), English sea captain, who led an expedition to support the English African company and took Goree and Cape Coast Castle from the Dutch (1663–4). Later he defeated them off the North Foreland, sacking the island of Terschelling and destroying 150 Dutch ships in the celebrated 'Holmes's Bonfire' (1666). In 1672, on the eve of the Dutch War, he launched an attack on the Dutch Smyrna fleet in the Channel.

HOLOWCZYN, BATTLE OF (4 July 1708), last victory of Charles XII of Sweden against the Russians under Gen. Menshikov. Although he split the Russian forces in two and forced them to retreat eastwards, a shortage of supplies checked Charles's pursuit and instead he turned southwards to link up with Mazeppa's Cossacks.

HOLSTEIN, FRIEDRICH (1837–1909), German foreign office official, who successfully opposed the renewal of the secret Reinsurance treaty with Russia, causing an alliance between France and Russia. He entered the Prussian diplomatic service in 1860 and became embittered because he had to give evidence at the trial of the German ambassador in Paris on the charge of purloining state papers, and was subsequently socially ostracized as a spy. He turned against Bismarck and took part in intrigues that led to his fall from power. From 1890 to 1906 he was the key figure in the direction of German foreign policy, and favoured a preventive war with France. Von Bülow dismissed him after the Algeciras conference. He was largely responsible for Germany's isolation and encirclement at the beginning of the 20th cent.

HOLSTEIN CRISIS (1848), caused by the Danish king's promulgation of a new constitution applicable also to the duchies of Schleswig and Holstein, of which he was duke. Prussian and German federal forces invaded the duchies and Jutland, but because of British and Russian opposition Prussia signed a truce at Malmö, which was considered in Germany to have been a betrayal of the national cause.

HOLSTEIN-GOTTORP, CHARLES FREDERICK, Duke of (1700–39), son of Charles XII's elder sister, and unsuccessful claimant to the Swedish throne. He was brought up in Sweden and was Görtz's candidate for the succession, but on Charles's death was easily put aside in favour of Ulrika Eleonora. He moved to Russia and married Peter the Great's daughter, Anna. From 1727 he lived at Kiel in Holstein-Gottorp, hoping to acquire Schleswig or the Swedish or Russian succession.

HOLSTEIN-GOTTORP, FREDERICK, Duke of (1671–1702), the ally of Charles XII of Sweden and husband of his sister,

Hedvig Sophia. He commanded Swedish troops in Germany and was killed while directing his section of the army in Charles's victory at Kliszow in Poland.

HOLSTEIN-GOTTORP, dukedom established in 1544 for a younger branch of the Danish royal house, with territory mainly in Schleswig. Its rulers later became allies of Sweden against Denmark, Charles X of Sweden marrying the daughter of one duke, and another marrying the sister of Charles XII. The Swedish alliance was renounced in 1720 and the lands of the duchy in Schleswig were then taken over by the Danish kings, but its lands in Holstein did not pass finally into Danish hands until 1773.

HOLSTON TREATY (2 July 1791) ended a period of warfare on the northern Tennessee frontier by establishing the Cherokee–American boundary. The area south of the Little Tennessee river was guaranteed to the Cherokee Indians, but the actual boundary was not determined until 1797.

HOLT, SIR JOHN (1642–1710), lord chief justice of England and an ardent supporter of civil and religious liberty. He is best known for the firmness with which he upheld common law against parliament. In the *Ashby v. White* case he declared that a vote was a piece of property, and as such subject to common law.

HOLWELL, JOHN ZEPHANIAH (1711–98), British colonial servant, prominent in Bengal after going to Calcutta (1732) and becoming chief surgeon and, from 1751, *zamindar* of the 24 *pargana*s. He was one of those in the 'Black Hole' on the night of 20 June 1756. His description formed the basis of a legend, the truth of which is now generally doubted, as is Holwell's general veracity. Holwell was acting governor of Fort William in 1760.

HOLY ALLIANCE (1815), originally a statement of intent, approved by all European powers, except Britain, Turkey, and the papacy, to regulate the affairs of Europe in accordance with the principles of the Christian religion. It degenerated into an understanding between the reactionary monarchies of Russia, Austria, and Prussia to uphold the principle of monarchy even where this involved intervention in the affairs of other independent states. Described by Metternich as 'a high-sounding nothing', the alliance had little practical significance. Austria preferred her own and French troops to subdue rebellions in Italy and Spain (1820, 1823) rather than to allow Russian troops to cross Europe. All semblance of unity between the alliance powers crumbled during the Greek Revolt (1821), when Russia acted with England and France, but without Austria, to secure Greek independence.

HOLY EXPERIMENT, William Penn's name for the ideal government he established in Pennsylvania (1681). It was a peaceful administration with no militia or provision for war, guaranteed civil liberty, religious freedom, and economic opportunity for all, and had a constitution and code of laws ratified by the people. It lasted for 70 years.

HOLY LEAGUE (1571), union of the Catholic powers of Venice, Spain, and the papacy, negotiated with great difficulty by Pope Pius V to curb the Turks in the Mediterranean. Throughout the spring of 1570 Pius pleaded with Philip II to join in a defensive alliance, but the latter delayed sending assistance to the Venetian fleet until Aug. 1570, while dissension among the Catholic commanders grew. Throughout the winter (1570–1) negotiations continued between the three powers for a formal alliance which was concluded on 15 May 1571. It was agreed that operations should be carried on both in North Africa and in the eastern Mediterranean. Despite the fall of Cyprus (1 Aug. 1571) the league's fleet, commanded by Don John of Austria, virtually annihilated the Turkish fleet at Lepanto (7 Oct. 1571). Disagreements then

weakened the alliance and in March 1573 Venice concluded peace with the Porte. Spain, left to fight alone, concentrated on North Africa until the Ottoman conquest of Tunis (1574) temporarily ended Spanish ambitions.

HOLY LEAGUE (1684), organized at Linz by Pope Innocent XI, an alliance of the empire, Poland, and Venice against Turkey, inspired by John Sobieski's victory at Vienna (1683). Innocent planned a three-fold attack in Hungary, Moldavia, and Greece. The Hungarian campaigns lasted for 16 years, during which time a huge mercenary army recovered Buda (Sept. 1686) for the Holy League and the imperial general Charles of Lorraine defeated the Turks near the old battlefield of Mohacs (1687), to restore southern Hungary to the Habsburgs. The War of the League of Augsburg, however, sapped the imperialist war effort (1689–97). Meanwhile Sobieski's attempts to reconquer the principalities of Moldavia and Wallachia failed (1686, 1691). In the Mediterranean the league was brilliantly successful. The fleet of Francesco Morosini, reinforced by Tuscan, papal, and Maltese ships, attacked the Ionian island of Santa Maura and in 1685 began the reconquest of Greece by taking Koroni. The Morea and Athens were retaken by the Venetians in 1687. The peace of Carlowitz (1699) successfully ended the Holy League's crusade, the Turks surrendering nearly the whole of Hungary to the Habsburgs.

HOLY OFFICE, the new Inquisition instituted in 1478 under Isabella of Castile as an instrument for guaranteeing orthodoxy and for welding the Spanish kingdoms into a unified state under the Crown. Initially, from 1480, it proceeded against the *conversos*, the Jewish Christian community, but from the mid-16th cent., when Abp Carranza of Toledo, the primate of the Spanish church, was condemned for heresy by its officials, until 1780, when it claimed its last victim in Seville for sorcery, the Holy Office was accorded great authority by Spanish monarchs.

HOLYOAKE, GEORGE JACOB (1817–1906), British Chartist, co-operator, and secularist. He was an engineer's son whose self-improvement led him into rationalism and in 1842 he was imprisoned for blasphemy. His personality and objectives were not suited to organizing a secularist 'movement', and by the 1850s he was pursuing an objective morality which attracted respectable support. But courtesy and moderation could not attract indignant working men, and from 1858 the coarser Bradlaugh took over secularist leadership. The mature Holyoake championed co-operative societies, but was never a socialist, and opposed private property only in land.

HOLYOAKE, KEITH JACKA (1904–), NZ politician and prime minister throughout the 1960s, who entered parliament in 1932 as a Coalition (Reform) member. As deputy-leader of the National Party (1947), he succeeded Sir Sidney Holland for a brief term as prime minister before the Labour government (1957–60). An able, conciliatory leader in cabinet, house, and party, Holyoake was less successful on platform and television, but was confirmed in office, with a reduced majority, at the Nov. 1969 elections.

HOLYROOD PALACE, Scottish royal residence situated at the eastern end of the Royal Mile, Edinburgh. The building was begun in 1501 by James IV (*reg.* 1488–1513) in readiness for his marriage to Margaret Tudor. After its partial destruction by the Earl of Hertford in 1544, it was restored, but was again partly destroyed during the Cromwellian occupation of the 17th cent. The present buildings mostly date from Charles II's reign, when they were reconstructed by Sir William Bruce.

HOMAGE, in western Europe, ceremony by which a man recognized himself to be a dependant of another person. In medieval feudal custom it became one of the two essential features of a ceremony by which men became military vassals of their superiors. The other main feature was the swearing of an oath of fealty.

HOMAYUN (1508–56), the second Mughal Emperor of India (*reg.* 1530–56), who succeeded his father, Babur. Difficulties were created by the hostility of his brother Kamran, who held Afghanistan and the Punjab. At first he was successful in conquering Malwa and Gujarat, but his expedition to Bengal against Sher Khan in 1537 failed, largely through his own inertia and unwisdom. After defeats at Chausa (1539) and Kanauj (1540), Homayun fled to Persia, where he was given shelter by Shah Tahmasp. With his help he took Kandahar, and overcame Kamran. In 1555 succession disputes among his Afghan supplanters enabled him to recover Delhi and Agra.

HOME, SIR ALEXANDER FREDERICK DOUGLAS-HOME, 14th Earl of (Scottish) (disclaimed in 1963) (1903–), British Conservative politician and prime minister (1963–4), who entered parliament in 1931. He became parliamentary private secretary to Neville Chamberlain in 1937, and was closely identified with the policies being pursued towards Europe up to the outbreak of the Second World War. Although a critic of the wartime government's policies towards Eastern Europe (he had voted against the agreement with Russia over Poland), he was parliamentary private secretary in the foreign office in the closing months of Winston Churchill's government.

In 1945 he lost his seat; in 1950 he was again elected, but was obliged to resign upon succeeding his father as 14th Earl of Home in 1951. He was, nevertheless, minister of state for the Scottish office in the Churchill government, and secretary of state for commonwealth relations (1955–60). He was also leader of the House of Lords (1957–60). In 1960 Macmillan appointed him foreign secretary, and he played an active role in the East–West detente for which Macmillan had worked. In 1963 he succeeded Macmillan as prime minister. He then disclaimed his peerages, and re-entered the Commons. He resigned as leader of the opposition a year after the Conservative election defeat of 1964, but remained prominently associated with foreign affairs in the Conservative shadow cabinets (1965–70). In the Heath administration of 1970 he again became foreign secretary.

HOME OWNERS LOAN CORPORATION in US, federal agency established in 1933 to refinance non-farm home mortgages. It was a successful part of the New Deal programme, and handled over 1 million loans (1933–6).

HOME RULE LEAGUES, militant Indian nationalist organizations of the First World War period. They were led by B. G. Tilak (1856–1920) and Mrs Annie Besant (1847–1933), who were concerned to invigorate the Indian National Congress by the re-entry of the 'extremists', who had been excluded since 1907. By Sept. 1915 Tilak and Mrs Besant had each published plans for separate home rule organizations, although both were clearly anxious to work within Congress, if possible. Following the Congress session (Dec. 1915), Mrs Besant agreed to wait until the following Sept. before starting home rule activities. Tilak, however, inaugurated his Indian Home Rule League (IHRL) in April 1916 in the Marathi-speaking areas of Bombay and the Central Provinces, and in the Karnatak. Tilak had no formal office in the IHRL but it was clearly under his direction. Mrs Besant's All-India Home Rule League (AIHRL) began in Sept. 1916 and operated throughout the country exclusive of the IHRL area. The AIHRL drew its main support and its basic organizational network from the Theosophical Society, which Mrs Besant also controlled. By the beginning of 1918 there were 32,000 members in the IHRL and about 27,000 in the AIHRL, but the growth of the AIHRL had come mainly in the latter part of 1917 after Mrs Besant's internment.

The leagues were mainly concerned with public agitation for an immediate grant of home rule for India and they attempted to bring pressure on the Congress to support this demand. They were defeated on this issue at the 1916 Congress session but their pressure began to have an effect and, after the death of several of the important moderate leaders, the influence of leaguers increased. Mrs Besant was president of Congress in 1917, but her influence, and the effectiveness of the AIHRL, declined during 1918. Tilak increasingly came to dominate Congress and the IHRL was, in effect, merged in that body by 1919.   PDR

HOMER (*fl.* 8th cent. BC), Greek poet, author of the *Iliad* and *Odyssey c.* 700 BC. The two monumental poems represent the culmination of a long period (12th–8th cents) of orally transmitted poetry concerned with the Trojan War (*c.* 1200) and its aftermath. Historical facts are heavily embroidered with poetic fancy and the social, economic, and political background of the poems is an unreal amalgam of Mycenaean (16th–12th cents) and Dark Age (11th–8th cents) elements. Nevertheless, without the *Iliad* the destruction of Troy VIIA would remain unexplained and the *Odyssey* can be used with fair certainty to illuminate the social and economic conditions of the Dark Age. Finally, the poetry itself remains as indubitable evidence of Greek experience *c.* 700.

HOMER, WINSLOW (1836–1910), US painter and a popular reporter-illustrator of the Civil War for *Harper's Weekly.* He developed a quasi-Impressionistic style in genre studies. His later paintings, particularly of the Maine coast, explored more profoundly the elemental forces of nature.

HOMESTEAD ACT (1862) in US, legislation providing a quarter section, 160 acres (0·68 sq. kms), of public land free of all charges except a small filing fee to all adults or heads of family who were or were about to become citizens, provided they had lived or worked on the land for five years. The act represented the successful culmination of a movement for free homesteads that dated back to the early 19th cent., and led to a renewed wave of emigration to the West.

HOMESTEAD STRIKE (July 1892), one of the most bitter labour disputes in US history. Strikers at the Carnegie Steel Co. plant at Homestead, PA, fired on barges carrying 300 Pinkerton detectives up the Monongahela river to protect the plant. A battle resulted, causing 14 deaths, numerous injuries, and the capture of the Pinkertons. For 12 days the strikers ruled the town until state troops were called in to restore order. The attempted murder of the plant manager, Henry C. Frick, by Alexander Berkman, an anarchist who had no association with the strikers, swung public opinion away from the Iron and Steel Workers union and the strike was broken. Unionization in US steel mills was delayed for another 40 years.

HONDURAS, BRITISH, colony on the Central American Caribbean coast, claimed by and known to Guatemala as 'Belize'. The name may be a Spanish corruption of Wallace, the Scottish buccaneer, who made his headquarters there (*c.* 1738). Cortés established a Spanish colony on the Honduran coast (1524) under Cristoval de Olid, but Spanish settlement did not extend to the Belize river area. The first British settlers were logwood cutters from Jamaica (1738). By the treaty of Paris (1763) Spain acknowledged these 'Baymen's' right to cut logwood. Efforts to force the logcutters out were prevented by a British force under Admiral Sir William Burnaby (1764). George III granted the Baymen local rights and (1765) Burnaby drew up a legal code. By the treaty of Versailles (1783) Spain confirmed the log-cutters' right to work the area bounded by the Hondo and Belize rivers. A further treaty (1786) extended the area southwards to the Sibun. In 1786 the first 'Superintendent' arrived from Britain. The inhabitants repulsed a Spanish attack (1798).

The 'Settlement in the Bay of Honduras' was declared British territory and the old form of government replaced by Crown Colony government (1862). When Guatemala became independent (1821) she inherited Spain's claim to Belize. The Anglo-Guatemalan Convention (1859) prescribed boundaries, provided for the building of a road between Guatemala city and the Belize coast and gave Britain territorial sovereignty. Britain subsequently repudiated any obligation to share the road's cost and Guatemala contended that Britain had voided the Convention by default. Negro slaves were introduced to Honduras and their descendants now comprise 40 per cent of the population. A slave rebellion occurred in 1765. Some 8 per cent of the population are descended from the 'Black Caribs', a Negro-Amerindian admixture, deported from St Vincent (1796). Unrestricted adult suffrage was introduced (1960), and internal self-government (1964). Independence, scheduled for 1968, has been postponed after failure to settle relations with Guatemala. A United Nations mediator, seeking to reconcile Guatemalan claims with self-determination, proposed a draft treaty (1968). Amid local unrest, the legislature rejected it.

R. A. Humphreys, *Diplomatic History of British Honduras, 1638–1901* (Oxford, 1961).   RH

HONE, WILLIAM (1780–1842), English writer and bookseller, who was devoted to the freedom of the press and the sale of cheap and informative literature. In 1817 he began the *Reformer's Register* and was three times tried for publishing satires against the government and the Church, but acquitted.

HONESTIORES, legal category of citizens of the Roman empire that included senators, *equites*, professional men, *decuriones* (local councillors in the *municipia*), soldiers, and veterans. The severest penalty that they could incur, and which only the emperor could order was deportation to an island, with loss of property and citizenship. All others, *humiliores*, were liable to be flogged, burned alive, thrown to the beasts, or sent to labour in the mines. Social discrimination in punishment, a practice of long standing, received legal sanction in edicts of Hadrian (AD 117–38) and his successors, so that 3rd-cent. lawyers could provide different scales of penalties for every offence. When citizenship became universal (211), only *honestiores* retained the old privileges of Romans, and in the later empire even these were often ignored.

HONG KONG STRIKE (1925–6), anti-imperialist strike which crippled Hong Kong for 16 months. It started after Chinese demonstrators in Canton had been fired on from the British and French settlement, shortly after the 30 May Incident in Shanghai. Chinese workers deserted Hong Kong, paralysing the colony.

HONGI HIKA (*c.*1780–1828), first NZ Maori chief to escalate tribal warfare by the use of muskets, which he obtained during a visit to England (1820). The round of his campaigns set off in the 1820s depopulated thriving areas of Auckland province. Paradoxically, he protected Marsden's first mission (1814) and later missionary stations.

HONGI-TOCHTEN, expeditions by fleets (*hongi*) of Indonesian galleys, sent by the Dutch annually from 1649 to destroy clove and nutmeg trees outside the Dutch centres of Amboina and Banda. They brought economic ruin to the original 'spice islands'—Ternate and Tidore.

HONJONG (1827–49), King of Korea (*reg.* 1834–49), whose reign is notable chiefly as a period when his queen's relations, the P'ungyang Cho family, wrested power at the court from the Andong Kim family, which otherwise dominated Korea for most of the 19th cent.

HONORIUS (d. 425), Western Roman Emperor (*reg.* 395–23), whose reign was disastrous for the western empire after the effective ruler, Gen. Stilicho, was murdered in 408. He made Ravenna his capital while Rome was sacked by Visigoths under Alaric. Much of Spain and Gaul was overrun by German tribes and control of Britain was lost.

HONORIUS III (*reg.* 1216–27), Pope, who consolidated the work of his predecessor, Innocent III. Honorius gave formal recognition to the newly founded Dominican and Franciscan orders; was much concerned with the affairs of his two wards, Frederick II Hohenstaufen of Sicily and Henry III of England; with the implementation of the decrees of the Fourth Lateran Council (1215); with the continuing problem of the Albigensians; and with the organizing of the Fifth Crusade (1218–21).

HONTHEIM, JOHANN NICHOLAS VON (1701–90), German bishop of Trier, who wrote under the name of Justinus Febronius and gave his name to the movement called Febronianism, the struggle of the Catholic German princes to curb the powers of the papacy over the Church during the 18th cent. In his book *De statu ecclesiae et legitima potestae Romani pontificis* (1763) he looked to the reunion of all Christians, Protestant and Catholic, by limiting the primacy of the papacy to its ancient limits and restoring the authority of oecumenical councils over the pope. The rights of the bishops and princes were also to be restored. His ideas provided useful ammunition for those who fought against Jesuit and ultramontane policies and he greatly influenced the ideas and actions of the Emperor Joseph II and his minister Kaunitz.

HOOCH, PIETER DE (1629–*c.* 1684), Dutch painter, who worked in Delft and Amsterdam, and whose genre paintings afford interesting sidelights on everyday life.

HOOD OF WHITLEY, SAMUEL HOOD, 1st Viscount (1724–1816), British admiral, who served in the American War of Independence and under Rodney defeated the French off Dominica (1782), thus reasserting British control of the Atlantic. He entered parliament (1784) and was lord of the admiralty (1788–93). He commanded the force which occupied Toulon (1793) and captured Corsica (1794), but was then recalled for political reasons.

HOOD, JOHN BELL (1831–79), Confederate general in the American Civil War, more renowned for boldness and courage than for strategic or tactical skill. After much valiant fighting in the VA campaigns (1862–3), he led a rash advance from GA deep into TN (1864), where his army was shattered by George H. Thomas at the battle of Nashville.

HOOFT, PIETER CORNELISZOON (1581–1647), Dutch poet and historian, a member of the Muiden circle, who wrote about the Dutch revolt against Spain in his *History of the Netherlands*. He helped to launch the Dutch Academy (1617), which produced his play, *Warenar*.

HOOKE, ROBERT (1635–1703), British philosopher and scientist, who became (1662) curator of experiments to the Royal Society. He invented the wheel barometer, the double-barrelled air pump, and investigated sound and optics. He was one of the first to look at a variety of objects under the microscope and his results are recorded in his book *Micrographia* (1665). His term 'cell' is still used, though with wider significance.

HOOKER, JOSEPH (1814–79), Union general in the American Civil War, whose early record earned him the nickname 'Fighting Joe'. This, together with a capacity for intrigue, made him commander of the army of the Potomac (Jan.–June 1863). He was beaten by Robert E. Lee at the battle of Chancellorsville, and was replaced by Gen. Meade just before Gettysburg. He later fought in the battles near Chattanooga and Atlanta.

HOOKER, RICHARD (1553–1600), English theologian, who was a pupil of Jewel, master of the Temple (1585), parson of Boscombe, Wilts (1591), and of Bishopstone, Kent (1595). Conflict with the Calvinist Travers, lecturer at the Temple, led to Hooker's masterpiece, *The Laws of Ecclesiastical Polity*. Books I–IV were published in 1593; V in 1597; VI and VIII in 1648; and VII in 1661—VI–VIII edited from drafts, perhaps tendentiously. To meet Puritan and Presbyterian attacks on the Church of England and their claim that ministry and worship must be entirely regulated by express scriptural commands, he investigated the sources of authority and the nature of divine and human law (I–IV), propounding a balanced appeal to reason, scripture, and tradition. V defends Anglican worship and sacramental theology, VI considers ecclesiastical discipline, VII vindicates episcopacy, VIII reviews Church–state relations and royal authority.

While his anti-Calvinist conclusions particularly assisted the Caroline development of Anglicanism, his irenical outlook and theological method have profoundly influenced its general character and history.

HOOKER, THOMAS (?1586–1647), American clergyman, who emigrated to Boston (1633), where he became well known as an eloquent preacher, then moved to Hartford (1636), taking many members of his congregation with him. He believed in government by authoritarian rule of church elders and magistrates, and became a powerful leader in the theocratic colony of Connecticut.

HOOKER, SIR WILLIAM JACKSON (1785–1865), British botanist, who was the first director of the Royal Botanic Gardens, Kew. The exchange of plants and seeds with other botanic gardens throughout the world were among his innovations. Hooker encouraged the writing of floras of developing overseas countries, producing that of North America himself. His son, Sir Joseph Dalton Hooker (1817–1911), who succeeded him at Kew in 1865, produced with George Bentham his *Genera plantarum* from 1862 and his *Flora of the British Isles*. He was a noted plant collector, first in southern South America and Australia and later in the Himalayas.

HOOKS AND CODS, PARTIES OF THE (Dutch, '*Hoeken en Kabeljauwen*'), the names given to two factions in the county of Holland in the 14th and 15th cents, which were responsible for chronic civil strife in the county. They first arose after the death without issue of Count William IV (1345). His sister Margaret, wife of the Emperor Louis the Bavarian, was enfeoffed with Holland, Zeeland, and Hainault by her husband, but her son, William, claimed a share. The Cods, representing mainly commercial and urban interests, supported William, while the noble-led Hooks favoured Margaret. The dispute was settled in 1354 when William was recognized as count. The succession dispute only brought to the surface long-smouldering class and faction conflicts and provided the excuse for open warfare. The last Vlardingen count, Floris V (d. 1296), resisted the nobility with the support of rising towns and was murdered by noblemen. Class consciousness was fostered early in Holland by the development of estates. The two parties persisted in Holland until the end of the 15th cent., taking advantage of succession disputes and the like to indulge in overt fighting. Only with the incorporation of Holland into the strong Burgundian state did they gradually disappear.

HOOPER, JOHN, bishop of Gloucester and of Worcester (1495–1555), English Puritan extremist, who fled to Zürich in 1539, returning to England after Henry VIII's death. He was consecrated Bp of Gloucester (1550) and later of Worcester under Edward VI. He was burnt at the stake under Mary Tudor (9 Feb. 1555), and in Foxe's *Acts and Monuments* is accorded recognition as a Protestant martyr.

HOORN, PHILIP DE MONTMORENCY NIVELLE, Count of (1518–68), member of the great nobility of the Habsburg–Burgundian Netherlands and a Knight of the Golden Fleece. He was governor of Guelders under Charles V and a member of the Council of State of the Netherlands under Philip II. With the Prince of Orange and the Count of Egmont he formed a league to oppose Cardinal Granvelle's ecclesiastical reforms and forced his withdrawal from the Netherlands (1564). After the Calvinist-inspired outbreak of violence in Antwerp, Ghent, and other cities (Aug. 1566), Hoorn and most of the high nobility took a new oath of loyalty to the Spanish Crown, but after Alva's arrival (1567) he and Egmont were arrested (Sept. 1567) and executed in the market square of Brussels (5 June 1568).

HOOVER, HERBERT CLARK (1874–1964), US mining engineer, philanthropist, and Republican president (1929–33), widely known as 'The Great Engineer' and 'The Great Humanitarian'. In Harding's and Coolidge's administrations (1921–8) he served as secretary of commerce. His election as president came as a fitting climax to what was regarded as the perfect American success story.

Born in IA, of Quaker parents, he was orphaned by the age of ten. After studying engineering and geology at Stanford University he embarked on a career in mining that took him all over the world and made him a millionaire by the age of 40. During the First World War he supervised US relief operations in London and Belgium, and in 1917 was appointed US Food Administrator in control of both domestic supplies and the European relief programme. When official US relief ended he continued to organize voluntary funds to fight European famine. All the money he received for his services during the war he devoted to charity, as he devoted all that he received throughout his governmental career. As secretary of commerce Hoover stood out from the general mediocrity of the Harding and Coolidge administrations, and under his guidance the department exercised a key role in the promotion of business efficiency and prosperity.

Hoover's rural background and his business associations made him an ideal presidential candidate to succeed Coolidge (1928). Republican prosperity ensured his election over the Democratic nominee, Alfred E. Smith, but as president he was soon faced with the collapse of the stock market and the beginnings of Depression. Rejecting the advice of those who recommended inaction, as well as those who urged an expansion of federal activities, Hoover sought to persuade bankers, businessmen, state governments, and private charities to play their part in stabilizing credit, stimulating production, and providing for the needy. When good times still failed to return he agreed to expand the use of federal powers and established the Reconstruction Finance Corporation (1932), but despite increasing public hardship he refused to allow the federal government to assume direct responsibility for the unemployed. Being preoccupied by the Depression, Hoover devoted little time to foreign affairs. When Japan invaded Manchuria (1931), his determination not to commit the US to any course which might lead to war found expression in the Stimson Doctrine (1932).

On his defeat by Franklin Roosevelt in 1932, Hoover retired to private life, but continued his voluntary work. In 1946 President Truman called on him to make a survey of world food needs, and he was later appointed chairman of the Commission on the Organization of the Executive Branch of Government which came to bear his name (1947–9; 1953–5). For three decades he was the elder statesman of the Republican Party, but his political activities were largely limited to appearances at national conventions, for to many Republicans he represented a past they preferred to forget. Before Pearl Harbor, he was a firm opponent of US involvement in the Second World War and in the party struggles of the postwar years he sided with Senator Taft and those who wished to reduce US commitment in Europe.

H. G. Warren, *Herbert Hoover and the Great Depression* (New York, 1959).   AJT

HOOVER, JOHN EDGAR (1895–), US lawyer and director of the Federal Bureau of Investigation. He was assistant director of the Bureau of Investigation (1921), became its director in 1924, and made it one of the most efficient criminal investigation services in the world. During the Second World War the bureau became increasingly concerned with internal security, a preoccupation which was intensified by the Cold War, and in 1947, at President Truman's direction, Hoover began a check on the loyalty of government employees. In the reaction against McCarthyism after 1953 Hoover survived charges of allegedly illiberal methods and criticism that he had exaggerated the internal communist threat.

HOOVER COMMISSION in US, commission established by Congress in 1947 to enquire into duplication and inefficiency in the federal government. Officially known as the Commission on Organization of the Executive Branch of the Government, it was headed by Herbert Hoover, the former president. A second commission (1953–5) was established during President Eisenhower's administration.

HOOVER MORATORIUM in US, proposal by President Hoover (2 June 1931) for the suspension of payments on inter-governmental war debts and reparations for one year from 1 July 1932. The moratorium was designed to facilitate Europe's recovery from the Depression without sacrificing the principle of full repayment of war debts, which President Hoover and most US citizens regarded as vital. The proposal was implemented.

HOOVERVILLES in US, shanty towns made of old packing cases and scrap metal which sprang up during the Great Depression. The name, which went into common use, was an implicit indictment of President Hoover's handling of the Depression.

HOPI INDIANS, American tribe whose members speak Shoshonean dialect. Spaniards dispatched by Coronado first encountered them (1540) in northern AZ. They had little contact with Europeans until Franciscans established missions among them (1629). The missions were destroyed in the Pueblo revolt against Spanish rule (1680) and the Hopi resisted reconquest. As Spanish power dwindled, they were threatened by encroaching Navajos, especially when Mexican rule replaced Spanish control of the South-west (1823). The US government established a reservation for the Hopi (1882) and they now occupy several villages north-east of Flagstaff, AZ.

HÔPITAL, MICHEL DE L' (1505–73), Catholic French statesman and chancellor of France (1560–8). Originally he was chancellor to the Duchess of Berry, but resigned in 1553 and became president of the *chambre des comptes* (1554). During the minority of Charles IX (1560–3) his influence was predominant in the French state. He expounded a doctrine of religious toleration for the Huguenots, believing such a policy to be politically wise, if the state was to be strongly united and civil war averted. In this respect he was a forerunner of the *Politique* party which emerged in the later years of the French wars of religion. As chancellor, L'Hôpital introduced a number of pacific measures, eg, the edicts of Amboise and Romorantin (1560), and when neither of these laws quelled religious strife, he convened a great council, from which came the July Edict of 1561. L'Hôpital upheld royal authority, however, as belonging to the divinely bestowed law-giver, and denied the right of resistance. He also was the first to enunciate the theory of *parlementaire* unity (1560) which was to be taken up in the mid-18th cent.

HOPKINS, ESEK (1718–1802), American naval commander, who started as a merchant seaman and became the commander of a privateer during the French and Indian War (1754–63). He led Rhode Island's military forces (1775) and became commander-in-chief of the Continental navy (1775), which consisted of eight converted merchantmen. The fleet raided British shipping in the Bahamas, but Hopkins, unable to carry out the orders of Congress, was censured and later dismissed from his command (1777).

HOPKINS, SIR FREDERICK GOWLAND (1861–1947), British scientist, who carried out at Cambridge fundamental research on amino acids and vitamins. He was awarded the Nobel Prize for medicine in 1929.

HOPKINS, HARRY LLOYD (1890–1946), US social worker and administrator who became executive director of the Temporary Emergency Relief Administration in New York (1931). Thereafter his career was intimately associated with F. D. Roosevelt and the New Deal. He was successively director of the Federal Emergency Relief Administration (1933), the Civil Works Administration (1933), the Works Progress Administration (1935), secretary of commerce (1938–40), and administrator of the Lend-Lease programme (1941). He was committed to the principles of social welfare and exercised considerable influence over the development of the New Deal. During the Second World War he frequently acted as the president's confidential envoy on overseas missions and accompanied Roosevelt to conferences at Casablanca, Cairo, Teheran, and Yalta.

HOPKINS, SAMUEL (1721–1803), American theologian, who became a Congregational minister and a disciple of Jonathan Edwards. His book, *System of Doctrines Contained in Divine Revelation* (1793), was the first systematic treatise by an American theologian and was influential in American religious life.

HOPKINSON, FRANCIS (1737–91), American politician, jurist, poet, and musician. He was a representative from NJ in the Continental Congress (1776), signed the Declaration of Independence (1776), and was judge of the Admiralty Court of PA (1779–89). He wrote political satires in prose and verse and the words and music of the first secular songs published in America.

HOPLITES, ancient Greek heavy infantry, whose equipment consisted of bronze helmet, corslet, greaves, round shield, iron thrusting spear, and short sword. Individual items, adapted perhaps by early Greek mercenaries from foreign models, appeared in Greece *c.* 750 BC and the whole panoply was developed by 650. The spread of hoplite armour among small farmers throughout Greece in 7th cent. and the superiority of hoplites in close formation (*phalanx*) over aristocratic cavalry, contributed towards the emergence of the tyrants (*c.* 650). Sparta based her leading position in 6th–5th cents on her well-trained citizen hoplite army. In 4th cent. the classical hoplite began to be eclipsed with the development of light-armed troops and more effective use of cavalry, particularly by the Macedonians.

HOPTON OF STRATTON, RALPH HOPTON, Baron (1596–1652), English Royalist commander in the civil wars, who held the west for Charles I (1643), and advanced into Hampshire (1644) before finally submitting to Fairfax in Cornwall (March 1646).

HORACE (65–8 BC), Q. Horatius Flaccus, Roman poet, who became virtually poet laureate of the Augustan regime. He was born the son of a freedman at Venusia in Apulia and educated at Rome, and Athens, where he joined Brutus' army and fought at Philippi (42). On returning to Rome he began to write poetry while working as a clerk and was introduced by Virgil to Augustus' associate Maecenas. His works include the Epodes in iambic metre; two books of Satires or Miscellanies and two books of Epistles, all of which throw valuable light on Roman society; the Carmen Saeculare, written at Augustus' command for the Secular

Games (17); the so-called *Ars Poetica*; and the four books of the Odes, his greatest achievement.

HORATII, legendary trio of brothers in Rome of the 7th cent. BC, whose defeat of the three Curiatii of Alba Longa was followed by the moving of the Alban population to Rome.

HORE-BELISHA, LESLIE HORE-BELISHA, Baron (1893–1957), British lawyer and politician who became Liberal MP for Devonport, which constituency he represented (after 1931 as a Liberal National) until 1945.

During the 1930s he held varied government posts: parliamentary secretary to the board of trade, financial secretary to the treasury, minister of state for transport—as such giving his name to Belisha beacons, drafting a new highway code, and starting driving tests for motorists—and secretary of state for war, carrying out a number of controversial and far-ranging reforms to modernize the army. He was a member of the war cabinet (1939–40) and minister of national insurance in the 1945 caretaker government.

HORMUZ, Iranian port and island commanding the entrance to the Persian Gulf. It enjoyed great prosperity through the spice trade from South-East Asia in the 14th–16th cents, came under Portuguese control (1507), and was recovered by Iran with the aid of the English East India Co. (1622).

HORN, ARVILD BERNHARD (1664–1742), Swedish statesman who served Charles XII as general, diplomat, and (1705) minister in Stockholm, but lost favour being thought too cautious and too politic. At the time of Charles's death he was anti-absolutist and supported the enthronement of Frederick, under whom he became the leading figure in the Council (1720–38). He reduced the national debt and stimulated industrial and commercial development along mercantilist lines. Abroad he favoured alliance with the western powers and a policy of peace, which caused his overthrow in 1738–9 by the War party, known as the Hats.

HORN, GUSTAVUS (1592–1657), Gustavus Adolphus's chief general in Germany. After Breitenfeld he joined his father-in-law, Axel Oxenstierna, in urging an advance on Vienna. He was in command at the battle of Nordlingen (1634), where he was defeated and taken prisoner by the imperialists. In 1643–5 he headed the invasion of Scania.

HORNER, FRANCIS (1778–1817), British politician, who with Francis Jeffrey and Sydney Smith, founded the *Edinburgh Review* (1802). He entered parliament as MP for Wendover (1807) and moved for the appointment of the Bullion Committee, of which he became chairman (1810). He opposed the Corn Law of 1815 and was becoming a leading opposition speaker, similar in general political opinions to Brougham, when he died.

HORNIGHK, WILLIAM VON (*fl.* 17th cent.), Austrian cameralist philosopher, son-in-law of Joachim Becher, the chemist and natural philosopher, who expounded in his pamphlet 'Osterreich uber alles—wann es nur will' (1684) the theoretical basis of the paternalistic, bureaucratic state of the Habsburg, Leopold I.

HORSE SACRIFICE, elaborate ancient Indian ceremony by which a horse was let free to roam about, closely followed by the king's army. All territory crossed by the horse was considered justly conquered and any opponents were dealt with. After a year the horse was caught and sacrified in a complicated rite. It was one of the legitimate means used by Indian rulers to extend their territory in a time when there was still much uncultivated land. It fell into abeyance after the Gupta period.

HORSESHOE BEND, BATTLE OF (27 March 1814). Andrew Jackson, commanding 3000 troops and some friendly Indians, attacked Creek Indians at Tohopeta on the Tallapoosa river in AL. Over 800 Creek warriors were killed. The battle resulted in the treaty of Fort Jackson (9 Aug. 1814) and broke the Indians' power in south-eastern US.

HORTENSIAN LAW, measure carried at Rome in 287 BC by the plebeian Q. Hortensius, who had been declared dictator after a secession of the people from the city. It provided that decrees (*plebiscita*) of the *concilium plebis* should be binding on the whole citizen-body and is usually taken as marking the end of the Struggle of the Orders.

HORTENSIUS, Q., HORTALUS (114–50 BC), Roman orator, consul in 69, and Cicero's greatest rival at the beginning of his career, as well as his opponent in the Verres case, though later frequently associated with him in supporting senatorial supremacy.

HO-SHEN (1750–99), Manchu bannerman and an example *par excellence* of mandarin corruption, nepotism, greed, and ambition in Ch'ing China. He rose rapidly to power from relatively humble origins. In 1776, when 26, he was appointed grand councillor and a minister of the imperial household. He had the complete confidence of the Ch'ienlung emperor and his position was further secured by the betrothal of his son to the emperor's youngest and favourite daughter in 1780. As the emperor became increasingly senile, Ho-shen practically dominated the political scene, holding as many as 20 offices concurrently, including the important and lucrative post of president of the board of revenue. Even after the abdication of the Ch'ien-lung emperor, Ho-shen remained in control of the administration of the empire, and the Chia-ch'ing emperor was allowed little say in matters of government. Following the death of the Ch'ien-lung emperor, he was arrested and ordered to take his own life. His ascendency and network of corruption undoubtedly had a permanently debilitating effect on the government and marked the beginning of the decline of the Ch'ing dynasty.

HOSPITALLER, KNIGHTS. The Knights of the Order of the Hospital of St John of Jerusalem, otherwise known as the Knights Hospitaller and Knights of Malta, was one of a number of nursing orders established between the 11th and 13th cents. It was founded (*c.* 1118) by Raymond of Le Puy at the hospital of St John in Jerusalem, with the specific task of caring for pilgrims and the sick in the Holy Land. Like the Knights Templar, it was a military organization but, unlike them, it had a companion order of sisters to care for women. The order was dedicated to fighting unbelievers and provided military stability in the crusader states, where it held major fortresses. It was ruled by a grand master and its headquarters and chief hospital was at Jerusalem until 1187. It remained in the Holy Land in the rump kingdom of Jerusalem until the fall of Acre (1291), after which it was reformed and established itself in Rhodes (1306–8) (which it defended against Moslem attacks) (1306–1523), then moved to Malta, which it ruled from 1530 to 1798, when the island was annexed by Napoleon. Since 1834 its headquarters has been at Rome.

HOSSBACH MEMORANDUM (5 Nov. 1937), report of a secret conference between Hitler and his military chiefs, held in Berlin. Those present were Blomberg, the war minister; Neurath, the foreign minister; and Fritsch, Raeder, and Göring, the commanders-in-chief respectively of army, navy, and air force. Hossbach, Hitler's adjutant, attended the meeting but took no notes and wrote his account of the proceedings from memory some days later. According to the memorandum, Hitler began by discussing the German *Lebensraum* problem, and then went on to consider a number of ways in which this might be solved by force. He sketched Germany's potential strategy in a variety of military situations that might be expected to arise in Europe, and predicted a

German invasion of Austria and Czechoslovakia in 1938 (though in the circumstances of a French–Italian–English war that did not in fact occur). Hitler described his conclusions as the fruits of four and a half years of thought, and stressed that Germany's problems could ultimately only be solved by force. The conference is sometimes said to have laid down Hitler's timetable for the Second World War; although this is a somewhat exaggerated interpretation of the proceedings, the meeting did mark the date at which Hitler openly committed himself to an aggressive foreign policy and military strategy. The new line became evident in the new mobilization orders subsequently issued to the army, which took account of the situations postulated by Hitler.

HOSTIENSIS (*fl.* 13th cent.). Henry of Segusia (Susa), known as Hostiensis (from Ostia, of which he was cardinal-bishop from 1262), was the greatest canon lawyer of his time. A product of the law school of Bologna and a civil as well as a canon lawyer, his *Summa* is a synthesis of Roman civil and canon laws and a work of profound influence which was regarded as a standard text for centuries.

HOTHAM, SIR CHARLES (1806–55), Australian naval officer, who in 1854 became lieutenant-governor of Vic. He was an able financial administrator, but found it difficult to interpret his gubernatorial duties while Vic. adapted itself for responsible government in a period of political, economic, and social uneasiness caused by the gold rushes to that colony.

HOTMAN, FRANÇOIS (1524–90), French Huguenot jurist and political writer. His most important treatise, *Franco-Gallia*, based on an analysis of the French constitution, was published in 1573 while he was in exile in Geneva. In it he emphasized the authority of the estates over that of the king and advocated the right of resistance. His other works include *Discours sur l'Estude des Lois* (1567), in which he stressed the importance of customary law as against Roman law.

HOUGHTON, JOHN (*c.* 1488–1535), prior of the London Carthusian monks. He was sent to the Tower in 1534 for refusing to take the oath of succession and supremacy. In April 1535 he and two other Carthusian priors were tried for treason, and after pressure had been exercised on the jury, condemned and executed at Tyburn.

HOUSE, EDWARD MANDELL (1858–1938), US businessman, political manager, and adviser to President Woodrow Wilson. He was deeply involved in Democratic politics in TX and was given the honorary title of 'Colonel'. In 1911 he met Woodrow Wilson and they became close associates. House worked to secure Wilson's presidential nomination in 1912 and, although he had no official appointment, when Wilson became president (1913), he served as his adviser and liaison with business and financial circles. In foreign affairs his influence was probably greater than that of Wilson's first secretary of state, W. J. Bryan. In 1915 and 1916 he served as the president's emissary to Europe, represented the US in the drawing-up of the pre-armistice agreement (1918), and was a member of the US delegation to the Paris Peace Conference. His compromises with the Allied powers over issues such as reparations were regarded by Wilson as a betrayal, and quarrels over the Versailles treaty terminated their friendship as abruptly as it had begun.

HOUSE OF BURGESSES, first representative assembly in North America. Called by Gov. Thomas Yeardly of the English colony in Virginia (1619), the House of Burgesses consisted of the governor, an appointive council, and elected representatives ('burgesses'). In the late 17th cent. the House of Burgesses became a bicameral body. From the beginning, the Virginia assembly claimed the right to initiate legislation, and by its control over the salary of the royal governor and other officials its powers were extended in the 17th and 18th cents. The House of Burgesses played a significant role in rallying opposition to British colonial policy (1765–75).

HOUSES OF PARLIAMENT FIRE (1834) in London destroyed the buildings, with the exception of Westminster Hall and the speaker's house, and many manuscript records and other material, much of it belonging to the House of Commons. The fire was thought to have started in a flue overheated by the burning (following the 1834 exchequer reforms) of the old tallies used as receipts. The buildings were replaced by the present Palace of Westminster, designed by Barry.

HOUSTON, SAMUEL (1793–1863), US politician, who served as a Democrat in the US House of Representatives (1823–7) and was elected governor of TN (1827). After resigning for personal reasons in 1835, he moved to TX and became an Indian trader. He fought for Texan Independence from Mexico, defeated Santa Anna at the battle of San Jacinto (1836), became first president of TX (1836–8, 1841–4), and a US senator (1846–59). As governor of TX (1859–61) he strongly opposed secession and resigned when his state joined the Confederacy.

HOUTMAN, CORNELIS DE (d. 1599), one of the leaders of the first Dutch expedition to the Indonesian Archipelago (1595–97). He was murdered on board his own ship off Atjeh.

HOWARD, HENRY (*c.* 1517–47), English soldier, courtier, and poet. As the eldest son of the Duke of Norfolk, he enjoyed the courtesy title of the Earl of Surrey, by which he was known. He served in Henry VIII's French and Scottish wars in the 1540s, but was executed on the king's orders on a trumped-up charge of high treason. The real reason was the jealousy of the Seymour family, who sought an influence with the Crown that the Howards were challenging. Surrey's poetry included a translation of some of the *Aeneid* into blank verse, and the introduction of the sonnet into English literature.

HOWARD, JOHN (1726–90), British philanthropist and Quaker, notable for his efforts to improve conditions in prisons. He particularly attacked the bad sanitary conditions and the system of paying gaolers out of fees extracted from the prisoners.

HOWARD FAMILY in England, Catholic family closely associated with Henry VIII's ecclesiastical policies. Katherine married him after being brought to his notice by the Catholic and conservative party hostile to Protestant influences at court. Henry married her after his separation from the Lutheran Anne of Cleves (1540). But Katherine, unchaste before her marriage, was guilty of considerable indiscretion after it, details of which were established by Abp Cranmer and the Protestant faction, and she and her lovers were executed.

HOWDEN (HOVEDEN), ROGER OF (d. ?1201), royal clerk who served as justiciar of the forest under King Henry II of England and accompanied Richard I on crusade. He was the most important chronicler of his time and probably author of the *Gesta Henrici Secundi*, a major source of information on Henry's reign, and was certainly the author of the *Chronica*, which is a revision and continuation of the *Gesta* up to 1201 and the leading source for Richard's reign.

HOWE, RICHARD HOWE, Earl (1726–99), British admiral, who resigned his command of the North American station in 1778 because he was dissatisfied with the political conduct of the American War of Independence. After the war he became first lord of the admiralty (1783–8) and vice-admiral of England (1792–6). He commanded the British fleet on the

'Glorious First of June' (1794). He was popular with his men and was chosen to pacify the mutineers at Spithead (1797).

HOWE, WILLIAM HOWE, 5th Viscount (Irish) (1729–1814), British MP and soldier who commanded a battalion at the siege of Louisbourg (1759) and at the capture of Quebec (1759). As a Whig, Howe represented Nottingham in parliament (1758–80). He was appointed to the command of all British troops in America (1775). In the ensuing American War of Independence he abandoned Boston (1776) and with his brother, Admiral Richard Howe, captured New York (1776) and Philadelphia (1777). After being criticized for failing to take action against colonial troops, Howe resigned and returned to Britain (1778). He and his brother stoutly defended their military policies in America.

HOWE, ELIAS (1819–67), US inventor of the first sewing machine, which he patented in 1846. The important features were that the eye of the needle was near its point and that a lock-stitch was made by two threads using a shuttle. The sewing machine rapidly came into use, being the first product of the Industrial Revolution devised to assist women's domestic work.

HOWE, JOSEPH (1804–73), Canadian journalist, orator, and politician. In 1827 Howe purchased the *Novascotian* and made it into one of the leading newspapers of British North America. His successful defence against a charge of criminal libel helped to establish the freedom of the press in Canada and led to his election to the NS assembly (1836). In the legislature he led a successful movement to establish responsible government for NS (1848). He became chief commissioner of railways (1854–7), prime minister of NS (1860–3), and lieutenant-governor of NS (1873).

HOWE, JULIA WARD (1819–1910), US writer, who wrote the patriotic 'Battle Hymn of the Republic', after visiting a military camp near Washington, DC (1861).

HOWE, LOUIS McHENRY (1871–1935), US journalist and political adviser to F. D. Roosevelt. He was associated (1906–12) with the attempt of reform Democrats to break the power of Tammany Hall, and worked for the state Saratoga Springs Commission (1909–10). He first met Roosevelt in 1911, worked with him in the 1912 presidential election campaign, and became one of his closest political associates. Roosevelt owed much of his subsequent political success to Howe's political acumen and devoted service.

HOWE FAMILY in Australia. George Howe (1769–1821), with his sons Robert (1795–1829) and George Terry (1803–63), contributed much to the beginning of printing and publishing in Australia. George worked in London on *The Times*, but in 1799–1800 was transported to NSW for shoplifting, where he produced the first book printed in Australia (1802) and eventually became government printer. In 1803 he began publication, with Robert, of the *Sydney Gazette and NSW Advertiser*. George Terry, born in Sydney, went to Van Diemen's Land and founded the *Tasmanian and Port Dalrymple Advertiser* in Launceston (1825).

HOWELLS, WILLIAM DEAN (1837–1920), US novelist, journalist, and literary critic. The success of his campaign biography of Lincoln (1860) gained him the post of consul in Venice, where he spent the Civil War years. *Venetian Life* (1866) was assembled from travel letters and commentaries on everyday life first published in the *Boston Advertiser*. His first novel, *Their Wedding Journey* (1872), was followed by *A Modern Instance* (1882), *The Rise of Silas Lapham* (1885), and *A Hazard of New Fortunes* (1889). Howells continued his study of social and economic problems in *A Traveller from Altruria* (1894) and *Through the Eye of the Needle* (1907).

As a critic his influence was profound. He wrote extensively for *The Nation*, *Atlantic Monthly*, of which he was editor-in-chief (1871–81), and *Harper's Monthly*. Howells produced over 100 volumes of novels, plays, poetry, and criticism, and was elected president of the American Academy of Arts and Letters in 1908.

Van Wyck Brooks, *Howells: his life and world* (New York, 1959).
Edwin H. Cady, *The Road to Realism* (Syracuse, 1956).

AW

HOXHA, ENVER (1908–), Albanian politician, leader of communist Albania, and framer of its independent course. Hoxha was born near the Greek frontier, and won a state scholarship to France, where he studied in Paris. He became associated there with left-wing Albanian émigrés and joined several political groups. From Paris he went to Brussels and in 1933 was studying law while serving as secretary to the honorary Albanian consul to Belgium. On his return to Albania he formed (1936) a communist discussion group with Koce Xoce, which was to be an important step towards the formation of the communist party. Not long after the Yugoslavs organized the Albanian party, Hoxha became one of its leading figures. In 1943 he was named its secretary-general and supreme commander of the Albanian resistance forces. But the Yugoslavs distrusted Hoxha because of his seeming unwillingness to subordinate himself to Yugoslav policy. While the Yugoslav favourite, Xoxe, was predominant, Hoxha maintained a cautious and circumspect attitude. He was rewarded with Soviet support in 1948, when Xoxe's career foundered on the Soviet–Yugoslav split. Hoxha's position remained powerful until efforts for a Soviet–Yugoslav rapprochement were begun. Saved once by the Hungarian revolution, Hoxha's position again became precarious in 1960. He could secure himself only by submitting entirely to the will of the Kremlin or by seeking a strong ally abroad. Choosing the second course, he turned to the Chinese. The definitive break with the Soviet Union came in Nov. 1961 and Hoxha's position was entrenched. At one point in the controversy he called Khrushchev 'the greatest counter-revolutionary, charlatan and clown the world has ever known' and thereafter Albania's relations with her European neighbours were soured.

JMK

HOYSALA DYNASTY, line of ancient Indian rulers in present Mysore who, after having subsisted in subordinate states for centuries, rose to imperial status by the end of the 12th cent. AD. From then till their decline (after *c.* 1335), the Hoysalas were an important factor in south Indian politics and culture, notably in art and architecture.

HROSWITHA (*c.* 935–*c.* 1002), German nun, author of six Latin 'comedies', which were intended as edifying substitutes for the plays of Terence, and in which material from the lives of the saints is presented in conjunction with elements of comedy and even farce; as such they form a link between the earlier imitations of classical drama and the later miracle plays. She was the only woman dramatist of the Dark Ages.

HSIA, name of a 'dynasty' alleged in Chinese literature to have existed before the Shang kingdom (traditionally 1766–1122 BC). While Hsia bore some importance in China's historical tradition, its existence has yet to be substantiated.

HSIEN-FÊNG, reign-title of I-chu (*reg.* 1831–61), fourth son of the Tao-kuang emperor and seventh Emperor of the Ch'ing dynasty. The Hsien-fêng reign (1851–62) was plagued by social and political unrest which expressed itself in the Muslim Rebellion in the south-west, the Nien Rebellion in the North China Plain, and the Taiping Rebellion in central and south China. The anti-foreign policy adopted by the emperor and his ministers led to further humiliations at the hand of the Anglo-French forces which took Peking in 1860, forcing the emperor to flee to Jehol, where he died the following year.

HSIEN-PEI, confederacy of Central Asiatic peoples. Rising from the north-east of China during the 1st or 2nd cent. AD, they took the place of the Hsiung-nu as the dominant ethnic element lying to China's north, whose towns and farmlands they raided. In the 4th and 5th cents groups of Hsien-pei peoples took over parts of north China and established a few short-lived dynasties, such as the Earlier Yen or Western Ch'in. One group, known as the T'o-pa, founded the more stable dynasty of Northern Wei.

HSI-HSIA, state established in north-western China by Tangut (Tibetan) tribes 1038–1227.

HSIN DYNASTY (AD 8–23), regime established in China by Wang Mang in the hope of replacing the Han dynasty.

HSIUNG-NU, nomad peoples of Central Asia sometimes identified with the Huns. After achieving a short-lived unity of leadership, *c.* 200 BC, the Hsiung-nu frequently launched raids into north China. Varied results followed the frequent wars with the Han dynasty, which was at times able to avert the danger of invasion by separating the Hsiung-nu into two groups.

HSÜ SHIH-CH'ANG (1855–1939), president of China during the early republic. He was closely associated with Yuan Shih-k'ai before and after the 1911 Revolution. In 1918 he became president, a rare civilian holder of this office. He backed the wrong side in the Fengtien–Chihli War (1922) and was forced to resign.

HSÜAN TSANG, Chinese devotee of Buddhism. From 629 to 645 he travelled to India and back by way of Central Asia, so as to procure copies of Buddhist sacred writings. On returning to Ch'ang-an he undertook the translation of 74 Buddhist works into Chinese from Sanskrit.

HSÜAN-TSUNG, title of a T'ang Emperor (*reg.* 712–55). The cultural brilliance and patronage of poets and painters that was practised at his court have led to the description of the reign as China's golden age. The reign ended in imperial ignominy and flight owing to the outbreak of An Lu-shan's rebellion.

HSÜN-TZU, collection of writings of the philosopher Hsün Ch'ing (340–245 BC). The book includes essays on specific themes or topics of government and sets a new style of logical argument and well-organized exposition. In view of the inherent wickedness of human nature, the *Hsün-tzu* stresses the need for education, discipline, and restraint by means of accepted conventions of behaviour.

HU FENG (1903–), Chinese literary critic and a disciple of the writer Lu Hsün, who stood for the right of the artist to creative freedom. As a Communist Party member, Hu accepted political discipline, but not restrictions on creativity. He clashed with Mao Tse-tung's view that literature must be the instrument of political utility. In 1954 Hu launched an attack on the sterility of contemporary writing, and was bitterly denounced; his chief prosecutor was Chou Yang. Hu was imprisoned, and has not been heard of since (1970).

HU HAN-MIN (1879–1936), disciple of Sun Yat-sen. He worked closely with Sun for many years and became the chief interpreter of Sun's political philosophy. He took over Sun's responsibilities in Canton when Sun went to Peking (1924), and but for the murder of Liao Chung-k'ai (1925), in which Hu's cousin was implicated, might have continued to lead the Kuomintang. Instead he was forced to leave China, and never recovered his position within the Kuomintang. He later attacked Chiang Kai-shek as a perverter of Sun's ideals.

HU SHIH (1891–1962), Chinese educator and diplomat. In 1917 Hu published proposals for the reform of the written Chinese language, and started the movement for the introduction of vernacular Chinese. He played a leading role in intellectual life, particularly during the 4 May Movement (1919), but stayed out of politics until the Anti-Japanese War started (1937). He was then sent as ambassador to the US.

HUANCAVELICA MERCURY MINE, in the Peruvian province of the same name, discovered during the latter half of the 16th cent. Huancavelica soon became a government monopoly. It formed an essential part of the Spanish mining system because mercury was needed for the amalgamation process of silver extraction from its ore, a process used in Peru and Mexico during the Colonial Period, but now obsolete.

HUANG HSING (1874–1916), Chinese revolutionary, who, with Sun Yat-sen, provided the leadership for the overthrow of the Ch'ing dynasty. While in Tokyo (1902–3) he studied military strategy, target-shooting, and politics, with the aim of overthrowing the Manchu government. On returning to Hunan, he founded the Hsing-chung Hui 'Revive China Society') and planned a rising in a number of cities in Hunan in Nov. 1904. Their failure led him to visit Japan a second time and it was there he met Sun Yat-sen. The two founded the T'ung-meng Hui ('United League') in 1905, Sun being its chief and Huang its second-in-command. During the next few years Huang made many various unsuccessful attempts to stage localized risings in south China and to convert the officers of the New Army, which he believed would be the key to overthrowing the Manchus. Late in 1910, Huang, Sun, and Hu Han-min (1897–1936), who had succeeded in converting some officers, planned an attack on Canton, supported with funds (180,000 Hong Kong dollars) raised in South-East Asia, Canada, and the United States. The rising (April 1911) ended in failure and Huang escaped to Hong Kong. However, a successful revolt at Wuchang organized by Huang's associates led to his appointment as commander-in-chief of the revolutionary army on his arrival at that city. After the establishment of the republic (Jan. 1912), Huang was made minister of war, but he soon disbanded his troops in order to form a united government under Yüan Shih-k'ai, to whom Sun had offered the presidency. Meanwhile, Huang, Sun, and others, by expanding the *T'ung-meng Hui,* formed the Kuomintang. As Yüan's anti-republican intentions became clear, the Kuomintang declared war on him and gave command of its forces to Huang. But Huang's troops failed him and he fled to Japan, where he broke with Sun over the policy of reorganizing the Kuomintang. Huang left for the US, where he spent two years raising funds for the anti-Yüan cause. After Yüan's death (6 June 1916), Huang returned to China and reconciled his differences with Sun.

HUANG TSUNG-HSI (1610–95), Ming loyalist who organized guerrilla warfare against the conquering Manchus in the 1640s. He retired in 1649 and devoted the rest of his life to scholarship. Among his numerous works was the first critical study of Chinese intellectual history. The *History of the Ming Dynasty,* compiled under Manchu auspices, drew heavily on his historical writings. Unlike most classical scholars, Huang interested himself in contemporary politics, and his political ideas later had an important influence on Liang Ch'i-ch'ao and other late Ch'ing reformers. Huang also wrote extensively on mathematics, calendrical science, geography, literature, and philosophy.

HUÁSCAR (d. 1533), son of the Inca monarch, Huayna Capac, he fought against his half-brother, Atahuallpa, for possession of the empire, but was defeated and executed.

HUAYNA CAPAC (d. *c.* 1525), last great Inca leader before the Spanish conquest. He ruled a huge empire stretching from northern Argentina and central Chile to the Ecuadorian–Colombian border. Huayna Capac made the mistake of dividing his empire between Atahuallpa and Huáscar, two of his sons. After his death civil war broke out between them and weakened Inca resistance to Spanish invasion.

HUBERTUSBURG, TREATY OF (1763), peace settlement between Prussia, Austria, and Saxony, which ended the Seven Years War in Europe and broadly speaking restored the status quo. It confirmed the arrangements of the treaty of Berlin (1745). Frederick II of Prussia was finally recognized in Silesia. In return, he recognized Austria's claim to the succession of Modena and promised to vote for the election of the Empress Maria Theresa's son Joseph as King of the Romans. He failed to gain Saxony, which had been his political objective in starting the war.

Hubertusburg tacitly recognized Prussia's position as a great European power, though it left Frederick politically isolated.

HUBMAIER, BALTASAR (d. 1528), Swiss theologian and one of the founders of Anabaptism who was tortured in Zürich for his views on believers' baptism (1525) and driven thence to Augsburg and Nikolsburg in Moravia, where he became the leader of a popular radical movement. Despite his tolerance and his support for the civil power, he and his wife were captured by the imperial authorities and taken to Vienna. Hubmaier was burnt and his wife drowned in the Danube for heresy.

HUDAYBIYA, AL-, village on the edge of the sacred terrain (*haram*) at Mecca. Here, in 628, the Prophet Muhammad negotiated a truce for ten years with the Meccans, who had opposed his mission. The Prophet agreed to withdraw from his proposed pilgrimage (*'umra*) to Mecca, which he deferred until the following year.

HUDSON, GEORGE (1800–71), English draper, politician, and railway promoter, who was largely responsible for the network of north-eastern England. He entered local politics in the 1830s, and by 1837 was chairman of the proprietors of the York and North Midland Railway. He then promoted the completion of the line from York to Edinburgh, and other lines in the region, and, for reasons of local patriotism, developed York as the centre of the system. At the height of the railway 'mania' (1844) he controlled 1016 miles (1630 kms) of railway. He was elected MP for Sunderland, where he was chairman of the dock company (1845–59). Hudson's financial control of his enterprises was increasingly casual, and he became bankrupt in the slump of 1847.

HUDSON, HENRY (*c.* 1550–1611), English navigator, probably grandson of the London alderman who helped to found the Muscovy Co. (1555). He was employed by the Muscovy Co. as commander of the *Hopeful* and set out to cross the north pole in search of the 'spice islands' (1607). He skirted Greenland and Spitzbergen, but was unable to find a north-east passage. A second expedition in 1608 also failed. In 1609 he took service with the Amsterdam Chamber of the Dutch East India Co. and as commander of the *Half Moon* crossed the Atlantic, seeking a north-west passage. Reaching NS, he sailed north to discover the river and bay which has since borne his name. In a second attempt to find a north-west route, once again under English auspices, he and his men in the ship *Discovery* spent the winter of 1610–11 in the frozen Hudson Strait. On the return voyage his crew mutinied and set him, his son, and seven others adrift in a boat (21 June 1611), after which they presumably drowned.

HUDSON BAY, vast gulf or inland sea in north-eastern Canada. It may have been discovered by John Cabot (1498), but it was first explored by Henry Hudson (1610). Exploratory voyages followed by Sir Thomas Button (1612), William Baffin (1615), Jens Munch (1619), and Luke Fox and Thomas James (1631), during which time the entire coast was charted.

Médard Chouart des Groseilliers, in the service of the British, built the first trading post on its shores at the mouth of the Rupert river (1668), and the Hudson's Bay Co. received a charter from King Charles II for exclusive trading rights (1670). Posts, primarily for fur-trading, were built at the mouths of the Nelson, Moose, and Albany rivers. France and Britain contended for control of the Hudson Bay area, and British suzerainty was recognized by the treaty of Utrecht (1713).

A period of cut-throat competition with independent traders and a rival Scottish group, the North West Co., led to the 'fur-traders war', which ended when the two companies merged (1821), creating a fur-trading monopoly stretching from Labrador to OR, from the Red River to the Yukon. Following Canadian confederation, the Hudson's Bay Co.'s territorial rights were transferred to Canada (1869). The company however retained its posts and trading rights and became a commercial corporation chiefly concerned with the fur trade and retail merchandising. In 1880 the Hudson Bay Railway was planned: construction began in 1910, was completed in 1931, and counteracted the monopoly held by the Canadian Pacific Railway.   BB

HUE, imperial capital of Viet-nam. It became the capital in 1802, following the unification of the country by Gia-Long; previous emperors reigned mostly at Hanoi. Much of the imperial city and palace survives as a national monument, though part was destroyed by fire when the Viet-minh retreated from the city and the French reoccupied it, in Feb. 1947. The city was the scene of an even more furious battle during the 'Tet Offensive' of 1968.

HUE, TREATY OF (1883–4), between Viet-nam and France. The first draft of the treaty negotiated by Jules Harmand in Aug. 1883, following French occupation of the Tongking Delta, was more severe than the second, negotiated by Patenotre in June 1884. By the latter, the one finally ratified, Viet-nam recognized French protection over Annan and Tongking, and stipulated arrangements for French control of those territories. The treaty was revoked by the Emperor Bao Dai in April 1945.

HUERTA, VICTORIANO (1854–1916), Mexican general and president. Huerta rose through the army during the regime of Porfirio Díaz. After being involved in financial scandals, he was retired by President Francisco Madero, and then recalled to put down a revolt led by Félix Díaz. In 1913 Huerta led a revolt against Madero, and seems to have been involved in his murder. After seizing the presidency, he proved to be reactionary and brutal. Uprisings led by Venustiano Carranza, Francisco Villa, and Emiliano Zapata weakened his government and gradually reduced the area under his control. His position was further eroded by his inability to win recognition from the US, and corruption within the regime alienated many of his original supporters. On 15 July 1914 he resigned and fled abroad. The Huerta episode is thought of as a hiatus in the Mexican Revolution.

In 1916 he was taken into custody by US authorities for allegedly attempting to mount a conspiracy against the Mexican government from US soil.

HUGENBERG, ALFRED (1865–1951), German lawyer, industrialist, and politician, who became an influential figure in the Ruhr industry and, in 1909, rose to the position of chairman of the Krupp *directorium*. At the same time he engaged in politics and became an exponent of the violently nationalist and expansionist Pan-German League. In 1915 he seized an opportunity of directly combining business with politics when, as chairman of the *Bergbau-Verein*, he used the industrial funds at his disposal to purchase the right-wing Scherl publishing house. He assumed the chairmanship of the Scherl board of directors and over the years assembled a huge press empire. By 1928 about 50 per cent of the German papers subscribed to Hugenberg's *Telegraphen-Union* news service;

he controlled four dailies and eighteen periodicals and, in 1927, acquired the country's biggest film company, the UFA. The papers published by his empire not only had a considerable share in arousing middle-class antagonism to the Weimar republic, but also helped Hugenberg to gain prominence within the DNVP. In 1928 the party chose him as its leader. Henceforth he used every means at his disposal to destroy the republic and laboured to bring about an alliance with Hitler. But when this was finally achieved in Jan. 1933 Hugenberg, now minister of food and economics in the Hitler cabinet, soon found that he had grossly misjudged his own power. By the end of June 1933 his resignation from the government was accepted and his political movement allowed to initiate its self-dissolution. Hugenberg, though retaining a Reichstag seat until 1945, passed into oblivion and died on his estate near Rinteln in 1951. Few people played a more decisive role in bringing Hitler to power.   VRB

HUGH CAPET (*reg.* 987–96), King of France. As the heir to the vast feudal lordship of his father, Hugh the Great, in northern France and a descendant of earlier kings, Capet was elected King on the death of the last Carolingian ruler, Louis V. This was in preference to the latter's relative, Charles, Duke of Lotharingia, because the imperial government in Germany feared Charles and preferred Hugh. He initiated the continuous rule of the Capetian dynasty.

HUGH THE GREAT, Duke of the Franks (d. 956), powerful French potentate in the second quarter of the 10th cent. He restored to the French throne in 936 the Carolingian Louis d'Outremer, but kept him almost powerless. Hugh's son, Hugh Capet, replaced the Carolingians as kings of France in 987.

HUGHES, CHARLES EVANS (1862–1948), US jurist, politician, and public servant. As Republican governor of New York (1907–10) he sponsored a wide range of reform legislation and investigated abuses in life insurance and in the gas and coal industries. He was appointed to the US Supreme Court (1910) and was the unsuccessful Republican presidential candidate in 1916. After Harding's election as president, Hughes became secretary of state (1921–5) and he was largely responsible for the achievements of the Washington Conference (1921–2). In 1926 he was appointed to the Permanent Court of Arbitration at The Hague and in 1928 was elected to the Permanent Court of International Justice. He was chief justice of the US Supreme Court (1930–4) during a period of constitutional crisis following a series of decisions often made by a narrow majority, the effect of which was to render important social legislation unconstitutional. He succeeded in preserving the unity and independence of the court in the face of political attack, opposed President F. D. Roosevelt's court reorganization plan (1937), and, in a series of decisions on which he spoke for the majority, led the court to a position of cautious approval of legislation designed to effect social and economic change. Though a defender of civil liberties and of freedom of speech and of the press, Hughes also believed in a constitutional jurisprudence that emphasized the stability and continuity of judicial decisions.

HUGHES, JOHN JOSEPH, archbishop (1797–1864), US Roman Catholic leader, born in Ireland. He emigrated to the US in 1817 and entered a seminary in MD three years later. After being ordained a priest (1826), and appointed to a parish in Philadelphia, he became a skilful polemicist for Catholic rights against Protestant nativism, was consecrated coadjutant bishop of New York (1838), and archbishop (1851). He strongly supported the Union cause during the American Civil War, served as an unofficial presidential agent in Paris, Dublin, and Rome, and played a major role in ending the New York Draft Riots (1863).

HUGHES, THOMAS (1822–96), British lawyer and Liberal politician, whose *Tom Brown's Schooldays* (1857) helped to corrupt Thomas Arnold's ideal of the Victorian public school by unduly stressing the importance of manliness and athleticism. But Hughes's Christian Socialism helped him to preserve the original ideal of co-operative production and education into an age which tended increasingly to dilute co-operation into a movement for co-operative retailing.

HUGHES, WILLIAM MORRIS (1862–1952), Australian politician and prime minister of Australia (1915–23), who sat continuously in colonial and Commonwealth parliaments (1894–1952) and was a member of all Commonwealth Labor governments till 1916, and of non-Labor governments between 1934 and 1941. He was born in London, where, after a childhood spent in Wales, he became a pupil-teacher. He moved to Australia in 1884 and, after some years of casual work in the bush, settled in Sydney. He was one of the organizers of the 'solidarity' Labor Party, and in 1894 was elected to the NSW parliament, and on federation to the Commonwealth House of Representatives. In 1900 he formed the Sydney Wharf Labourers' Union and became its secretary. Later he formed the Carters' Union and the Waterside Workers' Federation, and was president of both. He was the most powerful union leader of the decade in Australia, and also the chief publicist and organizer of the Labor Party, with a weekly column in the Sydney *Daily Telegraph*. As attorney-general (1910–13), he was the principal advocate of enlarged Commonwealth powers.

On the outbreak of war in 1914, Hughes became an ardent advocate of a maximum war effort. He eliminated German firms from the base metals industry and organized wheat, sugar, and wool production under a controlling body consisting of Commonwealth, state, and private members. After succeeding Fisher as prime minister late in 1915, he went to England, where he made speeches and organized bulk sales of Australian products, to provide transport for which he established the Commonwealth shipping line. He tried to introduce conscription by referendum, but was defeated. He then left the Labor Party (1916) and joined his former opponents to form the Nationalist Party, which was returned with a large majority. In 1918 he sat in the Imperial War Cabinet, and at the peace conference in 1919 was a fearless defender of Australia's interests. He was prominent in the Imperial Conference of 1921, but was displaced as prime minister in 1923. Though active in politics until his death, he never regained the lead, and did not hold office after 1941.

L. F. Fitzhardinge, *William Morris Hughes, a political biography*, vol. 1, 'That Fiery Particle' (Sydney, 1964).   LFF

HUGO, VICTOR MARIE (1802–85), French writer and representative of the generation of romantic artists and writers who regarded political involvement in the liberal and democratic revolutions of their day as the natural corollary of their art. Hugo supported the Greeks in their struggle for independence and violently attacked Louis Napoleon's Second Empire.

HUGUCCIO (d. 1210). Hugh of Pisa, otherwise known as Huguccio, was Bp of Ferrara (1190–1210) and the most famous of decretalists. He studied and taught canon law at Bologna, where Pope Innocent III was his pupil. He wrote a standard dictionary of legal and ecclesiastical terms (*Liber Derivationum*) as well as the *Summa super Decreta*, the greatest of all commentaries on the Decretals of Gratian.

HUGUENOTS, French Protestants who derived their inspiration from Calvin and whose numbers increased rapidly in the mid-16th cent. through the influence of Genevan ministers. By 1562 there were 2000 churches in France, organized in hierarchical synods and dominated by the great nobility, *eg*, Condé and Coligny. Their rivalry with the Catholic family of Guise, who dominated the government of Francis

II, led to the outbreak of the wars of religion. After Francis's death (1560) the influence of Coligny grew until the massacre of St Bartholomew (24 Aug. 1572), when he and thousands of fellow Huguenots were murdered at the instigation of the Duke of Anjou and the Guises, aided by the Paris mob and abetted by the municipal authorities. Intermittent civil war followed and the most famous Huguenot publication, *Vindiciae contra Tyrannos* (1578), justified Huguenot resistance to a tyrannical ruler. The leader of the Huguenots in the later stages of the civil war was Henry of Navarre, the heir to the French throne from 1584, and after his succession and conversion to Catholicism (1593) he granted concessions to them to reunite a war-torn country. The Edict of Nantes (1598) guaranteed the Huguenots freedom of worship and the protection of 100 fortified towns. This Calvinist state within a state appeared to some Frenchmen more dangerous to internal security than religious division, and after the Huguenots of La Rochelle—at first ineffectively helped by the English under the Duke of Buckingham—rebelled against the Crown and then surrendered to Richelieu's forces (1628), they were deprived of their political sovereignty (peace of Alais, 1629). Like the English Nonconformists and the German Jews, deprived of political rights they concentrated their energies on commerce and industry. By Louis XIV's reign there were some 1 million Huguenots in France. Being concerned to promote religious and political unity, he applied pressure on them to be reconverted to Catholicism. At first they were bribed with money from the conversion bureaux (1677) and with promises of exemption from the *taille*, but later their places of worship were demolished under Louvois's direction and they were submitted to the *dragonnades*. Finally, in Oct. 1685, Louis revoked the Edict of Nantes. Supported by learned divines, *eg*, Bossuet and Fénelon, he ordered the destruction of all their temples, the ending of their services, the closure of their schools, and compulsory Catholic baptism. Many Huguenots accepted conversion, though the secret practice of their religion continued. About 200,000 escaped abroad and settled in the United Provinces, Brandenburg, Switzerland, and England, where they made a significant contribution to intellectual and economic progress. Louis's treatment of the Huguenots also massed Protestant Europe against him in both the Wars of the League of Augsburg and of the Spanish Succession. Persecution of the remaining Huguenots continued, *eg*, the Calais affair, but became more sporadic as the 18th cent. progressed, until the first restoration of normal rights by Loménie de Brienne's toleration edict of 1787.   MKS

HUGUES, VICTOR (d. 1826), French colonial governor, who was sent by the Revolutionary government to the West Indies (1794), where he declared the emancipation of the slaves in St Lucia and Guadeloupe. By thus encouraging them to rise, he recaptured both islands (1794), which had been lost to the British earlier in that year. While he permitted French royalists to embark with the British garrison defeated at Basseterre, he massacred 300 left behind, executing, in all, over 100 royalists on Guadeloupe. As governor of French Guiana he commanded the troops defeated at Cayenne by an Anglo-Portuguese attack (1809). After Cayenne fell he returned to France, settled again in French Guiana as a planter, but eventually retired to France (1822).

HUKBALAHAP, or *Huk,* abbreviation of *Hukbo nang Bayan Laban sa Hapon* (People's Army Against Japan) in the Philippines. It was organized on 29 March 1942 by a military committee headed by Luis M. Taruc and Casto Alejandrino and originally consisted of peasants who fought their landlords under the leadership of Filipino communists. At first the leaders attempted to rally into a united front Filipinos from all social classes who would fight alongside the peasants against the Japanese occupation forces. Based in the provinces of central Luzon Island, a centre of agrarian unrest in the 1930s, the *Hukbalahap* was largely the outcome of a decade of struggle, preparation, and organization by the Communist

Party of the Philippines, founded in 1930 and outlawed in 1931. The party was linked to the Comintern through the Philippine Committee of the Communist International operating in Los Angeles, CA. In 1938 a US communist, James Allen, had been responsible for arranging the pardon of Filipino communists serving prison sentences, some of whom later joined the *Hukbalahap*. But during the Japanese occupation of the Philippines, the *Hukbalahap* came under the tutelage and financial support of the Chinese communists, who helped to organize them militarily.

Affiliated to the *Hukbalahap* was the *Pambansang Kaisahang Magsaka* (*PKM*) (National Union of Farmers), which served as a reservoir of manpower for the *Hukbalahap*. The *Huk*, though disarmed by the Americans after the liberation of the Philippines from the Japanese, continued their fight against landlords and also challenged the legitimate Philippines government. In the elections of 1946 they supported the Nacionalista Party's presidential candidate against the Liberal Party's M. A. Roxas, who became the first president of the Philippines, and also secured the election of some of their own leaders, including L. Taruc, to congress; but the latter were prevented from taking office because of accusations against them of poll frauds. On 6 March 1948 President Roxas declared the *Hukbalahap* and the *PKM* illegal. But after Roxas's death in the following month, his successor, President Quirino, granted a general amnesty to the *Huk*'s followers, after negotiations with Luis Taruc in June 1948. Nevertheless, Taruc returned to the hills two months later, and in the following year the *Hukbalahap* was reorganized as the *Hukbong Magpapalaya nang Bayan* (People's Liberation Army), also known as *Huk*. On 18 Oct. 1950 most of the membership of the Politburo of the Communist Party were captured by government forces, which weakened the movement. In June 1957 President Garcia signed a new Anti-Subversion Law, outlawing the CPP, the *Huk*, and 'any successors of such organizations'. Dr Jesus Lava, at one time the CPP's secretary-general and one of the Politburo members who escaped capture in 1950, was apprehended in May 1964. Two other leaders were removed in 1970: Faustino del Mundo, alias Commander Sumulong, was captured in Sept. and Pedro Taruc was killed the following month. Since the death or imprisonment of the old guard of the communist leadership, young *Huk* leaders have appeared in central Luzon and by 1970 the CPP was reorganized and the *Huk* renamed the *Bagong Hukbo nang Bayan* (New People's Army).   JS

HULAGU (HULE'U) (*c.* 1217–65), founder of the Mongol regime of the Il-Khans in Persia, was the son of Toluy, a son of Chingiz Khan. His brother, the Great Khan Möngka, sent him in 1253 against the heartlands of Islam. Hulagu reached the region of Samarkand in 1255. He then (1256) brought much of Persia under Mongol control and also took Alamut, the stronghold of the Assassins. In 1258 Hulagu sacked Baghdad, an event which brought to an end the Abbasid caliphate (first established in 750). The Mongols turned next against Syria, taking Aleppo and Damascus in 1260. News of the death (1259) of Möngka Khan now came to Hulagu, who withdrew most of his forces eastward into Persia. The troops that he left in Syria were defeated in Sept. 1260 at Ayn Jalut in battle against the Mamluks of Egypt. In 1262 Hulagu became involved in hostilities with Berke, the Khan of the Golden Horde, the object in dispute being the territories of the Caucasus.

HULL, CORDELL (1871–1955), US politician and statesman. He served in the TN state legislature (1893–7), and was elected to a local judgeship (1903). As a Democratic congressman in the US House of Representatives (1907–21, 1923–31), Hull distinguished himself as a liberal on matters relating to low tariffs, free trade, and income and inheritance taxes. From 1921 to 1924 he served as chairman of the Democratic National Executive Committee. In 1931 he was elected to the US Senate, but resigned to become F. D. Roosevelt's secretary of state, a post he held longer (1933–44) than any previous incumbent.

Soon after his appointment, Hull made efforts to improve international trade relations to counteract the international Depression. Although he was unsuccessful as chairman of the US delegation to the London Monetary and Economic Conference (1933), his prestige among federal legislators materially assisted the president in securing passage of the Reciprocal Trade Agreement Act (1934), which marked the beginning of the liberalization of US high tariff policies. Hull was also instrumental, with President Roosevelt, in evolving the 'good neighbor' policy towards Latin America, which resulted in the withdrawal of US Marines from Haiti (1934) and the cancellation of the Platt Amendment (1934). He strongly supported the Pan-American movement and personally attended the Pan-American Conferences at Montevideo (1933), Buenos Aires (1936), and Lima (1938).

He shared Roosevelt's belief in the undesirability of 'isolationist' legislation and worked within the state department and with Congress to secure discretionary legislation that would allow the US to give economic assistance to the victims of aggression.

In the Far East, Hull repeatedly attempted to secure 'parallel action short of war' between the western powers in an effort to stabilize the situation. Even before Japan's declaration of a 'new order in East Asia', Hull strongly defended China's sovereignty and opposed any violation of the Open Door or the Nine-Power Treaty (1922). As late as his talks with Kichisaburo Nomura and Saburo Kerusu (Nov. 1941) Hull proposed a relaxation of economic sanctions if Japan would withdraw her troops from China and Indo-China and agree to close any further political and military expansion in South-East Asia.

For his contribution to the Moscow Conference of Foreign Ministers (1943), and the conferences at Bretton Woods and Dumbarton Oaks (1944), which led to the establishment of the International Monetary Fund and the United Nations Organization, Hull was awarded the Nobel Peace Prize (1945).

Cordell Hull, *Memoirs*, 2 vols (New York, 1948).
Julius W. Pratt, *Cordell Hull* (New York, 1964).   FPK

HUMANISM. *Studia humanitatis* means the study of rhetoric, grammar, poetry, history, and moral philosophy, a teacher of which would be termed by *c.* 1500 a *humanista* (humanist). The distinction is made between sciences and a form of education which placed its main emphasis upon the expressions of the human spirit and imagination—originally by the Latin authors of the classical period (especially Cicero, Horace, Ovid, and Virgil), to whom were added in the 15th cent. the writers of classical Greece. In this sense important humanists could be found in the Carolingian period (*eg*, Alcuin) and during the 12th-cent. Renaissance (*eg*, John of Salisbury), though the term is most usually applied to the literary figures of the Italian Renaissance. The first influential Italian humanist was Petrarch, in the 14th cent. His attitude to the classical authors led to a reorientation of the view taken of them. For him the study of literature was an end in itself; the Latin authors were not to be read as exemplars merely of style and grammar, but as models for a new way of thought and life. This attitude created the new and ardent enthusiasm for all classical literature that led to a search for the lost Latin texts and produced in Italy after 1395 the revival of the study of Greek. The introduction of printing into Italy after 1462 encouraged the publication of critically established standard texts of the leading classical authors.

Thus the concepts of humanism came to be embraced by both Catholic and Protestant scholars throughout western Europe, its greatest exponent north of the Alps being Desiderius Erasmus, of Rotterdam. Other scholars included John Colet, Lorenzo Valla, Johannes Reuchlin, and Jacques Lefèvre d'Etaples.

The movement had a fundamental impact upon western European education, hitherto geared to the priest and the clerk. The ideal of the cultured gentleman re-emerged in humanist works, *eg*, Castiglione's *Courtier* (1528) and Elyot's *Boke of the Governor* (1531). Moreover, the study of political theory and history received a new impetus. In more practical terms, humanists penetrated influential administrative posts in the European states, *eg*, Alonso de Valdes. New humanist institutions were established, *eg*, Cardinal Ximenez's foundation of Alcala University and Guillaume Budé's *Collège de France*. Thus the rediscovered literature of Greece and Rome was incorporated into the curricula of European schools and universities for three centuries or more.

The detailed study of the Bible and the early Church Fathers, which revealed the errors and misconceptions of scholastic theology, and the preoccupation with inner spirituality, perhaps inherited from the *Devotio Moderna*, gave rise to charges of anti-clericalism and heresy against the humanists. Many scholars, *eg*, Thomas More, John Fisher, Juan de Valdes, the reforming bishop Giberti, and not least Erasmus himself, remained within the Catholic Church. However, for some, *eg*, Ulrich von Hutten, humanism provided intellectual ammunition in the battle against papal authority and in this respect humanism stimulated the development of Protestantism. It was not until more modern times that humanism moved away from Christianity and that the humanist began to be identified with the agnostic or the atheist.

M. P. Gilmore, *The World of Humanism, 1453–1517* (New York, 1953).

HUMANITARIANISM, broadly speaking, an 18th-cent. movement in western Europe, which condemned the cruelty and ignorance of contemporary life and found practical expression in many charitable works, foundations, and changes in the law. It was inspired by the revival in personal and devotional religion, *eg*, in the Quaker and Methodist evangelical movements in England, rather than by rational enlightenment. From the condemnation of the slave trade by Fox in late 17th-cent. England the humanitarian impulse in many philanthropists, *eg*, Oglethorpe and Coram, led to the establishment of charity schools, orphanages, and hospitals in the 18th cent. As the movement gathered pace, later philanthropists, *eg*, Wilberforce and Shaftesbury, turned their attention to the condemnation of social evils, *eg*, slavery and the slave trade, religious intolerance, harsh and outdated justice, the conditions in prisons, asylums, factories, and mines, and the battle for these reforms continued throughout the 19th cent.

In France humanitarianism inspired a number of social and economic reforms during the 1770s and the 1780s, which revealed the growing hostility to the barbarous aspects of the *ancien régime*.

In central and eastern Europe, however, social reforms were initiated not by individuals, but by the reigning benevolent autocrats, who were inspired by needs of state rather than Christian motives.

HUMBERT I (1844–1900), King of Italy (*reg.* 1878–1900). His tour of northern Italy and his visit to cholera-stricken Naples in the year of his accession contributed to the growth of national consciousness in Italy. But the Crown did not long remain a symbol of unity, for Humbert brought the monarchy into disrepute by his encouragement of Crispi's disastrous colonial adventures and associated it with reaction by his approval of martial law in Sicily (1898). However, the king himself was never a blind reactionary and he moderated the more extreme policies of some of his ministers.

HUMBERT OF SILVA CANDIDA (*c.* 1000–61), one of the instigators of the Hildebrandine reform movement. He was friend and adviser to Pope Leo IX (who made him cardinal of Silva Candida) and to his fellow Lorrainer, Pope Stephen

IX. His zeal for orthodoxy was extreme and led him to play a disastrous part in bringing about the final, formal, breach with the Greek Church in 1054.

HUMBLE PETITION AND ADVICE (1657), second constitution of the English protectorate. The first constitution—the Instrument of Government (1653)—had worked well for a time, but James Naylor's case showed the need for some constitutional check upon the House of Commons. The civilian Cromwellian party, led by Lord Broghill, which had opposed the military rule of the major-generals and wanted a further return to the ancient constitution, introduced a 'Remonstrance' (later the Petition and Advice) into the Commons in Feb. 1657). In its original form it offered the title of king to Cromwell, but after much hesitation and pressure from the army he refused it. In its final form, with modifications suggested by Cromwell introduced in the Additional Petition and Advice (June 1657), it left him with the title of lord protector, but with power to nominate his successor (by the Instrument the office had been elective). Authority was vested in the protector, a privy council, and a parliament of two houses. The new upper house, or 'Other House' as it came to be called, was to consist of nominated 'lords'. The Commons were to control their own elections, and the government was given an annual revenue of £1,300,000 of which £1 million was assigned to the upkeep of the army and navy.

HUMBOLDT, ALEXANDER VON (1769–1859), German scientist, who accompanied the French botanist Aimé Bonpland on his scientific journey to Cuba, Mexico, and South America during the years 1799–1804. Humboldt published voluminous reports of his travels, filled with perceptive observations and valuable statistical information, and these have been much used by historians in their descriptions of the late colonial period. During his stay in South America Humboldt also made the first soundings of the Pacific Ocean current which bears his name, and he introduced Peruvian guano into Europe.

HUMBOLDT, WILHELM (1767–1835), Prussian politician, minister of education (1809–10), and reformer of the Prussian educational system. He introduced compulsory primary education and the training of primary and secondary teachers. His chief interest was the reform of the grammar school curriculum, culminating in a leaving certificate entitling the holder to university entrance. The foundation of Berlin University took place under his aegis. Humboldt's influence on education was not confined to Prussia or the term of his ministry, but was widely responsible for the importance of classical studies in the development of secondary and further education in Europe in the 19th cent.

HUME, DAVID (1711–76), Scottish historian and philosopher, literary rival of Dr Johnson, who stands out as one of the great intellectuals of the 18th cent. After being a merchant's clerk in Bristol (1734), he settled in France to study (1734–9). He was a prolific writer, using clear, simple prose, and his publications include *Treatise on Human Nature* (1739), *Essays, Moral and Political* (1741), *The Enquiry concerning the Human Understanding* (1748), *Political Discourses* (1752), his highly successful *History of England* (1754–62), and *Natural History of Religion* (1757).

A sceptic and a free-thinker, his revolutionary theory of causation undermined all religion. He argued openly against the credibility of miracles in his famous *Essay on Miracles* (1748) and rejected even the deductive reasoning of the deists, like Voltaire. His empirical approach to matters made him a pioneer in the fields of history and economics. Tory and royalist though he was, and therefore hostile to popular movements aimed at undermining established government, he was yet aware of the significance of social progress. In economics he foreshadowed much of Adam Smith's philosophy. A friend of Holbach, to whose Paris house he was a frequent visitor, he was known in all the *salons* and ranks with the leading *philosophes*.

HUME, HAMILTON (1797–1837), Australian explorer and settler, who, with William Hilton Hovell (1786–1875), made an overland journey south-westwards from Sydney in 1824, discovering the Murray river and much fertile country en route to Corio Bay in Port Phillip.

HUME, JAMES DEACON (1774–1842), British civil servant and joint secretary to the board of trade (1828–40), who exercised a substantial influence on the development of commercial policy. As a Custom House official he had prepared a compact digest of customs regulations for Huskisson (1825). In the 1830s he became prominent as a doctrinaire free trader, giving evidence before select committees of the period, notably the Import Duties Committee (1840), and was thus one of the influences behind Peel's economic policy.

HUME, JOSEPH (1777–1855), British politician and leader of the Philosophic Radicals in the House of Commons (1819–c. 1849). He supported many causes, but is chiefly notable for his skilful management of the campaign for the repeal of the Combination Laws (1824–5), and for his life-long and determined attempts to reduce public expenditure.

HUMPHREY, HUBERT HORATIO (1911–), US Democratic politician, born in SD and educated at Denver College of Pharmacy and Minnesota University. He was a teacher of political science, and also mayor of Minneapolis (1945–9), then was elected to the US Senate (1948). He unsuccessfully sought the Democratic presidential nomination (1960), but was elected vice-president in 1964. A consistent liberal and a strong supporter of civil rights, he instituted the first Fair Employment Practices Commission in the US while he was mayor of Minneapolis. At the 1948 Democratic convention he led the fight for a strong civil rights plank that led to the walk-out of the Dixiecrats. As a senator he continued to fight for liberal reforms, and was an early advocate of the suspension of nuclear tests. As vice-president his unwavering support of President Johnson's Viet-nam policy cost him the support of many liberals, but won him the Democratic presidential nomination (1968). The split within the Democratic Party was heightened by the violence surrounding the Chicago Convention, which contributed to Humphrey's narrow defeat by Richard Nixon.

HUNAN PEASANT MOVEMENT, REPORT ON (March 1927), key statement of Mao Tse-tung's views on the revolutionary potential of the peasantry. The report was the result of a short tour of peasant organizations in Hunan, which Mao made as head of the Peasant Department of the Chinese Communist Party. He challenged the accepted Marxist tenet that the proletariat must lead the revolution, and saw no reason why, in an agrarian society, the poor peasants should not be the revolutionary vanguard. For this view, which was Mao's first attempt to devise his own political philosophy, he was rebuked at the 5th Congress of the Chinese Communist Party (April 1927).

HUNAYN b. ISHAQ (c. 808–73) was born at Al-Hira and studied medicine in Baghdad. Through his numerous translations from Greek into Syriac and Arabic, *eg*, the works of Galen and Hippocrates, he ensured that much of the learning of the Ancient World should come into the possession of the Muslims. Hunayn b. Ishaq collated various manuscripts of a given text in order to secure a sound basis for his translation.

HUNDRED. By 1000 at the latest, the English shires had been sub-divided, in Anglo-Saxon areas into hundreds and in Danish into wapentakes. The hundred was a territorial administrative unit with its own court which met every four weeks and continued to do so throughout the Middle Ages.

HUNDRED ASSOCIATES, THE, association of 100 wealthy shareholders, known also as Compagnie de la Nouvelle France or Compagnie de Richelieu, founded by Cardinal Richelieu (1627) at the suggestion of Isaac de Razilly, which undertook to establish 4000 settlers in New France and Acadia, pay the costs of administration, and support the work of the Church, in exchange for a 15-year monopoly of the fur trade. The company suffered a series of setbacks: the capture of its first and second fleets (1628, 1629) by the English, the fall of Quebec (1629), royal interference, and Indian wars. The company's charter was revoked in 1663.

HUNDRED DAYS (March–June 1815), the interlude between the Emperor Napoleon's escape from Elba and his defeat at Waterloo. This last bid for power began with a triumphant march from Fréjus to Paris. But Bonapartist enthusiasm was short-lived. The French people now regarded representative government as the indispensable heritage of the Revolution and they greeted Napoleon's attempt to create a constitutional government with well-founded disbelief. He soon brushed aside its deliberations. The allies were equally sceptical about his supposed abandonment of aggression. They pronounced Napoleon an outlaw and reformed the Grand Alliance for the invasion of France. After his defeat at Waterloo Napoleon went into a second and permanent exile on St Helena.

'HUNDRED DAYS' REFORM' (11 June–21 Sept. 1898), a response by radical scholars to China's humiliating defeat by the Japanese in 1895 and the subsequent division of the empire into spheres of influence by the foreign powers. It was the first major attempt at sweeping institutional reforms, the aim being to revitalize the dynasty under the emperor's leadership. With the help of several metropolitan officials, including the moderate Weng T'ung-ho (1830–1904), the reformers, under the leadership of K'ang Yu-wei, finally caught the attention of the Kuang-hsü emperor. On 11 June 1898 the emperor issued an edict endorsing the introduction of reforms and ordered provincial officials to recommend able men to serve at court. Soon afterwards, K'ang was appointed probationary secretary in the Tsungli Yamen, and several of his followers were summoned to Peking. Some 40 reform edicts were issued in the next three months, dealing with every aspect of government. Classical studies were to be replaced by current affairs in the imperial examination system; a university was to be established at Peking; monasteries were to be transformed into schools; and the study of science encouraged. Sinecures, including three governorships and many high offices at Peking and throughout the empire, were to be abolished. Orders were given to remove conservative officials, to curb corruption, and to institute a public budgetary system. A bureau of agriculture, industry, and commerce was to be established in Peking; inventions, medicine, and study abroad were to be promoted; and the laws were to be modernized as a first step towards getting rid of extra-territoriality. The army, navy, and police systems were also to be reformed.

These reforms hit hard at many vested interests, and the radicalism of the reformers, both in theory and practice, alienated such moderate allies as Chang Chih-tung (1837–1909) and Weng T'ung-ho. Consequently, few reforms were carried out, except in Hunan. Moreover, all the reformers, the emperor excepted, were Chinese; while the abolition of sinecure posts affected mostly Manchus and threatened the empress dowager's network of power. On 21 Sept., the empress dowager seized the emperor, put him in forced seclusion, and terminated the 'Hundred Days' Reform'. K'ang Yu-wei and Liang Ch'i-ch'ao fled to Japan, but six other reformers, including T'an Ssu-t'ung, attempted to rescue the emperor and were arrested and executed.

Meribeth E. Cameron, *The Reform Movement in China, 1898–1912* (Stanford, 1931). DP

HUNDRED FLOWERS (1957), attempt by the Chinese Communist Party to encourage constructive criticism, which produced instead bitter attacks on the party. By the beginning of 1957 Mao Tse-tung felt that communist rule in China was well enough established to allow criticism of the party from outsiders. He was worried that the party was becoming monolithic and bureaucratic. His key speech 'On the Correct Handling of Contradictions within the People' (Feb. 1957) called for understanding and reasoned settlement of problems among those who supported the party. The Hundred Flowers Campaign, launched soon afterwards, was designed to carry out this process. At the same time, a campaign for party rectification was started, aimed at eradicating bureaucracy and special privilege within the party. The peaceable settlement of contradictions which Mao had envisaged, with constructive criticism of the party, turned into a flood of bitter criticism, both from left and right, which was allowed to pour forth for six weeks, an unprecedented phenomenon in any communist country. After the flood had been stopped, the rectification campaign was turned into a campaign against those who had criticized the party, the Anti-Rightist Campaign. Severe reprisals were taken by the shaken party against its critics.

HUNDRED THOUSAND SONS OF ST LOUIS, name given to the French army which reinstated Ferdinand IV on the throne of Spain (1823). Ferdinand had been forced by insurrection to accept a liberal constitution (1822) and the Ultras wished to repress the rebellion and demonstrate the conservatism of the Restoration. After a bitter debate in France, Louis XVIII announced that 100,000 Frenchmen commanded by a prince of his family were ready to march in the name of the God of St Louis to preserve the throne of Spain for a grandson of Henry IV. The army, led by the Duc d'Angoulême, encountered no real resistance and by Oct. Ferdinand was back in power. For five years 45,000 French troops remained in Spain.

HUNDRED YEARS WAR, more properly a series of wars between England and France, in which three major phases can be distinguished.

(*a*) 1337–60. This first stage of the wars was fought essentially over the possession of the Duchy of Guienne, declared forfeit by the French Crown in 1337. Not until 1340 did Edward III raise the question of his claim to the French Crown. There were three major English victories: the sea battle at Sluys (1340), which gave the English control of the Channel for a generation; the battle of Crécy (1346); and the battle of Poitiers (1356), at which the French King, John II, was captured and which led to the treaty of Bretigny in 1360, which gave Edward virtually the whole of Aquitaine, together with Calais.

(*b*) 1360–1413. A period of confused and generally fruitless campaigns by the English, frustrated by Bertrand du Guesclin's refusal to fight a pitched battle, and of French attacks (after 1375) on the English coast. A period of peace came with the marriage of Richard II to a daughter of Charles VI (1396), largely because France was torn by civil war during the insanity of Charles VI and because of the insecurity of Henry IV in England.

(*c*) 1413–53. The war was renewed by Henry V's revival of his claim to the French Crown. The battle of Agincourt (1415), the greatest victory ever won by English arms in France, and the conquest of Normandy led the way to the treaty of Troyes (1420), by which all France north of the Loire was ceded to Henry, who married Catherine of Valois, Charles VI's daughter, and was recognized as Charles's heir. Henry's death a few months before that of Charles, and the succession of the baby Henry VI (1422), foiled a complete triumph for the English. The decisive intervention of Joan of Arc (1429–31), the return of Burgundy to its French allegiance (1435), and English weakness during the minority of Henry VI led to the gradual expulsion of the English, culminating in the battle of Castillon in 1453, which left only Calais in their hands. JG

HUNG HSIEN, Chinese dynastic reign name. Yuan Shih-k'ai chose this name, meaning 'Great Constitution', for the new dynasty, which he proclaimed on 1 Jan. 1916. It lasted only a few months. Yuan died in June that year.

HUNG HSIU-CH'ÜAN (1814–64), leader of the Taiping Rebellion, was the third son of a small Hakka farmer in Hua-hsien, about 40 kms north of Canton. Hung was sent to school at the age of seven in the hope that he would acquire the necessary academic degrees for membership of the scholar-gentry class, and his failure to do so at the provincial examination at Canton in 1837 brought on him a breakdown. During his illness, he was delirious, and had fits of rage. When he recovered, his appearance was said to have changed and a sense of mission to be apparent. After his third failure at the provincial examination, his attention was drawn to a missionary tract entitled 'Good Words to Admonish the Age', which seemed to provide an explanation for his illness. He now called himself the younger brother of Jesus Christ, and believed God had entrusted him with the task of proselytizing the world and slaying the demons, particularly the Manchus. In April 1844 Hung and one of his converts, Feng Yün-shan, began preaching in the border region between Kwangtung and Kwangsi. Owing to opposition, Hung returned to Kwangtung, but Feng stayed and founded the God Worshippers Society at Thistle Mountain, southern Kwangsi. For two months in 1847 Hung visited Canton and received religious instruction from the Rev. Issachar T. Roberts, an American Southern Baptist. This contact, and the reading of the Bible, enlarged his ideas but did little to change his belief. In 1849, when he rejoined the God Worshippers Society at Thistle Mountain, he found an organization strong enough to challenge the local authorities. In the first flush of victory over the government troops, Hung declared the Heavenly Kingdom of Great Peace and himself the Heavenly King. The Taipings, as these rebels were called, broke out of Kwangsi the following year, overran the southern and Yangtze provinces, and eventually established their capital at Nanking. In 1856 the Taiping cause was considerably weakened by an internal struggle for power and the murder of Hung's most able assistants. Thereafter, Hung delegated his power to his brothers and relatives, retired from active leadership, and placed his trust in divine guidance. From 1861 onwards Taiping military power declined rapidly, and Nanking eventually fell on 19 July 1864, Hung having committed suicide on 1 June.

Franz Michael, *The Taiping Rebellion, History and Documents*, vol. 1 (Seattle, 1966).   DP

HUNGARIAN REVOLUTION (1848–9), nationalist movement led by the nobility which became a war of independence. Since the union of the Hungarian lands with the Habsburg Crown in 1526 the Hungarians had had their own constitution and Diet. During the 1840s the Magyarizing movement within the Diet had introduced some liberal reforms, culminating in the March Laws of 1848, accepted by the Emperor Ferdinand. The Hungarians refused to accept his abdication in favour of his nephew, Francis Joseph, in Dec. 1848, and, led by Louis Kossuth, proclaimed their independence. The movement was defeated by Russian troops and Croats under Jellačič. The Hungarian constitution was suspended and Hungary ruled from Vienna until 1860.

HUNGARIANS, also called Magyars, nomadic Asiatic people who settled the area of modern Hungary (895–6). Their origin is unclear, but they probably came from the area between the Volga and the Urals. From about the 5th cent. they were driven west by other tribes and settled in the area north of the Black Sea in association with the Khazars and Turki peoples. After Pethcheneg pressure drove them up the Danube into Hungary, they became the terror of Europe, raiding far and wide. They suffered severe defeats in Germany and were christianized under St Stephen. By Stephen's

coronation in 1000 Hungary became a Christian kingdom of Europe.

HUNGARY, PEACE TREATY (1947). The frontiers of Hungary with Yugoslavia and Austria were restored by the peace treaty to those of Jan. 1938 and Hungary returned to Rumania the gains made by the second Vienna award. Hungary was to pay reparations of $300 million divided between the USSR ($200 million), Yugoslavia, and Czechoslovakia. The gains which Hungary had made by the first Vienna award (Nov. 1938) at the expense of Czechoslovakia, and by the second Vienna award (Aug. 1940) at the expense of Rumania were restored.

'HUNGRY FORTIES' in Britain, phrase devised in the early 1900s to describe the 1840s. There is no reason to believe that real wages were any lower in this decade than in the three preceding ones, and what evidence there is suggests that after sinking or stagnating between 1790 and 1820 they began to rise in the later 1830s or early 1840s. But the 1840s saw two sharp depressions in trade in which unemployment was probably high. There was also the potato famine of 1846–8. Potatoes were not only the staple diet in Ireland and in the Highlands of Scotland, but also an important item of cheap food in the large towns. It is in these aspects of the 1840s that the appellation 'hungry' may be justified.

HUNKANRIN, LOUIS (1887–1964), early nationalist leader in French-speaking West Africa. A courageous publicist, this Dahomeyan intellectual wrote for various nationalist newspapers, *eg*, *La Voix du Dahomey* and *Courrier du Golfe de Bénin*, and was one of the chief forerunners of later political movements.

HUNNE, RICHARD (d. 1514), English merchant, who, after challenging the clergy over the payment of a mortuary fee, was arrested in London on suspicion of heresy and was found hanged in the bishop's prison (1514). The coroner's jury accused the jailer and the bishop's chancellor of murder and the case caused riots in London and uproar in parliament, indicating growing anti-clericalism in pre-Reformation England.

HUNS, pastoral, nomadic people of Central Asian origin, who built up an empire stretching from the Caspian Sea to the Alps. They attacked a variety of German and Sarmatian tribes in southern Russia, driving them into the Roman empire from *c.* 370 onwards. The Huns reached their greatest power and realized their greatest territorial expansion under Attila (*c.* 434–53). After his death in 453 the Huns were defeated by a revolt of their own Germanic subjects in 454, which in turn led to a rapid and permanent disintegration of their empire.

HUNT, ATLEE ARTHUR (1864–1935), Australian Commonwealth public servant who was secretary to the departments of external affairs (1901–16) and home affairs (1916–21) and the first Commonwealth public service arbitrator. His was the successful attempt to formulate policy for the territory of Papua. His administration of the 'White Australia' laws took a liberal direction and his arbitration system was both comprehensive and permanent.

HUNT, RICHARD MORRIS (1827–95), US architect. He studied in Geneva and Paris, and became a highly successful architect of houses for the rich. Many, like the celebrated Vanderbilt mansions in New York (1881) and Asheville, NC (1896), were designed in the French Renaissance style that he made fashionable. Among his public buildings are the Naval Observatory in Washington, DC, and part of the Metropolitan Museum in New York.

HUNTER, JOHN (1728–93), Scottish anatomist and the founder of surgical pathology. He carried out animal experiments, including tissue transplantation, and kept a menagerie at Earls Court, London. He founded a museum in Leicester Square, which was destroyed in the Second World War.

HUNTER, JOHN (1737–1821), British admiral and second governor of New South Wales. During the administration of his predecessor, Gov. Phillip, he had experience as a magistrate in the new penal settlement, and also sailed on voyages of supply for the colony, which was not yet self-supporting. In England from April 1792, Hunter was favoured as Phillip's successor, but delay in the latter's departure from Sydney, and Hunter's arrival, made for future trouble between the naval governor and the rum-trading officers and ex-officers of the NSW Corps. Hunter proved no match for the latter, and his attempts to restrain a disorderly soldiery and its commercially minded officers were insufficiently supported by Portland, the secretary of state, who recalled Hunter at the end of 1799.

HUNTER, SIR WILLIAM WILSON (1840–1900), British colonial servant, member of the Indian civil service, and voluminous writer on Indian affairs. Six years after his arrival in India he published his *Annals of Rural Bengal* (1868). He was appointed to organize a statistical survey of the Indian empire and published *The Statistical Account of Bengal* (20 vols, 1875–7), and also prepared 23 volumes of *The Imperial Gazetteer of India* (1881–7). He was president of the Education Commission of 1882–3 and at the same time a member of the Indian Finance Commission. After his retirement (1887) he produced the Rulers of India Series, of which he wrote the volumes on Dalhousie and Mayo. His *History of British India* (2 vols (1899–1900), long remained a standard work.

HUNTER EDUCATION COMMISSION (1882–3), appointed to review the working of the system inaugurated in 1854 and to propose ways of extending and improving elementary education in India. It reported that, while higher and secondary education was popular and successful among the middle classes, especially in Bengal, primary education needed the strongest encouragement. It recommended that education should be increasingly left to private enterprise, supported by government grants. The exclusively literary character caused disquiet and the commission recommended that additional commercial and industrial training should be provided. It drew attention also to the importance of physical training and suggested that the educational system should be reorganized so as to attract better men. A proposal to get a moral textbook prepared was rejected by the government of India. Most of the commission's recommendations were accepted, but difficulty was experienced in getting municipal and district boards to spend money on elementary education.

HUNTINGDON, LUCIUS SETH (1827–86), Canadian Liberal politician, who opposed Canadian confederation. After confederation (1867), he advocated independence from Britain as the first step towards a commercial union with the US. He brought charges against the Conservative government of Sir John A. Macdonald, precipitating the 'Pacific Scandal' (1873), in which Macdonald and his party were charged with having accepted money from Americans in return for the charter to build the Canadian Pacific Railway. Macdonald's government fell, and Huntingdon became president of the council of the Liberal government of Alexander Mackenzie (1874) and postmaster-general (1875–8), but split the Liberal ranks by openly criticizing the 'Ultramontaine' clergy of Quebec. Defeated in the election of 1882, Huntingdon left Canada and spent the rest of his life in New York.

HUNTINGTON, COLLIS POTTER (1821–1900), US financier. He made his fortune as a trader in CA, after the gold rush (1849), and joined with Leland Stanford, Charles Crocker, and Mark Hopkins in building the Central Pacific Railroad. He and Stanford also built the Southern Pacific. The group were skilled lobbyists and rejected no means of furthering their own interests irrespective of the public interest.

HUNTZIGER, CHARLES (1880–1941), French general, chosen to sign the armistice of 1940. He later commanded the Vichy regime's 'armistice army', and was minister of war (1940–1).

HUNYADI, JANOS (c. 1387–1456), Hungarian soldier and nobleman. As governor of Transylvania, Hunyadi had a major role in the Hungarian offensive against the Ottoman Turks after 1437. The Hungarians and their allies were defeated, however, at Varna in 1444 and at Kosovo in 1448. From 1446 Hunyadi was regent of the Hungarian realm in the name of the young King Ladislaus V. He defeated the Ottoman Sultan Mehemmed II at Belgrade in 1456.

HURON INDIANS, name given by the French to a confederation of four Iroquoian-speaking American tribes and several dependent communities which called itself Wendat or Wyandot. Champlain found them (1615) in villages at the southern end of Georgian Bay and Lake Simcoe in Ont. The Huron traded with the French and were their allies against the Iroquois League, which destroyed the Huron confederacy (1648–50). The Huron then disintegrated into fugitive bands. The two largest settled in Que. (1649) and OK (1859), where they remain.

HURON TRACT, 1,100,000-acre, triangular area, fronting on Lake Huron for 60 miles (96·5 kms), purchased from the Crown by the Canada Co. (1826).

HURONIA, an area 40 miles (64 kms) long and 20 miles (32 kms) wide in southern Ont. It was once the most densely populated district in Canada, with a thriving trading and farming community of an estimated (in 1616) 30,000 Huron Indians, but its population was decimated by smallpox and influenza epidemics and by Iroquois raids (1648–9).

HURRIANS, ancient Middle Eastern people, about whom little is known. They probably came from the Caucasus and spoke a language of a type peculiar to themselves and the later Urartians. In the second half of the 3rd millennium BC they moved into northern Mesopotamia and Syria and also formed small communities in southern Mesopotamia. They established a number of small kingdoms too, as well as the powerful kingdom of Mitanni, which ruled northern Mesopotamia and Syria (16th–14th cents). Their separate identity was lost during the confused period of Mesopotamian history which preceded the establishment of Aramaean domination (c. 1000 BC).

HURTADO DE MENDOZA, ANDRÉS, Marqués de Cañete (d. 1560), Spanish viceroy of Peru and administrative reformer. His principal task was the pacification of war-torn colonial Peru. This he accomplished by exiling undesirables to unexplored areas and by fostering local industries.

HURTADO DE MENDOZA, GARCÍA (1535–1609), Spanish governor of Chile and viceroy of Peru, who campaigned against the Araucanian Indians of Chile.

HUS, JOHN (?1369–1415), Czech religious reformer, whose life and death inspired the Hussite movement in Bohemia. He advocated a moral reform of the Church, a return to its primitive purity, and the removal of what he saw as abuses. He condemned the wealth of the Bohemian Church and advocated the abolition of clerical property. In his belief that the Church must return to poverty and purity, he had many forerunners inside and outside Bohemia, including the English reformer John Wycliffe. He borrowed heavily from the ideas of these men, but did not adopt their systems. He had no intention of setting up a separate Bohemian Church and of breaking with Rome. He was supremely an academic theologian, who preached in Czech, appealing to anti-German sentiment in Prague University and in the country. King Wenceslas IV found it politically advantageous to support Hus and the Czech party. In 1409 the Czech 'nation' at the university was granted a predominant position by the king. A mass exodus of Germans followed and Hus became rector in the same year. His works were subsequently condemned by the Bohemian Church. The conciliar movement, which caused a split in the Bohemian clergy, increased religious and political confusion. Hus was given mass support when, in 1412, he attacked the sale of papal indulgences for an Italian war waged by the papacy. Thereby he began to challenge the pope's claim to be head of the Church. In 1414 he went to Constance to defend his beliefs before a general council of the Church, armed with a safe-conduct of King Sigismund, in the belief that he was still an orthodox Catholic. In Nov. 1414 he was arrested and in June 1415 he was condemned to death and burned. He was mistaken in his belief that the council was an assembly of theologians ready to debate his ideas with him; in fact, it was a court to try heresy. To the end Hus remained unrealistic. His death rather than his life gave rise to the most spectacular results in the Hussite movement. MH

HUSAYN (1668–1726), Safawid Shah of Persia (*reg.* 1694–1722), whose reign saw the collapse of the Safawid regime. The Ghalzay Afghan chieftain Mir Ways (d. 1715) established an almost independent state at Kandahar. Under Mahmud of Kandahar (d. 1725) the Ghalzay tribesmen invaded Persia in 1719 and again in 1722, crushing the Safawid forces then at Gulnabad and capturing Isfahan. Meanwhile, the Ottoman Turks and the Russians had intervened in the Caucasus area. An agreement reached in 1724 led to the partition, between these two powers, of large territories in north-west Persia and the adjacent lands. Mahmud of Kandahar, having deposed Husayn in 1722, kept him in confinement at Isfahan. He was executed in 1726 by Mahmud's successor, Ashraf b. 'Abd al-Aziz.

HUSAYN, ALI, b. ABI TALIB (626–80), son of the Prophet Muhammad's cousin, the Caliph 'Ali, and daughter, Fatima. After the death of his father (661), Al-Husayn lived in retirement at Medina throughout the reign of the Caliph Mu'awiya. He refused homage (*bay'a*) in 680 to the son of Mu'awiya, the Caliph Yazid I. Al-Husayn, in attempting to exploit to his own advantage the disaffection existing in Iraq against the Umayyad regime, met his death at the hands of the forces of Yazid I. His 'martyrdom' gave a great impulse to the development of the Shi'a faith.

HUSAYN IBN TALAL (1935–), King of Jordan (*reg.* 1952–) and effective ruler since 1953, who established a system of monarchical absolutism based on army support, to control the demands of the Palestinian element in the population, while pursuing a policy of rapid economic and administrative development.

HUSAYN–McMAHON CORRESPONDENCE (14 July 1915–30 Jan. 1916), exchange of ten letters between Sharif Husayn of Mecca and Sir Henry McMahon, British High Commissioner in Egypt in which Britain (McMahon's letter 24 Oct. 1915) agreed to recognize and support Arab independence in Arab areas of the Ottoman empire, subject to reservations concerning coastal Syria, Mesopotamia, and the acceptance of British advice, in return for Husayn's proclamation of the Arab Revolt. Disputes about the meaning of the agreement later led to great Anglo–Arab bitterness.

HÜSEYIN AVNI PASHA (?1820–1876). Ottoman general, politician, and Grand Vizier (1874–5). He was several times minister of war and was responsible for a major army reorganization, but is best known for his part in the deposition of Sultan Abdülaziz (30 May 1876).

HUSKISSON, WILLIAM (1770–1830), British politician, and a dominant influence on British commercial policy in the early 19th cent. He served in minor administrative offices (1795–1805) and, after Pitt's death (1806), became closely associated with Canning, resigning with him in 1809.

At the treasury, Huskisson developed his interest in financial policy and his public reputation was made by a pamphlet, 'The question concerning the depreciation of our currency stated and examined' (1810), attacking the Bank of England, and explaining why the Bullion Committee, of which he was a member, advocated a return to cash payments as soon as possible. Huskisson remained a strong advocate of this policy and was chairman of the Finance Committee of 1819 which recommended the return (1821). He supported agricultural protection in 1815.

With Canning's appointment as foreign secretary (1822), Huskisson became president of the board of trade and treasurer of the navy (1823–7). His work, together with Wallace's reforms of the Navigation Acts, and Robinson's budgets of 1824 and 1825, established the movement towards the freeing of trade, after 20 years of war taxation. Their policy brought some opening of colonial trade to foreign shipping, placed foreign ships on an equality with British ships, in British ports, in exchange for reciprocal benefits in foreign ports, and allowed the importation of silk manufactures, previously prohibited, on payment of a 30 per cent duty. Huskisson's standing in commercial circles was shown by his election as MP for Liverpool (1823–30).

With the collapse of a commercial boom (1826–7) these liberal measures, previously popular, encountered strong hostility, and the simultaneous revival of the anti-Corn Law agitation caused much division within the ministry. Huskisson's bill (1827) providing for a sliding scale was attacked by Wellington and shelved, but was finally passed in 1828.

Throughout the 1820s Huskisson, like Canning, accepted the need for Catholic emancipation and for some piecemeal improvement of the electoral system. After Canning's death (Aug. 1827), Huskisson remained as colonial secretary in the Goderich administration, but resigned, with the rest of the Canningites, from Wellington's administration on the question of East Retford (1828). He was run over and killed at the opening of the Liverpool–Manchester railway (Sept. 1830), during a conversation with Wellington that seemed to betoken a reconciliation between him and the Canningites.

Huskisson was more of an administrator than a political leader, and formed an admirable complement to Canning. Politically he was opposed to Peel, though Peel later adopted similar economic ideas. Such ideas were generally current in the 1840s, but Huskisson, with his expert interest in economics, had moved ahead of public opinion.

C. R. Fay, *Huskisson and his Age* (London, 1951). LMB

HUSSITE MOVEMENT, Bohemian revolutionary movement starting in the first decade of the 15th cent., named after its leader, John Hus, which produced an enduring religious schism. It had complex political and social as well as religious causes and drew momentum from accumulated Czech bitterness against German settlers and German influence in the country. There were many divergent streams within the movement, from the moderate Prague Utraquists, who advocated a reform of the Church, to the extreme Taborites, who sought to bring about a religious and social revolution. After 1419 the movement came under constant attack from various foreign enemies, which gave the extreme military brethren, who took the war into their enemies' lands, greater influence. The Hussites refused to recognize the Emperor Sigismund after his coronation as King of Bohemia in 1420, especially as he had been partly responsible for the burning of Hus as a heretic in 1415, and he organized several crusades against them. The wars lasted 15 years and was characterized by the brutality and destruction of a civil war. The Council of Basle, assembled in 1431 to deal with the Hussite heresy, failed to achieve a compromise and was forced in 1433 to concede communion in both kinds in Bohemia as a temporary measure. This, and doctrinal differences between the various groups, widened the divisions in the movement. A Catholic conservative party remained strong, especially among the German inhabitants and a section of the nobility. The destructive anarchy, the disturbance of economic life, and the extremism of the Taborites and their fellows gave increasing weight to a party of moderate 'politiques'. In May 1434 the extremists were defeated at Lipany by an allied army of the Utraquists and the Catholic League of Lords. This left the moderate Hussites in control. In 1436 Sigismund had to drop the charge of heresy, granted the demands of the Utraquists, and confirmed the rights of the country, and was restored to the throne. The Hussite Church remained in schism from Rome until it was suppressed in 1620. The movement left Bohemia economically weakened, strengthened the nobility politically and economically at the cost of the Crown, the serfs, and the Church, and destroyed a culture based on the co-existence of the Czech and German nationalities. MH

HUTCHINSON, ANNE (1591–1643), American religious leader, born in England, who married William Hutchinson, a merchant, and emigrated with him to the Massachusetts Bay colony (1633). In meetings, originally with groups of women, Mrs Hutchinson advocated a religion based on an individual's direct knowledge of God's grace rather than one based on obedience to laws of the state and church. She was supported by important civil and religious leaders, but Gov. John Winthrop labelled her an Antinomian and banished her and some of her followers from the colony. Mrs Hutchinson went to Rhode Island (1638), and following the death of her husband (1642) she settled on Long Island. She was killed in an Indian massacre.

HUTCHINSON, THOMAS (1711–80), British colonial governor, born in Boston, MA, and a descendant of Anne Hutchinson. He graduated from Harvard (1727), entered business, and served in the MA House of Representatives (1737–9, 1741–9) and in the Council (1749–65). He represented the claims of MA against NH in England (1740), was appointed a judge (1752), and was a MA delegate at the Albany Congress (1754). In 1758 he was commissioned governor of MA. He opposed the Sugar Act (1764) and Stamp Act (1765), but as a conservative he argued that parliament had the right to pass and enforce laws for the colonies. His views aroused hostility and a mob destroyed his mansion (1765). Hutchinson quarrelled with Samuel Adams and other popular leaders, and by refusing to grant clearance papers for a shipload of East India Co. tea, he precipitated the Boston Tea Party (16 Dec. 1773). He was replaced by Gen. Thomas Gage, and went to Britain (1774), where he died.

HUTH, HANS (d. 1528), German Anabaptist propagandist, who was one of Thomas Munzer's subordinates. After escaping from the peasant slaughter at Frankenhausen (1525), he moved to Nikolsburg, Moravia, where with Jacob Widemann he led a fanatical splinter movement with an apocalyptic, millenarian philosophy. Huth was imprisoned by the lords of Lichtenstein, but escaped and made his way to Augsburg (1527). After again being arrested, he died in mysterious circumstances.

HUTTEN, ULRICH VON (1488–1523), German nationalist, humanist scholar, and leader, with Franz von Sickingen, of the anti-papal movement of the imperial knights in the early 16th cent. He published many works, including *Ars Versificatoria* (1511), *Triumphus Caprionis*, and *Epistolae Obscurorum Virorum* (1515). His edition of Laurentius Valla's *De Falso Credito et Ementita Donatione Constantini Magni* (1517) caused a sensation in humanist circles. He became acquainted with Luther (c. 1520), but the latter refused to become involved

in the turbulent political movement against the princes which Hutten led. After the knights' defeat at Landstuhl (1523) by an alliance of princes, he was exiled from the empire and with his death in Switzerland the political aspirations of his declining class ended.

HUTTER, JACOB (d. 1536), German Anabaptist leader, who was George Blaurock's successor in the Tyrol. He moved to the Austerlitz area of Moravia, where he joined Huth's former colleague, Jacob Widemann (1529). Under Hutter's leadership over 80 thriving communal settlements were established. In 1536 he was burnt for heresy.

HUTTON, SIR EDWARD THOMAS HENRY (1848–1923), Australian general and first Australian GOC, who organized the Australian army (1901–4).

HUXELLES, NICOLAS DE BLE, Marquis d' (1652–1730), French diplomat and soldier, created marshal of France (1703), who enjoyed the patronage first of Louvois and after 1702 of Mme de Maintenon. He was selected by Louis XIV as plenipotentiary at the Gertruydenburg discussions (1710), and later at the negotiations leading to the peace of Utrecht (1713). He was afterwards appointed governor of Alsace and Strasbourg.

HUXLEY, THOMAS HENRY (1825–95), British marine biologist, president of the British Association, and secretary of the Royal Society. He was noted for his power of research and gifts of exposition in lectures and papers. He championed Darwin and agnosticism against the Anglican bishops, led by Samuel Wilberforce, in the great debate at the Oxford Meeting of the British Association (1860).

HUYGENS, CHRISTIAN (1629–95), Dutch mathematician and astronomer who, in 1655, discovered by means of a 12-ft telescope, built by himself, a satellite of Saturn. He was the first man to explain the nature of Saturn's rings. His interests were diverse. He invented the balance spring which made efficient pocket-watches possible, and he also improved the pendulum clock. Although he attacked the Cartesian deductive method and advocated experiment to test theories, he held Cartesian views on cosmology. He was a member of the Académie Royale des Sciences, and was probably the greatest scientist after Newton in the second half of the 17th cent.

HYATT, JOHN WESLEY (1837–1920), US inventor, who in 1868 discovered the first synthetic plastic, celluloid. Although highly inflammable, it was commercially exploited, particularly for photographic films. It was not until the development of less inflammable plastics, notably 'Bakelite' by Baekeland, that these materials became important.

HYDARI, SIR AKBAR, NAWAB JUNG BAHADUR (1869–1942), British colonial administrator in India. After service in the Indian finance department (1888–1920), in which he had become accountant-general of Bombay, Hydari was finance and railway member of the Hyderabad Executive Council (1921–37) and president of the council (1937–41). He led the Hyderabad delegation to the Round Table conferences (1930–2) and the joint parliamentary committee (1933–4). He also played a crucial role in the negotiations between the states and the British Indian government concerning federation as chairman of the committee of Indian States' ministers (1934–41). He was information member of the viceroy's Executive Council (1941–2).

HYDASPES RIVER, BATTLE OF (326 BC), in north-west India (mod. Thelum river), Alexander the Great's last victory. Porus, the Indian king, held the east bank in strength, but Alexander crossed boldly, and after clever manœuvring broke the enemy with his cavalry, while his infantry held

Porus' elephants. Porus submitted, but Alexander's army refused to advance further.

HYDE, ANNE (1637–1671), daughter of Edward, 1st Earl of Clarendon. She was married (1660) to James, Duke of York, subsequently King James II (*reg.* 1685–8), and was the mother of Queens Mary II and Anne.

HYDE PARK DECLARATION (20 April 1941), agreement issued by the prime minister of Canada, Mackenzie King, and President Franklin D. Roosevelt of the US to share defence articles, increase US purchase of Canadian strategic materials, and allow certain Canadian imports to be charged to Britain's lend-lease account.

HYDERABAD, NIZAMS OF, rulers of Hyderabad state, the largest of the Indian states within the British Indian empire. They received from the British the honorific of 'Exalted Highness' and the title of 'Faithful Ally'. They consistently claimed equal status with the British as unbroken successors of the Mughal empire, but this was finally disallowed by Lord Reading's government in 1926. At the time of its incorporation with the new Indian state Hyderabad had an area of 82,000 sq. miles (213,000 sq. kms) and a population of over 17 million.

Hyderabad state grew out of the Mughal empire during its decline in the 18th cent. The first nizam, Chin Kilich Khan, was the son of a Turkish immigrant who rose high in the service of the Emperor Aurangzeb. In 1721 he became vizier of the empire, but in 1724 retired to the six Deccan provinces with his capital at Hyderabad. He received the titles of Nizam-ul-mulk and Asaf Jah and these became hereditary in his family. In 1738 the cession of Malwa to the Marathas cut Hyderabad off from Delhi, and left the new state independent in all but name. Until his death (1748) the nizam was preoccupied in defending his dominions from the Marathas, but he also extended them through the coastal Carnatic as far as Madurai in the far south.

In the succession troubles after the nizam's death, Hyderabad fell under French influence, the Nizam Salabat Jung being sustained, 1752–9, by the French general De Bussy with troops supported by the grant of the five northern sircars or districts bordering on the bay of Bengal. On De Bussy's withdrawal these districts passed by stages to the British on various conditions. Nizam Ali, the fifth nizam (1762–1803), spent most of his reign resisting the Marathas, then at the height of their power. After his great defeat at Khurdla (1795) by the Marathas he turned to the British and concluded a subsidiary alliance (1798), by which he received 6000 troops in return for an annual payment of 24 lakhs. The nizam's gains in the final war against Tipu Sultan (1798–9) were surrendered to the British in return for an increase of this force. This area was known as the Ceded Districts of the Madras presidency. In 1803 Hyderabad was protected from an attack of the Maratha chief Holkar by the victories of Sir A. Wellesley at Assaye and Argaon.

During the 19th cent. Hyderabad remained an aristocratic preserve often subject to exploitation. Sir C. Metcalfe (resident 1820–5) exposed and corrected some of its effects. Under Sir Salar Jung the administration improved and during the mutiny he kept Hyderabad loyal to the British. In 1853 the revenues of Berar were assigned to the British in settlement of debts, and this was converted into a permanent loan by Lord Curzon in 1903. The nizam refused to join either the British Indian federation proposed in the 1935 Government of India Act, or the Union of India in 1947 as a federal unit. In 1948 the state was absorbed by the Indian government's 'police action' and is now part of the Andhra state.

Imperial Gazetteer of India, vol. XIII, (Oxford, 1908).

TGPS

HYÈRES, BATTLE OF (Feb. 1744), naval action off Toulon in the War of the Austrian Succession. When the Franco-Spanish fleet emerged from its base it was pursued by a larger English force, but ill-feeling between the admiral and his second-in-command prevented a British victory.

HYKSOS, people of uncertain origin who migrated, probably from Palestine, into Egypt over a considerable period of time. Sometimes wrongly called 'shepherd kings', the name means literally 'rulers of foreign lands'. They gained control of northern Egypt (*c.* 1680 BC), making Avaris (probably at or near Tanis) their capital, and gradually dominated the whole country, although Egyptian kings continued to rule in Thebes. They seem to have adopted Egyptian customs and worshipped native gods as well as their own. After about 108 years of Hyksos domination the Egyptians, with the help of Nubian mercenaries, rose against them, finally, under the leadership of Aahmes, driving them out *c.* 1570.

HYMANS, PAUL (1865–1941), Belgian lawyer and politician, who was professor of comparative parliamentary history at Brussels University (1898–1914). He was elected a Liberal deputy in 1900, but at the same time continued his literary career. During the First World War he served as Plenipotentiary to Britain and then as minister of economic affairs. Although he also served as minister of Justice (1926–7) and minister without portfolio (1935), the key period of his career was his tenure of the foreign affairs ministry (1918–20, 1924–5, 1927–34, 1934–5). Because Belgium was a small power, recently ravaged by Germany, it was natural that her foreign policy should focus on the attempt to build a new international structure through the League of Nations. Hymans was one of the group of statesmen from the smaller states who worked hard to make the League viable. He had been a delegate to the Peace Conference in 1919, in 1920 was elected president of the League Assembly, and in 1922 of the Council. He was also Belgian representative at the Hague Conference (1929–30). In these varying capacities he played a leading part in the settlement of the Ruhr Question, the Dawes Plan, the economic union of Luxemburg with Belgium, and in the attempts to tighten up the security aspects of the league. By 1934–5, however, he was reduced to adopting old style power-politics, asking Britain for guarantees against Germany.

HYMNS, originally meaning acts of praise sung to God, were confined to metrical poems and excluded the psalms and canticles. The Latin metrical hymn was introduced into the western Church by St Ambrose and in the Middle Ages plainsong melodies were added. At the Protestant Reformation the hymn became the symbol of communal participation in religious services and this movement therefore inspired a great output of vernacular hymns, *eg*, by Luther, which carried on the medieval lyrical tradition and culminated in the Bach chorales. Wesley's Methodist movement and the religious revival of the mid-19th cent. were further stimuli to hymn writing. Hymns, in western forms, played a major part in the worship of the Christian Church in its missionary work in Africa and elsewhere. But later 20th-cent. developments brought musical art-forms of an indigenous nature, more familiar to the ears of participants.

HYNDMAN, HENRY MAYERS (1842–1921), British exponent of Marxism in England, whose *England for All* (1881) and Social Democratic Federation (founded, 1881) influenced many early socialists. His personal and political characteristics limited his appeal. For he was tactless, domineering, and doctrinaire, and his chauvinism, anti-Semitism, and distaste for liberalism and trade unions isolated him from the Labour Party's source of recruits. His writings, his dedication, and his personal generosity helped to create a working-class political party whose ideas improved upon pragmatic radicalism.

HYPERIDES (*fl.* 4th cent. BC), Athenian orator and politician, who, turning from forensic oratory to active anti-Macedonian politics, instigated the Athenian revolt from Macedon in the Lamian War (323), for which Antipater killed him.

HYPPOLITE, LOUIS MODESTIN FLORVILLE (1827–96), Haitian general and president (1889–96). He used the proceeds from a temporary coffee boom to expand public works.

HYSIAE, BATTLE OF (669 BC), defeat of Sparta's new 'Lycurgan' hoplite army by Pheidon of Argos, whose victory gave him control of Olympia (668) and much of the northern Peloponnese and enabled the Spartan *gerousia* to reassert its control over the *apella*.

HYTHE CONFERENCE (15–17 May 1920). The British and French prime ministers, Lloyd George and Millerand, with their respective financial ministers, met to discuss Germany's fulfilment of her treaty obligation to pay reparations for damage after the First World War. They wished to settle their own differences before the Spa conference on reparations, to which Germany, as well as their other allies, had been invited. The main point of dissension lay in France's claim to priority over Germany's other claimants. France was also reluctant to fix a sum representing Germany's total liability, as Lloyd George wished; she feared that at this stage the Allies might underestimate the German economy's capacity to recover from the war. Millerand was over-ruled on the question of priorities, largely through arguments that France's claim would be unacceptable to the British Dominions. A committee of French and British experts was set up to discuss the fixing of a minimum total debt owed by Germany, and to decide on the conditions of its distribution among the Allies.

The conference's communiqué mentioned the need to solve the reparations question in conjunction with that of inter-Allied debts. In the absence of a representative of the US, to whom both Britain and France were heavily indebted, this suggestion had little force. Lloyd George and Millerand returned to the question of war debts and reparations on 20 June 1920, when they met again at Hythe on the eve of a meeting with Belgium, Italy, and Japan at Boulogne. The two prime ministers decided to act jointly over settling their debts to the US.   ASJ

HYWEL DDA (*reg.* 915–50), Welsh King, who succeeded to his patrimony on the death of his father, and to Dyfed by marriage. Later he extended his rule to Gwynedd and Powys, becoming king of all Wales with the exception of the south-eastern kingdoms. Hywel admired the English King Alfred and his reign was marked by a long period of peace with the English, during which he paid homage to Kings Edward and Athelstan and frequently visited the Wessex court. It is not clear what part he played in codifying and adapting the diverse customs of the land into a system of law, the role traditionally ascribed to him, but the usual name given to Welsh medieval law, 'The Law of Hywel', suggests that some such unification was achieved during his reign over a united Wales. His laws survive in the British Museum and at Peniarth.

IAROSLAV OF KIEV (1024–54), Grand Prince of Kiev, who established himself as Prince of Kiev after the protracted civil war which followed the death of his father, Vladimir I, in 1015. His reign was a period of internal stability and consolidation, marked by the encouragement of religion and learning, which earned him the title of Iaroslav the Wise. He attempted to ensure the continuance of political stability by bequeathing a part of the Russian land to each of his surviving sons, but under the supreme authority of the eldest, as Prince of Kiev.

IBADAN, western Nigeria, became the capital of the Nigerian Federation's Western Region after that country's independence (1960). A principal city of the Yoruba, Ibadan greatly increased in importance during the 19th cent., when its people made a persistent bid for political supremacy among a large section of the Yoruba. It is the seat of a university.

IBADIS, Kharijite sect, originally Iraqi, but from the 8th cent. principally Maghribi. Though accepted in Ifriqiyya by Berbers contending for power c. 750, its leaders were expelled to Tahert on the central steppe, where their imamate, recognized as far afield as Tripolitania, was later extinguished by the Fatimids (909). Its chief members were oasis communities, especially after the Tahertis fled to the Saharan Mzab, although some nomads claimed adherence. They were leading agents in Saharan trade (9th–12th cents) but they declined as a sect by conversion to orthodoxy from the mid-11th cent., vanishing from the Ifriqiyyan Djerid, but remaining as a distinct community in the Mzab.

IBADIYYA, branch of the Khawarij movement. The sect, originating, perhaps, at Basra in the mid-7th cent., takes its name from one of its reputed founders, Abdallah b. Ibad al-Murri al-Tamimi. The Ibadi doctrines seem to have reached their definitive form under the guiding hand of Abu'l-Sha 'tha Jabir b. Zayd al-Azdi. Ibadi zealots, perhaps, became involved in the rebellion (701–2) of Abd al-Rahman b. Muhammad al-Ash 'ath. Soon afterwards Abu 'Ubayda Muslim b. Abi Karima al-Tamimi, the greatest of the Ibadi leaders, organized at Basra a centre for the training of Ibadi missionaries. The Ibadi expansion continued throughout late Umayyad into Abbasid times. Representatives of the Ibadi faith are still (1970) to be found in Oman, East Africa, Tripolitania, and southern Algeria.

IBAÑEZ DEL CAMPO, CARLOS (1877–1960), Chilean general and president, whose first term of office (1927–31) was characterized by suppression of the opposition and severe censorship. He was re-elected in 1952 and again resorted to emergency measures by declaring a state of siege. He was blamed for a crisis caused by a fall in the price of Chilean copper on the world market.

IBARRA, FRANCISCO DE (1539–75), Spanish explorer and conquistador, noted for his opening up of the province north of Mexico City, later called Nueva Viscaya (New Biscay).

IBERIANS, geographical name first used by ancient Greek writers to denote the people who dwelt along the coasts of southern France and the Iberian peninsula. In terms of modern archaeology, the most reliable evidence for cultural unity among the various localized and individual Iron Age 'Iberian' cultures of the Mediterranean seaboard lies in the classical root of their art and in the uniformity of their alphabet. Iberian pottery has been found throughout the western Mediterranean, and on Phoenician sites in North Africa.

IBERVILLE, PIERRE LE MOYNE, Sieur de (1661–1706), French naval officer, soldier, and governor, who entered the French navy (1673) and served in the expedition against the English in Hudson Bay (1686). He led an overland expedition in Nfld (1696) which captured St John's. He left Brest (1698) in command of an expedition to settle LA and established the first settlements there around Fort Biloxi (1699). Iberville returned twice to LA, founding Fort Maurepas (1699–1700) and Fort Mobile (1701–2). He was appointed governor of LA (1703), but never returned to the colony, being delayed in France by difficulties over supplies and transport. In 1706 he led a French fleet against the West Indies and captured Nevis and St Kitts.

IBN AL-ARABI (1165–1240), Muslim mystic, born in Spain, who travelled in North Africa and lived in Anatolia and Damascus. He had a considerable influence throughout the Muslim world, but particularly in Anatolia.

IBN AL-ATHIR (1160–1234), Arab historical chronicler, author of *Al-Kamil fi'l-Ta'rikh.* This was, in effect, an abridgement of *Al-Tabari,* with a continuation of the narrative to the year 1231, the section dealing with the period of the crusades being an original contribution of great value.

IBN AL-HAYTHAM (*c.* 965–*c.* 1039) (the Alhazen of the Latins), Arab mathematician and physicist, whose main achievement was a work on optics (*Kitab al-Manazir*) which greatly influenced the development of this subject in medieval Europe.

IBN BAJJA (d. 1138), Abu Bakr Muhammad b. Yahya (the Avempace of the Christians). He was well versed in the natural sciences and in medicine and was esteemed as a musician. His main achievements were as a philosopher and a commentator on Aristotle.

IBN BATTUTA, MUHAMMAD IBN ABDULLAH (1304–77), Muslim traveller, who spent 24 years travelling in Europe, Africa, and Asia. In 1325 he undertook the pilgrimage to Mecca, passing through North Africa and Upper Egypt and making a detour through Syria and Palestine. He spent some time studying in Mecca, visited Iraq, returned once more to Mecca, and then journeyed to southern Arabia and parts of the East African coast, where he visited Kilwa (1331). From the Persian Gulf he again visited Mecca and then went through Egypt and Syria to Asia Minor and the Crimea. After visiting Constantinople, he travelled to India, where he was appointed judge by the Sultan of Delhi. His portrayal of the latter's court is among the most striking descriptions which survive of that of any medieval Muslim ruler.

He was the head of a mission to the Mongol Emperor of China (1342), spent a year as judge in the Maldive Islands, and eventually reached Canton via Ceylon and Bengal. He returned to Mecca through Persia, Iraq, Syria, and Egypt, thence to Fez, where he was received in honour by the Marinid ruler Abu Inan (1349). He next undertook a mission to Spain in order to fight in the holy war in Andalusia, using the opportunity to meet scholars in Granada. He next travelled to the western Sudan, where he visited Mali (1352–3), and several important Saharan trading towns. His description of the court of the Malian Sultan Mansa Sulaiman (1339–60) is detailed and arresting. Having returned to Morocco, Ibn Battuta dictated his memoirs to Ibn Juzayy, a secretary at the Marinid court. The latter embellished the simple racy narrative of the traveller, but the personality of its true author is always apparent.

Ibn Battuta, *Travels in Asia and Africa*, trans. and selected by H. A. R. Gibb (London, 1929). HTN

IBN HAZM (994–1064), exponent of the Zahiri school of Muslim theology and jurisprudence and poet of platonic love. He wrote a book analysing and comparing various religious denominations and heresies.

IBN IYAS (1448–*c.* 1528), Mamluk historian, author of the *Bada'i al-Zuhur*, a chronicle describing the affairs of the Mamluk sultanate of Egypt and Syria during the last phases of its existence.

IBN JUBAYR (1145–1217), Arab traveller, who journeyed through Egypt, the Hijaz, Iraq, and Syria in 1183–5 and again visited the central lands of the Muslim world in 1189–91 and in 1217. His *Rihlah*, describing his experiences in 1183–5, is one of the most important travel accounts in Arabic literature.

IBN KHALDUN (1332–1406), politician and scholar, who divided an active life between the Maghrib and Egypt and was the author of a 'universal' history, the *Kitab al-Ibar*, with its introduction or *Muqaddima*. The work appears as an original application of Arabic Aristotelianism to the data of Muslim historiography, with particular reference to North Africa, and presents a remarkable model for the historical process.

Given the serial view characteristic of Semitic monotheism, progression is seen in terms of succeeding cycles reminiscent of classical thought. Assuming the determination of human behaviour by the economic and social environment, the basic cycle is a necessary development from the simplicity of nomadism to the complexity of urban life, which then reverts inevitably towards the desert by impoverishment arising from extravagance. The motor is a concomitant cycle constituted by the process of state formation and decline.

Asabiya, communal solidarity, strongest in simple societies, aims naturally at dominion. A group emerges to establish a dynasty, whose expenditure creates a city of increasing social and economic specialization. *Asabiya* then declines as the ruler becomes a dictator, so that the dynasty weakens and eventually falls to a fresh group, and so the process recommences.

Continuity through successive cycles is provided for by imitation, whereby the culture of one cycle contributes to its successor. The course of history thus becomes the progressive manifestation of constant factors operative within human societies. Such an analysis compels attention, though its use of historical data for sociological ends, and its determinism, may be criticized. There seems confusion between *asabiya* as a conservative force for the preservation of society and as a revolutionary force for change, so that the causes provoking its political activity are not entirely clear. The primacy of the state seems exaggerated, while a puritan definition of extravagance is a disappointing explanation of contraction after Ibn Khaldun's description of growth. In consequence, neither the inevitability of the two cycles, nor their identity, seem sufficiently demonstrated. Despite Ibn Khaldun's unusual perception of a reciprocity between various social activities, his characterization of the society controlled by a particular government as equivalent to a biological organism is unsatisfactory. Even as a working hypothesis, it may well

obscure the assessment of wider or longer trends. Certainly, with regard to the span of history, Ibn Khaldun tends to the familiar pessimism of Muslim historicism. Vision, approach, and observation seem more valid than the resultant form: but these, indeed, are valuable.

Ibn Khaldun, *The Muqaddima*, trans. E. Rosenthal (London 1958; abridged N. Dawood, London, 1967). MB

IBN KHALLIKAN (1211–82), chief *qadi* of Syria, born at Irbil and educated at Aleppo and Damascus. He is celebrated for his composition of the *Wafayat al-A'yan*, a remarkable collection of biographies (865 in all) of distinguished Muslims.

IBN MAYMUN (1135–1204) (the Maimonides of the Latins), astronomer, theologian, physician, and philosopher, of Jewish descent. He was born at Cordoba and lived from *c.* 1166 in Egypt. His main philosophical endeavours were directed towards the reconciliation of Jewish religious thought with Muslim Aristotelianism. The writings of Ibn Maymun, of which some were translated into Latin, long remained one of the principal avenues along which Jewish ideas passed into the possession of the Christians.

IBN MULJAM, a member of the Khwariji sect who murdered the Caliph Ali (661) at the instigation of his betrothed and in revenge for the death of his co-religionists, who had been killed at the battle of Nahrawan (658).

IBN RASHIQ (1000–*c.* 1063 or 1073), Arab poet who lived most of his life at the Zirid court in Qayrawan. He also wrote works on the science of poetry and is perhaps the most influential of the classical Arab literary critics.

IBN SAUD DYNASTY, family which became rulers of most of Arabia. Originally established at Dar'iyya in the Wadi Hanifa, Nejd, in the 15th cent., the family remained of only local importance until 1745, when the then ruler, Muhammad ibn Sa'ud (d. 1765), linked his fortunes with the religious reformer Muhammad ibn Abd al-Wahhab and made the Saudi dynasty the secular vehicle and beneficiary of the puritanical, religious revival of Wahhabism. Under the next rulers (Abd al-Aziz I ibn Sa'ud (1721–1803), who reigned 1765–1803, and Sa'ud II ibn Sa'ud (1748–1814), who reigned 1804–14, the Saudi dynasty extended its power over much of Arabia including the Hijaz, while Wahhabi forces raided deep into Syria and Iraq. The Saudi power was challenged and eventually crushed by Egyptian forces (1811–18) and Abdullah I ibn Sa'ud was sent to Istanbul for execution. Egyptian control soon weakened and Turki ibn Sa'ud (d. 1834) regained control of Nejd (1825), Al-Hasa, and Oman. During the reign of Turki's son and successor, Faysal ibn Sa'ud (1834–65), the Egyptian attack was renewed and Faysal surrendered and was imprisoned in Egypt (1838–43). Although Egyptian forces withdrew to the Hijaz, by 1841 internal rivalries had weakened the Saudi dynasty which, under Faysal's successors, became eclipsed by the Rashidis in the later 19th cent. The fortunes of the dynasty were restored during the long rule of Abd al-Aziz II ibn Sa'ud (?1879–1953), when Saudi authority became established throughout the modern state of Saudi Arabia, and enormous oil reserves were discovered. Abd al-Aziz was succeeded by his son, Sa'ud IV ibn Sa'ud (*reg.* 1953–64), who was replaced by his brother Faysal II ibn Sa'ud in 1964. MEY

IBN SINA (980–1037), Muslim philosopher and physician (the Avicenna of the Christians). He was born at Bukhara and buried at Hamadhan. Among his most famous works are the *Kitab al-Shifa* (Book of Healing), a philosophical encyclopaedia, and the *Qanun fi'l-Tibb*, a codification of Greco-Muslim medical learning, which was translated into Latin and thereafter often printed in Europe during the time of the Renaissance and subsequently.

IBN TAGHRIBIRDI, ABU'L-MAHASIN (1411–69), author and the son of a high official at the court of the Mamluk Sultans of Syria and Egypt. He wrote *Al-Nujum al-Zahira*, a valuable chronicle of Egyptian affairs from the Arab conquest to 1453.

IBN TAIMIYYA (1263–1328), Arab, Hanbali theologian, and jurist, who lived in Mamluk Syria and Egypt and was noted for his hostility to the Mongols, his emphasis upon strict observance of orthodox Islamic practice, and his rigorous opposition to all heretical sects. His teaching greatly influenced the 18th-cent. Wahhabi movement.

IBN TUFAYL (d. 1185), Muslim philosopher trained in the Aristotelian tradition. He was well versed in medicine and became the vizier and also the court physician to the Almohad Abu Ya'qub Yusuf (d. 1184). His most important work was a philosophical romance, *Hayy ibn Yaqzan*.

IBN TUMART (d. 1129), Mahdi of the Almohads. He was born in the Anti-Atlas and travelled to the east (1105–10) to study Ash'arite theology. He returned *c.* 1119 and used his native Berber tongue to preach a puritan moral and a monotheistic theology from Mahdiya to Bougie, where he encountered and recognized his future caliph, Abd al-Mu'min. After denouncing the Almoravids in Marrakesh, he retreated to the High Atlas (*c.* 1121), where he rallied the tribes with the help of local leaders and proclaimed himself Mahdi, his base being at Tinmel (1125). At the time of his death he had organized the Almohad community and begun its rebellion against the Almoravids.

IBO, people of southern Nigeria, numbering in 1970 about 8 millions. Traditional Ibo communities, highly successful in farming and trading as they are today, comprised patrilineages organized around a central market and shrine—usually to *Ale* the Earth Goddess. Lineage heads (*okpara*) exercised ritual authority with the ancestral *ofo* stick. But status achieved through wealth or membership of the higher grades of title societies and age sets was also important. Intractable problems were placed before oracles. Those of Arochuku, Igweke Ala in Umunoha, and Agbala of Awka drew supplicants even from places beyond Iboland. The *mbari* shrines of mud-sculpture were an obvious sign of Ibo artistic tradition. The Igbo-Ukwu bronze sculptures suggest a tradition of great antiquity. Oral tradition ascribe the Ibo kingdoms of Onitsha, Aboh, and others west of the Niger to Benin influence. The sacred priest kings of the Umueri (the possible owners of the Igbo bronzes) are similarly derived from the Igala kingdom.

IBRAHIM BIN ABUBAKAR (*reg.* 1895–1959), Sultan of Johor, Malaya. Although forced to accept a British adviser in 1914, Ibrahim continued his father's tradition of personal rule, aided by many influential friends in London. He was the Malay ruler most reluctant to accept the 1957 independence arrangements.

IBRAHIM PASHA (1523–36), Ottoman Grand Vizier, was born at Parga in Epirus. He reorganized the Ottoman administration of Egypt (1524–5), and thereafter had a major role in the great events of the reign, including the Ottoman siege of Vienna (1529). His dominance of affairs aroused against him continuing intrigues which eventually led to his execution.

IBRAHIM PASHA (1789–1848), Egyptian soldier and eldest son of Muhammad Ali, commanded the Egyptian forces in the Greek War (1824–8) and Syria (1831–40), and succeeded his father as Pasha of Egypt.

IBSEN, HENRIK JOHAN (1828–1906), Norwegian writer, famous for his historical plays, lyrical dramas (including *Peer Gynt*), and social plays, the first of which was *Pillars of Society* (1878). His influence on radical thought and the psychological drama has been world-wide.

Ibsen's early life was embittered by poverty and lack of recognition, and his attitude to his own country was much influenced by its failure to support Denmark in 1864. He lived (1864–92) mainly outside Norway, and though the setting of his dramas was Norwegian, their interest lies chiefly in the unfolding of individual character.

ICELAND, first settled by Irish hermits, probably in the 8th cent. Norsemen discovered it in the mid-9th cent. The first major settler was Ingolf, traditionally in 874, and the settlement was largely complete before 950. Settlers came mostly from south-western Norway and the British Isles and brought many Celtic slaves. At first Iceland was ruled by pagan priest-chieftains, the descendants of early settlers, who claimed loyalty from those to whom they had distributed land. A national legal code was established on the Norwegian model (*c.* 927) and the national assembly (*Althingi*), with legislative and judicial authority, was founded *c.* 930. There was no executive power. The law and law-enforcement largely represented an attempt to provide substitutes for blood-feuds. Christianity was adopted by law (*c.* 1000) under pressure from Norway, which supplied almost all Iceland's timber and cereals. Deprived of its legal basis, paganism vanished rapidly, except as a literary tradition. The heathen priest-chieftains frequently became Christian priests or, later, employed priests for their own churches. Their authority was thus little impaired. Isleif Gizurarson was the first Icelander to be ordained bishop (*c.* 1056) and his son, and successor, Gizur established the first permanent see. The first recorded book in Icelandic was written in *c.* 1117. The spread of education among the chieftains ensured the rapid development of vernacular literacy, thus preserving much pagan tradition. Iceland therefore developed a rich vernacular literature in the 12th and 13th cents, preserving earlier poetry and in prose reaching unsurpassed heights. By the 13th cent. the chieftainships had been concentrated in relatively few hands and Iceland was ravaged by increasingly destructive feuds. The Norwegian King Hakon the Old (1217–63) manipulated these to gain influence and his rule increasingly appeared the only remedy. For these and economic reasons he was able by 1262 to assume the authority of the chieftains and to levy taxes. In 1376 Iceland, with Norway, came under Danish rule. The association continued for six cents. The power of the *Althingi* declined and it was temporarily (1800–43) abolished altogether. From the mid-19th cent. a national movement gained strength. In 1918 Denmark recognized Iceland's independence under a common king, and in 1944 full independence was achieved, with the dissolution of Danish ties, the proclamation of a republic, and the election of a president.

V. Stefansson, *Iceland* (London, 1939).
J. S. Griffiths, *Modern Iceland* (London, 1969).   PB

ICELANDERS, BOOK OF (*ISLENDINGABOK*), second draft of what is reputedly the first history book written in Icelandic. It was composed (1122–34) by Ari the Wise (1068–1148), and seems to show the influence of Bede. Although brief, it is sober and careful and of the greatest historical importance. It outlines the history of Iceland to 1118, with special reference to legal, chronological, and ecclesiastical matters.

ICELANDIC *LANDNAMABOK*. The Book of Land-takings (*ie*, settlements) describes the settlement of Iceland, giving the names and genealogies of major settlers and to some extent also those of their descendants. It also recounts many incidental stories. It was probably based on 12th-cent. written sources but survived in several versions, and was put together as an outline of the genealogical information essential to the Icelandic legal system. It is a major source for the early history of Iceland.

ICELANDIC LAWSPEAKER, only official of the Icelandic republic. He was elected and probably paid by the priest-chieftains for a period of three years, during which time he recited the whole law, one-third at each meeting of the Icelandic court, the *Althingi*. He was to recite the procedural law of the *Althingi*, however, each year, and to supervise its performance. Everything pronounced as law by the Law-speaker had full force, unless challenged at the time. Many lawspeakers were re-elected for further terms of office and some acquired great personal ascendency. The office came to an end in 1271, after Iceland came under the Crown of Norway and the *Althingi* lost its supreme legislative powers.

ICENI, native British tribe ruled by a Belgic house and occupying territory in south-west Norfolk and north-west Suffolk when the Romans invaded (AD 43). At first they were not conquered but recognized as a client kingdom allied to Rome. Trouble occurred in 47, when the Romans disarmed them, and again in 60, when King Prasutagus died without male issue. Then the treaty lapsed and after the Roman failure to maintain the kingdom's independence, despite the nomination of the Emperor Nero as joint heir with Prasutagus' daughters, Queen Boudicca led a widespread revolt in the east and south-east, which was suppressed with difficulty by Suetonius Paulinus. Caistor-by-Norwich (Venta Icenorum) became their administrative centre.

ICKES, HAROLD LE CLAIRE (1874–1952), US politician, reformer, and governmental administrator. He was chairman of the Cook County Progressive Committee (1912–14), the Illinios State Committee (1914–16), and a member of the national executive of the Progressive Republican Party (1915–16). He helped to manage Charles E. Hughes's presidential campaign (1916), and supported Hiram Johnson's bid for the Republican presidential nomination (1924), but became increasingly out of sympathy with the Republican Party in the 1920s and in 1932 supported the Democratic presidential candidate, F. D. Roosevelt. Ickes became the first of several prominent Republicans to join the successive Roosevelt administrations and, as secretary of the interior (1933–46), became one of the New Deal's boldest spokesmen and champions. He was also head of the Public Works Administration (1933–9) and controller of coal and petroleum during the Second World War. He was the author of *The New Democracy* (1934), *Back to Work* (1935), *Freedom of the Press Today* (1941), *Autobiography of a Curmudgeon* (1943), and the posthumous *Secret Diary* (1953–4).

ICONOCLASM, religious and political movement, inaugurated by Leo III the Isaurian, which on its religious side sought to extirpate the veneration of sacred images as idolatrous, and on its political side to enhance the power and standing of the military classes in the Byzantine empire and to diminish the power and pretensions of the Church. The controversy tormented Byzantine society for a century. Leo banned image-worship in AD 726, destroying vast numbers of icons representing Christ, the Blessed Virgin Mary, and sundry saints. The Iconoclasts had the older Judaic and early Christian tradition on their side and many Asian subjects of the empire supported their policy, especially the Armenians, from whom were reunited the best Byzantine troops. The condemnation of image-worship was bitterly opposed by most of the clergy and especially by the monks and was resented by the populace of Constantinople and other Greek towns. Iconoclasm also strained relations with the papacy at a time when the last remnants of Byzantine Italy were under severe pressure from the Lombards; thus it contributed to the formation of a Frankish–papal alliance which culminated in the coronation of Charlemagne as emperor in Rome in 800. The opponents of iconoclasm won a notable victory when a Council held at Nicaea in 787 defended images, chiefly on Christological grounds. But Leo the Armenian, who came to power after the empire had been disastrously defeated by the Bulgars, reintroduced the iconoclast decrees. It was not until 843 that the controversy lost its violence, when a synod called by Theodora, the widow of Emperor Theophilus, confirmed the canons of the Council of Nicaea.

IDAHO, 43rd member state of the US, admitted 1890. ID's mountains and forests, part of the Oregon country discovered by Meriwether Lewis and William Clark (1805–6) and confirmed as part of the US in 1846, were an obstacle to early settlement, except by missionaries and fur traders, and few of the thousands of settlers on the OR trail chose to stay in ID. In 1855 and 1860 the Mormons established communities in ID as part of the elaborate defensive network of Salt Lake City, but in 1860 the discovery of placer gold attracted a large mining population and led to ID's separation from Washington territory in 1863. The present boundaries of ID were formed by the separation of MT (1864) and the transfer of another sector to WY (1868). The mountainous terrain and relative isolation which delayed its settlement and admission to the Union have limited the growth of ID's population, but it has a flourishing farming industry, beef cattle, wheat and potatoes being of particular importance, and is a leading producer of silver, lead, and zinc. It is also increasingly popular as a vacation area.

IDRIS (*reg.* 1887–1916), Sultan of Perak, Malaya. After being rewarded with the sultanate for his pro-British attitude during the turbulent 1870s, Idris made it into a dignified and stabilizing institution. He was a champion of educational and administrative opportunities for Malays, and an effective critic of the centralizing trend of British policy after 1895.

IDRIS ALOMA (*reg.* 1569–99), King of Bornu in north-west Nigeria, succeeded to the throne as a minor and had to deal with the Bulela of Kanem. In the course of seven campaigns he seems to have secured a durable settlement. He also campaigned against the non-Muslim peoples of the southern frontier and against the Ngizim of western Bornu, and raided Kano and Agodès. These wars secured metropolitan Bornu, while much of Tchad and the Hausa region became tributary or protected areas—while, along the northern Desert trade routes, the king's authority extended as far as the Fezzan. These successes stemmed from a reformed and strengthened administration. Guns and mercenaries were obtained from North Africa. Diplomatic missions were sent to Istanbul in 1577 and to Morocco in 1583. The fugitive rulers of Songhay sought refuge in his domains in 1593. Idris was a great Islamizer. The *Sharia* was enforced, and mosques and palaces were built of burnt brick. Aloma was killed fighting on the southern frontier, and it was left to his successors to consolidate his achievements.

IDRISI, AL (1100–*c.* 1165), Muslim geographer, who was born at Ceuta and studied at Cordoba. He lived for a long time in Palermo, at the court of the Norman King Roger II. In 1154 he completed the 'Book of Roger', *ie*, a description of the world.

IDRISIDS, 9th-cent. Moroccan dynasty. The founder, Idris, was a refugee from Abbasid persecutions in the east, who established descent from the Prophet as the criterion of nobility in Morocco. The dynasty's principal achievement was the foundation of Fez.

IEMITSU (1604–51), 3rd Tokugawa *shōgun* (*reg.* 1623–51). He succeeded his father, Hidetada, and presided over the completion of the Tokugawa system. During his reign the practice of *daimyō* attendance at Edo was regularized and Japanese contacts with the outside world were reduced to a minimum.

IETSUNA (1641–80), 4th Tokugawa *shōgun* (*reg.* 1651–80). His reign was marked by administrative stabilization and by a change in emphasis from military power to Confucianism as the foundation of Japanese government.

IEYASU (1542–1616), 1st Tokugawa *shōgun* (*reg.* 1603–5) and third of the great 16th-cent. unifiers of Japan. He was the son of a minor *daimyō* named Matsudaira, who claimed descent from the Minamoto family, and spent much of his early life as a hostage at the castle of the powerful Imagawa Yoshihira. After Imagawa's defeat by Oda Nobunaga (1560) Ieyasu allied himself to the latter, defending his rear while he gained control of Kyoto. At the same time he consolidated his own increased domains. After Nobunaga's death Ieyasu held his own against Hideyoshi before accepting the latter's suzerainty. He assisted Hideyoshi in besieging the Hojo family in Odawara, and partly as a reward, partly as a precaution, was transferred to the Kantō plain by Hideyoshi, being granted lands which produced nearly one-twelfth of Japan's total rice yield. This provided an excellent base for Ieyasu in the struggle which followed Hideyoshi's death, although diplomacy played almost as large a part as military resources in his victory at Sekigahara (1600) and his consolidation of power thereafter. By 1603 he was able to revive the office of *shōgun*, a title he made over to his son, Hidetada, in 1605, thus ensuring the latter's smooth succession. The most important of Ieyasu's measures to confirm Tokugawa supremacy was the wholesale confiscation of many of his enemies' domains and their redistribution in such a way that the Tokugawa family and its vassals controlled two-thirds of the country, including the strategic centre. When Ieyasu died in 1616, a year after the destruction of Hideyoshi's heirs at Osaka, the absence of any challenge to Tokugawa power showed the thoroughness of his work.

IFE, ancient Yoruba town of western Nigeria, remembered in Yoruba traditions as being the first of their kingdoms, and the one from which their great 'founding ancestor', Oduduwa, sent out his sons to reign over 'junior' Yoruba states. Its foundation is fairly well attested by archaeological evidence as being some time before AD 1000. This evidence bears on the dating of many pieces of remarkable sculpture, in bronze and terracotta, which have been found at or near Ife over the past half-century. Most of these pieces, or the larger of them, probably represent early rulers and kinsmen of rulers, and are preserved in a museum near the palace of the *oni*, or traditional King of Ife. Though always of great spiritual and social importance to Yoruba community life, Ife seems never to have become the centre of a political unity among the many Yoruba states.

IFNI (1500 sq. kms), on the west Sahara coast, has (1970) a population of 56,500 Arab and Berber nomads. Ifni has been a Spanish province since 1958 and is ruled by a Spanish governor-general.

IFRIQIYYA (from Africa), the name of the Roman province round Carthage. It is medieval Arabic for the region from Tripoli through Tunisia to eastern Algeria.

IGLESIAS, PABLO (1850–1925), founder of the Spanish Socialist Party. He developed the Printers' Association, of which he was president, from an old-fashioned craft union into a militant organization to resist employers, which staged the first effective strike in Restoration Spain (1882). Inglesias's task was hampered by the rival popular appeal of anarchism in Spain, but his organizing ability ensured the slow growth of socialism through its paper *El Socialista* and the UGT (*Union General de Trabajadores*). However, the party never gained widespread working-class support until it began to act in conjunction with the republicans in 1909. This gained Iglesias a seat in the Cortes and implicated his party in a broad attempt to reform the whole political structure of Spain.

IGNATIEV, COUNT NIKOLAI PAVLOVICH (1832–1908), Russian soldier, politician, and diplomat, who negotiated the treaty of Peking with China (1860) and headed the Asiatic department of the foreign office (1861–4). As ambassador to Constantinople (1864–77) he established a predominant influence over the sultan and followed a Pan-Slavist policy aimed at establishing a Russian-dominated Slav federation, contractory to Gorchakov's agreement with Austria and Germany. Through his agents he encouraged the Serbs to declare war, and his influence over Alexander II led to the Russo-Turkish War (1877–8).

The treaty of San Stefano was his greatest success, creating, independently of the European powers, a large Bulgaria under Russian influence. He also proposed control of the Straits through a secret Russo-Turkish agreement. The Congress of Berlin partly reversed these gains. He was minister of the interior (1881–2).

IGOR (*reg.* 913–44), Grand Prince of Kiev, traditionally held to be the son, or more probably the grandson, of Rurik, the first Varangian ruler of Kievan Russia. His reign is notable for his campaigns on the Caspian Sea (913–14, 943–4) and against the Byzantine empire (941, 944). He subjugated the Slav tribe of the Drevlianians, by whom he was killed in 944 for trying to extort excessive tribute.

IGUALA, PLAN OF (1821), compromise proposal for Mexican independence issued at the small town of Iguala by Agustín de Iturbide. After the deaths of Miguel Hidalgo and José Morelos, the struggle for independence was carried on by Vicente Guerrero and other guerrilla leaders. Iturbide, who was sent to crush them, began instead to negotiate. The result was the Plan of Iguala, which sought to reach a compromise between the beliefs of the conservative Creoles and the rebels.

Although Mexico was to become independent, it would retain ties with Spain and would remain a monarchy. Catholicism would remain as the state religion, and a new constitution would be drawn up by an elected congress under the supervision of the army. The compromise was successful in that its conciliatory tone brought it the support of many of those who had formerly opposed independence. It was also used by Iturbide as a means to accelerate his rise to power.

II, NAOSUKE (1815–60), Japanese politician of the late Tokugawa period and the most powerful of the *fudai daimyōs*. He led the conservative majority of this group in 1858 in rejecting the idea of broadening the Tokugawa political structure. Simultaneously he accepted foreign demands for trade, with the aim of safeguarding the *bakufu* from external threat, but without gaining the emperor's prior approval. When these actions aroused criticism Ii punished his opponents severely, but his attempt to revive Tokugawa authoritarianism ended with his assassination.

IKEDA, HAYATO (1899–1965), Japanese politician and prime minister (1960–4). To heal the divisions within the nation and the Liberal-Democratic Party which his predecessor, Kishi, had caused, he followed a compromise policy, at the same time laying great stress upon economic advancement.

IKHSHIDIDS, dynasty ruling in Egypt during the 10th cent. The founder of the regime was Muhammad b. Tughj, who became the effective master of Egypt from about 935 and, in 937, received from the caliph the title of Al-Ikhshid. Ibn Tughj came into conflict first with Muhammad b. Ra'iq, the powerful *āmir al-umarā* at Baghdad, then (after 944) with the Hamdanid amir of Aleppo, Sayf al-Dawla. Muhammad b. Tughj died in 946. Two of his sons succeeded him in the years 946–66, but all real power was in the hands of the eunuch Kafur, who himself became the ruler of Egypt in 966–8. In 969 the forces of the Fatimid Caliph Al-Mu'izz took over Egypt and thus brought the Ikhshidid line to an end.

IKHWAN, Muslim religious fraternity of puritanical character established among the Bedouin tribes of eastern Arabia in and after 1912 by Abd al-Aziz ibn Sa'ud. The Ikhwan were settled in religio-military colonies which became the nuclei of villages and towns, thus facilitating the conversion of Bedouin nomads to settled agriculture. One of the most important elements in the victorious Saudi campaigns in Arabia, the Ikhwan's military power was eventually broken (1929–30) after they had challenged the king's authority.

IKHWAN AL-SAFA, 'The Brethren of Sincerity', an association flourishing at Basra and Baghdad during the late 10th cent. Its members devoted themselves to philosophical and scientific studies, but constituted also a religio-political opposition, of extreme Shi'i views, ranged against the existing governmental order.

IKKŌ UPRISINGS, series of attempts (c. 1460–1580) by dedicated (Ikkō) followers of the Shinshū sect of Buddhism in Japan to resist the power of local lords. Many such attempts were successful, most notably in Kaga, which a Shinshū community controlled for nearly a century. The success of Nobunaga and the surrender of the chief Ikkō fortress at Osaka (1580), however, led to the re-establishment of *daimyō* authority everywhere.

ILAHI ERA, calendar introduced by the Emperor Akbar (1584) in connection with his religious cult. It was a solar year, reckoned from 1556, the year of Akbar's accession. It began with the Persian *nauroz* or new year, using the Persian names for months, with some variation of length to avoid intercalation.

ILBERT BILL (1883), named after the politician who introduced it, was intended to remove racial discrimination in India. In the districts outside the Presidency towns cases against European British subjects were heard only by Englishmen. The object of the bill was to allow Indian judges and magistrates in the districts to try Europeans, which was contrary to the Criminal Procedure Code of 1873. It was vehemently opposed by the non-official European element, especially the planters, who boycotted Ripon's viceregal entertainments and insulted him. Eventually a compromise was effected under which Europeans were entitled to claim that they should be tried by a jury, half of the members of which were to be Europeans. Racial discrimination did not come to an end until 1923, when similar rights were accorded to Indians. The importance of the controversy is that it intensified racial antagonism and caused educated Indians to realize the value of combination and organization.

ILCHINHOE, 'Association for United Advance', in Korea (1904–10), advocated union between Japan and Korea. The prime mover was Song Pyongjun, who had advocated pro-Japanese policies since 1884, and been exiled to Japan in 1895. He returned with the Japanese armies in 1904 and enlisted the support of two survivors of the Independence Club and Yi Yonggu's faction of the Tonghak (Ch'ondogyo). The Ilchinhoe ran its own newspaper, *Kungmin Sinbo*. Song joined the Yi Wanyong cabinet, which worked under the Japanese resident-general, Itō Hirobumi, from 1907, and the society was dissolved upon the Japanese annexation of Korea in 1910.

ÎLE DE RÉ, island off the coast of the French department of Charente Maritime and scene of the Huguenot wars of the early 17th cent. It was fortified by Vauban.

ILI DISPUTE, between China and Russia, began with Russian occupation (1871) of the Ili river valley in Chinese Turkestan in an attempt to forestall Yakub Beg and British influence in Eastern Turkestan. The Russians, confident that the weak Ch'ing government would not be able to restore control of the area, which was plagued by the Muslim Rebellion (Kansu and Shensi) and general disorder, promised its return as soon as Chinese authority was re-established in that area. With the recovery of Chinese Turkestan in 1878, the Ch'ing government demanded that Russia should evacuate Ili. However, during the ensuing negotiations, the Ch'ing diplomat, Ch'ung-hou, made such extensive territorial and trade concessions, that both he and the agreement signed were denounced by the Ch'ing government, which now threatened war. Beset with domestic and foreign difficulties at this point, the Russians agreed to renegotiate. The resulting treaty of St Petersburg (1881) provided for the return of most of the Ili valley to China, tax exemption for Russian traders in Mongolia, an indemnity to be paid by the Chinese, and some other commercial privileges.

ILJ ALI (*fl.* 16th cent.), corsair renegade, last successor of Barbarossa as *beglerbeg* of Algiers (1568–87), and an Ottoman admiral after Lepanto (1571). Algiers, Tunis, and Tripoli became separate *pashalik*s after his death.

IL-KHANS, name given to the Mongol rulers of Iran and surrounding areas (1256–1353). Following the campaign of Chingiz Khan in Transoxania (1219–22), Mongol forces became established in parts of Iran, Khurasan, Transcaucasia, and Asia Minor. In 1251 the Great Khan, Möngka (*reg.* 1251–9) decided to consolidate these conquests and sent an expedition (1253–8) under his brother, Hulagu (d. 1265), which resulted in the destruction of the Abbasid caliphate and the establishment of the Il-Khanid dynasty. Under Hulagu and his son and successor Abaka (*reg.* 1265–82) the Il-Khans were powerful and feared by their neighbours, but a period of weakness supervened after the death of Abaqa, before the accession of the remarkable and versatile ruler, Ghazan Khan (*reg.* 1295–1304), during whose reign Islam was adopted as the official religion in place of the variety of Shamanism, Buddhism, and Christianity which had hitherto prevailed. Ghazan's reign was also distinguished by vigorous frontier campaigns and by splendid building. This last feature was continued during the more peaceful and prosperous reign of his brother Öljeitü (*reg.* 1304–16), but internal unrest again became pronounced under Öljeitü's son, Abu Sa'id (*reg.* 1317–35), and after his death local rebellions broke the power of the central government, the rule of the Il-Khans disintegrated, and various local dynasties emerged, *eg*, the Jalayirids and Muzaffarids. The external relations of the Il-Khans were characterized by a long struggle with the Egyptian Mamluks for control of Syria, lasting until 1313, in the course of which the Il-Khans repeatedly and unsuccessfully sought alliances with the Christian powers of the west; and by a prolonged struggle with the rulers of the Golden Horde for control of the Caucasus. Domestically, the Il-Khan period was one of apparent economic decline, aggravated by continued internal strife, and, at the end of the period, the appearance of the Black Death. The Il-Khans made their capitals at Maragheh and later Tabriz, but they habitually continued to live in nomadic encampments, *eg*, at Sultaniyah.
MEY

ILLINOIS, 21st member state of the US, admitted 1818. The area was part of the French empire in North America until it was transferred to Britain in 1763. In 1778 it was captured by George Rogers Clark and subsequently incorporated in the Northwest territory (1788). After being reorganized as part of Indiana territory (1800), in 1809 it was organized as a separate territory including what is now WI. It was inhabited by the powerful Algonquian Indians, from one tribe of which, the Illiniwek, IL derives its name; Indian land claims were not finally cleared until after the Black Hawk War (1832). The first wave of settlement, after the war of 1812, came largely along the river system from the South, and so paved the way for early statehood. Later, eastern migration was stimulated by construction of the Erie canal (1825) and the final defeat of the Indians. IL, a wealthy agricultural state with a huge industrial and financial complex centred in the north around Chicago, still reflects the different cultural influences of its early settlement.

ILLINOIS CENTRAL RAILROAD, major mid-western US system, originally projected (1836) as a local railroad from

Galena to Cairo, IL. It was the first railroad to be allotted a congressional land-grant (1850) and by 1860 had linked Chicago to New Orleans. Its methods of advertising and settling land were later adopted by Western land-grant railroads.

ILLINOIS COMMAND, administrative district of New France, established after explorations by Jacques Marquette and Louis Joliet (1673). It was made part of French Louisiana in 1717, ceded to Britain (1763), and governed from Quebec (1774) until it was transferred to the US in 1783.

ILLINOIS INDIANS, confederacy of American Algonquian tribes, comprising the Cahokia, Kaskasia, Michigamea, Moingwena, Peoria, and Tamaroa, formerly occupying parts of WI, IL, IA, and MO. They were first encountered by the French (1667). Wars with other tribes and liquor obtained from the French reduced their numbers. After a Kaskasia Indian murdered the celebrated Ottawa chief, Pontiac (1769), a war of vengeance decimated the confederacy. By 1800, there were only about 150 Illinois left. The survivors sold their lands (1833) and moved to the Indian Territory, where they joined two other tribes.

ILLUMINISTS, or Alumbrados, Spanish sect existing *c*. 1512, predating the Protestant Reformation and originally consisting of the followers of Isabel de la Cruz, a Franciscan sister, and Pedro de Alcaraz. Illuminism, an aberrant form of mysticism, gained ground in the Spanish towns, *eg*, Toledo, especially among friars and nuns, but it was condemned and suppressed by the Inquisition (Sept. 1525), although the spiritual fervour which inspired the movement was revived in the mysticism of the later 16th cent.

ILLYRIA, ROMAN, area covering at its maximum much of modern Yugoslavia and parts of Austria and Hungary. Piracy in the Adriatic by Illyrian tribes resulted in wars with Rome in 229 and 219 BC and Roman hegemony over the Dalmatian coast, with extension inland after 168. Further conquest up to the middle Danube came under Octavian (Augustus) between 35 and 11 BC. Illyria was divided into two provinces, Dalmatia and Pannonia, in the 1st cent. AD, but the name Illyria continued to be used with reference to a much larger customs area. During the 4th to 6th cents Illyria was the name of a territorial prefecture covering most of the Balkans. Some vigorous soldier emperors, among them Aurelian, Diocletian, and Constantine, were of Illyrian origin.

ILLYRICUS, MATTHIUS FLACIUS (1520–75), Dalmatian leader of the Gnesiolutherans, the German Protestants who bitterly disputed the theological interpretations of Melanchthon and his followers, the Philippists, after Luther's death (1546). In his collective work *The Centuries of Magdeburg* (1559–74) Illyricus claimed that the Lutheran church was the true historical heir to the early apostolic church.

ILOKANO REVOLT, uprising in 1762 in Ilokos, one of the colonial administrative divisions of the Spanish Philippines, in Luzon island. During the Spanish period a number of revolts broke out in this area, usually in protest against the abuse of power by the government-appointed local Spanish representative, the *alcalde mayor*, who collected tribute and recruited forced labour through the local Filipino chieftains. The most widespread and serious of the Ilokano revolts was that led by Diego Silang, which took place during the first year of the British occupation of Manila (1762–4), a development in Asia of the Seven Years War (1756–63). The immediate aims of the revolt were the abolition of tribute and forced labour and the overthrow of the *principalia* or local elite, to whom the *alcalde* had left the exercise of his powers. The revolt broke out in Vigan on 14 Dec. 1762, after Silang's return from Manila, where he had been impressed by the ease with which British forces had defeated the Spaniards. The rebels removed the *alcalde mayor*, and

drove Bp Ustariz from Vigan. The latter had earlier issued an interdict against the rebels, which probably contributed to the final suppression of the revolt, since it caused a number of Silang's followers to withdraw and kept others from joining his movement. The bishop fled to the northern part of Ilokos, and from there called the people to arms against the rebels. Meanwhile, Silang established an independent government centred on Vigan and immediately abolished tribute and forced labour, although he imposed new taxes. After Simon de Anda, head of the Spanish government in areas unoccupied by the British, had sent Silang an ultimatum to surrender, the latter decided to offer his services to the British and took an oath of allegiance to the King of England on 13 May 1763. The British gave him the titles of *alcalde mayor* and *sargento mayor*, with authority to appoint his subordinate officials. On 23 May 1763 Silang was assassinated. The uprising continued under the leadership of Silang's wife and his uncle Nicolas Carino, until it was quelled by a Spanish military force in Sept. 1763.   JMSa

ILTUTMISH, SHAMSHADDIN (d. 1236), the 2nd Sultan of Delhi (*reg.* 1211–36). He was a Turk of noble birth who was sold as a slave to Qutb-ad-din Aibek. His ability secured him rapid promotion and the key governorships of Gwalior and Budaon. On Aibek's death (1210) Iltutmish defeated his son and inaugurated the Delhi Slave dynasty (so called from their origin before manumission). Iltutmish found the sultanate much reduced by revolt and dissension and his first care was to restore his authority. He recovered Bengal, Gwalior, and the Punjab in a series of campaigns and then added Malwa and Sind and the Rajput fortress of Ranthambor. In Delhi he completed the Qutab Minar from its first storey, probably as a tower of victory. During his reign much anxiety was caused by raids of the Mongol followers of Chingiz Khan.

ILYMINSKY, NIKOLAI IVANOVICH (1822–91), Russian teacher and Oriental traveller, who was director of Kazan Teachers' Training College (1870). Ilyminsky's teachers spread Orthodox Christianity among the Muslim tatars and encouraged the growth of literacy by developing native languages.

IMAD SHAHI DYNASTY of Berar, founded by Fathullah Imad Shah, a Hindu converted in youth, who became the governor of the Bahmani province of Berar and for a time was vizier of the Bahmani kingdom. After the death of Mahmud Gawon, he retired to his province and declared his independence in 1490. He had three successors, and the state was then absorbed (1574) by Ahmadnagar.

IMAM, one who serves as a guide or example (cf. the Arabic verb 'amma', to precede). The word has several shades of meaning. At first the Imam of the Muslims, the one who led them in the ritual of prayer, was the Prophet Muhammad himself, and, after his death, the caliphs or the delegates acting in their name, *eg*, the governors of the provinces. The title also denotes the mosque officials who guide the faithful in prayer. It is sometimes accorded, moreover, to Muslim scholars of high distinction, *eg*, the great theologian Al-Ghazali. The term reached its most notable development among Shi'is, who restricted it to certain descendants of Ali, who were regarded as divinely guided rulers, and later, in Safawid Iran, as themselves divine.

IMHOTEP (*fl.* 2700 BC), architect of the Egyptian King Djozer, for whom he designed the Step Pyramid, the first known building constructed entirely of stone. Later, the fame of his writings and knowledge of healing led to his deification.

IMMIGRATION INTO AUSTRALIA. By 1891, 83 per cent of the 1 million Australians born overseas had come from the British Isles and until after 1945 this percentage was maintained. This was primarily due to economic and political ties with Britain, though the gold-rushes of the 19th cent. brought other Europeans. Another important feature of immigration policy before 1945 was severe restriction on the entry of non-Europeans for permanent settlement. The deep-seated conflict between European and Chinese diggers in the goldfields was heightened by the policy of the Federal government by which all political parties agreed to what became widely known as (but was never officially designated) the White Australia Policy.

Two major policy changes followed the Second World War, an event which had demonstrated Australia's vulnerability to invasion. Political parties agreed that the population should be quickly increased, if possible to 25 million by the year 2000, to 'deter any future aggressor'. As the 1930s low birth rates limited Australia's capacity, a large-scale immigration programme was launched. During a period of 25 years, nearly 3 million immigrants were brought from Europe, about one-half coming from continental countries because the British government was unwilling to negotiate agreements involving the loss of so many of its people.

The other policy change was the progressive relaxation of restrictions on entry of non-Europeans with special qualifications. Sensitivity and concern about increasing difficulties which the restrictive policy had caused in relations with Asian countries were combined with increasing confidence in ability to control the economic and social consequences of its relaxation. By 1970 a professional, English-speaking Asian offered a job in Australia found it relatively easy to enter for permanent settlement. RTA

IMMIGRATION INTO NEW ZEALAND. Before British annexation of NZ in 1840, the Maoris' fearsome reputation and the long sea voyage discouraged European immigrants, who in 1839 numbered fewer than 2000. The NZ Co. and the associated Otago and Canterbury groups sent about 17,000 emigrants to NZ in the years 1840–53 under their various schemes of 'systematic colonization', and thus provided the first considerable nuclei of European population, apart from Europeans already established at Auckland. A steady intake under provincial immigration schemes was overshadowed by the gold-rushes of the 1860s, which brought over 200,000 immigrants, mostly to Otago, though only about half this number remained. An even larger number was added to NZ's population by the immigration policies of 1870–84, the net gain being about 160,000; in the peak year—1874—38,000 immigrants arrived. Soon after this, a prolonged period of depression began and it was not until this receded c. 1900 that government-assisted immigration was resumed. By 1914 another net increase of about 120,000 was registered. After 1918, Massey's government set out to aid Britain during the Depression by taking large numbers of assisted immigrants, until depression fell on NZ itself, leaving a net gain of 70,000.

Following the Second World War, NZ embarked on its largest schemes of organized immigration, over 190,000 immigrants coming between 1951 and 1964. For 125 years immigration was practically all European and overwhelmingly British. Sharing the Australian colonies' alarm about 'Asiatics', NZ, from the 1880s, adopted a 'White NZ policy'. After the Second World War, NZ received more continental Europeans, as well as Pacific Islanders from her own territories. From the mid-1880s, natural increase predominated over immigration as a population source.

IMMIGRATION INTO THE UNITED STATES. Apart from Negroes, Orientals, Mexicans, and Puerto Ricans, Europeans comprised more than half the immigrants who ever crossed oceans in search of new opportunities from the 15th cent. onwards. This European emigration to the US totalled more than 35 million people, though several million went back to their own land. As the US became more fully developed and economic opportunities became more numerous; as traditional agriculture and industries in Europe became dislocated; as knowledge spread more easily; and as transport systems (especially railways and steamships) improved, the scale of immigration grew. In the 1840s nearly 1½ million entered; in the 1880s over 5 million; and in the first decade of the 20th cent. nearly 9 million. Within this main trend, fluctuations occurred as the US experienced prosperity or depression. Thus immigration was very high in some years (eg, 1847–54; 1869–73; 1880–4; 1887; 1893), and low in others (eg, 1858–62, 1876–9; 1894–7). It was again high just before the First World War, over a million people arriving between 1905 and 1914.

From the 1830s to the 1850s almost all immigrants were British, Irish, or German, but then, until the early 1890s, these were joined by Scandinavians and Canadians. Thereafter, to the 1920s, most were Italians, or Poles, Slovaks, Croats and other Slavs, or Magyars, Greeks, and Russian Jews. Immigrants did not settle equally in all parts of the country. In 1890 there were fewer in the entire South than in New York city. Agriculture and urban work in the Middle West attracted many north-west Europeans. Eastern cities always received a high proportion, and especially when textiles, iron, and steel, and other industries were increasing. Irish were prominent in dock labour and railway construction, French-Canadians in cotton mills, Slavs in mining and heavy industry, Welsh in coal mining, Italians in building, and Jews in the clothing trades.

All immigrants—even the British, who had no language problem—set up their own shops, clubs, newspapers, churches, and other institutions. This practice continued as long as the group was reinforced by newcomers from Europe, even though at the same time the children of earlier immigrants were becoming assimilated; but as soon as reinforcement stopped, ethnic institutions and languages began to decay.

In the 1920s immigration was greatly reduced by federal legislation. Between 1931 and 1945 no year saw as many as 100,000 enter, and in the worst years of the Depression more people went back to Europe than arrived. After the Second World War, skilled workers from north-west Europe, refugees from central and eastern Europe, Canadians, and Mexicans, combined to make up an immigration figure that often reached 300,000 a year. In a society changing rapidly towards white-collar work, and urban or suburban living, such numbers have not been enough to perpetuate communities of the old type. What remain are ethnic preferences in the choice of a marriage-partner, religion, and politics. The old languages and the foreign-language press were declining by 1970 among the later immigrant groups, and among Germans and Scandinavians were almost extinct.

IMPEACHMENT, in England, process of trial in parliament generally reserved for high crimes and misdemeanours beyond the reach of normal process and for offenders whom no other authority would prosecute. On a motion by the House of Commons for the impeachment of any person, articles of impeachment are drawn up by a Committee of that House and exhibited to the House of Lords, through which a copy is supplied to the accused requiring him to answer them. Trial is by the House of Lords, each peer having an equal place as judge of law and fact; verdict is by a majority. The process was used first against Lord Latimer and others in the Good Parliament of 1376, and in several cases in the Merciless Parliament of 1388: it was well established by the end of the reign of Richard II. In the Stuart and early Hanoverian periods it was much used, but the last cases were the famous and lengthy trial of Warren Hastings in 1788 and that of Lord Melville in 1806. The modern practices of the collective responsibility of cabinets and the resignation of governments following an adverse vote of censure in the House of Commons have resulted in the process falling into disuse. JRLS

IMPERATOR, Roman term meaning 'commander-in-chief', which became from 2nd cent. BC a special title conferred on a victorious Roman general by the acclamation of his troops.

Julius Caesar used it as a permanent title and Octavian made it part of his nomenclature as a forename (Imperator Caesar), but this usage did not become regular until the time of Vespasian. Since under the empire all military honours belonged to the emperor and all victories were won in his name, imperator also appeared after the emperor's name, with a number indicating how many such salutations he had received after victories of the Roman armies.

IMPERIAL DEFENCE, SELECT COMMITTEE ON, to co-ordinate defensive policy for the British empire, was handi-capped initially by the self-governing colonies' reluctance to surrender any independence to Westminster or to share the expenses involved. In 1904 the prime minister, A. J. Balfour, reorganized the committee, which was expanded after the German threat to Agadir (1911). During the First World War its functions were absorbed by smaller bodies such as the war council, but it was re-established (1919), its secretary becoming cabinet secretary, a new appointment which brought about the keeping of cabinet minutes. A sub-committee of imperial chiefs of staff was developed in 1924 to consider new problems, such as the role of the RAF and anti-aircraft defence. The organization held good until 1939, when a war cabinet system on Lloyd George's model, strengthened by the chiefs of staff organization, helped towards the achievement of victory in the Second World War.

IMPERIAL FEDERATION LEAGUE (1884–93), pressure group in Britain for the furtherance of Imperialist ambitions launched by W. E. Forster, backed by many influential statesmen, writers, and propagandists, including Lord Rosebery, W. H. Smith, J. A. Froude, J. R. Seeley, and James Bryce. The league seized the opportunity of Queen Victoria's Golden Jubilee (1887) to urge that the prime ministers of the self-governing colonies visiting London should confer on imperial problems with the British ministers concerned. This Colonial Conference (1887) was the origin of all later Colonial and Imperial Conferences. Though supporting ventures such as the Colonial and Indian Exhibition and the foundation of the Imperial Institute, South Kensington, the members of the league failed to agree on a constructive policy and broke up.

IMPERIAL FREE KNIGHTS, in German *Reichsritter*, class of lower nobility enfeoffed with their lands by the emperor and subject to him alone. Instead of taxation they gave 'free gifts' to the emperor. They were especially numerous in the south and west of the Holy Roman empire.

IMPERIAL LEGISLATIVE COUNCIL, constituted by the Indian Councils Act (1861). Until the Montagu–Chelmsford reforms (1919) legislative powers were, to a large extent, concentrated at the centre. In 1861, for purposes of legisla-tion, the governor–general's council was reinforced by 12 additional members, not less than half of whom were to be non-officials. The first three non-official Indians were the Maharaja of Patiala, the Raja of Benares, and Sir Dinkar Rao, of Gwalior. In 1892 the number of additional members was raised to 16. The council had the right of interpellation and to discuss the budget. In 1909 the number of members was increased to 60, of whom 28 were to be nominated offi-cials, 5 nominated non-officials, and 27 non-officials elected by various bodies. In 1919 the Imperial Legislative Council was merged with the Indian Legislative Assembly and for the first time there was no official majority.

IMPERIAL MARITIME CUSTOMS in China, customs service managed by Westerners on behalf of the Chinese government, was the outgrowth of the Shanghai Foreign Inspectorate system. The latter was an improvisation by Rutherford Alcock, British consul at Shanghai, for the collection of customs duties on behalf of the Chinese government, which had temporarily lost control of the city to rebels in 1853.

The Foreign Inspectorate began its operations in mid-1854 under inspectors nominated by the British, American, and French consuls. Its success was its recommendation for its continuation, and, after the Anglo-French War (1856–60), its extension to all treaty ports. Its name was duly changed to the Chinese Imperial Maritime Customs Service. The development of this new institution, as well as that of its predecessor, owed much to a British consular officer, H. N. Lay (1832–98), who served as its first inspector-general (1861–3). Lay was succeeded in 1863 by Robert Hart, who remained in office for 45 years. The insistence on honesty and efficiency by both Lay and Hart turned the Maritime Customs Service into an important revenue collector for the Ch'ing government. Customs duties, increasing with trade, rose from 7 million taels in the 1860s to 22 millions in the early 1890s and to 35 millions in the early 1900s. The Maritime Customs was thus able to perform the function of servicing the payment of war indemnity between 1860 and 1866, and thereafter contributed towards financing modern-izing projects such as the Foochow Navy Yard, the Kiangnan and the Tientsin arsenals. The dependability of the Maritime Customs presented itself naturally as the security for the loans floated by Chinese government agencies. After the Sino-Japanese War (1895) and the Boxer Rising (1900) practically all of the revenues collected by the Maritime Customs were pledged to meet China's loans and indemnities.

The role of the Maritime Customs Service went beyond that of a duties-collecting agent, however. It completed the charting of the China coast and the Yangtse river begun by the British navy, erected lighthouses and other aids to naviga-tion, and provided general harbour facilities. It was also responsible for the creation of the Imperial Post Office in 1896, which eventually became an independent organization in 1911. In addition, it represented China in 28 international trade exhibitions. Its commercial reports remain the only accurate account of China's foreign trade.

Foreign personnel dominated the Maritime Customs throughout its history. It employed 400 Westerners and 1400 Chinese in 1875. The numbers increased to 700 and 3500 respectively in 1895. More than half of the Westerners were British. Control of the Maritime Customs reverted to the Chinese in 1933.

Stanley F. Wright, *Hart and the Chinese Customs* (Belfast, 1950).   DP

IMPERIAL PREFERENCE in the British Empire, economic policy advocating a modified form of protection enabling imports from the colonies to enter Britain at a lower rate of duty or duty-free. Joseph Chamberlain fervently believed in an Imperial Zollverein or Free Trade within the empire, the only section of his aims for a unified empire at the Colonial Conference (1897) which interested the colonies, but which would have meant abandoning Free Trade. His programme of Tariff Reform was a godsend to the Liberals and split the Conservatives, who lost the general election (1906). His arguments were defeated by Asquith, who de-clared that Free Trade meant a 'big loaf against the little loaf', no duties on food, maintenance of employment and international goodwill. In the World Depression Chamber-lain's policy finally won acceptance when the National govern-ment had to adopt Imperial Preference (1931) and sign the Ottawa Agreements (1932), between Britain and the Dominions, which was extended to the Crown Colonies (1933). Britain obtained more meat, butter, bacon, and grain from the Dominions and exported more machinery, cars, and textiles to them. The General Agreement on Tariffs and Trade (1947) recognized Imperial Preference, a crucial factor in later British approaches to trade agreements with EFTA and the European Economic Community.   JRA

IMPERIAL SERVICE TROOPS, recruited in the Indian states, officered by Indians and supervised by British officers. It was Dufferin who, as viceroy (1884–8), accepted the offer of certain princes to place troops at the disposal of the paramount power. In 1922 the title was changed to Indian State Forces. They fought with distinction in both World Wars.

IMPERIAL WAR COUNCIL, the *Hofkiergsrath* of the Holy Roman empire, a central office instituted under the Emperor Ferdinand in 1556 with responsibility for all problems of military organization and appointments and the general direction of wars involving the empire. It did not, however, control supply and finance, which were under separate bodies, the *Generalkriegskommissariatamt* and the *Hofkammer.* The war council's powers were increased however by Prince Eugène, who became its president in 1703 and carried out reforms to improve and enlarge the standing army. The council, under the presidency of Count Haddik, was retained by Joseph II, who carried out other further administrative reforms.

IMPERIALISM, the desire, for varied motives—economic, strategic, aggressive, missionary, or colonizing—to build up an empire. Far from being unique to one country, imperialism, in varied forms, can be detected throughout history. Many imperial powers have imposed alien cultures on their subject peoples; others have been content with political domination, while yet others have carried out a process of racial and political assimilation.

In the Ancient World, Chinese, Middle Eastern, Persian, Greek, and Roman empires all exercised their sway, for differing periods of time over varied races, and left behind a cultural imperial legacy. With the decline of power at the centre, the empires, symbols of self-confident aggression, fell apart, often leaving behind a vacuum for new nations seeking aggrandizement.

In the Middle Ages imperialism sometimes went hand-in-hand with religious zeal, as witnessed in the territorial ambitions of Islam or the papacy. With the rise of modern nation states however, these supranational entities faded. The European voyages of discovery in the late 15th and 16th cents, stimulated by economic and religious imperialism, gave to Spain and Portugal in particular, valuable possessions in the New World and Asia. In the process, organized empires, such as those of the Incas and Aztecs, were destroyed.

The British empire, starting from colonizing motives, often with religious freedom as well as economic advantage in mind, developed from the 17th cent. For over a hundred years Britain's chief European rivals for land in America and India, the most important spheres of influence, were the Dutch and French. However, the work of Chatham, Wolfe, Clive, Hastings, and others had created British imperial hegemony by 1763, and by 1800 colonizing activity in Australasia had begun.

Meanwhile, in eastern Europe, tsarist Russia was building up an empire contiguous with the homeland: Siberians, Caucasians, Central Asians, Cossacks, Mongols, and Tatars gradually came under the sway of St Petersburg and the Orthodox Church.

Napoleon's imperialistic ambitions faded at Waterloo, but in many former French-occupied countries a legacy of law and order and sound government remained.

By 1815 Britain had acquired large territorial gains and the Victorian era began and continued in a mood of confident superiority, typified by the 'John Bull' attitude of Palmerston. Cobden, and to some extent Gladstone, saw colonialism as unnecessary, since the advent of free trade could bring great prosperity through 'informal empire'. In 1847 Disraeli had suggested an Imperial Union—an embryonic idea which he later developed. In 1868 Dilke's 'Greater Britain' stimulated interest in Britain's imperial achievements, and in the next year the Royal Colonial Institute was founded. Thus, after a period of relative disinterest, the states of Europe began to extend their control over vast areas of the world. The 'New Imperialism', which in Britain reached its height in the 1880s and 1890s, had begun.

The European watershed of 1870 saw Britain, France, Germany, Belgium, Portugal, and Italy contenders for imperial gains. The 1878 Congress of Berlin, the 'Scramble for Africa' beginning in 1884, the Fashoda Crisis of 1898, and the Anglo-Boer War of 1899 were all landmarks in this rivalry. British motives as expressed by Disraeli, Salisbury, and Rosebery tended to favour the strategic advantages, Kipling encouraged romanticism, while Chamberlain and Rhodes looked to economic gains. It was estimated by J. A. Hobson in 1902 that territorially, one-third of the British empire was acquired between 1870 and 1900. Despite all the economic arguments, 75 per cent of Britain's overseas trade in 1901 was, however, still with foreign countries.

Im 1880 the only important French dependencies were Senegal, New Caledonia, Algeria, Cochin-China, the French West Indies, and the Island of Reunion. Under Jules Ferry in the following years French rule was extended to Tunisia, Annan, Tonkin, Madagascar, West and Equatorial Africa. French imperialism never received full-scale support at home, yet prestige and economic factors led to centralized, assimilatory control from Paris.

By the 1880s Bismarck's imperial ambitions had created extensive fields of German influence in New Guinea, South-West Africa, West Africa, and East Africa. By the Heligoland treaty of 1890 and subsequent arrangements, Germany made agreements with Britain, France, and Italy which completed the partition of East and Central Africa by 1891.

European imperialistic ambitions contributed to the causes of the First World War, and this was followed by a gradual loosening of the bonds of empire, and the evolution of the British empire into the Commonwealth. The desire for independence among the developing nations greatly accelerated the process. Imperialism became, for left-wing politicians, a derogatory term implying exploitation, tied-aid, and political capitalist pressure.

The Second World War enlarged the overseas responsibilities of the US and after 1945 a massive aid programme was developed. Nevertheless, the US found itself losing credit in the Third World as the 1950s progressed. The activities of the Central Intelligence Agency, the long and expensive struggle in Korea, and later in Viet-nam, all aroused America's critics. In 1962 the US secretary of state, Robert McNamara, expounded the modern version of the Monroe Doctrine—that the US would intervene militarily whenever their national interest was threatened. At least half of the Federal budget is devoted to defence for this purpose. Since the beginning of the Cold War American imperialism, usually in the form of economic aid, has invariably been directed towards the anti-communist bloc.

The post-war situation in Europe similarly saw the USSR anxious to keep its hold over its satellites. Resistance in East Berlin in 1953, Poland and Hungary in 1956, and Czechoslovakia in 1968, was soon subdued by Moscow. Less overt Soviet imperialism, seen in the form of aid, was given extensively to Nasser's Egypt, and is (1970) providing general support for the Arab cause in the Middle East.

In 1970 20th-cent. imperialism, ingenious and more subtle than in the 19th cent., was still a potent factor in world politics.

H. M. Wright, *The New Imperialism* (Boston, 1966).
Louis Heren, *The New American Commonwealth* (London, 1968).   MEB

IMPERIUM, fundamental constitutional concept in ancient Rome denoting supreme military and judicial power which belonged to the kings, and after their expulsion to the consuls, military tribunes with consular power (445–367 BC), praetors, dictators, and *magistri equitum.* Under the republic, magisterial *imperium* was progressively limited, especially by the principle of collegiality, by the laws guaranteeing appeal to the people against a capital sentence, and because a proconsul's or pro-praetor's *imperium* was valid only within his province. In special cases *imperium* was conferred on private persons and in the 1st cent. BC extraordinary grants for specified terms of years were made, *eg*, to Pompey against the pirates and Mithridates (67–66). Augustus received such a grant in 23 BC, giving him *imperium* specifically superior to that of other magistrates, and it was voted by the Senate to succeeding emperors on their accession.

IMPEY, SIR ELIJAH (1732–1809), British colonial official, who was appointed chief justice of the Supreme Court at Calcutta (1773). He was educated at Westminster School, where he was a contemporary of Warren Hastings. In 1775, when Hastings prosecuted an Indian called Nand Kumar for conspiracy and forgery, Impey presided at the trial. Nand Kumar was sentenced to death and hanged—a penalty that has been denounced as a judicial murder. There seems to be no doubt that Nand Kumar was guilty, but it was felt that a fine or term of imprisonment would have been fairer. In 1777 Impey also favoured Hastings in the dispute over his alleged resignation. He also sentenced Philip Francis to pay heavy damages in the *Le Grand* case. There were constant conflicts between the Supreme Council and the Supreme Court until Impey was made president of the new *Sadr Diwani Adalat* (1780). Because this was considered irregular, Impey was recalled (1782). An attempt to impeach him was unsuccessful.

IMPORT DUTIES REPORT (1840) in Britain, by the Select Committee condemning Protection and advocating Free Trade. The committee, which met during a period of disastrous Whig finance in a severe industrial depression accompanied by high wheat prices, argued that Protection was a tax on the community as a whole, limiting the consumption of foodstuffs, keeping up the price of corn, and stifling initiative in industry needing to conquer fresh markets. It attacked the labyrinth of the tariff in which 16 out of 1150 dutiable articles realized £22,018,000 out of a total revenue of £22,963,000 (1839–40) and predicted a great rise in revenue if duties were repealed. Relations with foreign countries would be more friendly, industry would flourish, and landlords share in the general prosperity if Corn Laws were abolished.

The report charted Britain's progress towards Free Trade, though Sir Robert Peel had not read it before introducing his first budget (1842) and Gladstone was acutely conscious of some of its fallacies.

IMPÔT UNIQUE, proposed scheme for a single, universal direct tax in France during the *ancien régime*. Inspired by the reforms of Colbert and Vauban's *dîme royale*, it was championed by successive financial reformers, *eg*, Michel Amelot early in the 18th cent., the controller-general Bertin after the Seven Years War, and Mahy de Cormère in the immediate pre-revolutionary period. The proposal faced strong opposition from vested interests in the outlying provinces of France, from the commercial, manufacturing, and municipal bodies and, in the later years of the *ancien régime*, from the farmers-general. Finally, a project to implement the tax was adopted by the National Assembly (1790).

IMPROVEMENT COMMISSIONERS in Britain, ad hoc bodies, established by local acts of parliament, to supplement the limited powers of the local authorities. General acts imposing new duties on borough corporations and JPs in Quarter Sessions were very rare in the 18th and early 19th cents, and in any case the growth of new urban areas made the creation of new authorities necessary. The first body of improvement commissioners was established in 1662 to supervise cleansing, lighting, sewerage, and nuisance removal in London and Westminster. Similar acts became frequent in the later 18th cent. and by 1800 there existed about 300 bodies of commissioners, 100 of them in the metropolitan area. Their composition varied, but they usually consisted of ex officio members, the mayor and corporation and the justices, together with the principal inhabitants, and perhaps

elected representatives of the ratepayers at large. They had fixed rating and borrowing powers. Improvement commissioners were not established after 1835, but the existing bodies were only gradually superseded by the local government reforms of the 19th cent.

IN EMINENTI (1643), papal bull promulgated by Urban VIII to condemn Bp Jansen's controversial work, the *Augustinus*, but which failed to suppress Jansenism in France.

INCAS, the rulers, and by extension the inhabitants, of one of the most advanced ancient Indian civilizations of America. The Incas, a small group of herders in the Peruvian highlands, settled around the valley of Cuzco, possibly in the 12th cent. Between then and 1532 they showed qualities of social organization and military superiority by which they gradually expanded their territory to include much of modern Ecuador, Peru, and Bolivia, and parts of Argentina and Chile.

The empire was organized on rigid hierarchical lines, with the Inca, who was considered to be a child of the sun, as supreme authority. Minute regulations governed the day-to-day activities of the masses, and dissident groups were controlled by terror and forcible dispersal. A system of roads and runners ensured logistical readiness against attack and massive fortifications protected their garrisons.

In the arts they showed high skill in architecture, pottery, and weaving. The Peruvian city of Cuzco remains a monument to their mastery of building construction in an earthquake zone.

Civil war over the Inca succession between Atahuallpa and Huáscar weakened the Incas' resistance to the Spanish invasions led by Francisco Pizarro and Diego de Almagro. In less than a year (1532–3), many Incas had been killed and the Spaniards had taken complete control.   MJM

INCENSE ROAD, name given to a series of ancient trade routes running northwards from South Arabian ports, along which eastern spices, particularly frankincense from the Minaean and Sabaean kingdoms of South Arabia, were carried.

INCHIQUIN, MURROUGH O'BRIEN, 1st Earl of (Irish) (*c.* 1614–74), Irish soldier and statesman, who fought for both parliament and the king in the Irish rebellion. On being appointed vice-president of Munster (1640), he took up arms against the Irish (1641) on behalf of Charles I. Though formally approving the Ormonde truce of 1643, he did not think it favourable to the cause of Irish Protestants. In 1644 he visited Oxford and urged the king to make peace with parliament. Gradually he edged away from Ormonde's pro-Catholic policy and joined the parliamentary forces and was made president of Munster. In 1648, discontented with parliament's treatment of his army, he declared for the king and concluded a truce with the Irish, which Ormonde converted into the peace of 1649. Charles II created him lord-president of Munster (1649), but he was forced to flee in the face of the Cromwellian invasion. After being raised to an earldom in 1657, he returned at the Restoration (1660) but thereafter was politically unimportant.

INCH'ON LANDINGS (15 Sept. 1950), seaborne landings by the US 10th Corps on the west coast of Korea which outflanked the North Korean armies, who were simultaneously attacked frontally along the Pusan perimeter, more than 100 miles (161 kms) to the south-east. This achieved the first objective of the United Nations in the Korean War—the destruction of the North Korean forces which had invaded South Korea. The landings can be justified by their success, but the plan was hazardous, and its success is attributable entirely to poor North Korean intelligence.

INCONFIDÊNCIA MOVEMENTS, conspiracies resulting in unrest during the Brazilian colonial period which demonstrated the dissatisfaction of the local inhabitants with the

Portuguese imperial system in Brazil. The most famous of these movements was centred on the province of Minas Geraes in 1789. Here the unrest had republican overtones and was also connected with slavery.

INDEMNITY ACTS in Britain, legislation passed annually from 1727 until 1828, enabling Nonconformist Dissenters who managed to gain office to avoid the stringency of the Corporation Act (1661). They were permitted to take the Anglican sacrament after, instead of before, election to town corporations and were thus able to take some part in public life at a time when other dissenters, *eg*, Roman Catholics, were still excluded. The indemnity acts ended when the Test and Corporation Acts were repealed.

INDENTURED SERVANTS, Europeans who, from the 16th to the 19th cents, were sent to overseas colonies and required to provide labour for the purchaser of their indenture (a work contract usually to meet the cost of transportation) for a stipulated period of time, after which the servant would be considered a free citizen.

INDEPENDENCE CLUB in Korea (1896–8), aimed at restricting foreign interference in Korean internal affairs. Its promoter, So Chaep'il, was a naturalized American, who never held office in the club. At its formation it included several shades of opinion, and its first chairman was a government minister, Yi Wanyong. The club was given the building which had been used for the reception of envoys from China, and the gate by which those envoys entered Seoul was renamed 'Independence Gate'. The club propagated its ideas through public meetings, and through Korea's first regular newspaper, *Tongnip Sinmun* (*The Independent*). It was successful in persuading King Kojong to return to his palace from the Russian legation, where he had taken refuge from the Japanese a year earlier. Soon after this, however, all government officials, including Yi Wanyong, resigned from the club. The young members who remained, including Syngman Rhee, were outmanœuvred by the government, which set up a rival 'Empire Club', offered government posts to some members, used gangs to provoke incidents involving the Independence Club, and arrested many of its members.

INDEPENDENCE HALL, former Pennsylvania State House, in Philadelphia, preserved as a memorial to the American Revolution. In this building, the meeting-place of the Second Continental Congress (1775–7), were held the debates on the Declaration of Independence and the Articles of Confederation. It also housed the Philadelphia Convention (1787) and was the second site of the Federal government (1790–1800).

INDEPENDENT LABOUR PARTY in Britain, founded in 1893 by a diverse group of working-class and left-wing organizations. Its aim was to secure the representation of the working classes independently of the existing political parties. But its growth was slow. It was unsuccessful in the elections of 1895 and it had to face competition from other socialist groups as well as from the Liberal Party. Its real opportunity came in 1900, when, in alliance with the trade unions and the other socialist societies, it formed the labour representation committee, to become the Labour Party six years later. James Ramsay MacDonald, one of the ILP delegates to the founding conference, was elected secretary of the new Labour Party.

In 1906 the ILP shared in the general success of the Labour Party, and Keir Hardie, until then the sole ILP MP, was joined by, among others, MacDonald and Philip Snowden. The ILP acted (1906–14) as a 'ginger-group' within the Labour Party, constantly urging a greater degree of independence from the Liberals than the leadership of the Labour Party thought was possible. After the outbreak of the First World War in 1914 much of the ILP found itself at odds with the rest of the Labour Party over attitudes to the war—MacDonald himself resigned the leadership of the Parliamentary Labour Party.

But if the war rather isolated the ILP, it brought it some thousands of new members, many of them from the middle class and many of them former Liberals or radicals who had withdrawn their support from the war, and who found in the ILP a new political home. But at the same time, the strategic position of the ILP within the larger Labour Party was weakened after the introduction of Labour's new constitution in 1918. This decisively strengthened the power of the trade unions and permitted individual and direct membership of the Labour Party. The latter was a blow at the ILP and it was recognized as such.

Thus the history of the ILP from 1918 to 1932 was one of increasing separation from the main body of the Labour movement. The ILP's base was found more and more to be in the west of Scotland, and throughout the 1920s it had a series of disputes with the trade unions over social and economic policy. Despite the opposition of the unions the ILP persisted in clinging to its policy of the 'Living Wage' and it came out strongly against the Mond–Turner talks on industrial conciliation. The ILP's official policies in this period assumed the imminent collapse of capitalism and it began to demand that its MPs should subscribe to these policies rather than those of the Labour Party, a demand intolerable to the Labour Party and a violation of its standing orders.

The differences between the ILP and the Labour Party increased during the second Labour government, and the fall of the government did not in any way reconcile the ILP to the larger party: Henderson and the 'loyal' leaders were thought to be as much tainted with compromise as MacDonald. In 1932 the ILP disaffiliated itself from the Labour Party. Thereafter it declined rapidly, though it remained strong on Clydeside, and in 1945 won four Glasgow seats.

INDEPENDENT SOCIAL DEMOCRATIC PARTY in Germany (USPD), founded in 1917 by the anti-war minority of the German Social Democratic Party (SPD), as a result of the first open schism in German socialism since the 1880s. It included many of the leading intellectuals of the old party (Karl Kautsky, Eduard Bernstein, Rudolf Hilferding, Rosa Luxemburg), but was weaker in politicians of the first rank. Its chairman and leading figure, until his murder in Nov. 1918, was Hugo Haase, previously co-chairman of the SPD. Until the end of the First World War the party stood for a negotiated peace and for international socialist action to that end. Prepared itself to take action in Germany, it was partly responsible for the general strike of Jan. 1918. During the war it had about half as many members as the SPD.

The USPD inherited the quasi-revolutionary tradition of pre-war German social democracy and, after the Russian Revolution, moved further to the left. The German Revolution of Nov. 1918, though not the work of socialists, precipitated it into positions of importance and sometimes power. It joined with the SPD on nominally equal terms to form the Provisional Government (10 Nov. 1918), and attempted to turn the revolution in a socialist direction. But the SPD, committed not to revolutionary action but to democratic institutions, proved the dominant partner. Ineffective in government and under pressure from its radical wing, the USPD withdrew from the coalition at the end of Dec. In the elections of Jan. 1919 to the National Assembly it secured only 7·6 per cent of the vote (SPD, 41 per cent). During the succeeding months of civil war (Jan. to May 1919) the revolutionary state and city governments in which the USPD had played a role were suppressed by force.

Nevertheless, the USPD, benefiting from military brutality and from Germany's continuing economic and international crises, grew rapidly in 1919 and 1920. During these years it, rather than the small Communist Party, was the characteristic left-wing radical party. At its apogee in 1920 it had 900,000 members. In the elections of June 1920 it received nearly 5,000,000 votes (18·8 per cent) and elected 81 members of the Reichstag, making it, after the SPD, the second largest German party. By this time, however, the party was itself divided over the question of an alliance with the successful Russian revolutionaries in the Third International. At the party's Halle conference in Oct. 1920 the party split. The majority amalgamated with the Communist Party two months later, providing it for a time with the mass membership it had been unable to secure for itself. The minority, with about 300,000 members, continued the USPD for two years. Unable to find a role between the Communist Party on its left and the SPD to its right, and in conditions of declining membership and finance, the party reunited with the SPD in Sept. 1922. A few thousand members maintained the USPD as a tiny socialist splinter party until 1931.

DM

INDEPENDENT TREASURY ACT (1840) in US, legislation by which a system of sub-treasuries was created for the handling of federal funds. The act, which was supported by the Van Buren Democrats as an alternative to the Bank of the United States, established sub-treasuries in New York, Boston, Philadelphia, Washington, DC, Charleston, St Louis, and New Orleans. It was repealed by the Whigs (1841), but re-enacted by the Democrats in 1846 and the system continued until creation of the Federal Reserve System (1913). The sub-treasuries were finally abolished in 1920.

INDEPENDENTS, English Puritans who rejected both prelacy and the Presbyterian system of synods in the exercise of judicial and administrative powers. They were not direct heirs of the Brownist movement (which after 1580 tried to secede from the Elizabethan Church) nor were they true separatists. Although they asserted the right of individual congregations to worship according to God's Word, as the sole test of truth, their apologists in the 1640s professed 'a middle way between that which is called Brownism and the Presbyterial government as it is practised'.

The first truly Independent Church in England was set up in Southwark (1616) by Henry Jacob, a one-time Brownist who had belonged to exiled separatist groups at Middelburg and Leyden. He now desired the sort of organization later advocated by Independent spokesmen at the Savoy Conference (1657–8). This has been described as a 'decentralized Calvinism' in which congregations might be grouped for local convenience, but would not be subordinate to any higher ecclesiastical authority. At the same time they did not repudiate all connection between Church and state. Up to a point they were tolerant, but the congregations saw themselves as groups of true Christians who looked to the civil power to repress licence and disorder and punish such manifest 'errors' as prelacy, popery, and denial of the Trinity. This alliance with the magistrate distinguished Independency from the dangerously anarchic tendencies of Brownism.

The removal of Abp Laud and episcopacy (1641) brought home many Independents who had fled to Holland, but the movement was still small and ineffectual, particularly in parliament, until the covenant with the Scots (1643). This was a necessary measure to win the civil war and had, as its price, the Westminster Assembly's attempt to impose a Presbyterian system. Toleration, meaning the rejection of synodal discipline and rigid doctrinal tests, then became a major issue. Presbyterians feared the anarchic consequences of any loosening of the ties between Church and state, while Independents feared that Presbyterianism would frustrate true religion by substituting one intolerant Erastianism for another. In this struggle the Independents sought the help of Levellers and other radical allies whose social and political ideals were abhorrent to the army officers, who mostly came from the lesser gentry. But in their mistrust of King Charles I the officers were eventually converted to republicanism, and by Pride's Purge (1648) the Independents at last gained control of parliament.

Its traditional rejection of separatism then made Independency respectable. Oliver Cromwell's guiding light was godliness and religious experience, and the civil power was invoked to protect 'God's people, who are as the apple of His eye'. By taking over the parochial system and its ancient endowments, Puritan ministers won the support of local gentry who had a vested interest in tithes and patronage and could confidently look to the law to suppress fanatics and extremists; while the ministers themselves, unhampered by bishops, synods, or other central organization, could conscientiously regard themselves as representatives of their congregations. In parishes where the incumbent was not of their persuasion, Independents were free to organize their own local societies.

At the Restoration the Clarendon Code (1661–5) drove all dissenters underground until the Toleration Act (1689) gave them liberty of private worship, although they were still proscribed politically. Under the stimulus of Methodism the various congregational bodies grew in numbers and enthusiasm, and this was followed in the 19th cent. by a tendency towards combination, the Congregational Union of England and Wales being formed in 1831.

In the British American colonies their organization had always been tighter. Between 1620 and 1640 some 25,000 Puritans emigrated to escape Anglican persecution, and in these new lands the elders of the Church enforced a stern civil and religious orthodoxy. In the spirit of the old separatists Roger Williams denounced this subservience to political and doctrinal authority, and in 1654 he obtained freedom for his Rhode Island settlement, but it was many years before liberty of conscience and organization was recognized in the New England provinces.

M. M. Knappen, *Tudor Puritanism* (Chicago, 1939).
G. Yule, *The Independents in the English Civil War* (Melbourne, 1958).

MMR

INDEX, catalogue of books which are regarded as dangerous to the faith or morals of Roman Catholics. Books were condemned at the Council of Nicaea (325), more frequently after the invention of printing, and, under the formal title of *Index librorum prohibitorum*, from 1559 onwards.

INDEX LIBRORUM PROHIBITORUM, list of books, judged immoral or heretical first by the Holy Office and later (1587) by the Congregation of the Index, which Catholics were forbidden to read. The first papal Index was commissioned by Paul IV (1555–9) in 1559, but proved too severe; a modification was recommended by the Council of Trent and in accordance with this decision Pius IV (1559–65) commissioned a new list (1564). It remained in 1970 as the official list of books which Catholics might not read.

INDIA CONCILIATION GROUP, committee, mainly of Quakers, which was formed (31 Oct. 1931) at the time of Gandhi's visit to London for the second Round Table Conference, and which sought to maintain contacts between Indian and British politicians and administrators. The group worked for many years from the Friends' House, Euston Road, London, with Carl Heath, the secretary of the Friends' Council for international service (1919–35), as chairman, and Agatha Harrison (1885–1954) as secretary throughout. The group played a particularly important intermediary role during the visit of the Cabinet Mission to New Delhi (1946), as they had close contacts with the ministers concerned.

INDIA OFFICE, name given in 1858 to the establishment of the newly appointed British secretary of state for India. There had been (1784–1858) two offices in London occupied with Indian affairs, the East India House in Leadenhall Street and the Board of Control at Westminster. The India Office was one of the departments of the home civil service and it housed the Council of India. The cost of the establishment was defrayed from Indian revenues. In relation to

India the India Office may be said to have combined the functions of a treasury, war office, home office, board of trade, civil service commission, and foreign office. Its various departments corresponded to the committees into which the Council of India was divided. After 1935 its premises became the commonwealth relations office. The library and records office are (1970) in Blackfriars Road, London.

INDIAN ADMINISTRATIVE SERVICE, successor to the Indian Civil Service (ICS) as the administrative cadre from which superior administrative officers for state and central governments in India are selected. It was formed in Oct. 1946, and the first entry examinations were held in July 1947. War-service candidates and those promoted from the civil services of the provinces and the princely states were also taken into the new service. Members of the ICS who continued in service after independence became part of the IAS establishment, but they retained special privileges of service and emoluments and generally continued to hold the highest posts. Annual competitive examinations and promotions from subordinate services continue to be the main sources of recruitment, but there has throughout been a shortage of recruits and two special recruitment boards (1948, 1956) have been established to provide a wider range of candidates. The ICS numbered about 1300 at independence, but the IAS, in order to meet a much wider range of administrative, developmental, and managerial tasks, was twice as large by the late 1960s. All members of the IAS are allotted to state cadres on appointment and are seconded to the government of India or centrally controlled public service enterprises. Unlike the ICS, judicial appointments are not made from IAS cadres, and diplomatic appointments are the responsibility of a separate (foreign) service.

INDIAN AFFAIRS, OFFICE OF, office of the US Department of Interior in charge of all government dealings with the Indians. Indian affairs were conducted by the War Department until 1824, when a Bureau of Indian Affairs was created within that department. The office of Commissioner of Indians was created (1832) to give management of all Indian affairs to the bureau and a Department of Indian Affairs was created (1834) within the War Department. The present office (1970) was transfered to the Department of the Interior (3 March 1849) placing it under civilian control for the first time.

INDIAN ARMY, term which officially came into use with Kitchener's reorganization (1903) to distinguish British-officered Indian regiments from British line regiments serving in India. The Indian army sprang from the guards enrolled for the protection of the factories of the East India Co. and, until 1860, included regiments of Europeans enlisted for Indian service, as well as regiments of Indians.

In 1748 the French presence in Madras caused the company to organize a force for the defence of its possessions. This was done by Capt. Stringer Lawrence, who, in addition to the Madras European regiment, enlisted 2000 sepoys. In 1759 the sepoy forces were organized into battalions each under a native commandant and two British subalterns. This was the real foundation of the Indian army. The three presidential armies of Bengal, Madras, and Bombay developed independently. There was a great expansion of the Bengal army under Clive and the number of sepoy battalions rose from one in 1757 to 19 in 1764. In 1765 the number of Madras sepoy battalions increased from 7 to 10. The growth of the Bombay army was much slower. In 1796 the single-battalion native infantry regiments were formed into regiments of two battalions, of which Bengal had 12, Madras 11, and Bombay 6. In addition, Bengal and Madras each maintained four regiments of regular cavalry. One serious defect was that European officers were absent for long periods from their regiments and were seconded to various staff appointments and to the political service. By 1824 the numbers had grown rapidly and the two-battalion regiments of native

infantry were divided into single-battalion regiments, of which Bengal had 68, Madras 52, and Bombay 24. There were also regiments of native cavalry, both regular and irregular. In 1835 Bentinck drew attention to serious defects and even declared that the Indian army was the least efficient and most expensive in the world. Then in 1857 came the Mutiny.

After 1858 the company's European troops were transferred to the service of the Crown and in 1860 they were amalgamated with the British army of the line. Until the Mutiny, military officers in civil and political employment had been retained on the establishment of their regiments, blocking the promotion of those who remained with the regiment. From 1861 such officers became members of a staff corps. To render service with native troops more attractive the officers of each of the three presidency establishments were also graded in the Staff Corps. In 1903 Kitchener renamed the Staff Corps, together with the Indian troops, the Indian army.

In 1917 Indians were made eligible for the King's Commission. There was a radical reorganization of the Indian army in 1922. Indianization was accelerated in 1924 by the formation of 8 units (later 16) completely Indianized, without British officers. In 1934 an Indian Sandhurst was opened at Dehra Dun. The Indian army was composed of many classes and races, and so organized after 1858 as to inhibit mutinous combination. The most martial were the Sikhs, Punjabi Musalmans, Pathans, Baluchis, Dogras, Rajputs, Jats, Garhwalis, and Marathas. From 1815 Gurkhas from Nepal were recruited and eventually formed 10 regiments. The record of the Indian army in both World Wars was a proud one.

The Army in India and its Evolution (Calcutta, 1924).

CCD

INDIAN ASSOCIATION, formed in 1876 and not to be confused with the smaller British Indian Association. It was established in Calcutta by S. N. Banerjea as a political organization to represent the educated middle classes. Branches were started at Lahore, Meerut, Allahabad, Cawnpore, and Lucknow, but Madras remained aloof. The main object of the association was the unification of the people of India on the basis of common political interests, an idea derived largely from Mazzini. They drew attention to Indian grievances and protested against the lowering of the age limit for entrance to the Indian civil service (1876). They also demanded simultaneous examinations in England and India. They protested against the Vernacular Press Act (1878) and drew Dufferin's attention to the need for reforming the Provincial Legislative Councils (1884). They were opposed to the Partition of Bengal (1905). The importance of the association is that it paved the way for the Indian National Congress.

INDIAN CIVIL SERVICE may be traced back to the writers, factors, and merchants of the East India Co., who were known as civil servants to distinguish them from the company's naval and military officers. Whereas Clive's conquest of Bengal made the company a territorial power, the measures of Warren Hastings and Cornwallis converted its mercantile employees into the Indian Civil Service (ICS). When the company required Hastings to take over the revenue administration (1772) he knew that the English collectors were corrupt and oppressive, but his freedom to censure them was limited by his need to placate powerful interests in England. Cornwallis was not similarly encumbered and he organized the ICS on a footing of probity and efficiency. By establishing a liberal scale of salaries he eliminated the root cause of private trading and corruption. The company insisted that their servants should sign contracts or covenants promising to serve honestly, and not to engage in private trade or receive presents, hence the term Covenanted Civil Service. In time, they ceased to be merely agents of a commercial concern and had to discharge the functions of magistrates, judges, ambassadors, and governors of provinces. Wellesley realized that they should be well educated, especially in the history, languages, laws, and customs of the people of India. He therefore proposed the establishment of a college at Fort William, but it was opposed by the directors, who, in 1806, established a similar college in England at Haileybury. In 1853 the covenanted civil service was thrown open to competitive examination.

The Indianization of the ICS proceeded very slowly. Despite pledges made in 1833, and a royal proclamation (1858) that neither race nor religion should debar the peoples of India from employment in the government of the country, little was done to ensure this. Competitive excellence at examinations held in London was to be the criterion of eligibility. It was not until 1864 that an Indian, S. N. Tagore, brother of the poet Rabindranath, won a place by examination in the ICS. Admission of Indians was made more difficult in 1876 by the lowering of the maximum age of entry from 23 to 19. In 1889 the age was again raised to 23. With the growth of Indian nationalism the pace of Indianization increased. Out of a total ICS membership of 1100–1200, some 60 were Indians in 1909, 240 in 1929, and 540 in 1939. Although the ICS was one of the best services in the world, it was also expensive to maintain and had the defects of all rigid bureaucracies.

L. S. S. O'Malley, *The Indian Civil Service, 1601–1930* (London, 1931).
E. Blunt, *The I.C.S.* (London, 1937). 　　　　　　　CCD

INDIAN COMMISSION in the US (Board of Indian Commissioners), independent body created in 1869 as a part of President Grant's attempt to clear up abuses in the Office of Indian Affairs. It shared control with the Interior Department over the disbursement of Indian appropriations and was given full power to inspect all work of the office.

INDIAN CONFEDERATE BRIGADE, consisted of two regiments of Cherokee and one of Creek Indians, led by Brig.-Gen. Albert Pike during the American Civil War. They fought at the battle of Pea Ridge, AR (7 March 1862), after which all but one regiment, led by the Cherokee general Stand Watie, faded away. This regiment harassed Unionists in the Indian Territory throughout the war and Stand Watie was the last Confederate general to surrender.

INDIAN CONSTITUENT ASSEMBLY. Elected in mid-1946, the assembly was boycotted by the Muslim League and did not begin to operate effectively until after partition, when the representatives of areas included in Pakistan left to form a separate assembly. A constitution for the new Indian Union was debated in the assembly (1947–9) and proclaimed on 26 Jan. 1950. Until the completion of the first general elections to the new parliament (1952), the assembly also operated as a provisional parliament for India.

The original members were elected by provincial legislators, voting in General, Muslim, and Sikh categories. There were 296 members representing the British Indian provinces and provision was made for 93 members to represent the princely states. After the Pakistani representatives departed, some 300 members remained. The Congress controlled the assembly from the outset but took steps to secure the election of some prominent non-Congressmen, notably Dr B. R. Ambedkar. Dr Rajendra Prasad was the president of the assembly, and Jawaharlal Nehru, Sadar Vallabhbhai Patel, and Maulana Abul Kalam Azad between them controlled the key committees. Other members were important in the drafting of the constitution, especially Dr Ambedkar and Sir Benegal Narsing Rau, ICS, who was constitutional adviser to the assembly.

The constitution which emerged from the assembly's 165 days of debate gave India a republican government and provided for a federation to include the former princely states, which had, by then, been integrated into India. The head of state was to be a president elected by a college of all legislators at the centre and in the states. He was armed with emergency powers to assume control, on the recommendation of the state governor, of any state where parliamentary government had become impossible. The constitution endorsed the parliamentary form of government which had been developed to a limited extent within the earlier constitutions drawn up by the British. Bicameral legislatures were provided at the centre and in all states and the majority party within the lower houses formed the government. The executive was controlled by a prime minister, at the centre, and chief ministers, in the states, at the head of cabinets. Elections to the lower houses, the central Lok Sabha or 'House of the People' and the state Vidhan Sabhas, or Legislative Assemblies, were to be direct and on the basis of adult suffrage. Of particular importance in the constitution were Part III, which assured the fundamental rights of citizens and gave protection to minorities and special privileges to scheduled castes (untouchables) and scheduled tribes, and Part IV, which set out the directive principles of state policy, particularly on economic and social matters. On the contentious issue of the future official national language the constitution provided that Hindi would be the official language, but that English would continue to be used for a period of 15 years.

G. Austin, *The Indian Constitution: cornerstone of a nation* (London, 1966).
B. N. Rau, *India's Constitution in the Making* (Calcutta, 1960). 　　　　　　　PDR

INDIAN LAW COMMISSIONS. The first, on which Lord Macaulay sat, was appointed in India (1833) to begin the codification of the laws. Progress was slow after the departure of Macaulay. As a result of its labours the Indian Penal Code was finally produced in 1860. There was a second commission in England (1853) which led to the Code of Civil Procedure (1859) and the Code of Criminal Procedure (1861). A third commission was convened in 1861.

INDIAN MUTINY (1857–8), revolt of the sepoys of the Bengal army and a revolt of certain discontented sections of the civilian population. Its causes were social, religious, economic, political, and military. It is impossible to underestimate the increasing pace of westernization after 1818. Missionaries challenged the religious beliefs of Hindus and there was a widespread belief that the British were striving to break down the caste system. Change threatened the supremacy of the Brahmans. Dalhousie's annexations, especially that of Oudh, produced a discontented aristocracy and a disbanded and disgruntled soldiery.

The mutiny broke out in the Bengal army because here Indians were organized and serious defects in army administration existed. As commanding officers possessed no adequate powers of punishment (for there were then no summary courts-martial) discipline was poor. High-caste sepoys had been enlisted whose prejudices interfered with their military duties. The distribution of European troops was unstrategic and they were hopelessly outnumbered. Furthermore, the disasters of the First Afghan War (1838–42) had destroyed the traditional belief in the invincibility of the company's forces.

The pretext for the revolt was the introduction of the new Enfield rifle, to load which the cartridges had to be lubricated and their ends bitten off by the sepoys. It seems to be true that the grease used was tallow of unknown origin or a mixture of pigs' lard and cows' fat, an insult to both Muslims and Hindus. To a certain extent it was a Muslim revolt. Muslims remembered their former greatness, the emblem of which, the Mughal emperor, lived at Delhi as a miserable puppet.

The mutiny was confined to Upper and Central India. It did not spread to Madras, and the Punjab remained loyal. Few important Indian princes joined the mutineers. The Mughal emperor and his sons, and Nana Sahib, the adopted son of the deposed Maratha peshwa, were implicated. The extension of the revolt was gradual and resulted from gross British incompetence in the early stages. The mutiny broke out at Meerut in May 1857, when the 3rd Cavalry refused to use the greased cartridges. The cavalry and infantry slew their European officers and released the prisoners who had refused to use the greased cartridges. The officer commanding at Meerut was long past the age of efficiency. The mutineers marched to Delhi, which was taken, and all Europeans were shot or cut to pieces in the streets. This was the beginning of the atrocities. The Punjab held out under John Lawrence, Herbert Edwardes, and John Nicholson. Punjab forces took Delhi after five days of bloody fighting (Sept. 1857). This was the turning-point in the mutiny. Then followed the terrible massacre of the women and children at Cawnpore. After this the mutiny was suppressed with medieval ferocity. By the middle of 1858 order had been restored in Rohilkhand, Central India, and Bundelkhand.

T. Rice Holmes, *A History of the Indian Mutiny* (London, 1913).

S. N. Sen, *Eighteen Fifty-Seven* Delhi, 1957).   CCD

INDIAN NATIONAL ARMY, formed by Subhas Chandra Bose (4 July 1943) in Singapore from among 40,000 Indian prisoners of war and volunteers from the resident Indian population. Bose was supreme commander of the INA as well as head of state of the provisional government of free India, which he established (21 Oct. 1943) and which declared war on Britain and the US (25 Oct.). The Japanese were unsure of the utility of the INA and only after considerable argument was Bose able to send a brigade to the Manipur front (Feb. 1944). This group crossed into Indian territory (March 1944), capturing several posts and participating in the attack on Imphal. Bad weather, shortages, and the withdrawal of Japanese air support forced them to fall back. The INA headquarters were shifted to Bangkok (April 1945), but the bulk of the force remained in Burma and was captured (May 1945). The attempt by the government of India to prosecute three leading INA officers in Delhi caused widespread popular sympathy for the force. The government had to remit the sentences of life transportation that had been imposed upon them.

INDIAN NATIONAL CONFERENCE first met at Calcutta in Dec. 1883. Representatives were invited from all parts of India. The conference discussed questions relating to education, the separation of the judicial and executive functions, and the need for more Indianization. After 1885, its place was taken by the Indian National Congress.

INDIAN NATIONAL CONGRESS, major Indian nationalist organization. Founded (1885) as a means of drawing together regionally based, well-educated political groups, it had become by the 1930s a strong and broadly based mass movement. After independence it continued as the Congress Party and held power at the centre and in almost all states until the late 1960s.

Initially the annual session was the focus of Congress activity and it continued to be important as a national forum even after independence. The key to Congress strength, however, lay in the parallel development, by the 1920s, of a strong and representative 'All-India Congress Committee' with a compact executive 'Working Committee', and a hierarchy of branches down to village and town-ward level. In 1920 membership was made possible with a 4-anna membership fee and Congress provinces were established on a linguistic basis in order to strengthen local organization. This structure was retained, with some modifications, until the party's increasingly important parliamentary functions in independent India made reorganization necessary (1948).

The development of Congress policy and strategy can be seen in three broad phases (1885–1919, 1920–47, 1948–   ).

In the first phase Congress was primarily a means of rallying support for demands for a greater share in government and the liberalization of government policies. Leaders such as Surendranath Banerjea, Pherozeshah Mehta, and Gopal Krishna Gokhale sought political advances by demonstrating their reasonableness and ability. Such policies came increasingly under attack from those, like Bal Gangadhar Tilak, who favoured more aggressive means of extracting concessions from the British. From an open rupture between the two groups (1907) the gradualists emerged in control. By 1914 there was growing disillusionment with gradualist policies and the Home Rule Leagues of Tilak and Mrs Besant sought to revitalize the movement. When constitutional change became imminent (1918) there was a division within Congress and the more moderate leaders left to form the National Liberal Federation.

The emergence of Mohandas Karamchand Gandhi and his lieutenants, especially Jawaharlal Nehru, Vallabhbhai Patel, Rajendra Prasad, and C. Rajagopalachari, marked the beginning of the second major phase of Congress activity. Gandhian agitational strategy was central to the movement in this period and the major campaigns, non-co-operation (1920–2), civil disobedience (1930–4), and individual *satyagraha* (1940–1) demonstrated a widening support for Congress. There was a continuing debate in the movement concerning participation in the legislatures. These were officially boycotted on occasions (1920–3, 1929–34, 1939–45), but in the Swaraj Party period, under the leadership of Chittaranjan Das and Motilal Nehru (1923–9), and following the introduction of provincial autonomy (1937–9), Congressmen did gain election to the councils and began to make significant contributions to legislative activity. In 1920 Congress defined its aim as the attainment of *swarajya* or 'self-rule', but by the end of the 1920s it demanded *purna swaraj*, 'complete independence'. In the 1930s, other strategies emerged to challenge that of Gandhi. The Congress Socialist Party, which looked to the mobilization of peasant and worker support, was organized (1934) and the rise of Subhas Chandra Bose by the end of the 1930s opened the possibility of a shift to more militant action. The Socialists were never able to control the organization, however, and Bose was forced from the Congress (1939). At the outbreak of war Congress offered to support the British government if immediate and effective Indian control of the war effort were conceded. This condition was not met and there followed the individual *satyagraha* campaign (1940–1) and the more violent 'Quit India' movement (1942).

After independence the Congress party dominated Indian politics until the late 1960s. Tension between Patel and Nehru ended with Patel's death (1950). Until Nehru died (1964) he was the dominant influence in the party. The Socialists left the Congress (1948), but Nehru succeeded in committing it nominally to socialist goals. Its size, past importance, and control of resources enabled the Congress to remain dominant until the late 1960s. By then, however, its diversity of membership had set in motion a process of internal fissuring and in 1969 a schism occurred to bedevil the future of the party.

P. Sitaramayya, *History of the Indian National Congress*, 2 vols (Bombay, 1947; reprinted Delhi, 1969).

S. A. Kochanik, *The Congress Party of India: the dynamics of one-party democracy* (Oxford, 1968).   PDR

INDIAN OCEAN TRADE. Apart from the trade inside the enclosed seas, like the Persian Gulf and the Red Sea, Indian Ocean trade began in the 6th or 7th cent. BC, probably as a result of improvements in shipbuilding. The external trade expanded with the prosperity of the Mediterranean in Hellenistic and Roman times. It may have contracted during the decline of the west in the 5th, 6th, and 7th cents, but expanded again with the revival of western Asia under the Baghdad caliphate. The arrival of the Portuguese, followed by the Dutch, French, and English, introduced the new route round Africa and increased the competitiveness of the trade. The Cape route took an increasing share with the development of the steamboat (1842), until the opening of the Suez Canal (1862) restored the old route through the Mediterranean.

The principal ports have varied, but in their time, Chu'an Chow, Malacca, Quilon, Goa, Cambay, Ormuz, and Aden were all places of exchange as well as ports of entry. The merchants were Phoenicians, Alexandrian Greeks, Arabs, Persians, and Indians, and later Portuguese, Dutch, French, and English. Trade with the west consisted of luxuries and rarities, such as spices, sandalwood, perfumes, and precious stones, in exchange for gold, silver, and glass. The trade included the cloth, beads, timber, and ironware of India; the gold, ivory, millet, tortoiseshell, mangrove poles, rhinoceros horn, and slaves of Africa; the dates, copperware, incense, salt, and pearls of the Arab world, and the porcelain and silk of China.

INDIAN PLANNING COMMISSION, established (March 1950) to enable the government of India to supervise Indian economic development. The decision to have a central planning authority was taken in Dec. 1946, but problems within the interim government and divisions within the Congress high command delayed a definite start until 1950. The commission then established was given the task of assessing resources for development, formulating a national 5-year plan, and assessing progress. The first plan covered the period 1951–6. There have been three subsequent plans, although the third (1962–7) had to be severely curtailed because of financial difficulties, and the fourth (1967–72) was delayed by the difficult circumstances following the war with Pakistan. The plans cover the activities of both central and state governments, although states control their own plans. A National Development Council, comprising all state chief ministers, and the planning commission, co-ordinates centre-state activities.

The commission has gradually grown in size since its creation and its membership has acquired an increasingly ministerial character. Initially there were five members, of whom only the prime minister was in the cabinet. By the 1960s there were five or six ministers and seven non-ministerial members. The prime minister is ex officio chairman. Jawaharlal Nehru was chairman continuously, 1950–64, when the cabinet secretary also acted as secretary to the commission.

INDIAN REFORM SOCIETY, formed in London in 1853 by John Dickinson, a British humanitarian, with John Bright as chairman. Its aim was to assist British enterprise in India, especially the production of non-slave-grown cotton. The report of the Indigo Commission (1860) undermined Radical sympathy for the planters.

INDIAN REMOVAL, name given to the US government policy of relocating eastern Indians west of the Mississippi. Thomas Jefferson first put forth the idea of removal to Congress in 1803 and included a provision for an exchange of Indian lands in the act organizing the Louisiana Territory (1804). Numerous treaties provided for immediate or ultimate removal, but it was not until 1825 that a definite removal policy providing for the transfer of eastern Indians to trans-Mississippi regions was adopted. The plan was to facilitate the advance of white settlement and to fix a permanent Indian frontier beyond the 95th meridian. The policy was originated by John C. Calhoun as secretary of war in 1823, announced by President Monroe (1825), and carried out on an extensive scale by President Jackson. Congressional enactment of the Removal Bill (1830) gave the president further power to transfer any eastern Indian tribe to the trans-Mississippi region. During Jackson's presidency (1829–37) 94 treaties extinguishing Indian land title and removing tribes were concluded.

Under treaty terms the Five Civilized Tribes—Creek, Chocktaw, Chickasaw, Seminole, and Cherokee—gave up their lands in the southern states and were transported to the Indian Territory (1825–40). Indians who rejected treaties were forcibly removed and an estimated 4000 out of 14,000 Cherokees lost their lives while being sent westward (1838). Two Indian wars were the direct result of the removal policy. The Black Hawk War (6 April–2 Aug. 1832) along the Upper Mississippi broke out when the Sac and Fox Indians sought to reoccupy their ceded lands in Wisconsin Territory and Illinois. In Florida the Second Seminole War (Nov. 1835–14 Aug. 1843) erupted as a reaction to removal.

By 1840 over 100,000 Indians had been removed west of the Mississippi, either peacefully or forcibly, and the land east of the Mississippi was cleared of most of its Indian population, but the hoped-for permanent Indian barrier proved to be an illusion as white settlement pushed towards the 95th meridian.

G. Foreman, *Indian Removal* (Norman, OK, 1932).
W. Hagan, *The Sac and Fox Indians* (Norman, OK, 1958).
                                                                                          DHP

INDIAN REORGANIZATION ACT (1934) (Wheeler–Howard Act), in US, which ended individual land allotments and provided for a return to tribal ownership of surplus lands hitherto open to sale. The act was designed to establish Indian political and economic home rule, to protect the Indian against the encroachments of whites, and to improve Indian education.

INDIAN RESERVATIONS, lands set aside for Indian tribes by the US government. Reservations began in 1786, but there were few before 1830, when a concerted removal policy led to the concentration of Indians on reserved lands. After the Civil War a reservation policy was introduced for all Indians. They were established by treaty, agreement, Act of Congress and Executive Order. The lands were tribal lands and were to be held in common by the members of the tribes. The Dawes Act (1887) and later acts modified this policy, but over 39 million acres (158,000 sq. kms) of reservation land still remain (1970) in the US, of which more than 19 million (77,000 sq. kms) are in AZ.

INDIAN TERRITORY included all of the present state of OK, US, except the Panhandle. It was originally land obtained from the Osage and Kansa Indian tribes in June 1825 and set aside as a home for the Five Civilized Tribes. From 1866 other tribes were assigned lands in the territory and eventually over 40 different tribes were located there. In 1889 2 million unassigned acres (8100 sq. kms) were opened to white settlement and organized as Oklahoma Territory (2 May 1890). At the same time, the laws of AR, so far as was applicable, were extended over Indian Territory. In 1907, when OK became a state, the Indian Territory ceased to exist.

INDIANA, 19th member state of the US, admitted in 1816. The area was part of the French empire in North America until 1763, when it was transferred to Britain. It came under US control following George Rogers Clark's capture of Vincennes in 1779. Organized as part of the North-west territory (1787), IN was made a separate territory in 1800, following the reduction of the British and Indian threat by the victory at Fallen Timbers (1794) and the treaty of Greenville (1795). It was reduced to almost its present size by separation from MI (1805), but its population increased rapidly after the final defeat of the Indians and British at the battle of the Thames (1813). By 1815 its population had reached 60,000, and statehood came the following year. A leading industrial state, its north-western section bordering on Lake Michigan is part of one of the densest concentrations of heavy industry in the world, but it is at the same time one of the leading agricultural states of the Union.

INDIANS IN FIJI were introduced by Sir A. H. Gordon. Altogether 62,000 casual and plantation labourers were indented, chiefly from the United Provinces and Madras Presidency (1879–1916), and many free Gujeratis and Punjabis made the passage after the Indian government banned further indentures (1917). Renewed agitation in India ended in Fiji's cancellation of all remaining indentures (1920), but only 40 per cent returned home. Resultant racial difficulties in Fiji were exacerbated by the limited area available, the strong racial, cultural, and religious differences of Fijian and Indian, and population trends that favoured the Indian sector.

INDIANS IN SOUTH AFRICA were originally brought there between 1860 and 1911 as indentured labourers for Natal's sugar plantations. Many stayed on as market gardeners, servants, and labourers; a small number of merchants migrated from India in their wake. The Indians differ in region of origin, language, caste, and religion, the majority being Hindu.

As Indian numbers increased, intense anti-Indian feeling developed in Natal; after Natal had received self-government (1893), Indians were openly discriminated against. In the Transvaal republic and Orange Free State (where they were few) they had no legal or political rights. It was Indian disabilities in the Transvaal which led Mohandas K. Gandhi to perfect his techniques of non-violent resistance. Through his endeavours, Indian Congresses were formed in Natal and the Transvaal to fight anti-Indian legislation. These united in 1917. Congress remained a cautious body, fighting Indian grievances on a narrow front until 1946, but thereafter joined in campaigns with the African National Congress.

INDIGENISM IN LATIN AMERICA, 20th-cent. movement in the Indo-American countries which attempts to establish the Indian as an important part of the national culture by reviving study of his past civilization and attacking the degradation to which he has been subjected since the European conquest. The Mexican Revolution (1911–17) gave great impetus to this kind of thinking and writing. Painters such as Diego Rivera and José Clemente Orozco also extolled the Indian past.

Since the revolution divisive issues within the movement have included the question of whether the Indian should be incorporated into modern western life, or should remain aloof and try to revive his former life-style.

INDIGO, important article of Indian export in the 18th and 19th cents. It had been grown and used as a dye in India from very early times. Large areas were under cultivation in Bihar and Bengal and riots broke out in 1860 because the planters tried to force the *raiyat*s to grow indigo. They realized, however, that it would be more profitable to grow oilseeds and cereals. Another cause of trouble was the capricious weather of Bengal which led to fluctuations in the supply of indigo, the raising of which required laborious weeding. The cultivators' discontent found expression in the famous Bengali drama *Nil-Darpan.* Christian missionaries went so far as to say that not a chest of indigo reached England without being stained with human blood. A commission appointed to enquire into complaints found them substantiated. The industry declined after 1897 because of the increasing use of German synthetic dyes.

INDIVIDUALISM, emphasis upon the social and spiritual importance of the single human being, stimulated by the humanist revival of classical studies in the Renaissance and possibly further encouraged by the teachings of Protestant reformers, *eg,* Luther. In the field of political theory individualism reached its apogee with 19th-cent. liberalism.

INDOCHINA WAR (1946–54), between the Viet-minh and the French colonial government in Indochina. After a period of growing tension, the war began in earnest in Dec. 1946 when, despite the presence of French troops, the Viet-minh tried, but failed, to take over Hanoi. The first phase ended about March 1947, when the French had control of the major towns and many lowland areas, notably the Tongking delta. Later in 1947 they conducted operations against the Viet-minh base area in northern Tongking, but were unable to eliminate the Viet-namese army. In the next two or three years the Viet-minh, under the military leadership of Vo Nguyen Giap, consolidated their position in the countryside, especially in the north and centre of the country. In the south the Communists were less strong, and the French came to terms with the nationalist sects known as the Cao-Dai and Hoa-Hao. By 1950 the Viet-minh were strong enough, with Chinese assistance, to step up their pressure on the French, who suffered serious setbacks when they were forced to evacuate Cao-Bang and Lang-Son in Oct. 1950. French fortunes recovered to some extent under the leadership of Gen. De Lattre de Tassigny (1950–1), and the French were able to defeat the Viet-minh in battles at Vinh-Yen (Jan. 1951) and Mao-Khe (March 1951). But the Viet-minh recovered by the end of the year, and early in 1952 De Lattre de Tassigny died. During 1952–3 fighting became concentrated in western Tongking and north-eastern Laos. In mid-1953 Gen. Navarre devised a new plan for defeating the Viet-minh, which included the creation of a large base at Dien-Bien-Phu, on the Tongking–Laos border. Gen. Giap's first response to this plan was to conduct diversionary operations in central and northern Laos and around Kartum, in order to disperse French troops. Then in Dec. 1953 he laid siege to Dien-Bien-Phu, which fell in May 1954. By then negotiations were about to begin at Geneva, and this psychological defeat made the French more anxious than ever to end the war. The cease-fire agreement, in effect a Viet-minh victory, was signed on 20 July 1954.

D. Lancaster, *The Emancipation of French Indochina* (London, 1961). RBS

INDOCHINESE COMMUNIST PARTY, principal Communist (Stalinist) organization in Viet-nam (1930–45). It grew out of the 'Association of Revolutionary Youth' founded by Nguyen Ai Quoc (Ho Chi Minh) at Canton in 1925. In the absence of its founder, that organization split in 1929 on the issue of whether to declare itself openly communist. In 1930, at a conference in Hong Kong, Nguyen Ai Quoc healed the breach, drawing all communist groups together into a new Indochinese Communist Party, which shortly afterwards organized the Nghe-An revolt in Viet-nam itself. As a result of this and other disturbances in 1930–1, the principal communist leaders were executed or imprisoned, and it was only after the release of some of the leaders by the French 'Popular Front' government in 1936 that the party again began to flourish. Driven underground once more in 1939, its chief leaders fled to south China, returning only to a jungle-base in Tongking in 1941, where they founded the Vient-minh. The party was formally dissolved in 1945, to please the Nationalist Chinese then occupying northern Viet-nam, but later it re-emerged as the Lao-Dong party.

INDOCHINESE UNION, government framework of French Indochina (1887–1945). It originally included the colony of Cochin-China and the protectorates of Cambodia, Annam, and Tongking, the Protectorate of Laos being added in 1893. The Union, at first a very loose organization, was reshaped by Paul Doumer, governor-general (1897–1901), to become the principal executive authority in economic, financial, political, and military affairs throughout Indochina. It came to an end in 1945, when the Japanese, who had occupied the country militarily since 1942, overthrew the French administrative authority. The status of the Indochinese states was ambiguous from then until the creation of the Associated States of Viet-nam, Cambodia, and Laos in 1949.

INDO-EUROPEAN, name usually applied to a group of languages and occasionally, misleadingly, to a racial group, otherwise called Aryans. The demonstration in 1816 by Franz Bopp of the relationship of Sanskrit to Greek led to the development of the concept, although, since the discovery in 1915 that Hittite and other ancient Anatolian languages were also connected, scholars have preferred the term Indo-Hittite. The original homeland of the Indo-European speakers has been the subject of much dispute. Europe, India, Central Asia, and southern Russia have been claimed. It is possible to date Indo-European movements into Greece and India shortly after 2000 BC and into Iran *c.* 1500 BC. Recent discoveries indicate penetration into Asia Minor as early as the end of the third millennium BC. The absence of written records makes the question of their second-millennium movements into western Europe much more speculative. Little that is positive can be said, although some well-known hypotheses, *eg*, that they were nomads or that they were driven to wander by some major climatic change, can be discarded.

INDONESIAN REGIONAL REVOLT, major rebellion of the 1950s against the Indonesian government. Its causes lay in dissatisfaction in the islands outside Java with Java's political domination; the discontent of exporters over Djakarta's attempts to impose stricter economic controls; and the alarm of pro-Western politicians at the increasingly nationalistic stand of the government, which at the end of 1957 seized Dutch property and which was rapidly moving away from parliamentary government to 'Guided Democracy'. The revolt drew military support from the close identification of some territorial commanders with the civilian interests of their areas and from their participation in illegal export activities. Moreover, the efforts of the army chief of staff to strengthen central military control met with resistance from regional commanders anxious to preserve their freedom of action.

In Nov. 1956 military officers in West Sumatra formed the Banteng Council, which soon took charge of government in the area. Regional commands and councils were subsequently proclaimed in other disaffected areas. In April 1957 Indonesia was declared to be in a state of emergency and was placed under martial law. Finally, several prominent Masjumi and Indonesian Socialist Party leaders went to Padang, West Sumatra, where on 15 Feb. 1958 they proclaimed the Revolutionary Government of the Republic of Indonesia (PRRI). They were joined by rebels in the largely Christian area of northern Sulawesi (Celebes), who formed the Universal Struggle (*Permesta*) movement. The insurgents received some foreign aid via Malaya and North Borneo, but although they had considerable Western sympathy they received little concrete support, partly because of the prompt and effective military campaign launched against them. The rebellion was broken in a few months, but sporadic fighting continued for several years.   RTM

INDULGENCE, DECLARATIONS OF (1662, 1672, 1687, 1688) in England, royal measures taken by Charles II and James II to relieve the hardships of the dissenters and to win their support by suspending the enforcement of legislation upholding the supremacy of the established Church.

The first declaration (Dec. 1662) was a tentative announcement of Charles II's intention to seek the approval of parliament for the use of the royal dispensing power, but it brought a furious reaction from the Commons.

In March 1672, two days after the declaration of war against the Dutch, Charles issued another declaration of indulgence, suspending the penal laws against both Catholics and Noncomformists, in line with the secret treaty of Dover (1670). The king desperately needed money for the Dutch War and a reassembled parliament forced him to withdraw the declaration in return for voting £1,200,000, while the Country Party extremists forced through the Test Act (1673), further thwarting royal indulgence towards Catholics.

After failing to persuade parliament to repeal the Test Act, the Catholic James II issued a declaration of in-dulgence (14 April 1687), which was intended to suspend the application of that act for all dissenters and to destroy the privileged position of the Anglican Church, through the use of the royal prerogative. On 7 May 1688 another declaration was published and ordered to be read from all parish church pulpits. This blatant use of the suspending power resulted in the case of the seven bishops, and their acquittal was the signal for the invitation to William of Orange to oust James II.

INDULGENCES. In Roman canon law an indulgence is a remission, whether immediate or after death, of the temporal punishment due after pardon for the committing of a sin. It is conditional on the sincere repentance by the sinner, manifested by the performance of some good work, usually prayer, and is expressed in terms of remission of a set number of days of punishment. A plenary indulgence, *ie*, complete remission of punishment, can be granted only by the pope.

The granting of indulgences can be traced back to the early Church but in the 11th cent. the practice developed of granting an indulgence for the performance of a specific good work, such as going on a crusade or contributing money to the building of a church, hence the notorious indulgence for the rebuilding of St Peter's, Rome, which provoked Luther's Wittenberg Theses, and the notion that indulgences could be bought. Similarly, the granting of indulgences in prospect led to the notion that they were permissions to sin, although no indulgence was effective without true repentance. The possibility of such erroneous ideas continuing to circulate was removed by the Council of Trent, which tightened up the regulations and forbade any trafficking in indulgences.

INDULGENCES, SALE OF, practice of selling documents offering commutation of penance for money payments, which by the later Middle Ages had been perverted by papal agents, *eg*, the Dominican Tetzel, for financial gain. The abuse was condemned by Martin Luther (31 Oct. 1517) and led to the first open conflict between Luther and the Church authorities.

INDUS VALLEY CIVILIZATION, ancient civilization (*c.* 2150–1750 BC) of the Indus valley and adjoining areas. Excavations have brought to light the ruins of two great cities: Harappa (Punjab) and Mohenjo-daro (Sind), and more than 60 other ancient settlements along the Indus, the Makran coast, the Gulf of Cambay and, in the north, up to east of Delhi. The cities, relatively well preserved in the dry climate, each comprise a citadel and a lower town, divided into rectangular blocks by streets. All houses have bathrooms and drains. In Mohenjo-daro a large public bath, fed by wells and provided with two flights of stairs for easy access, is noteworthy. The presence of granaries at all the sites is another interesting feature. The stability of the Indus Civilization can be inferred from the absence of major change during four centuries, except for some apparent decline just before its end. Equally interesting is its homogeneity, as all sites, extending over more than 1000 miles, are very similar. This, and the predominance of the great cities, may suggest a high degree of centralization. As only a few weapons have come to light conditions may generally have been peaceful. There is evidence of intensive commercial contact with Mesopotamia, where many Indus valley seals have survived. The main port may have been on the Gulf of Cambay where, at Lothal, a large dock, connected with the gulf by a canal, was discovered.

The high level of civilization also follows from the knowledge of script of a pictographic type. Despite the discovery of some 2500 inscribed seals, no attempt at decipherment has yet been generally accepted. The language of the Indus people, as well as several fields of their civilization, therefore still remains completely unknown. The seals have, however, provided some information on such things as flora and fauna, and religion. Thus it has been suggested with some plausibility that a three-headed deity in a yoga-like attitude and surrounded by animals represents an early form of the Indian god Shiva. From this one could infer some continuity from the Indus times to later Indian civilization.

It is believed that the Indus Civilization developed after mountain tribes had descended from Baluchistan and eastern Afghanistan to settle in the valley. Its apparently sudden end soon after 1750 BC is attributed to the destruction by Indo-Aryan tribes of the Indus cities. On account of chronological problems (it seems difficult to date the Indo-Aryan invasions much earlier than the 13th cent.) caution is still necessary.

Sir Mortimer Wheeler, *The Indus Civilization* (Cambridge, 1968).   JG de C

INDUSTRIAL DISPUTES INVESTIGATION ACT (1907) in Canada. Under this act, before a strike or a lockout could be declared in public utilities, a three-man investigating body, representing labour, employer, and public, had to report to the government. Public opinion was usually sufficient to enforce their recommendations. The law was declared *ultra vires* of the Canadian constitution by the privy council (1925).

INDUSTRIAL GROUPS, name given to Australian trade unionists organized to check the growth of communist influence within particular unions after the Second World War. Strongly supported by Roman Catholic elements with the Australian Labor movement, industrial groups were later opposed by the ALP leader, H. V. Evatt, as allegedly aiming at Church domination of the movement. They thus formed one cause of the Labor split of the mid-1950s, and of the emergence of the Australian Democratic Labor Party.

INDUSTRIAL REVOLUTION, phrase coined by Arnold Toynbee to designate the drastic economic and social changes that took place in Britain between the years 1780 and 1820 and subsequently in various other countries. It involved the establishment of a factory system, large-scale production, the exploitation of water- and steam-power, the creation of a wage-earning class working under factory discipline, and eventually the growth of large industrial towns. Though the food production of the country had to be adapted to feed the growing industrial population, many sectors of the economy, including agriculture, remained unmechanized until much later. Recently the tendency has been to emphasize not so much the outward forms of industrial organization, but the rapid and self-sustained economic growth manifest in the change.

At various times attention has concentrated on the social and political results of the industrial transformation: on its effect on the distribution of political power, on the standard of living and social hegemony of the working classes, and on problems of social and political organization in urban communities. Since 1945 the attempts of some undeveloped countries to achieve economic growth have attracted attention to the causes and processes of industrialization, in particular the accumulation and availability of capital, the growth of large-scale demand, and improvements in transport and technology. In this study the British Industrial Revolution has a special significance, for it was not only earlier than that of any other country, but also predominantly produced by native resources. Whereas industrial revolutions in other countries have involved borrowing money, techniques, or labour from already developed countries, it was on local capital, the use of entrepreneurship and of native sources of power and skilled labour that Britain industrialized herself. Yet this self-contained achievement should not be overstressed. The wealth that made it possible had been developed by exploiting colonial resources and by trade, and the Industrial Revolution itself relied on foreign markets, and to some degree on foreign raw materials. It also appears to have benefited from foreign as well as native scientific advances, and on a population growth that was common to most of western Europe at that time.

T. S. Ashton, *The Industrial Revolution, 1760–1830* (Oxford, 1957).
M. W. Flinn, *The Origins of the Industrial Revolution* (London, 1966).   RMM

INDUSTRIAL WORKERS OF THE WORLD, revolutionary labour union founded in Chicago, IL (1905). The IWW concentrated on organizing unskilled and migratory workers in the shipping, lumber, fruit-growing, mining, and textile industries. Its charter emphasized abolition of the wage system, industrial unionism, and class conflict. Believing in direct action, the IWW led many strikes, the most successful being a textile strike in Lawrence, MA (1912). The use of violence resulted in counter-violence and after a number of federal prosecutions the union was virtually eliminated as an influence on American labour by 1920, although a small organization still exists in Chicago and unionists still sing the songs for which the movement was famous. At its peak membership never exceeded 100,000, but branches were established as far afield as Britain, Australia, New Zealand, Mexico, Canada, South Africa, and Norway.

The Wobblies, as they were called, laid the groundwork for the mass organization of unskilled and foreign-born in the CIO of the 1930s and 1940s. They also contributed a number of new strike methods, such as the sit-down and chain-picketing.

INFANTICIDE in India. Two kinds were suppressed by the British in India. Female infanticide, practised by the Rajputs because marriage settlements on daughters were expensive, was declared murder in 1795, though it persisted as late as 1870. The Hindu practice of throwing children into the sea at Saugor island was suppressed in 1802.

INFLUENCE OF THE CROWN in Britain, phrase used especially in the 18th cent. to denote the use of Crown patronage as a means of exerting government influence on parliament, and especially on the House of Commons and elections to it. The appointment of MPs to Crown offices was regarded by the opponents of Crown influence as a dangerous threat to the independence of the Commons. There were many attempts in the century after 1680 to exclude placemen from the Commons, or at least to restrict their number. Sir Robert Walpole's Excise Bill (1733) was opposed on the grounds that it would increase Crown influence; Dunning (1780) blamed the influence of the Crown for the disasters of the American War of Independence. Burke claimed that his Civil Establishments Bill (1782) would reduce the influence of the Crown by 50 places.

On the other hand, the influence of the Crown performed an important function: it provided a link between the government and the Commons at a time when most ministers were in the Lords. But the strength of the link must not be exaggerated, although it is sometimes said that influence performed something like the function which cabinet and party performed later. It must be emphasized that the influence of the Crown was neither large enough nor reliable enough in its effects to give any 18th-cent. government the certainty of majority Commons support.   BK

INGOLDSBY, SIR RICHARD (1617–85), English politician, who fought in the English Civil Wars as colonel of a foot regiment in the New Model Army and signed the death-warrant of Charles I. He was MP for Buckinghamshire in the 1654 and 1656 parliaments and supported Richard Cromwell (1659). After the latter's fall he negotiated with Charles II's agents, seeking a royal pardon in the event of a restoration. To this end he arrested Gen. Lambert (22 April 1660) and brought him to London, for which he was thanked by the Commons and created a Knight of the Bath at Charles

II's coronation. He was MP for Aylesbury in the four parliaments of Charles II's reign.

INGOLF ARNARSON (or BJORNOLFSSON) (*fl.* 9th cent.), first major settler of Iceland. He and his foster-brother, Hjorleif, were reputed to have landed in either 870 or 874 after an earlier exploratory voyage. Hjorleif was killed by mutinous slaves, but Ingolf finally settled at Reykjavik and laid claim to much of south-western Iceland.

INGOLSTADT UNIVERSITY, medieval institution in Bavaria, which remained Catholic after the Reformation and became a centre for the counter-Reformation after the establishment of a Jesuit college there with the assistance of Duke Albert V (1550–79).

INITIATIVE, in Switzerland, constitutional device which gives the citizens, as well as the legislature, the right to initiate legislation. Combined with the referendum, the popular initiative spread through Switzerland during the 1860s, reaching the last canton by 1921. By involving the people directly in the business of state, the referendum and the initiative superseded parliamentary government in favour of pure popular sovereignty.

INKERMANN, BATTLE OF (5 Nov. 1854), Anglo-French victory during the Crimean War. In a confused and disorganized battle, leading to 11,000 Russian and 4000 allied casualties, the Russians failed to use reserves and the long siege of Sevastopol resulted.

INLAND REVENUE COMMISSIONERS (1849) in Britain, were created by the consolidation of the Board of Excise and the Board of Stamps and Taxes. Their appointment consolidated a long process of fiscal rationalization which began with economical reform in the 1780s.

INNESS, GEORGE (1825–94), US landscape artist, who portrayed a calm and intimate landscape in pictures such as *Delaware Water Gap* (1861) and *Peace and Plenty* (1865). His later works, including *Grey Day, Goochland* (1884), showed a renewed preoccupation with diffused light and form akin to that of the French Impressionists.

INNOCENT III (1161–1216), Pope (*reg.* 1198–1216). His pontificate is the apogee of the medieval papacy. Of outstanding intellect, cool temperament and shrewd judgement, he brought the theory of papal power (*plenitudo potestatis*) to its fulfilment. For him the pope stood midway between God and man, with absolute moral and spiritual authority over the princes of the world. He was the arbiter of the destinies of Europe; Sicily, England, Ireland, Aragon and Portugal all became papal fiefs under him. He made (1199) and unmade (1209) Otto of Brunswick as emperor, putting his own ward, Frederick II, in his place. By interdict and excommunication (1208–13), he forced John of England to accept his nominee, Stephen Langton, as Abp of Canterbury. He annulled Magna Carta conceded by King John, though a subsequent re-grant by Henry III (1216 and 1217) was accepted by Innocent's successor. He called the Fourth Crusade (1202–4), initiated the Albigensian Crusade (1209), and supported St Francis and St Dominic. He also called the greatest of all medieval general councils, the Fourth Lateran Council (1215). No pope before or since has so exemplified the universality of papal power as did Innocent III.

INNOCENT IV (*c.* 1190–1254) Pope (*reg.* 1243–54), and canonist, whose *Commentary* on canon law, written while he was pope, is an important step in the development of the theories of papal authority, temporal as well as spiritual. His pontificate marked the triumphant climax of the long papal struggle against the empire and especially the house of Hohenstaufen. Innocent was able to thwart the policies of Frederick II in Italy and on his death in 1250 to restrict his son to the kingdom of Sicily, thus removing permanently the threat to papal temporal independence posed by the link between Sicily and the empire. It marked also an important stage in the secularization of the papacy; the need for money to finance the struggle with the Hohenstaufen led him to continue the policies of his predecessor, Gregory IX, of exploitation of the revenues of the Church and to make an enormous increase in the practice of papal provisions to benefices throughout Christendom.

INNOCENT X (1572–1655), Pope (*reg.* 1644–55), known for his condemnation of both the ecclesiastical settlement of the peace of Westphalia in the bull *Zelo Domus Dei* (Nov. 1648) and the five propositions of Bp Jansen's *Augustinus* in the bull *Cum occasione* (May 1653).

INNOCENT XI (1611–89), Pope (*reg.* 1676–89), who was elected in succession to Clement X. An austere reformer, he opposed nepotism, moral laxity, and financial corruption in the Holy See and condemned the obscure mysticism of Quietism. His pontificate was marked by the Turkish threat, against which he won John Sobieski's support (1683) and created the Holy League of Poland, Venice, and the Habsburgs (1684), and also by bitter conflict with Louis XIV over the *régale temporelle* and *régale spirituelle* of the French monarchy, in which he proved to be a determined opponent. His bull *Paternae charitati* (1682) castigated the French clergy for submitting to the Gallican Articles. After a period of deadlock the threat of schism developed as Innocent refused to admit the Marquis de Lavardin as French ambassador to Rome (1687). French troops invaded the papal enclave of Avignon (Oct. 1688) and the situation was only saved by Innocent's death.

INNOCENT XII (1615–1700), Pope (*reg.* 1691–1700), who was champion of Italian neutrality. He reached a compromise with Louis XIV on the Gallican issue, confirming in their sees (1692) those French bishops who had not taken part in the national assembly of 1682 and later also confirming the participants (1693). Under pressure from Louis XIV and Bp Bossuet he condemned Fénelon's *Explication des Maximes des Saints* and Quietism (12 March 1699).

INNOCENT XIII (1655–1724), Pope (*reg.* 1721–4), elected when an old and sick man to avoid a repetition of Clement XI's long pontificate (1700–21). He recognized the Stuart pretender, James, to the English throne, promising him financial aid if Catholicism was re-established in England. He adopted a severe policy towards Jesuits whose missionary policy, deviating from Catholicism, he distrusted.

INONU, ISMET (1884–   ), Turkish soldier and politician. He was Atatürk's chief lieutenant during Turkey's struggle for independence and later prime minister (1923–4, 1925–7). He succeeded Atatürk as president (1938–50) and leader of the Republican People's Party, and again became prime minister (1961–5) when civilian rule was restored following the 1961 coup.

INOUE, KAORU (1835–1915), Japanese politician. He served as vice-minister of finance and minister of public works before wrestling with the problem of treaty revision as foreign minister (1879–87). Hostile popular reaction to his proposals forced his resignation, but he later served as acting prime minister and as *genrō*. His connections with Itō Hirobumi and the Mitsui company gave him considerable influence.

INQUILINO, Chilean variant of *péon*, a tenant on a large semi-feudal estate, or a tenant farmer.

INQUISITION, in its origins a series of separate diocesan attempts to deal with heretics. It obtained some unity under St Dominic and his order, when he employed it to combat the widespread heresy of the Albigensians in southern France. From here, it spread usually under the direction of the Dominicans, into the rest of France, and especially Spain, where religious orthodoxy was rendered difficult by the presence of the Moorish community. No type of inquisition was allowed to function in England, except for the trial of the Knights Templar in 1310. By the late 15th cent. it had become an organ of the Spanish Crown and in general had become a repressive and corrupt organization which was often employed against rival religious orders and political opponents. In 1542, as part of the counter-Reformation movement in the Catholic Church, a Roman Inquisition was set up. It was used particularly by Pope Paul IV and Pius V in the 16th cent. Technically it remains (1970) as an institution under the presidency of the pope to check doctrinal error and publish the Index.

INSTITUTES OF A CHRISTIAN RELIGION, religious treatise by John Calvin, dedicated to Francis I of France and published in Basle in 1536. Its main themes are the submission of man to God and the doctrine of election. The *Institutes* were revised in 1539, translated from Latin into French in 1541 (thus encouraging the spread of Calvinism in France), and enlarged in the editions of 1543, 1550, and 1559.

INSTITUTIONAL REVOLUTIONARY PARTY (PRI), dominant government party of Mexico. In 1929, after the death of Álvaro Obregón, the heirs of the Mexican Revolution organized their first political party and named it the National Revolutionary Party (PNR). Over the years this party has changed its aims, and, from time to time, its name, but it has remained firmly in power. The first change came in 1938, when Lázaro Cárdenas reorganized the party and renamed it the Party of the Mexican Revolution (PRM). In 1946, to stress that the party had carried out many of its promised reforms, and was an accepted part of Mexican government, the name was changed to Institutional Revolutionary Party (PRI).

INSTRUCTION (*NAKAZ*) (1767) in Russia. It was written by Catherine II for the guidance of a legislative commission of all classes, except serfs, which was to draft a new legal code for Russia. The document was not a detailed legal programme applicable to the Russian empire, but a restatement of the ideas of Montesquieu and Beccaria and was intended more to impress Europe by portraying Russia as a European enlightened monarchy than to produce results.

Censored and condensed by Catherine's advisers, the published version ranged from Russian history and monarchical absolutism to the nature of law, education, and punishments. It proposed not to emancipate the serfs, but to give them legal rights against their masters and limited serf proprietary rights.

INSTRUMENT OF GOVERNMENT in England, constitutional device proposed by the more conservative generals after the failure of Barebone's Parliament, whereby Cromwell became lord protector for life (Dec. 1653). The intention was to provide a regime acceptable both to the army and the electorate. The franchise was redistributed to disfranchise family-dominated borough seats and increase the number of county seats. Small dependent freeholders were disfranchised in favour of independent men of property, real and personal. However, the Instrument nominated to the executive (council) a majority of the generals, also for life, so that parliament, which was to meet every three years, had no effective control. An army of 30,000 men and considerable religious toleration were guaranteed by the constitution. When parliament assembled (Sept. 1654) it attempted to assert its own supremacy and the subsequent dissolution of Jan. 1655 opened the way for the rule of the major-generals.

INSUBRES, Gallic people who, entering Italy by the Ticinus valley *c.* 400 BC, defeated the Etruscans settled round Mediolanum (Milan), which became their capital. No direct confrontation with Rome took place until 225 BC, when the Roman northward expansion induced the Insubres to join with Boii and Gaesati for a mass invasion of Etruria. After initial success against Roman arms, they were routed and retired, to lose Mediolanum and their independence in the Roman campaign of 223–222. They joined Hannibal when he invaded Italy in 218, but their assistance was meagre; in campaigns between 200 and 196 the Romans crushed them and established Italian settlers at Mediolanum.

INSURANCE, MARINE, IN THE MIDDLE AGES. The introduction of marine insurance was preceded by a variety of devices designed to lessen the risks of maritime trade. One such device was a 'sea loan' which was not repayable if the ship or cargo financed by it were lost through misadventure. Search for more comprehensive and cheaper methods of lessening risks produced marine insurance proper, which was probably first practised at Genoa. It was used to insure the earliest regular Genoese sea voyages to Flanders, beginning *c.* 1298. In the course of the 14th cent. it became a normal feature of Italian and Catalan sea ventures.

INTEGRALISTA PARTY (BRAZILIAN INTEGRALIST ACTION), founded by Plinio Salgado as a Brazilian fascist and nationalist party. Its sympathies with the German Nazi Party led to its being banned (1937) by President Getulio Vargas.

INTELLIGENTSIA, term which originated in Russia in the 1860s to describe a European-educated minority which was totally alienated from the autocracy and normally ignorant of Russian realities, and which held radical and oppositional views. They formed a distinct, idealistic group, scorning state service, bound together by a common interest in the universities, literature, and radical journals, and devoted to ideas, social problems, and the people.

Under Nicholas I the intelligentsia were mainly 'conscience-stricken nobility'. When, however, Boborykin coined the term 'intelligentsia' and it became associated with the nihilist sons of Turgenev's *Fathers and Children* (1862) they were chiefly students of various social origins (*raznochintsy*) and adopted the more radical ideas of populism and later Marxism.

INTENDANT OF FINANCE, French royal official of the *ancien régime* with general control of financial administration. The office was originally performed by *maîtres des requêtes*, but as the work became more specialized in the 16th cent. the *intendants* became more important than the other *maîtres* and sat in the *conseil d'état*. Under Francis I there were two *intendants* of finance, but their number rose to four in Louis XII's reign and then reverted to two under Colbert. For most of the 18th cent. there were six, until their offices were suppressed by Necker in 1777, though their functions survived to the Revolution.

INTENDANT, OFFICE OF, French royal appointment during the *ancien régime* whose holders were concerned with broad matters of justice, finance, and police in the provinces on behalf of the central government. The office appeared in the 16th cent., first as an extraordinary commission, with the chief function of collection of the *taille*, but it became more regular and permanent under Henry III (1575–89). In Henry IV's reign (1589–1610) the tasks of the *intendant* were numerous, *eg*, the supervision of dissident elements in the provinces, the organization of alms and relief in times of famine or disease, the representation of the Crown at provincial estates, the task of advising the king on varied local problems (*eg*, fiscal, military, and administrative), and of enforcing laws which were being flouted. Under Louis XIII the *intendants*' powers continued to grow, and the office was used by Richelieu to counteract the authority of the great nobility in the provinces. Louis XIII conceded that the *intendants* should not be resident in their jurisdictional areas and that their decisions should be subject to appeal in the courts. However, as the fiscal demands of the king whom they represented increased steadily, they appeared to be the instruments of an authoritarian government. Opposition came to a head in the *Fronde* when the *intendants'* commissions were revoked by edict as being outside the law (July 1648). Re-established as the pillars of royal government in the provinces by Louis XIV's minister, Colbert, they continued to supervise an unlimited range of matters throughout the 18th cent., *eg*, justice, police, the army, agriculture, industry, public works, roads, waterways, universities, and colleges.

The *intendants* were almost always professional judges, drawn from the ranks of the *maîtres des requêtes*, and were originally men of comparatively humble birth. Unlike many offices in the *ancien régime*, theirs did not become venal, but they did increase in social and economic importance to the extent that in the tax scale of 1695 the *intendants* were superseded only by the dauphin, princes of the blood, royal ministers, and the tax farmers-general.

J. H. Shennan, *Government and Society in France, 1461–1661* (London, 1969). JHS

INTENDENCIES IN SPANISH AMERICA. As part of the Spanish Bourbon reforms in the second half of the 18th cent. the Spanish Crown redivided the American colonies into new administrative units called intendencies, modelled on French royal administration. The reform was designed to eliminate corruption at the local level and increase royal revenue. As far as these aims were concerned the intendencies were a success, but they created resentment and discontent among many members of the Creole petty bureaucracy.

INTER-AMERICAN ARBITRATION ACT (1929), agreement among the American nations signed in Washington, DC. All disputes were to be settled by an inter-American court. Many of the participating nations gave only conditional approval, and the act has not always been implemented.

INTER-AMERICAN COMMISSION ON TERRITORIAL ADMINISTRATION (1940), set up in Havana to administer European colonies in the New World which might otherwise have changed hands as a result of the Second World War. The fall of France and the Netherlands led the US and other American governments to fear a German seizure of French and Dutch colonies. The commission was designed to prevent this.

INTER-AMERICAN CONFERENCES, series of meetings between the nations of the Americas to express their solidarity and resolve conflicts. The first conference attended by all the Latin American states was held in Washington, DC, in 1889. Although these conferences have been essentially disappointing, especially from the Latin American point of view, their achievements include the setting up of the Pan-American Union, and the creation of the Organization of American States (OAS), a regional group within the UN. The 1961 meeting, anti-Cuban in tone, laid the basis for the Alliance for Progress. Many critics have felt that the conferences are used by the US government to impose conformity upon the Latin American nations.

INTER-AMERICAN DEFENSE BOARD (1942), organized in Rio de Janeiro as a response to the threat of German and Italian attack during the Second World War. The board now (1970) acts as an adjunct of the Organization of American States, and seeks military co-operation among the American nations.

INTERDICT, form of ecclesiastical sanction which forbids the use or practice of religious rites or services, such as the saying of mass or solemnization of marriages. The most celebrated use of the interdict was against England by Pope Innocent III between 1208 and 1213.

INTERIM OF AUGSBURG, theological statement of 30 June 1548 by which the Emperor Charles V attempted to reach agreement with the Protestants at the Diet of Augsburg (1547–8); but neither the Catholic nor the Protestant princes would accept this compromise.

INTERLOPERS, independent English merchants who traded in the East in defiance of the East India Co.'s monopoly. In the 17th cent. the company regarded them as little better than pirates, which they sometimes were, but had to make terms with some of them. Thomas Pitt, governor of Madras (1697–1709), and founder of the Pitt family fortune, had been an interloper.

INTERNAL IMPROVEMENTS in US, programme to develop inter-state transportation links through state and federal aid. In the early years of American nationhood the improvements demanded were on a small scale and were undertaken by private groups. When private financing became insufficient, local and state aid was sought and generally given by the well-settled states of the eastern seaboard. Frontier regions, unable to support expensive construction works, requested federal help. This demand raised the constitutional dilemma of whether, in the absence of specific constitutional provisions, Congress could use public funds for internal improvements. The first federal appropriation for inter-state construction work was made for the Cumberland road (1806). Gallatin, secretary of the treasury, presented a report (1808) on a comprehensive system of federally financed canals and roads, but no action was taken. In 1816 Madison vetoed the Bonus Bill which would have provided for internal improvements and Monroe (1822) and Jackson (1830) both vetoed similar bills on the grounds of unconstitutionality. Despite such executive vetoes, Congress subsidized many canal and road projects during the 1820s and 1830s, but federal grants fell far short of the money supplied by individual states, especially in the 1830s, when a craze for internal improvements resulted in an over-expansion of roads and canals that was ended only by the financial panic of 1837.

In the 1840s many transportation ventures were undertaken by private enterprise, but pioneer efforts in railroad construction were given local and state support. With the territorial expansion of the nation in the 1840s, railroad surveys and a federal plan to build transcontinental wagon roads focused the attention of Congress on the increasing need for federal support of internal improvements. In 1851 a new era of federal aid began, when Congress granted 2·5 million acres (10,100 sq. kms) of public land to help finance the Illinois Central Railroad. In the following 20 years some 131,350,534 acres of public domain were given as subsidies and large loans were also made to US railroads, particularly the transcontinentals. These generous grants, together with assistance from local governments, were mainly responsible for the expansion of the railroad network in the west during the second half of the 19th cent. In the 20th cent. the use of the motor car has called for heavier expenditure on a highway system, both at the local and the national level, and the cost of constructing and maintaining transport links is now apportioned among the local, state, and federal authorities.

George R. Taylor, *The Transportation Revolution, 1850–1860* (New York, 1951).
Robert E. Riegel, *The Story of the Western Railroads* (New York, 1926). MW

INTERNAL MACEDONIAN REVOLUTIONARY ORGANISATION (IMRO). IMRO was founded in 1893 to promote the liberation and independence of Macedonia from the Turks. Originally it was a genuinely Macedonian organization whose ranks were open to all regardless of nationality and whose slogan was 'Macedonia for the Macedonians'. It competed with the Society of Saint Sava (1886), a Serbian national organization, the Ethnike Hetaerea (1893), which strove for union with Greece, and the Supreme Macedo-Adrianopolitan Committee (1895), which favoured union with Bulgaria. After a period of secret preparation IMRO opened a campaign of terror and violence against the Turkish authorities in 1897. In Aug. 1903 this campaign culminated in IMRO's seizure of the Monastir vilayet and an attempt to liberate all Macedonia. The Turks quickly and severely suppressed the rebellion, but the powers imposed the Murzsteg reform programme upon the Porte in Oct. 1903. Repressive policies by the Turks and competition from rival organizations drove IMRO into a close relationship with the Bulgarian government. During the Balkan Wars and the First World War IMRO placed itself at the disposal of the Bulgarian army and administered Serbian Macedonia. Reliance upon Sofia produced division among IMRO leaders, a federalist group opposing an annexationist faction. The annexationists, strengthened by the patronage of the Bulgarian government and profiting from disenchantment with the treaty of Neuilly, easily became the dominant element. IMRO had degenerated into a purely terrorist organization which bedevilled Bulgarian politics throughout the 1920s. It played a leading part in the coup of June 1923 which toppled the Agrarian regime. Under the governments of Alexander Tsankov and Andrei Liapcev IMRO enjoyed a virtual free hand. It took harsh reprisals against its opponents and settled its internal differences in violent fashion. At this time IMRO was led by Vancho Mihailov and was entrenched in its stronghold in the Petrich district near the Yugoslav frontier. Not until the military coup of 19 May 1934 were strong measures taken against IMRO by the Bulgarian government. Georgiev's government used the army and quickly broke IMRO's power. But IMRO, long subsidized by Italy, joined with Yugoslav, Hungarian, and Italian terrorist groups in a number of conspiracies, the most important of which was the assassination of King Alexander of Yugoslavia.   JMK

INTERNATIONAL, FIRST (1864), Working Men's Association, founded in London by Karl Marx to provide a means of co-operation between all the working-class societies of Europe. Its programme was deliberately general to avoid dissent and representatives attended from Britain, France, Germany, Belgium, Switzerland, Italy, and Spain. But after Bakunin and the anarchists joined the movement in 1869 conflict arose between the Marxist concept of socialism as an authoritarian, centralized movement and the anarchists' dislike of organization and discipline. Bakunin was expelled in 1872, but the international had lost its impetus and was dissolved in 1876. Its failure encouraged the participation of Marxists in national politics, first evident in the growth of the Social Democratic Party in Germany.

INTERNATIONAL, SECOND (1889), Working Men's Association, arising from the large assembly of socialists in Paris for the centenary of the French Revolution. Anarchists were excluded and the international embarked on a long series of congresses providing an effective forum for debate, the exchange of information, and the promotion of international understanding. By 1910, with a permanent base in the International Socialist Bureau in Brussels, the movement had 896 delegates representing 23 nationalities. But its support for the Russian revolution of 1905 was the nearest it came to true international solidarity. There was controversy over the role socialists should play in national politics and the attitude they should adopt to war. But the arguments in favour of a general strike or a full-scale revolution appeared academic in 1914 when most socialists rallied to their national governments. The international's most enduring decision was its proclamation of May 1 as Labour Day.

INTERNATIONAL ATOMIC ENERGY AGENCY (IAEA), agency of the UN established in 1957, with headquarters in Vienna, with responsibility for the development of atomic

energy for peaceful purposes. It has set up a number of important laboratories in Austria and a Centre for Theoretical Physics at Trieste.

INTERNATIONAL BANK FOR RECONSTRUCTION AND DEVELOPMENT (WORLD BANK), established in 1945 after successful negotiations at the Bretton Woods Conference (July 1944). The purpose of the bank is to assist economic development by providing capital in the form of loans. Its capital comes from members' subscriptions and from loans raised on the open market. The bank supports only projects which it believes to be good investments on normal economic grounds. Its reputation has both facilitated the raising of capital and encouraged private investment in projects which the bank has studied.

INTERNATIONAL BRIGADES, THE, formed under the influence of the Comintern for action during the Spanish Civil War. National Communist parties were asked to supply volunteers, who were then sent to Spain via Paris, where the organization was run by the future Marshal Tito. On 14 Oct. 1936, the first volunteers arrived at Albacete for training under the leadership of the French communist, André Marty. The air section was run by André Malraux and the military commander was Gen. 'Emilio Kléber', a Rumanian communist.

The first units arrived in Madrid on 7 Nov. and consisted of German and Italian anti-fascists, together with some British, French, and Polish volunteers. They were used as shock troops or to save key positions in important actions such as at the battles of Jarama and Guadalajara, the Brunete offensive, and the battle of Teruel. Hence, the International brigades' losses were severe and over a third of its members lost their lives.

Figures vary, but the total number of volunteers appears to have been nearly 40,000, although there were never more than 18,000 at any given time. The volunteers were organized into five brigades, numbered XI, XII, XIII, XIV, and XV. They came from all over Europe and Great Britain and from South and North America. They came for personal reasons, but all shared the ideal of fighting fascism. It would seem that a large proportion of them were either communists before they came or joined the party while in Spain. France supplied most volunteers, about 10,000, Germany and Austria about 5,000 each, and Italy 3,350. The rest were from a variety of countries.

By Jan. 1938, as a result of heavy losses and because the work of training the republic's army was over, the International brigades were incorporated into the Republican army. After Munich (1938), the Russians began to think of a rapprochement with Germany. This, together with the fact that many of the volunteers had been replaced by Spaniards and that the non-intervention committee was calling for the withdrawal of volunteers, led to brigades being pulled out. On 15 Nov. 1938, a farewell parade was held in Barcelona at which a moving oration was made by La Pasionaria. Of the volunteers who survived the Civil War and then the Second World War, those from Eastern Europe were purged and many of those from the West were ostracized during the Cold War.   PP

INTERNATIONAL CONFEDERATION OF FREE TRADE UNIONS, founded in 1949 in resistance to a communist attempt to dominate the World Federation of Trade Unions (founded in 1945). It immediately became a much larger organization than the rump of the WFTU which was left, with unions in some 53 countries and a membership of 50 million.

INTERNATIONAL DEVELOPMENT ASSOCIATION, established in 1960 to provide development loans on 'softer' grounds than the World Bank (IBRD). Its purpose is to finance projects in developing countries where the economic return is less immediate or less certain than would be necessary to justify private or even bank investment. Its resources are drawn in part from members' subscriptions, in part from transfers from the World Bank—the latter being derived from its successful operation as a development bank.

INTERNATIONAL FINANCE CORPORATION (IFC), established 1956 as an affiliate of the World Bank. The IFC recruits private capital and provides experienced management to assist the development of economically viable private enterprises in developing countries.

INTERNATIONAL LABOUR ORGANIZATION (ILO), established by the treaty of Versailles 1919. The ILO has a continuous history and became one of the Specialized Agencies of the UN. Its establishment was the result of the hopes and successful pressures of labour organizations which, ideally, would have set up a 'labour parliament' with legislative powers. While the ILO has been closely associated with the League and with the UN it has maintained its autonomy from both: in the inter-war years it retained the membership of Japan after Japan had left the League, and the US joined, although not a member of the League.

The representation of members in the ILO has taken a distinctive tripartite form—governments, employers, and workers each being represented in the proportion 2 : 1 : 1. Its main achievement, particularly in its early years, has been to establish rules for the protection of labour in the form of conventions and recommendations. After 1954 it played an important part in the provision of technical assistance to developing nations.

INTERNATIONAL NEWS SERVICE (1906–58), news gathering agency established by the US newspaper publisher, William Randolph Hearst. In 1958 it merged with the United Press to form United Press International.

INTERNATIONAL SUGAR AGREEMENT (1953), adopted at the United Nations Sugar Conference, London, effective for five years from Jan. 1959, with provisions for renewal. Designed to assure supplies and markets, the agreement regulates production and export quotas related to world prices and limits permitted stocks. It was renewed and was still valid in 1970.

INTERNATIONAL WHEAT AGREEMENT (1949), understanding reached between the major countries engaged in the trade of wheat, to ensure supplies of wheat at stable and equitable prices and a guaranteed market. It has been renewed at four-yearly intervals since then.

INTERREGNUM, THE GREAT GERMAN, period between 1250 and 1273 when no candidate could win general acceptance as emperor. In Germany it was marked by deep disorder. It was called 'the fearful emperor-less time' and was characterized by a loss of faith in Germany's future. It was the longest of several periods of civil war and disputed succession which enabled powerful princes to become even more powerful. It was ended by the intervention of Pope Gregory X, who needed a German ruler as a counterweight to the Angevin Charles of Sicily.

INTERSTATE COMMERCE COMMISSION (1887–) in US, federal agency established by the Interstate Commerce Act (1887) to regulate in the public interest railroads engaged in inter-state or foreign commerce. Its original limited authority was extended to common carriers in other forms of transportation and was considerably strengthened by a series of later acts. The 11 members of the commission are appointed by the president, subject to the advice and consent of the Senate, for seven-year staggered terms, and not more than six may be members of any one political party.

'INTOLERABLE ACTS' (1774), American nickname for four laws passed by the British parliament. The Boston Port Act closed the port of Boston, MA, until the tea destroyed in the 'Boston tea party' (16 Dec. 1773) had been paid for. The Massachusetts Government Act suppressed town meetings and increased the appointive power of the royal governor. The Act for the Impartial Administration of Justice allowed royal officials accused of capital crimes in MA to be tried in Britain or in another colony. Finally, the Quartering Act authorized colonial governors to requisition buildings as needed by royal troops. The passage of these laws was a major cause of the outbreak of revolution in the British North American colonies.

INUKAI, TSUYOSHI (KI) (1855–1932), Japanese politician, who was an important figure in the development of political parties in Japan. His unbroken election success in Okayama gave him a strong political position, but his unwillingness to compromise meant that he rarely held office. In 1912–13 he figured prominently in the movement to protect constitutional government which overthrew Katsura, and for many years he was a supporter of Sun Yat-sen. In 1929 he became president of the Seiyūkai, forming his only cabinet after the Manchurian Incident (1931). His attempt to find a moderate solution to this problem led to his assassination by fanatical young officers in the notorious 15 May incident (1932), which ended party cabinets until 1946.

INVALIDES, hospital in Paris for discharged soldiers, commissioned by Louis XIV and built by the architect Libéral Bruant (1670–7). The enormous complex of buildings includes the church of St Louis des Invalides, the burial place of Napoleon, with its magnificent dome constructed by Jules Hardouin-Mansart (1648–1708) in the years 1675–1706, a blend of classical and Italian baroque architecture. It is now the headquarters of the Paris military district.

INVERGORDON MUTINY (1931) in Scotland. In Aug. 1931 Ramsay MacDonald formed his National government after most of his Labour colleagues had refused to implement cuts in public expenditure, thought necessary to 'balance the budget' and avoid devaluation. On 14 Sept. sailors at Invergordon refused to sail in protest against their proposed pay cuts. The news of this prompted a run on the pound which forced the chancellor of the exchequer, Snowden, to suspend the gold standard after all (and thus redress the overvaluation caused by the ill-advised return to gold in 1925). The pay cuts for public employees were reduced in severity.

INVERLOCHY, BATTLE OF (1645), victory of James Graham, Marquis of Montrose, and his small force of Royalists over the Lowland Covenanters and Campbells under the Marquis of Argyll. The battle, fought near the head of Loch Linnhe in Scotland, ended the power of the Campbell clan for some years.

IOLCUS, Greek city in Thessaly of considerable importance in the Mycenaean period (16th–12th cents BC) and home of Jason, leader of the Argonauts.

IONA, island and monastery, off Mull, Scotland, founded (563) by Columba, descendant of powerful provincial princes in Ireland, who organized a small community on the island. From there he travelled to Inverness and converted King Brude of the Northern Picts to Christianity. The conversion of the people followed, and for several centuries missionaries went from Iona to teach throughout Scotland. In 635 Aidan was sent at the request of King Oswald to convert Northumbria. Iona was several times sacked by the Vikings. In the reign of Kenneth MacAlpine, who united the Scottish and Pictish kingdoms in the 9th cent., some of the relics of Columba were moved to the ecclesiastical centre of Dunkeld. Iona is the burial place of many early Scottish kings. The island remains (1970) a place of pilgrimage. The later abbey church was restored in the 20th cent. by the Church of Scotland.

IONESCU, TAKE (1858–1922), Rumanian statesman identified with the Entente during the First World War and the Little Entente after it. He entered parliament as a Liberal in 1884, but soon joined the Conservatives. As minister of culture he was embroiled in an affair involving the payment of state subsidies to Rumanian institutions in Transylvania. In 1908 he left the Conservative Party over the issue of agrarian reform and founded the Conservative Democratic Party. Ionescu led much of the interventionist activity during the early years of the First World War. He joined the national coalition formed at Jassy after Rumania's initial setbacks (Dec. 1916), but resigned over the decision to open talks with the Central Powers for a separate peace (Feb. 1917). After resigning, he went to Paris, where he was prominent in pressing the Rumanian national cause before the Paris Peace Conference. While serving as minister for foreign affairs in Averescu's cabinet (1920–2), Ionescu negotiated Rumania's alliances with Yugoslavia and Czechoslovakia which formed the basis of the Little Entente.

IONIAN ISLANDS consist of seven major islands—Corfu, Cephalonia, Zante, Santa Maura, Ithaca, Cythera, and Paxo—and their islet dependencies. They all came under the rule of Venice during the course of the 15th cent. The Venetian regime established the Roman Catholic Church, while affording the islands a wide measure of autonomy. The Greek and Italian aristocracies intermingled with one another and accepted Roman Catholicism, but the lower classes continued to speak Greek and worship in the Orthodox faith. By the treaty of Campo Formio (1797) the islands fell to revolutionary France. But a Russo-Turkish agreement in 1800 established the independent Septinsular Republic. The independence of the Ionian islands ended with the treaty of Tilsit (1807), which returned them to France. Until 1815 the islands were governed as a part of the province of Illyria. The treaty of Paris (1815) placed them under British protection. A constituent assembly promulgated a constitution in 1817 and administrative, judicial, and educational reforms followed. Meanwhile, sentiment in favour of union with the kingdom of Greece mounted and in 1848 parliament voted a resolution in favour of immediate union. Britain finally ceded the islands to Greece in 1864, after King Otho's abdication.

IONIAN REVOLT (499–494 BC), abortive rising of the Ionian Greeks of western Asia Minor against the Persians, their rulers since 540. Widespread discontent with Persian-backed tyrants and Persian exactions of ships, men, and tribute exploded through the personal machinations of Aristagoras, tyrant of Miletus. Though assistance from Greece was inadequate and short-lived, the rising spread to nearby islands and as far as Byzantium and Cyprus, but the Ionians were weak on land and disunited and their fleet's defeat at Lade ended the revolt. Though severe on some cities, especially Miletus, Darius allowed democracies and eased the tribute, and Xerxes included Ionians in his Greek expedition of 480–479. The revolt, however, strengthened Persian determination to conquer Greece, and led directly to the expedition to punish Eretria and Athens for sending help (490), but the homelanders learned well the lessons of Ionian disunity.

IONIANS, Greek ethnic group resident during the Mycenaean period (16th–12th cents BC) in southern Greece, later (11th–10th cents) driven eastwards by the Dorians into eastern Attica, the Cyclades, Chios, Samos, and the adjacent Asiatic coast from Phocaea to Miletus. The Asiatic Ionians, including those of Chios and Samos, established c. 700 a common religious and political centre at Mycale, henceforward regarding themselves as *the* Ionians. Among them emerged the oral epic poetry that culminated in the *Iliad* and *Odyssey* (c. 700) and later (6th cent.), especially at Miletus, the first Greek philosophy. Economically prosperous from c. 600, they were generally politically subservient to whatever power controlled their hinterland, but in the 5th cent. they were dominated by Athens, who exploited the tradition that Codrus' sons had led the original migration eastwards.

IOWA, 29th member state of the US, admitted 1846. It was first explored by Joliet and Marquette in 1673 and was part of the territory ceded to Spain by the treaty of Fontainebleau (1762), then returned to France in 1800 and acquired by the US in the Louisiana Purchase (1803). Organized as part of the Missouri territory (1812–21), the Michigan territory (1834) and the Wisconsin territory (1836), it was not open to settlement until the Indians had been removed by the Black Hawk Purchase (1833) and subsequent cessions in 1837, 1843, and 1847. It was organized as a territory in 1838.

IOWA INDIANS, one of the American Siouan tribes, apparently stemming from the Winnebago nation north of the Great Lakes. The French, who gave them firearms, reported them on the headwaters of the Des Moines river in 1700, and Lewis and Clark found them on the Platte river in 1704. The Iowa were important as fur traders. They ceded their lands (1824) and now live on reservations assigned to them in KS (1836) and OK (1890).

IPATIEFF, VLADIMIR NIKOLAIEVICH (1867–1952), Russian-American chemist, whose studies from 1900 of high-temperature catalytic reactions are fundamental to the petrochemical industry. In 1930 Ipatieff left Russia and worked subsequently in the US. By then it had become of prime importance that the quality of petrol used as a motor car fuel was improved. Ipatieff showed how this could be effected by the conversion of the hydrocarbon mixtures. His work was also important in the development of aviation fuel during the Second World War.

IPHICRATES (c. 415–353 BC), Athenian general, who by effectively deploying light-armed peltasts against less mobile hoplites achieved a notable victory over Spartan forces in the Corinthian War (390). After mercenary service in Thrace and Syria following the King's Peace (387), he returned to Athens, where he succeeded Timotheus as general and prevented Spartan invasion of Corcyra (373). He co-operated with Callistratus in seeking either quick military success or peace with Sparta. After the peace (371) and the Theban defeat of the Spartans at Leuctra, he failed against the Thebans and around Amphipolis and withdrew to Thrace. After returning to command the Athenian fleet once more in the Social War he was defeated at Embata (356).

IPSUS, BATTLE OF (301 BC), in Phrygia, the defeat by Lysimachus and Seleucus of Antigonus Monophthalmus, involving in all 134,000 infantry, 20,500 cavalry, and 555 elephants. Antigonus was killed and his power broken, but his son, Demetrius Poliorcetes, who charged too far, escaped and for 18 years remained an independent prince.

IPSWICH PROTEST (1687), American colonial statement, originating in Ipswich, MA, against taxes levied by the English governor, Sir Edmund Andros.

IQBAL, SIR MUHAMMAD (1876–1938), Muslim poet, philosopher, and politician. His major philosophical poems, written in Persian, were 'Asrar-i Kudi' (1915) and 'Rumuz-i Bekhudi' (1918), translated later as 'The Secrets of the Self' (1920) and 'The Mysteries of Selflessness' (1953). These works contain the core of his view that for the Muslim the self could only be realized within the community, but that, at the same time, the community could only exist as the expression of self-affirming individuals. His 'Javid-Namah' (1932), 'The Book of Eternity', modelled on Dante, contained some of his most profound poetry. He also wrote three volumes of Urdu poetry. His philosophical views were further developed in a series of lectures, *The Reconstruction of Religious Thought in Islam* (1930).

Iqbal played an active part in Punjab and Muslim League politics as an elected member of the Punjab legislative council (1927–30), president of the Muslim League (1930), and a delegate to the Round Table Conference (1931). As Muslim League president, he put forward for the first time (1930) the idea of a separate Muslim state in north-western India. Nothing emerged from this suggestion immediately, but it was the basis of the idea of Pakistan. It had an increasing appeal in the face of the widening cleavage between the Muslim League and the Congress.

IQTA, granting of state lands in parts of the Muslim world in return for taxes, tithes, or services. The term might denote the assignment of an entire province to a governor as a kind of appanage; or the allotment of revenues deriving from land as an income, or a pension to a given individual. Later, the word was extended in meaning to include the farming out of taxes, customs duties, and tolls; and, still later, to denote a fief assigned to a soldier in return for services in time of war. This latter development of iqta in the sense of military fief was in progress above all during the time of the Buyids and the Seljuks, ie, in the 10th–12th cents.

IRALA, DOMINGO MARTÍNEZ DE (d. 1557), Spanish conquistador and governor of Paraguay from 1539 until he was replaced by Alvar Núñez Cabeza de Vaca in 1542. Within two years he and his followers had removed Cabeza de Vaca, and Irala ruled as governor from then until his death, almost independent of the authorities in Spain. He encouraged marriage between Spaniards and the local Guarani Indians, and laid the basis for the self-sufficiency of the region.

IRAQ PETROLEUM COMPANY, name adopted (1929) by the former Turkish Petroleum Co., which was itself the name adopted (1912) by a company first formed in 1911 to reconcile British, German, and Ottoman interests in Iraqi oil. After the First World War Ottoman and German interests were replaced by US and French. The Red Line Agreement (1928) gave a 23·75 per cent share each to US and French interests, 47·5 per cent to Anglo-Dutch interests, and 5 per cent to Calouste Gulbenkian's interests. With its associated companies (Mosul Petroleum Co. and Basra Petroleum Co.) the Iraq Petroleum Co. continued to dominate Iraqi oil production, despite the confiscation of 99·5 per cent of its concession area by law in 1961.

IRAQ REBELLION (1920), basically a tribal rising, with some nationalist overtones, centred among Shi'ite tribesmen of the mid-Euphrates and directed against British rule. It affected one-third of Iraq and lasted from July to Oct. before order was restored. The rebellion was a major factor in Britain's decision to withdraw to a treaty relationship with Iraq.

IRAQI REVOLUTIONS. The Hashemite government, which had survived several revolutionary attempts, fell (14 July 1958) during a military coup, planned and led by Brig. Abd al-Qarim Kassim (Qasim). The 1958 revolution was partly the outcome of discontent among civilian political opponents of the regime, who formed a clandestine coalition in 1957 and who criticized the Hashemites for their restrictive domestic political policies and their pro-Western external alignment, but more particularly it was the work of a Free Officer movement within the army. In the coup Faysal II, most of his family, and some leading politicians were murdered. The new revolutionary regime proclaimed a republic and adopted a policy of neutralism and Iraqi nationalism abroad and moderate social and economic reform at home. The dominant figure was Kassim, who successfully played off Arab nationalists against communists and neutralized both. He failed however to win influential support and alienated civilian politicians, intellectuals, religious leaders, and the Kurds. Disaffection and the spread of Ba'thist ideas in the

army eventually led to a further successful coup (9 Feb. 1963) and the execution of Kassim. Abd al-Salam Aref, once Kassim's principal supporter and later opponent, became president and was succeeded after his death in 1966 by his brother, Abd al-Rahman Aref. The Aref governments did not carry through any radical internal economic and social reorganization and political power remained with factions of the army. In a further coup (17 July 1968) Aref was replaced by Gen. Ahmad Hassan al-Bakr.   MEY

IRENAEUS (AD 130–200), bishop of Lyons from c. 178. He came from Asia, where, in early life, he studied under Polycarp. In the persecution of 177 he carried a letter concerning Montanism from Gaul to Rome, and later rebuked Victor, Bp of Rome, for his attitude in the Quarto-deciman controversy. He wrote five books *Against the Heresies*, which refute the Gnostics and Marcion, and an apologetic work, *Proof of the Apostolic Preaching*. As a constructive Christian thinker he had an all-embracing vision of the restoration or summing up (*recapitulatio*) of the whole universe and mankind in Christ.

IRENE (*reg.* 797–802), Byzantine Empress, wife of Leo IV, who died young. She became sole regent during the minority of her son Constantine VI. Capable, domineering, and popular, Irene filled the principal offices of state with her own supporters. In a palace revolution Constantine asserted his authority and resumed an active Iconoclast policy until 979, when Irene overthrew him, had him blinded, and immured him in a monastery. Thereafter she reigned as empress until 802, when she, in her turn, was incarcerated in a nunnery by Nicephorus. Her reign is chiefly notable for her encouragement of Charlemagne to be crowned emperor at Rome in 800, exploiting the fact that there was no emperor in the East.

IRETON, HENRY (1611–51), English soldier and politician, who married Oliver Cromwell's eldest daughter, Bridget, and served in the Civil War. At Naseby, Ireton, in command of the left wing, was driven from the field by Prince Rupert. By 1646 he had emerged as a political thinker and leader in his own right. He tried to act as mediator between the army and the Commons, and worked for a negotiated settlement with Charles I, drawing up the Heads of the Proposals (1647). He was a strong opponent of the Levellers, fearing that their claims for a wider suffrage would undermine respect for property. In the second Civil War he lost his sympathies for Charles and became a regicide. In 1649 he served under Cromwell in Ireland as a major-general and stayed, when Cromwell left, as lord deputy and acting commander-in-chief. He died in Limerick shortly after the siege.

IRGUN ZVAI LEUMI, revisionist Zionist underground military organization, also known as Etzel, from its initials, originally formed (1937) for defence against Arabs and which subsequently operated against British mandatory authority. Under Menahem Beigin it was responsible (1947–8) for massacres of Arabs before its absorption into the regular Isaeli forces.

IRISH FREE STATE ACTS (1922), Recognition of the Irish Free State by the British government was accompliished in three acts of parliament passed in 1922. The Irish Free State (Agreement) Act of March accorded force of law to the treaty of 1921 which had ended the 'Black and Tan War' between Britain and Sinn Fein, and provided for elections to a constituent assembly in the South of Ireland. The Irish Free State (Constitution) Act of Dec. recognized the Free State constitution passed by that body and empowered the Irish parliament to apply to Ireland acts which already applied to other Dominions. The Consequential Provisions Act recognized the already-extant position between North and South, by providing that the Government of Ireland Act (1920) should not operate outside Northern Ireland, and by making provision for Northern Ireland to vote itself out of the Free State. This it did, the day after the Act was passed, and so the constitutional position of Northern Ireland was established in the form it still retained in 1970.

IRISH HOME RULE, self-government for Ireland, urged by the Home Rule Association, a parliamentary pressure group founded by the moderate Dublin professor, Isaac Butt (1870), which aimed at repeal of the Act of Union (1800) and the creation of a Dublin parliament. After winning 59 seats in the 1874 election, it was taken over by the more dictatorial and efficient Charles Stewart Parnell, who obstructed the routine work of the Commons by continually focusing attention on mounting Irish discontent. Gladstone realized that his dis-establishment of the Irish Church and attempts to create harmony between tenant and landlord on English lines were not enough and was converted to Home Rule (1885). Parnell had ordered the Irish living in England to vote Conservative, but the Liberals won the 1885 election by a majority of 86, the Irish securing just that number ('the 86 of '86'), and so became the arbiter in parliament.

Gladstone's first Home Rule bill proposed a separate Irish parliament and executive in Dublin with subjects relating to the Crown, peace and war, defence, foreign relations, customs and excise, trade, post office, and coinage reserved for the Westminster government. Representation of Ireland by MPs at Westminster, a controversial issue, was to be ended. An accompanying bill provided for land purchase by Irish tenants which would help them and aid English landlords to sell out their estates and escape any harsh measures an Irish government might take. The bill was defeated after grave debate (343 votes to 313), with 93 Liberals voting against Gladstone. The Liberal split was fatal to the bill, Lord Hartington supporting the English landlords, and Joseph Chamberlain opposing a Parnellite Ireland that would destroy his vision of imperialism and of active, reforming local government. Lord Randolph Churchill stressed the threat of Roman Catholic supremacy overwhelming Protestant Ulster. Surrender to terrorism was resented. Determined on Home Rule as the only just solution, Gladstone introduced his second bill (1893), which differed only in allowing 80 Irish members to come and vote at Westminster on imperial or Irish affairs. Piloted through under considerable uproar, it passed the Commons (307–267 votes) but was overwhelmingly rejected by the Lords (419–41 votes).

Land Purchase acts did much to ease the land problem, but Irish nationalist pressure increased and was reflected in the growth of Sinn Fein. In 1912 the Liberals under Asquith, encouraged by the success of the Parliament Act limiting the Lords' powers, introduced a third Home Rule bill, hoping to make the moderate nationalist leader, John Redmond, into the 'Irish Botha'. The bill divided Ireland rapidly into two armed camps, the resistance of Protestant Ulster hardening under Sir Edward Carson, supported by the Conservative-Unionist party leader, Bonar Law. Private armies came into existence in North and South and civil war threatened. The bill passed the third Commons reading but with the outbreak of war in Europe was suspended indefinitely.

After more terrorism and bitter fighting, Lloyd George's Coalition government passed the Government of Ireland Act (1920), providing for separate parliaments for Ulster and the South, and negotiated the Irish Free State treaty (1921), renamed as independent Eire by De Valera (1937) and recognized as a republic (1949). Bitterness between North and South, Protestant and Catholic, still persisted in 1970.

N. Mansergh, *The Irish Free State* (London, 1934).
N. Mansergh, *The Irish Question 1840–1921* (London, 1965).
JRA

IRISH INVASION (1798), French attempt to exploit incipient rebellion in Ireland which failed because it was not synchronized with the Irish rebellion. The first invasion force was sent off in Feb. 1797, but landed in Pembrokeshire, where it

was captured. The English authorities thereupon took vigorous action to repress rebellion in Ireland. A second invasion force under Humbert landed in Co. Mayo in Aug. 1798, too late to gather Irish support, and on 10 Oct. a second force, which included Wolfe Tone, was captured in Lough Swilly.

IRISH LAND LEGISLATION (1870–1903) reflected the British government's attempts to solve the problems of the Irish peasants' land hunger and absentee landlords. Gladstone's first attempt in his Land Act (1870) to compensate evicted tenants for any permanent improvements they had made on their farms and to prevent evictions was neither popular nor successful. His second Land Act (1881)—the 3 F's—gave tenants fair rent, fixity of tenure, and free sale of any improvements made on their holdings, and set up land courts to hear tenants' appeals. This commendable bid to create harmony and 'dual ownership' between tenant and landlord on English lines was inadequate, but Lord Ashbourne's Act (1885), the first state-assisted scheme of land purchase, pointed the way to a solution. The Tories followed liberal lines in Balfour's (1891) and Wyndham's Land Purchase Acts (1903), the latter dealing with entire estates, instituting a thorough-going system of peasant proprietorship by a large cash contribution from the Westminster parliament to buy out the landlords. The scheme worked well until the 1930s, when the Free State government appropriated the peasants' repayments.

IRISH NATIONAL LAND LEAGUE (1879), association formed to agitate for reduction of tenants' rents and ultimately to create peasant proprietorship by the state's expropriation of the landlords. Parnell was president and two Fenians, Davitt and Brennan, were secretaries. The league was a vital part of a double-pronged Irish attack: in Ireland through the widespread distress of the peasants; in England through MPs in the House of Commons like Parnell and Davitt. Campaign funds poured in from the US and Australia. Measures like 'boycotting' and 'moonlighting' were adopted to force the government to act. The league survived prosecution for conspiring (1881) and saw the beginning of its eventual triumph with Gladstone's land legislation. Parnell, himself a landlord, encouraged all opposition to landlords short of physical violence and used the league's formidable pressure for his own political ends. This caused quarrels with Davitt, who gave land nationalization, not Home Rule, priority.

IRISH PALE, that part of Ireland which lay under direct English rule, until the complete subjugation of Ireland under Elizabeth I. The extent of the Pale varied considerably according to the strength or weaknesses of the monarchy, but by *c.* 1500 it embraced much of the modern counties of Dublin, Louth, Meath, and Kildare.

IRISH REBELLION (1798) demonstrated the failure of Grattan's Irish parliament. Both the Presbyterians of Ulster and the mass of Roman Catholics were dissatisfied with it, and between 1795 and 1798 the United Irishmen of Ulster—strongly organized and influenced by Jacobinism—and the Roman Catholic Defenders became militant. With the failure of Fitzwilliam's expedition (1795) they lost faith in the possibility of reform by constitutional means. The threat of French invasion provoked repressive measures by the English, which in turn led to a premature rising. The rebellion degenerated into affrays between Protestants and Catholics, and the decisive defeat by the English took place at Vinegar Hill (June 1798).

IRISH REPUBLICAN ARMY, grew out of the force organized by the Irish Republican Brotherhood under Tom Clarke and Patrick Pearse to fight the Easter Rising in 1916. In the years of the 'Black and Tan War' (1919–21) the IRA functioned as the military wing of Sinn Fein and organized guerrilla raids against British troops and institutions. When civil war broke out in Ireland in 1922 over the acceptance of the 1921 treaty and 'Free State' status, the same tactics were repeated by the 'Irregulars', the soldiers fighting on the intransigent Republican side of De Valera, who took over the title of IRA. When De Valera's party became the government in 1933, the IRA in turn was proclaimed an illegal organization, as it continued guerrilla attacks in Northern Ireland. Although quiescent immediately after the Second World War, the IRA again ran a campaign of attacking policemen and border posts (1956–1961). The outbreak of serious trouble in Northern Ireland in 1968 caused a split in the IRA. The official leadership in Dublin had embraced militant socialism and was accused by the breakaways, who called themselves 'Provisionals', of neglecting the threatened Catholics in the North. The Provisionals helped to organize the movement of arms into Belfast and Londonderry, and in 1970 two members of the Fianna Fail government in Ireland were accused (and later acquitted) of having taken part in the illegal import of arms for use in the North. Throughout the period 1919–70 the IRA did its best to live up to the role of a dedicated subversive organization depicted by the Ulster Unionists in the interest of maintaining their Protestant working-class support.

IM

IRISH REVOLUTION (1782) gave legislative independence to the Irish parliament, which had previously been subordinate to Westminster. During the American War of Independence Irish exports of foodstuffs and woollens to America and France became illegal, and economic distress was generally blamed on subordination to English commercial policy. The Irish volunteer movement, originally formed to counteract any threat of invasion, and led by Grattan and Flood, began to demand legislative independence. They were supported by the parliamentary opposition in England, and when Lord Rockingham came to power in 1782 he repealed Poyning's Law (1495) and the act of 1719, which together subordinated the Irish to the English legislature.

IRISH RISING (1803). Robert Emmet plotted to paralyse Ireland by seizing government offices in Dublin. This, at a time when Napoleon was threatening invasion of England, was a further reminder of the threat to security presented by Irish disaffection.

IRISH UNION (1800) regulated Anglo-Irish relations till 1921. The Irish rebellion of 1798 had shown the lack of popular support for Grattan's Irish parliament. In 1799 Pitt proposed its abolition as a means of restoring order. The Protestant ascendancy would lose their parliamentary interests, but would gain security from the existence of a permanent Protestant majority at Westminster. The Catholics, able since 1793 to vote, but not to sit in parliament, would be won over by the promise of Catholic emancipation. These arguments were supported by the offer of peerages and direct bribery. Castlereagh was Pitt's principal agent in the negotiations and the Act of Union was passed by the English and Irish parliaments in 1800. Under it Ireland was given 100 seats at Westminster, which the Irish MPs were to use to great effect in the later 19th cent. The settlement was undermined by George III's refusal to countenance the Catholic emancipation which Pitt had intended should accompany it.

IRNERIUS (c. 1050–c. 1130), founder (1084) of the school of glossators at Bologna. He introduced the use of the marginal gloss in the study of Roman civil law.

IRON ACT (1750), in Britain, allowed pig and bar iron from the British American colonies to enter Britain free of duty. Slitting mills, steel furnaces, and plating mills were not to be erected in the colonies. This part of the act, however, was ignored by them.

IRON AGE, AFRICA, period of (mainly tropical) African development between the era which introduced ferrous technology, about 2000 years ago, and the late 19th cent., so called because iron tools and weapons were a decisive factor in promoting the spread of the comparatively very small populations of Late Stone Age Africa. Such implements helped to improve food supplies and facilitated the settlement of nomadic peoples.

If the population of sub-Saharan Africa was only a few million people at the outset of the Iron Age, as seems likely, it was probably not less than 150 million by the 19th cent., having spread across and settled in the whole of the habitable continent, evolving in the process its own characteristic socio-political systems and cultures.

The origins of this Iron Age are variously defined. Some historians trace its spread across sub-Saharan Africa by diffusion from North Africa, the Nile valley (notably Meroe), and possibly Axum; others argue for a mainly independent growth by local invention or adaptation. The earliest sub-Saharan culture known to have made iron implements is that of Nok, a transitional culture from the Late Stone Age centred round the lower course of the Benue river in middle Nigeria. Radio-carbon datings suggest that iron objects were being made here in the first half of the 3rd cent. BC. Other datings indicate the onset of an Iron Age in central–southern Africa soon after zero AD. By about AD 500 many peoples in western, central, eastern, and southern Africa were making iron tools and weapons. Five centuries later the greater part of sub-Saharan Africa had come within the scope and range of Iron Age development.

This development is interpreted as including the growth and ramification of peoples; the progressive sub-division of labour and its consequent effects, such as the evolution of centralizing forms of rule among a large number of peoples; the use of mineral technology for the production of gold and other metals, whether for local use or export; and, generally, the onward course of history up to the crisis and upheavals of the 19th cent. which culminated in European colonial dispossession and the close of this long period of Iron Age growth.

B. M. Fagan, *Southern Africa during the Iron Age* (London, 1965).

M. Posnansky, *Prelude to East African History* (Oxford, 1966).

BD

IRON GUARD, indigenous Rumanian fascist movement prominent during the 1930s and a partner in government in 1940–1. Originally the Iron Guard was the political section of a wider movement, the Legion of the Archangel Michael. The legion was founded in 1927 and the guard in 1930, both by Corneliu Zelea Codreanu. Under his leadership the movement was marked by conservative nationalism, religious mysticism, and cultivated primitivism. These qualities were manifest in the guard's rabid anti-Semitism and anti-communism, fascination with death, and perverted populism. It prided itself on the lack of a programme, insisting that the nation needed leaders, not programmes. Although frequently dissolved by the government, the guard participated in elections under a variety of names. By 1937 it had become a mass movement, polling 16·5 per cent of the vote. The *déclassés* and *Lumpenproletariat* supplied its most active members, but this should not obscure its appeal to other disaffected elements in society, including the peasantry, bureaucracy, and working class. Carol II turned on the guard after establishing his dictatorship in 1938, arresting the leaders on charges of conspiring with foreign powers against the state. These allegations were exaggerated, though the guard received some financial backing from Germany and Italy. In 1939, a year after Codreanu had been shot in prison, the guard struck back, assassinating Armand Calinescu, the prime minister and strong man of Carol's regime. And the next year Carol was compelled to bring the guard, now led by Horia Sima, into his government. After forcing Carol's abdication, Gen. Ion Antonescu granted the guard a share of power in the National-Legionary state (Sept. 1940–Jan. 1941). During this brief spell the guard unleashed a wave of terror, inciting pogroms and settling scores with old enemies. But Antonescu's alliance with Germany required internal stability, and in Dec. 1940 he sought to bring the guard to heel with German support. Antonescu's campaign met fierce resistance and culminated in a pitched battle lasting three days in which the army broke the strength of the guard.

JMK

IRON INDUSTRY in the Middle Ages. The collapse of the Roman empire in the West led to a decline in the output of iron goods in Europe, but there was no loss of technical knowledge. Some of the weapons produced in the Frankish territories in the Dark Ages rival in their combination of flexibility with endurance the best modern work. The general expansion of European economy after the 11th cent. stimulated the growth of the iron industry. The iron ore was processed in a multitude of low furnaces, each of which could only be used for a short time. They were widely dispersed all over Europe and most of them served only local needs. Long-distance trade in iron and iron goods was slow to develop and was usually restricted only to specially valuable articles. Technological improvements from the 13th cent. onwards brought a gradual change in the prospects of the industry. First of all water power came to be widely employed in hammering the ores and in driving the bellows used in furnaces. There was general progress in the mining of all types of minerals, which by the 15th cent. made deeper deposits of iron ore accessible to exploitation. Most important of all was the introduction of high-temperature furnaces, which were invented in the later 14th cent., either in northern Spain or in Germany. These were more permanent structures and it was possible to achieve in them temperatures high enough to melt the ore. This made it possible to extract most of the pure metal present in the ores and the total output of the industry greatly increased. Furthermore, cast-iron objects could be produced for the first time. The European production of iron and steel expanded considerably after c. 1450.

EBF

IRON KNOB, rich deposit of iron ore in South Australia, discovered in 1891. By 1915 it had become the main source of ore for Australia's steel industry.

IRONSIDE, WILLIAM EDMUND IRONSIDE, 1st Baron (1880–1959), British soldier who was supposedly the model for John Buchan's fictional character, Richard Hannay. He was British commander-in-chief of the Allied troops based on Archangel in the Russian Civil War (1918–19). On the outbreak of the Second World War he was appointed chief of the imperial general staff in succession to Gort, who went with the British Expeditionary Force to France. In May 1940 Ironside was relieved by Field Marshal Sir John Dill.

IRONSIDES in England, name given to the cavalry regiment of Oliver Cromwell in the English Civil war of the 17th cent. It was originally given to Cromwell himself by Prince Rupert after the battle of Marston Moor.

IROQUOIS INDIANS, linguistic family of North American Indians, including the Huron (Wyandot) Tionontati, Neutral, Erie, Susquehanna, Nottoway, Meherrin, Cherokee, the Tuscarora confederation, and the League of the Iroquois (Mohawk, Oneida, Onondaga, Seneca, Cayuga). Their ancestral home was the southern US, but they ranged as far north as Canada. Their first European contacts were Jacques Cartier (1534) on the Gaspé Peninsula; Hernando de Soto, who found the Cherokee (1540) in eastern Tennessee; Capt. John Smith, who found the Susquehanna on Chesapeake Bay (1608); and the Dutch, who discovered the league Iroquois (1609) in New York. Inter-tribal wars, pressure from expanding European settlements, and US government policy defeated and dispersed the Iroquois, or caused them to be assimilated by other tribes. Only the league Iroquois, the Cherokee, and the Huron survive (1970).

IROQUOIS LEAGUE, also known as the Five (later Six) Nations, league of Iroquoian-speaking tribes formed in the mid-16th cent. to keep peace among them. The members were the Mohawk, Oneida, Onondaga, Seneca, Cayuga, and, from 1722, Tuscarora. After obtaining firearms from the Europeans, they established an empire over other tribes in north-eastern America. The Iroquois were England's allies against the French, except for groups which seceded from the league to join the French. The league was neutral in the American War of Independence, but individual tribes fought for both sides. In the years after the war, defeated and dispersed, they settled in Canada, New York, WI, and OK, where they still remain in 1970.

IRREDENTA. The Mazzinian republicans in Italy felt that unification was incomplete without the strategically valuable, Italian-speaking territories of Trentino and Trieste, the *terra irredenta*, which Austria had retained in 1866. The Italia Irredenta Society was founded in 1876 to agitate for their inclusion in the Italian state, but it had little influence, since it had neither official nor socialist support. Conflict with Austria over the provision of an Italian-speaking university and the treatment of Italian minorities sparked off a fresh wave of irredentist activity early in the 20th cent. This combined with the aggressive nationalism of D'Annunzio to contribute to the deterioration in Austro-Italian relations which caused Italy's refusal to act with the Triple Alliance in 1914. The aims of the irredentists were fulfilled, in part, when Italy occupied Trentino and Trieste in 1918.

IRVING, WASHINGTON (1783–1859), US lawyer and writer, whose early work included the satirical *Letters of Jonathan Oldstreet, Gent.* (1802–3). He established his reputation with the burlesque *History of New York, by Deidrich Knickerbocker* (1809). After moving to Europe in 1815 he wrote *The Sketch Book of Geoffrey Crayon, Gent.* (1819), which includes two famous stories, 'Rip Van Winkle' and 'The Legend of Sleepy Hollow'. He increased his popularity with two further books of romantic sketches, *Bracebridge Hall* (1822) and the *Alhambra* (1832), and returned home (1832) as a celebrity. Later he was appointed minister to Spain (1842–5). On his return to the US (1846) he devoted himself to writing, producing, among a variety of lesser works, a monumental *Life of Washington* (5 vols, 1855–9).

ISAAC I COMNENUS (c. 1005–71), Emperor of Byzantium (reg. 1057–9), who ruled with the support of the military magnates in Asia Minor. His reign was spent in efforts to set the imperial finances on a better foundation and to make good the neglect which the army and the defences of the empire had suffered under the preceding domination of the civil bureaucracy. His high-handed methods aroused against him the ill-will of the churchmen and of the bureaucrats—an alliance which compelled him to abdicate in 1059, the rest of his life being spent as a monk.

ISAACS, SIR ISAAC ALFRED (1885–1948), first Australian-born governor-general of Australia (1930–6). After a short time as a country school teacher, he studied law and was called to the Victorian bar (1882). He became a member of the Vic. Legislative Assembly (1892–1901) and was attorney-general of Vic. (1894–1901). He played a prominent part at the Constitutional Convention (1897–8) which drafted the Commonwealth constitution, and was a member of the Commonwealth House of Representatives (1901–6) and attorney-general of the Commonwealth (1905–6). He was appointed a justice of the high court of Australia in 1906 and became its chief justice in 1930. In 1930, after a controversy over the propriety of the appointment of an Australian, he became governor-general of the Commonwealth.

ISAACS, JORGE (1837–95), Colombian novelist, whose work *María* (1867) is the most famous romantic novel of Latin America.

ISABEL (1846–1921), Princess of Brazil, daughter of Pedro II, and regent of Brazil. The abolition of slavery was passed during her regency. She was exiled with her father in 1889 after his fall from power.

ISABELLA (d. 1358), Queen, daughter of Philip IV the Fair of France and wife of King Edward II of England. Her relations with Edward deteriorated rapidly after 1322, and while on an embassy in France (1325–6) she took as her lover Roger Mortimer, with whom she invaded England in Sept. 1326, deposing Edward II and ruling England in the name of her son, Edward III. When Edward overthrew and executed Mortimer in 1330 she was allowed to remain free.

ISABELLA (d. 1435), Queen, daughter of Stephen III of Bavaria and wife of the mad Charles VI of France. The court was dominated by her extravagance and her quarrel with Valentina Visconti, wife of the king's younger brother, the Duke of Orléans. Her irresponsible political manœuvring inflamed the struggle between the dukes of Burgundy and Orléans which turned into a disastrous French civil war.

ISABELLA (1451–1504), Queen of Castile (*reg.* 1474–1504), daughter of John II of Castile by his second wife, who married on 19 Oct. 1469 Ferdinand of Aragon. She became queen on the death of her brother, Henry IV (1474), and helped to forge the basis of the powerful nation state of Spain. She inherited a kingdom weakened by civil strife, which was to last another five years (1474–9), until the withdrawal from Castile of Alfonso V of Portugal and Henry IV's daughter, Joanna, whose claims he supported. By the Agreement of Segovia (1475) Isabella assumed the internal government of Castile, leaving her husband control of foreign policy. With political understanding and intelligent co-operation, together they built up a strong, centralized state, reinvigorating existing institutions to suppress disorder and disunity, eg, the Santa Hermandad (1476) and the Inquisition (1478). In 1476 Isabella acquired the mastership of the military order of Santiago with its enormous revenues and areas of jurisdiction and in 1480 the nobility was forced to surrender those crown lands seized since 1454.

Isabella revealed her gifts for organization during the successful crusade against the Moors in Granada (1481–92). A grateful papacy rewarded the Catholic monarchs by permitting the Crown to dominate the wealth, patronage, and reform of the Spanish Church. To deal with the Moorish problem, Isabella initiated the policy of forced conversion or expulsion (1502).

Though she supported the powerful sheep farmers of the *Mesta* at the expense of arable farming and industry, she understood the importance of overseas trade and patronized Christopher Columbus's first voyage of discovery (1492).

Isabella produced four daughters and a son, whose marriages were carefully planned for dynastic advantage to cement alliances with Portugal, England, and the Habsburgs. On her death her testament gave the Crown of Castile to her insane daughter, Joanna, wife of Philip, the Habsburg heir.

ISABELLA II (1830–1904), Queen of Spain (*reg.* 1833–68). Her effective reign (1843–68) ended in revolution hastened by her continued loyalty to the Moderates and refusal to appoint a ministry of Progressives.

ISABELLA CLARA EUGENIA, Infanta, Archduchess (1566–1633), daughter of Philip II of Spain and his third wife, Elizabeth of Valois. Her claims to the French throne were unsuccessfully pursued by her father (1590–2) before her marriage to her cousin, the Archduke Albert (1598), when she became joint sovereign ruler of the Netherlands with him. After the death of her husband without heirs (1621) this gracious, gifted, and popular princess continued to rule the Netherlands, although technically the provinces had reverted to the Spanish Crown. Isabella's authority was, however, increasingly superseded by the new rulers of Spain,

the young Philip IV and his favourite, Olivarez. Though starved of money, she struggled hard to retrieve the United Provinces and to direct the Spanish war effort in the Thirty Years War, but she was forced to pawn her jewellery and to raise exceptional levies from the people. She was eventually superseded by the Cardinal-Infant Ferdinand (1633).

ISAGORAS (*fl.* 6th cent.), Athenian archon in 508 BC, possibly related to the Philaids and after the expulsion of Hippias (510) an opponent of the Alcmeonid Cleisthenes. The Spartan King Cleomenes I supported him in two unsuccessful attempts (508, 506) to frustrate Cleisthenes' reforms.

ISCHIA (Pithecusae), island off Cumae, the site of the earliest post-Mycenaean Greek settlement in the West *c.* 750 BC, when traders from Eretria and Chalcis were attracted by metals available from the Etruscans.

ISHAQ II IBN ASKIA DAWUD (*reg.* 1588–91), ninth *askia* of Songhay, who came to power in the middle of a civil war. Though he was able to defeat *balama* Sadiq, the revolt greatly weakened the empire. At the close of 1589 the Moroccan sultan, Al-Mansur, claimed the right to tax salt from the Saharan mines of Taghaza, traditionally a Songhay prerogative. Ishaq's angry reply served as *casus belli* and in March 1591 a small Moroccan force armed with muskets defeated Ishaq's much larger army of bowmen and mounted lancers at Tondibi, north of Gao. Songhay never recovered and the Niger Bend fell to the rule of Moroccan pashas based at Timbuktu.

ISHPUINUS, Urartian King (*reg. c.* 828–785 BC), associated on the throne with his son Menuas, who greatly extended his kingdom by annexing the area south of Lake Urmiah and the Assyrian territories on the Upper Tigris and Upper Zab. He built fortifications, towns, and irrigation canals.

ISIDORE (*fl.* 15th cent.), Greek monk and metropolitan of Moscow. He was appointed by the patriarch of Constantinople in opposition to a Russian nominee, to attend the Council of Florence (1439), where the Orthodox agreed to union with the Latin Church in order to prevent Turkish supremacy in Constantinople. In spite of his promises to Basil II, Isidore subscribed on behalf of the Russian Orthodox to union with the Latin Church, substituting the pope's name for that of the orthodox patriarchs in the Liturgy. On his return to Moscow, Isidore was deposed and arrested, but later escaped. As from this period two patriarchates were established in Russia, one in Moscow, and one in Kiev (for Lithuania) with Roman Catholic allegiances. The resulting uniate church has survived to this day.

ISIN, Amorite kingdom of Sumeria which, for a time (*c.* 2000–1924 BC), dominated the region. It was conquered by Rim-Sin of Larsa (*c.* 1794).

ISKANDAR MUDA (*reg.* 1607–36), Sultan of Atjeh who pursued a policy of conquering or destroying the key commercial centres of the Malacca Straits—Deli (1612), Aru (1613), Johor (1613), Pahang (1618, 1630, 1635), Kedah, and Perak (1619–20). Eventually the defeat of his massive expedition against Portuguese Malacca in 1629 ended his successes. Iskandar centralized power internally, and kept European traders under tight control. In religion he favoured the syncretic monism of his Sufi adviser, Sheikh Shamsuddin of Pasai.

ISKANDAR SHAH (*reg. c.* 1403–24), founder and first Ruler of Malacca, Malay Peninsula. Historians generally agree that this is the name adopted by the Javanese prince Paramisora (or Parameshwara) after his conversion to Islam. After unsuccessful attempts at founding an independent centre at

Singapore and later at Muar, he chose Malacca as his base, from where he exercised some control of shipping in the Straits with the help of the 'Ceilates', who were probably fishermen and pirates. He maintained himself by playing Java (Majapahit) against Thailand (Ayuthaya). The Malay Chronicles, however, connect Iskandar Shah with Palembang, once the capital of the empire of Shriwijaya.

ISLAM, religion founded in western Arabia by the Prophet Muhammad (570–632). Muhammad's 'flight' (Hijra) from Mecca to Medina in AD 622 (the starting date of the Muslim calendar) marks the beginning of the political power of the Muslim community, which, at his death, extended over much of Arabia. Under his first four successors as leaders of the Muslim community (the so-called Rashidun caliphs) Muslim power was confirmed in Arabia (under Abu Bakr, 632–4), and carried by Arab armies into Syria, Iraq, Egypt, and Iran (particularly under Umar, 634–44). Internal dissension within the Muslim community led to the murder of the third caliph, Uthman (644–56), and continued strife during the rule of his successor, Ali (656–61). After the death of Ali power passed to the Umayyad family, whose capital was at Damascus, and under whose rule Muslim forces drove through North Africa and Spain and into Central Asia. Umayyad rule was brought to an end by family, tribal, and personal rivalries, and the discontent of the new converts to Islam (Mawalis) over the preference given to Arabs. It was replaced by the Abbasid dynasty in 750, whose capital was at Baghdad. The political unity of the Muslim community was, however, lost. Spain remained under Umayyad rule and other areas soon passed under the authority of new dynasties. The Arabs (though not Arabic) lost their pre-eminence in Islam and Iranian and Turkish peoples came to dominate political life. Islam had already become the religion of the majority of the peoples of the Middle East through voluntary, not forced, conversion. After the Byzantine defeat at Manzikert (1071) Asia Minor also became Islamized. Islam also spread widely outside the area of the Middle East. In India pockets of Islam were established in Sind by conquest and in western India by the activities of traders from the 8th cent., but the main impetus to the spread of Islam in northern India was provided by the conquests of Muslim rulers from Afghanistan and Central Asia from the 11th cent. These rulers established the Delhi sultanate (13th–16th cents) and the Mughal empire (16th–19th cents). Aided by Muslim political dominion, Islam spread into western India (Gujarat) and eastern India (Bengal) and through the Bahmanid dynasty established a foothold in the northern Deccan, which was subsequently enlarged in southern India by the Mughul, Aurangzeb (1658–1707). The main agents of conversion in India, however, were not the Muslim warriors, but the Sufi (mystic) traders and missionaries who won over many low-caste Hindus. Muslim traders and missionaries were also the agents of Muslim penetration of South-East Asia, where, although Muslim settlements existed from the 8th cent., substantial conversion began in the 13th cent. and grew rapidly in the 15th cent. after the conversion to Islam of the ruler of the great commercial centre of Malacca. Through Malacca Islam spread into Malaya, Sumatra, and Java and into other areas of South-East Asia, including the Philippines. Although some Muslim settlements were established in south China at an early date, the principal focus of Islam in China was in the north-west, where it was adopted by Turkish and other minorities and won some Chinese converts, particularly in and after the Mongol period (13th–14th cents). In Africa Islam spread among the pagan Berbers of the north and through the agency of traders and such political movements as that of the Almoravids into the western Sudan. In the 13th cent. the adoption of Islam by the ruler of the Mali empire set an example which was repeated by later dynasties on the upper Niger. But as a mass religion Islam in West Africa owed most to the work of the Sufi missionary orders, *eg*, the Tijanniya, Qadiriyya, and Ahmadiyya, which operated with great success under the

British and French colonial administrations. In East Africa Islam spread much more slowly, possibly owing to its association with the slave trade. It is generally supposed that a major reason for the attraction of Islam in black Africa has been the Muslim emphasis on racial equality, a feature reflected in its recent growth among the Negro population of the US (the Black Muslims). Islam had least success in Europe. Although widespread in Spain, it was extirpated after the Christian reconquest, while in south-east Europe it remained as a substantial element only in Bosnia and Albania after the collapse of Ottoman rule. In the Crimea and the Ukraine Islam was largely replaced by Christianity in the 18th and 19th cents. It is estimated that about one-seventh of the world's population (over 500 million) are Muslims, the largest numbers being in Pakistan, Indonesia, India, the Middle East (including the Muslim areas of the USSR and the CPR), and in North and West Africa. About 85 per cent of Muslims are nominally Sunnis, following one of the four main legal schools (Hanafi, Maliki, Shafi'i, and Hanbali), although, through the activities of the Sufi *tariqa*s, many non-Muslim practices have been incorporated into popular belief. Nearly all the remainder are Shi'is. Shi'ism originated in a political dispute about the succession to the caliphate, but through concentration on the semi-divine status of the Caliph Ali and his descendants, acquired a distinct messianic character. The largest Shi'ite sect is that of the so-called 'Twelvers' of Iran and Iraq. The 'Seveners', or Isma'ilis, who produced the Fatimid dynasty of Egypt and the sect of the Assassins, include the followers of the Aga Khan. Throughout history Islam, particularly in the Middle East, has been much more an institutionalized way of life than a mere matter of personal belief. The most significant change in the 19th and 20th cents has been the erosion of its position in law and education and its progressive limitation to the area of personal belief, despite the opposition of powerful Muslim political movements, such as the Muslim Brotherhood.

H. A. R. Gibb, *Mohammedanism* (Oxford, 1968)   MEY

ISLAMABAD, capital city of Pakistan, situated to the north of Rawalpindi. It was begun in 1960 after a commission set up by President Ayub Khan to examine its possibilities had reported favourably, and was scheduled for completion in 1975. The design was prepared by the Doxiadas group.

ISLAND TERRITORIES OF NEW ZEALAND. During the later 19th cent. some NZ politicians, notably Grey, Vogel, Stout, and Seddon, developed plans for NZ expansion in the Pacific islands, which met with British, Australian, and foreign opposition. The island groups which eventually came under NZ control formed only a small fraction of those it was hoped to acquire. They were acquired in haphazard fashion, and, far from forming a commercial empire, they required substantial subsidies from NZ. The only 19th-cent. acquisition was the Kermadecs (1886), the nearest island group to NZ and without native inhabitants. The most important of NZ's island territories, the Cook Islands, were proclaimed (with the island of Niue) part of NZ in 1901, and granted self-government in free association with NZ in 1965. The Tokelau group, formerly part of the British Gilbert and Ellice Islands, was transferred to NZ control in 1925, and became New Zealand territory in 1949.

ISLE OF MAN PURCHASE ACT (1765), in Britain, ended the Duke of Atholl's lordship for £70,000 and so enabled George Grenville's ministry to curb extensive smuggling between Man and the mainland of Britain.

ISLE OF ORLEANS, approximately 2800 sq. miles (7168 sq. kms) of land on the east bank of the Mississippi river which includes the city of New Orleans. It was first owned by France, then passed to Spain (1763), and then again to France (1803). As the isle controlled the mouth of the Mississippi river it impeded American trade until it became US territory (1803).

ISLEIF GIZURSSON, bishop (d. 1080), member of an Icelandic chieftain family, who was educated in Germany and ordained as a priest. Returning to Iceland (c. 1030) as both chieftain and Christian priest, he was the first scholar to combine native traditional culture and European learning. He founded Iceland's first school on his family estate at Shalaholt. He was the first native bishop of Iceland (1056–80) and he profoundly influenced the development of medieval Icelandic civilization.

ISLES, LORDS OF THE, title held by the MacDonalds of Islay in the west of Scotland in the late 14th and 15th cents. They gave some degree of cohesion to the clans of Argyll and the Hebrides but, of uncertain loyalty to the Crown, they were finally destroyed by James IV in the 1490s and superseded by the Campbells under the chief of the Campbells, appointed lord of Argyll in 1457.

ISLINGTON COMMISSION, Royal Commission on the Public Services in India (1912–14), called after its chairman, Lord Islington. The commission, which included three Indian members, the most notable of whom was G. K. Gokhale, and nine British members, was appointed in Sept. 1912 and visited India in the following two winters to collect evidence. Its tasks were to enquire into the recruitment, training, pay, and conditions of the services, and to consider the question of Indian entry into the Indian civil service. In its report (Aug. 1915) the commission called for increased Indian entry to the ICS, both by additional direct recruitment and by promotion from the provincial services. It recommended that examinations for entry should be held simultaneously in both London and India.

The report remained largely a dead-letter because of the First World War. It was not published until 1917 and the announcement of further constitutional changes (Aug. 1917) altered the position from which the commission had reported. The Lee Commission (1923) was therefore set up to look at the superior civil services in India, with terms of reference almost identical to Islington's 12 years before.

ISMA'IL I (d. 1524), head of the Shi'i religious order known as the Safawiyya and the founder of the Safawid regime, which endured in Persia until 1722. With the aid of his adherents, recruited in no small degree from amongst the Turcoman tribes of Asia Minor, he was able, in 1499–1503, to overcome the Aq Qoyunlu princes, who had dominated hitherto much of Persia, Azerbaijan, and the Caucasus region, defeating them in the battles of Shurur (1501) and Hamadan (1503). Shah Isma'il extended his control thereafter into Kurdistan (1507–8) and also drove the Uzbeg Turks out of Khurasan in north-eastern Persia (1510). At the battle of Chaldiran in 1514 the Ottoman Sultan, Selim I, routed the forces of Shah Isma'il and thus set a limit to the westward advance of Safawid influence in Asia Minor.

ISMA'IL BEY GASPRINSKII (1851–1914), Russian Muslim reformer and writer, and member of a Crimean Tatar family. Besides editing *Terjüman* from 1883, he contributed largely to educational reform, developed a common Turkish language as a means of unifying Turkish Muslims, and was the first advocate of Pan-Turkism.

ISMA'IL PASHA (1830–95), second son of Ibrahim Pasha and ruler of Egypt (*reg.* 1863–79) as Pasha (1863) and Khedive (1867). His reign was a period of large public investment and expansion of cotton cultivation and trade, but his financial borrowings led to bankruptcy (1875), the imposition of European financial control, and encroachments on his political authority. When Isma'il attempted to resist this process (1879) he was deposed by the Ottoman government, following Anglo-French representations.

ISMA'ILISM. A decisive split occurred amongst the adherents of the Shi'a movement during the time of the sixth Alid Imam, Ja'far al-Sadiq (d. 765). The more moderate elements recognized Musa (d. 799) as the lawful Imam in succession to his father, Ja'far. The line of imams running through Musa would number 12 in all—whence the designation of Ithna 'Ashariyya (Twelver Shi'a) later applied to their adherents. The more extreme elements gave their allegiance, however, to Isma'il (d. 760), the oldest son of Ja'far al-Sadiq. Around Isma'il and his descendants there developed religious doctrines compounded of Muslim beliefs and of ideas drawn from earlier religions and from neo-Platonic thought. The Isma'ili imams were regarded as divine and infallible. The Koran was held to contain two meanings—one external, and one hidden—which the imams alone could interpret to the faithful. Working as a secret, subversive organization against the established order, the Isma'ilis sought through their missionaries to canalize to their own advantage all the discontents—social, economic and political—so strong within the Muslim world of the 9th–10th cents. Out of their activities arose the Fatimid caliphate in North Africa (909–69) and later in Egypt (969–1171). A further division of allegiance occurring within the Fatimid movement in 1094 led to the emergence of the Nizari Isma'ilis, best known through the activities of the Assassins working from such centres as Alamut and Masyaf during the 12th–13th cents. The Isma'ili beliefs took root also in India, and still survived in 1970.

ISMAY, HASTINGS LIONEL ISMAY, Baron (1887–1965), British soldier. After service in India and Somaliland he was assistant secretary to the committee of imperial defence (1925–30). He became deputy secretary (1936) and secretary (1938). With the reorganization of the defence secretariat following the outbreak of the Second World War he became head of the military section of the war cabinet secretariat, and in 1940 was appointed chief of staff to Winston Churchill, who was minister of defence. In this role Ismay sat on the chiefs of staff committee, whose secretary he was, and played a crucial part as intermediary and frequently mediator between the prime minister and the chiefs of staff, as well as supervising the complex system of cabinet and defence committees set up to meet the demands of the war. He remained as chief of staff to Attlee after the 1945 general election, retiring from the army at the end of 1946. In 1947 he went to India as chief of staff to Mountbatten, then viceroy, and played an important role in the events surrounding the granting of Indian independence and the partitioning of India and Pakistan. He was (1951–2) secretary of state for commonwealth relations in Churchill's administration, and in 1952 became the first secretary general of the North Atlantic Treaty Organization, a post from which he retired in 1957.

ISOCRATES (436–338 BC), Athenian orator and stylist, who established schools in Chios and Athens, in which he taught rhetoric and the importance of historical perspective to political aspirants, displaying in his own writings an elaborate and complex style which permanently influenced Greek and Roman rhetoric. Eschewing active politics himself, he exercised influence through pamphlets and the support of public figures, *eg,* Timotheus. He was critical of Spartan imperialism and saw Athens as the natural leader of a united Greece against Persia, *eg,* in his *Panegyricus* (380), but becoming disillusioned with Athenian politics he eventually placed his hopes for unity in the leadership of Philip II of Macedon, *eg,* in his *Philippus* (346), and lived to see Philip's victory at Chaeronea (338).

ISOPOLITEIA, ancient Greek term for a mutual grant of potential citizenship to each other's citizens by two states, as opposed to *sympoliteia,* the sharing by two or more states of a common federal citizenship.

ISRAEL, CREATION OF (1948). After the failure in Feb. 1947 of negotiations between Jews and Arabs, Britain referred the

Palestine question to the United Nations. A special session of the General Assembly (9 May 1947) appointed a committee (UNSCOP), which recommended (1 Sept.) partition. An ad hoc special committee accepted this and a resolution to give effect to partition passed the General Assembly (29 Nov.) by 33 votes to 13 with 10 abstentions. On 11 Dec. Britain announced the termination of the mandate on 15 May 1948. British forces were progressively withdrawn, leaving Jews and Arabs to fight for possession of Palestine. The state of Israel was proclaimed (14 May 1948) and admitted to the UN in May 1949.

ISSUS, BATTLE OF (Nov. 333 BC), in north-west Syria, Alexander the Great's first victory over the Persian imperial army, which had moved down to the coast behind him. After careful dispositions and clever manœuvres, Alexander's cavalry won the battle, putting Darius III to flight. The victory opened Syria, Palestine, and Egypt to Alexander.

ISTIQLAL (Independence) **PARTY** in Morocco, emerged in Jan. 1944 from the reformist Kutlat al-Amal al-Watani (National Action Bloc) and at once published a manifesto calling for an end to the French Protectorate over the country. Its outstanding intellectual personalities in the years that followed were the traditionalist thinker Allal al-Fassi and the radical Mehdi Ben Barka. Morocco's first independent government in 1956 was headed by Ahmad Balafrey.

ISTRI, Illyrian tribe dwelling in antiquity in the promontory at the head of the Adriatic (mod. Istria). After Aquileia was colonized by Rome (181 BC), the Istrians were subdued by Manlius Vulso and Claudius Pulcher in 178–177.

ITAGAKI, TAISUKE (1836–1919), Japanese politician and leader of the people's rights movement in early Meiji Japan. After playing an important part in overthrowing the Tokugawa, he served in the Meiji government, but opposed its treatment of the samurai class and its domination by Satsuma and Chōshū, and resigned when the invasion of Korea was called off (1873). Returning to Tosa, he founded Japan's first political party, the Aikokukōtō. In 1881 Itagaki became president of the Jiyūtō, and his oratory helped to make it the first genuinely nation-wide party. In 1898 he became home minister under Itō, but after the failure of his collaboration with Okuma in a short-lived coalition (June–Nov. 1898), he turned from politics to public welfare work.

ITALIAN COMMUNES. In antiquity Italian towns were the centres of regional government and places where the notables of each region preferred to live. This preference persisted in Italy throughout the Middle Ages. The revival of economic prosperity in Italy from the 11th cent. onwards stimulated rapid growth of numerous existing towns and the appearance of some new ones. Where strong territorial states developed in the 12th cent., in the south of Italy, controlled by the Norman kings of Sicily, towns were not allowed to have their own autonomous governments. But in much of central and northern Italy the more important towns achieved in the course of the 12th cent. a considerable measure of independent power. By force or purchase, these municipalities acquired the sovereign powers previously vested in their bishops or other lords. These communes successfully subdued many of the neighbouring nobles, compelled them to live permanently within the town walls, and began to build up territorial states comprising considerable stretches of the surrounding countryside. A powerful ruling class developed in many of the communes, representing a mixture of former landed nobles and of men enriched by trade. The Emperor Frederick Barbarossa was defeated in 1176 by the league of the Lombard cities and his grandson, the Emperor Frederick II, tried in vain between 1236 and 1250 to destroy this Lombard League. Thereafter, northern and central Italy was divided between city-states owing only nominal allegiance to popes or other territorial rulers. One of the chief features of

the history of these communes from the 12th cent. onwards was the frequent fighting between neighbouring towns. This inter-urban rivalry was one of the main reasons for the emergence in many towns of despotic governments headed by military adventurers or members of the leading town families. Such despotic governments became very common in the course of the 14th and 15th cents. As the more powerful city-states gradually absorbed most of their neighbours, the number of autonomous territories was greatly reduced, so that by the 15th cent. Italy was divided between a relatively small number of urban states—Milan, Genoa, Venice, Florence, Siena, and Bologna being the most important.

MH

ITALIAN WARS, series of intermittent military campaigns in seven phases, spread over 65 years and fought on Italian soil between the French Valois kings and the Habsburgs, aided by their various Italian allies and Swiss mercenaries. Italy was the scene of this conflict because of its economic and cultural wealth and the relative equality but defencelessness of the five dominant states: Milan, Venice, Florence, Naples, and the papacy. The wars began with Charles VIII's invasion of Naples (1494) and ended with the treaty of Cateau-Cambrésis (1559).

The political equilibrium which Italy had enjoyed from the peace of Lodi (1454) was upset by the deaths of Lorenzo de Medici of Florence (1492) and Ferrante of Aragon, ruler of Naples (1494). Charles VIII's Angevin claim to the Neapolitan throne was supported by Ludovico Sforza, while Florence backed the Aragonese Alfonso of Naples. Charles's remarkable march through Florence, Rome, and Naples ultimately ended in failure after the inconclusive battle of Fornovo and provoked an alliance between the empire and Spain, who were later joined by the Venetian republic, Milan, and the papacy (League of Venice, 1495) and cemented by the marriage of the Archduke Philip to Joanna, heiress to Aragon and Castile.

Charles VIII's successor, Louis XII, was obsessed with dreams of conquest in Italy and claimed the duchy of Milan through his grandmother, Valentina Visconti. His forces occupied Milan (1499), and defeated and captured Ludovico Sforza at Novara (1500). They then invaded Naples, Louis dividing the conquered kingdom with Ferdinand of Aragon until the French were driven out by the Spaniards (1504). French power was, however, entrenched in Milan. After suppressing the Genoese rebellion (1507), Louis came to terms with the Emperor Maximilian, pledging the partition of Venetian territories through the League of Cambrai (1508). Coveting the former papal cities in Romagna, Julius II joined the league and on 10 May 1509 Louis XII's army crossed the Adda and inflicted an overwhelming defeat upon the Venetians at Agnadello. Having regained the Romagna cities however, Julius changed sides (1510) and worked to build up the anti-French Holy League (1511). In the battle of Ravenna (1512) the evenly matched armies of France and the league faced each other, but victory, which went to the French was marred by the death of their leader, Gaston de Foix. A further blow was their defeat by Swiss mercenaries at Novara (1513), after which the French withdrew from Milan, leaving the duchy to Massimiliano Sforza and Florence to the Medici.

A third French expedition entered Italy in Aug. 1515 under Francis I. Facing the opposition of the Holy League, Francis crushed the Swiss infantry, who formed the spearhead of the Milanese defences, at the battle of Marignano. With the Eternal Peace of Fribourg (1516) he ended their effective role in the wars, at the same time acquiring the duchies of Milan, Parma, and Piacenza. However, France's success was short-lived. The rivalry between the two youthful rulers, Francis I, and Charles of Spain and Burgundy, focused itself on the imperial election (1519), and Charles's success initiated a period of conflict centred on Italy. Charles, allied with Pope Leo X, seized Milan (1521), reinstated the Sforzas, and retook Parma and Piacenza. Despite Swiss assistance, the French, under Lautrec, were defeated at Biococca (1522), and lost Genoa. These imperial successes, followed by the invasion of southern France, prompted a secret alliance between France, Venice, Florence, and the papacy (1524). A French army again entered Milan (1524), but it attacked the imperial forces near Pavia and suffered a humiliating defeat (24 Feb., 1525). Francis was captured and taken to Madrid and renounced all his Italian claims. Habsburg pre-eminence prompted the formation of the Holy League of Cognac (1526), by which Rome, Venice, Florence, and Milan supported the French cause. In May 1527 the imperial army sacked Rome, causing Clement VII to flee and ensuring imperial domination of the papacy for some time. Another French invasion of Milan and Naples was undermined by the defection of Andrea Doria of Genoa to the Spanish-Imperial cause (1528), and the defeat at Landriano (1529). By the treaty of Cambrai (1529) Francis once more renounced his Italian claims.

After a period of relative tranquillity, the death without heirs in 1535 of Francesco Sforza of Milan provoked a short conflict (1536–8). Francis I revived his claims to the duchy and appealed for help to the advancing Turks, while Charles V, as suzerain ruler of Milan, resisted the French advance into Savoy and Piedmont by invading Provence. Pope Paul III's intervention produced the truce of Nice (June 1538), which gave Savoy and two-thirds of Piedmont to France, a valuable gateway into Italy. The investiture of Milan upon Charles's son, Philip, and the assassination near Pavia of two French agents returning from Constantinople (1541) provoked the last war between Francis and Charles (1542–4). Despite French victories at Nice (1542) and Ceresole (1544), Francis was deserted by his allies and sued for peace at Crespy (1544), renouncing his claim to Naples. He died in 1547, but though his successor, Henry II, renewed the dynastic rivalry, his main interest lay in northern Europe. Pope Paul IV persuaded Henry to break the truce of Vaucelles (1556) and to undertake another Italian campaign (1557). French forces under Guise crossed the papal states and attacked Naples, while Philip II of Spain negotiated a Florentine alliance. The recall of Guise to the Netherlands ended this brief epilogue to the Italian wars. In 1559 the treaty of Cateau-Cambrésis ended French claims to Italy and confirmed Spanish domination.

M. L. Bush, *Renaissance, Reformation and the Outer World* (London, 1967).   MKS

ITALIANS IN SOMALIA (1885–1960). Italy's interest in the Somali area became important in 1885 when an Italian official, Cecchi, was sent to Zanzibar to determine the sovereignty of the Juba valley, and a commercial treaty was concluded with the Zanzibari Sultan. A local Italian trader, Filonardi, subsequently signed treaties of protection with the sultanates of Obbia and Mijertain in 1889, an Italian protectorate over the eastern Somali coast being proclaimed later in the year. An Anglo-Italian protocol defining the frontiers between the British and Italian spheres followed in 1891. The Italian protectorate was given the name of Benadir, and entrusted in 1893 to Filonardi, who ran it on behalf of a chartered company, the Royal Italian East Africa Co., in return for a subsidy of 350,000 lire. The Italians advanced inland up the Juba river towards the major trading centre of Lugh, which fell to Italy in 1895. Filonardi's company proving both inefficient and excessively paternalistic, the protectorate was transferred, in 1896, to another private company, the *Società Anonima Commerciale Italiana del Benadir*. Subsequent scandals concerning slavery and slave trading led to the Italian government's taking over direct control in 1905. A series of military expeditions (1908–14) extended Italian rule, from a 30-km-wide strip along the coast to some 160–200 kms inland, and a system of indirect rule was established.

Italian Somaliland was one of the two bases for Mussolini's invasion of Ethiopia in 1935, and, after Italy's entry into the Second World War, was occupied by South African forces in 1941. In 1947 Italy accepted the forfeiture of this and other colonies as part of the peace settlement, but in 1950 the United Nations granted her a ten-year trusteeship over the territory, which became an independent republic in 1960.

R. L. Hess, *Italian Colonialism in Somalia* (Chicago and London, 1966).   RP

ITALY, PEACE TREATY (1947), peace treaty signed with Italy at the end of the Second World War (Italy being in the anomalous position of having fought as an ally of Germany, then—from 1943—against Germany).

The treaty made minor frontier adjustments with France; ceded to Yugoslavia the Zara enclave and the Italian islands off the Dalmatian coast; ceded the Dodecanese islands (including, among others, Rhodes, Patmos, and Cos) to Greece; and established the free territory of Trieste, an arrangement which it proved impossible to carry out in practice. Italy gave up all rights to Libya, Eritrea, and Italian Somaliland. It recognized the independence of Albania and gave up its special rights in that country. It was to pay reparations to the Soviet Union ($100 million), Greece ($125 million), Ethiopia ($25 million), Yugoslavia ($125 million), and Albania ($5 million). Part IV of the treaty limited armaments and an annex specified the warships which Italy could retain, making provision for the transfer of others to the United Nations (the subject of subsequent revision and dispute between the USSR and the western powers). An Italo–Austrian agreement provided for the protection of the language and other rights of Germans in the South Tyrol.

ITAMARACA, BATTLE OF (Jan. 1640), defeat of a combined Spanish-Portuguese armada off the coast of Brazil by a Dutch fleet. The battle insured Dutch supremacy in the West Indies for many years and contributed to the decline of the Spanish American empire.

ITATA AFFAIR (1891). Chilean opponents of President Balmaceda, who bought military equipment in the US, and had it loaded on to the vessel *Itata*. The ship was stopped and escorted back to the US by the USS *Charleston*, causing bitterness among the revolutionaries.

ITHNA ASHARIYYA (the 'Twelvers'), name given to those Shi'is who recognize a series of 12 Imams extending from the first of the line, Ali al-Murtada, through Ja'far al-Sadiq and Musa al-Kazim, to Muhammad al-Mahdi, the last Imam, who disappeared under obscure circumstances c. 873–4.

ITŌ, HIROBUMI (1841–1909), Japanese statesman. Itō played a more important part than any other individual in the shaping of modern Japan. Born of low samurai rank in Chōshū, he was a pupil of the nationalist Yoshida Shōin and in 1861 took part in an attack on the British Legation. In 1863 he travelled illicitly to England with Inoue Kaoru, returning the following year convinced of the futility of trying to expel foreigners. His services during the Meiji Restoration were rewarded with office and he soon became, with Okuma Shigenobu, one of Okubo Toshimichi's protégés. The rivalry for leadership which developed after Okubo's assassination (1878) ended in victory for Itō in 1881. Thereafter he stamped his mark on political life by supervising the drafting of the Meiji constitution and by serving as prime minister four times. It was during his second ministry that Japan secured treaty revision and defeated China. During the 1890s Itō became convinced of the need for governments to collaborate with political parties, and, notwithstanding the opposition of most of his fellow *genrōs*, he negotiated with the Kenseitō for the formation of a new party, the Seiyūkai, with himself as president (1900). This experiment was not entirely satisfactory and in 1902 he allowed Yamagata to manœuvre him out of party politics. During his remaining years Itō devoted himself mainly to foreign policy, assisting in reconciliation with

Russia and moderating army demands for a complete military take-over in south Manchuria. In 1909 he was assassinated by a Korean nationalist after endeavouring, as resident-general, to maintain a Japanese protectorate rather than annexe the country. He did much to raise Japan from a backward and vulnerable state to a major power, but was always aware of the need for caution and compromise in international relations. He was raised to the rank of prince in 1907.   RLS

ITUZAINGÓ, BATTLE OF (1827). In this Argentine armies defeated larger invading forces of Brazilians in the Argentine province of Corrientes.

ITZCÓATL (*fl.* 15th cent.), Aztec Ruler who spread Aztec power throughout the central valley of Mexico.

IVAN I (*reg.* 1328–41), Grand Prince of Moscow, nicknamed 'Kalita' ('money bags'), one of Russia's most able and successful negotiators with the Tatar invaders of the Golden Horde. He was the first Prince of Moscow to whom the Tatars entrusted the collection of tribute from the Russian lands. Ivan Kalita's rule marks a significant turning point in Russia's history, in so far as the central seat of power and administration became established in Moscow. Its significance was consolidated under Ivan by the visible investiture upon it of political power arising from the prince's newly acquired role of collector of Tatar tribute, and of power 'eternal' symbolized by the establishment of a new seat for the metropolitan of the Church, transferred under Ivan in 1326 from Vladimir to Moscow. At a later stage the Moscow prince was to evolve into tsar of all Russia.

IVAN III (1462–1505), Grand Prince of Moscow (*reg.* 1462–1505), whose reign marks a strategic epoch in the development of Russian autocracy, during which the essentially regional powers of the grand prince of Moscow gave way to the power of the 'tsar and autocrat by the Grace of God of all Russia' (as eventually formulated by Ivan's son, Vasily III). Control of Russia from the princely throne of Moscow was achieved by Ivan III first by expansionist aggression against other Russian princedoms, then against Russia's foreign neighbours, the most important being Russia's former invaders, the Tatars. Ivan fortified his position internally by improving the machinery of government through establishing the *boyarskaya duma* (boyars' council), an administrative organization which eventually paralysed the tsar's vassals in the grip of the autocrat. Ivan trebled the extent of his lands by acquiring the provinces of Riazan, Yaroslavl, Tver, Rostov, Novgorod, and Pskov. In the west, on the Polish–Lithuanian frontiers, lost Russian lands were recovered under a truce in 1503. Ivan's second marriage in 1472 to Zoe Paleologus, the orphan niece of the last Byzantine emperor, was approved by the pope as an attempt to revive the Church Union of the Council of Florence. Its main effect, however, was to raise the prestige of the growing Muscovite autocracy. To political supremacy and military conquest was added the ceremonial mystique of Byzantium.   AK

IVAN IV (1530–84), Tsar of Moscow (*reg.* 1533–84), known as *Ivan Grozny* ('the Terrible'), son of Vasili III and Helen Glinsky, succeeded as tsar at the age of three, and ruled for over 50 years, establishing a reputation for ruthlessness and cruelty.

After his mother's death (1538) Ivan's childhood was unhappy and insecure. At the age of 16 he declared his intention of being crowned tsar and marrying Anastasia Romanovna, a member of a leading *boyar* dynasty (1547). In choosing his own advisers he picked able men, mostly from the middle ranks of society—the Metropolitan Makary, Sylvester, the court chaplain, and Adashev, the chamberlain. In 1550 he summoned the *Zemsky Sobor* in order to initiate widespread reforms, *eg*, the remodelling of Ivan III's code of law, and alterations in the system of local administration.

In 1552 Ivan led an expedition against the Khanate of Kazan, besieging the capital and forcing it to surrender (1552). Its capture was a symbol of Muscovy's destruction of Tatar domination and the beginning of her eastward advance beyond the Urals into Siberia, which was perhaps the most lasting achievement of Ivan's reign. A request from the pro-Muscovite faction in the Khanate of Astrakhan that Ivan should nominate a prince to rule that Tatar state (1553) led to the annexation of the province in 1556, making Muscovite control of the Volga basin complete.

During Ivan's reign significant contacts were also made with the west. The advent of the merchant-explorers, Chancellor and Jenkinson, initiated trade with England and gave encouragement to foreign experts to settle in Russia. The founding of Archangel (1584) on the White Sea gave Muscovy an outlet for maritime trade. Ivan also sought a Baltic outlet and marched into Livonia, whose ruling military order was in decline (1558). It was this action, in defiance of the advice of Sylvester, Adashev, and the *boyar* Kurbsky, that caused the latter to desert Ivan for the court of his enemy, the Grand Duke of Lithuania.

Despite early successes in the Livonian venture (1558–63), Ivan's sense of personal isolation grew, and in 1564 he decided to leave Moscow and stage a confrontation with the *boyar*s from the monastery of Alexandrovskoe. The metropolitan of Moscow urged Ivan's return, to which the tsar agreed, on condition that he should be allowed absolute authority (1565). From then onwards Ivan created a police state, the *oprichnina*, centred on territories confiscated arbitrarily from the *boyar*s, with its own court, offices, army, and police, and initiated a period of gross personal licentiousness and cruelty, alternating with spells of abject repentance. After Anastasia's death (1560) Ivan remarried six times. The Metropolitan Philip was deposed, exiled, and then strangled on Ivan's orders (1568). He killed his cousin, Prince Vladimir (1569), and fatally struck his son and heir, Ivan (1584). The power of the *boyar*s was curbed by the replacement of hereditary ownership of land (*votchina*) by personal and conditional ownership (*pomestie*), based on service to the state. He ordered the savage destruction of Novgorod by the *oprichniki* (1570).

In these years (1565–84) Ivan's external enemies increased in strength. The Crimean Tatars began to harass Astrakhan, and then Moscow (1571). The union of Lublin (1569) threatened the position of Orthodox Russians in Lithuania and brought Poland into the Livonian war. Ivan's attempt to secure Esthonia caused war with Sweden (1575), but the Muscovites were defeated at Wenden (1578) and lost Polotsk (1579), Ostrov (1581), Narva (1581), and the old Russian towns on the Gulf of Finland. A ten-year truce was concluded with Poland (1582), by which Ivan surrendered Livonia, and a three-year truce with Sweden (1583), marking the ultimate failure of his attempt to establish a hold on the Baltic.

I. Grey, *Ivan the Terrible* (London, 1964).   MKS

IVAN V (1666–96), Tsar of Moscow (*reg.* 1682–96), second son of the Tsar Alexis Romanov and his first wife, Maria Miloslavsky, succeeded his elder brother Fedor III jointly with his half-brother Peter, through a *coup d'état* engineered by his elder sister, the regent Sophia, and the *streltsy* corps (1682). A sickly and incompetent youth, he married Praskovia Saltykov, by whom he had three daughters, including Catherine, later Duchess of Mecklenburg, and Anna, later Empress of Russia (1730–40). While Ivan was certainly a tsar, the effective rulers of Russia during his reign were Sophia and, later, Peter.

IVAN VI (1740–64) Tsar of Russia (*reg.* 1740–42), son of Anton Ulrich of Brunswick-Lüneburg and Anne, niece of the Empress Anna (1730–40), was declared the latter's successor in her will (Oct. 1740), but was arrested in a *coup d'état* arranged by the guards regiments in favour of Peter I's daughter, Elizabeth (5 Jan. 1742), and imprisoned in the fortress of Schlüsselburg, where he was assassinated by his jailers.

IVERNOIS, SIR FRANÇOIS D' (1757–1842), Swiss political economist, who published many historical and statistical works (1783–1836). Although a liberal, he opposed the French Revolution, fearing its effects on Geneva's integrity. He was condemned to death, escaped to England, and published pamphlets criticizing the continental system and the French government. He became a British citizen and in 1794 was knighted by King George III, who entrusted him with various diplomatic missions. He also represented Geneva at the Congress of Vienna.

IVES, CHARLES EDWARD (1874–1954), US composer, who wove together band and folk music with sounds from the objective world in conflicting rhythms and dissonant patterns, making him one of the innovators of 20th-cent.-music. Among his major works are the Second Piano Sonata: *Concord, Massachusetts 1840–60* (1915–19) and Symphony No. 3 (1901–4).

IVORY COAST (322,500 sq. kms), independent republic in West Africa, until 1960 a province of French West Africa. Government is by a council of ministers and a National Assembly elected by adult suffrage, as is the president. The Baoule and Senufo form important elements in the population (1970) of 3,830,000.

IVRY, BATTLE OF (14 March 1590). King Henry IV of France defeated the forces of the Catholic League under the Guise leader, Charles, Duke of Mayenne, but he was unable to follow up his success by capturing Paris.

IWAJUKU FINDS, archaeological discoveries in Gumma prefecture (1947) which first rendered beyond doubt the existence of a pre-pottery culture in Japan. They have stimulated a considerable amount of investigation, the results of which have established the date of Japan's earliest habitation as being at least 150,000 BC.

IWAKURA MISSION (1871–3), Japanese embassy which visited America and Europe. It was of major importance in the Meiji government's understanding of the problems facing Japan in her transformation into a modern state. The mission was a very large one, comprising in all 106 members of the government including Okubo Toshimichi, Kido Kōin, and Itō Hirobumi. Its leader was Iwakura Tomomi, a court noble, who had played a vital role in associating the emperor with Satsuma and Chōshū and who exercised great influence until his death in 1883. Although his background was extremely conservative, Iwakura was as impressed as the other members of the mission by what they saw, particularly in industrial areas. They realized that they could not hope for immediate revision of the unequal treaties (notably the Ansei treaties) and that they must make economic development and domestic reform their first priorities. When the envoys returned home, therefore, they successfully fought the other leaders' plan for an invasion of Korea. The ensuing resignations of Saigō Takamori, Itagaki Taisuke, Eto Shimpei, Soejima Taneomi, and others meant that one important result of the mission was the strengthening of the influence of Okubo and Iwakura in the Meiji government.

IWO JIMA, BATTLE OF (19 Feb.–17 March 1945), battle in Second World War for the tiny island of Iwo Jima in the western Pacific. US marines wiped out a Japanese force of about 23,000 men, sustaining among themselves almost 20,000 casualties, including over 4000 killed.

IZVOLSKY, ALEXANDER PETROVICH (1856–1919), Russian diplomat and foreign minister (1906–10), who shifted the focus of Russian policy back to Europe and restored relations with Japan by agreements (1907, 1910) which delimited their respective spheres of influence in Asia. He negotiated a convention with England regarding Tibet, Persia, and Afghanistan (1907) which removed friction on the north-west frontier of India and opened the way to European co-operation, but which he declared was not meant to be anti-German in spirit.

Izvolsky hoped to use the Austrian annexation of Bosnia-Herzegovina (1908) to summon a European conference and open the Straits to Russian warships, but his plans failed. As ambassador in Paris (1910–16) he followed an anti-German policy, worked for the consolidation of the Triple Entente, and negotiated the Constantinople agreements (1915).

J

JA JA (or Jo Jo Ubani) (1821–91), Head of the Opubu (Anna Pepple) House at Bonny (1861–9). After civil war (1869) in Bonny, Ja Ja and his supporters founded a new settlement at Opobo, where he guarded his commercial interests against African and European intruders. In 1887 he was deported by the British government to St Vincent in the West Indies for opposing free trade in his domain.

JAABAEK, SOREN PEDERSEN (1814–94), Norwegian journalist and politician who championed the cause of the peasantry and, in the economic crises of the 1870s, encouraged emigration of Norwegians to the US through giving information about America in his papers.

JABARTI, AL-, ABD AL-RAHMAN IBN HASAN (1755–1825), author of a valuable Arabic chronicle, *Aja'ib al-Athar*, which deals with events in Egypt and Syria (1688–1821).

JABIR IBN HAYYAN (GEBER) (*fl.* 8th cent.), Muslim writer from Kufa, around whose name was gathered a large corpus of treatises, chemical and alchemical, constituting the outline of an experimental science derived mainly from the physics of Aristotle.

JABOTINSKY, VLADIMIR ZEEV (1880–1940), Russian journalist, dissident Zionist, and leader of the Revisionist opposition to Weizmann. He was converted to Zionism by the news of pogroms. He attended the sixth Zionist Congress in Basle (1903) and from that time on was totally committed to the Zionist cause, although frequently quarrelling with its other leaders. With the outbreak of the First World War he wanted a clear and definite position to be taken up on the side of the Allies, since his belief in Palestine as a home for the Jews made Turkey (in his view) an implacable enemy. He joined the British army and worked successfully to persuade the British government to establish a Jewish legion (Aug. 1917). He fought in Palestine with one of the Jewish battalions. At the end of the war he organized self-defence units—the Haganah—and accepted leadership of them. The part played by these units in the Jerusalem riots (1920) led to his arrest. He was sentenced to 15 years' penal servitude, but amnestied. He travelled to Britain, then to the US to raise funds and conduct propaganda. He was appointed to the executive of the Zionist Organization (1921) but resigned (Jan. 1923) in protest against the leadership's acceptance of the Churchill White Paper. He left the World Zionist Organization and led an opposition group of 'Revisionists' who urged that Zionist effort should be devoted to the immediate creation of a Jewish state supported by organized, mass immigration of Jews from eastern Europe. The Revisionists were more extreme in their territorial demands (on both sides of the Jordan) and their belief that a Jewish state must be established before agreement with the Arabs could be achieved. Jabotinsky and the Revisionists established in 1935 a New Zionist Organization (which was dissolved in 1946) and an offshoot of the Revisionists formed the Stern group of terrorists, taking Jabotinsky as their inspiration after his death.

J. B. Schechtman, *Rebel and Statesman* (New York, 1956).

WK

JACINI, STEFANO, Count (1886–1952), Italian politician, writer, and agriculturalist. He was active in the Catholic Modernist movement, and editor of the magazine *Rinnovamento* (1907–9). During the Second World War he co-ordinated North Italian and French resistance workers, and was minister of war (June–Dec. 1945). He was responsible for the emigration treaty with Argentina (1948).

JACKSON, ANDREW (1767–1845), US politician, soldier, and seventh president of the US. After serving as US congressman and senator from TN (1796–8), he became a judge of the state supreme court (1798–1804). During the War of 1812 he led the TN militia to victory over the Creek Indians at Horseshoe Bend (1814), and made himself a national hero by routing the British at the battle of New Orleans (8 Jan. 1815) just before news of the peace treaty of Ghent reached the US. In 1818 he invaded FL during the Seminole War and aroused indignation in some quarters at home as well as abroad by hanging two British citizens as spies. He again became a senator from TN (1823–5), and was a presidential candidate in 1824. He had the highest number of votes in the electoral college, but lacked an overall majority in a four-cornered contest, and was defeated by John Quincy Adams when the election was decided by the House of Representatives. However, he was elected president in 1828 and served two terms (1829–37).

His presidency symbolized many of the developments taking place in American politics and society in the direction of greater democracy, equality, and individual opportunity. He gave a new dimension to presidential leadership, taking the initiative in policy-making and using the veto far more than his predecessors. His two greatest policy achievements were his firm stand for the Union in the nullification crisis with SC (1832–3) and his destruction, after a long struggle, of the Second Bank of the United States. During the 1830s a new two-party system of Jacksonian Democrats and Whigs emerged.

Jackson was a personal symbol of the rise of the American west and of the new democratic spirit of the age.

J. W. Ward, *Andrew Jackson, symbol for an age* (New York, 1955). PJP

JACKSON, SIR CYRIL (1863–1924), British social worker and educationist, who worked in England and Australia. He was head of the Education Department of Western Australia (1897–1903), and reorganized public education on progressive lines during the expanionist period following the colony's rich gold discoveries. In England he became chief inspector of the Board of Education, chairman of the London County Council, and of several commissions dealing with unemployment, relief work, and child labour.

JACKSON, HELEN HUNT (1830–85), US writer and advocate of justice for the American Indian. After the death of her husband in the American Civil War she began to write children's stories, poems, and essays. Later, she was attracted to the cause of the Indians. In *A Century of Dishonor* (1881), an attack on the government's Indian policy, and *Ramona* (1884), a sympathetic novel of Indian life, she gave wide publicity to the Indians' plight and was appointed a Commissioner of Indian Affairs in July 1883.

JACKSON, THOMAS JONATHAN (1824–63), US soldier and Confederate general, known as 'Stonewall' because of his resistance at the first battle of Bull Run (1861). After graduating from West Point (1846), he served in the Mexican War (1846–8), taught at the VA Military Academy (1852–61), and joined the Confederacy (1861). As commanding general in the Shenandoah valley (1861–2), he proved a brilliant tactician, and ably assisted Gen. Lee in northern VA (1862–3). He was accidentally shot by his own men at Chancellorsville (2 May 1863) and died a few days later.

JACKSONIAN DEMOCRACY in the US, political movement, named after President Andrew Jackson, which flourished during the 1830s and 1840s. It represented a move towards a more popular, egalitarian form of democratic politics, as shown by the increasing use of the spoils system, especially as a party instrument, belief in rotation in office, development of party-nominating conventions, adoption of new styles of electioneering, and Jackson's reliance on the informal advisers of his 'Kitchen Cabinet'. The Jacksonian Democratic Party was challenged in the 1830s by the emerging Whig Party, which won the election of 1840 partly by adopting the style and methods of the Jacksonians.

Jacksonian Democracy has been traditionally regarded as the political expression of the rise of the west, but recent historians have either challenged or complemented this interpretation by suggesting that the movement reflects the rise of an urban working class in the north-eastern cities, the ambitions or frustrations of small entrepreneurs, or the tensions between the Jeffersonian ideals of the past and the rich opportunities offered by economic progress. Certainly, the movement was closely connected with the social, religious, intellectual, and literary movements of the day, which supported a wide variety of reforms and demanded the removal of obstacles to individual freedom and opportunity.

JACOB, JOHN (1812–58), British soldier, who raised the Scinde Irregular Horse. In 1848 he was appointed political superintendent of Upper Sind, where he revolutionized Napier's administrative arrangements. He negotiated a treaty with Kalatin (1854), and raised 'Jacob's Rifles' in 1858, armed with rifles of his own design.

JACOBABAD, TREATY OF (8 Dec. 1876), between the British and the Khan of Kalat in Baluchistan. As a result, Quetta became a British military base.

JACOBIN, originally, a word which designated those deputies of the French National Assembly and other Frenchmen who were members of a club which began to meet in Paris in the disused convent of the Dominican (or 'Jacobin') fathers in the rue Saint Honoré at the end of 1789. This was the successor of the earlier Club Breton, formed at Versailles around a nucleus of Breton deputies to the states general. From this came the society first known as the 'Société de la Révolution', then as the 'Société des Amis de la Constitution' and finally, in Sept. 1792, after it had long been referred to as the Jacobin Club, as the 'Société des Jacobins, amis de la liberté et de l'égalité'. It was by then the established centre of radical political activity in the Revolution. Its subscription was high and its membership well-to-do, but it nevertheless played a great part in the popular political movement. It was the place at which the radical leaders among the deputies could speak to the public, who were provided with galleries in the church of the convent in which, eventually, the club met every day. Robespierre, in particular, made use of this platform for the publicizing of his views. The club was also the centre, as 'mother society', of a network of patriotic societies throughout France, communicating to them its views on the latest events by circular, and receiving from them in return news of the doings of the revolutionary activists in the provinces. Schism and purge maintained the club's purity as the Revolution progressed and from the end of 1793 it was virtually Robespierre's instrument. This led, inevitably, to suspicion of it after his downfall and it ceased to exist in Nov. 1794. Nevertheless, the term 'Jacobin' went on being used to indi-cate a person of known left-wing views in France. In other countries it was used more loosely still to mean at first any sympathizer with the French, and, later, anyone with advanced and possibly terroristic political views. In this way it generated into a generalized term of political abuse in the first half of the 19th cent.

C. Brinton, *The Jacobins* (New York, 1930).
J. M. Thompson, *Robespierre*, 2 vols (Oxford, 1935).   JMR

JACOBITE REBELLION (1745), led by the Young Pretender, Prince Charles Edward, against the Hanoverian rule in Scotland and England. The Prince, grandson of James II of England and son of James, the Old Pretender, expected French aid because the War of the Austrian Succession was in progress. Impatient of waiting for it, he landed in the Outer Hebrides in July 1745. He had one ship, seven companions, and a few thousand weapons, then after some hesitation the Cameron and MacDonald clans joined him in raising his standard on the mainland at Glenfinnan. At Perth they recruited the organizing genius of the rebellion, Lord George Murray, and by Sept. had occupied Edinburgh and driven back a government army under Sir John Cope at Prestonpans.

The prince hoped that by invading England he would commit the French invasion forces assembling at Dunkirk, so in Nov. he marched south with a force of about 6000, took Carlisle and continued through Preston and Manchester, reaching Derby on 4 Dec. So far from gaining support for the Jacobite cause in the traditionally Catholic north-west, his force was steadily reduced by desertion, and although from Derby it was only six days' march to London there was little hope that the rebellion would succeed if the Highlanders were caught by the armies of Gen. Wade and the Duke of Cumberland. The French force was held in Dunkirk by two naval squadrons. Accordingly a retreat to Scotland began on 6 Dec. Though harassed by Cumberland near Penrith the rebels reached Glasgow almost unscathed by Christmas.

By Jan. 1746 Charles Edward had gathered sufficient Highland reinforcements to defeat a government army at Falkirk, but the Duke of Cumberland pursued him through the Highlands and in April inflicted the bloody defeat of Culloden which ended the rebellion. In the savage pacification of the Highlands which followed, nearly 100 leaders were executed after being tried for treason, the authority of the chieftains was taken away, the clan system broken up, bagpipes and kilts forbidden, and, with the Highland clearances by chiefs who converted lands formerly held in trust for their clans to profit-yielding property, the whole way of life of the Scottish Highlands was permanently changed.

Sir Charles Petrie, *The Jacobite Movement* (London, 1949).
Winifred Duke, *Lord George Murray and the Forty Five* (Aberdeen, 1927).   HNBM

JACOBITES, in Britain, supporters of a political and religious movement holding to the hereditary succession of the House of Stuart. After the dethronement of King James II in 1688 loyalty was extended to his son, James, and grandson, Prince Charles Edward. In England there were many supporters of the Jacobite cause among the Tory Party, and active resistance to the Hanoverian succession was expressed in Scotland. The Jacobite bishops of the Scottish Episcopal Church refused to pray for William of Orange in the state prayers and the Church was then disestablished. Many of the clergy went into exile as did the Non-jurors in England.

Sympathy for the Jacobite cause was strongest in the Highlands of Scotland, and this was shown in the Risings of 1715 (after the death of Queen Anne) and 1745. Many Highland chiefs led their clansmen into battle in the Stuart cause and paid for their loyalty with loss of life and property. As a political force the Jacobites were crushed after the retreat from Derby of Prince Charles Edward and the battle of Culloden Moor in 1746. Violent reprisals against the Highlanders were taken by the Duke of Cumberland; all weapons were seized and the wearing of clan tartans forbidden. By the end of the 18th cent. Jacobitism had disappeared as a political force.

JACQUARD, JOSEPH MARIE (1752–1834), French textile engineer, who developed a machine for weaving net (1801). For this he was awarded a patent and a small pension, which allowed him to study at the Conservatoire des Arts et Métiers with a view to perfecting a mechanism for pattern weaving. Although it was not entirely reliable until modifications by Breton and Skola were incorporated, subsequently the draw loom was generally accepted and still remains (1970) the only means of weaving complicated patterns.

JACQUELINE OF BAVARIA (1401–36), Countess of Holland, Zeeland, Hainault, last representative of the Wittelsbach rulers of the Netherlands, who struggled with her cousin, Philip the Good of Burgundy, for possession of her lands, which she inherited in 1417. Her husband, John of Brabant, whom she deserted to marry Humphrey, Duke of Gloucester, ceded his rights to Philip. In 1424 she invaded Hainault, which Philip had occupied, with Gloucester, but in 1425 he deserted her and she was captured by Philip. She escaped to Holland, where she stirred up her noble supporters in the 'Hooks' party, initiating a civil war, as the towns and 'Cods' supported Philip. Again defeated, she came to terms with Philip in the treaty of Delft (1428), by which she recognized Philip as her heir. In 1432 she again attacked Philip, who deposed her, acquiring her lands permanently.

JACQUERIE (May–June 1358), most serious peasant rising in medieval French history. It occurred mainly in the region north of Paris, and was started by the ravaging of the countryside by bands of French and English soldiers. The rising developed into an outbreak of class war in which the peasants, with some support from townsmen, were aligned against the nobles. The peasant rebels killed noblemen and their families. Ruthless repression followed, marked by indiscriminate slaughter of thousands of villagers and townsmen, without much attention to justice or law. It spread fears of similar risings in other countries, such a danger being mentioned in an English parliamentary debate in 1377.

JACQUINOT, LOUIS (1898–   ), French lawyer and politician, who was elected (1932) deputy of the Meuse and in 1940 became under-secretary of the interior in Reynaud's government. He resigned (May 1940) to serve in the Second World War. After the defeat of France in 1940 he joined De Gaulle in London. He was appointed commissioner, and then minister, of marine by the Algiers committee. After the war he held a series of cabinet posts under the Fourth and Fifth Republics, and was the minister responsible for marine, overseas France, scientific research, and Sahara and overseas dependencies.

JADIDISM, reform movement among Russian Muslims in the late 19th and early 20th cents. Beginning as a movement for the modernization of Muslim schools and, to a lesser extent, law, its supporters advanced political demands, embracing Pan-Islamism and Pan-Turkism after 1905. The movement was strongest in Kazan, the Crimea, and Russian Azerbayjan, and also was important in Turkestan, where it was associated with similar movements, eg, the Alash Orda in Kazakhstan.

JADWIGA (1373–99), Queen of Poland (reg. 1383–99). By consenting to marry Jagiello of Lithuania (Ladislas II of Poland), she made possible the union of the two countries and the conversion of the pagan Lithuanians. A pious and educated woman, she left a large bequest for the re-establishment of Cracow University, which had decayed since the death in 1370 of its founder, King Casimir the Great.

JAFFNA, or Yapapatuna, a peninsula in northern Ceylon and centre of an important Tamil kingdom (end of 13th cent.–1620). The kings are best known by their title, Aryachakravartin. Founded during the breakdown of Sinhalese central authority in the 13th cent., Jaffna developed into a major power during the 14th cent. and remained so till the middle of the 15th cent., when it was occupied by the Sinhalese under Prince Sapumal (1449–66). After this brief period it regained its independence till it was occupied by the Portuguese in 1597, by whom the last ruler of Jaffna was executed in 1620. The kingdom of Jaffna was economically important on account of the pearl fisheries and culturally as a centre of Tamil civilization in Ceylon.

JAGAN, CHEDDI (1918–   ), Guyanese politician, of East Indian extraction, who was educated in British Guiana and the US. He formed (1950), with Forbes Burnham, the Peoples' Progressive Party, which won the 1953 election. Their partnership foundered on personal rivalry, growing racial bitterness, and clashes over controversial labour legislation, culminating in the suspension of the constitution and Jagan's imprisonment (1954) for six months. In 1957 Jagan's party was again triumphant and, on full internal self-government being granted (1960), he became prime minister. He opposed Guiana's entry into the West Indies Federation. Further internal disorder, culminating in a general strike, led to new constitutional proposals, and in 1964 on the basis of proportional representation Jagan's Peoples' Progressive Party became the largest—though still a minority—party and lost power. As leader of the Opposition Jagan boycotted the negotiations which led to Guyana's independence (1966).

JAGANNATH, form of the Indian god Vishnu, worshipped especially at Puri, where twice a year festivals attract many thousands of pilgrims from all over India. The construction of the present temple is attributed to King Anantavarman Chodaganga in the 11th and 12 cents.

JAGAT SETH, title of the head of the Hindu banking house of the Seths, awarded to them by Nawab Alivardi Khan of Bengal (reg. 1740–56). The Seths had become wealthy by financing the large transit and foreign trade of Bengal in the earlier part of the 18th cent. Their ability to provide loans gave them political influence. When Nawab Siraj-ud-daulah insulted them (1756–7) by threatening them with circumcision they conspired with the British to secure his removal. Mir Kasim (1760–3) removed the Seths from Murshidabad to his new capital, Monghyr, and this was one of the points at issue between him and the East India Co. After his defeat by the British in 1763 Mir Kasim, suspecting the Seths of complicity with the East India Co., had the two leading members, Mahtab Rai and Sarup Chand, shot.

JAGIR (lit., taking or holding a place or position), form of land tenure under the Muslim governments of India. The essence of the tenure was the right of the grantee to collect and retain the revenue of the land and to perform the functions of government. The grant was used to reward faithful service and to attach important persons to the state. Under the Mughals it was extensively used to support the *mansabdari* system of imperial service, *jagir*s being allotted to provide the salaries attached to the *mansab*s. The grant of a *jagir* could be conditional or unconditional, for a term of years, for life or hereditary. Any *jagir* could be revoked for failure to observe the required conditions. Unconditional grants often became independent chieftainships. Common conditions were military service or police and administrative duties.

JAGUNÇOS in Brazil, rural gunmen and assassins employed in former times in political and clan wars by landowners in the north-east of the country. Private armies of jagunços resisted federal troops in 1896 and opposed the Prestes Column (1924–7). After the 1930s, with easier access into the region by state police forces, jagunço armies gradually disappeared.

JAHAN SHAH (d. 1467), Chieftain ruling over the Qara Qoyunlu Turcomans. Having submitted to the Timurid, Shah Rukh (1434), he was appointed governor of Azerbayjan. In the years after 1447 Jahan Shah wrested most of Persia from the Timurids.

JAHANGIR, NURUDDIN MUHAMMAD (1569–1627), Emperor of the Mughal dynasty (*reg.* 1605–27). Jahangir was the eldest son of the Emperor Akbar, born, it was said, as a result of the prayers of the saint Salim Shah Chishti, at Sikri, which Akbar made his new capital. His mother was a Rajput princess.

On his accession Jahangir suppressed rebellion by his eldest son, Khusrau, and secured his position by promising to support Islam. This meant the end of Akbar's cult and of the patronage of the Jesuits. Though lacking his father's brilliance, Jahangir was a man of talent, well versed in the arts as well as in politics and war. His patronage of both painters and architects was extensive and sensitive. In particular, his love of nature gave a naturalistic twist to the Mughal school of painting which permanently affected it. With these qualities he combined the hot temper of his race, a cruelty which could be savage, and his family's propensity for drink. These habits undoubtedly shortened his life and would have wrecked his reign, but for the influence of Nur Jahan, whom he married in 1611. Her ability gave her much influence in the state, enhanced by the appointment of her father, Itim-ud-daula, and her brother, Asaf Khan, to high office.

Jahangir continued the policy of imperial expansion. Mewar, the surviving independent Rajput state in Rajasthan, capitulated in 1614. In 1616, Ahmadnagar, in the Deccan, was taken and half its kingdom annexed, and in 1620 Kangra, a key fortress in the northern foothills. In the north-west, however, the Persians recovered Kandahar. The reign also saw the development of relations with Europe. Though Jahangir renewed friendly relations with the Jesuits from Goa, he resented the Portuguese stranglehold over Mughal commerce at Surat, and their control of the pilgrim traffic to Mecca. The English defeat of the Portuguese at Swally (1612) removed this fear and provided the basis of privileges granted to Sir Thomas Roe's embassy (1618) after long negotiation.

Like his father, Jahangir suffered towards the end of his reign from troubles about succession. His surviving son, Khurram, rebelled, and though he was defeated, the reign ended in a tangle of plot, counter-plot, and frustration.

Beni Prasad, *History of Jahangir* (London, 1922).   TGPS

JAHILIYA, Arabic word meaning 'time of ignorance', which is used to denote the Arabia of the period preceding the rise of Islam.

JAHIZ, AL- (*c.* 776–*c* 868), writer whose works were of a religio-political nature. In religion he was an adherent of the Mu'tazila and in politics an apologist on behalf of the 'Abbasid caliphate. One of the best known of his works is the *Risala fi Manakib al-Turk*, a treatise on the Turkish soldiers who served as the guards of the Caliph. Al-Jahiz composed also a 'Book of Animals' (*Kitab al-Hayawan*).

JAI SINGH I (d. 1666), Raja of Jaipur, commonly known as Mirza Raja. He held high office under Shah Jahan and Aurangzeb, and was responsible for the defeat and submission of the Maratha chief Sivaji, and for arranging his visit to the Mughal court (1666).

JAI SINGH II (d. 1743), Raja of Jaipur, descendant of Jai Singh I, who held high Mughal office. He built the city of Jaipur (1728), removing his capital there from Amber, and giving its name to his state. He was an astronomer and erected observatories at Jaipur, Delhi, Ujjain, Mathura, and Banaras. He also corrected Hindu astronomical tables.

JAINISM, important Indian religion founded in the 2nd half of the 6th cent. BC by Mahavira. It is therefore roughly contemporary with Buddhism, but, unlike the latter, did not develop into a world religion. It remained within the fold of Hinduism and has, at present, about 1½ million followers. Jainism lays stronger emphasis on non-violence than any other Indian religion and, for members of the monastic order, on asceticism which was not rarely carried to extremes, such as fasting to death.

Although Jainism emerged in eastern India, it later found a centre at Mathura (Punjab) and, from the early cents. AD, developed mainly in Saurashtra, Gujarat, and the western Deccan, where it enjoyed the patronage of many kings of the Chalukya and Rastrakuta dynasties. It found strong support also among prosperous merchant classes. Its importance in Indian history is therefore much greater than the number of its adherents might suggest.

JAINTIA, KINGDOM OF, situated on the present Indian–East Pakistan border, from the Surma river northwards in Assam. A Khasi kingdom, it maintained its independence though defeated by the Ahoms early in the 18th cent. On the Burma invasion (1824) the raja sought British assistance. After his sacrifice of three British subjects to Kali (1832), the plains of the state were annexed (1835), whereupon the raja abandoned the remaining hill country.

JAIPAL (JAYAPALA) (*reg. c.* 985–1001), King of the Shahi dynasty, who, after several campaigns, brought western Punjab and eastern Afghanistan under his control. He is remembered for his unceasing efforts to resist the Muslims of Ghazna. He was, however, unsuccessful and, after being defeated by Mahmud of Ghazna (1001), committed suicide.

JAIPUR, present capital of the Indian state of Rajasthan, with a population of around 400,000. It was formerly, from its foundation (1728), the capital of the Rajput state of that name. Previously known as Amber, Jaipur had a close connection with the Mughal empire from the time of Homayun. The rajas held high office and they intermarried freely with the imperial house. Raja Bahar Mal's daughter married the Emperor Akbar and his son, Bhagwan Das, enjoyed Akbar's confidence. Rajas Man Singh, Jai Singh I and II all held high office. After Jai Singh II's death (1743), succession disputes, Maratha incursions, Pindari raids, and the detachment of Alwar to form a new state (1790), greatly weakened Jaipur. In 1818 it recognized British suzerainty.

JALAL AL-DIN MANGUBIRDI (*reg.* 1220–31), Khwarazm Shah, who was compelled to abandon Khwarazm (the lands along the lower Oxus) before the relentless advance of the Mongols. Jalal al-Din continued to resist the forces of Chingiz Khan in the region of Ghazna, but without much success, being obliged in 1221 to take refuge in India. He returned to Persia in 1225 and, finding that Khwarazm was now closed to him, sought to fashion for himself a new dominion in Azerbayjan and the adjacent areas.

JALAL AL-DIN RUMI (1207–73), known as Mawlana (Mevlana), mystical poet of Islam, from whose teaching and practice arose the Mevlevi order of dervishes. The most influential works of Jalal al-Din were his *diwan*, a corpus of poems written in Persian, but with some items composed in Turkish and Greek; and above all his Mathnawi (Mesnevi), a poetical exposition of the basic ideas of mysticism.

JALAYIR, originally the name of a Mongol tribe. This expression is used to denote one of the succession dynasties which arose from the disintegration of the Mongol regime of the Il-Khans in Persia. After the death of the last Il-Khan, Abu Sa'id, in 1335, the first of the Jalayirid princes, Hasan, established himself at Baghdad in 1338 and managed to hold the city until his own death in 1356. The Jalayirid regime—extended now to embrace much of Azerbaijan and Western Persia—was at its height in the reigns of Uways (*reg.* 1356–74) and Husayn (*reg.* 1374–82). Internal discord and the westward advance of Timur Beg led thereafter to the decline of the Jalayir state. Baghdad itself fell to the Qara Qoyunlu Turcomans in 1412. Jalayirid princes continued to hold out, however, in Mesopotamia until 1432.

JALULA, BATTLE OF (AD 637), on the Diyala river. The Arabs drove the Persian forces eastward in the direction of Hulwan and so assured to the Muslims firm control over most of Iraq.

JAMA'AT-I-ISLAMI, 'the Islamic movement', founded (1941) by the Indian Muslim philosopher Maulana Sayyid Abul Ala Maudoodi (1903–   ). Maudoodi advocated an austere Islamic orthodoxy and sought to create a tightly disciplined group which would work for the creation of a state in which *islam*, 'submission to God', would be the fundamental constitutional principle. He was strongly opposed to the nationalist programmes of both the Congress-oriented *Jamait-ul-Ulema-i-Hind* at Deoband and the All-India Muslim League, because nationalism seemed to him to undermine the concern for religious values in Islam. After partition he was forced to go to Pakistan because of the situation at his Indian base at Pathankot. The *Jama'at* has continued in India, but has been more significant in Pakistan, where it has been in continual opposition to the government of the day and has increasingly come to act as a political party, contrary to Maudoodi's original intention. Since 1947 Maudoodi's career has been stormy. He was first imprisoned (1948–50) for opposition to the Kashmir struggle, then again—and sentenced to death by a military court for his part in sectarian riots in Lahore (1953). He was reprieved by the government after a public outcry. The *Jama'at* was banned (1958–62) following the *coup d'état* in Oct. 1958 and again briefly (1964), when Maudoodi was imprisoned because of his continued opposition to the policies of President Ayub Khan.

JAMAICA, island in the West Indies, discovered by Columbus (1494) and settled by the Spanish (1509), who named it Sant'Jago. They exterminated the native Arawaks whom they replaced with Negro slaves. Jamaica was later captured by the English, led by Admiral William Penn and Gen. Robert Venables (1655), and put under military rule until 1661, when Lord Windsor established the constitutional basis that was to last for the next two centuries, namely that the governor should be assisted by a nominated Executive Council, with provision for planter interests to be represented in the elective Assembly. In 1728 an agreement was reached whereby Jamaica undertook to pay £8000 per annum to the Crown, but any further taxes would require the approval of an annual vote of the legislature. By 1700 the twin bases of the Jamaican economy had been firmly established, the sugar plantations and the slave trade organized by the Royal African Co. (formed in 1672). The 19th cent. witnessed severe setbacks to the Jamaican economy: the slave trade was abolished (1807); an act emancipating the slaves was passed (1833), its economic impact on the planters being partially alleviated by compensation at the rate of £19 per slave; and tariff protection for colonial produce in the British market was abolished. Economic troubles were reflected in growing tension between the various interests on the island, evidenced in 1865 by the Morant Bay Uprising of Negroes which was savagely suppressed by the authorities. As a consequence, Gov. E. J. Eyre was recalled, the constitution abolished, and Jamaica put under a Crown Colony government (1866); this was modified by stages, however, to increase the representative element (1884, 1895). The system came under increasing attack in the 1920s and in 1930s and became a cause of civil unrest. In 1944 a new constitution established a house of representatives elected by universal suffrage, from which a two-party system evolved, Norman Manley's People's Nationalist Party and Alexander Bustamante's Labour Party. The Jamaican economy received an essential stimulus in the late 19th cent. by the development of the banana trade and after the Second World War further diversification into

bauxite mining and tourism proved beneficial. Furthermore, the island profited greatly from help under the Colonial Development and Welfare Act. In 1958 Jamaica entered the federation of the West Indies, but in 1962, with the Labour Party under Bustamante returned to power, it pressed for secession and the federation collapsed. Jamaica became independent (Aug. 1962), with formal backing from Britain.

P. Abrahams. *This Island Now* (New York, 1957).
S. H. Olivier, *Jamaica, the Blessed Isle* (London, 1936).

BD

JAMAICA PROGRESSIVE LEAGUE was founded (1936) in the US by Jamaican exiles with the objective of replacing Crown Colony government in Jamaica by self-government based on universal suffrage. Though originally a middle-class movement, it became increasingly committed to improving working-class conditions, and became affiliated (1938) to the People's National Party.

JAMAICA TRADES AND LABOUR UNION, Jamaica's first trade union, founded in 1907 and affiliated to the American Federation of Labor. It was re-formed (1918) and in the 1920s battled for legal rights. In the 1930s its aggressive unionism led to increased disturbances, from which there emerged the People's National Party and the Jamaica Labour Party, backed by the unions.

JAMAICA WELFARE LIMITED, community development scheme, established (1937) and run by middle-class Jamaicans independent of government agencies on funds from the United Fruit Co.

JAMAL AL-DIN AL-AFGHANI (1839–97), principal spokesman of the doctrine of Pan-Islamism. Though of Persian origin he habitually passed as a Sunni Afghan, and, despite his strong emphasis on the importance of Islam, was probably personally indifferent to religious belief. He travelled widely in Afghanistan, India, Egypt, the Ottoman empire, Iran, and Europe, advocating that Muslim peoples should modernize their societies and unite to resist the encroachments of Europe. Although often regarded as an advocate of constitutionalism, his support for that doctrine appears to have derived more from hostility to particular monarchs, *eg*, Nasir al-Din Shah of Iran, rather than from any conviction concerning its ultimate desirability.

JAMES OF HEREFORD, HENRY JAMES, Baron (1828–1911), British lawyer and Liberal politician. He became MP (1869), solicitor-general (1873), and attorney-general (1873–4, 1880–5), and carried through the Corrupt Practices Act (1883). A staunch opponent of Home Rule (1886, 1893), he joined the Unionist cabinet as chancellor of the duchy of Lancaster (1895–1902).

JAMES I (1208–76), King of Aragon (*reg.* 1213–76), ended Aragon's participation in the freeing of Spain from Moorish domination by conquering Valencia (1238). He established the Mediterranean as the area for future Aragonese expansionist activity by annexing the Balearic islands (1229–35) and encouraging the development of Catalan commercial interests, which during most of the 14th cent. were to dominate Mediterranean trade.

JAMES II (1633–1701), King of Britain (*reg.* 1685–8), second son of Charles I and Henrietta Maria. He was captured by the Parliamentarians at Oxford (1646), but escaped (1648) to join his brother, Charles, in exile. He served in the French army under Turenne (1652–5) and when driven out of France by Mazarin's agreement with Oliver Cromwell, he entered the service of Spain and fought at the battle of the Dunes (1658).

Returning to England at the Restoration (1660), James was appointed lord high admiral. This office, and his marriage to Clarendon's daughter, Anne Hyde (1660), gave him some influence over the policies of Charles II. James fought in the Dutch War, being present at Lowestoft (1665) and Southwold Bay (1672), and supported the naval reforms of Samuel Pepys. James also introduced schemes to improve the training of officers and reorganize discipline, as well as encouraging commercial companies such as the Royal African Co. Though the Test Act (1673) forced him out of office because of his Catholicism, James continued to advise and influence his brother.

His conversion to Catholicism (in the 1660s) gave James a new driving force in life and strengthened his authoritarian political opinions. Though he agreed to allow his daughters, Mary and Anne, to be educated as Protestants and for Mary to marry the Protestant champion, William of Orange (1677), his own second marriage was to a Catholic, Mary of Modena. As it became clear that Charles would die without legitimate issue and that James would succeed, a movement began to exclude him from the throne. During the Exclusion crisis (1679–81) James was forced into exile, first at Brussels and later at Edinburgh, whence he exercised (1681–5) viceregal powers, ruling with predictable intolerance.

Yet his succession to the throne (1685) was well received, parliament stressing its loyalty and voting him adequate supply. The two rebellions against him, Monmouth's in the south-west and Argyll's in Scotland, were easily suppressed, but allowed James an excuse to build up a large standing army. James's short reign emphasized his lack of tact, his extreme views, and his intolerance. His basic aims were the introduction of a more absolute system of government, and toleration for Catholicism. Various events helped to bring about his rejection by his people—the assembly of his army on Hounslow Heath to overawe London; his introduction of Catholic officers, circumventing the Test Act by the use of the dispensing power; the pliant judiciary under Judge Jeffreys; the attack on the Church of England's supremacy by the Declaration of Indulgence; and the tampering with local and central government, affecting the political supremacy of the ruling Anglican elite; all these helped to bring about the Revolution of 1688, the final factor being the birth of a Catholic heir. James fled to France, returning briefly to fight in Ireland until the battle of the Boyne (1690), and thereafter spent the remainder of his life in exile at St Germain.

F. C. Turner, *James II* (London, 1948).
David Ogg, *England in the reigns of James II and William III* (Oxford, 1955).   AW

JAMES I (1394–1437), King of Scotland (*reg.* 1406–37). At the age of 14 James was captured by the English on his way to France. His father, Robert III, died a month later and while he was kept in honourable captivity in England, Scotland was ruled by two successive Dukes of Albany as 'governors'. During his imprisonment James accompanied Henry V abroad on his French campaigns. He was an able monarch, responsible for many judicial reforms and for an attempted modification of the Scottish representative assembly on the lines of that of England. He also successfully subdued the Highlanders. The personal ambition of Walter, Earl of Atholl, a distant relative of James's, led to James's assassination, but there was also a good deal of discontent among the nobility with his financial policies. He was the author of the poem 'The Kingis Quair' and founder of St Andrews University.

JAMES II (1430–60), King of Scotland (*reg.* 1437–60), succeeded his murdered father, James I. He became effective ruler only when he had both attained his majority and tamed the powerful Douglases (1455). Taking advantage of the Wars of the Roses, he made war on England, but was killed while besieging Roxburgh castle.

JAMES III (1452–88), King of Scotland (*reg.* 1460–88). In his minority the country was governed successively by the queen mother and Bp Kennedy and, after 1465, by the family, who seized the young king. After the fall of the Bo₂ in 1469, James's own rule became unpopular because he did not choose his favourites from the great nobility. Alexander, Duke of Albany, was declared King of Scotland by the English and subsequently James found himself in conflict with the Humes, a powerful border family, and was murdered after a battle near Stirling by an unknown hand. He was a great patron of the arts. His marriage to Margaret of Denmark led to the Cession of Orkney and Shetland to Scotland in 1569.

JAMES IV (1473–1513), King of Scotland (*reg.* 1488–1513), was brought to the throne by nobles who rose against his father, James III, and defeated and killed him at Sauchieburn. James himself dealt firmly with an incipient rising in the following year, and in 1491 with a conspiracy to carry him off to England. Having thus strengthened his position, he gradually extended the Crown's authority. He subdued the formidable Donald Dubh and the other chiefs of the western isles, where the king's writ was respected for perhaps the first time. He cleared the east coast of pirates and laid the modest foundations of a navy. He took musters in each shire for the levying of local forces, and with the help of Lowland chiefs he was able to garrison and control the Highlands.

These achievements gained Scotland greater recognition abroad, and James was able to assume the trappings of a Renaissance prince. He civilized his court, patronized the arts, and dabbled in surgery and astronomy. He also moved towards a policy of friendship with England, where Henry VII was anxious to be at peace with Scotland, and gradually convinced James that this was in Scotland's interest too. When the pretender Warbeck was seeking allies, James received him at his court, found him a Scottish bride, and made a token foray into England (1495–6). His English-hating nobles were always recommending such expeditions, and truces and alliances between the two kings were frequently interrupted by skirmishes at sea and by border raids. But the peace concluded in 1499 was more enduring and James married Henry's daughter Margaret (1503), a union which 100 years later brought a Scottish king to England.

After 1509 the peace was broken by the ambitions of Henry VIII, and James was drawn into the complex diplomacy of men much subtler and more experienced than himself. Pope Julius II had already named him 'Protector of the Christian Faith' (1507), and he now found himself flattered by rulers who needed the Scottish alliance in their struggle for supremacy in Italy. In these affairs James was quite out of his depth, and he slowly blundered into war after Barton had been killed in a privateering skirmish off the Downs (1511). With Henry and his main army engaged in France (1513), he revived the 'auld alliance' and crossed the border. After capturing a handful of towns he was routed by Surrey at Flodden and killed with some 10,000 of his men. He was succeeded by the infant James V, the only one of his six legitimate issue to survive him.   MMR

JAMES V (1512–42), King of Scotland (*reg.* 1513–42), was only a year old at his accession and his mother, Margaret Tudor, was regent until her marriage to the Earl of Angus (1514). Nobles who disliked her pro-English policy brought over from France the Duke of Albany, James's cousin and the heir-presumptive, and for some years the French and English factions struggled for possession of the king's person. In 1524 he was pronounced fit to govern under the supervision of Margaret and the council, but he was kept in confinement by Angus (1526–8) until he escaped and drove Angus into England.

James then began to reassert the authority of the Crown, much weakened during his minority, and he angered the nobility by widespread confiscations, claiming the forfeiture of estates held by minors. He also had trouble in the turbulent western isles, and it was not until 1540 that he was able to subdue them.

In 1537 James was married in Paris to Madeleine, daughter of Francis I, and on her death in the following year he married Mary of Guise. This French alliance weakened his friendly relationship with Henry VIII, with whom he had made a treaty in 1534, and he further displeased his uncle by refusing to countenance the Reformation. Henry wished to be on good terms with Scotland, for fear of an invasion in the event of war with France or Spain, and he hoped to strengthen the relationship by persuading the Scots to repudiate the pope. But Paul III had already sent gifts to James as a favoured son of the Church (1537) and under the influence of the Francophil Cardinal Beaton, Apb of St Andrews, the reforming party was discouraged.

Henry sent Sir Ralph Sadler to Scotland to explain the advantages of a religious reformation based on the confiscation of ecclesiastical property, but Sadler could only extract a promise from James that he would confer with Henry at York. But James, alleging fears for his safety, failed to do so, and Henry decided that, with France and Spain once again at war, it was time to teach the Scots a lesson. In August 1542 an English raiding party was annihilated at Haddon Rig, and in Oct. Norfolk, son of the victor of Flodden, led another unsuccessful expedition. But James's counter-attack was a disaster, his numerically superior forces being defeated at Solway Moss (1542). James died shortly after hearing the news a few days after the birth of his daughter, Mary Queen of Scots.   MMR

JAMES I and VI (1566–1625), King of Scotland (*reg.* 1567–1625) and England (*reg.* 1603–25). He was the son of Mary Queen of Scots, by her second husband, Henry Stuart, Lord Darnley. During his minority a series of regents struggled for power until in 1578 the Earl of Morton was driven from the regency and James (aged 12) nominally took over the government. For several years, however, he remained a puppet of various factions. In 1583 he escaped from the Protestant party and began to pursue a policy of freeing himself from factious politics and establishing his claim to the English throne, *eg*, he concluded an alliance with England (1585–6) to which he remained true despite his mother's execution (1587) and Queen Elizabeth I's refusal to recognize him as her successor. In 1589 he married Anne of Denmark. James's attempt to balance himself between the factions ended when Catholic extremists (the Earls of Bothwell, Huntly, and Erroll) forced him into the Protestant and Presbyterian fold. By 1603 he had firmly established his rule in Scotland.

James's experience in Scotland and his theory of the divine right of monarchy (expounded in his two books: *The True Laws of Free Monarchies* and *Basilikon Doron*, published 1598–9) did not fit him for the problems he faced when he succeeded Elizabeth I on 24 March 1603. By insisting upon his prerogative rights he drew from the English parliament ever-increasing counter-claims, *eg*, the Apology of the Commons (1604). The English disliked his favours to impecunious Scots, while his use of court decisions, *eg*, Bates's Case (1606), to undermine parliament's legislative supremacy and taxation rights, offended their political and constitutional sensitivities. His ecclesiastical policy of 'no bishop, no king' at the Hampton Court Conference (1604), which failed to establish a comprehensive religious settlement, alienated the English Puritans, who were forced into an alliance with the House of Commons. The general impecuniousness of his court doubled Elizabeth I's debts in four years, though parliament did not appreciate his financial needs. The result was that when his ablest minister, Robert Cecil, Earl of Salisbury, proposed the Great Contract (1610–11) as a solution to James's monetary problems, it failed because of parliament's lack of support. The death of Salisbury was the turning point in James's reign, and the government became increasingly influenced by favourites and factions, *eg*, Robert Carr, Earl of Somerset, and George Villiers, Duke of

Buckingham. The failure of the Addled Parliament (1614) led James to adopt unpopular financial expedients, *eg*, the sale of monopolies and the Cockayne Project (1614–17), which had disastrous effects on trade.

James's pro-Spanish foreign policy and his refusal to help directly his son-in-law in the Palatinate not only greatly offended his subjects' Protestant sensibilities, but also succeeded in fusing the various sections of discontent into a formidable opposition to his government, which manifested itself in the parliaments of the 1620s. The 1621 parliament was dissolved after attacking the government and claiming to dictate foreign policy. James's pro-Spanish policy was reversed by Buckingham and Prince Charles after their failure in Madrid to negotiate a Spanish marriage (1623). James, however, died before this change had much effect on his government. He left a considerable legacy of political resentment against the Stuarts which increased under his son, Charles I, although to some extent the parliamentary opposition at the end of Elizabeth I's reign was ready enough to oppose a new sovereign however benevolent in his policy.

D. Matthew, *James I* (London, 1967).
D. H. Willson, *James VI & I* (London, 1956).   CJ

JAMES, Saint (*fl.* 1st cent. AD), Jesus' brother, with St Peter leader of the Church in Jerusalem from an early date, and later its ruler until he was killed by the Jews in AD 62. Held in high repute among Jewish Christians, he was later known as 'the Just'. Tradition identified him with the son of Alphaeus, known as 'James the Less'.

JAMES, Saint (*fl.* 1st cent. AD), 'The Great', Jesus' Apostle and brother of John, a member of the inner group of disciples who were present at the Transfiguration and at the Agony in the Garden of Gethsemane. Because of their ardent zeal, James and John were nicknamed by Jesus 'Boanerges', *ie*, Sons of Thunder. James was martyred by Herod Agrippa I in AD 44 and was revered in Spain as a saint during the Middle Ages.

JAMES, HENRY (1843–1916), US writer, born in New York, brother of William James, with whom he had a close relationship. He was educated in New York, London, Paris, and Geneva, and entered Harvard Law School in 1862, but left after a year, and from 1865 contributed reviews and stories to American periodicals. After visiting Europe (1869, 1872–4), he settled in Paris (1875), where he became friends with Turgenev and Flaubert. In 1876 he moved to England, where he spent most of the rest of his life, either in London or at Lamb House, Rye. In 1915 he became a British subject.

His early writings were chiefly concerned with the impact of European civilization on American life. To this period belong his first major novels, *Roderick Hudson* (1875) and *The American* (1877), and some of his best-known short stories, *eg*, 'Daisy Miller' and 'An International Episode'. In 1881 came the novel which is central to James's literary fame, *The Portrait of a Lady*, which depicts a young American woman among Europeans and expatriated Americans. After *Washington Square* (1881) and *The Bostonians* (1886), studies of the American character in its own environment, James turned to a more English milieu. To this period belong *The Tragic Muse* (1890), which concerns the pursuit of the arts against the background of contemporary England; *The Spoils of Poynton* (1897); *The Awkward Age* (1899); and a few unsuccessful ventures into playwriting. In *The Wings of the Dove* (1902), *The Ambassadors* (1903), and *The Golden Bowl* (1904) James returned to international themes. He was constantly concerned with structural consistency in his novels, and believed that nothing should remain which was not represented as a perception or experience of a character. This, together with his mastery of a complex and powerful prose style, make him an important figure in the history of the modern novel. To the last period of his life belong his impressions of America after 20 years, *American Scene* (1906), *A Small Boy and Others* (1913), and *Notes of a Son and Brother* (1914).

JAMES, THOMAS (*c.* 1593–1635), English explorer who sailed from England (1631) to find the North-west Passage. He explored James Bay, the southern lobe of Hudson Bay.

JAMES, WILLIAM (1842–1910), US philosopher and psychologist, who was a brother of Henry James, the novelist. In 1872 he obtained a teaching position at Harvard, where he remained for most of his life. In his most important psychological work, *The Principles of Psychology* (1890), he propounded some original and important theories, maintaining that psychology should be treated as a science, and that enquiries about the mind must begin from a careful study of mental processes. He also made important contributions to understanding the emotions, with the 'James–Lange' theory, and the memory, reasoning, habit, and several other key psychological concepts. In his *The Varieties of Religious Experience* (1902), he argued that religious experience was capable of scientific explanation, but that this, in itself, did not invalidate the claims made on religion's behalf. As a philosopher, James was an empiricist. Among his important contributions was his advocacy of Pragmaticism, the theory that we should accept as true that which we find in practice to work. His main philosophical works were *The Will to Believe* (1897), *Pragmaticism* (1907), and *A Pluralistic Universe* (1909), the latter an attack on rationalist metaphysics.

R. B. Perry, *The Thought and Character of William James*, 2 vols (Boston, 1935).   GAJR

JAMES ISLAND, on the Gambia river estuary in West Africa. It was a European trading base in Senegambia when agents of the Duke of Courland (a principality of the southern shore of the Baltic Sea) built a small fort there in 1651. It acquired its present name when an expedition of the chartered Royal African Co. seized the fort for Britain in 1661 from a Courland garrison, then numbering only seven men and two women. After that it was rivalled as a Gambian trading base only by the French station at Albreda, built in 1681.

Anglo-French hostilities late in the 18th cent. led to French seizure of James Island in 1778, but the British regained it a year later; a peace settlement of 1783, abolishing the British protectorate of Senegambia, confirmed the British in possession of the island and handed St Louis, on the Senegal estuary, back to the French. In 1816 the British transferred their base to St Mary's Island, at the very mouth of the river, and built there a new settlement which they named Bathurst, afterwards to be the capital of the Gambia territory.

JAMESON, SIR LANDER STARR (1853–1917), British doctor and South African politician. He went to South Africa in 1879 and practised at Kimberley. He became associated with Rhodes in the diamond industry and helped him establish the British South Africa Co. in 1889. Jameson followed the pioneer column into Mashonaland (1890), and was appointed first Administrator of what became Rhodesia. In 1893 he engineered a war against the Ndebele, and conquered Matabeleland.

Jameson had connections with gold-mining interests on the Witwatersrand. The English in the Transvaal (the Uitlanders) were restive under Kruger's government, and Jameson took their talk of rebellion seriously; he persuaded Rhodes and Joseph Chamberlain, in Britain, to do so too. At the turn of 1895–6, anticipating rebellion on the Rand, and without waiting for Rhodes's consent, Jameson invaded the Transvaal from Bechuanaland with 500 armed white men. At Doornkop this force surrendered to Kruger's troops and Jameson was sent back to Britain, where he was convicted and imprisoned under the Foreign Enlistment Act. Never-

theless, he returned to South Africa and entered Cape politics. He became prime minister of the Cape (1904–8) and was leader of the opposition in the first Union parliament (from 1910) until his permanent return to England in 1912.

J. van der Poel, *The Jameson Raid* (London, 1951).
I. Colvin, *The Life of Jameson* (London, 1923).   AEA

JAMESTOWN, established (1607) by the London Co. under the leadership of John Smith on the James river in Virginia, was the first permanent English settlement in America. The House of Burgesses of Virginia, first representative governing body in America, met here in 1619, and Jamestown remained the capital of Virginia until 1699, when it was moved to Williamsburg. Little remains of the colonial settlement.

JAMSHEDPUR, major Indian steel town situated in the Chota Nagpur region of Bihar, chosen because of its proximity to iron and coal deposits. The town was built on the site of a village, Sakchi, by the Tata organization. It is named after the founder of the company, Jamshedji Nusserwanji Tata (1839–1904). The project was begun in 1908 and production began shortly before the First World War. The capacity of the works has increased steadily and by the 1960s the plant produced some two million tons of steel a year. The population—5000 in 1911—had risen to over 300,000 by 1970.

JANA SANGH, major Hindu nationalist political party in India, formed in Oct. 1951 by Syama Prasad Mookerjee (1901–53) and leaders of the *Rashtriya Swayamsevak Sangh*. It aimed to represent Hindu political interests more effectively than the existing communalist organizations, such as the Hindu Mahasabha and the *Ram Rajya Parishad*. Its founders, alarmed by the consequences of partition and the communal rioting in West Bengal and East Pakistan (1949–50), felt strongly that Indian, and especially Hindu, interests were being allowed to go by default by the Congress government, led by the 'secularist' Jawaharlal Nehru. Mookerjee himself had resigned from Nehru's cabinet, in which he had been minister for industries since 1947, on these issues. He and the RSS leaders hoped that Sadar Vallabhbhai Patel would assume control in the Congress, but when Patel died (Dec. 1950), they decided to organize themselves. The *Bharatiya Jana Sangh*, 'the Indian People's Party', was formed with Mookerjee as its president, branches being established in the north Indian states.

Although the party was formed in time for the first general elections, it was not in a position to challenge Congress. None the less, Mookerjee's campaign in the north Indian towns, where there were large groups of refugees, brought it 3 per cent of the national vote—more than was achieved by the older communal parties put together, and three seats in the Lok Sabha and 35 in the state assemblies. Mookerjee's death in June 1953 while in detention in Kashmir, as the result of a Jana Sangh *satyagraha* campaign, was a great loss to the party. Attempts to merge with the Hindu Mahasabha later that year failed, but the party went on to enlarge its membership and to improve its electoral performance steadily. By 1967 it had trebled its share of the national vote and had 35 Lok Sabha and 264 state assembly seats, results which gave it the opportunity to take a leading part in coalition governments in several northern states for a time. The RSS has continued to play an important part in the party's development and to espouse Hindu nationalist causes, such as *Akhand Bharat*, a reunited India. But it also has well-developed economic and social policies and has sought alliances with various groups, such as businessmen and peasants. By 1970 it had eclipsed the Hindu Mahasabha and was probably the most securely based of all the right-wing non-Congress parties, even though the Swatantra Party had a slightly larger representation in the legislatures.   PDR

JANBERDI AL-GHAZALI (d. 1521), Mamlūk amir, who suffered defeat at the battle of Gaza against the Ottomans. He made submission later to the Ottoman Sultan Selim I, who appointed him to be beglerbeg of Sham (Syria), with his seat at Damascus. On the death of Selim I in 1520, Janberdi al-Ghazali rose in revolt against the Ottomans but his forces were routed and he himself was slain.

JANE SEYMOUR (c. 1509–37), Queen consort and third wife of King Henry VIII of England and sister of Protector Somerset, was lady-in-waiting to Catherine of Aragon and Anne Boleyn. She married Henry in 1536, 11 days after Anne's execution, but died shortly after giving birth to the future Edward VI. As queen she favoured the Catholic party, Luther describing her as 'an enemy of the gospel'. She reconciled Henry with his daughter Mary and during the Pilgrimage of Grace urged him to restore the smaller monasteries.

JANID, Muslim dynasty from Astrakhan, of Turco-Mongol origin, which established itself in Bokhara (1599) in succession to the Shaybanids and ruled much of Central Asia, during the 17th and 18th cents.

JANISSARIES. The Ottomans, in the time of Murad I (*reg.* AD 1362–89), or even a little earlier, raised a corps of foot-soldiers recruited from slaves, captured in war or acquired through purchase and gift. A further source of recruitment came into being under Bayezid I (*reg.* 1389–1403)—the devshirme or child tribute levied on the non-Muslim subjects of the Ottoman state, above all on the Slavs. The devshirme seems to have been discontinued during the interregnum after the battle of Ankara in 1402. Murad II (*reg.* 1421–51) was to revive and consolidate this device and also to strengthen the slave troops belonging to his household, among them the corps of foot-soldiers known as Yeni Çeri ('New Troops'), ie, the Janissaries. The 15th and 16th cents saw, among the Janissaries, the introduction and increasing use of firearms. The great wars against Persia (1578–90) and against Austria (1593–1606) imposed on the Ottomans, and in particular on the troops of the central regime, a rate of loss so high that the traditional sources of recruitment sufficed no longer to make good the wastage. The Ottomans had therefore to allow the recruitment of Muslim-born subjects of the sultan and also to expand greatly the forces included in the imperial household. One result of this change was the gradual falling of the devshirme into desuetude. At the same time, there was a marked growth of indiscipline and revolt among such troops as the Janissaries. Although good material was still to be found in the corps during the 17th and 18th cents, the old excellence was in large measure lost. The Janissaries became now more dangerous to the sultans than to the enemies of the Ottoman empire. Continuing defeat in war against Austria and Russia compelled the Ottomans at last to create for themselves armed forces organized on European lines. The introduction of a programme of radical reform under Selim III (*reg.* 1789–1807) foreshadowed the end of the Janissaries. Sultan Mahmud II, in 1826, crushed an attempted revolt among them and brought the corps to an end. VJP

JANKAU, BATTLE OF (1645), defeat by the Swedish army, under Field Marshal Lennart Torstenson, of a combined Imperial-Bavarian force near Tabor, 56 kms south-east of Prague. The Austrian cavalry commander, Count von Goetz, was killed and the survivors of Gen. Werth's Bavarian cavalry fled to Prague. Torstenson, however, was forced to relinquish his siege of Prague through lack of supplies and withdrew to the Elbe.

JANSENIUS, CORNELIUS (1585–1638), archbishop of Ypres, who devoted himself to the study of the early Church Fathers, especially of St Augustine, and wrote the controversial work, the *Augustinus* (1640). This challenged the doctrine of free will and expounded a concept akin to predestination. His ideas were popularized in France by his friend, the Abbé de Saint Cyran, and gave rise to the Jansenist movement within the Catholic Church in France and later in Italy.

JANSZOON, WILLEM (*fl.* 17th cent.), Dutch navigator who made the first authenticated discovery of northern Australia. Sailing from Bantam, he crossed the straits separating Australia from New Guinea and penetrated the Gulf of Carpentaria, though he thought that these two land masses were one and the same.

JANUARY EDICT (1562) in France, moderate royal decree expressing the religious policy of Catherine de Medici and her advisers, Beza and Coligny. It granted the French Huguenots full freedom of worship outside towns and the right of private worship within them. They were also permitted to hold synods and their pastors were given official recognition, subject to an oath of loyalty to the crown. However, this pro-Huguenot edict was unacceptable to the Catholic Guise faction, who challenged the settlement by the massacre of Huguenot worshippers at Vassy (1 March 1562).

JAPANESE PEACE TREATY (8 Sept. 1951), signed between Japan and 47 of the 51 states which had declared war on Japan; it constituted a major advance in the establishment of US–Japanese relations. The Soviet Union did not sign the treaty: neither the Nationalist nor the Communist Chinese were invited to attend the San Francisco Conference which preceded the treaty; India objected to the provision of the treaty that the US should retain a trusteeship over the Bonin and Ryukyu Islands, and wanted the return of Formosa to China; Burma objected to the reparations clause as being insufficient. Subsequently, diplomatic relations between the Soviet Union and Japan were re-established by a joint declaration (19 Oct. 1956), which was less than a peace treaty.

The treaty re-established Japan as a sovereign state (Art. 1), reduced to the four main islands by the renunciation of any claim to Korea, Formosa, the Pescadores, the Kuriles, and Sakhalin (Art. 2). A compromise formula on reparations provided for subsequent negotiations between Japan and those Allied Powers whose territories it had occupied. The text (Art. 14) ran:

> It is recognized that Japan should pay reparations to the Allied Powers for the damage and suffering caused by it during the war. Nevertheless, it is also recognized that the resources of Japan are not presently sufficient, if it is to maintain a viable economy, to make complete reparation for all such damage and suffering and at the same time meet its other obligations.

The peace treaty was accompanied, on the same day, by a security treaty between the US and Japan. The US occupation of Japan was thus formally ended by the peace treaty, but US troops remained in Japan under the terms of the security treaty. WFK

JARDIN DES PLANTES in France, botanical garden, originally the *jardin du roi*, started in Paris in the early 17th cent. in imitation of those of Padua, Bologna, and Leyden medical schools. With its formalized baroque layout, the Paris botanical garden became the model for those of other European cities and reflected the widespread interest in botany and medicine.

JARMO, ancient site in northern Iraq. Tools, jewellery, and other remains of a farming village community, dating from the 5th millennium BC, have been excavated.

JARNAC, BATTLE OF (1569), on the Charente, a victory for the Catholics under Anjou during the French Wars of Religion. Condé, the Huguenot leader, was killed after surrendering, but although Coligny, his successor, was defeated at Moncontour later in the year, the Huguenots received favourable terms at the peace of St Germain (1570).

JASMUND, BATTLE OF (25 May 1676), major sea battle fought between the Danish and Swedish navies in the Dutch war with Louis XIV, in which they took opposite sides. The Danish admiral, Niels Juel, defeated the Swedes off Jasmund peninsula, Rügen island.

JASON OF PHERAE (d. 370 BC), Tyrant, who, after overcoming Polydamas of Pharsalus, was elected *tagus* (leader) of Thessaly (*c.* 375) and created a powerful army which inspired elsewhere fears that he intended to dominate Greece. Jason was hostile to the Spartans, who supported Polydamas, and was briefly a member of the Second Athenian Confederacy and the Thebans' ally in 371 when they defeated the Spartans at Leuctra. His ambiguous behaviour during that campaign and subsequent manœuvres, especially concerning Delphi, threatened Theban control of central Greece. But his assassination cleared the way for the Theban invasion of the Peloponnese (370–369) and his successor, Alexander, failed to maintain his position against Theban intervention.

JASSY, PEACE OF (1792), ended the Ottoman–Russian war begun in Aug. 1787. The Sultan ceded to the tsar the fortress of Özi (Oczakow) and the lands situated between the Bug and Dnestr rivers; he also formally recognized once more, the Russian annexation of the Crimea carried out in 1783.

JATAKAS, THE, collection of Buddhist stories in which the protagonist is invariably a former incarnation of Lord Buddha, sometimes human, more frequently animal. Although the nucleus of many *jatakas* may go back to great antiquity, it is now believed that social and economic data contained in them reflect conditions in the early cents AD.

JATS, sturdy agricultural and pastoral people inhabiting the north Indian plain from the banks of the Chambal to those of the Sutlej. They first appear after the great Huna and associated invasions of the 5th and 6th cents AD. They were mainly Hindu and founded the states of Bharatpur and Dholpur in the 18th cent. But many became Muslims and still more Sikhs, of which community they are the main constituent element.

JAURÈS, JEAN (1859–1914), French socialist politician. He served briefly as a centrist deputy in the Chamber (1885–9), but became a socialist and went on to serve as a socialist deputy (1893–7, 1902–14). He was a humane socialist who was influenced by, but not obsessed with, Marxism, and was one of the leading independent socialists, notable for his willingness to work with non-socialist parties. After losing his seat through his support for Dreyfus, he participated in the formation of the SFIO (1905). By his work in the press, parliament, and the international socialist movement he became the dominant figure in French socialism. He was assassinated on the eve of the First World War.

JAVA SEA, BATTLE OF (17 Feb.–1 March 1942), naval engagement between Allied and Japanese forces during the Second World War. US, British, and Dutch units under the command of the Dutch admiral, Karel Doorman, suffered a decisive defeat while fighting a delaying action after the fall of Singapore.

JAVID BEY (Mehmed Cavit) (1875–1926), Turkish politician who was a member of the Committee of Union and Progress, and served as minister of finance and public works in several Ottoman cabinets. He was executed for allegedly conspiring to assassinate Atatürk.

JAVORINA, village of 300 inhabitants in Spisz county in the Carpathian mountains, assigned, with 43 villages, to Czechoslovakia by the Ambassadors' Conference on 6 Dec. 1920. The Poles disputed the settlement, and, although Javorina was of little economic or strategic value, both governments claimed that this dispute prevented the rapprochement they desired. Compromise was hampered both by Polish bitterness over Czechoslovakia's 'seizure' of the Teschen mines while Poland fought Russia in 1920, and by the difficulties of a Czech government conceding Slovak territory. When the League of Nations encouraged the governments to a minor economic compromise on 6 May, 1924, the way was cleared for a short-lived detente.

JAWHAR AL-SIQILLI (*fl.* 10th cent. AD), was of Christian (perhaps of Sicilian) origin and born under Byzantine rule (whence his alternative designation as Al-Rumi), and was brought as a slave to Al-Qayrawan in Ifriqiyya. He became one of the ablest soldiers of his time, asserting Fatimid control over the Maghrib (958) and reducing Egypt to Fatimid obedience in 969. Jawhar, in the same year, established immediately north of the old capital of Egypt, Al-Fustat, a new quarter named Al-Qahira (Cairo). He built (972) the great mosque called Al-Azhar.

JAY, JOHN (1745–1829), American lawyer and politician, was a delegate to the Continental Congress (1774–9), and president of the Congress (1778–9). He joined Franklin in Paris (1782) for the peace negotiations with Britain. His intervention may have helped to thwart Franklin's hopes for the cession of Canada, but his advice that America should sign preliminary peace articles independently of France and Spain probably hastened the formal end of the war. As secretary of foreign affairs (1784–90) Jay was primarily concerned with negotiations with Britain and Spain over territorial issues and the right of navigation on the Mississippi. He was increasingly aware of the weaknesses of the national government under the Articles of Confederation and became a leading advocate of the constitution of 1787 and contributed five of *The Federalist* papers. As first chief justice of the US Supreme Court (1789–95), he continued to emphasize the superior claims of nationalism over state rights. In 1794 he negotiated the unpopular but valuable Jay's treaty. He served as governor of New York (1795–1800).

JAYAVARMAN II (*reg. c.* 802–50), Ruler of the Khmer (Cambodian) kingdom in the period which saw the beginnings of the ascendancy of Angkor. After ruling at two other places, he established in 802 a new capital at Mahendrapavarta (Phnom Kulen, near Angkor) and declared his independence of 'Java'. He established the *devaraja* cult, and during his reign brought a large part of the Lower Mekong basin under his rule. He is also known in inscriptions as Paramesvara.

JAYAVARMAN VII (*reg.* 1181–*c.* 1219), Ruler of the Khmer (Cambodian) kingdom at Angkor. He was founder of the Bayon temple and of Angkor Thom, in whose architecture the face of the Bodhisattva Lokesvara figures so prominently. He was a Mahayana Buddhist and claimed to be a living Buddha. During his reign the Khmer empire reached its greatest extent: he was accepted as suzerain by Champa, by Lao princes on the Mekong, and by the Mons of the Menam basin.

JAYHAWKERS in the US, violent pro-Northern and anti-slavery elements in KS before and during the American Civil War. Having fought against MO 'border ruffians' in the 1850s, they made ruthless and destructive raids into MO during the war under the leadership of James H. Lane and Charles R. Jennison.

JAY'S TREATY (1794) in US, an attempt by George Washington, as president, to settle outstanding differences between the US and Britain. The American special envoy to London, John Jay, was only partly successful. He secured British agreement to the evacuation of the military posts in the north-west by 1796, entry for American vessels to Britain's East Indian ports, and also, for ships under 70 tons, to her West Indian islands, and the setting up of joint commissions to settle the ME boundary dispute and claims arising from the British seizure of American vessels. Nothing was decided, however, on the questions of impressment, the Indians, or the general issue of neutral rights on the high seas. Throughout the US the terms met with fierce criticism, but Washington, believing them to be the best then obtainable, risked his political reputation in support of the treaty.

JAZZ, distinctive, largely improvisational Afro-American musical idiom which developed in the LA region of the US in the late 19th cent. Stemming from a fusing of elements drawn from African, European, and West Indian musical traditions, jazz is allied to the work-song, the blues, and particularly to the syncopated piano style of ragtime which flourished between *c.* 1895 and 1915.

Jazz first came to prominence in New Orleans, where at the turn of the century Negro brass bands were using military marches, church hymns, and popular songs as a basis for improvisation. The melody was generally played by trumpet or cornet, trombone and clarinet weaving accompaniments, and a string bass, drums with guitar or banjo providing the regular rhythmic pulse. Towards the end of the First World War the new music radiated swiftly to Chicago, Kansas City, New York, and Los Angeles, all of which became important centres of jazz development.

By the late 1920s the polyphony of the New Orleans ensemble was being usurped by the jazz arrangement, designed for greatly augmented bands. However, a gradual reaction against the stereotyped formulae of many large swing bands contributed to the emergence of be-bop or bop music, the next stage in the development of jazz. The experimental nature of the playing of such musicians as Charlie Parker and Dizzy Gillespie was greatly to expand the harmonic and rhythmic vocabulary of jazz in the years to follow.

Almost all major jazz innovations have been brought about by soloists. In 1948 the trumpeter Miles Davis made a series of recordings with unorthodox instrumentation in which he succeeded in creating new and interesting textures. His work at this time typified the transition from the declamatory, frenetic approach of be-bop to the more relaxed and indirect style of 'cool' jazz.

The 1960s have seen further experimentation, as in the jazz of such men as Albert Ayler and Ornette Coleman in which a theme statement sets up a mood or general area of pitch in which the soloist is free to ignore the substructure of the piece as he improvises. Basic time has become less important, since tempos may change abruptly and the phrasing of solos and accompaniments has become increasingly complex.

Jazz is continuing to develop and the rich legacy of its recordings accumulated over half a century constitutes a significant part of American life and culture.

F. Newton, *The Jazz Scene* (London, 1959).
G. Schuller, *Early Jazz, its Roots and Musica Development* (New York, 1968). MWM

JEANNE D'ALBRET (1528–72), Queen of Navarre (*reg.* 1555–72), daughter of Margaret of Valois and Henry II d'Albret, married Antoine de Bourbon (1548), and on his accession became queen. She became an ardent Calvinist and turned her realm into a Protestant fortress. She played a large part in the Wars of Religion and was the mother of Henry IV.

JEANNENEY, JULES (1864–1951), French politician, who was deputy of Haute-Sâone (1902–9) and senator for the same district (1909–44). He was secretary of state for war in Clemençeau's cabinet (1917–20). In 1932 he became president of the senate and played an important role in the events of the Popular Front and the defeat of France in the Second World War. As one of the more prominent politicians of the Third Republic he provided the continuity that Gen. De Gaulle desired and as a result he was appointed minister of state in the Provisional government of 1944.

JEBEL MOYA, site in the central Sudan containing extensive ancient cemeteries, the date of which has been disputed; present evidence suggests that they were contemporary with Meroitic culture.

JEBTSUNDAMBA KHUTUKTU, title of the supreme dignitary of the Lamaist Church in Mongolia. In 1639 the Tushetu Khan Combodorji, ruler of one of the three Khalkha khanates, had his son (b. 1635) recognized as the first Jebtsundamba Khutuktu. The Khutuktu's position was somewhat analogous to that of the Dalai Lama in Tibet, and he soon became the focus of Mongol loyalties. The office was hereditary, each new incumbent being 'discovered' as a reincarnation of the preceding one. Of the eight Khutuktus the most important were the first (d. 1723), the second (d. 1758), and the eighth (d. 1924). During the lifetime of the first, the Lamaist Church in Mongolia took firm root and evolved into the greatest civilizing influence until modern times. It also preserved its independence of control from Tibet. The second Khutuktu was implicated in the rebellion of Chingunjab, and is thought to have been murdered by the Manchus. The last Khutuktu became the first, and only, King of Mongolia in 1911. After his death in 1924 a People's Republic was set up. Unsuccessful attempts were made to discover a ninth Khutuktu.

JEFE POLÍTICO, Spanish for 'political chief', and in many Latin American countries the local civil representative of the national government. Historically such men have often wielded great power in villages and small towns. In some parts of Latin America the term has come to mean local political 'boss' as a consequence.

JEFFERSON, THOMAS (1743–1826), American statesman, scholar, and 3rd president of the US. Jefferson graduated from William and Mary College (1762) and was elected to the Virginia House of Burgesses (1769–75). He became a member of the anti-British faction and (1774) composed his *Summary View of the Rights of British America*, denying any parliamentary authority over the colonies. As a delegate to Congress (1775), he became a member of the committee that drafted the Declaration of Independence, of which he was the chief author, but he left Congress in the following year to become a member of the Virginia House of Delegates (1776–9) and governor of the state (1779–81). During this period Jefferson was the force behind the Virginia 'reformation', a vast body of reform legislation, of which the principal achievements were the abolition of land-holding in fee-tail, the abolition of primogeniture (1785), and the establishment of religious freedom (1786). He retired from public life in 1781 to prepare his *Notes on the State of Virginia* (1785), which established his reputation as a scholar. Returning to Congress (1783), he advocated the adoption of the dollar unit and prepared the way for the Ordinance of 1787. In 1785 he succeeded Franklin as US minister to France and in 1789 accepted the secretaryship of state in Washington's first administration. He soon clashed with Hamilton, both on specific issues of economic and foreign policy and on matters of political principle. Jefferson abhorred Hamilton's supposed leanings towards monarchy, opposed, as unconstitutional, his proposal for the establishment of a Bank of the US, and wished to pursue a policy of sympathetic neutrality towards France. In 1793 Jefferson resigned and became a leader of the opposition Democratic–Republican factions. He was elected vice-president to the Federalist, John Adams, but took no active part in administration, though he was politically active and in reaction to the Federalist Alien and Sedition Acts (1798) drafted the Kentucky Resolutions which attacked the acts as unconstitutional and outlined the fundamentals of a doctrine of nullification. He was elected president in 1800. His inaugural address was conciliatory in tone and indicated the need for retrenchment in the economy and reconciliation with his Federalist opponents. The greatest achievement of his first administration, however, was, ironically, the Louisiana Purchase (1803), which involved just that extension of the government's implied powers which he had opposed over the bank bill. Jefferson's second term (1805–9) was plagued with the problems of neutrality in the face of British and French wartime restrictions on trade. His policy of economic coercion embodied in the Embargo Act (1807) was unpopular and ineffectual. He devoted his retirement to the furtherance of popular education, the promotion of a university for Virginia (chartered 1819), and an enthusiasm for architecture. His buildings for Virginia University marked the peak of the classical revival in the US.

Dumas Malone, *Jefferson the Virginian* (Boston, 1948).
Merrill D. Peterson, *Thomas Jefferson and the New Nation* (New York, 1970).   DBS

JEFFERSONIAN DEMOCRACY, democratic theory of government developed by the American statesman, Thomas Jefferson. Jefferson's idea of democracy derived intellectually from his acceptance of the doctrine of 'natural law', and the inalienable rights of man, concepts basic to his *Summary View of the Rights of British America* (1774), and the Declaration of Independence. But in practice he was influenced more by his experience as a landowner in a predominantly agrarian society. While a belief in the common man runs throughout his writings, by the common man he meant the landed yeomanry of the US, suitably educated and endowed with freedom of religion and the press. This class, as he wrote to Lafayette, was not 'the *canaille* of Paris', Jefferson never explicitly attempted the introduction of universal white male suffrage, and his draft constitution for Virginia (1776) contained both a property qualification for voters and a system of checks and balances to protect minority rights against an 'elective despotism'. He has been portrayed as the advocate of periodical rebellion, the leader of the Virginia 'revolution' which abolished primogeniture, entail, and restrictions on religious freedom, but he was neither by upbringing nor inclination a revolutionary democrat. Except for the religious issue, there was little opposition to his reforms, even from the Virginia aristocracy. No revolutionary could have been as satisfied as Jefferson was with the 1787 constitution or the *Federalist* papers. Yet there were fundamental differences between Jefferson and the Hamiltonian Federalists. Jefferson feared Hamilton's encouragement of industrialization, for the destructive effect it would have on his favoured yeomanry, and on American social and political life. As long as there was free land to be taken up, he argued, Americans would remain virtuous, but 'when they got piled upon one another in large cities, as in Europe, they will become corrupt as in Europe'. His policy when in office was suited to farmers' interests, and opposed to those of Hamilton's mercantile and manufacturing elite. In his first inaugural address he argued for the limitation of the function of government, a strict construction of the constitution, the safeguarding of minority rights, and freedom of trade. His greatest single achievement when in office, the Louisiana Purchase (1803), necessitated an unwelcome extension of government's 'implied powers', but safeguarded farming interests on the Mississippi and opened up a vast area for agricultural settlement. Jeffersonian Democracy was clearly only appropriate as long as the US remained an agricultural society. Nevertheless, subsequent US political parties and factions have frequently appealed to its principles, often quite out of their original context. Jeffersonian means were employed by proponents of slavery; Jeffersonian ends attempted by the Populists, who were prepared to use Hamiltonian means in their achievement. The traditional connection between free land and uncorrupted political democracy was developed by the historian, Frederick Jackson Turner, at a time when industrialization, not agrarianism, had become the norm, illustrating the extent to which Jeffersonian Democracy had developed into a powerful tradition in US politics.

C. M. Wiltse, *The Jeffersonian Tradition in American Democracy* (Chapel Hill, 1935).
R. Hofstadter, *The American Political Tradition* (New York, 1948).   DBS

JEFFREY, FRANCIS (1773–1850), Scottish critic, judge, and MP who, with Sydney Smith, Brougham, and Horner founded the *Edinburgh Review* (1802). During Jeffrey's editorship (1803–29) it became a leading forum for Whig opinion, with a circulation of 10,000 copies. Its well-paid contributors included Mackintosh, Macaulay, and Carlyle. Jeffrey was a notoriously caustic critic, unsympathetic to contemporary giants like Scott, Coleridge, Wordsworth, and Shelley. He was politically orthodox, disliking both Cobbett's radicalism and the Utilitarians' philosophy. As lord advocate (1829–34) he supervised Scotland's reform bill. Afterwards he became a court of sessions judge.

JEFFREYS OF WEM, GEORGE JEFFREYS, 1st Baron (1648–1689), Lord Chief Justice of England, who was notorious for his severity in criminal cases. As recorder of London (1678–1680) he sentenced those falsely accused in the Popish Plot, but resigned after obstructing petitions for the summoning of parliament. He used *Quo Warranto* procedure to compel the surrender of the City's charter, and conducted the trials of Russell and Algernon Sidney after the Rye House Plot. In 1685, when he was made a baron and lord chancellor, he presided at the trial of Oates and at the 'Bloody Assize' after Monmouth's rebellion. Jeffreys decided in favour of the Crown's dispensing power and supported James II's revival of the court of high commission. He also advised the committal of the seven bishops (1688). On James's abdication he tried to escape but was seized, disguised as a sailor in a Wapping ale-house, and died in the Tower.

JEHLIČKA, FRANTISEK (1879–1939), Slovak nationalist, who, in 1919, tried to persuade the Paris Peace Conference to grant Slovakia autonomy. Embittered by the hostile Czech reaction to this proposal, he returned to Hungary despite his earlier criticism of the policy of Magyarization. Until he died in exile he abused Czech rule in various ways and demanded Slovak independence under Hungarian protectorship. This programme was never representative of Slovak feeling and when, in 1933, Jehlička accompanied Count Bethlen on a revisionist propaganda tour of England, he was denounced as a traitor by Slovak deputies in the Prague parliament.

JEHOVAH'S WITNESSES, Protestant sect, founded in Pittsburgh, PA (1872), by Charles Taze Russell. The Church holds that Armageddon and the end of the world are near and that only those who obey Jehovah will survive. It has branches in 95 countries, and a membership of more than 1,200,000.

JEKYLL, GERTRUDE (1843–1932), British gardener and author. At Munstead Wood in Surrey, she put into practice her revolutionary ideas of using ornamental plants in informal situations. She emphasized that plant texture and form were as important as flower colour in garden planning and 'invented' the herbaceous border.

JEKYLL, SIR JOSEPH (1663–1738), Welsh judge and politician, who was brother-in-law of Lord Somers, of the Whig Junto, chief justice of the county palatine of Chester (1697) and master of the rolls (1717–38). He was active in Whig politics and author of a drastic measure aimed at curbing the excessive gin-drinking in Britain. His act, increasing the tax on a gallon of gin from 5s to £1 and the retailer's licence from £20 to £50, made him highly unpopular with the London mob; it was widely evaded and was repealed in 1743.

JELLAČIČ, JOSEPH (1801–59), Hungarian soldier, who was the victor of the battle of Schwechat, which prevented Hungarian insurgents from aiding the Vienna Revolution. In 1848 he became Ban (chief executive officer of the elected Sabor) of Civil Croatia, and was placed in command of the Military Frontier. It was thought that he combined loyalty with patriotism and could thus well control an area infected with Slav nationalism. The vacillating policy of the Emperor Ferdinand II caused him to delay his invasion of Hungary to quell the insurrection; but in Sept. 1848 he led his troops to intercept the Hungarian force going to relieve the Vienna revolutionaries.

JELLICOE, JOHN RUSHWORTH JELLICOE, 1st Earl (1859–1935), British sailor, who served in the Egyptian War (1882), the relief of Peking (1900), and was a member of the committee that instigated the design of the first Dreadnought battleships. He commanded the Grand Fleet in the First World War and fought the battle of Jutland (31 May 1916). Though his tactics were severely criticized at the time, it was later accepted that he achieved a strategic victory which rendered the German high seas fleet ineffective for the rest of the war. He was succeeded by Beatty in Nov. 1916.

JEMAL PASHA (Ahmed Cemal) (1872–1922), Ottoman soldier and politician and member (with Enver and Talat) of the triumvirate which dominated Ottoman politics (1913–18). During the First World War he commanded the IVth Army in Syria and was responsible for the stern repression of Arab dissident movements.

JEMAPPES, BATTLE OF (6 Nov. 1792), in the province of Hainaut, Belgium, during the Great French Wars. It opened the way to French occupation of Brussels and all the Austrian Netherlands. Gen. Charles Dumouriez, commanding 40,000 French troops, routed the entrenched Austrian army of 14,000 under Duke Albert of Saxe-Teschen.

JENA, BATTLE OF (14 Oct. 1806), French victory over Prussia, whose army fought without waiting for possible Russian aid. It led to the fall of Berlin and was an important victory for Napoleon.

JENKINS, ROBERT (*fl.* 18th cent.), British sailor, who claimed to have been involved in an episode with Spanish coastguards off Havana, during which his ship, the brig *Rebecca*, was seized and his ear torn off (9 April 1731). In 1738 Jenkins was examined before a committee of the Commons and his case created a national outcry against Spain, being one pretext for the War of Jenkins' Ear.

JENKINS, ROY (1920–), British politician, who entered parliament in 1948 and held minor office in the last days of Attlee's government. When Labour returned to office in 1964 Jenkins was made minister of aviation, then in 1965 entered the cabinet as home secretary.

In Nov. 1967, after the devaluation of the pound and the resignation of James Callaghan, he became chancellor of the exchequer. His policy was one of careful control of public expenditure and personal consumption, together with the fullest support of the export industries. He also began the disentanglement of the pound from its international role. In the immediate term his policies were successful and he endowed his successor with a large surplus on both visible trade as well as payments. But these achievements were bought at the price of low economic growth and almost stationary levels of consumption.

In 1970 Jenkins was elected deputy leader of the Labour Party. It may be said that he represents an intellectual tradition within the Labour Party which may perhaps be called Fabian (he is a former chairman of the Fabian Society), and his political manner recalls that not of a traditional Labour figure but of Asquith, whose biography he wrote.

JENKINS' EAR, WAR OF (1739–48), fought between Britain and Spain, originally in the Caribbean; later it became merged with the War of the Austrian Succession. It began ostensibly as a war of revenge against the atrocities of the Spanish coastguards, whose crimes included the tearing off of an English captain's ear, but in reality it was fought to open

up Spanish colonies to British trade and extend British colonial sovereignty.

Britain's war effort was directed against the Spanish colonies with naval expeditions by Admiral Vernon, Anson's circumnavigation (1740–3), and attacks on Spanish Pacific settlements. Though no decisive British gains were made, Spanish trade and naval communications were seriously dislocated. With the outbreak of the War of the Austrian Succession, hostilities widened to involve the Anglo–French colonial rivalry in India, Canada, and the Caribbean. Hostilities were ended by the treaty of Aix-la-Chapelle (1748), but none of the important outstanding colonial or commercial issues were settled.

JENNE, town in Mali on the Niger–Bani flood-plain, reputedly founded in the late 8th cent. Its early history is obscure, but *c.* 1200 its ruler is said to have adopted Islam. During the 14th and 15th cents the town and its populous dependencies formed a semi-autonomous province in the Mali empire. From the early 15th cent. Jenne became famous as a centre of commerce and learning. Gold from the Begho (Akan) area was exchanged there for Saharan salt and Mediterranean products brought down the Niger from Timbuctoo.

During Songhay expansion Sunni Ali added Jenne to his domains (*c.* 1472); later it fell to the Moroccan pashas (1592). In the 19th cent. it fell first to Ahmad Lobbo (1830), then to Al-hajj Umar (1863), and finally to the French (1893).

JENNER, EDWARD (1749–1823), English physician, pupil of John Hunter, who investigated a dairymaid's belief that those who had contracted cowpox, a mild disease, were immune to smallpox, a fatal or disfiguring one. His development of vaccination against smallpox was a major factor in the declining death-rate. In recognition of the value of his work parliament awarded him £30,000 (1802, 1807).

JERICHO, city of Palestine, strategically situated on the Jordan river. Excavations have revealed a number of towns, the earliest possibly dating from *c.* 6800 BC. Owing to erosion of the later layers of the site, it has not yet been possible to date with certainty the city reputedly destroyed by Joshua.

JEROME, Saint (*c.* AD 345–419), Christian scholar, born at Stridon, near Aquileia. He was educated locally and at Rome before serving as a minor court official under Valentinian I. He was converted at Augusta Treverorum (Trier) to the ascetic life (*c.* 370), and visited the Syrian desert and Constantinople. He then settled at Bethlehem with a group of supporters and devoted himself to a vast programme of writing. Among his most famous and influential works are his Commentaries on biblical books, his Letters (many of which are treatises in themselves), and his Latin translation of the Bible, the Vulgate. Jerome took a leading part in the theological disputes of his day.

JERSEY, EDWARD VILLIERS, 1st Earl of (1656–1711), English diplomat, who was envoy to The Hague (1695) and plenipotentiary at Ryswick (1697). After being ambassador-extraordinary to Paris (1698–9), Jersey was secretary for the southern department and plenipotentiary during the signing of the second Partition treaty (1700). He was lord chamberlain (1700–4), but did not again hold office after being dismissed for opposing Godolphin's foreign policy. Although he was suspected of Jacobite intrigues, just before his death he was nominated as plenipotentiary for the negotiations at Utrecht.

JERUSALEM, KINGDOM OF (1099–1187, 1192–1291), fluctuating area of Palestine established as a kingdom in 1099 after the First Crusade, at its greatest extending from Aqaba to Sidon and exercising loose sovereignty over Tripoli, Antioch, and Edessa. It was a colonial state into which a multi-national nobility and an amalgam of Western feudal practices were transplanted. The Crown was nominally elective and the nobility very powerful, inhabiting impressive castles and fulfilling feudal obligations grudgingly. Papal influence was often strong. There was little effective government organization and its exposure to Muslim attack gave it the rough-and-ready characteristics of a frontier settlement. Hereditary kingship was never firmly established, the title frequently passing to the husbands of heiresses: between 1192 and 1205 three husbands of Isabella, daughter of Amalric I, reigned as kings. The kingdom suffered also from factional strife among his barons, the rivalry and selfishness of the military orders, on which the defence of his kingdom largely depended, and the feuds of privileged Italian merchants, who colonized and exploited its ports. After the fall of Jerusalem (1187) a rump kingdom was restored by the Third Crusade, but it was restricted to a thin coastal strip. Successive Muslim rulers robbed it of more lands and fortresses until the fall of Acre (1291) brought it to an end.

JERVOIS, SIR WILLIAM FRANCIS DRUMMOND (1821–1897), British soldier and colonial governor, who, as governor of the Straits Settlements (1875–7), initiated a short-lived policy of direct rule in the Malay states which was discredited by the Perak War, to which it contributed (1875). Later, as governor successively of South Australia (1877–82) and New Zealand (1882–9), he advised in both areas on coastal defences. He had been inspector-general of fortifications at the war office (1856) and was associated with British defence policy throughout his career, both as consultant and writer.

JESUIT ESTATES ACT (1888), province of Quebec law to compensate the Society of Jesus for Canadian property confiscated in 1773. The act led to an outbreak of religious and sectional conflict in Canada.

JESUIT *RELATIONS*, annual reports by the Society of Jesus on its North American missions. The *Relations* form a valuable source for records of missionary effort, the privations of the early settlers, natural history, and geography, and for Indian life, customs, and beliefs. The first report was prepared by Father Pierre Biard (1616) and they were printed annually (1632–73). A complete edition in English, French, and Latin was edited in 1901 by R. D. Thwaites.

JESUITS, SUPPRESSION OF (1773). The political importance of the Jesuit order had declined from the mid-17th cent. In the 18th cent. anti-curialist feeling led to opposition to the Jesuits in several countries. The hostility of Joseph I's minister, Pombal, led to their expulsion from Portugal in 1759. In France, pro-Jansenist sympathy engendered by the bull *Unigenitus* and the unfavourable publicity of the case of Lavalette culminated in the order's suppression in 1764. A strong anti-Jesuit party grew up in Rome itself, and despite Clement XIII's defence of the society's constitution (1765) the order was suppressed in Naples and Spain in 1767 and in Parma in 1768. Finally, after Clement XIII's death (1769), pressure from the united Bourbon monarchs persuaded Clement XIV to dissolve the order by the bull *Dominus ac Redemptor* (1773), with disastrous effects upon Catholic educational institutions. The society was re-established by Pius VII in Aug. 1814.

JESUS CHRIST (*fl.* 1st cent. AD), founder of the Christian religion, born probably between 9 and 6 BC. His mother, Mary, and her spouse, Joseph of Nazareth, were pious Jews and Jesus was brought up as a carpenter. His ministry began *c.* AD 27–29 when he was baptized by John the Baptist. His main scene of activity was in Galilee and the neighbouring districts of north Palestine, from which he went to Jerusalem, where he was crucified. St John's Gospel, however, states that there were earlier visits to the Holy City. Jesus taught about the imminent coming of the Kingdom or Reign of God, and referred to himself as the Son of Man. His teaching concerning the Fatherhood of God was in harmony with the message of the Kingdom. The Church saw in his life, death, and resurrection a unique act of God.

JET ENGINE. Though the idea of jet propulsion has been known for many centuries, it was not until the 20th cent. that technology was sufficiently advanced to permit the construction of a successful engine. The earliest successful work on developing a gas-turbine engine suitable for aircraft propulsion was carried out in Germany by Hans von Ohain and Max Hahn at Gottingen; they produced a centrifugal-flow jet engine that powered a Heinkel He 178 which became the first jet-propelled aircraft to fly, on 27 Aug. 1939. Simultaneously with this work, but independently of it, an engine of the same type was being constructed in Britain by Frank Whittle, who had taken out patents for it in 1930; his Gloster E 28/39 first flew on 15 May 1941. By the end of the Second World War the Germans had a squadron of jet-propelled Messerschmitt Me 262 fighters in operational service, and the British had just started to use the new Gloster Meteor in action against flying bombs. Both aircraft flew at speeds far faster than those of the conventional piston-engined aircraft. In the period after the war Whittle's design was the most widely used, following the British decision to share their information with their wartime allies, the US and Russia. The Second World War also saw significant strides forward in the application of jet propulsion to rocketry: the Germans carried out successful trials with their rocket-propelled fighter, the Me 163 Komet, and the ram-jet powered V1 flying bomb and the V2 rocket were both used operationally. Refinements in the design and construction of jet-propelled aircraft followed in rapid sequence after the war. The first civil jet aircraft to enter regular service, in May 1952, was the De Havilland Comet.   NRB

JEUNESSE COMMUNISTE RÉVOLUTIONNAIRE (JCR) in France, one of several Trotskyite groups that emerged in France in the 1960s. Its leadership, headed by Alain Krivine, consisted of a group of left dissidents purged from the communist students' union during the latter stages of the Algerian War. Krivine felt that the Communist Party was trying to limit and confine the student movement to suit its own ends. The JCR had no ambitions to be a mass party and instead concentrated on building up a hard core of revolutionary cadres. Its doctrine emphasized the Trotskyite belief that the primary need was to create a disciplined *avant-garde leadership*. The JCR took a leading part in the political disturbances of May 1968. It was less violently inclined than many of the other left factions and did everything it could to avoid a direct confrontation with the police. It did, however, join the fray once the fighting started and was later banned by the government.

JEUNESSES COMMUNISTES in France, organized in 1920 as the youth wing of the newly formed French Communist Party. Many veteran communists came up through the JC, the most notable being Jacques Doriot, the leader of the young communists in the 1920s. They first attracted attention by organizing a series of anti-militarist demonstrations against the occupation of the Ruhr. They had considerable success in subverting members of the Ruhr army of occupation. Although the JC's were overwhelmingly bourgeois in origin, they nevertheless were a radical influence on the Communist Party. They had their own journal, *L'Avant-Garde Ouvrière et Communiste*, which was influential among Paris university students.

In 1945 the *Jeunesses Communistes* were dissolved and replaced by a front organization which was intended to have a wider appeal to the non-communist left.

JEUNESSES PATRIOTES in France, one of several right-wing leagues that sprung up after the victory of the *Cartel des Gauches* in 1924. It was organized by Pierre Taittinger in Oct. 1924 and attracted right-wing university students in the professional faculties. The *Jeunesses patriotes* consciously modelled themselves on the fascist movement of Mussolini. Like other neo-fascist groups it took part in the riots of 6 Feb. 1934 and other disturbances of the 1930s.

JEVONS, WILLIAM STANLEY (1835–82), British economist and exponent of marginalistic analysis. His *Theory of Political Economy* (1871) outlined his concept of a 'final degree of utility', a technique for measuring the extent to which the satisfaction derived from a commodity diminishes in proportion as its availability increases.

JEWISH AGENCY, title, formally adopted in 1929, of an organization established to represent the interests of the Jewish community in Palestine. It grew out of the Palestine Office (1908–18), whose functions were given to the Zionist Commission (1918) and the Zionist Executive (1921). After 1948 the Jewish Agency became an international body coordinating the work of overseas Jewish communities in Israel.

JEWISH WAR (AD 66–70), unsuccessful revolt of the Jews against the Romans in Palestine, of which Josephus' account survives. At Jerusalem the Jews put up a gallant resistance against the Roman army of three legions commanded by Vespasian and his son Titus. Recent excavations have shown that they died almost to a man. Jerusalem was destroyed in the siege, Jewish worship in the Temple was forbidden, and the tax formerly paid by Jews throughout the *diaspora* for the support of the Temple, was made a compulsory payment to Rome.

JEWS, THE. People descended from the inhabitants of Judaea, including those Judeans who remained in Babylon after the exile (597–538 BC) and those who practised Judaism scattered through the Near East and the Mediterranean world. While Judaea (later called Palestine) remained their centre, that country contained a decreasing proportion of the people, reduced finally to less than 10,000 by *c.* 1800. Modern Zionism stimulated a return from 1880 onwards. During the Babylonian exile their religion developed as a discipline of daily living rather than a sacrificial temple worship. Under a remarkable religious leader, Ezra (5th cent. BC), they began to develop a system of interpreting their religious laws and teaching them to the whole people, which made Judaism adaptable to the widest variety of environments. This enabled unity to be maintained in spite of ever-increasing dispersion.

In Judaea they consolidated their position in tranquil obscurity until the time of Alexander the Great who entered Jerusalem in 332 BC. He drew some hundreds of thousands to his new city of Alexandria. After his death Judaea became part of Egypt until 198 BC, when it was conquered by Syria. As a result of a Syrian attempt to destroy Judaism, the people revolted under the Maccabees in 167 BC, established their independence, and sustained it until the country was absorbed by Rome in 63 BC. Roman insensitivity led to continual unrest and finally to two wars. In the first the Temple at Jerusalem was destroyed (AD 70), and in the second the city was sacked (AD 135) and Jews forbidden to live in it. Many thousands were reduced to slavery and carried by the Roman armies to Europe—hence the earliest Jewish settlement in north-western Europe at Cologne.

Judaism was, however, a tolerated religion, and in the 2nd cent. a patriarchate was established at Tiberias with nominal authority over all Jews in the empire. It was gradually extinguished when the empire became Christian in the 4th cent. Thenceforth Christian hostility was a central feature of Jewish life, so that Jews welcomed the Arab conquests. Jerusalem was captured in 637. For some centuries they prospered in both eastern and western caliphates, especially in Spain and Cairo. As Arab political control passed either to various Turkish peoples or to Puritanical movements within Islam between the 9th and 13th cents, the whole Arabic-speaking civilization declined, and, apart from brief periods, conditions of Jewish life changed to oppression and stagnation which continued into modern times.

In the 11th cent. the centre of Jewish life passed from the Islamic world to European Christendom. Its increasing consolidation and prosperity allowed Jewish communities to develop a special contribution to its economy by their dispersion and trading experience. Trading involved possessing actual coin, and they became useful as lenders of money. As they had no status except as the private property of rulers, they played a special role in the money market. The rulers fixed their 'usury' according to their own needs, and took most of the profits, often by direct confiscation.

During the medieval period they were ruthlessly harried by the Church. False accusations were raised against them, such as that of the ritual murder of Christian children and the poisoning of wells. They were herded into ghettoes. Massacres, expulsions, and the destruction of their religious life drove them gradually eastwards, where Poland and Russia offered a refuge, because they needed their services. The Inquisition, begun in the 13th cent. and notorious in Spain in the 15th, completed their decimation in western Europe. They were expelled from Spain in 1492 and Portugal in 1496.

The 16th-cent. revival of learning opened a new period, and the shift of the trading centre from the Mediterranean to the Atlantic seaboard consolidated it. Fugitives from Spain found a commercial haven in south-western France, in the Low Countries, and in England. New communities appeared in the Americas, and trade with the Levant and the Far East offered scope for Jewish developments. The ancient communities stagnating within Islam received some new vitality from the European exiles, though it quickly passed. From this period it is usual to distinguish the northern communities as Ashkenazim, and those of Spanish origin as Sephardim, but now the names have social rather than scientific significance. There were also linguistic differences. Hebrew had become a language of religious activity only, and the Ashkenazim spoke Yiddish, a dialect of Medieval German, and the Sephardim Ladino, a dialect of Spanish.

The gradual secularization of political life in the 17th cent. led to toleration and finally to complete emancipation in western Europe, beginning in France in 1789. But most Jews lived by that time under Russian domination, where endemic persecution continued. After the murder of Alexander II in 1881 it grew to pogroms, expulsions, and flight. Hundreds of thousands fled annually to the West, especially to the US, though industrial centres in western Europe and elsewhere received a substantial quota. Great Jewish charities sprang up to aid the refugees, and it was their pride that none fell on public funds. 19th-cent. expansion and pioneering led to substantial Jewish contributions. In the 17th cent. Jews had transformed the economy of Germany (the Court Jews), and in the early 19th cent. that of Rumania. Now, as equal citizens throughout the Western World, they became able to show their skills in music as well as banking, in culture and entertainment as well as industry. The House of Rothschild became the symbol of this transformation.

Emancipation, however, brought strains within the community itself. The unity of the ghetto was broken and the hold of traditional orthodoxy weakened by progressive synagogues. The result was the appearance of a movement towards unity as a nation (Zionism). Greeted at first with scepticism and even alarm by many, it was strengthened by the emergence of a new anti-Semitism, based on conservatism, racialism, and jealousy. Zionism won increasing support, and in 1917 the British government recognized its roots in Jewish history and favoured the establishment of a national home in Palestine. Anti-Semitism reached its peak in German National Socialism. Six million perished in the Nazi Holocaust (1941–5). The National Home justified its existence in the eyes of the vast majority of the Jewish people by being alone able to give a home and the hope of rehabilitation to the survivors.

Thus, the state of Israel (founded in 1948) became a haven and refuge to which mass migration of Jews took place.

Cecil Roth, *A Short History of the Jewish People* (London, 1953).

James Parkes, *A History of the Jewish Peoples* (London, 1964).

JEWS, NATURALIZATION ACT (1753), in Britain, facilitated the naturalization of wealthy foreign Jews by a private bill. It modified the oaths of supremacy and allegiance. The Lords accepted it easily, but Tories vehemently opposed it in the Commons, although Pelham contended that it would attract Jewish capital investment. Outside parliament popular bigotry, fomented by financiers jealous of Jewish competition, assailed the bill. The act was repealed almost immediately, for the Duke of Newcastle believed the sustained public outcry would blight the administration's prospects at the approaching general election. The affair showed the strength of 18th-cent. religious prejudice, and how public opinion could cow even an unrepresentative legislature.

JEWS, RELIEF ACTS (1858, 1866), in Britain, measures allowing full Jewish participation in parliament. By the 1830s Jews had attained wealth and respectability in the City of London, whence came much of the pressure for their emancipation. The Liberal Party championed the interests of religious minorities, and the first Jewish emancipation bill was introduced in 1830. Jews attained several high positions in the city, which in 1847 and on four subsequent occasions chose Baron Lionel de Rothschild as its MP. The parliamentary oath excluded him, however, and opposition came mainly from the Conservative-dominated House of Lords. In 1858 Jews were admitted into the House of Commons, whose new form of oath omitted the words 'on the true faith of a Christian', and by the Parliamentary Oaths Act (1866) Jews were admitted to the House of Lords. The first Jewish peer, Sir Nathan de Rothschild, was created Lord Rothschild in 1885.

JHANSI, Rani of (d. 1858), widow of the Maratha ruler of Jhansi, whose country was annexed to British India in 1853, in accordance with the doctrine of lapse. Her resentment at this policy led her to join the mutineers in 1857. The extent to which she was responsible for the massacre of Europeans is controversial. She defended Jhansi and when it was taken continued the struggle from Kalpi. Her forces were eventually defeated by Sir Hugh Rose at Marar and Kotah. She was killed in battle.

JIBRIL GAINI (*c.* 1840–1903), Nigerian Mahdist leader and supporter of Hayat al-Din, who carved out the small state of Bormi (*c.* 1885–1902), in north-eastern Nigeria.

JIBUTI, main port of the Territoire Français des Afars et des Issas, formerly French Somaliland. It became important at the end of the 19th cent. with the construction of the Addis Ababa railway.

JIDDA, TREATY OF (1927), by which Britain recognized the complete independence of Saudi Arabia (so ending its subordinate status under the treaty of Qatif, 1915), in return for undertakings concerning British Muslim pilgrims to Mecca, the suppression of the slave trade, and the position of the Persian Gulf states.

JIHAD, expression which, deriving from the Arabic 'jahada' (to labour for a given end), came to mean a striving for the most laudable of objectives, *ie,* for the extension of the Muslim faith, even by force, over the non-Muslim world. To the Muslims the lands subject to their rule constituted the 'Abode of Islam' (Dar al-Islam)—beyond which stood the territories outside Muslim control, *ie,* the 'Abode of War' (Dar al-Harb), where dwelt the heathen and the infidel. *Jihad* was held to be a religious obligation incumbent on all Muslims. It was one of the gates of paradise: the Muslim who fell as a warrior of the *Jihad* was a martyr on behalf of Islam and assured therefore of salvation. *Jihad* was also perpetual in character. No enduring peace could be made with the heathen or the infidel; only a truce designed to serve the immediate interests of the Muslim state.

The spirit of *Jihad* found expression on the frontiers of the Muslim world, where it assumed the character of an endless *ghaza* (cf. Italian 'razzia'), *ie,* of raiding which the *ghazis*—soldiers of the *ghaza*—carried out into the non-Muslim lands, *eg,* from Turkestan against the heathen peoples of the steppe; along the border zones which, extending from northern Syria through Mesopotamia into Armenia, separated the empire of Byzantium from the empire of the caliphate; or in the Balkans, where the rise of the Ottoman Turks can be viewed as the gradual movement of a *ghazi* frontier north-westward from Asia Minor to the lands along the Danube river.

JIM CROW, formerly generic name for an American Negro, deriving from a minstrel show of 1828. Its common usage implied discriminatory legislation enforcing racial segregation. By 1900 Jim Crow laws had proliferated throughout the Southern, and some Northern, states and affected public transport, theatres, hotels, hospitals, prisons, cemeteries, schoolbooks, and the use of Bibles in courtrooms.

JIMÉNEZ DE QUESADA, GONZALO (1495–1579), chief Spanish conqueror of the Chibcha region around Bogotá in modern Colombia. In 1536, lured by reports of Chibcha gold and emeralds, Jiménez led his expedition from the Caribbean coast through hostile Indians and tropical forest to the Magdalena river. There vessels were built, and with these Jiménez reached the upper highlands after an eight-month journey. He marched into the valley of Bogotá and there two rivals confronted him: Sebastián de Belalcázar, conqueror of Ecuador, and the German, Nikolaus Federmann, from Welser-dominated Venezuela. Rather than resort to force, the three agreed to let the Spanish Crown arbitrate their case. The least quarrelsome of the conquerors, Jiménez made no demands, contented himself with an honorary title, and lived the rest of his long life peacefully in Colombia, organizing vain schemes for the conquest of mythical El Dorado.

JIMÉNEZ OREAMUNO, RICARDO (1859–1945), President of Costa Rica for three terms (1910–14, 1924–8, 1932–6) who shaped the National Republican Party. He favoured expanded trade with the US and nationalized Costa Rican insurance companies. During his last term banana workers received protective legislation.

JINDYWOROBAK, Australian literary movement founded in 1938 by Rex Ingamells (1913–55). The poets associated with the movement, which flourished mainly in the 1940s, demanded the development of an indigenous Australian culture.

JINNAH, MUHAMMAD ALI (1876–1948), Indian Muslim politician and governor-general of Pakistan (1947–8), known as *Qaid-i-Azam,* 'the great leader'. Although chiefly remembered as 'the creator of Pakistan', separatism was the very reversal of his earlier policies. His first 30 years in politics were spent in trying to draw Muslims into a united nationalist movement. He opposed the initial Muslim League campaign for separate Muslim electorates (1906–9) and when he joined the league (1913) he tried to modify its pro-government and separatist policies. The Lucknow Pact (1916) was concluded during his presidency. He was a leading nationalist spokesman in the Montagu–Chelmsford discussions and a member of the Imperial Legislative Council (1910–19), but resigned in protest against the Rowlatt bills (1919). On his election to the central Legislative Assembly

(1923), he established himself as a leading opposition spokesman. He served on the Reforms Enquiry (Muddiman) Committee (1926–7), but in the twenties he was not able to exert his previous influence on nationalist or Muslim politics. *Satyagraha*, which he would neither condone or adopt, forced him from the Congress front rank in 1920, and conservative Muslim opposition to his policies reduced his political stature. Though he presided over the special Muslim League session at Calcutta (Sept. 1920) and voiced Khilafat sentiments, he played no major part in the Khilafat movement and it was only when the league reappeared in the mid-1920s that he came to the fore once again. He then devoted himself primarily to the league because he came increasingly to see Muslim security as being dependent on a strong separate political organization which could ally itself with the Congress on more or less equal terms. His eagerness to bring Congress and Muslims together was his undoing, for conservative Muslims regarded his conciliatoriness as excessive. In fact, his efforts during the negotiations at the All-Parties Conference, his 'Delhi Proposals' (1927), and his 'Fourteen Points' (1929) made sweeping Muslim demands that were unacceptable to Hindus. None the less, Shafi split the league and Jinnah was forced to go to Britain in voluntary political 'exile', though he took part in the Round Table Conferences (1930–2).

On his return to India (1934) he assumed the presidency of the moribund Muslim League and, with the aid of able lieutenants, had by the mid-1940s built it up into a political party with an indisputable claim to have a dominant voice in Muslim affairs. His initial strategy (1934–7) was still to strengthen the league, so that Congress and the league could ally themselves, and in the Legislative Assembly, and in the campaign for the provincial elections (1937), he kept the league in line with Congress policy. Congress insistence on merger rather than alliance after 1937 was a rejection of this strategy, however, and when Congress tried to increase its own weak Muslim following by a 'Muslim mass contact campaign', Jinnah appealed to communal sentiment as the means of defending his own and the league's political position. By skilful manœuvring and a preparedness to use to the full the communal fears aroused by some Congress provincial governments, Jinnah greatly increased the league's following and its importance in the overall Indian political situation alongside the Congress and the British government. His call for the celebration by Muslims of a 'Day of Deliverance' (22 Dec. 1939) following the resignation of the Congress ministries, served to demonstrate this increased strength. This was the effective beginning of the separatist phase of Jinnah's career.

Faced with the possibility of a British decision to transfer power because of the war, the league spelt out its bargaining position—the creation of independent Muslim states in north-western and north-eastern India—in its Lahore resolution (March 1940). Thereafter the demand for Pakistan was not relaxed and no means was found to circumvent it. Jinnah was prepared, together with the Congress, to accept the Cabinet Mission's proposals (1946) as a basis for discussion, but he retracted when Nehru cast doubts on Congress's sincerity and he called instead for a 'Direct Action Day' (16 Aug.) as a means of impressing the British with the strength of Muslim feeling and power. In the negotiations which followed he made use of every possible occasion, backed as he was by an overwhelming league victory in the elections for Muslim seats in 1945–6, to polarize the situation between Hindu and Muslim, Congress and league. He was able to withhold the league's participation in the Interim government until he gained the sole right to nominate Muslim members. In such circumstances, partition became unavoidable.

Jinnah refused to have Mountbatten as the joint governor-general of the two new dominions. He himself took this office in Pakistan and until his death in Sept. 1948 he effectively ruled the country. The prime minister and the cabinet were not so much a government as a group of advisers whom he consulted if he wished. Foreign affairs, and in particular questions of relations with India, were almost his exclusive domain. His loss to his country was very great, for he was a major figure who was able to transcend the local and regional interests of the new nation. The power of his name even in the 1960s was shown by the decision of the Combined Opposition parties to support his aged sister, Miss Fatima Jinnah, in the presidential elections against Ayub Khan (1964).

H. Bolitho, *Jinnah: the creator of Pakistan* (London, 1954).
C. H. Philips and M. D. Wainwright (eds), *The Partition of India: policies and perspectives, 1935–1947* (London, 1970).

PDR

JÍVAROS, in Ecuador, refers to several related tribes on the eastern piedmont of the Andes which stubbornly resisted intrusion by Ecuadorian nationals and foreign missionaries alike. Among their customs was that of shrinking the decapitated heads of their enemies.

In Puerto Rico 'jívaros' are the rural peasantry of the mountainous interior.

JIZYA. The words jizya and kharaj were used, during the time of the first Caliphs, to denote the collective tribute which the Arabs raised from each particular region of the new Muslim empire. Under the late Umayyads, and above all, after the reign of Umar II (*reg.* AD 717–20), the term jizya began to assume the more specialized meaning of a capitation tax levied on the non-Muslim subjects (*dhimmi*s) of the caliph. The jizya, according to the legal theorists, was to be a graduated tax amounting to four dinars for the rich, two dinars for the middle-class elements, and one dinar for the poor—women, children, the aged, and the sick being exempted from payment.

JOAD, CYRIL EDWIN MITCHINSON (1891–1953), British civil servant and philosopher. Before 1939 he was a leading light in various pacifist organizations. On the outbreak of the Second World War he became a member of the BBC radio Brains Trust, which had an enormous wartime listening audience. He was a prolific writer on various aspects of philosophy, history, religion, and politics.

JOAN OF ARC, Saint (?1412–31), called 'the maid of Orleans', a French patriotic leader who claimed to have been visited by saints who instructed her to free France from the English and help the dauphin, Charles, to be crowned king. She had an obsessive belief in her own mission and was able to convince others. In 1429 she accompanied the French army which raised the siege of Orléans. Thereafter Charles was crowned in Rheims in Joan's presence, removing all doubts as to his legitimate right to the throne. After this she took part in military operations, but had little effect on high policy. In May 1430 she was captured by Burgundian forces and handed over to the English, who had her tried by a packed court as a heretic. A full record of the trial survives. She recanted her heresy, but relapsed and was burned at Rouen (30 May 1431). She was beatified in 1909 and canonized in 1920.

JOANNA LA BELTRANEJA (1462–1530), daughter of Henry IV of Castile, popularly known as *La Beltraneja*, after her reputed father, the court favourite, Beltran de la Cueva. On Henry's death (1474), she claimed the Castilian throne, helped by her husband, Alfonso V of Portugal. In the civil war of succession which followed, most of Andalusia and New Castile, and several towns in Old Castile supported her, but the cause of Isabella and Ferdinand eventually triumphed (1479), after which Joanna withdrew to a convent. The failure of her claim ended the possibility of a peaceful union of Castile and Portugal.

JOANNA THE MAD (1479–1555), daughter of Isabella of Castile and Ferdinand of Aragon. In 1496 she married the

Emperor Maximilian's son, the Archduke Philip, and gave birth in 1500 to the child who was the future king of Spain, and the Emperor Charles V, ruler of the vast Habsburg territories. In 1504, though already mentally ill and incompetent to rule, Joanna succeeded her mother as Queen of Castile. She retired in 1509 to the seclusion of Tordesillas for the remaining years of her life.

JOB, patriarch (*fl.* 16th–17th cents), Moscow metropolitan and follower of Boris Godunov, who was consecrated the first patriarch of All Russia. On the death of Tsar Feodor (1598) he presided over Boris's elevation to tsar and crowned him (20 Feb. 1599). He was deposed shortly after Boris's sudden death (1605) and was forced to retire to a monastery.

JÖCHI (d. *c.* 1226), eldest son of Chingiz Khan and ruler of an apanage of the Mongol empire, which extended over the area of modern Kazakhstan, western Siberia, and included Khwarazm.

JOFFRE, JOSEPH CHARLES CÉSAIRE (1852–1931), French marshal. After a successful career in the colonies and the Paris garrison, he was made chief of staff (1911) because of his reliable republican sympathies. He was responsible for some of the failures of the offensive planning in the First World War, but retrieved his reputation by his victory on the Marne (1914). This earned him great popularity and made it difficult to dismiss him when his unsuccessful offensives ground to a halt. Eventually (1916) he was forced to retire and rewarded with a marshal's baton and a mission to the US.

JOGJAKARTA in Central Java, Indonesia, the seat of the Sultan of Jogjakarta and of the Prince Pakualam. In this area have been located a number of kingdoms and royal residences, from as early as the 8th cent. The present city was founded in 1755, and is known officially as Ngajogjakarta Adiningrat. Its ruling sultans have borne the name Hamengkubuwana since the 18th cent.

JOGUES, ISAAC (1607–46), French Jesuit missionary, who came to New France (1636) and served in the Huron missions. In 1642 he was captured by Iroquois but ransomed by Dutch traders (1643). He returned to Canada (1644) and began a mission to the Mohawk Indians (1646), who murdered him. He was canonized in 1930.

JOHN, OF AUSTRIA, DON (1545–78), natural son of Emperor Charles V, who served his half-brother, Philip II of Spain, as a naval and military commander. Although educated for the priesthood, he commanded the royal forces in the Granada war against the Moriscoes (1568–70) and crushed the rebels. Yet he made his reputation as the general in command of the great fleet of the Holy League against the Turks. Leaving Messina (Sept. 1571), he sighted the enemy in the Gulf of Corinth and defeated them at the battle of Lepanto (7 Oct. 1571), capturing 117 ships and securing western Europe from Ottoman attack. Don John now dreamt of relieving Constantinople and Jerusalem, but was ordered to lead the reconquest of Tunis, which he achieved with an expeditionary force of 20,000 men (Oct. 1573), though he was unable to prevent its recapture by the Turks in 1574.

After succeeding Requesens as governor-general of the Spanish Netherlands in the midst of the Netherlands revolt, he entered Luxemburg on 4 Nov. 1576, when the Pacification of Ghent was on the point of being concluded. In Feb. 1577, by the Eternal Edict, he accepted the Pacification, and after the Spanish troops had withdrawn from the Netherlands according to its terms (March 1577) he was able to enter Brussels (May 1577). But being restless for military action and frustrated by lack of supplies, he repudiated the Pacification, left Brussels, and seized the fortress of Namur (July 1577). This bold step ended hopes of a reconciliation with the rebellious states. The states general withdrew their

allegiance to him (Dec. 1577) and proclaimed the Archduke Matthias as the new governor-general.

Meanwhile, Don John had conceived another adventure. He hoped to liberate Mary Queen of Scots from her English prison, win the throne of England, and claim her hand in marriage. Adequate supplies from Spain being denied to him, he negotiated with the pope and the Catholic party in France. Then, in Jan. 1578, reinforced by some 3000 Spanish soldiers, he left Namur and swept into Brabant, where he won the battle of Gembloux. In Spain, Philip's confidence in Don John was poisoned by the scheming Perez, who accused him of treason and instigated the murder in Madrid of Don John's secretary, Juan de Escobedo (March 1578). Don John died of typhus in his camp, still hoping for military reinforcements.

J. Lynch, *Spain under the Habsburgs*, vol. I, *Empire and Absolutism, 1516–1598* (Oxford, 1965).   MKS

JOHN I, Duke of Brabant (1259–94), called 'the Victorious', who succeeded to the duchy in 1267 on the deposition of his elder brother, Henry III. After 1280 he came into conflict with Guelders and its allies, Luxemburg and Cologne, over possession of the vacant duchy of Limburg, which had long been coveted by his house to gain control of the major Rhenish trade routes. The war against Guelders (1283–8) culminated in John defeating his enemies at Worringen near Bonn (5 June 1288), by which he secured Limburg and dealt a severe blow to the power of the Rhenish princes. He founded the military and economic power of Brabant.

JOHN III, Duke of Brabant (1312–55), last duke of his house, who ruled Brabant at the height of its power and wealth. A war-like and clever man, he resembled his grandfather, John I, and continued his policies of building a strong Brabançon state and acquiring new territories. After 1332 he was faced by a great coalition of his enemies under John of Luxemburg, supported by France. John was eventually able to defeat this by a mixture of diplomacy and war, as he was able to rouse the patriotic loyalty of his subjects, and emerged stronger than before. In 1347 he came to an agreement with the house of Luxemburg, under which his heir, Joanna, married Wenceslas, step-brother of the Emperor Charles IV, in return for which Charles renounced all imperial claims to Brabant. On his death Brabant and Limburg passed to the Luxemburgs.

JOHN THE FEARLESS (1371–1419), Duke of Burgundy (*reg.* 1404–19) second duke of his house to rule in the Netherlands. He tried to use his dominions as a base for dominating the kingdom of France, where the rule of the insane Charles VI encouraged French royal princes to squabble for power. In 1407 John removed his chief rival, Duke Louis of Orléans, by assassination, which started a civil war which continued until 1435. This encouraged King Henry V of England to invade France. In association with Queen Isabella, the wife of the mad Charles VI, John captured much of northern France and recaptured Paris in 1418, but was murdered in 1419 by Isabella's own son, the future Charles VII. This murder forced John's heir, Duke Philip the Good, to ally himself with the English and assured to Henry V the control of northern France, which lasted until 1435.

JOHN I TZIMISKES (*reg.* 969–76) who showed himself to be an able soldier during the campaigns of conquest against the Muslims. In 971 he brought the Bulgars under Byzantine control and, at Silistria on the Danube, crushed the forces of Svjatoslav of Kiev. In 974–5, he carried out two campaigns in Syria and Palestine, which took him as far south as Tiberias, Nazareth, and Caesarea.

JOHN II KOMNENOS (*reg.* 1118–43), Byzantine Emperor, who won a decisive victory over the Pechenegs in 1122.

Much of his reign was spent in a long and successful endeavour to drive back the Muslims in Asia Minor, taking skilful advantage of the tensions existing between the two main Turkish dynasties in the area, the Seljuks of Rum (at Konya) and the Danishmends (at Siwas). In 1137–8 he extended Byzantine control over the Christian kingdom of Lesser Armenia and over the Latin state of Antioch.

JOHN III VATATZES (*reg.* 1222–54), Byzantine Emperor at Nikaea, who, in 1225, forced the Latins at Constantinople to relinquish most of the territories which had fallen to them in north-west Asia Minor after the Fourth Crusade of 1204. In Europe he was able to regain control over much of Thrace and Macedonia, Thessaloniki falling to him in 1246. His successes paved the way for the subsequent Byzantine recovery of Constantinople (1261).

JOHN VI KANTAKUZENOS (*c.* 1292–1383), Byzantine Emperor (*reg.* 1347–54). On the accession of John V Palaiologos in 1341, John Kantakuzenos laid claim to the throne. A civil war ensued, deriving from the conflict of rival factions, but also embracing discords of a religious and social character. With the assistance of the Ottoman Turks John VI became emperor in 1347. His reign was a time of continuing warfare, above all with the Serbs and the Genoese. In 1354 John V compelled John VI to abdicate. During the years of his retirement as a monk, John Kantakuzenos wrote a number of theological works in defence of the Hesychast doctrines, the acceptance of which within the Orthodox Church he had done much to secure. He also wrote a famous chronicle covering the events of 1320–56.

JOHN II (*reg.* 1406–54), King of Castile, weak monarch who typified the failure of the Castilian Crown to control the nobility in the later Middle Ages. He surrendered power to his favourite, Alvaro de Luna, and became a patron of Castilian letters.

JOHN (1167–1216), King of England (*reg.* 1199–1216), youngest son of King Henry II, who succeeded his brother Richard I after the latter's accidental death. John was an able, intelligent man, sharing his father's interest in the development of a sophisticated administration and legal system. But he was not a competent warrior and his suspicious and selfish character made him widely unpopular. He inherited extensive territories in France exhausted by long years of warfare under Richard, but was unable to defend them against King Philip of France when the war restarted in 1202, and lost everything north of the Loire in 1202–4. Thereafter he withdrew into England to prepare a war of revenge. By 1213 he had again accumulated a large war treasure and powerful allies on the continent, but his methods of raising money had aroused bitter opposition in England. Furthermore, John relied too much on his mercenary captains, who were hated by the English magnates. Also, he had drifted into a conflict with the papacy by refusing to accept Stephen Langton, the choice of Pope Innocent III, as Abp of Canterbury. From 1208 to 1213 England was under a papal interdict and John appropriated the revenues of his ecclesiastical opponents. John believed himself surrounded with conspiracies and a suspected plot to kill him in 1212 persuaded him to make his peace with the papacy in 1213. This enabled John to renew the war in France, but his allies were defeated at Bouvines (1214) and John had spent his war treasure to no purpose. His opponents in England rose in rebellion, profiting from his lack of funds to hire mercenaries. To gain a temporary respite, John had to concede in June the Great Charter of Liberties (*Magna Carta*). The civil war soon restarted and its outcome was still uncertain when John died. His disappearance paved the way for peace, as his opponents hated and feared John personally, but were ready to accept the rule of his infant heir, Henry III.

JOHN I (1316–1316), King of France (*reg.* 14–19 Nov. 1316), posthumous son of Louis X, who lived only five days. His uncle, the regent, thereupon usurped the Crown, as Philip V, to the exclusion of the infant king's sister, a step which began to establish the custom of male succession (the Salic Law).

JOHN II (1319–64), King of France (*reg.* 1350–64), son of King Philip VI. In 1356 he led a superior army against Edward the Black Prince at Poitiers, but the battle ended in his defeat and capture. For four years he remained a prisoner in London until, by the treaty of Bretigny (1360), he was released for the promised payment of 3 million gold crowns and in return for ceding to England south-western France south of the Loire. When his second son, a hostage for the ransom, broke his parole and escaped, John chivalrously returned to captivity and died in London. John 'the Good', in whose reign France sank to an unexampled state of dissension and wretchedness, lacked political sense. His generous award of Burgundy to his brave youngest son, Philip, gave rise to a dynasty which was to be a major threat to the French monarchy in future years.

JOHN III (1502–57), King of Portugal (*reg.* 1521–57), succeeded his father and was married to Catherine, sister of Charles V. He supported the extreme clerical party, introduced the Inquisition (1533), and received the Jesuits (1540). He attempted to exploit the Portuguese trade in spices, particularly pepper, which were in high demand in Europe, but weakened his finances by borrowing against expected profits that were not always realized. Ambitious colonial schemes in China and Malaya were frustrated. The Gujerats were stubborn enemies in India, where Da Gama was sent as viceroy (1524), and a grandiose design for Brazil, where John divided the coastline into 12 captaincies, broke down under native attacks and the reluctance of Portuguese noblemen to assume the necessary responsibilities. Portugal lacked the money and manpower to execute John's far-flung ambitions, and his schemes were gradually deflated by the inefficiency and corruption of his proconsuls.

JOHN IV (1604–56), King of Portugal (*reg.* 1640–56), came to the throne through a French-assisted revolt against the 60-year Spanish occupation. The French hoped to control Portugal as a base against Spain, but John maintained his independence despite the hostility or indifference of other powers. His ill-considered support for King Charles I of England exposed him to the attacks of the Commonwealth navies under Blake, and he was forced to open his country's trade to English merchants. Internally he strengthened the throne by dispensing with the *cortes* and councils and ruling through his personal secretaries. The formation of the Brazilian Trading Co. (1649) to protect merchant shipping with armed convoys led to the recovery of some of the trade that had been lost to the Dutch and English East India Cos. John's daughter, Catherine of Braganza, married King Charles II of England in 1662.

JOHN V (1689–1750), King of Portugal (*reg.* 1707–50), succeeded at a time when Portugal had already deserted Louis XIV and made the Methuen treaty with England (1703). His marriage to a sister of the Archduke Charles strengthened his ties with the Grand Alliance. The wealth of Brazil made John financially independent of the *cortes* and enabled him to emulate the magnificence of other European monarchs. He was interested in music and learning, and endowed museums and libraries, founded an academy of history, and built the palace and monastery at Mafra in imitation of the Escorial (1717–31). From the pope, who gave him the title of 'most faithful majesty' (1707), he secured several privileges and endowments, including the right to appoint his own cardinals. In his last years John became insane and the country was administered by regents.

JOHN III (1537–92), King of Sweden (*reg.* 1568–92), second son of Gustavus I, and a believer in a reunion of churches. He deposed his elder brother, Eric XIV, with the help of his younger brother, Duke Charles, and the nobles, whose powers he had to confirm by charter. He unsuccessfully planned a compromise with Rome, to be based on a liturgy which he devised himself and imposed on the Swedish clergy. His marriage to the sister of Sigismund II of Poland, a Catholic, resulted in his son's election to the Polish throne (1587) as Sigismund III, an appointment which the father later tried to terminate. John, who was no soldier, brought the Seven Years War against Denmark to an end, but in a long war with the Russians his commanders secured Sweden's hold on Estonia.

JOHN XII (937–64), Pope (*reg.* 955–63), succeeded his father, Alberic II of Spoleto, as absolute ruler of Rome in 954. In 955 he had himself made pope. A worthless person of scandalous reputation, his pontificate was significant for his appeal for aid to Otto I, whose entry into Italy (961) and imperial coronation by John began the long and momentous connection between the German kingdom, the empire, and the papacy. He was deposed in 963.

JOHN XXII (1249–1334), Pope (*reg.* 1316–34). His pontificate was marked by the final breach with, and condemnation of, the Spiritual Franciscans, by a bitter quarrel with the emperor, Lewis of Bavaria, and by his own views on the Beatific Vision, which led to grave doubts of his own orthodoxy. Despite all this, John's pontificate showed him to be one of the major popes. He made the last medieval additions to the canon law, the *Clementines* and *Extravagentes*, and he reorganized papal finances, laying the foundation of the great financial prosperity of the popes during the Avignon period.

JOHN XXIII (*c.* 1360–1419), Pope (*reg.* 1410–15), rose to prominence as an extortionate official of Pope Boniface IX, who made him a cardinal and ruler of Bologna. As Baldassare Cossa he was a leading force in the Council of Pisa (1409), which the cardinals had summoned to end the Schism, and so his election as successor to the first Pisan pope, Alexander V, was as politically inevitable as it was ecclesiastically scandalous. Unable, however, to wrest the political initiative from those working for the conciliar reform of the Church, John became a virtual prisoner of the Council of Constance, which finally deposed him for piracy, murder, rape, sodomy, and incest. After four years in confinement, he submitted to Martin V, who made him a cardinal.

JOHN XXIII (1881–1963), Pope (*reg.* 1958–63). He served in the First World War in the medical corps and then as a chaplain. After the war he worked in Rome (1921–5) and was appointed titular archbishop and apostolic delegate to Bulgaria (1925), then (1934) to Greece and Turkey. At the end of the Second World War he became papal nuncio to France (1944). He was elected pope in succession to Pius XII, and was expected to play the limited role of a man of nearly 80, who had been regarded as a compromise candidate. Instead, he played an active part, summoning the Second Vatican Council (1962) which began a wide movement of reform in the Church. He captured the public imagination of the world by the warmth of his personality and his obvious interest, particularly in those who suffered. He also took important steps towards a closer union between the Roman and other Christian Churches, receiving in audience the Greek patriarch, the Abp of Canterbury, and the Moderator of the Presbyterian Church of Scotland.

JOHN THE BAPTIST (*fl.* 1st cent. AD), son of Zacharias, a Temple priest, and Elizabeth, a kinswoman of Jesus' mother. He appeared *c.* AD 27 as a mission preacher by the Jordan river, demanding repentance (*ie*, an altered mode of life) and baptism in view of the imminent coming of the Messiah. He attracted large crowds, and his dress was reminiscent of the Old Testament prophets. Three of Jesus' 12 apostles had been his disciples and Jesus himself suggested that he was, like the great Elijah, come to earth again. Later his denunciation of Herod Antipas led to his imprisonment and death. His influence 20 years later is, however, attested by the Acts of the Apostles. He is highly revered among the Mandaeans, who may have some remote connection with his original followers.

JOHN BIRCH SOCIETY in US, semi-secret militant anticommunist organization founded by Robert Welch (1958) and named after John Birch, an American allegedly killed by Chinese communists in a border incident after the end of the Second World War. An influence in national politics, its right-wing views find their greatest support in strong chapters in the Western states.

JOHN CASIMIR, Count Palatine (1543–92), second son of Count Frederick III and one of the leading Calvinist princes in 16th-cent. Europe. While acting as regent and administrator for his young nephew, Frederick IV, after the death of Ludwig VI in 1583, he restored Calvinism as the state religion of the palatinate. He also intervened on the Calvinist side in the civil disorders of neighbouring states. With his German horsemen (*reiter*) he supported the Huguenots in the second French Civil War (1567–8). In 1578, at the invitation of the Calvinist citizens of Ghent and subsidized by Elizabeth of England, he supported the rebellion in the southern Netherlands against the Spanish authorities, but achieved little and returned to the palatinate in 1579.

JOHN CHRYSOSTOM, Saint (AD 345–407), Christian writer. He was born and educated at Antioch in Syria, and became Bp of Constantinople (398). There, his outspokenness on moral and political questions, particularly his criticisms of the court of Theodosius II, led to his deposition by a church council (403), and exile. Having been temporarily recalled to placate his supporters, he was again exiled (404) and died in a remote spot by the Black Sea. Named Chrysostom, 'The Golden-mouthed', for his eloquence as a preacher, he left many works, particularly sermons, theological treatises, and letters from exile on the ascetic life.

JOHN FREDERICK THE ELDER, Elector of Saxony (1503–1554), succeeded his father, John the Steadfast, of the Ernestine line of the house of Wettin, to the electoral title (1532) and together with Philip of Hesse led the Protestant League of Schmalkalde against the Emperor Charles V. A determined Lutheran, he prevented Melanchthon from negotiating Church unity with Francis I (1535) and rejected Pope Paul III's scheme for a general council (1537) and the doctrinal agreement of the Diet of Regensburg (1541). In 1546 he was attacked by his ambitious cousin of the Albertine line, Maurice, Duke of Saxony, and invaded Maurice's duchy in the spring of 1547, but his armies were shattered by the imperial forces under Alva at the battle of Mühlberg (24 April 1547). He was captured and tried for rebellion, but his death sentence was commuted to imprisonment. Meanwhile, his lands were overrun by the troops of Maurice and Ferdinand, Archduke of Austria, and the emperor transferred his electorate to Maurice. He was released at the latter's instigation after the treaty of Passau (1552).

JOHN GEORGE (1585–1654), Elector of Saxony, son of Christian I, succeeded his brother, Christian II, in 1611 and ruled throughout the Thirty Years War (1618–48). A Lutheran, he was the leader of the Protestant constitutionalist group of German princes and tried to pursue a policy of peace and neutrality. He not only declined to accept the Bohemian Crown in defiance of the Emperor Matthias, but gave his vote to Archduke Ferdinand, rather than the Protestant elector palatine, Frederick V, and tried to arrange a peaceful solution of the Bohemian revolt at Eger (April 1619). His respect for the German liberties led to his forming a military alliance with Ferdinand against Frederick, but his annexation of Lusatia as a reward for this assistance undermined his reputation in Protestant eyes (1620–3). As a sincere constitutionalist he deplored the transference of the palatinate to Maximilian of Bavaria (1621) and that of the duchy of Mecklenburg to Wallenstein (1628), and above all the imperial challenge of the Edict of Restitution (1629). However, he equally distrusted the intervention of foreign powers in a German conflict and only the sack of Magdeburg persuaded him to make an agreement with Gustavus Adolphus of Sweden (1631). His leadership of the Protestant princes was undermined by the humiliating rout of the Saxon contingent under his leadership at Breitenfeld (1631). Rejecting the advice of his wife, Magdalena Sybilla, and his general, Von Arnim, he sided again with the emperor (peace of Prague, 1635) to settle the problem of the German lands without Swedish interference. After his lands were terrorized by Torstenson's army he came to terms with the Swedes (truce of Kötschenbroda, 1645). At the Münster–Osnabrück negotiations he engineered a compromise settlement based on the 1624 position (1646), but after the war his leadership of the Protestant princes was lost to Frederick William of Brandenburg.

JOHN OF JOINVILLE (d. 1319), Seneschal of Champagne, biographer of King Louis IX of France, and historian of Louis's first crusade (1248–54), of which his *Histoire de St Louis* is a detailed and vivid account.

JOHN, OTTO (1909–   ), German security chief (1950–4) suspected of defection to East Germany in 1954. During the Second World War John had worked in the *Abwehr* (counter-intelligence), but took part in the July Plot (1944) and managed to escape abroad, returning to Germany to become head of the Office for the Protection of the Constitution in 1950. In 1954 he disappeared into East Germany for 17 months, and when he returned (1955) he was tried and imprisoned for treason. John always denied that he left West Germany voluntarily, and claimed he was kidnapped. Attempts (1963, 1966) to secure a retrial failed, and he had not, by 1970, been officially rehabilitated.

JOHN OF SALISBURY (c. 1115–80), one of the greatest scholars of the 12th cent., a Latinist and one of the early Aristotelians, his *Metalogicus* being the first medieval work based on the complete Aristotle. He was educated at Paris and Chartres, numbering Peter Abelard and Gilbert de la Porrée among his teachers. After a period at the papal curia when he collected material for his *Historia Pontificalis*, a notable work of contemporary history, he served the abps of Canterbury, went into exile with his friend Thomas Becket, and was an eye-witness of Becket's assassination at Canterbury in 1170. He was Bp of Chartres (1176–80). His other writings include the *Policraticus* (Book of the Statesman) written for King Henry II, Lives of St Anselm and of Becket, and an edition by himself of over 300 of his letters which constitute an invaluable source for the history of his times.

JOHN SCOTUS ERIGENA (*fl.* 9th cent.), medieval philosopher and one of the earliest schoolmen. Nothing is known of him before his arrival at the court of Charles the Bald in 845, possibly as a refugee from the Viking attacks on Ireland. In 851 he completed his *De Predestinatione*, which was condemned at the councils of Valencia (855) and Langres (859). Around 860 he was commissioned by Charles to make a translation (from the original Greek) of the work known as the Pseudo-Dionysus (*Corpus Areopagiticum*), sent to Charles by the Byzantine emperor in 827. In Scotus's translation it was to be the basic and most influential text in western mystical thought. Its neo-Platonism deeply influenced Scotus's own work, the *De Divisione Naturae* (862–6). Its doctrine is elusive and obscure, but its message is clear: reason must be guided by faith, but faith must be illuminated by reason. This principle was taken to heart.

It governed scholasticism and motivated the logic and dialectic of the schools of the 11th and 12th cents.

JOHN SIGISMUND (d. 1620), Elector of Brandenburg, son of Joachim Frederick, succeeded as elector in 1608. In 1591 he married Anne, eldest daughter of the King of Prussia, and through her Brandenburg acquired the predominantly Protestant duchies of Cleves, Mark and Ravensburg, which John Sigismund claimed in 1608 and received by the treaty of Xanten (1614), after his conversion from Lutheranism to Calvinism, and in addition the throne of Prussia (1618), which he held as a fief of the Polish Crown.

JOHN SIGISMUND (1540–71), King of Hungary (*reg.* 1540–71), infant son of John Zapolyai I and Isabella, daughter of Sigismund I, King of Poland. Shortly after his father's death and his own birth, the anti-Habsburg nationalist party, with Turkish connivance, proclaimed him King of Hungary.

JOHNSON, AMY (1903–41), British aviation pioneer. Her most famous feat was her solo flight from Britain to Australia in May 1930, in 19½ days. It was the ninth such flight since 1919, but the first by a woman. She served in the Second World War, and was killed on a flying mission.

JOHNSON, ANDREW (1808–75), US politician and 17th president of the US, who succeeded on the assassination of Abraham Lincoln. Born in NC, he moved to TN (1826), where he worked as a tailor and became active in local and state politics. He served in the US House of Representatives as a Democrat (1843–53), was governor of TN (1853–7), and a US senator (1857–62). In Congress, he was a champion of the Southern yeoman farmer and an early supporter of the homestead bill. He was the only Southern senator to support the Union during the Civil War and was appointed military governor of TN (1862–4). As a War Democrat and a Southerner, he was chosen as Lincoln's vice-presidential running-mate in 1864, to balance the ticket. On his accession to the presidency (April 1865), his stubborn adherence to Lincoln's moderate policy of reconstruction, which in the event favoured the white South and failed to help or protect the freed Negro, created a rapidly widening breach with the majority of Republicans in Congress, both radicals and former moderates. His vetoes on important measures, including the Freedmen's Bureau Act and the Civil Rights Act (1866) and the Reconstruction Acts (1867), were over-ruled by two-thirds majorities in Congress. His dismissal of the secretary of war, Edwin Stanton, in defiance of the Tenure of Office Act provided the pretext for impeachment proceedings against him in Congress (1868). This, the only attempt to impeach a president, failed by only one vote, and Johnson completed his presidential term. He was elected a senator a few months before his death and thus became one of only two ex-presidents to serve in Congress. Self-taught, sturdy, courageous, and obstinate, Johnson aggravated the formidable problems of reconstruction both by the policy he pursued and by his political mistakes.

E. L. McKitrick, *Andrew Johnson and Reconstruction* (Chicago, 1960).   PJP

JOHNSON, EDWARD (1598–1672), American soldier and writer, who emigrated from England (1630) to Massachusetts Bay and founded Woburn. He published *A History of New England, The Wonder Working Providence of Sions Savior in New England*, which was the earliest general history of the Bay colony. It was written from the viewpoint of the devout Puritan. New England leaders were depicted as Christ's soldiers marching against the wilderness and its barbarians.

JOHNSON, HIRAM WARREN (1866–1945), US lawyer and politician. As governor of California (1911–17) he introduced a wide range of progressive measures, such as the initiative, referendum, recall, Blue Sky law, and the eight-hour day for women. In 1912 he was chosen by Theodore Roosevelt as vice-presidential candidate on the Progressive ticket. He was a leading candidate for the Republican nomination for president in 1920, and challenged Coolidge for the Republican nomination (1924). As senator from CA (1917–45) he supported progressive measures during the 1920s, particularly the Swing–Johnson Bill of 1928, authorizing the construction of the Boulder Dam. In 1932 he refused to support the party ticket and endorsed F. D. Roosevelt, but in the late 1930s became disillusioned with the New Deal.

In foreign affairs, Johnson was a leading isolationist. He played a prominent role as an 'Irreconcilable' in the controversy over US membership of the League of Nations (1919–20), sponsored the Johnson Act (1934), banning American loans to nations in default of their war debts, and supported mandatory neutrality legislation during the 1930s. He vigorously opposed F. D. Roosevelt's foreign policy, which he felt certain would involve America in the Second World War.

JOHNSON, SIR JOHN (1742–1830), American United Empire Loyalist, who fled (1776) from his native Mohawk valley to Canada to organize and lead the King's Royal Regiment of New York. He remained in Canada after the American War of Independence and was active in Lower Canadian politics.

JOHNSON, LYNDON BAINES (1908–), US politician and 36th president of the US, who was educated in TX, where he taught for two years before going to Washington, DC, as secretary to a TX congressman (1932). As an ardent supporter of the New Deal, he was appointed Texan director of the National Youth Administration (1935), and was elected to the US House of Representatives (1937). In 1948 he was elected by a narrow majority to the US Senate, where he served as Democratic whip (1951–3) and party leader (1953–61). An instinctive and astute politician, his power and influence within Congress was considerable. He worked closely with the Republican President Eisenhower after 1955, and as a moderate southerner was able to help secure passage of the first civil rights acts (1957, 1960) since Reconstruction. Defeated by John F. Kennedy for the 1960 Democratic presidential nomination, he was asked to become vice-presidential candidate, partly in order to help the party in the South. As vice-president, he was given responsibilities in a number of spheres, including space research and equal employment opportunities, and undertook a tour of South-East Asia (1961), but was never close to the president, nor his entourage. He succeeded to the presidency on Kennedy's assassination (Nov. 1963).

Committing himself to a continuation of his predecessor's policies, he was able to secure passage of Kennedy's proposals on civil rights and taxation (1964). Elected in his own right in a landslide victory over Barry Goldwater (1964), he successfully launched his own 'Great Society' programme of domestic reform, but began to come under attack from liberal Democrats over US intervention in the Dominican republic (1965) and escalation of the war in Viet-nam. Protest against the war merged into campus revolts which, together with the crisis in the Negro ghettoes, provoked a dangerous polarization in the nation. With the announcement of the candidacies of Eugene McCarthy and Robert Kennedy for the Democratic nomination, Johnson decided not to seek re-election in 1968, but direct confrontation between the administration and its critics came at the Chicago presidential convention, where, despite the apparent verdict of the Democratic primary elections, Johnson's Viet-nam policy, and his candidate, Hubert Humphrey, were endorsed amid unprecedented violence. He left office bitter at what he regarded as betrayal by elements in the party from whom he felt he had inherited his Viet-nam policy, but still hopeful that posterity might remember him as 'the man who saved

Asia and Viet-nam, and who did something for the Negroes of this country'.

Eric F. Goldman, *The Tragedy of Lyndon Johnson* (London, 1969). AJT

JOHNSON, RICHARD (1753–1827), British clergyman, who was the first to serve in Australia. He sailed to the NSW penal settlement in the first fleet and conducted the first divine service in Sydney in Feb. 1788. He worked harmoniously with governors Arthur Phillip and John Hunter, but was very critical of Francis Grose as lieutenant-governor and at all times had difficulty in reconciling his evangelical desire to reform convicts with his responsibilities as chaplain of the settlement. He returned to England in 1800.

JOHNSON, SAMUEL (1696–1772), American philosopher, who was ordained as an Anglican minister in England (1722). He opened the first Anglican church in CT (1724), and was the first president of King's College, Columbia (1754–63). He wrote *Elementa Philosophica*, which expounded the ideas of the English philosopher George Berkeley. This was the earliest textbook of philosophy published in America.

JOHNSON, SAMUEL (1709–84), English journalist, critic, and lexicographer, the son of a bookseller in Lichfield, Staffs. After failing as a local schoolmaster, Johnson went to London, where for several years his main employment was as a literary hack. But his abilities gradually began to make themselves known and in 1747 he was commissioned by a group of booksellers to prepare a Dictionary of the English Language, a task that occupied him for the next eight years. Meanwhile, his fame grew, partly on account of the breadth of his scholarship and partly because of his powers of conversation. He was welcomed in intellectual circles and his contributions to *The Rambler* (1750–2) and *The Idler* (1758–1760), a magazine, almost all of its contributions written by himself, his sole novel, *Rasselas* (1759), and his *Lives of the Poets* (1779–81) were received with high praise.

Much of what is known about Johnson derives from the classic biography (1791) by his friend, the Scot James Boswell, who recorded the progress of their association in considerable detail.

JOHNSON, SAMUEL (1846–1901), Anglican pastor at Oyo and author of the *History of the Yorubas* (completed 1897, first published 1921), a classic record of the Yoruba peoples' traditions preserved in royal houses at Oyo, and expressed in biblical prose.

JOHNSON, SIR WILLIAM (1715–74), Irish-born American fur trader and administrator. He managed Mohawk valley lands for his uncle Peter Warren, and set up a trading post on the Mohawk river at Amsterdam, New York (1758). Johnson owned a domain of 100,000 acres (405 sq. kms), which was a gift of the Mohawk tribe, and was the wealthiest colonist of his day. He associated with the Indians as equals, protected their hunting grounds, wore their clothes, spoke their language, and had their trust and respect. He controlled the Iroquois confederacy which was the key to the west, and was important in the struggle with the French. Johnson won the battle of Lake George (1755) against the French. He was appointed superintendent of Indian Affairs (1756–74).

JOHNSON–REED ACT (1924) in US, legislation restricting immigration to 150,000 annually after 1 July 1927; national quotas thereafter were to be determined by the ethnic composition of the US in 1920. During the transition period quotas were fixed at 2 per cent of the foreign-born recorded at the 1890 census. Both plans were designed to favour immigrants from north-west Europe.

JOHNSTON, ALBERT SIDNEY (1803–62), US soldier and Confederate general, who rose to command successive military departments in the West (1856–61). During the Civil War he led Confederate forces and was killed while securing victory at Shiloh (6 April 1862).

JOHNSTON, SIR ALEXANDER (1775–1849), British lawyer, who became chief justice of Ceylon (1811–20), and played a large part in improving the island's judicial system. He introduced trial by jury. On his return to Britain he was a founder of the Royal Asiatic Society.

JOHNSTON, GEORGE (1764–1823), Scottish-born officer of the NSW Corps, who had previously served in the American War of Independence, and is best known for his part in the deposition of Gov. William Bligh (1808). While temporarily in command of the corps, he yielded to pressure by the rebels, deposed Bligh, and assumed office as lieutenant-governor. Though cashiered at a London court-martial (1811) he was nevertheless permitted to return as a settler to NSW, where he was a successful farmer.

JOHNSTON, SIR HARRY HAMILTON (1858–1927), British explorer, writer, and administrator in Africa. He travelled widely in tropical Africa (1883–1900), extending the frontiers of the British empire. By 1888, his action against Ja Ja of Opobo had confirmed British power in the Niger delta. He originated the phrase 'Cape-to-Cairo' as a stimulus to British expansion across Africa from south to north, and contributed to the partial realization of this dream between 1891 and 1896, as the first British consul-general in Malawi, and in his wars against the Arab slavers and their African allies. His conclusion of the Uganda Agreement in 1900 simplified temporarily British administration in Uganda but, by the nature of its land settlement, created difficult problems for the future. Although he was a convinced imperialist, Johnston acquired an increasingly pro-African point of view in his later years. An indefatigable artist and author, he wrote and illustrated 38 books, several of them on Africa.

JOHNSTON, JOSEPH EGGLESTONE (1807–91), US soldier and politician, who became quartermaster-general of the US army, but resigned to join the Confederacy. He commanded Confederate forces in northern VA (1861–2) and also in the west, where he conducted the retreat before Gen. Sherman (1864–5). He served as US congressman from VA (1879–81) and US commissioner of railroads (1887–91).

JOHNSTON PLAN (1953–5), for regional development of the Jordan river system was put forward by the British mission under Eric Johnston. Based upon the earlier Main plan, it offered hopes, ultimately shattered, of a settlement of the Arab-Israeli dispute through regional economic co-operation.

JOHOR–RIAU SULTANATE, leading Malay state in the Malacca Straits region after the Portuguese conquest of Malacca (1511). Sultan Mahmud of Malacca (1488–1528) re-established his court at Bintang, in the Riau archipelago, but the Malay capital moved constantly between there and various sites on the Johor river because of destructive attacks from the Portuguese (1526, 1536, 1587), Atjeh (1564, 1613, 1623), and Djambi (1673), before finally returning to Bintang (early 18th cent.). As a point of exchange of Chinese goods and the tin, pepper, and spice of the Malay archipelago, Johor–Riau achieved considerable prosperity, especially in the late 16th cent. From the late 17th cent., however, its loosely held Malay dependencies in the peninsula and eastern Sumatra gradually fell away or came under Bugis control. Riau itself was effectively ruled by a Bugis *Raja Muda* (viceroy) from 1721, in recognition of the Bugis' expulsion of Minangkabau invaders.

The sultanate was divided by Raffles, who installed a discarded heir to the throne as Sultan Hussein of Johor (1819), in order to provide a British title to Singapore without directly denying Dutch claims over Riau. This division was recognized by the treaty of London (1824). Riau became a minor Dutch Residency, where the sultanate was eventually abolished (1911). On the mainland the British pensioned Raffles's incompetent protégé, while the more energetic Temenggong family opened Johor to Chinese pepper and gambier farmers. This family's great influence, and good relations with British Singapore, were eventually rewarded with the title Sultan of Johor (1885).

JOINT-STOCK COMPANIES in Britain, business associations in which the common stock or share capital is divided between a group of shareholders. The largest and oldest was the East India Co., founded in 1600 as an offshoot of the Levant Co. After the Restoration (1660) the joint-stock companies were the instruments chosen by the Crown for colonial expansion, *eg*, the East India Co., the Royal African Co. (successor of four previous African companies dating back to 1553), and the Hudson's Bay Co. founded in 1670. In 1662 an act protected shareholders of such companies by limiting their legal liability to the nominal value of their holdings. The companies were able to attract surplus capital from a wide public, often outside the mercantile community. Their monopolistic privileges were often a target for criticism, but without the vast resources necessary for long-distance trading, *eg*, the construction of forts and armed ships to protect their trade, which only the monopolistic joint-stock companies could command, expansion of trade would have been impossible. In 1694 the Bank of England was formed, and by legislation of 1707 and 1708 received a monopoly of joint-stock banking in England. This situation ended in 1826 and 1833, when changes in the law enabled other joint-stock banks to be formed, *eg*, the London and Westminster Bank (1834).

Early in the 18th cent. the companies boomed and by 1717 the share capital of the 12 largest had risen to over £20 million, half of which was the capital of the South Sea Co. (founded 1710). The great financial and speculative crash of the South Sea Bubble (1720) weakened faith in the system of joint-stock companies, though the great trading and insurance companies survived, scarred but fundamentally sound. After 1720 the foundation of joint-stock companies was controlled by the so-called 'Bubble Act', a panic measure resulting from the collapse. It prohibited the formation of new joint-stock companies unless sanctioned by a private act of parliament or a crown charter. It never affected the already established public companies, and the act was readily circumvented by the creation of unincorporate joint-stock associations. It was repealed in 1825. With the reform of the law controlling public companies in the 19th cent., *eg*, the Registration Act (1844), a rapid growth of joint stock companies followed which helped to change the face of Britain, financing such developments as the railways.

W. H. B. Court, *A Concise Economic History of Britain from 1750 to Recent Times* (Cambridge, 1954).
C. Wilson, *England's Apprenticeship, 1603–1763* (London, 1965).   CJ

JOINVILLE, TREATY OF (31 Dec. 1584), secret agreement concluded between Philip II of Spain and the Guises, reviving the Holy League in France. Philip's ambassador, Bernardino de Mendoza, promised Spanish subsidies to bolster the policy of the eradication of Protestantism and the prevention of Henry of Navarre's succession to the French throne.

JOLIET, LOUIS (1645–1700), Canadian-born discoverer of the Mississippi. In May 1673 he and Jacques Marquette set out to navigate the Mississippi past the mouths of the Illinois, Missouri, Ohio, and Arkansas rivers, and established that it flowed south. Joliet made further explorations in Hudson Bay (1679) and on the Labrador coast (1694). He was appointed royal hydrographer and pilot for the St

Lawrence (1690) and the seigneurie of Joliet in Beauce county, Quebec (1697).

JOLIOT-CURIE, FRÉDÉRIC (1900–59), French politician and scientist, who was a student of Paul Langevin and Marie Curie and married the latter's daughter. He and his wife were awarded the Nobel Prize (1935) for their discovery of artificial radioactivity and the fissionable properties of uranium. In the late 1930s he directed the National Centre for Scientific Research. He escaped abroad after the defeat of France (1940) in the Second World War. After the Liberation he sat in the consultative assembly of 1944 and resumed his position at the National Centre for Scientific Research. He also participated in the *conseil du plan*, represented France on the United Nations Atomic Energy Commission, and was a member of the French atomic energy authority. In 1956 he succeeded his wife to the chair of nuclear physics and radioactivity at the Sorbonne.

He was one of the Communist Party's most influential intellectuals. In the 1930s he played a leading part in the League of Anti-Fascist Intellectuals and in the League for the Rights of Man. He joined the Communist Party in 1942 and was dismissed from the atomic energy authority in 1951 after the break-up of *tripartisme*.

JOLY, CLAUDE (1607–1700), French cleric and lawyer, who published (1653) his *Recueil des Maximes*, a bold discussion of the rights of the sovereign and people, in which he expounded an extreme *parlementaire* view of royal authority, asserting that the king was subject to the magistrates in matters of justice and the law.

JOLY DE FLEURY, GUILLAUME (1709–87), French politician, who was a member of one of the most respected *parlementaire* families in Paris. Entering the *parlement* of Paris in 1729, he was *avocat-général* (1731–40) and *procureur-général* (1740–71). In May 1781 he agreed to serve Louis XVI as controller-general of finances in succession to Necker, on condition that he would soon succeed Micromesnil as keeper of the seals. By increasing indirect impositions and levying a third *vingtième* to pay for the American War he provoked widespread opposition from the *parlements* and the court, and was dismissed in March 1783.

JOLY DE FLEURY, GUILLAUME-FRANÇOIS (1675–1756), French magistrate, who was *avocat-général* of the *parlement* of Paris and later proved a worthy successor to d'Aguesseau in the office of *procureur-général* (1717).

JOLY DE LOTBINIÈRE, SIR HENRI GUSTAVE (1829–1908), Canadian politician, who became prime minister of Quebec (1878–9) and minister of inland revenue for Canada (1897–1900) under Sir Wilfred Laurier, and ended his career as lieutenant-governor of BC (1900–6).

JŌMON CULTURE, Japan's first major culture. It derives its name from the distinctive cord pattern (*Jōmon*) which decorates the richly designed and highly artistic pottery of a people that inhabited Japan from at least 3000 BC, and possibly much earlier. They lived mainly by hunting and gathering shellfish, and the refuse in the shell mounds outside their sunken-pit dwellings has left sufficient traces for archaeologists to divide *Jōmon* culture into five phases. It eventually gave way to the *Yayoi* culture, which introduced rice cultivation into Japan (*c.* 300–100 BC).

JOMSBORG, Viking market-town with an attached citadel, now Wollin, on one of the mouths of the Oder. It was founded (*c.* 950) almost certainly by Norsemen, probably in connection with the eastward trade routes to the Norse kingdom of Russia. In later medieval times Jomsborg was thought to have been the home of a legendary band of celibate and highly-disciplined vikings (*Jomsvikings*).

JONAS, JUSTUS (1493–1555), German Protestant reformer, professor at Wittemberg, and friend of Martin Luther, whom he accompanied to Worms (1521). He worked in the reformed church in Saxony as Luther's assistant and preached his funeral sermon (1546).

JONCKHEER, EFRAIM (1917–), Netherlands Antilles politician. He was founder-president of the Democratic Party (1944) in Curaçao, served in the colonial assembly (1945–54), and became prime minister of the Netherland Antilles (1954–68). He was appointed minister plenipotentiary of the Netherlands Antilles at The Hague in 1968.

JONES, ERNEST (1819–69), British Chartist leader, who joined the O'Connorite Chartists in 1846. In 1848 he was imprisoned for two years for advocating the use of force. Jones gave to the Chartists his popular *Chartist Songs* (1846), his oratory, his important *People's Paper* (1852–8), and his extraordinary single-mindedness and self-denial. But he was an advocate of socialism at a time when the British working classes were reluctant to listen and his influence diminished.

JONES, INIGO (1573–1652), English architect, who studied in Italy. He has a significant place in the history of the English theatre as the first designer to use a proscenium arch and the originator of spectacular scenic devices. On a second visit to Italy (1613–14) he studied the work of Palladio and brought the pure Renaissance style into English architecture. He was surveyor of the king's works (1615–40), and built the Queen's House at Greenwich and the Banqueting Hall at Whitehall and laid out the piazza at Covent Garden. In the Civil War he was a royalist and was captured at the siege of Basing House (1645) and fined. Later he rebuilt part of Wilton House for the Earl of Pembroke.

JONES, JOHN PAUL (1747–92), Scots-born naval officer in the service of the American Continental navy. In command of the *Ranger*, he successfully harried English ports and shipping (1777–8) and was given a small squadron. With the ageing *Bonhomme Richard* as his flagship, he attacked a large British convoy off Flamborough Head (23 Sept. 1779), forcing the escorting frigate *Serapis* to surrender. After the war Jones acted variously as an American agent in Paris and a rear-admiral in the Russian navy.

JONES, THOMAS (1870–1955), British civil servant, who was appointed Insurance Commissioner for Wales, probably at the suggestion of Lloyd George, who was also responsible for his appointment to the new cabinet secretariat in 1916. He was assistant secretary, and later deputy secretary to the cabinet, under Hankey, and was largely responsible, with Hankey, for creating the style of a department which had no pre-war precedents on which to base its activities. He had very close relationships with Lloyd George, Bonar Law, and Baldwin, as prime ministers, and exercised considerable influence over them, but was less successful in influencing Ramsay MacDonald. His diaries throw great light on the views and character of all these men, and on the cabinet in action.

JONES, SIR WILLIAM (1746–94), Welsh orientalist, who served as judge of the Supreme Court at Calcutta (1783–94). He founded the Bengal Asiatic Society in 1784 and was president until his death. Although his translation of Kalidasa's *Sakuntala* and other oriental works showed some defects, he was a pioneer who introduced eastern thought and literature, especially Sanskrit, to the west.

JONES LAW (1916) in US, also known as the Philippine Autonomy Act, was intended to reassure the Filipinos of America's intention not to occupy the Philippines permanently. The main intent of the law was to grant all legislative power to the Filipinos, subject only to veto by an appointed American governor-general and in certain cases by the US president. The law gave the people of the Philippines a large control of their domestic affairs as a preparation for their complete independence. It was considered by Filipinos as a compact between the people of both countries on the method of government and sovereignty. The law also stipulated that the governor-general could act in domestic affairs only with the advice of the cabinet, which would be composed of Filipinos, except for the secretary of public instruction, who was also the American vice-governor. These provisions were in keeping with the three major principles embodied in the Jones Law: that the government was to be in the hands of Filipinos as far as possible; that American sovereignty over the Philippines was not to be impaired; and that the US government was to grant independence to the Philippines as soon as a stable government was established.

JONSON, BEN (1572–1637), English dramatist and poet. His principal comedies were *Everyman in his Humour* (1597), *Everyman out of his Humour* (1598), *Volpone* (1606), *The Alchemist* (1610), and *Bartholomew Fair* (1614), all of them combining an idiosyncratic satire with social realism. Jonson also wrote masques for the court, poems and epigrams, and a prose work, *Timber* (publ. 1640). He was a friend of all the principal writers of the day, including Shakespeare, and from 1616, when James I gave him a pension, he was virtually poet laureate.

JORDANES (*fl.* 6th cent.), Gothic priest who wrote a history of the Goths (*The Origin and Exploits of the Goths*), which is almost certainly an abridgement of a lost *History of the Goths* by Cassiodorus (493–526), a Roman noble who was counsellor to the Ostrogothic king of Italy, Theodoric. It is an important and early, though uncritical, account of one group of the Scandinavian peoples who had migrated into Russia and subsequently, in late 4th cent. AD, were driven into the Balkans and western Europe by the Huns.

JOSEPH I (1678–1711), Holy Roman Emperor (*reg.* 1705–11), elder son of Emperor Leopold I and his third wife, Eleanor of Neuburg, who was elected King of the Romans in 1690 and succeeded his father in the Habsburg territories in 1705. At his accession he faced two major threats. In western Europe Austria was engaged, as a member of the Grand Alliance, in the War of the Spanish Succession (1702–13), to oust Louis XIV's grandson, Philip V, from the throne of Spain and to replace him by Joseph's younger brother, Archduke Charles. In eastern Europe, where lands reconquered from the Turks in the preceding 20 years had been settled by Germans of the Habsburg empire, Joseph faced a serious revolt (1704–11), led by Francis Rakoczi, for the independence of Hungary and Transylvania. By 1711 the Hungarian rising had been suppressed, while in the west Prince Eugène won a victory at Turin (1706), Naples was occupied by Count Daun (1707), and with Marlborough, Eugène shared the victories of Oudenarde (1708) and Malplaquet (1709), though Philip V remained firmly established on the Spanish throne. A patron of music and the theatre, Joseph held a brilliant court at Vienna. He carried out useful internal reforms, *eg*, the creation of a new permanent committee of nine officials to control foreign affairs.

JOSEPH II (1741–90), Emperor (*reg.* 1765–90), co-regent from 1765, known as 'the revolutionary emperor' because of his sweeping reforms. He is often regarded as the most sincere and radical, albeit the least successful, of the Enlightened Despots.

In childhood Joseph reacted against the traditional royal education in religion, music, dancing, and hunting, to which he was subjected by his pious mother, preferring mathematics, natural science, and law. Martini, his teacher, was one of the greatest influences upon his life. He also learned to admire the works of the French Enlightenment, especially those of Voltaire.

He was twice married, first to Isabel of Parma, and then (1765), reluctantly, to the ugly Josepha of Bavaria. Both wives died of smallpox, leaving Joseph an embittered widower.

On his father's death, his mother, Maria Theresa, retired from public life and Joseph assumed effective power, though he relied on his chancellor, Kaunitz. He set about making minor financial and social reforms and ceded to the state the large private fortune bequeathed by his father; whereupon Maria Theresa, emerging hastily from seclusion, reassumed control and made Joseph co-regent.

Joseph, influenced by Beccaria and Sonnenfels, drew up a programme of radical reform and also travelled widely— to Bohemia, Italy, Hungary, France, Russia, and the Netherlands. Maria Theresa's death (1780) enabled him to implement his concept of enlightened government. He strove to create a centralized, unified, and efficient bureaucracy for his scattered territories, and in ten years issued 6000 decrees, regulating a multitude of petty matters. He completed the codification of the civil and criminal laws and introduced many legal reforms, *eg*, abolition of the death penalty. Aristocratic privileges and serfdom were also abolished (1781) and education was made compulsory. Emergent capitalism was protected and all taxes equalized on the basis of land (1789), in accordance with Physiocratic ideas. Commercial treaties were entered into with Morocco, Turkey, and Russia and friendship sought with America. Delighting in the suppression of the Jesuits, Joseph aimed at creating a national Church on Febronian principles, granting religious freedom to all churches and reducing the number of monasteries on the grounds of their non-productivity. He also curtailed the power of the pope in his lands and turned the clergy into state officials.

Joseph was determined to assert Habsburg leadership in Germany and to consolidate his hereditary dominions. He tried to engineer Habsburg claims to part of Bavaria (1777) and was thus involved in a short, unsuccessful war with Prussia (1778–9). He agreed with Catherine II to partition the European lands of the Ottoman empire (1781), and planned to exchange the Austrian Netherlands for Bavaria, but dropped this idea when confronted with French and German hostility, voiced through the *Furstenbund*. Austrian hopes of opening the Scheldt were also thwarted by French mediation.

The closing years of his reign saw Joseph reluctantly involved in war with Turkey (1788) and facing a hostile Anglo-Prusso-Dutch combination, as well as insurrections in the Netherlands (1787), Hungary (1789), and the Tyrol (1790). Far from appreciating the enlightenment which prompted his social and administrative reforms, Joseph's subjects bitterly resented interference on rationalist grounds with longstanding traditions.

Saul K. Padover, *The Revolutionary Emperor* (London, 1967).

MKS

JOSEPH I (1714–77), King of Portugal (*reg.* 1750–77). His reign was marked by the complete ascendancy of his chief minister, the Marquis de Pombal. Joseph had neither inclination nor ability for political matters, and after the Lisbon earthquake (1 Nov. 1755) was content to leave the task of government to Pombal, who alone kept his head and organized the country's recovery. Pombal, to whom Joseph gave absolute control, attacked the two forces which obstructed modernization and social change—the nobility and the Society of Jesus. The former tried to overthrow Pombal by attempting to assassinate the king (1758), but the plot failed. Pombal took his revenge on the two leading noble houses and also attacked the Jesuits, who were believed to be implicated in the plot. The order was expelled by royal edict (1759) and the authority of the Inquisition was also broken (1769).

Although Joseph's influence at home was slight, in foreign affairs he continued the tradition of preserving good relations with Britain.

JOSEPH, CHIEF (*c.* 1840–1904), American Indian leader. Upon becoming a chief (1871) of the Nez Percés, Joseph refused to recognize the treaty of 1863, by which his people's rights to the Wallowa valley of OR were surrendered. US troops tried to remove them to the Lapwai Reservation in Idaho (1876) and the Nez Percé resisted. After several battles, Joseph decided to lead his band to Canada and began a march which turned into a running battle over 1700 miles (2740 kms) of OR, ID, and WY, and ended at the battle of Bear Paws in northern MT, 50 miles (80 kms) from Canada. There Joseph surrendered in 1877 and was taken to Fort Leavenworth, KS. After being removed to Indian Territory (1878), he was sent to the Colville Reservation in northern WA (1885). Chief Joseph encouraged his people to seek education and live peaceably.

JOSEPH (*fl.* 17th cent.), patriarch of the Russian church who preceded Nikon, and like him, encouraged Greek scholars to come to Russia as ecclesiastical teachers.

JOSEPH FERDINAND (1692–99), Prince of Bavaria, son of Max Emmanuel, Elector of Bavaria, and his wife, Maria Antonia, daughter of Emperor Leopold I and the Infanta Margaret Theresa, who was the younger daughter of Philip IV of Spain. Although only a child, he was recognized as the rightful claimant to the Spanish throne and empire on the anticipated death of Charles II of Spain, both by the first Partition treaty (Oct. 1698) signed by England, the United Provinces, and France, and by Charles II's will of Nov. 1698, which promised Joseph Ferdinand the entire Spanish possessions. His sudden death in Feb. 1699 added fresh complexities to the Spanish succession question.

JOSEPH, PÈRE, FRANÇOIS LE CLERC DU TREMBLAY (1577–1638), French diplomat, popularly known as the *Eminence Grise*, the friend and mentor of Richelieu. He began his diplomatic career in 1619 and gave Richelieu military advice at the siege of La Rochelle (1628). Acting as a roving ambassador, he went as the French agent to the Diet of Regensburg (Ratisbon) with a brief to negotiate a settlement of the Mantuan succession with Emperor Ferdinand II. The news of Louis XIII's serious illness persuaded him to conclude the peace of Regensburg (13 Oct. 1630), later repudiated by Richelieu in favour of the treaty of Cherasco (1631). However, after intriguing with the Catholic electors, led by Maximilian of Bavaria, Père Joseph engineered the dismissal of the able but unpopular imperial general, Wallenstein (3 Aug. 1630). He reassured Richelieu during political crises, *eg*, 1636, and died consoled by the premature news of the French capture of Breisach (18 Dec. 1638).

JOSEPHINE, Empress (1763–1814), first wife and Queen of Napoleon I, whom she married in 1796 after her first husband, the Vicomte Alexandre Beauharnais, had been executed. The marriage was stormy, partly because of her flagrant infidelities; she was repudiated in 1809 for failing to produce an heir, but continued to influence the emperor until her death.

JOSEPHUS (*c.* AD 37–100), Jewish historian of priestly descent and learned in Jewish law. He commanded the Jewish forces in Galilee in 66–67 and was taken prisoner by the Romans. During the siege of Jerusalem he acted as interpreter to Titus, whom he accompanied to Rome, where he assumed his family name, Flavius, and later received citizenship and a pension. His *Jewish War*, probably written originally in Aramaic, summarizes events from the time of Antiochus IV Epiphanes and provides a largely eye-witness account of the war. His other great work, the *Antiquities of the Jews*, traces the history of the Jews from the creation to the end of the Jewish War.

JOULE, JAMES PRESCOTT (1818–89), English brewer and physicist, who established the equivalence of heat and mechanical energy and performed (1839–49) a multitude of ingenious measurements on the conversion of mechanical (and electrical) energy into heat. He established accurately for the first time that a given amount of mechanical energy always produces the same amount of heat, no matter what means of conversion is used. It was on this work that the basic physical law of the conservation of energy (the first law of thermodynamics) was based. Later Joule worked with William Thomson (Lord Kelvin) on a classic series of delicate experiments to verify predictions of the young science of thermodynamics about the behaviour of expanding gases.

Though he was elected FRS (1850), he never held an academic appointment, remaining a brewer all his life.

JOURNAL DES DÉBATS (1789–1914) was founded in France during the French Revolution by F. J. Baudouin. In the 1840s it supported the policies of Guizot against the Catholic party.

JOURNAL DES SAVANTS in France, literary, philosophical, and scientific weekly, first published in Jan. 1665, which devoted much space to summaries of books and reported the business of the scientific societies. Its editor, Denis de Sallo, fell foul of the *parlement* of Paris and in Feb. 1665 the *Journal* was closed down, though its publication was renewed in 1666.

JOURNÉES (1789), the periodic risings of the Parisian *sans-culottes*, which affected the course of the French Revolution for five years.

JOVANOVIĆ, ARSO (1905–48), Montenegrin soldier and communist political figure, who took the Kremlin's part in the Soviet–Yugoslav dispute of 1948. He joined the Partisans in the Second World War and served as their chief of staff until 1946. When the Yugoslav leadership debated their policy towards the Soviet Union in 1948, he opposed the adoption of an independent course. Allegedly he was shot while attempting to flee Yugoslavia to Rumania.

JOVELLANOS, GASPAR DE (1744–1811), Spanish intellectual and civil servant in the reigns of Charles III and Charles IV, whose career illustrated the gulf between the enlightened paternalism of his generation in Spain and the radicalism of France. Jovellanos was the main inspiration behind a programme of agrarian reform which was the most constructive attempt to deal with the poverty of rural Spain before the 20th cent. His book *Informe* (1795) argued the case for creating a free market in land by abolishing entail and selling Church estates. But Jovellanos was essentially a moderate; he opposed the Inquisition yet remained a devout Catholic. He thwarted Romana's attempted military dictatorship (1808), but advocated the inclusion of a house of lords in the new constitution. The moderate politicians of the 1830s called themselves 'Jovellanistes'.

JOWETT, BENJAMIN (1817–93), British classical scholar, broad churchman, and master of Balliol College, Oxford (1870–93). His prominent part in the 1850s in the reform of the civil service and of Oxford University, his contribution to the controversial *Essays and Reviews* (1860), and his close interest in his pupils, many of whom later became famous, made him a national figure.

JOXE, LOUIS (1901–), French civil servant, diplomat, and politician, who started his political career in 1932 as an undersecretary of state in the ministry of foreign affairs. In 1934 he left the public service to become inspector of foreign services for the *Agence Havas*. In 1942 he was arrested and interned in Algeria because of his pro-Gaullist sympathies. He was released by De Gaulle and became secretary-general of the committee of national liberation (1942–4). In 1944 he became secretary-general in the provisional government and in 1946 director-general for cultural affairs. In 1952 he went to Moscow as ambassador and in 1955 to Bonn. In 1956 he returned to Paris to become secretary general of the French foreign office. Like many other civil servants, he became a politician in the Fifth Republic and was appointed minister of national education and minister in charge of Algerian affairs in 1960. In the latter capacity he conducted the negotiations that resulted in the Evian Agreements (March 1962) and the independence of Algeria. In 1963 he became minister of state and in 1967 minister of justice.

JOYCE, GEORGE (b. 1618), English soldier in Fairfax's horse regiment during the civil wars. In June 1647, when the army and parliament quarrelled, Cornet Joyce's popularity with the soldiers led to his being charged, with Oliver Cromwell's connivance, to bring Charles I from Holmby House to the army's headquarters at Newmarket. After the Restoration (1660) he fled to Rotterdam.

JOYEUSE ENTREE, name given to the Brabantine charter of liberties which, after 1354, regulated the relations between the Dukes of Brabant and their subjects. It arose out of the concessions made by Duke John III to ensure the succession of his daughter Jeanne and her husband, Wenceslas of Luxemburg. It was confirmed by them on their first entry into their capital of Brussels in 1356 (hence the name). It guaranteed the necessity of securing the consent of the estates of Brabant to taxes, war, and other important political decisions. The ill-advised attempt of Emperor Joseph II to abrogate this charter led to the Belgian revolt (1789–90).

JUAN, JORGE (1713–73), and **ANTONIO DE ULLOA** (1716–95), Spanish naval officers who accompanied a French expedition sent to Quito in 1735 to measure an arc of the meridian at the Equator. They remained in South America until 1744, and later wrote the famous *Noticias secretas de América,* a document harshly critical of colonial conditions in general and of the colonial bureaucracy in particular. Although supposedly a confidential report for the Crown only, the manuscript was published in London (1826). Ulloa also published his *Relación histórica del viaje a la América Meridional,* and was later governor of the Huancavelica mercury mine in Peru.

JUAN FERNÁNDEZ ISLANDS, small group of Pacific islands 644 kms off the Chilean coast. These islands, now Chilean, were first discovered by the Spanish explorer Juan Fernández. Alexander Selkirk, a Scottish sailor, was set ashore on the largest island of the group and managed to survive there (1704–9). His account of his life there provided material for Daniel Defoe's *Robinson Crusoe.*

The islands have been in turn a pirates' haunt, a Chilean place of political exile, and a criminal detention centre.

JUAN JOSE OF AUSTRIA, DON (1629–79), Spanish soldier, who was a natural son of Philip IV of Spain by Maria Calderva and governor of the Southern Netherlands. He pursued a military career, suppressing the Catalan revolt (1652), but failing in the battle of the Dunes (1658) and in the reconquest of Portugal (defeated at Amexial, 1663). Excluded from the governing junto of Charles II's minority (1665), he fled to Catalonia (1668), whence he led a successful *coup d'état* to oust the queen mother's Jesuit confessor and political adviser, Father Nithard (1669). Being unable to exploit his success, he allowed the queen mother and her Andalusian favourite, Fernando de Valenzuela, to recover power, until he was recalled by the discontented nobility to head the government (1677), which he led ineffectually until his death.

JUAN YÜAN (1764–1849), Chinese scholar and official and a native of Yangchow, Kiangsu. He was noted for his administrative ability as governor and governor-general of various provinces, although he was criticized for his lenient policy towards foreign traders at Canton (1817–26). He became Grand Secretary in 1835 and was awarded the title of Grand Guardian of the Heir-Apparent in 1838. He was also a noted antiquarian, writer, and compiler, in the fields of classical literature, local history, epigraphy, poetry, and mathematics.

JUAN-JUAN, confederacy of Mongol nomad groups. Arising north of China's great wall during the 5th century, the Juan-juan extended their influence west as far as Turfan. In the middle of the 6th cent. they were overtaken by the T'u-chüeh (Turks), some of their own vassals.

JUÁREZ, BENITO PABLO (1806–72), president of Mexico (1858–62, 1867–71, 1871–2), leader of the opposition to the French intervention (1862–7) and of the struggle for the restoration of the republican form of government. Juárez is regarded in Mexico as the outstanding political personality of the 19th cent. He was born in Guelatao, Oaxaca, of Zapotec origin, and was fortunate to have received some education. He began his career as a lawyer (1832–46), was briefly a member of the federal congress, and became governor of Oaxaca (1847–52). In 1853 he was exiled because of his opposition to Santa Anna in the successful revolt against whom (1855) Juárez played a vital role. He served as minister of justice in the new government formed by Gen. Juan Alvarez.

During his ministry the Juárez Law was promulgated, abolishing ecclesiastical courts and ending the jurisdiction of military courts in civil cases. Juárez was appointed by President Ignacio Comonfort to head the Supreme Court (1857). With the initiation of the War of Reform (1858–60), he became de facto chief executive and operated from Veracruz while the Conservatives held the capital. After the war (1861) Juárez became constitutional president, but was forced to retreat northward by the French invasion (1862–7). Though Maximilian was declared emperor in Mexico City (1864–7), Juárez refused to resign and never ceased to conspire against the French intervention.

As co-ordinator of the anti-French struggle, Juárez supervised the operations that led to the defeat of the French (1867) and ordered the much-criticized execution of Maximilian. The victory of the republic resulted in the election of Juárez to the presidency for two further terms, during which he adopted a strong-handed approach which alienated some of his earlier followers.

Ralph Roeder, *Juárez and His Mexico,* 2 vols (New York, 1947).   HDS

JUBA I (*reg. c.* 60–46 BC), King of Numidia and son of Hiempsal II. He sided with Pompey in the civil war and, after the Pompeians were defeated by Caesar at Thapsus in 46 BC, was rejected by his subjects and, with Scipio and Cato, he committed suicide. His former kingdom became the Roman province of Africa Nova.

JUBA II (*reg.* 25 BC–AD 24), King of Mauretania and son of Juba I. As a child at the time of his father's death, he was taken to Rome and brought up by the sister of Octavius. After being married to Cleopatra Selene, daughter of Anthony and Cleopatra, he was installed by Augustus on the throne of an enlarged Mauretania. Lacking any real power, he devoted himself to study and the embellishment of his kingdom with works of art.

JUBILEES (1887, 1897), in Britain. Queen Victoria's Golden and Diamond jubilees were great national celebrations of the years of progress and prosperity under her rule. The first Jubilee was the occasion of a thanksgiving service at Westminster Abbey attended by princes and representatives from many parts of the world, bonfires blazed from Land's End to the Shetlands, a royal volunteer corps paraded at Buckingham Palace, the army was reviewed at Aldershot, and the navy at Spithead. The first colonial conference was held for prime ministers from the self-governing colonies and was the forerunner of all imperial and commonwealth conferences.

The Diamond Jubilee was celebrated enthusiastically with genuine popular affection for the queen, the symbol of the age. The colonial conference was attended by prime ministers of 11 colonies, but Joseph Chamberlain failed to secure practical agreement on closer unity for the empire. Rudyard Kipling sounded a warning note of humility at this apogee of imperialism in his 'Recessional'.

JUDAH, southern part of Israel, which became independent in *c*. 922 BC. Judah came under Assyrian and later Babylonian control, and Nebuchadrezzar II destroyed Jerusalem and deported many of its people to Babylon (586). It subsequently came under Persian, Greek, and Roman rule and under the latter the Jews were gradually dispersed throughout the empire and the country was renamed Palestine.

JUDAR PASHA (d. 1603), eunuch from Las Cuevas in Granada, brought up at the Sa'dian court in Marrakesh. He was granted the rank of pasha by Sultan Ahmad al-Mansur and put in charge of a small force sent to overthrow the Askias of Songhay (1591). With 4000 men, many of Spanish origin, he crossed the Sahara and defeated Askia Ishaq II's forces at Tondibi, thanks largely to the possession of firearms. He was first Pasha of Timbuctoo and, though later dismissed, remained loyal to the sultan till his triumphal return to Marrakesh (1599) with a rich caravan of booty.

JUDICIAL REVIEW in the US, procedure allowing the examination or review by the courts, in cases actually before them, of legislative statutes and executive or administrative acts. It consists essentially of two types of review, sometimes known as 'pure' and 'federal' judicial review. The former involves the power of federal courts to decide whether or not actions of organs of the national government are consistent with the US Constitution, and so declare such actions valid or invalid. The latter involves both the power of the courts to review state government actions and invalidate them if they conflict with the US Constitution, and the power of the US Supreme Court to review and, if necessary, over-rule state court decisions as being inconsistent with the US Constitution, which is 'the supreme law of the land' (Article 6, Section 2). Of less significance is the power of state courts to invalidate state legislation in conflict with the constitution of that state.

Although not specifically embodied in the US Constitution, judicial review was fundamentally an outgrowth of colonial and Revolutionary political philosophy, attaining recognition in several state cases between 1778 and 1787. The doctrine was not, however, universally accepted in the Revolutionary era, since it seemed to be in direct conflict with the notion of legislative ascendancy. The 1789 Judiciary Act recognized that federal judicial review was implicit in the judicial articles of the US Constitution and in the creation of a federal system, Section 25 providing for appeals from state courts to the federal judiciary in particular circumstances. Pure judicial review was not specifically recognized in this legislation, and was not asserted firmly by the US Supreme Court until *Marbury v. Madison* (1803), when Chief Justice Marshall, in declaring a section of the 1789 Judiciary Act unconstitutional, asserted that it is 'emphatically the province and duty of the judicial department to say what the law is'.

Federal judicial review was also extended when the US Supreme Court, under Chief Justice Marshall, declared an act of a state legislature to be in conflict with the Constitution in *Fletcher v. Peck* (1810), and affirmed the right of the Supreme Court to review judgments of state courts if a national constitutional issue is involved, as in *Martin v. Hunters Lessee* (1816) and *Cohens v. Virginia* (1821).

After *Marbury v. Madison* the court did not again declare an act of Congress unconstitutional until the Dred Scott case (1857). In the post-Civil War period a number of state statutes were invalidated, and in the period 1890–1937 a large number of federal laws were declared unconstitutional, especially during the early years of the New Deal. Since 1937 the court has been reluctant to challenge national statutes directly, though not executive or administrative actions. State courts have also exercised the power of judicial review, but the relative ease in amending most state constitutions has made this less frequent and less significant.

R. K. Carr, *The Supreme Court and Judicial Review* (New York, 1942).
H. E. Dean, *Judicial Review and Democracy* (New York, 1966). JDL

JUDICIARY ACTS (1789, 1801, 1914) in US, legislation in compliance with Article 3 of the US Constitution. The 1789 Judiciary Act created a federal court structure and defined the jurisdiction of the various courts. Section 25 of the act provided for appeals from state courts to the federal judiciary in certain cases, a provision of major significance in the development of the federal system.

The 1801 act, a Federalist party attempt to retain control of the federal judiciary, created new district and circuit courts and ended circuit-riding by Supreme Court justices. The Jeffersonians repealed the act and passed a new Circuit Court Act (1802), re-establishing six circuit courts and reviving participation by Supreme Court justices.

The 1914 Judiciary Act, a moderate response to Progressive demands for the recall of judges and of judicial decisions on constitutional matters, increased the opportunity to appeal state court decisions to the Supreme Court. The 1925 Judiciary Act gave the Supreme Court increased authority to reject certain cases, requiring that petitions for writs of *certiorari* to affirm lower court decisions be granted on the affirmative vote of at least four justices.

JUGURTHA (*reg.* 118–105 BC), King of Numidia and grandson of Massinissa. He was the illegitimate son of Mastanabal and, after his father's death, he was educated and finally adopted by his uncle, Micipsa. On the latter's death he first shared the kingdom with Micipsa's two sons, Hiempsal I and Adherbal, but later succeeded in killing them both, thus provoking the armed intervention of Rome. He at first obtained the support of Bocchus I, King of Mauretania, but was finally delivered by him into the hands of the Romans and, after being paraded in triumph, was strangled.

JUGURTHINE WAR (111–105 BC), fought by Rome against Jugurtha of Numidia, who attempted (118) to take over the kingdom by murdering one rival and attacking another, who appealed to Rome. The Senate tried to avoid warfare by sending commissions which Jugurtha flouted. Political agitation and Jugurtha's massacre of Italian traders at Cirta (112) resulted in a declaration of war. A series of defeats caused widespread discontent with senatorial leadership, which was not allayed by the successes of Q. Caecilius Metellus, who deprived Jugurtha of eastern and central Numidia (109–108), and Marius was given the command by popular vote (107). Jugurtha was defeated near Cirta (106), then betrayed by his father-in-law and ally, Bocchus of Mauretania, taken as prisoner to Rome, and murdered.

JUIN, ALPHONSE (1888–1967), French soldier and marshal of France (1952). He fought in Morocco (1912–14), and on the Western Front in the First World War, where he was seriously wounded. After a short spell at the war college he went to Morocco and served as Lyautey's chief of staff.

During the Second World War he covered the retreat to Dunkirk, then became commander-in-chief of the Vichy forces in North Africa. After the Allied landings (1942) he joined de Gaulle and served in Italy. After the war he was appointed resident-general in Morocco (1947–51). He then commanded the Central European sector of NATO forces (1951–56).

He repeatedly and publicly criticized the governments

which he served as chief military adviser. His outspoken criticism of the European defence community in 1954 (when the French government was seeking its ratification) led to his dismissal. He welcomed De Gaulle's return to power, but soon took to criticizing his Algerian policy.

JULIA (1) (d. 54 BC), daughter of Julius Caesar by Cornelia, married Pompey (59), as a sign of her father's political alliance.

JULIA (2) (39 BC–AD 14), only child of the Roman emperor Augustus, who married her to various potential successors, her cousin Marcellus (25 BC), M. Vipsanius Agrippa (21), and the future Emperor Tiberius (12). In 2 BC Augustus accused her of immorality and banished her to the island of Pandateria, where she died.

JULIA DOMNA AUGUSTA (d. AD 217), wife of the Roman emperor Septimius Severus and mother of Caracalla and Geta. She was the first of the Syrian empresses to exercise political influence under the Severan dynasty (193–235).

JULIA MAESA AUGUSTA (d. AD 226), sister of Julia Domna, was instrumental in the proclamation of her grandson Elagabalus as Roman emperor (218). She was also implicated in his assassination and in the accession of Alexander Severus (222).

JULIA MAMAEA AUGUSTA (d. AD 235), cousin of the Roman emperor Caracalla and daughter of the powerful Julia Maesa, herself influential in persuading the Emperor Elagabalus to adopt her own son Alexianus, in frustrating Elagabalus' plots against him, and in making him emperor, as Alexander Severus, after Elagabalus' assassination (222). She remained powerful throughout her son's reign and accompanied him on expeditions to the east (231–3) and to the Rhine (233–5). But her influence was resented by the army and she and her son were murdered by the supporters of Maximinus.

JULIAN (reg. AD 361–3) (Fl. Claudius Julianus, 'The Apostate'), Roman Emperor, who was appointed Caesar in Gaul by his father, Constantius II, but rebelled against him. He became emperor after Constantius' premature death. He reformed the administration and, openly revealing his pagan beliefs, took indirect measures against Christianity, but died during a campaign against Persia before any long-term effects could be felt. Julian was the author of numerous works which have survived or can be reconstructed, in particular a neo-platonic hymn to the gods, a diatribe against the Christians, and speeches and letters which are of great interest for the events and thought of his time. Although a successful general, he was inclined to impulsiveness and over-ambition, as on his Persian campaign; and his austere personal tastes were regarded by many as unsuitable for the dignity of the imperial position. He was succeeded by Jovian.

JÜLICH-BERG, fragmentary secular duchy of the Holy Roman empire, straddling the lower Rhine near the Netherlands, originally two separate counties which rose to importance in the 13th–14th cents. They were joined in 1423, when Duke Adolf of Berg acquired Jülich, and were later linked with the principalities of Cleves, Mark and Ravensburg, when Duke John III of Cleves inherited Julich and Berg (1511) through his marriage with Mary, daughter of William IV of Jülich and Berg. His heirs reigned until 1609, when Jülich-Berg was inherited by the Protestant Counts Palatine of Neuburg. On this occasion the duchy became the centre of a succession dispute and almost a *casus belli* between the Protestant and Catholic powers of Europe. Peace was preserved after the death of Henry IV of France, and the treaty of Xanten (1614) confirmed the now Catholic duke, Wolfgang William of Neuburg, in possession of Jülich-

Berg, while Cleves, Mark, and Ravensburg devolved upon the Hohenzollerns of Brandenburg.

During the 17th cent. Jülich-Berg was occupied by the Spaniards in the Thirty Years War and ravaged by the French in Louis XIV's wars of 1672–89. In 1690 the two principalities were linked with the palatinate, when the Elector John William, of the house of Neuburg, became Duke of Jülich-Berg (1690–1716), and their chief function as a valuable recruitment ground for the palatine armies emerged during the War of the Spanish Succession. The elector and his successor, Charles Philip, ruled Jülich-Berg from the palatinate as absolute princes on the Brandenburg pattern.

Another succession crisis loomed when the Hohenzollern Frederick William I, in anticipation of the extinction of the Neuburg line, sought imperial guarantees for his claim to Jülich-Berg (1725–7, 1738). When the house of Neuberg died out in 1742, however, the duchy came into the possession of Charles Theodore, of Pfalz-Sulzbach, elector palatine (reg. 1742–99), who also succeeded to the electoral throne of Bavaria in 1777. On his death in 1799, Jülich-Berg, as a small part of the greater palatine–Bavarian inheritance, passed to the Wittelsbach, Maximilian Joseph I. Over-run by Napoleon's armies, Jülich on the west bank of the Rhine was absorbed into France, while Berg on the east bank was later incorporated into the Confederation of the Rhine (1806). At the Vienna settlement (1815) the former duchies were part of the Rhineland territories awarded to Prussia, and became part of the North German Confederation (1866) and Bismarck's German *Reich* (1871).

F. L. Carsten, *Princes and Parliaments in Germany* (Oxford, 1959). MKS

JULIUS II (1443–1513), Pope (reg. 1503–13). Lacking the true spirituality for his calling, but a soldier, diplomat, and politician of forceful personality, he succeeded in restoring papal authority in central Italy by balancing the interests of France and the empire. After securing the imprisonment of Cesare Borgia, he personally led his troops against Perugia (1506) and then Bologna (1507). His next objective was the secular republic of Venice, against whom he built up the League of Cambrai (1508), joining the alliance later to recover the former papal cities of the Romagna (1509).

After the suppression of Venice, he made peace (Feb. 1510) to concentrate on checking France, whose power was established in northern Italy. Julius imprisoned a French cardinal in the dungeons of Sant' Angelo, which caused Louis XII to retaliate by summoning a general council at Pisa (1 Sept. 1511), thus reviving the challenge of the conciliar movement. The pope's response was to call the Fifth Lateran Council to meet under his leadership in April 1512. In addition, Julius had negotiated the anti-French Holy League, whose Swiss mercenaries drove the French from Milan (Novara, 1513).

Julius was also a noted patron of the arts. Bramante was his choice of architect for the reconstruction of St Peter's. Michelangelo was commissioned to sculpt the tomb which was to be his lasting memorial, but the ceiling of the Sistine Chapel, also the work of Michelangelo, and Raphael's frescoes in the pope's private apartments, are perhaps the greatest tributes to his patronage.

JULIUS III (1487–1555), Pope (reg. 1550–5), who was papal legate during the 1st period of the Council of Trent (1545–7). Professing a desire for peace, but in reality playing the traditional game of power politics to uphold the papacy's independence, he was responsible for the recall of the council for a second session at Trent (1551–2).

JULIUS CAESAR, C. (100–44 BC), Roman dictator, whose victory in the Civil War (49–45) effectively ended Republican government. He was born into an impoverished and politically obscure branch of a Patrician family, and his ruling passion throughout his life was the assertion of his personal prestige and power. His early career was devoted to winning popular favour, and in the sixties he was associated with Crassus in a number of abortive propaganda demonstrations appealing to the classes, which had suffered under Sulla's regime, and he was suspected of involvement in Catiline's conspiracy. He was quaestor (69), aedile (65), and in 63 was elected pontifex maximus despite competition from the two most senior members of the Senate. He was praetor in 62 and governed Further Spain (61) with some success. On his return he was opposed by Cato and his faction, and formed the First Triumvirate with Pompey and Crassus. He was elected consul for 59, when he secured by violent means the passage of measures in favour of his two associates and secured for himself the command in Gaul, which he subdued during the next nine years. The alliance with Pompey and Crassus was renewed at Lucca (55) and Caesar's Gallic command prolonged for a further five years. But the deaths of Julia, Pompey's wife and Caesar's daughter (54), and of Crassus (53) broke the alliance and Pompey joined Cato and his faction, who out-manœuvred Caesar politically. To maintain his power and prestige he invaded Italy (49), defeated Pompey at Pharsalus (48), and the remnants of the Republican forces in Africa (47–46) and Spain (45). In 46 he became dictator for ten years and in 44 for life and passed a number of measures of reform. His rule was popular with the people, but he was assassinated (15 March 44) by an aristocratic conspiracy led by Brutus and Cassius. Though he was an accomplished orator and an artful stylist, his political flair and generalship have generally been over-rated.

M. Gelzer, *Caesar, Politician and Statesman*, tr. by P. Needham (Oxford, 1968).   DCE

JULIUS, SIR GEORGE ALFRED (1873–1946), English-born consulting engineer, who worked in Australia. He invented the automatic totalizator for racing tracks and was foundation chairman of the Commonwealth Council for Scientific and Industrial Research (1926–45).

JULY EDICT (1561) in France, royal ordinance issued in answer to the Huguenots' petition for toleration (June 1561). It was the work of the chancellor l'Hôpital, and laid down tentative terms for the maintenance of religious peace and the repression of civil unrest and gave the Huguenots qualified toleration, until it was superseded by the Edict of St Germain.

JULY MONARCHY (1830–48), Orleanist monarchy which was created as a result of the July Revolution. The revolution itself was largely the work of Bonapartists, republicans, and discontented liberals and the rather conservative July monarchy was foisted on Paris by the politicians. It has been described as the rule of the financiers or of the *grande bourgeoisie*, but, as its name suggests, it lacked precise social characteristics and drew its support where it could find it, mainly from the landed and official classes.

Its institutions were little different from those of the Restoration, although the franchise was extended, the hereditary status of peers abolished, and the constitutional position of the monarchy clarified by revision of the charter. Few measures were taken against the partisans of the old monarchy, who, except for the demonstration at St Germain l'Auxerrois (1831) and the attempt of the Duchess of Berri to raise a revolt in the Vendée (1832), caused little trouble to the new regime. The major opposition came from the left, which inspired a series of plots and minor risings in Paris and the provinces. To combat this, the king called in Casimir Périer, who dealt firmly with the Lyons *canuts* and also helped to deal with the Belgian crisis (1831). The challenge from the left was finally mastered by savage repression in Lyons and Paris (1834), although Bonapartists and republicans continued to conspire and there were several attempts on the king's life.

Périer's death was followed by a period of ministerial instability, caused partly by the king's dislike of authoritarian ministers and partly by the growth of a new internal opposition. After a number of experiments, including the ministry of Thiers, who led the country to the brink of war over Egypt (1840), Louis Philippe secured a conservative ministry under Soult and Guizot (1840) with which he could work in harmony. Profiting by the growth of prosperity and a rather cynical manipulation of elections, the regime established itself, encountering no real problems except over education, and even gaining a certain amount of popularity over the Spanish marriages (1845). Nevertheless, the combination of an economic depression with a campaign for parliamentary reform produced an inflammable situation which the regime proved unable to deal with. The July monarchy has been harshly judged by some historians, but it saw the development of industrialization, and parliamentary life, and avoided diplomatic entanglements. Its great failing was its refusal to face up to the social problem.

E. L. Woodward, *French Revolutions* (London, 1934; reprinted, 1962).   CHC

JULY PLOT (1944), to assassinate Hitler and form an anti-Nazi government, was mainly the work of the military resistance in Germany and included men like Beck, Witzleben, Stülpnagel, Rommel, Tresckow, and Olbricht. The attempt was made only after lengthy planning and was carried out on 20 July 1944 by Klaus Schenk von Stauffenberg, a young officer long active in the resistance, who planted a bomb in a conference room in Hitler's headquarters at Rastenberg. Owing to a series of unpredictable accidents, the attempt failed literally by a hair's breadth, for although several of the conference participants were killed, Hitler himself escaped with only light injuries. Stauffenberg, however, assuming that Hitler had in fact been killed, gave his colleagues in Berlin the signal for proceeding with the coup. In various centres in Germany and abroad the opposition, working with regular troops, began to organize the arrest of leading SS and NSDAP officials and the take-over of the machinery of government. But the coup was doomed as soon as communications between Hitler's headquarters and the outside world had been restored and it was known that he had survived, for this rallied the wavering loyalties of many key officers. One of these, Gen. Fromm, was released from the rebels' captivity in Berlin by a squad of loyalist soldiers, and initiated counter-measures. He ordered the summary execution of five of the ringleaders, including Stauffenberg, and in Berlin and elsewhere Nazi control was quickly re-established. By the same evening Hitler had broadcast a speech over the radio, and the plot had more or less collapsed.

The vengeance that was wreaked was severe even by Nazi standards. A Gestapo commission undertook a wide-ranging investigation into the plot, and between July 1944 and the end of the war thousands of people with little or no connection with it had been executed after trials that were a mockery of justice, or had simply been thrown into concentration camps, murdered, or driven to suicide.

The failure of the July Plot effectively wiped out the German resistance. Had it been successful, the coup might well have come off too, as the example of the smooth take-over of power by the conspirators in Paris suggests. The plot had the support of a large number of key army officers and well-known conservative political figures, who had mainly been won over to the cause by their desperate concern at Hitler's disastrous conduct of the war. However, behind this important but somewhat equivocal leadership, there stood the mass of socialist, communist, and Christian opponents of Nazism, whose resistance had begun long before the Second World War and the threat of defeat, and derived from a more profound and sincere hatred of Nazism than many of the disgruntled officers could claim.

H.-A. Jacobsen, *July 20 1944: the German opposition to Hitler as viewed by foreign historians* (Bonn, 1969).
T. Prittie, *Germans against Hitler* (London, 1964).   AJC

JUNE DAYS (1848), episode in the French Revolution of 1848, in which the working-class radicals were crushed by the army and the National Guard. The events resulted from the desire of Falloux and the Assembly to close down the National Workshops—which were regarded as an expensive communist innovation—although they supported a third of the adult male population of Paris. There was agitation throughout June, when the National Guard was permanently mobilized, and the final confrontation, desired by both sides, came on Friday 23 June, after the Assembly had ordered the dissolution of the Workshops, offering the workers the alternatives of joining the army or undertaking forced labour.

Barricades went up all over the eastern sections of Paris, but Cavaignac and the government forces were slow to act, partly because he hoped to allow the rebels to expose themselves and make it possible to crush them. Cavaignac sent out three columns on the Friday evening, but they made little progress save in the north of the city. The heaviest fighting came on the Saturday, where Lamorcière in the north came under heavy pressure, which was relieved by National Guard from the provinces, who showed a keen desire to deal with the 'reds'. The politicians were alarmed by the lack of progress, but Cavaignac secured full powers and declared a state of siege. By Sunday the rebels were surrounded in a gradually decreasing area in the east of Paris, and their misfortunes were compounded by their failure to co-ordinate their actions or to counter-attack when they had repulsed an assault on the barricades. Fighting grew fiercer and fires broke out as Lamorcière and the other commanders pressed forward, and while some workers fought to the death, others capitulated. The last vestiges of resistance were extinguished on the Monday by the indiscriminate shooting of some 3000 prisoners. The government forces lost some 5500 killed and wounded; how many insurgents perished is not known, but at least 9000 were killed in the fighting, more were massacred, and some 4000 were deported. These repressive measures made a considerable impact on popular opinion and embittered class relations for generations.

P. Robertson, *Revolutions of 1848, a social history* (New York, 1965). CHC

JUNG BAHADUR (1816–77), prime minister of Nepal in 1845. He sent a force of Gurkhas to the support of the British in the 1857 Mutiny.

JUNÍN, BATTLE OF (6 Aug. 1824), initial encounter in the successful campaign of Antonio José de Sucre to dislodge Spanish royalist forces from the Peruvian highlands. Sucre's victory at Junín paved the way for the final battle of Ayacucho (9 Dec.), which assured Peruvian and Bolivian independence.

JUNIUS, LETTERS OF (1768–72), appeared in the English press attacking Grafton's administration in terms which indicated both rancour and inside knowledge of the political and fashionable world. The identity of the author is still unknown but he has been variously identified with Edmund Burke, John Wilkes, George Grenville, and others, the two most likely candidates being Philip Francis and Lord Shelburne.

The Letters at first appeared anonymously, and the first to be signed with the name of Junius appeared in Nov. 1768. The writer attacked not only the policies, but the private lives of ministers. He supported Wilkes over the Middlesex election, but advocated strong action against the American colonists. Junius showed a particular hatred of Grafton, Bedford, Sir William Blackstone, and Lord Mansfield. His chief importance lay in his convincing the politically influential classes that Grafton was a threat to liberty at home and to pre-eminence abroad.

The arguments in favour of the authorship of Francis are largely circumstantial. He was a school-fellow of Henry Sampson Woodfall, later the publisher of the Letters. Moreover, his post as a clerk at the war office gave him access to information which Junius certainly possessed. A letter to Wilkes seems to show that he had seen a paper which was in Francis's desk at the time, and he was angry at the latter's enforced resignation. Junius's silences correspond roughly with Francis's absences and there is some similarity of handwriting. Francis did not directly deny authorship, which was supposedly revealed by the publication of Taylor's *Discovery of Junius* (1813) and *Junius Identified* (1816), and he left a copy of Junius's collected letters sealed up for his wife after his death.

Against the identification of Francis as Junius may be reckoned the lack of wit and polemical talent in his other writings. Shelburne showed more intellectual ability and had inside knowledge of the administration. Moreover, Junius began to write soon after Shelburne had been forced out of the cabinet on the insistence of the king and the Bedford party, and the letters coincide with his known views.

C. W. Everett, *The Letters of Junius* (London, 1927).

VEC

JUNKER GEORG, pseudonym of Martin Luther, when he set aside his Augustinian habit and dressed as a bearded knight, while in hiding from the imperial authorities at Wartburg castle (1521–2).

JUNKER PARLIAMENT (1848) in Prussia, nickname given by its liberal opponents to a meeting held in Berlin by the Association for the Protection of Property and the Advancement of the Welfare of All Classes. Its purpose was to prepare counter-measures against the government's proposals to end the tax exemption of the nobility and the manorial obligations of their tenants. It consisted of Junker noblemen, who had already founded a newspaper, the *Neue Preussische Zeitung*, generally known as the '*Kreuzzeitung*'. The association successfully bid for the support of the lower classes against the liberals.

JUNKERS, East German landowning nobility, who, in the wake of a series of wars, *eg*, Thirty Years War, Northern War, Seven Years War, in the 17th–18th cents consolidated their demesne farms into vast estates and reduced the once free peasantry of the lands east of the Elbe to serfdom (*Gutsherrschaft*). In the 19th cent. the power of this class, unshaken by the liberal revolts of 1848–9, was enshrined in the constitution of Bismarck's German Reich (1871).

JUNOT, JEAN ANDOCHE, Duc d'Abrantes (1771–1813), French general, who acted as Napoleon's commander in Portugal, where he was beaten by Wellesley at Vimiero (1808).

JUNTA, Spanish term meaning council, committee, or conference which, in Spanish-speaking countries, has come to mean collective government, usually of a nation, by a few individuals working in concert. Typically, a national junta will consist of about four military officers who have seized power, and who will attempt to govern together until a leader emerges.

JUNTO, THE WHIG in England, group of leading politicians who represented the most important element in the Whig party after 1688, and in Queen Anne's reign supplied the party with much of its driving force and organization. Although the group as such had existed before 1696, it was then that the term 'Junto' was first applied to them. Previously they had been known as 'Court Whigs' or 'Modern Whigs'. In 1696 the Junto consisted of four of the ablest and most ambitious Whigs in parliament; *eg*, Sir John Somers, Charles Montague (later Lord Halifax), Lord Thomas Wharton, and Edward Russell, Earl of Orford. In 1702 the Junto lords were joined by the Earl of Sunderland. Of the five, only Orford and Wharton had had a serious role in politics before the 1688 Revolution.

The unsuccessful attempt to impeach Somers, Halifax, and Orford in 1701 for their part in the conclusion of the partition treaties testifies to the importance which their opponents placed on them. Yet their significance to the Whig party has been exaggerated, for they did not dominate the whole parliamentary party. The Junto did, however, lead the largest and most disciplined of the Whig groups in the Commons, and during Anne's reign had the firm support of a majority of Whig peers.

Though neither drawn together by compatible personalities, nor united by kinship, the Junto shared a strength of principles, an outstanding sense of loyalty, and a mutual quest for power virtually unknown outside their circle. Disagreements, however, were far from uncommon, and they sometimes did not act politically as a coherent group, eg, when forced out of office (1699–1700), they resigned individually.

Their exceptional loyalty to their followers and their regard for party ties gave them a considerable cohesive force which was further cemented by their various individual and complementary talents. Somers, the leading figure of the Junto, was the most distinguished lawyer of his age, possessing the sharpest intellect in the party, and his integrity and moral strength were widely acknowledged. Halifax, though the least reliable because of his restless ambition, was a superb debater with an unequalled grasp of financial affairs. Orford, while ceasing to be an active parliamentarian under Anne, provided a large personal following in the Commons from among naval officers and admiralty officials. He also gave the Junto the benefit of his unrivalled personal naval experience. Sunderland, despite his occasional indiscretions, brought to his task of parliamentary management an unfailing energy and zeal. Being the son-in-law of the Duke of Marlborough, he had valuable political connections. Wharton had a reputation as the unrivalled master of the art of electioneering and had the large personal fortune necessary to pursue the art, a fortune which he unquestioningly exhausted in the interest of the 'honest party'.

The Junto lords, working as closely in parliament as out of it, displayed unprecedented skill in electoral and parliamentary management. They went further than anyone else towards solving the main problems facing party leaders in Anne's reign: those of getting their supporters to attend parliament, and then of persuading them to endorse their policies.

G. S. Holmes, *British Politics in the Age of Anne* (London, 1967).
J. H. Plumb, *The Growth of Political Stability in England 1675–1725* (London, 1967). CJ

JUNTO CLUB, a mutual improvement society organized (1727) in Philadelphia by Benjamin Franklin. Originally organized for artisans, it came to have an important cultural influence. It founded the first public library in America (1731).

JURANTS (1712) in Scotland, members of the Scottish kirk who accepted the oath of allegiance to the reigning British monarch imposed by the 1712 Toleration Act in Scotland. The act threatened to bring about a schism between the jurants and the non-jurants until a modified oath was introduced in 1719.

JURIEU, PIERRE (1637–1713), French Huguenot theologian and polemicist, who was professor of Hebrew at Sedan (1674–81), before fleeing to the United Provinces to escape persecution for his *Politique du clergé de France* (1681). There he wrote innumerable religious and political works, attacking the religious policy of Bossuet and the scepticism of Bayle. In *Les vœux d'un patriot* (1688) he produced a critical history of Louis XIV's government.

JURISDICTIONS in Brandenburg, grant of legal right to exercise authority on civil and criminal matters in the first instance and to receive fines and services, through which the Brandenburg rulers allied themselves to the Junker class while the latter acquired greater authority over the peasantry.

JUROS in Spain, originally annuities granted by the Spanish Crown out of state revenues as a token of favour. They were used by Ferdinand and Isabella as a means of raising loans to finance the Granada war (1481–92). Under Charles V (1519–56) the practice of issuing these state bonds at stated interest rates developed so rapidly that it created a *rentier* class in Castile and had highly inflationary consequences. By the end (1598) of Philip II's reign the *juros* had virtually been transformed into a consolidated debt. In the 17th cent. they were used as the basis of forced loans by a financially bankrupt crown.

JUSSIEU, DE, BROTHERS, eminent 18th-cent. botanists who also practised medicine. The eldest brother, Antoine (1686–1758) and the second brother Bernard (1699–1777), were associated with the Jardin des Plantes in Paris and wrote many scientific works. The youngest, Joseph de Jussieu (1704–79), went to Peru and travelled widely in South America for 36 years.

JUSSIEU, ANTOINE LAURENT DE (1748–1836), French botanist, who was director of the Paris Jardin des Plantes. His *Genera Plantarum* used a system of classification that was neither based upon the Aristotelian system of habit, nor upon an artificial type such as Linnaeus's, but upon a 'natural' system. It was so in the sense that it reflects his understanding of nature at a time when a flood of new plants was appearing, needing to be named and classified, from many parts of the world. De Jussieu's classification was based mainly upon floral characters, grouped into 100 'ordines naturales', many of which are accepted as intact families of plants in 20th-cent. botany.

JUSTI, JOHANN HEINRICH VON (1705–71), Austrian minister of public works under Maria Theresa, and one of the chief exponents of Cameralism.

JUSTICE PARTY, 'non-Brahman' political organization in Madras, founded (1916) as the South Indian Liberal Federation, but known as the Justice Party after its English-language newspaper, *Justice* (founded 1917). It was a successful attempt by the landowning and mercantile 'non-Brahman' castes to exploit the idea of an oppressed 'non-Brahman' community in order to get special treatment in representative political institutions and in government employment. This meant opposition to nationalist agitation for reforms, which were represented as Brahman attempts to secure control in a self-governing Madras, together with a campaign for communal representation for 'non-Brahmans'. The 'non-Brahmans' were able to control the Madras legislature from 1921 to 1926 and to secure privileges for 'non-Brahmans' in employment. Increased Congress efforts to attract 'non-Brahman' support, together with growing conflict between the heterogeneous collection of castes which made up the 'community', eroded Justice Party support by the time of the 1926 elections and the party lost its majority. It was still further weakened by the formation of the Tamil-oriented 'Self-Respect Movement' led by E. V. Ramaswamy Naicker (1879–), which set out to mobilize lower-caste and untouchable 'non-Brahmans'. There were later Justice Party ministries (1930–6) while Congress remained outside the legislature, but these were much less effective. Naicker gave the almost moribund party new life when he became president (1938) and made it the basis for his campaign for an autonomous south Indian federation (*Dravidisthan*). In 1944 he and C. N. Annadurai renamed it the *Dravida Khazagam* (Dravidian Federation).

JUSTICES ITINERANT, also justices in eyre (Old French from the Latin *iter* = journey), they appear first in the only usrviving Pipe Roll (1130) of King Henry I of England. They did not become a regular feature of the English legal and judicial system until 1166. From that year they appeared, with scarcely an exception, annually. Under Richard I and John their visitations were less regular. They ceased altogether between 1209 and 1218 and thereafter were normally septennial. The realm was divided into a number of circuits, each visited by a group of justices whose original function was to deal with judicial and financial matters at full meetings of the county courts and in particular to expedite the hearing of cases and to keep a close eye on sheriffs and other local officials—indeed, after 1194 sheriffs were forbidden to sit on the eyre in their own counties. In time the 'articles of the eyre' came to include all matters concerning the king's interests.

JUSTICES OF THE PEACE in England, local magistrates, who in the first instance were simply guardians of the peace, being responsible for law and order, but they soon became burdened, mainly during the 16th cent., with a succession of other functions which made them the pivot of all local government. The institution can be traced back to the late 12th cent., when Hubert Walter, the justiciar of England, required certain knights in the counties of England to assist in the keeping of the royal peace. An act of 1327 gave statutory sanction to an existing system whereby the men designated to execute the law were local knights and gentry, who might be expected to command respect in their localities. A statute of 1361 transformed simple keepers into 'justices of the peace' by the permanent extension of their powers, giving them definite authority to determine felonies and trespasses. The authority of the JPs was gradually extended beyond criminal matters to cover economic and administrative affairs. By the end of Elizabeth I's reign they were the chief institution of local government in the counties, with 309 statutes referring to them, eg a 1531 act put the whole burden for the administration of the poor law on JPs. The formal qualifications of the JPs, who were appointed by the lord chancellor, had been settled in the Middle Ages. They had to be the most sufficient knights, esquires, and gentlemen of the land, were not to be in the service of another, had to be resident in their counties, and had to hold lands of a minimum value of £20 per annum (the property qualification for knighthood). No legal expertise was required, though many JPs were either barristers or had spent some time at the Inns of Court. The office, though virtually unpaid and voluntary, attracted the most important landowners because of the rewards of power and local prestige it conferred.

The main duty of the JP remained the enforcement of the criminal law by powers derived from the commission of the peace, which was revised in 1590 to give JPs a general authority to enforce all statutes and ordinances for keeping the peace, while it also conferred jurisdiction over all crimes except treason and gave powers to try such crimes on indictment. In practice, virtually all serious crime, from murder downwards, was the concern of the JPs. They were also supposed to carry out certain socio-economic functions, eg, supervision of the maintenance of highways, enforcement of recusancy laws, regulation of wages and prices in times of dearth, and control of the apprentice system. The system in general was brutally inefficient, but it did work in one major respect. Because the JPs came from the classes that benefited from law enforcement, it united the gentry in serving the Tudor regime in its pursuit of a stable government.

The basic institution altered little from Tudor times until the 20th cent. Though the County Councils Act (1888) took most of the responsibilities of local government away from the JPs, their jurisdiction was extended to many more serious offences. Up to the First World War the bench reflected county society as it had always done, but it was less exclusive and was recruited on a broader basis. In 1906 the property qualification was abolished. In 1911 advisory committees were established in the counties to advise the lord chancellor on the selection of JPs. Women became eligible for the bench

in 1918. In 1966 a period of compulsory training was introduced for new JPs.

G. R. Elton, *The Tudor Constitution* (Cambridge, 1962).
E. Moir, *The Justice of the Peace* (London, 1969).   CJ

JUSTICIA in Aragon, medieval institution which existed to protect subjects against royal and private injustice. The chief judge or *justicia* headed a court of 21 judges, five appointed by the Crown and 16 nominated by the *cortes* of Aragon. From the late 15th cent., the office of *justicia*, originally a life appointment, became a hereditary privilege of the Lanuza family. In the face of growing royal authority it provided a challenge to royal jurisdiction, and after the capture and execution of the *justicia* Juan de Lanuza for supporting the rebel Pérez (1591), Philip II of Spain made the office dependent upon royal pleasure, while all the judges were henceforth to be nominated by the Crown.

JUSTICIALISM ('*justicialismo*'), official doctrine of Argentine Peronism after 1949. It was first promulgated by Juan Perón before a philosophical congress. 'Justicialism', together with the Declaration of Economic Independence (1947), offered *ex post facto* legitimization of policies already undertaken, often on opportunistic grounds. Its values were authoritarianism and social justice (emphasizing the roles of the regime's twin props, the military and organized labour). It aroused a populistic creole nationalism, in calculated rejection of the cosmopolitanism of Argentina's former rulers (who were characterized as '*vendepatrias*'). In economics, 'justicialism' lay between collectivism and free-enterprise capitalism.

JUSTICIAR, CHIEF (or JUSTICIAR OF ENGLAND). Under the Norman kings of England, the term 'justiciar' was used in a general sense to mean a justice or judge. As the title of a particular office, it has been claimed to date from 1109 and Roger, Bp of Salisbury, certainly performed many functions later regarded as proper to the chief justiciar. The first clear reference to the 'justiciar of England' came in 1159, when the office was held jointly by Robert, Earl of Leicester, and Richard de Lucy. The justiciar was the chief and most powerful minister of the Crown. He was the chief legal and administrative official and usually acted as regent in the king's absence. In the period of the fully developed justiciarship, its powers were immense, as was shown by such men as Ranulf Glanville (1179–89), William Longchamp (1189–91), Hubert Walter (1193–8), and Geoffrey Fitzpeter (1198–1213). The justiciarship came to its zenith under Hubert de Burgh (1215–32), but the dangers of so powerful an office also became apparent and it was not filled after 1234. The baronial opposition to Henry III revived it after capturing power in 1258 and its last holder, Hugh Despenser, was killed by the royalists at Evesham in 1265.

JUSTIFICATION BY FAITH, Christian doctrine, emphasized by Martin Luther, that man's salvation could not be achieved by good works, but only by the individual's simple faith in God.

JUSTINIAN I (c. 500–65), Byzantine Emperor (reg. 527–65). Originating from the Latin-speaking Balkan provinces, he served as chief executive to his uncle, Justin I, becoming emperor on the latter's death. His personality dominated his epoch and his contemporaries together with the extraordinary figure of Theodora, his consort, on whom his personal dependence was considerable. A man of autocratic temperament marked by occasional hesitations, Justinian was a devout if rather sombre-minded prince, who regarded the imperial office as properly a vehicle for promoting the orthodox Christian theology. A good judge of men, he was served by a number of outstanding soldiers, jurists, and administrators. During a succession of major wars he held the eastern frontier against Persia, at great cost, and achieved the brilliant if shortlasting reconquest of Africa, Italy, and south-eastern Spain by Belisarius and Narses. Thus in his reign the political unity of imperial Graeco-Roman civilization was temporarily restored. Another achievement (also impermanent) was a reconciliation between the Eastern and Western Churches. The emperor's orthodoxy led him both to persecute Monophysite and other heretics in Constantinople and to regard his western campaigns as crusades against Arianism. The two lasting monuments of his career were the cathedral church at Constantinople and the revision and codification of Roman Law under the direction of Tribonian. Justinian had great abilities and enormous energy to support his grandiose schemes, but appears to have lacked human warmth. In the history of Procopius, his contemporary, he appears as a moral monster. His conquests were almost ruinous in execution and temporary in effect, but it can be argued that they secured the empire an essential breathing-space and thereby promoted its survival into succeeding centuries.   RP

JUSTO, AUGUSTÍN PEDRO (1876–1943), Argentine general and president 1932–8, prominent in the coup of 1930 and the subsequent militarization of Argentine politics. As president, Justo successfully combated economic depression by preserving the traditional British connection. However, his policies provoked a strong nationalist reaction.

JUSTO, JUAN BAUTISTA (1865–1928), Argentine physician, socialist intellectual, and politician, who was among the founders of the Argentine Socialist Party and its organ *La Vanguardia* (1896). Justo, as deputy (1912–24) and senator (1924–8), was an influential critic of Argentina's subservience to foreign capital and markets.

JUTE INDUSTRY, important Indian industry before 1947 because India had almost a world monopoly of raw jute. Jute cloth was manufactured in India by the 16th cent. Regular export of raw jute to Dundee, Scotland, began in 1838, but the manufacture of jute on a large scale in India did not begin until 1855. There was great expansion after 1894 and by 1908 the output of India's mills surpassed that of Dundee's. During the First World War jute was urgently needed for war purposes, and the manufacture of sandbags brought great wealth to owners of Dundee jute mills. Its effect on the social and economic life of Dundee in the 19th and 20th cents was significant. Cheap Irish labour was shipped round the north of Scotland and poured into the city, and back-to-back tenements were built to house the jute workers. Cholera, cheap spirits, and bad drains increased the evils of long hours and bad housing. Women worked in the jute mills and stunted physical growth was characteristic in Dundee. The city suffered badly in the Depression of the 1930s, but jute was again in demand in the Second World War. Jute became a major factor in the economy of East Pakistan after partition in 1947 and a trade relationship with Scotland was maintained.

JUTES, continental Germanic tribe who invaded Britain in the 5th cent. They came from Jutland and settled in Kent and on the Isle of Wight. They mingled with other tribes and a distinctive Jutish element in Kentish culture is difficult to detect.

JUTLAND, BATTLE OF (31 May 1916), largest naval battle of the First World War, in which the British fleet under Jellicoe lost three battle-cruisers and three cruisers, and the Germans under Scheer, one old battleship, one battle-cruiser, and four cruisers. British strategy aimed to preserve command of the sea by forcing a decisive engagement, but the Germans, hampered by numerical inferiority and the timidity of high command, could only hope to reduce the odds by decoying part of the enemy into action against superior numbers. The battle resulted from one of several abortive attempts to achieve this.

On 31 May both fleets were steaming on a converging course, unaware of each other's presence. Contact between the battle-cruisers at 2.20 p.m. led to a general engagement, Scheer finding himself at 6.15 confronted by the entire British fleet, deployed across his line of advance. Covered by his destroyers, he escaped by turning away sharply into the gathering dusk. Although fighting continued sporadically during the night, inadequate admiralty intelligence prevented Jellicoe from renewing contact the following morning.

Although the Germans inflicted heavier losses than they received, they failed to alter the overall situation in their own favour: British command of the sea was confirmed and thereafter the Germans, increasingly demoralized, remained in harbour.

A number of British technical and tactical weaknesses were demonstrated during the battle; also it showed that communications were inadequate for controlling large numbers of ships in battle. Jutland was the first naval action in which an aircraft was successfully launched at sea. The battle had major importance in that it was the one occasion in the whole war when final victory or defeat might have been decided in one day.   RJVL

JUVENAL (Decimus Junius Juvenalis) (*c*. AD 58–138), Roman satirist, whose satires, written after 100, are the most violent surviving from Roman literature, and were largely inspired by genuine moral disgust at the life of the wealthy classes in Rome, and also at the tyranny of Domitian, under whom Juvenal apparently spent some time in exile. Allowing for the exaggerations conventional to the satirist, his work is useful as a source for various aspects of Roman life, *eg*, the material squalor of the poor (of whom he was one), relations between client and patron, and aristocratic snobbery. His reputation has been greater since the Renaissance than in antiquity.

JUXON, WILLIAM (1582–1663), archbishop of Canterbury, friend and protégé of Abp Laud, who was successively vice-chancellor of Oxford University (1627), where he initiated the reform of the University statutes known as the Laudian Code, and Bp of London (1633), lord high treasurer (1636), and lord of the admiralty (1636). He was present with Charles I at the Newport negotiations (1648) and throughout his trial and execution (1648–9). He was deprived of his see for the next decade (1649–59), during which time he lived quietly on his Gloucestershire estate. He went to the see of Canterbury at the Restoration (1660). In his last years he was responsible for the rebuilding of the great hall of Lambeth Palace and the improvement of St Paul's Cathedral, London.

KAAHUMANU (?1768–1832), favourite consort of Chief Kamehameha I of Hawaii. She was his effective successor in 1819 and made Hawaii a literate, Christian state. As an imperious leader, opposed by whites and disaffected native leaders for her vigorous puritanism and anti-catholicism, she preserved Hawaiian unity in a crucial, formative period.

KABALEGA (1850–1923), King of Bunyoro-Kitara (reg. 1870–99), who asserted the supremacy of royal power backed by his army, and strove to revive the fortunes of his ancient kingdom. His efforts were cut short by British intervention. He was banished in 1899.

KABIR (c. 1440–1518), son of a Muslim weaver at Banaras, who became the disciple of the Hindu mystic Ramananda. An ecstatic poet of great power, he preached brotherhood and devotion to God without regard to caste or creed. A sect of Kabirpanthis arose to follow his teaching.

KABUKI, popular Japanese dramatic form. It emerged in the 17th cent. from somewhat disreputable origins, losing its association with prostitution only when the *bakufu* introduced some controls, including a ban on women, to prevent its corruption of the samurai class. Essentially, however, it was patronized by merchants and townspeople, who loved its exuberance and colour. The subjects of *kabuki* plays ranged from historical legends to thinly disguised contemporary events. Dance and music were incorporated, but the most striking feature of *kabuki*, which the hereditary tradition still maintains unchanged (1970), was the highly skilled depiction of women by actors specializing in such roles.

KABUL, RETREAT FROM, disastrous retirement of the British–Indian garrison from Kabul, Afghanistan (Jan. 1842). The entire force of 4500 troops and 12,000 camp followers was wiped out by Afghan tribesmen.

KACHINS, or Jinghpaws, war-like Tibeto-Burman race, numbering some 250,000, and inhabiting the mountainous far north of Burma. Their southward migration was still in progress when the British annexed Upper Burma (1886). Under the British, the Kachins were indirectly administered through their own headmen and chiefs, and much recruited into Burma regiments of the Indian army. In the Second World War, British-officered Kachin guerrillas successfully resisted the Japanese in the only part of Burma never to be overrun. After independence the quasi-federal Union of Burma included a separate Kachin state. There is now (1970) a strong Kachin nationalist movement.

KADALIE, CLEMENTS (1896–1951), African trade unionist, who was born in Nyasaland and educated at the Livingstonia mission. He worked his way to the Cape, where he founded the Industrial and Commercial Workers Union (1919). This developed into South Africa's most successful black trade union movement, claiming at its height 100,000 members. During his visits overseas he established links with the ILO and the British trade unions. By 1930 the movement he founded had disintegrated through financial and organizational difficulties and struggles among the leadership.

KADAR, JANOS (1912–   ), Hungarian politician, who joined the Young Communist Federation (1931) and the Communist Party (1932). He spent the Second World War in the Soviet Union and then returned to Hungary to become a secretary of the central committee of the Communist Party. He was appointed minister of the interior (1948) and was responsible for the arrest of Rajk. He was himself imprisoned (1951–3). He was appointed first secretary of the party (July 1956) and collaborated with Imre Nagy (July 1956). During the Hungarian revolution he abandoned Nagy and joined the Russians, returning with them to Budapest. Since being established in power after Soviet Russia's suppression of the Hungarian revolt, he has succeeded in pursuing a policy of relative independence from the Soviet Union.

KADIRI (or Kediri, also Daha), city in east Java, Indonesia, capital of an empire (c. 1100–1222). According to tradition, it developed out of one of the two halves into which Airlangga had divided the Javanese state (c. 1045) by gradually absorbing the other state. Though its actual power was limited to east Java, Kadiri apparently exercised some vague supremacy over other islands in eastern Indonesia. Its best-known ruler is Jayabhaya (1136–57). The Kadiri period is especially renowned for the great achievements in Old Javanese literature, notably the composition of ornate epic poetry.

KAFFA (KEFE), ancient Theodosia, located on the southern shore of the Crimea. It rose to prominence as a commercial centre during the domination there of the Genoese (13th–15th cents). It continued to be a prosperous place under the rule of the Ottoman Turks, who took possession of it in 1475. Kaffa—thereafter known as Feodosiya—became Russian in 1783, when the Tsarina Catherine II annexed the Crimea.

KAFFRARIA, BRITISH, between the Keiskamma and Kei rivers, contains East London and Kingwilliamstown. It became a separate British colony in 1847, and was annexed by the Cape Colony in 1866.

KAFUR, ABU'L-MISK (d. 968), eunuch who, after the death of Muhammad ibn Tughj (AD 946), became the real force behind the Ikhshidid regime in Egypt and at last ruled there in his own name (966–8).

KAGANOVICH, LAZAR MOISEYEVICH (1893–   ), Russian politician who was one of Stalin's principal lieutenants. He joined the Bolshevik Party (1911) and led the Bolshevik seizure of power in Gomel. Under Stalin he had a long and continuous career in posts of importance in the party. He twice directed the party organization in the Ukraine (1925–8, 1946–7). He was a member of the central committee (1924–57) and (from 1930) of the politburo, and secretary of the central committee (1928–39) and of the Moscow party committee (1930–5). Under Stalin's direction he played a leading part in organizing the collectivization of agriculture and the great purge. Throughout the Second World War he was a member of the state defence committee.

In the last years of Stalin's life he was eclipsed by Malenkov. But after Stalin's death he again came to prominence as an opponent of Khrushchev. He had acquired considerable power during his long career in overcoming the crises of Stalinist rule and conducting purges and he had long experience of heavy industry and transportation. He opposed

Khrushchev on most of the issues where Khrushchev took the initiative—the relaxation of Stalinist control, the reform of the industrial structure, agricultural policy, and industrial development. He stood for the Stalinist tradition of primacy in heavy industry, especially steel, and for Bolshevik purity. With Molotov and Malenkov he thus ranked as one of the most important members of the 'anti-party' group. After their defeat (1957) he was expelled from the central committee and for a time was made manager of an asbestos plant in the Urals.

KAGOSHIMA BOMBARDMENT (1863), attack by British ships on the main town of Satsuma in southern Japan, to avenge the murder of a British merchant. Although not completely successful, it helped convince Satsuma leaders of the futility of a *jōi* ('expel the foreigner') policy.

KAGWA, SIR APOLO GULEMYE (d. 1927), Ganda politician and writer of the early colonial period, who became chief minister (*katikiro*) of the kingdom of Buganda shortly before the imposition of British rule in Uganda. His rise to power followed the war of succession in Ganda (1888–92), when opposing armies were mobilized on a basis of rivalry between Catholics and Protestants. Kagwa supported the Protestant side, which eventually won. He welcomed the coming of the British, seeing them as arbitrators in internal disputes, and negotiated the treaty of 1900, which not only established British colonial rule upon a durable basis, but also ensured a considerable autonomy for the Buganda kingdom. He recorded much Ganda oral history in written form.

KAHINA, AL-, legendary prophetess, who led Berber resistance to the Arab conquest of the eastern Maghrib (*c.* 700).

K'AI-FENG, capital city of China during the northern Sung dynasty (960–1126). It is situated in the present province of Ho-nan; during the Ming period a Jewish community lived there.

KAISERSWERTH, German town on the east bank of the Rhine river in the archbishopric of Cologne, which was controlled by the French at the beginning of the War of the Spanish Succession. It was besieged by Prussian, Palatine, and Dutch soldiers of the Grand Alliance (April–June 1702). The siege was the first military operation of the war in northern Europe and preceded by one month the official declaration of war on France.

KAKATIYAS, THE, Hindu dynasty that ruled the state of Warangal in the Telugu country of east central India. It arose (*c.* 1190) on the break-up of the Chalukya empire of Kalyan. They waged war with the Hoysalas and the Cholas. In the early 14th cent. their power was broken by the Sultans of Delhi.

KALADIAN KULUBALI (*c.* 1652–82), Bambara warrior leader, whose great-grandson, Mamari (1712–55), founded the state of Segu in the Western Sudan.

KALAHOM, name of the ministry of defence in Thailand. It was first recognized as a separate unit of administration in the kingdom of Ayudhya in the 15th cent., having general superintendence over military affairs. Its head, also called *Kalahom*, directly commanded four great armies and subsidiary departments. By 1700, its military responsibilites in the northern and eastern provinces having been assumed by the *Mahatthai*, the *Kalahom* was given full civil administrative powers in west and south Siam, thus restoring its parity of political power with the *Mahatthai*. For most of the following two centuries it was controlled by members of the Bunnag family. It was reorganized as a military ministry in the years 1889–94, its provinces being transferred back to the

Mahatthai, and now (1970) includes departments of the army, navy, and air force.

KALB, JOHANN DE (1721–80), American soldier, who was born in Germany. After long service in the French army he came to America (1768) as a French secret agent. He became a brigade commander in the Continental army, served with Washington at Valley Forge (1777–8), and under Gen. Gates in the Carolina campaign, where he was killed.

KALBITES, amirs of Muslim Sicily, who were appointed viceroys of the Fatimids (970), but became substantially independent. From their capital, Palermo, they completed the conquest of the island from the Byzantines, advancing into southern Italy and routing the Emperor Otto II near Stilo (982). In the 11th cent. factions and local separatisms typical of Sicilian history under the Muslims undermined their authority, leading to civil war, which overthrew the dynasty in the 1030s and divided the island into some four principalities, whose quarrels provided the opportunity for the Norman conquest (1060–91).

KALEB (*fl.* 6th cent.), ruler of the Aksumite empire, who conquered part of South Arabia and later became a monk.

KALENJIN, collective name given to a number of pastoralist people occupying the Rift Valley in Kenya, such as the Elgeyo, the Kipsigi, the Marakwet, the Nandi, and the Tugen. In so far as the name denotes a political grouping it is a product of competition for scarce resources (especially land) during the first half of the 20th cent., not only between the Kalenjin and neighbouring African agriculturists such as Kikuyu, but also with European settlers. When the Kenya African independence movement split into two in 1960, most Kalenjin support accordingly went to the Kenya African Democratic Union (KADU), rather than to the Kenya African National Union (KANU) in which Kikuyu politicians figured more prominently.

KALIBAPI, abbreviation of *Kapisanan sa Paglilingkod sa Bagong Pilipinas* ('Association for Service to the New Philippines'); it was established during the Second World War (Dec. 1942) by an executive order of the chairman of the Executive Commission, the central administrative organization of the Philippines during the Japanese occupation, before the establishment of the republic in 1943. Its purpose was to support the administrative policies of the Japanese Imperial Forces in the Philippines, and to promote the establishment of the Greater East Asia Co-Prosperity Sphere. All existing political parties, as well as civic professional organizations, were merged into the *Kalibapi*; and membership was a qualification for employment in any public or private institution. Under the wartime Philippine republic, the organization increased its membership to 1,500,000 early in 1944. As the war in the Pacific was drawing to an end, the *Kalibapi* became increasingly a centralized, authoritarian party with paramilitary potential. It ceased to exist in 1945, when the Americans reoccupied the Philippines.

KALIDASA (*?fl.* 4th–6th cents AD), Indian poet and playwright, whose work reflects classical Hindu ideals in their purest form, much of it being based on traditional accounts of the past which are no longer available.

KALININ, MIKHAIL IVANOVICH (1875–1946), Russian politician who was one of the early members of the Russian Social Democratic Party (from 1897), and became president of the Soviet Union (1937–46). He supported Lenin when the party split (1902), although he did not accept Lenin's denunciation of the First World War or approve his intention to seize power (in 1917). He was appointed a member of the central committee (1919) and of the politburo (1926). He does not appear to have played any decisive part in the formulation of policy, but was a consistent supporter of Stalin, and thus remained a member of the politburo throughout the purges.

KALISCH, BATTLE OF (1706), engagement in the Great Northern War between 10,000 Swedes under Gen. Mayerfeld and 30,000 Russians and Poles under Prince Menshikov, in which the former were defeated with considerable losses.

KALKA, BATTLE OF (1223), first recorded battle between the Russians and the Tatars, fought on the Kalka river, which flows into the Sea of Azov. A coalition of Russian princes, fighting in alliance with their former enemies, the Polovtsi nomads, was decisively defeated. The Tatars, however, retreated to Asia without following up their victory, and did not undertake the systematic conquest of Russia until 1238.

KALM, PETER (1716–79), Swedish scientist trained by Linnaeus, who was sent by the Royal Academy of Science at Stockholm to visit the American colonies (1748–51). He wrote an account of his journey, *Travels into North America*, which dealt with botanical studies, and included perceptive observations of the people and institutions.

KALMAR, STATUTES OF (1587) in Sweden, enactments agreed to by Sigismund III at the request of the Swedish aristocracy before he left Sweden to become King of Poland. They were designed so that the union of the crowns should not endanger Sweden's independence nor prejudice the Lutheran Church there. The rights of the Church were guaranteed, Catholic propaganda was forbidden, and Sweden was to be governed by an aristocratic regency council of seven during Sigismund's absence.

KALMAR, UNION OF (1397), dynastic union of the three Scandinavian kingdoms which had a long influence on their history. It was created by Margaret, Queen of Denmark and Norway, who had also been elected Ruler of Sweden (1389). In 1521 Sweden, under Gustavus Vasa, succeeded in breaking away from the union, which was dominated by the Danish monarchy and council. Norway was united with Denmark until 1814.

KALMUK, Turkish name for the Oirat Mongols of western Mongolia and Turkestan, who established the great 17th-cent. nomad kingdom of Jungaria in the upper Ili valley. The state reached its apogee under Galdan (*c.* 1644–97), but was destroyed by the Manchus in 1758. Another branch of the Kalmuks, established on the Volga in the 17th cent., attempted to migrate to China in 1771 and became the victims of a massacre by the Kazakhs celebrated by De Quincey.

KALOMO CULTURE, early Iron Age culture of central Zambia noted for its fixed village sites on mounds occupied on a rotational basis by cattle-keepers and farmers.

KALYANI INSCRIPTIONS in Burma, erected (1472–92) near Pegu by King Dammazedi. They standardized the form of ordination for monks used on the Kalyani river in Ceylon.

KAMAKURA PERIOD, era of Japanese history when the major centre of government was at Kamakura, south of present-day Tokyo. It had been Minamoto Yoritomo's headquarters during his war against the Taira clan (1180–5), and he remained there in order to maintain control over his followers, who mostly held land in the Kantō area. The first century of Kamakura rule was a period of good government for three main reasons: first, the ability of the Hōjō regents; second, the control exercised over their branch families by the *bakufu*'s chief supporters; and third, the fact that Yoritomo's constables (*shugos*) and stewards (*jitōs*) did not replace but supplemented existing authorities. Thus the stability of the country rested on a balance between Kamakura and

Kyoto, although power tended to swing towards the new feudal regime, especially after the retired emperor, Go-Toba's, unsuccessful challenge of Kamakura (1221). Eventually the resentment of one branch of the imperial line at Kyoto did result in the destruction of Kamakura (1333), but the essential causes lay elsewhere. Population increase, the penetration of samurai life by money and Kyoto influences, the weakening of family ties and the development of local loyalties, and the burden of defence preparations during and after the Mongol invasions (1274, 1281), all combined to create a general dissatisfaction which could only be solved by war. The achievements of the period were considerable: the introduction and spread of the most important popular Buddhist sects, as well as Zen; the development of a literature concerned with the exploits of the samurai class; a certain degree of social liberation; a rapid extension of commerce and communications; and, generally, the growth of a more distinctively Japanese style of civilization.

KAMARAJ NADAR, KUMARASWAMY (1903–), Madras politician, renowned as a 'king-maker' in the Congress Party during the 1960s. After entering Congress in 1920, Kamaraj became an influential provincial figure in the Tamilnad Congress Committee, first as secretary (1936–40) and then president (1940–54). After being chief minister of Madras from 1954–63, he resigned in fulfilment of the 'Kamaraj Plan' for the revitalization of Congress organization and became national president of the party. In that position he was responsible for the selection of two successive prime ministers, Lal Bahadur Shastri (1964) and Mrs Indira Gandhi (1966).

KAMCHATKA, Siberian peninsula, lying between the Sea of Okhotsk and the Bering Sea, first explored by Russian cossacks in Peter I's reign (1697) and settled by the Russians in the 18th cent., despite a native rebellion of 1730. The naval base of Petropavlovsk and the town of Bolcheretsk were established in the 18th cent., and in the 19th it became a centre for the fur trade. Kamchatka was first strengthened and valued as a base for the consolidation of Russian power in the Far East when Muravev-Amursky (1809–81) was appointed governor-general of Eastern Siberia (1847–61).

KAMEHAMEHA I (1753–1819), High Chief of Hawaii island, who founded the Hawaiian kingdom. He was attacked in 1782 by local foes bent on eliminating the ranking chief Kiwalao, and, in 1791, his rival Keoua. In 1785, as Kiwalao's successor, he resumed the inter-island feud with Kahekili of Maui–Oahu, and in 1795, after the latter's death, overthrew his sons in two battles. He became ruler of the archipelago and divided the land in feudal style among tributary chiefs supervised by governors. He adapted western technology, encouraged commerce, and acquired wealth in money, guns, and ships. Much of his prosperity was due to sandalwood sales. His consort, Kaahumanu, became effective ruler on his death.

KAMEHAMEHA III (1814–54), King of Hawaii (*reg.* 1825–1854), who adopted in 1840 a civil code and representative institutions as a basis for international recognition, accorded in 1843. He introduced universal private landownership (1848). Although induced by renewed French threats (1849) and local white agitation (1853) to seek US annexation, he was encouraged by Anglo-French protests to keep his throne. He was a benevolent ruler, well served by ex-missionary advisers, and his reign was marked by liberty and progress.

KAMENEV, LEV BORISOVICH (1883–1936), Bolshevik revolutionary and politician, who was born in Kiev, of Jewish parents. In 1902 he became a member of the Leninist faction of the Russian SDP. In 1914 he undertook the dangerous work of encouraging the Bolshevik deputies in the Duma to declare their hope that Russia would be defeated in the First

World War, which had just broken out. He was arrested and imprisoned. In 1917 he escaped and arrived in Petrograd before the return of Lenin. With Stalin he directed the Bolshevik Party in a policy of co-operation with the provisional government. With Zinoviev he continued to oppose Lenin's extreme line for the rest of the year without, however, forfeiting Lenin's trust. He felt strongly that it would be folly to provoke a Bolshevik revolution. In the famous meeting of the Bolshevik leaders on 23 Oct. 1917 he voted against the motion that 'an armed uprising is inevitable and the time is perfectly ripe'. He carried his opposition to the length of publishing an article in the newspaper, *Novaya Zhizn*, attacking the decision of the Bolshevik leaders and revealing their revolutionary plans. Lenin was infuriated by this breach of discipline, but this did not prevent Kamenev from continuing to take an independent line in the hectic days immediately after the Nov. 1917 revolution. He proposed the abolition of the death sentence; and he also suggested that the Bolsheviks should form a left-wing coalition government which would exclude Lenin and Trotsky. The adoption of such comparatively tolerant attitudes made Kamenev a useful negotiator between the party and the outside world. In Feb. 1918 he was sent to London to sound out the British government's attitude towards the new order in Russia. After meeting a few MPs he was deported. When Lenin fell ill, Kamenev joined Stalin and Zinoviev in an attempt to resist Trotsky's rise to power. But as soon as Kamenev had served his turn, Stalin undermined his position. At the 14th Congress (1925) he was shouted down by the disciplined Stalinists when he attempted to defend the Leninist axiom of collegiate rule. After this he was deprived of his place in the politburo and of the office of chairman of the Moscow Soviet and was reduced to the position of ambassador to Rome. In a desperate attempt to prevent Stalin's consolidation of power he joined forces with Trotsky, but he was compromised by the latter's fall and expelled from the party (1927). Although he was readmitted in the next year, he never recovered power. In 1933 he was alleged to be involved with the group known to be opposed to further collectivization, but he was allowed to appear at the 17th Congress in order to confess his past errors. The death of Kirov (1934) enabled Stalin to use Kamenev as an important defendant in the show trial of Aug. 1936. He was induced to admit in open court to a series of crimes, including a Trotskyite plot to overthrow Stalin. In his testimony he involved other leading Bolsheviks. He was shot immediately after the trial. After 1956 Soviet authorities admitted that he was not guilty.

L. Schapiro, *The Communist Party of the Soviet Union* (London, 1964).
R. Conquest, *The Great Terror* (London, 1968).   GS

KAMIL, AL- (*reg*. 1218–38), Ayyubid Sultan of Egypt and Syria. After three years of conflict (1218–21) he was able to expel the forces of the Fifth Crusade from Damietta in Egypt. Later, he warded off the threats of the Hohenstaufen Emperor Frederick II, but in 1229 yielded to him Jerusalem, together with Bethlehem and Nazareth, in return for a guarantee of peace between the Christians and the Muslims. His main endeavour was directed towards the establishment of his own control over the local dynasties (Ayyubid, Zangid, etc.). He ruled over much of Syria and Al-Jazira (Mesopotamia), a complex and difficult task which remained unfinished at the time of his death.

KAMINIEC (Turkish: Kaminçe), important fortress in that region of the western Ukraine called Podolia. The Ottomans conquered the fortress from Poland in 1672, but had to return it to the Poles at the peace of Carlowitz in 1699. The town now belongs (1970) to the USSR under the name Kamenetz Podolski.

KAMMERGERICHT, margrave's supreme court of justice in the Old Mark of Brandenburg, held in Berlin from 1516 and increasingly superseded by the privy council of Brandenburg-Prussia from the 17th cent.

KAMMU (737–806), Emperor of Japan (*reg*. 781–806), the last to rule unchallenged as well as to reign. It was he who moved the capital from Buddhist-dominated Nara to Heian.

KAMURASI (*reg*. 1852–69), King of Bunyoro-Kitara, father of Kabalega. It was during his reign that Europeans first visited Bunyoro.

KANAKAS, name given to some 57,000 South Sea islanders recruited as labourers in the sugar and cotton industries of Qld and NSW (1874–1904). Legislation by the Australian Commonwealth parliament prohibited their further recruitment and provided for their repatriation by 1907.

KANAUJ, ancient city in Uttar Pradesh, India, about 40 miles north-west of Kanpur. It rose after the Gupta period, when it became the capital of the Maukhari dynasty, and developed into one of the greatest political and cultural centres of northern India in the 7th cent. in the reign of Harsha. During the 8th cent. Kanauj became the focus of the ambitions of Indian princes. In the beginning of the 9th cent. it was chosen by the Pratiharas as their capital. It remained a great city for the next two centuries, but was taken and partly ruined by Mahmud of Ghazna (1018). Although it later became the residence of kings of the Gahadavala dynasty it gradually declined, so that in 1970 little of its former greatness remained.

KANCHI or Kanchipuram (mod. Conjeevaram), ancient Indian city of (1970) about 100,000 inhabitants, 47 miles (75 kms) south-west of Madras. It was the capital of the Pallava empire (4th–9th cents AD) and remained one of the main centres of the Chola empire (*c*. AD 890–1245). Though later its political importance declined, it continued to flourish as a religious centre. The Kailasanath temple there is among the most impressive of Pallava foundations.

KANDYAN CONVENTION (1815). When the British put an end to the ancient kingdom of Kandy, an agreement was made with the Kandyan chiefs transferring the kingship to King George III of Britain and guaranteeing the maintenance of their rights, privileges, and powers and the inviolability of the Buddhist religion.

KANDYAN KINGDOM, the last of the Sinhalese kingdoms of Ceylon (1591–1818), takes its name from the term Kande-uda-pas-raṭa (the five districts in the hills). The name, Kandy, a later British derivative, came to be applied to the ancient hill-capital, Senkadagala. The kingdom was located in the hill-country in the centre of the island, but also extended over parts of the maritime region. Though mountain ranges tended to break up the political unity of the region, resistance to foreign invasion welded the chiefs and people into a kingdom. For many centuries little-known independent and semi-independent rulers controlled the mountain valleys. But it was only with the death of Rajasinha I of the Sitavaka kingdom (1593), who struggled to gain control of the maritime region from the Portuguese, that Vimaladharmasuriya I, who had proclaimed himself ruler of the hill-country in 1591, became the focus of opposition to the foreigner. The political history of the Kandyan kingdom, thereafter, consists of the unsuccessful attempts of the kings of Kandy, first, to expel the foreigner from the maritime regions and later, to avoid being conquered. The Dutch came to the assistance of Rajasinha II (*reg*. 1635–87) but captured the Portuguese colony for themselves in 1656. The British ousted the Dutch in 1796. Repeated attempts to invade or conquer the hill-country failed because of the terrain, which lent itself to guerrilla warfare. A dynastic change, however, by which a scion of the Nayakkar dynasty of Madura in south India succeeded to the throne, caused a gradual rift between the court and the chiefs. This eventually led to the betrayal of Sri Vikrama

Rajasinha to the British and the signing of the Kandyan Convention (1815), by which the chiefs ceded the kingdom to Britain. An abortive rebellion (1817–18) finally ended the semblance of independence which the chiefs hoped to enjoy.

The kingdom was based on a feudal socio-economic structure, linked to a service-tenure land-holding system. Buddhist religious practices and beliefs prevailed throughout. The kingdom preserved for over two centuries the ancient cultural traditions of the Sinhalese people.   LSP

KANDYAN REBELLION (1817–18). The Kandyan chiefs and the Buddhist *sangha* (clergy) had not really understood the terms of the Kandyan Convention (1815). They found their powers and influence curtailed by having British officials set in authority over them, and disliked the coming of Christian missionaries. In 1817 a rebellion broke out in a remote part of the province in favour of a pretender to the throne, and was supported by most of the chiefs. It was put down with considerable difficulty, Gov. Brownrigg having to call for reinforcements from India, and two chiefs were executed. In a proclamation Brownrigg declared that the rebellion had abrogated some provisions of the convention relating to the chiefs' privileges.

This was the only serious rebellion against British rule, though in 1848 another pretender appeared and disturbances broke out in two Kandyan districts, because of the imposition of new taxes. These uprisings received no general support, but were put down with unnecessary severity.

KANDYAN WARS. After the Portuguese had occupied the kingdom of Kotte in Ceylon (1597), the only independent kingdom left was that of Kandy, in the mountainous interior, access to which was only possible by narrow paths through dense jungles, so that invaders were liable to be ambushed and their communications cut. On five occasions the Portuguese attempted invasions, but these all either failed or achieved only temporary success. Sometimes the Kandyan kings invaded the Portuguese-held territory, and one of them, Rajasinha I (*reg.* 1628–35), laid siege to Colombo, which was relieved only just in time by reinforcements from Goa.

During the Dutch occupation relations with the kings of Kandy, though not good, were less bitter. Fighting occasionally took place on the borders. In 1766 a Dutch expedition failed, and in the next year another penetrated to the city of Kandy, but could not hold it. A British expedition in 1804 succeeded in taking Kandy, but most of the garrison fell ill and were ultimately massacred. In 1815 an expedition launched with the secret co-operation of some Kandyan chiefs was successful, and the king was driven out.

KANE, ELISHA KENT (1820–57), Arctic explorer and surgeon in the US navy. He served in the first Grinnel expedition (1850–1), sent to search for Sir John Franklin, who had been missing since 1845. Kane published (1853) an account of the voyage, which helped to raise funds for a second Grinnel expedition, which he himself commanded (1853–5). Relying on his theory of there being an open Polar sea, Kane reached Baffin Bay (1853), and pushing through Smith Sound, discovered Kane Basin, an important milestone in Polar exploration. His sleigh parties discovered the Humboldt Glacier and the Kennedy Channel and also sighted the north section of Ellesmere Island, which Kane named Grinnel Land, after the expedition's patron. He was forced eventually (1855) to abandon his ship, which became trapped, and made an epic overland journey down the Greenland coast, where Hartstein's relief expedition picked up the survivors.

KANELLOPOULOS, PANAYIOTIS (b. 1902), Greek politician, who gave up an academic career in 1935 to found and lead the National Unionist Party. After taking part in the Albanian and Italian campaigns, he went into exile during the Second World War, serving as premier and minister of defence in the Greek government-in-exile. He returned to Greece in 1944 and accepted the plebiscite on the king's return. Kanellopoulos held ministerial positions in 1944 and was briefly prime minister in 1945. He served (1947–50) in various governments and in 1951 organized the Popular Unionist Party, together with Stephanopoulos. In that same year he allied his party with the Greek Rally for electoral purposes and subsequently was minister of defence in the Papagos government. After a brief spell as a professor at Athens, he returned to politics as deputy prime minister in the government of Karamanlis. When in 1963 Karamanlis retired to Paris Kanellopoulos became leader of the National Radical Union (ERE). Later that year the king summoned Kanellopoulos to form a coalition with the Centre Union, but Papandhreou refused to participate. However, an agreement was reached whereby the Centre Union would desist from attacks on the king and withhold the plebiscite on the monarchy. In April 1967 Kanellopoulos formed a government in advance of the election. But, after failing once again to reach a firm understanding with the Centre Union, he was forced to resign and parliament was dissolved. Soon afterwards the army seized power. On 27 Sept. 1967 Kanellopoulos publicly denounced the ruling junta.

KANEM, area of the Tchad republic to the north-east of the lake. The name, derived from a Tubu word meaning south, was originally applied to most of the region south of the Tibesti mountains by Arab geographers, who first mentioned it in the 9th cent. as being inhabited by the nomadi Zaghawa. Between the 9th and 11th cents the Saifawa emerged as the most powerful of a number of small kingdoms. They extended their rule over the areas both west and east of Lake Chad and as far north as Fezzan. Weakened by internecine wars, they were driven from Kanem late in the 14th cent. Their main foes, the Bulela, established a state in Kanem which is mentioned by Leo Africanus under the name Gaoga.

Most of Kanem was recaptured by Idris Katagarmbe (1504–25), but it was not until the reign of Idris Aloma (1569–99) that the Bulala were finally crushed. A Bornu governor, Dala Afuno, was placed at Mao, probably early in the 17th cent.; he or his successors fought with the fugitive Tunjur from Darfur. Later in the century the area was raided by Baghirmi, but remained under Bornu until a succession dispute over the governorship enabled Wadai to intervene (c. 1800). It was raided by Al-Kanemi, together with forces from the Fezzan and from c. 1846 was devastated by continuous warfare between the Awlad Sulayman Arabs, who had fled there from the Fezzan, and their neighbours. Sanusiyya influence became strong in the 1890s; the first military confrontation between that brotherhood and the French occurred at the battle of Bir Alali in 1901.

KANEMI, AL-, MUHAMMAD AL-AMIN (1775–1837), first Shehu of Bornu, born in the Fezzan of mixed Arab–Kanembu parentage and educated at Ngazargamu as a scholar-merchant. Returning to Bornu by way of Darfur and Wadai, he attracted a number of followers and established a school at Ngala in 1799. He was joined by the Shuwa and Kanembu peoples when he went to the aid of the Saifawa, who had been driven from their capital by the Fulani jihadists under Gwoni Mukhtar. He was successful in driving away the Fulani from most of metropolitan Bornu by a combination of diplomacy and military skill. He entered into relations with the British government and was host to the Denham, Clapperton, and Oudney Expedition (1823–5).

K'ANG YU-WEI (1858–1927), Chinese reformer and political thinker of late Ch'ing period, who came from Canton. During a visit to Hong Kong and Shanghai in the early 1880s, he was much impressed by the orderliness and efficiency of the British-dominated municipal governments. Subsequent reading of Western works in translation convinced him of the necessity of reform in China along Western lines. His ideas influenced Liang Ch'i-ch'ao, who became his supporter. Reforms such as those advocated by K'ang were anathema to the traditional order, but K'ang eventually found justification for them in the 'Modern Text', which consisted of classics and commentaries outside the mainstream of Neo-Confucian orthodoxy, reinterpreting them to show that Confucius himself was a reformer. The reform movement, in which K'ang was an important figure, was far from impressive until 1895, when China was humiliatingly defeated by the Japanese, revealing all the inadequacies of 30 years of 'self-strengthening'. In 1897 the German seizure of Kiaochow and the subsequent 'scramble for concessions' revived the sense of crisis. K'ang was brought to the attention of the Kuang-hsü emperor, whose support enabled him to initiate reforms (the 'Hundred Days' Reform') in June 1898. These reforms were quashed by the Empress Dowager Tz'u-hsi, the young emperor's political powers being no match for the deep-rooted control of Tz'u-hsi. Aided by the British, K'ang fled to Japan, but six of his colleagues were executed. In Japan, K'ang and Liang Ch'i-ch'ao organized Chinese students in support of reforms under the Manchu emperor, while Sun Yat-sen and the revolutionaries worked for the overthrow of the Manchus. K'ang then made a world tour, visiting overseas Chinese communities and rallying them to the support of a truly constitutional monarchy. K'ang remained a loyal monarchist, even after the Republican Revolution (1911), and his advocacy of Confucianism as the state religion alienated him from the progressive elements of the Republican period. Thus K'ang, the leading reformer of imperial China, became a Confucian conservative in the 20th cent.

Lo Jung-pang (ed.), *K'ang Yu-wei, a biography and a symposium* (Tucson, 1967).   DP

K'ANG-HSI, reign-title of Hsüan-yeh (1654–1722), 2nd Emperor of the Ch'ing dynasty of China. (*reg.* 1661–1722). He assumed personal rule at the age of 13. Under him the unification of the Manchu empire was completed, relations with Russia were improved by the treaty of Nerschinsk (1689), and Outer Mongolia was brought under Manchu control by force in 1696. Through his intervention, Tibet was also brought under Ch'ing suzerainty (1720). However, K'ang-hsi's crowning achievement was winning the support of the Chinese gentry-literati by sponsoring Confucian learning, employing large numbers of scholars, mainly from the Lower Yangtse region, the stronghold of Sung and Ming traditions, for the compilation of large-scale scholastic and artistic works. For the same purpose, six grand tours of the south were made. K'ang-hsi continued the employment of Jesuit missionaries at the imperial court, particularly making use of their scientific knowledge in fields such as calendrical methods, astronomy, mathematics, and geography. However, the challenge of the pope to his authority (the Rites Controversy) led to persecution of Christians.

KANGHWA, Sack of, by the French Far Eastern fleet in Oct. 1866, in retaliation for the killing of nine French priests in a massacre of Korean Catholics. Admiral Rose, having failed in an attack on Seoul, landed on Kanghwa Island, burned Kanghwa city, and removed treasures stored there since 1637.

KANISHKA (*reg.* AD 78–102), King of the Kushan dynasty, who ruled over large parts of northern India and Pakistan as well as parts of Afghanistan and Central Asia. His capital was at Peshawar. The precise year of Kanishka's accession is still controversial, many scholars preferring a date about half a century later. The Kushans were a branch of the Central Asian Yüe-chi tribe originally belonging to the western confines of the Chinese empire, but they had migrated into eastern Iran (Bactria) by the end of the 2nd cent. BC and occupied parts of India in the 1st cent. AD. This period is important as being one of intensive contact between India, Central and Western Asia with important developments in art (the so-called Indo-Greek art of Gandhara and the oldest Buddha images), religion (the beginnings of Mahayana, the 'Great Vehicle' of Buddhism), and other fields. Although

Kanishka survived in tradition as a great patron of Buddhism, his coins show also effigies of Hindu and Iranian deities.

KANO, city and emirate in northern Nigeria, and of the Hausa *Bokwai*. Traditionally, the site was first settled by Dalla, who gave his name to the hill in the city; his descendant, Barbushe, a powerful magician, is said to have gathered people together so as to form a town. The dynastic history began with the coming of the Kutumbawa with Bagauda, grandson of Bayajidda, or his grandson Gijinmasu, who imposed themselves on the descendants of Dalla. Gijinmasu began building the first city wall *c.* 1100. Hunters and smiths were important in the early period, and recent research has shown that iron was smelted near Dalla as early as the 17th cent. The rulers expanded their authority over the neighbouring towns until in the 15th cent. Kano had become one of the major states of the region.

Islam probably came in the early 15th cent., but it was in the reign of Rumfa (1462–99) that Wangarawa scholars settled there and the North African juris-consult Al-Maghili visited the town. Leo Africanus (*c.* 1520) mentioned Kano as being subject to Songhay. The 16th–18th cents were occupied with wars against Katsina and Jukun, in which the latter occupied the city at least twice. Like its neighbours, it was a tributary to Bornu in the 17th and 18th cents. In 1807 Alwali, the last Kutumbawa ruler, was driven away by the local leaders of the Fulani jihad. First Sulayman and then Ibrahim Dabo (1819–46), in whose line the throne has continued, succeeded. At this time the city succeeded Katsina as the major entrepôt of the region, trading with North Africa, Ashanti, Timbuctoo, and Chad. The country was disrupted by a civil war between the grandsons of Dabo in 1893–4 and in 1903 the city was occupied by the British. It was, in 1970, the capital of Kano state.

KANSAS in the US. 34th member state of the US, admitted in Jan. 1861, a mid-western region of prairie and plain, occupying the geographic centre of the continental US. It was visited by Coronado in the 1540s, was later crossed by Spanish and French Indian traders, and became part of the US by the Louisiana Purchase (1803). Although designated as permanent Indian territory by the Federal government, the opening of the Santa Fé and Oregon Trails through the region stimulated white settlement, and the position of KS on the western border between Southern slave states and the free-soil North made it a focus of sectional rivalries. After the passage of the Kansas–Nebraska Act (1854), undeclared war between irregulars from both North and South broke out, and 'Bleeding Kansas' threatened the stability of the union. Both factions sought to establish a state government, but popular rejection of slavery facilitated the entry of the state of KS into the union. After the Civil War Abilene and Dodge City, the western termini of the railroads, became important cattle towns to which western cattle were driven for shipment to eastern markets. But the state's prosperity was founded on wheat farming and despite the establishment of the aircraft industry there during the Second World War, and the recent exploitation of petroleum deposits, its economy is still primarily agricultural.

KANSAS–NEBRASKA ACT (1854) in the US, attempt to solve the problem of slavery in the US territories by application of the doctrine of popular or squatter sovereignty. The measure, sponsored by Stephen A. Douglas, organized the territories of Kansas and Nebraska without any restrictions on slavery, thus leaving the decision on this question to the local inhabitants and effectively repealing the provision of the Missouri Compromise (1820), which divided slave and nonslave territory at the 36° 30′ line. The Act was intended to foster both Douglas's presidential ambitions and the construction of a railroad to the Pacific, as well as to settle the controversy over the extension of slavery; in fact, it aroused a strong 'Anti-Nebraska' coalition in the North, which led to the formation of the Republican Party, turned 'Bleeding

Kansas' into a battleground between pro-slavery and anti-slavery forces, and provided a stepping-stone on the path to Civil War.

KANT, IMMANUEL (1724–1804), German philosopher, who was born at Konigsberg in East Prussia, where he spent his entire life, teaching at the university. His major works included *The Critique of Pure Reason* (1781), *The Fundamental Principles of the Metaphysics of Ethics* (1785), and *Religion within the Bounds of Reason alone* (1793). As a philosopher Kant allowed his thought to range into the speculative fields of science, mathematics, and theology. He influenced 19th and 20th-cent. philosophers in Germany and Britain, *eg*, J. G. Fichte, G. W. F. Hegel, and T. H. Green. Protestant theologians have drawn upon his metaphysical thought (*eg*, William Temple, Abp of Canterbury), although in his own lifetime Kant's views on Lutheranism caused minor difficulties with political authority in Prussia.

KANTEMIR, ANTIOCH DMITRIEVCH, Prince (1709–44), Russian politician and poet, who helped to persuade the Empress Anna to reassume the title and powers of an autocrat and dismiss the Supreme Privy Council (1730). He was a satirist, who modelled his works on those of the French poet, Boileau.

KANTEMIR, DMITRI, Prince (1673–1723), Moldavian *boyar*, who was appointed *hospodar* of the principality of Moldavia (1710). He entered into secret negotiations with Tsar Peter I (1711) and signed two treaties with him, one a military alliance against the Turks, and the other guaranteeing himself a safe refuge in Russia. After the disastrous Russian campaign on the Pruth river (1711), for which Kantemir failed to provide Moldavian support, he fled to the Ukraine.

KANVA DYNASTY, ancient Indian dynasty of only four kings, supposed to have reigned in parts of northern India, according to the Puranas (texts dealing with religion, cosmology, etc., but also often containing semi-historical portions), but unknown to more reliable sources.

KÁNYA, KÁLMAN (1869–1945), Hungarian politician and diplomat, who was Austro-Hungarian minister in Mexico (1909–19). He was later minister in Berlin (1925–33). As Hungarian foreign secretary (1933–8), his policy was tortuous. He hoped to regain the territories lost in 1919, and cultivation of German friendship appeared the only chance of realizing this, but he feared the consequences of dependency upon Germany and tried simultaneously to maintain the goodwill of Britain. Despite shrewd diplomacy, he satisfied neither country and was dismissed through German pressure for showing 'weakness' over the partition of Czechoslovakia.

KAPITZA, PETER (1894–   ), Russian physicist who worked at Cambridge in the 1920s, becoming (1930) professor of the Royal Society Mond Laboratory. His published work was mainly on magnetism and low temperatures and he received rewards from Britain, the US and the USSR.

KAPP, WOLFGANG (1858–1922), Prussian civil servant and politician, who was leader of the unsuccessful right-wing *putsch* against the newly founded German republic in March 1920. Kapp, an extreme nationalist and conservative, supported expansionist aims in the First World War, and founded, with Tirpitz, the German Patriotic Party (1917). His behaviour as provisional 'chancellor' during the attempted *putsch* was indecisive, and after its collapse he fled to Sweden. He returned to Germany voluntarily to face trial (1922), but died during the preliminary investigations of the case.

KAPP *PUTSCH* (1920), attempted right-wing revolt against the newly established Weimar republic in Germany. It followed moves by Noske, defence minister in Bauer's social democrat government, to disband the irregular troops (*Freikorps*) still fighting in the Baltic area, and to discharge regular officers and men in accordance with the disarmament provisions of the Versailles treaty. By March 1920 disaffection with the government was strong among both these groups of soldiers, many of whom saw little future in returning home to civilian life and unemployment. A harsh blow to the new republic's prestige was the failure, on 12 March, of a libel action brought by the finance minister, Erzberger, against the arch-conservative Helfferich, which ended in the latter's effective victory and the former's humiliation. This was the signal for revolt, and early next morning Lüttwitz's troops and the irregulars of Ehrhardt's brigade seized Berlin. The legal government retired to Dresden, and Kapp proclaimed himself chancellor. The army officers' corps, led by Von Seeckt, refused to offer armed resistance to the *putsch*, but the workers called a national general strike, and in Berlin civil servants refused to co-operate and prevented access to state finances. Kapp, isolated in Berlin and denied even the bourgeois support he had counted on, realized that his *putsch* was doomed to failure. After a futile attempt to negotiate a compromise with the legal government, he resigned and fled, on 17 March, and the occupying troops left Berlin.

The *putsch* itself was a total failure, but it indicated a profound hostility to the republic among conservatives and nationalists that was far from transient. In later years similar movements attracted the middle-class support needed for effective protest against the democratic republic, and culminated in National Socialism.

KAPPEL, BATTLE OF (11 Oct. 1531), defeat of a force of 2500 Protestants of Zürich canton by the superior army of the Catholic cantons (Zug, Uri, Unterwalden, Lucerne, and Schwyz), some 8000 strong. The Protestant reformer, Ulrich Zwingli, who was acting as army chaplain, was killed and the hegemony of Zürich within the Swiss confederation ended.

KAPPEL, 1st and 2nd PEACE OF (1529, 1531), attempts to settle the political problems arising from the religious division in the Swiss cantons. After building up the Christian Civic League by which he hoped to establish an evangelical Swiss confederation headed by Zürich, the Protestant reformer Zwingli was forced to make peace with the Catholic cantons (26 June 1529). The terms of this settlement were respected by neither side, and Zwingli's attempt to subjugate the Catholic cantons by military force led to his death in the battle of Kappel (Oct. 1531). A second peace restored the status quo and left the confederation divided into Catholic and Reformed cantons (1531).

KARA KHITAI, Tungus or Mongol peoples who established (916) the Liao dynasty in northern China. After their expulsion by the Jurjens (*c.* 1125), a branch settled in the upper Ili valley and established a loose rule over Kashgar, Khotan, and parts of western Turkestan which endured until 1211.

KARAKORUM, Mongol town on the Orkhon river and capital of the Mongol empire (*c.* 1230–60). It declined rapidly after Khublai removed the capital to China, but was restored after 1368, then in the 15th cent. lost all importance.

KARAMANLI, pashas of Tripoli (1714–1835), dynasty of Janissary origin, whose founder seized control after a rebellion against Ottoman authority (1711). A period of some power and prosperity under the founder, Ahmad (*reg.* 1714–1745), led to the incorporation of Cyrenaica and the Fezzan with Tripolitania. Loss of control by Ahmad's successors led to civil war, which was ended by the accession of Yusuf (1795), who took advantage of the Napoleonic wars to promote a profitable trade with Britain, and to build up a fleet with which to threaten shipping in the central Mediterranean. Falling into debt to the European factors controlling the export of cattle and corn, his reign was brought to an end by bankruptcy (1832), a possible European take-over being forestalled by rebellion, which led to the recovery of the country by Turkey (1835).

KARAMZIN, NIKOLAI MIKHAILOVICH (1766–1826), Russian thinker and historian. His negative reactions to the French Revolution and his historical studies made him a leading conservative influence in the reign of Alexander I. His most important works are *Letters of a Russian Traveller* and *History of the Russian State*. His *Memoir on Ancient and Modern Russia*, written for Alexander's sister, was an attack on Alexander's foreign involvements and, by implication, Speransky's administrative projects. Later, his ideas on Russian absolutism and his nationalist interpretation of Russian history were to influence the Slavophiles.

KARANKAWA INDIANS, small tribe near Matagorda Bay, TX, where the French explorer La Salle found them (1687). Their relations with white settlers were hostile, and by 1840 only 100 were left. They were apparently exterminated in an attack by ranchers (1858).

KARBALA, on the Euphrates river in Iraq. Here Husayn, second son of the Caliph Ali (d. AD 661) and grandson of the Prophet Muhammad, met his death in conflict with the forces of the Umayyad Caliph Yazid I on 10 Oct. 680. The martyrdom of Husayn did much to foster a rapid and enduring development of the Shi'ite faith.

KARDAN, PEACE OF (1534), settlement between Emperor Charles V's brother, Ferdinand, and the German princes (29 June 1534), by which the former accepted the fait accompli of Duke Ulrich's restoration to Württemberg in return for his recognition by the Elector of Saxony and his associates as the King of the Romans. Although Württemberg was to be held by Duke Ulrich as an Austrian fief, Ferdinand recognized the secularization of Church lands and the establishment of the Lutheran faith there.

KARDELJ, EDVARD (b. 1910), Yugoslav communist politician and the party's leading theoretician. When Tito took control of the Yugoslav party and set about reorganizing it, Kardelj was one his close associates. He was a well-known publicist and wrote under the pseudonym of 'Sperans', particularly about the national question with regard to Slovenia. During the Second World War he directed Partisan activity in Slovenia and served as vice-president of AVNOJ (Antifascist Assembly of National Liberation of Yugoslavia). He became vice-president of the Yugoslav government in 1945 and led the delegation to the peace conference at Paris in 1946. He became minister of foreign affairs in 1948, and, together with Djilas and Bakaric, represented Yugoslavia in the last discussions with Stalin at Moscow before the split with the Soviet Union. He later held numerous high positions in both the party and the state. As a prominent member of the 'old guard' he sat, in 1970, on the council of federation and its executive body, a senate or upper house. After the fall of Djilas he was closely identified with policies of decentralization.

KARDIS, PEACE OF (1661), confirmation of the preliminary peace concluded at the end of 1659 at Valiesar. It restored the status quo between Russia and Sweden after the Northern War (1655–60). Although Tsar Alexis had invaded Livonia and captured certain Baltic fortresses, *eg*, Dorpat, in the early stages of the war, he failed to take Riga and the Swedes held on to the Gulf of Finland. By the Kardis settlement Russia surrendered all her gains in the Baltic provinces, including Ingria and Karelia.

KARELIA, region spanning the eastern border between Finland and Russia, an important centre for forestry and related industries. The eastern part of the region was for long a source of friction between Finland and Russia, being politically a Russian territory, but culturally and linguistically related to Finland. In 1918 the Karelian national convention decided to request union with Finland, but in 1920, under the treaty of Tartu (Dorpat), Finland ceded eastern Karelia to Russia, with the assurance that it would have a large measure of autonomy. In 1921 Finland alleged that Russia was failing to observe this undertaking, and in 1922 Russia had to suppress a Karelian anti-Soviet uprising that had to some extent been fomented by Finland. Finland appealed to the League of Nations, which handed the case on to the International Court of Justice, but as Russia refused to co-operate in the court's proposed investigation of the Finnish complaints, the case had to be dropped. In 1923 Karelia was made an autonomous republic within the Soviet federation.

In 1938 Russo-Finnish talks began over territorial exchanges in the area, demanded by Russia, but these broke down in March 1938. Russia reconvened them in Oct., offering to cede some 9050 sq. kms of Karelia in exchange for Finnish cessions which would improve the strategic position of Leningrad. Finland refused the offer and hostilities broke out on 29 Nov. The Winter War was ended by the peace treaty of March 1940, in which Finland was forced to renounce most of western Karelia to Russia. Although a joint German–Finnish campaign temporarily won back the Karelian isthmus in 1941, Russia eventually regained the military initiative, and under a treaty of Sept. 1944 Finland was forced to accept again the 1940 frontiers. Most Finns left Karelia after its cession, and the area was repopulated by Russian settlement.

KAREN NATIONAL DEFENCE ORGANIZATION (KNDO), military wing of the Karen National Union (KNU). The KNDO was formed as part of the Karen revolt against the Burmese in the civil war after the independence of Burma. For a while, the KNDO, joined by the Kachins, dominated the greater part of Burma. In 1949 the initiative passed to the government and by 1954–5 the operations of the defeated KNDO degenerated into banditry. In 1962, when the army seized power, the KNDO rebellion revived. But on 12 March 1964 an uneasy peace was established between the Burmese and the Karens.

KARENS, Tai-Chinese race, the second largest indigenous minority community in Burma, numbering probably 2 million. They established themselves below and on the southern spurs of the Shan plateau. In the hills three Karenni or Red Karen states were recognized by the British as being independent. However, the majority of Karens were in the Papun, Thaton, Amherst, and Toungoo districts, though groups made their way elsewhere, particularly into the delta of the Irrawaddy. During the British period many Karens of the delta and of the Toungoo, Thaton, and Amherst districts became Christians and gained a good education in mission schools. They were influential out of proportion to their numbers, since they comprised only one in six of the whole community.

The Karens have little history. Until the missionaries came they were an illiterate, primitive people, seldom able to develop any permanent political organization beyond the village. They were particularly 'loyal' to the British, partly on religious grounds, but mainly because the British were their best protection against the Burmese, with whom there was long-standing enmity. This loyalty was shown by the British-officered resistance movement against the Japanese (1942–5). By the end of the war some 12,000 Karen guerrillas were in arms. When Burma became independent, civil war broke out and there was a strong Karen rebellion, mainly by the Karen National Defence Organization (KNDO). But Karen units in the Burmese army remained loyal to the government, although they fought their own people. Meanwhile, the government established the Karenni (later Kayah) State, and took action to create the Karen State in 1951. This consisted mainly of the Papun and Thaton districts, with Pa-an as its capital. By 1954–5 the rebellion was largely suppressed.

When the army seized power in Burma (1962) rebellion flared up again. On 12 March 1964, however, an agreement was negotiated between the government and the KNDO, the basis of which was that the government would consider inclusion within the Karen State (renamed Kawthulay) of areas of Karen population in the predominantly Burmese Irrawaddy and Tenasserim divisions. An uneasy peace subsisted in 1970, based on an understanding that the government would not meddle too much in Karen affairs.

KARIM KHAN ZEND (d. 1779) of the Lur tribe, ruled Iran from 1750 onwards without taking the title shah. He established his power first in western Iran during the anarchy which followed the death of Nadir Shah (1747) and, from his capital at Shiraz, gradually extended it throughout Iran, except for Khurasan.

KARKOTA DYNASTY, line of kings of ancient Kashmir (c. AD 700–855). During this period, especially from the reign of Lalitaditya (reg. 733–69), Kashmir grew into a strong power which intervened in the Gangetic valley (as far as Kanauj) and opened direct relations with China. This period was also a great age of temple building in Kashmir.

KARLSEFNI, THORFINN (fl. 12th cent.), Icelandic explorer, who was one of the earliest Viking explorers of America, which had first been sighted (c. 1000) by Leif Eiriksson. His expedition (1107–11) started from Greenland and represented an attempt to establish a settlement. It was unsuccessful because of the hostility of the natives.

KARLSRÜHE, capital city of Baden, the most notable example of 18th-cent. European town planning. Designed to replace Durlach, the whole town was built symmetrically as one huge star radiating from the palace of the margrave, Charles William.

KARMA (lit., 'deed'), the (especially) morally qualified deed which inevitably produces consequences—rarely in this, almost always in future, life, the shape and quality of which is in fact determined by the sum-total of such deeds. Belief in karma is common to nearly all Indian religions. It is important to the historian because it may have strongly influenced actions by historical figures, but especially because it has basically affected the points of view inherent in Indian sources.

KARNAK, part of Thebes, on the right bank of the Nile, where a complex of temples of the god Amun was built up from the time of the Middle Kingdom (c. 2134–1786 BC) until the Roman period.

KAROLYI, ALOYS (1825–89), Austrian diplomat, who failed to win Russian support for Austria against Napoleon III in 1858 and was unable to prevent the breakdown in relations between Austria and Prussia which preceded the Seven Days War (1866). However, after Austria's defeat, Karolyi secured a favourable settlement at the preliminary peace of Nikolsburg. He was one of Austria's leading delegates at the Berlin Congress (1878) and ended his career as ambassador in London (1878–88).

KARTAL (KAGHUL), BATTLE OF (1 Aug. 1770). The Russian general Count Peter Rumyantsev routed the Ottoman forces under the command of the Grand Vizier Khalil Pasha—a triumph which led to the Russian occupation of Ismail and Kilya on the Danube river.

KARTINI, RADEN ADJENG (1879–1904), Indonesian writer and early advocate of Javanese cultural modernization, who became the symbol of enlightened Indonesian womanhood. Her father, a progressively inclined Central Java regent, gave her a Western type of education which made her conscious of the gulf between Javanese tradition and Western modernity, and of the contradiction between European democratic ideals and the subordinate position of colonial Indonesians and of women in her day. She discussed these problems in a series of letters to the liberal Dutch educator, H. Abendanon, which were published after her death. They contributed much to initial Dutch sympathy for colonial reform. Kartini Day is now celebrated in Indonesia as a national holiday in honour of women.

KASHMIR, or the state of Jammu and Kashmir, largest of the former Indian states. On the west and north-west it is bounded by Pakistan and Afghanistan. To its south lies the East Punjab. On the east it is bounded by Chinese Tibet, while its northern frontiers are conterminous with those of Chinese Turkestan. Its early history is obscure. In the 14th cent. AD its Hindu rulers were overthrown by Muslim invaders. At the beginning of the 19th cent. it was conquered by Ranjit Singh, the Sikh ruler of the Punjab. In 1846, at the end of the First Anglo-Sikh War, it was handed over to Gulab Singh, a Hindu Dogra raja. His descendants ruled until the abdication, in Dec. 1952, of Maharaja Sir Hari Singh.

Kashmir has often been unfortunate in its rulers, whose policy was to fleece the peasantry and live in luxury. This was particularly true of its late Dogra rulers and their Brahman advisers, the Kashmiri pandits. In 1931 revolts against the maharaja's rule led to a British commission, which reported that the Kashmiri pandits had acquired a stranglehold over all state employment and the Muslims, who formed the vast majority of the population, were not being given a fair share in the administration of the country.

After the partition of the Indian sub-continent in Aug. 1947, Kashmir became a bone of contention between India and Pakistan. Tribesmen from the frontier of Pakistan threatened its capital, Srinagar, which was saved by the intervention of Indian airborne troops. At the same time, the ruler of Kashmir signed an instrument of accession to the Indian union. In 1948 India brought the dispute before the United Nations Security Council but, so far, all efforts to find a solution have failed. Pakistanis contend that Kashmir belongs to Pakistan because of the communal balance of its population, and because of its contiguity to Pakistan. In Aug.–Sept. 1965 the Kashmir dispute erupted into a war between India and Pakistan. United Nations Security Council and Russian diplomatic intervention achieved a cease-fire.

M. Brecher, *Struggle for Kashmir* (New York, 1953).
A. Lamb, *Crisis in Kashmir, 1947 to 1966* (London, 1966)

CCD

KASIRAM DAS (fl. 16th cent.), author of the Bengali version of the ancient Indian epic the *Mahabharata*, who worked in a period which shows, in several respects, renewed interest in classical Indian culture.

KASKASIA, French mission station established in the Illinois country by Gabriel Marest (1703), a Jesuit. It was the first permanent white settlement in the Mississippi valley.

KASSIM (QASIM), ABD AL-QARIM (1914–63), Iraqi soldier, born in Baghdad who, as a brigade group commander (1958), planned and led the coup which overthrew the Hashemite monarchy and by which he himself became the dominant figure in Iraqi politics (1958–63). Although to the outside world his actions seemed strange, they are logical when viewed as part of a constant struggle to pursue an Iraqi nationalist policy, based on moderate economic and social reform, against opposition from Arab nationalists, communists, Kurds, and former privileged groups. Although Kassim maintained his position with great skill at first, his ultimate failure to win the support of any substantial influential group and to retain control of the army led to his overthrow and execution (9 Feb. 1963).

KASSITES, people speaking a language of the Asianic group, from the Zagros region, who invaded Mesopotamia in the 2nd millennium BC, captured Babylon (*c.* 1530), and extended their control to Sumer. Little is known about them, but they seem to have adopted Mesopotamian culture and to have been well accepted by the subject peoples. The Kassite dynasty was overthrown by the Elamites (*c.* 1162).

KATANGA, secessionist movement in the large region of that name situated in the south-east of Congo (Kuishasa) republic, established in July 1960 and briefly led by Moise Tshombe with foreign financial help.

KATAYAMA, TETSU (1887–), Japanese politician and Japan's first, and (in 1970) only, socialist prime minister. His coalition cabinet survived less than a year (May 1947–March 1948).

KATHERINE HOWARD (*c.* 1520–42), Queen consort and fifth wife of King Henry VIII of England, whom he divorced for adultery.

KATHERINE PARR (1512–48), Queen consort and sixth wife of King Henry VIII of England, had been twice widowed and was about to marry Sir Thomas Seymour, brother of Henry's third queen, when Henry himself claimed her (1543). During his absence in France (1544) she was regent. She took a kindly interest in her three royal step-children and was admired for her learning. Her enemies accused her, unsuccessfully, of heresy. After Henry's death (1547) she married Seymour, but died in the following year, after giving birth to a daughter.

KATIPUNAN, abbreviation of *Kataastaasan Kagalanggalang Katipunan Ng Mga Anak Ng Bayan* ('Highest and Most Respected Association of the Sons of the Country'), a Philippine secret society founded by Andres Bonifacio on 7 July 1892. The *Katipunan* also referred to as K.K.K., favoured a revolution if reforms could not be attained by peaceful means. Its ideas were embodied in the *Kartilla ng Katopunan* ('The *Katipunan* Primer'). It was governed by a supreme council, of which Bonifacio became president in 1896; below it were organized provincial councils, and under them popular councils, whose members were elected by majority vote. Because it was a secret society, the *Katipunan's* members took assumed names, and wore hoods during meetings and initiation rites, which resembled those of the freemasons. Originally, the *Katipunan* was open only to men; later, a women's section was formed. The discovery of the K.K.K. caused the premature outbreak of the Philippine revolution in the same month. The *Katipunan* directed the revolution until it was replaced by a new revolutionary government at the Tejeros Convention in March 1897.

KATKOV, MIKHAIL NIKIFOROVICH (1818–87). Russian writer, and professor of philosophy at Moscow University (1845–50). He was a member of the Stankevich circle, a friend of Belinsky, and an advocate of constitutional monarchy. He supported the emancipation (1861) and the zemstvo and judicial reforms, but after the Polish uprising (1863) his liberalism gave way to fervent nationalism. He exercised a conservative influence on the court. He published Pan-Slavist works and was a member of the Moscow Slavic Benevolent Committee, but was primarily a nationalist and supporter of imperialist expansion.

KATŌ, KŌMEI (TAKAAKI) (1860–1926), Japanese diplomat and politician, who was four times foreign minister. He played a considerable part in forming the Anglo–Japanese alliance (1902) and was responsible for the 'Twenty-One Demands' presented to China (1915), the extreme nature of which was due partly to Katō's desire to restore the foreign ministry's control over foreign policy. Ousted from the cabinet (1915), Katō became an advocate of liberal policies, and president of the newly organized *Kenseikai* party (1916), to which he attracted the financial support of the Mitsubishi Co. In 1924 he formed a *Kenseikai–Seiyūkai* coalition ministry, and in 1925 a *Kenseikai* cabinet. His legislation included manhood (over 25 years) suffrage and a peace preservation law under which the police suppressed the most radical parties.

KATSINA, city and emirate in northern Nigeria, one of the Hausa *Bokwai*, traditionally founded by Kumayo, grandson of Bayajidda, who married the daughter of the last Durbawa ruler of the area. The new dynasty, the Larabawa, ruled until the 15th cent., when the last king was killed in a wrestling bout with Muhammad Korau from Yandoto, a great centre of learning. His descendants ruled until 1807, when they were forced to move to Maradi in Niger, where their descendants still rule. Islam was introduced in the reign of Korau, his son Ibrahim Sura (1493–6) was host to the jurisconsult Al-Maghili and corresponded with the polymath Al-Suyuti. Leo Africanus records the subjugation of the city to Songhay, but it had gained its independence by 1554 only to fall under Bornu hegemony. The 16th and 17th cents saw a series of wars between Kano and Katsina which seem to have ended with the Jukun invasions. In the 18th cent. the city was the major entrepôt of the Sudan trading with North Africa, Egypt, Chad, and Ashanti; it was likewise the intellectual centre of the region. The present dynasty dates from 1906 when the Fulanic dynasty was deposed by the British resident.

KATSURO, TARŌ (1847–1913), Japanese soldier and politician. During his military career he was active in the establishment of a general staff (1878), but his principal achievements were political. As Yamagata Aritomo's main Chōshū protégé, he became army minister (1898) and then prime minister (1901), a position he held for more than seven out of the next ten years, largely owing to his compromise with the *Seiyūkai* party. During his first cabinet, the Anglo–Japanese alliance was signed (1902) and the Russo–Japanese War was fought. But his third administration failed owing to the *Taishō* political crisis (1912–13).

KATYN GRAVES, discovered by German troops during the Second World War. Berlin radio announced (13 April 1943) that some 10,000 Polish officers had been murdered and buried at Katyn by the Russians. Though this was an exaggeration, the report in essence appears to have been true. As a result, the Polish government in exile in London broke off diplomatic relations with the Soviet Union (26 April 1943).

KAUFMAN, KONSTANTIN PETROVICH VON (1818–82), Russian general and administrator in Central Asia. After service in the Caucasus and Poland, he became governorgeneral of Turkestan (1867) and conquered and annexed to the Russian empire the khanates of Khiva, Bokhara, and Khokand.

KAUNDA, KENNETH DAVID (1924–), president of Zambia, who, having embraced the cause of African emancipation, joined (1949) the Northern Rhodesia National Congress, led by Harry Nkumbula. In 1953 he became Congress secretarygeneral, but in 1958 broke away from Nkumbula's leadership, and founded the Zambia National Congress. This was later banned and Kaunda was detained by the British authorities. He was released in the midst of a country-wide agitation against the white-dominated Federation of the Rhodesias and Nyasaland (1953–63) and against continued colonial rule.

Kaunda at once took over the leadership of the United National Independence Party, the successor to the Zambia National Congress, and became the country's acknowledged leader, and its prime minister. After its independence in 1964 he became president.

KAUNITZ, WENZEL ANTON, Prince von (1711–94), Austrian statesman and counsellor and servant of Maria Theresa and Joseph II. He was Austrian representative at the peace conference of Aix-la-Chapelle (1748) and served in Turin and Brussels before being sent to Paris as ambassador (1750), where he set about achieving a rapprochement between Austria and France and the diplomatic isolation of Prussia, with the ultimate object of achieving the recovery of Silesia. In 1753 he was made Austrian chancellor and in Aug. 1755 renewed the fitful Franco–Austrian negotiations. The news of the Westminster Convention (Jan. 1756) enabled him to conclude the first treaty of Versailles with France, which consisted of a convention of neutrality and a defensive alliance. Kaunitz then worked to convert the defensive into an offensive alliance by persuading Louis XV to participate in the destruction of his former ally, Frederick II. Frederick's invasion of Saxony (1756) enabled Joseph to achieve this in the second treaty of Versailles (1757). Thus Kaunitz, known as 'the coachman of Europe', drove France into that shift of alliances called the Diplomatic Revolution.

Despite Austria's failure to recover Silesia in the Seven Years War which followed, Kaunitz never gave up his schemes for the aggrandizement of the Habsburg empire. To this end he fought Frederick II of Prussia by both military and diplomatic means for some 30 years, planned to dismember Turkey, placated Russia, and participated in the first partition of Poland. He also strengthened the internal administration of the empire by setting up a Council of State (*Staatsrat*) to consider all the internal affairs of the diverse provinces from the centre (1761). In 1770 Kaunitz met Frederick II at Neustadt and encouraged Prussia to take a share of Poland in the hope of recovering Silesia as a *quid pro quo*, but was nearly out-manœuvred when Frederick co-operated with his old enemy, Catherine II of Russia, in a scheme to dismember Poland. Rather than be excluded, Kaunitz persuaded Maria Theresa and Joseph II to join in the partition scheme, from which Austria received Galicia and the important salt monopoly of central Europe.

Meanwhile, Kaunitz manipulated the Russo-Turkish balance of power in south-east Europe. In 1771, to prevent Russian expansion, he made a convention with the Porte, promising Austrian guarantees of the territorial integrity of the Ottoman empire in return for a large annual subsidy. After the War of the Bavarian Succession, however, he and Joseph decided to break the dangerous Russo–Prussian alliance and draw closer to Russia. Kaunitz arranged a meeting between Joseph and Catherine (1780), which led to their co-operation in the Turkish War (1787–92). As an old man, Kaunitz counselled Leopold II to modify Austrian foreign policy and seek reconciliation with Prussia and Poland and the maintenance of the status quo with Russia and France.

Kaunitz had tried to caution Joseph against the reopening of the Scheldt river, on the grounds that it was not economically worthwhile and would provoke a European war. He also advocated the pacification of the rebels in the Netherlands (1787) and supported Joseph's liberal reforms, *eg*, the Edict of Toleration.   MKS

KAVAD I (*reg.* 488–531), Sassanian King of Iran during a weak period in its history. He was placed on the throne by the Ephthalites, supported the Mazdakites against the nobility, but was deposed, then reinstated by the Ephthalites (499), on whose support he subsequently depended for his security. He fought campaigns against the Romans and Huns.

KAVEL, AUGUST LUDWIG CHRISTIAN (1798–1860), Prussian Lutheran pastor, who resisted Calvinist pressure by King Frederick William III and, aided by George Fife Angas,

led 200 of his former congregation to South Australia in 1838. Kavel's successful leadership contributed to the substantial SA German settlement, later some 8000 strong. He was followed in 1841 by Gotthard Daniel Fritzsche (1797–1863), who also ministered in SA until a doctrinal dispute between them (1845) split the SA Lutheran community.

KAWA, site of Kushite town and temples, known in Pharaonic and Napatan times as Gem-aten. The temples have been excavated, the earliest being found to date from the Egyptian New Kingdom and to have been built by Tutankhamun, though it is possible that he merely restored an earlier building. Taharqa carried out much work here, building a large temple dedicated to Amun, which he embellished with precious metals and surrounded with gardens of exotic trees, and in which he set up inscriptions. The occupation of Kawa continued until late Meriotic or X-group times, when it was destroyed by fire.

KAY, JOHN (d. 1764), British textile engineer, who invented the flying shuttle (1733), an improved loom mounted on wheels, which doubled the width of cloth that one man could weave and therefore accelerated the output. Popular hostility to his invention drove him to France (1753), where he died in poverty (1764).

KAYASTHA CASTE, one of the highest castes, mainly in north-eastern India, especially Bengal, the members of which have been engaged in clerical duties from the 6th cent. AD.

KAY-SHUTTLEWORTH, SIR JAMES PHILLIPS (1804–77), British physician, educationist, civil servant, and writer, whose early experience as a doctor gave him an understanding of social needs. He served as a poor law commissioner in East Anglia (1835) and became secretary to the committee of council on education (1839–49), which administered the annual state grant under the Education Act (1833) given to voluntary schools. This required him to introduce the system of school-inspection. Kay-Shuttleworth's concern for teaching standards led him to found a training college at Battersea (1839) on which the subsequent training of teachers in the country was modelled. He served (1861–5) on the central relief committee during the Lancashire cotton famine and on various scientific commissions.

KAZAKH, Turkish people inhabiting the area embraced by modern Kazakhstan (USSR). The name was applied to Uzbek tribesmen who separated from their leader, Abu'l Khair (1412–68). During the 17th cent. the Kazakhs became divided into three 'Hordes'. In 1730 the Khan of the Little Horde accepted Russian suzerainty and this and subsequent treaties formed the basis of a Russian claim eventually enforced by conquest after 1847. Subsequent Russian peasant immigration and the forced settlement of the nomadic Kazakhs, particularly during collectivization (1928–32), changed the demographic composition and economy of the area which became Kazakhstan (1926). Kazakh hostility to Russian encroachment, symbolized by the popular hero, Kenesari (d. 1847), took on new nationalist forms in the 20th cent. A short-lived independent government was founded (1917) by the Kazakh party, which was known as the Alash Orda.

KAZAN, town on the Volga and capital of the Tatar state of that name (c. 1445–1552), which emerged after the collapse of the Golden Horde. Wars with Russia and continual internal commotions, partly induced by Russian and Crimean Tatar interference, characterized its history. In 1521 Khan Sahib Girey and his Crimean relatives attacked Moscow and forced that state to pay tribute to the Crimea. After unsuccessful campaigns in 1548 and 1550, Ivan the Terrible finally captured Kazan in 1552 and incorporated it in the Russian state. It remained an important Turkish Muslim cultural centre within Russia.

KAZEMBE, trading empire of Central Africa on the Luapula river. The rulers of Kazembe were 17th- and 18th-cent. immigrants from the Lunda empire, attracted eastward to seek salt mines, copper industries, and a commercial opening to the Portuguese on the lower Zambezi. Kazembe became the focus of three different trading systems—the slave trade to the Atlantic via Mwata Yamvo's Lunda, the ivory trade to Zanzibar, and the trade of the Bisa and Yao to the northern Mozambique coast. In the 19th cent. Kazembe escaped the disruptions caused by Ngoni invasions, but was superseded as the major commercial power in the eastern Congo by Arabs and Nyamwezi.

KEARNY, STEPHEN WATTS (1794–1848), US soldier, who served in the War of 1812 and the Mexican War (1846–8). He captured Santa Fé (1846) and advanced to CA where he became involved in a conflict of authority with John C. Frémont.

KEBBI, area and once a state in north-western Nigeria. It became prominent early in the 16th cent. when its ruler, Kanta Kota, shook off Songhay tutelage (1516). From its walled capital, Leka, and later Surame, Kebbi could withstand both Songhay and Bornu, acting as a buffer between Songhay and the Hausa states. After the Moroccan invasion of Songhay (1591), Kebbi gave refuge to the fleeing Askias. It endured as a state until the late 17th cent., when internal weakness led to its being divided among the rulers of Aïr, Gobir, and Zamfara.

KEBLE, JOHN (1792–1866), English clergyman and writer, whose assize sermon in Oxford (1833) initiated the Oxford Movement, in which he, J. H. Newman, and E. B. Pusey defended the Catholicity of the Church of England and upheld the apostolic succession of bishops. The publication of a series of *Tracts for the Times* (1833–45) led to them and their followers being called Tractarians. Although never aspiring to high office within the Church and remaining a country incumbent, Keble's influence was considerable. He edited the *Works* of Richard Hooker (1836) and published several pamphlets and works of devotion, while his *Christian Year* (1827) was the major achievement in verse of one who had been professor of poetry at Oxford (1831). Keble College, Oxford, was founded (1870) in his memory.

KEDAH SULTANATE, in north-west Malaya. Although southern Kedah was an ancient centre of trans-Peninsula trade, the Muslim sultanate appears to date from the 15th cent. The Atjehnese, Portuguese, and Dutch competed for monopoly of its pepper and tin, but the most lasting political influence was that of Siam, exercised through Ligor (Nakhon Sithammarat). Kedah leased Penang to the British (1786) in the vain expectation of receiving protection against Siam. Nevertheless, Britain accepted the Siamese devastation of Kedah in 1821, and acknowledged Siamese suzerainty until this was transferred to Britain by treaty (1909). Earlier (1905) Kedah had been forced by near bankruptcy to accept from Siam a British 'financial adviser'.

KEFAUVER, CAREY ESTES (1903–63), US politician, who was Democratic congressman from TN (1939–49) and US senator from TN (1949–63). He fought for the rights of the individual against big business, big government, and organized crime. He sponsored the Kefauver–Celler Bill (1950), tightened anti-trust curbs, and, as chairman of a Senate subcommittee (1950–1), conducted much-publicized investigations into the drug industry and into organized crime. He was Adlai Stevenson's vice-presidential candidate (1956).

KEIR, JAMES (1735–1820), Scottish soldier and industrial chemist, who founded the Tipton Alkali Works (1780), which may be regarded as the beginning of the scientific chemical industry. By 1781 he had developed a process for the commercial manufacture of caustic soda from waste sulphates which was succeeded by the process devised by Nicholas Le Blanc (1742–1806).

KEITA, lineage of ancient Mali whose chiefs gradually overcame rival clans and emerged under Sundiata (d. *c.* 1255) as the leaders of an expanding empire.

KEITEL, WILHELM (1882–1946), German field marshal and chief of the armed forces (OKW) in the Second World War. Having been a staff and training officer, in 1925 he joined the defence ministry, became a departmental head in 1929, and in 1935 head of the Armed Forces Office (*Wehrmachtsamt*). In Feb. 1938 he was appointed chief of the OKW after the dismissal of Blomberg and the abolition of the war ministry, Hitler having deliberately raised him from his relatively obscure status to this high rank because of his reputation as an industrious and submissive subordinate. In the Second World War Keitel fully lived up to Hitler's expectations; he seldom voiced an independent opinion on military strategy and remained totally subservient to Hitler, thus helping Germany to lose the war. After the defeat of France, he conducted the cease-fire negotiations in Compiègne subsequently being given the rank of field marshal (July 1940). In May 1945 he signed the German capitulation in Berlin. He was one of the major defendants at the Nuremberg trials, where he was charged with war crimes and crimes against humanity, and with planning and waging a war of aggression. He was sentenced to death in Oct. 1946.

KEKULÉ, VON STRADONITZ, FREDRICH AUGUST (1829–1896), German chemist, who postulated (1858) that the atoms making up a molecule were arranged in a specific way and in 1865 proposed the cyclic formula of benzene. The foundation of structural organic chemistry enabled each organic compound to be assigned a precise and individual representation. Despite later modifications, structural formulae based on Kekulé's concepts continue to guide chemists, as they have done over the last century, in the synthesis of new compounds.

KELANTAN SULTANATE, in north-east Malaya, after being weakened by constant internal divisions, accepted Siamese suzerainty throughout the 19th cent., but appealed to Britain when, after 1898, more direct rule was imposed. The ensuing conflict was resolved by an Anglo–Siamese agreement (1902) whereby Siam appointed an 'Adviser' to Kelantan of British nationality. Siamese rights were transferred to Britain in 1909.

KELLOGG, FRANK BILLINGS (1856–1937), US lawyer, politician, diplomat, and statesman, who rose from humble origins to become a wealthy lawyer and statesman of high international reputation. He worked as janitor and office boy in a Rochester, MN, office in exchange for instruction in law and was admitted to the bar in 1887. During Theodore Roosevelt's presidency, Kellogg established a reputation as a 'trust-buster'. He acted as special counsel to the Interstate Commerce Commission in an investigation of the Harriman Railroads and he prosecuted such companies as the Western Paper Trust and Standard Oil. He was elected Republican senator from MN in 1916, but lost his seat in 1922. In 1923 he was appointed ambassador to Britain, where he helped to negotiate the Dawes Plan. As secretary of state (1925–9), his most celebrated achievement was the Kellogg–Briand Pact, which outlawed war as an instrument of national policy, and for which he was awarded the Nobel Peace Prize (1929). He served on the Permanent Court of International Justice at The Hague (1930–5).

KELLOGG–BRIAND PACT (1928), multilateral treaty condemning recourse to war for the settlement of international disputes and renouncing war as an instrument of national policy. It was signed in Paris (27 Aug. 1928) by representatives of 15 nations, including the US. The treaty grew out of a proposal by the French foreign minister, Aristide Briand, for a bilateral agreement between the US and France. Partly in order to avoid making an entangling alliance, the US secretary of state, Frank B. Kellogg, translated the proposal into a multilateral instrument, which was ratified by the US Senate (Jan. 1929) and was eventually adhered to by 62 nations. Containing no provisions for sanctions, it rested solely on the moral force of world opinion.

KELLS, BOOK OF, finest of the Hiberno-Saxon illuminated manuscripts, predominantly Irish in its decoration, dating from *c.* 800. Its origin is uncertain (possibly Iona). Known also as the Gospel-book of St Columba, it was later kept at Columba's monastery at Kells.

KELLY, NED (1855–80), leader of the Kelly gang of Australian bushrangers. After a battle with the police, in which the gang wore home-made armour, all were killed except Kelly, who was caught and later hanged.

KELLY, WILLIAM (1811–88), US ironmaster who shared with his English contemporary, Henry Bessemer, the discovery that steel could be made by blasting air on to molten iron. He experimented with the process from 1851 and commercial production began in 1864.

KELVIN OF LARGS, WILLIAM THOMPSON, Baron (1824–1907), Scottish mathematician, physicist and inventor, who was professor of natural philosophy at Glasgow University (1846–99) and chancellor (1904). He (1851–4) formulated the two great laws of thermodynamics and evolved the theory of electric oscillation, the foundation of wireless telegraphy. In 1866 he superintended the successful laying of a cable across the Atlantic. He was interested in problems of measuring and generating electricity, and in electric lighting. He acquired a large fortune from a shrewd application of his inventions. He was president of the Royal Society in 1890–4.

KEMALISM, term commonly employed to describe the policy pursued by Mustafa Kemal Atatürk (1881–1938) as president of Turkey (1923–38). According to Atatürk's own manifesto (1931), it was based upon six principles—republicanism, nationalism, populism, statism, secularism, and revolution. Republicanism found expression in the abolition of the sultanate (1 Nov. 1922) and the proclamation of the Turkish republic (29 Oct. 1923); nationalism in the prolonged attempt to inculcate a sense of Turkish national identity through the rewriting of history, the remodelling of language, and the renunciation of Pan-Islamic, Pan-Turkish, and Pan-Ottoman aims; populism in the assertion that political authority derives from the will of the people, although, with some abortive exceptions, it was thought premature to permit the people to express their will through a democratic system and political power remained in the hands of Atatürk and his Republican People's Party; statism in the comparatively unsuccessful attempt to industrialize Turkey after 1930 through state initiative; secularism by the abolition of the caliphate (3 March 1924), the adoption of a completely secular system of civil law (1926), the abolition of the fez (1925), and the romanization of the alphabet (1928); revolution in the continuous radical changes which characterized the whole period, for, although Atatürk built upon the foundations laid by the Ottoman reformers, his policy was unique in its radical rejection of the past and emphasis upon total modernization.

KEMP, JOHN (*c.* 1380–1454), became Abp of York (1426), a cardinal (1439), and Abp of Canterbury (1452). He served twice as lord chancellor, his combined terms of office lasting ten years. He favoured peace with France, helped to put down Cade's rebellion in Kent in 1450, and upheld the royal authority of Henry VI in face of the growing Yorkist challenge. He was a moderating influence on the eve of the

Wars of the Roses and might have averted the Civil War if he had lived.

KENDALL, AMOS (1789–1869), US newspaperman and politician, who became an influential Democrat in KY. He supported Jacksonian policies in the Washington *Globe,* served in Andrew Jackson's informal 'Kitchen Cabinet', and was postmaster-general under Jackson and Van Buren (1835–1840). During the Civil War he supported the Union cause.

KENILWORTH, DICTUM OF (1266), name given to an English royal ordinance settling the terms on which the rebels against King Henry III were to be readmitted to royal allegiance after the Barons' Wars (1263–6). It laid down a system of fines, by which the rebels were allowed to redeem their properties according to the degree of their guilt. By its comprehensive review of all possible land tenures, it provides one of the most systematic and coherent statements of the English land law in the 13th cent.

KENNAN, GEORGE FROST (1904–   ), US diplomat, who was first chairman of the policy planning staff in the state department (1947), and US ambassador in Moscow (1952–1953). He retired to Princeton (1953), published several volumes of a major study of Soviet–American relations, then returned to government service as US ambassador to Yugoslavia (1961–3). He was the chief author of the containment theory (1946–7).

KENNEDY, EDWARD MOORE (1932–   ), US politician, fourth son of Joseph P. Kennedy, who helped to run his brother John F. Kennedy's senatorial campaign (1958) and presidential campaign (1960). He was elected to the US Senate for the rest of John F. Kennedy's uncompleted term (1962) and re-elected as senator from MA (1964). He became assistant majority leader in the Senate (1969) and was a prospective candidate for the Democratic presidential nomination until his political image was damaged by his involvement in a mysterious and fatal car accident on Chappaquidick Island off Cape Cod, MA in July 1969.

KENNEDY, JAMES (d. 1465), Scottish statesman, who became Bp of Dunkeld in 1437 and was Bp of St Andrews (1440–65), founding there the college of St Salvator in 1450. He acted as regent for the young King James III.

KENNEDY, JOHN FITZGERALD (1917–63), 35th president of the US, second son of Joseph P. Kennedy. Educated at Princeton, Harvard, and the London School of Economics, his senior thesis at Harvard, an analysis of British policies at the time of the Munich agreements (1938), was published as *Why England Slept* (1940). He then studied at the Stanford University Graduate School of Business (1940–1). As a naval lieutenant during the Second World War he was decorated for his role as commander of a torpedo boat (PT109) during the Solomon Islands campaign (1943). Elected as a Democratic congressman from MA (1946), and re-elected 1948, 1950, he established a record as a moderate liberal on domestic issues, a strong supporter of the Truman Doctrine, and a believer in a more aggressively anti-Communist China policy. Elected to the US Senate (1952), in an election year in which the Republican presidential candidate, Dwight D. Eisenhower, carried the state, he assumed an ambivalent position during the McCarthy era. During a long convalescence after a number of serious spinal operations, he wrote *Profiles in Courage* (1956), a study of political leadership which was awarded a Pulitzer Prize (1957). He narrowly missed the Democratic vice-presidential nomination (1956) and was re-elected to the Senate (1958). As a candidate for the presidential nomination in 1960, he built up a powerful political organization, won an impressive series of primary elections, and gained the nomination on the first ballot. In his acceptance speech he introduced his programme under the title, the New Frontier. In a carefully conducted campaign against the better-known Republican candidate, Richard M. Nixon, his political style, effective organization, and youthful image, confirmed by a series of television debates with Nixon, gave him a narrow victory.

His administration rapidly acquired a glamorous aura that appealed to large sections of the American people and increased his public support, but he failed to persuade Congress to accept a number of important domestic reform measures. In foreign affairs his achievements were more substantial. After the initial setback of the abortive Bay of Pigs invasion of Cuba (April 1961) he held profitable meetings with Khrushchev in Vienna (June 1961). The relationship established between the two leaders did not, however, prevent construction of the Berlin Wall in the summer of 1961, and the Cold War continued. The introduction of Soviet missiles into Cuba (1962) resulted in the Cuba missile crisis in Oct., when Kennedy imposed a naval embargo on Soviet shipments to Cuba and war seemed imminent. After an exchange of notes, the USSR agreed to withdraw the missiles in exchange for an American agreement to respect the territorial integrity of Cuba. Perhaps one of Kennedy's greatest achievements was the conclusion of the Nuclear Test Ban treaty (1963) in the more relaxed international atmosphere following the Cuban crisis. Kennedy worked for international co-operation between the US and other countries, launched the Peace Corps and the Alliance for Progress (1961), and supported the Trade Expansion Act (1962). In Viet-nam the administration continued to support the South Viet-namese regime, increased the amount of US aid, and strengthened the number of American economic and military advisers in South Viet-nam. While on a political tour of Texas, President Kennedy was murdered in Dallas on 22 Nov. 1963.

Arthur M. Schlesinger, Jr, *A Thousand Days* (Boston, 1965). Theodore C. Sorensen, *Kennedy* (New York, 1965).   FPK

KENNEDY, JOSEPH PATRICK (1888–1969), US financier, public official, and father of John F., Robert F., and Edward M. Kennedy. During the 1920s he was an investment banker (1919–24) and financier of motion pictures in Hollywood (1926–30). By 1930 he had become a multi-millionaire. In 1932 he supported F. D. Roosevelt's presidential election, was appointed first chairman of the Securities and Exchange Commission (1934–5), chairman of the United States Maritime Commission (1937), and US ambassador to Britain (1937–40). After some initial success in London, his dispatches and public comments about Britain's chances of survival became increasingly pessimistic and more stridently isolationist in their tone. Kennedy's resignation under pressure from Washington (6 Nov. 1940) effectively ended his public career.

KENNEDY, ROBERT FRANCIS (1925–68), US politician, third son of Joseph P. Kennedy. He won a reputation as an investigator with the Criminal Division of the US Department of Justice (1951–2), and then as an assistant counsel with a Senate sub-committee on investigations, under the chairmanship of Senator Joseph McCarthy (1953–4) and Senator John McClellan (1954–7). Later, he served as McClellan's chief counsel (1957–60) for the Select Committee on Improper Activities in the Labor or Management Field, which helped to expose irregular activities in the Teamsters' Union. After assisting his brother, John F. Kennedy, in the 1960 presidential campaign, he was appointed US attorney-general and became known as an uncompromising defender of minority group civil rights. He resigned from President Johnson's administration (1964), was elected US senator from NY, and became one of the most outspoken critics of Johnson's South-East Asia policies. Following the success of Senator Eugene McCarthy in the NH Democratic primary election (1968), Kennedy announced his own candidacy for the US presidency. He won a number of state primaries, but immediately after victory in CA he was murdered in Los Angeles.

KENNETH I MACALPINE (*reg.* 844–60), King of Scotland, who secured Galloway (834) and, by 844, ruled most of central Scotland. He broke the power of the Picts and established Dunkeld as his capital.

KENNETH II (*reg.* 971–95), King of Scotland, who extended his kingdom north of Fife, established the importance of Brechin, and made serious, if unsuccessful, attempts to secure Lothian from Northumbria.

KENSEIKAI, Japanese political party, founded in 1916. It was a successor to Ōkuma's *Kaishintō* and Katsura's *Dōshikai*. In 1927 it merged with the *Seiyūhontō* to form the *Minseitō*.

KENSINGTON STONE, slab of rock found (1898) on a farm near Kensington, MN. It is inscribed in runic letters and has an account of a journey from Vinland made by Norse explorers who camped near the site of its discovery (1362). There have been many historical and philological arguments over its authenticity, which remain (1970) unresolved.

KENT, Hubert de Burgh (2nd Earl of (1st of 2nd creation)) (d. 1243), justiciar of England (1215–32). Born of a knightly family from Norfolk, he rose to be chamberlain (1200–5) and Earl of Kent (1221). After John's death (1216), he governed England with the regent William Marshal on behalf of the infant Henry III. From the time of Marshal's death in 1219 until his own fall from power in 1232 he was the effective ruler of England. His rise to wealth, title, and power excited the envy and hatred of many people, who caused his downfall, but he was loyal and hard-working and tried to govern the country with justice.

KENT, JAMES (1763–1847), American jurist, who was judge of the New York supreme court (1798), chief justice (1804), and chancellor of the state court of chancery (1814–23). Adapting English practice to the American situation, Kent was the founder of equity jurisprudence in the US. His *Commentaries on American Law* (4 vols, 1826–30) became a standard Federalist interpretation of the law and the constitution.

KENT, WILLIAM (1684–1748), English architect, painter, sculptor, and garden designer. He was closely associated with Lord Burlington in popularizing the Palladian revival in Britain. Holkham Hall, Norfolk, is his finest surviving building and Rousham, Oxfordshire, his best garden. Its significance lies in its being in the transitional style between the 17th-cent. vista garden (*eg*, Versailles) and the 'natural' English landscape school of the mid-18th cent., originated by Kent.

KENT, conquered in the 5th cent. by Germanic invaders, traditionally led by Hengest and Horsa, was settled by the Jutes. Aethelbert, King of Kent, was converted to Christianity in 597 by Augustine, who was sent by Pope Gregory the Great, and became the first Christian Anglo-Saxon ruler. Proximity to the continent made Kent a rich kingdom and it was always one of the leading centres of Anglo-Saxon art and culture. The presence of the archbishopric of Canterbury in Kent enhanced its political significance and in 825 it was annexed by the kingdom of Wessex.

KENTIGERN, Saint (?518–603), missionary who, according to 12th-cent. sources, worked in Scotland, chiefly in Glasgow. He probably also visited Wales.

KENTISH KNOCK, naval battle off (1652), defeat of a Dutch fleet under Cornelius de Witt by an English fleet under Robert Blake in the first Anglo–Dutch War (1652–4). Many of De Witt's captains refused to fight towards the close of the action, being hostile to De Witt, who had recently replaced Tromp, on personal and political grounds.

KENTISH PETITION (1701) in England, presented to parliament by five representatives of Kentish freeholders. Parliament had been reluctant to meet the demands of King William III for military preparations against the threat of Louis XIV and this petition was an attempt to influence its attitude. The petitioners urged the Commons to vote supplies to provide for the religion and safety of the nation, and assist the king's allies. The petition offended the Tory members, who, suspecting a Whig plot, imprisoned the petitioners and begged the king to take measures to prevent a disturbance. These events inclined Defoe to present his *Legion's Memorial*, asserting the right of the nation to control its representatives in parliament. The Kentish petitioners were released when the parliamentary session came to an end (July 1701).

KENTUCKY, region west of the Alleghenies, bounded on the north and west by the Ohio river. In prehistoric times, KY had an ancient agricultural and hunting civilization and was a hunting and battle ground for Indians before the white men came. The great Warrior's Trace ran diagonally across the region and the Shawnees from OH and the Cherokees from the south hunted and fought back and forth across the area. It was called 'the dark and bloody ground' by the first white settlers because of its sanguinary history. French and Spanish explorers probably saw the region in the 16th cent., and there are records of explorations of Thomas Batts from VA (1671), John Peter Salling (1742), and the Baron de Longueuil (1739). Richard Henderson, of NC, formed the Transylvania Co. (1774) and purchased from the Cherokees a region between the Kentucky and Cumberland rivers. Daniel Boone was hired to carve out the Wilderness Road, which ran from the back country of NC to KY. Henderson's efforts to have his settlements recognized as a colony by the Continental Congress failed. James Harrod, of PA, brought in settlers to establish Harrodsburg, and Harrod county became a county of VA (1776). The chief outlet for KY's whisky, hemp, flour, and tobacco was down the Mississippi to LA, which was owned by Spain. An unsuccessful conspiracy led by James Wilkinson sought to make KY a part of Spanish territory, but by 1787 the Mississippi was opened to free navigation, which was guaranteed by a treaty with Spain (1795).

By the close of the American War of Independence KY had a population of some 25,000 settlers, who became dissatisfied with their governance by the eastern states. VA gave up jurisdiction over its KY counties (1789) and Congress admitted KY to the union (1722).

T. D. Clark, *A History of Kentucky* (New York, 1937).

KENTUCKY AND VIRGINIA RESOLUTIONS (1798) in US, protests adopted by two state legislatures in response to the Federalist Naturalization, Alien and Sedition Acts (1798). The purpose of these acts had been as much to repress Republican opposition and criticism as to keep out undesirable foreigners, and Republican leaders denounced them as violations of the Bill of Rights and as being unconstitutional. While the Resolutions, drafted by Jefferson and Madison respectively, may have been as propagandist as the acts themselves, they raised an important issue of constitutional theory, the 'states rights' doctrine. The Kentucky Resolution declared that whenever Congress exercised powers not specifically delegated to it, each state has an equal right to judge for itself the method of redress, and called upon other states to declare the acts void and join in requesting their repeal. In the Virginia Resolution, Madison referred to the 'interposition' of state authority between the aggrieved citizen and the federal government.

KENYA (225,000 sq. miles) (583,000 sq. kms), in East Africa. Arab traders made settlements in the territory in the 10th cent. Later, the Portuguese built a fort at Mombasa (1511), German missionaries arrived in 1848, and Kenya became a British sphere of influence, administered by the British East Africa Co. in 1888. In 1920 Kenya was recognized as a British Crown colony, its capital being Nairobi. During the Second World War Italian troops briefly invaded in the north (1940–1). Kenya became independent within the British Commonwealth in 1963 and a republic in 1964. The population of almost 10 million (1970) includes Kikuyu, Luo, Masai, and a proportion of European settlers who remained after independence.

KENYA, THE 'WHITE HIGHLANDS' IN, area of 15,800 sq. miles (41,000 sq. kms) in western Kenya, rising to altitudes between 4920 ft and 9840 ft (1500 and 3000 metres), proved suitable for European settlement, and the Uganda Railway, completed from Mombasa to Kisumu in 1902, provided transport for agricultural products. Sir Charles Eliot, commissioner in charge from 1900, encouraged settlers so as to make the railway profitable. Much of the area, though Kikuyu, Kamba, and Masai tribal land, was relatively unoccupied at the time, famine and disease having driven Africans elsewhere. 'Empty' land was declared Crown land, to be sold or leased to settlers, who began to arrive from Britain and the dominions in the 1900s. Leadership tended to be provided by the British aristocracy, among whom were Lord Delamere, and later Lords Francis Scott and Cavendish-Bentinck.

Several governors came under influence of white settlers, who aimed at complete racial discrimination on their farms. In 1903 Indians were excluded from the Highlands, and in 1904 African farming was confined to native reserves, which left the Highlands exclusively white. African labour was required, however, and settlers got the colonial government to pass measures, especially the 'Northey circulars' of 1919, which virtually imposed forced labour. They then demanded elections that would have led to white self-government, but after Indian and African protests Britain declared such a policy to be contrary to the provisions of the Devonshire White Paper (1923). But until after the Second World War settlers, who produced 90 per cent of the country's wealth from cash crops and mixed farms, remained the strongest political force. The Mau Mau rising (1952–5), caused some of them to leave and by 1959 the Highlands were declared open to all races. After independence, African resettlement schemes cleared some Highland areas of settlers, many of them being bought out by means of a British loan to Kenya. Others, among them some 600 British farmers, became Kenya citizens and remained (1970) important producers.

KENYA AFRICAN DEMOCRATIC UNION (KADU), formed (1960) by Ronald Ngala and Masinde Muliro, in opposition to KANU. Its main political influence occurred in the period before and immediately after independence (1963).

KENYA AFRICAN NATIONAL UNION (KANU), chief nationalist organization, formed in 1960, through which Kenya Africans strove for and won their independence. Its policy underlined the vital importance of Kenya's independence and the release of Jomo Kenyatta from the British, while assuring immigrant groups of their right to identify themselves with the independence struggle. KANU duly formed the first independent government in 1963, and afterwards remained the dominant force in Kenya politics.

KENYA PEOPLE'S UNION (KPU), opposition party formed in 1966 by the former vice-president of Kenya, Oginga Odinga, and other KANU dissidents. It was banned by the government in 1969.

KENYATTA, JOMO (1891–), president of Kenya, of Kikuyu origin, and one of the founding figures of African nationalism. In 1921 he was involved in the politics of emancipation, becoming secretary of the influential Kikuyu Central Association and publishing a Kikuyu-language newspaper, *Muigwithania*. As a spokesman of African grievances, Kenyatta was sent to London to petition the British government for the right to open independent schools. On returning to England in 1931, he studied at London University (1933–6) and published *Facing Mount Kenya* (1937), one of the earliest attempts at a systematic rehabilitation of African culture from an African standpoint. In 1946 he returned to Kenya and in 1947 became president of the newly formed Kenya African Union. In 1952 he was arrested on charges of having organized the Mau Mau conspiracy, and was sentenced to seven years' imprisonment. On his release in 1961, which was due to the insistent pressure of the majority nationalist party, the Kenya African National Union, he took over leadership of his country's affairs.

KEOKUK (*c.* 1780–1848), American Sauk Indian, who led a faction against Black Hawk during the Black Hawk War (1832). Contrary to the desires of the Sauk, the US government made him their chief after the War.

KEPA, TE RANGIHIWINUI (MAJOR KEMP) (1823–98), a NZ Maori officer of friendly Maori troops who won a notable success in bush campaigns against dissident Maoris (1864–9).

KEPLER, JOHANNES (1571–1630), German astronomer, discoverer of the laws of planetary motion, who went in 1594 to teach mathematics at Graz in Austria. The attitude of the Archduke Ferdinand towards Protestants eventually forced him to leave, and he joined Tycho Brahe in Prague in 1600. Tycho died the next year, and Kepler inherited both his post of court mathematician and his mass of astronomical observations. His duties included the giving of astrological advice and the completion of the great Rudolphine Tables of planetary positions begun by Tycho, for which he made extensive use of the newly discovered logarithms. From 1600 onwards he was interested especially in the observations of Mars, whose rather eccentric motions are particularly difficult to account for in terms of circular orbits. He eventually discovered that all the observations could be fitted to a high degree of accuracy on the assumption that the appropriate orbit is an ellipse (with the sun at one focus) rather than a circle; with this hypothesis all the other planetary motions also fall into place. This law and the second (that the line from sun to planet sweeps out equal areas in equal times) were published in 1609; the third (that the square of the period of revolution is proportional to the cube of the distance from the sun) followed in 1619. These laws paved the way for Newton's discovery of universal gravitation.   JMS

KEPPLER, WILHELM (1882–1960), German economist, who was an adviser to Hitler. He was asked by Hitler in 1932 to build up an informal association of industrialists sympathetic to Nazism. This group, known later as 'The Himmler Circle of Friends', included some of Germany's most prominent industrialists, who worked for Hitler's appointment as chancellor in 1933, cooperating with the regime afterwards. He also became Göring's personal adviser on the Four Year Plan (1936), and was involved in the economic exploitation of occupied territories. After the Second World War he was sentenced to ten years' imprisonment at the Nuremberg trials, but was released in 1949.

KER, JOHN OF KERSLAND (1673–1726), Scottish trader and adventurer, who became a government spy (*c.* 1707). In 1713 he went to Austria and in 1720 approached Emperor Charles VI with a scheme for a chartered trading company based on Ostend, which would give the imperial treasury 3–6 per cent profits of the projected trade with the East Indies, China, and Africa. His plan led to the formation of the Imperial and Royal Co. of the Austrian Low Countries (Dec. 1722), but after its failure Ker returned to London.

KERAK, AL-, town in Jordan, situated east of the Dead Sea, site of the great Crusader castle of 'Crac de Moab'. The fortress was built in 1142 and fell to the Muslims in 1188. It

was of great importance, since it threatened the routes leading from Syria to Egypt and to the Hijaz.

KERENSKY, ALEXANDER FEDOROVICH (1881–1970), Russian lawyer, politician, and prime minister in the Provisional government (1917), who entered the fourth *Duma* (1912) and took his seat as a member of the Trudovik Party, a small group slightly to the right of centre. In 1917 he became a Socialist Revolutionary but his political affiliations were never strong. He considered himself above party and relied for his influence on his powers of oratory. He entered the provisional government as minister of justice and simultaneously became a deputy chairman of the Petrograd Soviet. This gave him an opportunity to dominate both organizations. In May 1917 he became minister of war and the navy and the major figure in the cabinet. His policy was to restore the morale of the army so as to allow Russia to enter peace negotiations with strengthened bargaining power. But an increasing lack of military discipline left Kerensky with little more than words with which to spur the unwilling soldiers forward. Prince Lvov's government collapsed, and in July Kerensky became prime minister. His cabinets, which were dominated by moderate socialists, became increasingly impotent because of the growing influence of extreme left- and right-wing groups. He attempted to rally public opinion by summoning rapidly constituted assemblies such as the Moscow state conference (Aug.) and the pre-parliament (Oct.), but his impotence was shown by the ease with which the Bolsheviks seized power. Kerensky fled to Pskov, tried to rally loyal troops, narrowly avoided capture, and then went into exile. He lived first in Paris and, after 1940, in the US.

KERLEREC, LOUIS BILLOUART (1704–70), French naval officer, who was governor of Louisiana (1753–63), which he successfully administered until his recall to France, having been accused of misgoverning the colony. As a result he was exiled and died without being able to prove his innocence.

KERMA, centre of an indigenous Nubian culture during the period *c.* 2000–1500 BC. The archaeological remains consist of two *deffufas* (mounds) which have been excavated. The eastern *deffufa* was a burial mound with a central chamber in which an important local chief had been buried; in a corridor were found the remains of over 200 people, mostly women and children, who had been buried alive to accompany the chief in the after-life. This was not an Egyptian form of burial, and the main occupant of the mound is thought to have been a local ruler rather than an Egyptian governor, as was suggested by the excavator (Reisner). The western *deffufa* was a trading post; material found there implies that it was an entrepôt for trade with Egypt. The people of Kerma had a distinctive culture which is also found occasionally in Upper Egypt. The pottery was of a highly polished black-topped red ware. Other examples of their artistic achievements are to be seen among the grave goods from the eastern *deffufa* and the trade goods in the western one.

Contemporary with the Kerma settlement were a people known as the C-Group, who were in some sense connected with Kerma, but not of it. Their culture was different and remains of it are to be found in Nubia, but not so far south as Kerma. The C-Group people also made fine pottery, but of a different kind, which depended on incised patterns for decoration; they also imported pottery from Egypt. This is mostly found as grave goods, four or five pots being placed around the stone cairn which covered an oval-shaped grave containing a contracted burial. Other grave goods, such as daggers with carved handles, fine jewellery, and small faience bowls, were all of Egyptian origin, and the C-Group clearly had close links with Egypt.

G. A. Reisner, *Excavations at Kerma* (Cambridge, MA, 1923).
A. J. Arkell, *A History of the Sudan to 1821* (London, 1961).
                                                                                                    MS

KERTANAGARA (*reg.* 1268–92), King of East Java, Indonesia, ruling from Singhasari (25 miles (40·2 kms) south of Surabaya). His reign marks a turning point in Javanese history. While earlier rulers may have aspired to build a great Indonesian empire, Kertanagara actually took measures to achieve this end, partly in response to threats by the Mongol Emperor of China, Khublai Khan. Kertanagara's conception appears to have been that of a confederation of Indonesian states under the aegis of Singhasari. This new policy, involving administrative changes and strange rituals, antagonized certain Javanese circles. These, led by Jaya-katwang, viceroy of Kadiri, raised a revolt and took Singhasari by surprise. Though Kertanagara was killed in the fighting, it is fair to assume that the subsequent achievement of Indonesian unity in the empire of Majapahit owes a great deal to Kertanagara's policies.

KESARI, weekly paper in Marathi, first published in 1881. It was supplemented by an English weekly, the *Maratha.* Its editor and proprietor, G. B. Tilak, violently attacked the British government and strongly opposed the Age of Consent Bill. In 1897 he alleged that British soldiers had committed various offences while employed on plague duty in Bombay. In 1908 he was prosecuted for his inflammatory articles and sentenced to 18 months' imprisonment, during which the *Kesari* was edited by C. B. Khadilkar and, after Tilak's death (1920), by N. C. Kelkar.

KESHAB CHANDRA SEN (1838–84), Indian social and religious reformer, who joined the Brahma Samaj in 1857. The younger members, under Sen, who desired more rapid social reform, formed the Bharatvarshiya Brahma Samaj.

KESSELDORF, BATTLE OF (15 Dec. 1745), victory of the Prussians, west of Dresden, over the Austro-Saxon forces under Marshal Rutowski. The imperial offensive in the war of the Austrian Succession thus collapsed and Maria Theresa accepted the treaty of Dresden.

KESSELRING, ALBERT (1885–1960), German field marshal and air force commander in the Second World War. After service on the Western Front in the First World War, he joined the general staff (1916) and in 1926 was transferred to the high command as a specialist in aerial warfare. In 1935 he was appointed *Reichswehr* delegate to the newly created Luftwaffe, and later became chief of staff. In the early years of the Second World War he commanded the First Air Fleet in the Polish campaign (1939) and the Second Air Fleet in the west (1940) and against Russia (1941). He was given the rank of marshal in 1940. At the end of 1941 he was appointed to the command of the south-west military sector, and from his base in southern Italy conducted aerial operations against Allied strongholds in the Mediterranean. Despite his failure to secure German air supremacy in this theatre, he managed to avoid the disgrace or transfer that were the fates of some of his colleagues. After the Allied landings in Italy, he organized the strategic withdrawal of his sector's troops in Nov. 1943 to a line north of Naples, and put up a tenacious resistance there until March 1945, when he replaced Von Runstedt as commander-in-chief on the western (Rhine) front. At the end of April his command was extended to the entire southern sector.

In 1947 Kesselring was sentenced to death by a British tribunal for his part in the notorious massacres of Italian civilians in 1944, but his sentence was later commuted to one of life imprisonment, and he was released in 1953.

KET, ROBERT (d. 1549), English farmer from Norfolk, who, with his brother William, led a rebellion of Norfolk peasants against the enclosure process. The rebels encamped at Wymondham and attacked Norwich (1 Aug. 1549), but were soon afterwards suppressed by the earl of Warwick and his German mercenaries at Dussindale (27 Aug.). The Ket brothers were captured and later executed, but their rebellion hastened the downfall of Protector Somerset.

KETTLER, GOTTHARD (*c.* 1558–95), Westphalian nobleman, and last master of the Order of the Livonian Knights (1559–1562). After the collapse of Livonia before the Russian invasion, Kettler negotiated at Vilna the subordination of his order and the lands of Livonia, except Riga, to Sigismund II Augustus of Poland (1561–2), while acquiring for himself, as a vassal of the Polish king (1562–95), the duchy of Courland.

KETU (Fr. Kétou), some 96·5 kms north of Porto Novo on the Dahomey coast, in history the westernmost of the states of the Yoruba people, situated in the easterly part of Dahomey. Of its list of 48 kings remembered by tradition, the 38th began his reign *c.* 1748. The town of the state still (1970) exists, and has a well-preserved fortified gateway in its otherwise ruined walls.

KEW GARDENS in England, Royal Botanic Gardens established in 1841, and comprising private gardens belonging to George III and his mother, Princess Augusta. Some of the dowager princess's original garden features survive, notably Sir William Chambers's chinoiserie pagoda. The palm house was built to designs of Decimus Burton (1844–8). Under its first director, Sir William Hooker, Kew became a foremost centre for taxonomic botany. The living and herbarium collections of plants are still second to none. Acting as a quarantine and propagating base, Kew has been instrumental in the economic development of several former British colonies, *eg*, in the introduction of para rubber (*Hevea brasiliensis*) to Malaysia.

KEYNES, JOHN MAYNARD KEYNES Baron (1883–1946), British economist who taught at Cambridge both before and after serving at the Versailles peace conference in 1919. At Versailles, he was a strong critic of the policy of reparations, his *Economic Consequences of the Peace* (1919) being a vigorous exposition of contemporary European economics. In the 1920s and 1930s his publications on finance had a beneficial effect upon the thinking of those concerned with grave social problems, *eg*, unemployment. During the Second World War, he played a major role in budgetary policy, and his contribution at the Bretton Woods Conference in 1944 led to the setting up of the International Monetary Fund and International Bank. He also participated in lease–lend discussions with the US.

KEYSER, HENDRIK CORNELISZOON DE (1565–1621), Dutch sculptor, town architect for Amsterdam (1612), and a master of the Dutch Renaissance style. His architectural masterpieces in Amsterdam include the South Church (1603–14), the first Protestant church in the Netherlands, the East India House (1606), the Exchange (1609), and the West Church (1620). His mausoleum of William the Silent at the church at Delft (1614–21) was probably his best piece of sculpture.

KHABAROV, YEROFEI PAVLOVICH (*fl.* 17th cent.), Russian cossack explorer, who encountered the Chinese on his expeditions to the Amur valley (1649–51), and after whom the city of Khabarovsk was named.

KHADDAR **OR** *KHADI,* hand-spun and hand-woven cloth, the product of the spinning-wheels (*charkha*s) which Gandhi made a central part of the economy of his Constructive Programme. Gandhi talked of *khaddar* even in South Africa, but it was in the 1920s that he made his most determined effort to establish it. In 1924 he urged Congress to require all members, under a 'yarn franchise', to spin 2000 yards (1970 metres) of yarn per month and to wear *khaddar* at all times. The yarn franchise was not accepted by Congress, but habitual wearing of *khaddar* was adopted. Gandhi established the All-India Spinners' Association (1925) under Congress auspices, to develop *khaddar*, and he later added the All-

India Village Industries Association (1934) to link it with the wider development of village economy.

KHA'IR BEG (c. 1522), Mamluk amir who in 1517 received from the Ottoman Sultan Selim I the office of beglerbeg of Misr (Egypt). Kha'ir Beg, ruled in effect as a vassal of the Ottoman sultan, continuing at Cairo the traditions and practices of the former Mamluk regime.

KHAKSARS, 'humble ones', an Indian Muslim volunteer organization founded (1931) by Allama Mashriqi (1888–1963). Dressed in a brown uniform and carrying a spade (*belchah*) as tool, weapon, and symbol, *Khaksars* met every evening for drill and physical training and at camps for 'battle' training. The movement became increasingly active by the late 1930s and there were clashes with police in Lucknow (Aug. 1939), when *Khaksars* tried to intervene in Shia–Sunni disputes there, and again in Lahore (March 1940), when they defied a ban on processions imposed by the Unionist government. Mashriqi was imprisoned until June 1942 and then released and interned in southern India. The movement itself was banned in 1940 and again from June 1941, although it did in fact remain active until partition.

KHALID IBN AL-WALID (*fl.* 7th cent. AD), soldier involved in the rapid expansion of the Muslim state after the death of the Prophet Muhammad (AD 632). Khalid overcame (632–3) the movement of resistance against Muslim rule known as Al-Ridda, especially at the battle of Aqraba in 633. His most brilliant campaigns occurred in 634–6, during which time he gained memorable victories over the Byzantines at Al-Ajnadayn (after a march across the Syrian desert) and on the Yarmuk river—victories which brought Syria under Muslim control.

KHALIFA ABDULLAHI (Abdallah ibn Muhammad al-Ta'a'ishi (d. 1899)), Sudanese from nomadic Baqqara tribe of Darfur, who was the principal lieutenant and eventual successor, as Khalifa, of the Mahdi, Muhammad Ahmad. He transformed the Mahdist state into a secular autocracy. After his defeat at Omdurman (1 Sept. 1898) he maintained resistance in Kordofan until his defeat and death at Umm Diwaykarat.

KHALIQUZZAMAN, CHOUDHRY (1889–   ), Indian Muslim, and later Pakistani, politician. He took a leading part in nationalist politics from 1916 onwards, as joint secretary of the Muslim League (1916–26) and a leading Khilafat worker, then as secretary of the Swarajya Party and foundation secretary of the Nationalist Muslim Party (1929) under Dr Ansari. He grew increasingly sceptical of Gandhi's tactics during civil disobedience, however, and drifted away from Congress in the 1930s. His concern was to find a viable Muslim platform which, while nationalist in outlook, would guarantee Muslim political interests. To this end he formed a 'Unity Board' of nationalist but non-Congress Muslims and he placed this organization behind the revived Muslim League (1936). As a highly successful local politician in Lucknow city, of which he was municipal board chairman for some 16 years (1922–5, 1929–32, 1936–46), his electoral work for the Muslim League was a crucial factor in the league's accession of strength in the last decade of British rule. While he was influential in the inner councils of the league, however, he was overshadowed publicly after 1938 by Liaquat Ali Khan, whom Jinnah preferred as his chief lieutenant. A supporter of partition, Khaliquzzaman none the less decided to remain in India in Aug. 1947. After election to the Indian Constituent Assembly, he became the leader of the Muslim group from July. Later that year he went to Pakistan at Gandhi's request, in an effort to persuade Hindus not to leave, but he then decided not to return to India. He was president of the Pakistan Muslim League (1948–51), and for a time governor of East Pakistan (1953–4), as well as Pakistan's ambassador in Indonesia (1955–6).

KHALJI (or KHILJI) DYNASTY, THE, Turkish family of the Khalji tribe domiciled in Afghanistan, who ruled the Delhi sultanate (1290–1320). On the murder of Qaiqabad (1290), the last sultan of the Slave dynasty, Firoz Shah, an elderly noble, was elected to the throne with the title of Jalal-ud-din. He repulsed the penultimate Mongol invasion of India (1292). In 1296 he was murdered by his nephew, who had acquired ample treasure by a raid into the Deccan, and assumed the title of Ala-ud-din. His reign (1296–1316) was a time of rapid expansion. Gujarat (1297) and Malwa (1305) were annexed, the Rajput fortresses of Ranthanbor and Chitor (1301, 1303) were captured, and a series of raids into south India, yielding great booty, were conducted by Malik Kafur. The last Mongol invasion was repulsed (1299). The Khalji régime was severe towards the Hindus, but enriched Delhi with fine buildings. With the murder of Ala-ud-din's son Qutb-ud-din (1320), the dynasty ended.

KHALKHYN GOL, BATTLE OF (1939), also known as Nomonkhan, was the culmination of a series of conflicts between Japanese troops in Manchuria and Soviet and Mongol forces. The Japanese were defeated, and the battles marked the end of their ambitions in this border area.

KHALSA, word of Arabic derivation meaning pure, sincere, or free. It was used in north India in two senses: (*a*) as a revenue term, indicating land revenue directly collected by government officers without an intermediary; (*b*) as a collective term for the Sikh commonwealth, *ie*, the brotherhood of the pure or liberated.

KHAMA III (*c.* 1830–1923), King of the Ngwato in Botswana. He was a Christian who welcomed the establishment of a British protectorate over Bechuanaland in 1885.

KHAMA, TSHEKEDI (1905–59), son of Khama III. He acted as regent over the Ngwato for his nephew Seretse Khama (1925–49).

KHAMI, Rhodesian citadel probably built and occupied by the 18th-cent. Rozwi, using well-established stone building techniques associated with the Zimbabwe culture.

KHAN, Turkish title, a contraction of Qaghan (cf. Arabic Khaqan). Under the Mongols a distinction was made between Qaghan, reserved now for the supreme lord over all the Mongol empire, and Khan, used to denote a prince ruling over a portion of that empire. In the course of time the term Khan ousted Qaghan and Khaqan from popular usage.

KHANDAQ. In AD 627 the Meccans, still hostile to the Prophet Muhammad, attempted to take Medina, where the Prophet had found refuge in 622. This attempt was foiled largely through the construction at Medina of a trench (khandaq) and a rampart—the fighting which occurred along these defences being known thereafter as the 'Battle of the Trench'.

KHARAJ, a term which, in the time of the first caliphs, was used (as was also the word jizya) to denote the collective tribute which the Arabs raised from the various regions of the new Muslim empire. Under the late Umayyads, and above all after the reign of Umar II (*reg.* AD 717–20), the term kharaj acquired the more specialized meaning of a land tax, the rate of taxation being higher for non-Muslims than for Muslims. Conversion to Islam—then beginning to gather momentum—meant therefore a notable fall in the revenues of state. This situation was resolved through the use of a legal fiction, *ie*, the land, not the proprietor, paid the tax. Henceforth all land designated as kharaj land paid the higher rate of taxation irrespective of the religious allegiance (Muslim or non-Muslim) of the man who held it.

KHARDA, BATTLE OF (1795), in which the Nizam of Hyderabad was defeated by the Marathas. This prompted the nizam to enter into a subsidiary alliance with the British in 1798.

KHAROSTHI, type of script derived from Aramaic, but adapted to the writing of Indian languages. Unlike Brahmi script, which was used almost all over the Indo-Pakistani sub-continent in ancient times, Kharosthi is limited to part of the Punjab, the north-west of the sub-continent and part of Chinese Turkestan (c. 3rd cent. BC–4th cent. AD).

KHAWARIJ ('the ones who went out'), name given to those Muslims who, rejecting the arbitration between Ali and Mu'awiya, abandoned the cause of Ali and established thereafter a religio-political movement, aggressive in character, but destined to ultimate failure, not least on account of its internal discords and its fissiparous nature. Ali was obliged to use force against the dissidents, whom he defeated on the Nahrawan canal in Iraq (AD 659). The Kharijite faith continued, however, to gain ground, taking root in Mesopotamia, in central Arabia, and in Persia. The Khawarij of Kirman and Fars represented an extreme form of the movement (Azraqi —ie, deriving from Nafi' ibn al-Azraq). Their resistance to Umayyad rule was so fierce as to call forth all the skill of the able soldier Al-Muhallab ibn Abi Sufra, who waged a series of brilliant, but bitter, campaigns against them during the reign of the Caliph Abd al-Malik (reg. AD 685–705). After that time the Kharijite movement, in Persia, remained influential only in the remote province of Sijistan. The doctrines of the Khawarij also found much favour among the Berbers of North Africa during the 7th–10th cents AD. Remnants of the old Kharijite faith—adherents now of the Ibadi sect—are to be found (1970) in Algeria, Tripolitania, Oman, and Zanzibar.

KHEDIVE, title of Persian origin, borne by the Muhammad Ali dynasty in Egypt (1867–1914).

KHILAFAT MOVEMENT (1919–24), attempt by Indian Muslims and nationalist Hindu sympathizers to secure the Holy Places of Islam against allied incursions during the conclusion of peace negotiations with Turkey. It coincided with the non-co-operation movement and marked the peak of Hindu–Muslim unity in the quest for Indian freedom. Its roots lay in the development of pan-Islamism in the later 19th and early 20th cents, but its immediate course was the threat which Turkey's defeat implied to the position of the Ottoman sultan, who was also the caliph (*Khalifa*, in India) or 'successor' of the Prophet, and hence the spiritual head of the Islamic world.

The movement began with the formation of the 'Association of the *Ulema* (or learned doctors) of India', the *Jamiat-ul-Ulema-Hind*, and the holding of *Khilafat* conferences in 1919. At once Gandhi accepted its religious importance to the Muslims and its strategic value in the forging of Hindu–Muslim unity and strengthening of the nationalist movement. In Nov. 1919 he presided over a conference in Delhi at which interest was shown in the possibility of a Muslim boycott of the government as a means of securing the Holy Places. At a further meeting (Jan. 1920), attended by the leading Indian pan-Islamists, Abul Kalam Azad and the Ali brothers, he obtained a general agreement that his plan of non-violent non-co-operation should be adopted by the *Khilafat* movement. However, the *Khilafat* Committee was by no means unanimous in its acceptance of the plan. Only after Muhammad Ali had led—without success—a deputation to London to place the Muslims' views before the British government (Feb. 1920) did the committee formally adopt non-co-operation (28 May). After an unsatisfactory meeting with the Viceroy in June, the committee backed Gandhi's ultimatum whereby non-co-operation would begin on 1 Aug. 1920 if the committee's demands for revision of the peace treaty terms were not met.

Under the aegis of *Khilafat* large numbers of Muslims joined in non-co-operative activities late in 1920 and early in 1921, and there was a considerable show of Hindu–Muslim unity, although even Gandhi was cautious in judging its depth. There were also specifically Muslim facets of the movement. The Muslim National University, the *Jamia Millia Islamia*, was founded by a breakaway faction from the Aligarh Muslim University in Dec. 1920. In July 1921 the Ali brothers used a *Khilafat* conference in Karachi to launch an appeal for Muslims to refuse to serve as troops for the British, a cry which, when they were arrested in Sept., Gandhi made the basis for further protest. But while these activities gave strength to non-co-operation, the Moplah rising (Aug. 1920) and the subsequent communal fears which it aroused, marked the beginning of the end of effective co-operation, despite Gandhi's efforts to dissociate the Moplah outrages against Hindus from the non-co-operation movement.

As Hindu–Muslim co-operation became more difficult in India, events in Turkey were working to undermine the whole basis of the *Khilafat* movement. Mustafa Kemal's government separated the caliphate from the Turkish state in Nov. 1922 and 15 months later (March 1924) abolished the caliphate and exiled Abdul Majid, the last Ottoman sultan and caliph. The rationale of the *Khilafat* movement was thus removed. Although the Ali brothers continued the *Khilafat* Committee as an anti-British organization, they became increasingly critical of the Congress and of Gandhi.

Aziz Ahmad, *Islamic Modernism in India and Pakistan 1851–1964* (London, 1967).
C. Khaliquzzaman, *Pathway to Pakistan* (Lahore, 1961).

PDR

KHIVA (Khwarazm), country on the lower Amu Darya (Oxus) delta and the centre of the power of several dynasties. The last of these was the Khongrat or Inek dynasty, whose leader, Iltüzer, assumed the title khan (1804). The khanate of Khiva was continually threatened by internal rebellion and external enemies, who included Bokhara and Russia. The Russian expedition of 1839–40 failed, but in 1873 the khanate was conquered, a large part annexed, and the remainder placed under Russian protection. The last khan was deposed in 1920 and the Khorazmian People's Soviet Republic founded, which was divided (1924) between the new Turkmen and Uzbek Republics.

KHMELNITSKY, BOGDAN (c. 1595–1657), leader of the Zaporozhie cossacks in their revolt against Catholic Poland (1648–54). Coming from Ukrainian gentry stock, he fled from Polish injustice to the Zaporog fastness (1547) and was elected hetman in 1648. With military support from the khanate of Crimea he twice defeated the Polish armies at Zheltya Vody and Kherson, while the cossacks swept through the Ukraine, encouraging the peasants to rebel against their Polish overlords and perpetrating vicious anti-Jewish pogroms. In 1649 Khmelnitsky defeated the Polish prince, Jeremy Wisniowiecki, at Pilava, ransomed the city of Lvov, and surrounded the forces of King John Casimir at Zborov. Deserted by his Tatar allies, he concluded an agreement with the Poles, which excluded the Polish armies from the Ukraine and recognized the autonomous cossack army of 40,000 men, but confirmed the existence of serfdom in the Ukraine under Polish lords. But the peace was short-lived. In a renewed war between the Poles and the cossacks, Khmelnitsky was again deserted by the Tatars, and being defeated by John Casimir at Beresteczko (June 1651), was forced to accept the treaty of Belaya Tserkov. He had appealed repeatedly to Tsar Alexis for help, but envisaging the prospect of war between Poland and Muscovy if he defended the Ukrainian cossacks, Alexis delayed his decision, while the *zemsky sobor* considered the plight of their coreligionists intermittently for two years (1651–3). Finally, in Jan. 1654, after negotiations between Khmelnitsky and

Buturin, Alexis's envoy, the treaty of Pereyaslavl was agreed, confirming the rights and privileges of the Zaporozhie cossacks, the Ukrainian gentry and towns, in return for the fundamental concession of the recognition of the tsar's sovereignty over the cossacks. After the outbreak of war between Muscovy and Poland, Khmelnitsky was alarmed by Alexis's decision to transfer his attention from Poland to the Baltic, and entered into negotiations with Charles X of Sweden and the Transylvanian prince, George Rakoczy II, to partition Poland. He died shortly afterwards.

KHMER, name of the people of Cambodia, and of their language. The earliest Khmer kingdom, known to the Chinese as Chen-la, was established in the 6th cent.

KHOIKHOI, more commonly known as Hottentots, pastoral peoples encountered by Europeans when they rounded the African continent at the end of the 15th cent. Their origin is obscure, but current opinion holds that they are of African negroid stock, probably being identical with the hunter-gatherer Bushmen of San, and have a long history of differentiation in the southern part of Africa; their culture probably changed through contact with Early Iron Age farmers and metal-workers. Although in historic times they lived west of the Kei river through South-West Africa and along the Orange river, archaeological and linguistic evidence suggests they were once far more widespread. At the time of the Dutch settlement at the Cape (mid-17th cent.), they were organized in many bands of varying strength which were unable to unite effectively against white encroachment. The usual stereotype of the rapid crumbling of Khoikhoi society before the whites, underestimates, however, the reactions displayed by the Khoikhoi, which ranged from outright resistance to complete assimilation.

They waged war against the Dutch twice in the 17th cent., and during the 18th cent. many joined the San bands which raided Boer farmers and in the last quarter of the century succeeded temporarily in pushing back the settlers' frontier. At the same time, the loss of their land and cattle led many Khoikhoi to become a class of rightless servants on white farms, especially after 1713, when their numbers were severely reduced by smallpox. The desertion of these labourers in 1799 to the Xhosa made the frontier war in 1799–1802 particularly formidable for whites. On the Cape Eastern frontier many merged with the Xhosa people to form such groups as the Gqunukwebe, a process which went back long before the advent of the white man. Yet others moved out of the white orbit to the Orange river.

By the 19th cent. most Khoikhoi groups had lost their independence and replaced emancipated slaves as the main source of labour in the Cape. Very few pure Khoikhoi are still (1970) in existence, with the exception of the Nama of South-West Africa, though they form the most substantial base of the Cape Coloured population, as well as of certain Bantu-speaking groups.

M. Wilson and L. M. Thompson, *The Oxford History of South Africa* (Oxford, 1969).
J. S. Marais, *The Cape Coloured People* (Johannesburg, 1957).
                                                                                                                                SM

KHOKAND, independent Uzbek khanate in the Farghana valley (modern Uzbek SSR), founded in the late 18th cent., which reached its greatest extent under Madali (*reg.* 1822–42). It was annexed by Russia (1875).

KHORANA, HAR GOBIND (1922–), Indian-American biochemist, co-winner of the 1968 Nobel Prize for Medicine, who in 1970 manufactured the first synthetic gene, future developments of which, it was hoped, would lead to the treatment of diseases caused by gene deficiencies, and possibly also to the reproduction of people with defined characteristics by the manipulation of genes.

KHOTIN (Polish, Choczim; Turkish, Hotin), town situated on the Dniester river and now belonging to the USSR where John Sobieski, King of Poland, defeated the Turks (1673).

KHOVANSKY, Prince (d. 1682), Russian officer in the *streltsky* who tried to exploit his services to the regent Sophia during a guards' rebellion in Moscow (May 1682) to further the cause of the Old Believers, with whom he sympathized. Foreseeing further popular unrest, Sophia summoned him to the Trinity Monastery, where he was summarily executed.

KHRUSHCHEV, NIKITA SERGEYEVICH (1894–), Russian politician, who became first secretary of the party and prime minister. He joined the Red Guard during the revolution and later joined the Communist Party (1918). He immediately assumed a leading political role, first with the army during the civil war, then at the Donets Institute and in the town of Yuzovka (later named Stalino, now Donetsk). He became secretary of the party committee in Kiev (1928) and then went (1929) to the Industrial Academy in Moscow for further training in engineering. There he kept up his political work as well.

After leaving the academy (Jan. 1931) he played an increasingly important role in the Communist Party and thus in the government of the Soviet Union, the more so since his responsibilities were in the two most important areas, Moscow and the Ukraine. He was second and then first secretary of the Moscow town party organization (1932–5), then first secretary of the Moscow province (1935–8). He also became a member of the central committee of the CPSU (1934) and was elected to the supreme soviet (1937). He was then appointed first secretary of the Ukrainian Communist Party (1938) and so, just before the outbreak of war, became responsible for the largest non-Russian republic of the USSR. At the same time he became a candidate member of the Politburo, to which he was elected as a full member in March 1939. Subsequently he was able to argue that his election to the Politburo came too late for him to know about Stalin's purges in the 1930s. He remained in the Ukraine throughout the war and was directly concerned with its varying fortunes—the annexation of Polish territory in 1939, the defence of Stalingrad, the direction of resistance to the Germans from behind the lines, and the restoration of Soviet authority after the expulsion of the Germans (Nov. 1943). He was responsible for reconstruction after the war and for the suppression of nationalist opposition which had shown itself during the German invasion.

He returned to Moscow as first secretary of the provincial party organization (Dec. 1949) and took an important, though not the leading, part in the 19th party congress (1952). After Stalin's death he was one of the principal contenders for power and was made first secretary of the CPSU (Sept. 1953). He established his supremacy over Stalin's apparent heir, Malenkov, by tactics resembling those which Stalin used—through his control of the party organization and by taking over the policies of his rival—but Malenkov, rather than being purged, was allowed to resign (Feb. 1955). He was replaced by Bulganin, who was in turn deposed, Khrushchev taking over the premiership himself (May 1958).

Once he was in power his career was marked by distinctive characteristics which Djilas had observed in Khrushchev's personality long before—a directness of approach, and concern with immediate and practical problems. From this stemmed his interest in agriculture—the cinderella of the Stalinist economy. Before Stalin's death he had been an authority on agricultural administration and had tried unsuccessfully to group collective farms into *agrogorods* (agricultural towns). In power, he fought to maintain expenditure on agriculture and to develop the fertilizer industry. He also tried to restore and increase the primacy of the party as an instrument of government. This meant, on the one hand, the demotion of the secret police, and on the other, a more central role for the party in economic administration.

Khrushchev also gave a distinctive turn to Soviet foreign

policy. He effected a reconciliation with Yugoslavia (May 1955) and sought to reformulate Soviet relations with the countries of Eastern Europe, in spite of the upheaval of the Polish and Hungarian risings (1956). He travelled abroad in a way that Stalin had never done—he attended the Geneva Conference (1955), went to Belgrade (1955), and visited all the capitals of the Soviet bloc, going twice to Peking. He also visited Britain and France, went to Paris for the abortive summit (1960), and to Vienna to meet Kennedy (1961). He visited the US (1959) and attended the UN in New York (1960). He actively sought a detente with the US, although his attempt to do so while scoring some major success in diplomatic affairs produced the crises of Berlin (1958–61) and Cuba (1962).

In several major respects Khrushchev thus departed from the policies of Stalin. In addition, he made a formal and sweeping denunciation of Stalin at the 20th party congress (Feb. 1956) which was 'scooped' by US intelligence and published in the West. He made enemies among the old Stalinists, particularly Kaganovich and Molotov, and he also created opposition by various attempts at reform, both domestic and of foreign relations. He surmounted a major challenge to his leadership in the presidium of the party (June 1957) and thereafter tried systematically to demote the 'anti-party' group who had opposed him. But his failure to produce a striking success for any of his major policies (his gamble over Cuba may have been the most important) accumulated opposition. His opponents organized themselves to deprive him of power and, having learned lessons from the experience of 1957, succeeded in doing so (12–14 Oct. 1964). He was deprived of office and went to live in retirement.

Carl A. Linden, *Khrushchev and the Soviet Leadership* (Baltimore, 1966).
Michel Tatu, *Power in the Kremlin* (London, 1969).   WFK

KHUANG APHAIWONG (1902–68), prime minister of Thailand (1944–8) and leader of the Democrat Party after the Second World War. He was a descendant of a ruling family of western Cambodia. He studied engineering in France, took a leading part in the revolution of 1932, and was prominent in successive governments (1937–48).

KHUBLAI KHAN (1215–94), grandson of Genghis Khan, succeeding as great Khan of the Mongols in 1260. He was the first of the Mongol khans to be established as emperor of a dynasty in China, the Yüeh (from 1279). He realized the need to apply traditional Chinese methods of government so as to secure the co-operation of Chinese officials and the material welfare of the empire. His forceful personality was largely responsible for the early success of the Mongol dynasty.

KHUFRU (*fl. c.* 2590 BC), (Cheops), Egyptian King who built the Great Pyramid at Giza.

KHUMARAWAYH (AD 864–96), Amir of Egypt (*reg.* 884–96), who succeeded his father, Ahmad ibn Tulun. In the first years of his reign he was involved in a conflict with the caliphate. Agreements made in 886 and 890 confirmed him as Amir of Egypt, with control over Syria and the march-lands of Al-Jazira (Mesopotamia), for a term of 30 years. After a successful reign marked, however, by a financial expenditure which strained the resources of the Tulunid regime, Khumarawayh was killed during a palace intrigue.

KHUTBA, sermon which the imam delivers in the mosque during the course of the Friday service at noon. This address contains a prayer offered on behalf of the ruling head of state, the mention of whose name in the khutba constitutes in the Muslim world one of the traditional prerogatives denoting sovereign status.

KHWARAZMSHAHS, title born by a powerful Muslim dynasty based on Khiva (Khwarazm) in the Amu delta, the independent power of which was established by Qutb al-Din Muhammad (*reg.* 1098–1127), although he was still nominally dependent on the Seljuks. Under his successors Atsiz (*reg.* 1127–56), Il-Arslan (*reg.* 1156–72), Tekesh (*reg.* 1172–1200), and Muhammad (*reg.* 1200–20), the Khwarazmshahs established themselves as the inheritors of Seljuk power in the eastern Middle East until their state was destroyed by the Mongols.

KHWARIZMI, AL- (780–*c.* 850), mathematician (*ie,* from the region of Khwarazm (Khiva), to the south of the Aral Sea), who compiled a series of astronomical tables and wrote treatises on arithmetic and algebra. His works introduced into Europe the Arabic numerals or algorisms, a word derived from his name. His major treatise, *Hisab al-Jabr wa'l-Muqabala*, made known to the Christians the science of algebra and continued to be (in Latin) the principal textbook on mathematics employed in the universities of Europe until the time of the Renaissance.

KHYBER PASS, most northerly of the five mountain passes between Peshawar and Quetta connecting Central Asia with the Indo-Pakistan sub-continent. A railway was opened through the pass in 1925.

KIANGNAN ARSENAL in China, established at Shanghai (1865) by combining previous enterprises of Tseng Kuo-fan and Li Hung-chang, as China's first modern arsenal. It soon became one of the biggest and most impressive in the world, manufacturing field guns, small arms, and ammunition, as well as constructing warships. The Arsenal school conducted a training programme and also undertook the translation of Western works into Chinese. Its growth, however, was hampered by shortage of funds, maladministration, and corruption.

KIANGSI SOVIET, main centre of the Chinese communist movement between 1928–1934. The Soviet grew out of a base established by Mao Tse-tung and Chu Te in 1928, after the setbacks suffered by the Communist Party in 1927. Mao expanded his area of control over wild and inhospitable regions of southern Kiangsi province, and was gradually joined by the urban-oriented members of the party, who found conditions increasingly difficult in the cities. A Central Soviet was set up in 1931. The area was constantly harassed by Kuomintang troops, who launched five campaigns against the area between 1930 and 1934. The last was successful in dislodging the communists, who were forced to abandon the Soviet and move off on the Long March. Although Mao was not firmly established in his leadership during this period, it was nevertheless crucial to the acceptance within the party of his ideas of a peasant-based, Chinese-style communism.

KIAOCHOW (Tsingtao), Chinese port situated on the southern coast of Shantung peninsula. It was leased (after occupation by force) to Germany for 99 years in March 1898, thus precipitating the general 'scramble for concessions' by the Western powers. The lease also included railway and mining rights in the province of Shantung, the resulting installations to be guarded by German police. The Germans lost Kiaochow and related privileges to Japan in 1914. It was agreed at the Washington Conference (1921–2) that Kiaochow should be returned to China.

KICKAPOO INDIANS, American tribe first encountered by the French (*c.* 1667) in WI. After helping to destroy the Illinois confederacy (*c.* 1765), they moved south into conquered territory in IL and IN. They fought against the US in the War of 1812 and the Black Hawk War (1832). After ceding their lands (1809, 1819), they moved to MO, and then KS. A small party moved to Mexico (*c.* 1852) and were given lands in Chihuahua, from which they harassed border settlements. Some were induced to return to Indian Territory 1873) and about a third of the tribe still (1970) lives in OK.

KIDD, WILLIAM (*c.* 1645–1701), Scottish pirate, reputedly the son of a covenanting minister, emigrated to America and harassed French shipping. In 1696 he was commissioned to repress piracy and reached Madagascar, but he was accused of turning to piracy on his own account, was arrested on his return to Boston, and sent to England for trial. He was hanged at Wapping on a charge of murdering a sailor. Some of his spoils, estimated at £70,000, were recovered and used for the purchase of the Queen's House at Greenwich.

KIDINNU (*fl.* 4th cent. BC), Babylonian astronomer. By observation and study of records he calculated astronomical phenomena and gave the exact duration of the solar year to within 4 minutes and 32·65 seconds.

KIDO, KŌIN (TAKAYOSHI) (1833–77), Japanese political leader. He was a high-ranking Chōshū samurai, who negotiated the anti-Tokugawa alliance with Satsuma (1866) and thereafter played a major role in Meiji Restoration politics. He was among the first to advocate the adoption of a modern constitution and was also a prime mover in establishing central control over the *hans* (feudal domains) (1869–71). He did much to check Satsuma domination of government.

KIEL, DIET OF (1526), in Denmark, meeting of the estates which marked a step towards establishing the Lutheran reformation in the country. Frederick I persuaded the bishops and prelates to accept the authority of the Abp of Lund instead of the pope with regard to appointments, and papal revenues were to go to the royal treasury.

KIEL, TREATY OF (1814), transferred Norway from the Danish to the Swedish Crown, but left the ancient Norwegian possessions of Iceland, Greenland, and the Faeroes in Danish hands. Swedish Pomerania, ceded in partial compensation, was exchanged with Prussia for Lauenburg (1815).

KIEL CANAL, from Kiel Bay to the Elbe, constructed (1887–1895) to link the Baltic and the North Sea and enlarged (1907–1914) to take dreadnoughts. It proved to be of strategic importance in both World Wars.

KIENTHAL CONFERENCE (April 1916), second conference of socialists, organized by the Zimmerwald committee, established the year before. It followed a pattern similar to that of the first conference, with Lenin in a minority (12 out of 44 delegates supported him) in extremist opposition to the First World War and an attempt to split the International. The majority wanted to bring pressure on their governments to end the war without annexations.

KIEV, 'mother of the Russian cities', was the capital of the earliest Russian state, known as Kievan Russia (878–1240). Its origins are obscure, but it seems that it was already a flourishing town when it was captured by the Varangian adventurers Askold and Dir, *c.* 860. In the 12th cent. it declined in political and economic importance and in 1240 was devastated by the Tatars.

KIEVAN MONASTERY OF CAVES, monastery in Kievan Russia, founded some time in the first half of the 11th cent. by a Russian-born hermit named Antony, who had spent some time at Mount Athos, Greece. It derives its name from the fact that its first inhabitants lived in caves in a hill above the Dnieper river. In the second half of the 11th cent., under the Abbot Theodosius, it became the leading centre of ascetic life and cultural activity in Kievan Russia.

KIGERI IV RWABUGIRI (*reg. c.* 1860–95), Mwami (King) of Rwanda. During his reign he expanded Rwanda's borders, reorganized its army, centralized its political institutions, kept the coastal traders at bay, and negotiated relatively lenient terms with German colonialists.

KIKUYU, African society of over 1 million, speaking a Bantu language, and occupying highland country in central Kenya. Although traditionally agricultural and organized in clans and age-sets, by 1970 they had become conspicuous in Kenya's economic and political life.

KIKUYU CENTRAL ASSOCIATION, political organization created in 1924 and proscribed by the Kenya colonial government in 1940. It aspired to advance the interests of Kikuyu particularly and indigenous East Africans generally and perpetuated Kikuyu leadership in African political organizations. Its founders and leaders were usually mission-educated and Nairobi-based, and some became prominent in politics after the Second World War. It was strongly opposed by government and by appointed chiefs.

KILBURUN (KINBURN), Ottoman fortress situated opposite Oczakow, at the end of the peninsula projecting into the Black Sea near the mouths of the Dniester and Bug rivers. Russian troops captured Kilburun in 1736 and again in 1770. The fortress was ceded to Russia under the terms of the peace of Kuchuk-Kainardji signed in 1774.

KILIJ ALI PASHA (d. 1587), known to the Turks as Uluj Ali and to the Italians as 'Occhiali', last of the great Kapudans (High Admirals) who commanded the Ottoman fleet in the golden age of Turkish naval achievement. He was a Christian captive who became a Muslim and served under the famous corsair Turghud Ali Re'is (Dragut). After distinguished service at Jerba (1560), Malta (1565), and Lepanto (1571), he carried out the formidable task of building a new Ottoman armada (1571–2). In 1574 he shared in the Ottoman conquest of Tunis. Under the designation of Kilij Ali he held the office of Kapudan (1572–87).

KILLIEKRANKIE, BATTLE OF (1689), fought in Scotland between Jacobite Highlanders and government troops, led by Mackay. The Highlanders' charge overwhelmed the government forces, but the Jacobite leader, Claverhouse, was killed. The leaderless Jacobites roamed the Highlands until they were defeated at Dunkeld (1689).

KILMAINHAM TREATY (1882), agreement between the Irish Home Rule Party leader, Parnell, and the Liberal prime minister, Gladstone. Parnell was released with Dillon and O'Reilly from Kilmainham Gaol, where he had been in custody for six months, after promising to use his influence to end violence and disorder in Ireland. In return, Gladstone, through his envoy, Chamberlain, undertook to introduce a bill to pay off the arrears of rent owed by some 100,000 Irish tenants. Until these debts were paid they could not take advantage of the 1881 Land Act, and were liable to eviction. The bargain was intended to replace coercion by co-operation, but Gladstone's hopes of peace were soon wrecked by the Phoenix Park murders. Parnell's imprisonment in Kilmainham helped him to avoid publicity while his mistress, Mrs O'Shea, was expecting his child, but also gave him an aura of martyrdom for sympathizers, especially in the US.

KILMUIR, DAVID PATRICK MAXWELL FYFE, Earl of (1900–67), British lawyer and Conservative politician, who became an MP in 1935. During the Second World War he was solicitor-general (1942) and then attorney-general (1945) in the Churchill coalition. As deputy to Sir Hartley Shawcross he assumed much of the burden of the trial of Nazi war criminals at Nuremberg in 1946. He later held office as home secretary (1951–4) under Churchill. In 1954 he became lord chancellor (1954–62). He was one of the victims of Macmillan's purge of his cabinet in 1962.

KILSYTH, BATTLE OF (15 Aug. 1645), Royalist victory in the English Civil Wars, when James Graham, Marquis of Montrose, overwhelmed the Scots Covenanters, whose 6000 infantry were mown down.

KILSZOW, BATTLE OF (1702), victory of Charles XII of Sweden over Augustus of Saxony-Poland during his invasion of Poland. As a result of this and further victories, Charles persuaded the Poles to depose Augustus in favour of Stanislas Lesczynski.

KILYA (KILIYA), situated in Bessarabia on the northern edge of the Danube delta, important both as a fortress and as a commercial centre, located at one end of the trade routes extending from the Black Sea, through Moldavia and Poland, to the Baltic Sea. The Ottomans took Kilya from Moldavia in AD 1484. Russian forces occupied the fortress in 1770 and again in 1790 and 1807. Kilya was ceded to Russia under the terms of the peace of Bucharest (1812).

KIM IL-SUNG (1912–　), name adopted by Kim Songju while leading a band of anti-Japanese guerrillas in Manchuria in the 1930s. He appeared with the Russian army of occupation in Korea in Aug. 1945, was given control of the administration which they set up, and named prime ministers of North Korea in 1948. During and after the Korean War his position was precarious, but in 1958 he initiated the cultural revolution in which, during the next ten years, his rivals were eliminated and North Korea was transformed into a communist state centred on his person and aiming to be completely self-reliant.

KIM KU (1875–1949), Korean soldier, and pioneer (1894–1919) of Korea's independence. By 1945 his Korean Restoration Army in China numbered 3000. After the Second World War he fought for political power in Korea and refused to accept the division of the country. He led the extra-parliamentary opposition to Syngman Rhee.

KIMATHI, DEDAN (1920–56), leader of African nationalist insurgents during the Kenya Emergency of the 1950s, who became known (though not to themselves) as 'Mau Mau'. Kimathi, a Kikuyu member of the Kenya African Union, emerged as a skilful military commander, and was obliged, largely through the lack of other political leadership, to assume political responsibilities as well. He fought a defensive campaign in the Aberdare Mountains against large British forces, and was successful for a long time; at the same time, he attempted to unify and organize the insurgents by means of a 'forest parliament' intended to prefigure the legislature of an independent Kenya. His capture in 1956, and subsequent execution, was crucial in bringing hostilities to a close. But the revolt he had led ensured the later success of the nationalist cause.

KIMBANGU, SOMON (d. 1951), leader in the growth of proto-nationalist messianic movements among village Africans of the Belgian Congo, Angola, and French Congo during the late colonial period. He was accepted by a large number of Kongo villagers as a prophet and redeemer. Long before his death, the ideas of 'Kimbanguism' were being relayed by other messianic leaders such as André Matswa, Simon-Pierre Mpadi, and Simão Toco. Such men formed their own dissident churches, which provided fertile soil for the growth of nationalism.

KIMBERLEY, JOHN WODEHOUSE, 1st Earl of (1826–1902), British politician who, as colonial secretary in Gladstone's ministries (1870–4, 1880–2), was responsible for granting self-government to the Boers after their defeat of the British at Majuba Hill (1881). He supported parliamentary reform and Home Rule and became leader of the Liberal Party in the House of Lords (1891–1902). He achieved his highest ambition by becoming foreign secretary (1894–5) under Rosebery.

KIMWERI YE NYUMBAI (c. 1800–67), King of the Shambaa, whose small but prosperous state was situated along a range of hills lying inland from the northerly coast of modern Tanzania. He was one of a fairly large number of 'small kings' who emerged in East Africa, notably in Tanzania, during the troubled times of the middle of the 19th cent. and showed political wisdom.

KINDI, AL- (fl. 9th cent.), writer who served under the Caliphs Al-Ma'mun (reg. 813–33) and Al-Mu'tasim (reg. 833–42) as a translator into Arabic of Greek philosophical and scientific works. In his own writings Al-Kindi sought to reconcile the ideas of Plato and Aristotle. He also wrote influential treatises on optics and on music.

KINDRED, in Anglo-Saxon England this was a family unit which embraced fourth cousins. It acted as a mutual benefit society and had the obligation to pursue the blood-feud against another kindred if one of its members were slain by a member of that kindred.

KING, EDWARD (1829–1910), English theologian and bishop. As principal of Cuddesdon theological college (1863–73), professor of pastoral theology at Oxford (1873–85), and Bp of Lincoln (1885–1910), he identified himself with the Tractarian movement in the Church of England. Charges of ritualism were brought against him by the evangelical Church Association under the Church Discipline Act (1840). A court, set up by E. W. Benson, Abp of Canterbury, decided largely in his favour (1890). Subsequently, the extreme bitterness of party divisions within the Church of England gradually declined.

KING, ERNEST JOSEPH (1878–1956), US sailor, who was the principal American naval strategist in the Second World War. He was commander of the Atlantic Fleet (1941) and became commander-in-chief of all US naval forces after Pearl Harbor (Dec. 1941). He was later chief of naval operations (1942–5).

KING, GREGORY (1648–1712), English herald and statistician. He was employed at the Royal College of Arms (1677–1694) and then entered the treasury. His *Natural and Political Observations upon the State and Condition of England* (1696) was a demographic survey of the population of the country (which he estimated at 5½ million in 1688), and its geographical distribution, classified according to income and occupation.

KING, MARTIN LUTHER, Jr (1929–68), US Negro Baptist minister and civil rights leader. He was born in Atlanta, GA, where his father was a Baptist preacher, and became pastor of churches in Montgomery, AL, and in Atlanta. When Mrs Rosa Parks, a Negro, refused to give up her seat to a white passenger on a bus in Montgomery (1955) her arrest produced a boycott of the bus service by local Negroes which lasted for 381 days. King directed the boycott committee, despite the bombing of his home by white terrorists, which brought him national prominence. He became president of the Southern Christian Leadership Conference (1957), advocating non-violent confrontation as a weapon of social protest. He was frequently arrested, beaten, and imprisoned, but never doubted that his philosophy and strategy could effect a change in American racial relations.
In 1960, while in prison in GA, he gained the support of the Democratic presidential candidate, John F. Kennedy, and in 1964 abandoned his political neutrality by urging Negroes to ignore Barry Goldwater, the Republican presidential nominee. During the March on Washington (1963) King delivered the keynote address, 'I have a dream', one of the greatest orations delivered in this century. In 1966 he

led demonstrations in Chicago against segregation in housing and discrimination in employment and was organizing a 'Poor People's March on Washington' at the time of his murder in Memphis, TN (4 April 1968). His death was followed by a wave of Negro violence which he would have condemned.

King's strength lay in the Negro churches of the South and his methods undoubtedly hastened desegregation in Southern schools and public facilities. But when directed at Northern cities, where the Negro church is less organized and racial problems more complex, King's appeal was limited and his movement faltered. Even before his death, his leadership and ideas had been challenged by a younger generation of black militants, born in the ghettoes, who reject nonviolent integration and endorse some form of black separatism. Yet King unequivocally condemned the rhetoric and ideology of 'black power' as 'racism in reverse'. His death removed the one black leader capable of restraining the forces of violence which afflict racial relations in the US. In 1964 he was awarded the Nobel Peace Prize.

Martin Luther King, Jr, *Why We Can't Wait* (New York, 1964).
David L. Lewis, *King: a critical biography* (New York, 1970). JW

KING, PHILIP GIDLEY (1758–1806), English sailor and governor of NSW, who was sent by Gov. Arthur Phillip to command the subsidiary settlement at Norfolk Island (1788), of which he became lieutenant-governor (1791–6). He succeeded Gov. John Hunter in 1800 and did much to give economic stability to the penal settlement and to extend its frontiers by land and sea exploration.

KING, RUFUS (1755–1827), US politician, who represented MA in the Continental Congress (1784–8) and was a delegate to the Philadelphia Convention (1787). As a US senator from NY (1789–96, 1813–25) he advocated Federalism and opposed the expansion of slavery. He was US minister to Britain (1796–1803), federalist vice-presidential candidate (1804, 1808), and presidential candidate in 1816.

KING, WILLIAM LYON MACKENZIE (1874–1950), Canadian prime minister. In 1900 Sir William Mulock invited him to become Canada's first deputy minister of labour, and he was largely responsible for the drafting of the Industrial Disputes Investigation Act (1907). A seat on a Royal Commission (1907) following race riots against oriental immigrants in BC led to his appointment as a member of the British delegation at the Shanghai Opium Conference (1909). King entered parliament as a Liberal (1908) and became Canada's first minister responsible solely for labour. He lost his seat in the Conservative landslide of 1911 and was not returned again until 1921. During the First World War he worked on labour relations for the Rockefeller Foundation, then was chosen to succeed Sir Wilfrid Laurier as Liberal leader (1919), thereafter becoming prime minister and foreign secretary (1921), offices which he retained, with only a brief interval, until 1930. In 1926 Governor-General Byng refused King's request for a dissolution of parliament. Arthur Meighen, the Conservative leader, took office, but was defeated and a dissolution was granted. King was returned to power and helped to draft the Balfour Declaration at the Imperial Conference (1926). He misjudged the economic effects of the 1929 stock market crash and was defeated at the polls (1930), but returned to office (1935) and remained there until his retirement (1948). In 1939 King promised there would be no conscription, but public opinion forced a referendum to be held (1942) in which the voting was solidly for conscription, except in Quebec. King passed vague legislation, but did not act upon it until faced with a cabinet revolt (1945). He was a very adroit politician and was able to prevent a split between English and French Canadians during the Second World War.

R. M. Dawson, *William Lyon Mackenzie King . . . 1874–1923* (London, 1959).
H. B. Neatby, *William Lyon Mackenzie King . . . 1924–1932* (London, 1963). AJS

'KING ACROSS THE WATER', Jacobite toast to the exiled Catholic Stuart line. When drinking the loyal toast Jacobites would pass their drink over a glass of water, signifying their true allegiance.

KING GEORGE'S WAR (1744–8), the American phase of the War of the Austrian Succession. This conflict, named after George II of England, mainly a series of border actions, was between English and French colonists, with their Indian allies playing a prominent role. 4000 New Englanders under William Pepperell captured Fort Louisbourg in NS(1745). The Iroquois in the Mohawk valley, aroused by William Johnson, fought the French. The treaty of Aix-la-Chapelle (1748) brought a temporary peace and returned Louisbourg to France. The war decided nothing but increased the bitterness and rivalry between the French and English settlers.

KING OF THE ROMANS, title of the heir of the Holy Roman emperor of the German nation.

KING PHILIP (1611–77), American Indian chief, who became the chief of the Wampanoag Indians on the death of his father, Massossoit (1662). After three of his warriors were executed by whites for raids on English settlements (1675), the Wampanoag, joined by the Nipmuck and Narragansett Indians, began a series of attacks upon white settlements which led to King Philip's War (1675–7).

KING PHILIP'S WAR (1675–6), named after King Philip, chief of the Wampanoag Indians, was the bloodiest of the 17th-cent. wars between American colonists and Indians. Massassoit, father of King Philip, had been friendly to the white colonists, but their increase in numbers and expansion in territory alarmed the Indians and they sought to exterminate the white men. The Indians conducted a series of raids in western MA, wiping out at least 12 settlements (1675–6). The settlers organized the New England Confederacy and their militia gradually gained the upper hand, but not until 1720 did the New Englanders regain the western frontier, which they had penetrated 50 years earlier. The Narragansetts were nearly annihilated in the winter of 1675–6 and the Nipmucks in RI were subdued in the following spring.

KING WILLIAM'S WAR (1689–97), North American phase of the War of the League of Augsburg, fought by Britain and her American colonies against France and her Indian allies. The English and French fought in the Hudson Bay region, the Iroquois and French fought in NY, and Canadian privateers preyed on Yankee fishermen and traders. The British seized Port Royal in NS (1690), but it was recaptured in the following year. The treaty of Ryswick (1697) terminated the war without territorial changes in North America.

KING–CRANE COMMISSION (1919), committee led by Henry C. King and Charles R. Crane to investigate public opinion in the territories of the former Ottoman empire. It recommended US mandates for Syria, Palestine, Armenia, Turkey, and (by implication), a new Constantinople state, and a British mandate for Mesopotamia. Its report, not published until Dec. 1922, was disregarded.

KING'S (QUEEN'S) BENCH, Court of, in England, last Court to emerge as an independent body from the Norman and early medieval King's Court (*Curia Regis*). It thus retained its connection with the administration of government.

As the last of the Courts of Common Law to develop, it learned from the mistakes of its predecessors and largely avoided their rigidity, complexity, and expense. There were initially four judges, of whom one was first appointed chief justice in 1268. From the time of Edward III the court remained at Westminster and did not follow the king, but individual judges were already holding Assizes on the established circuits as Justices in Eyre (*in itinere*). The court's original jurisdiction was criminal, and cases were heard either on Assizes or 'at bar', at Westminster.

The civil jurisdiction developed from the criminal: first, all actions based on the unlawful use of force were deemed to be 'against the King's Peace' and so triable by the court, and second, the court developed the legal fiction that the defendant to an action was a prisoner in the Marshalsea, a prison subject to the court's control. The flexibility with which its writs could be adapted to changing social needs and the comparative speed and cheapness of its procedure ensured the growth of the court's jurisdiction at the expense of the other Courts of Common Law.

The court exercised a supervisory jurisdiction over all other courts by the prerogative writs of *mandamus*, which directed a court to carry out an act within its jurisdiction: 'prohibition', which forbade a court to carry out an act beyond its jurisdiction; *Quo varranto*, which enquired into the general basis of a court's claim to jurisdiction; and *certiorari*, which enabled particular proceedings in any court to be investigated. A further prerogative writ, that of *habeas corpus*, enabled the court to enquire into the legality of the detention of any person by any court or other person, and where appropriate to order his release. With modernized procedures, these powers are still (1970) exercised by the King's Bench Division of the High Court of Justice.

The court played a notable part in the struggle to establish, principally in the 17th cent., the independence of the judiciary from royal and executive control. Coke (chief justice, 1611–16) delivered judgments which vitally affected the political situation of his day, and in 1688 the trial at bar of the Seven Bishops resulted in an acquittal in defiance of King James II's known wishes.

Since the establishment of the King's Bench Division in place of the three Courts of Common Law, the number of judges has been progressively increased, to 40 in 1970. The judges of the division sit in London to hear civil cases and exercise their administrative control (by a Divisional Court, normally of three judges), and on Assizes to hear civil cases and try criminal cases.

W. S. Holdsworth, *History of English Law* (London, 1922–1938). JRLS

'KING'S BOOK' (1543) in England, book of instructions, entitled *Necessary Doctrine and Erudition for any Christian Man*, which substituted Catholic orthodoxy for the tentative Lutheranism of the 'Bishops' Book' (1537). It was principally the work of the bishops, though greatly influenced by King Henry VIII. For the rest of the king's reign the Church of England restored traditional dogma and practices, merely replacing papal by regal authority. It was thus a Church Catholic in doctrine, but Protestant in government.

KING'S EVIL (scrofula), so called because in England and France kings were supposedly vested with power to cure the disease by royal touch, as a result of the anointing at their coronation. In England the custom dated from Edward the Confessor and the last sovereign to practise it, apart from Stuart pretenders, was Anne, who touched Samuel Johnson.

KING'S FRIENDS in Britain, expression current particularly in the first part of George III's reign to describe those politicians whose main concern was for a strong executive at a time of chronic political instability, but who were repre-

sented by the Rockingham whigs as a clandestine group of royal advisers, used by the king to thwart policies of which he did not approve. This charge was seized upon by 19th-cent. historians to support their thesis that George III tried to destroy the balance of the constitution by an undue increase in royal power.

The reality was somewhat different. Rockingham particularly resented the king's failure in 1766 to use his personal influence to support repeal of the Stamp Act (1765) and in the same year there was a meeting of minor MPs to discuss ways of securing a more stable administration. They blamed 'party' for the instability and concluded that the king, as permanent head of the executive, should exert himself more to achieve some continuity. These so-called King's Friends were not a closely knit group. They had no leader and there is no evidence that they exercised undue influence on the king or were used as a royal pressure group. Although George was unenthusiastic about the repeal of the Stamp Act, he did not oppose it.

The vacillating policy over the Stamp Act illustrated the very evil which gave the King's Friends cause for concern. Between 1760 and 1766 there were such frequent changes of ministry that it was difficult to pursue a consistent policy. They were in a difficult position, for in the absence of a modern party system or an independent civil service, loyalty to one's patron was a necessary prerequisite to a successful career in politics. This was particularly frustrating to the talented administrator who needed some security of tenure and was therefore tempted to look to the king for support if his patron resigned. The King's Friends were not the sinister, subversive force depicted by Burke, but capable men anxious to reinforce the executive so that government could continue. SH

KING'S PEACE (?387 BC), treaty dictated by the Persian king Artaxerxes II and imposed by the Spartans on their Greek enemies in the Corinthian War. It recognized Persian rule of the Asiatic Greeks and the independence of all other Greek states, the latter being the essential principle of subsequent 'Common Peace' treaties.

KINGSLEY, CHARLES (1818–75), English cleric, novelist, and historian, and an ardent follower of F. D. Maurice and the Christian Socialists, who was professor of modern history at Cambridge (1860–9). His many writings included *Westward Ho!* (1855) and *The Water Babies* (1863). His Protestant energy was said to typify Victorian 'muscular Christianity'.

KINGSTON, CHARLES CAMERON (1850–1908), Australian lawyer and politician, who was colonial prime minister of SA (1893–9). He helped to draft the federal constitution and as a member of the first Commonwealth government was an ardent reformer in the fields of industrial arbitration and women's rights. His influence was considerable in Liberal-Radical and Labor circles.

KINO, EUSEBIO FRANCISCO (*c.* 1645–1711), Italian Jesuit missionary and explorer who went to Mexico in 1681. He explored and mapped the areas of lower CA, Sonora, and southern AZ, going as far north and west as the Gila and Colorado rivers. He established many missions and introduced cattle farming

KINSALE, BATTLE OF (1601), defeat of a Spanish force of 4000 men under Juan d'Aguila, which landed at Kinsale in southern Ireland to reinforce the Earl of Tyrone's rebellion against Elizabeth I (1601). Charles Blount, Lord Mountjoy, forced the Spaniards to surrender before turning back to crush the Irish rebels.

KINSKY, FRANZ ULRICH, Count (1634–99), Bohemian diplomat, who served the Emperor Leopold I as a diplomat in Poland and as vice-chancellor of Bohemia (1664). Later he became a member of the Imperial Privy Council (1675), imperial plenipotentiary at the Nymwegen (1676) and Ryswick (1697) peace negotiations, grand chancellor of Bohemia (1683–99), and a member of the commission set up to reorganize Hungary, after its recovery from the Turks (1684).

KINWUN MINGYI (1821–1908), chief minister of the Hlutdaw under King Mindon, who visited Europe on a diplomatic mission, and became head of consultative body set up by the British after the annexation of Upper Burma (1886).

KIOWA INDIANS, American tribe, who were the allies of the Comanches. They were found on the upper Yellowstone and Missouri rivers by the American explorers Lewis and Clarke. They harassed settlements in Mexico and TX on the North Platte river (1805), and may have killed more whites in proportion to their numbers than any other tribe. Under their first treaty with the US government (1837), they received lands in OK, where they remained.

KIPLING, RUDYARD (1865–1936), British writer whose experiences in India as a child and later as a journalist influenced his view of the British Empire. His works included *Barrack-room Ballads* (1892), the *Jungle Books* (1894, 1895), *Puck of Pook's Hill* (1906) and *Rewards and Fairies* (1910).

KIPPING, FREDERIC STANLEY (1863–1949), British organic chemist, who is remembered internationally for his work in developing organic derivatives of silicon. The silicones, as these compounds are now called, have exceptional properties of water-repulsion and high-temperature stability. During and after the Second World War they became widely used, particularly as greases, hydraulic fluids, synthetic rubbers, and water repellents.

KIRGHIZ, Turkish people long established in Turkestan who became localized in the 16th–18th cents in the area of modern Kirgizia. During the 18th and 19th cents they were usually called Kara Kirghiz to distinguish them from the Kazakhs, to whom the Russians applied the name Kirghiz. The Kirghiz came under Russian control in 1864 and raised a formidable rebellion in 1916. The Kirghiz Autonomous oblast created 1924 was raised to the status of an ASSR (1926) and SSR (1936).

KIRHOLM, BATTLE OF (1605), defeat of the Swedes, who under Charles IX had attacked Livonia and besieged Riga, by Polish forces led by John Charles Chodkiewicz. The Swedish army retreated to Sweden, but Sigismund III of Poland was unable to profit from this great victory because of the threat of civil war.

KIRICHENKO, ALEKSEY ILLARIONIVICH (1908–), Russian politician, who joined the Communist Party in 1930 and rose to a position of leadership in the Odessa party organization (1949). He became a member of the central committee (1952), and was close to Khrushchev during his rapid rise to membership of the Presidium (1955). Kirichenko fell from favour in 1960.

KIRINA, BATTLE OF (*c.* 1234), in which the Keita chief, Sundiata, overcame the Soso tyrant Sumanguru Kanta and emerged as ruler of an independent Mali.

KIRK O'FIELD, house outside Edinburgh to which Mary Stuart brought her husband, Lord Darnley, to recuperate from smallpox. While Mary and her court were at a wedding a violent explosion wrecked the building. The strangled body of Darnley and that of his servant were found in the grounds, both being believed to be the victims of foul play by a group of Scottish lords led by James Bothwell (10 Feb. 1567).

KIROV, SERGEI MIRONOVICH (1886–1934), Soviet politician, who joined the Bolshevik Party in 1904 and played an active underground part, especially in the Caucasus. In 1921 he headed the party in Azerbayjan. He was elected (1922) to the central committee and, as a trusted Stalinist, was appointed (1926) to head the party in Leningrad. This was an important post, since the Leningrad party machine had to be purged of Stalin's Zinovievite enemies. In 1930 he was elected to full membership of the Politburo. He was ruthless, efficient, and the finest orator in the party since the departure of Trotsky. He was an enthusiastic supporter of the first Five-Year Plan, but he probaby became an advocate of less harsh measures as the plan reached its conclusion. He voted against the execution of Riutin and his accomplices in 1932. At about the same time he showed his independence in the seizure of food supplies for the inhabitants of Leningrad. His popularity in the party increased; the 17th Congress elected him into one of the central committee secretaryships (1934) and accorded him ovation second only to that given to Stalin. The latter perhaps feared him as a rival for the leadership; more probably he foresaw that Kirov could lead the opposition to the intensified efforts required by the second Five-Year Plan. On 1 Dec. 1934 Kirov was shot by a party member, Nikolayev. Officially it was asserted that Nikolayev was acting for the Zinovievites. Many years later Khrushchev hinted that the murder had been organized by Stalin; it has also been suggested that Nikolayev's act was that of an isolated terrorist protesting against the regime. The murder gave Stalin the excuse to unleash his Great Terror.

R. Conquest, *The Great Terror* (London, 1968).
L. Schapiro, *The Communist Party of the Soviet Union* (London, 1964).   GS

KIRWAN, SIR JOHN WATERS (1869–1949), Irish-born Australian journalist and politician, who won prominence during the Western Australian gold-rush of the 1890s as editor of the *Kalgoorlie Miner*. His goldfields 'Separate to Federate' campaign helped to carry Western Australia into the Australian Commonwealth and Kirwan into its first parliament (1901–3). He was a member of the WA State Legislative Council and its president (1926–46).

KISALE CULTURE, earliest known Iron Age culture of southeastern Congo (*c.* 7th cent. AD). Evidence for it is based on finely worked pottery, implements, and metal ornaments from a necropolis at Sanga.

KISAN SABHAS, 'peasant associations' in India. Though *sabhas* were organized in the United Provinces and Bihar as early as 1917 and were active during the non-co-operation movement (1920–2), their growth on an all-India scale dates from the 1930s. The first All-India Kisan Congress (April 1936) brought together regional groups which had developed during and after the civil disobedience movement (1930–4) as a result of the work of congressmen, notably Professor N. G. Ranga in Andhra and Swami Sahajanand Saraswati in Bihar. The second congress at Faizpur (Dec. 1936) elected Ranga as president and Sahajanand as secretary of the All-India Kisan Sabha. Henceforth relations between Congress and the *kisan sabha* movement became increasingly strained. *Sabha* demands for radical agrarian reforms grew so insistent that in 1938 the Congress ruled that congressmen should not join *sabhas*. During the Second World War the All-India Kisan Sabha came increasingly under communist control and immediately after independence police action forced it underground. It re-emerged as an important element in the Communist Party of India (1952–3), though its strength varied widely in different regions.

KISELYOV, GENERAL COUNT PAVEL DMITRIYEVICH (1788–1872), Russian politician and minister of state domains under Nicholas I. As military governor of Moldavia and

Wallachia he introduced peasant reforms. He was appointed to the new ministry (1837) after an investigation set up to study peasant conditions following the cholera epidemic (1830–1) and subsequent bad harvests and unrest. The ministry established new machinery of local government, was concerned with agricultural reform and education, and ran schools and hospitals. Kiselyov's aim was to establish a class of prosperous free peasants on Crown land and he saw his work as a model for landowner's serfs. Although the reforms caused resentment and resistance and a new land tax failed, his work influenced the Emancipation Act (1861).

KISH (mod. Tell Akhimer), Sumerian city and one of the most important centres in Early Dynastic times (c. 2700 BC). Later Sumerian kings took the title 'king of Kish'. Kish came early under Semitic control.

KISHI, NOBUSUKE (1896–), Japanese politician. His modification of Occupation policies after the Second World War provoked the formation of a large-scale protest movement (1959–60), his plans for revision of the Japanese–American security treaty offending resurgent nationalist sentiment and seeming at the same time to endanger Japan. Although he was able to persuade parliament to agree to the treaty's revision, Kishi lost support within the Liberal-Democratic Party, and the enforced cancellation of President Eisenhower's visit compelled him to resign, though he still retained some influence as the brother of Satō Eisaku, prime minister from 1964.

KITA, IKKI (1883–1937), Japanese politician, whose *Outline Proposal for Japan's Reconstruction* (*Nihon Kaizō Hōan Taikō*) combined elements of socialism with emphasis on the importance of the emperor and the army and had considerable influence on some extremist army officers. Kita himself, after aiding the Chinese nationalist movement, organized several Japanese ultra-nationalist societies; but his hostility to big business went too far for the army's leaders and, after being accused of complicity in the 26 Feb. 1936 Tokyo mutiny, he was executed.

KITARA, original name of an extensive but loosely organized empire in central and southern Uganda, at the height of its power during the 15th cent.

KIT-CAT CLUB in England, exclusive social centre for Whig politicians in the early 18th cent. The members were leading representatives of the influential sections of the Whig party in both houses of parliament, who met together to co-ordinate party policy and preserve discipline and unity.

KITCHEN CABINET in US, political term originally applied by opponents of President Andrew Jackson to a group of unofficial political advisers who between 1829 and 1831 were said to be more influential than the regular cabinet. Among its most prominent members were Amos Kendall (1789–1869), Duff Green (1791–1875), and Francis Preston Blair, sr (1791–1876).

KITCHENER OF KHARTOUM AND OF BROOME, HORATIO HERBERT KITCHENER, 1st Earl (1850–1916), British soldier and administrator. His military career began as a cadet with the French army during the Franco–Prussian War (1870–1). He served in Egypt and the Sudan (1882–98), taking part in the Gordon relief expedition, reorganizing the Egyptian police, and training her army. He won the battle of Omdurman (1898) in the Sudan. In 1900, he went to South Africa, succeeding Lord Roberts as commander-in-chief in the Boer War, where he organized the controversial 'blockhouse and drive' strategy, together with concentration camps.

He was commander-in-chief in India (1902–9), where his particular achievement lay in reforms in army hygiene, sanitation, and victualling. On the outbreak of the First World War, he was already a member of the committee of imperial defence, and became war minister (1914–16) in Asquith's government, being the first serving officer to hold the post. His recruitment policy, with the poster bearing his portrait and the slogan 'Your country needs you', was the major factor in Britain having 67 divisions of infantry in the field by 1916. He was drowned when HMS *Hampshire*, in which he was sailing to Russia, was torpedoed in May 1916.

KIZIL-BASH (lit. red head, from their red head-gear), name applied to a confederation of seven Turkoman tribes (Ustajlu, Shamlu, Tekelü, Baharlu, Zu'l Kadr, Qajar, and Afshar), which formed the basis of the power of the early Safawid rulers of Iran.

KIZIMKAZI, small settlement on the south-west coast of Zanzibar, with the oldest inscription on the east coast of Africa, dated 500 AH (AD 1107), in the mosque, rebuilt in 18th cent.

KLAGENFURT BASIN, in Carinthia, territory of 1950 sq. kms with a population in 1920 of 150,000, whose possession was bitterly disputed by Austria and Yugoslavia (1918–20). The Great Powers at the Peace Conference (1919) were disunited over the affair: the Italians supported Austria's claims both because an Austrian Klagenfurt would give Italy a direct railway link with Vienna, and because of Italian–Yugoslav rivalry. The others, though fearing the political consequences of depriving Austria of more territory, were reluctant to risk future Yugoslav irredentism through ceding the overwhelmingly Slovene lands to her. Yet they were also unwilling to divide a balanced economic unit.

In May 1919 Yugoslav aggression, and the possibility of Italian intervention, forced a decision; and an American proposal for a plebiscite in two zones was accepted by the Supreme Council, to the annoyance of Italy. On 10 Oct. 1920 the vote took place in the southern zone, which accounted for a substantial part of the Basin. A majority of 7000 opted for Austria, although 70 per cent of the population were Slovenes. (10,000 Slovenes voted for Austria.) By a previous arrangement this rendered a vote in the predominantly German zone unnecessary, for it was assumed that Germans would choose Austrian nationality. This vote showed that Slovene national consciousness was not as developed as the Yugoslav government had claimed, but it could be attributed also to a desire to preserve the economic unity of the basin, and a fear of the compulsory military service that was in force in Yugoslavia.

KLAMATH INDIANS, Lutuamian tribe formerly living along the Klamath river in OR and CA. They joined the Modoc in ceding their lands to the US government (1864) and now (1970) live on a reservation on Klamath Lake, OR.

KLEIN-SCHNELLENDORF, TREATY OF (Oct. 1741), military convention suspending hostilities between the Empress Maria Theresa and Frederick II of Prussia during the War of the Austrian Succession. The Prussians were to be allowed to besiege Neisse and occupy Silesia, while the Austrian army was to be free to withdraw to defend Bohemia against a Franco-Bavarian attack and drive their armies from Upper Austria. It was further agreed that the terms were to be kept secret, pending negotiations for a definitive peace treaty, but hostilities between the two powers were renewed shortly afterwards, when Frederick's army attacked Moravia (1742).

KLONDIKE GOLD-RUSH, movement into Canadian North-West Territory after the discovery of gold by George Washington Carmack at Rabbit (Bonanza) Creek, a tributary of the Klondike river (1896). In April 1897 1500 people were encamped on the Yukon flats near Eldorado Creek, where richer deposits had been discovered, and Dawson City was founded. By 1898, Dawson had 25,000 inhabitants, and even though the rush proper ended in 1899 there were still 30,000 in 1900, but by 1930 the population was less than 1000.

KLOSTER-SEVEN, CONVENTION OF (8 Sept. 1757), signed by George II's son, the Duke of Cumberland, two weeks after his defeat by the French in the Seven Years War at the battle of Hastenback. Cumberland's mixed force of German mercenaries was ordered by King George II of England to defend Hanover, but was forced to retreat to Stade on the North Sea. No reinforcements being forthcoming from England, Cumberland had to capitulate to the French and to agree to the disbanding of his mercenary army. Hanover and Brunswick were left to the mercy of the French, leaving Prussia open to invasion. George II, furious at this humiliation, recalled his son and dismissed him.

The convention was later repudiated by Britain and a new treaty was signed (April 1758) with Frederick II, granting him an annual subsidy of £670,000 to sustain an Anglo-German army, commanded by Prince Ferdinand of Brunswick, to defend Hanover and Prussia from the French.

KLUGE, HANS GUNTHER VON (1882–1944), German field marshal in the Second World War. He served on both the Western and Eastern Fronts, and in June 1944 was appointed to the Command of the West Front. He hesitated to give his support to the anti-Hitler clique, and in July 1944 refused to co-operate with them after the attempt on Hitler's life had failed. In August Hitler dismissed him after Kluge had refused to defend a hopeless position. Shortly afterwards he committed suicide, fearing that the Gestapo were about to arrest him for his part in the July Plot.

KLUSHINO, BATTLE OF (1610), victory of the Poles under Stanislas Zolkiewski over a force of Russians led by Tsar Shuisky and 5000 Swedes under James de la Gardie. As a result of the battle Shuisky was deposed and the Poles occupied Moscow.

KNÄRED, TREATY OF (1613), peace settlement between Christian IV of Denmark and Gustavus Adolphus of Sweden mediated by James I of England. The settlement, which favoured the Danes, ended the war of 1611–13. The Swedes renounced their claims to expansion into Danish territory and agreed to pay 1 million *riksdaler* within six years to release the Alvsborg area from Danish control. Denmark was to display the Three Crowns on the royal insignia. The one concession to Sweden was the abolition of the tolls hitherto paid by Swedish ships passing through the Sound.

KNATCHBULL, SIR EDWARD (d. 1730), English politician and diarist, who was a supporter of Bolingbroke and the Tories. His diary provides a valuable record of political events in the reigns of Anne and George I.

KNELLER, SIR GODFREY (*c.* 1646–1723), English portrait painter, who studied in Amsterdam. In 1674 he came to England, where he painted hundreds of portraits, notably of members of the Kit-Cat club. Kneller was the first to attempt to establish a painting academy in England.

KNIBB, WILLIAM (*c.* 1800–75), British Baptist pastor in Jamaica, who was arrested for incitement to rebellion in the slave uprising of 1831. He came to England to argue the case for slave emancipation. After slavery was abolished (1833), he returned to Jamaica, where he was instrumental in creating free villages for former slaves driven off their old estates by high rents.

KNIBBS, SIR GEORGE HANDLEY (1858–1929), Australian physicist and statistician, who became NSW director-general of technical education (1905). As Commonwealth Statistician,

he created the Commonwealth Bureau of Census and Statistics and was responsible for the Commonwealth *Year Book*. He was later director of the Institute of Science and Industry (1921–6), precursor of the Council for Scientific and Industrial Research.

KNIGHTHOOD, may be described as the condition of being a knight in a chivalric rather than in a merely military sense. The utilitarian nature of early knighthood is seen in the making of knights in the earlier Middle Ages. It was then a simple matter of a grant of land (the fief, fee, or benefice) with which he maintained himself, his equipment, horses, and necessary attendants, and there was a simple ceremony of investiture with the arms of a knight which continued well into the 12th cent. (cf. the episode of the grant of arms to Harold by William of Normandy depicted in the Bayeux Tapestry).

With the growth of courtly practice and chivalry in the 12th cent., the idea of knighthood became a conscious one, clothed with mystical, romantic, and quasi-religious trappings. An elaborate ritual evolved, including a ritual bathing and clothing and a nocturnal vigil preparatory to the investiture. The knight was expected to behave in a manner worthy of his knighthood, to show reverence for ladies of noble rank, for religion, and for the code of chivalry, and was to fight—at least, against another knight—according to strict etiquette of knightly honour. The knight should be of gentle birth and, by the 13th cent., except on the field of battle, was raised to knighthood only by a ruling prince.

The elaboration of knighthood increased in the 14th and 15th cents as the knights declined in importance as a military force. The concept of knighthood was intimately connected with that of chivalry and courtliness or courtesy, of which it was the most obvious manifestation, just as the tournament, which often accompanied the making of a knight, especially of a royal house, was the most obvious means for knighthood to manifest itself.

From the end of the 13th cent. knighthood came to acquire political importance in England, where men sat in parliament as 'knights of the shire'. As a mark of favour knighthoods continued to be conferred by the British sovereign upon subjects within the empire and commonwealth. By 1970 the practice of conferring knighthood had been extended to a wide area of achievement (*eg*, music, letters, scholarship, sport). JG

KNIGHTS OF LABOR (1869–1917), largest of the early labour unions in the US. It was organized in Philadelphia (1869) by a group of garment workers led by Uriah S. Stephens (1821–82). The Noble and Holy Order of the Knights of Labor, though open to all workers, operated at first as a secret society because of hostile public opinion. Its leaders, wishing to replace the wage system by the 'Universal brotherhood of labor', tried to avoid industrial warfare.

The union's growth was slow and it had only 19,000 members when its practice of secrecy was abandoned (1881). The period of its greatest growth was in the 1880s, when, under the leadership of Terence V. Powderly, it advocated specific reforms, such as the eight-hour day, and condemned monopolies. Its maximum membership (702,924) was achieved in 1886. By 1893 this figure had declined to 74,635 owing to Powderly's lack of aggression, his objection to strikes, and public reaction to the Haymarket riot (1886). The union was officially ended in 1917, but the craft unionism of the American Federation of Labor had long before replaced it as the strongest force in US organized labour.

KNIGHTS OF ST CRISPIN in US, society of boot and shoe makers, founded in Milwaukee (1867). It followed a reactionary and unsuccessful policy of maintaining the apprenticeship system under guild control, and opposed the introduction of machinery. From its maximum membership of 50,000, organized in 327 lodges (1871), it declined rapidly.

KNIGHTS OF THE GOLDEN CIRCLE, secret order formed during the 1850s in the American Mid-West, to support pro-slavery policies and the conquest of Mexico. During the Civil War the order was composed mainly of 'peace' Democrats opposed to Lincoln. When reorganized as the Order of American Knights (1863) and the Sons of Liberty (1864), the society had a maximum membership of 200,000.

KNIGHTS OF THE WHITE CAMELIA, US secret society for the maintenance of white supremacy. Originating in New Orleans (1867) and opposed to 'Radical Reconstruction', the Knights, like the Ku-Klux-Klan, employed violence and intimidation to deprive Negroes of the franchise.

KNIGHTS WAR (1522–3), uprising of the discontented and impoverished German knights (*reichsritter*) who wanted to secularize Church lands for their own economic benefit in defiance of the Emperor Charles V, and under the banner of anti-clericalism. Led by Franz von Sickingen and Ulrich von Hütten, the knights declared war on Richard von Greiffenklau, the wealthy Abp of Trier, in Aug. 1522, and fighting began in Sept. The princely rulers of Hesse and the Palatinate rallied to the archbishop's support and the knights were defeated at Landstühl after being spurned by Martin Luther. Sickingen was killed, Hütten exiled, and the political power of the knights destroyed for ever.

KNOCKNANOSS, BATTLE OF (13 Nov. 1647), episode in the Cromwellian conquest of Ireland, when the Earl of Inchiquin, having swept through Munster, defeated Lord Taafe's Catholic army near Kanturk. A force of Antrim Highlanders, under Alastar 'Colkitto' MacDonnell and attached to the Catholics, advanced too quickly and was cut to pieces.

KNOCKTOE, BATTLE OF (1504), Kildare's victory in Galway over the western chiefs under Ulric Burke of Clanricarde. Kildare had been reappointed deputy (1496) after being imprisoned for his support of Perkin Warbeck, and he ruled Ireland in the interests of his own family, the Geraldines. With an English force from the Pale to give respectability to a domestic enterprise, he routed Burke and was made a Knight of the Garter.

KNOLLYS, SIR FRANCIS (?1514–96), Elizabethan politician, who opposed the government of Mary I and exiled himself to Germany. His friendship with Elizabeth I and William Cecil later gained him many offices, *eg*, treasurer of the royal household (1571–96). Though close to the government, he never wavered in his consistent championship of Puritanism.

KNOW-NOTHING PARTY, US political party of the 1850s, officially named the American Party in 1854. It was formed from a number of nativist secret societies, such as the Native American Association (1837) and the Order of the Star Spangled Banner (1849), as a reaction to the immigration of large numbers of Irish Catholics and Germans. Members swore not to vote for any candidates for office who were not American-born Protestants. The term Know-nothing derived from the practice of members claiming they knew nothing when asked about the party. After the Whig disaster of 1852, many anti-slavery Whigs allied themselves with the Know-Nothings and in 1854 managed to elect a number of state and local officials, senators, and Congressmen. However, they had little influence on legislation, and with the rise of the Republican Party most of the defecting Whigs found a more compatible political home. Millard Filmore ran a poor third as the Know-Nothing presidential candidate in 1856, and by 1860 most of the party's members had drifted to one or other of the major political parties.

KNOX, HENRY (1750–1806), American soldier and politician, who served in the American War of Independence. He displayed great competence in the handling of artillery and

was promoted major-general (1781). He was a founder of the Society of the Cincinnati (1783–), an organization of officers, and was secretary of war (1785–94).

KNOX, JOHN (*c*. 1505–72), Scottish Calvinist theologian, who established the Protestant Reformation in Scotland.

He studied theology and law at Glasgow University (1522) and took minor orders, but almost nothing is known of his life in the years 1523–44, until he became a disciple of the Scottish Lutheran, George Wishart, whom he accompanied on a preaching tour of Lothian (1545). He was profoundly affected when Wishart was burnt at the stake for heresy (1546) and approved the murder of his mentor's persecutor, Cardinal Beaton (1546). After being captured by royalist forces at the siege of St Andrews castle (31 July 1547), Knox was exiled and condemned to the French galleys by the regent, Mary of Guise. He settled in England during Edward VI's reign, was appointed a royal chaplain, and was favoured by the Earl of Warwick, who offered him the see of Rochester. On Mary Tudor's accession he fled to Dieppe (1554) and thence to Switzerland, where he met Calvin and Bullinger for the first time. He then moved to Frankfurt, but after disputes with his fellow Marian exiles, led by Dr Richard Cox, he returned to Geneva, where he studied under Calvin (1554–5) to become a pastor. In 1555–6 he returned to Scotland, where he preached widely as an advocate of the Calvinist faith, but he was condemned to further exile and went once more to Geneva (1556). There he began translating the Bible into English and published *The first Blast of the Trumpet against the Monstrous Regiment of Women* (1558), in which he sought to justify the right of resistance and attacked Mary of Guise and Mary Tudor, and inadvertently annoyed Queen Elizabeth I of England.

In May 1559 Knox was invited to return to Scotland by his supporters. His inflammatory preaching at St John's Church, Perth, where he called for the substitution of Protestant worship for the old Catholic forms, the confiscation of ecclesiastical property, and the downfall of the French regime, provoked a general insurrection led by the Protestant nobles, who called themselves the lords of the congregation. He appealed urgently to Elizabeth I for help and as a result military and naval assistance was sent to the Protestant lords (1560). Support for Knox's religious teachings grew, particularly after the death of Mary of Guise (June 1560), when he and Maitland of Lethington took over the effective government of Scotland. His Calvinist confession of faith was adopted by the Scottish parliament (17 Aug. 1560), and after the return of Mary Stuart to Scotland (1561), he repeatedly denounced the queen and her court and survived accusations of treason (1563). Between the deaths of Rizzio (1566) and Darnley (1567), Knox retired to England and wrote his *History of the Reformation in Scotland* (1566). After Mary's abdication he preached at the coronation of James VI (29 July 1567) and exercised considerable political influence until Moray's death (Jan. 1570), retaining his direction of ecclesiastical affairs during the regencies of Lennox (1570–1) and Mar (1571–2).

G. Donaldson, *The Scottish Reformation* (London, 1960).
MKS

KNOX, PHILANDER CHASE (1853–1921), US lawyer and politician, who was appointed US attorney-general (1901–4). He served as US senator from PA (1904–9), and as President Taft's secretary of state (1909–13) became identified with the policy of 'Dollar Diplomacy'. On returning to the Senate (1917), he opposed ratification of the treaty of Versailles.

KNOX, WILLIAM (1732–1810), British official and under-secretary for the American colonies (1770–82), when Shelburne abolished the office. Knox served in GA and eastern FL as British agent until his open defence of the Stamp Act (1765). His influence on North's American measures during the American War of Independence was considerable, but his projected loyalist colony in ME proved too costly. Knox, a strict mercantilist, drafted the 1783 order-in-council excluding America from the British West Indies trade, and suggested New Brunswick's creation as a refuge for dispossessed loyalists.

KNOX, WILLIAM FRANKLIN (1874–1944), US newspaper publisher and politician, who bought (1931) the Chicago *Daily News*, which he made an organ of opposition to the New Deal. In 1936 he was nominated Republican vice-presidential candidate. In view of his Republican sympathies, his appointment to F. D. Roosevelt's cabinet as secretary of the navy (1940), was a surprise, but the appointment was designed to lessen political tensions at a time of international crisis, and he served with great ability and success.

KNUDSEN, AANON GUNERIUS (1848–1928), Norwegian Liberal politician who was a republican before independence (1905) but served Haakon VII as prime minister (1908–17), keeping Norway out of the First World War.

KOCH, ROBERT (1843–1910), German bacteriologist. After serving as a surgeon in the Franco–Prussian War, he began research into the causative organisms of infectious diseases. He and his pupils discovered 11 such organisms in 12 years. Koch published his postulates (1881) relating to the specificity of an organism after his work on anthrax (1876). He studied cholera and plague in India, rinderpest in South Africa, sleeping sickness in Uganda, and malaria in New Guinea. His discoveries of tubercle bacillus (1882) and cholera virus (1884) changed attitudes towards these diseases and their means of spread. He was awarded a Nobel Prize in 1905.

KOCH-WESER, ERICH (1875–1944), German politician and co-founder and leader (1919–30) of the German Democratic Party. He twice held cabinet office, as interior minister (1919–21) and minister of justice (1928–9), but he was unable to give his party and the democratic centre the strong leadership that was needed in an era of extremist politics. He resigned in 1930 after the failure of his attempt to amalgamate the party with elements of the conservative People's Party.

KŌDŌHA (lit. 'Imperial Way faction'), unofficial group of officers in the pre-war Japanese army. Although eventually out-manœuvred by the *Tōseiha* ('Control faction'), the *Kōdōha* had an important impact on Japanese policies and politics in the 1930s. It was supported mainly by extremist officers, who objected to parliamentary government and resented the privileged position of War College graduates. Its leaders, notably Generals Araki and Mazaki, were mainly concerned to end the near-monopoly by Chōshū of senior military posts, to oppose the general staff's tendency to rate economic planning above traditional valour, and to prepare for war against Russia. Despite Araki's appointment as war minister (1931), however, the *Kōdōha* was no match for its more realistic and better-placed rivals and eventually lost influence (1934–6).

KÖGE BIGHT, BATTLE OF (30 June 1677), victory of the Danish fleet under Niels Juel over the Swedish navy under Evert Horn, south of Copenhagen. In the campaign in which this battle was fought, and which was part of the greater Franco–Dutch conflict of 1672–8, the Danes were helped by a squadron of Dutch ships.

KOGURYO, ancient state in south-eastern Manchuria and northern Korea, formed by five tribes who apparently broke away from the Puyo confederacy in central Manchuria and moved south to the upper Yalü. Here they emerged, at some date prior to the 1st cent. AD, when they are first noticed by Chinese historians, as a tribal aristocracy ruling a subject population of primitive agriculturalists. Raids on the adjacent lowlands brought Koguryo into conflict with the Chinese colonists of Liaotung, and in the following four centuries of intermittent warfare the Koguryo capital, a mountain fort to the north of the Yalü, was twice destroyed by invading armies (245, 342–3). After the collapse of Chinese rule in Korea in the 4th cent. AD, the kings of Koguryo gradually extended their power southwards, particularly under King Kwanggaet'o (390–412). This led to hostilities with the southern state of Paekche and the Japanese Yamato kingdom, which had established a sphere of influence in southern Korea. This was the most prosperous period in the history of Koguryo; Buddhism was introduced from China in 372, and in 427 the capital was moved from the Yalü valley to P'yong-yang, the former headquarters of the Chinese commandery of Lo-lang. From the same period date the large tombs, richly ornamented with murals, which form the most outstanding of Koguryo's material culture.

Koguryo was not only strong enough to dominate Korea and Manchuria, but also weathered a number of invasions from the newly reunited empire of China under the Sui and T'ang dynasties early in the 7th cent. Nevertheless, Koguryo failed to annex the independent states which had grown up in southern Korea, and it was one of these, Silla, which combined with T'ang China to bring down the kingdom in 668.

W. E. Henthorn: *Korea, the Mongol Invasions* (Leiden, 1963). KHJG

KÖHLER, HEINRICH (1878–1949), German politician who was elected to the Reichstag in 1913. He made his political career in the *Land* government of Baden, where he served as finance minister (1920) and prime minister (1923–4, 1926–7). As *Reich* finance minister in Marx's last cabinet (1927–8), he was responsible for the revision of the civil service salary system; this included large pay increases which, despite misgivings about the extra expenditure, Köhler regarded as necessary to revive the strained loyalty of the civil service. After the Second World War Köhler returned to political life, and as economic minister in Württemberg was active in Germany's reconstruction.

KOISO, KUNIAKI (1880–1950), Japanese soldier and politician, who succeeded Tōjō as prime minister (July 1944). He was unable to control the services effectively or respond to the wishes of the 'peace party' and was forced to resign (April 1945).

KOJONG (*reg.* 1213–59), 23rd King of the Koryo dynasty in Korea. He was devoted to Buddhism and under his patronage the third and surviving Korean *Tripitaka* was printed. Kojong was controlled almost throughout his reign by military dictators of the Ch'oe clan, who removed the court to Kanghwa island in 1232, so as to avoid the Mongol invasions. For over 20 years the mainland was devastated, until the Ch'oe were overthrown in 1258, and Kojong agreed to the Mongol demand that he should return from Kanghwa; but he died before he could do so.

KOJONG (*reg.* 1863–1907), 26th King of the Yi dynasty in Korea. He was under the regency of his father, the Taewongun, till 1873, and after that under the domination of his queen, a member of the Min family. From 1876 onwards Japan and the Western powers enforced the opening of Korean ports, and in 1894 a Tonghak rising, directed against influential foreigners, took place. The reaction which followed the murder of Queen Min by pro-Japanese elements (1895) placed Korea under Russian domination for 10 years (1895–1905), and at the same time Kojong assumed the title of Han emperor. By the time of his abdication in 1907 Korea had passed finally under Japanese influence.

KOK, ADAM (d. 1875), chief of South African mixed Khoikhoi–white group, the Griqua, who were forced by whites to move from the Orange river to Griqualand East in 1861.

KOKODA TRAIL, THE, across the Owen Stanley mountains in New Guinea, the scene of bitter jungle fighting in the Second World War. Japanese forces, having captured Rabaul, sought to cross from their base at Buna-Gona on the north coast to Port Moresby on the south, but were checked by relatively small Australian forces when only 35 miles (56·3 kms) from Moresby. In the second half of 1942 reinforced Australian troops drove the Japanese back to their northern base, heavy casualties being inflicted on both sides.

KOKOVTSOV, VLADIMIR NIKOLAYEVICH, Count (1853–1942), Russian politician of conservative, but not reactionary, views. As minister of finance (1906–11) he negotiated the French loan of 1906. He was prime minister (1911–14).

KOKUMINTŌ party in Japan, founded in 1910. It played an active part in the movement for protection of constitutional government which overthrew Katsura (1912–13), but it soon disintegrated.

KOLA NUT. West African trade in this popular chewing nut, in some sense the forerunner of tobacco, whose smoking in pipes began to spread only in the early 17th cent., was for long an important element in the general network of long-distance trade in western Africa. Kola was produced in the forest belt, especially in the central part of modern Ghana, and was traded southward to the coast and northward to the Sudan, as well as being consumed locally. In the 18th cent. it continued to out-rival tobacco; the heart of its trade at that time was at Salaga, the principal market-centre linking the central forest country of Ashanti and its neighbourhood with the towns of Hausaland and the Middle Niger.

KO-LAO HUI ('Brothers and Elders Society'), founded in the Ch'ien-lung period (1736–95), in south China, as a politically oriented secret society with religious overtones. Its main aim was to overthrow the Ch'ing, and restore the Ming, dynasty. During the 1890s and the 1900s it was particularly active in anti-foreign, anti-missionary, and anti-Manchu risings. The revolutionaries who eventually overthrew the Ch'ing dynasty owed much of their success to Ko-lao hui support.

KOLBERG HEATH, BATTLE OF (1644), indecisive naval action in which the Danes, commanded by King Christian IV, prevented a Swedish seaward assault under Admiral Klas Fleming on Copenhagen. Christian lost an eye and the Danes suffered many casualties, but the Swedes withdrew to Kiel and later escaped past the Danish fleet.

KOLCHAK, ALEKSANDR VASILYEVICH (1873–1920), Russian sailor and politician. After joining the navy he had some experience of Arctic exploration. He served during the siege of Port Arthur (1904–5) and was promoted to the command of the Black Sea fleet in 1916. After the Feb. 1917 revolution he showed sympathy with the objectives of the provisional government, but he was unable to retain discipline in his command and he resigned it in July 1917. He went to the US and after the Bolshevik revolution he returned to Siberia to take command of the anti-Bolshevik forces. This decision was probably the result of persuasion by the British government. After the overthrow of the Socialist Revolutionary-controlled Ufa Directory Kolchak set up his own government at Omsk and proclaimed himself Supreme Ruler of All Russia, a title which was recognized by the other White leaders and by the French and British governments. He acted as a dictator, but claimed that his objective was 'victory over Bolshevism . . . so that the people may choose the form of government which it desires'. However, he lacked political or military skill and never won the confidence of the Siberian peasants, whose partisan bands continually impeded his operations. He relied chiefly upon Czech troops under the command of Gajda. Kolchak's offensive of 1919 failed to link up either with the British troops in Archangel or with the forces of Denikin in southern Russia. By the end of the year Red forces had driven him out of Omsk and he retreated along the Trans-Siberian railways. All movements on the line were controlled by the Czechs and at length they handed Kolchak over to a radical regime in Irkutsk (Jan. 1920). This arrangement enabled the Czechs to evacuate their troops more rapidly. Kolchak was shot by the Reds.

E. Varneck and H. H. Fisher, *The Testament of Kolchak and other Siberian Materials* (Stanford, 1953).
D. Footman, *Civil War in Russia* (London, 1962).   GS

KOLLIN, BATTLE OF (1757), Austrian victory during the Seven Years War, when Count Daun's army, 54,000 strong, marching to relieve Prague, was intercepted by Frederick II's 34,000 Prussians. The Austrians occupied the heights between Kollin and Chotzewitz and successfully withstood the Prussians' attack, and inflicted heavy losses on them. The Prussian siege of Prague was abandoned.

KOLLONTAI, ALEXANDRA MIKHAILOVNA (1872–1952), Russian revolutionary, female emancipationist, novelist, and diplomat. She was the daughter of a general and after some experience of revolutionary circles in the 1890s she joined the Bolsheviks in 1904. She later became a Menshevik, but maintained a friendly correspondence with Lenin. She belonged to the Zimmerwald 'left' and wrote the pamphlet 'Who needs the War?' (1915). In 1917 she rejoined the Bolsheviks and proved to be an effective agitator among the sailors of the Baltic fleet during the First World War. In 1918 she opposed the signature of the peace of Brest-Litovsk, but she worked loyally as commissar of public welfare, a task which involved the attempt to feed hordes of starving children. In 1921 she and Shliapnikov led the workers' opposition faction of the Communist Party. Their opposition to Lenin's leadership centred on the role allotted to the trade unions. Lenin dismissed Mlle Kollontai's views as those of an anarcho-syndicalist. Her career was damaged by her adherence to the workers' opposition; she lost her place in the secretariat of international women and was directed into diplomacy. Later she was minister in Norway and in Mexico and, in 1930, became minister and later ambassador to Sweden, being the first woman to hold this rank. In 1940 she played an important part in the peace negotiations between Finland and the Soviet Union. She wrote copiously and in her novels and stories advocated the 'winged Eros' theory of sex relations. Lenin disapproved, but her ideas had some influence during the period when the Soviet authorities were trying to erode family ties. In her novel, *Free Love*, a Bolshevik wife discovers that she can no longer love her husband, not merely because he is unfaithful to her but because he cannot dissociate himself from his bourgeois past. In the end the heroine triumphs over jealousy and throws herself into party work. Martov said: 'There are only two real communists in Russia, Lenin and Madame Kollontai.'

A. Kollontai, *Free Love*, tr. by C. J. Hogarth (London, 1932).
A. Kollontai, *The Workers' Opposition* (London, 1924).   GS

KOLOWRAT, FRANCIS ANTON, Count (1778–1861), Austrian politician, who became minister of state for the interior in 1825 under Francis II, continued in this post under Ferdinand I, and also became a member of the Council of Regency. He was a specialist in state finance, but achieved little in this direction. Though not a liberal, he supported the development of Czech culture and, as an opponent of Metternich, received much liberal support. He effectively undermined Metternich's influence after 1835.

KOLYMA RIVER, most remote river of north-eastern Siberia, 2484 kms long, rising in the Kolyma mountains, and flowing into the East Siberian Sea. Its estuary was the departure point for Dezhnev's expedition through the Bering Straits.

KONATÉ, MAMADU (d. 1956), nationalist leader in the French territory of Soudan (afterwards Mali). He formed the Union Soudanaise in 1946 as a territorial branch of the Rassemblement Démocratique Africain, and laid the political foundations for the territory's independence.

KONBAUNG DYNASTY in Burma, founded (1752) by Alaungpaya. Subsequent rulers were Naungdawgyi (*reg.* 1760–3), Hsinbyushin (*reg.* 1763–76), Singu (*reg.* 1776–82), Bodawpaya (*reg.* 1782–1819), Bagyidaw (*reg.* 1819–37), Tharrawaddy (*reg.* 1837–46), Pagan (*reg.* 1846–53), Mindon (*reg.* 1853–78), and Thibaw (*reg.* 1878–85). The capital was originally Shwebo and later Ava, Amarapura, and Mandalay. The growth of European interest in trade with Burma and neighbouring countries brought the dynasty into contact with Europeans, especially the British, with whom it ultimately came into conflict. Mindon alone appreciated the seriousness of European expansion, and was willing to negotiate with an approach to realism. The dynasty fell when Britain annexed Upper Burma (1886).

KONEV, IVAN STEPANOVICH (1897–), Russian soldier and marshal of the Soviet Union, who joined the Bolshevik Party and the Red Army in 1918, and took part in operations against Kopchak. He commanded the Transbaikal Military District (1938–41), but during the Second World War transferred to the Western Front, where he had a distinguished career, taking part in the battle for Smolensk and commanding the battles which resulted in the liberation of Kharkhov and Kirovograd. He replaced Zhukov as commander-in-chief land forces (1946–55), then was commander-in-chief of the Warsaw Pact forces until his retirement in 1960.

KONG (Kpon), old trading town in the central Ivory Coast, West Africa, was one of a number of small states founded after *c.* AD 1400 (though much later in the case of Kong) by Mande-speaking dyula merchants as relay stations in the long-distance trade, whether in kola, ivory, gold, cottons, or other goods. Dyula 'companies', linked by strong religious ties, were accustomed to nominate one of their number as their chosen leader—eventually their king—and to raise their own troop of guards for convoy duties along the trading trails. The earliest leader in Kong is remembered as Seku Wattara, who is said to have come from the Macina region south of the middle Niger. Like other dyula towns, Kong remained commercially important until late in the 19th cent. and is still (1970) a market of considerable local importance.

KONGO, powerful kingdom founded in the south-western corner of the Congo basin (*c.* 14th cent.). It later accepted many European influences (16th cent.), but from the 17th cent. was seriously reduced by conflicts with the Portuguese colony of Angola, into which it was finally incorporated (late 19th cent.).

KÖNIGSBERG, TREATY OF (1656), peace treaty forced upon the Elector Frederick William I of Brandenburg by Charles X of Sweden after his triumphant military campaigns of 1655, culminating in his invasion of Brandenburg. The settlement, which converted East Prussia into a fief of the Swedish Crown, gave the Swedes privileged access to the Prussian ports of Memel and Pillau and half their customs revenues, and marked a stage in the fulfilment of Swedish hopes of Baltic domination.

KÖNIGSMARCK FAMILY, noble Brandenburg family which became Swedish by adoption. Count Hans Christoph (1601–1663), a general of the Swedish Crown in the Thirty Years War (1618–48), was the victor of Wolfenbüttel (1641), the conqueror of Prague (1648), and Swedish governor-general of Bremen and Verden. His elder son, Konrad Christoph (1634–73), was killed at the siege of Bonn (1673) and his younger son, Count Otto Wilhelm (1639–88), fought under Turenne before taking part as general of the Venetian armies

in the attack on Athens, then held by the Turks, in which the Acropolis was damaged (1687). He died of wounds in 1688. Karl Johann (1659–86), elder son of Konrad Christoph, also fought for Louis XIV until 1685, and then likewise took Venetian service, and died campaigning on Euboea. His sister, the beautiful and talented Maria Aurora von Königsmarck (1662–1728), was a mistress of Augustus II of Poland-Saxony and later became abbess of the convent of Quedlinburg (1698). She was the mother of Maurice de Saxe (1696–1750), the last scion of the family. Konrad Christoph's third child, Philip Christoph (1665–94), a colonel in the Hanoverian guards, was the ill-fated lover of Sophia Dorothea, wife of the Elector George of Hanover (later George I of Britain), upon whose orders Philip was murdered (1 July 1694).

KONOE, FUMIMARO (1891–1945), Japanese politician, who was three times prime minister (1937–9, 1940, 1941). He was closely connected with the escalation of Japanese aggression against China and the deterioration of Japanese–American relations. Because of his aristocratic birth and good standing with the army he was chosen to form a government of national unity (June 1937), but proved a weak leader, and was unable to curb the drift towards a completely militaristic foreign policy. He himself proclaimed a new order in East Asia based on Japanese hegemony (Jan. 1938), although he later attempted to avert war with the US by vainly proposing a personal meeting with President Roosevelt; and in the latter stages of the Pacific War he was a leading advocate of peace negotiations. He committed suicide (Dec. 1945) to avoid trial as a war criminal.

KONYA, BATTLE OF (27 Dec. 1832), victory by Egyptian forces under Ibrahim Pasha over Ottoman forces. It opened the way to Istanbul and by thus forcing the sultan to seek Russian help, led to the treaty of Unkiar-Skelessi (8 July 1833).

KOO, WELLINGTON (1887–), Chinese diplomat, who served a succession of governments, both war-lord and Kuomintang. He was best known for his presentation of China's claims against Japan over Manchuria at the League of Nations in the 1930s.

KOOTI, TE (*c.* 1830–93), NZ Maori resistance leader who was embittered by European injustice and especially by his imprisonment in the Chatham Islands (1866–8). Escaping to NZ, he led guerrilla campaigns with skill and ferocity until he was forced to withdraw into the isolated King Country (1872). There he was left unmolested, and pardoned in 1883. He founded a religious millennial movement, the Ringatu cult.

KÖPRÜLÜ, AHMED (*reg.* 1661–76), Ottoman Grand Vizier during whose tenure of office the Ottomans engaged in a brief war with Austria. Although defeated at the battle of St Gotthard, Ahmed Köprülü secured favourable terms from the Emperor Leopold I at the peace of Vasvar (1664), by which the Ottomans acquired the Hungarian fortresses of Grosswardein and Neuhausel. After a memorable siege of Candia in Crete, Ahmed Köprülü brought to a successful end the conflict begun with Venice in 1645—Crete became an Ottoman possession in 1669. The grand vizier conducted a war (1672–6), against Poland which, at the peace of Zurawna, gave to the Sultan the province of Podolia in the western Ukraine, together with the fortress of Kaminiec.

KÖPRÜLÜ, HÜSEYN (*reg.* 1697–1702), Ottoman Grand Vizier, who was called to the highest office in the empire after the defeat of the Ottomans by Prince Eugene in the battle of Zenta. Hüseyn Köprülü's main purpose was to bring to an end the long war which had begun with the Ottoman siege of Vienna in 1683. He achieved this aim with the peace of Carlowitz (1699), by which Austria received almost all the old Hungarian realm; Poland regained control of Podolia, with the fortress of Kaminiec; Venice retained her conquests in Dalmatia and in the Morea; and Russia acquired Azov. Hüseyn Köprülü also strove to reform the administration of the Ottoman empire.

KÖPRÜLÜ, MUHAMMAD (*reg.* 1656–61), Ottoman Grand Vizier, came to high office at a time when the empire was beset with grave internal discord and involved in war (1645–69) with Venice. The new grand vizier, acting with implacable severity, crushed all opposition to his rule. By strengthening the defences of the Dardanelles and retaking the islands of Tenedos and Lemnos, Muhammad Köprülü was able to ensure that the Venetian fleet would not break through into the Sea of Marmara. In addition, he reduced Transylvania to a close dependence on the Porte, capturing (1660) Grosswardein fortress. Perhaps the most notable success of Muhammad Köprülü was to ensure the transference, after his own death, of the Grand Vizierate to his son, Ahmed Köprülü.

KÖPRÜLÜ, MUSTAFA (*reg.* 1689–91), Ottoman Grand Vizier, called to the highest office in the empire at a time when the war of 1683–99 was going badly for the Muslims. The new grand vizier—incorruptible and indefatigable—showed himself to be an able statesman and administrator, restoring efficient rule and assembling fresh troops for a vigorous counter-offensive against the Christians. Under his guidance the Ottomans drove the Imperialist forces from Serbia and in 1690 recaptured the great fortress of Belgrade, which had been in Christian hands since 1688. The Ottoman assault encountered, however, a serious reverse in 1691, when at the battle of Szalákemen, Ludwig von Baden gained the most brilliant success of his career. During the battle, Mustafa Köprülü was killed.

KORAN (QUR'AN), utterances which the Prophet Muhammad gave to the people of Mecca and Medina as a direct revelation from Allah. After the death of the Prophet (AD 632) the first caliph, Abu Bakr, ordered Zayd ibn Thabit of Medina to gather together the various portions of the Koran and to make a complete text of them. Difficulties arose later in the time of the third caliph, 'Uthman (*reg.* 644–56), which necessitated a revision of the version derived from Ibn Thabit. In 651 Zayd ibn Thabit established a definitive text based on a copy which Abu Bakr himself had owned.

To the Muslims the Koran is the actual Word of God, co-eternal with him, uncreated and passed to Muhammad from an archetype existing in heaven. It constitutes the last and most perfect revelation given by Allah to mankind. The Koran is divided into *sura*s or chapters. Of these *sura*s the ones which Muhammad enunciated at Mecca deal with the oneness of Allah, his attributes, and the retribution which will be visited on man, if he remains unrepentant of his wrong-doing. The *sura*s made known at Medina after the *Hijra* from Mecca in 622 are concerned with theological dogma, religious ceremonies such as public prayer, pilgrimage, fasting, and alms-giving, and with the prescriptions relating to civil and criminal affairs (*eg*, marriage, divorce, inheritance, slavery, murder, theft, etc.). The influence of the Koran has been immense—and not alone as a book of scripture. It has served as the textbook which most Muslims have used in their learning of Arabic and as an instrument for acquiring a liberal education. It has served also to establish and maintain a written Arabic intelligible throughout the Muslim world from Morocco to Iraq, and a spoken Arabic which, despite differences of dialect, is also comprehensible, at least in no small measure, throughout the Arab lands.

VJP

KORANA, group of Khoikhoi, who apparently retreated from the whites at the Cape to the Middle Orange river, whence in the 19th cent. they raided much of the Highveld. Armed with guns and on horseback they closely resembled the Griqua, as they did also in their form of government. In 1879 they were defeated by colonial forces after a long period of dispossession and warfare.

KOREAN WAR, THE, resulted from the division of Korea in 1945 into Russian-occupied North Korea and American-occupied South Korea. From 1948 both claimed sole legality as the government of Korea, and each was recognized by most countries in the appropriate Cold War bloc. The occupying troops withdrew in 1949, and border clashes subsequently grew in scale. At dawn on 25 June 1950, eight North Korean divisions crossed into the South and advanced rapidly, taking the capital, Seoul, within three days. Although the legal position was unclear, President Truman decided that it was morally right that the US should help South Korea. He authorized Gen. MacArthur, American commander-in-chief, Far East, to give support, and referred the matter to the UN Security Council. The council, which at the time Russia was boycotting, was able to set up a United Nations Command (UNC) to meet North Korean aggression. Fourteen other nations sent forces, precipitating for the first time the question of whether a limited war could be fought in the nuclear age.

By August the UNC had halted the North Koreans at the 'Pusan perimeter'. On 15 Sept. they counter-attacked frontally and landed simultaneously in the communists' rear at Inchon. Within two weeks the North Korean armies in the South had been destroyed, and the General Assembly authorized the UNC to implement the 1947 policy of unifying Korea. By the end of Oct. the North Korean state had virtually ceased to exist. However, when the UNC launched its 'home by Christmas' offensive on 24 Nov. 1950 Chinese troops attacked in force. As the UNC withdrew from North Korea and the Chinese advance continued into South Korea, MacArthur publicly advocated attacking China. Attlee and Truman conferred in Washington in Dec. and the UN's objectives were again revised. Again the military objective was to be to defend South Korea, and reunification was made a political objective. Truman dismissed MacArthur. Further Chinese offensives in April and May 1951 failed disastrously, and in June the UNC regained all occupied South Korean territory.

As the two armies regrouped, Russia hinted at the possibility of a cease-fire, and the UNC was quick to respond. Negotiations opened on 8 July 1951. The communists managed the cease-fire talks very astutely, but the greatest obstacle to agreement was the refusal of some 50,000 prisoners in the South to be repatriated. The cease-fire was not agreed until July 1953, after Eisenhower had threatened to widen the war in Dec. 1952 and the death of Stalin in March 1953. By the end of 1969, the Military Armistice Commission had met 300 times at Panmunjom, but the Geneva Conference having failed to settle any of the political problems in 1954, North and South Korea entered 1970 still technically at war with each other.

David Rees, *Korea: the limited war* (London, 1964).   WES

KOREMATSU v. US, 323 US 214 (1944), US Supreme Court case concerning the conviction of a Japanese-American who had remained on the West Coast contrary to military exclusion orders. The majority opinion of the court deemed that the exclusion policy was constitutional in time of war and did not imply racial discrimination.

KORFANTY, WOJCIECH (1873–1939), Polish politician, who played an important role in the Polish national revival in Upper Silesia and sat in the Prussian Landtag (1904–18) and the Reichstag (1903–12). He was prominent in the Upper Silesian risings of 1920 and 1921, which led to the province's division and the granting of most of its industrial areas to Poland. In independent Poland Korfanty was a leader of the Christian Democratic Party. After the May coup, he clashed increasingly with Pilsudski and in 1930 was imprisoned for a short time. He later lived in exile in Czechoslovakia (1935–9).

KORNILOV, LAVR GEORGYEVICH (1870–1918), Russian soldier, whose republican sympathies earned him the command of the Petrograd Military District after the Feb. 1917 revolution. He distinguished himself by stabilizing the front after the failure of Brusilov's offensive. In July 1918 Kerensky appointed him commander-in-chief of all the Russian armies, but he was unable to prevent Riga from falling to the Germans (Aug. 21). The fall of this city created a situation of terror, which Kornilov meant to exploit in order to further his own aims. These were to suppress the Soviet and the Bolshevik Party and to reinstitute the death penalty behind the lines. Kerensky needed Kornilov's help to prevent a Bolshevik rising in the capital, and the two agreed that troops should be sent for this purpose. But shortly afterwards Kerensky discovered that Kornilov had already made troop dispositions for the purpose of seizing power in Petrograd and overthrowing the Provisional government. Consequently (26 Aug. 1917) Kerensky ordered Kornilov to lay down his command. Kornilov refused and ordered his 'Savage Division' to capture Petrograd; he announced that the Provisional government had fallen under German control. But the fighting power of Kornilov's troops was dissolved by the obstruction of the railwaymen and the words of the agitators. His commander, Krymov, committed suicide, Kornilov allowed himself to be arrested (4 Sept.). But Kerensky gained little from the failure of Kornilov's efforts; he had been forced to allow the Soviet to form a Red Guard. Kornilov escaped in Dec. 1917 and formed the first anti-Bolshevik units. He was killed in April 1918, leading an attack on Yekaterinodar.

GS

KORYO, Korean dynasty from which the western name of the country is derived. It was founded by Wang Kon, lieutenant of the bandit leader Kung Ye, who succeeded his master as an independent war-lord in 918, and received the abdication of the last nominal King of Silla in 935. Since the traditional social order had largely broken down in the wars which accompanied the fall of Silla, Wang Kon and his successors, once they had gained control of the country, were able to remodel Korean institutions on Chinese lines. Kaesong, the Koro capital, was planned like a Chinese city, and with the increasing influence of Neo-Confucianism from China historical works such as the *Samguk-sagi* were composed in imitation of Chinese histories. Koryo was celebrated for its celadon porcelains and the invention of movable-type printing.

In extending their power northwards to the Yalü, the kings of Koryo clashed with their northern neighbours, the Khitan, who sacked Kaesong in 1011. The prolonged northern threat led to the government being taken over—from the late 12th cent. onwards—by a succession of military leaders, the most famous of whom were of the Ch'oe clan, who moved the court to Kanghwa island in 1232 to escape the Mongol invasions. When the Ch'oe fell from power in 1258, the Koryo king, Kojong, surrendered to the Mongols, and for the next century Koryo remained under their control, contributing heavily in ships and men to the Mongol invasions of Japan in 1274 and 1281. The collapse of Mongol rule in China caused repercussions in Korea, where the last Koryo ruler was deposed by one of his generals, Yi Songgye, in 1392.

KHJG

KOSCIUSZKO, THADDEUS (1746–1817), Polish soldier, who went to America (1776), where he served under Washington and became a friend of Lafayette. He returned to Poland at the end of the American War of Independence (1783), and in the Russo–Polish War (1791–3) served under Poniatowski, but was forced to take refuge in Dresden. On 24 March 1794 he raised the standard of independence at Cracow, having returned to Poland to lead a mass revolt against the Russian partition. After varying military success he was defeated and

taken prisoner at Maciejovice (10 Oct. 1794), but was released two years later by the Tsar Paul and allowed to return to Poland. When Napoleon's armies reached Poland (1806), Kosciuszko declined to serve under him. At the Congress of Vienna (1814–15) he tried to obtain the independence of Poland from Russia.

KÖSE DAGH, BATTLE OF (1243), fought near Erzinjan in Asia Minor, resulted in the Mongols crushing the forces of the Seljuk sultanate of Rum, the sultanate being reduced later to dependence on the Mongol regime of the Il-Khans, established in Persia after 1256.

KOSHALA, ancient Indian kingdom corresponding to part of modern Uttar Pradesh. Country of the mythical hero Rama in remote times (according to the epic the Ramayana), it had developed into a large kingdom by the 6th–5th cent. BC. It was ruled by Prasenajit (Pasenadi) in the time of Lord Buddha. In the latter half of the 5th cent. it declined and was absorbed by its eastern neighbour, Magadha. Among its important towns were Shravasti (Saheth-Maheth) and Ayodhya (Oudh).

KOSOVO (Kosovo Polje—'The Field of the Blackbirds'), in Serbia, was the scene of two battles (1389, 1448) between the Ottoman Turks and the Christians. In 1389 Sultan Murad I overcame Lazar, Prince of Serbia, in an encounter that proved decisive in the Ottoman conquest of the Balkans and in which both Lazar and Murad I lost their lives. The second battle of Kosovo was fought between the Ottoman Turks and the Hungarians under John Hunyadi, who attempted unsuccessfully to make good the disaster which the Christians had suffered at the hands of the Turks in 1444 at the battle of Varna.

KOSSUTH, LOUIS (1802–94), Hungarian revolutionary and nationalist, who promulgated the Hungarian declaration of independence of 1849. He was originally a lawyer, but turned to journalism after deputizing for a magnate in the Hungarian Diet, reports of whose proceedings he circulated. In 1837 Kossuth was arrested and imprisoned for treason; on his release he edited *Pesti Hirlap* and launched an agitation for peasants' rights, the taxation of nobles, and Hungary's independence of Austria. While minister of finance in Batthany's government (1848) he established a separate Hungarian coinage. When the government resigned, Kossuth ruled as a dictator and on 19 April 1849 declared that the Habsburgs had forfeited the Hungarian throne; this precipitated Russian intervention and Kossuth fled to England. The peasants nevertheless attributed their emancipation to him and continued to revere him, though liberals, conservatives, and communists alike considered him to be devoid of principles and self-seeking. The xenophobic nature of the patriotism he aroused delayed Hungarian constitutional rights by making them suspect to non-Magyars.

KOSTOV, TRAICHO (1897–1949), Bulgarian communist politician, who was purged because of his nationalist sympathies. He remained in Bulgaria during the Second World War and afterwards emerged as one of the most influential leaders. In 1944 he assumed control of arrangements for the economic recovery and social reconstruction of the country. He was a member of the central committee and the Politburo and headed important ministries and committees, as well as serving as deputy premier. In 1949 he found himself in the middle of the contest between the indigenous communists and those trained in Moscow. Like Gomulka in Poland, Rajk in Hungary, and Patrascanu in Rumania, he was charged with pursuing a nationalist and anti-Soviet policy. He was tried in Dec. 1949 and shot after putting up a courageous and resolute legal defence.

KOSYGIN, ALEKSEY NIKOLAYEVICH (1904–   ), Russian politician and prime minister of the Soviet Union. He joined the Red Army in 1919 and the Communist Party in 1927. He became chairman (mayor) of the Leningrad City Soviet (1938), USSR minister of textiles (1939–40), deputy chairman of the USSR council of ministers (1940–53), and a member of the Politburo (1948).

His career suffered a check as a result of Zhdanov's death (1948), although he escaped the purge to which many of Zhdanov's protégés fell victim at the hands of Malenkov. He became minister for the consumer goods industry (1953) and, after Malenkov's fall from power, was a candidate member of the Presidium of the central committee (1957) and then became first deputy prime minister (1960).

In the period of Khrushchev's dominance he showed considerable independence. He resisted Khrushchev's promotion of the party and the intrusion (as Kosygin regarded it) of the party into the affairs of the state apparatus, of which he was a leading member. He was himself a reformer, but opposed Khrushchev's more radical initiatives and stood for practical reforms at the base, in the sphere of factory management, rather than sweeping changes imposed from above through the intervention of the party.

When Khrushchev fell Kosygin became chairman of the USSR council of ministers—that is, prime minister (Oct. 1964), and initiated a period of conservative, middle-of-the-road policies, avoiding the extremes both of Stalinist concentration on heavy industry on the one hand and the forceful development of consumer goods industries on the other. WK

KOTELAWALA, SIR JOHN (1896–), Sinhalese politician and landowner, who entered the Ceylon state council (1931) and became minister of communications and works (1936). He was active in the formation of the United National Party (1947) and became minister of transport and works in D. S. Senanayake's cabinet. When Bandaranaike quitted the government (1951) Kotelawala became leader of the House of Representatives. On Senanayake's death (1952) he was not chosen as prime minister, as he had expected, but was appointed to that office two years later, when Dudley Senenayake, who had succeeded his father, gave up the office. Kotelawala took a more active interest in international affairs than his predecessors, and arranged a meeting of five Asian prime ministers in Colombo (1954), which was a precursor to the 1955 Asian conference at Bandung. Here he gained some notoriety by a strong attack on communism.

In 1956, the Buddhist *jayanti* (2500th anniversary of the Buddha's enlightenment) year, by which time he and his party had lost popularity, he called a general election in which he was defeated. He then retired from politics.

KOTOSHIKIN, GRIGORI (d. 1667), Russian bureaucrat in the department of foreign affairs, who fled first to Poland, then to the empire, and finally to Sweden (1664), where he wrote *On Russia in the Reign of Alekcei Mikhailovich*, a revealing and critical account of Russian life and society in the 17th cent.

KOTTE, name of an ancient kingdom in Ceylon (*c.* 1370–1597) and its capital (also called Jayavardanapura), situated in the south-eastern outskirts of present Colombo, where there still (1970) remain a few ruins. Originally a stronghold and centre of a semi-independent kingdom, it was made the capital of a state which, during part of the reign of Parakramabahu VI (1412–67), controlled the entire island. The Kotte period is particularly remarkable for unprecedented Sinhalese literary activity. After the death of Parakramabahu VI, however, decline set in and the state disintegrated in the 16th cent.

KOWLOON, peninsula across the harbour (approx. 1 mile (1·6 kms) from the island of Hong Kong, was ceded by China to the British by the treaty of Tientsin (1858). It became a residential, and later, business district of the British Crown Colony.

KOZLOV, FROL ROMANOVICH (1908–1965), Russian politician, who joined the Communist Party in 1926 and was given a technical education. He rose rapidly in the party apparatus as a result of the great purge, became second secretary of the Kuybyshev district committee, then rose further in the important Leningrad apparatus, becoming secretary of the city committee (1949–52), then of the district committee (1952–1953), and then first secretary (1953–7). He was a strong supporter of Khrushchev in the challenge offered to Khrushchev by the anti-party group (June 1957), after which he became chairman of the RSFSR council of ministers (1957–8), then first deputy chairman of the USSR council of ministers (1958–60), and a secretary of the central committee of the CPSU (1960–4). Although rewarded by Khrushchev for his part in the 1957 crisis, his base in the Leningrad organization gave him considerable independence. After the Cuba fiasco (Oct. 1962) he became increasingly the leader of the conservative opposition to Khrushchev, particularly over relations with China and policy towards Yugoslav 'revisionism'. Thereafter (1963–5) his career was hampered by ill-health.

KRAPF, JOHANN LUDWIG (1810–81), German missionary and explorer, who went to Ethiopia (1837) and then to East Africa (1844) on behalf of the Church Missionary Society. He sought to start a chain of mission stations across Africa, to found a colony for freed slaves at Mombasa, and eventually to promote an African clergy. In 1846 he was joined by John Rebmann. Separately they made a series of explorations inland, Rebmann being the first European to see Mt Kilimanjaro, while Krapf discovered Mt Kenya. Their map showing these mountains, and a great lake further inland which they had heard about, aroused great interest and led to Burton and Speke's expedition of 1857. Their mission work, however, had only meagre success. Rebmann stayed at Rabai almost uninterruptedly for 30 years, but had few followers. Krapf wrote a Swahili grammar and dictionary, and translated the New Testament into Swahili. He was interpreter for Lord Napier's expedition to Ethiopia (1867).

KRAUS, KARL (1874–1936), Austrian writer, journalist, satirist, and editor of the periodical *Die Fackel*, whose major preoccupation was the purity of the German language. He was intensely aware of the significance and influence of words, hence his passionate campaigns against National Socialist propaganda, which he attacked as a perversion of language designed to camouflage inhuman facts. Kraus remained almost unknown outside the German-speaking world and the vital intellectual environment to which he belonged was destroyed by Nazism. But his satirical insight, his ability to unmask equivocation and intellectual confusion, and his moral integrity ensure him a place among the important thinkers of the 20th cent.

KREDIT-ANSTALT, largest and most important of Austria's banks founded in 1856. The Kredit-Anstalt was also the financial focus of the Danube region and an essential link in the world financial system. Its virtual collapse in 1931 was thus of direct importance to the entire world, and heralded the most intense period of financial chaos ever experienced. On 12 May 1931 the Austrian government revealed that it had been forced to vote the Kredit-Anstalt 100 million Schilling (£4 million) in order to save it from insolvency. This provoked a crisis of confidence among the bank's internal and foreign creditors, who began to withdraw funds, and the government was left with no other choice than to underwrite the bank's entire debt. The social democrats protested strongly against the national finances being embroiled in those of a private concern, and the cabinet disintegrated. Attempts to secure French aid failed, and it is still unclear whether France herself had, by withdrawing funds from the bank, provoked the crisis in protest against the proposed customs union between Austria and Germany. On 16 June the Bank of England granted short-term credits of £6 million, but no long-term relief was possible until President Hoover's announcement (20 June) of a moratorium on international debts began to put the situation into a world perspective and offered some hope of solution. The crisis reverberated throughout Europe, being especially damaging to Germany. It revealed the futility of relying on narrow national policies and on a vague belief in the ultimate rationality of capitalism to solve the world-wide economic depression.

KREISAU CIRCLE, anti-Nazi group in Germany, named after its meeting-place, the family estate of its principal member, Count H. J. von Moltke. The group, which began to meet in 1940 and numbered about 20 persons, was a loose association of men of widely differing origins and views, *eg,* conservative officers like Von Trott and Von der Schulenberg; progressive liberals from aristocratic backgrounds, like Von Wartenburg and Von Moltke; the right-wing social democrats Mierendorff and Haubach; and the left-wingers Leber and Leuschner, as well as representatives of both the Protestant and Catholic clergy. Despite its heterogeneous membership, the group was united by a common belief in ultimate standards of democracy, social co-operation, and freedom under the rule of law, and its overall character could be broadly described as Christian Socialist. Von Moltke, as its moving spirit, aimed at uniting in his group the various elements in the anti-fascist movement, with the object of discussing the type of society and government to be established after the overthrow of Nazism. Several lengthy drafts of these plans survive. Hence, although some members of the circle maintained contact with the more active centres of resistance in the army and elsewhere, the Kreisau circle was not itself involved as a group in violent acts of opposition, and accordingly some tension existed between those who believed in the need for urgent and decisive action, and those who remained uncertain of the morality of using violence, even against a tyranny. The circle began to break up after Jan. 1944, when Von Moltke was arrested. In June the left-wing members were arrested, following contacts with Gestapo-infiltrated communist resistance groups. The circle's dissolution came in the wake of the July Plot, in which several Kreisau members were involved, and which marked the final collapse of organized resistance in Germany.

KREMLIN, central citadel of Moscow, begun in the 12th cent., which includes palaces and churches within its walls, the seat of government in Muscovy and Russia for 800 years. Built on rising ground and bounded by the Moskva river and its tributary, the Neglinka, it was first fortified with wood in 1156 and with stone walls in 1367 to withstand Mongol and Lithuanian attacks. In the reign of Ivan III (1462–1505) it was embellished by the addition of cathedrals, towers, and palaces, built by Italian artists and technicians whom Ivan introduced, *eg,* Fioravanti, Novi, Ruffo, and Solario, creating the Kremlin's familiar architecture. As Moscow grew, the Kremlin was surrounded by the Belygorod (White Town), an area of shops and houses of nobles and merchants.

Although Peter the Great transferred his capital to St Petersburg, Moscow remained the centre of culture and enlightenment in Russia.

Inside the Kremlin, the Arsenal, begun in 1701, was completed in 1735 and the Menshikov Tower of the Church of the Archangel Gabriel was built by Zarudnej (1705–7).

During the 1812 French occupation of Moscow by Napoleon an unsuccessful attempt was made to blow up the Kremlin. In the 19th cent. the magnificent Armoury and Grand Palace were added. The latter housed the sessions of the Supreme Soviet after the Communist Revolution until in 1961 a new building was erected overlooking the Moskva river.

Today (1970) the churches are museums, the treasures of the tsars are on view to the public, and outside the Kremlin walls in Red Square are the Mausoleum of Lenin and the memorials to various leaders of the USSR. The name 'Kremlin' has become, in international terms, synonymous with the Soviet government.

KREMSIER CONSTITUTION (1849), draft constitution for the Austrian empire, of a federal type, drawn up by a committee of the Constituent Assembly elected by universal suffrage after the 1848 revolution. The constituent assembly was dissolved by Schwarzenberg without its having accepted the draft constitution, and unified central administration of all lands, including Hungary and Lombardy-Venetia, was introduced in its stead.

KRIEBEL, HERMANN (1876–1941), German politician. As an early associate of Hitler, he helped to form the *Deutscher Kampfbund,* or German Combat Union (1923), a federation of patriotic armed units, and played an important part in the military preparations for the Nov. *putsch* (1923). He was tried with Hitler and others, and sentenced to five years' imprisonment, but was released in 1924. Later, he was active in the Carinthian militia (1926) and in China as adviser to Chiang Kai-shek (1929). In 1934 he became German ambassador to Shanghai.

KRIPALANI, ACHARYA JIWANTRAM BHAGWANDAS (1888–   ), Indian nationalist politician. Although from Sind, Kripalani worked mainly in Gandhian village-uplift and educational projects in Bihar, the United Provinces, and Gujarat in the 1920s. His most important period of Congress service came as general secretary (1934–46). After being elected president (1946), he resigned in protest against his treatment by the new Congress ministers, particularly Vallabhbhai Patel. Further alienated by his failure in the Congress presidential elections of 1950, he formed the Congress Democratic Front to espouse socialist objectives within the party and later (May 1951) resigned to form the *Kisan Mazdoor Praja Party,* which later merged with the Socialist Party to form the Praja Socialist Party. Kripalani was president of the PSP (1952–4), but left the party in 1960; he has been a member of the Lok Sabha almost all the time since 1952. His inability to establish lasting links with any organization has limited his influence.

KRISHAK PRAJA PARTY in India, 'Cultivators and Tenants Party', formed by the Bengal Muslim leader, A. K. Fazl-ul-Huq (1936). The party was the more radical wing of the *Nikhil Banga Praja Samiti* (All Bengal Tenants Association) which Huq had helped to found in 1929 and of which he became president in 1935. Efforts by the leaders of the newly revived Muslim League in Bengal to draw the KPP into alliance were not successful and as a result neither group gained a clear majority of Muslim seats in the general elections (Feb. 1937). A coalition ministry was formed with Huq as chief minister, but with only one other KPP minister, as against four Muslim Leaguers and five non-Congress Hindus. The ministry took up many of the agrarian and educational proposals of the KPP programme, but their implementation was slow and Huq gradually lost the support of a large section of the KPP; he himself joined the Muslim League in 1938. When he broke with the league (1941), however, he was able to form a new 'Progressive Coalition' ministry with KPP and Hindu support which held office until 1943. The KPP was decisively beaten by the Muslim League in the general elections in 1946.

KRISHNA, legendary Indian hero of the Yadava clan, born in Mathura (Punjab), the son of Vasudeva and Devaki. Pursued by his wicked uncle, King Kamsa, he grew up among the cowherds of Brindaban. While still a child he showed tremendous force. As a youth he was mostly among the cow-girls, making love and playing his flute. He subsequently killed Kamsa and founded a new kingdom in Dvaravati (Saurashtra). With his brother Balarama he destroyed many demons and other enemies, and took an important part in the Mahabharata war. In his old age he retired to a forest, where he was accidentally killed by a hunter.

It is impossible to determine the historical nucleus of these stories. From the 3rd cent. BC (if not earlier) Krishna had been fully deified and was regarded as a manifestation of Vishnu. In the *Bhagavadgita* Krishna reveals a famous doctrine that glorifies devotion and has had enormous influence in India. To the historian the Krishna legend is important mainly because it may sometimes have provided a model for historical figures.

KRISHNA MENON, VENGALIL KRISHNAN (1896–), Indian diplomat and politician, who came to England (1924) and was appointed (1927) joint secretary of the Commonwealth of India League in London. The league, which he remodelled as the India League (1930), became a useful channel for Congress lobbying in Britain, aided by Krishna Menon's contacts within the Labour Party and his position as a Labour councillor in St Pancras (1934–47). He was a close friend of Jawaharlal Nehru in the mid-1930s, and was drawn into the negotiations for Indian independence (1946–1947); he was made independent India's first High Commissioner in London (1947–52). He then became, in turn, deputy leader and leader of the Indian delegation to the United Nations (1953–7), where he was noted, in particular, for his defence of the Indian position on Kashmir. Elected to the Rajya Sabha (1953), he became minister without portfolio in the government of India (1956) and then, after his election to the Lok Sabha for North Bombay, became minister for defence (1957). He was eventually forced to resign after the Chinese attacks (Oct. 1962).

KRISHNAVARMA, PANDIT SHYAMAJI (1857–1930), Indian revolutionary organizer and journalist, who came to London in 1897 and gradually established a political circle among Indian students. He started *Indian Sociologist* (1905) as the journal for the Indian Home Rule Society (1905) and provided scholarships to bring politically active students to England—the most notable being V. D. Savarkar. In 1907 he set up 'India House' to serve as a centre for revolutionary training, but later that year, because of police surveillance, was forced to flee to Paris and India House came under Savarkar's control. Krishnavarma continued to publish *Indian Sociologist* while in Paris, but he became increasingly isolated from the revolutionary movement, first because of his embarrassed disclaimers of any personal involvement in the assassination of Sir Curzon Wyllie (1909) and, later, by his inactivity in Geneva during the First World War. He resumed publication of *Indian Sociologist* from Geneva after the war, but he no longer had any influence in Indian affairs.

KRLEŽA, MIROSLAV (1893–), Croatian novelist, playwright, and critic, the leading Croatian literary figure of the 20th cent. Before the Second World War he edited numerous radical journals and played a prominent part in the cultural life of Yugoslavia. His works reflected a morbid sense of social reality as well as a positive sense of humanitarianism. Many of his writings dealt with the decline of the old order, particularly its bourgeoisie. Among his best-known works are the novel *The Return of Philip Latinovic* and a cycle of dramas, *Ballad of Petrica Kerempah and Glembaj*.

KROFTA, KAMIL (1876–1945), Czechoslovak historian, diplomat, politician, and foreign minister (1936–8), who was professor of history at the Charles University in Prague, and retained this position while he was successively minister to Vienna, Rome, and Berlin. He was a diplomatic protégé of Beneš, who appointed him foreign minister. He opposed the Munich settlement (1938), and in the government changes which followed it, he was replaced by the pro-Axis Chvalkovsky. He then returned to academic life. In 1943 he was imprisoned and brutally treated in Terezin; he died shortly after his release.

KRONSTADT, Russian naval base, fortress, and, later, port, scene of the sailors' mutiny of 1921. It was built on Kotlin Island near the mouth of the Neva river on Peter the Great's orders (1704), to protect the seaward approach to the newly built city of St Petersburg.

KRONSTADT MUTINY (March 1921) in Russia. The naval base on the island of Kronstadt, near Petrograd, had provided the Bolshevik Party with some of the most enthusiastic supporters during the Revolution and the Civil War. But by 1921 its fanatical sailors had left and most of the garrison consisted of raw peasant recruits, who were sensitive to the rural disturbances which were occurring in many parts of Russia at that time. There had also been serious strikes in Petrograd and Zinoviev, the party leader in the city, was forced to use troops to maintain order. On 1 March 1921, at mass meetings at Kronstadt it was agreed to issue the following demands: freedom of speech and the press for all left-wing parties; fresh elections to the Soviet by secret ballot; freedom of assembly for trade union and peasant organizations; the withdrawal of all grain-requisitioning squads, and the re-establishment of a free market for the peasants. Lenin was now faced with the first organized revolt against his party from the left. Kalinin, the president of the Soviet Union, was dispatched to harangue the rebels and was lucky to escape unscathed. Trotsky and Gen. Tukhachevsky followed him with 60,000 loyal troops and Cheka men. Tukhachevsky, realizing that the ice would soon melt and make access to the island impossible, began to attack on 7 March. It took him ten days to storm the island. Lenin officially attributed the mutiny to White intrigues. The tenth congress of the party was in session during the mutiny, and Lenin's decision to adopt NEP—which contained changes in policy in line with the Kronstadt demands—was probably hastened by the mutiny.   GS

KROPOTKIN, PYOTR ALEKSEYEVICH, Prince (1842–1921), Russian anarchist and geographer. He was a member of the Russian Geographical Society and published works on Siberian geography and criticisms of Darwinism. In Switzerland (1871) he joined the International, siding with Bakunin against Marx. He was a member of the populist Chaikovsky circle, was imprisoned (1874), and escaped to Europe. He advocated the abolition of centralized states and the development of mutual aid communities. His books, *eg*, *The State, its part in history* (1898), *Memoirs of a Revolutionist* (1899), and *Mutual Aid* (1902), gave him a wide following. He returned to Russia after the February Revolution (1917), but opposed the Bolsheviks.

KROSZKA, BATTLE OF (1739), defeat of the Austrians under Wallis by Turkish forces who besieged the fortress of Krozka near Belgrade, as a result of which Wallis and Count Neipperg concluded the unfavourable treaty of Belgrade (1739).

KRUGER, STEPHANUS JOHANNES PAULUS (1825–1904), South African politician, brought up in the strict Calvinist sect known as Doppers, who accompanied his family on the Great Trek to the Transvaal (1836). With Andries Pretorius, he sought an independent South African republic, of which Transvaal would be a part. He opposed the British annexation of the Transvaal (1877), secured the restoration of her independence (1881), and was president of the South African republic (1883–1900). Despite the economic advantages of gold-mining, Kruger was unable to achieve his objectives of a Boer South Africa. Anglo-Boer relations declined, war followed (1899), and Kruger left South Africa for Holland, and then Switzerland. Afrikaners regarded him as the symbol of their nationalist aspirations.

KRUM (d. 814), chieftain of the Pannonian Bulgars, who were ruled by the Avars until the destruction of the Avar state by Charlemagne in 791. This freed Krum's followers for a career of conquest in the Balkans, where in 803 he brought all the different groups of Bulgars under his rule. He later (811) trapped the main Byzantine army, the Emperor Nikephorus I being among the slain, but thereafter Krum's Bulgars failed to capture Constantinople.

KRUPPS, famous German industrial combine, founded in 1811 by Friedrich Krupp (1787–1826). It remained a family concern for five generations. Its success was built on the production of high-quality steel, backed by continuous technical research, and, after the 1860s, on the massive manufacture and indiscriminate sale of armaments. By 1870 the works at Essen employed some 8000 people, their steel trust financed the German Navy League (1898), and, by 1914, when the firm had expanded into mining and shipbuilding, and workforce numbered 80,000. In the First World War the firm had a virtual monopoly of German arms production. The postwar limitations on German armaments, however, forced Krupps to change over to peaceful manufactures such as agricultural and railway machinery. Its declining fortunes made the chairman, Gustav Krupp von Bohlen (chairman 1909–43), an ardent supporter of Hitler, both before and after 1933, when the firm became a major contributor to Germany's rearmament programme. During the Second World War, Krupps was intimately involved in the exploitation of the occupied territories and the use of slave labour. As a result, Gustav's son Alfried (1907–67) was sentenced at the Nuremberg trials to 12 years' imprisonment and the forfeiture of his fortune; the firm itself was ordered to be dispersed (1947). However, in 1951 Alfried was released, his fortune returned to him, and compensation of £25 million paid to him for the sale of part of the firm. Although he was ordered to disperse the rest of his empire within five years, Alfried claimed he could find no buyer, and the firm prospered under him until it was badly hit by the Ruhr recession in the mid-1960s. Because of the threat to its 102,000 jobs, the firm was offered massive credits by the German government, on condition that the holding was converted into a social and charitable foundation. In 1967 Alfried died and his son renounced his inheritance. In 1968 the foundation was constituted and the Allied order on dispersal finally lifted.

B. Menne, *Krupp, or the Lords of Essen* (London, 1937).
AJC

KSHATRIYAS, THE, second of the four ancient Indian classes (varna) following, at least in theory, the priestly class of the Brahmans. They are not really a caste, but comprise a number of true castes, among which Rajputs are predominant. All kshatriyas are entitled to wear the sacred cord and are bound to a certain way of life including standards of chivalry.

KU K'AI-CHIH (c. 345–411), earliest Chinese painter whose style and work can be conjectured. He came from the lower Yangtse valley. In his portraits and landscapes he tried to capture spirit, as well as appearance, and in the latter to express Taoist ideas. What are probably copies of two of his horizontal scrolls are preserved, entitled 'Admonitions of the Instructress to Court Ladies' (British Museum) and 'The Nymph of the Lo River' (Freer Gallery, Washington).

KU YEN-WU (1613–82), Chinese scholar of the early ch'ing period. There had been a growth of interest in textual studies in late Ming, and the fall of the dynasty was the occasion for many, including Ku, to devote their energies to scholarship rather than to serve their Manchu conquerors. With an encyclopaedic knowledge and lucid writing style, Ku made original contributions in such fields as phonetics, geography, epigraphy, history, and textual criticism. His reputation was enhanced by his extensive travels, and numerous friends who wrote in praise of him, but especially by his conspicuous loyalty to the fallen Ming dynasty.

KUANG-HSÜ, reign-title of Tsai-t'ien (1871–1908), Emperor of the Ch'ing dynasty of China (*reg.* 1875–1908). He was the ninth of the dynasty and was chosen by the Empress Dowager Tz'u-hsi to succeed to the throne. He being a minor, rule was left in the hands of Tz'u-hsi and her co-regent, the Empress Dowager Tz'u-an (1837–81). Despite Tz'u-hsi's domination, Kuang-hsü, under the influence of the imperial tutor, Weng T'ung-ho, grew up to be a man of considerable character and strong moral convictions. However, even after 1889, when he assumed personal rule, Kuang-Hsü was unable to shake off Tz'u-hsi's control, as was shown by the failure of the 'Hundred Days' Reform': Tz'u-hsi's coup of 22 Sept. 1898 led to Kuang-hsü's confinement and her resumption of power. One result of this change was the court's support for the Boxer Rising, to which the young emperor was strongly opposed. Tz'u-hsi died on 15 Nov. 1908, the death of Kuanghsü having been announced as having occurred the day before. The sequence of events suggests that Kuang-hsü did not die a natural death. What could have been a successful reign was thus marred by the personal ambition of the Empress Dowager Tz'u-hsi.

KUBITSCHEK, JUSCELINO (1902–), Brazilian physician, politician, and president of Brazil (1956–61). He entered politics in 1933, served in congress (1934–7, 1946–50), as mayor of Belo Horizonte (1940–5), and governor of Minas Gerais (1950–5), before reaching the presidency. As a president he promised 'fifty years of progress in five', and promoted the rapid development of transport, power, food production, and industry. His administration was accused of widespread graft, and criticized because of inflation and heavy foreign borrowing. Kubitschek's major achievement was the construction of Brasília, which became the capital of Brazil in 1960. As an advocate of inter-American co-operation for economic development, he proposed Operation Pan America, which anticipated the Alliance for Progress. Kubitschek, who in 1964 was a senator from Goiás had his mandate and political rights cancelled by the revolutionary government.

KUCHEK KHAN (d. 1921), Iranian revolutionary leader of the Gilan peasant movement and of Muslim sympathies, who reluctantly allied himself with Russian Bolsheviks and established the Soviet Republic of Gilan (1920). He later broke with the communists and his regime was overthrown by Iranian forces (1921).

KUCHUK-KAINARDJI, TREATY OF (1774). By this treaty Russia imposed on the Ottoman empire a peace settlement of great significance for the future. Russia gained large territories in the Kuban and along the Terek river; Azov at the mouth of the Don; the fortresses of Kerch and Yenikal'e, which controlled the strait leading from the Sea of Azov into the Black Sea; and the lands situated between the Bug and Dniester rivers. She also obtained freedom of navigation on the Black Sea, and the right to send merchant ships through the Bosphorus and the Dardanelles, as well as the privilege of building an Orthodox church at Istanbul and the right to make representations on behalf of 'those who serve it'. The Porte was to hand over to the Russian government war indemnities amounting to 4½ million roubles. More important still, the Tatar khanate of the Crimea, until then subject to the Ottomans, was to become an independent state, the sultan retaining only certain rights of a religious nature. The clauses relating to the Tatars foreshadowed the annexation of the Crimea to the Russian empire—an event which came about in 1783. By the treaty, Russia secured a firm hold on the northern shore of the Black Sea. It broke the exclusive control which the Ottomans had long exercised over those waters. Through the clauses concerned with the Orthodox church at Istanbul, it bestowed on the Russian government a pretext for intervention almost at will in the internal affairs of the Ottoman empire.

KUFA, AL-, situated not far from Najaf in Iraq, was at first an Arab cantonment established c. AD 638. It soon attained the dimensions of a large town, becoming a main base for the Arab campaigns in Persia. Al-Kufa also demonstrated a strong inclination towards the Shi'a, *ie*, towards the cause of the Caliph Ali (*reg.* 656–61) and his descendants—an inclination so strong in fact that the Umayyads founded in Iraq at Wasit (AD 702) a new base for their Syrian troops, hoping thus to control the turbulence of Al-Kufa, and also of Basra. Under the Abbasids Al-Kufa was from time to time involved in revolts of Shi'i origin, as in 815 and 870. It later suffered considerable damage from the raids of the Qaramita (924–5, 927, 937) and thereafter fell into a gradual decline.

KUFIC, form of Arabic script developed at Al-Kufa in Iraq and used above all for the Koran, for official documents, and for inscriptions on monuments and coins.

KÜHLMANN, RICHARD VON (1873–1948), German diplomat and politician. He joined the German diplomatic service in 1899 and, after working in a variety of overseas posts, was appointed counsellor at the London embassy in 1909, where he served until the outbreak of the First World War. His attempts to improve Anglo-German relations in this period were based on the belief that Germany's colonial ambitions could be satisfied by means of peacefully negotiated agreements with Britain, if Germany were prepared to make commensurate concession in her foreign policy.

After the outbreak of war (1914) Kühlmann held posts in Stockholm, Constantinople, and The Hague, and in Aug. 1917 was appointed secretary of state for foreign affairs, holding this office under both Michaelis and his successor, Hertling. He conducted the peace negotiations with Russia at Brest-Litovsk (1917–18), where he supported a moderate rather than an expansionist settlement. At the same time, he backed attempts then being made through the Vatican to reach a negotiated peace with Britain, arguing that Germany should use the renunciation of Belgium as her main bargaining point. His policies, however brought him increasingly into conflict with Ludendorff and the Supreme Command. On 24 June 1918 he made a speech in the Reichstag in which he emphasized the inevitability of a diplomatic solution to the war—an accurate assessment of the situation, but not one which he had been authorized to make officially. Ludendorff seized on this incident as an excuse to force Kühlmann out of office and end the threat of a compromise peace settlement. On 8 July 1918 Kühlmann was dismissed by the Kaiser, this being one of the final acts of Ludendorff's dictatorship.

KUJULA KADPHISES (*fl.* 1st cent. AD), first Kushan King. In a series of campaigns he conquered Bactria and the Kabul area, and extended his kingdom to the Indus. He controlled most of the navigable course of the Oxus river.

KUKAWA, former capital of Bornu in north-eastern Nigeria. It was built (*c.* 1814) by Al-Kanemi and became an important commercial centre. It was sacked by Wadai in 1846 and by Rabih in 1893, and was replaced as capital by Maiduguri.

KUKIYA, capital of the Za and Sunni dynasties of Songhay (western Sudan) before the Songhay state became established at Gao *c.* 8th–9th cents. Its nucleus is thought to have been on the island of Bentia, to the south of modern Ansongo.

KU-KLUX-KLAN in US, secret organization, originally a social movement, founded in Pulaski, TN (1865–6). It quickly became a quasi-political society, led by an ex-Confederate general, Nathan B. Forrest, for the maintenance of white supremacy in the South. At Nashville, TN (1867), it was organized into the 'Invisible Empire of the South', led by a Grand Wizard, with subordinate Realms, Provinces, and Dens headed by Grand Dragons, Titans, and Cyclops. Its curious terminology was designed to arouse fears among the superstitious, and the Klan thrived on organized resistance to the congressional Reconstruction programme. Many Southerners saw it as a defence of the principles of Ameri-

canism, and it succeeded in thwarting many of the main aims of the Freedmans Bureau and attempts to guarantee Negro rights.

Disguised in white robes and masks, members of the Klan terrorized, and sometimes lynched, Negroes who persisted in voting Republican, and persecuted Southern whites who opposed their views. The Klan was formally disbanded in 1869, but its activities continued, and Congress passed the Ku-Klux-Klan Acts (1870, 1871, to enforce the 14th and 15th Amendments. Though sections of these acts were declared unconstitutional, the power to punish private interference with individual voting rights was accepted. Congressional committee investigations (1871–2) produced extensive evidence of the Klan's activity in several Southern states but, with the end of Reconstruction and the regaining of political power in the South by white Southerns, its activities declined.

The Klan was revived in 1915 by William Joseph Simmons as a more nativist organization. The scope of its hostility was broadened to include such enemies of 'true' religion and patriotism as Catholics, Jews, Communists, and recent immigrants. It developed from a group of some 2000 members (1917) into a national organization numbering some 5 million which, by 1925, had exerted strong political influence in a number of states, from ME to TX; it also had considerable support in the expanding industrial cities throughout the nation. The burning of fiery crosses, the apparent acceptance of violence, and finally a series of scandals began to falsify the Klan's claims of moral leadership. Although its combined rural and urban strength had enabled it to exercise considerable influence at the Democratic national convention in 1924, by 1928 it was unable to prevent the nomination of a Catholic, Alfred E. Smith. It continued to lose ground during the Depression, and after considerable Federal pressure was formally dissolved in 1944, though in the South it maintained a scattered pattern of intimidation to prevent Negroes from voting. Its activities increased as the civil rights movement in the South gained momentum and the Klan re-emerged openly in the 1950s, following the US Supreme Court's attempts to help Negroes by outlawing segregated schools. However, its methods were crude and its leaders no longer part of the Southern political elite. Disowned and vulnerable, it was investigated by the House Un-American Activities Committee in the mid-1960s.

S. F. Horn, *Invisible Empire, the story of the K.K.K. 1866–77* (Boston, 1939).
J. M. Mecklin, *The Ku Klux Klan: a study of the American mind* (New York, 1924). JDL

KULAKS, Russian term of abuse referring to rich peasants or village money-lenders, and often applied to Lenin's category of rich peasants who hired labour. They benefited from Stolypin's reforms (1906–10). In the 1930s they were eliminated as a class.

KULELI INCIDENT (1859), abortive conspiracy to assassinate Sultan Abdülmecid (1839–61). The incident, though often held to be the first attempt to democratize the Ottoman empire, was really the work of traditional opponents of westernization.

KULINISM, type of hypergamy in Bengal (traced back to the 12th cent. AD) whereby Brahmans used to marry their daughters, for reasons of prestige, to men of the highest Brahman sub-caste: the Kulins. This practice led to a particular form of polygamy and to various excesses.

KULTURKAMPF (1871–87), name given to Bismarck's anti-Catholic policy carried out in alliance with the National Liberal Party in the Prussian Landtag and in the Reichstag. It originated in fears of ultramontanism after the declaration of papal infallibility and in suspicion of the loyalty of many of the Catholic groups in the German empire.

Although a Protestant state, accession of territory from Poland and on the Rhine had given Prussia a population one-third of which was Catholic, and among the Polish elements religion was closely connected with Polish nationalism. Outside Prussia, Catholic states had tended to side with Austria in the German Confederation. Protestant Prussians, therefore, often thought Catholics un-German. The situation was aggravated by sympathy for many Old Catholics expelled from their posts and by the election of more than 50 Catholic (Centre Party) candidates to the Prussian Landtag in 1870 and 57 to the Reichstag in 1871. To confirm the worst suspicions of Protestants and Liberals, the Centre Party leader, Windthorst, proposed in the Reichstag that Germany should intervene in Italy on the pope's behalf.

Bismarck reacted by abolishing the Catholic section of the Prussian ministry of education, which had been set up in 1850, and eliminating Catholic supervision from Catholic schools. In 1872 the Reichstag expelled the Jesuits from Germany. Then the May Laws were passed in Prussia, dissolving all religious orders except those engaged in nursing, and requiring state approval of any candidate for clerical office. Clergy could be dismissed by the state and civil marriage was made compulsory throughout the empire. This resulted in widespread imprisonment of priests, and even bishops, for ignoring the laws, and many sees were made vacant. At the same time, the strength of the Centre Party in the Reichstag was increased. When Pope Pius IX died (1878) Bismarck began to move away from his National Liberal allies, the laws were gradually relaxed, and by 1887 there was a Prussian ambassador to the Holy See and the Kulturkampf had ended.

The end came for a number of reasons—partly because Bismarck was finding the National Liberals unco-operative about protection, which was necessary to Prussian agriculture, confronted with the importation of prairie wheat, and unco-operative also about army finance—and partly the Prussian Conservatives disliked the effect of the May Laws on their own Lutheran schools. Furthermore, Bismarck was worried by the growth of Socialism and needed the Centre Party's support. Chiefly, the laws were ineffective. They were strengthening the Centre Party and passive resistance continued. Bismarck was always opportunist, never doctrinaire, and knew when to retreat.

Ralph Flenley, *Modern German History* (London and New York, 1953).   DMK

KUM, city in Northern Persia which for centuries has been a centre for caravan traffic, and in modern times became a link-point for traffic to and from Tehran, Isfahan and Iraq. A shrine was built there in the 17th cent. by Shah Abbas.

KUMARAJIVA (AD 350–409), Buddhist monk and scholar, originally from Kucha (Sinkiang). He studied in Kashmir and later went to China, where he made Chinese translations of Sanskrit works on Buddhist monastic discipline. His career is an example of the lively cultural intercourse between India, Central Asia, and China in his time.

KUMASI, capital of Asante in central Ghana, founded in the reign of Osei Tutu (c. 1697–c. 1731). It prospered during the Asante empire, but fell to British forces in 1901.

KUMBI SALIH, site in southern Mauritania, thought to be the merchants' suburb of a royal city of ancient Ghana. Parts have been excavated, revealing a mosque and stone houses. Its area suggests that it had a maximum population of about 20,000.

KUN, BELA (1886–1937), Hungarian politician and communist dictator, who came from a middle-class Jewish family in eastern Hungary. After being active in politics and journalism he served in the First World War and was captured on the Russian front in 1915. After the Russian revolution he was trained by Lenin, supplied with funds for political work, and sent back to Hungary.

Later he was expelled from the Social Democratic Party and briefly imprisoned. On his release (March 1919) he led a Communist–Social Democratic coalition government. Though nominally commissar for foreign affairs, he was, in fact, dictator and his government carried through a programme of confiscation, collectivization, and anti-clericalism. Kun was unable to establish a popular or stable government and Hungary was invaded by Rumanian armies which he was unable to resist. His regime came to an end (Aug. 1919), and he was interned, then allowed to go to Russia. When he left, he went to Vienna (1928). After an unsuccessful attempt to renew revolution in Hungary he was again arrested and again allowed to go to Russia. He disappeared in the great purge of 1936–8. In 1956 he was praised by *Pravda* and thus became one of the first important figures to be rehabilitated after being liquidated in the purge.   GE

KUNG, Prince (1833–98), personal name of I-hsin, brother of the Hsien-feng Emperor of China. In 1860, when the Anglo-French forces took Peking, Hsien-feng fled, leaving Prince Kung to negotiate with the British and French representatives. He was thus responsible for the signing of the Peking Convention and the ratification of the treaties of Tientsin. His first contact with foreigners also affected his anti-foreign attitude. In 1861, he proposed the creation of the Tsungli Yamen, of which he was placed in charge, to deal with foreign affairs. On the death of the Hsien-feng emperor in the same year, he was made prince counsellor, while Tz'u-hsi and Tz'u-an became co-regents of the child emperor, Kuang-hsü. For much of the next 24 years, Prince Kung was in charge of foreign affairs, dealing particularly with foreign ministers resident in Peking, in addition to his duties as head of the Grand Council. In 1884, he as well as other members of the Grand Council and the *Tsungli Yamen*, were replaced by more belligerent elements, who accelerated the conflict with France.

KUNNERSDORF, BATTLE OF (1759), Prussian defeat in the Seven Years War, inflicted by a joint army of 80,000 Austrians and Russians under Generals Loudon and Saltykov. Frederick II's army attacked the Russian flank, capturing 180 guns, but was later routed by the Austrian artillery with the loss of 20,000 men.

KUNTA, Arab tribe widely dispersed along the southern Saharan fringes. Their origin is obscure, though they claim descent from Uqba ibn Nafi. In the 15th cent. they were encamped around the Tuwat oasis and from there dispersed southwards, their major camps now being in the Azawad area north of the Niger Bend.

From the late 15th cent. one family, descendants of Ahmad al-Bakka'i (d. *c.* 1515), became famous for its scholars and saints. Al-Bakka'i's son, Umar al-Shaikh, is said to have introduced the Qadiriyya brotherhood to the southern Sahara, and Al-Maghili is traditionally associated with him in this. Certainly the Kunta were the main propagandists of the order and were the custodians of Islamic learning in the area after the decline of Timbuctoo in the 17th cent.

The 18th cent. produced two great Kunta scholars, Sidi Mukhtar (1729–1811) and his son Muhammad (*c.* 1765–1826). Both were prolific authors and the father's works in particular influenced Uthman ibn Fudi. Muhammad's son Ahmad al-Bakka'i, himself a scholar and poet, was the protector of the German traveller Barth during his stay in Timbuctoo (1853).

KUNWAR SINGH (d. 1858), Rajput chief of Jagdispur and unsuccessful leader of the 1857 revolt against the British in Bihar.

KUO MO-JO (1892–   ), Chinese writer and cultural administrator. Kuo went through a romantic period in the 1920s, when he was leader of the Creation Society. He later developed his talents in many spheres, including archaeology and classical Chinese scholarship. Kuo occupied many key literary and cultural posts under the Chinese Communist administration, notably that of head of the Chinese Academy of Sciences.

KUO SUNG-TAO (1818–91), Chinese scholar and China's first resident minister abroad. His mission as minister to London (1877) originated in the presentation of a letter of apology to the British government over the Margary affair (1876). While in England, he came to realize the need for China to modernize herself, not only militarily, but also in her political, legal, and educational systems. Kuo's diary, which embodied these ideas, was published and distributed by the *Tsungli Yamen*. But conservative opposition soon led the court to suppress the work. Kuo returned to China in 1879, and, to avoid conservative hostility in Peking, lived in retirement for the rest of his life in his native Hunan.

KUOMINTANG, the Chinese Nationalist Party. Sun Yat-sen founded the Kuomintang's precursor, the *Hsing Chung Hui* ('China Revival Society') in 1895 and developed it into a revolutionary republican party. Sun and his followers staged a series of uprisings against the Manchu emperor; the party was known successively as the *Tung Meng Hui* ('Alliance Party') and the Kuomintang. After the 1911 Revolution which overthrew the dynasty, Sun was briefly president, but was forced out of office by the chief holder of military power in China, Yuan Shih-k'ai. There followed many years of largely abortive political activity, during which Sun tried to gain a secure base for the Kuomintang, chiefly in his native Kwangtung province. Sun's persistence was finally rewarded in 1923, when the Kuomintang at last established a secure hold over Canton, and started in earnest the massive task of reunifying China. With the help of Soviet advisers, and with the active co-operation of the fledgling Communist Party, progress was made in training a party army, and in extending political work. Sun himself died in 1925, a year before the Northern Expedition to reunify China was launched. Control of the Kuomintang passed not to the man who was generally regarded as Sun's heir, Wang Ching-wei, but to the military leader, Chiang Kai-shek. Under Chiang, China was superficially reunified (by 1928), but the Kuomintang also became increasingly authoritarian, right-wing, and army-dominated. The social and political reforms which Sun had outlined in his Three People's Principles were not carried out, nor was China's economy rehabilitated. Chiang was preoccupied with his crusade against the communists, launched with the Shanghai Purge (April 1927), and subsequently with the fight against the Japanese, whose encroachment upon China from 1931 on eventually developed into full-scale war (1937–45). The Kuomintang lost its revolutionary dynamism, and reverted to conservatism; Chiang's New Life Movement harked back to the anachronistic Confucian virtues. By the end of the Anti-Japanese War this conservatism had degenerated into corruption and incompetence, leaving the Kuomintang ill-prepared to fight the communists in the Civil War (1946–9). After its expulsion from the mainland (1949), the Kuomintang retired to Taiwan, where its repressive political and social policies continued, but with a much more successful economic policy; Taiwan is now (1970) one of the most prosperous Asian states.

DCML

KURAL, THE, one of the most beautiful works of the classical Tamil literature of south India, composed by Tiru-valluvar (*c.* ?7th cent. AD). It is a collection of well over 1000 stanzas, each concisely expressing a complete idea. Together they represent a treasure of practical wisdom in a religious spirit.

KURBSKY, ANDREI MIKHAILOVICH, Prince (1528–83), Russian *boyar* general and political adviser to Ivan IV, who, after disagreements, fled from his military command in Livonia and took refuge with Ivan's enemy, the Grand Duke of Lithuania. He later exchanged some polemical letters with the tsar and wrote a history which shed interesting light on Ivan's reign.

KURDISTAN. The autonomous Kurdish state envisaged in the abortive treaty of Sèvres (1920) did not materialize and Kurds came to form a minority notably in Turkey, Iran, and Iraq. Kurdish revolts occurred in all these countries, but particularly in Iraq, where endemic disturbances developed into a major rebellion (1960) led by Mulla Mustafa Barzani and comprising both tribal and nationalist elements. Autonomy for the Kurdish areas of Iraq was demanded. Civil war, punctuated by truces in 1963, 1964, 1966, and 1970, ensued. In 1970 a new general agreement conceding most Kurdish demands was achieved.

KURDS, name given to a group of peoples, Iranian in descent or Iranized, who inhabit the eastern extension of the Taurus range and also the Zagros mountains. The Kurdish dialects fall into two main sections, northern and southern, the line of division running approximately from Lake Urmiya to the Great Zab and along that stream to the Tigris. To the southeast are found the related dialects of the Zagros area, Lakki and Luri. After the advent of Islam, the Kurds attained from time to time a position of prominence within the Muslim world. A number of Kurdish dynasties came into being, *eg*, the Shaddadids (951–1174) in Armenia; the Marwanids (990–1096) in Diyar Bakir; and above all the Ayyubids (1169–1250) ruling over Egypt and Syria—the first of this line being the famous Salah al-Din (Saladin). The Kurds, existing as a complex of small semi-autonomous principalities, had also a role of some importance in the long Ottoman Safawid wars of the 16th and 17th cents. The 19th and 20th cents saw the rise of a Kurdish nationalism which, though disappointed of success in the years following the First and Second World Wars, still survived with a tenacious vigour in 1970.

KURIGALZI II (*fl. c.* 1345–1324 BC), Kassite King who protected Sumer by a campaign in Elam. He built extensively, *eg*, a still-visible ziggurat near Baghdad.

KUROPATKIN, ALEKSEI NIKOLAYEVICH (1848–1921), Russian soldier and politician, who was minister of war (1898) after service in the Balkans and the Caucasus. Later he became commander-in-chief during the Russo–Japanese War (1904–5), but resigned after defeat at Mukden. He commanded the Northern Front in the First World War until he became governor of Turkestan (1916).

KURRU, EL, the earliest of a group of royal Kushite cemeteries lying near Napata. The earliest burials were covered by mounds, the later ones by *mastaba*s or pyramids.

KUSH, name used by ancient Egyptians for the territory lying south of Aswan. It was probably the indigenous name of the area, and was first used in Egyptian texts of the XIIth dynasty. In Pharaonic times it became an important part of the Egyptian empire; its governor, who was given the title of 'Royal Son of Kush', was one of the senior Egyptian officials. His capital in New Kingdom times seems to have been at Amara West. The name is also given to the indigenous state which developed at Napata after the end of Egyptian domination, and subsequently flourished at Meroe.

KUSHANS, people of Central Asia, of first importance in the 1st cent. AD. Under a number of strong kings, the greatest of whom was Kanishka, they formed a powerful kingdom stretching from Mathura in India to beyond the Oxus, and including Bactria, Herat, and Seistan. They had many trading and cultural connections with the Romans and brought Central Asian and Chinese influences into Iran and

India. Since they controlled parts of three important trade routes, they were a serious commercial threat to Iran. The Sassanian King Shapur I conquered the Kushans and deposed the dynasty. Shapur II (309–79) destroyed the kingdom after it rebelled.

KUTAMA, Berber people of the Petite Kabylie, whose rebellion (905) brought the Fatimids to power in North Africa, and who for a century supplied the dynasty in the Maghrib and Egypt with soldiers.

KÜTAYHA, CONVENTION OF (8 April 1833), by which the Ottomans, following their defeat by the Egyptians at Konya, recognized Muhammad Ali as governor of Syria and Adana.

KUTNA HORA, SILVER MINES OF, in German Kuttenberg. A medieval Bohemian mining city, the site of major silver deposits and a mainstay of Bohemian finances. The products of its mint enjoyed the prestige of an international currency. The mines were worked mainly by Italian and German companies.

KUTUSOV, MIKHAIL ILLARIONOVICH, Prince (1745–1813), Russian field marshal, who was commander-in-chief at Borodino and ordered the abandonment of Moscow to Napoleon (1812). He was one of the founders of Russian military science. He served in Russo–Turkish wars (1790) under Suvorov, commanded a Russian army in Austria in the War of the Third Coalition against Napoleon, and defeated the Turks in the war (1811–12) which led to the peace of Bucharest. He was not popular with Alexander I, but nevertheless was recalled as commander-in-chief (1812) after the fall of Smolensk, though he continued Barclay de Tolly's policy of retreat. He led the Russian army in pursuit of Napoleon, and died in Silesia.

KUUSINEN, OTTO VILGELMOVICH (1881–1964), Russian politician, who joined the Bolshevik Party in 1904, was a member of the Finnish revolutionary government (1918), and was made head of the puppet Finnish government established by the Russians at the time of the Russo–Finnish War (1939). He was a member of the Presidium of the central committee of the CPSU during its enlargement after the 19th congress (1952–3). He strongly supported Khrushchev in his clash with the anti-party group (June 1957) and as a result was brought back into the Presidium and appointed to its secretariat. His prestige as an old Bolshevik was valuable to Khrushchev at a time when he was engaged in conflict with Molotov and Kaganovich. Kuusinen continued to support Khrushchev, both at the 22nd congress and in his writings.

KUWAIT AGREEMENT (23 Jan. 1899), by which Sheikh Mubarak of Kuwait undertook not to alienate any territory or receive foreign representatives without British consent. It was designed to prevent the establishment of Russian influence. The agreement marked the beginnings of British control over Kuwait.

KUWAIT CRISIS. Following the termination of the 1899 Anglo–Kuwaiti agreement (which had established de facto British protection over Kuwait), President Kassim revived (June 1961) an older Iraqi claim to Kuwait. In response to Kuwaiti appeals for assistance, British and Saudi Arabian troops were sent to meet the possibility of an Iraqi attack. These forces were later replaced (Sept.–Oct. 1961) by a composite Arab force. President Kassim claimed that he had never intended to pursue the claim other than by peaceful means, and the evidence supports this statement. The principal effect of the episode was to weaken the Kassim regime in Iraq. Kuwait was admitted to the Arab League (20 July 1961) and the new Iraqi regime abandoned the claim (1963).

KWAKIUTL INDIANS, tribe native to and still (1970) living on northern Vancouver Island and in BC. They were possibly encountered by whites as early as 1640, and were frequently visited by English and American explorers and traders after 1775.

KWANGGAET'O (Jap., Kōtai-ō) (*reg.* 390–412), King of Koguryo in Korea. He conquered Liaotung in the time of the Mujung Yen dynasty and extended his control southwards into the Korean peninsula, reducing the kingdom of Silla to vassal status and clashing with Japanese forces in Paekche and Mimana. The inscribed stele erected to his memory by his successor King Changsu (412–91) constitutes the earliest Korean historical text.

KWANGSI CLIQUE, longest surviving regional war-lord clique in Republican China which was active during the period 1925–49. The clique, led by Li Tsung-jen and Pai Ch'ung-hsi, co-operated closely with the Kuomintang until 1929, then broke with the Nanking government and maintained an independent regional administration in the province of Kwangsi. There was a partial reunion during the Anti-Japanese War (1937–45), but the Kuomintang was never able to subjugate the clique completely. The clique was an example of the 'new warlordism' which appeared after the technical elimination of China's war-lords in 1928.

KWANTUNG ARMY, Japanese army of occupation in the territory of Kwantung in southern Manchuria, annexed by Japan after the Russo–Japanese War (1904–5). Its duty of protecting Japanese railway zones in southern Manchuria involved it in Manchurian politics. In 1928 certain Kwantung army officers blew up the train of Chang Tso-lin, the Manchurian war-lord, an episode which led to the resignation of the prime minister, Yanaka, and foreshadowed the 1931 Mukden Incident.

KYANZITTHA (*reg.* 1084–1112), third King of Pagan dynasty, son of Anawrahta. He is remembered as the builder of the Ananda Pagoda.

KYD, THOMAS (*c.* 1558–*c.* 1594), English dramatist, who wrote *The Spanish Tragedy* (*c.* 1592), a blank-verse Senecan melodrama which, despite its crudities, was extremely popular and set a fashion for plays of revenge. Among other uncertain attributions to Kyd is a lost play about Hamlet.

L

LABARNAS I (*reg. c.* 1680–1650 BC), Hittite King, the first recorded and possibly legendary. It was claimed that he conquered western Asia Minor and made the Mediterranean his frontier.

LABELLE, ANTOINE (1833–91), French Canadian priest who opened up new regions of Canada. Having enlisted public support for the idea of settlement he was appointed deputy minister of colonization for the province of Quebec (1888). He was the founder of 860 settlements.

LABIAU, TREATY OF (20 Nov. 1656), agreement between Charles X of Sweden and Frederick William I of Brandenburg-Prussia, by which the Swedes recognized the sovereign independence of the elector in his duchy of East Prussia, previously a Swedish fief, and surrendered their share of the customs revenues of the Prussian ports of Memel and Pillau, which they had acquired ten months before by the treaty of Königsberg.

LABIENUS, T. (d. 45 BC), Roman politician and general, who, after carrying (63) a law to restore popular election to the office of Pontifex Maximus, in consequence of which Julius Caesar was elected, served with Caesar in Gaul (58–51). But on the outbreak of the Civil War (49) he joined Pompey and died at the battle of Munda.

LABOR PARTY IN AUSTRALIA. By 1859 trade unions in Australia reached sufficient maturity to pay some 'Labor' MPs, but organized parliamentary activity began only in 1891, when the NSW legislative assembly elected 36 members pledged to support measures beneficial to wage-earners, including a national bank. Political rather than industrial action was encouraged by failure of the maritime and shearers' strikes in the early 1890s. Labor governments of brief duration followed—in Qld (1899) and in the Commonwealth (1904). There the first decade after federation was an era of Liberal–Labor alliance, Alfred Deakin's term as prime minister with Labor support confirming protection and establishing industrial arbitration, preference for unionists, old age, and invalid pensions. An Australian navy and compulsory military training were also introduced as agreed Liberal–Labor policies.

Such collaboration ended in 1908, but between 1910 and 1916 Labor governments under Fisher and, later, Hughes established the Commonwealth Bank and an Australian note issue, began the transcontinental railway, developed land and income taxation, and created military, naval, and air force colleges. Voluntarily recruited expeditionary forces were sent overseas, but Hughes's conscription proposal (twice defeated, in 1916 and 1917 referenda) split the party. The official ALP was in opposition from 1916–41, except for 1929–31, when, however, the Scullin government was hampered in its Depression policies by a hostile Senate.

Curtin and Chifley Labor governments (1941–9) successfully organized the wartime national effort and launched post-war reconstruction, economic development, and revolutionary immigration policies. Curtin enacted a form of conscription (1943) without splitting the party; Keynesian financial ideas were adopted; the Commonwealth Bank was brought under direct government control; and the objectives of full employment and social security were largely achieved.

Chifley, however, lost public support over attempted bank nationalization; this, combined with industrial unrest and the increasing unpopularity of continuing wartime controls, put Labor out of Commonwealth office for over two decades.

In external affairs Labor had been largely isolationist between 1919 and 1939, except for some intellectual support for the League of Nations; from 1942 H. V. Evatt, as minister for external affairs, led the party from isolationism into strong support of UN activity, including intervention in the Korean War (1950–3). Demographically, the ALP's late 19th- and early 20th-cent. support from low-income Roman Catholics increased after 1916 because Irish-Australians opposed conscription. Formation (1955) of the substantially Catholic Democratic Labor Party lessened Catholic working-class support for the ALP—appreciably in Qld and markedly in Vic.—but the ALP nevertheless remained the party through which most Roman Catholic MPs entered politics.

ALP leadership in opposition passed successively after Chifley's death to H. V. Evatt (1951–60), A. A. Calwell (1960–7), and E. G. Whitlam (1967–). The party supported ANZUS, reluctantly accepted SEATO, and opposed Australian participation in, and use of conscription for, Viet-nam; it was unenthusiastic about giving the US Australian bases for control of nuclear submarines and intercontinental ballistic missiles.

The ALP rarely obtained less than 40 per cent of the votes cast in post-war Commonwealth and state elections, often gaining more than the Liberal and Country parties combined. It was nevertheless excluded from Commonwealth office by DLP preferences and, in some states (Qld, SA, and WA), by unfavourable distribution of electorates. In NSW and Tas. the party had very long periods in power after the Second World War.

L. F. Crisp, *The Australian Federal Labour Party, 1901–1957* (London, 1955). KEB

LABOUR PARTY IN BRITAIN, name first used after 29 of the Labour Representation Committee's (LRC) 50 candidates were returned at the Jan. 1906 general election, and set up their own separate parliamentary organization. It marked the start of massive trade union political involvement. Unlike the Conservative and Liberal parties, the Labour Party originated outside parliament, and consisted of affiliated organizations, not of individual members.

Labour's growth, from two MPs and 51 affiliated bodies with 375,931 members (1901), to 30 MPs and 233 affiliated organizations comprising nearly a million members (1906), stemmed from the Taff Vale judgment (1901), as a result of which trade unions again felt themselves to be at the mercy of the courts and politicians. Furthermore, unemployment intensified the wish for direct parliamentary labour representation. Instead of embracing full socialism, the LRC advocated old age pensions, slum clearance, industrial reform, and women's suffrage. By-election wins at Clitheroe, Woolwich, and Barnard Castle, and steady successes in municipal elections provided encouragement.

Although the committee stressed its complete independence, a Liberal–LRC agreement (1903) helped it greatly. Sixteen LRC candidates succeeded (1906) against only Conservative opposition, and eight in two member constituencies with only one Liberal candidate each. The committee's parliamentary fund, levying (compulsorily from 1904) affiliated societies at the rate of 1d per member, promoted labour unity. Sponsored candidates received a quarter of their election expenses and, if elected, £200 per annum, provided they kept the party's rules. The Miners' Federation, however, remained aloof until 1909. Its 14 MPs comprised most of the Lib-Labs (trade union-sponsored MPs who still sided with the Liberals).

The new Parliamentary Labour Party elected Keir Hardie as their first chairman, and Arthur Henderson as Whip. Their immediate successes included an act (1906) enabling local authorities to provide school meals (free for needy children). The Trade Disputes Act (1906), giving unions full legal protection, finally embodied the text of a Labour private member's bill. Later, when the Osborne Judgment (1909) temporarily jeopardized Labour's existence, and syndicalist sentiment grew among trade unionists, the party appeared becalmed. Liberal social reforms, and the party's own lack (until 1918) of a firm socialist commitment, left Labour's pre-1914 role undefined.

In Aug. 1914 Ramsay MacDonald resigned the leadership of the Parliamentary Party on finding his anti-war sentiments repudiated by the majority of Labour MPs. His successor, Arthur Henderson, accepted an electoral truce for the war's duration, and some Labour MPs held office in the Coalition.

The first Labour government, formed in Jan. 1924, was soon dissolved, following a judicial dispute involving Sir Patrick Hastings, the attorney-general. The depressing economic situation was partly responsible for Labour's electoral victory in 1929. By the autumn of 1930 unemployment figures exceeded 2 millions, but the government rejected Sir Oswald Mosley's far-reaching plans. Loan terms from foreign banks were not acceptable to the unions and in Aug. 1931 MacDonald resigned, but resumed office as the head of a Coalition government—an act strongly criticized by his more militant socialist opponents.

Meanwhile, new men rose in prestige in the party in the 1930s such as Attlee (leader from 1935), Cripps, Bevin, Morrison, and Dalton. With the outbreak of the Second World War the party showed little of its 1914 pacifism and in 1940, on Chamberlain's resignation, Labour joined the Coalition under Churchill.

The 1945 general election saw a great Labour victory—393 MPs returned. This gave Attlee, who became prime minister, a clear majority of 146. This was the first Labour government with any real power, possessing members of widely different social backgrounds. Extensive nationalization, the establishment of the National Health Service, and independence to India were the most noticeable achievements.

The 1950 election result was the closest for 100 years—making a dissolution necessary in 1951. The Conservatives then returned to office for the next 13 years. For eight years Hugh Gaitskell led the Opposition—often against bitter attack from his party's left wing. In 1964 and 1966 Labour returned to office under Harold Wilson. Rising inflation, industrial unrest, and balance of payments difficulties were some of the economic problems facing the country and in the 1970 general election, despite the psephologists' forecasts, Labour, having won only 287 seats, had to concede victory to the Conservatives under Edward Heath.

Carl F. Brand, *The British Labour Party: a short history* (Stanford, 1964; London, 1965).
H. Pelling, *A Short History of the Labour Party* (London, 1961). MRB
MEB

LABOUR PARTY IN NEW ZEALAND was formed in 1916, when a divided Labour movement closed its ranks to oppose wartime conscription, rising prices, and labour regulations. Leadership was mainly from the left; the platform of gradual socialism more from the right. During the 1920s industrial and political Labour were sometimes at odds, and the party's 'usehold' land policy repelled farmers. Depression united the party and a programme of welfare and economic plan-

ning (with some adaptations from Social Credit) widened Labour's appeal to the point of victory in 1935. Guaranteed prices for farmers (1936), compulsory unionism (1936), and social security (1938) provided an electoral basis for continued power to 1949, in spite of a serious split on monetary policy (1940). The Labour government's wartime controls, prolonged after 1945, irked a more affluent electorate, and further ground was lost in the industrial strife of 1949–51. The party was mostly in opposition in 1945–70.

LABOUR PARTY OF SOUTH AFRICA, formed in 1910, represented privileged white workers. In 1924 the party entered into a pact with Hertzog and so brought the first Afrikaner nationalist government to power. Later, it lost much of whatever popular support it had among whites. Its more right-wing supporters tended to join the United Party, and, after the Second World War, its more left-wing supporters the Liberal Party. In the general election of 1948 the party secured only six seats, and by 1970 had altogether disappeared from the parliamentary scene.

LABOUR REPRESENTATION COMMITTEE (1900) in Britain, formed to 'establish a distinct Labour group in parliament' by trade union, Fabian, Independent Labour Party, and Social Democratic Federation (SDF) delegates. They created a permanent 12-man committee, with Ramsay MacDonald as secretary, to sponsor Labour and associated parliamentary candidates. These, if elected, would have their own Whips and pursue policies beneficial to labour, collaborating where necessary with another party. The SDF seceded (1901) because the LRC had no specific socialist commitment. Affiliated bodies contributed according to membership. Only two LRC candidates were elected in 1900; but in 1906, spurred by the Taff Vale decision (1901) and the MacDonald–H. Gladstone electoral pact, 29 succeeded, and became the Parliamentary Labour Party.

LABOUR REPRESENTATION LEAGUE (1869) in Britain, promoted by the trade unions, worked for the election of MPs, municipal councillors, etc. from the working class, who after 1867 comprised an electoral majority. It also sought the registration of working-class voters, irrespective of political bias, and established a central record of labour candidates. Its chief problems were financial, *eg*, the meeting of election expenses, and maintenance of MPs. The league generally failed to persuade Liberal constituency parties to adopt labour candidates. Two miners, Burt and Macdonald, were returned (1874), but by 1880 the league was practically defunct.

LA BOURDONNAIS, BERTRAND FRANÇOIS MAHÉ DE (1699–1753), French admiral and colonial governor, who went to India as a child (1709). In 1725 he led the French force which captured Mahé. He became governor of the Isles of France (Mauritius) and Bourbon (1735–40). In 1741 he improvised a fleet to attack the British on the Coromandel coast (1746). Driving away a British squadron under Capt. Peyton, he took Madras (21 Sept.), but then quarrelled with the French governor of Pondicherry over the ransoming of the town. His fleet was dispersed (13 Oct.) and he returned to the Isles. On his way home he was captured by the British and later spent three years in the Bastille.

LABOURERS, STATUTE OF (1351) in England, legislative measure passed as a result of the first visitation of the Black Death (1348–9). A shortage of labour, particularly of agricultural labour, threatened a sharp increase in wages. An ordinance of 1349 and the statute of 1351 tried to keep wages at pre-plague rates and to insist on completion of contracts by labourers. These restrictions were among the complaints of the peasants in the revolt of 1381. The statute ceased to be rigidly enforced after 1390, the justice of the peace in each county being henceforth empowered to fix maximum wages in the light of changing local conditions.

LABRADOR, English province in North America, originally inhabited by Eskimos. It was probably visited by the Norse in the 10th and 11th cents, and possibly by John Cabot (1498). French fishermen were in the area from about 1500. 'Labrador' appears on a map (*c.* 1500), the name having been originally applied to part of Greenland in honour of a Portuguese 'Lavrador' or landowner. The coastline was explored by Cartier (1534), Bourden (1657), and Joliet (1694). Extensive concessions to merchants from New France encouraged settlement. Labrador was ceded to Britain (1763) and jurisdiction given to Nfld (1763–4, 1809–25), and to Que. (1774–1809). In 1825 Labrador was divided between Nfld and Que., which gave rise to prolonged boundary disputes settled by the British privy council (1927). Sir Wilfred Grenfell's missions (1892–1935) helped the growth of fishing co-operatives. Labrador became part of the dominion of Canada when Nfld became a province (1949).

LA BRUYÈRE, JEAN DE (1645–96), French moralist and writer, who frequented the society of the Paris salons. He became famous in 1688 with the publication of his *Caractères de Theophraste ou les Mœurs de ce Siècle*, a series of maxims and observations on life, although his satires of certain social types, *eg*, the idle nobleman and the stupid office-holder, and his criticisms of aspects of the French state, *eg*, the widespread use of judicial torture, offended some contemporaries. None the less, he was elected to the French Academy in 1693. On his death, he left an unfinished series of Dialogues on Quietism.

LABY, THOMAS HOWELL (1880–1946), Australian physicist who worked in the field of radio-activity, organized national projects with the Radio Research Board, and developed an optical industry during the Second World War.

LACERDA, CARLOS (1914–), Brazilian politician and journalist, conservative congressman (1954–60), and governor of Guanabara (1961–6), who achieved notoriety for his unrestrained attacks on presidents Vargas, Kubitschek, Quadros, and Goulart. He played a major role in the revolution of 1964. His political rights were cancelled by the revolutionary government in 1968.

LA CHALOTAIS, LOUIS-RÉNÉ DE CARADEUC (1701–85), French procureur-général of the *parlement* of Brittany, who achieved notoriety during its political conflict with the king's governor, the Duc d'Aiguillon, in 1765–6. La Chalotais was arrested by D'Aiguillon and exiled, while Louis XV repudiated the concept of *parlementaire* solidarity.

LA CHÉTARDIE, Marquis de (d. 1758), French diplomat who served as envoy in Berlin (1729–39) before being sent to Russia to establish a rapprochement between that country and his own (1739). He helped to arrange the *coup d'état* by which Tsarina Elizabeth assumed the throne (Dec. 1741), but was expelled from Russia in 1744.

LACHINE, Canadian town, originally named Saint-Sulpice, a seigniory given to Robert La Salle (1667). It was renamed in mockery of his dream of finding a route to China. Settlement began in 1675, but the Iroquois massacred the inhabitants (1689). The first Lachine Canal was built (1821–4) to facilitate the fur trade.

LACOLLE, BATTLES OF (1814, 1838), fought in the Canadian village of Lacolle, Que. In the first battle the British, under Maj. R. B. Handcock, drove off an invading American force led by Gen. James Wilkinson. The second battle was fought during the rebellion of 1837, when a rebel force led into Lower Canada from the US by Cyrille-Hector-Octave Côté, was defeated by militia from Lower Canada.

LACOMBE, ALBERT (1827–1916), French Canadian Catholic missionary, who organized a Métis settlement near Fort Edmonton (1861–72), extending his ministry to the Cree and Blackfoot Indians. He was used as a government emissary to the Indians during the North-West Rebellion (1885).

LACONIA GRANT. In 1629 John Mason and Sir Ferdinando Gorges received a grant from King Charles I of England to found an agricultural community in the region called Laconia, on the banks of the Merrimack river. Settlements were made there and Laconia, with other grants, became the colony of New Hampshire.

LA COSA, JUAN DE (1460–1510), Spanish navigator and geographer, master of the *Santa Maria* on Columbus's first voyage (1492–3), and his companion on the second (1493). He was pilot for expeditions to the north coast of South America (1499–1500, 1500–2, 1507–8) and made the first large map of the New World (1500). He was killed by Indians near Cartagena.

LA COURT, PIETER DE (1618–85), Dutch merchant and political economist, who supported the ideals of mercantile republicanism against the monarchical Orange tradition. In his most famous work, *The Interest of Holland* (1662), he advocated economic and religious freedom.

LA CRUZ, ISABEL DE (*fl.* 16th cent.), Spanish Franciscan sister, leader of the Illuminists (*Alumbrados*) in Alcala and Toledo, who was arrested by the Inquisition (1524).

LADE, BATTLE OF (494 BC), off Miletus, western Asia Minor, the victory of the Persian fleet which effectively ended the Ionian revolt, the Greeks being crippled by the treachery of the contingent from Samos.

LADINO, Spanish term whose varied meanings depend upon the context and region of its use. It can refer to ancient Spanish, though in Spain it was used in the Middle Ages to describe an Arab who spoke Castilian. In Latin America it denotes a person who is crafty and sly. In Cuba, it applies to an acculturated African. In Peru and Argentina, it means an Indian who speaks colloquial Spanish. In Guatemala, it usually describes anyone who, regardless of ancestry, lives in the European rather than in the Indian style.

LADISLAS II (1140–73), King of Bohemia (*reg.* 1158–73), Premyslid Duke of Bohemia. He was a strong supporter of Emperor Frederick I and a loyal prince of the empire and was rewarded with the title of king in 1158. The title lapsed on his death and did not become hereditary until 1198.

LADISLAS II (*reg.* 1386–1414), King of Naples, member of the Hungarian Angevin ruling house who successfully reasserted the family's claims to Naples in 1399. He tried to unify much of Italy under his rule and secured control over Rome and its pope. His death ended a threat to Florence and other independent city-states.

LADISLAS I (*reg.* 1320–33), King of Poland, creator of the reunited Polish kingdom in the 14th cent. He became the leader of the resistance (1291–1305) to several kings of Bohemia, who coveted the Polish Crown. In 1306 Ladislas managed to establish himself as Duke of Cracow and in 1320, with papal consent, he was crowned King of Poland. When he died his state was still gravely menaced by Bohemia and the Teutonic Order.

LADISLAS II (1348–1434), King of Poland (*reg.* 1386–1434), originally a pagan Grand Prince of Lithuania bearing the heathen name of Jagiello. He became a Catholic under the name of Ladislas and married Queen Jadwiga of Poland in 1386, after whose death in 1398 he remained King of Poland, leaving Lithuania to a succession of relatives. He overcame all the threats to the precarious confederacy between Poland and Lithuania; the conversion of the Lithuanians to Christianity was gradually completed, and the combined Polish and Lithuanian armies defeated the Teutonic Order at Tannenberg (1410), from which dates its decline as a military power. In 1413 the Catholic Lithuanian nobles were given the privileges of the Polish nobility. Jagiello secured the recognition of his son, Ladislaw III, as heir to the Polish throne, but he had to make concessions to the nobles which imposed permanent limitations on the Polish monarchy.

LADISLAS III (1424–44), King of Poland (*reg.* 1434–44), King of Hungary (*reg.* 1439–44). In 1444 the papal legate, Cesarini, persuaded him to break a truce recently made with the Turks and lead another crusade, during which, at the battle of Varna, both Ladislas and Cesarini were killed.

LADISLAS IV (1595–1648), King of Poland (*reg.* 1639–48), who succeeded Sigismund III. His reign was marked by constant Turkish threats. He strengthened his country by a marriage alliance with France.

LAELIUS, C., Roman politician, soldier, and writer in the 2nd cent. BC. After serving at Carthage and in Spain (149–5), he became consul in 140, and his unsuccessful proposal of land reform anticipated the law of Tiberius Gracchus, whom, however, he strongly opposed (133). Cicero's *Laelius* (or *On Friendship*) commemorates his prominence in the cultural circle of Scipio Aemilianus.

LAËNNEC, RENÉ THÉOPHILE HYACINTHE (1781–1826), French physician, who invented the stethoscope. He interpreted the normal and adventitious breathing sounds heard with it in his *Traité de L'Auscultation médiate* (1818).

LA FARGE, JOHN (1835–1910), US artist, who specialized in mural painting and stained glass, of which he became the leading US designer. His water-colours of the Orient and books such as *Reminiscences of the South Seas* (1912) were widely popular and influential.

LA FAYETTE, MME MARIE MADELEINE PIOCHE DE LAVERGNE, Comtesse de (1634–93), French authoress, who became a friend of most of France's leading literary figures, including La Rochefoucauld and Mme de Sévigné. Her classic romantic novel, *La Princesse de Clèves*, was one of the earliest works of fiction and is characterized by a detailed analysis and study of character.

LAFAYETTE, MARIE JOSEPH PAUL (1757–1834), French soldier and statesman, of noble family and radical views, who became a hero of the American War of Independence (1777–1782), played a leading part in the French Revolution (1789–1792), and led opposition to the Bourbon and Orléans monarchies (1818–34). He was commissioned in the continental army (1776), arrived at Philadelphia (1777), and served with distinction at Brandywine. He became a friend of Washington, who appointed him a divisional commander, in which capacity he planned an invasion of Canada, but it foundered from lack of support. He fought at Monmouth Court House (1778) and helped to obtain a Franco-American treaty of friendship and commerce, acting as liaison officer when the French fleet arrived. In France, whence he returned in 1779, he pleaded for more assistance for the American cause, and supervised abortive preparations for the invasion of England. After returning to America (1780), he took a leading part in the Yorktown campaign (1781) as commander of the light division.

From 1782 Lafayette campaigned in France for political and social reform and improved conditions for the peasants on his own estates, and demanded a national assembly. On the summoning of the states general (1789), he led the patriot party as a deputy. He also put forward a draft of the Declaration of the Rights of Man and forwarded its adoption. As vice-president of the National Assembly he supported the storming of the Bastille. He also organized the National

Guard in Paris, and commanded the regular army. He was able to maintain order while reform proceeded, but he refused to make an alliance with Mirabeau, which might have saved the constitutional monarchy. He declined to organize the National Guard on a national basis, but presided at the Champ de Mars (1790) over *fédérés* and troops of the line.

Although a republican, Lafayette accepted the constitution of 1791 and retired on the election of the new legislative assembly, supposing the revolution to be at an end. He was appointed a lieutenant-general and given command of the troops fighting against Austria (1792), and he created a mounted artillery unit, which was to assist Napoleon's later success. After the attack on the Austrian Netherlands had failed, Lafayette returned to Paris to defend the monarchy, but his troops deserted him and he was proscribed. He fled, was arrested by the Austrians, and held captive by the Prussians, then released into American custody (1797). He returned to France during the consulate (1799), but was disenchanted with Bonaparte and retired to his estates, though during the Hundred Days he became vice-president of the Chamber of Deputies.

Lafayette became an opposition deputy under the Bourbons (1818) and maintained contacts with liberals in Europe and Latin America. After being defeated in 1824, he returned to the US on a triumphal visit as the 'hero of two worlds' and 'America's marquis'. In France, he was re-elected as a deputy (1827) and briefly resumed command of the National Guard during the 1830 Revolution. He was a reluctant supporter of Louis Philippe. He continued to press for the abolition of slavery and freedom of the press, and from 1832 openly opposed the regime.

LAFITTE, JACQUES (1767–1844), French politician, who became a leading Orleanist, and served briefly as prime minister and minister of finance (1830–1).

LAFLÈCHE, LOUIS-FRANÇOIS-RICHER (1818–98), French Canadian Catholic bishop and an opponent of Liberalism, who helped define Ultramontane principles in Canada. He hoped for the creation of a French Canadian nation and was bitterly disappointed by papal condemnation of clerical intervention into Canadian politics (1897).

LA FLESCHE, FRANCIS (1860–1932), American Indian ethnologist. After being a clerk in the Bureau of Indian Affairs (1881–1910), he produced (1910–30) a number of important studies of the Osage and Omaha Indians.

La Flesche's sister, Susette (Bright Eyes) (1854–1903), was considered the foremost Indian woman of her time. She lectured in the US (1879–85) and in Britain (1886), and later settled on the Omaha reservation in Nebraska, where she wrote and illustrated stories of Indian life.

LA FOLLETTE, ROBERT MARION (1855–1925), US politician and WI lawyer. As a progressive Republican, he clashed with the leaders of the Republican Party of Dane County, of which he became district attorney in 1880. In 1884 he was elected to the US House of Representatives, where he served until 1891. Through his fight against the entrenched political groups, he won the governorship of WI by acclamation (1900). The programme which he introduced became known as the 'Wisconsin Idea' and served as a model for progressive government in other states. It embraced the direct primary, control of railroads by a state commission, opposition to political bosses, and the employment of technical experts.

In 1906 La Follette was elected to the US Senate, where he served three terms. As a progressive leader in the Senate, he opposed the Payne–Aldrich tariff and advocated the physical valuation of railroads as a basis for rate-making. During Wilson's presidency he supported the president's progressive measures, and sponsored the Seamen's Act (1915), which gave seamen the same rights as industrial workers.

In 1911 he drafted the programme for the National Progressive Republican League, and in 1912 campaigned for nomination as the Progressives' presidential candidate. He became ill, however, and Theodore Roosevelt was nominated instead.

In foreign policy, La Follette was an uncompromising isolationist. He opposed the armed merchant ship bill (1917) and voted against America's entry into the First World War. Although he supported the war effort, he was denounced as a traitor and was censured by the WI state legislature. He condemned the treaty of Versailles as being vindictive, unjust to Germany, and a betrayal of America's ideals, and opposed the League of Nations, which he regarded as likely to involve American soldiers in disputes abroad.

After the war he was a leading figure in the Progressive bloc in the Senate, and sponsored a demand for an enquiry into the Teapot Dome affair and other transactions of President Harding's administration. In 1924 he ran for president as a Progressive, won 5 million votes, and carried the state of WI in the electoral college.

After his death the powerful political machine which he had built up was maintained by his two sons, Robert M. La Follette, jr, senator from WI (1925–47), and Philip F. La Follette, who served as governor of WI for three terms during the 1930s.

Belle C. and Fola La Follette, *Robert M. La Follette*, 2 vols (New York, 1952).
Robert M. La Follette, *Autobiography* (New York, 1913).

LA FONTAINE, JEAN DE (1621–95), French poet, whose fame rests on his *Fables* (1668–78), modelled on those of Phaedrus and Aesop. They were translated into many languages and still give pleasure by their freshness and subtle reflections on human behaviour.

LAFONTAINE, SIR LOUIS-HIPPOLYTE (1807–64), Canadian lawyer and statesman. As leader of the French Canadian reformers he formed ministries with Robert Baldwin (1842–3, 1848–51). During the second Baldwin–Lafontaine ministry, Lafontaine introduced the Rebellion Losses Bill (1848), which established responsible government in Canada.

LA GALISSONIÈRE, ROLAND, Comte de (1693–1756), French admiral, with wide philosophical and scientific interests. As governor of New France (1747–9) his policy of building forts did much to strengthen the colony's strategic position. He defeated a British fleet at Minorca (1756).

LA GASCA, PEDRO DE (1485–1567), Spanish bishop and colonial administrator, who led the royalist opposition to the rebellion of Gonzalo Pizarro in Peru. His defeat of Pizarro re-established royal authority in Peru, and Pizarro's execution saw the end of the arbitrary government of the original conquistadors.

LAGASH, Sumerian city (mod. site, Tell Luh), north of Shatra, whose most notable rulers were Eannatum (*c.* 2550 BC), who conquered all or part of Elam and some Sumerian cities, and Gudea, who rebuilt the city (*c.* 2100).

LAGGAN ARMY, THE, in Ireland, bands of Protestant settlers in the north-west of Ireland who united in 1642 under the command of Robert Stewart and his brother. They garrisoned Londonderry and Enniskillen which became Protestant 'cities of refuge' from the Irish Catholic rebellion.

LAGOS, island and city, in Nigeria, West Africa, a centre of Afro-European trade. During the 19th cent. it became a centre of British influence on the coastland of the Niger river and its delta, Britain's first consul for the Bights of Benin and Biafra, John Beecroft, being appointed there in 1849. Annexed to Britain in 1861, Lagos was to prove the main springboard for British invasion of the mainland. It grew much in importance during the colonial period, when it provided the capital. After the independence of Nigeria

(1960), Lagos continued to be the capital of the Nigerian Federation and was by 1970 a large, wealthy, and expanding modern city.

LAGOS, BATTLE OF (1693), naval engagement off southern Portugal during the War of the League of Augsburg, when a convoy led by Admiral Rooke was attacked by a French fleet commanded by the Comte de Tourville, and 100 merchant ships were lost.

LA GUARDIA, FIORELLO HENRY (1882–1947), US politician and mayor of New York city, known as the 'Little Flower'—he was five feet two inches tall. La Guardia was one of the most dynamic and colourful reform mayors in American history. Born of Italian immigrant parents in New York, he served in the consular service in Budapest, Trieste, and Fiume (1901–6), worked as an interpreter at Ellis Island, the immigration arrival centre in New York (1907–10) and devoted himself to the immigrant cause. On being elected to the US House of Representatives (1917), thus becoming the first Italo-American congressman, he took leave of absence in order to serve as a bomber pilot in the First World War. As a Republican congressman (1917–21, 1923–33) he supported progressive legislation and sponsored the Norris–La Guardia Anti-Injunction Act (1932). Having a sympathetic understanding of the ethnic complexity of New York city, he was able to form a coalition of different immigrant groups behind his reform programme and as mayor of New York (1933–45) he won the reputation of being aggressively determined to introduce efficiency and honesty into civic government. He helped to improve the amenities in New York by sponsoring the provision of parks, health clinics, public housing developments, bridges, and La Guardia airport. He also eliminated many unneeded employees from the city's payroll. In 1946 he served as director-general of UNRRA.   PGB

LAHARPE, FRÉDÉRIC CÉSAR (1754–1838), Swiss politician, who played an important part in establishing the Helvetic republic (1798) and was its first president (1798–1800). He was for some years tutor to Tsar Alexander I.

LAHARPE, JEAN FRANÇOIS (1739–1803), French writer and literary critic. At the time of the Revolution, which he welcomed, he became a political journalist and editor of *La Mercure*. The views expressed in it caused him to be arrested and he was only saved from execution by Thermidor. He was a bitter conservative critic of the Directory, who exiled him at Fructidor (1797). On his return to France (1799), he published his main work, *La Lycée ou cours de littérature*, a survey of 18th-cent. literature from a pre-romantic point of view.

LA HOGUE, BATTLE OF (1692), between the French and an Anglo-Dutch force fought in the English channel in the War of the Grand Alliance (1689–97). The Comte de Tourville, with 44 ships, attacked and held his own against an Anglo-Dutch fleet, more than twice as large, under Edward Russell (later Earl of Orford), Sir John Ashby, and the Dutch commander Philips van Almonde. The same night (19 May) the French withdrew, but became separated, and though 20 ships escaped, 15 were destroyed by the allies in the next three days.

LA HONTAN, LOUIS ARMAND, Baron de (1666–1715), French soldier and author, who went to New France (1683) and served with distinction against the Iroquois and the English. His colourful but unreliable *Nouveaux Voyages . . .* (1703) contains descriptions of New France.

LAHORE, leading city of the Punjab. It first appears in the 7th cent. AD in the account of a visit by the Chinese monk Hiuen Tsang. In Mahmud of Ghazni's time (997–1030) Lahore passed to the Muslims with the Punjab, of which, from 1200, it became the political centre. Under the sultans of Delhi it was taken by the Mongols (1241) and put to ransom (1246). Under the Mughals it was the capital of the Punjab, and under Akbar (1556–1605) and Jahangir (1605–1627) was for some years a royal residence. With the Mughal collapse it passed (1767) to the Sikhs and became the capital of Ranjit Singh's (1790–1839) Sikh kingdom until its annexation by the British (1846). It remained a prosperous and growing city and became successively the capital of the British Punjab, the Pakistani province of the Punjab, and in 1955 of West Pakistan.

LAHORE RESOLUTION (23 March 1940), passed by the Lahore session of the All-India Muslim League (22–24 March), declared terms for the settlement of the constitutional problem in India. In substance, though not explicitly, this was the 'Pakistan' resolution. It reiterated the league's rejection of the federal scheme of the Government of India Act (1935) and specified the 'basic principles' of a constitution acceptable to the Muslims: 'The areas in which the Muslims are numerically in a majority, as in the North-Western and Eastern zones of India, should be grouped to constitute "Independent States" in which the constituent units shall be autonomous and sovereign.' In other areas, where Muslims were in a minority, the constitution was to provide 'adequate, effective and mandatory' safeguards for their interests. Henceforward, despite bitter denunciation by the Congress and the Hindu Mahasabha, the demand for separate Muslim states was the basis of league policy. At its Madras session (1941) the league wrote the substance of the Lahore resolution into its constitution and the 'Muslim League legislators' convention (April 1946) during the Cabinet Mission negotiations reaffirmed the resolution.

LA HUERTA, ADOLFO DE (1881–1955), Mexican revolutionary politician who served as provisional president in 1920. He attempted to raise a revolt against Álvaro Obregón and Plutarco Calles (1924), but it was defeated and as a consequence he spent many years in exile.

LAIBACH CONGRESS (1821), continuation of the Congress of Troppau (1820), at which the rift in the European Congress system became apparent. Austria was authorized to put down the rebellion in Naples against King Ferdinand, but whereas Austria, Prussia, and Russia claimed the right to quash revolution anywhere, Britain considered that the intervention was justified only because of Austrian interests in Italy and Austria's treaty (1813) with King Ferdinand.

LAIBON, title of ritual leaders among the Masai of East Africa. Of great antiquity, the office of such leaders was to preside over ancestral shrines and ensure the spiritual welfare of the various sections of the Masai among whom they functioned. Some of them acquired political importance during Masai resistance to colonial enclosure.

LAINEZ, DIEGO (1512–65), Spanish Jesuit, one of the six followers who met Loyola in Paris (1534) and formed the brotherhood that became the Society of Jesus. At the Council of Trent, Lainez, a subtle theologian, led the conservative group that opposed compromise with Lutheran doctrines. He defended the Jesuits against Pope Paul IV, who hated everything Spanish and wanted to suppress them. On Loyola's death Lainez (1556) succeeded him as general of the order.

LAISSEZ-FAIRE, political and economic doctrine by which the role of the state in economic and social affairs is confined to a minimum, on the theory that the free action of private enterprise must be beneficial to all. It has often been attributed to Jeremy Bentham. This is erroneous, for Benthamite thought gave emphasis to the position of the legislator and to the collection of factual knowledge on which he was to act. The period in which laissez-faire was dominant in Britain was 1820–70, but at this period it is difficult to distinguish

between the results of this principle and the effects of a desire to economize on government expenditure, the lack of a bureaucracy, and the stress on religious individualism. Moreover, in this period there were survivals of earlier regulation from the mercantilist period, and the initial stages of social and economic control made necessary by the new industrialized society, so that, though the concept of laissez-faire was of great importance, at no point can it be regarded as an exclusive and dominant policy.

LAJPAT RAI, LALA (1865–1928), Indian nationalist politician, and a leading Arya Samajist in the Punjab, whose main concerns were with education and social welfare work, until he became involved (1904) with attempts to promote a more militant line of action in the Indian National Congress. He was an active agitator in the Punjab over local agrarian grievances (1907) and was deported by the government for a short time. At the Surat Congress session (1907) he attempted to prevent the breach between 'moderates' and 'extremists', but gradually drifted away from Congress because of his dissatisfaction with 'moderate' leadership. Having been caught in England by the outbreak of war, he went to the US, where he published several books on Indian social and political questions and established an Indian Home Rule League (1917) with a journal called *Young India*. He returned to India (1920) with a considerable reputation and was elected president of the special session of Congress (Sept. 1920), called to consider Gandhi's non-co-operation programme. Though never convinced of the utility of the entire programme, he did nevertheless join the campaign and was imprisoned (1922–3). After his release he helped the Swarajya Party in the Punjab and was eventually (1925) himself elected to the central Legislative Assembly as a Swarajist. By this time, however, he was becoming increasingly concerned with Hindu nationalist groups. As the founder of the Servants of the People Society (1921), he was active in the *shuddhi* and *sangathan* campaigns of the Hindu Mahasabha in the mid-1920s, and presided over the Mahasabha in 1925. He broke with the Swarajya Party (1926) and joined Malaviya in forming the 'Independent Congress Party', which undermined the Swarajist position in the elections of that year. He was a leader of the campaign to boycott the Simon Commission.

LAKE OF DELHI, GERARD LAKE, 1st Viscount (1744–1808), British general, who served in America, Ireland, and against the French. He went to India (1800) in command of the East India Co.'s forces. In the Second Anglo-Maratha War he took Aligarh, Delhi, and Agra, and defeated Sindhia at Laswari (1803). He defeated Holkar in 1804, but failed to capture Bharatpur in 1805.

LAKE ERIE, BATTLE OF (10 Sept. 1813), occurred during the 1812–14 War. A British fleet was defeated by superior American forces under Commodore Perry in Put-in-bay. This made it impossible for the British to hold Detroit and so ensured possession of the south and west shores of the Great Lakes by the US.

LAKE GEORGE, BATTLE OF (1755), fought by American colonial militia and Indians under the command of William Johnson against French and Indian troops under Baron Dieskau. It was the only British victory in 1755.

LALAING, GEORGE DE, COUNT RENNENBURG (d. 1581), Walloon nobleman, who was *stadtholder* for Friesland, Groningen, Drente, and Overyssel the states general (1578), and an associate of William of Orange, despite his own Catholicism. He led the capture of Kampen and Deventer (1578) during the Dutch revolt, but later abandoned his support for the Union of Utrecht (1580).

LALEMENT, JÉRÔME (1593–1673), Jesuit missionary in Canada, who went to Quebec (1638) as superior to the Huron Missions. He moved the mission headquarters to Fort

Sainte-Marie-aux-Hurons (1639) and established subordinate missions in other villages. He was appointed (1659) vicar general and superior of the Jesuits in Canada.

LALIBELA (*fl.* 13th cent.), Zagwé Emperor of Ethiopia and reputed builder of the monolithic rock-hewn churches in the place which bears his name.

LALLY, Comte de (1700–66), French general who was appointed (1756) governor-general and commander-in-chief of French India, with a mandate to expel the British. He arrived (April–May 1758) with the fleet of Admiral d'Aché. Displaying great vigour, though also rashness and lack of tact, he took Fort St David and Cuddalore. But D'Aché refused to support an attack on Madras and an ill-judged attack on Tanjore for the purpose of plunder was repulsed. After recalling the Marquis de Bussy from the Deccan, Lally besieged Madras for two months until it was relieved by a British squadron (16 Feb. 1759). At Wandiwash (Jan. 1760) he was defeated by Col. Coote with British reinforcements and Bussy was captured. Lally was then besieged in Pondicherry, which capitulated (14 Jan. 1761). On his return to France he was confined in the Bastille and executed for dereliction of duty (1766).

LALOR, PETER (1827–89), Australian politician, who led the Eureka rebellion at Ballarat in 1854. Later he was elected to the Vic. Legislative Council (1855), and then to the new Assembly (1856). Despite Eureka, he was a conservative in politics, holding minor portfolios before becoming speaker (1880–7).

LAMACHUS (d. 414 BC), Athenian general who was prominent in the great Peloponnesian War. In Aristophanes' comedies he was the typical militarist. Jointly commanding the expedition to Sicily with Nicias and Alcibiades (415), he failed to carry his plan for direct assault on Syracuse and supported Alcibiades' idea of diplomatic offensive. After Alcibiades' recall, Nicias agreed to Lamachus' plan, but did so too late for a successful assault. Lamachus' death in action during the Athenian attempt to wall off Syracuse virtually doomed the expedition by leaving the sick and dilatory Nicias in sole command.

LA MAR, JOSÉ DE (1788–1839), Peruvian soldier, who became president in 1827 after the overthrowing of a council organized by Simón Bolívar, who returned and defeated La Mar in the field. Subsequently he himself was overthrown by opponents.

LAMARCK, JEAN BAPTISTE PIERRE ANTOINE DE MONNET, Chevalier de (1744–1829), French biologist, whose work included botanical studies and many contributions to zoological systematics. In *Philosophie Zoologique* (1809) he developed a theory of evolution which stressed a continuity of descent, thus cutting across systematic classification. This theory of the inheritance of acquired characters gained support after the publication of Darwin's *Origin of Species* (1859), but was later discredited by 20th-cent. research into genetic inheritance.

LA MARFÉE, BATTLE OF (6 July 1641), defeat near the Meuse river of French royal forces under Maréchal de Châtillon by Louis de Bourbon, Comte de Soissons and a force of Spaniards. Soissons headed an unsuccessful rising to overthrow Richelieu, in the course of which he was killed. Most of the other rebels made their peace with Louis XIII.

LA MARMORA, ALFONSO FERRERO (1804–78), Italian general and statesman, who distinguished himself during struggles for independence (1848). As Sardinian war minister he was responsible for the reconstruction of the Piedmontese army, which he commanded in the Crimea (1855), and in the war of 1859 against Austria. He was accused of treason after his defeat by the Austrians at Custozza (1866) and defended himself by publishing (1873) documents relating to secret negotiations between Prussia and Italy before the battle.

LAMARTINE, ALPHONSE MARIE LOUIS DE PRAT DE (1790–1869), French romantic poet and politician. He served as a diplomat (1820, 1825), a deputy (1831), and leader of the liberal opposition (1843). He proved an ineffective head of the provisional government (1848) and was defeated when he stood for the presidency.

LAMB, JOHN (1735–1800), American revolutionary and a leader of the Sons of Liberty in New York. He helped to form the Committee of Correspondence, and led those who seized the New York Custom House (1775). He commanded troops in the American War of Independence and later was collector of the port of New York.

LAMBARDE, WILLIAM (1536–1601), English antiquary whose *Perambulation of Kent* (1570) was the earliest county history and a model of its kind. He collected material (1730) for a general history of England, but abandoned the idea on learning that Camden was similarly engaged. His *Eirenarcha* (1581) became a standard authority on the duties of English justices of the peace.

LAMBERT, Saint (d. 705), member of a family of counts, who became Bp of Maastricht (*c.* 670). He was murdered by local notables at Liège. The erection of his shrine there in 718 was followed by the transfer of the seat of the bishopric to Liège, which became an important city. His successor, St Hubert (d. 727), who enjoyed the support of the Carolingian dynasty, completed the conversion of the eastern Netherlands.

LAMBERT, JOHN (1619–83), English parliamentary general during the Civil Wars, who fought against Prince Rupert at Marston Moor (1644) and commanded a regiment in the New Model Army. He was major-general of the north, and showed courage and tactical judgement at Preston (1648), Dunbar (1650), and Worcester (1651). Lambert concealed his religious opinions and politically he always supported the authority of the army. Thus he assisted Ireton in preparing the Heads of Proposals (1647), approved of the dissolution of the Rump and Barebone's parliaments (1653), and drew up the Instrument of Government which made Cromwell Protector. But he opposed the scheme to turn the protectorate into a hereditary monarchy (1656) which would have re-established constitutional and civilian rule, and following the failure of Richard Cromwell he attempted to reassert the army's control (1659–60). His men deserted him as Monk marched southwards, and eventually he was sentenced to death, but the sentence was commuted to life imprisonment and he was consigned to Guernsey.

LAMBERT DE LA MOTTE, PIERRE (1624–79), apostolic vicar in Siam. He held the titular bishopric of Beirut and directed the early work of the French Society of Foreign Missions in Siam and Indo-China (1662–79).

LAMBETH CONFERENCES, assemblies of bishops of the world-wide Anglican communion held about once every ten years (the first was in 1867) at Lambeth Palace under the presidency of the Abp of Canterbury. The original demand for such a conference came from a group of clergy of the Anglican Church in Canada concerned at the effects of the Bp Colenso case and the publication of *Essays and Reviews* (1860). The idea of a council to define doctrine against liberal theological views was abandoned because of opposition. The first conference, under Abp Longley, was attended by 76 bishops out of a possible 144 and issued an Address to the Faithful. The resolutions passed are not binding, but are significant expressions of the opinions of the bishops. Conferences, which have grown steadily in importance and influence, are attended by some 300 leaders and emphasize modern problems such as Christian Reunion through the Ecumenical Movement, the family, birth control, and international relations.

LAMERIE, PAUL DE (*c.* 1688–1751), gold and silversmith, who was born in the Netherlands, but went to London as a Protestant refugee, was apprenticed to Pierre Platel and registered his own mark in 1712. He developed the rococo style made fashionable in France by Meissonier, and his ornamental plate, cups, and *épergnes*, all with elaborate scroll-work, are noted for their broken lines and asymmetric design.

LAMIAN WAR (323–322 BC), disastrous attempt of Athens and other Greek states to throw off Macedonian rule after Alexander the Great's death (323). At Athens, despite Phocion's opposition, Hyperides and other democratic leaders, supported by the exiled Demosthenes, proclaimed a liberation movement which the Aetolian League and other states in central Greece and Peloponnese soon joined. Antipater, the Macedonian regent, was defeated and temporarily besieged at Lamia in southern Thessaly, but in the summer of 322 the Athenians were twice beaten at sea and Craterus joined Antipater from Asia. In Sept. they decisively defeated the Greeks at Crannon in Thessaly. Antipater granted moderate terms to most of the rebels, but he dissolved the so-called League of Corinth and put an end to Athenian democracy, stationing a garrison in Piraeus, and executing Hyperides, Demosthenes, and others.

LAMMENAIS, FELICITÉ ROBERT DE (1782–1854), French religious thinker, philosopher, and politician. He became a priest (1817) and made his name by his writings on the relationship of Church and state, culminating in his advocacy of their separation, so as to leave the Church free to exercise greater moral authority in society (1828). Lammenais's increasingly liberal Catholicism was propagated in *L'Avenir* (1830), and his major work, *Paroles d'un croyant* (1834), led to his condemnation by the papacy (1834). Eventually he broke with the Church and became a social republican, was elected to the Constituent Assembly (1848), and was placed under police surveillance (1852).

LAMOIGNON FAMILY, influential French legal family, who established themselves at Basville in 1559 and entered the ranks of the *parlement* of Paris about that time, rising to a dominant position in the presidential order in the 17th–18th cents. Guillaume de Lamoignon (1617–77) was a famous First President under Louis XIV, but perhaps the most celebrated representative of the house was Chrétien Guillaume de Lamoignon de Malesherbes (1721–94), minister to Louis XVI, who was a victim of the French Revolution.

LAMORCIÈRE, LOUIS CHRISTOPHE LÉON JUCHAULT DE (1806–85), French conservative soldier and politician, who served in Algeria, played a large part in repressing the June Days (1848), and served as minister of war (1848) and as an unsuccessful commander of the papal army (1860).

LAMPSACUS, ancient Greek city-state founded by Phocaea on the south shore of the Hellespont (Dardanelles), *c.* 650 BC. Successively subject to Persia, Athens, Sparta, and Persia again, it became the site of one of Alexander the Great's mints. It was largely dependent on Pergamum in the 3rd cent., and, with Smyrna, the first Greek city to appeal to Rome against the aggression of Antiochus III of Syria (197).

LAMU ARCHIPELAGO, group of islands consisting of Lamu, Pate (once called Rasini), Manda, Ndau, and Kiwaiyu, off the north Kenya coast: probably the Pyralaon Isles of the *Periplus* (2nd cent. AD). They are inhabited by Swahili speaking people and are where the pre-Omani culture has best survived. The principal centres are Lamu; and Faza, Siyu, and Pate, all on Pate island. Manda, now abandoned, was in existence in the 9th cent. AD; Lamu and Pate, according to tradition, were founded in the 7th cent. The origins of Siyu and Raza are unknown, but they are said to have been re-settled from the mainland in the 16th cent. Lamu was a republic; Pate was governed by a sultan, and the other towns by sheikhs.

All were involved continually in conflict with the Portuguese in the late 16th and 17th cents. Lamu, the largest and most wealthy, with the best harbour, normally avoided political activities. Manda and Faza were destroyed in 1587 and Pate in 1678 and 1688. In the late 17th cent. Faza was the ally of the Portuguese, and Pate the leader of the opposition. In the first half of the 18th cent. Pate was at its height, but in the second half was ruined by a long civil war and by Mombasan intrigues. In 1812 the forces of Pate and Mombasa were defeated by Lamu, with great slaughter. Later the archipelago accepted the rule of the Sultan of Oman. Subsequently there were intermittent, unsuccessful attempts by the Sultans of Pate and the Sheikhs of Siyu to recover their old independence, but these ended in 1863.

LAN CHANG, kingdom in Laos, founded (1353) at Luang Prabang by Prince Fa Ngum with Cambodian aid. By the end of the 14th cent. it covered most of northern and central Laos. Subsequently its extension southwards, and increasing conflict with Burma and Ayudhya, forced the transfer of the capital to Vientiane (1563). Internal strife followed the death of King Soulignavongsa in 1694, and by 1707 the kingdom had disintegrated into three states, centred on Luang Prabang, Vientiane, and Champasak. 'Lan Chang' means 'million elephants'.

LANCASTER, HENRY OF GROSMONT, Duke of (1st of 1st creation) (?1299–1361), soldier and friend of King Edward III of England and a founder-member of the Order of the Garter. 'Good Duke Henry' was the chief founder of Corpus Christi College, Cambridge (1352), and author (1354) of the religious tract *Le Livre de Seyntz Medicines*. His lands and titles descended to his daughter, Blanche, and her husband, John of Gaunt, the third son of Edward III. After 1413 the dukedom of Lancaster was merged in the Crown.

LANCASTER, JOHN OF GAUNT, 2nd Duke of (1st of 2nd creation) (1340–99), third surviving son of King Edward III of England. His marriage to Blanche of Lancaster in 1359 made him Duke of Lancaster in 1361 and the richest man in England. The mortal sickness and death (1376) of his eldest brother, Edward the Black Prince, the senility of Edward III, and the accession of the child Richard II (1377) made him virtual ruler of England from *c.* 1373. He was not popular and was the target of attack from the Good Parliament in 1376 and of the Peasants' Revolt in 1381. He was also the object of the hostility of orthodox churchmen because of his patronage of John Wycliffe and the focus of the general suspicion attached to 'the over-mighty subject', yet he was in truth a man of loyalty and a moderating influence. His absence in Spain (1386–9) to lay claim to the Crown of Castile as the inheritance of his second wife, Constance, left a vacuum that was filled by the Lords Appellant, one of whom was his own son, Henry Bolingbroke, the future Henry IV. By his third wife, Katherine Swynford, who had been his mistress, he was the father of John Beaufort, Earl of Somerset, the ancestor of the Tudors, and Henry, Cardinal Beaufort.

LANCASTER, THOMAS, 2nd Earl of (*c.* 1278–1322), first cousin of King Edward II and the wealthiest magnate in England. He was a man of mediocre ability but great ambitions and a leading opponent of Edward II. Lancaster's feuds with other magnates allowed Edward to defeat him in a brief civil war in 1321–2. After being captured at Boroughbridge, Yorks, he was executed.

LANCASTER, JOSEPH (1778–1838), English Quaker educationalist. He opened a school at Southwark (1801), where, for reasons of economy, he developed the monitorial system by which older children taught younger. This he publicized (1803), but though supported by the British and Foreign School Society, Lancaster fell into debt and emigrated to the US (1818). His system had a great influence on 19th cent. British education.

LAND, EDWIN HERBERT (1909–   ), American inventor, who developed (1937) a material, Polaroid, used in safety glass and spectacles to reduce reflected sun-glare. He later devised the polaroid Land Camera (1947), which produced a positive photograph less than a minute after it had been taken, making it a valuable tool in industrial and scientific photography.

LAND ACTS in the US, series of acts passed to regulate the disposal of the public domain. The Land Act of 1796 re-enacted the rectangular survey system of the Ordinance of 1785 and stipulated that the land be sold at public auction in minimum units of a section (640 acres) at a minimum price of $2 per acre. It was an immediate failure because the land unit was too large and full payment was required within a year, at a time when money was scarce. The Harrison Land Act of 1800 amended and democratized the 1796 Land Act, reflecting demands on the frontier for farmsteads. It authorized minimum purchases of half a section, made the credit system more flexible—although it still retained the minimum price per acre and the auction system—and established four land districts along the Western frontier, each with its own land office. This act was designed to discourage speculators and encourage settlers, but was not very successful, since the typical frontiersman was still too poor to afford land and the credit system only promoted speculation. Nevertheless, the Harrison Act served as a model for similar legislation until the passage of the Land Act of 1820, which abolished the credit system for purchasing public land, reduced the minimum price to $1·25 per acre, and the minimum purchase to 80 acres. The demands of settlers were not, however, fully met until passage of the Pre-emption Acts (1830, 1841), and more particularly the Homestead Act of 1862.

LAND APPORTIONMENT ACT (1930) (amended 1941) in Southern Rhodesia, the equivalent of the South African Natives Land Act (1913), enforced legal segregation between Africans and whites. It granted whites nearly 40 per cent of the land (and the best agricultural land), the remainder being either African reserved land, or unallocated land. By 1961 most of the unallocated land had been granted to Africans, and the constitution of that year contained a new Land Apportionment Act, which made the segregation of land between Africans and whites even more rigid. The major element in apartheid had thus been introduced long before the crises of the 1960s in Rhodesia.

LAND APPORTIONMENT ACTS (1913, 1936) in South Africa, Native Land Acts which laid the basis for segregation in land ownership in rural areas. The 1913 act set aside areas to be reserved solely for African ownership outside which Africans could not acquire land without the approval of the governor-general. These reserves consisted of those lands still in African hands at the beginning of the 20th cent.—in all some 7 per cent of the land for $\frac{17}{24}$ of the population.

The act also contained provisions governing Africans living on European-owned lands as tenants or 'squatters'. Although intended as a consolidating measure, it made different provisions for each of South Africa's four provinces. The Cape was excluded completely, because of the link between land ownership and the African franchise, which could only be altered by a two-thirds majority of both Houses of Parliament. The worst effects were felt in the Orange Free State, where many Africans were evicted from white-owned farms. Although some whites viewed the Land Act as an act

of trusteeship the major pressures behind it were: European fears that Africans were buying land increasingly at the expense of 'poor whites', the demand for African labour, and the obsolescence of earlier 'squatting' arrangements as South African agriculture became more efficient.

The act was intended as an interim measure until further land could be set aside, but it remained unchanged until the Native Land and Trust Act (1936). This aimed at providing additional land for Africans as compensation for the abolition of the Cape African franchise under Hertzog's Representation of Natives' Act of 1936. The full quota of lands (12 per cent) released by the government for African occupation has still (1970) not been acquired, largely because of the reluctance of whites to part with land intended for Africans. These areas, however, form the territorial basis of the Nationalist government's Bantustan policies.

Africans always opposed the Land Apportionment Acts; the South African Native National Congress (NNC) was first able to mobilize mass support on this issue in 1913. The inequitable distribution of land in South Africa has ensured a constant supply of cheap black labour for her white-owned farms, factories, and mines.

C. M. Tatz, *Shadow and Substance in South Africa* (Natal, 1962).   SM

LAND BANKS in England and the American colonies were schemes by which land, rather than cash, would be made the reserve against which notes and credit could be issued. There were several such schemes in the 1690s. Though none succeeded in England, several were established in America. The most famous English Land Bank was created by Nicholas Barbon and Hugh Chamberlayne and encouraged by the Tory politicians, Robert Harley and his brother-in-law, Paul Foley. It was founded in 1696 for the purposes of publicity on the credit of land as opposed to moneyed interest symbolized by the Bank of England (1694), a Whig creation. Its sponsors were men of imagination rather than reputation and the squires to whom it was intended to appeal preferred a more orthodox banking system. In consequence, Harley's National Land Bank proved a failure.

Land banks in colonial America were declared illegal (1740) by the British parliament. This produced much litigation and ruined some stockholders. Nevertheless, many flourished until a few years before the Revolution (1776).

LAND BOOM IN AUSTRALIA (1880–90) affected every colony in eastern Australia, and especially Vic. Money borrowed publicly and privately from England and Scotland was spent largely on over-priced suburban land and railway development, building of ornate mansions, and financing speculative companies, many of them fraudulent. The boom thus created, and the subsequent depression, are nevertheless traceable to the activities of a relatively small group of speculators, bankers, and politicians.

In July 1891 the Imperial Bank went into liquidation and scores of other major financial institutions did the same. British investors refused to renew their loans. Vic.'s biggest bank, the Commerical, itself a heavy overseas borrower, was forced to call in overdrafts. Many building societies suspended operations as a result. Major frauds were proved against the Federal Bank, headed by the colony's prime minister, and a general banking collapse followed, stock exchange prices dropping by £36 million in one year.

During three years of serious depression the population of Melbourne decreased by 50,000. There were thousands of bankruptcies, some leading citizens committed suicide, and others, convicted of fraud, were imprisoned. It took more than a decade before there was a full recovery, during which time Melbourne lost its financial leadership to Sydney. Reconstruction policies included tighter controls over the banking system, a stronger Companies Act, and alterations to insolvency procedures to prevent frauds.

LAND QUALIFICATION ABOLITION ACT (1858) in Britain, abolished the property qualification for MPs prescribed by statute in 1711.

LAND REFORM IN CHINA, important aspect of social revolution in China. The reform of traditional patterns of land tenure has been a matter of vital social and political significance and has largely determined the success or failure of China's recent governments. Sun Yat-sen's vague schemes for granting land to the tillers, and improving the abject conditions of China's peasant population (85 per cent of the whole), were not implemented by his successor as leader of the Kuomintang, Chiang Kai-shek. The Kuomintang, which drew much of its support from landlords, had been alarmed by the force of the peasant movement in the mid-1920s, and refused to tolerate the idea of substantial land reform. During the 20 years of Kuomintang rule (1928–49), rural conditions declined—from an already low level. When the communists came to power in 1949, they already had considerable experience in the practice of land reform. They redistributed land on a per capita basis, taking from the rich and giving to the poor. This was welcomed by the millions of peasants, who owned land for the first time, but produced a great deal of dislocation, and a drop in production as the size of individual land units fell. To counter this, and to foster the development of the collective, socialist spirit, co-operatives were set up (1955), in each of which several hundred people pooled their land, tools, and animals, and were rewarded for their labour on a points system. Before this could really prove itself, it was replaced during the Great Leap Forward (1958) by the commune system, under which much larger units were organized, which took on many responsibilities of local governments, as well as of production. Emphasis was put on communal living (mess halls, nurseries, etc.); individualism and desire for personal gain were discouraged. This system, with major modifications, still existed in 1970.

LAND REFORM IN JAPAN (1946), American-imposed reform during the post-Second World War Occupation (1945–52). It dramatically reduced the scale of tenancy in Japan. Absentee landlords were forced to sell all their land to the government and, except in Hokkaidō, no landlord was permitted to own more than 7½ acres. As a result, 5 million acres (20,300 sq. kms) became available for resale to previous tenants at low interest over 30 years. With purchase made even easier by rapid inflation, the proportion of land cultivated by tenants decreased from 46 per cent to 12 per cent.

LAND SETTLEMENT IN NEW ZEALAND. The mission stations of Northland gave NZ agriculture its most solid beginnings before 1840. Thereafter, the NZ Co. and its associates established what were intended to be concentrated settlements for small agricultural farmers (1840–53). By 1850 it was clear that NZ's future lay in pastoralism, and Australian sheep shipped across the Tasman by squatters multiplied quickly on native grasslands. Grey's miscalculated land regulations of 1853 enabled pastoralists to lock up great areas in sheep runs. Thereafter, land policy (1853–76) varied from one province to another. Eager for revenue or under pressure from run-holders, provincial governments alienated large blocks which were used for grazing sheep, or held for speculative sale. In the depressed 1880s many great properties stagnated; they could be neither developed nor subdivided, with profit. Radical demands for 'bursting up the big estates' resulted in limited legislation (1892–4) for state repurchase and subdivision, principally on leasehold. Meanwhile, small farming had been slowly advancing in the North Island, and returning prosperity (c. 1895) encouraged private subdivision in all provinces. By 1914, the sheep run had long been replaced by the family farm (sheep, mixed, or dairy) as the characteristic NZ rural holding, extensive aggregation being illegal (1907). NZ farmers' greatest need, development capital, was first successfully met by a system of state advances (1894). The outcome of a long debate on land tenure con-

firmed freehold as the NZ norm, and state tenants optionally purchased their farms on easy terms (1912). Developments after 1914, though great in terms of production, were within existing patterns. Special laws (of varying success) put returned soldiers of both World Wars on the land, assisted Maori farmers, and improved Crown land for subdivision. Attempts to stabilize land values and check speculation (a recurring NZ problem) were unpopular and short-lived (1943–50), running up against the strong individualism of NZ farmers.   WJG

LAND TAX in Britain, direct imposition first introduced in the period 1693–7 which became the most important single source of government revenue in the 18th cent. During wartime it was levied at 4s in the pound and was resented by landowners who bore a disproportionate burden compared with businessmen, who invested their wealth in government stock. In the 19th cent. its place as the principal direct tax was taken, at first temporarily and later permanently, by income tax; the principle of a land tax has continued in the form of rates.

LANDA, DIEGO DE (d. 1579), Franciscan friar and bishop of Yucatan, who typified the best and the worst aspects of the 16th-cent. Spanish missionary effort in America. He was a devoted champion of the Indian, and he recorded his impressions of Maya culture in *Relación de las cosas de Yucatán* (1566). However, during his tenure as bishop (1572–9) Landa did not hesitate to apply severe physical punishment in an effort to eliminate heathen practices among the baptized but scarcely converted Maya.

LANDAMMAN, Swiss official and chief magistrate, the main administrator of a region who was originally the agent of an absent lord. The name was given to elected headmen of the forest cantons from the early 14th cent. The position often became hereditary, giving its holders the status of 'nobility' in Swiss communities.

LANDAU, French-held fortress in the upper Rhine valley which was besieged by Louis William, margrave of Baden, commander of an imperial force during the war of the Spanish Succession. Marshal Catinat, unable to send reinforcements, resigned himself to the loss of the town, which surrendered on 12 Sept. 1702.

LANDEN (or Neerwinden), **BATTLE OF** (1693), fought near Liège between the Dutch and English under William III and the French under the Duc de Luxembourg in the War of the Grand Alliance. William's forces were heavily outnumbered but, as at Stienkirk the previous year, though he fought obstinately and inflicted severe losses, he was able to make an orderly retreat. After their victory, the French took Charleroi, but their advance into the Netherlands was checked when William recovered Namur (1695).

LANDFRIEDE (lit., 'land peace'), German institution designed to curtail endemic private wars and brigandage, especially by noble robbers. They were local confederations sworn to preserve peace. In 1235 Emperor Frederick II for the first time proclaimed a national *Landfriede* throughout Germany. More restricted regional leagues became particularly important in the 14th and 15th cents in south-western Germany, where the cities took the lead in the formation of the Swabian League in 1376 and the Rhenish in 1381.

LANDON, ALFRED MOSSMAN (1887–), US politician and a liberal Republican governor of KS (1933–7). He was the Republican nominee for president in 1936, but was defeated by Franklin Roosevelt, winning only ME and VT.

LANDRATE, local government officials selected from the nobility in Prussia, Pomerania, Magdeburg, and Brandenburg at the turn of 17th–18th cents and introduced into Russia by

Peter I (1713). In Brandenburg they were given considerable powers over the countryside in matters of taxation and military administration (1702) and were chosen by the ruler. In Russia they acted as a check upon the provincial governors.

LANDRIANO, BATTLE OF (1529), victory for the imperialists under De Leyva over a French force trying to capture Milan. Six weeks later the treaties of Barcelona and Cambrai acknowledged Charles V's supremacy in Italy, a setback for Wolsey, who had allied England with the French. One consequence of the imperial victory was the papal decision to adjourn the court at Blackfriars, London, then considering the claims of Henry VIII for a 'divorce' from Charles V's aunt, Catherine of Aragon.

LANDSBERG LEAGUE, association of south German principalities presided over by the dukes of Bavaria in the 16th–17th cents.

LANDSTÄNDE, provincial Estates which arose in most German principalities during the later Middle Ages. They normally comprised representatives of the clergy, nobility, and towns and also, occasionally, of the peasantry. They were called into being by princes, chiefly as a way of securing extraordinary taxes. Some of these Estates acquired considerable power in the Middle Ages, but in the modern period they tended to atrophy in the face of the growing absolutism of the princes, though a few retained importance until the 18th cent.

LANE, SIR ALLEN (1902–70), British publisher, founder of Penguin Books. In 1935 he decided to reissue successful books by well-known authors in a paperback format. The idea itself was not new, but he planned to publish books that were cheap—6d (2½p)—but well produced. His first ten books, by authors such as Hemingway, Linklater, and Maurois, were not immediately successful. Three months later another ten were issued, and within six months he and his brother had formed Penguin Books Ltd, with a capital of £100. By the spring of 1937 more than 100 titles were in Penguin. The time was right for his new venture—a new reading public who could afford a cheap book were aroused by the great debates on peace and war, democracy and fascism. Penguin specials, on a variety of topics, sold up to 250,000 copies. He attracted the interest of intellectuals and the result was a new series, the Pelican. When the Penguin Co. went public in 1962 the shares were over-subscribed 160 times and Lane became a millionaire.

In Oct. 1960 he deliberately challenged the censorship laws in the *Lady Chatterley's Lover* Case. In 1969 Penguin published its 3000th novel—James Joyce's *Ulysses*. Lane dominated the company and fiercely maintained its autonomy, resisting a series of take-over bids. His death was immediately followed by a merger between Penguin books and the Longman Group. CPC

LANE, JAMES HENRY (1814–66), US politician, who became a free-soil leader in KS during the struggle over the state constitution (1855–7), raising a militia against the pro-slavery forces. As a Republican US senator (1861–6) he advocated the emancipation of slaves and enrolment of black troops in the Union armies.

LANFRANC (*c.* 1000–89), archbishop of Canterbury, who was born and educated in Italy, came to study theology in France and became the prior of Bec in Normandy, where he developed a distinguished school. King William I of England made him abbot of his new foundation at Caen and induced him to become the primate of the English Church (1070). He was zealous in the cause of internal Church reform, but saw no need for increased papal interference in provincial churches. He thus combined active suppression of the evils denounced by the Gregorian reformers (such as clerical marriage and simony) with hostility to the political conse-

quences of the Gregorian programme. He was upheld by William I in asserting claims to the supremacy of Canterbury over the archbishopric of York. As head of the whole English Church he supported William's refusal to accept undue papal interference in English affairs or the claims of the papacy to special overlordship of England.

LANG OF LAMBETH, COSMO GORDON LANG, Baron (1864–1965), British clergyman, who became Abp of York (1909–28) and of Canterbury (1928–42). He played a major part in church–state relations in the first half of the 20th cent., being associated with the royal commission on divorce (1909–12), the national mission of repentance and hope (1916), the prayer-book controversy (1928), and the abdication of King Edward VIII (1936).

LANG, JOHN DUNMORE (1799–1878), Australian Presbyterian minister and politician, who emigrated to NSW from Scotland, built Scots Church, Sydney, and became known as the 'Father of Australian Presbyterianism'. He was a vigorous supporter of immigration and introduced hundreds of settlers to Australia. As a member of the NSW Legislative Council from 1843 and of its new Assembly (1859–69), he sponsored progressive legislation. He founded the Australian College in Sydney, published 23 books, and edited three newspapers. He was an early advocate of Australian independence.

LANG, JOHN THOMAS (1876–), Australian Labor politician, who was a NSW MP (1913–46), state party leader (1923–39), prime minister (1925–7, 1930–2), and Commonwealth MP (1946–9). His first government's introduction of the 44-hour week, child endowment, widows' pensions, and extended compensation for workers created much goodwill among trade unionists, but his proposed repudiation of overseas loan interest during the Depression, and his opposition to deflationary recovery plans, put NSW at odds with the Commonwealth and other states. In 1932 the governor, Sir Philip Game, dismissed Lang and in an ensuing state election Labor lost and the party split.

Lang's popularity with trade unions and his tight organization of an American type of political machine, gave him unprecedented influence over the Labor movement in the early 1930s. But electoral success eluded Labor in both state and Commonwealth politics and union leaders turned against him. Unity was restored in 1939, when Lang was replaced as state leader by W. J. (later Sir William) McKell. With a small band of violently anti-communist followers, Lang continued to embarrass the ALP and sat in the Commonwealth parliament as an independent Labor member in opposition to J. B. Chifley. He subsequently devoted himself to his newspaper, the *Century* (founded 1938), but exercised no appreciable influence over post-war Australian affairs.

LANGEVIN, SIR HECTOR-LOUIS (1826–1906), Canadian lawyer, author, and politician. He was a prominent member of the Liberal-Conservative Party, held several government posts (1864–73, 1878–91), was implicated in the Pacific Scandal (1873), and resigned (1891) after being found guilty of negligence during Senate investigations into charges of corruption.

LANGEVIN, PAUL (1872–1946), French physicist. During the First World War he played an important part in the development of submarines and submarine detection. In the inter-war years he campaigned for a moral and intellectual liberation of France through a scientific, and at the same time humanistic, communism. He pursued his aims as vice-president of the Ligue des Droits de l'Homme. He took part in the first anti-fascist meetings with Henri Barbusse and Romain Rolland and later became vice-president of the Comité de Vigilance des Intellectuels Antifascistes. During the Second World War he joined the Communist Party.

LANGO, people of northern Uganda, numbering about a quarter of a million of mixed origin, Itese and Luo. They speak a Luo dialect, and came to occupy their homeland mainly after 1500.

LANGPORT, BATTLE OF (10 July 1645), prelude to the surrender of Bristol by the royalists in the English Civil War. After the battle of Naseby, Fairfax and Cromwell marched to the south-west, where Lord Goring attempted to defend Bridgwater. Cromwell's cavalry proved decisive at Langport and most of the royalists surrendered. Bridgwater fell on 23 July and Bristol on 11 Sept.

LANGSIDE, BATTLE OF (13 May 1568). After Mary Queen of Scots had escaped from Lochleven Castle her forces and those of the Hamiltons were defeated by the Earls of Moray and Morton and the 'confederate lords' representing her infant son, King James VI. After the battle the queen fled to England.

LANG-SON INCIDENT (1885), during the Sino-French War. In March 1885, during fighting against Chinese regular and irregular forces, on the Tongking–Kwangsi border, the French were forced to evacuate the town of Lang-Son, which they had occupied. News of the disaster reached the French Assembly on the eve of a debate on Indo-China. The prime minister, Jules Ferry, was defeated and forced to resign, although in the end the French were able to hold on to Tongking.

LANGTON, WALTER (d. 1321), English cleric, who was Bp of Coventry and of Lichfield. He served as treasurer and chief adviser to King Edward I of England. Later, he was brought to trial by Edward II, and found guilty of abuse of his office, but was subsequently recalled to the king's service.

LANKA SAMA SAMAJ PARTY in Ceylon, Trotskyist party in the House of Representatives which was founded (1935) by a group of young intellectuals educated at British and American universities, the most prominent of whom were N.M. Perera and Philip Gunawardana. Both were elected to the state council in 1936. During the Second World War they and several other leaders were placed in detention and the party was declared an illegal organization. After the war it gained considerable influence among the urban proletariat, and in the 1947 general election ten of its members were returned to the House of Representatives, where, with a splinter Trotskyist group and three other communists, they formed a small but articulate opposition. The party gained a few more seats at the 1952 election, but was split between the followers of Perera and Gunawardana. In 1964 Mrs Bandaranaike sought the LSSP's support and Perera became minister of finance, an appointment which helped to split her party, the Sri Lanka Freedom Party.

LANNOY, CHARLES DE (c. 1482–1527), Flemish nobleman, lord of Mangoval, Molembais, and Sanzelles and knight of the Golden Fleece, who was the trusted counsellor of the Emperor Charles V. He was appointed viceroy of Naples (April 1522) and commanded the forces of the anti-French coalition which defeated Francis I at Pavia (1525). Lannoy personally conducted the captive French king to Spain and negotiated the treaty of Madrid between the two countries (1526). He visited Francis at Cognac (1626) to plead for the ratification of the Madrid treaty and was later ordered back to Italy by Charles V to conduct further diplomatic negotiations.

LA NOUE, FRANÇOIS DE (1531–91), French Huguenot commander in the French Wars of Religion, who wrote *Discours politiques et militaires* (1587). He served with Coligny (1569) and Louis of Nassau (1572), led the defence of La Rochelle (1572–3), and died of wounds at Lamballe.

LANSBURY, GEORGE (1859–1940), British socialist politician and Christian pacifist. Lansbury was elected (1892) to the Board of Guardians in Poplar, a poor district of London's East End. He signed the minority report of the Poor Law Royal Commission (1905–9), supported women's suffrage, and edited the *Daily Herald*. In the 1920s Lansbury embodied 'Poplarism', *ie*, payment by certain Guardians of generous scales of outdoor relief to the unemployed. As first commissioner for works (1929–31), he gave London the Serpentine Lido in Hyde Park. He survived Labour's 1931 election débâcle and led the Opposition (1931–5), but resigned when Bevin persuaded the party conference to approve League sanctions against Italy after Mussolini invaded Abyssinia.

LANSDOWNE, WILLIAM PETTY, 1st Marquis of (1737–1805), British politician, who was, during his public life, the Earl of Shelburne. His administration (July 1782–April 1783) ended the American War of Independence. Shelburne, a supporter of Chatham, inspired by his arrogance and alleged duplicity a distrust of his abilities. At the board of trade (1763) and as secretary of state (1776–8), Shelburne urged conciliation of the Americans. In 1782 he clashed with Fox over responsibility for the peace negotiations. As Rockingham's successor, he advocated parliamentary and economic reform, retrenchment and freer trade, but failed to attract enough support from patriotic independent MPs to outweigh the hostility of rival factions and general dislike of the peace terms.

LANSDOWNE, HENRY PETTY-FITZMAURICE, 3rd Marquis of (1780–1863), British Whig politician, who entered the House of Commons (1802) and became chancellor of the exchequer in the Ministry of the Talents (1806–7). He consistently supported Catholic emancipation and advocated the abolition of slavery. He was one of the Whigs to join Canning in 1827, entering the cabinet first without office and then becoming home secretary, which he remained under Goderich (1827–8). He played an important part in the passage of the 1832 Reform Act in the House of Lords. He held office as president of the council under Grey (1830–4), under Melbourne (1834, 1835–41), and again under Russell (1846–52). In the 1840s and 1850s he was leader of the Whigs in the House of Lords. In 1852 and again in 1855 he declined to lead an administration, preferring to serve in the cabinet without office under Aberdeen (1852–5) and Palmerston (1855–8).

LANSDOWNE, HENRY CHARLES KEITH PETTY-FITZMAURICE 5th Marquis of (1845–1927), British politician, who left the Liberal Party over Home Rule after being appointed governor-general of Canada by Gladstone. He became viceroy of India (1884–94). As secretary for war (1895–1900) he incurred blame for the army's unpreparedness at the beginning of the Boer War. He succeeded Salisbury as foreign secretary (1900–5), determined to retrieve his reputation, and helped to negotiate the Anglo-French entente (1904) after the failure of earlier approaches to Germany. He led the Conservative majority in the Lords, agreeing with Balfour to wreck or heavily to amend Liberal government bills passed in the Commons. As the holder of great estates in Ireland, he was ready to reject Lloyd George's budget (1909) with its implications for land taxation. He urged that the Crown's right to create peers should be restricted and that there should be 350 lords elected by hereditary peers and MPs, in addition to nominees of the Crown. As minister without portfolio in Asquith's coalition government (1915–16), he opposed Home Rule and advocated a negotiated peace with Germany (1917).

LANSING, ROBERT (1864–1928), US lawyer and statesman, who founded the *American Journal of International Law* (1907). As US secretary of state (1915), he disagreed with

President Wilson's advocacy of the League of Nations and resigned (1920).

LANSING–ISHII AGREEMENT (2 Nov. 1917), exchange of notes between the US secretary of state and the Japanese special ambassador in which, despite a confirmation of the principles of the Open Door policy with regard to China, the US recognized Japan's 'special interests in China, particularly in the part to which her possessions are contiguous'. The agreement, regarded by Japan as recognition of her claim to Manchuria, caused considerable embarrassment to the US and was cancelled by a further exchange of notes (30 March 1923) following the Washington Conference (1921–2).

LANSKOY, SERGEI STEPANOVICH, Count (1787–1862), Russian minister of the interior during the reforms of 1860s. He was associated with the Decembrists in his youth and was an ardent advocate of Emancipation. He exercised a liberal influence on Alexander II.

LAO-DONG ('WORKERS') PARTY, in Viet-nam, ruling party of the Democratic Republic of Viet-nam (North Viet-nam) since 1951. The Indo-Chinese Communist Party was formally dissolved in 1945, owing to Chinese (Nationalist) pressure, but continued to exist in secret, and in March 1951 was refounded as the 'Workers' Party. Its structure and organization have developed in much the same way as 'the Party' in other communist countries.

LAOS, FRENCH ANNEXATION OF (1893). The three successors to the Lao kingdom of Lan Chang were brought under Thai hegemony between 1777 and 1840, especially firmly following the revolt of Chao Anou (1826–8) and the destruction of Vientiane. Luang Prabang was too weak to withstand the invasions of Chinese brigands in the 1870s and 1880s, and King Oun-Kham escaped their sack of Luang Prabang (1887) only with the aid of the French vice-consul, Pavie. By pressing claims against Thailand for Lao territory by military incursions (1889–93), the French provoked Thai resistance, which led to the Paknam Incident (1893); following which Laos east of the Mekong river was annexed as a French protectorate. Further provinces opposite Luang Prabang and Pakse were gained by a second treaty with Thailand (1904).

LA PEROUSE, JEAN FRANÇOIS DE GALAUD DE (1741–88), leader of an epic French scientific expedition to the Pacific (1785–88), who was lost with his two ships at Vanikoro, near Santa Cruz (c. July 1788). Traces of them were recovered in 1826.

LAPIS NIGER (Latin 'black stone'), marble slab erected, perhaps in the 1st cent. BC, over the putative grave of Romulus or Tullus Hostilius in the ancient Roman forum. On it is the oldest known Latin inscription, dating to c. 500 BC. Though too fragmentary to be deciphered, it appears to relate to augurs' ritual.

LA PLATA, UNITED PROVINCES OF, federation of Argentine provinces (1813), created by the constituent assembly at Buenos Aires. With pretensions to succeed to the Spanish viceroyalty of La Plata, the federation sought but failed to incorporate the peripheral areas that later became Uruguay, Paraguay, and Bolivia. It was beset by internal conflict between the centralizers and modernizers of Buenos Aires (*unitarios*) and the traditionalist autonomists of the interior provinces (*federales*), not all of whom were represented when the federation declared Argentine independence at Tucumán in 1816. A centralizing constitution (1819) provoked only anarchy, and failed. The federation was revived (1826) under Buenos Aires auspices with a new constitution and with Bernardino Rivadavia as president. He, however, was compelled to resign the following year. Under his successor, Rosas, Argentina came to be governed through a system of inter-provincial pacts, and styled itself the 'Argentine Confederation'.

LA PLATA, VICEROYALTY OF, territorial division of Spanish America composed of modern Argentina, Paraguay, Bolivia, and Uruguay. Erected in 1776 to forestall Portuguese encroachment from Brazil, the viceroyalty disintegrated during the Latin American struggles for independence, a process virtually completed in 1828, when Uruguay gained independent status.

LA POLE, WILLIAM DE, OF HULL (d. 1366), English merchant who helped to finance Edward III's early campaigns in France (1338–40) and was one of the main organizers of the companies of English businessmen who financed Edward's expedition of 1346–7, which ended in the capture of Calais. By his unscrupulous proceedings and excessive profiteering, Pole aroused much hostility at court and was twice imprisoned by Edward and mulcted of some of his gains. His eldest son, Michael, was summoned to the House of Lords in 1365. Under Richard II he became lord chancellor. Pole's descendant, John, Earl of Lincoln, was recognized as heir to the throne in 1484 by his uncle, King Richard III, but was killed at the battle of Stoke in 1487 by King Henry VII.

LAPPS, people speaking a Finno-Ugrian language, who have co-existed with Norsemen in Scandinavia throughout recorded history, and probably also prehistorically, since the archaeological record shows no cultural break. The Norsemen have, however, continually driven them further north and further inland. They were and remained a nomadic people, dependent upon the reindeer and upon hunting and fishing. Their pagan religion much influenced Norse paganism, especially the cults of Odinn and Freyja. It was probably a major source of Norse magic.

LA PRENSA, Argentine daily newspaper, founded in 1869 by José C. Paz. It was for decades the most august organ of the enlightened Argentine oligarchy and incurred the enmity of Juan Perón because of its Anglophilia and its defence of liberal economics and individual rights. It was closed in 1951, expropriated, and given to the General Confederation of Labor in the following year. Its restoration to its owner, Alberto Gainza Paz, in 1955, seemingly symbolized the close of the Peronist interlude.

LA REVEILLIERE-LEPEAUX, LOUIS MARIE (1753–1824), French republican, member of the states general (1789) and deputy to the convention in 1792, where he voted for the death of the king. He was a member of the executive directory (1795), presiding over the department of science, morals, and religion, and showing great hostility to the Catholics. He acted with Barras in the *coup d'état* of 18th Fructidor (Sept. 1797), but when the directors split he found himself in a minority and resigned (June 1799).

LARGILLIÈRE, NICOLAS DE (1656–1746), French portrait painter who worked in London as assistant to Sir Peter Lely. He returned to France at the downfall of the Stuarts (1649) and made his home in his native Paris, where he continued to be court painter.

LARGO CABALLERO, FRANCISCO (1869–1946), Spanish politician and trade union leader, who succeeded Iglesias as leader of the UGT (*Union General de Trabajadores*), and sought to base the Socialist Party firmly on union strength. His co-operation with De Rivera and his acceptance of the ministry of labour in Azana's government (1931–3) made him unpopular with the extreme left. But disillusionment with bourgeois democracy led him to found a revolutionary alliance of working-class parties which engineered the abortive October Revolution (1934). Largo Caballero's dislike of anarchism made it impossible for him to emerge as leader of a united proletariat and his suspicion of communism ruined his brief attempt to lead the popular front during the Civil War (1936). But he enjoyed immense prestige and the contradictions in his career reflected the complexities of Spanish left-wing politics rather than lack of consistency in himself.

LARISA (or Larissa), in antiquity the chief city in Thessaly, north-eastern Greece. It was dominated by the aristocratic Aleuadae and supported the Persian invasion of 480–479 BC. Despite Spartan hostility, it defied its rivals, Pharsalus and Pherae, until the latter's domination under Jason (c. 375–370). Later, it called in Philip II of Macedon against Pherae (357–352), and was a firm ally of Macedon until Rome's victory in the Second Macedonian War (196). Thereafter it became the capital of the new Thessalian League organized by Rome and remained of some importance through the Middle Ages until it was taken by the Turks in 1393.

LA ROCHE-FLAVIN, BERNARD DE (*fl.* 17th cent.), French political theorist and magistrate in the *parlement* of Toulouse, who in his *Treize Livres des Parlements* (1617) propounded the theory of the constitutional limitations imposed upon the exercise of royal sovereignty by the legal authority of the *parlements*.

LA ROCHEFOUCAULD, FRANÇOIS, PRINCE DE MAR-SILLAC, Duc de (1613–80), French nobleman and *frondeur*. As a young man he became involved in plots against Richelieu on behalf of Anne of Austria. Later, he intrigued against Anne and Cardinal Mazarin, playing a conspicuous part in the Fronde of the princes, which was cut short by his being seriously wounded at the Porte Saint-Antoine. After being exiled to his estates (1653), he returned to Paris in 1656, having been granted a pension from Fouquet. He passed the rest of his life enjoying the literary society of the salons. He was a regular visitor to the rooms of Mme de Sablé, the Hôtel de Rambouillet, and the Hôtel de Nevers, where he met Mme de la Fayette, with whom he later enjoyed a life-long friendship. In 1662 he published his *Mémoires* and in 1665 his *Reflexions ou Sentences et Maximes Morales*, a series of well-known aphorisms.

LA ROCHEJACQUELEIN, HENRI DU VERGER, Marquis de (1772–94), French leader of the insurgent loyalists in La Vendée (1791), who was repeatedly successful against the Convention.

LA ROCHEJACQUELEIN, LOUIS DE (1777–1815), émigré French marquis, who fought for England in St Domingo and on returning to France (1801) refused offers to serve Napoleon and became the leader of the legitimists in La Vendée and Guyenne. On Napoleon's return from Elba he again took refuge in England, but returned to organize resistance in La Vendée, and died in battle at Mathes (1815).

LA ROCHELLE, French Atlantic seaport, in the old province of Poitou. It was the most important Huguenot stronghold from the mid-16th cent. and became an independent city-republic with considerable privileges by the Edict of Nantes (1598). Its city council of 100 members, an oligarchy of merchant-shipowners, controlled the city, which posed an increasing threat to the absolutism of French kings. Richelieu therefore instigated the siege of La Rochelle, whose citizens waited in vain for English help under the Duke of Bucking-ham, and finally surrendered (28 Oct. 1628). Jean Guiton, the indomitable mayor, was exiled, the walls and towers of the city's defences were razed and its privileges abolished. A royal declaration of 1669 restricted Protestant worship and decreed the destruction of 13 churches; from 1685 the city was subject to the dragonnades. None the less, it enjoyed considerable economic prosperity in the 17th cent. as the West Indian trade increased rapidly.

LA ROCHELLE, BATTLE OF (June 1372). An English fleet carrying important reinforcements for their army in Aquitaine was destroyed off La Rochelle by Castilian allies of the French. Henceforth English sea communications with their outposts in France were permanently in jeopardy, the English army in Gascony was defeated, and in Aug. 1372 the French recaptured La Rochelle and wide stretches of territory. It proved the decisive conflict in the second phase of the Hundred Years War during the last years of the reign of King Edward III of England, who lost most of his earlier conquests.

LA ROCHELLE, PEACE OF (1573), compromise settlement at the end of the fourth civil war in France (1572–3) between Charles IX and the Huguenots, besieged by the Duke of Anjou in La Rochelle. Peace was needed so that Anjou could take up the Polish Crown. The royalists abandoned the siege and allowed the Huguenots freedom of worship in the three towns of La Rochelle, Nîmes, and Montauban (6 July 1573).

LA ROCQUE, FRANÇOIS DE (1886–1946), French soldier, businessman, and political figure. After retiring from the army in 1928, he went into business, then, with the backing of the industrialist, Coty (1931), became president of the Croix de Feu. Under his leadership it evolved from an ex-servicemen's organization into a para-military political movement, which took part in the demonstrations of 6 Feb. 1934. The movement lacked a clear ideology, but was nearer traditional nationalism than fascism. It was dissolved by the government in 1936, and La Rocque then formed the Parti social français, a political party which used constitutional methods. He also bought a newspaper, the *Petit Journal*. During the Second World War he at first supported Pétain, but was later arrested by the Germans. On his return to France he was mildly penalized.

LARRETA, ENRIQUE RODRÍGUEZ (1875–1961), Argentine novelist whose *La gloria de Don Ramiro* (1908) is a study of the psychology of the Spain of Philip II.

LARS PORSENNA (*fl.* 6th cent. BC), Etruscan King of Clusium or Vulci, who according to the tradition sought to reinstate the exiled Tarquinius Superbus to the Roman throne in 509 BC, but was repelled by Horatius Cocles. The legend conceals the fact of renewed Etruscan occupation. The subsequent defeat of Lars by Aristodemus of Cumae and the Latins at Aricia in 506 spelt the decline of Etruscan power in Italy.

LARSA (mod. Sankara), city of south Mesopotamia, which became the centre of an Amorite kingdom whose ruler, Gungunum (c. 1932–1906 BC), conquered other Sumerian cities. Larsa was taken by Hammurabi of Babylon (c. 1763).

LARUT WARS, fought for the control of tin mines around Taiping, Malaya. The *Ghee Hin* Chinese society was driven out of Larut by the rival *Hai San* society (1861–2), but the position was reversed in subsequent fighting (1872–4), which led to British intervention in the Malay state of Perak (1874).

LA SALLE, RENÉ-ROBERT CAVELIER, Sieur de (1643–87), French explorer, who emigrated to Canada and probably went on expeditions south of Lakes Ontario and Erie (1669–1673), and may have discovered the Ohio river (1671). He helped to build Fort Frontenac (1673) and was given its command (1675). The French government gave him a grant of nobility with the right to establish new seignories in the west (1677). He built (1678) the *Griffon*, the first commercial ship to sail the Upper Great Lakes (1679). In Green Bay the *Griffon* was loaded with furs with which to pay La Salle's creditors, but the ship was never seen again. Unaware of the loss, he travelled south and built Fort Miami on the St Joseph river (IN) and with Henri de Tonti he constructed Fort Crevecœur on Lake Peoria, IL (1680). In 1681 La Salle, Tonti, and Jacques Bourdon set out with a party of over 50 and descended the Mississippi river to the Gulf of Mexico. On 9 April 1682 La Salle raised a cross and took possession of the region watered by the Mississippi, naming it Louisiana in honour of Louis XIV. La Salle returned to Lake Peoria and instructed Tonti to build Fort Saint-Louis-des-Illinois, the first permanent post in the IL region, and directed two men to build another fort on the present site of Chicago. Pressing on into the Ohio valley, he continued trading (1682–3), but the IL forts were removed from La Salle's control when La Barré replaced Frontenac as governor of New France (1682). Having sailed to France (1684), La Salle induced the government to return his forts and he was made governor of LA. He sailed with four ships and 400 men to establish the new colony (July 1684). The expedition landed in TX, having missed the mouth of the Mississippi (1685). Failing to find the river by ship, La Salle attempted to reach the Mississippi by marching eastward. He was murdered by his own men near the Trinity river in TX.

Francis Parkman, *La Salle and the Discovery of the Great West* (Boston, 1879).　　　　GFO

LA SALLE, SAINT JEAN BAPTISTE, DE (1651–1719), French cleric, who was the founder of the Frères des Écoles Chrétiennes. He devoted himself to developing popular Catholic education for boys. His lay brothers were responsible for many innovations in the curriculum, and were recognized as a religious congregation (1725). Their work for Catholic education finally led to La Salle's canonization (1900).

LAS CASAS, BARTOLOMÉ DE (1474–1566), Dominican friar, historian, and champion of the natives of the Americas. Las Casas sought his fortune on Hispaniola and later in the conquest of Cuba. He was successful in winning lands and Indian labour for use in the gold pannings. It was not until 1514, at the age of 40, that Las Casas doubted the morality of the system. He gave up his lands and Indians, and for 52 years fought for the natives of America.

He found powerful patrons in Spain, among them Cardinal Jiménez de Cisneros. Although appointed 'Protector of the Indians' Las Casas was too late to save the natives of the West Indies from virtual extermination. To prevent similar events on the mainland, he proposed that African slaves be imported, an idea he later repudiated, and that small farmers from Spain should be used as colonists. He himself tried unsuccessfully to establish a trial settlement in Venezuela. Discouraged by its failure, he retired in 1520 to become a Dominican, and his next eight years were spent in seclusion writing his *History of the Indies*.

In the 1530s Las Casas resumed the fight, proposing that persuasion rather than force be used to extend the American empire. In 1537 he tested his method in an area of Guatemala which the Spanish had failed to conquer. He was at first successful, but rival priests and settlers forced their way into the area and caused an Indian revolt. Even Las Casas's newly acquired dignity as Bp of Chiapas was insufficient to stem the tide.

A greater disappointment followed. In 1542 Las Casas's arguments persuaded Charles I to promulgate the New Laws, legislation designed drastically to modify the *encomienda* system of Indian tribute and labour. The attempt failed in the face of colonial resistance, and, although the intent of the New Laws was slowly implemented in succeeding decades, this was of small comfort to Las Casas.

In 1547 he left America and spent the rest of his life writing in Spain. His most famous work was the *Very Brief Recital of the Destruction of the Indies*, which described the treatment of the aborigines in gruesome detail. Las Casas challenged the eminent humanist Juan Ginés de Sepúlveda, who justified the Spanish conquest by arguing that the Indians were inferior beings.

Las Casas's successes were Pyrrhic victories. Sepúlveda's ideas were never published in Spain, but the tide of Spanish conquest rolled on. His *Very Brief Recital* infuriated the colonists, and its many foreign editions helped to foster the Black Legend of the Spanish conquest, but it did nothing to improve the lot of the Indians. The courage and determination of Las Casas are beyond dispute, but his unyielding idealism assured that more practical men would shape the future of Latin America.

Lewis Hanke, *The Spanish Struggle for Justice in the Conquest of America* (Boston and Toronto, 1965).
Henry R. Wagner, and Helen Rand Parish, *The Life and Writings of Bartolomé de las Casas* (Albuquerque, 1966).
　　　　FPB

LAS CASES, EMMANUEL AUGUSTIN DIEUDONNÉ JOSEPH, Comte de (1766–1842), French historian, who, after emigrating to England during the revolutionary period, became fascinated by Napoleon's genius and insisted on accompanying him into exile at St Helena. His account of Napoleon's conversations, *Mémorial de Sainte-Hélène* (1823), fostered the idea that Napoleon was a benevolent ruler who had been misunderstood in the chancellories of Europe.

LASKI, JOHN (or A LASCO) (1499–1560), Polish Protestant reformer, who organized the Calvinist Church of Emden and stayed in London during Edward VI's reign at Cranmer's invitation. He left England on Mary Tudor's accession and in 1557 returned to Poland to spread Calvinism and work for the creation of a national Polish evangelical church.

LAS NAVAS DE TOLOSA, BATTLE OF (1212), decisive defeat of the caliph Nasir by Castile, which led to the collapse of Almohad power in Andalus and the fall of most of Muslim Spain to the Christians.

LASSALIE, FERDINAND (1825–64), German politician, economist, and leader of the early socialist movement in Germany. In 1863 he founded a workers' political party (later the Social Democratic Party). He differed from Marx in that his socialism was national, and in thinking it possible to improve the condition of the working class without revolution. His friendship with Bismarck foreshadowed Bismarck's later social policy. His law of wages, derived in part from the classical economists, stated that, in an expanding capitalist economy, wages inevitably remained at subsistence level.

LASSUS, ORLANDO DE (c. 1530–94), Netherlands composer of the 16th cent., who ranks with Palestrina and Byrd. He entered the service of the Gonzaga viceroy of Sicily and was taken to Italy (1544). Later, he returned to Antwerp, though he spent most of his working life in Munich at the court of the dukes of Bavaria. He is known for the quantity and quality of his vocal compositions, *eg*, madrigals and motets, both sacred and secular.

LASTMAN, PIETER (1583–1633), Dutch portrait painter, who led the Italian-Baroque movement in Amsterdam in the 1620s and in whose studio the young Rembrandt was apprenticed to learn the art of painting (c. 1623).

LASWARI, BATTLE OF (1 Nov. 1803) in the Second Anglo-Maratha War, when the British, under Lake, defeated Sindhia's forces.

LAT DIOR (c. 1842–86), *damel* (ruler) of Cayor, Senegal. Born into the Geedy royal matrilineage, he was elected *damel* in 1862, but fled to Saloum (1864–8), in the face of French troops. The ruler of Saloum, Ma-Ba Dyakhou, converted him to Islam (1864), and after returning to Cayor he became *damel* again (1871). He refused to let the French take the Dakar–St Louis railway through Cayor (1882) and four years later was killed in an encounter with French troops at Dyaqlé. It was under his influence that Islam gained a significant hold on the Wolof masses.

LA TÈNE CULTURE, typical late Iron Age phase of Celtic culture, associated with a distinctive art-style and named after a site on Lake Neuchâtel in Switzerland. It began in the 5th cent. BC in the general area of the middle Rhine and Marne and it is characterized by imports of both Greek and Etruscan manufacture, the latter connection being reinforced by the Adriatic outlet for barbarian trade provided *c.* 500 by the Etruscan foundations in northern Italy. Evidence for chariotry as a military tactic from early La Tène times onwards suggests connections also with eastern Europe.

LATERAN AGREEMENTS (Feb. 1929) (Patti Lateranensi), consisting of a treaty between Italy and the Vatican, a Concordat and a financial settlement, signed by Mussolini and Cardinal Gasparri. The 1871 Law of Guarantees was abrogated. The Vatican recognized the Italian state. Italy recognized the Vatican City state as an independent, neutral international power, and paid 750 million lire compensation for the seizure of the papal states in 1860–70. Italy undertook to protect the Vatican from offensive political or religious occurrences in Rome; the Catholic religion was to be the sole religion of state; marriage was to be regulated by canon law; religious instruction to be given in schools; and Catholic schools and non-political activities of Catholic Action allowed. Bishops were to take an oath of loyalty to the king, but be Vatican appointments.

Mussolini thus secured acquiescence or loyalty to his regime from most Catholics. The Vatican could maintain its influence in education, and, through Catholic Action, counteract unpalatable fascist doctrines. The agreements were incorporated into the 1948 Republican Constitution, Article 7, through a Christian Democrat–Communist agreement. The 1969–70 Italian political crisis largely hinged on the Christian Democrats' reluctance to contravene or alter the Concordat in allowing divorce, as demanded by left-wingers.

LATERAN COUNCIL (1215), greatest general council before that of Trent, marking the zenith of medieval papal reform. It was convoked by Pope Innocent III and attended by over 1200 prelates. It passed a large number of canons concerning ecclesiastical organization and the duties of the clergy. Its theological decrees included the first official definition of the doctrine of transubstantiation. By prohibiting the clergy from participating in judicial ordeals it promoted the disappearance of these primitive legal procedures (in England after 1219).

LATERAN COUNCIL (1512), general church council summoned by Pope Julius II (19 April 1512) to counteract the influence of the general council which Louis XII of France had called at Pisa (1511). It lasted for 12 sessions, the first beginning on 3 May 1512 and the last on 16 March 1517, and was dissolved by Leo X in 1517. A triumph for the papacy, before Julius II's death the council had condemned the Pisa gathering and had agreed on spiritual sanctions against Louis and the kingdom of France. Later, Louis sent an embassy to the council in an attempt to end the Gallican conflict. Some urgent Church reforms were tackled. A bull of 5 May 1514 was issued to deal with the abuses of the *commendam*, greater penalties were introduced for blasphemy, sorcery, and superstition, and the Camaldolese monks, Quirini and Giustiniani, produced a programme for the American missions, union with the Eastern Christians, and measures to remedy the ignorance of the clergy and laity. However, most of the council's decrees were not implemented because of papal irresolution from Leo X to Clement VII.

LATHAM, SIR JOHN GREIG (1877–1964), Australian politician and chief justice of the high court of Australia (1935–52), who had succeeded S. M. Bruce in 1929 as leader of the Nationalist Party in the Commonwealth parliament but, two years later, stood down to allow the former Labor minister, J. A. Lyons, to become leader of the United Australia Party and prime minister. He was widely respected as attorney-general and minister for external affairs and, later, as chief justice (with a wartime interlude as Australia's first minister to Japan, 1940–1). He was active in honorary public service, as chancellor of Melbourne University and foundation president of the Australian Elizabethan Theatre Trust.

LATIFUNDIA, Roman term, first known from the 1st cent. AD, but commonly applied in modern times to the large ranch type of farms, worked largely by slaves, which were formed on public land in Italy in the 2nd cent. BC by land-owning nobles, who by buying out citizen peasant-farmers created a dangerous drift from the land. Tiberius Gracchus' legislation (133) reduced the size of estates and slave-gangs were mostly replaced in the 1st cent. BC by demobilized veterans as free tenant-farmers (*coloni*). In the history of later periods the term latifundism is used of similar land tenure systems, in which large estates are under-utilized, only marginally profitable, worked by semi-servile or underpaid labour, and used as an asylum for capital. Such systems are still (1970) characteristic of much of Latin America and of some parts of Spain and Italy.

LATIMER, HUGH (1485–1555), bishop of Worcester and Protestant martyr, burnt by Mary I at Oxford. His advocacy of Henry VIII's 'divorce' won him protection in high places and he was able to air his radical views. He became a bishop in 1535, but resigned in opposition to the Six Articles (1539) and was for a time imprisoned. Under Edward VI he did not resume his see, but became an itinerant preacher, supporting religious change but denouncing oppressive landlords responsible for enclosure, exorbitant rents, and 'the decay of husbandry'. On Mary's accession Latimer was condemned as a heretic and in his own words died, with Bp Ridley, 'to light such a candle . . . as [I trust] shall never be put out'.

LATIN AMERICAN CENTRALISM AND FEDERALISM, political principles which primarily characterized the conflicts of the 19th cent. Centralists advocated strong centralized government, stemming from the old colonial capitals where local officials would be appointed. Centralists were supported by the Church hierarchy and some provincial landowners, who sought the protection of the capital. Federalists advocated weak central government and strong state and local governments, and the election of local officials. Extreme federalists argued that government rested with the states; extreme centralists would have created provinces (on the French model) rather than states (on the US model). 19th-cent. liberals were usually federalists, while 19th-cent. conservatives were frequently centralists.

LATIN AMERICAN FREE TRADE ASSOCIATION (LAFTA), first agreed to in 1960. LAFTA began to function in 1962 and most Latin American countries were members by 1970. LAFTA's member nations hoped in 1970 that the institution, copied to some extent from the European Free Trade Association, would help to eliminate all mutual trade barriers by 1973.

A basic problem which troubled LAFTA was that most Latin American states exported unprocessed agricultural products or minerals to the industrialized nations of the North Atlantic, and so historically did not trade much with each other. Trade within the area increased rapidly in the 1960s, but remained only a small fraction of total Latin American trade. Another complaint concerned the uneven distribution of benefits. Some countries' LAFTA exports expanded dramatically, notably those of Mexico, but other nations felt that the plan had been disappointing. In spite of these obstacles, however, in 1970 the member nations were still adhering to their original proposals.

LATIN EMPIRE OF CONSTANTINOPLE, was established after the fall of Constantinople to the Fourth Crusade in 1204. It was organized on the feudal pattern normal in western Europe and embraced a number of subordinate principalities, notably the kingdom of Thessalonica and the small states founded at Bodonitza, Athens, and in the Morea. The Latin empire was often engaged in conflict with the Bulgarians and with the Byzantines of Nikaea. Constantinople resisted successfully an attack carried out in 1236–37 by the combined forces of the Bulgarian tsar, John Asen II, and of the Nikaean basileus, John III Vatatzes. It fell, however, to Michael Palaiologos, assisted by the Genoese, in 1261—an event which marked the end of the Latin regime.

LATIN LEAGUE, political association of communities in Latium, near Rome, first important in checking the southern advance of the Etruscans in the late 6th cent. BC. At this time the Romans were excluded from the league, which included the cities of Aricia, Tusculum, Cora, Tibur, and Ardea, but after they clashed with the Latins at Lake Regillus (499 or 496), a treaty negotiated by Spurius Cassius allowed them entry on equal terms to face the common foe, the Aequi and the Volsci. Rome gradually gained the leadership in the 5th cent., and though the Latins exploited the Gallic invasion (390) to reassert their independence, their opposition was repressed by 358. After a final revolt (340–338) the league was dissolved, the cities being given higher status than other allies ('Latin rights'), but not the Roman citizenship.

LATIN RIGHTS, the status (*ius Latii*) of those members of the Latin League, *eg*, Ardea, Signia, and Sutrium, to whom Rome did not award full citizenship at its dissolution in 338 BC. Theoretically equal with Rome, they were, however, now each allied to Rome only and not to each other, and so became de facto politically inferior, holding an intermediate position between full Roman citizenship and the status of allies (*socii*). This intermediate status, extended subsequently to other communities, allowed trade with and intermarriage between Roman citizens, but not with other Latin cities. Inhabitants of such Latin towns could attain Roman citizenship by holding office in their communities or by taking residence in Rome and leaving a son at home. Between 89 BC, when all Italy received full citizenship, and AD 212, when the entire empire obtained it, communities abroad were frequently accorded the *ius Latii* as a mark of privileged status.

LATIN UNION (1865), monetary union formed between France, Belgium, Italy, and Switzerland, to which Greece, Serbia, Rumania, and some South American states later adhered. A fixed amount of silver was to be coined yearly in order to protect members against the relative appreciation of silver to gold due to gold discoveries in Australia and California. In 1873, owing to the depreciation of silver, the members agreed to suspend the free coinage of silver, thus dropping the double standard of gold and silver and virtually placing their currencies upon the gold standard.

LATITUDINARIANISM, movement in the Anglican Church emanating from Cambridge after the Restoration (1660), which stressed the virtues of charity, free enquiry, and tolerance. Its early adherents included John Tillotson, later Abp of Canterbury, and Edward Stillingfleet, later Bp of Worcester. It flourished in the comparative torpor of the 18th-cent. Church of England, but declined in the more fiercely divided Anglicanism of the 19th cent.

LATROBE, BENJAMIN HENRY (1764–1820), US architect, born and trained in England, who emigrated to the US (1796) and is regarded as the first professional American architect. His Bank of Pennsylvania in Philadelphia (1799–1801) helped to launch the Greek Revival in the US. He was appointed surveyor of public buildings by President Jefferson (1803), helped to design the Capitol, the White House, and other official buildings, and advised Jefferson on his plans for Virginia University. Among his other notable buildings are the Roman Catholic cathedral in Baltimore (1804–18) and St John's Church in Washington, DC (1816). Latrobe is also supposed to have introduced the Gothic Revival with

Sedgley, a house in Philadelphia (1799–1800). In all his work he was concerned with a commitment to rationality in architecture and a belief that function should largely dictate form.

LA TROBE, CHARLES JOSEPH (1801–75), Australian official who was superintendent of Port Phillip (1839–51) and first lieutenant-governor of Vic. (1851–4). His organization of the independent administration of Vic. was efficient and understanding—notably in dealings with diggers on the goldfields—by contrast with the efforts of his successor, Gov. Sir Charles Hotham.

LATTRE DE TASSIGNY, JEAN-JACQUES (1889–1952), French soldier and marshal of France, who served on the Western Front (1914–15) in the First World War, then in the Riff War in Morocco (1921–5). In the Second World War after 1940 his sympathies were with De Gaulle, but he remained under Vichy command until 1942, when he attempted to establish a bridgehead in the south of France for allied forces to cross from North Africa. He was imprisoned, but escaped and was brought to England by the RAF. He commanded the invasion of the south of France (Aug. 1944) and took part in resisting the German Ardennes offensive. After the war he served as commander-in-chief of the Brussels treaty forces at Fontainebleau (1948–50). He was appointed (1950) commander-in-chief and high commissioner in Indo-China.

LATVIA, independent Baltic republic (1921–40), area 64,700 sq. kms, population 2 million, comprising the old provinces of Livonia and Courland. Before declaring her independence in Nov. 1918 Latvia had undergone periods of Polish, Swedish, and finally Russian rule. In 1919 the Red Army invaded the Baltic states, as did German irregular troops, and it was not until mid-1920 that Latvia freed herself from foreign occupation. A democratic republican constitution was adopted and international recognition achieved (1921).

With a variety of national minorities forming 24 per cent of the population, Latvian politics were confused, and the existence of a bewildering number of parties and political blocs hindered stable government. Although the social democrat bloc held the largest number of seats in the *Saeima* (parliament), it was split among various factions and participated in no more than three of the 18 ministries formed (1918–34), the rest being dominated by the conservative–agrarian bloc. Fascist tendencies in politics began to appear early in the 1930s, and when (1934) the *Saeima* approved a social democrat motion to dismiss all fascists employed in the public service, the right-wing prime minister, Ulmanis, dissolved the *Saeima* and established an authoritarian regime. He later assumed the presidential powers (1936), and introduced a fascist form of government under his own dictatorship.

Up to the outbreak of the Second World War Latvia pursued a neutral foreign policy, in common with the other Baltic states, though in the late 1920s a series of non-aggression pacts was negotiated on Russia's initiative. After 1934 Ulmanis's government tried to avoid entanglement with Russia, and looked for security to an entente of the Baltic states, and later to Germany, with whom a non-aggression pact was signed (1939).

The Nazi–Soviet pact of Aug. 1939 placed Latvia in the Soviet sphere of influence. Despite Russian assurances that she had no designs on Latvia or the other Baltic states, she forced Latvia (Oct. 1939) to sign a pact of mutual assistance, whereby Russia was allowed to establish military bases on Latvian territory. In June 1940 the Soviet Union accused Latvia of having violated this pact, and invaded the country. Under Vyshinksy as commissar, Ulmanis headed a puppet government, but in July he was deported and a communist regime installed and in Aug. the country was annexed to the Soviet Union.

Latvia was invaded by Germany in 1941, the Germans being greeted at first as liberators. In the autumn of 1944 the Russians again occupied Latvia. Soviet rule was re-established under the 1940 constitution, and the country again incorporated into the Union.

J. Rutkis, *Latvia: country and people* (Stockholm, 1967).
A. Bilmanis, *A History of Latvia* (Princeton, 1951).   AJC

LAUD, WILLIAM (1573–1645), archbishop of Canterbury. After being president of St John's College, Oxford (1611), dean of Gloucester (1616), and Bp of St Davids, he won influence at court through his friendship with Buckingham and under King Charles I his advancement was rapid. He controlled ecclesiastical appointments and was made dean of the Chapel Royal and Bp of Bath and Wells (1626), privy councillor (1627), Bp of London (1628), Chancellor of Oxford (1630) and Abp of Canterbury (1633).

He opposed the Calvinist idea of predestination and wholeheartedly supported episcopacy and the preservation of a decent order and reverence in the services. He also organized visitations in his province to discipline clergy who were openly defying the law. He demanded the use of the surplice and a proper ceremonial; clergy were to read only the service laid down in the prayer-book and the altar was to be railed at the east end. He drove the money-changers from St Paul's Cathedral, London, reformed the statutes and discipline of his university, ordered bishops to reside in their sees and tried to increase clerical stipends.

Yet Laud was narrow and personally unattractive, repelling many who were in sympathy with his ideals. He also provoked opposition by trying to revive the medieval status of the Church as the arbiter of faith and morals. He used the Crown's ecclesiastical supremacy to crush dissent, often appearing in person in the conciliar courts to punish the conventiclers and pamphleteers who defied his edicts. His enemies naturally, but unjustly, denounced him as a papist while he was making further enemies at court by denouncing the queen's Catholic confessors and her way of life.

The whole edifice of his authority collapsed when he and Charles raised a rebellion by imposing a prayerbook on the Scots. Laud was impeached and committed to the Tower (1641), where he was kept for more than two years without trial. A charge of treason being impossible to sustain, he was condemned by attainder and executed.

H. R. Trevor-Roper, *Archbishop Laud* (London, 1962).   MMR

LAUDERDALE, JOHN MAITLAND, Duke of (Scottish) (1616–82), secretary for Scotland (1660–80). He was an active Presbyterian who became involved in English affairs after the Solemn League and Covenant (1643), for which he was one of the Scottish commissioners. In 1645 he tried to mediate with King Charles I for a Presbyterian settlement in the Uxbridge negotiations. Though still working for Presbyterianism, he gradually shifted to the king from parliament and was largely responsible for the Engagement (1647) which Charles I signed. After the second Civil War he became a friend of the Prince of Wales (later Charles II), and accompanied him on his invasion of England (1651). He was captured at Worcester (1651) and imprisoned till 1660. On the Restoration of Charles II, he was appointed secretary for Scotland. He soon out-manœuvred his enemies and emerged as the most powerful man in Scotland. The fall of Clarendon (1667) strengthened his position in England, and saw the fulfilment of his 'nationalist' policy of excluding English influence from Scottish government. His Scottish administration was often marked by arbitrary rule and cruel repression which led to continuous demands from the English opposition for his removal, but his undeviating loyalty to Charles enabled him to survive. He alone of the Cabal survived its dissolution. Lauderdale's attempt to turn Scotland into 'a citadel for his majesty's service' was closely bound up with his attempt to gain a political union with

England (1669–70) which failed because of the opposition of the king and the English nation. Later, Lauderdale's government grew more brutal. His fall in 1680 was welcomed.

M. Lee, *The Cabal* (Urbana, 1965).
W. C. MacKenzie, *John Maitland, Duke of Lauderdale* (London, 1923).   CJ

LAUDERDALE, JAMES MAITLAND, 8th Earl of (Scottish) (1759–1839), Scottish lawyer, politician, and economist. His *Inquiry into the Nature and Origin of Public Wealth* (1804) contains one of the first references to the concept of utility.

LAUFFELDT, BATTLE OF (2 July 1747), victory of Marshal Maurice de Saxe over an Anglo-Dutch force under the Duke of Cumberland at Lauffeldt, near Maastricht, during the War of the Austrian Succession. The French field commander marched his troops 80 kms in two days to relieve the fortress and broke the allied lines in a surprise attack.

LAURANA, FRANCESCO DA (d. 1502), Dalmatian sculptor whose works display a wide variety of styles, adapted to his particular commissions, from the classical reliefs on the triumphal arch of Alfonso of Aragon to the rough and expressive late Gothic of the Calvary at San Didier at Avignon.

LAURANA, LUCIANO DA (1420–79), Dalmatian architect, famous for his contribution to the building of one of the earliest and most perfect palaces in the Renaissance style, constructed at Urbino by Duke Federigo. The original design may have been due to others, including perhaps Alberti and Piero della Francesca, but Laurana was the architect in charge (1468–72) when the palace was mainly built.

LAUREL, JOSE PONCIANO (1891–1959), Filipino politician, lawyer and scholar, who served his country for almost three decades in the executive, legislative, and judicial branches of government. He was appointed under secretary of the interior in 1922, and secretary (1923). He was elected a senator in 1926 and during the last three years of his term he assumed the position of majority floor leader. As a member of the constitutional convention which met in 1934, he is referred to as one of the 'Seven Wise Men' who drafted the Philippine constitution. Under the Commonwealth government he became an associate justice of the Supreme Court and in 1941 was concurrently acting chief justice of the Supreme Court and secretary of justice. During the Second World War, he was successively commissioner of justice, commissioner of the interior, chairman of the Preparatory Commission for Philippine Independence, and president of the republic of the Philippines (1943). After defending himself against charges of treason after the Second World War, Laurel was set free under President Roxas's general amnesty (1948). In 1949 he was defeated in the presidential election and in 1951 headed the list of successful senatorial candidates. During the last years of his life, believing that the fundamental objective of education should be nationalism and patriotism, Laurel founded (1952) the Lyceum to provide a 'university of the masses'.   JMSa

LAURENS, HENRY (1724–92), American merchant, planter, and statesman, who became a moderate leader of the Revolutionary movement in the South, was elected to the first Provincial Congress (1774), and served on many important committees in the Continental Congress (1777–80). He was captured by the British (1780), but was exchanged for Lord Cornwallis two years later; whereupon he joined Franklin, Adams, and Jay in Paris and played a valuable part in the peace negotiations. He represented American interests in England in an unofficial capacity in 1783–4.

LAURIER, SIR WILFRED (1841–1919), Canadian politician of Roman Catholic, French-speaking background. He began his career as editor of *Le Défricheur* (1866), which was banned by Bp Laflèche for its anti-clericalism. He served in the Quebec Legislature (1871–4), and in 1874 entered the Dominion House of Commons. In 'Discours sur le Liberalisme politique', a speech delivered to the Club Canadien of Quebec (20 June 1877), he moderated his political beliefs so as to identify himself with the British liberal tradition rather than with the doctrinaire anti-clericalism of France. The speech had an immediate effect and Laurier was appointed minister of inland revenue (1877–8) in the Mackenzie government, and in 1887 became party leader. He was the first French Canadian and Roman Catholic prime minister of Canada (1896–1911), and during this period was the dominant figure in Canadian politics, winning increased majorities in 1900 and 1904. Having resolved the ethnic conflict created by the Manitoba Schools controversy (1897), he was faced with the problem of Canada's relationship with Britain. He tried to balance loyalty to the empire with French Canadian fear of British domination. At the Imperial Conferences (1897, 1902, 1907), though he supported preferential tariffs, he avoided further Canadian commitment to Britain, but was strongly attacked by the nationalists, led by Henri Bourassa, for the decision to send troops to South Africa (1899). Laurier rejected a direct contribution to the British navy (1907), but aroused Imperial sentiment among English Canadians as well as anti-Imperial feeling among French Canadians by the compromise which established a small Canadian naval force (1910). The Liberals, split by the American Reciprocity agreement, were defeated (1911). Laurier's greatest achievement, which was helped by increased prosperity, was perhaps the rapid settlement of the West, encouraged by vigorous recruitment and assistance to settlers. He continued as liberal leader in opposition, supporting the Borden government until the conscription issue (1917), when he refused to join the Union government. In the bitter election which followed, the Liberals were again divided and Laurier tried to reconstruct the party.

Sir John S. Willison, *Sir Wilfred Laurier and the Liberal Party* (Toronto, 1926).

LAURIUM, MT, 35 kms south-east of Athens, site of silver-mines exploited by the Athenians down to *c.* 100 BC, and especially from *c.* 483—when the use of new rich veins provided the wealth with which to build a large fleet to oppose the Persians—until 413, when the Spartans occupied Decelea in the great Peloponnesian War.

LAUSANNE, TREATY OF (1923), peace settlement between the Allies and Turkey after the First World War. The delay in its negotiation was due to the emergence of the Turkish nationalist movement and the 'Turks' refusal to accept the treaty of Sèvres, which the Allies had tried to impose on Turkey (1920). At the end of 1918 an armistice had been concluded between the Allies and the Ottoman empire—which was then occupied by British and French troops, the pre-war Young Turk movement, which had striven for a national revival, having disintegrated—and the Allies set up a reactionary puppet government in Constantinople. They were, however, unable to reach agreement on Turkey's fate, and in May 1919 Greek forces seized the initiative by occupying Izmir and the surrounding area. The Constantinople government prevented organized Turkish resistance, fearing that it might turn into a national revolution directed against itself. Despite this, the call to resist Greece did form a new rallying-cry for nationalist forces, which gathered under Mustafa Kemal.

Meanwhile, the Sèvres treaty was under negotiation, and was signed on 10 Aug. 1920. It amounted to the mutilation of Turkey, for she was to lose outright the Arab areas—Armenia, the Kurdish region, southern Anatolia, and European Turkey—and to retain only a nominal sovereignty over the Greek-occupied area. The Kemalist forces redoubled their military struggle against the Allies and Greece, and liberated the country from Greek troops in three campaigns (1920–2). At the same time, the nationalists forged ahead with their political organization, evolving policies and programmes, and setting up a rival government in Ankara (1920).

In Oct. 1922, after the defeat of the Greek army, Britain and Turkey signed an armistice, the French, Italian, and Russian governments having already begun to make their peace with Kemal separately. A peace conference opened in Lausanne in Nov., and the treaty was signed on 24 July 1923. Under its terms, Turkish sovereignty was re-established in all Turkish territories, Kemal having already abandoned any claim to the Arab areas. An exchange of population between Greece and Turkey was agreed (a somewhat savage but nevertheless effective means of solving the vexed problem of national minorities), the straits were demilitarized, and the Ottoman debt distributed among the succession states.

The Lausanne treaty fulfilled most of Kemal's demands, and achieved the reversal of the Sèvres terms, which had in any case been dangerously harsh. Because the Lausanne treaty was negotiated and not imposed, and represented the aspirations of Turkey herself rather than the unrealistic attitudes of the Allies, it proved one of the most successful and durable of the post-war settlements.

B. Lewis, *The Emergence of Modern Turkey* (London, 1968). H. N. Howard, *The Partition of Turkey 1913–23* (London, 1931). AJC

LAUSANNE CONFERENCE (1932), between Germany and the First World War Allies, to discuss the possibility of abolishing German reparations payments. It took place against a background of world financial and economic chaos, then reaching its climax, and followed the expiration of the one-year Hoover moratorium on international debt repayments, and Germany's subsequent announcement (Nov. 1931) that further payments of reparations would jeopardize her economy. In Dec. an advisory committee of the Bank of International Settlements met at Basle, and reported that Germany would in fact be unable to pay her next annual instalment, due in July 1932. A conference on this problem, and on the general situation in international debts, was proposed for Jan. 1932.

But it was postponed for six months, owing to disagreements between the main reparations creditors, Britain and France. France was anxious lest Britain should agree to the German call for a total abolition of reparations, while Britain was hoping that a delay of some months would encourage the US to adopt a more flexible attitude to the debt situation, and perhaps join in the conference. When it was finally convened in June, however, the US did not attend. Britain, as chairman, tried at first to secure the cancellation of all reparations, but in the face of French opposition, a compromise was agreed. Germany's unpaid debt was assessed at some three billion RM (£150 million), and bonds to this value were to be deposited by her with the Bank of International Settlements, it being agreed that they would be marketed after three years at a guaranteed price of 90 per cent par or more. By this means it was hoped that Germany's credit would be strengthened, and in effect the plan amounted to the sacrifice of most of the Allied claims in the interests of this achievement. However, ratification was to depend on the conclusion of a settlement between the US and her debtors over the adjustment of war debts owed to her, *ie*, the European Allies could not afford the abolition of reparations unless at the same time their own war debts were remitted. But despite representations to the US, including in Dec. 1932 a solidly argued British statement supporting the remission, the US Congress refused to agree. Shortly afterwards the US opted out of international efforts at financial and economic stabilization with the result that the Lausanne proposals were not ratified and therefore did not come into force. Germany's debt remained unpaid, and was ultimately abrogated unilaterally by Hitler.

W. A. Lewis, *Economic Survey 1919–39* (London, 1949).
AJC

LAUZON, JEAN DE (1584–1666), governor of New France (1651–6). When the Co. of New France (the Hundred Associates) was founded (1627) he became president of its first board of directors. He gained the seigniory of Lauzon, near Quebec (1636).

LAVAL, PIERRE (1883–1945), French politician and leading figure in the Vichy government, who started his political career as a socialist, having joined the party in 1903, and entered the chamber as deputy for a working-class Paris constituency in 1914. During the First World War he advocated a compromise peace with Germany, thereby earning a reputation for defeatism that lost him his parliamentary seat in 1919, although at the same time he was regarded by the police as a dangerous revolutionary. After the war he began a move away from socialism that was to culminate in his conversion to fascism. He re-entered the chamber in 1924 as a moderate associate of Caillaux and the radicals. In 1925 he became minister of works, and was also secretary to Briand, whose policy of reconciliation with Germany he supported. The dominant motif in Laval's politics, consistent throughout his career, despite violent shift from one end of the party spectrum to the other, was his passionate attachment to peace—a policy which resolved itself in collaboration with Germany during the Second World War.

After two brief periods of ministerial office (1926, 1930), Laval became prime minister after a government crisis (1931–2). Later, as foreign minister (1934–6), he was responsible for delaying the conclusion of the Franco-Soviet pact, signed in May 1935, but not ratified until after Laval's fall. From the middle of 1935 he was also acting prime minister, his acceleration towards the right being shown by his patronizing an influential neo-fascist movement and adopting a pro-Mussolini line in the Abyssinian War. After the Hoare–Laval plan to partition Abyssinia, he was forced out of office by public disgust.

Laval remained in the background for the next four years, though vociferous in his support of the appeasement policy. After the fall of France in June 1940, he was active in the creation of the Vichy government. He advocated French co-operation in the Nazi plan for a European 'New Order', arguing that France had little to gain from an intransigent hostility to Germany, and that even a future dominated by Germany was preferable to a communist and Russian-dominated Europe. In Oct. 1940 he was appointed foreign minister, but in Dec. Pétain dismissed and imprisoned him, after discovering that Laval had been involved in a plot to deprive him of power. Laval engineered his own return to power in April 1942, when he became Pétain's deputy and effective head of the regime. In this position he tried to mitigate the severity of German rule in France, though he became increasingly powerless as time went on. In Aug. 1944 he tried to dissociate himself from Germany and assemble a new government in preparation for the impending liberation of France, but the attempt failed and he fled to Spain. A year later he was forcibly returned to France, and in Oct. 1945 was executed for treason.

G. Warner, *Pierre Laval and the Eclipse of France* (London, 1968).
AJC

LAVAL DE MONTMORENCY, FRANÇOIS-XAVIER (1623–1708), Roman Catholic bishop in New France. He was born in France, educated in Jesuit colleges, and went to Canada as vicar apostolic of New France and titular Bp of Petraea (1659). He became involved in a long dispute with the archdeacon of Rouen, who had hitherto exerted jurisdiction over the Church in New France. When the pope created Laval Bp of Quebec (1674), control passed from Rouen to Quebec. He quarrelled with successive governors over his opposition to the sale of brandy to the Indians and his determination to maintain episcopal control of ecclesiastical affairs. He founded the seminary of Quebec (1663), a junior seminary (1668), and an industrial school (1678).

LA VALETTE, JEAN PARISON DE (1494–1568), French general, governor of Tripoli (1537) and founder of Valetta, capital of Malta. He was elected grandmaster of the order of Malta (Aug. 1557) and successfully defended the island against a severe siege by the Turks (May–Aug. 1565).

LAVALLEJA, JUAN ANTONIO (1778–1853), Uruguayan patriot and leader of the '33 immortals' who invaded Uruguay from Buenos Aires (1825) in order to incite a revolt against Brazilian rule. Their action led to war between Argentina and Brazil, and ultimately (1828) to Uruguayan independence.

LAVARACK, SIR JOHN DUDLEY (1885–1957), Australian soldier, who was chief of the Australian general staff (1935–1939). During the Second World War he commanded the 7th Division, 2nd AIF (1940–1), 1 Australian Corps (1941–2), and 1st Australian Army (1942–4). He was governor of Qld (1946–57).

LA VÉRENDRYE, PIERRE GAULTIER DE VARENNES, Sieur de (1685–1749), fur trader and explorer in New France. With his four sons he sought to extend the fur trade and find a route to the Pacific (1731–43). A chain of forts established by them in the west became centres of the fur trade and restricted the supply of furs to the English Hudson's Bay Co. Their explorations helped to open up the western plains of Canada. In 1738 La Vérendrye reached the Missouri river; and his sons may have reached the Rocky Mountains (1743).

LAVO (LO-HU, LOPBURI), western outpost of the Cambodian empire of Angkor before the 13th cent., and a centre of Theravada Buddhism. It may have had a substantial Mon population by the 7th cent. After being intermittently independent in the 12th and 13th cents, it became an important provincial centre in the kingdom of Ayudhya and in the 17th cent. became the summer residence of King Narai.

LAVOISIER, ANTOINE LAURENT DE (1743–94), French chemist and founder of modern chemistry, who discovered the composition of water and the process of combustion as reaction with oxygen.

LAW, ANDREW BONAR (1858–1923), British politician, leader of the Unionist Party (1911–21), and prime minister (1922–3). He was educated in Glasgow and became an iron merchant. He entered politics (1900) as a Conservative-Unionist, supported Tariff Reform, and replaced Balfour as leader (1911) after the latter's weak handling of the House of Lords crisis (1909–11). Law championed Ulster's resistance in the crisis (1912–14) and entered Asquith's coalition as colonial secretary (1915–16). He helped to oust Asquith (1916) and as Lloyd George's chancellor of the exchequer introduced National Savings. Lloyd George relied greatly on his advice in the most successful political partnership of the war. Law withdrew the party's support from Lloyd George after the war and in 1922 won the election and the premiership, from which ill-health forced him to retire after seven months. His cabinet was the most aristocratic of the period, and Law himself was a great debater, an able financier, and a stubborn fighter. He was a man of moderation, who became known, perhaps unfairly, as the unknown prime minister.

LAW, JOHN OF LAURISTON (1671–1729), Scottish financier and speculator, son of an Edinburgh goldsmith and banker, on whose death he moved to London (1691). Law fell into debt and was imprisoned for killing an opponent in a duel, but escaped to Amsterdam (1695) and travelled in Europe, where he studied finance. He returned to Scotland with financial proposals for a bank in Edinburgh and presented the Scottish parliament with a memorandum, 'Considerations on Currency and Commerce' (1700), in which he advocated the use of paper money, but his scheme was rejected. He then spent some years on the continent as a gambling adventurer, where he became friends with the Duke of Orléans, regent of France (1716). Through Orléans's patronage Law obtained letters patent with which to found a private bank (May 1716), then received the concession of the trade monopoly in Louisiana which enabled him to establish the Western Co. (*Compagnie de l'Occident*) in Aug. 1717. The bank, of which Law was made a director, was transformed into a royal bank (4 Dec. 1718); branches were formed in the provinces, and it was given the right to issue paper notes and collect taxes, hitherto in the hands of the Farmers-General. Law then took over the national debt, offering the *rentiers* shares in his company, while in 1720 the bank and the trading company were officially merged. Despite opposition from politicians and financiers, *eg*, the Paris brothers, Law's trading company was granted the total monopoly of French trade and became the Co. of the Indies (*Compagnie des Indes*), and by 1720 his 'system' had reached its apogee and he controlled the French economy. He became a naturalized Frenchman, was converted to Catholicism, and finally was appointed controller-general of finances (5 Jan. 1720). Yet despite the stimulus which his schemes provided for commercial life, the actual volume of commerce was insufficient to support his complex 'system'. In March 1720 the crash came, Law fled to Brussels, his company was liquidated, and many were ruined.

LAWES, SIR JOHN BENNET (1814–99), British agricultural scientist, who in 1843 established a factory for producing superphosphate, which was the foundation of the synthetic fertilizer industry. Concurrently with these industrial interests he carried out, in collaboration with J. H. Gilbert (1817–1901), extended field trials on the mineral requirements of important crops, at his family estate at Rothamsted. In 1872 Lawes established a trust for the continuation of the work there, which became a foremost international agricultural research station.

LAWN TENNIS ASSOCIATION (1888), body which formulated the rules for the new game of lawn tennis pioneered by Major Wingfield, who patented 'a new and improved portable court for playing the ancient game of tennis'. The association developed from the All England Croquet and Lawn Tennis Club and began the annual Wimbledon championships in 1877 with 22 competitors.

LAWRENCE OF THE PUNJAB AND OF GRATELY, JOHN LAWRENCE, 1st Baron (1811–79), viceroy and governor-general of India (1864–9). He entered the East India Co.'s civil service in 1830 and spent most of his early service as magistrate and collector in the Delhi area. After the annexation of the Punjab (1849) he served with his brother, Henry, on the Punjab Board of Administration, where they differed over policy. Whereas Henry favoured leniency to the Sikh aristocracy John wanted to base British rule on a prosperous and contented peasantry. In 1853 John was made chief commissioner of the Punjab, where he reorganized the administration, created a police force, and built roads and canals. During the Mutiny he kept the Punjab loyal and sent a Sikh army to relieve Delhi. Fortunately Canning rejected Lawrence's unsound proposal to evacuate Peshawar during the Mutiny.

Lawrence was in England as a member of the secretary of state's council (1859–64), when he became viceroy. In 1864 he authorized the annexation of the Bhutan Duars. He also had to deal with the Orissa famine of 1866 and another in upper India (1868–9). He laid the foundations of a more humane famine policy and enunciated the principle that it was the duty of officers to prevent death from starvation. He created a department of irrigation, held an enquiry into the state of the Oudh peasantry, and helped secure peasant rights with the Punjab Rent Act (1868). His frontier policy was one of non-interference in Afghan affairs and he made no attempt to recognize Sher Ali as amir until his power had been firmly established. He believed that the Indus should be the boundary of India and opposed any advance beyond it. This policy of 'masterly inactivity' lasted until Lytton's viceroyalty (1876–80).

R. Bosworth Smith, *Life of Lord Lawrence*, 2 vols (London, 1883).   CCD

LAWRENCE, DAVID HERBERT (1885–1930), English novelist and poet, who was the son of a Midlands miner. He worked first as a clerk and then as a teacher in Nottingham before going to London in 1908. His first book, *The White Peacock*, was published in 1911, and by 1913, with the publication of *Sons and Lovers*, he had established himself as a writer. Other works included *The Rainbow* (1915), *Kangaroo* (1923), *The Plumed Serpent* (1926), and *Lady Chatterley's Lover* (1928). Seeing man as a 'thought-adventurer', Lawrence offered in his books an account of his own feelings and perceptions, magnified by his powerful style so that they emerged in writing as emotions of often shattering violence. There was a resurgence of interest in his work in the 1960s, in a society less restricted by taboos on the discussion of sex that had earlier obscured an assessment of its literary merits.

LAWRENCE, ERNEST ORLANDO (1901–58), US nuclear physicist, who built a high-energy particle accelerator (1930), the cyclotron, to initiate and study nuclear reactions. Advances in nuclear physics since have largely stemmed from the use of this and related instruments. In 1939 Lawrence was awarded the Nobel Physics Prize. With his collaborators he pioneered important applications of some of the artificial radioisotopes produced.

LAWRENCE, SIR HENRY MONTGOMERY (1806–57), British soldier and colonial official in the service of the East India Co. who took part in the First Burmese War, the First Afghan War, and the First Sikh War. After a period in the revenue department he was transferred to the political service in the Punjab. He was Resident in Nepal (1843–6). After the annexation of the Punjab (1849) he was president of the Board of Administration. He died of wounds in the siege of Lucknow (1857).

LAWRENCE, THOMAS EDWARD (1888–1935), British soldier, scholar, and diplomat. He went to Mesopotamia with a British Museum archaeological expedition (1911) and also worked for a War Office survey, using the opportunity to travel throughout Syria and Mesopotamia. On the outbreak of the First World War he was given a post in the war office, then sent by Kitchener (1915) to Egypt to work with a skeleton military intelligence service. He played an important part in instigating the Arab revolt against Turkish rule and begged leave to go to Jidda. From there he went inland, established a close relationship with Emir Faysal, and for the rest of the war organized and inspired the revolt under Faysal's leadership. In swift and dramatic desert actions he succeeded in breaking Turkish communications by blowing up the Hejaz railway, ranged north into Syria, and then struck south to open a route to Aqaba (Aug. 1917) and finally, with the consent of Gen. Allenby, advanced with Faysal to reach Damascus before the British (1918). After the war, he went to Paris to try to influence the decisions of the peace conference, but failed to do so; Faysal was obliged to leave Damascus and Syria was placed under French mandate. Lawrence was elected a Fellow of All Souls College, Oxford (1919), then appointed by Winston Churchill to the colonial office as adviser (1921). He left in 1922 and sought anonymity by enlisting in the ranks of the RAF, then joined the tank corps (1923), again in the ranks, and was transferred back to the air force (1925). In 1927 he changed his name to Shaw. He left the RAF in 1935 and shortly afterwards died from an accident on his motor-cycle. His books include the *Seven Pillars of Wisdom* (1926), an account of the Arab Revolt, and a translation of the *Odyssey* (1932).

LAWSON, HENRY (1867–1922), Australian poet and short-story writer, and a central figure in the Australian literary tradition. His prose, which distilled the ethos of the 1890s, included *While the Billy Boils* (1896) and *Joe Wilson and His Mates* (1901).

LAYARD, SIR AUSTEN HENRY (1817–94), British archaeologist, politician, diplomat, and author, who excavated Nimrud and Nineveh (1845–52). He was under-secretary for foreign affairs (1852, 1861–6) and commissioner of works (1868–9). As ambassador in Istanbul (1877–80), he was an advocate of British support for the Turks against Russia and of reform in the Ottoman empire. He published *Early Adventures in Persia, Susiana and Babylonia* (1887).

LAZARUS, EMMA (1849–87), US poet and essayist, whose sonnet celebrating the unveiling of the Statue of Liberty (28 Oct. 1886) was engraved on its pedestal. She was a supporter of Judaism and of aid for Jewish immigrants. Her works include *Admetus and Other Poems* (1871) and *Songs of a Semite* (1882).

LE DYNASTY, reigning dynasty in Viet-nam from 1428 to 1789, with some interruption in the 16th cent. Founded by the hero Le Loi, after the expulsion of the Chinese, who had occupied the country for 20 years (1407–27), the dynasty reached the peak of its power under Le Thanh-Tong (1460–97). In the early 16th cent. the imperial clan lost power to a number of other clans, notably the Nguyen, Trinh, and Mac, and a rebellion in Tongking in 1516 almost led to its overthrow. During the next ten years, power came into the hands of Mac Dang Dung, who in 1527 overthrew the emperor and founded his own dynasty (1527–92). But the Mac could only control Tongking, and the southerly province of Thanh-Hoa remained loyal to the Le. With the aid of the Trinh and Nguyen clans, a new Le emperor was proclaimed in Thanh-Hoa in 1532; and in 1592 the Le supporters finally defeated the Mac and restored the Le at Hanoi. By this time, however, real power lay with the Trinh and the Nguyen. The remaining period of Le rule (1592–1789) was one in which the emperor had only religious and ceremonial functions, the kingdom being divided between the Trinh, in control at Hanoi, and the Nguyen, at Hue. The dynasty was finally overthrown, as were the Trinh, as a result of the Tay-Son rebellion, which began in 1773.

LEAGUE FOR SOCIAL RECONSTRUCTION in Canada, political movement founded in 1932. The league was concerned about social inequalities accentuated by the Depression. It helped to found the co-operative Commonwealth Federation (1932), which was influenced by the League's *Social Planning for Canada* (1935). The League's publication *Social Purpose for Canada* (1961) influenced Canadian policy in the 1960s.

LEAGUE OF COMMUNISTS OF YUGOSLAVIA (Savez Komunista Jugoslavije—SKJ), formerly the Communist Party of Yugoslavia (KPJ), founded (April 1919) as the Socialist Workers' Party of Yugoslavia (Communist), an amalgamation of various left-wing socialist groups. This party announced its adherence to the Comintern and in June 1920 changed its name to the Communist Party of Yugoslavia. In the elections of Nov. 1920 the party won almost 200,000 popular votes and 58 seats in the Constituent Assembly, in which it became the third largest party; unlike most other parties, which were regionally based, it won support from all areas. The party was banned in Dec. 1920, and remained illegal throughout the inter-war period. With its leadership

in exile, the party was riven by factions, which repeated Comintern intervention did nothing to reconcile. Indeed, under Comintern influence the KPJ not only came out in favour of the dismemberment of Yugoslavia, but after 1928 adopted a policy of armed insurrection, which resulted in many arrests, reducing the party's numbers to a few hundreds in all. Both these tactics were abandoned in the mid-1930s; and with the appointment of Josip Broz (Tito) to lead the party inside Yugoslavia, its fortunes improved. By 1940 it numbered over 6000 members. But its real growth came from its leadership of the Partisan resistance to the Germans during the Second World War, from which it emerged in a position that enabled it to grasp power quickly. The success of the Partisans gave Tito his own military and administrative cadres with which he successfully challenged Stalin in 1948–9. Under the impact of this conflict the Yugoslav party developed its own critique of Stalinism as a bureaucratic form of state capitalism, and reached conclusions about its own practice, 'workers' self-management' (later, 'social self-management' being adopted as a general principle of economic and social organization, and the role of the party being redefined. The party (now renamed the League of Communists—SKJ) was to 'guide' and not to 'rule', ie, to withdraw from direct interference in day-to-day decision-making, relying instead on the persuasive powers of its members at their places of work. Ultimate power still rested with the party, but the rein on which it ran the country was looser and the political atmosphere correspondingly freer than in any other communist state. Internationally, the SKJ was somewhat isolated from the world communist movement, and its relations with the Soviet party fluctuated widely.   RKK

LEAGUE OF NATIONS, international organization established in 1920 under Part I of the treaty of Versailles. Its formation was foreshadowed in the last of President Wilson's Fourteen Points (1918), and was regarded by him as indispensable to the preservation of peace and security in the post-war world. However, contrary to Wilson's hopes the US Congress refused (1920) to ratify the Versailles treaty or join the league. Both in practical terms and in spirit, this was a poor augury for the future of the league as a world peacekeeper.

The 26 articles of the league covenant bound member nations to respect each other's independence, and committed them to reject war as a means of settling international disputes. These were to be submitted to the league or other arbitrators, who were to report within six months. If arbitration failed, a further three months was to elapse before resort to war, the intention being to enforce a cooling-off period in acute situations. Under the controversial Article 16, sanctions could be enforced against any state failing to observe these provisions, or committing acts of aggression, and these sanctions varied in severity from the severance of trade relations to the use of armed force. Further clauses provided for the registration of international treaties, in an attempt to prevent a revival of the secret diplomacy which was held largely responsible for the 1914 war; for arms reductions; and for the observance of elementary human rights by signatory nations. The league assembly, consisting eventually of 54 member states, met annually in Geneva. The council, comprising Britain, France, and Russia as permanent members and 12 other nations in rotation, met about three times a year. The league maintained various international organizations such as the ILO and the Court of Justice at The Hague, and devoted major efforts to the resettlement of refugees.

Although the league represented a genuine effort to enforce international standards of diplomatic behaviour, in practice it soon showed grave weaknesses. The defection of the US at the start was a major blow. The organizational structure proved to be too loose, since the league lacked an international military force and member nations declined to limit their sovereignty by concessions to international authority. However, it was not the internal weakness of the league alone which hindered its efficacy, but the gravity of international problems arising from the deficiencies of the post-war peace settlements, which formed a chronic threat to the status quo.

The league's first clear failure, after initial successes in the 1920s, was its impotence in the face of Japan's aggression in Manchuria (1932). Japan, on being condemned by the league, simply withdrew her membership; a course later followed by Nazi Germany (1933), and by Italy (1937) after the feeble attempt to impose sanctions after her aggression in Abyssinia. By the time war broke out (1939), nations had ceased to rely on collective security through the league, but had returned instead to the traditional system of defensive alliances and power blocs. Germany's eastern European annexations (1938), which led to the Second World War, marked the final demoralization of the League. It was officially dissolved in April 1946, when it was replaced by the United Nations.

F. P. Walters, *A History of the League of Nations*, 2 vols (London, 1952).
G. M. Gathorne-Hardy, *A Short History of International Affairs* (London, 1950). AJC

LEAGUE OF THE RHINE (1658), alliance of German princes of the Rhine area, formed by the efforts of the Elector of Mainz and Cardinal Mazarin to defend 'German liberties' and French interests against the Habsburgs. Although its German members turned a blind eye to French conquests in the Low Countries in 1657–9, Louis XIV's aggression against the Dutch and France's invasion of Franche-Comté (1668) undermined the league.

LEAKAGES SCANDAL (1954), or *'affaire des fuites'*, right-wing attempt in France to discredit the cabinet of Mendès-France. The leakages themselves were reports that appeared in the Paris press of secret meetings of the Defence Council between July 1953 and Sept. 1954. Although the information leaked did have some military value in the context of the Indo-China war, its significance was inflated out of all proportion and the incidents used in a right-wing smear campaign directed principally against the minister of the interior, Mitterand, who was accused of responsibility for the leakages. A key figure in the affair was the recipient of much of the leaked information, a journalist called Baranès, who was both a communist and a police spy, and it remained uncertain which role he was playing at the time. Members of the police force were undoubtedly implicated, and obstructed a proper investigation into the scandal and the allegations against Mitterand. A judicial tribunal eventually conducted an enquiry, though its authority was marred by a bias against Mitterand, so that much information of material importance was discounted. It finally found (1956) the two secretaries of the Defence Council, Turpin and Labrusse, guilty of leaking the reports, but their sentences were light and their guilt adjudged nominal.

The scandal occurred against the background of the French defeat in Indo-China and her mounting colonial troubles, and her history of internal instability and disunity since the war; it was exploited as part of the deliberate strategy of fascist, Poujadist, and ultra-nationalist elements in the state to destroy the credibility of the democratic alternative to authoritarian government in France.

LEAVIS, FRANK RAYMOND (1895–), English scholar, critic, and editor of the influential critical journal *Scrutiny* (1932–53). He has given his name to a school of literary criticism characterized by a 'practical' approach to literature and insistence on rigidly high standards in both creative and critical writing. These principles, and his belief in the universality and inseparability of areas of knowledge, have given him a wide controversial fame. They provoked persistent conflict with his main critic, Lord Snow, whose concept of the 'two cultures' Leavis rejected.

LEBANESE CONSTITUTIONAL BLOC (1932), political grouping conceived by Bishara al-Khuri and launched (1934) in opposition to Émile Eddé and French domination. Its name was changed (1955) to Constitutional Union when an attempt was made to convert it into a mass party.

LEBANESE CRISIS (1958), political struggle in Lebanon between President Chamoun and opposition politicians organized as the National Front (1957), which became an international incident. Muslim opponents of Chamoun condemned his pro-Western policy and advocated the accession of Lebanon to the newly formed United Arab Republic. An armed insurrection broke out in May. Following the July Iraqi revolution, Chamoun appealed for US help, and US marines landed on 15 July. On 31 July Gen. Fu'ad Shihab was elected to succeed Chamoun and, after further Christian–Muslim clashes (Sept.–Oct.), arranged a compromise settlement and the departure of US forces.

LEBANESE NATIONAL BLOC, political grouping which emerged in 1930s under the leadership of Émile Eddé. Raymond Eddé, son of Émile, tried unsuccessfully to convert it into a mass party in mid-1950s.

LEBANESE NATIONAL PACT (1943), unwritten agreement between the Muslim Al-Sulh family and Bishara al-Khuri by which Muslims agreed to support Lebanese independence in return for Christian recognition of its Arab nature. It later developed into an elaborate system for dividing political power and offices among the Lebanese religious communities, *eg*, six Christian to five Muslim deputies, the president a Maronite, the prime minister a Sunni Muslim, the speaker of the chamber a Shi'ite, etc. The pact became the basis first of the struggle for independence against France and, subsequently, of Lebanese political life.

LEBANESE PROTOCOL (1861). Following the sectarian Lebanese civil war (1858–60) and the 1860 massacres of Christians in Syria, European diplomatic pressure, applied chiefly by France, which sent troops to Lebanon (1860), forced the Ottoman government, although it had already restored order, to concede a new form of government for Lebanon. The Règlement Organique (1861) made Mount Lebanon into an autonomous Ottoman province under European guarantee, with a Christian Ottoman governor (mutasarrif), assisted by a council representing the various religious communities. As amended (1864), the protocol provided the successful basis for the government of Mount Lebanon until 1914 and paved the way for its ultimate separation from the rest of Syria.

LEBENSRAUM, German word for 'living-space'. The term was adopted by the Nazi Party as a political slogan, and referred to the demand for additional territory to compensate for Germany's alleged over-population and to create a rational politico-economic unit. A policy of eastwards expansion was envisaged, both because the supposedly agricultural nature of Germany's economy and culture demanded the acquisition of the plains of eastern Europe, and because a strategic and historical right to these areas was claimed. The policy was largely, if temporarily, realized by occupation and annexation in the Second World War.

LEBER, JULIUS (1891–1945), German social democrat and member of the anti-Nazi resistance. He was a newspaper editor who belonged to the moderate wing of the SPD and had been active in the movement to remodel German socialism before 1933. He was arrested after the Nazi take-over, but released in 1937 and devoted himself to resistance work, co-operating closely with the military opposition. He was executed in Jan. 1945.

LEBNA DENGEL (*reg.* 1508–40), Emperor of Ethiopia before the major invasion of Ahmad Gragn. He came to the throne as a child, and his foreign policy was at first framed by his grandmother, Empress Eleni, who tried to obtain allies against the Muslim principalities to the east, then increasing in strength because of the advent of firearms. A Portuguese diplomatic mission arrived in 1520, but Lebna Dengel, who was over-confident of his strength, failed to conclude an agreement, whereupon, in 1527, one of the Muslim leaders, Ahmad Gragn, invaded Ethiopia. Lebna Dengel became a fugitive, fleeing from province to province.

LEBON, PHILLIPE (1767–1804), French pioneer of gas lighting, who produced gas from sawdust and burnt it in his 'Thermo-lampe' which he exhibited in 1799. He also designed a gas engine.

LEBRUN, ALBERT (1871–1950), French politician and last president of the Third Republic who was elected to the Chamber of Deputies in 1900. He held office as minister of colonies in Caillaux's cabinet of 1911 and again in those of Poincaré (1912) and Doumergue (1913). During the First World War he was minister of blockade and then minister of liberated regions in Clemenceau's government. He became president of the Senate (1931) and president of the republic (1932) after the assassination of Paul Doumer. He was a worthy but undistinguished politician who made no attempt to influence the course of events during and after the collapse of France. He was arrested by the Germans in 1943.

LEBRUN, CHARLES (1619–90), French artist, decorator, and director of the Royal Academy of Painting and Sculptures. His works include the decoration of the *Galerie des Glaces* at Versailles.

LECANUET, JEAN (1920–   ), French lawyer and Catholic politician. In 1951 he was elected a deputy and became (1956) secretary of state to the president of the Council of Ministers. He was *chargé de mission* under Pflimlin (1958), was elected a senator in 1959, and, under the Fifth Republic, played a leading part in trying to form a moderate centre movement independent of Gaullism. In the Senate he was leader of the Centre Démocratique (1960–3) and national president of the Movement républicain populaire (1963–5). In Dec. 1965 he was the Centre Démocratique candidate for the presidency of the republic. On the first ballot he received 15·5 per cent of the popular vote, coming third after De Gaulle and Mitterand, who alone (under the electoral law) could compete in the second ballot. He was re-elected to the Senate in 1968.

LECH, BATTLE ON THE (955), victory over the Hungarians, won near Augsburg by Otto the Great, which removed their threat from the south-eastern borders of Germany. It gave Otto the prestige necessary for him to be crowned emperor and laid the foundations of the Christian kingdom of Hungary.

LE CHAPELIER, *LOI DE* (1791), passed by the middle-class French Constituent Assembly and not repealed until 1884. It made combinations of workers illegal.

LECHÍN OQUENDO, JUAN (1914–   ), leader of the Bolivian tin miners union, politician, and Bolivian vice-president. Lechín played a large part in bringing the tin miners into the National Revolutionary Movement (MNR), which seized power in Bolivia in 1952. As minister of mines and petroleum, he became a key figure in the running of *Comibol*, the new government mining corporation.

While vice-president of Bolivia, Lechín broke with Victor Paz Estenssoro, the president and MNR party leader. After Paz and the MNR fell from power in 1964, there were various attempts to reconcile MNR leaders with Lechín. He opposed the military regimes which governed Bolivia (1964–70), although his control over the Bolivian mining unions seemed to have weakened.

LECKY, WILLIAM EDWARD HARTPOLE (1838–1903), Irish historian, politician, and philosopher, author of *History of England in the Eighteenth Century* (1878–90), which became a classic, and of the *History of European Morals* (1869). He entered parliament (1895) as MP for Dublin University and opposed Home Rule.

LECLANCHÉ, GEORGES (1839–82), French engineer, who invented (1867) an electrolytic cell, which could provide an intermittent electric supply, as required.

LECLERC, CHARLES VICTOR (1772–1802), French general and brother-in-law of Napoleon. He was sent to the colony of Sainte Domingue (Haiti) to crush Toussaint L'Ouverture's rebellion (1801). Though at first successful, his army was weakened by guerrilla warfare and yellow fever and British blockades increased his logistical and supply problems. He withdrew to Tortuga Island and died there of yellow fever. The survivors of his expedition were defeated and returned to France.

LECLERC, DE HAUTECLOQUE, PHILIPPE (1902–47), French general, who, after joining De Gaulle in 1942, went immediately to Equatorial Africa, re-established the Free French forces, and led a spectacular march from Fort Lamy to join the Eighth Army at the Mareth Line (1943). Later, he trained the 2nd Armoured Division. He received the German surrender in Paris (Aug. 1944) and led the French entry into Strasbourg (Nov. 1944). Later he was commander-in-chief in Indo-China (1945–6).

LECLERCQ, CHRESTIEN (b. 1641), Recollet missionary to New France. He was the first missionary to the Micmac Indians, where the system of hieroglyphics invented by him is still (1970) employed. His *First Establishment of the faith in New France . . .* (1691) is an important source for early Canadian history.

LECŒUR, AUGUSTE (1911–   ), French trade unionist and communist leader. At the age of 13 he was a miner. He joined the Communist Party and during the Spanish Civil War commanded a battalion of the International Brigade. In 1938 he became a member of the Central Committee of the French Communist Party. During the Second World War he was secretary in charge of organization of the clandestine Communist Party. After the Liberation he became Mayor of Lens and a deputy in the two Constituent Assemblies (1945–6) and the National Assembly (1946–55). In both Gouin's and Bidault's cabinets (1946) he was under-secretary of state for industrial production. He retained the post of secretary in charge of organization in the Communist Party and was regarded as the third most important leader, after Thorez and Duclos. But in 1954 he was removed from office, accused of deviationism, insufficient self-criticism, and failure to establish cells amongst industrial workers. In 1958 he joined the Socialist Party (SFIO).

LECOMPTON CONSTITUTION (1857), proposed constitution for the US state of KS adopted by a convention of pro-slavery factions. It sought to legalize the institution of slavery within KS, and was rejected by the electorate (1858). President Buchanan's attempt to secure the admission of KS as a state of the Union under this constitution was rejected by the US Congress and contributed to the further fragmentation of the Democratic Party.

LE COQ, ROBERT (d. 1373), bishop of Laon (1351–60) and leader of the opposition to the French regent, Duke Charles (the future Charles V), during the captivity in England of King John of France (1356–60). Le Coq became the leading adviser of King Charles of Navarre, who was trying to supplant his cousin, John. Le Coq, in alliance with the Parisian leader, Etienne Marcel, dominated the Estates-General, held in Paris in Oct. 1356. An opportunity seemed to exist for a lasting improvement of the French government and for putting an end to the worst abuses of the French fiscal system, but the selfish intrigues of Charles of Navarre destroyed the popularity of his party and enabled Duke Charles, after 1358, to recover control of the government. After the return of King John to France in 1360, Le Coq was excluded from the general amnesty and died in exile.

LE CREUSOT, industrial centre in the Saône-et-Loire department of France. Its development in the 19th cent. was largely the work of the Schneider family. Iron and steel making were the foundation of Le Creusot's prosperity, and engineering and other industries were added later. The town was the scene of major strikes at the end of the Second Empire, and of a short-lived revolutionary Commune in 1871.

LEDRU-ROLLIN, ALEXANDRE AUGUSTE (1807–74), French radical republican politician, who became a deputy (1841) and was an unsuccessful minister of the interior (1848). He was eventually exiled (1851) and subsequently tried *in absentia* (1857) for his opposition to Louis Napoleon. He returned to sit in the National Assembly (1874), but with reluctance, because of his radicalism.

LE DUAN (1908–   ), Viet-nam politician of the Democratic Republic of (North) Viet-nam, born in Central Viet-nam. He became associated with the communists in or before 1930. He spent many years in prison before 1945. During the 1950s he became increasingly prominent in Hanoi, and in 1960 emerged as first secretary of the Lao-Dong ('Workers') Party. He was an advocate of a firm line in the conflict in South Viet-nam in the 1960s, and he probably enjoyed greater influence than his rival, Truong Chinh. In 1969 he was the principal contender for the succession to leadership, following the death of Ho Chi Minh.

LEDYARD, JOHN (1751–89), American explorer, who joined Capt. Cook's last voyage to the Sandwich Islands (Hawaii) (1776), and published an account of the journey (1783). He believed that the American states would eventually reach the Pacific Ocean and tried to organize an expedition to explore the Pacific north-west, but failed to raise enough money to do so. He crossed Europe on foot to Irkutsk in Siberia (1787), where he was temporarily imprisoned as a spy.

LEE OF ASHERIDGE, JANET BEVAN (née LEE), Life Baroness (1904–   ), British politician, who became MP for North Lanark at the age of 24 in 1929. Unlike her husband, Aneurin Bevan, she stayed outside the Labour Party for some years after the Independent Labour Party became disaffiliated in 1932. In Wilson's government she was minister for the arts (1964–70) and succeeded in obtaining increasing public support for the arts in spite of a worsening economic situation. On losing her seat in 1970 she became a life peeress.

LEE, CHARLES (1731–82), American soldier, born in Britain, who served as a British general in the French and Indian war He settled in VA (1773), was commissioned as a major-general in the American forces, and was a rival of George Washington for the supreme command in the American War of Independence. Lee disregarded Washington's orders after the battle of White Plains (28 Oct. 1776) and also his order to retreat after the battle of Monmouth (28 June 1778). He was court-martialled for disobeying orders and permanently suspended because of his criticism of Washington and Congress (1780).

LEE, JOHN (1733–93), English lawyer and Whig politician, who represented the Middlesex petitioners who supported John Wilkes in opposing Luttrell's election to parliament (1769). He also represented Admiral Keppel at his court-martial (1779). Lee was solicitor-general in the Rockingham

and Portland administrations, and became attorney-general in the latter (1783).

LEE, ROBERT EDWARD (1807–70), US Confederate general and member of a notable Virginian family. He graduated from West Point Military Academy (1829), served in the Mexican War (1846–8) as an army engineer, was superintendent of West Point (1852–5), and commanded the Texas military department (1857–61). He refused command of the Union forces at the outbreak of civil war, returned to VA, and was appointed President Davis's military adviser (1861–2). As commander of the Army of Northern Virginia (1862–5) he conducted a series of defensive campaigns that place him among the great military strategists, brilliantly out-manœuvring Gen. Hooker at Chancellorsville (May 1863) and delaying Gen. Grant's thrusts towards Richmond during the Wilderness campaign (May–July 1864). After being appointed general-in-chief of Confederate forces (Feb. 1865), he surrendered to Grant two months later at Appomattox. After the war, Lee became president of Washington College (now Washington and Lee University).

LEE, WILLIAM (*fl.* 16th cent.), English inventor of the knitting machine (1589), one of the earliest industrial inventions which was widely used in hosiery production.

LEE COMMISSION, Royal Commission on the Superior Civil Services in India under Lord Lee, which reported in March 1924. The commission's task was to find a way of meeting demands for more rapid Indianization and of solving the problems posed by the falling-off in British recruitment and the premature retirement of officials disgruntled by the Montagu–Chelmsford reforms. With regard to Indianization, it recommended increased Indian recruitment through both examinations and promotion from provincial services, so as to make the Indian civil service 50 per cent Indian by 1939. Also, by placing certain specialist services under direct provincial control, it allowed for much more rapid Indianization in such spheres as education, agriculture, and certain engineering and medical services. At the same time, the commission looked for increased recruiting in Britain and recommended changes designed to make the service more attractive to British recruits. Although the commission included four Indian members, its recommendations were strongly attacked in the central Legislative Assembly. A resolution introduced by Motilal Nehru, for the rejection of the report, the end to all recruitment in Britain, and the complete control of administrative services in India, was carried by the Assembly. Despite this opposition, the commission's recommendations were accepted by the government and quickly implemented. Substantial improvements in recruitment were reported as a result and there was also a steady increase in Indian appointments, although the target for 1939 was not in fact achieved.

LEE FAMILY, American family from Virginia, whose progenitor was Richard Lee (d. 1664), a wealthy tobacco planter. Four Lee brothers were statesmen during the revolutionary period: Richard Henry, Francis Lightfoot, William, and Arthur. Richard (1732–94) protested against the Stamp Act, helped to form the Committee of Correspondence, was a member of the Continental Congress, and signed the Declaration of Independence. Although he opposed the Federal constitution, he was a senator (1789–92) and helped pass the Bill of Rights. Francis (1734–97) was a member of the Continental Congress, signed the Declaration of Independence, and supported the adoption of the Federal constitution. William (1739–95) founded a business house in London, and was a diplomatic agent of the Continental Congress whose aim was to win support for the American cause, and attempted to arrange a treaty with the Dutch. Arthur (1740–92), an agent for the Continental Congress, arranged for the French to furnish arms to America, helped to arrange a Franco-American alliance, and was commissioner to Spain and Prussia. Henry (Light Horse Harry) Lee, a cousin of the four brothers, and a revolutionary hero, was the father of Robert E. Lee (1807–70), general-in-chief of Confederate armies in the Civil War, who graduated from the US Military Academy and served with honour in the army. Lincoln offered him the command of the Union army, but he chose to fight on the side of the Confederacy. The forces of the Confederacy were at first successful under his able leadership, but were finally defeated and he surrendered at Appomattox (April 1865). His sons, George Washington Custis Lee, and William Henry Fitzhugh Lee, were general officers in the southern forces.

Burton Jesse Hendrick, *The Lees of Virginia: biography of a family* (Boston, 1935).   DJF

LEE KUAN YEW (1923–), prime minister of Singapore (1959–). He was a founder and secretary-general (1954–) of the Singapore People's Action Party (PAP). When the PAP won the 1959 election with strong pro-communist support, Lee became chief minister. He chose to fight the pro-communist challenge within his own party on the issue of independence through merger with Malaysia, which proved a popular one. The dissidents left the PAP and formed the Barisan Sosialis (1961), which was narrowly defeated in the Malaysia referendum (1962) and the following election (1963).

As Singapore's leader within Malaysia (1963–5) Lee was increasingly driven into an opposition role, which took on a strong ethnic character during 1965. The resulting Chinese–Malay tension led to Singapore's expulsion from Malaysia (9 Aug. 1965). Lee quickly made a virtue of necessity as prime minister of a small republic. He successfully initiated a vigorous 'survival' policy involving multi-lingualism, industrialization, and the creation of an army. Though his foreign policy was nominally non-aligned, he retained Commonwealth defence links and a favourable climate for foreign investment.

LEEDS, THOMAS OSBORNE, 1st Duke of (1632–1712), English politician, normally known by his earlier title of Earl of Danby, who entered parliament in 1665 and was appointed lord treasurer (1673). Until 1679 he was the chief minister of King Charles II. His financial ability was undoubted, and for the first time since the Restoration (1660) the annual revenue exceeded parliamentary estimates. Equally noteworthy was his management of the House of Commons. In foreign affairs he differed from his royal master in being pro-Dutch and especially pro-Orange. He sought to end the third Anglo-Dutch War and did much to bring about the marriage of Mary, elder daughter of James, Duke of York, to William of Orange (1677), but he never won Charles II to his point of view. On the contrary, he found himself playing a part in policies of which he did not approve. Thus, in the Commons, articles of impeachment were presented against him, following the disclosure that as lord treasurer he had been involved in the conclusion of a subsidy agreement with Louis XIV. But the Lords refused to commit him, and early in 1679 Charles II dissolved parliament. A general election was held and the new Commons seemed intent on pursuing the impeachment, so Charles granted Danby a pardon under the great seal, a procedure voted illegal by the Commons. They now proposed to bring in a Bill of Attainder against Danby, who at this point resigned and was removed to the Tower of London, where he remained until 1684. His political career seemed to have come to a premature close, for he was not appointed to office again under Charles or James II. During James's reign, he had a part in bringing about the Revolution (1688), communicating with William of Orange (1687) and with those who invited William to England. After the revolution he was appointed president of the council. When the ministry became predominantly Tory (1690) he retained his position, and was generally regarded as the king's leading minister. By 1694 his influence was already waning. New articles of impeachment were levelled against him (1695), alleging malpractices regarding his conduct towards the South Sea Co. Though the charges were substantiated he was not removed from the presidency of the council until 1699, by which time his political career was virtually finished. He spoke on the Sacheverell issue as late as 1710.

A. Browning, *Thomas Osborne, Earl of Danby* (Glasgow, 1944).   BM

LEEDS, FRANCIS OSBORNE, 5th Duke of (1751–99), British politician. After opposing North, and serving Rockingham as ambassador to Paris (1782), he became Pitt's foreign secretary (1784–91), but resigned when Pitt retracted his Oczakov ultimatum to Catherine II of Russia.

LEE-ENFIELD RIFLE, rapid-firing service rifle developed in 1895. Although it was the finest military rifle of its day, supplies of the Enfield were limited during the First World War by its unsuitability for mass production.

LEEWARD ISLANDS, West Indian islands colonized by British and French private companies in the 1620s. The British group of St Kitts, Nevis, Anguilla, Antigua, Barbuda, and Redonda were appropriated to the British Crown in the 1660s, at first under the governor of Barbados and then, as a separate colony (1671), under Sir Charles Wheler. From 1670 to 1711 a general assembly functioned intermittently, but the island retained individual legislatures under a common executive, a constitution which persisted largely unchanged until 1871. The islands prospered as sugar plantations, while Antigua in the 18th cent. developed as a major naval base. The Leeward Isles Act (1871) set up a federal colony comprising the presidencies of Antigua (with Barbuda), Dominica (which in 1940 was transferred to the Windward Islands group), Montserrat, the Virgin Islands, St Kitts (with Anguilla), and Nevis, the last two forming a single presidency after 1882. 20th-cent. attempts to develop the islands' economies have met with limited success.

LEFÈVRE D'ETAPLES, JACQUES (1455–1536), French humanist scholar and theologian, whose work proved an inspiration to French Protestants. As early as 1512 he published an edition of the Pauline epistles with a commentary that anticipated Luther in its assertion of justification by faith. He respected the institutions of the Church, but called for reform, doubted the sacrificial character of the mass, and stressed its memorial aspects. Lefèvre was librarian of the monastery of St Germain des Prés, but at the end of 1520, after being condemned by the Sorbonne, he and his followers took refuge with his former abbot, Guillaume Briçonnet, in the diocese of Meaux, where he was eventually made vicar-general. In 1523 he published a French translation of the four Gospels and four years later one of the Old Testament. Driven from Meaux, he went to Strasbourg (Oct. 1525), but returned to France in April 1526. After Francis I's violent reaction to the placards (1534), he fled from France again and died, aged 82, at Nérac, the court of Marguerite of Angoulême (1492–1549), the king's sister. One of his pupils was Guillaume Farel.

LEFORT, FRANÇOIS JACOB (1656–99), Swiss-born soldier and diplomat, who served in France and Holland before settling in Moscow. He gained the favour of Peter I and was eventually appointed commander-in-chief of both the Russian navy and the army (1691). He also organized and led the Russian Grand Embassy which toured Europe (1697–8).

LEFT COMMUNISM in Russia, doctrine of an opposition group within the Bolshevik Party, led by Bukharin. It was at first inspired by distrust of the Brest-Litovsk treaty (1918). The group's opposition was largely emotional. Its members reiterated the principles of Bolshevism and emphasized the dangers of capitulation to imperialism which they saw arising from acceptance of the treaty. The practical advantages to be gained from an end to the war were such that their support in the party dwindled and they were in a small minority when the treaty was accepted by the seventh Party Congress and by the Congress of Soviets (March 1918). They kept up their opposition to Lenin on other issues for a few months, and urged extreme measures, including workers' control and widespread nationalization. After the summer (1918) they no longer existed as a distinct group, but their tradition continued to inspire the opposition to Stalin until the expulsion of Trotsky (1927).

LEGAL TENDER CASES, 8 Wallace 603 (1870) and 12 Wallace 457 (1871), US Supreme Court cases concerning the Legal Tender Act (1862) which made fiat money issued during the Civil War legal tender for the payment of debts. In the first of these, by a 4–3 decision, Chief Justice Chase declared the act invalid with regard to contracts made before its passage, as a violation of the due process clause of the Fifth Amendment and the obligation of contracts. The decision was announced just before President Grant appointed two new Supreme Court justices. In 1871 other cases concerning the act came before the court and in the *Second Legal Tender Cases* the initial decision was directly over-ruled. This led to allegations that Grant had deliberately packed the court.

LEGALISM IN CHINA, the principles of government deriving from Legalist thinkers, principally Shang Yang, Shen Pu-hai, and Han Fei. Legalists, as opposed to Confucianists, held that government should be exercised for the enrichment and strengthening of the state and its rulers, and not for the benefit of the population. The power of government rests on the effective enjoyment by a ruler of his pre-eminent situation, and on the rigorous implementation of devices such as punishments and rewards with a view to discouraging crime and encouraging service to the state. The population must be kept in obedience to the laws of the state, which must be exercised impartially and the male members must be conscripted for service in the army or as labourers, in accordance with state needs. At the same time, agriculture must be promoted as being the primary productive occupation of the people, who should be prevented from transferring their energies to commerce, which was of less benefit to the state. Shang Yang introduced many of these principles into the government of the kingdom of Ch'in, where he served as a senior statesman from 361 to 338 BC. The successful adoption of these methods resulted in the expansion of Ch'in, and, finally, the formation of the first Chinese empire in 221 BC. Although many Legalist principles were retained in subsequent imperial governments, they were not generally recognized as such, but were kept under the guise of Confucianism.

LEGATUS, ancient Roman military officer, usually a senator with experience of warfare, appointed by provincial governors and generals to serve on their staffs, with no fixed range of duties. Caesar employed his *legati* to command individual legions and in the first two centuries of the empire each legion (except those in Egypt) was commanded by a *legatus legionis* of praetorian or quaestorian rank. The governors of the imperial provinces were regularly *legati Augusti propraetore*. Three new legions raised by Septimius Severus were put under the command of equestrian prefects and Gallienus removed senators from all military commands.

LEGAZPI, MIGUEL LÓPEZ DE (*c*. 1510–72), Spanish conqueror of the Philippine Islands who led an expedition from Mexico in 1563 in a conquest that was virtually bloodless. Legazpi began the trade in Oriental silks between Latin America and the Philippines employing the famous Manila Galleon.

LÉGER, ALEXIS (1887–   ), French diplomat and secretary-general of the ministry of foreign affairs, who began his career as secretary to the French legation at Peking (1916). He was a political adviser at the Washington Conference (1921) and *chef de Cabinet* (1925–32) at the foreign office under Aristide Briand. During this period he was deputy director for Asian affairs (1925), deputy director and then director of political and commercial affairs (1925–33), and delegate at the Hague Disarmament Talks and the London Naval Conference (1930). He was secretary-general of the ministry of foreign affairs (1933–40).

As secretary-general Léger believed that it was necessary to restrain German and Italian expansion by defensive alliances, but his views were overridden by ministers whom he served, particularly Laval (1935) and Bonnet (1938–9).

In 1940 Léger was one of Reynaud's closest advisers and one of the firmest in advocating total prosecution of the Second World War. However in May 1940 Reynaud dismissed him, and then offered him the ambassadorship in Washington, which he refused. He left France for the US and remained there until 1958, working in the Library of Congress.

In 1958 he returned to France and in 1960 he was awarded the Nobel Prize for poetry. His literary works were published under the pseudonyms of Saintléger Léger and Saint-John Perse. Among his better-known poems are 'Éloges' (1911), 'Exil' (1944), 'Pluies', 'Neiges' (1945), 'Vents' (1946), and 'Amers' (1957).

LEGHORN, Tuscan entrepôt port 96 kms from Florence, which was one of the great commercial centres of Europe in the 18th cent. Its prosperity dated from the 15th cent. and until 1737 it was ruled by the Medici, and then came under Habsburg influence (1738). Dependent for its prosperity on British, French, Dutch, and Genoese shipping, it remained a free port until 1868.

LEGION, major unit of the ancient Roman army. In the early republic both of the consular armies consisted of two legions, each comprising 4200 infantry divided into 30 maniples and 60 centuries. The number and size of the legions greatly increased during the Punic Wars, and under Marius (107–101 BC) the legion became 6000 strong and the cohort replaced the maniple as the tactical unit. Augustus established a standing army of 28 legions, each 5000 strong, which was reduced by the losses in the battle of the Teutoburg Forest (AD 9) to 25. The total number of legions never exceeded 30 until Septimius Severus raised three new ones. The size of the legion was reduced by Constantine the Great to only 1000 infantry.

LÉGION DES VOLONTAIRES FRANÇAIS CONTRE BOLCHEVISME (LVF), body recruited by the Germans during their occupation of France in the Second World War. It was formed in July 1941 and directed by a committee drawn from the collaborationist parties. It was never officially recognized by the Vichy government, consequently its recruits came exclusively from the Occupied zone. Its members wore German uniforms and it was registered in the *Wehrmacht* records as a German unit, but as an experiment in military collaboration it was a failure. The Germans had hoped to recruit over 50,000 soldiers, but there were never more than 20,000 members and although they served on the Eastern Front the Legion's role was minimal.

LÉGION D'HONNEUR (1802), instituted by Napoleon as First Consul, who wanted to use it to create an order of merit for public servants in France.

LÉGION TRICOLORE in France, established by the Vichy government in response to German demands for military collaboration in the Second World War. In contrast to the *Légion des volontaires français contre bolchevisme* (LVF), it was a recognizably French unit, recruited from both zones and clothed in French uniforms. It was commanded by Gen. Bridoux, a regular French officer. After the Liberation the *Légion Tricolore* provided important evidence in the conviction of various Vichy politicians for collaboration.

LEGION'S PETITION, English political pamphlet written by Daniel Defoe (1701), attacking the Tory House of Commons and claiming that the people had a right to control parliamentary proceedings. This manifestation of extra-parliamentary opinion was sparked off by attempts to persuade the Commons to support William III's European policy.

LEGISLATIVE ASSEMBLY, FRENCH (1791–2), met in Oct. 1791 as a consequence of the constitution accepted by Louis XVI a month earlier. It was elected indirectly and represented the interests of the French middle class. Its deliberations were dominated by the issues of the war and the role of Louis in the new constitution. Although strong republican elements developed within the assembly, the destruction of the monarchy (Aug. 1792) was not its work, but that of the Paris Commune and clubs, who held the real power from the Storming of the Tuileries until the Assembly was replaced by the more democratic Convention (Sept.).

LEGITIMISM, French royalist political movement that supported a clerico-aristocratic society and the claims of the Bourbon pretender to the French throne (1830–83). It began after the July revolution, when many leading personalities of the Restoration era either refused to take the oath of allegiance to the new regime or were excluded from office. At first, it was a rather negative movement characterized by the satires of the salons of the Faubourg St Germain, by the retreat from politics—the so-called *émigration intérieure* of the nobility—and by the failure to respond to the Duchesse de Berri's attempted rising in the Vendée (1832). When the Comte de Chambord became the head of the movement (1844), after a dispute over the succession, there was an active legitimist press, a number of deputies such as Berryer and Fallaux, and a tradition of military service in the cause of ultra-conservative monarchy in Portugal. Their programme, largely inherited from the Ultras, embraced a dogmatic belief in Church, aristocracy, and Crown, and a preference for local and corporative organizations over centralized and elective ones. Chateaubriand and others tried unsuccessfully to liberalize this policy. Alliance with the Orleanists proving impossible, Legitimists played little part in the revolution of 1848, although the elections of 1849 showed their strength in the south and west.

Legitimists were again excluded from political life under the Second Empire, and did not return to prominence until the elections of 1870. The Comte de Chambord visited France in June 1871 and proclaimed the need for decentralization, local liberties, parliamentary government, and aid to the working class. Yet though he was willing to promise there would be no return to the *ancien régime*, he could neither abandon the white flag of the Bourbons and all it stood for, nor come to terms with the Orleanists. This was a misjudgement, because from July 1871 elections began to go against the Legitimists and they began to lose touch with the new France. A further attempt at restoration was made in 1873, when the Comte de Paris secured an equivocal understanding with Chambord, and Broglie replaced Thiers as prime minister. There was a royalist majority of 26 and a restoration was only thwarted by Chambord's insistence on the white flag (Oct. 1873). Chambord came to Versailles during the following month to persuade MacMahon to proclaim him to the National Assembly, but the marshal refused even to see him. Similarly, the Assembly rejected La Rochefoucauld's call for a restoration (1874) and the two branches of royalism split, enabling the republic to be consolidated. A final attempt was made on 16 May 1877, when Broglie and MacMahon dissolved the chamber and tried unsuccessfully to obtain a royalist majority. Successive elections destroyed legitimist strength. On the death of the childless Chambord

(1883), most royalists accepted the claims of the Orleanist Comte de Paris, but a few turned to the Spanish Bourbons, while leadership of the conservative forces in France passed into other hands.

S. M. Osgood, *French Royalism under the Third and Fourth Republics* (The Hague, 1960).
R. Remond, *The Right Wing in France from 1814 to de Gaulle* (PA, US, and Oxford, 1966). CHC

LEGNANO, BATTLE OF (1176), defeat of Frederick I by an army of the Lombard League, which ended his dream of predominance over northern Italy. The defeat, followed by the capture of the imperial camp, was partly due to the failure of Frederick's cousin, Duke Henry the Lion, to give promised support.

LEGUÍA, AUGUSTO BERNARDINO Y SALCEDO (1863–1932), banker, president, and dictator of Peru, who devoted his early life to finance and to representing American and British companies in Peru. He also engaged in export dealings and the formation of a steamship line. After serving as minister of the treasury he was elected president (1908–12), and rationalized the disbursal of the national revenue, encouraged a national steamship line, railway expansion, and domestic consumption of guano. He was exiled to London and in 1919 returned as the candidate of the upper class and the army. Known as the 'Oncenio' or 11-year rule (1919–30), his rule saw a widening of the gulf between the rich and the poor. He shaped a new constitution which made the state a regulator of national institutions. With the onset of world Depression his economic projects suffered and in 1930 a military uprising forced him from power.

LEHMAN, HERBERT HENRY (1878–1963), US politician and philanthropist. As Democratic governor of New York (1932–1942) he sponsored social welfare measures, was director-general of the United Nations Relief and Rehabilitation Administration (1943–6), and served in the US Senate (1949–57).

LEHNZWANG (lit. 'the obligation to enfeoff'), the custom under which the German emperor was bound to grant away fiefs falling vacant through lack of heirs or the banning of their holder, within a year. This obligation was recorded in the *Sachsenspiegel* of the early 13th cent. It was designed to prevent an emperor accumulating land in his own hands. Strong emperors like Frederick II successfully ignored it, while others, like Rudolph I of Habsburg and Henry of Luxemburg, evaded it by enfeoffing their eldest sons.

LEIBNITZ, GOTTFRIED WILHELM, Baron (1646–1716), German philosopher and mathematician who worked in Paris (1672–6), where Huygens encouraged him to pursue his mathematical enquiries and where he evolved, independently of Newton, differential and integral calculus.

Little of Leibnitz's work was published in his lifetime, and his philosophical system was largely developed in articles and correspondence. He consistently complained of poverty and neglect, and it was only after his death that his enquiring spirit and vast and catholic learning began to be properly appreciated, *eg*, his belief in the importance of subconscious mental processes has benefited modern psychology.

His philosophy, as set forth in *Théodicée* (1710) and *La Monadologie* (1714), followed that of Plato in accepting the superiority of final over mechanical causes. Leibnitz conceived the universe as 'a pre-established harmony' in which monads, the ultimate units of being, although having the power of spontaneous activity, move in harmony with each other and with God, who is the prime cause. Only these individual substances are indivisible and real, and the phenomena of the material world are merely consequences of this reality. The existence of evil Leibnitz explained as an imperfection in a world not absolutely perfect, but the world that God had chosen, out of conceivable alternatives, was 'the best of all possible worlds'. This view caused Leibnitz to be accused of a facile optimism, which Voltaire satirized in *Candide* (1759).

His philosophical belief in a unity in the midst of variety led him to seek its practical realization in the contemporary world. He called on princes to subsidize research to prepare an encyclopedia to contain the whole of human knowledge, a universal language to facilitate communication, a universal method of logic for the examination of ideas, and the codification of regional laws into a universal system. He also sought to unite the Catholic and Protestant Churches and to settle the differences between the Protestants themselves. The only outcome of these endeavours was the foundation of the Berlin Academy (1700).

When Louis XIV threatened Germany, he urged the settlement of local disputes and the formation of a Rheinbund to resist attack. He also put forward a scheme for ending the constant warfare in Europe by uniting all the nations in a crusade against the non-Christian peoples. To France he offered Egypt as a bait whose possession would undermine the trading position of the Dutch. Louis summoned him to Paris (1672) to explain his ideas, and the *Consilium Aegyptiacum* which he wrote for the occasion may have influenced Napoleon I's eastern venture in 1798.

B. Russell, *An Exposition of Leibnitz's Philosophy* (London, 1937).   MMR

LEICESTER, SIMON DE MONTFORT, 6th Earl of (2nd of 2nd creation) (*c.* 1208–1265), son of Simon, leader of the Albigensian crusade. King Henry III of England recognized Simon's claim to the earldom of Leicester and granted Simon his sister, Eleanor, in marriage. At first the great favourite of Henry, he emerged in the 1250s as one of the most ardent baronial reformers. He contributed to the Provisions of Oxford (1258) and when Henry violated these Simon became, though a Frenchman, the champion of English liberties. Idealism, desire for reform, and personal ambition motivated him. His victory over Henry III at Lewes (1264) left him virtually sole ruler of England. In his short rule he called the famous parliament, to which burgesses were first summoned, in an attempt to broaden the basis of his flagging support (1265). He lost the support of many nobles, including the powerful Earl of Gloucester, and was defeated and killed by the royalists at Evesham.

LEICESTER, ROBERT DUDLEY, 14th Earl of (1st of 4th creation) (1533–88), English courtier, who was implicated in the succession plot of his father, the regent Northumberland (1553), but he was pardoned and was master of the ordnance at the capture of St Quentin (1557).

Dudley and Queen Elizabeth had been acquainted before her accession and it is likely that for a time there was a strong attachment between them. His wife, Amy Robsart, died (1560) in circumstances that suggested—falsely, according to the latest evidence—that he had had her killed, and when Elizabeth was gravely ill with smallpox (1562) she named him protector of the realm. Cecil and other conservative statesmen were alarmed and resentful at the favour shown to him, and the Spanish ambassador wrote of him as 'the king that is to be'. But Elizabeth's heart did not rule her head, and she saw the danger in Dudley's arrogant presumptions. Although she never lost her personal affection for him, she seldom allowed him any real influence in public affairs, especially as his support for Puritanism and an aggressive, evangelistic foreign policy would have disturbed the delicate balance of power.

She made him an earl (1564) as an inducement to Mary Queen of Scots to marry him, but neither party was enthusiastic about the match, although it might one day have brought Leicester or his son to the English throne. His subsequent amours, particularly his liaison with Lord Sheffield's widow, and his marriage (1578) to the Countess of Essex,

infuriated the queen, and his amorous adventures were viciously exposed in the anonymous *Leicester's Commonwealth* (1584). In a dilettante way he encouraged the arts and was patron of one of the earliest theatrical companies, of which James Burbage was the manager. His entertainment of Elizabeth at Kenilworth (1575) remains famous.

Leicester was one of the instigators of the Bond of Association (1584), formed to encompass the death of Mary Stuart, and when Elizabeth at length abandoned her neutrality and sent an expedition to Holland (1585), she put Leicester in charge of it. He behaved with characteristic optimism and incapacity, announcing that he would expel the Spaniards within a year and accepting the title of Supreme Governor of the United Provinces. This angered Elizabeth, who was opposed to any irrevocable commitment, and he was recalled (1586).

When the Spanish invasion threatened, Elizabeth made him captain-general of the forces at Tilbury, and he is credited with the inspiration of persuading her to address the troops in one of her memorable orations. He died a few days after the Armada was defeated.

E. Jenkins, *Elizabeth and Leicester* (London, 1961).   MMR

LEICESTER OF HOLKHAM, THOMAS WILLIAM COKE, 1st Earl of (1754–1842), of Holkham, Norfolk, British MP (1776–84, 1790–1832), great landowner in Norfolk and Derbyshire. He was one of the most successful estate improvers of the period. Among his achievements were an increase in the yield of arable land through marling, manure fertilization, drill husbandry, and crop variation, and an improvement in the breeding of pigs, sheep, and cattle.

LEICESTER HOUSE GROUP in England comprised Sir Robert Walpole's Whig opponents who, in George II's reign, used the traditional enmity between Hanoverian kings and their heirs to form a party round Frederick, Prince of Wales and so deflect charges of faction. The group included some of parliament's ablest men, *eg*, Carteret, Pulteney, Cobham, and his 'boy patriots', including William Pitt and Lyttelton. They caused the rejection of Walpole's Excise Bill (1733), promoted war with Spain (1739), and finally ousted Walpole himself (Feb. 1742). The ministry then gradually recruited Leicester House men, including Pitt (1746). The Prince of Wales's death (1751) meant the end of Leicester House as a focus of political opposition for some years.

LEIF EIRIKSSON (*fl* 11th cent.), son of Eirik the Red, the discoverer of Greenland. Leif was largely responsible for Greenland's religious conversion, which took place in 1000 on the instigation of King Olaf Tryggvesson of Norway, as in Iceland. After being blown off course on a voyage from Norway to Greenland, Leif sighted America. He soon set out again from Greenland to explore this new discovery. There he found self-sown vines, and so called the country Vinland (Wineland).

LEIPZIG, BATTLE OF (16–19 Oct. 1813), the 'Battle of the Nations', resulted in an overwhelming defeat of Napoleon by the armies of the Fourth Coalition, and his rapid evacuation of Germany.

LEIPZIG, DISPUTATION OF (1519), between John Eck, a Catholic theologian of Ingolstadt, and Luther and his friend Carlstadt. Luther's original position had not been essentially revolutionary, but in debate with Cardinal Cajetan at Augsburg (1518) he had been led to challenge papal supremacy and appeal to general councils as a higher authority. At Leipzig Eck, a subtler disputant, drew from him an admission that even councils might err, since scripture was the only infallible guide. He finally asserted that some of the beliefs for which Hus had been condemned were truly Christian and not heretical. The next year he said that even

Paul and Augustine were Hussites, and took his stand on the infallibility of the Bible against all ecclesiastical authority.

LEIPZIG, INTERIM OF (1548), called by the Elector Maurice of Saxony following the Augsburg Interim of Charles V, an intended compromise which dissatisfied the Protestants by making only tentative concessions. At Leipzig Melanchthon secured the adoption of moderate Protestant views, but the Interim alienated rigid Lutherans by accepting certain Catholic ceremonies as 'indifferent' to salvation and sanctioning the authority of popes and bishops when not abused.

LEIPZIG CONVENTION (1630), meeting of Protestant princes, independent nobles, and towns, called by John George, elector of Saxony, and George William, elector of Brandenburg, to present an ultimatum to Emperor Ferdinand II to annul the Edict of Restitution and to restore the constitutional rights of the German rulers.

LEISLER, JACOB (1640–91), American politician, born in Germany, who went to America (1660) and became prominent in New York politics. He was a leader of the movement to force out Francis Nicholson, governor of New York, who had been appointed under King James II. Leisler himself served capably as governor of New York (1689–91), but was accused of treason by the English and was hanged. The English parliament later reversed the verdict of his guilt (1693) and paid an indemnity to his heirs.

LEITH, CONCORDAT OF (1572) in Scotland, compromise between those who supported the structure of the Roman Church and the Protestant reformers. Episcopal sees which fell vacant were to be filled by bishops nominated by the Crown, but examined and admitted by a 'chapter' composed of ministers. New bishops were subject to the General Assembly of the reformed church in all spiritual matters. The system was abused under the regent Morton and led to the second Book of Discipline, which condemned episcopacy.

LEJRE, near modern Roskilde in Denmark. Archaeological and literary evidence indicate that it was probably a major centre in pre-Viking times. It is reputed to have been the site of the great hall Heorot of *Beowulf* and the seat of the legendary King Hrolf Kraki. It had been a major cult-site, as well as a royal cemetery, for many cents.

LELAND, JOHN (*c*. 1506–52), English antiquary, who was chaplain and librarian to Henry VIII (1530) and king's antiquary (1533). He toured England (1534–42), searching ecclesiastical libraries for manuscripts of historical interest.

LELANTINE WAR, long conflict *c*. 700 BC between Chalcis and Eretria for possession of the Lelantine plain, noteworthy for the extensive participation of other Greek states. Chalcis was supported by Samos, Erythrae, Thessaly, and probably Corinth; Eretria by Miletus, Chios, and probably Megara. Such alliances arose during the expansion overseas and concomitant intensification of local conflicts between neighbours among the over-populated, emergent 8th-cent. Greek city-states. Enemies at home remained enemies abroad, wherever colonization or trade was attempted, and hostile pairs of neighbours joined other such pairs to form loose associations of common friends against common enemies. Thus in Sicily Chalcidians joined Corinthians in opposing Megarians as well as Eretrians, whereas in the Black Sea and its approaches Milesians co-operated with Megarians, but not with Chalcidians.

LELY, SIR PETER (1618–80), Dutch-born painter who came to England in 1641. Throughout the troubled period of the Civil Wars, the Protectorate, and the Restoration he painted notable figures of all parties, *eg*, Charles I and Oliver Cromwell. He also painted numerous pictures at the court of Charles II.

LEMIEUX ACT (1907) in Canada, named after its author, it was largely drafted by W. L. Mackenzie King. The act prohibited strikes and lock-outs in public utilities until after investigation by a conciliation board. The act was declared *ultra vires* by the privy council (1925).

LENA, one of the great rivers of Siberia, rising near Lake Baikal in Central Asia and flowing into the Arctic Ocean. It was first discovered by Cossack explorers searching for furs (*c*. 1630), who gradually ousted the Yakuts natives and established the fortified settlement which became the city of Yakutsk (*c*. 1632).

LEND-LEASE ACT (1941) in the US, legislation providing for the lending, lease, transfer, or exchange of 'defense articles' to countries whose security the president deemed necessary to the defence and security of the US. After being introduced into Congress with the symbolic number HR1776, the year of the Declaration of Independence, the bill passed both houses in March 1941. It transformed the nature of American neutrality in the Second World War, and represented the logical culmination of President F. D. Roosevelt's 'arsenal of democracy' speech of the previous Dec. Over $50,000 million was eventually spent on Lend-Lease.

L'ENFANT, PIERRE CHARLES (1754–1825), French-born American army engineer and city planner, who went to America (1777) and fought in the American War of Independence. At President Washington's request he submitted plans for the proposed national capital, but his radial scheme, influenced by the pattern of Versailles, proved too expensive to implement fully and Washington terminated his services (27 Feb. 1792). However, his scheme was revived in the later replanning of Washington, DC

LENIN, VLADIMIR ILYICH ULYANOV (1870–1924), Russian politician. Religion and discipline were the basis of his upbringing, but this changed when he went to Kazan University, from which he was expelled at the end of his first term, having been accused of political agitation. This was probably caused by the execution of his elder brother, Alexander, a populist terrorist. From then onwards Lenin virtually educated himself, chiefly by reading the works of Marx. By 1891, when he passed his law examinations, he was already involved with the St Petersburg underground, where he learnt much from Plekhanov and Martov. In 1895 he was arrested and spent 14 months in prison in St Petersburg. Here he began his first major work, *The Development of Capitalism in Russia* (1899). Afterwards he was exiled for three years to Siberia; this again was a period of creative leisure. He enjoyed hunting, his health was excellent, and he married Nadezhda Krupskaya. They spent their honeymoon translating the Webbs' *Theory and Practice of Trades Unionism*. After his return he began to reorganize the Russian Social Democratic movement, the aim of which was the seizure of power by conspiratorial and revolutionary means. In adopting this aim, which he pursued single-mindedly for the rest of his life, he admitted his debt to Tkachev and Nechaev. His chief enemies were those within the movement who saw the proletarian cause developing along democratic or trade union lines. In 1900 he went to Switzerland, where he founded the newspaper *Iskra* (*The Spark*), which later appeared in Munich. Through the paper's secret distribution network he won control of the Russian underground. His position he made clear in a pamphlet, 'What is to be done?'—the title of which he borrowed from his favourite novelist, Chernyshevsky. His insistence on establishing the party upon a small disciplined nucleus of active and committed revolutionaries disgusted most of the émigré Social Democrat leaders. After the party's Brussels–London Congress (1903) he was isolated and dismissed from *Iskra*'s editorial board. In Russia, however, he still had much influence in the underground and soon started a new subversive paper, *Vperyod* (*Forward*).

He played little part in the 1905 revolution (although he returned briefly to Russia from Geneva, where he was living at the time) and was at first suspicious of the Soviet movement since it had been created not by the party but by the workers themselves. Later, with characteristic realism, he saw that the Soviets could be used as a disguise by the party. He was an uncompromising enemy of the Dumas and in this was an unexpected ally of the Tsarist government—a striking example of the community of views between the two authoritarian extremes of Russian political life. But in the decade between the Russian revolutions his cause made no advance. Many of his comrades were disgusted by the cynical way in which he financed the Bolshevik centre—by organizing bank raids, accepting subventions from millionaires like Morozov, and by marrying off a comrade to an heiress. He was unable to prevent the Okhrana (Tsarist secret police) from riddling the Bolshevik Central Committee with its agents. His attitude towards the First World War, which he saw simply as opportunity for exploiting the aims of the party, offended the patriotism of the European socialists. At Zimmerwald (1915) he rejected the majority's proposal for an early peace without conquests. By the end of 1916 he was almost entirely isolated from the other Russian exiles. He was living in poverty in Zürich and even such optimism as his was not proof against his apparent failure. However, a reversal in his fortunes began during 1917, when after the February revolution the German government transported him to Petrograd. He was provided with German money, but he used it in his own interests. In the 'April Theses' he struck a characteristically uncompromising line: no co-operation with the Provisional government. Partly by skill and partly by luck, he avoided being drawn into the revolution until the Provisional government became thoroughly discredited; then he persuaded his comrades, many of whom were hesitant, that the moment had come to fulfil the purpose of the Bolshevik Party and to seize power by revolutionary and non-democratic means. After the Nov. revolution he became chairman of the Soviet of people's commissars and his career became merged with the progress of the new communist state. In Aug. 1918 he was seriously wounded by a terrorist; in Aug. 1922 he suffered a stroke, from which he never fully recovered. During the last weeks of his life he dictated his political 'Testament', in which he warned his comrades against Stalin's ambition. By a curious irony (for which Stalin was largely responsible) the embalmed body of this militant atheist now provides the Russians with an object of pseudo-religious veneration.

D. Shub, *Lenin* (London, 1966).
D. W. Treadgold, *Lenin and his Rivals* (New York, 1955).
GS

LENINGRAD, SIEGE OF (Sept. 1941–Jan. 1944). During the Second World War Leningrad was cut off from the rest of Russia by Von Leeb's Army Group North, aided by the Finns. The front was stabilized on the southern outskirts of the city early in Oct. through the ruthless direction of the Red Army's chief trouble-shooter, Zhukov, and by the shift in weight of the German assault to the Moscow front. From then onwards Hitler dismissed the possibility of taking Leningrad by storm and a regular siege began by which it was hoped to starve the 3 million inhabitants and 500,000 troops into submission. Supplies could only be got in, and the population evacuated, by air or across Lake Ladoga, where an ice-road war formed during the winter of 1941–2. It is probable that by the spring of 1942 a million people had died of hunger and the overall death rate may have reached a million and a half. Resistance was reinforced by intense local patriotism, by a rational calculation of the population's fate if the Germans should capture the city, and by Zhdanov's ruthlessly efficient party organization. Repeated attempts at a break-out failed, then in Jan. 1943 the Leningrad front, under Govorov, was united with that of Volkhov, south-east of Lake Ladoga, under Meretskov; thereafter supplies could

reach the city by rail. The Germans did not begin to retreat however, until Jan. 1944, when they were slowly driven southwards after maintaining a siege lasting about 900 days. Their failure to capture the city did not have the same overall strategic impact on the war as did the Germans' disaster at Stalingrad, but it did involve the diversion of their strength from more decisive areas at several crucial periods, particularly the summer of 1942.

LENNOX, ESMÉ STUART, 1st Duke of (Scottish) (c. 1542–1583), Franco-Scottish diplomat and politician, who was sixth Seigneur D'Aubigny and cousin of Mary Queen of Scots' second husband, Lord Darnley. Sent to Scotland as an agent of the Guise family to restore Catholicism, he became a favourite of the young James VI, who bestowed on him the ducal title (1581). He secured the condemnation of the Earl of Morton for Darnley's murder, but was expelled from Scotland after the Ruthven Raid (1582) and died in France.

LENNOX FAMILY, of Celtic or Saxon origin; the original Earls of Lennox were politically prominent in medieval Scotland. After a period of rival claims in the late 15th cent., the title was confirmed to Sir John Stewart of Darnley (1488). The eldest son of the 13th Earl, Lord Darnley, married Mary Queen of Scots and was the father of James VI. The title reverted to James VI (1571), who granted it to his paternal uncle (Darnley's younger brother) Charles. In 1580 the earldom was given to Esmé Stuart (c. 1542–83), grandson of the 12th Earl, and in 1581 he was created Duke of Lennox. His son, Ludovic (1574–1624), was created Duke of Richmond (1623). He was succeeded, in his Scottish titles only, by his brother Esmé (d. 1624), but Esmé's son, James (1612–55), the 4th Duke of Lennox and a fervent royalist, was also created Duke of Richmond (1641). In 1675 the dukedoms of Lennox and Richmond were bestowed by Charles II on Charles Lennox (1672–1723), his illegitimate son by the Duchess of Portsmouth. Thereafter the Lennox titles were held by the dukes of Richmond.

LENOIR, JEAN JOSEPH ÉTIENNE (1822–1900), French inventor of the first gas engine, patented in 1860, and the first to be a practical success.

LE NÔTRE, ANDRÉ (1613–1700), French landscape gardener, who produced, firstly at Vaux-le-Vicomte for the financier Nicholas Fouquet and, after the latter's arrest, for Louis XIV at Versailles, the ultimate development in vista gardens. Versailles is his masterpiece, which neither was nor ever could be really completed, because innovation and change were continually required. Such gardens, stretching to the horizon, were conceived as vast stage-sets to reflect the formal and stylized society of the court. Le Nôtre's style was copied all over Europe in the 17th cent. and the mode continued to the end of the 18th cent. in some of the states of eastern Europe long after 'natural' gardens led garden fashion in the west.

LENS, BATTLE OF (2 Aug. 1648), victory of the Prince of Condé over the Austro-Spanish forces under Archduke Leopold William, younger brother of Emperor Ferdinand III, in the closing stages of the Thirty Years War. Condé doubled back to surprise the imperialist troops 17 kms north-east of Arras, and killed, wounded, or captured almost all of them, thus forcing Ferdinand to conclude the peace of Westphalia (1648).

LEO III (c. 680–740), first Byzantine Emperor of the Isaurian dynasty (*reg.* 717–40), who seized the throne after a period during which several short-lived rulers had reigned and chaos had descended on the empire. He resisted an Arab siege of Constantinople, reorganized the bureaucracy, restored the imperial treasury, and developed the themes as units of civil and military government. This valuable work was carried further by his able son, Constantine V. Leo became notorious as a religious innovator, initiating the Iconoclast controversy with which his name is indelibly linked. A decree of 726 forbade the worship of images and Leo followed this with a wholesale destruction of cult-objects representing Christ and the saints. Iconoclasm was originally a movement for the puritanical reformation of a religious observance which seemed to Leo and his supporters to have degenerated into idolatry. However, political motives developed, Leo being concerned to check the growing autonomy of the Church, with its vast estates and centres of popular assembly associated with icons of special fame. The movement was resisted by the common people, as well as the monasteries, but found support among the imperial armies, recruited chiefly from Asiatics influenced by the Semitic prejudice against graven images. Iconoclasm split the empire, alienated the remaining Western provinces, opened a new breach with the Western Church, and guaranteed permanently the Greek character of Byzantine civilization. These momentous consequences have tended to overshadow Leo's real achievements as a capable and vigorous ruler.   RP

LEO VI (d. 912), Byzantine Emperor (*reg.* 886–912), much of whose reign was spent in conflict with the Bulgars and the Pechenegs. He carried to completion—in the form of a code known as 'Basilica'—the work of legal reform begun in the time of his father, Basil I. The decrees of Leo VI himself are also of great importance and cover a wide range of ecclesiastical and secular matters. He was the author of liturgical poems and orations and of a valuable treatise (the *Tactica*) on the art of warfare.

LEO I (*reg.* 440–61), Pope, whose pontificate made explicit the papal claim to universal authority over the Church. During the barbarian invasions of the 5th cent. he persuaded (451) Attila the Hun not to ravage Rome, but a similar appeal to the Vandal Geiseric in 455 was not successful.

LEO III (*reg.* 795–816), Pope, whose pontificate was notable for his appeal to Charlemagne against his enemies in Rome, which led to Charlemagne's visit to Rome and his imperial coronation by Leo in St Peter's on Christmas Day 800. This event revived the empire in the west, later known as the Holy Roman empire.

LEO IX (1002–54), Pope (*reg.* 1049–54), cousin of the Emperor Henry III, who secured his election to the papacy. His pontificate marked the beginning of the great Hildebrandine or Gregorian reform of the papacy. He introduced into the curia a group of young reformers, including Humbert of Silva Candida, Frederick of Lorraine (later Stephen IX), and Hildebrand (later Gregory VII). By a series of synods and councils held in Italy, France, and Germany, he made the papal presence felt and initiated a programme of reform against simony and clerical marriage and for the independence of the clergy from secular control. His pontificate ended in defeat by the Sicilian Normans at Civitate (1053) and the formal schism with the Eastern Church in 1054, but the impulse given by Leo to the creation of a reformed papacy was of permanent importance.

LEO X (1475–1521), Pope (*reg.* 1513–21), last of the true Renaissance popes and a devoted patron of science and the arts. He occupied the papacy in the opening stages of the Protestant Reformation. His main concern was the advancement of his family by diplomacy and intrigue, through which he hoped to set his brother on the throne of Naples and his nephew in the duchy of Milan; he thus became involved in the Franco-Spanish power struggle in Italy. After concluding a treaty with Spain (1515) Leo changed sides when the French victory at Marignano resulted in Francis I becoming Duke of Milan, and made peace with France, yielding Parma and Piacenza in return for a French guarantee that the Medici should retain Florence. He met Francis at

Bologna (Dec. 1515) to settle the discordant relations between the French Church and the papacy, formally reassuming control over the former, but ceding to the French monarchy considerable control over some 600 ecclesiastical appointments in return for the abolition of the Pragmatic Sanction of Bourges, embodied in the bull *Pastor Aeternus* (1516).

His relations with the Habsburgs were equally volatile. He supported the respective anti-Habsburg candidates, Frederick the Wise of Saxony and Francis I, in the election for King of the Romans (1518) and emperor (1519), but gradually moved towards an imperial alliance with Charles V as relations with France cooled. His promise to crown Charles as emperor in return for the latter's protection of the Medici family interests by the acquisition of Milan, Parma, and Piacenza was sealed in their treaty of 29 May 1521, and later Leo rejoiced in the entry of an imperial–papal army into Milan. Portugal and England were also favoured nations. He promoted Wolsey to be a cardinal (1515) and papal legate (1518) and bestowed upon Henry VIII the style of Defender of the Faith (1521). To Portugal he gave papal blessing to all discoveries and future conquests which might be made by sailing eastwards (1514).

Leo showed little zeal for reform and dissolved the 5th Lateran Council without making much effort to fulfil its reforming decrees. His financial policy contributed to anti-papal and anti-clerical feeling. Professing a desire for a crusade against the Turks, he instructed his agent at the Diet of Augsburg, Cardinal Cajetan, to raise a special tax (1518), while he himself sold offices and sinecures to augment his annual revenues. A bull of 1515 announcing an indulgence to collect funds for the building of the basilica of St Peter's led ultimately to Luther's condemnation of indulgence in the 95 theses (1517). He tried to deal with the Lutheran problem by mediation and by granting concessions to loyal rulers, but after the publication of *Exsurge Domine* condemning Luther (15 June 1520) Charles V delayed action until the Diet of Worms (Jan. 1521). A second bull (3 Jan. 1521), excommunicating Luther, failed to suppress the new movement and within days of Leo's death (Dec. 1521) Luther re-entered Wittenberg from his hiding place.

L. von Pastor, *The History of the Popes from the Close of the Middle Ages* (London, 1891–1953).   MKS

LEO XIII (1810–1903), Pope (*reg.* 1878–1903). Despite his failure to end the international isolation of the papacy and to achieve a formal reconciliation between Church and state in Italy, Leo greatly enhanced the prestige of his office and gave it new relevance by ranging the Church on the side of social reform and encouraging the emergence of Christian democracy, a political creed which provided an increasingly popular alternative for the middle-class, which was dissatisfied with liberalism and fearful of socialism. In a series of great encyclicals Leo reaffirmed the traditional teaching of the Church, but stated that democracy was as acceptable as any other form of government. He encouraged examination of working-class conditions and the full participation of Catholics in public life.

LEO AFRICANUS (?1490–?1540), born Al-Hasan ibn Muhammad al-Wazzan, in Granada. After the *Reconquista* (1492) his family fled to Fez, where he grew up and studied. In early life he travelled in Morocco and the Middle East and accompanied an uncle on a mission to Askia Muhammad I of Songhay. He later visited the Sultan of Fez and went on to Agadès, Bornu (via northern Hausaland), returning home via Nubia and Egypt. Numerous other missions took him over much of North Africa and the Middle East. On returning from Egypt in 1518 he was captured by Christian corsairs, presented to Pope Leo X, and subsequently baptized by him. Later, he taught Arabic in Bologna, and possibly returned to Morocco and to his Muslim faith. His *Description of Africa*, written in Italian and published posthumously in Venice (1550), is a unique source for the geography, sociology, and history of North Africa and its Saharan hinterlands in the early 16th cent. and formed the chief authority for most other cosmographies and maps dealing with these areas down to the early 19th cent.

LEOFRIC (d. 1057), English soldier, who, in the last generation before the Norman conquest, was one of the most powerful men in England. He represented the only effective opposition to the power of the house of Godwine and in 1051 supported King Edward the Confessor against Earl Godwine. Leofric founded the monastery of St Mary, Coventry, and was the husband of Lady Godiva. In the crisis of 1066 his grandsons, Edwin and Morcar, earls of Mercia and Northumbria, failed to join King Harold at Hastings, though this may have been due not to treachery, but to the exhaustion of their resources after their recent defeat by a Norwegian invader. After Harold's death they tried to oppose William of Normandy, but were defeated.

LEON, ALONSO (d. 1691), Spanish soldier, who was governor of Coahilla, and led five expeditions into Texas. He discovered Robert La Salle's abandoned colony at Matagorda Bay. He took formal possession of Texas for Spain (1690).

LEON, DANIEL DE (1852–1914), radical US labour leader, who joined the Socialist Labor Party (1890), became editor of the *Weekly People* (1892), and later of the *Daily People* (1900). He opposed the conservatism of the American Federation of Labor, and helped to found the International Workers of the World (1905).

LEON, FRAY LUIS DE (1527–91), Spanish humanist, Augustinian theologian, and poet. While he was professor of theology at Salamanca University, he was arrested by the Valladolid Inquisition on suspicion of heresy (1572), partly because of his friendship with Arias Montano and other Hebrew teachers, and was tortured and imprisoned for five years, then released on Cardinal Quiroga's orders (Dec. 1576). He was reinstated in his chair and promoted to Augustinian provincial of Castile, but died a few days later. Leon wrote a life of St Theresa and a group of lyrical poems (1631), on which his modern reputation rests.

LEONARDO DA VINCI (1452–1519), Italian artist of the Renaissance. The beginnings of his many-sided interests are to be found in his period of apprenticeship in the Florentine studio of Andrea Verrocchio (1469–75). In 1481 he sought the patronage of Lodovico, Duke of Milan, and included engineering and architecture among his qualifications. At Milan he made suggestions for the roofing of the cathedral and for a revised city plan, and was employed on many practical enterprises. He also painted his *Last Supper* (in the convent of St Maria della Grazie in Milan) and his *Virgin of the Rocks*. He returned to Florence (1499) and became absorbed by a project to link the Tuscan cities by canals. He also painted his *Mona Lisa*, the portrait of a wife of a Florentine merchant. His last years were spent under the patronage of King Francis I of France. His repeated failure to complete projects was not due to impatience, but to his perfectionism, the distraction of an excessive number of commissions, his fascination with techniques, and his concern with theoretical studies. His love of experimentation led to the partial and premature disintegration of some of his paintings (especially the *Last Supper*), as it also contributed to the eerie light which fills his later paintings and makes his landscapes different from those of any of his predecessors. His portraits are unique for their psychological insight.

LEONIDAS (d. 480 BC), Spartan Agiad King (*reg.* 490–480), whose famous fight to the death with 300 Spartiates against the Persian army at Thermopylae won the Greeks precious time and strengthened their morale for later battles.

LEONTINI, ancient Greek city in eastern Sicily founded from Sicilian Naxos *c.* 730 BC at the southern end of the Symaethus (Simeto) plain, 40 kms north-west of Syracuse. Leontini, primarily an agricultural community, flourished for two centuries before its subjection early in the 5th cent. to Hippocrates of Gela and subsequently to Hieron of Syracuse. In its many later attempts to throw off Syracusan control Leontini contributed to both Athenian (427–424, 415–413) and Roman (215) intervention in Sicily against Syracuse. The city was finally destroyed by the Saracens (AD 848).

LEOPARD'S KOPJE CULTURE, second stage of the Iron Age in western Rhodesia. It gradually superseded the Gokomere culture from late in the first millennium, and is associated with pottery innovations and the growth of mining before the advent of stone builders.

LEOPOLD VI (d. 1230) Duke of Austria, who represented the high point of Babenberg rule in Austria. He kept out of the quarrels between the emperors and popes, was a great benefactor of the Church, and made his court into a leading cultural centre.

LEOPOLD I (1640–1705), Holy Roman Emperor (*reg.* 1658–1705), second son of Emperor Ferdinand III. He had been intended for an ecclesiastical career until the death of his elder brother, Ferdinand, King of the Romans (1654), resulted in his election to the crowns of Hungary (1655) and Bohemia (1657). His elevation to the imperial title was largely due to the efforts of the Electoral Abp of Mainz and was unanimous despite French support for the elector of Bavaria. Leopold married, first, the Infanta Margaret Theresa, second daughter of Philip IV of Spain (1666), by whom he had one child; then Maria Antonia; and after her death (1673), Eleanore Magdalene of Neuburg, by whom he had two sons, the future Emperors Joseph I and Charles VI.

Leopold succeeded to the imperial throne at a critical time, when Austria's ally, Poland, had been attacked by Charles X of Sweden and George Rakoczy, Prince of Transylvania (1657), while the Ottoman Turks under Muhammad Käprülü posed a new threat by overrunning Transylvania (1658). After the conclusion of the Northern War (1660) Leopold engaged in two wars with the Turks (1662–4, 1682–99) with wide fluctuations of fortune, *eg,* the victory at St Gotthard (1664) and the Turkish siege of Vienna (1683). The first ended in the 20-year truce of Vasvar (1664) and the second in the triumphant treaty of Carlowitz (1699), which confirmed the Habsburgs in possession of Hungary and Transylvania, except the Banat of Temesvar.

Hungary proved an intermittent problem. The revolt of 1670 was firmly suppressed, the Magyar leaders, Zrinyi and Frangepan, being executed and the Hungarian constitution replaced by direct Austrian rule. However, oppression, dearth (1679), and plague (1678–80) provoked further rebellion in Bohemia (1680) and Hungary (1681) and Leopold was forced by Count Imre Thököly to restore the Hungarian constitution. After the fall of Budapest (1686) Hungary was gradually subjected again to Habsburg rule through the dictatorship of Kollonics and the *Hofkriegsrat*. Archduke Joseph was crowned king in Pressburg (1687), while the Hungarian diet accepted the right of hereditary succession in the Habsburg male line. Though recognizing the ruling prince, Leopold also retained suzerainty over Transylvania. Another major problem for Leopold was Louis XIV's challenge to him for the hegemony of Europe. Under the influence of the francophile Prince Lobkowitz, Leopold signed treaties of neutrality with Louis (1667, 1671) which lasted until France threatened the empire's Rhine frontier (1673). Leopold then joined in the Dutch War (1674) to reduce France to her 1660 frontiers, but was forced to accept the peace of Nymwegen (1679) and cede Freiburg to France. Louis's *réunion* policy forced Leopold to break the truce of Ratisbon (1684) and join the League of Augsburg (1686), after which he entered the Nine Years War (1689–97), by which he succeeded in regaining the right bank of the Rhine. His last years were spent in further conflict with Louis XIV over the Spanish inheritance, which he claimed for his younger son, Charles. In 1701 Leopold joined the Grand Alliance and Vienna was later saved at Blenheim (1704) from Franco-Bavarian attack.

Leopold sought to fulfil the ideal of the paternalistic, bureaucratic state. The establishment of a standing army and the creation of a central council of imperial ministers, the *Geheime Conferenz* (1669), provided some centralization, and the reorganization of the military administration (1681) improved the imperial defence system. The long period of war and the overriding influence of the Jesuits may have hindered cultural development in the territories over which he ruled, although this pious and dutiful ruler was himself interested in books, the theatre, and music. He died while Austria was still involved in the Hungarian revolt of Francis Rakoczi (1703–1711) and the War of the Spanish Succession (1701–13).
                                          MKS

LEOPOLD II (1747–92), Holy Roman Emperor (*reg.* 1790–1792), son of the Emperor Francis I and Maria Theresa. He was an enlightened despot and was created Grand Duke of Tuscany in 1765, making this former Medici possession into one of the best-ruled states in Europe. Inspired by the Physiocrats, he abolished serfdom, revised the criminal code, removed internal customs barriers, and abolished guilds. He was concerned for the welfare of his subjects, and his constitutional proposals, embodied in the Charter of 1782, were remarkable for their democratic ideals.

After succeeding his brother Joseph II as emperor by a combination of force and concession, Leopold restored stability to those provinces of Hungary and the Netherlands that were in revolt at Joseph's death. He skilfully manipulated the diets, persuading them to confirm some reforms and rescind other measures. He protected the non-privileged classes and had embarked on constitutional reforms in Bohemia and Hungary when he suddenly died.

Leopold's foreign policy was peaceful and conciliatory. He extricated Austria from the costly Turkish war and tried to avoid direct conflict with France.

LEOPOLD II (1797–1870), last Grand Duke of Tuscany (*reg.* 1824–59). Although a mild and progressive ruler he found it difficult to adjust himself to the new forces of liberalism and nationalism. He granted a constitution (1848) and declared for a federal union of Italy, which was denounced (1849) both by Sardinia and by the pope. With the triumph of the democratic party Leopold retired from Florence. Though restored by the Austrian army in the following year, he never regained his former prestige and in 1859 chose to abdicate rather than make an alliance with Sardinia. In 1860 Tuscany was annexed by Sardinia and in 1861 became part of the new kingdom of Italy.

LEOPOLD I (1790–1865), King of the Belgians (*reg.* 1831–65), son of Francis, Duke of Saxe-Coburg, uncle of Queen Victoria. He served with distinction in the Russian army (1805–1818) under Alexander I. In 1816 he married Princess Charlotte, heir-presumptive to the English throne, and although she died in 1817, he remained in England until 1830. He continued to be interested in English affairs and corresponded frequently with his niece. He refused the Crown of Greece, offered to him in 1830, but was elected King of the Belgians in June 1831. In 1832 he married Louise of Orléans, daughter of Louis Philippe, thus assuring himself of French assistance in his eight-year battle to establish the new nation in the face of the resolute hostility of the Dutch. After 1839 Leopold was free to concentrate on the building of the new state and it is a testament to his wisdom and moderation that Belgium avoided revolutionary disruption in 1848. His political influence throughout Europe was considerable.

LEOPOLD II (1835–1909), King of the Belgians (*reg.* 1865–1909). Throughout his life his main interest was in African exploration and colonization, and it was as a result of the expeditions he sponsored that the European 'scramble for Africa' was inaugurated. In 1867 he founded the International African Association (later renamed International Association of the Congo) and commissioned Stanley to explore the Congo river basin. At the Berlin Africa Conference (1884–5) this area was recognized as the Congo Free State and Leopold's personal possession. Leopold thus 'owned' the Congo in his own right, and under his rule its inhabitants were exploited with such barbarity, even for those days of colonial expansion and oppression, that a public outcry was aroused. He was forced by public pressure to set up an enquiry (1904–5), which produced a report critical of his administration, and in 1908 the Congo was annexed to the Belgian state. However, he ruled Belgium with statesmanship, managing to preserve her neutrality in the Franco–Prussian War (1870–1), and steering a hazardous course through the anti-clerical crises of domestic politics. He was succeeded by his nephew, Albert I.

LEOPOLD III (1901–), King of the Belgians (*reg.* 1934–51), succeeded his father, Albert I. As commander of the Belgian army in the Second World War he ordered its capitulation to Germany on 28 May 1940, a decision which was neither approved by his government nor popularly supported. While Leopold insisted on staying in Belgium throughout the war, and went into German captivity, his ministers went into exile in London. After liberation (1944) the Belgian parliament proclaimed Leopold's brother Charles regent, subsequently (July 1945) deciding to make Leopold's restoration dependent upon a majority vote in parliament. In 1946 Leopold appointed a commission of enquiry into his conduct during the war, and its report published in 1947 absolved him from the major charge of collaboration with the Germans. A national referendum followed (1950), in which 58 per cent of the population, mainly the Flemish group, voted for his return, but riots followed which created a dangerous situation that led to Leopold's abdication in favour of his son Baudouin (1951).

LEOPOLD III, Margrave of Austria, Saint (1095–1136). In 1122 he negotiated the concordat of Worms, which ended the Investiture Contest. He showed great political realism, refusing to become an emperor and keeping his lands immune from general German troubles.

LEOPOLD WILLIAM, bishop, Archduke of Austria (1614–61), son of Emperor Ferdinand II (1578–1637) and governor of the Spanish Netherlands (1647–56). His father chose an ecclesiastical career for him and he was made Bp of Olomouc and Breslau. Appointed imperial commander-in-chief by his elder brother, Ferdinand III, in 1640, he proved a disastrous choice, being soundly defeated by the Swedes under Torstensson at the second battle of Breitenfeld (1642) and later by the French under the Duc d'Enghien at Lens (1648). Meanwhile, he had been appointed governor of the Netherlands (1647) to preserve the links between the Spanish and Austrian Habsburgs. Although joined by Turenne and Condé after the peace of Westphalia (1648), Leopold had little military success in the Netherlands, and his pro-Jesuit policy alienated many Jansenist sympathizers, eg, Jacob Boonen, Abp of Mechlin. He was replaced as governor by Don Juan Jose of Austria (1656).

LEOTYCHIDAS II (d. *c.* 469 BC), Spartan Eurypontid King who succeeded the deposed Demaratus in 491 and in the second Persian invasion of Greece commanded the Greek navy which in 479 drove the Persians from the Aegean, destroying their fleet at Mycale. He subsequently failed to remove the pro-Persian Aleuadae from Thessaly, and was exiled (?476) on suspicion of taking bribes.

LEPANTO, BATTLE OF (1571), defeat of the Turkish navy in the Gulf of Corinth by a smaller force under Don John of

Austria. After the Turks had taken Cyprus (1569), the pope formed a league that included Spain, Venice, the Genoese under Doria, and other Italian states. The victory was not followed up, and Don John attacked Tunis instead of going on to Constantinople; but the battle ended the legend of Turkish invincibility at sea.

LEPCIS (less correctly **LEPTIS**) **MAGNA,** ancient Phoenician and Roman city on the Libyan coast, founded in the 5th cent. BC. It was a wealthy city when Rome conquered North Africa (mid-2nd cent. BC) and its prosperity, derived from trans-Saharan trade and local agriculture, increased. It became a Roman colony under Trajan (c. AD 109). Its fortunes were at their height under Septimius Severus (193–211), a native of Lepcis. In the 4th cent. it became the capital of Tripolitania, but declined under Vandal rule. Magnificent remains of the Roman city survive.

LÉPERO, derogatory term applied individually or collectively to the beggars, petty thieves, and vagabonds who infested the larger cities of Latin America during the colonial era and much of the modern period.

LERDO DE TEJADA, MIGUEL (c. 1814–61), Mexican Liberal politician of the 'Reform' period, sponsor of important legislation attacking the landed position of the Church and the clergy in Mexico, and secretary of the treasury (1855–9). Lerdo initiated the most influential law concerning the Church during the Reform period (1855–67). It (1856) denied the Church or any other corporation the right to own land in excess of its basic financial requirements. Lerdo supported legislation subjecting the religious orders and the Church to government regulation.

LERDO DE TEJADA, SEBASTIÁN (1825–89), president of Mexico (1872–6), and a leader of the Reform period. He was a Liberal politician and a supporter of President Benito Juárez. He rose from being a lawyer to be a judge of the Supreme Court (1855–7) and a cabinet minister (1857–67). He was among Juárez's closest associates during the War of Reform (1858–61) and the French intervention (1862–7). Following the restoration of the republic he became chief justice of the Supreme Court (1867–72). He succeeded to the presidency when Juárez died in office (July 1872), and was president from 1872 to 1876. Gen. Porfirio Díaz conspired successfully against Lerdo (1876), who had hoped to serve for a second term, but failed to rally enough support and was forced into exile.

LERMA, FRANCISCO GOMEZ DE SANDOVAL Y ROJAS, Duke of (1553–1625), Spanish statesman and powerful favourite of Philip III. With vast royal patronage at his disposal, Lerma demoralized the Cortes and councils with bribes, pensions, and gifts of office, and amassed a huge personal fortune.

Having watched the breakdown of the aggressive and doctrinaire policies of the previous reign, Lerma decided that Spanish influence might be less expensively maintained by the traditional Habsburg policy of dynastic marriages. He made peace with England (1604) and a truce with the Dutch (1609). He had to keep a force in the Mediterranean to contain Venice and the Berbers, and in Italy he was troubled by the ambitions of the Duke of Savoy. But relations with France were smoother after the death of Henry IV (1610), and in 1615 the Infanta Anne was married to Louis XIII, and Philip, the Spanish heir, to Louis's sister.

Lerma's domestic policy was less successful. In 1609 the Moriscoes, the Christianized Moors whom Philip II had deported from Granada (1570) and settled in other regions, were expelled. Forming about a quarter of the population, they were hard-working and prosperous, but the Spaniards frowned on intermarriage and there was no real prospect of integration. The Moriscoes were expelled on ideological grounds, regardless of the possibility of unfavourable economic consequences.

Prices meanwhile were rising because of inflation, and as early as 1599 the government had begun to debase the coinage in a hopeless attempt to balance expenditure. Crown lands were sold, the *alcabala* rose from 10 per cent to 14 per cent, and trade was further crippled by an excise ('the millions'), and by tolls so obstructive that goods were only sold at their place of manufacture. The indiscriminate charity of the Church merely encouraged the mendicant mentality which Cervantes satirized in *Don Quixote*.

If Lerma understood these difficulties, he only aggravated them by his acquiescence when Philip, after the death of his wife (1611), sank into morbid religiosity. Yet it was through the mutterings of friars and confessors that Olivares, Lerma's ambitious rival, weakened Philip's confidence in his favourite. When his own son was inveigled into the plot to remove him, Lerma claimed a cardinal's hat from Paul V to comfort his retirement (1618), leaving it for others to decide whether it was in Spain's interest to join in the Thirty Years War.

J. H. Elliott, *Imperial Spain* (London, 1963).   MMR

LERNA, ancient pre-Greek settlement near Argos, famous for its monumental House of Tiles (40 kms × 19 kms) built in the second half of the 3rd millennium BC and destroyed sometime before the intrusion of Greek-speaking peoples, c. 2000.

LERROUX, GARCÍA ALJANDRO (1864–1949), Spanish politician and prime minister, who became leader of the extremist Radical Republicans in Barcelona (c. 1900). He roused the city's workers by inciting them to kill priests, burn churches, and overthrow the rich. But during the Barcelona insurrection of 1909 the Radicals stood aside. This betrayal and their corruption lost them much support to the anarchists.

Lerroux became henceforth a mild Republican whose appeal was to the middle classes. With the advent of the republic (1931) he seemed an obsolete survivor from the days of *caciquismo*, but, because the Radicals were the second largest party, with 90 seats, Lerroux became foreign minister. He resigned (Oct. 1931) when Azaña was made prime minister in preference to himself. In 1933 he became the advocate of 'a republic for all Spaniards' and when in the elections of that year the Radicals gained 104 seats, he became prime minister. During his two ministries (Nov. 1933–April 1934, Oct. 1934–April 1935) he steered a moderate course, hoping to curtail the republic's dependence on revolutionary parties. He hoped also to bring over the mass of Catholics and monarchists by showing that the republic could protect the Church and property. Agrarian reforms were slowed down and church schools allowed to operate normally. After the Asturian rising (1934) Lerroux tried to subdue the right's call for revenge. Two financial scandals in 1935 brought his government down and in the Feb. 1936 elections his party failed to win a seat. Though he endorsed the June rising of that year, his anti-clerical reputation kept him in exile, where he wrote his account of the republic, *La Pequeñe Historia*.

LESAGE, ALAIN RENÉ (1668–1747), French dramatist and novelist, who went to Paris (1692) to study the Spanish language and Spanish literature. He wrote dramas, eg, *Turcaret* (1709), and novels, eg, *Le Diable Boiteux* (1707), his masterpiece being *Gil Blas* (1715).

LESCOT, ELIE (1883–), Haitian lawyer, diplomat, and president (1941–6), who governed during a period of economic crisis. His administration was plagued by riots. He was accused by opponents of conducting an elite regime and was overthrown and exiled in 1946.

LESCZYNSKI, STANISLAS (1677–1766), King of Poland (*reg.* 1704–9, 1733–4). He was the pawn of Charles XII of Sweden, by whom Augustus II of Poland-Saxony was deposed in favour of Stanislas (1704). Augustus's reununciation was reinforced by the treaty of Altranstädt (1706), but Sweden's defeat at Poltava forced Stanislas to leave Poland, which was recovered by Augustus (1709). For the next 16 years (1709–25) he lived in obscure exile at the Hôtel Weber at Wissembourg, Alsace, the recipient of a small pension bestowed upon him by the regent of France, the Duke of Orléans. After the marriage of his only daughter, Maria, to Louis XV of France, Stanislas lived at the Château de Chambord in a style befitting the king's father-in-law (1725–33) until the death of Augustus of Poland-Saxony (1733) renewed his prospects of the Polish throne. At the instigation of the anti-Habsburg faction of ministers, led by Villars, Chauvelin, and Belle-Isle, Stanislas was reluctantly granted three million francs by Fleury with which to recover the Polish Crown. Disguised as a merchant, he travelled incognito through the Holy Roman empire and on reaching Poland was elected king (12 Sept. 1733). However, Saxon forces, supported by imperial and Russian troops, overran Poland and forced Stanislas and his supporters, including the Princes Czartoryski and Poniatowski, to flee to Danzig, whence he escaped across Prussia in a farm cart, leaving his followers to face a four-month siege before capitulating to Augustus III of Saxony. Stanislas again abdicated (Königsberg, 1734). At the end of the War of the Polish Succession (1733–8) Stanislas confirmed his cession of Poland to Augustus, but through French diplomatic pressure was compensated with the duchy of Lorraine and Bar (1738), whose reigning duke, Francis III, moved to Tuscany, while France received the reversion of Lorraine. Stanislas settled down at his provincial court at Lunéville, but was forced to leave it temporarily in face of the Austrian advance after Dettingen (1743) and he died there in 1766.

His daughter, Leszcynska Maria (1703–68), married (1725) Louis XV of France, bore him ten children, and was a strong Jesuit supporter.

LESDIGUIÈRES, FRANÇOIS DE BONNE, Duc de (1543–1626), French nobleman, who replaced Montbrun as Huguenot leader in the Civil Wars (1575), and became a marshal of France under Henry IV (1608). Under Louis XIII he helped to negotiate the treaty of Montpellier (1622), abandoned Protestantism in favour of Catholicism, and was rewarded with the office of constable of France.

LÈSE-MAJESTÉ, basic principle of the law of treason, which regarded any offence against the person of the sovereign as punishable by death. In England, the vagueness of the offence at common law, and the consequent arbitrariness of judicial decisions, led to a statute of Edward III (1352) which defined *lèse-majesté* as compassing the king's death, levying war against him, or adhering to his enemies. In times of political disorder further definitions were evolved to meet new emergencies. In the reign of Henry VIII a case of poisoning was held to be a treasonable act against the sovereign.

LESOTHO (17,000 sq. kms) in south Africa, formerly the British High Commission Territory of Basutoland, became independent in 1966 as a constitutional monarchy within the British Commonwealth. A general election under adult suffrage elects a senate and national assembly of 60 members, which provides a prime minister and cabinet responsible to the monarch. Most of the 967,700 people are Sotho.

LESSEPS, FERDINAND DE (1805–1894), French diplomat and friend of Sa'id Pasha, from whom he obtained a concession (20 Nov. 1854) for the construction of the Suez Canal, the successful completion of which owed much to De Lesseps' skill and tenacity. His attempt to repeat his success by building a Panama Canal (1879–89) ended in disaster.

LESSER ARMENIA. The advent of the Seljuk Turks gave rise in the years after AD 1064 to a movement of Armenians westward into Byzantine Asia Minor—a process which was accelerated following the Seljuk defeat of the Byzantines at Manzikert in 1071. This westward migration of Armenian elements led to the emergence of a Christian kingdom of Lesser Armenia, embracing Cilicia and the mountains north of that area and including such towns as Sis, Mamistra, Adana, Tarsus, and Ayas (Lajazzo). Under Leo II (1187–1219), who acquired from the emperor and the pope the title of king, and under Hethoum I (1226–69), Lesser Armenia was at the height of its influence. The Armenians sought to defend themselves against the Muslims through alliances with Antioch, with Cyprus, and above all with the Mongols. The eviction of the Latins from Syria (completed in 1291) and the decline of the Mongol regime of the Il-Khans in Persia (above all, after 1304) exposed the Armenians to the pressure of the Mamluks, who had ruled since 1250–60 over Egypt and Syria. Mamluk troops ravaged Cilicia in 1266, 1274–5, 1293, 1322, and 1337. Ayas fell to them in 1347; Adana and Tarsus in 1359. With the Mamluk capture of Sis (1375) the kingdom of Lesser Armenia came to an end.

LESSING, GOTTHOLD EPHRAIM (1729–81), German philosopher, poet, and critic, famous for his tragedy *Emilia Galeotti* (1772) and the drama *Nathan the Wise* (1780), which he wrote in the cause of toleration. Lessing helped to make German into a literary language.

L'ESTRANGE, SIR ROGER (1616–1704), English journalist and pamphleteer, who was an ardent royalist during the Civil Wars, and was appointed censor or surveyor of the press (1663). He started the *Intelligencer* (1663) and the *Observator* (1681), both political periodicals. Becoming suspected of Catholic sympathies, he was forced to flee to the United Provinces (1680–1) and was later deprived of his office (1688) and imprisoned (1688, 1695–6).

LE TELLIER, MICHEL DE LOUVOIS (1603–85), secretary of state for war and chancellor of France under Louis XIV (1677–85). He was patronized by, and served, Mazarin and Anne of Austria as an outstanding administrator. After Fouquet's dismissal he, Lionne, and Colbert, who had been his secretary, became Louis XIV's counsellors. He continued the work of Sublet de Noyers in carrying out sweeping military reforms over a period of 20 years and founded the *intendants de l'armée*, who introduced an efficient administrative despotism into the army. Most of his reforms of discipline, recruitment, training, and command were carried out jointly with his son, Louvois, who succeeded him as minister for war after Le Tellier had been promoted to be chancellor. His administrative talents were far from confined to military matters and as a member of the *conseil d'en haut* he was consulted by Louis XIV on all important political problems.

LE TELLIER, PÈRE MICHEL (1643–1719), French Jesuit confessor of Louis XIV, who succeeded Père de La Chaise in 1709. He persuaded Louis to raze the Jansenist abbey of Port-Royal-des-Champs.

LE THAI-TO (1385–1433), first Emperor of the Le dynasty (*reg.* 1428–33). He was formerly known as Le Roi and was a native of the province of Thanh-Hoa, then one of the more southerly areas of Dai-Viet. He led a resistance movement (1418–27) against the Chinese government which had been established following the Ming conquest of Viet-nam in 1407. His campaigns are remembered especially because of his guerrilla war methods, in which the capture of the capital came only after he controlled the whole country. After his victory, he deposed the last emperor of the Tran dynasty and seized the throne for his own clan. As emperor he was assisted by the celebrated poet Nguyen Trai.

LE THANH-TONG (1442–97), Emperor of Viet-nam (*reg.* 1460–97), whose reign is sometimes called the golden age of Viet-namese Confucianism. Early on, he succeeded in bridging the gulf which had previously existed between military and scholastic officials, permitting the latter a greater role in government than they had ever enjoyed before. There followed a thorough overhaul of government institutions, on Confucian principles, and there was regular recruitment of officials by examination. Le Thanh-Tong's reign is also noted for the development of Confucian literature, as well as for the military successes of 1470–1, which led to the fall of the Cham city of Vijaya and the annexation of a substantial area of Champa. But the balance of political forces achieved by Le Thanh-Tong could not be maintained by his successors, and the next century saw division and civil war in Viet-nam.

LETICIA DISPUTE. Leticia, a wedge-shaped territory bordering on the Amazon river in the south, was awarded to Colombia under the terms of her treaty with Peru (1922), only to become the source of a dispute between the two countries when Peruvians entered Leticia and ejected Colombian government officials (1932). Sporadic fighting developed and both governments became increasingly belligerent. The Peruvian president, Luis Sánchez Cerro, was murdered (April 1933), and thereafter the Peruvian government became more conciliatory. The Leticia territory was transferred by both sides to an international commission, which a year later returned it to Colombia.

LETRADOS, Spanish jurists, trained at one of the universities of Castile, and usually drawn from *hidalgo* (gentry) or bourgeois backgrounds. They were widely used as bureaucrats by Isabella and Ferdinand and their successors to counteract the power of the great nobles.

LE TROQUER, ANDRÉ (1884–1963), French lawyer and socialist politician under the Third and Fourth French republics. He was elected socialist deputy in the popular front victory (1936) and in 1940 vehemently opposed French capitulation. He became the Socialist representative on the *Conseil Nationale de la Résistance* (CNR). At the Riom trial (1942) he defended Leon Blum. After playing an important part in reorganizing the clandestine Socialist Party he left France for Algiers and joined De Gaulle's National Committee. He became minister of war (1945) and president of the National Assembly (1954). When the Left Coalition was disrupted after the defeat of the European Defence Community, Le Troquer lost the presidency of the Assembly, but regained it in 1956 and held it until the end of the Fourth Republic. He was opposed to De Gaulle's return to power in 1958 and at one time hoped to succeed René Coty as president of the republic and constitute a government of a 'republican majority' including the Communists. He left political life shortly after De Gaulle's return to power (1956).

LETTER OF MAJESTY, imperial edict granted by Emperor Rudolph II in 1609, recognizing freedom of worship for the Protestants of Bohemia and guaranteeing the ecclesiastical property of both Catholics and Protestants. It was confirmed by the Bohemian Diet as a fundamental law in 1619, but was abolished by the Emperor Ferdinand II in 1627.

LETTER OF MARQUE, commission to the captain of a merchant ship or a privateer to take reprisals on an enemy's ships or property.

LETTER TO A DISSENTER (1687), written by George Savile, Marquis of Halifax (1633–95). It was provoked both by James II's Declaration of Indulgence (4 April 1687), which suspended all penal laws against Catholics and Protestant dissenters, and by addresses from nonconformists pledging their support to the King. It warned the dissenters not to trust James, as he was turning to them as second best, having failed to win over the Anglicans—if he gained their support he would sooner or later turn on them and destroy them.

LETTOW-VORBECK, PAUL VON (1870–1964), German general, who saw service in the Boxer Rising, China, and South-West Africa (1903). He was appointed commander of German colonial troops in the Cameroons (1911) and of colonial troops in German East Africa (1914). Although lacking reinforcements or supplies, he kept a much larger force in action against him throughout the First World War. But in 1915 he lost Bukoba, and in 1916–17 Gen. Smuts, adding South African troops to the British and Indian forces, captured most of German East Africa. Smuts failed to capture Von Lettow-Vorbeck's column, which the latter led skilfully in guerrilla fighting for the rest of the war. In 1919 he returned to Germany, and was leader of a corps named after him, until its disbandment. He sided with Kapp in the latter's unsuccessful putsch (1920) and was then obliged to retire. He wrote *Meine Erinnerungen aus Deutsch-Ostafrika* (1919).

LETTRE DE CACHET, French royal order, sealed with the private royal seal, issued during the *ancien régime* for the arrest and imprisonment of an individual. The system was abolished in 1790.

LETTRE DE JUSSION, French royal order to the *parlements* during the *ancien régime* demanding the immediate and unqualified registration of royal legislation.

LETTRE DE JUSTICE, authorization of the *parlements* for a case to be brought before it during the *ancien régime* in France.

LEUCTRA, BATTLE OF (July 371 BC), defeat 16 kms southwest of Thebes in central Greece by a smaller Theban army under Pelopidas and Epaminondas of the Spartans and their allies, under King Cleombrotus, who were advancing from the west to ensure the independence of the Boeotian cities from Thebes, in accordance with a newly agreed peace treaty. This victory, the result of a tactical innovation—the use of a deep wedge of hoplites to break the opposing line—established Theban power in central Greece, destroyed the legend of Spartan invincibility, and within two years led to the defection of many of Sparta's Peloponnesian allies and an invasion of Laconia.

LEUSCHNER, WILHELM (1890–1944), German social democrat politician and leading member of the anti-Nazi resistance, who had been minister of the interior in Hessen (1928–33) and deputy chairman of the German trade union confederation (1932–3). He was arrested in 1933 and after his release (1935) organized trade union resistance cells in Germany and established secret contacts with British trade unions. He was arrested and executed after the failure of the July Plot (1944).

LEUTHEN, BATTLE OF (1757), Prussian victory in the Seven Years War over an Austrian army of 90,000 under Prince Charles of Lorraine and Count Daun. The Austrians lost 20,000 prisoners and 134 guns and five days later (10 Dec.) Breslau surrendered to Prussia. Leuthen exemplifies the success of the oblique battle order in overcoming a superior enemy force.

LEVANT (from the French 'lever', to rise), the name often used to note the coastal lands of the eastern Mediterranean and in particular of Syria and Asia Minor.

LEVANT COMPANY, English company granted a monopoly of trade with Constantinople and the eastern Mediterranean, founded when William Harborne went to Turkey (1580) to request the sultan to grant privileges to English merchants. Originally the Turkey Co., it received its more familiar title when incorporated with the Venice Co. (1591). It maintained a resident ambassador in Constantinople, and its principal depots were at Smyrna, Aleppo, Alexandria, and Tunis. Trade was largely in currants, for which lead, textiles, and fish were exchanged. The company captured much of the

Mediterranean trade from Venice, but was later in conflict with the East India Co. about their respective spheres of operation. Although it slowly declined, it continued to trade until early in the 19th cent.

LEVELLERS, THE, in England, 17th-cent. agitators and pamphleteers who urged parliament and the generals (1648–1649) to adopt more radical measures than the latter wished to countenance. John Lilburne, William Walwyn, Richard Overton, and John Wildman were the leaders of the Levellers, who were an amorphous group and appealed to varied economic and social interests.

The end of the Civil War offered an unprecedented opportunity for the reframing of the constitution and the rejection of the notion of a balance between king, lords, and commons. The Levellers emerged as a symbol of the discontent felt by parliament's more radical supporters at its intransigence in refusing petitions and imprisoning without trial, since, as Lilburne argued, parliament's sovereignty derived from the people and therefore should be representative of the people. Their philosophy, an amalgam of pleas for the historic rights of free-born Englishmen and a claim to the natural rights of men, soon embraced a catch-all reform programme: abolition of the monarchy and the House of Lords, redistribution and extension of the franchise, the abolition of excise and of the privileges of corporations, law reform, and demands for arrears of pay and indemnity for the army. This programme appealed to the small masters and apprentices of London and to the army's rank and file, whose elected representatives, the agitators, co-operated with civilian Levellers to produce, in Oct. 1647, a written constitution, the Agreement of the People, which assumed, in opposition to the generals' Heads of the Proposals, the end of the monarchy and called for biennial parliaments. Cromwell and the generals, already at odds with the House of Commons, and unwilling to let the army slip from their control, debated these matters in the army council, which, since June had become representative of all ranks. The extension of the franchise was the vital issue of the Putney debates. Although Levellers spoke as if in favour of manhood suffrage, in fact, their notion of a 'free Englishman' was limited to those able to dispose of their own labour. This excluded wage labourers, apprentices, and servants, as well as paupers and criminals. The generals claimed the Levellers' position to be far more democratic and destructive of property rights than was the case. The debates ended inconclusively.

The king's flight in Nov. 1647 reunited the ranks behind Cromwell, who easily suppressed the Leveller mutiny at Ware. After the Second Civil War, Cromwell needed the Levellers' support for a time, to keep the army united, but the Levellers disliked the Rump and its council of state as much as they had the king and privy council. Lilburne was imprisoned again, mutinous troopers were court-martialled, and in May 1649 the most serious Leveller-led mutiny was crushed. The destruction of Leveller influence in the army was final. The leaders turned to other matters or faded into obscurity.

The Levellers were not communistic utopians, as were the Diggers, who called themselves 'the true levellers', nor successful politicians, for their support was never united. They did, however, sway events some way in the direction they desired and earned the right to be regarded as the precursors of the British parliamentary reform movement.   DS

LEVEN, ALEXANDER LESLIE, 1st Earl of (Scottish) (?1580–1661), Scottish soldier, who gained his military experience in the Swedish army and rose to become fieldmarshal (1636). He returned to Scotland (1638) as a supporter of the Covenanters, and was made lord general of the covenanting army (1639). He successfully invaded England in the second Bishops' War. In 1641 he accompanied Charles I to Scotland, and was created Earl of Leven at the request of the Scottish parliament. In 1643 he commanded the Scottish army sent to help the English parliament, and led the Scottish troops at Mar-

ston Moor (1644). He entertained Charles I at Newcastle (1645–7), and on returning to Scotland in 1647 continued in office, though his age curtailed his active service. He opposed the Engagement (1648) and the invasion of England. He was appointed to command the army sent against Cromwell's invasion of Scotland, but was defeated at Dunbar (1650). He was captured and imprisoned in England (1651–4).

LEVERS' PACIFIC PLANTATIONS LTD, firm which acquired extensive British and German concessions in the Solomon Islands (1905–6) for copra production. With other firms, Levers' brought the infant British colony useful early revenues, but its activities were restricted at various times by local anarchy and depopulation, by government refusal (1911) to admit indentured Indian labour, and by the Second World War (1942–5).

LEVI, CARLO (1902–), Italian painter, writer, and senator. For co-ordinating the liberal anti-fascist *Giustizia e Libertà* movement in Turin he was 'confined' to Lucabia in southern Italy (1935–6). His book *Christ Stopped at Eboli* (1947) was a major contribution to the understanding of problems in southern Italy. Other documentary memoirs and articles by Levi reveal the problems of Italy's underdeveloped areas, and advocate reforms, as well as giving support to activists like Danilo Dolci.

LEVIATHAN, THE (1651), English political treatise by Thomas Hobbes, in which he argued that fear is the basis of society. In a state of nature the life of man is 'solitary, poor, nasty, brutish, and short', and since his object is preservation, he covenants to surrender his individual rights to a sovereign power which unites the multitude in a single person, or commonwealth. Hobbes thus denied both the divine origin of kingship and the theory of conditional obedience depending upon a revocable contract. His treatise persuaded some royalists that it was expedient to submit to Oliver Cromwell.

LÉVIS, FRANÇOIS-GASTON, Duc de (1720–87), French soldier, who succeeded to the command of the French forces in Canada on the death of Montcalm (1759). At the battle of Sainte-Foye (April 1760) he defeated the British forces, but was unable to recapture Quebec or prevent the capitulation of Montreal.

LEWANIKA (d. 1916), Ruler of the Lozi kingdom, who restored the strength and unity of the state after ejection of the Kololo and maintained it in face of advancing British interests to remain paramount chief under the protectorate.

LEWES, BATTLE OF (May 1264), in the south of England, site of the first major battle of the English Barons' War (1263–5). For nearly a year there had been indecisive fighting, interspersed with fruitless negotiations, but at Lewes Simon de Montfort, the baronial leader, defeated and captured King Henry III of England and his son Prince Edward. This gave Montfort control over the English government for over a year, when Edward escaped from captivity and killed Montfort at the battle of Evesham (Aug. 1265).

LEWIS, ESSINGTON (1881–1961), Australian industrialist, who was executive head of Broken Hill Proprietary Co. (1921–52). After visiting Japan in 1934, he became convinced that a Pacific war was imminent and expanded Australia's steel industry and also started the manufacture of military aircraft in Melbourne. He was Australia's director-general of munitions (1940–5).

LEWIS, SIR GEORGE CORNEWALL (1806–63), English politician, writer, and administrator. He served on commissions enquiring upon affairs in Ireland (1833) and Malta (1836–8) and became a poor law commissioner for England and Wales (1839–47). He was editor of *The Edinburgh Review*

(1852–5), Liberal chancellor of the exchequer (1855–8), home secretary (1859–61), and secretary for war (1861–3).

LEWIS, JOHN LLEWELLYN (1880–1969), US labour leader, who, after holding various offices in the United Mine Workers Union (1909–20), became its president (1920–60). He was a persistent advocate of improvements in miners' wages and conditions. Following a disagreement with the American Federation of Labor over industrial unionism, he was instrumental in forming the Committee for Industrial Organization (1935), and was its first president (1935–40). In 1936, being well aware of the potential political power of organized labour, he supported F. D. Roosevelt, but broke with him because the president refused to accept any political obligation to Lewis. In 1942 he withdrew his union from the CIO after disagreement with its new president, Philip Murray, and subsequently (1946) reaffiliated it to the AFL, but withdrew it from the Federation after differences about signing the non-communist affidavit of the Taft–Hartley Act (1947).

LEWIS, (HARRY) SINCLAIR (1885–1951), US novelist, who achieved popularity with *Main Street* (1920), an attack on the drabness and complacency of Mid-western middle-class society. He became internationally famous with *Babbitt* (1922), a satirical study of the US businessman. After *Arrowsmith* (1925), *Elmer Gantry* (1927), and *Dodsworth* (1929), the power of his work declined, although such books as *It Can't Happen Here* (1935), an account of a totalitarian revolution in the US, had a considerable impact. Lewis was the first American to be awarded the Nobel Prize for Literature (1930).

LEWIS AND CLARK EXPEDITION (1804–6), first US expedition to explore the northern part of the Louisiana Purchase and to make accurate and scientific observations of the region and its inhabitants. President Jefferson appointed his private secretary, Meriwether Lewis, to lead the expedition and Lewis invited his friend William Clark to share command. The party of 34 soldiers and 10 civilians trained in frontier techniques during the winter of 1803–4, and left St Louis in May 1804. They travelled by boat up the Missouri to the Mandan villages in what is now North Dakota, where they established winter quarters. On 7 April Lewis and Clark, with 26 soldiers, 2 interpreters, and an Indian woman guide, moved on up the Missouri towards the unknown West. They reached the Great Falls of the Missouri (13 June 1805), crossed the Continental Divide with help from friendly Shoshone Indians, followed the Clearwater to the Snake, and so reached the Columbia. On 7 Nov. 1805 they saw the Pacific Ocean. After spending a miserable winter at Fort Clatsop, near modern Astoria, they began the return journey late in March 1806. In order to make a more intensive exploration of the country, the party split into two groups after crossing the Rockies. They successfully regrouped near the confluence of the Yellowstone and the Missouri and moved rapidly down-river to St Louis, which they reached on 23 Sept. 1806. Despite great hardship and difficulty the 4000 miles had been successfully traversed. The party had not only discovered several usable passes through the Rockies, but, by their careful and detailed observations of the terrain, its flora, fauna, and Indian population, had contributed immeasurably to knowledge of the West.   AB

LEX REGIA (1665), Danish absolutist constitution, compiled by Schumacher (Griffenfelt) for Frederick III. It was made known at the time of the king's death in 1670, published in 1709, and remained valid until 1849. The only legal limits to royal power were the obligation not to cede national territory, change the official religion, or alter the succession.

LEX VILLIA ANNALIS (180 BC), Roman law which fixed the sequence of magistracies required for a public career and the age-qualifications for office. A man had to be quaestor,

aedile (optional), praetor, and consul in that order, and two years had to elapse between the tenure of each office.

LEXINGTON AND CONCORD, BATTLES OF (19 April 1775), first battles of the American War of Independence. Gen. Gage, commander of the British garrison at Boston, having learned that the colonists were gathering arms at Concord, sent a detachment to seize them. Paul Revere and others had aroused the countryside, and a group of Minutemen lined up across the common at Lexington to stop the British. The 'shot heard round the world' was fired and eight Americans lay dead. The British soldiers continued their march to Concord, where they were met by a group of angry farmers. When the British regiment began its return to Boston it was fired upon by Americans along the way and 273 British soldiers were killed. The Americans lost 93 men.

LEY, ROBERT (1890–1945), German chemist and politician. He joined the NSDAP in 1924 and became *Gauleiter* of Cologne (1925–32), where he acted as an important contact man between the Nazi Party and employers and banking circles. He displayed unqualified loyalty to Hitler and to the end was part of his intimate circle. In 1928 he was released for political reasons from his job as a food chemist with I.G. Farben. He was deputy to the Prussian Landtag from 1928 and to the Reichstag from 1930. In 1932 he replaced Gregor Strasser, whom he had opposed since 1925, as chief of the party organization. After the dissolution of the German trade unions in 1933, Ley was appointed leader of the German Labour Front, which ultimately embraced more than 25 million members. His repeated attempts to extend the power of the Labour Front in the economy and the state were frustrated by Schacht, Göring, and Hess. After 1936 he backed the mounting demands made on workers under the Four-Year Plan, and, through the Labour Front, administered the scheme of forced labour. He sponsored the 'Strength Through Joy' programme of regimented leisure and was one of the brains behind the *Volkswagen* (people's car) project. He also helped to organize the Nazi educational system. He was captured by American forces at the end of the Second World War and hanged himself while awaiting trial as a war criminal in Nuremberg.

LEY JUÁREZ (1855), in Mexico, law, formulated by Benito Juárez, which limited the jurisdiction of ecclesiastical and military courts in civil cases. Reaction to the law caused a strengthening of the conservative alliance between the Church and the army.

LEY LERDO (1856), in Mexico, law limiting the right of civil and ecclesiastical corporations to possess more land than was required to fulfil their needs. Indigenous communities were affected, besides the Church.

LEYDEN, UNIVERSITY OF, Dutch Protestant university founded in 1575 as a memorial to the raising of the Spanish siege of the city during the Eighty Years War (1574). Although its roots were in French culture, and among its founding scholars were the Frenchmen Louis Cappel, Guillaume Feugueray, and Joseph Scaliger, Leyden soon became a great international community, with many English and Scots students, and the chief centre of Dutch philosophy, science, and arts in the 17th–18th cents. Through the teaching of Hermann Boerhaave during the early 18th cent. it became the leading medical school in Europe.

LHASA, TREATY OF (7 Sept. 1904), imposed on Tibet after the Younghusband expedition. It provided for the promotion of commerce between India and Tibet. No foreign power was to be granted concessions for railways, roads, or mining rights. Tibet was to pay an indemnity of 75 lakhs of rupees and the British were to occupy the Chumbi valley until it did so. Later, the indemnity was reduced to 25 lakhs and the occupation of the Chumbi valley to three years. Chinese assent to the treaty was secured in 1906.

LHASA UPRISING (1959), culmination of Tibetan discontent aroused by increasing Chinese military and political activity. After the Dalai Lama's departure, Tibetan irregulars attacked Chinese positions around Lhasa, but were quickly dispersed. Guerrillas, who for some years had been active in eastern Tibet, continued the fight and have probably never been completely suppressed. The uprising provoked the Chinese to assert control over the Tibetan government.

LI, prescribed rule in traditional Chinese Society for human behaviour, designed to ensure that correct social distinctions are maintained, that persons react to one another in ways compatible with their status or relationship, and that ceremonies are carried out with due solemnity and reverence. *Li* features conspicuously in Confucianism as a means of regulating society and promulgating education.

LI HUNG-CHANG (1823–1901), politician, diplomat, and reformer of late Ch'ing China and a native of Anhwei. In 1853 Li and his father, then officials in Peking, were ordered by the throne to return to Anhwei to organize militia against the Taipings. Li's success led to his rapid rise in rank and reputation, and in 1858 he joined Tseng Kuo-fan's camp in Kiangsi. In 1861 Tseng ordered him to organize an army of Anhwei men to put a halt to the revival of Taiping activities in Kiangsu province and to protect the commercial wealth of Shanghai. With the aid of the Ever Victorious Army, Li and his men, known as the Huai Army, contributed significantly to the rebels' defeat. In 1870 Li was appointed governor-general of Chihli, the most important provincial post that he was to hold for the next 25 years. He was also concurrently the Commissioner of Trade for the Northern Ports. As such, he became involved in almost all the major issues relating to foreign affairs. His experience in these matters convinced him of the need to strengthen China against further Western encroachments. Thus he was instrumental in the development of arsenals, mining, telegraphy, the navy, and railways from the 1860s onwards. He also encouraged indigenous enterprises in order to wrest the China market from foreign control. The most successful of these enterprises was the China Merchants' Steam Navigation Co. established in 1872. However, Li's attempts at modernization were hampered by the lack of funds, conservative opposition, lack of support from Peking, and his own inability to root out corruption even within his own administrative machine.

Li's downfall was brought about by Japanese ambitions in Korea, which had traditionally acknowledged Chinese suzerainty. Tensions built up between the Chinese and the Japanese eventually erupted in the Sino-Japanese War (1894–5). The ignominious defeat of the Chinese revealed the inadequacies of China's effort at 'self-strengthening', in which Li played an important part. Although he was allowed to keep his official posts, he was stripped of his honours, and was given the task of negotiating the peace settlement with Japan. Owing to an attempt on his life during the negotiating, the terms of the treaty of Shimonoseki were less harsh than the original Japanese demands.

On his return to China Li was relieved of his posts. In 1896, however, on the occasion of the tsar's coronation he was sent to Russia, and then to Europe and North America, where he met the heads of state in Germany, England, and the US. While in Russia, he negotiated an agreement whereby Russia secured the right to build the Chinese Eastern Railway through Manchuria, short-cutting the Trans-Siberian Railway by several hundred miles. In 1899 Li was appointed governor-general of Kwangtung and Kwangsi. In this capacity, he and several other governors-general declared south China neutral during the Boxer Rising, thus saving a large part of China from being plunged into a suicidal war against the powers. In 1901 Li was recalled to Peking to negotiate the Boxer Protocol.

In many ways Li served the dynasty well, despite conservative opposition, bureaucratic inertia, and unrestrained rivalry among the powers in China. Undoubtedly, he was part of a corrupt system, and some historians blame him for establishing the pattern for the development of regional power and of that of the war-lords of a later period, and for creating a milieu suitable to their existence.

Stanley Spector, *Li Hung-chang and the Huai Army, a study in nineteenth-century Chinese regionalism* (Seattle, 1964).
                                                                                    DP

LI LI-SAN (?1900–), Chinese Communist Party chief (1928–30), associated with extreme left tendencies. Li made his career in the communist movement as a labour organizer. After the Kuomintang attack on the Communist Party (1927), he suggested the promotion of urban insurrections, which was gradually accepted as official party policy. Li gradually won control of the party organization, in the absence of the official party chief, Ch'ü Ch'iu-pai, in Moscow, but was disgraced in 1930, when a series of urban risings failed disastrously. He spent the next 15 years in Moscow. The failure of Li's plan stimulated the peasant-based policies of Mao Tse-tung.

LI SHIH-MIN (*reg.* 627–49), second of the T'ang Emperors, who had the title of T'ai-tsung. A man of strong character, bravery, and determination, he consolidated T'ang dynastic strength and China's system of government and reasserted Chinese prestige in Central Asia.

LI SSU (?280–208 BC), statesman of the Ch'in kingdom and dynasty, said to have studied in company with Han Fei under Hsün Ch'ing. He played a significant part in applying the practical principles of legalism to the unification of China (221 BC) and the government of the first of the Chinese imperial dynasties. Li Ssu helped to realize the concept of a single authority ruling all under Heaven, rather than the coexistence of a number of states owing nominal fealty to the King of Chou, while conducting their own independent governments and disputing territories between one another. The emerging structure of imperial government included central authorities and a provincial system whose officials were appointed from the centre. Li Ssu applied strict punishments of state to enforce discipline and is said to have proposed and effected the destruction of early literature by burning, so as to prevent criticism and reference to past precedent. To facilitate the conduct of government the Chinese script was standardized and simplified; and attempts were made to standardize the currency, encourage agriculture, and discourage attention being given to secondary occupations, such as commerce. Li Ssu's career ended in disgrace and death during the confused situation that followed the death of the first Ch'in emperor.

LI TA-CHAO (1889–1927), Chinese politician and a central figure in the establishment of the communist movement in China. Li, a progressive Peking intellectual, was associated with the magazine *New Youth,* and was founder (1919) of the Marxist Research Society. In 1921 Li's group of Marxists, together with Ch'en Tu'hsiu's Shanghai group, founded the Chinese Communist Party. Li continued to base himself in war-lord-dominated Peking, and did not play an active role in party organization; but his influence on specific issues, notably the formation of a CCP–Kuomintang alliance, was great. His principal role was as an intellectual leader; he was responsible for introducing large numbers of young Chinese, including Mao Tse-tung, to Marxism. In 1927 Li was arrested by troops of the war-lord Chang Tso-lin, who then controlled Peking, and was executed.

LI TSUNG-JEN (1890–1969), Chinese general and leader of the Kwangsi Clique. He and his associate, Pai Ch'ung-hsi, won control of their native province, Kwangsi, in 1925, and used it as a base from which to help the Kuomintang, and after 1929 from which to attack it. In 1936, in the interests of unity against Japan, there was a reconciliation between the clique and the Kuomintang. Li won fame during the Anti-Japanese War as an able and patriotic commander, but spent much of the time in enforced idleness because of Chiang Kai-shek's distrust of him. In 1948 he was elected vice-president, against Chiang's wishes, and became acting president when Chiang retired (Jan. 1949). At the end of the Civil War, Li went to the US, where he stayed until 1965. In that year he returned secretly to Peking, where he was welcomed and his previously anti-communist attitudes forgotten.

LI TZU-CH'ENG (*c.* 1605–45), Chinese bandit leader, who rose against the declining Ming dynasty after a severe famine in Shensi province in 1628. Having established themselves in the mountains of southern Shansi, his bands conducted raids in the northern and Yangtse provinces as far as Szechwan. In April 1644 Li captured Peking and proclaimed himself emperor while the last Ming emperor hanged himself on Prospect Hill, overlooking the Forbidden City. Li's record of banditry and the peripatetic nature of his bands precluded his development of an effective government, and being thus handicapped, he fell victim to the better-organized Manchus, who were helped by a Chinese brigade-general, Wu San-kuei. For this reason, Wu is reviled in modern China as the arch-traitor and Li as the exponent of Chinese patriotism.

LI YUAN-HUNG (1864–1928), president of China (1916–17, 1922–3). When the 1911 revolution broke out at Wuhan, Li, a local commander, fortuitously became head of the Republican government formed there. In 1912, when Yuan Shih-k'ai became president, Li was appointed vice-president, and succeeded Yuan on his death (1916). He soon resigned, after unsuccessfully dabbling in war-lord politics. He was briefly recalled five years later, to replace Hsü Shih-ch'ang.

LIANG CH'I-AO (1873–1929), Chinese reformer, political thinker, and publicist. Liang, a native of Kwangtung province and a child prodigy, studied under K'ang Yu-wei, with whom he played a vital role in the reform movement in the 1890s. Liang was also much influenced by Western missionaries, especially Timothy Richard (1845–1919). Between 1895 and 1898 Liang edited several newspapers, helped K'ang to organize study societies, and lectured on the subject of reform. He was particularly successful in Hunan, where, at the invitation of the provincial governor, he became chief instructor in the new School of Current Affairs. During the 'Hundred Days' Reform' (1895), Liang acted as a vital link between K'ang and the Kuang-hsü emperor, who, for fear of opposition from the Empress-Dowager Tzu-hsi, was unable to appoint K'ang to a position of power. After the failure of the 'Hundred Days' Reform', Liang fled to Japan.

Japanese victory in the Russo–Japanese War (1904–5) inspired another wave of reform in Ch'ing China. Some regarded Japan's success as a victory for constitutionalism over monarchism. Liang, now more familiar with Western ideas through Japanese translations, advocated nationalism, liberty, and equality as the indispensable ingredients of a modern state. These ideas were expounded in journals he edited, and posed a serious challenge to Sun Yat-sen's revolutionary cause. In the end, Liang failed to gain acceptance by the Ch'ing court or to defeat Sun's influence elsewhere. Not only was revolution more appealing to the young, but Liang himself believed in democracy, to which end he regarded constitutional monarchy as simply a means.

After the 1911 revolution Liang and a student of his, the former military governor, Ts'ai Ao, opposed the dictatorial Yüan Shih-k'ai, while his teacher K'ang, true to his Confucian heritage, supported Yüan's monarchical ambitions. During the First World War Liang became disillusioned with the unbalanced achievement of Western materialism and science, and urged a return to the spiritual civilization of China. His studies of the political thought and intellectual trends of China's past greatly enriched the 'intellectual revolution' of 1917–23.

Joseph R. Levenson, *Liang Ch'i-ch'ao and the Mind of Modern China* (Cambridge, MA, 1959).   DP

LIANG-SHUI or 'Double Tax' system, principle of taxation introduced in China in 780, after some decades in which the *chün-t'ien*, or equal field system, had failed to collect the necessary revenue and the imperial economy had been disrupted by the An Lu-shan and subsequent rebellions. In the Han empire tax had been collected from the land in kind and on a per capita basis, usually in coin; and in the Wei, Sui, and early T'ang periods it had been associated with the state scheme for the allocation of land, and based on the number of individuals of certain categories. Under the change of 780, a large number of taxes that had been introduced in the interim period were amalgamated by the imposition of the Double Tax, so-called because it was collected twice annually; and the basis for assessment was henceforth landholdings that were actually, and not only nominally, in the possession of landowners. This fundamental change marked a new period in China's economic history which was characterized by the growth of a new and more widespread practice of landlordism and tenantry.

LIAO CHUNG-K'AI (1878–1925), Kuomintang politician and party organizer. Liao, an early disciple of Sun Yat-sen was responsible for implementing the Kuomintang–Communist alliance in the early 1920s, and for supervising the reorganization of the Kuomintang along Leninist lines. He was murdered in 1925, by unknown but presumably right-wing agents. In retrospect, his murder seemed to be the first move of the right wing of the Kuomintang to eradicate left-wing influence.

LIAO DYNASTY (947–1125), founded in north China by the Ch'i-tan (Khitan) people. The dynasty was ended when the Jürched leaders set up the Chin dynasty, but it survived in east Turkestan as the Western Liao (1124–1211). The name Cathay is derived from the ethnic term Ch'i-tan.

LIAQUAT ALI KHAN, Nawabzada (1895–1951), Muslim League leader in India and prime minister of Pakistan (1947–1951), whose earliest political activities were in the United Provinces legislative council (1926–40), where he established himself as an able and forceful Muslim spokesman. He did not take a leading part in the reconstruction of the Muslim League prior to the 1937 elections, but soon afterwards he emerged as Jinnah's chief lieutenant and secretary of the league. In this position, which he retained until partition, he was a major influence on the wartime and post-war negotiations. He ran the Muslim League election campaign for the central Legislative Assembly (1945) and when the league finally agreed to join the Interim government (1946), Liaquat led the Muslim League bloc as Finance Member. He used this office, with the help of Chaudhuri Muhammad Ali, to give the league a strong position in the confrontations with the Congress which took place within the government.

At partition he assumed the post of prime minister and his role became doubly important after the death of Jinnah. He guided Pakistan through the difficult years of hostility with India (the late 1940s) and in 1950 he made, with Jawaharlal Nehru, a genuine effort to improve relations between the two countries with the so-called 'Delhi Pact'. He was also responsible for the earliest moves to draw up a constitution for Pakistan, although he was not able to get either widespread agreement or prompt action. His assassination in Oct. 1951 was a serious blow to hopes of stable government in Pakistan.

LIBANIUS (AD 314–93), rhetorician and teacher at Nicomedia and Constantinople, and from 354 until his death at his home city, Antioch. He was educated at Athens and was a convinced supporter of paganism and of Greek culture, being a friend of Julian the Apostate and refusing throughout his life to learn Latin. He was a successful teacher, numbering John Chrysostom among his pupils, and became a bold spokesman on public issues, particularly those affecting his own city and class. His numerous letters, speeches, and pamphlets are important to the social history of his time.

LIBBY, WILLARD FRANK (1908–), American chemist, who perfected (1945–7) a method of dating objects up to 45,000 years old by using the radioactive isotope carbon-14. The scientific principle involved is that this isotope is produced continuously by the interaction of cosmic rays with atmospheric nitrogen and should always be found in the carbon dioxide of the air. As a consequence of the incorporation of carbon dioxide into plant tissues and the dependence of animals on plant life, a small amount of carbon-14 will be present in all living creatures and carbon-containing products of life. On the death of an organism this process ceases. Thereafter, owing to the radioactive decay of carbon-14, the ratio of this isotope to the total amount of carbon present will decrease with time at a known rate, enabling the age of an object to be determined. This technique has proved invaluable for dating archaeological remains unequivocally, *eg*, the Dead Sea Scrolls, and for this work Libby was awarded the Nobel Chemistry Prize (1960).

LIBEL ACT (1792) in Britain, introduced by Fox, gave the jury responsibility for pronouncing on both fact and law in libel cases. By reversing the traditional view, reaffirmed by Mansfield, that the jury should decide on the fact of publication and the judge should decide whether it constituted a libel, the act saved many from condemnation for seditious libel during the French revolutionary wars. It provided a permanent safeguard for the individual in times of political controversy.

LIBERAL CATHOLICISM, 19th-cent. European movement to reconcile Catholicism with the liberal-nationalist tenets of the French Revolution, had two aspects: the nationalist (where Catholics were ruled by foreign non-Catholics and the clergy were identified with the nationalist movement) and the liberal (in mainly Catholic countries). The nationalist aspect was predominant in Belgium, Poland, and Ireland, and only in Belgium was there any truly liberal movement. The popes exhorted clergy and people to obey their rulers, remembering the excesses of the French Revolution.

The German movement was essentially one of education of the laity and of intellectual study. After the Congress of Mainz (1848) bishops sought to educate new voters in their responsibilities and this bore fruit during the *Kulturkampf*.

The most controversial aspects of Liberal Catholicism were to be found in France, the home of the Revolution. The father of the movement was Lamennais, an inspired but excessively impetuous writer. After pushing the Vatican into a decision against his journal, *L'Avenir*, submitting to it, and then publishing *Paroles d'un Croyant*, he apostasized. A more moderate movement under Lacordaire, Montalembert, and Dupanloup won freedom for Church schools (*Loi Falloux*) while effectively rejuvenating and de-Gallicanizing the French Church, and Frédéric Ozanam founded the Society of St Vincent de Paul in which the laity worked to relieve suffering and secure social justice.

The Mennaisian stage of the movement occurred at a time when liberals were radical, anti-clerical, and at loggerheads with governments everywhere. It could not hope for success in making liberalism a dogma of the Church, but only Lamennais's impatience procured its condemnation. Pius IX, acclaimed in 1846 as the 'liberal' pope, condemned liberalism in the Syllabus of 1864, but Dupanloup showed that this applied to a specifically Italian situation of liberal expropriation of ecclesiastical property. The real substance of what most liberal Catholics were seeking—Church involvement in

social justice—came with the papal encyclicals *Rerum Novarum* (1891) and *Quadragesimo Anno* (1931).

The association of the Church with Nationalism lessened as many Catholic countries obtained national independence. The separation of Church and state, for which Lamennais campaigned, became the rule in most countries with the fall of the old dynasties. Nevertheless, despite the triumph of the ideas of the French Revolution, the Church continued to be associated with the Establishment and with middle-class respectability in many countries.

A. R. Vidler, *Prophecy and Papacy* (London, 1954).
G. P. Gooch, *French Profiles* (London, 1961).   DMK

LIBERAL PARTY IN AUSTRALIA, established (1944) as a 'nation-wide political movement' after the disintegration of the United Australia Party, fought its first Commonwealth election in 1946, under the leadership of its founder, R. G. Menzies, winning seven seats from the Australian Labor Party with a nation-wide vote of 24·3 per cent. After three years in opposition, and with a House of Representatives enlarged from 75 to 123, it was elected to govern in coalition with the Country Party (74 seats to the ALP's 48 and one Independent) and it remained in government under Menzies (1949–67), Holt (1967–8), and Gorton, from 1968.

Divisions of the Liberal Party functioned in all states by 1945, its federal council being comprised of equal representatives from the several states, with a strong professional secretariat co-ordinating activities of state divisions and maintaining contact with state office-holders. There is, however, no uniformity in state party structure.

The Liberal Party has no systematic and clearly defined philosophy and no single authoritative text. Its founder asserted that 'Liberal' was adopted because 'we were determined to be a progressive party, willing to make experiments, in no sense reactionary, but believing in the individual, his rights, and his enterprise, and rejecting the Socialist panacea'. The party platform seeks an Australian nation 'in which an intelligent, free, and liberal Australian democracy shall be maintained by parliament controlling the executive and the Law controlling all'. Freedom of speech, religion, and association and freedom of citizens to choose their own ways of living and of life, 'subject to the rights of others', were asserted, together with protection of the people against exploitation and initiative and enterprise were presented 'as the dynamic force of reconstruction and progress'.

Electoral support for the party varied substantially. During 1969–70 the Liberal Party was in government at the Commonwealth level and in every Australian state. In most instances after 1949, however, its ability to form the government was greatly influenced by the role of the Democratic Labor Party and the Country Party in the distribution of preferences.

K. West, *Power in the Liberal Party* (Melbourne, 1965).   GSR

LIBERAL PARTY IN BRITAIN, leading political party (1868–1918), which won the general elections of 1868, 1880, 1885, 1892, 1906, and 1910 (twice), took office on six occasions under Liberal prime ministers and was included in Coalition governments under the Liberal leader, Lloyd George (1918–1922). The Liberals were the successors of the Whigs. They insisted that aristocratic rule could not go on for ever and ensured that the successors of the landed class should be a section of the aristocracy reinforced with middle-class talent to form an administrative elite. They appeased the underprivileged by democratic reforms.

The party, which began in the 1860s, owed much to the philosophies of Jeremy Bentham and John Stuart Mill, and claimed inspiration from men like Charles James Fox and Adam Smith. The death of Palmerston (1865) provided an opportunity for changes overdue since the 1840s in a rapidly developing industrial society. Gladstone embodied the crusading spirit which united popular and parliamentary

Liberalism, Whigs and middle-class Radicals, Anglicans and nonconformists, offering sound, reforming government in the aristocratic tradition, clothed in the new oratory of goodwill.

His first Liberal ministry (1868–74) was the greatest. It passed Forster's Education Act, Cardwell's Army Reforms, and the Universities Tests Act, introduced the secret ballot, legalized trade unions, and opened the civil service to competitive examination. The party created democratic Britain, supported parliamentary reform (1867), passed the Third Reform Act (1884), ended corrupt electoral practices (1883), and introduced the equal, single-member constituencies (1885). Gladstone's watchwords, Peace, Retrenchment, and Reform, meant Free Trade budgets, economy, and a foreign policy that, while recognizing the necessity for empire, aimed at European national self-determination, which triumphed in the treaty of Versailles (1919).

The Liberals created the first American type of party machine, the National Liberal Federation (1877). The split over Home Rule (1886) weakened the party, which lost both Whigs and Radicals, like Chamberlain, and opened the way for the emergence of the Labour Party, which by 1922 had overtaken the Liberals in parliament, having 142 seats against their 117. Gladstone's Newcastle Programme (1891) pushed the party towards the Celtic fringe, the radicalism of Wales and Scotland, with which were allied the Irish Home Rulers. After 1886 it never won an English majority except in the 1906 landslide. Having previously proclaimed free enterprise, the party now saw the need for assuming social responsibilities and through the great ministries (1906–15), in a predominantly nonconformist parliament, laid the foundations of the welfare state, old age pensions, national insurance, minimum wages, trade boards, a Trades Union Act, and also curbed the Lords' traditional power to veto Commons legislation. Home Rule for Ireland and the Disestablishment of the Church of Wales were frustrated by the war.

The party's decline came through the wartime split into factions loyal to Asquith or loyal to Lloyd George, who supplanted him as coalition war leader (1916–22), the abandonment of Free Trade by 1931, and the successful advance of socialist policies. Individual Liberals held office in coalitions (1931–45), but despite signs of a post-war revival led by Joseph Grimond (1956–67) in the popular vote, it could not hold more than 13 seats. Its programme in 1970 included co-ownership in industry, liberty of the individual, electoral reform, self-government for Wales and Scotland, and entry into the European Common Market.

J. Vincent, *The Formation of the Liberal Party 1857–68* (London, 1966).
T. Wilson, *The Downfall of the Liberal Party 1914–35* (London, 1966).   JRA

LIBERAL PARTY IN CANADA. After the formation of the Conservative Party (1854), reform groups formed several short-lived alliances which were sometimes loosely called the Liberal Party. But the creation of a permanent all-embracing reform party was delayed by opposition to Confederation. After Confederation (1867) Liberal forces came together and elected Alexander Mackenzie as parliamentary leader (6 March 1873). Mackenzie formed a government (1873–8), but although the party won a parliamentary majority of 80 (1874) discipline was difficult to maintain. Lacking cohesion, the Liberals were defeated (1878) and Edward Blake became the new leader (1880). Little ground was gained in the 1882 and 1887 elections. The Liberal Party was increasingly influenced by Wilfred Laurier, whose *Discourse on Political Liberalism* (1877) was the clearest expression of principle for the next generation. Laurier distinguished between political and philosophical liberalism and identified himself with the traditions of British rather than French liberalism, whose doctrinaire anti-clericalism he opposed. Laurier became party leader (1887) and formed a Liberal government (1896–1911), which was characterized by policies of compromise and moderation. He sought to reduce tensions between French

and English-speaking Canadians and to increase Canadian independence in imperial affairs. In 1911 the Liberals were severely split and defeated after 18 leading members, led by Clifford Sifton, left the party. The Liberals seemed in further disarray when several party leaders joined Borden's Union government to bring about conscription, which Laurier opposed (1917). Many later returned and W. L. Mackenzie King became leader of a reunited party after Laurier's death (1919). With wide experience of labour problems King helped to restructure Liberal thinking on social reform. After elections in 1921, 1925, and 1926 King was able to form ministries with support of the Progressive Party. He was defeated (1930), having failed to alleviate the effects of the Depression. The Liberals were soon returned to power and under King's leadership they won substantial majorities in the elections of 1935, 1940, and 1945. On his retirement (1948), King was replaced by Louis St Laurent, who won the elections of 1949 and 1953. After 22 years in power (1935–57) the Liberal Party was defeated by the Conservatives, led by John Diefenbaker (1957). Lester B. Pearson became leader (1957) and the Liberals formed ministries after the 1963 and 1965 elections. Pearson resigned and under the leadership of Elliot Trudeau the Liberal Party won the 1968 election.

J. W. Dafoe, *Laurier, a Study in Canadian Politics* (Toronto, 1968).   GFO

LIBERAL PARTY IN NEW ZEALAND occupied a central position in NZ's political development. Practically all early NZ politicians claimed to be 'Liberals', 'Conservative' being a derogatory term. Grey's abortive 'Liberal Party' (1876–9) somewhat tarnished the name, but Ballance firmly appropriated it after his 1890 election victory. His party's great rural slogan was 'bursting up the estates', but Liberalism appealed to urban labour with industrial legislation. This country–town harmony was successfully sustained under Ballance (1891–3) and Seddon (1893–1906), the latter founding the Liberal and Labour Federation (1899). Growing economic tension split the party under Ward (1906–12), who suffered serious losses to the right among 'free-hold' Liberals, and could not contain Labour. The Liberal Party, shorn of its left wing, became a dwindling alternative to Reform on the right, though reviving briefly as 'United' in 1928.

LIBERAL YELLOW BOOK (1928), set out the British Liberal Party's proposed solution to the problem of unemployment, which in 1929 stood at $1\frac{1}{4}$ million. It was the outcome of the Liberal industrial enquiry, established in 1925, with finance from the Lloyd George Fund. Those concerned with the enquiry included Lloyd George, Philip Kerr, Herbert Samuel, and John Simon, representing the politicians, and B. S. Rowntree, W. T. Layton, and J. M. Keynes, representing the economists. The 'Yellow Book', published in 1928 as *Britain's Industrial Future*, was a survey of Britain's post-war economy and advocated large-scale government planning as a solution to unemployment. Public boards were proposed for industry, and an economic general staff within the government and the expansion of joint industrial councils were advocated. The Bank of England's powers over credit were to be used to maintain a steady flow of trade, and a large programme of national development, *eg*, of roads, houses, garden cities, and the extension of electricity, the reclamation of land and afforestation—was to provide work. A special committee under Lloyd George produced a manifesto, 'We Can Conquer Unemployment', which caused a sensation when it appeared in March 1929. This formed the basis of the 1929 Liberal campaign. In many ways the Liberal policy foreshadowed the New Deal in the US. Impressive though the programme was, it failed to restore the Liberal Party's fortunes in the general election of 1929.   CPC

LIBERIA, independent Negro state in West Africa, 43,000 sq. miles (111,000 sq. kms) in area, with a population (1970) of nearly 2 million. The republic was proclaimed in 1847, many of its inhabitants being freed slaves brought from the US by the American Colonization Society. During the Second World War the US used Liberia as a military and air base, and later improved health, agricultural, and educational services in the country. Its peoples are mainly Kru and Grebo.

LIBERTINES in Holland, section of the regent class in the late 16th cent., of whom the most prominent was D. V. Coornhaert, who inherited the Erasmian and tolerant traditions of the northern Netherlands and were opposed to ecclesiastical interference in the state. Their opponents were the Precisians, a faction of the Calvinist preachers and their artisan and petty bourgeois supporters, who identified Church with state and found support from the English governor-general, the Earl of Leicester.

LIBERTY, STATUE OF, figure of a woman holding an uplifted torch, originally called *Liberty Enlightening the World*, erected on Bedloe's Island in Upper New York Bay (1884–6). It was designed by Frederic August Bartholdi, and built of copper sheets, and was a present from the French people to the US. With a total height, including pedestal, of over 300 feet (91·5 metres), it became a landmark for immigrants entering New York and was made a national monument in 1924.

LIBERTY BELL, historic bell, cast in London (1751), in Independence Hall, Philadelphia, US. It was hung in the Pennsylvania State House and was rung to proclaim the Declaration of Independence (1776). Repeatedly damaged and recast, it cracked while being tolled on Washington's birthday in 1846. This was the last time it was rung.

LIBERTY PARTY in the US, earliest anti-slavery political party, which held its first national convention at Albany, NY (1 April 1840), and nominated an ex-slaveholder, James G. Birney, for the presidency. The party, composed of moderate abolitionists favouring political action, played an important part in the election of 1844, when Birney's 62,300 votes helped to defeat Henry Clay. It was opposed to the annexation of TX and in 1848 merged with the Free Soil Party.

LIBERUM VETO, Polish nobility's right of dissent or veto in the national assembly which developed in the 17th cent. It could be used by an individual deputy in the name of democratic liberty, but often proved detrimental to the confederation's interests, *eg*, Sicinski's veto of the Polish–Cossack treaty (1652), and was abolished in the constitution of 1791.

LIBRARIES (PUBLIC) ACT (1850) in Britain, promoted by the radical MP William Ewart and Edward Edwards, the first librarian of Manchester public library. It enabled boroughs with 10,000 or more inhabitants (population clause repealed 1866) to set up a public library with the consent of two-thirds of the ratepayers at a special meeting. The rate was not to exceed $\frac{1}{2}$d (1d after 1855), nor was it to be spent on the purchase of books. By 1860 25 towns had established libraries.

LICENSING ACT (1662) in Britain, part of the Clarendon Code, which instituted a system of censorship of the press based on parliamentary authority and exercised a narrow ecclesiastical spirit. By its terms the number of master printers in England was to be allowed to dwindle to 20 and no more were to be admitted without the approval of the Abp of Canterbury and the Bp of London. No book was to be published without a licence from a censor appointed, according to the subject, by the appropriate civil or ecclesiastical authority. Printing presses were only to be allowed in London, Oxford, and Cambridge. The act prevented the printing of or importing of books containing doctrines contrary to those of the Church of England, or against the governors of Church and state. It was originally enacted for two years, but was successively renewed until 1679, when it was replaced by a proclamation ordering the seizure of libellous books and authors. It was renewed in 1685, and again in 1693 till 1695. Roger L'Estrange was appointed (1663) to enforce the regulations, which he did by frequent prosecutions.

LICENSING ACT (1872) in Britain, legislative attempt to curb drunkenness. After seriously underestimating the publicans' capacity to resist temperance legislation in 1871, the home secretary, H. A. Bruce, in 1872 introduced a more moderate measure—shortening drinking hours and increasing penalties for drunkenness and adulteration. Although a non-party measure, it added to the unpopularity of Gladstone's first administration and helped to align an urban 'interest' behind Conservatism. Thus an indirect effect was to broaden the base of what had hitherto been a predominantly landed party. It also provided an opportunity for rallying the mass electorate behind aristocratic traditionalism and opposition to state interference.

LICET AB INITIO, papal bull published by Pope Paul III on 21 July 1542, reconstituting the Holy Office of the Inquisition in Rome as the central punitive body with authority over all western Europe.

LICHFIELD HOUSE COMPACT (1835), alliance between the various whig factions in Britain, supported by Daniel O'Connell, which led to the reunion of the Whig Party, the defeat of Peel's first administration (1834–5), and the resumption of power by Lord Melbourne.

LICINIO-SEXTIAN LAWS (367 BC), passed in Rome by the tribunes C. Licinius and L. Sextius, perhaps the most important single body of economic and political legislation ever decreed at Rome in the plebeian (popular) interest. The political legislation decreed that one consul must be a plebeian, and L. Sextius himself became the first plebeian consul in 366, thus effectively opening all magistracies to all citizens. The economic measures limited the amount of public land tenable by an individual, thus checking the growth of a landlord class, and freed the working population from a perpetual burden of debt by deducting interest paid from the capital debt and by prescribing repayment of the balance within three years.

LICINIUS (d. AD 325), Roman Emperor (*reg.* 308–24), who was appointed by Galerius as his colleague and eastern emperor (Augustus), and succeeded him at his death (311), making an alliance with Constantine the Great and suppressing the rival Augustus, Maximinus Daia (313). He lost territory to Constantine after a brief war (314); and, when hostilities were resumed (323), he was defeated at the battle of Chrysopolis and shortly afterwards executed, Constantine becoming sole emperor.

LIDICE, village near Prague in Czechoslovakia, annihilated by Gestapo forces in June 1942 in reprisal for the assassination by two Czechs of Reinhard Heydrich, chief of the Security Police (SD) in Germany and deputy protector of Bohemia and Moravia. All the male inhabitants of the village were shot, the women and children deported to concentration camps, and the buildings razed. The incident symbolized the unparalleled barbarity of Nazi rule in Europe.

LIE, TRYGVE HALVDAN (1896–   ), Norwegian politician and first secretary-general of the United Nations. He was a member of the Norwegian Labour party and after the conquest of Norway by Germany he emigrated to London with the government (1940) and did much to enhance the office by the active part that he played in the UN's affairs. Neutrality did not come naturally to him—he was opposed to the establishment of the UN in Switzerland, which he saw as a neutral country unsuited for an 'active, "trouble shooting" world organization'. By supporting the UN's action in Korea he earned the unceasing hostility of the USSR (which had voted for his appointment). He sought to protect the UN from the US when US citizens in the secretariat were under attack by Senator McCarthy. The Soviet Union's hostility towards him resulted in deadlock when the renewal of his term of office came to be discussed. The Soviet Union refused to accept his reappointment and the US would accept no other candidate. In the event, his term of office was extended for three years (1951). None the less, he resigned in Nov. 1952.

LIEBIG, JUSTUS (1803–73), German chemist and professor of chemistry in Giessen University, where he had a profound influence upon the progress of chemistry, by providing practical instruction in the subject. The rapid growth of chemistry in Germany owed much to the influence of the Giessen school and Liebig's work in chemical education. He made notable advances in organic chemistry and also in agricultural and physiological chemistry.

LIEBKNECHT, KARL (1871–1919), German politician and founder of the German Communist Party, who became well known in the first decade of the 20th cent. for his agitation against militarism and the danger of war. When the First World War broke out in 1914 he was the first member of the Reichstag openly to oppose support of the German war effort on socialist grounds. Thereafter his courageous agitation made him a symbol and an inspiration for the growing anti-war movement. However, his conviction, shared by the Spartacus Group, of which he and Rosa Luxemburg were the principal leaders, that the war must end in international proletarian revolution, placed him too far in advance of German working-class opinion, and he was more admired than followed. In May 1916 he was arrested and imprisoned for nearly 30 months, being released two weeks before the end of the war. He quickly became once more the most active and popular revolutionary agitator in Berlin. As a leader of the Spartacists he opposed the socialist Provisional government and sought to prepare working-class opinion for its forcible overthrow and the establishment of a 'dictatorship of the proletariat' based on workers' and soldiers' councils. At the end of 1918 he played an important role in the foundation of the German Communist Party, whose aim this was. But the party failed at first to attract much support, and while he was still striving to broaden the basis of his revolutionary movement by agitation, he was drawn into a futile uprising originated by others—the famous Spartacus Week of Jan. 1919. In the course of its bloody suppression he was arrested and murdered by a band of soldiers.

LIÈGE, city situated at the confluence of the Meuse and Ourthe rivers, and bishopric within the Holy Roman empire. It was temporarily annexed by the house of Burgundy (1468) and because of its proximity to France's eastern frontier became a key area in the struggle between the Habsburgs and the French houses of Valois and Bourbon. For some 200 years from 1581 it was held by Bavarian princes, who were also electoral archbishops of Cologne and thus remained within the Catholic orbit. Under the electors Maximilian Henry and Joseph Clement Liège was involved on the French side in Louis XIV's wars against the Emperors Leopold and Joseph (1672–1713) and the city was stormed by Marlborough (1702). It remained an imperial enclave in the 18th cent., was overrun by Napoleon, and was incorporated first into the kingdom of the Netherlands (1815) and then into the modern state of Belgium (1830). It was a centre for coal and iron mining from the 15th cent. and remains (1970) the industrial heart of Belgium.

LIEGNITZ, BATTLE OF (1241). In 1241 the Mongols launched their first invasion of western Europe. Three armies converged on Hungary, while a fourth moved through southern Poland. Henry the Pious, Duke of Cracow, the most powerful of the Polish princes, intercepted it at Liegnitz in Silesia, with a smaller army, without waiting for Czech reinforcements. His force was annihilated, but the heavy losses

suffered by the Mongols may have contributed to their decision to move south-east, rejoining the other Mongols in Hungary.

LIEGNITZ, BATTLE OF (1760), Austro-Russian defeat in the Seven Years War by a Prussian army one-third their size. Frederick II with 30,000 men awaited attack from a superior army, under Daun and Tsernichev, which advanced to reinforce Loudon's Austrian force, when the latter marched into the middle of the Prussian lines and was routed.

LIEUTENANT-GENERAL OF POLICE, chief civil official of the Paris region, a post created by Louis XIV (1667) whose incumbent was responsible for all matters relating to the security and salubrity of the capital. The first holder was Nicolas de la Reynie, who carried out sweeping reforms (1667–97).

LIEVEN, DOROTHEA, Princess de (1784–1857), was born De Benkendorf, of an old Livonian family, and married the Russian diplomat, Prince de Lieven, ambassador to England (1812–34). She was a prominent figure in political society in England and, after her husband's death (1836), in Paris. Her comments on English and French politics and politicians are entertaining and illuminating, though not unbiased. Her correspondence with Earl Grey (published 1890) is an important source of information on 19th-cent. politics and diplomacy.

LIFE INSURANCE in Britain. The first commercial organization for life insurance was the Equitable Society of London, which started operations in the 1760s, but annuities had been in use as a means of raising money for government since 1692. Neither of these means was based on any sound knowledge of life expectancy, but they created an interest in this subject. The first life-table of any actuarial value was that of Northampton, made in 1780, and subsequent tables gave an improved insurance structure in the 19th cent. Insurance was important as a means of effecting savings and British insurance of all kinds played a valuable part in the structure of invisible exports of the late 19th cent.

LIFE PEERAGES ACT (1958) in Britain, legislative measure which empowered the Crown to confer on any person a peerage for life, carrying the right to sit and vote in the House of Lords. The act created (1) life barons, (2) life baronesses, thus admitting women to the Lords for the first time. Some 200 life peerages were created up to 1970, but no hereditary peerages after 1964. As a result a better party balance existed in the Lords, as the number of hereditary and life peers regularly attending the House was about equal. Life peers therefore could, in time, come to dominate the House, and the principle of hereditary peerages—except perhaps for members of the royal family—fall into disuse.

LI–FOURNIER CONVENTION (1884), established jointly by Li Hung-chang and Captain F. E. Fournier, was an attempt to settle Sino–French differences over Annam. It recognized the independence of Annam, traditionally a tributary state to China. However, both the French and the Chinese governments refused to ratify the convention, and the Sino–French War resulted.

LIGA FEDERAL, short-lived federation (c. 1816) established by José Artigas to counter the growing influence of Buenos Aires within the United Provinces of La Plata. It was ended by the Portuguese invasion in the same year of Artigas's own Banda Oriental (Uruguay).

LIGA LITORAL (1831), inter-provincial pact between Buenos Aires (1831) and the *caudillos* of Santa Fé and Entre Rios. It was the basis of the de facto confederal system under which Argentina was ruled until 1853, but it proved ineffectual as a check upon Buenos Aires' growing economic hegemony in the area.

LIGA UNITARIA, coalition of nine Argentine interior provinces formed late in the 1820s to oppose the 'federalism' of Rosas of Buenos Aires and his *caudillo* colleagues of the littoral provinces. It collapsed after 1831 after the capture of its military leader, José María Paz.

LIGDAN KHAN (1592–1634), last Mongol Emperor (*reg.* 1604–34). By the end of the 16th cent. the Mongol empire had been broken down into a number of khanates or princedoms, though the ruler of the Chahars was still nominally emperor. Ligdan Khan seems to have wished to reunite the Mongols under his rule, but his autocratic and violent methods estranged many princes, who threw in their lot with the emerging Manchu power. Ligdan died an obscure death in the Kukunor area. He is remembered as a patron of the Lamaist religion and the organizer of an ambitious programme of translation of the scriptures.

LIGHT, FRANCIS (1740–94), British colonist and founder of the first British colony in Malaya, at Penang (1786). As a private trader in Phuket (southern Siam), Light attracted the attention of the East India Co. to Penang. Since the 1750s the company had been seeking a safe commercial and strategic base in the Malay archipelago. Light negotiated the lease of Penang from the Sultan of Kedah, and superintended the new colony.

LIGNY, BATTLE OF (16 June 1815), fought two days before the battle of Waterloo as Napoleon tried to drive a wedge between the Anglo-Dutch army of the Duke of Wellington and the Prussian army under Blücher. The Prussians, though decisively defeated, were not destroyed, nor was the line with Wellington cut and Blücher was able to make his appearance at Waterloo.

LIGONIER, JOHN LOUIS LIGONIER, Earl (1680–1770), British soldier of French Huguenot origin, who left France after the peace of Ryswick (1697) and served as a British cavalry officer under Marlborough in the War of the Spanish Succession (1702–13). As an old man, he fought under Wade in the War of the Austrian Succession (1742–8) at Fontenoy (1745), Roucoux (1746), and Lauffeldt (1747), where he was captured. He was appointed commander-in-chief to replace Cumberland in the Seven Years War (1757).

LIGOR, Malay name of Nakhon Si Thammarat in peninsular Thailand. It was the centre of the state of Tambralinga by the 8th cent. and was a gateway through which Theravada Buddhism reached Indo-China. After being fought over by Burmese, Cambodians, Malays, and Thai since the 11th cent., it was incorporated into the kingdom of Ayudhya in the 17th cent.

LIGUE NATIONALISTE, LA, founded (1903) by Oliver Asselin, advocated separate schools for French Canadian Catholics, French as an official language, immigration limitations, conservation, railroad nationalization, provincial autonomy, and a nationalistic foreign policy. The league reached its greatest strength in 1911, when it opposed Sir Wilfred Laurier's naval bill.

LIGURIANS, earliest inhabitants of western Europe of whom history speaks. According to Rufus Festus Avienus (*Ora maritima*), the territory formerly occupied by the Ligurians extended from the Mediterranean to the Atlantic seaboard and the Channel, before they were invaded, overthrown, subjugated, and chased away, first by the Celts or Gauls, in a wave of westward expansion of Bronze Age Indo-European peoples. The Ligurians were driven back into Provence south of the Durance river and east of the Rhone, the western Alps, the upper reaches of the Po valley, Liguria and Apuania in

Italy, where the Romans further reduced them. The bloodgroups of inhabitants of Liguria show such similarities to those of the Basques that they must be related to that pre-Indo-European relict of the Neolithic Mediterranean race. H. d'arbois de Jubainville showed that it was possible to trace the former extent of Ligurian territory by means of the 'fossil' place-name endings *asco, -asca, -anca, -enco*, which are found in great numbers in Piedmont, Lombardy, western Switzerland, and also in south-eastern France (Manosque, Lambesc, Tarascon, Matisco = Mâcon), and in Corsica, which is a test case, because Gauls never colonized that island.

LIKIN, commercial transit tax in China, instituted on the initiative of the provinces of the Ch'ing empire during the decade beginning in 1853, to meet the expenses for suppressing the Taiping rebels. The *likin*, however, was continued after the Taipings were suppressed, and constituted a major source of government income. But the control of the *likin* never passed out of the control of the individual provinces; only a small amount of what was received was reported to Peking. The *likin* thus contributed much to growing provincial power in the late Ch'ing period and to lining the pockets of provincial administrators; however, many modernizing projects owed their survival to this tax. The *likin* was not abolished until well into the Republican period.

LILBURNE, JOHN (1615–57), English agitator and pamphleteer with a flair for publicity and an ingrained opposition to authority. He was imprisoned by Charles I, fought for parliament, but deserted after refusing to take the covenant, and as a Leveller defied Cromwell. His *Agreement of the People* (1647) was a characteristic statement of Leveller doctrines. He was banished to the Channel Islands (1654–5) and finally became a Quaker.

LILIENTHAL, DAVID ELI (1899–   ), US lawyer and government official, who made a decisive contribution to the development of the Tennessee Valley Authority during his period as director and chairman (1933–46). His concept of 'centralized, large-scale production combined with decentralized, grassroots responsibility' shaped the nature of the experiment in federal–state–local co-operation. He served as chairman of the US Atomic Energy Commission during its formative years (1946–50).

'LILLIBURLERO', originally a password used by the Irish Catholics in 1641, was the refrain of a scurrilous ballad by Lord Wharton (1686) when Tyrconnel became viceroy in Ireland. It was taken up by the revolutionary armies in 1688 and was said to have 'sung King James out of three kingdoms'. 'Lilliburlero' was sung by certain commando units in the Second World War.

LILYBAEUM (mod. Marsala), chief Carthaginian town in Sicily, founded in 396 BC to replace the sacked city of Motya. It was blockaded unsuccessfully by the Romans in the First Punic War from 250 BC, and surrendered by the treaty of Catulus. It became the second city of the Roman province of Sicily, and was administered by one of the two quaestors assigned to it.

LIM YEW HOCK (1914–   ), Singapore politician and chief minister of Singapore (1956–9), who led the Singapore delegation to London (1957) which negotiated full internal self-government.

LIMA, DECLARATION OF (Dec. 1938), adopted by a conference of American foreign ministers, in which they resolved to defend American principles against foreign intervention. They agreed that a threat to their mutual peace, security, or territorial integrity would demand that the foreign ministers should confer on the problem.

LIMANTOUR, JOSÉ IVES (1854–1935), Mexican financier, finance minister (1893–1911), and leader of the *científicos* (or 'scientifics') (1895–1911), during the last years of Porfirio Diaz's dictatorship. As finance minister he instituted policies aimed at economic stabilization and nationalization. Among his more important accomplishments were the nationalization of the railroads, the abolition of the traditional sales taxes (*alcabalas*), and the consolidation of government debts. He also supervised the growth of state banks and the transition to the gold standard. After the revolution (1910), Limantour handled negotiations with Francisco Madero, then went into permanent exile in Paris.

LIMERICK, PEACE OF (1691) in Ireland, civil articles of surrender obtained by Patrick Sarsfield, Jacobite commander of the city, from Godbert de Ginkle, William III's commander, which ended the king's reconquest of Ireland. They were signed by the lords justices and subsequently ratified by William III and Mary (1692) and by the Irish parliament, though not until 1697. The peace included three stipulations: (*a*) a measure of religious toleration for the Catholic population of Ireland; (*b*) security of life and property for Jacobite officers and men remaining in Ireland and submitting to the new government; (*c*) similar security for the civil population of Limerick and other Jacobite towns. William tried to administer the peace fairly, and of almost 1300 persons who claimed benefit only 16 were refused. Both the Irish and English parliaments, however, interpreted the peace narrowly, implementing a series of penal laws against Catholics upon its ratification. Yet the treaty still protected many Jacobite landowners, though nearly a million acres were confiscated by 1700.

LIMERICK, SIEGES OF (1651, 1691), at the end of the Irish rebellion and William III's reconquest of Ireland. In 1651 Hugh O'Neill (nephew of Owen Roe O'Neill) was besieged in Limerick by the English army led by Cromwell's son-in-law, Henry Ireton. O'Neill yielded in Oct., and Ireton died a few weeks later.

In 1690, after the defeat of the Boyne, James II's Irish army under the Earl of Tyrconnel fell back on Limerick pursued by the armies of William III (from Dublin) and John Churchill (from Munster). William's first attempt to take the town failed, and he departed for England, leaving Ginkle in command. In 1691 the command of the Irish army was taken over by Patrick Sarsfield, Earl of Lucan, on the death of Tyrconnel. After taking Athlone, Ginkle concentrated on Limerick (4 Sept. 1691) and Sarsfield decided to treat, the help expected from France having failed to arrive. On 3 Oct. a treaty was signed between him and Ginkle and the chief justices.

LIMES, Latin word originally meaning a path or track, particularly one suitable for troops, which came to mean first a road with fortified posts and later a fixed frontier system; it is generally used in the last sense by modern archaeologists and historians, being applied particularly to the frontiers of the Roman empire as fixed by the Flavian and later emperors, covering natural barriers (*eg*, the Rhine and Danube rivers) and artificial constructions (*eg*, Hadrian's Wall) with their supporting systems of forts, watch-towers, forward posts, and roads.

LIMITED LIABILITY ACTS (1855, 1862) in Britain, landmarks in the growth of Victorian business enterprise. Promotion of companies had been handicapped by the perils of unlimited liability, which might make an individual shareholder liable to lose all his property through the failure of a company in which he held an interest. After earlier attempts to introduce a degree of limited liability and registration, the Limited Liability Act (1855) and the Joint Stock Companies Act (1856) were passed. General limited liability came with the Consolidating Act (1862), which removed anomalies and stimulated the investment of capital by the middle-class.

Half the companies formed at this time did not survive ten years and the dangers of over-speculation were shown in the failure of the reputable firm of Overend and Gurney, which caused a run on the banks and a request to suspend the Bank Charter Act (1844). Yet without the security and confidence given by limited liability the great expansion of commerce at home and overseas would have been impossible. It also widened a gap between ownership and management.

LIMMU, Assyrian name for five royal officials who presided at the New Year festival for the first five years after the king's accession year and gave their names to the years. By the use of *limmu* lists, dates have been established fairly accurately for the first part of the 1st millennium BC.

LIN PIAO (?1908–   ), Chinese communist marshal, and since 1968 declared successor to Mao Tse-tung. Lin was educated at the Whampoa Academy in Canton, and joined the Communist Party at a very early age. He rose to prominence in the Red Army, and before he was 30 was commanding an army corps on the Long March. He was not active in the field during the Anti-Japanese War (1937–45), but achieved great success in the Civil War (1946–9), when he was commander in Manchuria during the first and most crucial stage of the war. Lin represented the guerrilla tradition in the Red Army; in Manchuria he implemented Mao Tse-tung's policy of 'encircling the towns with the countryside', *ie*, of strangling the towns by isolating them from their surrounding countryside. After 1949, when the Communist government was established, Lin, who may have been ill, held a series of high but apparently nominal posts. When Marshal P'eng Te-huai was disgraced (1959), Lin returned to active service; he took over the Defence Ministry, and set about creating a more politically conscious army. His efforts were apparently opposed by other military leaders, notably Lo Jui-ch'ing, the chief of staff, who wanted a more professional, mechanized army. In 1965 Lin was responsible for the abolition of ranks throughout the army. When the Cultural Revolution started (1966), Lin emerged as one of Mao Tse-tung's few supporters in the top echelons of party and army. He won for Mao the support of certain sections of the army—support that was essential for carrying out the Revolution. His devotion to Mao was rewarded when he was named as Mao's 'closest comrade in arms', and then as his successor.

LIN SHU (1852–1924), Chinese poet, painter, and translator. Despite his coming from a very poor family, Lin received a classical education. Although unfamiliar with foreign languages, he rendered 159 Western works into Chinese with the help of translators, including social novels, biographies, plays, and detective stories. He thus contributed significantly to the introduction of Western culture and ideas into China. However, he remained a strong advocate of the classical language and was much opposed to the vernacular favoured by progressive intellectuals of the May Fourth Movement.

LIN TSE-HSÜ (1785–1850), Chinese official from Fukien. In his early career as a provincial official during the 1820s, he earned a reputation as an able and incorruptible official, particularly in judicial matters, water conservancy, and social relief. He was appointed governor-general of Hupei and Hunan in 1837. In the 1830s the declining Ch'ing dynasty was faced with a serious opium problem. As governor-general, Lin's policy was to suppress the opium trade; at the same time he put forward suggestions for curing addicts. The success of his policy in Hupei and Hunan led the Taokuang emperor to appoint him Imperial Commissioner, with plenipotentiary powers to examine the opium situation at Canton, and to put an end to it. While he was there, Lin pursued a dual policy of suppressing opium smoking in Kwangtung and stopping the opium trade. The British traders, who handled the bulk of imported opium, were doubtful of Lin's sincerity, and regarded his initial success as a temporary setback for the trade. They were soon disillusioned; Lin blockaded their factories until they surrendered their entire stocks of opium, which was then destroyed under his personal supervision. This line of policy, combined with his lack of knowledge of the local situation and of international relations, contributed to the outbreak of hostilities which followed. However, Capt. Charles Elliot, the British superintendent of trade, who pursued British policy with an equal disregard for Chinese tradition, was also responsible for the bad relations that ensued. War broke out, and the arrival of a British squadron followed.

For his failure in dealing with the British, Lin was exiled to Ili. However, the flooding of the Yellow river just at this time led the emperor to order him to Kaifeng to control the river. This he quickly did, but the court refused to reduce his sentence of exile. While serving it, he was put in charge of colonization in Sinkiang by the military governor there. In 1845, Lin, having opened vast areas of land to cultivation, was pardoned and appointed an acting governor-general. Two years later he was made governor-general of Yunnan and Kweichow, where he reduced the long-standing enmity between the Muslims and the Chinese. In 1848 he retired to his native Fukien for reasons of health.

Both as an individual and as a bureaucrat, Lin was renowned for his loyalty and patriotism. Although the wisdom with which he handled Sino-British relations can be questioned, he must be credited with securing the first Chinese translation of sections of international law and with inspiring a number of Chinese officials to interest themselves in Western weapons, steamship building, and maritime defence.

Chang Hsin-pao, *Commissioner Lin and the Opium War* (Cambridge, MA, 1964).   DP

LINACRE, THOMAS (*c.* 1460–1524), English scholar and physician, who studied at Florence and in Venice and took a medical degree at Padua. He returned to England and lectured on Greek and medicine at Oxford, was tutor to Prince Arthur (1500–1), and was appointed physician to Henry VIII (1509). He also became tutor to Princess Mary (1523) and wrote a Latin grammar, but his works of scholarship were less important than his medical treatises, especially his translations from Galen. He founded lectureships in medicine at Oxford and Cambridge and helped to establish the College of Physicians (1518).

LIN-AN, also known as Hangchow or Kinsai. After fleeing from the northern invaders, the Sung dynastic house established its capital here in 1127, and a thriving emporium arose. The city is situated in the present province of Chekiang.

LINCOLN, JOHN DE LA POLE, 14th Earl of (7th creation) (*c.* 1462–87), nephew of King Richard III of England, was recognized as his heir after the death of Richard's son, Edward, in 1484. After the overthrow and death of Richard III, Lincoln became the hope of the English Yorkists. Their rising against Henry VII in 1487 was crushed at the battle of Stoke (16 June), where Lincoln was killed.

LINCOLN, ABRAHAM (1809–65), 16th president of the US, who was brought up in the backwoods of KY and IN, before settling in New Salem (IL) as a mill manager and storekeeper (1831–7). He studied law, became a licensed attorney (1836), and served in the IL legislature (1834–41). As a Whig congressman from IL (1847–9), he became so unpopular for his attacks on President Polk's administration that he did not stand for re-election. Within four years he had achieved success as a circuit lawyer, and returned to politics in opposition to the Kansas–Nebraska Act (1854). In 1856 he joined the new Republican Party, and was considered as a possible vice-presidential candidate. In 1858 he stood in IL as Republican candidate for the Senate in opposition to Stephen A. Douglas, and began his campaign with the famous Springfield speech (16 June) in which he said that 'A house

divided against itself cannot stand. I believe this government cannot endure permanently half slave and half free.' Challenging Douglas to a series of public debates, he adopted a moderate stance on slavery, disavowed abolitionism, but sought to oppose the extension of slavery and show inconsistencies in Douglas's position. Although Lincoln lost the election, he had by now become a national figure and in 1860 received the Republican presidential nomination. Already in his Cooper Union speech in New York (27 Feb.) he had formulated the issues for the campaign, stressing above all the exclusion of slavery from the territories. He was elected in Nov. by a substantial majority in the electoral college, though with a minority of the popular vote, but he kept silent until his inauguration, despite the secession of the lower South. Nevertheless, he made it known that he opposed compromise over the extension of slavery. In his inaugural address (4 March 1861) he denounced secession and emphasized the perpetual nature of the Union, but denied that he intended any interference with slavery in the states and adopted a conciliatory tone. As president he was faced almost immediately with the Fort Sumter crisis, and his decision to reprovision the garrison was taken by the South as an act of war. Congress being in recess until July 1861, Lincoln was forced to act on his executive authority. He summoned the militia, proclaimed a blockade, suspended *habeas corpus*, and prepared for war. While his handling of the military aspect of the Civil War is open to criticism, the Union's early misfortunes were due more to congressional interference with the army and the doubtful quality of the higher command. Once Lincoln had found, in U. S. Grant, a general who could win battles, he gave him unreserved support. Preserving throughout a calm and tolerant attitude to his opponents, he resisted radical pressures. The Emancipation Proclamation (1863) was issued only when he judged the time to be ripe, and he emancipated only slaves in Confederate territory, thus avoiding alienating the border states. His plans for reconstructing the Union after the war were conciliatory and he vetoed the radical Wade–Davis bill (1864). In the Gettysburg Address (19 Nov. 1863) Lincoln gave one of the most eloquent statements of his democratic faith and belief in the Union. After re-election (1864) with a popular majority of over 400,000 he once again advised his countrymen (4 March 1865) against vindictiveness towards the South. On 14 April 1865 he was shot by John Wilkes Booth whilst watching a play at Ford's Theatre in Washington, and died the following morning.

J. G. Randall, *Lincoln the President*, 4 vols (New York, 1945–55).
D. Donald, *Lincoln Reconsidered* (New York, 1956).   DBS

LINCOLN–DOUGLAS DEBATES (Aug.–Oct. 1858), series of seven public debates between Abraham Lincoln and Stephen Douglas, whom Lincoln was challenging for election as US senator from IL. The debates centred around the issue of slavery's extension, Lincoln insisting that this was a moral question which could not remain unresolved. 'This government', he had already argued in his House Divided speech (16 June), 'cannot endure permanently half slave and half free.' Douglas was more pragmatic. 'If each state will only agree to mind its own business,' he declared at Quincy (13 Oct.), 'this republic can exist forever divided into free and slave states.' In a debate at Freeport (27 Aug.), Lincoln tried to force his opponent into repudiating either his belief in 'popular sovereignty' or the Dred Scott decision. Douglas sidestepped this challenge with his 'Freeport doctrine', which, it has been supposed, won him re-election to the Senate but lost him support in the South, and therefore the presidency of the US in the election of 1860.

LINDBERGH, CHARLES AUGUSTUS (1902–   ), US aviator, who made the first solo trans-Atlantic flight (20–21 May 1927). He flew his single-engined monoplane, *The Spirit of St Louis*, non-stop from New York to Paris, a feat that captured the imagination of his generation. The kidnapping and death of his infant son (March 1932) shocked public opinion and led directly to the passage of the so-called Lindbergh Act (1934), making kidnapping under certain circumstances a federal crime. Lindbergh became an airline consultant, and made several exploratory flights seeking trans-Atlantic and trans-Pacific air routes. He spent some time in Europe during the 1930s, returned to the US an avowed neutralist, and joined the America First movement (1940–1), which sought to strengthen America's defence and at the same time keep the country out of the Second World War. After Pearl Harbor, however, he served with the US air force and flew a number of combat missions in the South Pacific. His book *The Spirit of St Louis* (1953) won a Pulitzer Prize for biography (1954).

LINDISFARNE GOSPELS, dating from the early 8th cent., are the finest English example of Hiberno-Saxon decorative art. The Gospels are remarkable also for their fine version of the Vulgate text. A 10th-cent. colophon states that they were produced by Eadfrith, Bp of Lindisfarne (698–721).

LINDLEY, JOHN (1799–1865), English botanist, who pioneered the Royal Horticultural Society, organizing in the 1830s exhibitions of flowers and fruits. These were the first flower shows in the country. As an eminent botanist and horticulturist he was frequently asked by the government to enquire into horticultural matters of national importance. He reported upon the Royal Gardens at Kew in 1838, recommending that they be handed over to the nation, and was sent by Sir Robert Peel to advise upon the Irish potato famine (1845).

LINDSAY, JOHN VLIET (1921–), US politician and mayor of New York city (1965–), was elected to the US House of Representatives (1958) as an independent Republican candidate from Manhattan. He was re-elected in 1960 and 1962 and gained national prominence by refusing to support Barry Goldwater, the Republican presidential candidate in 1964. He was elected mayor of New York city as a non-partisan Republican (1965), and became a symbol of young progressive Republicanism. Though refused renomination by his own party, he confounded the major parties by being re-elected as an independent (1969).

LINDSEY, BENJAMIN BARR (1869–1943), US judge and publicist, won an international reputation as an authority on juvenile delinquency. He was a promoter of the juvenile court system, introduced the practice of putting boys on their honour, and was instrumental in CO legislature's passing of the first contributory delinquency law, which holds negligent adults and employers accountable. The unorthodox views contained in his book *Companionate Marriage* (1927) heightened the controversy with which he was surrounded and he was forced to resign. He moved to CA (1928) and served in the state superior court (1928–43). He published his autobiography, *The Dangerous Life*, in 1931.

LINEAR B, name applied to a system of syllabic signs found on clay tablets discovered *c.* 1900 at Cnossos in Crete and dated to *c.* 1400 BC. Similar tablets, dated to *c.* 1200, were later found in the Greek Peloponnese at Pylos. Those found at Cnossos, when deciphered, revealed the language as Greek, and thus provide the evidence for its earliest known use. The tablets appear to be palace inventories of royal possessions and revenue at Greek Pylos and Greek-occupied Cnossos and reveal an economy heavily centralized around the palace and controlled by a developed bureaucracy. A similar syllabic system of writing, known as Linear A, and discovered so far only in Crete, represents an earlier and as yet undeciphered non-Greek language.

LINIERS, SANTIAGO ANTONIO MARÍA DE (1756–1810), expatriate Frenchman who twice in 1806–7 led the citizens of Buenos Aires in successful attempts to frustrate a British invasion. He was appointed acting viceroy by the Spanish Crown (1807–9).

LINKÖPING MASSACRE (1600), execution of four Swedish nobles after a trial organized by the future King Charles IX. It was the most notorious of his ruthless measures against supporters of ex-King Sigismund.

LINLITHGOW, JOHN ADRIAN LOUIS HOPE, 1st Marquis of (1860–1908), governor of Vic. (1889–95), and first governor-general of the Commonwealth of Australia (1901). His early resignation resulted from misunderstandings, which were the government's fault rather than his, about the scale of expenditure appropriate to his position.

LINLITHGOW, VICTOR ALEXANDER JOHN HOPE, 2nd Marquis of (1887–1952), viceroy of India (1936–43). After service in the First World War, he was civil lord of the admiralty (1922–4) before going to India to inaugurate the new constitution embodied in the Government of India Act (1935). In the latter half of his viceroyalty the process of assimilating the constitution was overshadowed by the Second World War, which imposed new administrative demands on India and drastically altered political conditions. Linlithgow had had considerable administrative experience and direct contact with India through his chairmanship of both the royal commission on Indian agriculture (1926–8) and the joint select committee on Indian constitutional reform (1933–4), which dealt with the Government of India Bill when it came before parliament. As viceroy he was successful in executing one of the two main purposes of the new constitution, provincial autonomy. But he failed to bring about the other, Indian federation. He secured the Congress's acceptance of office in July 1937 and he could be satisfied that the provincial constitutions operated everywhere from 1937 to 1939 and thereafter in the 'non-Congress' provinces. But much of the credit for this must go to the provincial governors and the provincial politicians rather than to the government of India, which was itself still cossetted against the strains of responsible government. The negotiations with the princes for accession to the federation failed, partly because of the home government's reluctance to allow Linlithgow to use either pressure or financial inducements.

The war then brought its own problems. Linlithgow's declaration of hostilities on India's behalf and without any consultation offended nationalist Indian leaders, and in the ensuing three years he was unable to induce them to cooperate with the government. His first offer (Oct. 1939) of a new constitution after the war in return for support for the war effort was rejected by the Congress, which claimed immediate independence, and by the Muslim League, which sought to rid itself of the unpalatable prospect of a Hindu-dominated federation. His attempt to increase the scope of the proposals in his 'August Offer' (1940) was undermined by Winston Churchill's interference, by the determination of Congress to hold out for more extensive concessions, and by the league's adoption of the 'Pakistan' scheme in March 1940. Linlithgow's government dealt effectively with the 'individual satyagraha' against the war (1940–1) and in 1940 he was able to expand the membership of his executive council to 15, including 11 Indians, which he did as an earnest of his intentions, and a means of attracting support for the war effort. But he made no headway with the basic political problems. Within his government there was a firm belief that Congress could—and indeed should—be broken rather than won over and this doubtless had some effect upon his judgement. When the Cripps proposals of April 1942 were rejected by Congress and League leaders and Congress decided upon its 'Quit India' campaign, the government moved against the leadership and imprisoned them for the rest of the war, then moved in considerable force against the 'rebels' of Aug. 1942. As a result, India was quiescent by the end of Linlithgow's viceroyalty, but its political problems were no nearer solution.

The contribution made to the war effort by Linlithgow's government was more successful. The army was expanded from 175,000 to 2 million men and, in the period 1940–3 India was able to meet the bulk of Eastern Group's supply demands. Although India's domestic economy benefited from this increase in demand, there were less fortunate episodes, notably the mismanagement which resulted in famine in Bengal in 1943. This was by no means Linlithgow's fault, for under provincial autonomy it was the Bengal government's responsibility to take the steps necessary to avoid famine; but given his experience on the royal commission on agriculture and his even wider experience of agricultural marketing and prices in Britain (1923–36), Linlithgow might have been expected to act more expeditiously.

On his return to Britain he played little part in public life but was lord high commissioner of the general assembly of the Church of Scotland (1944, 1945) and chancellor of Edinburgh University.

C. H. Philips and M. D. Wainwright (eds), *The Partition of India. Policies and Perspectives 1935–1947* (London, 1970).
R. Coupland, *Report on the Constitutional Problem in India* London, 1943).   PDR

LINNAEUS, CAROLUS (1707–78), Swedish naturalist who introduced binomial nomenclature for each species of plant and animal: the name of the genus followed by that of the species, *eg, Homo sapiens*, defined by published diagnostic description based on a type specimen. There are 250,000 plant species and 1,500,000 animals. Without Linnaeus's binomial system biology would be in chaos; medicine and veterinary science of parasite-caused diseases would be impossible, for no workers would know which species others were researching on.

LIN-YI, Chinese name for a kingdom which flourished in present-day Central Viet-nam from the 3rd to the 6th cent. It was the predecessor of the Hindu kingdom of Champa.

LINZ, TREATY OF (1645), agreement between Emperor Ferdinand III and the Calvinist Prince George Rákoćzy I (*reg.* 1630–48) of Transylvania, after the latter had fought against the empire in defence of the Hungarian Protestants. He extracted far-reaching guarantees of Transylvanian sovereignty and religious toleration for Protestants of noble birth and for all townsfolk in royal Hungary.

LIONNE, HUGHES DE, MARQUIS DE BERNY (1611–71), French diplomat and chief minister of state under Louis XIV. He was sent by Cardinal Mazarin to Madrid on a secret peace mission (1656), and though not immediately successful, was chosen to accompany Mazarin to the Isle of Pheasants for the Franco–Spanish negotiations which led to the treaty of the Pyrenees (1659). He was responsible for the marriage contract between Louis XIV and the Infanta Maria Theresa and in particular for the famous clause by which the latter renounced her claim to the Spanish Crown on the conditional payment of a dowry of 500,000 gold *écus*. Lionne also took a leading part in the negotiations for the creation of the League of the Rhine (1658) and for the restoration of peace among the Baltic countries (1660). After Mazarin's death (1661) he was in effective charge of the department of foreign affairs under Loménie de Brienne and in 1668 he bought the office of secretary of state for foreign affairs from the Briennes. In the same period he was a member of the *conseil d'en haut* and was entrusted by Louis with many delicate diplomatic missions, *eg,* to negotiate an agreement with the Dutch concerning French annexation of the Spanish Netherlands (1662), and a Franco–Swiss treaty (1663) which ensured the safety of the narrow corridor of Gex between Franche-Comté and Savoy and enabled Swiss volunteers to enter France to serve in the French army. At the same time, he evaded the demand that Louis XIV should guarantee the existing status of Franche-Comté which the French later occupied (1668, 1674). He played an important part in working out French claims to the Spanish Netherlands by the law of devolution, and helped Louis to achieve a temporary settlement of the Jansenist controversy, when the four French bishops who had refused to accept the anti-Jansenist formulary of 1656 were reconciled to Clement IX (1668). At the end of his life he worked for an alliance of north German states to replace the moribund League of the Rhine.

LIPPMANN, WALTER (1889–   ), US newspaper columnist and political writer, who became a founding editor of the progressive weekly, *The New Republic* (1914). He welcomed America's entry into the First World War and helped to establish Col. House's 'Inquiry' into the terms of peace. But the treaty of Versailles (1919) was a profound disappointment to him and induced a scepticism about progressive idealism which marked such later writings as *Public Opinion* (1922), a disenchanted analysis of modern democratic practice, and *The Good Society* (1937), a critique of the pretensions of collectivist social planning. In world affairs, he became an advocate of 'realism', arguing that the US should protect her national interests and maintain the balance of power, but avoid ideological crusades and limitless commitments. His editorials in the New York *World* (1921–31) and his syndicated newspaper columns (1931–67) carried his commentary on current events to a wide audience.

LIPSIUS, JUSTUS (1547–1606), Dutch Latinist scholar of the Netherlands Renaissance, a native of Brabant, who became professor at Louvain and Leyden universities. He was known for his editions of Tacitus and Seneca and also wrote *De Militia Romana* (1598).

LIPSKI, JÓZEF (1894–1958), Polish diplomat, who entered the Polish diplomatic service in 1918, and served in London, Paris, and Berlin (1918–25). He then worked in the foreign ministry in Warsaw (1925–33), where he became the leading expert on Western European problems. From 1933 to 1939 he served in Berlin, first as minister, then as ambassador, and was an enthusiastic exponent of Beck's policy of achieving friendly relations with Nazi Germany. After the Second World War he lived in the US.

LIRCAY, TREATY OF (1 May 1814), signed on the banks of the Chilean river of the same name between the Spanish and the Chilean leader, Bernardo O'Higgins, by which the latter agreed to accept Spanish sovereignty and the former agreed to evacuate the country. Neither side honoured the treaty.

LISA, MANUEL (1772–1820), Spanish-American fur trader, who held a monopoly on the fur trade with the Osage Indians, led a fur-trading venture into the upper Missouri region (1807), and built Fort Manuel at the junction of the Big Horn and Yellowstone rivers. He formed the Missouri Fur Co. with members of the Chouteau family (1809).

LISBOA, ANTONIO FRANCISCO (O ALEIJADINHO) (1730–1814), Brazilian architect and rococo sculptor. He was a crippled mulatto who worked in the province of Minas Gerais and built some of the loveliest churches in Brazil.

LISBON, TREATY OF (13 Feb. 1668), settlement by which the regent of Spain, Mariana of Austria, acting on behalf of the three-year-old Charles II, recognized the independence of Portugal after the War of Independence (1640–68).

LISBON EARTHQUAKE (1755), greatest natural disaster of the 18th cent. The earth tremors occurred on a Sunday morning, on the feast of All Saints (1 Nov.). Within 15 minutes two-thirds of the city of Lisbon collapsed in ruins, its low-lying areas were swept by a tidal wave, and by evening the remains were engulfed in flames. Churches toppled on their packed congregations, monasteries, convents, public buildings, and private homes were crushed alike. The dead were estimated at some 60,000. In the ensuing panic Joseph I's minister, Pombal, took control of a demoralized people and during the following 20 years rebuilt Portugal's capital.

LISELOTTE (1652–1722). She was Elizabeth-Charlotte of Bavaria, Princess Palatine and Duchess of Orléans, and daughter of the Elector-Palatine, Karl Ludwig. She became the second wife of Philippe of Orleans and thus sister-in-law to Louis XIV of France (1671). It was through this Protestant German princess, sister of the deceased Elector Charles, that Louis claimed the palatinate in 1685. Her son, the Duke of Orléans, became regent of France (1715–23).

LISOLA, FRANZ PAUL, Freiherr von (1613–74), imperial diplomat and publicist, born in Franche-Comté, whose pamphlet, 'Le Bouclier d'État et de Justice' (1667) gave warning of impending French aggression under Louis XIV. By his diplomacy he helped to break the alliance between Brandenburg and Sweden in favour of Austria's ally, Poland (1657), and as imperial envoy in London he worked for an anti-French coalition (1668), though this did not materialize until 1673.

LISTER OF LYME REGIS, JOSEPH LISTER 1st Baron (1827–1912), British doctor, who advanced surgery with asepsis in operating theatres by using carbolic acid (1865). He devised many surgical instruments and introduced the catgut ligature. He also popularized the rubber drainage tube in treating Queen Victoria (1871).

LIT DE JUSTICE, ceremony during which the King of France attended *parlement*, reassumed the powers delegated to it, and ordered the registration of one or more edicts or ordinances which the court had hitherto refused to accept.

LITERACY TESTS IN THE UNITED STATES, devices employed mainly by state governments as a suffrage qualification. The right of states to require such tests was upheld by the US Supreme Court in *Williams v. Mississippi* (1898) and in *Lassiter v. Northampton County Board of Elections* (1959), and in 1968 19 states still had some form of literacy test. The court has, however, also recognized that such a test might be used for discriminatory purposes. Evidence of this in some Southern states has given rise to demands that objective educational criteria be used as evidence of having fulfilled the literacy requirement. The Voting Rights Act of 1965, as extended in 1970, suspended literacy tests in all states until Aug. 1975. Literacy tests have also been used as a means of restricting immigration. Congress unsuccessfully sought the enactment of such tests for immigrants in 1896, 1913, and 1915, and in 1917 a bill was passed over President Wilson's veto excluding aliens over 16 who were unable to read.

LITERARY CLUB in London. 'The Club', founded in 1764, was the apogee of the literary elite in the reign of George III. It was dominated by Dr Johnson and its membership included Garrick, Sheridan, Gibbon, Adam Smith, Boswell, Burke, and Fox.

LITHUANIA, independent Baltic republic (1922–40), area 55,600 sq. kms., population (1970) 2,500,000. For centuries it was a part of Poland and later of Russia; its independence was proclaimed in Nov. 1918. The first years of Lithuania's independence were occupied with clearing Bolshevik and German troops from the territory and establishing firm borders. By 1920 all foreign troops had been expelled, but Lithuania was unable to regain her capital, Vilna, whose seizure in 1920 by Poland was recognized internationally in 1923. Using the Polish action as a model, Lithuania herself seized Memel (1923), thus securing a trade outlet on the Baltic, though at the same time incurring German hostility. Quarrels with Poland and Germany dominated Lithuanian

foreign relations until the Second World War. In 1938 Poland forced her, under threat of invasion, to abandon her claims to Vilna, and in March 1939 she was also obliged to surrender Memel to Germany.

Lithuania's domestic politics were fairly stable until 1926, before which time mainly Christian-democrat governments achieved much-needed agrarian reforms. In 1926 a centre-left coalition came to power, but its generally liberal policies, and especially its pro-Russian foreign policy, provoked a right-wing coup by the *Tautininkai* or nationalist bloc, which established a repressive dictatorship under its leader, Voldemaras. In 1929 he was forced to resign, but the regime of his successor, Tubelis, was no less authoritarian, and the country gradually moved towards fascism. The 1930s were a period of rising internal tension, but popular opposition to the dictatorship was severely repressed, and in 1938 a new corporatist and one-party constitution was promulgated.

Before 1939 Lithuania sought collective security through agreements with the other Baltic states, and a degree of reliance on Russia, and at the outbreak of war (1939) she declared her neutrality. However, under the secret Nazi–Soviet pacts of Aug. and Sept. 1939, Lithuania was assigned to the Russian sphere of influence, and in Oct. Russia began to put pressure on her. Lithuania was forced to accept a treaty whereby, in exchange for the return of Vilna (then under Russian control), she allowed Russian troops to be stationed on her territory. In May 1940 Russia provoked a new crisis with Lithuania, as a result of which the country was occupied by the Red Army. Elections were held and a puppet government established, and on 3 Aug. Lithuania was formally incorporated into Soviet Russia.

In the summer of 1941 Lithuania was occupied by German troops during their invasion of Russia, and remained under German control until Aug. 1944, when she was liberated by Russia. She suffered heavy losses of population under German rule, particularly through the extermination of Jews. After the war, Lithuania was reincorporated into the Soviet Union, though the cause of Lithuanian independence is still championed by small groups of exiles in the west.

C. R. Jurgela, *History of the Lithuanian Nation* (New York, 1948).
E. Senn, *The Emergence of Modern Lithuania* (New York, 1959). AJC

LITTLE BIG HORN, BATTLE OF (25 June 1876), decisive victory of American Indians over the US Cavalry. The battle, fought on the Little Big Horn river in south-central MT, was a part of the Sioux War (1875–6). Three columns of US troops converged on the camp of Sitting Bull and Crazy Horse. Upon reaching the junction of the Rosebud and Yellowstone rivers, Gen. A. H. Terry, commanding one of the columns, sent Lt-Col. George A. Custer south along the Rosebud to cut off the Indians' retreat. Custer, coming upon the encampment and thinking it small, attacked. He and 265 men of the 7th US Cavalry were overwhelmed by 2500 warriors and were annihilated. The victory did the Sioux little good and by the end of Oct. 1876 they all surrendered, except for a few under Sitting Bull, who fled to Canada.

LITTLE ENTENTE, THE (Aug. 1922), name applied to the mutual defence arrangement entered into by Czechoslovakia, Rumania, and Yugoslavia, which consolidated three earlier arrangements made between the individual pairs of states (1920–1). The alliance was directed towards maintaining the territorial gains made by each member at the expense of Austria-Hungary at the end of the First World War and formally recognized by the treaties of St Germain and Trianon. The treaty, in addition to co-ordinating defence policy, provided for economic and political co-operation, and in the following years steps were taken to convert the alliance into a more broadly based association. The members agreed (1929) to the treaty's automatic renewal every five years and signed an additional agreement for the pacific settlement of their disputes. The apogee was attained (Feb. 1933) with the establishment of a permanent council and secretariat directed to meet three times a year in order to concert the policy of the alliance; further collaboration was facilitated in the following year by the creation of an economic council.

Though specifically united by a mutual fear of Hungarian revisionism, the anxiety was not shared equally by the three members. Yugoslavia was more concerned with containing Italian ambitions in the Adriatic, and Rumania feared Russian designs on Bessarabia, which she had lost to Rumania in 1918. Until the early 1930s the Little Entente was able to rely on the tacit, and later on the formal, support of France against both Italy and Hungary; but with Hitler's rise to power (1933) and the ensuing German–Italian rivalry over Austria, there followed a reorientation of alignments, which reflected and emphasized already existing divergences within the Little Entente. Czechoslovakia, aware that her own security was endangered by the growing German threat to the independence of Austria, welcomed Franco-Italian rapprochement. By contrast, Yugoslavia and Rumania saw Germany's revival as a dominant power as a useful counter-weight to Italy and Russia. Thus while lip-service continued to be paid to the principles of the Little Entente, its original *raison d'être* failed to maintain the unity of the three members, who tended more and more to move in independent directions. The assassination of King Alexander of Yugoslavia in Marseilles by a Croat terrorist served to strain Franco–Yugoslav relations and further to undermine the Little Entente. As Rumania and Yugoslavia edged towards Germany, so Czechoslovakia moved closer to France, and the signing of the Russo–Czech treaty shortly after the signing of the Franco–Russian pact (1935), emphasized the widening rift in the alliance. The last conference was held in 1938, but the German occupation of Czechoslovakia signalled the end of the Little Entente, which was formally concluded by Rumania and Yugoslavia (Feb. 1939).

Though unable to withstand the pressure of European politics in the 1930s, the Little Entente had played an active role in League affairs and serves, despite its failings, as an early example of a regional organization designed to further both the security and economic welfare of its members.

WFK

LITVINOV, MAXIM MAXIMOVICH (1876–1951), Soviet diplomat, politician, and foreign minister. In 1898 he joined the SDP and he was imprisoned for running a secret printing press in Kiev. In 1902 he organized the escape for himself and several of his companions, then went into exile and eventually met Lenin in London. His Bolshevik companions called him '*papasha*' because he was solid, calm, and dependable. Lenin sent him to Riga, where he acted as link with the Bolshevik underground in Russia. During the 1905 revolution he ran arms and edited the Bolshevik paper *Novaya Zhizn*. After this he lived mostly in London, where he earned his living as a clerk in a publisher's office. In 1914 he married an Englishwoman, Ivy Low. In 1918 he was appointed as the first Soviet representative to the British government. But his position was not recognized by the foreign office; after being imprisoned he was at length exchanged for his counterpart in Moscow, Sir Robert Bruce Lockhart. In 1921 he was appointed deputy commissar for foreign affairs and quickly gained a reputation outside the Soviet Union as a humorous, shrewd, and capable diplomat. He accompanied Chicherin to Genoa (1922), where he formed a friendship with Barthou, the French foreign minister. In 1924 he headed the Soviet delegation to London which negotiated the formal recognition of the Soviet Union by Britain. He spoke at Geneva at the meetings of the Preparatory Disarmament Conference. Later he gave his name to the Litvinov pact (1929), which was a regional affirmation of the Kellogg pact. He was commissar for foreign affairs (1930–9), and was closely associated with the Soviet attempt to create a system of collective security against Germany and Japan.

After a visit to Washington (1933) during which he established cordial relations with President Roosevelt, he persuaded the US to recognize the Soviet Union. In 1934 he negotiated a Franco–Soviet pact and also took the Soviet Union into the League of Nations. He appeared frequently at Geneva, where he denounced the failure of the Western powers to consolidate plans for collective security. He also criticized the policy of non-intervention in the Spanish Civil War. The Munich conference (Sept. 1938) represented a victory of the Western appeasers and consequently the failure of Litvinov's policy. In May 1939 Molotov took his place as commissar and the Soviet Union made preparations to take a different line. Litvinov was brought out of semi-retirement to be ambassador to the US (1941–3), but his appointment was abruptly terminated when Soviet–American relations deteriorated as a result of the discovery of the Katyn forest massacre.

M. Beloff, *The Foreign Policy of Soviet Russia*, 2 vols (London, 1949).

L. Fischer, *The Soviets in World Affairs, 1917–1929*, 2 vols (Princeton, 1951).   GS

LIU PANG (*reg*. 202–195 BC), founder and first Emperor of the Han dynasty. He is known under the posthumous titles of Kao-tsu. Rising from unprofessional and non-aristocratic origins, during the civil wars of 210–202, he succeeded in winning control of key areas in western China and eventually in eliminating all other pretenders to power.

LIU SHAO-CH'I (1900–), Chinese Communist Party leader, and most prominent victim of the Cultural Revolution. Liu was a school-mate of Mao Tse-tung in Hunan, and like him, a radical. His early work in the Communist Party was as a labour organizer, in which capacity he continued to operate clandestinely after the Communist Party was outlawed in 1927. In 1932 he moved to the Soviet area in Kiangsi. He made the Long March to Shensi (1934–5), and on his return took part in underground labour organization in the cities of north China. After the start of the Anti-Japanese War he moved to the Communist capital, Yenan, and started to make a name for himself as a political theorist. His first major polemical work, 'How to be a good communist', was published in 1939. Liu emphasized the need for austerity and self-discipline; he claimed that a communist's class status was determined more by attitude than by birth—in contrast to Mao's line, in which stress was laid on birth as the key factor. Liu gradually came to act as official party spokesman, and as party secretary. In 1949, when the new administration was set up, he was one of its most influential members. His authority over the party apparatus was enormous, though from 1954 Teng Hsiao-p'ing was officially party secretary. In 1959 Mao was forced to resign as chairman of the People's Republic; the havoc created by the Mao-sponsored Great Leap Forward had incensed the more pragmatic of China's party and government leaders, who now gathered around Liu. Liu embarked on a series of cautious policies, designed to restore order and prosperity. For the next seven years Mao, who retained overriding prestige as leader of the party, searched for ways to remove Liu and his 'counter-revolutionary' supporters. Eventually, in 1966, he launched the Cultural Revolution, using as his 'shock-troops' the loyal and malleable Red Guards. Liu and his supporters were swept from office, though not without a stubborn fight. Liu himself was denounced as 'the top party person in authority taking the capitalist road'; he is now believed to be under house arrest in Peking. Until personal animosity destroyed their relationship, Liu's austerity and respect for organization was an effective foil to Mao's romantic revolutionary ideas, and to his impetuosity.   DCML

LIU YUNG-FU (1837–1917), Chinese leader of the 'Black Flags', a group of bandits in Tongking, who aided the Chinese in their resistance against French expansion in Viet-nam.

After the Chinese defeat in 1884, Liu and his men were forced to withdraw within China's borders. In 1895, when China was defeated in the Sino–Japanese War, and had to cede Taiwan to the Japanese, Liu fought against the Japanese without success.

LIUDPRAND OF CREMONA (d. 972), imperial historian, who left Italy (*c.* 956) and went to the court of Otto I of Germany. He wrote a history of Italian and German affairs (887–949), but is best known for the *Legatio*, an account of his unsuccessful embassy to Constantinople in 968 on behalf of Otto I.

LIUTPRAND (*reg.* 712–44), King of the Lombards, who consistently attacked the remnants of Byzantine power and eventually captured the Byzantine capital, Ravenna (751). He also repeatedly menaced Rome, but being a Catholic, was restrained by religious scruples from a decisive attack. His consolidation of a powerful Lombard state led, after his death, to an alliance between the papacy and the Franks and the latter, under Charlemagne, destroyed the Lombard kingdom in 774–5.

LIVERIES, ACT OF (1504) in England, was intended to prevent private wars in England by forbidding the giving or taking of indentures. During the Hundred Years War, when the procedure of the feudal levy was insufficient to keep regular forces in the field, the Crown indented with the nobility for the supply of men, and the greater lords made similar contracts with lesser landowners. When the English were evicted from France, the nobles had at their disposal small armies which they employed in private quarrels. The Wars of the Roses were prolonged by mercenaries and adventurers who took their lord's 'livery', which included food and keep as well as apparel, and were 'maintained' by him in lawsuits arising from acts committed in his service. A series of statutes in the 15th cent. showed the failure of successive governments to prevent this practice, and in his efforts to control the barons, Henry VII passed acts in 1487 and 1495 before the more effective measure of 1504 put an end to the armed retainer.

LIVERPOOL, CHARLES JENKINSON, 1st Earl of (1727–1808), British politician of great influence at court and in parliament in the reign of George III. His talents were noted by Lord Bute and he served as under-secretary of state (1761) and joint secretary to the treasury (1763). A leader of the King's Friends in the Commons, he was out of office under Rockingham (1765), but served Grafton as vice-treasurer of Ireland and a privy councillor (1772), and Lord North as secretary for war (1778). The younger Pitt made him president of the council for trade and the plantations (1786) and chancellor of the Duchy of Lancaster. He established the family fortunes by becoming clerk of the pells in Ireland and master of the mint (1775).

LIVERPOOL, ROBERT BANKS JENKINSON, 2nd Earl of (1770–1828), British politician and prime minister, under whose administration the French Wars were successfully concluded by the treaty of Paris (1815). He guided the Tory Party away from policies of repression pursued in time of war and civil disorder to one of social reform after 1822. He was astute in his choice of ministers and in managing his cabinet and party, believing opposition to catholic emancipation to be necessary to party unity.

Liverpool was an MP from 1790, when he succeeded to his father as Lord Hawkesbury (1803). He was foreign secretary under Addington (1801–4) and conducted the peace negotiations with France, though he foresaw a renewal of the war and opposed the surrender of Malta. On Pitt's return he became secretary (1804–6) and leader of the House of Lords. He led the opposition to the Ministry of the Talents and helped to precipitate its fall by persuading George III to refuse a dissolution which might have produced a Commons favourable to Catholic emancipation. He was home secretary (1807–9), foreign secretary (1809), and secretary for war and the colonies (1809–12), and dealt with the reorganization of the London police, and the maintenance of order in Ireland. He also successfully advocated the evacuation of Walcheren and supported Wellington in the Peninsular campaign. On the assassination of Perceval, the prime minister, Liverpool succeeded him. By treating Catholic emancipation as an open question he was able to recruit a strong cabinet, though Canning was excluded from it.

Liverpool's position was strengthened by Napoleon's failure in Russia (1812) and Wellington's success at Waterloo (1815). He supported a moderate policy towards France in order to maintain the stability of Europe. This policy Castlereagh, the foreign secretary, pursued at the Congress of Vienna and at later conferences.

In 1815 Liverpool approved the acquisition of territories required for the establishment of British naval and colonial supremacy, and in the interests of his Far Eastern policy opposed Russian designs on Turkey. He supported the Spanish policy pursued by Canning as foreign secretary, which he saw as being helpful to British commercial interests in South America. At home, unrest caused by economic distress was intensified by Liverpool's government, which passed the Corn Law of 1815, and replaced income tax by indirect taxation (1816), thus raising prices. A series of disorders culminating in the massacre of Peterloo resulted in the suspension of *habeas corpus* (1817) and the coercive Six Acts (1819), while the royal divorce bill (1820) involving George IV's wife increased the government's unpopularity. After the reconstruction of 1822, when the administration was strengthened by Canning's inclusion, Liverpool encouraged the reforms sought by ministers such as Huskisson and Peel. At the board of trade Huskisson reduced duties on imports and Peel, as home secretary, reformed the penal code, prisons, and the police. Liverpool bequeathed the leadership to Canning at a time of increasing national prosperity and ministerial popularity.

W. R. Brock, *Lord Liverpool and Liberal Toryism* (London, 1967).
                                                                    VEC

LIVERY COMPANIES, so called from the distinctive costume of their members, developed in London from the medieval guilds and formerly controlled their respective crafts (mercers, grocers, fishmongers, goldsmiths, etc.), supervising conditions of apprenticeship and standards of work. Their influence declined after the 16th cent., but they still elect the mayor and sheriffs of the City of London—a situation unique in the election of municipal officers—and their wealth is mainly devoted to charitable and educational purposes. There are still (1970) about 80 livery companies, some founded in the 20th cent.

LIVIA DRUSILLA (58 BC–AD 29), wife of the Roman Emperor Augustus and daughter of M. Livius Drusus Claudianus, the adopted son of M. Livius Drusus (tribune 91 BC). She married Tiberius Claudius Nero, by whom she had two sons, the future Emperor Tiberius, and Drusus. Nero divorced her in 38 BC so that she could marry Octavian. With their marriage the Roman aristocracy realized that Octavian might defeat Antony. Augustus valued her advice on matters of state, and on Tiberius' accession (AD 14) she attempted to gain an equal share in the government. Although thwarted, she retained immense influence until her death.

LIVINGSTON FAMILY in US. Robert Livingston (1654–1728) went to New York from Scotland (1663) and became a wealthy fur trader. His descendants were prominent in the affairs of New York as colony and state. Robert R. Livingston (1718–75), his grandson, was justice of the New York Supreme Court and chairman of the Committee of Correspondence. Robert R. Livingston (1746–1815), the former's son, was a lawyer, a member of the Continental Congress, and one of five appointed to the committee that drafted the Declaration of Independence. He was Jefferson's minister to France and conducted negotiations for the Louisiana Purchase. Edward Livingston (1764–1836), son of Justice Robert R. Livingston, practised law in New York and was mayor of New York city (1800–3). Because of financial swindles by some of his officials he resigned his office, made good the deficit, and moved to New Orleans, where he practised law. He was secretary of state under President Jackson (1831–3), and minister to France (1833–5). He drew up a penal code for LA, which was not accepted there, but became the model of state penal codes in the US and elsewhere. Peter Van Brugh Livingston (1710–92) and Philip Livingston (1716–78), nephews of the first Robert Livingston, were patriot leaders during the American War of Independence. Their younger brother, William Livingston (1723–90), was NJ's first state governor. William's son, Henry Brockholst Livingston (1757–1823), served in the American Army and was associate justice of the US Supreme Court (1806).

F. Van Rensslaer, *The Livingston Family in America and its Scottish Origins* (New York, 1949).   DJF

LIVINGSTONE, DAVID (1813–73), Scottish Christian missionary, doctor, and explorer in Africa. From 1840, when he went out to South Africa for the London Missionary Society, to his death in Zambia in 1873, Livingstone's explorations, covering a third of Africa, and his writings and speeches about them, captured the imagination of Europe and America. More than anyone else, he convinced the white world of the opportunities in Africa for social service, economic gain, and the advancement of learning, at a time when Europe and America were ready to move increasingly into Africa.

In his first major expedition of 1853–6, alone save for a few African followers, Livingstone crossed Africa from Loanda in the west to Quelimane in the east and discovered the falls on the Zambesi which he named after Queen Victoria. His second expedition of 1858–63 was sponsored by the British government and Livingstone was made consul at Quelimane for the east coast and interior districts. He reached Lake Nyasa in 1859, and conducted two explorations of the Ruvuma river, proving that it was useless for the penetration of the interior. Although often contrasted unfavourably with the heroic achievements of his first major expedition, this journey stimulated Scottish missionary and colonizing activity in Malawi. On his third venture into the interior, from 1865 to 1873, Livingstone travelled again with only a few followers, seeking the sources of the Nile. He never found them; but he contributed significantly to European geographical knowledge, reaching Lakes Mweru and Bangweulu and the upper Congo river. The sensational encounter at Ujiji in 1871 of Livingstone and the Welsh-American, H. M. Stanley, with his relief expedition, quickened the interest of the outside world in Africa.

Livingstone considered that Christianity could only be spread in those parts of Africa which he had visited by the stamping-out of the Arab slave trade and the introduction of commerce and industrialism. In spite of his paternalism and Victorian prejudices, Livingstone believed seriously in the Africans' capacity to advance into the modern world. In this sense, he was a forerunner not only of European imperialism in Africa, but also of modern African nationalism.

George Seaver, *David Livingstone* (London, 1957).
George Shepperson, *David Livingstone and the Rovuma* (Edinburgh, 1965).   GS

LIVINGSTONIA, missionary venture in Malawi, started in 1875, by the Free Church of Scotland, and named after David Livingstone. It has had a profound effect on African education and political consciousness inside and outside Malawi.

LIVIUS ANDRONICUS (*c.* 284–204 BC), father of Latin literature, a Greek from Tarentum, who translated the *Odyssey* into Latin, and wrote tragedies and comedies on Greek models. None of his works survives.

LIVIUS DRUSUS, M., THE ELDER (*fl.* 2nd cent. BC), Roman politician, who as tribune (122 BC) outbid C. Gracchus, probably while the latter was absent in Africa, and undermined his support among the people. He was subsequently consul (112) and governor of Macedonia, being the first Roman commander to reach the Danube (111).

LIVIUS DRUSUS, M., THE YOUNGER (*fl.* 1st cent. BC), Roman politician, who precipitated the Social War, and son of the elder Livius Drusus. As tribune (91 BC) he tried to recover for the Senate the support of the Italian allies by proposing their enfranchisement. The proposal was included in a composite bill which also dealt with the foundation of colonies and a reform of the *Quaestio de rebus repetundis* which favoured the Senate. But in attempting to satisfy all classes Drusus merely alienated them. Violent agitation led to the invalidation of his legislation, he himself was murdered, and the exasperated Italians rebelled.

LIVONIAN ORDER, military order founded by Albert of Bremen and confirmed by the pope in 1204. It was intended to convert the pagan Latvians. Most of the knights were exterminated in 1236 by the Russians under Alexander Nevsky and the survivors joined the Teutonic Order.

LIVRE TOURNOIS, money of account used in France from the 16th cent., the equivalent of the pound sterling in England, the lira of the Italian states, the guilder of Holland, the florin of the Spanish Netherlands, and the gulden of the German states. It was convertible into gold and silver coins at a variable rate.

LIVY (Titus Livius) (?59 BC–AD 17), Roman historian from Padua, whose 142 books covered Rome's history from its foundation to 9 BC; of these, Books 1–10 and 21–45 have survived, recording the events of 753–293 and 219–167 BC. Lacking personal experience of politics or warfare, he was a poor critic of his sources, but he consulted a wide range of writers and transmitted their information honestly. Believing that the didactic purpose of history was to chart Roman moral virtues in politics, warfare, and private life, he shaped his source-material to highlight the moral attributes of the leading figures of each age. This central aim of characterization is achieved by constant emphasis on the psychological, particularly through the convention of inserting composed speeches at apposite historical junctures. His literary gifts in both stirring narrative and speech composition have lent a perennial appeal to his history, the most important single document by which Republican aristocratic attitudes can be assessed.

LLANEROS, occupants of the sparsely populated plains of Venezuela. Large bands of *llaneros*, led by José Tomás Boves and José Antonio Páez, played an important role in the wars of independence against Spain, and various Venezuelan dictators have at times used their support. The name *llaneros* is also given to the plainsmen of neighbouring Colombia.

LLANOS (lit. 'plains'), word used to identify the vast Orinoco plains in Venezuela and Colombia, often considered the local equivalent of the 'far west'. In the past, inhabitants of the llanos have been used as tough cavalry for various causes.

LLERAS CAMARGO, ALBERTO (1906–), Colombian politician, diplomat, and president (1945–6, 1958–62), who headed a government of national reconciliation. During his term of office Colombian rural violence decreased.

LLORENZ, JUAN (d. 1520), Catalan leader of the *Germanias* movement in its early stages (1519–20), originally a weaver in Valencia, which he hoped to turn into a republic on the Venetian model.

LLOYD, HENRY DEMAREST (1847–1903), US lawyer, journalist, and reformer, who attacked monopolies in general, and Standard Oil in particular, in *Wealth Against Commonwealth* (1894). He advocated the public ownership of monopolies. His book anticipated the muckraking journalism of the Progressive era.

LLOYD, JOHN SELWYN BROOKE (1904–   ), British lawyer and politician who entered parliament (1945) as MP for Wirral, becoming a junior minister under Eden at the foreign office (1951–4). He was foreign secretary (1955–60) and, as such, was involved in the Suez crisis (1956). He was appointed chancellor of the exchequer in 1960, and in 1961 his emergency budget contained proposals for a National Economic Development Council and constituted a major step towards the introduction of a Prices and Incomes policy. In the following months the economic difficulties continued and the standing of the Macmillan government declined. In July 1962 Macmillan dismissed several senior ministers, including Lloyd. After some months on the back-benches he was made lord privy seal and leader of the house. After the Conservative defeat in 1964 he remained active in the Conservative Party. In 1970 he was elected speaker of the House of Commons.

LLOYD GEORGE OF DWYFOR, DAVID LLOYD GEORGE, 1st Earl (1863–1945), British Liberal politician and prime minister, who lost his father at an early age and was brought up in a Caernarvonshire village by his uncle, a shoemaker and Baptist lay preacher. He qualified as a solicitor and also became a champion of Welsh nonconformity against the Anglican ascendancy. He represented Caernarvon Boroughs uninterruptedly as an MP (1890–1945). In parliament he was a prominent opponent of the Anglo-Boer War and of Balfour's Education Act. In Dec. 1905 he became president of the board of trade and in 1908 chancellor of the exchequer. His People's Budget (1909), which introduced supertax and taxation of land values, provoked a constitutional crisis with the House of Lords. He devised the first scheme of National Health Insurance and, with Winston Churchill, of Unemployment, thus initiating the welfare state.

In Aug. 1914 he appeared as leader of the anti-war group in the Liberal cabinet, but was converted to support of the First World War by the German invasion of Belgium. As minister of munitions (1915–16) he transformed industry and negotiated with labour for the needs of war. In Dec. 1916 he urged a more efficient conduct of the war and, when Asquith resisted this demand, provoked a political crisis which ended with himself becoming prime minister. He instituted a war cabinet, insisted on convoy for merchant shipping, and secured a unified military command under Foch. He was rightly regarded as the man who won the war.

In Dec. 1918, his Coalition supporters having triumphed in the general election, he took a leading part in the Paris peace conference and thereafter attempted to revise the settlement. He built Homes for Heroes and defeated the miners' demand for coal nationalization. In Dec. 1921 he concluded the treaty which established the Irish Free State. His government fell in Nov. 1922, after the Chanak crisis, when the Conservatives ceased to support him. Thereafter he made an uneasy reconciliation with Asquith and was (1926–31) nominally leader of the Liberal Party. In 1929 he put forward the first plans for a creative economic policy ever propounded by a responsible British politician. He opposed the National government of 1931, first over economic, and then over foreign policy. In 1940 he refused to join Churchill's government, partly on account of his own age and partly from the hope of securing a negotiated peace with Hitler. He was created an earl shortly before his death in 1945. He was the most creative British statesman and most effective demagogic speaker of his time, arousing unparalleled devotion and also unparalleled detestation.

G. M. Thomson, *David Lloyd George* (London, 1948).
Tom Jones, *Lloyd George* (London, 1951).   AJPT

LLOYD'S COFFEE HOUSE in London, centre of maritime insurance and for a time (1696) a place from which *Lloyd's News* (later revised as *Lloyd's List*) was published. This contained special information about shipping. The name of Lloyd's is still (1970) used by the great exchange which emerged from these humble beginnings.

LLYWELYN I (ABIORWERTH) (1173–1240), Prince of Gwynedd. By 1197 he was master of the whole of Gwynedd, as it had been under Owain Gwynedd, his grandfather. He married Joan, illegitimate daughter of King John of England, but his relations with the king were unstable. Taking advantage of John's quarrel with the barons, with whom he sided, he had, by 1218, extended his power to Powys and parts of Deheubarth. The latter part of his rule was almost wholly peaceful and he succeeded in retaining the lands he had won. He pursued a policy of peace with his English neighbours, marrying his children into powerful marcher families, and attempting to create a feudal state in Wales, uniting diverse kingdoms owing homage to him while he, in turn, paid homage to his overlord, the king. He provided for the continuance of his policy when he named his son, Dafydd, as his sole heir, whom Henry III recognized in 1229, as did the Welsh lords in 1238. Llywelyn's reign was marked by a spirit of unity, resulting in the development of the legal code and in the idea of allegiance to the state.

LLYWELYN II (d. 1282), Prince of Gwynedd and grandson of Llywelyn I (Ab Iorwerth). After the death of his uncle, Dafydd (1247), Llywelyn was left with a Gwynedd which was a mere fragment of what it had been under his grandfather, but by 1257 he had regained much of what had been lost. In 1258 the allegiance of the other Welsh princes was transferred to him from the king (Gruffydd ap Gwenwynwyn submitted in 1263) and he proclaimed himself Prince of Wales. Henry III, preoccupied with his own affairs in England—Llywelyn was an ally of Simon de Montfort—recognized the title (though Llywelyn continued to owe him homage) and confirmed Llywelyn in his position by the treaty of Montgomery (1267), the zenith of Llywelyn's career. His policy now became more aggressive; he attempted to extend his power, both territorially and politically, refused to pay homage to Edward I, provoked the marcher lords, and remained intransigent and uncompromising, failing to realize that the situation in England had changed. Edward defeated him in 1277, the treaty of Aberconway leaving him only his lands west of the Conway and the now empty title of Prince of Wales. War again broke out in 1282 and in an affray near Builth Llywelyn was killed. His death marked the end of Welsh independence.

LO JUI-CH'ING (1907–?1966), Chinese communist military leader. Lo became chief of staff of the People's Liberation Army (1959) and was concurrently head of the secret police. His immense power, and his advocacy of a professional army, brought him into conflict with Mao Tse-tung and his supporters. He was one of the first people to be denounced in the Cultural Revolution, and was reported to have committed suicide.

LOAYSA, DON GARCIA DE, Cardinal (1480–1546), bishop of Osma (1525–32), archbishop of Seville (1539–46), and Spanish confessor of the Emperor Charles V. Loaysa was also president of the India board, a member of the council of state which advised Charles on matters of general policy concerning Spain and Germany in the 1520s, and imperial representative in Rome (1530).

LOBANOV ROSTOVSKY, ALEXEI BORISOVICH, Prince (1824–96), Russian ambassador in several European capitals (1878–95). As foreign minister (1896) he negotiated a treaty with Japan which established the Chinese Eastern Railway and a joint condominium in Korea.

LOBANOV–YAMAGATA AGREEMENT (1896), defined Russian and Japanese aims in Korea as the insurance of its independence through a policy of co-operation. Secret clauses limited the entry of troops of either country into Korea.

LOBENGULA (*c.* 1833–94), King of the Ndebele (*reg.* 1870–1894). He was the son of Mzilikazi. By the 1880s he was being harassed by white concession hunters, who hoped to find a second Rand north of the Limpopo. In 1888 he granted a mineral concession to Rhodes's agent, Rudd. The following year the British South Africa Co. was formed to exploit this concession, and in 1890 the first whites misused it to settle in Mashonaland, to the east of Matabeleland. Lobengula went to great lengths to avoid a confrontation with the whites, but in 1893 the company declared war, defeated the Ndebele armies, and captured their capital, Bulawayo. Lobengula fled.

LOBKOWITZ, WENZEL EUSEBIUS VON, Prince (1609–77), Bohemian nobleman and the most influential statesman in the Habsburg empire during the early years of the Emperor Leopold I's reign (1658–1705). He was a member of the Imperial Privy Council (1645–74), of which he became president (1668), but his pro-French inclinations aroused suspicions of treason and he was dismissed and exiled by Leopold in 1674.

LOCAL GOVERNMENT ACT (1888) in Britain, greatly simplified county administration and extended the elective principle, already applied to municipal government in 1835, to the counties. The act created 62 administrative counties in England and Wales, each under an elective council, modelled on that of the boroughs. Almost all the administrative powers of the justices of the peace (except those concerning licensing and the police) were transferred to the new councils. Larger boroughs (minimum pop. 50,000) became county boroughs, independent of county administration, and London was treated as a county with 28 metropolitan boroughs. The act began the process (carried further in 1894) of linking smaller administrative units (urban and rural districts) with the new councils. School boards remained outside the county administrative structure until 1902, and boards of guardians until 1929.

LOCAL GOVERNMENT BOARD (1871) in Britain was constructed by joining the local government section of the home office and the medical department of the privy council to the poor law board. It resulted from the report of Disraeli's commission of 1869, which recommended a single supervising authority and a single local health authority in each area. The first president of the board was Sir James Stansfeld (1820–98), who had a seat in the cabinet. He had formerly been president of the poor law board, and maintained its traditions, with the result that Sir John Simon's medical department was overshadowed and increased powers to enforce sanitary laws were renounced owing to local opposition. The local government board also became associated with a campaign against extravagance, a feature of the poor law, so that legitimate expenditure on reform was threatened. The board was replaced by the ministry of health (1918).

LOCALISMO (or 'localism'), political phenomenon in Latin America, whereby local loyalties take precedence over national loyalties, and thus inhibit the development of strong central government and nation states. *Localismo* was the cause of the prolonged federalist–centralist struggles in 19th-cent. Latin America.

LOCARNO TREATIES (1925), agreements reached after the First World War. In Oct. 1925, Germany, Britain, Italy, France and Belgium agreed to protect national frontiers, and submit disputes to arbitration. There were also separate arbitration agreements between Germany and individual nations, *eg*, Poland and Czechoslovakia. The treaty, signed in Dec. 1925, was violated by Germany's Rhineland invasion (1926).

LOCHAU, AGREEMENT OF (1551), anti-Habsburg alliance negotiated between the French ambassador, Jean de Fresse, Bp of Bayonne, and the German princes, led by Maurice of Saxony and Hans of Küstrin, at Lochau Heath (5 Oct. 1551). Henry II of France was to grant military subsidies to the princes against Charles V, in return for the right to rule as imperial vicar over Cammerich, Metz, Toul, and Verdun.

LOCHLEVEN, CASTLE OF, where Mary Queen of Scots was imprisoned by the 'Confederate Lords' after her surrender at Carberry. She was forced to resign the Crown to her infant son James, and to appoint her half-brother, the Earl of Moray, regent (24 July 1567). In May 1568 Mary escaped from Lochleven.

LOCKE, JOHN (1632–1704), English philosopher, whose upbringing in London and in Oxford during the troubled years of the Civil Wars and the Commonwealth led him to devote his life to a consideration of the role of the individual in society in terms of personal freedom, education, religion, and government.

He became (1666) personal physician and secretary to the Earl of Shaftesbury and because of this was later forced to leave the country, with his master, for supposed complicity in the various plots to keep James, Duke of York, from succeeding his brother, Charles II. While living in Holland, Locke met William of Orange. When William became king (1689) he appointed Locke a commissioner of appeals (1689–1704) and a member of the council of trade (1696–1700).

Locke's philosophical views were recorded in *Letters concerning Toleration* (1689, 1690, 1692), *Essay concerning Human Understanding* (1690), *Two Treatises of Government* (1690), *On Education* (1693), and *The Reasonableness of Christianity* (1695).

He was the apologist of the English Revolution of 1688, combating the theory of the divine right of kings with that in which the ruler was bound, in contract, to his people. His thought influenced economists such as Adam Smith, philosophers such as Berkeley and Kant, and had a lasting effect on political theorists, on the makers of the American constitution, and on educationists.

LOCOFOCOISM, US political movement comprising the radical wing of the Democratic Party, originated in New York in 1835, and gained some support in MA and PA. The Locofocos were hostile to privilege and attacked monopolies, corporations, banks, and paper money. They took their name from the 'loco-foco' match, used to light their first meeting.

LOCRIANS, tribe of central Greece, which was divided, perhaps at the Dorian invasions (*c.* 1100 BC), into two parts, the Opuntians living on the east coast south-east of Thermopylae and the Ozolians on the north shore of the Corinthian Gulf, including Naupactus. They co-operated in founding Locri near the southern-most tip of Italy (*c.* 670 BC). Both surrendered to the Persians after Thermopylae (479) and later, after a brief alliance with Athens (457–447), supported Sparta in the great Peloponnesian War (431–404), the Ozolians remaining her allies until the battle of Leuctra in 371. Thereafter, both joined Thebes, suffered in the Third Sacred War (356–346), and then supported Philip II of Macedon.

LODGE, HENRY CABOT (1850–1924), US historian and politician. He received the first Ph.D. in political science granted by Harvard (1876). He was assistant editor of the *North American Review* (1876–79), lectured on US history at Harvard and published biographies of *Daniel Webster* (1882), *Hamilton* (1882), and *Washington* (1888). He was a prominent Republican, an ardent nationalist, a congressman from MA (1886–93) and senator (1893–1924). As a member of the Immigration Restriction League (1894), he was its spokesman in Congress, urging the adoption of a literacy test for immigrants. He supported annexation of the Philippines, was a protectionist and opponent of free silver, and helped to draft several tariff measures, including that of 1909. He opposed women's suffrage and the direct election of senators, but supported civil service reform, helped to frame the Sherman Anti-Trust Act (1890) and the Pure Food and Drug Act (1906), and voted against adoption of the 18th Amendment. Lodge opposed President Wilson's peace policy and, as chairman of the Senate Foreign Relations Committee, led the attack on the Versailles treaty and on US participation in the proposed League of Nations (1919–20). He helped to secure the presidential nomination of Warren G. Harding in 1920, and was a delegate to the Washington Conference (1921–2).

LODI DYNASTY, THE (1451–1526), last rulers of the Delhi sultanate. After Taimur's Indian raid and capture of Delhi (1398) the sultanate disintegrated. The feeble rule of the Sayyid kings was replaced (1451) by Buhlol Khan Lodi, the most powerful of the Punjab chiefs. Buhlol was a vigorous ruler who re-established the Delhi sultanate from the Indus to the borders of Bengal. But it was a loose confederacy of Afghan and Turkish chiefs controlled by a vigorous personality, rather than a Turkish-controlled bureaucratic empire. Buhlol found his actual authority restricted to an area around Delhi, the nominal empire being ruled by virtually independent fief-holders. He was threatened by wealthy Jaunpur in the east and by Malwa in the south. The struggle with the Sharqis of Jaunpur went on for most of the reign. At first Jaunpur was clearly the stronger and Delhi was twice threatened by Husain Shah Sharqi. In the intervals between Sharqi attacks Buhlol was able, by force and dexterity, to establish his authority over his feudatories. With the resources of the Punjab and the Delhi *doab*, he was then able to capture Jaunpur. In 1486 he drove out the Sharqis and made his son Barbak Shah viceroy.

On Buhlol's death (1489) his second son succeeded, as Sikandar (1489–1517). He also was a man of energy and resource, and he continued his father's policy of a loose rein in a firm hand in dealing with the nobles. He suppressed a rebellion led by his brother Barbak in Jaunpur, gained control of Bihar, made a treaty with Husain Shah of Bengal, and extended his dominions southward. The present city of Agra was founded by him on the site known as Sikandarabad. His reputation was only tarnished by his religious bigotry. On his death (1517) he was succeeded by his eldest son, Ibrahim. His attempts to enhance the royal authority led to disaffection. Though he suppressed rebellions by Jalal Khan Lodi and the Afghan nobles, their discontent found a focus in Daulat Khan Lodi, governor of the Punjab, who invited Babur to India. Ibrahim was defeated and killed at Panipat (18 April 1526) and the empire passed to the Mughals.

K. S. Lal, *Twilight of the Sultanate* (London, 1963).   TGPS

LODI, BATTLE OF (10 May 1796), fought during Napoleon's pursuit of the retreating Austro-Sardinian army under Gen. Jean de Beaulieu. The bridge over the Adda, defended by the Austrian rearguard, was successfully stormed by Gen. André Masséna; the destruction of the Austrian artillery force which followed opened the way for Napoleon's entry into Milan.

LODI, TREATY OF (1454), between Milan and Venice, which was eventually accepted by their allies, put an end to several decades of intermittent warfare for predominance in northern Italy. The 40 years of relative peace which followed witnessed a remarkable flowering of Italian art and culture.

LOGAN, JAMES (1674–1751), Irish-born American scientist who came to Philadelphia (1699) as secretary and confidential adviser to William Penn. He established a vast estate and traded and fostered friendly relations with the Indians, carried on botanical experiments (*eg*, he demonstrated for the first time the fertilization of corn), and wrote on optics and was a follower of Newton. He bequeathed his large scientific library to the city of Philadelphia.

LOGOTHETE, title given to various leading financial and administrative officials of the Byzantine empire. Of particular importance was the *logothetēs tou dromou*, who functioned in effect as the chancellor of the empire. The *logothetēs ton sekretōn*—an appointment instituted in the time of Alexius I Comnenos (*reg.* 1081–1118)—became known later as the Grand Logothete, who supervised all the civil affairs of the Byzantine state.

LOGSTOWN, American Indian village on the Ohio river, originally settled by the Delaware and Shawnee Indians (*c.* 1747) and by the Iroquois, Nipissing, and Abnaki (1749). It was abandoned (1750) and reoccupied later by Mingo, Mahican, Ottawa, and other tribes supporting the English in the French and Indian War. It fell vacant (1758) after serving as an important trading rendezvous and the site of a treaty (1752) between the Virginia Commissioners and tribes of the region.

LOHARA DYNASTY in Kashmir (1003–1155), originally from Lohara (south-west Kashmir, probably around modern Punch). The Lohara rulers succeeded the energetic but unscrupulous Queen Didda, herself a Lohara princess, who married into the previous dynasty. The best-known ruler was Harsha (*reg.* 1089–1101). He tried to introduce strong central authority, but is mainly remembered for his iconoclastic zeal, a rare propensity among Hindus. The Lohara period was generally one of decline and rebellions.

LOI FALLOUX (1850) in France, act of the Second Republic which restored the position of the Church in education. It was based on a report of the Comte de Falloux who, when minister of education (1848–9), summarized the discussions of several commissions. Although the bill was modified and passed (March 1850) after he had retired from office, it kept his name. It allowed the creation of a private sector of education alongside state education. The new sector was subject to few controls, while the power of the Church in state education was considerably increased. Although a more limited act than many Catholics wanted, it was bitterly unpopular with the anti-clericals.

LOISEL, ANTOINE (1536–1617), French lawyer in the *parlement* of Paris, who sought to unify French customary law as the basis for a single code of law. He published the *Institutes Coutumières* or *Manuel de plusieurs et diverses règles, sentences et proverbes du droit coutumier et plus ordinaire de la France* (1607) at the end of Guy Coquille's *Institution du droit français*.

LOK SABHA, 'the House of the People', the lower house of the Indian parliament. The House has 525 members, who are elected directly on adult suffrage from all the states and territories of the Union for a term of five years. Seats are reserved for Scheduled Castes and Tribes. The proceedings are controlled by a speaker and parliamentary procedure is modelled on that of the British parliament, with a strong committee system and a daily question hour which brings cabinet ministers into the House. The Congress Party won a majority—although a decreasing one—in the *Lok Sabha* at each of the four general elections up to 1967.

LO-LANG (Korean, Nang-nang), Chinese colony in the north-western coastal plains of Korea, established after the conquest of the old Choson state by Han China in 108 BC. Its headquarters were at P'yong-yang, the former capital of Choson. Lo-lang outlasted the other Chinese settlements of the peninsula, and survived well into the 4th cent. Rich grave-goods have been recovered from the tombs of its colonists, which include the splendidly decorated tomb of Tung Shou, possibly the last Chinese governor of Lo-lang, dated 357.

LOLLARDS, name of uncertain origin, applied generally to religious enthusiasts in England in the late 14th and 15th cents, and specifically to those who held a number of heretical beliefs, among which were commonly found denial of the miracle of Transubstantiation in the Eucharist and of papal authority, and rejection of pilgrimages and the veneration of saints. The unifying principles of Lollardy in the narrower sense were adherence to the Scriptures, interpreted literally, and disbelief in the sacerdotal character and authority of Christ's ministers. All the essential Lollard doctrines are found in the writings of John Wycliffe, but Wycliffe himself was an academic theologian who took few or no steps to reach a popular audience. However, his Oxford disciples propagated his teaching outside the university, and their action was probably decisive in the rise of Lollardy. Down to the rebellion of Sir John Oldcastle in 1414, the movement attracted some gentry. Thereafter most Lollards were of humble status, many being artisans or clerics of the poorer sort. Women were prominent in the movement. Books were important in disseminating and sustaining Lollardy. Bishops were responsible for detecting it and trying suspects, but after 1401 they were obliged to hand over obdurate or lapsed heretics to the secular arm for burning. Recantations were common, executions few. Although Lollardy existed in certain places where Protestant ideas gained an easy hold, and Wycliffe came to be revered by the Reformers, the Lollards themselves seem to have had little or no influence in the Reformation.

K. B. McFarlane, *John Wycliffe and the Beginnings of English Nonconformity* (London, 1952).   BFH

LOLME, JEAN LOUIS DE (1741–1807), Swiss lawyer and constitutional theorist. His work *La Constitution de l'Angleterre*, published in Amsterdam in 1771 (translated into English in 1775), was immediately regarded as an authoritative exposition of the principles underlying the balanced 18th-cent. English constitution. De Lolme, a citizen of Geneva, went to live in England in 1769, after supporting the claims of the citizen body during the constitutional troubles of 1766–7. He compared the English constitution favourably with republican forms because it gave the House of Commons greater powers than republican assemblies had. Of these powers, the most important was the power to initiate legislation.

LOMBARD LEAGUE, properly the 'Society of Lombardy', a name given to two alliances of Lombard communes. The first, formed in 1167, was intended to resist Frederick Barbarossa's attempt to restore imperial authority in Italy and was prompted by resentment against his German officials. It came to include most Lombard cities and came under the leadership of Frederick's greatest opponent, Pope Alexander III. The league rebuilt the city of Milan, earlier destroyed by Frederick, defeated him decisively at Legnano in 1176, and forced him at the peace of Venice (1177) to recognize the autonomy of the Lombard cities, in return for their acknowledgement of imperial sovereignty. Thereafter the league broke up. It was revived in 1226 out of fear of Frederick II's growing power in Italy. Frederick won a great victory over the Lombard cities at Cortenuova in 1237, but could not disarm their opposition. The second league contributed considerably to the final failure of Frederick's dream of controlling all Italy.

LOMBARDO TOLEDANO, VICENTE (1894–1969), Mexican politician and labour leader, who was organizer of the Popular Socialist Party (1947–8). He was a professor of the Mexican Popular University (1917–21), and professor at Mexico University (1918–33). He had also been secretary of the Federal District's government (1920) and governor of Puebla (1923). He founded the General Confederation of Workers and Peasants (1932), supervised the creation of the Mexican Federation of Labour (1936), and organized the Confederation of Workers of Latin America, which included several Latin American trade unions.

Lombardo's importance declined when Mexican labour rejected his pro-Soviet leadership (1946) and the pro-US Inter-American Federation of Labour was formed (1948).

LOMBARDS, Germanic tribe, settled in early 6th cent. on the Lower Danube, who, in 568, invaded Italy. Unlike the previous Germanic invaders, they established themselves permanently and their ferocity and cruelty reduced much of Italy to extreme misery. The Lombards were unable to conquer the whole country and the division of Italy into a multitude of states dates from their invasion. They were originally Arians, but became converted to Catholicism during the 7th cent. The Lombard state reached the height of its power under King Liutprand (*reg.* 712–44). The popes summoned the Franks to save Rome from a Lombard conquest and Charlemagne destroyed the Lombard kingdom in northern Italy in 774–5.

The name was often given in medieval Europe outside Italy to Italian merchants, irrespective of whether they came from Lombardy or other parts of Italy (*eg*, Lombard Street in London). In Europe north of the Alps it also became one of the terms used for holders of pawnbroking shops. Important Italian merchants did not dabble in such petty money-lending, which was largely left to lesser men, many of whom really originated from Western Lombardy.

LOMONOSOV, MIKHAIL VASILIEVITCH (1711–65), Russian scholar, who became the first notable Russian poet and also broke new ground in the fields of philology, history, economics, and science. The son of a peasant shipbuilder from Archangel, he obtained some education in Moscow before being sent to study at Marburg University under J. C. Wolf. On returning to Russia he began his career at the St Petersburg Academy of Sciences, where he became professor of chemistry and the first Russian academician. He did fundamental research into Russian philology, combining outdated Church Slavonic with non-literary spoken Russian in order to create a new literary language which became the vehicle for the great output of literature in the 19th cent. Fiercely patriotic and an outspoken critic of Russia's neglect of her own scholars in favour of foreigners, he became involved in two famous intellectual conflicts, first when he wrote a critique of Gerhard Mueller's dissertation on Russia's origins (1750) and later with A. L. Schloezer, one of the founders of modern German historiography, who was appointed professor of history and fellow academician in 1765. In 1750 Lomonosov started his own researches into Russian history and in 1758 completed his *Ancient Russian History to 1054* and in 1759 the *Short Russian Chronicle*. In addition, he made himself proficient in physics and mineralogy.

LONARDI, EDUARDO (1897–1956), Argentine general and leader of the anti-Peronist rising (1955) and provisional president of the military regime which followed. He was soon forced from office because of his conciliatory policy toward Peronists and his association with Catholic nationalist groups.

LONDON, in England, modern capital, bears evidence of Celtic settlement, suggested origins for its name being Llyn Dun (Celtic lake fort) or Lud (Celtic river god). After the Claudian conquest of AD 43 effective settlement began. Roman Londinium, centred on later Cornhill, soon became the focus for land and sea traffic and a natural centre for British trade and administration. The sack of AD 60, during Boudicca's rebellion, and the fire of the 120s was followed by extensive rebuilding of the forum and basilica. At Cripplegate a fort was built and a wall was constructed (c. 200) to enclose the occupied area of about 325–80 acres on two low hills, divided by a stream. Londinium was then larger than most Roman cities north of the Alps with a thriving port and civic amenities. Lack of adequate written evidence still puts our reliance on archaeology for 4th- and 5th-cent. development. Traditional Roman deities and Mithraic cults flourished, yet Londinium became a centre of early Christianity, sending a bishop to the Synod of Arles in 314. Political turbulence in the 4th cent. necessitated the building of bastions on the wall but expansion continued, beyond the Fleet, into Southwark and Westminster. One estimate gives the population of this city of wood, stone, and brick, the residence of the civil governor, as 50,000 when most prosperous.

The 5th-cent. Roman withdrawal makes London's fate for the next 200 years very vague. Continental unrest led to a decline in trade flowing through London, which was probably a British refuge against the new invaders, the Anglo-Saxons. Much of the site fell into decay but habitation continued. After Augustine's arrival in England in 597 London's importance increased and Aethelbert of Kent is associated with the founding of a church near the present St Paul's Cathedral. Literary sources, eg, Bede, indicate the revived trade passing through. Its importance during the 9th-cent. Viking attacks was crucial and in 886 Alfred, according to his biographer, Asser, rebuilt the defences and used the city as a stronghold against the invaders. The largest town in England with thriving palaces and monasteries, vigorous commerce and political activities, 11th-cent. London had an assured national supremacy. After the battle of Hastings William of Normandy realized the importance of winning London and on Christmas Day, 1066, his coronation took place in Edward the Confessor's new Westminster Abbey. The next step was his charter protecting the citizens' rights. By Henry I's reign the city was divided into wards under aldermen, and during the civil war of Stephen and Matilda a vital political role was played when London put its own army into the field. Recognized as a commune in 1191, the growth of the powerful guild system (by 1377 at least 50 craft guilds existed) protected the city's independence. Despite a preoccupation with trade, London was inevitably involved with the newly created parliament and political events such as the 1381 Peasants' Revolt, Richard II's deposition in 1399, and Jack Cade's rebellion in 1450. Commercial prosperity, however, usually made the citizens support the forces of law and order.

Medieval London attracted Germans, Gascons, Flemish, and Italians in considerable numbers. Normally excluded from guilds, they built up their own enclaves and in 1517 a bitter demonstration broke out against French and Lombard traders. Along the river expansion took place, affluent mansions, eg, Savoy Palace, provided homes for the rich. Monastic dissolution led to much property distribution and rebuilding. Muscovy, Levant, and East India companies were founded with an important business centre in Sir Thomas Gresham's Royal Exchange in Cornhill. The Tower, witness of so much Tudor upheaval, ceased to be a royal residence in Elizabeth I's reign. Court patronage supported London's theatre—a playhouse in Shoreditch, and the Globe.

By 1605 London's population was around 75,000 within the walls and 150,000 in the suburbs. The Guildhall, Royal Exchange, livery halls, civic buildings, St Paul's, and 87 parish churches were destroyed in London's worst fire (1666), soon after the Plague (1665), along with over 13,000 houses. Civic initiative was responsible for far-sighted rebuilding during which Sir Christopher Wren rebuilt St Paul's and 49 other churches.

London in the 18th cent. was a city of elegance in architecture and leisure in the coffee houses. But it was also an age of squalor and sporadic viciousness. Loyal to the Hanoverians during the Jacobite rebellions, Londoners vocally expressed themselves for Wilkes, against Popery in the Gordon Riots, and against Jacobin sympathizers during the French Revolution.

By 1820 the whole character of London had changed. The population, of over 1,000,000, was bringing in all the surrounding villages, numerous bridges and turnpike roads eased entry into the capital and congestion of the port was eased by the opening of new docks. In 1851 the Great Exhibition in Hyde Park put Britain on show to the world. Social services were created to cope with vast urban problems and the Metropolitan Police Force became the guardians of the peace. Gradually the worst slums, round Shaftesbury Avenue, Charing Cross, and the south-east, were eliminated. In 1888 the Metropolitan Board of Works was replaced by the powerful London County Council, which in turn was superseded in 1965 by the Greater London Council. In 1890 the world's first electric underground railway was opened in London. The First World War saw little loss of life in the capital but the Second World War caused extensive air damage, the docks, the City, and the East End suffering particularly. Recovery followed, however, and the 1961 census revealed a population in Greater London of 8,171,902. Attempts were being made in 1970, by administrative decentralization to the provinces, to ease the transport and housing problems of an ever-growing capital.

Ivor Brown, *London* (London, 1965).
Michael Harrison, *London Growing* (London, 1966). MEB

LONDON COMPANY (1606), trading company which was granted a charter by the English Crown to colonize America. It was permitted to plant colonies anywhere from SC to NY and made its settlement at Jamestown, VA (1607). The company was annulled by King James I of England (1624) and its powers and interests were thereafter vested in the Crown.

LONDON CONFERENCE (1814), visit by the Tsar of Russia and the King of Prussia with their ministers and the Austrian minister, Metternich, to the prince regent in London, after the conclusion of the first peace of Paris, at which some of the outstanding questions arising from the French Wars were settled.

The enlargement of Holland, by giving her the former Austrian Netherlands, was agreed, and Britain returned all the Dutch colonies captured during the wars, except the Cape of Good Hope and Guiana, for which Britain promised to pay £2 million, to be spent on building fortresses on the French frontier. Sweden received £1 million indemnity for renouncing claims to Guadeloupe. The powers agreed also that each should keep 75,000 troops mobilized until the peace was signed.

It was agreed that the Congress of Vienna should open on 1 Oct. 1814.

LONDON CONFERENCE (1864), initiated by Britain to save the Danes from humiliation by the armies of Austria and Prussia during the Schleswig-Holstein conflict. Palmerston hinted at action in support of the Danish king, but was hampered by lack of support from queen and cabinet, and the preoccupation of his potential ally, Napoleon III of France, with Mexico. Owing to the cleverness of Prussia's representative, Bismarck, and the stubborn resistance of the Danes, war was renewed in June and the Danes crushed.

LONDON CONFERENCE (1867) decided the future of Luxemburg, whose neutrality had been guaranteed in 1839. Luxemburg was ruled by the King of Holland, but Napoleon

III wished to enhance his prestige by annexing it on payment of an agreed indemnity. Prussia had a garrison in Luxemburg which was a member of the Zollverein and linked to the German Confederation, but Bismarck assented to the annexation provided that Prussian public opinion was not aroused, though in this event he demanded the right to garrison the duchy. Napoleon's policy was revealed to the powers by the Dutch king, opposition mounted, and at the subsequent conference he withdrew his claims. The independence of Luxemburg, which was not to join the German Confederation, was again guaranteed. Napoleon's humiliation led him to reorganize the army and to begin negotiations for alliances with Austria and Italy, preliminaries which marked the approach to the Franco-Prussian War (1870).

LONDON CONFERENCE (1871) nullified the Black Sea clauses of the treaty of Paris (1856) and restored Russian rights to a Black Sea fleet.

LONDON CONFERENCE (1884), unsuccessful attempt to check the antagonism between France and Britain resulting from Britain's assumption of sole control over Egypt to safeguard their joint financial interests, formerly administered by a system of dual control. Britain also valued her position in Egypt for the protection it afforded the route to India, and the conference broke up without result, except to confirm the diplomatic revolution whereby Britain and France were estranged for 20 years, after being friendly since 1815. France even drew temporarily closer to Germany in the so-called Continental League, before finally settling for a more permanent relationship with Russia to end her isolation in Europe.

LONDON CONFERENCE (1–7 March 1921), arranged after the First World War to present Germany with the Allies' reparations bill and schedule of payments. These had not been fixed in the Versailles treaty, which laid down that the Reparations Commission should establish the total bill by 1 May 1921, and that in the interim Germany and the Allies should discuss ways and means of payment. The Allied conference at Paris in Jan. 1921 resulted in the so-called 'Paris Resolutions' on payments which were to be the basis of discussion with Germany at London. These set out a scheme of annual gold payments extending over 42 years, totalling 226 milliard gold marks, and incorporated a 12 per cent tax on German exports. These resolutions greatly disappointed the German government, which had been hoping for a provisional arrangement incorporating deliveries in kind. In turn, Germany's counter-proposals, offered at the opening session of the London conference, antagonized Allied opinion and demonstrated how little communication had been established on reparations questions between the former belligerent powers.

Germany's foreign minister, Simons, in a speech on 1 March 1921, quoted Germany's long-term debt in the values of the day: thus the Paris resolutions' total of 226 milliard became 50 milliard. Simons then claimed that 20 milliard, required by the Versailles treaty to be paid into the reparations commission by 1 May 1921, had been paid in full, a claim disputed by the Allies. This left a mere 30 milliard as Germany's reparations debt. There was an additional proviso that Germany's ability to pay must depend on a favourable result in the plebiscite in the minerally and industrially rich border province of Upper Silesia. The Allies considered this to demonstrate a lack of good faith in the German counter-proposals.

With questionable legality, the Allies threatened to impose sanctions if Germany rejected their proposals. On 8 March 1921, the day after the close of the abortive conference, they occupied Düsseldorf, Duisburg, and Ruhrort on the right bank of the Rhine, and prepared to erect a new Rhine customs barrier. On 5 May the Allies delivered the London ultimatum, based on the Paris resolutions and the reparation commission's estimate of Germany's total debt, and threatened to occupy the Ruhr. The German government, under Fehrenbach, resigned rather than accept these terms. A new government under Wirth approved them, however, but by the end of 1921 found itself unable to meet the ultimatum's schedules and faced with the necessity of negotiating yet another agreement with the Allies.   ASJ

LONDON CONFERENCE (Nov.–Dec. 1947), last of the conferences of the foreign ministers of the US, USSR, Britain, and France to discuss the German question after the Second World War. It took up problems left unsettled at the previous conference, held in Moscow (March–April 1947). Molotov demanded acceptance of the figure of $10,000 million for reparations due to Russia from Germany and attacked the Western powers for their construction of a German state based on Marshall aid. Bevin and Marshall insisted that the Russian zone should be open to trade and the economic unity of Germany thus established in accordance with the Potsdam agreement. Molotov's participation became increasingly vitriolic until the American delegation published a reply to the Russian charges and brought the conference to an end (15 Dec.). Its failure was followed by an intensification of the Cold War, resulting in the Czech *coup d'état* (Feb. 1948) and the Berlin blockade (June 1948).

LONDON CONVENTION (1840), signed under Palmerston's guidance by Britain, Austria, Prussia, and Russia. They agreed to force a settlement on Mohammad Ali of Egypt, who was threatening the stability of the Turkish empire. Mehemet was to receive Egypt as an hereditary possession and Southern Syria for life, but to give up Crete, Northern Syria, Mecca, and Medina, and return the Turkish fleet, which he had captured. Mehemet was given 20 days to accept these terms, but, supported by France, he rejected them. The sultan, against Palmerston's wish, deposed him and he capitulated after the bombardment of Acre and the prospect of a British naval attack on Alexandria, retaining his rights as Pasha of Egypt. The French government under Thiers threatened war, but backed down and with other powers accepted the Straits Convention (1841).

LONDON CORRESPONDING SOCIETY, founded in 1792 by Thomas Hardy. It was one of several radical societies that sprang up in Britain, inspired by the French Revolution. The society enjoyed widespread working-class support, and envisaged fundamental reforms, thus foreshadowing the great working-class movements of the 19th cent. Its participation in the Edinburgh Convention (1793) and success in evoking nation-wide sympathy for the struggle in France, led to the indictment of several of its leaders for high treason (1794). Their triumphant acquittal was the high point of the society's influence, for disillusionment with the work of the convention was already widespread before its suppression in 1799, a victim of the government's exaggerated fears of Jacobinism.

LONDON DOCK STRIKE (1889), major strike for a wage of 6d an hour; its success was a landmark in Britain, indicating the power of trade union action by unskilled workers. It also gave expression to international working-class solidarity, for at a crucial point it was sustained by funds received from labour organizations in Australia.

LONDON, FIRE OF (1666). Early on Sunday, 12 Sept. 1666, a fire broke out by accident in Pudding Lane. Fanned by an easterly wind, it rapidly developed into an inferno. The upper storeys of houses projecting over the streets, and the houses themselves being made of wood and plaster, the fire spread quickly. Within five days more than 400 acres had been devastated, and more than 13,000 houses reduced to ruins. St Paul's, the Royal Exchange, all the halls of the livery companies, and nearly 90 parish churches were destroyed. Casualties, however, were few, fewer than 20 people being killed. The fire also cleared London of the last remnants of infection from the Plague (1665). The cost of restoring the buildings ran into millions of pounds. Sir Christopher Wren's overall plan of reconstruction was not accepted, but the incomparable skyline he created did not disappear until it was obliterated by the property developments in the 1960s.

LONDON GAZETTE, first newspaper, other than newsletters, to be published in England. It was begun as the *Oxford Gazette* in Nov. 1665 (the court was then at Oxford, owing to the Plague) by Henry Muddiman, under the direction of Sir Joseph Williamson. It was later renamed and is still (1970) published as the record of official appointments, etc.

LONDON MISSIONARY SOCIETY, founded in 1795 by Anglicans and Congregationalists as an undenominational evangelical society. Its first missions were sent to Sierra Leone, Tahiti, and, under a Dutchman, Van der Kemp, to South Africa in 1798. Madagascar later became a field for LMS endeavours. In South Africa the society, under John Philip, was influential in liberalizing the Cape Colony's policy towards Africans and coloured people, but its main field of activity was in Botswana. Its station at Kuruman was founded in 1817, and directed by Robert Moffat (1820–70). Livingstone began his career in Africa as an LMS missionary in 1841. Sechele and Khama were among the more prominent Tswana whom the society converted to Christianity.

Its work in the Pacific included the training of Polynesian teachers, who were already at work before the arrival of European missionaries. It was the first Pacific mission and the most successful. It pioneered the study of oceanic language and culture.

LONDON NAVAL TREATY (1930). After the failure of the Geneva Naval Conference (1927), the subsequent disarmament deadlock was not broken until Jan. 1930, when a new conference was convened on Anglo-American initiative. The London Conference was attended by the signatories to the Washington naval treaty (1922), *ie*, US, Britain, France, Japan, and Italy; its purpose was to move towards the goal of disarmament initially by improving on the provisions of the Washington treaty. The main reasons for the success of this conference, as against that of 1927, were that Britain had reduced her cruiser demand, and Japan was persuaded after some difficulty to accept a tonnage ratio higher than that allowed at Washington, though less than she had demanded in 1927 (70 per cent of the US level, compared with the 60 per cent agreed in 1922). However, France argued that her scattered colonies necessitated a large defence fleet, and finally refused to accept the major part of the treaty, as did Italy.

The treaty was divided into two sections. One was signed by all five powers and amounted to a confirmation and very limited extension of the Washington treaty. The other part was accepted only by the US, Britain, and Japan, and limited the tonnages of smaller, non-capital ships which had not been included in the Washington treaty. Hence, only the second part of the 1930 treaty amounted to a genuine advance in disarmament, and the considerable limitations it imposed were strongly criticized in each of the countries concerned as endangering national security.

The 1930 treaty remained in force until 1936, when its provisions were incorporated in a new London naval treaty.

LONDON NAVAL TREATY (1936), arms agreement concluded between Britain, France, and the US, but not effective until mid-1937, owing to delays in ratification. The treaty was intended to replace that of 1930, which was due to expire at the end of 1936, and imposed mainly qualitative limitations on naval armaments, *ie*, on the size and gun calibre of individual ships. Advance exchange of information on construction programmes was also agreed. The treaty was later

accepted by Italy, but not by the other major naval power, Japan, and hence its effectiveness was limited.

LONDON PROTOCOL (1830) granted independence from the Turkish empire to Greece from Aspropotomo to the Gulf of Lamia. Following the treaty of Adrianople the Turks agreed to accept the protocol, but it was rejected by the Greeks on territorial grounds. For fear of Russian influence in the area, British policy under Wellington and Aberdeen was to keep an independent Greece divided and weak, but Palmerston achieved a settlement by accepting Greek boundaries that included Arta and Volo, and guaranteed a loan to assist Greece and her newly appointed king, Otto I, by the treaty of London (1832).

LONDON PROTOCOL (1877), demands made on Turkey (31 March 1877) after the failure of the Constantinople Conference. The powers requested Turkish reform and peace with Montenegro, and Ignatiev's original draft was modified by Britain to include Russian as well as Turkish demobilization. The protocol's rejection by the Porte led to the Russo-Turkish War (1877–8).

LONDON RADICAL REFORM ASSOCIATION, founded in 1829 as a non-party movement to work for annual parliaments, universal suffrage, and a secret ballot. The association was particularly successful in stirring up popular enthusiasm for reform during the excitement following the July Revolution in France and the death of King George IV of Britain in 1830. It contributed to the atmosphere of emergency in which the Reform Bill (1832) was passed.

LONDON, TREATY OF (1518), between England, France, Spain, the emperor, and the pope, sealed a 'universal Christian peace' which enabled them to make a combined campaign against the Turks. The peace was immediately broken on the death of the Emperor Maximilian three months later.

LONDON, TREATY OF (1604), ended the Anglo-Spanish War begun in 1585. The English refused to recall troops from Holland or to abandon trade with the Dutch. They were allowed free commerce with the Spanish possessions in Europe, and would not accept the principle that Spain had a prescriptive right to forbid them to trade in the Spanish New World.

LONDON, TREATY OF (1661), peace settlement between Portugal and the United Provinces to conclude the war which had developed over Portugal's recovery of Brazil after the rising of 1654.

LONDON, TREATY OF (1824), regulating Dutch and British spheres in Asia. It was necessitated by the impossibility of forcing British traders and officials to return to their modest pre-war role in the Malay archipelago after Holland's possessions had been restored at the end of the Napoleonic wars. Under the treaty Dutch possessions in India and Malaya were exchanged for British possessions in Sumatra, and established the Straits of Malacca and Singapore as the effective boundary between the political spheres of influence of the two powers. Acrimony quickly arose because of the treaty's ambiguity about intended safeguards for British commerce, and over Borneo.

LONDON, TREATY OF (1827), signed by France, Britain, and Russia. It confirmed the Protocol of St Petersburg (1826) between Britain and Russia, which provided for joint or separate intervention if the Sultan of Turkey failed to accept their proposals for settling the Greek revolt on the basis of Greek autonomy. The French required that the protocol be changed to a treaty before they would adhere to it. Metternich disapproved of rebellion, so neither Austria nor Prussia signed the treaty. In addition to the provisions of the protocol, the treaty provided for the dispatch of a naval force to compel an armistice, and this led to the battle of Navarino. The sultan finally acceded to the treaty of London as part of the treaty of Adrianople. Britain's main purpose was to prevent Russia intervening alone, but was also prompted by pro-Greek sentiments in Britain herself.

LONDON, TREATY OF (1839), between Britain, France, Russia, Prussia, and Austria, whose infraction by Germany caused Britain to declare war in 1914. The treaty was a consequence of the Belgian revolution, and the powers recognized Belgium as an independent and perpetually neutral state and guaranteed its frontiers. At Britain's insistence, France and Germany signed an extra treaty reinforcing the neutrality of Belgium during the Franco-Prussian War. Bethmann-Hollweg, the German chancellor, referred to the treaty in 1914 as a 'scrap of paper', an epithet which united the British government in favour of war.

LONDON, TREATY OF (1852), agreement by which the five European powers and Sweden–Norway recognized Christian of Glücksburg as heir to all territories then united under the King of Denmark.

LONDON, TREATY OF (1913). The major powers of Europe, alarmed by the successes of the Balkan League against Turkey, met to discuss a settlement, but could do little more than register the results of the First Balkan War. Thus, the treaty of London divided European Turkey between the allies in the league and secured an independent Albania to make the settlement acceptable to Austria. While apparently demonstrating the continued vitality of the concert of Europe, the settlement, in fact, marked the triumph of Balkan nationalism. The Balkan powers did not find it necessary to submit the treaty of Bucharest (1913) for European approval and the European powers did not act in concert on the issue of the crisis caused by the assassination of the Archduke Ferdinand at Sarajevo in 1914.

LONDON, TREATY OF (1915), secret agreement in the First World War between Britain, France, and Russia, and the hitherto neutral Italy, whereby Italy agreed to enter the war on the Allied side in exchange for a guarantee of territorial gains after the war.

Italy had, since 1882, been a member of the Triple Alliance with Germany and Austria, but was not obliged to go to war on her allies' behalf unless informed in advance of their intention to engage in hostilities. In the summer of 1914 Austria had deliberately kept Italy in the dark over her proposed action against Serbia, fearing Italian opposition. On 3 Aug. Italy proclaimed her neutrality in the growing conflict, on the justifiable ground that Austria had violated the terms of the alliance.

From the beginning of the war, efforts were made by both sides to encourage Italian participation, and there were proponents of both causes in Italy itself. However, the main current of feeling was in favour of Italy throwing in her lot with whichever side promised the greatest rewards. Negotiations were conducted with Austria on the basis of Italian support in exchange for the *Irredenta* territories in the north, *ie*, areas on the Austrian frontier claimed by Italy, but Austria regarded this demand as excessive. At the same time, Italy was in contact with the entente powers in London, with whom she eventually reached agreement on 26 April 1915. In exchange for an undertaking to declare war on the Central Powers within one month, Italy was promised the *Irredenta* that Austria had refused her, and in addition, part of the Dalmatian coast, part of Albania near Valona, the Dodecanese islands, some Turkish territory in Asia Minor, African colonies, and a share in any war indemnities. These extensive concessions were offered by the Allies because their armies were not having the immediate success they had hoped for, and it was believed that Italy could strike a decisive blow against Austria and swing the balance against the Central Powers. In the event, Italy's part in the war was somewhat less than glorious, and the military hopes of the Allies were disappointed. Moreover, in 1918 the Bolshevik government in Russia revealed the terms of the secret treaty. President Wilson refused to honour it, as the vast territorial concessions struck directly at the principles of national self-determination on which he believed the post-war settlement must be based. Thus at the Paris Peace Conference (1919) the awards to Italy were considerably reduced, much to her chagrin.

W. W. Gottlieb, *Studies in Secret Diplomacy* (London, 1957). R. Albrecht-Carrié, *Italy at the Paris Peace Conference* (New York, 1938).   AJC

LONDON UNIVERSITY (1836). University College, London was founded in 1826 by a committee composed predominantly of radicals and utilitarians, including Grote, Thomas Campbell, the poet, and Lord Brougham. The college, then known as the University of London, taught a wide variety of subjects, but excluded theology, and King's College was founded, by those who wished to see theology included, in 1829. By a royal charter of 1836 the two colleges, together with some of London's medical schools, were made parts of a new London University which was empowered to grant degrees, and in 1858 the university's scope was enlarged to allow it to grant degrees to persons other than students of the constituent colleges. This formed the basis of its large external department. During the 19th cent. the university, as distinct from the colleges, had no teaching functions, and was an examining body only. An act of 1900 ended this dualism, and London University was recast as a teaching body with faculty boards and teachers appointed by the university. At the same time, later foundations, including Bedford College, Royal Holloway College, and the London School of Economics and Political Science, were incorporated into the system.

London University enabled many colleges in Britain and the empire and Commonwealth to take external degrees. During the 20th cent. most of these institutions became independent and awarded their own degrees. But London University still (1970) offers the facility of external study for thousands of external students.

LONDON WORKING MEN'S ASSOCIATION, one of the working men's associations which gave rise to Chartism. It was founded in July 1836 by some London working-class radicals, among them Lovett, James Watson, John Cleave, and Henry Hetherington. Its purpose was to unite 'the intelligent and influential portion' of the working classes in favour of equal political and social rights. It attached great importance to education and a cheap press. In the next two years the association published many pamphlets, notably 'The Rotten House of Commons' and 'Address on National Education', and sent 'missionaries' to encourage the foundation of similar associations in the provinces. In 1837 it prepared a list of radical political demands and, after a conference with radical MPs, a joint committee was formed to redraft the demands as a parliamentary bill. In the event, the redrafting was largely done by Lovett, with help from Francis Place. It was published as the People's Charter (May 1838) and distributed to all provincial associations. The LWMA elected seven members to attend the Chartist Convention, which met in 1839, but after this had no further influence over the Chartist movement, being superseded by more extreme organizations and losing its own more extreme members. It did not cease to exist, but reverted to its educational activities.

LONDONDERRY, ROBERT STEWART, 2nd Marquis of (Irish) and Viscount Castlereagh (1769–1822). British foreign secretary, who laid the foundations of 19th-cent. foreign policy. He was chiefly responsible for forcing the Act of Union through the Irish parliament (1800) and became secretary for war in Pitt's final administration (1805). While holding the same post under Portland (1807–9), he was the chief advocate of continental expeditions, including those to Spain (1808) and Walcheren (1809). The disaster of the latter and Castlereagh's bitter quarrel with Canning, the foreign secretary, led to the government's collapse. He returned to office, however, in another Tory government under Liverpool, acting as foreign secretary and leader of the Commons (1812). Being determined to keep the anti-French coalition together and to maintain British involvement on the continent, he personally intervened at Châtillon (1813) to ensure this. At the Congress of Vienna (1815), with little reference to London, Castlereagh worked closely with Metternich to achieve a balance of power and security against France and Russia. The decision of the powers to meet in periodic congresses afterwards was largely his work, but he became increasingly suspicious of their attempts to suppress revolutionary and nationalist movements by international action, which he made clear in his state paper of 1820. His diplomatic achievements were overshadowed at home by the unpopularity and abuse from which he suffered as the chief spokesman in the Commons for the government's repressive domestic policy.

LONDONDERRY, RELIEF OF (1689), turning point in James II's attempt to retain Ireland against William III. James, landing in Ireland in the spring of 1689, enlisted the aid of the Earl of Tyrconnel and many Irish supporters. On 17 April he besieged Londonderry, but the Protestant garrison under Maj. Henry Baker held out for 105 days; until relieved by a naval force under Col. Percy Kirke. James abandoned the siege (30 July) and three days later his followers were routed at Newton Butler near Enniskillen.

LONG, HUEY PIERCE (1893–1935), US politician, who served as railroad commissioner (1918–21) and public service commissioner (1921–6) in LA before being elected governor (1928). He taxed powerful state oil interests to finance educational and highway improvements, and, having narrowly escaped impeachment for corruption (1929), established virtually dictatorial control over LA. Though elected US senator (1930), he retained the governorship for two years until he felt secure enough to concentrate on national politics. Being impatient with the New Deal, he launched his radical 'Share-Our-Wealth' plan (1934), prepared to form his own political party, and presented a growing political threat to President F. D. Roosevelt. He was murdered whilst attending a meeting of the LA legislature. A controversial figure, he justified his malpractices and disregard for democratic procedure as being in the interests of the poor.

LONG ISLAND, BATTLE OF (27 Aug. 1776), engagement in the American War of Independence, when 20,000 British and German troops under Gen. William Howe surrounded American fortifications on Brooklyn Heights and inflicted heavy casualties on an American force of 5000. Gen. Washington, seeing that the position was untenable, skilfully withdrew Gen. Israel Putnam's troops to Manhattan Island.

LONG MARCH (1934–5), epic march of the Chinese communists across 6000 miles (9650 kms) of China. In 1934, Kuomintang pressure forced the communists to abandon the Kiangsi Soviet area; about 100,000 people, mainly soldiers, set out on foot to seek sanctuary in China's wild western regions. They were pursued by Kuomintang troops, and constantly harassed. Their worst battles, however, were against nature, as they crossed vast swamps and mountain ranges. Early on the march, at Tsunyi, a conference was held which gave Mao Tse-tung control of the party; but when the march reached Szechwan in July 1935, a quarrel broke out between Mao and Chang Kuo-t'ao. Chang led one section of the march towards Tibet, while Mao led the bulk into Shensi, where the Chinese communists had their major headquarters

for the next decade. The casualties of the march were appalling: only 20,000 of the original marchers reached Shensi, though their numbers were increased by recruits who joined en route. Until the Cultural Revolution, the veterans of the march occupied positions of special esteem in China.

LONG PARLIAMENT (1640–60) in England, last parliament of King Charles I which remained legally in being throughout the interregnum (1649–60). The second Bishops' War forced Charles to call a parliament which met on 3 Nov. 1640. The king was in a weaker position than he had been in April (Short Parliament), and the leaders of the Country party had meanwhile decided to remove the king's ministers and make arbitrary government impossible in future. The opposition to the king was bound together by a belief in a Catholic plot engineered by his advisers. The court's conduct over the next two years gave ample grounds for such a belief and enabled John Pym, the Country's leader, to marshal his followers effectively. Between Nov. and May 1641 the Country party removed various royal ministers, including Abp Laud and the Earl of Strafford, and at the same time passed reform statutes which formed the basis of the parliamentary revolution: the king was to be obliged to meet parliament every three years; he would not be able to dissolve parliament without its own consent; the prerogative courts, eg, Star Chamber, were to be abolished; and ship money was to be declared illegal. Pym believed that the reform statutes would eventually be set aside unless the opposition could ensure the appointment of ministers who would abide by them. Control of the executive, and with it the control of the armed force and religion, therefore became vital issues.

The second session saw the break-up of the Country party over this question of control, and the formation of the Royalist and Parliamentary parties which were to fight the Civil War. The abortive Root and Branch Bill (May 1641), the rebellion in Ireland (Oct. 1641), and the subsequent Grand Remonstrance (22 Nov.) gave the king a party headed by the 'Constitutional royalists', eg, Edward Hyde. Charles, however, lost control of the City of London to Pym, and when the Commons impeached the bishops with the Lords' support, he panicked. His unsuccessful coup, when he tried to arrest five leading MPs (3 Jan. 1642), ended any hopes of reconciliation between the two sides. During the next nine months there occurred a struggle over the control of forces to be raised for the relief of Ireland, and a paper war of manifestos and counter-manifestos. In March parliament passed the Militia Ordinance and prepared for conflict. On 6 June parliament enunciated the doctrine that the king's person was distinguishable from his office, and the functions of his office could be exercised by parliament. Parliament itself was soon driven to policies quite as arbitrary as any of the king's, eg, levying of forced loans by distraint.

Helped by the Scottish alliance (1643), and its superior economic and financial resources, the parliament forces won the war. Many of parliament's supporters, however, had become disillusioned and a political split developed between the Independents and the Presbyterians (roughly the war and peace parties respectively). The new Model Army came under the control of the Independents, and though parliament, increasingly dominated by Presbyterians, continued to govern, the ascendancy of the army in politics was assured by 1647. In 1647–8 the army claimed to represent the nation more than the remains of the Long Parliament (the Caroline MPs had been expelled during the war). The evident lack of war aims and parliament's refusal to meet the army's arrears of pay became a grievance. Parliament desperately tried to find a settlement with the king, but Charles played off the army against parliament. The resulting collision led to the expulsion of MPs hostile to the army. After the second Civil War parliament tried again to settle with the king. This proved too much for the army, which, by Pride's Purge (6 Dec. 1648), excluded most Presbyterian MPs, thus reducing the Long Parliament to a Rump. As such it continued to govern the country until the forcible dissolution in 1653. It was restored for a short time in 1660.

G. Davies, *The Early Stuarts* (Oxford, 1937).
J. P. Kenyon, *The Stuart Constitution* (Cambridge, 1966).
CJ

LONGBOW, THE. Until the late 13th cent. the standard form of bow was the short cross-bow, whose range and power were very limited. The longbow was first developed in Wales and, although in its original form was not much more effective than the cross-bow, its potentialities were much greater. Under Edward I and his successors the longbow rapidly replaced the cross-bow as the standard weapon of the English foot soldier, and the archer supplemented the knight as one of the mainstays of English armies. The longbow was made of yew, maple, or oak and in its fully developed form in the mid-14th cent. was up to six feet long and could fire up to twelve arrows a minute (as against the cross-bow's two) and had a range of up to a quarter of a mile. At shorter distances its arrow could pierce chain mail. The longbow was essentially a defensive weapon. It could not be used on horseback and for its best effect required suitable terrain and an attacking enemy. Under these conditions it was used with stunning effect against the Scots at Halidon Hill (1333) and Neville's Cross (1356) and won the victories of Crécy (1346), Poitiers (1356), and Agincourt (1415) against the French.

LONGFELLOW, HENRY WADSWORTH (1808–82), US poet and scholar. After studying in Europe (1826–9), he established himself at Bowdoin College, ME, as teacher and scholar, and published articles and textbooks, his first prose work being *Outre-Mer* (1835). By 1854 he had become internationally famous as the author of 'Voices of the Night' (1839), 'Ballads and Other Poems' (1842), 'The Spanish Student' (1843), and 'Evangeline' (1847). 'Hiawatha' (1855) increased his popularity still further, as did 'The Courtship of Miles Standish' (1858). The death of his wife (1861) turned Longfellow away from creative work to translation, and, assisted by James Russell Lowell and C. E. Norton, he produced a version of *The Divine Comedy* (3 vols, 1865–7). His poetry, affirmative, melodic, and full of popular sentiment, subscribed perfectly to contemporary middle-class tastes, but today his work commands little attention.

LONGFIELD, MOUNTIFORT (1802–84), Irish judge and economist, whose *Lectures on Political Economy* (1834) investigated marginal utility as a factor in the determination of value.

LONGJUMEAU, TREATY OF (1568), agreement ending the second French civil war. The Amboise edict, favourable to the Huguenots, was reimposed and Charles IX's government agreed to pay off the Huguenots' allies, the German knights of John Casimir of the palatinate. The treaty proved abortive, however, being soon repudiated by the Guises and the Duke of Anjou (the future Henry III).

LONGO, LUIGI (1900–), Italian politician and head of the Italian Communist Party (PCI). He was a member of Gramsci's group and became leader of PCI youth movements, directing clandestine anti-fascist operations. The Comintern sent him as political commissar to the 2nd International Brigade in Spain (1936), then as inspector-general for all brigades, under the pseudonym of 'Gallo'. After internment in France and Italy, he became politico-military commandant of Garibaldi's partisans in northern Italy, and vice-commander for the Committee for National Liberation (1944–5). As vice-secretary general of PCI and a deputy (1946), he was a loyal supporter of Togliatti, whom he succeeded in 1964, but he failed to command the same authority. He got the PCI to declare itself in favour of the Czechs' liberal experiments in 1968 and opposed to Russia's interference.

LONGSTREET, JAMES (1821–1904), US soldier and Confederate general, who served in the Mexican War (1846–8), commanded the Confederate 1st Corps under General Lee, and fought in GA and TN (1863–4). At the end of the Civil War he became a Republican and held a number of federal appointments in the South.

LONGUEUIL, CHARLES LE MOYNE, Baron de (1656–1729), French Canadian soldier and administrator who was sent on embassies to the Iroquois (1696, 1704, 1711). He was governor of Trois-Rivières (1720) and helped to get the Iroquois to consent to the rebuilding of the fort at Niagara (1721). He was appointed governor of Montreal (1724–9) and also administrator of New France (1725–6).

LOOKOUT MOUNTAIN, BATTLE OF (23 Nov. 1863), 'Battle above the Clouds' in the American Civil War, fought for control of the railroad centre of Chattanooga, TN. 10,000 Union troops under Gen. Hooker drove 2000 Confederates off this key height south of the city.

LOOS, BATTLE OF (25 Sept.–19 Oct. 1915), the British contribution to the Allied autumn offensive of 1915 during the First World War. The French commander-in-chief, Joffre, planned to attack both shoulders of the great salient formed by the German front in France, the left with 30 French divisions in Champagne, the right with 17 French and 9 British divisions in Artois. Haig, who commanded the First Army, objected that the terrain chosen for the British attack, on the northern outskirts of Lens, was unsuitable, and both he and Sir John French, the British commander-in-chief, considered that the British heavy artillery was inadequate, that there were insufficient reserves of ammunition, and that the Territorial and 'New Army' divisions on which the offensive was to rely, needed more training. They were overruled by their government in the interests of Allied solidarity. After four days' preliminary bombardment had sacrificed any chance of surprise, the first use of chlorine gas by British troops enabled them to achieve some success on the first day, but the impetus of the attack was quickly checked by the difficulty of bringing up reinforcements and supplies across the devastated battlefield, and by German counter-attacks from the flanks, and repeated 'pushes'; the last on 13 Nov. could not recover it. The whole offensive achieved nothing. The British lost about 60,000 killed, wounded, and missing—three times the German total.

LÓPEZ, CARLOS ANTONIO (1792–1862), Paraguayan lawyer and president. He came to prominence upon the death of Paraguay's great dictator José Francia (1840) and was chosen as president in 1844. Through his manipulations of the constitution and the obedience of a subservient congress López was able to perpetuate himself in office for 18 years. His internal policies, while more eclectic than those of Francia, were basically the same. In foreign affairs, however, his changes were substantial. Isolationism was gradually abandoned and foreigners and foreign trade were encouraged. Assuming a role in the River Plate area, Paraguay signed treaties with Brazil and the US.

On López's death the nepotistic basis of his regime became obvious when his son, Francisco Solano López, automatically inherited the presidency.

LÓPEZ, FRANCISCO SOLANO (1826–70), president and dictator of Paraguay (1862–70). At an early age he held various important posts given him by his father, Carlos Antonio López. In Europe he met Eliza Lynch, who was to be his mistress and confidante until his death. When his father died (1862), he assumed the presidency and ruled in dictatorial fashion. He placed great emphasis on Paraguay's military preparedness and her international role in the River Plate area. These policies have provoked great debate, his supporters claiming that he was alert to the aggressive designs of his powerful neighbours, Argentina and Brazil, and his opponents asserting that his policies were over-ambitious and a sign of megalomania.

Brazilian–Uruguayan hostilities (1864) caused López to declare war against Brazil. To come to the aid of his reluctant ally Uruguay, López marched his army across Argentinian territory. Soon all three River Plate nations, Argentina, Brazil, and Uruguay, had resolved their mutual difficulties, and had declared war on Paraguay in the protracted and bloody War of the Triple Alliance (Paraguayan War). López was soon forced into a defensive position and though he showed a callous disregard for the sufferings of his countrymen, he displayed great skill in his defence of the Paraguayan heartland.

Gradually allied forces fought their way up the river system, with huge losses on both sides. In 1869 organized Paraguayan resistance collapsed and the remnants of López's army began a guerrilla war. On 1 March 1870 he himself was ambushed and killed by a Brazilian detachment.

The war was a disaster for Paraguay. Large border areas were lost to Argentina and Brazil, who kept an army of occupation in the country for the next six years; the population was reduced by about half, to some quarter of a million, and almost all the country's able-bodied men disappeared—some historians have claimed that as few as 28,000 were left. Paraguayan demographic recuperation was surprisingly rapid, but development was crippled for many years. In spite of the war, many Paraguayans have considered López to be a national hero.

Charles J. Kolinski, *Independence or Death! the story of the Paraguayan war* (Gainesville, FL, 1965).   MJM

LÓPEZ, JOSÉ HILARIO (1800–69), general and president of New Granada (approximately modern Venezuela, Colombia, Panama, and Ecuador). López, who was noted for his anticlericalism, expelled the Jesuits and instituted civil marriage. He also abolished slavery in New Granada (1851).

LÓPEZ CONTRERAS, ELEAZAR (1883–), Venezuelan general and president. He was a follower of the dictators Cipriano Castro and Juan Vicente Gómez and was elected president for seven years on the latter's death (Dec. 1935). López Contreras shortened his own term of office to five years, and refused re-election in 1941.

LÓPEZ MATEOS, ADOLFO (1910–70), lawyer and president of Mexico (1958–64). He was elected to the federal senate (1946) and soon became chairman of the Foreign Relations Committee. He headed the Mexican delegation to UNESCO and managed the presidential campaign of Adolfo Ruiz Cortines (1952), who appointed him minister of labour and social welfare (1952–7). López Mateos won the presidency (1958) for the following term. He refused to break off diplomatic relations with revolutionary Cuba and sought to relieve rural discontent with a massive distribution of lands. He brought Mexico into the Latin American Free Trade Agreement (LAFTA) and encouraged the growth of exports. He was recognized as a competent administrator and politician and was personally popular.

LÓPEZ PUMAREJO, ALFONSO (1886–1959), Colombian diplomat and president (1934–8, 1942–5), whose programmes imposed new taxes on the rich and helped organized labour. He sponsored a new Liberal constitution (1936). His second term was troubled by an economic recession, a fall in coffee prices, and financial scandals. He resigned in 1945 and later represented Colombia at the UN and in various foreign countries.

LORD DUNMORE'S WAR (1774), American Indian war. VA claimed land in the Ohio territory which was disputed by hostile Indians. Two expeditions, one under Lord Dunmore, governor of VA, and the other led by Gen. Andrew Lewis, were sent against Indians in the Ohio river valley. At the Battle of Point Pleasant Lewis defeated the Shawnee Indians. Their chief, Cornstalk, gave up Shawnee title to lands south and east of the Ohio river.

LORD'S DAY ACT (1906) in Canada, law prohibiting most kinds of Sunday work, excursions, and performances where fees were charged. The Laurier government introduced the bill under pressure from the Lord's Day Alliance. The act was opposed by Roman Catholics, who regarded the measure as a restriction on personal liberty. Resentment was expressed at mass meetings in Quebec and Montreal. Antagonisms aroused by the act led to growing support for Henri Bourassa and the nationalist movement.

LORDS, HOUSE OF, in Britain, extension of the great council (*magnum concilium*) of the post-Conquest kings of England. When parliament emerged in the 13th cent., it was essentially as meetings of this great council augmented by the attendance of representatives of the boroughs and counties, the future House of Commons. Summons to attend was by individual writ addressed to a named person and, although certain groups of people—earls, bishops, greater barons—would be summoned to every parliament, so also would a number of lesser lay lords and certain royal officials, who would not necessarily be summoned again. Despite later constitutional law, before the 15th cent. the receipt of an individual writ did not create its receiver a peer of the realm with hereditary rights of attendance. In the course of the 14th cent. there emerged something like a fixed customary membership (over a hundred in all) of the House of Lords, consisting of all earls and barons (now a rank of society rather than a description of mode of tenure of land), the episcopal bench, and the heads of certain great monastic houses. Receipt of an individual writ of summons was now virtually an hereditary right. Even so, the House was dominated by the spiritual lords until the reign of King Henry VIII. But after the dissolution of the greater monasteries in 1539, power passed to the lay peers, who were increased in numbers by the Tudors, whilst the 27 abbots disappeared from the Lords. Membership of the House remained fairly constant until the reign of King George III (*reg.* 1760–1820), when there were many new creations of peers, and there have been numerous additional creations in the 19th and 20th cents. In 1707 16 representative Scottish peers were added to the House and in 1800 28 Irish representative peers. Lords of appeal in ordinary were given the right to sit in 1887. There are now (1970) about 950 peers. The membership of the House has been much affected by 20th-cent. legislation: life peerages were instituted in 1958—though there were earlier precedents apart from the law lords—and women, whether life baronesses or hereditary peeresses, can now sit (1958, 1963). By 1970, the rapid creation of life peerages was changing the character of the Lords; as no hereditary peerages were created after 1964, the hereditary principle appeared to be becoming obsolete.

The Lords were and are hereditary counsellors of the Crown. They can initiate legislation, but usually act as a revising chamber for bills emanating from the Commons. Their former absolute veto on bills is now (1970) merely suspensive (Parliament Acts, 1911 and 1949). After 1911 they lost the power to reject, even temporarily, a money bill. But they retained extensive judicial functions as a court of appeal, exercised through the lords of appeal in ordinary under the Appellate Jurisdiction Act (1876).   LGRN

LORDS LIEUTENANT in England, usually peers, though sometimes commoners, who were the official representatives of the Crown in a county or counties. With their deputies and sheriffs, they were responsible for the musters of the militia and for levies for service outside the county. They were also supposed to exercise a general supervision over the collection of taxes, the suppression of recusancy, and see that the JPs enforced the statutes of the realm or the orders of the privy council.

The lords lieutenant originated from the military needs of the Tudors. Henry VIII appointed temporary deputies in the north and west called lieutenants. It soon became customary to issue ad hoc commissions to local nobles to be responsible for military forces. After 1550 the Duke of Northumberland regularly sent lieutenants into the counties to deal with disturbances. By 1600 England was divided into regular areas, each with its lieutenant. The local magnate was usually linked to the court, and assisted by deputies who normally did the work. The lords lieutenant, controlled by the privy council, soon grew to be the formal heads of their localities. The lord lieutenant and his deputies still (1970) represent the Crown, though now in a purely honorary capacity.

LORDS OF THE ARTICLES, THE, Scottish parliamentary steering committee. It was developed by James VI in the 16th cent. to the point where it took over virtually all the legislative powers of the parliament, under the guidance of the privy council. Consequently, the Scottish parliament never dared to promulgate anything which the Crown opposed. The constitutional settlement of 1689 abolished the Lords of the Articles.

LORDS OF THE COMMITTEE in England, title of the 'cabinet council' under Queen Anne when the queen herself was not present. The queen sat at the regular weekly meetings of the 'cabinet council', which acted as a kind of second chamber to the inner council or lords of the committee.

LORDS OF THE CONGREGATION in Scotland, nobles and lairds, calling themselves 'the Faithful Congregation of Christ Jesus', whose military power enabled the Reformation, under the guidance of John Knox, to triumph in Scotland. Knox began winning such men to his cause in 1557, when a group of Protestant lords, known as the 'First Band', signed a covenant to 'apply our whole power, substance and our very lives' to establishing the reformed faith. Many later converts were motivated by both economic and political interests. Some of the lesser lairds resented paying church tithes, while a significant group, led by the Earls of Argyll, Morton, and Arran, felt neglected in state affairs by the French queen regent, Mary of Guise; there also existed a general anti-French feeling. Military operations began in the summer of 1559, and by Oct. the lords had 'suspended' the regent. To secure their victory, however, they had needed the assistance of England, whose fleet had cut supplies to the regent's French army. The treaty of Edinburgh (1560) excluded the French from Scottish affairs and laid the foundation of an English alliance. Parliament accepted Knox's Confession of Faith (June 1560) and the Protestant religion.

LORIS-MELIKOV, Count General **MIKHAIL TARIELOVICH** (1825–88), Russian politician and commander in the Russo-Turkish war (1877–8). He was head of an investigating commission into terrorism (1880) and minister of the interior (1880–1). His very limited proposals for administrative reform, involving consultative commissions with some elected members, in no way limited autocracy. They were accepted by Alexander II, but rejected by his successor.

LORRAINE, CHARLES ALEXANDER, Prince of (1712–80), Empress Maria Theresa's brother-in-law and Austrian general, who was a successful governor of the Austrian Netherlands (1744–80).

LORRAINE, duchy straddling the upper Moselle river, lying between Champagne, Alsace, and Franche-Comté, the heart of the Middle Kingdom during the early Middle Ages and from the 9th to 20th cents a source of disagreement between the rulers of France and Germany. Occupied by Rudolph I of Burgundy (888), it passed under German control (888–911), then came under French influence (911–25), and returned to German rule under Henry I (925). As an imperial fief on France's eastern flank it became, from the late 12th cent., the object of French expansionist aims, eg, it was occupied by French forces in 1444 and was also overrun by the Burgundians under Charles the Bold (1473). Falling under Habsburg influence early in the 16th cent., it became a key point in Spanish communications with the Low Countries, and Duke Charles IV supported the Austro-Spanish Habsburg bloc in the Thirty Years War (1618–48). Although by the peace of Westphalia (1648) France gained the enclaves of Metz, Toul, and Verdun, first promised in the treaty of Cateau-Cambrésis (1559), and the Spaniards agreed to dismantle the fortress of Nancy by the peace of the Pyrenees (1659), Louis XIV and Cardinal Mazarin were thwarted in their desire to obtain the whole duchy, which continued to expose France's eastern frontier to the Habsburg empire. Louis bribed the impecunious Duke Charles to cede Lorraine to the French Crown on generous terms (treaty of Montmartre, 1662), but the agreement was never implemented and French possession of the duchy by force was cancelled by the treaty of Nymwegen (1678). Finally, in the second Partition treaty (1700) Louis made a secret agreement with William III that Leopold Joseph of Lorraine should be asked to exchange his duchy for Milan; but after Louis accepted Charles II's second will this arrangement fell through. By the treaty of Vienna (1738), Cardinal Fleury negotiated a territorial exchange by which Lorraine's Duke Francis received Tuscany in return for ceding his duchy to Louis XV's father-in-law, Stanislas Leszczynski, and on the latter's death in 1766 Lorraine reverted to France. It was retained by the French even at the Congress of Vienna (1815), but was restored to Germany after the Franco-Prussian War (by the treaty of Frankfort, 1871), to be returned again to France at the end of the First World War (1918).

LORRAINE MOTIONS (1713) in Britain, anti-Jacobite parliamentary addresses to Queen Anne, proposed by the Whigs and moved by Wharton in the Lords (30 June 1713) and Stanhope in the Commons (1 July 1713), pressing for the removal of James, the Old Pretender, from Bar-le-Duc in Lorraine, lest the safety of the Protestant succession in Britain be jeopardized.

LOS COBOS, FRANCISCO DE (c. 1477–1547), Andalusian-born imperial secretary under Emperor Charles V, who became the effective governor of Spain (1522–47). He got his first post in the royal secretariat (1501) through the patronage of Queen Isabella's secretary, Hernando de Zafra, and was promoted in Ferdinand of Aragon's service through his competence and industry. After being the chief assistant to Ferdinand's secretary, Lope Conchillos, he went to Brussels in 1516 to seek employment under Charles, Duke of Burgundy. There he secured the favour of Chièvres, who appointed him royal secretary. He returned to Spain with Charles and from 1523, when he became secretary of all the royal councils except those of Aragon, War, and Orders, he became a rival of the Grand Chancellor Gattinara for political power, until the latter's death in 1530 left him supreme. Cobos travelled abroad with Charles V (1529–33), acting as his principal adviser and constantly advocating a policy of peace, to avoid straining Spanish finances. From 1533 until his own death he remained in Spain, where his financial expertise gave Spain smooth and efficient government. During these years he established the central archive of official documents at Simancas and built up a trained professional staff, eg, Juan Vazquez de Nolina, Alonso de Idiaquez, Gonzolo Perez, and Francisco de Eraso, all men from the lesser municipal gentry. He prepared the Crown's financial estimates, pruned sinecures, and negotiated loans.

LOSSOW, OTTO HERMANN VON (1868–1938), German soldier, who commanded the Bavarian section of the German army in 1923 at the time of the Hitler putsch. When the French occupied the Ruhr (1923), the German army gave support and training to various para-military formations—mostly of an anti-Republican character—in order to have reserves available in case of war. The Bavarian army was particularly active in this. When Stresemann's new coalition government prepared to give up passive resistance to the French in Sept. 1923, the Bavarian government was opposed to such a policy and hoped for a nationalist coup in Berlin. The Berlin authorities ordered Lossow to suppress the Nazi *Völkischer Beobachter* for an attack on Gen. von Seeckt, but Lossow refused. Seeckt demanded that Lossow should resign, but the Bavarian government supported him and on 22 Oct. 1923 Bavarian troops were required to give allegiance only to their Bavarian officers. However, Lossow was not prepared to risk all-out war with Berlin; he and the Bavarian state commissioner, Gustav von Kahr, preferred to await developments in northern Germany. Hitler and his more radical followers rejected this policy and on 8 Nov. seized Kahr and Lossow at a meeting in the *Bürgerbräukeller*. Lossow agreed to collaborate with Hitler and Ludendorff in a march on Berlin and was released. Later that night the Bavarian army was ordered to resist Hitler and the putsch quickly collapsed. Lossow claimed to have been bluffing Hitler, but it is possible that he was actually uncertain about his attitude and that more forceful officers in his entourage tipped the balance against Hitler. Lossow was discredited by the affair and resigned.

'LOST GENERATION', THE, term loosely applied to certain disillusioned young US intellectuals who came to maturity during and just after the First World War. They were attracted to the European capitals, especially to the artistic excitement of Paris and the varied personalities and experiments of Joyce, Gertrude Stein, Cocteau, Aragon, Pirandello, and others. 'You are all a lost generation,' Gertrude Stein said to Hemingway in Paris, and he recorded the statement in his preface to *The Sun Also Rises* (1926). This novel, which concerns a typical expatriate group of the 'lost generation' and Fitzgerald's *Tender is the Night* (1934), perhaps the most accurate analysis of its spiritual climate, epitomized the disillusionment of the group.

LOSTWITHIEL, BATTLE OF (2 Sept. 1644), royalist victory in Cornwall during the English Civil Wars, when King Charles I and his Cavalier army surrounded the rear of a parliamentary force commanded by the Earl of Essex. Essex lost most of his infantry and artillery, but escaped with his cavalry, while the king wheeled round and marched towards London.

LOS VELEZ, PEDRO FAJARDO Y CORDOBA, 3rd Marquis of (*c.* 1530–80), Spanish nobleman, soldier, and diplomat, who became the aristocratic figurehead of the Eboli faction in liaison with the effective leader, Antonio Perez, after the death of the Prince of Eboli (1573). He served Philip II as councillor of state (1575), and was party to Juan de Escovedo's murder before falling from royal favour (1578).

LOTHAIRE I (*reg.* 840–55), Emperor, eldest son of Emperor Louis the Pious and the prime mover in causing the civil wars that hastened the disruption of his father's state during the last decade of Louis's reign. After the death of Louis (840), Lothaire was defeated by his younger brothers, Charles of France and Louis the German, and forced to accept a partition of the Carolingian dominions under the treaty of Verdun (843). Lothaire was left with the Middle Kingdom, running from the North Sea to central Italy and comprising the ancestral lands of the Carolingian family, their capital of Aachen, and control over Rome. Lothaire also kept the imperial title, but he was no longer regarded as overlord by Charles and Louis, who ruled the states approximating to the future France and the future Germany respectively. On Lothaire's death, his kingdom was parti-

tioned among his sons and the non-Italian territories were in 869 divided permanently between France and Germany.

LOTHAIRE III (*reg.* 1125–37), Emperor, puppet prince elected by his fellow-princes on the death of the last Salian emperor, Henry V, to demonstrate their right of free election. He had great possessions in Saxony and spent his reign fighting against Henry's nearest relatives, the Hohenstaufen, who regained the kingship after Lothaire's death.

LOTHIAN, PHILIP HENRY KERR, 11th Marquis of (Scottish) (1882–1940), diplomat and politician, who was brought into politics by Lloyd George. He worked closely with the cabinet secretariat, and as the prime minister's personal adviser on foreign and imperial affairs (1916–21) was involved in the Versailles negotiations. He always regarded the treaty as a mistake and believed it would cause future world problems. After 1921, though he remained closely connected with the Liberal Party, he spent much of his time in writing and travelling in the cause of better relations with the empire and the US, rather than involvement in Europe. He was organizing secretary of the Rhodes Trust (1925–39) and, as under-secretary and then as chairman of the Indian Franchise Committee (1931–2), was involved in the plans for Indian self-government. He was a fervent believer in the appeasement of Germany in the 1930s and worked actively to promote better personal relations with the German leaders. The last year of his life was spent as ambassador to the US, where his knowledge of the country was useful in laying the foundations of the Lend-Lease treaty and the subsequent alliance in the Second World War.

LOTTO, LORENZO (1480–1556), Venetian painter, famous for his sensitive portraits, *eg, The Protonotary Apostolic Juliano*. Perhaps the most spiritual of the great Renaissance masters, he left the worldliness of Rome to seek refuge at Bergamo (1512), where he became a pantheist.

LOTZER, SEBASTIEN (*fl.* 16th cent.), Swabian reformer from Memmingen, whose unofficial programme of 12 articles voiced the demands of the German peasants in the Peasants' War (1525). They included the ending of social and economic oppression, *eg*, by the abolition of serfdom, and religious freedom. Although Lotzer's demands were moderate, the peasant movement was discredited by more extreme reformers.

LOUBET, ÉMILE (1838–1929), French politician and president of the Third Republic (1899–1906), who was elected after a long career in local government and the Senate. He upheld the republic during the last phase of the Dreyfus affair.

LOUCHEUR, LOUIS (1872–1931), French engineer, politician, and author of the *loi Loucheur* (1928), the foundation of France's modern housing policy. The law encouraged the construction of moderate-rent flats, of the type today known as HLM's, by making long-term state loans to housing organizations. Loucheur was a Radical deputy and a minister in several governments, specializing in economic and social questions. He also represented France in reparation negotiations and at the League of Nations.

LOUDON, JOHN CLAUDIUS (1783–1843), English landscape designer and horticultural writer, whose *The Suburban Gardener and Villa Companion* and *Encyclopaedia of Cottage, Farm and Villa Architecture* met the horticultural needs of the rising middle-classes in the 19th cent. His wife, Jane Loudon (1807–58), wrote *Ladies Companion to the Flower Garden*.

LOUDON, PEACE OF (1616), settlement between Marie de' Medici, queen-regent of France, and the great nobles, *eg*, Henry II de Bourbon, the Prince of Condé, and Henri,

Duke of Rohan, who had raised a rebellion in south-west France in protest against the queen mother's ultramontanism and her choice of foreign favourites as advisers. After three months' negotiations she agreed to dismiss Concini and accept Condé into her council.

LOUIS DE MALE (1330–84), Count of Flanders, last of the medieval native counts of Flanders (*reg.* 1346–84). A policy of neutrality in the war between England and France secured a revival of Flemish prosperity. Louis restored to Flanders most of the territories lost since the 12th cent., including Artois, southern French Flanders, and Antwerp. By the marriage of his heiress, Margaret, to Philip of Burgundy, the brother of King Charles V of France (1369), he laid the foundations for the creation of the Burgundian state, destined to become one of the strongest European powers in the 15th cent.

LOUIS THE PIOUS (*reg.* 814–40), Emperor and only legitimate son of Charlemagne to survive his father. He thus succeeded to the whole Carolingian inheritance, but he was incapable of preserving it. He encouraged the reform of Frankish monasteries by his friend Benedict of Aniane and supported Agobard, Abp of Lyons, in his efforts to replace judicial duels and ordeals by more rational legal procedures. But he lacked the military capacity or the formidable and ruthless personality of his father. Charlemagne had found it difficult in his last years to control his over-extended state, and, under Louis, it began to disintegrate rapidly. Civil wars that broke out after 830 over the partition of the Carolingian dominions between Louis's sons served only to reveal the extent of disruption that was already occurring, though the internecine fighting that followed (830–43) hastened the demoralization of the Frankish aristocracy. The final partition of the Carolingian state occurred in 843, three years after Louis's death.

LOUIS IV (*reg.* 1314–47), Emperor, whose reign is famous for his prolonged conflict with the papacy, which never accepted his imperial election. In 1328 he briefly occupied Rome, but was soon expelled. Because of the papal opposition to him, Louis maintained a remarkable group of men persecuted for heresy, including several spiritual Franciscans, the scholastic William of Ockham, and Marsilio of Padua, whose anti-papal *Defender of the Peace* is one of the most important medieval treatises on the state.

LOUIS THE GERMAN (d. 876), first Carolingian King of the eastern Frankish kingdom created by the partition of Verdun (843). He was thus the first king of what was to become medieval Germany. In 869, on the partition of the middle kingdom of Lotharingia, he acquired territories west of the Rhineland, which in the 10th cent. formed a bone of contention between France and Germany, but finally became an integral part of the German empire. Under Louis, important dynasties of margraves guarding the frontiers of Germany began to overshadow the Carolingian kings. One of these, the margraves of Saxony, finally rose to the kingship in 919.

LOUIS IV (921–54), King of France (*reg.* 936–54), son of the deposed King Charles the Simple. He lived in exile in England at the court of his uncle, King Athelstan. On the death of King Raoul of France, who had supplanted Louis's father, Louis was restored as King of France. His reign showed that lack of sufficient lands doomed the last Carolingians to failure, despite their personal ability. Louis was overshadowed by Hugh the Great, Duke of the Franks, whose son, Hugh Capet, supplanted the Carolingians in 987.

LOUIS VI (1081–1137), King of France (*reg.* 1108–37), whose *Life*, written by Suger, his life-long friend and chief adviser, makes him one of the best-known Capetian kings. He concentrated on being unquestioned master within his own royal domain and was the first Capetian to reduce to impotence the turbulent baronage of the region between Paris and Orléans, which formed the core of the personal royal territories. By arranging the marriage of his heir, Louis VII, to Eleanor, the heiress of Aquitaine, he left his dynasty as the predominant power in France, though this did not prove a permanent achievement.

LOUIS VII (*c.* 1121–80), King of France (*reg.* 1137–80), first king of the Capetian line to succeed to a secure inheritance. He lost his initial advantage by divorcing his wife, Eleanor, in 1152 and allowing her to take her great inheritance of Aquitaine (all south-western France south of the Loire) to her second husband, Henry II of England. Louis henceforth faced the danger of the huge Angevin empire in France, though, fortunately for him, it was never part of Henry's purpose to destroy the French king's power. Louis was a devout man and a just ruler. His great personal prestige and the consolidation of an efficient administration within the royal territories prepared the way for the achievement of his son, King Philip Augustus, in breaking up the Angevin empire in 1202–5.

LOUIS VIII (*reg.* 1223–6), King of France and heir of King Philip Augustus. His short reign was very successful. A conquest of Poitou from its English lord (1224–5) was followed by an invasion of Languedoc, where he hoped to reap the benefits of the earlier Albigensian crusades which had ruined the power of the counts of Toulouse. But he died during this campaign and his widow, Blanche of Castile, had great difficulty in safeguarding the power of her minor children.

LOUIS IX (1214–70), King of France (*reg.* 1226–70), better known as St Louis, was the greatest of the medieval kings of France. He fulfilled one of the ideals of medieval kingship: he was a pious and just king (the other ideal was a warrior king). St Louis became the creator of French royal absolutism. His authority was supreme, but the fact that he was answerable to God for his actions had a real meaning for him. His duty was to rule his people well. Before Louis, no permanent central judicial court existed in France. He made the Crown the foundation of justice and earned the reputation of the best judge in Christendom. After 1254 he abolished the barbaric judicial duel in cases heard before the royal justices. The quality of the royal administration was greatly improved. The *parlement* of Paris developed into a central judicial court. Local government greatly benefited from the introduction of the practice of periodic enquiries by impartial royal commissioners, first sent out in 1247, and employed regularly after 1254. In his dealings with foreign powers he showed a desire to act justly. In the treaty of Corbeil with Aragon (1258) he accepted the boundary of the Pyrenees, though he could have claimed land to the south. Likewise, he made a just settlement with Henry III in England in 1259. Towards heretics Louis's attitude was strikingly harsh, even by 13th-cent. standards. His chief aim was to launch a great crusade against the Muslims. The Egyptian crusade (1248–54) ended in disaster. Louis was recklessly brave, but was a hopeless general and was captured with much of his army. This failure did not daunt him. In 1270, already a sick man, he embarked on another crusade and died outside Tunis, which he was besieging.

LOUIS X (1289–1316), King of France (*reg.* 1314–16), eldest son of Philip the Fair. He faced leagues of hostile nobles in the provinces on his accession, but temporarily subdued their discontent by sacrificing his father's finance minister and granting local charters of liberties. He died soon after an abortive campaign in a war with Flanders (1315).

LOUIS XI (1423–83), King of France (*reg.* 1461–83), son of Charles VII. As heir to the Crown he was treacherous and disloyal and during the last years of his father's life was in exile in Burgundy. Louis's main task as king was to restore the authority of the Crown, seriously weakened during the Hundred Years War. To this end he subdued the great nobles, curbed the independence of the towns, and added extensively to the royal domain. This centralizing policy, based on a growing bureaucracy, was not achieved without setbacks and humiliations, but Louis was adept at outmanœuvring his enemies. He thus began a process which Richelieu and Louis XIV were to complete. In his foreign policy he was equally skilful, breaking the power of the Burgundian state and exploiting to his own advantage the needs of the rival factions in England during the Wars of the Roses. Louis was one of the ablest French kings, but in character he was crafty, cruel, avaricious (his taxation was a crushing burden), and morbidly superstitious.

LOUIS XIII (1601–43), King of France (*reg.* 1610–43), eldest son of Henry IV and Marie de Medici, who succeeded to the throne as a child after his father's murder. Before his majority (1614) Marie de Medici acted as regent. She was dominated, however, by an Italian favourite, the Marshal d'Ancre, and his wife, Leonora, while the nobility, led by Condé, Soissons, Bouillon, and Mayenne, schemed against the Crown. Louis's betrothal to Philip III's daughter, Anne of Austria, was concluded in the Franco-Spanish peace treaty of 1612, and was followed three years later by their marriage at Bordeaux when the pair were 14 years old.

His sense of isolation led him to seek the friendship of the royal falconer, later the Duc de Luynes, who with the king's approval arranged a palace coup, the murder of d'Ancre, the trial and execution of his wife, and the exile of the queen mother to Blois (1616–17). Further aristocratic unrest (1619–20) led to a reconciliation between the youthful king and his mother through the good offices of Richelieu, Bp of Luçon, and a military clash at Ponts-de-Cé on the Loire, in which Louis directed the royalist campaign with courage. After Luynes's death (1621) Louis ruled with the advice of the royal council, but found the constant decision-making an intolerable strain. Though he continued throughout his life to be informed and to participate in all matters of government and showed some interest in military affairs, he gladly handed over the direction of policy to Richelieu and withdrew to enjoy his favourite sports—hunting, riding, tennis, and boating.

Richelieu was the driving force (1624–42) behind the royal administration, while the king presided over the gradual establishment of an absolute monarchy. On Louis's behalf Richelieu tackled the three major problems of the French Crown: the rivalry with Spain, which led to the declaration of war (1635) and involvement in the Thirty Years War; the independence of the Huguenot communities, curbed after 1628; and the continual intrigue of the nobles and princes of the blood who hatched a series of plots against the cardinal, *eg*, the Chalais conspiracy (1626), the plots of Soissons, Gaston, and Montmorency (1632, 1637, 1641), and the Cinq-Mars plot (1642), which involved Louis's favourite. After the Day of Dupes (10 Nov. 1630) Marie de Medici fled to Brussels, never to return to France.

The ambitions of Gaston were stilled by the birth of a dauphin (5 Sept. 1638) and of a second son to Louis and Anne (1640). In 1642 Louis led the French army against Spain in the conquest of Roussillon, but within months of Richelieu's death (4 Dec. 1642) he became seriously ill. In his will he entrusted the regency to Anne of Austria, with the guidance of a regency council, presided over by Mazarin, while Gaston of Orléans was to be lieutenant-general of the realm.

O. Ranum, *Richelieu and the Councillors of Louis XIII* (Oxford, 1963). MKS

LOUIS XIV (1638–1715), King of France (*reg.* 1648–1715), elder son of Louis XIII and Anne of Austria, known as Louis *le dieudonné* and *le roi soleil*, who succeeded to the throne at the age of five (1643). During his minority he was guided by his mother, the regent, and her chief minister, Cardinal Mazarin. He learnt the realities of power politics at an early age when his childhood was disrupted by the civil disorders of the *Frondes* (1648–52).

On 7 Sept. 1651 Louis was declared of age and in the decade before Mazarin's death (1661) he studied the triple roles of judge, soldier, and statesman, traditional to French monarchy, with the counsel of Turenne, Le Tellier and Mazarin. He was married (1660), according to the terms of the peace of the Pyrenees, to the elder daughter of Philip IV of Spain, the Infanta Maria Theresa, who bore him a son, the dauphin, Louis (1661–1711), through whom Louis was later to claim the Spanish empire for his second grandson, Philip of Anjou.

After Mazarin's death (1661) Louis ruled without a single favourite minister, but with the advice of various royal councils, of which the *conseil d'en haut* was the most important and included his ministers of state, *eg*, Le Tellier, Lionne, Fouquet (until his arrest in Sept. 1661), and later Colbert, Louvois, Pomponne, and Colbert de Croissy. Louis constantly consulted his ministers and relied heavily on their conscientious devotion, but he alone took critical decisions and assented to all lesser administrative matters. Deeply conscious of the obligations as well as the divinely bestowed authority of kingship, he gave expression to the theory of the divine right of kings, while the excessive arbitrariness widely attributed to him, especially in his later years, arose from his defence of his own and his nation's rights.

Louis's obsession with the greatness of France led him to undertake aggressive commercial and foreign policies. His chief enemy was the Dutch republic, against whom he undertook a series of wars (*eg*, the Dutch War, 1672–8, the War of the Grand Alliance, 1689–97; and the War of the Spanish Succession, 1701–13), which also involved England from 1689. He also had to contend with the powerful Habsburg state under Leopold I, which posed a considerable challenge to French power after the reconquest of Hungary and Transylvania from the Turks (1686), and, in the person of Archduke Charles, provided the allied claimant to the Spanish empire after 1700. The possession of the Spanish Netherlands preoccupied Louis from the time of his father-in-law's death (1665) and led him to undertake the War of Devolution (1667–8). Although he concluded partition treaties with Leopold (1668) and William III (1697, 1699) to divide the Spanish inheritance, he repudiated these on the death of Charles II of Spain, whose second will bequeathed Spain and the empire to Philip of Anjou. Louis's attempt to create a Franco-Spanish Bourbon bloc led to the formation of the Grand Alliance of England, the United Provinces, and the Habsburg empire, which enforced the division of the Spanish possessions by the treaty of Utrecht (1713).

Louis also presided over the cultural ascendancy of France within Europe. A patron of the arts, he freely commissioned the services of the leading artists of the day, from Molière and Racine to Le Nôtre and Le Brun. The château of Versailles, which housed his brilliant court, not only provided an outlet for artistic talent, but became the model for all other European rulers. Louis's concern for French greatness also led him to support Colbert's economic paternalism, by which trade, industry, overseas exploration, communications, and naval power were assiduously encouraged. His determination to preserve the unity of the French state and the independence of the French Church in the Gallican tradition led him into conflict with the papacy over the question of the *régales* in the years before 1693 and into involvement in the Jansenist controversy, where he sought papal assistance. His suppression of the Huguenots (1685) was inspired by an outburst of religious orthodoxy.

His last years were saddened not only by military disasters but by the successive deaths of members of the royal family (1701–13). His fears for the French succession caused him to recognize the rights of his legitimized bastard sons, Maine and Toulouse, his surviving grandson, Philip, having renounced his claim on succeeding to the Spanish throne.

However, when Louis died, five days before his 77th birthday, he was succeeded by his five-year-old great-grandson, who became Louis XV.

J. B. Wolf, *Louis XIV* (London, 1968).   MKS

LOUIS XV (1710–74), King of France (*reg.* 1715–74), succeeded his great grandfather, Louis XIV, at the age of five. The first years of his reign were dominated by the regent, Philip of Orléans, but in Feb. 1723 Louis was declared of age and assumed the government. Two years later he was married to Maria Lesczynska, daughter of ex-King Stanislas of Poland. In 1726 he appointed as chief minister his former tutor, Cardinal Fleury, upon whom he relied heavily and whose diplomatic skills gave France the reversion of Lorraine and Bar, the inheritance of Louis's father-in-law. After Fleury's death in 1743 Louis decided to act henceforth as his own first minister and to make all effective decisions. France entered the War of the Austrian Succession and Louis headed the French army which invaded the Netherlands (1744). While concluding the peace of Aix-la-Chapelle (1748) he failed to appreciate the potentiality of France's overseas empire. When courted by the Austrian ambassador, Kaunitz, he allowed France to be drawn into the Seven Years War in support of Maria Theresa, while the struggle between Britain and France for control of India and North America was neglected. The promotion of the Family Compact with France's Bourbon neighbour, Spain, failed to stave off the loss of India, Canada, and the West Indian islands of Granada, St Vincent, Dominica, and Tobago.

Louis's domestic policy was marked by increasing financial disorder and by occasional outbursts of royal activity, *eg*, interference in the Jansenist controversy of the 1730s and the repudiation of the *parlement* of Brittany (1766). His reign was noted for the influence of two royal mistresses, the Marquise de Pompadour and Mme Du Barry. Despite his attempted assassination (1757), Louis was popular until the last decade of his life, when naval and military failures abroad and royal inconsistency brought the monarchy into growing disrepute. The last years of his reign were marked by the philosophical undermining of absolutism and established religion. Political conflicts with the *parlements*, especially that of Paris, underlined the discrepancy between the theory and practice of royal government.

P. Gaxotte, *Louis XV and his Times* (London, 1934).
                                                                      MKS

LOUIS XVI (1754–93), King of France (*reg.* 1774–93), succeeded his grandfather, Louis XV. His reign saw the defeat of England in the American War of Independence, the French Revolution, and the destruction of the *ancien régime*, including the French monarchy itself. Yet it opened in an atmosphere of hopefulness. Turgot, the controller-general, pressed forward with a programme of reforms designed to rationalize the French fiscal system and stimulate the economy. But he ran into opposition from entrenched interests, against whom Louis failed to support him, and he was dismissed (1776). This episode showed one of Louis's persistent failings: he was unwilling to use his authority to support ministers whose programmes traversed vested rights and traditional social assumptions and attitudes. In such situations he was always likely to succumb to pressure from the court circle; blame for this was often assigned—not always justly—to his wife, Marie Antoinette, who came to be seen as a nefarious influence diverting the king from his duties to his subjects; a view which in the end proved fatal to her, and in some measure damaging to him. Louis's worst personal shortcoming was a lethargic and conservative disposition which, by itself, explains much of his inaction.

Events in France grew graver through the 1780s. Necker, the finance minister, was dismissed and dealt a grave blow to public confidence by the publication of a tendentious statement of the national credit position. Then came the ruinous expense of the American war. The operation of the ordinary fiscal system, always inequitable, was rendered harsher than usual by a deepening economic crisis, which by 1789 had reduced some parts of France to near famine. A succession of ministers attempted structural reforms, but, more and more, legal privilege appeared to stand in the way of financial reform. When Louis at last acquiesced in the expedient of summoning the states general (1789), it seemed for a moment that he might place himself at the head of a reform movement. But almost as soon as the states general met, Louis lost the initiative. He began to squander his great popularity by too evident a reluctance to accept political and social reform at the expense of the privileged classes. From this point, the king's story is one of growing isolation as the goodwill and trust of 1789 were dissipated and compromised. It was increasingly clear that Louis only acquiesced in the great revolutionary measures of reform because he felt himself coerced. The belief grew that the court was the centre of an aristocratic pro-Austrian faction; the king's flight to Varennes was virtually the end of his moral authority. The rising of 10 Aug. 1792 led to Louis's suspension from the throne as France's constitutional monarch. Characteristically, his unwillingness to rely on force to save himself lost him any hope of survival and also led to the massacre of the Swiss Guards who, until his orders to cease fire, had held their own. On 21 Sept. the monarchy itself was abolished and France became a republic. In Dec. Louis's trial before the Convention began. A small, but absolute, majority voted for the death penalty and on 21 Jan. 1793 Louis was beheaded. His queen was not beheaded until the following October.

B. Fay, *Louis XVI, or, the end of a world* (tr. London, 1968).
G. Lefebvre, *The Coming of the French Revolution* (tr. by R. R. Palmer, Princeton, 1949).   JMR

LOUIS XVII (1785–95), de jure King of France, who never reigned. He was Louis XVI's only son and was kept a prisoner after the death of his parents. Rumours of escape circulated and a crop of pretenders appeared. In fact, he died of scrofula.

LOUIS XVIII (1755–1824), King of France (*reg.* 1814–24). As Louis, Comte de Provence, he played an ambiguous role early in the Revolution, while his flight to Coblenz (1791) and his ostentatious and selfish policies helped to induce the execution of his brother, Louis XVI. None the less, he proclaimed himself lieutenant-general (1791), regent (1793), and king (1795) on the death of Louis XVII, when he issued from Verona a rigid and maladroit declaration which made a restoration inconceivable. His next years were therefore spent in exile in eastern Europe (1797–1807) and England (1807–14), where he was persuaded to be more moderate when he was eventually called to the throne (1814). His mistakes prompted the Hundred Days, which made him adopt a much harsher line for a time, until the excesses of the Chambre Introuvable made him dissolve it (1816) and return to a policy of moderation with Decazes and Richelieu. His failing health and the murder of Berri (1820) later threw power to the Ultras, and in his last years he had little influence.

LOUIS I (1326–82), King of Hungary (*reg.* 1342–82), King of Poland (*reg.* 1370–82), whose reign was a high point in Hungarian history. He ruled through a council, minimizing the importance of the Diet, and favoured the lesser nobility and the towns at the expense of the magnates. Population expanded and prosperity increased. A university was founded at Pest. He expanded Hungary more than any other monarch, acquiring the northern Balkans and becoming King of Poland. Most of his conquests were lost soon after his death and his dominions were partitioned between his two daughters. He owes his fame to his temporary successes rather than to any lasting achievements.

LOUIS II (1506–26), King of Hungary and Bohemia (*reg.* 1516–26), son of Wladislas Jagiello, who succeeded his father shortly after being betrothed to Mary, grand-daughter of Emperor Maximilian (1515), while his sister Anne married Archduke Ferdinand, Mary's brother. On Louis's refusal to pay tribute to the Turks, war broke out (1521) and on 29 Aug. 1526 Louis's army was defeated and he himself drowned in the battle of Mohacs. His death left Hungary open to Turkish occupation, while his thrones were inherited by Ferdinand of Habsburg.

LOUIS PHILIPPE I

LOUIS PHILIPPE I (1773–1850), King of the French (*reg.* 1830–48). He was the Duke of Orléans and became the first constitutional monarch of France. As a revolutionary general he served with distinction at Valmy (1792), Neerwinden, and Jemappes. After a period spent in Switzerland (1793–4) he travelled widely in Europe and America (1795–8), then settled in England. Though he was reconciled with the Bourbon princes, he kept aloof from émigré activities. In 1809 he married Princess Marie Caroline of Naples and settled in Sicily. On the fall of Bonaparte he returned to France, tried to organize resistance to the Hundred Days, but fell foul of the Bourbons again, first by retiring to Twickenham rather than Ghent (1815), and later by attacking the White Terror (1815), which made him retire to England.

On his return to France (1817) he lived quietly, and was not a full party in the intrigues of Thiers and other Orleanists against Charles X. He was drawn reluctantly into the July crisis (1830), when he seemed, to the conservative politicians who wished to preserve the structure of society, a safe choice because he was both of royal blood and popular for his revolutionary career and his hostility to the Bourbons. He proved an able ruler at first, although loath to accept the direction of his prime ministers, because he wished to be 'the cab driver', as he put it. Eventually he was able to come to a harmonious working arrangement with Guizot (1840) and thereafter took less part in public affairs. However, he seems to have become complacent, or disillusioned by satire and family bereavement, and made little or no attempt to resist the February Revolution (1848). He abdicated and then fled to England.

T. E. B. Howarth, *Citizen King, the life of Louis Philippe, King of the French* (London, 1962).   CHC

LOUIS QUINZE

LOUIS QUINZE, decorative rococo style which flourished in France under Louis XV (*reg.* 1715–74) in reaction against the Palladian style of the previous reign. In architecture, it meant the building of smaller, less classical châteaux; in painting, the voluptuous colouring of Boucher, the gaiety of Lancret and Pater, and the delicacy of Watteau; and in ceramics, the dainty porcelain of Sèvres. But Louis Quinze principally denotes rococo in furniture and interior decoration, beginning with the transitional work of Robert de Cotte during the Regency (1715–23). It came to its full brilliance with Charles Cresset and Meissonier, and in the last years of the reign was more restrained under the influence of Jean François Oeben. Louis Quinze is distinguished by curves, scrolls, and bronze ornamentation, with an emphasis on comfort, daintiness, and exquisite visual appeal. In this style may be found the supreme examples of the commode, the chaise-longue, the cabriole, and the bergère.

LOUISBOURG

LOUISBOURG, French fort on Cape Breton, Canada, captured by New England militia in 1745 in the British interest during the War of the Austrian Succession. It was restored to France in 1748 in return for Madras. During the Seven Years War it was again captured by British forces (1758). The fortifications were destroyed in 1760.

LOUISE OF SAVOY

LOUISE OF SAVOY (1475–1531), daughter of Philip, Duke of Savoy, and wife of Charles of Orléans, Count of Angoulême (1458–95), whom she married in 1490; she was the mother of Francis I, King of France. She was widowed at the age of 20, but she wielded considerable influence during Francis's reign as queen mother. She intrigued against the Constable

de Bourbon, precipitating his flight and ruin (1523), and acted as regent during the king's absence in Italy (1515) and during his captivity in Madrid (1525–6). She negotiated a Turkish alliance (1525) and the treaty of Cambrai (1529) with Margaret of Austria.

LOUISIANA

LOUISIANA, French and Spanish province in North America, located between the Mississippi river and the Rocky Mountains and including land on both banks of the lower Mississippi. Louisiana may have been first visited by the Spaniard Alonso de Piñeda (1519). The survivors of the Narváez expedition (1528) undoubtedly traversed the province, as did Hernando de Soto. Finding no precious metals, the Spanish made no attempt at colonization. After the discovery of the Mississippi (1673) during Louis Joliet and Jacques Marquette's expedition from New France, Robert La Salle led an expedition from the Great Lakes and reached the river's mouth (9 April 1682). He planted a cross and claimed the land drained by the river for France, naming it 'Louisiana' in honour of Louis XIV. In France he obtained permission to colonize Louisiana (1684), but on his return he failed to find the Mississippi. After La Salle's death (1687) the idea of colonizing Louisiana was taken up by the sieur D'Iberville and his brother, the sieur De Bienville. In three expeditions forts were established—at Bilox (1699), Maurepas (1699–1700), and Mobile (1701–1). Iberville was appointed governor (1703), but died (1706) before returning to Louisiana. Bienville has been called the 'Father of Louisiana' because of his work in the colony. He was administrator (1703–17) and governor (1717–25, 1732–43). The province was granted to Antoine Crozat (1712–17), and in 1718 to a company financed by the Scottish-born banker John Law, who launched his notorious 'Mississippi Scheme'. When the 'Bubble' of speculation burst (1725), Law withdrew and the company surrendered its charter (1731) and the French Crown assumed direct control. Bienville had established New Orleans (1718) and it soon became the centre of French rule in the lower Mississippi. The French government largely neglected Louisiana and it was ceded to Spain after the Seven Years War (1763). Resentment within the colony prevented the first Spanish governor, Don Antonio de Ulloa, taking formal possession and he was forced to flee (1768). The revolt was swiftly suppressed by Alejandro O'Reilly (1769) and Spanish laws and institutions introduced. Spanish rule was liberal and tolerant, French colonists being given positions of authority. After US independence the Spanish feared American expansion into Louisiana. The Spanish used control of the mouth of the Mississippi as a bargaining counter by closing it to American traders. Spanish plans were overtaken when Napoleon forced Spain to return Louisiana to France by the treaty of San Ildefonso (1800). But, facing revolts in Haiti and war in Europe, Napoleon abandoned his hopes for a new colonial empire. He sold the colony to the US by the Louisiana Purchase treaty (1803), which included a vast largely unmapped area from the Mississippi to the Rockies and from the Gulf to Canada. W. C. C. Claiborne took formal possession of Louisiana (20 Dec. 1803) and became its first governor. The southern part of the province became the Territory of Orleans, which, with additional territory, was made the state of Louisiana (April 1812). The northern part, the Louisiana Territory, was retitled the Missouri Territory (1812).

E. A. Davis, *Louisiana, the Pelican State* (Baton Rouge, 1959).   GFO

LOUISIANA PURCHASE

LOUISIANA PURCHASE (1803), acquisition by the US from France of over 1 million sq. miles (2,590,000 sq. kms) of territory west of the Mississippi, extending northwards to Canada, westwards to the Rocky Mountains, and including New Orleans. The area, held by Spain since 1763, was transferred to France by the secret treaty of San Ildefonso (1800). In 1802 the right of deposit of goods for transhipment at New Orleans, granted by Spain in Pinckney's treaty (1795), was withdrawn and there was a real danger that France might use her newly acquired control over the mouth of the Mississippi to curb development of the American West, drawing the US inevitably into the European conflict. 'The day that France takes possession of New Orleans,' declared President Jefferson, '... we must marry ourselves to the British fleet and nation', and he sent James Monroe to Paris to try to buy New Orleans. Fortunately, Napoleon had already decided to give up the whole of Louisiana. The fate of the French army sent to quell the rebellion in Haiti (1801) had left him without the means to defend Louisiana against British attack, and he preferred to strengthen the US as a potential rival to Britain, and at the same time fatten his war chest. Talleyrand therefore offered the whole of the territory acquired from Spain to Robert Livingston, the US minister in Paris, for a sum variously put at $12–15 million. According to a strict construction of the constitution, the Federal government had no authority to acquire new territory or, as the treaty of acquisition provided, to offer full citizenship to its inhabitants, but in the circumstances Jefferson swallowed his principles and asked the Senate to ratify the treaty.　　　　　　　　　DBS

LOUVOIS, FRANÇOIS MICHEL LE TELLIER, Marquis of (1641–91), French statesman, who became Louis XIV's secretary of state and minister of war jointly with his father, Michel Le Tellier (1662), until he assumed sole command of the war ministry (1677). His administrative ability and relentless devotion to the service of France made him the king's most favoured minister in the 1680s.

Louvois carried out jointly with his father a series of far-reaching military reforms which established the superiority of the French armed forces in Europe. These reforms included the improved instruction of officers, the formation of the *compagnies de cadets* as officer-training corps for the younger sons of the nobility, the checking of officer corruption over payroll musters, the reorganization of supply services, the rationalization of weapons, and the development of an engineer corps. To improve discipline he revised the court-martial system, introduced the regular inspection of regiments by inspectors-general, and the use of uniforms. The *ordre du tableau* regulated the military hierarchy and established the superiority of military rank over social status. By the advent of the Dutch War (1672) a disciplined army of 120,000 had been built up and the authority of the state over the armed forces had been established.

Louvois' arrogance created hostility in many quarters. He was hated by Condé and Turenne, and by Mme de Montespan and Mme de Maintenon. He combined with another personal enemy, Colbert, to overthrow the rival minister for foreign affairs, Pomponne (1679). He was accused by contemporaries of fomenting Louis XIV's wars and religious discord so as to remain indispensable to the king. The chamber of reunion at Metz, which he directed, ruthlessly pursued French claims in Lorraine and Bar (1680–3) and was crowned by the destructive invasion of the Spanish Netherlands (1683) and the seizure of Luxemburg (1684). Louvois ordered the devastation of the palatinate (1688) and the destruction of Heidelberg and the electoral castle (1689). and he encouraged an increasingly severe policy towards the Huguenots, eg, the dragonnades (1684). His ruthlessness extended even to his family. When his eldest son, Courtenvaux, proved incapable of managing the war department, Louvois dismissed him in favour of his fourth son, Barbésieux. Louvois's sudden death (16 July 1691) deprived Louis XIV of a gifted minister.

C. F. M. Rousset, *Histoire de Louvois et son administration politique et militaire*, 4 vols (Paris, 1863–4).　　　MKS

LOUVRE, THE, French royal palace on the northern bank of the Seine near the Tuileries and the Pont-Neuf. The medieval buildings were replaced under Henry IV by a new palace begun in 1594. From the mid-17th cent., when the royal family moved to the more convenient Palais-Royal, it was used for receptions, parties, and theatrical performances. Le Vau added a southern wing with a dome endowed by Mazarin, and a façade of classical simplicity, designed by Claude Perrault (1613–88), was constructed in preference to an extravagant baroque front planned by Bernini (1667). Building ceased c. 1683, as Louis XIV's interest became centred on Versailles and from the 19th cent. the Louvre became an art gallery and museum.

LOVAT, SIMON FRASER, 11th Baron (Scottish) (c. 1667–1747). His career was one of intrigue in troubled political times, and he maintained contacts with the exiled James II while serving William III. On the accession of Queen Anne (1702) he entered Jacobite service, promising to raise a Highland army. His plotting produced a political crisis between James Douglas, 2nd Duke of Queensbury, and the Duke of Atholl, but no army, since the Highlanders suspected him of being a double agent. After fleeing to France, Fraser was arrested and kept under surveillance until 1713.

He escaped and returned to Scotland and raised his clan for George I during the Jacobite rebellion of 1715. For this he was rewarded with a full pardon and restoration of estates, but soon became reassociated with the Jacobites and during the attempt of 1719 had to explain his conduct to the government in London. During the 1745 rebellion he mobilized support for the Jacobites and his clan fought at Falkirk and Culloden. He was captured, tried (1747), and executed, being the last peer to be so dealt with for high treason.

LOVEJOY, ELIJAH PARISH (1802–37), US journalist, who campaigned against slavery. He edited the St Louis *Observer* (1833–6), a Presbyterian newspaper which often discussed the slavery question. When censured at a public meeting which denied the 'moral right' of abolitionists to discuss slavery 'either orally or through the medium of the press', Lovejoy defended his constitutional right to freedom of expression. He was forced to move to IL after an editorial attack on a mob that had burned a Negro sailor. At Alton, IL, he published the *Alton Observer* as an abolitionist newspaper. His press at Alton was destroyed three times by mobs and Lovejoy was killed (7 Nov. 1837) defending his fourth press. His murder was said by John Quincy Adams to have produced 'a shock as of an earthquake throughout this continent', and convinced much Northern opinion that abolitionism and civil liberties were related issues. Ironically, this first abolitionist martyr was also a rabid anti-Catholic and believed that slavery and Catholicism were synonymous.

LOVEK, capital of Cambodia in the 16th cent., after the Khmers had abandoned Angkor. It became the capital under Ang Chan (reg. 1516–66), but was sacked by the Thai in 1594, and itself abandoned.

LOVETT, WILLIAM (1800–77), English radical, Chartist, and educationalist, who was secretary of many radical movements (1830–48). He was active in the unstamped press agitation and became (1836) secretary of the London Working Men's Association, a body which pursued his life-long objective of elevating his class through banding together its more respectable and earnest members. Lovett helped to draft the Charter and, like many Chartist leaders, was imprisoned (1839–40). He had always denounced attacks on the middle-class and defended the new poor law, and his prison experience convinced him that O'Connor would never promote the necessary alliance between radical middle and working classes. In 1841 he launched his own campaign for an educational brand of Chartism, but without much success. He realized the important role education might play and, as manager of a radical London school, he was able to put into practice the ideas of the phrenologist George Combe, and develop a curriculum which stressed music, physical exercise, diet, and the social and natural sciences.

In his old age Lovett continued to blame the aristocracy for working-class self-indulgence and for foreign wars, and shared Cobden's belief in the civilizing influences of democracy and international trade. But he also blamed drink for the failure of radical remedies to produce his longed-for utopia, and firmly repudiated socialism in his important and moving *Life and Struggles* (1876). His high-mindedness—his life-long stress on the importance of cleanliness, punctuality, and self-education—seriously limited his influence with a working class which preferred less puritanical leadership.

G. D. H. Cole, *Chartist Portraits* (London, 1941).   BHH

LOW, SIR DAVID (1891–1963), NZ-born British political cartoonist. After working on the Sydney *Bulletin*, he came to London and joined the Conservative *Evening Standard*, where (1927–50), his left-wing views notwithstanding, he became one of the paper's main attractions and a powerful Labour propagandist. He originated 'Col. Blimp' as an epitome of reactionary conservatism and was especially severe on the administrations of MacDonald and Baldwin. After leaving the *Standard* he went to the *Daily Herald* (1950) and then to the *Manchester Guardian* (1953).

Low was the outstanding British cartoonist of his generation, his work being characterized by its biting wit, the cruel likeness of his caricatures, and his remarkable powers of draughtsmanship.

LOW, SIR HUGH (1824–1905), British colonial servant and Resident of Perak, Malaya, whose cautious, understanding approach to reforming Malay society established the model for 'rule by advice' in Malaya, and ensured the survival of the Malay sultanates within the colonial system.

LOWELL, JAMES RUSSELL (1819–91), US man of letters and diplomat. His marriage in 1844 to Maria White, an ardent reformer, aroused in him an interest in contemporary reform movements. He won recognition with *A Fable for Critics* (1848), a humorous attack on the leading literary personalities of the day, and with *The Biglow Papers* (1848), in which, through the character and rustic dialect of Hosea Biglow, he criticized the Mexican War. After the death of his wife (1853) his interest in reform declined, and he succeeded Longfellow as professor of modern languages at Harvard (1855). He was a founder of *The Atlantic Monthly*, and its first editor (1857–61), contributing articles under the pseudonym of Hosea Biglow which championed the Unionist cause during the Civil War. These, later collected as *The Biglow Papers: Second Series* (1867), mark the end of his best work, although he continued to make regular and influential contributions to *The North American Review*. He was a Republican and was appointed US minister to Spain (1877–1880), and to England (1880–5).

LOWELL, ROBERT TRAILL SPENCE jr (1917–   ), US poet, closely concerned with his New England heritage and the spiritual values of his adopted faith of Catholicism. His major books of poetry are 'Lord Weary's Castle' (1946), 'Life Studies' (1959), 'Imitations' (1961), and 'For the Union Dead' (1964).

LOWENHAUPT, ADAM LUDWIG, Count (1659–1719), Swedish soldier, who took Austrian service and fought against the Turks in Hungary before his participation in the Great Northern War (1700–21). In 1704 he saved Riga from the Russian and Saxon–Polish forces and won victories at Jakobstadt and Gemauerthof (1705). Advancing from Livonia with 18,000 men to reinforce Charles XII, he was attacked by the Russians at Lesnaya on the Sozh river (29 Sept. 1708), losing two-thirds of his army. Although he managed to join Charles on the Lower Dnieper, after the Swedish defeat at Poltava he surrendered to Menshikov (1709) and spent his remaining years a captive in Russia.

LOWER CANADA, one of the provinces created by the British Constitutional Act (1791). The act established government by a lieutenant-governor with appointed executive and legislative councils and an elected House of Assembly. As in Upper Canada, there was an increasing demand for 'responsible' government. With a largely French-speaking population the reform movement was complicated by ethnic differences. Relations were damaged by Edward Ellice's attempt to get Upper and Lower Canada united by British act of parliament (1822), which aroused fears of a permanent English majority in the legislature. Reforms recommended by the British parliament's Canada Committee (1828) were regarded by reformers as too slow and the Ninety-Two Resolutions passed by the Lower Canada Assembly (1834) revealed the growing colonial grievances. Disillusionment at the failure of constitutional methods sparked off the rebellion of 1837. Lord Durham's *Report* precipitated the Act of Union (1840) which united Upper and Lower Canada.

LOWESTOFT, BATTLE OF (1665), North Sea engagement early in the second Anglo-Dutch War (1665–7). The two fleets, commanded by James, Duke of York, and Van Tromp, each had more than 100 ships, and a conclusive English victory was only prevented by a storm and Van Tromp's seamanship in getting most of his fleet back to harbour.

LOWTH, ROBERT, bishop (1710–87), English Hebrew scholar, whose recognition of the use of parallelism in Hebrew poetry was of major importance in Old Testament studies.

LOYALISTS, American colonists who upheld the British cause during the American War of Independence. They represented all classes, but were mostly the wealthy, Anglicans, and office-holders. Loyalist sympathies were strongest where British arms were most successful, as in New York and New Jersey. Eighty thousand loyalists left the country, many going to Canada, where they were called United Empire Loyalists. Others settled in the West Indies. Those who could not leave took the oath of allegiance after the war and were excluded from the professions and public office. Thirty thousand served in the British army and many acted as spies for the British and supported their cause with money. Confiscation of Loyalists' property helped to finance the American revolutionary cause. The peace treaty (1783) called ineffectually for the return of this property.

LOYALTY ISLANDS, in the Pacific, an annexe of New Caledonia, the scene of several sandalwood massacres (1842–5). The islands were occupied by London Missionary Society teachers (1841–2) and English missionaries (1854). The intrusion of French Marist priests (Uvea, 1857; Lifu, 1858) led to bitter tribal conflict, followed (1864) by French annexation and the proscription of the Lifu mission—reversed by a commission of the Second Empire in 1869. A new outbreak of violence on Maré (1886) caused the expulsion of one missionary and the remaining one retired in 1922, when the mission was transferred to French Protestant interests.

LO-YANG, capital city of China at times during the Han, T'ang, and other dynasties. The city acted both as a centre of Buddhist establishments and as a scene of commercial activity. It is in the present province of Ho-nan.

LOYOLA, IGNATIUS, Saint (1491–1556), Basque nobleman and founder of the Society of Jesus. His early career was spent as a soldier. He was wounded at the siege of Pamplona (1521) and while recovering in his father's castle he occupied himself by reading a famous life of Christ by the 14th-cent. Carthusian, Ludolph of Saxony, and a series of lives of the saints, works which had a profound effect upon him and inspired him to his true vocation. After he had recovered from his injuries he set out on a pilgrimage to the Holy Land, pausing en route to lead the primitive life of a hermit in a cave near Manresa (1522–3). During this self-inflicted solitude he composed the *Spiritual Exercises*, a devotional programme of spiritual reform. Later, Loyola visited Italy and Jerusalem (1523–4). He next sought to educate himself fully, attending the Spanish universities of Alcala, Burgos, and Salamanca (1525–7), during which period he was twice imprisoned by the Inquisition for suspected illuminist activities and forbidden to preach for three years.

He continued his studies in Paris and gathered round him a small group of dedicated admirers, six of whom—Le Fevre, Lainez, Salmeron, Bobadilla, Rodriguez, and Francis Xavier—accompanied him to the chapel of St Denis on Montmartre, where they dedicated themselves to poverty, chastity, and total obedience to the papacy, should their committal to a missionary crusade to the Holy Land prove impossible (15 Aug. 1534). In 1535 he and his friends left Paris for Italy, but after ordination in Venice (1537) they were prevented from undertaking a crusade by the war between Venice and Turkey. Instead, they won a great reputation for their work with the sick and the poor of Rome during the harsh winter of 1538–9.

Finally, Loyola and his friends offered their services to the pope, proposing the formation of an order of regular clerics dedicated to an active missionary, pastoral, and educational programme. In Sept. 1540 Pope Paul III promulgated the bull *Regimini militantis ecclesiae* which established the Society of Jesus, and shortly afterwards Loyola was elected its first general, with full control over the order and its appointments. In Rome Loyola supported the establishment of the Holy Office (1542) and showed a special interest in education. He founded the Rome College in 1550 and the German College in 1552. Although the order faced abolition in 1555 on the election of his enemy, Paul IV, to the papacy, it survived Loyola's death (1556), by which time it had expanded to over 1000 members in 11 provinces. Loyola was canonized by Gregory XV in 1662 and he must be regarded as the most formative influence on the Counter-Reformation.

J. Brodrick, *The Origin of the Jesuits* (London, 1940).
J. Brodrick, *St Ignatius Loyola: the pilgrim years* (London, 1956).   JHS

LOYSEAU, CHARLES (1566–1627), French jurist and political theorist, who examined the social order and institutions of France in his two main works, *Cinq Livres des droits des offices* (1610) and *Traité des ordres et simples dignitez* (1613).

LOZI, people of the Upper Zambesi flood-plain who evolved a centralized state (*c.* 1650). It was briefly overrun in the 19th cent. by the Kololo, migrants from the south, but later the state regained its independence, and later still became the Barotseland protectorate within Northern Rhodesia.

LU HSÜN (1881–1936), pseudonym of Chou Shu-jen, Chinese writer. His first collection of short stories, *Outcry*, was published in 1923. The best-known, *The Story of Ah Q*, describes a decaying wretch who lives in a world of delusion, refusing to accept his destitution, or to escape from it. The story is an allegory on decaying, feudalistic, superstition-ridden China. Lu Hsün became increasingly left-wing during the 1930s, and gathered around him a circle of younger writers and critics. His passionate involvement with the fate of the nation, and his pessimism, illuminated by a faint gleam of hope, were enormously influential.

LÜ THAI (*reg.* ?1347–74), King of Sukhothai in north Thailand. He was a pious Buddhist and an able monarch and fought hard to gain his patrimony and to defend his kingdom against encroachments by Ayudhya to the south.

LUANDA, capital of the Portuguese overseas province of Angola. The city was founded in 1575 on a wide bay with important shell fisheries. It rapidly became the leading port for the export of slaves from central Africa, often shipping 10,000 and more slaves per year. It was also the starting point of the Portuguese chain of forts up the Kwanza valley, built during the 17th cent. In the mid-20th cent. the European population was rapidly increased by Portuguese immigration and the extension of other European and US business interests.

LUANG PRABANG, royal capital of Laos, which had become a centre of Lao settlement by the 8th cent. and was the seat of the kingdom of Lan Chang (1353–1563). It became independent after the dissolution of Lan Chang (*c.* 1700), and gradually fell under Thai domination, and a Thai commissioner resided at the court of King Oun-Kham (*reg.* 1872–87). The French protectorate (1893) properly applied only to Luang Prabang and its northern provinces, while the centre and south were directly administered from Vientiane. After the Second World War the Kingdom was unified.

LUBA AND LUNDA STATES, a series of states with similar patterns of political organization which had organized many of the peoples of the southern half of the Congo basin by the 19th cent. The earliest known Luba states probably flourished in the 14th–15th cents among the lakes of Katanga, an area of important development at least since the 8th cent. The economic basis of Luba political sophistication was probably hunting and fishing, as well as farming and the artisan industries associated with the copper resources of neighbouring peoples.

In the 16th cent. the concept of state formation was adopted by the neighbouring Lunda, who had probably begun to experience the opportunities offered by European traders on the Atlantic coast. By judiciously allowing a small fraction of the unskilled labour of the empire to be exported for sale to Europeans, the early rulers of Lunda were able to acquire a level of luxurious living which greatly enhanced the prestige they gained from adopting a Luba type of monarchical government. The expansion of the Lunda sphere of influence took place in two phases, the first being due to refugees who escaped the tutelage of the Mwata Yamvo to establish Lunda-like kingdoms of their own, such as Kasanje, and possibly Lozi and Bemba. The second phase was introduced by 'governors' sent out to control satellite kingdoms who were brought under the Lunda political umbrella and required to pay tribute to the Mwata Yamvo and to channel their external trade through his markets.

This Luba–Lunda political and economic system extended from the fringes of Angola in the west to the fringes of Mozambique in the east, and controlled the external economy of much of central Africa. It began to crumble in the mid-19th cent. when the pattern of trade was radically altered by the sudden growth of the ivory trade, which the Lunda were ill-equipped to master. They lost to Bemba, Nyamwezi, and Arabs in the east, and to Cokwe in the west. The Cokwe finally overran the whole metropolitan area and destroyed the power and prestige of the empire, which survived into the colonial period only as a small state in western Katanga.

Jan Vansina, *Kingdoms of the Savannah* (Madison, 1966).
Richard Gray and David Birmingham, *Pre-Colonial African Trade* (London, 1970).

LUBBE, MARINUS VAN DER (1909–34), Dutch communist, who was tried and executed by the Nazis for setting fire to the Reichstag on 27 Feb. 1933. Originally it was assumed that the Nazis had themselves caused the fire as a political move, and that Van der Lubbe was merely a scapegoat. This seemed likely because of the difficulty that one man would have had in starting such a destructive fire, and because of Van der Lubbe's behaviour at his trial, which suggested that he was incapable of such a well-planned action. However, later evidence suggested that he had a decisive part in the incident. He is said to have gone to Berlin (Feb. 1933) with the intention of stimulating the workers' movements to a revolutionary protest against the Nazi regime, and that his setting fire to the Reichstag was one of a series of attempts by him to provoke a popular uprising by some sensational act. Throughout his trial he reiterated that he was guilty and claimed to have had a political motive. Although his part in the affair remains in dispute, the incident was exploited by the Nazis to raise the spectre of communist revolt and strengthen their power.

LÜBECK, free imperial city on the Baltic coast. It formed the eastern terminus of an overland trade route south of the Jutland peninsula to western Germany and the Netherlands devised to avoid shipments around Jutland, which were precarious because of Scandinavian hostility and endemic piracy. Lübeck was founded by Saxon dukes in the middle of the 12th cent. By early in the 13th cent. it was the centre of German resistance to the Danes and of the eastward expansion of German towns. In the later Middle Ages it was the head of the Hanseatic League. Its central position made it the natural promoter of Hanseatic unity against the separatist tendencies of the cities of the eastern Baltic and the western group in the Rhineland and the Netherlands. The decline of the league and of Lübeck came in the 16th cent.

LÜBECK, TREATY OF (1629), ended Danish intervention in the Thirty Years War. Wallenstein was anxious to keep Christian IV and Gustavus Adolphus of Sweden apart, and he therefore exacted only the abandonment of Christian's claims to German bishoprics for his family and of the directorship of the Lower Saxon Circle, to which he had been elected in 1625.

LUBECKI-DRUCKI, KSAWERY (1778–1846), Polish statesman of Russian princely extraction, was responsible for the restoration of the Polish finances after the Napoleonic Wars. He encouraged industrial development and established the Land Credit Society (1825) and the Bank of Poland (1828). He defended Polish autonomy, but opposed the 1830 revolution, and after his failure to negotiate with Nicholas I, left Poland and spent the last years of his life in St Petersburg.

LÜBKE, HEINRICH (1894–   ), West German politician and Christian-Democrat president of the German Federal Republic (1959–69). He was obliged to resign under pressure of allegations that, as an architect, he had collaborated with the Nazis in the construction of forced labour camps during the Second World War. The allegations were denied, but his resignation high-lighted the importance attached in the 1950s and 1960s to such accusations in West Germany.

LUBLIN, UNION OF (1569), constitutional merger of Poland with Lithuania and the latter's dominions in East Prussia, White Russia, and the Ukraine, carried out at the Diet of Lublin. Thus a vast multi-racial, multi-lingual, and multi-religious state, stretching from the Baltic to the Dniester, was created under Sigismund II Augustus, the last of the Jagiellon kings. The terms of the union included an elective monarchy, to be chosen in a single *sejm* or national assembly, a common coinage, and freedom of office and movement for the Russo-Lithuanian nobility, as was already enjoyed by the Polish nobility. The union had been anticipated by the personal link between the two kingdoms formed by the Jagiellon dynasty since 1385, but the aggression of the Crimean Tatars and Muscovy against Lithuania created the need for closer union.

LUCA, VASILE (1898–c. 1953), Rumanian communist politician, of Hungarian origin. After the First World War he joined communist groups in Rumania, and in 1924 became secretary of the regional organization centred on Brasov. In 1928 he became a member of the central committee, but later (1933–9) was imprisoned for political offences. He was again arrested in 1940, but soon afterwards was freed by the Red Army and taken to Moscow, where he became associated with the Rumanian bureau. He returned to Rumania in 1944 as one of four party secretaries and as minister responsible for industry and finance. In 1952 he was purged with the other Muscovite leaders and is believed to have died in prison.

LUCAN (M. ANNAEUS LUCANUS) (AD 39–65), Roman epic poet and nephew of Seneca the younger, who was also a member of Nero's literary coterie. He died after Piso's conspiracy against Nero. His 'Pharsalia', an epic on the Roman civil wars, is interesting for its Stoic outlook and nostalgia for the extinct republic.

LUCAYAN INDIANS, tribe of Arawakan speakers, the first natives encountered by Columbus when he landed at San Salvador in the Bahamas (1492). A peaceful people with an estimated population of 45,000, they were exterminated before 1600 by Spanish colonists who captured them as slaves to replace the decimated tribes in other Spanish settlements.

LUCCA, Italian city in northern Tuscany. An independent commune after 1160, it always resisted the attempts of Florence to conquer it and remained a republic until the French captured it in 1797. In the 13th cent. the bankers of Lucca were among the leading European financiers and the Lucchese firm of the Riccardi helped to finance the conquest of Wales by King Edward I. In the later Middle Ages Lucca was the chief European centre for the manufacture of the finest silks. After the 16th cent. its trade and industry declined.

LUCCA, CONFERENCE OF (56 BC), between Pompey, Caesar, and Crassus, was precipitated by the threat of L. Domitius Ahenobarbus to recall Caesar from Gaul if he were elected consul for 55, and by Pompey's growing estrangement from Caesar and Crassus. The Triumvirate was renewed and it was decided that Caesar's command in Gaul should be prolonged for another five years, that Pompey and Crassus were to be consuls for 55, and that they should have Spain and Syria respectively as their proconsular provinces.

LUCE, HENRY ROBINSON (1898–1967), US magazine publisher, who founded (1923) the news magazine *Time*, which became renowned for its brisk incisive style and its emphasis on personalities. Among his later publications were *Fortune* (1930–   ), *Life* (1936–   ), and *Sports Illustrated* (1954–   ). He acted as editor in chief of all his magazines, the total circulation of which had reached 12·5 million by 1967. He was also influential in Republican politics, and his wife, Clare Boothe Luce, spent two terms in Congress (1943–7) and was US ambassador to Italy (1953–7). As a staunch protagonist of US power in world affairs, he used his journals to mount partisan attacks on President Truman's policy towards China after 1945.

LUCERNE, TREATY OF (1510), agreement between the Swiss cantons and Pope Julius II whereby the Swiss agreed to provide 6000 men for five years to do military service for the Holy See in return for an annual payment of 1000 *gulden* to each canton. The treaty was fulfilled in 1512–13, when Swiss mercenaries drove the French out of Italy.

LUCIUS VERUS (L. AURELIUS VERUS AUGUSTUS) (AD 130–69), Roman Emperor (*reg.* 161–9). His father, L. Ceionius Commodus, was adopted by Hadrian, but predeceased him. Hadrian then adopted the future emperor Antoninus Pius, who in turn adopted Lucius Verus and the future emperor Marcus Aurelius. When Antoninus died in 161, Marcus Aurelius shared imperial power with Lucius, who was younger—the first time there had been joint emperors. He was overshadowed by Marcus, being weak and ineffective, and was only nominally an emperor.

LUCKNOW PACT (Dec. 1916), also known as the 'Congress–League Scheme', a statement of the united Indian nationalist demands for constitutional reforms agreed to at simultaneous meetings of the Congress and the Muslim League in Lucknow in the United Provinces. It embodied concessions from both sides. The Congress accepted separate electorates for Muslims, while the League endorsed more extensive constitutional changes than it had hitherto contemplated. The agreement gave the Muslims substantial weight in the provincial legislative councils in Muslim minority provinces. However, it reduced the clear Muslim representation in the Punjab and Bengal to 50 per cent and 40 per cent respectively; this was to cause a split in the League's ranks in both provinces and to cause considerable political discomfort to the Bengal Muslims, in particular in the 1920s. The pact proposed legislatures with 80 per cent directly elected members, executives with at least half of the members elected Indians; provincial autonomy, and executive governments at both the provincial and national levels that were bound by resolutions of the legislatures. The agreement was a major step forward for the Indian nationalist movement, although the Congress's concession of separate electorates might be judged a mistake in the ultimate cause of Indian unity. The constitutional reforms of 1919 did not meet the demands of the pact, but the scheme of communal representation was accepted with only minor amendments.

LUCRETIUS CARUS, T. (*c.* 99–55 BC), Roman poet, author of the 'De Rerum Natura', a didactic poem in six books, expounding Epicurean philosophy, designed to free men from religious superstition and fear of death.

LUCULLUS, L. LICINIUS (*c.* 117–56 BC), Roman general, and Sulla's quaestor (87). He raised a fleet from Egypt and Syria and campaigned successfully against Mithridates VI of Pontus in the Aegean. Remaining in Asia as proquaestor until 80, he was, with Sulla's support, elected aedile for 79. As praetor in 78, he governed Africa (77–75), and as consul (74) received an extraordinary command against Mithridates. His successful campaigns and sound administration were undermined by his political enemies, who spread disaffection among his troops, and in 66 his command was transferred to Pompey. After a triumph in 63 and bitter opposition to Pompey's demands in 61–60, he retired into elegant luxury.

LUDDITE DISTURBANCES in England. Luddites claimed to be imitators of one Ned Lud or Ludlam, an apprentice, who was alleged to have destroyed a stocking frame in a rage. They were organized groups of workers who destroyed machinery (1811–12) in a period of high prices, unstable employment, and low wages. Their attacks were on shearing frames and gig mills in the West Riding of Yorkshire, on steam-powered looms in Lancashire and Cheshire, and on improved lace machines and 'cut-up' stocking frames in the Midlands. The damage was well organized and highly selective, and to some degree successful in discouraging the installation of labour-saving machinery. It ceased when the government brought in and applied the death penalty for such offences. There is some evidence that the organizations involved had links with early trade unions, but none of the outbreaks in different areas were co-ordinated.

LUDENDORFF, ERICH (1865–1937), German general and politician, who, entering the army in 1882, reached the rank of major-general by 1914. He won fame during the First World War in the western offensive by capturing Liège, and was then transferred to the east as Hindenburg's chief of staff. In the winter of 1914 his strategies led to a series of victories, *eg*, at Tannenberg and the Masurian Lakes, which lent him the prestige and aura of heroic infallibility on which he later built his political power.

Ludendorff had great authority (1916–18) which grew out of the eclipse of the civilian government by the military leadership. By 1916 slaughter and stalemate had soured the early optimism and enthusiasm of the German people, and the precarious national unity of 1914 was threatening to collapse. Working-class bitterness at their appalling living conditions was shown by strikes and demonstrations, while the deteriorating military situation had begun to weaken the morale and loyalty of the upper and middle classes. The Kaiser and his government shared in the general opprobrium,

and in Aug. 1916 William II bowed to national feeling by appointing Hindenburg chief of general staff, *ie*, giving him, in effect, the supreme command. Ludendorff was appointed chief quartermaster-general, a new rank which gave him equal status and responsibility with Hindenburg. He converted this military command into a political dictatorship by claiming that his military responsibilities gave him a legitimate interest in any policy which bore on the conduct of the war. Using the threat of resignation as a foolproof means of blackmail, he was able to dictate government policy, and thus Bethmann-Hollweg (1917) and Kühlmann (1918) were both forced from office because Ludendorff refused to work with them. The harsh terms of Brest-Litovsk, the resumption of unrestricted submarine warfare, and the neglect of Reichstag opinion in matters like the democratization of government and the opening of peace negotiations, were all policies adopted through Ludendorff's influence.

His power collapsed after the success of the Allies' summer offensive in 1918. On 29 Sept. he proposed the formation of a more broadly based government to negotiate an armistice, hoping for terms which would allow Germany to reopen hostilities if the Allies tried to impose an unacceptable peace. However, it soon became obvious that the war-weary nation could not offer further resistance, and on Oct. 26 Ludendorff resigned and fled to Sweden.

After the war, he was politically powerless, but was active in nationalist and racist circles. In 1920 he played a minor part in the Kapp putsch. Attracted to the embryonic Nazi movement by Hitler, who hoped to profit from the general's prestigious name, he participated in the Munich putsch in Nov. 1923, but was acquitted at the trial that followed it. He was a member of the Reichstag (1924–8), and in 1925 stood as Nazi presidential candidate, but received only 200,000 votes. After this disappointment he broke with Hitler and founded his own right-wing anti-Semitic group, the *Tannenbergerbund*. He remained on the fringes of extremist politics until his death.

D. J. Goodspeed, *Ludendorff* (London, 1966).
A. Rosenberg, *Imperial Germany: the birth of the German Republic* (Boston, 1964).   AJC

LUDLOW, EDMUND (*c.* 1617–92), English politician, parliamentary general, and republican, who served in the Earl of Essex's lifeguard until 1646, when he was elected MP for Wiltshire in the Long Parliament. He was a chief promoter of Pride's Purge (1648), a regicide, and a member of the first council of state of the Comonwealth. In 1651 he was sent to Ireland as second-in-command to Ireton and as one of the commissioners for the civil government. He succeeded Ireton as commander-in-chief (1651). Upon his return to England (1655) he was arrested because of his refusal to recognize Cromwell's protectorate, but was allowed to retire to Essex. As an MP in Richard Cromwell's parliament (1659), he helped to organize the end of the protectorate. He was in the restored Rump and its council of state, and was appointed commander in Ireland again (1659). He opposed the Restoration (1660) and escaped to Switzerland, where he remained until his death, except for a short visit in 1689, when the English authorities forced him to return to exile.

LUDLOW RESOLUTION (1937), proposed amendment to the US constitution, requiring a national referendum, except in the case of invasion, before a congressional declaration of war could become effective. Introduced in the House of Representatives by Louis Ludlow, it commanded wide support in the country and was only defeated (209–188) after severe pressure had been exerted by President F. D. Roosevelt.

LUGAL, Sumerian name, 'great man', for the ruler, probably of a number of cities. At first elected, they later became hereditary rulers.

LUGAL-ZAGGE-SI (*c.* 2400–2371 BC), *ensi* of Umma, who conquered Sumeria and claimed to have conquered all

Mesopotamia and Syria. He was defeated and his empire taken by Sargon of Akkad.

LUGARD, FREDERICK JOHN DEALTRY LUGARD, Baron (1858–1945), British colonial servant whose name is inseparable from the history of modern Nigeria. His first experience of colonial administration was acquired on the North-west Frontier and in Burma. He then filled various quasi-military roles (1888–98), *eg*, four years in Nyasaland and Uganda in the service of the British East Africa Co.; leader of an expedition to Nikki (1894) for the Royal Niger Co., and of another to Bechuanaland (1896) for the British West Charterland Co.; and was Commissioner (1897–99) for the Nigerian hinterland, where his object was to raise the West African Frontier Force and contain French penetration. He married Flora Louise Shaw (d. 1929), *The Times* correspondent on colonial affairs, who had the ear of influential lobbies in Westminster and Whitehall and who coined the name 'Nigeria'.

Like many that followed him to the Muslim emirates of the north, Lugard was a 'Northerner' before he was a 'Nigerian'. His greatest work and satisfaction lay in Northern Nigeria, where he created the expedient of indirect rule on the pre-colonial administrative structure of the Hausa/Fulani kingdoms. Translated into practice, the principles of indirect rule became the favoured system of Native Administration, erected on the four pillars of Native Authority, Native Treasury, and Native Courts, with the District Officer as adviser and supervisor, but never as an executive. Lugard's unshakeable belief in the efficacy of his indirect rule, and in the superiority of emirate administration, blinded him to their potential limitations in the context of other political cultures and dazzled him into rejecting a real chance, however difficult, to unify the country rather than simply to amalgamate the administrations. The lost chance—whether for 'good' or 'bad'—was to be poignantly recalled, along with a similar chance lost at the time of the 1958 Minorities Commission, by Nigerian leaders during the constitutional rethinking in Nigeria's crisis years (1966–70).

Lugard was the architect of the most comprehensive and coherent system of administration in Britain's colonial history. The new historiography generated by African independence has, in general, not extinguished his achievements.

Margery Perham, *Lugard*, 2 vols. (London, 1956, 1960).
Lord Lugard, *The Dual Mandate* (London, 1922).

AHMK-G

LUGDUNUM (mod. Lyons), important Roman colony in Gaul, founded on a Celtic site in 43 BC. It became the capital of the province Gallia Lugdunensis and in 12 BC the centre of the imperial cult for all Roman Gaul except Narbonensis. It was intermittently the site of an imperial mint. It was economically and strategically important because of its situation at the junction of the Rhone and Saone, and was severely damaged in a civil war in AD 197, but survived till the end of the Roman empire, when it became the capital of the Burgundian kingdom.

LUGO, ALONSO DE (c. 1500–c. 1546), *Adelantado* or official leader of the colonization of New Granada, and son of Pedro Fernández de Lugo, founder of Cartagena. Lugo used his influence at court to gain the appointment, thereby thwarting the ambitions of Jiménez de Quesada, but his rule (1542–5) was stormy, and he returned to Spain.

LUKÁCS, GEORGE (1885–   ), Hungarian philosopher and literary critic, whose vast output, spanning more than 60 years, embraced philosophy, aesthetics, and literary criticism, as well as political writings. He became a Marxist after the Russian Revolution, was deputy people's commissar for public education in Bela Kun's short-lived Hungarian Soviet Republic (1919), and then went into exile in Vienna, where he edited the extreme-left journal, *Kommunismus*. In 1923 he published his essays, *History and Class Consciousness*. After the Second World War, when he returned to Hungary, Lukács published some major books of literary criticism, including *Goethe and his Age* (1947), *Thomas Mann* (1948), and *The Historical Novel* (1955), as well as studies of Russian, French, and German Realism. He also published a critique of existentialism, *Existentialism or Marxism?* (1947), and an interpretation of the history of German philosophy as a pointer to the emergence of Hitler, entitled *The Destruction of Reason* (1954). In 1956 he was briefly minister of culture in Nagy's government, but, after the Revolution's suppression, was out of favour for about a decade. He wrote *The Meaning of Contemporary Realism* (1958) and then devoted himself to major works on aesthetics, ethics, and social theory.

LUKE, Saint, Gentile evangelist and physician and, according to tradition, author of the Third Gospel and *Acts of the Apostles*. He accompanied St Paul on his second missionary journey from Troas to Philippi (AD 49) and on his third from Philippi to Jerusalem (53) and went with him to Rome (61), where he stayed during St Paul's captivity. He may have been one of the first members of the Christian community at Antioch and, according to the Anti-Marcionite Prologues, was unmarried. He wrote his Gospel in Greece and died aged 84.

LULLY, JEAN-BAPTISTE (1632–87), Florentine-born French violinist and composer and Master of the Royal Music at Louis XIV's court (1662–87). He developed the *ballet de cour*, collaborated with Molière in comedy-ballets and with the librettist, Quinault, in a series of operas, the first of which was *Fêtes de l'amour et de Bacchus* (1672).

LUMIÈRE, AUGUSTE (1862–1954) and **LUMIÈRE, LOUIS** (1864–1948), photographic pioneers. The Lumière brothers were prolific investigators of the science of photography and gave the first satisfactory demonstration of the projected image to a paying audience (1895) in Paris. The design of their equipment, which was both a camera and a projector, incorporated a claw movement with a 35-mm film, which is still the basis of modern ciné equipment. They introduced (1907) the Autochrome process, the first commercially successful direct colour photographic process.

LUMUMBA, PATRICE (c. 1925–61), first prime minister of the republic of Congo (Leopoldville-Kinshasa), who was prominent in the Belgian Congo's brief pre-independence agitations. Lumumba emerged as the only Congolese leader who stood squarely for an all-Congo nationalism as distinct from the regionalism of his principal opponents. Though a prime minister of energy and courage, he was swept away in the chaos and intrigue which accompanied independence in 1960. Early in 1961 he was seized by those who wished or had been ordered to oust him, handed over to the Katanga secessionists, and murdered.

LUNA, ALVARO DE (d. 1453), favourite of John II of Castile, who assumed virtual control of the monarchy. He fought to curtail the power of the Castilian nobility, whose intrigues led to civil war and their own defeat at Olmedo (1445). Succumbing finally to pressure from the nobility, John had Luna executed.

LUNAR SOCIETY, included as members Boulton, Watt, Erasmus Darwin, Galton, Priestley, and Josiah Wedgwood, who met to discuss natural and applied science, philosophy, education, and psychology. The society, which began c. 1765, received its name (c. 1776) from the time of meetings at full moon. It declined after the Birmingham riots (1791), which were partly directed against scientists.

LUND, Swedish city from the 10th cent. AD onwards, which became a bishopric in the mid-11th cent., and the seat of the primate of all Scandinavia in 1163. It was reduced to a bishopric in 1536.

LUND, BATTLE OF (1676), Swedish victory which enabled Charles XI to reconquer Scania from the Danes. The losses were the heaviest of any inter-Scandinavian battle.

LUND, TREATY OF (1679), ended the Scanian War without loss of territory by Sweden to Denmark, as provided by the Peace of Fontainebleau, already imposed on the Danes by Louis XIV of France. A Swedish–Danish alliance followed.

LUNDY'S LANE, BATTLE OF (25 July 1814), engagement in the War of 1812, near Niagara Falls. US forces under Gen. Jacob Brown, invading Canada, met British troops in a five-hour battle. Both sides claimed victory, but the British remained in command of the field.

LUNÉVILLE, TREATY OF (1801), peace between France and Austria. France acquired the left bank of the Rhine from Switzerland to Holland; the Swiss, Dutch, Cisalpine, and Ligurian republics were recognized; Venice and the Dalmatian coast with eastern Lombardy up to the Adige was kept by France; the Duke of Parma received Tuscany; and the King of Naples was compelled to maintain a French garrison at Taranto. The treaty was a diplomatic success for Napoleon and left Britain the sole survivor of the Second Coalition.

LUNG-SHAN, neolithic archaeological site in east China. Finds include characteristic black pottery dating from perhaps after 1500 BC.

LUO peoples of East Africa, variously divided, but united in their language origins, live in western Kenya under the name of Luo and under other names, and corresponding groupings, in northern and north-eastern Uganda. They appear to have derived from an area of ancient and initial growth and dispersal in the Bahr al-Ghazal (south-western Republic of the Sudan) some time before AD 1000, and most probably much earlier. At some point that is certainly distant these 'original Luo' gave rise to migrations which produced some of the leading peoples of the southern Sudan (Nuer, Dinka, and others). Other migrations took ancestral Luo groups southward into what is now northern Uganda, where they may have arrived c. AD 1300, into north-western Kenya c. AD 1500, and into the present area of Luo habitat in western Kenya c. AD 1700. Originally stock-raisers, a number of Luo groups have developed a successful agriculture, possibly by symbiosis with Bantu agriculturalists among whom they settled. In Kenya in 1970 the Luo formed a large element in the population, and took a leading part in the country's affairs.

LUO UNION, political and social organization of the Luo people of Kenya, was launched in 1946 by Oginga Odinga, Richard Arina, and Walter Odede. In subsequent years it strove, as other ethnic associations were doing, to raise the level of education by collecting funds for classrooms and books and sending students to study abroad. Still later, it became an important factor in the wider movement of Kenya nationalism.

LUPERÓN, GREGORIO (1839–97), Dominican political figure who was one of the leaders of the second Dominican independence movement against Spain (1863). He later led the faction or party known as the 'Blues' in the internal strife in the republic in the 1870s and was provisional ruler in 1879.

LUPUS OF FERRIÈRES (c. 802–65), pupil of Raban Naur at Fulda, who became abbot of Ferrières in 840. He was a close associate of the Emperor Charles the Bald and the scholars Einhard and Hincmar of Rheims and a major figure in the later stages of the Carolingian Renaissance.

LUQUE, HERNANDO DE (d. 1532), Spanish priest and partner with Francisco Pizarro and Diego Almagro in the explorations which led to the conquest of Peru. Resident in Panama, Luque took no active part, but seems to have raised most of the initial capital for the ventures.

LURISTAN BRONZES, large number of bronze and iron objects, mostly weapons, pins, and horse and chariot trappings, found in tombs at Luristan in Iran. They show both Mesopotamian and Scythian influences and probably date from the 8th and 7th cents BC, though some may be forgeries.

LUSIGNAN. In 1191 King Richard I of England, en route for Palestine, took Cyprus from the Byzantines. In 1192 he handed the island to Guy de Lusignan, King of Jerusalem, who ruled it until 1194. Amalric, the brother of Guy, was the real architect of Lusignan rule in Cyprus, reigning there until 1205 and acquiring from the Emperor Henry VI the title of king in 1195, the coronation being carried out in 1197. The direct Lusignan line became extinct in 1267, the House of Antioch-Lusignan holding the throne of Cyprus thereafter until 1474. Lusignan Cyprus reached its apogee under Hugues IV (1324–59) and Peter I (1359–69), this latter monarch being celebrated for his attempt to revive the crusade against the Muslims and for his capture, in 1365, of Alexandria in Egypt. Later the Genoese dominated (1373–4) the affairs of Cyprus. In 1426 the Mamluks of Egypt and Syria invaded the island, crushed the Cypriot forces at Kherokoitia, and compelled the king, Janus, to recognize the sultan as his overlord. The last Lusignan died in 1474. His mother, Catarina Cornaro, of Venetian origin, ruled Cyprus until 1489, when it passed into the possession (1489–1571) of the Signoria.

LUSITANI, ancient tribe of western Spain (now Portugal) which showed mounting opposition to Rome (193–139 BC), reaching its climax under Viriathus, who forced the Romans briefly to recognize their territory as independent. After forming part of the province of Further Spain, Lusitania became an imperial province under Augustus (?27 BC).

LUSITANIA, British passenger liner sunk off Ireland by a German U-boat on 7 May 1915, with the loss of 1198 lives, including 198 American citizens, ie, neutrals. The incident provoked severe anti-German riots in England, and led the US to threaten diplomatic action against Germany. The Kaiser, William II, later banned unrestricted submarine warfare, but it was reintroduced in Jan. 1917 and contributed largely to America's entry into the First World War a month later.

LUTE, pear-shaped, plucked string instrument of oriental origin, which became known throughout western Europe during the crusades, flourished particularly in the 16th cent., but fell into disuse during the 18th cent.

LUTFI PASHA (reg. 1538–41), Ottoman Grand Vizier of Albanian origin. As grand vizier he showed himself to be an able statesman. After 1541 he devoted himself to historical and related studies. His most important works are a chronicle of the Ottoman empire (*Tawarikh-i Al-i Osman*) and a valuable treatise of guidance for high officials engaged in public affairs, the well-known *Asaf-name*.

LUTHER, HANS (1879–1962), German politician and chancellor (1925–6) during the Weimar republic. After serving as minister of food under Cuno (1922–3) he was appointed finance minister in succession to Hilferding and held this post under Stresemann and Marx until 1925, when he formed his own cabinet. His major achievement in this period was the reform of the currency and stabilization of the budget after the catastrophic inflation of 1923–4. Following the prolonged government crisis of 1924, Luther managed to form a cabinet in Jan. 1925, in which the Nationalist Party was for the first time strongly represented. With Stresemann as his foreign minister, he signed the Locarno pact in Dec. 1925, but resigned immediately afterwards in the face of right-wing criticism. However, it proved impossible for an alternative government to be formed, and Luther returned to office in Jan. 1926. He remained chancellor until May, when he was forced to resign after a dispute over the sensitive constitutional issue of Germany's post-1918 national colours. He was later president of the Reichsbank (1930–3) and ambassador to the US (1933–7).

Luther belonged to no political party, and believed ideally in a strong presidency supported by a cabinet of non-party experts, *ie*, the so-called *Fachregierung*. His inability to understand or operate the machinery of parliamentary government was highly detrimental to its standing, and he typified the failure of many conservative though non-Nazi politicians to appreciate the importance of maintaining and strengthening the organs of democratic government in the precarious republic.

LUTHER, MARTIN (1483–1546), German Protestant reformer, who studied law, and both the Old and New Testaments, in particular the Psalms and the Epistle to the Romans, at Erfurt University. He then became an Augustinian monk and a professor at Wittenberg University. On a visit to Rome (1511) he was dismayed by its wealth and spiritual emptiness, compared with the transparent pieties of the Augustinian mystics on whom he pondered in his cell.

When the Dominican Tetzel came to Germany (1517) to sell indulgences for the remission of sin, Luther exhibited 95 theses attacking, in principle, the efficacy of justification by works. It was an offer of academic disputation, a typical Augustinian protest against the scholastic ascendancy won for the Dominicans by the massive authority of Aquinas. It might have remained a purely domestic quarrel if the ecclesiastical authorities, alarmed at the sudden decline in the traffic in indulgences, had not ordered Luther to retract.

When examined at Augsburg (1518), Luther said that general councils had an authority superior to the pope's, but in a disputation with Eck at Leipzig (1519) he declared that councils too were capable of error and that some of the 'heresies' attributed to Hus were conformable with the gospel. Luther was convinced by now that the gospel was the only true source of doctrine, and that salvation was offered to believers through the love and goodness of God.

In 1520 he wrote three pamphlets that set the Reformation on its course. *On the Liberty of a Christian Man* asserted that faith was the only means of salvation; *On the Babylonish Captivity of the Church* renounced all but three of the seven sacraments; and the *Address to the Nobility of the German Nation* urged the princes to cast off the unscriptural supremacy of Rome and personally undertake the reform of their churches. When Leo X issued a bull condemning him as a heretic, Luther solemnly burnt it, along with the decretals and the books of canon law.

He was duly excommunicated, but political circumstances were in his favour. The Emperor Charles V was at odds with the pope, and the German princes were always anxious to defy papal authority. At the Diet of Worms (1521) the princes prevented Luther's outright condemnation, and Frederick of Saxony harboured him at Wartburg castle, where he translated the New Testament into German.

Although Luther quarrelled with Erasmus over the freedom of the will and lost support by his savage attack on the peasants' revolt (1524–5), German patriotism and Charles V's vast conflicting interests ensured the survival of his movement. At Marburg (1529) he fell out with the Zwinglians over the doctrine of the Real Presence, but, for the diet of 1530, his colleague Melanchthon prepared the placatory Augsburg Confession, accepted by the majority of German Protestants as a declaration of their faith. In the subsequent years of warfare and political manœuvre Luther ceased to be in the forefront of events, but the movement that bore his name continued to be unmistakably his. He preached widely, composed catechisms and hymns, completed his translation of the Old Testament (1534), and in the company of his wife,

a recalcitrant nun, delivered the *Table Talk* from which his dutiful disciples compiled a supplementary scripture.

Doctrinally, Luther always denied any revolutionary intent and protested that he was reviving pure Christianity freed of later glosses and corruptions. He rejected transubstantiation, but asserted a consubstantial Presence at the Eucharist. Three of the sacraments, baptism, the Eucharist, and private confession, were retained, as were vestments and certain Catholic ceremonies, but the clergy were released from celibacy, the communion cup was given to the laity, the Bible and liturgy were translated into the vernacular, the intercession of saints was no longer sought, and endowments were diverted for pastoral and educational purposes.

The core of Lutheran doctrine is the authority of scripture and the attainment of salvation through faith. Luther rejected the conception of a God constructed in man's image and required to be comprehensible by reason, since God is neither rational nor human. Salvation depends upon God's overflowing grace, which may seem arbitrary and by human standards unjust, but it is not a debt that God owes to man as a reward for good behaviour. God is not a judge working out his obligations by a mechanical process. He is love and his grace is given to those who believe in him.

R. H. Bainton, *Here I Stand* (London, 1952).
G. Ebeling, *Luther: an introduction to his thought* (London, 1970).   MMR

LUTHULI, ALBERT JOHN (1898–1967), chief of the Groutville African community in Natal, and a devoted Christian, who became president of the African National Congress in South Africa in 1952. Despite his being banned by the Nationalist government, he was able to attract mass support for Congress for the first time. In 1960 he received the Nobel Peace Prize.

LUTTER, BATTLE OF (1626), near Brunswick, defeat inflicted on Christian IV of Denmark by the Imperialists under Tilly, who made skilful use of his artillery.

LÜTTWITZ, WALTER VON (1859–1942), German general and military leader in the unsuccessful Kapp putsch of March 1920. Though originally loyal to the new republic's government, he resented the enforced disbandment of the *Freikorps* and was persuaded to participate in Kapp's venture. His troops occupied Berlin for four days until the putsch collapse, when he fled abroad. He was allowed to return to Germany in 1925.

LÜTZEN, BATTLES OF (1632, 1813), near Leipzig. In 1632, during the Thirty Years War, the forces of Wallenstein were defeated in a hard-fought battle in which Gustavus Adolphus met his death. On 2 May 1813, in the French Wars, the combined Russian and Prussian armies under Wittgenstein and Blücher met Napoleon's advance guard south-east of Lützen. Napoleon forced his opponents to withdraw after inflicting heavy casualties on them, but his own losses prohibited a vigorous pursuit.

LUWIANS, Indo-European-speaking people related to the Hittites and settled by the 2nd millennium BC in southern Anatolia. Their language survived the destruction of Hittite power in the 12th cent. and is recognizable in the neo-Hittite hieroglyphic inscriptions of Syria (12th–8th cents) and in classical Lycian. Possible earlier affinities have been seen with the undeciphered language of Linear A in use on Crete during the first half of the 2nd millennium.

LUXEMBOURG, FRANÇOIS-HENRI DE MONTMORENCY-BOUTEVILLE, Duc de (1625–95), French soldier, who fought against the French Crown during the Fronde and for a time served in the Spanish army. For this reason he was distrusted by Louis XIV, owing much of his advancement to the patronage of Condé. During the Dutch War (1672–8) he served on the Rhine and in Flanders and commanded the French forces at St Denis (1678). He later fell from favour and for a time (1680) was imprisoned in the Bastille. On the outbreak of the War of the League of Augsburg he was denied command until 1690. Thereafter his career was marked by successive military victories—at Fleurus (1690), the siege of Mons (1691), and of Namur (1692), Steinkirk (1692), and Neerwinden (1693).

LUXEMBURG, ROSA (1870–1919), Polish Socialist leader, who was influential in both Polish and German social democracy. She was a fervent internationalist and revolutionary, who helped to split her native Polish party over the nationalist issue and opposed revisionism. She took part in the Russian revolution (1905), but, unlike Lenin, advocated the general strike and mass action as revolutionary weapons.

In her critique of Marxist economy, *The Accumulation of Capital* (1903), she pioneered the theory of imperialism as a necessary stage of capitalism. With Karl Liebknecht, she founded *Spartakusbund* and the German Communist Party (1918). She welcomed the Bolshevik revolution, but in her fragmentary essay on it expressed fear of the consequences of a policy of terror. She was murdered in Jan. 1919.

LUXEMBURGS, German family who began as minor counts in Luxemburg (eastern Netherlands) and rose to great power through the election of Count Henry as German emperor (*reg.* 1308–13). His principal achievement was to procure the marriage of his heir, John, to the heiress of the kingdom of Bohemia. Henry's grandson, Charles, was elected emperor in 1347. The dynasty ended in 1437 with the death of Charles's son Sigismund, whose territorial claims passed to the Habsburgs.

LUYNES, CHARLES MARQUIS D'ALBERT, Duc de (1578–1621), French courtier and favourite of the young Louis XIII. He conspired in the murder of Concini (24 April 1617) and helped Louis to seize control of France from the queen mother, Marie de Medici, who was subsequently exiled to Blois (1617). He became constable of France (1621).

LY DYNASTY, reigning dynasty of Viet-nam (1009–1225). Its founder, Ly Thai-To (*reg.* 1009–28), established the capital at Thang-Long (mod. Hanoi), and reformed the army and the taxation system. Further organization of the kingdom was carried out by his successors, and the state which they created proved strong enough to resist a major Chinese attack in 1077. Tribute was sent to the Sung capital, but there was no further question of direct Chinese administration. The 11th cent. saw two wars with Champa, to the south, as a result of which the Chams lost territory to the Viet-namese in 1069. In the 12th cent. the Chams were assisted by the Khmers, and in 1128, 1138, and 1150 attacks were made on Viet-nam from Angkor, but without serious effect. In the later 12th cent. the imperial clan declined in power, and after their reliance on Tran Ly to suppress a revolt in 1209 the Tran family became increasingly prominent. In 1225 the Ly gave way to the Tran dynasty. During the Ly period there was a gradual increase in the importance of Confucianism, but it was not yet the dominant orthodoxy of the Viet-namese court. The period was more significant for the prominence of *Mahayana* Buddhism, which was extensively practised by the imperial clan. Many pagodas were built, and on several occasions monks were sent by the emperor to obtain Buddhist texts from China.

LY THUONG KIET (1019–1105), Viet-namese soldier, who was related to the Ly dynastic house. In 1068–9 he led an attack on Champa which resulted in the acquisition of three Cham provinces by Dai-Viet. He was responsible for preventing a Chinese conquest of Dai-Viet in 1077. From 1082 till his death he was governor of the southerly province of Thanh-Hoa and defeated a serious Cham attack in 1104.

LYALL, SIR ALFRED COMYN (1835–1911), British colonial official in India (1856–87), who was appointed governor-general's agent in Rajputana (1874). He became foreign secretary to the government of India (1878–81), and lieutenant-governor of the North-West Provinces (1882–7). He served on the India Council (1888–1903). He wrote *The Rise and Expansion of the British Dominion in India* (1893) and *Asiatic Studies* (1882, 1889).

LYAUTEY, HUBERT (1854–1934), French soldier, colonial administrator, and marshal of France (1921). He became Galliéni's chief of staff during the Tonkin campaign of 1894, went with him to Madagascar (1897), and saw the French enclosure of that island. In 1904–6 he served in Algeria, but his life's work was in Morocco, where he became French resident-general (1912–16, 1917–25), and which he transformed into a French protectorate. An intelligent authoritarian administrator, his paternalist concepts about the French civilizing mission were to form the basis of many of the principles of French colonial doctrine, applied elsewhere after the First World War.

LYCURGUS (*fl.* 12th–8th cents BC), legendary Spartan lawgiver. He was credited with (5th–4th cents) creating the political, military, social, and economic structure of classical Sparta. Some time in the 7th cent., in consequence of Sparta's recent conquest of Messenia, Spartan institutions underwent considerable reform. Possibly the reformers then first appealed to the authority of Lycurgus as the traditional, but conveniently obscure, Spartan lawgiver. This precedent was followed by many subsequent reformers at Sparta, *eg*, Agis IV and Cleomenes III (3rd cent.). Political theorists from the 4th cent. onwards added to the confusion. By Plutarch's time (*c.* AD 100) the Lycurgan tradition comprised, in some complexity, Spartan reform programmes of widely different date and purpose.

LYCURGUS (d. 324 BC), Athenian orator, who maintained the spirit of resistance to Macedon after Philip II's victory in 338. He reconstructed the Lyceum, Gymnasium, and theatre of Dionysus, and proposed official preservation of the tragedies of Aeschylus, Sophocles, and Euripides.

LYDIA, kingdom of Asia Minor, prominent in the 7th and 6th cents BC. Having conquered a number of Ionian cities, Lydia enjoyed great prosperity, based on trade between east and west, in furtherance of which coinage was developed. The last Lydian king, Croesus, was deposed by Cyrus II (547).

LYGDAMIS (*fl.* 6th cent.), Tyrant of Naxos, ancient Greek city-state in the Aegean, established *c.* 540 with Peisistratus' help in return for his assistance in establishing Peisistratus at Athens (*c.* 545). Subsequently he was friendly with Polycrates of Samos (*c.* 535–522). Lygdamis was expelled from Naxos by the Spartans in 525.

LYLY, JOHN (?1554–1606), English novelist, dramatist, and politician. He wrote the novel *Euphues* (2 parts, 1578–80) and his creation of the style 'euphism' and his plays, *eg*, *Endimion* (1591), were the first high comedies written in English prose. He was an MP (1589–1601) and supported the bishops in the Martin Marprelate controversy.

LYNCH, ELIZA ALICE (or ELISA ALICIA) (1835–86), Irish mistress and adviser of the Paraguayan dictator, Francisco Solano López. López met her in Paris and took her back to Paraguay (1854). She bore him several children and accompanied him into battle during the War of the Triple Alliance.

LYNCH, JACK (1917–   ), Irish politician and prime minister of the Republic of Ireland after 1966. He became prime minister as a compromise candidate in 1966 and his principal problem was to strike a balance between the traditional militancy of his Fianna Fail party in the demand for a United Ireland and the constraints imposed by the de facto existence of Northern Ireland. A detente between North and South had been heralded by talks between Lynch's predecessor, Sean Lemass, and the Northern premier, Terence O'Neill, in 1965; but the crisis in the North beginning in Oct. 1968 soon developed along traditional lines to reopen the division between North and South. Lynch at first succeeded in combining the maximum appeal to republican sentiment with the minimum of embarrassing commitment of Irish resources when he twice asked the United Nations to intervene in Northern Ireland or when he set up refugee centres and field hospitals near the border. Lynch's position was, however, seriously challenged in early 1970 when two of his senior cabinet ministers were dismissed and later charged (but acquitted) in connection with the illegal importation of arms to Northern Ireland. The effect on the solidarity of the government and the Fianna Fail party was not, however, as great as might have been expected.

LYNCH, SIR THOMAS (d. ?1684), English colonial governor of Jamaica. On the conclusion of peace with Spain (1667), he was charged with the task of suppressing piracy. Lynch was appointed lieutenant-governor in 1670 and governor in 1682.

LYNDHURST, JOHN SINGLETON COPLEY, Baron (1772–1863), English lawyer and judge, who achieved fame by his successful defence of several radicals. He served the Tory Party as solicitor-general (1819), attorney-general (1824), master of the rolls (1826), and lord chancellor (1827–30). He was appointed by Grey to be chief law baron, his judgments being acknowledged as brilliant; at the same time he advised on opposition to the reform bill (1832) and other Whig measures, and assisted in the reform of the criminal law. He resumed office under Peel (1834, 1841–6), retiring as lord chancellor on the fall of the administration.

LYNE, SIR WILLIAM JOHN (1844–1913), Australian politician, who entered NSW politics in 1880, and was prime minister (1899–1901). He served under Edmund Barton in the first Commonwealth ministry and held various portfolios (1901–9).

LYONS, DAME ENID MURIEL (1897–   ), Australian politician. She was the widow of the Australian prime minister J. A. Lyons and became the first woman member of the House of Representatives (1943–57) and the first woman Commonwealth minister (1949–57). She was later a member of the Australian Broadcasting Commission.

LYONS, JOSEPH ALOYSIUS (1879–1939), Australian politician, who was a Tasmanian Labor MP (1908–29) and prime minister (1923–8). He left state for Commonwealth politics in 1929 and achieved cabinet rank under J. H. Scullin, after the ALP's electoral victory in that year. He left the ALP in 1931 after disagreeing over economic depression policies and became prime minister in a coalition with Nationalists, as head of United Australia party governments (1931–9).

LYONS, second city of France after Paris. It owes its importance primarily to its favourable position at the junction of the Rhone and Saone rivers. A leading city of Roman Gaul (called *Lugdunum*), it became permanently part of the kingdom of France in 1312. As a base for French military enterprises in Italy and as the chief residence of the Italian merchants trading in France, Lyons, between 1494 and 1560, became one of the most important European business centres, especially for the marketing of silks and other textiles. In the 17th and 18th cents an important native silk industry was developed. In 1793 the city was destroyed for leading provincial revolts against the Jacobin dictatorship at Paris, but it was repopulated and rebuilt after 1794. In the 19th cent. it became a leading industrial and financial centre of France

and the Credit Lyonnais emerged as one of the greatest European banks.

LYONS, TREATY OF (1601), peace settlement which Henry IV of France concluded with Charles Emmanuel of Savoy to prevent Spanish intervention in the Savoy war. Henry agreed to withdraw from Italy, ceding Saluzzo to Savoy, but received the French-speaking territories of Bresse, Bugey, Valrouey, and Gex, just north of Lyons.

LYSANDER (d. 395 BC), Spartan admiral, whose skill and effective co-operation with the Persians led to the final defeat of Athens in the great Peloponnesian War. Temporarily superseded after success at Notium (407), he returned in 405 to win a decisive victory at Aegospotami, and after driving the Athenians from the Aegean reduced Athens to surrender (404). After a triumphant return to Sparta, he lost influence through the unpopularity of his policy towards Athens' liberated subjects and was prevented from suppressing the democratic movement at Athens against the Thirty Tyrants (403). He supported Agesilaus' claim to the kingship, but Agesilaus, when successful, repudiated him (396). He may have influenced the Spartans in provoking the outbreak of the Corinthian War and led an invasion of Boeotia, but was defeated and killed at Haliartus.

LYSIAS (c. 459–c. 380 BC), leading Athenian orator, member of a wealthy Syracusan family living in Athens. After instruction in rhetoric from Tisias at Thurii, he returned to Athens (413), where he owned property and 120 slaves who made shields. He lost them and his brother Polemarchus in the Thirty Tyrants' coup (vividly described in his speech against Eratosthenes) and fled to Megara (404). Returning after the democratic restoration, he became a professional forensic speech-writer, composing over 200 (some 30 are extant) distinguished for clarity rather than emotion and skilfully adapted to his clients' character. In Olympic oration (388) he urged pan-hellenic unity.

LYSIMACHEIA, Greek city strategically situated on the isthmus of the Thracian Chersonnese (Gallipoli), founded by Lysimachus, who suppressed the neighbouring town of Cardia to obtain inhabitants (309 BC). After Lysimachus' death Lysimacheia was possessed in turn by Seleucus, Ptolemy Ceraunus, the Gauls, Ptolemy III, the Aetolian League, and Philip V, and in about 200 it was overcome and destroyed by Thracians. Antiochus III rebuilt and his possession of it caused friction with Rome. After his defeat, Lysimacheia passed to Pergamum (188); it was eventually destroyed by Thracians (c. 144).

LYSIMACHUS (c. 355–281 BC), Macedonian officer of Alexander the Great, who, after Alexander's death, became satrap of Thrace, and after consolidating his control proclaimed himself King of Thrace and thereby a joint successor to Alexander (306). A member of the coalition against Antigonus Monophthalmus, he joined Seleucus and Cassander in defeating him at Ipsus (301), after which he acquired much of western Asia Minor. In Europe he joined Pyrrhus of Epirus in expelling Demetrius Poliorcetes from Macedonia, which he added to his kingdom (287). After being challenged in Asia Minor by Seleucus, he died in battle at Corupedion. Lysimachus' career typifies the energetic self-seeking of the first successors of Alexander the Great.

LYTTELTON OF FRANKLEY, GEORGE LYTTELTON, 1st Baron (1709–73), English politician, who became secretary to Frederick, Prince of Wales (1737). As an active member of the Commons, he attacked Sir Robert Walpole, and opposed Carteret on Walpole's fall. On Carteret's own fall (1744) Lyttleton was appointed a lord of the treasury in the Broad Bottom administration, but resigned on Pelham's death (1754). His friendship with William Pitt the Younger ended with his refusal to oppose Newcastle. He became chancellor of the exchequer in 1755, but resigned with Newcastle in 1756, and was created Baron Lyttelton. He became reconciled with Pitt (1764) in order to oppose Bute. He later advocated stronger measures against the American colonists and supported Wilkes. His powerful political connections—the Pitts and the Grenvilles—explain his importance in parliament.

LYTTON, EDWARD ROBERT BULWER-LYTTON, 1st Earl of (1831–91), British colonial servant, diplomat, and man of letters, who was viceroy and governor-general of India (1876–80). He held diplomatic appointments in Belgrade, Vienna, Copenhagen, Athens, Lisbon, Madrid, and Paris, and declined the governorship of Madras. Disraeli later appointed him as viceroy of India, where he was confronted by severe famine (1876–8) in Mysore, the Deccan, Madras, and northern India. The 'temple' or reduced ration was introduced, but abandoned as being insufficient. A Famine Commission was appointed and its recommendations were embodied in a famine code. Lytton owed much to his able finance minister, John Strachey, on whose advice he abolished the internal customs line from Attock to the Deccan. Against the advice of his executive council, he reduced import duties on imported textiles, thereby favouring Lancashire goods. He developed the system of financial decentralization initiated under Lord Mayo. He passed the Vernacular Press Act (1878) to suppress abusive criticism of the government of India, but it was repealed four years later. He favoured a forward-looking policy on the north-west frontier rather than one of non-intervention. He supported Robert Sandeman's advance into Baluchistan and the occupation of Quetta. The refusal of Sher Ali of Afghanistan to allow a British mission to cross the frontier at Ali Masjid furnished Lytton with his famous *casus belli* for the Second Afghan War (1878–80). By the treaty of Gandamak (1879), Yakub Khan agreed to accept a British Resident at Kabul. Within a few months Cavagnari and his escort were massacred. This led to the second phase of the war, when British troops under Lord Roberts occupied Kabul.

Lytton was ambassador to France (1887–91). He wrote poetry under the name of Owen Meredith.

B. Balfour, *The History of Lord Lytton's Indian Administration* (London, 1899).   CCD

LYTTON REPORT (1932), League of Nations commission of enquiry in Manchuria, arising out of the Mukden incident. The Japanese invasion of Manchuria (Sept. 1931) presented the first major test for the league. China appealed to the League Council under Article XI of the Covenant, a procedure requiring a solution acceptable to both sides. The proposal to send a commission of enquiry, delayed while unsuccessful attempts were made at conciliation, was finally adopted (21 Nov.), at the Japanese suggestion, instead of the more drastic alternative of invoking Article XV, under which one side could be condemned as an aggressor. The five-man commission, chaired by the 2nd Earl of Lytton and representing Britain, France, Germany, Italy, and the US, did not leave till 3 Feb. 1932. In that month Japan invaded Shanghai and China did invoke Article XV, but the investigations under that article were carried out by a separate committee. The Lytton Report appeared on 2 Oct. 1932. It rejected the pretexts for the Japanese invasion of Manchuria, denied the independence of Manchukuo (a puppet state set up by Japan), and recommended the establishment of a genuinely autonomous state in Manchuria under Chinese sovereignty. By the mid-1930s the report came to be viewed by critics of the National government as a formal league condemnation of Japan on which Britain, and Sir John Simon in particular, had failed to act. However, the report acknowledged that Japanese economic rights had suffered from Chinese inability to maintain order. Even had Japan been condemned as an aggressor, sanctions were militarily impossible. Japan asked for six weeks to study the report, which was not discussed by the League Council until Nov. and was adopted by the assembly in Dec. But world opinion was preoccupied by the Disarmament Conference and the American Depression. Japan invaded Jehol in Feb. before leaving the league in March 1933.

LYUBECH, AGREEMENT OF (1097), attempt to settle disagreements between the branches of this Russian princely family, which had led to protracted civil wars. This was especially so in the first part of the reign of Svyatopolk II (1093–1113), owing to the breakdown of the arrangements made by Iaroslave the Wise for the division of the Russian state among his descendants. Under the Lyubech Agreement each member of the princely family was guaranteed the right to his patrimonial inheritance.

LYUH WOON-HYUNG (1883–1947), Korean communist, who proclaimed a 'Korean People's Republic' in Aug. 1945; but no major politician joined his 'government' and the occupation authorities refused to recognize him. He was subsequently almost a lone moderate in a period when extremists dominated Korean politics, and he was assassinated in 1947.

MA AL-AINAIN, Muhammad al-Mustafa (d. 1910), scholar and teacher. Technically the Moroccan sultan's rice-regent (*khalifa*) in the western Sahara from 1858, he became the de facto ruler of the Saharan town of Smara, which he began to build as his capital just before 1900. He formed the Ainiyya fraternity which established branches in Morocco, and attempted to unite the schools of Muslim mysticism into a new eclectic order. He pursued an activist policy of armed resistance to French expansion from Mauritania, and subsequently transferred his headquarters to Tiznit in southern Morocco. In 1910 he made a bid for Muslim allegiance in Morocco, but his supporters were defeated at Tadla near Fez. Smara, still unfinished, was sacked, and its library burnt.

MA'AFU HENELE (Ma'afu'otu'itoga) (*c.* 1816–81), Tongan high chief in Fiji, who was appointed (1853) by his royal cousin Taufa'ahau (George Tupou I) as governor of the turbulent eastern Fiji Tongan warrior population. He challenged the rising power of Cakobau (Mbau), but later became heir to Taufa'ahau's own Fijian ambitions (1869) and (1871) his viceroy. This uneasy relationship ended with the British annexation (1874) and Ma'afu's appointment as Roko Tui.

MA'ARRI AL, ABU L-ALA (AD 973–1057), Arab poet, who wrote the 'Luzumiyat' and the 'Risalat al-Ghufran' (a treatise on forgiveness). It has been claimed that the 'Risalat' influenced Dante's *Divine Comedy*.

MAASTRICHT, fortress situated 89 kms east of Brussels, giving control of the Meuse river (Maas) and communications with the Rhine. It was captured during the Thirty Years War by Frederick Henry of Orange after a siege which the imperial commander, Count Pappenheim, tried in vain to relieve (Aug. 1632). During the Franco-Dutch War (1672–8) it became one of France's main objectives. Maastricht belonged to the Elector of Cologne, but was garrisoned by the Dutch, and was besieged and captured by the French (June 1673). The siege, the first in history to be directed by a trained engineer, Sebastien le Prestre de Vauban, was a masterpiece of military art.

MABILLON, JEAN (1632–1707), French Benedictine scholar and historian of the Congregation of St Maur at Saint-Germain-des-Prés. His *De Re Diplomatica* (1681) laid the foundation of the science of diplomatics; he also wrote *De Liturgia Gallicana* (1685), the history of the order of St Benedict (1703–39), and edited St Bernard's works (1667).

MABINOGION, general title given to eight prose tales in medieval Welsh which are the only remnants of a once extensive corpus of stories now known only through brief references in other sources. The eight tales of the *Mabinogion* are of different origins and dates. The earliest are *The Four Branches of the Mabinogi* (mid-11th cent.), which is largely mythological in content, and *Culhwch and Olwen* (early 11th cent.), which is one of the earliest Arthurian tales. *The Dream of Rhonabwy* (13th cent.) is the only other native Arthurian story in Welsh, but this is literary rather than traditional in conception. Three Arthurian romances, also of the 13th cent., *Peredur, The Lady of the Fountain, Geraint and Enid*, bear a strong resemblance to three romances by Chrétien de Troyes and may show French influence. The remaining two tales, *Lludd and Llevelys* and *The Dream of Maxen*, are imaginative speculations on the traditional early history of the Welsh. Apart from their literary qualities, these tales are important for the light they throw on the origins of the medieval romances.

MAC CUU (d. 1736), Chinese adventurer who, following the collapse of resistance to the Ch'ing dynasty in south China in the 1680s, took to the seas and established himself at Ha-Tien on the Gulf of Siam. He received recognition from the Cambodian king, and in the early 18th cent. made Ha-Tien into an important entrepôt. His son, Mac Thien Tich, ruled there (1736–77), during which time Ha-Tien became increasingly a dependency of the Viet-namese; it was finally absorbed into Viet-nam in the Tay-Son period.

MAC DYNASTY, reigning dynasty of northern Viet-nam (Tongking) (1527–92). Mac Dang Dung, having emerged as the most powerful figure at the Le court in 1520–1, seized the throne and established his own dynasty in 1527. He made his son emperor, but was himself the effective ruler until his death in 1541. He was unable, however, to control the southern provinces, where the Le dynasty was restored in 1532, and the power of the Mac was therefore always limited to Tongking. There were short wars between the rival dynasties in 1559–60 and in the 1570s. Finally, in 1592 a Le army, led by Trinh Tung, recovered Hanoi; and after four more years of fighting, the Mac were forced to retreat to Cao-Bang in the far north. They were saved from liquidation by Chinese protection, which enabled them to survive at Cao-Bang until 1677. Not a great deal is known of the internal politics of the Mac period, since the chronicles were written by Le supporters, whose main concern was with their own dynasty.

MACADAM, JOHN LOUDON (1756–1836), British engineer, whose main achievement was in concentrating on well-drained and well-organized repair of roads, at relatively low cost. His name is perpetuated in the word 'macadamize', although other leading engineers of this period also made roads of small stones bonded together by the weight of traffic. Macadam's most original work was his attempt to consolidate the Turnpike Trusts round London into a coherent road system, but the coming of the railways ended this by destroying the economic basis of the trusts.

McADOO, WILLIAM GIBBS (1863–1941), US lawyer and politician, who became active in Democratic politics. He helped to manage Woodrow Wilson's presidential campaign (1912) and served in his cabinet as secretary of the treasury (1913–18). He also served as first chairman of the Federal Reserve Board and was director-general of railroads (1917–1919). He was a leading contender for the Democratic nomination for president in 1920, and in 1924 he led for over 100 ballots at the Democratic convention before losing to John W. Davis. He moved to CA (1922) and came to dominate the state Democratic Party. His support for F. D. Roosevelt on the fourth ballot at the Democratic national convention in 1932 ensured Roosevelt's nomination. He served as US senator from CA (1933–8).

MACANAZ, MELCHIOR RAFAEL DE (1670–1760), Spanish lawyer and the first general intendant of Aragon (1711), who tried to reform the fiscal and administrative systems of Spain in the early Bourbon period (1707–13), but was exiled by Guidice (1715) to Bayonne. He is also known for his political *Testament of Spain* (1740), which expressed the Spaniards' guilt at their imperial tradition.

MacANDREW, JAMES (1820–87), NZ politician, who was twice superintendent of Otago province (1860–1, 1867–76) and colonial minister of public works (1877–9).

MACAO, small peninsula about 100 kms south of Canton, the base of Portuguese traders and missionaries in China from 1535. For the privilege, the Portuguese paid an annual fee to the Chinese local authorities. The Portuguese appointed officials to govern the area as though it were a colony. During the decades before the Opium War, other Western traders also operated from Macao; but after the opening of the treaty ports (1842) its importance declined. In 1887, Macao formally became a Portuguese colony, and remained so in 1970.

MACAPAGAL, DIOSDADO (1910–   ), Philippine lawyer, politician, and president of the republic of the Philippines (1961–5). He was legal assistant in the office of the president of the Philippine Commonwealth until the outbreak of the Second World War. During the war he raised funds for the guerrillas. Later, as a member of the department of foreign affairs, he successfully negotiated with the British for the transfer of the Turtle Islands to the Philippines in 1948. He was elected congressman of the first district of Pampanga (1949) and proposed several laws for social reform. He became vice-president in 1957. As president, he decontrolled the peso, pressed forward the passage of the Agricultural Land Reform Code in 1963 (an improvement of the 1955 Land Reform Act), and embarked on a five-year socio-economic programme. He also proposed 'Maphilindo'—an alliance of Malaysia, Indonesia, and the Philippines—and filed the Philippines' formal claim to North Borneo (Sabali). He lost the presidency to F. E. Marcos in 1965.

MacARTHUR, DOUGLAS (1880–1968), US general, who rose to be chief of staff (1930–5). After retiring, he became military adviser to the Philippine government (1935–7), was recalled to active service in 1941, and appointed commander of US forces in the Far East in the Second World War. As Supreme Allied Commander in the south-west Pacific (1942–5), he led the successful campaigns which culminated in the recapture of the Philippines. In 1945 he became commander of the occupation forces in Japan and presided over Japan's postwar recovery. He was commander of UN forces in Korea (1950), but his public disagreement with President Truman over military strategy led to his dismissal in 1951. He returned to the US for the first time in 15 years to a hero's welcome, and in the ensuing congressional investigation of US policy in the Far East lent his weight to Republican attacks on the administration.

MACARTHUR, JOHN (1767–1834), New South Wales Corps officer, rum trader, pastoralist, and protagonist in the struggles with NSW colonial governors before, during, and after the Bligh mutiny. He was also a founder of Australia's merino wool industry. His fleeces attracted British clothiers and won him the patronage of Lord Camden, through whom he obtained 5000 acres (20 sq. kms) of the colony's finest Cowpastures land. After retiring from the army he devoted himself to his flocks. Colonial quarrels led him to spend a long period in England (1809–17), during which he developed the British market for his wool. He returned to Australia in 1817 and by the mid-1820s 'Camden Park' was recognized as the show place in the colony's wool industry. His wife, Elizabeth Macarthur (1769–1850), left a vivid correspondence which is a valuable original source for early colonial history.

MACARTNEY, GEORGE MACARTNEY, Earl (Irish) Lord (1737–1806), British colonial servant and diplomat. He was envoy extraordinary to the Empress of Russia (1764–7) and on his return became chief secretary for Ireland. In 1775 he was appointed governor and captain-general of Grenada, the Grenadines, and Tobago, but was forced to surrender to the French (1779). As governor of Madras (1781–5) his relations with Warren Hastings illustrated the difficulty of the governor-general in controlling the subordinate presidencies. In 1792 he was sent as ambassador to China, but failed to procure commercial concessions. In 1795 he went on a confidential mission to Louis XVIII. He was governor of the Cape of Good Hope (1797–8).

MACARTNEY, SIR SAMUEL HALLIDAY (1833–1906), Scottish-born physician and diplomat, who served under the Chinese government. He went to China as a military physician in the British forces in the Arrow War. Later, he fought the Taiping rebels, first with the 'Ever-Victorious Army' and then under Li Hung-chang. He was instrumental in helping the latter to found the Kiangnan arsenal. In 1876, he accompanied Kuo Sung-tao's mission to Britain and became councillor and English secretary to the Chinese legation in London (1876–1906).

MACAULAY OF ROTHLEY, THOMAS BABINGTON MACAULAY, Baron (1800–59), British historian and Whig politician, who became commissioner of bankruptcy (1828), MP (1830), commissioner and secretary of the Indian board of control (1832), and legal adviser to the supreme council of India (1833). After a term in India (1834–8), Macaulay became secretary of state for war (1839–41) and paymaster-general (1846–7) when the Whigs returned to power. From 1823 he contributed essays to *The Edinburgh Review*. His *Lays of Ancient Rome* (1842) and collected essays (1843) were well received, but his greatest success was the *History of England to the Death of William III* (1848–61). As a historian Macaulay showed powers of vivid narration and his stress on constitutional and material progress accorded with the spirit of the times, encouraging popular interest in history.

MACAULAY, HERBERT SAMUEL HEELAS (1864–1946), Nigerian civil engineer, journalist, and politician. He represented African views on such controversial issues as the liquor traffic and British land policy in West Africa. After playing a leading part in the Apapa land case (1909–21), he defended the House of Docemo in the latter's clash with the government (1925–31). He founded the first Nigerian National Democratic Party (1923) and was its leader and later its national president (1944–6).

MACAULAY, ZACHARY (1768–1838), English Evangelical clergyman, who was the driving force within the Clapham Sect, the British and Foreign Bible Society, and the Church Missionary Society. He championed the cause of freedom for slaves, for whom he urged the use of Sierra Leone as a home.

MACAULAY'S EDUCATION MINUTE (1835) supported the Anglicists against the Orientalists. T. B. Macaulay, the legal member of the governor-general's council, favoured an English education for Indians in preference to a study of the ancient learning of the Hindus and Muslims. English was to be the chief medium of instruction and western science and literature the chief subjects of study. The minute exerted a lasting influence on education in British India.

MACBETH (*reg.* 1040–57), originally a ruler of Moray in north Scotland, who slew Duncan, King of the Scots in 1040, and seized the kingship for himself. In 1057 he was slain by Malcolm, son of Duncan, who succeeded as King Malcolm III. Macbeth became a figure of folklore and legend and was immortalized by Shakespeare's tragedy.

McCALLUM, SIR HENRY (1852–1919), British colonial servant, who was governor of Ceylon when the first instalment of constitutional advance for many years was conceded (1910), following a memorandum from the Ceylon National Association to the British government, which he forwarded but did not recommend. Two members each of the Legislative Council were elected by the European and Burgher communities and one, on a very restricted franchise, for an 'educated Ceylonese' seat.

McCARREN INTERNAL SECURITY ACT (1950) in US, legislation to control communist activities, named after its sponsor, Senator Patrick A. McCarren, of NV (1876–1954), and passed in reaction to the Cold War, and to revelations of communist infiltration within the US. The act established a Subversive Activities Control Board, provided for the registration of communist and 'front' organizations, prohibited the employment of communists in defence work, and excluded aliens belonging to totalitarian organizations. The act was passed over President Truman's veto.

McCARREN–WALTER IMMIGRATION AND NATIONALITY ACT (1952) in US, legislation to codify immigration laws, named after its sponsors, Senator Patrick A. McCarren of NV (1876–1954) and Representative Francis E. Walter of PA (1894–1963). The general provisions of the 1924 immigration act were maintained, with the annual quota from each immigration area fixed at one-sixth of one per cent of the 1920 US population originating from that area. The total ban against orientals was lifted, but new grounds for the exclusion of 'subversives' were added, and provision made for the deportation of immigrants with 'Communist or Communist front' affiliations, even after they had become citizens. The act was passed over President Truman's veto.

McCARTHY, D'ALTON (1836–98), Canadian politician (1876–98) who broke with the Conservatives when he opposed the Jesuits Estates Act (1889), and thereafter became a leader of anti-Catholic and anti-French opinion.

McCARTHY, JUSTIN (1830–1912), Irish politician, historian, and writer. He made a reputation as a novelist with *Dear Lady Disdain* (1875) and *Miss Misanthrope* (1878), but it was his *History of Our Own Times* (1879–97) which won him general recognition. He entered politics as MP for County Longford (1879) and became vice-chairman of the Home Rule Party under Parnell, for whom he won Londonderry (1886). When the crisis over Parnell's leadership arose, McCarthy became chief of the anti-Parnellites. 46 MPs seceded under him, only 26 remaining with Parnell (1890), and in the next general election his party won an overwhelming majority (1892). He had no strong political ambitions, preferring to write, and he resigned the Irish leadership in favour of John Dillon.

McCARTHYISM in US, anti-communist 'witch hunt' which dominated the early 1950s and was associated with Senator Joseph McCarthy (1909–57). He was an obscure WI circuit judge who, with the aid of an embellished war record, won election to the Senate in 1946. He remained politically insignificant until he announced in a speech at Wheeling, WV (9 Feb. 1950), that he held in his hand a list of 'card-carrying communists' in the US state department. McCarthy's allegations were dismissed by a committee of investigation, but served as the catalyst for a number of tensions in American society. His early charges were not unlike those made by other Republicans who sought to link the failures of US foreign policy, especially in Asia, with treason in high places; a view that was given credibility by the Hiss case (1948–50) and the arrest of the Rosenbergs for atomic espionage (1950). The theme of '20 years of treason' under the Democratic Party, with which McCarthy delighted the 1952 Republican convention, was echoed by many during the campaign. But by this time McCarthyism had generated a momentum of its own which could not be stopped by the Republicans' return to power. From the immunity of the Senate he continued to make unsubstantiated charges, and as chairman of the Permanent Subcommittee on Investigations of the Senate Committee on Government Operations (1953–5), launched over 150 investigations. Although these were virtually without result they created widespread fear and disrupted the work of agencies such as the US Information Service. Such was McCarthy's power that in 1953 he was able to negotiate an agreement with Greek shipping interests to prevent trade with communist countries. This move, which he had no authority to make, was unchallenged by either Secretary Dulles or President Eisenhower. The administration also failed to challenge his access to highly classified information, which he claimed came in an unending stream from his 'Loyal American Underground'. However, when he began to attack the US army (1954) he went too far; the administration closed its ranks and the Senate censured McCarthy for unbecoming conduct. Although he still retained a popular following, his influence in Washington was lost as quickly as it had been won.

Richard H. Rovere, *Senator Joe McCarthy* (London and New York, 1959).
Earl Latham, *The Communist Controversy in Washington from the New Deal to McCarthy* (Cambridge, MA 1966).   AJT

McCLELLAN, GEORGE BRINTON (1826–85), US engineer, soldier, and politician. At the outbreak of the Civil War he organized the Army of the Potomac and became general-in-chief (1861–2), but proved over-cautious in the field. He was Lincoln's Democratic presidential opponent (1864), but carried only three states and afterwards resumed his career as a civil engineer. He served as governor of NJ (1878–81).

McCLURE, SIR ROBERT JOHN LE MESURIER (1807–73), British naval officer who discovered the western entrance to the North-west Passage whilst searching for Sir John Franklin (1850).

McCLURE'S MAGAZINE (1893–1929), US monthly published and edited by Samuel S. McClure (1857–1949). Articles by Lincoln Steffens, R. S. Baker, Ida Tarbell, and others (1900–12) gave the magazine a reputation for popularizing progressive reform.

McCORMICK, CYRUS HALL (1809–1884), US agricultural engineer. The first workable reaping machine, made in 1826 by a Scot, Patrick Bell (1799–1869), was only moderately successful and no firm would manufacture it. In 1833 McCormick patented a harvester of a somewhat different design six months after another had been patented by a fellow American, Obed Hussey (1792–1859). The two men became bitter rivals in the commercial exploitation of their machines, which was stimulated by the decrease in labour during the American Civil War and the consequent necessity for farmers to use machinery. McCormick's firm eventually emerged as the principal American manufacturer. His son, Cyrus Hall McCormick jr (1859–1936), became president of the International Harvester Co.

McCORMICK, JOSEPH MEDILL (1877–1925), US journalist and politician. As a Republican US congressman (1917–19) and senator (1919–25) from IL, he opposed the League of Nations and the Versailles treaty, sponsored the measure that created the Bureau of the Budget (1921), and supported the proposed 'Great Lakes to Gulf waterway'.

McCULLOCH, SIR JAMES (1819–93), Australian politician, who was prime minister of Vic. (1863–8, 1868–9, 1870–1, 1875–7). Under the influence of David Syme, he facilitated the passage of protectionist legislation and weakened the position of the upper house. By tacking social reforms on to financial measures and by alleged abuse of Gov. Darling's support, McCulloch attracted conservative criticism, but he himself swung to the right during the close of his career.

McCULLOCH, JOHN RAMSAY (1789–1864), British journalist, civil servant, and economist. He gave powerful support to Francis Place in his struggle for the repeal of the combination laws (1823–4). His *Principles of Political Economy* (1825) stated, with little modification, Ricardo's analysis of value and of distribution and his theory of wages. But, like John Stuart Mill and Nassau Senior, he advocated a larger sphere of state intervention than some of the first generation of philosophical radicals.

McCULLOCH v. MARYLAND, 4 Wheaton 316 (1819) in the US, Supreme Court case concerning the second Bank of the United States. At issue was the constitutionality of a tax levied by the MD legislature (1818) on the bank's Baltimore branch. The state courts upheld the act, and the bank appealed the case to the US Supreme Court. Chief Justice Marshall, voicing a unanimous decision, upheld the constitutional power of Congress to charter a bank and to have exclusive control over it, denied the right of MY to interfere with the federal government by taxing its agencies, and declared the state law unconstitutional. The long-term significance of this controversial decision lies in Marshall's unequivocal assertion of national sovereignty and the doctrine of implied powers, a broad construction of the US constitution giving the federal government certain implied powers as well as those specifically enumerated.

MacDONALD, JAMES RAMSAY (1866–1937), British politician and first Labour prime minister (1924, 1929–31), who was chiefly responsible for making Labour a party of government. He was born in Scotland and was largely self-educated. He became an evolutionary, undoctrinaire socialist and joined the Independent Labour Party (1894). As secretary of the Labour Representation Committee (1900–6), his skill, industry, and tact contributed to its growth, and in 1906 to its electoral success. He was himself elected at Leicester. As party chairman (1911–14), MacDonald opposed Britain's entry into the First World War and resigned when most of the Labour Party supported it. He was subsequently accused of equivocation and endured public obloquy and electoral defeat (1918).

On being elected for Aberavon (1922), he again became party leader and was, therefore, leader of the Opposition. His moderation and lack of any clearly defined socialistic creed reassured an electorate which saw Labour on the brink of power. He formed a minority government—with liberal forbearance (Jan. 1924)—in which he was foreign secretary as well as prime minister. As an advocate of collective security through the League of Nations, he worked with Briand on the Geneva Protocol and supported the Dawes Plan for revised German reparations. Under his administration Soviet Russia received de jure recognition and a guaranteed loan. MacDonald eschewed co-operation with the Liberals, which pleased most of his supporters. He preserved Labour's identity, but was defeated in a general election (Oct. 1924), and thus the prospect of early radical action was brought to an end.

In 1929 Labour took office as the largest party. The problem of unemployment overshadowed a disarmament-orientated foreign policy. MacDonald's idealistic aspirations could not compensate for his confused thinking and lack of constructive statecraft. During the 1931 financial crisis, a cabinet split was caused by the proposal to cut unemployment benefits by 10 per cent. Instead of resigning, MacDonald formed a National government (1931), which devalued the pound and won a 'doctor's mandate' in an electoral landslide. Labour, with only 52 seats, formally expelled the isolated 'traitor'. Ironically, MacDonald was now nominal head of a Conservative-dominated government, which introduced the means test (1931), increased tariffs (1931–2), and sanctioned British rearmament (1935). In June 1935 he was succeeded

as prime minister by Baldwin, and two years later MacDonald left the government.   MRB

MACDONALD, SIR JOHN ALEXANDER (1815–91), Scottish-born Canadian politician, who was elected to the Upper Canadian House of Assembly as a Tory (1844) and was receiver-general in the Draper–Sherwood ministry (1847–8). He played an important part in the negotiations between the old-style Tories and the Liberal reformers which led to a Liberal–Conservative, later Conservative, Party (1854). In the Macnab–Morin government Macdonald became attorney-general for Canada West. Macdonald proposed (1858) a federal union of the whole of British North America, and this became official Conservative policy. He formed a ministry with George E. Cartier (1858–62). Two years of unstable governments led to the formation of a coalition, which included Macdonald and was committed to confederation. Macdonald played a large part in the Charlottetown and Quebec Conferences (1864) and led the Canadian delegation to a final conference in London (1866). When the British North America Act went into operation (1 July 1867) Macdonald became first prime minister of the Dominion of Canada. Nova Scotian resistance was broken by taking Joseph Howe into the government and increasing the federal subsidy (1869). The Hudson's Bay Co. lands were acquired (1870) and the province of Man. established. BC (1871) and PEI (1873) also joined. Macdonald's attempt to secure the building of a transcontinental railway ended in the Pacific scandal (1873) and the fall of his government. He returned to office in 1878 and chartered the Canadian Pacific Railway (1880); the transcontinental route was completed in 1885. As a firm believer in centralized government, he fought a long battle with Sir Oliver Mowat over provincial rights, which Mowat won. More serious was his government's neglect of the NWT resulting in the disturbances of 1869–70 and the rebellion of 1885. In 1891, reversing his former policy of trying to negotiate a treaty of reciprocity with America (he had tried unsuccessfully to do so in 1871 and 1887), he attacked reciprocity as the first step towards annexation by America, and won a general election on this policy, but over-strained himself.

D. G. Creighton, *John A. Macdonald*, 2 vols (Toronto, 1952, 1955).   AJS

MACDONALD, JOHN SANDFIELD (1812–72), Canadian politician, who entered the House of Assembly (1841) as an independent and reformer. He was solicitor-general (1849), speaker (1852–4), and prime minister (1862–4). Although an opponent of Canadian Confederation, he accepted it, once achieved, and became the first prime minister of Ont. (1867–71).

MacDONALDS OF GLENCOE, Scottish clan which was late in taking the oath of allegiance to the government of King William III. Highland troops of Argyll's regiment, the clan enemy of the MacDonalds, were quartered in Glencoe and after a week of hospitality, massacred their hosts (1692), including the chief of the MacDonald clan, Alexander.

MacDONOUGH, THOMAS (1783–1825), US naval officer, who won the battle of Plattsburg (11 Sept. 1814) in the War of 1812. In gratitude, Congress awarded him a gold medal and NY and VT granted him lands overlooking the battle area.

McDOUGALL, ALEXANDER (1731–86), American soldier and politician, who helped to organize the Sons of Liberty in New York. He was a major-general during the American War of Independence and a member of the Continental Congress.

McDOWELL, IRVIN (1818–85), US soldier, who served in the Mexican War. He commanded Union forces on the

Potomac (1861) and the Rappahannock (1862), but was reprimanded and relieved of his comand following a Union defeat at the second battle of Bull Run (Aug. 1862).

MACEDONIA, KINGDOM OF, in northern Greece, important in antiquity from the 4th to the 2nd cent. BC, when, under Philip II, it subjected the city-states of Greece; under Alexander the Great and his successors, overthrew Persia and spread Greek civilization over the near East; and under Philip V provoked the Romans to expand into the Greek world. It was inhabited by a semi-Greek people under kings claiming descent from Heracles, and before Philip II's accession (359 BC) was only occasionally significant in Greek history (eg, under Perdiccas II in the great Peloponnesian War). Philip II unified and enriched the kingdom and built up a powerful army. He then won control of Greece (338) and initiated the conquest of the Persian empire, carried out by his son Alexander (reg. 335–323). In the Wars of the Successors, Macedonia lost its primacy in the new Hellenistic world as powerful independent kingdoms were established in Egypt and Syria, but was itself comparatively unaffected until c. 295. A period of invasions and instability, including a Gallic raid (279–277), ended with the reign of Antigonus Gonatas (276–239), who until c. 250 maintained a degree of control over Greece, which was regained by Antigonus Doson (224). His successor, Philip V, provoked Rome by an alliance with Syria and aggression in Greece. Defeat in the Second War (197) confined Philip to Macedonia, but his avoidance of further trouble with Rome gave the kingdom a last period of prosperity, before Perseus' disastrous foreign policy brought the Third War and its division into four republics (168).

MACEDONIA, ROMAN, province of the Roman empire organized in 148 BC, after the Fourth Macedonian War, out of the four short-lived Macedonian republics, the extreme south of Illyricum and Epirus, Greece being added in 146. Greece became a separate province in 27 BC and Epirus c. AD 140. Macedonia was important for the land route from the Adriatic to the Hellespont (Via Egnatia), and was a frontier province, where governors were often involved in warfare, until Augustus' advance to the Danube. Thereafter, it flourished peacefully until the troubled period of the 3rd cent., when it was frequently ravaged by barbarian raiders. Its chief cities were Beroea, Philippi, and Thessalonica.

MACEDONIAN QUESTION. By the end of the 19th cent. Macedonia was the last major European province left to the Ottoman empire. Unlike other areas, no single element predominated in the population. Bulgars formed the largest section and there were substantial Greek, Albanian, Vlach, and other groups; they were of mixed religions—Muslims and Christians of Catholic, Bulgarian, and Greek Orthodox persuasions. Accordingly, claims were advanced to parts of Macedonia by Bulgaria, Greece, and Serbia and attempts made to foment revolutions in Macedonia. Through the connections of the Great Powers with the parties involved, the issue became a question of international diplomacy. In 1912 the three Balkan powers with Montenegro reached agreement on the partition of Macedonia and launched the Balkan Wars (1912–13), as a result of which the area was partitioned between them, part being detached to form Albania. Bulgarian dissatisfaction with the division remains (1970) a continuing source of conflict.

MACEDONIAN WARS (214–205, 200–196, 171–168, 149–148 BC) between Macedon and Rome were important stages in Rome's conquest of the Greek world. The First War, following the alliance of Philip V of Macedon with Hannibal, involved little direct confrontation; Rome sought the friendship of Aetolia, of Attalus I of Pergamum, and of Peloponnesian cities, to prevent Philip lending aid to Carthage. The war was confined to Greece, and the treaty of Phoenice (205) left Philip's

power unimpaired. The Second War was declared by Rome (200 BC) partly from resentment at Philip's earlier policy, partly under pressure from the Aetolians, Attalus, and the Rhodians because of Philip's aggressive pressures in the Aegean. This philhellenic gesture, according with Rome's interests of having no powerful eastern rival, won her Greek support. Flamininus ended the war with a victory at Thessalian Cynoscephalae (197); the peace confined Philip to his kingdom, which Rome was anxious to keep intact to preserve the balance of power. Philip until his death (179) remained at peace with Rome, and on accession his son Perseus renewed the alliance. But his increasing influence in Asia and Greece led Eumenes of Pergamum to lay complaints at Rome (172), and the Third War was declared (171). Rome's initial failures caused her allies (Rhodes, Pergamum, the Achaean League) to waver; only with the arrival of the consul for 168, Aemilius Paullus, did the Romans clinch the victory at Pydna. Perseus was captured and brought to Rome, and Macedonia partitioned into four republics. Eventually, a rising under Andriscus, who claimed to be Perseus' son, led to the Roman annexation of Macedonia (147).

MACEDONIANS (867–1056), most famous of all the dynasties which ruled the Byzantine empire. Under the guidance of the Macedonians, and above all in the later years of Basil II (reg. 963–1025), Byzantium attained the summit of its power and splendour.

MACEK, VLADKO (1879–1964), Croatian national leader, who (1928–41) strove to achieve Croatian autonomy without resorting to extremism. In 1928 his demands for federalism antagonized King Alexander, who retaliated by proclaiming a dictatorship emphasizing 'Yugoslavism', and subsequently imprisoned Macek. Macek claimed that the new regime did nothing for Croatia and after Alexander's assassination (1934) he negotiated with Prince Paul, but because he too refused Macek's demands, he co-operated with the democratic Serbs and in 1937 became leader of a united opposition. Nevertheless, his nationalism and distrust of most Serbian politicians proved stronger than his democratic sentiments and in Aug. 1939 he exploited the authoritarian government's fears of the country becoming divided in the event of war, which appeared imminent, and concluded an agreement with the government whereby Croatia was granted autonomy and Macek himself became deputy prime minister. Similarly, two years later, he supported Yugoslavia's adherence to the Tripartite Alliance and only reluctantly continued to serve in the government after the coup d'état. Yet he was not pro-German and refused to head the puppet state of Croatia. He was, however, still unable fully to co-operate with the Serbs, many of whom manifested intensely anti-Croat feelings. For Macek, the fratricidal strife between Serbs and Croats (1941–5) was tragic, but not wholly unexpected. He was unsympathetic to Tito's regime, and in 1945 emigrated to the US.

MACEO, ANTONIO (c. 1845–96), leader of the Cuban struggle for independence against Spain (1867–8). After the collapse of the revolt, Maceo visited Jamaica, the US, Haiti, the Dominican republic, Honduras, Mexico, and Panama in search of money and support for the rebels. In 1890 he was allowed to return to Cuba by the Spanish authorities, but soon became involved again in local revolutionary activities and was forced to leave for Costa Rica. There he organized an invasion of Cuba by exiles, which reached Cuba in April 1895. Soon Maceo became, with Máximo Gómez and José Marti, a principal leader of the revolt in which he was killed during a skirmish. Cuban independence was achieved two years later.

MACEWAN, SIR WILLIAM (1848–1924), Scottish surgeon, who studied the growth and transplantation of bone in man and deer. He was a pioneer in lung surgery and devised a hernia repair (1886). From 1876 he specialized in brain surgery, summarizing his work in *Pyogenic Diseases of the Brain and Spinal Cord* (1893).

McGEE, D'ARCY (1825–68), Canadian journalist, poet, and politician. He was implicated in the abortive 1848 Irish rebellion and fled to America, where he founded the *Nation* (1848–50) and the *American Celt* (1851). In 1857 he moved to Montreal and entered Canadian politics (1858). He became president of the council in the Sandfield Macdonald–Sicotte ministry (1862–3), but later joined the Conservatives and was minister of agriculture in the Taché–J. A. Macdonald government (1864–7). He was a delegate at both the Charlottetown and Quebec Conferences (1864) and spoke in favour of confederation. His opposition to the Fenians' efforts to create disloyalty among Irish immigrants led to his assassination.

McGILLIVARY, ALEXANDER (*c.* 1759–93), American Indian chief of the Creek nation, son of a Scots trader and a half-breed. McGillivary was educated in Charleston, SC, and became a partner in a company trading in the Creek country. He rose to a high position among the Creeks and was elevated to the chieftainship (1783). Calling together the representatives of 34 Creek towns, he persuaded them to repudiate the treaty of Augusta (Nov. 1783) and to agree to sell no more land without the tribe's consent. For ten years he helped the Creeks maintain a united front and played the Spanish, British, and Americans off against each other for the benefit of the Creeks. The treaty of New York (7 Aug. 1790), which he successfully negotiated with the US, gave the Creeks a guarantee of their hunting lands.

McGILLIVRAY, WILLIAM (1764–1825), Canadian fur trader who entered the service of the North-West Co. (1784) and became its chief director (1804). During the War of 1812 he commanded a company of voyageurs. He directed the North-West Co.'s opposition to the Red River Settlement (1814–16) and was captured when Lord Selkirk seized Fort William. In 1812 the North-West and Hudson's Bay Cos merged, and McGillivray joined the new joint board.

McGREGOR, SIR WILLIAM (1846–1919), Scottish doctor and colonial official, who served in the Seychelles (1873), Mauritius (1874), and Fiji (1875–88), where he became well known for his work in the measles epidemic (1875) and the threatened smallpox outbreak (1879), vaccinating 60,000 Fijians. He was acting governor of Fiji (1885) and successively administrator and lieutenant-governor of British New Guinea (1888–98), governor of Lagos (1899–1904), Nfld (1904–9), and of Qld (1909–14). He founded the Suva Medical School.

McGUFFEY, WILLIAM HOLMES (1800–73), US educationist, who was president of Ohio University (1829–43) and professor of moral philosophy at Virginia University (1845–73). His *Eclectic Readers*, six schoolbooks for elementary grades (1836–57), which sold over 122 million copies, played a major role in shaping American education and culture.

MACHADO Y MORALES, GERARDO (1871–1939), Cuban general and dictatorial president of Cuba (1925–33). He served in the Cuban wars of independence and thereafter used the Cuban Liberal Party as a vehicle for reaching power. His regime was noted for its repression, secret police, and brutality, and there were many uprisings against his rule. In 1933 he lost the support of the Cuban army and resigned.

MACHAULT, JEAN BAPTISTE, SEIGNEUR D'ARNOUVILLE (1701–94), French minister under Louis XV, who tried to extend the French tax structure to include the privileged classes. He was *intendant* of Valenciennes before being appointed controller-general of finances in 1745. In 1749 he introduced the *vingtième*, a permanent direct tax on all three estates, similar to the English land tax, in order to revive the finances after the demands of the war of the Austrian Succession. His radical plans were bitterly opposed by many nobles, the clergy, and the *dévot* party at court, who together with Machault's enemy, Count d'Argenson, the war minister, forced the suspension of the tax (1751) and brought about Machault's appointment as secretary of state for the marine instead of controller (1754). Although he was also made chancellor in 1756, he was soon sacrificed by Louis XV to *parlementaire* hostility (Feb. 1757).

MACHIAVELLI, NICCOLO (1469–1527), Florentine diplomat, historian, and political philosopher, who was secretary of the Florentine republic (1498–1512) and conducted its diplomatic affairs with such skill that he was sent on a number of foreign embassies, *eg*, to Paris (1504) and to the Emperor Maximilian (1507). He was opposed to the restoration of the Medici family, and was imprisoned and tortured on their return to power (1512), but was eventually freed (1514). He spent the rest of his life writing poetry, plays, *eg*, the *Mandragola*, and numerous treatises, *eg*, the *Discourses* (1512), the *Art of War* (1519–20), and the *History of Florence* (1525). His most famous work, however, was an appraisal of government as seen through Italian politics, *The Prince* (written in 1513, published in 1532). His doctrine came to be known as machiavellianism and marked him out as the first modern political theorist. In *The Prince* he expounded the thesis that in order to preserve the integrity of the state a ruler should not feel himself bound by any moral scruples, based on justice or humanity, but only by the three criteria of political action: the need to grasp the necessities or realities of the state; the importance of showing strength or force; and the desirability of exploiting chance events and making pragmatic decisions, thus controlling all political situations.

McILWRAITH, SIR THOMAS (1835–1900), Australian politician and prime minister of Qld (1879–83, 1888, 1893), originally a Scots engineer who had worked the Vic. railways. In domestic politics he represented the sectional interests of squatters and, as a nationalist, supported the federal movement.

MACINTOSH, CHARLES (1766–1843), Scottish inventor of a process of waterproofing fabrics, which he patented in 1823. This consisted of applying a solution of rubber in naphtha, a byproduct of coal tar distillation, to two pieces of cloth, which were then pressed together to form an impermeable fabric. Subsequently, in Manchester, he started the manufacture of the garments which still bear his name.

MACINTOSH, WILLIAM (*d.* 1825), American Indian chief, who led the Lower Creeks in Andrew Jackson's campaign against dissident Creeks (1813). He was executed by his people for signing the treaty of Indian Springs (1825), which ceded Creek lands to the US.

McKAY, DONALD (1810–80), US shipbuilder who developed and perfected the fast sailing vessels known as clippers. He launched *Stag Hound* in 1850 and thereafter his ships, among them *Flying Cloud* (1851), *Sovereign of the Seas* (1852), and *Lightning* (1855), achieved a pre-eminent reputation for fast, long-distance voyages.

McKAY, HUGH VICTOR (1865–1926), Australian inventor and manufacturer, who devised a horse-drawn machine (*c.* 1885) that stripped, threshed, winnowed, and cleaned wheat. In Ballarat, and then in Melbourne, McKay manufactured his harvesters on a large scale and by the early 1900s was exporting them to South Africa and South America.

McKELL, SIR WILLIAM JOHN (1891–   ), Australian politician and governor-general, the first to be appointed (1947–1953) while still active in politics, he had succeeded J. T. Lang in 1939 as NSW Labor leader. As a member of the state legislature (1917–47), he held ministerial office (1920–2, 1925–7, 1930–2) and was prime minister of NSW (1941–7). In 1956, he served on the Malayan constitutional commission.

McKENNA, REGINALD (1863–1943), British Liberal politician who, as chancellor of the exchequer (1915–16), introduced the McKenna Duties which were intended to reduce the imports of luxuries in wartime. Their introduction implied the abandonment of Liberal Free Trade principles. The duties were continued after the First World War, abolished by Snowden, restored by Churchill the following year (1925), and retained when Protection was brought back in 1932.

McKENNA DUTIES in Britain, revenue-raising duties on the importation of certain foreign manufactured goods: motor cars and motor cycles, musical instruments, films, watches and clocks. They were first imposed by Reginald McKenna, Liberal chancellor of the exchequer in Britain's wartime coalition government, in his budget for 1915. The duties were criticized by many Liberals as a breach of their Free Trade philosophy. The original intention was to raise money and conserve foreign exchange rather than to protect British products, and they were an *ad valorem* tax, imposed at 33 per cent, which brought in about £3 million a year to the exchequer. While the duties were accepted at first as a necessary wartime expedient, reasons were put forward for retaining them after the war: the needs of the exchequer, the threat of increased international competition on the British economy, and the beneficial effects of protective measures on employment in Britain. They were abolished in the budget of 1924 by Philip Snowden, first Labour chancellor of the exchequer, as a part of a consistently free trading approach to tariff policy, which also included his refusal to renew the expiring Safeguarding of Industries Act, first imposed in 1921. There was criticism of Snowden's action by employers and by Conservative politicians, who drew attention to the considerable rise in imports which followed the abolition of the duties. They were reimposed, together with the renewal of Safeguarding, in Winston Churchill's Conservative budget of 1925, although they were then imposed selectively, as a part of a general policy of Imperial Preference. They were not affected by the Ottawa Conference or the Import Duties Act (1932) and remained in force as reimposed in 1925.

MACKENZIE, SIR ALEXANDER (1764–1820), Canadian politician, explorer, and fur trader. On 3 June 1789 he left Fort Chipewyan and, travelling by the Slave river, Great Slave Lake, and an unexplored river, later named in his honour, reached the Arctic Ocean in mid-July. He had hoped to reach the Pacific, however, and in 1793 he tried again, leaving the fork of the Peace and Smoky rivers, crossing the Peace River Pass, and arriving at Dean Channel on the Pacific (22 July 1793). He served in the House of Assembly of Lower Canada (1804–8).

McKENZIE, SIR JOHN (1838–1901), NZ politician and land reformer. Both in Otago and colonial politics, he denounced the aggregation of great estates by 'dummying' and other malpractices. As Liberal minister of lands (1891–9), he put thousands of small farmers on Crown and re-purchased freehold land, mostly as state leasehold tenants. Wielding political power second only to Seddon's, he resisted radical attacks on his popular land policies.

MACKENZIE, SIR THOMAS (1854–1930), NZ politician and Liberal prime minister (1912). He represented the interests of farmers and business men in parliament.

MACKENZIE, WILLIAM LYON (1795–1861), Canadian radical politician and journalist, who was born in Scotland. He went to Canada (1820) and set up (1824) a newspaper, the *Colonial Advocate*. His attacks on the ruling clique, known as the Family Compact, led to a raid on his office and the destruction of some of his equipment (June 1826), for which he was awarded substantial damages, and he became the hero and leader of the provincial radical reformers. He was elected to the House of Assembly (1828), but expelled (1831) for libelling the House, and although re-elected five times, was not allowed to resume his seat. He became mayor of the new city of Toronto (1834), sold his paper, and was re-elected to the Assembly (1835), where he was the main inspiration of the *Seventh Report of the Committee on Grievances*. The defeat of Mackenzie and the reformers in the 1836 election drove him into extra-constitutional opposition, and he divided his time between editing the *Constitution* (founded 1836) and organizing armed revolt. The attempted revolt in Upper Canada (Dec. 1837) was a fiasco. Mackenzie fled to America and established a provisional government (14 Dec. 1837–13 Jan. 1838) on Navy Island, above Niagara Falls. He was arrested by the US authorities for violating their neutrality laws and imprisoned for 18 months (1839). After his release he supported himself by journalism and writing, but became disillusioned with America and returned to Canada after the amnesty of 1849. He was again elected to the House of Assembly (1851), but found few supporters and retired from public life (1858). He was the grandfather of William Lyon Mackenzie King.

William Kilbourn, *The Firebrand* (Toronto, 1956).   AJS

McKINLEY, WILLIAM (1843–1901), US politician and 25th president of the US. He fought on the Union side throughout the Civil War and served in the House of Representatives (1877–84, 1885–91). He was a leading advocate of high protective tariffs and as chairman of the Ways and Means Committee (1889–90) was largely responsible for the McKinley tariff (1890). He was governor of OH in 1891 and 1893, and in 1896 became Republican president. His cautious pro-business administration passed the Dingley Tariff (1897), and also became embroiled in the Cuban question. Though he gave in to popular clamour for war with Spain (1896), McKinley was at first reluctant to annex territory, but became convinced of the necessity of retaining the Philippines. Negotiations (1900) for the construction of an isthmian canal, the Platt Amendment (1901), and promulgation of the 'Open Door' policy towards China, heralded the emergence of the US as an active world power. McKinley was re-elected president in 1900. On 6 Sept. 1901 he was shot by an anarchist, and died eight days later.

McKINLEY TARIFF (1890) in the US legislation named after congressman William McKinley of OH that significantly raised duties to an average of 49·5 per cent in order to protect domestic industry. The act also provided a bounty for domestic sugar producers of two cents a pound, which upset the Hawaiian sugar industry, and it authorized a reciprocal raising of tariffs by executive agreement to meet discrimination by foreign nations.

McLEAN, SIR DONALD (1820–77), NZ politician, government land purchaser, and native secretary, who secured large blocks of Maori land by patient negotiation, being skilled in Maori language and customs. In the later 1850s his methods under settler pressure were suspect, especially in the controversial Waitara purchase (1859), which led to war. As superintendent of Hawke's Bay (1863–9) and government agent (1868–9), McLean wielded unrivalled influence on the east coast, then subject to Maori guerrilla raids. While native minister (1869–76), he sought successfully to end hostilities with dissident Maoris.

MACLEOD, IAIN NORMAN (1913–1970), British politician. After service in the Second World War, he joined the Conservative research office. In 1950, he entered parliament as MP for West Enfield and became one of the 'One Nation' group of Conservatives. He was minister of health (1952–5), minister of labour (1955–9), and colonial secretary (1959–61).

At the colonial office he scored his greatest triumph by making the ideological break-through necessary for his party to carry out the policy of de-colonization which Harold Macmillan had expressed in his 'wind of change' speech—the more so since independence was accompanied by the assurance of African majority rule—and he won the understanding of both Africans and Europeans. He was chairman of the Conservative Party (1961–3), leader of the House of Commons, and chancellor of the duchy of Lancaster (1961–3). He supported Butler as Macmillan's successor as prime minister, and when Lord Home was chosen, he refused to serve under him. From 1963 to 1965 he was editor of *The Spectator*. When the Conservatives went into opposition he was appointed to the 'shadow' cabinet (1964) and after their electoral victory (1970) was made chancellor of the exchequer in Heath's administration. He died suddenly on 20 July 1970.

McLOUGHLIN, JOHN (1784–1857), Canadian frontiersman, who entered the service of the North-West Co. (1803). He favoured the merging of the North-West and Hudson's Bay Cos, became an important member of the new organization (1821), and was appointed general superintendent of the Columbia district (1824). From his post on the Columbia river he befriended American missionaries and settlers. He remained in OR when it became US territory (1846) and came to be known as the 'Father of Oregon'.

MacMAHON, MARIE EDMÉ PATRICE DE, Duc de Magenta (1808–93), marshal of France, who became second president of the Third Republic. He served with distinction in Algeria, the Crimea, and Italy (1859), but was defeated in the war with Prussia and surrendered at Sedan (1870). He later commanded the Versailles forces against the Commune (1871), and replaced Thiers as president (1873). At first he supported the *Ordre Morale*, but later tried to dissolve the Assembly in order to aid a restoration (1877). His failure led to his resignation in 1879.

McMAHON, WILLIAM (1908–), Australian politician who became an MP in 1949, and was minister for labour and national service (1958–66), at the treasury (1966–9), and thereafter minister for external and foreign affairs.

MacMAHON LINE, marking the north-eastern frontiers of India with Tibet and China, proposed in the Simla Convention (1914), was drawn up at a tripartite conference between British, Tibetan, and Chinese representatives (Oct. 1913–July 1914), presided over by Sir Henry MacMahon, foreign secretary to the government of India. The Chinese government refused to ratify the convention and never accepted the validity of the line. In the late 1950s their rejection of it was a cause of open conflict between China and India.

MacMICHAEL MISSION (Oct.–Dec. 1945) to Malaya. Sir Harold MacMichael's task was to obtain the consent of the nine Malay rulers to the British Crown's legal establishment of the new constitutional framework, known as the Malayan Union. He was also instructed to investigate, and if necessary replace, any ruler who had compromised himself by co-operating with the Japanese occupation forces. The high-handedness and speed with which the rulers' signatures were obtained drew strong protests from Malays and former Malayan administrators, and later most of the rulers publicly regretted having given their consent.

MACMILLAN, MAURICE HAROLD (1894–), British politician and prime minister (1957–63). He entered parliament as a Conservative MP in 1924. He opposed appeasement, and was one of a group of Conservative back-benchers who wanted to replace laissez-faire policies with qualified government intervention in the economy. His wartime offices included those of parliamentary secretary to the ministry of supply (1940), under-secretary at the colonial office (1942), and minister resident in Algiers (1942), where he began a

long-standing friendship with Gen. Eisenhower. He then became head of the Allied Commission in Italy (1943), and later was secretary for air (1945).

In Nov. 1945 he joined the Conservative shadow cabinet and in 1951, as housing minister, he surpassed his pledge to build 300,000 houses. He then (1954) became defence minister and (1955), under Anthony Eden's premiership, spent nine months as foreign secretary, and was then transferred to the treasury, where he took traditional deflationary measures such as raising the bank rate and tightening hire-purchase conditions. By July 1956 he had achieved a £144 million surplus. He also introduced Premium Bonds and tentatively embarked on a voluntary incomes policy.

As foreign secretary, Macmillan was largely responsible for the Baghdad pact, which showed his fear of communist influence. As chancellor of the exchequer he played a crucial part in the Suez operation. He opposed taking the Canal dispute to the United Nations. In Oct. 1956, when Eden was considering a settlement, he strongly advocated invasion. Officially he advised on the cost of such a move and on probable American reactions, which he utterly miscalculated. The suggestion that American disapproval of Suez, expressed in financial pressure, caused the Anglo-French retreat, is denied in his memoirs.

Following Eden's illness, Macmillan became prime minister (1957) and adopted a policy of 'retreat from Suez'. Instead of acting independently in the Cold War, he tried to establish warmer relations with Presidents Eisenhower and Kennedy, and closer contacts with Russia. His 1959 Moscow visit and the 1960 Paris summit conference were spectacular examples of this policy. Macmillan's persistence in summit discussion may ultimately have helped to retard the nuclear arms race, although his administration worked in a contrary direction by exploding Britain's first H-bomb.

He presided over major transformations in Britain's imperial role, *eg*, the dissolution of the Central African Federation. He was largely responsible for the emergence of new African nations within the Commonwealth and deeply regretted South Africa's leaving in 1961.

In internal policies he veered between inflation and deflation. In instituting an incomes commission, and economic planning machinery, he went far beyond previous Conservative programmes.

The 1961 sterling crisis led him to adopt unpopular financial measures, and his 'purge' of older ministers in 1962, which was succeeded in 1963 by the Profumo scandal, did nothing to improve his image. External difficulties included the US cancellation of the 'Skybolt' missile programme, revealing the weakness of Britain's proposed 'independent' nuclear deterrent. Macmillan's subsequent Nassau meeting with Kennedy contributed heavily to France's veto of Britain's Common Market application. In Oct. 1963, illness forced him to resign. Subsequently he became chancellor of Oxford University, wrote his memoirs, and returned to his family's publishing firm.

A. Sampson, *Macmillan, a Study in Ambiguity* (London, 1967).   ASJ

MACMILLAN COMMITTEE in Britain, appointed in 1930 by Snowden, the Labour chancellor of the exchequer, to enquire into banking, finance, and credit and to examine the effect of credit policy on unemployment. It reported in 1931, proposing a certain amount of management of the money supply. A minority report signed by J. M. Keynes and Ernest Bevin added a proposal for extensive public investment to stimulate consumption as a means of tackling the Slump.

The report had practically no immediate impact; its proposals shocked Snowden, whose devotion to Gladstonian principles of economy and balanced budgets was total. He preferred to act on the recommendations of the May Committee of 1931, which proposed sweeping cuts in public expenditure.

What the Macmillan Committee did was to give wider currency to Keynes's views on the need for deficit budgeting and encouraging consumption during a slump. The co-operation on the committee between Keynes and Bevin led to the adoption of some Keynesian ideas by the Labour party. In 1927 Snowden had called the Keynes-inspired Liberal Yellow Book 'the economics of Bedlam'. After 1931 Snowden was expelled from the Labour Party, and the now very small parliamentary party was dominated by Bevin through the TUC. Thus the Macmillan Committee played its part in increasing the acceptance of Keynesian views which finally became economic orthodoxy in the 1950s.   IM

MACNAGHTEN, SIR WILLIAM HAY (1793–1841), British colonial official in the political service of the East India Co., who influenced Auckland in the policies which led to the First Afghan War (1838–42). He was treacherously murdered by Akbar Khan, the son of Dost Muhammad, Amir of Afghanistan, during an interview with him.

McNAMARA, ROBERT STRANGE (1916–   ), US business executive, who resigned as president of the Ford Motor Co. to become President Kennedy's secretary of defence (1961), and continued to serve under President Johnson. He became (1968) president of the World Bank.

McNARY–HAUGENISM in US, plan devised to enlist government aid in support of farm prices, embodied in a series of congressional bills introduced by Senator Charles L. McNary, from OR, and Representative Gilbert N. Haugen, from IA (1924–7). Although the details changed, certain features remained constant, notably a two-price system for selected agricultural goods. The plan envisaged a high domestic price, bearing the same relation to other commodity prices that had prevailed in 1905–14, and a low foreign price. A government corporation was to be set up to buy on the American market at the computed 'parity' price, and sell abroad at the current world price. The loss involved would be covered by an 'equalization fee', to be paid, under the original scheme, by the farmers, but later assessed on the processing and sale of farm products. Although the bill passed through Congress in 1927, it was vetoed by Coolidge as being economically unsound and an improper use of the taxing power.

MACON'S BILL (1810) in US, legislation designed to safeguard US commerce which was adopted by Congress during the Napoleonic Wars. It replaced the Non-Intercourse Act (1809), which ended the embargo policy of 1807 and opened trade by American shipping to all countries except Britain and France. Macon's bill proposed the reopening of commercial relations on an exclusive basis with whichever of the European belligerents was prepared to recognize America's neutral rights.

MACPHERSON, SIR JOHN (1745–1821), British colonial official in the service of the East India Co. He sailed for India in 1767 as purser on one of the company's ships, and returned to England (1768) on a secret commission from the Nawab of the Carnatic. In 1770 he was appointed a writer in the company's service, but was dismissed (1776) for his earlier activities on behalf of the nawab. He was reinstated by the Court of Directors and appointed a member of the Bengal council. He succeeded Warren Hastings as governor-general (1785–6); his administration was extremely corrupt.

MACQUARIE, LACHLAN (1762–1824), Scottish-born Australian governor. After becoming an ensign (1777), he served in Canada, US, Jamaica, and India (1788), saw service in England, then went to NSW (1809). There he succeeded the deposed governor, Bligh (1810), and set about restoring order, encouraging exploration, and employing convicts in various public works. His policy of treating deserving ex-convicts as the equals of immigrants and officers was disapproved of

locally and caused criticism in the House of Commons, which, with pressure for economy after the Napoleonic Wars, led to a commission of enquiry (1819). Macquarie repeatedly offered his resignation, but did not leave the colony until 1822.

MACRINUS, M. OPELLIUS (AD 164–218), Roman Emperor (*reg.* 217–18), who, as praetorian prefect of Caracalla, replaced him by a *coup d'état* in Syria. Macrinus, an equestrian by birth, made an honest attempt to rule, but never enjoyed widespread support and was easily overthrown by the proclamation of Elagabalus, inspired by Julia Maesa at Emesa.

MACRO, NAEVIUS SERTORIUS (d. AD 38), prefect of the praetorian guard at Rome under the emperor Tiberius, who facilitated the succession of Caligula (37), but aroused his suspicions and was forced to commit suicide.

MACROBIUS (*fl. c.* AD 430), author of the *Saturnalia*—imaginary conversations of learned men of the late 4th cent. AD—and of a commentary on Cicero's *Dream of Scipio*, and other works. If he is identical, as seems likely, with a praetorian prefect of 430, the *Saturnalia* are of less direct value than used to be supposed as evidence of the intellectual history of the 4th cent., being rather an idealized recreation of that age. Macrobius' works possess great antiquarian erudition and, with the contemporary commentary on Virgil by Servius, are a mine of information on early Roman religious practice; they also show the nature of literary criticism of his own day.

MACROSSAN, JOHN MURTAGH (1832–91), Irish-born Australian politician, who settled in northern Qld. As colonial MP from 1873, he was a supporter of Thomas McIlwraith, under whom he held cabinet office, and an opponent of the future chief justice, Samuel Walter Griffith. He supported the federal movement but advocated a separate state in northern Qld.

MADAGASCAR, island situated 483 kms off the Mozambique coast of Africa, the two main towns of which are Antananarivo in the centre and Fort Dauphin on the south coast. It was first discovered by the Portuguese (1505) and became a strategic base for buccaneers in the Indian Ocean during the 17th cent. A French attempt to settle the island failed (1675), but it was later annexed by Choiseul to compensate for French losses in India (1768). In the 19th-cent. grab for Africa, Madagascar was reoccupied by France (1885) and annexed in 1896. It remained a French colony until 1946, then became a territory of the French Union (1946–58), and then an autonomous republic within the French community. The complete independence of the Malagasy republic from France was declared in 1960.

MADAME, informal title given to the wife of the eldest brother of the reigning French monarch under the *ancien régime*.

MADARIAGA, SALVADOR DE (1886–   ), Spanish diplomat, scholar, and author, who was a railway engineer in Spain, before becoming a journalist in London (1916). He worked (1921–7) in the secretariat of the League of Nations. After three years at Oxford he left (1931) to serve the newly established Spanish republic, becoming Spanish ambassador to the US (1931–2) and later to France (1932–4). He also served as education minister (1934) and as the republic's permanent delegate to the League of Nations (1931–6). A passionate liberal and individualist, he avoided committing himself to either side in the Spanish Civil War (1936–9), and later managed to make his peace with Franco. His published works include books on Spanish and Spanish-American history, novels, literary criticism, and political and philosophical studies.

MADEIRA ISLANDS, area of 797 sq. kms, off the north-west coast of Africa in the Atlantic Ocean, with a population of

(1970) 270,000. The islands were discovered by European sailors in the 14th cent., settled by the Portuguese in 1419, and have remained an administrative part of metropolitan Portugal, except for brief British occupation during the French Wars (1801–2, 1807–14).

MADERNA, CARLO (1556–1629), Italian Baroque architect, who was architect to Pope Paul V. His facade for the church of S. Susanna (1603) employed columns to give an effect of light and shadow in the characteristic Baroque style. At St Peter's he lengthened the western nave, introduced bays and lateral chapels to give the cathedral its cruciform design, and built the facade as a setting for papal ceremonies.

MADERO, FRANCISCO INDALECIO (1873–1913), Mexican revolutionary leader and president of Mexico (1911–13). His book, *The Presidential Succession in 1910* signalled the beginning of an active opposition to President Porfirio Díaz, which came to focus on the presidential candidacy of Madero himself. He was imprisoned before the election, then went into exile in TX, where he issued a revolutionary proclamation (Oct. 1910), declaring himself provisional president. After some setbacks, he gained the support of regional revolutionaries in both the North and the South, and Porfirio Díaz was forced into exile. Madero's political liberalism was not the answer sought by the revolutionaries, who found his programmes lacking in social content. He was elected president (Oct. 1911), but failed to remove Porfirian elements from the government and reactionary generals from the army. The regional revolutionaries again took up arms, forcing Madero to rely on army leaders to restore control over the countryside. Gen. Victoriano Herta soon emerged as the arbiter of power and together with Felix Díaz, a relative of Porfirio, and the US ambassador, Henry Lane Wilson, had Madero removed from office (1913). Shortly afterwards he was shot; Huerta was suspected of complicity in the murder.

MADISON, JAMES (*c.* 1750–1836), US politician and 4th president of the US, who was drawn into a political career by the current disputes with Britain. He was a member of the Virginia Convention (1776), served also in the first Assembly under the new constitution, in the governor's council (1778), and as a delegate to the Continental Congress (1780–3). There, in the debate on the proposal to change the basis of state contributions from land values to population, he suggested the 3/5 ratio of free persons to slaves, a ratio later adopted in the federal Constitution of 1787. On returning to VA (Dec. 1783) he was elected to the House of Delegates, where he championed development of the state's resources and the right of the West to an outlet via the Mississippi river. He also advocated a national commercial policy and was prominent in bringing about the Annapolis and Philadelphia Conventions (1786, 1787). He served again in Congress (Feb.–May 1787), and as a member of the Virginian delegation in Philadelphia formulated a number of proposals designed to strengthen the central government; these were incorporated in the Virginia Plan of 29 May 1787. Not all were adopted, nor was Madison thoroughly satisfied with the new constitution, but he strongly supported its ratification, and collaborated with Alexander Hamilton and John Jay in writing *The Federalist* papers in its defence. When the constitution came into effect (1789), Madison, who was by then a leading member of the House of Representatives, became increasingly concerned about Hamilton's financial policies, and joined the emergent Democratic–Republican opposition. He retired from public life (1797), but being opposed to the Alien and Sedition Acts, he drafted the Virginia Resolution (1798) in which he argued that states could interpose their own authority in order to prevent an arbitrary use of federal powers. Jefferson, a close friend of Madison's, appointed him as secretary of state (1801). His main task was to protect American interests in the face of British and French disregard for the rights of neutrals on the high seas during the Napoleonic wars. His reasoned objections to the British orders-in-

council and the French decrees being ignored, he and Jefferson resorted to the ineffective Embargo policy (1807–9). As Jefferson's chosen successor in the White House (1809–17), Madison was confronted with the continuing dilemma over foreign policy. He was tricked by Napoleon into issuing a proclamation of commerical non-intercourse with Britain (1810), and was subjected to pressure for war from expansionists in the West. Finally, on 1 June 1812, he advised Congress to declare war against Britain. From the first, the war effort was mismanaged and, except in the West and parts of the South, unenthusiastically supported. Peace was formally made by the treaty of Ghent (Dec. 1814) and the great American military victory in the war, the battle of New Orleans that did so much to strengthen nationalism in the following decade, was won two weeks after the treaty was signed. Federalist opposition to the war helped to discredit the party, but its demise was hastened by Republican adoption of many of its principles, which included the establishment of a national bank and a protectionist tariff. The second Bank of the US was established (1816) and Madison signed the tariff act of 1816. On his retirement from the presidency he left national politics, succeeded Jefferson as rector of Virginia University (1826), served in the VA constitutional convention (1829), opposed secession during the nullification crisis (1832–3), and lived quietly on his estate at Montpellier, devoting himself to the preparation of his notes on the Federal Convention of 1787.

I. Brant, *James Madison*, 6 vols (Indianapolis, 1941–61).
A. Koch, *Jefferson and Madison—The Great Collaboration* (New York, 1950).   DBS

MADIUN AFFAIR (1948), confrontation between Indonesian armed forces loyal to the republic and the followers of the Indonesian Communist Party. It resulted from the culmination of tensions between right and left in the revolutionary republic, as successive retreats in the war with the Dutch, economic chaos, Cold War pressures, and a decline in revolutionary élan made co-operation between the republic's diverse ideological and social groups increasingly difficult. Further strain was added by attempts to demobilize armed units considered unreliable by Hatta's conservative government, and by the efforts of the communist leader, Musso, to force the republic into an anti-imperialist war; left-wing soldiers mutinied and seized the city of Madiun and the communist leaders declared their solidarity with the mutineers. The ensuing struggle, which was brief but bloody, caused violent religious conflicts in the villages and most of the communist leaders were killed. With the Dutch invasion of the republic at the end of the year the remaining communists were granted an amnesty, but to many the party seemed to have turned against the republic in its hour of need.

MADRAS, CITY AND PRESIDENCY OF. Madras city was founded (1639) when Francis Day obtained from the last ruler of the Vijayanagar state at Chandragiri permission to build a fortified factory. The headquarters of the East India Co. were moved there from Masulipatam (1641) because of harassment by the Muslim Kings of Golkonda. During the next century the company's trade grew steadily, especially in textiles, and the settlement survived successive threats from the French (1672), the Dutch (1674), the Mughal general, Daud Khan (1702), and the Marathas. From 1742–99 Madras was involved in a series of wars. The French captured it (1746) after a week's siege; a second attack (1759) was repulsed by Gov. Pigot. The fort was afterwards largely rebuilt and the city spread southwards over the hitherto desolate Choultry plain. Though twice threatened by Haidar Ali (1769, 1780), who ravaged the countryside, it remained intact and was finally secured by the defeat of Tipu Sultan (1799).

The annexations following the Mysore wars and the absorption of the Carnatic state (1801) gave Madras a large hinterland. It became the capital of south India and grew steadily in importance. To the crowded Indian city called Black Town (renamed George Town, 1906), to the north of the fort, was added a spacious European and official quarter which gave Madras the aspect of a garden city. The Nawab of the Carnatic's descendants, known as Princes of Arcot, added an unusual Muslim element to a south Indian city. Trade facilities were improved by the construction of a pier (1862) and an artificial harbour (1881), and the impressive marina or esplanade was built (1884). With Indian independence Madras became the capital of the new state of Tamil Nad (1956), but it has continued to grow and now (1970) has a population of nearly two millions.

The Madras presidency began when the Madras factory was made independent of Bantam (1653) and given control of the Bengal stations (1658). Madras had little territorial jurisdiction until it acquired a *jagir* (land tenure carrying the right to revenues), in 1753 from the Nawab of the Carnatic and the Northern Sarkars in 1759 from the Nizam. The former areas were leased to revenue farmers and the latter left to local chiefs. Real administration began with annexations from Tipu Sultan (1792, 1799), cessions from the nizam (1800), and the absorption of Tanjore (1799) and the Carnatic (1801). Madras became noted for the *rayatwari* settlement of the land revenue by Sir Thomas Munro, which set a new pattern of revenue administration in British India. Throughout the 19th cent. until 1947 the Madras Presidency covered the whole of the Indian peninsula south of the Kistna except for the Mysore state. Since 1956 its Telugu, Kannada, and Malayalam-speaking areas have been removed, leaving it a Tamil-speaking state. During the premiership of Kamaraj Nadar (1954–63) the new state made striking progress.

C. S. Srinivasachari, *History of Madras* (Madras, 1939).
                                                              TGPS

MADRASA (theological college). One of the first important examples of this institution was the Nizamiya, which the famous vizier of the Seljuk sultans Alp Arslan and Malik Shah, Nizam al-Mulk, founded at Baghdad in AD 1065–7. The institution became disseminated thereafter throughout the Muslim world. Its role, in the time of its rise to prominence, was to act as a centre of orthodox Muslim conformism and to counter the heterodox doctrines of the Isma'ili movement, which had made notable progress during the course of the 10th and 11th cents. The madrasa included facilities for the accommodation of students and the granting of scholarships. It often contained other amenities in the form of libraries, kitchens, baths, and hospital accommodation. The curriculum embraced studies relating to religion (the Koran and the Hadith); to law (the Shari'a); and to language and literature.

MADRID, PEACE OF (1526), an agreement by which Francis I of France was sworn on his honour as a knight after his defeat by the Spaniards at Pavia (1525). He was released on condition that he bound himself to surrender Burgundy and Tournai to Charles V, renounce his claims to Italy and the suzerainty of Artois and Flanders, and restore to the Duke of Bourbon his forfeited lands and titles. Francis also promised to marry the emperor's sister Eleanor, but he repudiated the whole of the treaty as soon as he was free.

MADRID, TREATY OF (1670), confirmed England's possession of Jamaica following its capture by Cromwell (1655). It had been held against Spanish attacks by a combination of merchants, planters, and privateers, and after its formal cession, Sir Henry Morgan, a notorious buccaneer, was made lieutenant-governor in the hope of his being able to suppress piracy in the area.

MADRID TREATY (1801) between Napoleon and the Spanish government was a diplomatic setback to Britain. Spain transferred LA in America to France and promised to attack

Portugal, England's ally (War of the Oranges). Napoleon promised that Charles IV's son-in-law should rule the newly created kingdom of Etruria in Italy.

MADRID TREATY (1880) assured most-favoured nation treatment to all the European powers in Morocco. France regarded Morocco as a logical extension of her North African interests, but Britain wanted to see it reformed and independent, and Germany's aim was to develop a strong commercial interest in the area. This open-door policy ensured that Morocco would become a focus of international controversy.

MADRIGALS, originally short amatory lyrics fashionable in Italy, set to music in the 16th and early 17th cents as contrapuntal part-songs, sometimes accompanied by viols. Leading composers of madrigals included Monteverdi and Palestrina in Italy, and Byrd, Morley, and Gibbons in England.

MAECENAS, C. (d. 8 BC), Roman diplomatist and voluptuary, and Augustus' minister of information and culture. He claimed to have been born into the ancient Etruscan nobility, and was an early adherent of Octavian. He was with him at the battles at Philippi (42), represented him in the preliminary discussions to the treaty of Brundisium (40), was sent by him on a diplomatic mission to Antony (38), and helped to negotiate the treaty of Tarentum (37). In the service of Augustan propaganda Maecenas organized his famous literary circle, which included Horace and Virgil. Although he held no public office, he was one of Augustus' closest advisers until, in 24, he betrayed to his wife, Terentia, the impending exposure of the conspiracy of Terentius Varro; after this his influence declined.

MAELRUAIN OF TALLAGHT (d. 792), founder of the monastery of Tallaght, Leinster, and a leader of the ascetic reform movement of the Culdees (vassals of God) in the 8th cent. His extant *Teaching* shows that he laid great emphasis on chastity, fasting, and personal devotion.

MAETSUYKER, JOHAN (1606–78), Dutch colonial official and governor-general of the Dutch East India Co. (1653–78). During his administration the company had to deal with troubles in Macassar, West Sumatra, and Java, where the rebellion of Trunadjaja broke out; and in 1662 the company lost its position on Formosa.

MAFIA, term denoting the societies, or 'families' of Sicilian underworld 'gentlemen' who for some 100 years illegally dominated, and to some extent still (1970) exercise control of, the island. The word's origin is obscure, but debatably Arabic: extra-legal societies opposed to foreign rulers had been rife for centuries, but the term became prevalent (among non-Sicilians) from the 1860s, covering groups of anti-aristocratic middlemen. From the 1870s *mafiosi* took control of elections by means of promises, influence, and intimidation, linking themselves with the central government in Rome.

World-War conditions facilitated monopolistic business control by the Mafia and army deserters proved useful as killers and intimidators. By the 1920s *mafiosi* controlled many Sicilian estates, and had become increasingly opposed to peasant and labour organizations. Though partly curbed by fascists, like the prefect, Cesare Mori, the Mafia, under Calo Vizzini, helped the Allied invaders in 1943, and consequently were placed in power as local officials. After briefly flirting with the Separatist movement, the Mafia allied itself with Christian Democracy, and by using bandits like Giuliano, eliminated trade unionists and communists. *Mafiosi* have been respected by Sicilians as 'men of honour', upholding concepts of loyalty, family honour, the vendetta, the ideal of silent suffering, and non-co-operation with officialdom (while also stopping much petty crime). Through infiltrating national and local government, the police, and Church, *mafiosi* have made themselves virtually immune from conviction, nobody daring to testify against them.

Mafia societies have seldom been centrally united. Since the 1950s, murderous fights between 'families', loss of local respect for drug trafficking and prostitution, challenges from Danilo Dolci and others, have encouraged greater official control and the establishment of a parliamentary anti-Mafia commission (1962–   ) before which some witnesses have dared to testify. As a result a few of the leading *mafiosi* have been banished or imprisoned. Similar associations loosely linked to the Sicilians exist (1970) elsewhere, notably the US 'families' of *Cosa Nostra*, linked by the drug trade.

MAFIA ISLANDS, group of small islands off the mouth of the Rufiji river in Tanzania, perhaps the Menouthias mentioned in the *Periplus of the Erythraean Sea* (c. AD 150). Excavations on the site of the town of Mafia Kisimani, on Chole Island, indicate that this was an important trading centre from the end of the 11th to the beginning of the 14th cent. A close association between Mafia and Kilwa has been shown by the presence of large quantities of the small copper coins made at Kilwa during that period. Extensive ruins of the 18th cent. town of Kua, destroyed by the Sakalava of Madagascar early in the 19th cent., have survived on the island of Juani.

MAGADHA, area and state in ancient India, corresponding approximately to modern Bihar. In contrast to the most ancient centres of South Asian civilization in the Indus valley and Punjab, Magadha had grown by the 6th cent. BC into a great political centre. Its capital, originally Rajagriha (mod. Rajgir), was later shifted to Pataliputra (Patna), which remained the most important centre in eastern India till the 6th cent. AD. Unorthodox religions, notably Jainism, Buddhism, and Ajivika doctrines, flourished in Magadha in the earlier centuries. The two greatest empires of ancient India, those of the Mauryas and the Guptas, were based on Magadha. After the 7th cent. AD, however, it was overtaken by Bengal in the east and Kanauj in the west.

MAGDALA, BATTLE OF (1868), between Tewodros II of Ethiopia and an Anglo-Indian expeditionary force led by Sir Robert Napier. It was the culmination of a long dispute between the emperor and the British government, resulting from the latter's failure to answer a letter from Tewodoros or heed his request for craftsmen. The emperor was provoked into imprisoning the British envoy Cameron and other Europeans, whereupon the British despatched an expedition of 12,000 men who crossed Tigre province with the co-operation of the local ruler and assaulted Tewodros's mountain fortress of Magdala on 13 April. The emperor committed suicide and the British withdrew.

MAGDEBURG, CENTURIATORS OF, Protestant chroniclers, followers of the German theologian Flacius Illyricus, who produced an ecclesiastical history (1559–74) which was highly critical of the Roman Church. Its strictures were answered by the *Annales ecclesiastici* (1588–1607) of the Vatican librarian, Cardinal Baronius.

MAGDEBURG, THE RAZING OF (1631). Magdeburg was a city-bishopric of central Germany, secularized in the mid-16th cent. and captured by the imperialists in the Thirty Years War. It was held by Bietrick von Falkenberg for the Protestant administrator, Christian William, brother of the elector of Brandenburg, and besieged by Tilly and Pappenheim, who attacked it (17 May 1631) and destroyed the outworks (19 May). The city council was about to surrender when the imperial army stormed the city (30 May), plundered it mercilessly, and left only the great Gothic cathedral standing among the ruins. The destruction shocked Protestant Europe and caused Saxony to join Gustavus Adolphus in the war.

MAGELLAN, FERDINAND (1470–1521), Portuguese sailor, whose discovery of the straits which bear his name, and of the Pacific Ocean, place him among the world's greatest explorers. After serving Portugal in Morocco and the East Indies he became dissatisfied with Manuel I's treatment and offered himself to Spain. Under Charles V's patronage he set out from Seville with five ships and reached the Moluccas by the western route (Sept. 1519). After being shipwrecked and faced with a mutiny off the Patagonian coast, he pressed on and for over a month sailed through the waters between the South American mainland and Tierra del Fuego, a distance of some 375 miles (603 kms), until he reached the ocean which seemed to him to deserve the name of Pacific. With a starving crew he eventually reached the Philippine islands, but died together with 40 of his men, in a battle with Indians at Matan. The remnants of his expedition returned to Spain under the command of Sebastian del Cano.

MAGENTA, BATTLE OF (1859), at which the Austrians, fighting to defend the Milanese, were defeated by the French, with the support of Garibaldi and his 'Hunters of the Alps' during the Austro–Sardinian War. As a result, the Austrians retreated towards the Quadrilateral until they decided to make a stand at Solferino.

MAGHILI, AL-, MUHAMMAD IBN ABD AL-KARIM (d. 1504), Berber scholar, of Tlemcen, who spoke against the Jews and their wealth in North Africa at a time of Muslim humiliation. His activities brought him into conflict with Sultan Sa'id of Fez, who suspected his ambitions. He retired to Tuwat, where he instigated a massacre of the rich Jewish community. The *qadi* of Tuwat opposed him and he sought refuge farther south. He visited first Takedda, then Kano, where he advised Sultan Muhammad Rumfa (1463–1499), and finally Gao, where he answered questions on Islamic government posed by Askia Muhammad I. He later returned to Tuwat, where he died. His writings had an important influence on Uthman ibn Fudi in early 19th-cent. Nigeria.

MAGI, priesthood of Median origin, important in ancient Persia. They performed certain rites, interpreted dreams, tended tombs, and educated young men. Having adopted Zoroastrianism, they became its defenders against later religions such as Christianity.

MAGINOT LINE. Work on this elaborate system of fortifications on the Franco–German frontier was begun in 1930, when André Maginot, a veteran of Verdun, was minister of war, but it had been under discussion since the end of the First World War and he was not solely responsible for it. It was inspired by the successful use of the fortifications built after 1871 in resisting attacks during the First World War, and it was intended to ensure that the newly regained territory of Alsace-Lorraine, the Lorraine industrial complex, and the direct route to Paris, could be defended in any future war without the fearful loss of French lives that characterized battles like Verdun. Each of the continuous chain of interconnected subterranean fortresses was designed to withstand for three months the fiercest assault without assistance from outside. The most modern weapons were mounted with carefully planned interlocking fields of fire. Barracks, storerooms, hospitals, gymnasia, power-stations, and underground railways were installed, some of them at a depth of 62 metres, and which are now regarded as proof against nuclear attack. By 1935 over 7000 million francs had been spent—more than twice the sum originally appropriated—and the line was still unfinished. This huge investment made it impossible, and seemingly unnecessary, to equip the French armed forces with the most modern aircraft, tanks, and artillery, while the sense of security engendered by the Line fostered the apathetic military and diplomatic attitude subsequently known as the 'Maginot mentality'.

The Franco-Belgian border was not fortified on anything

like a comparable scale because of the cost, the difficulty of constructing a line of fortifications through the Lille–Valenciennes industrial area, which straddles the border, and the diplomatic danger of making Belgium feel left out in the cold. Besides, it was always intended to fight and defeat the Germans in a battle of movement in Belgium when they attacked there, as they had done in 1914. An attempt was made to follow this plan in 1940. The Maginot Line was still largely intact when France surrendered (1940).   PJBD

MAGISTER EQUITUM, ancient Roman extraordinary official, the 'master of the cavalry', subordinate to and appointed by a dictator.

MAGLOIRE, PAUL (1907–), Haitian general and president (1950–6), who played a leading part in the revolution of 1946 which removed the mulatto president, Elie Lescot, and replaced him with the black Dumarsais Estimé. When Estimé was overthrown in his turn (1950), Magloire emerged as the strongest political figure and was appointed president for a six-year term. His presidency was marked by relative prosperity and an emphasis on expanding trade and education, but it was marred by financial scandals, gaudy display, and arbitrary imprisonment of some of Magloire's opponents. Suspicion that Magliore intended to perpetuate himself in office beyond his constitutional term led to his overthrow and exile.

MAGNA CARTA in England, of fundamental importance to the development of law and government in all those countries (including the US) which have developed legal and constitutional systems based upon English usages. The occasion of Magna Carta was a baronial revolt against King John in 1215, but its causes lay deep in the legal and administrative developments of the preceding half-century. Henry II and his sons had created a precociously sophisticated and effective system of law and government. John's baronial opposition did not wish to undo this achievement, but they wanted to assure that this formidable governmental machine would not be used in an excessively arbitrary fashion, as seemed to be happening under John. In the summer of 1214 John had suffered a crushing defeat in France, he had no allies, except the pope, and his financial reserves were spent, so that he could not afford to hire mercenaries. This last consideration determined the timing of the baronial uprising, which started early in 1215. With the support of Abp Stephen Langton of Canterbury, who acted as a friendly mediator, they forced upon John a negotiated agreement resulting in the issue of Magna Carta on 19 June. The charter is conventionally divided into 61 clauses. The first confirmed the liberty of the Church and was interpreted as a guarantee of free elections of bishops and heads of monastic houses. A group of clauses specified that general taxes require consent of a baronial council and contain the first formulation of a principle that resulted ultimately in parliamentary consent to taxation. The 39th clause, requiring that freemen should be judged by their equals according to the law of the land, was from the start regarded as one of the most vital provisions of the charter. Taken as a whole, the charter embodies the principle that even the king must recognize certain legal rights of his subjects. John's submission to it was an unwilling one and he soon procured its abrogation by Pope Innocent III, thus contributing to the resumption of the civil war. After his death in 1216 the regents for his young son reissued the charter in a modified form as the means of pacifying the realm. Reissued on several occasions in the 13th and 14th cents, it became the touchstone of the king's good intentions.   JG

MAGNESIA, BATTLE OF (190 BC), in western Asia Minor in the Hermus valley. It was the decisive victory of the Romans under Lucius Scipio and Scipio Africanus over Antiochus III of Syria, who subsequently accepted severe peace terms in the treaty of Apamea.

MAGNUS III (*reg.* 1093–1103), King of Norway and son of Olaf III Kyrre. In contrast with his father's peaceful policies, he led three expeditions to England and Scotland, and established Norse sovereignty over Orkney and the Hebrides. He was killed in battle in Ulster.

MAGNUS VI (*reg.* 1263–80), King of Norway who was renowned for his creation in 1276 of a common law for his kingdom. His reign saw the cession of the Hebrides to Scotland in 1266.

MAGNUS, JOHANNES (1488–1544), Swedish historian and Abp of Uppsala who opposed the Reformation in Sweden and the secularization of Church property. He retired to Rome in 1526, where he wrote his *History of the Goths and Swedes*.

MAGNUS MAXIMUS (d. AD 388), Roman general, who was proclaimed emperor in Britain, overthrew Gratian (383), and ruled the west until he was defeated and killed by Theodosius near Aquileia. His reign is chiefly notable for the execution of the Spanish heretic, Priscillian.

MAGONIDS (6th–4th cents BC), leading family in early Carthage, named after their first important member, Mago, a general in Sardinia *c.* 550 BC. Its earlier figures included his sons Hasdrubal (died in battle, *c.* 500 BC), and Hamilcar (defeated by the Greeks in Sicily, 480 BC). It also included the explorers Hanno and Himilco (*c.* 450 BC). During the 5th cent. the Magonids' quasi-monarchical position was limited by constitutional changes, but the family remained influential in the 4th cent. when Hanno 'the Great' was prominent (*c.* 367).

MAGSAYSAY, RAMON (1907–57), president of the republic of the Philippines (1953–7). He took part in guerrilla activities in the Zambales province (1941–5). After the Second World War he was elected representative of his province in 1946, a victory which was due in part to his personal and direct methods of political campaigning.

In between his election as a congressman and his becoming president of the republic, Magsaysay was chairman of the Committee on Guerrilla Affairs and chairman of the House Committee on National Defense. He was appointed Secretary of National Defense at the height of the *Huk* activities in 1950, and within a month practically all the members of the Politburo were captured. The following year he encouraged the establishment of a civic organization called the National Movement for Free Elections (NAMFREL), which was responsible for a comparatively clean local election in 1951 and restored the people's faith in their government. After he became president, many important *Huk* leaders surrendered to him, including Luis Taruc. Magsaysay preferred to win the *Huk*'s trust in the government rather than to use military force.

His victory over Quirino in 1953 marked a basic change in the Philippine political scene. A number of politicians belonging to the older generation were replaced by new and vigorous men. As president, he opened his official residence to the public; created a Presidential Complaints and Action Committee, which facilitated the hearing and solution of problems brought to it by individuals; persuaded Congress to pass the Land Reform Act (1955); and encouraged the establishment of co-operatives and credit facilities to facilitate his land resettlement programme. He also initiated a community development programme, which was directly supervised by a Community Development assistant under the office of the president.

M. Gray, *Island Hero. The Story of Ramon Magsaysay* (New York, 1965).   JMS

MAGYARS, people of Mongolian origin from the highlands of Central Asia, who migrated westwards in the 9th cent. and settled in the fertile plain of the middle Danube (later Hungary and Transylvania), where they form the dominant ethnic group.

MAHABAD, centre of Kurdish area of western Iran, where (15 Dec. 1945) the Kurdish republic of Mahabad was proclaimed under Qazi Muhammad, who was supported by Iraqi Kurdish rebels under Mulla Mustafa Barzani and the USSR. The republic was crushed by Iranian government forces (Dec. 1946).

MAHABAT KHAN (d. 1634), title of Zamana Beg, a leading nobleman in the reigns of the Mughal emperors Jahangir and Shah Jahan. He was active against Mewar (1608) and in the Deccan (1610), but later fell from favour for 12 years. In the complicated political moves at the end of Jahangir's reign, Mahabat Khan at first sided with the emperor, defeating his rebellious son, Prince Khurram. But, becoming jealous of the Empress Nur Jahan's influence, he arrested Jahangir (1626), but was overcome by Nur Jahan's partisans. Under Shah Jahan he was raised to the rank of Khan Khanan (chief noble) and captured Daulatabad.

MAHABHARATA, great ancient Indian epic in 18 books (*parvan*), existing in numerous different versions. Its basic topic is the struggle between two branches of the Bharata clan—on the one hand the five Pandava brothers, on the other the 100 Kauravas—which culminated in the great battle of Kurukshetra, near present-day Delhi. The main plot is, however, frequently interrupted by long episodes, often of a didactic nature, which are only loosely connected with the story. The epic was for many centuries recited (and probably elaborated) by bards and was not written down until the early centuries AD. It spread all over South Asia and became popular also in South-East Asia (a partial Old Javanese translation is dated as belonging to the end of the 10th cent.). The influence of the epic on the standards of conduct of historical figures in India cannot be overestimated.

MAHAICA REBELLION (Aug. 1823), slave revolt in British Guiana, instigated by a slave, Jack Gladstone. It was suppressed by British troops at the battle of Bachelor's Adventure. Many slaves were flogged and hanged, and a white minister, John Smith (1790–1824), was imprisoned. Smith died in gaol and became an important martyr-figure among British abolitionists.

MAHAJANA EKSATH PERAMUNA (People's United Front), name assumed before the 1956 general election in Ceylon by a coalition formed between Bandaranaike and Gunawardana. When the latter broke away he, and his followers, continued to use the name.

MAHAMUNI IMAGE of Buddha, originally at Dinnyawadi in Akyab, is said to be a contemporary likeness of the Buddha. Anawrahta, having failed in an attempt to move the image to Pagan, desecrated it instead. Bodawpaya brought it to the Arakan Pagoda in Mandalay (1785). The image was dismantled, brought by sea to Taungup, carried overland to Padaung, and then taken up the Irrawaddy to Mandalay.

MAHAN, ALFRED THAYER (1840–1914), US naval officer and historian, who spent many years at sea, lectured in naval history and tactics at the Naval War College (1886), of which he was president (1886–9, 1892–3), and retired in 1896. He served on the Naval War Board during the Spanish–American War (1898). His many writings, most notably *The Influence of Sea Power Upon History: 1660–1783* (1890), examined naval strategy and advocated the necessity of a large navy for any country aspiring to world leadership. His views, reiterated and expanded in a series of books and articles, including *The Interest of America in Sea Power,*

Present and Future (1897), exerted considerable influence on Theodore Roosevelt and other leading American politicians, and had an enthusiastic reception in England and Germany before the First World War.

MAHARASHTRA, state of the republic of India, and historically the region in which the Marathi language is spoken. It is roughly coterminous with the main mass of the Deccan lavas above the Ghats and stretches from the Satpura range as far south as Bijapur and from the Western Ghats to Nagpur. The origin of its inhabitants, the Marathas, is controversial, but they are probably a mixed ethnic group. Little is heard of them until, under Sivaji, they spearheaded the Hindu reaction against Aurangzeb in the 17th cent. Claims of the upper-class Marathas to a Rajput origin are unsupported by evidence. For political reasons Sivaji himself hid his Kunbi origin and had a Rajput pedigree fabricated by an accommodating Brahman. The backbone of his army was formed by the Mawalis, or the hillmen of the central Deccan, who were expert guerrilla fighters. For regular campaigns on the plains he employed another class of infantry, called Hetkaris, recruited from part of the Konkan. He also depended on numerous forts, and the flat-topped Western Ghats were natural citadels.

The country of Maharashtra formed part of Asoka's empire. It was visited by the Chinese pilgrim, Hiuen Tsang. In the 7th cent. AD it was under the sway of the Chalukya monarch, Pulakeshin II. Later, it came under the Rashtrakutras, Yadavas, and the Delhi sultanate. It formed part of the Bahmani kingdom, and, on its disintegration into the five Deccan sultanates, was partly in Ahmadnagar and partly in Bijapur. The main historical importance of Maharashtra is that the expansion of its people was one of the causes of the decline of the Mughal empire. They were also the determined opponents of British paramountcy in India until their final defeat in 1818, when Maharashtra was incorporated in Bombay Presidency.

J. C. Grant-Duff, *A History of the Mahrattas*, 2 vols (Oxford, 1921).   CCD

MAHATTHAI, ministry of interior in Thailand, created as a separate administrative unit of the kingdom of Ayudhya in the 15th cent. It was responsible for civil administration and its head, usually known as *Chaophraya Chakri*, controlled four subordinate departments: treasury, palace, lands, and capital. Though a powerful ministry in its early days, it had declined by the 17th cent. and its subordinate departments became independent; control over the southern and western provinces was transferred to the *Kalahom*. It was reformed in 1894, when under Prince Damrong Rajanubhab it again became a ministry of provincial administration in a highly centralized government.

MAHAVAMSA, Pali chronicle of Ceylon describing the history of the island from *c*. 500 BC to AD 349. It was compiled by the Buddhist monk Mahanama, 'for the serene joy and emotion of the pious' (early 6th cent. AD). In spite of a certain bias in favour of the Buddhist order, the *Mahavamsa* represents an admirable record of the past based upon careful use of sources. These consisted mainly of Sinhalese glosses attached to the Buddhist canonical texts. Whenever there were no reliable data available, local legends of doubtful historicity were used, but this is usually indicated in the text. A striking feature of the *Mahavamsa* is its adherence to a consistent chronology. The original *Mahavamsa* was several times extended by additions called Culavamsa, bringing the account down to the 19th cent.

MAHAVIHARA MONASTERY, oldest and most respected Buddhist monastery in Anuradhapura, Ceylon, founded in the middle of the 3rd cent. BC. It remained the centre of orthodox Theravada Buddhism and enjoyed great influence and prestige.

MAHAVIRA (*fl.* 6th cent. BC), historical founder of Jainism, born at Kundapura in present-day Bihar, India. He was a contemporary of the Buddha.

MAHDI, AL-, Abbasid Caliph (*reg.* 775–85), the son of the Caliph Al-Mansur whose reign saw a resumption of warfare with Byzantium, the Empress Irene, in 782, being constrained to promise an annual tribute to the caliph. It also witnessed the outbreak of a dangerous rebellion in Khurasan under a certain Al-Muqanna' (the Veiled One).

MAHDI, AL-, Arabic expression meaning 'the rightly guided one', *ie*, guided by Allah. To the Shi'i Muslims the term indicates the hidden imam who has gone into concealment and who will return to restore the dominance of truth and justice on earth. The word has also served as a title or designation attributed to historical figures, *eg*, to the first Fatimid Caliph Ubayd Allah al-Mahdi (*reg.* 909–34); or to Muhammad Ahmad ibn Abdallah al-Mahdi, the leader of the Mahdist movement which developed in the Sudan during the years after 1881.

MAHDI, THE (Muhammad Ahmad ibn Abdallah (*c.* 1841–1885), Sudanese religious leader of Dunqulawari origin, who announced (1881) that he was the expected Mahdi, sent by God to usher in the rule of righteousness. He began a revolt against Egyptian rule on the island of Aba on the White Nile and later moved to southern Kordofan, where he attracted a large following to his movement, known as the Mahdiyya.

MAHDIYYA, religio-political movement in the Sudan in the later 19th cent. under the leadership of the Mahdi (Muhammad Ahmad *c.* 1841–85). In its religious aspect the movement resembled other movements, *eg*, Wahhabism, which aimed at purifying Islam, although it also had strong eschatological overtones. In its political aspect it aimed at the destruction of Egyptian rule in the Sudan. The followers (Ansar) of the Mahdi included religious disciples, disgruntled former slave traders, and the Baqqara nomads. With their aid the Mahdi first established control of Kordofan (1881–3) and then extended his power northwards, following his defeat of Hicks Pasha (5 Nov. 1883). The provinces of Darfur and Bahr al-Ghazal came under his control and the Beja tribes of the east rallied to his support through a compact between the Mahdi's agent, Uthman Diqna (d. 1926), and a local religious leader, Shaykh Al-Tahir. Khartoum was captured (26 Jan. 1885). Under the Mahdi's successor, the Khalifa Abdallahi, the rigid theocratic character of the movement was submerged beneath a more formal, secular state organization. The Khalifa overcame the opposition of the relatives of the Mahdi (the Ashraf) and the settled peoples (Awlad al-balad) and appointed his own kinsmen and supporters to the principal offices of state. He created a new military force dependent upon himself, in order to be less dependent upon tribal support, and also an elaborate administrative system. His efforts to extend the Mahdiyya outside the Sudan failed. Although he had some success against Abyssinia, he was defeated by the Italians in Eritrea (1894) and his invasion of Egypt was defeated at Tushki (Toski) (3 Aug. 1889). In 1896 Egyptian forces under Kitchener advanced into Dongola and began to construct a railway line to facilitate the reconquest of the Sudan. The Mahdists were defeated at the Atbara river (8 April 1898) and near their capital, Omdurman (1 Sept. 1898). Sporadic Mahdist opposition continued for some years after the Sudan came under British control. Under the leadership of the Mahdi's posthumous son, Sayyid Abd al-Rahman al-Mahdi (?1885–1959), the religious community revived and with British support and in opposition to the Mirghani family (leaders of the Khatmiyya sect) became identified with the moderate Umma party, which sought the achievement of gradual Sudanese independence in co-operation with the British.

P. M. Holt, *The Mahdist State in the Sudan 1881–98* (Oxford, 1958).
A. B. Theobald, *The Mahdiyya* (London, 1951).   MEY

MAHERERO, SAMUEL (1856–1923), succeeded his father, Maherero, as chief (*reg.* 1890–1904) of the Herero people in South-West Africa in 1890 at a time of increasing pressure from German settlers and administration. Though at first compliant, in Jan. 1904 Maherero led his people in revolt against the Germans and a brutal war ensued which triggered off a revolt of other African groups in South-West Africa. The Herero were defeated by Gen. von Trotha, who had virtually decreed their extermination. After the battle of Waterberg (Aug. 1904) Maherero and his army, followed by the mass of his people, fled across the desert. Though some reached the Bechuanaland protectorate, many thousands died of thirst. After the war, all their lands in South-West Africa were confiscated and the surviving Herero, forbidden to keep cattle, became a reservoir of labour for the white settlers. It is estimated that they were reduced from 80,000 to 15,000.

MAHICAN INDIANS, American Algonquian tribe discovered by the Dutch (*c.* 1664) on the Upper Hudson river, at war with the Mohawk, who forced them to remove to Stockbridge, MA.

MAHINDA (*fl.* 3rd cent. BC), son (or brother?) of the ancient Indian king, Ashoka, who became a Buddhist monk and converted the King of Ceylon, Devanampiya Tissa, to Buddhism, which henceforward became the established religion of the island. Although the extant accounts contain many miraculous features, there is no reason to doubt the main lines of this tradition.

MAHMIL, Arabic name for the decorated litters sent on the annual pilgrimage (Hajj) to Mecca in order to show the splendour and prestige of the states (*eg*, Egypt, Syria, Iraq), by whom they were sent. The mahmil was borne on a camel that was led, not ridden. It would seem that the custom, although there is mention of it earlier, was in fact established on a firm basis during the reign of the Mamluk Sultan Baybars (AD 1260–77).

MAHMUD (d. 1529), Sultan of Malacca (*reg.* 1488–1511), succeeded Ala'uddin Riayat Shah after a struggle for the throne. Both Malay and Portuguese sources describe Mahmud as proud and cruel, but it is likely that this unfavourable image can be partly attributed to the Portuguese conquest of Malacca in 1511. On the other hand, Malacca appears to have reached the peak of its power and prosperity during his reign. The fall of Malacca revealed serious weaknesses in the state, notably dissensions between the different groups comprising the population of this cosmopolitan city. Mahmud continued the resistance against the Portuguese from other centres on the peninsula. After his death in Pahang, his son Ala'uddin founded Johor, which continued most of the traditions of Malacca.

MAHMUD II (1784–1839), Ottoman Sultan (*reg.* 1808–39), son of Abdülhamid I. He succeeded Mustafa IV. Shortly after his accession, the reforming grand vizier, Bayrakdar Mustafa Pasha, was overthrown and killed (Nov. 1808) and power passed to the anti-reforming traditionalist groups of the ulema and the Janissaries. Mahmud began cautiously to reassert the power of the central government over independent local governors and notables, but the essential precondition of a major reform was the establishment of a new professional army. His orders to begin this provoked the revolt and subsequent destruction (15 June 1826) of the Janissary corps, and so opened the way to a radical reform of

Ottoman institutions. The new army was developed, military colleges opened, and European instructors introduced. Reforms in the administration included training in foreign languages. The feudal (*timar*) system was abolished and religious endowments (*waqfs*) were placed under government control. Although his reign ended in disastrous defeat by Muhammad Ali of Egypt, Mahmud laid the foundations of the centralizing reform movement which was continued in the Tanzimat.

MAHMUD OF GHAZNA (969–1030), Muslim ruler in Afghanistan and ruler of Khurasan (*reg.* 999–1030) in succession to his father, Sebuktegin (d. 997). Mahmud led 17 raids into northern India in the name of Islam, winning the title Ghazi and enormous plunder, which he used to ornament his capital at Ghazna. His most famous raid (1025–6) resulted in the sack of the Hindu temple of Somnath. He also extended his power into Transoxania, Iran, and Iraq. His destruction of Hindu power in northern India paved the way for the creation of the subsequent Muslim dynasties.

MAHMUD SHEVKET PASHA (1856–1913), Ottoman general, born in Iraq, who, as commander of the IIIrd Army in Macedonia, crushed the 1909 counter-revolution and became the dominant figure in Ottoman politics. His attempt to assume the role of the patriotic soldier-statesman, standing above politics, was cut short by his murder.

MAHSUDS, Pathan tribe from Waziristan (West Pakistan), who, especially under the leadership of the Mulla Powinda (d. 1913) and his son Fazl al-Din, continually opposed British authority on the north-west Indian frontier and were the objects of several expeditions after 1860.

MAIDS OF TAUNTON, English schoolgirls who on their teachers' instructions innocently paraded an embroidered banner when Monmouth came to Taunton before the battle of Sedgemoor (1685). Certain courtiers and ladies-in-waiting were authorized by the queen, Mary of Modena, to keep the girls in prison until their wealthy parents paid a ransom for their release. The agent in this transaction was George Penne (not, as stated by Macaulay, William Penn, the Quaker).

MAIDUGURI, capital of the North-east State of Nigeria and railhead, is the stronghold of Kanuri areas of the great region of Bornu. It was founded only in 1907, when the Shehu of Bornu was induced to abandon Kukawa on Lake Chad in favour of a village 120 miles (193 kms) south, astride the important trade and pilgrim route between Kano and the Sudan. Maiduguri became the most dynamic emirate town in Northern Nigeria. Often called Yerwa, it ranks among the famous Kanem/Kanuri capitals, from Kauwar and Njimi in the first millennium to the walled city of Birni Ngazargamu, which lasted for 350 years, to Kukawa, founded by El Kanemi in 1814 and ransacked by Rabeh in 1893. Ibn Battuta, Clapperton, and Barth wrote informative and accurate descriptions of the life and culture in the Kanuri capital.

MAIESTAS TRIALS, important in ancient Roman history. From 103 BC an increasing number of actions in the political field which were held to be injurious to the *maiestas* (majesty) of the Roman state were made criminal offences. Later, as the welfare of the emperors became identified with that of the state, any real or assumed threat to their person or standing became treasonable. The lack of precision in defining offences led to abuses, even when there were real plots. Many *maiestas* trials, mostly of senators, under Tiberius, Claudius, Nero, and Domitian, resulted from, and exacerbated, general mistrust between emperor and Senate.

MAILLEBOIS, JEAN BAPTISTE FRANÇOIS DESMARETS, Marquis de (1682–1762), French soldier, who served under Villars (1703) and fought in the Wars of the Polish and Austrian Successions. He repulsed the imperialist forces in Italy (1733–4) and conquered Corsica (1739), fought in Germany (1741–2), and jointly commanded the Gallispan armies in Italy (1743–6). He defeated Charles Emmanuel of Savoy at Bassignana (1745), but after disagreement with the Spanish commander-in-chief was himself defeated at Placentia (1746), retreated from Italy, and was replaced by Belleisle (1746).

MAIMAN, THEODORE HAROLD (1927–), US physicist who (1960) was the first to generate a laser beam. The underlying principle had been postulated in 1917 by Einstein, that by irradiation with light of a certain frequency an excited atom could be stimulated to release its excess of energy in the form of light. Lasers have been used for precision mensuration, high-speed cutting of various materials, and for delicate welding, including reattachment of the retina of the human eye.

MAINE, LOUIS AUGUSTE DE BOURBON, Duc de (1670–1736), eldest illegitimate son of Louis XIV and Mme de Montespan, who was legitimized (1673) and later endowed with the governorship of Languedoc and much royal property. His right to the French succession was recognized by royal edicts of 1714 and 1715, and Louis's last will entrusted Maine with the care of the future Louis XV and the royal household, as well as giving him a place on the proposed council of regency. However, after Louis XV's accession his succession rights were rescinded by parlementary edict. Maine and his wife, Louise Bénédicte de Bourbon-Condé, were subsequently involved in the plot of Philip V's ambassador Cellamare, against the regent Orléans, and were disgraced (1718).

MAINE, SIR HENRY SUMNER (1822–88), British jurist and historian, who held legal chairs at both Oxford and Cambridge at various periods between 1847 and 1888. He was also legal member of the Supreme Council in India (1863–9) and a member of the Council of India (1871–88). He published *Ancient Law* (1861) and *Village Communities* (1871).

MAINE, 23rd member state of the US, admitted in 1820. Possibly visited by the Cabots (1498–9), it was frequently explored in the early 17th cent. and was first settled by Pierre du Guast (1604). The first English settlement at Sagadahoc (1607–8) was short-lived, but its patron, Sir Ferdinando Gorges, persevered. Successive royal patents, referring to the 'Province of Main' (1606) and 'Mayn-Land' (1629), gave Gorges title to the area. The province was bought from his heirs by MA (1677), under whose jurisdiction it remained until statehood was achieved as part of the Missouri Compromise (1820). Its northern boundary was finally determined by the Webster–Ashburton treaty (1842). Because of its extensive forests and good natural harbours, MA was for long a major centre of US shipbuilding. Paper pulp is now the state's major industry. Maine's 2500 lakes and its mountains and forests have made it a popular recreation and vacation area.

MAINE, USS, American battleship, whose sinking by an explosion from an unknown source in Havana harbour (15 Feb. 1898) was an important cause of the Spanish-American War (1898). 'Remember the *Maine*' became a popular slogan of the war.

MAINTENON, MADAME DE, FRANÇOISE D'AUBIGNE, Marquise de (1635–1719), French widow of the poet Scarron (d. 1660), and the second and morganatic wife of Louis XIV of France. She was born in prison at Niort, where her father was held as a debtor, and was converted to Protestantism by a relative but reconverted by a sister of the Ursuline convent of St Jacques. Mme de Montespan chose her to take care of the royal bastards (1669) and when they were legitimized (1673) she and they were summoned from the rue Vaugirard court. Through Louis's generosity she bought the château and estate of Maintenon (1675), by which time jealousy had developed between her and Montespan, who was later to be replaced as royal mistress by Mlle de Fontanges (*c.* 1678). Mme de Maintenon's friendship with the king continued and some time after Maria Theresa's death (1683) she and Louis were secretly married. Before 1700 her influence with the king was limited to ecclesiastical appointments, but later she was consulted more frequently and had a profound effect upon the king's conduct by her constant preaching about the divine retribution which would follow from continuing sinfulness. After Louis's death (1715) she retired to the convent of St Cyr, where she and the king had jointly founded a school for girls (1684).

MAINZ, JOHN PHILIP, Elector of (1605–73), German ecclesiastical prince of the family of Schönborn, associated with the young philosopher Leibnitz, who after doing military service for the emperor against the Turks was elected Bp of Wurzburg (1642), and electoral Abp of Mainz (1647). He was also arch-chancellor of the empire, an office which he exercised responsibly. In 1654 he formed the Rhenish Confederation, an alliance of German princes, and after the interregnum following Emperor Ferdinand III's death (1657–8) he secured the election of Leopold I (1658) on condition that the new emperor would not interfere in the Franco–Spanish War still continuing in the Low Countries, which might risk the peace of Germany.

MAINZ, major German city at the confluence of the Rhine and the Main. It prospered from the trade carried by both rivers and was a centre of medieval textile manufactures. Gutenberg developed his printing enterprise at Mainz, which was the seat of one of the three German electoral archbishoprics.

MAINZ ACCORD (1621), treaty agreed during the Thirty Years War between the delegates of the princes and cities of the Protestant Union and Ambrogio Spinola, the Spanish commander on the Rhine, by which the Union promised to disband their army on condition that their neutral rights would be guaranteed by the Spaniards. This document was the last gesture of the Protestant Union, which was never to act corporately again after the assembly broke up (May 1621).

MAIPÚ, BATTLE OF (1818), fought in Chile between forces led by José de San Martín, who had invaded the country from Argentina, and the remaining garrisons loyal to Spain. The latter were decisively defeated on 5 April, and the independence of Chile was assured.

MAISKY, IVAN MIKHAILOVICH (1884–), Soviet diplomat, politician, and author, who became a Menshevik and was imprisoned after the revolution of 1905. He emigrated to London (1912), where he formed a friendship with Litvinov. He returned to Russia (1917) and in 1921 he joined the Communist Party. He served (1925–7) as counsellor at the Soviet Embassy in London and later (1932–43) as ambassador. Later he was a deputy minister for foreign affairs (1943–1946). He wrote many books, several of which have been translated into English: *Before the Storm* (1944), in which he describes his early life; *Journey into the Past* (1962), which shows him to be a keen observer of the English scene in the pre-1914 era; *Who Helped Hitler?* (1962), and *Memories of a Soviet Ambassador* (1964). The last two books present a controversial view of the motives of British politicians and of the British governing class during the years of appeasement.

MAISTRE, JOSEPH, MARIE, Comte de (1754–1821), French publicist, diplomat, and political philosopher, born at Chambéry. He went into voluntary exile after the French annexation of Savoy (1792), and from 1802 to 1817 he was Victor Emmanuel's envoy in St Petersburg. One of the most powerful leaders of the neo-Catholic and anti-revolutionary movement, he attacked anything which tended to undermine tradition, autocracy, and, above all, papal authority. His greatest works are *Considérations sur la France* (1796), *Du Pape* (1817), and *Les soirées de Saint Petersburg* (1821).

MAITLAND, SIR THOMAS (1759–1824), British colonial official and second governor of Ceylon (1805–11), who effected major improvements in the colony's administrative, financial, juridical, and military organization.

MAITLAND, WILLIAM (*c.* 1528–73), known as 'Secretary Lethington' (from his estates), Scottish politician, who supported Mary Queen of Scots and urged her claims to succeed Elizabeth I on the English throne. Although he welcomed Mary's marriage to Darnley, Maitland later regretted that event and was in sympathy with those who murdered Darnley. In the years of disturbances that followed Mary's subsequent flight to England (1568), he held Edinburgh Castle against English forces which had come north to secure James VI's position on the Scots throne. With the surrender of the castle (1573), Mary's hopes were ended, while Maitland's death in prison probably saved him from being executed by his enemies in a divided Scotland.

MAITRAKAS, ancient Indian royal dynasty (*c.* AD 500–730) that ruled in Valabhi (Saurashtra) and controlled important areas round the Gulf of Cambay. It rose during the decline of the Gupta empire. and remained in power until the raids by the Arabs of Sind. The Maitraka empire is of special significance in the history of Buddhism and Jainism.

MAIWAND, BATTLE OF (27 July 1880), at a village west of Kandahar, when Afghan forces under Ayub Khan (d. 1914), fourth son of Amir Shir Ali, defeated British forces under Gen. G. R. S. Burrows. Although Ayub was subsequently defeated by Gen. Roberts (1 Sept. 1880), after Roberts's famous march from Kabul, Maiwand became celebrated as a great national victory in Afghan history.

MAIZE, historical diffusion in Africa. It is most concentrated in parts of Central Africa, the Kenya Highlands, Uganda, Rwanda-Burundi, the highlands of the Cameroon, western Nigeria, and lower Dahomey (the place of highest concentration), and may have come to tropical Africa by one or both of two routes: first, across the Sahara from the Middle East; and second, across the Atlantic from the Americas. The millets and sorghums have been known in Africa for a long time and some writers have asserted that maize too was grown before Columbus discovered America. Indeed, design on pottery found at Ife, identified as maize, has been tentatively dated as AD 1100. The earliest Portuguese report of maize in West Africa was in 1502; but there is no direct evidence of its introduction by the Portuguese. They are known to have grown maize on the island of São Tomé, and may have done so on other islands.

In the 17th cent. maize was reported to be important on the coast between Liberia and the Niger delta. It was common even in the interior, and in the Gambia and Niger valleys, from the 18th cent. In the Congo basin and Angola, linguistic and oral evidence indicates its introduction by the Portuguese apparently in the 16th cent.; by the mid-17th cent., maize had penetrated deep into Central Africa. It was known in Ethiopia in the 16th cent., according to Portuguese sources, and became important in other parts of East Africa, probably in the 18th cent., but reached Uganda only late in the 19th cent.

MAJALLA (MECELLE), Ottoman code of civil law, promulgated 1869–76, and largely the work of Ahmed Cevdet Pasha (1822–95). Although influenced by European codes, it was based upon the Sharia and long remained the foundation of civil law in the Ottoman empire and its successor states.

MAJAPAHIT, name of the most powerful ancient Indonesian empire (1293–c. 1512), centred in the modern village of Trawulan, Mojokerto, East Java. It was founded by Prince Vijaya (later King Kertarajasa) initially as a base from which he could conduct the resistance against both the Chinese invaders and his Javanese rival Jayakatwang.

The first period (to 1329) was one of consolidation, and during the second (1329–1364) Majapahit gradually assumed control over most of present Indonesia and Malaysia, and exerted influence far beyond. This period, immortalized by Prapancha in the *Nagarakertagama*, is one of splendour unprecedented in Indonesian history. The chief architect of greater Majapahit was Gajah Mada, the courageous and shrewd minister, first of Queen Tribhuwana (*reg.* 1329–50) and later of King Hayam Wuruk (*reg.* 1350–89). Gajah Mada's death in 1364 marked the beginning of the third period of nearly a century (to c. 1450), during which Majapahit remained a big power but was unable to prevent the emergence of virtually independent states within its realm, which recognized only the formal overlordship of Majapahit (eg, Malacca). After the middle of the 14th cent. the authority of Majapahit became gradually confined to eastern Java. In this period (c. 1450–c. 1512) the empire began to disintegrate with the establishment of Muslim sultanates on the north coast of central and eastern Java. Although Majapahit lingered on for over half a century it retained only a shadow of its former glory.

The circumstances surrounding its disappearance are obscure. A late tradition of its conquest in 1478 by a coalition of Muslim coastal sultanates conflicts with other evidence. Thus, the Portuguese attest to the existence of Majapahit after the fall of Malacca (1511), but this is also the last unambiguous reference.

The main importance of Majapahit in political history is that for a brief period most of the Indonesian archipelago was brought under one state. It may thus, in retrospect, be regarded as the beginning of the development leading to Indonesian statehood. Economically, it is important in that it established a pattern of Javanese shipping, especially with Borneo and eastern Indonesia. It also led to the spread of Javanese cultural influence in and outside Indonesia (Philippines and mainland South-East Asia). Its importance to later generations is reflected in the attempts of later dynasties, notably that of Muslim Mataram, to trace their ancestry, as well as the symbols of statehood and various institutions, back to Majapahit.

Th. Pigeand, *Java in the 14th Century. A study in Cultural history* (The Hague, 1960–3).   JG de C

MAJI MAJI, rebellion which broke out in southern Tanganyika in 1905 in opposition to German colonial rule. The area was politically disunited, being thinly populated by many diverse societies, and had been affected by Ngoni migrations and slave-raiding activities during the 19th cent. A badly conceived and mismanaged scheme had been introduced in the Rufiji valley whereby the people were obliged to cultivate cotton. Nevertheless the revolt spread far beyond the affected area and took the German authorities completely by surprise.

During the months before the outbreak, and in the early weeks of the rebellion, an important basis of co-operation in many areas was the influence of a religious cult, Kolelo, which also provided the rebels with hopes of success. Water was administered to initiates in the belief that it would ensure immunity to bullets—hence the name given to the rebellion, Maji Maji, from the Swahili word *maji*, meaning water. The rebellion, which lasted over two years, was terminated largely by famine. There were probably some 75,000 African casualties. The combined effect of the rebellion and the Herero-Nama rebellion in South-West Africa obliged the German colonial authorities to revise their policies and act with greater circumspection.

MAJID BIN SAID (*reg.* 1856–70), Sultan of Zanzibar and son of Said bin Sultan. He continued his father's policy of friendship with Britain and co-operation with Indian merchants in the commercial exploitation of East Africa.

MAJOR-GENERALS, THE (1655–7), chiefs of a system of English local government and military security instituted by Oliver Cromwell. Penruddock's Rising (1655) resulted in the Royalists being subjected to severe restrictions enforced by a new type of local military organization. England and Wales were divided into 11 districts, each commanded by its own major-general. They were nominally appointed to supervise the reorganized militia, but also to act as tax collectors, policemen, and agents of an intended reformation of public morals—something close to Cromwell's heart. Their existence supplemented existing local government, eg, the JPs and county committees, by providing for the enforcement of the poor law, laws against enclosure, etc. Though they varied in their effectiveness, the major-generals were generally disliked, not only because they suppressed horse-racing, cock-fighting, plays, brothels, and alehouses, but because they represented an encroachment of the central authority on local affairs. They were detested by the gentry. The hatred of militarism which they engendered erupted in the House of Commons in Dec. 1656, when a Militia bill was brought in suggesting a decimation tax on Royalists which would pay for the system. The bill was rejected and Cromwell allowed the system to disappear.

MAJORIAN (*reg.* 457–61), Roman Emperor in the West, who was elected by the Senate and proclaimed by the armies. Despite administrative reforms and some military successes in Gaul and Spain against rebellious barbarian auxiliary troops, the general disintegration of the Western empire continued. Majorian led an expedition against the Vandals in Africa. He was defeated and on his return to Italy was forced to abdicate. Five days later he died, having almost certainly been assassinated by order of Ricimer, the Suevian commander of the barbarian troops in Italy. Amid the confusion of the times and the last convulsions of the Western empire, Majorian stands out as an exceptionally brave and attractive figure.

MAKABULOS, FRANCISCO (1871–1922), Philippine revolutionary from Tarlac—one of the first Philippine provinces to be placed under martial law by the Spanish government. Makabulos founded a short-lived government based on the 'Makabulos Constitution', after the revolutionaries had moved to Tarlac from Malolos in Bulacan province, where they met and formulated a constitution for the first Philippine republic of 1899. This was the culmination of Makabulos's revolutionary activities. He had served under Spanish colonial rule successively as mayor of a *pueblo cabeza de barangay*, or village head, lieutenant-treasurer, and fiscal. He also joined a secret society called the *Katipunan*. He was appointed by the revolutionary government's Central Council in Luzon to be one of 12 brigadier-generals, and became responsible for the support given to the revolutionary cause by his own province and the neighbouring province of Pangasinan. After the Americans occupied the Philippines in 1898, he became a peaceful citizen, produced a few plays, and joined the *Lapiang Democrata*, or Democratic Party.

MAKARIOS, archbishop (1913–), Cypriot political leader, who entered the monastery of Kykko in 1926 as a novice. In 1948 he was consecrated a bishop and two years later was elected archbishop or ethnarch of the Orthodox Church in Cyprus. He was a convinced Greek nationalist, and organized a plebiscite on *enosis* (union with Greece) in Jan. 1950 which resulted in a 96 per cent majority in favour of union. In 1951 Makarios met Gen. Grivas and joined him on a revolutionary committee. After Papagos reneged on his promise to promote union and the appeal to the United Nations failed (1954), Makarios found resistance to Grivas's plans to use force increasingly difficult. Later, however, he came to an agreement with Karamanlis and Sir John Harding, governor of Cyprus, which allowed for internal self-government with a guarantee of eventual self-determination. But further proposals from the British were rejected and in 1956 Makarios was exiled to the Seychelles islands. He was released in 1957 and returned to Athens, where in 1958 he rejected proposals for a partnership with the British. Fears of the partition of Cyprus led Makarios to accept a scheme for an independent Cyprus without *enosis*. An agreement was concluded in Feb. 1959 and in Aug. 1960 a republic was proclaimed and Makarios chosen as its president. Neither the Greeks nor the Turks were satisfied with the arrangement. The troubles of 1964–5 between the two communities led Makarios to establish a unitary state and abolish rights given to the Turkish population. His desire to alter the constitution framed at Zürich led him to establish loose relations with the Soviet Union and its allies.

JMK

MAKARY, Metropolitan of Moscow (*fl.* 16th cent.), Russian scholar and principal adviser of Tsar Ivan IV and a member of his Chosen Council, who compiled the *Lives of the Russian Saints*. He advised Ivan to assume the title of *tsar* in 1546 and inspired him with ideas of the high dignity and the responsibilities of a Christian ruler.

MAKASSAR SULTANATE, 17th-cent. commercial centre in South Celebes (Indonesia), which became a centre for Malay and Portuguese spice trade to the Moluccas in the 16th cent. Despite considerable Christian (Portuguese) influence, it accepted Islam in 1603, and immediately thereafter conquered the neighbouring Bugis people. The height of Makassar's prosperity was achieved after the Dutch conquest of Malacca (1641), when, as the largest Indonesian port free of the Dutch monopoly, it became the centre of Portuguese activity. Its political authority then embraced Sumbawa and eastern Borneo as well as South Celebes. Makassar's power ended with its conquest by the Dutch captain, Speelman, aided by rebellious Bugis (1668). It remained, however, the most important Dutch–Indonesian administrative centre in eastern Indonesia.

MAKEMIE, FRANCIS (1658–1708), American clergyman, who organized the first presbytery of the Presbyterian Church in Philadelphia (1706), and preached from the Carolinas to New York. He was arrested and imprisoned in New York (1707) for preaching without a licence, but the court freed him. His case resulted in the enactment of laws preventing religious persecution.

MAKERERE UNIVERSITY COLLEGE, Kampala, Uganda, oldest centre for higher education in East and Central Africa. It was established in 1921 as a college for technical training in applied sciences, and soon began to concentrate on academic instruction. In 1950 London degree courses were instituted in arts and sciences. During the early 1960s, other colleges were established at Nairobi and Dar es Salaam, and in 1963 the University of East Africa was set up, to which the three colleges were affiliated, and which offered its own degrees. The University of East Africa ceased to exist in 1970, when each college became a national university. As the only centre for higher education in East Africa for many years, Makerere produced a high proportion of East Africa's new leaders.

MAKURIA, one of the kingdoms of medieval Christian Nubia, which stretched from the third Nile cataract to 'El Abwab', which is thought to be near modern Kabushiya. Its capital was at Old Dongola.

MALACCA SULTANATE (*c.* 1400–1511). The beginnings of Malacca on the Malay peninsula date back to the first years of the 15th cent., when Prince Parameshwara (or Paramisora), who was probably a Javanese, settled in Malacca, at that time

a village of fishermen and pirates. Its subsequent development into the greatest commercial centre of South-East Asia, especially from the middle of the century, must no doubt be attributed to the energy of its population, but can be fully understood only in the context of other developments of the time. Majapahit, which had dominated the Straits for the preceding century, was paralysed owing to an internal conflict. A show of force by the Chinese (the maritime expeditions of Cheng Ho) created new opportunities; the expansion of Islam new loyalties. In fact, the founder of Malacca himself became a Muslim later in life.

The first 40 years represented a period of consolidation during which Malacca sought Chinese help against the Javanese of Majapahit and the Thai of Ayutthaya, both of which claimed some form of suzerainty over the new state. By maintaining its independence Malacca laid the foundations of its later expansion.

In 1446 a new sultan, Muzaffar Shah, succeeded to the throne after bloody intrigues. Assisted by his prime minister (*bendahara*), Tun Perak, and his admiral (*laksamana*), Hang Tuah, of legendary fame, he inaugurated an era of a Greater Malacca. By different campaigns, which were continued through the reign of the next sultan, Mansur Shah (1456–77), the southern part of the Malay peninsula as well as important ports on the east coast of Sumatra were brought under the control or influence of Malacca. Political supremacy, as in the time of Srivijaya a few centuries earlier, enabled the rulers to concentrate most of the trade of the area in Malacca. It thus developed into the greatest mart of South-East Asia. Among the numerous products traded or exchanged at Malacca were Indonesian pepper and spices, Chinese silk and porcelain, and Indian cotton cloth.

Meanwhile the population became more and more cosmopolitan. While the Malays constituted the ruling class, a considerable part of the population, if not the majority, was non-Malay, being predominantly Javanese and Tamil. Among the Malays the classical Malay language, based on the official language of Srivijaya but enriched by numerous words borrowed from Arabic, developed into an excellent vehicle for literature and administration.

The prosperity of Malacca made it a prime target of the Portuguese, who first came into contact with Malacca in 1509. Subsequent conflicts led to a Portuguese expedition in 1511 occupying the city after a long siege. This meant the end of the Malacca sultanate, although it was continued in Johor, which, in many respects, followed the traditions of Malacca.

R. O. Winstedt, *A History of Malaya* (Singapore, 1962).

JGdeC

MALACHY (d. 1148), Irish Church reformer, who was Abp of Armagh (1129–37) and in 1139 was appointed papal legate in Ireland. He worked continuously for reform of the Irish Church on continental lines and introduced the Cistercians into Ireland. His friend, St Bernard of Clairvaux, wrote a valuable *Life of Malachy*.

MALAGA, BATTLE OF (24 Aug. 1704), only full-scale naval engagement of the War of the Spanish Succession between a French fleet of 50 ships, under the Count of Toulouse, and an Allied fleet of 53 ships under Sir George Rooke. Tactically the battle was indecisive; the French, whose objective had been the recapture of Gibraltar, withdrew to Toulon, though they claimed a victory.

MALAGASY, REPUBLIC OF (595,790 sq. kms), island off the east coast of Africa formerly the French colony (1898–1960) of Madagascar. Most of the 6 million inhabitants belong to the Marina group. Since achieving independence in 1960, Malagasy elects by adult suffrage a president for a seven-year term and a national assembly for five years. The republic's economy is (1970) largely agricultural.

MALAGASY PEOPLES. The population of Madagascar (1970) consists of a mixture of African and Indonesian peoples, who arrived by sea over a long period of time. There is no indication of any lithic inhabitants on the island, and it is apparent that the earliest voyagers were iron-age peoples. Those who came from Indonesia arrived therefore after the development of iron-age cultures in Indonesia, but probably before the introduction of Hinduism, there being no traces of this religion on Madagascar. This puts the date of the Indonesian origins between the 1st and 5th cents AD. A similar date of arrival is suggested for African peoples. As well as later Indonesians and Africans, there have been Arabs, Europeans, Indians, and Chinese.

The Malagasy language is by origin Indonesian, with some Bantu influence. Traditional religious practices centred round ancestor worship, and the social structure was based upon large patrilineal clans. Later, a caste system related to slavery developed in some parts of the island. Before the 19th cent. Madagascar was politically fragmented.

The Malagasy peoples first came into contact with Europeans (Portuguese) in the 16th cent. During subsequent centuries, trade in guns and slaves with the British, French, and Dutch encouraged the rise of strong states in Madagascar. One of these, Merina, rose to a position of dominance in the 19th cent. By this time Christianity, which was introduced by the British London Missionary Society, had become influential. By the 1960s there were over 6 million Malagasy, almost half of whom were Christian, and a very large proportion were educated in both Malagasy and French.

H. Deschamps, *Madagascar* (Paris, 1951).   AEA

MALAITA, populous island in the British Solomons, inhabited by some 60,000 mixed bush and salt-water people (Melanesians) which long resisted Christian missionaries. In the 1940s the island was convulsed by a 'nativistic' movement culminating (1947) in a march of 9000 on Auki and the arrest of nine district leaders. In 1951 a new Federal Council Movement won the concession of an elective, subsidized, consultative Malaita Council.

MALAKA, IBRAHIM GELAR DATUK TAN (?1897–1949), Minangkabau (West Sumatran), who was an early leader of the Indonesian Communist Party. He was exiled (1922) by the colonial authorities and went to Moscow, where he pleaded unsuccessfully with the Communist International for co-operation between Islam and Communism against Western imperialism. The International sent him to the Far East, where he attempted to organize and co-ordinate communist efforts in South-East Asia. He tried in vain to prevent the Indonesian communists from attempting their revolt of 1926–7, and argued the need for a more nationally oriented, long-term approach to revolutionary warfare. Following the revolt, he established a secret organization, PARI, aimed both at creating an Indonesian revolutionary underground and at promoting South-East Asian unity on a Pan-Malay basis.

Tan Malaka's regionalist and nationalist inclinations caused him to drift away from orthodox communism. He returned to Indonesia during the Second World War, and after the declaration (1945) of Indonesia's independence became politically active, leading a radical nationalist opposition to both President Sukarno and the left-wing government coalition, insisting that there should be no compromise with the returning Dutch. He was arrested and imprisoned (1946–1948). On his release he established the Murba (Proletarian) Party, a radical nationalist group. He was killed during the final clash with the Dutch.

MALAN, DANIEL FRANÇOIS (1874–1959), South African politician and prime minister, who before entering politics was a minister of one of the Dutch Reformed Churches. He was the first editor of the Afrikaner nationalist newspaper, *Die Burger*, founded in 1915. His career, like that of many of

his extreme nationalist colleagues, showed him as a skilful opportunist as well as a determined ideologue. In 1927, though still a provincial figure, he could say with warmth that 'England today' was 'the mother of our freedom'. But the steady growth of Afrikaner separatism soon found him talking a different language. In 1934 he was among those who refused to follow Gen. Hertzog into a coalition with the English-speaking followers of Smuts, and he rapidly became one of the chief spokesmen of anti-English sentiment among the Afrikaans-speaking population.

At the outset of the Second World War he was among those who rejected the Allied cause and, for a while, looked to a Nazi victory as a means of establishing an Afrikaner national state. By 1942, however, he was again singing another tune, declaring that 'the Afrikaner who bases his hopes on a German victory is an untrustworthy coward'. The end of the war found him vigorously campaigning for an Afrikaner Nationalist victory at the polls, and by the time this was achieved (1948) he and his followers had adopted the extreme racist attitudes which were to characterize the apartheid system, founded by Malan as prime minister of the first Afrikaner Nationalist government. For him, as for his colleagues, all arguments in favour of moderation or reform of non-racist policies were tantamount to 'communism', and thus were a form of a treason to the state they were determined to establish.   BD

MALARIA (in the Pacific), anopheline-borne, largely coastal disease restricted between 0–20° S and W of 170° E (Buxton's line), *ie*, to Melanesia. Diffused eastwards from Indo-Malaysia—as the attenuation of anopheline species in this direction suggests—it probably reached its present limit (Aneityum, New Hebrides) by the 15th–16th cents, gradually driving the indigenous Papuan inland and checking or frustrating the westward expansion of the maritime Micronesians and Polynesians—hence the mixed nature of the modern island 'Melanesian'. A serious impediment to European contact, particularly in the missionary period, the disease had a notable effect on the progress of the Solomons–New Guinea campaign (1942–4).

MALASPINA, ALEJANDRO (1725–1809), Spanish navigator who led a notable scientific survey (the results of which are still largely unpublished) of the Galapagos, Tonga, parts of North America, and the Philippines (1789–94).

MALAVA, republican tribe (*gana*) of ancient India, originally from the Punjab, but later settled in south-east Rajasthan, where they were brought under the control of the satraps of Ujjain (2nd cent. AD). In the 3rd cent. they again became independent and then issued numerous coins until the middle of the 4th cent., when after being defeated by Samudra Gupta, they were incorporated into the Gupta empire as an autonomous unit. Many scholars believe that the famous Vikrama Era, starting in 57 BC, was originally a tribal era of the Malavas.

MALAVIYA, PANDIT MOHAN (1861–1946), Indian nationalist politician and Hindu leader of the Congress in the United Provinces. He was a member of the Congress from 1886, and between 1902 and 1930 was never out of the UP legislative council or the central legislature for long. His reputation as a nationalist spokesman, which his minority report to the Indian Industrial Commission (1916–18) further enhanced, was formidable, but his major campaigns were concerned with the protection and furtherance of Hindu interests. At the turn of the century he campaigned for the use of Hindi and was the dominant force in the creation of Benares Hindu University (1916), of which he was vice-chancellor (1919–39). He presided at special sessions of the Hindu Mahasabha (1922, 1924, 1926) and at the regular session of 1923, and he took an active part in the *sangathan* movement to strengthen unity within the Hindu community. In the mid-1920s, as Hindu–Muslim relations deteriorated, he sought to swing the Congress to the defence, as he saw it, of Hindu interests, and he went so far as to organize an 'Independent Congress Party' (1926) to contest elections against official Congress (*ie*, Swarajist) candidates. Although disagreement with new policies within the Mahasabha caused him to break with that body in 1928, he remained the chief Hindu spokesman within the Congress and his influence on negotiations with Muslims at the All-Parties Conference (1928) and the second Round Table Conference (1931) ensured that there would be no compromise on the principle of joint electorates. He was, therefore, adamant in his opposition to the Communal Award (1932), and when Congress refused to denounce its terms unequivocally, he left the Congress and formed a new Congress Nationalist Party to fight the award. He was active as a municipal councillor in Allahabad and was also a prominent journalist, playing a leading part in establishing both the *Leader* of Allahabad and the *Hindustan Times* of New Delhi.

MALAWI (119,000 sq. kms) in south central Africa, until 1964 the British protectorate of Nyasaland, now (1970) an independent republic within the British Commonwealth. A president and parliament are elected for five-year periods by adult suffrage. Nyanja and Tumbuka groups predominate in a population of 4,042,400.

MALAY PIRACY, characteristic of many parts of the Indonesian archipelago in the 18th and 19th cents. In traditional Malay states at their zenith there was a close relationship between trade and politics. The ruler who could attract the largest share of the shifting international trade became powerful, and used this power to destroy rival ports and force local trade to use his own. But the legitimate trade and power base of these states was undermined by monopolistic Europeans, particularly the Dutch (from *c*. 1620). As the old Malay capitals decayed, the line became further blurred between unsystematic political pressure to regain trade, and simple piracy.

Certain politically disorganized areas, like northern and western Borneo, and eastern and north-western Sumatra, became especially notorious in the 18th and 19th cents as the home of vagrants who lived by piracy and fishing. But European powers frequently regarded any form of interference with their trade as piracy, even where political motives were paramount. Early in the 19th cent. this led usually to the burning of one of the coastal villages by a European gunboat, while later it was often advanced as the grounds for more permanent European intervention.

MALAYAN EMERGENCY (1948–60), period of counter-insurgency against the Malayan communists. When their trade union activity was curbed by repressive British action (1948), the predominantly Chinese communists of Malaya returned to jungle warfare, in which they had had valuable experience fighting the Japanese. They attempted to apply Mao Tse-tung's strategy, but never succeeded in advancing from terrorist attacks to the establishment of liberated areas.

British and Malayan troops checked their initial threat to the towns, but only began to succeed in eliminating terrorism after 1952, when Gen. Templer isolated the armed communists by resettling rural Chinese, while initiating rapid steps towards Malayan independence. Although the Baling talks between elected Malayan leaders and the communists (1955) were abortive, guerrilla strength was reduced to about 500 men along the Thai border by the end of the emergency (1960). The emergency cost the lives of 6700 communists, 519 Commonwealth troops, 1346 police, and 2473 civilians. At its height, about 40,000 troops, 61,000 armed police, and 250,000 home guards were in action against about 3000 guerrillas.

MALAYAN UNION, abortive British blue-print for post-war Malaya. The White Paper of Jan. 1946 on the subject proposed a union of the former Federated and Unfederated Malay States and the Straits Settlements, excluding Singapore. Administration was to be centralized under a governor assisted by Legislative and Executive Councils in a manner similar to a Crown Colony. Equal rights of citizenship were to be granted to people of all races born in Malaya. The scheme foundered on strong Malay opposition, expressed through the first mass Malay movement, UMNO. It gave way to the Federation of Malaya in Feb. 1948 without ever having become fully effective.

MALAYU, originally the name of an ancient state in modern Djambi, central Sumatra, Indonesia (7th cent. AD). At the end of the 7th cent. it was eclipsed by Srivijaya, but revived by the middle of the 13th cent. In the 14th cent. it became powerful as a subordinate ally of Majapahit under King Adityavarman; the centre of the state was then shifted to Pagerruyung, West Sumatra.

Besides its precise connotation, Malayu was sometimes used as a vague term for indicating the island of Sumatra or the Malay-speaking areas in general, but from the 15th cent. the name became confined to the southern part of the Malay peninsula, then the centre of Malay civilization.

MALCHUS (*fl.* 6th cent. BC), Carthaginian general who defended the Phoenician colonies in Sicily against the Greeks, but was defeated by native tribes in Sardinia. He was later executed for attempting to return from exile.

MALCOLM III (*c*. 1031–93), King of the Scots (*reg.* 1058–1093), son of King Duncan I, who was killed by Macbeth in 1040. He in turn slew Macbeth in 1057 and Macbeth's son in 1058. In *c*. 1070 Malcolm married the devout Margaret, grand-daughter of King Edmund Ironside of England, who promoted the spread of more civilized usages at the Scottish royal court and in the Church. Malcolm submitted to William I of England in 1072, but was eventually killed in a raid into England. Four of his sons reigned successively after him and his daughter Matilda (d. 1118) became the wife of King Henry I of England.

MALCOLM IV (1141–65), King of Scotland (*reg.* 1153–65), who succeeded his grandfather, David I. For most of his reign he was a minor, yet he managed to keep at bay the powerful Macbeth family, who threatened him in the north, and fend off trouble from the west, stimulated by Fergus of Galloway. Relations with the English were less successful. He surrendered (1157) to Henry II border territories, won by David I and left to his successor, William the Lion (*reg.* 1165–1214), the task of freeing Scotland from English subjugation.

MALCOLM, SIR JOHN (1769–1833), British soldier and colonial official in India, who fought against Tipu Sultan and the Marathas. As envoy to Persia (1799–1801), he drew up a political and a commercial treaty; he was resident in Mysore, and at the court of Sindhia (1801–5) drafted the treaties at the end of the Second Maratha War, and in 1818 arranged for the abdication of the peshwa. He was governor of Bombay (1827–30). His publications included a *Memoir of Central India* (1823) and a *Political History of India* (1826).

MALCONTENTS, name given to those Catholic nobles in the southern Netherlands who, from 1578, opposed William of Orange, turning to the French Duke of Alençon for leadership. They included Lalaing, Montigny, and Hèze and they fought for the Catholic religion and the pacification of Ghent. Originally anti-Spanish, they were won back to allegiance to Spain by Alexander Farnese's diplomacy and military successes and also by their loathing for popular dictatorship and Calvinist extremism.

MALDIVE ISLANDS, 1087 small islands in the Indian Ocean with a population (1970) of 104,000. The islands, formerly under British protection, became independent in 1965. The sultan is head of state, and there is a House of Representatives elected by adult suffrage.

MALEBRANCHE, NICOLE (1638–1715), French Cartesian philosopher, who entered the Congregation of the Oratory in 1660 and devoted himself to theology until his study of Descartes led him to apply Cartesian theory to theology and he became Descartes's chief disciple. In his most famous work, *De la Recherche de la Vérité* (1674–5), he stressed that everything requires divine support to exist and all perception comes through union with God. This led him into controversy with Antoine Arnauld, but Malebranche had a positive influence upon philosophers such as Pierre Bayle, David Hume, and George Berkeley.

MALENKOV, GEORGIY MAKSIMILIANOVICH (1902–), Russian politician and prime minister of Russia, who was first a commissar in the Red Army (1919) and joined the Communist party (1920). He was for a time attached to the central committee and to Stalin's personal secretariat (1925). He directed the party organization in Moscow (1930–4) and was responsible for the management of party cadres throughout the Soviet Union at the time of the great purge (1934–9). In 1939 he became a member of the central committee and then a candidate member of the Politburo (1941). Throughout the Second World War he was a member of the state committee for defence (1941–5). As a mark of service, and of Stalin's favour, he was made a full member of the Politburo (1946) and a deputy prime minister.

He became increasingly prominent and in 1952 presented the report of the central committee to the 19th party congress—thus assuming a position which appeared to designate him as Stalin's successor. After Stalin's death (March 1953) he became prime minister and was the leading member of the 'collective leadership' established at that time. He introduced a number of measures of reform designed to make concessions on the domestic front while at the same time strengthening the state apparatus as the directing agency of the economy. He was also associated with the detente in foreign policy.

He was, however, an opponent of Khrushchev in the struggle for power. In contrast to some of the Stalinist 'old guard', he was a rival in the promotion of moderate reforms. His position at the head of the state apparatus put him at a disadvantage in relation to Khrushchev, who headed the party apparatus, and his reforming policies were not of the sort to produce quick results. He asked to be allowed to resign, making a confession of his failures (a new feature of Soviet politics), and was replaced by Bulganin (Feb. 1955). He continued in opposition to Khrushchev and was one of the members of the Presidium which nearly succeeded in ousting him (June 1957). As a result, he was expelled from the central committee and appointed manager of a hydro-electric station in East Kazakhstan.   WK

MALESHERBES, CHRÉTIEN GUILLAUME DE LAMOIGNON DE (1721–94), French statesman, magistrate, and member of the great *parlementaire* family of Lamoignon. He was a patron of the enlightenment, a member of the academies of Sciences and *Belles Lettres*, as well as of the *Académie Française*. As director of the publishing trade or chief censor (1750–63), he gave unofficial protection to the *philosophes*, whose ideas he admired. In 1763, when president of the *Cour des Aides*, he called for a meeting of the states general. He was later exiled for protesting against Maupeou's appointment of superior councils in place of the disbanded *parlement* of Paris. On being recalled by Louis XVI to succeed La Vrillière as minister of state at the head of the king's household, he served with Turgot, who had replaced Maupeou and Terray. Turgot and Malesherbes recalled the *parlements* and restored the *Cour des Aides*. In May 1775 Malesherbes presented Louis with a plan of fiscal reform, but it was ignored, and two months later he resigned. In 1788 he unsuccessfully pleaded with the king that he should lead a movement for constitutional reform. Malesherbes was executed on the orders of the Committee of Public Safety (22 April 1794).

MALI, empire in West Africa, which reached its apogee in the 13th–14th cents. Its early nucleus was on the upper region of the Niger river and the empire appears to have grown out of the gradual dominance of the Manding clan of Keita over its two chief rivals, the Konaté and the Tara-ure (Traoré). At an uncertain date, but probably in the 11th cent., an early ruler was converted to Islam. Though some of his successors recanted, the 13th- and 14th-cent. rulers made Islam the royal cult and several went on pilgrimage to Mecca.

The real founder of the Mali empire was Sundiata. He defeated the Soso chief Sumanguru (c. 1234), and thus opened the way to northward expansion into savannah lands bordering the Sahara. Ghana had long since declined and Mali now succeeded it as the major power of the Western Sudan. Being in control of caravan termini, such as Walata, and later Timbuctoo, Mali could profit fully from the alluvial gold produced along the tributaries of the Niger and Senegal rivers. This was exported to North Africa in exchange for Saharan salt and Mediterranean products—cloth, beads, copper, and horses.

During the reign of Mansa Musa (1312–37), Mali reached the height of its prosperity and territorial expansion. To the west its domains extended to the Gambia; in the east it controlled the Niger Bend up to Gao. Diplomatic relations were established with the Marinids of Fez, and Musa was received in Cairo by the Mamluk sultan, Al-Nasir (1324), while making a pilgrimage to Mecca. The wealth and prestige of Mali is reflected by its appearance on European maps from 1339.

In the reign of Sulaiman, Musa's brother (1341–60), Mali was visited by Ibn Battuta, whose description of court ceremonial reveals a rich blend of Islamic and indigenous pomp. He also spoke warmly of the ruler's justice and the security of travel in his lands.

After Sulaiman's reign a succession of internal struggles weakened the huge empire. Governors of outlying provinces made themselves independent, and by the late 15th cent. the rising power of Songhay had overrun the northern and eastern provinces while three rival clans contested power at the centre. The 16th cent. saw further decline and contraction of the Mali empire and by 1600 it had disintegrated into a conglomeration of petty chieftaincies.   JOH

MALI, REPUBLIC OF (1,240,021 sq. kms), in West Africa has a population (1970) of 5 million, chiefly Bambara, Fulani, Songhay, and Tuareg people. It was formerly a province of French West Africa, and became an independent republic in 1960. Since an army coup of 1968, it has been ruled by a president who is head of the national liberation council and rules by decree.

MALIETOA LAUPEPA (d. 1898), titular chief of Upolu, Samoa (Pacific), was self-styled 'king' from 1868 to 1869 and king in Steinberger's brief constitution (1875–6). He fell foul of local lineage rivalries and foreign pressure and was deported (1887–9) by the local German consul because of his pro-British leanings. Subsequently he regained office with German backing.

MALIK, ADAM (1917–), Batak (Sumatran) radical nationalist politician and journalist, who founded the Indonesian news service, *Antara*, in 1937. Until 1966 he was prominent in the Murba Party, whose members were followers of Tan Malaka. Malik served (1963–6) as minister of trade under Sukarno's regime, and thereafter as minister of foreign affairs under Suharto.

MALIK IBN ANAS (c. 715–95), Muslim jurist, whose great work, the *Kitab al-Muwwatta*, a corpus of legal and religious traditions as exemplified in the practice of the Hijaz, became the canon for the particular *madhhab* or school of Muslim law designated as Maliki and to be found (1970) throughout most of North Africa (except Lower Egypt), and in eastern Arabia.

MALIK SHAH (*reg.* 1072–92), Seljuk Sultan, during whose reign the Great Seljuk Sultanate reached its apogee. The Turks, at this time, overran much of Byzantine Asia Minor, establishing there the Seljuk sultanate of Rum, with its centre at Konya; and also laid the foundation of a brief-lived Seljuk regime in Syria. Under Malik Shah, as under his father, Alp Arslan (*reg.* 1063–72), the main business of government rested in the capable hands of the famous Vizier, Nizam al-Mulk. After the death of Malik Shah dynastic discord and internal rebellion began to undermine the domination of the Seljuks.

MALIKI 'school' (*madhhab*) of Islamic law, takes its name from Malik ibn Anas (d. 795), a scholar of Medina, whose *Kitab al-Muwwatta* forms the basis of Maliki legal thought. The work was transmitted by a number of pupils, some of whom added their own views. Malik's own ideas also found expression through the *Mudawwana* of Sahnun (d. 854), a jurist of Qairawan (Tunisia).

It was particularly in North Africa and Spain that Maliki teachings took root, first at Qairawan and later in Tlemcen, Fez, Cordoba, and Toledo. Under the Almoravids (1069–1147), it was the official rite of north-west Africa and Spain and its rulings were rigorously enforced. Though out of favour under the Almohads, it came into its own under their successors, the Marinids, from 1269. To this day it remains the law-school of all Africa west of the Nile, with the exception of Lower Egypt.

In North Africa the most favoured Maliki text became the *Risala* of Ibn Abi Zaid (d. *c.* 996), while in West Africa the *Mukhtasar* of the Egyptian scholar, Khalil ibn Ishaq (d. 1374), gained enormous popularity after it was introduced to Timbuctoo early in the 16th cent. This work, with its numerous commentaries and glosses, was avidly studied in West African centres of scholarship and formed a major legal source for Uthman ibn Fudi (d. 1817) when he codified the laws relating to *jihad* and the government of his Sokoto-based state.

MALINDI, Arab settlement on the Kenya coast. It was in existence in the 12th cent. AD, and was visited by a Chinese fleet in 1417. It was the headquarters of the Portuguese Captain of the Coast (1512–93), was abandoned in the second half of the 17th cent., reoccupied in 1848 by settlers from Lamu and Zanzibar, and burnt in 1896 during the Mazrui rebellion.

MALINOVSKY, RODION YAKOVLEVICH (1898–1967), Russian soldier and politician, who was a marshal of the Soviet Union and minister of defence. He was active in the civil war, joined the Communist party (1926), and graduated from the M. V. Frunze Military Academy (1930). During the Second World War he distinguished himself at the battle of Stalingrad (1942). The army under his command occupied Rumania and Hungary. He then commanded the Transbaykalian army group fighting against Japan (1945). In 1952 he was made a candidate member of the central committee of the CPSU. He was appointed minister of defence after the dismissal of Zhukov (1957).

MALLET DU PAN, JACQUES (1749–1800), Swiss political writer of moderate royalist views who was patronized by Voltaire and in 1779 began to publish his *Annales Politiques Mémoires Historiques* in Geneva. He was employed by Panckoucke during the early years of the Revolution to report debates of the French assembly for the *Mercure de France*. In 1792 Louis XVI sent him as an envoy to the Emperor Leopold II and King Frederick William II of Prussia. He deplored the death of the child-king Louis XVII in prison (1795), which ended the hopes of constitutional monarchists

like himself, and retired to Switzerland, until Napoleon's conquest of that country forced him into exile in Britain, where he founded the successful *Mercure Britannique* (1798).

MALLIA, Minoan city in northern Crete, 27 kms east of Cnossos. The palace dates from *c.* 2000 BC, was rebuilt and enlarged *c.* 1750, and finally destroyed *c.* 1400. The surrounding town flourished (*c.* 1700–1400) and was partially reoccupied after the destruction of 1400.

MALMESBURY, JAMES HARRIS, 1st Earl of (1746–1820), British diplomat, who held posts at Madrid (1768–72), Berlin (1772–6), and St Petersburg (1777–82). In 1784 he was appointed minister at The Hague, where he was instrumental in overthrowing the republican party in favour of the House of Orange and in negotiating the Triple Alliance of 1788 between Britain, Holland, and Prussia. He seceded from the Whig Party in 1793 and in that year was sent on a futile mission to try to hold Prussia to the First Coalition against France. In 1794 he achieved a fresh alliance with Prussia and negotiated the marriage between the Prince of Wales and Princess Caroline of Brunswick. His efforts to negotiate peace with France (1796–7) failed. Nevertheless, successive foreign ministers, including Canning, sought his advice and guidance as a diplomat.

MALMESBURY, JAMES HOWARD HARRIS, 3rd Earl of (1807–89), British politician. As foreign secretary in Lord Derby's first and second administrations (1852, 1858–9) he recognized the French Second Empire and maintained good relations with Napoleon III. He was lord privy seal (1866–8, 1874–6).

MALMÖ, TREATY OF (1848), seven-month armistice in the Dano–Prussian War, under which Schleswig-Holstein was administered by a joint commission of Danes and Prussians. Its acceptance was bitterly opposed by the Liberals in the Frankfurt parliament.

MALOUET, VICTOR PIERRE (1740–1814), governor of French Guiana (1776–8), who tried to revive the decaying colony by draining the coastal lowlands and encouraging the planters to drink less rum and grow more sugar. Their hostility forced him to retire prematurely.

MALPIGHI, MARCELLO (1628–94), Italian anatomical scientist, who taught at the Bologna University as professor of medicine and carried on the work begun by Harvey. He launched the science of histology and cytology and made fundamental discoveries by examining the liver, kidney, the cortex of the brain, and the tongue. He first revealed the uriniferous tubules which begin in the cortex of the kidney as dilated bulbs and were called Malpighian corpuscles after him. With the aid of a microscope he also discovered the functioning of the blood capillaries in the lung of a frog, published in *De Pulmonibus* (1661). Amongst his other studies were those of the taste buds of the tongue and the development of larvae; he also wrote a treatise on the silk-worm. Many of his papers were published in the *Philosophical Transactions* of the Royal Society.

MALPLAQUET, BATTLE OF (1709), fought in northern France during the War of the Spanish Succession between the forces of the grand alliance, commanded by the Duke of Marlborough and Prince Eugène of Savoy, and the French army, led by Marshals Villars and Boufflers. Villars left his fortified lines, offering battle to halt the siege of Mons. He deployed his army on a strong natural site and, by using extensive earthworks, made his position formidable. However, Marlborough was determined to seize this chance to destroy the last field army of France and end the war, but only after much bitter fighting were the French positions stormed. Though Villars was wounded, the French retired in good order, unmolested by the allied forces.

It is difficult to adjudge the victors of Malplaquet. The allies drove the French from prepared defences and were able to complete the siege of Mons. But their victory cost 16,000–18,000 troops to France's 11,000. The battle had a profound effect on public opinion in England. The Tories, proposing peace, made full use of the loss of life to support their arguments. In the general election of 1710 the Tory peace policy was endorsed.

MALRAUX, ANDRÉ (1901–   ), French writer and politician, who was a supporter of revolutionary movements before the Second World War. In the Spanish Civil War he organized the foreign volunteer air force which fought for the Republican government. In the Second World War he fought in France (1939–40), and was captured by the Germans, but escaped and became a leader of the clandestine forces in central France. After the Liberation he commanded a regular brigade. At this time, he became an admirer of De Gaulle and was a minister in his government (1945–6). He then directed the propaganda activities of De Gaulle's Rassemblement du peuple français (RPF) movement, and again became a minister when De Gaulle returned to power (1958). As minister for cultural affairs (1959–69) he made his mark by a policy of conserving France's artistic heritage and giving active state patronage to the arts. His novels *Man's Estate* (1933) and *Days of Hope* (1937) were based on his experiences in China and Spain in the 1920s.

MALT TAXATION in Britain was one of the reasons for a general dislike of excise and was a source of friction between England and Scotland in the early 18th cent. It had been established on Scottish beer (1713), contrary to the Act of Union (1707), although it was not levied until 1725. In June 1713 it led to an unsuccessful move by the Scots in parliament to repeal the union. When it was eventually imposed at half the English rate, it caused the Shawfield riots (1725).

In England, malt taxation was burdensome on the poorer classes, especially when it was raised very sharply in 1802 and 1803, so that the cost of the grain was approximately doubled. It remained high until after the French Wars. There was also a duty on beer, making fermented liquor heavily taxed. In 1830 the beer duty was taken off, but the tax on malt remained as a handicap to the brewing industry until 1880.

MALTA, SIEGE OF (1565). Sultan Suleiman, in 1565, made a determined attempt to capture Malta from the Knights of St John, who had held the island since 1530, after their eviction from Rhodes by the Turks in 1522. A great fleet, numbering about 200 vessels and bearing some 30,000 men, left Istanbul in April of that year. The main Turkish assault was directed against the Fort of St Elmo, which eventually fell, but the defences at St Angelo and Il Burgo held out until the arrival of reinforcements from Messina induced the Turks to abandon this memorable siege.

MALTA TRADE ACT (1814) regulated trade between Malta, Britain, and other British colonial dependencies.

MALTHUS, THOMAS ROBERT (1776–1834), British clergyman and economist, who was the first man to attempt a comprehensive enquiry into the relationship between population and the state of society. His *Essay on the Principle of Population as it affects the future Improvement of Society* (1798) was written to refute the optimistic theories of Godwin, Condorcet, and Rousseau, as to the condition of mankind if freed from artificial restraints. The *Essay*'s main theorem is that population tends to increase more rapidly than the means of subsistence available to it. The rate of population growth was lessened by various positive checks—wars, epidemics, famines—and by the preventive check of moral restraint and foresight. Other factors operated as bounties on population, notably poor relief, which, for this reason, was likely to defeat its own purpose. The *Essay* ran through

several editions in Malthus's lifetime, and in 1830 he published *Summary View of the Principle of Population* in order to correct misrepresentations and to emphasize that his object was 'to improve the conditions of the lower classes'. Malthus was professor of history and political economy at Haileybury East India College, a friend of Ricardo, and an active member of the Political Economy Club. He wrote several general economic treatises, notably *Principles of Political Economy* (1820).

MALUS INTERCURSUS (1506), Francis Bacon's name for a provisional trading agreement conceded to Henry VII of England by Philip of Flanders when a storm drove him into an English harbour. It permitted English exporters to retail their cloth in the Netherlands without paying local tolls, but Philip died before it was ratified and it was probably never effective.

MALVANA CONVENTION (1597), agreement obtained by the Portuguese captain-general of Ceylon, Azavedo, from representatives of the Sinhalese, to the succession to the throne of Kotte of the King of Portugal on the death of King Don Juan Dharmapala, on condition that the rights, customs, and privileges of the Sinhalese should be maintained.

MALVY, LOUIS-JEAN (1875–1949), French politician, who was responsible as minister of the interior (1914–17) for order within France during the First World War. In 1917 French morale reached its nadir with mutinies, strikes, and agitation for a compromise peace. Malvy, being sympathetic to this demand, refused to take the firm action demanded by the war party, and became the target of a press campaign which forced him to resign. He was also alleged to have personal links with spies and traitors. When Clemenceau came to power, Malvy was arrested, tried, and sentenced to five years' exile (1918). In 1924 he was amnestied and returned to politics. His attitude was widely supported in the Radical Party, and he again became minister of the interior for a short time (1926). Until 1936 he was chairman of the finance commission of the Chamber of Deputies.

MALWA, plateau in western India, part of the state of Madhya Barat, important especially for communications between Gujarat and Maharshtra on the west coast, and the Gangetic valley. The oldest known state in this area was Avanti (from the 5th cent. BC), whose capital was at Ujjayini (Ujjain), one of the great cultural centres of ancient India, notably under the satraps of Ujjain (*c.* AD 100–380) and the Guptas (380–500). Malwa again became important under the Paramaras of Dhar (*c.* 950–1180). Throughout the centuries Malwa was famous as a centre of Sanskrit literature.

MAMAIA CULT, in Tahiti (Pacific), directed against the newly founded Protestant Church (1815). Despite its advocacy of sexual licence and political anarchy, the cult declined rapidly after the decimation of its (unvaccinated) adherents in the smallpox epidemic of 1841.

MAMALLAPURAM, ancient Indian port and important archaeological site (*c.* AD 600–900), also called Mahabalipuram or the 'Seven Pagodas', 32 miles (51·5 kms) south of Madras. There are a large number of monuments: cave temples, a shore temple, a vast rock sculpture in high relief depicting the descent from heaven of the Ganges river, and eight monolithic shrines. They are splendid examples of the art of the Pallava empire, an offspring of northern Indian Gupta style, but with its own genius and vigour. It exerted strong influence upon the art of Ceylon and South-East Asia.

MAMELUCO, term used in Brazil to designate the offspring of a white and an Indian. It is sometimes more loosely employed to embrace all offspring of mixed blood, including those of Negro and white, Negro and Indian, etc.

MAMERTINES, 'sons of Mamers' (the Sabellian Mars), Italian mercenaries who, after fighting for Agathocles of Syracuse against the Carthaginians in Sicily, seized and held Messana (288–264 BC). They then precipitated the First Punic War by first receiving a Carthaginian garrison as protection against Syracuse and subsequently inviting Rome to expel the Carthaginians.

MAMILIUS, C., LIMETANUS (*fl* 2nd cent. BC), Roman politician, who as tribune in 110 instituted an investigation into allegations that Jugurtha had bribed members of the Roman nobility during the Jugurthine War.

MAMLUK, Arabic participle meaning 'owned', in the sense of being a 'slave'. The word was used to denote above all slaves acquired and trained to serve as soldiers—as, for example, the Turkish slave troops whom the Caliph Al-Mu'tasim (*reg.* AD 833–42) recruited into his service, or the slave soldiers of Kipçak Turkish and later of Cerkes (Circassian) origin who constituted the warrior elite in the Mamluk sultanate of Egypt and Syria (1250–1517). Comparable expressions employed at a later date, *eg*, in the Ottoman empire, are ghulam or qul.

MAMLUK SULTANATE (1250–1517), ruling in Egypt, Syria, and the Hijaz. By origin the Mamluks were mercenary slave soldiers in the service of the preceding Ayyubid dynasty (1169–1250), which they displaced. The regime was continually replenished by fresh slaves from the Kipçak steppes and, after 1400, predominantly from the non-Muslim peoples of the Caucasus, *ie*, Circassians. The slave soldiers were trained in the households of Mamluk lords. It is customary to divide the Mamluk rulers into the Bahri or River (Nile) Sultans, who ruled until 1382, and the Burji or Citadel Sultans, who ruled thereafter. Hereditary succession was usual among the Bahris, but died out among the Burjis. The real power of the Bahri Mamluks was established under Baybars I (*reg.* 1260–77) and sustained by the rulers Qalawun (*reg.* 1279–90) and his son, Al-Malik al-Nasir Muhammad (*reg.* 1293–1340, with two interruptions). Their rule was noteworthy for the final defeat of the Mongol Il-Khans and the Crusaders in Syria. The best known of the Burji Mamluks were Barquq (*reg.* 1382–99) and Barsbay (*reg.* 1422–38). During the 14th cent. much wealth accrued to the Mamluks through their dominance of the trade routes of the Levant. This prosperity, the existence of a strong, locally recruited bureaucracy, and the absence of a sustained challenge by a powerful enemy, ensured the long survival of the Mamluk regime despite the continual factional struggles among the Mamluk lords. But in 1516–17 the Mamluks came into conflict with the expanding Ottoman state, were easily defeated, and the sultanate was brought to an end, although the Mamluk lords continued to play a major role in Egypt until the early 19th cent.   VJP

MA'MUN, AL- (AD 786–833), Abbasid Caliph (*reg.* 813–33). After the death of his father, Harun al-Rashid, in 809, Al-Ma'mun, then governor of Khurasan, became involved in a conflict with his brother the Caliph Al-Amin, ascending the throne himself on the death of his brother in 813. Not until 819, after six years of further confusion in Iraq, did Al-Ma'mun at last leave Khurasan and return to Baghdad. His reigns saw the outbreak (816) of a dangerous rebellion, under Babak, in Azerbayjan; the emergence (822) of the Tahirid line of amirs in Khurasan; and renewed warfare (830–33) against Byzantium. Al-Ma'mun supported the doctrines of the Mu'tazila. He also established at Baghdad a famous Bayt al-Hikma (House of Wisdom), where, among other learned activities, scholars devoted themselves to an enterprise of vast importance for the future—the translation of numerous works, above all philosophical and scientific in character, from Greek into Arabic.

MANAGING AGENCY SYSTEM, one of the reasons why India's economic development in the 19th and 20th cents was commercial rather than industrial. Since British companies in London needed managers in India with a first-hand knowledge of Indian conditions, they employed Indian firms on a commission basis as managing agents. The system was much criticized. By concentrating industrial control in family groups it favoured excessive conservatism and discouraged enterprise. However, it did provide capital, and progress would have been slower without it.

MANCHESTER, EDWARD MONTAGUE, 2nd Earl of (1602–71), English parliamentary general and Presbyterian politician. He was the eldest son of the 1st Earl, and was created Baron Kimbolton in 1626, but was known generally by his courtesy title of Viscount Mandeville. At the beginning of the Long Parliament he was leader of the opposition to Charles I in the House of Lords and with five MPs was charged with treason by the king in Jan. 1642. In Nov. 1642 he succeeded to the earldom. In 1643 he was appointed major-general of the Eastern Association, with Oliver Cromwell as his second-in-command. As a member of the committee of both kingdoms, he also helped administer the war. He was attacked by Cromwell in parliament for his 'backwardness to all action'. Their quarrel resulted in the self-denying ordinance (1645) and Manchester lost his commands. He took a leading part in the frequent negotiations for an agreement with Charles I, and was custodian of the great seal (1646–8). Having opposed the king's trial (1649), he retired during the Commonwealth. He actively assisted the Restoration, unsuccessfully hoping to bring back Charles II on Presbyterian terms. He became speaker of the Lords in 1660.

MANCHESTER GUARDIAN, British Whig-Liberal newspaper, founded in 1821, whose greatest editor, C. P. Scott (1846–1932), adapted it after 1872 into an instrument for modernizing the Liberal Party. It recommended Liberal co-operation with Labour, opposed the Boer War, and attained a national status which was confirmed by its change of title to *The Guardian* in 1959.

MANCHESTER SCHOOL in England, a radical group which emerged in the 1840s, taking its name from the association of its leaders, Cobden and Bright, with Lancashire industry. At home its members supported the Anti-Corn Law League by agitation in the country and in parliament, hoping by this means to raise the standards of the working class without raising wages and manufacturing costs. The Manchester school advocated a policy abroad based on moral considerations directed towards peace and free trade, so that the benefits of commerce and cultural improvement might be world-wide. It opposed imperialism and gunboat diplomacy, especially as practised by Palmerston, which it associated with a corrupt aristocracy. The movement was united in deploring colonial empire as useless and a cause of war, but it was divided on international co-operation (Cobden) and isolationism (Bright). Its influence was evident in the Little England movement and in the liberal–pacifist opposition to the Boer and First World Wars.

MANCHESTER SHIP CANAL. The scheme for this, put forward in the 1880s, met considerable resistance in parliament, from Liverpool and from railway interests, both fearful of competition. The canal, which opened in 1893, was not profitable to its shareholders, but by bringing ocean-going ships to Manchester city, it encouraged industry there and in the areas along its course. The competition obliged Liverpool to improve the Mersey as a waterway, and there is no reason to think that her trade suffered in the long run.

MANCHUKUO, puppet republic established by Japan (1931) in the part of China formerly known as Manchuria. P'u Yi, the last Emperor of China, was nominal head of state.

MANCINI, MARIE (1639–1715), niece of Cardinal Mazarin, whose romance with the young Louis XIV of France (Dec. 1658–June 1659) encouraged Mazarin to arrange a dynastic marriage between Louis and the Infanta Maria Theresa (1659). Though Marie was exiled to Brouage, near La Rochelle, and Louis was sent to Chantilly to recover from his infatuation, a clandestine correspondence continued until Sept. 1659. She later married the constable of Naples, and died in obscurity (1715).

MANCO CAPAC (*fl.* 14th cent.), Inca Ruler, the first whose historical existence can be reliably authenticated. According to legend, Manco Capac, and his relatives and followers, emerged from some caves to the south-east of Cuzco and, after many adventures, founded the city.

MANCO CAPAC II (*c.* 1500–44), Emperor of Peru, whom Pizarro recognized in 1533. Manco pretended to collaborate with him, but in 1536 led a native revolt which threatened to take Cuzco. After being defeated in 1537, he fled to the mountains, but continued to harass the Spanish until he died.

MANDALAY, second-largest town in Burma; its population is around 200,000 (1970). It was the last capital of the Burmese kings (1857–86). The fort and palace survived the British annexation intact, but the palace was destroyed and the fort suffered considerable damage in the Second World War. Since independence, both have been extensively restored. There are a number of sacred monasteries and pagodas in the city.

MANDAM INDIANS, American tribe, first encountered by the French (1738) along the Heart river, ND, and by the Americans in the upper Missouri river valley (1804). The Mandam signed a peace treaty with the US (1825) and were placed on a reservation (1870) in ND and MT. Theories that the Mandam were descendants of Ohio mound builders or of Welsh explorers of the 12th cent. AD, have been denied by anthropologists. These theories were probably fostered by the fact that the Mandam language is only loosely related to that of their Sioux neighbours and, unlike other Plains tribes, the Mandam lived in permanent communities and dwelt in conical-shaped huts.

MANDATES, name given to the ex-German and ex-Turkish possessions which were administered by the victorious powers after the First World War, and applied by extension to the overall system. The basic idea, apparently originating with the South African, Smuts, and the American, George Louis Beer, was that suitable powers should rule the colonies of the defeated countries in the name of the League of Nations, to which they would be responsible for the enlightened government of those territories. In practice, apart from small adjustments, these colonies were administered by the powers which had captured them and the system was an ingenious and flexible compromise between the results of wartime promises to the natives (as well as inter-Allied pacts), a desire not to return the areas to the defeated powers—and also to gain some recompense for wartime sacrifices—and at the same time to fit in with Allied war aims. This was especially clear in the 5 Nov. 1918 statement, on 'no annexations'. In practical terms, joint rule was impossible and the territories were therefore attached to single powers, the mandators, but under League supervision.

The varying combinations of motivation, particularly as regards the nature of promises given to native leaders, produced three types of mandate. Group A was formed out of the former Turkish Middle Eastern provinces north of Arabia. Their independence was provisionally recognized, as was their need for support until they were able to stand alone in the modern world. Thus the task of educating Iraq, Transjordan, and Palestine for independence was given to Britain, and of Syria and Lebanon to France, although no such clear responsibility was given to the mandatories of the other territories. In Group B, comprising Germany's former colonies in Central Africa, Togoland, and the Cameroons were partitioned between Britain and France (who received the larger part); Tanganyika also went to Britain, and Ruanda-Urundi to Belgium. In Group C, ex-German Pacific territories, Samoa went to New Zealand, New Guinea and eventually Nauru to Australia, and the islands north of the equator to Japan, and South-West Africa to South Africa. It was held that these could best be administered as integral territories of the mandator, subject to the same safeguards in the interests of the natives, if not their wishes, as in Group B. A Permanent Commission was instituted to supervise the system, and especially to receive annual reports from the mandators—but neither the commission nor the league possessed coercive powers. In fact, as an experiment in international law and, more important, in the solution of the practical problems of colonial administration, the scheme was far from being a failure. Iraq gained nominal independence and membership in the league in 1932, and Syria and Lebanon in 1941. The standard of government did not always immediately carry on where the Germans in particular had left off, especially in Central Africa, but a tricky international problem had been solved and more than lip-service was paid to the humanitarian and progressive ideals of the scheme's originators. The Mandate system was superseded in 1945 by UN trusteeship.   KM

MANDEL, LOUIS GEORGE (1885–1944), French politician, who began his career as secretary to Clemenceau. He was elected deputy for the Gironde (1919) and, with the exception of the years 1924–8, retained his seat until 1940. For most of the inter-war period he was one of the most effective critics of French foreign policy, but his facility in making political enemies deprived him of a seat in the cabinet until 1934. He then became minister of post, telegraph, and telephones and retained this position in four cabinets. During his term of office the postal service, which was notoriously inefficient, was much improved, but deep hostility was aroused in his subordinates.

As the international situation degenerated after 1936, Mandel came to symbolize firmness towards Germany, and in doing so earned the undying hatred of his former political friends on the right. He opposed the remilitarization of the Rhineland, and, as minister of colonies in Daladier's cabinet, was opposed to Munich (1938). Reynaud wished to make him minister of the interior in his cabinet of March 1940, but Mandel himself felt that the hatred towards him meant that he could only become truly effective if the situation became desperate. He accepted the post of minister of colonies, then on 5 June became minister of the interior. As the most resolute opponent of the armistice he tried to rally the rapidly disintegrating government, but failed and left for Morocco to continue the war from the colonies. On arrival there, he tried to contact British officials, but was arrested and returned to France. He was at first interned by the Vichy government and then in Nov. 1942 handed over to the Germans. After the murder of Philippe Henriot by the Resistance, Mandel was transferred to the custody of the Milice, by whom he was killed on 7 July 1944.

MANDELA, NELSON ROLIHAHLA (1918–), African nationalist leader in the republic of South Africa. In 1952 he helped to lead a widespread movement of passive resistance to racist regulations and, in 1956, was among 156 South Africans of all races charged with high treason, but acquitted four years later.

When the African National Congress was outlawed after the Sharpeville incident, Mandela became one of its underground leaders. In 1961 he issued a call for a national political strike, and, when the latter was defeated, announced the formation of *Umkonto we Sizwe* (Spear of the Nation) as an armed wing of the African National Congress. Abroad in 1961–2, he appealed for support, and on returning to South Africa was arrested after a further period of 17 months' clandestine activity. He was sentenced to five years' imprisonment for leading the 1961 strike and for having left the country illegally. In 1963 the chief leaders of the African National Congress, including Mandela (despite the fact that he was already in prison), were charged with sabotage and conspiracy to overthrow the government. The accused were sentenced to life imprisonment on Robben Island, off the Cape of Good Hope.

MANDEVILLE, JOHN DE, fictitious name assumed by a Belgian writer whose *Boke of wayes to Jerusalem et of marveylys of Inde . . . (c.* 1357), translated into many languages, incorporated much of the medieval lore about the known world and contained many descriptions of marvels.

MANDING, peoples of West Africa, also sometimes called Mandingo, Mandinka, Mande, etc. The term Manding is perhaps more correctly used to refer to a linguistic sub-group of the Niger–Congo family, including in it not only Mandinka (Malinke, Dyula, and Bambara), but also Mende, Vai, Soninke, Ligbi, and many other small language groups. Historically, the name Malinke was applied to members of the leading warrior clans of the Manding people in Mali; Dyula was the name for the trading lineages, and came to be synonymous with 'Muslim', while Bambara indicated peasants and 'pagans'. Manding society also recognized a servile caste-like system whose members were either pre-Manding groups of the area or other absorbed peoples; their occupations included forging, leatherwork, medicine, fishing, etc.

Several important states were founded by Manding peoples; notably Mali (*c.* 1100–1500), the Bambara states of Kaarta (1670–1854), and Segu (1750–1861), and the empire carved out by Samori (d. 1900).

MANETHO (*c.* 300 BC), Egyptian priest, who wrote a history of Egypt, dividing the period from *c.* 3100–343 between 30 dynasties. The historical part is lost, but four versions of the King List remain, and, despite many inaccuracies, form the basis for Egyptian chronology.

MANFRED (*c.* 1232–66), King of Sicily (*reg.* 1258–66), illegitimate son of the Emperor Frederick II and the most gifted of his children, who was able, after his father's death in 1250, to retain control of the emperor's professional army and to maintain himself as the effective ruler over Frederick's kingdom of Sicily. Papal attempts to dislodge him having failed, he crowned himself king in 1258 and proceeded to rally an anti-papal party in central and northern Italy. His Tuscan opponents, led by Florence, were defeated at Montaperti in 1260. The papacy in desperation turned to a brother of Louis IX of France, Charles of Anjou, who, financed by the papal bankers, invaded Manfred's dominions in 1266 and in a lightning campaign defeated and killed him at Benevent, thus ending Hohenstaufen rule in Italy.

MANGALORE, TREATY OF (11 March 1784), between the British and Tipu Sultan, which restored peace on the basis of a mutual cession of conquests. The treaty ignored the existing treaty of Salbai and interests of the Nawab of the Carnatic.

MANGAREVA or Gambier's Island in the eastern Pacific, discovered by James Wilson in 1797 and a notable early source of pearls and pearlshell.

MANGAS COLORADAS (1793–1863), American Mimbreño Apache Indian chief, who raided and harassed settlements in south-western NM and formed an alliance with Cochise to resist reoccupation of the area by whites during the American Civil War. He was taken prisoner by CA militia and killed while in captivity.

MANGIT, Mongolian tribe conquered by Chingiz Khan, the name of which was subsequently borne by an important tribe of the Golden Horde and by a dynasty established in Bukhara which exercised de facto power (from *c.* 1747) and later ruled (1785–1920).

MANGUNKUSUMO, TJIPTO (1885–1943), Indonesian politician and pioneer of radical nationalism. With other students of Javanese aristocratic origin, he founded the moderate *Budi Utomo* in 1908. He then sought to establish more radical organizations, uniting Eurasians and native Indonesians behind a demand for independence, but his efforts were frustrated by growing Eurasian conservatism and harassment by the Dutch. His revolutionary activities led to his being exiled in 1927. After the abrogation of Dutch rule in 1942 he was allowed to return.

MANHATTAN, island in New York Bay about 12·5 miles (20 kms) long and 2·5 miles (4 kms) wide, bounded by the Hudson, Harlem, and East rivers. It was discovered in 1524 by Verranzo, and sold two years later to the Dutch, who named it after its original Indian inhabitants. It was part of the Dutch settlement of New Amsterdam until it was conquered by the English in 1664, when the colony was renamed New York. The city of New York did not extend beyond Manhattan until 1874, but its prime location had already made it the dominant city of the eastern seaboard. In 1898 it became one of the five boroughs of an enlarged New York city, and is the commercial, financial, and cultural centre of the US.

MANHATTAN PROJECT (1942–7), name given to the US programme to develop an atomic bomb. Under the command of Gen. Leslie R. Groves, the Manhattan Engineer District sustained a vast scientific and industrial effort at a number of universities and at research establishments such as Oak Ridge, TN; Hanford, WA; and Los Alamos, NM. British and Canadian resources were also pooled in the common endeavour. The first successful explosion of a nuclear device took place at Alamogordo, NM (16 July 1945).

MANICHEANS, followers of the Iranian teacher Mani (d. *c.* 274), who preached a religion based on Zoroastrian, Babylonian, and Christian ideas. Mani was encouraged by Shapur I, but on the latter's death opposition, especially from Zoroastrian priests, led to his execution and the persecution and dispersion of his followers. The Manichean movement grew in Central Asia, Syria, and Egypt, and spread to North Africa, Armenia, China, and southern France, where, under the name of Cathari or Albigensians, they were persecuted in the Middle Ages.

MANIFEST DESTINY in the US, term used to describe a longstanding expansionist tradition which conceives of the right and duty of the American people to extend the benefits of their democratic civilization throughout the American continent. While the spirit of Manifest Destiny may be perceived in the first Puritan settlements in Massachusetts Bay, the phrase belongs more properly to the popular clamour for territorial acquisition in the 1840s and 1850s. In July 1845 John O'Sullivan prophesied in his *United States Magazine and Democratic Review* the 'fulfilment of our manifest destiny to overspread the continent allotted by Providence for the free development of our yearly multiplying millions', and in Dec. he again spoke of Manifest Destiny in the *New York Morning Review* in supporting the annexation of TX. The phrase was eagerly adopted by congressmen in their debates on the three major territorial issues then facing the US—the annexation of TX, the OR boundary, and the war with Mexico. Of these, the first two were settled peaceably, but the Mexican war, deliberately engineered by President James K. Polk, involved a more aggressive reading of the concept. It required the American people to consider how far they were prepared to accept the full consequences of victory, and take over the whole of Mexico. Democrats and Whigs supported the prosecution of the war, but were less united over its aims, Southerners being fearful of including mixed races in the US population, Northerners of opening up new areas for slavery's extension. President Polk and Congress eventually settled for the northern third of Mexico, out of which were carved CA and the states of the south-west. Ultra-expansionists looked beyond the continent. In 1850 *De Bow's Review* declared that 'We have a destiny to perform, a "manifest destiny" over all Mexico, over South America, over the West Indies and Canada', and envisaged US penetration of China and Japan. Further attempts at territorial expansion were focused on Cuba, but without immediate success. However, Cuba, and those other key Spanish possessions, the Philippines, were at the centre of a second outburst of enthusiasm for Manifest Destiny in the 19th cent. when jingoists like Capt. A. T. Mahan, Theodore Roosevelt, and Rev. Josiah Strong, advocated an imperialist policy for the US in strategic and moral terms, and the US embarked on the Spanish American War (1898). The American people, however, accepted a colonialist role *vis-à-vis* the Philippines only with reluctance, and US imperialism in the 20th cent. has generally taken the form of indirect influence rather than direct rule.

A. K. Weinberg, *Manifest Destiny* (Baltimore, 1935).
F. Merk, *Manifest Destiny and Mission in American History* (New York, 1963).   DBS

MANILA, situated on Luzon in the Philippine Islands, first discovered by the Spaniards in 1521 and part of their colonial empire from the 1560s to 1898. The trade between Manila and Acapulco, primarily in Chinese silks, led to a drain of American bullion which caused the Spanish government to intervene in the 17th–18th cents. Manila was captured by the British in 1762 and restored to Spain by the peace of Paris (1763), then ceded to the US at the conclusion of the Spanish–American War (1898).

MANILA BAY, BATTLE OF (1 May 1898), engagement between US and Spanish naval forces during the Spanish–American War. Commander George Dewey's squadron, consisting of four cruisers and two gunboats, based on Hong Kong, attacked a larger but less powerful Spanish fleet of ten vessels under Admiral Montojo in Manila Bay; the shore batteries were silenced and all the Spanish ships sunk or seriously damaged. Manila was then blockaded, and surrendered on 13 Aug.

MANILA GALLEON, or *Nao de China*, a term referring to ships plying annually (1593–1815), between two trading ports within the Spanish empire: Manila, the capital of the Philippines, and Acapulco in Mexico. Under Spain's mercantilist policy, the Spanish government, through royal decrees later codified in the Laws of the Indies, monopolized trade relations between these ports. It limited the weight of each ship, the value of the goods it carried, and the number of ships making the outgoing and incoming voyages; the laws were often violated. Manila, the terminal point of trade in the East, served only as an entrepôt. To this city merchants from China brought silk and spices, which constituted the main cargo of the Manila galleons, in which they were reshipped to Acapulco; there they were exchanged mainly for Mexican silver, sometimes for European goods, such as Flemish ware. The galleons, built by Chinese and Filipino workmen at the Cavite shipyard close to Manila, frequently took an eastward rather than the westward route, even if it took five or six months, because the Manila merchants preferred it. Initially, the Manila-galleon trade was meant to provide income for the entire Spanish community of the city. However, it soon came to be controlled by a small group of traders who bought the *boleta,* a ticket entitling its holder to cargo space in the galleon. The Manila–Acapulco galleon trade prospered until it was faced with competition from the Spanish government's

20-year experiment of direct trade between Manila and the mother country, following the end of the British occupation of Manila. At about the same time, Manila was opened to other foreign traders dealing with 'goods of the Indies'. By 1785 the Spanish king chartered the Royal Co. of the Philippines, and gave it special trading rights and privileges. All these developments, and also the Mexican campaign for independence during the Napoleonic Wars, eventually brought an end to the trade between Manila and Acapulco.

W. L. Schurz, *The Manila Galleon* (New York, 1959).

                                                                                                    JMS

MANIN, DANIEL (1804–57), Italian patriot and statesman, who was recognized as leader of liberal opinion in Venice from 1831 onwards. He was thrown into prison because of his political opinions (1847), but was rescued by the mob in the revolution of 1848 and elected president of the Venetian republic. He was the inspiration behind the heroic five-month defence of Venice and was excluded from the amnesty when the city fell, and escaped to Paris, where he died.

MANIOPOTO, REWI (c. 1815–94), NZ Maori warrior chief, who was the leading advocate among the Maori king's supporters of armed resistance to British encroachment. He commanded the king's forces in the Waikato War (1863–4).

MANIPLE, formation of the ancient Roman army. Each legion was made up of 30 maniples, each consisting of two centuries. By 100 BC the maniple had been replaced by the cohort as the normal tactical unit, but was retained for administrative purposes.

MANITOBA, western province of Canada, lying between Ontario and Saskatchewan. The area was the scene of the Hudson's Bay and North-West Cos' rivalry. The first agricultural settlement was made by Lord Selkirk in the Red River valley (1812). When the Hudson's Bay Co. sold its territorial rights in Man. to the new Dominion of Canada, there was an unsuccessful uprising in the Red River colony, led by Louis Riel (1869–70). The province of Man. was founded in 1870 and its territory expanded in 1912. The Man. constitution was drafted with the growth of a large French population in mind, but the Anglo-Saxon majority was not threatened, despite the arrival of Icelanders (1875) and Ukrainians (1896).

MANIU, IULIU (1873–1955), Rumanian politician, and a founder member of the Rumanian National Party, who served on its executive committee from 1896. He was a deputy in the Hungarian parliament at Budapest, representing his co-nationals. During the First World War he served with the Austro-Hungarian forces in Italy, and was then transferred to Vienna. With the collapse of the imperial war effort he made his way to Transylvania, where he took part in discussions among Rumanian national leaders about the policy to be adopted. They decided to unite the country with the Rumanian kingdom and Vaida-Voevod delivered the key speech in the Hungarian parliament. In Nov. 1918 a 'directing council' was established to govern Transylvania, Maniu being at its head. In 1918–19 he arranged the union of Transylvania with Rumania. As leader of the National Party, during the period of Liberal rule in Rumania (1920–8), he became a leader of the opposition forces. He was behind several efforts to unite his party with Mihalache's Peasant Party and in 1926 this was done and Maniu became the leader of this new political unit. In 1928 the National-Peasants won the elections and he formed a government, but before its measures could take effect the Depression struck Rumania and Carol's return caused political chaos. The National-Peasants had negotiated arrangements for Carol's return to the throne which he had left in 1926. Maniu stipulated that Mme Lupescu must not accompany the king to Rumania, but otherwise favoured his return. When Maniu discovered that Mme Lupescu was living with the king he resigned. Of all the problems facing his government this was perhaps the least serious, but morally the most highly charged. Maniu resigned crippling the National-Peasant Party by this somewhat irresponsible action. He served as prime minister only once more and only briefly. By 1933 the National-Peasants were out of office and never regained power. The party declined during the 1930s, a chauvinist element having defected and all opposition being crushed by dictatorships. Maniu's questionable move of making an electoral alliance with the fascist Iron Guard did nothing to stop this decline. Initially he endorsed the foreign policy of Marshal Antonescu—a reaction to the shock of the partition of Transylvania—but later became an opponent of the regime. This was perhaps his finest hour. He urged the king to oust Antonescu in 1944 and from then on became the rallying point for the forces of democracy in Rumania. He led the opposition to the communists against unequal odds and in 1947 was arrested and tried. At his trial he conducted a brave defence but was given a life sentence. He died shortly after his imprisonment.

JMK

MANGKUNEGARA, name of the line of subsidiary Princes of Surakarta, Central Java, whose position was independent of the authority of the Susuhunans of Surakarta. In the 1740s Mangkunegara I (Mas Said) rebelled against the Susuhunans Pakubuwana II and III, and against his father-in-law, Pangeran Mangkubumi (after 1755, Sultan Hamengkubuwana I of Jogjakarta), who were aided by the forces of the Dutch East India Co. In 1757 he was granted lands and an independent position at Surakarta, where he ruled (1757–96). Mangkunegara II succeeded him (1796–1835), and was in turn succeeded by Mangkunegara III (1835–53). Mangkunegara IV (1853–81) is remembered for his promotion of and contributions to Javanese literature. The last prince of the line was Mangkunegara VIII, inaugurated in 1944. His administrative area, the Mangkunegaran, was incorporated into the republic of Indonesia shortly after the revolution of 1949.

MANLEY, NORMAN WASHINGTON (1893–1969), Jamaican lawyer and statesman who was the leading barrister in Jamaica (1921–55) and the first West Indian to appear before the judicial committee of the privy council of England (1951). He supported his cousin, Sir Alexander Bustamante, until 1938, when Manley founded the People's National Party. He was chief minister (1955–62) and led Jamaica into the short-lived West Indian Federation. His party was defeated in 1962 and Manley was in opposition till his retirement in 1969.

MANLIUS CAPITOLINUS (*fl* 4th cent. BC), Roman leader who, according to tradition, was aroused by the sacred geese, and saved the Capitol from a Gallic night-attack (390 BC). He is said subsequently to have fomented class-revolution, but this is patently anachronistic.

MANN, HORACE (1796–1859), US politician and educationist, who served in the MA legislature (1827–37) and the US Congress (1848–53). As secretary of the Massachusetts Board of Education (1837–48) he reorganized the state public school system, instituting longer terms, higher teaching salaries, and new methods of instruction, and established the first state normal school in the US at Lexington (1839). He published and edited the *Common School Journal* (1838–48), advanced the principle of non-sectarian education, supported the reform movements of his day, and as president of Antioch College (1853–9) infused his ideas into higher education.

MANN, THOMAS (1875–1955), German novelist and liberal critic of National Socialism. *Buddenbrooks* (1901) is his best-known work. He supported Germany in the First World War, but settled in the US (1939), and later became an American citizen. His last years were spent in Switzerland. Mann's wartime and post-war attempts to rouse Germany's conscience against Nazism caused much resentment. His huge literary output included *The Magic Mountain*, the tetralogy *Joseph and his Brothers, Doctor Faustus*, and the *Confessions of Felix Krull, Confidence Man.*

MANN ACT (1910) in US, legislation named after Congressman James R. Mann (1856–1922) of IL, prohibiting the transportation of women across state lines for immoral purposes. It is often called the White Slave Act.

MANN–ELKINS ACT (1910) in US, legislation, named after Congressman James R. Mann (1856–1922) of IL, and Senator Stephen B. Elkins (1841–1911) of WV, which strengthened the powers of the Inter-state Commerce Commission and gave it jurisdiction over telephone, telegraph, cable, and wireless systems.

MANNERHEIM, CARL GUSTAF (1867–1951), Finnish soldier and president of Finland (1944–6), who joined the Russian army in 1887, explored Asia on horseback (1906–8), commanded a cavalry regiment in the First World War, and led the Finnish War of Independence against the Bolsheviks (1918). He again led Finnish troops against superior Soviet forces (1939–40, 1941–4) and was elected president in Aug. 1944.

MANNING, HENRY EDWARD, Cardinal (1808–92), British Roman Catholic, who was Abp of Westminster. His tact and untiring industry helped to counteract the anti-papal feeling aroused by the pope's creation of a Catholic hierarchy in England (1850). Manning was converted to Catholicism after 20 years as a clergyman in the Church of England, during which he moved steadily towards the Tractarian position. As head of the Catholic hierarchy in England, he did much to integrate Catholicism into British life, placating the old Catholic families and allaying Protestant suspicions. He seemed less opposed to liberalism than many British Catholics, and promoted social causes (*eg*, protection of children and temperance), especially amongst the London poor. He arbitrated successfully in the London dock strike (1889). Manning was an uncompromising supporter of Ultramontane principles and his persuasive skill at the Vatican Council (1870) greatly helped the upholders of papal infallibility. Yet in Britain he did more than anyone else to moderate the 'foreign' image of his Church.

MANNIX, DANFIELD, archbishop (1864–1963), Australian Roman Catholic, who was a controversial figure in the 20th-cent. public life of Australia, as well as one of the country's most influential prelates. Most of his early career was spent at Maynooth, which he left in 1912 to become Co-adjutor Abp of Melbourne. Though he did not succeed Abp Carr until 1917, Mannix's vigorous leadership of the second anti-conscription campaign of that year against the prime minister, W. M. Hughes, won him a position of significant political influence. This extended beyond the ranks of Irish-Australian Catholics, whose champion he had always been.

During the 1920s the ill-organized Labor opposition in the Australian Commonwealth parliament came to look to Mannix for guidance in matters which many Protestants thought beyond the archbishop's proper field of faith and morals. When Labor returned to office in Canberra (1929), almost all senior members of J. H. Scullin's cabinet were Roman Catholics. In the later 1930s, however, the combined effects of world economic depression, internal divisions in the Labor movement, and forces at work overseas, ended this collaboration between Church and party. In 1941, the reunited Labor Party was returned to office by a 'lapsed' Catholic, John Curtin, who in 1945 was followed by J. B. Chifley, another Catholic.

By the 1950s increasing communism in the trade unions, the counter-offensive of the Mannix-supported 'Movement', and the advent to Labor leadership of Dr H. V. Evatt in 1951 again focused public scrutiny on the archbishop. By publicly declaring, in effect, that a vote for Evatt was a vote for communism, he ensured victory for the anti-Labor Liberal and Country parties through votes of supporters of a right-wing Labor splinter group, the Democratic Labor Party, in which Roman Catholic influence was strong. In the early 1960s, however, a sharp divergence in interpretation of Church policy was evident between the archbishopric of Melbourne and the mother see of Sydney. Mannix nevertheless continued in active control of his see until his death four months before his 100th birthday.   FA

MANO, PHYA (*Phraya* Manopakonnitithada; personal name, Thongkon) (1884–1948), prime minister of Siam from June 1932 to June 1933. He studied law in England, and served in Thailand's ministry of justice before the coup of 1932, in which he played a leading role. He died in exile at Penang.

MANOR, term which appears in the English Domesday Book (1086) to describe an estate of a single owner, comprising both his own land, known as the demesne, and the holdings of his dependent peasants, who were obliged to help in cultivating the demesne and who paid the lord rents in money and kind. This type of estate, which has affinities with some of the agrarian institutions of the Roman empire, developed in western Europe during the Dark and early Middle Ages. There are traces of it in England in the laws of Ine (7th cent.) and it may have been present—one among several Anglo-Saxon forms of agrarian organization—from an even earlier period. The manor was never universal, and, where it was present, its two most characteristic features— a demesne and a dependent peasantry—show many differences from place to place. Originally such estates were organized merely to provide sufficient supplies of food and other necessaries for the lords and their peasants. Manors could be adapted to intensive production for the market, as happened on a large scale in England in the late 12th and 13th cents. The supply of labour was also affected by the growth of the market, and by the 13th cent. much hired labour, not all of it entirely free, was used on the demesnes, but the old type of labour services may have been intensified on some demesnes in this period.

The disappearance of the manor was nearly as slow a process as its growth. It began as soon as a market for produce and labour developed outside a manorial context, in the towns, but the time of greatest difficulty for lords came in the 14th cent., when a scarcity of labour and a widespread revulsion of the peasantry against the severer forms of dependence made the manorial type of production, already in decline, virtually impossible to maintain. A manor, in the full Domesday sense, was a rarity in England by the 15th cent., although a manorial terminology continued to be used in estates records until the end of the Middle Ages.   BFH

MANSA MUSA (*reg.* 1312–37), ruler of the Mali empire. During his reign Mali was at the height of its power and prosperity. He established diplomatic relations with the Marinids of Fez, and while on pilgrimage (1324) was received by the Mamluk Sultan Al-Nasir in Cairo. The amount of gold spent by him and his retinue in Cairo was so great that it caused a devaluation from which Egypt took several years to recover.

When he returned to Mali he took with him some scholars, including the Grenadine poet Al-Sahili, who died in Timbuctoo. Egyptian creditors pursued him, and from this period there was generally increased trade between Mali and Egypt. Musa's fame reached Europe; the name 'Melly' appeared on a map in 1330 and in 1375 the seated figure of 'Musa Melli, Lord of the Negroes' adorned a Majorcan map made for Charles V.

MANSA SULAIMAN (*reg.* 1341–60), Sultan of Mali, brother of Mansa Musa. He probably gained power by deposing the latter's son, Magha, who reigned only four years. After Sulaiman's death, Magha's son, Mari-Djata II, in turn deposed Sulaiman's son, to whom power had passed. Henceforth conflict between these and other branches of the Keita dynasty greatly weakened the Mali empire. Sulaiman's reign, however, was one of peace and prosperity, though he had a personal reputation for avarice. The empire was still extensive, and included Walata and Timbuctoo, and perhaps Gao. Ibn Battuta's account of the Mali capital in 1352–3 stresses the importance of Islam there, though at the court many non-Islamic practices evidently persisted.

MANSABDAR (lit. 'the holder of a command') term applied to the official nobility of the Mughal empire. There were 33 grades of officers, commanding from 10 to 10,000 men, distinguished by the horsemen to be supplied, horses per man, and months per annum for which pay could be drawn. The horses belonged to the government. *Mansabs* of 1000 or over carried the status of *amir* or noble. The *mansabdars* were usually paid by assignments on the revenue from specific areas of land. These assignments were often changed and advances were recovered at death, usually leaving little for relatives. The *mansabdars* were thus dependent on the government and formed the effective imperial civil-cum-military service. The system was developed by the Emperor Akbar. In the higher ranks 70 per cent were of foreign origin and half the rest were Hindus.

MANSART, JULES HARDOUIN (1646–1708), French architect of Versailles, great-nephew and pupil of François Mansart, architect to Louis XIII, whose surname he adopted. He built a château at Clagny for Mme de Montespan (1674), and supervised (1676–1708) the building of Versailles, and designed the palace, its colonnade, the cathedral, the orangery, and the Grand Trianon, and with Le Brun decorated the principal rooms. He also built the dome of the Invalides in Paris and the Institut of St Cyr, laid out the Place des Victoires and the Place Vendôme, and made additions to St Germain, the Palais Royal, and Orléans cathedral.

MANSFELD, ERNEST, Count von (1585–1626), German mercenary soldier in the Thirty Years War who joined Frederick of Bohemia's cause, but was defeated at Sablat by the imperial forces (1619). After making his peace with the emperor (Oct. 1620) he returned to Frederick's service (1620–2), then joined Christian of Brunswick in the Netherlands (1622–4) and later sought James I's help in London (1624). He was then sent by Christian of Denmark to Silesia to divert Wallenstein's Catholic forces but was defeated by the latter at the Dessau bridgehead (25 April 1626) and fled to Brandenburg. He moved thence into Silesia and Moravia, and while marching towards Dalmatia he died.

MANSFIELD, WILLIAM MURRAY, 1st Earl of (1705–93), British politician and judge who was solicitor-general and attorney-general, and acted as leader of the Commons under the Duke of Newcastle. He was also chief justice of the King's Bench (1756–88). He reversed on a technicality (1768) the decision whereby John Wilkes was outlawed and was responsible for improvements in mercantile law, court procedure, and the law of evidence.

MANSFIELD, DAVID MURRAY, 2nd Earl of (1727–96), British diplomat and, as Viscount Stormont, a representative peer of Scotland until he succeeded his uncle in the British peerage (1793). He was lord Chief justice of Scotland (1778), secretary of state (1779–82) during the Gordon riots, and twice lord president of the council (1783, 1794–6). He opposed British intervention in the war between Turkey and Russia (1791), and supported the British declaration of war against France (1793).

MANSTEIN, FRITZ ERICH VON (1887–   ) (also known as Von Lewinski), German field marshal who served in the

First World as a staff officer. At the outbreak of the Second World War he commanded army group A on the Western Front, and his strategy of a surprise attack through the Ardennes was later adopted by Hitler. He was promoted to general (1940) and later field marshal (1942) and commanded the 11th Army in Russia. Later he headed the army group South and led the Crimean campaign (1942). At Stalingrad he refused to save his army from destruction by rejecting Hitler's orders, though later there was an open dispute with him and in 1944 Manstein was transferred to the reserve.

MANSUR, AL-, ABU JA'FAR (*reg.* AD 754–75), the 2nd Abbasid Caliph, had been governor of Azerbayjan, Armenia, and Al-Jazira in the reign (750–4) of his brother Abu'l-Abbas al-Saffah. On his accession to the throne Al-Mansur had to face a revolt of his uncle Abdullah ibn Ali in Syria—a revolt suppressed through the vigorous intervention of Abu Muslim, who had done much to bring the Abbasids to power. Al-Mansur, distrusting the great influence and prestige of Abu Muslim, above all in Khurasan, had him killed in AD 755. The death of Abu Muslim led to a rebellion of his adherents in Khurasan under a certain Sunbadh. More formidable still were the Shi'i revolts (AD 762–3) of Muhammad ibn Abdallah ibn al-Hasan in the Hijaz and of his brother Ibrahim at Basra. With these dangers overcome, Al-Mansur resolved to establish a new garrison town for the Khurasani troops, who constituted the real strength of Abbasid rule. This resolve led to the building of Baghdad, which was begun in AD 762. It was Al-Mansur, in fact—a clever, unscrupulous, and energetic monarch—who established the Abbasid regime on a sure foundation.

MANSUR, AL- (*reg.* AD 946–53), 3rd Fatimid Caliph. On his accession to the throne Al-Mansur had to deal with a great revolt then in progress among the Berber tribesmen. Order was restored in Ifriqiyya, the rebellion crushed, and its leader, the Kharijite Abu Yazid, slain in AD 947. Measures followed which did much to strengthen Fatimid influence over the western Maghrib.

MANSVELDT, EDWARD (d. 1666), Dutch pirate, based in Jamaica, who as leader of the Port Royal buccaneers, and with the connivance of the English governor, molested Spanish shipping in the Caribbean. He seized Providence Isle from the Spaniards (1665), and also attacked Cuba and Nicaragua (1665).

MANTEGNA, ANDREA (1431–1506), Mantuan painter, who was influenced by both Donatello and Jacopo Bellini, and became one of the leading artists in Venice. After 1459 he was chiefly attached to the court of the Gonzaga lords of Mantua. His fascination with antiquity is clearly to be seen in his *San Sebastian* (*c.* 1455–9), in which the saint is tied to a classical column among fragments of ancient ruins. Another distinctive characteristic of Mantegna's work was his wonderful perception of the Italian landscape.

MANTEUFFEL, EDWIN VON (1809–85), Prussian field marshal and first German governor of Alsace-Lorraine, who supported William I's army reforms, and fought in the Austro-Prussian and Franco-Prussian wars. In 1879 he became governor of Alsace-Lorraine, where his policy of conciliating the pro-French population met with little success.

MANTINEA, ancient Greek city-state in central Peloponnese, near modern Tripolis. It was allied to Sparta in the Peloponnesian League from the 6th cent. BC, and remained loyal when the other Arcadians supported Argos (*c.* 466), and sent help to Sparta after the earthquake and helots' revolt of 464; but in the great Peloponnesian War it temporarily joined Argos and Athens (420–418). After further intransigence in the Corinthian War, the city was besieged by the Spartans

(384) and on surrendering was broken up. It was rebuilt after the Spartan defeat at Leuctra (371), and supported the Thebans' invasions of the Peloponnese (370–369), but fought with Sparta and Athens against them at the battle of Mantinea (362).

MANTINEA, BATTLES OF (418 BC, 362 BC). In the great Peloponnesian War the Spartans and their allies, under King Agis II, defeated the Argives, Mantineans, and their allies, including 1300 Athenians. By this victory the Spartans re-established their authority in the Peloponnese after the troubles following the peace of Nicias (421).

In 362 a second battle of Mantinea was won by the Thebans and their allies under Epaminondas fighting against Sparta, Athens, and other Peloponnesian states. The Thebans were seeking to regain their hegemony after the defection of Elis and Mantinea, but their victory was frustrated by Epaminondas' death, and a Common Peace treaty followed, which recognized the status quo.

MANTUA, Italian city in eastern Lombardy, famous as the birthplace of the poet Virgil. It achieved considerable importance as an independent buffer state between the duchy of Milan and the territories of Venice. Members of its native dynasty, the Gonzagas (1328–1708), managed to preserve their rule for centuries. In the later 15th cent. Mantua became a centre of Renaissance art, Mantegna being Ludovico and Francesco Gonzaga's chief court painter. Under the rule of the Austrian Habsburgs (1708–97, 1814–66) the city became one of the most formidable military centres in Italy, and part of a network of fortresses assuring Austrian control over Lombardy. It was one of the main bases for Radetzky's Austrian army in 1848, allowing it to retain a foothold in Lombardy and ultimately to defeat the Italians and to re-establish Habsburg domination in northern Italy.

MANTUAN SUCCESSION, WAR OF THE (1628–31), conflict over the succession to the north Italian duchies and imperial fiefs of Mantua and Montferrat, which developed on the death of the ruler, Vincent II (Dec. 1627). The claimant with the strongest hereditary right was the French Duke of Nevers, Charles of Gonzaga, but the ruler of Savoy claimed Montferrat, while Spain supported another claimant, the Duke of Guastalla, in order to challenge French domination of Milan and the strategic routes through the north Italian plain. With encouragement from Ferdinand II and the Spanish minister, Olivares, the Spanish governor of Milan, Don Gonzalo de Cordoba, led a joint Spanish–Savoyard occupation of Montferrat and besieged the key fortress of Casale (March–April 1628). This drew strong papal protests and pleas to France for help from the Duke of Nevers. In Jan. 1629 a French army under Louis XIII marched towards the Alps and seized Suza, the fortress commanding the Alpine pass into Italy, forcing Charles Emmanuel of Savoy to come to terms. However, imperial forces, freed by Wallenstein's successes in the Thirty Years War, seized the Valtelline and besieged the fortress of Mantua, while Spanish forces under Spinola laid siege to Casale, and Charles Emmanuel repudiated his French alliance. The French therefore occupied Pinerolo and invaded Savoy, and the imperial cause was further damaged by the deaths of Spinola and Charles Emmanuel (1630). Ferdinand therefore sought a general settlement of the war at the diet of Regensburg, where Richelieu's plenipotentiary, Father Joseph, agreed to Spanish occupation of Casale and Pinerolo in return for Nevers's succession in Mantua (Oct. 1630). Gustavus Adolphus's successes in the Thirty Years War, however, enabled Richelieu to repudiate the Regensburg terms and to conclude a more favourable settlement. The treaty of Cherasco (March 1631), which concluded the war, confirmed Nevers's succession in Mantua as an imperial feudatory, gave the pro-French ruler of Savoy a small part of

Montferrat in compensation, and reaffirmed France's control of Pinerolo, while Spain gained nothing from Olivares' intervention.   MKS

MANU, mythical hero of ancient India, often regarded as the first man or the first king. The most authoritative of Indian lawbooks, the *Manava Dharmashastra*, is attributed to him although, in its present form, it can be assigned to between the 2nd cent. BC and the 2nd cent. AD.

MANUCCI, NICCOLO (1639–*c.* 1717), Venetian traveller in India, whose memoirs, though often unreliable, form a classic record of the Emperor Aurangzeb's India and of European adventuring there.

MANUEL I KOMNENOS (*reg.* 1143–80), Byzantine Emperor, whose reign saw the Byzantines engaged in conflict with the Normans of Sicily. After being defeated at Brindisi in 1156 the emperor made a truce (1158) under the terms of which he agreed to withdraw his forces from southern Italy. He obtained from Serbia in 1159 and from the crusading state of Antioch in 1172 a recognition of his own position as their suzerain. In the east Manuel strove to continue the endeavours of his father, John II, and grandfather, Alexius I, to drive back the Turks in Asia Minor. At Myriokephalon, however, in 1176 he suffered a disastrous reverse which marked the end of the Byzantine reconquests of territories in Asia Minor.

MANUEL I (1469–1521), King of Portugal (*reg.* 1495–1521), son of Ferdinand, Duke of Viseo, succeeded his childless cousin, John II in 1495, then proceeded to consolidate royal power on the lines adopted by his neighbours, Ferdinand of Aragon and Isabella of Castile. He ceased to call the Cortes after 1502, enjoying considerable financial independence through the flood of wealth which poured back to Portugal from her overseas conquests. Manuel patronized Vasco de Gama's voyage to India (1497–9) and during his reign Portugal acquired enormous tracts of land in the New World, *eg,* Brazil (1500) and the Far East, *eg,* Sumatra (1510) and Goa (1511). He not only financed this remarkable expansion, but appointed members of his royal household, *eg,* Almeida and Albuquerque, to govern the empire. In 1501 he assumed the title of 'Lord of the Conquest, Navigation and Commerce of Ethiopia, Arabia, Persia and India'.

MANYŌSHŪ (lit. 'Collection of a Myriad Leaves'), the earliest anthology of Japanese poetry (*c.* 760), written in Chinese characters used phonetically. The 4516 poems are not only a landmark in the development of written Japanese, but also bear witness to a strong poetic tradition pre-dating Chinese influence.

MANZIKERT, BATTLE OF (1071), in Armenia, not far from Lake Van where the Turks, under the Seljuk sultan, Alp Arslan, routed the forces of the Byzantine Emperor Romanos Diogenes IV, who was captured during the battle. Alp Arslan, his main attention being directed towards Syria, did not want a sustained conflict with Byzantium, and therefore released Romanus IV on generous terms. This encounter can be taken to mark the beginning of the long and complex process which was to transform Asia Minor into a Muslim and a Turkish land.

MANZONI, ALESSANDRO (1785–1873), Italian poet and novelist, whose *I Promessi Sposi*, set in 17th-cent. Italy, has been acclaimed as one of the most notable novels in Italian literature. Despite his Catholicism, he was a strong supporter of Italian unification. He participated in the Milanese revolt (1848) and became a senator of the new Italian kingdom in 1860.

MAO TSE-TUNG (1893–), leader of the Chinese Communist Party and chief protagonist of the Chinese People's Republic. Mao was born in the south Chinese province of Hunan, and his education, which was frequently interrupted, included a grounding in the classical Chinese tradition, and an introduction to Western ideas. From the 1911 Revolution, in which he served briefly as a soldier, he was involved in revolutionary activities in his native province. In 1918 he went to Peking, where he became a librarian, and came into contact with the early protagonists of Marxism in China, in particular Li- Ta-chao. After his return to Hunan (1919), Mao moved gradually towards Marxism, and within a year had embraced it completely. He represented his province at the founding of the Chinese Communist Party in 1921. His work during the following years was varied: he was first a labour organizer, then co-ordinated CCP and Kuomintang policies during the heyday of the alliance between the two parties. From 1925 he became increasingly involved in the peasant movement, especially in Hunan, and his report on it (1927) is a vital document for the study of his political ideas. He was at this stage out of line with the city-oriented policies of the leadership of the party, and his individualism did not go uncriticized. But the chaotic situation within the party after the reverses of 1927 allowed Mao to pursue an independent policy, since he had only intermittent contacts with the CCP centre. With a small band of followers, he set up a base in the mountains on the borders of Hunan and Kiangsi, which was eventually expanded into the Kiangsi Soviet (1930). This area became the main region of communist activities; as its importance grew, so did Mao's within the party, though he still met with fierce opposition from the official party centre. Not until 1935, after the Soviet had been abandoned, did Mao win undisputed leadership over the party. The Long March took the communists from Kiangsi to Yenan, where they were to remain for the next decade. Mao set about forming the party into a peasant-based, highly disciplined organization, which was used in conjunction with the efficient guerrilla communist forces to mobilize the peasantry of north China against the Japanese and against the Kuomintang in a revolutionary nationalist movement. From this strong foundation laid during the anti-Japanese War, the communists expanded during the Civil War (1946–9), eventually winning control of the whole of China. Mao's role was increasingly that of the visionary leader, the creator of general policy lines, rather than that of the executive. Particularly after the establishment of the People's Republic (1949), he became the focus of a considerable personality cult. There is some evidence that this was not entirely of his own choosing, but was forced upon him by more pragmatic subordinates, chiefly Liu Shao-ch'i, who felt that his revolutionary romanticism, while essential for galvanizing the nation, was not helpful to practical administration. Twice Mao broke out of the restraints placed upon him, during the Great Leap Forward and the Cultural Revolution. The extreme voluntarism characteristic of these two movements was effective in producing revolutionary energy, but also created enormous confusion, and led, in both cases, to a reversion to more sober policies, though without any significant reduction in Mao's own prestige. He has remained the inspirational leader of the Chinese communist movement.

S. R. Schram, *Mao Tse-tung* (London, 1966).
J. Ch'en, *Mao and the Chinese Revolution* (London, 1965).   DCML

MAORIS, THE NEW ZEALAND. The first inhabitants of NZ are thought to have left eastern Polynesia between AD 750 and 950; a second wave arrived between AD 1150 and 1250. There is argument about how they accomplished their 2000-mile (3220 kms) sea-migration—whether accidentally or intentionally; by one-way or two-way voyages; by single canoes or by 'fleet' (according to Maori tradition). It has been suggested that they paddled, rather than sailed (which would have simplified the problem of navigation) and that occasional canoes still reached NZ as late as the 17th cent., when the *kumara* (sweet potato) was first introduced by Polynesian voyagers, either from Tahiti or the Marquesas.

The NZ Maoris had no idea of themselves as a nation, being divided on a basis of kinship and territory. The *whanau* (extended family) merged into the *hapu* (sub-tribe), *iwi* (tribe), and *waka* (ancestral 'canoe' group). This complex structure was sometimes disrupted to the point of local anarchy by internecine feuds. The chief (*ariki*, *rangatira*) exercised great authority (*mana*), but within a framework of strong communal life and landowning. Maori neolithic culture evolved many special characteristics in isolation from the rest of Polynesia. In cooler NZ, clothing and building developed markedly, and craftsmanship reached its peak in the curvilinear carving of house facings. Religion became less a matter of worship than of invoking aid in personal and tribal crises and undertakings, to each of which was attached a ritual supervised by the appropriate *tohunga* (priest).

Modern scholars have distinguished between an Early (also 'Archaic' and 'Moa Hunter') Maori period to *c*. 1350, and a Classic Maori period to *c*. 1800. The former was marked by sparse population, semi-nomadic life, less strife, and moa-hunting—the latter by developed agriculture based on the culture and storage of the *kumara*, greatly increased numbers, tribal warfare for resources, the elaborate *pa* (fort), and cannibalism. The transition has been variously ascribed to steady evolution, to climatic change affecting *kumara* culture, to new migrants introducing the previously unknown *kumara*, and (transposing the period of change itself to *c*. 1800) to early European contacts. At this later point the Maori population was about 250,000, all but a small number living in the North Island.

The arrival of European sailors (*c*. 1790) brought fatal diseases to the Maoris, as well as demands for women, alcohol, iron tools, and muskets, and provoked both brutal reprisals and acquisitive desires. With the new weapons, ambitious chiefs exacerbated tribal conflict to the level of wholesale slaughter. By 1830 the lives of many tribes were disrupted and their morale shattered. Appeals to the missionaries were widespread, though this is now thought to have been largely a quest for literacy. Many influential chiefs looked for salvation from tribal anarchy to the treaty of Waitangi (1840), which appeared to give British protection without infringing Maori rights.

Sparse British settlement and weak government existed largely on Maori sufferance and because of the Maoris' eagerness for European techniques. However, by the mid-1850s, they were in a minority; there was acute European pressure on their land and racialist attitudes to an 'inferior' people had developed among Europeans. Maori attempts to stop tribal land-sales and promote inter-tribal union under the Maori King (1858) aroused European hostility, and thus helped to bring about the wars of the 1860s. Nothing more than regional combination was achieved, and later resistance was largely crushed by Maori 'friendlies'. Maori frustration erupted briefly in the savage Hauhau movement (1864–8) and guerrilla campaigns of Te Kooti (1868–70), and gave rise to some millennial movements. Land confiscation (1863), private land purchase (1862–92), and the tactics of land dealers reduced both Maori land and population (about 42,000, 1896).

Maori schools (1867), parliamentary representation (1867), and local government (1902), though all inadequate, helped to reduce racial tension, along with lessening European land-hunger. Maori resilience confounded the prophets of extinction, and a Young Maori Party, formed in 1897, provided new leadership. Tribal land incorporations showed how Maori tenure and European farming could be combined, and Ngata inaugurated state assistance for Maori land development (1929). The Ratana Church (1925), in political alliance with Labour from 1931, long monopolized the four Maori electorates. After 1945 the Maori population rose to 220,000 (1970), the urban proportion by then reaching over 50 per cent. The old official policy of 'assimilation' (1881) was disavowed in favour of 'integration' (1960), of which the clearest expression was the Maori Education Foundation (1961).

J. Metge, *The Maoris of NZ* (London, 1967).
E. G. Schwimmer, *The Maori People in the 1960s* (Auckland, 1969).   WJG

MAORI KING MOVEMENT, THE NEW ZEALAND, founded in the later 1850s to halt both the disintegration of Maori tribes and the sale of land to European agents. Borrowing an alien symbol of power for Maori ends, Wiremu Tamihana led Waikato and other tribes in electing Te Wherowhero as Potatau I (1858). The king's *mana* (authority) was placed over his supporters' land. Though Kingites claimed that their movement was defensive only, Grey tried to break it in the Waikato War (1863–4). Thereafter, the 'King Country', largely unmolested, flourished successfully behind its self-imposed *aukati* (border). However, under increasing European pressure, King Tawhiao opened the King Country (1881–5), a step followed by further land sales and tribal decline. Though the king's territorial *mana* was abandoned, and attempts to establish supporting political institutions failed, royal election continued. The king (or queen) has remained a principal symbol of Maori racial identity.

MAORI (ANGLO-MAORI) WARS IN NEW ZEALAND, precipitated by European settlers' increased demands for Maori land purchase in the 1850s. Maoris, spiritually rooted in their tribal lands, feared for their own future as a distinctive people, and attempts were made to form 'leagues' to prevent land-selling. Especially in Taranaki, they resisted both pressure on tribes (or sections of them) to sell, and also investigation of tribal tenures, taking their stand on the treaty of Waitangi. However, when Wiremu Kingi used his chieftainly *mana* to forbid negotiations for the controversial Waitara purchase (1859), the governor (Gore-Browne) treated his action as defiance of British sovereignty. The Maoris' obstruction of surveyors led to the Taranaki War of 1860–1, and, after an uneasy interval, to the Waikato War of 1863–4, which involved the Maori king's supporters. Though skilled in bush (forest) skirmishes, Maori warriors could not sustain long campaigns, nor advance far from cover. Their attempts to fortify and hold positions (*eg*, Rangiriri, 1863, Orakau, 1864) invariably failed against superior numbers and equipment, and hostilities virtually ceased when they fell back into the bush-clad interior. The later campaigns of the Hauhaus (1864–8) and of Te Kooti (1868–70) amounted to a series of savage, usually improvised, guerrilla raids. These were ended largely by patrols of 'friendly' Maori troops, and hostilities petered out by 1872. The main burden of crushing Maori resistance fell on imperial troops (11,000 in 1864), who acquitted themselves reasonably well in unfamiliar circumstances, in spite of colonists' criticisms. Many imperial soldiers disliked both the nature and the object of their campaigns. Some colonial troops, especially forest rangers, distinguished themselves in guerrilla expeditions. The British government, seeing the wars as an imperial responsibility, was later disillusioned by the colonial government's chicanery, and withdrew its troops (1866–70), thereby compelling the introduction of more moderate policies.

                                                      WFG

MAPUNGUBWE CULTURE, rich iron-age culture in the Middle Limpopo valley, South Africa, carbon-dated in its middle-stages to between 1380 and 1420, and characterized by fine pottery, gold remains, and stone buildings. It may have been an extension of the Zimbabwe empire in Rhodesia.

MAQDISI, AL- (AL-MUQADDASI) (*fl*. 10th cent.), Arab geographer, who travelled through most of the lands subject to Islam and wrote (985) an account of what he had seen, entitled *Ahsan al-Taqasim*, a work full of valuable information.

MAQRIZI, AL- (1364–1442), historian writing in the time of the Mamluk sultanate of Egypt and Syria. His fame rests on the *Khitat*, a work historical, topographical, and antiquarian in character relating to Egypt and the adjacent lands. He also wrote a chronicle, *Itt'az al-Hunafa*, dealing with the affairs of the Fatimid caliphate.

MAR, JOHN ERSKINE, 23rd Earl of (Scottish) (1675–1732), Jacobite leader, who was a commissioner for the Union of Scotland and England (1705–7), and supported the Old Pretender in 1715. He took part in the battle of Sheriffmuir (1715) and thereafter fled to France when the Jacobite rebellion failed.

MARAT, JEAN PAUL (1743–93), extremist French politician and editor of the *Ami du Peuple*, who was murdered in his bath by Charlotte Corday. He was one of the Jacobin leaders who called for the execution of profiteers and the setting up of a dictatorship to resolve the problems of a disintegrating society in France.

MARATHA CONFEDERACY, result of the expansion of the Marathas under the Peshwas of Poona after the death of Sivaji (1680). The generals in the outlying areas, Holkar of Indore, Sindhia of Gwalior, and the Gaekwar of Baroda, sought greater independence. After the Maratha defeat at Panipat (1761), such centrifugal tendencies were much in evidence. This impaired the strength of the Marathas in their struggle with the British, who were able to play the members of the confederacy off against each other.

MARATHA WARS, with the British for paramountcy in India, were three in number and took place during the governors-generalship of Warren Hastings, Lord Wellesley, and the Marquis of Hastings. The first war (1775–82) resulted from the action of the Bombay government, which championed the claim of Raghoba to the peshwaship of the confederacy. This ended with the treaty of Salbai (1782). Wellesley's treaty of Bassein (1802) with the peshwa, Baji Rao II, led to the second war (1803–5), but Wellesley was recalled before he could crush the power of the Marathas. It was left to the Marquis of Hastings to do this in the final Maratha War (1817–19), which resulted in British paramountcy in India.

MARATHON, BATTLE OF (490 BC), in Greece 27 kms northeast of Athens, the first Greek victory of the Persian Wars, won by some 10,000 Athenian and 1000 Plataean hoplites over a Persian expedition of about 25,000 men under Datis and Artaphernes, which had crossed the Aegean and sacked Eretria and intended to reduce Athens. Herodotus' account leaves much obscure, but, after the Athenians had blocked the Persian advance inland for some days, the Persians embarked their cavalry, probably for an alternative landing near Athens, or perhaps to anticipate the arrival of Spartan reinforcements. The Athenians attacked and defeated the Persian infantry, driving the survivors on to their ships. This victory proved the Greek infantry's superiority and greatly encouraged further resistance to Persian invasion.

MARBURG, COLLOQUY OF (1529), held at his castle by Philip of Hesse, in an effort to settle the difference between Lutherans and Zwinglians on the manner of the divine presence in the Eucharist. Agreement was reached on lesser issues, but Luther, accompanied by Melanchthon, took his stand on the words 'Hoc est corpus meum' and would not admit that *is* might mean *is a sign of.* Zwingli and Oecolampadius were equally insistent that the elements were simply memorials of the body and blood of Christ, and the conference, so far from achieving unity, emphasized this essential difference. Melanchthon still hoped for reconciliation, but the articles which Luther based on the Marburg Confession merely reasserted his own views.

MARBURY v. MADISON, I Cranch 137 (1803), US Supreme Court case in which the court for the first time declared an act of Congress unconstitutional, and established its own power of pure judicial review. William Marbury was one of several Federalist judicial appointments made by President Adams on the eve of Jefferson's becoming president. His commission as a justice of the peace for the District of Columbia had been signed and sealed, but not delivered when Jefferson took office. Jefferson believed the appointment to be invalid, and ordered Madison, his secretary of state, to withhold the commission. Marbury, acting under Section 13 of the Judiciary Act (1789), applied to the Supreme Court for a preliminary writ requiring Madison to show cause why a writ of mandamus should not be issued directing him to deliver the commission. Madison ignored the preliminary writ and Chief Justice Marshall handed down an opinion on Marbury's application (1803). Without debating whether the Supreme Court had jurisdiction of the case, Marshall asserted that Marbury had a right to the commission and the laws afforded him a remedy, but the proper remedy was not a Supreme Court writ of mandamus, because Section 13 was unconstitutional, Congress having no authority to alter the court's original jurisdiction. Marshall's opinion was an attack upon Jefferson's administration, and a bold statement of the general theory of judicial review. Although this decision limited the Supreme Court's powers, its effect was to enhance its potential political power.

MARCEL, ETIENNE (d. 1358), French merchant, who became the chief Parisian magistrate (provost of the merchants) in 1355 and a revolutionary leader in the great crisis of the French monarchy in 1356–8. The French king had been captured by the English on 19 Sept. 1356 and his young son Charles, was unable to control the estates general of northern France, which assembled at Paris on 17 Oct. Marcel, who had political allies among the nobles and prelates, reduced Charles to a helpless figurehead, his friends being imprisoned and some even massacred by Parisian mobs. This outbreak of violence, and a revolt of peasants north of Paris, who were encouraged by Marcel, discredited his leadership. He was murdered on 31 July 1358, whereupon Charles was able to restore control over Paris and to begin the re-establishment of the royal authority in France.

MARCELLUS, M. CLAUDIUS (d. 208 BC), Roman general, who, with Scipio Africanus and Fabius Cunctator, was one of their three great commanders in the Second Punic War. He fought in the First War, and as consul against the Insubres (222). He also fought (216–214) against Hannibal in Italy, and was instrumental in saving Nola. The next three years he spent in frustrating Carthaginian plans in Sicily, becoming notorious for his sack of Leontini (214) and capture of Syracuse (211). After fighting three further campaigns of attrition in Italy, and being consul for the fifth time, he was killed in ambush near Venusia.

MARCELLUS, C. CLAUDIUS (42–23 BC), son of C. Claudius Marcellus (consul, 50) and Octavia, Augustus' sister. Augustus intended Marcellus as his heir and he was married to Augustus' daughter Julia (25), but he died prematurely.

MARCH, ROGER MORTIMER, 1st Earl of (1st of 1st creation) (*c.* 1288–1330), one of the leading baronial opponents of King Edward II of England. After their disastrous defeat in 1321–2 he was imprisoned in the Tower of London, but managed in 1323 to escape to France. There, in 1325, he joined Edward's queen, Isabella, and together in Sept. 1326 they invaded England with a small force of exiles and mercenaries. Rapidly deserted by his friends, Edward II was captured in Nov. His heir, Edward III, aged 14, was proclaimed king in Jan. 1327, Mortimer becoming the effective ruler. A gradual estrangement between him and his former confederates led to a brief civil war against Henry, Earl of Lancaster, in 1328–9. Edward III, who was friendly with

Lancaster, became alarmed for his own safety and arranged for Mortimer's seizure in Oct. 1330. In Nov. he was executed. His grandson was restored to the earldom of March in 1354. The Yorkist kings and all the rulers of England from Henry VIII onwards are his descendants.

MARCH FIRST MOVEMENT (1919), turning point in Korean nationalism. Korea had not been capable of resisting foreign aggression between 1880 and 1910, but sought peaceful means of nullifying the Japanese annexation after 1910. In Jan. 1919 an appeal to the Versailles Peace Conference failed, as did a memorial by Koreans in Japan in Feb. On the occasion of the funeral of King Kojong, 33 representatives of the protestant Christian churches, the Ch'ondo-gyo, and the Buddhists signed a declaration of independence, 21,000 copies of which were printed and read throughout the country at noon on 1 March 1919. During the following two months the Japanese killed 7500 Koreans, wounded 16,000, and imprisoned 47,000 in one of the most brutal episodes of modern colonialism.

MARCHAND, JEAN BAPTISTE (1863–1934), French colonial soldier and explorer, who was involved in the Fashoda incident (1898), affecting Anglo French relations in the Sudan. He commanded colonial troops in the First World War.

MARCHFELD, BATTLE OF THE (1278), site of the defeat and death of King Ottokar II of Bohemia by an Austrian and Hungarian army under Rudolph of Habsburg. It was a decisive battle and marked the end of his dreams of a 'Great Bohemia', comprising Bohemia, Moravia, Silesia, Austria, Carinthia, Carniola, and Styria. It also marked the beginning of the rise of the house of Habsburg to preeminence.

MARCHMONT, PATRICK HUME, 1st Earl of (Scottish) (1641–1724), Scottish Whig chancellor, who supported the Presbyterian Church and the Hanoverian settlement in the early 18th cent. He unsuccessfully introduced an Act for the Abjuration of the Pretender (1702) and was replaced by the Earl of Seafield in 1703.

MARCHMONT, ALEXANDER HUME-CAMPBELL, 2nd Earl of (Scottish) (1675–1740), Scottish politician, who sat as an MP in the last Scottish parliament (1706) and supported the union with England. He was in sympathy with the Hanoverian succession (1714), defended Berwickshire during the 1715 Jacobite rebellion, and was employed by George I as envoy to Denmark (1715–21). He was lord clerk register of Scotland (1716–33). He sat in the House of Lords from 1727 onwards as a Scottish representative peer and opposed Sir Robert Walpole's excise scheme.

MARCO POLO BRIDGE INCIDENT (July 1937), first clash in the open war between China and Japan, sometimes declared to be the first encounter of the Second World War. The incident, which followed a series of clashes in the undeclared war between Japan and China which had been going on since 1931, occurred at a strategic river crossing near Peking, and was created by the Japanese in order to give them grounds for attacking Peking. After the incident, war started in earnest.

MARCOMANNI, early German tribe which migrated in 8 BC from the upper Main to Bohemia and formed a powerful kingdom under Maroboduus. The Roman Emperor Augustus failed to destroy them, but they became less dangerous. Between 168 and 180 they led attacks on the Roman empire, but in the 3rd and 4th cents declined again in importance, some of them being settled within the empire or serving as soldiers. In the 5th cent. they left Bohemia for southern Germany, where they were called Baiuvarii, giving this name to Bayern (Bavaria).

MARCONI, GUGLIELMO (1874–1937), Italian inventor, who in 1896 sent the first recorded message through space by electromagnetic waves. In 1901 he succeeded in transmitting and receiving signals between Nfld and Cornwall. The rest of his life was spent in the scientific and commercial development of wireless telegraphy, telephony, and broadcasting. He was awarded (1909) the Nobel Prize for Physics.

MARCONI AFFAIR (1912) in Britain. The buying of shares in the US Marconi Co. by Lloyd George, chancellor of the exchequer, and other ministers, a few weeks after the British government's acceptance of the British Marconi Co.'s tender for an imperial wireless chain, led to allegations of ministerial corruption. The ministers concerned were exonerated at an official enquiry, but in a minority report were accused of grave impropriety, having acquired shares through the offices of the attorney-general's brother, a member of the company. The Conservative opposition refused to accept Lloyd George's apology for his error of judgement and forced a vote in the Commons, hoping to bring about his resignation, but the motion was defeated.

MARCOS, FERDINAND (1917–   ), president of the Philippines (1965–9), the first to be elected for a second term (1969–73). He was called to the bar while facing a trial for murder, in which he successfully conducted his own defence. He served with distinction in the Second World War and in 1949 was elected to Congress. As leader of the minority party in the House, he proved to be an excellent parliamentarian, and preserved the two-party system by maintaining an alert and active opposition. Twice he was re-elected to the House of Representatives, where he concentrated on the development of government incentives in commerce and industry; the elevation of the farmers' living standards through government aid; the protection and extension of civil rights; and the improvement of ethical standards in politics and the civil service. He continued to campaign for legislation in these spheres when he was elected senator (1959). In 1963 he became Senate president, but later moved from the Liberal to the Nacionalista Party, which adopted him as its candidate for the presidency in the 1965 election. He emphasized the need for self-sufficiency, self-improvement, and hard work to improve the economic and social conditions of the people, and of nationalism at home and abroad, as well as greater initiative in independent Asian leadership.

MARCUS AURELIUS (AD 121–80), Roman Emperor (*reg.* 161–80), whose reign marks the end of the most successful period of the Roman empire. Born M. Annius Verus, he was adopted by his uncle Antoninus Pius in 138, when the latter was adopted by Hadrian, and married his daughter Faustina in 145. He was at Antoninus' side during much of his reign. From 161 to 169 he shared imperial power with the unsatisfactory Lucius Verus. Marcus, a convinced Stoic and man of high principles, was forced to spend most of his reign at war instead of in peace as he wished to spend it. In 162 the Parthians attacked Syria and Cappadocia; in a counter-attack, nominally under Verus, Seleucia and Ctesiphon were captured, but during operations a disastrous plague was introduced into the empire. In 168 or 170 the Marcommani broke through the Danube frontier and penetrated as far as Verona; wars to repel them and other invaders continued till 174, and were renewed in 177. Marcus sought to relieve the damage done to the empire by war and plague, but with limited success. Some persecutions of Christians are known to have occurred in his reign. His *Meditations*, a private or semi-private book of philosophical and ethical common places, survives.

A. Birley, *Marcus Aurelius* (London, 1966).   BHW

MARCY, WILLIAM LEARNED (1786–1857), US lawyer and politician, who had a distinguished career in NY state politics before entering the US Senate (1831). He originated the term 'spoils system', in defending Van Buren's appointment as minister to London (1832). After being governor of NY (1833–8), Marcy was secretary of war (1845–9), then secretary of state (1853–7), and negotiated 24 treaties, notably the Gadsden Purchase treaty (1853), and a Reciprocity treaty with Britain (1854).

MARDONIUS (d. 479 BC), Persian general, and son-in-law of King Darius I who was prominent in the Persian Wars with Greece. After taking command in western Asia (492), he carried out Darius' new policy of establishing democracies in the Ionian Greek cities, but abandoned an expedition to attack Greece from the north when his fleet was wrecked off Mt Athos. He took part with Xerxes' invasion of Greece and, when the king returned to Asia (autumn 480), assumed command of the Persian army based on Thebes, but was defeated and killed at Plataea.

MARDUK, patron god of Babylon, elevated to head the pantheon by Hammurabi (c. 1792–1750 BC), who had genealogies and the Epic of Creation rewritten to accommodate him.

MARDYCK, French fortified harbour, which, with its larger neighbour, Dunkirk, provided a haven for French privateers in the War of the Spanish Succession. Its fortifications were to be razed according to the peace of Utrecht (1713), and Stanhope secured a similar guarantee in the Triple Alliance (1717), but disputes over the implementation of these treaties continued well into the 18th cent.

MARE CLAUSUM, name given to the doctrine of a closed sea in the 16th–17th cents controversy arising from the demands of different states to exclusive dominion over areas of open sea. Spain and Portugal laid claim to whole oceans; England restricted her claims to the Channel and the North Sea. It is also the title of a book by John Selden (published 1635), which asserted 'that the sea by the law of nature or nations is not common to all men, but capable of private dominion or property as well as the land'.

MARE LIBERUM, name given to the doctrine of an open sea in the 16th–17th cents controversy over the control of the seas. It is also the title of a book by Hugo Grotius (published 1609). Cornelis van Bynbershoek in *De dominio maris* (1702) put forward the formula which solved the controversy, restricting dominion over the sea to the actual distance from land which fell within cannon range, *ie*, three nautical miles.

MARENGO, BATTLE OF (14 June 1800), fought during the French Wars. The Austrian army, led by Melas, attacked Napoleon's forces at Marengo, 4 kms east of Alessandria, and, catching the French off their guard, broke their line and forced them to fall back 6·4 kms to San Giuliano. Their defeat seemed certain, but the arrival of a fresh corps under Desaix put new heart into the French, who mounted a counter-attack which checked the Austrian advance, and when night fell the Austrian forces fled from the field in disorder.

MARGARET (c. 1045–93), Queen of Scotland, granddaughter of Edmund Ironside, and Stephen the Good of Hungary, and sister of Edgar Atheling. After living in Hungary and in England, her family escaped from William the Conqueror and fled to Scotland.

In 1070 Margaret married King Malcolm III of Scotland, of which three of their sons became kings. Their daughter became the queen of Henry I of England. As queen, Margaret—in consultation with Abp Lanfranc—was instrumental in bringing the ancient Celtic Church in Scotland into touch with Christian thought in Europe. She introduced new customs and manners into the Scottish court, she encouraged monastic development, and education, and she

was concerned with conditions of slaves-of-war in lowland households. At Queensferry she organized hostels for pilgrims to St Andrews, and also cared for the needy. Her biographer, Bp Turgot, testifies to her life of Christian devotion, which led to her canonization by Pope Innocent IV (1250).

MARGARET (1489–1541), Queen of Scotland, eldest daughter of Henry VII who married James IV (1503) and on his death at Flodden (1513) became regent for their son, James V. On her marriage to the Earl of Angus (1514) she was compelled to surrender the regency to the heir-presumptive, the Duke of Albany. She withdrew temporarily to England (1515) and for some years was engaged in a bitter struggle for the possession of the young king, supporting one faction after another. Margaret lacked the characteristic Tudor sagacity and control, and was discredited when she divorced Angus and married Methven (1528). She helped to negotiate a treaty with England (1534), but was prevented from escaping there after an unsuccessful attempt to divorce Methven (1537). Her great-grandson by her first marriage became James I of England and VI of Scotland.

MARGARET (1522–86), Duchess of Parma, natural daughter of the Emperor Charles V, and half-sister of Philip II, who appointed her governor-general and regent of the Netherlands after he had left to ascend the Spanish throne (1559–1567). Her mother being Flemish, Margaret was born and brought up in the Low Countries, and at first she governed with the co-operation of the native nobility. Instructed by Philip to follow the advice of Cardinal Granvelle, she was forced to make concessions to the nobles over the enforcement of decrees against heretics (1566), and though she successfully exploited the reaction to an outbreak of iconoclasm (Aug. 1566), she wanted to make moderate concessions to the Calvinists (1567). But she was over-ruled by Philip, and replaced by the Duke of Alva, then recalled (1567). In 1578 Philip planned to reappoint her, but her place was taken by Alexander Farnese, her son by her marriage to Ottavio Farnese, Duke of Parma.

MARGARET THERESA (1651–73), younger daughter of Philip IV of Spain and Elizabeth of France. She became the first wife of the Emperor Leopold I (1666), but died when still young. Her daughter Maria Antonia married Maximilian II Emmanuel of Bavaria (1685) and the child of this marriage, Joseph Ferdinand (1692–9) became the most acceptable candidate for the Spanish succession, since Margaret Theresa had never renounced her hereditary rights.

MARGARET OF ANGOULÊME (1492–1549), Queen, sister of Francis I of France and grandmother of Henry IV. She married, first, Charles, Duke of Alençon (1509), and after his death, Henry d'Albret, King of Navarre (1527), their daughter being Jeanne d'Albret (b. 1528). Margaret was a patroness of Christian humanism and Renaissance literature, and her court at Angoulême became a refuge for reformers seeking protection against religious persecution, among them Rabelais and Lefèvre d'Etaples. She herself published a number of works, including the *Heptameron*, a novella or prose tale adapted to a didactic purpose, based in form on Boccaccio's *Decameron*.

MARGARET OF AUSTRIA (1480–1530), daughter of Emperor Maximilian I and Mary of Burgundy, who was a generous patron of letters and the arts and a considerable politician. She was betrothed as a child to Charles VIII of France for a dowry of Artois and Franche-Comté (1482), but was later repudiated by the French (1491) and married to Juan of Castile, son of Ferdinand and Isabella, who died almost immediately. The young widow then married Philibert of Savoy (1499) and after his death (1504) became regent of the Netherlands during Charles V's minority (1507–15). During this time she negotiated the Franco-

Imperial alliance against Venice, known as the League of Cambrai (1508), and a treaty with England (1508), and also acted as foster-mother to the young family of her brother, Philip the Fair (d. 1506), which included the future Emperor Charles. Margaret relied heavily on the Piedmontese statesman, Gattinara, and her relations with the native nobility, *eg*, the Duke of Aerschot, were sometimes strained. On Charles V's accession to the Spanish throne, she again became governor of the Netherlands and retained this position for the rest of her life (1518–30). One of her last political acts was the negotiation of the peace of Cambrai with Louise of Savoy (the Ladies' Peace, 1529).

MARGARET OF NORWAY (1353–1412), Queen, Regent of Scandinavia, was the daughter of Valdemar IV of Denmark and wife of Haakon VI of Norway. Her son, Olaf, succeeded to the Danish throne on her father's death in 1376. In the later 1380s she secured the sovereignty of all three Scandinavian kingdoms. Olaf had become King of Norway when Haakon died (1380) and on Olaf's death (1387) Margaret secured both the Danish and Norwegian thrones for herself. In 1389 she won the support of a faction in Sweden, defeating King Albrecht. Her position was never formalized, in that a woman could not rule in Sweden. The Union of Kalmar (1397) saw the crowning of her great-nephew, Eric, as king of all three countries. During his minority—and until her death—Margaret was the effective ruler. Her main interest was Denmark, and Copenhagen emerged as the centre of administration. Although the period was one of financial and economic growth in northern Europe, largely through the work of the Hanseatic merchants, Norway prospered least and her national pride suffered. By the 1430s the union had collapsed.

MARGARET OF SAVOY (1589–1655), Spanish princess, who was appointed governor of Portugal by Olivares and Philip IV (1634), but was expelled (1640) by the Portuguese at the outset of their rebellion against the Spanish.

MARGARET OF VALOIS (1553–1615), Queen, daughter of Henry II and Catherine de' Medici, who became the first wife of Henry of Navarre (1572). This Valois–Bourbon alliance, planned to settle the religious and civil strife in France, was vitiated by the St Bartholomew Massacre (1572), separation (1576), and finally divorce (1599).

MARGARET OF YORK (1446–1503), Duchess of Burgundy, sister of King Edward IV of England. She was married to Duke Charles the Bold of Burgundy as part of the Anglo-Burgundian alliance against France. After his death at the battle of Nancy (1477) she played a vital part in preventing the French annexation of the Netherlands, thus preserving the independent existence of the Burgundian state. In 1477 she procured the intervention of Maximilian, son of the Habsburg Emperor Frederick III, and ensured the marriage of Maximilian with Mary, the only daughter and heiress of Charles. After Mary's death in 1482, Margaret again acted as the main representative of the Burgundian dynasty, governing the Netherlands during Maximilian's frequent absences abroad and bringing up Mary's children until they were of age to rule the Netherlands. She was an enemy of King Henry VII of England, who had killed her brother, Richard III, and was the main inspiration of all the Yorkist conspiracies against Henry.

MARGARITA PHILOSOPHICA, compilation of knowledge at the opening of the 16th cent. by Gregorious Reisch (d. 1525), published in 1503. The classics of philosophy are treated under nine headings: Grammar, Logic, Rhetoric, Arithmetic. Music Geometry, Astronomy and Astrology, Natural Philosophy, and Moral Philosophy.

MARGRAVES OF BRANDENBURG, rulers of the mark or frontier region of Brandenburg on the Middle Elbe, which had been founded as a bishopric by Otto I in the mid-10th cent. After being overrun by heathen Slavs, the mark first enjoyed a continuous existence under the Ascanian house of margraves, founded by Albert the Bear (1134). From the death of the last Ascanian margrave, Woldemar (1319), there was a succession of weak margraves of the house of Wittelsbach and Luxembourg, whose real interests lay further south in Germany. In 1412 Frederick of Hohenzollern acquired the title of margrave of Brandenburg and three years later was elevated to the position of elector (1415), from which time the mark of Brandenburg was merged in the possessions of this ambitious princely family from which the imperial house of Germany sprang.

MARI (mod. Tell el-Hariri), ancient Mesopotamian city commanding the main trade routes up the Euphrates to the west. It had periods of importance in Early Dynastic times (c. 2700 BC), as a provincial city under the Third Dynasty of Ur (c. 2113–2004) and as capital of an Amorite kingdom (c. 1900–1800).

MARIA THERESA (1717–80), Empress (*reg.* 1740–80). She was the Archduchess of Austria and elder daughter of the Emperor Charles VI. Her succession to the Habsburg possessions in default of a male heir was established by the Pragmatic Sanction. In 1736 she married Francis, Duke of Lorraine. In 1740, on the death of her father, she succeeded to her hereditary lands, though her claim was not universally accepted and led to the War of the Austrian Succession.

In 1741 Maria Theresa was crowned Queen of Hungary, appearing with her baby son in her arms to receive the acclamation of the assembled estates. In 1745 her husband was elected Holy Roman emperor. Maria Theresa ruled the Habsburg lands until 1765, when, on Francis's death, she shared authority in the co-regency with her eldest son, the Emperor Joseph II (1765–80).

After being forced to accept the alienation of Silesia, seized by Frederick II at the opening of the Austrian Succession War, Maria Theresa embarked on a policy of domestic reform, inspired by fear of Prussian aggression (1748–56). The army was reformed, the centralisation of the administrative system begun, and the economy overhauled by her capable ministers, *eg*, Haugwitz and Chotek. Meanwhile, the chancellor and foreign minister, Kaunitz, her devoted servant and lifelong friend, prepared for the recovery of Silesia by diplomatic means, cultivating the friendship of Austria's traditional enemy, France (1749–55), and creating the reversal of alliances (1755–6) which led to the treaty of Versailles (1756). Maria Theresa's fears were justified when Frederick II's army invaded Saxony (1756) and precipitated the Seven Years War (1756–63). France and Russia supported Maria Theresa, but despite victories at Kolin and Landshut, her troops suffered defeats at Leuthen, Leignitz, and Torgau and she was forced to accept the status quo of 1756. Henceforth, disillusioned by the futility of war, Maria Theresa strove to maintain international peace, though she never lost her hatred of Prussia. In her later years she was preoccupied by the partition of Poland (1772) and Russian expansion at Turkey's expense. Though opposed to the suggestion of Poland's dismemberment, she allowed Kaunitz and Joseph to participate in it.

Maria Theresa, a pious and devoted Catholic in her personal life, showed signs of that independence from papal intervention which was known in her son's reign as Josephinism. The wealth and organization of the Church was put at the disposal of the state. She was an imperious and dominating personality of limited intelligence and lacked her son's determination to carry out rational and humane reforms.

E. Crankshaw, *Maria Theresa* (London, 1969).
G. P. Gooch, *Maria Theresa and Other Studies* (London, 1951). MKS

MARIA I (1734–1816), Queen of Portugal (*reg.* 1777–1816), and eldest daughter of King Joseph Emmanuel. She ruled jointly with her husband, Pedro III, but both were weak-minded and control of affairs was seized by Maria's mother, Mariana Victoria. After Pedro's death the queen became demented and her second son, John, was declared regent (1792).

MARIA CRISTINA (1806–78), Queen Regent of Spain, daughter of Francis I of Naples and fourth wife of Ferdinand of Spain. On the death of Ferdinand (1833), she became regent for their daughter, Isabella III. She was forced to give up her regency (1840) as a result of the Carlist War (1833–9), but returned in 1843. The revolution of 1854 again drove her into exile.

MARIA THERESA (1638–83), Queen of France, elder daughter of Philip IV of Spain and Elizabeth of France. She married Louis XIV in 1660 and the marriage treaty, concluded in the peace of the Pyrenees (Nov. 1659), provided for a dowry of 500,000 escudos, full payment being a condition of Maria Theresa's renunciation of all claims to the Spanish throne.

MARIANA OF AUSTRIA (1634–96), daughter of the Emperor Ferdinand III and second wife of her uncle, Philip IV of Spain, whom she married in 1649. She bore two sickly sons, the second of whom lived to become Charles II of Spain. Becoming regent and guardian of Charles on Philip's death (1665), she was influenced by her Austrian Jesuit confessor, Father Nithard (1607–81), and by an Andalusian favourite, Fernando de Valenzuela. During her regency (1665–75) and for the rest of her lifetime, Spanish prestige and power reached their nadir.

MARIANA, JUAN DE (1535–1624), Spanish Jesuit theologian and political philosopher. His famous treatise, *De Rege et Regis Institutione* (1599), attacked absolutism and advocated constitutional monarchy. He also defended tyrannicide (1599) and criticized the effect of the Jesuit order upon Spanish education and the methods of the Inquisition. In 1601 he wrote a general history of Spain. His outspokenness led to his arrest by the Inquisition and his being charged with treason for having criticized Philip III's fiscal policies in a treatise on money (1609); but after a year's imprisonment Mariana was released, though his treatise was put on the Index.

MARIANA ISLANDS, called by the navigator Magellan the Ladrone (Robber) Islands. They extend northwards from Guam in the northern Pacific. In 1564 they were annexed by Spain and were used as a staging post by the annual Manila galleon. A Jesuit mission to Guam (1668) eventually won native (Chamorro or mixed Micronesian) confidence, but was deported (1769) after being involved in a local campaign against Spanish misrule. In the 19th cent. Guam was a major watering place for vessels outward bound from Australia, and in 1898 was ceded to the US, the remaining islands in the chain (with other Spanish Micronesian islands) going to Germany. In 1914 the group (except Guam) was occupied by Japan, which secured, after the First World War, the mandate over them. Guam fell to Japan (1942) in the Second World War, but was recaptured with the rest of the group in July 1944. As a major military base it became an unincorporated Territory of the US, the other islands being absorbed into the separate trust territory of Micronesia.

MARIÁTEGUI, JOSÉ CARLOS (1895–1930), Peruvian radical, who helped to organize the Peruvian Socialist Party. He sought to resurrect pre-Spanish socialism in Peru in order to form an Inca-oriented nation.

MARICA (MARITSA), BATTLE OF (1371), on the Maritsa river, near Çirnomen, when the Ottoman Turks forced the Serbian princes in Macedonia and the adjacent lands to become the vassals of the Ottoman beg.

MARIE ADELAIDE OF SAVOY (1685–1712), Duchess of Burgundy, daughter of Victor Amadeus, duke of Savoy, and sister of Marie-Louise, Queen of Spain, who came to France in 1696, according to the treaty of Turin, to marry Louis XIV's eldest grandson, the Duke of Burgundy. She had three children, including the future Louis XV of France.

MARIE ANTOINETTE (1755–93), Queen, daughter of the Emperor Francis I and Maria Theresa, and wife of Louis XVI of France. She was guillotined nine months after her husband. In 1770 Marie Antoinette was married to the then Dauphin and came to Versailles as the pledge of Choiseul's Franco-Austrian alliance. She proved to be irresponsible, meddlesome and extravagant. After the Revolution broke out she and the royal family fled from their confinement in the Tuileries towards France's eastern frontier and her native Austria, to be halted at Varennes and returned to Paris as prisoners (1791). She continued to scheme for the restoration of the monarchy until her trial and execution by the Revolutionary Tribunal (Oct. 1793).

MARIE DE' MEDICI (1573–1642), Queen, and daughter of the Grand Duke of Tuscany, who married Henry IV (1600) of France after the death of his first wife, Marguerite of Valois.

Marie was excluded from state affairs until Henry was assassinated (1610) on the eve of a war with Spain. The Paris *parlement* then declared her regent for her nine-year-old son, Louis XIII, and in seven years she put the clock back on Henry's reforms. Sully was edged into retirement and replaced by two Florentine adventurers, the waiting-woman Leonora Galigai and her husband, Concini, who was promoted to be Maréchal d'Ancre. When Condé raised the nobles against them, Marie twice bought them off (St Menehould, 1614, and Loudun, 1616) with substantial bribes from the wealth amassed by Sully's prudent administration.

Meanwhile, she had withdrawn from Henry's anti-Habsburg league, which immediately collapsed, and instead sought an agreement with Spain. Marriages took place (1615) between Louis and the Infanta Anne of Austria and between Marie's daughter Elizabeth and Philip, the Spanish heir.

Four years of improvident misrule led to the summoning (1614) of the last states general to meet before the Revolution. The third estate, dominated by lawyers, provincial officials and others of the professional classes, attacked the exorbitant pensions enjoyed by the nobility, who themselves were critical of the *paulette*, a tax permitting the hereditary transmission of judicial and civic offices. The third estate also attacked the ultramontanism of the clergy, and in this atmosphere of internal bickering the states general was unable to achieve many reforms. It was, however, united in opposing the government's financial administration, and Jeannin, the finance minister, was forced to produce what passed for accounts. A special court was set up to supervise the finances, and the Crown agreed to reduce the pension list and check the purchase system by suspending the *paulette*.

In 1617 Louis determined to escape from his mother's influence, and she was forced to withdraw to Blois after Concini had been murdered and his wife executed on a charge of sorcery. But Luynes, the king's new favourite, was no more efficient than Concini, and after a rising of some of the nobility in alliance with the Huguenots (1620), Marie was allowed to maintain a small court at Angers and was admitted to the royal council. This did not satisfy her, however, and she continued to intrigue for the recovery of her power. Her particular enemy was Richelieu, formerly her protégé, and on the Day of Dupes (1630) her son Gaston of Orléans and the queen joined her in a conspiracy to overthrow him. The plot failed and she was exiled to Compiègne. After escaping to Brussels she lived for a time in England, where her daughter Henrietta Maria was Charles I's queen.

MARIE DE FRANCE (*fl.* 12th cent.), earliest known medieval European poetess, who wrote in French and was virtually the creator of the lay as a poetic form. This was originally a lyric to a song based on ancient legends and was used by Breton minstrels. Two of her poems, 'Chevrefoil' and 'Lanival', are significant to Arthurian literature and her work as a whole marked a major advance in chivalric literature.

MARIE GALANTE, small island in the French Antilles, a dependency of Guadeloupe, and since 1946 a département of France.

MARIE-LOUISE (1791–1847), Empress of the French, daughter of Archduke Francis, later Francis I, Emperor of Austria. She was the second wife of Napoleon I (1810) and bore him one son, who was created King of Rome.

MARIE-LOUISE (1688–1714), Queen of Spain, daughter of Victor Amadeus, Duke of Savoy, and first wife of Philip V, whom she married in 1701 at the age of 13. She was Regent of Spain while her husband was absent in Italy during the War of the Spanish Succession.

MARIENBURG, TREATY OF (June 1656), between Frederick William I of Brandenburg-Prussia and Charles X of Sweden. It counterbalanced the effects of the treaty of Königsberg (Jan. 1656) between the two powers, by granting the elector four provinces of western Poland lying between Prussia and Brandenburg in return for armed support for the Swedish king. In accordance with the terms of the Marienburg treaty, a well-organized Prussian force of 8500 men joined with the Swedes in the decisive defeat of the Poles at the battle of Warsaw (July 1656).

MARIGNANO, BATTLE OF (1515), in Lombardy, victory for Francis I of France over the hitherto invincible Swiss mercenaries, who were fighting for Milan and the Emperor. Francis seized Milan, where Ludovico Sforza abdicated, and was ceded Parma and Piacenza by Pope Leo X, who also agreed to the Concordat of Bologna (1516), surrendering to the Crown the right to make certain ecclesiastical appointments.

MARIGNY, ENGUERRAN DE (d. 1315), French official of King Philip IV, who was the minister most closely associated with the king's financial exactions. He was especially unpopular at the time of Philip's death (1314), having mismanaged the war against Flanders. Philip's successor, Louis X, allowed Marigny to be tried and executed.

MARILLAC, MICHEL DE (1563–1632), French politician, keeper of the seals (1626), and one of Richelieu's chief aides. He was a friend of Cardinal Bérulle and St Francis de Sales and a spokesman for the *dévot* party in the government. He conspired with Marie de Medici and Anne of Austria against Richelieu in the Day of Dupes (1630) and was consequently disgraced and imprisoned.

MARIN, LOUIS (1871–1960), French politician, who made nationalism the guiding principle of his political life. He entered parliament in 1905, and in the inter-war years was leader of the Fédération républicaine. In the 1920s he supported the policy of exacting heavy reparations from Germany, and consistently opposed all concessions made to the Germans. He was a minister in several governments, notably those of Poincaré (1926–8) and Doumergue (1934). In 1940 he served under Reynaud, and unlike most conservative politicians he opposed the armistice and refused to accept the Vichy government. He later joined De Gaulle in London, and returned to political life for a time under the Fourth Republic.

MARINA, DONA, also **LA MALINCHE or MALINTZÍN** (*fl.* 16th cent.), mistress, counsellor, and interpreter to Cortés, daughter of an Aztec chieftain who was sold into slavery among the Maya. She was given to Cortés in 1519. Her knowledge of the Aztec language and culture were invaluable to him during his conquest.

MARINETTI, FILIPPO TOMASO (1876–1944), Italian poet, novelist, dramatist, and founder of the Futurist movement. He was educated in France and Italy and wrote in both languages initially. *Destruction* (1904) made his name. A Manifesto (1909) launched the Futurist Movement in Paris and was followed (1912) by his Manifesto concerning Italian Futurist poetry, advocating liberation from academic values and the past, and a life and art of free spiritual expression and violent action. His futurist groups led Italian nationalist agitations from the 1911 Libyan adventure onwards. With Mussolini, he led ex-servicemen's attacks on socialists, and in 1919 was a founder member of Mussolini's *Fascio*. Though he stopped supporting fascism in 1920, when it dropped its anti-clericalism and began to show conservative tendencies, he remained a partial admirer of the movement, and became a Fascist Academician.

MARINI, GIAMBATTISTA (1569–1625), Italian poet, patronized in France by Marie de Medici, whose works typify the extravagant and artificial stylism of baroque poetry and gave rise to a school of poetry known as 'Marinist'.

MARINIDS, of Fez, dynasty arising from a coalition of tribes in eastern Morocco, which profited, as treacherous allies of the Almohads, from the failure of an expedition against Tlemcen (1248), whose object was to take control of northern Morocco. The Marinids' capital was at Fez. Under Abu Yusuf they put an end to the Almohads in Marrakesh (1269), inheriting from them their involvement in Spain, but they were barred by the Banu Abd al-Wadd in Tlemcen from expansion to the east. For 20 years Abu Yusuf allied himself with Granada to prevent Castilian encroachment. His son Abu Ya'qub, however, abandoned Spain to attempt the capture of Tlemcen, but was murdered towards the end of an eight-year siege (1307), when a period of dynastic quarrelling ensued.

This first century of Marinid history saw the establishment of the Sufi brotherhoods as an important social and political factor in capital and country; it culminated in a revolutionary period in the mid-14th cent. which affected the entire Maghrib. The ambitious Abu'l Hasan reacted to attempts by the Banu Abd al-Wadd in Tlemcen to expand eastwards at Hafsid expense by capturing the city (1337). He was decisively defeated in Spain (1340), and in 1347 he overran the Maghrib as far as Tunis, only to be defeated by Tunisian tribes. He was ousted by his son Abu Inan, who repeated his conquest, but with no more success (1357). The result was a long period of weak government in Morocco and the central Maghrib.

The Marinids of Fez, unable to arrest the spread of local autonomy, fell into the hands of viziers, and became subject to the intrigues of Granada and Castile. From 1399 both Castile and Portugal made expeditions to Morocco, which led to the Portuguese capture of Ceuta (1415). Popular indignation against the Marinids led to their being put aside by the Wattasids, who controlled an enfeebled central authority as mayors of the palace until the last of the Marinids, Abd al-Haqq, reasserted himself (1458), only to perish at the hands of the mob (1465). MB

MARION DU FRESNE, MARC-JOSEPH (1724–72), French sailor, who carried Prince Charles, the Young Pretender to the British throne, to France in 1746. He later served in the French India Co. and, on his retirement from it, settled in Mauritius. In 1771 he undertook to locate Terra Australis—a largely fruitless mission which led to his death in a massacre at the Bay of Islands (NZ).

MARITIME POWERS, European powers, notably England and the United Provinces, whose seaboard enabled them to take the lead in overseas trade and colonization.

MARIUS, C. (157–86 BC), Roman politician and general, who in spite of senatorial opposition, attained great power and prestige. His reforms of military organization contributed greatly to the collapse of the Republican government. He came from Arpinum and was of Italian origin. He served at Numantia in Spain, was tribune in 119, and married Julia, aunt of Julius Caesar. In 115 he was praetor, and as governor of Further Spain (114) was moderately successful. As *legatus* of Metellus Numidicus in the Jugurthine War (109–108) he took advantage of agitation in Rome against the conduct of the war to secure the consulship (107) and by popular vote the command in Numidia. Through the treachery of Bocchus of Mauretania he captured Jugurtha and thereafter was repeatedly elected consul (104–101) to command in Gaul against the Cimbri and Teutones, whom he eventually destroyed at Aquae Sextiae (102) and Vercellae (101). His reorganization of the Roman army prior to these campaigns increased its effectiveness, but the abolition of the property qualification for service created a body of semi-professional soldiers who later proved only too ready to follow eminent generals who turned against the state. Opposition from the nobility, whose acceptance he desired, drove him into alliance with Saturninus, whom he suppressed as consul in 100. He later served in the Social War, in which he defeated the Marsi (90). He had Sulla's command against Mithridates VI of Pontus transferred to himself, but fled when Sulla marched on Rome. After returning to Italy in 87, he joined Cinna, instituted a reign of terror at Rome, and appointed himself to a seventh consulship (86), but died a few days later.   DCE

MARIVAUX, PIERRE DE CARLET DE CHAMBLET DE (1688–1763), French novelist and dramatist, whose works, of which the most famous is *Le Jeu de l'amour et du hasard* (1730), show his subtle wit and affectation of style, later known as *marivaudage*.

MARJ DABIQ, BATTLE OF (Aug. 1516), near Aleppo, where the Ottoman sultan, Selim I, routed the forces of the Mamluk sultan of Egypt and Syria, Qansawh al-Ghawri—a victory which brought all Syria under Ottoman control.

MARJ RAHIT. After the era of conquest which followed the death of the Prophet Muhammad in AD 632 tribal feuds began to divide the Arab warriors who dominated the Muslim empire. In the conflict which broke out on the death of the Umayyad Caliph Yazid I in 683, the Qays or northern Arab faction supported Ibn al-Zubayr as a claimant for the office of caliph. The Umayyads, with the aid of the Kalb or southern Arab faction, crushed the Qays, under Al-Dahhak ibn Qays, at Marj Rahit, north of Damascus, in Aug. 684. It was a fateful moment for the Umayyad house, which, having identified itself with one particular group, lost the neutral position that it had hitherto striven to maintain.

MARK, Saint, John, evangelist and cousin of St Barnabas. He is possibly the unnamed young man in his own account of Jesus' arrest. He went with St Paul on his first missionary tour but, to the latter's annoyance turned back. Later he was in Rome with St Paul and St Peter, and, according to Papias (c. AD 140), was Peter's interpreter and wrote down accurately, —although not in order—everything he remembered of Jesus' life and deeds. Mark's Gospel was thus probably written in Rome c. AD 65. According to Eusebius, Mark later went to Alexandria and was its first bishop. This, however, may be a reminiscence of the arrival of his Gospel in the city.

MARK, COUNTY OF, small German state lying in the valley of the Ruhr river, which belonged to the duchy of Cleves until the death of the childless duke, John William (1609), whence it passed to John Sigismund, Elector of Brandenburg.

MARKOVIC, SIMA (1888–?1936), Yugoslav politician, who founded (1919) the Yugoslav Communist Party. He turned to communism after an earlier interest in anarcho-syndicalism and socialism. During the troubled 1920s and 1930s he was three times secretary-general of the party and often served as chief delegate to international conferences. In 1936 he was accused of fomenting dissension and was expelled from the party.

MARLBOROUGH, JOHN CHURCHILL, 1st Duke of (1650–1722), British soldier and statesman, who owed his early advancement to his sister, Arabella, who was for a time the mistress of James, Duke of York, to whom Churchill became page (1666). Through the duke's favour he was commissioned as an ensign in the Foot Guards (1667) and later served at sea with the duke at Tangier, and in Flanders under Marshal Turenne. He received the public thanks of Louis XIV after distinguishing himself at the siege of Maastricht.

On his return to England (1678) Churchill's advancement was rapid, mainly owing to the Duke of York's influence, and also to his own marriage to Sarah Jennings (1678), a close friend and confidante of Princess Anne. During the Exclusion Crisis Churchill shared the fortunes of the Duke of York, who was the cause of much discontent. For his support of his master he was rewarded with the Scottish barony of Ayemouth (1682) and a colonelcy in the Guards. On the accession of James II he was given an English peerage, as Baron Churchill of Sandridge, and the rank of general (1685). During Monmouth's rebellion he was second-in-command to Feversham and played a prominent part in the victory at Sedgemoor (1685). However, his friendship with James II cooled as a result of the king's attack on Anglican supremacy, and, in the Revolution of 1688, he deserted and joined the forces of William of Orange. After serving in Ireland, where he captured Cork and Kinsale, and in Flanders, he fell from favour (1692), being suspected of Jacobite sympathies.

He returned to the king's good graces, however (1698), and was appointed a privy councillor and governor to Prince William of Gloucester. He was also appointed commander-in-chief of the English forces in Holland and plenipotentiary to the states general (1701). On the accession of Anne he became commander of the army and a political manager in Godolphin's ministry. For a decade his prestige, patronage, and power were enormous and he exercised almost viceregal powers. Largely at the insistence of Anne, he was appointed captain-general of the allied armies in Flanders (1702) and plenipotentiary to The Hague. His military career was supreme and his admirers boasted that he never fought a battle he did not win or besiege a town he did not capture. His victories included Donauwörth (1704), Blenheim (1704), Ramillies (1706), Oudenarde (1708), Malplaquet (1709), and the taking of a host of towns, including Lille (1708). For these victories he was lavished with honours, among them a dukedom, the princedom of Mindelheim, and great riches, while a grateful nation gave him Blenheim Palace in Oxfordshire.

Marlborough does not easily fit into party classification. He was a political manager supporting a war policy. However, when he lost the support of Anne his importance diminished, and he fell from power through refusing to support a Tory peace policy. He was personally attacked for peculation and left the country to avoid further scandal (1712). He returned, however, in 1714 and was restored to all his former offices by George I. But his mental faculties began to decline and during the rest of his life he played little part in public affairs.

W. S. Churchill, *Marlborough, His Life and Times*, 4 vols (London, 1933–8).

MARLBOROUGH, SARAH, Duchess of (1660–1744), wife of John Churchill, whom she married in 1678, and confidante of Queen Anne. After service in the household of James, Duke of York, Sarah was appointed a lady of the bedchamber (1683) and began a long period of personal dominance over Anne, to whom their friendship meant more than family ties, since she was persuaded to abandon her father, James II (1688). On Anne's accession (1702) Sarah was appointed to numerous offices. She became the chief link between the queen and Marlborough, placing her dominance over the queen at her husband's disposal. However, various quarrels brought the friendship to an end (1710) and both Marlboroughs were dismissed from office (1711). Sarah outlived her husband to preside over the completion of Blenheim Palace.

MARLOWE, CHRISTOPHER (1564–93), English dramatist, son of a Canterbury shoemaker. His plays include *Tamburlaine* (c. 1587), *Dr Faustus* (c. 1588), *The Jew of Malta* (c. 1592), and *Edward II* (1593). His development of blank verse as a dramatic medium had an important influence on Shakespeare. Marlowe was casually employed as a government spy, and his death in a tavern brawl may have been politically inspired.

MÁRMOL, JOSÉ (1817–71), Argentine writer of the romantic period, best known for his historical novel *Amalia* (1851–5), a vigorous and detailed denunciation of the dictator Rosas, from whose tyranny Mármol himself was forced to flee.

MARMONT, AUGUST FREDERIC LOUIS VIESSE DE, Duc de Raguse (1774–1852), French soldier and one of Napoleon's marshals. He later became a supporter of the restoration. His first encounter with Napoleon was at Toulon (1793). He became his aide-de-camp and served with distinction in Italy (1796–7) and Egypt (1798–9). After Brumaire he was made a councillor of state, but also continued his military career. He was appointed governor of Dalmatia (1806), duke (1808), and marshal (1809). After conducting some undistinguished campaigns, he excelled himself during Napoleon's final resistance, but then negotiated secretly with the allies and surrendered Paris (1814). He followed Louis XVIII to Ghent, then served as minister of state (1817), and as governor of Paris (1821), being responsible for the city's unsuccessful defence in July 1830. In the same year he followed King Charles X into exile.

MARNE, BATTLES OF (1914, 1918). The first battle of the Marne (5–11 Sept. 1914) halted Germany's advance into France and ended her hopes of a rapid victory in the First World War. On 30 Aug. Von Kluck, commander of the German First Army, believing the British Expeditionary Force had been destroyed at Mons and Le Cateau, turned south-eastwards to assist Von Bülow's Second Army in dealing with the French Fifth Army, which he now regarded as the Allies' effective left wing. While Moltke was digesting this abandonment of Schlieffen's plan for an advance outside Paris, Maunory's Sixth French Army, formed from troops withdrawn from the Lorraine offensive, and rushed to Paris by rail and thence to the front in taxicabs, attacked Kluck's right and rear on the Ourcq on 5 Sept. Kluck halted his south-eastwards advance and wheeled back to the west to face this threat, opening a wide gap between his army and Bulow's. Into this gap the BEF advanced on 7 Sept. as part of an Allied general offensive on the Marne. The Germans, confused and exhausted, retreated behind the Aisne, where they fortified themselves in much the same positions as they were to hold until 1918.

The second battle (15 July–2 Aug. 1918) proved to be the last German offensive of the war. In 1918 Ludendorff attempted to destroy the British army—which, since Passchendaele, he had regarded as his chief opponent—by using new infantry and artillery tactics and troops released by the collapse of Russia. After the springtime failure of direct attacks at St Quentin and on the Lys, he planned in the summer to attract Allied reserves southwards by advancing from Rheims towards Paris before striking a decisive blow in Flanders. This plan he called *Friedensturm*—'Peace Offensive'. Though the diversion on the Marne achieved considerable success, penetrating closer to Paris than had any attack in 1914, the elastic defence of the French had halted it by 17 July and on

the 18th they counter-attacked against the Germans' right flank on the Ourcq, and compelled them to retreat. French losses were 112,000 and German about 170,000. The Flanders offensive was abandoned, and the strategic initiative passed to the Allies.   PJBD

MARNIXE, PHILIP DE, Lord of St Aldegonde (1540–98), Brabantine Calvinist nobleman, publicist, and poet, who became a leader of the Dutch revolt against Spain and a councillor of William of Orange (1569). He and his brother, Jean (1537–67), were converted to Protestantism after a visit to Geneva (1560) and joined with the Count of Brederode and Louis of Nassau in the Compromise, a league of nobles pledged to force the Spanish king, Philip II, to end the Inquisition's policy of persecution in the Netherlands. After Jean had been killed by government forces at Osterweel, outside Antwerp (1567), Philip led the movement in Holland which established William of Orange as *stadtholder*. He was appointed burgomaster of Antwerp by William (1583), but returned to Zeeland when the besieged city surrendered to the Spaniards (1585) and cut short his political career. He spent his last years translating and writing theological works.

MARONITES, Roman Catholics of the Syro-Antiochene rite. Their spiritual head—under the pope—is the Maronite patriarch resident near Beirut. The Maronites speak Arabic, but their liturgical language is Syriac. At first, the Maronites would seem to have followed the Monothelite faith, derived from Sergius, patriarch of Constantinople, which affirms that there was in Christ a divine, but not a human, will. William of Tyre notes that in AD 1182 the Maronite patriarch sought to bring about a union with the Latin patriarchate of Antioch. A stable and developed relationship with the Roman Catholic Church came into being during the 16th cent. through the work of a Jesuit, John Eliano. Pope Gregory XIII, in 1584, established a Maronite College at Rome. Antagonism between Muslims and Christians in 1859–60 led to the intervention of Europe in the affairs of the Lebanon—an intervention which secured for the Maronites an autonomous status under the Ottoman sultan. In 1920 the Maronites obtained self-government under the protection of France. The independent state of the Lebanon was established in 1944. The Maronites constitute the most numerous of the religious groups in the republic. Maronite communities are also to be found in Egypt, in southern Europe, and in North and South America.

MAROONS, originally slaves freed by Spaniards (1654) to harass the English occupiers of Jamaica. The British were unable to dislodge the Maroons from their mountain centres and in the 18th cent. Maroons, joined by escaped slaves and under the leadership of Cudjoe, raided plantations, defeated English military forces, and in 1738 were granted semi-autonomy and rights to their own territory. During the Morant Bay rebellion (1865) the Maroons supported the British governor against the Jamaican rebels. Though marriage out of the group has been common in the last century, Maroons are still (1970) a recognized communal society in Jamaica.

MARPERGER, PAUL JACOB (1656–1730), German political economist and writer, who produced studies of commercial enterprise in most parts of Europe in the early 18th cent. He became a member of the Berlin Academy and was commercial adviser to the Elector of Saxony (1724).

MARPRELATE, MARTIN, pseudonymous English author of seven pamphlets issued from a secret press (1588–9), satirizing bishops and advocating a Presbyterian system. Their ribald jocularity and pungent style were more effective than the efforts of the 'Anti-Martinists', including Lyly and Nashe, who replied for the Church. Of the supposed authors, Penry was executed, Udall died in prison, and Job Throckmorton successfully denied complicity. The pamphlets did much to ridicule the cause of Elizabethan Puritanism.

MARQUESAS ISLANDS, 12 drought-prone, high islands in the eastern Pacific, settled by war-like Polynesias (*c.* AD 400). The southern four were discovered by Mendana (1595), the northern-most by Ingraham (1791). As whaling and sandal-wood centres and privateering bases the group attracted numerous castaways. After Protestant missionary efforts by the London Missionary Society and the Hawaiian Missionary Society (1853–80), a belated conversion was effected by (Catholic) Picpus fathers landed by Dupetit-Thouars (1838), who also established a protectorate, and finally annexed the group with 200 soldiers (1842). The resultant military regime was replaced (1881) by a civilian administration which struggled unavailingly against depopulation, though this was modified by miscegenation.

MARQUETTE, JACQUES (1637–75), French Jesuit missionary, who founded the mission of Sault Ste Marie (1668). In 1669 he went to La Pointe-du-Saint-Esprit on Lake Superior to minister to Huron and Ottawa Indians, re-establishing the mission at Michilimackinac after Sioux attacks rendered the original mission untenable (1671). Marquette and Louis Joliet were probably the first French to sail on the Mississippi river (1673). They went down the river to its confluence with the Arkansas river and proved that the Mississippi was not a passage to the Pacific Ocean.

MÁRQUEZ, JOSÉ IGNACIO DE (1793–1881), Colombian lawyer and president (1837–41), who secured diplomatic relations with both Ecuador and Venezuela, which had broken away from Colombia to become independent republics.

MARRAKESH, city founded by the Almoravids about AD 1070 at the foot of the High Atlas, has given its name to Morocco. It was the North African capital of the Almoravids and Almohads. Although superseded by Fez as the seat of the dynasty with the advent of the Marinids in the 13th cent., it remained the capital of an often independent south, and in the 16th–17th cents was the residence of the Sa'dians.

MARRIAGE ACT (1753) in Britain, laid it down that no marriage was valid that had not been solemnized by an Anglican clergyman after the banns had been called on three successive Sundays in the parish church. The royal family, Jews, and Quakers were excepted, but not Protestant dissenters of other sects, or Roman Catholics, who were thus penalized. The act ensured that records of marriages would be more reliable, and it put an end to hasty Fleet marriages, by which disreputable clergy would marry for a small fee anyone who required it, so putting at risk eligible heirs to property.

MARRIED WOMEN'S PROPERTY ACT (1870) in Britain, which was extended in 1882 and in 1893, granted to married women the rights of separate ownership over every kind of property, so that their status became in this respect similar to that of the unmarried. This reform was promoted from 1855 by Barbara Bodichon, and since increasing numbers of women met the property qualification for the parliamentary franchise, the issue of female suffrage arose during the framing of the 1884 Reform Act.

MARROQUÍN, JOSÉ MANUEL (1827–1908), Colombian intellectual and president (1900–4), who assumed the presidency when President Sanclemente was overthrown in a civil war. During Marroquín's term of office an uprising in Panama, assisted by the US, led to its secession from Colombia.

MARSAGLIA, BATTLE OF (1693), fought between the French troops of Marshal Catinat and the forces of Victor Amadeus, Duke of Savoy, during the War of the League of Augsburg.

In a bloody battle Catinat defeated the Savoyards and was able to raise the siege of Pinerolo.

MARSDEN, SAMUEL (1764–1838), English missionary, the second Anglican clergyman to arrive in NSW, Australia (1794). Besides his missionary activity in the Pacific, especially in NZ, he did important work as a farmer and sheep-breeder in NSW. He was often accused of neglecting his pastoral duties and of extreme severity as a magistrate and was frequently in conflict with John Macarthur. He also opposed Lachlan Macquarie's 'emancipist' policy and quarrelled with the latter's successor, Gov. Brisbane. Despite all this, he was known as the 'apostle of NZ'.

'MARSEILLAISE' (1792), French marching song composed by Rouget de Lisle for the volunteers from Marseilles at the outbreak of the war with Europe. It was declared the French national anthem (1795), but was banned under the First Empire and the Restoration Monarchy.

MARSHALL, ALFRED (1842–1924), British economist, whose aim was to bring classical theory up to date by applying to it the criteria of marginal analysis. He adopted what he called a method of partial equilibrium, designed to isolate certain phenomena and their relationships from their economic context. In the *Principles of Economics* (1890) Marshall used this approach to elucidate the problems of the firm and of price-formation, and to study the distribution of income and its relationship with social welfare. His other important works of a less systematic character were *Industry and Trade* (1919) and *Money, Credit and Commerce* (1923).

MARSHALL, DAVID SAUL (1908–), Singapore politician and first chief minister (1955–6), who resigned after constitutional talks in London became deadlocked over the control of Singapore's internal security. The Labour Front Party which he had founded remained in power until 1959.

MARSHALL, GEORGE CATLETT (1880–1959), US soldier and politician. After a career which included service in the Philippines (1913–16), France (1917–19), and China (1924–1927), he was assigned to the planning division of the general staff (1938). As a general and chief of staff (1939), he supervised military planning before Pearl Harbor and was the principal allied strategist in the Second World War. In 1945 he was sent to China by President Truman in an unsuccessful attempt to find a political solution to the Chinese civil war. He served as secretary of state (1947–9) during the formative period of the policy of 'containment', and was particularly involved in the creation of the European Recovery Program (1947). As secretary of defense (1950–1) after the outbreak of the Korean War, he was criticized by extremists for allegedly betraying US interests in Asia. In 1953 he was awarded the Nobel Peace Prize.

MARSHALL, JOHN (1755–1835), US politician, lawyer, and jurist, who fought in the American War of Independence, practised law, and became a member of the VA Assembly (1782–91, 1795–7). He declined the position of attorney-general, offered him by President Washington (1795), but served as a special envoy to France (1797–8), was elected to US Congress as a Federalist (1799–1800), appointed secretary of state by President John Adams (1800–1), and served as chief justice of the US Supreme Court (1801–35). At the time of his appointment the court had not yet established itself as the authoritative interpreter of the US constitution and he set himself a joint objective: to reinforce the trend towards a stronger national government, and in so doing establish the position of the Supreme Court. He viewed the constitution as an instrument of national unity which did not merely define specific powers, but also possessed implied powers. Five major decisions, among many of importance during his term as chief justice, illustrate Marshall's views and his influence on the constitutional development of the new nation.

Marbury v. Madison (1803) affirmed the constitutional power of the court to undertake judicial reviews of federal as well as state statutes. *Fletcher v. Peck* (1810) and the Dartmouth College case (1819) established judicial barriers against governmental attacks on property rights, and *McCulloch v. Maryland* (1819) gave judicial sanction to the implied powers doctrine and to a broad interpretation of national governmental authority, a view strengthened in *Gibbons v. Ogden* (1824) with regard to federal commerce powers. There is little doubt that Marshall, as a shrewd politician, was often affected by political as well as legal argument, and he was often in conflict with Republican and Democratic administrations. Yet he had the almost total loyalty of his fellow justices on the Supreme Court, so dominating it that in his 34 years of service he wrote about half the opinions, and dissented only eight times.

A. J. Beveridge, *The Life of John Marshall*, 4 vols (Boston, 1916–19). JDL

MARSHALL, SIR JOHN HUBERT (1876–1958), British archaeologist and director-general of the Archaeological Survey of India (1902–31). He was appointed by Lord Curzon to reorganize the almost moribund Archaeological Survey and established the basis of modern Indian archaeological work in the conservation of ancient monuments and in epigraphical services. He instituted the series of annual reports on archaeological work in the sub-continent. His earliest areas of investigation were the Buddhist sites of Taxila and Sanchi, to both of which he published guides, and in the 1920s he directed the excavations at Mohenjo-daro, which established the outlines of the Indus Valley civilization.

MARSHALL ISLANDS, two parallel chains of typhoon-prone, North Pacific atolls, discovered by Loiasa (1526) and Saavedra (1527) and named after their British rediscoverer in 1788. Intermarriage with white convicts and traders and depopulation in the 19th cent. radically modified the original Micronesian strain (15,000 in 1886). In the 1860s the islanders accepted Protestantism at the hands of the Hawaiian Evangelical Mission, but the Sacred Heart Mission (1899) made little impact. In 1878 the trading post at Jaluit became a German coaling station. In 1886, with prior British assent, Germany occupied the islands, the *Jaluitgesellschaft* (a Hernsheim–Godeffroy combine) exercising effective power until 1906, when the commissioner came under direct imperial control, US missionaries withdrawing in favour of German Protestants. In 1922 the Japanese mandate reversed the German tradition of indirect rule and later (1935) militarized the group. In the Second World War the islands were the scene of bitter fighting. In 1946 the US occupied the group as a strategic trusteeship territory, administered by the navy (1946–9) when a bicameral legislature was established under civilian control. The controversial hydrogen bomb tests at Bikini (1946) and Eniwetok (1958), though less destructive than the typhoon 'Ophelia' (1958), rendered the island uninhabitable until 1968.

MARSHALL PLAN, in the US, programme of economic aid for Europe, publicly proposed by the secretary of state, George Marshall, in a speech at Harvard in 1947. The plan, dependent on the initiation and co-operation of European governments in agreeing on a joint programme, encouraged the formation of the Organization for European Economic Co-operation and came into effect as the European Recovery Programme (1948–52).

MARSHALSEA PRISON, in Southwark, existed from the 14th cent. for people convicted in the court of the steward and marshal of the household. Those guilty of offences on the high seas were also committed there, but from the time of Elizabeth I it was mainly used for debtors, among whom was the father of Charles Dickens, whose visit to the Marshalsea provided him with material for his description of it in *Little Dorrit* (1855). It was pulled down in the 19th cent.

MARSHMAN, JOHN (1794–1877), English Baptist missionary and journalist, who edited the earliest Bengali weekly newspaper, the *Samachar Darpan* (1818).

MARSIGLIO OF PADUA (c. 1275–1342), political thinker, who was rector of Paris University in 1313, but had to flee from France in 1324 after the publication of his principal work, the *Defender of the Peace*. He spent the rest of his life under the protection of the German emperor, Louis of Bavaria, who was at war with the papacy, and also harboured William of Ockham and several spiritual Franciscans. He was inspired by an intense hatred of the papacy which he regarded as the chief disturber of the peace of Italy (hence the title of his chief work defending the peace against papal disturbers). This is the starting point for his advocacy of the subjection of the Church to the state and for restricting the clergy to purely spiritual functions. In justifying this predominance of lay power, he is the first thinker to state clearly the doctrine of sovereignty, which in every state is vested in the supreme legislator, from whom all executive authorities derive a delegated power. Marsilio's attempt to apply these ideas during his imperial master's brief occupation of Rome (1328) ended in disaster. His writings continued to be secretly circulated and were probably known to all the leaders of heretical movements during the rest of the Middle Ages. They were first openly published by the Swiss Protestants in 1521.

MARSIN, FERDINAND, Comte de (1656–1706), French soldier, in the War of the Spanish Succession, who was Louis XIV's commander on the Danube. He was defeated with Tallard at Blenheim (1704), and was mortally wounded and captured at Turin (1706) by Prince Eugène's forces.

MARSTON MOOR, BATTLE OF (2 July 1644), largest battle of the English Civil War, fought near York. In the summer of 1644 York, the Royalists' northern stronghold, was besieged by the Parliamentarians and the Scots. Charles I sent his nephew, Prince Rupert, to relieve William Cavendish, Marquis of Newcastle, and his Royalist forces. Rupert, by out-manœuvring his opponents, relieved York, while the Parliamentarians, under Sir Thomas Fairfax, and the Scots, under Alexander Leslie, Earl of Leven, retired to Marston Moor, seven miles (11 kms) to the west, where they were reinforced by cavalry under the Earl of Manchester and Oliver Cromwell. The Royalist forces numbered 11,000 infantry and 7000 cavalry and the allies had 18,000 infantry and 9000 cavalry. Inconclusive skirmishing took place early on 2 July, but at 6 p.m., as Rupert began to disengage, the Parliamentarians attacked. All the Royalists, except Lord Goring's cavalry on the left flank, were overwhelmed, chiefly by Cromwell's cavalry. Newcastle, who lost most of his army, retired and went into exile. York surrendered on 16 July and the north was lost for the king.

MARTABAN, port at the mouth of the Salween river, opposite Moulmein. It was the capital of the kingdom of Pegu (1287–1363), and became a Portuguese trading port (1519–1613).

MARTEN, HENRY (1602–80), English politician, who was an MP for Berkshire in the Long Parliament. He was expelled from the Commons and imprisoned for advocating Charles I's deposition (1643). On being readmitted to parliament in 1646, he associated with the Levellers outside the House. Though active at the king's trial, concurring in his execution, and being prominent in the establishment of the republic, his influence declined after 1649. He was opposed to Cromwell's rise and disappeared from political life during the protectorate, but he returned with the Rump Parliament in 1659. In 1660 he surrendered to Charles II, and though found guilty of treason was not executed, but spent the rest of his life in prison.

MARTÍ, JOSÉ (1853–95), Cuban poet, journalist, and propagandist of the Cuban struggle for independence against Spain, whose early revolutionary activities led to his imprisonment. He was afterwards deported to Spain as a political exile, but was allowed to attend Madrid and Saragossa Universities. Being unable to return to Cuba, he joined the growing community of his exiled compatriots in New York city and supported himself by journalism, writing articles on US economics, culture, and politics. While he felt some affection towards his second homeland, he dreaded the effects of its size and commercialism on the small Latin American nations. His energies were principally devoted to the fomenting of revolution in Cuba, and he was involved in fund raising, the purchase of armaments, pamphleteering, and military planning. He founded (1892) the Cuban Revolutionary Party and in 1895 was one of the leaders of the insurrection against Spanish rule. After his return to Cuba he was killed by Spanish troops in the first days of the fighting.

In the Cuba of 1970 Marti's works and ideas were considered to be intellectual precursors of the Cuban Revolution of 1959.

MARTIAL (M. VALERIUS MARTIALIS) (*c.* AD 38–102), Roman poet, who, though born in Spain, spent most of his life in Rome. His *Epigrams* in 12 books cover many topics and provide some incidental information on Roman life, though he lacked Juvenal's powers of social criticism.

MARTIN IV (*reg.* 1281–5), Pope, former chancellor of King Louis IX of France, who owed his election to Louis's brother Charles of Anjou, King of Sicily. Charles had been obstructed by previous popes and needed one who would be a dependable supporter. In 1282 Charles was faced with the disastrous Sicilian rising, which was supported by the King of Aragon. Martin excommunicated all the opponents of Charles and even preached a crusade against Aragon. Charles's nephew, King Philip III of France, obeyed Martin's call and invaded Aragon in 1285, but suffered a defeat and died during the retreat from Spain.

MARTIN V (1368–1431), Pope (*reg.* 1417–31), member of a powerful Roman family, the Colonna, whose election as pope at the council of Constance ended the Great Schism. His pontificate was largely concerned with countering the effects of the schism and in restoring papal authority in the papal states.

MARTIN, LUTHER (*c.* 1748–1826), American lawyer and politician, who became state attorney-general (1778–1805, 1818–22) of MD. He was a delegate to the Philadelphia convention (1787), and being opposed to the establishment of a strong central government he refused to sign the new constitution of 1787, but later became a Federalist. He defended Supreme Court justice Samuel Chase against impeachment (1804), and Aaron Burr, tried for treason in 1807.

MARTIN, SIR WILLIAM (1807–80), NZ chief justice (1841–1857), and founder of the colony's judicial system. He was also a champion, especially in the early 1860s, of Maori interests threatened by European encroachment.

MARTIN, WILLIAM ALEXANDER PARSONS (1827–1916), American Presbyterian missionary and educator from IN, who spent most of his life in China. His Presbyterian training enabled him to respect Chinese civilization, and he saw Christianity as an enrichment of Confucian thinking. This liberal approach led to his translation into Chinese of Henry Wheaton's *Elements of International Law*, which the Chinese used to their advantage. He broadened the curricula of the *T'ung-wen Kuan*, of which he was professor of English and later president (1869). When the Peking Imperial University was established during the 'Hundred Days' Reform' (1898),

he became the dean of Western studies. Martin thus contributed greatly to the introduction of Western knowledge in China, and in 1898 he was made a mandarin of the 2nd class. He was also a Membre de l'Institut de Droit International. Among his books on China, *A Cycle of Cathay* deserves mention.

MARTIN v. HUNTER'S LESSEE, I Wheaton 304 (1816), US Supreme Court case that reaffirmed the court's right to review state court decisions. The case arose because the VA Court of Appeals refused to accept an earlier reversal by the Supreme Court of their decision to uphold a state law denying the right of an alien to inherit real property.

MARTINEAU, HARRIET (1802–76), English writer, whose first successful publication was *Illustrations of Political Economy* (1832), which was a collection of stories with a moral designed to reconcile the reader to the working of economic laws. Later came *Forest and Game Law Tales* and a novel, *Deerbrook*. Her visit to the US (1834–6) converted her to the abolitionist cause. Later, an illness from which she was cured by mesmerism led her to write *Letters on the Laws of Man's Social Nature* (1851). She was also attracted to Comte's philosophy, which she popularized and condensed in *Positive Philosophy* (1853).

MARTINET, JEAN (d. 1672), French soldier and inspector-general of infantry, whose introduction of a strict military discipline left an indelible mark upon the French army.

MARTÍNEZ, MAXIMILIANO HERNÁNDEZ (1882–1962), president and dictator of El Salvador (1931–44), who modernized the army, used press censorship and government spies, and exiled or imprisoned thousands of his opponents. In 1932 rural workers, protesting at his regime and their own low wages, marched on the capital, San Salvador. Convinced that they were led by communists intent on overthrowing the government, Martínez ordered the army to restore order, and in the ensuing disturbance hundreds were killed. Martínez nevertheless supported social and economic improvements for the working class. He also signed trade agreements with the US. He perpetuated his rule by remaking the constitution several times. He fell from power, however, as the result of a nation-wide strike.

MARTÍNEZ, TOMÁS (1812–73), president of Nicaragua (1857–67), who combined forces with Costa Rica to repel American filibusters led by William Walker (1858). He opposed all ideas of confederation, about which he fought with his neighbours, and suppressed demonstrations in its favour.

MARTINI, SIMONE DI (called **MARTINO**) (1284–1344), Sienese painter whose decorative works were influenced by the Gothic style. The oldest surviving Italian painting of a purely secular inspiration was his mounted portrait of a Sienese general (1328). He also worked for King Robert I of Naples, and painted frescoes in the Lower Church of St Francis at Assisi and at Avignon.

MARTINIQUE, Caribbean island discovered by Columbus (1502), and established as a French colony by Pierre Belain (1635). It later passed to the French Crown (1672) and except for the years when it was held by the British (1762, 1794–1802, 1809–14) it has since been a French possession. Sugar planting began there in 1650 and sugar has remained its staple crop. The island became a département of France in 1946, its executive government being conducted by a prefect and appointed officials and legislative authority being vested in a general council of 36 members, elected by popular vote. It is represented (1970) in the French national assembly by three deputies and in the senate by two senators.

MARTINITZ, JAROSLAV (1582–1649), Catholic Bohemian administrator, son of a minor court official of an old Bohemian family, who was one of the victims in the Defenestration of Prague (1618). He was a supporter of the Counter-Reformation in Bohemia and was appointed imperial deputy-governor of Prague by the Emperor Matthias (1617). His refusal to sign the Letter of Majesty earned him the enmity of the estates. After the defenestration episode at the Hradschin palace he fled in disguise to Munich and thence to Passau, but returned to Bohemia in 1621 and was promoted by the Emperor Ferdinand II to membership of the imperial privy council (1628–49).

MARTINUZZI, GEORGE (UTJEŠENOVIĆ, JURAJ) (1482–1551), bishop of Nagyvared (Grosswardein), who, on the death of John Zápolya, governor of Transylvania, in 1540, became regent in the name of Zápolya's infant heir, John Sigismund, and in 1541 obtained Sultan Suleiman's assent to the prince's ruling over Transylvania under Ottoman protection. In 1551 Martinuzzi made an agreement with Ferdinand of Austria which placed Transylvania under Habsburg control. He was afterwards raised to the archbishopric of Esztergom (Gran) and made a cardinal, but was forced into a role so ambiguous that it resulted in his murder.

MARTY, ANDRÉ (1886–1956), French sailor and politician. In 1919 his leadership of the Black Sea Mutiny of the French fleet led to the recall of the fleet and of the Franco-Serbian expeditionary force in southern Russia. Both his role in the mutiny and his imprisonment made him a martyr to the extreme left in France. He was amnestied in 1923 and elected a Communist deputy for Seine-et-Oise in 1924. As one of the most intransigent figures in the party he led the opposition to the Popular Front policy in 1935. His role as inspector of international brigades in the Spanish Civil War earned him the nickname 'the butcher of Albacete' among his opponents. In 1953 he was excluded from the party for 'left deviations'.

MARTYR, PETER (c. 1457–1526), Italian humanist and historian who became the director of the palace school at the court of Isabella of Castile, making it a centre of humanist learning. He established the new school of critical historiography in Spain.

MARVELL, ANDREW (1621–78), English poet and politician. who held office under the protectorate, celebrating Cromwellian achievements in verse, eg, the 'Horatian Ode upon Cromwell's return from Ireland' (1650). His works range from political satires to love poetry.

MARWAN II (reg. AD 744–50), Umayyad Caliph, had been governor of Armenia and Azerbayjan before his accession. Syria, hitherto the main support of the Umayyad domination, was now rent with tribal feuds. Marwan restored some degree of order there in 744–6, but deemed it wise to raze a number of the more important fortifications (eg, at Hims, Damascus, and Jerusalem) as a precaution against further rebellion. The eastern half of the Muslim empire was in a state of confusion. Marwan had to undertake a vigorous campaign (746–7) against the Khawarij in Al-Jazira (Mesopotamia) and Iraq. In 747 there began the great revolt in Khurasan which led to the establishment of the Abbasid regime. Marwan II, defeated by the Abbasid forces on the Great Zab river in Jan. 750, fled for refuge to Egypt, but was overtaken there and slain. He was the last Umayyad caliph.

MARWANIDS, amirs of Kurdish origin who rose to prominence in the region of Diyar Bakir during the years which followed the death of the Buyid prince, Adud al-Dawla. The real founder of the Marwanid regime was Abu Ali al-Hasan ibn Marwan (d. AD ?997). The Marwanids reached the apogee of their power in the time of Abu Nasr (1012–?1061). The Seljuk Turks overran Diyar Bakir in 1085–6 and the last Marwanid disappeared from the scene in 1095–6.

MARX, KARL HEINRICH (1818–83), Prussian-born philosopher and prophet of international revolutionary communism. He was the son of a Jewish lawyer and a rabbi's daughter, who had become Lutherans. Marx studied law at Bonn and Berlin Universities, where he was profoundly influenced by the dialectical philosophy of Hegel. He started a paper, the *Rheinische Zeitung*, at Cologne, which in 1843 was banned for its attacks on the Russian government. In the same year (that of his marriage to Jenny von Westphalen, daughter of a high official in Trier, whose devotion sustained him through many misfortunes) Marx went to Paris, where he met Friedrich Engels, a cotton manufacturer's son, who came to be his life-long partner. In Paris (1843–5) he read Proudhon and socialist writers, but at the request of the Prussian government was expelled from France for contributing to another seditious journal, *Vorwärts*. He went first to Brussels, where he castigated Proudhon's *Philosophie de la Misère* as *Misère de la Philosophie* (1847), and then, via Cologne, to London (1849), which became his permanent home.

On the eve of the February Revolution in Paris (1848), he wrote, with Engels, the *Communist Manifesto*, a masterpiece of political propaganda. In it he advocated the expropriation of landed property, a high, graded income tax, abolition of the right of inheritance, the establishment of a state bank to centralize credit, nationalization of transport, increasing state ownership of factories, state education, the ending of children's factory labour, and the duty of all to work. It attacked the state as an instrument of oppression, and religion and culture as capitalist ideologies in a system whose competition would lead to over-population and downfall. 'Workers of the world unite! You have nothing to lose but your chains!' became the revolutionary slogan.

Marx now began to study economics and history in the Reading Room of the British Museum, developing his theories of class struggle and inevitable revolution, coloured by his observation of mid-19th-cent. industrial England. During this period, in which he published his *Critique of Political Economy* (1857), he received money from Engels and from his own journalism. In 1864 he founded the International Working Men's Association, later known as the First Communist International. As its secretary, he mediated between English trade unionists and European workers, and saw the IWMA (1873) split into two anarchist factions, one headed by himself, the other by Bakunin. In 1867 he published the first volume of his most important work, *Das Kapital*, the second and third volumes of which were edited by Engels after his death (1885, 1894). It has been variously described as a treatise on economics, a philosophy of history, a system of laws of sociology, a moral and political indictment of capitalism, and the Communist Bible.

Ignoring poverty, and despite declining health, he watched for and urged on the revolution, which he did not live to see, and which eventually came, not in industrialized England, but in Russia (1917). He was the implacable foe of Tsardom, the greatest enemy of freedom, against whom, in his view, even the British empire might be strengthened as a counter-balance. He hated Napoleon III, welcomed the Paris Commune (1871), and accepted German unity, though he was hostile to Prussian and Bismarckian hegemony. In the American Civil War he vigorously supported the North and despite his contempt for the bourgeoisie, owed something to its liberal, humanitarian traditions.

G. Lichtheim, *Marxism: a historical and critical study* (London, 1961).
K. Marx, *Das Kapital*, ed. F. Engels (London, 1867, 1885, 1894).

MARX, WILHELM (1863–1946), German chancellor and leader of the Centre Party in the Weimar republic, who succeeded Stresemann as chancellor in Nov. 1923, having secured the support of the social democrats in the Reichstag for his bourgeois coalition government. He was given emergency powers to overcome the economic chaos which was gripping Germany following the inflation. After elections in May 1924, Marx formed his second cabinet, whose members were the same as in his first, the Nationalists refusing to join while Stresemann remained as foreign minister. Marx pursued reconstructionist policies, and with Stresemann and Luther attended the London Conference (Aug. 1924) and accepted the Dawes Plan, which rationalized Germany's reparations and ended the occupation of the Ruhr. His government was defeated in a Reichstag vote on the plan, and after a general election in December, Marx resigned.

In April 1925 he stood as coalition candidate for the presidency, but was defeated by the nationalist, Hindenburg. In May 1926 he again became chancellor, but failed to bring the SPD into his coalition because of the objections of Stresemann's People's Party. A period of relative stability followed, marked by economic recovery and by Stresemann's successful policy of gradual national reassertion. The latent political disunity of the country led, however, to the defeat of the government in Dec. 1926 by a joint Nationalist and SPD vote in the Reichstag, and, after the reconstitution of Marx's government in Jan. 1927, to the final collapse (Feb. 1928) of the coalition over the issue of confessional schools. The Centre Party lost support in the elections in May, and Marx did not return to power. In Dec. he resigned the party leadership, but remained a Reichstag deputy until 1933.

MARX BROTHERS, US comedians, born in New York city, who appeared in vaudeville and musical comedy, on radio and television, and established an international reputation with such films as *Duck Soup* (1933), *A Night at the Opera* (1935), and *A Night in Casablanca* (1946). They portrayed a dislocated world in which logic and reason were sometimes refined, but more often reduced to absurdity by verbal fantasy and instinctive action.

MARXISM began with Marx and Engels as a theory intimately linked with practice, aiming to explain the past and the present, and mould the future. It sought to situate industrial capitalism as the penultimate stage in mankind's historical progress and reveal the inner dynamics of capitalist society, thereby providing an internationally united working class with theoretical guidance in the practical task of revolution—overthrowing capitalism and building international communism. In 19th-cent. Europe overthrowing capitalism was the major problem. In the contemporary world, where capitalism seems relatively secure and communism far from international, versions of Marxism serve as official ideologies for the various socialist states, as party ideologies and forms of protest and criticism in capitalist societies, and as a major political force in many of the diverse societies of the Third World. The versions differ, as they have throughout the history of Marxism, each interpreting and developing the original doctrines in different ways for different purposes.

The original doctrines (whose sources include Hegel and Feuerbach, the classical Political Economists and French socialism) stress economic factors as being ultimately decisive in explaining other social developments (the view known as 'historical materialism'), class conflict as the crucial motor of historical change, and (increasing) economic exploitation as the central feature of capitalism. These doctrines were developed by Marx in close collaboration with Engels (see especially their two-volume *Selected Works*), though Engels was rather more positivist in spirit than Marx and applied their ideas to the natural sciences (see his *Dialectics of Nature*): Engels was really the father of that general, all-embracing philosophical approach which the orthodox came to call 'dialectical materialism'.

Marx began from a general humanistic moral critique of the alienation of man, which, in his view, reached an extreme form under capitalism (see especially the Paris Manuscripts of 1844), but he made that critique concrete by turning from philosophy to political economy (see *Capital*): alienation under capitalism was based on economic exploitation of the proletariat by the ruling bourgeoisie. The worker produced commodities for the market, but in effect became a commodity himself, selling his labour-power and creating surplus value on behalf of a diminishing number of owners of capital for minimal wages. The dynamics of the system were cumulative: a falling rate of profit, deepening crises, increasing class polarization, and class consciousness. The (inevitable) consequence was a revolutionary transformation of society, to be brought about by collective action. Certain factors might hinder this development (*eg*, the influence of the ruling ideology, the power of the state, etc.), but they could only delay it. Moreover, all features of society under capitalism were linked to its central contradiction, between capitalists and workers, which would ultimately cause its collapse, as previous types of society, such as Feudalism, had collapsed, when the developing forces of production had come into irreconcilable conflict with obsolescent relations of production. Marx and Engels were less than explicit about the exact nature of the proletarian revolutions and about the classless, truly human society that would succeed it: they concentrated on establishing the theoretical and political preconditions for revolution, by developing Marxist theory, enhancing class consciousness, and trying to set up an international organization of the working class (the 'International').

By the turn of the century Marxism had indeed been adopted by various working-class movements, especially in Germany, where the increasingly bureaucratized Social Democrat Party proclaimed revolutionary aims while remaining inactive in practice. Some Marxists, led by Eduard Bernstein, thought this approach futile and sought to 'revise' Marxism by stressing the possibilities of evolution rather than revolution, and arguing for income redistribution and reformist politics. Official Marxism in Western Europe was, moreover, badly damaged by the outbreak of war in 1914, when almost all the supposedly internationalist socialist parties joined their respective national war efforts.

However, various radical forms of Marxism had emerged which foreshadowed future developments, among them the anarcho-syndicalists in France, Rosa Luxemburg and others in Germany, and the Russians, including Plekhanov, Trotsky, and Lenin. With the Russian Bolshevik Revolution of 1917 and the end of the First World War, many of these radical forces came together with some of the old socialists to form communist parties in various countries, while in Russia itself Leninism developed Marxism into the ideology of a revolutionary elite party imposing a workers' revolution on a society in which capitalism itself was not yet far advanced. Thus political action itself had the task of creating the preconditions of socialism. Thenceforth official Marxism became the ruling and conservative ideology of the first Workers' State, developing from Leninism to Stalinism and through the Khrushchev period to the present; and, apart from China, the international communist movement followed where Russia led. However, in the 1950s, with the rise of Mao's China (and North Viet-nam and North Korea), the independent development of Yugoslavia, the Revolution in Cuba, and a period of abortive polycentrism in Eastern Europe, a certain conflict between official Marxisms ensued, each using the original doctrines to maintain and develop differing social systems. The conflict between the Russians and Chinese versions continues (1970) and will probably increase.

Yet throughout this period, ever since Rosa Luxemburg attacked the elitism of Lenin, there have been dissident Marxist currents, notably that of Trotsky, who was expelled from the USSR by Stalin and thereafter became Stalinism's most bitter critic, and more recently within Poland and Czechoslovakia. Non-communist societies have seen a continuing Marxist influence extending beyond the official communist parties, though the old social democratic and socialist parties have increasingly abandoned their residual adherence to Marxist tenets. This influence is to be found among many critics of capitalism (such as Jean-Paul Sartre and Herbert Marcuse) and among many Third World leaders and ideologists (such as Frantz Fanon); and, in general, it still serves in these societies as a theoretical basis for radical social criticism and political action. Moreover, Marxism offers a particular way of looking at society and history, focusing on social change through conflict (especially between classes) and on the socio-economic determinants of belief-systems, politics, law, etc. Consequently, its influence on the study of history and on the development of the social sciences (especially sociology) has been considerable. Marxist ideology has been of immense importance as a social and political force during the last century, adapting the original ideas of Marx and Engels to diverse conditions and purposes; while Marxist theory, drawing on those original ideas, continues to have much explanatory power in the study of society.

K. Marx and F. Engels, *Selected Works*, 2 vols (Moscow, 1962).
G. Lichtheim, *Marxism: a historical and critical study* (London, 1961).   SL

MARY I (1516–58), Queen of England (*reg.* 1553–8), only surviving child of Henry VIII and Catherine of Aragon, was provisionally betrothed to Francis I (1517) and Charles V (1522), received the intensive education customary at Renaissance courts, and was sent to Ludlow (1525) as governor of Wales.

On Henry's separation from her mother, she was statutorily declared illegitimate (1534) and suffered years of estrangement and humiliation, during which she adhered unwaveringly to her Catholic faith. An act of 1543 placed her next in succession after Edward and his heirs, and she remained in England throughout his reign, steadfastly refusing to recognize the new religion.

Despite Northumberland's conspiracy to prevent her succession, Mary was declared queen at Cambridge (1553) and brought to the throne by the widespread acclamation of a country disturbed by the pace of recent changes. Had she been content to restore the religious position as it stood at the time of her father's death, her popularity would have lasted, but she aimed at the restoration of papal supremacy and Catholic doctrine.

She began cautiously by releasing imprisoned Catholics and repealing the ecclesiastical legislation of the previous reign, but parliament refused to restore the monasteries' confiscated lands, and Wyatt's unsuccessful rebellion indicated the alarm felt at the queen's decision to marry Philip, the Spanish heir (1554). The old ceremonies and Latin services were restored and married clergy were ejected from their livings, and with the arrival of Pole as cardinal and legate (Nov. 1554), Mary proceeded to the fulfilment of her mission.

A third and more amenable parliament petitioned Pole, now Abp of Canterbury, 'to call us home again into the right way from whence we have all this long while wandered and strayed abroad', and on the condition of its acknowledging papal supremacy, the country was absolved from the sin of schism. Mary then repealed most of the anti-catholic legislation passed since 1529 and revived the old statute for the burning of heretics.

In the next few years some 300 people were burned, including Hooper, Latimer, Ridley, and Cranmer. It is hard to say who was chiefly responsible for the persecution. Certainly it was not the Spaniards, who deplored its effects and tried to slow it. Mary herself, crippled by illness and heartbroken at her barrenness and her husband's desertion, was so far unheeding that she may not have known what was happening. But since she cared more about souls than about bodies, she would not have disowned a policy that in practical terms was destroying her cause. The government's intention and hope was that the leading Protestants would refuse martyrdom, as Cheke did, and others who applauded from the sidelines. But those who stayed were willing to die, and their example built their faith upon a rock.

In a last tragic irony her Spanish marriage led the dutiful daughter of Rome into a war against the pope. The fall of Calais was the end of the era.

H. F. M. Prescott, *Mary Tudor* (London, 1952).   MMR

MARY (1542–87), Queen of Scotland (*reg.* 1542–67), queen consort of France, daughter of James V and Mary of Guise. She succeeded in infancy and was betrothed to Edward VI. But after the battle of Pinkie (1547) she was sent to France (1548) and married the Dauphin, who reigned for 17 months as Francis II (*reg.* 1559–60). On his death, the Guises lost influence in France and Mary returned to Scotland.

In the same year her mother, the regent, had died, and the French had been expelled from Scotland with English help. For a while Mary ruled with sense and moderation, and did not attempt to reverse the Reformation or recover the Church's lost estates, so long as she was allowed to observe the Catholic faith with reasonable discretion. Her ambition was to secure the English throne, which she had already claimed on the ground of Elizabeth I's illegitimacy. She sent Maitland of Lethington, her shrewdest adviser, to London to persuade Elizabeth I to name her as the heir, only to be met with the English queen's refusal to make any announcement about the succession. Mary's hand was sought by many, among them Don Carlos, heir to the Spanish empire. His insanity brought marriage negotiations to an end, and eventually (1565) she married Darnley, a grandson of Margaret Tudor, and, in his own right, a claimant to the English throne. Their son was James VI and I.

Mary now threw off her earlier restraint and prepared to reintroduce Catholicism in Scotland. Darnley was persuaded by the Protestant lords to join them in assassinating Rizzio, Mary's Italian secretary, and after a pretended reconciliation, Darnley was himself murdered at Kirk O'Field (Feb. 1567). Meanwhile, Mary had become infatuated with Bothwell, an unscrupulous Scottish noble, and after an intimidated court had acquitted him of Darnley's murder, she married him in a Protestant ceremony (May) 12 days after he had been divorced from his former wife. Knox and the nobles rose in protest, and after surrendering at Carberry Hill (June) Mary was imprisoned at Lochleven and compelled to abdicate (July). The next year she escaped, but after a further defeat at Langside she fled into England and demanded Elizabeth's protection. It suited many parties in Scotland to have Darnley out of the way, but Mary's complicity in his murder was out of character and incapable of legal proof. It has been contended that she acted to frustrate a conspiracy being organized against herself, and that her marriage to Bothwell was forced upon her against her will. But it was this more than any other factor which cost her her throne.

Elizabeth meanwhile had to do something about her unwelcome guest, and a commission of enquiry, at which the casket letters—an extremely dubious source of evidence— were produced, was discreetly equivocal, deciding (1569) that while the rebellious lords had done nothing to impair their loyalty, no crime had been 'sufficiently proven' against Mary. Officially, Elizabeth could not countenance rebellion, but neither could she restore freedom of action to a dangerous rival to her throne. She therefore detained Mary in England without trial.

Her intention probably was to wait until Scottish passions had cooled and then restore Mary on conditions that would guarantee her good behaviour and safeguard the Protestant religion. But the opportunity never came, since Mary became the focus of all the forces that aimed to depose Elizabeth and restore Catholicism in England. She was moved for safekeeping from one castle to another, while the Spaniards and the English Catholics hatched a series of plots for her release —those of the Northern Earls (1569), Ridolfi (1571), Throckmorton (1583), and Babington (1586). Elizabeth steadily resisted the advice of council and parliament that Mary should be executed. Crowned heads should not come under the axe, and Mary's death, by simplifying the issue for Philip of Spain, might create more problems than it solved. When at last she signed the warrant for the execution at Fotheringay (1587), matters were taken out of her hands before she could change her mind.

Mary's sufferings have inspired a passionate hagiography,

since she has cast a spell on historians to which her contemporaries were immune.

Lady Antonia Fraser, *Mary Queen of Scots* (London, 1969).
MMR

MARY (1631–60), eldest daughter of Charles I of England, who married William II (1626–50), Prince of Orange, in 1641. A week after her husband's death from smallpox, she gave birth to a son, the future William III of England.

MARY OF AUSTRIA (1505–58), Queen of Hungary, daughter of Philip the Fair and Joanna the Mad, who was married (1523) to Louis II of Hungary and Bohemia, but had no children. After his death (1526), when the crowns of both countries passed to her brother, Archduke Ferdinand, Mary served her elder brother, Charles V. As regent of the Netherlands, she ruled with firmness for almost a quarter of a century (1531–55), despite mounting economic and religious discontent. She resigned when Charles abdicated from the imperial throne (1555).

MARY OF BURGUNDY (1457–82), Duchess of Burgundy. As a young girl she was unexpectedly thrust into the position of the ruler of the Burgundian states by the death of her father, Duke Charles, at the battle of Nancy (1477). This disaster was followed by the French invasion of all her territories and a general revolt of her subjects in the Netherlands. Her marriage to the Habsburg Archduke Maximilian (the future emperor) saved her main territories in the Netherlands and considerable internal concessions pacified her subjects, but the duchy and county of Burgundy, the cradle of her dynasty, were annexed by France. On her death, she left two small children, the future Emperor Charles V being her grandson.

MARY OF GUISE (1515–60), Queen, wife of James V of Scotland (1538) and mother of Mary Queen of Scots, who became regent of Scotland on her husband's death (1542). She was a vigorous opponent of the Reformation and in her last years faced the revolt of John Knox backed by English forces. She died shortly before the conclusion of the treaty of Edinburgh (1560).

MARY OF MODENA (1658–1718), Queen of James II of England, born Marie Beatrice D'Este, daughter of Alfonso IV, Duke of Modena. She married James, then Duke of York, in 1673. Contrary to contemporary popular opinion, she had little religious or political influence upon her husband. Between 1675 and 1682 she bore five children, none of whom survived. On 10 June 1688 her son, James Francis Edward, the future Old Pretender, was born. On William of Orange's invasion she escaped, with her son, to France, and urged James to follow. Her influence over her husband increased in exile and before her death her son had made a bid to secure the throne (1715) in the Jacobite 'rebellion'.

MARY TUDOR (1496–1533), Queen of Louis XII of France and youngest surviving daughter of King Henry VII of England and Elizabeth of York. Though already married by proxy (1508) to the future Emperor Charles V, Thomas Wolsey arranged her marriage to Louis XII in 1514 upon intimation from Emperor Maximilian I that he wished to withdraw from the contract. Louis died in 1515 and Mary secretly married Charles Brandon, Duke of Suffolk. Suffolk was pardoned for his temerity on Wolsey's intercession and upon payment of a heavy fine. Mary had three children, one of whom, Frances (b. 1517), was the mother of Lady Jane Grey.

MARYLAND, English colony on the east coast of North America. It was probably visited by Verrazano (1524), and was first inhabited by peaceful Indians, who engaged in agriculture. The Indians gradually withdrew as the white man came. MD was included in the London Co. grant and a trading post was established there (1631), but the London Co. authority was superseded by a charter granted to Cecilius Calvert, Lord Baltimore (1652), who named the colony in honour of Queen Henrietta Maria, wife of Charles I. The grant extended from the Potomac river to the 40th parallel and inland to the source of the river. The colony was designed as a refuge for English Catholics, but from the first settlement (1633) Protestants outnumbered Catholics. The Maryland Toleration Act (1649) recognized any Christian Trinitarian religion. However, a Protestant revolt overthrew the Catholic proprietors (1654), but they were restored with the aid of VA forces (1660). MD became a royal colony (1688), the Church of England was officially recognized, and Annapolis was made the capital. Free schools were established in each county (1723). Split by the 200-mile-long (320 kms) Chesapeake Bay, the colony developed a plantation culture on the eastern shore, but the north and west were tied economically to the north. The boundary dispute with PA was settled in 1732. The boundary was surveyed (1763–7) by Charles Mason and Jeremiah Dixon and became the historic Mason–Dixon Line, delineating the American South from the North. MD supported the American Revolution, and became the 7th state to enter the American union (1788).

M. P. Andrews, *History of Maryland* (New York, 1929) DJF

MASAFINT period (lit. 'era of the princes'), time of internal disunity in Ethiopia in the late 18th and early 19th cents.

MASARYK, JAN (1886–1948), Czech diplomat and politician, son of Thomas Masaryk. Although born and educated in Prague, he later lived in the US (1907–18). When the state of Czechoslovakia was created he returned to Prague, and entered the diplomatic service, afterwards working in Washington, London, and again in Prague before becoming minister to Britain (1925–38). He resigned after Munich (1938), but in 1939 returned to London. During the Second World War, from July 1940, he acted as foreign minister of the Czech government in exile in London, and in 1941 became deputy prime minister. He concentrated his efforts on the US, attending the UNRRA conference at Atlantic City (1943) and, in 1944, the international labour conference at Philadelphia. In Aug. 1945 he signed the UNRRA agreement, which was to benefit the post-war Czechoslovakia by about $264 million. Meanwhile he had returned to Prague in May behind the forces of the Red Army and Svoboda's liberated Czechs. From then on the cornerstone of Czech policy was the Soviet alliance, although, as his father's son, Masaryk naturally hoped that the country could remain open to influence from both East and West. Nevertheless, Russian backing was crucial in resolving the tension with Poland over Teschen (the Czechs acquired Teschen and the Russians Ruthenia), and supporting the expulsion of the German minority from the country. After the communist take-over in Feb. 1948 Masaryk remained briefly at the foreign ministry. There are grounds for suspecting that his death was not accidental, as was officially stated at the time.

MASARYK, THOMAS GARRIGUE (1850–1937), first president of Czechoslovakia, born in Moravia, though of Slovakian parentage. He was a professor in the Czech University of Prague (1882–1914). His approach to politics was always western-oriented—although he studied and wrote on Pan-Slavism and the Russian tradition—his wife was American, and in practical terms he was a radical and a nationalist. He was a member of the Vienna Imperial parliament (1891–3), and, as a leader of the so-called 'Realists', was closely associated with the Young Czech movement and championed workers' rights, female education, and national self-determination for Czechs, though within a federal empire. In 1908 he defended some Croats accused of treason at Agram (Zagreb), and in 1909 produced evidence which proved that forged documents emanating from the Austrian foreign office were designed to discredit South Slav political leaders. Between 1900 and 1918 he founded the Populist Party, on a platform of universal suffrage, an eight-hour day, and autonomy within the empire. When the First World War broke out he turned decisively towards the western powers as protectors of the Czechs' future, unlike others who turned to Russia, and in Dec. 1914 escaped to Italy, where he began a long campaign to persuade the Allies of the value of Czech autonomy—although at first he did not see this in terms of a complete Habsburg collapse. His aim in 1915 was a state formed of Bohemia, Moravia, Silesia, and Slovakia; Ruthenia he thought the Russians would claim. By Sept. 1918 all the Allies had recognized Czechoslovakia as an allied and independent state. A visit by Masaryk to the US in 1918 was particularly important for winning over the Slovakian and Ruthene colonies there to his plans. In Oct. 1918 the Czech national council set up by Masaryk in Paris in 1916 became the provisional government, Masaryk being its president. He returned to Prague in Dec. 1918 and subsequently was re-elected twice, remaining president until his resignation in Dec. 1935. During these years he gave general guidance on practical political affairs, but more significantly, by sheer force of his integrity, acted as a focus of admiration and, by extension, of national self-respect, being acclaimed by not only Czechs as the Platonic ideal of a philosopher-statesman.

R. W. Seton-Watson, *Masaryk in England* (London, 1943). Paul Selver, *Masaryk* (London, 1940). KM

MASCATES, Portuguese word meaning 'peddlers'. In Brazilian history the expression refers to the civil war in the captaincy of Pernambuco (1710–11), when the sugar planters of Olinda protested against the royal decision to grant city status to the nearby port of Recife, occupied largely by Portuguese-born merchants. The Crown's actions were upheld. The term is also identified with the 'rags-to-riches' tradition of Arabic-speaking immigrants (*Turcos*) to Brazil in the late 19th and early 20th cents, who began as itinerant peddlers, invested their savings in shops, and eventually became industrialists. Some of the largest family fortunes in Brazil were amassed by such immigrants, who started as peddlers.

MASHAM, LADY ABIGAIL (d. 1734), favourite of Queen Anne, who gradually usurped Sarah Churchill's place in the affections of Queen Anne. She was thus in a position to break the power of Sarah's husband, the Duke of Marlborough. Robert Harley, another relative of Abigail, was able through her to gain access to the queen. Once Harley had achieved power (1710), he ignored Abigail, who then gave her support to his rival, St John. The death of Anne (1714) marked the end of Abigail's influence.

MASINA, town (Ke-Macina) and district of the Niger floodplain in Mali. In the 15th cent. the area was inhabited by nomadic Sanhaja from Tishit and pastoral Fulani were moving in. In the 16th cent. Masina was ruled by Fulani chiefs, apparently as a client state of Songhay. During the Moroccan pashalik (post-1592) Masina maintained a semi-independent status, but by 1725 was dominated by the Bambara state of Segu. In the early 19th cent. a Fulani religious leader, Ahmad Lobbo (d. 1844), established a theocratic state based on Masina which, though overrun by Al-hajj Umar in 1862, was not finally destroyed until the French occupation (1893).

MASJID ('a place where prostration is made')—whence the English word mosque (cf. Italian: *moschea*). Masjid, the general term for a mosque, is to be distinguished from the designation Jami'. Among the most notable features of a mosque are the pulpit (minbar) and the niche (mihrab), indicating the direction of prayer (qibla) towards Mecca. The official staff serving a masjid—their number depending

on its importance and endowments—would include an imam (the leader of prayer) and might also embrace a sheikh (the preacher of sermons) and a mu'adhdhin (responsible for calling the faithful to prayer), as well as dignitaries (qayyim) appointed to supervise the servants (door-keepers, water-carriers, etc.) of the mosque.

MASJUMI (MADJELIS SJURO MUSLIMIN INDONESIA), founded in 1943 as a mass organization uniting Indonesian Muslims behind the Japanese war effort. It was reorganized into a political party after Indonesia's declaration of independence (1945). The party was controlled by Muslim modernists, notably Muhammad Natsir and Hadji Agus Salimm, and resentment of this caused the defection in 1952 of the traditionalist *Nahdatul Ulama* group. The general elections of 1955 showed the *Masjumi* to be the largest Indonesian religious party and the only party with solid strength outside Java. The late 1950s saw a rapid decline in *Masjumi*'s prestige owing to the involvement of some of its leaders in the Indonesian (PRRI) Revolt of 1958, its compromising stand on the Darul Islam Revolt, and its favourable view of capitalism and the West. In 1960, having refused to accede to the terms laid down by Sukarno for Guided Democracy, it was banned. Efforts to rehabilitate it after Sukarno's fall in 1965 were rejected by Suharto's government, but in 1968 a new group, the *Partai Muslimin Indonesia*, was permitted to appeal to the former *Masjumi* clientele.

MASON, GEORGE (1725–92), American politician and philosopher, whose liberal ideas were embodied in the VA declaration of rights (1776), and were used by Jefferson in drafting the Declaration of Independence. The VA declaration was used as a model for other states and formed the basis of the first ten amendments to the US constitution. It also influenced the French Declaration of the Rights of Man. Mason was a member of the federal Constitutional Convention (1787) and opposed its ratification because it lacked a bill of rights, and because it sanctioned the institution of slavery.

MASON AND DIXON LINE in US, boundary line between PA and DE on the north and MD and WV on the south, was surveyed by the English astronomers Charles Mason (1729–1786) and Jeremiah Dixon (1733–79). The Mason and Dixon Line (1763) came to designate the boundary in the US between slave and free states, and the North and the South. The area south of the line is sometimes known as 'Dixieland', and is important in US social history.

MASONS in the Middle Ages. The art of the mason began to come into its own with the ambitious building programmes which began on a large scale in Europe in the 11th cent. AD. It was the masons who envisaged grandiose concepts of building and decoration, and it was they who developed the practical organization which lay behind both lay and ecclesiastical building projects. Medieval masons were often wealthy and literate and enjoyed a fairly high social status. They were widely travelled, sophisticated professional men, and attended periodic congresses of their craft. They were organized on a lodge basis, the lodge being a body which upheld the regulations of their craft. Masons' marks cut on stone show that there was some degree of official control among the masons. A highly developed organization grew up in Europe, based on the precepts of the Strasbourg Lodge; in England the king's master mason exerted considerable influence. All this tended towards the creation of an architectural profession which was responsible for magnificent buildings, and for the rapid spread of new architectural concepts.

MASSACHUSETTS, English North American colony, named after the Indian tribe found along its coast. It was explored by Bartholomew Gosnold (1602), charted and described by John Smith (1614), and first settled by the Pilgrims at

Plymouth (1620). Massachusetts Bay colony was founded by the Co. for Massachusetts Bay under royal charter (1628), and, during the 'Great Migration' (1630–40), 25,000 Puritans emigrated to the bay. Their leaders set up a Puritan commonwealth with franchise limited to male property-owners who were Church members. Some prominent freemen left the colony because of the religious restrictions and established the colonies of Rhode Island and New Hampshire. Other Massachusetts Bay colonists settled along the Connecticut river valley. The Boston Latin School was established (1635) and Harvard College (1636), the first institution of higher learning in America. A law was passed (1641) establishing schools of reading and writing in every town of 50 or more inhabitants, the first law in the English-speaking world requiring the establishment of schools.

MA led the way in the American colonies in working out a plan of self-government. The voters elected the governor and the General Court, or legislature, became a bicameral body in 1644, the members being chosen by ballot in each town. A judicial system developed, following the English model. Precepts of the Bible were used by the judges, as well as English common law. A code of laws known as the 'Body of Liberties' was adopted (1641).

MA made little effort to enforce the English Navigation Acts, and its charter was annulled (1684) and the Dominion of New England was formed with Sir Edmund Andros at its head. The English revolution of 1688 resulted in the collapse of the Dominion of New England and MA resumed its self-government. The colony received a new charter (1691) and became a Crown colony, the governor being appointed in England. Because of the poor soil, fishing and shipping became the chief sources of livelihood and a lucrative China trade developed, which flourished until the Embargo Act of 1807. Citizens of MA, partly because of the restrictive Townshend Acts, were active in fomenting rebellion against England and the first battles of the American War of Independence were fought at Lexington and Concord. A state constitution was ratified by the people (1780). MA entered the federal union in 1788.

G. L. Haskins, *Law and Authority in Early Massachusetts. a study in tradition and design* (New York, 1960).
A. B. Hart, *The Commonwealth History of Massachusetts*, 5 vols (New York, 1927–30).   DJF

MASSACHUSETTS BAY COMPANY, London company granted land and trading rights between the Merrimack and Charles rivers from the Council of New England (1628). Reconstituted by royal charter (1629), the company's charter was transferred to America by the Puritan stockholders and it became the basic constitution of the colony. The charter was withdrawn (1684) because the colony had coined money without authority, denied freedom of worship, and refused to obey the Navigation Acts. The company government continued until the Dominion of New England was established (1686).

MASSACHUSETTS BODY OF LIBERTIES (1641), document drawn up by Nathaniel Ward and adopted by the General Court as the basic law of Massachusetts Bay colony. Based on English common law, it was in force for seven years and was then superseded by the Massachusetts General Laws and Liberties (1648). The latter contained 100 laws defining legal procedures and judicial safeguards, and was the first printed codification of law in British America.

MASSACHUSETTS CIRCULAR LETTER (1768), American protest statement, drafted by Samuel Adams, approved by the Massachusetts assembly, and sent to other North American colonies. The letter denounced the British American Imports Duty Act (1767) which levied a tax on imported commodities. The assemblies of Massachusetts and Virginia were dissolved for endorsing the letter, which helped to cement American opposition. The British govern-

ment subsequently repealed (1770) all duties except the tax on tea.

MASSACRE OF THE KINSMEN, practised by a new king of Burma to eliminate contenders for the throne. The most notorious massacre was that of some 75 relatives by King Thibaw on his accession in Mandalay (1878).

MASSÉNA, ANDRÉ (1756–1817), French soldier, and one of Napoleon I's marshals. His reputation as a military genius was made in the French Revolutionary and Napoleonic wars. He distinguished himself during Napoleon's Italian campaigns (1796–7), gained a crushing victory over Suvorov at Zürich (1799), brilliantly defended Genoa (1800), and was created marshal of the empire in 1804. He took command of the army in Italy (1805), where he defeated Archduke Charles at Caldiero (1805), and overran Naples. He was made Duke of Rivoli in 1808 and his brilliant generalship at Aspern-Essling (1809) and Wagram (1809) earned him the title of Prince of Essling (1809). But his reputation was shattered when he was defeated in Spain (1810) by the Duke of Wellington. He forced Wellington back upon his lines at Torres Vedras, but after five months had to retreat into Spain. With some justification he blamed the failure of the Spanish campaign on the disobedience of Ney, Junot, and others of his subordinates, but he never received another field command. At the Restoration he adhered to the Bourbons and refused to support Napoleon during the Hundred Days (1815).

MASSEY, VINCENT (1887–1967), Canadian politician and diplomat. He served in the Canadian army during the First World War, became minister without portfolio in Mackenzie King's government (1925), and, although he failed to get elected to parliament, attended the Imperial Conference in London (1926). He was the first Canadian minister to Washington (1926–30), president of the National Liberal Federation (1932–5), and Canadian High Commissioner in London (1935–46). He was chairman of the Royal Commission on National Development in the Arts, Letters, and Sciences (1949) and the first native-born governor-general of Canada (1952–9).

MASSEY, WILLIAM FERGUSON (1856–1925), NZ politician and prime minister, who emigrated from Northern Ireland to NZ in 1870. After setting up as a small farmer near Auckland, he entered parliament (1894) as a 'farmers' advocate', opposing Seddon's alleged 'socialism', and seeking 'justice for Auckland'. He was elected leader of the opposition (1903), and his party, named 'Reform' in 1909, won a close election in 1912. Massey became prime minister. Though the long Liberal period was thus ended, he maintained Liberal policies, and suppressed rising Labour militancy by his strong handling of the 1912–13 strikes. During the First World War he supported his pledge (1914) to aid Britain, but was ill-prepared to face the actual costs of war. Reluctantly he formed a National government (1915) with Ward, and together they attended Imperial war cabinets and the peace conference (1919). This experience confirmed Massey's strong feelings of imperialism, which persisted in peacetime. The onset of depression (1921), the chronic problems of farmers, and the rise of Labour were among post-war difficulties that confronted him at the time of his death in office.

MASSILIA, ancient Greek city (mod. Marseilles) established by Phocaeans c. 600 BC. Despite Carthaginian and Etruscan opposition, it prospered in the 6th cent. through the exchange of Greek pottery, bronzeware, etc. for Spanish silver and British tin. A Massiliot treasury was built at Delphi. In the 5th and 4th cents Massiliot seamen reached the Niger mouth and the British Isles. As an early ally of Rome against Carthage (3rd cent.), Massilia in the 2nd cent. increasingly needed Roman help against Ligurian attacks. It was overshadowed by the establishment of Gallia Narbonensis as a Roman province (121) and later stripped of territory by Julius Caesar for supporting Pompey (49). It declined rapidly under the empire.

MASSILON, JEAN BAPTISTE (1663–1742), French orator, a member of the congregation of the Oratory, who was made Bp of Clermont in 1717. His eloquence was such that he was invited to preach a series of ten sermons for Lent (his famous *Petit Carême*) before Louis XIV, in which he warned the king of the dangers of arbitrary government.

MASSINISSA (c. 258–148 BC), King of the Massylii (*reg.* 208–148 BC), who reigned over the Eastern part of Numidia situated between the Ampsaga river and Carthage. He first fought against the Romans in Spain, but during the Second Punic War allied himself with Rome and, after defeating Syphax, King of the Masaesylii, annexed most of Western Numidia. Throughout his long reign he continued to enlarge his kingdom at the expense of the Carthaginians, who were deprived by the treaty imposed upon them by Rome in 201 BC of any adequate means of defence. On Massinissa's death, the succession was divided principally between his three sons, Micipsa, Gulussa, and Mastanabal.

'MASSIVE RETALIATION' in US, controversial doctrine of defence policy stated by the secretary of state, Dulles (12 Jan. 1954). Designed to cut defence costs, the concept envisaged primary reliance upon massive nuclear striking power rather than local defences to deter aggression. It provoked protest both at home and abroad and was subsequently modified.

MASSON, SIR DAVID ORME (1858–1937), Australian biologist, who played a leading part in the establishment of the Commonwealth Institute of Science and Industry (1920) and the Council for Scientific and Industrial Research (1926).

MASSOSSOIT (1581–1662), American Indian chief of the Wampanoag Algonquins, and the father of King Philip. He received the English 'Pilgrim Fathers' with kindness (1621) and kept a pledge of peace with them until his death.

MASTERS OF REQUESTS, French judicial officers, closely associated with the *parlement* of Paris in its formative years.

MAS'UDI, AL-, ABU'L-HASAN 'ALI (d. AD 956), author of a large historico-geographical work, an epitome of which, extending to the year AD 947, has survived under the title of *Muruj al-Dhahab wa Ma'adin al-Jawhar* (*Prairies of Gold and Mines of Gems*).

MASULIPATAM, TREATY OF (May 1759), concluded between Col. Forde and Salabat Jung, Nizam of Hyderabad. Forde was sent by Robert Clive from Bengal to seize the Northern Sarkars, then part of Hyderabad state and under French control. The treaty marked the nizam's recognition of Forde's success.

MATAMBA, kingdom of the southern Congo basin founded in the 17th cent. by an Angolan dynasty to resist Portuguese invasion and dominate the westward trade-routes from the Lunda empire in Katanga.

MATANZAS, BATTLE OF (1628), defeat and capture of the Spanish treasure fleet and convoy in the Cuban harbour of Matanzas by Piet Heyn's Dutch Atlantic squadron. This blow to Spanish pride led to the trial and execution in Cadiz of the Spanish fleet commander, Admiral Juan de Benavides, for dereliction of duty (1633), while the Dutch used their windfall of some six million pesos to finance another invasion of Brazil (1630).

MATAPAN, BATTLES OF (1717, 1941). The battle in 1717 was an indecisive action between the Venetian and Turkish fleets in the course of the Austro-Turkish War of 1716–18. It demonstrated the declining importance of the galley, which had hitherto dominated Mediterranean naval warfare.

That of 1941 was a pursuit and night action between the British Mediterranean Fleet, commanded by Admiral Cunningham, and an Italian force under Admiral Iachino. Forewarned by intelligence, the British intercepted the Italians off Crete on 28 March. The Italians withdrew towards their coast, pursued by three British battleships and the carrier HMS *Formidable*, whose aircraft attempted to slow down the Italian battleship, *Vittorio Veneto*. Though crippled she escaped, but three Italian cruisers were sunk in a night engagement.

MATARAM, area of Central Java surrounding the present city of Jogjakarta. It was formerly the name of an ancient kingdom of the 8th and 9th cents in that area; later it was the name of the last Islamic kingdom of Central Java, beginning in the late 16th cent. and represented in the 20th cent. by the Sultans of Jogjakarta, the Susuhunans of Surakarta, and the Princes Pakualam and Mangkunegara.

MATCH-GIRLS PROTEST (1871) in London, a march to Westminster organized by girl employees of Bryant and May's factory to force Robert Lowe, the chancellor of the exchequer, to withdraw his budget proposal to raise £1 million from a match tax. The cabinet had, in fact, already decided to drop the proposal, but the incident helped to shake Lowe's parliamentary reputation and to discredit Gladstone's first Liberal administration. In 1888 match girls at the same factory organized a strike which achieved both recognition of their union and an improvement in the wages and conditions among some of the lowest-paid workers. The strike was a forerunner of the 'New Unionism' of the 1890s, the extension of unionism to the unskilled.

MATHER, COTTON (1663–1738), American clergyman, writer, and scientist, who was the best-known New England writer of his day. In his *Political Fables* (1692) he defended the new Massachusetts charter. During the Salem witchcraft trials (1692) he agreed with the judges, but urged them not to rely on 'spectral evidence' and advocated fasting and prayer rather than ruthless punishment in the treatment of those convicted of witchcraft. His *Magnalia Christi Americana* (1702) was a history of Church development in pioneer America. He also wrote on natural history and was elected to the Royal Society after describing the hybridization of Indian corn, which was the first account of a plant hybrid, and was important in the history of botany. He was interested in medicine, too, and was a pioneer advocate of smallpox inoculations. In his *The Christian Philosopher*, a book of Newtonian physics, he sought to reconcile religion and science.

MATILDA (1102–67), Empress, sole surviving daughter of King Henry I of England and recognized as his heiress in 1126. Previously she had been the wife (1114–25) of the German Emperor Henry V and hence her title as empress. The unpopularity of her second husband, Count Geoffrey of Anjou, was a major reason for the refusal of the English and Norman barons to honour their promises to Henry I to accept her as his successor and to prefer her cousin Stephen. Matilda's husband was soon able to conquer Normandy, but her attempt to recover England, where she landed in 1139, made little headway, partly because her haughty attitude alienated many of her supporters. When her cause seemed to triumph in 1141 and she was about to be crowned queen at Westminster, an uprising of Londoners compelled her to flee and she was never again in control of London. She left England in 1147, never to return, but her son, Henry II, succeeded in establishing himself as Stephen's successor.

Until her death Matilda continued to exert much political influence on Henry.

MATILDA OF TUSCANY (1046–1115). As countess of Tuscany and owner of huge estates in central Italy, she was one of the most powerful and reliable allies of the papacy in its struggle with the Emperors Henry IV and Henry V. In the winter of 1076–7 Pope Gregory VII took refuge in her castle at Canossa, and it was outside it that early in 1077 Emperor Henry IV sought papal absolution. At her death she left her lands to the papacy.

MATIWANE, (c. 1800–29), chief of the Ngwane, an Nguni-speaking South African group. He came into conflict with Shaka and Moshweshwe, and was put to death by the Zulu King Dingane.

MATOPE (reg. c. 1450–80), second Ruler of the central African empire of Mwenemutapa, founded by his father, Mutota (d. c. 1450), in the lands between the Zambezi and Limpopo rivers. It was formed by the Karanga branch of the Shona-speaking group of peoples, and in Shona oral history is said to have undergone a great extension under Matope's powerful rule, and to have included most of central Mozambique as far as the seaboard, where fruitful trading contacts were expanded with the Swahili of ports such as Sofala.

MATOS, NORTON DE (b. 1867), Portuguese colonial administrator and, during the First World War, successively minister of colonies and of war. As governor-general of Angola (1912–15) he set himself to displace various forms of internal slavery still existing in the colony by a contractual method which soon degenerated, however, into a system of forced labour. He was high commissioner for Angola (1921–4) and again met with severe opposition from settler and business interests and was driven to resign. During this period, however, he was successful in extending civilian colonial administration to regions previously under military government.

MATRA, JAMES MARIO (d. 1806), English sailor, author, and diplomat. He was a member of the crew of Capt. James Cook's *Endeavour*, and the author of a plan (1783) for settling American loyalists in eastern Australia. This, and other proposals, attracted official attention and contributed to NSW's foundation as a convict settlement. Matra was later British consul at Teneriffe (1772), secretary of the British embassy at Constantinople (1778), and consul-general (1786) at Tangier. His surname is variously spelt 'Magra', 'Magoa', 'Macgrath', and his Christian name is given as 'Jean' or 'Maria'.

MATSWA, ANDRÉ (d. 1942), African agitator of northern Congo origin, active during the 1920s in anti-colonial protest among Africans of the French colony of Moyen Congo (since Congo/Brazzaville) and neighbouring areas. As with other leading figures of his type, he framed his protest and won numerous supporters within the context of messianic belief, equating the power of evil with European domination, and preaching the need for active opposition to the latter. Finding him a threat to their security, the French colonial authorities arrested him in 1930 and exiled him to Chad. Later they brought him back to Moyen Congo, where he died in prison at Brazzaville.

MATTEI, ENRICO (1906–62), Italian industrialist and politician, who became financial organizer of resistance movements in northern Italy (1943–5) during the Second World War. In 1953 he established a large state-controlled holding company, National Hydrocarbons Trust (ENI), with exclusive rights in the Po valley for oil explorations. He gradually made Italy an international oil power and his agreements for cheap Russian oil (1959) established new

political–economic trends. He was a Christian Democrat deputy (1948–53).

MATTEOTTI, GIACOMO (1885–1924), Italian socialist politician, who became a founder of socialist organizations in the Po valley after the First World War. He was elected a deputy (1919) and supported Turati's revisionist socialism, becoming secretary of the Unitary Socialist Party in 1924. By a speech (30 May 1924) denouncing fascist violence and electoral manipulation, he infuriated the fascists. He was kidnapped and stabbed by *squadristi* on 10 June, but his body was not found until 16 Aug. His disappearance created fascism's most serious crisis. Lukewarm supporters deserted Mussolini, but on 26 June he received a Senate vote of confidence. Some of his opponents seceded from the Chamber (the Aventine Secession), but failed to make the king dismiss Mussolini, although he eventually admitted ultimate responsibility. He then launched into his full dictatorship. Though anti-fascists had failed to exploit the wave of indignation, some drew inspiration from Matteotti's courageous stand.

MATTHEWS, ZACHARIAH K. (1901–68), black South African academic, who became president of the Cape branch of the African National Congress (1949) and helped to formulate much of Congress's policy in the 1950s. When the Nationalist government took over control of the University College of Fort Hare, he resigned his chair in anthropology and he spent the last years of his life in exile.

MATTHIAS (1557–1619), Emperor (reg. 1612–19), younger son of the Emperor Maximilian II and brother of the Emperor Rudolph II. As a young man Matthias was appointed governor of the Low Countries (1578–81) and later of Austria and Hungary, granting a treaty of toleration to his Protestant subjects (1606). With Protestant support he tried to secure the deposition of his brother Rudolph on the grounds of his mental incapacity, and in 1608 a compromise was reached by which Matthias took possession of Hungary, Moravia, and Austria, and in May 1611 was elected King of Bohemia. He pursued a policy of religious compromise, though he made peaceful attempts to reassert absolutism in the Habsburg lands. In his old age, having no offspring, he adopted his cousin, Ferdinand of Styria, as his heir and it was the latter's election to the throne of Bohemia that precipitated the Thirty Years War, the start of which was followed soon afterwards by Matthias's death.

MATTHIAS CORVINUS (reg. 1458–90), King of Hungary, son of the Hungarian military hero, John Hunyadi, Matthias was proclaimed king by his fellow magnates as a reaction to a long line of foreign rulers. By means of a large standing army and cavalier treatment of the constitutional rights of his lands, he carried out sweeping reforms and was able to conquer part of the Bohemian state and wrest Austria from the Emperor Frederick III.

MATTHYS, JAN (d. 1534), Dutch Anabaptist, a baker of Haarlem, who became leader of the sect in the Netherlands after Melchoir Hofman's imprisonment. In 1534 he moved to Münster, where he took over the town council with his chief disciple, Jan Bockelson. He was killed shortly afterwards during an outbreak of violence in the town.

MATVEEV, ANDREI ARTAMONOVICH (1666–1728), Russian diplomat at The Hague from 1699, who was involved in abortive negotiations for Russia's entry into the Grand Alliance in the War of the Spanish Succession.

MATVEEV, ARTAMON SERGEIVICH (d. 1682), Russian politician and favourite of Tsar Alexis, who became a *boyar* and head of the department of foreign affairs (1671). He was a convinced 'westernizer', and was married to a Scotswoman. His home in Moscow was the centre for the social and intellectual elite and it was here that Tsar Alexis met his second wife, Natalia Naryshkin, Matveev's ward. Under Tsar Fedor II Matveev was exiled to Pustozersk, near Archangel, but was recalled at the beginning of the reign of Ivan V. He was stabbed to death in the *streltsy* palace revolt (1682) which resulted in the Tsarevna Sophia's regency.

'MAU MAU', the name (origin obscure) given to an African independence movement centred in Kikuyu country (1952–5). Regarded by government and settlers as Kikuyu 'tribal atavism', and by its members as a national liberation movement, it changed the direction and pace of political change in Kenya. The government emphasized the oathing techniques and violence of the rebels, but played down its own previous refusal to respond to constitutional pressure for reform. The government declared an emergency, detained suspected leaders, organized Kikuyu loyalists, and besieged the rebels in the forests, inflicting over 11,000 casualties, as against only 95 white fatalities. Nevertheless, *'Mau Mau'* demonstrated the inadequacy of the existing political structure and forced colonial authorities to admit and accept the need for political change.

MAUÁ, IRINEU EVANGELISTA DE SOUSA, Baron of (1813–89), Brazilian financier, founder of *Banco do Brasil*, and congressman from Rio Grande do Sul. As a youth he found employment in Rio de Janeiro with a British commercial firm, and subsequently enjoyed excellent relations with British financial circles. In 1850 he began his career as banker and contractor. He is closely identified with the modernization of Brazil, having introduced gas lighting and public transport in Rio de Janeiro, and the first railroad in Brazil (for which he was ennobled), in the 1850s. Mauá's banks advanced substantial sums to the imperial regime. His over-extended financial empire collapsed in 1875, when he was refused a loan by the Brazilian government.

MAUKHARI DYNASTY, ancient Indian dynasty, first attested in Kotah state (Rajasthan) in the 3rd cent. AD. A later branch of the Maukharis came to control the upper Gangetic valley (capital Kanauj) during the decline of the Guptas early in the 6th cent. AD. For a century they were subsequently involved in an intermittent struggle with the Later Guptas of Bihar. The last independent Maukhari king Grahavarman, killed in an attack by Sasanka from southwest Bengal, was succeeded by his brother-in-law, Harsha (Harshavardhana), who in this manner united his own inherited kingdom (Thanesvar) with that of the Maukharis of Kanauj, and thus laid the basis of a great empire. The main importance of the dynasty apparently consists in their efforts to restore and maintain some kind of Brahmanic orthodoxy.

MAUMEE INDIAN CONVENTION (Aug. 1793), meeting of American Indians in the North-west Territory. The Indians, encouraged by British agents, demanded, unsuccessfully, US withdrawal from Indian lands.

MAUNG GYEE, SIR (1886–), Burmese lawyer and politician, who was a member of the Legislative Council and minister for education (1923). He attended the Burma Round Table Conference, was nominated to the Senate (1937) and later as president. During the Japanese occupation in the Second World War, he was a judge of the Supreme Court.

MAUPEOU, RENÉ NICOLAS CHARLES AUGUSTIN (1714–1792), French minister, who served the house of Bourbon in the *ancien régime*, and was chancellor (1768–92). In 1768 he persuaded Louis to appoint the abbé Terray as controller-general and together they took over the government on Choiseul's downfall. In tackling the immediate problem of financial reform, they were brought into direct conflict with the *parlements*, guardians of tradition. Maupeou took the initiative and after provoking the *parlement* of Paris into rejecting royal authority, he exiled the magistrats to the Auvergne by *lettre de cachet* and abolished their offices, setting up new courts in six new areas of jurisdiction. The *Grand Conseil* alone was retained as a special tribunal for Crown matters and as a court of peers, and was known as the *Parlement Maupeou*.

Despite growing hostility, Maupeou proposed to follow this up by complete reform of the French judicial system, but the death of Louis XV (1774) cut short his career. The young King Louis XVI, facing popular pressure and on the advice of Maurepas, restored the *parlements* and dismissed Maupeou, who retired from political life. Many of Maupeou's planned reforms were put into effect after his death by his former secretary, Lebrun, who was third consul during the Napoleonic Consulate.

MAUPERTIUS, PIERRE LOUIS MOREAU DE (1698–1759), French mathematician, astronomer, and geneticist. In 1736–7 Maupertius went to Lapland on an expedition to measure the length of a degree of latitude in order to verify existing mathematical theory, and later (1738) he published a book, *On the Figure of the Earth*. In a series of essays, written in 1741–51, he expounded a complete evolutionary explanation of the organic world which anticipated the ideas of Darwin.

MAURA, ANTONIO (1853–1925), Spanish politician and conservative prime minister (1903–4, 1907–9, 1918–19), who shared Silvela's desire for the political regeneration of Spain. Revolution imposed from above was to end the system of electoral management and re-establish sincerity in politics. But Maura could not accept that republican, socialist, or liberal views represented 'sincere' opinion and the liberals rejected the concept of political revolution without modernization and social reform. Maura's intransigence made him the most hated prime minister of the Restoration. He resigned when he lost royal support (1909) and split the conservative party, the only sure safeguard of the monarchy, by launching a direct appeal to Catholic Spain. This created 'Maurism', which began as a movement among conservative youth, but degenerated into a focus for violence.

MAUREPAS, JEAN FRÉDÉRIC PHELYPEAUX (1701–81), French minister, who was secretary for both the king's household and the Marine under Fleury and effected many reforms (1726–43), which enabled the French navy to hold its own for most of the Seven Years War (1756–63). He continued as secretary of state after Fleury's death until he fell into disgrace over an epigram upon Mme de Pompadour (April 1749). For the rest of Louis XV's reign he remained out of office. He was recalled in 1774 to guide Louis XVI in decision-making and made some effort to meet the need for financial reform. He suggested the physiocrat, Turgot, as controller-general, but abandoned him as opposition to his reforming Six Edicts mounted (1776). He later dropped Saint-Germain, whose military reforms aroused hostility from the officer class, and forced the resignation of Necker, whose excessive borrowing plunged the royal finances more deeply into debt (May 1781).

MAURETANIA, name given by the Romans to the country of the *Mauri* (Greek *Maurousioi*), who, from at least the middle of the 4th cent. BC, had inhabited the region of the Maghrib, which today constitutes northern Morocco. The first King of Mauretania of whom there is adequate historical record, Bocchus I (*reg.* 118–81 BC), betrayed his ally, Jugurtha of Numidia, to the Romans (105) and was rewarded with much of Numidia, the name of Mauretania thereafter being applied to all North Africa up to the Ampsaga river (Oued el Kebir). Bocchus I's successors were client kings of the Romans, who in 25 BC installed their own nominee, Juba II: on the death of Juba's son, Ptolemy, in AD 40, Mauretania was annexed by Rome and divided into two provinces, Mauretania Caesariensis (capital Caesarea, mod. Cherchell) and Mauretania Tingitana (capital Tingis, Tangier). A few Roman colonies were established, but immigration was not extensive. Large areas of mountainous country remained little touched by Roman civilization.

The chief products of Mauretania were animals for the arena, timber, and corn. Christianity spread rapidly throughout the country in the 4th cent. In 429 Mauretania fell to the Vandals, who crossed from Spain. Gradually it relapsed into a complex of mixed Berber and Roman communities until the Arab conquest in the 7th cent.

MAURIAC, FRANÇOIS (1888–1970), French Catholic writer and political commentator. His best-known novels have the bourgeois life of Bordeaux as their background. His literary works also included verse, plays, and criticism. He was a member of the French Academy, and received the Nobel Prize for Literature in 1952.

Mauriac distinguished himself from most Catholic intellectuals through criticizing Mussolini's conquest of Abyssinia and Franco's campaigns in the Spanish Civil War. He was also exceptional among writers of his background in his firm opposition to the Vichy regime, and had works published by the clandestine presses of the Resistance. When De Gaulle returned to power Mauriac became an enthusiastic admirer and exponent of his policies.

MAURICE (*reg.* 582–602), Emperor, last member of the Byzantine imperial dynasty of Justinian I, who succeeded his father-in-law, Tiberius II. He successfully defended the Asiatic frontiers, but could not stem the movements of the Slavs into the Balkan peninsula. He tried to improve internal conditions by practising religious toleration and limiting expenditure, but his attempts at economy, including a cut in army pay, angered the troops, who murdered him. They proclaimed as his successor Phocas, a soldier who proved unfit to rule.

MAURICE, Count of Nassau and Prince of Orange (1567–1625), son of William the Silent. After his father's murder (1584), he was elected *stadtholder* of the provinces of Holland and Zeeland (1587), and subsequently (1589) of Utrecht, Overyssel, and Gelderland, through the influence of Oldenbarneveldt. He also became captain-general of the forces of the United Provinces and their military commander in their war of independence against Spain. It was upon the skill with which he checked the Spanish advance under Parma and consolidated the rebels' position in the northern provinces that Maurice's fame rests. He led the offensive (1590–1606) by which large parts of Groningen, Overyssel, and Drente were conquered, and also took valuable enclaves in Gelderland, *eg*, Nymwegen (1591), and Brabant, *eg*, Breda (1590) and Gertruydenberg (1593).

Maurice was one of the great military innovators of the 16th cent. He carried out reforms in the organization of his fighting forces, introducing the battalion (550 men) to counteract the Spanish *tercio*. He ensured organized regular payments to his men to preserve discipline, and insisted on regular drilling. His scientific methods of siege warfare were derived from lectures at Bruges by Simon Stevin, the mathematician, and it was this interest which led him to found a school of engineers at Leyden University (1600). He also shared with the merchants of Amsterdam an active interest in Dutch expeditions to Brazil and the Far East.

Maurice resisted Philip II's peace offers (1598) and as leader of the war party agreed reluctantly to the 12-year truce with Spain which Oldenbarneveldt negotiated in 1609. In the religious controversy between the Remonstrants and the Calvinists, known as the Gomarists, he supported the latter and helped to secure Oldenbarneveldt's execution and Grotius's imprisonment (1619). In the conflict with the Habsburgs which reopened in 1621 he continued to lead the new republic. In 1610 he had led a Dutch force in support of the Protestant Union to intervene in the Julich–Berg dispute. In 1624 he sought help from both England and France, though the price of French aid was his connivance at the

suppression of the Huguenot rebels. In 1625 he tried in vain to relieve Breda, which he had captured 35 years earlier, but died just before the town surrendered to Spinola and the Spanish army. He was succeeded by his younger brother, Frederick Henry.

P. Geyl, *The Revolt of the Netherlands* (London, 1958).
P. Geyl, *The Netherlands in the 17th Century* (London, 1961).
MKS

MAURICE, JOHN FREDERICK DENISON (1805–72), English clergyman, historian, and social reformer. A Unitarian upbringing, a refusal to accept the 39 articles at Cambridge, and, subsequently, a cautious acceptance of Anglicanism, led him to devote his ministry to the rejection of sectarianism and parties within religion. His unorthodoxy was expressed in *Theological Essays* (1853), which cost him his professorship (1840–53) at King's College, London.

He had already become interested in Christian socialism and devoted much of the 1850s and 1860s to the Co-operative movement, to writing tracts, *eg, Tracts for Priests and People* (1861), to the Working Men's College in London, and to education in slum areas. He became professor of moral philosophy at Cambridge in 1866.

MAURICE DE SAXE (1696–1750), scion of the house of Wettin, last heir of the great Swedish family of Königsmarck, and the illegitimate son of Maria Aurora von Königsmarck and Frederick Augustus, Elector of Saxony and King of Poland. He was also a Lutheran prince and a marshal of France.

As an ensign in the Saxon army, he saw service in the war of the Spanish Succession, being present at the sieges of Tournai (1709), Douai and Aire (1711), and at Malplaquet (1709), which instilled in him a life-long hatred of unnecessary bloodshed. Between periods of residence at the Saxon court he campaigned in Pomerania during the later stages of the Great Northern War and served as a volunteer under Prince Eugène at Belgrade (1717–18) in the Austro-Turkish War. Meanwhile, in 1711 his father bestowed on him the title of Count of Saxony, and in 1714 arranged his marriage to a Saxon heiress, Countess Johanna-Victoria von Löben (1714), a union which ended in divorce (1720).

In 1720 Maurice moved to Paris, where with the influence of the Dowager Duchess Elizabeth-Charlotte of Orléans, he became a protégé of the French regent, entered the French army, and purchased a colonelcy. He also took as his mistress the leading French actress of the day, Adrienne Lecouvreur. Maurice's greatest ambition was the acquisition of a crown and in 1725 he left Paris for Moscow, in pursuit of the duchy of Courland. To achieve his aim he needed Russian support and he was advised to marry either Anna Ivanovna, the niece of Peter I of Russia and widow of the previous Duke of Courland, or Peter's daughter, Elizabeth. Although he was created Duke-elect (1726), Maurice faced the hostility of Peter's favourite, Prince Menshikov, and strong opposition from the Polish nobility, who prevented Frederick Augustus from supporting his candidature. He prevaricated over the marriage and eventually was expelled from Courland with his motley force (1727); after which he returned to Paris until Adrienne's death (1730). While recuperating in Poland (1732), he wrote his *Rêveries*, a manual of war.

During the war of the Polish Succession, which followed his father's death (1733), he fought with the French at Kehl (1733) and Philippsburg (1734). His military reputation was, however, crowned in the War of the Austrian Succession (1740–8), when Louis XV made him a marshal of France (1744). In 1741 he captured Prague, a triumph which enabled France's ally, the Elector of Bavaria, to win the Bohemian throne (Dec. 1741). Maurice then took the fortress of Egra (1742) and afterwards made a brief and rapid visit to Moscow to propose marriage to Tsarina Elizabeth Petrovna, in a last attempt to secure Courland. His suit was unsuccessful, and on returning to the war, he was given command of the French forces in Alsace, where he contained the Austrian army (1743). He led the French advance into the Netherlands (1744) and won the battles of Fontenoy (1745), Roucoux (1746) and Lauffeldt (1747), and captured Bergen-op-Zoom. He retired to Chambord after the peace of Aix-la-Chapelle (1748).

J. M. White, *Marshal of France* (London, 1962).   JHS

MAURITANIA, ISLAMIC REPUBLIC OF (1,169,000 sq. kms), in West Africa, with a population (1970) of 1 million, chiefly Arabo-Berber. It was formerly part of French West Africa, and became independent in 1960, electing by adult suffrage a national assembly and president for five years.

MAURITIUS (2000 sq. kms), islands in the Indian Ocean with a population (1970) of 773,600. It was formerly a British colony and became in 1968 an independent member of the British Commonwealth. The legislative assembly of 62 members is elected by adult suffrage.

MAURRAS, CHARLES (1868–1952), French writer and founder of the neo-royalist Action française movement, who was the most distinguished and influential thinker of the modern French right. Maurras was at first influenced by the Provençal literary revival, and remained faithful to a 'Mediterranean' classicism throughout his literary career. He rose to political celebrity through the Dreyfus Affair, when he emerged as the most intransigent of the anti-Dreyfusards. The Action française movement was founded at this time, and espoused the politics of direct action, while Maurras used its newspaper to expound his ideas.

His nationalist doctrine was based on his own interpretation of France's national tradition. He saw monarchism and Catholicism as an essential part of the tradition (though not himself a Catholic believer), while denying true 'Frenchness' to 'alien' groups like Jews and freemasons. In practice, authoritarianism, anti-Semitism, and violent hostility to democracy were the main features of the creed.

Maurras's considerable influence in traditional conservative circles was weakened when the pope condemned his movement (1926), and the Action française was overtaken in the 1930s by newer extremist movements. But he retained an important personal following, especially among intellectuals. The 'National Revolution' in the early years of the Vichy regime was partly inspired by Maurras's ideas, and this was one reason why he supported Pétain, despite the fact that he himself had formerly been strongly anti-German. Although Maurras took little part in public life under the regime, he was rightly seen as one of the underminers of the Third Republic, and was condemned to life imprisonment after the Second World War.   RDA

MAURUS HRABANUS (c. 780–856), leading ecclesiastical adviser of Emperor Charlemagne and a pupil of Alcuin. As abbot of Fulda (822–42), he increased its influence. In his last years he was Abp of Mainz. As a poet, and a voluminous author, of grammar books, biblical commentaries, and an encyclopedic dictionary, he was the major figure to bring the Carolingian renaissance to Germany.

MAURYA DYNASTY or Moriya, one of the greatest dynasties of ancient India (c. 320–180 BC), founded by Chandragupta (*reg. c.* 320–296) after he had overthrown the Nandas and defeated the Greek satraps appointed by Alexander the Great in Sind and Punjab. By vigorous campaigns Chandragupta subsequently established his authority from his capital, Pataliputra (present Patna in Bihar), to the west coast and the Indus valley. This expansion later brought him into conflict with the Greeks, Alexander's successors, in Bactria. Chandragupta accepted, however, a compromise and concluded a treaty with Seleukos Nikator (305–304 BC) resulting in the dispatch to Pataliputra of the Greek envoy, Megasthenes. Internally, Chandragupta gave the newly founded

empire a strong centralized administration, assisted in these efforts, according to tradition, by the master-mind of Indian statecraft, Kautilya.

These policies were continued by the next ruler, Bindusara (*reg. c.* 296–268), whose reign was apparently unexciting. The third Maurya, Asoka (*reg. c.* 268–231), initially pursued a similar policy by conquering and annexing to the Maurya empire Kalinga (mod. Orissa) and maintaining friendly relations with the Greeks. After some ten years, however, Asoka initiated an entirely new line of policy.

Some time after Asoka's death decline set in owing to a combination of internal dissent and Greek attacks. In c. 185 BC a *coup d'état* by Pushyamitra Shunga ended the Maurya empire.

For about a century the Mauryas controlled most of the Indo-Pakistani sub-continent, which they brought under a centralized administration carried out by a hierarchy of officials. This was made possible by the existence of a network of highways and by the use of script, unattested in earlier periods, for public proclamations. The oldest extant Indian art also dates back to the Maurya period. Above all, this was a time of lively contact between India, the Middle East, and the Mediterranean.

R. Thapar, *Ashoka and the Decline of the Mauryas* (Oxford, 1961).   JGdeC

MAUSOLUS (d. 353 BC), vassal King of Caria (south-western Asia Minor) in the Persian empire, who assisted Athens' rebellious allies in the Social War (357–355). He offers the best example in his own century of a hellenized oriental ruler, using Greek for his inscriptions and moving his capital to Halicarnassus, where he built lavishly. To what he erected his widow added his massive tomb, the Mausoleum.

MAWALI (sing. **MAWLA**), term to describe a non-Arab who embraced Islam and became affiliated, as a client, to one or another of the Arab tribal elements constituting the dominant warrior caste in the Muslim empire created after the death of the Prophet Muhammad in AD 632. The non-Muslims in the empire had a status inferior to that of the Arabs. Islam was, however, a universal faith promising equal status to all its adherents. Conversion to Islam therefore seemed to offer to the non-Muslims a means to free themselves from their disabilities (*eg*, higher rates of taxation, social disadvantages, etc.). A large-scale conversion would, however, undermine the dominance of the Arabs in the empire. In practice, conversion did not bring to the Mawali that equal status, as Muslims, with the Arab warrior elite which it was their wish to achieve. It was thus that in their disillusionment the Mawali—and above all the Persians, conscious of their superior cultural heritage over the Arab nomads from the desert—turned more and more into various movements of opposition directed against the Arab domination, as embodied in the regime of the Umayyad caliphs, and in particular to the Khawarij and the Shi'a. The disaffection prevailing amongst the Mawali was indeed one of the main factors which brought about the downfall of the Umayyads in the great revolution of AD 750.

MAWSON, SIR DOUGLAS (1882–1958), Australian Antarctic explorer and geologist. As a member of Shackleton's Antarctic expedition (1907), he reached the South Magnetic Pole with Edgeworth David (1908). He himself led Australasian and British–Australasian polar expeditions (1911–14, 1929–31). His interest in the Adelaide System of Precambrian rocks in the Flinders Ranges, and in geological changes traced through central Australia, led to a geotectonic concept of the evolution of the Australian continent.

MAX, Prince of Baden (1867–1929), last chancellor of the German empire (1918). His appointment followed Ludendorff's decision in Sept. 1918 to ask for an immediate armistice through a new government acceptable to the Allies, so that her exhausted armies could recover and then, if necessary, resume hostilities. Max agreed that Germany must enter peace negotiations in a strong position, but after sending his Peace Note on 5 Oct. he tried to procrastinate once it became clear that the Allies would accept no terms that might permit a German recovery. In spite of his dismissing Ludendorff, the arch-militarist and reactionary, Max got little support, largely because his equivocations over the armistice negotiations were incompatible with the war-weary mood of the German people. Moreover, although Germany's constitution and government were partially democratized and Max was theoretically supported by a centre-left majority in the Reichstag, his own cautious liberalism was out of place in the increasingly revolutionary atmosphere of German politics. He was unable to persuade the Kaiser to abdicate, which was vital to prove to the German people and the Allies that the government was on the road to a liberal democracy. Amid mounting proof that his people were dissatisfied with its bourgeois government, Max tried to forestall the leftward movement by a false announcement that the Kaiser had agreed to go. On 9 Nov., when the SPD members of his cabinet resigned, the government's fate was sealed. To preserve a fictitious legitimacy, Max handed over his powers to the social democrat, Ebert; at the same time he rejected Ebert's suggestion that he should serve as his deputy.

MAXENTIUS, M. AURELIUS VALERIUS (d. AD 312), son of the Roman Emperor Maximian, who ruled Italy in defiance of the legitimate emperors, Galerius and Licinius. He was defeated by Constantine the Great at the battle of the Milvian Bridge and drowned in the rout. At first Maxentius was supported by the Senate, and was able to overcome a revolt in North Africa. But after his death his name was vilified as that of a savage and oppressive ruler.

MAXIM GUN, single-barrelled, automatic machine-gun, developed in 1881 by Sir Hiram Maxim and adopted by the British army in 1888. It was used with devastating effect against massed formations in the First World War.

MAXIMIAN (M. AURELIUS MAXIMIANUS) (d. AD 310), Roman Emperor (*reg.* 285–305), who, as a colleague of Diocletian and cofounder of the Tetrarchic system, governed the west, with Constantius as his Caesar, and devoted himself to military restoration. He resigned unwillingly with Diocletian in 305, and retired to southern Italy. But in 306, when his son Maxentius was proclaimed Emperor at Rome, he resumed the title Augustus, and supporting Maxentius, co-operated with Constantine (307–9) in Gaul. After breaking with Maxentius, and later with Constantine, he was besieged at Marseilles. In due course he surrendered and was pardoned, but after a final attempt to capture the throne (310), he committed suicide.

MAXIMILIAN, Duke, later Elector of Bavaria (1573–1651), eldest son of Duke William V, of the Wittelsbach family, who succeeded to the compact duchy in the Upper Danube basin on his father's abdication (1597) and became the second most powerful German Catholic prince of the early 17th cent. He proved one of the most effective instruments of the Counter-Reformation. To curb the growth of Protestantism within the empire, he suppressed heresy within his own state, forcibly intervened against the citizens of Donauwörth (1608), and founded the Catholic League of ecclesiastical princes (1609) as a counter-balance to the Protestant Union during the Jülich–Berg crisis. He saw the league, however, not simply as a bulwark of Catholicism, but as a political counterpoise to Habsburg domination. He represented the constitutionalist spirit among the German princes, and when Frederick of the Palatinate accepted the Bohemian Crown he insisted that military measures be taken to unseat him. Thus the Bavarian army, under Count Tilly, was sent to expel Frederick from Bohemia, which it did at the battle of the White Mountain (1620), for which Maximilian received the

lands of the Upper and Lower Palatinate east of the Rhine, the title of elector (25 Feb. 1623), and the revenues of Upper Austria. Tilly's forces later defeated the Danes at Lütter (1626), forcing Christian to retire to Holstein.

However, during the next few years Maximilian was alarmed by the Emperor Ferdinand's arbitrary actions and military success. He objected because the Edict of Restitution was not submitted to the imperial diet for approval, and he regarded as unconstitutional Ferdinand's dismissal of the Duke of Mecklenburg and the cession of his duchy to the new imperial general, Wallenstein. Equally, he deplored the subservience of German to Spanish Habsburg interests in the Thirty Years War. Thus he succumbed to French diplomatic overtures at the diet of Ratisbon, forcing the emperor to dismiss Wallenstein and to restore Tilly to the command of the imperial forces (1630). Sweden's entry into the war proved disastrous for Maximilian. His army was destroyed and his duchy reduced to a pitiable state (1632–5), although after Gustavus Adolphus's death Bavarian military power was rallied under generals Franz von Mercy and Johann von Werth, who defeated the French several times (1643–5) and became the mainstay of the imperial position. While peace negotiations were held at Münster, Maximilian suffered further military defeats, *eg*, Jankau (1645) and the devastation of Bavaria (1646). By the peace of Westphalia he surrendered the Lower Palatinate to Frederick's son, but was confirmed in his possession of the imperial title and the Upper Palatinate (1648).

A ruthless if benevolent despot, Maximilian built up his financial reserves and created the standing army which sustained his war effort (1620–48), and encouraged education and the arts, though he exposed his peasantry to untold suffering. He married, first, a princess of Lorraine, who died childless, and secondly (1635) Archduchess Maria Anna, daughter of Ferdinand II, who gave him a son and heir, Ferdinand Maria (1636–79).   MKS

MAXIMILIAN II EMMANUEL, Elector of Bavaria (1662–1726), son of Elector Ferdinand Maria, who succeeded to the electoral throne in 1679. Pro-French in sympathy, he became a pensioner of Louis XIV and agreed to vote for him as the next Holy Roman emperor after Leopold I. Maximilian was soon drawn to Vienna, however, by the promise of the hand of Maria Antonia, daughter of the emperor and his Spanish wife, Margaret Theresa (1685), and he accepted a command in the imperial armies in Hungary, winning for himself the reputation of a dashing soldier by his capture of Belgrade (1688). After signing the treaty of Augsburg he fought on the imperial side in the War of the League of Augsburg (1689–1697), during which he was appointed governor of the Netherlands (1692).

Maximilian became involved in the disputed Spanish succession when his young son, Joseph Ferdinand, was named as heir in the partition treaty of 1698 and in Charles II of Spain's first will. But after the death of Joseph Ferdinand (1699) and the subsequent accession of Philip of Anjou to Spain (1701) Maximilian recognized him as Philip V and renewed his former French ties, while his brother Joseph Clement, electoral Abp of Cologne, put his lands at the disposal of France. In the ensuing War of the Spanish Succession the two brothers sided with France, Maximilian opening his campaign (1702) with the capture of Ulm on the Upper Danube. In May 1703 he joined with the French under Marshal Villars, planning to occupy the Tyrol, and won the first battle of Hochstadt (Sept. 1703), though later he quarrelled with Villars. The allied assault on Bavaria, and the defeat of the Franco-Bavarian forces at Donauwörth and Blenheim (13 Aug. 1704) were disastrous for Maximilian. He retired to Brussels, but was forced to retreat in the Netherlands (1705), was defeated at Ramillies (1706), and he and his brother were placed under the imperial ban (April 1706). After seeking refuge in France, he was restored to his Bavarian lands by the treaty of Baden (1714), but Louis failed to achieve his recognition as sovereign prince of the

Netherlands. Though a colourful and able ruler, Maximilian's constant involvement in war cost Bavaria the leadership of the German states.

H. Holborn, *A History of Modern Germany* (London, 1965).
MKS

MAXIMILIAN I (1459–1519), Emperor (*reg.* 1493–1519), Archduke of Austria and eldest son of Emperor Frederick III and Eleanor of Portugal, who was elected king of the Romans (1486) and inherited the Habsburg lands of Austria, Tyrol, Styria, Carinthia, Carniola, and the Upper Rhine on the death of his father in 1493. He assumed the title of emperor-elect in Trent Cathedral, but his plans for a papal coronation were never fulfilled.

Maximilian enjoyed a reputation as a humanist patron, *eg*, he founded the *Collegium Poetarum et Mathematicorum*, and as a soldier and a sportsman. Though obsessed by illusions of imperial grandeur, his charm and ability masked the fundamental weaknesses of his inheritance. The notorious poverty of the Habsburg Crown hampered his ambitious foreign policy. His first marriage (1477) at Ghent, to Mary of Burgundy, the greatest heiress in Europe, brought him many problems. While regent of the Netherlands after her death (1482) he faced the hostility of the Flemish burghers, who disliked his attempts to centralize government in contravention of the Great Privilege of 1477 and showed it by seizing him at Bruges (1488). The Burgundian inheritance also involved him in conflict with France, both in northern Europe (1477–82), where he enjoyed early success, *eg*, Guinegatte (1479), and in Italy, where he found his original enemy, the Venetians, were less formidable than the triumphant French. Encouraged by Ferdinand of Spain, he therefore joined the League of Venice, which was pledged to drive the French from Italy (1495), though he was delayed in Germany through the inadequacy of his supplies. His later attempts to check French ambitions in Italy were doomed by financial inadequacy. The 1496 campaign proved useless. He was forced to invest Louis XII of France with the imperial fief of Milan at the treaty of Blois (1504), hitherto held by Ludovico Sforza, the father of his second wife, Bianca Maria Sforza. He wavered over joining the Holy League (1510–12), and his final campaign in Milan (1516) ended in his unpaid troops mutinying. Venice, too, remained hostile and, despite the League of Cambrai (1508), his forces were defeated by the Venetians at Friuli (1508) and failed in the siege of Padua (1509).

Maximilian's reign was also marked by other failures. The Swiss war (1499) culminated in the defeat of his German troops at Dornach and the peace of Basle, by which he accepted the fact of Swiss independence. The German constitutional movement, led by Berthold of Henneberg (d. 1504), prevented Maximilian from harnessing the resources of the Reich to Habsburg interests, but equally the plans for federal *reichsreform*, debated at the Reichstag of Worms (1495), were largely blocked. His Habsburg interests prevented him from acceding permanently to an imperial government controlled by a council or *reichsregiment*, representing the German estates, and in 1502 he abolished it. Thus he was involved in protracted and usually unsatisfactory negotiations with the Reichstag, which hampered his freedom of action and left unfulfilled his hopes for a crusade against the Turks. In the War of the Landshut Succession (1504), however, he successfully asserted his imperial authority to restrain Rupert of the Palatinate and obtain Kufstein for the Habsburgs.

Though he achieved little as king and emperor, as Archduke of Austria Maximilian initiated Habsburg autocracy and aggrandizement. He strengthened authoritarian government within the Habsburg lands by the creation of the *Hofrat*, a central treasury, and through the principle of separation of functions. After the death of Matthias Corvinus (1490), he invaded Hungary and forced Wladislas Jagiello to return Austria to the Habsburgs and to agree that if he died without heirs Hungary should pass to them (1492). Maximilian thereafter exercised a close protectorate over Hungary and in 1506 concluded a second agreement providing for a double marriage between Wladislas's children and his grandchildren. This was confirmed when he met the Jagiello kings of Poland and Hungary at Vienna (1515), who accepted the marriage of Louis of Hungary-Bohemia to Mary of Habsburg and Louis's sister, Anne, to the Archduke Ferdinand. The death of Louis at Mohacz (1526) resulted in the union of Austria–Bohemia–Hungary under Ferdinand of Habsburg and the fruition of Maximilian's dynastic plans.

Meanwhile Habsburg prestige had been enhanced by the union of Maximilian's children by Mary of Burgundy with the royal houses of Castile and Aragon. His son, Philip (1478–1506), was married in 1496 to the Infanta Juana, and his daughter, Margaret (1480–1530), to the Infant Don Juan (1497). Despite the latter's premature death (1497) and Ferdinand of Aragon's remarriage (1505), the Spanish Crown eventually passed to Philip's son, Charles, Duke of Burgundy (1516). Maximilian's negotiations for Charles's election as King of the Romans were cut short by his own death.

R. W. Seton-Watson, *Maximilian I* (London, 1902).   MKS

MAXIMILIAN II (1527–76), Emperor (*reg.* 1564–76), eldest son of the Emperor Ferdinand I and Anne of Hungary, who was elected King of the Romans in 1563, despite a Habsburg family agreement of 1551 giving precedence to Philip of Spain, and was also chosen King of Bohemia and Hungary before his father's death in 1564, when he gained the archduchy of Austria and the imperial crown. He was educated by Lutheran tutors and preferred a policy of compromise and toleration to the strict religious orthodoxy of his Spanish Habsburg cousin. Thus, in 1568, in return for taxes to pay for anti-Turkish defences, he granted a degree of toleration to the Lutheran nobility of Austria, permitting them to follow the Confession of Augsburg and, from 1571, to use a new litany. Nor did he try to stamp out Protestantism in Hungary. Although less favourable to Calvinism, which was growing in the empire, he tried to persuade Philip II to end the reign of terror in the Netherlands (1568) and later (1575) mediated at a conference at Breda between representatives of Philip's governor, Requesens, and deputies of the estates of Holland and Zeeland.

Conscious of the strength of Habsburg family ties, which were to make him heir-presumptive to the Burgundian and Spanish lands from 1568, he married his cousin, Maria, a daughter of his uncle, Charles V, while his own daughter, Anne of Austria, was married to Philip II as his fourth and last wife. On the other hand, he hoped for peaceful reconciliation with the Valois and gave another daughter, Elizabeth of Austria, in marriage to Charles IX of France (1570).

Anxious, too, to avoid war with the Turks and with the principality of Transylvania, which was under Turkish suzerainty, he failed to exploit the death of Suleiman the Magnificent (1566) or to send help to the Hungarian defenders of Szigetvar, and signed an eight-year truce with Selim III (1568), by which he agreed to pay an annual tribute of 30,000 ducats and to recognize the right of Transylvania to elect its own successor, subject to Turkish confirmation.

Maximilian's hesitation lost the Polish candidature for his son Ernest (1572), but when the Polish throne again became vacant (1575) he pressed his claim against Stephen Bathory of Transylvania. While the latter took the initiative, Maximilian prepared to invade Poland, but died suddenly. He left six sons, of whom his eldest, Rudolph, became his sole inheritor.

B. Chudoba, *Spain and the Empire* (Chicago, 1952).   MKS

MAXIMILIAN (FERDINAND MAXIMILIAN JOSEPH) (1832–1867), Emperor of Mexico (*reg.* 1864–7), and brother of Emperor Francis Joseph of Austria. He married (1857) Princess Carlotta of Belgium. As archduke, Maximilian could have inherited the Austrian Crown, had he refused the Mexican throne proffered by the French emperor, Napoleon III, on behalf of the Mexican conservatives. Maximilian was an intelligent, liberally educated Habsburg.

Napoleon III responded to the entreaties of Mexican clerical-conservatives, who desired a monarch for Mexico at all costs, having lost the War of Reform (1858–60) to the liberals. The French for their part were anxious to collect debts and expand their empire, and their invasion of Mexico (1862) cleared the way for Maximilian's acceptance and his arrival in Mexico (June 1864). But he was hampered by Juárez's refusal to surrender or to resign the presidency, and by the clerical-conservatives' refusal to compromise in their demands on the empire. He refused to return Church lands confiscated by the liberals, and he tolerated a free press. He did restore slavery, however, but refused to compromise with the reactionary ecclesiastical hierarchy. The forces of Juárez in the North and the displeasure of the US, increasing as the Civil War drew to a close, forced the French gradually to withdraw their military support for the empire. Napoleon III had European priorities of greater importance by 1866 and he responded to a US threat by abandoning Maximilian. However, the emperor stayed on, hoping to the last for Mexican support against the liberals, but was forced to surrender (1867), and, following a court-martial, was shot at Querétaro.　　　　　　　　　　　　　　　　　　HDS

MAXIMINUS, C. IULIUS VERUS (d. AD 238), Roman Emperor (*reg.* 235–8), who overthrew Severus Alexander and governed for three years, at the same time campaigning successfully in the north. When challenged by the proclamation at Rome of Balbinus and Maximus, he advanced to meet them, but was murdered by his own troops at Aquileia.

MAXIMUM (29 Sept. 1793), decreed by the French Convention, fixing the price of essential goods, including food. The Jacobin government had no alternative but to give way to this demand of its supporters, the *sans-culottes*, who had been suffering severe economic distress since before the outbreak of the Revolution. After the fall of the Jacobin dictatorship, the *maximum* was quickly lifted and the market given free play.

MAXTON, JAMES (1885–1946), Scottish politician, who came to the fore during the First World War when he called for a general strike on Clydeside. He was chairman of the Independent Labour Party on several occasions between the wars and sat in the House of Commons from 1922 until his death. He was always to the left of labour politics, and led the ILP after it split from the Labour Party in 1932. He wrote *Lenin* (1932) and *If I Were Dictator* (1935).

MAXWELL, SIR JOHN GRENFELL (1859–1929), British soldier, who served overseas almost continuously from 1879 until the First World War. He was with Kitchener in the Sudan, became military governor of Pretoria during the Anglo-Boer War, and commanded British forces in Egypt (1908–12, 1914–16). He was sent to Ireland during the Easter Rebellion (1916) and there acted with sound judgement in difficult circumstances.

MAY COMMITTEE in Britain, departmental committee of enquiry, set up in March 1931 by the chancellor of the exchequer, Philip Snowden, to report on the deteriorating state of government finances and to propose ways of meeting the deficit. It was appointed in response to a demand by the Liberal Party, but Snowden welcomed the committee as a way of getting authoritative backing for his own economic policy (opposed by Labour MPs) and increased taxation (opposed by Conservatives). Economies were made necessary by the continuing drain on the exchequer to meet the deficit of the unemployment insurance fund in a time of rising unemployment.

Sir George May, the chairman, was secretary of the Prudential Insurance Co.; four of his colleagues were businessmen, and two represented labour. In July two reports were issued, together with proposals dealing with a budget deficit of £120 million in the current year. They made a gloomy analysis of Britain's trading position and caused a crisis of confidence in sterling. The majority report called for economies of £97 million by cuts in unemployment payments and the salaries of government employees. The minority report, signed by the two trade union members, made little impact, as it accepted the deficit of £120 million and merely suggested different plans to meet it, with fewer economies and more taxation. The reports were discussed during Aug. by a cabinet committee whose failure to agree on what action to take caused the break-up of the Labour government on 23 Aug. The final measures, introduced by Snowden in the National government's Economy Bill, were based heavily on the findings of the May Committee, and were half-way between the majority and minority reports.

MAY 4TH MOVEMENT (1919), political and cultural movement in China, which began as a series of student protests in Peking and other cities against concessions granted to Japan in China under the terms of the Versailles treaty. The demonstrations, directed specifically against pro-Japanese politicians, forced the Chinese government to withhold its signature from the treaty. After the first outburst, a new spirit of patriotism generated by the demonstrations developed into a general movement by the educated youth for wholesale rejection of the past, and for the introduction of modern, western ideas to strengthen China. The movement gradually polarized itself into political and cultural wings; the political wing became increasingly radical, and many of its members became interested in Marxism, while the literary wing concentrated on language reform and the creation of a vernacular literature.

MAY 30TH MOVEMENT (1925), Chinese workers' movement. British police in Shanghai shot dead a number of Chinese workers taking part in a communist-organized demonstration. The incident aroused national protest, and strikes in foreign-owned enterprises. Further killings of demonstrators in Canton led directly to the Hong Kong strike. The movement extended political participation from students to workers and merchants for the first time.

MAYAS, peoples indigenous to the Yucatan peninsula, consisting of most of modern Guatemala, and British Honduras. Of uncertain antiquity, Maya culture during its classical period (*c.* AD 325–925) was the most impressive of the Indian high civilizations. In the Petén area of lowland Guatemala, the Mayas evolved a ceremonial civilization centred in great temple cities—Copán, Palenque, Piedras Negras, Uaxactún, and Tikal. These were city-states, ruled by priests and nobles, supported by maize-growing peasants, and politically largely autonomous. The principal buildings were temple-pyramids and massive, many-chambered community houses used by priests and novices. The notable features of these buildings include an unsurpassed richness and inventiveness of sculptured decoration, and the roofs supported by corbelled vaulting, which are unique among the Amerindian peoples, who did not discover the true arch. Most interesting and characteristic of all are the commemorative stelae or calendar stones. These great monolithic shafts, covered with glyphs and sculpture figures in relief, reveal much about Maya chronology, largely because Maya religion was preoccupied with astronomy to measure time, to predict the future, and to fix propitious dates for sacrifices and major undertakings. A numerous and highly trained priesthood collected extensive astronomical knowledge, and the resulting calendar was complex and remarkably accurate. Since the Mayas, alone among Amerindian peoples, also possessed an embryonic form of writing, using glyphs or symbols and not mere pictographs, they recorded on their stelae astronomical and calendric information and (presumably) historical data. At present, only the calendric glyphs can be reliably deciphered to tentatively date Maya sites. The Mayas were also remarkable mathematicians, using a system of numeration by position involving the concept of zero.

In the 9th cent. the temple cities were abandoned, and often suddenly, as half-finished buildings attest. The cause was perhaps a peasant revolution, when the burden of building temples and supporting an increasingly esoteric priestly hierarchy grew intolerable. Whatever the cause, the Maya cities of lowland Guatemala were swallowed up by the forest.

The cities of northern Yucatan, peripheral during the Classic Period, survived only to fall prey to foreign infiltration and conquest. During this period (975–1200), Mexican groups entered the area, perhaps as mercenaries, and came to rule. A league of cities was established, dominated first by Chichen Itzá (to *c.* 1200) and then by Mayapán (to *c.* 1440), which controlled the whole of northern Yucatan. The Mexicans brought with them Toltec religion and culture, *eg*, the feathered serpent god, Quetzalcoatl (Kukulcán), human sacrifice, and militarism. The invaders were also great, though unimaginative, builders. By the 15th cent., when the hegemony of Mayapán ended and the area split into warring fragments, the Mexican rulers had become absorbed by the Mayas, but the cost was an alarming cultural decline. Disorder and progressive barbarization preceded the arrival of the Spaniards. For all that, conquest was stoutly resisted, and the last Maya outpost in the Guatemalan jungles did not fall until 1697. Maya accomplishments were then almost forgotten until they were rediscovered in 1839–41 by the American diplomat, John L. Stephens.

Sylvanus G. Morley, *The Ancient Maya* (Stanford, CA, 1957). J. Eric Thompson, *The Rise and Fall of Maya Civilization* (Norman, OK, 1954).   FPB

MAYENNE, CHARLES DE GUISE, Duke of (1554–1611), scion of the French noble house of Guise, who succeeded to the leadership of the family and of the Holy or Catholic League on the murder of his brothers, Henry, Duke of Guise, and the Cardinal de Guise (Dec. 1588). The league recognized Mayenne as lieutenant-governor of France, repudiating Henry III, but he was defeated by Henry of Navarre at Arques (1589) and Ivry (1590) and lost the support of the league's popular wing by arresting several members of the Committee of Sixteen in Paris (1591). He had hopes of the French Crown for himself, but these were not supported by the league's paymaster, Philip II of Spain. In 1593 Mayenne summoned the states general on Philip's request to establish the succession rights of the Infanta Isabella Clara Eugenia, but Henry of Navarre's conversion to Catholicism thwarted this move. Mayenne submitted to Henry with other Catholic nobles and dissolved the league (1594).

MAYFLOWER COMPACT (21 Nov. 1620), document drawn up and signed by the 41 male adult Pilgrims on the *Mayflower*, anchored off Cape Cod, in North America. The compact joined them in a civil body with the right to make laws and appoint officers for the general good of the colony. The only record of the document is in an anonymous journal of the voyage, *Mourts Relation*. It remained Plymouth colony's basic charter until 1691, when the colony was absorbed by MA.

MAYHEW, HENRY (1812–87), British author, journalist, and social investigator. He was, with Mark Lemon, the first editor of *Punch* (1841), and later published 76 letters about the London poor as part of the *Morning Chronicle's* nationwide survey of poverty (1849–50). Mayhew was uniquely qualified to capture the confidence of the poor, from whom he obtained superb interviews, reported verbatim. His survey (republished 1861–2) shocked polite society. Although ill-constructed, inconclusive, discursive, and faulty in its statistics, it attacked the political economy of the day so vigorously that the *Morning Chronicle* grew alarmed and discontinued the series. As a pioneer of systematic social investigation, Mayhew showed a compassionate sensitivity towards the realities of working-class life.

MAYHEW, JONATHAN (1720–66), American minister and patriot, whose liberal theological views brought him into controversy with Jonathan Edwards, and caused him to be excluded from the Boston Association of Congregational Ministers. He shared in the theories of liberty of his friends, James Otis and John Adams, and his sermon, 'The Snare Broken', on the Stamp Act, gave religious sanction to civil disobedience and urged the uniting of the colonies in opposition to Britain.

MAYNE, CUTHBERT (1544–77), English Catholic seminary priest (*ie*, one trained on the continent rather than in England), who was martyred under Elizabeth I. He was trained at William Allen's seminary at Douai, and returned to his native West Country (1576), where he was arrested, tried, and executed for high treason (1577).

MAYNOOTH COLLEGE GRANT (1845), proposal by Sir Robert Peel to conciliate the powerful Irish Catholic clergy by increasing the longstanding subsidy to the Catholic College at Maynooth from £9000 to £26,000 a year. The suggestion split the cabinet and delayed Peel's final decision. Gladstone felt compelled to resign the presidency of the board of trade on a point of principle, since he had condemned the original grant in his book on *Church and State*. The issue created a storm in England, where Catholic Emancipation and the Oxford Movement seemed to threaten the Anglican Church. The Tories' Romantic Young England Movement broke up over the question of the grant. The bill was passed in April 1845, Gladstone surprisingly voting for it. Peel's bid to appease Irish Catholicism was overtaken by the threat of famine and the Corn Laws crisis (1845–6).

'MAYNOOTH, PARDON OF' (1535), in Ireland, execution of the survivors, 'as an example to others', of the siege of Maynooth during the rebellion of Lord Offaly by the lord deputy, Sir William Skeffington. The 'pardon' served as a precedent for the rest of the Tudor Irish wars.

MAYO, RICHARD SOUTHWELL BOURKE, 6th Earl of (Irish) (1822–72), chief secretary for Ireland on three occasions before becoming viceroy and governor-general of India (1869–72). In 1869 he established friendly relations at Ambala with Sher Ali of Afghanistan. He developed roads, railways, and canals, created a department of commerce and agriculture, and improved Indian finances by introducing financial decentralization. He founded the Mayo College of Ajmir for the education of the sons of Indian chiefs. He was murdered by a Pathan convict while visiting the Andaman Islands.

MAYORAZGO, legal device employed in Spain and colonial Latin America whereby a landed estate was entailed, thus limiting succession to the eldest son or nearest kinsman under the rule of primogeniture as an inalienable inheritance. Holders automatically acquired noble status, and the device helped to perpetuate a landholding aristocracy.

MAYSVILLE ROAD VETO (1830) in US, issued by President Jackson to defeat a congressional bill authorizing federal aid for a road from Maysville to Lexington, KY. Jackson argued that it was unconstitutional for the federal government to aid schemes of a local nature, the Maysville road falling entirely within the state of KY.

MAZARIN (GIULIO MAZARINI), Cardinal (1602–61), Italian-born French diplomat and politician, who served France for 19 years, as the leading minister during Louis XIII's last months, the regency of his widow, Anne of Austria, and the first decade of Louis XIV's reign. He was educated at Rome by the Jesuits and became a captain in the Pontifical Guard (1624). His first venture into diplomacy was the negotiation of a papal truce in the Mantuan conflict (1630) between Spain, France, and Savoy. After winning

Richelieu's favour he came to Paris as nuncio-extraordinary (1634), and though recalled to Rome (1636–9), he so impressed Richelieu that he was invited to return to France (1639), becoming a naturalized citizen (1640) and receiving a cardinal's hat (1641). Before his death (1642) Richelieu had recommended Mazarin to Louis XIII as his successor, which advice the king accepted by naming him a member of a future council of regency. In fact, after Louis's death (1643) Anne of Austria became sole regent, but she ruled throughout Louis XIV's minority with Mazarin's advice, showing both respect for his opinions and affection for him personally. It is generally thought that a secret marriage took place between them, and the queen-regent appointed him supervisor of the young king's education.

Mazarin has been blamed for that complex outburst of opposition—popular, *parlementaire*, and aristocratic—known as the *Frondes* (1648–52). The financial burden of the Thirty Years War and Richelieu's autocratic government had alienated the office-holders and the privileged, but it was the foreign cardinal-favourite who inherited the odium. He and his finance minister, d'Hemery, were condemned in a flood of pamphlets during the episode called the *Mazarinades*. He submitted to the *parlementaire* demands of June 1648, but with the court fled to St Germain (Jan. 1649). Though forced to arrest the leaders of the aristocratic opposition, Condé, Conti, and Longueville (1650), he was unable to regain control of the kingdom, was driven from Paris, declared a corrupt counsellor, and took refuge in Cologne. Only after Anne declared Louis XIV of age (7 Sept. 1651), and the pro-Condé rebellion in Paris ended in the battle of St Antoine (July 1652), was royal authority restored. Mazarin returned to the capital in March 1653.

In the sphere of foreign policy his success was more conspicuous. From 1643 he worked for the fruitful conclusion of the Thirty Years War at the Münster negotiations, for the isolation of Spain from the empire, and for the acquisition of the Spanish Netherlands by France. By the peace of Westphalia (1648) France received the sovereignty of Metz, Toul, and Verdun, Alsace on the left bank of the Rhine, and Philippsburg and Breisach on the right bank, and assumed the role of guarantor of the German constitution. Later he intervened in the imperial election of Archduke Leopold, delaying the proceedings for a year and goading the German princes to insist on a capitulation limiting Leopold's authority (1657–8). He also gave French support to the anti-Habsburg League of the Rhine. Mazarin brought about a further shift in foreign policy by opening negotiations with Cromwell and concluding a treaty with England (Oct. 1655), which resulted in Anglo-Spanish hostilities. Simultaneously, Lionne was sent to Madrid to conclude secret terms with Spain (1656), but these negotiations proving abortive, the Franco-Spanish war continued. Peace negotiations were restarted in Nov. 1658, leading to Mazarin's meetings with Don Haro on the Isle of Pheasants and the conclusion of the peace of the Pyrenees (Nov. 1659). This was Mazarin's final diplomatic coup. France won Roussillon, Cerdagne, and nearly all of Artois. A marriage was arranged between Louis XIV and Philip IV's elder daughter, Maria Theresa (1660), through which their grandson, Philip, Duke of Anjou, was subsequently to succeed to the Spanish empire (1701). Although the status quo was restored in Italy by the treaty, Mazarin won the alliance of the Duke of Modena and Spanish power was patently crumbling there.

Mazarin's death ended half a century of ministerial domination and initiated another of Louis XIV's personal governments.   MKS

MAZDAKITES, followers of Mazdak in 5th-cent. Iran, who wanted economic and social equality. The movement caused, or may simply have been blamed for, violent social disturbances and was suppresed (*c.* 528).

MAZEPPA, IVAN STEPANOVICH (1644–1709), Russian soldier and hetman of the Ukraine Cossacks, who won the confidence of Peter the Great. In 1705 he opened negotiations with Stanislas Leszczynski of Poland and later (1708) sided with Charles XII of Sweden and openly declared himself against Peter. He joined Charles on the Dneiper with minimal forces, but was unable to prevent Menshikov from storming the Cossack fortress of Baturin, and in the following year fled with Charles to Ochakov after the Swedish defeat at Poltava (July 1709).

MAZORCA, political police organization (1830s–1852) of the Argentine dictator Juan Manuel de Rosas, notorious for its ubiquity and brutality. The name derives from the Spanish for 'ear of corn', denoting unity; but it was also said to imply '*más horca*' ('more gallows').

MAZRUI, Omani family who provided nine governors of Mombasa (1736–1837). Originally appointed by the Sultan of Oman, they made themselves independent in 1741. Their dominions included a strip of coast 40 miles (64 kms) north and 60 miles (96 kms) south of Mombasa, and the island of Pemba. In their efforts to maintain their independence the Mazrui obtained unofficial British protection from 1824 to 1826, but were evicted from Fort Jesus, Mombasa, in 1837. The survivors fled to Gazi and the last governor's son, Mbarak bin Rashid, from the time he became of age until his expulsion by the British in 1896, was in intermittent revolt.

MAZYADIDS, line of Arab amirs established at Al-Hilla in Iraq. The Banu Mazyad belonged to the tribe of Asad and lived west of the Tigris in the region extending from Al-Kufa to Hit. Their chief, Abu'l-Hasan Ali, received from the Buyids the title of amir in AD 1012–13. Under Sadaka ibn Mansur ibn Dubays (?*reg.* 1086–1108), the Mazyadids extended their domination over much of southern Iraq, including Basra. Their regime ended in 1163.

MAZZINI, GIUSEPPE (1805–72), Italian patriot and republican, who joined (1830) the Carbonari, but six months later was betrayed and banished from Italy. In March 1831 he established a new revolutionary society, 'Young Italy', which aimed at the unification of Italy under a republican form of government. Mazzini hoped to elevate Italian patriotism to a new moral plane, but he failed to interest Charles Albert in leading the movement for independence and after two abortive revolutionary expeditions (1833–4), he retired to Switzerland (and in 1837 to London), where he became the most untiring political agitator in Europe. 'Young Europe', which he founded in 1834, aimed at a republican brotherhood of nations working together in Christian harmony. In 1848 he returned to Italy to liberate Milan and in March 1849 he became head of the triumvirate which controlled the Roman Republic. When the republic fell (1849), he returned to London, where he planned risings at Mantua (1852), Milan (1853), Genoa (1857), and Leghorn (1857). Unable to accept unification under the monarchical leadership of Sardinia, he never again openly returned to Italy and continued to fight what had become a lost cause. A utopian idealist, he had great organizing ability and in the early stages of the Risorgimento he unified and vitalized the struggling aspirations of the Italian peoples; but his solution of a republic without foreign assistance was not in accordance with political realities and Italian unity was eventually achieved by the *realpolitik* of Cavour.   MR

MBOYA, THOMAS JOSEPH (1931–69), Kenyan politician, who was a Luo from Rusinga Island, Lake Victoria. He was a prominent trade union leader, and became secretary-general of the Kenya Federation of Labour and treasurer of the Kenya African Union. He was not an active supporter of the '*Mau Mau*' rising, but first showed his ability as a leader in the Mombasa dock strike (1955), when he secured a negotiated settlement. As an elected member of the Kenya

Legislative Council, he played a principal part in the negotiations with Britain that led to self-government and independence (1963); after which he became minister of justice and constitutional affairs. He helped to form the Kenya African National Union and was its secretary-general. He was later concerned with plans for Kenya's economic future and was minister of economic planning and development at the time of his murder on 5 July 1969.

MEADE, GEORGE GORDON (1815–72), US soldier, who fought in the Seminole and Mexican wars. In 1863 he succeeded Joseph Hooker as commander of the Army of the Potomac, defeated Lee at Gettysburg (1–3 July 1863), but was criticized for allowing him to escape. He held command in the South during Reconstruction.

MEAL TUB PLOT (1679) in England, Catholic plot designed to prove that the Popish Plot was really a 'Presbyterian plot' against the monarchy and the Catholics. It is based on forged treasonable letters planted to incriminate the Earl of Shaftesbury, but it backfired, and the discovery of papers similar to the forged letters in the meal tub of a famous catholic midwife, Elizabeth Cellier, confirmed suspicions of a plot to defame the Whigs.

MEANJIN PAPERS, Australian literary journal founded (1940) by C. B. Christesen (1912–), first published in Brisbane, later in Melbourne, where its name was changed to *Meanjin Quarterly*. It published, often for the first time, virtually all the major Australian writers of its period.

MEANS TEST in Britain, imposed by the National government (Sept. 1931) as part of the cut in government spending. These cuts were the culmination of the international monetary crisis (1929–31). The Slump, with its long-term unemployment problem, meant that the existing insurance provision was inadequate. A system of transitional payments was therefore devised. Orthodox financial opinion decreed that the cost of these should be met without borrowing or large increases in taxation. Thus those who applied for benefit had to submit to a means test to prove their needs.

Although financed by the treasury, the means test was administered by the former Poor Law administrators operating at local level; this caused differing local rates of relief and consequently further bitterness. The means test was welcomed by Conservatives and Liberals, but given a hostile reception by Labour, who condemned it as an attack on already poverty-stricken workers and saw it as a further sign of Ramsay MacDonald's 'betrayal' of socialism. It was made uniform by the Unemployment Act (1934) and was finally ended in that form by the Labour government (1948).

MEANY, GEORGE (1894–), US labour leader who became president of the New York State Federation of Labor (1934–1940). His skill in public relations and knowledge of labour's problems won him the position of secretary-treasurer of the American Federation of Labor (1940–52). During the Second World War he was active on government boards and after the war led the fight against US affiliation with the World Federation of Trade Unions. He was elected president of the AF of L (1952–5) and worked for the reunification of the US labour movement. A merger with the Congress of Industrial Organizations was agreed (1955) and he was elected president of the combined AF of L–CIO (1955–).

MECCA (MAKKA), perhaps the 'Macoraba' of Ptolemaeus (cf. South Arabian *miqrab*, a temple), situated in the Tihama region of the southern Hijaz, some 50 miles (80 kms) from the Red Sea. Mecca, even before the rise of the Prophet Muhammad, was a religious centre venerated throughout western Arabia. The town was under the control of the Arab tribe of Quraysh, who acted as the guardians of the religious shrine known as the Ka'ba. It grew prosperous through the pilgrimages made to the Ka'ba, and its location on the important commercial route extending from the Yemen northward through the Hijaz to Palestine.

MECHANICS INSTITUTES in Britain, were established in Glasgow and Birmingham at the end of the 18th cent. to provide mainly technical instruction for craftsmen and others working with machinery. They received support in their early years from Francis Place, Henry Brougham, and Thomas Hodgkin, and in 1823 the London Mechanics Institute was founded. Each institute was self-supporting and possessed a reading-room and library. The *Mechanics Magazine* was first published in 1827. By 1851 there were over 700 such institutes, whose lectures and courses were cultural as well as technical.

The movement afforded a means of self-education and self-improvement for working and lower middle-class men which was not provided for them by the state until the beginning of the 20th cent. It also established a pattern of local control which continued when adult education classes and public libraries were provided.

MECKLENBURG, German duchy which became Lutheran (1549) and during the Thirty Years War was taken from Wallenstein by the Swedes, to whom Wismar was ceded in 1648. The duchy was subdivided in 1701.

MEDES, Iranian peoples first mentioned in an Assyrian record of a campaign in c. 836 BC. They were settled near Lake Urmiah in the Hamadan region. At first they were organized in tribes with fortified towns and castles and mainly fought each other. The Assyrians made frequent raids against them, perhaps to obtain horses, for which the Medes were famous. An attempt was made (c. 700) to unite the Medes, but this was probably thwarted by the invasions of Scythian and Cimmerian tribes into the region at this time, and it was not until c. 673 that the Median chief Kashtaritu (Greek, Phaortes) united the Medes and made Hamadan their centre. In c. 625 the Scythians conquered Media, which remained their vassal for 28 years, during which time Cyaxares, the Median king, reorganized the army, annexed the land round Lake Urmiah, and finally drove out the Scythians. The Persians subsequently submitted to the Medes and in 612 the Assyrian empire was destroyed with the help of Babylonia, and the eastern provinces of Assyria were annexed. In 585 the frontier with Lydia was fixed on the Halys river, and about the same time Urartu probably fell to the Medes. The eastern extent of the empire is unknown, but it seems probable that conquered lands were only loosely governed. The last Median king was Astyages, who was defeated by Cyrus the Great (549) and the Median empire became part of the Persian empire. Little archaeological work has been done in the area of ancient Media, but it seems likely that Median institutions and customs strongly influenced later Persian developments.   JKG

MEDICI, COSIMO DE' (1389–1464), Florentine banker, patron of the arts and de facto ruler of Florence who founded a dynasty that ruled Tuscany until 1737. He discovered that he could only preserve his business position by securing and keeping political power. His rivals had imprisoned and exiled him in 1433, but lucky electoral change allowed him to return in 1434. He exiled his opponents and thereafter so manipulated the Florentine constitution that his supporters continued to dominate the government. His son Piero (d. 1469) and his grandson Lorenzo (1449–92) succeeded him in effective control of the state. As a munificent patron of scholars and artists he was associated with many of the enterprises that made Florence the leader of Renaissance Italy in arts and learning. The buildings that he created or helped to finance included the church of San Lorenzo (the parish church of the Medici), built by Brunelleschi, the Dominican convent of San Marco, which Cosimo also endowed with a splendid library, and the monastery at Fiesole.

MEDICI, GIOVANNI DE' (1360–1429), Florentine banker and founder of the great fortune of his family, which enabled his son Cosimo to become the virtual ruler of Florence in 1434. In 1397 Giovanni created an independent bank, which specialized in transacting papal financial business at Rome. He became one of the richest Florentines, but avoided political entanglements. Although personally without intellectual interests, he ensured an excellent education for his sons, which contributed to Cosimo's subsequent political success.

MEDICI, LORENZO DE' (1449–92), Florentine banker who was the third member of his family to be the virtual ruler of Florence, a position based not on the holding of any formal office, but on effective control over the state. To maintain it the Medici had continually to manipulate the existing constitution and their position depended essentially on the willing collaboration of a large group of the wealthier Florentine families as well as acceptance by the rest of the population. Lorenzo's grandfather, Cosimo (d. 1464), had first achieved this position in 1434. When Lorenzo succeeded to it in 1469, on the death of his father, Piero, it seemed outwardly beyond challenge. But he was less wise than his predecessors in avoiding the appearance of power as well as having its substance and he excessively abused his position. In 1478 a plot to assassinate him failed but his brother was killed. By the time of Lorenzo's prematurely early death the regime was very unpopular and his son Piero was easily overthrown in 1494 when the approach of a French army encouraged the malcontents to change the government. Lorenzo also allowed the Medici Bank, the source of Cosimo's great wealth, to fall into decline. He wrote some fascinating Italian poetry and was a discriminating patron of scholars. The period of his rule was one of great progress in the arts and in learning in Florence.

MEDICI, PIERO DE' (1470–1503), Florentine leader and eldest son of Lorenzo de' Medici, who succeeded (1492) on his father's death to his position as the virtual ruler of Florence. He rapidly alienated many of the leading Florentine families, on whose support his father's rule had depended. When in the autumn of 1494 King Charles VIII advanced into Italy, Piero was taken by surprise. He failed to collaborate with his allies in resisting the French and in a panic hastened to the French camp in Oct. 1494, where he offered to open the principal Florentine fortresses and harbours to the French. The outraged Florentines refused to agree to this and, after a futile attempt to raise partisan support, Piero fled from Florence with his brothers on 9 Nov., thus ending 60 years of Medici rule. He was killed while fighting for the French nine years later.

MEDICI CHAPEL, 16th-cent. funerary chapel in honour of four of the Medici, designed by Michelangelo, and one of the first Mannerist buildings in Europe. On the lid of the sarcophagi are statues representing Day, Night, Dawn, and Evening, and not the Virtues, as was traditional. It is the first and only funerary chapel of the Renaissance in which pagan and Christian themes are completely fused.

MEDINA, known before the advent of Islam as Yathrib (the Jathrippa of Ptolemaeus), lies in a well-watered area of the northern Hijaz, near the mountain range which separates the Najd from the Tihama. Like Mecca, Yathrib was situated on the commercial route running from the Yemen through western Arabia to Palestine. It was also an agricultural centre of considerable importance. Yathrib, in the period before the arrival there (AD 622) of the Prophet Muhammad, was under the control of the Arab tribes of Aws and Khazraj. Also present in the town itself and in the adjacent lands were several Judaized Arab tribes—the Banu Qaynuqa, the Banu Nadir, and the Banu Qurayza. Yathrib, at this time, was rent with the feuds between the Aws and the Khazraj, the Jewish elements maintaining a precarious balance of power in the area.

MEDINA ANGARITA, ISAÍAS (1897–1953), Venezuelan general and president of Venezuela (1941–5), a transitional figure between the old Venezuelan *caudillos*, such as Cipriano Castro and Juan Vicente Gómez, and the later liberal democrats. As such, he was disliked by both sides. In 1945 he was overthrown by followers of the Democratic Action Party (AD), which had combined with some elements of the army.

MEDINA DEL CAMPO, medieval Castilian town, whose importance in the 15th–16th cents rested on its great wool fairs and its role as a financial centre for foreign exchange. Although badly burned during the revolt of the *Communeros* (1520), it none the less gained economically by the integration of all the Castilian fairs there (1567–8) and enjoyed considerable prosperity until the late 16th cent. When the wool markets of northern Europe were disrupted by Philip II's wars and the Spanish economy became increasingly dependent upon Seville's monopoly of American treasure imports, Medina del Campo began to decline. It never recovered from the royal bankruptcy of 1596 and the transference of the court from Valladolid back to Madrid (1606).

MEDINA ZAVALA, JOSÉ TORIBIO (1852–1930), Chilean historian and bibliographer, noted for his works on the early press in Latin America and his biographies of emminent Chileans.

MEDINACELI, JUAN FRANCISCO TOMAS DE LA CERDA, Duke of (d. 1691), Valencian grandee, who succeeded Don Juan José as the first minister of Charles II of Spain (1680). As president of the council of the Indies he tried to introduce economic and colonial reforms, continuing an unpopular deflationary policy, but the appointment of the Count of Oropesa as president of the council of Castile (1684) led to his resignation (1685).

MEDINA-SIDONIA, ALONSO PEREZ DE GUZMAN, Duke of (1550–1615), Spanish grandee, son-in-law of the Princess of Eboli, captain-general of Andalusia, and successor to Admiral Santa Cruz as commander of the Spanish armada in the Enterprise of England (1588). Medina-Sidonia has been made the scapegoat for this disaster, but modern scholarship suggests that he was a brave and conscientious leader, though inexperienced at sea. He successfully brought the great Spanish fleet up the English Channel to Calais roads, but was unable to rendezvous with Farnese because of the shallow waters, and with his ships badly damaged by English gunnery and fireships led the retreat homewards via the northern coasts of the British Isles. He arrived at Santander a sick man (23 Sept. 1588) with the remnants of his battered fleet, and though he recovered Philip II respected his promise never to send him to sea again.

MEDISM, ancient Greek pejorative term for collaboration with the Persians, whom they identified with the Medes. In the Persian Wars most northern and central Greek states 'medized' during Xerxes' invasion (480), chiefly because resistance was hopeless; but some elsewhere threatened 'medism' to further local rivalries, *eg*, Aegina against Athens (491) and Argos against Sparta (480–79). Individuals or groups within states likewise sought Persian help, *eg*, the Thessalian Aleuadae, Demaratus of Sparta, and Hippias of Athens. After victory (479), the Greeks abandoned threats to punish 'medizing' states, and from the great Peloponnesian War (431–404) onwards leading states unashamedly sought and used Persian support, while acknowledging Persian rule of the Asiatic Greeks.

MEDITERRANEAN AGREEMENTS (1887), informal diplomatic exchanges between Britain, Austria–Hungary, and Italy, the first of which committed them to the preservation of the status quo in the Mediterranean, the Aegean, and the Black Sea, and the second to the status quo in the Near East and the free passage of the Black Sea straits. The first agreement was mainly directed against France, giving Britain diplomatic support in Egypt and encouraging Italy's hope for Tripoli. The second was anti-Russian. Bismarck welcomed British support for his fellow members of the Triple Alliance (1882). But the agreements, the nearest that Britain came to an alliance with a group of powers in peacetime, were not only tenuous, but short-lived. They were abandoned after 1892, but had achieved the result of encouraging the rapprochement between France and Russia which was the nucleus of a second armed camp in Europe.

MEDWAY DISASTER, THE (1667), in England. Towards the end of the Second Anglo-Dutch War, in June 1667, a Dutch fleet under De Ruyter anchored off the mouth of the Thames river. It was able to do so with impunity because the English government, in the interests of economy, had not fitted out a fleet for operations in that campaign. On the morning of 23 June a detachment under Van Ghent burst through the boom or chain at Gillingham and burnt six ships of the line, towed two others away, the *Unity* and the flagship *Royal Charles*, and did much other damage. The whole incident was seen as a national humiliation by the English and as a tremendous victory by the Dutch. The following month the treaty of Breda was signed, bringing the war to an end.

MEERUT CONSPIRACY CASE (1929–33), trial of 32 Indian trade union leaders and officials, most of whom were connected with the Communist Party of India and some with the Indian National Congress. The prosecution was brought by the government of India to break communist influence among Indian workers. It dragged on for more than three years, and eight months elapsed before appeals arising from it were heard. The sentences, ranging from 3 years' rigorous imprisonment to transportation for life, were drastically reduced on appeal, 3 years' rigorous imprisonment becoming the maximum sentence. The trial disrupted the Communist Party for a time, but new leaders emerged and the platform with which the communists were provided by the court probably increased their standing and popularity.

MEGACLES, recurrent name in the ancient Athenian Alcmeonid family and by *c.* 420 BC regarded at Athens as the aristocratic name *par excellence*. The earliest known Megacles, who was archon *c.* 632, was responsible for the murder of Cylon. His grandson, Megacles, married (*c.* 570) Agariste, daughter of Cleisthenes of Sicyon, and led the men of the coast against Peisistratus. After the latter's victory, *c.* 546, he went into exile. In the 5th cent. a Megacles was ostracized (486), another's grand-daughter, Isodice, married Cimon, and yet another's daughter, Deinomache, married Cleinias and bore Alcibiades (*c.* 450). Later the name appears as that of an Olympic victor (436) and as secretary to the Treasurers of Athena (428).

MEGALOPOLIS, ancient Greek city, near the site of the modern town. It was built in 370 BC as the centre of the new Arcadian League and to protect southern Arcadians against Sparta. After the early break-up of the league, it remained an independent city-state, relying first on Theban help, and then on Macedonian. After it had joined the Achaean League (235), it was attacked by the Spartans Cleomenes III (228, 223) and Nabis (204–203). Nevertheless it played a leading role in Achaean politics, especially under Philopoemen, until the Roman annexation (146 BC).

MEGARA, ancient Greek city-state on the isthmus of Corinth. Early rivalry with Corinth over borderland and colonial sites in Sicily (*c.* 730–700 BC) resulted in a loose alliance between Megara and Miletus and the establishment in the 7th cent. of important colonies in the Black Sea and its approaches, *eg*, Byzantium. The tyrant Theagenes attempted unsuccessfully to interfere in Athens through his son-in-law Cylon (*c.* 630), and soon after 600 Salamis was lost to Athens.

In the 5th cent. Megara at first sought an Athenian alliance against Corinth (*c.* 460), but later changed sides (446). Despite exclusion from Athenian-controlled markets by the 'Megarian Decree' (432), repeated Athenian incursions, and the occupation of Nisaea (424–410), the Megarian oligarchs remained true to Corinth. In the 4th cent. Megara prospered and became a refuge for early followers of Socrates.

MEGARIAN DECREE (*c.* 432 BC) promulgated by the Athenian people was inspired by Pericles and prohibited the Megarians from trading at any port in the Athenian alliance. It was one of the immediate pretexts of the great Peloponnesian War.

MEGASTHENES (*fl.* 4th–3rd cents BC), Greek who stayed at the court of the Indian king, Chandragupta Maurya, at Pataliputra (mod. Patna) as an envoy of Seleucus Nikator (*reg.* 312–280 BC), probably after the treaty concluded between the two kings in 303. Megasthenes wrote an account of India which is now lost, but from which numerous quotations were made by later Greek and Roman authors. On the basis of these fragments it seems that Megasthenes, though taking a sympathetic interest in India, was credulous and lacked understanding. The fragments are therefore more important for the knowledge they supply of Greek attitudes towards India than for any other information.

MÈGE MOURIÈS, HIPPOLYTE (1817–80), French inventor, who won (1869) the government's prize for an acceptable and economic substitute for butter, of which there was a shortage. Improvements by F. Bonder in 1872 rendered the product more palatable; it was called margarine, because of its pearly texture (Latin *margita*, a pearl). Margarine manufacture was soon established throughout Europe and the US.

MEHEMMED I (*reg.* AD 1413–21), Ottoman Sultan, son of Bayezid I. After the battle of Ankara against Timur Beg in 1402, Mehemmed established himself at Amasya in Asia Minor. The years 1402–13 were a time of interregnum, when the Ottomans had no universally recognized sultan. Mehemmed, during these years, was involved in a conflict with his brothers and rivals for the throne, 'Isa Çelebi, Süleyman Çelebi, and Musa Çelebi. His success in defeating them and in reuniting the Ottoman territories under his own control was due in no small degree to his close identification with the old traditions of the Ottoman state. As sultan, Mehemmed I still had numerous difficulties to face, above all the great revolt of Shaykh Badr al-Din and the continuing disturbances centred around a claimant for the throne, said to be a son of Bayezid I and known to the Ottomans as Dözme (False) Mustafa—disturbances which continued after the death of Sultan Mehemmed well into the reign of his son and successor, Sultan Murad II.

MEHEMMED II (*reg.* AD 1451–81), Ottoman Sultan, first raised to the throne late in 1444, when his father, Murad II, went into retirement. Tensions at the Ottoman court led Murad II to resume (1446) the office of sultan, Mehemmed being relegated to Manisa in western Asia Minor. These tensions arose in no small measure from differences of outlook between the elements of the central regime, representing the older traditions of the Ottoman state, and the slave elements of the imperial household advocating a vigorous drive towards consolidation within the empire.

Mehemmed II, once he had become effective sultan on the death of Murad in 1451, identified himself with the more forward-looking elements around the throne. In 1453 he achieved the conquest of Constantinople—a triumph which earned him the name of Fatih (the Conqueror) and united in the most effective manner possible the two halves, Asiatic and European, of the Ottoman empire. The conquest of 1453 marked the start of a process of renovation which, in the course of 100 years and more, transformed the dilapidated Constantinople of Constantine XI into the splendid metropolis of Süleyman the Magnificent.

In a long series of campaigns Sultan Mehemmed brought under Ottoman control the Morea (1458, 1460), Serbia (1459), and Bosnia (1463). A war against Venice (1463–79) gave to the Ottomans Negroponte (1470) and much of northern Albania, including Skutari (1478–9). In Asia Minor the sultan made an end of the last Turkish principalities surviving there—Kastamuni (1461) and Karaman (1464–5). The Greek empire of Trebizond, established in 1204, fell to the Ottomans in 1461. Mehemmed II, at the battle of Otluk Beli in 1473, drove back a dangerous intrusion of the Ak Koyonlu Turcomans into Asia Minor. On the Lower Danube Wallachia had been reduced to obedience in 1462. Now, in 1475–6, the sultan subdued the resistance of Moldavia. His forces also occupied Kaffa in 1475, the Khan of the Krim Tatars becoming (at least in name) a vassal of the Ottomans. In the last years of the reign the sultan's troops were repulsed in an attempt (1480) to take the island of Rhodes from the Knights of St John, but were successful in their attack (also in 1480) on Otranto in Apulia. Mehemmed II, over and above this vast labour of territorial consolidation, sought to define the basic institutions of the Ottoman state—an endeavour which found expression in the decrees issued during the course of his reign. Nor was Mehemmed less active in his efforts to strengthen his armed forces, fostering among them an extended use of gunpowder and cannon which enlarged greatly the Ottoman practice of war. The reign of Mehemmed II, a time of remarkable achievement and consolidation, ushered the Ottoman empire into its golden age.

P. M. Holt, Ann K. S. Lambton, and B. Lewis (eds.), *The Cambridge History of Islam*, vol. 1 (Cambridge, 1970). D. M. Vaughan, *Europe and the Turk. A pattern of alliances, 1350–1700* (Liverpool, 1954).   VJP

MEHEMMED III (*reg.* AD 1595–1603), Ottoman Sultan. His accession to the throne saw the last enforcement of the 'law of fratricide', which enforced on a new sultan the execution of all his brothers and their male children. Nineteen of the sons of Murad III suffered death in 1595. The reign of Mehemmed III coincided with the great war of 1593–1606 against Austria. Sultan Mehemmed went on campaign himself in 1596, his forces capturing in that year the Hungarian fortress of Eger (Erlau) and defeating the imperialists at the battle of Mezö-Kerestes. Thereafter the war declined into a series of sieges, which brought to the Ottomans only one further gain—the fortress of Kanizsa, conquered in 1600.

MEHEMMED IV (1641–92), 19th Ottoman Sultan (*reg.* 1648–87) in succession to his father, Ibrahim, whose reign saw both the great revival of Ottoman fortunes under the Köprülü viziers and the disastrous defeats which followed the repulse at Vienna (1683).

MEHEMMED V (RESHAD) (1844–1918), 36th Ottoman Sultan (*reg.* 1909–18) in succession to his brother Abdülhamid II, whose reign witnessed the establishment of the domination of the Committee of Union and Progress and the defeat of Ottoman forces in the First World War.

MEHEMMED VI (WAHID AL-DIN) (1861–1926), 37th and last Ottoman Sultan (*reg.* 1918–22), whose policy of full collaboration with the victorious Allies in the First World War led him into conflict with, and ultimate deposition by, Atatürk and the nationalists.

MEHEMMED SOKOLLU, Ottoman Grand Vizier (1565–79), was of Bosnian origin and entered the service of the sultan as a recruit from the devshirme or child tribute levied on the non-Muslim peoples of the Ottoman empire. He rose to be Kapudan Pasha (High Admiral of the Ottoman fleet) in 1546–50. As Beglerbeg of Rumeli he fought in the campaigns of 1551–2 on the Hungarian front, which led to the Ottoman capture of Temesvár. As Grand Vizier he accompanied Sultan Süleyman on the Szigetvár campaign of 1566 and, in the reign of Selim II, guided the Ottomans to success in their great naval conflict (1570–4) with Venice and Spain. Mehemmed Sokollu, one of the ablest of the Ottoman grand viziers, was assassinated in 1579.

MEHTA, SIR PHEROZESHAH (1845–1917), Indian politician, who, with Tyabji and Telang, carried on a ceaseless campaign for reforms in every branch of the administration. He was an advocate of municipal reform, became chairman of the Bombay corporation (1884), and took an active part in the proceedings of the Indian National Congress, of which he became president in 1890. In 1893 he became a member of the governor-general's legislative council.

MEIGGS, HENRY (1811–77), US railroad builder, who constructed spectacular railways through difficult terrain in South America.

MEIGHEN, ARTHUR (1874–1960), Canadian politician and prime minister, who entered the Canadian parliament (1908) and was solicitor-general (1913–17), secretary of state (1917), and minister for the interior (1917–20). He succeeded Sir Robert Borden as prime minister (1920) and leader of the Conservative Party, but was defeated in the general election (1921). He was again prime minister in a short-lived government during the constitutional crisis when Byng, the governor-general, refused Mackenzie King's request for a dissolution of parliament (1926). After a second defeat at the polls (1926) Meighen retired, but returned as a senator and minister without portfolio in R. B. Bennett's government (1932). He was re-elected as Conservative leader (1941), but was defeated when he stood for election to the Commons.

MEIJI (1852–1912), Emperor of Japan (*reg.* 1867–1912), whose personal name was Mutsuhito. His reign marked Japan's emergence as a modern state, but his own part in this transformation is obscure. Although governmental affairs rested in the hands of samurai leaders, any opposition to their plans by the emperor would have created difficulties. On occasion disputes between government leaders forced him to choose between competing policies, and in retrospect his decisions appear well judged.

MEIJI CONSTITUTION, first modern Japanese constitution. Its place in Japanese political history has caused considerable controversy. Drafted by Itō Hirobumi (1882–9), who had studied in Europe, and promulgated by the Emperor Meiji (1889), it rejected popular sovereignty and severely restricted the rights of the Diet. It did, however, give the Diet power to curtail budget increases, an important factor in a period of inflation and international crisis. Given Japan's authoritarian tradition, the constitution was not illiberal. Under it, political parties gained a strong foothold among the elites which controlled Japan, even if the parties were forced to modify their original aims. The constitution was amended several times, notably by the extension of the franchise from 1 per cent of the population (1889) to all males over 25 (1925). It was replaced after the Second World War by a completely democratic, US-drafted constitution (1946).

MEIJI RESTORATION (1868), major turning point in modern Japanese history. It began as a *coup d'état* by a coalition of opponents of the Tokugawa *bakufu* acting to restore the long-usurped authority of the emperor, and led to the radical political, social, and economic changes which enabled Japan to modernize itself and become a major world power. The basic force behind these changes was nationalism. From 1800 many samurai were concerned about the military and technological gap between Japan and the West and feared for their national independence. During the 15 years which followed Perry's first expedition (1853) to Japan, therefore, there were continual proposals of political reform, notably by Tokugawa collaterals, *tozama daimyōs*, and their retainers, who insisted that national safety required a more broadly based central government which could utilize all available ability. The *fudai daimyōs*, however, who dominated the *bakufu*, were unwilling to see substantial changes in the Tokugawa system. Not only did it give them a privileged position, but it had maintained peace for two centuries, and they could thus rely on some support from moderate elements who feared that sudden changes might lead to anarchy. The authority of the *bakufu* was undermined, however, by the demands of the Western powers and the presence of foreign traders. When, eventually, the *bakufu* attempted to reestablish its position by securing French help, the two most powerful south-western *han*s, Satsuma and Chōshū, in whose councils younger samurai of lower rank had now become prominent, formed a coalition to overthrow the *bakufu*. On 3 Jan. 1868 they seized control of Kyoto in the name of the young Emperor Meiji and with some help from other *han*s quickly defeated those Tokugawa supporters who opposed them.

That the Meiji Restoration did not amount solely to the revival of an older form of imperial government or the establishment of a new *bakufu* under Satsuma or Chōshū, as many expected, was due to two main factors. One was the need for unity in the face of external threat, the other the fact that feudal institutions had been undermined during the two preceding centuries. In particular, the growth of a money economy had created a frustrated lower samurai class whose remuneration was low and whose expectation of a position appropriate to their ability slight. At the same time, a considerable number of rural entrepreneurs had emerged, who welcomed the new opportunities presented by foreign trade. The aspirations of these two important groups were reflected in, and gave strength to, the plans of a group of samurai reformers within the new Meiji government, whose most important figures were Ōkubo Toshimichi (Satsuma) and Kido Kōin (Chōshū). Only they offered a real solution to Japan's basic problems and it was in accompaniment to their rise to power that Japan abandoned within a few years most of its feudal trappings and established the foundations of a modern state.

M. B. Jansen, *Sakamoto Ryoma and the Meiji Restoration* (Princeton, 1961).

W. G. Beasley, *The Modern History of Japan* (London, 1963).
RLS

MEINDERS, FRANZ VON (*fl.* 17th cent.), German diplomat under the Great Elector of Brandenburg, who negotiated the peace of St Germain (1679) and the Franco-Brandenburg alliances of 1679 and 1681.

MEINECKE, FRIEDRICH (1862–1954), German historian and philosopher, who was a professor at Strasbourg (1901–6), Freiburg (1906–14), and Berlin (1914–28) Universities. He was also editor (1896–1935) of the influential *Historische Zeitschrift* (*Historical Journal*) in succession to Treitschke. After the Second World War he helped to found the Free University in Berlin, and became its first rector (1947). Meinecke, a philosopher of history in the tradition of Ranke, Dilthey, and Troeltsch, believed in the interdependence of the state and ethics, the inseparability of values and ideas from historical description, and the advancement of a German culture distinct from that of the western Enlightenment. His book *Cosmopolitanism and the Nation State* (1907) was a landmark in writing on the history of ideas. However, his optimistic interpretation of the morality of power could not survive the break-up of his traditional world after the First World War, and in his later works, *The Nature of Raison d'état* (1924) and *The Origins of Historicism* (1936), a certain pessimism was evident in his attempts to reconcile the brutal realities of power with his own ethical standards.

Politically, Meinecke was a patriotic liberal before 1914 and a supporter of Bethmann-Hollweg during the war. After 1919 he supported the new republic with sincerity, but without much intellectual enthusiasm. His attitude to the Nazis was somewhat equivocal, since he genuinely abhorred the nature of Nazi rule, yet approved of much of Hitler's foreign policy. This equivocation was reflected in his short book, *The German Catastrophe* (1946), in which his genuine attempt to interpret the origins of the Nazi dictatorship was combined with a certain naïveté as to the responsibility of Germany herself.

MEISSEN, Saxon town on the Upper Elbe, north-west of Dresden, where Augustus the Strong of Saxony-Poland founded the first porcelain factory in Europe (1710), which gave rise to a new European industry. Through the inventiveness of J. F. Boettger and modellers like J. G. Kirchner and J. J. Kaendler, who made the Swan service for Count Bruehl, Meissen figures and services became highly fashionable and were copied throughout Europe, *eg*, at Hoechst, Berlin, and Vienna, with the help of workers who had left the Meissen factory. The occupation of the town by the Prussians in the Seven Years War (1756) was a blow to the factory, and though it enjoyed a revival under Count Camillo Marcolini and the French modeller, Acier, it never regained its unchallenged lead in porcelain manufacture.

MEISSNER, OTTO (1880–1953), German civil servant and state secretary under Ebert, Hindenburg, and Hitler. He joined the office of the president (1919) and was appointed state secretary (1923). He remained in office after the conservative Hindenburg replaced the social democrat Ebert (1925), and by 1932 was to some extent involved in the movement towards authoritarian government which culminated in the appointment of Hitler as chancellor in 1933. Meissner was the supreme example of the submissive bureaucrat who, although not an active Nazi supporter (he did not join the NSDAP until 1937), sympathized with its superficially nationalist and conservative aims and co-operated with the regime, discovering too late the real nature of Nazism. Meissner was probably more powerful in real terms before 1933 than afterwards, when his authority and sphere of influence shrank in comparison both with that of his governmental colleagues and of party officials, leaving him little more than ceremonial and formal duties. He was tried by a US tribunal in 1949 as a Nazi war criminal, but was acquitted, and devoted his retirement to writing his memoirs.

MEKNES (MIKNASA), city of north Morocco, which takes its name from a local people and is famous for the vast rebuilding by Mulay Isma'il in the 17th cent.

MELANCHTHON, PHILIP (1497–1560), German humanist and reformer and associate of Martin Luther, who systematized the Lutheran faith and acted as its diplomatic representative. While professor of Greek and Hebrew at Wittenberg he published a handbook of Greek grammar (1518) and wrote the first systematic statement of Protestant theology, the *Loci Communes* (1521). In 1530 he wrote, with the help of George Spalatin, the famous *Augsburg Confession*, a document of moderate and conciliatory tone, which provided a classic statement of Lutheranism on behalf of seven princes and two free cities for the emperor and the representatives at the imperial diet of Augsburg (June 1530).

He tried to achieve reconciliation with the Catholic body at discussions held at Worms, Hagenau, and Regensburg (1539–41, 1546) and later wrote a Protestant confession for the Council of Trent (1551). His influence on the Protestant reformation was not confined to Germany, *eg*, it could be seen in the Church Ordinance of 1539 which established the Danish reformed church and through the work of Laurentius Petri, Abp of Uppsala, who had studied at Wittenberg, and George Norman, the German Lutheran, who became the superintendent of the Swedish church,

Melanchthon's thought deviated only slightly from Luther's, but after the latter's death (1546) a controversy developed within the Lutheran fold between the inflexible Flacius Illyricus and the Gnesiolutherans, who supported him, believing that outward forms of religion mattered fundamentally, and the Philippist supporters of Melanchthon, who modified Luther's eucharistic teaching, rejected the essential importance of religious ceremonial, and asserted a doctrine of synergism, *ie*, that human will can co-operate with divine grace in the act of conversion.   MKS

MELANESIAN LABOUR TRADE (in the Pacific), in reality a massive, largely voluntary migration of New Hebrideans, Solomon Islanders, etc., to Samoa, New Caledonia, Fiji, and Qld, began with an appeal for cotton pickers for Towns's new Qld plantation (1863) and similar properties in Fiji (1864). It developed rapidly with the swing to sugar in Australia (1868) and Fiji (1874), and the opening of nickel mines in New Caledonia (1877). Most recruits opted for Fiji and Qld (1546 and 4687 respectively in 1883), the number employed in the latter colony rising to 11,443 in 1883, and in all, 61,271 between 1863 and 1904. Increasing racial tension in Qld after 1880 and the crucial musket ban of 1883–4 temporarily halved recruitment, though there was some recovery before the passage of the Australian Immigration Restriction Act (1901), which forced all but 700 of the 6839 remaining to go home by 1904. The movement played an important role in the Melanesian economy and provided a lingua franca, pidgin English, which aided later political development.

MELBA, DAME NELLIE (1861–1931), Australian soprano, born Helen Porter Mitchell in Vic., who studied in Melbourne, London, and Paris, adopted—in honour of her home city—the stage-name by which she is remembered and began (1887) her career as an operatic and concert performer.

MELBOURNE OF KILMORE, WILLIAM LAMB, 2nd Viscount (Irish) (1779–1848), British politician and prime minister, who entered the House of Commons in 1806, joining the Whig opposition under the leadership of Fox. He was greatly influenced by Canning, whose coalition ministry he joined (1827) as secretary for Ireland, and this partial alienation from the Whigs was increased when he not only accepted office under Goderich, but also remained for a short time in Wellington's administration. On his father's death in 1828 he inherited the title, entered the House of Lords, and on the formation of Earl Grey's reform ministry (1830) became home secretary. He succeeded Grey as prime minister (1834), but was dismissed by William IV after only a few months. He formed his second administration (1835) after Peel's resignation. With the accession of Queen Victoria (1837), his personal position was strengthened as the young and inexperienced sovereign came to rely not only on his political judgement, but on his friendship. But his government was never a strong one, grew weaker after 1837, and fell in 1841.

MELCHETT, ALFRED MORITZ MOND, 1st Baron (1868–1930), British politician and industrialist, son of a Jewish émigré who, with his partner, built up the great chemical company of Brunner, Mond & Co. As a director of this company from 1895, and later as managing director, Mond developed his ideas on industrial organization. He saw that the age of laissez-faire capitalism, where a large number of companies competed for profits, was over. He favoured rationalization involving the concentration of production in each sphere into large corporations which would dominate the market for a product, while economizing through bulk buying and large-scale production. His efforts culminated in the establishment (1926) of Imperial Chemical Industries Ltd, with a capital of £95 million and close involvement in many other industries. Mond favoured conciliation between capital and labour and pioneered profit sharing. In 1927, at

discussions between himself and Ben Turner, the president of the TUC, he attempted to open a new chapter in industrial relations, following the general strike of 1926.

He entered parliament as a Liberal MP in 1910, and rose to cabinet rank under Lloyd George (1916–22). During the 1920s he broke away from the Liberals and accepted the need for tariffs to protect industry. He was an enthusiastic Zionist and active in raising funds for the cause.

MELCOMBE, GEORGE BUBB DODINGTON, 1st Baron (1691–1762), British politician and patron, who had immense influence through his control over some boroughs. His patronage gained him posts in several ministries, as commissioner of the treasury (1724–41), and treasurer of the navy (intermittently 1744–62). He was created Lord Melcombe shortly before his death.

MELFI, CONSTITUTIONS OF (1231), first major code of law issued by a western European ruler in the Middle Ages. Their author, Emperor Frederick II, was attempting to codify the welter of feudal Byzantine and Islamic customs current in his kingdom of Sicily into a coherent rational system. The emphasis on the imperial authority as the source of law is a salient feature (Frederick's official name for the code being *Liber Augustalis*), but so is the insistence on the principles of the equality and subjection of all under the law.

MELFI, TREATY OF (1059), between Pope Nicholas II and the Norman rulers of southern Italy, by which they received their lands as papal fiefs and were thus transformed from outlawed brigands into territorial princes, sanctified by papal authority. The treaty was promoted by the Roman reform party which was anxious to secure support independent of the emperor and the Roman aristocracy, and reversed all previous papal policy.

MELGAREJO, MARIANO (1820–71), Bolivian dictator (1864–71), who sold large sections of Bolivia to neighbouring powers, embezzled public funds, and suppressed all opposition. His exploits make him a prototype of the barbarous *caudillo*.

MELLO FRANCO, AFRÂNIO DE (1870–1943), Brazilian politician and lawyer, who represented Brazil at the League of Nations until 1926, and was a member of the World Court (1923–9). As foreign minister of Brazil (1930–3), he arbitrated in the Leticia dispute between Peru and Colombia.

MELLON, ANDREW WILLIAM (1855–1937), US financier and diplomat, who built up a vast financial and industrial empire and incorporated the Mellon National Bank (1902). He was active in Republican Party politics, being secretary to the treasury (1921–31). He was convinced of the need to encourage business and stimulate investment by tax reductions and government economy, a policy which appealed to the upper and middle classes, but was opposed by progressives, First World War veterans, and farmers. His commitment to a high tariff impeded the repayment of European war debts, and he failed to foresee the onset of the Depression, to which his policies may well have contributed. He served as US ambassador to Britain (1932–3), and in 1937 presented his art collection as the nucleus of the National Gallery of Art in Washington, DC.

MELORIA, BATTLE OF (6 Aug. 1284), one of the decisive naval battles of medieval history, in which the Genoese, under Benedetto Zaccaria, lured the Pisan fleet to destruction off the island of Meloria near the mouth of the Arno river, west of Pisa. Pisa was blockaded and then captured. This marked the end of her importance as one of the great naval powers of the Mediterranean. The Pisan economy also suffered a heavy blow, though Pisa retained its independence until the capture of the city by Florence in 1406.

MELOS, ancient Greek island city-state in the south-western Aegean, settled by Dorians from Laconia in the 10th cent. BC. In the 5th cent. it long remained outside the Delian League and Athenian domination, but its sympathy and, probably, co-operation with the Spartans in the great Peloponnesian War provoked Athenian attacks in 426 and in 416, when, during the interlude of peace, the city was taken and its population killed or enslaved (416).

MELVILLE, HENRY DUNDAS, 1st Viscount (1742–1811), British politician and authority on Scottish and Indian affairs. At 24 he became solicitor-general for Scotland (1766), entering parliament (1774) as MP for the Midlothian; later he briefly represented the borough of Newtown, Isle of Wight, and later Edinburgh. He was appointed (1781) chairman of the secret committee to report on the causes of the war in the Carnatic, condemned the Indian administration, and tried unsuccessfully to procure the recall of Warren Hastings (1782). He was Lord Advocate of Scotland (1775–1783) and served under Pitt as treasurer of the navy (1784–1800), and as member, and finally as president (1793–1801), of the Board of Control for Indian Affairs. Later he became secretary for war (1794–1801) and first lord of the admiralty (1804–5).

His enemies said he had three passions in life—Scotland, his party, and himself. This verdict has been modified by recent research, which has cleared him of the charge of general corruption in the manipulation of the Scottish elections (1774–1811). Neither was he guilty of embezzlement in the use of navy funds. He certainly made extensive use of the Indian patronage at his disposal and he was accused of filling India with Scotsmen. But the exodus from Scotland to India had started long before the Board of Control was formed.

Dundas unsuccessfully introduced a bill in 1783 for the regulation of the government of India. In this he proposed the centralization of the civil and military authority under the governor-general in council with a strong supervising authority in London. He also favoured a permanent settlement of the land revenues and the extension of British sovereignty in India at the expense of Mughal sovereignty. He vehemently opposed both Fox's India bill (1783) and Burke's charges against Warren Hastings on the Rohilla war. But he voted for Hastings's impeachment on the Benares charge. In 1806 Dundas was himself impeached for malversation of public money, but was acquitted.

H. Furber, *Henry Dundas, First Viscount Melville, 1742–1811* (London, 1931).

C. H. Philips, *The East India Company 1784–1834* (Manchester, 1940). CCD

MELVILLE, ANDREW (1545–1622), Scottish divine and scholar, who influenced the curriculum of Glasgow and St Andrews Universities. He was instrumental in the production of the *Second Book of Discipline* (1581), which established the Presbyterian form of Church government in Scotland and rejected episcopacy. As such he, rather than John Knox, was technically the founder-figure of Scottish Presbyterianism. This brought him into conflict with King James VI and I, who later had him confined to the Tower of London (1607–11) for ridiculing Anglican ritual. On his release he became a professor at Sedan (1611–22), and took no further part in the bitter controversies between the exponents of Presbyterian and episcopal forms of church government, which far outlasted his lifetime.

MELVILLE, HERMAN (1819–91), US writer, who worked as a clerk, schoolmaster, and sailor, besides living for a time (1842) among cannibals. *Typee* (1846), based on his encounter with them, and *Omoo* (1847), its sequel, brought him instant recognition. In 1851 came his masterpiece, *Moby-Dick*, which combined an exciting narrative with a symbolic examination of man's quest for absolute meaning in a world of ambiguous and conflicting values. His later work was less

successful; he became a customs inspector (1866–85) and wrote poetry. *Clarel* (1876), *John Marr and Other Sailors* (1880), and *Timoleon* (1891), were all published privately. Melville, though virtually unknown at the time of his death, came to be regarded as one of the greatest of US writers, and *Moby-Dick* as one of the world's classics.

MEMEL (Klaipeda), area on Germany's north-eastern border, renounced by her under Article 99 of the Versailles treaty (1919). It comprised the Baltic port of Memel and a strip of land along the right bank of the Niemen river, some 112 kms long and 16–32 kms wide. Its population totalled 150,000, the inhabitants of the town being mainly German-speaking, while those of the rural hinterland formed a Lithuanian minority.

In 1919 the area was placed under the provisional administration of a French High Commissioner appointed by the Allies, their ultimate intention probably being to assign it to Lithuania once the frontiers of the new Baltic states had been settled. The port was indispensable to Lithuania, as it was an important trade centre and her only possible outlet to the sea. Fearing that it might be made independent and fall under Polish influence, Lithuania annexed the territory (1923). The Allies eventually recognized the annexation, and Memel became part of Lithuania, with its own Diet and directorate, and a governor nominated by Lithuania.

In the first elections (1925) the German parties won 94 per cent of the votes and 27 of the 29 Diet seats, a pattern that was repeated in all subsequent elections. The composition of the Diet was highly unwelcome to Lithuania, and through her governor she made persistent attempts to override the German majority and obstruct its policy of rapprochement with Germany. In Dec. 1926 the pro-Lithuanian party seized power in a coup, and for much of the period till 1939, despite the permanent German majority in the Diet, Memel was ruled either by a minority Lithuanian directorate or directly by the governor. This state of affairs, though not unconstitutional, was nevertheless ultimately damaging to Lithuania, as it invited Germany's hostility and drove the German Memellanders into the arms of the growing Nazi movement. Nazi influence made itself felt as early as 1928, when some Memellanders joined the NSDAP, and in 1933 two crypto-Nazi parties were founded. By 1935 the pro-Nazi parties dominated the German group in the Diet and began to work for Memel's return to Germany. The governor and the pro-Lithuanian party took countermeasures, *eg*, the dismissal of German public officials and the settlement of immigrants from Lithuania, but with little hope of altering the situation in view of Germany's growing power and influence. In March 1939, within a week of Germany's seizure of Czechoslovakia, Hitler issued an ultimatum to Lithuania, demanding the surrender of Memel. Lithuania had no choice but to give way, and on 23 March Memel was incorporated into the German Reich. It remained in German hands until Oct. 1944, when it was occupied by the advancing Russian armies. After the Second World War it was incorporated into the Soviet Union as part of the Lithuanian SSR. AJC

MEMEL CONVENTION (1924). In Jan. 1923 Lithuania, suspecting a Franco-British move to make Memel a self-governing territory, like Danzig, incited an uprising in the town and then sent in troops, which quickly overwhelmed the small French garrison. France was preparing to occupy the Ruhr and could spare no troops for the Memel crisis, so negotiations for a settlement were initiated. These ended in deadlock, Lithuania objecting especially to any Polish share in the administration of Memel harbour. In Sept. the League of Nations took responsibility for the problem, and a compromise settlement drafted by its commissioners was accepted by the parties. Memel became self-administering under Lithuanian sovereignty. Lithuania guaranteed unrestricted trade and transit through the port, and in exchange Polish representation on the harbour board was withdrawn.

MEMNON (d. 333 BC), Greek mercenary captain from Rhodes, who fought for Persia against Alexander the Great, commanded a contingent at the Granicus (334), defended Halicarnassus, and was threatening Alexander's rear with the Persian fleet when he died.

MEMPHIS, city of ancient Egypt, 17 miles (27·3 kms) south of Cairo, built, probably by Menes, at the junction of Upper and Lower Egypt. It was the capital of the Old Kingdom. Nearby, at Sakkara, Abusir, Giza, and Dahshur, are many pyramids and other buildings dating from the Old and Middle Kingdoms.

MENANDER (c. 342–292 BC), Athenian writer of 'New' comedy. Only fragments survived from about 100 plays that he wrote before 20th-cent. discoveries, eg, the complete *Dyskolos* and nearly complete *Samia*. His comedy of situation and manners influenced Roman, Restoration, and modern drama.

MENCKEN, HENRY LOUIS (1880–1956), US journalist. He wrote for the Baltimore *Evening Sun* (1905–48). With his contributions to the magazine *Smart Set* (1908), Mencken began vitriolic attacks on the prevailing values in American society, particularly those of the middle class, which he delighted in calling the 'booboisie'. He denounced the genteel tradition in American literature, and strongly supported naturalism, championing such writers as Theodore Dreiser, Sherwood Anderson, and Eugene O'Neill. As joint editor, with George Jean Nathan (1882–1958), of *Smart Set* (1914–1923) and the *American Mercury* (1924–33), he became the spokesman for intellectual protest during the 1920s, but during the Depression his '*Smart Set* cynicism' became less popular and his influence negligible. His greatest contribution to American letters was the *American Language* (1919), a massive study of the development of the English language in the US.

MENDANA DE NEYRA, ALVARO DE (1542–95), Spanish sailor, who discovered the Solomons (1568) and on a long-deferred return voyage the Marquesas (1595) and Santa Cruz (1595).

MENDE, ERICH (1916–), German politician and co founder of the Free Democratic Party (FDP) in 1945. As a member of the *Bundestag* since 1949, and successively manager (1951), parliamentary chairman (1957), and leader of the FDP, Mende represented the right wing of the party, eg, by opposing its official policy of eastern detente. He was deputy chancellor and minister for all-German affairs in the CDU–FDP coalition (1963–6).

MENDEL, GREGOR JOHANN (1822–84), Austrian Augustinian monk and science teacher, who began (1857) to collect and observe the numerous varieties of the garden pea. He made many crossings between varieties and recorded his observations on the nature of the progeny. He continued his observations over a period of seven years, then presented his results and his general conclusions, now known as Mendel's Laws. Although his paper was forgotten until 1900, his discovery of the basic principles of heredity was the origin of the science of genetics.

MENDELÉEFF, DMITRY IVANOVICH (1834–1907), Russian chemist, who (1868–70), while writing a textbook of chemistry, attempted to systematize the properties of the elements he was describing. As a result, he formulated an important scientific generalization, the Periodic Law of the Elements. This law brought order to existing information and directed further research towards the existence and properties of elements then unknown, predictions of which were soon fulfilled.

MENDERES, ADNAN (1899–1961), Turkish lawyer, cotton planter, and politician, who left (1945) the ruling Republican People's Party to form, with others, the Democratic Party, which won the 1950 elections. During the first half of his term as prime minister (1950–60) Turkey made rapid economic progress, but inflation and increasing payments deficits in the latter half increased criticism of the government, which the Democrats countered by more authoritarian measures to suppress opposition. Menderes's popularity, especially in rural areas, remained high and was enhanced by his escape from an aircrash (1959). The Democrats won the 1954 and 1957 elections by substantial majorities, but opposition still increased, notably in the army, and the Democratic government was overthrown (27 May 1960) by an army coup. The Democrats were put on trial and Menderes with two other ministers was executed (Sept. 1961).

MENDÈS-FRANCE, PIERRE (1907–), French politician, who became a Radical deputy (1932) and was the most active prime minister of the Fourth Republic. His government (1954–5) was an important episode in its history.

During the Second World War he was arrested by the Vichy government, but escaped to London and joined the Free French air force. He was a member of De Gaulle's provisional administration in Algiers (1943), then minister of national economy after the Liberation. But he resigned (1945) when his colleagues refused to back his plan for stabilizing the economy by a programme of austerity and controls. Later, he represented France on the International Monetary Fund and at the World Bank.

Mendès-France's government was based on his personal popularity and authority rather than on a firm party coalition. He had the courage to take unpopular decisions and to challenge vested interests, eg, the alcohol lobby. He signed the Geneva agreements which ended the Indo-China war, set on foot Tunisian independence, and forced the French parliament to vote on the European Defence Community. The confusion caused by the defeat of the EDC, and the beginnings of the Algerian war, helped to cause Mendès-France's fall.

He then tried to reinvigorate the Radical Party and turn it into an instrument of modernization and reform. The 'Mendesists' captured control of the party for a time, but it split, and Mendès-France resigned (1957). He was later a member of the small Parti socialiste unifié. He played little part in the politics of the Fifth Republic, sitting in parliament only in 1967–8.   RDA

MENDIETA MONTEFUR, CARLOS (1873–1960), Cuban radical politician and provisional president (1934–5), much of whose life was spent in political opposition to the regimes in power. He fought on the rebel side during the Cuban struggle for independence against Spain, and then opposed the dictatorships of Menocal and Machado, and the regime of Grau San Martín. His provisional presidency was ended by his enforced resignation.

MENDIZABEL, JUAN ALVAREZ (1790–1853), Spanish politician and financier who joined Riego's revolution (1820) and on its failure emigrated to London, where he acquired a fortune and financed thel iberal restoration of Maria II of Portugal. He returned to Spain (1835) to become minister of finance under Toreno, who hoped his radical reputation would pacify revolutionary elements. As prime minister (1835–6) during the Carlist War he aimed to unite the country by absorbing provincial revolutionary juntas into legal provincial deputations and gave official posts to local leaders. His attempt to revise the Royal Statute to secure a more liberal franchise led to moves for his dismissal from an alliance of the Crown and conservative liberals. As a result, he was forced to join Calatrava and those who eventually created the Progressive Party. He hoped to finance a conscript army by a British loan with customs concessions as an inducement, but Palmerston foresaw French opposition and the failure of the scheme. The speculation in Spanish bonds collapsed (1835) and the army of 100,000 men grew ill-equipped and mutinous. Mendizabel's attack on Church property was intended to secure credit and pay off the National Debt. In 1836 he converted monastic property into national bonds and proposed the sale of land endowments of the secular Church and abolition of tithes, driving many devout Catholics into opposition and further dividing Progressives and Moderates. Mendizabel was dismissed (1837), but returned under Calatrava to take charge of the treasury. He instigated the military service laws (1837), but his financial mismanagement resulted in the government's disintegration and he returned to power only briefly in 1843.

MENDOG (d. 1263), founder of the first important Lithuanian principality centred on Nowogròdek, who embraced western Christianity. He was killed with his sons and their death was followed by a pagan reaction in Lithuania.

MENDOZA, ANA DE LA CERDA, Princess of Eboli (1540–1591), daughter of Diego Hurtado de Mendoza, viceroy of Catalonia, and wife of Ruy Gomez de Silva, whom she married in 1553. After her husband's death (1573) she became involved in the intrigues of Philip II's secretary, Antonio Perez. After falling foul of Philip she and Perez were arrested (1579), thus ending the influence of the Eboli faction. For the rest of her life she was confined to an apartment of her palace at Pastrana.

MENDOZA, ANTONIO DE (1490–1552), Spanish colonial official, who was the first viceroy of Mexico (1535–50). He brought stability to the strife-torn colony, successfully thwarting the ambitions of Cortés (among others) and establishing the foundations of the viceregal institution. Mendoza was a tireless champion of the Indian. He sought to contain the greed of the Spanish *encomenderos*, although he wisely refrained from promulgating the celebrated New Laws (1542–3), and he encouraged the clergy to found educational institutions for the natives. In addition, he sponsored the ill-fated Coronado expedition, drafted a comprehensive mining code for the colony, and introduced the merino sheep. He was viceroy of Peru (1551–2).

MENDOZA, BERNARDINO DE (d. 1600), Spanish diplomat and Philip II's last ambassador to Elizabeth I (1578–84), who was expelled from England for his complicity in the 1583 Throckmorton plot to depose Elizabeth in favour of Mary Stuart (Jan. 1584). He became ambassador in Paris, where he continued to organize a spy service, was party to the Babington conspiracy (1586), and acted as paymaster to the Catholic League in France.

MENDOZA, DIEGO HURTADO DE, Duke of Infantado (1461–1531), Castilian grandee, head of the house of Mendoza, whose wealth and power, based on his estates in Guadalajara, posed a permanent challenge to the Catholic kings in Spain. He became deeply involved in factional strife with the Count of La Coruna and plotted against Cardinal Ximines, but later supported Charles V in the *communeros* revolt.

MENDOZA, DIEGO HURTADO DE (1503–75), Castilian soldier, diplomat, and humanist poet, who was appointed ambassador to Venice in 1539, was imperial orator at the Council of Trent (1545), governor of Siena (1547), and imperial representative in Rome (1549). He also wrote verse and produced a history of the Morisco war in Granada, in which he had fought as a military commander (1572).

MENDOZA, PEDRO DE (*c.* 1487–1537), leader of the first (1535) Spanish expedition to the Rio de la Plata and founder of Santa María de Buenos Aires, soon destroyed by the Indians.

MENELIK II (1844–1913), King of Shoa (*reg.* 1865–89), Emperor of Ethiopia (*reg.* 1889–1913). He was the founder of modern Ethiopia, and grandson of King Sahle Selassie of Shoa. As King of Shoa he built up its military strength and succeeded after 1880 in obtaining large quantities of firearms. The French and Italians, then establishing themselves on the Red Sea and Gulf of Aden, both supplied him with weapons in the hope of gaining his friendship. After the death of the Emperor Yohannes, ruler of northern Ethiopia, Menelik claimed the imperial throne, and signed the Uccialli treaty of peace and friendship whereby Italy recognized him as emperor (1889). Article XVIII, however, varied in its Amharic and Italian versions: the former stated that Menelik might use Italy's good offices in his negotiations with Europe; the latter version made this obligatory. The Italian government claimed that this gave it a protectorate over Ethiopia, but Menelik repulsed an ensuing Italian invasion, winning a decisive victory at Adowa in 1896.

Menelik actively pursued a policy of unification and modernization. In the last quarter of the century he gained control of the southern provinces, and, after the defeat of Italy, devoted himself increasingly to the establishment of new institutions, among them a national currency, telephone and telegraph services, a railway, roads, banks, schools, hospitals, and a printing works. He also established the country's first governmental cabinet.

MÉNENDEZ DE AVILÉS, PEDRO (1519–74), Spanish sailor and colonist who was commissioned by Philip II to set up a colony in Florida. He sailed from Spain with 11 ships and a large number of colonists, founded St Augustine, the first white settlement in Florida, and attacked the French garrison at Fort Caroline. He visited America again (1569–70), but failed in his efforts to establish settlements.

MENES (*fl. c.* 3100 BC), first King of a united, ancient Egypt and the one with whom Egyptian history is usually taken to begin. He is thought to have founded Memphis.

MENGER, CARL (1840–1921), Austrian economist and founder of the Austrian 'psychological school'. In his *Grunsaetze der Volkwirtschaftslehre* (1871) he made certain basic criticisms of the classical theory of value. In particular, he saw the utility of a commodity as deriving simply from the judgement expressed by a person feeling the need for it. All commodities which are capable of satisfying a need are useful, and are goods. But goods acquire an economic significance only if they are scarce, so that their supply is insufficient to meet the need for them.

MENG-TZU, text including the teachings of the philosopher Meng K'o (Mencius, ?372–289 BC). He was a follower of Confucius and is often regarded as the second principal teacher of Confucianism. The form of the *Meng-tzu* is similar to that of the *Analects of Confucius*, and contains Mencius' replies to questions, his statements of principle, and dialogue with rulers. To Confucius' stress on humanity, Mencius added the importance of duty to other members of society, together with his belief in the fundamental goodness of human nature. He insisted that government must be conducted for the benefit of those governed rather than for that of the government, and enjoined the adoption of fair means of taxation and the avoidance of imposing unnecessary burdens on the population.

MENNONITES, Anabaptist communities of north-west Europe, especially strong in Holland, who drew their inspiration from the Swiss Brethren of Zürich and were led by Menno Simons (1492–*c.* 1561), a renegade priest, turned reformer.

MENOCAL, MARIO GARCÍA (1866–1941), Cuban politician and president and dictator of Cuba (1913–21), who was a conservative and efficient administrator. His government, however, was constantly supervised and harassed by the US. During his regime sugar production began to increase rapidly.

MENOMINEE INDIANS, American Algonquian tribe, first encountered by the French (1634) along the Menominee river in WI and MI. They ceded their lands to the US government (1854) except for a reservation on the Wolf river, WI.

MENON, VAPAL PAGUNNI (1894–1966), Indian administrator and historian. After nearly 20 years' service in Madras, where he made his mark in the administration of the reforms introduced in 1919, Menon moved to the Reforms Office of the government of India (1933). His control of this office (1942–7) gave him a position of great importance during the negotiations for India's independence and which he recorded in his book, *The Transfer of Power in India* (1957). At independence (1947) he became Sardar Patel's right-hand man in another major exercise in diplomacy and policy-making, the integration of the princely states into the Indian Union. As secretary of the Ministry of States (1947–8) and as adviser thereafter while Patel lived, he was the effective arbiter of the princes' fortunes, as he recorded in his volume, *The Story of the Integration of the Indian States* (1956). After Patel's death he was briefly governor of Orissa (1951).

MENSHEVISM, term, from the Russian word for minority, used after 1903 to denote the non-Leninist section of the RSDLP, although there was no formal separation until 1912 and a Menshevik Party was founded only in 1917. The word is misleading in that it was the majority faction for much of the period 1903–12 and controlled the main party newspaper, *Iskra*, after 1903.

Its most important leader was Julii Martov, who had been a close associate (1895–1903) of Lenin. At the second party congress he supported Lenin against the Bund and the Economists (despite early Bundist affiliations) but split the *Iskra* board and the party by opposing Lenin's proposals for party membership. While agreeing with the need for an organized party, Martov and the Mensheviks wanted a broader based workers' party rather than a body of disciplined revolutionaries. They favoured more initiative being given to local committees as against a strong central organization.

The Mensheviks were closer than Lenin to the ideals of Western Social Democracy and always envisaged a two-stage revolution and a long period of bourgeois government, during which the party would strive to forward the economic and educational needs of the proletariat and establish, first, a democratic government and, eventually, socialism. The division, not seen as permanent in 1903, widened with the 1905 revolution, when the Mensheviks attempted to build up a mass party, supported strikes, and co-operated with the liberals and the Duma. They were influential in the Petrograd Soviet in 1905, and dominated the soviets in 1917 until Sept. They were an association of groups rather than an organized party, and included most of the great names of Russian Social Democracy—Plakhanov, Potresov, Axekod, and, occasionally, Trotsky. They were especially influential in Georgia, where there was a Menshevik government during the Revolution. Differences of opinion increased disunity. Potresov and the 'liquidators' advocated the abolition of a centralized, conspiratorial party and a legal labour movement on European lines. This was opposed by Plekhanov and Martov. Martov and Trotsky's internationalist and defeatist line on the First World War was opposed by a right wing, led by F. I. Dan, which joined the Provisional government in the summer of 1917. The Mensheviks opposed the Bolsheviks' seizure of power, claiming that Russia was too backward to establish socialism, and under Martov's leadership tried to function as a legal opposition. The party was suppressed in Russia in 1922.

I. Getzler, *Martov* (Cambridge, 1967).
L. Schapiro, *The Communist Party of the Soviet Union* (London, 1960).   BJW

MENSHIKOV, ALEXANDER DANILOVITCH, Prince (1672–1729), Russian soldier and politician, who became one of Peter I's principal advisers on military and diplomatic affairs and accompanied him on his tour of Holland and England (1697–8). In the Great Northern War with Sweden he won renown for his victory at Poltava and was created a field marshal and prince on the battlefield. He was then sent to Poland to reinstate Peter's ally, Augustus, as king (1709). Among Menshikov's many appointments were membership of the war ministry, the governorship of Izhera and the presidency of the Military College. He introduced Peter I to his future wife, Catherine Skavronsky, whom he had captured at Marienburg, and secured the throne for her on Peter's death (1725). As the leading member of the Supreme Privy Council he controlled the government during her reign until he was banished to Siberia by a noble clique (1727).

MENTANA, BATTLE OF (3 Nov. 1867), fought north-east of Rome during the Italian Wars of Independence over the control of Rome. The withdrawal of French troops from the city (1866) encouraged Garibaldi to make another attempt to capture it. Napoleon III, seeing the danger, hurriedly reversed his decision, with the result that Garibaldi faced the combined force of French and papal troops. The Garibaldians were routed, the volunteers proving no match for the papal Zouaves and the French regulars, equipped with *Chassepot* rifles. Garibaldi was captured and exiled to the island of Caprera, and Rome was not finally annexed to Italy until 1870.

MENTUHETEP KINGS, three Egyptian kings of the XIth dynasty. Mentuhetep I (*reg. c.* 2060–2009 BC), ruler of Thebes, reunited and pacified the country after a period of anarchy, and fought campaigns against Libyans, Nubians, and Semites. (Hayes (*Cambridge Ancient History*) designates this king Mentuhetep II and his successors Mentuhetep III and IV, but most authorities accept that he was the first king of that name belonging to the dynasty.) The reigns of Mentuhetep II (*reg. c.* 2009–1997) and Mentuhetep III (*reg. c.* 1997–?1991) appear to have been spent peacefully in building, quarrying, and the reopening of trade.

MENZIES, SIR ROBERT GORDON (1894–   ), Australian lawyer, politician, and prime minister (1939–41, 1949–66). He entered state politics in 1928 and became successively attorney-general, minister for railways, and deputy prime minister from 1932, but in 1934 transferred to the Commonwealth field. This brought cabinet rank at Canberra and succession to the United Australia Party leadership on the death of A. H. Lyons.

Menzies's wartime premiership (1939–41) was marked by a steady growth in political power of the reunited Labor Party, led by John Curtin, by increasing friction within the UAP–Country Party alliance, and by factious opposition to the prime minister from within his own party and from the press.

After a short period in office under the CP leader, Arthur Fadden, Menzies used his years as leader of the opposition (1941–9), during the ALP administrations of Curtin and Chifley, to create a new Liberal Party to replace the UAP. This party he led to victory in 1949, thereafter holding office continuously until his retirement in 1966. Menzies defeated the Labor policy of bank nationalization, but failed in attempts to proscribe the Communist Party. He continued and extended Chifley's programme of post-war reconstruction, national development, and social security, and increased British and European immigration and encouraged university expansion.

He was a brilliant tactician in domestic politics, combined great skill in parliamentary debate, and made use of mass media. In international affairs he was less successful and was less sensitive to Australia's changing role in the world after 1945.

MEOS, THE, turbulent pastoral tribe, inhabitants of the ill-defined tract known as Mewat, south of Delhi, and adjacent areas of Rajasthan. The majority are Muslims, known as Mewatis, while the Hindu Meos claim to be Rajput. They are said to have entered the area in the 11th cent. and their last outbreak of violence was during the Indian uprising (1857–8).

MERCANTILISM, expression used towards the end of the 18th cent. to explain a trading economy which had operated in Europe for 200 years, in particular, during the century of economic expansion (1660–1760).

Mercantilism aimed at making individual nations wealthy through encouraging exports and limiting imports. In practice this meant stimulating the export of manufactured goods and the import of raw materials while discouraging the import of foreign manufactures. As a monetary policy mercantilism sought the accumulation of gold and silver, which were regarded as essential expressions of national wealth, and of a favourable trade balance, though this became less important after the second half of the 17th cent. The system only worked to the advantage of specific 'interests'. Since its aims were geared to the material wealth of those who pursued them, it appears as an aggressive instrument and a contributory factor to Europe's wars in the period.

Particular features of mercantilism were evident in certain countries. In England—and Scotland, after 1707—the system was identified with the encouragement of merchant shipping through numerous Navigation Acts. It governed the economic relationship between England and her colonies, ultimately contributing to the American Revolution. In France, under Colbert, mercantilist principles were applied towards the creation of a powerful state and the defeat of her enemies. In Prussia, Frederick the Great embarked upon a policy of land reclamation and the encouragement of skilled immigrants. Although many conventional aspects of mercantilism were absent in the Netherlands, the importance of gold and silver was constantly emphasized.

Contemporary works on mercantilism included Thomas Mun's *Englands Treasure by Foreign Trade* (1622) and Matthew Decker's *Essay on the Causes of the Decline of Foreign Trade* (1739). The first major attack upon its doctrines came in Adam Smith's *The Wealth of Nations* (1776). Thereafter mercantilism declined in the changing conditions created by the Industrial Revolution. GMDH

MERCATOR, GERHARDUS (Gerhard Kremer) (1512–94), Flemish geographer, included in an atlas in 1569 'Mercator's projection', maps in which the meridians of longitude were at right angles to the parallels of latitude. This assisted navigators by giving a correct compass-bearing between points. Mercator's cartography was scientifically based on mathematics and astronomy, and he published numerous maps, one (1540) introducing the name America.

MERCENARY TROOPS, soldiers who offer themselves for hire. In the ancient world the Assyrian and Persian empires, while recruiting their armies and fleets chiefly from subject peoples, hired mercenaries of good fighting quality from free Greek states. Greek mercenary soldiers became especially important in the 4th cent. BC, when they were widely used by rebellious Persian satraps (*eg,* Cyrus the Younger), by the Persian kings to suppress revolts and resist invasion (*eg,* by Darius III against Alexander the Great), and by certain Greek states (*eg,* by Phocis in the Third Sacred War); and they were extensively employed by the Hellenistic kings in the 3rd–2nd cents. Mercenaries were also an essential part of the fighting forces of Carthage, but Rome made little use of them until the 3rd cent. AD, when barbarian communities were settled within the empire so that their fighting men could be recruited into the imperial army as *foederati.* They emerged later to replace the feudal military organizations of western Europe in the 12th and 13th cents. The Italian mercenaries of the later Middle Ages, the German *Landsknechte* of the 15th and 16th cents, and the Swiss infantry, who still (1970) form the Vatican guard, are the most famous examples. The development of national armies in the 19th cent. largely removed the need for mercenaries, though their role in relation to Africa is significant.

Pre-colonial Africa knew various forms of institutional military service, including that of mercenaries. Certain societies, though a minority, maintained groups who specialized in the arts of war and were available at a price for the convoy of trading caravans or other defensive duties; they might also on occasion be used on offensive raids. Such activities were always on a small scale, but increased in significance during the late 18th cent., at least in West Africa, under the pressures of the Atlantic slave trade and its ever-growing demands for war captives who could be sold into American slavery.

During the colonial period (*c.* 1500–*c.* 1900) the European colonial powers found it relatively easy to recruit African volunteers for paid military service on a long-term basis, it being the almost invariable practice to use such troops outside their areas of origin. During the First World War the French conscripted some 200,000 African troops for use in other theatres, mainly on the Western Front. The British mobilized, by methods little different from conscription, about 350,000 unarmed porters for use in their campaigns against the Germans in Tanganyika; some 42,000 of these died. The same semi-mercenary role was fulfilled by large numbers of Africans in the Second World War. Even in the 1960s the Portuguese had called up some 30,000 Africans or more for active service against nationalist guerrilla movements in Angola, Guinea-Bissau, and Mozambique. Most of these troops were not mercenaries in the proper sense of the word, though in many cases a mercenary element remained.

TTBR, BD

MERCIA, one of the leading Anglo-Saxon kingdoms which derived its name from the Mercians or 'boundary folk' bordering on the predominantly Celtic country further to the west. Its centre was in the upper Trent valley, but it came to embrace all the English midlands. It was converted to Christianity only in the third quarter of the 7th cent. The great age of Mercian supremacy in England was in the 8th cent. It rested on the agrarian development of the central Mercian regions and on the wealth brought by the closeness of London and Kent with their flourishing trade to the continent. King Offa of Mercia (758–96) was treated as virtually an equal by Charlemagne. The Mercian supremacy was ended by Egbert of Wessex in 925 and Mercian independence was ended altogether by the Viking invasions. Its last king, Burgred, fled in 874. A Danish army brought its eastern portions under Scandinavian settlement, while the south-western provinces became a dependency of Wessex. After the reconquest of the whole of England in the 10th cent. by the West Saxon kings, Mercia became one of the major earldoms into which the country was subdivided until the Norman Conquest.

MERCIER, HONORÉ (1840–94), Canadian politician and founder of the Parti National (1871), which sought to overcome clerical opposition to liberalism. He was solicitor-general in Que. under Henri Joly (1879), whom he succeeded as leader of the provincial Liberals (1883). He became prime minister of Que. (1886); his legislative programme included the passing of the Jesuits Estates Act (1888).

MERCIER DE LA RIVIÈRE, PIERRE PAUL (1720–93), French author and physiocrat, who in his book *L'ordre naturel et essentiel des sociétés politiques* (1767) discussed the meaning and justification of despotism.

MERCŒUR, PHILIPPE EMMANUEL DE LORRAINE, Duke de (1558–1602), French nobleman descended from the Dukes of Brittany, who supported the Guise faction and the league against Henry of Navarre in the later stages of the French civil war (1589–98). With Spanish help he led the revolt in Brittany until 1598, when he made peace with Navarre at Angers (20 March), giving his only daughter in marriage to the Duke of Vendôme, Henry's illegitimate son. He later joined the imperial forces of Rudolph II against the Turks (1599).

MERCURIO PERUANO, bi-weekly journal founded in 1791 as the organ of the Society of Friends of the Country of Peru. It features articles by leading Peruvian technologists describing such things as empirical methodology and the influence of climate upon civilization. It is still (1970) published.

MERCURY SPACE PROJECT in US (1961–3), manned space programme. Following Commander Alan B. Shepard's initial sub-orbital flight (5 May 1961) the project continued with a series of five flights that included that of Lt-Col. John H. Glenn (20 Feb. 1962), the first US manned orbital flight, and culminated in the 22-orbit flight of Maj. L. Gordon Cooper (May 15 1963).

MEREDITH, JAMES HOWARD (1933–), first Negro to graduate from Mississippi University, whose enrolment (1962) produced violence and a dramatic confrontation between state and federal authorities. Meredith's dignity and courage gained him an international reputation.

MERGENTHEIM, BATTLE OF (1645), victory of the Austro-Bavarian forces over the French in the closing stages of the Thirty Years War. Led by Generals von Werth and Mercy, the imperialist troops inflicted heavy casualties on Turenne's army on the Tauber river, south of Wurzburg. Turenne retreated to the Rhine with only a third of his force.

MERICI, ST ANGELA (1474–1540), Italian founder of the Ursuline order of nuns (1535), who worked all her life for the poor, sick, and ignorant in the Brescia area of Lombardy, carrying out the practical reforming spirit of the Oratory of Divine Love. Like Loyola, she rejected the pattern of an enclosed order, seeking only to give spiritual instruction to women and girls in society, though from the end of the 16th cent. the society developed into a general teaching order.

MERINA, Hova kingdom in central Madagascar, which in the 19th cent. united many of the Malagasy peoples. It was overthrown by French forces (1895–6).

MÉRINDOL, DECREE OF (1540), order of the *parlement* of Aix by which the French Alpine community of Mérindol was massacred for its Calvinist sympathies, in accordance with Francis I's policy of exterminating heretics.

MERODE-WESTERLOO, EUGÈNE JEAN PHILIPPE, Count of (1674–1722), Flemish mercenary soldier, who served as a cavalry officer first in the French, and then the Habsburg, army, rising to the rank of field marshal, in the War of the Spanish Succession. His memoirs provide a useful insight into military life at the turn of the 17th cent.

MEROE, situated on the east bank of the Nile about 130 miles (209 kms) north of Khartoum, was the residence of the kings of Kush from the 6th cent. BC until at least the 4th cent. AD, when it may have been conquered by the Axumites. It gives its name to the later culture of Kush from c. 300 BC. The site of the town contains the ruins of temples, palaces, and domestic dwellings, while 2 miles (3·2 kms) to the east are three groups of pyramids marking the graves of rulers and their families. There are also extensive cemeteries containing the graves of ordinary citizens.

Meroe is famous as an early iron working site, and many mounds of slag are to be seen among the ruins of the town. Excavations have shown that iron was being worked as early as 500 BC, and the extent of the workings and the comparatively early date have led many to suggest that it was from Meroe that the technique of iron working was diffused

through Africa. This suggestion remains unproven. While Meroe may well have been a centre of diffusion, it need not have been the only one.

The culture of Meroe was deeply influenced by that of Egypt, and the changes brought about by Hellenistic and Roman elements in Egypt were also reflected at Meroe. Though always subject to changes in artistic tradition from the north, there was a strong indigenous character in Meroitic culture that may also have been influenced by cultures further east, Persian and Indian elements being discernible in certain art forms. Of special interest is the fine painted pottery, of the first few centuries AD, which has no equal in Egypt.

The town of Meroe, standing at the mouth of the Wadi Haward, was well placed to control the area between the Nile and Atbara rivers, the 'Island of Meroe' in which the major monuments of this civilization are to be found.

P. L. Shinnie, *Meroe—A Civilization of the Sudan* (London, 1967). MS

MEROITIC WRITING, used to write the Meroitic language, was developed by the Kushites when knowledge of Egyptian, which was in general official use in Napatan times, had faded. It was in two forms, hieroglyphic and 'cursive', and the signs, obviously based on Egyptian models, had alphabetic values. The earliest known Meroitic inscription, in hieroglyphs, is that of Queen Shanakhdakhete (?reg. 180–170 BC) found at Naqa, near Meroe. It was through the discovery of an inscription at Wad ben Naqa, in which the names of Netekamani and Amantari were given in Egyptian and Meroitic hieroglyphs, that the phonetic values of the latter were established. Meroitic 'cursive' gradually replaced the hieroglyphs and, after the time of Netekamani (? reg. c. 12 BC–AD 12), hieroglyphs were hardly used. Although the phonetic values of this Meroitic alphabet are known, and inscriptions can therefore be read, they cannot be translated because Meroitic words are not yet understood.

MEROVINGIANS. King Merovech of the Salian Franks, who succeeded to the throne in the mid-5th cent. AD, gave his name to the first dynasty to rule over the Frankish kingdom. Kings such as Childeric I and Clovis laid the foundations of the kingdom, but the dynasty produced no outstanding rulers to follow them. From the 7th to the early 8th cent. disorders within the kingdom allowed the state to fragment and enhanced the power of the 'mayors of the palace'. The usurpation of Pepin II in 687 effectively brought Merovingian power to an end, the dynasty being replaced by that of the Carolingians, although Merovingian kings continued to rule nominally until the deposition of Childeric III by Pepin III in 751.

MERRIMAN, JOHN XAVIA (1841–1926), South African politician who entered the Cape Colony parliament in 1869 and with brief intervals remained a member until 1923, serving in five ministries and in the last of these as prime minister from 1908 until the Union in 1910. Although bitterly anti-imperialist during the Boer War, he became one of the architects of the Union.

In South African politics Merriman was a liberal. But there was never a liberal party in the Cape Colony, and liberalism was expressed chiefly in attitudes to Africans and other non-whites, especially on political rights. Before enclosing many Africans within its boundaries the Cape Colony had acquired a constitution granting the vote to all males on a comparatively low socio-economic qualification. As the Cape expanded, Africans were enrolled as voters. The liberals were those who, from principle or expediency, supported this practice of politically integrating Africans within the white polity. In this group Merriman was an outstanding personality, his liberalism being a complex mixture of moral principle and political expedience. In his old age he criticized the racial policies and practices of Botha's and Smuts's governments in the early years of the Union.

P. Lewsen (ed.), *Correspondence of J. X. Merriman*, 4 vols (Cape Town, 1960–9). AEA

MERRYMAN, EX PARTE, 17 Fed. Cases 9487 (1861), US circuit court case in which Chief Justice Taney challenged Lincoln's suspension of *habeas corpus*. Taney, having failed to get the military to produce Merryman in court to ascertain the cause of his imprisonment, wrote an opinion denying the president's right to suspend *habeas corpus* and asserted that this could only be done constitutionally by Congress.

MERS EL-KEBIR, naval base adjoining Oran, at which during the Second World War a British naval force, under the command of Admiral Somerville, sank a large part of a French fleet (4 July 1940). The incident resulted from British determination to prevent the French fleet falling into German hands, but its immediate cause may well have been a misunderstanding between Somerville and his French counterpart (Admiral Gensoul), who rejected the choice offered to him of joining the British, or sailing his fleet either to a British port or to a French port in the West Indies. The incident was followed by the Vichy government's severance of diplomatic relations with Britain.

MERV, oasis on the lower Murghab river, the centre of a thriving town before its destruction by the Mongols (1221). It subsequently became a base for Turkmen tribes engaged in slave-raiding. In 1884, Merv was annexed by Russia, an event which aroused fears in Britain known as 'Mervousness'.

MESNAGER, NICOLAS LE BAILLIF, Comte de St Jean (1658–1714), French diplomat, originally a merchant of Rouen, who purchased the expensive office of *secrétaire du roi* and became first deputy to the council of commerce (1700). His commercial knowledge led to his appointment as a special envoy to Spain, the United Provinces, and then to England, where he conducted preliminary peace negotiations with Henry St John (1711). He was one of the three French plenipotentiaries who signed the peace of Utrecht (1713).

MESOAMERICA, area encompassing central and southern Mexico, Guatemala, British Honduras, El Salvador, and part of Honduras, which archaeologists consider to have constituted a cultural unity in pre-Columbian times.

MESOPOTAMIAN CAMPAIGN. Following the entry of the Ottoman empire into the First World War, a British–Indian expeditionary force was landed at Basra (Nov. 1914) to protect the Abadan oil installations and preserve the loyalty of local chiefs at Kuwait, Muhummerah, etc. The Chief Political Officer, Sir Percy Cox, advocated an advance to Baghdad and, although the government at first opposed this policy, a northward movement was made in 1915 under Maj.-Gen. C. V. Townshend (1861–1924). An attack on Baghdad was ordered (Oct. 1915), but Townshend's forces were repulsed and besieged in Kut, where they surrendered (29 April 1916). A fresh campaign was launched (Dec. 1916) under Maj.-Gen. Stanley Maude (1864–1917), which captured Baghdad (11 March 1917). In the latter part of 1917 and in 1918 a further advance was made towards Mosul, which was occupied, despite Ottoman protests, after the Armistice of Mudros.

MESOPOTAMIAN RELIGION. There is not enough specific evidence as yet to give a precise picture of Mesopotamian religion, but it seems to have been basically Sumerian, adopted and adapted by other peoples. Among a large number of deities worshipped, the principal triad were Enlil (god of air and life), Enki (god of earth and sweet water), and Anu (god of heaven). These were later supplanted to some extent by national gods like Marduk of Babylon and Ashur of Assyria. The statue representing the god was of central importance and it was cared for by many priests, who centred their activities on the temple. The kings, as earthly representatives of the gods, were closely involved in religious affairs, but there is no evidence that the ordinary people were deeply concerned in a personal way other than in the ritual and ceremonies.

MESSALLA CORVINUS, M. VALERIUS (64 BC–AD 8), Roman soldier, statesman, orator, and patron of literature. After service with Brutus and Cassius at Philippi (42) he joined Antony, but transferred his allegiance to Octavian, with whom he was consul in 31. He fought against Sextus Pompey (36), in Illyricum and Pannonia (34–33), against the Alpine Salassi (34–33), and against Antony at Actium. As pronconsul in Gaul he conquered the Aquitani, triumphing in 27. He was the first permanent commissioner of the water supply (11), proposed the title *Pater Patriae* for Augustus (2 BC), gained fame as an orator and historian, and was the patron of the poet Tibullus.

MESSANA, ancient Greek city in north-eastern Sicily (mod. Messina), originally named Zancle by its Chalcidian founders from Cumae, *c.* 725 BC. Its importance lay in its position, which gave it control of the straits between Italy and Sicily. It founded Mylae (8th cent.) and Himera (*c.* 650). In 5th cent. it was won by Anaxilas of Rhegium, himself of Messenian descent, and renamed Messana (*c.* 493). From 461 it was independent and prosperous. After being destroyed by Carthage in 396, it was refounded by Dionysius I and remained substantially under Syracusan control until it was seized by the Mamertines, Campanian mercenaries of Agathocles (288). Hiero II's attempts to recover the city resulted in the First Punic War and Messana's eventual subjection to Rome.

MESSENE, ancient Greek city in the Peloponnese, founded in 369 BC as the capital of the newly liberated Messenia. Its well-preserved city walls provide a magnificent example of 4th-cent. Greek fortifications.

MESSENIAN WARS, series of conflicts in which Sparta won and maintained control of Messenia, the fertile land of the south-western Peleponnese. First conquered and made helots *c.* 730–710 BC, the Messenians rebelled unsuccessfully in the 7th cent. and again in the 5th (*c.* 464–455). Spartan power depended heavily upon the exploitation of Messenia. Already in the 7th cent. fear of further Messenian revolt produced reactionary reform at Sparta and by the 5th cent., as full Spartan citizens decreased in number and Athens began to support Messenian resistance, *eg*, by the occupation of Pylos (425) in the great Peloponnesian War, the need to preserve control of Messenia strongly influenced Spartan policy. After the Spartan defeat at Leuctra (371) Messenia was finally liberated by Epaminondas and the Thebans in 369, but the Spartans would not recognize its independence and it achieved security only with the Macedonian conquest (338).

MESSERSCHMIDT, WILLY (1898–), German scientist and chief designer of the *Bayerische Flugzeugwerke* from 1926, and head of the firm, renamed Messerschmidt A.G. (1938–45). He was responsible for the design and manufacture of the various types of aircraft which bore his name and saw service with the Luftwaffe during the Second World War.

MESSINA CONFERENCE (June 1955), renewed the movement towards European unity after the failure of the project for a European Defence Community, and led eventually to the establishment of the European Economic Community and Euratom. The conference was attended by the foreign ministers of the six members of the European Coal and Steel Community. It produced a resolution stating that 'the time has come to make a fresh advance towards the building of Europe . . . first of all in the economic field', if Europe intended to 'maintain her position in the world, regain her influence and prestige and achieve a continuing increase in the standard of living of her population'.

The conference established an inter-governmental committee (the Spaak committee) which prepared the treaties of Rome. A British 'representative' attended the meetings of this committee for the first few months—his appellation being carefully chosen to indicate a status between that of delegate and observer. The ending of his participation (Nov. 1955) indicated the British decision, reaffirming that with regard to the Schuman plan, not to join the Europe of the Six.

MESSINES, BATTLE OF (7 June 1917), British attack preliminary to their main offensive at Ypres, designed to secure the southern end of the heavily fortified ridge dominating the Salient. It was regarded as one of the most successful attacks of the First World War. Although artillery preparation had taken 18 days, Plumer's Second Army had reached all its objectives by nightfall of the first day, thanks to the detonation at dawn of 19 mines containing almost 200 tons of ammonal which in the course of the previous year had been placed in tunnels dug as much as 200 feet (62 metres) under the German position. The British lost 24,000 men, the Germans 28,000

MESTA, powerful association of Castilian sheep-farmers, originating in the 13th cent., who came to control the production of merino wool, Castile's chief export, and who therefore had immense influence over the Spanish economy from the 15th cent. The *Mesta* was granted wide privileges in a series of ordinances culminating in the law of land lease (1501) which gave it the right to use in perpetuity and at fixed rents any land it had once used as pasture, and in return paid a tax to the Crown. By the 1520s the Mesta's flocks numbered $3\frac{1}{2}$ million head of sheep, and under the stimulus of the price revolution and the American market wool production boomed until the mid-16th cent., after which time it steadily declined. Though it became a decadent institution, the *Mesta*'s privileges survived until the reforms of 1834–6.

MESTIZOS, Latin Americans of mixed Spanish and Indian blood. They were originally illegitimate offspring of conquistadores and Indian women, and occupied a subordinate (but legally equal) position in colonial society. The mestizo predominates (1970) in many Latin American countries, and his handicaps are more social and economic than racial.

METAURUS RIVER, BATTLE OF (207 BC), first decisive Roman victory in Italy in the Second Punic War, in which the consul Claudius Nero, after forced marches from southern Italy, joined his colleague Livius Salinator on the Adriatic coast north of Ancona and defeated Hasdrubal, who had marched from Spain to relieve Hannibal. Livy's estimate of the Carthaginians' losses (56,000 dead, 5400 prisoners) are too high to be credible, but this Roman victory killed Hannibal's remaining hopes of success.

METAXAS, IOANNIS (1870–1941), Greek soldier and politician. After serving as assistant chief of staff during the Balkan Wars (1912–13), he became chief of staff in 1915 and emerged as a strong opponent of Venizelos. A memorandum which he wrote in order to dissuade the government from undertaking a campaign in Asia Minor eventually proved to be correct in its forecast of events, and Metaxas resigned in protest against Venizelos's pro-Entente policy. When Venizelos returned to Athens in 1917 Metaxas was exiled to Corsica. In the 1920s he entered politics as an ultra-royalist. His participation in various governments, especially that of Tsaldaris, provoked the republican opposition into the coups of 1933 and 1935. After the return of the king in 1936 and the fall of parliamentary government, Metaxas was named as prime minister by the king without consultation with the party leaders. That same year the dictatorship of the '4th August regime' was established by royal decree. The left-wing parties and trade unions were suppressed, reforms were promised (but never carried out), and Greece came under martial law. Metaxas, despite his unpopularity and lack of political skill, survived because of the opposition's weakness and unswerving support given him by the king. In 1941 he rejected the Italian ultimatum and took Greece into the Second World War.

METAYAGE in France, common method of land-holding under the *ancien régime*, in which the produce of the land was divided equally between the owner and the leasehold tenant.

METCALFE OF FERN HILL, CHARLES THEOPHILUS METCALFE, Baron (1785–1846). British colonial official. During service in India he negotiated (1809) a treaty with Ranjit Singh of Lahore which extended British influence to the Sutlej. Two years later he became Resident at Delhi. He had great influence over Lord Hastings, until he attempted to expose the shady transactions of the Palmer Co. in Hyderabad. He was acting governor-general (1835–6), but offended the Court of Directors of the East India Co. by removing restrictions on the press. After leaving India he became governor of Jamaica (1839–42), where by sound diplomacy he ended the refusal of the Jamaican legislature to co-operate with the executive consequent upon the West India Prisons Act. He ended his career as governor-general of Canada (1843–5), where he successfully resisted the Lafontaine–Baldwin ministry's demand for responsible government (1845).

METELLUS NUMIDICUS, Q. CAECILIUS (d. ?91 BC), Roman general, who as consul (109) was in command during the Jugurthine War. After campaigning successfully for two years (109–108), he was supplanted by his seditious *legatus*, Marius. As censor in 102 he tried to exclude Glaucia and Saturninus from the Senate and went into exile rather than swear the oath to maintain Saturninus' agrarian law (100). His recall in 99 became a political issue between the oligarchy and its opponents.

METHODIOS (*c.* 825–85), archbishop of Belgrade who, with his brother, Cyril, sought in 860 to convert the Khazars to the Christian faith. Cyril and Methodios undertook a remarkable labour of proselytization which brought within the Christian Church not only the Slavs located in the region of the Danube, but even their neighbours as far as southern Poland, and which, continuing through the efforts of their disciples, exerted a deep influence on the later religious and cultural development of the southern Slav peoples. The brothers visited Rome in 868, and there won the support of Pope Adrian II for their mission. After Cyril's death (869), Methodios returned to the Slavs as Abp of Belgrade. The claim of the German Church to ecclesiastical control over the lands where Methodios was active led to friction in the years after 870, and Methodios had to make a second visit to Rome (880) in order to defend the work which he and his brother had carried out among the Slavs.

METHODISM, world-wide family of Protestant churches owing their origins to the work of John Wesley (1703–91), son of an Anglican clergyman. Wesley's disciplined search for godliness at Oxford University led him to muster a group of sympathetic men, including his brother, Charles, and George Whitefield, whose systematic quest for piety and charity earned them the nickname 'methodists'.

Wesley extended his acquaintance with current mysticism, particularly through contact with Moravians such as Peter Böhler. After his return from unsuccessful missionary service among the colonists of Georgia, America, he experienced, on 24 May 1738, an evangelical conversion that inaugurated his life's work for the conversion of Britain. Travelling extensively, preaching wherever possible, and writing prolifically, he established numerous societies throughout Britain, often composed of those untouched by the Church of England. His intention was apparently to form societies within Anglicanism, yet not only the rejection of his work by many of the clergy, but his own actions, such as the setting apart of laymen as preachers, and the presbyteral 'consecration' of Dr Thomas Coke to the superintendency of the Methodist work in America, made him like a man rowing a boat, who looks fixedly in one direction, but moves in another.

Wesley witnessed the rapid growth of his movement, often through scenes of extraordinary enthusiasm adjudged vulgar by his sophisticated contemporaries. Converts were gathered into classes, and met regularly for mutual encouragement or reproval. Where no sympathetic clergyman was to be found, travelling preachers had pastoral oversight of the societies. Methodist orthodoxy was fixed by Wesley's four published volumes of sermons and his 'Notes on the New Testament'. His theology was anti-Calvinist, separating him from Whitfield, but his positive emphasis was on the genuine possibility of Christian perfection for all faithful men. The societies learned their theology through Charles Wesley's hymns, John's books, and the itinerant preachers' sermons.

Wesley's autocracy, essential for the early growth of his societies, was enshrined in the self-perpetuating senatorial government of the 'Legal Hundred', which he instituted in 1784. After his death, his creation began to disintegrate. The New Connexion, the Primitive Methodists, and the Bible Christians were among the separated groups. The road to reunion lay through a slow liberalizing of the Wesleyan Conference, and, in the latter half of the 19th cent., led by men like Hugh Price Hughes, through a growing Methodist emphasis on the social implications of the gospel. Reunion of some of the Churches in 1907 was followed by a British act of parliament (1932) which legally reunited the divided body.

Following the Abp of Canterbury's appeal in 1947 for serious exploration of the possibility of reunion based on the Lambeth Quadrilateral (1888), Anglican and Methodist representatives produced joint schemes for the consideration of their Churches. Twice the Methodist Conference has expressed its willingness to implement such a scheme but the Church of England, by a narrow majority, rejected it in 1970.

Methodism initially spread from Britain through the migration of laymen to the colonies, from America through Africa and Ceylon, to Australia. Soldiers, craftsmen, and traders established societies which were later incorporated in more formal structures. Wesley's appointment of Thomas Coke to the superintendency of the American work recognized the importance of the societies already there. Against Wesley's advice, Coke styled himself 'bishop', so that Methodism in the US is (1970) episcopal, but in a non-catholic sense. In Canada and in southern and northern India (1970), Methodism disappeared through incorporation in autonomous, national, and united churches. Autonomous Methodist Conferences, springing often from direct missionary work, existed in 1970 in many countries, and the World Methodist population (1970) was about 40,000,000, of whom a quarter were to be found in the US. A World Methodist Council provided a regular consultative forum.

S. Andrews, *Methodism and Society* (London 1970).
Davies and Rupp, *A History of the Methodist Church in Great Britain* (London, 1965). PDob

METHODIST SECESSIONS in Britain occurred because of conservative religious, political, and social tendencies in 19th-cent. Wesleyan Methodism. The Methodist New Connexion (1797) stressed congregational independence and lay leadership. Primitive Methodism (1812) was led by Hugh Bourne and William Clowes, whose evangelizing camp meetings were initially suspected of fostering undue emotionalism and (wrongly) of cloaking sedition. It was strongest in rural areas and the Durham coalfield, where it produced numerous trade union stalwarts. The Bible Christian Society (1815) worked in West Country villages bypassed by Wesleyanism. The United Methodist Free Churches (1857) repudiated the long-lasting ascendancy of Jabez Bunting, who appeared to be making Conference an instrument of autocratic centralization.

METHUEN TREATIES (1703–4), agreements between England and Portugal. Portugal concluded a defensive treaty with England and the Dutch republic and an offensive treaty with England, the Dutch republic, and Austria, both on 27 May 1703; and a commercial treaty with England alone, on 7 Jan. 1704. Under the terms of the defensive and offensive treaties, the Austrian Archduke Charles was to be proclaimed King Charles III of Spain. Accordingly, the conquest of that country was to be undertaken by an army of 28,000 Portuguese and 18,000 allied troops, of whom each of the main allies was to provide one-third, and a naval force was to be stationed on the Tagus. Finally, King Pedro II was to be granted a yearly subsidy by the Allies. The English signatory was Paul Methuen, English minister at Lisbon; but most of the negotiating had been undertaken by John Methuen, Paul's father, at that time entrusted with this special mission. The commercial treaty provided for Portuguese wines to be allowed into England at a preferential rate of duty, one-third less than that imposed on French wines. In return, English wollen cloth was to be readmitted into Portugal on preferential terms.

METICS, resident aliens of free status in ancient Athens, which as a commercial centre for trade and manufacture from the early 6th cent. BC officially encouraged several thousand settlers to engage in trade and ancillary services, giving them legal protection, but not civic rights. Though prohibited from marriage with citizens, from land tenure except by special grant, and from litigation except through a citizen patron, they nevertheless paid taxes and were liable for military service.

MÉTIS, half-breeds, generally the result of unions between French Canadian fur traders and Cree or Ojibwa Indian women. They were strongest in north-west Canada, where they were encouraged, for various reasons, by the North-West Co. and the Catholic missionaries. The *Métis* never properly settled, but followed the buffalo or the fur trade. They were used by the North-West Co. to oppose the Red River Settlement and took part in the Seven Oaks battle (1816). In the 1840s they fought the Sioux for buffalo hunting rights and won a decisive battle at Grand Cocteau. In the Red River Rebellion (1869–70) and the North-West Rebellion (1885) the *Métis*, under Louis Riel, unsuccessfully attempted to prevent the encroachment of white Canadians on their lands. *Métis* settlements survive in Sask. and Ont. and in the 1960s some joined dissident Canadian Indian 'Red Power' advocates.

METOCHITES, THEODORE (*c.* 1260–1332), Byzantine scholar and grand *logothete* (chancellor) under the Emperor Andronikos II Palaiologos. He was the author of poems, letters, and treatises, philosophical and rhetorical in character, which contain valuable information on the events of his own time.

METTERNICH, CLEMENS WENCESLAS LOTHAR, Prince (1773–1859), Austrian politician, who presided over the Congress of Vienna. After entering the Austrian service (1801), he became foreign minister to Francis II after the battle of Wagram. He negotiated the marriage of the emperor's daughter, Marie-Louise, to Napoleon, ensured that Austrian troops played only a nominal part in the Russian campaign, and, as soon as the retreat from Moscow began, persuaded the emperor to sign the treaty of Reichenbach and join the Allies. He was the diplomatic leader of the final campaign against Napoleon, but mistrusting Russian presence in central Europe, sought an early peace with a relatively strong France. After the battle of Leipzig he supported the Frankfurt proposals, which Napoleon's procrastination rendered fruitless.

After the Congress of Vienna, he opposed any changes to the settlement and supported the Congress system to repress revolution and the Carlsbad decrees to halt liberalism in Germany. Within the Austrian empire he favoured a limited form of representation, but the emperor disliked change and postponed the introduction of reforms. From 1825 Kolowrat took over the internal administration of the empire and at the death of Francis (1835), Metternich lost all influence over such matters under the Council of Regency. He favoured adhesion to the Zollverein, but was defeated by the combined opposition of Austrian industrialists and Magyar landowners and by the Prussian refusal to admit non-German lands.

The liberal views of France under the July Monarchy and of England threw the three eastern powers together. Metternich's attempts to strengthen Austrian power were frustrated by lack of finance, so that the Austrian armed forces were increasingly starved to the detriment of their efficiency. Meanwhile Polish nationalists were using the Free State of Cracow as a base and Metternich was finally compelled to annex it, in breach of the Vienna settlement, in order to forestall the Russians.

The 1848 revolution in France set Europe aflame and in March the Regency Council and mob violence in Vienna compelled Metternich to resign.

The significance and the value of Metternich's work were disputed in his own time and have been since. His pompous and complacent manner offended his contemporaries; his moderation and subservience to the emperor have led to doubts as to his importance and principles; Whig historians condemned him as an arch-reactionary; while the disintegration in 1918 of Europe's greatest multi-national state is frequently blamed on his policies. Much criticism of him is due to a mistaken notion of his position. The zenith of his power came near the beginning of his career. After 1818, when he had to act primarily as foreign minister to the autocrat of an impoverished state which had many responsibilities, his work required an empirical approach and was naturally of a defensive nature. In this he showed skill and integrity, and fidelity to the principles of equilibrium, stability, and the preservation of peace and order. After 1825, especially after 1835, his influence upon events was small.

Algernon Cecil, *Metternich* (London, 1947).
Henry F. Schwarz (ed.), *Metternich, the 'Coachman of Europe'* (Boston, 1962).   DMK

MEURON, PIERRE FREDERIC DE (*fl.* 18th cent.), commander of a Swiss mercenary regiment owned by his brother, and hired by the Dutch in the closing years of their occupation of Ceylon. The regiment was secretly bought by the British, which greatly eased their capture of Colombo (1795). Subsequently, De Meuron entered the British service and proved a valuable administrator.

MEVLEVI (MAWLAWI), order of dervishes deriving from the great mystic, Jalal al-Din Rumi (d. AD 1273). Music and dancing were important in its ceremonies and practices. The order was set on a durable foundation in the time of Sultan Walad, its sheikh (1283–1312).

MEXICAN REVOLUTION, violent movement (1910–17) which ended the Porfirian dictatorship (1911) and made possible the constitutional conventions of Aguascalientes and Querétaro and the revolutionary constitution of 1917. The revolution contained the seeds of subsequent tendencies, such as agrarian reform, economic nationalism, and socialist and secular education for the masses.

The revolution began as a movement for political reform, but demands for socio-economic change were soon heard. The election of 1910 was 'won', possibly by fraudulent means, by the dictator, Porfirio Díaz, while Francisco Madero, his liberal opponent, languished in prison at San Luis Potosí. Madero fled to San Antonio soon afterwards, and from there proclaimed a revolutionary plan against the Porfirian regime. In Chihuahua and in Morelos men such as Pascual Orozco, Francisco (Pancho) Villa, and Emiliano Zapata heeded his call. Díaz resigned and fled to Paris. Madero installed a conservative provisional government and tolerated the existence of the Porfirian army, errors which contributed to the loss of Zapata's support in the south.

With Madero's election to the presidency (Oct. 1911), came further disaffection. The lack of peace in rural areas occupied the attention of the president, who now began to use the Porfirian army against Orozco in the north and against Zapata's agrarian revolutionists.

Gen. Victoriano Huerta soon saw that the president was trapped between the social revolutionaries and the reactionary army and decided to eliminate him. Following the 'tragic ten days', Madero was shot, probably at Huerta's instigation, and Huerta emerged victorious (1913). The US ambassador and an important part of the foreign community had connived in these developments. Huerta now faced Zapata and a new threat from the north—the Constitutionalists, who were loyal to Venustiano Carranza. In Washington President Wilson refused to recognize Huerta and allowed arms to reach his enemies.

Carranza ignored Zapata and allied his movement, which was pledged to avenge Madero's death, to the armies of Francisco Villa and Álvaro Obregón in the north. This alliance was tenuous from the beginning. Villa, whose cavalry constituted the strongest force in Mexico, was not trusted by Carranza, the 'First Chief', who was surrounded by urban advisers who little understood the social dynamics of the movement that was under way. The allies defeated Huerta's army, however, and he fled (1914).

The split between Villa and Carranza now came to the fore, with Obregón supporting Carranza (1914–15). Villa took the capital (Dec. 1914), but he was unable to establish a government, though he did win the favour of Zapata. Obregón's victory over Villa at Celaya (1915), in the bloodiest engagement of the revolution, assured Carranza's dominance over all other factions. He was recognized as de facto president (1915) and, with Obregón's support, and in spite of Zapata's continued opposition, was legally elected president (1917–20). During his struggle against Villa, Carranza had received US support, but as president was unable to compromise when faced with US demands. For this reason, Washington refused to recognize his government. For the advantages it gave him during the revolution Carranza had hesitantly accepted the need of social reform; he was now called upon to provide a constitution which would embody his government's aims. He summoned a constitutional convention, which met at Querétaro (1917). Such a constitution was not to Carranza's liking, and though he accepted it, he refused to enforce it. It produced a document providing for labour legislation, agrarian reform, economic nationalism, and public education and it also advocated anti-clerical policies.

F. Tannenbaum, *The Mexican Agrarian Revolution* (Washington, DC, 1929).   HDS

MEZÖ-KERESTES, BATTLE OF (Oct. 1596) (Turkish: Haç Ovasi, meaning Plain of the Cross), fought not far from the Hungarian fortress town of Eger (Erlau). The Ottomans, after a desperate conflict which brought them to the verge of defeat, routed the imperialist forces ranged against them. The Christians had made a great effort to expel the Ottomans from the Hungarian realm; Mezö-Kerestes marked their failure.

MFECANE or DIFAQANE, African term for the wars in southern Africa between 1818 and 1828, whose cause lay in the empire-building activities of Shaka-Zulu in Natal and Zululand. The Mfecane changed the demography of the subcontinent and had social, political, and economic repercussions as far afield as Mozambique, Malawi, Zambia, and Tanzania.

The roots of the Mfecane are probably to be found at the end of the 18th cent., when population expansion and increasing trade with Delagoa Bay led to the formation of a number of new corporate kingdoms in northern Zululand. Conflict between them culminated during the rule of Shaka, chief of the Zulu people, and as warfare spread defeated chiefdoms ricocheted in all directions. Among the first to leave were the Ngwane, under Sobhuza, who moved across the Pongola river to form the Swazi nation. They were followed by groups of the Ndwandwe people, under Soshangane and Zwangendaba, who carried the movement northwards to Mozambique, Malawi, and Tanzania.

Westward, the flight of the Hlubi and Nwane, under Matiwane, precipitated the turmoil on the Highveld, among many other Sotho groups. One of these, the Kololo, under Sebetwane, after prolonged migration, established a kingdom on the Upper Zambesi. Yet others were formed into the Basuto nation by Mshweshwe. In the Transvaal, one of Shaka's rebellious lieutenants, Mzilikazi, founded the Matabele kingdom before moving still further north to what afterwards became Rhodesia.

In Natal itself the African population was devastated by the passage of Shaka's armies and the hordes of fugitives, many of whom penetrated as far as the Cape colonial frontier. These were later to be regrouped and settled by the colonial authorities as the Mfengu.

The destructive aspects of the Mfecane were most immediately felt. Thousands were massacred or died of the famine which followed in the wake of marauding armies. Many refugees scrambled to safety in broken, barren, and hilly country, while others joined the invading armies or set off in turn in search of a fresh victim. Not surprisingly, the first whites to enter these devastated lands saw them as depopulated and awaiting white colonization. Yet out of this maelstrom new peoples and new states were born. To those who were not crushed by their advent, the invaders brought an example of military and political organization which was to enable them to withstand many of the later pressures—the Voortrekkers—and to resist newer invaders.

J. D. Omer-Cooper, *The Zulu Aftermath, A Nineteenth-Century Revolution in Bantu Africa* (London, 1966). SM

MIAJA MENANT, JOSÉ (1878–1958), Spanish soldier. Although trained at the Toledo Military Academy at the same time as the Fanjul–Goded generation, he neither made his career in Africa nor participated in later right-wing conspiracies. He avoided the Sanjurjo rising of 10 Aug. 1932. Although briefly a member of the anti-Republican *Unión Militar*, he was a moderate and loyal officer. In the spring of 1936 he identified himself with young Republican officers rather than with the Nationalist plotters, and in the July rising was head of the Madrid division.

Miaja figured briefly as minister of war in Martínez Barrio's emergency one-day ministry of 18–19 July, and reluctantly armed the workers for the defence of Madrid. Thereafter, he was the republic's most notable military figure. He led the unsuccessful attack on Cordoba (Aug. 1936) and was retired thereafter. He was recalled (Oct.) to take over the Madrid front and organized the defence of the city. When the seat of government was transferred to Valencia in Nov., Miaja was left in charge of Madrid.

He was sympathetic to the communists because of their resoluteness and efficiency, and became one of the channels through which their policies were put forward. After the fall of the Basque Provinces, he led the Republican offensive of Brunete in an attempt to cut off the besiegers of Madrid. In April 1938 he was made supreme commander of Central and South-west Spain. As the end of the war approached, he advocated resistance to the last man, but subsequently joined those who were ready to negotiate a surrender. After the war, he went to Mexico.

MIAMI INDIANS, North American tribe, first recorded by the French (1658) near Green Bay, WI. The Miami were involved in all the Indian wars in the Ohio valley until the end of the War of 1812. They ceded their lands to the US government by a series of treaties (1818–40) and moved west of the Mississippi, except for one group which remained on a reservation in IN. The rest were put on a reservation in OK (1867).

MIANI, BATTLE OF (17 Feb. 1843, fought near Hyderabad in Sind, when the British, under Napier, defeated the Amirs of Sind. This, and the victory at Dabo, led to the annexation of Sind.

MICHAEL VIII PALAIOLOGOS (*reg.* 1261–82), Byzantine Emperor, who was a leading collaborator with the Emperor Theodore of Nikaea (d. 1258) and in 1259 became co-emperor with Theodore's son, John IV. In 1261 Michael, with Genoese help, regained control of Constantinople, which had been in the hands of the Latins since 1204, deposed John IV, and became the sole emperor, thus founding the dynasty of the Palaiologoi, which was destined to rule the Byzantine empire until its end in 1453. Michael had to face numerous foes, above all, Charles of Anjou, the master of southern Italy. In order to meet this threat, the emperor sought to retain the support of Genoa and in 1274 even made the submission of the Greek Church to the pope. A formidable coalition embracing Charles of Anjou, the papacy, Venice, the Serbs, and the Bulgarians, was formed against Byzantium in 1281–2. The threat from this combination was averted, however, in March 1282 by a revolt in Palermo, later known as the Sicilian Vespers. Michael and his successors financed Charles's enemies in the ensuing war, in which the Aragonese conquered Sicily and ultimately broke the Angevins' power. During the long years of crisis Michael had shown himself to be an able statesman. His preoccupation with Balkan affairs had, however, its less fortunate side. It demanded a large expenditure of resources, which left the provinces in Asia Minor denuded of strength; a situation that accounted in no small degree for the speed and ease of the Turkish advance through the territories of the former Nikaean state to the Aegean Sea in the two decades following the death of Michael VIII.

MICHAEL (1922–70), King of Rumania (*reg.* 1926–30, 1940–7), son of King Carol and his first wife, Princess Helen of Greece. He first came to the throne as a child in 1926, when his father renounced his right to it for Mme Lupescu. A regency was named for the period of Michael's minority. When Carol returned to Rumania and took the throne in 1930 Michael was reduced to the rank of a crown prince. He again became king in 1940 when Carol and his entourage were forced to flee the country. He ruled during Antonescu's dictatorship, but was not wholly a party to it, most decisions being taken without prior consultation with the king. In 1944 Michael showed courage in accepting Maniu's advice to oust Antonescu. Thereafter he was under constant attack from the Rumanian Communist Party and its Soviet ally. After he boycotted Groza's government he became a rallying point for opposition to the communists. For the last two years of his reign he was in the anomolous position of a king in what was virtually a communist state. The anomaly ended when in 1947 he was forced to abdicate. After leaving Rumania he lived in Western Europe, primarily in Switzerland.

MICHAEL FYODOROVICH ROMANOV (1596–1645), Tsar (*reg.* 1613–45), son of Patriarch Filaret (Fedor Romanov) and great-nephew of Tsar Ivan IV. At the age of 16 he was elected tsar by a national assembly (*zemski sobor*) and with the unanimous support of the people was crowned in Moscow, thus founding the Romanov dynasty.

His accession coming at the conclusion of the Time of Troubles, during which he was forcibly separated from his exiled parents, Michael exercised an authority which was far less absolute than that of his predecessor, Ivan IV, or of his grandson, Peter I. The circumstances of his election and his youthfulness meant that he ruled in conjunction with the *zemski sobor*, and with favourites, *eg*, the Saltykovs, while his father was a Polish captive, and in the years 1618–33 he shared his authority with this energetic man, who was the supreme head of the Orthodox Church. In effect, during the first two decades of Michael's reign Filaret was the real ruler and while he lived efforts were made to reform the administration, encourage foreign trade, and end the war with Sweden and Poland, which had proved disastrous for Muscovy. Thus by the peace of Stolbovo (1617) Novgorod was restored to Russia, but the armistice of Deulino with Poland (1618) left the Smolensk and Seversk regions in Polish hands.

In Michael's reign Russia's relations with the western powers developed and Russia became less isolated from Europe. The English and Dutch helped the tsar to come to terms with Poland and Sweden because Muscovy would provide a good market for their goods. Louis XIII also sought an alliance for commercial reasons. After Stolbovo Gustavus Adolphus of Sweden looked for a Muscovite alliance against the Catholic powers, Poland, and the empire. Yet under Michael Muscovy fought two wars with Poland and one with Sweden, all unsuccessful and typified by the badly planned and inefficiently conducted Smolensk campaign (1632–3). The cost of these wars was ruinous. After his father's death it became clear that Michael had little strength of character and he left no conspicuous mark upon his country.

R. N. Bain, *The First Romanovs, 1613–1725* (New York, 1905).   MKS

MICHELANGELO BUONARROTI (1475–1564), Italian sculptor, painter, architect, and poet. He was apprenticed in 1488 to the Florentine fresco painter, Domenico Ghirlandaio. In Rome he carved (1496) his first major work, the St Peter's *Pieta*. He returned to Florence, already a famous sculptor; and in 1508 he began to paint the frescoes on the ceiling of the Sistine Chapel in the Vatican. He completed this colossal enterprise in 1512. From 1513 to 1516 he worked in Florence on the Julius Monument, the tomb of Julius II, which was to occupy his mind for 40 years through numerous changes in design. Over 40 figures were originally projected, but only three remain: the two *Slaves* at the base of the monument and the *Moses* from the upper story. In 1520 he began planning the Medici Chapel for Pope Leo X, on which work began in 1524. In the same year he was commissioned to design the Laurenziana Library (1530–4). In Florence Michelangelo's fortunes followed those of the Medici and the uncompleted nature of many of his works are witness to Florence's turmoil and unrest. He left Florence in 1534 to settle permanently in Rome. Two years later he started to paint the *Last Judgement* on the altar wall of the Sistine Chapel, and in this writhing mass of naked forms the Mannerist style makes its appearance. As in the Laurenziana Library, Michelangelo broke free from classical Renaissance canons of form and reversed classical rules. In 1547 he became chief architect of St Peter's and his plan for the dome (1557) prefigures the Baroque style. His influence on the next century and on his contemporaries was enormous.   LB

MICHELET, EDMOND (1899–1970), French businessman and politician, who was active in the Christian Democrat movement before the Second World War. During the war he participated in the Resistance and was arrested and deported to Dachau. He entered parliament in 1945, and was a minister in De Gaulle's government (1945–6). He sat at first as a member of the Catholic MRP party, but joined De Gaulle's RPF movement when it was founded (1947). He again served as a minister under the Fifth Republic (1958–1961, 1967–70).

MICHELET, JULES (1798–1874), French historian, who was a professor at the Sorbonne (1832), and at the Collège de France (1838), a post which he lost (1851) by his refusal to swear allegiance to Napoleon III. His works included *Histoire de France* and his *Histoire de la Révolution*.

MICHELS, ROBERT (1876–1936), German sociologist and author of *Political Parties: A Sociological Study of the Oligarchical Tendencies of Modern Democracy* (1911), which had an influence on political sociology, organization theory, and discussions about the viability of democracy.

MICHELSEN, PETER CHRISTIAN HERSLEB KJERSCHOW (1857–1925), Norwegian politician and businessman who played a major part in the securing of national independence in 1905; as prime minister he introduced a bill promising Norway a consular service separate from that of Sweden. Its rejection by Oscar II, King of Sweden and Norway, led Michelsen and his fellow ministers to secure the passage of a resolution through the Storting (parliament) that the monarchical union was dissolved. He then negotiated with the Danish prince, Charles, to ascend the throne of Norway as Haakon VII despite the republican tradition of Michelsen's own radical party.

MICHELSON, ALBERT ABRAHAM (1852–1931), US physicist, who (1887), together with Edward Williams Morley (1838–1923), carried out the experiment which showed that the velocity of light was unique. This result was in contradiction with Newtonian physics and led in 1905 to Einstein's formulation of the Theory of Relativity. In 1907 Michelson became the first US scientist to be awarded a Nobel Prize.

MICHIGAN, 26th member state of the US (admitted, 1837), occupying the peninsulas between Lakes Huron, Michigan, and Superior. The area that became MI was penetrated by French explorers and missionaries, who established permanent settlements at Sault Ste Marie (1668) and Fort Pontchartrain, later Detroit (1801). It passed to the British (1763), who ceded it to the US (1783), but did not evacuate Detroit until 1796. The region formed part of the North-west (1787–1800) and Indiana Territories (1800–5) before being organized as Michigan Territory (1805). Further territorial changes followed, and the Federal government required the solution of a boundary dispute with OH before admitting MI into the Union (1837). Expanding agriculture and commercial enterprise led to the indiscriminate exploitation of MI's forests during the 19th cent. but reforestation is now restoring the 'cut-over' land. The economy of the state was transformed during the 20th cent. by the growth of the automobile industry around Detroit.

MICHILMACKINAC, island in the straits between Lakes Michigan and Huron on which the French had a mission (1670) and a fort (1679). It passed under British control in 1761 and was granted to the US in 1783. The island was seized by Ojibwas during Pontiac's Rebellion (1763) and by British–Canadian forces in the War of 1812.

MICMAC INDIANS, Algonquian tribe inhabiting the Canadian Atlantic provinces, possibly encountered by the Norsemen (*c.* 1000) and probably by John Cabot (1497). They acted as middlemen between Europeans and other Indians. The French sent missionaries to the Micmac (*c.* 1600), and after the cession of Acadia to the English (1713) their friendship with the French caused disputes with the English until 1779. They are unusual in that they suffered no permanent decline in numbers as a result of European contact, and continue (1970) to occupy their original lands.

MICO TRUST FUND, established in England (1670) by Lady Mico's initial £1000 bequest to redeem Christian slaves from the Moors. Its dormant capital—£120,000 by 1827—was used to educate children in the former British slave colonies in the West Indies.

MICRONESIA, Trust Territory, made up of 2100 low and high, humid, volcanic, typhoon-torn islets, formerly the Mariana, Palau, Caroline, and Marshall Islands. It was discovered by Spanish navigators in the 16th cent., the various groups later passing successively under Spanish, German (1885), Japanese (1914), and US (1945) control, the area as a whole being accepted in 1947 by the US as a UN strategic trusteeship territory under naval and, in 1951, civil administration. The UN encouraged education, tourism, and constitutional development, and the first bicameral congress from the constituent groups met at Saipan in 1965.

MICROSCOPE. The first compound model was invented by Zacharias Janssen (1590) and the first single lens model by Anton van Leeuwenhoek (*c.* 1673). In 1611 Kepler suggested a compound microscope, which was to prove the prototype of the modern microscope, but it was left to Christoph Scheiner (*c.* 1628) to construct it. In 1684 Christian Huygens invented the two-lens eye-piece. Further improvements were carried out in the 19th and 20th cents.

MIDDLE EAST, term coined (Sept. 1902) by Capt. Alfred T. Mahan to denote an indefinite area around the Persian Gulf, which was given greater precision by *The Times* correspondent, Valentine Chirol, in a series of articles (Oct. 1902) later collected in a book (*The Middle Eastern Question*, 1903) in which it was used to designate the approaches to India from Iraq to Tibet. After the First World War the area thus designated was extended westwards at the expense of the term 'Near East' and during the Second World War came to include parts of North Africa. Despite its outdated strategic origin and its lack of geographical justification, the term has become applicable to a variable area ranging from Turkey to Aden and from Central Asia to Morocco.

MIDDLE EAST DEFENCE ORGANIZATION (1951), abortive proposal designed to provide for the 'modernization' of the Anglo-Egyptian treaty (1936) and to bring Turkey into a defence organization in the eastern Mediterranean, linked to NATO. The proposal offered a theoretical equality between the proposed member states (US, Britain, France, Turkey, Egypt), but in practice would have meant the retention of the British base in Egypt under a different flag. It thus ran counter to the desire of the Egyptian government to achieve its independence—demonstrated by its unilateral denunciation of the 1936 treaty two days before the MEDO proposal was put to it. Subsequently, the sensitivity of the new US administration to Egyptian nationalism prevented the proposal being revived.

MIDDLE EAST OIL. The mineral oil deposits of the Middle East, known and used from ancient times, became of immense importance in the 20th cent. as a result of increased world demand and the development of drilling techniques. Exploration by European concessionaires began in the late 19th cent. and the first major discovery (excluding the great Russian oilfield at Baku) came in 1908 in Iran. It was made by the D'Arcy interests, which formed the basis of the future Anglo-Iranian Oil Co. Small deposits were also found in Egypt, but the second most important area of development was Iraq, although for political reasons this was not exploited until after the First World War, when the Turkish (later Iraq) Petroleum Co. was reconstructed, began production (1925), and discovered a large oilfield in Kirkuk (1927). In the Arabian peninsula development was slower in Bahrayn (1932), Saudi Arabia and Kuwait (1938) and Qatar (1939). By the outbreak of the Second World War, despite the large known potential of the Middle East, its oil production had risen only from 1 per cent of world production in 1920 to about 6 per cent. A major expansion took place after 1945 in Iran, Iraq, and particularly in Saudi Arabia under the Arabian American Oil Co., especially after the completion (1950) of the Trans-Arabian Pipe Line to the Mediterranean (the first pipeline to it from Kirkuk had been opened 1934) and in Kuwait, which profited from the cessation of Iranian oil supplies (1951–4). Later developments in the Arabian peninsula included commercial production from the Kuwayt–Saudi Arabian Neutral Zone (1953), Abu Dhabi (1962), and Oman (1967), and, after 1957, from various offshore wells In 1965 the Middle East (excluding Libya) produced 27 per cent of world oil, had 60 per cent of proven reserves, and was the largest exporter of oil, supplying 55 per cent of West Europe's needs. Oil is by far the greatest Middle Eastern industry and includes refining (notably at the great refineries at Abadan (1913), Bahrayn (1937), Ras Tanura (1945), and Ahmadi (1949)) and transportation (both by pipelines and from enormous tanker terminals, *eg*, Kharg Island, begun 1960). Its economic and budgetary importance to producer and transit countries led to their demands for greater control of and shares in the profits of oil, which led to political clashes, especially in Iran (Abadan crisis, 1951–3), Egypt (1956), Iraq (1961), and in Syria over pipeline maintenance. New agreements giving producer countries a half-share of profits became the pattern (1950–2) and later agreements raised this in effect to 75 per cent. Although the Middle East oil industry was for some time dominated by seven major international companies operating through local companies which held concessions, new national or joint national–private companies came to play an increasing role. The Organization of Petroleum Exporting Countries (OPEC, founded 1961) also played a vital part in preventing the concessionaires from reducing the official 'posted' price of oil, despite a world oil surplus in the late 1950s.

S. H. Longrigg, *Oil in the Middle East* (Oxford, 1968).

MEY

MIDDLE EAST SUPPLY CENTRE, British regional organization established in Egypt (1941) to co-ordinate the production and distribution of basic commodities in the Middle East during the period of dislocation brought about by the Second World War. Joint British–US control was introduced in 1942 and the organization wound up in 1945.

MIDDLE KINGDOM, one of the three great periods (Old, Middle, and New Kingdoms) of ancient Egypt. It was ushered in by the Theban king, Mentuhetep I (*reg. c.* 2060–2009 BC) of the XIth dynasty, who united the country. The Middle Kingdom reached its apogee under the kings (all of whom were named either Amenemhat or Sesostris) of the XIIth dynasty (*c.* 1991–1786). It was a period of strong centralized government, of prosperity based on renewed trade, improved agriculture, extensive quarrying, mining, and building, and of artistic and literary achievement. Abroad, friendly relations were established with Syrian and Palestinian rulers, attacks were made on Libya, and part of Nubia was conquered. The Middle Kingdom was followed by a time of confusion which ended with the Hyksos invasions.

MIDDLE PASSAGE, that part of the triangular trade in which slaves were carried from Africa to America (16th–19th cents). The wretched conditions in slave ships in the Middle Passage led in the 19th cent. to European and American movements to abolish the slave trade.

MIDDLEMEN, class of merchant traders who emerged from the later Middle Ages as the intermediate link between artisans and craftsmen and the markets for their goods, both agricultural and industrial. Their emergence was closely linked with the growth of capitalism. In England middlemen developed from the early 16th cent., particularly to handle the rapidly expanding trade in finished cloth, despite Tudor legislation to restrict their activities. They often supplied the craftsmen with raw materials and also marketed the finished products. As a class middlemen acquired social and political respectability and were an essential element in the capitalist revolution of the modern age.

MIDDLESEX, LIONEL CRANFIELD, 1st Earl of (1575–1645), English politician and lord treasurer, whose early years were spent as a merchant, particularly in the cloth trade, and in 1613 he became surveyor-general of the customs. During the next few years he supplied advice and information to the privy council, allied himself with George Villiers (later Duke of Buckingham), and rose rapidly in his wake. He was successively made master of requests (1616), master of the great wardrobe (1618), master of the court of wards (1619), and a member of the privy council (1620). During his rise he managed to effect reforms in the departments under his control.

In the parliament of 1621 he proved himself one of the ablest of privy councillors, acting as an intermediary between James I and the Commons, and being instrumental in the impeachment of Francis Bacon. He was appointed lord treasurer (1621) and attempted to increase the royal revenues and decrease the king's expenditure. Though partially successful in his first aim, Middlesex failed in his second and became unpopular with both James and Buckingham, who defeated his programme of retrenchment. The deep rift between him and James and Buckingham led to the latters' encouraging the Commons in 1624 to impeach Middlesex as lord treasurer. He was accused of corruption and maladministration, found guilty on four charges, and sentenced to the loss of all his offices, to be imprisoned at the king's pleasure, and fined £50,000. In 1626 Charles I granted him a full pardon, and he spent the rest of his life in retirement.

M. Prestwich, *Cranfield: politics and profits under the early Stuarts* (Oxford, 1966).
R. H. Tawney, *Business and Politics under James I: Lionel Cranfield, as merchant and minister* (Cambridge, 1958). CJ

MIDDLESEX ELECTION (1768) in England, the most protracted and probably the most momentous of John Wilkes's assaults on the establishment politicians of George III's reign, from which may be said to date the birth of English radicalism.

Wilkes was elected MP for Middlesex soon after his return from France, still technically an outlaw facing charges of libel. By quashing the outlawry, only to imprison Wilkes on the original charge, Grafton's administration played into the hands of the radicals and constitutional reformers. After a fortnight of continuous rioting, to the cry of 'Wilkes and liberty!', a dozen of the mob were shot down by troops in St George's Field. Wilkes wrote an inflammatory pamphlet virtually accusing the secretary of state, Weymouth, of premeditated murder and was promptly elected alderman of the City of London. He was expelled from parliament and re-elected, unopposed, for Middlesex. After two more expulsions and unopposed re-elections, and ignoring the Commons' resolution incapacitating him from sitting again in that parliament, he won a fourth election, this time over a government candidate, Col. Luttrell. The Commons then declared Luttrell elected. By thus flouting the wishes of the Middlesex electors the administration transformed Wilkes's vendetta into a constitutional issue. The Commons had replaced election by co-option, and Wilkes's supporters could talk of the day when a co-opted majority might stifle the wishes of the people.

From this controversy, with the help of Horne Tooke, sprang the Society of the Supporters of the Bill of Rights, which brought new method into English politics. Between May 1769 and Jan. 1770 the king received petitions representing the signatures of about a quarter of the voting population. In 1774 Wilkes was allowed to take his seat in the Commons and in 1782, after many attempts, the House was persuaded to condemn its resolution incapacitating Wilkes. But before then Wilkes's radical fervour, always a somewhat shallow emotion, had deserted him, though his name was to become irretrievably linked with the parliamentary reform clubs which were to flourish in London and the provinces in the next half century. English radicalism had been given its first real focal point. SH

MIDDLETON, JOHN MIDDLETON, 1st Earl of (Scottish) (1619–74), Scottish soldier of fortune, who served with the Scottish army in England in the 1640s, commanding the cavalry at the battle of Preston (1648), where he was captured. Until that time he had been a zealous covenanter, but he then changed his opinions. He quarrelled with the Scottish government over their treatment of Charles II (1650), and was in command of the royalist cavalry at Worcester (1651), where he was again captured; later he escaped to France. In 1654 he led an abortive royalist highland rising. He returned to England with Charles II, was created Earl of Middleton, and appointed commander-in-chief in Scotland. His opposition to Lauderdale ended in his overthrow (1663). He was later governor of Tangier.

MIDHAT PASHA (1822–83), Ottoman politician and reformer, born in Istanbul, the son of a *qadi*. Midhat established his reputation as an administrator in the Danubian provinces (1865–9) and Baghdad (1869–72) and was briefly grand vizier in 1872. Thereafter he lost favour and decided some constitutional check upon the sultan was necessary. His opportunity to achieve this came in 1876, when he played a leading role in the discussions which followed the deposition of Abdülhamid II, and Midhat was appointed grand vizier (Dec. 1876). But in Feb. 1877 he was dismissed and exiled, and on his return (1881) was arrested, banished to Arabia, and later murdered.

MIDI, ill-defined region of south-west France which retained strong Roman influences, *eg*, tradition of written law, and was part of the Capetian kingdom from the early 13th cent. The foundation of the *parlement* of Toulouse (1443), with jurisdiction over the Midi, reinforced royal authority.

MIDIANITES, Semitic nomads who lived mostly in the area east of the Gulf of Akaba. They were conquered by the Hebrews (*c.* 11th cent. BC).

MIDLOTHIAN CAMPAIGNS (1879–80) in Britain, outstanding speeches made by W. E. Gladstone on his election campaigns in Nov. 1879 and March 1880 in southern Scotland and northern England. Despite his official resignation earlier, he was still the undoubted leader of the Liberal party. He denounced the foreign, colonial, and financial aspects of Disraeli's administration in passionate rhetoric which profoundly influenced the Liberals' victory in the election of April 1880. It was the first time that an eminent statesman had courted the British voters in this way. He delivered speeches at various places during his journey and at every railway stop at which he spoke the Liberals gained a seat. Midlothian was the great triumph of the Gladstonian principle that a government should act no less morally than a free and unselfish individual. It showed the importance of the new voters and of the key party workers, inspired by Gladstone's speeches. It also outlined new electoral strategies for the party caucus, the National Liberal Federation begun by Joseph Chamberlain (1877).

MIDWAY, BATTLE OF (3–6 June 1942), engagement in the Second World War between US and Japanese carrier-borne aircraft and naval units near Midway Island in the central Pacific. It was a major defeat for the Japanese and ensured the safety of Midway and Hawaii and helped to re-establish the balance of naval power in the Pacific.

MIESZKO I (d. 992), Prince of Poland. His Piast ancestors controlled some Polish tribes for at least a century before Mieszko's accession to power (*c.* 950). In 966, with German support, he introduced the western type of Christianity, thus ending any chance of Poland's adhering to the eastern Slavonic rite.

MIGRANT LABOUR in Africa. In the earlier stages of industrialization or in the more intensive production of agriculture in African countries, there was a large amount of shifting or migratory labour. In colonial times the plantations of the Ivory Coast and the Gold Coast (Ghana) attracted labour from the less fertile interior, and likewise the growing economy of Buganda was a magnet for migrants coming from elsewhere in Uganda Protectorate and beyond, such as Ruanda. Similarly, mining operations were a focus for migrant labour. The Copper Belt–Katanga region is a good example, but the best are the gold, diamond, and coal mines of South Africa.

Many millions of Africans have been migrant labourers over the past century. The social results have been disastrous, with the eroding of traditional values and authority, and the disruption of family life. But as the economies of these countries become more developed or their governments more xenophobic, so the demand for migrant labour lessens, and the numbers of each permanent labour force increases. This has not been the case in South Africa, at least in theory. Here the major centres of industry have been declared to be white areas, and all African workers involved in these urban complexes have been declared to be impermanent. Their place of residence is considered to be in the Bantu homeland or Bantustans.

At first, the mining industries of South Africa depended for their large labour force almost entirely upon migrancy. By 1904, 77,000 migrant workers were being recruited for the gold mines; by 1939 the figure had risen to 323,000. But increasingly more and more of these labourers were in fact becoming urban dwellers—so much so that many Africans had lived in towns for several generations. But the theory of separate development (Apartheid) demands that African urban workers be deemed to be transitory, and those who cannot find employment are liable to be 'endorsed out'. In this way a huge labour force which is de facto permanent has been declared de jure migratory, with all the consequent insecurity that this implies.

Lord Hailey, *An African Survey* (London, 1956).
S. van der Horst, *Native Labour in South Africa* (London, 1941). AEA

MIHAILOV, IVAN (1897–   ), Bulgarian soldier and politician, known for his close ties with Moscow and ability to survive political changes. He served with the Red Army for 20 years before returning to Bulgaria in 1945 and receiving the rank of major-general in the Bulgarian army. In 1950 he was deputy minister of defence, and also deputy prime minister. He remained in this post after joining the Politburo in 1954.

MIHAILOVIC, DRAZA (1890–1946), Serbian soldier and politician, who led the royalist resistance in Yugoslavia during the Second World War. He began the war in the Yugoslav army, assembling a resistance force in central Serbia in 1941, which came to be known as the Chetniks. Neither Mihailovic nor Tito was prepared to co-operate with the other and soon the two resistance groups were warring among themselves. Mihailovic was strongly anti-communist and favoured a restoration of the monarchy and Serbian hegemony in Yugoslavia. He also shrank from large-scale pitched battles with the enemy. In 1942 he was promoted to the rank of general and appointed minister of war by the royalist government-in-exile. Despite official sanction for his movement, his units were much less successful than Tito's Partisans. Unable to challenge the Partisans either politically or militarily, he turned to the enemy and collaborated with the Germans in order to defeat the Partisans. The Allies, on learning of his collaboration, gave their support to Tito, Mihailovic was discredited, and with his defeat prospects for a restoration in Yugoslavia were shattered. After the war he was captured, tried for treason, and executed.

MIHALACHE, ION (1883–   ), Rumanian politician, who founded the Peasant Party in the kingdom of Rumania in 1918 as the First World War drew to a close. In the Vaida-Voevod government (1919–20) he was minister of agriculture. His agrarian reform law was rejected by the Liberal opposition and caused the king summarily to dismiss the government. Mihalache again served as minister of agriculture in Maniu's National-Peasant government (1928–30). After Maniu's resignation he moved to the ministry of the interior and sought to dissolve the Iron Guard, but without success. As a patriot and monarchist, he shunned the extreme nationalism of the Vaida-Voevod section of the party and, together with Maniu, tried to preserve the National-Peasant ideal in the face of growing tensions. Once Vaida-Voevod left the party Mihalache refused to deal with him or his faction.

He continued his association with Maniu and led the opposition to the Carolist and Antonescu dictatorships. After a brief and abortive period of co-operation with the communists after the Second World War, the National-Peasants became the target of communist attacks. Mihalache was arrested in July 1947 and in Oct. was tried with Maniu and 17 others for espionage by a military court. He was found guilty and sentenced to life imprisonment.

MIHRAB, recess or niche in the wall of a mosque indicating the qibla, *ie*, the orientation towards Mecca which is to be observed during the performance of Muslim ritual prayer.

MIKHAILOVSKY, NIKOLAI KONSTANTINOVICH (1842–1904), Russian exponent of populist theories, through his writings for *Notes of the Fatherland* (*Otechestvennye Zapiskie*) and other journals in the 1870s and 1880s. He encouraged the 'going to the people' movement and was associated with Narodnaya Volya. In *What is Progress?* (1867–8) and *The Struggle for Individuality* (1871) he made a double plea for the full development of individual personality and the moral duty of the intelligentsia to serve society. Rejecting Marx's historical determinism, although influenced by his economics, Mikhailovsky's historical theory involved an immediate movement by Russia to socialism based on the peasant commune (*mir*) and workshop (*artel*), through which, rather than Western capitalism, individuality could develop. With V. Vorontsov and N. Danielson he led the debate with the Marxists in *Russian Wealth* (*Russkoe bogatstvo*) (1892–1904).

MIKLOUCHO-MACLAY, NICOLAUS NICOLEVITCH DE (1846–88), Russian biologist and explorer, who conducted anthropological investigations in New Guinea (1872), the Malay Islands, and New Guinea (1873–7). He settled in NSW (1878), and maintained a biology station at Watson's Bay until 1887.

MIKOLAJIZYK, STANISLAW (1901–66), Polish politician, who became active in the Peasant Co-operative Movement. As an associate of the exiled peasant leader, Wincenty Witos, he became prominent in the Polish Peasant Party and was one of the organizers of the great peasant strike of Aug. 1937. After the collapse of the Polish state, he played an important role in émigré politics, holding the offices of deputy-chairman (1940–1) and chairman (1941–3) of the exile parliament in London. On the death of Gen. Sikorski, he became prime minister of the government-in-exile (July 1943). He attempted unsuccessfully to induce the émigré politicians to accept the Curzon line as Poland's eastern frontier and having failed to do so, he resigned (Nov. 1944). After the Yalta agreement (Feb. 1945), by which the Communist government in Poland was recognized by the Western Allies, in return for broadening its political representation, he returned to Poland and became deputy prime minister, his hope being to prevent the new regime from becoming entirely communist. As leader of the recreated Peasant Party, he controlled the chief force that obstructed the communists' acquisition of complete power, and was consequently the target of a campaign by them to destroy the influence of his party. Its success forced him to flee from Poland in Oct. 1947. He settled in the US, where he was president of the 'Green International' of Peasant Parties.

MIKOYAN, ANASTAS IVANOVICH (1895–   ), Russian politician, who joined the Bolshevik Party (1915) and was active in Tiflis and Baku. He became head of the party organization in Nizhni-Novgorod (1921), then in the North Caucasus (1922–6). He was made a member of the central committee of the CPSU (1923), alternate member of the Politburo (1926–35), and full member (1935–66). He was appointed minister of home and foreign trade (1926–30) and minister of supplies (1930–4), then minister of food industry (1934–8). He was deputy chairman of the council of ministers (1937–55, 1957–8) and first deputy chairman (1955–7, 1958–64).

He strongly supported Khrushchev after Stalin's death and played a key role in the leadership crisis (June 1957). He sometimes prepared the way for important developments in Khrushchev's policy: he spoke critically about Stalin before Khrushchev at the 20th party congress (1956), travelled to the US in advance of Khrushchev's visit (1958), and to Cuba to mollify Castro (1962). He supported Khrushchev's economic reforms and his development of the consumer goods industries. At the same time, his seniority gave him independence of Khrushchev and he held back in the attempts Khrushchev made to suppress the anti-party group. When Khrushchev's leadership was again decisively challenged (1964) Mikoyan played a role as important as that which he played in 1957, but this time in preparing the ground for the overthrow of Khrushchev. He then became chairman of the Presidium of the supreme soviet (*ie*, president) for a brief period (1964–5) before retiring on grounds of age and health.

MILAN, OBRENOVIC (1854–1901), King of Serbia (*reg*. 1882–9), who ascended the throne in 1868 as a minor, with the title of prince. Through his country's defeat by Turkey (1876) and by Bulgaria (1885), and a commercial treaty with Austria (1881), he succeeded in reducing Serbia to the status of an economic and political protectorate of Austria, although he assumed the title of king. His unpopularity was such that he abdicated in 1889. Milan's main contribution was to the balance of power, for while Austria could count on an economically dependent satellite in the Balkans, she was less likely to resent Russian infiltration in that area.

MILAN, capital of Lombardy, situated in the centre of an immensely fertile region. It first rose to prominence in the 4th cent. as the capital of the Roman emperors in the West, then in 402 they withdrew for greater safety to Ravenna. Thereafter, Milan remained the leading Catholic centre of Italy. In 538 it was destroyed by the Arian Ostrogoths. The Arian Lombards, after their conquest of northern Italy in 568, established their capital at Pavia, while the archbishops of Milan became the virtual rulers of that city. Late in the 11th cent. their power was diminished by the rise of a self-governing commune: the struggle over the control of Milan precipitated the conflict in 1075 between Pope Gregory VII and the Emperor Henry IV, whose nominee to the archbishopric was being challenged. A century later control of Milan again seemed the key to the government of Lombardy by Emperor Frederick Barbarossa. After a siege of nine months (1161–2) Milan was starved into submission by Frederick and was utterly destroyed, only the churches being spared. It was soon rebuilt by a league of Lombard cities, created in 1167, and the Milanese were the leaders of the army which defeated Frederick at Legnano in 1176, thus ending his schemes for controlling Lombardy. After 1236 Milan was the foremost member of the reconstituted Lombard League, which combated Frederick II, again contributing to the failure of his attempt to dominate Italy. Thereafter, free from the threat of foreign dominance, Milan became the centre of an important state in central Lombardy which in the 14th and 15th cents, under the rule of the Visconti and Sforza dynasties, was one of the principal powers of Italy. Milanese Lombardy reached the summit of its prosperity in the later 15th cent. After 1499 Milan became the coveted prey of the French, the Imperialists, and the Spaniards, falling permanently to the Habsburgs in 1535 and remaining in their hands until 1859, when it was recovered by the new kingdom of Italy. By 1970 it had become the most important industrial city in Italy.   EBF

MILAN, EDICT OF (AD 313), published in the joint names of the Emperors Constantine and Licinius, and marking the triumph of Christianity over persecution. Preserved, in divergent forms, by Lactantius and Eusebius, it granted to both Christians and others full authority to follow 'whatever worship each man desired, whereby whatsoever Divinity

dwells in heaven may be benevolent and propitious to us and all who are placed under our authority'. Restitution was to be made in full to Christians, their property restored and their right of worship assured. It did not, however, 'establish' the Church as such.

MILAN, PERPETUAL PEACE OF (1516), otherwise known as the Eternal Peace of Freibourg, the settlement between Matthias Schinner and the Swiss and Francis I of France after the latter's victory at Marignano (1515). It defined the boundaries between Switzerland and the Italian state of Milan and recognized Francis's title as Duke of Milan.

MILAN DECREES (1807) reaffirmed and extended Napoleon I's declaration at Berlin (1806) blocking commerce between Britain and all areas of Europe which he controlled or influenced ('the continental system'). It followed the treaty of Tilsit (1807) by which the support of Russia was secured, and was answered by the orders in council of the same year.

MILAN PATRIOTIC SOCIETY, founded by the Emperor Joseph II to signify his approval of the economic reforms undertaken in Lombardy in the 1770s by the Habsburg governor, Count Firmian, on the advice of Pietro Verri, an economist and administrator. They included the reorganization of tariffs and abolition of the tax form (1773), and certain tax immunities. The reforms inaugurated a period of prosperity for Lombardy and reversed Milan's economic decline. Joseph made Verri president of the society, which was intended to promote the study of economic and social problems.

MILDMAY, SIR WALTER (?1520–89), English politician and financier who was chancellor of the exchequer (1566). His influence grew under Elizabeth I and he used it to shield Puritans from episcopal attack and often urged Elizabeth to intervene on behalf of the Protestants in the Netherlands.

MILETUS, ancient Greek city-state on the west coast of Asia Minor, established *c*. 1000 BC on an earlier Mycenaean site by Ionians from mainland Greece. The Milesians, who were under constant Lydian attack in the 7th cent., founded many settlements in the Black Sea, *eg*, Olbia, Sinope, and Trapezus. They were among the first Greek traders in Egypt and had commercial connections with Sybaris in southern Italy. In the 6th cent. Thales, Anaximander, and Anaximenes, all Milesians, were responsible for the beginnings of Greek physics and philosophy. Hecataeus, another Milesian, was the first Greek to attempt descriptive geography and critical history (*c*. 500). In the 5th cent. emigrant Milesian intellectuals were still influential, *eg*, Hippodamus and Aspasia. From 546 onwards Miletus was subject to Persia. She tried unsuccessfully to assert her independence in the Ionian Revolt (500–494) and later became subject successively to Athens (5th cent.), Persia (4th cent.), Alexander and the Hellenistic monarchs (4th–2nd cents), and finally Rome (from 129 BC).

MILITARY CONVERSATIONS (1906–14). Far-reaching discussions between the military staffs of Britain and France began during the first Moroccan crisis to consider means of co-operation should they both become involved in war with Germany. So Edward Grey, the British foreign secretary, authorized the talks with the permission of Asquith, the prime minister, and other ministers. Cabinet approval of the conversations was not sought, however, until 1912. Grey continually emphasized the non-binding nature of the discussions, though they were, in fact, calculated to deepen Britain's moral obligations, especially after naval talks began, with the British navy concentrated in home waters and the French in the Mediterranean. Similar British conversations with the Belgian military staff started in 1906. The Anglo–Russian talks envisaged after the Entente (1907) were eventually begun by the naval staffs in 1914, but made little progress. When the First World War broke out British naval plans had long been settled; whereas, despite the long Anglo–French discussions, no firm decision on the use of the British Expeditionary Force had been taken.

MILITARY FRONTIER (1522–1881), area 1610 kms long and of varying depth between the Habsburg lands and the Ottoman empire. It was settled by soldier-colonists exempt from manorial obligations, who held their land direct from the Crown. With the decline of Turkish power it became an area from which to recruit reliable soldiers cheaply. After 1770 it formed a permanent *cordon sanitaire* against bubonic plague, which was endemic in Turkey. After 1871 it was gradually assimilated into the civil administration.

MILITARY SERVICE ACTS (1916) in Britain. By late 1915 the British government, during the First World War, was under pressure from the army and right-wing opinion to introduce conscription. This was political dynamite for a coalition containing Liberal and Labour ministers, hence the attempt at compromise in the Derby Scheme of Nov. 1915, by which men 'attested' their readiness to be called up if necessary. Asquith, the prime minister, promised that no married man would be called up before a bachelor, and since only 50 per cent of men in both categories had actually 'attested', this was virtually a pledge for conscription of at least the unmarried—a pledge fulfilled by the first Military Service Act (Jan. 1916). It ended the voluntary system of recruitment and imposed compulsion on unmarried men aged 18–41. The Liberal opposition was less than had been feared and only Sir John Simon resigned. The act also set up rather clumsy local tribunals to investigate 'conscientious objectors', 16,000 of whom appeared in the course of the next three years. Because the act was not producing the necessary manpower fast enough, and was probably being unfairly implemented at the local level, the government was forced to supersede it with a second act (May 1916) which decreed universal military service for those up to the age of 41 in the United Kingdom, excluding Ireland. This time there was much greater political tension, Lloyd George, one of the main advocates, being opposed by McKenna, Runciman, Grey, and the Labour ministers. The coalition was in danger of collapse; but eventually the opposition backed down and the bill went through. Conscription was clearly of vital social importance not only in that it now involved one-third of the adult male population in the experience of modern war, but because it also helped open the way to the mass entry of female labour into industry and therefore to women's emancipation.   KM

MILITARY TACTICS in the Middle Ages. The collapse of the Western Roman empire in the 5th cent. left the Byzantines in possession of the only professional disciplined army combining cavalry and infantry and capable of well-organized siege tactics. Despite many disasters, it remained the best professional army of Christian Europe until the 11th cent. The armies raised by the barbarian rulers of western Europe were indisciplined and inadequately armed levies, usually fighting on foot with shield, sword, and spear in a traditional Germanic fashion. In the 8th cent. the Carolingian rulers of the Franks tried to create an elite of heavy armed cavalry and the spread of feudal institutions was the result of these military reforms. By the 11th cent. western European nobles usually came to fight on horseback and the mobile disciplined armies of heavy mailed cavalry dominated the European battlefields from the 11th to the 14th cents. Bodies of infantry were, however, needed to garrison castles and for sieges, as much of the warfare of this period resolved itself into a series of sieges. The 14th cent. saw a revival in the importance of infantry corresponding with the introduction of the English longbow on continental battlefields and the early use of cannon against fortifications. Disciplined archers, stiffened by bodies of dismounted armoured cavalry, were capable of smashing cavalry charges or of forcing the opposing armoured cavalry to dismount and fight on foot. In the late 14th and

15th cents the Swiss infantry fighting in phalanx with pike and halberd also played a significant part in ending the preponderance of heavy cavalry. The spread of cannon and handguns had important repercussions from the late 15th cent. onwards. Cavalry could still retain its value as a mobile shock force, but the wearing of armour ceased to be an adequate protection against cannon and arquebus missiles and more lightly armoured cavalry began to be used, especially in the later 16th and 17th cents. The best armies at the end of the Middle Ages depended on a skilful combination of cavalry, infantry, and artillery and on a considerable expansion of supply services.   JD

MILITIA, citizen reserve, with some degree of training, from which manpower can be drawn in emergencies. It is essentially local in character and recruitment, short in duration of service, and organized for local defence only. These characteristics distinguish the militia from a professional military force. The English militia can be traced back to the Anglo-Saxon fyrd, a tribal arrangement which imposed military service on every able-bodied free man. The fyrd continued during the Middle Ages below the level of the feudal military obligation, and survived in modified form into the 17th cent. The national defence levy was organized by the lords lieutenant on a county basis, and property owners were obliged to provide men and arms. Those called on to serve were allowed to call substitutes. In 17th-cent. England the militia was an important point of contention between the monarchy and parliament. The Militia Ordinance of 5 March 1642, by which the Long Parliament claimed control of the nation's militia forces and which was refuted by the king, was one of the main reasons why each side resorted to arms. The militia in the Civil War, however, proved a broken reed in the hands of parliament, mainly because of its poor training and local basis, *eg*, the London trained bands or militia had an incurable tendency to march home if a campaign lasted more than a few weeks. In consequence a professional fighting force, the New Model Army, was created to replace the militias. The prospect of a professional standing army, and with it the prospect of a continental type of absolute monarchy, led to the revival of political support for the militia in the late 17th cent. The militia in England became essentially a volunteer force after 1852, with the increasing importance of a regular, professional army. In 1907 the Territorial and Reserve Forces Act ended the system, but the name militia was applied to a special reserve in 1921 and revived by the Military Training Act (1939).   CJ

MILITIA, in US, now (1970) called the National Guard, body of armed forces within the states, formed by enlistments. The state governors are commanders-in-chief, except in time of war, when militias are incorporated into the regular armed forces. In colonial times war with the Indians was an ever-present danger and each community had its own militia, made up of all able-bodied citizens. Thus wars could be fought without professional troops and a standing army came to be considered an instrument of tyranny. Provincial militia were notoriously ill-disciplined and preferred to stay near their homes. There were short-term enlistments, and desertions were commonplace. It was largely with such an army that Washington fought the American War of Independence. The Federal Constitution gave Congress power to raise a regular national army, but the 2nd Amendment sanctioned state militias by specifying the right of the people to keep and bear arms. State-organized bodies of citizen soldiers evolved in the first half of the 19th cent. New York state militia assumed the name of National Guard (1824) and the National Guard Association of the US was formed (1878). The Dick Act (1903) made the National Guard the country's reserve force, federally equipped, but under state control. The National Defense Act (1916) made the National Guard subject to federal call, and the Reserve Forces Act (1955) revised the requirements and training of the National Guard. The militia have served in all US wars and police actions, and have frequently been called upon by state and federal officials to maintain order in local crises.

MILITIA ACT (1757), in Britain, reorganized the militia, on which the country depended for home defence, into an effective force, by making the counties responsible for providing a quota of trained men, chosen by lot, who could be enrolled in a national emergency. The act, passed on the insistence of Pitt the Elder, reawakened hostility to the idea of a standing army. But this was overcome by the imminence of the threat from France and in the course of the century the role of the militia was expanded to include service abroad.

MILITIA RESERVE ACT (1882) in Britain, by which members of the militia who agreed to enter the regular forces in a national emergency were allowed a small retaining fee in time of peace. Cardwell's reform of the British army had drawn the militia into closer association with the regulars for home defence, and eventually it was absorbed into the reserve and special reserve forces (1908).

MILL, JAMES (1773–1836), Scottish philosopher, who held the posts of assistant examiner (1819) and head of India House (1830). He became the centre of a group of philosophic liberals that included his son, John Stuart Mill, as well as Bentham and Ricardo. He expounded utilitarianism in government (1824), and his *Analysis of the Phenomena of the Human Mind* (1829) showed utility as the motive behind social progress and mental activity, blending it with associationist psychology. Mill encouraged educational advance by his support for London University (1828), and penal reform by his article on prisons in the *Encyclopaedia Britannica* (1823), which advocated reform through industry rather than simply by punishment.

MILL, JOHN STUART (1806–73), Scottish economist, philosopher, civil servant, and politician. In 1823 Mill founded the Utilitarian Society, coining the name subsequently used for followers of Bentham. In the *London Review*, which he owned (1837–40), the *Westminster Review*, and his book, *Utilitarianism* (1863), he both expounded and modified Bentham's ideas. He combined a belief in the classical principles of free competition with faith in utilitarian doctrines, but his approach to social and economic problems was also influenced by romantic thinkers like Coleridge and by French socialist thinkers like Saint-Simon. Mill was also a man of affairs: he was an employee of the East India Co. (1823–58) and an MP (1865–8). His political ideas, expressed in *On Liberty* (1859) and *Representative Government* (1861), mark a transitional stage in the development of British liberal thought. Mill's main concern was with individual liberty, which he saw as being threatened by the state, by public opinion, and by the tyranny of the majority. At the same time, the changes he made in successive editions of his *Principles of Political Economy* (1848) show his growing concern with social welfare, his belief that economic doctrine should be the handmaid of legislation, and his gradual enlargement of the sphere he thought proper for state intervention. In his later years he regarded himself as a socialist. His *Autobiography* (1873) is a document of great importance in the history of utilitarian and liberal ideas.   BK

MILLE, CECIL BLOUNT DE (1881–1959), US film producer and one of the founders of Hollywood as the centre of the US film industry. He joined (1912) Samuel Goldwyn and others in forming the film studio that eventually became Paramount Pictures. He produced over 70 films and was famous for spectacular historical 'epics' such as *The Ten Commandments* (1923; remade, 1956).

MILLENARY PETITION (1603) in England, moderate plea for Church reform presented by the Puritans to James I on his first entry into England. The authors claimed that it expressed the view of more than 1000 ministers. In studiously

moderate language it urged that some practices should be abolished, *eg*, the sign of the cross in baptism or the ring in marriage, and that others should become optional, *eg*, the surplice. James promised that a conference would be held at Hampton Court to discuss the matter, but later (1604) he rejected the demands for relaxation in ceremonial and declared he would have 'one doctrine and one discipline' in religion.

MILLER, SIR DENISON SAMUEL KING (1860–1923), Australian financier and first governor of the Commonwealth Bank of Australia (1912) after service (1876–1912) with the Bank of New South Wales. He determined the Commonwealth Bank's policy of operating as a savings bank and a trading bank without engaging in 'unfair' competition with the private trading banks. His long-term aim to develop the Commonwealth Bank into a central bank commanded wide support.

MILLER, PHILIP (1691–1771), English botanist, who was curator of Chelsea Physic Garden. His *Gardener's Dictionary* (1731) was the first English publication of its kind. As an experimental botanist his observations on the significance of insects in the pollination of flowers were well ahead of his time.

MILLET, term used to describe a Muslim group. It was neither racial descent nor language or cultural formation which determined in former times the status of the individual within the Muslim state. The determining factor was his religion. It was laid down in the Shari'a, the Sacred Law of Islam, that the ahl al-kitab, the peoples with a book (of scripture), should be allowed to retain the practice of their faith, a status inferior to that of the Muslims being, however, imposed on them (entailing higher taxation, various social disabilities, etc.). The freedom thus granted to practice a religion other than Islam embraced far more than the right to worship in a particular manner. It meant permission to live under one's own religious law—a permission which included attendance at church, the administration of ecclesiastical affairs, education, charitable purposes, and even privileges connected with justice and the collection of taxes. Moreover, non-Muslims did not have to serve in the armies of Islam, being exempted because of their payment of additional taxation which did not all on the Muslims, *eg*, a poll-tax (*jizya*). A Muslim state, such as the Ottoman empire, should be envisaged therefore as an amalgamation of different religious groups, *eg*, Greek Orthodox, Gregorian Armenian, or Jewish. Each group lived under its own religious head (bishop, rabbi) who served as a link with the Muslim authorities. Such a group was in fact a millet. The Muslims, too, constituted a millet like the other religious communities, the basic difference being that, as in the Ottoman empire, the supreme political power was vested in that Muslim millet. With this general situation in mind, it is not difficult to understand how the non-Muslim subjects of the Ottoman sultan retained through the long centuries of Turkish rule their own particular cultural and linguistic identities.   VJP

MILLIGAN, EX PARTE, 4 Wallace 2 (1966), case in which the US Supreme Court asserted its right to review, and if necessary nullify, the action of a military commission. The court declared unlawful the trial and sentence of Milligan for treasonable activities by a special military commission authorized by President Johnson.

MILLONES in Castile, indirect tax levied on basic foodstuffs and necessities, *eg*, wine, meat, oil, vinegar, candles, and soap, introduced by Philip II in 1590 as an extraordinary tax for six years and voted by the Cortes to meet the Crown's soaring costs. It was renewed and increased in 1596 and from 1600 became a permanent tax. Although the nobility and clergy were not exempt, they could evade or afford to pay it, but for the rest of the population this inflationary measure proved a great burden. Periodically ministers, *eg*, Olivares, tried to abolish it, but found no alternative source of revenue, so it was constantly renewed, despite a falling yield in the 17th cent. Under Charles III (1759–88) the millones was considerably reduced.

MILLS, ROBERT (1781–1855), US architect, who practised in Philadelphia, Baltimore, and Charleston (1808–30). After moving to Washington, DC (1830), he became architect of public buildings (1836–40), and built the Treasury (1836–9), the Patent Office (1836–40), and the old Post Office (1839). The Washington Monument, begun in 1848, was not completed until 1884 through lack of funds and of confidence in its design. Mills was devoted to the simplicity and austerity of classical models, and helped to establish Greek Revival architecture as the national style for American public buildings.

MILNER, ALFRED MILNER, Viscount (1854–1925), British administrator, politician, and colonial servant, who was chairman of the board of inland revenue (1892–7) and became British High Commissioner in South Africa (1897–1905). He saw the outbreak of the Anglo-Boer War (1899–1902) as a chance to achieve British supremacy throughout South Africa. After the war he set about reconstructing the gold-mining industry of the Transvaal. Because of a temporary shortage of cheap African mine workers, Milner imported Chinese labourers, and was criticized for doing so. With the years he modified his attitudes on the empire and became an advocate of imperial unity, imperial preference, and Egyptian independence. He opposed the Liberal budget policy (1909), and during the First World War held office in Lloyd George's coalition.

MILNER MISSION (1919–20), British mission of enquiry in Egypt, under the chairmanship of Lord Milner, which was appointed in May 1919 and recommended (Dec. 1920) the substitution of a treaty of alliance guaranteeing British interests in return for the British protectorate then existing over Egypt.

MILO, T. ANNIUS (d. 48 BC), Roman tribune (57), who organized gangs against those of Clodius to secure Cicero's recall from exile. He continued to fight Clodius in the streets and law courts and eventually murdered him at Bovillae (52). Pompey, as sole consul, had Milo condemned, despite Cicero's defence of him, and he retired into exile at Massilia. In 48 he returned to Italy to create further disorder, but was captured and executed.

MILOSLAVSKY, ILIA (*fl.* 17th cent.), Russian *boyar*, who dominated the government of Tsar Alexis (1645–76) and became the tsar's father-in-law on his daughter Maria's marriage to Alexis. He was head of the treasury department and the military administration in Russia. His fraudulent involvement in the manipulation of the copper currency (1656–62) resulted in his temporary disgrace (1662).

MILTIADES (*c.* 550–489 BC), Athenian soldier and political leader, who led the resistance to Darius' Persian invasion of Greece (490), defeating it with skilful tactics at Marathon. He was appointed naval commander against Persia in the Cyclades, and in the attack on Paros was fatally wounded.

MILTON, JOHN (1608–74), English poet and republican pamphleteer. His early poetry, written in the 1630s, includes 'Comus' and 'Lycidas'. He travelled abroad (1637–9), mainly in Italy, visiting Grotius and Galileo. In the 1640s and 1650s he wrote mainly political sonnets and pamphlets on various subjects, *eg*, against episcopacy (1641) and on the doctrine and discipline of divorce (1643). In 'Areopagitica' (1645) he defended the liberty of the press, and in the 'Tenure of Kings and Magistrates' (1649) the execution of Charles I. In 1649 he was appointed Latin secretary to the council of state of the Commonwealth, a post he retained until the Restoration.

He became blind and was assisted in his secretarial work by Andrew Marvell. At the Restoration (1660) he was arrested and fined. Sometime in the early 1660s he began to write his most famous work, 'Paradise Lost', the greatest epic poem in the English language, which he had begun to sketch out in 1642. The work was finished between 1663 and 1667. His last poems were 'Paradise Regained' and 'Samson Agonistes' (1671).

MILVIAN BRIDGE, BATTLE OF (AD 312), at Rome, in which Constantine the Great defeated the usurper, Maxentius, and initiated his career as a Christian emperor. Constantine attributed his victory to the Christian monogram, which, allegedly in response to a dream, he had ordered before the battle to be painted on his troops' shields.

MILYUTIN, Count General **DMITRY ALEKSEYEVICH** (1816–1912), Russian politician, who was the most liberal of Alexander II's ministers. His scheme of administrative reform (1879) would have limited autocracy and established a *rechtsstadt*. As minister of war (1861–81) he introduced universal military service and wide-reaching army reforms.

MILYUTIN, NIKOLAI ALEKSEYEVICH (1818–72), nephew and follower of Kiselyov and brother of D. A. Milyutin. As deputy minister of the interior, he was one of the chief liberal influences behind the emancipation of the serfs, though he retained a belief in autocratic control. After 1863 he carried out land reforms in Poland.

MIMANA, protectorate, between Paekche and Silla, established by the Japanese state of Yamato over Karak and other tribal principalities in southern Korea. Founded in 369 and garrisoned by Yamato troops, the protectorate came under pressure from Koguryo at the end of the century, and was eventually divided between Paekche, nominally an ally of Yamato, and Silla, which annexed Karak in 532.

MIN (1851–95), Queen of Korea (*reg.* 1866–95), as consort of King Kojong. In 1873, her family, the Min of Yohung, obtained Chinese recognition of her son Sunjong as crown prince and secured Chinese help in keeping the Taewongun (prince regent) out of power for about 20 years. The Japanese victory over China in 1894 ended Chinese domination of the Korean court, and might have ended the power of the court itself; but the murder of Queen Min on 8 April 1895, arranged by the Japanese consul Miura, united not only the progressives and the court in Korea, but also the liberals and the emperor in Japan. King Kojong himself gained a greater share of power following her death.

MINAEANS, South Arabian people who, in the second millennium BC, established a state which had its capital at Qarnaur, near Sana'a, Yemen.

MINAMOTO, YORITOMO (1147–99), Japanese feudal leader, who, as founder of the Kamakura *bakufu*, played a major part in the shaping of Japan's feudal institutions. He was exiled by Taira Kiyomori at the age of 12, and in 1180 raised the Minamoto standard in eastern Japan. After some perilous times the Minamoto forces emerged victorious from the Gempei (*ie*, Minamoto v. Taira) War, largely owing to the brilliance of Yoritomo's younger brother, Yoshitsune. The latter's success, however, was resented by Yoritomo, and when Yoshitsune accepted favours from the imperial court Yoritomo's hostility drove him to rebellion and death. Yoritomo's own abilities were political and administrative rather than military. He accepted as his vassals or housemen most of the leading warriors of east Japan and others elsewhere, and he used his military strength to secure from the court some important titles and governing powers. Chief among these were the office of *shōgun* (1192) and the permission to appoint constables (*shugōs*) in each province and stewards (*jitōs*) in each estate (*shōen*). It was not Yoritomo's intention to replace existing institutions, however, and much of his regime's success was due to the balance he achieved between Kamakura and Kyoto. His main concern was with control of the restless samurai, and to this end he set up the various boards and offices which comprised the Kamakura *bakufu*. After his death his sons were quickly dispossessed of power, but his institutional changes proved increasingly important as the samurai class came to dominate Japan.

                                                                          RBS

MINAMOTO CLAN played a leading part in the emergence of Japanese feudalism. Their descent from Emperor Seiwa (*reg.* 858–76) gave the Minamotos great prestige when they took up provincial governorships, and the outstanding military ability of Minamoto Yorinobu (968–1048), Minamoto Yoriyoshi (998–1075), and Minamoto Yoshiie (1041–1108) brought them the leadership of many of the growing *bushi* (provincial mounted warrior) bands, especially in eastern Japan. The Minamotos further increased their power by giving military assistance to the Fujiwara family, but eventually two unsuccessful clashes (1156, 1159) with their chief rivals, the Taira family, resulted in the death of all their main leaders. In 1180, however, the young Minamoto Yoritomo escaped from custody and began a war (1180–5) which, though as much a struggle between east and west Japan as between Minamoto and Taira, ended in the latter's downfall and the establishment of a feudal government under Minamoto rule.

MINANGKABAU, most populous region and people of Sumatra, characterized by matrilineal descent. Minangkabau is also distinctive in not having developed any monarchic sultanate, even though it accepted Islam in the 16th cent. and became a militant Muslim centre as a result of the *Padri* crusades (1803–38). It was rather an amalgam of semi-independent village republics (*nagaris*), surmounted by a triumvirate of hereditary rulers, each competent in a different sphere. Although deprived early in its history of its coastal outlets (*babs*), Minangkabau proper was little affected by the West before the Dutch conquest (1830–8). But from 1900 its people responded vigorously to Western education and Islamic modernism, and became prominent in Indonesian politics, business, and literature.

MINDON MIN (1814–78), King of Burma (*reg.* 1853–78), 9th of the Konbaung dynasty. Military reverses in the Second Burmese War led the Hlutdaw to depose Pagan Min and enthrone his half-brother, Mindon, who made peace with the British. But without risking his throne he could not conclude a treaty conceding Burmese territory and a frontier. After several years of disturbances on both sides of the de facto frontier friendly relations were established by the good sense and good will of Mindon and Sir Arthur Phayre, the British Commissioner of Pegu. In 1857 Mindon transferred his capital from Amarapura to Mandalay. In 1862 a commercial treaty was concluded between the British and Mindon. During the next 20 years England, France, and the US sought to expand their spheres of influence and trade in the far east. The great, unknown, and potentially exploitable area was China, to which it was hoped Burma would offer access. In Mandalay competition developed between the British from Lower Burma and the French from Indo-China. Mindon maintained friendly relations with the British, but wisely sought to balance British influence by negotiating treaties with the French and Italians also. Towards the end of his reign relations with the British deteriorated, the main causes of this being restrictions on trade arising from royal monopolies, the status of the Karenni States, and insistence upon British observance of Burmese court etiquette. Mindon was a good administrator and attempted, but without much success—for want of funds—to substitute a system of paying officials salaries for the traditional method of allocating the revenues of a district to them. He introduced a tax on property and wealth that was perpetuated by the British.   FSVD

MINERAL AND BATTERY WORKS, COMPANY OF, in Britain, chartered in 1568 and, with the Society of Mines Royal, the first industrial company in Britain. Its founder, William Humfrey, had also discovered 'calamine' or zinc in 1566, which made possible the native production of brass which was replacing bronze. The company was mainly interested in the mining and production of precious metals, lead, and copper, which was converted from ingots into plates at its 'battery works' in Nottinghamshire, and into wire at its mill at Tintern. Owned by the Crown, it was involved in the monopolies dispute in the early 17th cent. and was disrupted by the Civil War. It resumed operations in 1660, but with little success.

MINERAL DISCOVERIES IN AUSTRALIA. The mineral most commonly linked with Australia is gold, but the continent possesses a wide range of other minerals and is a major producer of iron ore, coal, silver, copper, lead, zinc, mineral sands, and also produces nickel, oil and natural gas, tin, and uranium.

Coal was first mined on the Pacific coast not far from Sydney during the convict period; in the steam era, Australia was a major coal exporter to Pacific ports from Valparaiso to Hong Kong; today, Japan is the main coal market. Copper was mined extensively from the 1840s, first at the SA fields of Kapunda and Burra, then at scattered fields from the rain forests of western Tas. (Mt Lyell, 1890s) to the tropics of northern Australia (Cloncurry, 1880s; Mount Isa, 1940s; Tennant Creek, 1950s). Tin mining first boomed in the 1870s at points scattered along a 2000-mile (3220 kms) stretch of the eastern coastal spine, then faded away, but was revived in the 1960s with the expansion of Renison Bell in Tas. into one of the world's largest tin mines. Iron ore was mined only intermittently until the growth of local steelworks in the First World War. The most stable of these early industries was silver–lead–zinc, which provided two of the greatest finds in Australian mining—Broken Hill (1883) and Mount Isa (1923).

These branches of mining, all begun in the 19th cent. and still important, were augmented after the Second World War. In the 1950s uranium, mineral sands, and bauxite became important, and in the 1960s oil (offshore in Bass Strait) and nickel (south-west Australia). The post-war discoveries, both of new and traditional minerals, were so extensive that Australia in 1970 produced most of its mineral wealth from fields which were either deserted or unknown only 20 years earlier.

The leading mineral export is now (1970) iron ore, which was originally thought to be so scarce in Australia that no exports were permitted before 1960. Even then, it was believed that less than 400 million tons of high-grade ore existed at Pilbara in north-west Australia, where the estimate by 1970 was over 15,000 million tons.   GB

MINES ACT (1842) in Britain, passed during Sir Robert Peel's administration (1841–6). Following the findings of the commission of 1840, it prohibited the employment of women and girls underground and set an age limit of ten to the employment of boys. Inspectors were to enforce the law and make reports.

MINES ROYAL, SOCIETY OF, in Britain, owned by the Crown, was mainly interested in the mining of precious metals and copper, the high price of which had led Elizabeth I's minister, William Cecil, to grant a patent for production in 1564 to Thomas Thurland, master of the Savoy in London, and Daniel Hochstetter, master miner and smelter of Augsburg. Mines were started in Cumberland, and in 1566 a court case led to the decision that in law a mine of base metal containing substantial quantities of gold or silver was a mine royal. In 1568 the society was incorporated, a second charter being granted in 1605. After 1580 the society's centre of mining moved to Devon and Cornwall, while smelting moved to Neath in South Wales. Statutes of 1689 and 1693 reversed the court decision of 1568 and copper and zinc mining was thrown open to private enterprise.

MING DYNASTY (1368–1644), China's last native imperial dynasty. The Ming was the only major dynasty of China to be founded in the southern part of the sub-continent, and was governed at first from Nanking before the capital was moved to Peking in 1421. The Ming period was characterized by the practice of orderly government, social stability, and the steady growth of cultured achievements. After a period of rule by the alien Mongol house, the Ming emperors took pride in their reassertion of native strength, their consolidation of imperial authority, and their use of military power. The institutions of central government were reshaped so as to permit the emperor's personal direction of state affairs. The administration of the empire was conducted with a new degree of regularity and governmental measures applied more widely than hitherto, *eg*, in such matters as registration of the population and the land and the organization of labour. The examination system was reconstituted to allow for the recruitment of talent to government service from less restricted groups of the population than hitherto. At the same time, the gentry were exercising an increasing influence on the maintenance of social hierarchies, local law and order, and the promotion of cultural standards.

The Ming period also witnessed far-reaching economic developments and changes. Commercial exchanges between the prosperous cities of the south and the north resulted in greater attention being given to transport, and a new system of taxation was evolved to take account of a more specialized and advantageous use of state labour and resources. The payment of tax in silver accompanied the use of paper money at first, but notes had almost ceased to circulate from the 16th cent. Technological advances were seen in the new quality of ceramics and the development of printing by movable type; intellectual movements comprising a reassessment of the Chinese classics and attention to questions of metaphysics and Buddhist theology were stimulated by philosophers of Neo-Confucianism. The weakening of the dynasty from the middle of the 16th cent. has been ascribed partly to the amount of attention paid by statesmen to ideological theory instead of to practical matters of state, to the growth of corruption, and to the tenure of power by eunuchs. In the 16th and 17th cents a movement for the reform of the conduct of politics and administration failed in its purpose, and the Ming dynasty broke down amid an outbreak of internal rebellions and the advance of Manchu forces from the northeast.

In foreign affairs the Ming governments were for long threatened by hostile Mongol groups in the north and countered such moves by renovating the Great Wall, launching expeditions into Central Asia, and following a policy of *divide et impera*. After a short experiment involving voyages to the west, led by Cheng Ho, Ming China received a growing number of commercial prospectors and missionaries from Europe, of whom Matteo Ricci is the best known. Attempts were made with varying success to maintain a policy of overlordship with the communities of Burma, Siam, Korea, and the court of Japan.

C. Hucker, *The Traditional Chinese State in Ming Times* (Tucson, 1961).
ML

MINGHETTI, MARCO (1818–86), Italian politician, leader of the 'dissident right', and prime minister (1873–6) who was responsible for the achievements of the right-wing governments in the 1870s. The united Italian state was firmly established by balancing the budget, maintaining law and order, and pursuing an independent foreign policy. But although Minghetti shared Cavour's belief that the state should take responsibility for social legislation, the post office savings bank, and the railways, his left-wing critics accused him of jeopardizing economic growth by unnecessary stringency. Minghetti also supported Depretis' policy of *trasformismo* (consensus politics) and the arbitrary police methods which made constitutional government so difficult to achieve in Italy.

MINH-MANG (1791–1841), second Emperor of the Nguyen dynasty of Viet-nam (*reg.* 1820–41). He was educated as a strict Confucian, and his succession represented a victory for the Confucian scholar-officials at the court of Hue. There followed extensive administrative reforms, and a strengthening of the examination system. An attempt to impose greater centralization in 1832 led to revolts in Tongking and in the far south (Saigon). But after their suppression, the dynasty was stronger than ever and by 1836 also controlled much of Cambodia, though the latter territory was lost after his death. The antipathy of the Confucian scholars towards Christianity led to increasing persecution of missionaries and their converts from about 1830; and to rejection of all diplomatic approaches by French and British envoys. A Vietnamese mission to France, sent by Minh-Mang at the end of his reign (1840), was rebuffed in Paris owing to pressure by missionaries. Under his successor, Thieu-Tri, the policy of persecutions was renewed. Though Minh-Mang was a scholar, he took no interest in Western learning.

MINIATURE PAINTING, small-scale paintings, especially portraits, derived from medieval manuscript illuminations which flourished in Europe from the 16th to the 18th cents. A great variety of techniques and materials were used. In 16th-cent. Italy Bronzino developed the method of using oil paint on sheets of metal, a method in which the English miniaturist Samuel Cooper excelled in the 17th cent. The 18th cent. saw the introduction of painting with water-colour on ivory. Portrait (and more rarely landscape) miniatures could be executed on glass, enamel, vellum, or even playing cards. Many famous oil painters attempted miniature painting, most notably Fragonard, Bronzino, and Cranach the Elder. The practice all but died out in the 19th cent.

MINISTERIALES, class of unfree servants, military and civil, employed in the Middle Ages by the Crown, the aristocracy, and the Church in the empire. They received land and office as an alternative to the established nobility, a motive which seems to have been especially strong in the case of the Church. The Salian monarchs used ministeriales in various positions of power and many rose high in the Church as a reward for service. Under Henry IV they became the backbone of royal government and they were indispensable to the Hohenstaufen state, though ultimately Frederick II sacrificed them to the territorial nobility. They also formed the professional core of royal armies. From early in the 12th cent. they began to form a class with common interests and enhanced their position by acquiring written titles to their lands. They were gradually emancipated and merged with the knightly class.

MINNESOTA, 32nd member state of the US, admitted in 1858. After its exploration by French adventurers and trappers, notably Radisson, Groseilliers (1654–60), and Du Lhut (1679–89), the region west of Lake Superior and east of the Mississippi passed to Britain (1763). It was ceded to the US (1783) and became part of the North-west Territory (1787). What is now (1970) western MN was acquired by the Louisiana Purchase (1803). Settlement began between the St Croix and Mississippi rivers on Indian land bought by the Federal government (1837), and, after successively forming part of Michigan, Iowa, and Wisconsin Territories, MN became a separate territory (1849) and a state (1858). During the later 19th cent. its population was increased by large numbers of immigrants from Europe, particularly Scandinavians and Germans, and its economy was based upon iron-ore mining in the Mesabi range, lumbering, and large-scale wheat production. Fluctuations in agriculture after the Civil War, together with industrial unrest, resulted in the state becoming a centre for Granger and Populist activities, and its radical tradition continued in the Farmer-Labor party after 1920.

MINOAN CIVILIZATION, pre-Greek civilization on Crete *c.* 2000–1400 BC. During the Early Palace Period (*c.* 2000–1700) Cretan naval supremacy, reflected in the later legend of Minos, resulted in the first unfortified palaces at Cnossos, Mallai, and Phaestus. Their arts, especially metalwork and pottery, advanced considerably. The development of Linear A writing and the extensive use of engraved stones, etc., as seals show a sophisticated palace bureaucracy. There was trade with Egypt, the Levant, and the Aegean islands, but little direct contact with the Greek mainland. After earthquakes (c. 1700) the palaces were rebuilt and decorated with impressive frescoes. During the Late Palace Period (c. 1700–c. 1400) new townships, eg, Gournia; mansions, eg, at Vathypetro; and palaces, eg, at Hagia Triada, appeared and trading posts were established in the Aegean at Thera, Melos, Rhodes, Miletus, and elsewhere. Minoan art became increasingly naturalistic. In the 16th cent. the Mycenaeans in Greece developed their own civilization in imitation of the Minoans and by c. 1500 had begun to replace Minoans in sea-borne trade, especially with Egypt. The massive volcanic eruption of Thera c. 1475 caused widespread destruction of Cretan palaces and towns; Mycenaeans occupied Cnossos and introduced more abundant weapons and the 'Throne Room'; Linear B was adapted from Linear A for writing Greek. Soon after 1400 the palace at Cnossos was mysteriously destroyed and was never rebuilt.

MINOBE, TATSUKICHI (1873–1948), Japanese constitutional lawyer and professor at Tokyo University. He developed a constitutional concept according to which the emperor was regarded as no more than the principal organ of state; the concept also lent theoretical support to the political parties in their struggle to establish responsible cabinets. In the 1930s Minobe's ideas came under ultra-nationalist attack and were officially suppressed, Minobe himself being driven from public and academic life.

MINORCA, second island of the Balearic group, less fertile than Majorca, but with a good harbour in Port Mahon. It was Spanish until the English took possession of it in 1708. They retained it by the treaty of Utrecht (1713), and thus won mastery of the Mediterranean trade. After being captured by the French in 1756, as a result of which Admiral Byng was court-martialled and shot, it was restored to Britain in 1763. It was recaptured by Spain in the American War of Independence (1782), and was briefly taken by the British under St Vincent in the French Wars (1798). Since that time it has belonged to Spain.

MINOS, legendary king of Crete in the 2nd millenium BC, whose navy is said to have controlled the Aegean, including the Athens of Theseus. He died in Sicily. His legend, containing dim memories of 'Minoan' Crete, was later revived as a supposed analogue to 5th-cent. BC Athenian imperialism.

MINSEITŌ, Japanese political party formed in 1927 mainly from the Kenseikai and led by Hamaguchi Yūkō and Wakatsuki Reijirō. It supported parliamentary government and international co-operation more strongly than any other major pre-war party.

MINTO, GILBERT ELLIOT MURRAY KYNYNMOUND, 1st Earl of (1751–1814), British colonial servant and politician, who was governor-general of India (1807–13). He was governor of Corsica (1794–6), then became president of the board of control (1806), but proceeded to India in the following year as governor-general. Because of the supposed French menace to India he despatched Malcolm to Persia, Metcalfe to Ranjit Singh at Lahore, and Elphinstone to the camp of Shah Shujah at Peshwar. Between 1810 and 1811 the French islands of Bourbon and Mauritius were taken, Amboyna and the Spice Islands were annexed, and an expedition captured Java (1811).

MINTO, GILBERT JOHN ELLIOT MURRAY-KYNYN-MOUND, 4th Earl of (1845–1914), governor-general of Canada (1898–1904) and viceroy of India (1905–10). He entered the British army (1867) and later served with the Turkish (1877); he also served with Roberts in the Second Afghan War (1879), at the Cape (1881), in Egypt (1882), and was military secretary to Lord Lansdowne, then governor-general of Canada (1883–8). He thus had some experience of both Canada and India before he returned to govern. In Canada he had to deal with a number of sensitive issues, eg, imperial preferences, the participation of Canadian troops in the Boer War, and the settlement of the Alaskan border. In India he inherited from Curzon the problem of the partition of Bengal. Though appointed by a Conservative administration, he worked well with the Liberal secretary of state for India, John Morley. The relationship which developed between the two men gave the period of Minto's viceroyalty its distinctive character. The 'Morley–Minto reforms' (1909), largely the product of Minto and his advisers, were the outstanding achievement of the partnership, though they fell far short of meeting the political needs of India at that time. The provision of separate electorates for Muslims, a major innovation of the period, owed much to Minto's initial handling of the Muslim deputation (1906) and his persistence in his correspondence with Morley. Minto's conservative proposal for Advisory Councils of Notables to represent landowners and/or princes was dropped from the reforms scheme in the face of Morley's disagreement and of practical difficulties in implementating the idea.

Minto had varied success in dealing with the problems of day-to-day administration which were posed by Curzon's legacy of a partitioned Bengal, the continued growth of a revolutionary movement in India, and the agitation in the Punjab, which gave rise to difficulties concerning the provincial government's handling of the situation. The anti-partition movement was contained, though less by effective government measures than by internal differences and the natural subsidence of feelings, and it was left to Hardinge, who succeeded Minto, to make the changes which ended the agitation (1911). The Punjab government was finally brought to its senses, although only after the deportation of Lajpat Rai and Ajit Singh, the leading agitators, had embarrassed all the governments concerned. The revolutionary movement continued to expand—Minto himself was the object of a bomb attack in Ahmadabad (Nov. 1909)—and as a result his government introduced a number of measures to give it new powers to deal with the press, political meetings and societies, and bomb-throwers.

Mary, Countess of Minto, *India, Minto and Morley, 1905–1910* (London, 1935).
S. R. Wasti, *Lord Minto and the Indian Nationalist Movement, 1905 to 1910* (London, 1964).   PDR

MINUIT, PETER (1580–1638), first director-general of New Netherland, America (1626–31). He was recalled to Holland to answer charges of maladministration, and later headed a group sent by Sweden (1638) to establish a colony on the Delaware river, where he erected a fort and trading post at Wilmington.

MINUTEMEN, Massachusetts colonial militia, or armed citizens, who agreed to be ready for an emergency at a minute's notice. They figured in the battles of Lexington and Concord, which began the American War of Independence.

MIR, usual name for peasant commune (*selskoe obshchestvo*) found in many parts of European Russia. It became the object of intellectual debate (c. 1847) for different reasons, by nationalist, slavophile, and populist thinkers and was misleadingly extolled as democratic by western observers. Its origin is disputed, but its redistribution functions probably do not normally predate the introduction of a soul tax (1724). Its main characteristics were joint ownership of land, which was often periodically redistributed between families through an egalitarian (if economically wasteful) strip system of tenure. Elected elders organized the joint responsibilities of the *mir* for taxes and various obligations to government and landowner. The system was retained, largely for fiscal and administrative reasons, at Emancipation, but under Stolypin's reforms (1906–11) its compulsory basis was abolished.

MIR JAFAR (*c.* 1691–1765), Nawab of Bengal (1757–60, 1763–5), who rose in the service of the usurping Nawab of Bengal, Alivardi Khan, to become the latter's commander-in-chief. A year after Alivardi's death (1756) he conspired with Robert Clive to overthrow Alivardi's grandson, Siraj-ud-Daulah. This aim was achieved in the battle of Plassey (1757). Thus Mir Jafar became nawab. His large presents and abolition of customs duties on the private trade of the East India Co.'s servants undermined their morale and introduced a period of open plunder in Bengal. On Clive's departure from India (1760), Mir Jafar was replaced by Mir Kasim, but was restored (1763) on the latter's defeat.

MIR KASIM (d. 1777), Nawab of Bengal (1760–3), son-in-law of Nawab Mir Jafar. He was disappointed at not being nominated as heir after the death of Mir Jafar's son, Miran, and persuaded Gov. Vansittart of Calcutta to depose Mir Jafar in his favour (1760). He proved a good administrator and organized an effective army, but was crippled by the bribery needed for his elevation and by the commercial exploitation of the East India Co.'s officials. An agreement with Gov. Vansittart on customs duties was disavowed by the Calcutta council and war resulted. After several defeats, Mir Kasim massacred the British factors who had tried to seize Patna, and fled to Oudh. After the Mughal defeat at Baksar (1764) he lost his treasure, became a fugitive, and died in obscurity near Delhi.

MIRABEAU, HONORÉ GABRIEL RIQUETTI, Comte de (1749–91), French politician, who dominated the debates of the National Assembly in the first years of the French Revolution. With few prospects of employment, yet aware of his own abilities, Mirabeau was delighted with the opportunity suddenly presented to him by the summoning of the states general in 1789. He was elected by the *tiers état* of Marseilles and from the first he stood out in the states general and National Assembly. He strove consistently to harness the revolutionary spirit and the king's fears to the cause of erecting a constitutional monarchy on principles similar to those of England. His failure arose on the one hand from the distrust of his talents and ambition shown by his fellow deputies and, on the other, from the unwillingness of the king (influenced strongly by the queen) to believe that the fate of the monarchy could safely be entrusted to the schemes of a man who appeared to be in the forefront of the revolutionary movement. Mirabeau desired above all a new role for the Crown, which he expounded in a series of secret notes to the court. The Crown (he argued) should accept a new role as the mouthpiece of popular feeling and should cut itself free from compromising and entangling associations with the privileges of the *ancien régime.* This was unacceptable to Louis XVI. At the same time, revolutionaries deplored Mirabeau's assertion that the Crown ought to be more than a figurehead and should be given real powers. Though Mirabeau left his mark on the form of the constitution, he failed in his primary purpose

O. J. G. Welch, *Mirabeau* (London, 1951).
E. Dumont, *Recollections of Mirabeau* (London, 1904). JMR

MIRAMBO (d. 1884), Nyamwezi chief, who spent part of his youth among the Ngoni, where he observed their military tactics. He became chief of a minor polity in Uyowa and expanded his authority to control all trade to the west of Tabora. Though the Arabs regarded him as a brigand, his intention was to obtain a larger share of trading profits. Of his military cam-

paigns, those which he initiated had the limited purpose of asserting and maintaining his control over the western trade route.

MIRANDA, SEBASTIÁN FRANCISCO DE (*c.* 1750–1816), one of the precursors of the Latin American struggles for independence. He was born in Venezuela, joined the Spanish army (1774), and was sent on a mission to Jamaica at the end of the American War of Independence (1783). There he was involved in financial irregularities and supplied military information to the Jamaican authorities. He was tried in his absence and sentenced to eight years' confinement in Oran. He escaped capture, and after unsuccessful attempts to get himself reinstated devoted himself to various forms of conspiracy.

He was in London (1785–1810), where his grandiose plans included one for a great free new nation in South America, presided over by a native prince of the Inca line. Britain was not disposed to provoke colonial revolts against Spain, but the younger Pitt, then prime minister, foresaw that if outbreaks came, it would be wise to harbour this spirited revolutionary. Miranda was accordingly subsidized by the treasury during most of his long stay in London. He also visited the continent, where his fluency in most European languages and his brilliant conversation won him a number of friends, among them Catherine of Russia. He identified himself with the French Revolution and soon became a French general, but was involved in a charge of treachery and found himself in jail.

On his release he returned to London, where he became associated with plots against Spain. In 1806, disgusted by England's caution, he returned to the US, found a few volunteers and a small vessel, and landed at the Venezuelan port of Coro. But few rallied to his cause, and he made his way back to London. However, when the Caracas *cabildo* created an independent junta in 1810, he returned in triumph to Venezuela and became commander-in-chief of the revolutionary army and virtually dictator. He was later overthrown by the Bourbon governor and on 26 July 1812 he capitulated to the patriot army. After two years spent in captivity at various places he died in prison at Cadiz.

W. S. Robertson, *The Life of Miranda*, 2 vols (Chapel Hill, NC, 1929). FPB

MIRBACH-HARFF, WILHELM VON (1871–1918), German diplomat, who became ambassador in Moscow (1918) after the conclusion of the Brest Litovsk treaty. He was assassinated by two members of the Social Revolutionary Party, helped by officials of the Cheka. His death was intended to split the Fifth Congress, then in session, and force a resumption of hostilities against Germany. It was followed by an attempted coup, which was suppressed, and the congress officially condemned the assassination.

MIRDASIDS, Arab dynasty which rose to prominence in Syria under Salih ibn Mirdas (d. AD 1029), a chieftain of the Kilab tribe, during the 11th cent. The Mirdasids, established at Aleppo, had to withstand pressure from the Fatimids of Egypt and from the Byzantines at Antioch. Internal discord and the arrival of the Seljuk Turks in Syria led to the breakdown of the Mirdasid regime after the death of the Amir Thimal (1061).

MIRÓ, ESTEBAN RODRIGUEZ (1744–95), Spanish colonial governor, who was governor of LA (1782–91) after serving in the Spanish army in Portugal and Flanders. His governorship was marked by intrigues to procure trade monopolies and to detach KY from the US. Miró encouraged agriculture and commerce, opposed the establishment of the Inquisition, and partially opened LA to US trade.

MIRZA, ISKANDAR (1899–1969), soldier, governor-general, and president of Pakistan (1955–8). After graduating from the Royal Military Academy, Sandhurst, Mirza served in the Indian army (1921–6) and then the political service (1926–46). He was in the defence department (1946–54), first of India and then of Pakistan. His political career began when he became governor of East Pakistan (1954); he was later minister of the interior, states and frontier regions. He was the last governor-general (1955–6), and with the inauguration of the new republic he became its first president (1956–8). On 7 Oct. 1958 he assumed direct control of the regime, which had been placed under martial law with Ayub Khan first as chief administrator and later (24 Oct.) as prime minister. But on 27 Oct. Mirza was forced to resign and leave the country, and Ayub Khan became president.

MISSI DOMINICI, Latin term for the royal envoys whom the Frankish king, Charlemagne, regularly sent on missions throughout his kingdom. They usually acted in pairs, a lay notable accompanied by an ecclesiastic. Charlemagne's predecessors had sent such missions out periodically. The innovation of Charlemagne consisted in making this the normal feature of his government and in an enormous increase in the duties of the envoys. They were expected to supervise the local officials. Charlemagne revived the practice of legislating for his whole kingdom and it became a major function of the envoys to enforce this legislation. After the decline of the power of Charlemagne's successors in the 9th cent. the practice of sending regular envoys was gradually discontinued.

MISSILE CRISIS IN CUBA, confrontation (1962) between the USSR and the US over offensive missiles on Cuban soil. On 1 Jan. 1959 a regime headed by Fidel Castro Ruz took power in Cuba. During the next four years Cuban relations with the US deteriorated, and those with the USSR were strengthened. Cuba joined the communist group of nations.

In 1962 the US government became aware of greatly increased imports of arms by Cuba, most of which were coming from the communist bloc. The discovery that these arms included missiles capable of reaching the US and much of the circum-Caribbean area precipitated an international crisis. On 22 Oct. 1962 President Kennedy demanded that the missiles be dismantled and removed from Cuban soil. To enforce this demand Kennedy imposed a blockade of the island and threatened to stop and search Soviet vessels heading towards Cuba. After some hours of tension a number of Soviet vessels bound for Cuba turned back to Europe, and the government of the USSR acceded to the US demands (Oct. 28), and began to dismantle the missiles.

Their removal caused some strain in the relations between Cuba and the USSR. Cuba also claimed that any system of international inspection would constitute a violation of her national sovereignty. To ensure that the missiles were not replaced, the US government continued to keep the island under high-altitude scrutiny from U2 planes and by other devices.

MISSION INDIANS, term applied to American tribes which settled at Franciscan missions founded in CA (1769–1823) in the area between San Francisco and San Diego. An estimated 100,000 Indians came under mission influence before the Mexican government secularized them (1834). Mission property was divided among the Indians, who were quickly deprived of it by whites. Their living conditions became intolerable, and their numbers dwindled rapidly to a few thousand.

MISSIONARY RIDGE, BATTLE OF (25 Nov. 1864), final engagement of the Chattanooga campaign in the American Civil War. Troops of the Union Army of the Cumberland, under Gen. George Henry Thomas, disobeyed orders to halt while advancing on enemy positions and overran the Confederate forces of Gen. Braxton Bragg. A week later, Bragg relinquished his command of the Army of the Tennessee.

MISSIONS AND MISSIONARIES IN NEW ZEALAND. The NZ Maoris, fearful of their own gods, but fascinated by the

European God and the material success of his adherents, in turn stimulated and frustrated Christian missionaries. After Samuel Marsden's first visit (1814), the Church Missionary Society maintained stations with difficulty, making few converts until the 1820s. A number of factors then led to a considerable Maori response as shown in baptisms. The standing and methods of missionaries improved and Maori confidence was gradually gained through agricultural instruction and peace-making between tribes. There was also widespread desire for literacy through mission schools. The establishment of Wesleyan (1823) and Roman Catholic (1838) missions spread Christianity more widely, but introduced sectarian conflict to Maori converts. Missionary advocacy was perhaps the major factor in Maori acceptance of the treaty of Waitangi (1840), but when European settlement and war subsequently destroyed most of its promised benefits, there was a drastic decline in missionary influence.

MISSISSIPPI, 20th member state of the US, admitted in 1817. The region east of the Lower Mississippi river, explored by De Soto (1540–1), was declared part of LA by La Salle (1682) and was first settled by D'Iberville near Biloxi (1699). It passed into British possession (1763), but was lost to the Spanish (1779). Although the US gained title to the area north of the 31st parallel (1795), the Spanish did not withdraw until 1798, whereupon Mississippi Territory was organized. The western part of the territory became the state of MS (1817), and settlement increased substantially following the removal of the Choctaw, Chickasaw, and Natchez Indians (1830–2). The state seceded from the Union (9 Jan. 1861), experienced bitter fighting during the Vicksburg campaign of the Civil War (1863), and was readmitted to the Union (1870). Its economy has long depended upon cotton cultivation. With the lowest per capita income and the highest percentage of Negroes of any US state, MS has experienced grave racial disturbances in recent times.

MISSISSIPPI BUBBLE (1720) in France, financial crash of the Compagnie de l'Occident, the trading venture started by John Law with the concurrence of the regent Orléans. The company aimed at developing the Mississippi basin, and to promote the scheme Lorient and New Orleans were founded. On the strength of the company's total monopoly 624,000 shares were issued, which the French public rushed to buy. When, by 1720, they had reached 40 times their face value some shrewd speculators, eg, the Duke of Bourbon, sold out. Law ordered the systematic reduction of the value of the shares to restore his system to solvency. But the public rushed to sell as frantically as they had rushed to buy, and the price of the shares crashed (1720). Law fled and many investors were ruined.

MISSOURI COMPROMISE (1819–21) in the US, first great compromise between North and South over the issue of slavery's extension into the territories. Before 1819 its extension had posed few political problems. With slavery banned from the North-west Territory by the Ordinance of 1787, new states from that area, such as OH (1803), were admitted automatically as free states, and it had proved possible to maintain the balance in Congress between free and slave states. However, with the expansion of short staple cotton production, slavery's extension became a live issue for which MO offered a convenient focus. As the first state after LA to be formed from the Louisiana Purchase, MO's status as a free or as a slave state might well have provided a precedent for future admissions from that area. In 1819 slave and free states were evenly matched at 11 each, but the admission of MO seemed bound to upset the status quo. While most of the territory was not suited to cotton production, its settlers had been allowed by Congress to hold slaves, and those who did expected to continue to do so. In Jan. 1819, when the House of Representatives began consideration of MO's application for statehood, Representative James

Talmadge, of New York, proposed an amendment to the enabling bill that prohibited the further introduction of slaves into MO, and declared all slaves born there after statehood to be free at age 25. The bill thus amended passed through the House by almost a straight sectional vote, only to be blocked by the Senate. When Congress reassembled in Dec. MO renewed its application, and at the same time ME (then part of MA) applied for admission as a free state. The House promptly passed the Maine bill, but in the Senate two amendments were attached, providing for the admission of MO without restriction of slavery, and prohibiting slavery for ever in any remaining part of the Louisiana Purchase north of latitude 30° 30′. In this form the Maine–Missouri bill passed the Senate in March 1820. The debates on the Compromise in many ways anticipated later arguments on the slavery issue which were to harden sectional attitudes; the appeal to the Scriptures by Senator William Smith of SC, the repudiation of the Declaration of Independence, with its assertion of human equality, by Senator Nathand Macon of NC, and above all the constitutional debate on the power of Congress to admit states under Article IV, section 3 of the constitution. To some the portents were clear. 'I considered it at once', wrote Jefferson, 'as the knell of the Union.'

G. Dangerfield, *The Awakening of American Nationalism* (New York, 1965).
G. Moore, *The Missouri Controversy 1819–21* (Lexington, 1953). DBS

MISTRA, ruined town in Greece, some 5 kms west of Sparta. Guillaume de Villehardouin, ruler of the Frankish state of Morea, founded Mistra as a fortress on Mt Tyagetos in 1248–9. It became Byzantine in 1262 and then, in 1348, the capital of the Despotat of the Morea, falling to the Turks in 1460. In the first half of the 15th cent. Mistra was a flourishing intellectual centre, famous especially for its Platonist scholars, some of whom considerably influenced the Renaissance of Greek studies in Italy.

MITA, forced labour system employed in the colonial Andean area, under which Indian communities were obliged in turn to contribute a fixed number of labourers for a fixed period of time at fixed wages for public purposes. Unskilled labour for the Peruvian silver mines was recruited in this way.

MITANNI, powerful kingdom formed by the Hurrians and an aristocracy of Indo-Aryans (16th–14th cents BC). Its power extended over much of northern Mesopotamia, northern Syria, and Armenia. During the 15th cent. it was involved in wars with Egypt, but by the end of the century these two countries were in alliance and in the 14th cent. a new enemy, the Hittites, attacked and finally devastated the country, though it was left to the Assyrians under Ashuruballit I (? *reg. c.* 1365–1330) to strike the final blow and share the remaining Mitannian territory with the neighbouring state of Alshe.

MITCHELL, JOHN (1680–1768), American physician and naturalist, who, by applying the plant classification system of Linnaeus discovered 25 new genera of plants. On being elected to the Royal Society (1748), Mitchell prepared a 'Map of the British and French Dominions in North America' which was used at the treaty of Paris (1783) and remained the standard North American map until the 19th cent.

MITCHELL, SIR THOMAS LIVINGSTONE (1792–1855), British soldier who served (1809–12) during the Peninsular War and became surveyor-general of NSW in 1828. He directed important surveys and undertook four exploratory journeys into the interior of Australia. He published accounts of his exploration in 1838 and 1848.

MITCHELL, SIR WILLIAM (1861–1962), Scottish-born Australian philosopher, who held the chair of mental and moral philosophy at Adelaide University (1894–1922), was vice-chancellor (1916–42), and chancellor (1942–8). He was praised by neo-Hegelian philosophers for his *Structure and Growth of the Mind* (1907). His most influential work was *The Place of Minds in the World* (1933).

MITHRAISM, cult of Mithras, a Persian and Indian Sungod, which spread rapidly over the Roman empire and reached Rome in 67 BC, becoming an imperial cult in the reign of Commodus (AD 180–192). Mithraic monuments are common in frontier regions of the empire, as the cult appealed chiefly to soldiers. It was a type of Mystery Religion, with rites of baptism and bread, water and wine consecrated by priests called 'fathers', and seemed to Tertullian the Devil's parody of the Christian sacraments, but the resemblances may be due to common affinities. Although a strong rival to Christianity in the first three centuries AD, by the 4th cent. it had been almost entirely superseded.

MITHRIDATES I (*reg.* 171–138 BC), Parthian King of Iran, who annexed (160–140) the area from Media to the Persian Gulf and from Mesopotamia possibly as far as Herat, Seistan, and the Indus river, and successfully held back Scythian invaders on the frontiers. Facing Seleucia on the Tigris, he built a large military camp, which grew into the capital city of Ctesiphon. Despite hostility from the Greek communities, he treated them well, accepting and using Hellenization.

MITHRIDATES II (*reg. c.* 123–87 BC), Parthian King of Iran, who restored the empire in the east by repelling Scythian invaders and reoccupying the area up to the Indus river. In the west he quelled a revolt of the western provinces and brought Armenia under Parthian control. In 92 Iran first confronted the Romans when the latter reached the Euphrates and refused an offer of alliance from Mithridates. The large number of coins found dating from his reign suggests a period of considerable commercial activity, and a treaty to facilitate trade through Iran was made with the Chinese emperor.

MITHRIDATES VI (120–63 BC), King of Pontus and Rome's strongest opponent in the east. On the death of his father, King of Galatia, Phrygia, and Paphlagonia (120), he fled from his mother and established himself on the shore of the Black Sea, subsequently occupying Colchis, Lesser Armenia, and eastern Pontus. Attacks on Cappadocia and Bithynia and his occupation of most of Asia Minor (88) brought him into conflict with Rome and he was slowly defeated by Sulla, Murena, Lucullus, and Pompey in the Mithridatic Wars. After final defeat, he fled to the Crimea and ordered one of his guards to kill him.

MITHRIDATIC WARS (88–63 BC), Rome's wars against Mithridates VI of Pontus. On Mithridates' seizure of Cappadocia, Bithynia, and the Roman province Asia (88), Sulla crossed to Greece (87) and twice defeated Mithridates' general there (86), Mithridates himself being out-manœuvred by Flavius Fimbria in Asia. Sulla's peace treaty with Mithridates (84) was temporarily broken by the aggression of Murena (83–82), who was defeated. In 74 Mithridates seized Bithynia, bequeathed to Rome by its late king, Nicomedes IV, and Lucullus waged a series of highly successful campaigns against him (73–68), but for political reasons he was superseded first by M. Acilius Glabrio (67) and then by Pompey (66), who drove Mithridates from Pontus.

MITRE, BARTOLOMÉ (1821–1906), Argentine soldier, journalist, historian, and president of Argentina. Having learned the professions of arms and political journalism in exile, Mitre returned to Argentina to fight alongside the victors at Caseros (1852), which ended Rosas's dictatorship. Thereafter, he identified himself with Buenos Aires in its secession from Urquiza's federal union and commanded the

Buenos Aires forces in their victory over Urquiza at Pavón (1861). The republic was thereby consolidated under Buenos Aires's hegemony, and Mitre became its first president (1862–8). His presidential programmes underlay much of Argentina's subsequent economic growth. Simultaneously, Mitre commanded the allied armies in the war against Paraguay (1864–7). Though defeated in two later attempts to regain the presidency (1874, 1891), Mitre remained an influential political manipulator. His literary versatility was shown through writings in the family newspaper, *La Nación*, and in two histories, *Historia de Belgrano . . .* (1859–76) and *Historia de San Martín . . .* (1887).

MITSUBISHI, Japanese *zaibatsu* (industrial combine), founded by a Tosa samurai, Iwasaki Yatarō, after the Meiji Restoration. Mitsubishi prospered, first in shipbuilding and foreign trade and later in other sectors of modern industry. His close relationship with Ōkuma Shigenobu made Mitsubishi an important financial supporter of the Kaishintō party, and later the Kenseikai and Minseitō. Though affected by the post-1945 Occupation economic reforms, Mitsubishi remains one of the largest Japanese companies, with a great diversity of interests.

MITSUI, Japanese *zaibatsu* (industrial combine), established in the 17th cent. It comprised one of the few older merchant families which made a significant contribution to Japan's economic modernization. By the 1920s Mitsui had become the largest *zaibatsu*, its various subsidiary companies employing over 1 million persons. Its wealth and importance made its directors natural targets for assassination attempts during the Depression, but Japan's move towards a war economy further increased Mitsui's importance. It continues (1970) to play a leading role in Japan's economy.

MITTERAND, ALEXANDRE (1859–1943), French lawyer and politician, who entered politics as Radical deputy for the Seine. Like his contemporary, Jean Jaurès, his concern for the condition of the working class led him from radicalism to socialism. In 1896 he advocated the socialization of the means of production, and the peaceful conquest of power by universal suffrage gave him a leading role in French reformist socialism.

His decision to join Waldeck-Rousseau's cabinet in 1899 precipitated a lasting doctrinal quarrel among the socialists concerning ministerial participation. As a result Mitterand was excluded from the Socialist party in 1904. He continued his career as minister of public works (1909) and minister of war in Poincaré's cabinet (1912–13) and in Viviani's cabinet (1914–15). In this capacity he supported the general staff in its opposition to parliamentary supervision. After the First World War he led the Bloc Nationale to electoral victory in 1919 and became *président du conseil* of the first post-war government. In 1920 he was elected president of the republic. Because of his interventions during his presidency on behalf of conservative governments and conservative policies he was forced to resign after the victory of the *Cartel des gauches* in 1924. He was elected senator in 1925, but ceased to play an active part in politics.   PMR

MIXED CONSTITUTION in Britain, one in which sovereignty does not reside in a single person or body. Britain retains the elements of a mixed constitution in that the sovereignty of the Commons is tempered by an independent judiciary and it is arguable that the civil service which is capable of influencing the policy of its minister has an element of independent authority. But the classic age of the mixed constitution was the 18th cent., when power was shared between king, Lords, Commons, and the judiciary, each of whom was, supposedly, prevented from usurping undue power by a built-in system of checks and balances. Analysed and admired by Montesquieu and Locke, the British constitution was alleged to function through a balanced mixture of legislative, executive, and judicial power.

There were checks and balances in the 18th-cent. constitution. The king was intimately involved in political processes. He had to choose his ministers from within parliament, but they then had the benefit of official patronage to secure control of the House of Commons. However, they had to contend with opposition created by private patronage. The predominance of aristocratic, propertied interests did not create a rift between Lords and Commons, since many MPs owed their seats to patrons in the Lords or belonged to the aristocracy themselves. The system worked through patronage, but the constitution contained many uncertainties. The absence of precise constitutional formulae meant that the extent to which power was shared depended on the outcome of the constant political conflicts, which were endemic in the mixed constitution.

Ultimately, the Commons' control of finance made it the central political forum. The king's government could not continue if he persistently chose ministers who could not command the Commons. The outcome of the 18th-cent. constitutional debates was an assault on patronage, which cleared the way for the development of the modern party system, in which royal power is largely ceremonial, since the monarch automatically appoints the leader of the majority party to head the government. An independent civil service has assumed responsibility for administering the king's government. Representative, parliamentary government has superseded the system in which power was shared, but government was in the interests of the few.

B. Kemp, *King and Commons 1660–1832* (Oxford, 1957).
R. Paevs, *Limited Monarchy in Great Britain in the 18th century* (London, 1957).   SH

MIZUNO, TADAKUNI (1793–1851), Japanese *daimyō* and political leader, who was the chief promoter of the *Tempō* Reforms (1841–3) which were intended to restore the Tokugawa *bakufu*'s finances after a decade of famines. His conservative measures, however, had less success than the contemporary reforms of several *hans* and the intense opposition they aroused forced their abandonment.

MKWATI (*fl.* 19th cent.), priest of the Shona god Wwari, and one of the main leaders of the Ndebele and Shona revolts (1896–7) against the British South Africa Co.'s settlers in Southern Rhodesia. He was apparently killed by his own people after their defeat by the whites.

MKWAWA (d. 1898), chief of the Hehe in south-central Tanzania (1880–98), who succeeded his father, Munyigumba. He had first to fight for the chieftaincy, and immediately afterwards to defend it against Ngoni attacks. By 1890, having established Hehe hegemony over all the neighbouring societies and assuring himself of the loyalty of his subordinates, he began to raid the caravan route further north. During these years a stone fort was built at Kalenga. In 1891, hostilities broke out between the Hehe and the Germans, and although the fort was captured in 1894, Mkwawa escaped and led guerrilla resistance for another four years. In 1898, when his forces had dwindled, he committed suicide rather than let himself be captured.

MOAB, Semitic state established east of the Dead Sea, *c.* 1200 BC. It was conquered by the Hebrews (*c.* 1000) and enjoyed only intervals of independence thereafter. In religion, language, and culture, the Moabites appear to have been akin to the Hebrews.

MOBERLY, WALTER (1832–1915), Canadian politician and engineer who explored BC (1858) to find a suitable transcontinental railway route. He assisted in laying out the new capital, New Westminster (1859), and supervised the construction of the Cariboo wagon road (1862–4). He was elected (1864) to the Legislative Council of BC, but resigned

(1865) in order to become assistant surveyor-general of BC. He discovered Eagle Pass (1868), through which the Canadian Pacific transcontinental railway was eventually routed.

MOCAMBO, in Brazil, a hiding place in the woods or jungle used by lawbreakers or runaway slaves. By extension, the term has come to mean any shack or hut in the woods, and also a thicket where grazing cattle are hidden from sight.

MOCH, JULES (1893–), French businessman, politician, and writer who entered parliament (1928) as a Socialist deputy and in 1936 became secretary-general of Blum's personal cabinet. He served in Blum's second, short-lived cabinet of 1938 as minister of public works and after the defeat of France in the Second World War he joined the Resistance.

After the war he served as minister of public works (1945–7) and minister of the interior (1947–50). In the latter capacity he became the *bête noire* of the communists as the breaker of the political strikes of 1947 and 1948.

Through serving as minister of national defence in Pleven's cabinet (1950–1) he developed an interest in nuclear policy and disarmament and was France's permanent representative (1951–61) to the United Nations Disarmament Commission. He also wrote several books on nuclear disarmament. In 1958 he served as minister of interior in Pflimlin's government, but his doubts about the loyalty of the police had much to do with Pflimlin's resignation and De Gaulle's investiture.

After 1961 Moch continued his political career as a member of both the *comité directeur* of the Socialist Party and of the Fédération de la Gauche Démocrate et Socialiste (1965–8), but devoted most of his time to writing.

MOCTEZUMA I (*c.* 1390–1464), Aztec Emperor (*reg.* 1440–1464), under whose aegis the empire expanded south into Guerrero and Oaxaca and east into Veracruz. Moctezuma strengthened the priestly hierarchy and expanded the scope of human sacrifice.

MOCTEZUMA II (1466–1520), Aztec Emperor (*reg.* 1502–20) at the time of the Spanish conquest. He successfully maintained Aztec hegemony, and appears to have been the first Aztec ruler to claim semi-divine status. He did little, however, to assuage rising discontent within the vassal states over Aztec tribute demands, aggravated by the pressure of an extremely dense population on the available land. Moctezuma's reaction to the Spanish threat was curious: a victim of his own fears and superstitions, he tried by threats and presents to dissuade Cortés from visiting Tenochtitlán, only to be forced to capitulate in the end. He soon became a prisoner and puppet of the Spaniards, was deposed by his exasperated nobility, and killed while attempting, at Cortés's insistence, to try to pacify his people.

MODEL, WALTER (1891–1945), German field-marshal and one of the pro-Nazi elements in the German Officer Corps. Hitler had noted as early as 1938 that Model, like Rommel, was more favourably disposed towards him and his plans than many more senior officers. In the latter part of the Second World War his loyalty was never suspect; indeed, he was one of the few generals whom Hitler allowed to argue with him, and was employed in attempts to retrieve desperate situations. He was a tough and aggressive leader of men rather than a planner, and distinguished himself as a tank commander. He commanded the 3rd Panzer Division in Guderian's *Gruppe* in the Kieve encirclement (Sept. 1941), and in July 1943 commanded the 9th army, which was to play a crucial role in the Kursk offensive. He questioned the wisdom of the attack, however, and won Hitler's special confidence when it collapsed. He superseded Von Manstein as commander of the Army Group in south-central Russia in March 1944, checked the Russian advance on his front, and organized a successful counter-attack outside Warsaw in

Aug. He succeeded Von Kluge as commander of Army Group B in northern France on 16 Aug., extricated his beaten forces from the Falaise pocket, and prevented the retreat towards Germany from becoming a rout. Acting energetically to foil Montgomery's bid to outflank him at Arnhem, he stabilized the front on the Siegfried Line. He argued against the Ardennes offensive, but loyally carried it out. Finally he was driven back across the Rhine early in 1945 and ordered by Hitler to stand fast in the Ruhr, where on 11 April he was surrounded with 325,000 men; on the 26th he surrendered and committed suicide.

MODEL PARLIAMENT in England, term applied by English historians to the parliament held by King Edward I in 1295 to procure supplies for the war with France. It was an exceptionally well-attended assembly at which knights and burgesses were present, as well as prelates and magnates. It was not the earliest parliament composed in this way, though some of its features (*eg*, the wording of writs of summons to elected representatives) did create enduring precedents. Quite unhistorically, it is treated by the modern law of peerage as the first parliament originating baronies by writ for the descendants of all the magnates personally summoned to it.

MODERADOS, moderate republicans who stood between Mexican liberals and clerical-conservatives throughout the 19th cent. They opposed both the liberals' anti-clericalism and the conservatives' authoritarianism. President Ignacio Comonfort was a leading moderate (1855–7).

MODOC WAR (1872–3), fought in southern OR and northern CA by a band of Modocs, who refused to come into the reservation. The members of a peace commission led by US Gen. Edward R. S. Canby were killed (11 April 1873) before the Indians surrendered. Four Modoc leaders were hanged and the others moved on to the reservation. This was the last Indian war in this area.

MODYFORD, SIR THOMAS (?1620–1679), English soldier, planter, and colonial governor, who fought in the Royalist cause in the early part of the English Civil War, before emigrating to Barbados (1647) as a planter. He later served the Commonwealth (1652–60) as a colonel of his regiment and supported Oliver Cromwell's plan for the 'Western Design', a project to destroy Spanish power in the Caribbean and take Jamaica. Modyford became governor of Barbados (1660), but resigned on the restoration of Charles II, from whom, however, he received a pardon for his service to the Parliamentary cause. He was governor of Jamaica (1664–70), whence he took with him 800 settlers from Barbados and introduced sugar planting. As governor, he granted commissions to buccaneers such as Sir Henry Morgan and Edward Mansveldt. When the peace of Madrid (1670) was made with Spain, Charles II ordered the suppression of the buccaneers, instructed Sir Thomas Lynch to replace Modyford, who was sent to England under arrest. Modyford was confined to the Tower (1671–4), but returned to Jamaica (1675) as chief justice.

MOERENHOUT, JACQUES ANTOINE (1796–1879), Belgian colonial official, who began as a pearl sheller and planter in the Tuamotu and Tahiti. He later became, successively, US and French consul, and director of native affairs under Gov. Bruat (1843).

MOESIA, Roman province south of the Danube, which covers much of modern Bulgaria. It was conquered by Rome in 29 BC, and in AD 44 constituted a separate province, later being divided by Domitian into two provinces. It was always important militarily and in the 2nd cent. the area regularly supported four or five legions. Most of the few towns developed round legionary fortresses, *eg*, Singidunum (Belgrade) and Novae (Svistov), though there were some old

Greek colonies on the Black Sea, *eg*, Tomis (Constanza). From the 3rd cent. Moesia was increasingly exposed to attacks by Goths, Huns, Avars, and later the Bulgars.

MOFFAT, ROBERT (1795–1883), Scottish missionary, who went to South Africa for the London Missionary Society in 1816, becoming in southern Botswana one of the most influential missionaries in South Africa (1821–70). He formed a close relationship with Mzilikazi, the Ndebele king, although Christianity had little effect upon the Ndebele nation until after its defeat by whites in Rhodesia in the 1890s. Moffat inspired David Livingstone, his son-in-law, in the earlier stages of his missionary activities and journeys.

MOGADISHU, most important of Benadir towns, said to have been founded by immigrants from Al Hasa (Persian Gulf) in the 9th cent. It was described by Ibn Batuta in AD 1332.

MOGUNTIACUM (mod. Mainz), Roman legionary fortress on the Rhine opposite its junction with the Main. It was garrisoned (*c.* 13 BC–3rd cent. AD), and a substantial walled town grew up alongside it. It was the capital of Upper Germany, and though plundered several times in the 4th and 5th cents survived as a medieval town.

MOHÁCZ (MOHÁCS), BATTLES OF (Aug. 1526, Aug. 1687), Hungarian town situated on the Danube where in 1526 the Ottoman Turks routed the Hungarians in a conflict which marked the end of the old Hungarian kingdom. In the second battle the Ottomans were defeated by the imperialist forces under the command of Charles of Lorraine and Maximilian Emmanuel of Bavaria.

MOHAVE INDIANS, large American tribe of the Yuman linguistic group, found by the Spanish, possibly in 1540, on both sides of the Colorado river in AZ. The US government took their lands without a treaty and established them (1865) in their present (1970) reservation in AZ.

MOHAWK INDIANS, war-like American tribe of the Iroquois confederacy, formerly occupying the Mohawk river valley in NY. They suffered severe defeats in inter-tribal wars before the Dutch arrived (*c.* 1614), who, in exchange for furs, gave them firearms, which enabled them and their confederates to establish an empire in the north-eastern US. The Mohawk sided with the British in the French and Indian War (1755–63) and the American War of Independence (1776–83). After the latter war, most of them fled to Canada, and were given lands in Ont., where they remain (1970).

MOHEGAN INDIANS, American tribe, probably a branch of the Mahican, who originally lived in the Thames river valley in CT. When the Pequot Indians were annihilated (1637), the Mohegan took control of their lands. An alliance with the English against other tribes strengthened their position, and at the end of King Philip's War (1676) the Mohegan were the only important tribe left in southern New England. The encroachment of white settlements reduced their numbers and territory and only a remnant of mixed blood survives (1970).

MOHILA, PETER (*fl.* 17th cent.), Russian scholar and Metropolitan of Kiev. From 1631 he organized the defence of Orthodoxy against Jesuit propaganda and sent young scholars to Lvov and to western Europe. By vigorously organizing education in Little Russia he did much to raise the intellectual level of the Orthodox Church in Muscovy.

MOHSIN-UL-MULK (1837–1907), Nawab, Sayyid Mahdi Ali, Indian administrator and the main figure in the Aligarh movement after the death of Sayyid Ahmad Khan. He was in the service of the British until 1874, when he resigned to serve under the Nizam of Hyderabad. He rose to be a political and financial secretary to the nizam's government. On retiring from Hyderabad in 1893, he settled in Aligarh, where, after Sayyid Ahmad's death, he became secretary of the Muslim Educational Conference.

MOLA VIDAL, EMILIO (1887–1937), Spanish soldier and last director-general of security under the monarchy. His right-wing sympathies kept him out of office during Azana's ministry, but he was appointed to command the Moroccan army when Gil Robles was minister of war.

On the advent of the Popular Front government in 1936, he reluctantly accepted the need for army intervention. He became head of the conspiracy for a rising to establish 'order, peace, and justice' and drew up plans for the occupation of various cities. He rejected perhaps the last opportunity to avoid war when he refused Martínez Barrio's offers of compromise in July 1936.

On 18 July Mola proclaimed a rising in Pamplona, to which command he had been transferred in March. He was part of the junta which ruled Nationalist Spain. In Aug. he led the Army of the North against the Basque province Guipuzcoa. After capturing San Sebastian in Sept., he turned to Madrid. He left the siege in March 1937 to continue the assault on the Basque country.

In April 1937, when Franco combined the Carlists and Falangists under his supreme command, Mola was passed over. On June 3 he was killed in suspicious circumstances in a plane crash.

MOLASSES ACT (1733) in Britain imposed heavy duty on all foreign sugar, molasses, and rum imported into North America. The act, which was highly unpopular in the American colonies, reflected pressures exerted in the House of Commons by the West Indian 'planters' lobby'.

The act was a failure, partly because the prime minister, Sir Robert Walpole, was diplomatic enough not to demand its effective enforcement. Its replacement, Grenville's Sugar Act (1764), was meant to be applied with authority. As such, it became one of the significant American grievances contributing to the outbreak of the War of Independence.

MOLESWORTH, SIR WILLIAM (1810–55), British politician, who held office under Aberdeen and Palmerston. He was a philosophical radical who opposed the transportation of criminals and advocated colonial self-government.

MOLIÈRE (JEAN BAPTISTE POQUELIN) (1622–73), French dramatist, who became Louis XIV's favourite playwright, his many comedies being performed before the court. His plays are noted for their humour and pointed social criticism, which later incurred for him the hostility of those sections of society whom he ridiculed. His principal works are *L'Avare*, *Les Précieuses Ridicules*, *Le Bourgeois Gentilhomme*, *L'École des Femmes*, *Le Tartuffe*, *Le Misanthrope*, *Le Medecin Malgré Lui*, *Les Femmes Savantes*, and *Le Malade Imaginaire*.

MOLINA LUIS (1535–1600), Spanish Jesuit theologian of the Portuguese Evora University, whose book, *Concordia Liberi Arbitrii* (1588), initiated a violent debate between the Jesuits and the Dominicans on the problems of grace and free will. His optimistic views of human nature were adopted as the official doctrine of the Society of Jesus in the later 16th cent. and his theological optimism became known as Molinism.

MOLINOS, MIGUEL DE (1628–96), Spanish priest, who lived in Rome (*c.* 1670–80) and founded the religious movement of Quietism or 17th-cent. Molinism. His writings include the *Defence of Contemplation*, *The Accord of Fatigue and Repose in Prayer*, and *The Spiritual Guide* (1675), in which he taught that true Christianity was a purely personal experience when the soul was in a state of quiescent peace with God. Under pressure from Louis XIV, who disliked the impact of French Quietists, and alarmed at suggestions that the movement fostered sexual immorality, Pope Innocent XI (1676–89) permitted the Inquisition in Rome to condemn Molinos and his writings for heresy (1687), and he was subsequently imprisoned for life.

MOLLET, GUY (1905–), French politician and trade unionist, who emerged as one of the youngest militants in the Section française de l'international ouvrière (SFIO) and in the Teachers' Union. In 1932 he became secretary of the union and an important figure in the Confederation générale du travail (CGT).

After serving in the battle of France in the Second World War he was captured and imprisoned in Germany (1940–2). He was repatriated for reasons of health and joined the Resistance. In 1946 he was elected deputy for Pas-de-Calais. As secretary of the Pas-de-Calais federation, one of the largest and most influential within the party, he played an important role in the internal affairs of the SFIO. In 1946 he led a coalition of the traditional centre and extreme left of the party against the secretary-general, Daniel Mayer, who favoured an appeal to non-Socialists. After Mayer's resignation Mollet became secretary-general of the party, a post he held until 1968.

For over 20 years Mollet exerted a dominating influence over his party, largely through his understanding of tactics, his support being based on the two large and usually united federations of Nord and Pas-de-Calais. After holding several cabinet posts (1945–51), he led his party out of the government in 1951, hoping that the 'cure' of opposition would arrest the party's electoral decline. After the election of Jan. 1956 he became *Président du Conseil*, and although his government was defeated in May 1957, the SFIO participated in Bourgès-Maunoury's and Gaillard's governments until May 1958.

In domestic affairs and in French West and Equatorial Africa his own government had pursued liberal policies, but in Algeria he followed a 'hard' line after the demonstration of 6 Feb. 1956 in Algiers. This was to be the origin of a disastrous split within the SFIO and set a valuable precedent for the French settlers of Algeria.

After the rebellion in Algeria on 13 May 1958 the Socialists reversed their decision not to participate in the cabinet. Mollet became convinced that the only alternative to De Gaulle was civil war and played a decisive part in persuading the SFIO to support De Gaulle. He became minister of state in De Gaulle's first cabinet (although not as a representative of his party). In Jan. 1959 he resigned from the government. During the Fifth Republic he managed to weather an open schism in the party and its electoral decline.

His hostility to Gaston Defferre in 1964 prevented the latter from becoming the official candidate of the left in the presidential election of 1965. Mollet resigned the secretary-generalship (1968), but has remained (1970) active in the new Parti Socialiste.   PMR

MOLLWITZ, BATTLE OF (April 1741), Prussian victory in Silesia over the Austrian forces of Maria Theresa in the War of the Austrian Succession, in which Frederick the Great fled prematurely from the battlefield. The conflict opened with the rout of the Prussian cavalry by the Austrians, but the Prussian infantry held firm and drove the enemy back by their accurate firing.

MOLLY MAGUIRES, secret society of miners active in the coalfields of PA, US, during the 1860s and 1870s. The society, an outgrowth of the Ancient Order of Hibernians, was open only to Irish Catholics. Members disguised in women's clothing and known as 'Molly Maguires', intimidated mine owners and officials in the anthracite coal mining areas from about 1865. The society was disbanded in 1877 after a number of its members had been hanged for murder on the testimony of James McParlan, a Pinkerton detective who had infiltrated the organization.

MOLOTOV, VIACHESLAV MIKHAILOVICH (1890–), Soviet politician and foreign minister. After joining the Bolshevik party when he was 16, he played an undramatic role in the underground. By Feb. 1917 he was a member of the Russian bureau of the central committee and editor of *Pravda*. The distrust which he expressed of the provisional government was later confirmed by Lenin. Molotov, who had attached himself to Stalin, advanced his career as that of his master proceeded. In 1921 he became a secretary to the central committee and in the next year an associate of Stalin in the general secretariat. In 1926 he became—and remained until 1957—a full member of the politburo. In 1927 he took charge of the Moscow party committee. He was chairman of the council of people's commissars (1930–40) and loyally supported Stalin during the strains and terrors of the 1930s. In May 1939 he was appointed commissar for foreign affairs (the first time that anyone of his rank in the party had been so placed) and he played an important part in the negotiations leading up to the Nazi–Soviet pact (Aug. 1939). As a member (1941–5) of the small state defence committee (GOKO) he had special responsibility for tank production in the Second World War. With the development of the Cold War after 1945 Molotov earned for himself a reputation in the West as the negotiator who always said 'No'. He retained his offices until 1957, but persistently opposed Khrushchev, who, being anxious to rid himself of Stalin's closest ally, arranged for him to be appointed ambassador to the Mongolian People's Republic.

MOLTKE, HELMUTH VON (1800–91), Prussian field marshal, who became chief of the general staff in 1858 and made it the focus of the Prussian army. His use of railways for deploying troops was chiefly responsible for Prussian victories in 1866 and 1870. He permeated the army with his ideas for training staff officers and his insistence on spells of regimental duty.

MOLTKE, HELMUTH VON (1848–1916), German general, who succeeded Schlieffen as chief of the general staff in 1906. His main concern was to adapt the Schlieffen plan to changing military circumstances, but when the First World War broke out Moltke proved a poor strategist. His inflexibility and inability to make quick decisions lost Germany the battle of the Marne and tied her troops unnecessarily on the left wing of the front. In the autumn of 1914 he was forced to resign, and was succeeded by Falkenhayn.

MOLTKE, HELMUTH JAMES VON (1907–45), German lawyer, who was a leading member of the anti-Nazi opposition in Germany, and inspirer of the Kreisau Circle. At the outbreak of the Second World War he joined the German general staff as an expert on international law. With his wife and Peter Yorck von Wartenburg, Von Moltke initiated the Kreisau Circle in 1940, and represented the most idealistic Christian-pacifist element within it. He was deeply involved in the group's efforts to plan post-war society in Germany, on the basis of a highly moralistic and anti-pragmatic Christian socialism. His pacifist beliefs prevented him from playing any part in the July Plot (1944); he had become convinced that violence was immoral under any circumstances, and could not condone the plan for Hitler's assassination. He was arrested in Jan. 1944, after attempting to protect another opposition activist from the Gestapo. Throughout his imprisonment and trial he displayed extraordinary courage, welcoming his inevitable execution as a chance for martyrdom in the cause of freedom and Christian morality. He was executed in Jan. 1945.

MOMBASA, Arab settlement on an island off the Kenya coast, first mentioned by Idrisi (late 12th cent.). In the 15th cent. it was the rising town of the coast, ruled by Shirazi sheikhs. In 1505 and 1528 it was destroyed by the Portuguese and was ravaged by marauding cannibals in 1589. It was the Portuguese northern headquarters (1593–1698), when it was taken by the Omani Arabs. In 1741 the Omani governor declared its independence, which was maintained by his successors until 1837. From then, it was governed by an officer appointed by the Sultan of Oman and after 1856 by the Sultan of Zanzibar, until the proclamation of the British Protectorate of Kenya in 1895.

MONAGHAN, SETTLEMENT OF (1591) in Ireland, by which Elizabeth I divided the Irish county between seven chief MacMahons and a McKenna. Monaghan was therefore not included in later plantations of Ulster. Under the Tudors the MacMahons had surrendered their lands in Monaghan to the Crown and had received them back under English law. The execution of chief Ross MacMahon (1589) had led to the return of the lands to the Crown.

MONARCHOMACHS, term coined by William Barclay in his *De regno et regali potestate* (1600) to describe those political theorists who justified the right of rebellion against a tyrannical king and emphasized the sovereign power of the people. These anti-royalist theories had been developed by the Huguenots after the St Bartholomew Massacre (1572) during the French Civil Wars.

MONASH, SIR JOHN (1865–1931), Australian general, who served in the First World War, commanding a brigade at Gallipoli (1915) and a division in France (1916–18). In May 1918 he took command of the Australian Corps. After the war he became vice-chancellor of Melbourne University (1923–31).

MONASTERIES, DISSOLUTION OF THE, in England, suppression of the monastic orders in England by parliamentary acts of Henry VIII's reign, at the direction of the vicar-general, Thomas Cromwell (1536–40). By the early 16th cent. monastic life in England was fairly moribund, and anti-clericalism sufficiently strong for Henry to carry through his ecclesiastical changes without serious opposition. The reform of clerical abuses and the dissolution of decayed monasteries figured among Cardinal Wolsey's many plans and he ordered the suppression of a few small houses after his agents had reported unfavourably upon their findings. The Crown's serious financial problems were a further stimulant to the secularization of Church lands. In Jan. 1535 Cromwell initiated a visitation of many monasteries which favoured dissolution. By an act of 1536 all those religious houses with an income of less than £200 a year were dissolved, probably about 275, affecting some 2000 clerics. The property passed to the Crown, to be handled by the newly created Court of Augmentations, the religious heads received pensions, and the monks and nuns were given the option of transferring to larger houses or of entering the ranks of the secular clergy. In the next four years the dissolution of the larger and richer monasteries continued in a piecemeal way. Some abbots were attainted for participation in the Pilgrimage of Grace (1536), their lands being seized by Crown commissioners. A few resisted, *eg,* Glastonbury and Reading, and were executed for treason, and their houses were dissolved. Others surrendered voluntarily, receiving handsome pensions, and by 1540 the process was complete.

A few estates were kept for the royal domain, a small number being granted by Henry VIII as outright gifts to loyal friends, but the majority were sold or leased to gentlemen farmers who rose from the ranks of successful yeomen, merchants, or craftsmen. This new landowning class was entrenched under a strong Crown as the last strongholds of papal authority in England were destroyed.

MONASTIC DEPARTMENT, *Monastyrskii Prikaz* or Russian government department responsible for the administration of the lay affairs of the Church, *eg,* it collected revenues from monastic estates. First founded by Tsar Alexis in 1649, it was closed by Tsar Fedor, but reopened in 1701 by Peter I, being subordinated to the Holy Synod in 1721.

MONCK OF BALLYTRAMMON, CHARLES STANLEY MONCK, 4th Viscount (Irish) (1819–94), British politician, who was called to the Irish bar (1841), was an MP (1852–8), and held office under Palmerston (1855–8). He was governor-in-chief of Canada and governor-general of British North America (1861–6). During his term of office Canadian–American relations were strained first by the '*Trent* affair' and later by raids from Canada by Confederate refugees during the Civil War, and by raids from the US by Fenians. Monck's efforts to further the cause of Confederation (1864–6) were recognized when he was appointed (1867) first governor-general of the Dominion of Canada.

MONCONTOUR, BATTLE OF (1569), victory of the Catholic forces of the Duke of Anjou over the Huguenots, led by Admiral Coligny, in the third French Civil War (1568–70). Although Coligny was wounded, the Huguenots survived to win the favourable peace of Saint-Germain.

MONDÉJAR, INIGO LOPEZ DE MENDOZA, 3rd Marquis of (1512–80), Castilian grandee, who succeeded his father in the hereditary position of captain-general of Granada (1543). During the 1550s his authority was increasingly undermined by the rival house of Fajardo. The Mondéjar family had been traditionally pro-Morisco and the influence of their enemies in Granada left the Morisco population unprotected against the activities of the Inquisition. He warned the government of the dangers of enforcing the pragmatic sanction of 1566–7 which led to the rebellion of the Alpujarras (1568–70). Although Mondéjar scored some successes at the beginning of the revolt, Philip II ordered him to hand over command of the royal armies to Don John of Austria.

MONDÉJAR, LUIS HURTADO DE MENDOZA, 2nd Marquis of (d. 1566), Castilian grandee, who was pro-Morisco and held the hereditary captaincy-general of Granada until 1543, when he was appointed viceroy of Navarre. He was also president of the Council of the Indies (1546) and president of the Council of Castile (1561–3).

MONDELET, CHARLES-JOESEPH-ELZÉAR (1801–76), Canadian pamphleteer, who wrote, under the pseudonym of *Pensez-Y-Bien,* four letters (1831–2) containing common colonial grievances and demanding that the Legislative Council of Lower Canada should either be made elective, or abolished.

MONDLANE, EDUARDO CHIVAMBO (1920–69), first president of the Mozambique Liberation Front (FRELIMO). He was born in Gaza province in southern Mozambique to a family with a long tradition of resistance to Portuguese colonial rule, and early in his career he embraced ideas of African advancement. He was expelled from South Africa as a 'foreign native' and went to Lisbon, and then to the US to seek a higher education. In 1962, after serving in UNO, he was invited by the leaders of Mozambique liberation groups, then coalescing to form a common front, to become their leader. This responsibility he discharged with success and courage, but he was murdered by his adversaries.

MONEY CHANGERS in the Middle Ages. Between the 10th and the 13th cents all medieval rulers, however insignificant, claimed the right to mint their own coins. With the appearance of autonomous towns (12th–13th cents) municipal coinages were also introduced. The existence of this multiplicity of coins of diverse quality and changeable value made the services of money changers indispensable. By the late 13th cent. in the more important business centres some of the changers were men of considerable means. They came to accept deposits of funds, on which they paid interest, and to extend credit to favoured customers. They were thus one of the groups that originated the practice of deposit banking. In the 1360s at Bruges in Flanders all the 17 money changers had accounts with each other, so that any of their customers could make transfers between all the banks in Bruges.

MONEYERS. The minting of coins was usually undertaken in medieval Europe by private businessmen acting under licences from one of the many territorial rulers or municipalities who arrogated to themselves the right to issue their own coinages. In the earlier Middle Ages many of the moneyers were important people who combined minting with other financial operations. With the emergence of the more powerful and centralized states, moneyers were reduced to an inferior position, though they were always well-remunerated and enjoyed important privileges.

MÖNGKA (d. 1259), Ruler of the Mongol empire (*reg.* 1251–9), and eldest son of Tolui Khan, who succeeded his cousin, Güyük, after a regency (1248–51) under Güyük's widow, Oghul-Ghaimish. Möngka's accession produced the first major split within the Chingizide family, the descendants of Jöchi and Tolui (Batu and Möngka) having combined against the descendants of Ögotei and Chaghatai, following whose overthrow they murdered supporters of the opposing faction. Möngka's reign inaugurated a period of Mongol expansion. Attacks were launched against the Sung empire in China under Möngka's brother and eventual successor, Khublai, and against the Abbasid caliphate in Iraq under a second brother, Halagu.

MONGOLIA, AUTONOMOUS. In 1911 the nobility of Khalkha (or Outer) Mongolia took advantage of the collapse of the Manchu dynasty in China to declare Mongolia an independent monarchy under the Jebtsundamba Khutuktu. Territorial ambitions provoked a clash with China, settled by the tripartite treaty of Khiakta (1915), signed also by Russia, which allowed Mongolia the status of autonomy under Chinese suzerainty, within frontiers approximately the same as those of the present-day Mongolian People's Republic. Russian influence was at first paramount, and some modernization was attempted. However, the collapse of Russia in 1917 facilitated the annexation of Mongolia by China in 1919. A confused situation, with the capital, Urga, occupied by White Russian troops under Baron Ungern Sternberg, was resolved in July 1921 by the intervention of revolutionary Russian troops and Mongol partisans. The Khutuktu was restored to the throne, with strictly limited powers regulated by the so-called 'Oath-taking Treaty'. His death in 1924 was followed by the establishment of the Mongolian People's Republic.

MONGOLS, nomadic people who established in the 13th cent. one of the greatest of the world's empires. The name Mongol was originally that of only one of the tribal confederations of Mongolia—that on the Onon and Kerulen rivers—but was later used to embrace many others, including the Tatars, Khongrats, Merkits, Oirats, Keraits, Naymans, etc. For centuries their activities troubled the rulers of China, but became truly formidable in the 13th cent., when they were united under Chingiz Khan (*reg.* 1206–27), organized on semi-feudal lines, and formed an invincible light cavalry army. After early campaigns against the Tangut state of Si-Hia and the Kara Khanids (1209), Chingiz attacked the Kin or Chin empire of northern China (1211) and captured Peking (1215). The campaigns against the Kins were continued under Chingiz's general, Mukali (d. 1223), and Mukali's son, Boru (d. 1228), and were completed in 1234. In 1252, further great campaigns were launched against the Sung dynasty of southern China under the direction of Khublai Khan (d. 1294). By 1258 he had completed the conquest of south-west China, including Yunnan and Annam.

The Chinese campaigns were resumed after the end of the struggle for power which followed the death of Möngka Khan (1259); the resistance of the Sungs ended (1279) and the Mongol (Yüen) dynasty (1271–1368) was established in

China. A second major area of conquest was indicated by Chingiz in the west. In 1219–23 he attacked Central Asia and made raids into Iran and the Ukraine. Under his successors the Mongol conquests were much extended. Batu (d. 1255), son of Chingiz's eldest son, Jöchi (d. 1226), led a campaign (1236–41) which penetrated almost to Vienna and resulted in the formation of the Golden Horde (1241–c. 1505). Halagu (1217–65), son of Tolui (d. c. 1232), directed operations which led to the capture of Baghdad (1258), the extinction of the Abbasid caliphate, and the establishment of the Il-Khanid dynasty (1258–1365) in Iran. At its greatest extent in the later 13th cent. the Mongol empire with its tributary states stretched from the Pacific almost to the Mediterranean and from south-east Asia to the Baltic. But the bonds of unity were already loosened. After Chingiz's death his empire was divided among his four sons, some shares being given to his brothers in Manchuria. One son, Ögetei (*reg.* 1229–41), was made Great Khan. But as the descendants of Chingiz acquired greater power within their apanages, dissension grew and the central authority was weakened. Conflict was narrowly averted by the early death of Ögetei's son and successor, Güyük (*reg.* 1246–8), but on the accession of his cousin Möngka (*reg.* 1251–9) a clash occurred when the descendants of Ögetei and Chaghatay and their followers were massacred by those of Tolui and Jöchi. After Möngka's death a further struggle for supremacy took place between two of Tolui's sons, Khublai and Arik-buka (d. 1266). The split widened when Khublai removed the Mongol capital from Karakorum to China, and Qaidu, a descendant of Ögetei, established his power in Central Asia and defied Khublai. In the west there was continued strife between the Golden Horde and the Il-Khans and between both and the Chaghatays of Central Asia, who supported Qaidu. After 1260 the empire had no unified political direction, although important links were maintained for economic, financial, and social reasons.

The Mongol empire should not be regarded as a great movement of the Mongol population. After their campaigns the vast majority of Mongols returned to Mongolia. A small aristocratic group alone held power in the apanages and states that grew up outside. The Mongols in China formed small nomadic groups outside the Chinese villages and towns. The bulk of the western clans were Turks. At its peak the Mongol empire was held together by its military strength, its remarkable communications system, and by the semi-divine status of the Chingizide family, which provided great continuity. The last of the successor states of the Golden Horde, the Crimean khanate, survived until 1783, the Mongol tradition in Central Asia continued until the extinction of the last Uzbeg khanate in 1920, while the Mughal (Mongol) dynasty in India (1526–1858) traced its origin through the Timurid Baber to Chingiz Khan. The main area of purely Mongol development was Mongolia, where, after the expulsion of the Yüens from China (1368), the Mongols created several short-lived empires under the Khalkhas and the Oirats (Kalmuks) until they passed under Manchu control.

Outer Mongolia gained autonomy in 1911 and independence in 1921.

C. R. Bawden, *The Modern History of Mongolia* (London, 1968).

E. D. Philips, *The Mongols* (London, 1969).   MEY

MONITOR, USS, ironclad warship, designed by John Ericsson. It was launched on 30 Jan. 1862 and had a system of revolving turret guns on a hull submerged for protection. On 9 March 1862, *Monitor* met the Confederate ironclad *Virginia*, formerly USS *Merrimack*, at Hampton Roads, VA, in an indecisive engagement, but one that revolutionized naval warfare. The *Monitor* later foundered and sank off Cape Hatteras (31 Dec. 1862).

MONIVONG (d. 1941), King of Cambodia (*reg.* 1927–41), during the period when French control was at its height.

MONMOUTH, JAMES SCOTT, Duke of (1649–85), illegitimate son of King Charles II and contender for the English Crown (1685). He was born at Rotterdam, the son of Lucy Walter, mistress of the exiled Charles II. On the death of his mother (1658), he was entrusted to William, Lord Crofts, by whose name he was for some time known. In 1662 he came to England, was created Duke of Monmouth (1663), and married a Scottish heiress, Ann Scott, Countess of Buccleugh. He took the name of Scott and was created Duke of Buccleugh in the Scottish peerage (April 1663). A staunch Protestant, he soon replaced his uncle, James, Duke of York, in the public's esteem. A rivalry developed between the two dukes as the king heaped offices on Monmouth, while James, having turned Roman Catholic, was forced to relinquish the admiralty by the Test Act. As captain-general of all the forces in England and Scotland, Monmouth gained great popularity by his defeat of the rebelling Covenanters at Bothwell Bridge (1679). Easily influenced, he fell under the spell of the Earl of Shaftesbury during the Popish Plot and the Exclusion Crisis, and was put forward as the Protestant candidate for the throne. Although Charles II refused to desert his brother and publicly denied that he had married Monmouth's mother, Monmouth refused to accept the king's decision not to exclude James. He lost all his offices and was banished. Returning without permission, he made a semi-royal progress in the south-west. Being deeply implicated in the Rye House Plot, he fled to Holland (1684), despite his being pardoned. On his father's death (1685), he was induced by friends and enemies to attempt an invasion of England. His pitifully inadequate force landed at Lyme Regis (11 June 1685), where he received considerable support from the local populace. Although he was proclaimed king at Taunton, his rebellion was doomed on his failure to take Bristol. Surrounded by royal forces at Bridgwater, he made a hazardous night attack at Sedgemoor (6 July). He was defeated, captured, condemned by an act of attainder, and executed on 15 July.

A. Fea, *King Monmouth* (London, 1902).
C. C. Trench, *The Western Rising* (London, 1969).   CJ

MONMOUTH PURCHASE, region in NJ from Sandy Hook to the Raritan river, for which Quakers and Baptists from Long Island and Newport were given a patent to settle by Gov. Nicolls (1665). They opposed the proprietary government, passed laws, administered justice, and held their own general assemblies. The patent was annulled (1672) because it was in conflict with a prior grant to Berkeley and Carteret.

MONNERVILLE, GASTON (1897–), French Radical politician, who was president of the upper house of the French parliament. He was born in French Guiana, and first entered parliament in 1932 as its representative, taking a special interest in colonial questions. He had a distinguished Resistance record. After the Second World War he was president of the Council of the Republic (1947–58) and of its successor, the Senate (1958–68). Under the Fifth Republic he became one of De Gaulle's strongest opponents, criticizing his authoritarian tendencies and neglect of parliament. His post was of considerable constitutional importance, since the president of the Senate acts as interim president of the republic during a vacancy.

MONNET, JEAN (1888–), French businessman and economist, who did much to shape the pattern of modern Europe, being a leader both in economic planning and European integration. He began his career in the family cognac business, and in the First World War helped to organize inter-Allied war supplies. He became deputy secretary of the League of Nations (1919–23), returned for a time to the family business, then entered international banking, advising various countries on economic development.

In 1938 the French government sent him to the US to purchase aircraft and he developed a joint Anglo-French buying organization. He then became head of the Anglo-French economic co-ordinating committee in London. He helped to inspire Churchill's offer of Franco-British union in 1940, and after the fall of France served on the British Supply Council in Washington. When the Allies liberated Algeria he went there and became one of De Gaulle's advisers.

His first post-war task as head of the French planning office (1945), was the initiation and working out of the 'Monnet plan'. He then developed the idea of the European Coal and Steel Community, and was the first chairman of its high authority (1952–5). He was also a supporter of the abortive European defence community, and his 'supranationalism' made him unpopular in some French quarters. He influenced the later development of European institutions as founder of the Action Committee for the United States of Europe. His own experience in Britain and America, however, gave his Europeanism a strong 'Atlantic' orientation.

MONNET PLAN (1947–53) in France, name given to the first economic plan in post-war France, embodying the ideas of Jean Monnet and supervised by him as head of the planning office. The plan aimed at the reconstruction of French industry on a modern basis, and concentrated on transport and a few basic industries. Its work was successful, and it is usually seen as one of the foundations of France's recent economic prosperity. The 'indicative' methods of Monnet's planning—setting targets of production and relating investment priorities to them—were followed in France's subsequent plans and widely imitated elsewhere.

MONNIER, HENRI BONAVENTURE (1805–77), French author and caricaturist of the July Monarchy, renowned for his *Mémoires de Monsieur Prudhomme* (1854).

MONOPHYSITISM, major theological controversy which racked the Eastern Church in the 5th cent. Schoolmen of Antioch held that Christ embodied two 'Natures', human and divine. Those of Alexandria took the view that Divinity was so tremendous as to absorb or obliterate mere Humanity: hence Christ had one Nature, the Divine. This conception became the Monophysite 'heresy' and is adhered to at the present time by the Coptic Church in Egypt and Ethiopia. Logically associated with this interpretation was the doctrine that the blessed Virgin Mary was 'mother of God' (*Theotokos*). On the other hand, Nestorious, Bp of Constantinople, declared that she should properly be acclaimed only as the mother of Christ. Beneath the wrangling of rival dogmatisms lay the intense competition for ecclesiastical power and prestige between the great sees of Antioch, Alexandria, and Constantinople. Cyril, Bp of Alexandria, gained the support of the Bp of Rome, who had an interest in belittling the authority of the see of Constantinople. Nestorius was condemned at the Council of Ephesus in 431. In 451 the Eastern Emperor Marcian, with the support of Pope Leo I, summoned a Council at Chalcedon which, while reasserting the primacy of the see of Constantinople in the East, approved the doctrine of *Theotokos* and upheld the Two Natures. Christians in Egypt and Palestine objected, blood was spilt, and the Monophysite Churches split from the Orthodox. In 482 the Emperor Zeno tried to heal the breach by proclaiming the single Nature of Christ, but Pope Silvanus promptly condemned Zeno's doctrine. Justinian I tried to preserve unity with the Monophysites by a fine-spun doctrine which held that Christ had two Natures within one, and forced this through the Council of Constantinople in 553. But the Monophysites of Egypt and Syria remained unreconciled, while the Western Church viewed Justinian's compromise with suspicion. As time passed Monophysitism, in the provinces where it was dominant, took the form of nationalist dissent, which contributed to the speedy conquest of Syria and Egypt by the Arabs in the 7th cent.   RP

MONOPOLIES, exclusive economic privileges, granted by European monarchs or ministers to individuals, companies, or corporations sometimes acting on behalf of the Crown, entitling the holders to the sole right to manufacture, export, import, or produce certain commodities, or to evade existing laws concerning their trade or manufacture, or to sell licences to others. In the paternalistic regimes of 16th–17th-cent. Europe monopolies were essential instruments of mercantilist economic policy, since they provided protection to new industries and trading interests and new sources of revenue for hard-pressed monarchs. They became a source of popular grievance, however, because they favoured the privileged few and forced up prices, and they were abandoned in Restoration England. It was not until 18th-cent. ideas of free trade spread in Europe that monopolies ceased to be granted.

MONROE, JAMES (1758–1831), 5th president of the US, who interrupted his studies at William and Mary College to fight in the American War of Independence. He was a member of the anti-Federalist group, a friend of Thomas Jefferson, and served with distinction in the VA legislature (1782, 1787–90), in Congress (1783–86), the Annapolis Convention (1786), and the VA ratifying convention (1788). As US senator (1790–4) he opposed the plans for a US bank and was severely critical of the Washington administration. He was appointed minister to France (1794), but had little success and on being recalled (1796), published his self-justifying *View of the Conduct of the Executive in the Foreign Affairs of the US* (1797). After serving as governor of VA (1799–1802), he was sent to France to assist in the negotiations that resulted in the Louisiana Purchase (1803). Neither of his next two missions, to Spain (1804) and Britain (1805–1806), produced satisfactory results. Although unsuccessful as rival to Madison for the presidency (1808), he accepted (1811) the secretaryship of state, hoping for a reconciliation with Britain, but these hopes were dashed by the outbreak of the War of 1812. He was elected US president (1816) and followed a cautious policy, modifying his earlier views to the extent of supporting internal improvements and abstaining from intervening in the debate on the Missouri Compromise (1820). His presidency was marked by several important achievements in foreign affairs, notably the Rush–Bagott agreement (1817), the ending of the Nfld fisheries dispute (1818), the acquisition of FL (1819), and his famous message of 2 Dec. 1823, incorporating the Monroe Doctrine. When he left the presidency he retired to VA, and served as president of the VA constitutional convention (1829–30).

DBS

MONROE DOCTRINE in the US, basic principle of US foreign policy contained in President James Monroe's message to Congress of 2 Dec. 1823 and largely written by John Quincy Adams, declaring that 'the American continents, by the free and independent condition which they have assumed and maintained, are henceforth not to be considered as subjects for future colonization by any European powers'. This statement of principle was in line with previous expressions of American independence from Europe contained in Washington's Farewell Address (1796) and Jefferson's First Inaugural (1801), but it arose directly from Russian claims to exclude all but Russian vessels from the north-west coast of America north of 51 degrees, and from fears of European reconquest of former Spanish colonies in Latin America.

Although the message met with an enthusiastic response in the US, it went largely unnoticed in Europe, and for the next 20 years had no appreciable effect upon relations between the US and either European nations or the Latin American republics. In the mid-1840s, however, the Doctrine was revived by President Polk, reacting to British and French intrigues over the annexation of TX (1845) and the threat of a British or Spanish protectorate over Yucatan (1848). Again, in the 1850s, the message was referred to frequently in discussions on the Central American question, and began to take on the status of a national principle. During the Civil War this principle was put to the test with France's attempt to

establish an empire in Mexico under Archduke Maximilian of Austria, an attempt frustrated in part at least by US diplomatic pressures in Paris. After the war, the Doctrine was given a still wider interpretation. In 1895 secretary of state Richard Olney applied it to the dispute between Venezuela and Britain, declaring that the US was entitled to resist any sequestration of Venezuelan soil, and in the Hay–Pauncefote treaty (1901) Britain accepted an interpretation of the Doctrine which precluded any country other than the US from controlling the projected trans-isthmian canal. President Theodore Roosevelt carried the main principle still further, and the Roosevelt Corollary (1904) transformed the Doctrine from a warning to Europe against interfering in Latin America into a justification for US intervention. After the 1920s, however, a new trend prevailed. The US presence had been withdrawn from Santo Domingo, Haiti, and Nicaragua by 1934, and in 1937 the chairman of the Senate Committee on Foreign Relations declared the principles of 1823 to be outmoded. At the Pan-American conference at Montevideo (1933), and again at Buenos Aires (1936), armed intervention in the internal affairs of the Latin American republics was repudiated, but this was replaced by a policy of co-operation. Out of the Havana conference (1940) came the famous declaration from the assembled republics that aggression against one of them should be considered aggression against all. After the Second World War the threat of ideological penetration of Latin America gave the Doctrine a new significance. The US took steps to cement solidarity amongst the American republics with economic aid, and, as over Cuba in 1962, to defend presumed hemispheric interests with armed force.

D. Perkins, *A History of the Monroe Doctrine* (Boston, 1963).
A. Alvarez, *The Monroe Doctrine; its Importance in the International Life of the States of the New World* (New York, 1924). DBS

MONROVIA, capital of Liberia, first and most important of the 19th-cent. West African settlements established for freed slaves from the US. It was sponsored by the American Colonization Society after two abortive attempts (1820–1) to make a settlement at Freetown in Sierra Leone. A group of black Americans reached Cape Mesurado, led by Eli Ayres, who signed a treaty with a local Bassa chief, in Dec. 1821. Cape Mesurado became the society's possession, and the new settlement was named after the US president, James Monroe.

This little American colony had inauspicious beginnings. Apart from problems of acclimatization, friction occurred with the settlers' African neighbours, the Dei, Mamba, Gola, and Kru, who resisted encroachment on their land. Another problem was unruliness among the settlers. Having been lately freed from slavery, they resented being again dominated by white masters (as they were until about 1841) in a land where they were supposed to be free.

However, the colony survived through the capability of its leaders, among whom was Jehudi Ashmun, the society's agent (1822–8), who won new land rights, introduced new crops, and encouraged farming. The colony, much expanded beyond Monrovia, was given a constitution setting up an advisory council of settlers to assist the society's agent. Meanwhile, other settlements were established along the coast: Maryland (1831); Edina (1833); Grand Bassa (1835); and Greeville (1838). In 1839 the last three united to form the Commonwealth of Liberia (to which Maryland acceded in 1857). Connections were then severed with the society, and on 26 July 1847, the Commonwealth became an independent republic.

C. H. Huberich, *The Political and Legislative History of Liberia* (New York, 1942).
P. J. Staudneraus, *The African Colonisation Movement, 1816–1865* (New York, 1961). TA

MONS, Mon-Khmer race, related to the ancient Cambodians, who entered Lower Burma from the east. They settled at first in Thaton, but in the 9th cent. they established the kingdom of Pegu. The Mons have now (1970) been largely absorbed by the Burmese, although they are slightly darker of skin. In 1941 they numbered 336,728, but they were probably more numerous, as many would allow themselves to be enumerated as Burmese. However, a certain racial consciousness survives and since independence (1948) a Mon nationalist movement has emerged.

MONS, BATTLE OF (24 Aug. 1914), fought in the First World War. The British Expeditionary Force's first battle in France, and the first battle fought by British troops on the Continent since Waterloo. Two British divisions, under Smith-Dorrien, held a good position behind the Mons–Condé canal against six German divisions from noon to nightfall, inflicting heavy losses with accurate rifle-fire. They checked the advance of Von Kluck's First Army, the pace-setter for the German right wing, for 24 hours. The next day a threat to their left flank, and the retreat of Lanrezac's Fifth French Army on their right, obliged the British to begin the famous retreat from Mons, which, with the battle of Le Cateau intervening, ended on the Marne on 6 Sept.

MONSIEUR, informal title given to the eldest brother of the reigning French monarch during the *ancien régime*.

MONSIEUR, PEACE OF (1576) in France, settlement some-times known as the treaty of Chastenoy, but also called after the younger brother of Henry III of France, it was the fifth peace treaty of the French Civil Wars and was concluded between the king and the Duke of Alençon who led the dis-contented Politique party in southern France with Condé and Montmorency-Damville. A humiliating peace for Henry III and highly favourable to the Huguenots, it granted Alençon the three duchies of Anjou, Touraine, and Berry, while the Huguenots were permitted freedom of worship throughout France, except in Paris, and several fortified towns as surety, eg, Angoulême, Niort, La Charité, Bourges, Saumur, and Mézières. The peace was short-lived, however, for, alarmed by the generosity of its terms, the Catholic party, led by the young Duke of Guise, formed the aggressive Holy League (1576).

MONT BLANC, France (Haute Savoie), highest peak in the Alps and in Europe, 4807 metres above sea level. It was first climbed on 8 Aug. 1786 by Dr Michel-Gabriel Paccard, and a porter, Jacques Balmat, both of Chamonix. Paccard had reconnoitred and studied the route for some years, and led the ascent. But the greed of Balmat, the envious malice of a rival, Marc-Théodore Bourrit of Geneva, the culpable silence of Horace-Bénédict de Saussure, who knew the truth but suppressed it, conspired to give the credit to Bal-mat. Only in 1957 was Paccard vindicated by means of numerous unpublished documents, by T. Graham Brown and Gavin de Beer, in *The First Ascent of Mont Blanc*. The conquest of Mont Blanc marks the beginning of the sport of mountaineering, which has spread to all continents.

MONTAGNAIS INDIANS, group of Canadian Algonquian tribes, discovered (1603) at the mouth of the Saguenay by Champlain, who enlisted them in an expedition (1609) against the Iroquois. They were important to the Europeans as fur traders, but contact with white civilization and epidemics reduced their numbers.

MONTAGNARDS (mountaineers) (1792–4), name given to the Jacobin deputies and their allies in the French Convention because they occupied the upper seats at the back of the Assembly.

MONTAGU, EDWARD WORTLEY (1713–76), British poli-tician and secretary at the congress of Aix-la-Chapelle (1748). He was the son of Lady Mary Wortley Montagu. His *Reflections on the Rise and Fall of the Ancient Republicks*

analyses the merits and defects of the English contribution and compares it with those of the ancient world.

MONTAGU, EDWIN SAMUEL (1879–1924), British poli-tician and secretary of state for India (1917–22). He entered parliament in 1906 and immediately became parliamentary private secretary to H. H. Asquith. His first administrative connection with India was as under-secretary of state (1910–1914). At once, he showed himself ahead of general thinking on the future of India, his speeches visualizing colonial self-government, a goal which his superiors insisted was impossible and for which they gave him no support. During the First World War Montagu was chancellor of the Duchy of Lancaster (1915–16) and minister for munitions (1916). He returned to Indian affairs in 1917 when on 20 Aug., as secretary of state for India, he announced Britain's intention of giving India eventual self-government. Later in the same year he headed a delegation to India to sound Indian and official opinion. The resultant Montagu–Chelmsford reforms (1919) provided less than he had perhaps originally hoped for, and certainly in operation they achieved less than he had expected. His contribution to the reforms was recognized by Indian politicians, who were concerned when he was forced to resign from the cabinet (1922) because of his action in publishing the government of India's criticism of the Turkish peace treaty. This proved to be the end of his political career.

E. S. Montagu, *An Indian Diary* (London, 1930).
D. Waley, *E. S. Montagu. A memoir* (London, 1964). PDR

MONTAGU, LADY MARY WORTLEY (1689–1762), English writer, whose letters over half a century provide a detailed commentary upon contemporary society. Those written while she lived in Italy (1739–62) provide a wealth of de-scription upon architecture, clothing, and customs.

MONTAGU–CHELMSFORD REFORMS (1919), constitu-tional changes, embodied in the Government of India Act (1919), which were carried through by the secretary of state, E. S. Montagu, and the Viceroy, Lord Chelmsford.

On 20 Aug. 1917 Montagu announced the government's intention to move towards responsible government in India. The following year, after discussions in India, he and Chelms-ford produced the *Report on Indian Constitutional Reform*, which outlined the scheme that was enacted in 1919. Despite recognition of Montagu's good will, the reforms were criticized from the outset by nationalist politicians. The Congress boycotted the elections to the first councils (Dec. 1920) and even the moderates, while they worked in the councils, urged the rapid expansion of the system. But al-though there were investigations by the Muddiman com-mittee (1924), no substantial changes were made until the replacement of the whole provincial system was effected in 1937.

The act enlarged the provincial legislative councils and established a bicameral central legislature comprising a broadly representative Legislative Assembly and a more re-stricted Council of State. The viceroy and the governors were no longer to act as presidents of the legislatures, and although there were still blocs of nominated officials and some non-officials, there were clear elected majorities in all legislatures. The governors retained a veto against these elected majorities in their right to 'certify' essential legislation, but this was a power which they had clearly to use with discretion. The elec-ted members were returned directly by voters in territorial constituencies for a term of three years (or five in the case of the Council of State). The property franchise provided an electorate of 5·5 million for the provincial legislatures and 1·5 million for the centre. These electoral changes provided, for the first time, an effective local basis for provincial party politics. Separate electorates were maintained for Muslims in all provinces and there was further recognition of communal representation in the provision of Sikh constituencies in

Punjab and 'non-Brahman' reserved seats in Madras and Bombay.

There was no element of responsibility in the central executive, although provision was made for an increase in the number of Indian members in the viceroy's executive council. All the executive councillors were selected by the viceroy, however, and were responsible only to him; although they sat in the legislature, none were elected members.

At the provincial level there was some move towards responsibility. All the major provinces were given governors who, in a system termed 'dyarchy' ('the rule of two'), were to preside over governments comprising two parts: an executive council and a ministry. It was for the governor to decide how far the two met in joint consultation, and the practice varied from province to province. The executive councillors, called the 'reserved side', were selected by the governor from among either officials or non-officials. As at the centre, they sat in the legislature as nominated members, but were entirely responsible to the governor. They had charge of those departments which were considered essential to the maintenance of British authority, *eg*, finance and land revenue, irrigation, the police, and the administration of justice. The ministers, on the 'transferred side', were, on the other hand, chosen by the governor from among the elected members of the legislative council, and they served at his pleasure. They had charge of the so-called 'nation-building' departments such as agriculture, education, public health, local government, and public works, which gave them politically useful local patronage and influence.

R. Coupland, *The Indian Problem, 1833–1935* (Oxford, 1968). S. R. Mehrotra, *India and the Commonwealth, 1885–1929* (London, 1965). PDR

MONTAIGNE, MICHEL DE (1533–92), French writer, whose fame rests upon his *Essays* (1580), in which he expressed his novel scepticism, regarding religion as an act of blind faith and all rational knowledge as a highly suspect basis for natural law. He became the leader of the new Pyrrhonists, whose number included the philosopher Pierre Charron (1541–1603).

MONTALEMBERT, CHARLES FORBES RENÉ DE (1801–70), French writer, historian, and leader of liberal Catholicism, who tried to reconcile the Church with democracy. He expounded his views in the newspaper *L'Avenir* (1830)—condemned by Pope Gregory XVI at the request of the ultramontane bishops—and then in *L'Univers Religieux* (*1833*). He was also prosecuted for founding a Catholic school in protest against the state monopoly of education (1831). Fear of revolution led him to assume the leadership of liberal Catholic support for Louis Napoleon (1848), but opposed the dictatorial measures of 1851 and attacked the regime in print and through the Académie Française (elected 1851). Montalembert's speech in favour of civil liberty and religious toleration—'a free church in a free state'—encouraged opposition to the policy of Pope Pius IX at the Congress of Malines (1863), though he reluctantly accepted the doctrine of papal infallibility (1870). His most famous historical work is *Les Moines d'Occident* (1860–7).

MONTALVO, JUAN (1832–89), Ecuadorian polemicist and essayist, known for his sustained opposition while in exile to the Ecuadorian dictator, Gabriel García Moreno, and for his claim that his pen had played a part in the dictator's assassination.

MONTANA, 41st member state of the US, admitted in 1889. The American north-west was probably traversed by the Vérendrye brother (1742) and was explored by Lewis and Clark (1804–6). British and American fur traders established trading posts early in the 19th cent., but US title to the region was recognized by the Oregon treaty (1846). The discovery of gold (1852) and subsequent rich findings at Alder Gulch (1862) and Last Chance Gulch (1863) led to an influx of prospectors, and to incorporation of the area within Idaho Territory (1863), and its organization as Montana Territory (1864). Pacification of the Sioux and Nez Percés Indians during the 1870s and the completion of the Northern Pacific Railroad (1883) opened up the territory, and statehood followed in 1889. MT's economy has depended upon mining, cattle farming, and wheat growing. The state is sparsely settled, with a population of only 700,000 in 1970.

MONTANO, BENITO ARIAS (1527–98), Spanish scholar, who edited the Antwerp Polyglot Bible (1569–73).

MONTAPERTI, BATTLE OF (1260), defeat of Florentine propapal militia by German mercenary cavalry supporting King Manfred. The battle, in which the Florentines were decimated, was followed by a proposal to destroy the city of Florence, but this was averted by Florentine exiles in Manfred's entourage. It gave Manfred control of central Italy, temporarily destroyed the papal party in Florence, and by showing the superiority of veteran troops over urban militia, promoted the rise of the *condottieri*.

MONTCALM DE SAINT-SERVAN, LOUIS-JOESEPH DE MONTCALM-GAZON, Marquis de (1712–59), French soldier. After a distinguished career in Europe, particularly during the War of the Austrian Succession (1740–8), Montcalm was appointed commander-in-chief of the French armies in Canada (1754). In the opening campaigns of the French and Indian War (1756–63) he captured Fort Oswego, with 1600 prisoners and 121 guns (Aug. 1756), and seized and destroyed Fort William Henry (1757). He conducted a brilliant defence of Fort Carillon (Ticonderoga) (1757), defeated Abercromby's numerically superior invading force (1757), and defeated the British at Montmorency, when Quebec was already under siege (1759). Despite these successes, however, the French were weakened by British control of the seas, which prevented supplies and reinforcements reaching them, and also by personal animosities between Vaudreuil and Montcalm. After Wolfe had scaled the Heights of Abraham (13 Sept. 1759) Montcalm immediately brought him to battle, but was mortally wounded and died the next day. Wolfe was also killed in the battle and the city fell (18 Sept. 1759).

MONTE ALBÁN, impressive ruins of a ceremonial city in the Mexican state of Oaxaca, which is credited to the Zapotec peoples. A considerable quantity of gold and jewels was discovered there in 1932.

MONTE CASSINO, ABBEY OF, mother house of the Benedictine order, founded (*c.* 529) by St Benedict. It was destroyed by the Lombards (*c.* 581) and not revived until 717. Its prestige and power grew until the beginning of the 12th cent., since when it has been honoured rather than influential. Some unique manuscripts were preserved at Monte Cassino, including the sole source of our text of parts of Tacitus, rediscovered in mid-14th cent. During the Second World War the abbey was occupied by German troops and captured by the British army only after prolonged fighting, in the course of which it was almost completely destroyed (1943–4).

MONTE CORVINO, GIOVANNI DI (1247–1328), Franciscan friar sent by Pope Nicholas IV in 1291 on a mission to the Mongol Khan Khublai in China by way of India. He was welcomed by Khublai's successor Timur, and made some converts and was appointed the first Catholic Abp of Peking (1307), where he died. Three extant letters describe his experiences in the East.

MONTECUCCOLI, RAIMONDO, Count (1609–80), Italian soldier, who entered imperial service during the Thirty Years War and served the Austrian Habsburgs during a long and distinguished military career. He defeated the Swedes in Silesia (1637), and though taken prisoner in 1639, later helped to drive the Swedish army from Bohemia (1646) and was created a marshal (1648). He commanded the Austrian force which supported Poland against Sweden in the Northern War (1657) and then led the Habsburg forces against the Turks in Hungary (1663–4). Although he abandoned the Hungarians under Miklos Zrinyi to their fate (1664), he checked the Turkish hordes advancing towards Vienna in the battle of St Gotthard (1 Aug. 1664). In 1668 he was appointed president of the council of war in Vienna and commanded the imperial armies on the upper Rhine against Louis XIV's forces in the Dutch War.

MONTEGO BAY CONFERENCE (1947) in Jamaica, presided over by Arthur Creech-Jones, the British colonial secretary, and attended by delegates chosen from the legislatures of all British Caribbean colonies. The conference affirmed in principle the idea of West Indies federal nationhood and set up the Standing Closer Association Committee, which presented (1949) a draft of a federal constitution which was eventually embodied at the London Conference of 1953. The Montego Bay Conference was the first major step on the road towards the federation, which was to last for only four years (1958–62).

MONTEJO, FRANCISCO DE (c. 1484–1550), Spanish explorer and conqueror, who travelled to Cuba (1514) and twice to Mexico with exploratory missions. After joining Hernán Cortés's army, he reached Mexico and was made an officer of the first town council formed at Veracruz. As an emissary of Cortés to the Emperor Charles V, he informed him of Cortés's activities. Having secured a permit for further conquest, Montejo fitted out an expedition of his own. Arriving at Yucatán, Mexico (1527), he met with prolonged resistance and was eventually forced to leave the region. He next went to Honduras, where he clashed with Pedro de Alvardo. Nevertheless, he was rewarded for his exploits with the title of governor of Yucatán and Honduras. He left his son to complete the military conquest of Yucatán province and to found the city of Mérida.

MONTES, ISMAEL (1861–1933), lawyer, general, and twice Liberal president of Bolivia (1904–9, 1913–17), whose regimes are generally regarded as peaceful interludes in the country's turbulent national history.

MONTESCLAROS, BATTLE OF (1665), fought near Villaviciosa on the Portuguese frontier and the decisive battle of Portugal's War of Independence from Spain (1640–68). A well-drilled force of Portuguese and English soldiers defeated a numerically superior Spanish army of 23,000 men, killing 4000 and capturing 6000. The news shattered Philip IV, who died within three months.

MONTESPAN, FRANÇOISE-ATHÉNAÏS DE ROCHECHOUART DE MONTEMART, Marquise de (1641–1707), French mistress of Louis XIV. After her legal separation from her husband (1674) she was given official recognition of her position. Louis spent vast sums on her and legitimized her various children. She was superseded in 1678, though she remained at court until 1691, after which she retired to a convent.

MONTESQUIEU, CHARLES LOUIS DE SECONDAT, Baron de la Brède et de (1689–1755), French political philosopher and publicist of the Enlightenment, whose *Lettres Persanes* (1721) was a witty satire on Church and state at the end of Louis XIV's reign. His most famous work, *Esprit des Lois* (1748), was a systematic treatise on social science, in which Montesquieu studied the facts of history and contemporary society and proclaimed the rule of law. He defended the privileges of various social groups as part of French fundamental law and as an effective barrier against arbitrariness

and despotism. He thus enhanced absolute monarchy, which, by permitting intermediate powers to play a role in the state, could never become despotic. His concept also enhanced the position of the aristocracy and of the *parlements*, the depository of all law, and drew attention to the rule of law embodied in the practice of the English constitution, particularly the separation of powers, which the Americans were to copy.

MONTEVERDE, JUAN DOMINGO (1772–1823), commander of the Spanish forces in Venezuela during the successful 1812 campaign against the American rebels led by Miranda. Monteverde was able to send Miranda as a prisoner to Spain, but erred in permitting Bolívar to leave the country to fight another day.

MONTEVERDI, CLAUDIO (1567–1643), Italian composer, whose contribution to music was the transformation of the *dramma di musica* into true opera, in the period after 1600, when he wrote *Orfeo* (1607), *The Rape of Proserpina* (1630), *The Return of Ulysses* (1641), *The Marriage of Aeneas* (1641), and *The Coronation of Poppea* (1642). He also developed the madrigal.

MONTEZUMA, CARLOS (c. 1866–1923), American Indian doctor and writer, who was captured when a band of Pima Indians raided his Apache village (1871) and taken to Chicago (1872). He became a graduate of Illinois University (1884) and Chicago Medical School (1889), served as a doctor in the Bureau of Indian Affairs (1889–96), and was author of *The Indian of Today and of Tomorrow* (1906) and *Let My People Go* (1914).

MONTFORT, SIMON DE (d. 1218), French soldier who participated in the Fourth Crusade (1202–4). Later, he led armies in southern France in the crusade against the Albigensian heretics with encouragement from King Philip Augustus, who was careful to abstain from intervening directly. Simon won for himself the county of Toulouse and the duchy of Narbonne. His younger son, Simon, won prominence in England as a brother-in-law of King Henry III and a leader of baronial opposition to the king.

MONTGOLFIER, JACQUES-ETIENNE (1745–99) and **JOSEPH-MICHAEL** (1740–1810), French inventors of the warm-air balloon. After experiments with smoke-filled paper sacks from their father's paper factory, and encouraged by Joseph Priestley, their first *Montgolfière* flew in June 1783. In Nov. 1783 the first free flight of a *Montgolfière* carrying passengers took place near Paris.

MONTGOMERY OF ALAMEIN, BERNARD LAW MONTGOMERY, Viscount (1887–), British soldier, who served in the First and Second World Wars. He commanded the third division in France and Britain (1939–40), then successively the 5th Corps, 12 Corps, and south-eastern army until 1942, when he was appointed to command the 8th Army in Egypt in succession to Auchinleck. He commanded the 8th Army in North Africa and Italy (Aug. 1942–Dec. 1945) and the 21st Army Group in north-western Europe (1944–5) acting as co-ordinator of Allied land operations in 'Overlord' (June–Sept. 1944). He accepted the German armed forces' surrender in the north on Lüneburg Heath (4 May 1945). He then commanded British occupation forces in Germany (1945–6), and was chief of the imperial general staff (1946–8), and chairman of Western European Union chiefs of staff committee (1948–51). Finally, he was the deputy NATO supreme commander in Europe (1951–8).

As a military theorist Montgomery emphasized the importance of training and leadership. He was predominantly an organizer and administrator, more at home in the defence or assault of prepared positions than in the fast-moving hurly-burly of modern mechanized warfare. He was appointed to high command when the material difficulties bedevilling the British forces in the earlier stages of the war had largely been overcome, and when the US entry into the war enabled the Allies to go on to the offensive in overwhelming strength. He owed his reputation chiefly to the British government's need for an all-British victory and to his ability to inspire the men under his command with a sense of mission and involvement in the huge war-machine. His generalship was cautious, painstaking, and inflexible. He has been criticized for his failure to use the 'immense material superiority' of the 8th Army utterly to destroy the German–Italian Panzer army at the second battle of Alamein. But his powers of organization and leadership were recognized when he was entrusted with reorganizing the US 1st Army after the German offensive in the Ardennes. After 1945 he played an important role in post-war European–Atlantic alliances.

PJBD

MONTGOMERY, RICHARD (1736–75), Irish-born colonial soldier in the British army during the French and Indian War, who settled in New York (1772). He led an invasion of Canada (1775), captured Montreal, and was killed in an assault on Quebec.

MONTGOMERY, TREATY OF (1267), concluded between King Henry III of England and Llywelyn II, prince of Gwynedd. Llywelyn was confirmed in all his conquests of other Welsh lordships, and also of several marcher lordships, since 1258. His overlordship of the other Welsh lords was recognized by the acceptance of his title of Prince of Wales. The treaty was undone by the defeats inflicted on Llywelyn by King Edward I in the war of 1276–7.

MONTMORENCY, ANNE, Duke of (1493–1567), Constable of France, who served Francis I, Henry II, and Charles IX. He fought with Francis in Italy, being present at the defeat of Pavia (1525), and helped to negotiate Francis's release by the treaty of Madrid (1526). Though he later fell from the king's favour (1540) he was reinstated by Henry II (1547) and on the outbreak of the French Civil Wars joined the Duke of Guise and Saint André in the triumvirate against Catherine de Medici (1561). Although his nephew, Coligny, was later to be associated with the Huguenots, Duke Anne supported the Catholic cause and was captured at Dreux (1562). He was mortally wounded fighting against the Huguenots at the battle of St Denis in the Second Civil War.

MONTMORENCY FAMILY, French noble house of dukes and peers, who from the 12th cent. traditionally held the office of constable of France. Matthew I of Montmorency (d. 1160) was the first constable of the family; his grandson Matthew II, the Great Constable (c. 1174–1230), distinguished himself at Bouvines (1214). In the 16th cent. the family took a leading part in French politics. Although Constable Anne supported the Catholic cause, his younger son, Henry, Count of Damville, joined the Politique party with his nephew, the Count of Coligny. Damville's son, Duke Henry (1595–1632), was, like his uncle, Duke Francis, a marshal of France. He was a distinguished soldier, but joined in rebellion with the Duke of Orléans against their common enemy, Richelieu. After trial by the *parlement* of Toulouse, he was executed on Richelieu's orders (30 Oct. 1632), while the lands and possessions of his family reverted to the Crown.

MONTONERA, irregular *gaucho* cavalry band in the early decades of Argentine independence. They were virtually indistinguishable from bandits, and frequently served the autonomist *caudillos* of the interior. They thus provided an effective military check to Buenos Aires's pretensions to dominance.

MONTPELLIER, PEACE OF (1623), treaty signed between the Duc de Rohan, leader of the French Huguenots in the Languedoc region, and the Duc de Lesdiquières, acting on behalf of Louis XIII. The terms constituted relative success for the French government. Although the Edict of Nantes was to be confirmed, all newly-erected fortifications, including those of Montpellier, were to be razed and Catholic worship restored everywhere except in La Rochelle and Montauban.

MONTREUX CONVENTION (1936), international agreement which superseded the Lausanne treaty in establishing a new regime for the Straits—a vital economic and strategic link, of concern to trading nations as well as the chief local powers, Russia and Turkey. Under the Lausanne treaty, full commercial passage had been guaranteed, unlimited freedom of movement had been given to warships in peacetime, and to neutrals in wartime, when Turkey was neutral; the Straits were demilitarized and under the control of an international commission. Russia had refused to ratify this agreement because she wanted the Black Sea safe from potentially hostile navies at all times, thus Russia and Turkey, deprived of sovereignty over this vital area, had a joint interest in treaty revision. After several vain attempts to raise the question, the Turks found a favourable opportunity in April 1936 to demand a conference. Because of Abyssinia, Britain wanted a supporter in the eastern Mediterranean; France was in favour of the extension of Soviet influence beyond the Black Sea; only Italy refused to attend Montreux from 22 June to 20 July, when the convention was signed. Turkey could probably have succeeded in unilateral repudiation of Lausanne, but Kemal recognized the value to smaller powers of trying to keep the framework of international legality intact, and this in turn influenced the Western Powers even more in his favour. However, the conference saw some hard bargaining between Russia and Britain over a limitation on the passage of warships. A compromise was finally found by which the size of fleets allowed into the Black Sea was related to that of the littoral powers. The result was that while Russia could send out ships of any number, only light vessels of other navies were allowed in. On 20 July Turkish troops re-entered the Straits area, and, not surprisingly, given the trend of international affairs, contemporaries in the West hailed the convention as a major success for the cause of peaceful treaty revision.

KM

MONTROSE, JAMES GRAHAM, 1st Marquis of (Scottish) (1612–50), Scottish general, who was originally one of the covenanting leaders (1638). His dissatisfaction with extremists in Scotland led him to identify himself with the royalists in the English Civil War which, by 1641, had deeply involved the Scots. He successfully led armies in Scotland against the covenanting forces and incurred the enmity of powerful lords such as Argyll and Huntly. He was eventually defeated at Philiphaugh in the borders (Sept. 1645) and fled to the continent. After the execution of Charles I (1649) he returned to Scotland and raised a small force in the highlands. Charles's son, the future Charles II, disavowed Montrose's cause, largely to placate Argyll, whose support he might one day need. Montrose was defeated at Carbisdale (April 1650) and executed.

MONTS, PIERRE DU GUA (or GUAST) Sieur de (?1559–1628), French colonizer, who served under Henry IV against the Catholic League and was appointed lieutenant-general of Canada and Acadia (1603) with a ten-year monopoly of the Canadian fur trade. Accompanied by Samuel de Champlain and the Baron de Poutrincourt, he established the first settlement in Acadia at Sainte Croix (1604).

MONTSERRAT, island in the Lesser Antilles in the Caribbean discovered by Columbus (1493) and colonized by the English (1632). It became part of the colony of the Leeward Islands (1671), with Sir Charles Wheler as governor, and developed flourishing sugar plantations. Montserrat belonged to the Leeward Islands federation (1871–1956) and was a member of the West Indies Federation (1958–62). It remains (1970) a British Crown colony.

MONTT TORRES, MANUEL (1809–80), Chilean politician, twice president of Chile (1851–61), and father of the Chilean president, Pedro Montt. Manuel Montt's progressive regime emphasized the importance of expanding education and commerce. Chile became a haven for exiled intellectuals from other Latin American countries. His tax reforms decreased Chilean dependence on regressive taxes such as the *alcabala* or sales tax. Tariffs were altered to protect Chilean industry, which grew rapidly during Montt's decade in office. Later he served as president of the Chilean Supreme Court, as a senator, and as a diplomat.

MONZON, TREATY OF (1626), agreements of 1 Jan. and 5 March 1626 between France, Spain, and the papacy to restore the status quo of 1617 in the Valtelline. The Spanish forts were to be razed and France was to have the use of the passes into and out of the Valtelline, which was to be restored to the Grisons. The peace was confirmed by the treaty of Barcelona (10 May 1626).

MOODY, DWIGHT LYMAN (1837–99), US evangelist, who became the most widely known evangelist of his day. With the organist and singer, Ira David Sankey, he made numerous tours of the US and also campaigned in England (1873–1875, 1881–4). He founded Northfield Seminary (1879) and Mount Hermon School (1881), was active in the YMCA, and his work with college students led to the Student Volunteer Movement which greatly stimulated the growth of America's foreign missions.

MOOK, BATTLE OF (14 April 1574), Spanish victory under Sancho Davila over the Dutch rebels and their German mercenaries at Mook Heide in the Meuse valley during the Dutch Revolt against Spain. A German–Dutch force of 15,000 men was out-manœuvred and defeated; among the casualties were Louis and Henry of Nassau, William the Silent's two brothers, and their cousin, Christopher of the Palatinate.

MOOKERJEE, SYAMA PRASAD (1901–53), Indian politician and founder of the *Jana Sangh* (1951). He was a member of the Bengal legislative council (1927–47) and finance minister (1941–2). He also served as vice-chancellor of Calcutta University (1934–8). Although he began his political career in the Congress, he gravitated towards the Hindu Mahasabha during the 1930s and he became president of the Bengal Mahasabha in 1941 and working president, under V. D. Savarkar, of the All-India Mahasabha in 1942. He opposed partition, but when this seemed inevitable he urged the need for the partition of Bengal to keep the Hindu majority areas within India. At independence he joined Nehru's cabinet as minister for industries and resigned from the Mahasabha (1948), advising it to concentrate on social and cultural work. He resigned from the government in April 1950 in protest against Nehru's handling of negotiations with Pakistan following rioting in West Bengal and East Pakistan and in the next year he emerged as the leader of a new Hindu-nationalist party, the *Jana Sangh*. He died while in detention in Kashmir, where he had gone to lead a *Jana Sangh satyagraha* campaign against Sheikh Abdullah's government.

MOORE, SIR HENRY MONCK-MASON (1887–1964), British colonial servant, who was governor of Sierra Leone (1934–7), of Kenya (1939–44), and of Ceylon (1944–8). He did much to ensure the smooth transition of Ceylon from colonial to independent status and became the country's first governor-general (1948–9).

MOORE, SIR JOHN (1761–1809), British politician and soldier, who served in the American War of Independence and in the French Wars. He held the Mediterranean command (1806) and went to Spain (1808), where he was mortally wounded after the retreat to Corunna (1809).

MOPLAHS, Muslim community concentrated in the southern *taluks* of Malabar district and comprising about 30 per cent of the population of Malabar. By the 19th cent. economic changes in Malabar had reduced the majority—originally traders and seafarers—to the position of tenants and labourers in the interior of south Malabar. They maintained a strong Islamic faith and in the 19th cent. rose in a number of fierce, local uprisings which gave them a reputation as 'fanatics'.

The largest and the most significant Moplah rising was in 1921 as part of the Khilafat movement. Influenced by Khilafat leaders and non-co-operation propaganda, the Moplahs began to gather in bands and to agitate against the British. The decision of the authorities to arrest certain leaders and to search an important mosque for weapons provoked a clash with a large band and several officials were killed. Rebellion spread throughout southern Malabar in Aug. 1920 and the Moplahs declared an independent 'Khilafat kingdom' under 'Raja' Ali Musaliar. Having removed the British administration, they turned on the Hindu landlords and moneylenders in what became one of the worst communal outbreaks in 20th-cent. India. Women and temples were attacked and men forcibly converted or murdered. These outrages shocked Hindus throughout the country and aroused communal bitterness. The Indian army required four infantry battalions, a pack battery, and armoured cars to retake Malabar and pacify the Moplah areas, and it was not until Jan. 1922 that this was done. There were tragedies in the handling of Moplah prisoners, notably the asphyxiation of 70 Moplahs in a railway truck (19 Nov. 1921).

MORA, JOSÉ MARÍA LUIS (1794–1850), Mexican politician and economist, whose formative role in Mexican thought from independence (1821) to the French intervention (1862) was considerable. Mora was education minister (1833–4) and minister plenipotentiary to London (1847).

MORA PORRAS, JUAN RAFAEL (1814–60), Costa Rican politician and president of Costa Rica (1849–59), who stabilized government after years of political upheaval. He fought an invasion by William Walker (1858) and afterwards reduced military power. His officers overthrew him, in reaction, and while attempting to return he was captured and executed.

MORACZEWSKI, JĘDIZEJ (1870–1944), Polish politician, who was one of the leaders of the Polish Social Democratic Party in Galicia (1893–1919). He was a strong supporter of Pilsudski's plan for setting up an independent Polish military force in Galicia to fight alongside the Central Powers against Russia. During the First World War he fought in the Legions and in 1917 assumed a leading position in Pilsudski's underground Polish Military Organization. In Nov. 1918 Pilsudski appointed Moraczewski as prime minister of his government. However, Pilsudski was concerned, above all, to reach agreement with his National Democratic opponents, and as a result Moraczewski's government, being somewhat radical, proved short-lived, and in 1919 he resigned.

In independent Poland, Moraczewski was a prominent member of the Polish Socialist Party (PPS) and a deputy-speaker in the Polish Lower House (1919–25). After the coup of May 1926, he attempted to win the support of the PPS for Pilsudski, and entered the cabinet in Oct. 1926 as minister for public works. But his support of Pilsudski aroused increasing opposition in the PPS and in 1928 he was expelled from the party. He established a pro-government trade union organization, but it was not successful. After Pilsudski's death, Moraczewski became increasingly disillusioned with the nature of the regime established by the marshal's successors and after 1936 was a strong critic of its totalitarian leanings.

MORAIS BARROS, PRUDENTE JOSÉ DE (1841–1902), Brazilian politician, early leader of the Republican Party in São Paulo, and third president of Brazil (1894–8). His term, racked by financial crisis and rebellion in the backlands of Bahia, was noted for the consolidation of civilian control over the government of Brazil.

MORAN, PATRICK FRANCIS, Cardinal (1830–1911), Abp of Sydney (1884). His appointment symbolized the Irish–Roman dominance of the Australian Roman Catholic Church. He sought with limited success to end sectarianism and establish Catholics harmoniously, and on an equal basis, in his vision of a great national society enriched by religion. He was prominent in public affairs and championed federation of the Australian colonies and social needs.

MORANT, SIR ROBERT LAURIE (1863–1920), British civil servant, who was permanent secretary to the Board of Education (1903–11) and subsequently secretary to the first minister of health. He entered the Board of Education in 1895 and was largely responsible for the preparation and drafting of the Balfour Education Act (1902). His work in the creation of local education authorities and the state education system was invaluable.

MORANT BAY UPRISING (Oct. 1865), civil disturbance in Jamaica, which began at Morant Bay and continued for 12 days before being suppressed by police and army units. Nearly 600 people were killed. Savage reprisals, including the execution of a planter-politician, G. W. Gordan, led to charges being made against Gov. E. J. Eyre, who, however, was acquitted.

MORAT, BATTLE OF (22 June 1476), site of a defeat suffered by Charles the Bold, Duke of Burgundy, in Switzerland. This was the second defeat inflicted on him by the Swiss and was decisive, Charles losing all his artillery and most of his infantry. The Swiss then took the offensive, attacked Charles's territories, and killed him at Nancy in Jan. 1477.

MORAVIA, hilly central European province adjoining Bohemia, Silesia, Austria, and Lusatia, within the medieval Hohenstaufen empire and the Habsburg fold from 1526 to 1918, when it was incorporated into the modern state of Czechoslovakia. Its chief town was Brünn (Brno) and the inhabitants were two-thirds Slav and one-third German.

MORAVIAN BRETHREN, evangelical Church established (1457) in Moravia by the followers of the martyr John Hus. Their missionary movement brought Count Nicolaus Zinzendorf to America (1741), where he attempted to found a colony in GA, and later did so at Bethlehem, PA. The Moravians stressed missionary work among the Indians more than any other religious body in the colonies and established churches and schools among Indians in PA and NY. They also spread into the West Indies. The Moravians stand for Christian unity, personal service, and are opposed to war. They have 70,000 members in the US (1970). Moravian College in Bethlehem, PA, founded in 1742, maintains their tradition of learning.

MORAVIANTOWN, BATTLE OF (5 Oct. 1813), British defeat during the retreat from Detroit in the War of 1812. Most of the British forces were killed or captured.

MORAY, JAMES STEWART, 16th Earl of (Scottish) (1st of 10th creation) (1531–70), regent of Scotland, half-brother of Mary Queen of Scots, and illegitimate son of James V. He joined the lords of the congregation and supported the Scottish reformation. He acted as adviser to Queen Mary on her return to Scotland (1561), but his favour with the queen waned over his support of John Knox and his opposition to Mary's marriage to Darnley. After an attempted coup (1565) he fled to England, but was pardoned and in 1566 returned to Scotland. He was appointed regent on Mary's abdication (1567), and took part in the defeat of her forces at Langside (1568). For the next two years he pursued a vigorous Protestant and anglophile policy despite substantial opposition from a section of the nobility, especially the Hamiltons, who supported Mary. In 1570 he was shot by James Hamilton of Bothwellhaugh.

MORAZÁN, FRANCISCO DE (1799–1842), general and president of the Central American Republic (1824–39). He helped to organize a government for the state of Honduras (1821), then led Central America in a civil war (1826–9). Afterwards, having been named president of the republic, he attempted to institute a strong executive and an independent judiciary. At first he received support from the British minister, Frederick Chatfield, but forfeited this when Central Americans became belligerent towards Britain because of her domination of Belize (British Honduras). The states of the republic later deserted Morazán over tariff and taxation issues and he went into exile. Later he was recalled to lead the revival of the republic, but was captured and executed (1842) in Costa Rica.

MORE, HANNAH (1745–1833), English writer and philanthropist. In her youth she was a playwright and a friend to Garrick, moving in society as a witty bluestocking. After the outbreak of the French Revolution of 1789, she devoted herself increasingly to good works as a member of the Clapham Sect. She encouraged the education of the poor through her Mendip schools (1789), where children were taught to read the scriptures and to be industrious, but not to write, and through the publication of cheap tracts.

MORE, SIR THOMAS (1478–1535), English lawyer, politician, scholar, and martyr, who studied at Oxford (1492–4) with Grocyn, Linacre, and Colet, and later associated with Erasmus, who wrote *The Praise of Folly* in his honour (1509). Together they worked on the dialogues of Lucian. More also translated a life of Pico (1510), wrote *Richard III* (1513), and after representing the Merchant Adventurers at Bruges, proposed an ideal commonwealth in *Utopia* (1516).

His reputation as lawyer and scholar decided Henry VIII to make him an ornament of his court, and he was made a privy councillor and Master of Requests (1518), accompanied his master to the Field of Cloth of Gold (1520), was knighted, and helped Henry with his book against Luther (1521). He was nominated speaker in the parliament of 1523 and became chancellor of the duchy of Lancaster (1525). But More was not deluded by these demonstrations of royal favour. In both *Richard III* and *Utopia* he had shown his awareness of the seamy side of Renaissance politics, and he correctly judged Henry's constancy by remarking that 'if my head would win him a castle in France, it would surely go'.

While he sincerely wished to reform the manifold abuses of the Church, More detested Luther and accepted papal supremacy as divinely instituted. At the request of Tunstall, Bp of London, he wrote two pamphlets against Tyndale and the Protestant reformers (1528–9), and on Wolsey's fall (1529) he became lord chancellor, being the first layman to hold the office.

He resigned on the day after the statutory submission of the clergy (1532), and was conspicuously absent from the coronation of Anne Boleyn, Henry's second wife. He was too important to be allowed to withdraw into private life and engage in academic controversy with heretics. After the failure of charges of taking bribes as chancellor and of omitting to denounce the Nun of Kent, he was summoned to take the oath appended to the Act of Succession (1534). He was willing to swear part of the oath, since he acknowledged parliament's right to alter the succession, but he would not allow that Anne's issue were legitimate. The new Treasons Act also permitted a retrospective charge of denying the royal supremacy, since it enlarged the scope of treason to include malicious words or even thoughts. So by refusing the succession oath More could, by implication, be accused of traitorous intent. He was therefore arrested. In the Tower of London he wrote *A Dialogue of Comfort Against Tribulation*. At his trial his inevitable conviction was doubly assured by the perjury of Rich, the solicitor-general. More was executed in 1535 and Henry VIII confiscated his estates and deprived his widow of her home. He was beatified in 1886 and canonized in 1935.

R. W. Chambers, *Thomas More* (London, 1935).   MMR

MORELOS Y PAVÓN, JOSÉ MARÍA (1765–1815), Mexican priest, *mestizo* revolutionary leader of the pre-independence era, and earliest revolutionary advocate of agrarian reform. Born in Valladolid, Michoacán, he saw the economic dislocation which accompanied changes in the mining industry of *Bajío* region. From *peón* origins, he progressed to become a student under Hidalgo at San Nicolás in Valladolid, then to a curacy nearby.

With Hidalgo's rebellion (1810) spreading across the *Bajío*, Morelos was sent to the south by Hidalgo to raise revolt. The capture and death of Hidalgo (1811) left Morelos in charge of the revolution and in battle with the Spanish-*criollo* loyalist forces he was highly successful. Southern Mexico gradually came under his protection, only the urban centres of Mexico City, Puebla, and Veracruz remaining in Spanish hands.

Morelos summoned the Congress of Chilpancingo (1813) which declared Mexico independent, and wrote a constitution which was tolerant and progressive. Since he advocated racial tolerance and mass democracy, the document called for universal suffrage, the termination of the system of *castas*, and the abolition of ecclesiastical and military privileges (*fueros*).

After Chilpancingo, the royalist counter-attack began to take effect, the rebels were slowly eliminated, and Morelos was finally defeated and executed (Dec. 1815). The political leaders of the mid-19th cent. and the social revolutionaries of the 20th looked to Morelos for historical justification of their programmes.   HDS

MORENGA, JACOB (d. 1907), leader of the Bondelswarts Nama during the uprisings in South-west Africa against the Germans (1903–7). After engaging in guerrilla warfare for several months, Morenga was defeated (1906).

MORENO, MARIANO (1778–1811), Argentine lawyer and revolutionary leader, who wrote *Memorial of the Landowners*, in which he argued against the retention of traditional Spanish commercial monopolies and in favour of free trade. The document embodies a vision of economic development—particularly pastoral and agricultural development—as the consequence of the free play of market forces, which made it a doctrinal source for later generations of liberal Argentine statesmen. Moreno served (May–Dec. 1810) as secretary of the first revolutionary junta, which, in the Spanish constitutional crisis, had wrested de facto sovereignty from the colonial authorities. Simultaneously, in the *Gazette of Buenos Aires*, founded to publicize the acts of the junta, he published his arguments in favour of an autonomous Spanish America, governing itself—conceivably still within the imperial framework—as congeries of representative democracies under liberal constitutions. After he resigned from the junta he undertook a diplomatic mission to petition Britain to aid the cause of independence in the La Plata provinces, but died on board ship.

MORESBY, JOHN (1830–1922), English sailor, who discovered Port Moresby and carried out the original survey of the Louisiade archipelago and south-eastern New Guinea, from China Strait to Huon Gulf (1873).

MORGAN, SIR HENRY (?1635–88), English buccaneer, who was kidnapped as a child at Bristol and sold in Barbados. He later joined the buccaneers in Jamaica and sailed against Cuba (1662) and the Dutch colonies with Mansveldt (1666). On Mansveldt's death, Morgan became 'admiral' of buccaneers. In 1668 Sir Thomas Modyford, governor of Jamaica, gave Morgan command of an expedition which attacked Puerto Principe in Cuba in order to fend off a projected Spanish attack on Jamaica. Morgan, without authorization, also attacked Maracaibo on the coast of South America (1669). Then, with official sanction he carried out his most famous exploit, the sack of Porto Bello and Panama (1671) with only 1000 men. Morgan's reputation was tarnished by acts of cruelty which attended these events. British foreign policy sought to placate Spanish feelings and Morgan and Modyford were recalled to London. As hostilities with Spain loomed up again, Morgan was knighted and sent as deputy governor to Jamaica, which office he held on and off until his death, his tenure dependent on the cordiality of his relations with successive governors and the vicissitudes of English foreign policy.

MORGAN, JOHN PIERPONT (1837–1913), US financier, who acted as agent in NY for his family's firm. During the Civil War he engaged in gold speculation and foreign exchange, but after gaining control of the Albany and Susquehanna Railroad from Jay Gould (1869), he became chiefly interested in railroad development and organization. By the 1890s he had control of the largest group of railroads in the US. In 1871 he established the New York house of Drexel, Morgan & Co., known after 1895 as J. P. Morgan & Co. After purchasing the steel interests of Andrew Carnegie, Morgan formed the US Steel Corporation (1901), and also came to control insurance companies, banks, and shipping lines. He excelled in combination and centralization in business and industry, and helped to stabilize financial conditions during the panic of 1907. A Congressional investigation by the Pujo Committee (1912) discovered that J. P. Morgan & Co. held 72 directorships in 47 large corporations but Morgan remained impervious to public criticism. His personal reputation was unimpaired and he stood as a symbol of concentrated wealth and acute, though harsh, business practice. He was a noted art and book collector, and his pictures were presented to the Metropolitan Museum of Art, and his books and manuscripts to the Pierpont Morgan Library in New York.

MORGARTEN, BATTLE OF (1315), defeat of the feudal army of Duke Leopold of Austria by the infantry of the three Forest Cantons. It opened a period of 150 years of intermittent warfare between the Habsburgs and the Swiss and founded the reputation of the Swiss footguards.

MORGENTHAU, HENRY, Jr (1891–   ), US public servant, who became a close friend of F. D. Roosevelt and, when Roosevelt became governor of New York (1929), served as chairman of his agricultural advisory commission and then as conservation commissioner (1930). After Roosevelt became president of the US Morgenthau was appointed chairman of the federal farm board (1933), governor of the farm credit administration (1933), and acting secretary of the treasury (Nov. 1933), following the illness of William Woodin. On Woodin's resignation (1935) Morgenthau became secretary and served until his resignation (1945). Although in favour of trying to balance the budget, he co-operated fully with Roosevelt's New Deal policies which frequently involved large budget deficits. He is perhaps most remembered for his advocacy of the Morgenthau Plan for the pastoralization of Germany. This, despite the objections of the secretaries of state and war, was adopted by Roosevelt and Churchill at the Quebec Conference (Sept. 1944) as the basis for post-war planning, but was later rejected.   DKA

MORILLO, PABLO (1778–1837), Spanish soldier, who harshly suppressed the independence movement in what is now Colombia and Venezuela. He took command of the Spanish army in 1815 and by the following year had retaken

Caracas, Cartagena, and Bogotá, holding them by repressive means, including mass executions. After Bolívar's victory at Boyacá (1820), Morillo signed a six-month armistice with him, handed over the Spanish army to his replacement, and returned to Spain that same year. When the armistice ended, Bolívar defeated the Spanish troops at Carabobo (1821), thus assuring the independence of the area.

MORIN, AUGUSTIN-NORBERT (1803–65), Canadian lawyer and politician, who was elected to the Lower Canadian Legislative Assembly (1830), and later formed the Hincks–Morin (1851–4) and the McNab–Morin (1854–5) administrations. He became a judge of the Supreme Court of Quebec in 1855.

MORÍNIGO, HIGINIO (1897–), Paraguayan soldier and president of Paraguay (1940–8), whose absolutist regime was beset by numerous revolts. He was finally overthrown by members of the opposition Colorado Party.

MORISCOES, Moors who remained in Granada after its conquest by Ferdinand and Isabella (1492). They were industrious and peaceful, and edicts of 1502 and 1526 ordering their acceptance of Christianity were not rigidly enforced. But further edicts were issued by Philip II, who left their enforcement to the Inquisition, and after a particularly severe regulation had banned their national customs, the Moriscoes rose in revolt (1567). After its suppression (1570) their estates in Granada were forfeited and they were forbidden to leave the new places of residence assigned to them. They worked diligently in the areas to which they were drafted, but Philip III decreed their total expulsion from Spain (1609–14).

MORLEY OF BLACKBURN, JOHN MORLEY, 1st Viscount (1839–1923), British politician, journalist, and author. He became editor of the liberal *Fortnightly Review* (1867–82), to which he attracted eminent contributors, and later of the *Pall Mall Gazette* (1880–3), and wrote a number of biographies, the best-known being his life of Gladstone (1903). He was chief secretary for Ireland (1886, 1892–5) and influenced Gladstone towards Home Rule. He also helped to force Parnell's resignation as leader of the Irish nationalists by emphasizing nonconformist objections to the scandal of the O'Shea divorce. He urged Campbell-Bannerman to take office in 1905 as Liberal prime minister, and subsequently assisted the Parliament Bill (1911) through the Lords. As secretary for India (1905–14) he introduced the India Councils Act which made these bodies partially elective and was the first step to self-government in India. Morley was inclined to pacifism, being pro-Boer in 1900, and later resigned from the government on the outbreak of the First World War.

MORLEY, MRS, pseudonym adopted by Queen Anne of Britain when writing to Sarah, Duchess of Marlborough ('Mrs Freeman'). The name was used so that the two friends could converse as equals, despite their difference in rank.

MORLEY, SAMUEL (1809–86), English politician and philanthropist, who generously supported agricultural trade unionism and the Reform League. He consolidated the Liberal loyalties of leading late-Victorian working men.

MORLEY, THOMAS (1557–1603), English composer, possibly a pupil of Byrd, who was organist of St Paul's Cathedral (1590). He published *A Plain and Easy Introduction to Practical Music* (1597) and *The Triumphs of Oriana* (1601), which included canzonets and madrigals.

MORLEY–MINTO REFORMS (1909), the constitutional changes introduced by the Indian Councils Act as a result of discussions between John Morley, the British secretary of state, and Lord Minto, the viceroy. The changes in legislative institutions were crippled by the over-cautiousness of both

Morley and Minto, but the reforms contained two important turning points in the political development of British India—the admission of Indians to executive councils and the provision of separate electorates for Muslims.

The appointment of Indian members to the secretary of state's India Council and the viceroy's executive council was not a part of the act because no specific parliamentary action was required to make such appointments. Minto, who was convinced of the importance of the move, supported Morley's appointment of two Indians to his council (June 1907) and as soon as a vacancy occurred insisted on the appointment of S. P. Sinha as Law Member (March 1909). In the act itself the principle of Indian participation was extended by provision for at least one Indian on the executive councils of Madras and Bombay.

The basic reforms of the legislatures were extensions to principles already laid down in 1892. The legislative councils were made more representative by the provision that non-official members should be elected by constituencies representing such major interests as landholders, chambers of commerce, and universities, as well as local bodies such as municipal and district boards. In a much more controversial move, the regulations of Minto's government provided for separate electorates for Muslims, so that they would have a guaranteed number of members, in addition to any who might be returned from the ordinary constituencies. This provision was only decided upon after considerable debate between Morley and Minto and protests from leading Hindu politicians. There was less difficulty in securing rights for the legislatures to discuss the budget and to debate a wider range of resolutions than hitherto, but even these concessions were hedged about so as to keep non-official opinion within easily controlled bounds. The provincial legislatures were given nominal non-official majorities, but these were of little significance, as they depended upon the support of nominated non-officials, who were necessarily under the thumb of the government.

The reforms were variously received. Muslims applauded the separate electorates, but the Congress was dismayed at their size and scope. It was also alarmed by the provision which allowed the viceroy to debar from membership of the councils anyone whose membership, because of his 'character and antecedents', might be contrary to the public interest. In essence, by refusing to face the possibility of genuine responsible or representative government at this time, Morley and Minto ensured that there would soon be need for further reform.

R. J. Moore, *Liberalism and Indian Politics, 1872–1922* (London, 1966).
S. R. Mehrotra, *India and the Commonwealth, 1885–1929* (London, 1965). PDR

MORNING POST (1772) in Britain, began as an advertising medium, but after 1795 it became a national daily newspaper, whose contributors included Coleridge, Southey, Lamb, and Wordsworth.

MORNY, CHARLES AUGUSTE LOUIS JOSEPH, Duc de (1811–65), French Bonapartist politician, diplomat, and businessman, who served as a soldier (1832–8), but preferred a business career as a sugar refiner and speculator. He was elected to the legislature (1842, 1849), organized the *coup d'état* as minister of the interior (1851), and later served as president of the legislature (1854) and as ambassador to Russia (1856–7).

MORO ALDO (1916–), Italian politician and prime minister (1963–8), who became a Christian Democrat (DC) deputy in 1946, under-secretary to various ministries (1947–8, 1955–9), leader (until 1968) of the Dorothean, centre, faction of DC, and secretary-general of DC (1959–64). As a skilful mediator, he prepared for centre-left coalitions, and eventually led four successive cabinets of DC, Republicans,

Social Democrats, and Nenni Socialists (PSI). These governments procrastinated over many domestic reforms, and Moro was blamed for DC electoral setbacks. As foreign minister, under Rumor (1969), he reached agreement with Austria over Alto-Adige problems.

MOROCCO (444,000 sq. kms), kingdom in North Africa with 13,726,000 inhabitants of Arab and Berber origin. Morocco included, after independence in 1956, the former territories of French and Spanish Morocco and the international zone of Tangier. The king rules through a House of Representatives elected by adult suffrage; he appoints the prime minister and cabinet and heads the army.

MOROCCO CRISES (1905, 1908, 1911), France, the dominant presence in the area, had to be cautious in extending her North African interests in Morocco, for relations between the sultan and the European powers were governed by the Madrid convention (1880), but Germany had growing economic ambitions there, and Britain favoured the preservation of Morocco as a neutral zone. These considerations encouraged Germany to make Morocco the focal point of European relations. Her aim was to undermine the recently concluded entente between Britain and France (1904), but the result of successive Moroccan crises was to forge the entente into a military reality.

In 1905 Germany appeared to win a decisive diplomatic victory. After the French had sent a mission to Fez to reform the sultan's administration, the Kaiser decided to pay a state visit to Tangier, urging France to agree to an international conference at Algeciras on Morocco. But all the powers at the conference (1906), apart from Austria, were prepared to support French dominance in the area, provided they were given economic access to it. The Tangier incident was a dangerous threat to peace. The Casablanca incident (1908) appeared to end the tension in Morocco. Germany, to distract attention from the Bosnian Crisis, complained about the French violation of the German consulate in Casablanca to arrest three German deserters from the Foreign Legion. The case was settled by the International Court at The Hague and Germany agreed to accept French dominance in Morocco, provided that German economic interests were not hampered.

A further crisis occurred in 1911 when France sent a military expedition to check the progressive deterioration of the Moorish government. Acting on the irresponsible advice of Kiderlen-Wächeter, the Kaiser sent a gunboat, the *Panther*, to Agadir on the pretext of protecting German lives and securing an exchange for the extension of French interests in Morocco. This was a grave miscalculation, for although France agreed to give Germany part of the French Congo, they were alarmed and offended. Britain, fearing that Germany might establish a naval base in the Atlantic, gave notice in Lloyd George's famous Mansion House speech, of their readiness to give France military support. For the first time arrangements were made to make British troops available on the French front in the event of war with Germany.
SH

MOROCCO EXPEDITION (1860) by Spain, followed a declaration of war provoked by a tribal attack on the Spanish enclave at Ceuta. British opposition to Spanish occupation of the Moroccan coast resulted in a treaty sanctioning the enlargement of the Ceuta enclave and the establishment of a fishery. In 1934 Spain occupied Sidi Ifni on the basis of this agreement. A Franco-Spanish protectorate over Morocco had been established in 1912.

MOROKA, JAMES S. (1891–), African (Orange Free State) doctor of medicine and nationalist leader in South Africa, who became politically active in the 1930s, and was president of the African National Congress of South Africa in 1949. He was partly responsible for formulating more vigorous policies of political protest and was arrested by the authorities, with 19 other leaders, after the passive resistance campaigns of 1952 and, like them, sentenced to nine months' imprisonment. At the trial, however, he decided to be represented by separate counsel, and was the only one who agreed to enter the witness box; this contributed to his political eclipse in 1953, when Congress elected Chief Luthuli as its president in preference to Moroka.

MORONE, GIOVANNI, Cardinal (1509–80), Bp of Modena, who carried out much needed changes in his diocese, forbidding pluralism and providing for the education of his clergy, arranging regular diocesan visitations, and transforming the role of the bishop in society (1529–50). He invited the Jesuit Salmeron to revive Catholicism in Modena, where the influence of the Protestant Renée, Duchess of Ferrara, had been widely felt during his absence as nuncio at the court of Ferdinand of Hungary. Morone was himself suspected of heresy and imprisoned in the castle of St Angelo by Paul IV (1557–9). After his release he was appointed as presiding papal legate at the concluding session of the Council of Trent (1563).

MORONI, GIAMBATTISTA (1510–78), Italian painter who moved from Brescia to Venice, where he was influenced by Lorenzo Lotto. His great masterpieces are *An Italian Nobleman* and his portrait of *The Tailor*, in which his considerable skill and human sympathy are shown.

MOROS, PACIFICATION OF, Spanish and US attempts to suppress opposition to their colonial rule by the Moros (the Spanish term for the Muslims of the Philippines), who were and are concentrated in Mindanao and the Sulu Islands. Spanish pacification campaigns in these areas date back to the late 16th cent. when the Spaniards tried to Christianize and collect tribute from the Muslims, whose resistance was regarded by the Spaniards as piratical. Despite periodic Spanish expeditions against the Moros, colonial control over Sulu and Mindanao was not effectively enforced outside fortified towns. In the second half of the 19th cent. increasing Spanish fears of British and French ambitions to expand into certain islands in southern Philippines, and also persistent Moro raids on Spanish-held territories, resulted in the dispatch to Mindanao and Sulu of the first steam warships to operate in the Philippines. After a series of expeditions against Sulu, a treaty was concluded on 26 July 1878, which extended Spanish power over Jolo by the establishment of a permanent outpost. After Spain ceded the Philippines to the US under the Paris treaty (1898), the Muslims of Sulu recognized US sovereignty in the Bates treaty (20 Aug. 1899). Pacification campaigns, however, were continued by the US against sporadic uprisings, and it was not until Dec. 1913, when F. W. Carpenter succeeded Gen. Pershing, that the 'Moro Province' came under a civilian governor. The province, established in 1903, embraced the five sub-provinces of Sulu, Lanao, Cotabato, Davao, and Zamboanga. On 22 March 1915 the Sultan of Sulu agreed to relinquish his political powers, but retained his spiritual leadership. The US administration paid him an annual stipend and awarded him some land in Jolo.
RBS

MOROZOV, BORIS IVANOVICH, Prince (*fl.* 17th cent.), Russian *boyar*, who wielded great power in the early part of Tsar Alexis's reign and married a sister of Alexis's wife. He belonged to the pro-Western circle at the Russian court and did his best to promote German influence with the tsar. Morozov became highly unpopular in Moscow because of his salt tax (1646) and after the 1648 rising he was dismissed and two of his assistants were executed. He later headed the department of foreign affairs, but was superseded by Ordin-Nashchokin in 1667.

MORRILL LAND GRANT ACT (1862) in the US, legislation sponsored by Senator Justin S. Morrill, of VT, which provided federal land grants for the establishment in each state of at least one college of the agricultural and mechanic arts.

30,000 acres (121 sq. kms) of the public domain were allocated for each US senator and representative to which the states and territories were entitled, and states with insufficient public land for the grant received an equivalent amount of land scrip, which could then be located in the public domain of other states. Almost 11 million acres (44,500 sq. kms) of public domain were distributed under the act and receipts from lands sold exceeded $15 million. The Morrill Act, extended in 1890 and 1903, is generally regarded as the single most important piece of educational legislation passed in the US, and many of the colleges endowed under the act have developed into major universities.

MORRIS, GOUVERNEUR (1752–1816), American politician and diplomat, who served in the New York provincial congress (1775) and the Continental Congress (1788–9). He acted (1781–5) as assistant to Robert Morris, the superintendent of finance, and planned the nation's decimal coinage system. As a delegate from PA to the Philadelphia Convention (1787), he argued the Federalists' case for a strong centralized government with a limited franchise. His antidemocratic opinions kept him out of high office, and he left politics to act as Robert Morris's business agent in Europe, arriving in Paris at the start of the French Revolution. Here he used his influence to improve Franco-American financial relations. In 1792 he was appointed US minister to France, but was recalled (1794) after Washington's dismissal of the French minister, Genêt. He served as US senator from NY (1800–2).

MORRIS, ROBERT (1734–1806), American financier and politician, who emigrated from England to America (*c*. 1747) and became a leading Philadelphia merchant and banker. He was a member of the Continental Congress (1775–8), signed the Declaration of Independence, after initial reservations, and as superintendent of finance (1781–4) organized the Bank of North America (1781–2). He borrowed from European countries, persuaded Congress to levy taxes, and issued notes based on his personal credit. He was a member of the PA General Assembly (1785–6), a delegate to the Annapolis Convention (1786), and, as a member of the Constitutional Convention (1787), supported a strong central government. As US senator from PA (1789–95), he was a strong Federalist and again helped to provide firm financial leadership in Congress. Longstanding accusations of improper financial activities for private gain impaired his public reputation and he was not given office in the Adams administration. He was once reputedly the richest man in the US, but speculations on western lands brought about his financial ruin and he was imprisoned for debt (1798–1801).

MORRIS, WILLIAM (1834–96), British socialist thinker, artist, craftsman, and poet. After leaving Oxford, he decided to become a painter. He believed passionately in beauty in everyday things, such as furniture, wallpapers, household goods, and printing. Like Ruskin, he felt that a society which allowed a gulf between rich and poor was unhealthy. Because only a healthy society would produce good art, he championed the working-class movement which must destroy the harmful, ugly results of capitalism. He joined the Social Democratic Federation (1883), then founded the breakaway, anarchist Socialist League (1884). He published his Utopian *News from Nowhere* (1891) and, as his emotional socialism began to wane, found increasing inspiration in the Middle Ages. His achievement and influence lay in his giving practical expression, in terms of craftsmanship and design, to many of his ideals.

MORRISON OF LAMBETH, HERBERT STANLEY MORRISON, Life Baron (1888–1965), British politician, who figured in London Labour politics and in the parliamentary party from Labour's formative years until 1959. Having served as mayor of Hackney, he was elected MP for Hackney South in 1923, but lost his seat after only one year. He returned to local politics and played an important part on the London County Council. In 1929 he was re-elected to parliament and became minister of transport. He instigated the public control of London Transport, although by the time the bill became law he was again out of parliament and back in London affairs, becoming leader of the LCC.

Within the Labour Party he influenced policy-planning. On his return to parliament in 1935 he steadily became more prominent. In the wartime coalition (1942–5) he became minister of supply, home secretary, and eventually minister of home security.

After Labour's election victory in 1945 Morrison was leader of the House of Commons and lord president of the council. In 1951 he succeeded Bevin as foreign secretary, but his attempt to succeed Attlee in the leadership of the Labour Party failed.

MORRISON, GEORGE ERNEST (1862–1920), Australian doctor, traveller, and journalist, who became correspondent of the London *Times* (1895–1912), and thereafter political adviser to the republic of China. After practising in Vic. he began (1893) a long period of travel and observation in Asia and was *The Times* Peking correspondent before and during the Boxer Rebellion, and war correspondent with the Japanese army during the Russo-Japanese war.

MORRISON, ROBERT (1782–1834), British Protestant missionary in China, who took up residence at Canton under the protection of the East India Co. in order to translate the Bible into Chinese. This he accomplished in 1824. He had less success in evangelization, however, making only 10 converts in 25 years.

MORROW, DWIGHT W. (1873–1931), US ambassador to Mexico (1927–30), who, during this period, resolved problems outstanding between the two governments about both oil and religion.

MORSE, JEDIDIAH (1761–1826), American clergyman and geographer, who was minister of the First Congregational Church, Charleston, MA (1789–1819), and opposed the spread of Unitarianism. His *Geography Made Easy* (1784), the first geography text published in the US, and its successor, *The American Geography* (1789), went through many editions.

MORSE, SAMUEL FINLEY BREESE (1791–1872), US artist and pioneer of electrical telegraphy. With extensive technical help from others he eventually constructed for the US Congress a successful telegraph line from Washington to Baltimore. His subsequent unjustified claims to have been solely responsible led to bitterness and litigation, which went against him. Nevertheless, he is remembered for the telegraphic code still in use, which was named after him.

MORSHEAD, SIR LESLIE JAMES (1889–1959), Australian soldier, who served in Gallipoli and in France during the First World War. He made his name in the Second World War by his defence of Tobruk and in the battles of El Alamein. He commanded the Allied forces in Borneo (1945).

MORTON, JAMES DOUGLAS, 4th Earl of (Scottish) (1st creation) (*c*. 1516–81), Scottish politician and regent of Scotland, who succeeded to the earldom through his marriage to Elizabeth, daughter of the third Earl of Morton. He was, at first, active in his support of the Scottish reformation, and was appointed (1563) chancellor to Mary Queen of Scots, favouring co-operation with England. He was leader of the group that murdered David Rizzio, Mary's secretary (1566). He joined the opposition to Mary on her marriage to Bothwell and was responsible for her imprisonment at Lochleven and, after her escape, her defeat at the battle of Langside (1568). He was an efficient administrator, built up the power of the central government, restored law and order, sought to restore episcopacy in the government of the Church and hoped thus to achieve a Protestant alliance with England. His growing power and sympathy with episcopacy led to opposition against him. By 1581 French influences and that of the young King James VI brought about his fall. He was tried and convicted of complicity in the murder of James's father, Darnley, and executed.

MORTON, JOHN (*c.* 1420–1500), English cardinal, who was master of the rolls and Bp of Ely. He was exiled by King Richard III, but returned to influence under King Henry VII, under whom he became Abp of Canterbury (1486) and chancellor (1487). It was probably he who supplied Thomas More with the material for his *History of Richard III*, which contributed to Richard's infamous reputation.

MOŚCICKI, IGNACY (1867–1946), Polish chemist and politician, who—with no political experience—was elected to the presidency as Pilsudski's nominee after the coup of May 1926. As president, he proved entirely compliant with Pilsudski's wishes. After the latter's death in May 1935, Mościcki emerged as a skilful politician and enjoyed some success in his attempts to frustrate Rydz-Śmigly and his supporters in their plans to introduce a more totalitarian regime. After Poland's defeat (1939), he fled to Rumania.

MOSCOW, capital and largest city of the Soviet Union, stands on the Mostva river with a population (1970) of over 7 millions. It covers an area of 87 sq. kms.

Archaeological research dates a settlement back to Neolithic times, but Moscow's first mention in Russian chronicles was in 1147. Nine years later a wooden Kremlin (citadel) was built and this became the centre of the new city. By the 13th cent. Moscow was an important trading centre and the heart of the principality of Moscow. To offset successive Tatar attacks, the Kremlin defences were extended and towards the end of the 15th cent. Moscow became the centre for a unified Russian state.

Despite periodic fires and external attacks, the commercial, ecclesiastical, and administrative importance of the city grew. However, tired of conservative opposition and *boyar* troubles, Peter the Great transferred the capital in 1712 to his new city of St Petersburg, but in the 18th cent. Moscow remained the centre of culture. In 1755, through the initiative of Lomonosov, Russia's first university was founded in Moscow.

In 1812 the city played a significant role in the war against the French. The burning of Moscow by its inhabitants deprived Napoleon's army of vital supplies and he was forced to retreat. Much rebuilding followed and Moscow became the centre of Russia's railway network. Towards the end of the 19th cent. Marxist activity and workers' movements led to much unrest in the city, and in Nov. 1917 Soviet rule was established in Moscow. In the following year the government and Central Committee of the Communist Party under Lenin moved from Petrograd to Moscow, which again became the capital of Russia.

In 1941 during the Second World War German invaders approached within 40 kms of the city but a Soviet counterattack saved the day. After the war Moscow underwent tremendous changes, with gigantic rebuilding programmes typical of the Stalinist era.

MOSCOW CONFERENCE (March–April 1947), meeting of the foreign ministers of the four powers (US, USSR, Britain, France) occupying Germany, at which Molotov sought to obtain reparations from Germany for Russia, Bidault security and coal for France, and Marshall and Bevin to stabilize Germany as a political and economic unit without accepting Molotov's plan for a strong central government. No agreement was reached, but Bevin argued that progress had been made in understanding the contentious points from all sides. Marshall, in contrast, expressed his concern over the deteriorating economic condition of Europe—which contributed to the formulation of the Marshall Plan (June 1947).

MOSCOW CONFERENCE (1957), meeting of representatives of communist parties at which Khrushchev sought to restore the unity of the communist world after the strains consequent on the 'de-Stalinization' congress (20th party congress, 1956). By the time the conference met (Nov. 1957) Khruschev had survived the leadership crisis (June) and removed from power some of those, including Malenkov and Molotov, who had opposed him. The conference ended with a declaration signed by 12 ruling communist parties. It condemned revisionism and referred to the 'invincible camp of socialist countries headed by the Soviet Union'. Tito did not attend the conference, nor did Yugoslavia sign the declaration—an indication of the limitations in the rapprochement between the two countries which had begun with Khruschev's visit to Belgrade (June 1955).

MOSCOW CONFERENCE (1960), of 81 communist parties which marked a stage in the development of the Sino-Soviet dispute. The Chinese party was represented. Nevertheless, the declaration which emerged from the conference was for the most part an expression of the Soviet point of view, with important concessions to the Chinese. It included the statement that 'war is not fatally inevitable' and that 'the democratic and peace forces today have no task more pressing than that of safeguarding humanity against a global thermonuclear disaster'. At the same time, the US was denounced as the most significant danger to peace. The differences between the Soviet and the Chinese views on the role of national liberation movements remained unresolved in the ambiguities of the declaration.

MOSCOW, RETREAT FROM (1812). During the French Wars, Napoleon I left Moscow on 18 Oct. after a month had been spent in the burnt and abandoned city. The Russians refused to negotiate and Kutusov's army prevented Napoleon from returning through undevastated lands to the south where supplies were available. Badly equipped and supplied, harried by the Russians' pursuit and by partisans, and tortured by the cold weather, the demoralized French army suffered enormous losses.

MOSCOW, THE THIRD ROME, politico-religious concept formulated by the Russian orthodox monk, Philotheus of Pakov, during the reign of Vasili III (*reg.* 1505–33). He argued that after the downfall of the first Rome, which ended with the schism of 1054, the second Rome, Byzantium, had succeeded as the citadel of the true Christian faith, only to succumb to reunion with the papacy (1439) and to the divine retribution of Turkish conquest (1453). This bequeathed to Moscow, the seat of the Russian Orthodox Church, the role of *civitas dei*, while its ruler, the tsar, was the only true ruler of all Christendom. Philotheus made this claim on the basis of the forecast of the prophets that 'Two Romes have fallen, but the third [Moscow] stands, and a fourth there will not be'.

MOSCOW, UNIVERSITY OF, or the Lomonosov State University, was founded in 1755 by its first curator, Ivan Shuvalov, a favourite of the Empress Elizabeth, with faculties of law, medicine, and philosophy. By the 19th cent. it had become an important educational centre. Today (1970) it includes a number of separate institutes of a scientific nature. There are over 30,000 students.

The People's Friendship University is also in Moscow. It was founded in 1960 for students from the developing countries. Its courses are largely scientific.

MOSHWESHWE (*c.* 1780–1870) Lesotho African leader, born into a minor chiefdom near the headwaters of the Caledon river on South Africa's high veld. He is thought to have come into contact in his youth with Mohlomi, who was attempting to create a large and more stable political unit in the region. Moshweshwe augmented his political power during the *Mfecane* (Time of Troubles), initiated by the Zulu King Shaka's revolutionary expansion. For more than a decade after 1818 the high veld was the scene of disruption and violence. Moshweshwe took refuge in mountain fortresses, first on Butha-Buthe, and from 1824 on Thaba Bosiu. His security attracted various refugee peoples, and he slowly built up the Sotho (Basuto) nation.

The Sotho, under Moshweshwe, were seldom free from the threat of invasion. During the *Mfecane* this came from the Ngwane, the Zulu, and the Ndebele. The Tlokwa also were major rivals until 1853. In the 1830s Lesotho was threatened by Griqua and other Khoikhoi peoples, and in the 1840s and 1850s by the trek Boers. Moshweshwe invited French Protestant missionaries to live in Lesotho in 1833 to attract white allies. Lesotho and the Orange Free State fought bitter wars (1858, 1865–8). The British High Commissioner intervened in the second, and proclaimed (1868) Lesotho a British Protectorate (Basutoland). Moshweshwe died two years later on Thaba Bosiu.

MOSLEY, SIR OSWALD (1896–), British politician who lost the chance of high office by becoming a fascist. He entered parliament as a Coalition Unionist MP for Harrow (1918) and was active in early attempts to form a 'Centre' party to perpetuate Lloyd George's coalition, but becoming disillusioned with the latter's policy in Ireland, and with the failure to build a 'Land fit for heroes' he moved to the left. He joined the Labour Party in 1924, and was returned as Labour MP for Smethwick in 1926.

He was an extremely able politician and an outstanding speaker, though his arrogance and ambition were disliked in inner party circles. With John Strachey and Allen Young, he produced a plan to eliminate mass unemployed and create a managed economy. As chancellor of the duchy of Lancaster in the 1929 Labour government he hoped this blueprint for a British New Deal, calling for a vast public works programme, might come to fruition, but it was rejected in May 1930, and Mosley resigned from the government. He decided that conventional politics offered him no chance of putting his views into practice and with four other MPs formed the New Party in March 1931. In the Oct. 1931 election all four lost their seats. A visit to Italy later that year confirmed Mosley's latent belief that fascism was what Britain required, and in Oct. 1932 he launched the British Union of Fascists.

At first the union's programme of economic reconstruction within an imperial framework was backed by Lord Rothermere, proprietor of the *Daily Mail*, and made rapid progress. But the provocative behaviour and violence of Mosley's followers at spectacular fascist rallies, coupled with Britain's economic recovery, Hitler's unpopularity with the British public, and Mosley's anti-Semitism, antagonized public opinion. He and his movement were discredited, and when the Second World War came he was interned under Regulation 18 B. After the war (1948) he returned to politics with his Union Movement, whose slogan was 'Europe a Nation'.

Sir Oswald Mosley, *My Life* (London, 1968).   RS

MOSQUERA, TOMÁS CIPRIANO DE (1798–1878), president of New Granada (1845–9), and then president of its offshoot, Colombia (1861–4, 1866–7). He first gained prominence as an army officer under Bolívar during the Latin American wars of independence. In national politics he became identified with the conservative landowners and the Church. Although he transferred his allegiance to the Liberal Party in 1860, his basic policies and attitudes changed little. His autocratic rule caused his overthrow in 1867.

MOSQUITO COAST, section of the Caribbean coast of Central America from Honduras to Costa Rica, the object of English smuggling and dyewood cutting in the 17th–18th cents. The smugglers contravened Spanish law and made allies of the Mosquito Indians of the region, a mixed group of Indians and Negroes. After Central American independence, the British minister to Central America, Frederick Chatfield (1829–52), continued to encourage British trade

there until a nationalistic taxation programme was introduced in 1893 by José Santos Zelaya, dictator of Nicaragua. An agreement was reached whereby Nicaragua would pay an indemnity for damages to British citizens and the same citizens would leave Nicaragua. British interest in the area was ended by treaty in 1906.

MOSSI people (approx. 2½ million), who inhabit the upper Volta basin, mostly in modern Upper Volta. They speak a language of the Gur group of the Niger–Congo family. Two kingdoms, Wagadugu and Yatenga, emerged in the 11th–12th cents. In the 14th–15th cents Yatenga, the more northerly, attempted expansion. Timbuctoo was sacked (*c.* 1330), raids made around Lake Dabo (1410) and Walata was attacked (1477). Songhay counter-attacks (1498, 1549, etc.) contained the Mossi, but neither destroyed nor converted them. From the 17th cent. Muslim traders penetrated Mossi country and some 19th-cent. rulers professed Islam. But the Sokoto and Masina *jihad*s left them untouched and their traditional political structure still (1970) survives.

MOSUL QUESTION. The Ottoman *vilayet* of Mosul, with its predominantly Kurdish population, was occupied by British forces (7 Nov. 1918) despite Ottoman protests, after the conclusion of the Mudros armistice (31 Oct. 1918). Under the Sykes–Picot agreement (1916) it had been proposed that Mosul should form part of a French sphere, but France later abandoned her claim (Dec. 1918). Under the Sèvres treaty (1920) it was contemplated that Mosul would eventually form part of an independent Kurdistan, but after that project was abandoned it was decided to incorporate it with the rest of the British mandated territory of Iraq—a decision not uninfluenced by the presence of substantial oil deposits in the area. The Turkish claim to Mosul lodged at Lausanne (1922–3) was opposed by Britain and referred to the League of Nations. A provisional frontier (the Brussels Line) was agreed and Britain took the opportunity to extend military control over the area. A League Commission of Enquiry recommended (July 1925) that Mosul should go to Iraq and that the Brussels Line should be the basis of the permanent frontier, and this was reluctantly accepted by Turkey (Anglo-Turkish-Iraqi treaty, 18 July 1926).

MO-TI (?470–390 BC), Chinese philosopher. His main teaching, as expressed in the *Mo-tzu*, was that human happiness should be spread universally without adherence to a defined social hierarchy, without incurring unnecessary extravagance, and without excessive attention to ritual. As opposed to the school of Confucius, the Mohists believed in the utilitarian value of goodness.

MOTLEY, JOHN LOTHROP (1814–77), US historian and diplomat, who was author of *The Rise of the Dutch Republic* (3 vols, 1856), *The History of the United Netherlands* (4 vols, 1860–7), and *The Life and Death of John Barneveld, Advocate of Holland* (2 vols, 1874). His historical writings reflected his love of political and religious liberty, frequently at the expense of balanced academic judgement. Motley was US minister to Austria (1861–7), but was recalled as a result of rumours that he and his staff had openly criticized President Andrew Johnson. His second mission, as minister to Britain (1869–1870), also ended in his recall, partly because of dissatisfaction with his handling of the *Alabama* dispute.

MOTOLINÍA (TORIBIO DE BENAVENTE) (d. 1568), Spanish Franciscan friar, whose *History of the Indians of New Spain* (1530), contains valuable information concerning both pre-Conquest Mexico and the conditions which prevailed during the early decades after the Spanish occupation.

MOTOORI, NORINAGA (1730–1801), Japanese scholar, whose studies of Japan's earliest records greatly advanced the 'National Learning' School (*Kokugaku*) and contributed to a revival of interest in the imperial line.

MOTOR CAR ACT (1903) in Britain, established the registration of cars, the licensing of drivers, a speed limit of 20 mph, lighting regulations, and penalties for reckless driving. On the application of local authorities the Local Government Board had power to reduce speed limits and to close roads to traffic. In 1905 a Royal Commission was appointed to enquire into the working of the 1903 act.

MOTT, LUCRETIA COFFIN (1793–1880), US Quaker, who was active in the women's rights and anti-slavery movements. She was a delegate to the World Anti-slavery Convention (1840) but, as a woman, was refused participation. In 1848 she helped organize the first women's rights convention held in the US.

MOTYA (mod. Mozia), Phoenician settlement in western Sicily, being a small island in a lagoon, it was first settled in the 8th cent. BC and increased in importance as Carthaginian power in the western Mediterranean grew. There was considerable contact between Motya and the Greeks of Sicily. It was captured and destroyed by Dionysius I of Syracuse (398) but was recaptured by Carthage in the following year. It was never rebuilt, being replaced by Lilybaeum (mod. Marsala) as the main Carthaginian base in Sicily. Significant archaeological remains survive (1970).

MOULIN, JEAN (1899–1943), French Resistance leader, who was a prefect at the time of the 1940 armistice, which he refused to accept. Instead he joined De Gaulle in London. He was sent to France in 1942 as De Gaulle's personal representative, and did much to bring together the different Resistance organizations and to rally them behind De Gaulle. He created the National Resistance Council, and was its first chairman (1943). He was betrayed to the Germans and died after being tortured. His remains have been transferred to the Pantheon in Paris.

MOULINS, ORDINANCE OF (1566) in France, programme of 86 articles of legal reforms, presented to an assembly of notables convoked at Moulins by Charles IX. This ordinance remained the basis of French law until the Revolution.

MOUND BUILDERS, term applied to builders of variously shaped earth and stone structures, used for burial, ceremonial, defence, and other purposes by native American tribes. It was first thought that mound builders were the ancient and more highly cultured ancestors of the Indians encountered by the European settlers, but there is evidence, which includes explorers' chronicles and artefacts found in the mounds, that Indians of the Mississippi valley were still using and probably constructing them in the 16th cent. A few tribes, including the Cherokee, Natchez, and Creeks, used their temple mounds up to the beginning of the 18th cent.

MOUNIER, JEAN-JOSEPH (1758–1806), French politician, who figured in the debates of the French National and Constituent Assemblies and proposed the actual wording of the Tennis Court Oath. He admired the British constitution and hoped to see France turned into a constitutional monarchy on the British model. By 1790, however, he had become alarmed at the course of the Revolution and left France, but returned under the Consulate and was made a councillor of state by Napoleon I (1805).

MOUNTAIN MEN, fur trappers and traders who roamed the Western Cordilleras of the US in search of furs, particularly beaver, between 1810 and 1840. Adopting much of the Indian way of life, men such as Jim Bridger and Kit Carson brought their furs to the annual rendezvous, usually held in a mountain valley in UT or WY, where they exchanged furs for supplies and trading goods brought out from St Louis. When the fur trade declined after 1840, the mountain men acted as scouts and guides for wagon trains moving west.

MOUNTBATTEN OF BURMA, LOUIS FRANCIS ALBERT VICTOR NICHOLAS MOUNTBATTEN, Earl (1900–), British sailor and last viceroy of India, who was the son of Admiral Prince Louis of Battenberg, first sea lord in 1914. Mountbatten entered the Royal Navy in 1913 and saw active service in the First World War, being present at Jutland in Beatty's flagship. After the war he specialized in the relatively new field of wireless communication. In 1939, at the outbreak of the Second World War, he became captain of HMS *Kelly* and in command of the Fifth Destroyer Flotilla. He was appointed (1941) to the command of the aircraft carrier HMS *Illustrious*, but was almost immediately chosen by Churchill to succeed Admiral Sir Roger Keyes as chief of combined operations, in the acting rank of vice-admiral and with a seat on the chiefs of staffs committee. In this post he played a major part in the development of equipment and techniques of amphibious warfare, both of the highly specialized commando type and in preparation for the major Allied landings in North Africa and Europe. He was (1943–6) supreme allied commander in South-East Asia, an acting admiral, and an honorary lieutenant-general and air marshal, with responsibility for the co-ordination of the extensive Allied operations against the Japanese which resulted in the containment of their aggression and their expulsion from Burma by the end of the war. In Feb. 1947 he succeeded Field Marshal Earl Wavell as viceroy of India, being entrusted by the British prime minister, Attlee, with the task of supervising the granting of independence and organizing the transfer of power. Faced with mounting disorder and communal strife, he was responsible for the decision to partition India and Pakistan; it is a measure of the esteem in which he was held as a result of his brilliant administrative handling of this difficult assignment that, at Nehru's request, he remained in India as governor-general after the granting of independence.

In 1948 he left India and resumed his career in the Royal Navy, holding appointments in the admiralty and as commander-in-chief Mediterranean before becoming first sea lord in 1955. In 1959 he became the first holder of the newly created post of chief of the defence staff, an office from which he retired in 1965.   NRB

MOUNTRATH, CHARLES COOTE, 1st Earl of (Irish) (d. 1661), English soldier who fought against the Irish rebels (1641–2), was made president of Connaught (1645), and assisted Ireton in the forcible pacification of Ireland (1649–1652). He sat in three Cromwellian parliaments and he and Broghill held Ireland for the Commonwealth. On the fall of Richard Cromwell, he recognized Charles II, invited Ormonde to return from Brussels, and secured Ireland for the royalists.

MOURA, CHRISTABEL DE (1538–1613), Portuguese adviser to Philip II of Spain, especially during his later years (1585–1598) and a member of the Alva faction, who rose to power in the secretarial committee under Mateo Vasquez de Leca (1580). He came to the Spanish court in the suite of Philip's sister, Juana, widow of John III of Portugal, and was Philip's agent for the bribing of the Portuguese nobility to support his claim to the Portuguese succession (1580). On Philip III's accession (1598) Moura was appointed viceroy of Portugal, but on his return to Madrid he lost political importance.

MOUVEMENT DE LIBÉRATION NATIONALE (MLN) in France, one of several movements which attempted to carry the spirit of the French Resistance into post-war political life. Formed by the fusion of a number of Resistance movements, the MLN represented the views of the non-communist left, and hoped for the creation of a French version of the British Labour Party. But it suffered from the rivalry of the communist-led Front national, and negotiations for a combination of the two movements failed. The MLN disappeared in 1945, but the UDSR political party was its direct heir.

MOUVEMENT DU 22 MARS (Movement of 22 March) in France, left-wing movement active in the French social disturbances of spring 1968. It originated in the faculty of letters of Nanterre (Paris), and was mainly a student body, the most prominent leader being Daniel Cohn-Bendit. The movement was linked with Trotskyist groups, but it represented a mood rather than a fixed set of beliefs, and favoured spontaneous direct action, *eg*, the occupation of buildings. It was dissolved with other extremist organizations in June 1968.

MOUVEMENT RÉPUBLICAIN POPULAIRE (MRP) in France, Christian Democrat party, founded in 1944, was at the height of its influence in its early years. There had been a small Christian Democrat party (the PDP) before the war, but the emergence of a left-wing Catholic movement with mass support was a new phenomenon, owing much to the experience of Catholics in the Resistance and to the growth of Catholic youth and trade union movements. The MRP seemed to mark a new departure in French politics by cutting across the old religious divisions.

The MRP won striking successes in the three elections of 1945–6, competing with the communists for the highest total vote. This was partly due to the reforming mood of the period and the Resistance record of the MRP's leaders, *eg*, Bidault, but there were also some adventitious factors. The disorganization of the traditional conservative forces, the MRP's anti-communism, and the idea that it was the party of 'fidelity' to De Gaulle, all helped it to attract votes. Its leaders' belief in economic and social reform enabled them to join with communists and socialists in the 'tripartite' governments (1945–7), and then to take part in virtually every government until 1954. The MRP's most distinctive contribution was perhaps in foreign affairs, for it was the most strongly pro-European of all French parties.

The year 1951 was a turning point in the MRP's fortunes. Its vote in the election fell from nearly 5 million to 2½ million, while the revival of conflict about state aid to Catholic schools drove a wedge between the MRP and the socialists. After this, the party tended to ally itself with centrists and conservatives, and seemed to lose some of its earlier idealism. It opposed the reforming government of Mendès-France, and was divided on colonial policy; a right-wing group led by Bidault eventually seceded. The MRP leader, Pierre Pflimlin, was the last regular prime minister of the Fourth Republic.

The MRP supported De Gaulle's return to power in 1958, and had ministers in his governments until 1962, when it broke with him over his European policy. The popularity of Gaullism caused a further dwindling of the MRP vote, now increasingly localized in traditionally Catholic areas. The party continued to find allies more easily among conservatives than on the left, and its leader, Jean Lecanuet, was the candidate of the centre in the 1965 presidential election. The MRP then became part of the Centre démocrate, led by Lecanuet. Although some of the hopes aroused by the creation of the MRP had not been fulfilled by 1970, it had succeeded in making progressive Catholicism a permanent and influential element in French public life.

P. Williams, *Crisis and Compromise. Politics in the Fourth Republic* (London, 1964). RDA

MOUVEMENT SOCIAL RÉVOLUTIONNAIRE (MSR) in France, political party which collaborated with the Germans under the Vichy regime. It was the organ of Eugène Deloncle, formerly leader of the Cagoule terrorist organization. The MSR joined with other collaborationist groups to form the Rassemblement National Populaire (1941).

MOVEMENT, THE, in Australia, formed in 1945, was a loose national alliance of Catholic actionists, particularly trade unionists. It was administered from Melbourne by B. A. Santamaria, with the object of fighting communism within the labour movement. In 1954–9 its activities led to major public disputes on the relationship between religion and politics, and to the disruption of the Australian Labor Party.

MOWAT, SIR OLIVER (1820–1903), Canadian politician, who entered the Canadian Legislative Assembly (1857) and became provincial secretary in the two-day Brown–Dorion government (May 1858). He was postmaster-general in the Macdonald–Dorion government (1863–4) and in E. P. Taché's Great Coalition (1864), but retired from politics to become vice-chancellor of Ont. University (1864–72). He was a delegate to the Quebec Conference (1864), where he defended the powers of the provincial governments in the new confederation, a struggle he continued successfully as prime minister of Ont. (1872–96) against the centralizing theories of J. A. Macdonald. He was appointed minister of justice in Laurier's government (1896) but resigned to be lieutenant-governor of Ont. (1897–1903).

MOYNE COMMISSION (1937–8), Royal Commission appointed to study British colonies in the West Indies. Its report (1945) favoured expansion of colonial self-government and increased British grants.

MOZAMBIQUE (784,032 sq. kms), east-central African 'overseas province' or colony of Portugal. Its population of 7 million (1970) includes several large groups, notably Nyanja, Makonde, and Ngoni, and about 1 per cent of Portuguese settlers. After 1964 African nationalists, using guerrilla methods, won control of parts of Delgado, Niassa, and Tete provinces.

MOZLEY, JAMES BOWLING (1813–78), British theologian and one of the leaders of the Oxford Movement, who made a major contribution to contemporary doctrinal issues.

MPANGAZITA (*fl.* 19th cent.), Chief of the Hlubi people, who moved from Natal to the Cape via Lesotho in the 1820s to 1830s. In the Cape the Hlubi merged with other refugee groups to form the Mfengu (Fingos).

MRIMA COAST, name given to the mainland opposite Zanzibar from the Kenya–Tanzania border to the Rufiji river. Its most important old settlements were Tongoni and Kaole (later Bagamoyo).

MROHAUNG DYNASTY, established 1433, last and most stable of the dynasties of Arakan. The dynasty was overthrown and Arakan annexed by the Burmese in 1785. Mrohaung was the capital.

MSIRI (*c.* 1830–91), a Nyamwezi who pioneered the opening of Nyamwezi (west-central Tanzania) caravans into the southeastern Congo, and gained control of important sections of the copper industry in the 1870s. Msiri established his capital at Bunkeya, near modern Jadotville, and built in that region a strongly centralized trading state by conquering or incorporating many of the small surrounding peoples. By the time of the Belgian conquest, his state of Garenganze was the major kingdom in Katanga. He was killed by members of a Belgian expedition in 1891.

MSTISLAVSKY, FEDOR, Prince (*fl.* 17th cent.), Russian *boyar* and president of the *boyars'* council until the Polish occupation of the Kremlin (1611), when he swore allegiance to Prince Vladislav. He led one of the *boyar* factions during the Time of Troubles, but declined to be a candidate for the throne, to which Michael Romanov was elected.

MU'AWIYA, IBN ABI SUFYAN (*reg.* AD 661–80), Umayyad Caliph of the house of Umayya. He was governor of Syria at the time of the murder of his kinsman, the Caliph Uthman (*reg.* 644–56). Mu'awiya, seeking to avenge the death of Uthman, came into conflict with the Caliph Ali (*reg.* 656–61), cousin of the Prophet Muhammad. The battle of Siffin (657) led to the arbitration of Adhruh (659), which in effect made Ali and Mu'awiya into candidates for the office of Caliph. Mu'awiya, in 660, accepted from his adherents a formal oath as caliph. On the death of Ali (661) Mu'awiya's claim to the caliphate was soon accepted throughout the Arab empire.

The reign of Mu'awiya saw a vigorous prosecution of the war against the Byzantines. Even before his accession to the throne, Mu'awiya, as governor of Syria, had created a strong Muslim fleet and with an efficient naval force at his command he occupied Cyprus in 649. The Arabs, in 655, defeated a Byzantine armada at the battle of the Masts (Dhat al-Sawari) off the coast of Lycia. As caliph, Mu'awiya established a line of communication running northwards through Rhodes (672) towards the Dardanelles. Muslim forces, advancing on land and by sea, attacked Constantinople in 668-9. A second and more formidable assault was made in 674-80 from an Arab base in the peninsula of Cyzicus—an assault which was at last abandoned on the death of Mu'awiya.

He had a number of able servants—eg, Amr ibn al-As, who governed Egypt, Al-Mughira ibn Shu'ba, who controlled Al-Kufa, and Ziyad ibn Abihi, who governed Al-Basra.

Mu'awiya was a shrewd statesman and an able administrator. Arab sources praise him for his tact in political affairs, a prudent mildness, and imperturbable self-control. He ruled the empire more as a tribal sheikh than as an authoritarian monarch. To the Byzantine historian Theophanes he was a *prōtosymboulos*, a first councillor. Mu'awiya exercised his power through a *shura* (council) of dignitaries, officials, and tribal chieftains, and through the Wufud, delegations which came to visit him from the provinces. One of his main achievements was to ensure that after his death his son, Yazid I (*reg.* 680-3), should succeed him as caliph, and thus he introduced the principle of an ordered and regular succession to the throne. To the Arabs of his time Mu'awiya embodied in himself qualities which made him an ideal *malik* (king).

J. Wellhausen, *The Arab Kingdom and its Fall* (Calcutta, 1927).   VJP

MU'AYYAD, AL-SHAYKH (*reg.* AD 1412-21), Mamluk Sultan of Çerkes (Circassian) origin. He was engaged (1412-1415) in reducing Syria to obedience. In 1418 the sultan undertook a campaign to restore Mamluk influence in the border zones of northern Syria, *ie*, over such important centres as Malatya and Tarsus. There was friction on the north-eastern frontier in 1420 with the Qara Qoyunlu Turcomans. His reign witnessed the definitive emergence of the Circassians as the predominant force within the Mamluk regime.

MUBARAK IBN SABAH (d. 1915), Sheikh of Kuwait (*reg.* 1896-1915), who came to power after murdering his two half-brothers, and pursued a policy of reliance on British protection to evade Ottoman influence and establish stable foundations for ultimate independence.

MUCIUS SCAEVOLA (*fl.* 6th cent. BC), legendary hero of ancient Rome, said to have been captured in 508 BC when attempting to assassinate Lars Porsenna, who was besieging Rome, and to have plunged his right hand into the furnace to demonstrate Roman intrepidity, thus earning the name Scaevola (Left-handed).

MUCKRAKERS, popular designation of a group of US reformers who exposed corruption in public life and in business and provided much of the impetus behind the progressive movement between 1900 and 1914. Their frequent resort to sensationalism led President T. Roosevelt to call them 'muckrakers' (1906), a reference taken from John Bunyan's *Pilgrim's Progress*.

MUDALIYARS, Sinhalese officials in charge of a district, used by the kings of Ceylon, the Portuguese, the Dutch, and —in the earlier years of their occupation—by the British. Later they lost their administrative functions, but retained an honorary position, which was much coveted. The chief (*maha*) mudaliyar was attached to the governor's secretariat.

MUDDIMAN COMMITTEE (1924), Reforms Enquiry Committee under the chairmanship of Sir Alexander Muddiman, Home Member of the government of India, which was appointed to report on the working of the Montagu-Chelmsford Reforms (1919) and to suggest what improvements might be made in their operation. The government conceded this enquiry only after a great deal of public pressure and the terms of reference were kept as narrow as possible. It acted as a useful sounding board for popular disillusionment with the reforms, and particularly the disillusionment of the first ministers in the provinces under dyarchy. The nine-member committee divided into a majority of five—including the chairman—which felt that it was too soon to pass judgement on the system and that, therefore, only minor adjustments were necessary—and a minority of four, including T. B. Sapru and M. A. Jinnah, which was convinced that dyarchy was completely discredited and that the urgent need was for a new commission, with wider powers, to draw up a more liberal constitution.

MUDROS ARMISTICE (30 Oct. 1918), agreement ending hostilities between the Allies and the Ottoman empire in the last weeks of the First World War.

MUELLER, SIR FERDINAND JAKOB HEINRICH VON, Baron (1825-1906), German-born Australian botanist and explorer, who was appointed (1853) government botanist in Vic. As director of the Melbourne Botanical Gardens (1857-1873), he was responsible for its remarkable collection of labelled specimens, while his explorations in Vic. and WA added considerably to botanical knowledge.

MUELLER, GERHARD FRIEDRICH (1705-83), Westphalian-born Russian historian who came to Russia as librarian at the Academy of Sciences (1725) and after taking Russian citizenship (1748) became professor and official historiographer there. He undertook the systematic collection of sources for a study of Russian history which became his life work, and from 1732 published an historical journal to collect treatises and documents as a prelude to his comprehensive survey. He travelled all over Siberia collecting material and took part in Bering's second expedition to Kamchatka (1733-43). In 1749 he was involved in a bitter conflict with Lomonosov over the Scandinavian origin of the Russian people and temporarily lost his post, though later he was reinstated and wrote his *Essay on Modern Russian History* and founded his major review (1755). He was director of the archives of the college of foreign affairs (1766-83).

MUFTI ('one who delivers a *fetwa*'), term used to denote those members of the *ulama* who, being trained in the law of Islam, acted not as judges (*qadi*), but as jurisconsults (*mufti*), giving authoritative decisions (*fetwa*) on problems of a legal character submitted to them. *Muftis*, in general, retained a private rather than an official status. Under the Mamluk sultans of Syria and Egypt, however, a *mufti* was appointed to represent formally each of the four *madhhabs* of Islam (schools of law). In the Ottoman empire, from the time of Suleiman the Magnificent (*reg.* AD 1520-66), the Mufti of Istanbul held the status of Sheikh al-Islam.

MUFTI OF JERUSALEM, Al-Haj Amin al-Husayni (1897-), former Ottoman officer, chosen as *Mufti* (1921) and president of the Supreme Muslim Council in Palestine (1922). By 1936 he was established as the leader of Palestinian Arab opposition to Zionism. For a time (1937-46), he lived outside Palestine, during which period he negotiated with Germany. He resumed his leadership of the Palestinian Arabs (1946) and was elected president of the Assembly and the Supreme Council of the All-Palestine Government (1948).

MUGHAL DYNASTY, THE, ruled India, or parts of it, from the accession of Babur (*reg.* 1526-30) to the third battle of Panipat (1761). Though called Mughal, the dynasty was really Turkish, comprising members of the Chagatay clan. Babur himself was sixth in descent from the Turkish conqueror, Taimur. He founded the empire by defeating the Lodi sultan of Delhi at Panipat (1526), and consolidated it by defeating the Rajputs (1527) and annexing Bihar before his death (1530). His son, Homayun (*reg.* 1530-56), conquered Gujarat (1534) and overran Bengal but was expelled from India after two defeats by the Afghan Sher Shah. He returned to reign for only six months (1555-6). His son Akbar (*reg.* 1556-1605) gave the empire its characteristic form, extending it from Kabul to the Bay of Bengal and south to Gujarat and the northern Deccan. After defeating the Rajputs (1566, 1567), he took them into political partnership, making his administration in some sense a national one. Rajputs were given high army commands, provincial governorships, and seats on his privy council, and they intermarried with the imperial family. The *jizya* tax on non-Muslims was repealed and Akbar developed a religious cult centred on himself. Though abandoned after his death, it added a religious reverence for the emperor's person, which lasted until the 19th cent. Akbar organized the empire into 12 provinces or *subah*s and controlled it through an imperial service of *mansabdar*s, directly dependent on the emperor. He was also, like Babur, a patron of the arts, especially painting and architecture, and virtually founded both the Mughal schools of painting and architecture with their Indo-Persian inspiration. With the help of the Hindu raja, Todar Mal, he reorganized the land revenue administration.

From Akbar the empire passed intact to his son Jahangir (*reg.* 1605-27), who maintained it, and his grandson Shah Jahan (*reg.* 1627-58), under whom it reached its zenith. Shah Jahan's son, Aurangzeb (*reg.* 1658-1707), succeeded after defeating his brothers in a war of succession. In the latter part of his reign he conquered the Muslim kingdoms of Bijapur (1686) and Golkonda (1687), but could not suppress the Marathas in western India or deal with a financial and agrarian crisis in north India. He alienated the Rajputs by interference and the Hindus by reimposing the *jizya* tax. On his death (1707) the country was beset by civil wars and revolutions until the reign of Muhammad Shah (*reg.* 1719-48). Under this weak ruler the empire began to break up. The Nizam of Hyderabad became independent (1724), the Marathas took Malwa (1738) and spread across central India, and Nadir Shah the Persian took and plundered Delhi (1739). After 1750 the invasions of Ahmad Shah the Afghan culminated in the decisive Maratha–Afghan battle of Panipat (1761) by which the empire was submerged. It now became a local kingdom which passed under the protection of the Marathas (1785), and the British (1803). The last emperor, Bahadur Shah II (*reg.* 1837-58), was exiled to Rangoon (1858), after being involved in the Mutiny of 1857.

S. M. Edwardes and H. L. O. Garrett, *Mughal Rule in India* (London, 1930).
Cambridge History of India, vol. IV, ed. Sir R. Burn (Cambridge, 1937). TGPS

MUGHULISTAN, Turko-Mongol Khanate, founded in the 14th cent. in the upper Ili area by tribesmen hostile to the Islamization which was taking place in western Turkestan. Under Tughluk-Timur (*reg.* 1348-62), the khanate exercised control over western Turkestan. Later, the area became dominated by the Dughlat family. It remained so until the 16th cent. and subsequently became incorporated in the Kalmuk empire.

MUGWUMP, term in US politics applied both to independent members of a political party and to those who temporarily desert their party of allegiance in particular campaigns. It was first used by Charles Anderson Dana (1819-97) in the *New York Sun* to describe those Republicans who deserted James G. Blaine in the presidential campaign of 1884.

MUHAJIRUN (the emigrants), name given to the Muslims who in AD 622 made the *Hijra, ie,* went out from Mecca, and, under the guidance of the Prophet Muhammad, settled in Medina.

MUHALLAB, AL-, IBN ABI SUFRA (*c.* AD 630-702), soldier who served the Umayyad caliphate. In 664-5 he carried out a raid into the region between Kabul and Multan. The great campaigns of his life saw him engaged in a conflict with the fanatical Azraki branch of the Khawarij movement in Persia. His first important success over them came in 686, at the battle of Sillabra. Not until 694, however, was Al-Muhallab able to unleash a major offensive against the Azrakis. In a series of hard-fought actions (694-6), he drove the Kharijites from Fars and Kirman. During the last years of his life he was governor of Khurasan, an office which passed on his death to his son, Yazid ibn al-Muhallab.

MUHAMMAD V, (*reg.* 1957-61), King of Morocco, who acceded to the throne as the sultan Sidi Muhammad ibn Yusuf (1927) during the French protectorate. He co-operated with the French until after the Second World War, but thereafter used his constitutional powers on behalf of independence. The French deposed him for obstruction (1953) but his restoration became a necessary condition of the agreement whereby Morocco became independent (1955). As a national leader, he was a dominant figure in politics, taking the title of king (1957) and becoming prime minister (1960).

MUHAMMAD (*c.* AD 570-632), the Prophet of Islam, was born at Mecca into the Banu Hashim, a clan of the tribe of Quraysh. His career as a prophet began when he was about 40 years old. The Meccan suras, or chapters, of the Koran set forth in impassioned language the oneness of Allah, the evils of idolatry, and the imminence of divine judgement. Muhammad's teaching alarmed the Quraysh, fearful that his message would mean the end of Meccan pre-eminence as a centre of pilgrimage and of trade. At Mecca the Prophet gained few converts to his new faith; nor was his attempt to win over the neighbouring town of Al-Ta'if more successful. An invitation came to him, however, from Yathrib (Medina), where the moderate elements, wearied of the feuds which divided the Arab tribes dominant in the town, appealed to Muhammad to act as an arbiter in their disputes. In 622 the Prophet and his adherents left Mecca and settled in Medina —an event known as the *Hijra.* At Medina the Prophet became the head of a new religion and also of a new state. The Medinese suras are concerned with dogma, ritual, prayer, pilgrimage, and the like, but deal in addition with matters of an administrative, political, and financial character. After the *Hijra,* Muhammad was involved in a conflict with Mecca which found expression in armed encounters at Badr (624), Uhud (625), and Medina (627). A truce made at Hudaybiya in 628 was but a prelude to the Medinese occupation of Mecca in 630. The last two years of the Prophet's life saw a rapid extension of Muslim influence among the great tribes of the Najd (the Ghatafan, the Tamim, etc.). Muhammad had brought into the world a new religion—Islam—purporting to be the last and most perfect revelation of Allah to mankind. He had also established a form of religio-political organization new to Arabia. The idea of blood-descent as a social bond, exemplified in membership of a given tribe, was a concept exclusive in character, birth alone determining the status of the individual. Islam was different—race, language, and cultural inheritance were irrelevant to membership within it. To be a Muslim, to belong to the Muslim state, nothing more was required than to profess allegiance to Islam. The Muslim faith was, in short, not exclusive, but universal in character. Given favourable circumstances—the

Arab conquests achieved in the two decades following the death of the Prophet—it was capable of an indefinite expansion into the stature of a world religion open to all men, Arab and non-Arab alike.

W. Montgomery Watt, *Muhammad at Mecca* (Oxford, 1953).
W. Montgomery Watt, *Muhammad at Medina* (Oxford, 1956).   VJP

MUHAMMAD ABDUH (1849–1905), Egyptian political, legal, and educational reformer and disciple of Jamal al-Din al-Afghani, who became *Mufti* of Egypt (1899). He was principally concerned with attempting a philosophical reconciliation between Islam and modern science and the reform of Muslim institutions in law, education, and government, and had a profound influence on the movement of Islamic modernism.

MUHAMMAD AL-AMIN (d. 1887), called Demba Debasi, Soninke marabout from northern Mali, who rebelled unsuccessfully against the French in a proto-nationalist movement.

MUHAMMAD ALI (1769–1849), Ruler of Egypt (*reg.* 1805–1848), who had been an Albanian soldier, and was born at Kavala in Macedonia. He was sent to Egypt (1801) as second-in-command of the Kavala contingent of the Ottoman forces which co-operated with Britain in the expulsion of the French. From the confused struggles which followed the withdrawal of British and French forces he emerged (1805) as Pasha of Cairo, securing recognition from the Porte. He crushed his Mamluk rivals in a celebrated massacre in Cairo (1 March 1811) and subsequent campaigns in Upper Egypt. His control of Egypt thus established, he began a career of expansion. His campaigns in Arabia (1811–18) resulted in the temporary destruction of Wahhabi power. He also won control of the Sudan (1820–6). In response to Ottoman requests, his forces subdued the Cretan revolt (1822–4) and played an important part in the struggle in the Morea and mainland Greece (1825–7). He later conquered Syria (1831) and held it until local revolts and European opposition forced him to withdraw (1840–1). In 1841 he was accorded recognition as hereditary Pasha of Egypt. His major achievements, however, were in domestic policy. He carried out a complete reorganization of the Egyptian governmental system, abolished hereditary tax farming, confiscated charitable endowments (waqfs), established a system of state monopolies in trade and industry, controlled agricultural production, sponsored the introduction of new crops (notably improving varieties of cotton), constructed irrigation works, and improved communications. He reorganized the Egyptian army, establishing for the first time the practice of conscripting Arabic-speaking Egyptian Muslims and introducing European weapons and tactics. He founded new schools with a western type of curricula and sent students to Europe to study. In short, he laid the foundations of a modern administrative and educational system, and revolutionized the Egyptian economy, despite the failure of his industrial schemes. He has been called 'the founder of Modern Egypt.'

H. Dodwell, *The Founder of Modern Egypt* (Cambridge, 1967).   MEY

MUHAMMAD AL-SHAIKH (d. 1504), founder of the Wattasid dynasty in Morocco (*reg.* 1465–1504). He escaped the massacre of his family by the Marinid Abd al-Haqq (1458) and went to Arzila. He captured Fez (1471) and made himself sultan (with the title sheikh), only to lose Arzila and Tangiers immediately to the Portuguese. Although he established his power in the north by substituting his followers for local leaders, he was unable to control the south or to contain the Christian threat, leaving Morocco at the time of his death on the brink of political revolution.

MUHAMMAD AL-SHAIKH (d. 1557), first Sa'dian Sultan of Morocco, who, after wars against the Wattasids, beginning

in 1545, ousted his elder brother, Ahmad, as leader of a south Moroccan movement against the Portuguese on the one hand and the Wattasids of Fez on the other (1541). After capturing the Wattasid sultan (1545) and Fez (1549), he claimed the caliphate, but was unsuccessful against the Algerian Turks, with whose aid the last Wattasid, Bu Hassun, defeated Muhammad and retook the capital (1554). Muhammad regained the city when the Turks left, in spite of an alliance between Bu Hassun and his brother Ahmad. However, he preferred Marrakesh as his capital, whence he intrigued with Spain against Algiers. He was murdered by Turks pretending to have deserted to his side.

MUHAMMAD ASKIA, ibn Abi Bakr (1443–1538), founder of the Askia dynasty of Songhay. He seized power following the death of Sunni Ali and after defeating Ali's son, Sunni Baru, at the battle of Angao (1493). Early in his reign he made the pilgrimage to Mecca (1495–7) and in Cairo was invested by the puppet Abbasid caliph, Al-Mutawakkil II, as his deputy for Muslim West Africa. On his return to Gao, he waged a *jihad* against the Mossi and sought the advice of Muslim scholars, both local and foreign. However, the Songhay system of title-holders, both civil and military, remained unchanged and administration followed largely traditional lines.

Askia Muhammad's main achievement was to consolidate the territorial expansion undertaken by Sunni Ali. He was also able to extend his authority westwards to Galem in Mali (1512) and eastwards to Agadès and Kano; but these successes were short-lived and by 1516 Kebbi had broken away and the Hausa cities withdrew their allegiance. Several expeditions were made against the Mossi, but none resulted in annexation of their territory.

During the latter years of his reign Muhammad went blind, but this fact was long concealed. Ultimately, the growing power of his palace chamberlain aroused the envy of his sons. The eldest, Musa, deposed his father (1528) and took power. The last decade of Askia Muhammad's life was spent in semi-captivity.

MUHAMMAD AT-TAHIR (d. 1903), b. Ahmed, 12th Amir al-Muminin or ruler of the Sokoto caliphate, who was faced with the threat of British and French aggression. Though part of the caliphate was occupied, the British gave him nominal recognition as overlord. In Feb. and March 1903 British troops under Kemball occupied Kano and Sokoto itself. At-Tahir fled eastward, intending to visit Mecca; joined by thousands of ordinary people, he stopped at the Mahdist centre of Bormi, the former capital of Jibril Gaini, whence British forces pursued and killed him, with hundreds of his men.

MUHAMMAD BELLO (1781–1837), son of the militant Muslim (Fulani) reformer Uthman ibn Fudi. Though only 23 at the outset of his father's *jihad* (1804) in what later became northern Nigeria, Bello played a leading role in its campaigns, particularly in the siege of Alkalawa (1808). He built a walled city at Gwandu (1807)—later headquarters of the western provinces—and founded the town of Sokoto (1809). In 1812 his father gave him control of the eastern provinces to the borders of Bornu and Adamawa, while his uncle Abdullah administered the west and south. On his father's death (1817), Bello became the first successor or caliph. The *jihad* continued during his reign, particularly against Zamfara and Gobir, and he had to deal with a serious rebellion, that of Abd al-Salam (1818). To strengthen his defences he built a series of fortresses (*ribat*) along the Sokoto and Rima rivers. His caliphate of Sokoto was one of consolidation. With the help of his vizier, Gidado dan Laima, he provided a firm administrative basis for the empire, rooted in Islamic practice.

He was the author of numerous Arabic works on sufism, government, medicine, etc., and wrote some poetry. His best-known work, *Infaq al-Maisur*, is a major source for the history of the Sokoto *jihad*.

MUHAMMAD GHURI (d. 1206), Turkish founder of the sultanate of Delhi and younger brother of the Sultan of Ghur. He was appointed governor of Ghazni (1174) and in 1186 he defeated the last Ghaznavid sultan and annexed the Punjab. After two battles (1191, 1192), he defeated and killed the Rajput raja, Prithvi Raj, at Tarain. He then left India in charge of his slave, Qutb-ud-din Aibek, who captured Delhi (1193). He assisted Aibek to defeat Jai Chand of Kanauj and allowed him to extend Muslim conquests to Gwalior, Bihar, and Bengal. On his brother's death (1203) Muhammad Ghuri succeeded to all the Ghurid dominions. He was murdered by a fanatic, whereupon Aibek became the first Sultan of Delhi and founder of the 'Slave Dynasty'.

MUHAMMAD IBN ABDULLAH HASAN (1864–1920), known by his enemies as the Mad Mullah, was an early Somali nationalist. As leader of the Salahiyya religious brotherhood in British Somaliland, he declared a holy war in 1899 against all infidels, his movement spreading rapidly through British, Ethiopian, and Italian territory. With an army of several thousand spearmen (Dervishes), he fought for over two decades against various British, Italian, and Ethiopian forces. He won to his cause a band of followers who, though badly armed, became masters of guerrilla warfare, and being more mobile than their enemies, were often victorious; a less conventional weapon was his gift for spontaneous poetry, much of which is still remembered, and which inspired his followers with exceptional valour. He was defeated only in 1920, when the British bombed his fort at Taleh.

MUHAMMAD IBN ABI AMIR (d. 1002), known as Al-Mansur bi-Allah (Victorious through the aid of Allah), was the dominant figure in Muslim Spain during the reign of the Umayyad Caliph Hisham II. Having reorganized the armed forces of the caliphate, Ibn Abi Amir used them to remarkable effect, capturing Zamora (981) and sacking Barcelona (985), Leon (988), and St Iago de Compostella (997).

MUHAMMAD IBN AL-QASIM (*fl.* 8th cent. AD), advancing in 710 through the Makran and Baluchistan, reduced to Muslim control in 711–12 the region of Sind in northern India, *ie*, the lower reaches and the delta of the Indus river. In 713 Muhammad ibn al-Qasim extended his conquests northwards into the Punjab as far as Multan. The Muslims made no further advance in India until the time of the Sultans of Ghazna (10th–11th cents).

MUHAMMAD IBN TUGHJ (d. 946), of Turkish descent, established in Syria and Egypt the regime of the Ikhshidids (AD 935–69). Having gained a firm control over the affairs of Egypt in the years after 935, he obtained from the Caliph Al-Radi in 939 the old Iranian title of Al-Ikhshid (prince). He then sought to extend his influence over Syria—an endeavour which brought him into conflict with the *amir al-umara* at Baghdad, Ibn Ra'iq, and with the Hamdanid amir of Aleppo, Sayf al-Dawla. By the time of his death he had reduced central and southern Syria to dependence on the Ikhshidid regime.

MUHAMMAD KORAU (*fl.* 15th cent.), founder of the Muslim dynasty of Katsina, in northern Nigeria, who waged war against the rising power of Nupe.

MUHAMMAD RASHID RIDA (1865–1935), Syrian writer, biographer of Muhammad Abduh, and founder of the Salafiyya movement. He settled in Cairo (1897) and published the journal *Al-Manar*, in which he advocated Muslim unity and institutional reform. In later years he advocated Arab nationalism, although always in subordination to Islamic unity.

MUHAMMAD REZA KHAN (1717–91), son of a Persian court physician, who moved to India and settled at Murshi-dabad. He married into the Nawab of Bengal's family and held office from 1756. When the Mughal emperor granted the *diwani* of Bengal to the English East India Co. (1765), Muhammad was appointed the company's deputy in revenue matters, as well as the Nawab of Bengal's deputy in judicial affairs. In trying to maintain the Mughal administrative system he clashed with the company's servants and was removed (1772) by Warren Hastings following charges against him of corruption. But the charges were not proved and he was restored as deputy to the Nawab of Bengal in criminal affairs (1775), holding this office until it was abolished by Cornwallis (1791).

MUHAMMAD REZA SHAH (1919–), 2nd Ruler of the Pahlevi dynasty in Iran (*reg.* 1941–) in succession to his father, Reza Shah, who abdicated (Sept. 1941). The Allied occupation of Iran during the Second World War limited his power and virtually destroyed the autocratic system built up by his father. As a result, from 1946, he was involved in a prolonged struggle with the rival political interests which dominated the parliament (Majlis) and eventually grouped themselves under the leadership of Muhammad Musaddiq (1880–1967). After the fall of Musaddiq (1953) and the repression of the left-wing Tudeh Party (1954), the Shah regained supreme power and established strict control over political and intellectual life. The 1954 oil agreement provided revenues which he used to promote policies of rapid economic development and political and military modernization. In 1962 an extensive land reform programme was inaugurated. This struck at the roots of the economic basis of the political power of the landlord politicians and paved the way for further social and economic development. In foreign policy the Shah, after 1954, followed a strongly pro-Western line. In 1955 he joined CENTO, but after 1962 improved relations with the USSR permitted the partial restoration of the traditional Iranian policy of neutrality.

MUHAMMAD RUMFA (d. 1499), 20th Ruler of Kano (*reg.* 1463–99). In his reign Islam became established, at least at the court. Abd al-Karim al Maghili wrote his *Mirror for Princes* for him and visited the city (*c.* 1493). At the same time, Abd al-Rahman Zagaite led a party of Wangarawa scholars to settle in Kano, and Egyptian and Timbuktu scholars also visited the city. Rumfa introduced many innovations. He built the *Gidan* Rumfa, still the palace of the emirs, twice extended the city walls, and appointed eunuchs to titled offices. Royal power and prestige were enhanced and military reforms introduced. Rumfa fought the first of a long series of Kano wars against Katsina.

MUHAMMADAN EDUCATIONAL CONFERENCE, founded by Sir Sayyid Ahmad Khan in 1886 to develop Western education among Muslims. It became a highly organized society with a network of branches throughout India. Sir Sayyid was succeeded as secretary by Mohsin-ul-mulk. There are now (1970) two branches, one at Aligarh in India, the other at Karachi in Pakistan.

MÜHLBERG, BATTLE OF (1547), on the Elbe in Saxony, in which the Protestant Elector of Saxony, John Frederick, leader of the army of the Schmalkaldic League, was defeated by the imperial forces, deprived of his title, and imprisoned. But Charles V gained no permanent advantage and issued the Augsburg Interim (1548) as an intended compromise on religious differences.

MUHLENBERG FAMILY, in America. Henry Melchior (1711–87) was a Lutheran clergyman and founder of the Lutheran Church in America. He was born in Germany and went to Philadelphia in 1742, where he founded several churches in PA. His three sons, all Lutheran clergymen, were prominent in the political and cultural life of early America. John Peter Gabriel (1746–1807) raised and led a regiment in the American War of Independence and served three terms in the US Congress. Frederick Augustus (1750–1801), also served in Congress. As first speaker of the House, his vote insured the ratification of Jay's treaty (1794). Gotthelf Henry (1753–1815) was the first president of Franklin College (1787). He was an accomplished botanist and described the flora of PA.

MU'IZZ, AL- (*reg.* AD 953–75), Fatimid Caliph. The earlier years of his reign saw the Fatimid state in Ifriqiyya engaged in hostilities against Muslim Spain (a naval raid at Almeria in 955) and against the western Maghrib (a campaign to Tahert, Sijilmasa, and Fez in 958). A major objective of the Fatimids had long been to gain control of Egypt. Their propaganda did much to undermine the Ikhshidid regime in power there. The forces of Al-Mu'izz, under the command of Jawhar al-Siqilli, occupied Egypt in 969. Attempts made thereafter to reduce Syria to Fatimid obedience met with only a limited success, mainly because of the resistance offered by the Qaramita (Carmathians). He moved to Cairo in 973, leaving the Fatimid territories in North Africa under the administration of the Berber chieftain, Bulukkin ibn Ziri.

MU'IZZ AL-DAWLA (Ahmad ibn Buwayh) (*reg.* AD 945–67), Buyid Amir, occupied Baghdad in Dec. 945, becoming thereafter *amir al-umara*. Mu'izz al-Dawla, with his brothers, Imad al-Dawla and Rukn al-Dawla, established the domination of the Buyids—Shi'i in their religious allegiance—over Persia and Iraq. Much of his reign was spent in conflict with the Hamdanid amirate of Mosul, which he reduced to dependence on the Buyid regime.

MUKDEN INCIDENT (1931), first major aggressive act of Japan in China, sometimes known as the Manchurian Incident. It stemmed from an explosion, probably planned by Japanese officers, on the Japanese South Manchuria Railway (18 Sept. 1931), which provided a pretext for the Kwantung army to take over first Mukden, the key city, and then the whole of Manchuria. The Wakatsuki cabinet attempted to check the army's action but finally recognized its failure by resigning. The Chinese government protested to the League of Nations, which sent the Lytton Commission to investigate. The commission's compromise solution was unacceptable to Japan, who withdrew from the league, thus striking the first blow towards its destruction.

MUKHERJEE, ASUTOSH (1864–1924), Bengali lawyer and educationalist, who was chief justice of the Calcutta high court (1920), a member of the senate of Calcutta University, and for a time vice-chancellor. He did much to develop the university by persuading wealthy Indians to make donations. He was a member of the Sadler Commission.

MULAVARMAN, name of one of the earliest known kings in Indonesia, who ruled in eastern Kalimantan (Borneo) in the 5th cent. AD. Though he was probably an Indonesian, his inscriptions, all in Sanskrit verse, which describe his munificence, testify to the predominance of Hindu cultural values in this part of the archipelago in an early period.

MULAY ISMA'IL (*reg.* 1672–1727), Alawid Sultan of Morocco, acceded shortly after the dynasty's establishment by Mulay Rashid. During his long reign he succeeded in dominating the entire country, defeating a tendency towards regional independence, although in fact he merely repressed the underlying tribalism. Meanwhile he recovered from European hands Larache, Arzila, and Tangiers, leaving only Ceuta and Melilla to Spain, and Mazagan to Portugal. In constructing the vast walled city of Meknes he created a symbol reminiscent of the Versailles of his contemporary, Louis XIV, to which it has been compared. His government compelled the country to support the military expenditure required to maintain Mulay's power, though it did so with increasing difficulty, and on his death the system broke down in disorder.

MULGRAVE, HENRY PHIPPS, 5th Earl of (1st of 2nd creation) (1755–1831), British soldier and politician, who was chief military adviser to the Younger Pitt (1794). He served as chancellor of the duchy of Lancaster (1804–5), foreign secretary (1805–6), and first lord of the admiralty (1807–10). He organized the Danish and Walcheren expeditions, and was master-general of the ordnance (1810–18).

MÜLLER, MAX (1823–1900), a German-born orientalist and philologist. He was a naturalized Englishman, whose life-work was the translating and editing of the *Rig Veda*. From 1875 he edited *The Sacred Books of the East*, translated by various scholars and published in 51 volumes.

MÜLLER, PAUL (1899–), Swiss chemist, who discovered (1939) that the chlorine-containing organic compound DDT was an effective insecticide. Commercial production was started in 1942 and since then DDT has been one of the most widely used insecticides for the control of insect-borne disease and for agricultural purposes. For its discovery Müller received the 1948 Nobel Prize for medicine and physiology. In recent years DDT-resistant strains of insects, and possible toxic side-effects of these insecticides to animals, including man, have emerged.

MULLER v. OREGON, 208 US 412 (1908), US Supreme Court case that established the constitutionality of an OR statute (1903) limiting the employment of women in certain industries to ten hours a day. The case is notable for the tactics of the attorney for OR, Louis Brandeis, who in defending the statute departed from traditional legal arguments and presented statistical and sociological data on the situation of women and the impact of long working hours. The court accepted Brandeis's argument and upheld the OR legislation, thereby confirming that the peculiar position of women distinguished this statute from others declared void.

MULUK AL-TAWA'IF, or 'party kings', were local dynasts of 11th-cent. Muslim Spain (Andalus), who divided that country among themselves after the fall, in 1031, of the caliphate of the Western Umayyads. Originally they were the leaders of military and aristocratic factions in Andalusian provincial centres which, thanks to the caliphate's prosperity, had grown beyond the power of central control exercised previously from Cordoba. Of these provincial centres the most important was Seville.

The many rival courts of the muluk Al-tawa'if gave rise to a more emphatic cultural diversification in Andalus, notably in prose and poetry. But the dynasts, being divided, could not meet the military challenge of Christian attack from northern Spain. After Toledo was lost to the Christians in 1085, an appeal for aid was sent to the Almoravid ruler of Morocco. The latter responded by despatching an army whose victory over Christian forces signalled the beginning of Almoravid rule in Andalus and an end to the dynasts.

MUN, THOMAS (1571–1651), London merchant, who formulated the classic statement of the national economic policy of mercantilism as a result of the economic crisis of 1622. His *England's Treasure by Foreign Trade* (*c.* 1628) expressed the need to counteract the economic activity of the Dutch merchants to ensure England's survival and prosperity. An earlier work, *A Discourse of Trade* (1621), showed genuine, if crude, scientific empiricism.

MUNCH, EDVARD (1863–1944), Norwegian painter whose work, largely expressionist, led the contribution of art to the cultural revival of Norwegian nationalism at the end of the 19th cent.

MUNCH, PETER ANDREAS (1810–63), Norwegian philologist and historian whose *History of the Norwegian People* in six volumes (1830) revived interest in the Middle Ages and the Norse language. His work represented an early contribution towards the 19th-cent. movement for complete independence from Sweden.

MÜNCHENGRATZ CONVENTION (1833), semi-secret agreement between Russia, Austria, and Prussia to concert their foreign policies. In Spain they supported Don Carlos and his party (Carlists) against Isabella and her party (Christinos), who were favoured by Britain and France. The British minister, Palmerston, believed, mistakenly, that the convention was aimed at the dismemberment of the Turkish empire, though Nicholas I had persuaded Austria of his acceptance of Turkish integrity and the status quo in the Dardanelles.

MUNDA, BATTLE OF (17 March 45 BC), near mod. Osuna, Julius Caesar's last victory over the Pompeian forces in Spain.

MUNDELLA, ANTHONY JOHN (1825–97), British politician and social reformer, who was vice-president of the Committee of Council on Education (1880–5), and introduced an act for compulsory elementary education which bore his name (1881). In 1886 and 1892–4 he served in Liberal cabinets as president of the board of trade, in which he created a labour department (1892). He was also chairman of the textile labour commission (1891–4).

MUNICH (1938), name applied to the four-power conference held in Sept. 1938 between Britain, France, Germany, and Italy in an attempt to resolve the crisis over Czechoslovakia. The situation, which had grown steadily worse since the crisis of May, seemed likely to deteriorate into war after the Nuremberg Rallies (12–15 Sept.), and in an effort to avoid this possibility the British persuaded the French to join them in inducing Czechoslovakia to transfer to Germany all territory where more than 50 per cent of the population were German-speaking (19 Sept.). With great reluctance the Czech government agreed (20 Sept.); but the following day at Godesburg Hitler declared that this proposal was no longer acceptable.

The war which Neville Chamberlain so dreaded now seemed imminent. A final attempt was made to resolve the situation peacefully. With Mussolini's assistance, Hitler was persuaded to agree to a meeting between Britain, France, Italy, and Germany which took place in Munich on 29 Sept. With precipitate haste and no prior meeting between Chamberlain and Daladier, terms far harsher than those discussed at Berchtesgaden were agreed to, whereby Germany was to annex the Sudetenland between 1 and 10 Oct.; plebiscites were to be held in disputed districts, and the four powers would guarantee the new frontiers of Czechoslovakia once territorial concessions had been made to Poland and Hungary. Under the threat of isolation, Czechoslovakia, which had been excluded from the meeting, had no alternative but to agree (30 Sept.). Chamberlain's desire for a peaceful settlement had thus been satisfied: war had been averted, and the agreement had been accompanied by an Anglo-German pact renouncing war as a means of settling their mutual disagreements. No plebiscites were held, however, and within six months German troops occupied Prague, (13 May 1939) and Czechoslovakia ceased to exist as an independent state.

The agreement was greeted with a great sense of relief by the overwhelming majority of British and French people. It was opposed, however, in the Commons by the Labour Party and a few dissident Conservatives. In the French Chamber only the Communist Party and a handful of other deputies voted against acceptance of the plan. Subsequently the name 'Munich' came to be used pejoratively to denote a cowardly concession to pressure or force.

MUNICIPAL CORPORATIONS ACT (1835), in Britain, Whig measure which dissolved 178 chaotically diverse corporations and replaced them by uniformly constituted elected bodies. Other towns were subsequently incorporated on the same terms, eg, Manchester and Birmingham in 1838. A

Royal Commission (1833–5), whose secretary was Joseph Parkes, investigated English and Welsh corporations (Scottish and Irish corporations underwent mild reform in 1833 and 1840 respectively). The earlier haphazard granting and development of corporate status discouraged generalization, but widespread abuses included co-optation; secrecy; religious intolerance; misappropriation of revenues; administrative sloth (both a cause and effect of 18th- and early 19th-cent. appointments of local ad hoc Improvement Commissioners); incompetent or corrupt officials, and confusion of executive, legislative, and judicial functions. Parliamentary electioneering caused the creation of corrupt freemen (who were often exempted from rates).

The subsequent act (not applicable to London and 67 small towns) established democratic elections, public council meetings, and an annual audit. Councillors, elected subject to a property qualification, served for three years, one-third of them retiring annually. Councillors chose aldermen, comprising one-quarter of the council, for six-year terms (a concession to the act's opponents). The council annually chose the mayor, and had to appoint a town clerk and treasurer. Corporations' functions included the administration of local revenues; police; the making of by-laws, and supervising street lighting under local private acts.

The act's 'levelling' radicalism left Benthamites like Chadwick dissatisfied. They preferred centralization and disliked retention of the old town and county division. At first the act's acceptance of the representative principle overshadowed its administrative possibilities, but municipalities gradually invoked provisions allowing them to assume extra functions, particularly in connection with sanitary matters. The requirement of treasury sanction for loans and disposal of municipal property introduced the principle of central control into an act which generally upheld local autonomy. After 1835 the Crown appointed borough magistrates in accordance with local wishes.

J. Redlich and F. W. Hirst, *History of Local Government in England* (London, 1958).
S. and B. Webb, *English Local Government from the Revolution to the Municipal Corporations Act*, vols ii and iii (London, 1908). MRB

MUNICIPIA, ancient Roman term denoting Italian communities with which Rome exchanged social rights (eg, those of intermarriage), but not political rights. Such *municipia* retained full local autonomy and the first were willing allies. Later this status was imposed by Rome on conquered peoples and came to denote an inferior and limited franchise. Many *municipia* received full Roman citizenship in the 3rd and 2nd centuries BC and all did so after the Social War, when the term came to mean any self-governing Italian town, apart from the colonies. Under the Empire citizen rights were awarded in similar fashion to romanized communities in the provinces and *municipia* spread throughout the Western empire.

MUNN v. ILLINOIS, 94 US 113 (1877), US Supreme Court case arising from an IL statute (1873) fixing rates for grain storage in city warehouses and aimed at preventing abuses of the monopoly established by elevator operators in Chicago. The operators claimed that the statute violated the due-process clause of the 14th Amendment, and Congress's power to regulate commerce. The IL Supreme Court upheld the statute, and an appeal was made to the US Supreme Court, of which a majority upheld the statute and supported a limited use of state police power when private property was devoted to a public use. Two justices dissented, asserting that any state regulatory power over property violated the due-process-of-law clause of the 14th Amendment. A majority of the court later came to accept this view.

MÜNNICH, BURKHARD CHRISTOPH, Baron (1683–1767), German-born Russian soldier, who served in the armies of France, Hesse, and Poland before coming to Russia (1721), where he rose to be commander-in-chief of all forces. He achieved power through the patronage of Peter I and was created a count (1728) under Peter II. With Biron and Ostermann he dominated the government of Tsarina Anna Ivanovna (1730–40) and during her reign was made a field-marshal and governor of St Petersburg (1732). He led the Russian forces in the Russo-Austrian war against Turkey (1735–9) and thrice invaded the Crimea, winning notable victories over the Turks at Stavuchany near the Pruth river, and at Khotin, and capturing Perekop (1736), Ochakov (1737), and Azov (1738), though the terms of the peace of Belgrade did not do justice to his successes. On Anna's death Münnich led a guards' coup which resulted in the arrest of the regent, Biron, and his exile to Siberia (Nov. 1740). Münnich was first minister in the government of the regent, Anna Leopoldovna of Brunswick-Luneberg, but resigned in March 1741, although in the palace revolt against the regent, led by Elizabeth Petrovna (25 Nov. 1741), he and Ostermann were both seized, tried, and sentenced to death. He was reprieved, however, and sent to Siberia, but was recalled to St Petersburg and restored to his honours when Peter III ascended the throne (1762).

MUÑOZ MARÍN, LUIS (1898–   ), Puerto Rican politician and the island's governor (1948–64), who organized the Puerto Rican Popular Democratic Party in 1938, claiming that a negotiated association with the US would give greater economic benefit to the island than either US statehood or complete Puerto Rican independence. For many years this opinion dominated the politics of the island. Muñoz's 'Operation Bootstrap' was a crash programme of economic development which offered inducements to US industry to establish itself in Puerto Rico. After 1968, when the statehood party won the governorship, the ideas of Muñoz and his followers came under increasing attack in Puerto Rico.

MUÑOZ RIVERA, LUIS (1857–1916), Puerto Rican politician, who opposed Spanish rule and became the leader of the Federal Party when the US took control of the island.

MUNRO, SIR THOMAS (1761–1827), British soldier and administrator in the service of the East India Co., who, after joining the company's army in 1780, served in the Second Mysore War (1780–4). After a spell as a revenue officer in the Baramahal, he rejoined the army and took part in the final Mysore War, when Tipu Sultan was killed at Seringapatam (1799). Later, he administered Kanara on the Malabar coast (1800–7). Munro was responsible for introducing the *rayatwari* system of land tenure into the Hyderabad Ceded Districts. The main principle underlying the *rayatwari* system was that of dealing directly with the *rayats* (peasants) instead of through oppressive go-betweens or farmers of revenue. After a period in England (1807–13), Munro returned to India and served in the Pindari and Maratha wars (1816–18), then became governor of Madras (1820–7).

It was his influence on the authorities in London that was chiefly responsible for the failure of the Cornwallis caste of officials to extend the Bengal *zamindari* revenue system to Madras. Munro belonged to an able group of officials, including Mountstuart Elphinstone, Charles Metcalfe, and John Malcolm, that broke away from the Cornwallis system. He favoured the increased employment of Indians in administration, and as governor of Madras he advocated that English officers and officials should learn the local languages and be acquainted with local customs and prejudices. He objected to official interference with Indian customs and religions and contended that the *rayats* must be protected from oppression, believing that the object of British rule should be to train Indians for self-government.

G. R. Gleig, *Life of Sir Thomas Munro*, 3 vols (London, 1830).
N. Mukherjee, *The Ryotwari System in Madras, 1792–1827* (Calcutta, 1962).   CCD

MÜNSTER, SEBASTIEN (1489–1552), German mathematician and scholar, who, in 1534, published a Hebrew Bible with a Latin translation.

MÜNSTER, north German town and bishopric, capital of Westphalia, and home of the notorious early Anabaptist communities (1534–5). At the end of the Thirty Years War (1646–8) it was the seat of peace negotiations between the Habsburg emperor and his allies and Louis XIV's representatives, which led to the peace of Westphalia (1648).

MÜNSTER, TREATY OF (1648), peace settlement which, with other treaties, was part of the peace of Westphalia, concluded between the Holy Roman empire and France and her allies after five years of negotiation in which the papal nuncio, Cardinal Chigi, and the Venetian statesman, Contarini, acted as mediators. The Emperor Ferdinand III formally acknowledged French sovereignty in the bishoprics of Metz, Toul, and Verdun, which had been 'protected' by France since 1559, property and sovereignty in Alsace on the left bank of the Rhine, and the citadels of Philippsburg and Breisach on the right bank.

A separate treaty signed at Münster ratified the peace between Philip IV of Spain and the United Provinces. Spain recognized the latter as a sovereign, independent state, with the right to conquer all Portuguese colonial territory to which they laid claim. The southern Netherlands remained Spanish, but Spain failed to procure the opening of the Scheldt river or official religious toleration for Catholics in the northern provinces.

MUNZER, THOMAS (1489–1525), Anabaptist reformer, born at Stohlberg, who began to preach his exaggerated ideas of Christian liberty at Zwickau (1520), where he clashed with both the civil authorities and the reformed Church. He led the radicals of southern Germany and in 1524 became involved in the Peasants' Revolt at Mühlhausen. After the rebels were routed at Frankenhausen he was captured and executed.

MUQANNA, AL- (the Veiled One) (*fl.* 8th cent. AD), head of a heretical religious movement which began at Merv in Khurasan, spread thereafter, in the form of a violent rebellion against the Abbasids, from Khurasan into Central Asia, and lasted from AD 776 to 789.

MURAD I (*c.* 1326–89), Ottoman Sultan (*reg.* AD 1362–89), whose reign was, for the Ottomans, a time of careful consolidation in Asia Minor and of rapid conquest in the Balkans. Through marriage alliance and purchase Murad I was able to acquire additional territories from the Turkish begliks of Germiyan and Hamid in Asia Minor. In the Balkans Adrianople (soon to become the capital of the Ottoman state and remain so until the conquest of Constantinople in 1453) fell to the Ottomans in 1362. A 'crusade' organized in response to an appeal from Pope Urban V and under the command of Amadeo di Savoia took Gallipoli in 1366, but the fortress passed once more under Turkish control in the following year. The resistance of the Serbian princes ruling over Macedonia was broken in 1371, when the Ottomans crushed them in a great battle fought near Çirnomen on the Marica river. The campaigns of the 1380s gave Sofia and Nish to the Ottomans. At Pločnik, however, in 1387 the Ottomans suffered a reverse which encouraged the Serbs to prepare a vigorous counter-offensive. This offensive was broken at the first battle of Kosovo (1389) in which both the Serbian prince Lazar and Sultan Murad lost their lives.

MURAD II (*c.* 1403–51), Ottoman Sultan (*reg.* AD 1421–51), whose reign began with conflict with another claimant to the throne, Dözme (False) Mustafa, said to be a son of Bayezid I, and also with the begs of the other Turkish principalities in western Asia Minor, notably Junayd, the beg of Smyrna. This conflict was resolved in 1425 in favour of the Ottomans.

Thessalonica, which the Byzantines had handed over to Venice in 1427, fell to Murad II in 1430. The second half of the reign witnessed the last great effort of Christendom to organize a 'crusade' which might throw the Ottomans out of the Balkan lands. Hungarian forces, under the command of John Hunyadi, defeated the Ottomans at Yalowaz, between Sofia and Plovdiv, in 1443, but then had to retreat in the face of determined resistance from the Muslims. Murad II now attempted to end the war (peace of Szegendin, 1444). The Hungarians soon repudiated this agreement, however, and began a new offensive. It ended in disaster, the 'crusade' being routed at the battle of Varna (Nov. 1444). Hunyadi's attempt in 1448 to avenge this defeat came to grief at the second battle of Kosovo. The reign was also notable for the fact that, although the corps of Janissaries had been instituted at an earlier date, and also the child tribute known as the devshirme, it was not until now that these institutions, under the careful reorganization of the sultan and his ministers, received their characteristic form.

MURAD III (1546–95), Ottoman Sultan (*reg.* AD 1574–95), whose reign coincided with the great Ottoman–Persian conflict of 1578–90. The Ottomans, hoping to resolve the tensions prevailing on their unstable frontier with the Safawids in eastern Asia Minor, set themselves a difficult objective—to achieve a permanent conquest of Azerbayjan and the adjacent lands of the Caucasus. After a series of expensive and hard-fought campaigns the Ottomans secured from Shah Abbas I (then preoccupied with internal difficulties) the cession of Azerbayjan, Shirvan, Daghistan, Georgia, Hamadhan, and Luristan in the peace settlement of 1590. In 1593 the Ottomans entered into an arduous war against Austria, which was to continue after the death of Murad III and ended in 1606.

MURAD IV (*c.* 1611–40), Ottoman Sultan (*reg.* 1623–40), whose reign began in intrigue and violence, with feuds and shifting alignments among those around the throne. In 1632 he took power into his own hands and resolved to crush all dissidence within the empire. His aim was to restore good order and efficient rule, and to revive the old traditions of the Ottoman state. He was an able soldier, his chief success being the reconquest of Baghdad from the Safawids (1638). He ended the long conflict between the Ottoman empire and Safawid Persia (1639), establishing between the two states a frontier which suffered little modification during the next 200 years and which still (1970) survives in large measure as the borderline separating Iraq and Persia.

MURAD V (1840–1904), Ottoman Sultan (*reg.* May–Aug. 1876), spent years in confinement under Sultan Abd al-'Aziz. After his accession to the throne, it soon became clear that he was unfit to rule, and he was deposed, in favour of Abd al-Hamid II.

MURASAKI, SHIKIBU (978–?1016), Japanese court lady and woman of letters whose novel, *The Tale of Genji* (*Genji Monogatari*), was the most distinguished of the various prose writings in Japanese by court ladies in the 10th and 11th cents and is generally regarded as Japan's most outstanding literary work.

MURAVEV-AMURSKY, NIKOLAI NIKOLAYEVICH, Count (1809–81), Russian administrator and governor-general of Eastern Siberia (1847). He was a liberal in outlook and supported Emancipation. He initiated imperialist expansion in the Far East and the explorations of Capt. Nevelskoy, which established Russia at the mouth of the Amur river. He negotiated the treaty of Aigun with China (1858) and founded Vladivostok (1860). Nicholas I allowed him wide powers independently of the Russian foreign office.

MURDOCH, PETER (1670–1761), Scottish businessman closely associated with the trading enterprise to the isthmus of Darien (1699) and with the expansion of Scottish trade to the Americas after the Union of England and Scotland (1707). As provost of Glasgow (1730) he was responsible for considerable municipal developments in the city.

MURDOCH, PETER (1795–1871), Scottish soldier and colonial pioneer, who fought at Waterloo and went out to NSW (1821) as superintendent of an agricultural station. He became (1826) land commissioner in Van Diemen's Land (Tasmania), providing important information for the British government upon the problems of convicts and of land-settlement. His son, George Brown Murdoch (1836–1906), built railways in Russia, India, and Australia.

MURDOCH, WILLIAM (1754–1839), Scottish inventor who worked for the Birmingham firm of Boulton and Watt, in which he eventually became a partner. While working as a mining superintendent in Cornwall he pioneered the locomotive steam engine half a century before the work of the Stephensons. He was the first man to produce light from coalgas (1792) and was acknowledged as the inventor of gaslighting by the Royal Society in 1808. Throughout his life he was constantly inventing, and the achievement of precision in the manufacture of machine-tools owed much to his work.

MURET, BATTLE OF (1213), most decisive engagement of the Albigensian crusade. Raymond VI, Count of Toulouse, had been excommunicated and deprived of his lands for refusing to repress the Albigensian heretics in his lands. His overlord, King Peter II of Aragon, intervened on his behalf. Peter was completely orthodox in religion, but he could not tolerate the crushing of his southern French vassals by a crusading army of northern French nobles, instigated by King Philip Augustus of France. The crusading leader, Simon de Montfort (d. 1218), surprised Peter's camp at Muret in an attack at dawn and killed Peter, thus ending the last chance of successful resistance to the crusaders.

MURFREESBORO, BATTLE OF (1862–3), near Nashville, TN, fought in the American Civil War. On 31 Dec. 1862 Rosecrans's 41,000 Union troops engaged 34,000 Confederates under Braxton Bragg. Both sides suffered heavy casualties in the four-day battle, and although neither gained a clear victory, Bragg subsequently conceded control of central TN.

MURIDISM, Muslim mystical (Naqshbandi) movement originating in Shirvan in the 18th cent. and brought to Daghestan, where, under the preaching of the first imam, Qazi Muhammad (d. 1832), it took the form of an anti-Russian *jihad*. After the murder of the second imam (Hamzad Beg, 1789–1834) the movement reached its peak under the third imam, Shamyl (*c.* 1796–1871) and manifested strong egalitarian tendencies. The movement lost its political importance after the surrender of Shamyl (1859), although his second son, Qazi Muhammad (1833–1902), became fourth imam.

MURIDIYYA, Muslim brotherhood, offshoot of the Qadiriyya, founded in Senegal by Ahmad Bamba (d. 1927). It had in 1970 nearly half a million adherents, mostly among the Wolof. At their head was the 'Grand Sérigne' Falilou Mbacké, son of the founder, whose headquarters were at Touba, where Ahmad Bamba is buried. The movement, which has been responsible for the conversion of many Senegalese to Islam, is dogmatically orthodox; but it has its own litanies and ceremonies and members swear absolute obedience to the Grand Sérigne. Economically, it has played an important role in ground-nut production, its members being encouraged to settle in farming communities and the virtues of agriculture being emphasized. Politically, the Murids form a solid bloc, since the masses must follow their chief's lead.

MURPHY, FRANK (1890–1949), US lawyer and politician, who served as chief assistant US attorney for the eastern district of MI (1919–20), judge of the recorder's court in Detroit (1923–30), mayor of Detroit (1930–3), and governor-general of the Philippines. He later became governor of MI (1936–8). He was a political associate of President F. D. Roosevelt, was appointed US attorney-general (1939), and then associate justice of the US Supreme Court (1940–9).

MURPHY RIOTS (1867–8), in Britain, fomented by the anti-Catholic lecturer, William Murphy, notably at Birmingham in June 1867 and at Manchester in Sept. 1868. The riots were politically significant because at this time Gladstone was committing the Liberal Party to the disestablishment of the Protestant Church in Ireland. Mid-Victorian anti-Catholic prejudice was strong enough to support several such lecturers, among whom Alessandro Gavazzi was the most famous.

MURRAY, GEORGE, Lord (*c.* 1694–1760), Scottish soldier, who fought in both Jacobite rebellions (1715, 1745). In 1745, as Prince Charles's general, he defeated the English at Prestonpans (1745). He was unsympathetic towards the plan to invade England and his reluctance led him to persuade Charles to retreat after they had reached Derby. He was responsible for the last Jacobite victory, at Falkirk, in Jan. 1746 and participated in the defeat by English forces at Culloden (April 1746). He spent the rest of his life on the continent.

MURRAY, JAMES (1722–94), British military commander at the battle of Quebec (1759) who defended the city against the Duc de Léves (1760) and became the first civil governor of Que. (1764–8). His policy towards the French Canadians was conciliatory.

MURRAY, PHILIP (1886–1952), Scots-born US labour leader, who worked in the PA coal fields. He was a member of the United Mine Workers' executive board (1912), and a vice-president (1920). He played an important part in the formation of the Committee for Industrial Organization (1935) and was chairman of the Steel Workers' Organizing Committee (1936). Murray succeeded John L. Lewis as president of the CIO (1940–52), and when the United Steelworkers of America was formed (1942), he became its first president.

MURRAY, SIR THOMAS (*c.* 1630–84), Scottish lawyer, who produced (1681) an edition of the complete statutes of Scotland still cited as an authority in the 20th cent. He became a senator of the college of justice in Scotland and, as such, styled himself Lord Glendoick, though this designation did not confer the status of a peerage.

MURSA, BATTLE OF (AD 351), in Pannonia (near mod. Osijek, Yugoslavia), Constantius II's defeat of the pretender Magnentius. For a time the enormous casualties seriously weakened Roman military strength.

MURSILIS I, Hittite King (*reg. c.* 1620–1590 BC) during the early period of expansion. He invaded northern Syria, destroying Aleppo when that city rebelled, and conquered Babylon, ending its First Dynasty. He was assassinated and, in the subsequent anarchy, his conquests were lost.

MURSILIS II, Hittite King (*reg. c.* 1345–1315 BC), who firmly established the empire by quelling rebellions in western Asia Minor, Syria, and eastern Anatolia, and by many campaigns against the tribes on the northern frontier.

MURTINHO TARIFF (1900) in Brazil, after the finance minister, Joaquim Murtinho, by whom it was introduced. Although it was hailed as a free trade measure, and was designed to increase federal government revenues, it raised duties on imports, thereby providing protection for Brazil's infant manufacturing industries.

MURZUQ, capital of the Fezzan from the 16th to the early 20th cent., founded by the Awlad Muhammad dynasty. It became an important caravan and pilgrim centre and on a number of occasions, it was sacked by the Turks. It was the seat of a British vice-consulate (1843–61).

MUSA ÇELEBI (d. 1413), son of the Ottoman Sultan Bayezid I (d. 1403). He was sent to the Balkans to oppose Suleiman Çelebi, the eldest son of the dead Bayezid. Having crushed Süleyman (1411) and made himself the master of the Balkan lands under Ottoman rule, he abandoned his allegiance to Mehemmed I, his brother. In 1413 Mehemmed crossed over to the Balkans, defeated Çelebi, and slew him.

MUSADDIQ, MUHAMMAD (1880–1967), Iranian politician, who emerged (1950) as the leader of a nationalist and democratic movement within parliament in opposition to the shah and British oil interests. In March 1951 he forcibly nationalized the oil industry and soon afterwards became prime minister. Economic difficulties and political disorders weakened his support in the Majlis and he came to rely upon government by decree and the support of the extremist religious parties and the left-wing Tudeh Party outside parliament. A clash with the shah eventually led to his downfall (1953) and imprisonment until 1956.

MUSAFIRIDS, dynasty of Daylamite origin, prominent in the 10th and 11th cents. There were two branches of them, one located at Tarom and the other dominant over much of Azerbayjan and Armenia, especially during the reign of Marzuban ibn Muhammad (*reg.* AD 941–57).

MUSAWWARAT ES SUFRA, Meroitic religious centre, consisting of a large enclosure and temples, founded about 500 BC. It was used throughout the Meroitic period.

MUSCOVY COMPANY, joint-stock commercial enterprise founded by a royal charter granted by Mary I and Philip to Sebastian Cabot and a group of London merchants (1555). The company was formed as a result of Richard Chancellor's contacts with the Muscovite court of Ivan IV (1554), which promised a lucrative trade in woollen cloth with Archangel, on the White Sea, in return for furs and naval stores. The hope of finding a north-east passage to China provided the enterprise a further stimulus. Despite Chancellor's death (1557), a useful trade was established, but his more ambitious successor, Anthony Jenkinson, had hopes that the company might gain a monopoly of trade with the Far East, carried overland via Persia and the Volga. This route was followed for over a decade, until its use was stopped by the Turks in 1580. The company then sought the north-east sea passage to China, and a fleet was sent under the command of Arthur Pett and Charles Jackman, assisted by William Borough and John Dee, but it was stopped by ice. By the late 17th cent. the Muscovy Co. was moribund, Archangel having been eclipsed by Riga. The founding of St Petersburg and the Russian government's restrictions on Archangel's trade further undermined the company's trade in the 18th cent.

MUSHKI, military aristocracy, famous as horse breeders, who formed a powerful kingdom (Greek, Phrygia) of Asia Minor (*c.* 1200–700 BC). They were centred in Cappadocia and controlled the trade routes to western Asia Minor. They were in frequent conflict with Assyria. The kingdom was destroyed by Cimmerian invasions.

MUSKET, term covering all smooth-bore infantry small arms before the adoption of rifles in the 19th cent. It was a clumsy and inaccurate weapon, originally developed from the arquebus of the late 16th cent. used in the Spanish army.

Improvements during the Thirty Years War reduced its weight, and in the late 17th cent. the flintlock replaced the matchlock.

MUSKHOGEAN INDIANS, important linguistic family of American Indians, which includes Creeks, Choctaw, Chickasaw, and Seminole. Spanish explorers in the 16th cent. found them occupying a large area of the south-east. Advancing white settlements pushed the tribes westward, and they finally lost their lands in the Creek War (1813–14) and the Seminole War (1834). By 1840 the Muskhogean tribes had been removed to Indian Territory.

MUSKIE, EDMUND SIXTUS (1914–   ), US lawyer and politician who served in the ME house of representatives (1947, 1949, 1951), was the first Democratic governor of ME (1955–9), and the first popularly elected Democratic US senator from ME (1959–   ). He was vice-presidential candidate of the Democratic Party in 1968, in which his stature was enhanced by an impressive, although unsuccessful, campaign. This, together with his easy re-election to the Senate in 1970, confirmed his standing as a possible Democratic presidential nominee in 1972.

MUSLIM BROTHERHOOD, religio-political organization founded in Egypt (1928) by Hasan al-Banna (1906–49) to oppose the spread of Western ideas and practices and to demand the restoration of rigid Islamic forms in private and public life. It was at first concerned primarily with social reform, but became more political and after 1934 expanded rapidly. After the Arab defeat in Palestine in 1948, members of the brotherhood, which had strongly supported the Palestinian Arabs' cause, adopted terrorist tactics against the Egyptian government. The prime minister, Nuqrashi Pasha, was murdered (Dec. 1948), for banning the society and soon afterwards, probably at the instigation of the court, Hasan al-Banna, the leader or Supreme Guide of the brotherhood, was murdered. His successor Hasan Isma'il al-Hudaybi, never commanded the same authority, and though the brotherhood continued to attract a very large following, and played a significant role in the anti-British activities of 1951–1952, it was hampered by factional disputes. After the Egyptian revolt (July 1952) the society emerged as the main rival of the Free Officers, who took the opportunity of an unsuccessful attempt on the life of President Nasser (Dec. 1954) to suppress the brotherhood. At its height in 1948 the brotherhood claimed 1,000,000 supporters in Egypt and branches in other Arab countries.

MUSSATO, ALBERTINO (1261–1329), Paduan lawyer who was one of the earliest Italian precursors of the Renaissance humanist movement. He was the first Italian humanist to imitate the plays of Seneca. His enthusiasm for recovering the legacy of the Roman civilization went hand in hand with passionate republicanism. He was one of the leaders of the vain resistance to Can Grande della Scala, the despot of Verona, who conquered Padua in 1328.

MUSSO (1897–1948), Indonesian communist politician, who worked for the Comintern in Moscow following the failure of the Indonesian communist uprising (1926–7). He returned in Aug. 1948, when relations between right and left in the revolutionary Indonesian republic were tense. His efforts to reorganize the Communist Party for an uncompromising national liberation struggle brought about a confrontation with the right-wing Hatta government. A series of local clashes between armed adherents of the two sides culminated in the 'Madiun Affair' (Sept. 1948), when the communist leadership under Musso declared its support for the military insurgents. The communists were quickly defeated and their chief leaders, including Musso, were killed.

MUSSOLINI, BENITO (1883–1945), Italian politician, founder of the Fascist movement, and dictator of Italy. His revolutionary ideas were based on those of Marx, Sorel, and Pareto. He turned to journalism and founded (1911) *Lotte di Classe.* In the same year he was imprisoned for attempting to frustrate preparations for war in Libya. His powers as an orator were first recognized at a Socialist Party congress at Reggio Emilia in 1912, and he was made editor of the socialist paper, *Avanti!*

In the First World War he rejected the party's policy of neutrality and advocated war against Germany as a prelude to social revolution. He was expelled from the party and from his editorial post and started a daily paper of his own, *Popolo d'Italia* (1915). He also joined the army and served at the front and was wounded.

After the war, he returned to journalism and in order to promote his nationalistic and syndicalist ambitions founded the Fascist movement in Milan (March 1919). Under pressure from various quarters he adjusted the movement's policies, making it into an anti-communist and more conservative, middle-class organization. He raised money for D'Annunzio's ill-advised adventure in Fiume (1919–20), but in 1921, having severed his tenuous connection with the extreme socialists, deserted him for Giolitti in order to secure parliamentary seats for the fascists. His growing image as a national demagogue, and the fascists' spectacular 'March on Rome' (23–28 Oct. 1922) forced King Victor Emmanuel to appoint him as the head of a coalition government. But he was indecisive about the fascists' programme, as well as over the crisis following Matteotti's murder (1924), and did not assume dictatorial powers until Jan. 1925. He then intensified attacks on the opposition, curtailed civil liberties, and created a one-party regime which ruled by decree and with the aid of the OVRA (secret police).

As 'Head of Government' (1926), it was Mussolini, not the king, who exacted the obedience of ministers and state officials, except in the army. In the 1930s, although the king and the pope were alternative focuses of loyalty, a well-organized personality cult emphasized 'Il Duce's' infallibility. Even after the regime became discredited Mussolini remained personally popular. Although he was a dynamic and sometimes affable showman, in private he was indecisive and tended increasingly to avoid council discussions, as well as criticism.

His definition of fascism, written with G. Gentile for *Enciclopaedia Italiana* (1932), emphasized the virtues of 'action' rather than the need for a new social order, and lacking a definite programme, he put personal power before socialist ideals. His domestic policies remained muddled. Corporate-state theories which left Italian society virtually unchanged, he regarded rather as propaganda than as practical social-economic solutions to Italy's problems. He personally helped to achieve the Lateran Agreements with the papacy (1932), and his foreign policy was influential, *eg,* the Yugoslav treaty (1924); resistance to German threats to Austria and support for the Heimwehr and Dollfuss; the Abyssinian conquest (1935–6); and sympathy with the Spanish nationalists.

Italy's change to a pro-Nazi policy led to the Axis pact. Mussolini became mesmerized by Hitler's successes, but lacked his genius and when Italy entered the Second World War she was ill-prepared for it. Before this, Albania was attacked (April 1939), then in June 1940 France left to Hitler's mercy. Finally, the king was replaced as commander-in-chief by Mussolini himself, and in Oct. 1940 Greece was assaulted. However, there was little public enthusiasm for this, and still less for Hitler's war on Russia. Mussolini failed, however, to dissociate himself from this and support for him continued to diminish. Ultimately, some members of the Grand Council voted against him, persuaded the king to dismiss him, and he was arrested (26 July 1943). But in a daring Nazi raid he was rescued (12 Sept.) and established as the head of a puppet regime, Reppublica Sociale Italiano (or Salò Republic), in German-dominated northern Italy. He made a few unimportant socialist gestures and executed some captive members of the Grand Council, including his son-in-law, Count Ciano (Jan. 1944). Faced with the Germans' withdrawal from Italy, he attempted to negotiate with Italian partisans, but was captured and shot by them (28 April 1945).

Elizabeth Wiskemann, *Fascism in Italy: its Development and influence* (London and New York, 1969).
Laura Fermi, *Mussolini* (Chicago and London, 1961). CFB

MUSTAFA II (1664–1703), 22nd Ottoman Sultan (*reg.* 1695–1703) and son of Mehemmed IV, who succeeded his uncle, Ahmed II. His reign saw the end of the long wars with Europe by the peaces of Carlowitz (1699) and Constantinople (1700).

MUSTAFA III (1717–73), 26th Ottoman Sultan (*reg.* 1757–73) and son of Ahmed III, who succeeded Othman III. During his reign there occurred the disastrous war with Russia which ended with the treaty of Küchük-Kainardji (1774).

MUSTAFA BARZANI (*fl.* 20th cent.), younger brother of Sheikh Ahmad of the historically rebellious Barzan tribe of Iraqi Kurdistan. In 1943 he established himself as the leader of Kurdish opposition to the Iraqi government. After the fall (1946) of the Kurdish republic of Mahabad, with which he had been associated, he fled to the USSR, returning to Iraq after the 1958 revolution to become leader of the Democratic Party of Kurdistan. He again clashed with the Iraqi government and became the principal leader of the long Kurdish revolt which began in 1961.

MUSTAFA KAMIL (1874–1908), Egyptian lawyer, journalist, and editor of *Al-Liwa* who demanded immediate British evacuation of Egypt and organized the Nationalist Party (1907). He was the first popular nationalist and became the inspiration of others.

MUSTAFA KEMAL ATATÜRK (1881–1938), Turkish soldier, politician, and founder of the Turkish republic. He served in Syria, Macedonia, Libya, and the Balkan Wars, and in the First World War commanded the Ottoman forces which repelled the Allied attack on Gallipoli (1915). In 1918 he led the VIIth Army in Syria against Allenby, emerging as the most successful Ottoman general of the war. In May 1919 he was appointed inspector-general of the IXth Army at Samsun in Anatolia and began to organize the Turkish national resistance to Allied attempts to dismember what remained of the Ottoman empire. Despite great difficulties, including his repudiation by the official Ottoman government, he eventually won international recognition of Turkey's independence at Lausanne (July 1923) and in the following Oct. was elected first president of the newly established Turkish republic. He carried through (1923–38) an extensive policy of reform from above, usually known as Kemalism, laying the foundations of a secular, western-oriented, modern, national state. He was ruthless, dictatorial, and gradually removed all his former associates, with the exception of his eventual successor, Ismet Inönü.

MUSTAFA PASHA (d. 1580), Ottoman soldier of Bosnian origin who rose to prominence under the Grand Vizier Ali Pasha (*reg.* AD 1553–5). In 1556 he became tutor to the future sultan, Selim II (*reg.* 1566–74), who raised him (1569) to the rank of vizier. He carried out the conquest of Cyprus in 1570–1 and was chosen, in 1578, to be ser'asker (commander-in-chief) of the Ottoman forces against Safawid Persia. After routing the Safawids at the battle of Çildir in 1578, he thrust eastward and occupied Tiflis in Georgia.

MUSTAFA PASHA, BAYRAKDAR (*c.* 1750–1808), Ottoman Grand Vizier (*reg.* July–Nov. 1808), who was an influential a'yan (notable) in Rumili and supported the reforms of Sultan Selim III (*reg.* 1789–1807). In 1808 he marched on Istanbul, deposed Mustafa IV, whom the reactionaries had made sultan in the preceding year, and set Mahmud II

(*reg.* 1808–39) on the throne. As grand vizier he called together at Istanbul a meeting of high dignitaries, officials, and a'yan from Rumili and Anadolu and secured their assent to a far-reaching scheme of reform. He was killed in a Janissary revolt.

MUTANABBI, AL- (AD 915–65), Arab poet, who found favour with the Hamdanid Amir of Aleppo, Sayf al-Dawla; with Kafur, the dominant figure behind the Ikhshidid regime in Egypt after AD 946; and with the Buyid Amir Adud al-Dawla in Persia. His ornate and figurative style made him one of the most popular and admired of all authors in the Arab world.

MU'TASIM, AL- (*reg.* AD 833–42), Abbasid Caliph, son of Harun al-Rashid. In 836 Al-Mu'tasim moved the seat of government from Baghdad to Samarra, where it was to remain until AD 892. His reign saw the end of the long rebellion (AD 816–37) of Babak in Azerbayjan, Armenia, and Persia. It witnessed also a great campaign into Asia Minor, which resulted in the capture of the Byzantine fortress of Amorion (Ammuriya). Al-Mu'tasim was responsible for a large recruitment of Turkish slave soldiers into the service of the Abbasid caliphate.

MUTAWAKKIL, AL- (*reg.* AD 847–61), Abbasid Caliph who turned against the doctrines of the Mu'tazila, which had enjoyed official support since the reign of Al-Ma'mun (*reg.* 813–33), and restored to favour the orthodox dogmas of Islam. He also opposed the adherents of the Shi'a and at the same time enforced on the Christians and the Jews the disabilities inherent in their position as non-Muslim subjects of the caliphate. His reign witnessed also a marked increase in the power and influence of the Turkish troops surrounding the throne. Al-Mutawakkil was killed as the result of a palace intrigue.

MU'TAZILA, religious and philosophical movement, rationalistic in spirit, which originated under Wasil ibn Ata (d. AD 748), who taught at Al-Basra. The Mu'tazila, developing as a school of speculative dogmatics, accepted the doctrine of free will. One of its beliefs was to attain a particular importance, above all in the reign of the Caliph Al-Ma'mun (*reg.* 813–33)—the idea of the creation of the Koran, as opposed to the orthodox view that the Koran was co-eternal with God and therefore uncreated. Al-Ma'mun raised this view to the status of an official dogma and established a mihna (inquisition) to act against all recalcitrant qadis and teachers of religion (chief among them was the uncompromising adherent of the orthodox creed, Ahmad ibn Hanbal). The mihna came to an end during the reign of the Caliph Al-Mutawakkil (*reg.* 847–61).

MUTESA I (d. 1884), King (*kabaka*) of Buganda during the period of initial contact between Africans and Europeans during the 19th cent., who welcomed Christian missionaries to his court. The first to arrive were from the Church Missionary Society of London in 1877; they were followed two years later by White Fathers from Algiers. Previously Mutesa had encouraged a syncretistic form of Islam, but when Muslim palace pages seemed to be developing a competing politico-religious loyalty, he had many of them put to death. Their Arab teachers he encouraged to stay, probably so as to enable him to benefit from a growing Ganda–Zanzibari trade in slaves, ivory, and firearms. He was the last independent ruler of Buganda.

MUTESA II (d. 1969), King of the Buganda kingdom in Uganda, who became a principal symbol of anti-colonial protest during the 1950s, following his deportation to London by the British protectorate government under Sir Andrew Cohen. When Uganda acquired political independence in 1962, Mutesa remained King of Buganda as well as becoming governor-general until he was removed for political reasons by the new republican government under its first president, Dr Milton Obote.

MUTINY ACT (1689) in England, legislative measure, subsequently passed annually by parliament, to fix the size of the military establishment and authorize the maintenance of military discipline by courts-martial. The act was originally both a measure to limit the power of the monarch over the army and to ensure the frequent meeting of parliament, both needs being regarded as essential after the English Civil Wars and the reign of James II.

MUTINY ACTS (1766, 1784, 1807), in Britain. The 1766 act, authorizing military commanders to requisition supplies from the American colonists, angered MA and NY, whose Assembly refused to comply unless these demands were made under the royal prerogative rather than by statute. The passage of the 1784 Act indicated the Younger Pitt's triumph in the House of Commons over Fox, whose threat to bring down the government by withholding essential supplies thus evaporated. The 1807 bill, proposing that English and Scottish Catholics be allowed to hold army commissions, including staff appointments, aroused strenuous resistance from King George III, causing the Ministry of all the Talents to break up.

MUTINY, FRENCH ARMY (1917), during the First World War, had a variety of causes: frustration; disillusionment with the length of the war and conditions on the Western Front, especially after the failure of Nivelle's much-vaunted offensive on the Aisne in April; the influence of the Russian Revolution and the presence of disaffected Russian brigades on the Western Front; badly organized rest and leave facilities; and a collapse of morale among the French people which led to defeatism being openly voiced behind the lines and the subjecting of troops on leave to anti-war propaganda. The mutiny began on 29 April in Champagne, and in the course of the next six weeks spread to 54 divisions. Nivelle was relieved of his command and replaced by Pétain, already popular as the defender of Verdun who regained the army's confidence. Improvements were made in leave arrangements and in conditions in the trenches and rest areas, and the mutineers were firmly but moderately treated—432 death sentences were passed, but only 55 were carried out. Throughout the mutiny the German high command knew nothing of what was happening and failed to attack at a time which would have been disastrous for the French; the British army under Haig embarked on the third battle of Ypres to divert German attention while the French army recovered and waited for the Americans. By the end of 1917 Pétain had successfully restored the confidence of the French army, and Clemenceau, newly appointed as prime minister, was setting about a parallel reconstruction of morale in France as a whole.   NRB

MUTINY OF THE *BOUNTY*, THE (1789), near the Friendly Islands, touches Australasian history at two points. The captain of the *Bounty*, William Bligh, whose crew mutinied against him, was to be the fourth governor of NSW and some of the mutineers eventually settled on Pitcairn Island. In 1856, their descendants by native women from Tahiti and elsewhere, some 87 adults and 107 children, were removed to Norfolk Island, replacing convicts withdrawn from that island in the same year.

MUTIS, JOSÉ CELESTINO (1732–1808), Colombian scientist, whose botanical project, the *Expedición botánica* (1783), though potentially of considerable importance, was never completed. It was to make a systematic collection of specimens and drawings of all the South American flora north of the Equator.

MUTOTA (*fl.* 15th cent.), first Ruler of the Mwenemutapa empire, who may have belonged to a Karanga (Shona) group

whose expansion was possibly inspired by commercial pressures.

MUTSU, MUNEMITSU (1844–97), Japanese politician, a figure of importance in the Meiji government's domestic political strategy in the 1890s. He was also foreign minister in Itō's cabinet which secured revision of the 'unequal treaties' and declared war on China (1894).

MUTUAL SECURITY ACT (1951) in US, legislation authorizing a programme of economic and military aid to foreign countries. The act abolished the Economic Co-operation Administration, replacing it with the Mutual Security Agency (1951–3). The functions of the MSA were later transferred to the Foreign Operations Administration (1953–5), the International Co-operation Administration (1955–61), and ultimately to the Agency for International Development (1961–).

MUZAFFAR JANG (d. 1751), grandson of the first Nizam of Hyderabad. On the latter's death (1748), Muzaffar aspired to the succession, but was compelled to submit to the Nizam's second son, Nasir Jang. On Nasir's assassination (Dec. 1750), he became, with French support, the third nizam, but was in his turn murdered.

MUZAFFARID, Persian house which rose to prominence after the death of the last Il-Khan, Abu Sa'id, in AD 1335. Mubariz al-Din Muhammad, the son of a high Il-Khanid officer, Sharaf al-Din Muzaffar (d. 1314), established himself at Yazd and brought under his control most of Kirman and Fars, including Shiraz and Isfahan. Internal discord weakened his regime after the deposition of Mubariz al-Din Muhammad in 1358. The great conqueror from Samarkand, Timur Beg, made an end of the Muzaffarid line in 1393.

MWATA YAMVO, traditional title of rulers of the Lunda (central Congo) empire. The first ruler to adopt the title was probably responsible for the beginnings of its spectacular commercial and imperial expansion, probably in the second half of the 17th cent. The Mwata Yamvos evolved a peculiarly stable and well-structured political system which included an influential queen mother, a bureaucracy modelled on the military hierarchy, centrally appointed provincial governors, and a disciplined force of mobile security and tax officials. Their empire dominated the central Congo trade to and from the Atlantic, just as their subsidiary Lunda kingdom, of the Mwata Kazembe, dominated this trade to and from the Indian Ocean.

MWENEMUTAPA (MONOMOTAPA), 15th-cent. empire stretching between the Zambezi and Limpopo rivers in present-day Rhodesia and named after the royal title of its ruler. It was founded by Shona peoples, some of whose leaders probably migrated into Rhodesia early in the second millennium AD, where they developed new technical skills and cultural values, notably the concept of large-scale state building. One key to the empire's economic growth was gold mining, an old-established industry which the Shona rulers were able to bring under more centralized control. Mining had been stimulated by the creation of opportunities for oversea exports to the Swahili trading cities of the East African coast, notably Sofala and thence Kilwa and Mogadishu. One objective of the early Shona rulers was probably to gain control over the routes to the coast, notably the Zambezi valley route to the north of Shona territory.

The first known kings of the Shona dominions who began this process of territorial expansion, and created the title Mwenemutapa, were Mutota and Matope, who, in the middle decades of the 15th cent., conquered most of present-day Rhodesia and dominated some of the neighbouring kingdoms in Mozambique. They established close communications with the Islamic trading system of the Zambezi valley; when this was replaced in the 16th cent. by Portuguese trade, later Mwenemutapas maintained close, though fluctuating, relations with the Portuguese instead. Later, the power of Mwenemutapa was confined to a small area in the northeast by expansion of the southern Shona empire under Rozwi leadership. This included the major mining centres and trading emporia of Mwenemutapa. Although the territorial survival of Mwenemutapa was restricted, a vivid religious memory enabled the Shona priests of its ancestor cults to organize a powerful resistance to the late-19th-cent. British colonizers.

E. Stokes and R. Brown, *The Zambesian Past* (Manchester, 1966).

Terence Ranger, *Revolt in Rhodesia* (London, 1968).   DB

MYCALE, BATTLE OF (479 BC), the destruction by the Greek fleet under Leotychidas of the Persian fleet beached below Mt Mycale in western Asia Minor, north-west of Miletus. The Asiatic Greeks rose in revolt against Persia and no Persian warship entered the Aegean for 84 years.

MYCENAE, ancient Greek city in the Peloponnese, first occupied by Greek-speaking peoples *c.* 2000 BC and most powerful in the 16th–13th cents. The Shaft Graves (16th cent.) discovered by Schliemann in 1876 contained an amazing wealth of ceremonial weapons, vases, gold, jewellery and face-masks, *eg*, the so-called 'Mask of Agamemnon'. Cretan, Anatolian, Egyptian, and central European influences can be detected. In the 15th cent. Cretan influence was dominant. Tholos tombs appeared and continued to the time when the massive 'Treasury of Atreus' and 'Tomb of Clytaemnestra' (14th and 13th cents) were erected. After Thera's eruption and the destruction of Cretan palaces (*c.* 1475) Mycenae flourished with its own 'megaron' version of a Minoan palace and, perhaps, loosely controlled mainland Greece and the Aegean, as suggested in Homer's *Iliad*. In the 13th cent. massive fortifications, including the 'Lion Gate', were constructed, but *c.* 1200, probably soon after Agamemnon's return from Troy, the city was destroyed by unknown invaders. After 1150 the site was temporarily abandoned, then in the 11th cent. came the Dorian occupation. Mycenae was of little subsequent importance, and in the 5th cent. was incorporated into the city-state of Argos.

MYCENAEAN CIVILISATION, earliest Greek civilization, revealed by a century's extensive excavation and the recent decipherment of its writing, Linear B. It began at Mycenae in the 16th cent. BC under the strong influence of Minoan Crete. Later, similar pottery, metalwork, and writing (*eg*, Linear B) at Pylos, Mycenae, and Thebes, monumental tholos tombs and elaborate 'megaron' palaces characterized many sites in mainland Greece, *eg*, Mycenae, Tiryns, Pylos, Athens, Thebes, and Iolcus. Their inhabitants, called collectively 'Mycenaeans', stood in feudal relationship to the *wanax*, or 'lord', of the local palace. The local lords, despite some evidence for fighting among themselves (*eg*, the destruction of Cnossos and Thebes in the 14th cent.), were perhaps under the loose suzerainty of the *wanax* of Mycenae, as is suggested in Homer's *Iliad*. In the 14th–13th cents Mycenaean trade flourished with Anatolia, the Levant, and even southern Italy and settlements were established at Miletus, in Rhodes, and in Cyprus. Contemporary Hittite records possibly refer to Mycenaeans and their land, *Ahhiyawa*. In the 13th cent. many sites (*eg*, Mycenae, Tiryns, Athens) were heavily fortified, but nevertheless mysteriously destroyed *c.* 1200. Refugee settlements thrived in central Peloponnese, eastern Attica, and elsewhere in the 12th cent. before Dorian intrusion (*c.* 1100) necessitated migration eastwards to Asia Minor.

MYLAE, BATTLE OF (260 BC), off north-east Sicily, victory of the new Roman fleet under C. Duillius over the Carthaginians. The battle was chiefly remarkable for the innovation of the *corvus* or iron grapnel, through which the Carthaginians lost 50 ships.

MYOCHIT or NATIONALIST PARTY in Burma, formed in 1938 by U Saw, who was more interested in power than policy. A coalition with other groups enabled its leader to become prime minister in 1940.

MYRIOKEPHALON, BATTLE OF (1176), near Phrygia. After AD 1081 the Byzantine emperors of the House of Komnenos strove to drive back the Turks, who had overrun much of Asia Minor in the years following the battle of Manzikert (1071). Their efforts had restored western Asia Minor to Byzantine control. This 'riconquista' came to an end, however, in 1176, when the Seljuk Sultan of Rum, Kilij Arslan II, inflicted a defeat on the Emperor Manuel Komnenos in this battle.

MYSORE, RENDITION OF (March 1881). In 1831 the administration of Mysore was taken over by the British because the Hindu ruler was adjudged incapable. On the maharaja's death in 1868, his adopted son was recognized as his successor. In 1881, when the new ruler attained his majority, Mysore was restored to him by the viceroy, Lord Ripon.

MYSORE WARS, between the British and the Muslim rulers of Mysore, were four in number. The first (1767–9) ended in favour of Haidar Ali, who practically dictated the peace terms. The second (1780–4), in the time of Warren Hastings, ended in a mutual restoration of conquests by the treaty of Mangalore (1784). By the treaty of Seringapatam (1792) at the end of the third war (1790–2), in the time of Cornwallis, Tipu Sultan was forced to cede half of Mysore. Finally, in 1799 Wellesley defeated and killed Tipu. Although the ancient Hindu dynasty was restored, Mysore was virtually placed under British control.

MYSTERY PLAYS. Medieval drama grew out of the musical additions to Church liturgy from the 9th cent. onwards, and was originally enacted inside churches. Mystery plays were among the most popular of these religious plays and were devoted to events recorded in the Bible, eventually performed out of doors, often close to a church. By the early 14th cent. religious drama had largely passed from the hands of the clergy to those of the laity. Trade guilds may have contributed greatly to this transition. In many places, as at York, the plays came to be managed by the municipalities. On the whole, the plays were simple and devotional.

MYTILENE, ancient Greek city-state on Lesbos in the eastern Aegean, settled by Aeolians in the 10th cent. BC, which first became prominent late in the 7th cent. as the home of the poets Sappho and Alcaeus. Fragments of Alcaeus' poems shed an interesting light on the collapse of aristocratic rule and the mediation of the 'law-giver', Pittacus (*c.* 600). After being subjected by the Persians (*c.* 517), it joined the abortive Ionian Revolt (499–444), was liberated after the Greek victory at Mycale (479), and became a founder member of the Delian League. It was a privileged ally of Athens, and twice revolted unsuccessfully in the great Peloponnesian War. Generally friendly to Athens in the 4th cent., it prospered peacefully under Macedonia and Rome, apart from an unsuccessful revolt against Rome in the first Mithridatic War (80 BC).

MZILIKAZI (*c.* 1800–69), head of the Kumalo, a small Nguni-speaking chiefdom in modern Natal. He became a regimental commander of the Zulu king, Shaka, in 1822, but the following year rebelled and fled with a small following to the Transvaal. There he gradually built up a formidable military state, out of Sotho as well as Nguni people. After their defeat in 1837 at Mosega by the Voortrekkers, Mzilikazi removed the Ndebele (as his people were called) north of the Limpopo to Matabeleland, and established a military state, whose numbers were swelled by many Shona-speaking people. At the time of his death the Ndebele kingdom was still independent of European rule.

N

NABATAEANS, Arab people who founded a kingdom in western Palestine, Petra being its capital, in the 5th cent BC, and became prosperous through control of the incense and spice routes running through their territory. They developed distinctive types of architecture, pottery, sculpture, and stone-dressing and had their own script. Before the kingdom's annexation by Rome (AD 105) they controlled an area from Damascus to the Red Sea and from Sinai far into Arabia.

NABIS (d. 192 BC), Spartan popular leader, who in the second Macedonian War gained Argos with the collusion of Philip V of Macedon. After the Romans had defeated Philip (196), their Greek allies incited them to attack Nabis and they deprived Sparta of its external possessions (195). In 193 he declared for Antiochus III of Syria, but was defeated and subsequently assassinated through Aetolian intrigues.

NABOBS, THE, English corruption of the Arabic word *nawab*, signifying deputy in the plural. The word was used (18th cent.) as a title for Mughal nobles, generally signifying a Mughal grandee. Hence it was anglicized to describe the East India Co.'s servants, often wealthy, arrogant, and ostentatious, returning from India after the battle of Plassey (1757). From this group the term was extended to the company's servants generally from the 18th until early in the 19th cent.

Before Plassey the company's servants were often prosperous and some were wealthy, but not many returned to Britain and there were too few to impress British society. They lived in or near the company's factories, and their chief amusement consisted of heavy eating and drinking in the company's garden. They liked processions 'with the country musick' and grasped any opportunity, such as a king's accession or a public treaty, for fireworks and firing salvos of cannon. Many adopted Indian habits in their homes and married Christians of Portuguese descent. Apart from engaging in the company's trade they were merchants on their own account, their contacts being chiefly with the Indian mercantile classes, with which, however, they had little cultural interchange.

The age of the opulent nabob began with Clive's control of Bengal (1757), the French wars in south India, and the company's involvement with the Nawab of the Carnatic. In the north fortunes were made and remade from private trade in favoured conditions, presents, contracts, and revenue corruption; in the south from contracts and speculation on the nawab's debts. Greater security and wealth enabled large town houses and garden houses to be built. Here such merchants as survived—and the mortality rate was high—lived on a scale comparable to that of an Indian nawab, with retinues of servants and much ceremony. Though aggressively British in most respects, they made fashionable Indian features such as cuisine and hookah-smoking. It was these men, on their return to Britain, who were first called nabobs. They were caricatured in Foote's play, *The Nabob* (1769), and Thackeray's Jos Sedley. After 1772 fortunes became less easy to make and Lord Cornwallis (governor-general, 1786–1793) enforced higher standards of conduct and official duty.

Up-country a new type of nabob appeared—the adventurer—who made a fortune serving Indian princes, or British civilians and soldiers serving in distant places for long periods. Count de Boigne (1751–1830), Sindhia's French general, was typical of the former and Sir D. Ochterloney (1758–1825) of the latter class. These men lived in state, added *zenana* quarters to their classical mansions, and sometimes married Indian women of good family.

The decline of the typical nabob class and style came from enforcement of discipline by Cornwallis, from successive retrenchments, from Evangelical influence in India (c. 1785), and from a rising standard of public duty.

H. H. Dodwell, *Nabobs of Madras* (London, 1926).
T. G. P. Spear, *The Nabobs* (Oxford, 1963).   TGPS

NABONIDUS (*reg. c.* 556–539 BC), King of Neo-Babylonia, who was deeply religious and especially devoted to the god, Sin. He spent ten years in the Arabian desert, possibly trying to establish control of the incense trade. He lost his kingdom to Cyrus II of Persia (c. 539).

NABOPOLASSAR (*reg. c.* 625–605 BC), King of Neo-Babylonia and Chaldean founder, who conquered all southern Mesopotamia, and in alliance with the Medes (612) destroyed Nineveh and ended the Assyrian empire.

NABUCO DE ARAUJO, JOAQUIM (1849–1910), Brazilian politician and diplomat, who led the campaign to abolish slavery in Brazil (1878–88). He was the first Latin American ambassador to the US (1905–10).

NACIONAL FINANCIERA in Mexico, principal development bank (*financiera*) (founded 1933), responsible for handling government investment and financing development through low-cost loans with only a minimal concern for profit.

NACIONALISTA PARTY in the Philippines, founded on 12 March 1907, to fight in general elections for a National Assembly. It consisted of a coalition of political groups that agitated for immediate independence from US colonial control and replaced the Federal Party, which had advocated statehood within the US. The Nacionalista Party, although divided several times, has remained one of the country's two leading parties. Its first split occurred in 1922 owing to rivalry between M. L. Quezon and S. Osmena. In face of the cabinet crisis of 1923, the two wings merged, then split again in 1933 over the question of the Hare–Hawes–Cutting Law, the first of two Philippine Independence Acts approved by the American government. The 'Antis' and 'Pros' coalesced in 1935 to participate jointly in the Commonwealth government. Another split occurred after the Pacific war, when the Liberal Party was formed by M. Roxas, who left the Nacionalista Party in 1946. Because of the intensity of the issues which caused the break, and the bitterness of the struggle for power, the split resulted this time in the establishment of a two-party system. However, both parties continue to consist of factions joined by personal ties of loyalty and little divides them on matters of policy.

NADIR KHAN (1883–1933), Afghan Ruler (*reg.* 1929–33) of Muhammadzay family, who led a tribal revolt (1929) against the Tajik bandit, Bacha-i Saqaw (Habibullah II), who had earlier replaced Amanullah. As ruler of Afghanistan, he re-established public security and began a cautious policy of modernization.

NADIR SHAH (1688–1747), Ruler of Iran (*reg.* 1736–47), from the Turkish Afshar tribe of Khurasan who became the chief supporter of the Safavid ruler, Tahmasp II (*reg.* 1722–32) in his struggle against the Afghan invaders of Iran. Nadir defeated the Afghans (1729), restored Tahmasp to his throne, and defeated the Ottomans who had invaded western Iran. His original intention seems to have been to content himself with semi-independent power in Khurasan, but Tahmasp's incapacity led Nadir to depose him (1732) in favour of his infant son, Abbas III (*reg.* 1732–6). Real power remained with Nadir, who was proclaimed Shah in 1736. His reign was marked by a long series of campaigns. Though he forced the Ottomans to abandon western Iran, he was unable to establish his own power in Iraq, and persuaded Russia to evacuate the northern provinces, occupied by them under the treaty of Ganja (1735). He conquered Afghanistan (1737–8), whence he launched his celebrated Indian campaign, culminating in the sack of Delhi (1739) and the capture of an enormous treasure, including the Koh-i-Noor diamond and the Peacock throne. He also fought in Turkestan and Daghestan and again against the Ottomans. His successes, like those of other great Asian conquerors, was based on his light cavalry, consisting of Turkish, Afghan, and Persian tribesmen. He seems to have had no settled plan for developing an enduring empire or pursuing a specifically 'Iranian' policy and after his assassination his empire collapsed. His attempt (1736) to replace Shi'ism with the Jafari rite, which he claimed to be a fifth Sunni school, also had little success.   MEY

NAEVIUS, CN. (*c.* 270–200 BC), Rome's first known native poet and dramatist, who wrote an epic on the First Punic War (of which 70 lines survive), many comedies based on Greek models, and at least two plays with Roman themes.

NAGARAKERTAGAMA, old Javanese text extolling the greatness of the Indonesian empire of Majapahit under King Hayam Wuruk (*reg.* 1350–89). It is woven round the account of a tour by the king through part of his realm. He was accompanied by the author of the text, Prapancha, then superintendent of the Buddhist order. The text contains numerous episodes of great historical value, notably those dealing with the city and empire, the royal family, earlier rulers, political and social institutions, and temples and monasteries. Though sometimes exaggerated, Prapancha's work (dated 1365) seems generally trustworthy wherever its data can be checked with inscriptions.

NAGAS, tribes on the north-east frontier of India between Assam and Burma, were ferocious head hunters and constant British punitive expeditions were sent against them (1835–1947). Their demand in 1970 for complete independence presented a difficult problem for India.

NAGY, IMRE (1896–1958), Hungarian communist politician, who became prime minister during the Hungarian revolt (1956). In the First World War he fought in the Austro-Hungarian army, was taken prisoner by the Russians, and joined the Bolsheviks and became a Soviet citizen. He returned to Hungary in 1919 and took a minor part in Bela Kun's revolution. He remained active in the illegal Communist Party in Hungary and then (1930) went again to the Soviet Union, where he remained until the end of the Second World War. As minister of agriculture (1945) he was responsible for substantial land reforms. He was minister of the interior (1945–6). He was relegated to the background during the period of Stalin's tight control over Eastern Europe, but remained as speaker of the Hungarian parliament (1947–53). After Stalin's death Nagy became prime minister (1953–5) and carried out a number of liberalizing reforms, including the abandonment of compulsory collectivization of agriculture and the release of political prisoners. He was ousted and deprived of his party membership in April 1955.

He was appointed prime minister (24 Oct. 1956) in an attempt to stem the revolt which had broken out in Hungary. Since he lacked control of the security service and was imminently threatened by the Soviet army, he sought to establish power on a broad base, and his government abandoned single-party rule so as to include representatives of the former smallholders' and other non-communist parties. During the uprising he telegraphed to the secretary-general of the UN, seeking recognition of Hungary's neutrality. But meanwhile the Russians found an alternative to him in the person of Janos Kadar and, finding himself unable to meet the onslaught of the Soviet army, Nagy sought refuge in the Yugoslav embassy (Nov. 1956). A few weeks later he left under assurances that he would be allowed to return home, but he was abducted by Soviet troops and in June 1958 the Soviet government announced that he had been tried and executed.   WK

NAHDATUL ULAMA, 'Islamic Scholars' Association', founded in 1926 as a traditionalist opposition to *Muhammadijah*, a Javanese Muslim social and educational association led by religious modernists. In 1943 the two were united in the *Masjumi. Nahdatul Ulama* remained a component of the *Masjumi* party until 1952, when it seceded, it being thought that its leaders were not given a sufficient part to play. The general elections of 1955 showed *Nahdatul Ulama* to be Indonesia's second religious party, its support being concentrated in eastern and central Java. Its strength was largely rural, leading elements being drawn from the agrarian religious and economic elite. With the banning of the *Masjumi* in 1960, it became the leading political mouthpiece for Islam, and under 'Guided Democracy' its leaders co-operated closely with Sukarno in public, but at the same time resisted pressure from the left. Ultimately they formed an alliance with the army against the Indonesia Communist Party, and after the 1965 coup *Nahdatul Ulama* adherents played an active role in the violent suppression of the communists.

NAHHAS PASHA, MUSTAFA AL- (1876–1965), Egyptian lawyer and politician, who succeeded Zaghlul Pasha as leader of the Wafd Party (1927) and was seven times prime minister of Egypt (1928–52).

NAHUAS, Mexican Indians, who speak the language of the same name. This language, perhaps the most important in Middle American history, was a variant of Uto-Aztecan and achieved its diagnostic characteristics in an area which extended from the western escarpment of the Sierra Madre northwards into Jalisco. Nahua-speakers entered the heartland of Mexico, the central highland, in two great waves. The earlier wave came *c.* 800 and the later after 1100. The language spoken by these two groups differed slightly in that the earlier group did not use the *tl* sound characteristic of the later Nahua speech. For this reason, linguists call the earlier dialect Nahuat and the later Nahuatl. The earlier group were known as Toltecs, and during the 9th–10th cents they established hegemony over a large part of central and southern Mexico. Their capital was Tula, to the north of the Valley of Mexico in the present-day state of Hidalgo. The Toltecs were highly militaristic, and this is reflected in the Nahua language, which has a specialized vocabulary of military and political terms.

In the 12th cent. Toltec power began to wane, and Tula itself was destroyed in 1168 by new groups of migrants from the north, some Nahua-speakers, some not, who have been grouped together under the name Chichimecs. A period of political chaos followed, which witnessed the rise to power of the city-state of Texcoco, built on the edge of the lake of the same name in the Valley of Mexico. Texcoco became the intellectual capital of Mexico and the home of the most polished Nahuatl, as the language is (1970) properly termed.

The 15th cent. saw the rise of another Nahua group in the Valley, the peoples later called the Aztecs. This group, based on their lake capital of Tenochtitlán, were (*c.* 1430) strong enough to make an alliance with Texcoco and Tlacopán.

This triple alliance, by the end of the 15th cent. dominated much of central and southern Mexico, and Tenochtitlán became the major partner, reducing first Tlacopán and then Texcoco to satellite status, only to succumb to the Spanish onslaught (1619–20).

The language, however, not only survived European conquest, but was spread more widely since the Spanish missionaries, confronted with a bewildering variety of native tongues, fostered the usage of Nahuatl to aid them in their labours. Thus, in 1970, Nahuatl was still widely spoken in Mexico.

M. León-Portilla, *Aztec Thought and Culture: a study of the Ancient Nahuatl mind*, tr. by J. E. Davis (Norman, OK, 1963).

E. R. Wolf, *Sons of the Shaking Earth* (Chicago and London, 1959). FPB

NAIDU, MRS SAROJINI (1879–1949), Indian poet and politician, who was associated with the Congress before the First World War and presided at the Cawnpore session (1925). She became a close follower of Gandhi and important as one of his organizers, *eg*, in the Salt March (1930) and at the Round Table Conference (1931). After independence, she was governor of the United Provinces (1947–9). She published several volumes of romantic poems on Indian themes which are now collected in *The Sceptred Flute* (1958) and *The Feather of the Dawn* (1961).

NA'IMA, MUSTAFA (AD 1655–1716), official historiographer (waq'a'-i nuwis) to the Ottoman sultan and author of a chronicle (1591–1659) on the Ottoman empire.

NAJAF, AL-, shrine situated in Iraq to the south-west of Al-Hilla, close to the former Al-Hira and Al-Kufa. It is revered by the adherents of the Shi'a as the place of interment of the Caliph Ali (*reg.* 656–61), the son-in-law of the Prophet Muhammad.

NAJD, AL-, name given to the inland plateau constituting the central area of Arabia, east of the Hijaz, and consisting largely of desert land. Here lived the tribal confederations that were prominent in the campaigns of conquest which the Arabs undertook after the death (AD 632) of the Prophet Muhammad.

NAJM-UD-DAULAH (d. 1766), Nawab of Bengal (1765–6), who was the eldest surviving son of the Nawab Mir Jafar after the death of his eldest son, Miran (1760). On Mir Jafar's death (1765) he became nawab, but remained a puppet ruler, Muhammad Reza Khan exercising power as his and the East India Co.'s deputy.

NALANDA, archaeological site of ancient India, *c.* 40 miles (64 kms) south-south-east of Patna, Bihar, not far from Rajgir (ancient Rajagriha). There are remains of a vast complex of buildings constituting an ancient Buddhist monastic 'university', with instruction in Buddhist thought and many other disciplines. Excavations have revealed eight strata testifying to a very long period of occupation (probably 5th cent. BC–13th cent. AD), though only from the 5th cent. AD as a centre of learning.

Structural remains of 12 monasteries have been discovered, with a temple, numerous stupas, and inscriptions. Perhaps the most interesting discovery is that of a copper-plate inscription of King Devapala (*c.* AD 860), mentioning the foundation by the Sumatranese King Balaputra of a monastery, presumably for pilgrims from Indonesia. Nalanda exerted great influence as a meeting place of Buddhist scholars from all over Asia. The influence of Nalanda is especially evident in the art, bronze technique, and script of Ceylon and South-East Asia.

NAMIK KEMAL (1840–88), Turkish writer, who criticized the Tanzimat reformers as shallow westernizers and advocated the adoption of a constitutional regime which he claimed to derive from Muslim theory. He first expressed the idea of Ottoman territorial patriotism in his play, *Fatherland or Silistria* (1873). His frequent clashes with authority led him to be permanently exiled on Chios.

NAMUR, BATTLES OF (1692, 1695), engagements in the War of the League of Augsburg to capture the key fortress of Namur at the junction of the Sambre and the Meuse rivers. The city, fortified by the Dutch engineer Van Coehoorn, was none the less taken by the French through the siege tactics of Vauban after 36 days' resistance (5 June 1692). It was retaken by William of Orange and Coehoorn with great loss of life (1 Sept. 1695).

NANA OF EBROHIMIE (*c.* 1852–1916), West African trader, who was prominent among those who resisted British colonial encroachment. He came from the Itshekiri country in south-eastern Nigeria, and succeeded his father (1883) as head of the most powerful trading organization in the western delta of the Niger, having a virtual monopoly of palm oil from Urhoboland.

By 1884 he had acquired political power and, as governor of the Benin river, was able to dictate his terms to Europeans. He signed a protection treaty (1884) with the British, but rejected any free-trade clause. Having outrivalled the Itshekiri traders and intrigued with European traders, he set the Niger Coast Protectorate administration against him. The British, failing to make him give up his authority, sent an expedition to destroy his headquarters at Ebrohimie and he was exiled (1894–1906).

NANA FADNAVIS (1741–1800), Chitpavan Brahman minister of the Peshwas of Poona. In the time of Warren Hastings he opposed Raghoba's attempt to become peshwa. By receiving St Lubin, a French agent, he forced Hastings to declare war on the Marathas. He was (1782–1800) the chief Maratha politician and his greatest rival was Mahadaji Sindhia. Nana's policy was to bolster the power of the peshwas and maintain the Brahman ascendancy at Poona, to recover the lost Maratha territories to the south of the Narbada, and to keep the peshwa free from English control. After his death the Maratha confederacy was weakened by internal jealousies.

NANA SAHIB (*fl.* 19th cent.), leader of the Indian Mutiny (1857). He was the adopted son of the ex-Maratha peshwa, whose claim for the continuation of the peshwa's pension was rejected. In the Mutiny, after Sir Hugh Wheeler's surrender at Cawnpore, he murdered men, women, and children. He was also responsible for the murder of the women and children imprisoned in the Bibighar at Cawnpore.

NANAK, GURU (1469–1539), founder of the Sikh religion. He was early attracted to the *bhakti* tradition of Hinduism, which emphasizes the oneness of God, the brotherhood of all believers, and the practice of loving devotion as the path to spiritual realization. He travelled widely and preached the irrelevance of all religions in the devotional worship of one God. His followers considered him a Guru or spiritual guide and he was followed by nine others. Under Nanak Sikhism was a quietist, tolerant, devotional sect. Later Gurus clashed with the Mughal authorities and the tenth, Guru Gobind Singh (1666–1708), completed the transformation of the body into a military religious community. Nanak's poems are included in the *Granth Sahib*, or holy book of the Sikhs.

NANCH'ANG UPRISING (1 Aug. 1927), military revolt marking the emergence of an independent communist army in China. It occurred at the key centre of Nanch'ang in central-south China shortly after the Kuomintang had turned against the communists. Communist-led units, notably those of Ho Lung, Yeh T'ing, and Chu Te, rebelled against Kuomintang units, and marched towards Kwangtung, hoping to re-establish a revolutionary base there. But their forces were routed; some moved into Kiangsi, to form the nucleus of the armed forces of the Kiangsi Soviet. Later, 1 Aug. became Army Day in communist China.

NAN-CHAO, independent state situated in the present (1970) Chinese province of Yün-nan from 740. Its institutions were based on the model of the T'ang government. In 751 Nan-chao armies succeeded in defeating T'ang forces, who remained on the defensive in the area. For long, Nan-chao exerted more influence in this part of southern China than the recognized Chinese dynasty; it persisted independently until c. 1253, when it was taken over by Mongol invaders.

NANCY, BATTLE OF (5 Jan. 1477), fought outside Nancy, the capital of Lorraine, which Charles the Bold of Burgundy was besieging. Although menaced by a superior Swiss army, he refused to withdraw and was killed, his entire army being massacred. This ended the period of great Burgundian power and Charles's only daughter, Mary, had great difficulty in preserving even the main parts of the Burgundian inheritance from annexation by Louis XI of France.

NAND KUMAR, Maharaja (c. 1720–75), Brahmin of the Murshidabad district, given his title by the Emperor Shah Alam. He assisted Warren Hastings in the prosecution of Muhammad Reza Khan (1772), but later made allegations against him, while Hastings in turn charged Nand with conspiracy. While this charge was pending he was convicted of forgery by the Supreme Court and hanged according to English law. The opponents of Hastings regarded this as a judicial murder.

NANDA DYNASTY, ancient Indian dynasty of nine kings, most of whom probably reigned jointly in the Gangetic valley during a period of 22 years (c. 342–320 BC). According to later tradition—there is hardly any contemporary evidence—the Nandas were immensely rich and greedy. They were overthrown by Chandragupta, the founder of the Maurya dynasty.

NANDI resistance to the establishment of British rule in Kenya occurred from c. 1893 until 1906, and was long remembered in that colony because, among other things, it held up the completion of the railway from the coast eastwards to Lake Nyanza at Kisumu. But its historical importance lies chiefly in its demonstration of the stubborn and skilful ways in which 'king-less peoples', who were relatively few in number (the Nandi section of the Kalendjin group probably numbered fewer than 50,000 people in 1900), could and did hold up the imposition of colonial rule. Though defeated by British forces in 1905, and again in 1906, the Nandi as a whole continued to resist in passive ways, refusing to send their children to school or to abandon their traditional methods of stock-raising, until late in the colonial period.

NANKING INCIDENT (March 1927), in China, struck terror into the hearts of all foreigners. It occurred as the city fell to Kuomintang troops marching on the Northern Expedition. The foreigners in the city were attacked and a few killed by unidentified soldiers. In retaliation, British and US gunboats lying off the city shelled the city and killed hundreds of Chinese.

NANKING, RAPE OF (Dec. 1937) in China, took place during her war with Japan (1937–45). The Japanese occupied Nanking and troops fell on the city and slaughtered at least 100,000 Chinese civilians and soldiers. This and other less well publicized episodes proved a powerful factor in the awakening of Chinese nationalism.

NANKING, TREATY OF (29 Aug. 1842), concluded the Opium War between Britain and China. It provided for the payment of an indemnity to Britain of $21 million (Mexican),

the abolition of the *Co-Hong* system; the opening of five ports to British trade and residence; the cession to Britain of Hong Kong; diplomatic equality; and a fixed tariff. Opium was not mentioned. The treaty of Nanking was the first to be signed by China with a Western nation in modern times, and foreshadowed an intensification of Western trade and influence in China. As its terms were imposed by the British at gunpoint, it is regarded by the Chinese as the first of the 'unequal treaties'.

NANSEN, FRIDTJOF (1861–1930), Norwegian explorer, scientist, diplomat, and humanitarian, who crossed (1888) the unknown interior of Greenland and, in his ship the *Fram*, explored (1893–6) the North Pole regions, verifying the hypothesis about the westward drift of the polar ice-pack.

He then became closely concerned with the cause of Norwegian independence and took a major part in securing the election of Prince Charles of Denmark to the throne as Haakon VII (1905). This led to his becoming ambassador to Britain (1905–8) and he was then elected (1908) to the chair of oceanography at Oslo University. Subsequently he played a diplomatic role in Norwegian relations with the US during the First World War. He had publicly defended, while in the US, the neutrality of Norway and became one of his country's representatives at the League of Nations. His concern was with world peace, repatriation of prisoners, and the resettlement of both White Russians, after the Civil War, and Red Russians, after the Volga–Ukraine famine (1921–2). He was also involved in relief work in Greece and Turkey. In 1922 he was awarded the Nobel Peace Prize.

NAN-YÜEH, the southern Yüeh. During the western Han period several independent communities had arisen south of the Yangtse river or on China's south-eastern coast. With the development of a policy of territorial and commercial expansion from c. 135 BC, Chinese diplomats, soldiers, and traders penetrated to these as yet unknown areas in an attempt to spread Chinese influence. Although the first contacts with the kingdom of Nan-yüeh, situated in present-day (1970) Kuang-tung, had occurred in c. 165 BC, it was only after the military intervention of 112 that Han administrative units were established and the area became regarded as part of the Chinese empire and subject to some measure of Han authority.

NAOROJI, DADABHAI (1825–1917), Parsi businessman, newspaper owner, scholar, and politician, who was appointed prime minister of Baroda in 1874 and member of the Bombay legislative council in 1885. He was the first Indian to be elected to the House of Commons (1892–5). He was president of the Indian National Congress in 1886, 1893, and 1906.

NAPATA, ancient Nubian city situated below the fourth cataract of the Nile, probably on the site of modern Merowe. It formed the southern-most limit of Egypt under the New Kingdom from the time of Thothmes III onwards. After their expulsion from Thebes (c. 950 BC) the High Priests of Amen fled to Napata and ruled there for a century. In the 8th cent. Napata became the capital of an independent Nubian (Kushite) state, the kings of which ruled Egypt (c. 715–656) as the XXVth dynasty.

NAPIER, SIR CHARLES JAMES (1782–1853), British soldier and conqueror of Sind, who was taken prisoner at Corunna. His victory at Miani (1843) led to the annexation of Sind, which he administered till 1847. He returned to India in 1849 as commander-in-chief of the East India Co. armies. Following a reprimand by Dalhousie for altering regulations concerning the allowances of Indian troops, he resigned and retired to England.

NAPIER, JOHN (1550–1617), Scottish mathematician, inventor of logarithms and a militant Calvinist, who was involved in activities as various as pamphlet writing and devising curious instruments of war to confound Philip II of Spain. From 1594 onwards he developed his theory of logarithms, publishing the first tables in 1614. Logarithms replaced multiplications by additions, giving a large increase in computational speed. They dominated the processes of calculation in astronomy, navigation, the sciences, and (chiefly in the mechanized form of the slide rule) engineering for nearly 350 years.

NAPLES, largest city of southern Italy with fine natural harbour. It attracted Greek colonists in antiquity. Its medieval importance dates from the 13th cent., when Frederick II made it the capital of his mainland territories and its importance was accentuated after the Angevin conquest of southern Italy in 1266. The new conqueror, Charles of Anjou, who distrusted the Sicilians, made Naples his capital and it remained the seat of the Angevin kings and of their Aragonese successors (after 1435). After the Spanish conquest in 1500, it was the residence of Spanish viceroys. It continued to grow under the Spanish rule, being one of the most populous cities of 16th cent.-Italy, and developed important textile and other industries. The presence of a vast population lacking adequate means of subsistence has remained the chief feature of Naples since that time to the 20th cent.

NAPOLEON I (1769–1821), Emperor of the French (*reg.* 1804–14), was born in Corsica. Until 1796 he signed himself in the Italian fashion—'Buonaparte'; the dynasty he founded is known by the French name he thenceforth used, 'Bonaparte'. After entering the French army he became an artillery officer and was a lieutenant when the Revolution broke out in 1789. Like many other officers of the army of the *ancien régime*, he did not find it difficult to transfer his loyalty to the constitutional monarchy. But by the time the monarchy fell, officers were few, owing to emigration. He was therefore soon promoted, and first made his mark in the summer of 1793, by his supervision of the artillery at the siege of Toulon, then occupied by the British. The fall of Robespierre led to his arrest for a short time (he had been associated with Robespierre's brother), but he was soon freed and began to work in Paris as a staff officer. He was now a general and in 1796 was appointed to command the Army of Italy. Two days before leaving to take up this post he married Joséphine Beauharnais. His Italian campaign remains an outstanding example of military science and art, foreshadowing the characteristics of his later strategy: rapid movement by separated detachments in order to achieve concentration by surprise at a decisive point, and the overthrow of an outnumbered enemy by these means. He probably never again enjoyed the advantages of so fine an instrument as the Army of Italy. Later, his skill, though always great (and shown outstandingly in his campaign in the spring of 1814), showed some deterioration; he tended to rely more and more on swamping his enemies with massed gunfire and huge infantry assaults. Though his military genius was the basis of his career and fame, he would probably not have stamped himself so firmly upon the imagination of his contemporaries had that genius not been linked to outstanding administrative and creative ability. It is no longer thought that the detail of many of the changes he introduced was his own; nevertheless, his use of the ideas of others in the remodelling of French institutions remains impressive. It has been said that what has endured of the Revolution is the part which was established by Napoleon, and this is substantially true. He assiduously cultivated the myth of omniscience and infallibility and his victories and domestic achievements were rewarded by phenomenal popularity. He exploited this in the plebiscites which sanctified his steps towards personal power—first, as Consul (1800) for life, and later as Emperor (1804). Possibly his major political achievement was the appeasement of religious hatreds in France by his Concordat with the papacy. His greatest mistakes were cumulative; he alienated many of the best elements in France by his growing absorption with the pursuit of personal and dynastic authority. He wore out the people's goodwill by his prolonged campaigns, and he destroyed his European achievements by creating new enemies. None the less, he carried the French Revolution throughout Europe and left his mark on its map and its institutions for the next 100 years. His private qualities were unattractive. He was intensely selfish, though he had the grace to show real regret at parting with Josephine, whom he divorced in order to marry the Austrian princess, Marie-Louise, in 1809. But he remains a fascinating and titanic figure with better claim than any other politician or soldier to be called the greatest figure in modern history.

F. M. H. Markham, *Napoleon*, 2 vols (London, 1963).
P. Geyl, *Napoleon, For and Against* (London, 1949).   JMR

NAPOLEON II, FRANCIS CHARLES JOSEPH, Duke of Reichstadt (1811–32), styled King of Rome, was the son of Napoleon I by Marie-Louise. During the Hundred Days he was proclaimed as Napoleon II.

NAPOLEON III, LOUIS-NAPOLEON BONAPARTE (1808–1873), Emperor of the French (*reg.* 1852–70), second son of Louis Napoleon and Hortense Beauharnais. After the July Revolution (1830) his liaisons with the *carbonari* led him to participate in the abortive Italian insurrections. The death of his elder brother in Italy, followed by that of the Duke of Reichstadt (Napoleon II) (1832), left him the only young Bonaparte and, although his uncles had a better claim to the title, he arrogated to himself the role of pretender by his abortive coups at Strasbourg (1836) and Boulogne (1840). After this last episode he was imprisoned at Ham, near Amiens, which he called 'his university' because he read widely there and wrote some influential pamphlets. He escaped (1846) and went to Britain, where (1848) he enlisted as a special constable. A growing Bonapartist movement in France secured his election to the Assembly (June 1848).

In the same year he was elected to the presidency by an overwhelming majority, and proceeded cautiously to consolidate support by touring the country and sponsoring the Roman expedition (1849). He installed his own men as ministers, supported the restoration of the full franchise and revision of the constitution, and when the Legislative Assembly cavilled at this, overthrew it by a coup (1851). In 1852 the empire was declared. It was consolidated by his marriage to Eugenie (1853) and later the birth of the Prince Imperial (1856). Napoleon actively assisted the country's economic expansion, and by bringing the notables back into politics, established a strong regime, which he began to liberalize in conformity with his fundamentally radical beliefs (1860). In his foreign policy, however, he was less successful. His interventions in the Crimea and Italy were not as rewarding as he had hoped, and his Mexican expedition was ill-judged, leaving France exposed militarily at a time when Prussia was unifying Germany. Although he remained personally popular, and his regime commanded vast electoral support, especially from the peasantry, it was not as strong as it appeared. By allowing power to pass to the court and the politicians, Napoleon, now ailing and exhausted, contributed to the regime's collapse in 1870. Napoleon did not long survive his defeat by Prussia and died in exile.

T. A. B. Corley, *Democratic Despot, a life of Napoleon III* (London, 1961).   CHC

NAPOLEONIC WARS, THE, may be considered as a continuation of the French Revolutionary Wars, in that the basic issue at stake in both was the preservation to France of a European hegemony which guaranteed the social and political system created by the French Revolution. But they also came to show more and more the imprint of Napoleon's personal ambition. They began with his liquidation of the war of the Second Coalition after the battles of Marengo and Hohenlinden. The peace of Lunéville with Austria followed in Feb. 1801 and soon France again faced only Britain. In March 1802 Britain too made peace by the treaty of Amiens, beginning the only period (14 months) between 1793 and 1814 when the two countries were not at war. Napoleon's European reorganization during this interval brought about the virtual extinction of the Holy Roman empire and a substantial consolidation of the state structure of Germany. In May 1803 Britain resumed war with France because of quarrels arising from the Amiens settlement. The French occupied Hanover and massed an army which threatened to invade Britain, though this was impossible so long as naval supremacy remained in British hands. The realization that France was not invincible, combined with distaste for many of Napoleon's changes (including the creation of the French empire), led to the formation of the Third Coalition in 1805. Austria, Russia, and Sweden joined Britain. Two great land victories (Ulm and Austerlitz) again forced Austria to make peace (treaty of Pressburg), but the annihilating victory of Nelson at Trafalgar (1805) confirmed British supremacy at sea. A further reorganization of Germany in France's interest and the installation of a French king at Naples followed. When in 1806 Prussia entered the war against France, she was defeated at Jena. Antagonized in part by French success in getting the Turks to attack them, the Russians now came to the help of the Prussians. After costly fighting, the treaty of Tilsit ended this phase of the war in 1807. Again, Britain was France's sole opponent and Napoleon sought to wound her through the Continental System; economic warfare against her was one motive for Napoleon's invasion of Spain in 1808. Soon, a large French army was tied down there by a guerrilla war and the presence of a British expeditionary force operating from Portugal. Napoleon's difficulties encouraged the Austrians, who once more declared war in 1809, but again had to accept a punitive peace. Thereafter, no continental fighting took place outside Spain until Napoleon launched his invasion of Russia in June 1812. It ended a few months later with a disastrous retreat; the tide had now turned. Early in 1813 Prussia and Sweden joined the Russians, British, Portuguese, and Spanish. Though still able to inflict sharp defeats on his enemies, Napoleon was now over-extended. In Aug. Austria again declared war. The battle of Leipzig (Oct. 1813) led to the collapse of the French position in Germany and Napoleon's retreat across the Rhine. Wellington crossed the Pyrenees in Nov. The final and decisive campaign, in which Napoleon showed exceptional brilliance, was a triumph for superior numbers. In March, the Allies entered Paris. The events of 1815, culminating in the battle of Waterloo, were the epilogue to the Napoleonic Wars.

D. Chandler, *The Campaigns of Napoleon* (London, 1967).
G. Lefebvre, *Napoleon* (London, 1969).   JMR

NAQA, site of a Meroitic town, temples, and cemeteries in the 'Island of Meroe'. Temple architecture and reliefs, dating from the 1st cent. BC, show a mixture of Egyptian and classical styles.

NAQSHBAND, MUHAMMAD IBN MUHAMMAD BAHA AL-DIN AL-BUKHARI (AD 1317–89), Sufi mystic, from whom derived the Naqshbandi order of dervishes which gained a wide influence, above all in Turkistan, Persia, and Asia Minor.

NARA PERIOD, era in Japanese history (710–85) when Nara was the capital city. Nara, near present-day Kyoto, was Japan's first permanent capital and its establishment marked the great advance brought about by the *Taika* Reform (*c.* 645–700). It not only reflected the increased strength of the Imperial system, but also testified to the religious and cultural developments which had been stimulated by intercourse with China. The excessive influence which came to be exercised over the city by the surrounding Buddhist monasteries, however, prompted the court to establish a new capital, first at Nagaoka (785–94) and then at Heian (Kyoto).

NARAI (1633–88), King of Siam (*reg.* 1657–88), known for his policy of alliance with France. He was the younger son of King Prasat Thong by a queen who was the daughter of King Song Tham (*reg.* 1611–28). His elder brother, Chaofa Chai, seized the throne in 1656 on the death of their father, only to be overthrown by Narai and his uncle, who reigned as King Si Suthammaracha (*reg.* 1657). In Nov. 1657 Narai attacked the palace, seized the throne, and gradually eliminated all his rivals.

Narai is known chiefly for his openness to the West. A considerable number of European adventurers entered his service, in the trading departments of the Phrakhlang and even as governors of coastal towns. He drove a hard bargain with the European merchants competing for Siam's trade, and his own ships sailed to India and China. He was hospitable to Catholic missionaries, and the French Society for Foreign Missions established its regional headquarters in Ayudhya. Encouraged by the Greek Constantine Phaulkon, who became the chief of his ministers in the 1680s, Narai sought in France an ally whom he could balance against the growing influence of the Dutch East India Co. and new threats from the English East India Co. Louis XIV of France was promised small territorial concessions and led by Phaulkon to think that Narai would turn Catholic. Accordingly, he sent an embassy to Siam in 1685. A second embassy from France (1687) was accompanied by a small garrison intended for Bangkok and Mergui, Siam's chief ports. But internal hostility against Phaulkon, the French, and the missionaries increased and erupted into rebellion when Narai fell ill in March 1688. Phaulkon was arrested and executed, the French driven out, and, on the death of Narai in July, the leader of the rebellion, Phra Phetracha, assumed the throne.

Narai was influential as a poet and patron of Thai literature, and his reign was the golden age of Thai classical poetry.   DKW

NARIM-SIN (*fl. c.* 2291–2255 BC), King of Akkad, whose reign was spent in continual military campaigns on the periphery of Mesopotamia, the largest campaign being directed against the Lullubi on the eastern frontier. His reign may have ended in a serious Gutian invasion.

NARAYAN, JAYA PRAKASH (1902–   ), Indian nationalist politician and *Sarvodaya* leader. He was one of the founders of the Congress Socialist Party (1934), took a leading part in guerrilla activities in northern India during the 'Quit India' movement (1942), but left the Congress with the socialists in 1948. He was active with the Socialist Party, but became increasingly involved with Vinoba Bhave's *bhoodan* (land-gift) and *sarvodaya* (welfare for all) movements and in 1954 he withdrew from party politics to devote himself to this work. He was the foremost protagonist for the creation of village-based, decentralized democracy in India and was prominent in efforts in the 1960s to improve Indian–Pakistani relations and to find a peaceful settlement to the Nagaland dispute.

NARCISSUS (d. AD 54), an ex-slave who became the wealthy and influential principal secretary of the Roman Emperor Claudius. In 48 he exposed Messalina's plot, but opposed Claudius' marriage to Agrippina the younger, and committed suicide when Nero became emperor.

NARESUAN (1555–1605), King of Siam (*reg.* 1590–1605), warrior king, who reconstituted the kingdom of Ayudhya after its capture by the Burmese in 1569. He was the eldest son of King Thammaracha, installed by the Burmese as king in 1569. Naresuan was taken as a hostage to Burma, feigned loyalty, and was allowed to return home and lead troops in his suzerain's assistance, but he turned against the Burmese

(1584) to assert Siam's and his father's independence. He and his brother led the Thai forces which resisted new Burmese invasions of Siam (1584–92). After succeeding his father as king, he ended the threat of invasion from Burma, defeated Cambodia, and brought Chiengmai under Thai suzerainty. In 1593 he even offered to assist China against Japan by sending a naval expedition. He was succeeded by his younger brother, Ekathotsarot.

NARIÑO, ANTONIO (1765–1822), Colombian patriot, who was arrested and exiled (1795) for circulating a Spanish translation of the French *Declaration of the Rights of Man and the Citizen*. He escaped, later returned to Colombia (1797), and was eventually pardoned by the government, only to be rearrested and sentenced to death for conspiracy in 1809. Political disturbances prevented his execution. He was freed and in 1811 elevated to the presidency of the new independent republic of Cundinamarca. In an effort to unite his countrymen against the Spanish he assumed dictatorial powers, but was defeated and captured in 1814. He was imprisoned in Spain (1814–20), escaped, and returned again to Colombia in 1820. Bolívar appointed him interim vice-president to preside over the constitutional convention at Cucutá. However, factional difficulties, mostly with Santander, soon led him to resign.

NARODNAYA VOLYA (People's Will), in Russia, populist revolutionary group formed (1879) after the splitting of Land and Liberty (*Zemlya i volya*). Its adherents believed in political revolution and seizure of the state as a means of establishing representative government and socialism. Under Zhelyabov and Perovskaya it concentrated on terrorism and was responsible for the assassination of Alexander II (1881).

NARRAGANSET INDIANS, American Algonquian tribe of New England, which formerly occupied most of Rhode Island. They were friendly to the whites at the outset, and helped Roger Williams to establish his colony (*c.* 1636), but then joined King Philip's War (1675) and were destroyed as a tribe. The survivors abandoned their lands and joined other tribes.

NARROW SEAS, SOVEREIGNTY OF, one of the major tenets of British naval strategy, from the mid-17th cent. onwards. The 'narrow seas' consist of the Irish Sea and the English Channel, especially the Straits of Dover.

NARSES (*fl.* 6th cent. AD), Byzantine eunuch and one of the few to attain high military rank. After the revolt of the Goths in Italy under Totila following the withdrawal of Belisarius to lead the imperial armies against Persia, he undertook what was to amount to the second reconquest of the peninsula in a decade. He fought a remarkable and successful campaign from his base at Ravenna, slew Totila, and defeated fresh hordes of Franks and other Germans invading from the north. By 554 Byzantine rule was firm over Italy from Sicily to the Alps.

NARVA, BATTLE OF (30 Nov. 1700), on the south bank of the Gulf of Finland in Esthonia. Charles XII of Sweden defeated Russian forces three times larger than his own in the Great Northern War. The battle encouraged Charles to enter Poland and Saxony, though his failure to consolidate his defeat of the Russians ultimately contributed to the battle of Poltava (1709), which ended his hopes of dominating northern Europe.

NARVAEZ, RAMON MARIA, Duke of Valencia (1799–1868), Spanish soldier and politician, who displaced Espartero as regent of Spain (1843), established a military dictatorship, and played a dominating role in Spanish politics. His rise to power illustrated the bankruptcy of the political situation in Spain. He headed the moderates, a group of oligarchs held together by fear of revolution, who wanted to safeguard the liberal constitution by a return to order. But Narvaez loved power for its own sake and maintained order by muzzling the press, using spies, and governing by decree. He made no contribution to the long-term stability of Spain.

NARVÁEZ EXPEDITION, Spanish colonial venture commissioned by Charles V. Panfilo de Narváez sailed with five vessels, 400 men, and 80 horses to found a Spanish colony in FL. The expedition, which landed near Tampa Bay (1528), was harassed by Indians and did not find the gold they sought. They constructed boats and set sail for Mexico, but all but Cabeza de Vaca and three others were lost at sea.

NASEBY, BATTLE OF (14 June 1645), decisive rout of Charles I's forces in the English Civil War at Naseby in Northamptonshire. The uncertain leadership of parliament's cause by the Earls of Essex and Manchester had produced military deadlock, so the New Model Army was formed with Fairfax as lord general and Cromwell in charge of the cavalry. It immediately located the king's army, defeated it, and captured everything but the royal cavalry, with which Charles fled.

NASH, JOHN (1752–1835), British architect, whose work epitomized the Regency style and changed the appearance of a considerable area of central London. Under the patronage of the Prince Regent, he planned Regent Street, Regent's Park, its adjacent terraces and canal, and the Royal Mews at Buckingham Palace (the frontage of which he redesigned). He also made alterations to the Royal Pavilion at Brighton and designed the Marble Arch.

NASH, SIR WALTER (1882–1968), NZ politician and Labour prime minister, who emigrated from England in 1909 and became secretary of the NZ Labour Party (1922–32). He entered parliament in 1929, and as minister of finance in the first Labour government (1935–49) introduced guaranteed prices (1936) and social security (1938). Labour returned to office in 1957 and Nash became prime minister. He was an able, orthodox financier and an administrator of phenomenal industry, who advocated an active, mediatory role for NZ in international affairs.

NASHVILLE, BATTLE OF (15–16 Dec. 1864), most complete Union victory in the American Civil War. After Sherman's invasion of GA, John B. Hood led 40,000 Confederates into TN to cut his lines of communication. Hood's much weakened army was nearly destroyed by a superior force under Gen. George H. Thomas.

NASHVILLE CONVENTION (3–12 June, 11–18 Nov. 1850) in US, meeting in TN of delegates from nine Southern US slave states to consolidate resistance against alleged Northern aggression. The convention advocated an extension of the Missouri Compromise line westward, denounced the 1850 Compromise, and called, unsuccessfully, for secession.

NASIR, AL-, Abbasid Caliph (*reg.* AD 1180–1225). Taking advantage of the discord existing amongst the Seljuks of Iraq, Al-Nasir sought, though without durable success, to restore some measure of power to the Abbasid Caliphate. He brought much of Iraq under his direct rule and then tried to extend his control into the western provinces of Persia—an endeavour which brought him into conflict with the Khwarazm Shah Takash (*reg.* 1172–1200) and his successor, Ala al-Din Muhammad (*reg.* 1200–20). Al-Nasir also attempted to strengthen his influence through his patronage of the futuwwa movement.

NASIR AL-DAWLA (d. AD 968), Hamdanid Amir of Mosul (*reg.* 929–67), who succeeded his father, Abu'l-Hayja, as head of the Hamdanid house. He held (942–3) the office of *amir al-umara* at Baghdad. Much of Al-Jazira (Mesopotamia) and northern Syria was now under his control. Attempts to extend his influence over Azerbayjan in 934 and 938 had led to no enduring result. He was later engaged in a long and unsuccessful conflict to avoid falling into dependence on the powerful Buyid regime established at Baghdad. In 967 he was deposed from the amirate of Mosul.

NASIR AL-DIN (1832–96), Qajar ruler of Iran (*reg.* 1848–96) in succession to his father, Muhammad Shah (*reg.* 1834–48). He failed to follow any consistent policy of reform in Iran, created a foreign debt (partly to finance his expensive foreign tours), and allowed British and Russian influence to increase. He was assassinated in 1896.

NASMYTH, JAMES (1808–90), Scottish mechanical engineer, who in 1839 invented and in 1842 patented the steam-hammer, which greatly increased the possibilities of large-scale forging without loss of precision. This machine was devised for making the driving shaft for the paddle-wheels of the iron-clad steamship *Great Britain*, being built by Isambard Kingdom Brunel (1806–59). However, these were discarded subsequently and replaced by screw-propellers. A variety of machine tools and machines, including steam locomotives after 1839, were made at Nasmyth's foundry at Patricroft.

NASSAU, JOHN, Count of (1535–1606), second son of William, Count of Nassau-Dillenburg, and younger brother of William of Orange, who succeeded to the family estates (1559), but later joined William in support of the Dutch revolt. Although a vigorous Calvinist, he became *stadtholder* of the predominantly Catholic province of Gelderland (1578–1580) and, as such, signed the Union of Utrecht (1579), but in 1580 he retired to Germany.

NASSAU, LOUIS, Count of (1538–74), third son of William, Count of Nassau-Dillenburg, and younger brother of William of Orange, who began his career as a cavalry officer and associated himself with the extreme confederates (1565) in the rebellion of the Netherlands against Spain. In 1566 he signed the Compromise of the nobles. He was summoned before the Council of Blood (Jan. 1568), and joined William in exile, but soon led an invasion of Groningen with a small band of men. After an initial success at Heiligerlee (April 1568) they were defeated by Alva's Spaniards at Jemmingen, whence Louis fled to Trier. In 1570 Nassau established a new centre of resistance at La Rochelle, and from there sailed to Flushing (April 1572), which he seized, and then attacked Mons. Plans for French aid being dashed by the St Bartholomew massacre, Louis held Mons against Alva's forces until late in 1572, and then withdrew to Germany. In 1573 he invaded Liège, taking St Trond, and in 1574 led another invasion. He was surprised by the Spaniards at Mook Heide (April 1574) and died in the battle, together with his youngest brother, Henry, and his cousin, Christopher of the Palatinate.

NASSAU AGREEMENT (Dec. 1962), on the provision of Polaris missiles to Britain by the US. The agreement had an important impact on Britain's application to join the European Economic Community. The need for a fresh agreement between Britain and the US arose from the decision of the US government to cancel the development of the Skybolt missile, it being more expensive than, and inferior to, Polaris. Macmillan's government attached importance to the possession of an 'independent' British deterrent and therefore wanted to negotiate a replacement for Skybolt, which it had been promised. President Kennedy's administration was concerned, however, about the proliferation of nuclear weapons. The agreement was a compromise, reached after Macmillan and Kennedy had conferred at Nassau in the Bahamas, by which the US would make Polaris missiles (without warheads) available for British submarines, provided that these submarines would be available for inclusion in a NATO multilateral force and would in all circumstances

be used for the international defence of the Western Alliance, 'except where Her Majesty's Government may decide that supreme national interests are at stake'.

The negotiations came in the middle of the Brussels talks that followed Britain's application to join the Common Market. They appear to have confirmed De Gaulle in his suspicion of the Anglo-American 'special relationship'. Polaris missiles were made available to France as well as to Britain, but on the same terms, which De Gaulle regarded as subordinating France (or Britain) to the US. The Common Market talks were broken off the following month (Jan. 1963) as the result of a French veto.   WK

NASSAU-DILLENBERG, HENRY OF (1483–1558), Burgundian nobleman, who was the elder son of John, Count of Nassau-Dillenberg and close friend of Charles, Duke of Burgundy, later the Emperor Charles V. In 1504 he inherited the seneschalcy of Brabant from his uncle, Englebert, and from his father he acquired the extensive family lands in Flanders, Brabant, Luxembourg, Franche-Comté, and Dauphiné, becoming also *stadtholder* of Holland, Zeeland, and Friesland (1515). By the treaty of Paris (1515), as a widower at 32 years of age, he married Claudine de Châlons, heiress to the sovereign principality of Orange, and their son, René, later inherited the title of Count of Nassau and Prince of Orange. By replacing Chièvres as first chamberlain to Charles V, Henry became the most important member of Charles's household. He accompanied the king to Spain and was appointed head of a new Spanish council of finance (1523) and a member of the council of state. He also served him as a diplomat and soldier. On the death of René at St Dizier (1544), the Orange inheritance passed to his cousin, William, later leader of the Dutch Revolt.

NASSER (GAMAL ABD AL-NASIR) (1918–70), Egyptian soldier and political leader, who distinguished himself during the Palestine War (1948) in the battle of Faluja. His long-standing conviction of the necessity of revolutionary changes in Egypt was increased by the war and he became the leader of a group called the Free Officers, which carried out the July 22–3 1952 revolution. He replaced Gen. Muhammad Neguib as prime minister (1954) and became president of the Egyptian Republic (1956) and of the United Arab Republic (1958). His domination of Egyptian politics until his death was complete and his prestige unrivalled within the Arab world.

NASSERISM, Western term used to denote first the policies of Egypt (the United Arab Republic) under President Abd Al-Nasir, and second, a generalized movement among Arabs, characterized by pragmatism and advocating a union, under Egyptian leadership, of Arab countries which have previously undergone a political and social revolution. Within Egypt, Nasserism aimed first at the achievement of political independence by eliminating foreign control. This was achieved by the agreement to end the British occupation of the Suez Canal Zone (1954) and the nationalization of the Suez Canal Co. (1956) and other foreign enterprises. Social revolution required the elimination of the power of former dominant groups in Egypt especially by land reform (holdings limited to 200 feddans, 1952; 100 feddans, 1961), nationalization, steeply graduated taxation, and a great expansion of social services, particularly health and education. In 1960–1 and after, a very extensive system of close state control over all aspects of national life was established. Political life had been brought under control at an early date but economic activities now followed suit and a major programme of centrally planned industrialization was launched. The National Charter (1962) set out the principles and directions of Egyptian policy. In foreign affairs Egyptian policy was characterized by neutralism (Nasser played an important role in the 1955 Bandung conference), opposition to Western influence in the Middle East (as exemplified particularly by the Baghdad pact, which induced Egypt after 1955 to lean more heavily upon the USSR), and deep involvement in the Arab world. Her participation in the 1948 Palestine War had already drawn Egypt closer into Arab affairs but it was the Suez War (1956) which made Nasser the leading statesman of the Arab world. With Syria he formed the UAR (1958) although Syria subsequently withdrew (1961) and Egypt became involved in the Yemen War (1962–7). Egypt also provided support for Arab revolutionaries in North Africa and other parts of the Arab world, both against western domination and against so-called reactionary Arab regimes. Egypt was forced to modify the last policy after her June 1967 defeat.

A. Abdel Malik, *Egypt. Military Society* (New York, 1968). P. Mansfield, *Nasser's Egypt* (London, 1965).   MEY

NAST, THOMAS (1840–1902), German-born US political cartoonist, who joined *Harper's Weekly* (1862) and over the next 24 years developed the cartoon as an influential political weapon. During the Civil War Lincoln described him as 'our best recruiting sergeant', and after 1865 he supported liberal causes and helped to overthrow the political machine of William Marcy Tweed (1872). He established the donkey and the elephant as respective symbols of the Democratic and Republican parties.

NASTASEN (*reg. c.* 335–310 BC), King of Kush, who lived at Meroe in southern Kush and was the last king to be buried at Nuri near Napata in northern Kush.

NASUTION, ABDUL HARIS (1918–), Indonesian soldier, of Batak origin, who served with distinction in the Indonesian revolution (1945–9) and later became army chief of staff. He was forcibly retired after the abortive coup of 17 Oct. 1952. In 1955 he returned to office, restored the authority of the army central command, and suppressed the Indonesian (PRRI) revolt of 1958. In 1962 he became commander of the armed forces. Under his leadership the army became the major opponent of the communists during the period of 'Guided Democracy'. After the 1965 coup Sukarno removed him from office; Suharto appointed him to the post of chairman of the People's Consultative Assembly, an office of dignity rather than influence.

NATAL, one of the four provinces of the republic of South Africa, situated on the south-east coast. At the beginning of the 19th cent. it was the homeland of Bantu-speaking Iron Age farmers known as the Nguni, who had largely absorbed the earlier hunter–gatherer population.

By the 1820s, when British traders settled at Port Natal, the Nguni chiefdoms had been incorporated by the Zulu empire. The traders were followed by Afrikaans-speaking Voortrekkers from the Cape, who defeated the Zulu, and created a republic in Natal. In 1843 the territory between the Tugela and the Umzimkulu was annexed by the British, and most of the trekkers moved on to the Highveld, to be replaced by predominantly British settlers. For most of the 19th cent. the extremely small settler population was engaged in a search for suitable export crops. Sugar and tea proved the most profitable, and from 1860 Indian indentured labour was imported to work the plantations.

From the outset, the British settlers were determined to control the multi-ethnic polity, and in 1893 they obtained self-government in which the non-white majority had no political rights. In 1897 Zululand was annexed to Natal, which was invaded during the Anglo-Boer War (1899–1902), and later received additional territory from the Transvaal. In 1910, after some hesitation, Natal, already long dependent on the Transvaal economically, became part of the Union of South Africa.

NATCHEZ INDIANS, American tribe first encountered by the French (1682) near Natchez, MS. They fought three wars with the French, in the last of which (1792) they were destroyed as a tribe. The French sold some of the Natchez into slavery, and scattered bands joined other tribes, including the Creeks, Cherokees, and Chickasaws.

NATCHITOCHES, French trading post in LA, established by Louis Juchereau de St Denis (1713), which served as a gateway for explorers, traders, and colonists throughout the 18th and 19th cents until the main channel of the Red River shifted (1850).

NATION, CARRY AMELIA MOORE (1846–1911), US temperance leader, whose enthusiasm for the cause led to her smashing up saloons with a hatchet, first used in Wichita, KS, in 1900. Her numerous fines for breach of the peace were paid for by the sale of souvenir hatchets, lecture tours, and stage appearances.

NATION, THE (1865–) in the US, weekly magazine of current affairs, literature, and the arts. Under its founder and first editor, Edwin L. Godkin (1831–1902), it established an impressive reputation for rigorous criticism and support for reform movements. This was sustained by later editors, particularly by Oswald G. Villard during the 1920s.

NATIONAL AERONAUTICS AND SPACE ADMINISTRATION (1958–), US government agency set up by Congress to pursue the peaceful and non-military exploration of space. NASA allocates contracts to the aerospace industry for both space and aeronautical projects and controls five research centres, three space-flight development centres, and three rocket-launching areas.

NATIONAL ASSEMBLY (1789), the Third Estate of the French estates general, who proclaimed themselves the National Assembly on 17 June, inviting the nobility and clergy, who comprised the other two estates, to join them. In doing so the middle class changed the medieval meeting of estates into a national representative assembly, in which their numerical superiority ensured their control. To stress their intention of giving France a constitution, the assembly changed their name again almost immediately (July) to the Constituent Assembly.

NATIONAL ASSOCIATION FOR THE ADVANCEMENT OF COLORED PEOPLE, in US, organization seeking equality for Negroes. The NAACP, originating in a period of acute racial tension (1909) signified a profound shift in American Negro aims and leadership. Specifically rejecting the conservative social thought of the dominant Negro spokesman, Booker T. Washington, a coalition of black 'radicals' and white liberal 'progressives' and socialists formed the NAACP with the declared aim of pressing for Negro constitutional rights through legislative and legal action. Its ultimate goals were the ending of racial segregation and discrimination, and it advocated increased industrial opportunities for Negroes and protection against lynching.

The inter-racial character of the NAACP ensured it a wider audience and greater financial support than could have been secured by an all-Negro organization. Apart from W. E. B. Du Bois, editor of its journal, *The Crisis*, and director of research, the first senior officials of the NAACP were whites. In 1921, James Weldon Johnson, the Negro writer, became executive secretary, and the NAACP came to be staffed largely by blacks.

Regarded as radical at its inception, the NAACP dominated the Negro protest movement up to the 1950s, drawing its support from the 'black bourgeoisie' of American cities. In 1964 it had a membership of 400,000 in 1600 branches or 'chapters' across the US. The NAACP effectively utilizes the structure of the Negro church, with many clergymen, particularly in the South, acting as branch presidents.

Its most characteristic activity has been litigation to secure enforcement of the 14th and 15th Amendments, and an early victory was secured when the Supreme Court over-ruled a discriminatory voting clause in the OK state constitution (*Guinn v. US*, 238 US 347, 1915). In 1952, to test the validity of segregated high schools, the NAACP carried five test cases to the Supreme Court. NAACP lawyers argued that states which ratified the 14th Amendment had understood it to preclude segregation in public schools. In accepting this interpretation, the court reversed its 'separate but equal' decision of 1896, ruling that 'in the field of public education the doctrine of "separate but equal" has no place. Separate educational facilities are inherently unequal' (*Brown v. Board of Education of Topeka*, 347 US 483, 1954).

Although attacked for being too dependent on white support, too elitist in its membership, too conservative in its strategy, and lacking in racial pride, the NAACP made the largest single contribution to Negro advancement. With increasing direct action protest by other Negro organizations in the 1960s the NAACP, despite internal dissension, supported 'sit-ins', marches, and boycotts, often paying bail and court costs for those arrested. In a literal and symbolic sense, the NAACP remains the 'custodian of the civil rights movement' in America.

C. F. Kellogg, *NAACP: a history of the National Association for the Advancement of Colored People*, vol. 1, 1909–20 (Baltimore, 1967).

L. Hughes, *Fight for Freedom: the story of the NAACP* (New York, 1962).   JW

NATIONAL CONGRESS OF BRITISH WEST AFRICA, organization founded (1928) to embrace educated Africans in all the British West African colonies. The inaugural conference was held at Accra in March 1920 and subsequent conferences in Sierra Leone (1923), Gambia (1925), and Nigeria (1929). Discussions at these conferences centred on judicial and constitutional reforms, higher education, Africanization of the civil service, etc. The principle of self-determination was often invoked and some of the leaders of the Congress even envisaged the political union of the four colonies. Though declining after Casely Hayford's death in 1930, the Congress had helped the awakening of nationalism in West Africa.

NATIONAL COUNCIL OF LABOUR in Britain, originally created before the First World War as the Joint Board on which sat an equal number of representatives of the Trades Union Congress, the General Federation of Trades Unions, and the Labour Party. The board was designed to co-ordinate and arbitrate in the activities of the Labour movement.

In 1922 the board was reorganized as the National Joint Council, having an equal number of representatives from the Trades Union Congress, the Parliamentary Labour Party, and the National Executive of the Labour Party, and was required to supervise the new joint departments of the Labour Party and the Trades Union Congress.

In 1934 the Joint Council was itself reorganized as the National Council of Labour and, as a mark of the now almost predominant influence of the unions in Labour politics, the Trades Union Congress was given as many representatives on the council as the two party bodies combined.

NATIONAL COUNCIL OF NIGERIA AND THE CAMEROONS (known after 1961 as the National Council of Nigerian Citizens), founded in 1944. Its first president was Herbert Macaulay, who was succeeded by Nnamdi Azikiwe (1946). During the 1940s and 1950s it preferred a unitary form of government to regionalism. From the 1950s onwards it allied itself with such minority parties as the Northern Elements Progressive Union (NEPU) to contest regional and federal elections. The basis of this coalition was broadened, during the controversial 1964 federal election, to include its former principal southern rival, the Action Group. The resultant coalition, the United Progressive Grand Alliance, unsuccessfully protested against the 1964 election results. However, between 1959 and 1964 the NCNC had been in coalition with the Northern People's Congress (NPC) in control of the Federal government of Nigeria.

NATIONAL DEBT in Britain, public debt of the central government of a state secured on the national revenue. It is normally divided into the 'funded debt', *ie*, the proportion which is converted into bonds and annuities, and the 'floating debt', *ie*, short-term debts sooner or later repaid from taxation. In England by the 1690s there was a mass of short-term debts and a growing proportion of long-term debts which came to be recognized as virtual permanent liabilities on which interest was paid from taxation. The national debt assumed a permanent form in 1692, and since 1750 has been managed by the Bank of England.

NATIONAL DEBT COMMISSIONERS (1786) in Britain, independent public servants appointed by the Younger Pitt to manage the sinking fund. Pitt was anxious to prove the efficiency of his financial and administrative reforms by reducing the national debt, especially after the forecast by a parliamentary committee that the current surplus of £1 million would continue. He arranged for this sum to be paid to the commissioners annually for the purchase of government stock. By reinvesting the interest they were expected to produce an annual income of £4 million from each £1 million within 28 years for the purpose of debt redemption. The plan, based largely on the ideas of Dr Richard Price, was feasible in times of peace, though the surplus was only achieved by unrealistically low naval estimates. But Pitt brought it into ridicule by persisting with annual payments to the commissioners during the Napoleonic wars even though such payments could only be raised by further loans at unfavourable rates of interest.

NATIONAL DEFENSE EDUCATION ACT (1958) in US, legislation providing federal funds to improve the teaching of mathematics, science, and foreign languages at all levels in the educational system. In addition to establishing state and institutional grants and loans, the act established a number of NDEA fellowships for graduate study, and represented federal acceptance of educational responsibilities on a scale previously unknown, largely because of a sense of national crisis resulting from the Soviet success in launching Sputnik I (1957).

NATIONAL DEMOCRATIC UNION (UDN) in Brazil, central political prty, founded in 1945. The UDN candidate for president, Jânio da Silva Quadros, was elected in 1960, but soon resigned. After this the UDN became less prominent, and like all Brazilian political parties suffered at the hands of the military.

NATIONAL EDUCATION LEAGUE in Britain, founded in Birmingham in 1869 by Joseph Chamberlain and others to campaign for free, compulsory, and non-sectarian elementary education. It opposed some aspects of the 1870 Education Act and gave Chamberlain a popular platform within the Liberal Party.

NATIONAL GALLERY (1824), in London, England, opened, under treasury control, in Pall Mall, and removed to Trafalgar Square in 1838. It acquired important paintings through gifts, bequests, and purchases, *eg*, of the Angerstein collection.

NATIONAL GOVERNMENT (1931) in Britain, coalition of the leaders of the Labour, Conservative, and Liberal parties formed on 24 Aug. 1931. Throughout July and Aug. 1931 there was a heavy run on the gold balances held by the Bank of England as a consequence both of the failure of two important central European banks, and the publication of an apparently independent report in Britain—the May report—predicting a large budgetary deficit. The resulting loss of confidence in London as a monetary centre was such that the Labour government felt obliged to turn to New York and Paris for financial assistance. This assistance, it appeared, would not be forthcoming unless heavy cuts were made in expenditure. Though the cabinet agreed to most of these, a large minority of ministers refused to accept cuts in unemployment benefits and on 23 Aug. 1931 the government broke up.

The prime minister, Ramsay MacDonald, thereupon formed a coalition government with the Conservative and Liberal leaders—on the grounds that only such a ministry could restore international confidence in London and implement distasteful budgetary cuts. The Conservative and Liberal parties adhered to the government but the vast bulk of the Labour Party went into formal opposition and MacDonald and the other Labour ministers who had joined him were expelled from their party.

In Oct. 1931, though it had not maintained the gold standard, the National government won an overwhelming electoral victory, though the real victory had gone to the Conservatives. In 1932 most of the Liberals withdrew and thereafter it remained a Conservative government in all but name. A general election was fought in 1935. Although, in theory, it sought a mandate for rearmament, the issues of the election campaign were largely domestic and economic. The National government was returned and, because of the Second World War, remained in power until 1945.

NATIONAL GUARD (1789) in Paris, civic militia drawn from the middle class, which was recruited by the municipal authorities in July to protect property from popular disturbances as well as the Revolution from the forces of reaction.

NATIONAL INDIAN ASSOCIATION in US, group formed in Philadelphia (1879), to improve conditions of the American Indians. It was the first organization to demand citizenship and lands in severalty for the Indians.

NATIONAL INDUSTRIAL RECOVERY ACT (1933) in the US, legislation that formed part of President F. D. Roosevelt's early New Deal programme. The act, designed to help economic recovery, temporarily suspended the anti-trust laws and provided for the drafting of legally enforceable codes of fair competition in an attempt to raise prices and stabilize production. Section 7(a) of the NIRA, hailed by the unions as labour's charter, guaranteed labour's right to 'organize and bargain collectively through representatives of their own choosing', and a National Labor Board under Senator Robert F. Wagner was established (1933) to enforce the labour provisions. Gen. Hugh S. Johnson (1882–1942) was appointed head of the national recovery administration, and at first had considerable success in mobilizing voluntary support for the codes. One of his successful publicity devices was the sign of the Blue Eagle, a symbol displayed by establishments participating in the codes, which was later used by opponents of the administration as an example of the allegedly fascist tendencies of Roosevelt. Title II of the NIRA established a Public Works Administration to stimulate construction projects and provide work relief. The act was declared unconstitutional by the US Supreme Court in *Schechter v. US* (1935).

NATIONAL LABOR RELATIONS ACT (1935), in the US, legislation during the New Deal, which greatly strengthened the role of organized labour. The act reasserted the right of labour to bargain collectively through representatives of their own choosing, and established a National Labor Relations Board to supervise elections and restrain employers from 'unfair labor practices' such as the dismissal of workers for union membership. It was often known as the Wagner Act, after its sponsor, Senator Robert F. Wagner of NY, who fought for the bill against the initial disapproval of the administration, and was upheld by the US Supreme Court in *National Labor Relations Board v. Jones and Laughlin Steel Corp.* (1937).

NATIONAL LABOR UNION (1866–72) in US, first attempt to bring together organized labour and unskilled workers in a national organization. Founded in Baltimore, and led by William Sylvis and Richard F. Trevellick, it sought to establish co-operatives and engaged in direct political action to achieve its aims, particularly the eight-hour working day.

The union collapsed after the failure of its National Labor Reform Party in the presidential election of 1872.

NATIONAL LABOUR PARTY, in Britain, consisted of those few Labour members who supported Ramsay MacDonald when he formed the National government following the monetary crisis of 1931. It served as a convenient label for MacDonald, Snowden, and Thomas, and the Labour men who supported their new government, when they fought the 1931 election at the head of the Conservative-dominated National government. It was never an independent political party, had no programme or ideology of its own, and became increasingly indistinguishable from the Conservative Party. Of its 20 candidates 13 were returned in 1931, having been expelled from the Labour Party with MacDonald. In the 1935 election its members were again treated as supporters by the National government, and not opposed by Conservatives in the 20 seats they contested. Eight were returned.

The last vestige of a *raison d'être* for the National Labour Party disappeared when MacDonald was succeeded as prime minister by Baldwin. In the next election, that of 1945, none of the former 'National Labour' members was returned.

NATIONAL LIBERAL FEDERATION in Britain, originated in 1877 at Birmingham after Joseph Chamberlain and Francis Schnadhorst persuaded 83 Liberal constituency associations of the advantages of federation. More soon joined. Though it was ostensibly intended to create a democratic forum of Liberal opinion, the NLF enabled many associations to rebuild on the Birmingham 'caucus' model. Here, the electoral ward was the basic organizational unit, and, despite appearances, relatively few activists controlled the machine, which proved highly successful in municipal and parliamentary elections. The NLF, approved by Gladstone, strengthened Liberalism's Radical element and contributed significantly to the Liberal victory in 1880.

NATIONAL LIBERAL FEDERATION OF INDIA. After meeting first (Nov. 1918) as the All-India Moderates Conference, it took this title in 1920. The Liberals feared that their constitutional activities would be circumscribed within the increasingly radical congress, but while their secession enabled them to act freely, it deprived them of the organizational support necessary for success in the popularly elected legislatures from 1920 onwards. There were local and provincial liberal associations as well as the NLF, but these were conference organizations rather than political parties. The last session of the NLF was held in 1945, after which its members and ideas were absorbed by other groups, especially the Congress.

Congress boycott (1920) made it possible for the Liberals to enter the legislatures and accept ministerial positions (1921–3), but they found that without sufficient party backing they were dependent upon official support, and the result was increasing frustration. When Congress contested elections (1923, 1926, 1937, 1946), the Liberals were routed. After 1923, therefore, the Liberals were concerned mainly in the discussions to resolve basic social and political problems, so that political advance could be made, or as intermediaries in the negotiations between Congress and the British governments. The Nehru report (1928), the Round Table Conferences (1930–2), and the Non-Party or Sapru report (1945) embodied their plans. These were important in the construction of the political institutions created after 1930, but they did little to bring about the transfer of power itself.

NATIONAL LIBERAL PARTY in Britain, group of 23 Liberal MPs, led by Sir John Simon, who split off from the official Liberal Party in Oct. 1931 to form the Liberal National Group. This title was changed to National Liberal in 1948. Of the 41 Liberal National candidates in 1931, 35 were elected, although none was opposed by official Liberal candidates. In 1932, following the Ottawa Agreements, the Liberals under Samuel left the National government, but the Liberal Nationals remained. Of the 44 candidates in 1935, none faced Conservative opponents and, except in Denbigh, were not opposed by Liberals. Sir John Simon was succeeded as leader of the party in December 1940 by Ernest Brown. Only 13 out of 51 candidates were elected in 1945, and Brown lost his seat. The Woolton–Teviot agreement of May 1947 urged the establishment of combined Conservative and Liberal National constituency associations. This took place, and since then the National Liberals have grown increasingly indistinguishable from the Conservatives. In the 1966 election, only two MPs were elected as 'Conservative and National Liberal'; in addition, two MPs elected as 'Conservatives' were adopted by joint associations. At the general election of 1970 the label 'National Liberal' was not used.

NATIONAL LIBERATION MOVEMENT in Ghana, Ashanti-based political party founded by dissident members of the Convention People's Party in 1954. It joined other parties in 1957 to form the opposition United Party.

NATIONAL PARTY in NZ, formed in 1936 by opposition members, on a platform of 'free enterprise' and resistance to Labour's policy of increased state activity. Little ground was gained under Adam Hamilton (1936–40), but under H. E. Holland (1940–57) the party won a majority of 46 seats in 1949. Holland's promise to 'make the pound go further' rebounded in the 1950s, years of inflation and uncertain affluence. Though the party was briefly ousted by Labour (1957–60), it held office throughout the 1960s under K. J. Holyoake, under whom it was committed to welfare policies and had become a 'middle of the road' party. Though the predominant post-1945 party, its electoral support (1949–69) averaged about 46 per cent.

NATIONAL PARTY of South Africa, formed in 1913 after Gen. Hertzog had been forced out of the South African Party because of his 'two-stream' policy for English and Afrikaans-speaking South Africans. The Nationalists rapidly gained in strength, especially after the First World War. In 1924 they came into power as part of a coalition with the predominantly English-speaking Labour Party, with the tacit understanding that the Nationalists would drop their plans for a republic if the Labour Party dropped its socialist demands. By 1929 the Nationalists were returned to power on their own, although in 1933, largely as a result of the world economic crisis, Hertzog formed a coalition with Smuts's South African Party.

When the two parties joined together in 1935 as the United Party, Dr D. F. Malan and 18 followers broke away and formed the Purified Nationalist Party, reverting to the call for Afrikaner unity and separation from English-speaking South Africans. They made little headway, however, until 1939, when the Nationalists were reunified as a result of a split in the cabinet over the question of South Africa's participation in the Second World War.

Though the Nationalists were torn by dissensions during the war, and their political authority was challenged by extra-parliamentary bodies such as the Ossewa Brandwag and the Greyshirts, they increased their representation in parliament. During this period the rural base of the Nationalists had been changing as a result of the continued urbanization of Afrikaners in the preceding 20 years, and the Purified Nationalists and Broederbond built up a network of institutions to bolster their economic position. In 1948 the Nationalists were returned to parliament by the white electorate on a minority of votes though with a majority of seats, the result of an electoral system weighted in favour of rural constituencies. After 1948 they consolidated their position and at each subsequent election had an increased majority. This has been partly the result of demographic factors and skilful propaganda and partly because of deliberate manipulation of the electoral machinery. Despite a split in their ranks, there seemed in 1970 little possibility of their being dislodged by constitutional means.

After 1948 they also vastly increased the scope, range, and rigidity of discriminatory policies directed against the powerless and subordinated non-white groups in the country, despite world-wide criticism which grew in intensity in 1968–70.   SM

NATIONAL PEASANT PARTY in Rumania, was formed by the fusion of the National Party with the Peasant Party. The National Party began in the 1870s as the Rumanian National Party of Transylvania and Hungary. Originally the champion of the Rumanian peasant against the Hungarian landlord, it came to represent the bourgeoisie and professional classes from whom its leadership was drawn. Iuliu Maniu and Alexandru Vaida-Voevod were the party's principal spokesmen. The party was established in the Rumanian kingdom in the last stages of the First World War by Ion Mihalache, Nicolae Lupu, and Constantin Stere. It was a radical party identified wholly with the peasantry and concerned chiefly with the promulgation of agrarian reform. The two parties formed a coalition in 1919–20 after the ruling Liberals had been rejected at the polls. The two parties differed in their attitude to the Liberals, though both opposed them. The National Party was opposed to the centralist policy of the Liberal Party and strove to secure autonomy for the annexed provinces. The Peasant Party regarded the Liberals as spokesmen for the landlord class, whose power it sought to break through agrarian reform. Talk of unifying the two parties was rife in the early 1920s and some efforts were made, especially in 1924, but the king obstructed the proposed fusion. The National Peasant Party was finally formed in 1926. Although it was in some ways an uneasy marriage, the personalities of Maniu, the party president, and Mihalache, the vice-president, kept the party together through the initial stages of union. The National Peasants won an electoral victory in 1928 and Maniu formed a government. The *leu* was stabilized, foreign capital was attracted to Rumania, and social reform was undertaken. But the opposition sustained a virulent campaign, stressing various scandals which were part and parcel of Rumanian politics under all governments and charging the government with mishandling the economy in the midst of the Depression. The National Peasants fell from power, however, not because of the strength of the opposition, but because of internal dissensions. There was a considerable desire within the party to bring King Carol back to Rumania and end the regency. After protracted negotiations Carol returned, but he broke his promise to Maniu and continued to live with his mistress, Mme Lupescu. Maniu resigned and political chaos followed. The National Peasant government stayed in office for a short time, then was replaced, and in 1932 Vaida-Voevod formed a new National Peasant government. He was the leader of an increasingly nationalistic section of the party which was becoming steadily dissociated from the main body, and particularly from its peasant faction. During his periods as prime minister (June–Oct. 1932, Jan.–Nov. 1933) he associated himself with the fascist Iron Guard and collaborated with the king at the party's expense. In 1934 the party split, Vaida-Voevod setting up a nationalist and quasi-fascist group outside it. The National Peasants were weak in opposition despite Mihalache's attempts to invigorate the party. But during the Second World War, when the other parties were discredited by close association with the military dictatorship, the National Peasant Party revived its fortunes. Despite Maniu's non-aggression pact with the Iron Guard (1937) and endorsement of Antonescu's foreign policy (1940–1), the party formed the chief opposition to the regime in 1943–4. Maniu persuaded the king to oust Antonescu in Sept. 1944, emerging as the most popular figure in the early post-war period, and after became the focus for opposition to the communists. But in 1946–7, after a tense period of bogus co-operation, the communists launched a full-scale assault on the National Peasants. The party was eliminated by the arrest and trial of its leaders in 1947.   JMK

NATIONAL PEOPLE'S PARTY in Germany, Deutsch-nationale Volkspartei (DNVP), ultra-conservative political party in the Weimar republic, founded in Nov. 1918, which was intended as a rallying-point for a conservatism on the defensive. It had heterogeneous membership—moderate and extreme conservatives, Christian Socialists, anti-Semites, Pan-Germans, and renegade Catholic Centrists and National Liberals, and it soon split into two factions: those on the one hand who demanded complete negativism towards the politics of the republic and an active effort to overthrow the existing state; and, on the other, a more moderate wing, which, while theoretically opposing the new state, was prepared to be pragmatic on certain issues.

Growing disillusionment with the republic brought the DNVP steady gains (44 seats in 1919, 71 in 1920, 95 in May 1924). When, in Dec. 1924, it became the second largest party in the Reichstag with 103 seats, its leaders, Oskar Hergt and Count Kuno von Westrap, took it into coalition governments with the People's Party and Centre (1925, 1927). On both occasions the party spokesmen agreed to respect the constitution and accept the basic purpose and methods of Stresemann's foreign policy. The apparent ascendancy of the party moderates was undermined, however, in 1928 by a sharp electoral reverse. The loss of 30 seats led to mutual recriminations by both wings of the party, to the election of Alfred Hugenberg as chairman (Oct. 1928), and to a policy of complete opposition to the republic. Hugenberg aspired to lead a united 'national opposition' comprising all anti-republican groupings on the right. He instigated (1929) a referendum against the Young Plan on reparations, sought and won the co-operation of Hitler, and through this alliance bestowed on him a political respectability which he could not otherwise have achieved so quickly.

The DNVP's unequivocal shift to the extreme right drove out the moderates. By July 1930 more than half of the deputies elected in 1928 had left the party and joined or founded small splinter parties. Despite electoral setbacks—a decline of 41 seats in 1930 and 37 in July 1932—Hugenberg's grip over the party was actually tightened by the moderates' departure. At its 1931 conference the DNVP adopted many of the trappings of a fascist party, calling itself the 'Hugenberg movement', accepting the 'leader principle', and forming an organization of 'toughs' (*Kampfstaffeln*). After a slight recovery in the Nov. 1932 elections (52 seats), Hugenberg agreed in Jan. 1933 to join a coalition with Hitler as chancellor. In the March 1933 elections the DNVP received 8 per cent of the vote (52 seats) and allowed Hitler, in view of the NSDAP's 43 per cent, to proclaim the victory of an absolute majority for the government of 'national revolution'. After voting for the enabling law, the DNVP disintegrated; many members, and the entire regional organization of Braunschweig, unable to see any significant differences with the NSDAP, went over to the Nazis. On 27 June 1933 the executive decided to dissolve the party. Hugenberg wished to preserve it, but this time the leader lacked followers.   ME

NATIONAL POLITICAL UNION in Britain, formed in 1831 on the prorogation of parliament by the radicals of the middle class to unite all political unions of the kingdom into one union. Its aim was to support the king and his ministers against the faction preventing parliamentary reform. The NPU organized a form of political strike by refusing to pay taxes, thus encouraging the Whigs and ending Tory hopes of passing a modified Reform Bill. The National Union of the Working Classes, which demanded manhood suffrage and fundamental economic reform, threw its meetings into confusion, with the result that all political associations not sanctioned by the government were banned.

NATIONAL REFORM UNION in Britain, formed in 1864 and led by Manchester middle-class radicals, demanded the ballot, redistribution of seats, and enfranchisement of men liable to pay poor rates. After 1867 it sought reform of the county franchise and land laws, Church disestablishment in England and Scotland, and a national and a secular education system.

NATIONAL REVOLUTIONARY MOVEMENT (MNR) in Bolivia, major radical political party which played a large part in national politics in that country after the 1940s. It was organized by diverse civilian and military groups which opposed the old elites who had brought the country into the disastrous Chaco War. Its early emphasis was on opposition to the three great tin mining companies, Patiño, Hochschild, and Aramayo, known popularly as 'la rosca' or 'the screw', which the MNR claimed 'owned' the country and ran it for their own benefit.

During the military regime of Gualberto Villarroel (1943–1946), MNR members obtained government positions, but after the violent overthrow of Villarroel most of the party's leaders fled into exile. An MNR revolt failed in 1949 after capturing some of the largest Bolivian cities, but the exiled party leader, Victor Paz Estenssoro, emerged from the presidential elections of 1951 with a surprising majority, in spite of his absence from the country. When the government attempted to annul the elections, the MNR seized power by means of a popular uprising (1952), and Paz became president of Bolivia.

Led by Paz, Hernán Siles Suazo, Juan Lechín Oquendo, and Walter Guevara Arce, the MNR government nationalized the tin mines, began a sweeping land reform, gave the vote to illiterates (which meant, in effect, the Indian rural majority of the country), and attempted to diversify the economy.

After 1960 factionalism rent the party and in 1964 it was overthrown by a military *coup d'état* led by René Barrientos Ortuño. Thereafter MNR leaders explored means of resolving their differences as a prelude to regaining power. The party's main opponent in 1970 was the resurgent Bolivian army.   MJM

NATIONAL SCHOOLS in England gave elementary instruction according with the principles of the established Church of England. They were run on the monitorial system under the auspices of the National Society for the Education of the Poor (1811). After 1833 they received a grant from the central government and after 1870 from rates administered by school boards. The National Society still (1970) exists and has, as its major concern, the role of the Church of England in the training of teachers and in the work of church schools.

NATIONAL SECURITY COUNCIL in US, advisory council established by the National Security Act (1947) to help the president in co-ordinating policies affecting national security. Apart from its advisory function, it directs the Central Intelligence Agency.

NATIONAL SOCIALIST GERMAN WORKERS' PARTY, extreme right-wing party appealing mainly to farmers, the urban middle classes, and ex-servicemen in Germany. It was founded in Jan. 1919 in Munich by Anton Drexler as the DAP (German Workers' Party) and in Sept. Adolf Hitler became a member. On 24 Feb. 1920 the party's 25-point programme was formulated and in Aug. its name was altered to the NSDAP (National Sozialistische Deutsche Arbeiter Partei). In June 1921 Hitler imposed his leadership on his more conservative colleagues; he then set out to create a mass movement, while avoiding alliances with similar groups in north Germany and Austria which would weaken his own position.

After the unsuccessful Munich putsch of Nov. 1923 the NSDAP was banned. During Hitler's imprisonment its disguised remnants were entrusted jointly to Röhm and Rosenberg. After his release Hitler was faced with a number of tasks: the assertion of his own supremacy and that of the Munich headquarters; the establishment of the 25 points as an unalterable doctrine; the defeat of socialist-inclined factions in north Germany; and the imposition of the policy of obtaining power legally against those in the SA (Sturm-abteilungen) who preferred to organize themselves for civil war. All this was successfully achieved. After its refoundation in Feb. 1925, the party grew steadily. Efforts were made to attract rural support, and from 1927, annual rallies were held in Nuremberg.

In 1925 there were 27,000 party members; 176,000 in 1929; 806,000 in 1931; and 3,900,000 in 1933, after Hitler had become chancellor. After 1935 membership was possible only through the Hitler Youth (Hitler Jugend). With the onset of the depression electoral support also increased, *eg*, 12 Reichstag seats in 1928, 107 in 1930, and 230 in 1932. Hitler won 13·42 million votes in the presidential election of April 1932. At no time, however, did the NSDAP win an absolute majority: the 288 seats won in March 1933 still had to be combined with the 52 won by Hitler's Conservative allies.

From July 1933 the NSDAP was the only legal political party in Germany, and in Dec. the 'Law for securing the unity of party and state' declared it to be the 'sole bearer of the will of the German Nation'. The party's organization, still based in Munich, consisted of a Deputy *Führer* (Rudolf Hess), a Party chancellery, headed by Martin Bormann, and 20 *Reichsleiter*. The local organization was divided into provinces (*Gaue*), areas (*Kreise*), branches (*Ortsgruppen*), and cells. The most important auxiliary organizations included the SA, SS (Schutzstaffel), and Hitler Youth. Other 'affiliated' organizations, *eg*, the Labour Front and the multitude of corporate bodies, were part of the apparatus designed to exercise total control of German life, but did not carry automatic membership of the party. Relations between party and state, and between different party organizations, were strongly influenced by the energy and ambitions of the personalities involved. The NSDAP was banned in 1945 and its revival made illegal by the fundamental law of the German Federal Republic.   RJVL

NATIONAL SOCIETY FOR THE EDUCATION OF THE POOR

in England, founded in 1811 to provide instruction in accordance with the principles of the established Church of England by means of the monitorial system, as developed by Andrew Bell. The society took over many existing charity schools and raised money for their support. By 1830 346,000 pupils were receiving elementary education in national schools. They studied the liturgy and catechism of the Church of England, and attendance at Sunday worship was often obligatory. The society had large resources of textbooks and equipment in its repository and established its own college for teacher-training at St Mark's, Chelsea (1841). After 1833 it shared a government grant for provision of new schools, provided that half the grant was raised by public subscription, and its secular instruction became subject to government inspection (1840). After the 1870 Education Act the society became more closely linked with the state system of education.

NATIONAL UNION OF CONSERVATIVE ASSOCIATIONS

in Britain, founded by the Conservative Party leaders in 1867 to enlist the newly enfranchised working classes and to keep the leadership informed of popular opinion. The union was carefully excluded from any control over the formation of policy, and from 1871 was simply the propaganda agency of the party's Central Office. The equivalent Liberal organization—the National Liberal Federation, founded in 1877—forced itself on the leadership from below, and always enjoyed more control over policy. Lord Randolph Churchill's partially successful attempts to democratize the union were intended to strengthen middle-class influence within the party, and eliminate electoral corruption, rather than to promote any particular social programme. The union encouraged Stanley Baldwin into legislating against the trade unions in 1927 and the national government into faster rearmament in the 1930s, but it has never dictated Conservative policy. Its conference continues (1970) to be the most important annual gathering of the Conservative Party.

NATIONAL UNION OF SUFFRAGE SOCIETIES in Britain,

formed in 1897, when various societies for the enfranchisement of women became united under the leadership of Mrs Henry Fawcett. The union encouraged declarations of support from MPs and the forwarding of private members' bills for women's suffrage. After 1909 it declined before the advance of the Pankhurst militants, who wished to influence the cabinet as a whole by more forceful means; but by 1913 a reaction had set in and the NUSS, by showing a responsible attitude, especially towards war work, played a major part in achieving votes for women (1918).

NATIONAL UNITED FRONT, short-lived Burmese political

group, formed in 1955, of left- and right-wing elements with little in common except hostility to the anti-fascist People's Freedom League.

NATIONAL URBAN LEAGUE in the US, formed in 1910 as

an inter-racial organization to help Negroes migrating from the rural South to Northern cities. It emphasized economic opportunities for blacks and secured support from white business and philanthropists. Under its executive director (after 1961), Whitney M. Young, the league also participated in direct action against racial discrimination.

NATIONAL WORKSHOPS, in France, ill-fated attempt by

the provisional government of the Second Republic (1848) to solve the problem of mass unemployment. Instead of Louis Blanc's far-reaching scheme involving state credits to industry, the unemployed were herded into *ateliers* in Paris. Some were given relief work, others received a dole. Thousands of unemployed came from the provinces to better their conditions. The workshops were ruinously expensive, and the amount of relief work was limited. The newly elected Assembly decided to close them, drafted the single unemployed into the army and sent the rest to drain swamps in the provinces. As a result, class hatred was intensified in Paris in the savagely suppressed June Days.

NATIONALIST MOVEMENTS in British Central Africa

during the colonial period occurred in the early years after the Second World War, but, like other such movements in Africa, were preceded by many years of more or less confused striving towards organizations, whether secular or religious, representative of African aspirations. On one side they emerged among urbanized Africans from many local movements concerned with self-help and cultural activities; on the other, although precise links were often obscure and contradictory in their influence, they were born among rural Africans in movements of dissident Christianity and messianic churches of the Ethiopianist sort. In Zambia they were greatly aided by early efforts at trade union organization among workers in the copper mines and towns of the Copperbelt.

Many of these influences were crystallized, after 1945, in ideas of political nationalism which generally took the form of 'congress movements', somewhat on the lines of the Indian National Congress, though seldom with any clear idea of ideological descent. Consistently frustrated by colonial authority, which none the less (in sharp distinction from Belgian and Portuguese colonial practice) allowed these movements to exist and even to grow, the congresses were given a powerful forward thrust by reaction from the Federation of the Rhodesias and Nyasaland (1953–63) dominated by white settlers.

In Nyasaland (Malawi) and Northern Rhodesia (Zambia), though in much less degree in Southern Rhodesia, where settler control was unhampered by any balancing influence from colonial authority, the congresses were able to mobilize large numbers of rural and urban Africans in support of general programmes aiming at African equality of opportunity and territorial independence. Where leadership was strong and effective, as with that of Hastings Banda in Nyasaland and Kenneth Kaunda in Northern Rhodesia, this new nationalism proved capable of determined and successful self-defence against colonial authority, and, by the beginning of the 1960s, had also won widespread sympathy in Britain; these achievements enabled them to gain their political objectives without any great upheavals.

C. Leys, *European Politics in Southern Rhodesia* (Oxford, 1959).

R. I. Rotberg, *The Rise of Nationalism in Central Africa* (Harvard and Oxford, 1966).   BD

NATIONALIST MOVEMENTS, in British East Africa, developed, as elsewhere in the colonial empires of the continent, from many different strands of thought and action. Early attempts to resist imperial enclosure—and the same applied to German encroachment south of Kenya, Italian encroachment north-east of Kenya in Somalia, and Belgian presence after the First World War in Ruanda-Burundi—gave way to a wide variety of associations, often clandestine or illegal, based on social or religious efforts at further resistance. Modern political nationalism dates from the early 1920s, notably in Kenya, where men such as Harry Thuku began to organize followers within the framework of the colonial system, pressing for concessions which varied from higher wages to European political withdrawal. Here, as elsewhere, the impact of the First World War, involving as it did the enrolment and death of large numbers of Africans in the campaign against the German general, Von Lettow-Vorbeck in Tanganyika, played a notable role in the development of a new political consciousness.

The Second World War deepened and accelerated the process. There quickly followed the growth of new political organizations in Kenya, Uganda, and Tanganyika, and these were again enlarged in popularity by repressive administrative measures, especially in Kenya, where white settlers' influence on colonial government was both strong and self-confident. The early 1950s were a period of rising tension, again especially in Kenya. But the tide of nationalism continued to rise, however much obstructed, and the late years of the decade brought a general recognition on all sides that the British would withdraw their political control; this occurred early in the 1960s.   BD

NATIONALIST MOVEMENTS in British West Africa were vigorous in all four territories (Gold Coast, Nigeria, Sierra Leone, and Gambia) after the Second World War, and increasingly successful in the early 1950s in attaining their aim of independence. They were the outcome of a long process of cultural resistance by a number of outstanding intellectuals over a long period before 1945. Though forming only a very small minority of the Africans of these territories, from whom they were often divided by their western education and style of life, these men—typical among whom was the Gold Coast lawyer, J. E. Casely Hayford—nourished a generous and far-reaching vision of emancipation, not only or especially for themselves, but for Africans in general. During the years between the World Wars they strove by writing and public speaking, by their work for bodies such as the National Congress of British West Africa, and sometimes by serving as nominated members in the colonial legislatures, where they found at least an occasionally useful platform, to build up public pressure for constitutional change, to induce a sense of public pride in the past of Africa's peoples, and to encourage belief in a post-colonial future.

As in East Africa, these movements gained new impetus from the consequences of the Second World War, in which large numbers of Africans served in British units, whether at home or overseas. Ex-servicemen gave a new and sharper edge to earlier demands for political change. This was sharpened again, during the 1950s, by the steady expansion of primary education. Increasingly, the content of political demands and the mode in which they were expressed turned away from the polite gradualism of earlier times. The politics of the elite became, at least to some extent, mass

politics. If the nationalist organizations themselves consisted largely of the elite and of reformers, they were now backed by a strong popular consensus of opinion. This was reflected in the leadership which now emerged, and carried these countries to independence.   BD

NATIONALIST MOVEMENTS in Portuguese Africa. As in most African colonies, these independence movements rest on a long history of resistance to European penetration and control, especially in the late 19th and early 20th cents, when Portuguese imperialism first began to result in a systematic occupation of inland territories which Portugal had long claimed. With no reformist choice open to them, various peoples continued to revolt against Portuguese rule throughout the colonial period, the largest of these revolts being in 1961 in Angola, in 1963 in Guinea-Bissau, and in 1964 in Mozambique. By 1966 the Portuguese armed forces in Africa numbered at least 120,000 metropolitan troops, reinforced by aircraft supplied by Portugal's allies, and were engaged in the largest colonial wars that Africa has known, with the exception of the Algerian campaign (1954–62). Yet by 1969 movements of armed resistance in these territories had established wide zones of self-rule defended by several thousand battle-trained troops, and installed new social institutions from elective committees to schools and hospitals.

These movements originated among small groups of educated Africans, themselves looking back to earlier cultural associations, such as the Angolan *Liga Africana* (not to be confused with another body of the same name, created in Lisbon in 1920 as part of the Pan-African movement elsewhere), who came together at Portuguese universities in 1948 and after. Notable among them were Mario do Andrade (Angolan, 1928–   ); Amilcar Cabral (Guinea-Bissau, 1925–   ); Agostinho Neto (Angolan, 1922–   ); Francisco Tenreiro (Angolan, 1921–63); and, in a slightly different grouping, Eduardo Mondlane. Out of their work came a variety of initiatives which eventually crystallized, after rooting in their respective countries, in the Partido de Independência de Guiné e Cabo Verde (PAIGC, founded Bissau, 1956), and the Movimento Popular de Libertaçao de Angola (MPLA, founded Luanda, 1956); the same upsurge of ideas also gave rise to movements of lesser importance, notably the União dos Poblaciones de Angola (UPA), formed in Kinshasa by Roberto Holden in 1961. Another movement, the Frente de Libertaçao do Moçambique (FRELIMO), was formed in Dar es Salaam in 1962 as a union between several earlier Mozambique groupings.

B. Davidson, *The Liberation of Guiné* (London and Baltimore, 1969).

E. Mondlane, *The Struggle for Mozambique* (London and Baltimore, 1969).   BD

NATIONALIST MOVEMENTS in Spanish West Africa. Three small groupings in Spanish Equatorial Guinea (Región Ecuatorial de España, consisting of the island of Fernando Po, with the smaller island of Annobón, and, on the adjoining mainland, of the territory of Rio Muni, with its three small offshore islands of the two Elobeys and Corisco: total population about 250,000) were successful in their campaign for political independence in mid-Oct. 1968. These were IPGE (Popular Idea of Equatorial Guinea), MUNGE (National Unity Movement of Equatorial Guinea), and MONALIGE (National Liberation Movement of Equatorial Guinea). In March 1969 Spanish forces intervened during a crisis which arose partly from disputes between local Spaniards and Africans, and partly from leadership conflicts. Economic troubles added to instability during the rest of 1969.

In Jan. 1969 Spain relinquished control of its small enclave of Sidi Ifni (population about 50,000) on the Moroccan seaboard in favour of Morocco, but retained the vastly larger though less populous territory of Rio de Oro (Spanish Sahara), which has only about 40,000 inhabitants. Nationalist trends in Rio de Oro have been complicated by the rival claims of Morocco and Mauritania. A nationalist movement in the Canary Islands also took shape in the 1960s.

NATIONALIST PARTY in Australia was created to accommodate those politicians, led by the prime minister, W. M. Hughes, who had left the Australian Labor Party after the 1916 conscription crisis. It held office in all states and the Commonwealth, its supporters including members of the pre-1916 Liberal Party, ex-Labor branches, rural organizations, and returned-soldier leagues. Its organization resembled that of the old Liberal Party, its finances being controlled by committees of businessmen, parliamentarians being held responsible only to their constituents. The end of the war revealed the party's inherited divisions, and the rise of an independent Country Party hastened its collapse during the later 1920s.

NATIONALIST PARTY in Indonesia (Partai Nasional Indonesia, PNI), principal secular party in Indonesia, founded in Nov. 1945. (An earlier party of the same name, started by Sukarno, existed from 1927 to 1931.) In the 1950s the PNI was the major rival of the Masjumi Party, and it came to rely on the communists for parliamentary support in this quarrel. The PNI was particularly identified with the Javanese bureaucratic elite. At the same time, it sought to attach itself as closely as possible to Sukarno, and in so doing assumed his Jacobin stance. It thus contained members of both populist and bureaucratic-conservative inclinations, which contradiction it has not yet (1970) resolved.

During the period of 'Guided Democracy' (1957–65) the PNI identified itself closely with that system, but found itself gradually declining in Sukarno's favour and in general reputation as an effective political machine. The party was attacked by the 'New Order' militants following the coup of Oct. 1965, and a substantial number of its more radical members were arrested, though the party itself remained legal. Only the PNI's more conservative leaders were allowed a say in its affairs, but as the only legal party identified with the Sukarno style it became a haven for Leftists and others opposed to the 'New Order'.

NATIONALIST PARTY in Viet-nam (Viet-Nam Quoc-Dan Dang), political group founded in 1927 by Nguyen Thai Hoc (1892–1930). The party was modelled on the Chinese Kuomintang. Its main strength lay in Tongking. Following the abortive Yen-Bay revolt of 1930, its leaders were executed or fled to China. The party re-emerged in 1945, when Chinese (Kuomintang) troops occupied North Viet-nam; but it could not sustain its role after their withdrawal in mid-1946, and again its leaders withdrew. After 1954 it became one of many political groups active in South Viet-nam, but later split into several factions.

NATIONALIZATION in Britain, concept which lacks almost entirely the element of workers' control (or even works representation) which a continental tradition of a socialist ideology or of active syndicalism might have produced. Instead, it has assumed the form of state ownership and management with a nominated workers' representation on a central board of directors.

The origins of such a concept are to be found in the plans drafted by the Miners' Federation, before the First World War, for the control of the coal mines, and adopted by the Labour Party in the 1930s. It was the miners who first suggested state ownership and management as the appropriate British form of 'socialism'. Despite the influence of syndicalism in certain sections of the miners' unions, there was no significant opposition to this from the miners or from the trade union movement generally. From the miners, the theory of state ownership seeped into Labour Party policy and found its first expression in Herbert Morrison's London Passenger Transport Act (1931). Though not passed by the Labour government itself, it was accepted in its substance by the

National government and did not provide for the representation of the transport unions.

By 1945 the Labour party had accepted nationalization (as state ownership and management was now called) for the coal mines, railways, the steel industry, transport, and, in a slightly different form, the Bank of England. All these were, in fact, nationalized (1945–51) in the manner envisaged before 1939. The Conservative government denationalized steel in the 1950s, but in 1966 it was renationalized by Wilson's government as a state-managed industry.

That nationalization had only overtaken economically declining industries, and has been justified on grounds of economic efficiency as much as social justice, does not, therefore, suggest that nationalization in its British form is either wholly or necessarily socialist in its origins.

NATIVE BAPTISTS, Jamaican blacks converted by zealous Baptist missionaries. So prominent were they in the 1831 rebellion under the leadership of Samuel Sharpe that the incident was termed 'The Baptist War'.

NATIVISM IN THE UNITED STATES, attitude of hostility towards foreigners of particular types, races, and creeds, especially evident when Americans have felt threatened by external dangers or by social tensions within their country. The Alien and Sedition Acts (1798) and the Know-Nothing Party of the 1850s embodied such prejudices, and nativism was revived in the late 1880s by the American Protective Association, an anti-Catholic organization originating in the Middle West. In the 1890s and early 1900s racial theories of Anglo-Saxon–Teutonic superiority became fashionable, and contributed to the movement to restrict immigration from southern and eastern Europe. During the First World War emotional nationalism, suspicion of a clash of loyalties among some foreign-born Americans, and fears of radicalism following the Bolshevik revolution, combined to produce the second Ku-Klux-Klan, the Red Scare of 1919, and development of a concept of 100 per cent Americanism that facilitated the further restriction of immigration during the 1920s. Subsequently, fear of the intrusion of alien ideologies contributed to the establishment of the Committee of Un-American Activities of the House of Representatives.

NATIVITY, DATE OF THE. The precise date of Jesus' birth is a controversial matter, since the Gospel writers were not concerned with it. Four different dates have been suggested, depending on the Gospel followed, viz. AD 1, 6 AD, 20–15 BC, and 9–6 BC. The last, deduced from St Matthew's, is the one commonly accepted in the Christian Church. As to the day, Clement of Alexandria suggesed 20 May; 25 Dec., first mentioned in the Roman Philocalian Calendar of AD 336, was probably chosen to oppose the feast of the *Natalis Solis Invicti*. In the East, 6 Jan., the Feast of the Epiphany, was more important until the mid-5th cent. AD, and in the Armenian Church it is still observed as Christmas Day.

NATURAL FRONTIERS, doctrine that the boundaries of a state ought to follow some well-defined natural line, *eg*, a river, such as the 'Oder–Neisse line' between Poland and East Germany, or a mountain range, such as the Pyrenees between France and Spain.

NATURAL LAW, system of right or justice common to all mankind and independent of positive or man-made law, and differently interpreted in different ages. To Aristotle the law of nature and natural justice could not be affected by man's laws. His views were coloured by his observance of Hellenic civilization, for he unquestioningly accepted the subordination of women to men, of slaves to citizens, and of barbarians to Greeks.

Religion and natural law were combined in the philosophy of St Augustine, who believed that man had freely lived in a state of innocence under a law of nature before his fall and subsequently in bondage under sin and positive law. In the

11th cent. natural law was equated with divine law, *ie*, the revealed law of the Old and New Testaments. To St Thomas Aquinas natural law was the eternal law of divine reason, which was unknowable to man because of its very origins from God, yet human law must attempt to be an application of natural law. Such thinkers as William Ockham favoured 'voluntarism', *ie*, divine will as opposed to divine reason as the source of law. They greatly influenced the Counter-Reformation, but Aquinas' ideas were more widely accepted.

Hugo Grotius, in the 17th cent., insisted on the validity of natural law outside any religious context, and applied the idea to international affairs, thus becoming the father of international law. To him the states themselves, but not the society within the states which was based upon a theory of social contract, were still in a state of nature and so bound by natural law which was independent of God and based upon man's own nature. Johannes Althusius introduced the ideas of Calvin into natural law: for him the doctrine of predestination was the basis of a law binding all people. Thomas Hobbes, in a similar way to Grotius, constructed a system of law by rational deduction from a fictitious 'state of nature' in which men were free and equal and were at war with each other. To him natural law was a 'general rule found out by reason, by which man is forbidden to do that which is destructive of his life'. He went on to enumerate a theory of social contract for the establishment of society. To John Locke the state of nature was a state of society with free and equal men observing the natural law, while Montesquieu thought natural laws were pre-social and superior to those of religion and the state. Self-preservation and compassion were the two main principles of natural law according to Rousseau, who postulated the idea of 'the noble savage'. To Immanuel Kant a system of right was not based on natural law or any state of nature, but upon the practical and moral reasoning of man himself.

The French Revolution (1789) saw the natural rights of man as liberty and equality, property, security and resistance to oppression, while the American Revolution established the equality of men as an inalienable political right. In the 20th cent. human rights have been based more upon man's common values, *eg*, F. D. Roosevelt's four 'essential human freedoms' (1941), of speech and expression, of worship, from want, and from fear, rather than upon natural law.   CJ

NATURAL PRODUCTS MARKETING ACT (1935) in Canada, law designed to initiate Dominion control over prices and marketing conditions. It was passed by R. B. Bennett as part of his Canadian version of Roosevelt's 'New Deal' and declared *ultra vires* of the Canadian constitution by the privy council in 1937.

NATURALIZATION ACT (1709) in Britain, enabled all foreign immigrants who so wished to become naturalized British subjects, provided that they took the statutory oaths of allegiance and received the sacrament in a church of any Protestant denomination. It was vigorously supported by the Whigs but caused a flood of Tory pamphlets. It was repealed by the Tories in 1712.

NAUKRATIS, ancient Egyptian city, south-west of Sais. Aahmes (*reg. c.* 1575–1550 BC) confined the activities of the Greeks living in the Delta exclusively to Naukratis and it became a prosperous trading and manufacturing city remaining so until it was supplanted by Alexandria.

NAUMBURG, CONFERENCE OF (1561), congress of Protestant German princes held to establish Protestant unity, which failed because the strict Lutherans or Gnesiolutherans disagreed on the issue of the Eucharist with the Philippist majority led by the Duke of Hesse.

NAUPACTUS, in Greece on the northern shore of the entrance to the Corinthian Gulf, was important in the Peloponnesian Wars (495–404 BC) as the Athenian base of operations against Corinth in north-western Greece. A surviving inscription, which provides important evidence for relations between Greek colonies and mother-cities, records the reinforcement of its original western (Ozolian) Locrian inhabitants with settlers from eastern (Opuntian) Locris (*c.* 460), but in 459 Athens gave it to Messenian refugees from Spartan subjection. After Athens' defeat they were expelled and replaced by Achaeans (399), whose later resistance to Philip II of Macedon induced him to give it to the Aetolians (338), who kept it until the Roman annexation (146 BC).

NAVAJO INDIANS, major American tribe in the American South-west, first encountered by the Spanish (*c.* 1629). Before the US government took possession of their territory, they fought other tribes and white settlers. Several military expeditions were sent with the object of trying to subdue them, and Col. 'Kit' Carson finally succeeded (1863) by killing their sheep and leaving them without means of support. A large part of the tribe was captured and imprisoned until 1867, when they were sent back to their country and supplied with new flocks. A treaty signed at Fort Sumner, NM (1868), gave them a reservation in AZ and NM.

NAVAL WARFARE in the Middle Ages. The first vessels specifically designed for naval warfare were the Mediterranean war-galleys, which used tactics such as ramming and the destruction of oars before closing in for hand-to-hand fighting. This type of vessel was relatively useless outside the sheltered waters of the Mediterranean, but continued in use there until the 17th cent. by the Venetians, Genoese, Turks, and to a lesser extent the French and Spaniards. Naval forces in northern Europe were impermanent, and there were no vessels specifically designed for sea-fighting. The normal ship in these waters was the single-masted, 'round' ship, perhaps fitted with a stern rudder (*c.* 1200). This sturdy, seaworthy, but not easily manœuvrable ship was merely provided with temporary wooden 'castles' bow and stern, and a contingent of soldiers in addition to its normal crew in order to turn it into a fighting vessel. The weapons carried by these ships were the same as those on land. The Byzantines used a projector for 'Greek Fire' which set ships alight. Otherwise, it was a case of hurling projectiles from ballistae and relying heavily on archers and cross-bowmen. In hand-to-hand fighting it was a matter of capturing a ship or sinking it by ramming or dropping objects from the 'castles' on to the opponent's deck, as at the battle off La Rochelle in 1372, when an English fleet was defeated by the Castilians. Tactics were rudimentary in the extreme, battles such as that which resulted in the English victory at Sluys (1340) being nothing more than land battles fought on floating platforms. Ships began to carry small guns from about 1350, and as vessels became larger and began to carry more sail, the two- or three-masted sailing vessel became the norm in northern and Mediterranean waters. By the second half of the 15th cent. the two towering castles began to sprout small guns, but they had no decisive effect on the techniques of naval warfare until the calibre of these weapons was drastically increased during the 16th cent.   DJ

NAVARINO, BATTLE OF (20 Oct. 1827), naval victory, during the Greek War of Independence when a combined Russian, British, and French fleet under Admiral Codrington defeated Ibrahim Pasha. The action followed Turkish refusal to accept the treaty of London (July) and was much criticized in Britain.

NAVARRA, PEDRO (*c.* 1460–1528), Spanish mercenary and engineer, who fought in the Italian Wars. He first won fame as a mine-layer in Florentine service at the siege of Sarzana (1488) and after Ravenna (1512) commanded the French artillery under Francis I. He fought at Novara, Pavia, and Bicocca, and was twice captured by the imperialists.

NAVARRE, Basque state straddling the western part of the Pyrenees, covering an area of *c.* 12,000 sq kms, at its peak in 1500. It was occupied by the Romans, but resisted the invasion of the Suevi and the Visigoths. However, it was conquered by Charlemagne, who took Pamplona, the chief town, in 728. After becoming an independent country in 831, it emerged as a kingdom in 860, and despite its being ravaged by the Moors under Caliph Abd Al-Rahman, enjoyed a brief supremacy among the Christian states of the Iberian peninsula under Sancho the Great in the 11th cent. In 1076 Navarre was united with the kingdom of Aragon and remained so until 1284, when the marriage of Queen Jeanne I of Navarre to Philip the Fair of France linked the country with France. In 1322 the daughter of Charles IV of France inherited the kingdom, and on the death in 1425 of Charles III of Navarre it passed to John II of Aragon, who had married Charles's daughter, Blanche. On John II's death in 1479 his grandson, Gaston de Foix, received the kingdom and thence it passed through his sister Catherine to John d'Albret. In 1512 Ferdinand of Aragon sent his armies under the Duke of Alba to occupy the greater part of the kingdom south of the Pyrenees to uphold the claims of his second wife, Germaine de Foix. John d'Albret was deprived of all but Lower Navarre, a small area in the north, while Upper Navarre was annexed first to the Aragonese Crown (1512), then to the Castilian Crown (1515), and was ultimately incorporated into the Spanish state under Charles V. Lower Navarre was inherited by John's daughter, Jeanne d'Albret, who married Anthony de Bourbon, Duke of Vendôme (1548), and under their son, Henry of Navarre, who inherited the French throne in 1589, it was incorporated into France. The title of King of Navarre was finally relinquished by Louis Philippe in 1830.   MKS

NAVAS DE TOLOSA, BATTLE OF (1212), victory for Alfonso VIII of Castile, aided by the Aragonese, which checked the resurgence of Muslim power under the Almohades in Spain and made possible further annexations of Muslim-held territory. It proved a turning point in the defence of Christian Spain against the Muslims.

NAVIGATION LAWS in Britain dated from 1381 and were designed to protect British shipping and thus promote trade and naval defence. Statutes in 1485, 1489, and 1532 aimed to restrict the import of Bordeaux wines and other commodities to English ships manned by English crews, and in 1540 Thomas Cromwell had an ambitious plan to replace Antwerp by London as the centre of the cloth trade in an act allowing foreign merchants exporting English cloth in English ships to be exempt from prohibitive duties and pay the same customs as the native merchants. But all these earlier measures languished because they were unenforceable against foreign retaliation and the Crown itself encouraged evasion by granting costly licences of exemption.

An effective Navigation policy began with legislation in 1650-1, renewed and extended in 1660-3, which forbade foreign ships to trade with the plantations, prohibited all imports not carried by English crews in English ships, or in the ships of the exporting country, and 'enumerated' certain colonial produce, *eg*, tobacco, sugar, cotton, that was to be brought only to English ports. These acts were chiefly aimed at the Dutch, who had established an extensive carrying-trade while the English were fighting a civil war.

Their competition was largely eliminated by the three Dutch Wars (1652-74), and a subsequent aim of the Navigation policy was to ensure that the mother country suffered no competition from colonial manufactures and had exclusive use of raw materials not produced at home. In practice this worked advantageously for the colonies in many ways, and was tacitly evaded by smuggling when it did not, until Grenville decided to tighten the commercial regulations and impose taxation on North America (1763-5). The American secession discredited the Navigation system, and concessions forced by the Irish (1780) and the US (treaty of Ghent, 1814)

prepared the way for general repeal. With Huskisson and Wallace at the Board of Trade, the Reciprocity of Duties Act (1823) permitted agreements to be made with individual countries for the mutual cancellation of trade embargoes. In the Irish potato famine (1846) the laws were suspended to allow the home consumption of goods brought in for re-export, and in 1849 they were repealed for all foreign trade. The coastal trade was opened to foreign vessels in 1854.

NAVY, ROYAL. Though the continuous history of the British Royal Navy dates only from Tudor times, it is possible to see its origins in the naval activities of King Alfred against the Danes, and certainly medieval kings used ships both for the transport of troops to and from the continent and for the defence of trade during the period of the wars in France. These ships, however, were rarely owned by the king; they were more usually provided by the Cinque Ports (in return for commercial privileges) and were merchant vessels temporarily converted to warships by the addition of wooden superstructures fore and aft. Kings Henry VII and Henry VIII were responsible for the establishing of a fleet of fighting ships designed as such, owned by the king, and supported by royal dockyards, its policy directed by the Admiralty Board and its administration by the Navy Board. Elizabeth's reign saw its further strengthening, notably during Sir John Hawkins's tenure of the office of treasurer of the navy. Under his guidance warships such as the *Revenge* were built, the first capable of sustained operations outside narrowly European waters: it was these ships that provided the backbone of the fleet that engaged the Spanish Armada and which were used with such skill by the 'Elizabethan seadogs' against the Spanish on both sides of the Atlantic. By 1603 the role of the navy in the defence of the country, in the defence of trade, and as an instrument of foreign policy had been firmly established.

The navy fell into relative disrepair under the early Stuarts, notwithstanding the skill of Phineas Pett, the greatest ship designer of his time. Under the protectorate and the later Stuarts, however, it was again revived and reformed, initially by Blake and his fellow 'generals-at-sea', who applied the lessons learnt from the New Model Army to the navy, and latterly by Samuel Pepys, the first secretary of the admiralty (1673-88). Between 1650 and 1688 the navy's disciplinary system, its conditions of service, officer entry, and promotion, and its pay and victualling and dockyard services, were thoroughly overhauled and regulated, and in the course of the First and Second Dutch Wars tactical procedures based on the line of battle were gradually evolved.

It was in the period of the wars against France between 1689 and 1815 that the Royal Navy's superiority at sea was most convincingly established. This arose from the series of great battles fought against French invasion fleets, culminating in Trafalgar in 1805, and from the extensive operations carried out in the waters of the Mediterranean, off the West Indies and American coasts and in the Indian Ocean under the command of such brilliant admirals as Rooke, Anson, Vernon, Hawke, Rodney, Howe, St Vincent, Duncan, and Nelson. It was in this period, too, that the strategy of naval warfare based on blockade was worked out, notably in the Seven Years War under the direction of the Elder Pitt. It is significant that, during this period when Britain acquired her extensive empire in North America, the West Indies, and India, the only major war to see great reverses, that of the American War of Independence, was fought during a time in which the navy was incompetently directed. The end of the French Wars left Britain undisputed mistress of the world's seas, a role she continued to perform for the next 100 years, a period sometimes misleadingly referred to as *Pax Britannica*. The years from 1815 to 1853 found Britain attempting to pursue a range of operations against the slave trade and piracy, in addition to her normal peacetime tasks, with a navy drastically reduced in size.

After the Crimean War the pace of change accelerated with

the transformation of the fleet from one based on wooden sailing ships to one of 'all big-gun' battleships by the early 20th cent. The transition was lengthy and laborious, and it was largely due to the dynamism of Admiral Sir John Fisher (first sea lord, 1904–9) and to the rising threat of the German fleet that the Royal Navy was sufficiently modernized in all its departments in time for the First World War.

The role of the Royal Navy in the two World Wars was prodigious: in addition to the normal naval tasks, defence of communications against attacks from submarines became of paramount importance. Since the Second World War the aircraft carrier has eclipsed the battleship, a change foreshadowed in the war itself. From 1970 Polaris submarines of the Royal Navy carried Britain's nuclear deterrent.

S. W. Roskill, *The Strategy of Seapower* (London, 1963).
M. Lewis, *The Navy of Britain* (London, 1948).   NRB

NAXOS, ancient Greek island city-state in the central Aegean, settled by Ionian refugees· from the Dorian invasions (*c.* 1000 BC). It collaborated with other Ionian states (*eg*, Chalcis) in colonial enterprises in the west (*eg*, Sicilian Naxos, the first Greek settlement on the island, *c.* 735). Its powerful 'tyrant', Lygdamis, supported Peisistratus of Athens and after the Spartans expelled him (*c.* 524), it remained a centre of resistance to Persia, defeating a substantial attacking force in 500. Though overrun by a Persian expedition sent against Eretria and Athens in 490, it still took part in the fight against Xerxes (480) and was freed in 479. It was the first member of the Delian League forcibly coerced by Athens (*c.* 470) and having later received an Athenian cleruchy (*c.* 450) it never recovered its importance.

NAXOS, BATTLE OF (376 BC), in the Aegean, victory of an Athenian fleet of 83 ships under Chabrias over 65 Spartan ships, which gave Athens naval supremacy until the Social War (357–355).

NAZCA, society which flourished on the south coast of Peru and which, after arduous campaigns, succumbed to the Incas (*c.* 1400). Nazca pottery is noted for its brilliant colour and conventionalized, abstract thematic design.

NAZIMUDDIN, KHWAJA (1894–   ), Indian politician, governor-general (1948–51), and prime minister (1951–3) of Pakistan. He was minister for education (1929–34) and the revenue member (1934–6) in Bengal. He served as home minister in Fazl-ul-Huq's ministry (1937–41), and then as leader of the opposition until Huq's dismissal (April 1943), which opened the way for his own appointment as chief minister. After the elections (1946), he was displaced by H. S. Suhrawardy and went to the central Legislative Assembly. He was the first prime minister of East Pakistan, but he became governor-general after Jinnah's death. Following the assassination of Liaquat Ali Khan, he assumed the post of prime minister of Pakistan, which he remained until his dismissal by the next governor-general, Ghulam Muhammad.

NAZI–SOVIET PACT (24 Aug. 1939), non-aggression treaty signed in Moscow by Ribbentrop for Germany and Molotov for Russia. Although inconsistent with the ideological hostility of the signatories, the treaty was dictated by logical considerations on both sides. German willingness to negotiate was helped by the fact that her alliance with Italy, though enlarged into a treaty of military assistance in May, promised little real benefit, as Italy was still weakly armed. In military terms the Russian pact offered Germany a temporary security in the east, while Russia herself would benefit from even a limited period of guaranteed peace to reorganize her armies after the drastic effects of the purges.

Cautious soundings had been made as early as April 1939, Russia having been rebuffed in her attempts to achieve a rapprochement with the Western Powers. As Germany's plans for the Polish campaign coalesced, negotiations began in earnest. On 23 Aug. Ribbentrop flew to Moscow, and the pact was signed early the next morning. The published treaty amounted to a simple non-aggression pact, but a secret protocol divided eastern Europe into Russian and German spheres of influence, foreshadowing the partition of Poland that took place in Sept.

Although the pact was of great diplomatic and military importance at the time, neither party totally trusted the other, but continued to act on the assumption that there would be a limited respite only. Russia might indeed have been won to the Western side earlier, had Britain not hoped to reach agreement with Germany in the belief that a future war could be confined to the east.

NDEBELE AND SHONA RISINGS. In the 1840s the Ndebele, under Mzilikazi, established control over the Shona of what became western Rhodesia, and exercised tributary rights over parts of the east. It was in the east—Mashonaland—that the pioneer column of Rhodes's British South Africa Co. settled in 1890. Three years later the settlers invaded Matabeleland, easily defeated the Ndebele, and captured Lobengula's capital, Bulawayo; Lobengula, Mzilikazi's successor, died soon afterwards. The settlers claimed land in Mashonaland by right of a dubious concession from Lobengula; they expropriated land and cattle in Matabeleland by right of conquest. The settlers despised the Shona, of whose long history they had no notion, and considered the Ndebele cowed by defeat. The administration that was established over both peoples was inefficient and crude. Africans resented this interference, the loss of land, and the demands made on them by whites for their labour. They blamed the outbreak of rinderpest (1895–6), which killed large numbers of their remaining cattle, upon the presence of the white settlers.

In March 1896 the Ndebele and Shona of western Rhodesia rose against company rule, and killed whites on outlying farms and besieged Bulawayo. In June of the same year some of the Shona groups of eastern Rhodesia likewise revolted. Several hundred whites were killed as a result of the uprisings, and for a time the safety of the settlers, and the continuance of company rule, were in jeopardy. Imperial troops had to be used to suppress the revolts. Rhodes intervened to stop the fighting against the Ndebele, making terms with some of their leaders in Aug. 1896, but the Shona held out, though by the end of 1897 they had been brutally subdued. Subsequently, administration of Africans in Rhodesia was reformed, but the fears and bitterness engendered by these revolts left their mark on inter-racial relations in Rhodesia for many years.

Contemporary whites mistakenly thought that there was mutual hostility between the Ndebele and Shona, but in fact the uprising in Matabeleland was inspired and partly organized by Mkwati, the priest of the Mwari cult. Mwari was the god of the Rozwi kings, who had ruled in Rhodesia before the coming of the Ndebele. The Shona revolt was organized by the representatives of another religious system, that of spirit (ancestor) mediums. There was much interchange between the two religious systems. The two main spirit mediums, Nehanda (a woman) and Kagubi, were captured by the whites and executed in Salisbury in 1898. Some features of the revolts, and of the organization behind them, have been perceived in the development of modern African nationalist movements in Rhodesia.

T. O. Ranger, *Revolt in Southern Rhodesia, 1896–7* (London, 1967).

NDONGO, Angolan kingdom which flourished in the 16th cent. as a salt- and later slave-trading empire, but was destroyed in the 17th cent. by invasions of Lunda and Portuguese.

NE WIN (1910–   ), Burmese soldier, chairman of the Revolutionary Council and head of the Burmese government. Originally known as Shu Maung, he joined the Thakin party

(1930) and was one of the 'Thirty Comrades'. He succeeded Aung San as commander of the Burmese National Army (1943). In 1949 at the nadir of the government's fortunes in the Civil War, he became commander-in-chief of the Burmese army. He was minister for defence and home affairs (1949–50) and head of the 'caretaker' military government (1958–61). In March 1962 he overthrew the government by a military coup and proclaimed himself chairman of the Revolutionary Council.

NEAR EAST (occasionally Nearer East), term which came into use in the 1890s to denote the area comprised by the Ottoman empire and its former territories in south-east Europe. It was gradually replaced in European usage by 'Middle East' after the First World War, although it retained its popularity in the USA. The *New York Times* formally but prematurely announced on 1 Nov. 1956 the end of its usage.

NEBBIA v NEW YORK, 291 US 502 (1934), US Supreme Court case which resulted in the sustaining of a New York statute setting up a state milk control board empowered to fix maximum and minimum milk prices. The majority opinion of Justice Roberts ignored precedents and allowed the exercise of state police powers according to a broad conception of the public interest.

NEBRASKA, 37th member state of the US, admitted in 1867. The region was acquired by the US as part of the Louisiana Purchase (1803) and was explored by Lewis and Clark (1804–6), Zebulon M. Pike (1806), and Stephen H. Long (1820). The Platte river valley became part of the Oregon Trail and a highway for settlers moving west in the 1840s and 1850s. It was organized as a territory by the Kansas–Nebraska Act (1854), and its modern boundaries were largely defined once the Dakota and Colorado territories had been established (1861). Statehood was postponed because of its financial cost until 1867. It developed largely as a farming area, gave strong support to the Populist movement in the 1890s and later to its native son, William Jennings Bryan (1860–1925), a secretary of state in Woodrow Wilson's administration. Nebraska's economy has always rested upon cattle ranching and cereal production with their attendant processing industries.

NEBUCHADNEZZAR II (*reg. c.* 605–562 BC), second King of the neo-Babylonian kingdom. For two years before his accession he fought the Egyptians in Syria-Palestine, defeating them at Carchemish (605). He spent much of his reign fighting to hold his conquests and in 587 captured Jerusalem, destroyed the temple, looted the city, and deported thousands of Jews to Babylon. He rebuilt Babylon on a grand scale with massive walls, a huge palace, and a ziqqurat. The account of his madness, given in the Bible, was erroneously based on a propaganda document about a later king, Nabonidus.

NECHO (NEKAU) (*reg.* 610–595 BC), Egyptian King, whose early conquest of Syria-Palestine (*c.* 609) ended in defeat by the Babylonians at Carchemish (605). At home, he encouraged trade, kept fleets in the Mediterranean and Red Seas and tried, unsuccessfully, to link the Red Sea with the Nile by canal.

NECKER, JACQUES (1732–1804), Geneva-born French banker and director-general of finances (1776–81) under Louis XVI, who effectively controlled the French economy during the critical period of the American War of Independence. He was skilled at borrowing money and the phenomenal increase in the royal debt from 93 million (1774) to over 300 million *livres* (1789) was largely his responsibility. After coming to Paris in 1762, Necker founded a banking house and married Suzanne Cuchod, whose literary salon was famous (1764). He also wrote two economic treatises and captured Maurepas's attention with his timely opposition to Turgot's ideas. As the controller-

general's assistant, Necker carried out certain long-needed reforms, *eg*, the abolition of *main-morte* and certain forms of judicial torture. His gift for propaganda, illustrated by the publication of his *Comte-rendu*, persuaded the French into believing he had achieved a budgetary surplus, but bold demands for economy and Maurepas's jealousy undermined his position. He was dismissed in 1781, but twice recalled to office by a desperate king (Aug. 1788 and July 1789). He was opposed by Mirabeau, who ended his political influence.

NEDERLANDSCHE HANDELMAATSCHAPPIJ, Dutch trading company established by order of King William I in 1824 and concerned with shipping between Holland and her East Indies colony, particularly in the days of the Culture System.

NEDIĆ, MILAN (1887–1946), Yugoslav soldier and politician. Before the Second World War he served the royalist governments as minister of war and chief of staff. During the war he became president of occupied Serbia, heading the 'government of national salvation' established by the Germans. He was afterwards tried and imprisoned for collaborating with the occupation forces.

NEERWINDEN, BATTLE OF (18 March 1793) near Brussels, defeat of the French forces under Dumouriez by the Austrians under the Prince of Coburg during the French Wars. It forced the French to evacuate Brussels and ended their hopes of a speedy victory in the Netherlands over Austria.

NEFERTITI, wife of the Egyptian king, Amenhetep IV (*reg. c.* 1367–1350 BC), depicted with him in murals at El-Amarnah.

NEGRÍN LOPEZ, JUAN (1889–1956), Spanish physiologist and politician. While a professor at Madrid University he built up a magnificent medical library. He joined the moderate and reformist wing of the Socialist Party, but the left-wing, under Largo Caballero, considered him to be simply a wealthy intellectual who had no ties to the workers' movement and was lacking in sympathy for the aims of Spanish socialism. He came to the fore in 1936, when the party's executive committee voted him into Largo Caballero's cabinet. As minister of finance he was concerned both with combating the disruption caused by the revolution in Republican Spain and with raising Spain's standing with the democratic powers. Thus, he sought to hinder the collectivization of agriculture and industry. He also developed the *carabineros*, the frontier guards attached to the ministry of finance, into a large armed force for use against extreme left-wing elements within the republic. This brought him closer to the communists, whom he admired for their efficiency. When Largo Caballero refused to endorse communist policy of destroying the anarchists and the Partido Obero de Unificación (POUM), the communists ousted him in favour of Negrín. In power (1937–9) Negrín became convinced of the need for co-operation with the Russians. His government was communist-dominated, a situation that he accepted for the sake of aid. By 1938 he had staved off the republic's collapse and it was his determination that largely made possible the Ebro offensive. After the fall of Catalonia, however, he became indecisive, faced with the alternatives of a surrender or a fight to the death. On 5 March 1939, he fled to France.

NÉGRITUDE, concept introduced by the Martinican poet, Aimé Césaire, as the 'simple recognition of the fact of being a Negro and the acceptance of this fact and of its culture and historical consequences'. The concept is also associated with the writings of the Senegalese poet-statesman, Leopold Senghor, and other African nationalists.

NEGRO MINSTRELS in the US, troupes of white American entertainers, popular from the 1840s, who presented farcical or sentimentalized sketches of the Negro, with blackened faces and wearing either ragged 'plantation' dress or formal dress as Northern urbanized dandies. Their decline was hastened by the coming of radio and cinema, though sophisticated derivatives have appeared in recent years.

NEHRU, PANDIT JAWAHARLAL (1889–1964), Indian nationalist politician, and prime minister of India (1947–64), known familiarly as *Panditji*. He was educated in Britain. He owed his political importance to his energy and political initiative. He was in the forefront of Congress campaigns from 1920 and was imprisoned on numerous occasions; he was quick to see the need for popular support for these campaigns and the relevance of a clear-cut social and economic programme to the winning of that support. In the late 1920s he emerged as leader of the Congress 'left wing' and the most important spokesman for secular nationalism in the Congress movement.

His political career began with his involvement with the Home Rule League and the Congress in 1918, when he also made his first contacts with Gandhi, for whom he became the chief lieutenant in the United Provinces. There were occasions when he disagreed with Gandhi over economic policy and what he regarded as the Mahatma's 'obscurantism', but he never repudiated his leadership and his action in supporting Gandhi at crucial times had a decisive effect on Congress development. As a member of the All-India Congress Committee from 1918, and of the Working Committee from 1920, he made the Congress the main basis for all his activities. He was secretary of the UP Congress committee (1920–2) and general secretary of the AICC (1923–5, 1927–9) before becoming president for the first time at Lahore (1929). He was president again, for two successive years (1936, 1937), in the crucial years of the introduction of provincial autonomy and again on the eve of independence (1946–7). After independence he and Sardar Patel disputed the leadership of the party until Patel's death (1950); after that Nehru assumed the presidency (1951–4) and thereafter kept his nominee in office.

As Gandhi's proclaimed 'heir-apparent' and the most popular of all Congress leaders, Nehru was the natural choice to lead the Congress in the Interim government (1946–7), although his only direct public administrative experience until then had been a brief term as chairman of the Allahabad Municipal Board (1923–4). In the Interim government he was vice-president, *ie*, virtually prime minister, and had charge of foreign and commonwealth affairs. After independence, he continued to hold these portfolios as prime minister until his death (1964). As an emergency measure he also took over the defence portfolio in 1962. His concern for international affairs dated from the 1920s and the international contacts of the Congress. Visits to Europe (1926–7, 1935, 1938) kept him in touch with international anti-imperialist movements and also gave him a basis for judging European developments. Of all Congressmen he was the most disappointed that events after the outbreak of war did not give Indian nationalists an opportunity to join the fight against fascism. He was in the forefront of the development of the policy of 'non-alignment' in Asia and Africa after independence, and was a major influence on the work of the Bandung conference (1955). It was also his influence which kept India in the British Commonwealth.

Nehru's personal views and actions were particularly important in two areas of Congress policy: the handling of communal relations, and the development of socialist programmes. He was an opponent of all communal and sectarian organizations and his policies in dealing with the Muslim League after 1937 made relations between the two parties very difficult. In two particular instances (although final assessment is not yet possible), his actions gave the league grounds for apprehension as well as the means to arouse communal fears. The first was his insistence that, while Congress would accept Muslim Leaguers if they wished to merge with Congress, they would not form coalition ministries with the league in the provinces in 1937; and the second was his apparent suggestion that the Congress would not feel bound by the Cabinet Mission's grouping

scheme once discussions started in the Constituent Assembly (1946). The effect of these actions was doubly unfortunate, for no one worked harder than Nehru for a non-communal nationalist movement and there can be no doubt that independent India's secular state owed much to Nehru's insistence.

He was the first Congress president to espouse socialist sentiments, and the draftsman of the Karachi resolution on fundamental rights (1931). He played a large part in preparing the way for the Congress Socialist Party (1934), but he was never a member of it and made it clear that he was not willing to split the Congress, or lose Gandhi's leadership, in order to make the Congress socialist. As a result, the CSP remained a splinter group within the Congress and eventually withdrew from it (1948). Although Nehru, as its leader was able to cajole the party into accepting the objective of a 'socialistic pattern of society' at Avadi (1955) and the programme of general co-operative farming at Nagpur (1959), in supporting socialist policies, it was no more than lukewarm. More practical was Nehru's work on economic planning. As the chairman of the Congress National Planning Committee from 1939, and as prime minister, he presided over the formulation of three 'five year plans'.

M. Brecher, *Nehru. A Political Biography* (London, 1959). J. Nehru, *An Autobiography* (London, 1936) and *The Discovery of India* (London, 1946). PDR

NEHRU, PANDIT MOTILAL (1861–1931), Indian nationalist politician, who took an early interest in Congress affairs and presided at provincial conferences (1907, 1909). However, it was not until the end of the First World War that he devoted himself fully to nationalist politics. He was a member of the United Provinces' Legislative Council from 1910 and played a leading role within Congress in the fields of electoral and legislative politics. He presided at the Amritsar session (1919) and although he had some misgivings, he supported non-co-operation at a special session in Calcutta (1920). After non-co-operation he joined with C. R. Das to promote the entry of Congress into the legislatures in order to 'non-co-operate from within', and in 1923 he became secretary of the Swarajya Party. He was elected to the central Legislative Assembly (1923), led the Swarajya group there, and on Das's death assumed the leadership of the party. Working closely with Gandhi, he was responsible for the Congress decision to accept the Swarajists as the 'constitutional' wing of the movement (1926). He took a leading part in the campaign against the Simon Commission and in the work of the All-Parties Conference (1928) and was chairman of the committee appointed by the conference to draw up a nationalist constitution and which produced the 'Nehru Report' (1928). As president of Congress (1928) he argued strongly for the acceptance of dominion status as a realizable goal, but found Irwin's dominion status declaration (Oct. 1929) unsatisfactory and supported the decision to start civil disobedience for 'complete independence', which was taken at Lahore under the presidency of his son, Jawaharlal Nehru (1889–1964).

NEHRU REPORT (1928) in India, report of a committee under Motilal Nehru which was set up by the All-Parties Conference in Feb. 1928 to draft a nationalist constitution for India. The conference was convened by the Congress as a means of bringing together all those who refused to co-operate with the Simon Commission. Under the constitution which the committee presented to a further meeting of the conference in Aug., India, as a dominion within the empire, was to have fully representative and responsible government at both the centre and in the provinces. The central government was to have an indirectly elected Senate and a directly elected House of Representatives and the provincial legislatures were to be also directly elected. All elections be on the basis of adult suffrage and through electorates, although there would be reserved seats for minorities for a period of ten years and in population. The conference amended these proposals in one significant respect: it was agreed that the question of reservation should be reopened after ten years. At the National Convention which was called in Dec. to discuss the final report, however, non-Congress Muslims rejected these proposals for representation and declined to take any further part in the convention.

Within the Congress, the report's proposal on dominion status was the most controversial issue. Many, including Jawaharlal Nehru, believed Congress should stand for complete independence. Eventually it was agreed to offer an ultimatum to the viceroy under which Congress would accept dominion status within a year or would launch civil disobedience in support of its demand for complete independence. Subsequently, the Lahore session of Congress (1929) declared that the Nehru Report had lapsed and prepared for civil disobedience.

NEILL, JAMES GEORGE SMITH (1810–57), British soldier and servant in the East India Co. During the Indian Mutiny (1857) he captured Allahabad on the way to relieve Cawnpore. He and his troops dealt with the mutineers with great severity. He was killed fighting in the advance on Lucknow.

NEIPPERG, WILHELM REINHARD VON, Count (1684–1774), Austrian soldier and diplomat, who served Charles VI and Maria Theresa. He concluded the highly unfavourable peace of Belgrade (1739) with Turkey, for which he was later imprisoned. He also fought at Mollwitz and arranged the terms of the Convention of Kleinschnellendorf (1741) with Frederick II of Prussia.

NEISSE, CONFERENCE (Aug. 1769), between the Emperor Joseph II and Frederick II of Prussia, to discuss the fate of Poland. Catherine II of Russia had engineered the election of her lover, Stanislas Poniatowski, to the Polish throne, making that country a Russian satellite. This alarmed Poland's neighbours, Prussia and Austria, hitherto arch-enemies. The Austrian minister, Kaunitz, anxious to check further Russian expansion, suggested a rapprochement with Prussia, to which Maria Theresa objected, but her son Joseph II over-ruled her and proceeded to Silesia, where the personal meeting took place. The conference achieved no significant result. It was followed by another meeting at Neustadt (1770), and ultimately (1772) by the First Partition of Poland.

NEKHTNEBEF (*reg.* 380–363 BC), Egyptian King, who inaugurated an immense building programme, notably on the island of Philae. He repelled a Persian invasion of the Delta (373).

NELSON OF THE NILE AND OF BURNHAM THORPE, HORATIO NELSON, Viscount (1758–1805), British sailor, who, after entering the navy in 1770, served in the West Indies (1778–87) and took part in engagements at Corsica (1794), Cape St Vincent (1797), Santa Cruz de Tenerife (1797), and Naples (1799), where he was made Duke of Bronte. At Aboukir Bay (1798) he destroyed Napoleon's hopes of success in the Middle East, and at Copenhagen (1801), with Sir Hyde Parker, crushed the Armed Neutrality of the North. In 1805 Nelson pursued the French fleet under Villeneuve to the West Indies and ended the threat of Napoleon's invasion of England by his defeat of the French and Spanish fleets at Trafalgar (1805), where he was mortally wounded. His contribution to the role of the navy in the French Wars was immense and his death was viewed by contemporaries as a major tragedy, scarcely offset by the victory he had won. In the annals of British naval history his fame and reputation are unique among the nation's distinguished sailors.

NELSON, SIR HUGH MUIR (1835–1906), Australian pastoralist and politician, who farmed for 30 years before entering the Qld legislature in 1883. He was prime minister

(1893–8) as part of the 'continuous ministry', and president of the Legislative Council (1898–1906). His term of office as prime minister was marked by strict financial retrenchment and excessive caution towards federation.

NELSON, OLAF FREDERICK (1883–1944), Swedish–Samoan businessman who led local opposition to paternalistic NZ administration in Western Samoa, culminating in the Mau movement (1927). He was twice deported (1928, 1933), but was repatriated in 1935.

NELSON, WOLFRED (1791–1863), Canadian physician and politician, who served as a regimental surgeon during the War of 1812, and was elected to the legislature of Lower Canada (1827–30). He visited France (1830–3) for further medical studies and on his return he was re-elected to the Assembly (1834) as a follower of L. J. Papineau. Nelson became one of the chief leaders of the rebellion of 1837. He won the battle of St Denis, but was defeated at St Charles and St Eustace and was captured trying to escape to America. He was exiled to Bermuda (1838), but was released and thereafter, until the amnesty of 1842, practised medicine in America. He sat in the Assembly (1844–51), became an inspector of prisons (1852), and mayor of Montreal (1854–6).

NEMEA, in Greece 24 kms south-west of Corinth, in antiquity the site of a famous sanctuary of Zeus and of one of the four great pan-hellenic athletic festivals. Near it in the Corinthian War (394 BC) the Spartans and their allies defeated the Thebans, Corinthians, Argives, and Athenians, and so offset their defeat at Haliartus (395) and deterred their enemies from further offensive action while Agesilaus' army was returning from Asia.

NEMIROV, CONGRESS OF (1737), abortive peace conference, arranged through British and Dutch mediation, between Russia, her ally, Austria, and their enemy, the Turks. It was held in the Ukraine with the object of settling territorial differences that had led to the Russo–Turkish war (1735–9). Charles VI made moderate demands for frontier rectifications, but Russia's claim to all land between the Kuban and Dniester rivers led the Turks to break off negotiations.

NEMOURS, LOUIS CHARLES PHILIPPE RAPHAEL D'ORLÉANS, Duc de (1814–96), French nobleman and second son of Louis Philippe, who refused nomination as King of the Belgians (1830). He served in Algeria (1836), and under the Third Republic he became a general (1871).

NEMOURS, TREATY OF (1585), agreement between Catherine de Medici, King Henry III of France, and the Duc de Guise, in which the king humiliatingly promised to abolish all previous pacificatory edicts relating to the Huguenots in order to wean the leadership of the Catholic League from Guise and Philip II of Spain (7 July 1585). This promise of Catholic repression forced Henry of Navarre to renew the civil war.

NENE, TAMATI WAKA (c. 1780–1871), NZ Maori chief, who played a decisive part in the Maori acceptance of missionaries and of British sovereignty (1840) and helped subdue the rebellious Hone Heke (1843–4).

NENNI, PIETRO (1891–), Italian journalist and politician, who supported Mussolini from the time (1911) of their mutual imprisonment. He joined the Partito Socialista (PSI) in 1921 and dominated the non-communist left thereafter. He edited *Avanti!* (1923–6, 1943–6) and *Nuovo Avanti!* (1930–9). During the Second World War he worked closely with Togliatti for Italian liberation, and planned the new constitution. He held office immediately after the war as deputy prime minister (1945) and foreign secretary (1946–7). After 1953 he led the PSI away from identification with the

Communist Party (PCI), seeking government power by an alliance with the Christian Democrats; this culminated in a centre–left coalition (1963–9), in which he was foreign secretary (1968–9).

NEO LAO HAK SAT ('LAO PATRIOTIC FRONT'), in Laos, political party formed in 1956 as the open political arm of the *Pathet Lao*, its aim being to contest elections.

NEO-CONFUCIANISM in China, intellectual movement whose origins can be traced to the renewed propagation of the ideals of a Confucian state and society, following the re-unification of China under the T'ang dynasty. The Neo-Confucians of the Sung period wished not only to resurrect the earliest of the Confucian ideals and to purge them of the misapprehensions of the intervening 1000 years, but also to extend them in terms of metaphysical concepts that had been engendered by Buddhism. They incorporated in their thought elements of Ch'an, or Zen, Buddhism, as well as some of the terms of Taoism; but the main emphasis of Neo-Confucianism was directed not towards immortality or the permanent values of an after-life, but to the practice of ethical and political ideas in the newly evolving social conditions of Sung, Yuan, and Ming China.

The scholars responsible for drawing renewed attention to the real meaning of the classical texts of Confucius in the contemporary age included Han Yü (768–824), Fan Chung-yen (990–1053), and Ou-yang Hsiu (1007–72). One permanent result of their activity was the selection of the Four Books for special emphasis, which was retained in Chinese education until the 20th cent. Chu Hsi (1130–1200) made a synthesis of the interpretations of these texts, and acceptance of his views as orthodox was required of candidates for the civil service examinations until the 17th cent. In metaphysics, Chu Hsi and his school postulated the existence of *T'ai-chi*, the single supreme ultimate or fundamental principle underlying all phenomena, and they discussed its relationship with created matter, and other traditional Chinese concepts such as *yin-yang* and the Five Elements.

Perhaps of greater significance was the reassertion of Mencius' view of the inherent goodness of human nature and of the application of Confucian ideals both to the administration of government and to the retention of a balanced social order, *ie*, the five ideal relationships between ruler and subject, father and son, husband and wife, brothers, and friends; the dependence of state authority on the practice of ethical qualities rather than on the imposition of force; the need of the state to recruit men of the best quality into its service, and the responsibility of such men to serve the state and criticize superior authority.

In Neo-Confucian thought, the universe constituted a moral and organic whole, comprehending the laws of nature and those of human relationships; social prescriptions ensured the maintenance of that whole with balanced contributions from individuals; enlightenment of a man's own perfect, but hidden, nature provided a harmony between human behaviour and the world of nature. In the 15th cent. a new departure from Chu Hsi's thought was brought about by the Neo-Confucianist school of Wang Yang-ming (1472–1529), which stressed the participation by Heaven and Earth as parts of one and the same realm of existence and the need to seek ultimate reality not, as Chu Hsi had taught, by the investigation of external phenomena, but by the development of an individual's intuitive faculties.

W. de Bary, *Sources of Chinese Tradition* (New York, 1960).

ML

NEO-HITTITES, ancient people of uncertain origin, who wrote Hieroglyphic Hittite. They probably moved from Asia Minor into northern Syria and the Taurus region on the fall of the Hittite empire (c. 1215 BC). They established a large number of independent states and enjoyed some prosperity before falling to the Assyrians in the 8th cent.

NEO-SOCIALISTS in France, name given to a group which was expelled from the French Socialist Party in 1933 and later moved towards fascism. The original point at issue was whether the socialists should join in governments with the Radicals, and the group was at first led by the moderate, Pierre Renaudel. But shortly afterwards, under the influence of Marcel Déat and Adrian Marquet, it evolved a distinctive authoritarian creed. Its slogan was 'Order, authority, nation', and it claimed to seek a middle way between capitalism and socialism. Marquet and Déat were members of governments in the 1930s. The neo-socialists supported the policy of appeasing Germany and opposed French participation in the Second World War. After France's defeat, Marquet was a minister under Pétain (1940), while Déat became a leading collaborator with the Germans.

NEPAL, the land of the Gurkhas, an independent kingdom on the north-east frontier of India. It is bounded on the north by Tibet, on the east by Sikkim, on the south by Bengal and Uttar Pradesh, and on the west by Kumaon and the Kali river. Along its northern frontier stretch the Himalayas. Its early history is legendary and obscure. Asoka is said to have visited the valley in the 3rd cent. BC. His pillar inscriptions at Nigliva and Rummindi show that the Nepal Tarai was within his dominions. In the 4th cent. AD Samudragupta, the Gupta emperor, claimed that the king of Nepal paid him tribute. The Gurkhas are said to have come originally from Rajputana in the 14th cent. They entered the country through the Kumaon hills and gradually extended their power over the whole of Nepal. This advance was facilitated by internecine struggles. In the 18th cent. Prithwi Narayan Sah was their most important leader. By 1769 he had overthrown the three Newar kingdoms of Bhatgaon, Katmandu, and Patan. He died in 1771 and his successors extended Gurkha rule over Kumaon, Garhwal, Palpa, and Sikkim. In 1791 they invaded Tibet, but were driven out by the Chinese.

The Gurkhas entered (1791–1801) into three commercial treaties with the East India Co. In 1802 Capt. Knox reached Katmandu as British Resident, but was forced to withdraw (1803). Constant aggression along the British frontier led to war (1814). By the treaty of Segauli (1815, though not ratified until March 1816) a British Residency was established in Katmandu. Early in the 19th cent. all real power passed to the hereditary prime minister of the Rana family and the kings of Nepal became state prisoners in the white palace at Katmandu until, in 1950, King Tribhuvana reached Delhi by air. The most important prime minister was Jung Bahadur (1816–77), who reformed the administration. During the 1857 Mutiny he sent troops to assist the British. Nepal also sent aid to the British during the Younghusband expedition of 1904 into Tibet, and supported Britain in both World Wars. In 1923 the British recognized the complete independence of Nepal. After the partition of India (1947) Nepal signed commercial and political treaties with India. In 1951 the ruler was forced to grant democratic reforms.

W. Brook Northey and C. J. Morris, *The Gurkhas* (London, 1928).

P. Landon, *Nepal*, 2 vols (London, 1928).

CCD

NEPAL WAR (1814–16) was caused by constant Gurkha aggressions across the British frontier. The first campaign in 1814 under Gen. Gillespie was unsuccessful. In May 1815 Gen. Ochterlony stormed the fort of *Malaun* and forced the Gurkhas to sue for peace. Further fighting was necessary before the Gurkha government ratified the treaty of Segauli in March 1816. The Gurkhas ceded Garhwal, Kumaon, and a large part of the Tarai, withdrew from Sikkim, and agreed to receive a British Resident at Katmandu.

NERI, PHILIP, Saint (1515–95), Florentine philanthropist, who moved to Rome (1533), where he became a priest (1551) and founded the Congregation of the Oratory (1564) to rehabilitate the priesthood in the service of lay society. The name *oratorio* for a form of musical composition came from the services held in his oratory.

NERO (AD 37–68), Roman Emperor (*reg.* 54–68), whose frivolity brought the line of Julio-Claudian emperors to an end. His mother, Agrippina the younger, promoted him after marrying the Emperor Claudius, whose death was attributed to her. At first she dominated Nero, but Seneca the younger and Burrus eventually undermined her influence. Playing on Nero's fundamental lack of interest in government, they provided a good administration until Burrus' death in 62. Boudicca's revolt in Britain was suppressed and trouble with Parthia prudently confined to skirmishing and diplomacy. After 62 Nero relied on less satisfactory advisers. Already he had procured the murder of his mother (59) in resentment at her interference, and of his wife, Octavia (62) in order to marry Poppaea. He alienated opinion in Rome and Italy by his enthusiasm for singing and playing the lyre in public, and was blamed for the fire of Rome in 64. A conspiracy to supplant him with Piso in 65 was followed by many executions. In 67 he toured the festival centres of Greece, where his philhellenism evoked some response, but opinion in the west hardened. In 68 Vindex rebelled in Gaul and Galba in Spain, and Nero, incapable of decisive action, committed suicide, deserted by everyone.

NERONOV, IVAN (*fl.* 17th cent.), Russian priest and vicar of Kazan cathedral in Moscow, who clashed with Patriarch Nikon over his Greek reforms and was anathematized by the church council of 1656, but in 1657 came to terms with its innovations.

NERSCHINSK, East Siberian town founded by the Russians in the mid-17th cent. In the 18th cent. it became the centre of the flourishing silver-mining industry of the Amur valley. It was also the point of departure for the caravan route to China, with whom the Russians concluded their first treaty at Nerschinsk (1689).

NERUDA, PABLO (NEFTALÍ RICARDO REYES) (1904–   ), Chilean communist poet and politician, whose radical poetry expresses his Marxist opinions. His influence on Latin American writers has been immense. He also served as a Senator representing the Chilean Communist Party.

NERVA, MARCUS COCCEIUS (AD 30–98), Roman Emperor (*reg.* 96–98). After a long career as a lawyer and a courtier under Nero, Vespasian, and Domitian, he was chosen emperor on the latter's assassination, being acceptable to the senate because of his age and cautious temperament. But he had no political and military prestige, and failed to check political vendettas or control the praetorian guard. His adoption in 97 of Trajan, a distinguished soldier, narrowly averted civil war. His brief rule nevertheless inaugurated a long period in which benevolent paternalism was the mark of imperial government.

NERVII, Celtic-Germanic tribe of Roman times inhabiting parts of Flanders and Hainault. They were defeated by Julius Caesar after a long campaign (57 BC), but became highly prosperous under the empire. Their capital, Bagacum (mod. Bavay, France), became an important centre and their territory contained pottery works and numerous villas. Nervian merchants traded in the Rhineland and provided six auxiliary cohorts for the army.

NESSELRODE, KARL ROBERT, Count (1780–1861), Russian politician, foreign minister (1822–56), and chancellor (1844). He was adviser to Alexander I at Paris and at Vienna and co-operated closely with Nicholas, describing himself as merely his monarch's instrument. His long tenure of office and his experience probably exercised a moderating influence, although he did not initiate policy. He was a conservative supporter of legitimacy and the status quo, worked with Metternich in the Holy Alliance, suppressed the Hungarian revolt (1849), and opposed Polish nationalism, Pan-Slavism, and Asian expansion.

His Balkan policy involved influencing Turkey by upholding the status quo between the countries as at the treaty of Unkiar Skelessi (1833). He failed later to prevent the Crimean War.

NESTOR, legendary Greek king of Pylos in the southwestern Peloponnese. In Homer's *Iliad* he appears as the aged leader of the Pylian contingent against Troy (*c.* 1200 BC) and valued adviser to Agamemnon. The splendid Mycenaean palace recently uncovered at Pylos and dated to 13th cent. BC lends support to the legend.

NESTOR, CHRONICLE OF, earliest Russian chronicle, covering the period from the legendary origins of Kievan Russia to the year 1116, and more generally known as the *Russian Primary Chronicle*. It was formerly thought to be the work of the monk Nestor, of the Kievan Monastery of Caves. However, recent scholarship suggests that it was a compilation which included some of his work. From the middle of the 11th cent. onwards it provides a valuable source, based on contemporary materials.

NESTORIANISM, important heresy of the 5th cent. in the Eastern Church. Nestorius (*fl.* 5th cent.) was appointed Bp of Constantinople in 425 by Theodosius II. He was a puritanical and intolerant prelate, and was denounced by his enemies as a heretic for arguing that Christ was truly man, to whom divinity was added as a distinct attribute. Hence the Two Natures were not mystically indivisible and the blessed Virgin Mary was mother of the man Christ, not of God. In a general council summoned on the instigation of Nestorius at Ephesus in 431 his faction was first defeated by Cyril, Bp of Alexandria, who upheld orthodox Trinitarianism. But with the arrival of certain bishops held up on the road, Nestorianism triumphed. The emperor accepted both rival formulations, then deposed both bishops. Cyril bullied and bribed the officers of the court to press for his reinstatement, but Nestorius was banished to Egypt. Nestorianism continued as a force in the East and churches of the sect were established in Persia and as far afield as Ceylon and China. Nestorian missionaries were characterized by a self-sacrificing fervour and an awesome austerity. By implication Nestorianism condemned much popular veneration of the Virgin and her various cult-objects and hence foreshadowed the Iconoclast episode of two centuries later. Nestorian rigour, both intellectual and moral, could not commend it to the urban mobs, who demanded the continued comfort of their observances, their venerated objects, and their superstitions.

NETEKAMANI (*reg. c.* 12 BC–AD 12), King of Kush, whose name, together with that of Queen Amantari, is found on many monuments. His reign appears to have been one of outstanding prosperity.

NETHERLANDS, THE, the Low Countries, which became the economic centre of northern Europe in the Middle Ages because of favourable geographical factors. The navigable rivers of the Rhine, Maas, and Scheldt formed an excellent communications network, the coastline was well endowed with natural harbours, and the rich low-lying pastures provided grazing lands for cattle and sheep. The abundant herring of the nearby North and Baltic Seas enabled the northern ports of the Netherlands to develop the fishing industry and a strong maritime tradition, while the hinterland abounded in metal ores which formed the basis of the mining and metal-manufacturing industries of the Liège district. By the later Middle Ages, therefore, the Netherlands was prominent for its flourishing cities, eg, Ghent, Bruges, Ypres, Antwerp, the centre of the European textile industry, and its domination of northern European culture.

Politically, the Low Countries consisted of a number of separate fiefs owing allegiance either to the kings of France, *eg*, the county of Flanders, or to the Holy Roman empire, *eg*, Brabant, and wedged between these two powers, but seeking the alliance of England for economic reasons. In 1369 Philip the Bold, the Valois Duke of Burgundy, inherited through his marriage to Margaret, heiress of the Count of Flanders, claims to Flanders, Artois, Nevers, Rethel, and Franche-Comté, which he secured in 1384. His grandson, Duke Philip, acquired the imperial provinces of Brabant, Limburg, Holland, Zeeland, and Hainault from a weakened empire, purchased the fortress of Namur (1421) and the province of Luxemburg (1443), and extended his influence over Utrecht and Liège by the appointment of a son and nephew to those sees. The annexation of the duchy of Guelders by Charles the Bold (1473) completed Burgundian control of the Netherlands. The marriage in 1477 of Charles's daughter, Mary of Burgundy, to Maximilian of Habsburg, the future emperor, and the deaths of Charles (1477) and Mary herself (1482) resulted in the Low Countries becoming a part of the Habsburg empire. Moreover, the marriage of Maximilian and Mary's son, Philip the Fair, to Joanna, daughter of Ferdinand of Aragon and Isabella of Castile, laid the foundation for Habsburg power in Spain, in whose affairs the Netherlands became embroiled in the 16th cent. United under Emperor Charles V, the 17 provinces of the Spanish Netherlands enjoyed a great material and spiritual flowering until the accession of Philip II (1555) initiated a violent revolt against centralization, exploitation, and religious persecution. The War of Independence ravaged and divided the Low Countries from the time of William of Orange's unsuccessful invasion of 1568 until the recognition of the sovereign independence of the seven northern Dutch-speaking provinces of Holland, Zeeland, Utrecht, Gelderland, Friesland, Gröningen-Drente, and Overyssel in 1648. While these became known as the United Provinces or the Dutch republic, the ten southern provinces retained their aristo-cratic Catholic character under first the Spanish Crown (1648–1713) and then under the Austrian Habsburgs (1713–94). On being reunited after the French Revolutionary and Napoleonic Wars by the decision of the Congress of Vienna (1815), they became the kingdom of the United Netherlands under the House of Orange, but two centuries of division were confirmed when, after the Belgian revolt (1830–1), the Low Countries were again divided into the kingdom of the Netherlands or Holland and the kingdom of Belgium under Leopold of Saxe-Coburg (1831).

Thereafter, the two countries pursued their separate courses. Both suffered in the two World Wars of the 20th cent. The eastern overseas interests of the Dutch disappeared after 1945 while Belgium's brief period of empire-building (*c*. 1880) ended in the African nationalist movements of the 1960s.

P. Geyl, *The Revolt of the Netherlands 1555–1609* (London, 1962).

P. Geyl, *The Netherlands in the 17th Century*, parts I and II (London, 1961).
MKS

NETO, ANTONIO AGOSTINHO (1922–   ), Angolan doctor and politician of African (Mbundu) parentage, who became a leading figure in the development of nationalism in the Portuguese African colonies. He was imprisoned for political reasons (1955–7) and rearrested (1960) for propagating nationalist opinions and interned on the island of Santo Antão in the Cape Verdes. He was subsequently removed to Portugal, but escaped in 1962 and took over the leadership of the Movimento Popular por la Libertacão de Angola (MPLA), then based on Kinshasa in the Republic of Congo. Later he devoted himself to the further development of the MPLA, notably in its military and political control of wide grassland regions in eastern and central Angola.

NEUFVILLE, NICOLAS III DE, SEIGNEUR DE VILLEROY (1543–1617), French secretary of state in the 16th cent., who held office almost continuously for 50 years from 1567. He was the son and grandson of royal servants who held, among other posts, that of treasurer of France. Nicholas himself became a secretary of finances in Catherine de' Medici's household in 1559 at the age of 16. He was sent to Spain, Rome, and Scotland on delicate diplomatic missions (1559–67) and in 1567 succeeded his father-in-law as secretary of state and quickly became a favourite of Charles IX and later of Henry III, under whom he rose to pre-eminence (1574–7). In the last years of Henry's life, during the complex period of civil war, Neufville's relations with the king deteriorated and in 1588 he was dismissed from office with other royal secretaries. He was reinstated, however, by Henry IV in 1594, and remained in office for a further 23 years, during which time he helped to direct foreign affairs.

NEUMANN, BALTHASAR (1687–1753), German soldier and architect of the late Baroque or Rococo period, who started his career in the artillery force of the Prince-bishop of Würzburg, was promoted to surveyor of works, and rose to the rank of colonel. He was sent to Paris, Vienna, and Milan to study architecture and built the new bishop's palace at Würzburg. Among his most famous buildings is the church of the fourteen saints (*Vierzehnheiligen*) in Franconia.

NEURATH, KONSTANTIN VON (1873–1956), German diplomat and politician, who joined the German diplomatic service (1901) and served mainly abroad. He was ambassador at Rome (1922–30) and later at London (1930–2). He was foreign minister in Papen's cabinet (1932–3). In common with other members of Hitler's first cabinet, he was retained in his ministry in order to lend respectability to the regime, and thus shared, passively rather than actively, responsibility for the entrenchment of the Nazi government. Hitler eventually replaced him with the more ruthless and dynamic Ribbentrop. Neurath, who became an NSDAP member in 1937, remained in the cabinet as minister without portfolio, and held a number of nominal government offices until March 1939, when he was appointed protector of Bohemia and Moravia (1941–3). He was sentenced to 10 years' imprisonment at the Nuremberg war trials, and was released shortly before his death.

NEUSS, SIEGE OF (1474–5). Neuss was a German town north-east of Cologne which formed a strong natural fortress. Charles the Bold, Duke of Burgundy, surrounded it in 1474. He was marching on Cologne, in revolt against its archbishop, Charles's ally, and decided to take Neuss first, though there was no military necessity for doing so. The unsuccessful siege lasted 14 months and proved a turning point in Charles's career. It prevented him from travelling with his army to join Edward IV of England, whose invasion of France started in the summer of 1475. This thwarted the only chance that occurred of a joint successful campaign against Louis XI of France. England soon made peace and ruin overtook Charles in 1476–7.

NEUTRAL ISLANDS, West Indian islands of St Lucia, Dominica, Grenada, St Vincent, and Tobago, whose ownership was in dispute between Britain and France. Their neutrality in 1732 was achieved by British and French nationals quitting the islands. Breaches of this agreement, which never seemed to offer a satisfactory solution to Anglo-French differences, were a contributory factor to the outbreak of the Seven Years War (1756–63), at the end of which Britain took all the islands except St Lucia.

NEUTRALISM, term which gained currency in the 1950s denoting a refusal to take sides in international conflict, particularly in the Cold War between the US and the Soviet Union. The term covers a wide spectrum of foreign policies ranging from those of Sweden, Finland, and Austria (whose neutralism bears a close similarity to the more legal concept of neutrality) to the anti-imperialist 'positive neutralism' of Nkrumah's Ghana.

Neutralism was first an important force in Western Europe, where a left-centre political grouping, especially in France and Western Germany, advocated a withdrawal of Europe from the Cold War as it developed between the US and the Soviet Union. Western Europe, it was argued, could not afford the expense of rearmament or the risks of military alliances and should seek security by acting as a mediatory 'third force'. This view, while it gained adherents among the Bevanite wing of the Labour Party, the German social democrats, and the French socialists was never generally accepted.

At the same time, the Indian government, inheriting a Gandhian tradition and believing India to have suffered as a result of imperialist wars fought across its territory, adopted a policy of 'non-alignment', indistinguishable from neutralism —a policy which was somewhat discredited by the experience of the war with China in 1962.

The finest flowering of neutralism came at the Bandung conference (April 1955), which brought together a group of countries, most of them newly independent, with a common interest in establishing their independence from the conflicts of the great powers. In addition, the conference opened the eyes of some rulers to the possible advantages to be gained from exploiting the interests of both sides in the Cold War— notably it served as the prelude to Nasser's purchase of arms from the Soviet Union.

The policy of neutralism is one which has had an important emotional appeal, particularly when it has been given the somewhat aggressive tones of anti-colonialism. From a more practical point of view it has brought the most tangible results to countries which, although weak in relation to the great powers, enjoy an advantageous geographical or political position or both—India, sheltered by the balance between the great powers; Egypt (until the 1967 war) because of its key position in the Middle East; and Yugoslavia as a communist state outside the Soviet bloc.

After Bandung other neutralist conferences were held, notably at Belgrade (Sept. 1961), without any durable or cohesive union being formed to bridge the widely differing interests of neutralist states.

P. Lyon, *Neutralism* (Leicester, 1963).   WFK

NEUTRALITY PACT (1870). Britain, Austria-Hungary, Russia, and Italy each agreed, on Britain's initiative, not to abandon neutrality in the Franco–Prussian War without first communicating with the others. The British government, unused to the role of bystander in European affairs, felt obliged to assert its authority. But the pact prevented Gladstone from protesting at the cession of Alsace-Lorraine to Germany without consulting its inhabitants.

NEUTRALITY PROCLAMATION (1793) in the US, declaration inaugurating what became the traditional policy of independence and neutrality in wars outside the western hemisphere. It was drafted by the attorney-general, Edmund Randolph, after news reached America of the outbreak of war between Britain and France, and signed (22 April) by President George Washington and the secretary of state, Thomas Jefferson. Although not using the word neutrality, the proclamation declared that the US would be 'friendly and impartial toward the belligerent powers', and warned American citizens against illegal activity and intervention in the war.

NEUTRALS, confederation of Canadian Iroquois Indian tribes, so-called by the French because they were neutral in the wars between the Iroquois and the Hurons. After the Iroquois destroyed the Huron (1648–9) they conquered the Neutrals (1650–1). Remnants of the Neutrals joined the Seneca villages in NY.

NEUVE-CHAPELLE, BATTLE OF (1915), during the First World War, Neuve-Chapelle was an independent British offensive, planned by Sir John French, and one of the early attempts to end the stalemate of trench warfare. The German line was broken, but it proved impossible to achieve a breakthrough because of the difficulty of bringing up reinforcements and the ability of the Germans to consolidate their position. A small advance was achieved at a cost of heavy casualties.

NEVADA, 36th member state of the US, admitted in 1864. The region east of the Sierra Nevada was claimed by Spain (1776), became part of Mexico (1821), and was ceded to the US by the treaty of Guadalupe–Hidalgo (1848). It was explored by the fur traders, Peter Ogden (1825) and Jedediah Smith (1826), and was surveyed by John C. Frémont (1843–5). Following settlement at Mormon Station, later Genoa (1849), the area was incorporated within Utah Territory (1850). The discovery of silver at the Comstock Lode (1859) brought an influx of prospectors. NV was rapidly organized as a separate territory (1861) and achieved statehood (1864). Because of its arid climate, the state's economy was largely dependent upon mining, and, having had little success in attracting related industries, it has the smallest population of any US state. The liberalization of Nevada's divorce and gambling laws (1931) led to the rise of Reno and Las Vegas, greatly increased its transient population, and brought new prosperity. Since the Second World War its unpopulated areas have been used as weapon testing grounds.

NEVERS, LOUIS GONZAGUE, Duke of (1539–95), French soldier and son of the Duke of Mantua, who was a leader of the Catholic League in the French Civil Wars, but was later reconciled to Henry IV (1590) and made superintendent of finance (1594).

NEVILLE'S CROSS, BATTLE OF (17 Oct. 1346), near Durham. In the autumn of 1346 the Scots invaded England in an attempt to divert King Edward III from the siege of Calais. At Neville's Cross their army was defeated by the northern English baronage and King David II was captured.

NEVIS, island in the Caribbean discovered (1493) by Columbus, and colonized by the British from St Kitts (1628). Sugar plantations were developed despite repeated attacks by French and Spanish. Nevis joined the Leeward Islands federation (1871–1956) and was a member of the West Indies Federation (1958–62). It remains (1970) a British Crown colony.

NEW BISCAY (Nueva Vizcaya), territorial division of colonial Mexico, which comprised roughly the modern states of Durango, Chihuahua, and Zacatecas.

NEW BRITAIN (in the Pacific), large island in the Admiralty group, inhabited by Melanesians, discovered by Le Maire (1616) and named by Carteret (1767). The 1878 armed reprisal by the Rev. G. Brown, a Wesleyan missionary, against murdered villagers made conditions safer for German copra traders (Godeffroys, 1873) who paved the way for German annexation (1884). Occupied (1914) by Australia ('C' mandate, 1920), the island was seized in 1942 by Japan but its impregnable base at Truk was finally neutralized by the US installation at Manus (April 1944).

NEW BRUNSWICK, Canadian maritime province, created in 1784 and one of the four original provinces to join the Dominion of Canada (1867). It was originally part of Acadia under the French. The area was ceded to Britain in 1713 and made part of NS. After the American War of Independence some 12,000 loyalists settled there (1783) and the province was established and named in honour of the British ruling house (1784). The first governor was Thomas Carleton, brother of Sir Guy Carleton. Large numbers of British immigrants arrived in the first half of the 19th cent., but the French-speaking element, only 2 per cent in 1867, had risen to over 40 per cent by 1970.

NEW CALEDONIA (in the Pacific), large reef-girt Melanesian island, off eastern Australia, named by Cook (1774). Shipwreck and cannibals claimed many early traders, and London Missionary Society teachers and Marist priests were expelled after an epidemic (1847), the latter returning with James Paddon in 1851. The island was covertly annexed by Admiral Despointes (1853) as a possible French convict colony. With Port de France (Noumea) as capital (1859), the first convicts arrived in 1864, Parisian communards and Algerian rebels following in 1872. A gold rush (1863), Jules Garnier's discovery of cobalt, manganese, and nickel (1865), and the establishment of Higginson's nickel company (1877), employing New Hebridean labour, caused European settlement (432 in 1860) to leap to 16,895 in 1877 and 23,500 in 1901. Chronic native resistance was suppressed with difficulty, many recalcitrants being deported to the Loyalty Islands and the Melanesian population declining to 27,000 by 1921. The island was a strategic US base in The Second World War.

NEW COURTIERS, concept of the perfect courtier combining new ethical, intellectual, military, sporting, and urbane standards with elegance, symbolizing the highest moral aspirations of the Renaissance. The ideal qualities were first set out in the influential dialogue *Il Cortegiano* (1528) by Baldassare Castiglione (1478–1529). It was translated into English (1561) by Sir Thomas Hoby and had great influence upon the manners of Elizabethan gentlemen, as well as upon English literature, *eg*, the works of Surrey, Wyatt, Sidney, and Spenser.

NEW DEAL, in the US, name given to the legislative programme (1933–9) of President F. D. Roosevelt. In his acceptance speech to the Democratic national convention (2 July 1932), Roosevelt pledged himself to a new deal for the American people. Its precise terms were undefined, and the nature of the New Deal has since been a source of debate among commentators and historians, but in his speech Roosevelt emphasized 'planned action', an 'enlightened international outlook', and a liberal philosophy aimed at achieving the 'greatest good for the greatest number'. Stressing the necessity for government intervention in the economy in order to cure the Depression, he stated that economic laws are made by men and not by nature. He stressed the right of men to work and to security, and the importance of a more equitable distribution of national wealth, and committed himself to a pragmatic policy. Ironically, in terms of what was to come, he urged the need for economy in government. Such themes were reiterated during the presidential campaign, and in his inaugural address (4 March 1933) Roosevelt renewed his commitment to a New Deal. During the first hundred days of his administration the programme began to take shape in the Agricultural Adjustment Act, the National Industrial Recovery Act, the Tennessee Valley Authority Act, and many other acts, including legislation to regulate banks, mortgage and loan associations, and the securities markets. The complex legislative programme, largely drafted by members of the 'Brain Trust', suggested that the New Deal was an attempt to plan the economy without resort to nationalization, to raise prices, stimulate employment, relieve distress by both direct and indirect relief, and conserve natural resources. Agencies such as the Public Works, Civil Works, and Works Progress Administrations involved deficit spending on a large scale, as principles of economy were sacrificed to the needs of people in distress. Unforeseen consequences, such as the dispossession of tenant farmers as a result of agricultural policies, have led some critics to suggest that the New Deal was at first committed to recovery rather than reform, and that only in the 'second' New Deal of 1935, stimulated by increasing political opposition and embodied in the Social Security, Labor Relations, and Revenue Acts, did the administration seriously begin to attempt the reform of American society. However, in stressing the need for 'bold, persistent experimentation' Roosevelt, who saw himself as only a 'little left of center', always relied upon co-operation rather than coercion and from the beginning recovery and reform elements were intertwined as, for example, in the Tennessee Valley policy. Political considerations were always important in influencing the precise nature and timing of legislation. Although the economic depression was cured in the end by the coming of the Second World War, a measure of recovery was attained and the psychological and institutional effects of the New Deal were far-reaching. In international affairs the New Deal pursued the policy of the Good Neighbor and continued the traditional policy of avoiding entangling alliances, but sought to modify the prevailing concept of neutrality to enable the US to give economic support, short of war, to the democratic victims of aggression.

W. E. Leuchtenburg, *Franklin D. Roosevelt and the New Deal* (New York, 1963)
Broadus Mitchell, *Depression Decade* (New York, 1947).

DKA

NEW DEMOCRACY in China, key political policy of Mao Tse-tung, who outlined his ideas in an article, 'On New Democracy', published in 1940. Mao based his ideas on Lenin's concept of two revolutionary stages, a 'bourgeois-democratic' and a socialist stage; he expanded this concept to allow 'several revolutionary classes' to participate in the leadership of the first stage. The article's importance lay in the fact that Mao now felt secure enough, as a Marxist in his own right, to modify Lenin's ideas to suit the particular circumstances of China.

NEW ECHOTA, TREATY OF (Dec. 1835) in US, which ceded all Cherokee Indian land to the US in return for $5,600,000 and transportation of the tribe westwards. A majority of the Cherokee rejected the treaty, but it served as the basis for the Cherokee removal to the Indian Territory (1835–8).

NEW ECONOMIC POLICY. The adoption of NEP was announced by Lenin to the Tenth Party Congress in March 1921. Its predecessor, War Communism, had worked while the Civil War was in progress (up to the end of 1920) because the peasants had feared the result of a White victory, namely the restoration of private estates. But with the removal of this fear the peasants had revolted against the most objectionable feature of War Communism, the requisitioning of grain. The towns were not being fed and the urban population was pouring out into the country. Economic life was paralysed and the party was engaged in a war against the peasants. Consequently the essence of NEP was the conciliation of the peasantry. Grain requisitioning was abolished and replaced by a 10 per cent tax in kind. The purchase and sale of land was still prohibited, but peasants were allowed to lease land and to hire labour. Both individual and communal forms of land tenure were permitted. These measures certainly helped to alleviate the desperate conditions of 1921–2. By 1927 the total amount of grain produced was rather above the total for 1913; the peasant was enjoying a brief 'golden age'. The restoration of conditions of private trading for the peasant was accompanied by equivalent concessions in the industrial field. The capitalist market in light industrial goods was restored and the 'Nepman' merchant and manufacturer encouraged to enrich himself by supplying such goods as would attract the new peasant purchasing power. Such free market transactions were stimulated by the ending of the wild inflation of the War Communism period and the introduction of a stable new currency, the *chervonets*. Heavy industry remained under state control, but its products had to compete in the free market. This led to conditions of peculiar difficulty for heavy industry; capital was difficult to find and the peasant market did not easily absorb its products. The result was heavy unemployment in the industrial towns among the proletarian class which was the traditional backbone of the party. The 'scissors crisis' (1923) was a dramatic illustration of the imbalance between peasant and urban purchasing power. After the first shock, NEP had been accepted as a progressive means for the slow transition to socialism by most of the party leaders, with the exception of Trotsky. His desire to abandon NEP for a more dynamic plan helped to unite the other party leaders against him. But as soon as his challenge had been defeated (1927) Stalin began the moves against NEP which led at length to its total abandonment in the adoption of the first Five Year Plan (1929). Stalin's motives were probably mixed. In the economic field the continuation of NEP would have meant a dangerously slow tempo of industrial development. On the political front it was dangerous to allow the peasant to remain in control of agriculture. The inauguration of collectivization announced what was the most important result of NEP for the party, namely that it had given itself a breathing space for reorganization and unification.

E. H. Carr, *The Bolshevik Revolution*, vol. 2 (London, 1954).
E. H. Carr, *Socialism In One Country*, 2 vols (London, 1959).
GS

NEW ENGLAND, DOMINION OF (1688–9), consolidation of eight English colonies. Under the leadership of Joseph Dudley and later of Sir Edmund Andros, colonial assemblies were abolished, taxes and quit rents levied, and the Church of England given official encouragement. After the revolution in England (1689) Andros was imprisoned and the Dominion collapsed.

NEW ENGLAND COMPANY (1628), an English joint-stock venture to promote trade and colonization in North America. The company was given a patent to land along the MA coast between the Merrimack and Charles rivers, and took charge of the settlement of Salem, appointing John Endecott as governor. It was reorganized (1629) as the Massachusetts Bay Co.

The New England Co. (1649) was organized by the Society for the Propagation of the Gospel in New England to raise funds and provide workers to set up villages of 'praying Indians' on lands granted for the purpose. The company was led by John Eliot. King Philip's War (1675) largely destroyed this work.

NEW ENGLAND CONFEDERATION (1643), American colonial union of Massachusetts Bay, Plymouth, Connecticut, and New Haven for defence against the Dutch, French, and Indians. Boundary controversies were settled and the territorial integrity of each colony was guaranteed. A board of eight commissioners chosen annually by the respective legislatures could declare defensive and offensive war and had jurisdiction over Indian affairs and inter-colonial disputes. The confederation directed operations during King Philip's War (1675), but was dissolved when the Massachusetts Bay charter was revoked (1684). It was the first federation in America and pointed the way towards ultimate federation.

NEW ENGLAND WAY, religious and civil organization developed by the Puritans in Massachusetts Bay colony. Church and state were united, the magistrates were chosen by the ministry, and the franchise was limited to church members. The New England Way was proposed by Puritan elements in England (1640–60).

NEW FRANCE, French name for all land discovered, explored, or claimed by France in North America from the time of Giovanni da Verrazano's explorations along the Atlantic coast (1524). New France ended with the sale of LA to the US (1803).

NEW FREEDOM in the US, name given by Woodrow Wilson to the political philosophy articulated in his presidential campaign addresses of 1912. At a time when Americans were disturbed by the apparent concentration of economic and political power, Wilson emphasized the difference between his approach to this problem and that of his chief rival, the Progressive Party's candidate, Theodore Roosevelt. Roosevelt's 'New Nationalism' called for the assertion of the federal government's power to regulate the activities of large corporations in the national interest and to protect disadvantaged groups through social welfare legislation. Wilson, influenced by the traditions of Jeffersonian democracy and Cobdenite liberalism, alleged that such a programme would institutionalize the dominance of big business. American ideals would be corrupted by the 'philanthropy' of a paternalistic government and could be restored only through the abolition of special privilege and the revival of a competitive system which would provide opportunity for individual initiative. 'If America is not to have free enterprise, then she can have freedom of no sort whatever.'

The New Freedom and the New Nationalism were based upon different analyses of the rise of big business. Wilson adopted the view of his adviser, Louis D. Brandeis (whom he appointed to the Supreme Court in 1916), that the 'trusts' had been created through the unscrupulous use of economic power to control credit and markets, thus eliminating competitors and exploiting consumers. Roosevelt, like the publicist Herbert Croly (*The Promise of American Life*, 1909), saw large-scale business organizations as an inevitable result of technological advance and denounced 'trust-busting' as 'rural toryism'. But the theoretical clarity of this distinction became somewhat blurred when Wilson admitted that some corporations had grown large through their efficiency and explained gnomically that, though 'against the trusts', he was 'for big business'.

Certainly the doctrinal purity of the New Freedom did not long survive Wilson's attempt to put it into practice. Of the major reform legislation passed during his first term as president (1913–17), only the reduction of duties in the Underwood Tariff (1913) and the outlawing of certain trade practices in the Clayton Anti-trust Act (1913) clearly accorded with the philosophy of the New Freedom. The Federal Reserve Act (1913) and the establishment of the Federal Trade Commission (1914) represented concessions to the New Nationalist ideal of employing the government's authority to regulate economic activity for the common good. Welfare legislation like the Seamen's Act (1915) and the Child Labor Law of 1916 (declared unconstitutional by the Supreme Court, 1918), and such 'special interest' measures as the Farm Loan Act (1916) and the Adamson Act (1916) establishing an eight-hour day on inter-state railroads, were even more clearly contrary to the principles Wilson had enunciated in 1912. Nevertheless, the distrust of concentrated power, whether in the hands of big business or the national government, which was at the heart of the New Freedom, has always been an important strand in US thought.

Woodrow Wilson, *The New Freedom: a call for the emancipation of the generous energies of a people* (New York, 1913).
Arthur S. Link, *Woodrow Wilson and the Progressive Era, 1910–17* (New York and London, 1954). JAT

NEW FRONTIER in the US, term used by J. F. Kennedy, when accepting the US presidential nomination of the Democratic Party (1960), that came to symbolize the spirit of hope and expectation that pervaded his administration (1961–3). Kennedy's statement, that although the traditional frontier of the pioneers had long since been closed, Americans in the 1960s stood on the edge of a new frontier 'of unfulfilled hopes and threats', echoed F. D. Roosevelt's style in the 1930s. It later became clear that in many ways he saw his own legislative programme as an extension of the New Deal. The federal government accepted additional responsibility in such areas as the improvement of civil rights for minority groups, taxation reform, and the extension of social security coverage. In the field of foreign affairs Kennedy stressed the US commitment to the preservation of freedom, but gave a warning that there could not be an American solution to every world problem.

NEW GALICIA, political and judicial sub-division (*audiencia*) of colonial Mexico, centred in Guadalajara, whose jurisdiction in western Mexico was bounded by the Sierra Madre Occidental and stretched northwards through Durango and Chihuahua to New Mexico.

NEW GRANADA, name in colonial times of what is roughly modern Colombia. From 1717 (and, more permanently, from 1739) until independence, New Granada was also the name of a viceroyalty which included modern Colombia, Venezuela, Ecuador, and Panama.

'NEW GUARD', THE AUSTRALIAN, organization established on Nazi or Fascist lines which functioned in Sydney, NSW (1931–5), with the avowed objective of organizing paramilitary resistance to the debt-repudiation and other 'communist' policies of the Labor prime minister, J. T. Lang.

NEW GUINEA, AUSTRALIA AND. Australian interests in eastern New Guinea were aroused during the 19th cent. by naval and other visitors to its coasts, *eg*, Blackwood, Yule, Owen Stanley, Moresby, by occasional colonization proposals, by the activities of labour recruiters, and by signs of German interest in the islands, the western section of which was already within the Dutch sphere. In 1884, after prolonged Australian colonial pressure, Britain declared a protectorate over the south-eastern part of the island. Though German annexation of north-eastern New Guinea followed a month later, Britain's formal annexation of its protectorate did not take place until 1888. Thereafter it was administered jointly by Britain, Qld, NSW, and Vic. until 1906, when the Commonwealth of Australia accepted responsibility for the territory (then called Papua) and a tradition of benevolent administration was established under Sir Hubert Murray.

Australian troops seized German New Guinea during the First World War, after which Australia accepted responsibility for its administration as a 'C' class mandate, separate from Papua. Both territories became a battleground in the Second World War. A combined post-war administration launched new policies for development and welfare, Australia accepting positive responsibility for preparing 'Papua–New Guinea' for self-government. Substantial constitutional and administrative reforms were well received on the whole by the indigenous population (approx. 2¼ million) and the small Asian and European minorities. Continued attacks by the UN Trusteeship Council on the slow rate of political progress were more polemical than appreciative of the difficulties presented by the fragmented character of the indigenous society, the mountainous condition of the country, and the low level of material development.   JDL

NEW HAMPSHIRE, former English colony in North America. The area was visited by Champlain (1605) and John Smith (1614). The Council for New England (1620) received much of NH under royal grant and the first permanent settlement was founded by David Thomson at the mouth of the Piscataqua river (1623). Capt. John Mason and Sir Ferdinando Gorges were given rights to the territory between the Merrimack and Kennebeck rivers and later from the Merrimack to the Piscataqua (1623). Mason named the colony in honour of his home county in England, and is considered the founder of the colony. Portsmouth, the only NH seaport, was founded in 1630. The colony was settled, chiefly in the southern half, by families from CT and MA. NH was claimed by MA until 1679, when it became a separate royal colony. There was much conflict with the Indians and during wars with the French there were frequently raids on NH frontier settlements. The royal governor was driven out (1776) and the citizens were governed by a provisional constitution until 1784, when NH entered the union as a state.

NEW HARMONY in US, communistic settlement on the Wabash river, IN, founded by Robert Owen in 1825. New Harmony began as a co-operative enterprise and soon attracted a heterogeneous collection of settlers. On 5 Feb. 1826 the constitution of 'The New Harmony Community of Equality' was adopted. It provided for complete equality of labour and opportunity, common ownership of property, freedom of speech and action, and a law-making power vested in an assembly comprising all adult residents. But, lacking any real centre of authority, and with inadequate facilities, New Harmony quickly ran into difficulties and Owen admitted the failure of his experiment (May 1827). The settlement's weekly journal, the *New Harmony Gazette*, became, after 1829, the *Free Enquirer*, a vehicle for agnostic and socialist opinion.

NEW HAVEN COLONY (1638–60), English settlement on Long Island Sound, founded under the leadership of John Davenport and Theophilus Eaton. The colony was governed by a strict theocratic organization. It joined the New England Confederation (1643) and became a part of Connecticut colony when the latter received a royal charter after the Restoration (1660).

NEW HEBRIDES, THE, volcanic South-West Pacific archipelago inhabited by Melanesians, discovered by Quiros (1606) and charted by Cook (1774). Regular European contact was initiated by whalers (1800) and sandalwoders exploiting Dillon's find at Erromanga (1825). Early mission efforts ended disastrously in the martyrdom of John Williams at Erromanga (1839) and the expulsion of a new venture at Tanna (1842–3). In 1844 the sandalwooder James Paddon settled (till 1851) on Aneityum, where in 1848 John Geddie founded the Presbyterian mission. Presbyterian distrust of French intentions (1875) culminated in an Anglo-French non-annexation agreement (1878), challenged in 1882 by John Higginson's land-grabbing New Caledonia Nickel Co., which briefly hoisted the French flag at Efate and Malekula in 1886. Australian fears of French expansion aided the conversion of the Mixed Naval Commission (1887) into an Anglo-French Condominium (1907), which almost foundered in mutual recrimination by 1914 but dealt sensibly with post-war problems, including the John Frum cargo cult on Tanna. In 1970 an enlightened political programme was leading the group to eventual independence.

NEW HOLLAND, name given by 17th-cent. Dutch navigators to the western portion of *Terra Australis Incognita* which they discovered en route from the Cape to Batavia. It was sometimes used for the continent as a whole after British settlement in NSW on the east coast and gave place to 'Australia' early in the 19th cent.

NEW IRELAND, (in the Pacific), large Melanesian island off north-east New Guinea, discovered by Le Maire (1616), scene of a colonizing fiasco led by the French Marquis de Rays in 1880. Many settlers died of malaria, the remnant removing to Australia, Rays himself being imprisoned for four years in France. Annexed by Germany as a labour reservoir (1884) the island was seized by Australia in 1914 and became part of the 'C' mandate in 1920.

NEW JERSEY, former English colony in North America. NJ was first seen by white men when Verrazano sailed along the coast (1524). It was then inhabited by peaceful tribes of Algonquian and Delaware Indians. North-eastern NJ became a part of New Netherland (1609) when Henry Hudson explored and settled the area. When the English fleet, under Col. Nicolls (1664), took New Netherland from the Dutch, the territory between the Hudson and Delaware rivers was ceded to Sir George Carteret and Lord John Berkeley, and was named New Jersey because of Carteret's interests in the island of Jersey during the English Civil War. The proprietors found it difficult to collect quit rents and in 1672 deposed the appointed governor. East Jersey was initially settled by Puritans from New England, under a grant from Gov. Nicolls, of NY. West Jersey was purchased by two

Quakers, John Fenwick and Edward Byllinge. By 1679 East and West Jersey were purchased by a predominantly Quaker company led by William Penn. The new proprietors adopted a liberal constitution and under Robert Barclay, appointed in 1682, the colony prospered. The economy of East Jersey resembled the mercantile establishments and small farmholds of New England, while in West Jersey plantations and slaves were introduced.

During the American War of Independence loyalists furnished six battalions to the British, but the majority of the citizens upheld the Revolution. The area was strategically important and the major battles of Trenton, Princeton, and Monmouth were fought in NJ. A state constitution was accepted (1776) and NJ entered the union (1787).

J. T. Cunningham, *New Jersey: America's main road* (New York, 1966).   DJF

NEW JERSEY PLAN (1787) in the US, proposals for altering the system of government advanced by William Paterson (1745–1806) at the Philadelphia Convention. In response to the nationalist Virginia plan, it recommended amendment rather than abandonment of the articles of confederation, in order to strengthen the powers of Congress while retaining the federal principles of the sovereignty and equality of the states. Small states would be protected from domination by large states through equal representation in a unicameral legislature. Although the plan was rejected, the Connecticut compromise and subsequently agreed constitution embodied the principle of state equality in the upper house.

NEW KINGDOM, third great period (Old, Middle, and New Kingdoms) of ancient Egypt, which covered the XVIIIth–XXth dynasties (c. 1575–1087 BC), beginning with the expulsion of the Hyksos. Under a number of great kings, eg, Thothmes I and III, Seti I and Rameses III (ruling mostly from Thebes), who employed large, well-equipped professional armies, Egypt made conquests in Syria, Palestine, and Nubia and took large quantities of valuable commodities, especially from the last. Many great buildings were constructed, notably at Thebes and El-Amarnah. Administration, under royal control, was centralized and bureaucratic. At the end of the XXth dynastic period the Theban priests gained control of the Theban area and the kingdom was divided.

NEW LAWS OF 1542, legislation which represented the first effective limitation of the power of the Spanish conquerors over the Indian population of Latin America. There was a variety of reasons for the introduction of the laws. Among them were the Spanish Crown's determination to prevent the growth of a conquistador aristocracy, the bulls of Pope Paul III (1537), declaring the Indian a rational being and the continuous pressure exerted by Las Casas and his followers. Above all, disturbing reports of violence and anarchy following the conquest of Peru emphasized the need for comprehensive legislation to enforce royal authority.

The 54 articles of the New Laws, forming the first comprehensive code for the governance of Spanish America, were largely traditional. Only four articles were explosively contentious. In particular, Articles 31 and 35 abolished, in effect, the *encomienda* grants whereby the conquerors had been rewarded with the tribute and labour services of the natives. Some grants were now to be terminated immediately, especially those of individuals who had taken part in the recent civil wars of Peru, a clause which would have deprived virtually every Peruvian *encomendero*. All other *encomiendas*, on the death of their holders, were to escheat to the Crown. Further, Indian slavery was virtually abolished. Only Indians lawfully enslaved (eg, captured in rebellion) were to retain servile status, and future enslavement was completely forbidden.

This legislation came at a singularly inopportune time. In Mexico the Mixton Rebellion (1540–1) had recently been suppressed with great difficulty by the *encomenderos*, who were outraged by rumours of the New Laws. In Peru the distribution of *encomiendas* among the conquerors was barely completed. Bloody civil war among the Spanish had only recently ceased, Manco Inca was still at large, and now the government proposed to take away the conquerors' livelihood.

Knowing that colonial officials hesitated to enforce unpopular enactments, in 1544 the Crown sent out special commissioners to implement the New Laws. In Mexico, however, Viceroy Mendoza, attuned to colonial sentiment, prevented their proclamation and thus averted a major rebellion. For Peru, the first viceroy (Blasco Núñez) was appointed, and the Lima *audiencia* created, with express orders to enforce the New Laws. Blasco Núñez's blind adherence to his instructions provoked the armed insurrection of Gonzalo Pizarro, in which the viceroy himself was killed. This, the first major overt rebellion among New World Spaniards, was ruthlessly suppressed in 1548, but, in the face of colonial resistance, the Crown in the next ten years looked for the minimum concessions which would make the New Laws enforceable without sacrificing any major principle. The laws on Indian slavery remained. *Encomiendas* were retained, but *encomenderos* became entitled only to the tributes of their Indians and not to their labour. The Crown allowed grants to be inherited, thus assuring to the conquerors and their descendants an income in consideration of their past exertions, but *encomiendas* were never granted in perpetuity. In effect, the New Laws were the single most important step in the Crown's reconquest of Spanish America from its conquerors.

Lewis Hanke, *The Spanish Struggle for Justice in the Conquest of America* (Boston and Toronto, 1965).   FPB

'NEW LEARNING', the mainly Christian humanism of the Renaissance, which was 'new' in its respect for pagan antiquity. The Renaissance was a culmination rather than a rebirth, a goal as much as a starting-point. It fulfilled the slow maturing of the Italian genius, stimulated by the rediscovery of ancient learning and the desire to recreate a glorious past, and hastened in its final stages by geographical exploration and the invention of printing. It had little to do with the dispersal of Greek scholars after the fall of Constantinople (1453), by which time the native Latin culture was already reflowering. If the Renaissance can be defined at all, it was that moment, to which no particular date is assignable, when theology ceased to be 'queen of the sciences'.

In philosophy the new learning rejected the introvert nominalism of the universities, but it only did this in traditional scholastic ways, replacing the old curriculum with one that happened to be based on classical studies. But this revolution interacted with a general secularization of life. Piety and reverence were in decline, beauty was asserting its own independent values, and tradition was swept aside in the rush for self-expression. Machiavelli could even tell the truth about politics; a truth perhaps long recognized but never stated with such bluntness.

The Italian impulse was carried through Europe by the presses and by papal nuncios and tax-gatherers like Polydore Vergil. Scholarship led to ecclesiastical preferment, and Latin, the lingua franca, was a means to political and diplomatic careers. The new collegiate foundations adopted rhetorical disciplines in preference to the old theology. Oxford, which thanks to Humphrey of Gloucester was much richer in classical texts than ecclesiastical commentaries, was dedicated to the new learning, and More was unusual among the young scholars in not continuing his studies in Italy. *The Ship of Fools* (1494; English version, 1509), Erasmus's *Praise of Folly* (1509), and the *Letters of Obscure Men* (1515), in defiance of the effort to discredit Reuchlin in Germany, were typical humanist satires on the dead obscurantism of the past.

But liberation had its problems. Sensible scholars could reject such extravagances as the attempt to equate Christianity with Stoicism or to reconcile Genesis with Plato's

Timaeus, but students visiting Italy travelled through Florence and encountered Savonarola's denunciations of the godless libertinism of the age. Valla and Cusanus had exposed some papal forgeries, and Erasmus in his *New Testament* (1516) rediscovered Roger Bacon's glosses on some crucial passages in the Vulgate, which raised further doubts about certain features of the ecclesiastical establishment. Above all, the explorers were proving that the Christian world was not bounded by unnavigable oceans and the vast Mohammedan wastes. Conceivably, then, Christianity itself was just a local religion disseminated through the accident that the Judaean mountains sloped more gently towards the sea and therefore directed Jewish monotheism towards the Mediterranean.

Faced by awful possibilities, humanism became cautious and conservative. This indeed was its nature, because the new scholars were not particularly given to independent judgement or creative thought. They were quite unscientific, they worried overmuch about the Ciceronian perfection of their style, and where they had no classical exemplars to guide them, they dabbled in alchemy and astrology. Thus their training did not equip them to examine the Church as an institution or to question its basic ceremonies and doctrines. They simply believed that abuses could be cured by ridicule and the spread of learning.

In this they made some progress, and it was the only 'reform' with which they can be credited. Even Wolsey founded colleges. In Spain Ximenes established a university to edit the scriptures and train the clergy, and Reuchlin in Germany, and the communities of Valdes in Naples and Lefèvre and Briçonnet at Meaux, showed what learning and good intentions might achieve. It was the same in England, where Mountjoy's patronage attracted scholars like More, Erasmus, Linacre, Lily, and Colet, and allowed Henry VIII to think of himself as an enlightened prince.

But the humanists' encouragement of an informal, pietist, ethical Christianity was a fatal legacy to the future, and by their constant ridicule and their deference to pagan writers they devalued theology as a branch of knowledge and undermined respect for the learning and authority of the Church. Colet claimed to use classical scholarship as an instrument for interpreting scripture, and at least he founded a school (St Paul's, London), but he and his fellows never went to the root of the abuses they wanted to correct. When Luther made his protest, the scholars patronizingly welcomed such enlightenment in a monk, especially an Augustinian. But as soon as he began to speak of an invisible Church and the priesthood of all believers, his language was beyond their understanding.   MMR

NEW LIFE MOVEMENT in China, launched in 1935 as a movement of spiritual regeneration. It was Chiang Kai-shek's attempt to instill moral fibre into the demoralized Chinese people and arm them against the communist menace. It involved a return to Confucian virtues and laid great stress on modesty. Unfortunately, the virtues Chiang advocated were anachronistic, and were flagrantly abused by his own followers, and the movement eventually petered out.

NEW MEXICO, large area in south-western US, originally reaching from LA to CA. NM has been inhabited by man for at least 10,000 years. The earliest evidences of human life on the North American continent have been discovered here. The Hohokam and Salado Indians were farmers and irrigators in prehistoric times, and the Anasazi built cities. About 1000 years ago the war-like Navaho and Apache arrived.

Spanish explorations in the area began in 1525, Cabeza de Vaca being the first Spaniard to bring back reports of the area. Francisco Coronada (1540) explored as far north as Taos and west to the Grand Canyon. Spanish friars followed and small settlements of white men were established among the Pueblos. Juan de Onate's expedition established the first permanent settlement and Santa Fé was founded in 1610.

In 1680 the Pueblo Indians revolted and killed many settlers and priests and drove out the rest. Spanish troops under Diego de Vargas returned to NM in 1692 and by 1696 the whole province was under Spanish rule. Later the Spanish king confirmed the ownership of their lands to the Pueblos, which is the basis of their present holdings. By the end of the 18th cent. there were about 20,000 Spanish living in the province and about 10,000 peaceful Indians. The population was harried by the war-like nomadic tribes of Navaho, Apache, and Comanche.

In the 19th cent. trade with Missouri valley towns flourished and the Santa Fé trail became a major route to the west. During the Mexican War Gen. Stephen Watts Kearney entered NM and took formal possession of it for the US. Congress created the territory of NM on 9 Sept. 1850 and the territory of AZ, of the western half of NM, in 1863. The later 19th cent. saw the final defeat of the Navahos and the Apaches and their settlement on reservations. The Atlantic and Pacific railroad, later called the Atcheson, Topeka, and Santa Fé, reached Albuquerque in 1880. The population increased and cattle raising was introduced, causing much conflict with the sheep ranchers. On 6 Jan. 1912 NM was formally admitted as a state.

E. Fergusson, *New Mexico, a pageant of three peoples,* 2nd ed. (New York, 1964).
W. A. Beck, *New Mexico, a history of four centuries,* 1st ed. (Norman, OK, 1962).   DJF

NEW MODEL ARMY in England, professionally trained army which won the English Civil War for parliament. The victory of Marston Moor (1644) was not followed up, and the incompetence and indecision of the 'Presbyterian' generals, Essex, Manchester, and Waller, was exposed. Parliament decided to form a professionally trained army which would enable the war to be won on the battlefield. On 17 Feb. 1645 an ordinance was passed creating such an army of 6600 horse, 14,400 foot, and 1000 dragoons. It replaced the armies of the county associations, from which it drew many of its men, introducing the tactics and organization of the Swedish army of Gustavus Adolphus. Placed under the command of Sir Thomas Fairfax, with Oliver Cromwell as lieutenant-general of horse, the army was pledged to 'the defence of the king and parliament, the true Protestant religion, and the laws and liberties of the kingdom'. The myth that the army was an army of saints fighting for God's kingdom on earth was a contemporary creation of the junior officers and men who supported the Levellers. Many of the soldiers were pressed men, and many more enlisted for the pay, willing to follow their officers unquestioningly provided arrears of pay were forthcoming. Yet the army had the privilege of religious toleration, and the continuation of this liberty was always high on its list of demands. There were no questions about class or religion when a man enlisted, and though the officers were expected to take the Covenant, the common soldiers were not. Some officers were of low social origin, but most were men of substance. Despite the Covenant, it is correct to describe the New Model Army as an Independent force.   CJ

NEW NATIONALISM in the US, political reform programme advocated by former US president, Theodore Roosevelt, based on the principle that the national government was the best instrument for furthering progressive democracy. In radical speeches at Osawatomie and Denver (1910) and again in the 1912 election campaign, Roosevelt called for a 'new nationalism' to bring about a wide-ranging programme of political, social, and industrial reforms founded upon an augmentation of federal power. To some extent his ideas on social justice and the means for its achievement may have been influenced by Herbert Croly's *Promise of American Life* (1909), but there is a clear connection between the New Nationalism of 1910–12 and Roosevelt's messages to Congress in 1907 and 1908. Then he had demanded the extension of federal regulatory powers, especially over railroads and the activities of the stock market, and a better deal for labour, and had bitterly attacked the 'malefactors of great wealth' and the federal courts. In 1910 he went further in the same direction, and described the federal courts as one of the fundamental barriers to the securing of social justice, in that they had over-protected property rights, and had created a 'neutral area' in which lawless wealth could not be controlled by state action. His solution was to increase federal power, make the courts subordinate to Congress and the Chief Executive, and ensure that the community should have power to regulate property 'to whatever degree the public welfare should require'. In his bid for the presidency in 1912, he appealed to the social justice group of American progressives, and emphasized the social objectives of his programme, *inter alia* a minimum wage for women workers, a federal child labour law, and extended federal health and conservation schemes, thus anticipating much of what was achieved by Wilson's and F. D. Roosevelt's administrations.

G. E. Mowry, *The Era of Theodore Roosevelt* (New York, 1958).
G. Kolko, *The Triumph of Conservatism* (New York, 1963).
DBS

NEW NETHERLAND, Dutch North American possession, reaching from Albany, NY, to Gloucester, NJ. New Netherland was first explored by Henry Hudson (1609) and settled by the Dutch West India Co. in 1624. Peter Minuit, the first director-general, purchased Manhattan Island from the Indians for 60 guilders ($24), and founded New Amsterdam, later New York City (1626). The colony was controlled by wealthy patrons, who established feudal estates along the Hudson river. New Netherland was seized by the English (1664) and granted to the Duke of York.

'NEW ORDER' IN INDONESIA (1965). After the Oct. 1965 coup, the army and its anti-left allies demanded a New Order (*Orde Baru*) to replace Sukarno's Guided Democracy. Students organized in army-sponsored 'Action Groups' and younger officers prominent in the anti-communist campaigns sought an authoritarian modernizing regime with direct army responsibility for government. Although Suharto's government used New Order slogans, its reluctance to break with older political modes and personnel led to strained relations with these militants.

NEW ORLEANS, BATTLE OF (8 Jan. 1815), engagement in the War of 1812. US troops, under Andrew Jackson, decisively repulsed a British attack on New Orleans. American losses were light but British casualties were heavy. The battle, fought two weeks after the treaty of Ghent (24 Dec. 1814), had no effect on the peace terms, but made Jackson a national hero.

NEW PROTECTION in Australia, term given to the unsuccessful attempt (1908) by the prime minister, Alfred Deakin, with Labor's support, to combine fiscal duties levied on foreign competitors with the maintenance of reasonable wages and working conditions for employees.

NEW PROVIDENCE, small island in the Bahamas, settled by the English in 1656 and brought under royal control in 1717. New Providence was confirmed as British in the treaty of Versailles (1783) and welcomed many loyalists from the US.

NEW REPUBLIC (1914–) in the US, weekly magazine founded by Herbert Croly, and financed by the diplomat and businessman, Willard D. Straight (1880–1918), as a vehicle for liberal opinion. Walter Lippmann was associate editor (1914–17), and the former US vice-president, Henry Wallace, after his resignation as secretary of commerce (1946), served as editor until 1948.

NEW SHOREHAM ACT (1771) in Britain, enlarging the boundaries of the parliamentary borough of Shoreham, implemented proposals of a committee set up in 1770. It provided a model for piecemeal reform of boroughs found to have practised corruption at parliamentary elections.

NEW SOUTH WALES, Australia's 'mother colony', which developed from a penal settlement (1788) into the Commonwealth's most populous and industrialized state. The pastoral industry was NSW's mainstay before 1900, although sealing, whaling, and gold each had periods of importance, with wheat becoming significant in the 1880s. Small markets and overseas competition in the early 20th cent. kept the tariff-supported secondary industries relatively weak and unstable until the 1930s, but the Second World War and post-war development brought a rapid expansion, particularly of heavy industry, and intensified urban growth. By 1970 some 2,500,000 people—over one-sixth of the Australian population—lived in Sydney.

NEW SPAIN, term employed in the Spanish colonial period to designate variously central (Aztec) Mexico, the broader *audiencia* district of the same name, and, finally, the viceroyalty, which comprised all the Spanish provinces north of the Isthmus of Panama, the Antilles, and the Philippine Islands.

NEW STATES MOVEMENT IN AUSTRALIA, THE, was largely a reaction against increasing urban industrialization and metropolitan centralization in 20th-cent. NSW, but in Qld the movement dated back to attempted readjustment of conflicting regional economic interests within that colony in the 1860s. It was most marked in NSW in the New England and Riverina regions. The movement had two periods of striking activity; in the 1930s the New England agitation was linked with opposition to Labor ascendancy in Sydney under J. T. Lang; in the mid-1950s it was sufficiently strong to establish an unofficial constitutional assembly and, a decade later, to compel the NSW state government to hold a referendum of north-eastern residents on proposals for a separate state from Newcastle to the Qld border (April 1967). The result (No, 19,030; Yes, 168,239) suggested that, though regionalism was likely to remain a vigorous influence in late 20th-cent. economic development, constitutional decentralization had become a spent force in Australian politics.

NEW SWEDEN, colonizing venture undertaken in North America by the New Sweden Co. (1637). The Swedes made a settlement on the Delaware river at Wilmington. Control of New Sweden passed to the Dutch (1664), and then to England (1664).

NEW TESTAMENT, DANISH (1524), was followed by Christiern Pedersen's improved translation (1529) and by his Bible (1550), which was based on Luther's. This Bible also became established in Norway.

NEW TESTAMENT, FINNISH (1548), translation by Mikael Agricola, bp of Turku, the first writer to publish in the Finnish language.

NEW TESTAMENT, LUTHERAN (1522), Martin Luther's German translation of the New Testament, produced while he was in hiding in the castle of Wartburg (1521–2). It appeared in Sept. 1522 as the first stage in his German version of the Bible. By the time of his death (1546) his translation had reached 377 editions, making a considerable contribution to the evolution of a unified German language.

NEW TESTAMENT, SWEDISH (1526), translation by Olaus Petri and Laurentius Andreae, based chiefly upon the Vulgate and Luther's Bible. Together with the complete Bible (1541), it helped the development of the Swedish language.

NEW TOLERATION ACT (1812) in Britain relieved Protestant dissenters from the Church of England by repealing the Five-Mile and Conventicle Acts. It also allowed Quakers to affirm instead of taking oaths and protected nonconformist worship from outside disturbance. It was passed at the instigation of the Society for Protestant Religious Liberty.

NEW UNIONISM in Britain, movement of the left generated by the demands for political and industrial action of newly founded and expanded trade unions in the latter part of the 19th cent. Trade union membership had traditionally appealed to skilled workers organized by crafts rather than by industries, but after the success of the London dock strike (1889), unskilled workers were more willing to join unions, though there were few friendly benefits. Among the unions founded at this period were the National Union of Gasworkers and General Labourers (1889), the Dock, Wharf, and Riverside Labourers Union (1889), and the Navvies, Bricklayers' Labourers, and General Labourers Union (1890). Their maximum membership (1890–2) declined in periods of depression and industrial unrest, but the new unions survived to demand a legal minimum wage, an eight-hour day, and the right to work. They also believed that the government should provide work or maintain the unemployed. These demands could only be obtained by political action, and the new unionism appealed to socialists and to liberals disillusioned with their own party through the loss of Joseph Chamberlain's radical influence following the split on Home Rule. The Independent Labour Party, founded in 1893, induced the trade union movement to join forces with socialist groups and the Labour Representation Committee was formed (1900); in 1906 it became the Labour Party. Thus New Unionism led to the financial and ideological links between the unions and the Labour Party.

NEW YORK, former English colony in North America, bordering on Canada and extending from Lake Champlain on the east to Lakes Erie and Ontario on the west. Verrazano sailed into New York Bay (1524), Champlain explored Lake Champlain (1609), and Henry Hudson sailed up the Hudson and claimed the territory for the Dutch (1609). New Netherland was established by the Dutch (1623). An English expedition, under Col. Nicolls, took New Netherland (1664) and renamed it New York after the proprietor, the Duke of York (later King James II). The colonists in NY forced the duke to grant a Charter of Liberties (1683), but when he became James II these rights were revoked. New Yorkers ultimately won the right to participate in their government, but only a privileged few were granted the franchise and the government of the colony was less democratic than in any other English colony. French traders and missionaries explored in the north and west, but the activities of William Johnson, as a friend of the Iroquois Indians of NY, kept them loyal to the British. Much of the fighting in the French and Indian War took place in NY and in the Seven Years War decisive battles were fought at Ticonderoga, Crown Point, and Fort Niagara. Many great landowners were loyalists during the American War of Independence, but supported Continental Congresses and approved the Declaration of Independence. The British captured New York City (1776) and held it during the war, but the colony declared its independence and functioned from Kingston as its first capital. NY was the 11th state to ratify the Constitution (1788) and New York City was the first capital of the new nation (1789–90).

P. Eldridge, *Crown of Empire: the story of New York State* (New York, 1957). DJF

NEW YORK TIMES (1851–), leading US daily newspaper published in New York City. It was founded by Henry J. Raymond (1820–69) and gave a strong support to the Republican Party from 1854. After the American Civil War it campaigned for political reforms in New York and against corruption wherever it was found. Under the editorship of Adolph Ochs (1896–1935) the *New York Times* established an international reputation for accurate reporting and wide coverage of events. Its slogan, 'All the News That's Fit to Print', came to symbolize its commitment to responsible and objective journalism.

NEW YOUTH in China, monthly journal published in Peking, which was influential between 1915 and 1921. Its first editor was Ch'en Tu-hsiu, a founder of the Chinese Communist Party, who introduced through it new ideas to China, mainly from the West, and led the fight for the introduction of the vernacular language into written Chinese. It was the mentor of a whole generation of young Chinese, eager to break away from the stultifying traditional society. Although many of the Western ideas it advocated were inappropriate, it generated a new, enquiring state of mind crucial to reform and revolution.

NEW ZEALAND COMPANY, THE, played an important but controversial role in the early British settlement of NZ. It originated in the NZ Association (1837), formed by E. G. Wakefield to revive 'systematic colonization' after the failure of his South Australian scheme. Government opposition forced the association to reform itself as the joint-stock NZ Co. (1838). Hasty, ill-defined 'purchases' of Maori land were made in NZ and settlers despatched to Wellington (1840), all without government approval. Company land-claims and settlements were jeopardized by the proclamation of British sovereignty (1840), but the company was rescued by the grant of a charter (1841). Settlements were founded at Wanganui (1840), New Plymouth (1841), and Nelson (1842), but by 1843 the company was in recess. It was briefly revived in 1846, but surrendered its charter in 1850. Various factors helped to thwart the company and embitter its settlers, who denounced their parent body. These included its virtual commitment to land speculation and its concern for profits; absentee land-owing; a mistaken exclusion of pastoralism; and Maori resistance. Yet the company established the main foundations of British settlement in NZ with its 8600 emigrants (1839–43).

NEW ZEALAND, EXPLORATION OF. Following discoveries up to 1800, this was mainly by land, but many coastal features remained to be charted. Capt. Cook's two major geographical errors (or doubts) were cleared up by establishing the positions of Foveaux Strait (1804) and Banks' Peninsula (1809). D'Urville (1827) filled in the details of Cook's 'Blind Bay' in the course of his extensive coastal survey. The early explorers of the North Island were principally missionaries, eg, Marsden in North Auckland (1820); H. Williams (1831, 1839) and W. Colenso (1841–2) in traverses of the interior. Squatters in search of pasture and stock routes opened up the eastern grasslands of both islands. An important exploratory journey was that of W. M. Mitchell and E. Dashwood from Nelson to Canterbury (1850). The rugged, forested west coast of the South Island was the most difficult to explore and was the scene of T. Brunner's arduous journey (1846–8).

NEWBERRY, JOHN (1713–67), English manufacturer of patent medicines, journalist, and the first publisher of children's books, *eg, Mrs Margery* (or *Goody Two Shoes*). He was a friend and patron of such writers as Goldsmith and Johnson, and appears in Goldsmith's *The Vicar of Wakefield*.

NEWBURGH ADDRESSES (1783), petitions to Congress that were circulated anonymously to discontented officers in the American War of Independence gathered at Newburgh, NY. The officers were anxious to have their claims settled before demobilization, and the addresses advocated coercion of Congress by direct action. Washington, the commander-in-chief, succeeded in calming the officers, and resolutions were adopted to accept his advice and repudiate the addresses. Their authorship was later admitted by Maj. John Armstrong jr (1758–1843), subsequently a general and secretary of war (1813–14).

NEWBURN, BATTLE OF (1640), on the Tyne, conflict in the second Bishops' War. The Scottish army, under Alexander Leslie (later Earl of Leven), and stiffened by veterans of the Thirty Years War, met an English irregular force under William Seymour, Duke of Somerset, and routed it with a cannonade.

NEWBURY, BATTLES OF (1643, 1644), near Reading, Berks. Two conflicts in the English Civil War. On 20 Sept. 1643 the royalists sought to bar the way to the Earl of Essex's parliamentary army, returning to London after raising the siege of Gloucester. Charles I withdrew after the battle because his ammunition had been exhausted, leaving the road to London open and 6000 dead on the field.

On 27th Oct. 1644, in the second battle, a large parliamentary army failed to prevent the royalists from relieving the besieged Donnington Castle. This incident led to a parliamentary quarrel with Oliver Cromwell over military organization. As a result the New Model Army was formed.

NEWCASTLE (ON-TYNE), WILLIAM CAVENDISH, Duke of (1st of 1st creation) (*c.* 1593–1676), English soldier who was appointed by Charles I as governor of the Prince of Wales (1638). In the English Civil War he commanded the four northern counties (1642), raised the siege of York, and defeated the Fairfaxes at Adwalton Moor (June 1643). The Scottish invasion forced him to retreat to York, where he was relieved by Prince Rupert, who proceeded to fight at Marston Moor, contrary to Newcastle's wishes. Upon the royalists' defeat Newcastle abandoned the king's cause and fled to the continent, where he was admitted to Charles II's privy council in 1650. At the Restoration (1660) he regained his estates, which were burdened with debts, and was reinstated in his offices. He retired from public life in 1665, wrote books on horsemanship, several comedies, and was the patron of such writers as Dryden and Hobbes.

NEWCASTLE (UNDER LYME), THOMAS PELHAM-HOLLES, 1st Duke of (1693–1768), English Whig politician, party manager, and wealthy landowner, who threw the whole of his influence into securing the succession of George I and the triumph of the Whigs. In 1717 he was appointed lord chamberlain, his first official post. His long retention of ministerial office—over 40 years—won him great personal power and influence. He was secretary of state for the south (1724–48) and for the north (1748–54). He survived the fall of Sir Robert Walpole (1742), achieving even more power under his own brother, Henry Pelham, who became prime minister in 1743. On Pelham's death (1754) Newcastle himself became prime minister, though William Pitt (later Earl of Chatham) actually ran the government after 1757. In May 1762 Newcastle was replaced by George III's favourite, Bute. The last five years of Newcastle's life were spent mainly in opposition, except for a few months as lord privy seal (1765).

As the master of the systematic management of elections and the distribution of patronage to secure parliamentary support for a ministry, he won a unique reputation as the grand elector and caucus-leader to the Whig party in and out of parliament. His rise has been ascribed to his vast wealth and his borough influence, but it in fact derived from his official position under the Crown. His greatest electoral successes were in 1722, when the Whig majority of 200 was largely due to Newcastle's exertions, and in 1734, when the Whigs were returned in spite of adverse public opinion. Newcastle, however, had few political ideas beyond carrying on the affairs of the country through Whig majorities. Though he was the indispensable link between king and parliament,

by 1760 little was left of Walpole's office of prime minister. Pitt looked after foreign policy; otherwise there was no real government.

L. B. Namier, *England in the Age of the American Revolution* (London, 1930).
B. Williams, *Carteret and Newcastle* (Cambridge, 1943).   CJ

NEWCASTLE, HOSTMEN OF, in England, coal-shippers who were freemen of Newcastle and (from 1600) had a monopoly of the coal trade from the Tyne. They were the most influential group in northern society and the inner ring of hostmen, 'the Lords of Coal', controlled Newcastle politically and economically. During the Civil War their oligarchic rule tightened and a new corporation was established by a parliamentary ordinance (1645).

NEWCASTLE, PROPOSITIONS OF (1646) in England, during the Civil War, presented to Charles I during his captivity by the Scots. They represented a narrow spirit of revenge embodied in the remaining members of the Long Parliament, and were not the basis for any lasting settlement. Firmly based on the terms offered at Uxbridge (1645), they required that Charles swear to the Covenant, that a diluted form of Presbyterianism be established, that parliament should have complete control of the armed forces for 20 years, and that all the leading Royalists should be punished with varying degrees of severity. If Charles had accepted them, parliament would have gained the ascendancy in the body politic. Charles deferred his rejection as long as possible, hoping to play off parliament against the Scots, but he left it too long and parliament reached an agreement with the Scots whereby they left England and Charles was handed over to parliament.

NEWCASTLE COMMISSION (1858) in Britain, royal commission which surveyed educational developments since 1833. Its recommendation of payment by results, *ie*, giving government grants to schools whose inspectors found proficient in the 'three R's', damaged relations between the inspectorate and the teachers.

NEWCASTLE PROGRAMME (1891) in Britain, policies adopted by the Gladstonian liberals, some of which they attempted to carry out during Gladstone's last ministry (1892–4), in an effort to broaden the base of his support in the country after the split over Irish Home Rule. This proposal headed the programme, together with Church disestablishment in Wales and Scotland, showing the extent to which the Liberal Party, after the loss of Chamberlain and the defection of some members to the socialists, was becoming dependent on the 'Celtic fringe' for radical support. It was proposed to abolish plural voting, introduce triennial parliaments, and, in a bid for the rural vote, reform the land laws, purchase land for allotments, and create district and parish councils. The Local Government Act (1894) fulfilled this last provision, but a Lords' amendment limiting their financial responsibility made the new parish councils virtually powerless. The trade unions were to be won by payment of MPs, shorter working hours, and an Employers Liability Act. Asquith's Liability Bill would have become law had the Lords not rejected it (1894).

The Newcastle Programme illustrated the dilemma of late 19th-cent. liberalism; namely, how to steer an independent course between socialism and conservatism. The broad scope of the programme alienated as many interests as it placated. The brewers particularly resented a proposed local veto on the sale of intoxicating liquors. To the accusation that they were trying to be all things to all men, the Liberals replied that the programme illustrated the consistent application of liberal principles on a broad front. In the short term the Newcastle proposals were academic, since the Lords blocked the next Liberal government's attempts at reform. In the long run they warned of the demise of liberalism as an effective political force in the first half of the 20th cent.   SH

NEWCOMEN, THOMAS (1663–1729), British inventor of the atmospheric steam-pump. He was a Devonshire blacksmith, who, having studied a steam-pump invented by Papin, a Huguenot refugee, improved Thomas Savery's patent for using steam to extract water from mines (1705). Previously no mine-shaft was more than 120 yards (110 metres) in depth; Newcomen's 'fire-engine' was extensively used for draining mines and driving water-wheels until improvements were introduced by Watt, Murdoch, and Trevithick.

NEWFOUNDLAND, province of Canada (31 March 1949), comprising the island of Newfoundland in the mouth of the St Lawrence river and the surrounding islands (except the French-owned St Pierre and Miquelon) and the coast of Labrador with its adjacent islands. Norsemen may have visited the area (*c.* 1010) and Basque fishermen may have been there in the 15th cent., but John Cabot's voyage (1497) marks the beginning of European control. Sir Humphrey Gilbert claimed the area for Britain (1583). Spanish and Portuguese fishermen were ejected by Sir Bernard Drake (1585), leaving the British and French the only serious contenders, although the Spanish maintained formal claims to the area until the treaty of Paris (1763).

Nfld was ceded by France to Britain by the treaty of Utrecht (1713), but the French retained the right to land in order to dry and cure fish, a right which was a perpetual source of trouble until Britain extinguished the French privilege by purchase (1904). American fishing rights, another source of contention after the American War of Independence and the War of 1812, were ended by a decision of the International Court at The Hague (1910). A colony was established (1610) by the London and Bristol Co. at Cooper's Cove, but the company sold its interests (1617). Lord Baltimore attempted to found a colony, (1621), but after spending 1628 in Nfld decided he preferred Maryland.

The first British governor was appointed in 1729, though a resident governor was not appointed until 1817, after which Nfld was finally recognized as a colony rather than a fishery. At the Charlottetown Conference (1864) Nfld resisted confederation, and did so again in 1892 and 1894. Ultimately, economic difficulty led to the suspension of constitutional government and Nfld was governed by a commission under the British Colonial Office (1934–49). After Joseph Smallwood's vigorous campaign, 52 per cent of the electorate voted for confederation (1948), which occurred the next year.

R. A. Mackay (ed.), *Newfoundland: economic, diplomatic and strategic studies* (Oxford, 1946).   AJS

NEWFOUNDLAND FISHERIES. Fishing off the Nfld banks was started early in the 16th cent. by various countries and encouraged from the early 17th cent. by the governments of France and England as a training base for seamen. Most of this fishing was conducted by boats visiting seasonally, which sold their catch, salted, in the Mediterranean. Though the island was ceded to Britain at the treaty of Utrecht (1713), the French retained rights of access for fish drying, and this, with the clashes of US and British imperialism, provided occasional international disagreements in the 19th cent.

NEWGATE, in London, England, chief criminal prison from the 13th cent. onwards. It was several times rebuilt, being destroyed in the Fire (1666) and the Gordon Riots (1780). It ceased to house debtors after 1815, and was demolished in 1903.

NEWLANDS RECLAMATION ACT (1902) in US, legislation establishing a water policy for the arid lands of the West. The act, by which water was regarded as a national resource, provided for use of a proportion of receipts from the sale of public lands on irrigation projects and the construction of dams. A Reclamation Service was established, and by 1910 some 14 million acres (56,700 sq. kms) had been reclaimed.

A number of major dams, including Roosevelt, Hoover, Grand Coulee, Bonneville, and Shasta dams, were built under the act.

NEWMAN, JOHN HENRY, cardinal (1801–90), English theologian and scholar, who was brought up as an Anglican and became vicar of the University church in Oxford. He took the lead in the Oxford Movement, being the principal author of the many *Tracts for the Times* (1833–41), which argued the patristic tradition of the Church of England, *ie,* that Anglicanism came closer to the doctrines and philosophy of the early Christian fathers than did Romanism or non-episcopal protestantism. By 1839, however, Newman himself doubted this thesis and in 1845 he was received into the Church of Rome. He founded in Birmingham (1849) a branch of the Oratorian community of priests, and became rector of Dublin University (1854–8). He had already given his views on Christian education in *Idea of a University* (1852) and later wrote a book on his beliefs in *Apologia pro vita sua* (1864). Pope Leo XIII made him a cardinal (1879) and in the second half of the 19th cent. his influence was enormous in the revival of Roman Catholicism in England. He had also, in some measure, contributed to the acceptance of Catholic practices within the Church of England.

His brother, Francis William Newman (1805–97), was a classical scholar who wrote on religion—*History of Hebrew Monarchy* (1847), *The Soul* (1849), and *Phases of Faith* (1850). He became a Unitarian (1876) and played a prominent part in the activities of the British and Foreign Unitarian Association and also identified himself with various liberal and radical causes, *eg,* feminism and prohibition.

NEWPORT, CHRISTOPHER (*c.* 1565–1617), English sailor, who commanded expeditions to Virginia, to which he made five voyages (1607–11), on one of which he was shipwrecked on the island of Bermuda, which he claimed for England. His adventures are told in Jourdain's book *Discovery of the Bermudas*, which may have been source material for Shakespeare's play *The Tempest.*

NEWPORT ARTICLES (1648), peace treaty during the English Civil War between parliament and Charles I discussed in the Isle of Wight from Sept. to Nov. 1648. The 'Presbyterians' in parliament were determined to settle with the king before they became dominated by the army, but Charles was planning to escape and merely sought to spin out the negotiations, which eventually broke down over religion. Charles would only promise Presbyterianism for three years with toleration and a limited episcopacy.

NEWPORT TOWER, two-storey circular structure built of native stone in Newport, RI. Its origin was unknown and it was thought to have been a church built by the Norsemen. Recent excavations of William S. Godfrey of Harvard have revealed that its masonry and architecture are English in origin (*c.* 1640).

NEWSPAPERS, printed from movable type, originated early in the 17th cent. The first is said to have been the *Nieuwe Tydingen,* authorized at Antwerp in 1605. The first *English Coranto,* or news-letter, was produced at Amsterdam in 1621. The more regular newspapers which followed were bulletins of official announcements such as *The London Gazette* (1666) and the *Gazette de France,* founded by Richelieu. Later publications, such as *Lloyd's List* (1726), were specialist compilations of trade news. Though the 18th cent. saw a great increase in newspapers in most European countries, they consisted mainly of political articles and polemics, and were not reporting sheets. Freedom of the press meant freedom to comment, not the dissemination of information.

Modern newspapers date from the late 18th cent., when a wider public sought political and other information. *The Times,* established in 1788, has always been regarded as the senior British newspaper, and the *Observer* (1791) used to claim a similar primacy among Sunday newspapers. The 19th cent. saw a great increase in the number of newspapers and a steady growth in their circulation. The *Daily Telegraph* was the first to aim at mass-readership; the *Daily Mail* was the most dynamic and sensational. In England the trend has been towards an increasing domination of the London press at the expense of the provincial. In the US, where there is no single centre of publication, the distinctive feature is syndication, and in this the English press lords, such as Northcliffe and Beaverbrook, were outdone from the beginning by William Randolph Hearst. Until recently a readership of millions has been an exclusively British feature, but now the largest circulation in the world is that of a Japanese newspaper. All papers claim to present the news. All without exception also put forward some propaganda, political or otherwise.   AJPT

NEWSPAPER PUBLICATION ACT (1798) in Britain, which put publishers and editors under the close scrutiny of the magistrates. They were granted wide powers of search in order to prevent or punish the publication of seditious or blasphemous material, owing to fears of revolutionary influence from France.

NEWSPAPER TAXES REPEAL, in Britain, was achieved following a campaign by Lord Lytton, Milner Gibson, and Richard Cobden. In 1836 the stamp tax was reduced to a penny on a single sheet and abolished in 1855. It dated from 1712, when a tax of a penny was imposed, the government hoping by this means to combat the influence of popular newspapers by making them too expensive for the poorer classes to read. The French Revolution intensified fear of radical propaganda and the stamp duty rose from 1½d in 1789 to 4d (1815), with an added tax on advertisements lest they should subsidize the cost to the general reader. In spite of this many unstamped papers, often of a blasphemous and seditious nature, were published. After repeal of the stamp duty the annual circulation of newspapers rose from 29 million to 122 million.

NEWTON, SIR ISAAC (1642–1727), British mathematician, astronomer, and philospher, who became a member of the Royal Society in 1671, and was elected president in 1703, being re-elected every year after that for 25 years. He was appointed Warden of the Mint in 1695 and Master four years later.

As a result of his early work, he discovered the binomial theorem and the principles of the integral calculus. Later, he investigated the nature of light and made (1668) his first reflecting telescope. By 1684 he had established the law of gravitation, and in his greatest work, the *Principia* (1687), he set out his laws of motion and his ideas on universal gravitation.

NEY, MICHEL, DUC D'ELCHINGEN, Prince de la Moscowa (1769–1815), French soldier, who became a marshal under Napoleon I and skilfully commanded the rearguard in the retreat from Moscow (1812). His desertion to Napoleon during the Hundred Days led to his trial and execution by Louis XVIII's government to appease its royalist extremists.

NEZ PERCÉS INDIANS, western American tribe, identified as Chopunnish by the US explorers Lewis and Clark, who found them (1805) in an area which became part of ID, WA, and OR. They ceded most of their lands to the US (1855), but a large band under Chief Joseph refused to accept the treaty of cession. In the ensuing Nez Percé War (1877), US troops suffered several defeats before Joseph and his followers were captured and sent to Indian Territory. By 1885 they had been nearly wiped out by disease, and they were then returned to reservations in ID and WA, where they remain (1970).

NEZAHUALCOYOTL (1402–70), ruler form 1428 of the city-state of Texcoco (Mexico). In alliance with Tenochtitlán and Tlacopán, Nezahualcoyotl greatly extended the territories ruled by the triple alliance. Thus he established the base for the growth of the Aztec imperial confederation of central Mexico. He argued in vain against the increasing practice of human sacrifice by the Aztecs of Tenochtitlán.

NGAZARGAMU, capital of Bornu, founded by Ali Gaji (*c.* 1480), which became the commercial, political, and intellectual centre of the Saifawa caliphate. Many of its palaces and mosques were built of burnt brick. It was sacked and abandoned during the early 19th-cent. Fulani *jihad*.

NGHE-AN REVOLT (1930–1), most serious challenge to French authority in Viet-nam before 1940. The question, how far it was organized and controlled by the Indo-Chinese Communist Party, founded in 1930, and how far it was a spontaneous peasant rising, has never been answered. The revolt began in May–June 1930 with a series of demonstrations against taxation in southern Nghe-An and Ha-Tinh provinces. In Sept. there were attacks on the official posts of four sub-prefectures, and similar attacks followed before the year's end. Land was seized and soviets established. But attempts to march on the town of Vinh were halted, in some cases by use of aircraft. Calm returned early in 1931, but further outbreaks of unrest occurred in March–Aug. 1931, before the revolt was finally suppressed. There were also (1930–1) anti-French disturbances in Quang-Ngai province and in some parts of Cochin-China.

NGO DINH DIEM (1901–63), first president of the republic of Viet-nam (South Viet-nam), who was chosen (1933) as chief minister in Bao-Dai's attempt to create a constitutional regime; but the French refused to allow real autonomy and Ngo Dinh Diem resigned within a year. He spent the next 21 years in retirement, waiting for more propitious times; he refused to join the Viet-Minh in 1945 after the communists had murdered his brother. In June 1954 he became prime minister of the state of Viet-nam. With American support he defeated the opposition of the Binh-Xuyen and the Caodaists, and in Oct. 1955 instituted a referendum, which resulted in his becoming president of the republic of Viet-nam. He ruled South Viet-nam (1955–63), financially supported to a large extent by the US, but from 1960 his position was made increasingly insecure by a communist-led rebellion and he had to rely more than ever on his US allies. His unpopularity became evident in 1963, when a Buddhist revolt centred on Hue and Saigon expanded into a mass opposition movement. This was vigorously suppressed, but in Nov. 1963 the president was overthrown by the army, with US acquiescence. Throughout his rule much power lay with his brother, Ngo Dinh Nhu (1910–63), and the latter's notorious wife. Both brothers died in the course of the coup, though the manner of their deaths is not publicly known.

NGO QUYEN (*reg.* 896–944), Viet-namese ruler in the period when that country first became independent of Chinese rule. He was one of a number of generals who emerged in north Viet-nam following the break-up of the T'ang empire early in the 10th cent. When a southern Chinese army sought to conquer Tongking in 939, Ngo Quyen defeated it and proclaimed himself king: the event is regarded by the Viet-namese as the beginning of their effective independence of China.

NGOMO (*reg. c.* 1560–*c.*89), Ruler of the Mwenemutapa empire, who expanded relations with the Portuguese and accepted Christianity despite violent pressures to oppose foreign innovation and influence.

NGUYEN AN NINH (1900–43), Viet-namese nationalist, who was especially active in French Cochin-China. In 1923–4 he edited a French-language newspaper in Saigon, and later had founded a secret society with left-wing anti-French objectives. He was arrested (1928) and for several years was imprisoned. In 1936–7 he organized a strike movement and sought to create an All-Indo-China Congress. But in due course he was again arrested, and died in prison.

NGUYEN BINH KHIEM (1491–1585), Viet-namese scholar and hermit. After passing the Confucian examinations in 1535, he embarked on an official career, but in 1542 decided to retire. He spent the rest of his life as a hermit in his 'Refuge of the White Cloud' in Tongking, becoming celebrated for his poetry and skill in divination. He was consulted, at different times, by both sides in the conflict between the Le and the Mac.

NGUYEN CAO KY (1930–), South Viet-namese soldier and politician, who joined the French air force in 1952, and in 1955 became an officer of the newly formed Viet-namese air force. By 1964 he was its commander and from that position was able to enter Saigon politics, at that time dominated by the army. He was prime minister (1965–7) and vice-president from 1967. During those years he acquired a reputation as a belligerent anti-communist.

NGUYEN CONG TRU (1778–1859), Viet-namese official and poet who was a native of north-central Viet-nam and became an official under Minh-Mang (*reg.* 1820–41). His most notable public achievement was the opening up of new land for cultivation in southern Tongking.

NGUYEN DU (1765–1820), Viet-namese official and poet, who was a native of the province of Ha-Tinh (north-central Viet-nam), and became an official in the closing years of the Le dynasty, but refused to serve the Tay-Son emperor, Quang-Trung (*reg.* 1788–92). He reluctantly accepted office under Gia-Long (*reg.* 1802–20). He is noted principally as the author of the *Kim-Van-Kieu*, a verse-novel in the *nom* script of Viet-namese, which has come to be regarded as the national poem.

NGUYEN TRAI (1380–1442), Viet-namese official and poet, who was one of the few Tongking Confucian scholars to join with Le Loi and other natives of Thanh-Hoa in opposing the Ming occupation of Viet-nam (1407–27). He became a close adviser of Le Loi, and following the defeat of the Chinese wrote a famous declaration of Viet-namese independence. He retired from office in 1439, and three years later was executed by his political enemies for allegedly poisoning the Emperor Le Thai-Tong (*reg.* 1434–42).

NGUYEN TRI PHUONG (1800–73), Viet-namese soldier and official, who rose to prominence in the 1840s, and led (1859–60) the Viet-namese defence against French attacks on Da-Nang and Saigon. From 1866 till his death he was probably the most powerful figure at the court of Tu-Duc. In 1873, when a French force attacked Hanoi, he again led the defence, and died when the citadel fell.

NGUYEN TRUONG TO (1828–71), Viet-namese scholar, who was a native of Nghe-An province, where he was educated by missionaries. He studied in Italy and France (1858–63). As a Catholic he was unable to hold an official post higher than that of secretary to a provincial governor. Nevertheless, he submitted (1863–71) a series of memorials to Tu-Duc, recommending such reforms as the promotion of Western learning, the development of industrial resources, and greater impartiality in government. Little notice was taken of them at Hue.

NGUYEN TUONG TAM (NHAT-LINH) (1906–63), Viet-namese novelist and politician, who was a native of Tongking. After visiting France he became a founder of the *Tu-Luc Van-Doan* (Self-strengthening Literary Group) and during the 1930s and 1940s wrote many novels. He was a member of the *Viet-nam Quoc-Dan Dang* (Viet-nam Nationalist Party),

and became foreign minister in the coalition government (1945–6), but thereafter had to flee to China. In 1954 he chose to live in South Viet-nam, but became increasingly estranged from the regime of Ngo Dinh Diem. His suicide in 1963 was one of several acts of protest preceding Diem's fall.

NGUYEN VAN THIEU (1923–), Viet-namese soldier and second president of the republic of Viet-nam (South Viet-nam). He was a native of Central Viet-nam, and entered the French army as a cadet in 1948; subsequently he fought in the (pro-French) Viet-namese army against the Viet-Minh. He took part in the coup which overthrew Ngo Dinh Diem in 1963, and by 1965 had risen to be chairman of the (military) National Directory. In Sept. 1967, after two years as virtual head of state, he was elected president under a new constitution.

NGUYEN CLAN, powerful family in Viet-nam from the 16th to 19th cents. They came from the province of Thanh-Hoa, and like their rivals the Trinh, were prominent at the court of Le Thanh-Tong and in the succession conflicts of the early 16th cent. In 1532 Nguyen Kim took the lead in restoring the Le dynasty at Thanh-Hoa, with the help of the Trinh. But after his death in 1545, the Trinh gradually increased their influence, and by 1573 had forced the Nguyen into the relatively inferior role of governors of what is now Central Viet-nam. In 1600, following the Le restoration at Hanoi in 1592, the Trinh tried to eliminate Nguyen Hoang, but he escaped to the region of Hue, where he and his descendants remained virtual rulers until 1775. They resisted a series of Trinh attacks during the years 1627–73, and thereafter there was a century of peace between the two regions.

Like the Trinh themselves, the Nguyen formally recognized the powerless Le dynasty on the imperial throne; in 1702 their appeal to China for recognition as completely independent rulers of their territory was rejected. The Nguyen region was even less Confucianized than the north at this period, and Buddhism was patronized by several of the Nguyen rulers. As in the north, there was both missionary activity and persecution of Christians. Nguyen rule at Hue was brought to an end, for the time being, by the Tay-Son rebellion beginning in 1773, which was followed by a new invasion from the North in which the Trinh armies finally captured Hue. Survivors of the clan, however, escaped to the far south. After a period of conflict which involved his withdrawal to Bangkok in 1787, the last survivor, Nguyen Anh, established himself at Saigon in 1789. From there he gradually expanded his territory and army, until by 1801–2 he was strong enough to reconquer Hue and then to take Hanoi. He set himself up as the Emperor Gia-Long (1802–20) and founded the Nguyen Dynasty, which lasted until 1945.

RBS

NGUYEN DYNASTY, reigning dynasty of Viet-nam from 1802 to 1945, founded by Gia-Long (*reg.* 1802–20) and strengthened by his son Minh-Mang (*reg.* 1820–41). The dynasty proved unable to withstand French designs against Viet-nam in the later 19th cent.; under Tu-Duc (*reg.* 1847–83) Viet-nam lost its six southern provinces to France (1860–7), and had to accept the treaties of Saigon (1862, 1874). Shortly after his death, the court itself had to accept French protection, and there followed a succession of nominal emperors who reigned under firm French control. The last of the line, Bao-Dai (*reg.* 1925–45), abdicated in 1945.

NIAGARA CONFERENCE (May–June 1914) in US, sponsored by Argentina, Brazil, Chile, and the US. It attempted unsuccessfully to halt the Mexican civil war by suggesting that Victoriano Huerta should resign the Mexican presidency.

NICAEA, COUNCIL OF (AD 325), first Ecumenical Council of bishops summoned by the Emperor Constantine to deal with the Arian Controversy. Constantine's main interest was, however, to secure unity rather than a theological verdict. At the council, attended, according to tradition, by 318 bishops, St Athanasius was the leading champion of orthodoxy. It promulgated a creed which was probably a revision of the baptismal creed of Jerusalem, and which, with four anti-Arian anathemas attached, was agreed to by all the bishops present, except two. It also reached decisions on the Meletian schism in Egypt and the Paschal controversy.

NICE, TRUCE OF (18 June 1538), temporary agreement negotiated between the Emperor Charles V and Francis I by Pope Paul III at the end of the war of 1536–8. The truce was to last for ten years, but in the meantime the treaty of Cambrai was confirmed, both sides retaining their conquests in Italy. The truce was followed by personal negotiations at Aigues Mortes (July–Aug. 1538), where the two monarchs pledged themselves to fight against the Turkish infidel and Protestant heresy, but it collapsed when Francis again declared war on Charles (June 1542).

NICHIREN (1222–82), Japanese Buddhist, who was the founder of the *Hokke* or Lotus sect. He was the most militant of all Japan's religious leaders and his teachings had a strong nationalistic aspect. His belief that Japan had become the centre of Buddhist faith was strengthened by the Mongol invasions which he had predicted and the swift growth of his following was probably due as much to the national crisis as to his exceptional personality and energy. His attacks on other sects eventually led to his being sentenced to death, but the sentence was not carried out and he was exiled instead. His influence remains strong in modern Japan, as is evident not only in the activities of such sects as the *Soka Gakkai*, but also through those of ultra-nationalists such as Kita Ikki.

NICHOLAS I (*reg.* 858–67), Pope, whose pontificate was marked by his strong moral and spiritual leadership. He forced King Lothair of Lotharingia to take back his wife and in conflicts with French bishops he maintained the supremacy of the papacy over provincial churches. His letters and decrees gave the later medieval canonists some of the most important material for establishing the doctrines of papal supremacy in the Church and over secular rulers. He renewed the tradition of papal leadership in converting new areas of Europe to Christianity, winning, for a time, Bulgaria for the western Church and encouraging the introduction of Catholicism, using a Slavonic rite, into Bohemia and Moravia.

NICHOLAS II (*reg.* 1058–61), Pope, whose pontificate is a landmark in papal history: first, because his imposition on the papal throne against the candidate of the Roman nobility was a triumph for the Hildebrandine or Gregorian reformers; and second, because his decree at the synod of 1059 put the election of future popes into the hands of the college of cardinals.

NICHOLAS IV (*reg.* 1288–92), Pope, first Franciscan to achieve that office. His pontificate was marked by the sending of missions to Persia, China, and Ethiopia, by the grant of half the papal revenues to the college of cardinals, and by the reassessment (*Taxatio Papae Nicolai IV*) of liability for taxation of the English clergy, which remained in force until the Reformation.

NICHOLAS V (*reg.* 1447–55), Pope, whose pontificate marked the beginning of the rebuilding of Rome and the extension of the Renaissance there. He was a humanist, a collector of manuscripts, and a patron of the Greek scholars who fled to Italy when Constantinople was captured by the Turks.

NICHOLAS I (1796–1855), Tsar of Russia (*reg.* 1825–55), third son of Paul I, whose reign was dominated by a devotion to military values and order. He succeeded Alexander I, Grand-Duke Constantine having refused the throne, in the midst of the Decembrist uprising, the suppression of which initiated a reign renowned for its reactionary policies.

Nicholas, who was hard-working and had a strong sense of duty, ruled personally. He retained his predecessor's administrative machinery—senate, committee of ministers, and council of state—but real power lay with a series of ad hoc committees and the imperial chancery. The chancery's departments exercised control over the empire through censorship, the police, the army, and education. Nicholas emphasized the need to preserve autocracy as the only political system suitable for Russia; the importance of orthodoxy in religion and as a basis for life and education; and nationality, *eg*, in the Russification of non-Russian minorities. Nevertheless, the reign did produce certain reforms. Speransky's codification of law was completed (1833) and Kiselyov's reform of the state peasantry was encouraged by Nicholas. Though he realized the evils of serfdom, he advocated only gradual and piecemeal reforms, such as the prohibition of the sale of serfs without their families. There was considerable educational expansion.

In foreign policy Nicholas was a firm supporter of legitimacy and the status quo and opposed revolutionary and national-liberation movements in Europe. War with Turkey (1827–9) led to the treaty of Adrianople, which gave Russia territory at the mouth of the Danube and in the Caucasus and a protectorate over Wallacia and Moldavia. War with Persia led to the treaty of Turkmanchai (1828) by which Russia gained part of Armenia. In the Balkans, a policy of gaining influence in Turkey by supporting the status quo failed to prevent the Crimean War, partly occasioned by Nicholas's misunderstanding of British policy.

N. V. Riasanovsky, *Nicholas I and Official Nationality in Russia 1825–55* (Berkeley, 1959).
C. de Grunwald, *Tsar Nicholas I* (London, 1954).   BJW

NICHOLAS II (1868–1918), Tsar of Russia (*reg.* 1894–1917), was deeply influenced by the ideals of autocracy and orthodoxy inculcated in him by his father, Alexander III, and Pobedonostsev. His accession manifesto upheld these principles, disillusioning *zemstvo* leaders and others who had hoped for a more progressive policy. His reign was marked both by economic development and social change and by the growth of opposition and revolutionary parties. Nationalist movements among the non-Russian minorities constituted an important problem which the emperor did little to solve by Russification and anti-Jewish policies.

He encouraged economic development to strengthen the state and supported Witte's industrial policies and railway building. His encouragement of Russian expansion in the Far East, despite opposition from his foreign ministry, resulted in Russia's defeat in the Russo-Japanese War (1904–5). This and the revolution of 1905, which culminated in a general strike in Oct., forced Nicholas to grant a constitution and civil liberties and to establish the Duma. Nevertheless, he retained his autocratic title, never believed in Russia's transformation into a constitutional monarchy, and withdrew many of the concessions of the October manifesto.

The years 1906–14 were, however, marked by relative freedom in civil liberties and censorship, by a decline in revolutionary activity, by Stolypin's important peasant reform, and steady economic and educational improvements. The Franco-Russian alliance dominated foreign policy (although Nicholas preferred Germany) and was extended by an agreement with England in 1907.

After the outbreak of the First World War, Nicholas became his own commander-in-chief (1915), leaving government in the hands of the empress and Rasputin, and the royal family became increasingly isolated from the people and even from court circles.

The collapse of the government's authority made it impossible to suppress civil disturbances in Petrograd in Feb.

–March 1917, which, with the defection of the troops in the capital, led to Nicholas's abdication in favour of his brother, Grand Duke Michael. He was shot with his family by the Bolsheviks (1918).

R. K. Massie, *Nicholas and Alexandra* (London, 1967).
B. Pares, *The Fall of the Russian Monarchy* (New York, 1961).
                                                                    BJW

NICIAS (d. 413 BC), Athenian soldier and politician in the great Pelopennesian War and an opponent of the bellicose demagogue, Cleon. After Cleon's death, he brought about the peace of Nicias and an alliance with Sparta (421). He was appointed commander, with Alcibiades and Lamachus, of the expedition to Sicily (415), although he deplored it. He proposed a demonstration of force and withdrawal, but Lamachus, who favoured a direct attack on Syracuse, supported Alcibiades' suggested diplomatic offensive. After Alcibiades' recall (415) Nicias made a direct attack, but Lamachus' death (414) exposed his limitations and the insufficiency of his resources. Reinforcements under Demosthenes came too late and after the Athenian army had surrendered Nicias was killed.

NICIAS, PEACE OF (421 BC), treaty concluded by Athens and Sparta during the great Peloponnesian War. The Spartans failed to induce some of their allies to accept concessions to Athens which were included in the treaty and fighting recurred in the Peloponnese in 420–18 but not until 413 was the treaty formally abrogated.

NICODEMISTS, term applied by Calvin to those Italians of the early 16th cent. who conformed outwardly to Catholicism in matters of worship, but who were indifferent or secretly hostile to Catholic dogma.

NICOLA, ENRICO DE (1877–1959), Italian lawyer and politician who was elected as provisional head of state by the Constituent Assembly (June 1946), and assumed the title of president of the new republic (Jan.–May 1948). He was the first president of the Constitutional Court (1956–7), but resigned when ministers failed to fulfil the court's decisions.

NICOLAS, AUGUSTIN (1622–95), French soldier, diplomat, author, and lawyer. In the light of his experience as a magistrate in the *parlements* of Besançon and Dijon he was highly critical of the French system of justice, and particularly of the use of torture.

NICOLE, PIERRE (1625–95), French Jansenist and author, who helped to establish Port-Royal (1647) and became involved in theological controversies with Fénelon, Mme Guyon, the Quietists, and the Jesuits in the 17th cent. His ideas were summarized in his *Permanence of the Church's Faith Concerning Communion* (1669–74).

NICOLLET, DE BELLEBORNE, JEAN (?1598–1642), French explorer, who accompanied Champlain to Canada (1618) and was sent by him to work among the Algonquin and Nipissing Indians as an interpreter. While employed by the Co. of One Hundred Associates, he discovered and explored Lake Michigan as far as Green Bay. He also ascended the Fox river as far as an Indian village west of Lake Winnebago, where he concluded an important treaty with the tribes (1634).

NICOLLS, RICHARD (1624–72), English soldier, who served in the royalist cause during the Civil War. After the restoration of Charles II (1660) he was appointed to settle the affairs of New England and take New Netherland from the Dutch. He seized the colony without a shot being fired and changed the name of the province and the city to New York, after the Duke of York, who was its proprietor (1664). Under Nicolls the 'Duke's Laws' became the first code of law for New York. He was an efficient administrator and respected by both the English and the Dutch.

NICOLSON, SIR HAROLD GEORGE (1886–1968), British diplomat, author, and journalist, who entered the foreign office (1909). He was a member of the British delegation to Paris in 1919 and later served in Persia and Germany. He joined (1930) the staff of the *Evening Standard*, and briefly was associated with Sir Oswald Mosley's New Party, standing (1931) as a parliamentary candidate, but breaking with Mosley when the incipiently violent and militaristic tendencies of his movement became apparent. He represented (1935–45) West Leicester as a National Labour MP and in the last years of peace was a prominent opponent of the appeasers. His literary output ranged from criticism and journalism to biographies, history and contemporary affairs, and works on diplomacy.

NICOMEDES IV (*reg.* 94–74 BC), King of Bithynia, who was ejected from his kingdom by Mithridates VI of Pontus and restored by Rome (92). His raids on Pontus caused the first Mithridatic War (88). He was again restored to his throne by Rome (84), and was visited by the young Julius Caesar (80–79). On his death he bequeathed his kingdom to Rome, thus occasioning the third Mithridatic War.

NICOMEDIA (mod. Izmit) (88 kms south-east of Istanbul), founded (*c.* 264 BC) by Nicomedes I of Bithynia in extensive fertile territory on the main route from the Balkans to the Near East. Later it became the capital of the Roman province of Bithynia, whose assembly met at the temple of Augustus, begun in 29 BC. Nicomedia prospered greatly and accumulated titles of honour. Although sacked by Goths in AD 258, it remained the fifth city of the empire, becoming the eastern capital under Diocletian (284–305), whose persecution of Christians began with the destruction of its cathedral (303). After Constantinople became the imperial residence (328), successive earthquakes hastened the decline of Nicomedia.

NICOPOLIS CRUSADE (1396), first of a series of international crusades organized to check the conquests of the Ottoman Turks in the Balkans. Like its successors, notably the Varna crusade of 1444, it ended in crushing disaster for the Christians, largely because of disunity among the crusaders and their underestimation of the Turks. The crusade was launched by King Sigismund of Hungary (the future Emperor Sigismund) and consisted chiefly of the followers of John the Fearless, Duke of Burgundy (1404–19). It attacked and annihilated Nicopolis, the chief Turkish fortress on the Danube. John of Burgundy was captured, but released after the payment of a huge ransom.

NICUESA, DIEGO DE (*c.* 1460–1511), Spanish leader of an unsuccessful attempt in 1509 to colonize the Central American coast. The survivors joined other Spaniards on the Panamanian Isthmus at Darién, where Nicuesa lost the struggle for leadership to Balboa and was turned adrift in a boat.

NIDAROS (later Trondheim), founded by Olaf Tryggvesson in AD 996, became an archiepiscopal see in 1182 and was the scene of the coronation of the Norwegian kings. It was the capital of Norway up to 1380.

NIEBUHR, REINOLD (1892–   ), US theologian, who was ordained (1915) as a minister in the Evangelical Synod of North America and served in Detroit (1915–28). As professor of Applied Christianity in the Union Theological Seminary, New York City (1928–60), Neibuhr exercised a profound influence. He was concerned with social ethics and the relation of the Christian faith to social and political groups. His thought combines the Social Gospel with biblical theology. His many influential writings include: *Moral Man and Immoral Society* (1932), *Faith and History* (1949), *The Irony of American History* (1952), and *Beyond Tragedy: essays on the Christian interpretation of history* (1961).

NIEM (NIEHEIM), DIETRICH OF (c. 1340–1418), German official of the Roman popes, whose experiences at the papal court made him into an ardent reformer and an advocate of reforms through the holding of Church councils. His *Dialogus de Schismate* (1410) was the first complete exposition of the conciliar programme and he was a leading figure in the calling of the council of Constance (1414–18) which ended the Great Schism.

NIEMÖLLER, MARTIN (1892–), German Protestant clergyman and leader of the Protestant opposition during the Third Reich. After serving in the German navy as a submarine commander during the First World War, Niemöller worked with the Protestant charitable organization, the Inner Mission, then moved to a parish in Berlin in 1931. His political views were conservative and patriotic. After the Nazis came to power, he attacked the pro-Nazi Protestants who attempted to impose Nazi dictates like the Aryan paragraph (forbidding Jews from holding office) on the Church. Thereafter he became one of the leaders of the Protestant opposition, known as the Confessing Church, which denied the right of the state to totalitarian control (1934). In 1935 the Confessing Church was itself split by an apparently conciliatory gesture from the Nazi regime. Niemöller led the 'radicals', who refused to co-operate with the new Government Ministry for Church Affairs. In 1937 Hitler adopted a tougher policy; Niemöller was arrested and, despite a court decision in his favour, he was interned in concentration camps until 1945. His resistance, though often misunderstood, made him famous both within and outside Germany. After 1945 he took a prominent part in the German Church and, internationally, in the World Council of Churches. He remained politically engaged and actively opposed West German rearmament.

NIEN FEI (1853–68), Chinese gangs of secret-society bandits in the border regions of Shantung, Honan, Kiangsu, and Anhwei provinces, whose origins can be traced back to the White Lotus Society in the late 18th cent. Stimulated by the Taiping Rebellion, but initially unco-ordinated, they rose against the Ch'ing. They soon achieved some degree of centralized organization, and their cavalry and guerrilla tactics proved successful against government troops. After 1864, they were joined by the Taiping remnants, and later established connections with the Muslim rebels in the northwest. They were suppressed in 1868 by the efforts of Tseng Kuo-fan, Li Hung-chang, and Tso Tsung-t'ang.

NIEN-HAO (lit. 'titles of years'), *ie*, expressions used for enumerating years in the Chinese calendar. From the 2nd cent. BC a particular year was designated as the first in a series, which would be denoted by the chosen expression; subsequent years were counted appropriately, *eg*, in 33 BC it was decided that the title for years beginning in the next year would be named *Chien-shih* (The New Establishment); years were henceforth designated as *Chien-shih* 1 (corresponding with 32 BC), *Chien-shih* 2 (31 BC), etc. *Nien-hao* were sometimes chosen for propagandist purposes or to publicize an emperor's qualities or achievements. At first they were changed every five years or so, and later their use was extended for a decade or two; but since the 14th cent. a single *nien-hao* was adopted for the complete length of an emperor's reign. For that reason, in speaking of the Ming and Ch'ing periods, the term is sometimes translated as 'reign-title'.

NIEUWPOORT, BATTLE OF (2 July 1600), Maurice of Nassau's victory in the Netherlands War of Independence against the Spaniards under Archduke Albert of Austria. Cut off from his base, Maurice was forced to fight the Spaniards on the beach south-west of Ostend, but the heavier musket fire and greater mobility of the Dutch won the day.

NIGER (1,189,000 sq. kms), in West Africa, formerly a province of French West Africa which became an independent republic in 1960. Hausa, Songhay, Fulbe, and Tuareg groups predominate in a population (1970) of over 3 million. A one-party system and adult suffrage is used to elect a president and a national assembly of 50 members.

NIGER DELTA, geographically, an area in Nigeria of crisscrossing creeks, marshy lands, and dense tropical forests. Fishing, farming, and trading are the principal occupations. Its people include the Kalabari, Bonny, Okrika, Opobo, Ogoni, Brass, Akassa, Ogbenya, Epie Atissa, Western Ijo, Diobu of Port Harcourt, and Ikwere of Ahoada. The predominant language is Ijo, spoken in several dialects.

The kings of the various Niger Delta city-states and their subjects had contacts with European slave and palm-oil traders, Christian missions, and British consular and other officials earlier than most other Nigerian peoples. Their commercial and political rivalries and conflicts were exploited by European merchants and their agents during the era of the slave trade, legitimate commerce, British consular jurisdiction, and administration. Even so, some Niger Delta city-states—*eg*, Bonny, Brass, and Opobo—flourished commercially until the end of the 19th cent. With British penetration into the interior and development of railways, which bypassed the old Delta trading centres, the city-states gradually declined economically. The history of the Delta in the 20th cent. until the discovery of petroleum is one of economic neglect and political frustration. This stimulated a demand by the Rivers Peoples League, founded in 1941, for the creation of a separate Rivers State, which was created in 1967 as one of the 12 states of Nigeria.

NIGERIA, FEDERATION OF (341,000 sq. miles—924,000 sq. kms), became independent of British rule in 1960. It originally comprised three regions, and then four, but the structure was greatly changed in the wake of military coups (1966). In 1967 the military government of Gen. Gowan initiated a new federation composed of 12 autonomous states and a central government with far-reaching federal powers, vested for the time being in a supreme military council with civilian participation.

NIGERIA, SECESSION WAR (mid-1967–Jan. 1970), began when the military ruler of the Eastern Region of the (first) Nigerian Federation, Col. C. O. Ojukwu, declared the independence of the Eastern Region as the State of Biafra. This followed upon the breakdown of the first federation's central government in 1966, and massacres later that year and in early 1967 of Ibo people living in the Northern Region (the Ibo being the largest ethnic grouping of the Eastern Region). During painful and protracted hostilities the secessionist government was able to secure military aid from several foreign governments, including those of France, Portugal, and South Africa, as well as from private sources in Western Europe and the US, and to win the recognition of several African governments, including those of Gabon, Ivory Coast, Tanzania, and Zambia. On its side, the military government of Nigeria was able to count not only on British and Soviet aid, but also on the firm support of the rest of Nigeria and on the ardent opposition to inclusion within the secession state of eastern minority groupings such as the Efik and Kalabari.

The war ended when the secessionist government collapsed in Jan. 1970, and Ojukwu took refuge in the Ivory Coast. This paved the way for reorganization of the Eastern Region into three new states of the reshaped Nigerian Federation: Rivers, South-East, and East-Central, the latter being the Ibo heartland. Though the war had brought much suffering and starvation to large numbers of Ibo people, many thousands of whom died, and had given rise to much bitterness in the rest of Nigeria, its ending showed the Nigerian government as both energetic and tolerant in its policies of alleviation and reconciliation.

NIGHTINGALE, FLORENCE (1820–1910), English pioneer of efficiency in the profession of nursing and its acceptance as a respectable calling for women. After training on the continent, she led British nurses in caring for wounded soldiers at Scutari during the Crimean War (1854–6), from which she returned with her health permanently impaired. She established the Nightingale training home for nurses, and wrote and advised on public and army health.

NIHAWAND, BATTLE OF (AD 642), to the south of Hamadhan, in which the Arabs crushed the last real counter-offensive that Sassanid Persia was able to direct against the invading armies of Islam.

NIHONGI (NIHON–SHOKI), second oldest Japanese book still (1970) extant. It was compiled by imperial command from various oral traditions and written in Chinese (720), giving a much fuller account of Japan's early history and mythology than the *Kojiki* (712). Up till 1945 its chronology, which dates the establishment of the imperial dynasty at 660 BC (nearly 1000 years too early) and approaches accuracy only after AD 400, was officially imposed upon Japanese scholars. Despite this, however, and despite its obvious bias and internal contradictions, the *Nihongi* remains an enormously important source for studying the origins of Japanese culture and politics.

NIKAEA. After the fall of Constantinople to the Fourth Crusade in 1204 a Byzantine succession state was established at Nikaea through the efforts of Theodore I Laskaris, who, in 1208, assumed the title of emperor. Under him and under John III Vatatzes (*reg.* 1222–54) the Byzantines of Nikaea created a regime strong enough to wrest most of western Asia Minor from the Latin empire of Constantinople and also to take over much of Thrace and Macedonia. The Nikaean state, as such, ceased to exist in 1261, when Michael VIII Palaiologos recovered Constantinople for the Byzantines and thus brought the Latin empire to an end.

NIKEPHOROS I (*reg.* 802–11), Byzantine Emperor, who carried out an important series of reforms in the finances and the armed forces of the state. His reign saw the Byzantines in conflict with the Muslims and he had to give (806) tribute to the Caliph Harun al-Rashid. Nikephoros I died in battle (811) against the Bulgars, led by their new ruler, Krum.

NIKEPHOROS II PHOKAS (*reg.* 963–9), Byzantine Emperor, who, in 960–1, wrested Crete from the Muslims (the definitive Byzantine occupation came in 964–5) and campaigned in Cilicia and Syria during the years 962–3, advancing as far as Aleppo. After his accession to the throne as co-emperor with Basil II and Constantine VIII (the sons of Romanos II) he overran much of northern Syria in 964–6, a prelude to the conquest of Antioch in Oct. 969. Nikephoros II was killed in Dec. of that year as a result of a palace intrigue in favour of John Tzimiskes, like himself, a soldier.

NIKOLSBURG, TREATY OF (1621), agreement between Bethlen Gabor, ruler of Translyvania since 1613, and the Emperor Ferdinand II during the Thirty Years War, by which the latter was forced to respect the religious freedom granted to Hungarian Protestants in 1609, and recognized Bethlen's title of Prince of Transylvania and Hungary, as well as his possession of a duchy in Silesia and an extended frontier. The treaty lasted until Bethlen's re-entry into the war in 1624.

NIKON, Patriarch (1605–81), Russian priest, who initiated the great schism or *Raskol* in the Russian Orthodox Church. He came of peasant stock from Nizhni-Novgorod and began as a priest, becoming a monk when his wife entered a nunnery after the death of their children. In 1646 he was chosen as archimandrite of the Novospassky monastery in Moscow, two years later became the metropolitan of Novgorod, and finally was appointed Patriarch of Moscow (1652) in the reign of Alexis. Nikon championed the Greek heritage in the Russian church and sponsored a programme of reform of the service books and the introduction of Greek practices through the synod of Moscow (1654). His reforms led to a bitter controversy with the zealots such as Avaakum and Neronov, who were backed by the mass of the Russian people. In 1656 a church council condemned these *Raskolnik* opponents of revision, Avaakum was exiled to Siberia and Nikon appeared to triumph. He had enjoyed the support of the eastern patriarchs and of Tsar Alexis, but his relations with the latter soon underwent a radical transformation. Considering himself co-sovereign with the tsar as Patriarch Filaret had been, Nikon asserted the independence of the clergy from the state. To overcome the tsar's opposition, he staged a spectacular gesture of renunciation in 1658 and retired to the monastery of New Jerusalem, which he had founded. Alexis, however, failed to recall him, and on his return to Moscow Nikon was expelled. Finally his case was referred to a church council in the presence of the patriarchs of Antioch and Alexandria at which he was condemned to a monastery and deprived of his patriarchate (1666). Released in 1681, he died in the same year, leaving a controversy between the Greek revisionists and the *Raskolniks* or Old Believers which smouldered for two centuries.

NIKOPOLIS, BATTLE OF (Sept. 1396), on the Danube river, where the Ottoman Turks, under Sultan Bayezid I Yildirim (the Thunderbolt), routed a large Christian 'crusade' embracing troops of Hungarian, French, Burgundian, and German origins.

NILE, BATTLE OF (1–2 Aug. 1798) (more correctly of Abukir Bay), in which the British Mediterranean fleet, under Admiral Sir Horatio Nelson, defeated the French fleet under Admiral Brueys, thus endangering communications between Napoleon I's troops in Egypt and France. Of 13 French ships of the line, nine were captured and two burnt.

NILES, HEZEKIAH (1777–1839), US journalist, whose *Niles' Weekly Register* (1811–36) supported protection for industry, internal improvements, and nationalism. He became associated with Henry Clay and the supporters of the American System and after 1829 joined the Whigs.

NILOTIC PEOPLES, peoples, famous for their tall and slender physique, who inhabit the region along the Nile south of about latitude 12°. They are essentially cattle-owning people, their culture and religious beliefs being closely identified with their flocks. Their societies are ordered largely on the basis of the cattle's requirements, leading, *eg*, to annual excursions in the dry season to better grazing grounds, where each family has its own rights, based on longstanding custom. Chief among these peoples are the Dinka, Shilluk, and Nuer; although physically and linguistically similar, their cultural and social traditions show considerable variations.

Lack of written evidence makes reconstruction of the history of these people difficult, but study of their oral tradition has thrown light on a complicated series of migrations in the southern Sudan and East Africa. There is some reason to think that at one time the northern-most group, the Shilluk, existed even further north, and that they may have been associated with the people of Meroe. They may also have played a part in the formation of the Funj kingdom.

NIMITZ, CHESTER WARREN (1885–1966), US sailor, who succeeded Admiral Kimmel as commander of the Pacific Fleet in Dec. 1941. He led US naval forces in the Pacific throughout the Second World War and was chief of naval operations (1945–7).

NIMRUD, Assyrian military capital, situated on a strategic position between the Tigris and Upper Zab rivers. It was strongly fortified and had a palace, built by Ashurnasirpal (*reg.* 883–859 BC), several temples, and a ziqqurat. It was excavated (1845–51) by Layard.

NINETEEN COUNTIES, THE, in NSW, were enclosed by boundaries fixed in Oct. 1829 within which settlers were to select land for occupation by purchase or lease. They became officially the 'settled districts' as distinct from the pastoral, 'squatting' areas outside the limits.

NINETEEN PROPOSITIONS (1642), one of the last opportunities for negotiation between Charles I and the Long Parliament before the outbreak of the English Civil War. They were published on 1 June and sent to the king at York. They abrogated the existing constitution by claiming the sovereignty of parliament in every sphere of government and the state, including foreign policy. They demanded that the king's council, officials, and judges should be selected by parliament; that the Militia ordinance (31 Jan. 1642), which placed the control of the army in parliament, should be accepted by the king; that the Church be reformed along Puritan lines; and that the recusancy laws be put into execution. On 18 June King Charles rejected the propositions, arguing that England was a mixed constitution of monarchy, aristocracy, and democracy.

NINETY-TWO RESOLUTIONS (1834), series of resolutions adopted by the Legislative Assembly of Lower Canada. They were drafted by A. N. Morin and moved by E. Bédard, both members of L. J. Papineau's extremist group, and set out the grievances of the province. Their indiscriminate criticisms of British rule and their advocacy of the elective principle alienated moderate reformers, and the resolutions mark the break between moderate and extremist reformers in Lower Canada, and an important step towards the rebellion of 1837.

NINETY-FIVE THESES (1517), Luther's challenge to academic disputation which launched the Reformation. In protest against the papal sale of indulgences, he nailed to the church door at Wittenberg (31 Oct.) 95 theological propositions critical of 'justification by works', alleging that the purchase of an indulgence could not remit the divine punishment of sin, nor affect the condition of souls in purgatory. The sale of indulgences immediately declined, and when ordered to retract, Luther asserted scripture as the final authority on doctrine.

NINEVEH, Assyrian city, north of Mosul, which became the administrative capital under Sennacherib (*reg.* 704–681 BC), who enlarged and fortified it. It was destroyed in 612 by the Medes and Babylonians. Excavations (1849–52) revealed 25,000 tablets, mostly archival documents and literary works from the 7th cent.

NINIAN, Saint (*c.* 360–*c.* 432), British chieftain's son, who went to Rome and was consecrated bishop (394) for work in Scotland. His church at Whithorn in Galloway became a centre for conversion of neighbouring Britons and Picts. St Ailred (1109–67), in his *Vita*, is the main source of knowledge of Ninian's work.

NIÑO, PEDRO ALONSO (EL NEGRO) (*c.* 1468–1505), Spanish navigator, who accompanied Columbus on his first, second, and (perhaps) third voyages. He led his own expedition (1499) to the Pearl Coast of Venezuela, and returned with pearls and dyewood, making it the most profitable Spanish voyage to that date.

NIPPUR, Sumerian religious centre, situated near Diwaniyah. The approval of its patron god, Enlil, was required for all kings of Sumer, thus making possession of Nippur essential for control of Sumer. It declined in importance after the Amorite invasions (*c.* 2000 BC). Excavations at Nippur from 1945 onwards have yielded much information on Mesopotamian religion.

NISH, CONVENTION OF (1923), agreement signed by the Bulgarian and Yugoslav governments. Strained relations between these countries were normal in the 1920s and early 1930s, as a result of the new frontiers which had emerged in the Balkans (1912–20). Ethnic patterns of course defied the reasonable drawing of frontiers everywhere in south-east Europe, but one of the most significant sources of grievance was the dispersal of Macedonians in Greece, Bulgaria, and Yugoslavia. The Internal Macedonian Revolutionary Organization (IMRO) had been founded as far back as 1895, its aim being autonomy within either the Ottoman empire or a Balkan federation. By 1918 the situation was very complex because much of Macedonia lay within the newly created state of Yugoslavia, but a large number of Macedonian refugees were living in Bulgaria, particularly in the south-west region at Petritch, the IMRO headquarters. Backed by the Italians, these Macedonians kept up constant pressure for Bulgarian action against the Yugoslavs, gaining publicity and influence by terrorism—thus their position with respect to Bulgarian politics and its relations with Belgrade was similar to that of the Palestinian refugee organizations in Jordan during the 1960s. They wielded considerable power in Sofia, not least because of their extreme ruthlessness, and naturally opposed any attempt at a rapprochement with Yugoslavia. The convention of May 1923 thus has a dual importance. It marked a brief period of attempted concord between the two governments, for they agreed to take joint action against the IMRO as a way to cement a general reconciliation, a policy which suited domestic needs in both Belgrade and Sofia. In Bulgarian history in particular it is more significant as the immediate cause of the June coup, led by the IMRO and connived at by King Boris, which destroyed the Agrarian Party's monopoly of power and toppled their leader, Stambuliski.   KM

NITHARD (d. 844), grandson of Charlemagne, who had charge of the military defence of the coast in the vicinity of the Seine against the Vikings. His *History of the Dissensions of the Sons of Louis the Pious*, begun in 841 at the request of King Charles the Bald, deals with events down to 843. Nithard being an educated layman who knew the art of war, the *History* is a unique source for the period and describes in great detail the conflict between Charles and his brothers.

NITHARD, JOHANN EBERHARD (1607–81), Austrian Jesuit confessor to Mariana of Austria, Queen Regent of Spain, who rose to considerable political power in Spain in the years 1665–9, but was overthrown by the rebellion of Juan José of Austria (1669).

NITHSDALE, WILLIAM MAXWELL, 5th Earl of (Scottish) (1676–1744), Scottish Jacobite, who, in 1712, anticipating the consequences of his support for the exiled Stuarts, resigned his estates to his son, William. He took part in the Jacobite rising and was captured at Preston (1715) and condemned to death (1716). His wife vainly petitioned George I for his pardon, and then helped her husband to escape from the Tower by disguising him as a woman. In 1718 he became a minister at the court of the exiled James III at Urbino. He died in poverty and obscurity in Rome.

NITTI, FRANCESCO (1868–1953), Italian economist and politician, who was minister of agriculture (1911–14), and later of finance (1917–19). His economic planning and loan raising aided Italy's post-war recovery. As prime minister (1919–20) he concentrated on food and land problems, insurance schemes, and stabilizing the economy, but he antagonized extremists by his moderation in foreign relations, *eg*, over Fiume, Dalmatia, and Albania. The democratic state was jeopardized by the failure of the socialists and *popolari* to accept Nerini's moderate proposals for reform. After 1924 he became, in exile, a leading anti-fascist. During the Second World War he was imprisoned by the Nazis (1943–5).

NIVEDITA, SISTER (d. 1911) (Margaret Noble), Irish disciple of Swami Vivekanada, whom she accompanied to the World Congress of Religions at Chicago (1893). She devoted her life to the poor and suffering in Calcutta.

NIVELLE OFFENSIVE during the First World War. This incorporated the second battle of the Aisne (16 April–1 May 1917). At the end of 1916 Joffre, his strategy discredited by Allied losses at the Somme and Verdun, was replaced as French commander-in-chief by Robert Nivelle. Nivelle, in a brief command earlier, had achieved considerable success, notably the recapture of Fort Douamont, with his tactical innovations.

Joffre's plan for 1917 was for continued attacks on the great German salient Lens–Rheims, by the British at Arras and the French on the Oise and in Champagne. The British were to bear the brunt of the offensive. Nivelle promised a decisive French victory by a 'rupture' of the German lines in Champagne, where the attack was strengthened with troops freed by extending the British front south of the Somme; the other attacks were retained as diversions.

The German withdrawal, in anticipation of a renewal of the Somme offensive, to the Siegfried (or Hindenburg) Line frustrated the important diversion on the Oise, but Nivelle insisted, against the advice of the army group commanders, that the other attacks be carried out. On 9 April 1917 the British attacked at Arras and captured Vimy Ridge; continuing assaults met with no further success and heavy losses were suffered. Nevertheless, the assaults were persisted with in order to relieve pressure on the French, whose main attack on the Aisne between Rheims and Soissons on 16 April failed. French losses were 120,000 men in the first two days and morale collapsed completely. Mutinies broke out and soon spread to the greater part of the army. On 15 May Nivelle was replaced by Pétain, who proclaimed his intention of standing on the defensive and waiting for the tanks and the help of US troops, newly committed to the war.

NIXON, RICHARD MILHOUS (1913–), US politician and 37th president who served in the navy during the Second World War and was elected as a Republican congressman from CA (1946). His subsequent work on the Un-American Activities Committee attracted national attention, and helped him to secure election to the US Senate (1950). His selection as Republican vice-presidential candidate (1952) helped to heal party unity after bitter struggles in the convention between the moderate and conservative wings of the party. As vice-president (1953–61) he was frequently the centre of controversy, but his loyalty and hard-hitting partisanship was in 1960 rewarded with the Republican presidential nomination. His narrow defeat by John F. Kennedy, followed two years later by heavy defeat in his attempt to become governor of CA, appeared to have ended his political career, and he moved to New York to practise law. He continued, however, to be politically active, established firm support throughout the country, and developed the party's 'southern strategy' to revive and consolidate the Republican strength that Eisenhower had revealed in the previously Democratic South. He won the presidential nomination (1968) and climaxed his remarkable career by narrowly winning the subsequent election. AJT

NIZA, FRAY MARCOS DE (d. 1558), Franciscan friar, who was sent to verify the reports of Cabeza de Vaca of unbounded wealth in New Mexico. He returned with tales of the 'Seven Cities of Cíbola', gleaming with gold and turquoise, and inspired the Coronado expedition of 1540.

NIZAM AL-MULK (d. 1092), Persian vizier, who directed the affairs of the Seljuk sultanate during the reigns of Alp Arslan (*reg.* AD 1063–72) and of Malik Shah (*reg.* 1072–92). His years of power witnessed an extension of the *iqta* system and of the institution known as the madrasa. He founded at Baghdad (1065–7) one of the most famous of the madrasas, the Nizam-

iya, which served as a model for later foundations of this kind. He was the author of a remarkable treatise on the art of government, the *Siyasat-Name*.

NIZAM SHAHI DYNASTY, THE, ruled the kingdom of Ahmadnagar (1490–1633). The first ruler, Malik Ahmad, son of the minister who induced the Bahmani sultan Muhammad to murder his minister, Mahmud Gawan, revolted from the Bahmani sultan Mahmud and fixed his capital at Ahmadnagar, named after himself. The dynasty was constantly engaged in local wars until it was overthrown by the Mughals. The second ruler, Burhan Shah (*reg.* 1509–53), allied his kingdom with the Hindu state of Vijayanagar, but his successor, Husain (*reg.* 1553–65), assisted in its overthrow. The Mughal attack was resisted by Chand Bibi, Queen dowager of Bijapur, but Berar was lost (1596) and after her death (1600) Ahmadnagar was taken. But most of the state remained and was finally absorbed by the Mughals in the reign of Shah Jahan (1633).

NIZAM-I JEDID. Under the impact of continuing defeat at the hands of Austria and Russia, the Ottoman Turks at last came to realize the need for a radical reform of their war machine on European lines. The first sustained effort to achieve this aim was made under Selim III (*reg.* 1789–1807). Sultan Selim sought to organize and train a number of regiments—foot, horse, and guns—using European weapons, drill, and instructors. These reforms were given the name of Nizam-i Jedid (the New Order). The experiment was extended later in the reign to the provinces and a provincial recruiting system brought into being. A revolt of the conservative elements at Istanbul, among them the Janissaries, led Selim III in 1807 to dissolve the Nizam-i Jedid forces (about 25,000 men in all), but the programme of radical reform survived the turmoil of 1807–8 and was resumed by Sultan Mahmud II (*reg.* 1808–39).

NIZAM-UL-MULK, title of the rulers of Hyderabad, Deccan, in India (1724–1948), signifying Regulator of the kingdom. The founder, Asaf Jah (d. 1748), received the title from the Mughal emperor. His successors always professing loyalty to him, it became the recognized title of the rulers. The nizams claimed to be allies, not subordinates, of the British Indian government, but this was denied by the viceroy, Lord Reading, in 1926.

NIZIB, BATTLE OF (24 June 1839), in northern Syria. Egyptian forces under Ibrahim Pasha defeated the Ottomans. This defeat, combined with the desertion of the Ottoman fleet to Egypt, a week later, rendered the Ottomans helpless and precipitated European intervention against Muhammad Ali of Egypt.

NJIMI, town in Kanem first mentioned by the geographer, Al-Idrisi (d. 1166). It later became the capital of the Saifawa rulers of Kanem. It was abandoned by Mai Umar (*reg.* c. 1394–98) as a consequence of the Bulala wars. Njimi was temporarily reoccupied by Idris Katargarmabe (*reg.* 1503–1526).

NŌ, form of Japanese drama. It was developed at the Ashikaga court by Kanami (1333–80), a Shintō priest, and his son Seami (1363–1443), but its themes are mainly those of popular Buddhism and its style owes much to Zen aesthetics. The combination of chanting, poetic language, and stylized dancing by masked actors makes *Nō* a unique feature of Japanese culture, but it has never been popular, and throughout the feudal period was appreciated only by a limited section of the samurai class. It is respected rather than enjoyed by most contemporary Japanese.

NO PEACE WITHOUT SPAIN, English war aim during the War of the Spanish Succession. It was declared in 1703 to induce Portugal's entry into the war, and it sought to place

Archduke Charles on the Spanish throne by military force. It was stressed in parliament throughout the war and it was not until the allied defeat at Brihuega (1710) and the succession of Archduke Charles to the imperial crown (1711) that the Tories declared the principle both politically undesirable and militarily unattainable. The aim was an obvious stumbling block to the Tory peace ministry, since it was difficult to repudiate a policy sanctioned by previous parliaments, and since the Whigs and the allies continued to support it. Despite a press campaign the Lords reaffirmed the old policy (1711) and 20 new peers had to be created before the Tory ministry could depend on the support of both houses of parliament in dropping this war aim.

NOAILLES, ADRIEN-MAURICE, Duc de (1678–1766), French soldier and diplomat, who served Louis XIV during the War of the Spanish Succession. He presided over the council of finance during Philip of Orléans's regency until the rise of John Law (1718). He later succeeded Berwick as marshal and commander of the French forces in the War of the Polish Succession (1733–8). He was less successful in the War of the Austrian Succession (1740–8), being defeated at Dettingen (1743). He was ambassador-extraordinary to Spain (1746–55).

NOAILLES, LOUIS ANTOINE, Cardinal de (1651–1729), French cleric, who became Abp of Paris (1695) and was a key figure in the long and bitter controversy over Jansenism from 1698. He was firmly opposed to the bull *Unigenitus* (1713), which condemned 101 propositions in Pasquier Quesnel's celebrated work, *Reflexions morales*, but he finally accepted it in 1728, by which time Jansenism had ceased to be a purely theological controversy. Noailles came from a well-known family descended from Antoine de Noailles, Admiral of France (1504–62). His brother, Anne Jules (1650–1708), and his nephew Adrien-Maurice (1678–1766) both became marshals of France.

NOBATIA, most northerly of the medieval kingdoms of Nubia, had its capital at Faras. At some time in the 7th cent. it became united with Makuria, the secular capital thereafter being Dongola; but Faras retained importance as a bishop's seat.

NOBEL, ALFRED BERNHARD (1833–96), Swedish inventor and founder of the Nobel Prizes. He made a fortune from dynamite and other explosives, with which he established three annual awards, one for science, one for literature, and one for the promotion of world peace.

NOBLE'S LAND BANK in Russia, founded in 1885 under the ministry of finance to give loans on favourable terms to Russian nobility. It failed to prevent the decline of the size of noble landholdings.

NOBLESSE D'ÉPÉE in France, imprecise term generally denoting those members of the aristocracy in the *ancien régime*, whose ancient lineage predated the age when French kings sold offices with titles of nobility and was coupled with a military career.

NOBLESSE DE ROBE in France, members of the aristocracy, sometimes called *robins*, who rose to prominence in royal service as lawyers and administrators in the 16th–17th cents and acquired titles of nobility with their offices.

NÓBREGA, MANOEL DE (1517–70), leader of the Jesuit contingent of a Portuguese expedition (1549) which established royal control over Brazil. Under Nóbrega's leadership, Jesuit missionaries pushed south to São Paulo and north to Pernambuco, their first concern being the protection of the Amerindian from exploitation.

NOBUNAGA (1534–82), Japanese *daimyō*, first of the three great unifiers of Japan in the 16th cent. His first achievement was his rout of the powerful Imagawa with only 3000 men at Okehazama (1560). He was among the first to see the potential of the musket, which had just been introduced into Japan, but his success rested not only on his new infantry, but also on his choice of able commanders, his marriage alliances, and his central position, which allowed him to seize Kyoto (1568) on the pretext of assisting a claimant to the shogunate. Nobunaga soon consolidated his national position by subduing the powerful religious orders and, after some setbacks, defeated his chief *daimyō* rivals, Takeda and Uesugi. In 1576 he built a fortress at Azuchi, where, following his earlier practice, he encouraged commerce. Another notable feature of his rule, caused partly by his struggle against the great Buddhist monasteries, was his friendly reception of Portuguese missionaries. At the time of his assassination by one of his generals, Akechi Mitsuhide, Nobunaga controlled almost half of Japan, thus leaving a solid foundation for Hideyoshi and Ieyasu to build on.

NOEL, LÉON (1888–), French civil servant and diplomat, who became an *auditeur* at the *conseil d'état* (1913), *Maitre des requêtes* (1924), and *préfet* of the Haut-Rhin département in 1930. He was ambassador to Czechoslovakia (1932–5), and then to Poland. In 1940 he assisted Gen. Huntziger at the armistice negotiations with Germany and Italy during the Second World War. After the war he returned to political life as a member of the *conseil de direction* of De Gaulle's *railliement du peuple français* in 1949 and as deputy for the Yonne (1951–5). He became president of the Fifth Republic's constitutional council in 1959 and, although a faithful Gaullist, declared as illegal the general's proposal that the president should be elected by universal suffrage.

NOGARET, JEAN LOUIS DE, Duc D'Epernon (1554–1642), French soldier, who was prominent in the Holy League during the French Civil Wars and became a dominating influence over Henry III. He was disgraced in 1588, and later tried to defy Henry IV in Provence, but surrendered (1595) for territorial compensation. On Henry's murder (1610) he seized power for Marie de' Medici and became colonel-general of infantry. In his old age he was suspected of conspiracy with the Comte de Soissons and was exiled to Loches (1641).

NOGARET, GUILLAUME DE (d. 1314), French lawyer and adviser to King Philip IV of France. He is best known for his enterprises against Pope Boniface VIII, in which he seems to have been inspired by a fanatical conviction that the pope was an evil influence on the Church. Nogaret was largely responsible for the arrest in 1301 of Bp Bernard Saysset of Pamiers on a charge of treason; thus he unleashed the final conflict between France and Boniface. In 1303 Nogaret was in charge of plans to kidnap the pope at Anagni, the raid being timed to prevent the excommunication of Philip by Boniface. Though it succeeded initially, Boniface was soon rescued, but died shortly afterwards. Nogaret was thereafter responsible for blackmailing Boniface's successors by threats of a posthumous trial of Boniface for heresy and other infamous charges. To avert this, Pope Clement V made various concessions to France, including the suppression of the order of the Temple. The French Templars were arrested in 1307 and their vast wealth seized. The order was dissolved in 1311 and many French Templars perished miserably.

NOGUÈS, CHARLES AUGUSTE PAUL (1876–), French soldier and colonial official. He was a close collaborator of Lyautey in Morocco and became director of *affaires indigènes* in Rabat in 1927. He was appointed (1936) resident-general in Morocco. When the Second World War broke out he became commander-in-chief of the French forces in North Africa. Despite his conviction that he could resist a German invasion of North Africa, and despite telegrams from numerous French colonial officials and Gen. De Gaulle asking him to lead the French resistance to the armistice, he defected to Pétain. His example brought most of the colonial officials into line. After arresting the parliamentarians on the Massilia and resisting the Allied embarkation in North Africa in 1942, he retired to Portugal.

NOMBRE DE DIOS, village on the Caribbean coast of Panama, which was an important port in the 16th cent. for the shipment of Spanish colonial products.

NOMINALISM derives from the controversy between the Platonic and Aristotelian schools of philosophy in the 4th cent. BC. Arriving in medieval Europe through the works of Boethius, it began to be important in the later 11th cent. A leading nominalist of that time was Roscellinus of Compiègne, a teacher of Peter Abelard, whose nominalist interpretation of the Trinity was declared heretical. There was an eclipse of nominalism in the first half of the 12th cent., but it was revived in a new form early in the 14th cent., especially by William Ockham. The nominalists, deriving from Aristotle, held that every object was unique and that any common quality that objects of the same kind might have can be expressed only through their common name (Latin *nomen*; hence, nominalism). Ockham particularly stressed the unique and individual quality of each and every object. Through him nominalism became a major school of philosophy, predominant especially at Paris in the later 14th and 15th cents, rivalling and opposing the realist school associated with Aquinas. In later centuries Locke, Hobbes, Berkeley, Hume, and the English utilitarians can all be described as nominalists.

NON-CO-OPERATION MOVEMENT (1920–2), major Indian National Congress campaign conducted under Gandhi's leadership to force concessions from the British government. Disappointment in India with the Montagu–Chelmsford reforms (1919) gave Gandhi an opportunity to win Congress' support for his programme of non-violent non-co-operation through the boycott of law courts, schools, and colleges, the new legislative councils, official functions, and foreign foods, and the renunciation of British titles. Gandhi based his campaign on the government's failure to deal adequately with the persons responsible for the Amritsar massacre (April 1919) and the Indian Muslims' concern over the fate of the Caliph (Khalifa) under the terms of the peace treaty presented to Turkey by the allied powers. To secure Congress' support for his programme he had to overcome the opposition of Tilak, who favoured a policy of Responsive Co-operation, *ie*, of using the councils while agitating for further concessions, and also to allay the misgivings of C. R. Das, M. A. Jinnah, Lajpat Rai, M. M. Malaviya, and Motilal Nehru. In his earlier campaigns he had recruited a group of regional lieutenants and had achieved general recognition of the validity of his methods; to this he now added the Khilafat Conference, which accepted non-co-operation in May, and the remnants of the Home Rule League, of which he became president in April. With this backing he initiated non-co-operation on 1 Aug., though he obtained official Congress support only in Sept. Congress candidates then withdrew from the legislative council elections and tried to persuade other candidates to withdraw and voters to boycott the polls.

The boycott of courts, colleges, and councils was more successful in drawing attention to Congress than in breaking down these institutions. The councils were elected and in the end the Congress boycott meant chiefly that non-congressmen gained the seats and whatever influence the new ministries had to offer. Measured in terms of the politicization of the country and the salutary effects of having taken independent action, the movement was more significant than the results of the boycott would suggest. After the boycott phase, when there was a danger of non-co-operation being side-tracked by other movements (as it nearly was in the United Provinces by peasant rioting), activity was maintained by meetings and demonstrations, and in March the Congress launched the 'Tilak Swaraj Fund' to collect 10 million rupees, enrol 10 million members, and distribute 2 million spinning wheels.

The government's policy was to restrict the movement by use of well-tried laws against meetings and 'seditious' speeches, but to avoid severe repression. The government of India (some provincial governments were not so patient) hoped that Gandhi would over-reach himself. The new viceroy, Lord Reading, talked to him in May, but without results. In some provinces steps were taken to organize moderates to broadcast counter-propaganda early in 1921, but the movement showed no signs of disappearing and indeed after mid-1921 there were indications—such as the Moplah outbreak in Aug. and violence in Bombay in Nov.—that it was getting out of control. The governments therefore took wider powers and many arrests were made. Gandhi, however, was left free, but attempts at mediation failed.

Non-co-operation was reaffirmed at the Ahmedabad session (1921) and Congress volunteer units were called for, Gandhi being given full executive powers to carry on the campaign. He decided to start a no-tax campaign in Bardoli taluk (Gujarat) in Feb. 1922, and to give it his personal supervision, but before this could begin the murder of several policemen at Chauri Chaura in the United Provinces led him to disband the movement. There was widespread criticism of this decision in Congress, which was confirmed by the Working Committee (12 Feb.), but Gandhi was concerned to prevent further violence, which he feared would simply lead to more vigorous retaliation by the government. He was arrested on 13 March and sentenced to six years' imprisonment.

D. G. Tendulkar, *Mahatma: Life of Mohandas Karamchand Gandhi*, 8 vols (Bombay, 1951–4).
Marquess of Reading, *Rufus Isaacs, 1st Marquess of Reading, 1914–35* (London, 1945).   PDR

NON-INTERCOURSE ACT (1809) in Britain, by which President Jefferson's embargo on American trade with the belligerents during economic warfare between Britain and France was enforced in order to avoid incidents on the high seas. The Americans were angered by the loss of lucrative trade, which was resumed briefly in 1809, and their government wished to lift restrictions, as did the French, provided that Britain relaxed the orders in council (1810). In 1811 Madison ordered the British to comply, an act which led to the Anglo-American War of 1812.

NON-INTERVENTION COMMITTEE (Sept. 1936–April 1939), in Europe, diplomatic device for preventing the Spanish Civil War from developing into an international conflict. Throughout 1936–9 there were widespread fears, especially in Western Europe, that the presence of volunteers of different nationalities on opposing sides could precipitate a general war. In Aug. 1936 a non-intervention agreement was signed by the major powers, and a committee set up, largely through British and French pressure, to supervise the working of this agreement. The committee met for the first time on 9 Sept. 1936 and was dominated from the first by the personalities and policies of Corbin (France), Grandi (Italy), and Maisky (USSR). Ribbentrop later admitted that a better name would have been 'intervention committee' because it failed so obviously to throw even the slenderest cloak of respectability over the activities of Italy, Germany, and Russia in supplying equipment and men in large quantities. Negotiations were mostly futile because none of the governments took them seriously There were schemes for observation at the frontiers and ports, for mediation, and for the withdrawl of volunteers—but all failed. Between July 1938 and its final dissolution on 20 April 1939 the committee did not meet. Its concern for appearances may have prevented the situation getting out of hand, and gave the powers, none of whom wanted a general war, room for manœuvre. Thus it had a role similar to that of the UN, after 1945, though it lacked moral force or authority.

NON-JURORS, beneficed clergy of the Church of England and of the Episcopal Church in Scotland who refused to take the oaths of allegiance to William III and Mary II because they believed in the doctrine of non-resistance and that James II was the rightful king. There were about 400 in England and Wales, including Sancroft, Abp of Canterbury, and four others of the seven bishops imprisoned in 1688. Because so few of the major ecclesiastical figures in England emerged as non-jurors, the Church of England, as an Anglican established church governed by bishops, continued unchanged from pre-revolution (1688) days. In Scotland, however, the entire Scottish episcopate, and most of the clergy, rejected William III. Thus a Presbyterian form of government became the established Church of Scotland and the episcopal church suffered severely under penal laws which were not repealed for over a century (1792). The differing ways in which the churches of the two nations had gone was a major issue in negotiations for Union in 1707, the Presbyterianism of the Scots being secured in the Act of Union.

NON-PARTISAN LEAGUE (1915–24) in the US, agrarian movement in the US north-west. It arose out of wheat farmers' resentment against the monopoly control over the wheat trade exercised by the Minneapolis Chamber of Commerce, but embraced other agrarian grievances. It was led by A. C. Townley, a bankrupt ND farmer and Socialist Party organizer, and was formed by the alliance of the Equity Co-operative Exchange, farmers, and socialist leaders. Its programme included demands for state-owned elevators, mills, and packing houses, state rural credits, hail insurance, and taxation reform. The movement's greatest success was in ND, where its candidate, Lynn J. Frazier, won the Republican Party primary, was elected governor (1916), and secured enactment of its programme by the state legislature (1919). The league's influence spread into other mid-western and western states with programmes modified to meet local conditions. Accusations of disloyalty during the First World War and accusations of socialism during the post-war Depression led to a waning of its influence. By 1924 its organization had disappeared, although some elements persisted within the major political parties in ND and in the Farmer–Labor Party in MN.

NON-REGULATION PROVINCES, areas of British India where, in contrast with earlier territorial acquisitions, complicated codes of English law were not imposed, *eg*, the Punjab after its annexation in 1849.

NONSUCH, TREATY OF (1585), by which Queen Elizabeth I of England took the Dutch under her protection. She rejected the sovereignty of Holland and Zeeland, which would probably have involved England in perpetual war with Spain, and offered the treaty of Greenwich solely for the relief of Antwerp, but the city soon fell to Parma. The general treaty of Nonsuch was at once concluded, by which Elizabeth provided at her own cost an army of 5100 foot and 1000 horse for the Dutch under a high-ranking commander for as long as the war lasted. Flushing and Brill were to be handed over to England as cautionary towns until English expenditure was repaid by the Dutch. The Earl of Leicester was eventually sent as commander and Sir Philip Sydney as governor of Flushing.

NON-VIOLENCE, basic Indian principle prohibiting, on religious grounds, the killing of living beings. It is connected with belief in transmigration of the soul, which is believed to create a bond between all creatures. In the application of this principle, however, there are great differences depending on the period, area, social group, and sect. In general, there

was a tendency for non-violence to become less flexible as time went by; it was more strictly interpreted in the Middle Ganges valley than in many other areas and observed more strictly by Brahmans than by many lower castes; in some sects, notably the Vaishnava and the Jains, non-violence was absolute, whereas it was qualified among others. Moreover, it was always much more pronounced in its application to cows (and, *eg*, snakes) than other animals. The classical texts mention or imply important exceptions: war, the royal hunt, certain sacrifices, and the ancient custom of slaughtering a cow for an honoured guest. In spite of all these qualifications and exceptions non-violence has been through the ages an important factor that has given Indian history some of its distinctive features.

NOOTKA SOUND DISPUTE (1789–90). Capt. Cook's discovery of Nootka Sound (1778), a small natural harbour off Vancouver Island, led to the establishment of a small British trading settlement (1787). In 1789 a Spanish squadron under Martinez took possession of the Sound, claiming a prescriptive right by prior discovery of all territory on the Pacific coast up to 60° latitude. The British government, led by the Younger Pitt, repudiated this claim on the grounds of effective occupation and hastily endeavoured to fit out a fleet. Spain, unable to secure the support of the French revolutionary government, was forced to back down and after exhaustive negotiations agreement was reached (Oct. 1790) on navigation of the North Pacific and use of Nootka Sound.

NORDLINGEN, BATTLES OF (1634, 1645). In 1634, in the decisive engagements of the Thirty Years War, Sweden's hopes of controlling the empire were shattered and the position of German Protestants was endangered. Imperial forces under Archduke Ferdinand and his cousin the Cardinal-Infant, numbering 33,000 men, shattered the smaller Protestant force of 25,000 under Duke Bernard of Saxe-Weimar and Count Gustav Horn. The Swedes lost 17,000 men and all their artillery. Horn was captured and Bernard fled towards the Rhine. Eleven years later, in the same war, a French victory under Enghien (later Condé) and Turenne over the imperialists led by Marshal Franz von Mercy took place at Allerheim, south-east of Nordlingen. Although Mercy was killed it was a pyrrhic victory for the French, who were unable to pursue the enemy, allowing the Bavarians to retreat to Donauwörth.

NORE MUTINY (1797) in Britain, naval mutiny led by Richard Parker (May 1797) a month after the Spithead mutiny, at a critical point in the French Wars. The sailors of the North Sea fleet demanded a fairer division of prize money and the modification of the brutal disciplinary regulations. They threatened to blockade the Thames and to take the more drastic step of surrendering the ships to the enemy. The mutineers were not, however, united behind Parker and gradually gave way to the authorities, leaving their ringleader to surrender himself and be hanged for treason (July).

The suppression of the mutiny enabled reinforcements to be sent to Admiral Duncan, who spent the summer bluffing the Dutch at Texel with his single-ship blockade.

NORFOLK, THOMAS HOWARD, 8th Duke of (3rd of 3rd creation) (1473–1554), English statesman and uncle of queens Anne Boleyn and Katherine Howard. He became the brother-in-law of Henry VII by his marriage to Anne, daughter of Edward IV (1495). He was appointed lord high admiral of England (1513) and also led the van of the English army at Flodden and was created Earl of Surrey (1514). He successively became lord deputy of Ireland (1520), lord treasurer (1522), Duke of Norfolk (1524), and president of the council (1529). He favoured Henry VIII's divorce from Catherine of Aragon. Though his eminent position was shaken by the fall of Anne Boleyn (1536), his military abilities rendered him almost indispensable to Henry. In 1536 he put down the Pilgrimage of Grace. He was hostile to the religious reforms of Thomas Cromwell, and after the latter's fall (1540) he led the conservative group in the council in opposition to Cranmer, the Earl of Hertford (later Duke of Somerset), Lord Lisle (later Duke of Northumberland), and the rest of the Protestant group. In 1542 he led the English army to Scotland, and in 1544 to France. His position was, however, weakened by the fall of Katherine Howard (1542), and he was arrested as an accessory to his son's treason (1546). Though his son, the Earl of Surrey, was executed (1547), and Norfolk himself condemned by act of attainder, he was saved from execution by the death of Henry VIII. He remained imprisoned during Edward VI's reign, but was released by Mary I and restored to his dukedom (1553).

NORFOLK, THOMAS HOWARD, 9th Duke of (4th of 3rd creation) (1538–72), English soldier and courtier, son of Henry Howard, Earl of Surrey (who was executed in 1547). He succeeded his grandfather as duke in 1554. He commanded the English forces sent to Scotland in 1559–60, and in 1568 presided over the enquiry into the quarrel between the Scots and Queen Mary who had fled to England. Though favoured by Elizabeth I, he became jealous of the Earl of Leicester and of William Cecil and following the death of his third wife he readily listened to suggestions that he should marry Mary Queen of Scots. He was arrested (1569), and was only released on the suppression of the rising of the Northern Earls (1570). He soon allowed himself to be drawn into the Ridolfi Plot to place Mary on the English throne. Its discovery led to his execution in 1572.

NORFOLK, ROGER BIGOD, 7th Earl of (5th of 2nd creation) (c. 1245–1306), one of the main baronial opponents of King Edward I of England. He was the son of Hugh Bigod, the chief justiciar of England during a period of baronial rule, and a descendant of one of the leaders of the rebellion against King John in 1215. He may have been influenced by this tradition of opposition to the Crown. Edward I mishandled him over various personal matters and in the greatest crisis of the reign, in 1297, Norfolk emerged as the leader of the opposition which demanded the abandonment of excessive royal exactions and of unwise and unprofitable wars that were making them necessary. Edward I had to make important concessions, but never forgave Norfolk and in 1302 forced him into an agreement that disinherited Norfolk's relatives, so that on his death the earldom passed into Edward's hands.

NORFOLK ISLAND, territory of the Commonwealth of Australia, 930 miles (1500 kms) north-east of Sydney, discovered by Capt. James Cook (1774) and used intermittently as a penal settlement (1788–1855). In 1856 194 descendants of the *Bounty* mutineers were transferred from the Pitcairn Islands. Under colonial office control until 1900, when it passed to NSW, Norfolk Island became a Commonwealth territory in 1914 and in the 1966 census had a population of 1147.

NORFOLK REBELLION (1549) in England, widespread revolt of both agrarian peasants and urban artisans, small tradesmen, and semi-skilled workmen against economic inflation, led by Robert Kett (or Ket) and often known as Kett's Rebellion. The rebellion began as a protest against enclosure on 20 June 1549 in the village of Attleborough in Norfolk, where some villagers threw down the hedges of a local landlord who had enclosed part of their common land. Further disturbances centred round Wymondham. These disorders arose from the unrealistic social policy of the protector, the Duke of Somerset, who had a genuine concern to protect the commons from exploitation. In 1548 his follower, John Hales, had introduced three bills on enclosure into parliament and had aroused fierce opposition from landlords. Somerset had had to resort to administrative action. Hales's commission on enclosures set to work and the idea grew that the 'Good Duke's' government was on the side of the commons and

that it would support them in redressing their grievances. They were thus encouraged to riot.

A considerable amount of enclosure had taken place in Norfolk in the early 16th cent. and the gradual encroachment on the peasants' common rights was a serious grievance. Coupled with anger at inflation and rackrenting, it caused the peasants to throw down hedges. The leadership of Robert Kett, a local landlord, turned these riots into a rebellion. He wanted to alter the traditional (and unique) method of large-scale sheep-farming in Norfolk by the foldcourse system (this was the landlord's right to pasture his sheep on the peasant's land in return for manuring it). Kett wanted to prevent abuse by restricting a landlord's grazing to that necessary for the provision of his household. Other agrarian grievances figured large in Kett's demands and he clearly expected government support for his manifesto against the peasants' exploitation by the gentry. He regarded himself as acting on the king's behalf in his effort to remedy the local situation in Norfolk.

Having marched on Norwich, Kett encamped with his 16,000 followers on Mousehold Heath just outside the city (12 July). The Norfolk gentry made little attempt to disperse them, and opinion in Norwich itself was divided. Consequently the city authorities co-operated with Kett. On 21 July the turning point in the rebellion occurred. The government herald arrived to offer pardon to the rebels if they dispersed, thus shattering any illusions of government support. Kett's authority, which had hitherto restrained the camp, was unable to prevent an unprovoked attack on Norwich and on 23 July the city fell. On 30 July the Marquis of Northampton arrived with 14,000 men, but was forced to withdraw. John Dudley, Earl of Warwick, was then put in command of a new levy of 12,000 troops and arrived at Norwich on 23 Aug. His pardon was rejected by the rebels. Warwick was reinforced by 1000 mercenaries and proceeded to cut Kett's supply lines. The rebels thus forced into battle were cut down by Warwick's cavalry (about 3000 being killed) at Dussindale on 27 Aug. Kett was captured, condemned for treason and hanged. About 50 others were also executed.

S. T. Bindoff, *Ket's Rebellion* (London, 1949).
A. Fletcher, *Tudor Rebellions* (London, 1968).   CJ

NORHAM, TREATY OF (1291), agreement settling the royal succession in Scotland. After the extinction of the main line of the Scottish ruling dynasty in 1290, all the main claimants to the vacant throne accepted the arbitration of King Edward I of England. Edward met them at Norham and insisted on being recognized as overlord of Scotland. Thereafter agreement was reached for considering the claims of the numerous competitors and in Nov. 1292 John de Balliol became the new king. His inability to accept the consequences of Edward's overlordship led in 1296 to war with England and Balliol's deposition.

NORICUM, Roman province covering much of Austria, with parts of Yugoslavia and Italy. Annexed c. 16 BC, it needed no legions till the late 2nd cent. AD. Many of its Celtic and Illyrian inhabitants became Roman citizens under the Emperor Claudius, but there were few large towns. In 5th and subsequent cents, Noricum was subject to Germanic and later Slav invasions contributing largely to the present population distribution in the area.

NORMA FUTURARUM ACTIONUM, scheme for the reorganization of the Holy Roman empire after the Thirty Years War, proposed by Gustavus Adolphus of Sweden. The plan came to nothing with the king's death in battle (1632), but it was unlikely that it would ever have been viable, because the agreement of all the German princes was highly improbable.

NORMALCY, in the US, term used by the Republican senator Warren G. Harding in a speech at Boston (14 May

1920), when he said that 'America's present need is not heroics but healing, not nostrums but normalcy'. In 1920 Harding became president of the US, and during the 1920s, a decade when the federal government seemed once again to have entered into an alliance with big business, the term was applied to Republican policies.

NORMAN, GEORGE (d. 1553), German Lutheran reformer, a disciple of Melanchthon, who was appointed superintendent of the Swedish church by Gustavus Vasa and carried out with great thoroughness (1539–44) the reformation of the Swedish church on German lines. Widespread revolts forced the king to rescind many of the 'German' edicts (1544), but Norman was retained as a political adviser.

NORMAN, ROBERT (*fl.* 16th cent.), English sailor and compass-maker, who wrote on magnetism in his work, *The Newe Attractive* (1581).

NORMAN COMMISSION (1896), British commission under the chairmanship of Sir Henry Wylie Norman, a former governor of Jamaica, to examine the causes of and remedies for the economic depression in the West Indies. Its chief recommendations were that the West Indies economy should diversify by the establishment of new industries, especially fruit cultivation for the US market, that there should be government investment in improving communications and in increasing land settlement, and that Britain should seek the abolition of the bounty system by which European sugar-beet production was being heavily subsidized. The abolition of the bounty system was agreed at the Brussels Convention (1903).

NORODOM (*reg.* 1859–1904), King of Cambodia during the first decades of the French protectorate. He was brought up in Bangkok, and felt a strong cultural attachment to the Thai, but politically he had to accept a French protection, which, while not allowing his country independence, saved it from final partition between Siam and Viet-nam. His reign began with a rebellion in 1860 by his brother, Si Vattha. After withdrawing to Bangkok, he defeated the rebels with the help of the French missionary Mgr Miche. Meanwhile the French had annexed Cochin-China, and in 1863 Norodom accepted French protection. After preventing him from accepting a summons to Bangkok by Rama IV in 1864, the French entered into negotiations with the Thai, who finally recognized the French protectorate over Cambodia in 1867. Norodom, meanwhile, with French help, survived another rebellion: that of Pu Kombor (1865–7). In 1872 Norodom visited Hong Kong, Canton, and Manila, and on his return began a series of internal reforms to meet the French desire to modernize the country; but he was not able to prevent the French from taking over a good deal of administrative power by the treaty of 1884. This move led to a new revolt, headed by Si Vattha, which was a serious threat to French rule in 1885–6 and was not finally ended until 1892. But once again Norodom maintained his position, and the French theirs.

NORODOM SIHANOUK (1922–   ), King of Cambodia (*reg.* 1941–55) great-grandson of King Norodom (*reg.* 1859–1904) who was chosen to be King of Cambodia at the behest of the French governor-general of Indo-China (April 1941). Shortly afterwards, the French lost control of Indo-China to the Japanese, and in March 1944 King Norodom proclaimed the independence of Cambodia, with Japanese approval. When the French returned in 1945, Cambodia had to accept the status of an autonomous state within the French Union, modified in 1949 by a treaty which established the Associated State of Cambodia, but still retained such matters as foreign policy in French hands. In early 1953 he began a 'crusade for independence', visiting Paris and the US in the hope of persuading the French to grant full independence to his country. He was not satisfied that this had been achieved until after the Geneva Agreements, ending hostilities against the French in Cambodia, in July 1954. In March 1955, having ousted his potential rival Son Ngoc Thanh, and having obtained approval for his policies in a referendum, the king abdicated (1955) in favour of his father; the latter reigned till his death in 1960, when a Regency Council was created. As a prince, Sihanouk founded a political party, the *Sangkum Ryaster Niyum*, or 'Popular Socialist Community', and won the election which followed. In Oct. 1955 he became prime minister. Although he handed over that office to subordinates at several periods in the following decade, he remained in firm control of Cambodia until 1970. His principal concern was to maintain Cambodian independence and neutrality, despite bad relations with both Thailand and South Viet-nam. To that end he sought a closer relationship with Peking; he also avoided too close a relationship with the US, and broke off diplomatic relations with Washington completely in 1965. He denied US allegations that he permitted Viet-namese communist forces to use bases in Cambodia during the Viet-nam War, but in March 1970 his political opponents at home overthrew his regime on precisely that issue. Prince Sihanouk retired to Peking, whilst his successors faced the problem of how to prevent Cambodia becoming a battleground between communist and anti-communist Viet-namese.

M. Liefer, *Cambodia—the search for security* (London, 1967).
                                                                    RBS

NORONHA, FERNÃO DE (*fl* 16th cent.), converted Jew resident in Lisbon who, in 1502, received the first contract from the Portuguese Crown to gather dyewood (brazilwood) in Brazil for sale in Europe upon payment of a royalty to the government, a system which endured until the 1530s.

NORQUAY, JOHN (1841–89), Canadian politician and prime minister (1878–86) of Man. who encouraged railway building and greatly increased the province's federal grant (1884). He resigned over a railway scandal (1886) although not personally involved.

NORRIS, BENJAMIN FRANKLIN (1870–1902), US journalist and author. As a newspaper correspondent he was expelled by the Boer government for his part in the abortive Jameson Raid on the Transvaal (1895), and later covered the Cuban campaign (1898) for *McClure's Magazine*. After 1898 he began publishing a group of novels that reflected his growing concern with social and economic forces and the influence of Zola. His *McTeague* (1899), a story of lower-class life and degradation in San Francisco, established his reputation. *The Octopus* (1901) was the first of a projected trilogy concerning the 'Epic of the Wheat', the struggle between farmers and the dominant railroad in CA. He died after completing the second of his trilogy, *The Pit* (1903).

NORRIS, GEORGE WILLIAM (1861–1944), US politician, who was a liberal US congressman (1903–13) and senator (1913–43) from NB. His crusade in the 1920s for government operation of the Muscle Shoals dam opened the way for the Tennessee Valley Authority. He was one of the surviving progressives who supported the New Deal and also endorsed F. D. Roosevelt's foreign policy despite his earlier opposition to American entry into the First World War and the League of Nations.

NORRIS, SIR JOHN (*c.* 1660–1749), English sailor and diplomat who served in the Wars of the League of Augsburg and Spanish Succession. His main achievements were in the Baltic. His first expedition to that region (1709) was to hamper French war supplies. After the War of the Spanish Succession he commanded several other expeditions to the Baltic. His mission was to safeguard British trade, Hanoverian interest, and preserve a balance of power during the Northern War. Thus he supported both Russia and Sweden at various times and similarly used his diplomatic talents as envoy extraordinary and minister plenipotentiary to St Petersburg (1718) and as a pro-Swedish mediator (1720, 1721). He later commanded the Channel fleet (1733–44).

NORRKÖPING, RIKSDAG OF (1604), settled the Swedish Crown upon the family of Charles IX and restricted its inheritance to Lutherans, who must not occupy any other throne. The Diet also completed the proscription of Charles's enemies.

NORTH, ROGER (?1585–?1652), English merchant who sailed with Raleigh to Guiana (1617). He was later appointed to command a new colony on the Amazon, returning with tobacco (1621), but was briefly imprisoned because of his clashes with the Spanish. He sailed (1627) to establish a new colony in Guiana but it soon collapsed.

NORTH, ROGER (1653–1734), British politician, lawyer, and author who was attorney-general to Mary of Modena, queen of James II. He gave up politics at the Revolution (1688) and his books, all published posthumously, included a life of his brother, Francis North, Lord Guilford.

NORTH, WAR OF THE (1655–60), complex struggle arising out of Charles X of Sweden's attack on Poland. Since Poland was already at war with Russia, Charles quickly overran the country, capturing both Warsaw and Cracow, but a Polish national resistance developed and in 1656–8 hostilities with Russia were suspended through the mediation of the emperor. In 1657 Charles's armies still held most of Poland, but war with Russia, Austria, and Denmark made his hold precarious. Next year his chief ally, Brandenburg, changed sides, with the result that Poland's only permanent loss was its sovereignty over the duchy of Prussia, which passed definitively to Brandenburg.

Charles then turned against the Danes. In Oct. 1657 his forces captured Frederiksodde, the fortress guarding Jutland, and on 30 Jan. 1658 he began the famous 13-day march which brought him across the ice of both Belts to Zealand. To save Copenhagen from imminent attack the Danes signed the peace of Roskilde, at which they sacrificed nearly half their territory. Nevertheless, Charles renewed the war in July, but the Dutch, in fear of Swedish control over the Sound, kept open the supply route for Copenhagen, which the Swedes vainly attempted to take by storm. England, and to some extent France, joined in the pressure against Sweden (Concert of The Hague), but it was chiefly Charles's sudden death that precipitated the ending of the war by the treaties of Oliva and Copenhagen. Its most durable result was Sweden's acquisition of the Danish territories east of the Sound.

NORTH ATLANTIC TREATY (1949), alliance between the US, Canada, and the countries of western Europe. It followed from the organization of the states of western Europe into a defensive alliance, the Brussels treaty (March 1948), and the readiness of the US to give support to such an alliance, as shown in the Vandenberg resolution (May 1948). The treaty was distinctive in the degree of commitment by the US and Britain to the defence of the continent of Western Europe, and in the extent of the military and civilian organization—NATO—which it established. The original signatories were Belgium, Britain, Canada, Denmark, France, Iceland, Italy, Luxemburg, the Netherlands, Norway, Portugal, and the US. They were later joined by Greece and Turkey (1952) and the German Federal Republic (1955).

NORTH ATLANTIC TREATY ORGANIZATION (NATO), established by the North Atlantic treaty in 1949 and including Belgium, Britain, Canada, Denmark, France, the German Federal Republic (from 1955), Greece (from 1952), Iceland, Italy, Luxemburg, the Netherlands, Norway, Portugal, Turkey (from 1952), and the US. The organization remained inter-governmental, its governing body being the NATO

Council. Ministerial meetings of the council have generally been held twice a year, attended by foreign, defence, or economic ministers, according to the agenda. Occasionally, heads of governments have attended. It functions continuously at the level of permanent representatives, of ambassadorial rank. The secretary-general of NATO acts as chairman of the council. The military side of the organization is headed by a Military Committee, consisting of chiefs of staff and, to provide continuous representation, a Military Representatives Committee. A Standing Group of British, French, and US representatives forms an executive group of the Military Representatives.

Military integration is established through three principal commands (European, Atlantic Ocean, and English Channel) and a Canada–US Regional Planning Group. The first Supreme Allied Commander Europe (SACEUR), appointed by NATO, was Gen. Eisenhower (1950).

Initially the civilian headquarters of NATO were established in Paris, and the military in Washington. After De Gaulle came to power (1958) the French government showed increasing opposition to the integrated institutions of NATO. The French Mediterranean fleet was withdrawn from NATO command (1959) and French naval officers withdrawn from all NATO posts and staffs (1964). The French government set a timetable for withdrawal from NATO (1966), with the result that the NATO Council and secretariat building was moved from Paris to Brussels. The Standing Group was wound up and the Military Committee moved from Washington to Brussels. The European command (SHAPE) moved to Mons in Belgium. France remained in 1970 a member of the North Atlantic Alliance, but reduced her participation in the organization to a minimum.   WK

NORTH BRITON, newspaper begun by John Wilkes (1762) by which he tested and asserted the freedom of the press in Britain. Attacks on the monarchy and George III's dependence on his mother and favourites culminated in no. 45 for 23 April 1763, in which the speech from the throne was described as a falsehood. General warrants against all concerned in its production were issued, Wilkes arrested, and his patron, Lord Temple, dismissed from office for defending him. Wilkes successfully asserted his privilege as an MP but his appeals for public support led him to repeat the libels. In Nov. 1763 the House of Common declared no. 45 to be a seditious libel, asserted that the privilege of the House did not extend to this offence, and also banned the publication. Thereupon Wilkes fled the country and the *North Briton* was not successfully revived, though a few editions were produced (1768–9) by the Wilkesite printer William Bingley.

NORTH CAROLINA, English colony in North America. A French expedition under Verrazano sailed along the coast of NC (1524) and De Soto explored its mountain area before discovering the Mississippi (1539). At the time of the first permanent settlement by white men there were 30 tribes and an estimated 30,000 Indians in Carolina. Sir Walter Raleigh planted a short-lived colony on Roanoke Island (1585–c. 1590). Charles I granted Carolina to Sir Robert Heath, but the area was first settled in the 1650s by colonists from VA. After the Restoration Charles II granted the region to eight proprietors, who divided up the land and ruled it like feudal lords. Settlements around Charleston in the South came to be called South Carolina, and in 1729 a separate government was set up by the proprietors for NC. The growth of the colony was slow because of unrest over the non-resident proprietors and there were trade and boundary disputes with VA. George II bought out the proprietors and NC became a royal province (1729). Under the royal governors there was a rapid growth in population and agriculture, and trade and industry developed. Thousands of Highland Scots, Scotch-Irish, and Germans emigrated during the pre-revolutionary period and settled chiefly in the mountainous west, which remained poor and backward and separated from the aristocratic eastern part. The back-country people, suffering from excessive taxes and dishonest officials, formed an association called the Regulators, which sought to obtain reforms, but their insurrection was unsuccessful (1777). NC was the first colony officially to declare its independence from Britain (1776) and furnished ten regiments and thousands of militia to support the revolution. NC became a part of the US by ratifying the federal constitution (1789).

H. T. Lefler and A. R. Newsome, *North Carolina: the history of a southern state* (Chapel Hill, 1954).   DJF

NORTH DAKOTA, 39th member state of the US, admitted in 1889. This northern region of the Great Plains was traversed by Vérendrye (1738) and opened up by fur traders, notably David Thompson of the Hudson's Bay Co. (1797). The south-western part of the future state was acquired by the US under the Louisiana Purchase (1803) and the remainder from Britain (1818). Dakota Territory, embracing present-day North and South Dakota, Montana, and Wyoming, was organized in 1861. Settlement, begun at Pembina (1812), was sparse until the Indians were brought under control (1863–6). Gold was discovered in the Black Hills (1876), and together with miners and speculators, large numbers of German, Scandinavian, and east European immigrants moved into the Territory, from the northern part of which the present state was organized (1889). ND has always been pre-eminently agricultural, with its rich Red River valley soil producing large crops of cereals and potatoes; but it also has large lignite resources and some oil and natural gas fields. State politics have been dominated by the Republican Party, although agricultural discontent also produced a 'radical' tradition that found expression in the Non-partisan League.

NORTH FORELAND, BATTLES OF (1653, 1666), naval engagements in the Anglo-Dutch wars of the mid-17th cent., fought off the south-east coast of England. The first battle, between the Dutch under Van Tromp and the English under George Monck, later Duke of Albemarle, was inconclusive, while in 1666 the Dutch under De Ruyter were trounced by Albemarle.

NORTH GERMAN CONFEDERATION (1867–71) was set up after the Austro-Prussian war, replacing the German Confederation (1815) and forming the basis of the German empire (1871). The King of Prussia was president of the confederation of all German states north of the Main river, and was responsible for the army, foreign policy and the appointment of the chancellor, the only minister responsible to the Reichstag. The Reichstag was elected by universal manhood suffrage, had to be called regularly, and shared control of the Budget with the Bundesrat, composed of delegates from the various states but dominated by Prussia, with 17 delegates. The Bundesrat was responsible for legislation. Austria, Bavaria, Baden, Würtemberg, and Hesse-Darmstadt were excluded from the confederation, but all except Austria were joined to Prussia by secret military treaties and to the confederation by the economic ties of the Zollverein. Six hundred years of Habsburg domination of Germany had come to an end.

NORTH WALES ASSOCIATION (1648), system of county defence organized by the Long Parliament in Aug. 1648, shortly after the victory of Preston which ended the English Civil War. The North Wales counties, except Anglesey, which was still unsubdued, were organized on the pattern of the West Wales Association of 1644, with a committee in each county.

NORTHAMPTON, BATTLE OF (10 July 1460), north of Oxford. During the Wars of the Roses Warwick captured King Henry VI. He owed his victory largely to the sudden defection from Henry of Lord Grey of Ruthin. After the battle Richard of York proceeded to London to claim the Crown and was recognized as heir to Henry VI instead of Henry's son Edward.

NORTHBROOK, THOMAS GEORGE BARING, 1st Earl of (1826–1904), English politician and viceroy of India (1872–6) who dealt with the Bengal famine of 1874, and had the Gaekwar of Baroda tried for an attempt on the life of the British Resident and deposed for misgovernment (1875). He resigned after differing with the Disraeli second administration (1874–80) over their Afghan policy and over the question of taxing Manchester cotton goods. He became first lord of the admiralty (1880–5) in Gladstone's second administration.

NORTHCLIFFE, ALFRED CHARLES WILLIAM HARMSWORTH, Viscount (1865–1922), British journalist and newspaper proprietor who created the popular press. He founded the *Daily Mail*, a halfpenny paper, in 1896, and the *Daily Mirror* in 1903. He acquired *The Times* in 1908 and made it powerful and profitable. His newspapers campaigned successfully to make Lloyd George prime minister in place of Asquith (1916) and he was one of the major influential figures in Britain throughout the First World War, initiating *The Times* fund for the sick and wounded and visiting British forces abroad. He undertook a mission to the US in 1917 and was director of propaganda for enemy countries in 1918.

NORTH-EAST PASSAGE, sea-route through the north of Scandinavia and Russia sought (1553) by the English seamen Willoughby and Chancellor to establish trade with China and the Far East. Their venture failed directly, but Chancellor made a successful overland journey from Archangel to Moscow which led to the establishment of Anglo-Russian trade. The passage was eventually made in 1878–9 by A. E. Nordenskiöld, and subsequently was used by Russian ice-breakers opening up routes for the Siberian timber industry.

NORTHERN EARLS, RISING OF (1569), last feudal rising in England, nominally led by Thomas Percy, Earl of Northumberland, and Charles Neville, Earl of Westmorland. Its aims were to resist the Elizabethan religious settlement and ensure the safety of Mary Queen of Scots, as heir to the English throne. Mary had arrived in England in 1568 as a prisoner, an event which led to a long series of conspiracies. One, concentrating around the discontent at court, was to marry Mary to the Duke of Norfolk, and to this the northern rising was tenuously linked. The capitulation of Norfolk led to the northern earls abandoning a rising fixed for 6 Oct. 1569, but the confusion and uncertainty engendered eventually provided sufficient encouragement to set it off.

The earls were desperate men who felt cornered by Elizabeth I's government. Northumberland had a deep concern for the Catholic religion. He also had bitter personal grievances against the queen, who was pursuing a policy of weakening the hold of the great magnate families over the northern marches. He and Westmorland had declined in wealth and status, yet both were unwilling to rebel and were leaders of revolt only by virtue of their position. The real promoters of the rising were lesser-known men who were enthusiastic supporters of the Catholic cause.

The summoning of the earls to London on 9 Nov. 1569 was the signal for the rising to commence. The earls controlled County Durham, and then marched south to Bramham Moor near Tadcaster in Yorkshire (21 Nov.). Large numbers joined from the North Riding and the rebel forces stood at 3800 foot and 1600 horse. Durham, however, was the heart of the rising, and it soon became apparent that, though all the country east of the Pennines was at the command of the earls, their appeals to the Catholic nobility had failed and they were powerless outside northern England. They abandoned their plan to release Mary from Tutbury and began to retreat to Durham. As they returned to their own estates their followers began to leave them. Their only successes were the capture of Hartlepool and Barnard Castle. The earls fled to Scotland, where they sought the shelter of clansmen who supported Mary.

The rising failed because of its incoherence and aimlessness, and because its support was geographically limited. The rising itself caused little bloodshed, but over 400 of the rebels were executed, including Northumberland (1572), who was betrayed by the Scots. Westmorland and some of the other leaders escaped to the Netherlands, where they lived as pensioners of Spain.

Many of the gentry involved in the rising were the earls' retainers. The horsemen, the real strength of the rebel army, were provided by their tenants, who joined the earls through bastard feudal allegiance, while the rest were bullied or bribed into joining, religious propaganda playing a not insubstantial part. The failure of the rising indicated that northern feudalism and particularism could not withstand Tudor centralization.

J. B. Black, *The Reign of Elizabeth* (London, 1959).
A. Fletcher, *Tudor Rebellions* (London, 1968).   CJ

NORTHERN ELEMENTS PROGRESSIVE UNION (NEPU)

in Nigeria, founded in 1945, though its formal inauguration, under the leadership of Aminu Kano, came in 1951. From 1956 it allied with the United Middle Belt Congress in opposition to successive governments of the Northern People's Congress in Northern Nigeria.

NORTHERN EXPEDITION

(1926–8), major military campaign by which Chiang Kai-shek and the Kuomintang reunified China. The expedition was launched from the Canton region, and moved rapidly north to the Yangtse region. Soviet advice and training played a key role in this early success. But in 1927 the Kuomintang–Communist alliance collapsed; the Kuomintang turned on the communists, and the expedition was halted. In 1928 Kuomintang forces pushed north again and took Peking. Many Kuomintang conquests however were 'won' by payment of bribes, and over much of China the old war-lords remained in power, though now with Kuomintang titles. The unification achieved was more nominal than real.

NORTHERN PEOPLE'S CONGRESS,

in Nigeria, had its origin as a cultural organization in Dec. 1949 but became a major political party in Oct. 1951. Its strongest supporters came from the emirs, other Native Authority officials, and leaders in the former Northern Region. Until Jan. 1966 Ahmadu Bello, *Sardauna* of Sokoto and prime minister of the Northern Region, and Abubakar Tafawa Balewa, former federal prime minister, were its leader and deputy leader respectively. It won regional elections in Northern Nigeria (1951 and 1965). At the national level, it formed several coalition governments until Dec. 1965. With other political parties, it was proscribed following the *coup d'état* of Jan. 1966.

NORTHERN RHODESIA AFRICAN NATIONAL CONGRESS,

earliest African nationality party in Zambia, founded in 1937 and revived in 1948. It dominated Zambian politics of the early and middle 1950s under the leadership of Harry Nkumbula.

NORTHERN SECURITIES COMPANY v. US,

193 US 197 (1904), US Supreme Court case arising from an anti-trust suit brought by US Attorney-General Knox. The Northern Securities Co. was set up by rival railroad groups as a holding company to purchase control of the Northern Pacific and Great Northern railroads, so avoiding further bitter competition between the groups. The US Department of Justice brought a suit in equity to dissolve the company.

The Supreme Court, by a 5–4 decision, held the Northern Securities Co. to be an unlawful combination as defined by the Sherman Act (1890). The majority opinion, dismissing arguments that the company was the product of a stock transaction that was not in itself commerce, asserted that the Sherman Act was aimed at all combinations in restraint of trade which directly operate in restraint of commerce, and could therefore apply to companies or corporations lawfully organized under state statutes.

NORTHERN TERRITORY, THE,

in Australia, 520,000 sq. miles (1,350,000 sq. kms) central section of the northern half of Australia. It was first part of NSW, later of SA, then administered by the Commonwealth from 1911. Large areas are desert; a beef cattle industry existed in northern pasture land from the 19th cent. but agriculture made little progress and known mineral wealth—copper, gold, uranium, bauxite, and iron ore—was yet to be fully exploited. Improved communications during the Second World War helped to stimulate post-war development for a 1970 population of 100,000, including nearly 30,000 aborigines. The territory's minimal representation in the Commonwealth parliament was offset by a partially elective legislative council in its major city, Darwin.

NORTHINGTON, ROBERT HENLEY,

1st Earl of (1708–71), British politician, lawyer, and judge, who served as lord chancellor (1761–6), and lord president of the council (1766–7). His resignation from Rockingham's administration led to the summoning of the Elder Pitt and Grafton to office on his advice to George III.

NORTHUMBERLAND, JOHN DUDLEY,

1st Duke of (1st creation) (c. 1502–53), English politician and son of Edmund Dudley, Henry VII's minister, executed by Henry VIII. In 1543 he was appointed a privy councillor and lord high admiral for life, and later governor of Boulogne (1545–7). He was created Earl of Warwick and lord high chamberlain on Edward VI's accession (1547) and accompanied Protector Somerset to Scotland. His military talents contributed to the victory of Pinkie. Warwick resented the power and the policies of Somerset and began to conspire for his overthrow. After his defeat of Kett's rebellion, he brought down Somerset (Oct. 1549) with the help of extreme Protestants and Catholics. Warwick soon disposed of the Catholics, however, and pushed the Reformation further than it had gone under Somerset. By packing the council with his supporters, he finally effected the removal of Somerset, who was executed (1552). Dudley was created Duke of Northumberland, by Edward VI, over whom he had complete domination and whom he persuaded to alter the succession in favour of his daughter-in-law, Lady Jane Grey. Having bullied the council into proclaiming Jane queen on the death of Edward, he took the field against the forces of Mary Tudor. In his absence the council reversed its decision and proclaimed Mary queen. Northumberland's troops deserted him, and he was arrested, tried for treason, and executed.

NORTHUMBERLAND, HENRY PERCY,

1st Earl of (1st creation) (1341–1408), who supported King Henry IV of England in his usurpation (1399), but by 1403 he and his son Henry (Hotspur) drifted into a revolt, apparently to get the Crown for their own family. While Hotspur was killed on the Welsh border, Northumberland was prevented from saving him by the army of his chief northern rival, the Earl of Westmorland. The magnates forced Henry IV to pardon Northumberland, but he rose again in 1405 and was later killed in a raid.

NORTHUMBRIA,

one of the leading Anglo-Saxon kingdoms which stretched at the time of its greatest extent from the Humber to the Forth and north-westwards into Galloway. In the 7th cent. it was the most powerful of the English kingdoms. The defeat of Northumbria by the Picts in 685 ended this period of military predominance. Thereafter, Northumbria was chiefly important in the 8th cent. as an outstanding centre of religion and learning. Northumbria had been originally converted by Scottish missionaries from

Iona, but Roman influence predominated from the later 7th cent. The result was a unique mingling of Irish and Mediterranean influences, symbolized by the works of Bede (d. 735), the greatest ecclesiastical historian of the Dark Ages, and the prominence of the school of York, whose leading teacher, Alcuin, was invited by Charlemagne to become one of his most influential advisers on religious and educational affairs. Northumbria was the first of the Anglo-Saxon kingdoms to fall to the Danes, who captured York, its capital, in 866 and established a Danish kingdom, which survived until 954.

NORTH-WEST COMPANY, syndicate of fur traders created to exploit the Canadian north-west. The first official adoption of the name was in 1783, when a 16-share partnership was established. The North-West Co. was always in keen competition with Hudson's Bay Co., at first outstripping its rival in the fur trade, but matters reached a head over the granting of land in the Red River valley by the Hudson's Bay Co. (1811) to the Earl of Selkirk. A colony was founded (1812) followed by North-West Co. attempts to destroy the settlement. Reprisals by Selkirk (1814–16) and protracted legal battles lasting until 1818 overstrained the North-West Co.'s finances and it merged with the Hudson's Bay Co. (1821).

NORTH-WEST FRONTIER, zone of mountainous country stretching from the Pamirs through Pakistan to the shores of the Arabian Sea. Before the incursions of Europeans by sea India was peculiarly susceptible to invasion from Central Asia. The vulnerable part of the frontier between Peshawar and Quetta was traversed by five mountain passes, the Khyber, Kurram, Tochi, Gomal, and Bolan. Century after century hordes of invaders entered India through these passes. Persian, Greek and Afghan, the forces of Alexander the Great and the armies of Mahmud of Ghazni, the hosts of Timur, Babur, and Nadir Shah and the troops of Ahmad Shah Durrani, all advanced by these routes, either to found kingdoms and remain as conquerers or to retire, leaving in their train plundered cities and devastated plains. The history of invasion proves that neither the Sulaiman range nor the Indus ever presented any real barrier to an enterprising general.

The conquest of Sind (1843) and the annexation of the Punjab (1849) made the British frontier roughly coterminous with the territories of the Baluch and Pathan tribes. It also brought the British into closer contact with the Amir of Afghanistan and led to complications with Russia. The British were faced with two distinct yet closely related problems: the imperial problem of the defence of India against invasion from Central Asia, and the local problem of tribal control. The arrival of Lord Lytton (1876) marked the end of the policy of 'masterly inactivity' associated with the Lawrence school. The Lytton school would have advanced into Afghanistan and defended the so-called scientific frontier, the Kabul, Ghazni, Kandahar line. This problem was settled by the demarcation, where possible, of the various frontiers and by the Anglo-Russian agreement of 1907. As for the local problem, there were two schools of frontier administration, the Sind system, under which outrages were suppressed by a strong military force, and the Punjab system, which depended more on an efficient political management of the tribes. When all attempts at conciliation failed, the British forced the tribes to come to terms by means of fines, blockades, and punitive expeditions. Punjab frontier policy also differed from that adopted by Robert Sandeman in Baluchistan, where the tribal chiefs were controlled by a system of allowances and by the occupation of Quetta. In the north this was impossible because there were no outstanding tribal leaders. Apart from the economic factor, Afghan intrigues, especially after 1890, were the most potent cause of unrest. By the Durand agreement (1893) a boundary was delimited, distinguishing the tribes which were inside British India from those that were under the Amir of Afghanistan. The tribal problem was also complicated by

gun-running in the Persian Gulf. After 1947 Pakistan became responsible for the defence and administration of the frontier.

C. C. Davies, *The Problem of the North-West Frontier* (Cambridge, 1932).

D. Dichter, *The North-West Frontier of West Pakistan* (Oxford, 1967).   CCD

NORTH-WEST FRONTIER PROVINCE, created by Lord Curzon in 1901 because it was desirable to place tribal policy more directly under the control of the government of India. Politically, the province was divided into two parts: the settled districts of Hazara, Peshawar, Kohat, Bannu, and Dera Ismail Khan; and the trans-border tribal tracts between the administrative and Duran boundaries. The head was a chief commissioner, who was assisted by officers of the political department. After the formation of Pakistan, the Province was incorporated in West Pakistan (1955). In 1970 Pathans were again demanding a separate frontier province.

NORTH-WEST ORDINANCE (1787), act of the US Congress (13 July 1787) which organized 'the Territory Northwest of the River Ohio' and set a precedent for the admission of new states into the Union. It provided for a system of limited self-government for the region. Congress was to appoint a governor, a secretary, and three judges for the territory, which would achieve full territorial status when populated by 5000 free white males. It could then elect a bicameral legislature and send a non-voting member to Congress. When the territory had 60,000 free inhabitants it would be eligible for statehood, and could be divided into between three and five states which would be admitted 'on an equal footing with the original states in all respects whatsoever'. Other provisions prohibited slavery, and established freedom of worship, public support of education, and trial by jury.

NORTH-WEST PASSAGE, sea-route through the North American continent to China and the Far Eastern trade, sought from the 16th cent. onwards. At first it was seen as a means of avoiding political conflict with the Spanish and Portuguese monopolies of Empire. English sailors who attempted to find such a passage included Martin Frobisher, John Davis, and Henry Hudson. The Hudson Bay Co. in the late 17th cent. also sought to establish a passage. Sir John Franklin's expedition (1845) failed—and all its members perished in the attempt. In the 20th cent. the passage was made possible by R. Amundsen (1903) and by H. A. Larsen (1940–2).

In 1958 the US nuclear submarine *Nautilus* sailed under the Arctic in four days. The first commercial vessel to complete the passage (Sept. 1969) was the American tanker *Manhattan*, while investigating the possibility of using the passage in the exploitation of the Alaskan oilfields.

NORTH-WEST TERRITORIES, Canadian lands north of 60° N between Hudson Bay on the east and Yukon Territory on the west, as well as islands lying between the mainland and the North Pole. The original NWT were the lands handed over by the Hudson's Bay Co. to Canada (23 June 1870), but since then the provinces of Man. (1870), Sask., and Alta (1905) have been carved out and Ont., Man., and Que. extended northwards (1912). A resident lieutenant-governor and an appointed council were established (1875), and after a gradual change to an elective council responsible government was established in 1897.

NORTH-WEST TERRITORY, name given by the American Continental Congress to the region east of the Mississippi river, north of the Ohio river, south of the Great Lakes, and west of Pennsylvania. The greater part belonged to France until 1763, when Britain received it by treaty. Under the treaty of Versailles (1783) the region was ceded to the US. The territory was claimed by NY, VA, CT, and MA, whose colonial charters had given their western boundaries as the Pacific Ocean. By 1800 all had given up their claims, Congress having given a pledge that the land would be administered for all the people. An ordinance of 1787 officially established the North-west Territory, set up a government of a governor and three judges, and specified that when there were 5000 free male voters a legislature would be formed. The first governor was Arthur St Clair and the capital Marietta, OH. In 1800 the territory was divided into territorial governments. Out of this area OH became the 17th state in 1803. MI became a territory in 1805 and a state in 1837. IL became a territory in 1809 and a state in 1818. IN became a territory in 1800 and a state in 1848, and WI, a part of Michigan Territory, became a state in 1848.

NORTON, CHARLES BOWYER ADDERLEY, 1st Baron (1814–1905), British conservative politician who derived from his Christian faith a life-long concern for social questions. He built a model village at Saltley, near Birmingham, in 1837, and in the 1850s promoted campaigns for the reform of juvenile delinquents and for education. But two periods of office, as president of the board of health (1858–9), and of the board of trade (1874–8), proved him to be an inefficient administrator and parliamentarian. His Local Government Act (1858), which produced strong criticism from Sir John Simon, abolished the General Board of Health, and was intended to abolish the central government's control over local sanitary bodies, although it did not achieve this. In 1875 his Merchant Shipping Bill was attacked, both by interested shipowners and by Samuel Plimsoll, whose violent tactics forced the unwilling government to include a load-line requirement. In a different field of activity, as under-secretary for the colonies (1866–8), he defended Gov. Eyre, and carried through the House of Commons the British North America Act (1867), which created the Dominion of Canada.

NORTON, JOHN (1606–63), English-born clergyman who settled in Massachusetts Bay colony (1635) and became minister of First Church in Boston (1656). He was the author of a book in Latin about church government, which was the first Latin book written in the colonies.

NORWAY, GERMAN INVASION OF (8 April–8 June 1940). Almost from the outbreak of the Second World War both sides displayed special interest in Norway. The sea route south through her territorial waters—'the Leads'—was a loophole in the British blockade, and Swedish iron ore, vital to Germany's war economy, was shipped through the Norwegian port of Narvik. The Allies hoped for a time to secure control of northern Norway and Sweden on the pretext of intervention in the Russo–Finnish War. After Finland's surrender they sought to achieve this by mining the Leads, hoping to provoke a German invasion of Norway while their forces stood by to come to her assistance. Meanwhile the German navy had long advocated the occupation of Norwegian bases in order to outflank Britain's naval position in the North Sea, but Hitler's decision to take action seems to have been prompted largely by a desire to forestall the Allies—whose readiness to violate Norwegian neutrality was shown by the seizure of the German naval auxiliary *Altmark* by HMS *Cossack* in Jossingfiord on 16 Feb.

Both plans were put into effect at the same time. On 8 April the British destroyer *Glowworm* encountered the German heavy cruiser *Admiral Hipper*, proceeding to land troops at Trondheim, and was sunk after ramming her. The Germans achieved their objectives with the seizure of Oslo, Kristiansand, Egersand and Stavanger, Bergen, Trondheim, and Narvik by troops landed from warships and supported by 1200 aircraft, although they suffered considerable naval losses. The Norwegian government continued to resist, and substantial Allied forces were landed to support them by a direct assault on Narvik and a pincer movement on Trondheim from Aandsalves and Namsos. The latter operation

failed, largely owing to German command of the air (Norway was out of fighter range of Britain), and Aandsalves and Namsos were evacuated by the beginning of May. After 10 May, when the Germans invaded France, Norway became a diversion which the Allies could not afford; though Narvik was taken at the end of May, it had already been decided to evacuate it, and the withdrawal of Allied forces and of the Norwegian government was completed by 8 June: in this operation one British aircraft carrier was sunk and one German battle cruiser damaged.

The seizure of Norway gave the Germans a strategic advantage in the maritime war which probably outweighed the heavy naval cost of taking it and the drain on German forces involved in its defence.　　　PJBD

NORWAY, INCORPORATION OF, IN DENMARK (1536), provision in Christian III's charter to the Danish Council. The Norwegian Council ceased to exist, and until 1660 its king was elected in Denmark. After the introduction of absolutism, however, the monarch had the same relationship to each of his 'Twin Kingdoms'.

NORWAY, THE SEPARATION OF THE CROWN OF (1905), caused by the growth of nationalist sentiments and occasioned by the veto imposed by Oscar II of Sweden-Norway upon the unilateral establishment of a Norwegian consular service. The Swedes yielded to the result of a plebiscite on separation, and the European powers welcomed a peaceful solution which put Prince Charles of Denmark, son-in-law of Edward VII of Britain, on the throne. He took the title of Haakon VII.

NORWEGIAN CONSTITUTION (1814), second-oldest European constitution still in force. An assembly of delegates at Eidsvoll, chiefly officials, used the French constitution of 1791 as their principal model for a limited monarchy with separation of powers and a restricted franchise. In 1884, however, ministers were made responsible to the parliament (*Storting*), and in 1913 Norway adopted universal suffrage.

NOSKE, GUSTAV (1868–1946), German journalist and politician, who played an important part in the German Revolution (1918–19) and in the foundation of the Weimar republic. In the winter of 1918–19, as defence minister, he achieved notoriety for his harsh suppression of left-wing extremists in Berlin and elsewhere who threatened to overthrow the conservative Socialist provisional government. In Feb. 1919 he became minister of defence but was forced to resign (1920) for failing to prevent the Kapp putsch. Later he was *oberpräsident* in Hanover, but was dismissed by the Nazis, who arrested him in 1944. Later he was released by the Russians.

Noske was typical of many SPD members who shaped the course of 20th-cent. German socialism. He was more concerned with the realities of party and trade union administration than with the abstractions of Marxist doctrine. Having supported Germany's First World War effort, he was taken by surprise when the monarchy collapsed and he resolved to resist any thorough-going alteration of the German social and economic system. Although his use of the traditional officer corps during the Revolution was a practical necessity in order to avert chaos, his memoirs betray a much deeper emotional commitment to German military values. It was this which led both him and others to neglect the growing danger of right-wing threats to the new republic.　　　RJVL

NOSTRADAMUS (1503–66), French physician and astrologer, born at Michel De Notredame, who established himself as a doctor at Aix and began to make his prophecies, which were widely believed. In 1555 he published his *Centuries*, a book of rhymed prophecies. Among his patrons were Catherine de' Medici and Charles IX.

NOTTINGHAM, DANIEL FINCH, 14th Earl of (2nd of 6th creation) (1647–1730), British politician, who championed

High Tory principles in religious issues during the reigns of William III and Anne. It is not easy to class him purely as a High Tory, since his career makes a mockery of party distinctions. He was a man of independent principles and an opponent of the exclusion of James, Duke of York, to the succession during the reign of Charles II. Nevertheless, his Anglican religious principles forced him into opposition during the reign of James II, yet he refused to give his support to William of Orange. During the Revolution (1688) he was sent by the peers as a commissioner to negotiate with William· after the latter's arrival in England. He remained loyal to James II until his flight and thereafter refused any contact with the Jacobites.

Henceforth he was willing to serve William III, though he only agreed to recognize him as king de facto, refusing any oaths abjuring the Pretender, as well as opposing the Association of 1696. His great influence in the Revolution Settlement was his sponsoring of the Toleration Act (1689), which allowed freedom of worship to Protestant nonconformists, but asserted the political supremacy of Anglicanism. However, his Comprehension Bill, to enlarge the boundaries of the Church of England to include the more reconcilable nonconformists, failed.

He was recognized for his honesty and sincerity by William III, and was appointed secretary of state (1689–93). But he found it impossible to work in such a politically mixed ministry. He was reappointed secretary of state in Queen Queen Anne's first ministry (1702–4), but quarrelled with Marlborough over the strategy of the Spanish Succession War. He was denied office in the Tory ministry of 1710 through the personal opposition of the queen.

As a High Church leader he championed a number of Occasional Conformity bills, including the *tack* of 1704, all without success. In opposition, he became a leader of the Hanoverian Tories, ignoring the rise of the High Church October Club and opposing the Schism Act.

On the death of Anne, Nottingham was named a regent until the arrival of George I (1714). He returned to office as lord president of the council (1714–16), but his political career came to an end with his dismissal for urging leniency for Jacobite peers after the 1715 Rebellion.   AW

NOVA CARTHAGO (New Carthage; mod. Cartagena), capital of the Carthaginian empire in Spain, founded by Hasdrubal in 228 BC on the site of Tartessian Mastia, on what was then a promontory between the bay and an inner lagoon that is now dry land. Its daring capture in the Second Punic War (209) was the first military success of Scipio (later Africanus). When Spain became a Roman province, Nova Carthago was overshadowed by Tarraco. Julius Caesar awarded the town Latin rights (45 BC), and it became a colony under Augustus. The city was sacked and destroyed by the Vandals (AD 425).

NOVA SCOTIA, most easterly of the Canadian mainland provinces. It was sighted by Cabot (1497) and Verrazano (1524) and several Europeans visited it in the 16th cent. The first permanent settlement was made by the French (1605), who named the area Acadia. The British name of Nova Scotia (New Scotland) dates from 1621 and the granting of a colonizing charter to Sir William Alexander, but the French remained dominant in the area until the British captured and garrisoned Port Royal (Annapolis Royal) in 1710. The mainland was ceded to Britain by France by the treaty of Utrecht (1713), but the French retained Cape Breton Island, upon which they built the stronghold of Louisburg. Louisburg was captured by British and colonial troops (1745), but exchanged for Madras and returned to the French (1748), then seized again during the Seven Years War (1758). The forced removal of the French settlers and the pacification of the hitherto hostile Indians brought peace to the area. Halifax was established (1749) and Lunenburg founded by French and German-speaking Protestants (1752). After the American War of Independence, over 30,000 loyalists and ex-soldiers

settled along the St John River and on Cape Breton Island (1783–4). NB was separated from NS and made into a new province (1784) and Cape Breton Island made a separate colony (reannexed by NS, 1820). In the 19th cent. large numbers of Scots settled in NS. The first NS legislature met in 1759 and was reformed (1838), responsible government being granted in 1847. It was mainly due to the efforts of the prime minister, Charles Tupper, that NS became one of the founding provinces of the Dominion of Canada (1867). Confederation was not popular, but when Joseph Howe joined the federal government (1868) the opposition lost its leadership. The Inter-Continental Railway (1876) connected NS with the rest of Canada, but the increased prosperity it brought to coal mining and steel manufacture did not compensate for the decline of shipbuilding. NS suffered during the late 19th and early 20th cents from a lack of federal aid, until the Rowell–Sirois Royal Commission (1937). The vital Atlantic convoys in both World Wars were assembled off NS, and Halifax was a key centre in the direction of operations during the battle of the Atlantic in the Second World War.

G. G. Campbell, *The History of Nova Scotia* (Toronto, 1949).   AJS

NOVA SCOTIA, BARONETS OF, unsuccessful scheme of titular honours to advance the plantation of NS, established by William Alexander, and chartered by Charles I (12 June 1625). Each baronet paid a fee of £150 and undertook to promote colonization and received his title and a land grant.

NOVALES MUTINY (1823), Philippine uprising led by Capt. Andres Novales, a Mexican serving in the Spanish army at Manila, three years after Mexico won her independence from Spain (1820). Novales, leading three or four hundred men, among whom were creole non-commissioned officers, took his stand in the town hall and declared himself emperor of the Philippines. The mutiny was immediately suppressed, and Novales and his Filipino second-in-command, Sergeant Mateo, were executed for rebellion. The arrival in Manila of a new governor-general, Juan Antonio Martinez, who brought with him a large group of peninsular officers, is considered to be the cause of the mutiny, for these recently arrived officers were intended to replace the officer corps of the Philippine regiment, most of whom were Mexicans and Philippine-born Spaniards. The latter viewed the move as a sign of racial discrimination. It is said that the mutiny inspired the Mexican and Philippine-born officers to exert greater efforts towards their fight for equality, autonomy, and better treatment from officials.

NOVARA, BATTLE OF (28 March 1849), fought in Lombardy, between the Austrian army under Radetzky and Charles Albert's Piedmontese troops. After hard fighting, the Austrian regulars defeated the Italians, who were routed and driven from the field.

NOVARA, BATTLES OF (1500, 1513). Two battles fought in Italy in the Italian Wars of the early 16th cent. In 1500 the French defeated the forces of Ludovico Sforza, of Milan. Sforza's Swiss mercenaries refused to fight against their fellow-countrymen in Louis XII's army, so the Milanese were overwhelmed. Ludovico was captured while escaping from the battlefield and spent the rest of his life imprisoned in the castle of Loches.

The Swiss were successful in 1513 over the French under Louis de La Trémouille (6 June). The Swiss surprised the enemy camp west of Milan, killing or wounding half the French and their German mercenaries and causing Louis XII to withdraw from Milan.

NOVAYA ZEMLA, twin mountainous Arctic islands lying between the Barents and Kara Seas, off the coast of Siberia. They were first discovered by William Barents, the Dutch navigator, on his expedition of 1596–7.

NOVEMBER TREATY (1855) gave Sweden-Norway an Anglo-French guarantee of its territorial integrity in relation to Russia, in return for an undertaking to cede no territory to that power. It arose out of the desire of the allies to attract support in the Crimean War, and was superseded by the Norwegian Integrity and Baltic treaties of 1908.

NOVGOROD, town on Lake Ilmen in north-western Russia, founded by Scandinavians in the 9th cent., which became an important trading centre, acting as an intermediary between northern Europe and the Byzantine world and was connected with the Hanseatic League. It was an independent city, under its own princes, until 1270, and then under its mayors, but lost its independence in 1570.

NOVIBAZAR, SANJAK OF, mountainous Ottoman district of strategic importance between Serbia and Montenegro, placed under Austrian control (1878) and divided between Serbia and Montenegro (1913).

NOVIKOV, NIKOLAI IVANOVICH (1744–1818), Russian publisher and educationist, who founded the first independent satirical journals and the first printing presses in Russia. He was imprisoned (1792–6) for criticizing the Empress Catherine's social policy.

NOVOSILTSOV, NIKOLAI NIKOLAYEVICH (1761–1836), Russian diplomat and administrator, who was a member of Alexander I's Unofficial Committee (1801–3), negotiated a treaty with England (1804), and was Imperial Commissioner in Warsaw (1815).

NOVOTNY, ANTONIN (1904–), Czechoslovakian politician, who joined the Communist Party in 1921 and was interned by the Germans during the Second World War (1941–5). He was appointed general secretary of the party (1951) at the time of the purge of Slansky and elected president of Czechoslovakia in 1957. He was forced to resign by the reform movement (Mar. 1968), was dismissed from the Presidium (April), and expelled from the party.

NOVUS HOMO, 'new man', opposite of *nobilis* (noble), Roman term for a man obtaining the praetorship whose family had never held the consulship. Very few such men reached the consulship in republican Rome. Those who did included Cato the Censor, Marius, and Cicero.

NOYON, TREATY OF (1516), treaty of friendship between Charles I of Spain and Francis I of France, negotiated by the Walloon statesman Guillaume du Croy, lord of Chièvres. The alliance destroyed the diplomatic isolation of France created by the Holy League (1511–13) and by the alliance of Henry VIII of England with Spain and the Burgundian Netherlands. It provided for Charles's marriage to Francis's one-year-old daughter, Louise, with the kingdom of Naples as a dowry, while France agreed to drop diplomatic support for Germaine de Foix, Ferdinand of Aragon's widow. The Noyon agreement was ratified by Charles's grandfather, the Emperor Maximilian, when he visited the Netherlands (3 Dec. 1516). Meanwhile an alliance between Charles, Henry VIII, and the pope (29 Oct. 1516) provided a counterpoise to the Franco-Habsburg treaty.

NTARE IV (*fl.* 18th cent.), *omugabe* (King) of Ankole, whose military success against Bunyoro enabled him to expand his kingdom.

NU, THAKIN (1907–), Burmese political leader, who became treasurer (1937) of the Thakin Party. In 1940 he was interned for anti-war activities, but was released after the Japanese invasion. He became foreign minister in Ba Maw's government under the Japanese (1943–5) and vice-president of the Anti-Fascist People's Freedom League (AFPFL)

(1945–7). In 1947 he became president of the Constituent Assembly that drew up the constitution for independent Burma. On 19 July 1947 Aung San and seven members of his cabinet were murdered. Thakin Nu, summoned by the governor, formed a new cabinet, and so averted the confusion that the assassinations had been planned by U Saw to create.

Thakin Nu negotiated the treaty of independence with Britain and became the first prime minister of independent Burma. He faced successively the civil war (1948–51); the trespass into Burmese territory of the Kuomintang forces expelled from China by the communists; the slump in rice prices that followed the cessation of the Korean War; and the growth of corruption and disunity within the AFPFL and of disillusionment in the country. In 1952 he abandoned the title of Thakin. He relinquished (1956) the premiership in order to reorganize and eliminate corruption from the AFPFL, but resumed office in 1957.

In Oct. 1958, faced with the disintegration of his party and renewed civil war, he called upon Gen. Ne Win to form an emergency military government. In 1960, the army having re-established order, a general election returned U Nu to power. In 1962, however, Gen. Ne Win overthrew the government by a military coup and U Nu, with other leaders, was imprisoned. In 1967 he was released on health grounds and on the condition—imperfectly observed—that he refrained from political activity. In 1968 he was appointed to the Internal Unity Advisory Body to advise on how to achieve national unity, with a view to drafting a new constitution. When in June 1969 the government rejected this body's recommendations and U Nu's plan for implementing them, U Nu, in Bangkok, publicly denounced the regime, then went to London and the US to repeat his denunciation and seek international support for his cause.

H. Tinker, *The Union of Burma* (London, 1961).
F. N. Trager, *Burma—from kingdom to republic* (London, 1966).   FSVD

NUBIA, Pharaonic impact on. Pharaonic Egyptian contact with Nubia begins in the Old Kingdom. An inscription of King Djer of the 1st Dynasty, near to Wadi Halfa, suggests that there were military campaigns *c.* 2000 BC. Subsequently there was Egyptian settlement at Buhen, where copper was smelted, and there are records of many trading caravans which travelled to Nubia.

By the time of the Middle Kingdom (*c.* 2000 BC) there was full-scale military occupation up to the second cataract, where a series of massive forts was built. The most southerly of these were the two forts at Semna and one nearby on the island of Uronarti which, together, formed the southern frontier defence of Egypt. At Uronarti a stele was erected by Sesostris III (*reg.* 1878–1842 BC), laying down regulations for administering the frontier. At the end of the Middle Kingdom these forts were abandoned and Egyptian occupation came to an end, the forts probably being sacked by the indigenous people known as the C-Group.

With the resurgence of the Egyptian empire in the XVIIIth dynasty (*c.* 1500 BC) the area was again occupied and the forts restored to use, but this time Egyptian occupation was more permanent. Egyptians penetrated much further south, reaching the fourth Nile cataract and beyond; and towns and temples were built throughout Nubia. An inscription at Kurgus is the furthest upstream of the Egyptian monuments at present known. The whole region became deeply imbued with Egyptian culture and, even after the withdrawal of Egyptian administration *c.* 700 BC, the traditional influence of Egypt was maintained, notably at Jebel Barkal. The early rulers of the local state of Kush, which developed at Napata, maintained the full panoply of the Egyptian Pharaohs, and a marked Egyptian character stayed with the culture of Kush throughout the period of its history.

W. B. Emery, *Egypt in Nubia* (London, 1965).
A. J. Arkell, *A History of the Sudan to 1821* (London, 1961).
                                                                    MS

NUBIAN CHRISTIANITY is first known from the missionary activities of Julian and Longinus in the second half of the 6th cent., when both orthodox and monophysite missions were at work. The faith spread rapidly, and by 580 even the southern town of Soba, 14 miles (22 kms) from Khartoum, was partly Christianized.

The advent of Christianity deeply influenced the culture of Nubia. Churches were built in many places, and sometimes elaborately decorated with frescoes, as at Faras. Ruins of over 100 churches are known, all markedly Byzantine in style, as were the frescoes which adorned them. The history of the period is not well documented, but it is known that there were originally three kingdoms, Nobatia, Makuria, and Alodia, and that the two former united in the late 7th cent. Nobatia was subject to sporadic attack from the Muslims of Egypt starting in 641, when a trade pact was made, until, in 1323, the capital at Dongola was seized and conversion to Islam officially achieved. During the greater part of this period there was much Arab penetration through the Red Sea route, and tombstones from the 10th cent. with Arabic inscriptions have been found in the Red Sea hills. Conversion from Christianity to Islam was a more gradual process than might at first appear, and there may well have been a substantial number of converts, at least in the northern kingdom, well before 1323.

Soba, the capital of the southern kingdom Alodia, was mentioned in the reports of medieval travellers, but beyond the fact that it was a flourishing town with fine buildings, churches, and monasteries, nothing is known of its history. After the defeat of Nobatia, contact with other Christian centres became tenuous, and the town is thought to have been destroyed by the Funj in 1504.

A. J. Arkell, *A History of the Sudan to 1821* (London, 1961).
                                                                              MS

NUBIAN LANGUAGE, African language, possibly related to the Nilotic group. It is known from documents of the 9th cent. onwards. It is still (1970) spoken from Diraw in Egypt to just below the fourth Nile cataract in the Sudan.

NUCLEAR TEST-BAN TREATY (Aug. 1963), signed in Moscow between Britain, the US, and the USSR, by which the signatories undertake 'to prohibit, to prevent, and not to carry out' nuclear explosions, except underground. The treaty is open to other countries to sign and by the time of its entry into force (Oct. 1963) it had 105 signatories. France and the People's Republic of China had not signed by the end of 1970.

NUFFIELD, WILLIAM RICHARD MORRIS, Viscount (1877–1963), British engineer and philanthropist. In 1893, aged 16, having had only an elementary education and with nine months' apprenticeship behind him, he opened a bicycle shop. Soon he produced a model of his own, and then a motor cycle. In 1904 he opened the first Morris garage, and in 1912, employing his purely empirical engineering knowledge, he began making cars at Cowley, Oxford. By 1923 production figures had made immense strides. After visiting Detroit in 1925, Morris founded the Pressed Steel Co. for manufacturing bodies which by 1926 employed 4000 workers. In 1937 he established Nuffield Mechanisations Ltd, which produced tanks and other armaments, and in 1938 an aircraft factory (taken over by Vickers in 1940). He was appointed unsalaried director-general of maintenance at the air ministry in 1939. In 1948 he produced the Nuffield universal tractor. After the Austin–Morris merger in 1952, he was the British Motor Corporation's chairman for six months and subsequently became its honorary president.

By the time he was 80, he had given away over £27 million. He was particularly interested in the medical profession and contributed enormously to research and hospital facilities in Oxford, London, Birmingham, Newcastle, Leeds, and Liverpool. He also established (1936) the Nuffield Trust for

assistance to the Special Areas, and in 1937 founded Nuffield College, Oxford, as a centre for research into the social sciences. As an employer he was among the first to initiate a welfare scheme, sports facilities, and paid holidays.   ASJ

NUIE (Cook's Savage Island, 1774), isolated South Pacific Polynesian island. After repelling John Williams (1830) the islanders accepted Christianity under a London Missionary Society Samoan teacher, Paulo (1849). The first resident European missionary, W. G. Lawes, arrived in 1861. In 1862–3 many islanders were recruited for labour in Peru, Tahiti, and Samoa. British protection was accorded in 1900, the island being annexed to New Zealand in 1901.

NULLIFICATION CONTROVERSY in the US (1832), crisis over the attempt by the SC legislature to 'nullify', or to refuse to recognize as binding on the state, the Federal tariff acts of 1828 and 1832. The state, and its principal spokesman, John C. Calhoun, had hitherto supported the union against the proponents of state sovereignty, but the decline of SC's economy in the 1820s changed their attitude, and they became increasingly inclined to blame the protective tariff for their misfortunes. In 1828 the state legislature printed and circulated Calhoun's *Exposition and Protest*, a development of the nullification doctrine appealed to in the Kentucky and Virginia Resolutions (1798) and by the Hartford Convention (1814). The state Nullification Ordinance (1832) declared the recent tariff acts unconstitutional, and President Andrew Jackson responded with a demand to Congress (1833) for a Force Act to enable him to coerce the state. Congress passed both the Force Act and a compromise tariff, SC rescinded the Nullification Ordinance and declared the Force Act void, and both sides claimed victory.

NULLUM TEMPUS ACT (1768–9), in Britain, extended a law of James I so that 60 years' possession of land secured it against subsequent claims by the Crown. The act followed a political storm over a dispute about an estate of the Duke of Portland, the beneficiary being a relative of the royal favourite of George III, Lord Bute.

NUMA POMPILIUS, traditionally the second King of Rome (715–673 BC), the priest-figure contrasting (as often in Indo-European cultures) with the preceding warrior-king Romulus. The religious innovations and building attributed to him were in fact the later legacy of the Etruscans. His alleged interest in the Pythagorean teaching of southern Italy is a Greek fiction. Likewise his role as father of laws and civilized manners has been imaginatively developed. His importance is as the symbolic figure to whom these accretions cling, the first known king of the settled Palatine community.

NUMANTIA, in northern Spain (near mod. Soria, 193 kms north-east of Madrid), capital of the Celtiberians, was besieged by the Romans for nine years, until Scipio Aemilianus forced the defenders to surrender through hunger (133 BC).

NUMIDIA. Although the term *Numidae* (Greek *Nomades*) was applied to a variety of peoples of North Africa from the beginning of the 3rd cent. BC, by the time of Massinissa (208 BC) Numidia meant the whole region inhabited by the *Masaesylii* and the *Massylii*, which was situated between Mauretania on the west, the *Gaetuli* on the south, and Carthage on the east. After the defeat of Jugurtha, Mauretania expanded its boundaries eastwards until, by AD 42, the term Numidia came to be applied only to that territory which lay between the Ampsaga river (Oued el Kebir) and *Africa Nova*.

NÚÑEZ, RAFAEL (1825–94), Colombian diplomat and president of Colombia (1880–2, 1884–8, 1887, 1888). During his second presidential term Núñez's authoritarian and conservative personality turned his regime into a virtual dictatorship. Abandoning his Liberal friends, he manipulated national politics (1884–94), emphasizing the need for a strong presidency, a centralized state, and close ties with the Catholic Church.

NÚÑEZ VELA, BLASCO (*c.* 1490–1546), first viceroy of Peru, appointed with the members of the first *audiencia* of Lima, by the Spanish Crown in 1544. The most important part of Núñez's mission was to implement the New Laws (1542–3) concerning the native population. He quarrelled with his *audiencia* colleagues and systematically alienated every sector of the colonial population by adhering with blind arrogance to his instructions. The result was to provoke Gonzalo Pizarro's rebellion, and Núñez was exiled to Panama. Desperate to retrieve the situation, he landed on the Ecuadorian coast instead. There he raised an army to oppose Pizarro, but fell in the battle of Añaquito.

NUÑO DE GUZMÁN, GONZALO (d. 1539), Spanish conquistador and governor, who was sent to head the royal government in New Spain (Mexico). He tried to correct abuses committed by Hernán Cortés, but resorted to illegal activities himself on an even greater scale. After leading a destructive expedition to the north, Guzmán was imprisoned for his crimes and then returned to Spain.

NUPE, part of modern Nigeria, formerly a kingdom in the low basin formed by the valleys of the Niger and Kaduna rivers. With other ethnic groups in the Niger–Benue confluence, the Nupe people furnished strong commercial links between northern and southern Nigeria in pre-colonial days.

NUR AL-DIN (d. 1174) succeeded his father, Zangi (d. AD 1146), as atabeg of Aleppo. He brought Damascus under his control (1154)—a triumph ominous for the Crusading states of Antioch, Tripoli, and Jerusalem, which had to face a united Muslim power in Syria. The great contention thereafter between the Latins and the Muslims was for the possession of Fatimid Egypt. Shirkuh, the able soldier commanding the forces of Nur al-Din, secured control of Egypt in 1169. On the death of Shirkuh (1169) his nephew, Salah al-Din (Saladin), succeeded him at Cairo. The years after 1169 saw the growth of tension between Nur al-Din and Salah al-Din.

NUR JAHAN (1573–1645), favourite wife of the Mughal Emperor, Jahangir. She came to court after her first husband's death and Jahangir married her (1610). As his confidential adviser she exerted much influence. Gold *mohurs* were coined in her name. Her father, Itim-ud-daulah (d. 1630), became vizier and her brother Asaf Khan (1571–1641) succeeded him. She lies buried in Jahangir's mausoleum at Lahore.

NUREMBERG, one of the most important German imperial free cities. By the 14th cent. it enjoyed a near monopoly of south German trade with Bohemia and Hungary and in oriental goods imported from Venice. It acquired a larger territorial state than any other imperial free city and it was famed for its consistent loyalty to the German emperors, being the seat of such central royal institutions as existed in Germany in the late Middle Ages and the 16th cent. Several imperial diets were held at Nuremberg. It also became a major cultural and artistic centre, the painter Albrecht Dürer (1471–1528) being the most famous of its many artists.

NUREMBERG, CONGRESS AND TREATY OF (1649–50), conference chiefly of military officers representing the belligerent countries in the Thirty Years War, at which detailed negotiations took place to give effect to the decisions of the peace of Westphalia (1648). The imperialists were represented by Field Marshal Piccolomini and the Swedes by Charles Gustavus of Zweilbrucken, and their brief was to organize the liquidation of mercenary forces and the transfer of territory.

NUREMBERG, DIETS OF (1522–4), three assemblies of the imperial governing council held in the absence of the Emperor Charles V to discuss plans for federal reform, the enforcement of peace in the empire, and problems of finance and defence. The diets failed to produce results because of disagreement among the German princes.

NUREMBERG, LEAGUE OF (1538), association of Catholic German princes formed by Matthias Held, Vice-chancellor to Emperor Charles V, on the model of, and to counteract, the Protestant schmalkaldic League. Its members included the Emperor, Archduke Ferdinand, the Dukes of Bavaria, Saxony, and Brunswick, and the Abps of Mainz and Salzburg.

NUREMBERG LAWS (1935) in Germany, collective name given to the two principal race laws of Nazi Germany, promulgated in Nuremberg at a Reichstag meeting held in the course of the party rally. They were the first major steps in the process by which Jews and other 'non-aryans' were systematically reduced to the status of persons outside the ordinary law of the land. The first of these laws, ironically entitled '*Reich* Citizen Law', deprived of citizenship all those not 'of German or related blood'; and the second, 'for the protection of German blood and German honour', made marriage or extra-marital relations illegal between Germans and Jews, forbade Jews to employ women aged 45 or under in their households, and withdrew from them the right to display the German flag. The laws were followed later by legal definitions of the term Jew and the various gradations of mixed ancestry, and orders which expelled Jewish civil servants from office. The initiative for this anti-Semitic legislation came from the Nazi Party itself, and the fact that it was adopted at the annual party rally proved Hitler's desire to stress its special significance, and indicated his distrust of the normal procedures of bureaucratic codification.

NUREMBERG RALLIES in Germany, conventions of the Nazi Party. Nuremberg was first used as the venue for these mammoth gatherings in 1927 and in 1933 was officially adopted as the permanent home of the rallies, and was given the honorary designation *Stadt der Parteitag*. The rallies were the apotheosis of the Nazi style of propaganda, characterized by marches of impressive size, and vast open-air gatherings in which mass enthusiasm was disciplined with military precision to create a triumphant annual affirmation of Hitler's leadership and Nazi rule.

Other ends were also served by these annual meetings, *eg*, communication between party leaders and ministers who otherwise rarely met, or the announcement of special policies, such as the Nuremberg racial laws (1935) and the Four Year Plan (1936). Party observers also used the occasions to report on opinion and morale. After 1933 the rallies became an annual event until 1939, when the 'Peace Rally' was cancelled owing to the preparations for war. None was held during the Second World War.

NUREMBERG TRIBUNAL, court established by the Allies to try Nazi war criminals after the end of the Second World War. The decision to bring the Nazi leaders to justice was taken in 1943, and an International Military Tribunal (IMT) was set up by the London Agreement (Aug. 1945). The tribunal sat at Nuremberg (Nov. 1945–Oct. 1946) and consisted of one member and one substitute from each of the principal Allies, viz. Lawrence (president) and Birkett from Britain, Donnedieu de Vabres and Falco from France, Nikichenko and Volchikov from the USSR, and Biddle and Parker from the US. The procedural rules of the court were based on Anglo-American practice. Lawyers from the four Allies provided the prosecution, while the accused were defended by German lawyers of their choice. Prosecution and defence counsel were in theory accorded equal treatment, but the former had access to far more documentary evidence.

The indictment had four counts: (*a*) conspiracy, (*b*) crimes against peace, (*c*) war crimes, and (*d*) crimes against humanity.

The 21 accused who faced trial in person were, with their sentences, as follows: Göring (*a–d*) death; Hess (*a* and *b*) life imprisonment; Ribbentrop (*a–d*) death; Neurath (*a–d*) 15 years; Raeder (*b–d*) life; Dönitz (*b* and *c*) ten years; Keitel (*a–d*) death; Jodl (*a–d*) death; Rosenberg (*a–d*) death; Frick (*b–d*) death; Schirach (*d*) 20 years; Kaltenbrünner (*c* and *d*) death; Frank (*c* and *d*) death; Funk (*b–d*) life; Streicher (*d*) death; Sauckel (*c* and *d*) death; Seyss-Inquart (*b–d*) death; Speer (*b* and *d*) 20 years; Papen and Schacht acquitted. In addition, Bormann was tried and sentenced to death *in absentio*, Ley was charged but committed suicide before trial, and Krupp was found unfit to plead. A group of Nazi organizations was also tried collectively, viz. the NSDAP leadership corps, the Gestapo, the SS, SD, and SA, the Reich government, and the general staff and High Command of the fighting forces. The first four of this list were subsequently found to be criminal organizations, with the effect that membership was considered an offence in itself.

The accused persons included the most important surviving members of the Nazi regime, but by no means exhausted the list of potentially suspect persons. It was originally intended to conduct a series of trials, but it was later agreed that subsequent trials would be held in each of the control areas by the occupying power. It was the US which, above all, continued the process, holding 12 further trials of 185 persons between May 1946 and April 1949.

Both at the time, and later, there were criticisms of the trials from Germans and foreigners. The gravest of these were that the tribunal consisted only of members of the victorious nations; that the trials were held under retrospective laws, which tried to assign individual responsibility for crimes deriving from international law; and that only German, and not Allied, war criminals were tried. Although these were valid points, it is nevertheless a fact that the Nuremberg trials were not simply show trials staged by the victors, but were genuine judicial processes. Justice was done, even if the circumstances in which it was seen to be done were not ideal, and the decision to hold the trials was a logical attempt to give practical expression to the ideal of international justice which the United Nations represented.

E. Davidson, *The Trial of the Germans* (New York, 1966). IMT, *Trials of the Major War Criminals*, 27 vols (Nuremberg, 1947–8).   AJC

NURHACHI (1559–1626), unifier of the Jurched tribes which eventually conquered China and established the Ch'ing (Manchu) dynasty in 1644. Already, at the age of 24, when he became a Jurched chieftain, Nurhachi had harboured thoughts of conquering China. Through marriages, military campaigns, and monopolization of the trade in furs, pearls, and ginseng, he soon established for himself a position of power and prestige. By 1613 he had conquered all but one of the Jurched tribes. All the tribes were then incorporated into the 'Banner System', which he devised in 1601 to put everyone under his rule into a military–administrative unit called the Banner. This total control enabled him, in 1616, to proclaim the Chin state and declare war on the Ming dynasty in 1618. A series of military successes followed until 1626, when he was wounded in action; he died seven months later.

Nurhachi was succeeded by his eighth son, Abahai (1592–1643), who carried on his father's unfinished work and died the year before the conquest of China.

NURI, last of the Kushite royal cemeteries in the area of Napata. It contained 82 graves, of which the majority were marked by pyramids.

NURI AL-SA'ID PASHA (1888–1958), Iraqi Arab politician, who was also an Ottoman soldier (1906–14). He joined Al-Ahd (1913), took part in the Arab revolt (1916–18), and subsequently served under Faysal in Syria (1918–20). After his return to Iraq he was almost continually active in government, as minister of defence for most of the 1920s when, with

Jafar al-Askari (d. 1936), he was largely responsible for the organization of the Iraqi army, and frequently as prime minister or foreign minister (1930–58), when his name became identified with the system of government in Iraq. His domestic policies were characterized by conservatism, the severe repression of radical opposition, and (after 1950) long-term economic planning. His foreign policy was based on alliance with Britain and support for Arab nationalism, particularly in the form of a Fertile Crescent Union. After 1945 the problems of combining a western alignment with hostility to Zionism led him into difficulties, which were magnified by the polarization of the Arab world, following the 1952 Egyptian revolution, into so-called revolutionary and monarchical regimes, personified by the struggle between Nuri and Nasser, and which contributed to the former's overthrow and murder.

NUSANTARA, Indonesian term (corresponding to Sanskrit Dvipantara), used both for 'the other islands' as seen from Java, and for the Indonesian archipelago in general. In the Indonesian national movement of the 20th cent. there was for some time hesitation as to whether Nusantara or Indonesia should become the name of the new state.

NXABA (*fl.* 19th cent.), chief of the Msene, a Nguni group that fled from Shaka. After years of wandering, Nxaba was killed in the late 1840s by the Kololo king, Sebetwane, in Barotseland.

NYAMWEZI, society of over 300,000 people, inhabiting west-central Tanzania, and speaking a Bantu language. The Nyamwezi have no tradition of unity, and the name itself was applied by non-Nyamwezi. Long before the expansion of the slave trade from the coast, they were active in long-range trade, mainly from Nyamweziland to the coast, but also as far inland as Katanga. In this trade they were entrepreneurs as well as porters, and some settled at the extremities of the trade routes. During the late 19th cent. several of the minor chiefs attempted to expand their authority over all the Nyamwezi. During the same period the Nyamwezi were frequently obliged to defend their trading network from Arab intervention.

NYANI, site in north-eastern Guinea on the Sankarani river, thought to have been the capital of ancient Mali. The results of recent excavations are awaited (1970).

NYE COMMITTEE in US, committee of the Senate, set up in April 1934 to investigate the munitions industry and traffic in arms. It was under the chairmanship of Senator Gerald P. Nye, a progressive Republican from ND, who had demanded the enquiry, following an indictment of the industry's activities during the First World War in a magazine article. The committee, having found some evidence to support the allegations, turned to a wider issue and investigated the influence of economic interests on US intervention in 1917. The committee alleged that J. P. Morgan and others had profited unduly from the war, and that President Wilson himself had been guilty of 'falsification' when he denied knowledge of secret treaties. The committee's revelations contributed to the demand for neutrality legislation in the 1930s, and during its two-year investigation (1934–6) caused considerable embarrassment to President F. D. Roosevelt and the Department of State.

NYKÖPING RIKSDAG (1611) gave full royal powers to 15-year-old King Gustavus Adolphus on his acceptance of a charter, drawn up by Oxenstierna. This safeguarded noble and other privileges, required the approval of the Council for new taxes and levies of soldiers, and demanded the due approval of Council and Estates for laws, treaties of alliance, and declarations of war and peace.

NYMPHENBURG, TREATY OF (1741), Hispano-Bavarian agreement, to which Prussia, Saxony, and above all France, acceded, creating an anti-Habsburg coalition pledged to the support of Charles Albert of Bavaria's candidacy in the imperial election and the partitioning of Maria Theresa's territories.

NYMWEGEN, TREATIES OF (1678–9), peace settlement which ended the Franco–Dutch War (1672–8), the result of negotiations held at the Congress of Nymwegen from 1676, which acknowledged French ascendancy in Europe. The Dutch peace party, hard-pressed by French military successes, came to terms with Louis XIV against the wishes of the *stadtholder*, William of Orange, in a peace treaty of 10 Aug. 1678, to which the Spanish government acceded. France gave back her Dutch conquests, *eg*, Maastricht, and Colbert's aggressive tariff was suppressed. Spain was made the scapegoat for this settlement, losing Franche-Comté and 15 fortified places in the southern Netherlands to France, including Cambrai, Bouchain, Valenciennes, Condé, Saint-Omer, Ypres, Cassel, and Mauberge. The frontier between France and the Spanish Netherlands was straightened by the restoration to Spain of a few towns, *eg*, Charleroi, Oudenarde, Courtrai, and Ghent, thus confirming the shadowy provisions of the peace of Westphalia, but providing Louis XIV with the legal basis for the *réunion* annexations to rationalize France's eastern frontiers.

Meanwhile, the emperor signed a separate treaty at Nymwegen with Louis (Feb. 1679) after the collapse of his autumn campaign on the Rhine (1678). The Habsburgs surrendered Freiburg, but retained Philippsburg. This was followed by separate treaties (St-Germain and Fontainebleau) with Denmark and Brandenburg, who were obliged to restore most of their Baltic conquests to France's ally, Sweden, a condition of the treaties of Nymwegen.

NYSTADT, TREATY OF (1721), ended Swedish predominance in the Baltic region. In attempting to mitigate the effects of Sweden's defeat in the Great Northern War, King Frederick of Hesse was handicapped by lack of an effective army or ally, and also by his need of Russian support against the rival claimant to his throne, Charles Frederick of Holstein-Gottorp: Swedish cessions to Russia included Livonia, Estonia, Ingria, and the Karelian isthmus with Viborg.

NZINGA (*c.* 1582–1663), Queen of the Angolan kingdoms of Ndongo and Matamba, who led the Mbundu people on the death of her brother (*c.* 1624), at a time when the Portuguese were making serious inroads into Ndongo. She sought a new base among refugees in Matamba from which to resist Portuguese invasions and, in the 1640s, won support from the Dutch, who captured Luanda from the Portuguese, but held it only briefly. Nzinga was eventually forced to come to terms with the Portuguese (1656).

OASTLER, RICHARD (1789–1861), British social reformer. As steward to the Thornhill family in Yorkshire, he wrote effectively against the evils of child employment in a letter entitled 'Yorkshire Slavery' in the *Leeds Mercury* (1830). Backed by some Tory and radical MPs and by groups of factory workers, he organized demonstrations for factory reform, notably a Ten-Hours Bill to limit hours of work for adults and children. With the help of Lord Shaftesbury this was achieved (1847). Oastler's advocacy of force where the law offered no redress and his opposition from outside parliament to the New Poor Law led to dismissal from his post (1838) and later his imprisonment for debt (1840–3). Oastler was a churchman and a protectionist who saw in the rising class of manufacturers a threat to social justice and the landed interest.

OATES, TITUS (1648–1705), English conspirator, who was the son of a parson. He himself, having been expelled from school and sent down from two Cambridge colleges without a degree, took holy orders and became a naval chaplain, but was soon dismissed. He then studied briefly at Catholic seminaries in Europe (1677), from which he was also dismissed, and on his return to England (1678) he alleged that a Catholic conspiracy existed to murder Charles II and enthrone the Duke of York. He was welcomed, for political reasons, by Shaftesbury, and since the duke and his advisers were avowedly Catholic the invention of a 'Popish Plot' had just enough plausibility to seem credible. For two years Oates enjoyed a pension and a state apartment; a bill was introduced in parliament for the duke's exclusion from the succession, and about 35 people were executed before Oates's fabrications were exposed. He was severely punished when York came to the throne as James II, but after 1688 was released and pensioned. Eventually, having joined the Baptist Church, he was expelled from one of its ministries for embezzlement.

OB RIVER in Russia, 3640 kms long, with its tributary the Irtysh, rises in the Altai mountains and flows northwards to the Gulf of Ob and the Arctic Ocean. It was first discovered by the Cossacks in their drive eastwards from the Urals in the late 16th cent. and proved a vital waterway for explorers and fur traders crossing Siberia.

OBANDO, JOSÉ MARÍA (1797–1861), liberal president of Colombia (1853–4), who was instrumental in the passing of the federal constitution (1853). Obando was deposed in 1854 and died in a civil war against his conservative opponents.

OBRAJES, textile mills common throughout most of colonial Spanish America. Despite government attempts to limit their number and size, the *obrajes* dominated the domestic market for coarse, cheap textiles of wool and cotton. Official efforts to regulate the deplorable working conditions in the mills likewise failed. The mill owners relied primarily upon the forced labour and peonage systems, and in part upon convict labour, and thus no racial category of the lower classes was exempt from a life of virtual servitude, with long hours and close confinement to the mill premises. Indian villages frequently owned *obrajes*, whose prosperity was balanced by exploitation of the native commoners by their overlords and by Spanish administrators. *Obrajes* were Spanish America's most important manufacturing industry until, with independence, most were ruined by competition from cheaper English textiles.

OBREGÓN, ALVARO (1880–1928), Mexican farmer, soldier, and president (1920–4). He joined Francisco Madero's federal army against Pascual Orozco's rebellion (1912), and led the Sonora resistance to Huerta's *coup d'état* (Feb. 1913). He also created the Army of the North-west, which was nominally aligned with the forces of Francisco Villa and under the command of 'First Chief' Carranza (1913–15). Obregón contributed substantially to the defeat of Huerta and captured Mexico City (Aug. 1914). Villa was now alienated from Carranza's leadership and Obregón supported the 'First Chief' successfully at Celaya against Villa (April 1915), reducing his importance and assuring Carranza of the presidency. After this Obregón returned temporarily to farming, until Carranza initiated an attempt to deny him the presidential succession. He then organized a *coup d'état* (April 1920) and was elected president. During his term of office he began to enforce the more important social provisions of the constitution of 1917. He publicly aligned himself with organized labour and settled outstanding oil and debt questions with the US. He also thwarted Adolfo de la Huerta's rebellion (1923) and imposed Plutarco Elias Calles as his successor.

With Calles's support, Obregón was re-elected president (1928), but was murdered (July) by a religious zealot (*cristero*) before taking office. Before his death he had pacified virtually all the dissident factions of the Mexican revolution.   HDS

O'BRIEN, ERIS MICHAEL (1895–   ), Australian churchman and historian, who pioneered Australian Catholic historical research with a biography of *John Joseph Therry* (1922) and *The Dawn of Catholicism in Australia* (1928). He also wrote *The Foundation of Australia (1786–1800): a study in English criminal practice and penal colonisation in the eighteenth century* (1932). He was auxiliary bishop to Cardinal Gilroy (1948) and was Abp of Canberra–Goulburn (1953–66).

O'BRIEN, JAMES BRONTERRE (1805–64), Irish radical and Chartist, who demanded the nationalization of land and the extension to the workers of credit based upon it. He was a member of the Working Men's Association, and wrote for O'Connor's *Northern Star* advocating violence, but after 1839 he stressed the need for middle-class support and advised moderation.

O'BRIEN, WILLIAM (1852–1928), Irish journalist and nationalist politician who founded and edited *United Ireland* in support of Parnell and the Land League, and was frequently imprisoned under the Crimes Act (1887–91). After brief retirement, following controversy over party leadership (1895–1900), he founded the United Irish League to assist conferences between nationalists and landlords (1902–3).

OBSERVATION, ARMY OF, mixed force of Hanoverian and Hessian troops commanded by the Duke of Cumberland, sent to guard the line of the Weser to protect Hanover and Prussia from French attack in the Seven Years War. After Cumberland's defeat at Hastenbeck (1757) he was replaced by Prince Ferdinand of Brunswick, while the army, stationed at Stade, was reinforced with English troops paid for by a parliamentary grant of £1,200,000. This force soon drove the French back across the Weser and the Rhine (1758).

OBSERVER, THE (1791), in Britain, oldest surviving (1970) Sunday newspaper. It was most successful and politically influential under the editorship (1908–42) of J. L. Garvin.

OCAMPO, MELCHOR (d. 1861), Mexican liberal politician and cabinet minister under Benito Juárez, who was governor of Michoacán (1846) and negotiator of the McLane–Ocampo treaty with the US (1859). He was an outspoken opponent of clerical privilege.

OCCASIONAL CONFORMITY, in England, practice whereby religious dissenters qualified themselves for public office by periodically attending an Anglican church and receiving the sacrament in accordance with the Corporation Act (1661) and the Test Act (1673). The Toleration Act (1689) gave dissenters a large degree of freedom of worship, but did not relieve them of the sacramental test for national or local government office. Towards the end of William III's reign occasional conformity incurred the disapproval of many, both in and outside parliament, and in Anne's reign three attempts were made, without success, to eradicate it. In 1711, following an agreement between the Tory Earl of Nottingham and the Whig lords, a fourth bill was introduced, into the Lords this time, and ultimately became the Occasional Conformity Act. It was repealed in the following reign.

OCCASIONAL CONFORMITY BILLS (1702, 1703, 1704, 1711) in England. High Tory attempts to end 'occasional conformity', the practice whereby nonconformists took communion in an Anglican church often enough to qualify for municipal and national office according to the Corporation and Test Acts, besides worshipping in their own conventicles. The Earl of Nottingham was the real instigator of the bill, which was introduced into the Commons by William Bromley in Nov. 1702. Politics as well as religious principles were involved, for the Tories aimed at depriving the Whigs of electoral asset of the nonconformist vote. The struggle was mainly fought on party lines, with the powerful Tory majority in the Commons being checkmated by the slender Whig majority in the Lords. In 1704, two bills having already failed, the high church zealots in the Commons tried to force a bill through the Lords by 'tacking' it to the Land Tax Bill, a constitutionally dubious expedient which split the Tory ranks and led to the bill's defeat. In 1711 Nottingham's fourth bill, a less severe one than the previous three, became law because of an arrangement with the Whigs by which they acquiesced in its passing in return for Nottingham's support against Harley's peace policy. The act was repealed in 1718.

OCHAB, EDWARD (1906–), Polish communist politician and president of the republic (1964–8), who joined the party in 1929 and was imprisoned by the Polish authorities (1932–1935, 1937–9). On the outbreak of the Second World War, he moved to the Soviet Union, where he was one of the organizers of the communist-dominated groupings created there, the Union of Polish Patriots and the Kościuszko division. From 1944 he was a member of the Central Committee of the Polish Workers Party and First Secretary of the Provincial Committee of the party in Silesia and Dąbrowa (1946–8). In 1948 he became a deputy member of the Politburo and in 1954 a full member. He also sat on the Secretariat of the Central Committee (1950–7). During the Stalinist period, he was one of the main opponents of Bierut, but nevertheless, succeeded him on his death in March 1956 as First Secretary of the party. At that time, the Stalinist system in Poland was breaking down and it was Ochab's willingness to hand over power to Gomulka that prevented an upheaval in Poland similar to that which occurred in Hungary. In 1957, he became minister of agriculture and in 1964 became president of the republic. He fell in 1968 as a result of the anti-zionist campaign, which he opposed, although he was not a Jew.

OCHINO, BERNARDINO (1487–1564), Italian Capuchin monk and reformer, vicar-general of the order (1538), and confessor to Pope Paul III (1541), who fled to Geneva to preach Protestant doctrines (1542), but quarrelled with Calvin and moved successively to Augsburg, London, Zürich, Basle, and Nuremberg, propagating his antitrinitarian views. His best-known work was *Tragedy or Dialogue of the Unjust Usurped Primacy of the Bishop of Rome* (1549).

OCHS, ADOLPH SIMON (1858–1935), US newspaper publisher and editor, who established the *New York Times* as one of the great newspapers of the world. In 1878 he purchased a half-interest in the *Chattanooga Times*. By avoiding sensational journalism, he established the paper's reputation for trustworthy news-reporting. In 1896 he acquired the *New York Times*. His policy of a wide news coverage and truthful reporting rather than editorial comment gave the *Times* an unsurpassed reputation for accuracy and reliability. The publication of the *Dictionary of American Biography* was made possible through the generosity of Ochs, who allocated $500,000 to the project.

OCHTERLONY, SIR DAVID (1758–1825), British soldier in the service of the East India Co. While Resident at Delhi he defended it against Holkar (1804). He served in the Nepal War (1814–16), which he brought to a successful conclusion, and fought in the Pindari and Maratha Wars (1817–18).

O'CONNELL, DANIEL (1775–1847), Irish landlord, lawyer, and politician, who led the national campaign to achieve Catholic Emancipation (1829) as a first step to repeal of the Act of Union. He founded the Catholic Association, which attracted strong support from priests and others, whose subscriptions brought in £1000 a week. He was elected MP for County Clare (1828), after defeating the president of the board of trade. As a Catholic, he could not sit in parliament until an Emancipation Bill was passed. Under the threat of civil war the prime minister, Wellington, consented to this being done. O'Connell's greatest work was at an end by 1830, though in 1835 he led the Irish party at Westminster in securing the Lichfield House Compact. When Peel became prime minister (1841) O'Connell tried to organize another mass movement for repeal, but at the Clontarf meeting (1843) Peel forced his surrender. Though his approach was too cautious for the more revolutionary Young Ireland Party, his methods of agitation influenced Liberal nationalistic movements in Europe, as well as members of the Anti-Corn Law League.

O'CONNOR, FEARGUS (1794–1855), Irish Chartist leader and a radical politician, whose aim was to unite Irish nationalism and English radicalism in one reforming movement. He therefore clashed with O'Connell. In Nov. 1837 he established the *Northern Star*, which soon became the leading Chartist newspaper. His oratory and Irish wit attracted north of England audiences to his meetings against the new poor law and the factory system and he quickly dominated the Chartist movement. He was imprisoned for libel (1840–1) and thereafter converted Chartism from a movement into a sect. His anti-intellectualism alienated the more talented Chartist leaders, but he always remained faithful to Chartism (though later his influence on the movement declined) and compassionate towards victims of the factory system. Through establishing working men in rural smallholdings under an ill-managed and ambitious land scheme (1846), he lost money.

O'CONNOR, RICHARD EDWARD (1851–1912), Australian lawyer and federalist, who was a member of the drafting committee which framed the Commonwealth constitution. He was a senator (1901–3) and later a member of the first bench of the high court.

O'CONNOR, RORY (1883–1922), Irish Republican leader, who fought in the Easter Rising, and thereafter became prominent in the IRA. Under the title of Director of Engineering he was in charge of attacks on property in Britain. When the Civil War broke out in 1922, over the acceptance of Lloyd George's treaty, he took the intransigent Republican side, and led the 'Irregulars' who occupied the Four Courts in Dublin. He was captured in Aug. 1922, and shot in Dec. as a reprisal against the shooting of a deputy by Republicans.

O'CONNOR, THOMAS POWER (1848–1929), Irish author and politician, who favoured Home Rule. At first he supported Parnell's wish to retain the Irish party leadership in the crisis (1890) precipitated by the latter's divorce scandal, but he bitterly attacked Parnell's manifesto to the Irish people (29 Nov. 1890). His writings included *The Parnell Movement* (1886), *Life of Parnell* (1891), and *Memoirs of an Old Parliamentarian* (1929). He later became the first president of the Board of Film Censors (1917), and, as such, his signature on the screen was known to millions.

OCTAVIAN (63 BC–AD 14), great-nephew and heir of Julius Caesar, better known as the first Roman Emperor Augustus, the name conferred on him in Jan. 27 BC.

OCTENNIAL ACT (1768), in Britain, limiting the duration of Irish parliaments. It temporarily placated Ireland's parliamentary opposition and made subsequent parliaments more responsive to public opinion.

OCTOBER CLUB, in England, back-bench pressure group of country MPs representing extreme High Tory opinions. It was important after the 1710 election, when it numbered about 150 members. The club was linked to the government by Henry St John, and was pledged to an anti-Whig vendetta and to force partisan Tory and Church policies on the government.

OCTOBRISTS in Russia, right wing of the liberal constitutional movement which split after the October Manifesto (1905) into Kadets and Octobrists. The Octobrists were prepared to co-operate critically with the government inside the Duma, but relations were never good. They were supported by the right wing of the *zemstvo* movement and by business classes. They were the largest group in the third and fourth Dumas, and joined the Progressive Bloc (1915). Their leader, A. I. Guchkov, was chairman of the third Duma and of the War Industries Committee (established 1915). He became minister for war and navy in the first Provisional government (1917).

OCZAKOW (Turkish Özi), Ottoman fortress of great strategic importance controlling, with the fortress of Kilburun, the mouths of the Dnieper and Bug rivers. The Russians took Oczakow in 1737 and again in 1788. Oczakow was ceded to Russia under the terms of the peace of Jassy (1792).

ODAENATHUS, SEPTIMIUS (d. *c.* AD 266), Syrian noble from Palmyra, who repelled Persian incursions after the capture of the Roman Emperor Valerian (260), helped suppress a rebellion against Gallienus, and was recognized by him as independent ruler of the east. After a successful campaign against Persia, he returned to Syria, but was murdered at Emesa, being succeeded at Palmyra as head of the kingdom by his wife, Zenobia, and son, Vaballath.

ODAL, allodial tenure, the primary system of land tenure in ancient Scandinavia. The status was acquired if land remained in the possession of a family for three or more generations or more than 30 years. Such land was theoretically inalienable. Attempts to reduce odal to feudal tenure by some kings were largely unsuccessful and were regarded as tyrannical, consequently the king's power traditionally extended to the people rather than to the land.

ODOACER (*c.* 430–493), barbarian ruler who formally ended the Roman empire in the West. He was possibly of Hunnish origin, and led the Germanic Heruli, commanding an army which (476) deposed the last Western emperor, Romulus Augustulus. It is significant of the continuing prestige of the empire that he would have preferred thereafter to be appointed Roman patrician by the Eastern Emperor Zeno, but he could not secure this and assumed the less embracing title of King of Italy. In 493 Italy was invaded by the Ostrogoths at Byzantine instigation and their leader, Theodoric, defeated and killed Odoacer.

O'DONNELL, LEOPOLD, Duke of Tetuan (1809–67), Spanish soldier and politician of Irish descent, who led the Liberal Union from 1856, aiming at the formation of a centre party which would appeal to all sensible men. His administration (1858–63) was the most stable and successful constitutional ministry which Spain had hitherto enjoyed.

O'Donnell served in the army of Queen Maria Cristina and, during the regency of Espartero, made repeated efforts for her restoration, leading the unsuccessful revolt of 1841 in Pamplona. He assisted the fall of the San Luis government by the Manzanares proclamation, which enlisted radical support (1854), and became war minister in Espartero's subsequent government. This marked the coalition of Progressives and moderate Liberals, and the exclusion of Democrats who constituted the Liberal Union. In the crisis of 1856 O'Donnell became briefly prime minister and restored control in Madrid with Regulars, who routed the National Guards, thus ensuring the defeat of the Progressives and Democrats.

During his long ministry O'Donnell showed himself favourable to constitutional reform and an extension of the suffrage, and thereby attracted some Progressives and weakened the remnant. The Cortes met, and the press was in general free, though some extreme opponents were outlawed. A period of prosperity saw the expansion of railways and industry, and foreign trade doubled (1852–62). The budget of 1859 envisaged a system of public works financed by loans and the continuation of disentailing laws and their extension to charitable foundations. O'Donnell's foreign policy included the expedition to Cochin-China, the temporary restoration of Spanish rule in San Domingo, and the Mexican expedition of 1861. His greatest triumph was the Moroccan War and the capture of Tetuan (1861), for which he received his dukedom. He dealt successfully with the Carlist *pronunciamento* of Ortega and the rising of La Loja, but his government disintegrated on its recognition of the Italian kingdom, which was repugnant to the Holy See and therefore to Catholic elements in Spain (1863). In 1865 he returned briefly to power. He attempted to attract Progressive support by restoring dismissed opposition professors, introducing a liberal press law, halving the property qualification for the franchise, and giving recognition to the Italian kingdom. However, his brutal suppression of the mutiny of the sergeants of St Gil gave Isabella II cause to dismiss him, and thus ended his attempt to save the Liberal Union from extremists from both left and right.

R. Carr, *Spain 1808–1939* (Oxford, 1966).   VEC

O'DONNELL, HUGH ROE (1572–1602), last of the old Gaelic Kings of Ireland, known as 'Red Hugh'. His imprisonment in Dublin Castle (1588–92) by the lord deputy, Sir John Perrot, made him an inveterate enemy of the English, and when he succeeded his father as head of the clan (1592), he planned to drive them out of Ireland. He gained control of Tyrconnell and most of Connaught, becoming famous through his victory of the Yellow Ford (1598). His support of his Spanish allies, who counselled attack in opposition to the cautious Hugh O'Neill, Earl of Tyrone, may have greatly contributed to the disastrous defeat of Kinsale (Dec. 1601), which effectively marked the end of old Ireland. O'Donnell retired to Spain.

O'DONNELL, NIALL GARVE (1569–1625), cousin, brother-in-law, and successor to 'Red Hugh' O'Donnell. He went over to England on Hugh's defeat (1601), and at his death (1602) was chosen chief of the O'Donnell clan by his own partisans in preference to Hugh's younger brother, Rory. He was not satisfied with the terms for a settlement granted by the English, and in 1608 was charged with complicity in Sir Cahir O'Dogherty's rising and was imprisoned in the Tower of London, where he died.

O'DONOJÚ, JUAN (1755–1821), last Spanish viceroy of Mexico, who negotiated (1821) the so-called treaty of Cordoba with the Mexican leader Iturbide, thereby accepting the Plan of Iguala. The Spanish government repudiated the pact, and O'Donojú died shortly afterwards, thereby paving the way for Iturbide to proclaim himself emperor.

ODRÍA, MANUEL (1897–   ), dictator and president of Peru (1950–6), whose authoritarian rule brought the country political stability, but perpetuated inflation. Odría seized power in a military uprising in Arequipa (1948), and crushed rebellious students led by the American Popular Revolutionary Alliance (APRA). After suspending the constitution (1948), he drove APRA and the communists underground and then stood for election as president for a six-year term. Having achieved office, he permitted congressional elections and even allowed a few socialists to take their seats. Later, in his zeal to destroy the APRA, he co-operated with communists. Though he voiced sympathy for the working classes, his social programme was confined to Lima, the tax structure remained regressive, and the building of schools and public buildings was confined mostly to the capital. Post-war inflation was accompanied by a doubling of foreign investment in the country. Odría ignored these ominous symptoms and finally a huge uprising organized in part by Christian Democrats and university students inspired an electoral campaign that resulted in his defeat at the polls. Seven years later he staged a comeback, but it was unsuccessful. Later, to the astonishment of the public, he accepted APRA's support in another bid to secure the presidency, in return for which they were to be allowed to retain their congressional seats. Elements of the regular army were suspicious of this move and staged a *coup d'état* before it could be made effective.
VCP

O'DWYER, SIR MICHAEL FRANCIS (1864–1940), British colonial servant, who served in the Punjab and North-West Frontier Province, where he was revenue commissioner (1901–8), and in the princely states before becoming lieutenant-governor of the Punjab in 1913. His firmness in dealing with the *Ghadr* movement there, the persistence of his recruiting campaigns during the First World War and his opposition to political reform made him notorious among nationalist politicians, whose suspicions of him were confirmed by his responsibility in the Amritsar massacre (1919). He remained a controversial figure after his retirement, adding fuel to the fire with his autobiography, *India as I knew it* (1925), and his letters to the press opposing further Indian reforms. He was murdered by an Indian during a meeting.

ODYSSEUS, legendary Greek king of Ithaca and the adjacent Ionian islands. In Homer's *Iliad* he appears as stalwart supporter of Agamemnon against Troy (*c.* 1200 BC). His fabulous wanderings in the *Odyssey* after Troy's fall are perhaps a reflection of Greek exploration at the time of the poem's composition in the 8th–7th cents.

OECOLAMPADIUS, JOHANN HUSSGEN (1482–1531), German reformer, who helped Erasmus to edit the New Testament in Greek. He entered a monastery at Altmünster to study Lutheran doctrines (1520) and later helped to introduce the reformed doctrines at Basle and Ulm. He wrote commentaries on the prophets, gospels, and epistles.

OEDIPUS, legendary Greek king of Thebes, notorious for parricide and incest with his mother. The story of his family and of the war with Argos perhaps reflects dim memories of Mycenaean Thebes in the 14th cent. BC and the circumstances of its destruction.

OERSTED, HANS CHRISTIAN (1771–1851), Danish physicist who discovered accidentally during a lecture demonstration in 1820 that a compass needle was deflected at right angles to a wire carrying a current. This touched off one of the most spectacular trains of discovery and invention in the history of science and technology. The unit of magnetic field strength is named after him.

OFFA (*reg.* 758–96), King of Mercia, raised the Mercian kingdom to greater political dominance in southern England than had ever been achieved before. Contemporary charters reveal the extent of his influence. His control of the wealthy trading area of London and Kent enabled him to deal on almost equal terms with Charlemagne and to negotiate a commercial treaty with him. The Saxon penny makes its appearance at this time. Offa gave his name to the great earthwork dyke running from Rhuddlan, Flintshire, to Chepstow, Monmouth, which was probably built in his reign to mark the Welsh-Mercian frontier.

OFFALY, REBELLION OF LORD (1534–5), in Ireland, was largely engineered by the pro-English council in Dublin and resulted in the fall of the Geraldine house of Kildare. In Feb. 1534 the Earl of Kildare was imprisoned in the Tower of London on the representation of the Dublin council. He left his eldest son, Thomas, Lord Offaly, as his deputy. Kildare's enemies in the council, particularly the Butler family, spread rumours that he had died in the Tower, the victim of Henry VIII. On 11 June the Offaly declared himself Henry VIII's enemy. However, the rebellion had little military significance. The murder of Abp John Alen, of Dublin, brought excommunication upon Offaly, who, having failed to take Dublin, retired to Maynooth and appealed to the emperor and pope against the king. In Oct. 1534 Offaly was proclaimed a traitor, and Sir William Skeffington was sent out as lord deputy with a large army. Maynooth surrendered in March 1535, and in Aug. Offaly unconditionally gave himself up. He was executed at Tyburn (Feb. 1537) with five of his Geraldine uncles, his father having died of natural causes in Dec. 1534.

OFFICE OF STRATEGIC SERVICES (1942–5) in US, intelligence and covert operations agency, established by President F. D. Roosevelt's executive order (1942). The OSS, under Maj.-Gen. William J. Donovan, acted both as an intelligence network for the Joint Chiefs of Staff and as a co-ordinating agency for clandestine activities within enemy zones of operation during the Second World War. It was succeeded by the short-lived Central Intelligence Group (1946), and then replaced by the Central Intelligence Agency (1947–   ).

OFFICIALITÉ in France, medieval ecclesiastical tribunal surviving throughout the *ancien régime*, presided over by a judge or *official*. It dealt originally with cases involving breaches of Church discipline and many civil actions, *eg*, legitimacy, marriage, heresy, and sorcery. From the 14th cent. the *parlement* of Paris began to undermine its authority on behalf of the Crown, *eg*, over heresy and blasphemy.

OGARYOV, NIKOLAI PLATONOVICH (1813–77). Russian poet and revolutionary of noble birth. He was a close friend of Herzen and co-editor of *The Bell* (*Kolokol*). In 1856 he left Russia and developed (1857–63) a theory of a centralized, disciplined revolutionary organization for the populist group Land and Liberty (*Zemlya i Volya*).

OGDEN, PETER SKENE (1794–1854), US fur trader, who led expeditions into Snake River Country, discovered the Humboldt river (1828), and was one of the first white men to visit the Great Salt Lake region.

OGDEN PURCHASE (1826), lands in western NY, US, bought by the Ogden Land Co. from the Indians of the area on condition that they moved west. In 1810 David A. Ogden had purchased the pre-emptive rights to these lands from the Holland Land Co. for 50 cents an acre.

OGÉ, JACQUES VINCENT (1755–91), Haitian mulatto, who led a revolt against the French colonists of Sainte Domingue in 1790, and was afterwards executed. His insurrection led to widespread unrest and revolts, and eventually to Haiti's independence.

ÖGETEI (d. 1241), Great Khan of the Mongol Empire (*reg.* 1229–41), and third son of Chingiz Khan, whom he succeeded. During his reign, Mongol forces extended their penetration eastwards into China and Korea, westwards into Iran under Chormaghan, and into Europe under Batu. Ögetei established the capital at Karakorum.

OGLALA INDIANS, American tribe and the main division of the Teton Sioux. With other bands of Sioux, they terrorized white emigrant trains and military outposts under their chiefs, Crazy Horse and Sitting Bull. They took part in the battle of the Little Big Horn (1876), in which Gen. George Custer's command was destroyed. After signing two treaties ending hostilities (1868, 1876) they retired to the Pine Ridge, SD, Indian agency.

OGLE, SIR CHARLES CHALONER (?1681–1750), British sailor, who fought against the French in the Mediterranean (1708). He commanded the Jamaica station (1732) and joined Admiral Vernon in attacks on Cartagena and Guantanamo (1741) and the Panama Isthmus (1742). After replacing Vernon, Ogle became an admiral and commander-in-chief of the British navy (1749).

OGLETHORPE, JAMES EDWARD (1696–1785), British politician, soldier, and philanthropist. His concern for the plight of English debtors led him to obtain a charter (1732) to found the colony of Georgia in North America. Under his direction English debtors and persecuted European Protestants found refuge in the colony. He forbade rum, Negro slavery, and large plantations. During conflicts with Spain, Oglethorpe led an unsuccessful attempt to seize St Augustine (1740), but he defeated a Spanish invading force (1742). After returning to England (1743), he served in the British army during the Jacobite uprising (1745). Oglethorpe's connections with Georgia ended when it became a royal colony (1752). His last years were spent on literary and anti-slavery endeavours.

O'HIGGINS Y RIQUELME, BERNARDO (1778–1842), leader of Chilean independence and the illegitimate son of Ambrosio O'Higgins, an Irishman who became first governor of Chile and then viceroy of Peru. He rose to prominence by leading a revolt against José Miguel Carrera, who had ruled Chile despotically (1811–14) while professing loyalty to the Spanish king Ferdinand VII. However, in 1814 royalist forces in southern Chile, reinforced from Spain, defeated the hastily combined troops of O'Higgins and Carrera at Rancagua and forced both rivals to seek refuge with José de San Martín on the other side of the Andes. After assembling an army in western Argentina for an invasion of Chile, San Martín chose O'Higgins to be his second-in-command, and, after an incredible march across the Andes and the victories of Chacabuco and Maipú, Chile's independence was won.

San Martín customarily refused all honours, and in 1818 O'Higgins became virtual dictator of the country. His five-year term in office was stormy. He gave little form to political life and although he promulgated vague constitutions (1818, 1822), he ruled by decree, without a congress, and named his own cabinet.

To upper-class Chileans his bastardy and alien birth were both unacceptable. He offended Catholics and conservatives alike by abolishing titles of nobility, making light of social distinctions, insisting upon the nation's right of patronage over ecclesiastical appointments, demanding tolerance for religious dissenters, and opening a cemetery for non-Catholics. His emphasis upon public education likewise angered the Church, while the wealthy opposed his improvements in sanitation, paving, and street lighting, since these necessitated higher taxes. Landholders were outraged by his feeble attempt at land reform by abolishing entailed estates, and the Carrera faction, which was implacably hostile, accused O'Higgins (perhaps correctly) of complicity in the execution of their hero and his brothers in Argentina.

Although he was at first applauded for supporting San Martín's Peruvian campaign, O'Higgins was discredited when the effort, largely fought by Chilean soldiers, failed, and finally, in 1822, a disastrous drought and earthquake eroded what little support he had left. Though he forced through his re-election as leader for another ten years, he was powerless to thwart a rebellion in 1823 led by Ramón Freire, and went into self-imposed exile in Peru.

Stephen Clissold, *Bernardo O'Higgins and the Independence of Chile* (New York, 1969)   FPB

OHIO, 17th member state of the US, admitted in 1803. The region north of the Ohio river and south of Lake Erie was explored by French adventurers during the 17th cent. and opened up by American traders and land speculators under the auspices of the Ohio Co. of Virginia (1747). Britain gained possession of the area (1763), added it to the province of Quebec (1774), and ceded it to the US (1783). After being established as part of the North-west Territory (1787), it was settled by New Englanders, members of the Ohio Co. of Associates, around Marietta (1788) and by CT settlers in the Western Reserve (1792). Indian resistance was ended by the battle of Fallen Timbers (1794), and Indian lands were surrendered to the US by the treaty of Greenville (1795). Incorporation of the Western Reserve within the territory (1800), increasing settlement, and popular dissatisfaction with governor, Arthur St Clair, led to demands for statehood, which were met in 1803. The state prospered with the building of canals and railroads—the Erie and Kalamazoo Railroad was one of the first constructed in the old west (1836). Expanding industry and an enlarged population enhanced OH political significance between 1869 and 1923, during which period seven US presidents came from the state (Grant, Garfield, Harrison, Hayes, McKinley, Taft, and Harding). During the 20th cent. heavy metal and machine production has centred on Cleveland, rubber industries on Akron, and glass manufacturing on Toledo.

OHIO COMPANY OF VIRGINIA, American and English land company formed in 1747 to speculate in western lands claimed by the colony of Virginia. The company employed Christopher Gist to explore the claims, make treaties with the Indians, and construct a road (1750–3). Efforts to move settlers into the area led to French opposition and the outbreak of the French and Indian War (1755–63). The proclamation of 1763 issued by the British government prevented settlement of the Ohio Co. lands and its grant was discontinued (1770).

OHIO GANG in the US, name given to a group of self-seeking OH politicians, led by Harry M. Daugherty, who guided the political career of Warren G. Harding and helped him to win the Republican presidential nomination (1920). After being rewarded with government appointments following Harding's election, they abused his naive faith in their integrity and were deeply involved in a number of scandals, notably the Teapot Dome.

OHM, GEORG SIMON (1787–1854), German physicist and discoverer of 'Ohm's law', whose discovery that the current in an electric circuit is proportional to the potential (far from trivial with the available experimental resources) was published in 1827, but largely ignored until the Royal Society of London presented him with its Copley Medal in 1841. He had still to wait a further eight years before gaining a university appointment at Munich in 1849. The unit of electrical resistance is named after him.

OHTHERE (OTTAR) (*fl.* 9th cent.), Norwegian traveller, who is the source of the first important medieval report of Scandinavian voyages. He visited (*c.* 890) the court of the English King Alfred, who incorporated his account of a voyage north to the White Sea and of other travels into an old English translation of the universal history of Orosius.

OIDORES (lit. 'they who hear'), judges in colonial Spanish America who served in the highest court of appeal, the *audiencia*, and who also possessed political power. The *oidores* were a highly specialized group upon whom the Spanish Crown placed heavy reliance. In law, the life of an *oidor* was comfortable and well-paid, but semi-monastic. A judge lived with his colleagues, was forbidden to take gifts and fees, to hold lands or Indians, or to engage in trade, all in the interest of impartiality. Even his dress was prescribed, and the only relaxation allowed in an onerous schedule was attendance at religious festivals. *Oidores* were usually peninsular Spaniards, but by the 18th cent. more were Creoles. Although a judge occasionally allowed himself to become too closely identified with local interests, as a group the *oidores* were the most consistently loyal and effective branch of the colonial bureaucracy.

OJEDA, ALONSO DE (1466–1510), Spanish explorer, who accompanied Columbus on his second voyage and in 1499 led his own expedition to the coast of Venezuela, accompanied by Amerigo Vespucci. Ojeda's later attempt to colonize the northern coast of Colombia (Urubá) was a failure.

OKAI KOI (?reg. *c.* 1646–77), King of the Ga kingdom of Accra. Under his rule, Accra grew into a commercial emporium. He was beheaded by the neighbouring King of Akwamu during an invasion.

OKHOTSK, SEA OF, in Russia, between the Kamchatka peninsula and the Asian coast of Siberia. It was discovered by the Russians in 1639, providing them with fishing grounds and an outlet to the Pacific Ocean, although its waters are ice-bound from Nov. to March.

'OKIES' in US, name given in the 1930s to the thousands of tenant farmers and farm workers who were forced off the land in OK, TX, and KS by mechanization, foreclosure, and soil exhaustion, and who migrated westwards to CA in search of work.

OKINAWA, BATTLE OF (1 April–21 June 1945), major amphibious invasion by US forces, during the Second World War, of the largest of the Japanese-held Ryukyu Islands between Formosa and Japan. Vigorous resistance by the garrison of over 100,000 men, and *kamikaze* attacks by Japanese aircraft on American shipping, made it one of the costliest engagements in the Pacific theatre.

OKLAHOMA, 46th member state of the US, admitted in 1907. The region was visited by Coronado (1541), La Salle, and Joliet late in the 17th cent., and was acquired by the US under the Louisiana Purchase (1803). From 1820 large numbers of Indians were moved westwards into the area. Under the Indian Removal Act (1830) and the Indian Intercourse Act (1834) the **Five Civilized Tribes** (Cherokee, Creek, Choctaw, Chickasaw, and Seminole) established semi-autonomous republics within Indian Territory, then comprising most of the future state. A further 20 tribes were later settled in the territory (1866). After the Civil War pressure from white 'boomers' led to the opening up of 2 million acres (81,000 sq. kms) of unassigned land in a series of land 'runs' from 1889. Together with the Panhandle region, these lands were established as Oklahoma Territory (1890). Indian Territory was reorganized along lines suggested by the Dawes Commission (1896), and the two territories combined as the state of OK (1907). Much of OK's agricultural land was ruined by over-production, but reclamation of the Dust Bowl has continued since the 1930s. The state is one of the chief producers of crude oil in the US.

ŌKUBO, TOSHIMICHI (1830–78), Japanese politician, who shaped the course of the Meiji Restoration. Although of low samurai rank, he became prominent in Satsuma politics as a result of the atmosphere of crisis following the opening of Japan to foreigners (1854–8). He played a vital role in securing *bakufu* acceptance of Satsuma's proposal for greater co-operation between the imperial court, the *bakufu*, and the great *daimyōs* (1862); and in 1866, when the *bakufu* had reacted against co-operation, Ōkubo helped to create the alliance between Satsuma and Chōshū which overthrew the *bakufu*. In the confusion which followed the Restoration, Ōkubo worked behind the scenes with Iwakura, an influential court noble, to establish a firm political basis for the new government. He accompanied Iwakura on his mission to the US and Europe (1871–3), becoming very conscious of Japan's need to modernize. This led him, on his return (1873), to oppose the plan for an invasion of Korea to which other leaders, including Saigō Takamori, his old associate, had become committed. His firmness was decisive in checking so risky an adventure, but in 1874 he agreed to an expedition to chastise the Formosan aborigines, and when this created difficulties with China, he himself achieved a satisfactory diplomatic solution by going to Peking (1875). In 1877, after the Meiji government had replaced samurai stipends by inconvertible bonds, Ōkubo was faced, as home minister, and 'strong man' of the government, with the difficult and complicated task of repressing a major rebellion which had broken out in Satsuma with Saigō at its head. Although the rebellion was crushed, it led to Ōkubo's own death the following year at the hands of an assassin who wished to avenge Saigō. By then, however, both the Meiji government and its reform policies were soundly established.

M. Iwata, *Okubu Toshimichi, the Bismarck of Japan* (Berkeley, 1964).   RLS

ŌKUMA, SHIGENOBU (1838–1922), Japanese politician, a samurai from Hizen, who played an active role in the Meiji Restoration and became, with Itō Hirobumi, a protégé of Ōkubo Toshimichi. When Ōkubo was assassinated (1878), Ōkuma's ability and experience as finance minister made him a leading figure in the Meiji government until 1881, when, possibly hoping to take advantage of rivalry between Satsuma and Chōshū, he proposed the immediate introduction of responsible parliamentary government, but was outmanoeuvred by Itō and dismissed from office. After this setback Ōkuma played a somewhat ambiguous role, generally supporting the *Kaishintō*, a political party which he founded (1882), but occasionally co-operating with his former colleagues. In 1888 he became foreign minister in Itō's cabinet, but his efforts to solve the thorny question of revision of the 1858 treaties ended when he lost a leg from a bomb attack by a fanatical nationalist. In 1898 he became prime minister, in coalition with Itagaki Taisuke, in the first party cabinet in Japan; but after the swift collapse of this government, Ōkuma devoted most of his time to Waseda University, of which he was founder and president. In 1914, however, he returned to politics and again became prime minister and it was his cabinet which took Japan into the First World War and presented the 'Twenty-One Demands' to China (1915).

OLAF GUTHFRITHSON (d. 941), King of Northumbria (*reg.* 940–41) and of Dublin (*reg.* 934–41). While ruling in Ireland he invaded England, but was defeated by Aethelstan at Brunanburh and fled to his Irish domains. He returned later and secured Northumbria by a treaty (940) with Edmund I.

OLAF SIHTRICSON (d. 981), King of Northumbria (*reg.* 941–52) and of Dublin (*reg.* 944–81), who succeeded his father, Olaf Guthfrithson, in the Northumbrian kingdom, where he reigned, apart from a brief period of expulsion, until 952. During his exile (944–9), he secured the kingship of Dublin from his brother, Blacare (d. 948). He dominated the Viking settlements in Ireland until he was defeated in 980 by the Ui Neill prince, Mael Sechnaill mac Domnall. The last months of his life were spent on pilgrimage to Iona.

OLAF I TRYGGVESSON (c. 964–c. 999), King of Norway (*reg.* 995–c. 999), whose early life was probably spent as a Viking plunderer on the English coasts. He became a Christian, returning to Norway and overthrowing the king. He encouraged Christianity in both the Oslofjord region and in his overseas possessions of the Orkneys, Faeroes, Iceland, and Greenland. He met his death at the hands of King Sweyn I of Denmark.

OLAF II HARALDSSON (c. 995–1030), King of Norway (*reg.* 1015–28), who was originally a follower of the Danish Viking leader, Thorkell the Tall. He was converted to Christianity in Normandy (c. 1013), captured power in Norway (1015), and virtually completed the conversion of Norway to Christianity, converting the pagan interior and north by force, and established a Christian legal code and a native episcopate. He actively promoted trade and rebuilt the town of Nidaros (Trondheim), which became one of the leading ports of Norway. He was driven out in 1028 by Cnut, King of Denmark and England, but returned with a Viking mercenary force in 1030, and was defeated and killed. A cult rapidly grew up around him and he was canonized in 1164, becoming the popular saint of medieval Norway.

OLAF III HARALDSSON (c. 1050–93), King of Norway (*reg.* 1066–93), whose reign saw the foundation of Bergen as the greatest northern port of the Middle Ages.

OLAF V (1903–), King of Norway (*reg.* 1957–), who became crown prince of the newly independent kingdom of Norway in 1907 when his father, Prince Charles of Denmark, accepted the throne as Haakon VII.

OLD AGE PENSIONS ACT (1908), in Britain, introduced the principle of relief of the elderly poor (not merely the destitute) out of general taxation. Persons over 70 with incomes under £31 10s 0d (£31·50) a year received a maximum sum of 5s a week. The act followed more than 20 years of advocacy by politicians such as Joseph Chamberlain and social investigators such as Charles Booth and Seebohm Rowntree. Opponents believed the bill was merely disguised out-relief, undermining thrift and the voluntary friendly societies. The scheme, contributory after 1925, escaped the stigma of relief under the poor law. By 1914, nearly 1 million people received pensions.

The Beveridge Report (1942) advocated a comprehensive plan to ensure freedom from want for all members of the community. By July 1948 most of the provisions were implemented. Old age pensions became payable after the minimum age of 60 for women and 65 for men. For five years after this age a limit was placed on a person's earnings for receipt of the full pension. The Insurance Act (1959) introduced a scheme of graduated pensions, whereby contributors were paid along with Pay As You Earn (PAYE) income tax. The aim was to ensure a pension level in retirement more in proportion to the income earned in working years.

OLD BELIEVERS in Russia, *Raskolniks* or Russian Orthodox schismatics, who were followers of Avvakum. They refused to accept the Greek reforms of Nikon in the mid-17th cent., and were cruelly persecuted by the tsarist state and by the official Orthodox Church until the edict of toleration (1905).

OLD CATHOLICS, group of Catholics who separated from the Church of Rome at various points in the 18th and 19th cents. In Holland there was some identification between a Roman Catholic minority challenging aspects of papal authority and the Jansenist controversy. This led (1724) to the schismatic creation of the Church of Utrecht, with its own archbishopric and the sees of Haarlem and Deventer.

These Dutch Old Catholics were joined, in 1870, by movements in Germany, Switzerland, and Austria whose members rejected the dogma of papal infallibility uttered at the Vatican Council by Pope Pius IX. In Germany, the Old Catholics were temporarily strengthened by political factors, *eg*, the struggle against papal authority led by Bismarck and known as the *Kulturkampf*. Eventually Bismarck made his peace with the Vatican (1887) and the Old Catholics continued their separate existence, influenced by J. J. Dollinger (1799–1890), the Bavarian church historian, who had been excommunicated in 1871. Dollinger pioneered conferences with the Orthodox, Anglican, and Lutheran churches at Bonn (1874–5) on the theme of Christian unity, though he never himself formally joined the Old Catholic Church.

Bishoprics were established in Germany and Switzerland in the 1870s, but continued governmental opposition in Austria delayed the creation of sees there until after the First World War.

Old Catholic groups were also established in Yugoslavia and Poland. Polish Old Catholics established a National Polish Church (1897) for Poles in Europe and in the US, while a small sect, the Mariavites, were briefly in communion with the Old Catholics (1909–24).

The Old Catholic Church, national in character and origins, is unified in its adherence to the Declaration of Faith issued at Utrecht in 1889. This professed identification with the Catholic faith of the early Christian Church and with the decrees of Oecumenical Councils up to AD 1000. It rejected 18th- and 19th-cent. papal formulae, *eg*, the Bull *Unigenitus* (1713), the Syllabus (1864), and the Vatican decrees (1870).

The Old Catholics have retained the apostolic succession and their orders are recognized as valid by the Church of Rome, the Eastern Orthodox Church, and the Anglican Church. This gives them a unique position in relation to the three great churches of the Christian world. During the Second World War this was of some advantage in terms of facilities for worship for chaplains and combatants on both the Allied and Axis sides.

The Old Catholics have remained small in numbers—under half a million in 1970—but they have retained high intellectual standards and a flourishing church life.

C. B. Moss, *The Old Catholic Movement* (London, 1947).

GMDH

'OLD DOMINION', title taken by the English colony of Virginia after Charles II, who in honour of the colony's support of the Stuart cause, placed the seal of the London Co. (Virginia) on his royal shield (1660).

OLD GLORY in the US, popular name for the US national flag attributed (c. 1831) to a Salem, MA, sea captain, William Driver.

OLD KINGDOM, first of the great periods (Old, Middle, and New Kingdoms) of ancient Egypt. It includes the IIIrd–VIth dynasties (c. 2700–2140 BC), when the pyramids were built at Giza, Saqqara, and Abusir. The country was united under kings ruling from Memphis and there appears to have been strong centralized government, but, in time, the high offices became hereditary, and by the end of the VIth dynastic period powerful provincial rulers had become independent and the Old Kingdom ended in disorder.

OLD OLIGARCH, name given to the otherwise unknown author of a political tract, 'the Constitution of the Athenians', preserved with Xenophon's works—a critical but not entirely unsympathetic appraisal of Athenian democracy (c. 431 BC).

OLDENBURG, HENRY (c. 1615–77), German philosopher, who was the first secretary and co-founder of the Royal Society (1660). As such, he inaugurated the *Philosophical Transactions* (1665). He had earlier attended sessions at the fashionable Montmor Academy in Paris and continued to correspond with several members, thus promoting links between English and continental scientists.

OLDENBURG FAMILY in Germany, noble house which became prominent in the 15th cent. and divided into several lines. The counts of Oldenburg were north German nobles whose line became extinct in 1667. Christian I, Count of Oldenburg (reg. 1448–81), was the founder of the ruling dynasty of Denmark and Norway. The family also produced dukes of Holstein-Gottorp, who, from the time of Duke Adolf (1586), ruled the duchy under the Danish kings until 1773. From this branch sprang the Russian line, when Peter III of Holstein-Gottorp became tsar (1762), and the Swedish line (1751–1818), founded when Adolph Frederick became king of Sweden (1751). The third son of Christian III of Denmark, Duke John of Eldenburg, founded the line of Holstein-Sönderborg in 1582.

OLDER, FREMONT (1856–1935), US journalist, who became managing editor of the San Francisco *Bulletin* (1895) and was a prominent figure in the CA progressive movement. In 1918 he became editor of the Hearst newspaper, the San Francisco *Call*.

OLDFIELD, THOMAS HINTON BURLEY (1755–1822), British parliamentary reformer and constitutional historian, whose *History of the Boroughs* (1792) and *Representative History of Great Britain and Ireland* (1816) provided theoretical justification for the attempts by the House of Commons in the 19th cent. to alter its own composition, repeal the Septennial Act, and to abolish royal influence.

OLDUVAI, important prehistoric site in Tanzania, about 1,800,000 years old, where skeletal remains of three types of early hominids, *Homo habilis, Zinjanthropus (Australopithocus boisei),* and *Homo erectus,* have been found. Stone tools were also found with *Zinjanthropus.*

OLGIERD, Grand Duke of Lithuania (d. 1377), who seized Vilna, the pagan Lithuanian capital, in 1345. The cornerstone of his subsequent successes was the life-long devotion of his brother, Kiejstut, who assumed the thankless task of defending Lithuania in the west against the Teutonic Order, while Olgierd was free to expand eastwards into Russia. But for this division of Lithuanian resources, Olgierd might have conquered Moscow, which he twice besieged and deprived of some of its dependencies. His victory over the Tatars in 1362 at Siniya Voda led the Tatar khan to move his capital further south to the Crimea, while Olgierd's territory extended to the Black Sea. At his death, he ruled over the largest European state of his time. His son, Jagiello, murdered Kiejstut in 1382 and, despairing of resisting the Teutonic Order singlehanded, allied Lithuania with Poland, becoming, on conversion to Christianity, King Ladislas II of Poland.

OLID, CRISTÓBAL DE (1492–1524), Spanish conqueror and lieutenant of Hernán Cortés in Mexico. He served in Cuba with Diego Velásquez, who commissioned him to explore Yucatán (1518), commanded a ship under Cortés, and distinguished himself during the evacuation of Mexico City (*la noche triste*). Later, Cortés sent him by sea towards

Honduras (1523), while Pedro de Alvarado, another lieutenant, travelled by land. Having landed on the Honduran coast, Olid rebelled against Cortés and defeated troops sent to imprison him. When Cortés himself entered the region, Olid reasserted his loyalty to the conqueror. He was murdered by his own men shortly afterwards.

OLIVARES, GASPAR DE GUZMAN, Conde-Duque de (1587–1645), Spanish politician, royal favourite and first minister under Philip IV from the latter's accession (1621) until his exile in January 1643. He came from the Andalusian aristocracy, entering the royal household through the patronage of the Duke of Lerma before rising to pre-eminence with the help of his uncle, Balthasar de Zuñiga. Conscious of Spain's imperialist heritage, he advocated bold strategies which proved impossible to realize. His domestic policy was directed towards greater efficiency and centralization of royal government under Castile and the redistribution of provincial contributions to the economy of the state. He therefore attempted reforms such as the Union of Arms, but his policies brought large-scale revolts in Catalonia and Portugal (1640–3). His foreign policy added to Spain's economic difficulties. After the renewal of hostilities against the United Provinces (1621) he strengthened Spain's army and navy and brought the country into the Mantuan War (1628–31). He provoked French entry into the Thirty Years' War (1635) in which Spain sided with the Emperor Ferdinand II, Philip IV's Habsburg uncle. Olivares' popularity declined rapidly after Spanish naval power was destroyed at the battle of the Downs (1639), Roussillon was overrun by the French and provincial rebellion broke out. At the queen's connivance he was dismissed, dying two years later in Toro. His extravagant patronage of artists and writers made the Spanish court a brilliant centre of culture but added to the government's financial embarrassment.

OLIVA, TREATY OF (1660), ended the war begun in 1655 by Sweden's attack on Poland. The Swedes gained no territory, but kept Livonia, and John Casimir abandoned his claim to the Swedish throne. The treaty also confirmed Brandenburg's sovereignty over the duchy of Prussia.

OLIVETTI, GINO (1880–), Italian politician, who was a 'liberal' deputy and an industrial leader under the Fascist regime. As secretary-general of *Confindustria,* he was influenced by Mussolini's increasingly conservative economic policies and his ruthless attitude towards strikers, and he advised (Oct. 1922) King Victor Emmanuel to appoint Mussolini as a minister. He signed the Palazzo Chigi (1923) and Palazzo Vidoni (1925) pacts which provided for *Confindustria* alone to represent industrialists, dealing only with fascist unions. He preserved some independence for *Confindustria,* however, and later led protests against Mussolini's financial policies.

OLLENHAUER, ERICH (1901–63), German politician who joined the German Social Democratic Party (SPD) and worked, during the Weimar years, in the party press and youth movement, becoming chairman of the latter (1928–33). In 1933 he emigrated and became a member of the SPD executive in exile (in Prague, Paris, and London). His German citizenship was withdrawn in 1935. On returning to Germany in 1946 he was elected deputy chairman of the SPD, and after Schumacher's death (1952), chairman, a position he retained until his own death. He was a member of the Bundestag from 1949, and was leader of the SPD parliamentary party during a period when it was subject to stress, electoral frustration, and internal change. The SPD abandoned doctrinaire policies on domestic and foreign issues and widened its popular appeal. After 1959, although Ollenhauer remained technically chairman of the party, Willy Brandt was proclaimed the party's candidate for the chancellorship.

OLLIVIER, OLIVIER ÉMILE (1825–1913), French politician and prime minister of the liberal empire. He was one of the first republicans in the imperial legislature (1857), an exponent of gradual liberalization, and eventually led the first responsible ministry (1870). He felt compromised by the Franco–Prussian War and went into retirement, producing a study of the liberal empire.

OLMECS, pre-Conquest Amerindian peoples associated with a distinctive art style centred in the forests of Tabasco and coastal Veracruz, and most notably at La Venta, in Mexico. Olmec style objects, however, have been found in the valley of Mexico, as far west as Guerrero, and as far south as Costa Rica. The style, which flourished *c.* 900–400 BC and even longer in some areas, is noted for its use of carved jade and its obsession with the jaguar. At present, little else is known with certainty concerning these peoples.

OLMEDO, JOSÉ JOAQUÍN (1782–1847), Ecuadorian poet, journalist, and politician, who was concerned with the coming of independence to his native land and to Latin America in general.

OLMSTED, FREDERICK LAW (1822–1903), US writer and landscape architect, who was commissioned by the *New York Times* to explore the economic and social condition of the American South. His observations, published as *A Journey in the Seaboard Slave States* (1856), *A Journey through Texas* (1857), and *A Journey in the Back Country* (1860), and collectively in *The Cotton Kingdom* (1861), became a classic portrait of the *ante-bellum* South. He was appointed superintendent of Central Park, NY (1857) and, together with Calvert Vaux (1824–95), redesigned the park. He was secretary-general of the US sanitary commission (1861–3) and later planned the campus of California University at Berkeley and what was later to become Yosemite National Park. He then founded, with Vaux, a landscape architecture firm that established a pre-eminent reputation in its field. Among his achievements were Prospect Park in Brooklyn, the Capitol grounds in Washington, DC, the campus at Stanford University, and landscaping for the World's Columbian Exposition in Chicago (1893).

OLMÜTZ CONVENTION (1850), meeting between Schwarzenberg (Austria) and Manteuffel (Prussia) at which Prussia accepted the Federal solution to the Hesse crisis and acknowledged Austria's superiority within the German Confederation. After the failure of the Frankfurt parliament, Radowitz had tried to build up a Prussian Union of Princes which would unify Germany and exclude Austria. He met with moderate success while Austria was engaged in quelling revolutions, but dilatoriness in preparing the constitution and getting it accepted gave Austria time to recover, to undermine the unity of the princes, and to call a plenary session of the Confederation. The committee set up by this plenary session called on Bavaria to settle the Hesse crisis. Prussia knew that Austria was backed by Russia, and had to withdraw. It was her greatest, and last, humiliation. The future of the Confederation was postponed for the Dresden Conference.

OLNEY, RICHARD (1853–1917), US lawyer and politician, who was appointed attorney-general (1893), was involved in the prosecution of the sugar trust (*US v. E. C. Knight Co.,* 156 U.S.I., 1895), and also that of Eugene Debs, during the Pullman strike (1894). Olney is best known for his vigorous defence, while secretary of state (1895–7), of the Monroe Doctrine in the boundary dispute between Britain and Venezuela. He negotiated the Olney–Pauncefote treaty of arbitration between Britain and the US, which failed to achieve ratification in the US Senate.

OLYMPIC GAMES, ANCIENT (776 BC), Greek pan-hellenic athletic festival, traditionally established in honour of Zeus under the supervision of Pisa, later Elis, at Olympia in north-western Peloponnese. The games, including running, the pentathlon (long-jump, sprint, discus, javelin, wrestling), chariot racing, etc., were celebrated every four years. During the late 5th and 4th cents they became the accepted occasions for repeated appeals for Greek unity against 'barbarians', *eg,* Persians. A list of victors, first compiled by Hippias of Elis *c.* 400, was later developed by Timaeus and Eratosthenes as the most convenient, comprehensive chronological scheme for Greek historiography. In AD 393 the festival was abolished by the Roman emperor Theodosius I.

OLYNTHUS, ancient Greek city on the Chalcidice peninsula, 49 kms south-east of Salonika, which, after becoming a centre of disaffection from the Athenian alliance (432 BC), resisted all Athenian attempts at repression during the great Peloponnesian War and emerged as chief city of the Chalcidian League. It was besieged and subjected (380), when the Spartans attempted to dissolve the league, but quickly liberated (378), only to be destroyed by Philip II of Macedon (348). Cassandreia, founded by Cassander on the site of nearby Potidaea (316), was meant as its successor. Excavations have revealed a fine example of 4th-cent. town-planning, throwing interesting light on domestic architecture of the period.

OMAHA INDIANS, American Siouan tribe, formerly living in NB and SD, where the US explorers, Lewis and Clark, found them (1804) on the Missouri river. They ceded their lands to the US (1854), but by law (1882) were given lands individually and later citizenship.

O'MALLEY, KING (*c.* 1858–1953), Australian Labor politician, who worked in North America and in South Australia before becoming a Tasmanian member of the Commonwealth parliament (1901–17), where he encouraged projects for social reform, including a national bank, established in 1911. He was minister of home affairs (1910–13, 1915–16).

OMAN REBELLION (1955), reassertion of independence by the Ibadhi mountaineers of interior Oman under the leadership of the so-called Imam Ghalib and his brother Talib of the Hinawi tribal federation, first with Saudi and later with Egyptian support. In 1957 British forces came to the aid of the sultan to put down a rising, the consequence of standing differences between the people of the interior and those of coastal Muscat.

OMBUDSMAN, Scandinavian term, adopted elsewhere in the 1960s to designate a commissioner who is appointed by parliament to investigate individual complaints against officials. A 'parliamentary ombudsman for justice' was first introduced by the Swedish constitution of 1809, which gave him wide powers of enquiry, including the right to attend the deliberations of both officials and judges. He was appointed for four years by a special committee of the Riksdag. The activities of the office were further defined in 1941 and the post became the most important organ of control on the part of the legislature, to which the official made periodic reports.

The Swedish system was copied in 1919 for the first independent Finnish constitution, and spread later to Denmark (1954) and Norway (1962). A parallel institution for safe-guarding the rights of citizens during military service likewise originated in Sweden (1915), reached other Scandinavian countries after the Second World War, and was in 1956 extended to West Germany. The civil office, however, did not spread beyond Scandinavia until 1962, when a New Zealand law provided for a commissioner or ombudsman to investigate complaints and, in default of action by the department concerned, to report the case to the prime minister and parliament.

In Britain the introduction of a new official to scrutinize individual grievances was promised by the Labour Party at the 1964 election, and in March 1967 a bill was passed with the approval of all parties, under which the parliamentary commissioner of administration began work the following month. The British system requires the complainant to approach the commissioner through an MP, to whom any action taken will be reported, but the commissioner also presents an annual general report to the House of Commons and may report specially to the same body in any case where his representations have not caused an evident injustice to be remedied.

D. C. Rowat (ed.), *The Ombudsman: citizen's defender* (London, 1965). TKD

OMDURMAN, BATTLE OF (1 Sept. 1898), in which Egyptian and British forces under Kitchener defeated the Sudanese forces of the Khalifa Abdallahi at Karari, 6 miles (9·6 kms) north of Omdurman, and so ended the Mahdist state in the Sudan.

OÑATE, JUAN DE (1549–1624), Spanish official and explorer, who was appointed governor of New Mexico (1595). He arrived at the confluence of the Rio Grande and the Chama rivers (1598), with a few hundred soldiers, settlers, slaves, and livestock. From this settlement he led expeditions over the whole area. The last was down the Colorado river to the Gulf of California. He returned to Mexico convinced that California was an island.

ONE BIG UNION in US, synonym for the Industrial Workers of the World (IWW), American syndicalist union founded in Chicago (1905). It was also the title of a short-lived Canadian union which, while sharing the IWW's class beliefs, contested its expansion in Canada. This union was active in western Canada (1919–22), but it lost support and by 1944 it was confined to Winnipeg.

ONE THOUSAND AND ONE NIGHTS (ALF LAYLA WA LAYLA), collection of Oriental tales, the nucleus of which derives from Al-Jahshiyari (d. AD 942). The final version, much expanded, dates from the time of the Mamluk sultanate. The tales are of varied origin, *eg*, of Persian, Arab, Indian, Greek, and Hebrew provenance. A French translation by Antoine Galland was published in 1704–17, and an English one by E. W. Lane in 1840. Sir Richard Burton's unexpurgated edition appeared in 1885–8.

ONEIDA COMMUNITY (1848–79) in US, religious settlement, practising primitive Christian communism, established in central NY state by John Humphrey Noyes (1811–86), a believer in 'perfectionism', the possibility of human sanctification. Members of the community (originally 51 in number, but eventually 300) held property in common, raised their children under communal care, practised 'complex marriage', and an elementary form of birth control. Harmony in group life was regarded as essential, and members attempted to remove the competitive spirit and subjected themselves to 'mutual criticism'. Although Noyes did not envisage economic self-sufficiency for the colony, it gained a reputation for the high quality of its manufactures, including animal traps and silver plate. Threatened with legal action because of its practice of polygamy and polyandry, the community adopted monogamy after 1879. In 1880 a majority of members decided upon the incorporation of the community as a joint-stock company.

ONEIDA INDIANS, American tribe, by tradition the second to join the Iroquoian Confederacy. They were included in a royal warrant (1687) protecting the confederacy. They remained neutral in the American War of Independence (1775–83), but dispersed afterwards. Most of them moved to WI (1846).

O'NEILL OF THE MAINE, TERENCE MARNE O'NEILL, Life Baron (1914–), Irish politician who entered Northern Ireland politics as a Unionist in 1946, holding various offices before becoming prime minister in 1963. He met the prime minister of the republic of Ireland (1965) and some improvement in the relations between the two countries was anticipated. During his premiership (1963–9) he introduced local government reforms which angered Protestant extremists, who resented them as concessions to Catholics. Amid growing agitation over the civil rights issue, O'Neill resigned in April 1969 and accepted a life peerage in the British House of Lords.

O'NEILL, EUGENE GLADSTONE (1888–1953), US dramatist who gained his reputation with *Beyond the Horizon* (1920), *The Emperor Jones* (1920), *Anna Christie* (1921), *The Hairy Ape* (1922), and *Desire Under the Elms* (1924). O'Neill's attack on contemporary materialism was powerfully expressed in *The Fountain* (1925), *The Great God Brown* (1926), and *Lazarus Laughed* (1927). He experimented with the stream-of-consciousness technique in *Strange Interlude* (1928) and adapted the Greek theme to the aftermath of the Civil War in *Mourning becomes Electra* (1931). Among his later plays were *The Iceman Cometh* (1946) and *Long Day's Journey into Night*. He was awarded the Nobel Prize for Literature (1936).

O'NEILLS, EARLS OF TYRONE, Ulster family which until the destruction of the Gaelic order in the early 17th cent., was one of the most prominent families in Ireland. The O'Neills traced their descent from Niall of the Nine Hostages (d. 405), the first King of Ireland, whose existence is an undisputed historical fact. The name O'Neill was first used by Domhnall O'Neill, grandson of Niall Glundub (d. 919), King of Ireland, and is thus one of the earliest European hereditary names. The first O'Neill to emerge as leader of the Irish against the English in the 16th cent. was Conn O'Neill (*c*. 1484–1559), inaugurated chief of the Tyrone O'Neills in 1519. In 1541 he submitted to Henry VIII and was created Earl of Tyrone for life. Hugh O'Neill (*c*. 1540–1616), second earl, is known as 'the great earl', and was inaugurated chief of the clan in 1593. He sought aid from Spain to drive out the English, and in alliance with Hugh Roe O'Donnell, defeated the English at the Yellow Ford. After the defeat of Kinsale (1601), he submitted to James I, who confirmed his title. By 1607 he found his position in Ireland untenable and in 'the flight of the earls' left for Spain. Sir Phelim O'Neill (*c*. 1604–53) and Owen Roe O'Neill (*c*. 1590–1649), nephew of the second earl, took a prominent part in the Irish Rebellion. Owen routed the English at Benburb (1646), but died before he could co-operate with Ormonde to face the Cromwellian invasion. Sir Phelim continued the fight, but was executed for treason. The O'Neills were less influential in Jacobite Ireland (1689–91), but were still prominent as soldiers. Their importance as a leading family came to an end with the failure of the Stuart cause in Ireland.

ONGANÍA, JUAN CARLOS (1914–), Argentine soldier, who became president (1966) with the support of the military junta that overthrew the radical regime of Arturo Illia (1963–6).

ŌNIN WAR (1467–77), one of the most destructive wars in Japanese history. Beginning as a conflict between the Hosokawa and Yamana families over the shogunal succession, it soon spread into the provinces. Much of Kyoto was destroyed during the war and the Ashikaga shogunate lost all that remained of its national authority.

ONITSHA, important commercial town on the Niger river and principal Christian missionary centre in Iboland. Its famous covered market, the largest in West Africa, was destroyed during the civil war (1967–70). The *Obis*, traditional rulers of Onitsha, claim links with the rulers of Benin.

ONN BIN JA'AFAR, DATO (1895–1962), Malayan politician. As a Johor official and journalist, he led the Malay opposition to the British 'Malayan Union' scheme (1946). He convened a Pan-Malayan Malay Congress (March 1946) on the issue, at which the first and greatest Malay mass movement, UMNO, was born. Despite his great influence as its first president (1946–51), he was unable to persuade UMNO to admit non-Malay members, which he believed to be the only way to achieve independence. The rival multi-racial Independence of Malaya Party, which he then founded (1951) was defeated at the polls.

ONNES, KAMERLINGH HEIKE (1853–1926), Dutch physicist and discoverer of superconductivity, who founded the famous low-temperature laboratory at Leyden University in 1894. He was the first to liquefy helium, and discovered the phenomenon of superconductivity in which the electrical resistance of a metal suddenly vanishes completely as it is cooled. He was awarded the Nobel Prize for Physics in 1913.

ONONDAGA INDIANS, American tribe of the Iroquois confederacy, formerly located in NY. Many joined the Catholic Iroquois colonies on the St Lawrence river, and by 1751 about half the tribe had moved to Canada, where they were allies of the French during the French and Indian War (1755–63). They sided with the British in the American War of Independence (1775–83), and the US forces burned their villages (1779). After the war they were forced to cede most of their lands in NY.

ONSLOW, RICHARD ONSLOW, 1st Baron (1654–1717), British Whig politician, who was a lord of the admiralty (1691–3), speaker of the House of Commons (1708–10), and lord of the treasury and chancellor of the exchequer (1714–15).

ONSLOW, ARTHUR (1691–1768), British politician and speaker of the House of Commons (1728–61), whose long tenure of office did much to establish the dignity and impartiality of the office.

ONTARIO, Canadian province, once part of Quebec, formerly known as Upper Canada and Canada West. It was first explored by the Frenchman Samuel de Champlain (1615) and visited by Jesuit missionaries preaching to Indians. Fur-trading posts were found in the 1670s at Fort Nouille (Windsor), Fort Frontenac (Kingston), and Fort Conti (Fort Niagara). After the American War of Independence loyalists settled along the St Charles, Ottawa, and Niagara rivers. By the Quebec Act (1774) the area was subject to French tenurial law. Opposition came from the British colonists, who also wished to free themselves from domination of Montreal and Quebec, and the Constitutional Act of 1791 was introduced, which divided Que. into predominantly British-settled Upper Canada and largely French Lower Canada. York (Toronto) was made capital of Upper Canada (1795). After the Napoleonic wars there was a sizeable migration of Scots and Irish to the Ont. frontier. It is from these immigrants, opposed to the oligarchic power of the Anglican Church and the provincial legislature, that support came for the short-lived rebellion of 1837. As a result of the Durham Report (1839), Canada West was created, providing for effective local government, abolishing the clergy reserves, and stimulating economic expansion. With the formation of the Dominion of Canada (1867), Ont. became a founding province. Provincial autonomy was emphasized by the Liberal prime ministers Oliver Mowat (1872–96 and Mitchell Hepburn (1933–40), while Conservative governments favoured cooperation with the national government.

J. E. Middleton and F. Landon, *The Province of Ontario—a history, 1615–1927.* 5 vols (Toronto, 1927–8).　GS

OPEN DOOR, THE, expression used to describe the principle of equal trading opportunities for the great powers in parts of Africa that was adopted by the Berlin Conference (1884–5). Later, as applied to the Far East, it became identified with US policies towards China after 1899. The American secretary of state, John Hay, in a note to the powers with spheres of influence and extra-territorial rights in China (6 Sept. 1899), pledged on behalf of the US equality of commercial opportunity in China and asked for similar guarantees in return. In a circular note (3 July 1900) he reaffirmed this position and committed the US to the preservation of Chinese territorial and administrative integrity. Hay's first note was drafted by W. W. Rockhill, his adviser on Far Eastern affairs, who was influenced by the views of Alfred E. Hippisley, a British subject with long experience of China, and the policy was based on the established 'most-favoured nation' principle that was characteristic of 19th-cent. commercial treaties.

OPEN SKIES PROPOSAL in US, suggestion made by President Eisenhower at the Geneva summit conference (July 1955) that the USSR and the US should permit mutual air surveillance of their defence installations to ease international tension and aid disarmament. The proposal was made in the 'spirit of Geneva', but proved impracticable.

OPEN-FIELD AGRICULTURE, term used for a system of farming where all the arable land, in the intervals between the growing of crops, is also used for the pasturing of the cattle and sheep of the village. This was essential in villages where sufficient permanent pasture was not always available and it also provided the method of fertilizing all the arable. This type of farming precluded the permanent fencing off of holdings of the individual landholders. In practice, their strips were often intermixed. It is a system of farming typical of the plains of northern Europe from Midland England to Russia and still (1970) persisted in some parts of Europe.

OPERA, musical dramatic entertainment, in which vocal solos and choruses with instrumental accompaniment play an essential and not merely an incidental part, the last great art form created by the Italian Renaissance. Originating in Florence at the close of the 16th cent., opera was first developed by Monteverdi and then by Lully, Purcell, Handel, and Scarlatti. Through the genius of Mozart, Vienna replaced Italy as the centre for European opera in the late 18th cent., but in the 19th–20th cents this art form developed further, with distinctive national character, in Italy, Germany, France, Spain, Russia, and England, in the hands of many composers, *eg,* Wagner, Verdi, Bizet, Puccini, Falla, Rimsky-Korsakov, and Britten.

OPERATION BARBAROSSA (1941), German invasion of the Soviet Union during the Second World War. Hitler decided to strike in 1941 because of fears of Stalin's Balkan ambitions and frustration at the apparent impossibility of conquering Britain. The invasion began on 22 June. The Russians had advanced from their prepared positions to occupy Poland and the Baltic States. They were in the middle of reorganization for tank warfare and were taken by surprise within 48 hours. Their air force was destroyed. The Germans relied on superiority of technique and equipment to offset a considerable inferiority of numbers—in tanks and aircraft, as well as men. They made their main effort in the centre, where *Panzergruppe* under Hoth and Guderian executed three successive encircling manœuvres. Over half a million prisoners were taken, and the Russian defences completely disorganized.

The unmechanized German infantry was slow to deal with the considerable numbers of Russians bypassed and cut off by the Panzers, who fought stubbornly on in their rear, while on the flanks stiff resistance was encountered outside Leningrad and Kiev. Hitler therefore ordered the advance to be halted while the flanks and rear were consolidated; Halder and Guderian, favouring a continued drive towards Moscow, opposed this order and delayed its implementation, so that, although the Russians lost 600,000 prisoners in the encirclement at Kiev alone, the flanks had not been stabilized when the advance in the centre was resumed in Oct. By then, the German troops were exhausted and their machines were wearing out; they were not prepared for winter fighting and the weather was deteriorating rapidly. They won another huge encirclement battle at Vyazuma, and leading elements reached the suburbs of Moscow on 2 Dec., but the main force ground to a halt in the forests in front of the city. Zhukov's counter-offensive with fresh troops from Siberia and the new T34 tank began on 4 Dec. Hitler's greatest gamble had failed. By losing the strategic initiative he ultimately lost the war.   PJBD

OPERATION FLASH (1942), attempt to assassinate Hitler during the Second World War. At the end of 1942, after the disasters of Stalingrad and Tunis, a group of German conspirators, led by Gen. Beck and Dr Goerdeler, decided to attempt to assassinate Hitler. His death—the flash— would be followed by the seizure of power by the military authorities in Berlin and other key cities. Plans for this operation were drawn up by Gen. Olbricht, head of the *Allgemeines Heeresamt*, and Col. Oster of the *Abwehr* (Counter-Intelligence Service) by Feb. 1943, but they were abandoned after the failure of earlier assassination attempts organized by Gen. von Trescow.

OPERATION GREEN (1938), German plan for the invasion of Czechoslovakia 'by 1 Oct. 1938', whose execution was forestalled by the Munich Agreement of 30 Sept. Preparations for this operation led to a crisis of Hitler's relations with the army. Forty of Germany's 45 regular divisions were assigned to deal with the Czechs' efficient army and formidable fortifications, and many senior officers, fearing a French invasion across the denuded Rhine frontier, opposed Hitler. In Aug. 1938 the chief of the general staff, Beck, resigned after failing to unite his colleagues in a public protest, and began plotting a *coup d'état* in which his successor, Halder, and the commander-in-chief, Von Brauchitsch, were involved. But this military opposition was temporarily abated when Chamberlain and Daladier failed to call Hitler's bluff.

OPERATION SEALION (1940), German plan during the Second World War for the invasion of England in Sept. 1940. Preparations for this undertaking began in July, when it became apparent that, though France had surrendered, the British intended to fight on. The German command had not thought out the implications of the plan. Even in ideal conditions the hastily assembled flotilla of canal barges could not have landed the necessary nine divisions on the south coast in less than ten days, let alone their artillery. The problem of supplies for this force had scarcely been considered. Owing to Germany's naval weakness, support for the troops ashore and protection against the Royal Navy were to be provided almost entirely by the Luftwaffe. Yet by mid-Sept. the Luftwaffe had not even succeeded in securing command of the air and the plan for invasion came to nothing.

OPERATION TORCH (1942), landing during the Second World War of some 100,000 US and British troops in Morocco (at Casablanca) and Algeria (at Oran and Algiers) on 8 Nov. 1942. It was intended to lead to the occupation of Tunisia as the first stage in the invasion of Italy, in order to divert German forces from Russia and north-west Europe and clear the Mediterranean route to the Far East. This 'Mediterranean strategy' seemed to offer more certain returns from the employment of the comparatively small forces available for offensive operations than an invasion of France early in 1943. The landings were successful, but the advance into Tunisia was delayed, and the Axis was enabled to consolidate a position there which was not taken until 13 May.

OPERATION VALKYRIE (1943), plan for military coup in Germany during the Second World War, to take effect after the assassination of Hitler. It was drawn up in the summer of 1943 by Col. von Stauffenberg, chief of staff of the Home Army, to whom executive direction of the conspiracy had passed after the failure of Operation Flash (1942). It was to take place on 20 July 1944, but local military commanders hesitated to act against the SS and Gestapo. Only in Paris, where many senior officers were involved in the conspiracy, were the orders implemented. When it became clear that Hitler was still alive the plot collapsed.

OPERATION WHITE (Sept. 1939), German plan for the invasion of Poland which provided for the first use in war of fast-moving armoured and mechanized forces closely supported by low-flying aircraft—the technique known as *blitzkrieg*. The Polish forces were outnumbered, except in cavalry, to which they attached an anachronistic importance, and which was badly deployed. They had very few tanks and a tiny air force. Thus they offered no effective resistance to German forces advancing from East Prussia to the north and from Bohemia to the south, which met near Lvov on 12 Sept. Germany's Russian allies began to advance from the east on the 17th. Warsaw fell on the 27th, and the last significant Polish forces surrendered on 5 Oct.

OPERATION YELLOW (1939), German plan during the Second World War for defeating France, prepared on Hitler's orders after 27 Sept. 1939. Army leaders, including Von Brauchitsch and Halder, doubted whether *blitzkrieg* tactics would succeed against France. Their hesitation prevented an attack before the spring of 1940, and they proposed only a limited campaign in Belgium and Holland. The French general Gamelin, anticipating the plan, sent 33 Allied divisions to support the Belgian and Dutch defence on the Breda–Antwerp–Namur line, while 44 divisions held the Maginot Line, leaving the Allied centre guarded only by five divisions, and the supposedly impassable Ardennes forests. In Feb. 1940, however, the German staff, at Hitler's insistence, adoped a bolder scheme devised by Manstein and Guderian. While 29 divisions under Von Bock provoked the Allied dash north, by invading Holland and Belgium, and 19 watched the Franco-German frontier, 45, under Von Rundstedt, were to drive south-westward into France through the Ardennes and west to the sea, encircling the Allies' main striking force in Belgium and north-eastern France.

The operation began on 10 May, and Panzer spearheads under Guderian and Rommel crossed the Meuse at Sedan on the 13th. German superiority in the air was not seriously challenged, and though they had fewer tanks than the Allies, they used them more effectively. Airborne and commando units secured key points in advance of the armoured columns, giving rise to fears of 'Fifth Columnists'. The morale of the French forces was poor, and their leadership confused. On the 20th the Germans reached the Channel at Abbeville and the encirclement was complete. Though their failure to attack the Dunkirk perimeter before the 26th permitted the evacuation of 227,000 British and 110,000 French troops, these were in no condition to fight again. The Allied field force was destroyed and France lay open to the advance south across the Somme, which began on 5 June. Marshal Pétain's government surrendered on 22 June.   PJBD

OPIUM MONOPOLY, important source of income to the British government of India, which controlled the manufacture and sale of opium to China and other countries. The right to produce opium had been farmed out under Mughal rule, but in 1797 it became a monopoly of the East India Co. Although a subject of frequent attack, this system survived till 1907, when an agreement was reached with China by which it was hoped to stop the import of opium into China within ten years.

OPIUM WAR (1839–42) between Britain and China. Despite its name, this was brought about by conflicts over diplomacy and commercial practices, as well as opium. Since 1600, British trade from the Cape of Good Hope to the Straits of Magellan was monopolized by the East India Co. During the

18th cent. the company's importation of Indian fabrics was curtailed by acts of parliament to protect Britain's growing textile industry. As a result, the company turned its attention to the importation of tea from China, which had to be paid for in specie, since China provided no outlet for British products. The balance of trade was finally redressed by the exportation of Indian opium to China by private merchants under the company's wing. Socially and economically, the opium trade had an undesirable effect on China. Confucian orthodoxy had never admitted the desirability of trade, and the British East India Co. had to operate under many restrictions. Trade was confined to Canton and to the Co-Hong merchants, who had overall responsibility for foreign merchants; only through them were merchants permitted to communicate with the Chinese authorities. In 1834 the company's monopoly was terminated, and the aggressive free-traders, now represented by the superintendent of trade appointed by the British government, demanded freer trade and diplomatic equality, but to no avail. Hostilities became unavoidable in 1839, when Commissioner Lin Tse-Hsü came to Canton to put an end to opium-smoking and the opium trade. Succumbing to Lin's demands, Capt. Charles Elliot, the British superintendent, surrendered all the opium in British possession; he refused however to sign a bond for future non-importation of the drug, and withdrew the entire British community to Macao. Unfortunately, the opium affair was complicated by the killing of a Chinese villager by British sailors in Kowloon. Dissatisfied with Elliot's handling of the culprits, Lin expelled the British, who retired to the almost barren island of Hong Kong, where much hardship was experienced. Minor hostilities eventually broke out when the British were denied the right to buy food in Kowloon.

In June 1840 a British expeditionary force arrived and blockaded Canton; it then proceeded north to Pei-ho, but was persuaded to return to Canton to negotiate. On 20 Jan. 1841 the Chinese were forced to sign the 'Ch'uan-pi Convention', whereby they undertook to cede Hong Kong, pay an indemnity of $6 million, and permit direct and equal intercourse between the officials of the two countries. The Convention was rejected by the two governments concerned. In Aug. 1841 the British—now under Sir Henry Pottinger—moved north again, occupying Amoy, Tinghai, Ningpo, Shanghai, and Chinkiang in quick succession. The Manchu government finally conceded and deputed Commissioner Ch'i-ying to negotiate what became the treaty of Nanking (29 Aug. 1842), and concluded the Opium War.

Chang Hsin-pao, *Commissioner Lin and the Opium War* (Cambridge, MA, 1964). DP

OPPENHEIMER, JOHN ROBERT (1904–67), US physicist, who was appointed (1943) director of the laboratory at Los Alamos, NM, where the first atomic bomb was designed and constructed and near which it was exploded. After the Second World War Oppenheimer remained a government adviser, was chairman of the Scientific Advisory Committee of the Atomic Energy Commission, and head of the Institute of Advanced Study at Princetown (1947–65). For technical and political reasons his committee advised against the intensive development of thermonuclear weapons, but was over-ruled by President Truman. This project succeeded, however, owing to later technical innovations, but in 1954, during Senator Joseph McCarthy's period of influence, Oppenheimer's loyalty was called into question. After interrogation, he was cleared by the Personnel Security Board (1954), but thereafter denied access to classified information because of his having had communist associations earlier on. This decision meant the end of his usefulness to the Atomic Energy Commission. The commission made some amends, however, for the treatment he had received by recommending the president to confer on him the 1963 Enrico Fermi award for his contribution in nuclear research.

OPPERT EXPEDITION (1868), attempt by Ernst J. Oppert, a Hamburg trader based in Shanghai, to rob a Korean royal tomb, having failed to trade with Korea. The attempt did not succeed, but confirmed Korea's mistrust of western intentions.

OPRICHNIKI in Russia, officials of the *oprichnina*, numbering some 6000 and appointed by Tsar Ivan IV (1565), mostly drawn from the gentry class or from foreign adventurers. They always wore black clothes and acted as trusted royal agents over the confiscated *boyar* estates. They soon acquired a reputation for excessive cruelty, but their reign of terror ended with their disbandment (1572).

OPRICHNINA in Russia (lit. 'a separate household' or 'private court'). In historical terms it was applied to the royal domain in central and northern Muscovy, created by Tsar Ivan IV in the mid-16th cent. from the patrimonial estates confiscated from the *boyars* or old nobility and distributed among the *dvoriane* or lesser gentry on condition that they gave loyal service to the tsar.

OPTIMATES, ancient Roman term, used especially by Cicero, for the supporters of the 'best men' in politics in the 1st cent. BC, who tried to defend the senatorial aristocracy against the *populares* (eg, Marius, Julius Caesar).

ORACLE BONES, in China. Large numbers of bones and shells used for purposes of divination (*c.* 1400 and 1100 BC) have been found at An-yang. Small grooves were scored on the bones, which were then applied to fire. The diviner interpreted the resulting cracks and frequently inscribed on the bone the text of the questions put to the oracle, together with its answer. These bones and shells formed the earliest examples of Chinese writing and include forms of characters that have remained unchanged.

ORACLES, GREEK, shrines of ancient Greek gods, especially Apollo, *eg*, at Delphi, Didyma, and Claros, and Zeus, *eg*, at Dodona, and as Zeus-Ammon at the Libyan oasis of Siwa, where the god's advice was sought and revealed by various ritual means. In the 8th–6th cents BC Apollo's oracle at Delphi played an important part in, *eg*, Greek colonization, the Lycurgan reforms in 7th-cent. Sparta, and the establishment elsewhere of tyrants, *eg*, the Cypselids at Corinth, and their subsequent overthrow by Sparta. Later, the oracle of Zeus-Ammon supposedly supported Athens' expedition against Sicily (415) and encouraged Alexander the Great's belief in his divinity (331).

O'RAHILLY, THE (d. 1916), Irish republican, who was a member of the secret Irish Republican Brotherhood. He was deputed to persuade Eoin MacNeill to found, in 1913, the Irish Volunteers to fight for Home Rule, and later helped to organize the Howth gun-running in July 1914. He was killed in Dublin on the last day of fighting in the Easter Rising.

ORAKAU, SIEGE OF (April 1864), incident in the NZ Maori Wars. About 300 dissident Maoris, under Rewi Maniopoto, constructed Orakau *pa* (fort) near Te Awamutu, and defied a British force of nearly 1500, in March–April 1864. When called upon to surrender, they returned the famous cry 'Ake, Ake! ('Never, never!'), and their womenfolk refused to leave them. The *pa* was then taken with heavy Maori losses.

ORANGE, small principality which from the 11th cent. formed an enclave in the ancient province of Venaissin, north of Avignon in the Rhône valley. It was ruled by the house of Baux (1174–1393) and the Burgundian house of Châlons (1393–1530) and passed, together with extensive lands in the Low Countries, to René, nephew of Philbert de Châlons, and on his death (1544) to his cousin, William, Count of Nassau, who thus became Prince of Orange. Thenceforward the principality was associated with the family of Orange-Nassau, the head of which became hereditary sovereign ruler of the Netherlands. Although Orange was twice occupied by Louis XIV's armies (1660, 1680), the title of Prince of Orange was granted to John William Friso of Nassau and his heirs by the treaty of Utrecht (1713), and it was not until the French Revolution (1789) that the principality was absorbed into France.

ORANGE FREE STATE, in South Africa. For centuries Bantu-speaking and Khoisan peoples lived between the Orange and Vaal rivers. By the 1830s the Griqua, Sotho, and others had established fairly extensive states. From 1836 Trek Boers moved into Transorangia. In 1848 British sovereignty was declared over the land between the two rivers. However, the Orange River Sovereignty was abandoned in 1856, and the independent Orange Free State was established under a president. This state gained land at the expense of the Sotho, but lost the diamond region around Kimberley to the British in 1871. The Free State became a British colony after the Anglo–Boer War (1899–1902), and formed a province of the Union of South Africa after 1910. The capital of the Orange Free State is Bloemfontein.

ORATORIANS, Catholic order of secular priests dedicated to moral and religious education, founded in Rome by St Philip Neri (1556). It was introduced into England by Cardinal Newman (1847) and Brompton Oratory was built soon afterwards. A French order, also for preaching and education, was founded by Bérulle (1611) and had considerable influence until the Revolution.

ORBELTELLO, BATTLE OF (1646), French naval victory over the Spanish in the Tyrrhenian Sea, between the Italian mainland and Corsica, in the Franco–Spanish War of 1635–1659. Under the command of the Duke of Brézé, the French fleet overcame the Spanish domination of the western Mediterranean and enabled French forces to take Elba and Piombino in Tuscany.

ORCAGNA, known as Andrea di Cione (*fl.* 14th cent.), Florentine painter and sculptor, whose paintings included the altarpiece in the Strozzi chapel of the Dominican church at Florence and the *Last Judgement* in Santa Croce at Florence. The most famous of his works was the inlaid marble tabernacle in the chapel of Or San Michele at Florence. He was in charge of the whole design of the chapel and in his last years controlled the work on Florence Cathedral.

ORCHOMENUS, ancient city in Boeotia, central Greece, home of the legendary Minyans and of considerable importance in the 2nd millennium BC. Schliemann uncovered (AD 1880) remains of the great tholos tomb known as the 'Treasury of Minyas' and subsequently found frescoes from the Mycenaean palace. Although Mycenaean finds were scarce, earlier pottery characteristic of the 20th–17th cents BC was found in abundance and first called 'Minyan'. Orchomenus was probably already in the Mycenaean period overshadowed by Thebes and later in the 5th and 4th cents failed to prevent Theban domination of the Boeotian League and her own eclipse.

ORD RIVER, THE, in the eastern Kimberley region of northwestern Australia, passes through spectacular gorges before entering cattle-grazing areas with agricultural potential. After preliminary experiments with tropical crops, this became the scene of dam-building projects in the 1960s with Commonwealth and state government money, a model township (Kununurra), subsidized cotton and sorghum farming, and plans have been made for hydro-electric development.

ORDAINER, LORDS, in England, group of magnates who were opponents of King Edward II. They were led by his cousin, Earl Thomas of Lancaster, who, in association with Abp Winchelsea of Canterbury, objected to Edward's alleged acts of misgovernment. They especially objected to his favourite, Piers Gaveston. In the parliament of Feb. 1310 they demanded sweeping reforms and Edward had to agree to the Ordainers' control of the royal council and to the preparation of reforming ordinances (hence the name of 'lords ordainer'). These ordinances (41 in all) were promulgated in Aug. 1311 and imposed serious limitations on Edward. Gaveston's breach of an ordinance reimposing his banishment led to his capture and murder by some of the Ordainers (1312), but the baronial opposition was split by this crime. During the next ten years there were a number of attempts to enforce one of the ordinances on Edward, but in 1322 he defeated his opponents and executed Lancaster and several other barons. This, and the brutal misuse of his victory, led to Edward's downfall in 1326.

ORDEAL, JUDICIAL, or trial by ordeal, custom first observed among the various Germanic tribes which settled in the territories of the Roman empire after the 5th cent. AD. It was a means by which the guilt or innocence of a person accused of a crime was supposed to be determined. Accused persons faced certain tests involving physical pain or disfigurement. If they emerged unscathed they were deemed innocent. Some leading churchmen regarded the ordeal with dismay, as a wrongful way of tempting God, and the Frankish emperor, Louis the Pious, prohibited it in his kingdom, but this was soon forgotten. The same motives led to its abolition by Pope Innocent III at the Lateran Council in 1215. In England the use of ordeals probably dates from the foundation of the Anglo-Saxon kingdoms. The Normans introduced an alternative form of trial by battle, but continued to allow Englishmen to use the ordeal. After the Lateran Council forbade the clergy to participate in ordeals in 1215, they could no longer be regarded as divine judgements. In England, therefore, the king, in 1219, suspended the ordeal, which was gradually replaced by trial by jury.

ORDENANZAS SOBRE DESCUMBRIMIENTOS, in Spain, enlightened legal code promulgated by Philip II in 1573 for regulating the conduct of the Spanish settlers in the American empire, on similar lines to the New Laws of 1542.

ORDERS IN COUNCIL (1807), British retaliation against Napoleon I's Berlin Decree during the French Wars. Neutral ships visiting enemy ports were ordered to call at some British port, pay customs duty, and buy a licence to proceed. While enabling Britain to control and profit from continental trade, the Orders helped to provoke a war with the US (1812–14).

ORDINANCE (1650), in England, proclaimed under the Commonwealth, forbade all trade with the royalist colonies and barred all foreign ships from trading with any English plantation in America, without a licence.

ORDINANCE OF 1649 in Russia, the *Ulozhenie* establishing a new Code of Law for Muscovy, drawn up for Tsar Alexis I on the advice of the Zemsky Sobor, or Council of the Land, to restore order after the Moscow rising of 1648. The code, which favoured the lesser nobility and townsfolk, bore heavily upon the peasantry by legalizing serfdom as a state institution.

ORDINARII, in Sweden, replaced bishops in the early Reformation period, as did superintendents in Denmark and Norway.

ORDINARY PROCEDURE in France, legal procedure, originating in feudal times, for dealing with criminal offences. It provided for public trial and the defence of the accused and did not involve the use of torture. From the 15th cent. the 'ordinary' gradually gave way to the 'extraordinary' procedure.

ORDIN-NASHCHOKIN, AFANASI LAVRENTIEVICH (d.1680), Russian politician and diplomat, who headed the department of foreign affairs in the reign of Tsar Alexis (1645–76). He came from a family of provincial gentry in the Pskov region, proved an able provincial administrator under Michael Romanov, and won recognition as commander of a small force sent to defend the Muscovite frontier against Livonia and Lithuania in the Russo–Polish War (1654). He was afterwards made governor of several of the annexed towns. In 1658 he negotiated an armistice with Sweden, believing that that country posed a more serious threat to Muscovy than Poland. Although embarrassed by his son's defection to Poland (1660), he continued to rise in favour. In 1665 he became governor of Pskov, where he organized Russian merchants on a basis of mutual co-operation to defeat German competition. In 1667 he negotiated the treaty of Andrussovo with Poland, which ceded the Smolensk and Seversk regions to Russia, with Kiev and the east Ukraine. A keeper of the seal and foreign minister (1667), he sought a Polish alliance to counteract the growing influence of Sweden and Turkey. He was an admirer of the west, and anticipated many of Peter the Great's reforms. His advanced ideas led to a difference of opinion with Tsar Alexis over the restoration of Kiev and in 1671 he resigned and retired to the Krypetsky monastery at Pskov.

ORDZHONIKIDZE, GRIGORIY KONSTANTINOVICH (1886–1937), Russian politician, who joined the Bolshevik Party in 1903 and in 1912 was made a member of the central committee. He was appointed extraordinary commissar in southern Russia (1917) then directed the party in the Caucasus (1920) and Transcaucasia (1921–6). He was a close supporter of Stalin and became chairman of the central control commission (1926), of the supreme council of national economy, and a member of the Politburo (1930). He was then appointed commissar for heavy industry (1932). His death during the great purge was assumed to be due to suicide and was attributed by Khrushchev to his inability to work 'normally' with Stalin, in spite of his devotion to him, or to share the responsibility for his abuse of power. This allegation was an important part of Khrushchev's attack on the anti-party group.

OREBRO, STATUTE OF (1617), in Sweden, rigorous penal legislation against Catholics and the political and religious supporters of Sigismund of Poland, introduced by Gustavus Adolphus and endorsed by the Swedish estates. The statute was analogous to the Elizabethan penal laws in England and was an extension and reinforcement of the Norrkoping decisions of 1604. There was to be no communication between Protestant Sweden and the Catholic exiles in Poland, Catholic Swedes being deprived of their civil rights and expelled as traitors. The statute did not in fact lead to wholesale bloodshed, but there were isolated cases of execution and imprisonment (1617–24).

OREGON, 33rd member state of the US, admitted in 1859. The north-west Pacific coast was visited by Spanish, English, and American ships during the 16th and 17th cents, and the region was explored by Lewis and Clark (1804–6). John Jacob Astor's Pacific Fur Co. founded Fort Astoria (1811), but British fur interests were dominant for the next decade. After long dispute, US title to the area was recognized by the Oregon treaty (1846). Settlement, begun in the Willamette valley (1834), increased with the flow of settlers along the Oregon Trail from 1842, and a provisional government was organized (1843). Oregon Territory was established (1848) and achieved statehood (1859). State constitutional amendments, known collectively as the Oregon System, instituted the initiative and referendum (1902), the direct primary (1904), and the recall (1908), and served as reform models for other US states. OR's economy is based upon lumbering and mixed farming, but vast hydro-electric power resources have increased industrialization since the 1930s.

OREGON TRAIL in the US, western emigrant route stretching from Independence, MO, to Fort Vancouver in the Willamette valley of OR. The main trail followed the Platte and its northern fork to Fort Laramie, where it left the plains and crossed the Rocky Mountains at South Pass. From Fort Bridger the route led to Fort Hall on the Snake, and thence by way of the Grande Ronde valley, the Blue Mountains, and the Umatilla valley to the Columbia. By the 1830s it had been established by fur traders as a passable route to the West Coast, and after 1842 became the great highway for pioneers moving into the Oregon Territory. The Great Migration, 1000 strong, gathered at Independence in the spring of 1843 and pioneered the use of wagons over the whole trail. So many settlers used the Oregon Trail throughout the 1840s and 1850s that it became a deeply rutted road. Although equipment improved and knowledge of the environment increased, the hardship of the 2000-mile (3250 kms) trek made it a hard test of endurance for western pioneers.

O'REILLY, ALEXANDER (Don Alejandro) (1722–94), Spanish soldier, who served in the War of the Austrian Succession and the Seven Years War. He was sent (1768) to Spain's province of Louisiana, where he crushed the revolt against the governor, Antonio de Ulloa, and reorganized the provincial government on Spanish colonial lines. On his return to Spain he was created inspector-general of infantry (1770).

ORELLANA, FRANCISCO DE (c. 1500–49), Spanish sailor, and first European to navigate the Amazon. He was lieutenant to Gonzalo Pizarro on the latter's disastrous expedition (1541–2) to the Ecuadorian *montaña* in search of El Dorado. After eight months, the company arrived without supplies at one of the smaller streams leading to the Amazon. Orellana was sent down-stream with 57 men in improvised boats to search for food. Eventually, Pizarro, despairing of his return, returned to Quito. Orellana, in the meantime, made his way over 2000 miles (3250 kms) to the mouth of the Amazon. From that point, in Aug. 1542, the expedition went to Santo Domingo and thence to Spain. Orellana returned to the area for further exploration, but his boat capsized and all on board were drowned.

ORESME, NICHOLAS (c. 1320–82), Norman mathematician and physicist who invented the notion of fractional powers, was founder of analytical geometry, and anticipated Copernicus in discerning the motion of the planets round the sun. He was an adviser to King Charles V of France and his writings include important memoranda on practical matters, especially the reform of the French monetary system. In 1378 he became Bp of Lisieux.

ORFORD, EDWARD RUSSELL, 1st Earl of (1st creation) (1653–1727), British sailor and Whig politician, who opposed James II. He corresponded with William of Orange and signed the Declaration inviting him to invade England (1688). After the Revolution, Russell was a leading member of the whig Junto, where his family name gave him a good deal of patronage, and was first commissioner of the admiralty (1694–9). After Torrington's defeat at Beachy Head (1690), Russell was appointed to arrest and supersede him. He crippled Jacobite invasion plans by destroying the French fleet off La Hogue (1692), though much of the credit must be given to Rooke for his action at Barfleur. However, Russell found it difficult to work with a predominantly Tory ministry and was dismissed for allegedly not following up the victory at La Hogue. He was recalled, however (1694), and served both at sea and in the admiralty and became a member of the cabinet. He commanded the first major English fleet to winter abroad (1694–5), when he led a squadron in the Mediterranean to immobilize the Toulon fleet and relieved French pressure on Catalonia.

Russell commanded the navy for the rest of the war (1694–7), but achieved no further victory of note. However, He was rewarded with a peerage, becoming Earl of Orford

(1697), and treasurer of the navy. An unsuccessful attempt to impeach him was made (1701) by the Tories because of his acquiescence in the Second Partition treaty of 1700, and an equally unsuccessful attempt was made by the Commissioner of Public Accounts to find proof against him (1703) of peculation. In Anne's reign Orford was the least effective member of the Junto. Though he attended the Lords regularly, he was seldom prominent in debate. However, he retained his personal following in the Commons and briefly regained office as first lord of the admiralty (1709–10). He was appointed one of the lord justices to rule until the arrival of George I (1714) and then once more became first lord of the admiralty. He resigned (1717) with Townshend and Walpole.

ORFORD, ROBERT WALPOLE, 2nd Earl of (1st of 2nd creation), 1676–1745), British politician who anticipated the role of prime minister. He was the third son of a Norfolk squire and entered parliament in 1701, became an efficient debater, and rose to be secretary at war (1708) and treasurer of the navy (1710) under the Whigs' wartime ministry. He managed the impeachment of the High Church Tory Dr Sacheverell, for which he earned the hatred of the Tory party, and he was consequently dismissed by Queen Anne (1710), impeached (1711), and sent to the Tower for corruption and malversation, afterwards being expelled from the Commons by a Tory parliament (1712). His career was retrieved, however, by the Hanoverian succession, and when his Whig brother-in-law and neighbour, Charles Townshend, was appointed first secretary of state after George I's accession, Walpole was rewarded with the paymastership and then was promoted to be first lord of the treasury and chancellor of the exchequer (1715). In 1717 he went into opposition with Townshend, opposing Stanhope's foreign policy and securing the rejection of the Peerage Bill (1719) by an eloquent speech. He also, perhaps surprisingly, opposed the repeal of the Occasional Conformity and Schism Acts (1718). In 1720 he was restored to office, being appointed paymaster-general by Sunderland, and his return to the treasury (1721) helped to restore national confidence after the South Sea Bubble.

Walpole used his position to attack the Tory High Church. He secured the exile of Atterbury, Bp of Rochester (1722), and muzzled the lower clergy by curbing the activities of convocation. Higher appointments in the Church were reserved for Whigs. He tried to avoid raising sectarian bitterness, however, and though he refused to repeal the Test and Corporation Acts lest the interests of established Church should suffer, he started the practice of passing indemnity acts from 1727.

His economic policy was directed towards winning support for the Hanoverian dynasty. He had started the Sinking Fund in 1717 and this he maintained as a means of lowering the national debt. He revised the tariff system, removing export duties, offering bounties, and abolishing duties on imported raw materials. Imports which competed with British products were prohibited or taxed. In 1723 he introduced the bonded warehouse system for excise duties on tea and coffee which successfully increased the tax yield and discouraged smuggling. In 1733 he proposed to extend the scheme to wine and tobacco to enable him to reduce the land tax, a burden on the landed squirearchy, but political opposition forced him to withdraw the plan. His colonial policy was also mercantilist in principle. The 1733 Molasses Act increased the restrictions upon the American colonies, although he allowed the legislation to remain a dead letter rather than provoke recalcitrant settlers.

Walpole established his position as chief minister, eliminating the competition of other able politicians, *eg*, Carteret, Chesterfield, Pulteney, Bolingbroke, and Pitt. He contributed to the development of the cabinet system and to the Commons as the seat of parliamentary power, although he never forgot the importance of royal favour. He used the existing political practices of patronage and bribery to manage the lower house, and his dexterity and ability guaranteed his success. His

main aim in the field of foreign policy was to isolate the Jacobites and give peace to Britain. Townshend and the king directed foreign affairs until the international crisis of 1725–7, but thereafter Walpole practised non-intervention, *eg*, in the Polish Succession War, and neglected the armed forces. His appeasement policy was attacked during the naval conflict with Spain (1739–40) and in the 1741 election his majority was considerably reduced. He resigned in Feb. 1742, was created Earl of Orford, and though he retired, was still consulted by George II. Though neither interested in, nor gifted at, the conduct of foreign affairs, he promoted the country's economic prosperity and preserved the Protestant Succession and Hanoverian dynasty, to which the laws and liberties of Britain were entrusted.

He was the father of the author and diarist, Horace Walpole.

J H. Plumb, *Sir Robert Walpole*, 2 vols (London, 1956–60).
MKS

ORFORD, HORACE WALPOLE, 5th Earl of (4th of 2nd creation) (1717–97), English politician, author, historian, and patron of the arts. Though he was an MP (1741–67) and held lucrative sinecures, he shunned active politics and from 1747 spent much time adorning his villa at Strawberry Hill in the Gothic style, where he established a printing press (1757) which produced Gray's *Odes*. His own novel, *The Castle of Otranto* (1764), made popular the Gothic horror story, and his *Historic Doubts on the Life and Reign of King Richard III* (1768) inaugurated controversy among historians. His journals and letters, published posthumously, are indispensable records of politics and society in his time. They include *Reminiscences* (1819), *Memoirs* (1845), *Memoirs of the Last Ten Years of the Reign of George II* (1846) and *Journals* (1859) *of the Reign of George III, and Letters* (1903–5).

ORGANISATION DE L'ARMÉE SECRÈTE (OAS), terrorist organization which opposed the ending of French rule in Algeria, active in 1961–2. The OAS began among the Europeans in Algeria, but later extended its activities to France itself. In Algeria it sought to create an atmosphere of terror. In France it specialized in bomb attacks on individual liberals, and was responsible for two serious attempts to assassinate De Gaulle. The movement was led by Salan, one of the four generals involved in the 1961 Algiers insurrection, and included many ex-officers. In 1962 Salan and Gen. Jouhaud were arrested and tried, but the OAS continued; many criticized the government for not acting more vigorously against it. In Algeria the OAS sought to create chaos in the last months of French rule and to carry out a 'scorched earth' policy, the result of which was to hasten the departure of the European population.

ORGANIZATION FOR ECONOMIC CO-OPERATION AND DEVELOPMENT, inter-governmental organization established in 1961 in succession to OEEC. Its membership of 21 nations comprised the industrialized market economy of North America, Europe, and the Far East and its members were: Austria, Belgium, Britain, Canada, Denmark, France, the German Federal Republic, Greece, Iceland, Ireland, Italy, Japan, Luxemburg, the Netherlands, Norway, Portugal, Spain, Sweden, Switzerland, Turkey, and the US. Member countries accounted for 19 per cent of the world's population, but 66 per cent of the world's industrial production and 90 per cent of development aid. Yugoslavia, Australia and Finland made special arrangements with OECD which enabled them to participate in some of its activities.

OECD seeks to promote economic development within member countries, to obtain the best results from aid to developing countries, and to develop trade. In the words of its official publication, it 'functions primarily as a forum for key policy officials of Member governments, as a producer of knowledge and as a workshop for building that knowledge into co-ordinated policies through a permanent exchange of views'. The organization is governed (1970) by a Council on which each member has one representative and which elects an Executive Committee.

ORGANIZATION FOR EUROPEAN ECONOMIC CO-OPERATION (OEEC), inter-governmental organization of Western European states, established to promote the renewal of trade with the assistance of Marshall Aid. The Marshall offer (June 1947) was followed by the establishment of a Committee for European Economic Co-operation, then by the organization of the same name (1948). The organization was successful in negotiating the removal of quantitative restrictions on trade and facilitating multilateral growth by establishing a European Payments Union, with US dollar support. It did not attempt to co-ordinate investment programmes in the countries receiving Marshall Aid. Nor—partly because of British opposition—did it grow into a close form of European union, as some had hoped. On the completion of its task of promoting Western European recovery, it was wound up in 1961 and succeeded by the somewhat different Organization for Economic Co-operation and Development.

ORGANIZATION OF AFRICAN UNITY (OAU), established in May 1963 by 31 states. By 1970 the number had risen to over 40. The organization's permanent headquarters are at Addis Ababa, Ethiopia. Its five principal aims are: to promote the unity and solidarity of African states; co-ordinate and intensify their co-operation; defend their sovereignty, territorial integrity, and independence; end colonialism in Africa; and promote international co-operation. Member states enjoy equal rights and undertake equal duties. The OAU operates through the Assembly of Heads of State and Government; a Council of Ministers; a General Secretariat; and the Commission of Mediation, Conciliation, and Arbitration, which seeks to settle disputes among member states peacefully. The 1963 Charter envisaged the establishment of the following commissions: Economic and Social; Educational and Cultural; Health, Sanitation, and Nutrition; Defence; Scientific; and Technical and Research.

ORGANIZATION OF AMERICAN STATES (OAS), established in 1948, is a regional organization within the United Nations set up at the ninth international conference of American nations held in Bogota (1948). Its aims are defined as mutual economic, social, and military aid, and the settling of regional disputes among the member nations. It has a permanent council which meets in Washington, DC. Its most important subordinate organization is the Pan-American Union, also centred in Washington, DC, which acts as its administrative structure and is an agency for cultural exchange.

The OAS has attempted, with varying success, to settle several American international disputes. Boundary disputes between Nicaragua and Honduras were referred to the International Court of Justice at The Hague and the decisions implemented peacefully by the OAS. The organization's anti-Cuban attitude, however, has resulted in disputes, and some critics have claimed that during the Dominican crisis of 1965 the OAS became little more than an arm of the US government.

ORGANIZATION OF CENTRAL AMERICAN STATES (ODECA), established in 1951, comprises Guatemala, El Salvador, Honduras, Nicaragua, and Costa Rica. Its aim was not political, but to develop a common market. It began with a meeting in San Salvador of the foreign ministers of the five states concerned, who foresaw consultations to maintain peace among the states, and to uphold non-intervention, judicial equality, and the principles of the United Nations. Its formal meetings began a few years later and by 1961 had had substantial success in creating a Central American common market. Later, a more formal political and judicial structure emerged; this was followed by the equalization of tariffs on many goods traded among the members, and the creation of a Central American Bank.

ORGAZ Y YOLDI, LUIS (1881–1946), Spanish soldier, of strong monarchist sympathies, who was one of the most persistent military plotters of the Second Republic. In 1931 he was involved in the founding of the *Círculo Monárquico*, a centre of monarchist opposition to the republic, and of the *Unión Militar Española*, the counter-revolutionary group in the army, and in 1936 was prominent in the preparations for a military rising. Although exiled by the Republican government to the Canary Islands, with Franco, he was able to help in the taking of Las Palmas on the first day of the rising. While the rebel army invaded Spain, Orgaz was left as commander in Morocco. At the beginning of 1937 he was made supreme commander of the Madrid front and commanded the attacks on the Corunna and Valencia roads. After his failure to take Madrid, he was relegated to organizing military academies for officers. Towards the end of the war he was given command of the army of the Levant.

ORIBE, MANUEL (c. 1796–1857), Uruguayan patriot and politician, one of Lavalleja's '33 immortals' of 1825. After Uruguayan independence (1828), he became leader of the *blanco* faction, which was friendly towards and aided by Rosas of Argentina. Oribe's forces besieged Montevideo (1843–52), but failed to capture it.

ORIENTALIZING POTTERY, Greek painted pottery of the 7th cent. BC. Its decoration is characterized by abundant eastern motifs, *eg*, lions, sphinxes, and floral friezes. It was most common at Corinth and constitutes probably the clearest evidence for oriental influence in 7th-cent. Greece.

ORIGEN (c. AD 185–254), scholar, teacher, and writer of the early Church, the first Christian theologian to produce a full interpretation of the Christian faith set against the widest intellectual framework. He was head of the Catechetical School in Alexandria when only 18 years of age, his advice and help being constantly sought by distant Churches, although some of his views were controversial. Following his ordination in Palestine, Origen was expelled from Alexandria (c. 230–1), and moved to Caesarea, where he continued his work. He is said to have dictated 6000 books, most of which were biblical commentaries or homilies and made pioneer investigations of the text of the Bible, which he asserted had both a 'bodily' and a hidden 'spiritual' meaning. The *Hexapla*, an edition of the Old Testament in six columns, took him 25 years to complete.

ORISSA, state of the republic of India, lying between Bengal and Andhra Pradesh. It has always been a stronghold of Hinduism. Its capital, Bhubaneshwar, is renowned for its temples; thousands of pilgrims also visit the temple of Jaganath at Puri. Orissa formed part of the ancient kingdom of Kalinga, conquered by Asoka (c. 255 BC). Its early history is confused before the Muslim penetration of southern India. In the 14th cent. it was included in Muhammad bin Tughluq's province of Jajnagar; under Akbar it was administered as part of Bengal. With the break-up of the Mughal empire it came under Maratha rule, but was conquered by the British (1803). It did not become a separate province until 1936).

ORKHAN (reg. 1326–62), Ottoman Beg, whose reign witnessed the surrender to the Ottomans of Nikaea (1331) and Nikomedia (1337), and the acquisition (1335–6) of the Turkish state of Karasu (ancient Mysia). Ottoman forces often took service with the warring factions in the Balkan lands and in 1354 occupied Gallipoli—an event which marked the beginning of an era of conquest for the Ottomans in south-east Europe, their advance gaining its full momentum in the reign of Orkhan's successor, Murad I.

ORKNEYS, ISLANDS OF THE, 70 islands off the north-east Scottish coast. Norse settlement, replacing earlier Irish and Pictish settlements, began in the second half of the 8th cent., but appears to have been much intensified at about the same time as the settlement of Iceland in the 9th cent. In the Orkneys, though not in Iceland, nor in the Shetlands and the Faroes, a great dynasty of earls was founded (c. 900), and the islands enjoyed considerable cultural and political independence from Norway. In the 10th and 11th cents the earl's court became an important cultural centre. In 1383 the islands came under the Danish Crown, together with Iceland, through the union of Norway and Denmark. In 1468–9 they were ceded to the Scottish Crown as pledge for a dowry, which was never paid, and remained Scottish possessions thereafter.

ORKOYOT, title of politico-religious leader of Nandi people in western Kenya. The institution evolved in the 19th cent., and facilitated the expansion and coherence of the Nandi.

ORLANDO, VITTORIO EMMANUELE (1860–1952), Italian politician and prime minister of Italy (1917–19), who had the task of restoring Italian morale after the defeat at Caporetto— a time of acute internal disharmony. He appointed Diaz as commander-in-chief instead of Cadorna and secured Allied divisions to assist the military effort against Austria. Meanwhile, Nitti made the first systematic attempt to tackle the economic and social problems of the war. Orlando, who governed well, was less decisive in his leadership after the armistice. He left the Versailles conference (1919) because Italy's inflated territorial demands were unacceptable to President Wilson, but returned on finding that the Allies were continuing negotiations without him. This blow to Italy's pride blinded many Italians to the considerable gains achieved as a result of the war.

ORLÉANS, HENRIETTA, Duchess of (1644–70), youngest sister of King Charles II of England, who was married to Louis XIV's younger brother and took a leading part, shortly before her death, in the secret negotiations with her brother that resulted in the Anglo-French treaty of Dover (June 1670).

ORLÉANS, GASTON JEAN BAPTISTE DE FRANCE, Duke of (1608–60), third son of Henry IV and Marie de' Medici and brother of Louis XIII of France, created Duke of Orléans (1626). He married, first, Marie de Bourbon, heiress of the Montpensier family (d. 1627), by whom he had one daughter, Marie-Louise of Orléans (1627–93), known as *La Grande Mademoiselle*. By his second wife, Marguerite of Lorraine, sister of Duke Charles, whom he married secretly in 1632, he had five more daughters. Relations between Gaston and Louis XIII were vitiated by jealousy and he entered into all the plots to overthrow Louis's minister, Richelieu, though his royal blood protected him from the punishment meted out to his associates, *eg*, Chalais (1626), Montmorency (1632), and Cinq Mars (1642). Deprived of the likelihood of the French succession by the birth of Louis XIV (1638), he became lieutenant-general of the kingdom during Louis's minority (1643–51), acquitting himself well against Spain in the Low Countries. He was deeply involved in the *Frondes* (1648–52), and retired into voluntary exile on his Loire estates (1652).

ORLÉANS, PHILIP (I) OF FRANCE, Duke of Orléans (1640–1701), second son of Louis XIII of France and Anne of Austria and brother of Louis XIV, usually known as Monsieur. He commanded the French forces in the Low Countries against the Dutch, defeating William of Orange at the battle of Monte Cassel (1677).

ORLÉANS, PHILIP (II) OF FRANCE, Duke of Chartres and of (1674–1723), son of Philip I of Orléans and his second wife, Elizabeth-Charlotte, princess palatine, who became regent of France on the death of Louis XIV (1 Sept. 1715)

for the duration of Louis XV's minority (1715–23). He fought first in Italy during the War of the Spanish Succession, where he was over-ruled by Marsin at the disastrous battle of Turin (1706), and later commanded the French forces in Spain (1707–8). He had Louis XIV's will set aside by making a bargain with the *parlement* of Paris and assumed the position of sole regent for the five-year-old Louis XV (1715). His own claim to the French succession led him to take action against Spain's chief minister, Alberoni, *eg*, over the Cellamare plot (1718), and French forces successfully invaded northern Spain (1719), forcing the dismissal of Alberoni. Spain came to terms, Philip V repeating his renunciation of the French succession (1720). Meanwhile, through the agency of his foreign minister, Dubois, Orléans overcame 40 years of Anglo-French and Franco-Dutch hostility by the Triple Alliance (1717). Thus he did much to reduce the universal European hatred of France, engendered by Louis XIV's wars, and contributed significantly to the creation of a system of collective security.

Orléans's name has been associated with the economic collapse of the Mississippi Co. and his patronage of John Law has earned him much criticism. Conscious of the economic bankruptcy of France, the heritage of the War of the Spanish Succession, he hoped to stimulate overseas trade and develop France's possessions in the New World. His support for Law's company and for his advanced ideas on credit indicated his flexible attitude towards monetary problems. Likewise, although his experiment in conciliar government, the *Polysynodie*, had to be abandoned (1718), this attempt to harness the political talents of the *noblesse d'épee* and *robe* avoided a repetition of the *Fronde* or the civil conflicts of Catherine and Marie de' Medici's regencies.

Dom Leclercq, *Histoire de la Régence* (Paris, 1921).   MKS

ORLÉANS, LOUIS PHILIPPE JOSEPH D' (1747–93), French Prince and father of King Louis Philippe, who was known as 'Philippe Égalité' because of his democratic views during the French Revolution. He was one of the liberal aristocrats who favoured constitutional reform and ultimately sided with the republican revolutionaries. In 1789 he became a member of the National Assembly and turned the gardens of the Palais Royal into a public pleasure gound, which became a centre for political agitators, *eg*, the Jacobin, Brissot; here, too, plots to replace Louis XVI by Orléans may have been hatched. Orleanist agitators contributed to the widespread disorders of 1789, *eg*, the march on Versailles. Louis Philippe joined the Mountain Party in the national Convention, and voted in favour of Louis XVI's death (Jan. 1793). He was himself guillotined in 1793.

ORLÉANS, FAMILY OF, in France, name of the cadet branch of the Valois and Bourbon dynasties. There were four distinct houses. The first holder of the title of Duke of Orléans was Philippe, fifth son of Philip VI of Valois (1336–75), who received it in 1344. On his death without heirs the title lapsed until Louis I of Valois (1372–1407), second son of Charles V, was made duke in 1392. His eldest son, Charles (1391–1465), the poet-courtier, was created duke in 1407 and was the father of Louis XII of France. Louis XII's grandson, the third son of Francis I, Charles (1522–45), was created Duke of Orléans in 1536 and commanded the French armies in the Low Countries (1542–4). The third line of Orléans sprang from Gaston Jean Baptiste (1608–60), third son of Henry IV and Marie de' Medici, who received the title in 1626; though he had daughters he had no sons to succeed him. The younger brother of Louis XIV, Philip (1640–1701), was therefore created Duke of Orléans on Gaston's death in 1660 and became the founder of the present house of Orléans. He was succeeded by his son Philip II (1674–1723), the regent of France during Louis XV's minority, whence the title passed to Louis, Philip II's son (1703–82), and the latter's son, Louis Philippe, nicknamed 'Égalité' (1747–93), who lost his life in the French Revolution (1789). His eldest son, Louis Philippe (1773–1850), was created Duke of Orléans in 1793 and was elected King of the French in 1830. The last holder of the title was Louis Philippe's son, Ferdinand Philip Louis (1810–42), who was killed accidentally before his father's death.

ORLEANS, HUGH OF (*c.* 1095–1160), French poet, who was the archetype of the Goliard or wandering scholar and has been identified with the anonymous Archpoet.

ORLÉANS, SIEGE OF (1429), incident which helped Joan of Arc to win her first success against the English. After withstanding a six-month siege, Orléans was relieved by a force led by Dunois, but inspired by Joan. This destroyed the reputation of the English for invincibility and became a turning point in the Anglo–French war. Joan's reputation as a worker of miracles was established and she was able to assure the coronation of Charles VII as King of France.

ORLETON, ADAM (d. 1347), English bishop, who was one of the leading opponents of Edward II and supported, first, Thomas of Lancaster and then Roger Mortimer. After fleeing to France (1324), he returned to England with Isabella and Mortimer and played a leading part in the deposition of Edward. He was successively Bp of Hereford (1317), Worcester (1327), and Winchester (1333).

ORLOV, ALEKSEI FEDOROVICH, PRINCE (1786–1861), Russian diplomat, who was head of the third department of Imperial Chancery (Nicholas I's security police) (1844–56). He was sent abroad on several important missions and was chairman of the Secret Committee on Emancipation (1856).

ORME, ROBERT (1728–1801), British historian and East India Co.'s servant, who went to Calcutta (1742) and was appointed a member of the Madras Council (1754–8). He was historiographer to the company (1769–1801). His *History of the Military Transactions of the British Nation in Indostan from the year 1745* (1763) is a standard work.

ORMONDE, JAMES BUTLER, 1st Duke of (1610–88), Irish soldier, who dominated Anglo-Irish politics from 1640. Although belonging to a Roman Catholic family, he was brought up a Protestant, having been made a royal ward (1619), and placed in the household of George Abbot, Abp of Canterbury. In 1640 he was appointed commander-in-chief of the Irish army. In the confused Irish Rebellion (1641–9) he led the Protestants against the Catholics and the Royalists against the Parliamentarians. The success of the Irish Confederacy forced him to conclude both the 'Cessation' (1643), by which the greater part of Ireland was surrendered to the Catholics, and the treaty (1646), which granted religious concessions and removed grievances. This 'Ormonde Peace' was denounced by the papal nuncio, Rinuccini, whose forces attacked Dublin. Ormonde thereupon signed a treaty with the English parliament (1647), surrendering Dublin. He then fled to France. In Sept. 1648 he returned to Ireland to try to unite all the factions for the king, and concluded 'the 2nd Ormonde Peace' (1649) guaranteeing freedom of religion. After Oliver Cromwell's invasion of Ireland, Ormonde returned to France (1650), where he lived (except for a secret mission to England in 1658) at Charles II's court-in-exile until the Restoration (1660). He was active in the negotiations preceding the Restoration, and afterwards was appointed a commissioner of the treasury and of the navy. In 1661 he was created a duke in the Irish peerage (and in 1682 in the English peerage). As lord lieutenant of Ireland (1662–9) he ruled in the interest of the country, but his somewhat irresponsible actions led to his dismissal after he had been threatened with impeachment by the Duke of Buckingham. He was later restored to

favour (1677) and reappointed lord lieutenant, but was replaced on James II's accession (1685).

W. Burghclere, *The Life of James, First Duke of Ormonde* (London, 1912).
T. Carte, *The Life of James, Duke of Ormonde* (Oxford, 1851).
CJ

ORMONDE, JAMES BUTLER, 2nd Duke of (1665-1745), Irish soldier, who succeeded his father as Earl of Ossory (1680), and served in the royal army against the Duke of Monmouth (1685). In 1688 he succeeded his grandfather as duke and joined William III against James II. He later served in William's army in Ireland and on the continent. He served Queen Anne as lord lieutenant of Ireland (1703–7, 1710–13), and in 1711 replaced the dismissed Duke of Marlborough as captain-general, and commanded in the Flanders campaign in the War of the Spanish Succession. He was on the point of taking office under Viscount Bolingbroke when Queen Anne died. Though he had been in touch with the Jacobite Duke of Berwick, he accepted George I's accession, but was deprived of the captain-generalship. His impeachment was moved in parliament on grounds of treason (1715), and he fled to France. He commanded two abortive attempts to invade Britain (1715, 1719), and finally settled in Spain.

ORMONDE PEACE (1646), between the Irish Catholic Confederacy and the Royalist forces in Ireland under James Butler, Marquis of Ormonde. Charles I's defeat at Naseby (July 1645) made him dependent on Irish aid, and he ordered his viceroy in Ireland to offer peace to the Confederacy. An agreement was reached in March, but was not published until July 1646. By it the Confederates offered Charles 10,000 men, while the king made concessions, *eg*, abolition of the court of wards, substitution of an oath of allegiance for the oath of supremacy, the admission of Catholics to all civil and military offices, and the removal of disabilities on Catholic education. These moderate terms were a triumph for Ormonde and were welcomed by a large part of the Confederacy. However, the papal nuncio, Rinuccini, denounced them and excommunicated those who favoured peace. The nuncio was supported by Owen Roe O'Neill, the victor of Benburb, who forced the assembly of the Confederacy to reject the peace (Feb. 1647). A similar peace offered by Ormonde was accepted in Jan. 1649.

ORNANO, MARSHALS D', Corsican soldiers in French service. Alphonse d'Ornano (1548–1603) served first Charles IX and then Henry IV, being created a marshal of France (1595) and governor of Guyenne. His son, Jean Baptiste (1581–1626), was also a marshal and fought with Henry IV in the Savoyard War (1600–1). He was later a close associate of Gaston of Orléans and was imprisoned by Richelieu on suspicion of conspiracy with Gaston (1625).

ORODES II (*reg. c.* 57–37 BC), Arsacid King of Iran, during whose reign the Parthians and Romans first came into conflict, when the Roman forces under Crassus were defeated by the Parthians at Carrhae (53). The Parthians conquered most of Asia Minor, Syria, and Palestine (40) but were soon forced to withdraw. Orodes was murdered.

OROMPOTO (*fl.* 16th cent.), Alafin of the Igboho period of Oyo history, who established Oyo independence of the Ibariba of Borgu and prepared the way for a return to Old Oyo. He was a great warrior and founder of the cavalry force which enabled the Oyo to create their famous empire.

OROPESA, MANUEL JOAQUIN ALVAREZ DE TOLEDO Y PORTUGAL, Count of (1642–1707), Spanish politician who was (1685–91) the pro-Austrian first minister of Charles II. He made determined efforts to check Spain's economic decline by reducing taxation and government spending, but was dismissed because of pressure by vested interests (24 June 1691). He was recalled briefly in 1697, but was again dismissed and exiled (1699) through pro-French pressure.

ORRERY, ROGER BOYLE, 1st Earl of (Irish) (1621–79), Irish soldier, politician, and author who fought in the Irish Rebellion (1641–9), first under Lord Inchiquin and then, when the latter declared for King Charles I, under Lord Lisle. He was made president of Munster by the English parliament (1648). Though he intrigued with Charles II (1649), he was soon in Oliver Cromwell's favour, and was appointed lieutenant-general in charge of the Irish ordinance (1651), a member of Cromwell's council (1653), and president of the Scottish council of state (1655–6). He led the civilian Cromwellian party in the 1656–8 parliament, and was behind the offer of the Crown to Cromwell. In 1658 he was a member of Cromwell's Upper House, and in 1659 of Richard Cromwell's council. Having secured Munster for the Royalists (Dec. 1659), he was appointed commissioner for Irish affairs, created Earl of Orrery, and lord president of Munster (1660). During this time he wrote several rhymed, heroic dramas and prose comedies. He attacked the government of Ormonde and on his downfall (1669) hoped to become lord lieutenant. Instead, he was impeached for treason (Nov. 1669) but not sentenced. He lost his Irish presidential powers (1672) when the Earl of Essex suppressed the provincial presidencies, and he never held office again.

ORRERY, CHARLES BOYLE, 4th Earl of (Irish) (1676–1731), soldier and writer, a grandson of Roger Boyle, 1st Earl of Orrery, who succeeded his brother in 1703. He became involved in the dispute over the antiquity of Phalaris, of which he published a new edition in which he defended Bentley. The dispute inspired Swift's *Battle of the Books.* Politically he was a strong adherent of the Tories. Orrery served in the battle of Malplaquet (1709), and in 1711 he was an envoy in Flanders and took part in the negotiations preceding the treaty of Utrecht.

ORRY FAMILY in France. Jean Orry (1652–1719) was a French banker of humble origin who was in charge of French munitions during the War of the Spanish Succession. He went to Spain to reorganize the finances for Louis XIV's grandson, Philip V (1702), but was expelled after the disgrace of his patron, Princesse des Ursins (1715), and retired to France to continue his lucrative speculations.

His son, Philibert (1689–1747), Comte de Vignory, was controller-general of finances under Louis XV (1730–46) and a minister of state from 1736. He was also author of the decree establishing an industrial code to regulate mining in France (1744).

Another son, Jean Henri Louis (*c.* 1691–1751), was a councillor of state and *intendant* of finances. He acquired a patent giving him monopolistic rights to establish the porcelain industry at Vincennes (1738), which was later transferred to Sèvres (1756).

ORSINI, FELICE (1819–58), Italian nationalist and ex-member of Mazzini's Young Italy, who was leader of a conspiracy to assassinate Napoleon III. Three bombs thrown at Napoleon III killed several people and Orsini was arrested and sentenced to death. From prison he appealed to Napoleon to help Italian independence, and Napoleon had the letter published. Orsini later met Cavour at Plombières.

ORSINI FAMILY, noble Roman family, powerful since the 11th cent., and from which came a number of popes, including Nicholas III (*reg.* 1277–80), as well as many cardinals, papal officials, and military leaders.

ORSZA, BATTLE OF (8 Sept. 1514), victory of the Polish-Lithuanian armies under Sigismund I over Grand Duke Vassily III of Moscow, following Muscovy's seizure of the important stronghold of Smolensk. Although Sigismund was unable to recover the latter, this victory forced the Emperor Maximilian, Vassily's ally, to come to terms by the treaty of Vienna (1515).

ORTEGA Y GASSET, JOSÉ (1883–1955), Spanish philosopher and political thinker, who studied at Madrid University and in Germany (1904–8), where he was influenced by the work of Nietzsche. He returned to Madrid in 1910 as professor of metaphysics. He acquired a high reputation both in Spain and abroad as a humanist philosopher and essayist.

Philosophically, he glorified individualism; for him the individual life was of more reality than abstract truths. This led in politics to a tendency to élitism and hero-worship, which was later to be taken up by extreme right-wing groups. Ortega was always preoccupied with the problem of Spain and he sought to expose the corruptness of the Restoration political system, for which purpose he founded the impartial and liberal paper *El Sol* (1917) and the review, *Revista De Occidente* (1923). His best-known work, *España Invertebrada* (1921), analysed the divisive nature of national forces. In general, his work created widespread intellectual discontent with the existing state of affairs in Spain. In 1931 he joined the Movement in the Service of the Republic and wrote an article predicting the end of the monarchy—'Delenda Est Monarquia'. To a large extent, he had created the climate of opinion which made the Second Republic acceptable. Yet he himself was not partisan and became disappointed with the factionalism of the republic.

In 1936 he went into voluntary exile, dividing his time between Europe and Argentina until 1945. He founded the Instituto de Humanidades in Madrid in 1948.

ORTELIUS, ABRAHAM (1527–98), Flemish merchant and geographer, whose world atlas, *Theatrum Orbis Terrarum* (1570), achieved great fame.

ORWELL, GEORGE (pseudonym of Eric Blair) (1903–50), British writer, whose experiences in the Indian police and studies of middle- and working-class life influenced much of his work. His *The Road to Wigan Pier* (1938) was a shrewd and sympathetic tribute to the British working class. Service in the Spanish Civil War fighting for the Trotskyite POUM led to his *Homage to Catalonia* (1938). His two most celebrated works were *Animal Farm* (1944), a satire upon the Soviet Union, and *1984* (1949), a general attack upon all forms of modern society.

OSAGE INDIANS, American Siouan tribe, first noted by the French explorer Marquette (1673) on the Osage river in MO, and later found by Lewis and Clarke (1802) in AR. They were constantly involved in inter-tribal wars, and helped the French to defeat the Fox (1714) at Detroit. The Osage began ceding their lands in 1808 and were given a reservation in OK (1870), where they later received land allotments (1906) and were made citizens.

OSBORNE JUDGMENT (1909), in Britain, prohibited the collection of a compulsory levy from trade unionists for political purposes, and thus deprived the Parliamentary Labour Party of vital financial support. After 1906 the Amalgamated Society of Railway Servants collected 1s 1d annually from each member, to establish a fighting fund for the return of railwaymen to parliament and to maintain them there. W. V. Osborne, secretary of the society's Walthamstow branch, obtained an injunction against the society and members of other unions followed suit; as a result 16 MPs lost the salaries paid to them by their unions. Judges' fears of the coercion of union minorities, and of interference with MPs' freedom and between them and their constituents, failed to impress trade unionists, smarting under the effects of earlier legal decisions. The payment of MPs (1911), and the 1913 act legalizing political levies, subject to dissenters' right to 'contract out', eased the position of the Labour Party's finances.

OSCAR I (1799–1859), King of Sweden and Norway (*reg.* 1844–59), son of Charles XIV John (Bernadotte). He sought to placate his Norwegian subjects by various concessions, *eg*, a half-share in the union coat of arms, and contemplated, in the year of revolutions (1848), a Scandinavian unity. There was British and French backing for the proposal as a counter-weight to Russian influence in the Baltic, but he died with nothing accomplished.

OSCAR II (1829–1907), King of Sweden and Norway (*reg.* 1872–1905), King of Sweden (*reg.* 1872–1907), whose reign began at a time when the Norwegian claims to total inde-pendence were being strongly pursued. By 1884 the king was forced to accept the principle of responsible government in Norway. It was a concession that proved insufficient and in 1905 the Norwegians dissolved the union, declaring that Oscar had ceased to be their ruler. Throughout his reign he was in sympathy with Germany's European policies.

OSCEOLA (1803–38), American Indian leader, sometimes called Powell. Osceola was not a Seminole chief by descent, but won his place by his ability in the First Seminole War (1835). In the Second Seminole War (1835–42) he ambushed and killed a US Indian agent, Wiley Thompson, and kept up a fight with US troops in FL.

OSEBERG, on the west coast of the Oslo-fiord in Norway, site of the most important of all Scandinavian ship-burials dating from the mid-9th cent. Although plundered in anti-quity, it contains a great variety of goods of the greatest beauty and artistic importance. The grave appears to be that of a queen. With her were buried another woman, 14 horses, three dogs, and an ox.

OSEI BONSU (*reg.* 1801–24), Asantehene (ruler) of the Ashanti empire, who completed constitutional reforms initiated by Osei Kwadwo, strengthened the powers of the kingship at the expense of hereditary nobles and provincial rulers, and improved the civil service. He crushed rebellions in Gyaman and Gonja, defeating the coastal Fante and their Assin allies in 1898, and the Akwapem in 1811–14. He thus safeguarded Ashanti trade and trade routes. In 1823–4 Osei Bonsu fought and defeated Wassaw and Denkyira, as well as a British supporting contingent.

OSEI KWADWO (*reg.* 1764–77), Asantehene (ruler) of the Ashanti empire, who undertook major constitutional reforms designed to meet the problems of a growing empire. Basic to these was the centralization of power in his own hands. He replaced the old aristocracy with men of lowly birth who were dependent on him for their advancement in the civil service, and dividing his government into departments under them. This required a reinforcement of military strength, and Osei Kwadwo established a new corps of unquestioning loyalty. His reforms proved of lasting value, and were later carried further by Osei Bonsu.

OSEI TUTU (d. *c.* 1712), founder of the Asante (Ashanti) Union of Akan clans, which gave rise to a powerful empire enclosing, during the late 18th cent. and much of the 19th cent., most of the present (1970) republic of Ghana in West Africa. This union was achieved in about 1695, when Osei Tutu, aided by a remarkable priest of the Akan, *Okomfo* Anokye, won the acceptance of his kingship by a number of leading Akan chiefs living in the gold-producing region of what is now central Ghana. The symbol of this acceptance, and the spiritually unifying power of the union to which it led, was a Golden Stool 'brought down from the sky' by Anokye, and from then onwards held to embody the health and welfare of all the now united clans. No king could ever sit on this sacred object, but obedience to the precepts for which it stood—above all, the legitimacy of the Asante Union and its living rulers—was believed to ensure the success and prosperity of the whole polity.

Osei Tutu welded the fighting forces of the several united clans into a single army and set about defeating the neigh-bouring Akan state of Denkyira, to which the Asante clans were formally in tribute, as well as asserting Asante primacy in other directions. Although at first defeated, his army over-came Denkyira's in 1701, and thereby ensured its safe access to European trade with the Dutch at Elmina and the English at Cape Coast.

O'SHEA, WILLIAM HENRY (1840–1905), Irish politician, who helped to arrange the Kilmainham treaty between Parnell and Gladstone (1882). His decision to bring a divorce suit against his wife, Katharine, in 1890, citing Parnell as co-respondent, precipitated the crisis in the Home Rule party's leadership.

OSIANDER, ANDREAS (1498–1552), German Protestant reformer, who (1522–48) established the Zwinglian theology in Nuremberg, the first free city in Germany with an official Protestant church. In 1549 Osiander left his pastor's post there to seek the patronage of a convert, Duke Albert of Prussia, and became a preacher and professor of theology in Königsberg.

OSMAN (d. 1326), founder (*c.* 1300) of the Ottoman *beglik* in north-west Asia Minor. The earlier years of his reign witnessed a gradual expansion of the Ottoman state in the area around Bursa, which fell after a long blockade in 1326.

OSMAN II (*reg.* 1618–22), Ottoman Sultan, whose reign saw the Ottoman empire engaged in a brief war against Poland. In 1620 a Polish force was defeated at Cecora near Iaşi (Jassy) in Moldavia. A later campaign (1621) against the fortress of Khotin was unsuccessful. Osman II lost his life in the course of a violent rebellion among the troops of the imperial household.

OSMAN PASHA, ÖZDEMIR-OGHLU (d. 1585), Ottoman soldier and Grand Vizier, who served as *beglerbeg* of Habeş (ie, of Massawa and Suakin on the western coast of the Red Sea) and also had a large share in the suppression of a revolt which threw the Yemen into confusion (1567–70). The most brilliant campaigns of his life came in the Ottoman–Persian conflict (1578–90). He won the battle of Çildir, which enabled the Ottomans to penetrate into Georgia, and later he secured access to Shirvan. He reduced Shirvan and Daghistan to Ottoman obedience, and using Derbend, on the western shore of the Caspian Sea, as his base, maintained a skilful defence against superior forces (1578–83). On the arrival of reinforce-ments he routed the Persians in a battle on the Samur river, a triumph which brought Daghistan and Shirvan under Otto-man control (1583). He then dealt with a revolt of the Tatars in the Crimea and returned to Istanbul, where Sultan Murad III made him grand vizier in recompense for his services. In 1585 he broke through into Azerbayjan in the face of a stubborn Persian resistance, occupied Tabriz, but died during the course of a withdrawal into Asia Minor.

OSMENA, SERGIO (1878–1961), Philippine politician, vice-president, and (later) president of the Philippine Common-wealth inaugurated in 1935. In 1907 he sat in the Philippine National Assembly and was unanimously elected as its speaker. He led the Nacionalista Party from then until 1922, when he gave place to Quezon. Osmena served under Quezon in the Commonwealth government (1935–41), and joined him in exile in Washington, DC, during the Japanese occupa-tion (1941–4). He succeeded to the presidency on Quezon's death (Aug. 1944). On returning to the Philippines in Nov. 1944, Osmena faced both social and economic problems caused by the Second World War, controversy over collabora-tion, and also dissent within his party. He lost the presidency to Roxas in the 1946 election.

OSMUND, Saint (d. 1099), nephew of William I and his chaplain and chancellor. He was Bp of Salisbury, built the cathedral at Old Sarum, introduced a prebendal system, and drew up an Ordinal and Consuetudinary for his diocese. It was known as the *Use of Sarum* and was adopted in many other English cathedrals.

OSNABRÜCK, TREATY OF (1648), peace settlement concluded between the Emperor Ferdinand III and Sweden and their respective allies, which was part of the general peace of Westphalia that ended the Thirty Years War. The treaty was the result of the congress held at the Westphalian town of Osnabrück (1642–8), where the imperial and Swedish diplomats negotiated while fighting continued. Denmark originally agreed to mediate the treaty, but the open hostility between that country and Sweden (1643–5) rendered this impossible. Axel Oxenstierna and Adler Salvius won for Sweden the secularized bishoprics of Bremen and Verden, the port of Wismar, West Pomerania and its offshore islands, and Stettin, thus giving the Swedes control of the Oder, Weser, and Elbe rivers. The sovereignty of the states of the empire was recognized, and their right of free assembly to conduct all imperial affairs, make laws, alliances, peace treaties, wage war or raise taxes was guaranteed. The religious provisions of the treaty were an amplification of the peace of Augsburg (1555), Calvinists being given the same privileges as the Lutherans under the Augsburg Confession.

OSORIO, OSCAR (1910–   ), El Salvador soldier, politician, and president (1950–6), who seized power, formed a new constitution, and organized the new Party of Revolutionary Democratic Union (PRUD). He attempted to diversify the coffee-based economy, instituted a social security programme, and created the Salvadorean Institute for the Development of Production (INSAFOP, 1955) which formulated plans for new agricultural exports and the expansion of light industry. Radicals suffered under his rule as he banned the participation of communists in politics and co-operated with Honduras in opposing a left-wing regime in Guatemala. Radical army officers banned him from the country later, but he returned when they were ousted by fellow officers more sympathetic to the US. In 1970 he was in the background of Salvadorean politics.

OSPINA PÉREZ, MARIANO (1891–   ), Colombian politician and president of Colombia (1946–50), who was the first conservative to be elected in over 20 years. His legislative proposals were hampered by a hostile congress and his hopes for a bipartisan approach to the nation's problems came to little.

OSPINA RODRÍGUEZ, MARIANO (1805–75), Colombian politician and president of Colombia (1857–61). Although essentially a conservative, he tried to govern according to the federal and Liberal constitution of 1858. Consequently, his government faced the constant problem of how to exert central control, and provincial revolts were common.

OSSERVATORE ROMANO, Vatican daily newspaper, founded in 1861. It publishes official texts and papal speeches and acts as a moral crusader as well as a literary news informer. The papal-appointed editor usually reflects orthodox curial positions without recording dissenting opinions. Its office provides the authorized Vatican information service to the Italian press. Its period of greatest influence was between the two World Wars, when it was the only informative 'independent' paper circulating in Italy under Fascism. By 1940 it had become too anti-Nazi in its criticism. Thus Pope Pius XII was forced to curtail its political news-comment. It guides (1970) centre-right Christian Democrat action.

OSSEWA-BRANDWAG (lit. the Oxwagon Sentinel), paramilitary organization founded in 1938 to perpetuate Voor-

trekker ideals and establish 'a free, independent Christian Nationalist Republican State' in South Africa. During the Second World War it was openly pro-Nazi and anti-Semitic and its extra-parliamentary political ambitions challenged the authority of the National Party. It merged with the National Party in 1948.

OSTEND COMPANY, THE, name generally given to an association of Flemish merchants trading with the east. Its formation was the result of the transfer of the Spanish Netherlands to Austria under the treaty of Utrecht (1713). When formed (1723), despite the opposition of Britain and Holland, the company drove a prosperous trade with Bengal and China, which included extensive smuggling into Britain. The company was suspended (1727) and then suppressed (1731), as Britain's price for the recognition of Maria Theresa as the emperor's heir. But its operations continued in the emperor's name until its station at Bankibazar was taken by the Nawab of Bengal (1744), probably on Anglo-Dutch instigation. An attempted revival (1775–85) ended in bankruptcy ten years later.

OSTEND MANIFESTO (1854), declaration by the US ministers to Britain, France, and Spain that unless Spain agreed to sell Cuba, the US would be justified in seizing it. The three ministers were pro-slavery Democrats who wished to annex Cuba in order to create new slave states. Although the manifesto was repudiated by President Pierce's administration, it helped to inflame further political tensions within the US.

OSTER, HANS (1888–1945), German soldier, executed by the Nazis for resistance activities. As chief of counter-intelligence (*Abwehr*) in the German High Command, he was uniquely equipped to help the resistance. In April 1940 he warned the Dutch of the impending German invasions of the Low Countries and Scandinavia, a treasonable step, but in his opinion vital to prevent a German and European catastrophe. His warning went unheeded, however, as the Allies were suspicious both of the validity of the information and of Oster's motives for passing it on. He later participated in the preparations for Hitler's assassination and the anti-Nazi coup, using the machinery of the *Abwehr* to aid and protect members of the opposition. In 1943 his name was uncovered in an official investigation into a resistance attempt to contact the Allies through the Vatican. He was arrested after the July Plot (1944), and was shot by the SS in Flossenburg concentration camp a month before Germany's capitulation.

OSTERMANN, ANDREI IVANOVICH, Count (1687–1747), German-born Russian politician and diplomat, who served Peter I, Catherine I, Peter II, and Anna Ivanovna. In 1703 Ostermann left his native Westphalia and came to Russia, being appointed first an interpreter (1708) and then a secretary at the Russian foreign office (1710). He helped to negotiate peace with the Turks (1711) and represented Russia at the Åland peace congress (1718–21) that led to the treaty of Nystadt with Sweden, after which he was created a baron. In 1723 he concluded a treaty with Persia and became vice-president of a reorganized foreign office. Under Catherine I he was vice-chancellor (1725), a member of the supreme privy council, and president of the commission of commerce. He pursued a pro-Austrian foreign policy and concluded an alliance with Austria (1726). Tsarina Anna granted him the title of count (1730) and relied increasingly upon him, and after her death he was the virtual ruler of Russia during the short reign of Tsar Ivan V (1740–1), when he persuaded the regent, Anna Leopoldovna, to overthrow Field Marshal Münnich, his main rival. However, his own disgrace followed immediately after Elizabeth Petrovna's *coup d'état* (Nov. 1741). He was condemned to death, but was reprieved and banished to Berezov in Siberia (1742).

OSTIA, the port of ancient Rome at the mouth of the Tiber river. Though the area was controlled by Rome from the 6th cent. BC, the site was not colonized until *c.* 350. It became important as a port in the Second Punic War (218–202) and in the expanding trade of the 2nd cent. After being sacked in the Civil War of 87 and by pirates (*c.* 68), it was restored and developed under Augustus and Claudius, who built a new harbour, to which Trajan and Hadrian added in the 2nd cent. AD, marking the zenith of Ostia's fortunes. Substantial ruins of public buildings and houses remain.

OSTRACISM, political institution of democratic Athens, whereby the people voted which citizen they wished exiled by writing his name on a potsherd (*ostrakon*). Ostracism could take place only on one appointed day in the year, if sanctioned at a preliminary meeting and if sufficient votes were cast. The exile normally returned with full rights after ten years, but could be recalled early. Ostracism, said to have been devised by Cleisthenes (508 BC) to prevent 'tyranny', was first used, probably by Themistocles, to remove Hipparchus, of the pro-Persian 'tyrant' family (487), Megacles (486), and Xanthippus (485). In 483 or 482, after disputes over policy, Aristides was ostracized, leaving Themistocles to use a silver surplus for building the fleet which opposed the Persians (480). Xanthippus and Aristides were recalled in 480 and later Themistocles himself was ostracized (?471), as were two opponents of Pericles and radical democracy, Cimon (461), who returned to a position of influence (451), and Thucydides, son of Melesias (443). The last known ostracism (417 or 416) was intended to decide between Nicias and Alcibiades, but their supporters united to exile Hyperbolus. Ostracism sometimes secured a firm decision on policy when Athens needed one, but could also frustrate democracy by depriving opposition of its recognized leaders. Similar systems existed at Syracuse after the early 'tyrants' (466) and at Argos.

OSTROGOTHS (East Goths), one of the Germanic tribes expelled from southern Russia by the Huns in the late 4th cent. After the collapse of the Hunnish empire in 454 they settled south of the Danube. Theodoric, one of their chieftains, after spending his youth as a hostage at Constantinople, unified the Ostrogothic groups in the Balkans and was encouraged by the Byzantine government to invade Italy, which by 493 he had conquered. He reigned until 526, always recognizing the superiority of the Byzantine emperors, and tried to maintain a political balance by appointing Romans to civilian offices and restricting Ostrogoths to the army. Justinian I determined to destroy the Ostrogothic kingdom ruled by Theodoric's less masterful successors and by 552 the Byzantine conquest was completed. By destroying the Ostrogoths, Justinian unwittingly facilitated the invasion of Italy by the more savage Lombards, who moved into Italy three years after Justinian's death (568).

OSTROGS in Russia, fortified settlements established at key points along river routes and portages as the Russians penetrated the hinterland of Siberia (16th–18th cents).

O'SULLIVAN, JOHN LOUIS (1813–95), US journalist and diplomat, who founded *The United States Magazine and Democratic Review* (1837), to provide a mouthpiece for original work of a Democratic outlook. Under O'Sullivan's editorship (to 1846) it attracted the best and liveliest writers of the day. He was an ardent nationalist who advocated territorial expansion and is generally credited as originator of the phrase 'manifest destiny' (1845). In 1849 he gave financial backing to Lopez's filibustering expeditions against Cuba, to his own loss and detriment. After serving as US minister to Portugal (1854–8), he continued to live in Europe and during the Civil War gave external assistance to the Southern cause.

OSUNA, PEDRO TELLEZ GIRON, Duke of (1579–1624), Spanish politician and sailor, who was viceroy of Sicily (1611–16) and of Naples (1616–20). He was constantly involved in intrigues and after being recalled in 1620 was confined to prison on the orders of Philip IV's ministers, Olivares and Zuniga.

OSWALD (*reg.* 634–41), King of Northumbria, who defeated the Welsh army which had slain Edwin of Northumbria. He established himself as overlord (*bretwalda*) of the southern English kingdoms. He had been in exile among the Scots and invited missionaries from Iona to convert Northumbria. He was slain in battle by Penda of Mercia.

OSWALD (d. 992), Dane who became Bp of Worcester in 961 and Abp of York in 972. He studied regular discipline at the reformed centre of Fleury. In England he supported the Benedictine monastic reform movement, restoring the fenland monastery of Ramsey, and revived monasticism in the diocese of Worcester, but failed to reintroduce Benedictinism into Northumbria.

OSWALD, LEE HARVEY (1939–63), former US marine who was accused of assassinating President John F. Kennedy, a charge he denied. He was born in New Orleans, LA, and spent four years in the USSR (1959–62), where he tried unsuccessfully to become a Soviet citizen. He was arrested on 22 Nov. 1963, and was himself shot by Jack Ruby, a local night-club owner, while in police custody in Dallas. The Warren Commission's report (27 Sept. 1964) proclaimed Oswald as the man who fired the shot that killed the president.

OSWIU (612–70), King of Northumbria (*reg.* 642–70), brother of King Oswald, killed by Penda of Mercia in 641. He himself defeated and killed Penda in 655 or 656, and became for a time the overlord of the other English kingdoms. At the Synod of Whitby in 664 Oswiu supported the Roman party in the Northumbrian Church, thus contributing to the subsequent prevalence in England of the Roman and not the Celtic Church usages.

OTAGO, settlement and province in NZ, founded as a Free Church of Scotland colony. The first group of emigrants arrived in 1848. The Otago block of 400,000 acres (1620 sq. kms) was to be sold in 60¼-acres (244,000 sq. metres) sections at £2 an acre, to form a concentrated 'Wakefield' settlement. William Cargill and Thomas Burns, the colony's leaders, failed in their aim to establish an exclusive Free Church settlement, but two-thirds of the first group were Presbyterians. The struggling province (1853) was economically transformed by the gold rushes of the 1860s, but retained most of its social characteristics. Later it became NZ's leading province in terms of population (1870–80).

OTBERT (d. 1119), bishop of Liège, who was an imperialist during the Investiture contest, consistently supporting the Emperor Henry IV. When Henry abdicated Otbert found a refuge in Liège. He created the great principality of the bishops of Liège.

OTHO, MARCUS SALVIUS (AD 32–69), Roman Emperor (*reg.* 69), who was once a friend of Nero. He supported Galba's rebellion against him in 68, but, being disappointed in his hopes of being made Galba's heir, organized a coup by the praetorian guard. He ruled for only three months before being defeated by Vitellius' army.

OTIS, ELISHA GRAVES (1811–61), US manufacturer and inventor, who invented (1852) a lift (or elevator) with a safety device to prevent it from crashing if its cable broke, and later patented the steam lift (1861). His work made possible the construction of safe passenger lifts and consequently the building of skyscrapers.

OTIS, JAMES (1725–83), American lawyer who became the king's advocate-general of the vice-admiralty court in Boston

(1760), but resigned in order to represent a group of Boston merchants in a challenge of the right of the superior court to issue writs of assistance (1761). The case was taken to the MA general court (legislature) and presented the first serious challenge to the authority of the British parliament over the American colonies. Otis claimed that the writs were acts against the MA constitution and therefore not within the power of parliament. He was later a member of the Stamp Act Congress (1765), advocating colonial representation in Britain's parliament. Although a prolific pamphleteer on the constitutional rights of the colonies, he took no part in the American War of Independence.

ŌTOMO, SŌRIN (YOSHISHIGE) (1530–87), Japanese *daimyō*, who ruled a substantial fief in Kyūshū. His conversion to Christianity (1578) was a major factor in the early success of the Jesuits in Japan.

OTRANTO, town in Apulia, captured by Ottoman forces (1480) under Gedik Ahmed Pasha. The death of Mehemmed II (1481) and the conflict for the throne which ensued between his sons, Bayezid and Jem, contributed to bring the Ottoman occupation of Otranto to an end. The Turkish garrison capitulated (Sept. 1481) to Christian troops blockading the town.

OTTAMA, U (1871–1939), Burmese nationalist politician, imprisoned by the British for his opposition to constitutional reforms and incitement to violence.

OTTAWA AGREEMENTS (1932), commercial treaties between Britain and her self-governing dominions and with India, NS, and Southern Rhodesia. The agreements, reached at an economic conference held at Ottawa, Canada, provided, by means of tariffs and quotas, for a system of imperial preference between Britain and the dominions.

OTTAWA INDIANS, American Algonquian tribe first visited by Champlain (1615) in Ont. They were French and Huron allies, noted for their trade between western tribes and the French. After the Iroquois destroyed the Hurons (1648–9), they attacked the Ottawa, who fled to the western shores of Lake Michigan. Most of them settled (*c.* 1700) on the MI peninsula, on Manitoulin island, and along Lake Erie, where they fought in Indian wars up to the end of the War of 1812. The chief, Pontiac, who led a war in the Detroit area (1763), was an Ottawa. By 1833, the Ottawa had ceded all their lands along Lake Michigan and moved to KS and OK. Some remained in MI and the Canadian Ottawa stayed on Manitoulin and Cockburn islands.

OTTERBURN, BATTLE OF (5 Aug. 1388), in Northumberland. The Scots defeated the English under Henry Percy (Hotspur). This led Richard II of England to seek a truce with France, Scotland's ally, thus ending the hostilities for the rest of his reign.

OTTO I (*reg.* 936–73), German King and effective creator of the powerful German kingship which dominated central Europe from the 10th to the 12th cents. In essentials this consisted of an adaptation of the Frankish system of government of Charlemagne and his 9th-cent. successors to the special circumstances of Germany. There was the same reliance on bishops, who were used as royal agents and whose great wealth was controlled: this in turn necessitated the control of all appointments of bishops and abbots. Counts were treated as royal officials, appointed and freely transferred by the king. Through bishops and counts Otto undermined the power of the dukes controlling the great tribal duchies, some of which were resumed into his own hands. In those that remained special counts palatine exercised the royal jurisdiction. Otto, like his father, King Henry I (*reg.* 919–36), was especially preoccupied with the ruthless raiding of the pagan Hungarians. Henry had countered this

by constructing elaborate frontier fortifications. Otto extended this network, but solved the problem by defeating the Magyars in 955 on the Lech river. Thereafter they ceased to raid Germany. In the west, Otto exercised a sort of protectorate over France, acting as an effective arbitrator in French conflicts. As a descendant of former margraves of the Saxon march he had a particularly powerful position on Germany's eastern border, where he strongly encouraged missionary activity among the heathen Slavs. German expansion east of the Elbe made great strides, though it suffered setbacks after Otto's death. Further to the east the newly emerging Slavonic states of Poland and Bohemia paid tribute to Otto. He was compelled to intervene in Italy to discourage Italian support for German malcontents. In 962 he was crowned emperor at Rome, thus linking the imperial title with German kingship. In the last decade of his reign he effectively controlled northern and central Italy and in 966 even replaced an unsatisfactory pope (John XII) by his own nominee. His successors were lesser personalities and less formidable military leaders, so that some of Otto's conquests were lost, but Germany remained the greatest European power.   MH

OTTO II (955–83), Emperor (*reg.* 973–83), son of Otto the Great, who continued his father's policy of relying heavily on the resources of the German Church. His schemes of Italian expansion were defeated by the Byzantines and he died in the midst of a great Slavonic uprising east of the Elbe, which destroyed much of his dynasty's achievements in the east.

OTTO III (980–1002), Emperor (*reg.* 983–1002), who succeeded his father, Otto II, and assumed personal rule in 999. He was the first German emperor to make Rome his effective capital. This he did in collaboration with his friend Pope Sylvester II.

OTTO IV (*c.* 1175–1218), Emperor (*reg.* 1198–1215), originally the Welf anti-king to Philip of Swabia and imperial candidate of the English party among the German nobility. He was crowned at Aachen in 1198, but failed to win much acceptance until after Philip's death in 1208. Later, his Italian ambitions brought him into conflict with the pope, and the Hohenstaufen party, in alliance with France, elected Frederick II as anti-king. Otto's power was ended by the defeat of the Anglo-imperial army at Bouvines in 1214 and he lost his throne.

OTTO I (1815–67), King of Greece (*reg.* 1832–62), second son of Ludwig I of Bavaria. He was nominated to the Greek throne at the Conference of London (1832). He began the organization of the country with a loan of £2½ million guaranteed by the powers and moved the seat of government from Nauplia to Athens (1835). He at first refused constitutional government, but yielded to the bloodless revolution of 1843. During the Crimean War, Greek opinion was pro-Russian and pressure from French and British forces to prevent an attack on Turkish territory (1854) increased discontent against Otto, who favoured the allies. In 1862 he was deposed and returned to Bavaria. He was succeeded by Prince George, second son of the King of Denmark.

OTTO, NICOLAUS AUGUST (1832–91), German inventor. After the Belgian-French engineer Jean Joseph Étienne Lenoir (1822–1900), had designed and constructed a gas engine that worked, numerous attempts were made to increase its efficiency and practicality. In 1876 Otto built the first successful four-stroke internal combustion engine. More than 30,000 were sold by his company during the following decade. It was the Otto engine that made the automobile and the aeroplane possible.

OTTO OF NORDHEIM (d. 1083), Saxon nobleman and one of the leaders of the Saxon revolts against the centralizing policies of Emperor Henry IV in the 1070s. After the revolt was put down at the battle of Langensalza in 1075, Otto was pardoned by Henry and made royal viceroy in Saxony.

OTTOKAR I (*reg.* 1198–1230), King of Bohemia, prince of the Premyslid dynasty who increased immensely the importance of Bohemia during the German civil wars after 1197. By supporting the Welf, Otto IV, he won a royal crown and became virtually exempt from duties to the empire by several subsequent changes of side.

OTTOKAR II (*reg.* 1253–78), King of Bohemia, perhaps the greatest of the Premyslid kings. During the Interregnum he used his position as the strongest and richest prince in the empire to win advantages from the rival candidates for the Crown, which he had ambitions to acquire himself. As a reward for his support of Richard of Cornwall he received the Austrian lands (1262), which he claimed by virtue of his first marriage to the daughter of the last Babenberg Duke of Austria. He incorporated Moravia into his possessions and hoped to unite Bohemia, Hungary, and Austria. He opposed the election of Rudolph of Habsburg (1273) and quickly came into conflict with him for possession of Austria, but was defeated. He died at the Marchfeld.

OTTOMAN CONSTITUTION (1876), first major constitution (ignoring the much less important 1861 Tunisian constitution) in the Middle East, modelled on the 1831 Belgian constitution and promulgated 23 Dec. 1876. It led to the summoning of the comparatively successful first Ottoman parliament (1877–8). The restoration of the constitution, which was suspended by Abdülhamid II, became the principal demand of the 1908 Young Turk revolutionaries.

OTTOMAN EMPIRE. The Ottoman state stems from *c.* AD 1300. Its name derives from Prince Osman (cf. Arabic: Uthman), who is regarded as the first of the Ottoman begs to achieve an independent status. The Ottoman Turks were not one of the nomadic hordes moving westward, committing rapine and leaving destruction in their wake. Two forces above all contributed to the growth of Ottoman power: first, the spirit of *jihad*, of war on behalf of the Muslim faith, which was embodied in the warriors of the ghaza, the raids into the lands of the infidel; second, the resources of 'High Islam'—all the principles and practice, political and legal, administrative and financial, evolved during centuries of Muslim rule and now available to transform the rapid conquests of the ghazi soldiers into the durable fabric of an empire. The rise and development of the Ottoman state can indeed be viewed as the gradual advance, north-west-wards from Asia Minor, of a *jihad* frontier which came to rest at last, in the 16th and 17th cents, along the distant Danube and which had behind it the apparatus of efficient and stable rule. The conquest of Constantinople in 1453 bound together the Asiatic and European territories subject to the Ottoman Sultan. Now it was that the empire entered into a golden age destined to endure until about the year AD 1600, and to find its most brilliant exemplification in the reign of Sultan Suleiman the Magnificent (*reg.* 1520–66). Thereafter the Ottomans found it difficult to counter the remarkable advances (not least in the field of war) which Europe was to make in the 17th and 18th cents. A sustained effort to reorganize the empire on European lines begun in the reign of Selim III (*reg.* 1789–1807) and culminating in the years of reform known as the Tanzimat (1839–76), failed to ensure the survival of the Ottoman state. Under the impact of war and with the growth of nationalism among the subject peoples, the Ottoman empire—a polyglot and multi-racial edifice—crumbled at last, the heartlands which were Turkish and Muslim emerging from the debris to become (1922–4) the modern Turkish republic.

P. Witteh, *The Rise of the Ottoman Empire* (London, 1938).
R. B. Merriman, *Suleiman the Magnificent 1520–1566* (New York, 1966).　　　　　　　　　　　　　　　　　　　VJP

OTTOMAN PUBLIC DEBT ADMINISTRATION, European-controlled organization which collected up to one-fifth of all Ottoman revenues and exercised a significant economic influence within the Ottoman empire (1882–1914). It was established as a result of the negotiations which followed the Ottoman bankruptcy (1875) and culminated in the Decree of Muharrem (1881), which reduced the Ottoman public debt from £191 million to £106 million and assigned certain revenues to provide for the interest.

OUDENARDE, BATTLE OF (1708), fought in Flanders during the War of the Spanish Succession, when allied troops, commanded by the Duke of Marlborough and Eugène of Savoy, defeated a French army, commanded by Marshal Vendôme and the Duke of Burgundy. The battle, which followed a 25 kms march by the allies, was an 'encounter action' rather than a 'set-piece'.

OUDH, part of the Indian state of Uttar Pradesh, important centre of Hindu civilization until its annexation to the Delhi sultanate in the 12th cent. It formed part of the Mughal empire until its nawabs asserted their independence after the death of Aurangzeb. Nawab Shuja-ud-daulah came into conflict with the British, but was defeated at Buxar (1764). By the treaty of Allahabad (1765) he entered into a subsidiary alliance with the British in Bengal. Warren Hastings's relations with the incapable Asaf-ud-daulah (1775–97) formed one of the charges against him on his impeachment. In 1801 Wellesley forced its ruler to surrender Rohilkhand and part of the Doab. Its annexation by Dalhousie in 1856 was one of the causes of the Indian Mutiny.

OUDH, BEGUMS OF, mother and widow of Shuja-ud-daulah, to whom he left enormous treasure and rich *jagir*s or assignments of the revenues from tracts of land. Because the Begums were implicated in Thait Singh's revolt (1781), Warren Hastings allowed their *jagir*s to revert to the nawab. This formed one of the charges on which Hastings was impeached.

OUDH TENANCY ACT (1868), attempt to improve the condition of the cultivators in Oudh and protect them from the *talukdar*s (holders of estates).

OUDINOT, CHARLES (1767–1847), French soldier and marshal of France, who served throughout the French Wars until 1814, and contributed to the French victory at Friedland (1807). His bravery was undoubted, but he lacked the capacity for independent command. He later became a trusted supporter of the restored Bourbons, led the first division of the French army which invaded Spain (1823), and, for part of the French occupation period, governed Madrid. He retired when the July monarchy began, but Louis Philippe made him governor of the Invalides (1842).

OUDONG, capital of Cambodia from 1618 to 1863. During this period Cambodia gradually declined under pressure of attacks by the Viet-namese on one side and by the Thai on the other. The country was saved from partition between them by French intervention after 1860. It was at French insistence that Oudong was abandoned in favour of the present (1970) capital at Phnom-Penh.

OUTRAM, SIR JAMES (1803–63), British soldier in the military and political service of the East India Co. While in Khandesh he recruited the first corps from the Bhil robber tribes. He was political agent in Gujarat (1835–8), and fought in the First Afghan War. While political agent in Sind he opposed Napier's policy towards its emirs. He was appointed resident at Satara (1845) and at Baroda (1847). As resident at Lucknow he carried out the annexation of Oudh (1856), of which he became the first chief commissioner. He served in the Persian War (1856–7) and played an important part in the suppression of the Indian Mutiny.

OUVIDOR GERAL, term for a circuit judge in colonial Brazil who exercised judicial and administrative functions over large districts (*comarcas*). *Ouvidores* heard appeals from decisions made by local justices, inspected the management of municipalities, maintained roads and river crossings, and prepared special reports on various subjects for higher authorities.

OU-YANG HSIU (1007–72), Chinese politician and man of letters, who was deeply involved in the politics of the Sung government. He took a bold stand on controversial issues such as the procedure for entering the civil service, reform of the examinations, and the maintenance of standards of administration. In one of his works he defended the existence of factions in politics. He believed in gradual and natural reform rather than the sudden change of institutions; towards the end of his career he expressed opposition to Wang An-shih's proposals, but took no active part against him. After suffering setbacks in his official career, he devoted much of his time to writing prose, *eg*, descriptive pieces, essays on political theory, and on historical concepts such as dynastic legitimacy. As an historian he is best known as the principal compiler of two standard histories, *ie*, the *New T'ang History* and the *New History of the Five Dynasties*.

OVANDO, NICOLÁS DE (1460–1511), Spanish governor of Hispaniola, who gave definite shape to Spanish rule in America. He extended (1502–8) Spanish control over the island and ruthlessly organized the natives into *repartimiento* work gangs for use in the gold pannings, a measure which hastened their extermination.

OVERBURY, SIR THOMAS (1581–1613), English poet, courtier, and protégé of Robert Carr, Viscount Rochester, James I's favourite. He opposed Rochester's marriage to Frances Howard, Countess of Essex, and on a trumped-up charge of disrespect to the king, having refused to accept a diplomatic appointment, was imprisoned in the Tower (1613). There he was slowly poisoned on Frances Howard's orders. The discovery of this led to the disgrace of Rochester and the Howards. Overbury was known for his didactic poem, 'The Wife' (1614).

OVERLAND ROUTE, name given to those routes to India which passed through the Middle East. From the 16th to the 19th cents the all-sea route via the Cape of Good Hope formed the principal passage from Europe to the East Indies. In the later 18th cent. the need for speedier communications led to the development of routes for mails through the Mediterranean and thence via Egypt and the Red Sea or via Syria, Iraq, and the Persian Gulf. The development of steam navigation in the 1820s and 1830s led to greater interest in these routes, marked by the activities of Thomas Waghorn in Egypt and the Euphrates Expedition in Iraq. By 1839 the Overland Route for mails through Egypt was well established and was rapidly developed for passengers by the reorganized (1840) Peninsular and Oriental Steam Navigation Co. (P & O). With the opening of the Suez Canal (1869) the supremacy of this route, even for freight, was confirmed. The so-called Alternative Route through Syria and Iraq continued to attract support with the abortive project for a Euphrates Valley railway (1856–7) and the German Baghdad railway (1899). In the 1960s work was begun on the completion of a continuous rail link between Europe and India through the Middle East. The need to protect these two routes has been regarded by many historians as the major factor in British policy in the Near and Middle East in the 19th and early 20th cents, inspiring support for the integrity of the Ottoman empire and Iran, the control of the Persian Gulf, and the occupation of Egypt (1882).   MEY

OVERLORD (1944), series of operations in the Second World War undertaken by the Western Allies to secure a footing in north-western Europe from which Germany might be directly assaulted. Overlord owed its success to effective co-ordination by the Allied command under Gen. Eisenhower, the US commander-in-chief, and to the massive material resources which were committed to it—especially air power.

On 6 June 1944 156,000 Allied troops were landed on the coast of Normandy between Quineville and the Orne. This invasion (Operation Neptune) was the largest amphibious assault ever undertaken. It involved the deployment of 1213 warships, 864 merchantmen, 4126 landing craft, and about 10,000 combatant and 1000 transport aircraft. The Germans had been led to expect the Allies' main effort in the Pas de Calais or in Norway. The transport system of north-western Europe was paralysed by an air offensive which had begun in mid-April.

No major port facilities were available until Cherbourg was captured (26 June), and despite the use of beaching vessels and prefabricated breakwaters, the build-up of Allied forces within the beachhead, under constant German attack, was necessarily slow. But from mid-July, while heavy British pressure, directed by Gen. Montgomery around Caen, pinned down the bulk of the German armoured forces, the US under Gen. Bradley began to advance south from St Lo with rapidly increasing momentum. On 30 July they broke out into open country at Avranches, and while columns raced to secure the French Atlantic ports the main force drove south to the Loire and then east. On 16 Aug. spearheads of Gen. Patton's Third Army reached Orléans, while the First Army pushed north to join the British in encircling the greater part of two German armies in a 'pocket' west of Falaise. This success was followed by a general advance to the Seine and the liberation of Paris (25 Aug.). By 1 Sept. the Allied armies were on the Somme.   PJBD

OVERYSSEL, Dutch-speaking province of the northern Netherlands, lying between Gelderland and Drente, which were part of the Habsburg empire after 1528 and one of the seven which broke away from the Spanish Crown. It joined the Union of Utrecht (1579) and later the republic of the United Provinces.

OVID, P. OVIDIUS NASO (43 BC–*c*. AD 17), Roman poet, whose enormous output includes poems on erotic technique, cosmetics, mythology, the Roman calendar and religion, and his own troubles in exile at Tomis (mod. Constanza) on the Black Sea, to which he was banished by Augustus in AD 8.

OVIEDO, the main agricultural, mining, and industrial town of Asturias, situated in the foothills of the Cantabrian mountains. It was the centre of the Oct. 1934 rising. In Feb. 1936 working-class militants celebrated the left-wing election victory by releasing the workers imprisoned in 1934. Nevertheless, Oviedo fell to the Nationalists on the second day of the Spanish Civil War.

OVIEDO Y VALDÉS, GONZALO FERNANDEZ DE (1478–1557), Spanish writer and first official historian of the Spanish empire in America. He accompanied Pedrarias Dávila's expedition to Tierra Firme (1514) and lived in the area for several years. His *Historia general y natural de las Indias* (first published in full, 1851–5) is of value for the study of the early decades of the Spanish conquest, despite Oviedo's low opinion of the native population and his enmity towards Las Casas.

OWAIN GLYNDWR (GLENDOWER) (*c*. 1354–*c*. 1416), leader of the last native Welsh rebellion and a descendant of the old ruling houses of Gwynedd, Powys, and Deheubarth. In 1400 he took up arms to settle a dispute with his neighbour, Reginald Grey, Lord of Ruthin, and this was the spark which set alight the last and greatest Welsh rebellion. The real causes lie deeper than this and reflect Welsh anger at foreign rule and a general social discontent stemming from economic depression. The rebellion spread rapidly, gaining popular support and taking on a national aspect. By 1404 Owain had won most of Wales and as 'Prince of Wales' set up law courts, summoned parliaments, and drew up plans for the creation of a Welsh Church independent of Canterbury. He attempted to consolidate his position by diplomacy, allying himself with the Mortimers and Percies: the Tripartite Indenture (1405) planned the division of the kingdom of England between these three parties. In the same year, Owain entered into an alliance with France. Thereafter his position grew weaker. His alliances came to nothing and in 1408–9 he lost his strongholds at Aberystwyth and Harlech. The revolt and its aftermath left Wales impoverished and embittered, but Owain remains a popular hero in Welsh history.

OWAIN GWYNEDD (*c.* 1100–70), prince of Gwynedd in north-west Wales, who, during the first period of his rule, in the reign of King Stephen in England, took advantage of the English civil wars to extend the boundaries of Gwynedd and to strengthen his hold on the south with the help of his ally, Rhys ap Gruffydd, of Deheubarth. Though he was defeated by Henry II in 1157, he had regained his previous position by 1165. He laid the foundations of a strong Gwynedd which, under the overlordship of the English kings, became the most powerful principality in Wales, all subsequent medieval Welsh movements for national independence stemming from it.

OWEN, JOHN (1616–83), English Puritan clergyman and Independent theologian who was Cromwell's chaplain and vice-chancellor of Oxford University (1652–8). He was the author of many theological and controversial tracts, including *Doctrine of the Justification by Faith Explained* (1677).

OWEN, ROBERT (1771–1858), British socialist writer, factory owner, and reformer. As sole manager and dominant partner of a cotton-spinning firm at New Lanark in Scotland, he made its factory famous for its good labour relations, and ancillary enterprises such as housing for its workers and progressive schools for their children. In his *New View of Society* (1812–13) he asserted the importance of environment in determining character. He also agitated for the limiting of factory hands' hours, which resulted in the Factory Act (1819). But, by publicly renouncing religion in 1817, and by his unorthodox views on the family, he alienated the powerful support he had hitherto enjoyed in government circles.

Owen went to the US, where he founded New Harmony, the first Owenite community, in IN (1824), and finally withdrew from New Lanark in 1829. He helped to promote the working-class co-operative movement (1829–34), and tried to establish (1834) a great national federation of trade unions. Henceforward, Owenism, always millenarian in tone, became a sectarian and decreasingly successful 'movement'. In Karl Marx's view, Owen's influence was beneficial in its day, but later did harm by his failure to recognize the importance of stimulating class-consciousness. Owenites exerted little influence over the early Labour Party, but posterity saw in Owen a pioneer of personnel management, town planning, and of educational and socialist theory.

OWENS COLLEGE in Manchester, England, founded in 1851 on the proceeds of a legacy from the English radical nonconformist, John Owens. It was an undenominational college for the teaching of modern and vocational subjects and formed part of the Victoria University (1884), on the dissolution of which Owens College constituted the nucleus of Manchester University (1903).

OXENSTIERNA, AXEL GUSTAFSSON (1583–1654), Swedish politician and chancellor of Sweden. In the early years of Gustavus Adolphus's reign he reformed the Diet, local government, and the Chancery, organized the development of towns and industry, and systematized the Estate of nobles.

He carried out the king's diplomatic projects both before and during the Thirty Years War, and led the armies which relieved him at Nuremberg in 1632. After his master's death in that year, he rallied the German Protestants (League of Heilbronn) and made the French alliance (1638) which led on to Sweden's gains at the peace of Westphalia. He also planned the successful attack on Denmark in 1643–5.

Although Oxenstierna was often regarded as the champion of noble privileges against both the monarchy and the peasants, he was first and foremost a servant of the Swedish state. When Queen Christina came of age (1644), her relations with the masterful counsellor who had dominated the regency were less close than her father's had been, but his power was never shaken.

OXFORD AND ASQUITH, HERBERT HENRY ASQUITH, 1st Earl of (1852–1928), British lawyer and politician, the last prime minister of a purely Liberal ministry (1908–May 1915) and prime minister of the wartime coalition (May 1915–Dec. 1916). He was well established at the bar before he entered politics. He served as home secretary under Gladstone and Rosebery (1892–5), and in the divisions within the Liberal Party over the Boer War, he belonged, with Haldane and Grey, to the Liberal imperialists. He became chancellor of the exchequer in Campbell-Bannerman's ministry (Dec. 1905).

On Campbell-Bannerman's resignation (April 1908) Asquith became prime minister. The Liberal Party was faced with successive crises over the House of Lords, Home Rule, industrial unrest, and the militant suffragettes. From these they emerged with a reduced majority but, thanks to Asquith's leadership, undivided. In foreign affairs Asquith was close to Grey, and though he had originally been an 'economist' in public finance, he accepted the need for massive expenditure on rearmament. Thanks to his skill, the cabinet was united in deciding that Britain should enter the First World War in defence of Belgium.

In the first years of the war, Asquith's position began to be challenged by the rise of Lloyd George, who became minister of munitions on the formation of the coalition government and built up a reputation as a dynamic administrator. With the failure of the Dardanelles campaign and heavy casualties and stalemate on the Western Front, discontent with Asquith's leadership grew among Conservatives and among a number of Liberal back-benchers. This, combined with a virulent press campaign accusing him of 'wait-and-see' tactics, forced him to resign (Dec. 1916), as did most of his Liberal colleagues, in favour of a predominantly Conservative coalition headed by Lloyd George. While the attack on Asquith was undoubtedly severe, it can be argued that after 1914 his powers of leadership declined.

Thereafter he was leader of the opposition. He gave a general support to the government, though he attacked it in the Maurice debate (May 1918). As a result of this attack he was challenged by a coalition candidate and defeated in the coupon election (Nov. 1918). He re-entered parliament, at a by-election, as MP for Paisley (1920) and led what was by now a small group of 26 independent Liberals. After the break-up of the coalition in 1922, these increased to about 56; and in 1924 a reunited Liberal Party, under Asquith's leadership, supported MacDonald's Labour government. Asquith was defeated again at Paisley (1924). He entered the House of Lords (1925) and resigned the Liberal leadership (1926).

J. A. Spender and C. Asquith, *Life of Lord Oxford and Asquith* (London, 1932).
Roy Jenkins, *Asquith* (London, 1964)   LMB

OXFORD AND MORTIMER, ROBERT HARLEY, 1st Earl of (1661–1724), English politician. After entering parliament (1690) he devoted much attention to financial matters and as leader of the New Country Party attacked the royal prerogative and urged a reduction of the land forces after the peace of Ryswick (1697). He was twice chosen as speaker of the Commons before the end of William III's reign. He was again made speaker in Queen Anne's first parliament (1702), retaining the chair even after his appointment as secretary of state for the north in Godolphin's ministry (1704) until the dissolution (1705).

Harley's growing Toryism and devious methods earned him the distrust of the Whig Junto and eventually of Godolphin and Marlborough. His poor showing in the Almanza debate in the House of Commons and at the trial of William Greg, a clerk in his office convicted of treason, led to his resignation (1708). However, he engineered the downfall of the Godolphin ministry (1710), and returned to power as chancellor of the exchequer and second lord of the treasury. He was the foremost minister in the new government. To crown his achievement, in the ensuing general election (1710) more Tories than Whigs were returned to the Commons, where he now commanded a majority. He escaped an attempt upon his life (1711), and, while recovering, was created Earl of Oxford and Mortimer, and appointed lord treasurer. There was a marked dissimilarity of temperament between Oxford and his great rival, Bolingbroke, and, in addition, certain matters of substance, such as the despatch of the Quebec Expedition (1711), accentuated the rift. Both agreed upon the need to end hostilities with France, but Bolingbroke played the more notable part in the negotiations preceding the conclusion of the peace of Utrecht. Late in 1713 and early in 1714 they indulged separately in Jacobite intrigues to safeguard their positions whenever the queen should die. In the summer of 1715 Queen Anne dismissed Oxford; within a week she herself was dead.

Unlike Bolingbroke, Oxford remained in England to face the Hanoverian succession. Articles of impeachment were drawn up against him (1715), mostly in connection with the making of peace with France. Before they had all been proceeded with he was lodged in the Tower, where he was confined for nearly two years. Eventually, the outstanding charges against him were dropped and he was released. He made several further appearances in the Lords, but played little part in politics otherwise. Oxford was the greatest bibliophile of his day in England. His collected books and documents form the nucleus of the Harleian manuscripts in the British Museum.

E. Hamilton, *The Backstairs Dragon: a life of Robert Harley, Earl of Oxford* (London, 1969). BM

OXFORD, PROVISION OF (1258) in England, new written constitution devised by a committee of English barons with the object of taking control of the government out of the hands of the ineffectual King Henry III. A magnate council assumed control. In 1260 Henry overthrew this regime and in 1261 obtained papal release from his oath of 1258, by which he had promised to maintain the Provisions, which the barons originally intended to enforce for seven years.

OXFORD, UNIVERSITY OF. By the 12th cent. Oxford was a centre of learning comparable with Paris and Bologna, and attracting in its early days scholars such as Grosseteste and Roger Bacon. In the next century came the emergence of colleges, the first three being University (1249), Balliol (1263), and Merton (1264). So began the communal life of small units of students and their teachers which was to be the essence of Oxford University. Colleges in the 14th cent. included Exeter (1314), Oriel (1326), Queen's (1340), and New College (1379). The university acquired its Divinity School and the library of Duke Humphrey in the 15th cent., the one an architectural gem, the other a repository of rare mss and the basis of the future Bodleian Library. Further collegiate foundations followed, and the university flourished under the intellectual stimulus of humanists such as Grocyn, Colet, and More. In a different way their contemporary, Cardinal Wolsey, made his mark on Oxford in his foundation of Cardinal's College. When Wolsey fell from power (1529),

his scheme lapsed, but was subsequently revived (1546) as Christ Church, to provide, as well, the cathedral church of the diocese of Oxford.

Oxford in the 17th cent. saw the chancellorship of Abp Laud and the civil war. Laud made the same demands of efficiency and order of the university as he was later to ask of the Church of England.

The Civil War brought Charles I to Oxford to use the city and university as his court and headquarters. In the calmer atmosphere of the Restoration (1660) the Clarendon Press and the Sheldonian Theatre were built.

Oxford shared in the 18th cent. in the general torpor to which English (but not Scottish) education sank. By contrast, the 19th cent. brought a period of fervent activity to Oxford. Reforms abounded, scholarship was encouraged, and discipline was enforced, while the Tractarians centred their religious movement in Oxford, Keble College (1868) being founded as a testimony to their sojourn and influence.

Modern Oxford has seen the foundation of the Rhodes scholarships, the admission of women, large extensions to the Bodleian Library, new laboratories, and the benefaction of Lord Nuffield in founding a graduate college (1937).

In changing times, set in an Oxford that had become a bustling industrial and commercial city, the university in 1970 stood in the forefront of western learning. Its teaching was in tune with the demands of a modern world, while its college quadrangles, enclosed behind busy streets, were havens of academic calm and reminders of antiquity.

Sir Charles Mallet, *History of the University of Oxford* (Oxford, 1927). GMDH

OXFORD MOVEMENT in England, High Church group centred at Oxford University which urged that the Church of England must reassert its position as a divine society reflecting the Early Christian Church, proclaim its infallible authority, and revive traditions of an age when its authority was unquestioned. The leaders were all young men, *eg*, John Keble, John Henry Newman, Edward Pusey, and Richard Hurrell Froude, who were disquieted by reforms such as Catholic Emancipation (1829) and the Reform Bill (1832) and believed that liberalism, progress, and the materialism of the early railway age spelt danger for the Church. John Keble's Assize Sermon in the University Church of St Mary's, Oxford (1833), on 'National Apostasy' sounded the first alarm at the Whigs' proposal to secularize part of the revenues of ten Irish bishoprics. The government withdrew the clause and followed precedent in uniting a number of sees; but to Keble the situation was critical, with parliament disavowing the sovereignty of God.

Newman gave the movement its greatest strength. His influential writings appeared in 'Tracts for the Times' (1833–1840) and their supporters were variously known as Tractarians, Newmanites, and Puseyites. Unlike the evangelical movement, it made no impact on the ordinary man, who saw no crisis. The Tracts were primarily for clergy, and preached the 'beauty of holiness' and emphasized the apostolic succession. Their appeal to history antagonized the evangelicals and lay critics, who said that logically the Tractarians should join the Church of Rome.

Newman's Tract 90 (1841) sought to prove that the Thirty-Nine Articles, to which every Anglican clergyman was bound to subscribe, contained nothing contrary to traditional catholic belief. A storm of opposition arose. Newman was disturbed by Oxford University's ban on Pusey's preaching and its censure of his extremist follower, Ward. Eventually, he himself was received into the Roman Catholic Church (1845), and many others of the clergy joined him. A second wave of secession followed the Gorham case (1851), in which a lay court upheld views on baptism opposed by Tractarians. As a result, Archdeacon H. E. Manning also went over to Rome. He and Newman ultimately became cardinals. Keble, Pusey, and their friends remained Anglicans, moulding the powerful Anglo-Catholic tradition within the Church.

The influence of the Oxford Movement, like that of evangelicalism, remained long after the deaths of its original leaders. Deep concern for the dignity and meaning of Holy Orders, the emphasis on ceremonial, the general improvement of professional and administrative standards, the enthusiasm for Church architecture reflecting the general revival of interest in the Middle Ages, all had a marked impact. The introduction of religious communities, the promotion of Anglican teacher training colleges, the emphasis on social responsibility seen in the establishment of 'settlements' in the slums, all showed the strengthening influence of the Oxford Movement within the Church. But the Church of England was weakened in some respects by the rift with the Evangelicals over subjects like ritualism and it had lost men equipped intellectually to meet the challenge of Darwinism.

The episcopal church in Scotland, relieved (1792) from the penal laws against it, showed the influence of the Oxford Movement in its own 19th-cent. revival.

O. Chadwick, *The Victorian Church*, 2 vols (London, 1966 and 1970).
G. Battiscombe, *John Keble* (London, 1963).   JRA

OXFORD PARLIAMENT (1681) ended the 'exclusion' crisis and ensured the ultimate succession of James II to the English throne after the 'Popish Plot'. Twice in 1679 elections returned parliaments favourable to Shaftesbury and the exclusionists, and a bill excluding James passed the Commons (1680), but was defeated in the Lords. A third election (1681) again gave Shaftesbury a majority, but Charles II called the parliament to Oxford, where Shaftesbury's London gangs would be unable to terrorize the members. Short of exclusion, Charles offered substantial concessions, but these were rejected and he dissolved parliament, having been assured of financial help from Louis XIV. The panic caused by the alleged Popish Plot had largely subsided and moderate opinion was now swinging to Charles's side in support of the constitution.

OXLEY, JOHN JOSEPH MOLESWORTH (?1785–1828), Australian explorer and sailor, who was surveyor-general of NSW (1812–28). He played an important part in exploring NSW, and in framing land regulations in a time of rapidly expanding settlement.

ŌYAMA, IWAO (1842–1916), Japanese soldier, politician, and a Satsuma samurai, who served as war minister in several cabinets and was commander-in-chief of the army in Manchuria during the Russo–Japanese War (1904–5).

OYER AND TERMINER, COMMISSIONS OF, Anglo-French designation still applied in England to commissions, *ie*, assizes, at which a commissioner (normally a judge of assize) sits 'to hear and determine', *ie*, to try and to judge, all treasons, felonies, and misdemeanours committed in the counties specified in the commission. In 1708 the Treason Act extended the system to Scotland for the trial of treason and misprision of treason.

OYLY, SIR JOHN D' (1774–1822), British civil servant in Ceylon, noted for his intimate knowledge of the Sinhalese and their language. After the capture of the Kandyan kingdom (1815), he was appointed resident at Kandy. He did his best to conciliate the chiefs and the Buddhist monks, but was unable to prevent rebellion breaking out in 1817.

OYO, name of the capital city of a north-western sub-group of the Yoruba people. Old Oyo, 35 miles (56 kms) south-west of Jebba, was founded late in the 16th cent.; modern Oyo, some 90 miles (144 kms) to the south, replaced it in 1837. Yoruba was originally the name of the sub-group only, but when it began to be applied to all the people of south-western Nigeria related to them culturally and linguistically, the sub-group came to be known as the Oyo. Their language formed the basis of written Yoruba language.

Old Oyo is reputed to be the sixth capital of the Oyo kingdom. It was located in the Guinea savannah region, just south of the Niger. Through Nupe and Borgu, Oyo traded with the Hausa, Kanuri, and Mandinka peoples. Old Oyo became an emporium for the exchange of goods from the Western Sudan and North Africa for goods from the forest zone and the Europeans on the Atlantic coast. From the north came horses, the basis of the cavalry force on which the Oyo founded an empire that became the most powerful political system in Yoruba land, embracing principally the Oyo, Igbomina, Egba, and Egbado, and with influence wherever the cavalry could penetrate, including Borgu, Nupe, and Dahomey. This empire flourished largely in the 17th and 18th cents under the control of the Alafin, its ruler, and his council of senior lineage chiefs, led by the Bashorun. Other dignitaries included the Eso, captains of the cavalry force led by the Are-ona-Kakanfo; members of the Ogboni council, a powerful secret society; and leaders of cult organizations, particularly that associated with the worship of Shango, the god of thunder and symbol of divine wrath, originally a deified Alafin of the mythological period.

The Oyo empire declined at the beginning of the 19th cent. owing to internal factions and external pressure from the Fulani. Old Oyo became deserted as the Oyo pushed southward into Egba and Ife territory. It was in this latter period that distinctive Oyo cultural traits spread among other Yoruba people of the forest zone, even more rapidly than in the days of Oyo imperial power. These included the *gangan*, the double-ended hand-controlled talking drum; the narrow-strip male-operated loom, as opposed to the female-operated broad loom; and the clothed *egungun* masquerades, as opposed to those at which grass or palm fronds are worn. The Oyo also helped to spread Islam. In the 19th cent., Ibadan rose rapidly in size, power, and economic significance and has since become the most important Oyo city.

J. F. Ade Ajayi and R. S. Smith, *Yoruba Warfare in the Nineteenth Century* (Cambridge, 1964).   JFAA

PA CHIN (1904–), pen-name of Li Fei-gan, Chinese writer, influenced by anarchism. His novels concentrated on the rebellion of youth against tradition and the overpowering authority of the Chinese family.

PABST, WALDEMAR (1881–1970), German soldier, said to have been responsible (1919) for the murder of Karl Liebknecht and Rosa Luxemburg, the two Spartacist leaders. He was involved in the Kapp putsch (1923), after which he became an Austrian citizen; he remained active in extreme right-wing politics.

PACHACAMAC, pre-Conquest shrine and ceremonial centre south of Lima in Peru. The centre long antedated the Incas, who fitted its god into their pantheon.

PACIFIC FUR COMPANY, founded in 1810 by the American, J. J. Astor, to develop the fur trade with China. Because of mismanagement and the War of 1812 the company's Fort, Astoria, was sold to the North West Fur Co., which had captured it in 1813, and the Pacific Co. ceased trading.

PACTA CONVENTA in Poland, medieval constitutional contract defining the personal obligations imposed on Polish kings; it was revived after the end of the Jagiellon dynasty (1572) at the election of Henry of Valois (1573). These obligations, constituting an additional limitation on the Polish monarchy, were confirmed in the king's coronation oath. They included the provision of an army and navy, the education of youths, and the payment of treasury debts, and lasted until the late 18th cent.

PADEREWSKI, IGNACY (1860–1940), Polish musician and politician, who achieved a world-wide reputation as a concert pianist. During the First World War he worked for the Polish cause as representative of the Polish National Committee in the US. In independent Poland he was prime minister (Jan.–Dec. 1919) and represented his country at the Versailles Conference. He was a strong opponent of Pilsudski and moved from Poland to Switzerland after the coup of May 1926. He was one of the principal sponsors of the liberal opposition group the 'Morges Front'. After Poland's defeat, he became chairman of the National Council, the parliament of the government-in-exile.

PADILLA, JUAN DE (c. 1500–44), Spanish Franciscan missionary, who went to New Spain (1528), accompanied Coronado into New Mexico (1540–2), and established the first mission in the remote south-west. He was murdered by Indians.

PADILLA, JUAN LOPEZ DE (1484–1521), Spanish leader of the *Communeros* uprising in Toledo (1520), who was defeated and captured at the battle of Villalar and executed the following day (1521). His wife, Maria Pacheco (d. 1531), led the defence of Toledo after his death, and when it fell, (1522), she took refuge in Portugal.

PADISHAH, exalted title (of Persian origin, with the sense of 'lord' or 'king') which was often used of the Ottoman sultan.

PADJANG, kingdom of Central Java in the 16th cent., the south-west of present-day Surakarta. The history of Padjang is difficult to unravel from the maze of semi-historical tales. Djaka Tingkir is said by the *Babad Tanah Djawi* to have become Sultan of Padjang in the 16th cent. Later in the century power passed to Mataram.

PADMORE, GEORGE (c. 1902–59), West Indian journalist and African nationalist, who migrated to the US (1924), and worked on the Harlem *Negro Champion*. He represented US communists at the Moscow Communist International meeting (1929) and organized the Hamburg International Conference of Negro Workers and remained there to head the International Trade Union Committee of Negro Workers and edit the *Negro Worker*. In 1933 he resigned from the Communist Party in protest at the dissolution of the International Trade Union Committee of Negro Workers. With others, he formed the Pan-African Federation (1944) and covered United Nations events in Paris (1948) for the US Negro press. He became personal adviser to President Nkrumah in Ghana (1957) and helped to establish the All-African Peoples Organization (1959).

PADRI **WAR** (1822–37), gradual Dutch conquest of the Minangkabau region of Central Sumatra. Three Minangkabau *ulama*, who returned from Mecca in 1803 after absorbing some Wahhabi ideas, acquired a militant following, known as *padri*s, evidently by analogy with the priests of the Christians. Their opposition to opium, alcohol, cockfighting, gambling, and non-Islamic dress led to a violent confrontation with the traditional aristocracy of certain areas, whose members appealed for help to the British (1818), and then the Dutch (1819), on the coast. The Dutch established a series of forts in central Minangkabau (1822–4), but made little progress towards permanent conquest until the end of the Java War (1830). Bondjol, the last *padri* stronghold, fell in 1837.

PADUA, Italian city, of pre-Roman origin, situated in eastern Lombardy in a prosperous agrarian region near Venice. In the Middle Ages it was a wealthy city and one of the leading cultural centres of Italy. In 1238 the Emperor Frederick II founded a university there, which became one of the most famous in Europe, being noted for its Aristotelian scholars. One of the earliest groups of Italian humanists flourished at Padua early in the 14th cent., inspired by the memory of the Roman historian Livy, who was born in the city. The native dynasty of the Carrara, which ruled Padua from 1318 to 1405, continued the tradition of patronizing scholars and artists. After the Venetians conquered the city in 1405, it was for over a century the intellectual and artistic centre of the Venetian state, and members of the Venetian aristocracy were usually educated at the university. A succession of outstanding artists worked at Padua, including Giotto, Mantegna, and Donatello.

PAEKCHE (Jap., Kudara), ancient state founded among the Han tribes of Ma-han in south-western Korea, by refugees from the Manchurian state of Puyo. By the mid-4th cent. Paekche had taken over Tai-fang, the southern-most of the Chinese colonies in Korea, and soon afterwards formed a close alliance with the Japanese state of Yamato, which had established the Milmana protectorate in 369. Paekche was strongly influenced by the Chinese culture of Tai-fang, and played a major role in transmitting that culture further east to Japan. Buddhism, introduced to Paekche from southern China by an Indian monk in 384, was brought to Japan by a Paekche embassy in 552. In spite of their alliance with Japan, the rulers of Paekche were obliged by strong pressure from Koguryo to shift their capital further and further south from the 5th cent. onwards. At the same time, they became involved in a series of wars with Silla, their neighbour to the east, and the kingdom fell (c. 660) before the combined onslaught of Silla and T'ang China.

PÁAZ, FEDERICO (1877–), president of Ecuador (1935–1937), whose rise to power was due to the Ecuadorian army, which thereafter dominated his regime. He attempted to improve the conditions of the rural poor and set up a national system of social security and at the same time to convince the army and the conservatives that the only way to stop violent social revolution was by radical reforms. He resigned because of undue army pressure and was succeeded by a military government headed by Gen. Alberto Enríquez.

PÁEZ, JOSÉ ANTONIO (1790–1873), Venezuelan politician. By 1810 he was a master of guerilla tactics, and a partisan of Simón Bolívar. As the latter's chief aide in Venezuela, he was invaluable in the defeat of rival *llaneros*, led by Boves, and in the expulsion of the Spanish. He was virtually master of Venezuela (1830–46), survived five uprisings, and attempted to organize the country. He encouraged agriculture and industry, promoted immigration, and founded a few schools, while skilfully avoiding clashes between Church and state. He was deposed in 1846 but returned to rule with great severity (1861–3).

PAGAN, on the Irrawaddy, 100 miles (161 kms) below Mandalay, capital of Burma (1044–1287) and at other times the headquarters of local chiefs. It is the outstanding architectural site in Burma, the remains of some 5000 pagodas from its golden age surviving in various states of preservation. The Ananda pagoda, built by King Kyanzittha (1091), is the best known and best preserved, but the Thatpyinnyu and Gawdawpalin are also much visited. In a few other pagodas there are preserved murals of great beauty and of far greater-delicacy than is achieved today. Despite strong Hindu influence (the Mahabodhi pagoda was built on the model of the temple of Bodh Gaya in Bihar), a distinctively Burmese style was successfully evolved at Pagan.

PAGE, SIR EARLE CHRISTIAN GRAFTON (1880–1961), Australian physician, politician, and founder and leader of the Country Party, who entered the Commonwealth parliament (1919). He was a skilled negotiator and political opportunist, who helped to unseat W. M. Hughes as prime minister (1923), and organized the medical profession's resistance to J. B. Chifley's national health scheme. He was deputy prime minister to S. M. Bruce (1923–9) and to J. A. Lyons (1933–1939). As minister for health in Menzies Liberal-Country Party coalition he organized the contributory hospital benefits scheme (1953).

PAGE, WALTER HINES (1855–1918), US journalist, publisher, and diplomat who crusaded for better social conditions in the South, edited *Forum* (1890–5), the *Atlantic Monthly* (1898–9), and the *World's Work* (1900–13), and was joint founder of Doubleday, Page and Co. (1900). As ambassador to Britain (1913–18) he advocated US participation in the First World War and was an outspoken anglophile.

PAGET OF BEAUDESERT, WILLIAM PAGET, 1st Lord (1505–63), English politician, who began his career in the household of Stephen Gardiner, Wolsey's secretary, and in 1540 was appointed clerk of the privy council. As secretary of state and clerk of parliament (1543) he attached himself to the Earl of Hertford (later Duke of Somerset), and Henry VIII in his last years relied heavily on both of them. As a friend of

Somerset, he was appointed comptroller of the king's household and chancellor of the duchy of Lancaster (1547), but he incurred the hatred of Warwick (later Northumberland) and lost his offices in 1551. He was later lord privy seal (1556–8). Paget's peerage was unusual in that he was a member of the House of Lords, styled himself 'lord', but did not hold any rank in the peerage.

PAHLEN COMMISSION (1883) in Russia, only attempt of Alexander III's government to examine the condition of Russian Jews. The commission's report, which was not implemented (1888), admitted the validity of Jewish complaints, urged an end to their repression, and advocated their treatment as full citizens.

PAHLEVI DYNASTY, Iranian dynasty founded in 1925 by Reza Khan and continued by his son, Muhammad Reza Shah. The dynastic name was chosen to suggest the glories of the pre-Islamic Iranian past.

PAI CH'UNG-HSI (1896–1967), Chinese soldier, who was commander in the Kuomintang camp, leader of the Kwangsi clique, and a longstanding opponent of Chiang Kai-shek. He participated with distinction in the Northern Expedition and in the final stages of the Civil War.

PAINAN TREATY (1663), whereby the Dutch East India Co. drew the port-states of central West Sumatra away from their vassalage to Atjeh, and obtained promises of a monopoly of their pepper exports.

PAINE, THOMAS (1737–1809), English radical and pamphleteer of the American and French Revolutions, who met Benjamin Franklin in London (1774) and decided to go to the American colonies. There he edited the *Pennsylvania Magazine* (1774–6). His pamphlet, 'Common Sense', was published early in 1776 and within three months 120,000 copies were sold. He made a strong appeal for independence from England and the organization of a federal government under Congress. When the American War of Independence began, he served as a soldier, and also wrote 'Crisis' (1776–1783), a series of propaganda pamphlets. He became the secretary (1777–9) to the committee of foreign affairs of the Continental Congress, but resigned to become clerk of the PA Assembly. After the war he returned to Europe (1787–1802), where he became involved in pamphleteering for revolutionary causes. In answer to Edmund Burke's *Reflections on the French Revolution* (1790), Paine wrote *The Rights of Man* (1791–2), a strong defence of republican government. The book was suppressed by the British government and Paine was tried and convicted, in his absence, for treason (1792). He meanwhile had fled to France, where he was elected to the French National Convention (1792). On the fall of the Girondists he was excluded from the Convention and imprisoned (1793–4). His *Age of Reason* (1794–6), attacking the principle of biblical revelation, created a great stir and lost him support in both Europe and the US, where he was denounced as an atheist.

He returned to the US in 1802 and spent the rest of his life on a farm in NY.

PAINLEVÉ, PAUL (1863–1933), French mathematician, who became prime minister of France. He was mainly interested in differential equations, but was also one of the first to theorise on the use of aircraft in war. He was brought into politics by Aristide Briand and served as minister of public instruction (1915–16), minister of war (1917), and *président du conseil* (1917). After the First World War he was one of the leaders of the *cartel des gauches* and in 1925 formed two short-lived cabinets. As minister of war (1925–9) he was largely responsible for the creation of the Maginot Line.

PAISLEY, IAN RICHARD KYLE (1926–), Irish Protestant minister, politician, and founder of the Free Presbyterian

Church of Northern Ireland. He came to prominence with the worsening of community relations in Northern Ireland in 1968, when demonstrations in favour of 'civil rights' for Catholics were met by violent Protestant counter-demonstrations. The promise of reform from the Northern Ireland prime minister, Terence O'Neill, led to a split in the ruling Unionist Party, which O'Neill tried unsuccessfully to overcome by calling an election in Feb. 1969. Paisley, running as a Protestant Unionist, came a close second in O'Neill's own seat, and later (1970) won it at a by-election after O'Neill's resignation. In the British parliamentary election of 1970 he was again elected, against the official Unionist.

PAIUTE INDIANS, name applied to several tribes living in the arid regions of the American far west. The Northern Paiute, called Snake Indians, were first encountered by Europeans in 1825. The Southern Paiute, called Digger Indians, were visited by the Spaniards in the 16th cent. Although generally friendly to the whites, there was some hostility after gold was discovered in NV and CA, and the Northern Paiute took part in the Bannock War (1878).

PAKHTOONISTAN, Pakistani movement, originated in 1947 by Khan Abdul Ghaffer Khan, for an autonomous Pakhtu-speaking state encompassing the North-West Frontier Province and other Pathan areas which wished to join. This was construed by the Pakistan government as evidence of disloyalty and Abdul Ghaffar was frequently kept under detention until he went into exile (1964). From the 1950s the scheme was supported by Afghanistan and the notion of a 'Greater Pakhtoonistan' which would draw together Pathans in both Pakistan and Afghanistan was put forward. Considerable friction ensued between the two nations and diplomatic relations were twice broken off (1955, 1961).

PAKISTAN, EAST, DISASTER (Nov. 1970), tidal flooding, associated with a typhoon, in the Ganges delta which caused the loss of over half a million lives. Ten million people were affected by the destruction of homes and crops and the hazards of disease. The tragedy drew attention, in political terms, to the indifferent relations between West and East Pakistan. Nations from all over the world showed more immediate practical concern for the East Pakistan victims than did the West Pakistani authorities.

PAKISTAN CONSTITUENT ASSEMBLY, originally formed under the British Cabinet Mission's proposals in 1946, contained Muslim members, most of whom were Muslim Leaguers. Shortly before the partition of India (1947), the members who represented the areas included in Pakistan were called together to form the first Pakistan Constituent Assembly. This body continued after partition, its members being increased from 69 to 79 to take account of boundary changes, the integration of the princely states, and the influx of refugees. The Assembly had the task of drawing up a new constitution and—sitting in another capacity—acting as the national legislature. The Government of India Act (1935) was also the interim constitution, which the Assembly had the power to amend where necessary.

The task of producing a final constitution proceeded slowly. The Objectives Resolution was finally agreed in March 1949 and the Basic Principles Committee was set up, with sub-committees to report on federal and provincial constitutions, franchise, and the judiciary. Fierce criticism greeted the first sub-committee report (on federal and provincial constitutions) and further investigations were needed before the Basic Principles Committee's report was finally adopted (Sept. 1954). It had no sooner been accepted than the Assembly was dismissed by Ghulam Muhammad, the governor-general, as part of an attempt to restore public confidence in Pakistan's central government.

A new body, the Second Constituent Assembly, was elected on the governor-general's orders in July 1955; this had 80 members, 40 each from East and West Pakistan. The new government, led by Iskandar Mirza, did not wait for the Assembly to prepare the constitution. Instead, it drafted a document, placed it before the Assembly (Jan. 1956), and, by strict disciplining of the debate, had it approved by 29 Feb. It came into effect in the following month. This 1956 constitution, which lasted until the imposition of martial law in Oct. 1958, provided for a president as head of state, elected by members of the National Assembly, and two Provincial Assemblies, all three of which had 310 members. At the centre and in the provinces were cabinets responsible to the assemblies. Iskandar Mirza became the first president and until arrangements could be made for full elections, the existing assemblies were transformed into those provided by the constitution.   PDR

PAKNAM INCIDENT (13 July 1893), Franco–Siamese clash in which two French gunboats forced their way past the forts at the mouth of the Chaophraya river up to Bangkok. It was followed by an ultimatum which resulted in the French annexation of Laos.

PAKUALAM, house of subsidiary Princes of Jogjakarta, Central Java, whose position was independent of the power of the sultans. Pangeran Natakusuma, half-brother of Sultan Hamengkubuwana II (*reg.* 1792–1812, 1826–8), was installed in 1812 as the first Prince Pakualam (*reg.* 1812–29) by Sir Thomas Stamford Raffles during the English administration of Java. He was succeeded by seven princes of the same name. The house of Pakualam gave a lead in both traditional Javanese culture and in modern affairs, eg, education, especially under Pakualam V (*reg.* 1878–1900). Prince Pakualam VIII (*reg.* 1938–) functions (1970) as the lieutenant of Sultan Hamengkubuwana IX in the administration of the Jogjakarta Special District, under the independent Indonesian government.

PAKUBUWANA, name of a series of rulers of the house of Mataram, Central Java, in the 18th–20th cents. Susuhunan Pakubuwana I (Pageran Puger, (*reg.* 1703–19) disputed authority over the kingdom of Mataram with Susuhunan Amangkurat III (Sunan Mas, *reg.* 1703–8). The Dutch East India Co. chose to recognize Pakubuwana I as the legitimate ruler in 1703. The 'First Javanese War of Succession' ensued and lasted until 1708, when Sunan Mas was defeated and exiled to Ceylon, and Pakubuwana I was secure in the court of Fartasura. In return for the assistance of the Dutch Co., Pakubuwana I was required to make a number of concessions. He was succeeded by his son Amangkurat IV (*reg.* 1719–27). The grandson of Pageran Puger became Pakubuwana II (*reg.* 1727–49). The first half of the 18th cent. saw almost continuous warfare and rebellion in Java, leading to Dutch intervention and subsequent demands for concessions to the Dutch East India Co. Pakubuwana II became involved in the Chinese War of the 1740s, and in return for Dutch assistance was ultimately required to sign over to the company those sections of Java's north coast not already under company control (1743–6). Late in his reign (1746) the court was moved from the fallen Fartasura to Surakarta. On his deathbed Pakubuwana signed a document which the Dutch interpreted as a relinquishment of his sovereignty over the entire kingdom (1749), although he may have had no such intention. Under Pakubuwana III (Sunan Swarga, *reg.* 1749–88) Mataram was divided into the two territories of Jogjakarta and Surakarta (1755). Thereafter, the Susuhunan title and the name Pakubuwana remained with the rulers of Surakarta. The last of the line, Pakubuwana XII, was installed in 1944 but his domain was subsequently incorporated into the independent republic of Indonesia.

PAL, BEPIN CHANDRA (1858–1932), Indian nationalist politician and journalist, who was founder-editor of *New India* (1901). After the partition of Bengal he became a leading exponent of *swadeshi* and the founder-editor of *Bande Mataram* (1906), although he dissociated himself from it as Aurobindo Ghose's influence grew. Pal was an advocate of complete independence outside the British empire, and was regarded as a dangerous agitator. He was briefly imprisoned in 1907. After a period in Britain (1908–11), he became a believer in imperial federation and although he continued to be active in Bengal, his influence waned after non-co-operation, which he opposed.

PALA DYNASTY (c. AD 750–1150), line of ancient Indian rulers of Bengal and Bihar, founded by Gopala, a local chief, who, in a time of internal chaos, was put or confirmed in royal authority by some sections of the people in order to restore normal conditions. During the long reigns of his successors, Dharmapala (reg. c. 785–825) and Devapala (reg. c. 825–865), the power of the dynasty was extended from the capital at Mudgagiri (Monghyr) over present Bengal and Bihar, while Pala influence was felt all over northern India.

After Devapala the empire shrank, mainly owing to campaigns by King Mahendrapala of the Pratihara dynasty of Kanauj (UP). A great empire was, however, temporarily re-established in the 11th cent. by Mahipala I. His death (1043) marks the beginning of a fast decline with frequent invasions by neighbouring rulers. Most of Bengal came under the power of the Senas, originally invaders from South India, Pala authority being limited to southern Bihar, where it persisted at least till the middle of the 12th cent.

The main fame of the Palas rests on their patronage of Mahayana Buddhism, as well as of art and architecture. While in most of India Buddhism was in decline after the Gupta period, the opposite tendency is apparent in Bihar and Bengal. The greatest centre of Buddhist scholarship was the monastery of Nalanda (south-east of present Patna), but Vikramasila (unidentified) and Somapura (Paharpur in East Bengal) were hardly less famous. These centres of learning attracted scholars from all over the Buddhist world. The *stupa* (pagoda) of Paharpur had great influence on South-East Asian architecture. In art, the Pala period is notable for the perfection achieved in bronze casting and for the numerous huge stone sculptures, both Hindu and Buddhist. Bengali culture of this period exerted great influence on the cultures of Ceylon, Burma, Cambodia, Indonesia, and Tibet.

JGdeC

PALACIOS, ALFREDO LORENZO (1880–1965), Argentine lawyer, university teacher, and politician, whose writings and speeches in Buenos Aires and La Plata Universities and in the national congress dealt largely with social legislation.

PALACKY, FRANTISEK (1798–1876), Czechoslovakian historian, politician, and protagonist of equal national rights within the Habsburg empire. He was invited to the Frankfurt Constituent Assembly, as Bohemia was part of the German Confederation, but refused to attend on the grounds that Czechs had never considered themselves part of the German nation. Instead, he chaired the Slav Congress in Prague, and was a member of the Kremsier Diet. After this, he retired from politics until 1861, when he became a member of the Reichsrat. His *Idea of an Austrian State* (1865–9) proposed a federal Austrian empire based on the historic provinces, not the nationalities. He had great influence on the resurgence of Czech culture and the thought of Masaryk and his generation.

PALAFOX Y MENDOZA, JUAN DE (1600–59), Spanish churchman and Bp of Pueblo (Mexico), who, briefly, was simultaneously viceroy, visitor-general, and inquisitor-general in that colony.

PALAIOLOGOS, last of the dynasties to rule—from 1261— over the Byzantine empire. Under the Palaiologoi the territories remaining to Byzantium came more and more to be governed as a series of appanages bestowed on princes of the blood. The Palaiologoi held the imperial throne until the Ottoman conquest of Constantinople in 1453. A Palaiologos continued to reign over much of the Morea down to the year 1460, when the Ottomans subdued that area.

PALAIS DE JUSTICE, area of the old royal palace on the Île de la Cité in Paris, which, after the erection of the Louvre and the Tuileries in the 16th cent., became the centre of the French legal system. At its height the palace housed the *parlement* of Paris, the *chambre des comptes*, the *cour des aides*, and the *cour des monnaies* and was essential not only to the processes of administration and the conduct of justice, but also to the social life of Paris. The site was used by Roman governors and Frankish kings, as well as by the Capetians. It has been frequently rebuilt—many of its older buildings were destroyed during the Commune (1871)—and is now a legal centre.

PALAIS ROYAL, in France, palace in the centre of Paris, built by Richelieu (1633) and bequeathed to the royal family (1643). It eventually became the home of the dukes of Orleans. Later it was altered to include shops and a circus and it played an important part in Parisian social and intellectual life, particularly during the Revolution. Later still it housed a number of government agencies, notably the Conseil d'État.

PALAMAS, GREGORY, Saint (1296–1359), Abp of Thessaloniki, who defended the Hesychast doctrines against the attacks of the Calabrian monk Barlaam. He was a prisoner in the hands of the Turks during the years 1354–5. Among his writings were treatises on Hesychasm and letters which throw valuable light on the events of his own time.

PALATINATE, German principality stretching across the middle and upper Rhine, and bordered by the ecclesiastical lands of Mainz, Trier, Speyer, and Worms, its capital being the ancient university city of Heidelberg on the Neckar. This Rhenish province was united under one ruler with the Upper Palatinate, a smaller and less fertile area lying just north of Bavaria between the Danube and the Bohemian Forest. The Palatinate had been acquired in 1214 by the Wittelsbachs, an old German noble family, and came to the fore in the 13th-cent. 'Interregnum' (1250–73), when as representatives of the lay princes of Germany the princes voted in the imperial elections. The constitutional title of elector and the shared right to act as regent during an interregnum was enshrined in the Golden Bull of 1356.

In 1449 the Palatinate was inherited by Frederick I (reg. 1449–76), the second son of Elector Louis III. Under him the principality became important and wealthy. While other German states developed representative estates, the lack of political conflict within the principality and its comparative affluence in the 15th cent. enabled the electors to rule with undivided authority. Frederick's nephew, Philip (reg. 1476–1508), who succeeded him, aligned the Palatinate with the kings of France against the Habsburg emperor. His son, Rupert, coveted the town of Landshut, but was defeated at the battle of Regensburg (1504) by the Swabian League, which resulted in the electorate's loss of several towns to Emperor Maximilian. Louis V (reg. 1508–44) and Frederick II (reg. 1544–56) preserved the Catholic religion in the Palatinate during the early years of the Reformation, but Frederick III (reg. 1559–76) imposed Calvinism upon his principality (1563).

Under Frederick IV (reg. 1583–1610) the Palatinate was the leading Protestant German state, the defender of German liberties, and the head of the Protestant Union (1608). His son, Frederick V (reg. 1610–32) married Elizabeth, only daughter of James VI and I of Scotland and England. Under the influence of Christian of Anhalt, Frederick accepted the offer of the Bohemian throne and was crowned king in Prague (4 Nov. 1619), only to lose both his kingdom and his electorate within two years. As the Bohemians were routed by Tilly's imperial–Bavarian army at the battle of the White Mountain (1620), Spinola's Spaniards occupied the Rhenish

Palatinate. Frederick, driven into exile, was placed under the imperial ban (29 Jan. 1621) and his principality was divided, the Upper Palatinate and the electoral dignity being bestowed on Maximilian of Bavaria and the Rhenish lands divided between Spanish and Bavarian administrations. Protestantism was systematically eliminated in the Upper Palatinate (1630–48) and during the Thirty Years War the principality was devastated and depopulated. By the peace of Westphalia (1648) the Rhenish Palatinate was restored to the Calvinist Zimmern line in the person of Frederick V's son, Charles Louis (1648–80). He tried to revive trade and agriculture by protectionist policies; he also encouraged immigration, settled religious strife, and improved education. He refounded the city of Mannheim (1652) and reopened Heidelberg University. By imposing taxes on wine, fruit, and meat, he financed a standing army and a military administration. Despite French aggression (1674), he had married his daughter Elizabeth Charlotte to the Duke of Orléans. On the death of his son and successor, Charles (*reg.* 1680–85), the Zimmern line died out and the Rhenish Palatinate passed to the Catholic Neuburg branch of the Wittelsbachs, although it was claimed by Louis XIV in his sister-in-law's name. Philip William's short reign (1685–90) witnessed the last deliberate devastation of the Palatinate during the 17th cent., when French armies reduced Mannheim to rubble and destroyed the university and royal palace of Heidelberg (1688). The Catholic Elector John William (*reg.* 1690–1716) reintroduced persecution of the Calvinist population, driving many to emigration, and in the 18th cent. the principality sank to the position of a minor German state. The only achievement of John William's reign was the reunification of the two Palatinates when Maximilian Emmanuel of Bavaria was deprived of the Upper Palatinate under the imperial ban (1706).

After the death of Charles Philip (*reg.* 1716–42) the Neuburg line also became extinct and the Palatinate passed to Charles Theodore of Sulzbach (*reg.* 1742–99), who later inherited Bavaria (1777). Towards the end of his reign the Palatinate was occupied by the French (1793–4), before being divided between France and her client state, Baden, in the Recession of 1803. At the Congress of Vienna (1815) the former electorate was shared between Bavaria, who gained the West Rhenish and Upper Palatinates, and Baden, which kept the East Rhenish lands. Thence the areas formerly constituting the Palatinate passed into the Bismarckian Reich (1871).

H. Holborn, *A History of Modern Germany: the Reformation* (London, 1959).
H. Holborn, *A History of Modern Germany: 1648–1840* (London, 1963). MKS

PALATINE HILL, chief of Rome's seven hills and the site of the earliest settlement (*c.* 9th cent. BC). In the 1st cent. BC it was a desirable residential area where Crassus, Cicero, and Mark Antony, among others, had houses. It became the site of imperial palaces built by Augustus, Tiberius, and Nero, whose Golden House extended across from the hill to the Esquiline.

PALAZZO BARBERINI, Italian Baroque palace in Rome, designed by Carlo Maderna and started in 1628 shortly before his death (1629). The facade was by Bernini and much of the decorative detail by Borromini, and its design bore the influence of the elegant architecture of northern Italy rather than traditional Roman austerity.

PALAZZO CHIGI, in Rome, 16th cent. palace of the Chigi family, which became (1923) the headquarters of the Italian foreign office. The *Confindustria* and fascist union officials agreed on a mutual recognition pact there in Dec. 1923.

PALEMBANG SULTANATE, Muslin and commercial centre in South Sumatra. It was the site of the ancient Buddhist empire of Sri Vijaya (*c.* 7th–13th cents) and Chinese pirates and Javanese (Majapahit) expansion in the 14th cent. In adopting Islam (15th cent.) Palembang became virtually independent, though, under Sura, a group of Muslim Javanese from Demak were able to establish a new dynasty (1544). Javanese cultural influences remained strong until they were challenged by Arabic influences in the 18th cent.

As an important centre for collecting pepper and Bangka tin, Palembang had a Dutch post from 1640. During the British invasion of Java (1811), Palembang massacred its Dutch garrison. A turbulent decade followed, as both Raffles and the Dutch attempted to regain a foothold. After a series of military expeditions (1819, 1821, 1825) the Dutch abolished the sultanate and ruled through district chiefs. Rubber and oil brought relative prosperity to Palembang in the 1920s.

PALERMO, important natural harbour on the north-western coast of Sicily which first became prominent as the capital of the Carthaginian territories on the island. It was conquered by the Romans in 254 BC and was a Hellenic city for over 1000 years. The African Muslims captured it in AD 835 and for over two centuries it was one of the greatest Muslim cities in the Mediterranean world. Another revolutionary change came with its capture by the Normans in 1071. As capital of the Norman state of Sicily, it remained a large cosmopolitan city, seat of a splendid royal court, and a centre of magnificent churches, romanesque in style, but decorated with Byzantine mosaics. A temporary decline came with the conquest of southern Italy by Charles of Anjou (1266), as he distrusted the Sicilians and made Naples, on the mainland, his principal capital. The great Sicilian rebellion against Charles, known as the Sicilian Vespers, which occurred at Easter 1282, started with the massacre of all the Frenchmen and other foreigners in Palermo, no longer a tolerant cosmopolitan community. It again became the capital of a separate Sicilian kingdom (1282–1435) and experienced in the 14th and 15th cents its last period of economic prosperity as a centre of sugar plantations and silk exports. With the passing of Sicily under Spanish rule early in the 16th cent. there began, for Sicily in general and especially for Palermo, a long period of economic decline which a succession of fierce popular revolts could never reverse. The last of these risings, in 1860, ended the rule of the Spanish Bourbons in Sicily.

PALERMO, BATTLE OF (1676), French naval victory in the Franco–Dutch War (1672–8) which challenged Dutch superiority in the Mediterranean and gave France a foothold in Sicily, then ruled by the Dutch republic's ally, Spain.

PALESTINE GUERRILLAS, Palestinian Arabs engaged in an armed struggle against Israel. Apart from Egyptian-trained *fedayin*, who attacked Israeli territory from the Gaza strip (1955–6), most Palestine activity against Israel before the 1960s was unorganized. Of those organizations which became prominent in the 1960s the most important was Al-Fatah, whose military wing, Al-Asifa, attacked Israeli territory on 31 Dec. 1964. The Palestine Liberation Organization (PLO) under Ahmad Shukairy was established in Egypt in 1964 as the official representative body of the Palestinian Arabs and formed the Palestine Liberation Army to assist in the conquest of Israel. After the June 1967 War the guerrilla organizations played a more active role, winning considerable support and prestige in their battle with Israeli forces at Karameh (21 March 1968). Under their leader, Ysir Arafat, the guerrillas dominated the PLO and their radical views influenced the policies of Arab states. In Jordan they became very strong. In 1970 they opposed the cease-fire agreement concluded by Israel, Egypt, and Jordan. One group, the popular front for the Liberation of Palestine, led by George Habbash, hijacked aircraft belonging to western airlines (Sept. 1970). This action led the Jordanian government to strike against the guerrillas. The ensuing civil war resulted in a considerable reduction of guerrilla power.

PALESTINE, JEWISH IMMIGRATION TO. Although some Spanish Jews entered Palestine in the 16th cent., immigration really began in the second half of the 19th cent. The immigrants came principally from the Russian empire, helped financially by rich west European Jews. By 1914 some 40,000 Jews had entered Palestine, of whom about 12,000 were in agricultural colonies. Immigration increased after the Balfour Declaration (1917) and the establishment of British rule. In the 1920s about 100,000 Jews entered, of whom 33,801 arrived in the peak year (1925), and about 20,000 left. The influx of immigrants decreased rapidly after 1925, and 1928 saw a small net outflow. After remaining at a low level (1930–2), immigration increased rapidly (1933–5), reaching a peak of 61,854 in 1936. Thereafter immigration was limited for political reasons and averaged some 17,000 a year (1936–9). These figures do not include illegal immigrants. The majority of Jews who entered Palestine between 1920 and 1939 came from eastern Europe, especially Poland, although after 1933 the proportion from Germany and central Europe increased, and in the period 1938–9 were in the majority. Immigration thereafter (1939–47) was heavily restricted, but after the establishment of the state of Israel (May 1948) all restrictions on the entry of Jews were removed (legalized in the Law of Return, 1950). Of 687,000 Jews who entered Israel between 1948 and 1951, nearly half came from Asia and Africa. Although this rate was not maintained, further substantial immigration of Jews, particularly from the Middle East, took place in subsequent years.   MEY

PALESTINE, PARTITION OF. Until 1936, Britons, Jews, and Arabs all envisaged the development of Palestine (excluding Transjordan) as a unitary state. In 1936, increasing Arab hostility to Jewish immigration and sales of land to Jews culminated in a general strike (April) and outbreaks of violence, which led to a rebellion in parts of Palestine (1937–9). The report of the 1936–7 Peel Commission, which was appointed to investigate the disturbances, recommended (July 1937) the partition of Palestine into three areas: a Jewish state (including part of coastal Palestine, Esdraelon, and Galilee); an Arab state (including Transjordan); and a mandated territory, consisting of Jerusalem and a corridor to the sea at Jaffa. The British government accepted the recommendations, which were also accepted—though with strong reservations—by the Zionists, but they were rejected by the Arabs. The 1938 Woodhead Commission, appointed to recommend detailed boundaries, reported, however, that partition was impracticable. The British government thereupon abandoned partition and after failing to secure Arab and Zionist agreement, put forward a new policy in the Palestine White Paper (17 May 1939) which proposed to limit Jewish immigration to a total of 75,000 in the period 1939–44 and thereafter to make further immigration dependent upon the agreement of the Arab population of Palestine. Although rejected by both Jews and Arabs, the White Paper remained official British policy until 1945, although Jewish immigration was allowed to continue at the rate of 16,000 a year after the quota had been reached. In the meantime, Jewish pressure was increased by the support of American Zionists in the Biltmore Programme (May 1942), which demanded unrestricted immigration and the establishment of a unitary Jewish Commonwealth in Palestine, and by the moral dilemma posed by the extermination of European Jewry in areas under German control (1939–45). Debate crystallized over the admission to Palestine of the 100,000 survivors of the German policy of genocide who were in camps in Europe. The Anglo-American Committee recommended (April 1946) the admission of these 100,000 and the ending of restrictions on Jewish land purchase. Britain rejected these proposals and put forward (July 1946) a new scheme of provincial autonomy in Palestine. After failing to achieve agreement on this basis, Britain decided (Feb. 1947) to refer the matter to the United Nations. The UN Special Committee on Palestine recommended (Aug. 1947) partition. This was accepted (29 Nov. 1947) by the General Assembly and on the termination of the mandate on 15 May 1948 the state of Israel came into being.

P. Sykes, *Crossroads to Israel* (London, 1965).
J. Marlowe, *Seat of Pilate* (London, 1959).   MEY

PALESTINIAN ARAB REFUGEES. During the disturbances and wars in Palestine (1947–9) many Arabs left the area eventually occupied by Israel. The exact number is disputed, but was in the region of 550,000. In addition, some Arabs whose homes were in Arab territory lost their livelihood because their lands, areas of employment, or markets fell into Israeli hands. These 'economic refugees' numbered some 200,000. In 1949 the Clapp Mission estimated the number of refugees at 726,000. Responsibility for their welfare was assumed by the United Nations through UNRWA. According to UNRWA statistics, the total number of refugees (including economic refugees) on 31 May 1967 was 1,344,576. This figure, which shows the substantial natural increase among the refugees, has been criticized for making inadequate allowances for refugees who had been 'absorbed' either through settlement or finding permanent employment in various Arab countries, and for imperfect recording of deaths. It has been estimated that 15 per cent of refugees were self-supporting and 15 per cent partially self-supporting. The refugees were divided as follows: Jordan 722,687 (232,686 in camps); Gaza 316,776 (201,828); Syria 144,390 (34,160); Lebanon 160,723 (75,316). The June war (1967) further aggravated the refugee problem. According to the Michelmore report (6 Dec. 1967) about 550,000 refugees remained in Israeli-occupied territory (equally divided between Gaza and the Jordan West Bank), 110,000 refugees fled from the west to the east bank of the Jordan, and were accompanied by some 120,000 inhabitants of the west bank, who thus became refugees for the first time. In addition, 16,000 Palestinian refugees and 100,000 Syrian residents left the Golan Heights, 55,000 United Arab Republic residents were displaced from east of the Suez Canal, and an unknown but much larger number from the west bank of the canal through the continuing hostilities.   MEY

PALESTRINA, GIOVANNI PIERLUIGI DA (1526–94), Italian composer of sacred music, who was master of a chapel at the Vatican. His *Missa Papae Marcelli* ensured the survival of polyphonic music in the mass at a time when the Council of Trent had discussed its prohibition. Palestrina wrote a great number of masses, litanies, and chants, and two books of madrigals. He anticipated the orchestral masses of Bach and the oratorios of Handel.

PALEY, WILLIAM (1743–1805), English scholar and divine, who expounded rational and utilitarian Christianity. His works include *Principles of Moral and Political Philosophy* (1785) and *Evidences of Christianity* (1794).

PALI CANON or *T(r)ipitaka*, holy texts of the Buddhists in Ceylon and South-East Asia. Though traditionally the words of Lord Buddha, the actual texts were written down in their present form in Ceylon (1st cent. AD). They are written in Pali, originally a popular language derived from an early form of Sanskrit in present Bihar and used in ancient times as a medium of communication between Buddhist monks all over South Asia.

PALLADIO, ANDREA (1518–80), Italian architect who studied the *De Re Architectura* of Vitruvius (1st cent. BC) and published *Four Books on Architecture* (1570) which inspired a revival of the classical style. He designed churches and villas in Rome, Vicenza, and Venice, and the 'Palladian' style influenced European architecture for the next 200 years, in Britain through Inigo Jones and his school.

PALLAS (d. 62), Roman ex-slave who became financial secretary to Emperor Claudius, and acquired enormous wealth. He supported Agrippina's marriage to Claudius, and Nero's succession, but Nero later dismissed him and allegedly had him poisoned.

PALLAVA DYNASTY, ancient Indian royal dynasty (*c.* 4th cent. AD) which controlled large parts of southern India, notably the east coast (Coromandel) from their capital at Kanchi (Conjeevaram). Pallava history has been reconstructed from numerous copper-plate charters, the earliest in Prakrit, but later in mixed or pure Sanskrit. Most of these are land grants to Brahmans.

It is no longer believed that the Pallavas were originally connected with the Pahlavas, *ie*, Parthians. They may have been a local family in the service of the Satavahanas of the northern Deccan, who made themselves independent after the disintegration of the empire of their overlords.

The Pallavas were involved in intermittent warfare with their southern neighbours, the Pandyas, and with the Chalukyas in the north. They were at the zenith of their power in the reign of Narasimhavarman I Mahamalla (*reg. c.* 630–68) and remained the dominating state in South India till their sudden collapse when their last king, Aparajita (*reg.* 879–97), was completely defeated by a coalition of other South Indian kingdoms.

Pallava administration shows a happy compromise between central authority and local autonomy. This stimulated social and economic developments, notably the rise of mercantile and military corporations. The main fame of the Pallavas rests, however, on their great achievements in art and architecture, as well as in Indian cultural expansion to parts of South-East Asia during their rule. The most impressive monuments left by the Pallavas are those of Mamallapuram. Pallava style, influenced by North Indian Gupta art, is both harmonious and vigorous. It is also during the Pallava period that we find evidence for the rise of Indianized kingdoms in South-East Asia. The type of script of the earliest South-East Asian inscriptions and other indications suggest that the Pallovas played an important part in the expansion of Indian ideas and traditions to this area. JG de C

PALMARES, REPUBLIC OF, settlement of fugitive Negroes in the Brazilian state of Alagôas, whose population of some 20,000 had a capital city, a king, and an organized government. Palmares flourished for over 50 years and was destroyed by the government in 1697.

PALMER RAIDS (Nov. 1919–Jan. 1920) in US, large-scale arrest of suspected radicals by the US Justice Department under A. Mitchell Palmer, marking the high point of the 'Red Scare'. During 1919, the apparent spread of Bolshevism in Europe, bombing incidents, the formation of the US Communist and Communist Labor parties, and a series of major strikes, had combined to create a fear of revolution among the American public. Since many of the known anarchists and communists in the US were aliens, they were liable to deportation, and in Dec. 1919 249 people (including Emma Goldman and Alexander Berkman) were sent to Russia aboard the transport ship *Buford*. On 2 Jan. 1920 over 4000 people were arrested in raids throughout the country, but, largely owing to the efforts of the assistant secretary of labor, Louis F. Post, only a few of these were eventually deported. Palmer sought to exploit public tension in furtherance of his presidential ambitions, but by the summer of 1920 the hysteria had abated.

PALMERSTON, HENRY JOHN TEMPLE, 3rd Viscount (Irish) (1784–1865), British politician and prime minister. His high-handed diplomacy made him popular at home, but not abroad. The coalition of Whigs and Peelites which he formed in 1859 became in later years the Liberal party.

He succeeded to an Irish peerage in 1802 and became an MP in 1807. He held office as lord of the admiralty (1807–9), secretary at war (1809–28), foreign secretary (1830–4, 1835–1841, 1846–51), home secretary (1852–5), and prime minister (1855–8, 1859–65). Though originally a Tory, he joined Grey's Whig government in 1830. As foreign secretary he faced the aftermath of the Belgian revolution at the Conference of London (1831) and finally, by 1839, secured a five-power guarantee of Belgium's independence. He supported the constitutional rule of the Queens of Spain and Portugal against the rival candidates of reactionary powers, and with French assistance formed the Quadruple Alliance (1834). He dealt with Greek independence by the London Protocol (1830). After Muhammad Ali's attack on the Turkish empire (1831), and the ensuing Russian triumph in the treaty of Unkiar-Skelessi (1833) he resolved the crisis by the London Convention (1840) and the Straits Convention (1841), though threatened with war by Muhammad's ally, France. He also protected British rights in Afghanistan against Russia and in the Far East against China in the Opium War (1840–2).

Palmerston's next period as foreign secretary (1846) was stormy. Anglo-French relations worsened after his opposition to the projected Franco-Spanish royal marriage. He offended Queen Victoria by recognition of the French republican government (1848) and his encouragement of liberal revolutionaries in Portugal, Spain, and Italy. The Don Pacifico incident (1850) infuriated Greece, her patron France, and all Liberal opinion, though Palmerston defended his conduct successfully in the Commons. While supporting the Austrian empire as a bastion against Russian influence, his comments on Gen. Haynau exacerbated Anglo-Austrian relations. His approval of Louis Napoleon's *coup d'état* without proper consultation with the queen or the cabinet led to his dismissal (1851). He secured the defeat of the government on the Militia Bill, and later returned to office as home secretary (1852).

On the collapse of Aberdeen's government during the Crimean War, Palmerston became prime minister (1855). The fall of Sevastopol and the ensuing peace of Paris brought him the prestige of victory. He dealt calmly with the Indian Mutiny (1857), but was defeated in the Commons over the *Arrow* incident (1858). Though victorious in a general election, he was briefly put out of office over the Conspiracy to Murder Bill (1858), returning to power in 1859. He supported Italian unification and refused to join France in a naval expedition to prevent Garibaldi's invasion of Naples. His conduct of the *Trent* and *Alabama* incidents, and his inability to support Denmark at the London Conference (1864) showed the restraining influence upon him of public opinion, his colleagues, and the queen. In his domestic policy he discouraged change, and Gladstone's Free Trade policy was hampered by the demands of foreign policy and defence. Palmerston died shortly after electoral victory (1865). In spite of his policy of intervention, he left Britain diplomatically isolated.

D. Southgate, *The Most English Minister* (London, 1966).
J. Ridley, *Lord Palmerston* (London, 1970) VEC

PALMYRA (Aramaic Tadmor), important city in antiquity, situated on an oasis astride the southern-most caravan route between Mesopotamia and Syria and formed by the amalgamation of 24 tribes, only superficially hellenized. Its spectacular ruins show its close links with Mesopotamia and Persia. After being raided by Mark Antony in 41 BC, it came under Roman influence after AD 17. Germanicus made customs regulations, a legionary legate paid a formal visit, and Vespasian built a road. After 167 it was garrisoned and *c.* 200, became a Roman colony, Palmyrenes serving in the Roman army as individuals and in units; extensive public buildings mark its prosperity. When Roman power in the East collapsed after the Persian capture of Emperor Valerian (260), Odenathus resisted the Persians and rebellious generals and won control of Syria. His family were already predominant in Palmyra, and on his nomination by Gallienus Corrector of all the Orient, he assumed the title King of Kings. He was murdered (266–7) and succeeded by his wife, Zenobia, and son, Vallabath, who occupied Egypt (270) and became respectively Augusta and Augustus. Their power was broken by the Emperor Aurelian (272) and Palmyra destroyed (273). It lost its eastern trade to Nisibis and never recovered, though it survived as a small garrison town and bishopric.

PAMIR COMMISSION (1873), Anglo-Russian agreement on Afghanistan's northern frontier, which was too imprecise and came under Russian pressure. An agreement (1887) defined the western sector, but Russian encroachments on the still undefined eastern sector in the Pamirs led to serious crises from 1895 and the partial delimitation of the frontier by the Anglo-Russian Pamir Boundary Commission (1895). Attempts to make China a party to the agreement failed and she rejected the delimitation of her frontiers with British India, Afghanistan, and Russia.

PAMPLONA, ancient Basque centre of Navarre, settled by the Romans and Visigoths, and sacked by the Franks (533), Charlemagne's forces (778), and the Muslims (938), which became the capital of the independent kingdom of Navarre (10th–16th cents. It was occupied by Ferdinand of Aragon and incorporated into Spain (1515). Its siege by the French (1521) provided the occasion for Ignatius Loyola's injury which resulted in his spiritual metamorphosis.

PAN CH'AO (*fl.* 1st cent. AD), Chinese soldier whose expedition of AD 94 effectively re-established Han prestige in Central Asia for a few decades.

PAN KU (d. *c.* AD 92), Chinese historian, who was co-author, with his father and sister, of the *Han-shu*, or standard history of the western Han period.

PANAETIUS (*c.* 185–109 BC), Greek Stoic philosopher from Rhodes, who, as a member of the cultural circle of Scipio Aemilianus, was largely instrumental in adapting Stoic doctrines to Roman ways.

PAN-AFRICANIST CONGRESS of South Africa broke away from the African National Congress in 1959 under the leadership of Robert Sobukwe over the question of collaboration with non-African groups in the liberation struggle. In the Western Cape and Southern Transvaal it stole the initiative from the ANC. It was banned (1960), but its activities were continued underground and in exile.

PANAGAL, RAJA SIR PANAGATI RAMARAYANINGAR (1866–1928), Indian 'non-Brahman' politician and leader of the Justice Party, who was the 'chief minister' of its ministry in the first of the reformed legislatures (1921–6). He also held the portfolio of local self-government. There was increasing criticism of his leadership and his alleged misuse of his powers of patronage. The decline of the Justice Party in the 1926 elections meant that he was subsequently unable to form a ministry.

PANAMA CANAL. The possibility of cutting a canal across the isthmus of Panama was first considered by 16th-cent. explorers and again by the Scot William Paterson, during the Darién colonizing project of 1698. The 19th cent. saw a series of schemes which culminated in the US assuming the financial burden of constructing a canal, which opened in 1915.

PANAMA CONGRESS, held in 1826 at the urging of Simón Bolívar. The conference was attended by only a few of the newly independent Latin American states. Attempts to set up regional confederations failed, but the Congress of Panama is regarded as the first concrete attempt at inter-American co-operation.

PANAMA SCANDAL (1893), one of a series of affairs that shook the confidence of the French people in the politicians of the Third Republic. The Panama Co. had promoted the sale of its shares by a lottery for which special legislation was required. Several politicians, including the radical leaders, Clemenceau and Floquet, were accused of accepting bribes from the company. Six ministers were put on trial and one was convicted. The republic was, in fact, in greater danger from the royalist, clerical, and military extremists who sought to destroy it, than from the corruption they exposed.

PAN-AMERICAN CONFERENCES, series of American international conferences to discuss common aims and problems. The purpose of the conferences generally has been inter-American solidarity, and success at achieving this has been mixed. The 1942 conference, held in Rio de Janeiro, managed to reach a fair degree of unanimity on pan-American attitudes towards the Axis powers and the Second World War. The one held at Punta del Este, Uruguay, in 1961 was instrumental in setting up the Alliance for Progress, despite emphatic opposition from Cuba. Some other conferences have had more nebulous results, and critics have accused the parties involved of indulging in pious but unimplemented expressions of vague goodwill. Others assert that many of the conferences, particularly those since 1900, have been 'managed' by the US.

PAN-AMERICAN HIGHWAY, incomplete highway running from the US–Mexican border to the Argentine. Its construction began in the 1930s and sections have been officially opened from time to time. The cost has far exceeded original expectations. In 1970 only one section remained to be built— the link which would join Panama and Colombia through a wild, unexplored jungle region inhabited by hostile Indians.

PAN-AMERICAN UNION, in existence since the end of the 19th cent. passed under the control of the Organization of American States when the OAS was established in 1948. The Pan-American Union acts as the administrative arm of the OAS, but its most important activities within recent years have been concerned with cultural and informational exchanges among the several American nations belonging to the OAS.

PAN-ARABISM, movement for the political union of Arabic-speaking peoples. The creation after 1918 of separate Arab states under European control encouraged thoughts of political union, which became significant after Arab states began to achieve independence. From the 1930s the lead was taken by Iraqis with various plans for Fertile Crescent unity, involving Iraq, Syria, Palestine, and Lebanon. A new factor was injected by the decision in 1944 to establish the Arab League, which became the major organization for co-operative Arab action. The creation of the league meant that other Arab states, notably Egypt, became involved in plans for union, and rivalry developed between Egypt and Iraq. In 1958 two federations came into being—the United Arab Republic of Egypt and Syria, with which the Yemen became associated, and the Arab Federation of Iraq and Jordan. The 1958 Iraqi revolution destroyed the second and the first was dissolved in 1961. In 1963 an attempt to unite Egypt, Syria, and Iraq failed, when the parties could not agree on the form it should take. Efforts continued, however, fostered by united hostility to Israel and by changes in regimes in various Arab states. In 1970 a new federation of Egypt, Libya, and the Sudan was announced, to which Syria subsequently acceded, but this had yet at the end of 1970 to be translated into practice. The repeated failures of attempts at union, despite the strong support in Arab countries, notably by political parties such as the Ba'th, has provoked much discussion about the reasons. Arab socialists have argued that union must be preceded by political, social, and economic revolution in Arab countries; others have expressed fears of Egyptian domination or the strength of regional and sectarian interests within Arab states.

                                                                                        MEY

PANATHENAEA, principal annual summer festival of ancient Athens, in every fourth year the Great Panathenaea, celebrated in honour of the patron goddess Athena's birthday. Athletic contests were added to music competitions in the 5th cent. BC, and the festival culminated in a civic procession which included a wheeled ship which carried as a sail a great woven robe for presentation to Athena Polias on the Acropolis. This was followed by sacrifice and feasting.

PANAY INCIDENT (12 Dec. 1937), crisis in US–Japanese relations following the sinking of an American gunboat, the USS *Panay*, and three Standard Oil tankers on the Yangtse river. This unprovoked attack by Japanese planes incensed the US government, but war between the two countries was ruled out by the isolationist mood of the American people and Japan's willingness to apologize and pay an indemnity, later set at $2,214,007.

PANCHAYATI RAJ, system of local self-government generally in use in India by the 1960s. The present (1970) form derives mainly from the recommendations of the Balwantray Mehta report on community projects (1957), which suggested that the then existing haphazard collection of district or *taluk* boards, development block 'advisory committees', and village *panchayat*s, should be replaced by a uniform three-tier system of representative bodies which would be provided with genuine powers and resources. Although there are some variations in different states, the general pattern is of a directly elected *gram panchayat* at the village level; a *panchayat samiti* at the development block level, comprising the chairmen of the *gram panchayat*s included within it, together with some co-opted legislators and officials; and the *zila parishad* or district council, comprising the chairmen of the *panchayat samiti*s and the co-opted members. The executive work of these bodies is carried out by the development officials at each level: the *gram sevak* or village-level worker, the block development officer, and the district planning officer.

PANCHAYATS, representative bodies of five or more persons by which Indian villagers regulated their communal affairs. Mountstuart Elphinstone in Bombay and Thomas Munro in Madras advocated their preservation where possible. They failed because the introduction of law courts under British rule undermined the authority of the village *panchayat*s, which had no means of enforcing their decisions, and villagers preferred to resort to the civil courts for the settlement of their disputes.

Caste *panchayat*s, which still function, deal with breaches of caste rules.

PANCHEN LAMA. The abbots of Tashilunpo monastery in Tibet have borne the title 'Panchen' (meaning 'great scholar') since the incumbency of Lopsang Chökyi Gyeltsen (1557–1662), tutor to the 5th Dalai Lama. Following the latter's pronouncement, subsequent abbots of Tashilunpo were chosen as successive reincarnations, ultimately of the Buddha Amitabha. They have frequently been associated with the Tibetan ambitions of the Chinese government, which attempted to use them as counterweights to the Dalai Lamas. The present Panchen Lama was selected by the Chinese Nationalist authorities in 1949, and did not follow the 14th Dalai Lama into exile. He was supported by the Chinese communist regime as a figurehead (1959–*c.* 1965), but then fell out of favour. There is some mystery regarding his whereabouts since about 1965. Most Panchen Lamas have been prolific authors.

PANDIT, MRS VIJAYA LAKSHMI (1900–), Indian nationalist politician and diplomatist, a sister of Jawaharlal Nehru. She was active in the Congress campaigns of the 1930s and became India's first woman minister, when she took the portfolios of local self-government and public health in the United Provinces (1937–9). After the war she led the Indian delegation at the United Nations (1946–50) and was elected president of the General Assembly in 1953. She was Indian ambassador to the USSR (1947–9) and to the US (1949–52), and then High Commissioner in London (1955–1961). She returned to Indian political life as governor of Maharashtra (1962–4) and then, after the death of her brother, as a member of the Lok Sabha from his seat (1964–8).

PANDO, JOSÉ MANUEL (1848–1917), Bolivian soldier, liberal politician, and president of Bolivia (1899–1904), who seized power by a *coup d'état.*

PANDYAS, ancient dynasty of southern-most India, perhaps from the 4th cent. BC, which is mentioned in classical Tamil literature (Sangam). During most of the time the Pandyas were, however, feudatories of dynasties ruling to the north of their country, notably the Pallavas and Cholas, but were independent and powerful in the 9th cent., and especially in the 13th cent., when they were the dominant power of South India. The ancient Pandya capital, Madurai, still testifies to the greatness of the Pandyas, though many of its monuments were built or renovated after the decline of the dynasty.

PAN-GERMAN LEAGUE, founded in 1894, was partly responsible for the growth of Anglo-German hostility early in the 20th cent., and was influential on the young Adolf Hitler. It had no official backing before 1933. The league tried to encourage national sentiment among Germans both at home and overseas, to preserve and support German culture, to further German interests, and to expand German frontiers, including those of her colonies. It received much financial support from industrialists, but before 1914 never had more than 20,000 members. Its main work was the circulation of propaganda. It had a wide following in Austria, where Schönerer stressed the superiority of Germans over Slavs and the evils of Semitic capitalism.

PANGKOR ENGAGEMENT (1874), precedent for British indirect control of the Peninsular Malay States. By its terms Britain recognized one of the rival chiefs as Sultan of Perak, and furnished a resident, whose advice 'must be asked and acted upon on all questions other than those touching Malay Religion and Custom'.

PANGUL, BATTLE OF (*c.* 1419), 25 miles (40 kms) north of the confluence of the Kistna and Tungabhadra rivers. It was fought between Firoz Shah Bahmini, Sultan of the Deccan, and Vira Vijaya, Raja of Vijayanagar. Pangul had been taken by the Hindus, Firoz besieged it for two years, and was then defeated by a relieving force.

PANIN, NIKITA IVANOVICH, Count (1718–83), Russian diplomat and ambassador to Sweden, who was head of the department of foreign affairs (1763–80) and Catherine II's chief diplomatic adviser. He was also tutor to the Grand Duke Paul. He was an admirer of the Swedish aristocratic constitution, and advocated an Imperial Council (1762), though this was never established, and he reorganized the senate.

In foreign policy his scheme for a Northern Accord to maintain the balance of power and peace in Europe never materialized. He aligned Russia with Prussia and, although he argued for an independent but friendly Poland associated with Russia, he implemented the partition of that country. His influence declined in his last years.

PANINI, semi-legendary author of the earliest Sanskrit grammar (*Ashtadhyayi*), probably of the 5th–4th cents BC. This work, the composition of which is based on remarkable mnemotechnic rather than systematic considerations, is notable for its astounding richness and for the keenness of phonetic and other linguistic observations.

PANIPAT, BATTLES OF (1526, 1556, 1761), three decisive battles in north Indian history. The first (1526) was fought between the Mughal leader, Babur, then ruler of Kabul, and the Sultan of Delhi, Ibrahim Lodi. Babur won by using the still novel artillery and by the clever use of Turkish cavalry tactics. The Lodi power collapsed and the battle marks the beginning of Mughal rule in India. The second battle (1556) was fought between Bairam Khan, the general and protector of Akbar, the young grandson of Babur, and Hemu, the Hindu general and claimant for the Delhi throne. Hemu's defeat and death re-established the Mughal power. The third battle (1761) was fought between Ahmad Shah Abdali of Afghanistan, and the Marathas led by the peshwa's cousin, the Bhao Sahib, who were totally defeated. This battle marks the end of effective Mughal rule.

PAN-ISLAMISM, movement for the political unity of Muslim peoples. The old idea of the unity of the Muslim community decayed with the decline of the Abbasid caliphate. It was given a renewed importance when, in the treaty of Kuchuk-Kainardji (1774), the Ottoman sultan first advanced a claim to religious jurisdiction over Muslims outside his territories. The implications of this claim were subsequently elaborated, notably by Abdülhamid II (*reg.* 1876–1909), who employed the doctrine of Pan-Islamism both as an internal cement for his empire and as a diplomatic weapon to influence European powers with large subject Muslim populations. At the same time the theory was given a different aspect by Jamal-al-Din al-Afghani (1839–97), who contemplated a union of Muslim states (particularly the Ottoman empire, Iran, and Afghanistan) to resist European encroachment. With this Afghani coupled ideas about the modernization of Islamic society. Under his successors, Muhammad Abduh and Rashid Rida, this led to the movement of Islamic modernism. Fears of a general Muslim rising troubled European governments until after the end of the First World War. But the abolition of the Ottoman sultanate (1923) and the caliphate (1924) removed the political focus from Pan-Islamism and such movements as the Khilafat agitation in India died out. Interest in cultural unity was sustained by organizations such as the World Islamic Congress and attempts to provide a political content have been made, *eg*, by King Faisal of Saudi Arabia. The enduring strength of Muslim feeling has been demonstrated by the Muslim Brotherhood and similar organizations.

MEY

PANJDEH CRISIS (30 March 1895), Anglo-Russian crisis arising from the Russian occupation of the Panjdeh oasis, claimed by Afghanistan. Fears for Indian security almost led Britain to war, but a compromise led to an agreement on the Russo-Afghan frontier (Sept. 1885).

PANKHURST, EMMELINE (1858–1928), British founder of the Women's Franchise League (1889) and, subsequently, of the more militant Women's Social and Political Union (1903). Her husband, Richard Marsden (1839–98), had advocated women's suffrage as early as the 1860s. Her daughters, Christabel (1880–1958) and Estelle Sylvia (1882–1960), were also identified with the cause. All three women participated in the campaign before the First World War, and shared with many others the experience of prison and hunger-strikes. In 1914 the organization and experience of the WSPU was geared to the war-effort. It remains arguable whether the campaign of the WSPU in peacetime or the contribution of women in the war was the greater factor in their attaining the vote in 1918.

Subsequently Emmeline left the Labour Party to become a Conservative, Christabel became a religious propagandist of the second coming of Christ, working largely in the US, and Sylvia founded the Workers' Socialist Federation in London (which grew out of the East End Federation of Suffragettes). Although strongly influenced by communism, she did not join the Communist Party. Much of her life's work was devoted to Ethiopian affairs, about which she wrote substantially (1945–60).

PAN-MALAYAN ISLAMIC PARTY (PMIP), largest opposition party in independent Malaya/Malaysia. It represents (1970) exclusively Malay and Muslim interests, and is strongest in the relatively isolated north-eastern states of Kelantan (whose state government it has controlled since 1959) and Trengganu.

PANMUNJOM TRUCE (27 July 1953), which ended the Korean War. Negotiations began on 8 July 1951 at Kaesong, but because of the propaganda advantages of Kaesong to the communists the talks were moved to Panmunjom on 6 Sept.

PANNONIA, Roman province south of the Danube covering parts of Hungary, Austria, and Yugoslavia. It was conquered under the Emperor Augustus and was always of great military importance, being garrisoned by three or four legions; legionary fortresses included Vindobona (Vienna) and Aquincum (Buda). An important strategic and trade route crossed the Danube at Carnuntum (Petronell). There were some rich villas north of Lake Balaton. The mixed population of Pannonia produced excellent soldiers. In spite of much strengthening of the defences by Valentinian, the province was overrun by the Ostrogoths, *c.* 400.

PANSLAVISM, name given to a current of opinion in eastern Europe in the 19th cent. which emphasized the brotherhood of Slavs. In Russia, where it was especially strong (1860s–1880s), it involved a belief in Russia's historic mission to liberate the southern Slavs from Turkish or Austrian rule and to attain Constantinople. It was never an organized movement, but incorporated both slavophile and nationalist expansionist ideas and has been described as a transition between earlier slavophilism and panrussianism.

Ivan Aksakov, a dominant figure, was a slavophile and head of the Moscow Slavonic Benevolent Committee (founded in 1858). The committee's Slavonic Ethnographic Exhibition in Moscow in 1867 has been regarded as the beginning of panslavism. Aksakov and Pogodin turned the earlier cultural and religious interests of slavophilism into political fields and stressed the divine duty of Russia to reunite the orthodox Slavs, oppressed by foreign and non-orthodox governments. In practice, this involved, as Gen. Fadeyev urged in his book, *Opinion on the Eastern Question* (1869), military campaigns against the Ottoman and Habsburg empires. Danilevsky, the other main theorist of the movement, stressed the messianic nature of orthodoxy, which he saw as destined to conquer and replace a western Catholic civilization.

The movement was joined and supported by people whose interests were nationalistic and imperialistic rather than slavophile. It acquired a considerable following among industrialists and found a powerful ally in the publicist, Katkov. It involved Russification of non-Russian minorities, including the Poles, who, as Slavs, though not orthodox, were largely excluded from panslav sympathy.

During the Near Eastern Crises (1875–85) the movement achieved considerable political influence. It was opposed by the foreign office, since the Asiatic department was panslavist in its sympathies, as was Ignatiev, the Russian ambassador in Constantinople, and as were his Balkan agents. As a purely political programme, which came nearest to success with Ignatiev's negotiation of the treaty of San Stefano at the end of the Russo-Turkish War (1877–8), panslavism involved forcible freedom of the Balkan Slavs, their unity in a federation under Russian domination (and for Russian political ends rather than Slav sentiment), and Russian control of Constantinople and the Straits. The Serbo-Turkish War (1876), in which Russian volunteers joined, and the resulting Russo-Turkish War, saw the height of panslavic popularity, especially in Moscow, and was the peak of Aksakov's career.

After the Russian failure to dominate Bulgaria (1885–6), the movement declined, but was revived, in a more moderate form, during the Balkan Wars and the First World War.

B. Sumner, *Russia and the Balkans 1870–80* (Oxford, 1937). H. Kohn, *Panslavism* (New York, 1953).   BJW

PANT, PANDIT GOVIND BALLABH (1887–1961), Indian nationalist politician, who was active in Congress from 1916. He achieved pre-eminence as a leader of Congress parliamentary organization in the United Provinces, first as leader of the Swarajya Party (1923–9), and then as chief minister (1937–9, 1946–55). He served in the Central Legislative Assembly (1934–6) and in the Constituent Assembly (1946–9). In 1955 he was home minister in the government of India (1955–61).

PANTHAY REVOLT (1855–73), revolt of the Muslim minority in Yunnan province, China, brought about by years of oppression and discrimination by the Chinese. The immediate cause of the revolt was a dispute with the Chinese over some mining properties. The leader of the revolt proclaimed a new Muslim kingdom, and with an army said to be 360,000 strong, captured 53 cities in Yunnan. The revolt was suppressed in 1873.

PANTHEON, finest surviving ancient temple in Rome. The present building was erected under Hadrian in AD 126 and replaces an early temple built by Agrippa (27 BC). Its exterior is undistinguished, but the superb interior with immense coffered dome and bold opening to the sky is a landmark in architectural history.

PANTURANIANISM, movement almost inextricably confused with panturkism. Strictly speaking, it grew out of the now much-disputed theory held by 19th-cent. Hungarian scholars that the Turkish, Mongol, Tungus, Finnish, Hungarian, and other languages belonged to the same family. This led to the advocacy of a political federation of the speakers of these languages to create a Turanian state stretching from Hungary to the Pacific. The movement never had much support outside a narrow academic circle; its aim was expressed by Ziya Gökalp in *Turan* (1911): 'The country of the Turks is not Turkey, nor yet Turkistan, Their Country is a vast and eternal land: Turan!'

PANTURKISM, movement to establish a political union of all Turkish speakers. It began in the late 19th cent. as an outgrowth of the Islamic reform movement in Russia, particularly among Turkish Muslims in the Crimea and on the Volga, who looked to the Ottoman empire for support and were influenced by panslavism. The leading figure was Isma'il Bey Gasprinskii (Gaspirali) (1851–1914), who attempted to create a common Turkish language. This was also one of the aims of the Russian Muslims, who strove for Muslim unity during the 1905 revolution. After the suppression of this movement (1907) many leaders emigrated to the Ottoman empire, where a feeling of Turkish cultural identity had already developed to some extent in response to the writings of European scholars in praise of Turkish history. This feeling is shown in the work of Ahmed Vefik (1823–91) and Süleyman Pasha (1836–92). Panturkism was given more specific form by the émigré Yusuf Akchoraoglu (Akchurin) (1876–1935), who had been educated in Constantinople and Paris and wrote (1903) an article, 'The Three Political Systems', in which he argued that panturkism (which he confusingly called panturanianism) was a better basis for the Ottoman empire than either panislamism or panottomanism. Panturkism, imperfectly distinguised from panislamism, played some part in Ottoman war aims (1914–18), especially under the influence of Enver Pasha (1881–1922), and it enjoyed a temporary revival in Turkey during the Second World War, when German successes against the USSR led to short-lived hopes of union with the Turkish territories of the USSR. Within the USSR panturkism had some influence (1918–28), particularly when supported by Sultan Galiyev (d. ? 1929), but the USSR's policy on nationalities prevented the emergence of a single Muslim–Turkish republic.
MEY

PAO HUANG HUI ('PROTECT THE EMPEROR' SOCIETY) in China, founded in June 1899 by K'ang Yu-wei after the failure of the 'Hundred Days' Reform'. It was an attempt to bring about a constitutional monarchy in Ch'ing China and had many branches in Chinese communities overseas, drawing support from merchants, students, and secret societies. In the end the society failed, while the more appealing revolutionary cause headed by Sun Yat-sen and Huang Hsing succeeded.

PAOLI, PASQUALE (1728–1807), Corsican soldier and patriot, who led a long revolutionary war against the republic of Genoa (1755–68). After calling in French troops, the Genoese sold the island to France for two million *livres* (1768). Paoli and his followers held out for a year.

PAPACY, THE, that office of universal authority over Christianity claimed by the bishops of Rome by virtue of their position as successors of St Peter. This authority was asserted as early as the late 1st cent. AD by Pope Clement I. The collapse of the imperial authority in the West in the 5th cent. made the popes pre-eminent in the western provinces of the Roman empire, outstanding popes like Leo I (mid-5th cent.) and Gregory I (*reg.* 590–604) acting as leaders of the Roman people and enjoying enormous personal authority. The claims of the papacy to act as an effective supervisor of all the provincial churches of Catholic Europe date, as a practical reality, from the 12th cent. They are the great legacy of the Gregorian reform movement in the second half of the 11th cent. Significantly the word papacy (Latin *papatus*) first appeared early in the 12th cent. In the period from the election of Gregory VII (*reg.* 1073–85) to the death of Innocent III (*reg.* 1198–1216), the moral, spiritual, and legal authority of the popes increased enormously. The idea of the pope as ʃuniversal ʃordinary (with episcopal authority over every bishopric) was clearly defined and regularly implemented. A body of well-organized Canon Law, defining and applying the papal supremacy, was elaborated by 1140 by Gratian and his pupil, Pope Alexander III (*reg.* 1159–81). This made a great contribution to the creation of a judicial system centred at Rome and operating locally through papal judges delegate, who reported their findings and recommendations to the pope. Papal interest and intervention in all the countries of western Christendom became normal and continual. They launched crusades against infidels (first in 1095) and heretics, excommunicated rulers (*eg*, Emperor Henry IV in 1076), summoned general councils, and, in the course of the 13th cent., began to control appointments to most bishoprics as well as to provide the incumbents of many lesser benefices (especially from mid-13th cent.). The papal *curia* was converted from merely the administrative office of the bishopric of Rome into the office of government and jurisdiction over the universal Church, drawing revenues from all western Christendom and employing an international staff. Until the Reformation, the papal authority, though repeatedly resisted, was never permanently rejected in any part of Catholic Europe.

Events in 16th-cent. Europe had four direct consequences on the papacy. The Reformation brought the rejection of papal authority by Protestantism. The rise of nationalism led successive popes into diplomatic relations with nation-states. The Catholic Church, through its meeting at the Council of Trent (1545–63), embarked on a programme of reform and administrative reorganization. Finally, there emerged a series of popes, *eg*, Paul III (*reg.* 1534–49), Paul IV (*reg.* 1555–9), Pius V (*reg.* 1566–72), Gregory XIII (*reg.* 1572–85), Sixtus V (*reg.* 1585–90), and Clement VIII (*reg.* 1592–1605), who gave, collectively, an austerity, scholarship, and efficiency to the papal office.

In political terms, the power of the papacy declined when the peace of Westphalia (1648), marking the end of the Thirty Years War, settled the immediate future of Europe without reference to papal wishes. Nevertheless, succeeding popes joined issue with European princes in whose countries movements threatened the Catholic tradition, *eg*, Jansenism in France.

During the 18th and 19th cents the papacy tended to be on the defensive, against secularist philosophers, nationalist Catholic princes, and dominant politicians such as Metternich. It was left to Pius IX (*reg.* 1846–78) to rally the spiritual forces of Catholicism, despite the political disasters of his reign, *eg*, territorial losses in his papal dominions. Under him the Vatican Council (1870) met while his successor, Leo XIII (*reg.* 1878–1903), gave to the life of the Church a positive theology and a sense of dedication in terms of social justice. With Pius XI (*reg.* 1922–39) and Pius XII (*reg.* 1939–58) there came a new awareness of the necessity for the papacy to pronounce on political and social questions of the times, and to offer wisdom to men in the desolation of two world wars. Pius XII's approach to non-Catholics towards co-operation in working for common human ideals pioneered the brief but significant pontificate of John XXIII (*reg.* 1958–1963). No pope in modern times made so great an impact on the Christian world as did John. Both he and his successor, Paul VI (*reg.* 1963–   ) brought a new dimension to papal activity—travel.

                                                                                       JG
                                                                                       GMDH

PAPADOPOULOS, GEORGE (1919–   ), Greek soldier, prime minister, and senior member of the military junta which ruled Greece after the *coup d'état* of April 1967. As a colonel of infantry specially trained in military intelligence and political warfare, he played a key role in the coup. After it he resigned from the army and became prime minister of Greece. His rule was inspired by an austere and conservative paternalism which sought to eradicate the influences of communism, immorality, and other dangers from all aspects of Greek life by the imposition of a severe discipline.

PAPAGOS, ALEXANDER (d. 1955), Greek soldier and politician, who led the attempt to restore the monarchy in Oct. 1935, when he kidnapped Tsaldaris, the prime minister, and overthrew his government. In the non-party government formed in Jan. 1936 he served as minister of war, but the king replaced him with Metaxas when Papagos refused to consider a coalition with the communists, who held the balance in parliament. Under Metaxas's regime Papagos was chief of staff, a post he held during the German invasion of Greece. Near the end of the civil war he became commander-in-chief and directed the battle at Mt Grammos which closed the fighting. In May 1951 he turned from military to political affairs and formed the Greek Rally. The party won a majority in the elections of Nov. 1952 and Papagos headed the government (1952–5). His equivocal attitude towards the Cyprus problem bedevilled his period of office.

PAPAL LEGATE, envoy of the pope to a secular ruler. The most important were the legates 'from the pope's side' (*a latere*) sent with full powers for a specific purpose. When the office of papal legate was conferred on a leading royal minister, as in the case of Cardinal Wolsey under King Henry VIII of England, it could lead to the exercise by such a legate of almost absolute powers over a national Church.

PAPAL PROVISIONS, appointments to ecclesiastical benefices by the pope by virtue of his full papal power (*plenitudo potestatis*). The papal right to do this was first made explicit under Innocent III and developed strongly under Innocent IV and Clement IV. The practice of provision grew phenomenally in the later 13th cent. In the early 14th cent. it threatened to usurp completely the rights of ecclesiastical patrons to fill the benefices in their gift. As early as 1245 there was an English and in 1247 a French protest at the practice. In England the Carlisle parliament of 1306 urged the king to forbid the practice and the Statutes of Provisors of 1351 and 1390, reinforced by the Statutes of Praemunire of 1353, 1365, and 1393, forbade both the request for and the receipt of a provision. Nevertheless, every vacant English bishopric from 1367 to the Reformation was filled, with royal connivance, by papal provision.

PAPAL REFORM COMMISSION (1536–7), committee appointed by Pope Paul III to study the causes and nature of the abuses within the Catholic Church and the means by which they might be remedied. The commission's nine members included both reforming cardinals, *eg*, Contarini, Caraffa, Pole, and a conservative faction. Its report, the *Consilium de Emendanda Ecclesia*, was presented to Paul in March 1537, and despite official efforts to keep its findings secret it was printed in 1538 and ran into 13 editions in 20 years. It criticized the religious orders and former popes, who had broken the Church's laws by permitting simony, pluralism, non-residence, and the abuse of dispensations, and recommended the urgent reform of clerical education, discipline, and moral standards. Some of its proposals were later implemented, both by Paul III and post-Tridentine popes, but the continuing financial needs of the papacy and the commission's failure to grasp the fundamental nature of the Protestant challenge limited its positive effects.

PAPANDHREOU, ANDREAS (1919–   ), Greek politician and son of George Papandhreou. As an economic adviser to his father's government, his apparent grooming for high office caused dissension within the Centre Union Party, of which he led the left wing, a group of some 30 deputies. His implication in the Aspida affair, an alleged military conspiracy, rocked his father's government and the party. As a result, he was exiled (Jan. 1968). He remained an implacable opponent of the dictatorship that has ruled Greece since the coup (1967).

PAPANDHREOU, GEORGE (1888–1968), Greek politician. During the First World War he was prefect of Lesbos and later governor-general of Chios. He entered parliament (1923) as a republican and achieved office in the same year. In 1926 he was briefly exiled by the Pangalos regime. On his return he served different governments in various ministerial capacities, but in 1936 was again exiled, this time for opposing the dictatorship of Metaxas.

As a staunch republican but an equally strong anti-communist, Papandhreou played a key role in thwarting communist designs in Greece during and after the Second World War. In May 1943 he skilfully manœuvred the communists into accepting the government of National Unity and the conditions it imposed on political life. He arrived in Athens in Oct. 1944 at the head of the government and for a short time persuaded the communist elements to co-operate. But when the government attempted to disarm the former resistance groups, civil war broke out.

Papandhreou, who served in several governments (1947–1951) put his anti-communism above his republicanism and accepted the decision of the plebiscite in favour of the monarchy. In 1935 he established the Democratic Party, which later became the Social Democratic Party. The party lost ground in the late 1940s and early 1950s and Papandhreou became joint leader and chief (1954) of the Liberal Party. A heavy defeat at the polls in 1958 prompted him to form a new party, the Liberal Democrats, which became the basis of the Centre Union, established in 1961. Despite an electoral defeat in 1961, Papandhreou's assault on the right held the Centre Union together and it became the opposition party. After the indecisive elections of Nov. 1963, following the fall of Karamanlis, Papandhreou formed a short-lived government and prepared for new elections early in 1964. The Centre Union emerged with a clear majority and Papandhreou formed a government. His policy of expanding free and compulsory education was much needed, but by attempting economic expansion and at the same time providing for social welfare, he caused severe economic difficulties. His position was also weakened by a renewal of trouble in Cyprus, his son's implication in the Aspidas affair, the conflict with the king over control of the army, and suspicion of his relations with the communists. In July 1965 he was compelled to resign, his party having begun to fall apart under pressure. As leader of the opposition (1966–7) his persistence forced the king to consider elections in the spring of 1967. It was the fear of a victory for Papandhreou that led the right-wing army officers to seize power on 21 April.

PAPEN, FRANZ VON (1879–1969), German diplomat and politician, who served during the First World War as military attaché in Washington and then as chief of staff with the Turkish army. He was a right-wing Centrist deputy (1921–1932) in the Prussian Landtag. In May 1932 he succeeded Brüning as Reich chancellor, his aim being to solve the political impasse by new elections and concessions to the Nazis. This resulted in more violence and an electoral swing which gave 230 seats to the NSDAP (31 July). Earlier (20 July), Papen had further weakened German democracy by suddenly deposing the Prussian government and replacing it with a Reich commissioner. A possible Nazi–Centre coalition to restore majority government was blocked by Hitler's insistence on his becoming chancellor and President Hindenburg's refusal to agree to this. New elections (6 Nov.) weakened the Nazis, but brought no solution; the army now feared a civil war in which it would have to defend Papen's grossly unrepresentative government against the majority of the nation. Papen therefore resigned (17 Nov.), but his successor, Von Schleicher, also failed to create a broader basis for government. Papen then reopened negotiations with Hitler and used his growing influence with Hindenburg to create a new Nazi–Conservative cabinet with Hitler as chancellor and himself as vice-chancellor (30 Jan. 1933). However, his hope of 'containing' National Socialism was soon shattered: in July 1934, after the Roehm purge, he resigned the vice-chancellorship. He was subsequently emissary and ambassador in Austria (1934–8) and in Turkey (1939–44). He was acquitted at the Nuremberg trials in 1946, but was sentenced to imprisonment by a German court. He was released in 1949.

PAPER MONEY, bank notes originally, and still theoretically, redeemable for gold upon presentation to the bank of issue. In the 17th cent. it was realized in western Europe that this was a means of enlarging trade and releasing a state from the fear of money scarcity. Thus, the issuing of notes became one of the essential functions of a bank. Though the note strictly required the bank to repay the depositor his deposit, experience showed that depositors did not all come back at the same time to claim their right, therefore it was possible for a bank to issue a value of notes larger than the value of cash deposited with it. This 'extra' issue, known as the fiduciary issue, enabled banks to supply additional money to the community at large, and to stimulate economic expansion. Outside Europe, paper money was known in China in the Sung and Yuan periods (11th–14th cents), and was commented upon by Marco Polo, but in due course it became unviable when issued without sufficient backing by copper currency so that it had to be abandoned during the early Ming period (c. 1450).

PAPERMAKING. Plentiful supplies of cheap paper were an essential prerequisite in the early days of printing. The art of making paper originated in China (5th cent. AD) and was brought into the Mediterranean by the Arabs in the 12th cent., when workshops producing expensive hand-made paper began to operate in Moorish Spain and Sicily. The use of watermills for supplying power to drive hammers for pulping rags was introduced in Italy in the 13th cent. At first, the making and distributing of paper was an Italian monopoly, but as the demands increased its manufacture spread to the rest of Europe. By the second half of the 14th cent. paper was in general use throughout Europe, and France began to rival Italy as a producer of paper. In the middle of the 15th cent. stronger and thinner paper made possible the use of printing presses. The first important English mills appeared in the reign of Henry VII (1485–1509), and in the 16th cent. papermaking also became an important Scottish industry which developed principally near Edinburgh.

Papermaking had a limited success in the American colonies until after the American War of Independence.

PAPIN, DENIS (1647–c. 1712), French scientist, who carried out some of the first experimental work on steam engines and boats.

PAPINEAU, LOUIS-JOSEPH (1786–1871), Canadian politician, who was elected to the Canadian House of Assembly (1808), called to the bar (1810) and on his re-election (1814), was made speaker (1815–22, 1825–6, 1828–37). He went to Britain to protest against the proposed Act of Union (1822) and returned a convinced opponent of the colonial system. He inspired the radical members of the Assembly to draw up the 92 Resolutions, demanding that elective institutions replace the British constitutional system (1834). Papineau's oratory, which was often violent and personal, inspired the *patriote* force which was crushed in the rebellion of 1837. Thereafter he lived in exile until 1844 and, although re-elected to the Assembly (1848), retired in 1854, by which time his influence had disappeared.

PAPIRIUS CURSOR, L. (*fl.* 4th cent. BC), Roman noble, who distinguished himself in the Second Samnite War by capturing and colonizing Luceria (316 BC). His son, of the same name, won a famous victory in the Third War at Aquilonia (293), which paved the way for peace in 290.

PAPPENHEIM, GOTTFRIED HEINRICH ZU, Count (1594–1632), Bavarian imperial cavalry soldier in the Thirty Years War, who suppressed a peasant revolt in Upper Austria (1626) and took part in the notorious razing of Magdeburg (1631). He was defeated at the battle of Breitenfeld (1631) and mortally wounded at the battle of Lutzen (1632).

PARAGUAYAN WAR (WAR OF THE TRIPLE ALLIANCE) (1864–70), between Paraguay and Argentina, Brazil, and Uruguay. Although territorial ambitions undoubtedly underlay the war efforts of Argentina and Brazil, primary responsibility for this protracted, savage, and pointless conflict lies with the Paraguayan dictator, Francisco Solano López. Paraguay had known only dictatorship since winning independence from Spain in 1811. Under Francia it had remained a hermit republic until 1840. Thereafter, however, under Carlos Antonio López and (after 1862) his son, Francisco, the country had progressed economically and had established one of Latin America's largest standing armies. Francisco, who became a general at 19, had observed military operations in Europe in the 1850s. As dictator, he conceived the ambition of uniting the La Plata basin under Paraguayan hegemony, a not unreasonable project given the internal weaknesses of Argentina, Brazil, and Uruguay, but the campaign to achieve this end was conducted with an ineptitude that was redeemed only by the endurance of the Paraguayan people, who remained loyal to López to the end.

López began by interdicting Brazilian river communications with the interior territory of Matto Grosso and dispatching an army to repulse a Brazilian intervention in Uruguay. López's forces had to cross Argentine territory, which it did in defiance of the country's wishes; Argentina was thus drawn into the conflict. On 1 May 1865 the three aggrieved parties formed the Triple Alliance, dedicated to the overthrow of López and the settlement of outstanding boundary disputes with Paraguay. The allies at length fielded an army ten times the size of Paraguay's; it was first commanded by Argentina's Bartolomé Mitre, then (after 1868) by the Brazilian Duke of Caxias. Early in 1866 the Paraguayans were forced on to the defensive, and the war became a grinding campaign of attrition, characterized by epidemics, atrocities, and huge losses in battle. López eventually went mad and ordered the execution of numbers of imagined internal enemies. On 1 Jan. 1869 Asunción fell to the allies, but guerrilla war continued until López was killed at Cerro Corá on 1 May 1870.

Brazilian troops occupied Paraguay until 1876. The nation lost approximately 55,000 sq. miles (142,000 sq. kms) of territory to Argentina and Brazil, and would have lost more to Argentina, but for the binding arbitration of President Hayes of the US. Paraguay's greatest disaster, however —from which it cannot yet be said to have recovered—was demographic. Estimates of the pre-war population vary from 0·5 million to 1·3 million; at the war's end it was no more than a quarter million, of whom some 28,000 were adult males. López remains one of Paraguay's national heroes.

C. Kolinski, *Independence or Death: the story of the Paraguayan War* (Gainesville, FL, 1965).   RCN

PARAKRAMABAHU I (*reg.* 1153–86), King of Ceylon, who brought the entire island under his control and governed it from Polonnaruva. He restored unity among the Buddhist sects and increased prosperity by great irrigation schemes. His external policy, entailing campaigns into South India and Burma, had no lasting success.

PARAKRAMABAHU II (*reg.* 1236–70), King of Ceylon, who reigned from Dambadeniya (near Kurunegala), restored Sinhalese authority and Buddhism over large areas occupied by the ruthless Indian invader Magha and the South-East Asian adventurer Chandrabhanu (from Chaiya in present southern Thailand). He is also remembered as a scholar.

PARAKRAMABAHU VI (*reg. c.* 1412–67), King of Ceylon, who reigned from Kotte (near modern Colombo). He succeeded in reuniting the entire island for a brief period. His reign is remarkable for the great development of Sinhalese literature.

PARAMARA DYNASTY (*c.* 850–1000), line of kings of Dhara (Dhar, Madhya Bharat, India), who originally ruled as feudatories of the Rashtrakutas, but later became completely independent. The greatest of them was Munja (*reg. c.* 973–95), patron of poets, himself a poet, and a military leader. After an audacious campaign against the Chalukyas he was taken prisoner and executed.

PARAMOUNTCY, or the conception of an empire covering the whole of India, can be traced back to the Vedic period. The Mughal conception of sovereignty was aggressive and, like the Hindus, the Mughals strove for paramountcy in the peninsula. Lord Wellesley was the first governor-general (1798–1805) to realize that the time had come for the British to stand forth as the paramount power. Because of his recall it was left for the Marquis of Hastings (1813–23) to complete his work. After the final defeat of the Marathas in 1818, the British were undoubtedly the paramount power and this was accepted by the Indian princes, though it was not until 1849 that the British political and geographical frontiers became roughly coterminous on the north-west frontier. The exercise of paramountcy was facilitated by the development of communications after 1858.

PARARATON, oldest extant Javanese chronicle, which describes the period from the early 13th cent. to the end of the 15th cent. Analysis has revealed that the *Pararaton* is actually a compilation of some earlier texts. The problem of its reliability is therefore complex and depends on the historical value of the texts on which the chronicle is based.

PARDO, MANUEL (1834–78), Peruvian politician and president of Peru (1872–6), who founded the Civilista Party and won a following among the progressive aristocracy of his day. As president he attempted to expand education and to make the army a professional body. However, he gradually alienated both army and clergy and in 1878 was assassinated.

PARDO Y BARREDA, JOSÉ (1864–1947), Peruvian politician and president of Peru (1904–8). While in office he improved treasury organization, advanced education, and introduced social legislation. Railway expansion and exploitation of natural resources by foreigners were also encouraged. When his term ended he surrendered power peacefully to one of his ministers.

PARDO, CONVENTION OF THE (1739), attempt to settle by compromise a number of financial and trade difficulties between Spain and Britain. An earlier convention of the Pardo (1728) had ended a short war between the two countries, but had left unresolved difficulties, and intermittent skirmishes occurred between the vessels of the two countries. The British public began to clamour for war, and a British sailor, Robert Jenkins, showed the House of Commons an ear he had lost in a Spanish skirmish. The British and Spanish governments, anxious to avoid war, agreed on a new convention, by which Spain paid reparations for all vessels damaged. The convention was intended as a preliminary to a genuine settlement of all outstanding grievances, but it was greeted with disapproval in Britain. It was eventually ratified by parliament (Feb. 1739), but rumours of a Franco-Spanish alliance soured relations between Britain and Spain. The British fleet was ordered to Gibraltar, upon which Spain refused to pay the reparations. Relations deteriorated quickly, and in Oct. 1739 war, known as the 'War of Jenkins' Ear', was declared. This merged into the wider War of the Austrian Succession (1740–8).

PARDONER, man licensed to give papal pardons and indulgences in return for financial contributions to certain good works (*eg*, the crusades or building a church). The office was much abused (*eg*, Chaucer's fictional Pardoner and the historical friar Tetzel, whose activities infuriated Luther in 1517) and was abolished by the Council of Trent in the 16th cent.

PARÉ, AMBROISE (1517–90), French army doctor, surgeon to three French kings, and author of the first major treatise on surgery, *La Methode de traicter les playes feutes par les arquebuses et aultres bastons a feu* (1545). He treated gunshot wounds with a vegetable preparation instead of boiling oil, stopped bleeding by ligaturing arteries, and introduced artificial limbs. The invention of printing enabled him to publish his achievements, and thus his influence spread.

PARENT, ETIENNE (1802–74), Canadian journalist and politician, who edited *Le Canadien* (1822–5, 1831–42), in which he advocated Canadian advancement through commercial development rather than radical political action. He served as under-secretary of state for Canada (1867).

PARETO, VILFREDO (1848–1923), Italian political economist and sociologist, who, after 1890, was, with M. Pantaleoni, the leading proponent of free trade. As professor of political economy at Lausanne (1893–1906) and in his writings, *eg*, *Manuale d'Economia Politica* (1906), he made profound contributions to mathematical abstract economic theories, studied the role, evolution, and conflicts of elites in government and society, and emphasized the power of 'myth' and sentiment rather than logic in rousing political enthusiasms. In his *Trattato di sociologia generale* (1916) he attempted a definition of the psychological motives influencing communities. He was a leading critic of Italian parliamentary democracy and condemned the corruption and weakness of its bourgeois ruling elite. Pareto encouraged Mussolini's bid for power (Oct. 1922), and just before his death was made a senator.

PARINDRA ('Greater Indonesia Party') in Indonesia, conservative nationalist grouping influenced by the Japanese example. It was founded in 1935 from a fusion of the *Budi Utomo* and the Indonesian People's Association (PBI). In 1939 it became united with the *Gerindo* and some smaller groups in the moderate nationalist front (GAPI). Although re-established after the Indonesian revolution, it lost all influence after its failure in the 1955 general elections.

PÂRIS, FRANÇOIS (1690–1727), Parisian who devoted himself to a life of Jansenist austerity and around whose grave miracles were alleged to take place, so that the government had to close the cemetery of St Médard in order to prevent disturbances (1732).

PARIS, MATTHEW (c. 1200–59), chronicler who, as a monk of St Albans, one of the leading English monasteries, was in frequent personal contact with the leading personages of his time, including King Henry III, the justiciar Hubert de Burgh, and many other notables. His *Chronica Majora* is the primary source for the reign of Henry III (especially 1235–1259) and is supplemented by a valuable collection of official documents, royal and ecclesiastical. A special feature of his surviving autograph manuscripts of this chronicle and of other works are the numerous charming illustrations drawn by him personally.

PÂRIS BROTHERS, in France, sons of an innkeeper from Dauphiné, who entered the army supplies business in the early 18th cent. and later became leading financiers. They were Antoine (1668–1733), Claude (1670–1745), Jean (1690–1766), and Joseph (1684–1770) the best-known, who was usually called Pâris-Duverney and was one of the leaders of the opposition to John Law.

PARIS, UNIVERSITY OF, one of the earliest universities in Europe. It was the most influential of all, the undisputed intellectual capital of western Europe until it declined in the religious and political troubles of the later 14th cent. Its origins were in the schools of Notre-Dame and Ste Geneviève, to which in the early 12th cent. teachers such as William of Champeaux, Peter Abelard, and Richard and Hugh of St Victor attracted the ablest students from all over Europe. The corporation of masters was recognized by King Philip-Augustus in 1200 and granted papal recognition, and independence from the bishop. The teaching was organized into four faculties (arts, canon law, medicine and theology). Among those who studied at Paris were Stephen Langton, Robert Grosseteste, Albert the Great, Thomas Aquinas, Duns Scotus, Roger Bacon, and Jean Gerson. In the 15th cent. the university began to decline and in the next century a serious threat was presented to it by the education offered by the Jesuits. During the French Revolution the university was suppressed, but with the post-Napoleonic era there came both a revival in scholarship and a concern with training for the professions. In the latter half of the 19th cent. the university shared in the general European interest in higher education, and in the 20th cent. new buildings and courses, splendid laboratory facilities and distinctive teaching contributed to a doubling of numbers between 1920 and 1950, and a world-wide intake of students.

PARIS COMMUNE (1871), in France, social democratic rising against the peace with Germany and the conservatism of the new republic. There had been a great deal of socialist and republican opposition in Paris, both to the empire and the government of National Defence, and the city voted firmly for the continuation of the war with Prussia. When the Assembly at Bordeaux ended both the moratorium on debts and the wages paid to the National Guard, which had enabled a large proportion of the population to exist during the siege, trouble flared up, and turned into open conflict when Thiers attempted to withdraw the artillery stationed in Paris. The government withdrew and a plebiscite was held on the action to be taken. As a result, in March a Commune was set up on the lines of that which had existed in the first French Revolution (1792–4). It was controlled by a committee comprising manual workers, intellectuals, employees, and small businessmen; the majority were old-fashioned Jacobins or Blanquist socialists, although there was a small

Marxist group which favoured a federal rather than a centralized executive. Their programme was limited to prosecution of the war, anti-clericalism, and limited workers' control.

The lack of clearly defined objectives, the divisions among the leadership, and the failure of the provinces to respond, made the Communards' task difficult. Their initial assault on the crucial forts of Mont Valerian was repulsed early in April, and the Versailles forces gradually tightened their grip on the city and by the end of April had imposed a strict blockade. Conditions became increasingly stringent, hostages were shot, and there were a number of social and political experiments—often modelled on the events of previous revolutions. The Versailles forces, commanded by Mac-Mahon, finally forced their way into the city on 21 May and after a week of bitter fighting they subdued the Communards, killing some 25,000 in the process. The Commune finished with the Communards burning the Hôtel de Ville, the Tuileries, and other public buildings. Their resistance was ended by the massacre in the cemetery of Père Lachaise on 28 May. Fierce repression followed, in which some 30,000 people were arrested, of whom 23 were executed, 13,000 imprisoned, and 7500 deported to New Caledonia. This ended the old Jacobin tradition and the revolutionary temper and leadership of Paris, but though it wiped out the working-class movement for a generation, it assumed a mythical, though not wholly justified, reputation as the first proletarian revolt and embittered class relations for several generations.

A. Horne, *The Fall of Paris, the Siege and the Commune* (London, 1965).   CHC

PARIS, PEACE OF (Feb. 1763), treaty signed by Britain, France, and Spain which ended the Seven Years War. It established Britain's colonial supremacy and determined the history of international relations during the next 20 years. By the treaty, Britain returned Havana and Manila to Spain, who had to renounce her rights to the Nfld fisheries, allow Britain wood-cutting claims in 'Honduras, and return Sacramento to Portugal. Spain also ceded FL to Britain, her only gain being LA from France. The French were restored to their Indian possessions of 1749, but these could no longer be fortified and French trade was henceforth dependent on British goodwill. France surrendered to Britain the entire province of Canada and all her lands east of the Mississippi, Cape Breton and all islands in the St Lawrence, Dominica, St Vincent, Tobago, the Grenadines, and Senegal.

The immediate result of the peace was Britain's isolation in Europe, while the French ministers, Choiseul and Vergennes, sought to avenge the loss of their country's overseas empire.

PARIS PEACE CONFERENCE (1919), held after the First World War, during which the peace treaties between the Allied and the Central Powers were evolved and finally concluded and the League of Nations established. Proceedings began in Jan. 1919 and were initially concerned with the more technical difficulties of membership, representation, and procedure. Thirty-two states attended, but the conference was from the start dominated by the great powers, the US, Britain, France, Italy, and Japan. This supreme council, formerly the supreme war council, though advised by specially established committees and experts, decided political issues largely on its own initiative, the results in many ways reflecting the particular aims of the personalities present. Japan played an insignificant role, for her delegation absented itself from discussions not relevant to the Far East and the immediate problem of the conference was, indeed, to reach a settlement with Germany. Italy's representative, Orlando, also played a lesser part than the remaining triumvirate—Wilson (US), Lloyd George (Britain), and Clemenceau (France).

Serious differences of opinion and overall objectives emerged among the Allies during protracted discussions. France was obsessed with the need for security against

Germany and found support among the newly created states of Eastern Europe, who were similarly determined to maintain their existence at the expense of the defeated powers. By contrast, Wilson's over-riding aim was the creation of the League of Nations and the evolution of an international order based on his idealistic principles. The British, anxious to demobilize, saw their security assured with the destruction of the German navy. Thus the various demands made on the Central Powers—especially Germany—for reparations and territorial concessions, and the imposition of a military occupation, reflected the limits to which Britain and the US would go in punishing the defeated states and to which France could be induced to limit her demands.

By Nov. 1919 the peace treaties of Versailles, St Germain, Neuilly, Trianon, and Sèvres had been concluded and the map of Europe and the Middle East accordingly redrawn in an attempt to satisfy the demands of national self-determination. The conference established the League of Nations, but embodied its covenant in each of the treaties, with unfortunate consequences, for when the US Senate refused to ratify the treaty of Versailles in particular, the US was thereby excluded from the league, whose possible effectiveness was thus immediately reduced. Moreover, the league inevitably suffered from its close association with Versailles, which the Germans considered to be a *diktat* without moral validity.

The conference was later much criticized for its shortcomings, and the treaties for their severity in attempting to mix justice with revenge. The peacemakers undoubtedly compromised the ideals of the Fourteen Points on which the conference was reputedly based. A distinction had clearly and inevitably been drawn between victor and vanquished but neither was satisfied. The league, despite its failings, did achieve some success; but by 1939 the gnawing dissatisfaction of all parties had eroded and finally destroyed both the failures and achievements of Paris.   JK

PARIS PEACE CONFERENCE (1946), meeting of the five members of the Council of Foreign Ministers (Britain, China, France, US, USSR), together with 16 other members who had actively waged war against the European axis powers—Australia, Belgium, Brazil, Byelorussia, Canada, Czechoslovakia, Ethiopia, Greece, India, Netherlands, New Zealand, Norway, Poland, South Africa, the Ukraine, and Yugoslavia. The conference drew up peace treaties with Bulgaria, Finland, Hungary, Italy, and Rumania. Draft treaties had been prepared in successive meetings of the Council of Foreign Ministers, but the conference dragged on throughout the summer (29 July–15 Oct.) as a result of Soviet intransigence on a number of outstanding points—intransigence which dissolved suddenly into acceptance. The frequently repeated *Niet* of Molotov and the repeated division, in voting, into 16 against the five communist members gave public demonstration of the growing division of the Cold War. None the less, agreement was finally reached and peace treaties were signed the following spring.

PARIS PEACE TALKS (VIET-NAM) (1968–   ), between representatives of the US and of North Viet-nam in May 1968. At first little progress was made, since the US insisted that it could only halt its bombing of the North in return for some reciprocal concession. In Oct. secret talks produced agreement. The US president, L. B. Johnson, announced the end of bombing (31 Oct. 1968) and the scale of North Viet-namese action in the South was reduced. Representatives of the National Liberation Front and of the South Viet-namese government were then admitted to the talks. There was, however, a further long delay taken up by wrangling over procedure, particularly over the shape of the conference table (as indicating the status of the delegations). The talks entered a new stage when agreement had been reached on these points (Jan. 1969). The US delegation was now led by Henry Cabot Lodge, formerly ambassador to Saigon (who had replaced President Johnson's delegate,

Averell Harriman), the South Viet-namese by Pham Dang Lam, the North Viet-namese by Xuan Thuy, and the NLF by Tran Buu Kiem. Little progress appeared to be made, since the US and South Viet-nam wanted to reach a military agreement and the North Viet-namese and NLF wanted the withdrawal of US troops and a political settlement. In the summer of 1969 the talks moved on to more substantial issues of political settlement as the NLF and North Viet-nam proposed the formation of a provisional coalition government, while South Viet-nam sought internationally supervised elections under the existing regime.

While the talks, as seen by the press and the public, made little headway, the situation in Viet-nam altered as a result of changes in US policy, which led to the gradual withdrawal of US troops and an attempt to hand over conduct of the war to South Viet-nam. The death of President Ho Chi Minh (Sept. 1969) may have increased North Viet-nam's desire to end the war. Contact was maintained between the two sides, presumably by secret talks; and while Ho Chi Minh was alive he replied to a letter addressed to him by President Nixon (Aug. 1969). In these circumstances the Paris talks ceased to be the centre of interest in the Viet-namese conflict.   WFK

PARIS SUMMIT CONFERENCE (1960), abortive meeting which was intended to be the high point of East–West discussions centring on the question of Berlin and Germany, but which, as a result of the U2 incident, broke up without any serious discussions taking place.

Khrushchev had precipitated a fresh crisis over Berlin by demanding (Nov. 1958) that the 'patently absurd situation' of Berlin should be ended, and stating that the Soviet Union would hand over its functions in Berlin to the German Democratic Republic. Khrushchev spoke, in words that amounted to less than an ultimatum, of the need to reach a settlement in six months, and eventually the crisis became tense when a wall was built (Aug. 1961) between the east and west zones in Berlin. But in the intervening period much diplomacy was carried on; Khrushchev visited the US and Macmillan worked strenuously to bring about a fresh summit meeting which might promote a general understanding in Europe. This took place in Paris (16 May 1960). It was attended by Khrushchev, Eisenhower, and Macmillan, but the shooting down of an American U2 photo-reconnaissance plane over the Soviet Union and the admission of the US government that it was gathering intelligence information, was used by Khrushchev as a pretext for breaking off the meeting, presumably because he had reached the conclusion that he would gain nothing substantial from it.

PARIS, TREATY OF (1259), ended the long war between the English and the French kings that had started in 1202. The main fighting occurred in the time of King John, who lost all his French possessions north of the Loire. His son, Henry III, for long would not admit the finality of these losses, nor of the further loss of Poitou in south-western France, captured by the French during Henry's minority (1224–5). Only a rebellion of Henry's barons, exasperated by the cost of his foreign ambitions, forced him in 1258–9 to negotiate a permanent settlement with Louis IX of France. This peace endured until 1294, when France resumed an aggressive policy towards Henry's son, Edward I.

PARIS, TREATY OF (1515), alliance between the new monarchs, Francis I and Charles I, who had recently succeeded respectively to the thrones of France and Spain. It was negotiated by Henry of Nassau to resolve possible sources of dispute, *eg*, the fiefs of Flanders and Artois (24 March 1515). A double marriage was arranged between Charles and Renée, daughter of Louis XII of France (altered in 1516 by the treaty of Noyon), and between Henry of Nassau and Claudine of Orange-Châlons, from which union was to spring the future house of Orange-Nassau.

PARIS, TREATY OF (1621), agreement between France, Savoy, and Venice to force acceptance of the treaty of Madrid

(1617), in so far as it related to the Grisons' control of the strategically important Valtelline pass.

PARIS, TREATY OF (1657), Anglo-French alliance signed by the English ambassador in Paris, Sir William Lockhart, and the French ministers, Brienne and Lionne, pledging mutual action to force Spain to accede to peace terms, concluded after the breakdown of Franco-Spanish negotiations in 1656. This union led to the capture of Dunkirk by the French and its cession to England as the price of her assistance.

PARIS, TREATY OF (1783), between the US and Britain which marked the formal end of the American War of Independence. Negotiations between the American peace commissioners, Benjamin Franklin, John Adams, John Jay, and Henry Laurens, and representatives of Britain and the other belligerent powers opened in Paris in 1782. Terms of peace between the US and Britain were agreed on 30 Nov. 1782, but did not come into effect until settlements had been reached between Britain and France, the ally of the US, and Spain, the ally of France. Conflicting multi-national questions delayed signature of the treaty of Paris until 3 Sept. 1783. The US gained full recognition of its independence from Britain, formal agreement on its northern boundaries with British North America, the evacuation of British forces with 'all convenient speed', and fishing rights in British North American waters. It was also stipulated that creditors on both sides should not be legally inhibited in the collection of pre-war debts, and that Congress should recommend to the states the restoration of confiscated loyalist property.

PARIS, TREATIES OF (1814, 1815), concluded peace between France and the allies, respectively before and after the Hundred Days. By the first treaty of Paris (May 1814), France retained her 1792 frontiers, and colonies except for ceding part of San Domingo (to Spain) and St Lucia, Tobago, and Mauritius (to England). The second treaty (Nov. 1815) exacted limited retribution for French complicity in Napoleon's final campaign. France was confined within her 1790 frontiers, had to pay a 700 million franc indemnity over five years, undergo a military occupation, and return works of art misappropriated by Napoleon.

PARIS TREATY (1856), between Russia, France, and Britain, ended the Crimean War. By the Black Sea clauses (denounced by Russia 1870) neither Turkey nor Russia might maintain a navy on the Black Sea, or an arsenal on its shores. Russia ceded Southern Bessarabia to Moldavia, while Turkey promised self-rule to Moldavia and Wallachia. The Russian protectorate over Orthodox subjects of the sultan was replaced by a European protectorate, a guarantee of integrity of the sultan's domains and by a provision for mediation by a third power in case of any dispute involving Turkey. The navigation of the Danube was opened to all countries and an international commission set up to regulate it.

The immediate effect of the treaty was an outbreak of revisionism in place of conservatism among great and smaller powers. France became adventurous; Britain isolationist. The old balance of power system was destroyed and a new one did not emerge until 1871.

PARK CHUNG-HEE (1917–), South Korean soldier and president of South Korea since 1963, who served in the Japanese army (1940–5) and in the South Korean army from 1946. He held various divisional commands, punctiliously avoiding involvement in politics, and was chosen by the colonels in 1961 to head the military junta, which they saw as the solution to the failure of Chang Myon's democracy. Park balanced the idealism of Col. Kim Chongpil, which the politicians saw as near-fascism, against the professionalism of the politicians, which the idealists saw as corruption, and formed the Democratic Republican Party in 1963. He won a narrow victory in the presidential election of 1963, and was re-elected with an increased majority in 1967. An amendment of the constitution to enable him to stand for a third term in 1971 was approved by a 2–1 vote in a referendum in 1969.

PARK, MUNGO (1771–c. 1805), Scottish doctor and explorer of West Africa. On his first expedition (1795–7) he established that the Niger river flowed eastward, and not, as previously believed by many European geographers, to the west (and into the Senegal river). He met his death during his second expedition (1805), probably at Bussa on the lower-middle Niger.

PARKER, MATTHEW (1504–75), English theologian and Abp of Canterbury. As a young man at Cambridge he studied the new ideas in the light of patristics and history, and his eventual conversion to Protestantism was the firmer for having been reasoned and gradual. He became chaplain to Queen Anne Boleyn (1535), who made him dean of a college in Suffolk for the training of secular priests. As master of Corpus Christi College (1544) and vice-chancellor (1545) he protected the collegiate endowments of Cambridge after the Chantries Act (1545). In 1547 Parker married Margaret Harlestone, an event which, together with his tentative support of Lady Jane Grey, compelled him in Mary's reign to take refuge in scholarly obscurity. During this time he made a study of Anglo-Saxon chronicles which convinced him on historical grounds that the Church of England was a true Church, now purged of medieval superstitions and innovations.

On Elizabeth I's accession Parker hoped to return to Cambridge to foster a spiritual recovery, but the queen and Cecil needed a man of his learning, moderation, and incorruptibility to pilot their settlement, and he reluctantly accepted the primacy of Canterbury, being consecrated (1559) by four Edwardian bishops without sees.

Parker believed that a Church's surest bulwarks were discipline and sound learning. He conducted a metropolitan visitation to enforce the injunctions of 1559 and remove superstitious practices, initiated the compilation of the Bishops' Bible (1563–8), and provided in the 39 Articles (1563) a body of doctrine which he supplemented with homilies and a revised catechism. But the disputed ornaments rubric appended to the prayer book had opened the 'vestiarian controversy' with Puritans and he issued the Book of Advertisements (1566), insisting only on the wearing of surplice and cope, in an attempt to enforce a seemly discipline and uniformity of worship.

In his struggle with the Puritans Parker was handicapped by the queen's inability to understand spiritual earnestness of any kind. She persistently refused to give him adequate support, and her readiness to appropriate or alienate ecclesiastical property hindered his efforts to promote an educated, well-paid clergy. A further obstacle was the open sympathy shown to the Puritans by influential courtiers like Leicester and by many of the bishops, who had been fugitives in the previous reign. After the vestments dispute he had to face Cartwright's campaign to replace episcopacy and the prayer book by a Genevan system of worship. He was unpopular with the Catholics, although he had tried to limit their persecution and he was increasingly saddened by the queen's irresolution, in the face of problems that became graver every year. If in the end he seemed to give up the struggle, his earlier firmness, and his insistence on the continuity of the doctrines and institutions of the Church, helped to justify the Anglican *via media*.

His *De Antiquitate Ecclesiae* (1572) was an account of the primates of Canterbury from Augustine to himself, and he left an invaluable collection of documents, including his own editions of Asser, Matthew Paris, Thomas Walsingham, and other chroniclers.

V. J. K. Brook, *Archbishop Parker* (London, 1962).   MMR

PARKER, THEODORE (1810–60), US Unitarian theologian, transcendentalist, and social reformer, whose sermon 'On the Transient and Permanent in Christianity' (1841) established him as a leading transcendentalist. He was later ostracized by many Unitarians because of his unorthodox views. In the 1850s he emerged as a major critic of slavery.

PARKES, SIR HARRY SMITH (1828–85), British diplomat, who represented Britain in the Far East at a period when British policy was considerably influential. He was arrested by the Chinese and threatened with execution during negotiations for the termination of the third Chinese War (1860). His rivalry with Leon Roches, the French minister, was an important factor in Japanese politics (1865–8), but although Parkes favoured reform of the Tokugawa system and had friendly relations with some south-western *hans*, he did not envisage the forcible overthrow of the *bakufu*. He gave valuable help to the new Meiji government, both in diplomacy and in the provision of British experts, but after 1873 his relations with it became less intimate. He was responsible for the treaty (1883) which opened Korea to British trade.

PARKES, SIR HENRY (1815–95), Australian politician, who was five times prime minister of NSW and the outstanding figure in Australian politics of his day. He emigrated from England in 1839 and entered Australian political life through movements to end convict transportation and secure self-government. He was editor of the liberal *Empire* (1850–8) and a member of the legislative council from 1854. His first term as prime minister began in 1872, and his last ended in 1891. He was a staunch free trader, helping to make his own views those of his colony. As a liberal he was the chief architect of universal elementary education in NSW, and a champion of constitutionalism in an age of political turbulence.

PARKINSON, JOHN (1567–1650), English apothecary to James I, who published *Paradisi in Sole Paradisus Terrestris* (*a Garden of all sorts of flowers which our English Ayre will permit to be nursed up*) (1629). It described 1000 plants. His later *Theater of Plants, or a Universall and complete Herbal*, described 4000 and for 50 years remained the most complete English treatise on the subject.

PARKMAN, FRANCIS (1823–93), US historian. After travelling Europe (1843–4) he made frequent trips into the forests around Boston to study Indian life. A 1700-mile horseback journey (1846) along the Oregon Trail provided him with further authentic materials about the Indians and he recorded his experiences in *The Oregon Trail* (1849). His life's work was a massive history of the struggle between England and France for control of colonial America. This was collectively known as *France and England in North America* (8 vols, 1851–92), and included *LaSalle and the Discovery of the Great West* (1869) and *Montcalm and Wolfe* (1884). The literary quality of the series, together with Parkman's impeccable research, made it a classic of American historical writing.

PARLEMENTS of France, though primarily royal institutions for dispensing justice, also possessed wide powers of law enforcement and administration. In addition, the *parlement* of Paris, which emerged from the *curia regis* in the mid-13th cent., and like the other courts lasted until 1790, developed political functions which gave it a central position in French government.

Originating with the need for a court to administer justice when the king was unable to do so personally, the *parlement* of Paris gradually evolved a sophisticated procedure, a complex organization of chambers housed in the Palais de Justice, and its own officers and personnel. A network of provincial *parlements* also developed with the expansion of the French state in the 14th–17th cents, and by the 1789 Revolution there were 13 official *parlements* and three supreme councils which were *parlements* in all but name, Arras (1530), Colmar (1657), and Perpignan (1660). Earlier *parlements* were established at Toulouse (1443), Grenoble (1456), Bordeaux (1467), Dijon (1476), Rouen (1499), Aix (1501), Rennes (1553), Pau (1620), Metz (1633), Besançon (1674), Douai (1686), and Nancy (1775). They were staffed by magistrates, many of whose offices became venal in the 16th and 17th cents, and a host of petty officials, barristers, solicitors, clerks, and ushers. The Paris *parlement* was organized in certain permanent chambers, the *grand'chambre*, and by the 17th cent. some five chambers of *enquêtes* and two of *requêtes*. They were each presided over by a president, the head of the *grand'chambre* being the first president. The most solemn assembly of the court was called a *lit de justice*, when the king presided in person, but when he was absent he was represented by the *procureur-général* and his assistants, who were also responsible for maintaining public order. From the 14th cent. the royal barristers were called the *avocats-généraux*, and these officials were collectively known as the *gens du roi* or *parquet*. In the performance of its judicial role, the *parlement* brought together into one coherent system a diffuse body of customary, Roman, and canon law.

Acting with the Crown's judicial authority, the *parlement* of Paris proclaimed, enforced, and preserved royal law in written form. This considerable achievement was matched by a growing political role, for the court was not simply the agent of French kings, dedicated to carry out the royal will: it also protected the subject against royal arbitrariness and guarded the traditional rights of the monarchy against the innovations of individual kings, and from the 15th cent. acts of royal arbitrariness were not infrequent. Opposition was chiefly effected through the practice of remonstrance against royal decrees, but became open conflict in the *Fronde* of the mid-17th cent.

In opposing the king, however, the *parlement* of Paris revealed one fundamental weakness. Unlike modern parliaments, its members were not elected, but derived their power from the Crown. Its members faced an increasingly difficult dilemma, since any attack made by them on the Crown's authority necessarily weakened their own position, especially under Louis XV and Louis XVI when the monarchy's prestige was in decline. *Parlementaire* hostility towards royal policy on Jansenism and towards Louis XV's apparent abdication of governmental responsibility to his ministers, stimulated the courts to declare the belligerent theory of *parlementaire* unity. Under pressure from Maupeou and in an effort to reassert his shrinking authority, Louis exiled the magistrates (1771), though they were reinstated by Louis XVI (1774). In 1788 the *parlement* of Paris reached the apogee of its popularity by challenging the authoritarianism of the Crown, but by insisting that voting should be by estate and not by simple majority at the forthcoming meeting of the estates general, the magistrates forfeited public sympathy. The courts were dissolved between Nov. 1789 and Oct. 1790, many of the magistrates losing their lives in the Revolution.

J. H. Shennan, *The Parlement of Paris* (London, 1968). JHS

PARLEMENTS, REVOLT OF (1787–8) in France, inspired by the attempts of Calonne and Brienne to undertake fundamental tax reforms, abolishing the exemption of the privileged classes. The *parlements* acted as guardians of the law and intermediaries between king and people. Calonne's attempt to evade their opposition by summoning an Assembly of Notables (Feb. 1787) failed. His successor, Brienne, tried to win *parlementaire* co-operation, but his edicts were rejected and were registered by *lit de justice*. The *parlements* demanded the summoning of the states general, but were exiled to Troyes (Aug. 1787), then in Nov. were recalled, having been promised that the edicts would be withdrawn. They continued to remonstrate against Louis XVI's government, which ordered the arrest of two magistrates and suspended the *parlements* (May 1788). The *parlements*, backed by the clergy and nobility, openly resisted the government and serious riots developed in the provincial capitals, forcing the king to capitulate (Aug. 1788). Louis XVI agreed to the convocation of the states general and Brienne and Lamoignon resigned. On 23 Sept. 1788 the *parlement* returned triumphantly to Paris amid popular rejoicing. The revolt ended with the registration of the declaration summoning the states general (25 Sept. 1788).

PARLIAMENT ACT (1911) in Britain, limiting the legislative powers of the House of Lords, was the sequel to the Lords' rejection and amendment of Liberal government bills, culminating in the rejection of the 1909 budget. The act did not alter the composition of the Lords, which had clearly been the mainspring of their conduct, and it took no step towards reform of the kind advocated by those who wished to make the Lords into a second chamber. The bill passed after two general elections (Jan. and Dec. 1910) and the king's explicit promise to create as many peers as should be necessary to force it through the Lords. The act defines 'money bills' and gives the speaker the duty of certifying them. It states that money bills not passed by the Lords within one month shall be sent to the monarch for his assent. Other public bills may similarly be sent for the royal assent if not passed by the Lords in three successive sessions, spread over two years. The only exceptions are bills to extend the maximum duration of parliament, which the act reduced from seven to five years.

The preamble states that the act is temporary, and shall last only until agreement is reached on the proper structure of a democratic second chamber. This has not yet been agreed. The introduction of life peerages (1958) did not lead to changes in the Parliament Act, and it has been amended (1949) only by reducing to one year the period for which the Lords can delay bills passed by the Commons.　　BK

PARLIAMENT ACT (1949) in Britain, legislative measure passed by the post-war Labour government, reduced the delaying power of the House of Lords to a single session. Its enactment was closely related to the government's programme of nationalization, especially of the iron and steel industry.

PARLIAMENT, PAYMENT OF MEMBERS in Britain. The House of Commons resolved in 1911 that MPs should be paid £400 a year from the exchequer. English constituencies originally had a common-law obligation to pay their members (on a rate fixed by a statute of 1323) and Welsh constituencies had a similar obligation under an act of 1544 (repealed in 1856). In practice, payment had generally ceased by the mid-17th cent., largely because, from the 16th cent., members began to offer their services free.

The possibility of a connection between payment and accountability, which made the idea of payment generally disliked, was an undoubted fact in the financing of certain members by trade unions early in the 20th cent. This, ironically, provided an argument for the 1911 proposal for payment from public funds. Lloyd George represented it as both a reversion to past practice and an adjustment to modern conditions, allowing men of small means, unable to retain their ordinary employment because of the increased volume of parliamentary business, to sit in parliament independently of pressure groups.

PARLIAMENTARIANS in England, party which supported and fought for parliament in the English Civil War. They developed out of the Country Party which had dominated the first two years of the Long Parliament. This latter party split into Royalists and Parliamentarians over the Grand Remonstrance (Nov. 1642), and the political basis of the parliamentary party was the insistence upon additional securities from the king, *ie*, control over ministerial appointments and the militia. They were not a homogeneous group and a division appeared in the early years of the war between a peace party, led by such people as Holles, a middle party under Pym, and later St John, and a war party led by Vane and others. Later these divisions developed into 'Independent' and 'Presbyterian' parties. Socially, the Parliamentarians differed very little from the Royalists, and their cause could never have prospered had they not included numerous members of the aristocracy and gentry.

PARLIAMENTARY DEBATES, REPORTING OF, in Britain, forbidden in the 18th cent., but in 1909 undertaken by parliament itself. Debating in secret was held to be a corollary of freedom of speech, and the reporting or publishing of debates was forbidden, as a breach of privilege, by resolutions of the Commons in 1641, and of both houses after 1689, and at intervals to 1770. The view that this prohibition did not cover publication during a parliamentary recess was contradicted by a Commons resolution of 1738, and reporting in daily newspapers was forbidden in 1762. Legal proceedings were from time to time taken against publishers of reports, but the last time this happened was in 1771, when Wilkes, Brass Crosby, and other officials of the city of London defied the House of Commons. Thereafter, reporting was tolerated by both houses, though it remained, as it still is, a matter of grace and not of right. The fullest reports were those in *The Times* and the *Morning Chronicle*. Reporters sat at the back of the Strangers' Galleries and were forbidden to take notes, but their lot was eased after 1835 in the new Houses of Parliament in which special reporters' galleries were provided.

There was still no idea that parliament itself should issue reports of its debates. In 1803 Cobbett, having finished his *Parliamentary History, 1066–1803* (36 vols), began to compile contemporary debates from newspapers, and in 1812 his work was taken over by the firm of Hansard. Their reports, known colloquially as 'Hansard', remained a compilation until 1878, when the firm was given a government subsidy and began to employ its own reporters. In 1892 its reports were authorized and the title was changed to *Parliamentary Debates: Authorised Edition*. In 1909 this became the *Official Report*, made by reporters employed by both houses and printed by the Stationery Office, and containing for the first time 'substantially' verbatim accounts of the proceedings. In 1943 it was decided to add the word 'Hansard' to the title 'Official Report'.　　BK

PARLIAMENTARY PAPERS in Britain. From 1801 for the House of Commons, and from 1804 for the House of Lords, all papers presented to parliament began to be bound in sessional volumes, classified, and indexed. House of Commons papers have been on sale from 1835 and House of Lords papers from 1854.

PARLIAMENTARY PRIVILEGE ACT (1770), in Britain, provided that, though the persons of MPs should continue to be privileged from arrest for offences committed outside parliament, no action in a court of law should be stayed by reason of parliamentary privilege.

PARMA, Italian city situated in the Lombardy plain, incorporated into Charlemagne's empire (773–4) and during the Middle Ages an imperial fief, which was long disputed between the Visconti and Sforza Dukes of Milan and the papacy. It was yielded by Pope Leo X to Francis I after Marignano (1515), but was recovered by Emperor Charles V after Pavia (1525). In 1545 Parma was created a duchy and bestowed on Pietro Luigi Farnese by his father, Pope Paul III. The Farnese family held it until, on the death of Duke Antonio (1731), the family became extinct in the male line. Parma then passed to the Spanish house of Bourbon by virtue of the marriage of Elizabeth Farnese to Philip V, and their son Don Carlos succeeded as duke in 1731. Four years later he became King of Naples and Sicily and Parma was then ceded to the Austrian Habsburgs by the treaty of Vienna (1735), only to return to the Spanish Bourbons in 1748, when the treaty of Aix-la-Chapelle bestowed it on Don Philip of Spain. In 1801 Louis, Duke of Parma, was made King of Etruria, while the duchy was united with Napoleonic

France until 1814, when it was conferred on Napoleon's second wife, Maria Louisa of Austria. From this time until the Parmesan revolt against the restored house of Lucca (1859), Austrian influence was paramount. When Duke Robert (1859) was deposed the duchy was incorporated first into the kingdom of Piedmont-Savoy (1859) and ultimately into a united Italy (1870).

PARMA, BATTLE OF (1734), indecisive battle in the War of the Polish Succession, fought between the French under Marshal Coligny and the Austrians under Field Marshal Mercy, who was killed in the fighting. The Austrians, who had suffered from weak leadership and inadequate direction from Vienna, were manœuvred out of Milan and the Po valley by the French (1735).

PARMENIDES (b. *c*. 510 BC), Greek philosopher from Elea in southern Italy, who founded the Eleatic school. His poems on truth and falsehood concerned argument from principles, but grammatical difficulties, as in failing to differentiate between existential and predicative uses of the verb 'to be', led him to deny the possibility of change and diverted philosophy from cosmic speculation.

PARMENIO (d. 330 BC), Macedonian military commander under Philip II and Alexander the Great. He was first heard of as defeating the Illyrians (356) and he led Philip's vanguard into Asia (336). He also commanded Alexander's left wing at Granicus (334), Issus (333), and Gaugamela (331). He was killed when his son, Philotas, was condemned for treason.

PARNELL, CHARLES STEWART (1846–91), Irish politician who became an MP in 1875 and at once embarked upon a policy to secure home rule for Ireland. He became (1879) president of the Land League, designed to reduce rents and end ownership by absentee landlords. By 1880 he was chairman of the home-rule group in the House of Commons and henceforth dominated Irish politics for fifteen years. His policy of having those who took the farms of evicted tenants 'boycotted' brought increased trouble in Ireland, coercive legislation by the British government and his own imprisonment (1881), until released under the Kilmainham treaty agreement. He was not an extremist, and had no sympathy for those who brought about the Phoenix Park murders in May 1882. While there was some chance of his ambitions for Ireland being fulfilled while Gladstone was in office, the return of a conservative government in 1886, combined with his own decline in health, weakened his influence. He was exposed (1887–90) to the publicity arising from ill-founded accusations that he had supported murder and violence. No sooner was his innocence in this established when he was the subject of further unwelcome publicity. Captain O'Shea cited him as co-respondent in a divorce suit. In the moral climate of the 1890s it was enough to break Parnell, and he lost the support of Gladstone and of the Roman Catholic Church. He was briefly married to Katherine O'Shea before his death in 1891. In fifteen years of parliamentary activity he had made Irish home rule a prospect rather than a pipe-dream.

PAROS, Greek island in the Cyclades, famous in antiquity for its marble, and birthplace of the poet Archilochus (*c*. 700 BC). It colonized Thasos (*c*. 680). In the conflict with Persia (490, 480–79) it supported the Persians, and both Miltiades in 489 and Themistocles in 480 tried to exact an indemnity, the latter successfully. Subsequently it joined both the Delian League (5th cent.) and the Second Athenian Confederacy (4th cent.). An important Parian inscription, the *Marmor Parium*, gives a list of significant events in Greek history down to 263, dated by Athenian kings and archons.

PARRINGTON, VERNON LOUIS (1871–1929), US scholar, whose reputation rests on his study, *Main Currents in American Thought* (3 vols, 1927–30), a survey of the origins and development of American letters. In his political sympathies he was a progressive liberal, and characterized his historical viewpoint as 'Jeffersonian rather than Federalistic'. His work influenced a generation of American historians and literary critics, and remains a major interpretation of the American past.

PARSIS, Persian Zoroastrians, who fled the country after the Arab conquest and settled on the coast of Gujarat in India during the 8th cent. AD. Traditional Parsi songs refer to the fact that Akbar, the Mughal emperor, was invested with the *Sudreh* and *Kusti*, the sacred shirt and thread-girdle, the symbols of Zoroastrianism. Under British rule large numbers of Parsis settled in Bombay, where, because of their wealth and business ability, they acquired great political and social influence. They probably are the most westernized of all Indian communities. The prohibitions regarding contamination of the sacred elements of fire, water, and earth are still scrupulously observed. Their most remarkable rite is the exposure of the dead on the so-called Towers of Silence.

PARSONS, SIR CHARLES ALGERNON (1854–1931), British engineer, who produced (1884) the first practical steam turbine, initially to generate electricity. From the start of the Industrial Revolution inventors had experimented unsuccessfully to effect this improvement in the use of steam power. However, the technological problems involved could not have been overcome at any earlier date. Parsons started his own business and also developed the turbine for marine propulsion. In 1897 the performance of his *Turbinia* caused a sensation at the review marking Queen Victoria's Diamond Jubilee. Within a decade steam turbines were being used extensively for powering both warships and merchant vessels. Most of the electricity now (1970) being consumed is still being generated by steam turbines.

PARSONS, ROBERT (1546–1610), English Jesuit, who, with Cardinal William Allen, organized Catholic resistance to the Elizabethan regime. He was a former fellow of Balliol College, Oxford, who became a Jesuit in Rome in 1575. He returned to England with Edmund Campion to organize the Catholics (1580). He left again in 1581 and was given the task of directing the Jesuit mission from abroad. He was in Spain (1588–97) and founded the seminaries of Valladolid, Seville, and Madrid for the training of English priests. After the death of Elizabeth I he favoured armed intervention in England to restore Catholicism.

PARTHENON, temple of Athena Parthenos on the Athenian Acropolis, designed by Ictinus and Callicrates, with sculptures by Pheidias (447–432 BC), which originally included the 'Elgin Marbles', now in the British Museum. It was planned by Pericles to glorify imperial Athens and was partly financed by the Delian League and it housed the treasuries of Athens and the league. It was later used as a Christian church and as a Turkish mosque, and was badly damaged by Venetian bombardment (AD 1687).

PARTHIANS, name given to the Parni, a Scythian tribe, which, led by Arsaces and Tiridates, settled in the ancient Iranian province of Parthia (roughly mod. Khurasan), *c*. 248 BC. They annexed Hyrcania (south-east of the Caspian Sea) and founded a dynasty, the Arsacids, which ruled an empire extending from the Indian frontier to the Euphrates, until *c*. AD 224. In north-west India, Parthians, known in Indian tradition as Pahlavas, ruled for a time during the 1st cent.

PARTI NATIONAL (1788) in France, 'patriotic' party which emerged in the winter of 1788 to champion the nation against both aristocratic privilege and royal despotism and to advocate constitutional reform. It included some wealthy nobles, *eg*, Condorcet, La Fayette, and Larochefoucauld-Liancourt, whose liberal ideas were formed during military service in America, some *parlementaires*, *eg*, Adrien Dupont, Hérault de Seychelles, and Lepelletier de Saint-Fargeau, and members of the bourgeoisie, some of whom belonged to masonic lodges and the Committee of Thirty. The party supported the viewpoint of the third estate, both before and during the meeting of the estates general (1789).

PARTI POPULAIRE FRANÇAIS (PPF) in France, political party founded in 1936 by Jacques Doriot and several other ex-communists attracted by fascism. Its appeal was broadened by the addition of several intellectuals of the extreme right, the best-known being Pierre Drieu La Rochelle. During the Second World War the PPF constituted the principal support for a policy of collaboration with the Germans. The party's paper *Le Cri du peuple*, vehemently criticized Pétain's government and the party was used by the Germans to exert pressure on the Vichy government. Many of its members fought on the Eastern Front against the Russians. Doriot joined the puppet government at Sigmaringen after founding a Comité de libération française.

PARTI QUEBEÇOIS in Canada, French Canadian political organization founded in 1968 by René Levesque and advocating an independent, socialist Quebec. In a Quebec election in 1970, the party got 23 per cent of the vote and elected seven members to the provincial legislature.

PARTI RÉPUBLICAIN DE LA LIBERTÉ (PRL) in France, conservative party formed after the Second World War. Its founders hoped that it would be able to unite the forces of conservatism, something not achieved before in France, but it did not succeed in this. The right was weakened at the time by the war record of many of its leaders and by the rise of the Catholic MRP party. The PRL obtained nearly 30 seats in the 1946 parliament, but later lost support to the Gaullist movement, and was unable to overcome the traditional independent-mindedness of French conservatives. In 1948 it joined with other groups to form the Centre National des Indépendants and in 1951 disappeared as a separate entity.

PARTI SOCIALISTE UNIFIÉ (PSU) in France, small French socialist party on the extreme left, formed in 1960 by the amalgamation of the Parti socialiste autonome, which had broken away from the SFIO socialist party over the latter's support for the Fifth Republic (1958), and the Union de la Gauche socialiste, a body including intellectuals and left-wing Catholics. The new party's most distinguished figure was Pierre Mendès-France, who had joined the PSU after leaving the Radicals. The PSU has often been internally divided, and has attracted little electoral support, but its intellectual vitality has given it a certain political importance. Its secretary, Michel Rocard, was a candidate in the 1969 presidential election.

PARTITION OF INDIA (Aug. 1947), simultaneous transfer of power in British India to two successor states, India and Pakistan. Pakistan comprised western territories, including the western Punjab, Sind, Baluchistan, and the North-West Frontier Province, and an eastern area, which included eastern Bengal and Sylhet. The remaining British Indian provinces became India. The Indian states were required to accede to one of the new dominions, which led to difficulties in the cases of Junagadh, Hyderabad, and Kashmir. The transfer of power was effective on 14–15 Aug. and the actual boundary, the 'Radcliffe Award', was made public on 17 Aug. The viceroy, Lord Mountbatten, became governor-general of India and M. A. Jinnah became governor-general of Pakistan.

The idea of a separate Muslim state was broached by Iqbal in 1930 and given more definite shape by Chaudhuri Rahmat Ali (1933). But it was not adopted by the Muslim League until the 'Lahore Resolution' (March 1940), which contemplated the inclusion of the whole of the Punjab and Bengal

in Pakistan. Though the Indian National Congress opposed partition, the 'Pakistan scheme' now became integral to negotiations for an Indian political settlement. The Cripps scheme (1942) provided for the 'secession' of provinces, but this did not satisfy the league. Rajagopalachari made a vain effort to get Congress to accept the scheme as the basis for Congress–League co-operation to secure an immediate transfer of power. Gandhi and Jinnah held inconclusive talks (1944) and meetings at Simla (1945) with Lord Wavell also broke down. The 'Pakistan scheme' gained considerable strength from the league's activities during the Second World War and in the first post-war elections (1945–6), which were fought on this issue in the Muslim constituencies, the league gained a decisive victory. The cabinet mission's 'grouping' proposals were the last chance to avoid partition, but they were a dead letter by mid-Aug. 1946.

Lord Mountbatten's appointment as viceroy (March 1947) with instructions to transfer power by June 1948 brought decisive action. The Unionist–Congress coalition government in the Punjab fell. Congress acceptance of partition provided that the predominantly Hindu areas of Bengal and the Punjab remained in India, while the continued evidence of Congress–League unwillingness to co-operate in the interim government was a further decisive step towards partition, for which Mountbatten declared on 3 June. The next day he announced that the transfer of power would take place in mid-Aug. The detailed work was done by H. M. Patel and Chaudhuri Muhammad Ali, who formed the 'steering committee' of the partition council which met under Mountbatten.

Partition brought an exchange of populations between the two new nations, which produced a major refugee problem and, particularly in the Punjab, violence and bloodshed. The migrations imposed severe strains upon the military forces on the border. The Punjab Boundary Force, in particular, was inadequate to deal with the situation, and Bengal also experienced difficulties.

While partition settled the immediate issues required for the transfer of power it gave rise to new problems, such as that of the canal waters in the Punjab and the difficulties for East Pakistan jute, which was denied access to the mills in Calcutta. While economic problems were gradually resolved others were less tractable. The maintenance of a balance between the widely separated territories of East and West Pakistan remained one of Pakistan's major problems. Sections of Indian opinion were, moreover, never reconciled to partition and the demands for reunification of the subcontinent ('Akhand Bharat'), which the Jana Sangh made one of its major themes, did nothing to improve relations between India and Pakistan. By 1970 there was little evidence of any improvement in such relations.

C. H. Philips and M. D. Wainwright (eds), *The Partition of India: policies and perspectives, 1935–1947* (London, 1970).
Chaudhuri Muhammad Ali, *The Emergence of Pakistan* (New York, 1967).
                                                                    PDR

PARTITION TREATIES, concerning Spain and her possessions. The intended partition treaty (1668) between King Louis XIV and the Emperor Leopold I had never come into operation because the eventuality, namely the death of Charles II of Spain, had not occurred. The first partition treaty (1698) and the second partition treaty (1700) were concluded between Louis XIV and William III, and represented their joint effort to solve the problem of the Spanish Succession after the impending death of the childless King Charles II. The problem involved both legal and political considerations. In 1698 the first three claimants were the dauphin, the electoral prince of Bavaria, and Leopold I. The dauphin derived his claim from his mother, Maria Theresa, elder daughter of Philip IV of Spain; but he was prepared to resign his right to his second son, Philip Duke of Anjou, or to his third son, Charles Duke of Berri. The electoral prince derived his claim from his grandmother,

Margaret Theresa, younger daughter of Philip IV. Emperor Leopold derived his claim from his mother, Maria Anna, younger daughter of Philip III; but provided that the validity of his claim were recognized in full he was prepared to cede it to his younger son by his third marriage, Archduke Charles. There were other claimants, *eg*, Louis XIV derived a claim from his mother, Anne, elder daughter of Philip III, but obviously he would not press it when his son had a better one. As for the renunciations, the explicit Bourbon case was that all such were invalid for those who renounced but more particularly for succeeding generations. The implicit case of the house of Austria was that the renunciations were binding upon those who had made them and upon their descendants. From an international angle, no settlement could expect wide acceptance which permitted the whole Spanish inheritance to go to any one ruler, whether Bourbon or Habsburg. So the first partition treaty was signed by representatives of France, the Dutch republic, and England on 11 Oct. 1698. The major portion was allocated to the electoral prince, namely Spain itself, the Spanish Netherlands, and the extra-European possessions. The dauphin was to receive Naples, Sicily, the Tuscan ports, Finale, and Guipuzcoa. The archduke was to receive simply the Milanese. On 6 Feb. 1699 the electoral prince died, and so a second partition treaty was signed on 13 March 1700. This time the major share was allocated to the archduke. But the dauphin was now additionally to receive the Milanese, which would then be exchanged for Lorraine. An Austrian Habsburg was to become King of Spain but the house of Austria now stood to make no gains in Italy, unlike the Bourbons, and regarded the second treaty with even greater repugnance than the first. Both partition treaties were unpopular in England because of the secret way in which they had been negotiated. The second treaty became irrelevant when Louis XIV decided to accept the terms of Charles II's will (1700).

BM

PARTITIONS OF POLAND (1772, 1793, 1795), territorial dismemberment of this large but politically anarchic country by her ambitious and more powerful neighbours, Russia, Prussia, and Austria. In accordance with 18th-cent. political practice, partition was an extension of the principle of the balance of power by which the great powers could maintain Europe's territorial equality through reason rather than by war.

The first partition resulted from the prolonged political crisis beginning with the death of Augustus III of Poland and Saxony (Oct. 1763) and the election of Stanislas Poniatowski, the ex-lover of the Empress Catherine II, as his successor (1764). Under him Poland fell under Russia's military domination. Russia was simultaneously plunged into a war with Turkey (1768–74), in which her forces had by 1771 achieved considerable success. To save Turkey from drastic dismemberment, Prince Henry of Prussia tried to divert Russia's attention towards the helpless kingdom of Poland and encouraged the Austrian government to participate in that country's division in order to preserve international peace (1771). Though deploring such an aggressive act, Maria Theresa of Austria finally assented, and in Aug. 1772 the partition treaties were agreed. Prussia gained the area lying between Pomerania and East Prussia, with Ermeland. Austria, already in possession of the Polish enclave of Zips, took a large triangle based on the Carpathians; while to Russia fell the regions east of the Dvina, the Druc, and the Dnieper.

The second partition arose from the Polish political revival, embodied in the new constitution of May 1791, proclaimed while Russia was preoccupied with another Turkish conflict (1787–92). In 1791 Prussia and Austria had concluded a convention in which the integrity of Poland's constitution and territory was guaranteed. When the alliance was renewed in 1792 the Prussians took advantage of the revolutionary situation in France to alter the clause relating to Poland, so that Austria and Prussia only agreed to respect a free consti-

tution. The Prussian government, far from wanting to uphold a strong, united Poland, was already contemplating another partition, which was brought nearer by the death of the Emperor Leopold (1 March 1792). Thus Prussia refused to honour the guarantee when, with the Turkish war successfully concluded, Catherine informed the Prussian and Austrian ambassadors of her intention to annul this constitution, and sent an army of 65,000 'to restore Polish freedom'. The Polish king acceded to Catherine's demands and a treaty between Russia and Prussia (23 Jan. 1793) established the second partition. Austria agreed to forgo her share of Polish territory in return for a promise of Russo-Prussian help in the acquisition of Bavaria. Prussia took Danzig and an area of western Poland with a million people, while Russia acquired Polish Ukraine, Minsk, and Vilna, an area with 3 million people.

The defeat of their army by Russia in 1792 encouraged the Poles to further rebellion at the earliest opportunity. Gen. Kosciuszko's arrival in Warsaw (March 1794) precipitated a widespread insurrection. Warsaw, which first withstood the Prussians (Aug. 1794), fell to Suvorov's superior forces (Oct. 1794). The three major powers then proceeded to divide the remaining Polish lands between them, though not without disagreement. Austria and Prussia disputed Cracow and Russia and Prussia disagreed on the latter's eastern frontier. However, the partition treaties (Oct. 1795) stipulated that Prussia should gain 900,000 people and Warsaw, Austria 1 million people and Cracow, and Russia an additional 2 million people. In the Convention of St Petersburg (1797) the term 'the kingdom of Poland' was finally suppressed.

H. H. Kaplan, *The First Partition of Poland* (New York, 1962).
R. H. Lord, *The Second Partition of Poland* (Harvard, 1915).

MKS

PASAI, or Samudra, oldest Muslim sultanate in Indonesia, founded at the end of the 13th cent. in north Sumatra near modern Lho Seumawe. Its first sultan, Malik-us-Saleh (d. 1297), was a Sumatranese chief who was converted to Islam by traders from the west, probably India. Pasai became, in turn, the centre from which Islam spread to Malaysia, Indonesia, and the southern Philippines (Sulu) during the next two centuries. In *c.* 1520 Pasai was still important, having some 20,000 inhabitants, mainly Bengalis, according to Pires. A few years later, in 1524, it was incorporated into Atjeh (Achin) by Sultan Ali Mughayat Shah.

The history of Pasai is known from inscriptions, the *Sejarah Melayu* ('the Malay Annals') and the *Hikayat Raja-raja Pasai* ('Story of the Kings of Pasai') which concerns its earlier days. This is probably the oldest extant Malay text of some length.

PASARGADAE, first capital city of Achaemenid Iran, northeast of Shiraz, on the road between Hamadan and the Persian Gulf. Cyrus II (*reg. c.* 559–530 BC) built temples and his own tomb there.

PASCAL, BLAISE (1623–62), French scientist and thinker, who made a name for himself by inventing a calculating machine and by his essays on cones and vacuums. He came under the influence of Port Royal and eventually was converted (1653) to a more rigorous form of observance. He modelled his life on the *solitaires* of Port Royal and supported Antoine Arnauld by attacks on the Jesuits in *Les Provinciales* (1656–7). As his health deteriorated he spent his last years in meditation, preparing his *Pensées*, which are a landmark of French spirituality.

'PASIONARIA, LA' (DOLORES IBARRURI) (1895–), Spanish political figure of humble origins who became involved in politics through her marriage to an Asturian miner. She was one of the early founders of the Spanish Communist

Party and became a member (1930) of its central committee. During the Second Republic she made a reputation through her speeches, and in 1934 played a heroic role in the Asturian rising. When the army rebelled in 1936 she broadcast a speech demanding resistance throughout Spain, exhorting women to fight and coining the battle-cry of the republic and of besieged Madrid, 'No Pasaran!' ('They shall not pass!'). Thereafter, she was broadcasting frequently, denying defeatist rumours, rallying communist resistance, and using her popularity to recruit troops and boost morale. In Aug. 1936 she visited Paris to try to get arms for the republic. At the end of the war she was head of the Communist Party. Later, she fled to France and then to Russia, where she still remains (1970), president of the Spanish Communist Party in exile.

PASISIR, northern coastal areas of Java, including Surabaja, Tuban, Pati, Demak, and Pamelang. This was the area in which was found the 16th-cent. kingdom of Demak. The Pasisir may have played an important role as intermediary in transmitting the Javanese culture of the Madjapahit kingdom after its fall (late 15th cent.) to the successor kingdoms of Central Java, Padjang, and Mataram. The Dutch East India Co. succeeded in gaining control of these areas from the Javanese rulers through a series of agreements in the course of the 17th and 18th cents.

PASKEVICH, IVAN FYODOROVICH (1782–1856), Russian soldier and associate of Nicholas I, who was a commander in the Persian and Turkish wars. His capture of Warsaw (1831) ended the Polish rebellion. He was viceroy of Poland and Prince of Warsaw (1831–56).

PASQUIER, ETIENNE (1529–1615), French lawyer, poet, and historian, who served as *avocat-général* to the Parisian *chambre des comptes* (1585–1604). His poetry was undistinguished but his literary criticism and especially his historical work, leading to the multi-volume *Recherches sur la France* (1596), which began the scientific study of French history through its sources, was very important. He was a supporter of Henry IV and left many volumes of letters which give a vivid picture of court and literary life.

PASSARO, BATTLE OF CAPE (1718), naval battle off the south-east coast of Sicily between a British fleet of 21 ships, under the command of Admiral Sir George Byng, and a Spanish fleet of 22 ships, whose commander, Don Antonio Casteneta, was killed in the fighting (11 Aug. 1718). The British destroyed or captured 15 enemy ships, and shortly afterwards the Spanish government submitted to the Quadruple Alliance and accepted the Utrecht settlement (1713), which its attack on Sicily (July 1718) had violated.

PASSAROWITZ, TREATY OF (1718), negotiated by the Emperor Charles VI and the Venetian republic with the Ottoman empire; it ended the war begun by the Turks in 1714. Turkey ceded Temesvar to Charles, thereby allowing the whole of historic Hungary to be united under Habsburg rule. The treaty also ended the Turkish threat to Europe and began the long process of Turkish decline. Though the Turks made occasional recoveries, henceforth they were largely on the defensive. The treaty contributed to the decline of Venice by restricting her overseas possessions to the Ionian Isles, Dalmatia, Corfu, and Istria.

PASSAU, TREATY OF (1552), peace concluded between King Ferdinand of Hungary, Charles V's brother, and the Protestant German princes, led by Maurice of Saxony. The treaty was the result of prolonged negotiations (May–Aug. 1552) which followed Maurice's invasion of the Tyrol and Charles's flight from Innsbruck to Villach in Carinthia (April). Meanwhile, the French seized Metz, Toul, and Verdun and the Turks threatened the security of Austria. Charles therefore ratified the Passau agreement on 15 Aug., holding out the promise of a religious settlement which recognized Protestantism. The peace thus marked a stage in the collapse of imperial authority and foreshadowed the peace of Augsburg (1555).

PASSCHENDAELE, village in Flanders, 9 kms north-east of Ypres, which became the final objective of the main British offensive in the autumn of 1917. It is more correctly known as the Third Battle of Ypres.

PASSFIELD, SIDNEY JAMES WEBB, Baron (1859–1947), British civil servant, politician, historian, and an influential member of the Fabian Society. In 1892 he ceased to be a civil servant and married Beatrice Potter (1858–1943), daughter of a rich industrialist. Subsequently, most of his work and writing was done with her. As a member of the London County Council (1891–1910), he helped to establish (1895) and develop the London School of Economics and Political Science, and in 1913 founded the *New Statesman*. Both he and his wife were members of the Poor Law commission (1905–9) and he wrote its minority report. After the First World War he wrote the Labour Party policy pamphlet, 'Labour and the New Social Order', a statement of the democratic aims of evolutionary collectivist socialism. He was an MP (1922–9), serving in the first Labour government as president of the board of trade and in the second as secretary of state for the dominions and colonies (1929–30) and for the colonies (1930–1). But he exerted far greater influence as a writer and propagandist than as a politician. The Webbs wrote two valuable books of historical research, the *History of Trade Unionism* (1894) and *English Local Government* (9 vols, 1906–29).

PASSIONISTS, Catholic order of clerks founded (*c.* 1730) by St Paul of the Cross and sanctioned by Pope Benedict XIV in 1741. Passionists fast three days a week, as well as in Advent and Lent, and in their missionary work they take a special vow to keep alive the memory of Christ's Passion. The order was introduced into England in 1841 and into the US a few years later.

PASSIVE OBEDIENCE, politico-religious doctrine of absolute obedience to princes, based on the teachings of St Paul in the epistle to the Romans and of the first epistle of St Peter about the Christian duty to obey rulers, even if they are heathens or tyrants. This concept was adopted by Martin Luther and propagated by the early Lutherans, eg, John Tyndale in his *Obedience of Christian Man*. However, from the mid-16th cent. the doctrine was abandoned by Protestant reformers as the danger of persecution and extermination appeared. The first break came in 1549–51, when extreme Lutherans, eg, Flacius Illyricus, took refuge in Magdeburg and issued a solemn declaration justifying resistance in defiance of the Leipzig Interim of 1548. The Marian exiles, John Knox and Christopher Goodman, also attacked passive obedience in their writings (1556–8), while in France Huguenot leaders published a number of works justifying the right of resistance, eg, Hotman's *Franco-Gallia* (1573), Theodore Beza's *Du Droit des Magistrats sur leurs sujets*, published anonymously in 1576 after the St Bartholomew Massacre, and the famous *Vindiciae contra Tyrannos* (1579).

PASSOS, JOHN RODERIGO DOS (1896–), US writer of Portuguese descent, whose experiences in the First World War provided material for *One Man's Initiation . . . 1917* (1920), and *Three Soldiers* (1921), both dealing with the effects of war on the sensitive individual. *Manhattan Transfer* (1925) marks the beginning of his sociological approach to the novel, epitomized in *U.S.A.* (1937), first published in separate volumes as *The 42nd Parallel* (1930), *1919* (1932), and *The Big Money* (1936). *District of Columbia* (1952), another trilogy, comprising *Adventures of a Young Man* (1939), *Number One* (1943), and *The Grand Design* (1949), reflects the rejection of his earlier political radicalism, as do *The Men Who Made The Nation* (1957) and *Mr Wilson's War* (1963).

PASTERNAK, BORIS LEONIDOVICH (1890–1960), Russian poet and novelist, born in Moscow of Jewish parents. After studying music in Moscow he went (1912) to Marburg to study philosophy. His first book of verse, *Twin in the Clouds*, was published in 1914 and his reputation as a poet was established with *My Sister Life* (1922) and *Themes and Variations* (1923). From the first his attitude towards the Bolshevik Party was ambiguous. He certainly admired Lenin, but showed little enthusiasm for the communist regime. In *Lieutenant Schmidt* (1927) he revealed a greater interest in the revolution of 1905 than in that of 1917. The emergence of Stalinism helped to silence Pasternak as a poet, though Stalin admired his work sufficiently to invite his views about other Russian poets. During the Second World War years Pasternak lived mostly in Moscow and afterwards he went to the writers' village at Peredelkino. There he completed *Doctor Zhivago*, which at first he hoped to publish in Russia. But official critics found it 'profoundly unjust . . . anti-democratic and without benefit to the people'. Pasternak therefore agreed to its being published first in Italy and later (1958) in England. It was an immense success and in 1958 he was awarded the Nobel Prize for Literature, but this brought a storm of official protest on his head. He was forced to renounce the prize and some of his views and was expelled from the Writers' Union, though he was still allowed to live at Peredelkino. On his death, although it was not officially announced, thousands journeyed to Moscow to pay their last respects.

PASTEUR, LOUIS (1822–95), French chemist and bacteriologist, whose work on the causes of fermentation of wine and milk led him to study micro-organisms affecting domestic animals and man. He devised the processes of pasteurizing milk and of inoculations against anthrax, chicken cholera, and rabies. His proof of the existence of atmospheric germs led Lister to apply the principles of asepsis in surgery.

PASTON FAMILY in England, prosperous Norfolk family of gentry whose unique and lively correspondence, dating chiefly from the third quarter of the 15th cent., provides an invaluable picture of their social class and of the local political conflicts during the Wars of the Roses.

PASTOR AETERNUS (1516), papal bull issued by Leo X, which revoked the Pragmatic Sanction of Bourges (1438), and asserted papal authority to call, adjourn, or dissolve a council.

PASTOR AETERNUS (1870), papal bull which defined papal infallibility. Catholics who did not accept the dogma formed the Old Catholic Church.

PASTORALIS OFFICII (1718), papal letters promulgated by Clement XI on the anniversary of the publication of *Unigenitus* (1713), which excommunicated all those Frenchmen who had failed to give their unqualified submission to the controversial bull. The letters were declared invalid by the *parlement* of Paris, which denounced them as contrary to Gallican tradition.

PASTORIUS, FRANCIS DANIEL (1651–1720), American politician and early anti-slavery spokesman, who became an agent for the Frankfort Land Co. (1683) and led a party of Mennonites from the Rhineland to PA. He laid out Germantown and was its first mayor. As a member of the Provincial Assembly (1687–91), he signed the Quakers' first protest against slavery, declaring it contrary to Christian principles.

PASTOUREAUX, RISING OF (1251). The capture of King Louis IX of France during crusade in Egypt led to a spontaneous rising of the peasants of north-east France to rescue their king. They had no resources and their 'crusade' degenerated into local pillaging. But the rising shows the peasants' deep devotion to Louis.

PASTRY WAR, term of ridicule for the fighting between France and Mexico in 1838. French citizens living in Mexico had suffered severe financial losses during the previous unsettled decade, and Mexico's unwillingness or inability to pay reparations caused the French government to send a fleet to Veracruz to enforce payment. The French seized Veracruz and with British help obtained a promise that the claim would be paid.

The name Pastry War was coined by Mexicans from a French claim that a French-owned baker's shop in Mexico City had been wrecked by exuberant Mexican soldiers.

PATALIPUTRA, ancient city on the site of modern Patna in Bihar, India, once the capital of the great Maurya and Gupta empires. Some of its ancient buildings have been brought to light by excavations. The Greeks (3rd–2nd cent. BC) knew the city as Pali(m)bothra.

PATANI SULTANATE, 17th-cent. Muslim commercial centre in Malay Peninsula and the northernmost centre of Malay–Muslim influence in the peninsula. By the 15th cent. Patani was Muslim. Its prosperity as a point of exchange for Chinese and South-East Asian traders increased with the fall of Malacca (1511). The Portuguese traded there, and the Dutch (1603–22) and English (1612–23) Cos made it the site of one of their earliest Asian factories. Patani declined with the establishment of alternative outlets for the China trade at Batavia (1619) and elsewhere. Except during one major rebellion (1628–36) or periods of Thai weakness, Patani generally sent the *bunga emas* of vassalage to Thailand, while establishing marriage alliances with independent Malay states. In the course of Thailand's recovery from the Burmese wars, however, Patani was twice conquered (1784, 1832), and on the second occasion subdivided into seven small states. Thailand continued to rule through Malay rajas until 1902, when Patani became a normal Thai province.

PATANJALI (*fl.* 2nd cent. BC), grammarian of Sanskrit and author of the *Mahabhashya*, a work of interest for some examples of grammatical rules reflecting political and other developments of the time.

PATEL, SADAR VALLABHBHAI JHAVERI (1875–1950), Indian nationalist politician, who was associated with Gandhi's *satyagraha* campaign in Kaira district, Gujarat (1918). By the late 1930s he had become the controller of the Congress organization and was the dominant figure of the first post-independence (1947) government. In Bardoli in 1928, he himself conducted what was probably the most successful of all *satyagraha* campaigns in support of the peasants' demands. He was chairman of the Ahmedabad municipal council for a short period (1924–8), but gained his administrative experience largely in the Congress itself, and as chairman of the parliamentary sub-committee which ran the election campaigns of 1937 and 1946. He was president of the Congress in 1931. As minister for home affairs, information and broadcasting in the interim government (1946–7), he also took the states portfolio (July 1947) and was responsible for integrating the states into the new union. He was deputy prime minister (1947–50), but was never able to displace Nehru in the Congress Party, although the presidential election in 1950, which was won by his nominee, Purushottamdas Tandon, might have given him a stronger position had he lived.

PATEL, VITHALBHAI JHAVERI (1873–1933), Indian nationalist politician and elder brother of Vallabhbhai Patel. He was one of the founders of the Swarajya Party (1923) and became the first elected president of the Central Legislative Assembly (1925–30), a position which he used on a number of occasions to support nationalist policies. In 1932 he came out openly in support of Subhas Chandra Bose's more radical and anti-Gandhian attitude.

PATENT OFFICE in Britain, administrative body dealing with the issue of 'letters patent', which confer some privilege, *eg*, nobility, or the exclusive right to make, use, or sell a commodity. In the 19th cent. it became the body which grants the patent of a discovery or invention, restricting its exploitation to the holder for a limited period. The office, originally under the lord chancellor, was transferred to the commissioners of patents (1850). An act of 1883 created the office in its present form, in which it is presided over by the comptroller-general of patents.

PATERNAE CHARITATI (1682), papal bull, in which Innocent XI denounced the acceptance of the Four Gallican Articles by the general assembly of the French Church. Louis XIV prorogued the assembly (June 1682) to prevent a further confrontation between the clergy and the papacy, but discord between France and the papacy continued.

PATERSON, WILLIAM (1658–1719), Scottish company promoter and financial speculator, who traded between the City of London and the West Indies. He became the leading figure in the mercantile group which negotiated with the government to produce a scheme for the Bank of England (1694). The bank, a finance company with 1300 shareholders, was to raise a government loan of £1,200,000 in return for special concessions and its incorporation as the first English joint-stock bank. However, Paterson failed to pay all his subscriptions, quarrelled over policy with his fellow directors, and resigned (1695).

With the object of founding a colony on the Isthmus of Panama he became involved in the Darién Co. Despite the withdrawal of the English half of the capital and his own impeachment by the Westminster parliament (1695), Paterson landed at Darién, where his wife died and he caught fever. He consistently blamed William III and the English for the overall failure of the Darién enterprise, but was paid his compensatory 'equivalent' after the treaty of Union (1707) between England and Scotland.

PATERSON, WILLIAM (1755–1810), Australian soldier, naturalist, and explorer, who was active, in the latter two roles, in South Africa and India before serving in the NSW Corps (1793). He succeeded Grose as administrator of NSW (1794–5) during the interregnum between governors Arthur Phillip and John Hunter, becoming lieutenant-governor (1799) and founding small settlements in Van Diemen's Land (1806–8). After learning of Gov. Bligh's deposition, Paterson maintained nominal control of NSW until Gov. Lachlan Macquarie's arrival.

PATHANS, Muslim tribes inhabiting southern and eastern Afghanistan and the north-west frontier of Pakistan. North of the Gumal pass the most important tribes are the Darwesh Khel Waziris, the Mahsuds, Turis, Orakzai, Afridis, Mohmands, and Yusafzai. British relations with these war-like tribes in the 19th cent. involved continual punitive expeditions.

PATHET LAO ('LAO NATION'), revolutionary movement led by Prince Souphanouvong, formed in 1950 as the Lao wing of the Viet-Minh.

PATINO, DON JOSE DE (1666–1736), Spanish politician and minister of Philip V and Elizabeth Farnese, who did much to revive Spain's strength in the decade 1727–37. After holding a temporary administrative post in Milan during the War of the Spanish Succession, he was promoted by Philip V to membership of the consejo de ordenes militares (1707) before becoming intendant for the province of Estremadura. Here he restored order among the Castilian troops fighting in the war and reformed the system of taxation. He was transferred to Catalonia, became interested in naval construction, and carried out vigorous economies which provided the resources for Philip's eventual victory in the peninsular campaign. In 1717 he became military and naval intendant in Cadiz and as president of the chamber of commerce he devoted himself to the revival of Spain's maritime power. He headed a commission of Spanish and English merchants to consider tariff reforms and built up the fleets for Alberoni's Sardinian and Sicilian expeditions (1717–18). After the latter's failure Patino was out of favour for some years, but on Ripperda's downfall (1727) he became minister for the marine and Indies and took over responsibility for the nation's finances, as well as becoming chief secretary of state (1729). During this period of office (1727–36) he supervised the construction of another fleet which took part in the recapture of Oran (1732) and reached a total of 33 ships of the line by the time of his death. He restored the arsenals and dockyards at Cadiz and Havana, established a training college for officers, and enforced the strict collection of Spanish American revenues. He also ensured an increase of taxation upon the cargoes from the Indies and raised the government's revenue by 50 per cent from 142 million *reals* at the beginning of Philip V's reign to some 211 million in 1737.

E. Armstrong, *Elizabeth Farnese, the Termagent of Spain* (London, 1892). MKS

PATIÑO, SIMÓN ITURI (1864–1947), Bolivian tin magnate, originally an Indian mule driver and trader who received a small tin mine as payment for a petty debt and transformed his holdings into a gigantic enterprise. His power in a small country such as Bolivia and his preference for living abroad alienated radicals within Bolivia, and his mines there were nationalized in 1952.

PATIO PROCESS, mercury amalgamation process for the extraction of silver from the ore. It was used extensively in Latin America, and introduced into Mexico in 1556 by Bartolomé de Medina, who may have invented it. The process, which permitted the exploitation of lower-grade ores than did smelting, quickly spread to other areas, reaching Peru in the 1570s. Its adoption made mercury, a royal monopoly, of the utmost importance for the maintenance of the silver industry in Spanish America. In the late 19th cent. the patio process gave way to the use of cyanide.

PATKUL, JOHAN REINHOLD (1660–1707), Livonian nobleman, whose opposition to Charles XII of Sweden helped to cause the Great Northern War. He opposed Charles XI's Reduction on behalf of the Livonian landowners, fled the country to escape a death sentence imposed in his absence (1694), entered the service of Augustus of Saxony (1699), and organized the Russo–Saxo–Danish coalition. In 1701 he transferred his services to Russia, tried to bring Prussia into the coalition, and became commander of a Russian corps, which he placed temporarily under Austria (Dec. 1705). But his intrigues, which were aimed above all at the preservation of noble privileges in Livonia, resulted in his arrest by Augustus. After the peace of Altranstädt (1707) Augustus handed him over to Charles XII, and although Charles's sister Ulrika appealed on his behalf, he was put to death as a traitor.

PATRAŞCANU, LUCREŢIU (1900–54), Rumanian communist, who was born in Moldavia and educated in France and Germany. He joined the Communist Party (1921), was primary spokesman for the communist lawyers, and defended various party activists, despite his frequent arrest. In 1933 he was elected to parliament as a deputy of the Workers and Peasants Bloc. During the Second World War he represented the Communist Party in plots to overthrow the military dictatorship of Marshal Antonescu. He represented Rumania at the armistice talks in Moscow (1944) and became minister of justice (1944–8). He was later accused of sympathizing with Tito and contemplating the introduction of Titoism into Rumania, for which he was detained and held without trial until May 1954. He was then tried, found guilty, and executed. In April 1967 his reputation was rehabilitated and his major writings were subsequently reissued in Rumania.

PATRE ET AVO CONSULIBUS in France, legal formula borrowed by French jurists from Roman law to define *parlementaire* claims to nobility, voiced by Henry IV in 1600 when he ordained that three successive generations of occupancy in certain honourable offices of state in France vested a man with hereditary nobility.

PATRIA BOBA, or 'foolish fatherland', a term of derision used mainly in Colombia to refer to the early days of national life after independence (approximately 1810–15), when inexperienced and selfish leadership made a farce of national government.

PATRIA CHICA, or 'little fatherland', in Latin America, expression of affection for the locality, province, or region of one's origin, as distinct from the ties which one feels with the nation state as a whole. The attachment of many Latin Americans to the 'patria chica' has been a serious obstacle to those who hope for the emergence of nationalism and centralized nation states.

PATRIARCHATE, grade in the ecclesiastical hierarchy, ranking above primate. Originally four patriarchs were recognized by the early Church—those of Rome, Alexandria, Antioch, and Constantinople. Jerusalem was added during the Crusades, and later new Patriarchates were established in Venice, Iberia, and, more importantly, in Moscow and in other branches of the Eastern Churches, *eg*, over the Maronites.

PATRICIANS, name of the Roman aristocratic class as distinct from the ordinary people (plebeians), believed by the ancients to be descended from the original senators (*patres*). Some scholars hold that they were ethnically different from the plebeians, being the original Latin settlers, or alternatively Sabine conquerors of the original population; others attribute their privileged position to economic advantages. Certainly, by 500 BC a caste system existed and the patricians monopolized religious offices, the Senate, and magistracies, and the cavalry arm of the army. In 445 their exclusiveness was broken when the *lex Canuleia* permitted intermarriage with the plebeians, and the Struggle of the Orders diminished their importance and their numbers; by the end of the 1st cent. BC only 30 patrician families survived. Though Julius Caesar, Augustus, and later emperors admitted members to the order, it had disappeared by the 3rd cent. AD.

PATRICK, Saint (d. *c.* 460), British missionary, to whom Ireland's conversion to Christianity is usually attributed, probably mistakenly, as parts of Ireland were likely to have been converted before his time. He was captured by Irish raiders as a boy, and spent many years as a slave in Ireland, but ultimately escaped. Later, he returned to Ireland in order to convert the population. His *Confession*, in which he tries to justify the conduct of his mission, is the only authentic piece of writing by a native of the British Isles in the 5th cent.

PATRIOT KING, THE IDEA OF A, English political essay written by Bolingbroke in an attempt to discredit Sir Robert Walpole's government and provide the Tories with a new political theory. Bolingbroke rejected divine right, but claimed that the king should govern with the help of the best possible men, irrespective of party or faction. The essay belonged to the period of Bolingbroke's retirement from active politics after 1735. It had some influence on George III's approach to kingship.

PATRIOT PARLIAMENT (1689), Irish parliament summoned by James II. It was almost entirely Roman Catholic in membership and its patriotism was that of the English inhabitants, the native Irish being poorly represented. It asserted the exclusive right of the Irish parliament to legislate for Ireland, and prohibited appeals from Irish to English

courts. It would have repealed Poynings's Law (which required Irish bills to be approved by the English council), but for James's opposition. It went on to repeal the acts of settlement, to remove all civil disabilities imposed on religious grounds, and enacted that clergy of any denomination should receive tithes paid by their own followers. By an act of attainder, which would have confiscated the property of over 2400 Protestants—almost all the Protestant landowners in Ireland—the parliament threatened the English Protestant interest with extinction. This act gave the Protestants an excuse for retaliatory measures when the relief of Londonderry snatched from James II the military victory which was needed to make the Patriot Parliament's programme effective.

PATROCÍNIO, JOSÉ DE (1853–1905), Brazilian journalist and abolitionist, who was instrumental in the formation of the Confederation of Abolition Societies in 1883. As owner-editor of *A Gazeta da Tarde*, and later *A Cidade do Rio*, he argued incessantly for the need for emancipation of all Negroes still in bondage. After the abolition of slavery (13 May 1888), he campaigned on behalf of social justice and against the death penalty.

PATRONS OF HUSBANDRY in US, farmers' organization founded in 1867 by Oliver H. Kelly as the 'National Grange of the Patrons of Husbandry'. It was organized into local lodges, or 'Granges', and admitted both men and women to membership, which by 1876 numbered 858,050. Its original aims were social and educational, but in the 1870s it became involved in the 'Granger' movement, which advocated government regulation of railroads and grain warehouses. Local Granges also organized co-operative enterprises, but with little success, and membership declined. In the 20th cent. it gradually revived, and in the 1930s and 1940s its advocacy of agricultural adjustment legislation, farm credit agencies, and a commodity-by-commodity approach to farm problems gave the Grange a renewed political importance as a lobby for the farming community.

PATROON SYSTEM (1629), land ownership scheme employed by the Dutch in their North American colony of the New Netherlands. Under the system, begun by Dutch West India Co., any member of the company who established a colony of 50 adults in the New Netherlands was given a tract of land and received the title of patroon. Nearly all of these colonies failed; two survived until the end of Dutch rule (1664), and one (Rensselaerswyck) until 1776.

PATTESON, JOHN COLERIDGE (1827–71), English clergyman, who became Bp of Melanesia. He worked in the South Seas under Bp Selwyn from 1855. After an episcopate of ten years he was murdered on the island of Nukapu in tribal revenge for the kidnapping of some of the inhabitants by white slave-traders. His death focused British attention on the social needs of Polynesia. His father, Sir John Patteson (1790–1861), was an English high court judge who was frequently employed as arbitrator in disputes involving the government.

PATTON, GEORGE SMITH (1885–1945), US soldier, who served with distinction in the First World War. In the Second World War he played a prominent part in North Africa and Sicily, and as commander of the US Third Army fought in Europe after D-Day (6 June 1944). Outcry against his criticism of denazification policies led to his being relieved of his command.

PAUKER, ANA (born Rabinovici) (1893–1960), Rumanian communist politician, who joined the Socialist Party (1915), participated in the German occupation of Wallachia (1917), and in the strike movement of Dec. 1918. She and her husband, Marcel Pauker, a left-wing intellectual, reorganized the journal *Socialism*. They stood on the left of the Socialist

Party and, when the party split in 1921, joined the newly formed Communist Party. She was arrested (1925), but escaped and fled to Moscow, where she joined the Comintern. She returned to Rumania (1934) and in 1935 became secretary of the party. Soon she was arrested again and sentenced to ten years' imprisonment, during which her husband was purged. In 1940 she was exchanged by the Rumanian government for a Bessarabian nationalist held by the Soviet government and again she went to Moscow. During the Second World War she was a member of the Rumanian bureau and organized the Tudor Vladimirescu division (1943) from among Rumanian prisoners of war in Russia. In 1944 she returned to Rumania at the head of the Muscovite faction of the party, and was made responsible for party organization, recruitment, and statutes. She became minister of foreign affairs (1947) and took charge of arrangements for collectivization within the Politburo. Together with other leading Muscovites she was purged by Gheorghiu-Dej in 1952, ostensibly for errors in organization and recruitment, but in reality for her subservience and reliance upon the Kremlin.

PAUL I (1754–1801), Emperor of Russia (*reg.* 1796–1801) and son of Catherine II. He maintained his own military court at Gatchina and reformed the army. As emperor, he was an enlightened autocrat and carried out administrative reforms, but he alienated the nobility by abolishing provincial assemblies and taxing landed estates. He joined the second coalition against Napoleon I, but quarrelled with Britain, and even planned to invade India. He was overthrown on grounds of insanity and killed in a conspiracy which brought Alexander I to the throne.

PAUL III (1468–1549), Pope (*reg.* 1534–49), in whose pontificate were laid the foundations of Catholic revival after the impact of the Protestant Reformation. He was devoted to the interests of his family, the Farnese. Despite his blatant nepotism, he encouraged the work of reformers such as Contarini, Caraffa, Pole, and Morone. He relied on the advice of the oecumenically minded humanist, Cardinal Sadoleto, was interested in overseas missions, and recognized the Syrian Christians of Malabar as Catholics. He added to the Vatican library and appointed Michelangelo as chief architect of St Peter's, Rome.

Among his other actions were the appointment of the reform commission of 1536, formal recognition of the Society of Jesus, establishment of the modern Roman Inquisition, and the opening of the Council of Trent (1545). This was dedicated to the removal of heresy, the reformation of morals, the restoration of religious peace to Europe, and the preparation of an anti-Turkish crusade. In 1536 Paul set up a commission to study Church reform, the result of which was the *Consilium delectorum Cardinalium . . . de Emendanda Ecclesia* (March 1537). Although for financial reasons he shrank from reforming the *dataria*, the office which issued dispensations and appointments to benefices, he took steps to end episcopal absenteeism and improve pastoral care. He recognized the significance of Ignatius Loyola's work and in his bull, *Regimini militantis ecclesiae* (1540), gave full approval to the Jesuits' charter of foundation. His bull, *Licet ab initio* (1542), reconstituted the Inquisition by setting up a committee of cardinals, the Congregation of the Holy Office, under Caraffa, with wide powers to pass doctrinal judgements and root out heresy.

Against a background of political and religious confusion in Germany and French hostility, Paul delayed the opening of the promised General Council from its original date (23 May 1537) to 13 Dec. 1545, when 31 bishops and under 50 theologians met at the imperial city of Trent. The council was interrupted in 1547 by a quarrel between Paul and Charles V over Parma and complicated by Charles's defeat of the Protestants at Muhlberg (April 1547). It was transferred to Bologna, much to Charles's annoyance, and while the emperor sought his own reconciliation with the Protestants at

Augsburg (1548), Paul formally prorogued the council. He died shortly afterwards.

L. von Pastor, *History of the Popes from the Close of the Middle Ages*, (London, 1908–28).   MKS

PAUL IV (1476–1559), Pope (*reg.* 1555–9), whose pontificate was noted for his uncompromising attitude to heresy. He was one of the commissioners appointed to examine the state of the Catholic Church (1536–7). After Contarini's death (1542) he became acknowledged leader of the Catholic reformers and his appointment as inquisitor-general of a reformed Inquisition gave him the authority to organize the full-scale persecution and extermination of heretics, both convinced Protestants and Catholic deviationists.

As pope he continued this crusade for Catholic purity and revival. To combat heresy he commissioned the first Index of prohibited books (1559), which included all the works of Erasmus and the vernacular translations of the Bible. He established the Jewish ghetto in Rome and proclaimed the eternal guilt of the Jewish race in the bull *Cum nimis absurdum* (1555).

His Neapolitan background made him a life-long enemy of Spain. His excommunication of Philip II and his implacable hatred of Ignatius Loyola were also prompted by hostility to Spain. Only Loyola's death in 1556 and the appointment of the acceptable Diego Lainez as general saved the Society of Jesus from abolition. Finally, Paul precipitated the last phase of the Habsburg–Valois conflict in Italy, though his actions ended with the re-establishment of Spanish supremacy there (1556) and in Sept. 1557 he retired from the war, while the Spanish viceroy of Naples, the Duke of Alva, besieged his states.

PAUL V (1552–1621), Pope (*reg.* 1605–21), whose pontificate was marked by attempts to restore the temporal power of the holy see and particularly his unsuccessful struggle with Venice over clerical jurisdiction, which led him to place the republic under papal interdict (1606). He alienated not only Venice, but Henry IV of France and James I of England by his extreme ideas of papal authority, reinforced by his dependence on Jesuit agents and the philosophy of Bellarmine's *De Romane Pontific* (1610).

PAUL VI (1897–), Pope (*reg.* 1963–), in whose pontificate the Church has faced the challenge of social and moral issues, *eg*, abortion, birth control, and a celibate clergy, and of the relations of the Catholic world with Protestantism, secular thinking, and non-Christian ideologies.

PAUL, Prince (1893–), Regent of Yugolsavia (1934–41), and cousin of King Alexander. On the king's assassination he was named as regent. He began by relaxing the dictatorship, but soon returned to authoritarian methods. He prided himself on the apparent settlement of the Serb–Croat problem with the conclusion of the Sporazum in 1939. But it proved an ephemeral success. His turn towards the Axis in the Second World War aroused considerable opposition and he resigned (March 1941) after his government had signed the Tripartite Alliance. He was interested more in art than in politics.

PAUL, Saint (d. *c.* AD 65), 'Apostle to the Gentiles' and the leading figure of the early Christian era, originally known as Saul. He was brought up a Pharisee and educated partly at Jerusalem, where he studied under the famous rabbi, Gamaliel. Within a few years of Jesus' crucifixion Paul came into contact with Christianity, which he strongly opposed, and assisted in the martyrdom of St Stephen. On the way to Damascus he experienced a conversion which changed his life; it is described in three accounts in the Acts of the Apostles. Three years after he returned from Arabia he became active in the Christian mission and went on three missionary tours. The rapid growth of Gentile Christianity, however, raised serious issues as to its relationship to the original Jewish

Christianity. St Paul went up to Jerusalem to discuss the question with the Apostles, and the decrees of this first Council were in principle a victory for his point of view. After an adventurous career, St Paul was placed under house arrest in Rome for two years, and was probably martyred during the persecution of Nero (*c.* 65). In his letters, St Paul laid the foundations for later Christian theology.

PAUL-BONCOUR, JOSEPH (1873–), French lawyer and politician, who was France's chief delegate at the League of Nations after the death of Briand (1932) and a champion of collective security. He first made his name as a lawyer by defending trade unionists and socialists, and in 1909 he entered parliament. He returned to politics after First World War service, and sat as a Socialist, but resigned from the party in 1931. He was prime minister (1932–3), then foreign minister in several later governments (1933–4, 1938). In 1940 he opposed the armistice and was one of the deputies who voted against giving full powers to Pétain. He was a senator for a few years under the Fourth Republic.

PAULETTE in France, name given to the *droit annuel*, a fiscal levy which made tenure of many official positions quasi-hereditary. During the Religious Wars offices had been freely sold by the Crown and the purchasers were able to pass them on to their heirs, provided they had resigned them at least 40 days before their death. This left some office-holders in precarious positions and encouraged their families to resort to fraud, such as concealing bodies after death until 40 days had elapsed. In order to overcome this, and to ensure adequate funds for the siege of Sedan, Henry IV accepted the suggestion of a noted financier, Charles Paulet, that he should sell dispensations from the 40-days clause in return for an annual payment of $\frac{1}{60}$ of the value of the office in question. The right to collect this was farmed out to Paulet himself (12 Dec. 1604) for 900,000 *livres*, nearly twice the income the Crown then received from the sale of offices. As it offered firm security—despite clauses in the contract allowing the Crown to dispossess unworthy holders—officials stampeded to pay the levy. Prices of offices rose and many nobles became alarmed at the social and political implications of selling security of tenure on such a scale. So the contract, which by then had been sold by Paulet, was suspended (1618), but the Crown's need for money led to its re-establishment (1620). Thereafter it was renewed every nine years and remained in existence until the end of the *ancien régime* with only minor variations (1638, 1709, 1722, 1771), although increasingly exemptions were granted during the 18th cent.

PAULING, LINUS CARL (1901–), US chemist, renowned for his fundamental work on the molecular structure of chemical compounds and the complex molecules of living tissue. After the Second World War he was a vigorous protagonist of nuclear disarmament. For his work in these areas he received two Nobel Prizes: for chemistry (1954) and for peace (1963).

PAULISTAS, residents of the city or state of São Paulo, Brazil, whose slave raids and gold-seeking expeditions in the 17th cent. into the interior of the South American continent laid the basis for the later territorial expansion of Brazil.

PAUSANIAS (1) (d. *c.* 470 BC), Spartan soldier and nephew of King Leonidas (from 479), who was briefly regent for his son Pleistarchus. In 478 he led a Greek fleet which liberated much of Cyprus and Byzantium, but his tyrannical methods induced the Ionian Greeks to seek the protection of the Athenians, who organized the Delian League (478/7). Being suspected of intriguing with the Persians, he was recalled (478), tried, and acquitted. He then returned and established himself as despot of Byzantium. He was expelled by Cimon, but later returned again to Sparta, where he became involved with seditious helots and was killed.

PAUSANIAS (2) (*reg.* 408–395), Spartan Agiad King, son of Pleistoanax, superseded Lysander as commander of the Peloponnesian army at Athens in 403 and organized the settlement by which democracy was restored there after the fall of the Thirty Tyrants. Later, after failing to support Lysander at the battle of Haliartus (395), he escaped the death sentence and instead was exiled.

PAUW, ADRIAN (d. 1653), Dutch politician and son of Reinier Pauw, both of whom were burgomasters of Amsterdam. In 1631 he became Grand Pensionary of Holland and took part in abortive negotiations between the states general of the northern and southern Netherlands (1632). He disapproved of Frederick Henry's idea of a French alliance (1635), and although he became reconciled to its necessity, he fell from power (1636). Later, as leader of the peace party, he became the Netherlands plenipotentiary at the Congress of Münster (1646–8) in the peace negotiations that led to the peace of Westphalia.

PAUW, REINIER (d. 1636), Dutch businessman and burgomaster of Amsterdam during the last years of the 12-Year Truce, who was one of the original directors of the Dutch East India Co. He was leader of the Contra-Remonstrants on the Amsterdam town council, and supported Maurice of Nassau against Oldenbarneveldt, over whose trial he presided (1619).

PAVELIĆ, ANTE (1889–1959), Croatian nationalist and leader of the extreme organization called the Ustasa, which he formed in the late 1920s. It was soon outlawed by the government and its activists took refuge in Italy and Hungary, whose governments were eager to weaken Yugoslavia by any means. Abroad, the Ustasa co-operated with other terrorist groups, which were subsidized by foreign powers. In 1941 Pavelić became the *poglavnik* (leader) of independent Croatia. The motto of his regime—'Ready for the Fatherland'—in practice meant 'no Serbs'. Ustasa bands murdered nearly 750,000 Orthodox Serbs and Jews in the lands they controlled. The brutal policy of the Ustasa, and Pavelić's acquiescence in the Italian annexation of Dalmatia, led many to join the Partisans, who were most effective in areas under Pavelić's authority. After the Second World War Pavelić escaped from Yugoslavia and settled in South America.

PAVIA, Italian city in the centre of Lombardy which became the capital of the Lombard kingdom (late 6th cent. to 774). After the annexation of the Lombard state by the Frankish king, Charlemagne, Pavia continued to be the centre of the royal government in northern Italy and successive kings were crowned here with the Lombard iron crown. The city was gradually eclipsed by Milan as the main political centre of Lombardy, and finally annexed by the Visconti lords of Milan in 1360.

PAVIA, BATTLE OF (1525), Spanish victory under the Marquis de Pescara and Duke Charles de Bourbon in the Italian Wars over Francis I of France, who had laid siege to the town of Pavia, south of Milan. After beating back a Spanish charge by artillery fire, Francis launched an unsuccessful counter-attack with cavalry, which broke under deadly musket fire. Francis himself was captured, and was taken from Italy to Madrid as a prisoner.

PAVIE MISSION (1879–95), concerned with geographical, cultural, and linguistic studies in Laos, Cambodia, and Thailand, led by Auguste Pavie, which provided an occasion for French intervention in Laos.

PAVILLON, NICOLAS (1597–1677), Bp of Aleth in Languedoc (1639), a friend of St Vincent de Paul and a zealous reformer, whose austere piety led him to become involved in the Jansenist controversy over the formulary condemning the

Augustinus (1661–8). He was eventually persuaded to participate in the peace of the Church (1668), though his new ritual for his diocese was condemned by the pope.

PAVÓN, BATTLE OF (17 Sept. 1861), in Santa Fé province, Argentina. The Buenos Aires army, commanded by Bartolomé Mitre, defeated the Argentine Confederation forces, led by Justo José de Urquiza. Buenos Aires thereupon became the capital of a new national government, of which Mitre became the interim and then the constitutional president.

PAVONIA MASSACRE (25 Feb. 1643), murder by William Kieft, Dutch governor of New Amsterdam, of over 100 Indians at Pavonia, NJ. This action caused open warfare between the Dutch and the Indians (1643–5).

PAW TUN, SIR (1883–1955), Burmese politician, who was elected to the Legislative Council (1925) and became home minister (1937), minister for lands and revenue (1939), and prime minister (1942). At the outbreak of the Second World War he accompanied the governor to India.

PAWNEE INDIANS, confederacy of American tribes, possibly encountered by the Spanish in KS (*c.* 1541) and definitely by French traders in NB (*c.* 1750). They were friendly to the whites from the outset. The Pawnee never fought the US, and during the Indian wars members of the tribe served frequently as army scouts. They ceded their lands in NB in a series of treaties (1833–76) when they moved to Indian Territory. They were given lands in OK individually and became US citizens in 1892.

PAYS D'ÉLECTIONS in France, constitutional term given to those provinces where tax collection was in the hands of royal officials known as *élus*, first appointed in the Vermandois (1355). By the 17th cent. they had spread throughout the central areas of France at the expense of the old provincial estates. The provinces were divided into new administrative areas known as *élections* (1380) staffed by an increasing number of officials who performed many duties until the reign of Henry III, when they were limited to purely fiscal tasks (1577). Thereafter, they were gradually superseded by the *intendants* who exercised untrammelled royal authority greater than that which the *élus* had acquired.

PAYS D'ÉTATS in France, constitutional term signifying provinces which retained their old form of government by estates, and, in theory at least, some measure of fiscal and general autonomy. By the 18th cent. only the peripheral provinces relatively newly added to the monarchy preserved this status, such as Artois, Brittany, Béarn, Corsica, Burgundy, Flanders, Languedoc, Provence, Navarre, and some of the other Pyrenean valleys. The other estates had vanished by the 17th cent. and even those which remained had often only nominal powers which only concealed the exercise of royal authority.

PAZ ESTENSSORO, VICTOR (1907–), Bolivian economist, diplomat, and president of Bolivia (1952–6, 1960–4). He was an early leader of the National Revolutionary Movement (MNR) and assumed the presidency of Bolivia after the revolution of 1952, led by the MNR. During his first term of office Bolivia's three largest tin-mining companies were nationalized, sweeping land reforms were introduced, and attempts made to bring the Indian majority into Bolivian political life. After serving as ambassador to Britain (1956–1960), Paz was re-elected to the presidency for a second term in 1960. He was elected for a third term in 1964, but shortly afterwards the MNR split and he was overthrown by a military coup, led by his vice-president, René Barrientos Ortuño.

PAZZI CONSPIRACY (April 1478), in Florence, attempt of the Pazzi family to end the Medici's rule in Florence by murdering the brothers Lorenzo and Giuliano de' Medici. The Pazzi were related to the Medici and had genuine grievances against them. The conspiracy was supported by Pope Sixtus IV, whose nephews were actively implicated in it. The attempt was particularly shocking as the Medici brothers were attacked in Florence cathedral during the High Mass. Giuliano died, but Lorenzo escaped and the people of Florence rallied to him. Summary execution of the assassins, who included the Abp of Pisa, brought upon Lorenzo a papal excommunication and there followed a bitter war between Florence and the papacy.

PEABODY, ELIZABETH PALMER (1804–96), US educationalist, reformer, and member of the Transcendental movement. She was a follower of Friedrich Froebel and opened the first English-speaking kindergarten in America in Boston (1860), propagating Froebel's ideas through her numerous writings and her editorship of the *Kindergarten Magazine* (1873–5).

PEABODY, GEORGE (1795–1869), US merchant, financier, and philanthropist, whose endowment created the Peabody Fund for general education and teacher-training in the South after the American Civil War. He also endowed the Peabody Institute in Baltimore and a number of natural history museums. He was resident in England after 1837 and gave huge sums of money for the erection of model working men's tenements in London.

PEACE BALLOT (1934–5) in Britain, term used to describe 'The National Declaration on the League of Nations and Armaments'. This was a nation-wide questionnaire organized by the national declaration committee (set up by the league of nations union following a successful local poll run by the *Ilford Recorder*) to demonstrate the strength of British public support for the league. This was a time when its prestige had been shaken by the Manchuria crisis, by Germany's departure from the league and from the disarmament conference, and was about to be tested by Mussolini's designs on Abyssinia.

One ballot, supported by the Labour and Liberal parties and denounced by the *Daily Express* as the 'Blood Ballot', was seen by some as pacifist, and indeed its first four questions produced overwhelming majorities in favour of the league and of reduction of armaments by international agreement. But one question on it showed that out of 11,559,165, over 10 million supported the collective application of economic sanctions against an aggressor, and 6,784,368 supported military sanctions (compared with under 2½ million who opposed them—and a similar number of abstentions). The results were seen by the organizers as an endorsement of collective security through the league of nations—a policy adopted by Baldwin in the general election of Nov. 1935.

PEACE CORPS (1961–) in the US, agency of the department of state by which volunteers are sent overseas 'to help foreign countries meet their urgent needs for skilled manpower'. The concept was endorsed by J. F. Kennedy in his 1960 presidential campaign and the agency, established by executive order in March 1961, was given formal congressional approval by the Peace Corps Act (Sept. 1961). Peace Corps workers have served in some 50 countries in Africa, Asia, and Latin America.

PEACE OF THE CHURCH (1668–9), name given to a brief of Pope Clement IX which led to a temporary settlement of the dispute in the French Church over the *Augustinus*. Four Jansenist bishops and the nuns of Port Royal refused to sign a formulary, drafted by the French hierarchy, which denounced the work. With Louis XIV wishing to obtain internal harmony because of the impending war against Holland the papal nuncio negotiated an arrangement by which a new formulary was signed and the papal bulls condemning the *Augustinus* were accepted, but only at the foot of a statement querying papal jurisdiction. The bishops signed on 23 Oct., but the scruples of the nuns led them to hold out until 15 Feb. 1669.

PEALE, CHARLES WILLSON (1741–1827), American artist, who painted many leading figures of the American Revolution. He was a founder of the Philadelphia Academy of Fine Arts (1805).

PEARCE, SIR GEORGE FOSTER (1870–1952), Australian politician and member of the Senate of the Australian Commonwealth (1901–38), who began his political career in WA, in trade union and federal movements, while working as a carpenter. He was chiefly notable as minister of defence (1908–9, 1910–13, 1914–21, 1932–4). Nevertheless, he attracted more public abuse than popular support. Labor supporters considered his desertion of the party over conscription in 1916 as an act of treachery, while secessionists in WA denounced his attitude as symbolic of Commonwealth injustice to the western state. Later, Pearce moved to the right, but retained his enthusiasm for Australian nationalism, and for the British connection, and a hatred of both communism and fascism. Besides helping to create the Australian armed forces and raise Commonwealth public service standards, he established the Australian diplomatic service.

PEARL HARBOR, inlet on the southern coast of the island of Oahu, Hawaii, used by the US navy as a base since 1911 and the main operating base of the Pacific Fleet since 1940. On 7 Dec. 1941 Japanese carrier-based aircraft made a surprise attack, damaging and sinking 19 vessels. Seven battleships out of a total fleet strength of eight were either sunk or put out of action, but all were eventually salvaged or repaired, except the *Arizona*. During the two-hour attack 2392 Americans were killed, 1355 wounded, and 960 afterwards recorded missing. The US declared war on Japan (9 Dec.). Following a broadcast to the American nation (10 Dec.), in which President F. D. Roosevelt called the attack the climax of a decade of international immorality, and declared that the war against the Axis powers was a world issue, the US also declared war on Germany and Italy (11 Dec.). Thus the US became a participant in the Second World War.

PEARSE, PATRICK (1879–1916), Irish rebel, who joined (1913) the Irish Volunteers formed to protect the Home Rule Bill, and at the same time was recruited by the Irish Republican Brotherhood, the descendants of the Fenians of the 1860s, who were planning an armed uprising. Pearse rose to prominence as the person who, unlike the planners of the Easter rising, such as Tom Clarke and Sean Macdiarmid, openly held a post in the Volunteers and could issue orders.

On Easter Sunday 1916 the IRB started the rising and proclaimed the Irish Republic in Dublin, in spite of Pearse's mobilization order being countermanded by Eoin McNeill, chairman of the Volunteers, and of the interception of a shipment of German arms. The inevitable failure of the rising did not perturb Pearse, who extolled the bloodshed of the First World War and thought Ireland must be cleansed and freed by blood; in a sense he was right, in that the execution of himself and his fellow rebels turned them from an unpopular minority into the first martyrs for Irish independence.

PEARSON, CHARLES HENRY (1830–94), English-born historian and Australian politician. After a teaching career as an historian at London and Cambridge (1855–71), he settled in Vic. (1874) and became an influential radical journalist and minister of education (1886–90). His *National Life and Character* (1893) was a volume of philosophical and political importance.

PEARSON, SIR CYRIL ARTHUR (1866–1921), British newspaper proprietor, who founded *Pearson's Weekly* (1890) and, in 1900, launched the *Daily Express*. He supported Joseph Chamberlain's tariff reform campaign. Blindness led him to give up his newspaper interests and devote his energies to the blind. He founded St Dunstan's home for blind ex-servicemen after the First World War.

PEARSON, LESTER BOWLES (1897–), Canadian politician, diplomat, and prime minister of Canada (1963–8), who was ambassador to the US (1945–6), and under-secretary of state for external affairs (1946–8). He was a consistent worker for peace, helped draft the United Nations Charter (1945), was instrumental in securing the UN Palestine partition resolution (1947), and served as president of the UN General Assembly (1952–3). He entered the Canadian House of Commons (1948) as a Liberal and served as secretary of state for external affairs (1948–57) and leader of the opposition (1952–63). In 1957 he was awarded the Nobel Peace Prize for his efforts to resolve the Suez crisis (1956). Having led the Liberal Party to victory (1963), Pearson became prime minister (1963–8), and then (1968) chairman of the commission on international development.

PEARY, ROBERT EDWIN (1856–1920), US sailor and Arctic explorer. On various expeditions to Greenland he made important meteorological, tidal, and ethnological observations, and discovered the 'Iron Mountain' meteorites (1897). After two unsuccessful attempts (1898–1902, 1905–6), he reached the North Pole (6 April 1909) with his Negro aide, Matthew Henson, four Eskimos, and 40 dogs. Frederick A. Cook claimed its prior discovery (on 21 April 1908), but Congress recognized Peary's achievement (1911).

PEASANT LAND BANK in Russia, established under the ministry of finance (1883) to make loans on favourable terms to the peasantry to encourage their purchase of land.

PEASANT PARTY in Croatia, the champion of Croatian political aspirations in inter-war Yugoslavia. The party was founded in 1905 by the Radic brothers, Antun and Stjepan. So long as Croatia was part of Austria-Hungary the party fared badly at the polls because the peasantry from whom it drew its strength was disenfranchised. With the creation of Yugoslavia the Croatian Peasant Party became the party of Croatia and enjoyed regular electoral success. The first sign that the party would be a force to reckon with came in the constitutional assembly in 1921. Stjepan Radic, sole leader of the party since his brother's death in 1919, had already disapproved of the union of Serbia and Croatia, advocating instead an independent peasant republic of Croatia. At the constitutional assembly he became so outraged by the Serbian drive for hegemony that he withdrew the Peasant Party from the assembly and allowed the constitution to be adopted in his absence. This was the first of many boycotts of parliament, the party's principal strategy. Originally the party was the voice of the peasantry; pacifism, agrarian reform, government economy, and an egalitarian rural ethic marked its programme. Increasingly the party became the champion of Croatian nationalism. When in 1923 Radic proposed the revision of the 1921 constitution his appeals were ignored and again the party boycotted the parliament. The contest was clearly now between the Croatian Peasant Party and the Serbian Radical Party. Radic returned to parliament in 1924 and joined the united opposition to Pasic's Radical government. But in 1925 Radic made a visit to Moscow. Pasic seized the opportunity to crush the opposition. The Croatian Peasant Party was banned as the instrument of a foreign power and Radic was sent to prison. Nevertheless, the party, though banned, won the majority of Croatian votes at the 1925 elections. Suddenly in 1925 Radic decided to co-operate with the Radical government, but the honeymoon lasted less than a year. Relations between Serbs and Croats and between the two parties grew worse. In 1928 Radic was murdered in parliament. Vladko Macek succeeded him as the party's leader. But the situation continued without change, the Croats ranged behind Macek demanded federalism, and the Serbs, aligned with Stojadinovic and the monarchy, intent on preserving the centralized structure. Macek advanced a constitutional proposal, which was rejected; whereupon he boycotted parliament. As a result of his condemnation of Alexander's authoritarian rule he was imprisoned, but was later released by Prince Paul, and continued vigorously to oppose the government. Pressure from abroad, especially from Italy and Germany, forced a solution of the problem. In Aug. 1939 Macek and Cvetkovic, the prime minister, signed the Sporazum, which gave internal autonomy to Croatia. But it was too late, for extreme nationalism had already gripped Croatia and nothing less than independence would satisfy leaders like Pavelic. The Croatian Peasant Party was overshadowed by the Ustasa during the wartime occupation of Yugoslavia and parliamentary opposition, though radical and often irresponsible, was replaced by terrorism.

JMK

PEASANTS' REVOLT (May–Nov. 1381), in England, series of risings whose name is appropriate only in the sense that many of the risings involved country-dwellers of the common sort. Artisans and labourers also took part, and few, probably, of the landholders implicated were proprietors; moreover, there were many urban risings. Disturbances occurred in most counties, but it was the home counties that were principally affected. The rebels came mainly from Kent, Essex, and in and around London, and possibly with the assistance of aldermen, who were at odds with the party in power in the city, they entered London on 13 June. King Richard II, then aged 14, met a gathering of them at Mile End on 14 June and at Smithfield the next day. He did not avert the executions of Abp Sudbury or Richard Hales, the treasurer, but he promised to issue charters manumitting serfs and pardoning rebels. The rebels scattered after the death of their leader, Wat Tyler, in an altercation with the mayor of London. The charters of manumission and pardon were revoked on 2 July, suppression of the revolt having already begun.

Interpretations of the revolt have been coloured by Froissart's belief that it was connected with the 'ease and riches' of the common people at this time. There is in fact little objective evidence to suggest that the real wages of the labouring classes had risen significantly since the Black Death (although actual wages had), and much to suggest that the intervening period had been difficult for small farmers, whether proprietors or tenants. The labour laws, perhaps the first statutes relating to the life of the common people to be enforced with any degree of stringency in medieval England, and the poll taxes of 1377, 1379, and 1380 were among the causes or occasions of revolt in town and countryside alike. The mainspring of the movement was a revulsion against the remnants of serfdom in England. The distinguishing features of this, as compared with earlier protests, were the scale of the risings of 1381 and their co-ordination; the clearly articulated attack on the principle of inequality before the law; and, finally, the concomitant assault on the idea of a hierarchically ordered society. If the chroniclers are to be believed, all of whom were hostile to the revolt, the rebels demanded the abolition, not only of serfdom, but of lordship itself, except, the lordship of the king.

BFH

PEASANTS' WAR (1524–5), series of uprisings of the independent yeomen and craftsmen in the south-west and central German states of the empire, caused by a combination of social, economic, and political grievances and religious frenzy. The revolt began in Stühlingen in the Black Forest (June 1524) and spread rapidly to Swabia, where the prosperous peasantry resented the growing power of the princes, the effects of inflation, and the enforcement of legal demands by landlords in defiance of ancient customs. They demanded

a series of reforms contained in Sebastien Lötzer's Twelve Articles of Memmingen, eg, the alleviation of feudal dues, redress of abuses concerning hunting, fishing, and grazing rights, and lay election of clergy. The nobility conceded some of these demands (April 1525), but meanwhile a more violent situation had spread to Franconia and Thuringia. In Franconia the peasantry was supported by certain members of the lesser nobility or landsknechts, among them Florian Geyer, Wendel Hipler, and Götz von Berlichingen, and inflamed by the ideas of Andrew Carlstadt, the Protestant radical. In addition to economic and religious reforms the rebels wanted a Peasants' parliament. In May 1525, however, an outburst of looting, arson, and murder was crushed by the forces of the Swabian League, commanded by George Truchsess. In Thuringia the leadership of the peasants and townsfolk fell to an Anabaptist fanatic, Thomas Münzer, who voiced extreme millenarian ideas in Mühlhausen. Luther, whose religious revolt had originally encouraged the rebels, denigrated the war in his notorious pamphlet, 'Against the Murdering, Thieving Hordes of Peasants'. The German princes rallied against Münzer and, led by Philip of Hesse and Duke George of Saxony, routed his 8000-strong peasant army at Frankenhäusen (May 1525). The revolts collapsed for lack of skilful and united leadership and henceforth the peasantry of southern Germany ceased to have political significance.

PECHENEGS (or PATZINAKS), Turkish people located at first in the region between the Volga and Ural rivers. After moving westward in the 10th cent. they helped to drive the Magyars into Hungary. Thereafter the Pechenegs occupied territories extending from the Dnieper to the Danube. With the Byzantine subjugation of the Bulgars under the Emperor Basil II (reg. 976–1025), the Pechenegs became the immediate neighbours of Byzantium. Their raiding southward across the Danube was henceforth frequent and severe. The Emperor Alexios I Komnenos (reg. 1081–1118) summoned against them another Turkish people from the steppe lands to the east, the Cumans. The power of the Pechenegs was broken at last in the victories which the Byzantines and their Cuman allies won over them in 1091 and 1122.

PECOCK, REGINALD (c. 1392–c. 1460), English scholar, who was successively Bp of St Asaph (1444) and Chichester (1450). He wrote several works aimed at winning the Lollards back to orthodoxy, but his writings, especially the New English Creed, antagonized the conservatives, who enforced his trial for heresy (1457), his resignation from his see (1458), and his confinement to the remote abbey of Thorney.

PEDERSEN, CHRISTIAN (1480–1554), Danish theologian and historian, who accompanied Christian II of Denmark into exile (1523). He returned home in 1532 and collaborated in translating the Bible into Danish, thus contributing to the creation of a national and theological literature in the vernacular.

PEDRO I OF BRAZIL (1798–1834), first Emperor of Brazil (1822–31), second son of Prince Regent João and Princess Carlota Joaquina, of the Portuguese royal house of Bragança. In 1807 he accompanied the court on its flight to Brazil, where he remained till 1831. He was largely ignored by his estranged parents, and received little instruction in the protocol, diplomacy, and self-discipline then regarded as essential for European royalty. But he was a natural leader of men, an excellent horseman, an accomplished musician, and a linguist. In 1817 he married the Archduchess Leopoldina of Austria.

In the wake of the liberal revolution in Portugal, King João VI returned to Lisbon in 1821, leaving Pedro as regent in Brazil. A growing spirit of nationalism in Brazil, coupled with a reactionary colonial policy by the Cortes in Lisbon, encouraged agitation for Brazilian independence. Upon the advice of his father, his wife, and his chief minister, José Bonifácio de Andrada e Silva, who feared for the survival of the monarchy, Pedro assumed the leadership of the independence movement. He was convinced that the co-equal status of Brazil and Portugal under one Crown could no longer be preserved and proclaimed Brazil's independence in the *grito de Ipiranga* on 7 Sept. 1822. Shortly thereafter he was crowned as emperor.

The calmness of the independence period lasted for about a year, during which the remaining Portuguese troops were expelled from Brazil and a constituent assembly was convoked to draft a national constitution. However, after 1823 a series of crises arose which Pedro was eventually unable to surmount. The most persistent problem was his Portuguese birth and his preference for advisers who were also Portuguese-born. His dismissal of the assembly and imposition of a constitution (1824) granting extensive political authority to the Crown antagonized many Brazilian politicians. In 1826, when João VI died, Pedro was acclaimed King Pedro IV of Portugal, but public reaction in Brazil quickly forced him to renounce the throne in favour of his daughter, Maria da Glória. The loss of Uruguay (1828) was attributed to Pedro, despite the fact that the Brazilian parliament had refused to vote funds for the successful prosecution of the war. Subsequent attempts to govern with an all-Brazilian cabinet were insufficient to overcome mounting hostility towards Pedro, and on 7 April 1831, after army commanders indicated they would no longer protect him, he abdicated in favour of his young son and departed for Europe. He spent his remaining years in a successful military campaign to restore his daughter to the Portuguese throne.

Sérgio Corrêa da Costa, *Every Inch a King* (New York, 1950).
REP

PEDRO II OF BRAZIL (1825–91), second Emperor of Brazil (*reg.* 1831–89), who succeeded on the abdication of his father, Pedro I, in 1831. A series of regents governed Brazil (1831–1840), which was threatened by disintegration as a result of provincial revolts. The boy-emperor acceded to the throne on 23 July 1840, when the parliament, seeking a symbol of national unity, declared him to be of age. In 1843 he married Princess Teresa Cristina de Bourbon of the Kingdom of the Two Sicilies.

Pedro II was intelligent, scholarly, and the epitome of Victorian propriety, having been carefully educated for his role as a constitutional monarch. He was a student of history and of modern and classical languages, the active patron of the Brazilian Historical and Geographical Institute, and a corresponding member of several foreign scholarly societies. He was said to have remarked that had he not been emperor he would have been a school teacher and took pride in being called the philosopher-king.

Pedro II ruled for nearly 50 years, longer than any other chief of state in Latin America. His reign was preoccupied in its early years with the gradual suppression of rebellions in various provinces and with the serious dispute with Britain over the illegal African slave trade. By 1850, however, the authority of the monarchy was established throughout the empire, the slave traffic was abolished, and under Pedro's benevolent tutelage Brazil entered upon four decades of domestic peace and material progress. In relations with its neighbours Brazil continued to intervene in Uruguayan affairs, participated in the overthrow of the Argentinian dictator, Rosas (1851–2), and bore the brunt of the fighting against the dictator Francisco Solano López in the Paraguayan War (1864–70). Pedro was prematurely aged and often in poor health as a result of the strain of the long war, and thereafter took less direct interest in politics, frequently travelling abroad for relaxation and medical treatment, leaving his daughter, the unpopular Isabel, as regent. His declining health coincided with a decline of the monarchy, and his failure to curb the Republican Party (founded in 1870) or to discipline insubordinate army officers in the 1880s, encouraged the regime's enemies. At the same time, his endorsement of the gradual abolition of slavery (1871) and of the emancipation of all slaves without compensation to their former owners in 1888, caused the politically powerful landholders to withdraw support from the government. In this situation the monarchy collapsed without resistance when a republican revolt broke out on 15 Nov. 1889. Pedro was deposed and sent into exile with his family. He died in Paris two years later.
REP

PEEL, SIR ROBERT (1750–1830), British manufacturer and politician who supported the Younger Pitt's reforms, campaigned for improvements in the working conditions of children, and instigated the Health and Morals of Apprentices Act (1802); he later proposed its extension to other children (1815). He was the father of Sir Robert Peel, the prime minister.

PEEL, SIR ROBERT (1788–1850), British politician and prime minister, under whose administration the Corn Laws were repealed and who, as home secretary, established the nucleus of the Metropolitan Police. He was a great parliamentarian, choosing to influence by reasoned demolition of his opponents' arguments, and was widely regarded, after the Reform Act (1832), which he disliked, as the ablest leader of the Commons and a 'model prime minister'. His administration (1841–6) was alive to contemporary social problems, as was he himself, and its repeal of the Corn Laws lessened class dissension.

Peel sat in the Commons from 1809 until his death. He was under-secretary for war and colonies (1810–12), chief secretary for Ireland (1812–18), and chairman of the currency committee (1819). As home secretary (1822–7, 1828–9) he reformed the criminal law and his Metropolitan Police Act (1829) created the model for borough and county police forces. His Irish experience left him opposed to Catholic emancipation, and he refused to serve in Canning's government (1827), but, becoming convinced of the necessity of emancipation, he introduced the Emancipation Bill (1829). He did not subscribe to Wellington's statement (1830) that no parliamentary reform was necessary, but he feared the 1832 act would damage the mixed constitution and alienate the working classes. He thought the right policy after 1832 was a conservative one: pragmatic reform and opposition to radicalism. He further defined his position in the Tamworth manifesto (1835), an address to his constituents in the election forced on him by William IV's dismissal of Melbourne. Peel's government held office for 100 days, then resigned after successive defeats in the Commons.

Peel used the word 'conservative' in a constitutional, not a party, sense, and was sometimes criticized in the 1830s for not consistently opposing the Whig government's measures. He refused to form a government in 1839, lacking the Queen's confidence and believing his support in the Commons not sufficiently decisive. The 1841 general election, however, provided him with a vote of confidence. His government (1841–6) revised and reduced the tariff, abolishing import duties on raw materials and food; introduced an income tax; passed the Bank Charter Act, an act regulating joint-stock companies, and a Factory Act; and instituted an enquiry that led to the Public Health Act (1848). The repeal of the Corn Laws (1846), passed by a combination of Whigs, radicals, and a section of conservatives, and in the Lords by Wellington's persuasion, ended protection, which Peel believed agriculture no longer needed. On the day the Lords passed repeal, Peel was defeated in the Commons by manœuvres by Disraeli and Bentinck. He resigned, refusing either to ask for a dissolution or to lead a Peelite party. For the next four years he pursued a non-party policy, but his stature in the country was high and it was generally assumed that he would again hold office. After his death, from a riding accident, the Peelites (including all his ex-ministers, except Stanley) gradually declined in number, but they remained an important factor in politics for more than 20 years.

A. A. W. Ramsay, *Sir Robert Peel* (London, 1928).
Norman Gash, *Mr Secretary Peel* (London, 1960).
BK

PEEL, THOMAS (1793–1865), Australian land-speculator, who was granted 250,000 acres in WA in 1829 in return for promotion of the Swan river settlements and investment there. He brought in some 500 settlers before his emigration scheme failed.

PEELITES in Britain, adherents of Sir Robert Peel, the former prime minister, as opposed to the protectionists, led by Disraeli and Bentinck, who split the Conservative Party on the repeal of the Corn Laws (1846). At the general election of 1847, 100 out of 330 Conservatives returned were Peelites; they included Gladstone, Graham, and Sidney Herbert. Though Peel declined to lead them formally, they had influence out of proportion to their numbers because of their talent. Refusing the overtures of both Russell and Derby in the crisis of 1851, they joined with the Whigs in the Aberdeen coalition (1852–5). They remained isolated and suspicious of Palmerston, but after his defeat and the fall of the Conservative government (1859), the Peelites joined his administration, Gladstone accepting office as chancellor of the exchequer. This coalition of Whigs, Radicals, and Peelites led to the emergence of the Liberal Party.

PEENEMÜNDE in Germany, experimental station on Usedom island in the Baltic, established in 1936 as a centre for the army's long-range rocket programme. The first successful firing of an A4 (V2) rocket took place there on 3 Oct. 1942. From 1942 development of the Luftwaffe's flying bomb (V1) was also undertaken there. British intelligence agencies had been aware of Peenemünde's connection with long-range weapons research since Nov. 1939, but rockets and flying bombs were not observed there on aerial photographs until 1943. Thereupon the station was bombed, on 17 Aug. 1943, but development of the V-weapons was almost complete; the raid had no effect on the V1 programme and delayed the V2 by only a few weeks. However, technical and supply difficulties prevented their being used against Britain until the summer of 1944.

PEERAGE, THE, originated in feudal times. A peer was a nobleman originally entitled to share in the legislative and judicial functions of a ruler; in this sense peers seem to have been limited to Britain, France, and, for a time, Japan.

Peers—as the name implies—are equals, though in Britain there are ascending orders of precedence from baron, viscount, earl, and marquis to duke. British peers have a right to a seat in the House of Lords; they had (until 1948) the right to trial by their peers; they still (1970) possessed the right of personal access to the sovereign, and exemption from jury service. The Crown alone, as the fountain of honours, has the power to create peers; since the 16th cent. new peerages have generally been created for political services. A peerage may become extinct, fall into abeyance, be forfeited for high treason, or (since 1963) be disclaimed. There were, in 1970, about 950 peers in Britain, most of whom held hereditary peerages. Since 1958 more than 200 life peers have been created (the Crown had always had the power to create life peerages, but rarely used it). After 1958 life peeresses were allowed to sit in the Lords and, after 1963, hereditary peeresses also were allowed to sit. Wives of peers are not included in this category. The eldest sons of dukes, marquises, and earls usually bear a secondary title of their fathers ('courtesy titles'), but they remain commoners.

The English peerage derives from the court or council of the Norman kings. It originated in the greater barons, who received a writ of summons at the pleasure of the Crown. In the Middle Ages a peerage depended on the tenure of land and gradually became hereditary; but in 1387 the creation of peerages by letters patent shifted the emphasis from land tenure to personal dignity. Until the reign of Edward III the peerage consisted of prelates, earls, and barons; dukedoms appeared in 1337, marquisates in 1385, viscounties in 1440.

The claim of prelates to be peers, though generally accepted in the Middle Ages, has gradually been questioned; by 1628 the bishops were regarded merely as 'lords of parliament' by the lay peers. But the two archbishops and 24 bishops of the Church of England still (1970) sit in the House of Lords.

In Scotland and Ireland the peerage was also feudal in origin. In Scotland the greater barons were summoned to court and their peerages, attached to land until comparatively late, in time became hereditary. In Ireland the peers were almost entirely of Anglo-Irish stock. Irish peers, moreover, had no tradition of privilege. The Acts of Union of 1707 and 1800 limited Scottish and Irish representation in the British House of Lords to 16 and 28 respectively. After 1963, however, all Scottish peers could sit in the Lords; but Irish peers gradually disappeared after the creation of the Irish Free State in 1922.

In France the peerage, whose origins are obscure, was not clearly defined until the 14th cent. A French peerage was a purely honorary distinction created by the Crown and without political significance. It was usually associated with a duchy. The old peerage disappeared at the French Revolution (1789). A revived peerage lasted only during the Bourbon restoration of 1815–48, though during those years the existence of a chamber of peers gave the peers a share in legislation.

In Japan a 'peerage' was deliberately created in 1884 as a result of western influence. The constitution of 1889 established a house of peers, which lasted until 1946.   LGRN

PEERAGE ACT (1963) in Britain, legislative measure which enabled hereditary peers to renounce their titles and stand for election to the House of Commons if they wished to do so. The first peers to take advantage of the act were Lord Stansgate (Wedgwood Benn, who had campaigned for the measure for some years) and Lord Altrincham (John Grigg). They were followed by Lord Home (Sir Alec Douglas-Home) and Lord Hailsham (Quintin Hogg). Douglas-Home became prime minister in the year of his renunciation.

PEERAGE BILL (1719) in Britain, legislative proposal to limit the House of Lords to existing peerages except for the replacement of extinct lines, the princes of the blood, and six new creations. The 16 Scottish elective representatives were to be replaced by 25 hereditary peers. The bill threatened the constitution by creating a house impervious to the wishes of the king and Commons. It was defeated in the Commons largely due to Sir Robert Walpole's opposition, but thereafter the royal prerogative of creation was sparingly used.

PEERS, THREAT TO CREATE, in Britain, device which twice persuaded the House of Lords to pass measures of which it disapproved (the 1832 Reform Act and the 1911 Parliament Act). On both occasions the government secured the king's promise to create enough peers to pass the bill in the Lords: about 40 creations would have been needed in 1832, and 400–500 in 1911. The threat was successful, the House of Lords acquiesced, and on neither occasion was there an actual creation. The House of Lords was thus in effect deprived of its legislative power and left with a choice between passing the bill with or without the creation of peers. On both occasions the use of the king's prerogative in this way was criticized as unconstitutional. But there was an important difference: in 1832 the threat was made (May 1832) after the Lords had rejected the bill; in 1911 the king's promise to create was obtained, but kept secret, in Nov. 1910. This was eight months in advance of its need, before the bill had been discussed in parliament, and before the general election (Nov.), held to discover whether the government's proposal to reform the Lords was 'the will of the nation'.

PEGOLOTTI, FRANCESCO (*fl.* 14th cent.), Florentine banker, who served the Bardi of Florence, the greatest European banking and commercial company of this period. As the head of the Bardi bank in Cyprus he became particularly well-informed about Asia and wrote *The Practice of Trade* (c. 1340).

PEGU, town on the Pegu river, 50 miles (80 kms) north of Rangoon, from time to time the capital of Lower Burma. It was also the kingdom of Lower Burma, which came to be known as the kingdom of Pegu, whether or not Pegu was its capital at the time, in the same way that the kingdom of Upper Burma became known as the kingdom of Ava. Early European contacts with Burma were mostly with the kingdom of Pegu, which for long became, to Europeans, synonymous with Burma. Pegu owed its importance to its rich rice lands, its central position in the Mon-occupied part of Burma, and its comparative accessibility from the sea. It is said to have been founded by King Thamala in AD 825 and was the capital of the Mon kingdom until 1057, when the Mons were conquered by Anawrahta and their kingdom incorporated in that of Pagan. When the Pagan dynasty was overthrown by the Chinese in 1287, the Mon kingdom of Pegu revived, though its ruling family was Shan until the accession of Dammazedi (1472), and though the capital was at Martaban (1287–1363) and Donwun (1363–9) before returning to Pegu. In 1539 the Mon kingdom was overthrown by Tabinshweti, of the Burmese dynasty and kingdom of Toungoo, who, however, made Pegu his capital, and set up a new kingdom of Pegu, intending to win the support of the Mons. Pegu remained the capital until 1635, when Thalun transferred it to Ava, which had in fact been incorporated in the Pegu territories since 1555, when it had been conquered by Bayinnaung. In 1740, when the power of the Toungoo dynasty in Ava was crumbling, the Mons proclaimed their independence and Pegu became their capital again. In 1747, however, the kingdom was finally incorporated into that of Ava, by Alaungpaya. In 1852 the British annexed what was left of the kingdom of Pegu; Arakan and Tenasserim had already been annexed in 1826. Pegu was discarded as capital in favour of Rangoon with its potentialities as a port.

G. E. Harvey, *History of Burma* (London, 1925).
D. G. E. Hall, *Burma* (London, 1950).   FSVD

PEIPING, name used for Peking (1928–49), when the capital of China was Nanking. The name of Peking was changed to indicate its lessened status.

PEIRIS, SIR JAMES (1856–1930), Singhalese politician, who advocated constitutional advance in Ceylon. Under the 1924 constitution he was elected vice-president of the legislative council.

PEISISTRATUS (*fl.* 6th cent.), Tyrant of Athens, who was resident at Brauron in eastern Attica and resolved regional conflict within Attica by leading the 'men across the hills' against the opposing groups of plain and coast. Both his first and second spells as tyrant (*c.* 560) were short, but after ten years in exile, collecting money and allies, he landed at Marathon and, probably with Philaid support, defeated his Alcmeonid and other opponents at Pallene (*c.* 546).

Posing as Athena's favourite and a second Theseus, he made Athens, with its tutelar goddess, Athena, the effective political and religious centre of Attica and encouraged Athens' urbanization by improving its water supply. A great temple of Athena Polias was built on the Acropolis and the Panathenaea festival established. Athens became the new home of Artemis' ancient cult at Brauron and was brought into close connection with Demeter's Mysteries at Eleusis. The festival of Dionysus at Eleutherae was transferred to Athens as the City Dionysia. The first Athenian coinage, introduced by Peisistratus or his sons, showed Athena's head and owl.

Abroad, Peisistratus encouraged Athens' Ionian connections by purifying Delos and establishing Lygdamis as tyrant of Naxos. Further north, he won Sigeum from Lesbos and sent the Philaid Miltiades to win the Chersonese. Peisistratus, the true founder of Athenian greatness, prepared the way for the final unification of Attica by Cleisthenes' tribal reforms (508) and for Athenian domination of the Aegean in the 5th cent.

PEIXOTO, FLORIANO (1839–95), Brazilian soldier and president of Brazil (1891–4), who was distinguished for his bravery in the Paraguayan War (1864–70) and became a field marshal (1889), with responsibility for the security of the imperial government. After suddenly adhering to the republican *coup d'état* that overthrew the monarchy on 15 Nov. 1889, he participated in the provisional government, became vice-president in Feb. 1891, and succeeded President Deodoro da Fonseca on his resignation (1891). He was immediately faced with a naval revolt and civil war in protest against his arbitrary rule and continued military control of the government. Under his command the republican forces were victorious and Peixoto confounded his critics by holding elections during the hostilities. At the end of his term he transferred power to his civilian successor, Prudente de Morais.

PEKING, capital city of China under the Liao, Chin, Yüan, Ming, and Ch'ing dynasties, and from 1949. The city, formerly called Yen-ching during the Ming and Ch'ing periods, was laid out and built in accordance with a new scale of grandeur and beauty, with a majestic series of imperial buildings that surrounded the Forbidden City. Peking formed China's intellectual and cultural centre during the Ming and Ch'ing periods. It is situated in the modern province of Ho-pei.

PELASGIANS, ancient Greek name for the pre-Greek aborigines of Greece. The term was used generally to describe the heterogeneous peoples of northern and eastern origin who inhabited Greece from the 6th to the 3rd millennium BC and spoke various languages, in particular one with distinctive suffixes in *-ssos* or *-nthos*, *eg*, *thalassa*, 'sea', and proper names, including, *eg*, Parnassus, Corinth. The Homeric poems contain memories of their presence in Thessaly, Epirus, and Crete; and Herodotus (*c.* 430) notes their survival in his time near Chalcidice and the Hellespont.

PELAYO (d. *c.* 737), King of Asturias, first head of the small Christian state established by refugees from the Muslim advance across Spain. His victory over the Moors in a minor encounter at Covadonga (718) symbolizes the beginning of the reconquest of Spain from the Moors.

PELICAN, THE, ship in which the English sailor, Sir Francis Drake, circumnavigated the globe (13 Dec. 1577–26 Sept. 1580). In 1578 it was renamed *The Golden Hind.*

PELLA (1) in northern Greece, 38 kms north-west of Thessalonika (mod. Salonika), capital and principal city of the Macedonian kingdom from *c.* 400 BC to its dissolution (167 BC). After the Roman annexation (148) Thessalonika became the governor's seat, but Pella received the status of Roman colony.

(2) Ancient Greek city in Palestine, near the river Jordan, 85 kms north of Jerusalem, a place of refuge of Jerusalem's Christian community during the Jewish War AD 66–70.

PELOPIDAS, of Thebes (*d.* 364 BC), soldier and politician in Thebes' brief period of primacy in Greece. He was leader of the exiles who freed Thebes from Spartan control (Dec. 379), and helped Epaminondas to develop Thebes' military power, defeating a Spartan force at Tegyra (375) and playing a prominent role in the decisive victory at Leuctra (371). After accompanying Epaminondas on his first invasion of the Peloponnese (winter 370–369), he sought to extend Theban influence in Thessaly and Macedonia. He won a brilliant and decisive victory over Alexander of Pherae, who had earlier treacherously held him prisoner (368–367), but in the pursuit Pelopidas was killed.

PELOPONNESIAN LEAGUE, alliance of ancient Greek states, chiefly in the Peloponnese, led by Sparta; it was a major factor in Greek international politics from the middle of the 6th cent. until 370 BC. It grew out of a series of separate treaties linking Sparta with individual states, to provide security against outside attack or internal revolution, beginning with Tegea, c. 560, and including all the Peloponnese, except Argos and Achaea; by c. 520 Aegina and Megara were also included, and after Corinth had opposed Cleomenes I's attack on Athens in 507 a procedure for consultation before joint action was established. The league formed the nucleus of Greek resistance to Persia in 480–479, and generally supported the Spartans against Athens in the 5th cent., though they had to coerce independent action by Arcadia and Tegea in c. 470 and by Elis and Mantinea in 421–418, when Corinth and Megara also were temporarily alienated by Sparta's acceptance of the peace of Nicias. After Athens' defeat (404), the Spartans became more tyrannical, taking harsh vengeance for earlier opposition on Elis (398), Mantinea (384), and Phlius (379), and after their defeat at Leuctra (371) the league virtually collapsed.

PELOPONNESIAN WARS (459–446, 431–404 BC), the great struggle between Athens and Sparta for the leadership of the Greek world, which ended with the defeat of Athens and the dissolution of her empire. The first war began when, in an atmosphere of mutual suspicion, the Athenians threatened Sparta's ally, Corinth, by accepting as their ally her neighbour, Megara, and settling Messenian refugees at Naupactus. In 457 they subjected Aegina after siege and, though a Spartan force aiming to strengthen Boeotian Thebes defeated them at Tanagra, themselves overcame the Boeotians two months later and won control of central Greece. Thereafter disaster against the Persians in Egypt and trouble in the Aegean slowed down the Athenian war effort, and in 451 a five-year truce was concluded. In 447 Boeotia broke free from Athens and in 446 Euboea revolted, and then Megara; the Spartans invaded Attica and the Athenians agreed to return all their conquered territories, except Aegina, under the Thirty Years Peace.

The second and great war followed renewed Athenian pressure on Sparta's allies, especially Corinth, through interference in Corcyra and action against Potidaea, and Megara, through the Megarian Decree. Sparta being dominant on land and Athens at sea, the antagonists were evenly matched, and, though the Plague (430–427) seriously weakened Athens, the Spartans failed to exploit this advantage or the revolt of Mytilene (428–427) and were ready to negotiate for peace after the Athenians' victory at Pylos (425). The Athenians fought on for a more decisive advantage, but defeat in Boeotia at Delium (424), and Brasidas' successes among their allies in Chalcidice (424–423), coupled with a general weariness induced them to accept the peace of Nicias (421). Its terms alienated some of Sparta's allies without securing reconciliation with Athens, but the Spartans' victory at Mantinea (418) restored their position and an uneasy peace followed. In 415, however, the Athenians, deluded by ambition, sent a large expedition to conquer Sicily. Its early successes induced Sparta to resume the war, but its eventual failure, involving a second comparable reinforcing armament, encouraged widespread revolts among Athens' naval allies and also Persian intervention. Harassed by the Spartan occupation of Decelea in Attica, and by the brief oligarchic revolution of the Four Hundred (411), the Athenians by prodigious efforts recovered their naval supremacy at Cyzicus (410). But they rejected Sparta's peace offers, and failed to win back all their allies, when in 407 the Spartan admiral, Lysander, acquired the wholehearted co-operation of the Persians through Cyrus, son of Darius II. Athens, now virtually bankrupt, frittered away a remarkable victory at Arginusae (406) through internal dissension and, after losing her whole fleet in a single battle at Aegospotami (405), surrendered in 404 following a siege.

Thucydides, *The Peloponnesian War*, tr. by R. Warner (London, 1954).　　　　　　　　　　　　　　TTBR

PELUCONES, Spanish nickname for the powerful conservative leaders in Chile who contested power with the Liberals in the years following Chilean independence (1818).

PELUSIUM, ancient Egyptian city on the coast of Sinai, which may have been built by the Hebrews in the time of Rameses II (*reg. c.* 1290–1224 BC). It was the site of a battle (525) in which the Persians defeated the Egyptians.

PEMBROKE, RICHARD FITZGILBERT, 2nd Earl of (1st creation) (d. 1176), known as Strongbow, leader of the Anglo-Norman force which began the conquest of Ireland in 1169–70, in answer to an appeal for aid from Dermot, King of Leinster. He was married to Dermot's daughter and succeeded to Leinster on the latter's death in 1171, but this brought the swift intervention of King Henry II of England. Richard had to submit in 1171 and to recognize Henry's suzerainty.

PEMBROKE, WILLIAM MARSHAL, 4th Earl of (1st creation) (c. 1145–1219), landless younger son of a minor English magnate. His outstanding characteristic was unswerving loyalty. He was one of the very few who remained loyal to Henry II in his last days, in the face of the victorious rebellion of Richard Cœur de Lion. When Richard became king he recognized Marshal's integrity by marrying him to the heiress of the earldom of Pembroke and thus made him a great magnate. When, on the death of King John in 1216, the country was rent by civil war and Prince Louis of France had invaded England, Marshal took control of the government and arranged for the coronation of John's nine-year-old heir, Henry III. The royalist notables unanimously elected him regent (*rector regis et regni*). His wisdom was responsible for the reissue of Magna Carta (previously repudiated by John), which won many from the side of the rebels, his military skill for the victory at Lincoln in 1217, and his moderation for the treaty of Lambeth (1217), which ended the French invasion and the civil war with a singular lack of vindictiveness. The two and a half years of his rule over England prepared the way for the remarkable period of internal peace during the rest of Henry's minority.

PEMBROKE, RICHARD MARSHAL, 6th Earl of (1st creation) (d. 1234), younger son of William Marshal, who had been the regent of the English kingdom during the first years of the minority of King Henry III. Richard succeeded to his father's earldom of Pembroke and English estates in 1231. He became a leading opponent of the high-handed and authoritarian government that Henry III appeared to be favouring in 1232–4, and drifted into a civil war, waged mainly in Wales and Ireland. Henry was persuaded in 1234 to abandon the unpopular advisers who were responsible for his objectional policies, but Richard was killed at the end of hostilities. His death was widely regarded as a setback to the scheme for creating a better royal government.

PEMBROKE, PHILLIP HERBERT, 23rd Earl of (4th of 10th creation) (1584–1650), English politician and colonizer, who was financed by the Courteen merchant syndicate. By letters patent he received Spanish-occupied Trinidad, Tobago, Barbados, and a non-existent island named as Fonseca (1628). The Earl of Carlisle protested that Barbados was within his prior grant, but Carlisle's claim was preferred (1629) and Pembroke's grant was never amended. When he sold it (1638) to the Earl of Warwick the dispute was revived, though when Carlisle's grant was re-examined (1645) it passed unchallenged. Pembroke fought for Charles I in the 'Bishops' War' (1639–40), but joined parliament before the Civil War, representing them in negotiations with the king (1645 and 1648), and was elected MP for Berkshire (1649).

PEMEX, state-owned oil monopoly of Mexico (Petroleos Mexicanos) which resulted from the expropriation of foreign operators (1938). At first, Pemex was merely an agency of the government through which oil was extracted and refined. Separate agencies were established for its distribution and to administer the industry. Pemex soon incorporated all these functions (1940). But it was faced with serious difficulties until after the end of the Second World War. By 1957 oil production had doubled and drillings had increased impressively. Off-shore operations began in the 1960s, and undersea reserves were found at least equal to those previously discovered. By 1970 the monopoly was also developing Mexico's natural gas reserves and constructing pipelines to major urban areas.

PENAL CODE REFORM, in Britain. This developed early in the 19th cent. as Benthamite utilitarians, Quaker and Evangelical humanitarians like Howard and Wilberforce, and the Whig lawyers Romilly and Mackintosh, made plain the confusion, barbarity, and ineffectiveness of the existing criminal law. Romilly secured the abolition of capital punishment for pickpockets (1808) and other piecemeal improvements. After his death (1818), Mackintosh and Buxton led the cause in parliament. Backed by a flood of public petitions which castigated the harsh penal code as an incubator of crime, they secured a Commons committee of enquiry (1819), which recommended simplification of the penal code and reform of the forgery laws.

As a penal reformer, Peel (home secretary 1822–7, 1828–1830) was considered deplorably slow and cautious by Bentham, who wanted a rigid criminal code and fusion of common and statute law. Yet Peel went beyond his radical critics in linking penal reform with police, prisons, and criminal law procedures. (He reformed many prisons, and the jury system, in 1823 and 1825 respectively.) Five statutes (1823) abolished the death penalty for miscellaneous offences, repealed the Waltham Black Act, increased judges' discretionary powers in sentencing, and ended roadside burials of suicides with stakes through their bodies. The procedure in criminal prosecutions was reorganized (1826), so as to prevent the quashing of prosecutions on purely technical grounds. Peel and his under-secretary, Hobhouse, also carried through amendments and simplification of the laws relating to theft, forgery, and malicious injury to property (1827). Obsolete anomalies were abolished.

The five statutes of 1827 demonstrated Peel's strength as a reformer. Covering three-quarters of all offences, they reduced the gist of 130 earlier acts to one small volume. About 100 felonies had been exempted from the death penalty. Yet much parliamentary and public opinion was ready for more sweeping mitigations of the law's severity. In the 1830s many more offences, including housebreaking and sheep stealing, were exempted from the death penalty, which, after 1838, was only exacted for murder or attempted murder. Transportation, already virtually in abeyance, was abolished in 1857.

L. Radzinowicz, *A History of the English Criminal Law and its administration from 1750* (London, 1948).   MRB

PENAL LAWS in England, anti-Catholic legislation, which barred Roman Catholics from public office, the universities, and the professions, imposed fines for recusancy, *ie*, failure to attend the services of the established Church of England, and made Catholic priests liable to the penalties of high treason if they remained in the country.

The Elizabethan government did not regard the Catholic threat with any importance before the arrival of Mary Queen of Scots (1568), the papal bull excommunicating Queen Elizabeth (1570), and the influx of seminary priests, dedicated to restoring England to the true faith, which began in 1577. The mildness of the recusancy law, imposed by the Act of Uniformity (1559), involving a weekly fine of 1s (5p) reflects the government's attitude. The change in the government's mood meant that fines were increased to the prohibitive figure of £20 a month, or two-thirds of the income from the recusant's estates. Treason penalties were extended to cover

such matters as withdrawing the queen's subjects from their allegiance (1581), and simply being a Jesuit or seminary priest (1585). A 1593 act compelled avowed Catholics to remain within 5 miles (8 kms) of their domicile and to register themselves there. It was, however, the priests who mainly suffered, recusancy laws being slackly enforced, and after 1590 persecution grew less.

James I added three new statutes: a new oath of allegiance, which remained in force until the 1640s, severe restrictions on Catholic wives and their Protestant husbands (1606); and he permitted authorities to tender the new oath to persons under 18 (1610). In the 17th cent., however, it was only rarely that the penal laws were enthusiastically or effectively enforced, for the Crown, except during the post-1605 Gunpowder Plot persecution, was unco-operative. Parliament, as always more vigorously Protestant than the Crown, continued to press for effective enforcement of the laws. The Long Parliament's new oath of allegiance (1643), which was more detailed and specific, was to be the model for the Test Acts of 1673 and 1678.

The attempts of Charles II and James II to suspend the penal laws by their Declarations of Indulgence (1672, 1687, 1688) led instead to the Test Acts, which imposed an anti-Catholic declaration on all office-holders (1673) and drove the Catholic peers from the Lords (1678), and led to James losing his throne (1688). The reign of James II, in which Catholics had shown how politically restrained they could be, benefited them in the long run. A panic measure forbidding recusants to come within 10 miles (16 kms) of London was enacted in 1689, but a tolerant minority in the Lords was able to block the enforcement of the penal laws. Catholics were, however, obliged to pay a double land-tax, but this was accepted in lieu of recusancy fines. A 1700 act made Catholics incapable of inheriting or purchasing land, but it was repealed by Savile's Act, or the Catholic Relief Act (1778), and the continued existence of Catholic nobility and gentry testified to its ineffectiveness. In 1723 additional levies were placed on recusants, but the failure of this measure led to no other such experiments.

Though penal laws were left on the statute book in the 18th cent. to quiet Anglican fears, their enforcement was exceedingly lax. It was only the French Revolution (1789) and the personal hostility of the monarchs, *eg*, George III, that prevented Catholics from achieving equal civil rights. This came in 1829 with the Catholic Emancipation Act.

G. R. Elton, *The Tudor Constitution* (Cambridge, 1962).
J. P. Kenyon, *The Stuart Constitution* (Cambridge, 1966).
                                                                                          CJ

PENDA (*reg. c.* 633–*c.* 656), King of Mercia, who was a pagan all his life and a formidable warrior. He gave a new cohesion to the previously ill-defined midland kingdom of Mercia. He also conquered Middle Anglia and repeatedly attacked other Anglo-Saxon kingdoms. He was defeated and killed by Oswiu, King of Northumbria.

PENDERGAST, THOMAS (1872–1945), US politician and one of a family who dominated MO politics for half a century. He was the key political figure in Kansas City, MO, in the 1920s and 1930s. He was the political mentor of President Harry Truman.

PENDLETON ACT (1883) in the US, legislation which provided the foundations for a professional Federal civil service. It was drafted by Dorman B. Eaton, secretary of the Civil Service Reform Association, and sponsored by Senator George H. Pendleton of OH. The Act provided for a bipartisan three-man Civil Service Commission with responsibility for drafting and administering competitive examinations to determine on a basis of merit the fitness of appointees to Federal office. The act also required the establishment of a classified civil service list, and prohibited the levying of political campaign assessments on Federal office-holders.

P'ENG CHEN (1902–), Chinese communist, who, after the communist advent to power (1949), became mayor and party chief of Peking. He exercised great influence in the capital, especially over the national press and in cultural affairs, creating for himself an 'independent kingdom' at the heart of the nation. He and his associates were regarded by Mao Tse-tung as particularly anti-Maoist, and were some of the first to be attacked in the Cultural Revolution.

P'ENG TE-HUAI (1897–), Chinese soldier and politician, who joined the Communist Party in 1928, after serving in a war-lord army. He had a distinguished military career and played a key role in the Korean War. P'eng's advocacy of a modern, professional army closely linked with the Soviet Union brought him into conflict with Mao Tse-tung. In 1959 he openly attacked Mao and his radical policies, particularly those associated with the Great Leap Forward. He was dismissed as minister of defence and put under house-arrest.

PENINSULA CAMPAIGN (1704–14), military operations in the Iberian peninsula during the War of the Spanish Succession, occasioned by the attempt of the Grand Alliance to challenge the Bourbon bloc in Spain. The allied armies, acting on behalf of Archduke Charles, were led by British commanders, the earls of Peterborough and Galway, and Gen. James Stanhope, the Portuguese general, Das Minas, and the imperial commander-in-chief, Count Guido von Starhemberg, while the opposing Bourbon forces of Philip V were commanded by Marshals Berwick and Vendôme. The conflict proved highly wasteful of life and resources and ended with Philip V's retention of the Spanish Crown. Though Archduke Charles, as Charles III, refused to surrender his claims to Spain, his forces were gradually ousted from the peninsula, while Britain's only permanent gain was Gibraltar, which was taken in the opening year (1704).

English amphibious attacks on Spanish territory, eg, at Cadiz and Vigo Bay (1702), which were the prelude to the peninsula campaign, aimed at establishing naval supremacy in the Mediterranean. The need for port facilities, however, compelled England to seek a Portuguese alliance. The Methuen treaties (May 1703) gave her the use of Lisbon harbour, but also committed the allies to military and financial subsidies for the Austrian candidate for the Spanish throne. Archduke Charles arrived in Catalonia on 22 Aug. 1705, to be proclaimed King Charles III in Valencia and Catalonia. After the allied forces under Peterborough had captured Barcelona (May 1706), Philip V escaped temporarily to France, abandoning Aragon to the cause of Charles III (June 1706). A successful attack by Galway's army on Madrid and Toledo (1706) again forced Philip to seek refuge in Navarre, but, hampered by conflicting advice, Charles failed to establish himself in the Castilian capital and quarrelled with Peterborough, who was subsequently recalled to England (March 1707). Galway therefore withdrew the allied troops to Valencia, allowing Philip to reoccupy Madrid.

In April 1707 the Grand Alliance suffered a decisive blow at Almanza, when Berwick's French and Castilian troops smashed Galway's smaller mixed force of Portuguese, English, Dutch, Germans, and Catalans. Despite the withdrawal of French forces, Philip's grip on the peninsula was consolidated by the occupation of Valencia and Aragon. Imperial troops under Starhemberg, released from the Italian campaign, replaced English forces, who concentrated more on amphibious operations, eg, Port Mahon (1708). Stanhope's victories at Almenara and Saragossa (1710) led to the second Allied occupation of Madrid (Sept. 1710) and Philip's retreat to Valladolid, but French reinforcements enabled the Bourbons to counter-attack. During the Allied retreat the Duke of Vendôme defeated Stanhope at Brihuega (Dec. 1710), and though Starhemberg repulsed the French attack at Villaviciosa Charles's forces were besieged in Barcelona.

The year 1711 proved the final turning point in the peninsula campaign. The death of the Emperor Joseph (April 1711) and the election of Archduke Charles to the imperial title undermined the allied war aim of No Peace without Spain and threatened the European balance of power as much as Philip V's occupation of the Spanish throne had done. The advent of a Tory administration in Britain, pledged to make peace, further sapped the allied war effort. The capture of the besieged city of Barcelona by Berwick (Sept. 1714) finally ended the war, leaving Philip V in effective possession of the peninsula.

G. M. Trevelyan, *England under Queen Anne* (London, 1930).

PENINSULA WAR (1808–13), struggle for control of the Iberian peninsula between France and Britain during the French Wars. Napoleon I's decision to impose a French king on Spain was a major mistake, for it provoked a rebellion of the Spanish people which gave Britain the chance of undermining the continental blockade and finally getting to grips with the French army by landing in Portugal to liberate the peninsula. Instead of withdrawing to the Pyrenees, Napoleon kept 300,000 men tied up in a hopeless struggle in Spain. His 'Spanish Ulcer' was of his own making and seriously weakened the French war effort when it was most extended by the invasion of Russia. After the retreat from Moscow (1812), Wellington was able to drive the French over the Pyrenees (1813).

PENINSULARES, term employed in colonial Spanish America to refer to Spaniards born in Spain, as distinct from American-born Creoles.

PENN, WILLIAM (1644–1718), English Quaker and colonist, son of Admiral Sir William Penn. At Oxford he came under the influence of Thomas Loe, a minister of the Society of Friends, and in 1668 he himself became a Quaker. He was several times arrested and imprisoned for his preachings and writings, but managed to escape more severe punishment through his father's influence at court, and later his own. On the death of Sir William (1670), Penn inherited a large fortune, and also a claim against the Crown for £16,000, in payment of which he agreed to accept a grant of land in the New World. Penn saw this as a chance to establish an asylum for Quakers and to experiment in applying Christian principles to the governing of a colony. His interest in American colonization arose through his ownership of East and West Jersey (1676). The charter establishing Pennsylvania (March 1681) gave him proprietary rights to the area, making him both landlord and ruler, with power to make all the colony's laws, as long as they were in keeping with English law. Penn arrived in Oct. 1682 and settled in Philadelphia, which his commissioners had selected as the site for the capital. Large numbers of Quakers arrived and by 1683 the population exceeded 3000. In that year, by the treaty of Shackamaxon, friendly relations were established with the native Indians. A body of laws prepared by Penn, combining humane government with a generous religious policy, was adopted in 1682 by an assembly of freemen. In 1684 Penn returned to England to use his influence to gain better treatment for Quakers. He went back to Pennsylvania (1699–1701), then once more to England, where he died after a series of misfortunes which forced him to mortgage the colony and spent some time in a debtor's prison. The proprietorship passed to his sons, John and Thomas Penn.

C. O. Peare, *William Penn* (Philadelphia, 1957).   DHP

PENNSYLVANIA, former English colony in North America, founded by William Penn in 1681. It was first visited by Henry Hudson (1609), explored by Etienne Brulé (1615–16), and settled by Swedes under Johan Printz (1643). When Penn was given a charter to the land (March 1681), several thousand Dutch, Swedish, English, and Welsh squatters were already there. Penn's charter gave him proprietary rights extending from the Delaware river west for five degrees of longitude and from the beginning of the 40th degree of latitude on the south to the beginning of the 43rd degree of latitude on the north. The limits of PA, as defined in the charter, overlapped NY and MD. Penn agreed to the 42nd degree of latitude as the northern boundary (1682), but a quarrel between PA and MD over the southern boundary lasted until the 1760s, when the Mason–Dixon Line established it as 19 miles (30·6 kms) south of the 40th parallel.

The colony was intended as a refuge for the English Society of Friends. By 1681 about 1000 colonists had come and within two years over 3000 emigrants had settled there. The site of the capital, Philadelphia, was established (1682) at the junction of the Schuylkill and Delaware rivers.

The government of the colony, based on Quaker principles, was unusually liberal for the times. The land was purchased from the Indians, with whom friendly relations, developed by fair dealings, lasted until Penn's sons tried to acquire Indian lands by fraud (1737). PA attracted a heterogeneous group of settlers and religious groups. By a liberal land policy and by advertising in Europe, Penn induced many members of persecuted minority sects in Germany to settle in PA. It is estimated that at the end of the colonial period (1775) about one-third of the population was German, one-third Scotch-Irish, and the remaining third mostly English Quakers.

PA was a proprietary colony throughout its existence, except for a short period (1692–4) after the English Revolution (1688), when royal control was established. Penn's legal system was modified when the Charter of Liberties was granted (8 Nov. 1701), and the charter remained as the constitution of proprietary PA. There was strong support for colonial rights in PA and the First (1774) and Second (1775–1781) Continental Congresses were held in Philadelphia, whence the Declaration of Independence was issued (4 July 1776). PA adopted a new state constitution during the American War of Independence (28 Sept. 1776), ratified the Articles of Confederation (1777), and became a state of the US.

W. F. Dunaway, *A History of Pennsylvania* (New York, 1948). DHP

PENNSYLVANIA DUTCH, term applied to Germans in PA. They are the descendants of Germans who settled in the area around Lancaster County in the early 18th cent. The term also refers to the dialect—a mixture of German and English—which these people speak.

PENNY POST, in Britain, instituted by the Post Office Act (1840), authorized a uniform charge of 1d for any weight up to $\frac{1}{2}$ oz to be carried anywhere in the British Isles. In 1871 the weight was raised to 1 oz and in 1897 to 4 oz, as part of the diamond jubilee celebrations. After the First World War the penny post was abolished and a basic rate of $1\frac{1}{2}$d substituted. Britain was the first nation to introduce postage stamps.

PENOBSCOT EXPEDITION (1779), unsuccessful attempt by American militia to take Castine on Penobscot Bay from the British, who had occupied it (June 1779). Nearly the whole trading fleet of MA, under the command of Dudley Saltonstall and Solomon Lovell, was lost.

PENOBSCOT INDIANS, American tribe of the Abnaki confederacy, formerly living on Penobscot Bay and Penobscot river in ME. They took part in all New England frontier wars, but eventually made peace (1749). They are one of the two important bodies of Indians remaining in New England.

PENROSE, BOIES (1860–1921), US lawyer and politician, who served in the state legislature (1884–97) and the US Senate (1897–1921). He was identified with the conservative wing of the Republican Party and was a strong advocate of protective tariffs. He opposed prohibition and direct election of senators, and was stigmatized by Theodore Roosevelt in 1912 as the worst type of political 'boss'.

PENRUDDOCK'S RISING (1655) in England, royalist rising in the west of England, led by John Penruddock against the Cromwellian protectorate. It provided the pretext for the establishment of the government of the major-generals. It was the small visible part of a far larger conspiracy which failed. The rebels, never more than 400 strong, were mostly minor gentry and their tenants and were in arms for only four days. Having captured Salisbury on 12 March, they marched to Dorset for recruits, and then to Devon. Oliver Cromwell commissioned John Desborough to go down as major-general of the west to deal with the situation, but it proved unnecessary. The rebels, tired and reduced by desertions, surrendered to a single troop of regular cavalry under Capt. Croke at Cullompton, Devon. Less than 20 rebels, including Penruddock, were executed.

PENSACOLA, Spanish post on the Gulf of Mexico, founded by Tristan de Luna in 1539. Pensacola was shortly afterwards abandoned and rebuilt (1698) as a protection against French encroachments. It was seized by the French (1719), but restored to the Spanish in 1723. When Britain obtained FL (1763), Pensacola became the capital of west FL. During the American War of Independence, Pensacola was captured by a Spanish force (1781) and was returned to Spain (1783). The British used it as a base in the War of 1812, and it was seized by the US general, Andrew Jackson, in 1814. It was restored to Spain in 1815 and became US territory in 1821. Possession of Pensacola was contested during the American Civil War and finally occupied by Federal troops (1862).

PENTECONTER, type of Greek warship of the 7th cent. BC and earlier, propelled by 50 oarsmen, 25 a side. It was replaced in the 6th cent. by the trireme.

PENTLAND RISING (1666) in south-east Scotland. Col. James Wallace, a Scottish Covenanter, led a revolt against the rule of John Maitland, Earl of Lauderdale, and the restoration of episcopacy in Scotland. The rebellion was quelled by Gen. Thomas Dalyell, who routed Wallace's army.

PEONAGE, labour system in Latin America, whereby advances of money or goods were made to the peon to bind him permanently by debt to his employer. It developed in the colonial period and was perhaps most firmly entrenched in Mexico. It ceased with the Revolution of 1910.

PEOPLE'S ACTION PARTY (PAP), ruling party in Singapore after 1959, founded by Lee Kuan Yew, Dr Toh Chin Chye, and other English-educated socialist intellectuals in 1954. The PAP at first occupied the anti-colonial extreme left of the political spectrum. Pro-communist support helped it to win three seats at the 1955 election and 43 out of 51 seats in 1959. Internal disagreements came to a head in 1961, when 13 MPs and a majority of the branch executives resigned and formed the pro-communist Barisan Sosialis. Though deprived of most of its Chinese-educated supporters, the PAP raised the popular issue of independence within Malaysia at the polls (1963) and narrowly defeated the Barisan. The PAP led the parliamentary opposition within Malaysia (1963–5), but failed at the mainland Malayan elections (1964). It achieved full control of Singapore after separation from Malaysia by winning every seat at the 1968 election.

PEOPLE'S LIBERATION ARMY in China, armed forces of the People's Republic. The Red Army, the forerunner of the PLA, was established during the Nanch'ang Uprising (Aug. 1927). The vicissitudes which the communist movement in China suffered before its final victory in 1949 meant that its forces had to be hardy, decentralized, and self-sufficient. The communist forces developed guerrilla techniques to a high point, and identified themselves very closely with the peasantry. During the course of the Civil War (1946–9) they also acquired great skill in conventional fighting, a fact which Western forces fighting in Korea were forced to recognize.

PEOPLE'S NATIONAL MOVEMENT in Trinidad, majority political party since 1956. It was inaugurated in 1956 by Dr Eric Williams with L. N. Constantine, the cricketer, lawyer, and politician, as party chairman.

PEOPLE'S NATIONAL PARTY in Jamaica, founded in 1938 by Norman Manley. It was Jamaica's majority party (1955–1962).

PEOPLE'S PALACE in London, complex of buildings opened in 1887 in Mile End Road to provide sports, arts, and musical facilities for the East End's population. It was modelled on the Palace of Delight in Walter Besant's novel *All Sorts and Conditions of Men* and under the management of the Drapers' Co. became largely educational in its function.

PEOPLE'S PARTY (GERMAN) (DEUTSCHE VOLKSPAR-TEI) (DVP), founded in 1918 by G. Stresemann and other right-wing members of the National Liberal Party of the Wilhelmine Reich, after attempts to form a broadly based middle-class party had failed. Stresemann's nationalist record, which made him unacceptable to the Democrats, turned out to be a source of strength. The DVP became a party of the urban bourgeoisie, which preferred the 'national-democratic basis' and pronounced anti-socialism of the DVP's programme to the Democrats' left-wing liberalism. The party adhered to the black, white, and red colours of the old Reich and, until 1922, opposed the policies of the republican governments. But it rejected the idea of a violent overthrow of the existing order. It has been called the party of the 'counter-evolution', aiming at the gradual liberation of Germany from the 'red shackles' of the Weimar system. In the Reichstag elections of 1920 the DVP gained 62 seats and its ties with industry soon pushed the party on to a course of 'national *Realpolitik*'. It shared government responsibility almost without interruption (1922–30). Throughout this period it succeeded in attracting between 8·7 per cent and 10·1 per cent of the vote. But whereas Stresemann himself developed more and more into a *Vernunftrepublikaner*, *ie*, a rationally, if not emotionally, convinced Republican, his followers were turning to the anti-Republican right. When he died in 1929 it became clear that only his tactical skill and prestige as party leader and foreign minister had prevented assertion of this tendency. For a brief period the DVP participated in Brüning's cabinet before it linked itself with the 'National Opposition' under the leadership of E. Dingeldey. By 1932, it was collaborating with Hugenberg's DNVP and held only seven seats. By combining with the Christlich-Sozialer Volksdienst and the Deutsche Bauernpartei, it recovered some ground in the elections of Nov. 1932, but again lost heavily in March 1933. The two deputies which the party sent to the Reichstag voted for the Enabling Act, and thus prepared for the party's final dissolution on 4 July 1933.

E. Eyck, *A History of the Weimar Republic* (New York, 1967).
H. A. Turner, *Stresemann and the Politics of the Weimar Republic* (Princeton, 1965). VRB

PEOPLE'S PARTY in Thailand, organized by the promoters of the revolution of 1932. It constituted itself as the provisional parliament of the new regime and drew up the constitution of 1932 which guaranteed the group's continuing power through an appointed legislature. It was initially a grouping of young army officers, lawyers, and civil servants and not properly a political party. After 1933 it was dominated by the army and disintegrated with the end of the Phibunsongkhram government (1944).

PEOPLE'S PROGRESSIVE PARTY in Guyana, left-wing party founded in 1950 by Dr Cheddi B. Jagan. It was the majority party in the legislature of British Guiana (1961–4).

PEOPLE'S UNITED PARTY, in British Honduras, political party based on trade unions and founded in 1950. In 1954 it became the majority part, and remained so in 1970.

PEOPLE'S VOLUNTEER ORGANIZATION, in Burma, ex-servicemen's organization, formed in 1945, allegedly to do social work; in fact, it was a private army to support Aung San and the Anti-Fascist People's Freedom League (AFPFL) politically.

PEPI I (*reg.* 2257–2204 BC), Egyptian King of the VIth dynasty, who built himself a pyramid at Saqqara, and founded and restored other buildings, notably at Heliopolis. He sent military expeditions to Palestine, using Nubian mercenaries for the first time.

PEPPERELL, SIR WILLIAM (1696–1759), American merchant, soldier, and politician, who served on the Council of Massachusetts (1727–59). He led 4000 militiamen in a siege of Louisbourg on Cape Breton Island (1744). With the aid of British ships which blocked the sea approaches Pepperell's troops captured the fortress, for which exploit he was to be made a baronet (1746), the first American to be thus honoured.

PEPPLE DYNASTY, from the 17th cent. rulers of Bonny, Nigeria, descended from King Perekule, who acquired fame as warriors and statesmen. Among them was William Dappa Pepple (Pepple V), who was deported by Consul Beecroft in 1854.

PEPYS, SAMUEL (1633–1703), English diarist, politician, and naval administrator who entered government service as a clerk to one of the tellers of the exchequer. He went on the voyage to bring back Charles II for his Restoration (1660), observing and recording it (and many other events of the 1660s) in his *Diary*, which was never intended for publication and which he had begun to keep at the beginning of 1660. That year also saw the beginning of Pepys's outstanding work in naval administration, which was to range from details of contracts to schemes of officering. He was clerk of the acts until 1673 and then secretary to the admiralty, the post which he held on and off until the Revolution (1688). The full effects of his work for the navy were not seen in his own lifetime. Although his period of office coincided with such unhappy episodes as the Medway Disaster, his own efforts were indefatigable. Apart from his attention to administrative minutiae, he was largely responsible for setting the navy upon the course which resulted in a professional status for officers by his insistence upon the relevance of experience, expert standards, and public honesty.

After his wife had died and he had given up writing his *Diary* (1669) he found time and opportunity to spread his talents more widely, entering parliament (1673) and twice in succession being elected president of the Royal Society. As a protégé of the Duke of York, he suffered imprisonment at the time of the popish plot crisis and was dismissed from his position as secretary. But before the end of the reign of Charles II he was once more in favour, and after the accession of James II he completed his work at the admiralty, brought to an end by the Revolution (1688). He was dismissed and imprisoned for a short time but spent the last years of his life in busy and fruitful retirement. BM

PEQUOT TRAIL, American Indian route from the Niantic river in CT eastward into RI. White settlers made it a road from New London to Providence (1691). It later became a part of the post road between New York and Boston, and is now (1970) a motor highway.

PEQUOT WAR (1637), American Indian conflict fought in southern CT after the Pequots murdered a trader. Whites surprised them at their fort on the Mystic river and killed over 600. The survivors fled, but most were hunted down and shot or sold as slaves. The remaining Pequots were dispersed and ceased to exist as a tribe.

PERAK SULTANATE, most populous state of Malaysia. Since its origin in the 16th-cent. sultanate it has remained the richest source of tin in the peninsula. This constantly attracted foreigners, the sultanate being relatively weak, and a large-scale influx of Chinese tin-miners in the 1850s exacerbated internal conflict and led the British to establish indirect control (1874). After a period of turbulence following the murder of the first British resident, (1875), the system adopted in Perak established the pattern for British residents in the Malay States.

PERALTA BARNUEVO ROCHA Y BENAVIDES, PEDRO DE (1663–1743), Peruvian scholar, who was professor of mathematics at San Marcos University, and its historian. He was also chief cosmographer and engineer of the viceroyalty, and a doctor of law. His scientific investigations and literary efforts were numerous, and included verse in many languages, neo-classical dramas, and an epic poem.

PERCEVAL, SPENCER (1762–1812), British politician and prime minister. He was solicitor-general under Addington (1802), and defended the ministry almost single-handed in the Commons. He retained office on the return of the Younger Pitt, but opposed the ensuing ministry of the Talents, on the collapse of which he served as chancellor of the exchequer under Portland, drafting the orders in council (1807–9). Portland became ill and Perceval succeeded him as prime minister though Canning, Castlereagh, and Sidmouth all refused to support him. He faced the prince regent's hostility, as well as a financial crisis caused by economic warfare and the ruinous expense of the Walcheren campaign. He persevered in supporting Wellington in the Peninsula campaign and his administration was strengthened by Castlereagh as foreign secretary. He was shot by a madman in the lobby of the Commons, the only British prime minister ever to be assassinated.

PERCY, SIR HENRY (Hotspur) (1364–1403), English soldier and son of Henry, Earl of Northumberland, who played a prominent part in the deposition of Richard II and the accession of Henry IV. He was, however, disappointed by Henry's treatment of him and rose in rebellion, in which he was backed by his father, by his uncle, the Earl of Worcester, and by Welsh rebels following Owain Glyndwr. The rebellion amounted to a bid for the Crown, but Hotspur was defeated and killed at the battle of Shrewsbury.

PERDICCAS II (*reg. c.* 450–413 BC), King of Macedon, who fought in the great Peloponnesian War. He changed sides frequently, doing most harm to Athens by encouraging the revolt of Potidaea and neighbouring states (432), by helping Brasidas to reach Chalcidice, and to begin wooing Athens' allies (424), and by frustrating Nicias' expedition to the same area (417).

PERDICCAS (d. 320 BC), Macedonian officer of Alexander the Great and regent of the empire after Alexander's death (323). He was opposed by Antigonus, Antipater, Craterus, and Ptolemy, whose separatist ambitions he attacked. He was assassinated while invading Egypt.

PÉRÉFIXE HARDOUIN DE BEAUMONT DE (1605–70), French cleric, scholar, and protégé of Richelieu, who was appointed preceptor to Louis XIV in 1644 and Abp of Paris in 1662. He was elected a member of the Academie française in 1654 and wrote a history of the life of Henry IV (1661).

PEREIRA, JOSÉ DE FONTES (1823–91), Angolan writer and polemicist, born in Luanda, of European and African parents. He was the chief single precursor of the Angolan nationalist movement which began to crystallize half a century after his death. With a few others, he used the relative freedom of the Luanda press in the later decades of the 19th cent. to denounce colonial policy and practice, and did so in a way that won him both fame and notoriety. In *O Cruzeiro do Sul* (*The Southern Cross*), a radical journal founded by Pereira in 1873, he campaigned against the abuse and exploitation of Angolans, whether black, mulatto, or white, and for many years was the leading spirit of a type of polemical journalism that was suppressed by Lisbon after his death, though not finally silenced until the introduction of Dr Salazar's *Estado Novo* in the early 1930s.

Though long forgotten, Pereira may now be seen to have played a role in the Portuguese African colonies comparable with that of his contemporaries in the British and French territories. Like them, he raised ideas of African equality and independence that were to attract the many poets and publicists in the African colonies. He thus stands at the head of all that torrent of aspiration and protest which burst forth in the late 1930s in the work of Balthasar Lopes and Manuel Lopes in the Cape Verde Islands; in the polemics of *O Brado Africano* in Mozambique and its progeny of poets and prose writers (such as Luis Bernardo Honwana, José Craveirinha, Marcelino dos Santos, and Noémia de Sousa in the late 1950s); and, again in the 1950s, in the work of Angolan writers and poets such as Mario de Andrade, Costa Andrade, Viriato da Cruz, and Agostinho Neto. It is through Pereira's work, that one may see most clearly that modern nationalism in the Portuguese African colonies has its roots in the humanist thought of the 19th cent.

D. L. Wheeler and R. Pelissier, *Angola* (New York and London, 1971).

M. de Andrade, *La Poésie africaine d'Expression portugaise* (Paris, 1969).   BD

PEREYASLAVL, AGREEMENTS OF (1654), settlement between Bogdan Khmelnitsky, the hetman of the cossacks, and Tsar Alexis of Russia, by which the cossack lands of the Ukraine were united with Russia. It was not a treaty of union between two equal powers, however, but an understanding that in return for the right to elect their own hetman and retain their existing property and judicial rights, as well as their towns' rights of self-government, the cossacks would swear an oath of allegiance to the tsar and recognize him as their sovereign overlord and protector. In practice, the cossacks were granted a considerable degree of autonomy, and the hetman was allowed to exchange embassies with foreign countries, except Poland and Turkey, the traditional enemies. The Ukrainians continued to strive for independence, but the agreement of 1654 was the first stage in their suppression as a political entity and their integration into Russia.

PEREZ, ANTONIO (1539–1611), Spanish politician, who became secretary of state for the northern department and secretary of the council of Castile (1566). After the death of Ruy Gomez da Silva (1573) he assumed the leadership of the Eboli 'peace' faction which opposed the supporters of the Duke of Alva, and for the next five years he exerted great influence upon Philip II. But he became involved in a political intrigue with Philip II's half-brother, Don John of Austria, exploiting the tense relations between the two. To avoid the revelation of his activities by Don John's secretary, Juan de Escovedo, he procurred the latter's murder (1578), but after Don John's death he fell from royal favour for exceeding his authority. He was arrested in July 1579 and for the next 11 years was held in intermittent confinement while a search was made for incriminating evidence against him. In April 1590 he escaped from Madrid to Aragon and received the protection of the Aragonese courts. He was then prosecuted for heresy by the Inquisition at Philip's instigation (May 1591), and was liberated by a rioting mob in Saragossa. He fled to Béarn, leaving the Aragonese people to face Philip's wrath and the loss of their constitutional privileges for supporting him.

PEREZ, GONZALO (1500–66), Spanish administrator who rose to power on the recommendation of Valdes and Los Cobos to become secretary of state to Philip II (1543–66).

PÉREZ JIMÉNEZ, MARCOS (1914–), Venezuelan soldier and president of Venezuela (1952–8), who reached power by means of a military *coup d'état* (1948) and following the death of the military leader, Carlos Degado Chalbaud in 1950. While Pérez Jiménez was standing for president in 1952, he had the counting of the votes stopped and declared that he had won. His presidency was authoritarian and arbitrary and he was overthrown by disaffected army officers in 1958 and left the country. He returned to Venezuela in 1964 and in 1965 was prosecuted and imprisoned for illegal activities and financial irregularities during his presidency. On his release he was elected to the senate. He has since tried to regain political power.

PEREZ MOSCAYANO, JOSÉ JOAQUÍN (1800–89), Chilean diplomat and president of Chile (1861–71), during whose term of office, which was relatively progressive and undisturbed, the mining industry developed rapidly.

PERGAMUM, Mysian city in Asia Minor whose importance began in the 3rd cent. BC, when it became the capital of the hellenized kingdom of the Attalids, who maintained their independence against the hostility of the Seleucids. In the 2nd cent. (under King Eumenes II) Pergamum came to control most of Asia Minor, thanks to Roman friendship. The Attalids exploited their rich kingdom and lavished expenditure on public buildings and facilities; sculpture flourished and a major library was established, making Pergamum a cultural centre. When the last king (Attalus III) died, he bequeathed his kingdom to Rome (133). Thereafter it was known as the province of Asia, and rapidly became impoverished through Roman plunder and extortion which ultimately reduced it to a mere provincial city.

PERIANDER (*reg. c.* 625–585 BC), Tyrant of Corinth, son of Cypselus, who made Corinth the most influential Greek state (*c.* 600). He took Epidaurus from his father-in-law, Procles, controlled Corcyra through his sons, established connections by marriage with Argives and Athenians, and cultivated the friendship of Thrasybulus, Tyrant of Miletus, the Lydian kings, and the Saite dynasty in Egypt. He wished to extend Corinthian influence from the West to the Aegean and so constructed a *diolkos* which enabled ships to be drawn across the isthmus; he also planned a canal.

PERICLES (*c.* 495–429 BC), Athenian statesman and politician, the son of Xanthippus, an Alcamaeonid aristocrat. He fostered 'radical' democracy and achieved prominence by prosecuting the conservative Cimon (463), and by supporting Ephialtes' reforms (462–461) and, after his death, extending them. Realizing Athens' limitations, he advocated the Thirty Years Peace with Sparta (445), by which Sparta's supremacy on land and Athens' at sea were recognized. The Thirty Years Peace and that of Callias with Persia (*c.* 448) enabled Athens to consolidate control of the Delian League, whose revenues Pericles used to subsidize Athenian public expenditure, *eg*, on the Parthenon. After defeating his political opponent, Thucydides, son of Melesias, by ostracism (443), he came to dominate public life and was elected *strategos* annually until 429. As Sparta's suspicion of Athens' growing power changed to hostility, Pericles advocated firmness; he agreed to a defensive alliance with Corcyra (433) and proposed the Megarian decree (432). Despite attacks on himself and his associates, *eg*, Anaxagoras and Aspasia, he reconciled the Athenians to defensive siege tactics against Spartan incursions when the great Peloponnesian War began (431). His funeral oration for the fallen, of which Thucydides gives a sketch, is a classic eulogy of Athenian democracy. But a period of public disenchantment caused Pericles' suspension and conviction for embezzlement in 430. Later he was reinstated, but died in the following year.

PÉRIER, CASIMIR PIERRE (1777–1832), French Orléanist financier, politician, and prime minister. After election to the Chamber (1817), he attacked Villèle's financial policy, and became a leader of the Orléanist group. He played a large part in the July Revolution (1830) and served first as president of the Chamber (1830), then as prime minister (1831). He was determined to be his own master and dealt ruthlessly both with his own colleagues and the troubles in Lyons (1831–2). He rallied the conservative forces of the new regime, but made little attempt to tackle the problems which faced it.

PERIOECI ('dwellers around'), in ancient Greece, were small, outlying communities which enjoyed internal autonomy, but whose external affairs were controlled by a larger adjacent community. Best known are the *perioeci* in Messenia and Laconia, who appear as subject to Sparta from the 8th cent. BC onwards. They were obliged to serve in large numbers in the Spartan army and remained generally loyal, although some joined in the helots' revolt in 464–455 and Cinadon's conspiracy in 398. Their early skill in pottery and metalwork (7th–6th cents) seems to have been lost by the 5th cent.

PERIPATETICS, school of ancient Greek philosophers founded by Aristotle, so called because of his habit of instructing senior pupils and researchers while strolling in the Lyceum. His successor at their head was Theophrastus.

PERIPLUS OF ERYTHRAEAN SEA, anonymous guide to the export–import trade of some of the main commercial centres along the seaboard of the western Indian Ocean, notably those of north-west India, East Africa, and the Red Sea, during the early Christian era. Written in Greek (*c.* AD 100), probably by a Graeco-Roman sailor or merchant, the *Periplus* is one of the earliest and best historical sources for knowledge of this trade and its participants.

PERKIN, SIR WILLIAM HENRY (1848–1907), English organic chemist, who, by chance, produced (1866) a mauve compound, which he thought might be used as a dye. Having had a favourable report on its possibilities, he persuaded his father to finance a factory to produce the dye, known as aniline purple. Through the interest of the French fashion houses mauve became immensely popular, and it was also used for the British penny postage stamp. The business prospered and eventually (1874) Perkin sold it and returned to chemical research. His discovery initiated the synthetic dyestuffs industry and stimulated the synthesis of numerous chemical compounds not found in nature.

PERKINS, FRANCES (1882–1965), US public servant, advocate of social welfare legislation, and the first woman US cabinet member. She became a social worker at the Hull-House settlement in New York, studied public health problems, and lobbied the state legislature in Albany for factory legislation, unemployment insurance, and legal protection for women employees. After working for the Consumers' League, the New York Committee on Safety, and the State Industrial Commission, she served as Industrial Commissioner of NY state (1929–33) and was closely associated with Gov. F. D. Roosevelt. She was appointed secretary of labor in Roosevelt's cabinet (1933), and served until 1945. Her influence can be traced in much of the legislation of the New Deal.

PERMANENT COURT OF INTERNATIONAL JUSTICE, established by Article 14 of the Covenant of the League of

Nations. The PCIJ came into existence in 1921 and was unique in that it was the first court permanently available to consider any international dispute for which the parties involved sought a juridical opinion.

A committee of jurists was appointed by the League of Nations (Feb. 1920) to prepare a charter for the proposed court, and presented a plan, which the Assembly approved (Dec. 1920). By Sept. 1921 enough members of the league had accepted the draft, and an attached protocol, for it to become the 'Statute' of the PCIJ. The statute prescribed the appointment and tenure of judges and the overall jurisdiction and administration of the court, whose sessions were thereafter held annually at The Hague (1922–39). The court was itself administered independently of the league; but its panel of judges, originally numbering 11, but later increased to 15 (1936), were appointed every nine years by the Council and Assembly of the league.

The PCIJ was competent to consider any inter-state dispute which the parties thereto submitted to its jurisdiction. No state was obliged to bring an issue before the court, and unless all parties to the dispute were prepared to do so, the court was not compelled to give an advisory opinion. Nor was a given opinion necessarily binding. The statute contained an 'optional clause' (Article 36), whereby states could agree in advance, either when ratifying the statute or when a dispute arose, conditionally or unconditionally, to be bound by the court's decision. The Geneva Protocol (1924) attempted to make jurisdiction compulsory, but failed to achieve the requisite ratification. On two occasions the US Senate defeated a move by the US government to adhere to the statute; but an American judge nevertheless sat on the bench of the court throughout its existence.

Much of the court's work involved disputes arising out of the peace treaties signed after the First World War. In some cases, as between Finland and Russia (1923), or Rumania, Bulgaria, and Hungary, the refusal of one party to go before the PCIJ rendered a decision impossible. By contrast, the Mosul Dispute (1926) was successfully settled between Iraq and Turkey. But much of the court's success derived from issues not themselves prominent in contemporary international affairs nor likely to arouse the susceptibilities of any Power. By its treatment of disputes involving individuals not officially representing their state, or from general maritime matters, for example, the court acquired an acknowledged respectability and bequeathed a wealth of dicta to international law. The work of the PCIJ was competent and largely successful, as is perhaps indicated by the fact that the Charter of the International Court of Justice, which succeeded the PCIJ in 1945, remained, with few minor changes, practically identical with the Statute of the Permanent Court.   JK

PERMANENT SETTLEMENT, introduced into Bengal, Bihar, and parts of Orissa by Lord Cornwallis in 1793, against the wishes of Sir John Shore, the ablest revenue officer of his day. Under this system the land revenue demand from the *zamindar*s (landholders and revenue collectors) was fixed in perpetuity and they became the hereditary proprietors of their holdings. It was extended to Benares in 1795. It failed to protect the peasantry from the demands of the *zamindar*s, but protection was afforded by various Bengal Tenancy Acts (1859, 1885, 1928, 1938, 1941). The permanent settlement was made without a survey or detailed valuation of the lands. Most of the advantages claimed for it could have been attained by a temporary settlement for a long term of years.

PERMISO SHIPS (lit. 'permission ships') resulted from the commercial privileges obtained by Britain from Spain, as embodied in the treaty of Utrecht (1713) and clarified in 1716. Under these agreements, the British South Sea Co. was allowed to send one merchant ship a year to the trade fair at Puerto Belo (Panama), formerly reserved for Spanish commerce. By means of this *permiso* ship the British engaged in very profitable, and largely clandestine, trade with Spanish America, additional supply vessels replenishing the cargo at night. These activities were resented by Spain, even though technically the ship's size was restricted; each annual sailing had to be expressly authorized, and the Spanish king shared in the profits. Resentment over this and other issues led to war between the two countries in 1739, and *permiso* ships ceased to exist.

PERNAMBUCO, north-eastern state of Brazil. The first Portuguese settlement on the Iguarassu river, founded (1526) by Christavao Jacques, was soon abandoned, but permanent settlements were started at the present capital, Recife (1535), and Olinda (1537) by Duarte Coelho Periera. Men from these settlements assisted in expelling the French from trading posts along the northern coast. Pernambuco was captured by the Dutch (1630), who held it until their expulsion in 1654. With three other states Pernambuco broke away temporarily from Brazil (1817) and in 1824 another separatist revolution established a new state called Federacao da Equador. Pernambuco, though reunited with Brazil, was often the scene of disorders and unsuccessful revolutionary movements (1831–48).

PERÓN, JUAN DOMINGO (1895–   ), Argentine soldier and president of Argentina (1946–55), who was typical of the 'new' Argentine officer corps. He took part in the military coup of 1930, though this led only to a decade of political fraud and stagnation, and was of benefit primarily to the traditional land-holding oligarchy. In the view of nationalists such as Perón, Argentina was being condemned to a neo-colonial status as a supplier of raw materials and foodstuffs, as a market for foreign manufactures, and as a complaisant recipient of foreign investment. All this was at the expense of newer and native Argentinian commercial and manufacturing interests which might have given the nation genuine economic independence. Perón's ideas, influenced by German military writers, were also affected in these years by his personal observations of fascism in Italy and Spain during his visits to these countries (1939–40).

During the early 1940s he became influential in a secret military lodge, the GOU, dedicated to an authoritarian nationalism. The GOU took part in the overthrow (1937) of the conservative military regime of Ramón Castillo and in subsequent ad hoc military governments, whose pro-German bias caused them increasing difficulties as the Second World War drew to a close. Meanwhile, Perón came to the fore as labour secretary, then as war minister and vice-president under Gen. Farrell (1944). Perón had begun to establish a political following of his own by manipulating unorganized urban labour and, through generous wage and welfare decrees and the help of ambitious unionists, he moulded the 'shirtless ones' (*'descamisados'*) into a powerful faction, which later rescued him from oblivion when in Oct. 1945 they thronged the streets of Buenos Aires and threatened civil war unless Perón was released from the prison to which the resurgent democrats had consigned him. Shortly after this Perón married his mistress Eva ('Evita') Duarte, who had helped to organize the demonstrations in his favour. Early in 1946, in a free and honest election, Perón became president.

During his two terms of office constitutional forms were never abandoned, but Perón was widely accused of corrupting the courts, legislatures, and universities. He censored the press, silenced or exiled political opposition, and curtailed civil liberties. His power rested upon the army, on organized labour, and on business interests which profited from his nationalistic policies. The army remained hostile, however, to his social and economic programmes and the trade unions were rigidly subordinated to the regime. Nevertheless, the real living standard of the working class rose markedly at first, and welfare facilities were greatly expanded, whereby labour gained a dignity hitherto unthinkable in Argentina's stratified society. In all this 'Evita' (who died in 1952) was invaluable, for she had a genuine rapport with the common people and considerable political skill. Perón's policies of nationalization and industrialization, financed by Argentina's enormous wartime and post-war export of foodstuffs, were at first reasonably successful. However, by the early 1950s mismanagement and corruption, expensive welfare legislation, inflation, and European recovery, had gravely damaged the Argentinian economy and eroded Perón's political support, which was further decreased by an attack by him on the Church (1954–5). In Sept. 1955, after an army revolt, Perón was deposed and went into exile. Subsequent regimes have, however, failed so far to assimilate his movement, and this has contributed to their instability.

R. J. Alexander, *The Peron Era* (New York, 1951).   RCN

PERÓN, MARÍA EVA ('EVITA') DUARTE DE (1919–52), Argentinian wife of Juan Perón, and a political leader in her own right. In Oct. 1945 she was influential in organizing the workers' demonstrations that prevented Perón's overthrow by Argentinian democrats. She was a handsome, flamboyant, gifted, and ruthless woman, whose special role was that of the regime's patroness and de facto political leader of organized labour. Through a charitable foundation which she controlled, she showered material benefits on the 'shirtless ones' ('*descamisados*'). Her early death provoked an outpouring of public grief unparalleled in Latin American history. It was indicative of her influence on the regime that Perón thereafter (1952–5) seemed to lose his political touch.

PERONNE, DECLARATION OF (1585), proclamation of the Holy League in France, inspired by Philip II of Spain and issued in the name of Cardinal de Bourbon, as a protest against Henry III's maladministration and favour towards Protestants and as a call to all true Catholics to fight (March 1585). Henry and Catherine de' Medici were unable to resist its demands and submitted by the treaty of Nemours.

PEROZ I (*reg.* 457–484), Sassanian King of Iran, whose reign was marred by famine, religious strife, and a Hunnic invasion. Furthermore, two expeditions against the Ephthalites ended in disaster. On the first, Peroz was captured and ransomed, and on the second he was killed, leaving Iran under the influence of the Ephthalites.

PERPETUAL EDICT (1577), short-lived agreement between the Spanish Crown, represented by Don John of Austria, and the estates general of the provinces of the Netherlands during the Dutch Revolt (12 Feb. 1577). Don John accepted the terms of the Pacification of Ghent, including the departure of all Spanish troops from the Low Countries within 20 days, in return for the estates' recognition of his authority as governor-general and the maintenance of the Catholic religion. After the evacuation of the Spanish soldiery by the 'Spanish road' to Italy, Don John was allowed to enter Brussels. However, the expression of unanimity in the edict was to prove tenuous. Divisions among the provinces and uncertainty of his own position caused Don John to seize Namur (July 1577) and to recall 3000 troops (Jan. 1578) which defeated the rebellious provinces at Gembloux, thus ending the Pacification.

PERRAULT, CLAUDE (1613–88), French doctor, scientist, and architect, who was noted for his designs for the east facade of the Louvre (1665) and for the Paris Observatory (1668–71).

PERROT, NICOLAS (*c.* 1644–1718), French explorer, who acted as interpreter to the French expedition which took formal possession of the territories (1674) extending along Lake Superior. He discovered lead mines in the upper Mississippi valley and helped to preserve friendship between the western Indian tribes and France.

PERRY, CHARLES (1807–91), English-born Australian clergyman and Bp of Melbourne (1847–76). He founded Melbourne and Geelong grammar schools and Trinity College (University of Melbourne). After returning to England, he helped to found Ridley Hall, Cambridge (1879). In Australia he promoted the recognition of laymen in colonial church government.

PERRY, MATTHEW GALBRAITH (1794–1858), US sailor, who headed a mission to Japan which made the first breach in the Tokugawa policy of seclusion. He arrived in Edo bay in July 1853 with four ships, and in his discussions he combined diplomacy with veiled threats of force. On his return to the US he secured a treaty (1854) which provided for the appointment of a consul and named three ports where US ships might reprovision.

PERRY, OLIVER HAZARD (1785–1819), US sailor during the War of 1812, who commanded naval operations on Lake Erie. His capture of the British fleet (10 Sept. 1813) secured the Americans' north-western flank.

PERSEPOLIS, capital of Achaemenid Iran, planned and started by Darius I (*reg.* 522–486 BC) and added to by later Achaemenids. The main buildings, palaces, halls, and so forth were erected on a large terrace. The city was destroyed during the Greek occupation (330).

PERSEUS (*c.* 213–166 BC), King of Macedon (*reg.* 179–168), son and successor of Philip V, who renewed his father's alliance with Rome, but later extended his influence in Thrace and Illyria, intrigued in Greece, and made diplomatic connections in the east. His alliance with the Seleucids of Syria led Eumenes of Pergamum to lay complaints at Rome against his imperial designs, and in 171 Rome declared the Third Macedonian War. After initial successes, his army collapsed at Pydna in 168 before Aemilius Paullus, who brought him as prisoner to Italy, where he died. His kingdom was partitioned into four republics.

PERSHING, JOHN JOSEPH (1860–1948), US soldier, who graduated from West Point (1886), fought against the Apaches (1886) and the Sioux (1890–1), served in Cuba (1898) and in the Philippines (1899–1903), was a military attaché in Japan during the Russo–Japanese War (1905), and returned to the Philippines to campaign against the Moro in 1906 and 1909. Success led to his early promotion and in 1916 he was given command of the American force sent into Mexico to pursue Pancho Villa. When the US entered the First World War Pershing was appointed commander of the American Expeditionary Force, and planned to place 1 million US troops in the field by 1918 and 3 million by 1919. He strongly opposed American soldiers being used merely as reinforcements on the Western Front and insisted in maintaining them as a separate and distinct force; he did, however, 'lend' troops to Foch to stem the German offensive in 1918, and in the St Mihiel salient and the Meuse–Argonne offensive the AEF played an independent role. After the war Pershing was appointed general of the armies (1919), a rank that had hitherto been given only to George Washington, and became chief of staff (1921–4). His stern bearing and strict discipline led him to be known as 'Black Jack'. He published *Final Report* (1919) and *My Experiences in the World War* (1931).

PERSIAN CONSTITUTIONAL MOVEMENT, Iranian movement leading to the grant of a constitution (1906). Resentment of misgovernment under the ruling Qajar dynasty increased in the later 19th cent. and there was strong opposition to foreign loans, to the influence of foreigners and to concessions granted to them. In 1890–2 the granting of a tobacco monopoly to a British firm led to riots, demonstrations, and a boycott of tobacco, as a result of which the concession was withdrawn. The agitation was led by the traditional religious classes (*ulama*), supported by merchants, certain innovating landlords, and a few Westernized intellectuals, and demands appeared in some foreign newspapers, eg, *Qanun*, published in London. (Similar papers were published in Istanbul, Cairo, and Calcutta.) After 1900 the agitation was taken up by secret societies (*anjuman*s). In April 1905 a group of merchants took sanctuary (*bast*) in the shrine of Shah Abd al-Azim to demonstrate against the government's policies and in Dec. 1905, 2000 religious leaders did the same and demanded the establishment of a 'House of Justice' and the dismissal of certain ministers. In June 1906 further and larger *bast*s occurred at the British Legation in Teheran and at a shrine at Qum, and in Aug. Shah Muzaffar al-Din (*reg.* 1896–1907) agreed to summon a national assembly (*Majlis*). It met (7 Oct. 1906) and drafted the first Iranian constitution (signed Dec. 1906 and elaborated Oct. 1907). Muzaffar's successor, Muhammad Ali Shah (*reg.* 1907–9), was determined, however, to destroy the constitution. He dissolved the *Majlis* (June 1908) and abolished the constitution, but widespread resistance in Tabriz, Gilan, and Isfahan led eventually to Muhammad Ali's expulsion (July 1909) and the opening of the second *Majlis* (15 Nov. 1909). An attempt by Muhammad Ali Shah to regain power with Russian support was defeated (1911), although Russian influence greatly limited the success of the constitutionalists.

P. Avery, *Modern Iran* (London, 1965).   MEY

PERSIAN COSSACK BRIGADE, military force of Iranian cavalry, led by Russian officers and NCOs, established (1879) by Nasir al-Din Shah. The brigade was responsible for the temporary overthrow of the constitution (1920). In the same year its Russian officers were removed and it became the chief instrument in Reza Shah's rise to power and the nucleus around which the new Persian army was created.

PERSIAN GULF. Although it had long been an important artery of trade between the Middle East and India and a valuable source of pearls, the Persian Gulf was of little international importance before the 19th cent. In earlier periods control was usually divided among the various Arab tribes which lived around its shores. At the end of the 18th cent. the area became of great concern in relation to British interests in India, when fears of a French invasion threatened both trade and communications. Thereafter British influence in the area was slowly but steadily extended. An agreement was signed with Muscat (1798) and a British resident established at Bushir; later he became the resident in the Persian Gulf. Attempts by an expedition (1819–20) to suppress piracy and maritime warfare in the gulf were unsuccessful. Better results were achieved, however, by mediation to establish a maritime truce (1835), which was renewed and extended in subsequent years and made permanent in 1853. As a result, Britain acquired substantial influence over the so-called Trucial states, and this influence was later extended to the rulers of Muscat and Bahrayn. An agreement with Bahrayn (1880) which gave Britain effective control of Bahrayni foreign relations marked a new stage in the extension of British influence, and similar agreements were concluded with the Trucial states (1887, 1892). Agreements not to annex territory without British consent were concluded with Muscat (1891) and Kuwait (1899) and in 1916 with Qatar. In May 1903 the exclusive system was in some degree extended to the Persian shore by Lord Lansdowne's declaration that Britain would oppose any attempt to establish a foreign base in the gulf. The extension of British influence there at this period was due to fears of Ottoman, French, German, and Russian encroachments. Ottoman control of Al-Hasa and the inclusion of most of the Persian coast in the 1907 neutral zone meant that British power in the gulf was still not supreme. Supremacy was achieved, however, with the elimination of Russian and Ottoman influence after 1917. In 1935 Bahrayn became a naval base for British vessels. After 1945 British influence declined rapidly. The abandonment of India (1947) removed the main prop of British power, although the great expansion of oil production in the gulf area provided a motive for Britain to retain her influence.

Nonetheless, the cost of maintaining that influence, the possibilities of which had become more and more limited, was eventually considered too great. In 1961 control over Kuwait was relinquished and in Jan. 1968 Britain announced that military forces would be withdrawn from the gulf by 1971.

J. B. Kelly, *Britain and the Persian Gulf* (Oxford, 1968).
Husain M. al-Baharna, *The Legal Status of the Arabian Gulf States* (Manchester, 1968).   MEY

PERSIAN WARS, conflicts between the Greeks and the Persians, more especially the latter's invasions of 490 and 480–479 BC, which threatened to overrun the whole Greek peninsula and strangle the development of Greek civilization. Cyrus I had subjected the Asiatic Greeks (540), after overthrowing their overlord, Croesus of Lydia. Later, Persian control was extended to the off-shore islands (*c.* 520), but when Darius I came westwards (513), he attacked only Scythia (mod. Rumania), though after his return the north Aegean coast was subdued. The Ionian Revolt (499–494) and the intervention in it of Athens and Eretria confirmed Darius' intention to subdue the Greeks' homeland. An invasion under Mardonius (492) was abandoned after his fleet was wrecked off Mount Athos, but in 491 Darius sent heralds throughout Greece demanding surrender, and in 490 an expedition under Datis and Artaphernes subdued Naxos and other islands, sacked Eretria, and aimed to subject Athens and reinstal Hippias as tyrant, but the expedition was defeated at Marathon. Revolt in Egypt and Darius' death (486) delayed a further Persian attempt; then Xerxes began preparations (*c.* 483) for a large-scale military expedition, using the land route and supported by a fleet, while the Greeks, forewarned, prepared for a united defence under Spartan leadership.

Xerxes set out late in 480, but lost many ships in storms off Thessaly and Euboea. Though his fleet failed to defeat the Greeks off Cape Artemisium, many northern Greeks surrendered and after breaking through Thermopylae, Xerxes overran Boeotia and sacked Athens, the Athenians taking to their ships or seeking refuge in Salamis and other nearby places.

While the Greek armies prepared to defend the Isthmus of Corinth, their fleet remained off Salamis and Xerxes was induced to attack it, only to be defeated by the greater fighting qualities of the Greeks in narrow waters. This victory secured the Peloponnese, but a powerful Persian army under Mardonius wintered in central Greece and in 479 reoccupied Athens. The Athenians rejected enticing offers from Mardonius and at length the army advanced from the isthmus and re-emphasized the superiority of the Greek hoplite, defeating Mardonius at Plataea, while the Greek fleet crossed the Aegean and destroyed the Persian fleet at Mycale. The homeland was now saved, but operations continued to secure the Aegean and liberate the Asiatic Greeks, the leadership being transferred (478) to the Athenians, who organized the Delian League. In *c.* 467 the league's fleet defeated a Persian expeditionary force at the Eurymedon river in southern Asia Minor and, though a Greek expedition to Egypt ended in disaster (454), the Persians agreed under the peace of Callias (449) to leave the Asiatic Greeks free and to keep out of the Aegean.

A. R. Burn, *Persia and the Greeks* (London, 1962).
Herodotus, *The Histories*, tr. by A. de Selincourt (London, 1965).   TTBR

PERSIGNY, JEAN GILBERT VICTOR FIALIN, Duc de (1808–72), French Bonapartist politician. He had been cashiered from the army because of his republicanism (1832), but was converted to Bonapartism and became one of its most earnest exponents. Napoleon III described him as 'the only Bonapartist'. He participated in both abortive coups (1836, 1840) and twice served as minister of the interior (1852–4, 1860–3). He also became ambassador to Britain

(1855–8, 1859–60). He was dismissed for his maladroitness, but was made a duke in compensation (1863).

PERSONAL LIBERTY LAWS in the US, enactments by various Northern states during the 1840s and 1850s which hindered enforcement of the Fugitive Slave Acts of 1793 and 1850. They provided legal aid for apprehended runaway slaves, prohibited their confinement in state prisons, and generally made it difficult for masters to retrieve their 'property'. The South considered these laws unconstitutional.

PERSONALISM (Spanish, *personalismo*), tendency in Latin American politics for loyalty to be given to individuals personally rather than to ideas or political parties which they may represent. Constitutional government and political parties of broadly similar ideologies have suffered as a result.

PERTH, JAMES ERIC DRUMMOND, 16th Earl of (Scottish) (1876–1951), first secretary-general of the League of Nations (1919–33), who previously had been private secretary to Grey, Asquith, Balfour, and Curzon. In creating the league's secretariat, he refused to staff it with officials of the governments of member states. He was Britain's ambassador to Rome (1933–8), though well aware that his former association with the league might prejudice Mussolini against him, and was criticized, especially by Eden, for his conciliatory approach to the dictator. During the Abyssinian crisis he tried to play down the differences between Britain and Italy, despite the fact that Eden thought a firm stand in support of the league, and against appeasement, more appropriate. Drummond was not opposed to conceding Mussolini some sort of protectorate over Abyssinia.

The claim of Ciano, Mussolini's foreign minister, that Drummond understood and even loved fascism was certainly exaggerated. He was a convinced supporter of Neville Chamberlain's 'new course' of neutralizing Italy through Mediterranean concessions. Eden's resignation following the Anglo-Italian agreement of 1938 caused Drummond few misgivings, if any. He returned to Britain shortly before the Second World War, during which he joined the ministry of information and became deputy leader of the Liberal Party in the House of Lords.

PERTH, FIVE ARTICLES OF (1618), imposed on the Scottish Church by James VI and I and Abp Spottiswoode of St Andrews. They enforced the observance of Christmas, Good Friday, Easter, and Pentecost; kneeling at communion, confirmation, the early baptism of children, and the reception of communion by the dying. The articles were ratified by the Scottish parliament on 4 Aug. 1621. James had already restored bishops to the church in 1610. This action of 1618 was an extension of his policy towards ending the authority of Presbyterian government and discipline. It was condemned by the General Assembly at Glasgow in 1638, by which time Charles I's extreme policies had led the Scots to reject episcopacy. In the confusions of 17th-cent. Scottish religious affairs, the bishops' restoration (1660) proved temporary.

PERTINAX, P. HELVIUS (AD 126–93), Roman Emperor (*reg.* 193), who was proclaimed after the murder of Commodus. He had had a distinguished military career and was respected for his moderation, tolerance, and seriousness of purpose. He attempted to restore order and financial stability, but offended the praetorian guard and after only three months of rule was murdered by them. He was succeeded by Didius Julianus.

PERUSIA, ancient Etruscan town (mod. Perugia), which, after fighting against Rome, became a loyal ally (295 BC). It was occupied by Mark Antony's brother, Lucius (41), and besieged, captured, and sacked by Octavian in the Perusine War. Under the empire it flourished as Augusta Perusia.

PERUVIAN–BOLIVIAN CONFEDERATION (1836–9), led by Andrés Santa Cruz of Bolivia with certain Peruvian liberals who were convinced that such a state would provide a better organization and military leadership for the two countries. The arrangement provided for three states, one of northern Peru governed from Lima, another in southern Peru at Arequipa or Cuzco, and a third in Bolivia, ruled from La Paz. Santa Cruz was to act as overseer of the states, each having its own executive and legislature. Peruvian opponents of the confederation having been defeated at the outset, they combined forces with Chile, whose government viewed the confederation as a threat to its security, and in the end the confederation was defeated in battle. It had effected few substantive changes in the government and economy of either Peru or Bolivia before it ended.

PERVUKHIN, MIKHAIL GEORGIYEVICH (1904–), Russian politician and diplomat, who joined the Communist Party (1919), then studied in Moscow and became an electrical engineer. For some time he was manager of a power station and then rose rapidly as a result of the great purge. He became first deputy commissar for heavy industry (1938), then minister of power stations and electrical industry (1939–40, 1953–5), and minister of chemical industry (1942–50). He was later chairman of the state planning committee (1956–7). His career made him a natural associate of Malenkov after the death of Stalin and he then took part in the challenge to Khruschev (1957). He suffered less as a result of so doing than the other members of the anti-party group. He was appointed ambassador to the German Democratic Republic (1959)—this being a form of exile rather than an honour—and remained an alternate member of the Presidium until 1961. Khrushchev's fall made his career more promising once again and he was made a member of Gosplan (1966).

PESCARA, FERDINANDO FRANCESCO D'AVALOS, Marquis de (1490–1525), Spanish nobleman and imperial commander in the Italian wars against Francis I. With Colonna he drove the French from Milan (1521) and Genoa (1522), and crossed the Alps with Bourbon to besiege Marseilles (1524). His skilful use of his arquebusiers broke the French at Pavia (24 Feb. 1525).

PESCHIERA, BATTLE OF (1848), Piedmontese victory against the Austrians under Radetsky on an island in the Mincio in Verona. The island was one of the four fortresses of the 'Quadrilateral', the chief strength of Austrian control of Italy until 1866. The Austrians subsequently regained control by defeating the Piedmontese at Custozza.

PESHWA, THE, chief minister in the *Ashta Pradhan* or Council of Eight of the Maratha raja, Shivaji (c. 1627–80). He was also known as the *Mukhya Pradhan*. He held the seal and had responsibility for administration. After Shivaji's death (1680) the office lost its primacy, but it was revived (1712) by his grandson, Shahu, who appointed Balaji Vishvanath Bhat. Shahu later made the office hereditary in the Bhat family and his decision to expand northwards gave the peshwa further authority as the minister responsible. After Shahu's death (1749) the peshwa became the de facto head of the Maratha state. The defeat of the peshwa (1818) by the British and the annexation of his dominions broke up the Maratha confederacy. The last peshwa, Baji Rao, died as a British pensioner (1853).

PESSAGNO, MANOEL (*fl.* 14th cent.), Genoese noble who was the effective creator of Portuguese naval power. He was a member of a wealthy merchant family, his brother Antonio acting for some years as the chief banker of King Edward III of England. Manoel was appointed (1317) as the hereditary admiral of Portugal. The first recorded oceanic expedition of the Portuguese, which explored the Canaries in 1341, was probably organized as a result of his influence.

PESSOA, EPITÁCIO DA SILVA (1865–1942), Brazilian lawyer, politician, and president of Brazil (1919–22), who was a member of the World Court (1924–30). He represented Brazil at the Paris peace conference (1919). While in Europe he was elected to complete the term of President Rodrigues Alves, who had died in office.

PESTALOZZI, JOHANN HEINRICH (1746–1827), Swiss educationist, who was brought up in Zürich in a stimulating intellectual atmosphere created by men such as J. J. Bodmer, J. J. Breitinger, and J. K. Lavater. He early felt the need for social and political change, and especially for improving the lot of the poor. He believed at first that he could achieve his aims by improving agricultural methods and in 1769 he bought some land at Birr. Then he took in some poor children, hoping that he could give them a basic education while they paid their way by weaving and helping on his farm. Both attempts were financial failures and in 1779 the children had to be sent away. Pestalozzi devoted most of the next 20 years to writing, then in 1798 he was called upon to open a home in Stans for orphaned and homeless children. There, and later at larger, fee-paying establishments in Burgdorf (1800–4) and Yverdon (1804–25), he began to develop his educational ideas, published in a series of books, *eg, How Gertrude teaches her Children* (1801) and *Swansong* (1825). Inspired by Rousseau in his youth, he saw child development as a natural process of growth. As this process began at birth, he stressed the active part that parents, and especially the mother, had to play in education. Their role, and later that of the teacher, was to ensure that experiences were presented to a child in 'psychologically ordered sequences'. At the same time, organization of classroom material had to take into account the needs and abilities of the individual child. A child personality had to be encouraged to emerge from within, not to be fashioned by external pressures. As Pestalozzi's fame spread, more and more visitors came to study his methods and helped to propagate his ideas. But, problems of administration became an increasing burden to him and in later years a cause of conflict among his followers which unjustly obscured the relevance of his ideas.

M. R. Heafford, *Pestalozzi. His Thought and its Relevance Today* (London, 1967). 　　　　　　　　　　　　MRH

PÉTAIN, PHILIPPE (1865–1951), French soldier and marshal of France. After holding staff appointments, he became a lecturer at the École de Guerre (1901–10). He was appointed a general because of his part in the first battle of the Marne (Sept. 1914) and won fame by his defence of Verdun (1916) and his restoration of order in the French army after the mutinies of 1917. He was commander of the French forces at the end of the First World War, was promoted marshal (1918), and was the dominant military figure in France between the two World Wars. When the Second World War came, he was ambassador to Spain, but was recalled to France and received full powers from the Assembly as 'Head of State' (1940). He personally directed the ill-fated Vichy regime until his replacement by Laval and the collaborators (1942). Although unhappy about the course of events, he made no attempt to resist the Germans' demands. After the war he surrendered to the Free French, and was subsequently condemned to death. The sentence was commuted, however, to life imprisonment.

PETER II (*reg.* 1196–1213), King of Aragon, who attempted to defend his brother-in-law, the Count of Toulouse, and other vassals in southern France against atrocities committed on a crusade organized by the Catholic Church to put down the Albigensian heresy. Peter's defeat and death at the battle of Muret permanently destroyed Aragonese hegemony in southern France.

PETER IV (1319–87), King of Aragon (*reg.* 1335–87), who took a determined stand against exaggerated demands for power by the nobility and firmly established the supremacy of the monarchy in Aragon, although he respected the basic constitutional rights of his subjects. He conquered Roussillon (1343), organized an expedition to Sardinia (1354), and accepted the overlordship of the duchy of Athens (1381).

PETER I (1334–69), King of Castile (*reg.* 1350–69), who spent his reign defending his throne against his bastard brother, Henry of Trastamara. In spite of support from England, he finally succumbed to Henry, who, having waged war against Peter with the support of Aragon, treacherously murdered him at Montiel.

PETER II (1648–1706), King of Portugal (*reg.* 1683–1706), who was the third son of John IV of Portugal and Dona Luisa. He ruled Portugal as prince regent from 1667, having secured the abdication of his elder brother, Alfonso VI, who was both physically and mentally handicapped, and married Alfonso's wife, Princess Marie Françoise of Savoy, whose existing marriage had been declared null and void. Peter sought peace and economic recovery for his country. He favoured a protectionist economic policy and curbed government expenditure, and by concluding peace treaties with Spain (1668) and the Dutch republic (1669), and later a commercial treaty with England (1703), he improved Portugal's financial condition. Despite his hopes of remaining neutral he was forced to side openly with the Grand Alliance in the War of the Spanish Succession (1701–13).

PETER II (1923–　), King of Yugoslavia (*reg.* 1934–44), who came to the throne when his father, King Alexander, was assassinated in Marseilles. A regency headed by Prince Paul ruled in Peter's stead. In 1941 when his armies surrendered to the German invaders he himself fled from Yugoslavia. He remained in exile throughout the Second World War, leading the royalists. Several conversations were held to effect an understanding with the Partisan resistance forces and in 1944 Peter urged his people to unite themselves behind Tito. The monarchy was formally abolished and the communist regime of Tito was confirmed by the elections of 1945, when the only candidates were Tito's popular front nominees.

PETER, Saint (*fl.* 1st cent.), foremost of the 12 Apostles, named first in all lists of them, who was present on all occasions recorded in the Gospels when only an inner group were admitted. By nature impetuous and ardent, he made the strongest professions of faith in Jesus' lifetime, though he deserted him on his arrest. Jesus called him the Rock-man and said that on him the Church would be built (the foundation of later papal claims). After Jesus' death Peter took the lead in organizing the Church in Jerusalem, preaching and performing miracles, and he opened the Church to Gentiles by admitting Cornelius. Little is known of his later years. He was probably martyred at Rome during the Neronian persecution (*c.* AD 65). A recently excavated tomb under St Peter's at Rome may be his.

PETER I the Great (1672–1725), Tsar of Russia (*reg.* 1682–1725), whose economic and administrative reforms, coupled with his patriotic ideals, transformed the country from a backward and lethargic nation into a European power. The son of Tsar Alexis and his second wife, Natalia Naryshkin, he ruled jointly (1682–9) with his half-brother, Ivan V, under the regency of Ivan's elder sister, Sophia. In 1689 he became sole ruler. His reign is regarded as a watershed in Russian history, not only because of what he achieved, but because of the changes he wrought in attitudes towards Russia, both within the country and outside it.

Almost all Peter's internal reforms arose out of his military requirements, for during most of his reign Russia was at war. In 1696 he captured Azov from the Turks and almost reached the Black Sea. In 1700 he joined Poland and Denmark in the Great Northern War against Sweden. Defeated that year at Narva, the Russians won the decisive battle of Poltava in

1709. In 1721 Peter signed the treaty of Nystadt with Sweden, acquiring the south-eastern Baltic provinces of Ingria, Esthonia, Livonia, and part of Karelia. A second Turkish campaign was less successful, ending in 1711 with Peter's capitulation at the Pruth river and the loss of Azov. In Central Asia he made important conquests along the south and south-western shores of the Caspian Sea.

Needing an ordered administration and money, he reorganized the central government, establishing a senate (1711) and a system of departments or colleges (1718). In the provinces he undertook three separate series of measures. The effectiveness of these changes was limited by official corruption and inefficiency and the lack of a bureaucratic tradition. The same deficiencies hampered his attempts to reform municipal administration on a two-gild foundation and to introduce a poll-tax (1718), a direct tax levied on all male peasants.

However, he did succeed in raising a formidable conscript army, armed and clothed by growing mining and textile industries, and in virtually founding the Russian navy. Early in his reign he envisaged Russia as a sea-power, appreciating the importance of her natural frontiers in the Baltic and Black Seas and in the Far East, in terms of security and trade. His Baltic fleet played a significant part in the defeat of Sweden.

Peter believed that in industry and commerce Russia lagged behind the West and that her security depended upon emulating western military and naval techniques. He travelled extensively in England, France, and the Low Countries and encouraged western experts to work in Russia. His attitude to the West antagonized the Russian Orthodox Church and his replacement of the Patriarchate by the Holy Synod (1721) marked a decisive break with the past. Henceforth the Church lost its authority over the tsar and became a secular government department. Its obscurantist, anti-western ideology was replaced by the idea of secular service to the state, to which, in 1721, the tsar himself took an oath of allegiance. In 1722 Peter instituted a Table of Ranks embodying the principle that service, military, civil or court, not birth, conferred rank and status.

PETER II (1715–30), Tsar of Russia (*reg.* 1727–30), only son of Tsarevich Alexis and grandson of Peter I, who succeeded Catherine I. At the age of 12 he was betrothed to a daughter of Prince Alexander Menshikov (1727), but under the influence of the Dolgoruky faction he later repudiated the Menshikov alliance and ordered the prince's arrest and banishment to Siberia. He became betrothed instead to Catherine, daughter of Prince Alexis Dolgoruky, and moved his court from St Petersburg to Moscow (1728), whence he devoted himself mainly to hunting. He died from smallpox on 29 Jan. 1730, the day fixed for his wedding, and thus ended the direct male Romanov line.

PETER III (1728–62), Tsar of Russia (*reg.* 1762). He returned to Prussia the territory won in the Seven Years War, freed the gentry from compulsory service, and secularized church lands. He was overthrown in favour of his wife, Catherine II, and probably killed.

PETER, HUGH (1598–1660), American clergyman, who abandoned Anglican orders, emigrated from England (1635), and became pastor of the church at Salem, which he reorganized after the departure of Roger Williams. He returned to England as agent for the colony (1641), took part in the English Civil Wars, and was an influential Independent. He was one of the few excluded from the Act of Indemnity on Charles II's restoration (1660) and was executed for his association with the execution of Charles I.

PETER DE DREUX (or MAUCLERC) (d. 1250), founder of the dynasty that ruled Brittany in the later Middle Ages and the creator of an effectively governed duchy. He was a relative of King Philip Augustus of France, who married him off

(1213) to the heiress of Brittany to assure Brittany's support in the war against King John of England (1213–14). During the minority of Philip's grandson, King Louis IX, Peter was inclined for a period to desert France for England (1230–1), but he soon reaffirmed his allegiance to France. His effective government involved him in conflict with the Breton clergy, which earned him his nickname of 'bad clerk'.

PETER THE HERMIT (d. 1115), French popular preacher. After Urban II launched the First Crusade for the reconquest of the Holy Land in 1095, Peter collected thousands of humble followers whom he led into the Balkans ahead of the knightly crusading armies. Peter's host, a lawless rabble, after committing great depredations in Christian territories, were shipped off by the apprehensive Byzantine government to Asia Minor, where most of them were massacred by the Turks. Peter survived to join the main crusade and to return to France in 1101.

PETER THE LOMBARD (*c.* 1095–1160), bishop of Paris, a number of whose sermons and commentaries on the scriptures survive. His chief work was the *Book of Sentences* (*Liber Sententiarum*), which became the standard text on scriptural interpretation for the rest of the Middle Ages and longer. It quickly became established as the chief manual of the theological faculty at Paris and elsewhere and, despite certain reservations about its contents, was upheld in its orthodoxy by the Fourth Lateran Council (1215).

PETER THE VENERABLE (*c.* 1092–1156), a nobleman from Auvergne who entered the abbey of Cluny in 1109 and became its abbot and the head of the Cluniac order in 1122. He was the last great abbot of Cluny. The leadership in monastic affairs had passed to Citeaux and to St Bernard of Clairvaux but Peter was still one of the most influential churchmen of his time. He was revered by men as different as Bernard and Abelard, whom he reconciled to each other. He sheltered Abelard at Cluny in the last years of his life.

PETERBOROUGH, CHARLES MORDAUNT, 3rd Earl of (1658–1735), English soldier and politician, who commanded the expedition to win Spain for Archduke Charles (1705) and by his successes committed England to a policy of 'no peace without Spain' in the War of the Spanish Succession.

PETERHOF in Russia, oldest of the Russian tsars' summer residences, situated on the southern shore of the Gulf of Finland, near Leningrad, and built by Peter the Great, who hired the best European architects, *eg*, Leblond. It suffered severely in the Second World War, but was later restored.

PETERLOO MASSACRE (16 Aug. 1819), in Britain, repression by the Manchester magistrates of an open-air meeting of 50,000–60,000 in St Peter's Field addressed by the radical orator, Henry Hunt. The magistrates ordered the yeomanry to arrest Hunt, and when they were resisted a troop of cavalry was sent in. In the panic that followed 11 were killed and about 400 injured. The incident caused great indignation throughout the country. The government accepted the view of its law officers that the meeting had been an 'illegal assembly', but decided that the legal position about public meetings must be clarified. This was done by the Six Acts passed in 1819.

PETERS, KARL (1856–1918), German explorer and writer, who founded the German Colonization Society (1884), explored parts of East Africa, and induced Bismarck to declare the annexation of German East Africa in 1885. In 1887 Peters signed a 'treaty of protection' with the King of Buganda, but this was nullified by the Heligoland exchange of 1890. In 1891 he became imperial high commissioner for the Kilimanjaro district, but was recalled in 1893 after being accused of a cruel and oppressive administration. These charges were upheld in the course of three enquiries (1897) and Peters was dismissed. In 1906 he was reinstated. He wrote *New Light on Dark Africa* (1891) and *The Eldorado of the Ancients* (1902).

PETER'S PENCE, STATUTE OF (1534) in England, parliamentary statute of the Henrician reformation, drawn up and passed during the first session of Jan.–March 1534, which stopped the payment of the small annual tax known as Peter's Pence to the holy see and transferred the granting of dispensations and licences from Rome to Canterbury.

PETERSBURG CAMPAIGN (June 1864–April 1865), operation in VA during the final stages of the American Civil War. The Union army under Grant invested Petersburg, but was repeatedly repulsed with heavy losses by Lee's troops. The Confederate line, extending 36 miles (57 kms, was eventually broken at Five Forks (1 April) and Lee withdrew westward.

PÉTION, ALEXANDRE SABES (1770–1818), Haitian mulatto soldier and president of southern Haiti (1806–18), who fought in the forces of Toussaint L'Ouverture, and then joined the opposition to him under Rigaud. When Toussaint defeated Rigaud, Pétion fled to France, but returned to Haiti with the French expeditionary force under Leclerc which was sent to defeat Toussaint (1802). He deserted the French cause, however, and fought with the army of independence under Jean Jacques Dessalines. After Dessalines' murder Pétion refused to recognize the authority of Henri Cristophe and set up an independent republic in the south. His elite regime was dominated by educated mulattoes, but it adopted laissez-faire policies towards the peasantry. Pétion allowed many of the former French estates to be broken up into small peasant properties. He also gave refuge to Simón Bolívar and helped him in his struggle to expel Spain from South America.

PETITION OF RIGHT (1628) in England, addressed to Charles I by parliament and intended to declare what the law was and to secure the benefit of it for individuals. Originally the Commons had proceeded with a bill reaffirming the validity of old statutes, but the king had refused to allow his prerogatives to be thus curtailed. Sir Edward Coke then suggested that the two Houses should join in a 'Petition of Right'. It was steered through the Commons by Thomas Wentworth, later Earl of Strafford, and the pressure of the Lords forced Charles to accept it. The petition began with a recital of statutes alleged to have been broken and of grievances for which redress was required. It asked: (*a*) that no man should be compelled to pay non-parliamentary taxation; (*b*) that no free man should be imprisoned without cause shown; (*c*) that soldiers should not be billeted on individuals against their will; and (*d*) that martial law should not be invoked in future. The petition had no immediate effect, except that forced loans were no longer exacted.

PETITIONS TO THE HOUSE OF COMMONS in Britain on matters of public policy began in the 17th cent. and are found from time to time in the first three-quarters of the 18th cent. *eg.*, the Kentish petition (1701), petitions against the excise bill (1733), and against the cider tax (1762), and the Feathers petition (1772). Numerous county petitions for economic reform (1779–80) established petitions as a new technique of political agitation. The number of petitions rose from 880 (1785–90) to 23,283 (1828–32) and, in spite of restrictions (1831, 1839, and 1842) on the time allowed for debate on petitions, reached a peak of 101,573 (1868–72). The number then fell rapidly to 24,414 (1907–12), 245 (1917–22), and 32 (1939–42).

PETKOV, NIKOLA (1889–1947), Bulgarian politician and leader of the *Pladne* Agrarians, a left-wing splinter group of the Agrarian party. He was not a communist, but admired the Russian revolution and certain Bulgarian communists. He believed in a coalition of communist and democratic forces and during the Second World War, when Dimitrov

(Gemeto) left Bulgaria, he became the leader of the *Pladne* group. He joined the Fatherland Front and collaborated with the communists until Sept. 1944. Then the communists turned on their opponents. Dimitrov returned from abroad and resumed the leadership, but threats and harassment soon forced him to resign. Petkov replaced him and became a deputy prime minister. However, the communists found him too stiff an opponent and put Obbov in his place. Petkov then united the opposition around him, for which he was arrested. His show trial and execution shocked the West and shamed the Bulgarian regime.

PETRA, capital of Edom and later of the Nabataean kingdom, situated to the west of the Jordan plateau. It was an important trading city on the routes from Aqaba to Gaza and Damascus. The surrounding rose-coloured rock was sculptured as facades of temples and dwellings.

PETRARCH (PETRARCA, FRANCESCO) (1304–74), Italian poet, who was especially famed for his love sonnets. With his Florentine compatriots, Dante and Boccaccio, he was one of the creators of the Italian literary language, based upon the dialect of their native Tuscany. Petrarch was the first great representative of the Italian Renaissance humanism. His father had been exiled from Florence in 1301 at the same time as Dante, and Petrarch was brought up at Avignon. There and elsewhere in France he made his first discoveries of rare and lost classical texts. His greatest discovery was the finding in 1345 of Cicero's *Letters to Atticus*, one of the two extant collections of Cicero's letters (the other, *Familiar Letters*, was rediscovered in 1392 by Salutati, an enthusiastic admirer of Petrarch). He thus inaugurated the modern critical study of Cicero and, largely through his influence, the early Italian humanism became, above all, a Ciceronian movement. Petrarch is also one of the originators of the typical humanist assumption that the period between the decline of the Roman empire and his own time was an era of ignorance and darkness from which the Italian humanists were rescuing Europe. He was inspired by a fanatical Italian patriotism and a sense of the unity of Italy which was to be asserted by recovering the glorious heritage of ancient Romans.

PETRE, SIR EDWARD (1631–99), English landowner, who became a Jesuit priest (1671), and, as such, was imprisoned for suspected complicity in the Popish Plot (1679–80). He was released, however, through James II's influence. Petre was vice-principal of the English province of the Society of Jesus (1679–83), and was deep in James's confidence. He was appointed a privy councillor in 1687 and the king's more extreme policies were attributed to him. In 1688 he fled abroad and thereafter had no further contact with James. He became head of the Jesuit College at St Omer (1693–7).

PETRI, LAURENTIUS (1499–1573), Swedish clergyman, who was the country's first Lutheran archbishop. He was consecrated in 1531, the apostolic succession being preserved, and held a synod at Uppsala, which completed the breach with Rome (1536). He sought to maintain a conservative type of Lutheranism under three kings, his ecclesiastical ordinances being finally approved by John III in 1571 and accepted in the next year by a church meeting at Uppsala.

PETRI, OLAUS (1493–1552), Swedish theologian and writer, who was leader of the Reformation in Sweden. He studied at Wittenberg and spread Lutheran theology among his fellow clergy at Strängnäs. In 1524 Gustavus I brought him to Stockholm, where he was immensely active. He was royal chancellor (1531–3), and had a life-long influence over the king, although his insistence upon episcopal authority led to his nominal condemnation for high treason (1540) and the exaction of a heavy fine.

PETROBRÁS (Petróleos Brasileiros, SA), Brazilian state petroleum corporation. Oil was first discovered in Brazil in

1939 at Lobato, Bahia, but production remained low through the immediate post-war years. In Oct. 1953, following an emotional propaganda campaign, the Brazilian congress created Petróleos Brasileiros, the government monopoly corporation better known as Petrobrás. Private domestic and foreign companies that refined and distributed imported petroleum were permitted to continue operations, but Petrobrás was given exclusive control over prospecting, drilling, refining, and transportation of Brazilian oil. The National Petroleum Council directs (1970) and supervises the activities of Petrobrás, which embrace every aspect of the petroleum industry from geological surveys to petrochemicals, including the operation of a tanker fleet and a nation-wide chain of petrol stations.

PETRONIUS (*fl.* 1st cent. AD), Roman author, part of whose *Satyricon*, a picaresque novel unique in Roman literature, survives. He was probably identical with Nero's friend and adviser on matters of taste and luxury, who was forced by him to commit suicide in AD 66.

PETROV AFFAIR, THE, in Australia. The defection in April 1954 of Vladimir Petrov, third secretary and MVD resident at the Russian embassy in Canberra, was an event of greater importance for Australian domestic politics than it was significant for international relations. Petrov's defection in which he was joined by his wife, an MVD clerk, was skilfully managed by the Australian security intelligence service and was exploited politically with great success by the prime minister, R. G. Menzies. A royal commission on Soviet espionage was highly publicized and the decision of the ALP leader, H. V. Evatt, to appear before the commission, served to emphasize divisions within his party and helped the government to secure re-election.

PETROVARADIN (PETERWARDEIN), BATTLE OF (Aug. 1716), north-west of Belgrade, on the right bank of the Danube, resulted in Prince Eugène, commanding the imperial forces, defeating the Turks.
  Petrovaradin was the site of a Turkish fortress besieged unsuccessfully by Christians in 1687 and in 1694.

PETROVICH, ALEXIS TSAREVICH (1690–1718), eldest surviving son of Tsar Peter I of Russia and Eudokia Lopukhin, who was brought up by his aunt Natalia after his mother had been forced to enter a nunnery. He himself was forced to marry Charlotte of Brunswick-Wolfenbuttel, a German princess, who bore him a son, the future Peter II. In 1716 he fled to Vienna, seeking the protection of Emperor Charles VI, but was tricked into returning to Russia. He renounced the throne in the cathedral of the Assumption in Moscow and received Peter's public pardon (13 Feb. 1718), but within months was tortured to death on his father's orders for alleged conspiracy (7 July 1718).

PETRUNKEVICH, IVAN ILYICH (1844–1928), Russian radical *zemstvo* leader, who during the 1860s advocated constitutionalism and organized a *zemstvo* congress (1878), although at this stage his supporters were in a minority. He attempted to launch a press campaign and also tried unsuccessfully to negotiate (1878) an alliance with Narodnaya Volya leaders, on condition that they abandoned terrorism. In 1879 he was arrested and exiled to Tver, where he continued his campaign for a constituent assembly. He was chairman and founder member of the Union of Liberation and a kadet leader in the first Duma (1906). He signed the Vyborg manifesto after the dissolution of the First Duma and after 1907 devoted himself to publishing liberal papers (*eg, Rech*).

PETTY, SIR WILLIAM (1623–87), English economist, politician, and statistician, who in a varied career was also a sailor, physician, professor of anatomy at Oxford and of music at Gresham College, London, inventor, and surveyor for the Cromwellian settlement of Ireland. In his writings he helped to establish the basis of modern economic thought, expounding the economic functions of the state, touching on the problem of the theory of value, and maintaining that the state should initiate public works to keep up a high level of employment.

PFLIMLIN, PIERRE (1907–), French lawyer and politician. As one of the young Catholic militants who hoped to create a powerful Christian democratic party in France, he was instrumental in founding the Movement Républicain Populaire (MRP). He was elected the party's deputy for Bas-Rhin in 1945, and national president of the MRP in 1956. He was minister of agriculture in eight cabinets (1948–52), and in Faure's cabinet (1955–6) and Gaillard's (1957–8) he held the more important post of minister of finance. Later, as *président du conseil* (1958) he paved the way for De Gaulle's accession by resigning. He joined De Gaulle's first cabinet, but again in 1959 he resigned. For a brief period in 1962 he was a member of Pompidou's cabinet, but he generally sided with the moderate and European opposition to De Gaulle. His interest in Europe, mirroring that of his Catholic colleagues, found an outlet as president of the consultative assembly of the Council of Europe (1963–6). After 1966 he concerned himself with regional development in Alsace and Lorraine as president of the Commission du Développement Économique Régional (CODER) for that area.

PHAESTUS, Minoan city in the Mesara plain of southern Crete. Its impressive palace, like that at Cnossos, was begun in *c.* 2000 BC and reconstructed more magnificently *c.* 1700. However, after its destruction in the 15th cent., following the eruption of Thera, it was not rebuilt. Excavations have revealed the earliest Linear A tablets (before 1700) and a round clay disc, 'the Phaestus Disc', inscribed with hieroglyphic symbols, as yet undeciphered.

PHALANX, ancient Greek formation of close-packed heavy infantry, notably employed in the Macedonian armies of Philip II, who first adapted and developed Greek *hoplite* methods, and by Alexander the Great and his successors. Its forward thrusting forest of 13-ft (4-m.) (later 18-ft, 5·5-m.) spears formed an impenetrable defence and was a useful foil to the heavy cavalry; Macedonian *phalanxes* were rarely mastered before being faced with the greater mobility of Roman legions, *eg*, at Cynoscephalae (197 BC), Magnesia (189), and Pydna (168).

PHALARIS (*fl.* 6th cent. BC), Greek tyrant of Acragas in Sicily. Little is known of him beyond the legend that he roasted his enemies alive in a hollow bronze bull, but Acragas flourished in his time. He was overthrown by Telemachus, an ancestor of Theron.

PHAM QUYNH (1892–1945), Viet-namese writer and politician, whose views fell between the traditional Sino-Vietnamese culture of earlier generations, and the French culture which led a younger generation to adopt modern ideas. He himself did much to propagate French culture, as editor of the review *Nam-Phong* (1917–34) and the newspaper *France-Indochine* (founded in 1920). Later, in 1933, he became chief minister in Bao-Dai's 'cabinet' at Hue, but was allowed little real power by the French. In 1945 he was executed by the Viet-Minh, for his collaboration with the French. He wrote many essays, and translated a number of French classics into Viet-namese.

PHAM VAN DONG (1906–), Viet-namese politician and prime minister of the Democratic Republic of Viet-nam (North Viet-nam). In 1926, while studying at Hanoi, he joined the Revolutionary Youth Association of Nguyen Ai Quoc (Ho Chi Minh) and spent some time at the Whampoa military academy, near Canton. He was sent to Saigon to organize communist cells, but was arrested in 1929 and sentenced to ten years' imprisonment; under the amnesty of the French Popular Front government he was released in 1936. He again became active as a communist organizer in Hanoi (1936–40), then fled to South China to join Ho Chi Minh. He was founder member of the Viet-Minh, and its leader during Ho's imprisonment in China (1942–3), and became minister of finance in the Hanoi provisional government (1945). In 1946 he was officially head of the Viet-Minh delegation to the Fontainebleau Conference, at which the French refused to accede to his demand for complete independence. In 1949 he became vice-president of the Viet-Minh government, and in 1954 led its delegation to the Geneva Conference which achieved an armistice and Viet-Minh control of half the country. On his return to Hanoi, he became prime minister (Sept. 1955), and as such was a leading spokesman for the Democratic Republic in its relations with the rest of the world.

PHAN BOI CHAU (1867–1940), Viet-namese nationalist. In 1904 he became a founder-member of the Duy-Tan-Hoi (Renovation Association), which also included Phan Chau Trinh. He went to Japan in 1905, and helped to smuggle the Viet-namese Prince, Cuong-De, who became pretender to the throne, out of Viet-nam to Tokyo. He was impressed by the ideas of Liang Ch'i-Ch'ao, and later by those of Sun Yat-sen, and wrote several nationalist tracts. In 1912, after the Chinese Revolution, he founded a nationalist organization at Canton, the Viet-Nam Quang-Phuc Hoi (Viet-Nam Restoration Society). During the next few years he travelled in northern Viet-nam and China in furtherance of the society's aims, until he was imprisoned by the Chinese (1918). He advocated terrorist methods, and was responsible for a bomb-plot in Hanoi in 1913. Later, while living in Shanghai in 1925, he was allegedly betrayed to the French authorities by the communists and put on trial at Hanoi. The sentence passed on him—life imprisonment with hard labour—led to an uproar among all sections of the Viet-namese, and he was eventually reprieved by the governor-general. He lived the rest of his life at Hue, virtually under house-arrest.

PHAN CHAU TRINH (1872–1926), Viet-namese nationalist politician, who became an official under the French protectorate. Clandestinely he was also a member of the Duy-Tan-Hoi (Renovation Association), founded in 1904. In 1908 he wrote a letter to the French authorities calling for reforms, but without effect. Later in the same year he was arrested for being implicated in peasant protests against taxes in various provinces of Central Viet-nam. He was imprisoned on Poulo Condare island, but released in 1911 and allowed to go to Paris, after an appeal by French politicians on his behalf. He remained in Paris until 1926, but shortly before his death was allowed to return to Saigon. His tomb and memorial shrine became a focus for nationalist demonstrations in the years after 1926.

PHAN DINH PHUNG (1847–95), Viet-namese resistance leader in the first years of French rule. He was a Confucian scholar who had passed the state examinations in 1877, but refused to accept the French protectorate and withdrew from the office he held in the government, in order to organize resistance in his native province of Ha-Tinh (North-Central Viet-nam). He refused to surrender to the French and later intensified his opposition (1893–5).

PHAN THANH GIAN (1796–1867), Viet-namese scholar, official, and ambassador. He was a native of South Viet-nam and the first candidate from that region to pass the Confucian examinations at Hue. In 1862 he undertook negotiations with the French which resulted in the first treaty of Saigon. He was sent (1863) on an embassy to Paris and then to Madrid, but failed to secure a return to Viet-nam of the three provinces surrendered by the treaty. In 1864 he was appointed governor of Vinh-Long and the three southern provinces

which remained Viet-namese. He failed not only to recover the lost territory, but also to prevent French annexation of the other three provinces (1867).

PHANARIOTS, population of rich and influential Greeks, residing at Fanar (name given to a suburb of Istanbul) during the 17th and 18th cents. They grew prosperous as tax-farmers and contractors, serving the Ottoman government, or as merchants in the Black Sea wheat trade. Their importance was much increased through the growing need of the Ottomans to exploit their diplomatic resources in their relations with Europe. Phanariot Greeks, drawing from their wide commercial and financial contacts a first-hand knowledge of the European scene, were of great value to the Ottomans as secretaries, agents, and interpreters. Through their wealth and prestige the Phanariots acquired a dominant influence within the Greek Orthodox Church, controlling its administration and influencing the appointment even of the Patriarch of Constantinople. It was from amongst the Phanariots (AD 1711–1821), that the Ottoman government chose the princes (hospodars) who ruled over the Danubian principalities of Wallachia and Moldavia.

PHAO SIYANON (1909–61), Thai police-general and close associate of Phibunsongkhram of Thailand. He was a leading figure in the later Phibun regime (1948–57), but was forced into exile after the coup of 1957.

PHARAOH, word meaning, literally, 'great house', which from about the XVIIIth dynasty (*c.* 1575–1308 BC) onwards was the title of the king of ancient Egypt. The term has come to be used for all ancient Egyptian kings. Each pharaoh had five names, one given at birth and four which he adopted on his accession. In theory he was thought to be the embodiment of the god Horus in life and of Osiris in death, but in practice he seems to have been judged and treated according to his merits. As high priest, the pharaoh participated in religious ceremonies, but most of his time was probably spent in the business of government. In this he was assisted by his principal minister, the vizier, to whom he delegated his duties as chief justice. The vizier dealt also with administrative business, was commandant of the capital, received tribute paid by foreign rulers, and settled boundary disputes. Under the vizier the most important department was the treasury, which collected taxes and dues, mostly in kind, stored them, and released them when necessary. Under the early kings the vizier was a royal prince, but later he was a nobleman, chosen for his ability and, from the time of Thothmes III (*c.* 15th cent. BC), there were two viziers. The country was divided into provinces called nomes, and originally ruled by independent princes, but these were replaced under the kings of the XIIth dynasty (*c.* 1991–1786) by royal governors who were responsible for, among other things, public works and the collection of dues. Each nome had its own militia which the king used in time of war.

PHARNABAZUS (d. *c.* 370 BC), Persian soldier and administrator, important in Greek history as satrap of Hellespontine Phrygia during and after the great Peloponnesian War. After the Athenian disaster in Sicily (413) he rivalled Tissaphernes, satrap at Sardis, in encouraging revolts of Athens' allies and Spartan naval action, but, when he eventually enticed the Spartans to the Hellespont (411), they were defeated at Cyzicus, and effective co-operation against Athens was delayed until Cyrus, son of Darius II, took charge (407). After Athens' defeat Pharnabazus, faced with Spartan invasions of Asia, urged Artaxerxes II to raise a fleet, with which he and the Athenian, Conon, defeated the Spartans at Cnidus (394) and broke up their Aegean empire. After the King's Peace (387–386) Pharnabazus was chiefly concerned with unsuccessful attempts to recover Egypt for Persia.

PHARSALUS, ancient city in Thessaly in north-eastern Greece, rival of the dominant Larisa (37 kms to the north) and of Pherae during its brief ascendancy under Jason (*c.* 375–370 BC). In the 5th cent. members of the leading Meno family were prominent in the city, usually as friends of Athens, and Daochus was *tagus* (leader) of the Thessalian confederacy during the great Peloponnesian War (431–404). Pharsalus was briefly garrisoned by the Spartans (*c.* 399–395), and remained friendly to them, but they failed to help Polydamas against Jason. Later, Cottyphus of Pharsalus supported Philip II of Macedon, who subjected all Thessaly in 352.

PHARSALUS, BATTLE OF (9 Aug. 48 BC), in Thessaly, Greece, in the Roman civil wars. Julius Caesar defeated Pompey and the Republican army, which lost 6000 men; a further 24,000 were captured.

PHAULKON, CONSTANTINE (1647–88), Greek sailor, who became a politician at the Siamese court of King Narai and superintendent of the kingdom's foreign trade. By 1685 he was a minister of state, and became virtually prime minister. He encouraged French hopes for the conversion of Narai and Siam to Christianity, while satisfying Narai's hopes for a French counterweight to Dutch and English power. This hastened the Siamese revolution of 1688, in which Phaulkon died.

PHAYRE, SIR ARTHUR PURVES (1812–85), British colonial official and author, who became principal assistant to Commissioner Tenasserim (1846), and later to Commissioner Arakan. In 1852 he became commissioner of the newly annexed and important Pegu Division. He accompanied the Burmese king's mission to India in 1854, and in 1857 was in charge of a mission to the court of Ava. In 1862, when the province of British Burma was constituted, Phayre became the first chief commissioner. He left Burma in 1867. Phayre was a Burmese scholar and wrote a *History of Burma* (1883), which was for a long time the only such volume in English.

PHEIDIAS (d. *c.* 432 BC), Athenian sculptor, famous for his work on the Parthenon and for his chryselephantine statue of Athena placed within it. He was a close friend of Pericles, and his exile for alleged embezzlement of precious materials (*c.* 437) was probably engineered by Pericles' enemies.

PHEIDON (*fl.* 7th cent. BC), King of Argos, Greece, who organized the emergent hoplites at Argos against the nobility and so, according to Aristotle, 'became a tyrant'. After defeating Sparta at Hysiae (669), he seized Olympia (668) and re-established Argive supremacy in the Peloponnese. He probably introduced a standard Peloponnesian system of measures, but, contrary to later tradition, was not the first Greek to coin silver.

PHÉLYPEAUX FAMILY in France, administrators who became virtually hereditary ministers under the *ancien régime*. The first to make a name for himself was Paul Phélypeaux, sieur de Pontchartrain (1569–1621), son of a councillor in the *présidial* court of Blois, who entered royal service (1583) and rose through the favour of Marie de' Medici to be secretary of state (1610–21). As his son was too young to succeed him, the secretaryship was bequeathed to his brother Raymond, sieur d'Herbault (1560–1629), the *trésorier de l'épargne*, who eventually became one of the first secretaries of state to specialize in diplomatic affairs, rather than merely sharing the business of government. His success, and the opposition of the Pontchartrain branch of the family to the treatment of Fouquet (1663), led to his descendants emerging as the senior branch of the family which it remained for some time. D'Herbault was succeeded as secretary of state (1629–39) by his son, Louis I, Comte de la Vrillière (1613–1685), whose successor was his own son, Balthazar (*c.* 1638–1700), Marquis de Chateauneuf, later secretary for Huguenot affairs (1681–1700); but neither he nor Louis I had the expertise and standing of d'Herbault. Chateauneuf's brother Raymond, Marquis de Phélypeaux (*c.* 1650–1713), served in the army (1671) and then in the diplomatic service, notably as envoy to Savoy (1699–1704). Later, after his partial disgrace, he served as governor of Canada (1709). It was left to D'Herbault's great-grandson, Louis II, Marquis de La Vrillière (1672–1725), further to develop the fortunes of the family as secretary for Huguenot affairs (1699–1725) and secretary-general to the council of regency (1715–48). He was succeeded by his son Louis III, Comte de St Florentin and later Duc de la Vrillière (1705–77), whose devotion to Louis XV earned him the reformed ministry of the royal household (1749–75), as well as the Huguenot portfolio, together with the rank of minister of state (1751). His association with the less savoury aspects of the reign of Louis XV led to his dismissal by Louis XVI. CHC

PHERAE, ancient city in Thessaly, northern Greece, which was overshadowed until the 4th cent. BC by Larisa (about 32 kms to the north-west), but then enjoyed a brief ascendancy under Jason (*c.* 375–370), who temporarily made Thessalian dominance in Greece seem possible. Alexander, his successor as 'tyrant', after opposing Pelopidas, had to acknowledge Theban supremacy (364), and later Lycophron was overthrown at Larisa's request by Philip II of Macedon (352), who secured Larisa the primacy in a Thessaly subject to Macedon.

PHIBUNSONGKHRAM, LUANG (1898–1964), Thai politician and prime minister of Thailand (1938–44, 1948–57), who, having become a soldier, was sent to France for advanced military studies, and there met other Thai students who later joined with him in planning the revolution of 1932. He became an active revolutionary and won a name for himself by suppressing Prince Boworadet's rebellion (1933). As minister of defence in Phahon's government (1934–8) he was increasingly enamoured of Japanese power. On becoming prime minister (Dec. 1938) he led a nationalist crusade against the Chinese minority, promoted irredentist claims against France and Britain, and brought Thailand into a close relationship with Japan. In 1941, when Japanese troops invaded Thailand, he established a personal dictatorship which lasted until the war began to turn against Japan. In Aug. 1944 his government was defeated. Taking advantage of the weakness of civilian government after the war, especially after the death of King Ananda, he organized a *coup d'état* (1947) and emerged from behind the scenes to take office as prime minister in April 1948. In the 1950s he favoured an alliance with the US. Under increasing pressure by his rivals and public criticism of the army's dominance, he attempted to win the people's support through elections, but popular revulsion against electoral corruption led to a coup which forced him from office (Sept. 1957) and into exile in Japan, where he died.

PHILADELPHIA CONVENTION (1787), meeting in Philadelphia, PA (May–Sept.) at which a new constitution for the US was drafted. It was proposed by the Annapolis Convention (1786), and summoned by the Continental Congress to find ways of strengthening the federal government through revisions of the Articles of Confederation. But the convention exceeded these instructions. All states except RI elected delegates, among whom were James Madison, James Wilson, Gouverneur Morris, Alexander Hamilton, Benjamin Franklin, Roger Sherman, George Mason, Luther Martin, and George Washington, who was elected president; thus the convention included a large portion of the country's leaders. General agreement that the central government should be strengthened, that there should be a balanced government of executive, legislature, and judiciary, that democracy should be controlled and slavery condoned, did not prevent extended debate on the nature and form of a new government. In particular, there was argument over the relative powers of the federal and state governments, and between large and small states which believed themselves to have opposed interests.

The Virginia Plan included the establishment of a national government which would be supreme over the states and whose legislature would be apportioned by population; thus it would have favoured the large states. The New Jersey Plan unsuccessfully proposed a more genuine federal system of state sovereignty and equality which would also protect the interests of the small states. Such differences required many compromises, including the Connecticut Compromise on representation, the 'federal ratio', by which slaves were counted as three-fifths of a person for the purposes of representation and taxation, a provision that Congress should regulate commerce but not impose an export duty nor prohibit the importation of slaves for 20 years, and postponement of the establishment of inferior courts for consideration by Congress. The final draft of the constitution, representing more nearly the views of the 'nationalists' than that of the 'federalists', was signed by only 39 out of the 55 delegates who attended the convention. Having been accepted by the Continental Congress, it was ratified by state conventions after a fierce but unequal struggle between its nationalist advocates, the Federalists, and their opponents, the Antifederalists (1787–8), and came into effect in 1789.

Max Farrand, *The Framing of the Constitution of the United States* (New Haven, CT, 1913).

Charles Warren, *The Making of the Constitution* (Cambridge, MA, 1928).

PHILAIDAE, ancient Athenian noble family, traditional rivals of the Alcmeonidae during the 6th and 5th cents BC. Under Peisistratus they won lasting influence in Thrace and the Chersonese. Miltiades, Cimon, and the historian Thucydides were all related to the family.

PHILBY, HAROLD ADRIAN RUSSELL (1912–   ), British spy who achieved notoriety as the 'third man' who assisted the escape of Burgess and Maclean, foreign office officials who, like Philby, worked for the Soviet Union. As an undergraduate at Cambridge University he was known to be at least a 'fellow-traveller', and possibly a member, of the Communist Party. From Cambridge he went to Vienna, where he saw the shelling of workers' flats by the army of Dollfuss (1933) and married Alice Friedman to enable her to escape. Returning to England, he gave the appearance of having moved sharply to the right in his political views. He worked as a free-lance journalist and with the BBC and went to Spain, where he became *The Times* correspondent with Franco (1937). Long before this however he had been recruited to work for the Soviet Union—the first contacts may indeed have been made at Cambridge.

He joined the British secret service—MI 6—in 1941 and was rapidly successful. He was appointed to organize a new section established (1944) for operation against the Russians. He served in Istanbul (1947–9) and in Washington (1949–1951). The defection (May 1951) of Burgess and Maclean threw suspicion on Philby, who was asked to resign. But no case was established against him and in response to a question in the House of Commons Harold Macmillan, as prime minister, made a statement clearing him (Oct. 1955). He became the *Observer* correspondent in Beirut (1956). However the suspicions of the British counter-espionage service, MI 5, had never been allayed and were presently confirmed, presumably by a defector from the Soviet Union. Philby disappeared from Beirut (23 Jan. 1963) and re-emerged in Moscow, where he said that he had 'come home'.   WK

PHILIP D'ALSACE (d. 1191), Count of Flanders, the most powerful vassal of the young King of France, Philip II (Augustus), whom he hoped to dominate. He arranged the king's marriage to his niece. When the king tried to shake off his tutelage, Count Philip organized against him a coalition of the leading vassals of the French Crown. He was defeated after a series of civil wars (1181–5) in which King Philip was saved largely by the support of Henry II of England.

Thus ended a grave threat to the continued power of the Capetian kings of France.

PHILIP THE BOLD (1342–1404), youngest son of King John II of France, who was given the duchy of Burgundy in 1363 and was married to the heiress of Artois and Flanders whose lands he inherited by feudal law. After 1380 he was one of the most influential men in France, his nephew, King Charles VI, being at first a minor and then becoming insane. By using French resources for his own ends Philip made Burgundy into one of the great powers of Europe. He inaugurated the policies that placed his descendants in control of the whole of the Netherlands.

PHILIP THE GOOD (1396–1467), 3rd Duke of Burgundy of the Valois dynasty (*reg.* 1419–67). Under his rule the Burgundian state attained the height of its importance as one of the leading European powers. In the war between France and England his personal sympathies lay with France. But his father, Duke John the Fearless, had been murdered in 1419 by the Dauphin Charles (subsequently King Charles VII of France) and this drove Philip into an alliance with England which lasted until 1435. His chief interest lay in adding the rest of the Netherlands to his country of Flanders, and this he largely accomplished between 1427 and 1439. But his dream of becoming the most influential of French princes, as both his father and grandfather had been, was frustrated by King Louis XI of France (*reg.* 1461–83). Louis began a relentless series of aggressions against Burgundy. Philip suffered from the first of these attacks and his successor, Duke Charles, was ultimately ruined and killed by Louis (1477).

PHILIP (M. IULIUS PHILIPPUS) (d. AD 249), Roman Emperor (*reg.* 244–9), was promoted praetorian prefect by Gordian III during his Persian campaign (242–4) and succeeded him by a *coup d'état*. He made peace with Persia and returned to the west. On the Danubian frontier he conducted wars against Goths and Carpi, and in 248 celebrated at great expense the millennium of Rome.

PHILIP I (1478–1506), King of Castile (*reg.* 1504–6), who was the son of the Habsburg Emperor Maximilian I and Mary of Burgundy. He married the daughter of Ferdinand of Aragon and Isabella of Castile, Joanna (21 Oct. 1496), who succeeded to Castile in 1504, and with the birth of their son, Charles (1500), he became the founder of the Spanish Habsburg dynasty. Though nominally the joint ruler of Castile with Joanna, Philip was absent in Flanders (1504–6), returning to Spain in June 1506 only shortly before his death.

PHILIP I (1052–1108), King of France (*reg.* 1060–1108), whose reign was one of the longest in French history, was an ineffective ruler, being overshadowed by his vassals. He was powerless to prevent the mightiest of them, William of Normandy, from conquering England, but he began the process of establishing royal authority within the territories which he personally controlled, and his son, Louis VI (*reg.* 1108–37), using this inheritance, became the first ruler of his house to make the monarchy again a considerable power in France.

PHILIP II (1165–1223), King of France (*reg.* 1180–1223) (called Augustus after his death), who may deservedly be regarded as the founder of French royal power. Under him France first emerged as one of the leading European states. His greatest achievement lay in increasing considerably the size of his royal domain and more than doubling his income. His greatest gains were won from the Angevin empire, embracing almost all of Western France, then ruled by the kings of England. While Henry II of England lived (d. 1189), Philip played off his sons against him. Henry's successor, Richard I, temporarily kept Philip in check, but Richard's brother, King John (*reg.* 1199–1216), was no match for Philip. John, besides being unpopular, was a mediocre general and in the crucial crisis of 1202–5 his financial resources were inferior to Philip's. In these few years Philip conquered all the Angevin lands north of the Loire, including Normandy and Anjou, the two cradles of the English dynasty. Only south-western France remained in English hands. John's attempt to recover his lost inheritance with the help of a coalition of relatives and of German allies (1213–14) ended in disaster when his confederates were defeated at Bouvines (1214). From this point France became the chief power in Europe and remained so until the 14th cent. Philip did not intervene directly in the south of France, but he encouraged his vassals to lead a crusade against the Albigensian heretics in Languedoc, which destroyed the power of the counts of Toulouse and other southern lords and paved the way for the annexation of Languedoc in the 13th cent. by Philip's successors. Philip's successes against foreign enemies were based on improvements in his internal government. He did little to improve royal justice, but he secured much support from towns by encouraging them to develop self-government.   DB

PHILIP III (1245–85), King of France (*reg.* 1270–85), who succeeded his father, Louis IX (St Louis), one of the greatest kings of France. Throughout Philip's reign his father's advisers continued to govern the kingdom and his father's territorial policies came to fruition under Philip, who, on the death of his uncle, Count Alphonse, in 1271, acquired the huge territories of Languedoc, Auvergne, and Poitou. His heir (the future Philip IV) married the heiress of Champagne, thus adding yet another great principality to the royal domain. Philip died on a crusade against Aragon in the service of the papacy.

PHILIP IV (1268–1314), King of France (*reg.* 1285–1314), succeeding his ineffective father, who perished on crusade in the service of the papacy. He was determined to pursue only French interests and to expand his power to the utmost. This meant especially the extension of direct control over his most powerful vassals, the King of England (who was also Duke of Aquitaine) and the Count of Flanders. Philip provoked a war with England in 1294 in order to annex Gascony. Count Guy of Flanders, similarly menaced, allied with England. The French conquered most of Gascony. They also in 1300 overran Flanders, but a popular rebellion drove Philip out in 1302. This disaster and his conflict with the papacy led Philip to make peace with England and to restore the French conquests in Gascony. The wars against Flanders continued. Some Flemish territory was annexed, but Philip died without defeating the Flemings. The expense of these wars against England and Flanders led Philip to tax the French clergy. Pope Boniface VIII, who wanted to tax the clergy for his own enterprises in Italy, tried to stop the exploitation of the clergy by secular rulers. But in 1297 Boniface gave way and Philip's success on this issue encouraged him into further aggressions against the papacy. In 1301 a French bishop of Pamiers was indicted for treason. Boniface threatened Philip with dethronement. On the eve of the king's expected ex-communication in 1303 Philip had Boniface kidnapped by his agents and the aged pope died of shock soon afterwards. His successor, Clement V, was Philip's puppet and moved the papal court to France in 1305. Philip's rule in France was efficient but oppressive. The financial demands necessitated by his wars created an immense strain on the French monarchy, leading to debasements of the coinage and heavy taxation. By 1314 leagues of protesting nobles and townsmen were formed in many parts of France, presenting unexpected opposition at the end of his life.   DB

PHILIP V (1294–1322), King of France (*reg.* 1316–22), who usurped the Crown, after the death of his infant nephew, John I, setting aside the claims of his niece, John's older sister. This was the first occasion on which the claims of a

woman to inherit the French Crown were ignored in favour of a male member of a younger branch of the ruling dynasty. On Philip's death, the claims of his daughter were similarly ignored through the forceful seizure of the Crown by Philip's younger brother, Charles IV. These two usurpations were the origin of a custom, later known as the Salic Law, restricting succession to the French Crown to males.

PHILIP VI (1293–1350), King of France (*reg.* 1328–50). When Charles IV died, the third successive king to leave only daughters, the Crown, in accordance with the principle of male succession (given a supposed antiquity as the Salic Law), was assumed by his cousin, Philip of Valois, a grandson of king Philip III. Philip's title was challenged by Edward III of England, who himself claimed the French throne through his mother, Isabella, the late king's sister. This, however, was less the cause than the symbol of worsening relations with England, which culminated in the outbreak of the Hundred Years War in 1337. The war began badly for France. At Sluys (1340) the French lost command of the sea and at Crécy (1346) Philip, after being defeated by Edward, managed to flee the field. The loss of Calais (1347) and the onset of the Black Death (1348–9) brought further troubles to a country overburdened by taxation. The king, reared in a tradition of extravagant chivalry, was not competent to rule in such challenging times. His one lasting success was to acquire Dauphiné for the French heir-apparent.

PHILIP (c. 1177–1208), German King (*reg.* 1198–1208), who when his brother, the Emperor Henry VI, died in 1197, was elected as king during the minority of Henry's three-year-old son, Frederick. Throughout Philip's reign Germany was torn by a civil war between himself (supported by France) and the Welf Otto IV, subsidized by England. He was murdered during a private quarrel.

PHILIP II (c. 380–336 BC), King of Macedon (*reg.* 358–336), father of Alexander the Great and architect of the Macedonian empire, won control of the Greek city-states and planned the invasion of Asia. He was elected regent to the infant Amyntas III (359), dealt speedily with five pretenders, one backed by Athens, and with Paeonian and Illyrian invaders, and was himself made king (358). With Athens distracted by the Social War (357–355), he took Amphipolis and founded Philippi near the mines of Mount Pangaeus. Using their mineral wealth, which soon amounted to 1000 talents yearly, he created a new army which outclassed the city-state citizen militias and formed the basis of Alexander's victories. It also backed Philip's shrewd diplomacy in Greece. By 352 he controlled Thessaly and much of Thrace, threatening both central Greece and the Hellespont. Though the Athenians checked him at Thermopylae, they could not save Olynthus from destruction (348) and, denied support by the mainland Greeks, accepted the peace of Philocrates (346). Philip may have wanted reconciliation with the Athenians, but his immediate subjection of Phocis outraged them and thereafter they supported Demosthenes, his opponent since 352. By 342 Demosthenes was rallying support in Greece. Philip's friends were removed from Euboea and Megara and, after he had unsuccessfully besieged Byzantium (340), war was renewed. Trouble in the Amphictyonic League enabled him to invade central Greece (339) and, although Thebes joined Athens, he defeated the Greek coalition at Chaeronea (338). All the Greeks, except Sparta, now came to terms and a common peace settlement, backed by Macedonian garrisons at key places, secured his control and Greek support for an attack on Persia. He was preparing this when he was murdered.

PHILIP V (238–179 BC), King of Macedon (*reg.* 221–179), whose ambitions provoked the Romans into extending their power in the Greek world. After forming an alliance with Hannibal against Rome (215), he fought the Romans sporadically on sea and land in the First Macedonian War until the treaty of Phoenice (205), which gave him minor territories. Subsequently he allied himself with Syria against Egypt. But his aggression in the Aegean, coupled with Roman resentment at his earlier alliance with Carthage, led Rome to declare the Second Macedonian War in 200. Philip, having been routed by Flamininus at Cynoscephalae in Thessaly (197), was confined by stringent peace terms to Macedonia, where he remained faithful to the Roman alliance during Rome's struggle with Antiochus (192–189), developing the prosperity of his own kingdom. After 185 he took a more anti-Roman course, supporting Perseus against his other son, the pro-Roman Demetrius, whose death he ordered.

PHILIP II (1527–98), King of Spain (*reg.* 1556–98). In 1548, after being regent of Spain (1542–8), he began a European tour from the Low Countries (April 1549). To cement the English alliance, which was considered vital to the defence of the Netherlands, he married Queen Mary I (25 July 1554), and received the kingdoms of Naples and Sicily and the duchy of Milan (1554) from Charles V, who shortly afterwards abdicated the sovereignty of the Low Countries (25 Oct. 1555) and the remaining Spanish dominions in the Old and New Worlds (16 Jan. 1556). Charles then (Sept. 1556) retired to Spain, leaving Philip to take control of his inheritance. He was soon faced with a renewal of the Valois–Habsburg conflict, but the victories at St Quentin (1557) and Gravelines (1558) and the invasion of the papal states (1557) enabled him to conclude the peace of Cateau-Cambrésis. The deaths of his childless wife, Mary, and of his father, had meanwhile altered Philip's position. He returned to Spain, the heart of his empire (1559), and to seal the Franco-Spanish peace settlement married Elizabeth of Valois, who bore him two daughters, Isabella Clara Eugenia and Catherine. After her death (1568) Philip married Anne, daughter of Emperor Maximilian II (1570), of whose five children only one son, the future Philip III, survived childhood.

Philip's character has been interpreted in widely differing ways by both contemporaries and historians. To some he seemed the reactionary bigot of the Counter-Reformation who tried to crush the forces of Protestantism in France, England, and the Low Countries; to others the Catholic crusader who curbed the infidel and the heretic alike and protected religious orthodoxy. Two considerations dominated his life and reign, religious faith and concern for Spain's national interests. His dedication to the Spanish Church, to religious uniformity, and ecclesiastical reform, by the extension of the Inquisition and the suppression of the Moriscoes in Granada (1568–70), his personal piety and the confidence he placed in theologians and confessors, were fundamental aspects of his reign. Yet Philip was no tool of the papacy, and his relations with successive popes were far from cordial as he fought to preserve the rights of provincial councils. He defended Spanish interests as energetically over matters of episcopal jurisdiction and the Crown's prerogative as on political issues.

Among his political achievements were the protection of Spain's colonial interests, the revival of the navy and the curbing of Turkish sea power at Lepanto (1571), the unification of the Iberian peninsula through his conquest of the Portuguese kingdom (1580), the maintenance of a strong, disciplined army, and the establishment of an absolute monarchy, which controlled the network of government through councils, central and regional. His capacity for hard work and his professional attitude to the art of statecraft were to his credit. His defence of his inheritance in the Netherlands could be justified. However, the economic basis of Spain's greatness was flimsy. Although the collapse of the Antwerp market, the bankruptcy of the Crown, and the piracy of French Huguenots and English seamen were matters difficult to control, the supplies of American bullion were never invested productively in the Spanish economy. Inflation was aggravated, agriculture neglected, and industry discouraged by heavy taxation and entrenched privilege. On the other hand, the exploitation of the Americas enabled Philip to devote his reign to constant warfare, to the suppression of the Dutch revolt, the protection of the Mediterranean, and the Enterprise of England. These and the rash intervention in the French civil wars collectively drained the Crown's resources and left an impossible inheritance to Philip III (1598).

J. Lynch, *Spain under the Habsburgs, 1516–1598* (Oxford, 1965).   MKS

PHILIP III (1578–1621), King of Spain (*reg.* 1598–1621), only surviving son of Philip II of Spain and Anne of Austria. He inherited the problems of a declining power, an economy which had been distorted by continuous war and the influx of precious metals from America. To these Philip added further burdens. He took little interest in government, but relied heavily on a self-seeking favourite, a Valencian nobleman whom he created Duke of Lerma (1599). Lerma ruled as first minister until he was superseded (1618) by his own son, the Duke of Uceda, and in his hands the economy deteriorated, *eg*, through the manipulation of the coinage, the sale of office, the court's extravagance, and the expulsion of the Moriscoes (1609). Although Philip concluded peace with England (1604) and a truce with the United Provinces (1609), he allowed Spain to become involved in the Thirty Years War (1618) in return for the Habsburg fiefs in Alsace, and Spanish armies invaded the Palatinate as a prelude to the renewal of the Dutch War of Independence (1621). Philip died without having taken any steps to avert the national decline, which even Lerma recognized when he appointed a special reforming junta (1618).

PHILIP IV (1605–65), King of Spain (*reg.* 1621–65), whose reign marked the continued decline of Spanish commerce and industry, and Spain's involvement in widespread European campaigns which resulted in government bankruptcies (1647, 1653). In political terms, successive disasters undermined Spain's international reputation. Olivares' attempt to regularize taxation and establish a standing army of all the Iberian kingdoms by the Union of Arms collapsed in 1626, at a time when the renewed revolt in the Netherlands demanded an efficient fighting force. In 1635 France declared war on Spain, committing Philip to greater involvement in Germany. To the drain of the Thirty Years War was added the divisive factor of the Catalan revolt of 1640, which proved to be for 12 years a running sore. It was followed closely by the rebellion of the Portuguese (1640), who executed Philip's representative, Miguel de Vasconcellos, and proclaimed the Duke of Braganza as King John IV. The United Provinces were irretrievably lost by the peace of Westphalia (1648) and the conclusion of the war with France (1559) resulted in the cession of Roussillon and Artois. Although external peace left Philip free to send his armies into Portugal, they were defeated at Amexial (1663) and Villaviciosa (1665).

Philip's daughter by his first marriage, Maria Theresa, was married to his former enemy, Louis XIV, according to the terms of the peace of the Pyrenees (1659). His second wife and niece, Marianna of Austria, bore him another daughter, Margaret Theresa (1651), who became the wife of Emperor Leopold I, and two sons, one of whom survived to become his successor, Charles II. Philip's patronage of the arts was a redeeming feature of a long reign of unmitigated political disaster.

PHILIP V (1683–1746), King of Spain (*reg.* 1700–46), who, as Duke of Anjou, was nominated as Spanish king in the will of Charles II. He thus became the first of the Spanish Bourbon line. He was the grandson of Louis XIV and his acquisition of the Spanish throne was a factor in the War of the Spanish Succession. Philip himself was a man of little consequence and the policies of his reign were created and conducted by Alberoni, his minister, and Elizabeth Farnese, his Italian wife.

PHILIP, Landgrave of Hesse (1504–67), the son of William II who succeeded his father as a minor (1509), ruling

Hesse for 58 years. He contributed to the destruction of the peasants' cause in Thuringia (1525) and crushed the Anabaptist regime in Münster (1535). In 1526 Philip was converted to Lutheranism and henceforth became one of the militant leaders of the Protestant Reformation in Germany. With the Elector of Saxony he formed the Protestant League in support of Luther (1526), and arranged the disputation of Marburg (1529), through which he hoped to conciliate the Lutherans and Zwinglians, and where two years earlier he had founded a new university, the first under Protestant auspices. In 1530–1 he organized the Protestant League of Schmalkalden to contain the power of the Catholic princes and three years later flaunted Protestant strength by securing French help to restore Duke Ulrich to the state of Württemberg in defiance of Emperor Charles V (1534). In 1540, however, he made a serious political mistake when he bigamously married Margaret of Saale with the consent of Luther and Melanchthon. This step caused a scandal in Europe and forced him to submit to the emperor (1541). He rejoined the Schmalkalden League in 1544, only to be taken prisoner at the battle of Mühlberg (June 1547), and held in confinement by a triumphant Charles V until Feb. 1552. He was liberated through the good offices of his son-in-law, Maurice of Saxony. His support for Melanchthon's view of the Eucharist at the conference of Naumberg (1561) deepened the rift within the Lutheran fold and when he died (1567) German Lutheranism was being challenged by the growth of Calvinism.

PHILIP, ANDRÉ (1902–70), French academic, economist, and politician who was elected (1936) Socialist deputy for Marseilles. After voting against full constitutional powers for Pétain in 1940 he withdrew from public affairs for two years and then joined De Gaulle in London. As commissioner for the interior (1942–3) he co-ordinated the efforts of the various Resistance groups in France during the Second World War.

As minister of finances and national economy in Gouin's cabinet (1946) and minister of national economy in Ramadier's, he came to personify the policy of nationalization of certain sectors of the economy, and his replacement by Robert Schuman at the ministry of finances signified the end of the era of the controlled economy.

Philip was the most deeply committed 'European' within the French Socialist Party and was chairman (1950–64) of the Socialist movement for the United States of Europe.

The Algerian war intensified a chronic hostility between him and the secretary-general of the Section française de l'internationale ouvrière (SFIO), Guy Mollet. In 1958 Philip was expelled from the party for his public criticism of its policy. He joined the new Parti Socialiste Unitaire, but resigned in 1962. After 1962 he supplemented his earlier books on the problems of industrial relations and control of the economy with several on the problems and prospects of democratic socialism.

PHILIP, JOHN (1775–1851), Scottish missionary, sent to the Cape Colony by the London Missionary Society as resident director and superintendent of missions in 1819. His belief that the apparent failure of the LMS missions resulted from the unsatisfactory status of the Khoikhoi (Hottentot) and coloured labouring class led him into direct conflict with white settlers. Through his first-hand knowledge of the South African situation, he influenced legislation regulating relations between white masters and their Khoikhoi servants, who were taking the place of emancipated slaves. With the passage of ordinance 50 of 1828 the legal emancipation of the Khoikhoi peoples of the Cape Colony was secured.

Philip next turned his attention (1830) to the Eastern Cape, where he advocated a policy of direct British annexation in order to prevent the dispossession of Africans by whites, and in order to bring administration, a police system, and the rule of law to the frontier. He advocated the geographical separation of blacks and whites in the annexed territories.

In the first half of the 19th cent. Philip directed many of the early French, German, and American missionaries to their mission fields in South Africa and was the major representative of humanitarian paternalism in the Cape (1819–51).

PHILIPHAUGH, BATTLE OF (13 Sept. 1645), victory of Gen. David Leslie and his cavalry detachment of 4000 Covenanters over the royalist forces of Montrose, encamped at Philiphaugh in Selkirk county during the English Civil War. The royalists were taken by surprise. Montrose and a few survivors fled to the continent and the royal cause was crushed in Scotland.

PHILIPPI, BATTLES OF (42 BC), in the Roman civil wars caused the defeat of Julius Caesar's chief murderers, Brutus and Cassius, by Mark Antony and Octavian. In the first battle (23 Oct.) Antony broke Cassius' line and captured and plundered his camp. Cassius committed suicide in despair, although on his right wing Brutus routed Octavian's troops. In the second battle (16 Nov.) Brutus, forced to give battle, was routed and committed suicide the following day.

PHILIPPINE COMMONWEALTH, government of the Philippines from 15 Nov. 1935 to 4 July 1946, when the US granted the country independence, as provided for by the Tydings–McDuffie Act (1934). In 1935, in accordance with the act, the Filipino people elected delegates to a constitutional convention to prepare the framework of the Commonwealth government and that of its successor, the republic. The government of the republic of the Philippines is autonomous, but the Commonwealth was subject to US control: the Philippines as such remained US territory with a US high commissioner representing the US president, who could pronounce on any law, contract, or order of the Commonwealth government. Laws affecting currency, coinage, foreign trade, and immigration were also subject to the approval of the president. The US government, whose Supreme Court had authority to review important cases tried by the Philippine Supreme Court, including those involving the constitution, had direct supervision over the Commonwealth's foreign affairs. Philippine trade relations with the US were also governed by provisions of the Tydings–McDuffie Act (amended in 1939 by the Tydings–Koscialkowski Act). Under the leadership of President M. L. Quezon and Vice-President S. Osmena, the Commonwealth reorganized the government, and provisions were made for national defence, educational reforms, and a programme of social justice. Other policies included the development of a national language and the promotion of economic development. In 1941 war broke out between the US and Japan, forcing the Philippine government into exile in Washington, DC. It was not re-established in the Philippines until early in 1945, after Manila's liberation from the Japanese. In 1946 an independent Republican government replaced the Commonwealth.   RBS

PHILIPPINE ORGANIC ACT (1902) also referred to as the Cooper Act. It was a sequel to the Spooner Amendment to the Army Appropriation Act (1901), which had vested the US president with power to direct officials to govern the Philippines until otherwise provided for by the Congress. The military government of the Philippines, established in 1898, was thus replaced on 4 July 1901 by a civil government. Under the Spooner Amendment, the US president provided for a temporary administrative structure to undertake the affairs of the civil government. Among the government agencies created were the Philippine Commission, which functioned until it was replaced by the Senate, under the Jones Law of 1916, the offices of the civil governor and vicegovernor, and four executive departments. All these changes were affirmed in the Organic Act of 1902, which gave direct charge of Philippine affairs to the Bureau of Insular Affairs of the War Department. The Organic Act also stipulated the establishment of an elective Philippine Assembly. In 1902

President T. Roosevelt proclaimed the restoration of peace and order in the Philippines; a census was published in 1905, and two years later the elected members of the National Assembly met. The Organic Law also gave the people of the Philippines the right to be heard in the US Congress through Filipino resident commissioners, who enjoyed the same privileges, except that of voting, as members of the House of Representatives of the US Congress.   RBS

PHILIPPINE REPUBLIC, description applicable to three governments of the Philippines, each with its own constitution, established at different times. The first was the Philippine republic of 1899, otherwise called the 'Malolos republic', after the 1899 Malolos constitution, inaugurated at Barasoain church in Malolos, Bulacan, on 23 Jan. 1899. The second was the republic inaugurated on 14 Oct. 1943, the 'Japanese-sponsored republic', whose constitution was prepared and promulgated while Japanese forces occupied the Philippines. The third, the present (1970) Philippine republic, was formally inaugurated on 4 July 1946, when the Philippines gained their independence from the US, as provided for by the Tydings–McDuffie Act (1934). In 1970 provisions were made for the amendment of the present republic's constitution in Republic Act No. 6132, stipulating the election to, and the holding of, a constitutional convention to be convened in 1971.

PHILIPPINE ROYAL COMPANY (Real Compania de Filipinas), monopolistic trading company chartered on 10 March 1785 by a decree of Charles III of Spain (*reg.* 1759–88); the king himself was among its investors. The company was established towards the end of Gov. Basco y Vargas's administration in the Philippines (1778–87). It was intended to undertake projects similar to those Basco y Vargas had initiated after the British occupation of Manila, and was the logical sequence of a trading scheme started the year after the withdrawal of British forces from Manila. The plan, by which direct trade was to be opened by way of the Cape of Good Hope between Spain and the Philippines, involved the sending of a war vessel loaded with goods on the outgoing and incoming trips between Cadiz and Manila. The first ship, sent to Manila in 1765, met with hostility from the Manila–Acapulco galleon traders, whose opposition continued until the last ship to sail under the plan made the 14th and final voyage in 1785.

Philippine trade had hitherto been oriented towards Mexico, but now, in altered conditions of world trade, it was hoped that the country would be financially self-sufficient and cease depending on an annual subsidy from Mexico. A significant article of the royal charter obliged the company to invest 4 per cent of its profits in the development of Philippine agriculture and manufacturing. As renewed in 1805, the charter provided for additional capitalization and privileges. The company was abolished in the early 1830s, however, having failed to achieve its purpose, despite its privileges, because of poor management and factors beyond its control. One reason was that the company failed to establish factories in other Asian ports. In 1789 the government temporarily opened Manila to foreign traders dealing in items from Asia, to assure the company of supplies of Asian goods. This arrangement was made permanent in the company's charter of 1805. These moves unintentionally infringed the Spanish government's monopoly trade in the Philippines and paved the way towards the opening of other ports of the country during the 19th cent.

H. de la Costa, *Readings in Philippine History* (Manila, 1965).   JAS

PHILIPPISTS, Lutheran supporters of Philip Melanchthon who were centred on Wittenberg University and became involved in a bitter dispute with the Gnesiolutherans over the nature of salvation and the importance of free will, from the 1550s to the 1570s, which reached a climax at the Altenburg Disputation (1568).

PHILIPPSBURG, fortress town on the right bank of the Upper Rhine near Karlsrühe and within the ecclesiastical lands of the Bp of Speyer and the Holy Roman empire, upon which Bourbon–Habsburg rivalry turned in the 17th–18th cents. The fortifications, built in the last stage of the Thirty Years War (1640s), were coveted by French, Swedish, and Spanish armies as the key to control Alsace and southern Germany. Richelieu claimed Philippsburg for the French at the peace negotiations in Westphalia (1646–8) and its possession strengthened France's Rhine frontier. In 1676 Philippsburg was captured by an imperial army under Duke Charles V of Lorraine, and at the peace of Nymwegen (1678) Emperor Leopold I retained the fortress. It was retaken by the French at the beginning of the War of the League of Augsburg (1688) and surrendered again to Leopold by the treaty of Ryswick (1697), to be garrisoned by imperial forces in the War of the Spanish Succession. After being besieged by Marshal Berwick's army in the War of the Polish Succession, Philippsburg fell to the French (18 July 1734), despite Berwick's death and Prince Eugène's attempts to relieve the town. Its significance receded in the later 18th cent. after France received the reversion of Lorraine (1766).

PHILISTINES, one of the Sea Peoples who settled in Canaan in the 12th cent. BC at Ashdod, Gaza, Ashkelon, Gath, and Ekron. They soon adopted Canaanite language and culture and were in frequent conflict with the Israelites. They disappeared from history during the Assyrian and other invasions of the 8th and 7th cents.

PHILLIP, ARTHUR (1738–1814), British sailor and first governor of NSW, Australia, who arrived at Botany Bay in 1788. He chose Port Jackson as the site of a penal settlement for 756 convicts who formed part of his expedition. He held the settlement together under adverse conditions and made it largely self-supporting, and took pains to promote good relations with Aborigines.

PHILLIPS, WENDELL (1811–84), US lawyer and abolitionist who, through his marriage, became associated with the wing of the abolitionist movement led by William Lloyd Garrison. Phillips delivered a famous eulogy (1837) to the murdered abolitionist editor, Elijah Lovejoy. At first he supported Garrison's disunionism, arguing that slavery was an evil and any compromise with evil was wrong, but he rejected Garrison's pacifism, believing that the Fugitive Slave Law should be resisted by force. He was deeply religious and saw slavery as a sin. After secession, Phillips urged on Lincoln's administration the moral necessity of emancipation. In 1865 he argued—against Garrison—that the American Anti-slavery Society should remain in existence to campaign for equal civil and political rights for the freedman. With the ratification of the 15th Amendment (1870) Phillips felt his work was done and turned to new causes, particularly those embodied in the demands of labour unions.

PHILO (c. 20 BC–c. AD 50), Jewish sage of Alexandria, who was the most important figure among the hellenistic Jews of his age, and the author of numerous exegetical, philosophical, historical, and apologetic works. Nothing, however, is known of his life, except that in AD 39 he took part in a mission to Rome to plead the religious rights of the Jews. He was eclectic in his religious outlook, and his greatest achievement was the development of the allegorical interpretation of Scripture which enabled him, through discovering Greek philosophy in the Old Testament, to bridge the gulf between the Greek and Jewish worlds. His philosophical mysticism strongly influenced the Alexandrian school of Christian theology late in the 2nd cent. AD.

PHILOCRATES, PEACE OF (346 BC), treaty between Philip II of Macedon and Athens and the Second Athenian Confederacy. It was perhaps intended by Philip to lead to a permanent reconciliation, but was discredited, when he invaded Phocis.

PHILOPOEMEN (252–182 BC), Greek soldier and politician of the Achaean League, who became well known locally and was a friend of Philip V of Macedon. He was Achaean *strategos* eight times, first in 208, when he defeated Machanidas of Sparta at Mantinea. Thereafter he encouraged Achaean independence of Macedon. After entertaining Roman envoys (200), he hoped to persuade Achaea to join Rome; when Aristaenus succeeded in doing so (198) he was in Crete. On returning to Achaea (194), Philopoemen opposed Flamininus and other Romans, who were infringing Achaea's local independence, although on major international issues he supported Rome. In 192 Sparta joined Achaea, thus initiating years of unrest which involved him in constant disagreement with Rome. He died while trying to prevent Messene from seceding. Philopoemen was a vigorous advocate of Achaean independence, and his insistence on it aroused the hostility of Rome, whose reaction was to curb it.

PHILOSOPHES, name given to the leaders of the French Enlightenment, most of whom were professional writers and propagandists rather than philosophers in the usual sense. They were critical of the existing state of affairs in France and urged scientific and national investigation into society and government, but they had no plan of political action. Condorcet described them as 'a class of men less concerned with discovering truth than with propagating it'. Their great work was the *Encyclopédie*.

PHILOSOPHICAL TRANSACTIONS, journal of the Royal Society in England, initiated by the society's first secretary, Henry Oldenburg in 1665. The journal consisted of discourses read by fellows at the society's meetings and letters or communications on scientific subjects from scholars in England and on the continent, eg, Newton and Van Leuwenhoeck. Its success was immediate and it was translated into Latin for Dutch readers, and for French by the Académie des Sciences.

PHILOTHEUS OF PSKOV (d. *c.* 1547), Russian monk who formulated in his letters the doctrine of the Third Rome under Vassily III (*reg.* 1503–33).

PHIPPS, SIR ERIC CARE EDMUND (1875–1945), British diplomat, who entered the diplomatic service in 1899, serving at Constantinople, Rome, St Petersburg, and Madrid. He was in France during the First World War, and was British secretary to the Paris peace conference (1919). He was minister in Vienna (1928–33), and also during this period was briefly a British delegate to The Hague reparations conferences. He then became ambassador at Berlin (1933–7) and afterwards at Paris (1937–9). He was thus a close observer of the rise of Nazi Germany to European predominance, and of the failures of both British and French governments as they sought to appease the dictators and avoid war. His traditional friendship for France and hostility towards Germany made it easy for him to comprehend the danger of Nazism. In Paris he watched the corresponding dissolution of French will-power. He felt himself unable to continue as ambassador in the changed conditions of the Second World War and resigned.

PHIPPS, SIR WILLIAM (1651–95), English soldier and colonial governor, who commanded an expedition (1687) which recovered Spanish treasure off Haiti. He led an expedition against Port Royal (1690) and an unsuccessful expedition to capture Que. (1691). As the first royal governor of MA (1692–4) Phipps set up a special court in Salem to try women accused of being witches.

PHLIUS, small ancient Greek city-state in the northeastern Peloponnese, 24 kms south-west of Corinth, an ally of Sparta in the Peloponnesian League from *c.* 555 BC. It was besieged and subjected by King Agesilaus (*reg.* 381–379) during the period of Spartan imperialism after the King's Peace.

PHOCAEA, ancient Greek city in Asia Minor established by Ionians (*c.* 1000 BC). In the 7th cent. Phocaeans followed the lead of the Samian, Colaeus, into the western Mediterranean. The foundation of Massilia (*c.* 600) was followed by that of several settlements on the route to Tartessus in southern Spain. When Cyrus conquered Ionia (*c.* 545), there was mass emigration from Phocaea to Corsica, but after their defeat by Carthaginians and Etruscans at Alalia the emigrants moved to Elea in southern Italy. The insignificance of Phocaea itself after Cyrus' conquest is shown by the fact that only three Phocaean ships were engaged in the Ionian Revolt (499–494).

PHOCAS (*reg.* 602–10), Byzantine Emperor, whose reign was one of the most disastrous in the history of the Byzantine empire. A brutal barbarian soldier, he led a revolt against Emperor Maurice and, after Maurice had been murdered, himself usurped the throne. His reign was beset by insurrections and foreign invasions. The Eastern empire was in near anarchy when the governor of Byzantine Africa, Heraclius, managed to save it by taking his fleet to Constantinople and replacing Phocas.

PHOCION (d. 318 BC), Athenian politician and soldier who, despite his military reputation, advocated reconciliation with Macedon. He took the leading part in negotiations with Philip II (338), Alexander the Great (335), and Antipater (322). He was executed for treason by the restored democracy.

PHOCIS, district in ancient Greece round the upper Cephissus valley north of the Corinthian Gulf. It was at first a tribal state, but from the 5th cent. BC a federation of cities, which by the mid-4th cent. numbered 22. It was subjected by the Thessalians in the 6th cent., but freed itself by rebelling (*c.* 490). In 480 it was ravaged by the Persians. It was successively allied to Athens (457–447), to Sparta in the great Peloponnesian War and in campaigns against Thebes down to 371, and to the Thebans, before its defiance of Thebes over Delphi led to the Third Sacred War (356), in which the Phocians achieved considerable success, and then were crushed by Philip II of Macedon (346).

PHOENICE, PEACE OF (205 BC), treaty which ended the First Macedonian War between Rome and Philip V of Macedon, the Romans having apparently abandoned interest in Greece, though the addition of some independent Greek states to the treaty provided a possible excuse for later intervention.

PHOENICIA, ancient Greek name for that part of Canaan between Tell Suquas and Acre, a narrow strip between the Lebanese mountains and the Mediterranean. The origin of the Phoenicians is undecided, but they spoke a Semitic language and had a Canaanite culture. Their early history is obscure, but Egyptian reliefs indicate the existence of their cities before 2500 BC. The principal cities, usually built on rocky promontories or islands, each with its own ruler, were Byblos (Jubayl), Sidon (Saida), Tyre (Sûr), Berytos (Beirut), Acre, and Arvad (Aradus). In the 12th cent. invasions by the Sea Peoples disturbed Phoenician development. Sidon, Arvad, and Byblos were destroyed, but later recovered, and, with Acre and Tyre, prospered until Assyrian intervention (late 9th–7th cents) brought a period of gradual decline, from which, owing partly to the competition of Greek and Carthaginian trade and the domination of Phoenicia by other great powers, they never fully recovered.

The Phoenicians quarried and built with stone, were

famous shipbuilders and craftsmen, who were often employed in other countries, and they cultivated as much land as possible, growing cereals, vines, olives, figs, date-palms, and pomegranates. Their main prosperity came from their manufacturing industries and extensive trade, to which they had turned probably because of the scarcity of land and the difficulty of communications over the Lebanese mountains. The principal industries were textiles (often dyed purple), glass, metalware (which was especially profitable, since the ores were little valued by the countries which produced them), carved ivory, wood, and jewellery. These goods, as well as timber, olive oil, and wine, were exported and there was also a considerable re-export trade which included ebony, slaves, and Egyptian papyrus. The raw materials for Phoenician industries were mostly imported, *eg*, metals from Spain, Cyprus, Asia Minor, and Ethiopia, ivory and ebony from India and Africa, and precious stones from Syria and Arabia. Almost all trade was conducted by sea.

From the 12th cent. onwards colonies were founded, either as trading stations or as sources of raw materials. Among the most important were those in North Africa (*eg*, Carthage, Utica, Leptis Magna, Hadrumentum, Tangier, Mogador), in Sicily, Malta, Sardinia, Ibiza, Minorca, Spain, Cyprus, Rhodes, and Crete. It is impossible to determine, for the period after the foundation (*c.* 814) and rapid growth of Carthage, whether a colony was founded from Phoenicia itself, from Carthage, or as a joint venture, especially since in the later period Carthage was the leading Phoenician city. Artistically, the Phoenicians copied Egyptian, Aegean, and Mesopotamian styles and their greatest legacy to mankind was their alphabet. It seems likely that the alphabetic idea came from elsewhere, perhaps Ugarit, but from it the Phoenicians invented an alphabet, of 22 abstract consonantal signs, which was adopted in Syria-Palestine and Greece and was the basis of most important later alphabets.

S. Moscati, *The World of the Phoenicians* (London, 1968).
JKG

PHOENIX PARK MURDERS (1882) in Ireland, were committed by Irish extremists, known as the Invincibles, in Phoenix Park, Dublin. Their victims were the new Irish chief secretary, Lord Frederick Cavendish, and Thomas Burke, the under-secretary. The murderers were hanged after a severe Coercion Act had been passed. British public opinion, horrified by the wave of terrorism, wrongly associated Parnell with it, though the exposure of the Pigott forgeries (1887) completely vindicated him.

PHONGSAWADAN, historical chronicles of Thailand. Of the royal chronicles of the kingdom of Ayudhya, the most important are the short, early version known as the *Luang Prasoet* (1680), which is chronologically accurate but lacking in detail; the extended Phan Chanthanumat version (1795); and the British Museum or Somdet Phra Phonnarat version (1807), on which later editions by Prince Paramanuchit and King Rama IV are based. For the Bangkok period there are chronicles of the reigns of Rama I to Rama IV by Chaophraya Thiphakorawong, and of Rama II and Rama V by Prince Damrong Rajanubhab.

PHOTIOS (*c.* 820–91), Patriarch of Constantinople, and a champion of the Greek Orthodox Church against the Church of Rome. Pope Nicholas I, determined to enforce his own supremacy over the Eastern no less than over the Western Church, excommunicated Photios in 863. At a synod held in 867 Photios condemned the interference of Rome in the affairs of the Greek Church. As Patriarch Photios did much to extend the religious influence of Byzantium among the Slav peoples, strongly supporting the work of Cyril and Methodios, the apostles of the Slavs. He was the author of numerous letters, homilies, and theological treatises. The circle of scholars associated with him played an important part in preserving ancient Greek literary and scientific texts.

PHOUMI NOSAVAN (1920–   ), Laotian soldier and politician. After the elections in 1960 he briefly dominated a right-wing government, but he provoked a renewal of civil war which ended in his defeat and eventual exile to South Thailand in 1965.

PHRACHAO SUA (*reg.* 1703–9), King of Siam. Earlier, as Prince Dua, he dominated the reign of his father, King Phetracha (*reg.* 1688–1703). The excesses and cruelty of his conduct gave him the name by which he is remembered—'King Tiger'.

PHRAKHLANG (or BARCALONG), Thai politician and minister of the treasury and of foreign affairs in traditional Thailand. The office existed in Ayudhya by the 15th cent., but was under the *Mahatthai*. Foreign trade and relations became an important part of the minister's functions. In the 18th cent. it controlled the southern and coastal provinces and retained control of the latter to 1892. Its foreign trade responsibilities ended with the Bowring treaty (1855), and treasury and foreign affairs were later separated as departments.

PHRATRIES, ancient Greek 'brotherhoods', consisting of one *genos* (family) or more, who combined to form a *phyle* (tribe). Acceptance into the phratry, *ie*, proven blood-kinship with the group, remained a necessary requirement for citizenship in most Greek city-states.

PHUMIPHON ADUNYADET (1928–   ), King of Thailand (*reg.* 1946–   ), succeeded his elder brother, Ananda Mahidol. He was the ninth king of the Chakri dynasty and second son of Prince Mahidol. His heir-apparent (1970) is Crown Prince Wachiralongkon (1952).

PHYSICIANS, ROYAL COLLEGE OF, in England, professional body for doctors which received disciplinary and licensing powers over the physicians of London by a charter granted by Henry VIII (1518). Its powers were confirmed when it became the king's college of physicians by a charter granted by Charles II (1663), which was replaced by another in 1687. The college's importance declined in the 19th cent. as the state stepped into the field of public health, *eg*, through the formation of the General Medical Council (1858) to control education for doctors.

PHYSIOCRATS, group of French economic and political thinkers who, in the second half of the 18th cent., aimed to construct a logical system of economic laws. Their leader was François Quesnay (1694–1774), whose *Tableau économique* was published in 1758, and among them were Dupont de Nemours, Le Trosne, Mercier de la Rivière, Turgot, and the elder Mirabeau. They based their theories on an appeal to *a priori* principles of natural law and reason which would, if not interfered with, produce good results. These principles, similar to those acccepted by the Scot, Adam Smith, were also the starting-point for the British school of classical economists. The Physiocrats' theories led them to advocate specific reforms, especially the abolition of the internal barriers, of feudal origin, which prevented the free circulation of goods, particularly of agricultural produce, and the imposition of an *impôt unique*. They realized, as Petty, Cantillon, and Sir James Stewart had done, that the increase of wealth was not entirely due to trade, as the mercantilists had thought. They believed that only those industries which added to the total volume of raw material, especially agriculture and mining, were truly productive, because they alone created a *produit net*, a real surplus over and above the cost of labour and interest on capital. This theory was rejected by Adam Smith and has never been generally accepted.   BK

PI Y MARGALL, FRANCISCO (1824–1901), Spanish federalist politician and second president of the Spanish republic (1873–4). He saw federalism as the only adequate safeguard for individual liberty within the state, a belief which won mass provincial support for the republicans and sympathy from the anarchists. But instead of imposing federalism by decree, he decided to wait for the Constituent Cortes to declare its support for a federal republic, thus causing bitter disappointment. The delay provoked provincial disputes and the collapse of army discipline. As a result, Pi's policy was discredited and he resigned.

PIACENZA, north Italian city on the banks of the Po river, in the Middle Ages an imperial fief disputed between Milan and the papacy. In 1545 it was given to Pier Luigi Farnese, Pope Paul III's natural son, and from that time its history was closely linked with that of the duchy of Parma. It was held by the Farnese family until 1731, then passed to the Spanish Bourbons (1731–8), the Austrian Habsburgs (1738–1748), and back to the Spanish Bourbons (1748–1801). With Parma it became part of Napoleonic France (1801–14) and from 1815 remained under strong Austrian influence until its incorporation into the kingdom of Piedmont-Savoy (1859) and Italy (1870).

PIANKHY (*reg.* 751–716 BC), Kushite King. On a granite stele at Jepel Barkal Piankhy inscribed the record of his conquest of Egypt, showing Kush to be a powerful state. His father, Kashta, initiated this conquest, and Piankhy and his successors extended their dominion over the whole country, becoming the XXVth dynasty of Egypt. Pankhy was a great lover of horses and probably it was he who instituted the custom of burying favourite horses in the royal cemetery at Kurru.

PIANO DI CARPINI, GIOVANNI DI (d. 1252), archbishop of Antivari and head of the first papal mission to the Mongols, whose empire had extended over much of northern and central Asia in the first half of 13th cent. He was sent by Pope Innocent IV to the Mongol Khan Kuyuk at Karakorum (1245–7), and wrote a well-informed *History of the Mongols*.

PIARISTS (Patres Piarum Scholarum), Catholic educational order of the Counter-Reformation started by Joseph Calasanctius in Rome (1597), who opened the first free school in Europe for poor children. The Piarists became an order of clerks regular (1621), devoted to the cause of youth, and were active rivals of the Jesuits in Italy, Spain, and Germany in the 17th–18th cents.

PIAST DYNASTY, native Polish dynasty which created the unified Polish state. It is traceable from the 9th cent. in its homeland of Great Poland (*Wielkopolska*), from which it gradually subdued the other Polish tribes. It consolidated its authority by introducing western Christianity in 966 under Mieszko I. His son, Boleslaw the Mighty, proclaimed himself king in 1024. Their descendants were the principal rulers of Poland until the main line died out in 1370.

PIAVE, BATTLE OF THE (June 1918), near Caporetto, Italy. In Oct. 1917 during the First World War the Austrians, with powerful German reinforcements, launched an offensive in Italy. The Italians were defeated at Caporetto and driven in confusion back to the Piave river, behind which they were reorganized, and stiffened with British and French troops and aircraft. Meanwhile the German force was transferred to the Western Front. In June 1918 the Austrians attempted to renew the offensive alone, but were heavily defeated by the Italians, losing about 150,000 men. In a military sense the battle of the Piave was not decisive, though it laid the foundations for the Italian victory of Vittorio Veneto in Oct, but, combined with the defeats suffered by the Central Powers elsewhere, it undermined the prestige of the Habsburg dynasty, and thus began the dissolution of the Austrian empire.

PICCOLOMINI, OTTAVIO (1598–1656), imperial soldier and diplomat, who fought throughout the Thirty Years War and ended it as a commander-in-chief. After a short period in Spanish service he joined Wallenstein as the commander of his bodyguard and distinguished himself at Lützen and Nördlingen. In 1634 he was made a field marshal, possibly as an indirect reward for his share in Wallenstein's assassination and became a member of the imperial privy council (1639–56). After the war he led the imperial negotiators at Nuremberg (1649–50).

PICHINCHA, BATTLE OF (24 May 1822), fought in Ecuador between insurgent forces led by Antonio José de Sucre and royalist Spanish forces outside Quito. Sucre's army won, and Ecuador was freed from Spanish domination.

PICKETT'S CHARGE in US, frontal assault by 15,000 Confederate troops, led by Gen. George E. Pickett, on the centre of the Union line at the battle of Gettysburg (3 July 1863) during the American Civil War. The charge was beaten back from the Federal trenches with Confederate losses of 6000 men.

PICO (DELLA MIRANDOLA), GIOVANNI (1463–94), Italian humanist, who was a member of a princely Lombard family, the rulers of Carpi. He lived chiefly in Florence, where he was much appreciated by Lorenzo de' Medici, and was a friend of the leading humanists. Coming under the influence of one of them, Ficino, the editor of Plato, and neo-platonists, Pico tried to combine into a unified system Platonic, Hebrew, and Christian doctrines. He argued that they represented different aspects of the same fundamental truths. When he sent a statement of these propositions to the pope he was cited for heresy, but died before action could be taken against him.

PICTON, SIR THOMAS (1758–1815), British soldier who served in the French Wars, participating in the capture of St Lucia (1796) and Trinidad (1797). He was appointed commander of the captured island of Trinidad and became its civilian governor in 1801. Later his governorship gave way to a commission of three (including himself). His replacement had been due to rumours of his permitting mild torture under Spanish law then existing in the island. In subsequent trials in England no judgment was delivered, the case being regarded in the same light as the trial of Warren Hastings 20 years earlier: a British official had moral responsibilities towards trustee peoples. Both the Hastings and Picton trials contributed to a new concept of imperial obligation.

Picton returned to active service in the Walcheren campaign (1809), fighting later in the Peninsular War. He was wounded at Quatre Bras (1815), but kept his injuries a secret and a few days later fell fighting at Waterloo.

PICTS, peoples who dominated eastern and northern Scotland in the early Middle Ages. They were among the most persistent attackers of late Roman Britain, though this was partly due to the pressure on the Picts of the Scots, who were moving from Ireland into western Scotland. No native Pictish sources have survived and nothing is known in detail of the Pictish language, so that their history is difficult to reconstruct. They were converted to Christianity in the 6th cent., chiefly by St Columba, the centre of whose activities was on the island of Iona. Pictland was divided into seven kingdoms and apparently ruled over by a high-king. The Picts were finally conquered in the 830s by Kenneth Mac Alpin, the ruler of the Scottish Dalriada, who had some claims by descent to the Pictish kingship. The Picts have left behind some fine but enigmatic artistic remains. Early Pictish ornamented stones are distinguished by the Pictish 'symbols' incised upon them, which are of uncertain significance. In the 8th and early 9th cents the Picts produced some remarkably fine cross slabs with naturalistic carvings of human figures and horses.

PIERCE, FRANKLIN (1804–69), US politician and 14th president of the US. He was elected to the NH legislature in 1829 and was speaker (1831–2). He served in the House of Representatives (1833–7) and the Senate (1837–42) as a Jacksonian Democrat. After taking part in the Mexican War, he led Democratic support in NH for the 1850 Compromise, and was the Democratic candidate for president in 1852. As president, he embarked on a policy of territorial acquisition, particularly with regard to Cuba, but news of his intentions was leaked prematurely in the Ostend Manifesto, and the project failed. In 1853 he carried through the Gadsden Purchase and by the Dallas–Clarendon Convention (signed 1856, but not ratified) persuaded Britain to withdraw from Central America, except for Honduras. Pierce became embroiled in a political storm after the Kansas–Nebraska Act (1854) and his willingness to support a pro-slave government for KS alienated Northern Democrats. During the American Civil War he was a violent critic of President Lincoln. He died in political obscurity.

PIERO DELLA FRANCESCA (*c.* 1410–92), Italian painter who combined a mastery of perspective and a remarkable capacity for spatial feeling with the ability to integrate a composition by his use of colour. His most notable works include the frescoes of the church of San Francesco in Arezzo (1452–9).

PIÉROLA, NICOLÁS DE (1839–1913), Peruvian businessman and journalist who was twice president of Peru. He founded the newspaper *El Tiempo* (1864) to foster Roman Catholicism and material progress. He encouraged the Dreyfus Contract (1869), a guano arrangement. He was in office at the time of the defeat of Peru by Chile (1883), and as president, for a second term (1894–8), he implemented new taxes and reorganized the army.

PIETISM, in Germany, protestant evangelical movement associated with the Lutheran, Philipp Jakob Spener (1635–1705). It had considerable influence and its principles were expounded at Halle University. It remained of some significance in Germany, but conflicted with orthodox Lutheranism. In England emphasis on personal devotion, as evidenced by bible-reading, prayer, and philanthropy, had some effect on Methodism and on the evangelical movement in the Church of England.

PIJADE, MOŠA (1890–1957), Yugoslav communist politician, who spent much of the period between the two World Wars in prison for political offences. In prison he met and influenced Tito. Pijade participated in the Partisan movement and after the Second World War joined the party leadership. At the height of the quarrel with the Soviet Union he wrote a pamphlet explaining the Yugoslav position. When Djilas was expelled from the leadership for criticizing communist society, Pijade bitterly attacked him.

PIKES PEAK, 14,110-foot (4310 metres) mountain in the Colorado Rockies in the US, located 60 miles (96 kms) south of Denver and 10 miles (16 kms) west of Colorado Springs. It was discovered by Zebulon Pike (1806) and first climbed by Edwin James and his party (14 July 1820). It became historically significant as a landmark for early trappers and traders. Discovery of placer gold in the upper tributaries of the South Platte (July 1858) brought a flood of prospectors to the region. Exaggerated reports of the goldfields' potentialities circulated widely in Missouri valley towns during the winter of 1858–9, and helped to generate the great gold-rush of 1859, whose slogan was 'Pikes Peak or Bust'. Only half of the 100,000 people who set out ever reached the mountains, and only 25,000 stayed on to establish Colorado Territory (Jan. 1861), despite the fact that after initial disappointments rich veins of gold were found in the vicinity.

PILAR, MARCELO DEL (1850–96), Filipino lawyer and political writer who was one of the leading spokesmen of the reformist group among his country's intellectuals in the propaganda movement of the late 19th cent. His tracts exposed the ills of his country and satirized the abuses of the friars. As part of his propaganda activities, he founded the *Diariong Tagalog* in 1882. In 1888 Del Pilar went to Spain, hoping to mitigate Spanish colonial abuses and to be better able to work for reforms through the Spanish Cortes. While in Barcelona he became editor of *La Solidaridad* (1889). Through this journal he sought to achieve reforms rather than inspire revolution, and assimilation to, rather than separation from, Spain. In recognition of his significance in the Philippines' campaign for independence, his remains were brought back to the Philippines.

PILBARA, large district in north-western Australia, associated with gold discoveries in the last part of the 19th cent., and with the exploitation in the 1960s of immense iron ore deposits.

PILGRIM FATHERS, small band of English religious Separatists from Scrooby, Notts, who, having severed all connection with the Church of England, fled to Holland (1608). Becoming dissatisfied with life there, they obtained a grant from the Virginia Co., and, financed by a group of London merchants, embarked from Plymouth (Sept. 1620) in the *Mayflower*, intending to found a colony in the New World. On the voyage a covenant was made uniting the members in a political and religious society. They arrived in Provincetown harbour (11 Nov. 1620), drew up the Mayflower Compact, and elected John Carver as their first governor. Abandoning their Virginia patent, they chose Plymouth harbour for a landing. Friendly Indians taught them how to fish and plant corn, but during the first winter 44 colonists died. In 1621 William Bradford became governor and in Nov. of that year the ship *Fortune* arrived, bringing supplies, more colonists, and a charter legalizing the colony. After ten years it had a population of 300 and in 1691 the colony joined the larger Massachusetts Bay colony.

The name 'pilgrim fathers' was coined by the American, Daniel Webster, in 1820.

PILGRIMAGE OF GRACE (1536–7) in England, spontaneous and conservative rising of the northern English counties, the most serious revolt in Tudor England, against the Reformation and spoliation of the monasteries. In the autumn of 1536 a rising occurred in Louth in Lincs, and soon spread across the Humber; by the end of Oct. 30,000 men had assembled at Pontefract. The rising followed interference by the Crown in local affairs and the destruction of the smaller monasteries in 1536. The rebels demanded that the old privileges of the Church be revived, that the suppressed monasteries be restored, that the king demand no taxes in time of peace, and that Abp Cranmer, Thomas Cromwell, and other ministers be surrendered to the rebels or banished. The leader of the main revolt in Yorkshire, Robert Aske, who gave the whole rising cohesion, proclaimed that he was not acting against the king, but against those who had undermined both Church and commonwealth.

The key to the military situation was Pontefract castle, which was held by Thomas, Lord Darcy, a discarded servant of the Crown. On 21 Oct., cut off from the royal forces by a rising in the town, Darcy surrendered and became a leader of the pilgrimage.

As the royal army, with the vanguard under the Earl of Shrewsbury, moved northwards, Aske intimated that he was prepared to negotiate. The Duke of Norfolk, acting for the king, met the leaders at Doncaster and agreed to a truce. At the end of Nov. the Pilgrims drew up a longer list of complaints for Norfolk's perusal. On 6 Dec. Norfolk, in order to gain time, promised on his own initiative a pardon for the rebels, the calling of a parliament, and the restoration of the monasteries. Aske and most of the leaders were content with this offer, and persuaded their followers to disperse.

In Jan. 1537 there was a further small rising, led by Sir

Francis Bigod, who had detected flaws in the royal pardon. He failed to win support, and Aske and the other leaders even helped the Crown to suppress the rising. This revolt gave Henry VIII the pretext he had been waiting for, and with forces now strong enough to deal with the dispersed rebels he moved against them. Aske and Darcy, together with about 200 others, were executed.

Many of the landowners in the revolt, including Aske, were servants of the Percy family, and the Percies themselves vigorously encouraged them. This was because Henry VIII had virtually disinherited the family by making himself heir to the Percy lands of the childless Earl of Northumberland. But the pilgrimage was more than an aristocratic conspiracy, for its roots spread deep into the soil of social discontent. Motives differed from area to area, but there was a general resentment against the financial exigences of the Crown and the religious policy of the government. Aske kept the religious issues to the fore, but the pilgrimage also represented the inarticulate fears of the population about the government's encroachment on traditional ways of life. The revolt failed because southern magnates, such as Norfolk and Shrewsbury, decided to support the king, and because Aske put his trust too readily in the king.

A. G. Dickens, *The English Reformation* (London, 1964).
A. Fletcher, *Tudor Rebellions* (London, 1968).   cj

PILGRIMAGES. The practice of pilgrimage originally arose from a devotion to the memory of Jesus, the early Christians undertaking journeys to Bethlehem and Jerusalem. The practice was accepted by the Church in the 3rd–4th cents and the medieval Church continued it. Journeys were undertaken in honour of God, for purposes of prayer, or in quest of assistance—especially in search of health. At a later date, pilgrimages from northern European countries were undertaken with the intention of securing relics of which Palestine and Rome were believed to have abundant supplies. The medieval mind also associated pilgrimage with the forgiveness of sins, and the expiatory pilgrimage as an act of obedience, even as an expiation for serious crimes such as murder, became commonplace. The Church also developed a system of indulgences, and pilgrimages were increasingly undertaken to a particular church or chapel in order to obtain the indulgence vested in that particular shrine, on which pious gifts were bestowed in return. Consequently, the number of pilgrimages was continually on the increase in the medieval world. The most popular places for voluntary and involuntary pilgrimages were, of course, Palestine and Rome, though the shrine of Santiago di Compostella in Spain became so popular in the 12th cent. that it almost rivalled them both. Pilgrimages are essentially associated with the Middle Ages, though they occasionally occurred in later centuries.

PILLNITZ DECLARATION (27 Aug. 1791), issued jointly by the Emperor Leopold II and Frederick William II of Prussia. It invited the European monarchs to join them in helping Louis XVI to re-establish monarchical government in France. The declaration assumed that the restoration of order in France was the concern of all the European rulers, but Leopold regarded it as a piece of calculated bluff and had few illusions about the possibility of implementing it. However, the presence at Pillnitz of Louis XVI's younger brother, the Comte d'Artois, and the former royal minister, Calonne, encouraged both the émigrés and the French nation to believe that it heralded military intervention by Austria and Prussia to suppress the Revolution. The declaration, therefore, increased tension both between France and her neighbours, and also within the new Legislative Assembly, where more extreme elements pushed France towards defensive hostilities.

PILSUDSKI, JÓZEF (1867–1935), Polish revolutionary politician and leader. He inherited the traditions of the 19th-cent.

Polish insurrectionists and became active in the Polish Socialist Party. During the Russo-Japanese War he tried unsuccessfully to persuade the Japanese to sponsor a rising in Poland, and in the 1905 revolution led a series of terrorist attacks on Russian government outposts. These failed to bring about his hoped-for-national uprising and Pilsudski became convinced of the need to create a military force that would exercise some influence in the war which he expected between Russia and the Central Powers. By 1914 he had established in Austrian Poland a legionary movement which had nearly 7000 members.

On the outbreak of the First World War he again tried unsuccessfully to foment a national uprising in Russian Poland. Its failure compelled him to co-operate with the Austrian authorities, to whom he remained true until the middle of 1916. He then began to turn towards the Germans, who established a rump Polish state in Nov. 1916. Pilsudski realized, however, that the Germans were interested only in a satellite Poland and his refusal to co-operate with them led to his arrest (July 1917). He returned to Poland in Nov. 1918 and soon assumed a dominant role in the new country, becoming head of state and supreme commander of the army. But his attempt to exploit the weakness of Russia, following the attempt to dislodge Byelorussia and the Ukraine from the Soviet Union, ended in near disaster. Internally, his opponents, the National Democrats, emerged as the dominant political force and were able, constitutionally, to limit the powers of the president drastically. As a result, Pilsudski refused to stand for the office of president and withdrew from public life (1923–6).

He returned to power in May 1926 as the result of a three-day civil war. Among the dictatorships of the 1920s his regime proved an exception. His interests lay in the army and foreign affairs and he had little concern for the day-to-day business of politics, so that it was only with difficulty that he had been persuaded to move against the constitution. Thus he attempted to operate a semi-constitutional 'guided democracy', in which parliament retained a fairly important position. The attempt failed and he clashed more and more often with politicians of the centre and left. Eventually, many of the opposition leaders were arrested (Sept.–Oct. 1930). After this, the regime became much more autocratic, though still not totalitarian. By 1926 Pilsudski was a sick man and was forced to delegate a good deal of his authority, particularly after 1930, to subordinates, who lacked his honesty, ability, and discretion. His continued belief that Russia was still the main enemy of Polish independence was his principal reason for underestimating the aggressive potential of Nazi Germany, which was to prove so disastrous a feature of Polish foreign policy in the 1930s.

H. Roos, *A History of Modern Poland* (London, 1966).
J. Rothschild, *Pilsudski's coup d'état* (New York, 1960). ABP

PIMA INDIANS, American tribes living in the Salt and Gila river valleys in AZ, first encountered by the Spanish (1694). They were friendly to the whites, and became a US responsibility under the terms of the Gadsden Purchase (1853). They still (1970) live on reservations established on their traditional lands.

PIN KLAO (*reg.* 1851–65), 'Second King' of Siam, who, in principle, reigned as the co-equal of his elder brother, King Rama IV, and not as a mere *uparaja*. He was the son of King Rama II.

PINAY, ANTOINE (1891–   ), French politician, who was elected (1936) to the chamber of deputies as a Radical Independent, and in 1938 as a senator of the Loire. After voting full powers to Pétain, Pinay joined the national council in 1941. Although compromised by his association with the government, his parliamentary ineligibility was cancelled in 1945 because of his services to the Resistance, and in 1946 he was elected Independent Republican deputy of the Loire.

In 1952 he was elected *président du conseil*. A world-wide drop in prices and Pinay's willingness to sacrifice long-term investment credits helped him to check the chronic inflation of the Fourth Republic and he became one of the most popular leaders of modern France.

During the 1950s Pinay held several cabinet posts, and was one of the first notables of the Fourth Republic to support De Gaulle in 1958. He was minister of finance in De Gaulle's cabinet, and in Michel Debré's, but resigned in 1960 over De Gaulle's European policy. Afterwards he interested himself in regional economic development in the Rhône Alpes *département*.

PINCKNEY, CHARLES COTESWORTH (1746–1825), American lawyer, soldier, and politician, who was educated in England and returned to America in 1769, where he served in the SC legislature and the Revolutionary army. He was a prominent member of the Federal Convention of 1787 and in 1796 went as US minister to France, only to be denied official recognition by the Directory. He was one of the three US commissioners to France during the XYZ affair (1797), and commanded (1798–1800) all US military forces in the South. He was the Federalist nominee for vice-president (1800) and president (1804, 1808).

PINCKNEY, CHARLES (1757–1824), American lawyer, diplomat, and politician, who fought in the Revolutionary War, was congressman from SC (1784–7), and a prominent member of the Philadelphia Convention (1787). He was three times governor of SC (1789–92, 1797–9, 1807–9), and also served in the US Senate (1799–1801), and was US minister to Spain (1801–5), where he won Spanish approval of the Louisiana Purchase, but failed to secure the Floridas. As a US congressman (1819–21) he was a leading opponent of the Missouri Compromise.

PINCKNEY, THOMAS (1750–1828), American soldier and diplomat who was educated in England, called to the English bar (1774) and returned to America to serve in the American War of Independence. He was governor of SC (1787–9), US minister to Britain (1792–5), and special envoy to Spain (1794–5). He negotiated the valuable treaty of San Lorenzo (Pinckney's treaty) (1795). He was a Federalist congressman from SC (1797–1801) and a major-general in the war of 1812.

PINCKNEY'S TREATY (1795), or treaty of San Lorenzo, resolved longstanding differences between the US and Spain over navigation of the Mississippi and the definition of the western and southern boundaries of the US. Spain had long been fearful of the threat to her sovereignty (the earlier Jay–Gardoqui negotiations having come to nothing) in New Spain should the US be granted navigation rights or the acquisition of territory. In 1795, however, Spain's separate treaty with France in July, and the ratification of Jay's treaty with Britain in Aug., made an Anglo-American alliance hostile to Spain a distinct possibility. Spain therefore gave in to all the American demands in a treaty signed for the US by Thomas Pinckney on 27 Oct. The US was granted navigation rights on the Mississippi, and the right of deposit at New Orleans free of duty for three years. The 31st parallel was recognized as the northern boundary of Spanish Florida, Spain agreed to restrain the Indians from border raids, and a commission was set up to adjudicate claims arising out of Spanish seizure of neutral American vessels.

PINDAR (518–438 BC), Greek choral lyric poet, noted especially for his *epinician* odes, of which 45 survive, written chiefly in celebration of victories at the great pan-hellenic athletic festivals. He was a Boeotian aristocrat and wrote mainly for aristocratic patrons, *eg*, the Aleuadae of Thessalian Larisa, and for 'tyrants' with aristocratic background, *eg*, Hiero I of Syracuse, whom he visited in 476. The swift brilliance of his poetry enshrines the mores of the aristocratic age which was eclipsed by Athenian democracy and the rationalist revolution of the later 5th cent.

PINDARIS, THE, bands of Indian robbers, united solely by the hope of plunder, who thrived in the anarchy that followed the decline of the Mughal empire. Their depredations increased under the British policy of non-intervention and disregard of border anarchy. In well-organized bands the Pindaris attached themselves to the Maratha armies, their strategic base being the valley of the Narbada. At first they confined their activities to Rajputana, but, urged on by the Marathas, they began to raid British territory. Lord Hastings, realizing it was essential to extirpate them, eventually persuaded Sindhia to co-operate in doing so, and the Pindaris were wiped out by British forces in 1818.

PINEAU, CHRISTIAN (1904–), French economist and politician. During the Second World War he was one of the most active socialist members of the Resistance and was instrumental in creating the clandestine newspaper *Liberation* and the resistance movement, Liberation-Nord. In 1943 he was arrested and deported to Buchenwald prison camp in Germany. After the war he held the unpopular post of minister of food and was the *rapporteur* for the law on the nationalization of the banks. He was several times minister of public works and was responsible for foreign affairs at the time of the Suez crisis (1956), when he supported military intervention. By negotiating with the Israelis, he ensured that France and Britain could invade Egypt on the most advantageous military terms. However, these involved the two countries in a disastrous political situation which Pineau did his best to rectify at the United Nations. Unlike most other ministers, he became increasingly enthusiastic about the invasion as its chances of success waned.

After 1958 he was a member of the *comité directeur* of the Socialist Party and one of De Gaulle's bitterest opponents.

PINKERTON, ALLAN (1819–84), US law enforcement officer and founder of the Pinkerton Detective Agency. He was born in Scotland, went to Canada (1842), and thence to the US, where he became a deputy sheriff in Kane and Cook Counties, ILL. He was appointed first detective of the Chicago police force, uncovered a plot to assassinate the president-elect, Abraham Lincoln (Feb. 1861), and organized an intelligence service for the Union army (1861–2). Thereafter he engaged in general detective work and was particularly active in industrial disputes in the 1870s and 1880s.

PINKIE, BATTLE OF (10 Sept. 1547), was fought near Musselburgh, Edinburgh. The English, under Protector Somerset, defeated a Scots army twice its size. The battle was fought as part of the English 'rough wooing' policy of securing Mary Queen of Scots as a bride for Edward VI. As such, it failed in its objective, the Scots queen being sent for safety to France (1548), where she remained until 1560.

PINKNEY, WILLIAM (1764–1822), American lawyer and diplomat, who became one of the leading advocates of his day. He served on several diplomatic missions to Britain (1796–1811), was US attorney-general (1811–14), and minister to Russia (1816–18). He represented MD in the US House of Representatives (1815–16), and the Senate (1819–22), where he championed the cause of the slave states in the debates on the Missouri Compromise. As an advocate his greatest achievements were in *McCulloch v. Maryland* (1818–19) and *Cohens v. Virginia* (1821) before the Supreme Court.

PINTURICCHIO (BERNARDINO DI BETTO) (*c.* 1454–1513), Perugian painter, who worked with Perugino on the Sistine Chapel at the Vatican (*c.* 1471–3). He became the favourite artist of Pope Alexander VI, for whom he decorated the Borgia apartments in the Vatican. Much of his work is to be found in churches and palaces of Rome.

PINYA, near Ava, capital of the chiefs of Myinsaing and Pinya from 1312 to 1364.

PINZÓN, MARTÍN ALONSO (c. 1440–93), Spanish sailor and master of the *Pinta* on Columbus's first voyage (1492). After Hispaniola was sighted, Pinzón separated from the group and led a private expedition which discovered gold deposits on the island.

PINZÓN, VICENTE YÁNEZ (c. 1460–1524), Spanish sailor and master of the *Nina* on Columbus's first voyage (1492). In 1499, anticipating Cabral by a few months, Pinzón coasted part of northern Brazil and Guiana, territory of which he was later made governor, though the appointment proved purely nominal.

PIOTRKOW, DIET OF (1562), abortive meeting of the Polish Diet, following Kettler's surrender of Livonia to Poland–Lithuania (1561), at which, in order to defend itself from Russia, the Livonian port of Riga was to swear allegiance to Sigismund-Augustus of Poland in return for the recognition of its privileges. The Diet was postponed and it was only after the conclusion of the Livonian War (Jan. 1582) that Riga's incorporation into Poland was recognized.

PIPIOLOS (in Spanish, 'small fry' or 'greenhorns'), derisive nickname for the Liberals in Chile who fought the conservatives or *pelucones* ('bigwigs'), in the years following independence from Spain.

PIRACY IN LATIN AMERICA, particularly prevalent in Spanish America in the 16th–17th cents as Spain's revenues in American silver rose and as her naval power steadily decreased. As the attacks of her English, Dutch, and French enemies multiplied, Spain resorted to a convoy system of merchant vessels escorted by warships to bring her revenues home and to supply her colonies. The convoy system rarely failed, but after *c.* 1620 Spanish power was insufficient to keep her rivals from seizing Jamaica, part of Hispaniola, and the Lesser Antilles. These became bases from which such men as Morgan successfully preyed on Spanish shipping. Increasingly, however, the piratical agents of the various European powers began to attack each other as much as they did the Spanish, and by *c.* 1700 piracy was forbidden and to a large extent effectively suppressed.

PIRELLI FAMILY, in Italy, were responsible for the creation and development of Italy's leading rubber company, which in 1970 provided 12 per cent of the European car market with tyres. Giovanni Battista (1848–1932), who had served with Garibaldi, started the Milan rubber factory in 1872, which later produced insulated cabling and linoleum. Piero (1881–1956), Alberto (1882–), and Leopoldo (1925–) later became presidents of the company, and Italian senators. Alberto, who dominated *Confindustria*, co-operated guardedly with Mussolini, and helped to renegotiate US debts (1925), but declined ministerial appointments until 1938, and prevented excessive government interference in industry. During the Second World War Pirelli officials financed Partito d'Azione partisans (1943–5), and Pirelli factory workers jeopardized the fascist war effort by striking. Leopoldo was (1970) a progressive reformer of *Confindustria*.

PIRI RE'IS (*fl.* 16th cent.), Ottoman sailor who, after service in the Mediterranean, was appointed to be Qapudan (admiral) at Suez in the Red Sea. He led (1551) an Ottoman squadron from Suez to the Persian Gulf, raided the Portuguese at Muscat, failed in an assault on their base at Hormuz, and then sought refuge at Basra, which had been under Ottoman control since 1546–47. On his return to Egypt with a mere remnant of his squadron, Piri Re'is was executed. He produced a *mappa mundi* which incorporates material drawn, it would seem, from a lost map by Columbus illustrating his discoveries in the New World.

PIRPUR REPORT (1938) in India, report by a Muslim League committee headed by the Raja of Pirpur, which alleged that the Congress governments set up in 1937 were guilty of systematic discrimination against Muslim minorities in matters of language, education, cultural rights, and political and legal treatment. The report was an important stage in the league's efforts to become the sole representative of the Muslim community and, at the same time, to emphasize Congress's efforts towards 'Muslim mass contact'.

PISA, principal harbour of medieval Tuscany, near the mouth of its chief river, the Arno. Early in the 11th cent. Pisa became one of the leading Italian maritime cities. A Pisan expedition played a crucial part in assuring the capture of Jerusalem by the First Crusade in 1099. Thereafter the Pisans rivalled the men of Genoa and Venice as the greatest sailors and richest merchants of the Mediterranean. The power of Pisa was broken by Genoa in 1284, when the city was captured, and in 1406 it passed permanently under the rule of Florence. The greatest glory of Pisa is its cathedral and the buildings grouped around it, including the famous leaning tower, built when Pisa was at the height of its wealth in the 12th and 13th cents. They form one of the finest assemblages of romanesque buildings in Italy. Important Roman remains found at Pisa influenced the school of 13th-cent. Italian sculptors assembled around Niccolo and Giovanni Pisano, and later Tino di Camaino. The penetration of classical themes and models into Florence in the late 14th and 15th cents was influenced by familiarity with Pisa's antique remains and the works of medieval Pisan artists.

PISA, COUNCIL OF (1511–12), called by Louis XII of France to reform the Catholic Church. Ostensibly it revived the classic doctrine that general councils were superior to the pope, but in practice used this as a gambit against the papacy in the Italian Wars.

Having formed the League of Cambrai (1508) as an instrument of papal aggression against Venice, Pope Julius II was so alarmed by the successes of his French ally that he began diplomatic manœuvres that led eventually to the creation of the Holy League (1511), whose aim was to drive the invader from Italy. It was in this context that Louis supported the French synods that met at Orléans and Tours (1510) to demand a general council to reform the abuses of the Church. In the absence of a positive response Louis decided to call such a council on his own initiative (May 1511). Julius replied by threatening to excommunicate anyone attending or conniving at such an assembly, and when it opened (Nov. 1511) only French ecclesiastics were present.

Henry VIII used the council as a pretext for breaking his treaty obligations to France; Spain and the German princes boycotted it; only the Emperor Maximilian offered it a cautious recognition. In Jan. 1512 the council left Pisa for Milan, and its fate was settled when Louis failed to follow up his victory at Ravenna in April. Gaston de Foix, the French commander, was killed on the field, and by the end of the year the council had fled to Lyons, where it became extinct. Julius had summoned a council of his own, the Lateran Council, in Rome, and the French had virtually been driven from Italy.

The collapse of the Pisan council meant the failure of the Gallican version of the Conciliar movement, which held that councils might be summoned without the approval of the pope, Pius II's bull *Execrabilis* (1460) notwithstanding. But the French gained more solid satisfaction when their unexpected victory at Marignano (1515) compelled Leo X to make the Concordat of Bologna and give substance to the largely theoretical concessions contained in the Pragmatic Sanction of Bourges (1438).   MMR

PISA, TREATY OF (12 Feb. 1664), agreement restoring normal diplomatic relations between Louis XIV and Pope Alexander VII after the affray in which the pope's Corsican guard assaulted the French embassy in Rome (1662), causing

Louis to withdraw his ambassador, invade Avignon, and threaten the papal states themselves. Alexander sent his nephew to France to apologize for the action of his guard, which he was forced to disband, and agreed to erect an obelisk in Rome in Louis's honour in order to gain the return of Avignon.

PISANELLO (ANTONIO PISANO) (*c.* 1395–*c.* 1453), Veronese painter whose work is distinguished by its sombre lighting as a background to brilliant colour and by his interest in animals and bright plants. He was attached for many years to the court of Ferrara and his greatest works include portraits of the members of its ruling Este family.

PISANI, VITTORE (d. 1380), Venetian soldier, who, though twice dismissed after previous defeats, was appointed (1379) to command the city's forces against the Genoese fleet blockading Venice. The Genoese were in turn blockaded and defeated in a battle in which Pisani himself died of wounds.

PISANO, NICCOLO (d. 1284) and **GIOVANNI** (d. *c.* 1314–19), Italian sculptors. Niccolo's earliest dated work is a pulpit for the Baptistry at Pisa (1260); his son Giovanni was already working with him by 1265. They deliberately modelled their reliefs and sculpted figures on classical models, including Roman sarcophagi found at Pisa. Niccolo's pulpits at Pisa and in Siena cathedral contrast with Giovanni's more dramatic and deeply etched compositions, notably the pulpits in the cathedrals of Pisa and Pistoria, which may reflect northern Gothic influences. Giovanni was also partly responsible for the elaborate facade of Siena cathedral, which in its use of sculpture imitates northern Gothic buildings more closely than was usual in Italy.

PISO'S CONSPIRACY (AD 65), unsuccessful attempt to replace Nero as Roman emperor by the senator Calpurnius Piso. Many important Romans, including Lucan and Seneca the Younger, were condemned for complicity in the plot and relations between Nero and the upper classes in Rome and Italy became embittered.

PISTOIA SYNOD (Sept. 1786), meeting of the clergy of the diocese of Pistoia, Tuscany, called at the instigation of Bp Scipione de Ricci, a leading Italian Jansenist. Tuscany was one of the centres of Italian Jansenism, which had enjoyed the encouragement of Duke Leopold. The synod sat for ten days and produced a number of Augustinian propositions, denying papal supremacy in matters of discipline and organization, and granting bishops disciplinary and educational rights over the regular clergy; it also approved of the Gallican Articles (1682). The synod marked the climax of the Italian Jansenist movement, but Leopold was not happy about its anti-curialist views, and urged Bp de Ricci to summon an assembly of Tuscan bishops. This condemned (1687) the Jansenist attitudes of the Pistoia synod, and after de Ricci's resignation from his see (1791) the bull *Auctorem fidei* condemned the synod and its actions (1794).

PITCAIRN ISLAND (in the Pacific), ancient Polynesian quarry uninhabited on Carteret's discovery (1767), occupied by nine *Bounty* mutineers under Fletcher Christian and six male and 13 female Society Islanders in 1790. In 1800 their survivors, decimated by disease, suicide, and mass murder, submitted to the reformed leadership of the last remaining mutineer, John Adams. On his death (1829) the islanders settled briefly in Tahiti (1831–2) before removing (1856) to Norfolk, a nostalgic 42 returning to Pitcairn in 1863, where they embraced Seventh Day Adventism (1887) and in 1952 came under the jurisdiction of the governor of Fiji.

PITHOU, PIERRE (1539–96), French lawyer and writer, of Calvinist background. After being forced into exile he emerged as a prolific legal commentator, a leading *politique* supporter of the Liberties Gallican, collaborating on the *Satire Ménippée* (1594) in defence of Henry IV. In the same year he wrote *Les Libertés de l'Église Gallicane*.

PITMAN, SIR ISAAC (1813–97), British inventor of shorthand, whose adaptation of existing methods became popular after 1840, was adopted in other countries, and virtually replaced all other systems.

PITT, THOMAS (1653–1726), English politician and British East Indian merchant, known as 'Diamond Pitt', who traded in opposition to the East India Co., but later became governor of Madras (1697–1709). He was MP for Old Sarum (1689, 1690), and in 1691 bought the manor of Old Sarum, thus securing control of a parliamentary seat for his family. His grandson was William Pitt, Earl of Chatham.

PITT, WILLIAM (the Younger) (1759–1806), British politician and prime minister, the youngest—at 24—ever to achieve the office (1784–1802, 1804–6) and son of the Earl of Chatham. His exceptional gifts and strong sense of public duty helped him to preside effectively over the restoration of Britain's economic fortunes after the loss of the American colonies (1783), and the administrative reorganization that was the necessary concomitant to recovery. Simultaneously, his India Act (1784), and the Canada Act (1791), laid a new foundation for the government of these colonies, and the Triple Alliance with Prussia and Holland (1788), followed by a diplomatic victory over Spain at Nootka Sound (1790), reinstated British prestige in the eyes of Europe. Thereafter Pitt's energies were absorbed in conducting the war with France, a task for which he was less well suited.

His main concern was with financial and administrative questions. As a disciple of Adam Smith, he encouraged the renewal of trade by increasing income from taxation and by the reduction of smuggling, while reducing the duty on tea from 119 per cent to 12½ per cent, negotiating a free trade treaty with France, and attempting to do so with Ireland. Pitt was not, himself, an innovator, but his persistent pursuit of administrative competence made him the central figure in such measures as the abolition of sinecures, the establishment of the consolidated fund, and the creation of the Audit Office and the Stationery Dept. He not only accustomed the country to a higher standard of efficiency in government, but imposed on his cabinet colleagues greater discipline and co-ordination, though he never asserted his views, or those of the cabinet in opposition to those of King George III. Against these achievements must be set his half-hearted support of parliamentary reform once he was in office, and his perhaps exaggerated response to the threat of revolution in a series of repressive anti-Jacobin laws (1792–1800).

Having reluctantly accepted the inevitability of war with France in 1793, Pitt relied heavily upon Henry Dundas for advice. The resulting policy was costly and inefficient, relying on subsidized coalitions in Europe and concentrating British efforts in the colonies. Pitt's second ministry again revealed that he lacked his father's ability to devise a comprehensive military strategy. Yet he alone of his European contemporaries gave his country the will to resist the encroachments of France. His own commitment to the struggle wore him out and he died in 1806.

J. Steven Watson, *The Reign of George III* (Oxford, 1960).
J. H. Rose, *William Pitt and the National Revival* (London, 1911).   SH

PITTACUS (*fl.* 7th cent. BC), *aisymnetes*, or elective 'tyrant', of the Greek city-state of Mytilene. His ten-year rule prevented further strife at Mytilene between aspiring 'tyrants' and reactionary aristocrats, including Pittacus's former friend and, later, most virulent detractor, the poet Alcaeus.

PITT'S INDIA ACT (1784), in Britain, extended the control of the British home government over the East India Co. The civil, military, and revenue affairs of the company were placed under a board of control in London, consisting of the chancellor of the exchequer, one of the principal secretaries of state, and four privy councillors. A secret committee of three directors was to transmit important orders to India. The company retained its rights of patronage, but the governor-general, governors, members of the Indian councils, and the commander-in-chief were appointed subject to the veto of the Crown. The court of proprietors lost the right to suspend or revoke any resolution of the directors. In India the supreme government was in the hands of a governor-general and a council of three. The act prohibited any extension of the British dominions in India and advocated a permanent settlement of the land revenues. Politically, it made for a more efficient administration of India than had been possible under Lord North's Regulating Act (1773), as the difficult governor-generalship of Warren Hastings had demonstrated.

PIUS II (1405–64), Pope (*reg.* 1458–64), who attended the Council of Basle, and was secretary to the anti-pope, Felix V. Becoming disenchanted, he left the council to enter the service of the Emperor Frederick III in 1442 and helped to promote his reconciliation with the Roman pope. He was made Bp of Trieste (1447), cardinal (1456), and pope (1458). His main interest was in raising a crusade. However, he failed to stir the secular princes to action and died while on the way to lead a forlorn crusade himself. The real significance of Pius was as a humanist. He was a patron of artists and scholars and himself a poet of distinction. He also wrote a history of the Council of Basle, a life of Frederick III, and the *Commentaries*, a remarkably candid and engaging work which is virtually an autobiography.

PIUS IV (1499–1565), Pope (*reg.* 1559–65), who succeeded Paul IV and whose pontificate saw the triumphant conclusion of the Council of Trent (1563). Through his legate, Cardinal Morone, he played off the imperial, Spanish, and French factions at the reconvened council (1562–3) and won the support of the Emperor Ferdinand I. In 1564 he issued a papal bull confirming the decisions of the council, which had finally ended conciliarism and implicitly recognized the supremacy of the pope. He implemented certain recommendations of the council, *eg*, he created the modern Index of immoral and heretical books (1564), and established a seminary for priests in his diocese of Rome (1565).

PIUS V (1504–72), Pope (*reg.* 1566–72), whose main aims were to put into effect the decree of the Council of Trent and to extirpate heresy. He supported the Roman inquisition and stamped out Italian Protestantism. He set up a congregation to work for the conversion of heretics in Europe and another to promote the faith in pagan areas (1568). He congratulated Alva on his policy of extermination in the Netherlands and helped Charles IX of France against the French Huguenots. He encouraged Philip II of Spain to declare war on Protestant England and issued the bull *Regnans in Excelsis* (1570), excommunicating Elizabeth and imposing upon all English Catholics the duty of rebellion. His crusade against the heathen Turks came to fruition with the creation of the Holy League (Venice, Spain, and the papacy) and the great naval victory of Lepanto (1571). In the post-Tridentine spirit, Pius also issued a revised Catholic breviary (1568) and missal (1570), reduced the expenses of the papal court, and enforced clerical residence and monastic discipline.

PIUS VI (1717–99), Pope (*reg.* 1775–98), is remembered for the programme of public works and the much-needed economic reform in the papal states that he initiated, but is better known for his antagonism to the French Revolution. In the early years of his pontificate Pius dealt with a complicated customs network by abolishing all internal duties, except in the Legations. He set up industrial training schools and started a programme of road construction and the draining of the Pontine marshes.

He faced two hostile movements: the anti-curialism of the Italian Jansenist movement, backed by Leopold of Tuscany and the Emperor Joseph II; and the anti-religious and schismatic actions of the French revolutionary leaders. Visits by Pius to Vienna in 1782 and by Joseph to Rome in 1783, and even the signing of a concordat in 1784, could not eliminate the divisions between traditional papal attitudes and the Josephism of the Habsburg rulers. The conflict between the state and Church in France broke out in 1790, when the Legislative Assembly reorganized the Gallican Church in the Civil Constitution of the clergy, and further imposed on all beneficed clergy an oath of loyalty to the new constitution, on pain of deprivation. Pius took no immediate action, fearful of provoking the annexation of the papal territories in France, Avignon, and the Venaissin, but finally on 10 March and 13 April 1791 he condemned the civil constitution and the other social and political reforms in briefs addressed to the French bishops. A number of the clergy consequently retracted their oaths and the majority of the bishops, unable to conform to the Assembly's demands, left France as émigrés.

In 1796, when French forces swept into Italy, Pius hastily signed an armistice with Napoleon, agreeing to cede Ancona, Bologna, and Ferrara. The Directorate felt these terms were too generous to the 'irreconcilable enemy of the Republic' and ordered Napoleon to crush the papacy. After the swift French occupation of Rome, Pius submitted to the treaty of Tolentino (1797), surrendering his claims to Avignon and the Legations, closing papal ports to the ships of the anti-French coalition, and agreeing to the payment of a huge indemnity. The killing of a French general in Rome (1798) led to more drastic action. Pius VI was formally deposed and expelled by the French and the Roman republic was set up in place of the papal monarchy. Eighteen months later Pius died in captivity at Valence. MKS

PIUS VII (1740–1823), Pope (*reg.* 1800–23). He became Bp of Tivoli (1782) and Bp of Imola and a cardinal in 1785. He was elected pope after the interregnum which followed the death in captivity of Pius VI (1799). Pius was allowed to enter Rome after the withdrawal of the French (1801) and concluded a concordat with Napoleon I, whom he consecrated as emperor in 1804. However, a rift occurred in 1808, when Napoleon annexed Rome and the papal territories to the empire. Pius retaliated by excommunicating him and in consequence was removed to exile at Grenoble, then to Savona and to Fontainebleau, where he remained until Napoleon's defeat. In 1814 Pius returned to Rome and regained all the former papal territories (1815). In later years he began a reform of papal administration, acted against secret societies, including the Masons and the Carbonari, restored the Society of Jesus (1814), and encouraged the Ultramontanes.

PIUS VIII (1761–1830), Pope (*reg.* 1829–30). He became Bp of Monatalto (1800), Bp of Cesena and a cardinal in 1816, and prefect of the Congregation of the Index in 1822. He was supported by the French in the papal election of 1829, and accepted the July Revolution in France, showing himself to have liberal inclinations.

PIUS IX (1792–1878), Pope (*reg.* 1846–78), a reformer turned ultramontane conservative. On his election he proclaimed a political amnesty, relaxed censorship, and began financial, legal, and constitutional reforms, which allowed lay elective representation (1847). He was forced by revolution to grant a fully democratic constitution (1848) then fled to Gaeta, whence he was restored by French intervention. Relations with Piedmont deteriorated, and Pius lost his chance to lead an Italian federation by his intransigence after the Austro-Sardinian War (1859–60). Though the papal states were overrun, Pius, protected by Napoleon III, remained an obstacle to Italian unification until the French withdrawal from Rome (1870) forced him to retreat within the Vatican state. His control of the Church was evinced by promulgation of the Immaculate Conception (1854), condemnation of modern political doctrines (1861), and of liberal catholicism in *Quanta Cura* (1864), and his summoning of the first Vatican Council, at which the doctrine of Papal Infallibility when pronouncing *ex cathedra* was established (1870).

PIUS X (1835–1914), Pope (*reg.* 1903–14), who became pope after long experience of parochial work. His pontificate was concerned with social questions, as indicated in his encyclical *Il fermo proposito* (1905), with political issues of Church and state, eg, his refusal to allow the Churches of France and Portugal to come under government control, and with theological reforms. These included a new codification of canon law, revision of the missal and breviary, decrees on sacred music, and a commission to revise the text of the Latin Bible. He was canonized in 1954.

PIUS XI (1857–1939), Pope (*reg.* 1922–39), whose pontificate belonged to the difficult years between the two World Wars. A large part of his life had been devoted to scholarship and he was concerned with the importance of education in the work of the Church, as shown in his encyclical, *Quadragesimo Anno* (1931). Politically, he ended the breach between the papacy and Italy in the Lateran treaty (1929), and he criticized severely the growth of totalitarianism and the persecution of Christians.

PIUS XII (1876–1958), Pope (*reg.* 1939–58), who came of a legal family with a record of papal service. He was ordained in 1899 and entered the papal secretariat in 1901. He was papal nuncio in Germany during the Weimar republic and drafted a concordat which, as secretary of state (from 1930), he revised on Hitler's accession to power (1933). He supervised the implementation of the concordat with Italy.

As pope he sought to halt the progress towards the Second World War, but lacked the power and influence to do so. Throughout the war, particularly after the entry of Italy (June 1940), he sought to use the Vatican's neutrality to promote relief work. After the war he took a much stronger line in opposition to communism than he had towards the Nazi and Fascist regimes, and the Holy See formally excommunicated members of the Communist Party (July 1949). He pronounced the dogma of the Corporal Assumption of the Virgin Mary during a jubilee year (1950) and proclaimed 1954 a Marian year to commemorate the centenary of the dogma of the Immaculate Conception.

PIZARRO, FRANCISCO (*c.* 1470–1541), Spanish conqueror of Peru, who was with Balboa when the Pacific was sighted, and then settled in Panama, having received an allotment of Indians. There had long been rumours of a rich kingdom to the south, and Pizarro determined to conquer the area. The first Pacific Coast expeditions (1524–8), while not notably successful, yielded enough to encourage Pizarro to sail to Spain to secure the support of Charles V. Cortés had arrived with Aztec gold shortly before, and Pizarro was named governor, captain-general, and *adelantado* of the kingdom he proposed to conquer. He returned to Panama and sailed at the end of 1530 with about 180 men, leaving his colleague, Almagro, behind to enlist further recruits.

After raiding in Ecuador, Pizarro reached the north coast of Peru, conquered the stronghold of Túmbez, and was there joined by reinforcements. With these, he pushed south, founded San Miguel (1532), and was then ready to strike at the heart of the Inca empire. In a daring move, he surprised and captured the Inca Emperor Atahualpa at Cajamarca in Nov. 1532; Cuzco was entered and sacked in 1533, and by 1535 the conquest of the Inca empire was complete. In all this Pizarro was aided by Inca factionalism, the product of a civil war concluded shortly before his arrival. The con-

queror was amply rewarded by the king, who made him a marquis and governor of an area stretching 270 leagues south from Quito. In 1535 Pizarro founded his capital city, Lima.

But a series of blunders began to make their repercussions felt. The first, condemned by many Spaniards, was the judicial murder of Atahualpa, despite his payment to Pizarro of a huge ransom in gold and silver. The natives' consequent hostility culminated in a revolt led by the puppet Inca, Manco, in which Cuzco was nearly captured and which was suppressed only with difficulty. A further problem was that of Pizarro's associate, Almagro. He had never been as richly rewarded as Pizarro, receiving only a stretch of 200 leagues south of Pizarro's governance, and, after a disastrous expedition (1535–7) to Chile, Almagro was determined to possess Cuzco. Pizarro refused to yield on this point, and the issue was resolved by force at the battle of Las Salinas (1538). Almagro lost and was executed, but his embittered followers (the 'men of Chile') remained.

Pizarro used the uneasy peace which followed to consolidate his rule, delegating the Chilean conquest to Valdivia and founding the city of La Plata (Sucre) in Bolivia. His enemies, however, now led by Almagro's mestizo son, plotted against him, and in June 1541 Pizarro was assassinated in Lima.

W. H. Prescott, *History of the Conquest of Peru* (London, 1905).   FPB

PIZARRO, GONZALO (*c.* 1506–48), Spanish explorer and brother of Francisco, whom he assisted in the conquest of Peru. He was appointed governor of Quito and led (1541) an expedition into the Amazon jungle which Orellana immortalized by his voyage to the river's mouth in search of supplies. He returned to Quito to learn of his brother's assassination and was with difficulty persuaded not to claim the latter's governance by force. In 1545, however, with the Crown's high-handed attempt to enforce the New Laws in Peru, Gonzalo put himself at the head of a revolt, defeated and killed the viceroy, and momentarily reigned supreme. Although urged by some to declare himself independent of the Spanish Crown, Gonzalo temporized. He was defeated in battle and later executed.

PLACARDS, term used to describe the edicts issued by the Emperor Charles V and Philip II in the Netherlands in an attempt to curb Protestantism, and posters displayed in Paris (17–18 Oct. 1534) by the reformers. The French placards, probably the work of F. A. Marcourt, pastor of Neuchâtel, possibly aided by Farel, deliberately attacked the mass in violent Zwinglian language, forcing Francis I to lend his weight to the attempt to eradicate Protestantism in France, thereby driving it underground and helping to prepare the way for the Wars of Religion.

PLACE, FRANCIS (1771–1854), English radical and influential political figure, though never an MP. He was an active trade unionist in the 1790s, an effective moderate in the London Corresponding Society, and (from 1801) a prosperous Charing Cross master-tailor. He was deeply influenced by Bentham and Godwin, but disagreed with Godwin's refutation of Malthus, and pioneered birth control. He strongly opposed Owenite socialism, and in 1841 pronounced competition 'the greatest stimulus to improvement'. His knowledge, especially of facts, and his personal library were regularly drawn upon by reformers, notably Joseph Hume. In later middle age he influenced various politicians, and in 1824 secured the repeal of the laws forbidding combinations of workmen. In 1831 he organized a partial run on the bank of England, which discouraged Wellington from forming a government.

Place's importance declined because few could live up to the high standards he prescribed. He helped to draft the People's Charter (1838), but was strongly opposed to

Chartism, which alienated working men from the middle-class radicals whom he felt they should follow. His distaste for aristocracy made him a prominent Anti-Corn Law Leaguer from 1840. His vast collection of mss are housed in the British Museum and are an invaluable source for the study of 19th-cent. radicalism.

PLACE BILLS in Britain, excluding Crown officers from, or limiting the number eligible to sit in, the House of Commons, had as their avowed object the independence of the Commons from Crown influence. The most extreme action against placemen—their total exclusion—was imposed in the Act of Settlement (1701), but modified by the Succession to the Crown Act (1705), which allowed holders of old, pre-1705 offices, to sit, provided they stood for re-election. This requirement of re-election lasted, with small modifications, until 1926. Meanwhile, revenue officers were totally excluded at the beginning of the 18th cent., and clerks of the main government departments in 1742. Reduction in the number of placemen in the Commons was finally achieved, not by place bills, but by the abolition of places as part of the administrative reforms of 1780–1830. But, by concentrating on the exclusion of government officials from parliament, place bills took a step towards the exclusion of the civil service from politics.

PLACEMEN in Britain, term commonly used to describe MPs who held office under the Crown. In fact, the value of placemen as a link between the elected MPs and the royally appointed ministers outweighed their importance as a channel of royal influence. They gave no 18th-cent. government a certainty of support in the Commons. They did not constitute a party united in support of a particular policy and, since most appointments were permanent, the actual number of placemen that any administration could appoint was limited. They regarded their offices, often court or household posts, small sinecures or semi-sinecures, as rewards for past services, not as bribes binding them in the future. Apart from some 40 placemen who held active administrative office, there were about 160 of them in the mid-18th cent. Their number fell to about 60 by the early 19th cent., and to about 20 by 1830.

PLAGUE, primarily a disease of rats, but one that also attacks human beings. There are two main types. In bubonic plague the infection usually enters through the skin and attacks the lymphatic glands, buboes form in the groin, the armpit or the side of the neck; death may occur on the third to fifth day. In pneumonic plague the infection enters through the lungs and death occurs, in untreated cases, after two, three, or four days. 'Septicaemic plague', which some bacteriologists have classified as a separate type, is probably a particularly virulent form of bubonic plague: the blood stream is attacked by bacilli on so massive a scale that death supervenes before buboes have appeared. In *pestis minor* the glands or the lungs are affected, but mildly. The plague bacillus, *Pasteurella pestis*, was identified by S. Kitasato and A. Yersin within a few days of each other at Hong Kong in 1894. In the Middle Ages it was widely believed that plague resulted from a corruption of the air, of which the remote cause was thought to be astrological. Fumigation of rooms, purgation, diet, and avoidance of baths were among the recognized precautions of the well-to-do. Anticipations of a germ theory are found in the context of plague from the 16th cent.

Bubonic plague can be transmitted by a number of human parasites, but *Xenopsylla cheopis*, a species of rat flea, is the commonest transmitter, and *Rattus rattus*, the black indoor rat, the most dangerous carrier of fleas. The flea is most prolific and potent when temperatures are between 20° and 25° C (68°–78° F) and the atmosphere relatively humid; the plague seasons in Europe have been warm, rather damp summers. The continuing home of the disease is in the central Asiatic plateau, whence it is agreed there had been three major excursions. The first attacked Europe in the reign

of the Emperor Justinian in the 6th cent. AD. The second occurred in the 14th cent. The first epidemic in this pandemic (1346–1350) in Europe later became known as the Black Death, 'black' signifying, not the discoloration of the skin which occurs in some victims, but 'terrible'. This is the worst demographic catastrophe known to have occurred in the Middle Ages. The latest epidemic in England was the London plague of 1665. The third pandemic started in Hong Kong at the end of the 19th cent. and spread in Europe as far as Scotland, where in Glasgow there were three outbreaks; a number of others which were possibly a plague occurred in Suffolk (1906–18); but Europe was virtually immune in this pandemic. Until the 20th cent. the mortality rate in plague epidemics was often extremely severe, but it was always uneven from place to place, and the worst sufferers were towns; the rat-carrier thrives in conditions of urban over-crowding, and inter-human plague is most readily transmitted by these. Except in the initial outbreaks of a pandemic, places only a few miles from the centres of infection have escaped; those who were able to avoided the disease by flight. Such resources as flight, better housing conditions, and recuperative powers after illness have made plague mainly a poor man's disease. Although it is impossible to separate plague from other diseases in most epidemics of the past, it has been, with them, an important regulator of the mortality rate in pre-industrial societies.   BFH

PLAGUE, THE GREAT (1664–5) in England, last major outbreak of the bubonic plague, a disease carried by the fleas that lived on the brown rat. It is reputed to have been brought to England from the Middle East via the Dutch republic in bales of imported merchandise. London in particular was badly affected. It is calculated that there were about 70,000 deaths there from plague during 1665, but other centres of population, such as Southampton, Norwich, and Newcastle, were also stricken. The plague was at its height in London in the late autumn of 1665, after a hard winter and a sultry summer. Measures to combat the disease proved of little avail because of the retarded state of medical knowledge and public health; some indeed, such as preventing the exit of people from houses in which the disease had been detected, may have contributed to the mortality rate. By 1666 the plague was on the wane. The fire of that year rid London of many of the infected houses.

PLANCK, MAX KARL ERNST LUDWIG (1858–1947), German physicist, celebrated for his derivation (1897–1901) of a fundamental scientific relationship, the quantum theory. From this many of the most significant developments in physics during the 20th cent. have stemmed. The Nobel physics prize was awarded to Planck in 1918.

PLANTATIONS DUTIES ACT (1673) in England, part of the Navigation or Old Colonial System and one of the acts passed to extend and make good deficiencies in the Navigation Act (1660). It imposed export duties on certain goods shipped from one plantation to another. This was to prevent the leakage of these goods into the European market from inter-colonial trade. It was the earliest direct tax (other than customs dues) on colonial produce not initiated by a colonial legislature.

PLANTIN, CHRISTOPHE (1524–97), French-born printer and publisher, who founded a business at Antwerp (1555) and published the Antwerp Polyglot Bible (1569–73). He later became printer to the states general and to the town of Leyden and Leyden University.

PLASSEY, BATTLE OF (23 June 1757), although little more than a cannonade, was decisive in transferring authority in Bengal from the Mughal nawab to the British East India Co. The episode began with a dispute between the Nawab of Bengal, Siraj-ud-Daulah, and the East India Co. (1756), the nawab having forbidden the fortification of Calcutta against French attack on the expected outbreak of European war. The young nawab, aware of recent French intervention in Hyderabad, attacked Calcutta, and after the desertion of Gov. Drake and senior councillors, captured it (20 June 1756). The survivors took refuge at Fulta to await help. The Madras government sent Clive to Calcutta, with troops recently arrived from Europe and intended for action against the French in South India. Admiral Watson's squadron was also dispatched, and 800 European and 1000 Indian troops. Clive occupied Fort William and Calcutta (2 Jan. 1757) and concluded a treaty (9 Feb. 1757), restoring the company's privileges and permitting it to fortify Calcutta and coin rupees current throughout Bengal.

But the situation remained unstable; the nawab was still powerful and the French were in Chandernagar. But the nawab was distracted by fear of the British and of Ahmad Shah Abdali the Afghan, now in north India, and allowed Clive to take Chandernagar (23 March 1757). Realizing the nawab's unpopularity and anxious to return his Madras troops, Clive entered into a conspiracy to place Mir Jafar, brother-in-law of the late nawab, Alivardi, and recently dismissed from the office of *bakshi* (paymaster), on the Bengal throne. This plot was supported by the Seth financiers, and by Siraj's Hindu officers. Mir Jafar was to pay large sums for the losses in Calcutta, and, by private agreement, to the chief British officers. Included in the plot was the deception of the banker, Amir Chand, who demanded too large a share of the expected loot.

The crisis came in June 1757. Clive marched from Calcutta (13 June) with 800 Europeans and 2200 Indians. After a night of indecision he met the nawabi army of 50,000 (23 June). Mir Jafar's contingent held aloof. A cannonade and an unauthorized advance were indecisive, but the nawab lost heart and fled. Mir Jafar was installed as nawab, while Siraj was captured and executed (2 July 1757). Henceforth the British were the de facto rulers of Bengal.

H. H. Dodwell, *Dupleix and Clive* (London, 1920).   TGPS

PLATAEA, ancient Greek city-state in southern Boeotia, 12 kms south of Thebes, which it consistently opposed. The Plataeans, allies of the Athenians from 519 BC, alone helped them at Marathon (490), and during Xerxes' invasion (480) fought on when the other Boeotian states, except Thespiae, had surrendered, receiving a guarantee of freedom from the Greeks after their victory in their territory (479). But in the great Peloponnesian War Plataea was besieged by the Spartans and the Thebans (429–7) and destroyed. It was refounded by the Spartans to restrict Thebes (382), but was destroyed again by the Thebans (373). The state was finally restored by Philip II of Macedon after Chaeronea (338) and rebuilt on Alexander the Great's decree (331).

PLATAEA, BATTLE OF (479 BC), Greek land victory in the Persian Wars. After wintering in central Greece, the Persians, under Mardonius, reoccupied Athens in the spring of 479. In response to Athenian appeals, the Spartan regent, Pausanias, led out the largest Peloponnesian League army ever assembled (about 26,500 hoplites) and, joined by 11,500 Athenians, Aeginetans, Plataeans, and Megarians, advanced to face Mardonius and his Greek allies across the Asopus river between Plataea and Thebes. Here he tried to provoke a battle, but was handicapped by Persian cavalry superiority. Herodotus' account is obscure, but a planned Greek withdrawal provoked a Persian attack which failed before the Greek, and especially Spartan, hoplites. Mardonius was killed, his camp overrun, and his army withdrew hurriedly from Greece.

PLATO (c. 429–347 BC), Athenian philosopher and follower of Socrates, who founded the Academy and, apart from the Socratic 'Apology' and various letters, wrote 25 extant works in dramatic dialogue. He was disenchanted by political conditions and concluded that successful government depended on rulers becoming philosophers and philosophers becoming rulers. He outlined a system in the *Republic* for educating rulers or 'guardians'. Interested in numbers, algebra, plane and solid geometry, astronomy, harmony, and dialectic, he produced significant discussions on epistemology and psychology and analysed the validity of general and specific terms, developing the theory of 'forms' or 'ideas'. Despite his failure in educating Dionysius II of Syracuse as a 'philosopher-king', Plato powerfully influenced contemporary and later educationalists, political theorists, and scientists, including Aristotle.

PLATT, THOMAS COLLIER (1833–1910), US politician and businessman, who was a New York Republican Party 'boss' and US congressman (1875–9). He was elected to the US Senate in Jan. 1881, but resigned five months later over a dispute with President Garfield about patronage. After consolidating his control of NY state politics, he returned to the Senate (1897–1909). He was largely responsible for Theodore Roosevelt's election as governor of NY (1898), and as vice-president of the US (1900), but with Roosevelt's accession to the presidency, Platt's influence declined.

PLATT AMENDMENT (1902), in US, imposed amendment to the Cuban constitution of 1902, written into a formal treaty between the US and Cuba. After the Spanish–American War, Cuba was required to write into its constitution a series of clauses drawn up by Senator Orville H. Platt of CT and passed by Congress as an amendment to the army appropriations bill. The amendment gave the US the right to intervene to preserve Cuban independence. It was always unpopular in Cuba and was ultimately repealed in 1934.

PLATTE RIVER TRAIL (1825–69) in US, route, 780 miles (1255 kms) long, from the Great Bend of the Missouri river in the vicinity of Independence, MO, up the Platte river and its northern fork to South Pass. This part of the central overland route across the plains was established by fur-traders in 1825 and became a great highway for western settlers.

PLATTSBURG, BATTLE OF (11 Oct. 1776), naval battle on Lake Champlain, during the American War of Independence. An American flotilla under Benedict Arnold engaged a British force, greatly superior in quality, under Sir Guy Carleton. Although his ships were completely destroyed, Arnold successfully delayed Carleton's advance towards the Hudson and forced his temporary withdrawal to Canada.

PLATTSBURG, BATTLE OF (11 Sept. 1814), naval battle during the War of 1812, also known as the battle of Lake Champlain. A British naval squadron covering British troops at Plattsburg, commanded by Gen. Sir George Prevost, was annihilated in two hours by a US fleet under Capt. Thomas Macdonough. Prevost's army retreated to Canada, leaving behind vast quantities of supplies and the US in undisputed control of Lake Champlain.

PLAUTUS, T. MACCIUS (c. 254–184 BC), Roman comic poet, 21 of whose plays substantially survive. He owed his success chiefly to his skill in grafting boisterous Roman humour on to the somewhat mechanical social satire of his Greek originals, and was himself imitated by Molière and Shakespeare.

PLAYFAIR OF ST ANDREWS, LYON PLAYFAIR, 1st Baron (1818–98), British scientist and politician, who held the professorship of chemistry at Edinburgh University (1858–69); he discovered the nitro-prussides and investigated hydrated salts. In parliament he held office as postmaster-general (1873–4), deputy speaker (1880–3), and vice-president of the council (1886). He also served on various commissions on agricultural diseases and pests.

PLAYFORD, SIR THOMAS (1896–   ), Australian politician who was prime minister of SA for a record term (1938–65).

He was associated with the development of secondary industry in SA and his Liberal and Country League government nationalized state electricity supplies, developed the Leigh Creek coal field, and expanded the activities of the SA housing trust. Playford vigorously advanced the state's interests in many conferences with Labor and non-Labor governments in Canberra.

PLAZA LASSO, GALO (1906–), Ecuadorian rancher, diplomat, and president of Ecuador (1948–52). During his administration efforts were made to modernize the country. Advanced agricultural techniques were tried, and some small beginnings were made at land reform. Lasso failed to regain the presidency after his term of office ended, and he turned to international diplomacy, serving as UN mediator in Cyprus, and as secretary-general of the Organisation of American States (1969–).

PLEBEIANS, body of ordinary citizens in ancient Rome, as opposed to the ruling caste (patricians). They were excluded at first from religious and political offices, and debarred from marriage with patrician families, but later they organized themselves into a powerful political corporation with their own officers (plebeian tribunes and aediles) and their own assembly (*concilium plebis*, legalized by 471 BC). Through this they were able to extract social, political, and economic concessions, so that by 287 BC the Struggle of the Orders was won.

PLEBISCITA, resolutions passed in ancient Rome by the *concilium plebis*, initially requiring to be confirmed by the Comitia Centuriata before becoming law. By 287 BC they had attained a wholly binding status.

PLEBISCITES, means of consulting a population on their preferred form of government. First introduced in connection with the French republican constitutions (1793, 1795), they were adapted by Napoleon I for all the major constitutional changes of his regime (1800, 1802, 1804, 1815), when he secured large majorities in his favour. The practice was revived and reformed by Napoleon III, who also secured large majorities in favour of his own constitutional innovations (1851, 1852, 1870). Plebiscites were used in Italy to decide on the annexation of various provinces to the new kingdom (1859, 1860, 1870), and on frontier issues under the terms of the Versailles treaty (1919), particularly in the Saar. French governments after the Second World War also used plebiscites.

PLEBS LEAGUE in Britain, founded in 1908 by a group of dissident Ruskin College students who objected to the growing influence of Oxford University upon the curriculum of the college. They were, to some extent, guided by the thought of Daniel de Leon, the leader of the American Socialist Labor Party, and also by syndicalism. The league advocated a genuine working-class education, free from the values of traditional British education, and it looked especially to the newer social sciences. The league had its own journal, *Plebs*. Branches were established in several parts of the country and it was under the inspiration of the league that the Central Labour College was founded.

PLEDGES in Britain, promises made by MPs to their constituents to use their position in parliament to initiate or support particular policies, the implications of which are that MPs owe more loyalty to their constituents than to any party or government and the wholesale adoption of which would mean the introduction of direct popular sovereignty.

The giving of pledges flourished at certain periods in the 18th cent., especially in the 1740s, when they were used as a means to try to further the 'patriot' programme of free elections, short parliaments, and place bills. Later in the century John Wilkes, advocating popular as opposed to parliamentary sovereignty, encouraged his constituents to give him explicit instructions to follow in the Commons. But pledges were really inconsistent with the accepted theory that MPs were the representatives, not the delegates, of the people, whose independence, once elected, was an essential prerequisite of a strong House of Commons. Moreover, in an age when patronage flourished, an ambitious MP would further his career by taking account of the wishes of his patron rather than his constituents.

It was in the 19th cent., when patronage had declined and the discipline of the modern party system had not yet emerged to take its place, that pledges, together with petitions and other means of impressing popular opinion on the politicians, really flourished. Political theorists and politicians, such as Romilly and J. S. Mill, who realized the implications of pledges, opposed them. So did the supporters of the 1832 Reform Bill. But since one of their chief arguments in favour of reform was that the popular voice demanded it, some constituents, encouraged by Francis Place and the National Political Union, felt that they had the right to make their individual voice heard through their MP. However, the growing power of the executive after the 1867 Reform Bill and the growth of the party system checked any long-term threat to representative government by popular sovereignty.

SH

PLÉIADE in France, leading group of Renaissance poets, gathered round Ronsard and Du Bellay. They included Baif, Belleau, Dorat, Jodelle, and Pontus de Tyard. Taking their name from the seven daughters of Atlas, they worked together to develop, decorate, and elevate French poetry to a position of equality with that of Italy.

PLEISTOANAX (*reg.* 458–408 BC), Agiad King of Sparta and son of Pausanias, who was exiled in 445 for allegedly taking a bribe from Pericles to abandon his invasion of Attica and conclude peace. He returned in 427 and helped to negotiate the peace of Nicias (421) in the great Peloponnesian War.

PLEISWITZ ARMISTICE (1813) after the retreat of the Russian and Prussian allies into Silesia from their defeat at Wurschen against the French and their allies. The British agreed by the treaty of Reichenberg to subsidize the Prussians and Russians and both sides used the interval to seek an alliance with Austria, mediator in the ensuing Congress at Prague.

PLEKHANOV, GEORGII VALENTINOVICH (1857–1918). Russian politician, Marxist thinker, and 'father' of Russian social democracy. He was a populist who worked with the proletariat rather than the peasantry, joined *Zemlya i Volya* (Land and Liberty), and on its split (1879) led the non-terrorist wing, Black Partition (*Chernyi Peredel*). In Europe he adopted Marxism and founded The Liberation of Labour (1883) with Vera Zasulich and Axelrod. He was active in the debate with the populists, and wrote *Our Differences* (1885) and *On the Question of the Development of the Monist View of History* (1894). He opposed economism and supported Lenin (1903), but soon joined the Mensheviks. In 1910 he set up a faction of 'party-minded' Mensheviks opposed to 'liquidationism'. He opposed the Bolshevik revolution (1917) and founded an opposition Unity group.

PLESSY v. FERGUSON, 163 US 537 (1896), US Supreme Court case which was a legal landmark in the establishment of civil rights. It involved the constitutionality of a LA law requiring separate railway coaches for whites and Negroes. In the majority opinion, Justice Brown affirmed that such a statute did not deprive Negroes of the equal protection of the laws, providing the Negro accommodation was equal to that available to whites. This 'separate but equal' doctrine was extended by the court later to include schools, and legitimized the development of segregation in public accommodation and educational facilities in many Southern states.

Justice Harlan, in a vehement but lone protest at this decision, insisted that 'our constitution is color-blind' and that the state statute was unconstitutional, but the court did not come to accept his view *in toto* for almost 60 years.

PLETHO, GEORGE GEMISTOS (*c.* 1355–1452), Byzantine scholar and philosopher who spent most of his life at Mistra in the Morea. He attended the Council of Florence in 1438–9 and helped to foster among the Italian humanists a new interest in the works of Plato, which led in the second half of the 15th cent. to the translation of all Plato's works into Latin (by Ficino at Florence).

PLEVEN, RENÉ (1901–   ), French politician, who joined De Gaulle in London in 1940 during the Second World War. He was a member of both the London and Algiers liberation committees and minister of colonies in the provisional government. His succession to the post of minister of finances in Nov. 1944 represented the victory of a laissez-faire inflationist financial policy over the deflationary austerity and currency control of Mendès-France.

Pleven was one of the founding members of the Union démocratique et socialiste de la Résistance (UDSR). He was minister of national defence and of foreign affairs in several cabinets and twice *président du conseil*. During the Fifth Republic he was a constant opponent of Gaullist policies, but returned to the Gaullist fold during the May–June crisis of 1968. After 1964 he was president of the council of regional economic development of Brittany.

PLEVEN PLAN, proposal by the French government as a reaction to US insistence that West Germany should be rearmed (Sept. 1950). The French sought to avoid the establishment of an independent German army and the Pleven plan was devised to create small units of mixed nationalities. The practical problems which this created soon led to the plan's modification, but its principle was extended in the military provisions of the abortive European Defence Community.

PLEVNA, SIEGE OF (July–Dec. 1877), crucial resistance of an Ottoman fortress in Bulgaria under the command of Osman Pasha, which delayed the advance of Russian forces to Istanbul, and gave time for British diplomatic intervention, thus contributing to the modification of Russia's terms at the Congress of Berlin (1878).

PLIMSOLL LINE marking the maximum load line on British merchant ships. Its adoption was largely the result of the sustained efforts of an MP, Samuel Plimsoll (1824–98). The Merchant Shipping Act (1876) required shipowners to mark the maximum load line on the side of their ships. The 1890 act laid the duty of enforcement on the board of trade. In 1906 the requirement was extended to foreign ships in British ports. The 1930 load-line convention, signed by 40 states, was incorporated in the Merchant Shipping Act of 1932.

PLINY THE ELDER (C. PLINIUS SECUNDUS) (AD 23–79), Roman official and writer, and who served in several posts in the imperial administration. His most important works were a lost history covering the years 41–71, a source for Tacitus and others, and the surviving *Natural History* in 36 books, completed in 77, a vast collection of miscellaneous information. Though often erroneous and superstitious, it nevertheless preserves much important information on many aspects of Greek and Roman history, art, technology, and medicine.

PLINY THE YOUNGER (C. PLINIUS SECUNDUS) (*c.* AD 61–113), Roman politician, writer, and nephew of Pliny the Elder, who was a senator and an orator and became a consul in 100. He also governed Bithynia (*c.* 111). His *Panegyric* on Trajan is of some importance as a historical source. His *Letters* provide much useful information on the social history of Rome and northern Italy and on Trajan's provincial administration, and reveal Pliny as one of the more enlightened senators of his time, as well as a conscientious landowner and administrator. The most famous *Letter*, written from Bithynia, concerns the attitude to be taken by the authorities to the early Christians.

PLOMBIÈRES MEETING (1858), between Napoleon III of France and Cavour, representing Sardinia (Piedmont). Napoleon agreed to join Sardinia in attacking Austria so as to end her domination of northern Italy, provided that Austrian provocation was engineered. The agreement envisaged an Italian federation of four states under the pope, French acquisition of Savoy and Nice, and a marriage alliance between the royal houses of Sardinia and France. With Russia's goodwill assured by Napoleon, the Franco-Sardinian secret treaty was signed and the Austro-Italian War followed (1859).

PLOTINUS (AD ?204–270), philosopher, probably born at Lycopolis in Egypt, who studied at Alexandria and was an important influence on later religious philosophy, both Christian and Islamic. He was the centre of an upper-class philosophical circle at Rome, and although in his preaching he advocated a withdrawal from the world, he helped his friends generously. He was refused permission to establish Platonopolis (or a Platonic 'republic') in Campania. Starting usually from a statement by Plato or Aristotle, he sought to direct his pupils to find a transcendental unity behind the infinitely varied manifestations of the sensible world. His writings were edited by his pupil, Porphyry, who divided them into six sets of nine treatises (*Enneads*), arranged by subject matter.

PLOUGHMEN'S FRONT, radical Rumanian peasant organization, founded by Petru Groza at Deva in Transylvania in 1933. In its original programmes radical demands were made on behalf of the peasantry. The Ploughmen's Front remained in the 1930s a small organization, barely heard of beyond the Deva region. It made some effort, under Groza's direction, to co-operate with the communists in the popular front movement. In 1944 the Ploughmen's Front fell under the influence of the communist party, which used it as an agrarian arm. After joining the National Democratic Front, its membership expanded rapidly in all areas of Rumania. It stood in the government bloc at the elections of 1946 and absorbed the dissident National Peasants in 1947. In 1948 the Front became united with the Democratic Popular Front and Groza held prominent positions in the new communist regime.

PLUG PLOT in England, industrial strike, initially of Staffordshire miners against wage cuts, but which, with Chartist and Anti-Corn Law League support, spread in Aug. 1842 to the textile and mining industries of Lancashire and South Wales. By removing plugs from factory boilers, the strikers hoped to make it impossible for blacklegs to work. As with the Newport Rising (1839), riots occurred, and the government took severe reprisals against Chartist leaders. The incident suggests that there was a close relationship in 1842 between the Chartist, trade union, and free trade movements, but henceforward the Anti-Corn Law League was careful to adopt more respectable tactics.

PLUMER, HERBERT CHARLES ONSLOW PLUMER, 1st Viscount (1857–1932), British soldier, who served in the Sudan and in the Anglo-Boer War, becoming quartermaster general (1903–5). In the First World War, as commander of the second army, he held the Ypres salient and won the battle of Messines (1917). He again held Ypres (1918) against the final German offensive. After the war he was made a field marshal and was commander-in-chief in occupied Germany (1918–19). Subsequently, he was governor of Malta (1919–24) and high commissioner in Palestine (1925–8).

PLUNKET, OLIVER (*c.* 1629–81), Roman Catholic primate of Ireland and Abp of Armagh, who was the last man to suffer martyrdom for his faith in England. He restored order and discipline to the Church in Ireland, while keeping on good terms with the English Protestants. In 1673, however, he went into hiding after renewed persecution. He was betrayed (1680), tried, and taken to London, where he was executed. He was beatified in 1920.

PLURAL VOTING BILL (1906) in Britain, by which electors with the right to vote in several constituencies were only allowed to vote in one. Previously those with property and businesses in several areas had exercised a disproportionate influence at a time when electorates were smaller and did not vote simultaneously. The House of Lords delayed the bill on the grounds that it should be accompanied by a redistribution of seats, thus embittering relations with the Liberal government and leading to the Parliament Act (1911).

PLURALISM, holding of more than one ecclesiastical benefice or office at the same time. The practice grew to scandalous proportions in the 13th cent. and was finally regulated by the bull *Execrabilis* (1317) of Pope John XXII, which forbade unlicensed pluralism. Papal dispensations perpetuated this irregularity up to the 16th cent., but earnest efforts were made to curtail it at the time of the Council of Trent in the mid-16th cent. It was also found to exist after the Reformation and was a factor in the 18th-cent. decline of the Church of England.

PLUTARCH (*c.* AD 46–126), Greek writer, who was born at Chaeronea, and became a friend of influential Romans, though he lived mostly in Greece. There survive from his copious output the so-called *Moralia*, an extensive collection of dialogues and essays on philosophical, religious, literary, and political subjects, and the *Lives* of Greek and Roman statesmen, mostly arranged in pairs on the basis of frequently very artificial comparisons. Although in many respects superficial, the *Lives* are full of anecdote and are highly entertaining, and if treated with suitable caution are of great value as historical sources.

PLYMOUTH BRETHREN, Christian sect established by a former Anglican priest, J. N. Darby (1800–82), at Plymouth in 1830. It was a loosely organized body whose teaching combined elements of Calvinism and Pietism. The Brethren's moral outlook was strongly puritanical. They adopted a fundamentalist outlook on the Scriptures and renounced many secular occupations and leisure pursuits. There was no organized ministry; each local church was self-governing and met every Sunday for the breaking of the bread. In 1849 the movement split into the Open Brethren and Exclusive Brethren, with many smaller sub-divisions. Though relatively few in number, the Brethren were always very active and included a few notable converts. Their influence was strongest in Britain, Western Europe, and the US, reaching a membership (1970) of about 90,000.

PLYMOUTH COMPANY, one of two English companies incorporated in the first Virginia charter of 1606. The Virginia Co. of Plymouth was granted the right to settle between the 38th and 45th degrees of latitude. Its first leader, Sir John Popham (1531–1607), made an unsuccessful attempt to found a colony on the coast of ME (1606). After his death Sir Fernando Gorges (*c.* 1566–1647) became the leader and, recognizing the value of the fishing and trade with the Indians, reorganized the project under a new company, the Council for New England.

PO CHÜ-I (772–846), Chinese poet, who lived when the T'ang dynasty had been weakened by rebellion and the government lacked its earlier discipline, vigour, and determination. He embarked on an official career and held several appointments in central and provincial government. He was able to combine the Confucian outlook needed by a scholar-civil servant with a devout faith in Buddhism which sustained him throughout his life. In his extensive poetry he appealed to personal emotions and to a love of nature; in addition to compositions in traditional styles, in one of which at least he is one of China's acknowledged masters, he reinstituted the ballad as a type of poetry designed to voice protests against contemporary political and social abuses. His work is characterized by its direct appeal to emotion and its simplicity of diction. He received appreciation very quickly particularly in Japan.

POBEDONOSTSEV, CONSTANTINE PETROVICH (1827–1907), Russian lawyer and statesman, who was also procurator of the Holy Synod (1866–1905). He upheld orthodoxy against other branches of Christianity and persecuted sects, old Believers, and Jews. He was a fervant upholder of autocracy and Russification, and an opponent of constitutionalism. Nevertheless, he favoured administrative reform, the abolition of the *mir*, and he encouraged primary education.

POCAHANTES (1595–1617), American Indian princess, the daughter of Powhatan, chief of a group of Virginian Indians. She is said to have saved Capt. John Smith from death at the hands of her people. Pocahantes was kidnapped by the English (1612) and taken to Jamestown, where she was held as a hostage until her father agreed to a peace settlement. She was converted to Christianity while a prisoner in the colony, and was baptized as Rebecca. John Rolfe, an English colonist, married her (April 1613) and they went to England (1616), where she was presented to King James I. She died of smallpox in a ship off Gravesend, while awaiting a passage home.

Thomas Rolfe (1617–63), her only child, was educated in England and returned to VA, where he acquired wealth and distinction. John Randolph, of Roanoke (1773–1833), was one of a number of distinguished Virginians descended from Pocahantes.

POCKET-BATTLESHIPS, British description applied to the three German *Panzerkreuzer* of the *Deutschland* class. In their construction, begun in 1928, use was made of welding and light alloys in an attempt to keep them within the 10,000-ton (10,200 tonnes) limit of the Versailles treaty (1919) on German warship displacement. Diesel engines gave them exceptional range. They were intended as ocean commerce raiders and said to be able to outrun or outfight any ship afloat, except for the three old British battlecruisers. Their achievements in the Second World War were considerable, but, like Germany's other ships, they justified themselves, not by what they did, but by requiring the British to be aware of them. The *Deutschland* (renamed *Lützow* in Nov. 1939) cruised in the North Atlantic in 1939 and sank three merchantmen, but spent most of the war off Norway and in the Baltic. She was destroyed by RAF bombers at Swinemunde on 16 April 1945.

The *Admiral Graf Spee* cruised in the Atlantic and Indian Oceans (Aug. 1939–Dec. 1940), but was cornered by the British cruisers *Exeter*, *Ajax*, and *Achilles* off the Plate river and driven into Montevideo, where she was scuttled on 17 Dec. 1940.

The *Admiral Scheer* cruised in the Atlantic and Indian oceans (1940–1), sinking 15 merchantmen. Subsequently she served in Norway and the Baltic. She was destroyed by RAF bombers at Kiel on 9 April 1945.

PODESTÀ, name of an official in the towns of northern and central Italy (lit. *rector*). In 1158 Emperor Frederick Barbarossa introduced them as imperial representatives with both judicial and executive functions. In the 13th cent., as imperial power in Italy collapsed, each town came to appoint its own *podestà* for varying terms of office. As he had to enforce law and order, a man with military experience was required and it was usually found safer to appoint a non-native nobleman. In spite of these precautions, some men used the office as a starting point for assuming permanent rule, as did Martino I della Scala at Verona (1260–77). The *podestà* invariably lived in an imposing fortified building and in many Italian towns the 'palace of the *podestà*' is the most impressive surviving medieval secular edifice.

PODGORNY, NIKOLAY VICTOROVICH (1903–), Russian politician and president of the Soviet Union, who joined the Communist Party in 1930, but did not become prominent until after Stalin's death. He made his career in the Ukraine, but his rise within the Ukrainian party occurred after Khrushchev had risen to leadership in the Presidium, so that he was independent of Khrushchev's patronage. He began his career as a member of the state apparatus, notably in the food industry of the Ukraine and the Soviet Union, where he held various posts at deputy minister level (1939–50). He was appointed first secretary of the Kharkov district committee of the Communist Party (1950–3), then second secretary of the Ukraine central committee (1953–7), and first secretary (1957–63). He was brought into the secretariat of the central committee of the CPSU after the eclipse of Kozlov and at the same time as Brezhnev (1963). In the rivalry which preceded Khrushchev's fall he proved weaker than Brezhnev and his election to the chairmanship of the Presidium of the Supreme Soviet (*ie*, the presidency) in succession to Mikoyan (Dec. 1965) was a means of excluding him from powerful office rather than a promotion.

POE, EDGAR ALLAN (1809–49), US author. Having failed to attract attention with three volumes of poetry, *Tamerlane* (1827), *El Aaraaf* (1829), and *Poems by Edgar A. Poe* (1831), he began writing short stories. 'MS Found in a Bottle' (1833) earned him the editorship of the *Southern Literary Messenger*, whose circulation he increased from 500 to 3500. In 1836 he moved to New York, where he published *The Narrative of Arthur Gordon Pym* (1838), and then to Philadelphia, where he edited *Burton's Gentleman's Magazine* (1839–40) and *Graham's Magazine* (1841–2), filling them with stories such as 'The Fall of the House of Usher' and 'Murders in the Rue Morgue'. He won critical recognition with *Tales of the Grotesque and Arabesque* (1840) and popularity with 'The Gold Bug' (1843), and in 1844 he returned to New York, where he became famous as the author of *The Raven and Other Poems* (1845) and *Tales* (1845). Response to his poetry ranged from derision to adulation by the French symbolists. Poe's tales contain the origins of modern detective, horror, and science-fiction writing and he has been acknowledged as having had a profound influence on the evolution of the short story.

A. H. Quinn, *Edgar Allan Poe: a critical biography* (New York, 1941).   EFAL

POGROM (Russ., destruction), anti–Semitic violence, especially marked in the Ukraine. Sometimes, as in the 1880s and in 1905, the authorities unofficially encouraged attacks on Jews to divert popular discontent. Pogroms were often initiated by Black Hundred organizations.

PO-HAI, state established (*c.* 700) in northern Korea and southern Manchuria, by tribes who had escaped from Chinese control after the fall of Koguryo in 668. Po-hai became a major emporium on the northern trade route from China to Japan, sending regular embassies to both the Chinese and Japanese courts. It was destroyed by the armies of the Khitan Liao dynasty in 926.

POINCARÉ, RAYMOND NICOLAS LANDRY (1860–1934), French lawyer, politician, and president of the Third Republic (1913–20). He entered the Chamber in 1887 and was minister of education (1893, 1895–6). His main contribution came in finance (1894–5, 1906). He continued to practise at the bar, was elected to the Senate (1903) and the Académie (1909), and formed his first ministry (1912–13).

Both as prime minister and as president (1913–20) he showed himself determined to maintain French interests in the face of German pressure, and proved an effective head of state during the First World War, calling on Clemenceau at the time of crisis (1917). He refused to stand for re-election and returned to active politics (which was unusual for ex-presidents) first as senator (1920), then again as prime minister (1922), when he was responsible for the occupation of the Ruhr, a move which led to his downfall. Two years later he was called back to deal with a desperate financial situation. His mere presence and the confidence it inspired, together with some limited reforms, stopped inflation and allowed him to stabilize the value of the franc (1926). He reformed his ministry when the Radicals withdrew (1928), but had to retire a year later because of ill-health.

POINCY, PHILLIPE DE LONGVILLIERS, Chevalier de (d. 1660), French colonial administrator whom Louis XIII appointed lieutenant-general of France's American possessions and governor of St Kitts (1639). At the request of French buccaneers on Tortuga he sent them (1640) their own governor. He arrested the governor of Guadeloupe, appointed by the Compagnie des Îles d'Amérique (1641), and substituted his own nominee. Shortly before his death he made a treaty with the Carib Indians, reserving for them the islands of Dominica and St Vincent. He was an amateur botanist and his name was given to the flowering Poinciana Regia tree.

POINSETT, JOEL ROBERTS (1779–1851), US diplomat and commercial agent, who served as consul-general in Buenos Aires, Chile, and Peru (1809–16), and as the first US minister to Mexico (1825–9). In Mexico he competed with Sir Henry Ward, the British minister, for influence during the Guadalupe Victoria administration. Poinsett lent his support to the pro-Victoria 'Yorkist' republican faction, which was strongly anti-Spanish in sentiment (1827–8).

His support for one faction in the impending civil conflict angered the opposition and he was expelled from Mexico (1829). He later served as US secretary of war (1837–41) and attracted Mexican suspicion of his motives in respect of TX. Poinsett became a symbol throughout Latin America of the meddling North American emissary.

POINT FOUR PROGRAM (1949) in US, policy announced by President Truman in his inaugural address on 20 Jan. 1949, making American scientific and technical knowledge available to 'peace-loving peoples' in underdeveloped areas. The program also envisaged capital investment in co-operation with other nations.

POISSY, COLLOQUY OF, meeting of the French clergy presided over by the regent, Catherine de' Medici, and the youthful Charles IX, at which the French bishops and Theodore Beza, representing the Calvinists, sought a theological compromise (9 Sept.–14 Oct. 1561). The proposed settlement was denounced by Laynez, the Jesuit general (25 Sept.), and rejected by the faculty of theology at the Sorbonne (9 Oct.), whereupon the council was closed (14 Oct.) without having fulfilled Catherine's hopes of religious unity. The Catholic faction, led by the Duc de Guise, the Cardinal of Lorraine, and the Constable Montmorency, withdrew from court, and when a measure of toleration was granted to the Huguenots by the Crown (Jan. 1562), the two religious camps moved towards armed conflict.

POITIERS, DIANE DE (1499–1566), widow of Louis de Brézé, Comte de Maulevrier (1521). She became mistress of Francis I and later of his son, Henry II. She had great influence over Henry and supported Anne de Montmorency, Constable of France, against the Guise faction at court.

POITIERS, city in western France, which was the most northerly point reached by the Muslim raids from Spain.

Here Charles Martel, the Carolingian ruler of the Franks, defeated the Muslim raiders in 732, inflicting the first of a series of defeats which by 760 had ended their rule in parts of France north of the Pyrenees.

POITIERS, BATTLE OF (19 Sept. 1356), victory of an English army, led by Edward the Black Prince, returning from a prolonged raid into France. It was intercepted by a much larger French army led by King John II. Fighting on the defensive, the English, through their use of archers, repulsed a succession of attacks. The indiscipline of the French, some of whom deserted, permitted the encirclement of the main French force and the capture of the French king. This overwhelming victory paved the way for the victorious peace of Bretigny in 1360.

POITIERS, EDICT OF (Sept. 1577), royal edict of Henry III, confirming the provisions of the peace of Bergerac which had ended the sixth French War of Religion earlier that year. It allowed the Huguenots only modest rights of organization, reducing their membership in the special judicial chambers for religious affairs attached to the *parlements*. It also banned all organization among local churches but extended the garrisoning of eight places of safety for six years. Calvinist worship was banned from a wide area around Paris and elsewhere was restricted to one surburban church per bailiwick. The edict was applied only for a short time, but was briefly reinstated in 1591.

POITIERS, SYNOD OF (1557–8), one of the most important formative assemblies of the French Huguenots, called by La Roche-Chandieu and others after dissension among the French churches. It issued edicts on the organization, worship, and deportment of French Calvinists and arranged for better contacts between local churches, in which the deacons were entrusted with enhanced authority over both pastors and laity, particularly where communion, marriage, and public morality were concerned. It also established congregationalism as the basic system of governance in the Calvinist Church and marked the beginnings of strict teaching on such matters as dancing and games.

POLARIS MISSILES, US navy ballistic weapons. The 1500-mile (2410 kms) range of model A-1 (developed in 1957 and operational in 1959) was extended to 2500 miles (4020 kms) with the A-3 (1963). It was designed to be fired from nuclear submarines. Polaris added flexibility to American second strike capability. It was made available to Britain at the Bahamas conference (Dec. 1962) and became the basis of Britain's nuclear deterrent.

POLDING, JOHN BEDE (1794–1877), English Benedictine, who became Australia's first Bp in 1834. He was a dedicated missionary of great compassion, who ministered personally to convicts and settlers all over NSW, and established the fundamentals of a religious system. He was appointed Abp of Sydney in 1842.

POLE, REGINALD (1500–58), Cardinal Archbishop of Canterbury, son of the Countess of Salisbury, niece of Edward IV, and therefore a Yorkist claimant to the English throne.

In a conciliatory gesture towards the Yorkists, King Henry VIII paid for his education in England and Italy and, although Pole was only a deacon, allowed him to draw substantial ecclesiastical revenues. At Henry's request Pole obtained from the Sorbonne a favourable verdict on Henry's 'divorce', but announced his own disapproval of it and refused the offer of the archsee of York or the see of Winchester. He returned to Italy and wrote *De Unitate Ecclesiae* (1536), a scathing attack on Henry's proceedings which cost him his English benefices, but induced the pope to make him a cardinal and legate for the recovery of England to the Catholic faith.

Pole was learned and scholarly, the friend of Contarini, Caraffa, and other Catholic reformers, but his doctrinal views were dangerously liberal, particularly on justification by faith, and doubts about his orthodoxy lost him the papacy after he had received two-thirds of the votes on the first ballot (1549).

Over the years he made numerous efforts to persuade France and the Holy Roman emperor to invade England, and Mary's accession gave him the opportunity to complete the mission to which he felt his life dedicated. He arrived in England in Nov. 1554, was elevated from deacon to archbishop in a single stroke, and replaced Cranmer at Canterbury.

Although he reluctantly had to recognize that the monastic lands and revenues were irrecoverable, Pole supported Mary and Bps Gardiner and Bonner in their stringent policies. Some historians have held Pole principally responsible for the Marian persecution, but he had more constructive ideas than the mere elimination of heresy. In 1555 he called a legatine synod which was intended to restore a reformed Catholicism from which greed and superstition would disappear, and to a new English prayer book would be added homilies, a catechism, and a vernacular version of the New Testament. These plans were interrupted by a sudden attack from his old friend, Caraffa, who had now become Pope Paul IV. He deprived Pole of his legateship and summoned him to face the Inquisition on charges of heresy. He did not go, but his health steadily declined and he died 12 hours after Mary, leaving ten vacant bishoprics to make the passage of the Elizabethan settlement easier than it might otherwise have been.

P. Hughes, *Rome and the Counter-Reformation in England* (London, 1940).
W. Scherk, *Reginald Pole, Cardinal of England* (London, 1950). MMR

POLICE in Britain, body of civil officers empowered to maintain law and order, enforce the law, and prevent and detect crime. The original police in England were the village constables, who formed a voluntary and amateur force under the control of the JPs. Their innate inefficiency has been immortalized in Dogberry, Shakespeare's night constable in *Much Ado About Nothing*. The first regular police and detective force was the Bow Street Runners organized in London in the mid-18th cent. under the chief magistrate at Bow Street. The modern police in Britain stem from the establishment of the metropolitan police in London by the home secretary, Sir Robert Peel (1829). The earliest county constabularies were created *c.* 1840, and consolidation and integration of county and borough forces continued up to the Police Act (1946). The present (1970) system is still a locally based one with national surveillance by the home secretary (for England and Wales) and the secretary of state for Scotland, though there has been a tendency to create wider administrative units, *eg*, the Thames Valley police force (1968).

POLICE ACTS (1829, 1839) in Britain, established a metropolitan police force with headquarters at Scotland Yard, and local forces under the direction of chief constables. Earlier the law had been maintained by parish constables, who were unpaid. All citizens were liable to serve, but usually a few were hired as substitutes. In towns, burgesses employed watchmen and London had no organization covering the whole area, though Fielding's Bow Street Runners constituted a police force to check highway robbery (1760). In spite of the prevalence of crime, fears that a police force directed by the government might lead to the subversion of liberty led a parliamentary committee (1816–18) to place its faith only in the laws, their impartial administration by the magistrates, and the good moral state of the population. However, alarm at the behaviour of the mob during the controversy over Queen Caroline led to the setting up of another committee, with Peel as chairman (1822). This suggested a police force under the control of the home office, which should patrol the London area. In 1829 the Metropolitan Police Act was passed, establishing headquarters under the control of a commissioner and assistants at Scotland Yard.

The result was some migration of criminals from the London area. The reformed municipal corporations began to appoint watch committees and police, though detection was made more difficult by the fact that many towns still had no police force, and improved communications after the growth of railways enabled miscreants to move to other areas where there were no facilities for their pursuit. In 1839 a Royal Commission, influenced by Chadwick's advocacy of crime prevention, recommended wider police areas, the transfer of constables to centres of crime, and better police training. By a subsequent act, justices were empowered to appoint chief constables for the direction of the police. In some areas citizens objected to the cost of this reform and no chief constable was appointed. Accordingly it was enacted (1856) that police forces must be co-ordinated by chief constables in each area and the home office was given powers of inspection over local forces. This gave rise to accusations that the liberty of the subject was endangered, until increased grants were made to the localities, and opposition ceased.

L. Radzinowicz, *A History of Criminal Law and its Administration from 1750*, 3 vols (London, 1948–56).   VEC

POLIGNAC, JULES DE, Prince (1780–1847), French politician, diplomat, and prime minister, who participated in Cadoudal's plot against Napoleon I. Its failure led to his imprisonment in Vincennes (1804–14). Eventually he escaped and joined the Comte d'Artois, whose piety and conservatism he shared. He was made a peer (1815), and was granted a papal princedom for his sympathies with the Church in 1820. He was ambassador to Britain (1823–9), but was recalled by Charles X to head an extreme conservative government. He pursued an active foreign policy, which led to the capture of Algiers (1830), but he mishandled the crisis of July 1830, for which the security measures were insufficient. He fled for his life, but was arrested, tried, and sentenced to perpetual imprisonment, but was released in 1836.

POLIGNAC, ABBÉ MELCHIOR DE (1661–1742), French cleric and diplomat, who served Louis XIV and Louis XV, and came from a noble family of military tradition. He was appointed ambassador to Poland (1695–7), but later retired, then was recalled to royal favour (1702). He was French envoy at the Gertruydenberg negotiations (1710) and led the French embassy at the Congress of Utrecht (1713); afterwards he became minister at Rome (1725–32). In addition, Polignac was a member of the French Academy, a cardinal (1712), and Abp of Auch (1726).

POLISH CORRIDOR, part of West Prussia ceded to Poland by Germany under Articles 27 and 87 of the Versailles treaty (1919). The corridor was contiguous with the province of Posen in the south, and had a northern seaboard some 64 kms long. Its population was predominantly Polish, plebiscites in two areas having resulted in the return of mainly German inhabitants to Germany (1920). The chief purpose of the cession of this strip of territory was to give Poland access to the sea. The most suitable port for Poland would have been Danzig, but this city was overwhelmingly German in population and character, and under the League of Nations' guarantee became a free city though it remained linked politically and commercially to Poland by special treaties. Poland later began to construct an alternative port on her own territory at Gdynia.

Despite all the arguments in favour of the corridor, there were grave political objections which made it one of the most threatening areas of dispute in post-war Europe. The principal problem resulted from the corridor's division of Germany into two parts, East Prussia being separated from the

rest of the country, an arrangement that was certain to prove unsatisfactory even though Germany's right of transit was safeguarded under Article 89 of the Versailles treaty.

No less dangerous was the anomalous position of Danzig, whose German population deeply resented Poland's special privileges there, and it was in this city that the main pressures for revision of the corridor system built up. After April 1933 Danzig was governed by a Nazi majority in the senate, and after about 1936 was no longer under even the league's nominal control. In Germany itself, however, Hitler had temporarily abandoned his irredentist policies in favour of co-operation with Poland as a counterweight to Russia. A German–Polish non-aggression pact was signed in Jan. 1934; and the demands which Germany put to Poland in 1938, and which eventually led to the hostilities which opened the Second World War, would not have amounted to a full revision of the Versailles system. They were confined to requests for the return of Danzig to full German sovereignty, and the cession of permanent road and rail links between Germany and East Prussia. It was not until Poland rejected these demands unconditionally that Hitler resumed his radical revisionist policies *vis-à-vis* the corridor. He renounced the non-aggression pact and declared his intention finally to solve the Danzig and corridor problems. This led directly to the outbreak of war in Sept. 1939. After the invasion of Poland the corridor was reincorporated into the Reich as the *Gau* Danzig-Westpreussen. At the end of the Second World War the territory was restored to Poland.

G. M. Gathorne-Hardy, *A Short History of International Affairs* (London, 1950).
I. Morrow, *The German–Polish Borderlands* (London, 1936).
                                                                          AJC

POLISH FOUR-YEAR DIET (1788–92), attempt to reform the constitution before the final partition of Poland. Polish anarchy was caused by the existence of an elective monarchy with nominal powers and the extensive liberties of the nobility, especially their role in the Diet, or *sejm*. For a measure to pass through the *sejm* there had to be unanimity, and one noble could dissolve it. All government and legislation was made impossible by this *liberum veto*, which provided an ideal weapon for foreign influence. After the First Partition (1772), King Stanislas Poniatowski and a group of enlightened nobles were determined on reform and at last assembled a *sejm* to achieve this (1788). A new constitution, influenced by the Revolution in France, was presented to the *sejm* (May 1791), providing for a limited hereditary monarchy, the abolition of the *liberum veto*, political equality for the middle class, protection for the serfs, and religious toleration. Russian intervention (1792) led to a new *sejm*'s reverting to the old constitution (1793) and further partitions, which destroyed both Poland and its *sejm* (1795).

POLISH GOVERNMENT IN EXILE. After Poland's defeat in 1939 at the outset of the Second World War, a government in exile—first in France and later in London—was formed, with Raczkiewicz as president and Sikorski as prime minister and commander-in-chief. A National Council was set up as a parliament. The government directed an army in exile, which fought with the Allied forces, and the clandestine Home Army in Poland herself. The government established diplomatic relations with Britain and with Russia (1941), under a formula which blurred the historic question of frontiers between Russia and Poland. In April 1943, following the Katyn graves incident, the Soviet Union severed relations. The British and US governments continued to support the 'London Poles', while the Russians supported an alternative exile group, the Lublin Committee. The Soviet military success in Poland enabled them to establish this group as the provisional government of Poland (Jan. 1945).

POLISH OCTOBER (1956), series of events by which the Stalinist system in Poland was liberalized and Wladyslaw

Gomulka was brought back to power. The undermining of the Stalinist system in Poland was the result both of the impact of events in the Soviet Union and of pressure within Poland for a change. Stalin's system of personal terror did not survive him and his death was followed by the establishment of the principle of collective leadership and the repudiation of the 'cult of the personality'. At the same time, the fall of Beria led to a weakening of the security apparatus. These changes initiated demands for similar reforms in Russia's satellites. Two other events in the Soviet Union also affected the Polish situation: Khrushchev's attempt from May 1955 to achieve a rapprochement with Yugoslavia, which appeared to legitimize the concept of 'separate roads to socialism', and his speech at the 20th Congress of the Communist Party of the Soviet Union denouncing Stalin's crimes.

In Poland itself, a desire for change was expressed by various groups. Writers and intellectuals wished to diminish the crude rigidities of Stalinism in the cultural field, and many party members were disillusioned with the way the country was being governed, in particular, at the way in which its interests were being subordinated to those of the Soviet Union. At the same time, many economists were demanding a more flexible economic system, based less closely on the Soviet experience of the thirties and more responsive to Polish conditions. These pressures built up (1953–6) and achieved a number of results: the economic system was modified and more attention was paid to consumer demand, the system of police surveillance was weakened, and censorship was relaxed. But it was only in 1956 that significant changes occurred. The death in 1956 of Boleslaw Bierut, the man most closely identified with Stalinism, made possible the election of Edward Ochab, a moderate liberal, as first secretary. The extent of popular discontent with the regime was made obvious in June, when riots broke out among industrial workers in Cracow, in which at least 53 people were killed. Although these began as a protest against economic conditions, they soon involved political demands.

Early in Oct., demands for change had achieved considerable force and enjoyed a wide measure of support in the party. Gomulka came to appear increasingly as the only man who could achieve the peaceful reform of the communist system. In spite of strong Soviet opposition he was elected first secretary of the party at the end of Oct. and set up a new and liberal politburo. He was able to convince the Soviet government that he would not let the situation get out of hand and was thus able to prevent a Russian invasion, such as had happened in Hungary, but this was at the cost of abandoning most aspects of the liberal programme. In 1970 Gomulka, the rebel of 1956, was one of the most orthodox of communist politicians.

K. Syrop, *Spring in October* (London, 1957).
R. Hiscocks, *Poland, Bridge for the Abyss* (Oxford, 1963).
                                                                    ABP

POLISH REBELLION (Jan. 1863) broke out when Polish radical groups centred on the City Committee rebelled against the Russian government and the Polish administration, headed by the Marquis Wielopolski, who, accepting de facto Russian rule, was trying to introduce a programme of reform. The radicals were opposed to this and aimed at complete independence. After attempts to assassinate the Grand Duke Constantine and Wielopolski (1862), the latter introduced conscription, which was the immediate reason for the revolt. It lasted for over a year, during which insurgent bands, supported by landowners, roamed the countryside. Its suppression was followed by land and administrative reforms introduced by N. Milyutin (1864).

POLISH REVOLUTION (1830–1), nationalist uprising in the kingdom of Poland, supported by Poles in Lithuania and the Ukraine, its object being independence from Russian control. Nationalist sentiments were stimulated by the French revolution (1830), and a revolt, started by a conspiratorial group led by Wysocki, turned into a popular uprising (Nov.) to which the army gave support. There were two unconnected and mutually hostile centres of revolt—the Patriotic Society, a version of Krzyzanowski's earlier society, which had been connected with the Decembrists; and Prince Czartoryski, who headed a new provisional, and later national, government. The Grand Duke Constantine advocated moderation, but Nicholas, the Russian emperor, demanded surrender and war ensued. Gen. Paskevich captured Warsaw in Oct. 1831. The eastern provinces were severely punished, but under the new Organic Statute parts of the 1815 constitution were kept, although the Polish army was abolished. A large emigration took place. The revolt aroused sympathy in Britain and France, but not among Russian radicals.

POLISH SUCCESSION, WAR OF THE (1733–5), European conflict which broke out when the Polish throne became vacant on the death of Augustus II (the Strong) in 1733. Spain, France, and Savoy-Sardinia supported the claim of Stanislas Leszczynski, Louis XV's father-in-law, while Russia and Austria championed a rival candidate, Augustus, son of the late king. The fighting started in Poland, where Field Marshal von Münnich laid siege to Danzig; despite French efforts to relieve the city through the Baltic, it capitulated to the Russians (2 June 1734) after Leszczynski had fled to Prussia. The main theatre of conflict then moved to Italy, where the Austrians were defeated at Parma (1734) and driven from Milan and the Po valley by the French and out of Naples by the Spanish (1735). There was also some action on the Upper Rhine, where the aged Prince Eugène was unable to stop the French from taking Philippsburg (1734). Although the fighting had petered out by 1735, three years of negotiations followed before the signing of the treaty of Vienna (1738), which gave the Polish throne to Augustus III.

POLISH–RUSSIAN WAR (1920–1). In April 1920 Marshal Pilsudski, the leader of the newly revived state of Poland, decided to take advantage of the apparent weakness of the Bolshevik regime, still engaged in the Civil War, and invaded the Ukraine in the hope of achieving a frontier more generous than that envisaged by the Versailles peace-makers (the ethnographic Curzon Line) or that offered by the Bolshevik government. By 7 May Polish troops were in occupation of Kiev, and the Allied governments, meeting at Spa, had despatched a note to the Bolshevik commissar for foreign affairs, Chicherin, demanding negotiations on the basis of the Curzon Line and pledging themselves to defend the Polish state, if necessary. But the presence of Polish forces on Russian soil aroused the fears of the Ukrainian peasantry of a revival of the earlier Polish domination of the area, and by the end of July the Poles had been expelled from Kiev and the Red Army had crossed the Curzon Line into indisputably Polish territory. This decision to take the war into Poland had not been reached without controversy in the Bolshevik leadership: Lenin, backed by the second congress of the Comintern then in session, argued for it in the belief that it would be supported by a rising of the Polish workers and that it would present an opportunity to take Bolshevism westwards and to link up with German revolutionaries, but Trotsky (supported initially by Stalin) opposed it on the grounds that Polish patriotism would be too strong. The main Russian army, commanded by Tukhachevsky, advanced on Warsaw, while a subsidiary force under Egorov and Budenny moved towards Lvov. But the Polish workers failed to rise, the Russian lines of communication became over-stretched, co-operation between the two armies broke down, and the Poles, assisted by a French force under Gen. Weygand, halted the Russians in a battle before Warsaw in August. The Red Army, peasant based, had little offensive capacity and by the end of Aug. had been driven back across the Curzon Line. An armistice was signed on 12 Oct., establishing a provisional frontier along the lines then occupied. This frontier, which was confirmed by the treaty of Riga on 18 March 1921, placed a substantial minority of White Russians and Ukrainians under Polish control, and added to Poland a strip of territory between Russia and Lithuania; it survived until 1939.

NRB

POLITBURO in Russia, sovereign committee of the Communist Party of the Soviet Union, its full name being political bureau of the central committee of the Communist Party. The name was first used in Oct. 1917, when the central committee appointed a politburo to direct the imminent Bolshevik revolution. But the politburo had to be founded again in 1919 as a part of the administrative structure created at that time. Six full members were elected and were charged with the task of attending to all urgent business. To meet the complaint that the politburo would divest the central committee of power, it was ordained that members of the central committee could attend meetings of the politburo, but would have no voting powers. Very soon the politburo came to dominate the executives of both the party and the state. Lenin complained that even minor matters of detail were brought for decision to the politburo; shortly after his death it was calculated that each member of the politburo would have to read 6682 pages of material per year in order to deal adequately with the agenda. Little detailed information about the politburo was released, but the work-plan for 1926 shows that the following matters were discussed: the condition of the war industry, the state budget, a report on exports and imports, wages, labour discipline, state and collective farms, and the reports of the North Caucasus party organization. The politburo remained small, but tended to increase slightly during the period of Stalin's leadership. During 1919–52, when death, both by natural and violent means, took a heavy toll of the party leadership, only 29 persons became full members of the politburo. During the first stages of his rise to power Stalin tended to back the central committee against the politburo. But as soon as he had defeated his opponents he filled it with faithful and, on the whole, competent lieutenants, each of whom specialized in some particular field, *eg*, Mikoyan in that of foreign trade, Beria in police work, and Khrushchev in agriculture. Stalin was not tied by politburo decisions. Important matters were settled either by him individually or with the help of whichever members he liked at the time. Sometimes he refused to allow politburo members to attend meetings. When the Soviet Union was struck by the crisis of the German invasion (June 1941) Stalin promoted Malenkov and Beria over the heads of six full politburo members to GOKO (State Committee of Defence). In 1952 Stalin abolished the politburo and replaced it with a presidium of 25 persons. Khrushchev alleged that Stalin intended to annihilate the former members of the politburo. Under Khrushchev the size of the presidium was reduced and its membership showed several important changes as compared with the Stalinist era: it was dominated by party functionaries, the police were no longer represented and economic experts were demoted. The name politburo was restored in 1966.

L. B. Schapiro, *The Communist Party of the Soviet Union* (London, 1964).
M. Fainsod, *How Russia is Ruled* (Cambridge, MA, 1965).
GS

POLITIAN (ANGELO POLIZIANO) (1454–94), Italian classical scholar and poet of the early Renaissance, who attracted the attention of the Medici, then rulers of Florence. He acted as tutor to the children of Lorenzo de' Medici (d. 1492), frequently carried out confidential missions for Lorenzo, and was recompensed by being nominated as a professor at Florence University (1480). He was the first Italian humanist to rival as a Greek scholar the most accomplished Byzantines, and the first to publish a satisfactory critical edition of the works of a major Greek writer, Homer. He was a pioneer in the historical study of legal texts, carefully collating the 6th-cent. text of Justinian's Civil Law with versions current in Italy of his own time. He applied the same historical approach to the study of many literary and philosophical writers, trying in particular to reconstruct the chronology of the works of Aristotle. Several leading scholars were his pupils, including some of the most accomplished English humanists of the early 16th cent., among them the teachers of Sir Thomas More.

POLITICAL LEVY in Britain, name by which a trade unionist's contributions to the funds of the Labour Party are known. The levy, which is reckoned as a per capita sum on all trade unionists affiliated to the Labour Party, is paid in the sum of an individual's union dues and passed on by the union to the party.

This method of financing the Labour Party has been the subject of a good deal of controversy, and, from time to time, judicial and legislative attack. In 1909, as a result of a decision in *Osborne v. the Amalgamated Society of Railway Servants*, the House of Lords ruled that it was illegal for a trade union to contribute any of its corporate funds towards a political party. This judgment was partially reversed in an act of 1913, which permitted the payment of the levy, but it also allowed an individual member to contract out of payment to the Labour Party if he wished.

This remained the procedure until 1927, when, following the general strike, the Conservative government replaced contracting out by contracting in.

It was not until 1946 that the legislation of 1927 was repealed by Attlee's government and the position established by the 1913 act restored. There had been no alteration in the law by 1970.

POLITIQUE TIRÉE DE L'ÉCRITURE SAINTE (1709), one of the principal works of J. B. Bossuet, the French theologian, regarded as the greatest exposition of the theory of the divine right of kings and its practice by Louis XIV of France.

POLITIQUES in France, a current of thought during the Wars of Religion which supported religious toleration as a lesser evil than civil war. A *politique* approach is usually said to have become visible in the mid-1560s, when the damage that religious conflict was doing to France was already apparent. The view was associated particularly with the chancellor, Michel de l'Hôpital, who on his retirement (1568) claimed to have acted only in the interest of the state and never in the interest of faction. The Montmorency family came to the same point of view and were instrumental in urging the marriage of Elizabeth of Valois to Henry of Navarre in order to secure some degree of religious unity at court.

The St Bartholomew massacre (1572) confirmed the emergence of the *politiques*, horrifying many good Catholics, who felt that alliance with the Huguenots was necessary for the safety of France. This feeling was strong in the *Midi*, where an assembly at Nîmes (1574) achieved an entente between *politiques* and Huguenots. This led to the Crown losing control of the area, which split into small quasi-independent states, notably in Languedoc, where Damville, one of the Montmorencys' sons, was uncrowned king. The aim of the *politiques* was to secure the reversal of the St Bartholomew attainders, call a genuine states general to reform the government, and indemnify the Huguenots both financially and through equal representation in the *parlements*. These ideas attracted Catholic noblemen alarmed by the influence of the Guise, merchants whose livelihoods were being destroyed by the war, and lawyers and officials who were horrified by the way in which religious conflict was bringing France to the verge of anarchy. Motives for joining the *politiques* were not always disinterested, for many malcontents like the Duc d'Alençon lent their support for their own ends, particularly in the hope of gaining control of Church lands, one of the *politiques*' beliefs being the necessity for the state to control the Church in France in order to curtail religious extremism. The ideas of the *politiques* were also expressed in a number of political writings, particularly by Bodin. He argued for absolute state authority and obedience to it (1576), and urged the compelling claims of the state and its sovereignty against religious anarchy.

The understanding between Huguenots and *politiques* began to break down in the 1580s with the rise of the Catholic League and even *politiques* found themselves unable to accept at first the idea of an heretical king (1589). Henry IV was forced to abjure his faith in order to secure the throne, although thereafter the *politique* spirit gave him full support. The *politiques* are best regarded not as an organized party, but as a loose collection of people with the same general outlook on politics and religion. An attitude of mind rather than a real movement, it contributed in the long run to the consolidation of the absolute monarchy in France rather than to the growth of toleration.

M. J. Tooley (ed.), *Jean Bodin: the Six Books of the Commonwealth* (Oxford, 1955). CHC

POLK, JAMES KNOX (1795–1849), US politician and 11th president of the US, who began his career as a lawyer in Columbia, TN, and became an active member of the Democratic Party. In 1824 he was elected to Congress, where he became a Jacksonian spokesman and was one of the leaders in the attack on the Bank of the United States. In 1835 he became speaker of the House of Representatives.

Jackson's retirement left Polk as the leading figure in his state's Democratic Party, and in 1839 he was elected governor of TN. Despite Jackson's constant support, Polk lost a bid for re-election in 1841 and again in 1843; his political career then almost seemed at an end. None the less, he sought to achieve his party's vice-presidential nomination in 1844. Unexpectedly, Martin van Buren failed to win the presidential nomination at the party convention, which was deadlocked between the major Democratic leaders. Finally a compromise choice had to be sought, and Polk was nominated for the presidency, the first 'dark horse' candidate in American history. The Whigs put forward Henry Clay, but Polk won by a narrow majority, largely because his expansionist views on TX were more popular than Clay's ambiguous attitude.

Polk is said to have entered the White House with four aims: the reduction of the tariff; the re-establishment of the Independent Treasury; the settlement of the Oregon dispute; and the acquisition of CA. Each of these he accomplished. His attention was necessarily given largely to foreign policy. The whole of the Oregon territory (jointly occupied with the British since 1818) had been claimed in the election campaign and Polk, after negotiations with the British, finally agreed to a compromise which divided OR along the 49th parallel (1846). One reason for his willingness to negotiate with the British was the troublesome state of American relations with Mexico. TX had been annexed by the US before Polk took office. Mexico refused to accept either the annexation or the boundary (the Rio Grande) claimed by the US. Polk sent an envoy to Mexico to try to resolve the dispute by negotiation and to buy CA and NM. The Mexicans refused to receive the envoy, and after a border incident had occurred, Polk declared that a state of war existed (1846). The American armies easily defeated the Mexicans, and by the treaty of Guadalupe Hidalgo (1848) the Rio Grande boundary was recognized and the US acquired CA, NM, and UT.

Polk did not inspire affection as a president, but he was a man of remarkable industry and determination, qualities which ensured that his single term was packed with accomplishments.

Charles G. Sellers, *James K. Polk, Jacksonian: 1795–1843* (Princeton, 1957).
Charles G. Sellers, *James K. Polk, Continentalist: 1843–1846* (Princeton, 1966). MJH

POLL TAX, extraordinary direct tax levied by many ruling princes of Europe on each individual 'head' or 'soul'. It was first levied in England in 1377 and led to Wat Tyler's revolt of 1380. A general poll tax was levied in 1513 and in 1641 and was used occasionally after the Restoration (1660). In France, where another direct tax, the *taille*, existed, the poll tax was introduced as an emergency measure by Louis XIV in 1695 and existed from 1701 until the Revolution, but since the clergy, many of the nobles and towns compounded, it bore heavily upon the middle classes and peasantry. The latter were also adversely affected by the introduction of the tax in the German states, and in Russia, where Peter the Great levied it in 1724 and where it lasted until the mid-19th cent.

POLLITT, HARRY (1890–1960), British trade unionist and political figure, who was secretary and chairman of the Communist Party of Great Britain. He made his name as a militant trade unionist and secretary of the Hands off Russia committee in 1919. He was also prominent in the National Unemployed Movement, assisted in the formation of local unemployed committees, and became secretary of that organization when it became the National Minority Movement (1924–9). He was a good orator and administrator, and was a natural choice for the comintern when it was decided to 'Bolshevize' the Communist Party in the late 1920s. In 1929 he became secretary of the party and, in alliance with Palme Dutt, was responsible for 'purging' it of a good deal of the old leadership.

On the whole, Pollitt was a leader entirely suitable to Moscow. He faithfully followed changes in comintern policy in the 1930s and was an outspoken defender of the show trials that began in 1936. However, he fell out with the Russian party in 1939 over attitudes to the Second World War. The British Communist Party supported the war at the outset and Pollitt only reluctantly submitted to Moscow's formulation of it as an imperialist one. He was for a short time replaced as secretary of the party by Gallacher, but returned to the post after the German invasion of Russia in 1941. He retained the secretaryship until 1955, when he became chairman of the party. He was several times an unsuccessful candidate for parliament, opposing Ramsay MacDonald in 1929, and also standing at East Rhondda, where he was narrowly defeated in 1945. He published several books, including *Looking Ahead* (1947).

POLLOCK, OLIVER (1737–1823), American trader and financier, who emigrated to Philadelphia from Ireland and traded with the West Indies. He moved to New Orleans (1768), and with the co-operation of the Spanish authorities he supplied ammunition to the US army during the American War of Independence, and advanced credits of $300,000.

POLO, MARCO (c. 1253–1324), Venetian traveller and author, whose father and uncle, both Venetian merchants, had travelled on a trade mission into Asia, being the first Europeans to visit the court of the Mongol Great Khan Khublai in China. Khublai had sent them back with an appeal to the pope for Christian missionaries. In 1271 they set out again for Khublai's court with Marco, travelling from Palestine through Persia and Central Asia. In 1292 they returned by way of the Malay Straits, Ceylon, and India. There is no record of how they spent the intervening two decades. Marco made notes of what appear to be first-hand descriptions of two journeys from Peking into south China and in the direction of Burma. It is clear that he travelled extensively in the khan's dominions and presumably in his service. Some years after his return to Venice Marco, while serving in the Venetian naval forces, was captured by the Genoese and while in prison wrote his *Description of the World* (in French), helped by a fellow prisoner, the romance writer, Rustichello of Pisa. This is not only a storehouse of practical information on trade-routes and Asiatic commodities, but a unique panorama of exotic animals, luxurious ways of life, and bizarre customs. Marco fired the imagination of the West with its first vision of the East.

POLONKA, BATTLE OF (1667), last battle of the Russo-Polish Wars of 1654–67, where the Poles, under Czarniecki, routed the Russian invaders and helped to bring about the treaty of Andrussovo.

POLONNARUVA or Pulatthinagara, capital of the Sinhalese kingdom (c. 1070–1215), situated 30 miles (48 kms) south-west of Trincomalee. This was perhaps the most splendid period of ancient Ceylonese history, especially during the reign of Parakramabahu the Great (1153–86), when the whole island was united. This splendour is still apparent from the ancient monuments, beautifully restored by the Archaeological Survey of Ceylon.

POLOTSKY, SIMEON SITIANOVICH (*fl.* 17th cent.), Russian Patriarch, who was tutor to Fedor II and Sophia, the children of Tsar Alexis. In 1666 he became head of a new theological school which laid special emphasis on Latin as the basis of Orthodox education. He is considered to be Russia's first secular poet.

POLTAVA, BATTLE OF (1709), in the Ukraine, at which Peter the Great defeated the army of Charles XII during the Great Northern War. The Swedes, who were besieging the town of Poltava, attacked the camp of the Russian relieving force and were repulsed with the loss of nearly 10,000 men. This defeat was due to several factors: Charles had been wounded some days before and had therefore transferred the command to Rehnskiold; an unexpected realignment of the Russian redoubts deprived the Swedes of the advantage of a surprise advance; and many Swedes felt demoralized by the hardships and disappointments of the preceding winter. Three days after the battle 14,000 Swedes surrendered, a dénouement which might have been avoided if Charles had not fled to Turkey.

POLYANOV, TREATY OF (1634), settlement ending the short Russo-Polish War of 1632–4, concluded near Vyazma on the Polyanov river. Under the treaty Poland abandoned the pretensions of Vladislav and recognized Tsar Michael Romanov as the legitimate ruler of Russia. However, the Russians were forced to pay an indemnity and Smolensk and other border towns remained Polish, though some of these were later recovered by Russia in the War of 1654–67.

POLYBIUS OF MEGALOPOLIS (c. 200–120 BC), Greek historian of Rome's struggle with Carthage. He was a political supporter of Philopoemen and later Hipparch of the Achaean League (169–168). After the Third Macedonian War he was taken as hostage to Rome where he lived in the household of Aemilius Paullus, becoming a friend of Scipio Aemilianus. Polybius wrote the history of the period 264–146 in 40 books, but his main theme was the rise of Rome to world dominion between 220 and 168. His history, being universal, allowed him to depict the interaction between Roman policies and those of other nations. He travelled widely to reinforce his reading with personal observation.

POLYCARP (c. AD 69–c. 155), Christian leader who was Bp of Smyrna in Roman Asia. He visited Anicetus, Bp of Rome, to discuss the date of keeping Easter. Soon after his return to Smyrna he was arrested during a pagan festival, but refused to recant his faith, claiming that he had served Christ for 86 years, and was burnt to death. Polycarp spent much of his time defending orthodoxy and combating heresies. Important letters to him from Ignatius of Antioch and from him to the Philippians have survived.

POLYCRATES (d. 522 BC), Tyrant of Samos. By his defeat of Lesbos and Miletus, his control of Rhodes, his friendship with Lygdamis of Naxos, his close association with Delos, and the possession of 100 warships and 1000 archers, he dominated the Aegean. Among those who graced his court were famous poets, *eg*, Anacreon, Ibycus; craftsmen, *eg*, Theodorus; architects, *eg*, Rhoecus; engineers, *eg*, Eupalinus; and doctors, *eg*, Democedes. His public works included the great temple to Hera, the famous water tunnel, and the harbour mole. After being friendly at first with Amasis of Egypt, as appears from Herodotus' well-known story of the ring and the fish, he later supported Cambyses' expedition against Egypt (525). A Spartan expedition against him failed (525), but later (c. 522) he was treacherously slain by the Persian satrap of Lydia, Oroetes.

POLYNESIAN MIGRATIONS into the Pacific began in pre-Christian times. Carbon-14 dates suggest arrival c. 400 BC in the Marquesas; 1000 BC in Tonga. Quiros's accidental settlement thesis (1597), revived by Sharp (1957), is vague about primary routes. Zuniga's (1803) and Heyerdahl's (1951) suggestion of American origin is vitiated by the Spanish introduction of the crucial sweet potato into Hawaii (c. 1574) and of both cotton and kumara into the Marquesas in 1595 by 52 named Peruvian Indians with Mendana. The recently resurrected Indo-Melanesian route, via New Guinea, rests on still meagre archaeological evidence, dubiously Polynesian in provenance. Buck's traditional route, based on adze types, etc., leads from South-East Asia (Formosa?) through Micronesia down the Gilbert and Ellice chain to Samoa–Tonga, and along the Line to Tahiti and the Marquesas, thence secondarily to Easter Island (AD 400) and NZ (7th–13th cents). Movements (13th–16th cents) from the Gilberts–Samoa–Tonga west into eastern coastal Melanesia were finally frustrated by malaria—hence the 'outliers' and the distinct cultural divide at 170° E (Buxton's Line).

POLYPERCHON (c. 380–c. 303 BC), soldier of Alexander the Great's army who was appointed regent of the empire by Antipater (319), but was soon made ineffective by Cassander, his authority being restricted to the Peloponnese.

POLYSYNODIE in France, system of aristocratic conciliar government established by the Duke of Orléans, regent for the child-king Louis XV, during the period of political reaction following Louis XIV's death (1715–18). The use of the traditional royal advisers, the nobility, had been advocated by such as the Duke of Saint-Simon and the Abbé of St Pierre, to counteract the excessive power of the secretaries of state. Orléans set up six councils under a regency council to deal with war, the navy, finance, home affairs, foreign policy, and religion. By 1718 the experiment appeared to be failing and the councils were suppressed.

POMARE I (c. 1745–1803), *ari'i nui* (titular paramount chief) of Tahiti (1767), who provoked opposition by his pursuit of temporal power. He was worsted in numerous campaigns by rival chiefs (1771, 1777), was restored by 1791 but again overthrown (1798) by his son and successor, Tu (Pomare II), whom he recognized (1799). He was a friend of foreigners and missionaries though he hated the religion they introduced. He did much to transform ancient Tahiti.

POMARE II (Tu) (c. 1782–1821), *ari'i nui* (titular paramount chief) of Tahiti. He was a despot alienating all Tahiti, and was driven out to Mo'orea. He finally sought supremacy as a Christian and overthrew his rival, Tati of Papara, in 1815.

POMARE, SIR MAUI WIREMU (1876–1930), NZ Maori leader and politician, who advocated fuller Europeanization, was a health officer among the Maoris (1900–11), and minister of health (1919–28).

POMBAL, SEBASTIÃO JOSÉ DE CARVALHO E MELLO, Marquis of (1699–1782), Portuguese politician and diplomat, who was ambassador at London (1739–45), and at Vienna (1745–49), secretary of state for foreign affairs (1749–56), and became prime minister in 1756. He reorganized the education, finance, and armed forces of Portugal and encouraged industry and colonial development. His adroit handling of the chaos which followed the Lisbon earthquake (1755) assured him of the complete confidence of King Joseph, which enabled him to attack successfully the tyranny of the Church. The Jesuits were expelled (1759) and the power of the Inquisition broken, but on the death of the king in 1777 Pombal was dismissed by the queen mother, Marianna Victoria, and forbidden to reside within 20 leagues of the court.

POMERANIA, SWEDISH (*Vorpommern*), dukedom on the Baltic coast, acquired by Sweden in 1648 (together with rights of representation in the Imperial Diet). Brandenburg gained the districts east of the Oder in 1679 and those east of the Peene (including Stettin) in 1720.

POMERIUM, Latin term for the demarcation of any city, but particularly applied to Rome itself. The earliest known pomerium contained all seven hills, except the Aventine.

POMESTIE in Russia, estate held in service tenure from the grand dukes of Muscovy and later from the tsars on condition that the dukes performed military or other state duties. Such estates were first granted extensively by Ivan III (*reg.* 1462–1505). They were extended under Ivan IV (*reg.* 1533–84) and from Peter I's time (*reg.* 1689–1725) their holders were known as *dvoryanstvo*.

POMPADOUR, JEANNE ANTOINETTE POISSON, Marquise de (1721–64), French patron of the arts and mistress and confidante of Louis XV. She used her connections in the world of finance, and her beauty, charm, and intelligence, to become the king's mistress from 1745 to 1751 and she retained the king's affection until her death.

Her political influence was limited, though she took some part in cementing the alliance between France and Austria (1756) and her protégé, the Duke of Choiseul, rose to be secretary of state for foreign affairs. She was responsible for the founding of the Sèvres porcelain industry and patronized the tapestry workshops at Gobelins, Aubusson, and Beauvais. Her favourite painter was Boucher. Her interest in architecture was shared by her brother, Marigny, the superintendent of buildings, and her name is associated with the *petite Trianon*, planned for her by Louis XV.

POMPEII, ancient city about 19 kms east of Naples. It was an Italian foundation strongly influenced from the 8th cent. BC by neighbouring Greek colonies and was a Samnite city from *c.* 400, until Sulla captured it in the Social War (89 BC) and made it a Roman colony. It was destroyed, with Herculaneum, in the great eruption of Mount Vesuvius (AD 79) and, like Herculaneum, preserved under volcanic ash. Excavation, begun in 1748, uncovered a storehouse of artistic treasures and information about living conditions in the 1st cent. AD.

POMPEIUS, CN., STRABO (d. 87 BC), Roman consul in 89 and father of Pompey the Great. After commanding in the Social War, in which he reduced Asculum, he maintained himself in his native Picenum, ignoring senatorial orders to disband his army, which murdered his successor. He played an equivocal part in Marius' attack on Rome.

POMPEIUS, SEXTUS (d. 35 BC), younger son of Pompey the Great. After fighting against Julius Caesar at Munda (45), he escaped and after Caesar's death raised a fleet and occupied Sicily. Eventually, he was defeated by Octavian's admiral, Agrippa (36), but escaped to Asia, where he was captured and killed.

POMPEY THE GREAT, Cn. Pompeius Magnus (106–48 BC), Roman soldier and politician of the last years of the republic. He was an opponent of Julius Caesar in the Civil War which started in 49. After fighting under his father in the Social War, he raised a private army in Picenum to assist Sulla's invasion of Italy (83–82). Sulla sent him to destroy the Marian forces in Sicily and Africa. Having helped to suppress Aemilius Lepidus' revolt (77), he was sent with proconsular *imperium* to campaign against Sertorius in Spain, returning in 71 to assist Crassus in ending the slave rebellion led by Spartacus. Backed by their respective armies, Crassus and Pompey, who was not qualified, obtained the consulships of 70 against senatorial opposition and eventually did away with Sulla's political reforms. Neither took a provincial governorship in 69, but in 67 Gabinius had unprecedented powers conferred on Pompey to deal with piracy, and in 66 Pompey took over Lucullus' command against Mithridates, whom he defeated.

After settling the East, Pompey returned to Italy (61), desiring alliance with the nobility, ratification of his eastern settlement, and land for his discharged veterans. The opposition of the nobility, led by Cato and Lucullus, drove him into unwilling alliance with Crassus and Caesar, who passed the required legislation as consul (59). Loss of popularity and Clodius' attacks made Pompey regret the alliance, but it was confirmed at the Conference of Lucca. He was consul again with Crassus (55) and thereafter governed Spain *in absentia* for five years through *legati*. The murder of Clodius led to his appointment as sole consul (52) and a growing rapprochement with the nobility caused his acceptance of the command of the Republican forces (50), which he evacuated from Italy on Caesar's invasion (49). He was defeated by Caesar at Pharsalus, and fled to Egypt, where he was murdered.   DCE

POMPIDOU, GEORGES (1911–), French politician and president of France. When De Gaulle chose him as prime minister (1962) he had had no previous ministerial or parliamentary experience. After graduating from the École Normale Supérieure, he became a schoolteacher (1935–44). At the time of the liberation he attracted the attention of De Gaulle and joined his personal staff. He then entered public service as an official of the *conseil d'état*, and later became a director of Rothschild's bank and various companies. During this period he remained a friend and adviser of De Gaulle, and in 1958 he again served briefly on his personal staff. He was chosen to succeed Debré as prime minister, and had to weather the political storm caused by De Gaulle's proposal to make the presidency elective. Pompidou's government was defeated in parliament on this issue, but De Gaulle maintained him in office and called an election (1962). In the subsequent years Pompidou proved an able interpreter of De Gaulle's policies, and was widely regarded as his likely successor. The social disturbances of 1968 seemed to shake his position, and he lost his post after the elections of that year. But when De Gaulle resigned from the presidency Pompidou was chosen as the Gaullist candidate and elected on the second ballot (1969).

PONCE DE LEON, JUAN (1460–1521), Spanish explorer, who accompanied Columbus on his second voyage (1493), and was governor of Puerto Rico (1509–12). He made a fortune in trade in the Caribbean, and received a patent from the King of Spain (1514) to colonize FL, which he had discovered the previous year. His second expedition (1521) landed on the west coast of FL with 200 settlers. He was killed by Seminole Indians and the colony was abandoned. He had, however, gained for Spain the first territory on the mainland of North America.

PONDICHERRY, chief of the French settlements in India, founded (1683) by François Martin, by purchase from the Raja of Gingi. After restoration by the Dutch (1697), who had taken it (1693), Pondicherry grew rapidly and became the chief French station in India. Governors Lenoir and Dumas continued Martin's work. Dupleix (1742–54) attempted to oust the British from south India by direct attack and Indian alliances. The struggle ended with the surrender of Pondicherry (Jan. 1761). It was restored (1763), but thereafter occupied by the British at each outbreak of war (1778, 1782, 1793, 1803). At the European settlement of 1815 Pondicherry was finally restored as an open town, which it remained until it was ceded to India in 1956.

PONDOLAND REBELLION (1960) in Transkei, South African republic. It marked an important point in African rural protest against the application of *apartheid* to South African areas previously treated as purely African in composition. This took the form of an administrative transformation of the traditional authorities of the Pondo (more properly, Mpondo) branch of the Southern Bantu group of peoples into so-called 'Bantu authorities'. These were to be closely tied into the *apartheid* system, were expected to preside over a Transkei 'Bantustan' or nominally autonomous Bantu state, and were accordingly resented by people who wished to retain chiefs whom they respected.

Pondo farmers refused to accept this *Gleichschaltung* into the *apartheid* system (as others, in one degree or another, were to do elsewhere). They organized a determined resistance expressed in protests, civil disobedience, demonstrations, and selective hut-burnings. Towards the end of 1960 the Pondo movement took over the full programme of the African National Congress and its supporters, so linking rural protest to the hitherto largely urban protests. The South African government declared a state of emergency, and deployed a force to crush the movement.

P'ONG TÜK, earliest historic archaeological site in Thailand, on the Meklong river, 40 kms north of Ratburi, where a Graeco-Roman bronze lamp, building foundations, and statuary and stucco pieces were found in 1927.

PONSONBY OF IMOKILLY, JOHN PONSONBY, Viscount (1770–1855), British diplomat who, as ambassador in Istanbul (1832–7), played a vital role, in collaboration with Palmerston, in the reconstruction of British policy on the Eastern Question.

PONTCHARTRAIN FAMILY in France, elder branch of the Phélypeaux family, which was founded by Paul (1569–1621), sometime secretary of state to Louis XIII. His son, Louis I, Sieur de Pontchartrain (1613–85), was too young to succeed his father as secretary of state, but served with distinction in the Paris *chambre des comptes*, rising to be its president (1650), but he lost all hope of government preferment by his opposition to the trial of Fouquet (1663). His son, Louis II (1643–1727), then a councillor in the *parlement* of Paris, also opposed the trial, but through the support of Louvois was later promoted to the first presidency of the *parlement* of Rennes (1677) and later, as comte de Pontchartrain, went on to serve with distinction as *intendant* of finances (1687), controller-general (1689), minister for the navy and the royal household (1690–9), and finally minister of state (1690) and chancellor (1699–1714). In 1714 he retired to the Oratory. He was one of the more respected members of the government of Louis XIV, whom he served diligently if without panache, and was able to preserve his family's pre-eminence in the state after the king's death. His son, Jerome, Comte de Pontchartrain (1674–1747), was a tactless and incompetent secretary for the navy and the royal household (1699–1715) and was forced to resign in favour of his son, Jean Fréderic, Comte de Maurepas, who was to prove almost as distinguished a servant of the state as his grandfather.

PONT-GRAVÉ, FRANÇOIS (1554–1629), French explorer and trader, who led a trading expedition up the St Lawrence river in Canada as far as Three Rivers (*c.* 1599). He ascended the river as far as the falls of Saint-Louis (1603). Pont-Gravé was given charge of Port Royal, a settlement in Acadia (1605–6), and of Quebec (1619–20).

PONTIAC'S REBELLION (1763–4), uprising of Indians in the upper Ohio valley of North America. Following the French surrender of Canada to Britain (1763), Indian leaders became fearful of British control of the fur trade and the presence of traders, land speculators, and settlers coming in after the French defeat. A prophet of the Delaware tribe began to spread a message among the tribes calling for a return to the old customs and a rejection of the white man's ways. Pontiac (*c.* 1720–69), an Ottawa chief, made use of the prophet's message to help to convert Indian unrest into a unified attack on the British. In a speech (27 April 1763) to assembled delegates from various tribes, he called upon them to drive the British out. Pontiac planned a surprise attack on Fort Detroit, but the plan was exposed, and he was forced to lay siege to the fort (7 May 1763). News of Pontiac's attack on Detroit spread rapidly among the Indians and a massive uprising began. Shawnees, Delawares, and Chippewas joined with the Ottawas and western forts were captured or destroyed. By the end of July only Forts Niagara, Pitt, and Detroit remained in British hands. Several British expeditions were crushed and the frontier was isolated. The unity of tribes which Pontiac viewed as essential to the entire rebellion began to break up as individual tribes accepted Sir William Johnson's invitation to a peace conference for the summer of 1764. The tribes which did not accept the invitation were defeated by British expeditions in Aug. and Sept. Fort Mackinac was rebuilt (Sept. 1764) and the British once again controlled the west. Pontiac raised the siege of Fort Detroit (Nov. 1763) and finally submitted (17 Aug. 1765) to George Crogham and signed the final peace (24 July 1766) with Sir William Johnson at Oswego. Pontiac's Rebellion led the British government to issue the Proclamation of 1763, which excluded white settlement in the Ohio valley. The Proclamation was resented by colonial land speculators and was a major source of friction between the British government and their North American colonists. Pontiac lived at peace until he was killed by a Peoria Indian warrior (1769).

F. Parkman, *Conspiracy of Pontiac* (Boston, 1851).
H. H. Peckham, *Pontiac and the Indian Uprising* (Princeton, 1947).   DHP

PONTIFEX MAXIMUS, head of the college of pontiffs in ancient Rome, who supervised priests, vestal virgins, and the *rex sacrorum*, and was responsible for the administration of all state cults. It is uncertain how he was chosen earlier, but from the 3rd cent. BC he was elected for life by vote of 17 tribes chosen by lot. Sulla entrusted the choice to the college itself, but in 64 BC Labienus restored the election to the commons. Later, the office was customarily held by the emperors.

PONTIUS PILATE (*fl.* 1st cent. AD), Roman governor of Judaea AD 26–36, under whom Jesus Christ was crucified. Jewish sources depict him as a time-server, as do the Gospels, which represent him as being at first well disposed towards Jesus, but finally yielding to mob violence through fear. Eusebius records a tradition that he committed suicide. Later legends develop this theme and also give the name of his wife as Claudia Procula. The Coptic Church reveres him as a martyr.

PONTOTOC, TREATY OF (20 Oct. 1832), negotiated between the US government and Chickasaw Indians in northern Mississippi. The Chickasaw ceded all their land east of the Mississippi river and agreed to move west.

PONTS DE CÉ (7 July 1619), skirmish on the Loire, in which the forces of Louis XIII dispersed troops raised by Marie de' Medici and the magnates with whom she was allied, without much fighting and before they could raise a large army. It was caused by the conflict between the queen mother and Luynes, the royal favourite, and could have led to a serious civil war.

PONTUS, district in north-east Asia Minor on the Black Sea coast, established as a kingdom (301 BC) by a Persian satrap, Mithridates, whom Alexander the Great had put in charge of the region. The territory was enlarged by subsequent kings, reaching its greatest extent under Mithridates VI. After his defeat by Pompey the kingdom was dismantled, part becoming a Roman province with Bithynia. The remainder was annexed in AD 64 and joined to the province Galatia-Cappadocia.

PONY EXPRESS (1860–1) in US, attempt to demonstrate the feasibility of all-the-year-round communication over the central overland route. The freighting firm of Russell, Majors, and Waddell established relay stations every 15 miles (24 kms) for horses and riders who, from 3 April 1860 until 24 Oct. 1861, carried mail over the 2000-mile (3200 kms) route from St Joseph, MO, to Sacramento, CA. The opening of the transcontinental telegraph eliminated the need for the pony express.

POONA, TREATY OF (1817), by which the Maratha peshwa, Baji Rao II, who was conspiring to form a Maratha coalition against the British, promised to abstain from anti-British activities. A further revolt resulted in his defeat and the abolition of the peshwaship.

POONA PACT (25 Sept. 1932) in India, agreement between Gandhi and B. R. Ambedkar which amended the Communal Award (Aug. 1932) in respect of the Depressed Class representation in the provincial legislatures. The award had given the Depressed Class electors the right to vote in both the general constituencies and in separate electorates in all provinces except the Punjab and the North-West Frontier Province. Gandhi, who objected strongly to this separation of the Depressed Classes from the Hindu community, began (20 Sept.) a 'fast unto death' in Yeravada prison in Poona to force the amendment of the award. Under this pressure, Ambedkar agreed to accept 148 reserved seats within the general constituencies in place of 71 separate seats under the award, with the proviso that for the first ten years the depressed class electors would be able to hold primary elections to choose the candidates who would appear at the general election.

POOR LAW in England, series of enactments culminating in the English Poor Law (1601), known as the 'Old Poor Law', and later amended by an act of 1834 which established the 'New Poor Law', which provided for minimal relief for the destitute. The breakdown of the medieval economy, which added a new element of instability to economic life, led to the first statute dealing specifically with poor relief (1531), which empowered JPs to license aged and impotent persons to beg. A statute of 1536, often regarded as the first English poor law, organized voluntary funds for the relief of those unable to work, and divided the poor into deserving and undeserving. London took the lead in poor relief, imposing a compulsory poor rate (1547), which was extended to a national scale (1572). The Elizabethan Poor Law was completed by the codification of the laws (1597–8), their re-enactment in 1601, and final permanent form of 1623. The parish was the normal unit of administration, and JPs entrusted the work to overseers appointed annually. Though the privy council established machinery to make the acts effective, there was only patchy success in application. With the outbreak of civil war all supervision disappeared and the local authorities were left to themselves. Not until 1834 was centralized supervision to return.

The Law of Settlement and Removal (1662) enforced the removal of any poor persons who threatened to become a burden on a parish back to their original place of settlement. Though amended by acts of 1685 and 1693, the law of 1662, which had only given statutory force to established local custom, remained the centre of poor law administration until 1834. The system, however, did not work very effectively and mobility of labour was not unduly restricted.

Further acts of 1723 and 1782 enabled the parishes to build workhouses, and to provide outdoor relief for able-bodied poor. The major change in the system before 1834 came in 1795 with the introduction of the Speenhamland system by the JPs of Berkshire, which quickly spread and was confirmed by parliament (1796). It provided that wages below what was considered to be an absolute minimum should be supplemented by the parish in accordance with the price of bread.

The Poor Law Amendment Act (1834) laid down that poor relief should be granted to able-bodied poor and their dependants only in well-regulated workhouses under conditions inferior to those of the poorest labourer outside. New machinery was established, consisting of independent parishes grouped in unions, each under an elected board of guardians, with a strong central authority in the Poor Law Commission. The system proved cruelly inadequate to a society in the process of industrializing itself, in which there was much genuine unemployment. Reforms carried out during the 19th cent., principally concerned the central authority, but the system remained essentially unchanged until well into the 20th cent.

Despite the important report of the 1909 royal commission on the Poor Law, when a majority advocated fundamental alterations in the system, and a minority its abolition, no action was taken till the Local Government Act (1929). The development of such measures as old age pensions and national insurance, however, reduced the necessity for a poor law. The Poor Law Act (1930) consolidated previous legislation and placed relief under the minister of health. The break-up of the Poor Law in the 1930s under the impact of massive unemployment was the prelude to its final replacement by the Welfare State after the Second World War.

J. R. Tanner, *Tudor Constitutional Documents* (Cambridge, 1930).
Sidney and Beatrice Webb, *English Poor Law History* (London, 1927–9).   CJ

POPE, ALEXANDER (1688–1744), English poet, a master of the rhyming couplet, in which he achieved consummate satirical and lyrical effects. His poetic genius is evident in the Essay on Criticism (1711), 'The Rape of the Lock' (1712), the translation of Homer (1715–26), 'The Dunciad' (1728), 'An Essay on Man' (1733–4), and numerous satires.

POPE, JOHN (1822–92), US soldier, who served in the Mexican War (1846–8) and commanded the Union army of the MS (1862). He was appointed to organize a new Union army of VA out of mixed federal forces from both the eastern and western theatres but failed to reconcile conflicting loyalties and was replaced after the second battle of Bull Run, or Manassas (Aug. 1862). He never again held field command, but later served as commander of the third military district in the South (1867) and of the important Department of Missouri (1870–83).

POPE-HENNESSEY, SIR JOHN (1834–91), British politician and colonial administrator, who was the first Roman Catholic Conservative to enter parliament (1859). He later held appointments as governor of the Labuan (1867–71), the Gold Coast (1872–3), the Bahamas (1873–4), the Windward Islands (1875–6), Hong Kong (1877–82), and Mauritius (1883–9). In Mauritius he was felt to be unduly sympathetic to French creole interests. He was therefore recalled to Britain and suspended but later returned (1887) thereafter being vindicated (1889).

POPHAM, SIR HOME RIGGS (1762–1820), British sailor, who served in the French Wars, and commanded the naval expedition against the Cape (1806). Later in the same year he led an unauthorized expedition which captured Buenos Aires in 1806. He was recalled and severely reprimanded for his action. The British were later expelled from Buenos Aires.

POPHAM, SIR JOHN (1531–1607), Elizabethan lawyer and politician, who held the offices of solicitor-general (1579), speaker of the House of Commons (1580), attorney-general (1581–92), and lord chief justice of the king's bench (1592–1607), during which time he presided over the trials of Sir Walter Raleigh and the gunpowder plotters.

POPISH PLOT, THE (1678), in England, most notorious of the conspiracies supposed to have been hatched by Roman Catholics. In Sept. 1678 in sworn depositions before a magistrate, Sir Edmund Berry Godfrey, Titus Oates, and Israel Tonge alleged that certain Catholic Jesuit priests had on 4 May 1678 at the White Horse tavern in the Strand plotted to assassinate King Charles II, murder Protestants, and place James, Duke of York on the throne. Shortly afterwards they appeared before the privy council, most of whose members (but not the king) believed Oates. They had given a copy of their charges to Godfrey, whose body was found on 27 Oct. pierced by a sword and bearing marks of strangulation. The mystery of his death has never been solved. But the panic arising from news of the so-called popish plot coalesced with mass hysteria resulting from the discovery of Godfrey's death. To the public it seemed that Godfrey's fate might lie in store for Protestants. Thus the whole popish plot scare had a tremendous political effect: it provided the background against which the events of the next two and a half years were played out. In such circumstances, it seemed not unreasonable that the Duke of York should be excluded from the succession. Ultimately passions died down, James was not excluded, and Charles II was able to do without parliament altogether for the last four years of his reign. As for Oates, he was convicted of perjury at the beginning of James II's reign, and was imprisoned until released after the Revolution (1688).

POPITZ, JOHANNES (1884–1945), German civil servant, politician, and finance minister (1932–44), who was executed by the Nazis for complicity in the resistance to Hitler. He was an expert in fiscal and tax affairs, and was originally attracted to Nazism by his belief that strong government was needed to achieve political and economic reforms after the depression of the 1930s. He became disillusioned with the regime, but stayed in office in the hope that he could exert a restraining influence, especially through his superior, Göring. He maintained contacts with the military opposition and the Kreisau Circle, and in 1943 tried to enlist Himmler's support for the resistance. He was arrested and tried after the July Plot (1944).

POPLARISM in Britain, form of financial strike by several Labour-controlled municipal authorities, both inside and outside London, in the 1920s. It took its name from Poplar borough council and board of guardians, which decided (1921) not to pay the borough's contribution to the London County Council on the grounds that they could not afford to pay these contributions and to maintain the large number of unemployed in Poplar. It was asserted by a number of East End councils that the burden of Poor Law payment should be shared by the richer boroughs of London. One result of the 'strike' was the imprisonment of the mayor of Poplar, George Lansbury, and most of the council in Sept. 1921.

POPOLO D'ITALIA, IL, Milan daily paper, founded in Nov. 1914 to encourage Italian intervention in the First World War against Germany. It became the leading interventionist organ. It was virulent in attacking its opponents, and reflected Mussolini's evolving views. Having raised money for D'Annunzio in Fiume (1919), it then dropped his cause. It was increasingly financed by industry. It was a major contribution to Mussolini's rise to power, and was his mouthpiece throughout his dictatorship, and reflected orthodox government views.

POPULAR FRONT in France, alliance of the Communist, Socialist, and Radical parties which won the 1936 election, then supported the Popular Front government of Léon Blum. This was the most important episode in French history in the 1930s, and showed the continuing vitality of democracy.

The movement towards a Popular Front began in 1934, when the right-wing riots of 6 Feb. seemed to show that fascism was a danger at home as well as abroad. Another factor was the worsening of the Depression and the failure of orthodox measures to cope with it. In all parties it was the rank-and-file which impelled the leaders towards an alliance, but the Popular Front would have been impossible if the Communist International, formerly hostile to alliances with social democrats and 'bourgeois' parties, had not changed its policy. The French communist leaders then became the keenest supporters of the alliance.

The Popular Front, consolidated in 1935, drew up a programme for the 1936 election, adopting as its slogan 'Bread, peace, and liberty'. The result was a sweeping victory for the left, achieved in an atmosphere of popular euphoria. Blum became head of a Radical–Socialist coalition, the communists supporting the government, but refusing to take office. The election was followed by a spontaneous wave of sit-in strikes, to end which Blum negotiated the 'Matignon agreements' between unions and employers, providing for general wage increases and the recognition of trade union activity. The subsequent social reforms of the Popular Front government aimed at improving the workers' standard of living and at reducing the power of big business (the '200 families'). The reforms included the 40-hour week, paid holidays for all workers, state control of the Bank of France, nationalization of some parts of the arms industry, and the creation of a wheat marketing board.

By 1937 the alliance was breaking up. The communists were alienated by Blum's refusal to intervene in the Spanish Civil War, while the radicals disliked his unorthodox economic policies. These were intended to stimulate production by increasing purchasing power, but their immediate effect was inflationary. The government encountered severe financial difficulties, was forced to devalue the franc, and eventually resigned (1937), the Senate having rejected Blum's plans for exchange control and other emergency measures. This marked the real end of the Popular Front experiment, although three further governments under Chautemps and Blum (1937–8) are described as Popular Front governments.

The Popular Front created hopes and fears which had a profound effect in France, and it is still surrounded by controversy. Although many of its reforms were long overdue, it may have contributed by deepening social divisions to France's defeat in the Second World War. It was also accused by its enemies of weakening France's military strength, but in fact it was under Blum that serious rearmament began. The Popular Front episode remains relevant to contemporary French politics because of the continuing division of the left. RDA

POPULAR FRONT in Spain, narrowly defined as the electoral coalition of republicans and socialists which triumphed in the Feb. 1936 elections. The term is also used to describe the period of rule by the Republican government (Feb.–July 1936), which was installed in accordance with the coalition's programme. The term can further be used to describe the loyalist side in the Spanish Civil War.

A popular front of workers was anticipated (1932) by Joaquín Maurín's Bloque Obrero y Campesino and later by Largo Caballero's Alianza Obrera (1934). This Alianza Obrera, the backbone of the Asturian rising of Oct. 1934, consisted of the local UGT, CNT, and the Communists. The working-class unity produced in Asturias was the real forerunner of the Popular Front.

In 1935 it was realized by the left that the electoral defeat of Nov. 1933 derived from its disunity. Azaña decided to take advantage of the emotional unity created by the right-wing government's persecution of the Oct. rebels and of himself. At the same time as he and Prieto attempted by a series of speeches to forge the necessary alliance, the Communist Party began to advocate a popular front. Partly out of the needs of the Franco-Russian alliance and partly out of a realization of the folly of the policy which had allowed Hitler to seize power without opposition, the Comintern was calling for working-class support of bourgeois democracy to defeat fascism. In Aug. 1935 Dimitrov, the general secretary of the Comintern, called for 'the formation of a joint people's front'.

When elections were called it only required eight days of negotiation to produce the popular front pact of Jan. 1936. Republicans, socialists, communists, the POUM, and the Catalan Esquerra agreed on a programme of a return to the social, religious, and educational reform of the republic's first two years; a speeding up of agricultural reform; amnesty for the victims of the post-Asturias repression, and freedom for working-class organizations—to be carried out by a left republican government supported by working-class votes. The CNT officially stood aside, but the rank-and-file voted for the popular front, which gained 4,838,449 votes against the right's 3,996,931. PP

POPULAR PARTY in Italy (Partito Popolare Italiano) founded in 1929 by Don L. Sturzo, as a non-confessional but Catholic-orientated party, theoretically independent of the Vatican and Catholic Action, though it was initially supported by them. Its policies included decentralization of government, land redistribution, support for Catholic unions and co-operatives, educational reforms, and economic expansion. It was successful at elections in 1919 and 1921 and joined coalition governments (1919–22). But inter-party disagreements contributed to overall government instability, which in turn facilitated fascist successes. By mid-1922 moderate party leaders, such as Sturzo and De Gasperi, belatedly joined its left-wingers in seeking socialist collaboration; the right-wingers (encouraged by Pius XI and Catholic Action) conditionally supported Mussolini, and in 1922 joined his coalition. Fascist intimidation, Vatican hostility, and electoral setbacks influenced the *popolari* in joining the 'Aventine' secession from parliament (June 1924), but the party hesitated to oppose Mussolini decisively. Its remaining members were unseated in 1926. Remnants of its members created the Christian Democracy Party in 1943.

POPULAR SOVEREIGNTY in US, theory of government implicit in US history since the American Revolution, but explicitly expounded by Senator Lewis Cass, of MI, in 1847 as a solution to the question of slavery expansion into the territories. Cass suggested that the people of a territory had the right to decide whether slavery should exist within their jurisdiction. Stephen A. Douglas, of IL, endorsed this principle and included it in that section of the Compromise of 1850 which organized the territories of UT and NM. When applying for statehood, either territory would 'be received into the Union, with or without slavery, as their constitution may prescribe at the time of their admission'. Douglas used the phrase itself in the Kansas–Nebraska Act (1854). The issue of popular sovereignty, termed 'squatter sovereignty' by its opponents, dominated the famous Lincoln–Douglas debates (1858) and was a contributing factor to the growing rift between the North and South which foreshadowed the American Civil War.

POPULARES, ancient Roman term for politicians of the 1st cent. BC, *eg,* Marius, Julius Caesar, who used the support of the people to combat the *optimates,* supporters of the senatorial aristocracy.

POPULISM (*Narodnichestve*), term, derived from Russian word for folk, used to describe a widespread, radical agrarian socialist movement in mid-19th-cent. Russia. It covered many personalities and as an ideology it had no coherent body of doctrine. Some historians describe it as encompassing the whole revolutionary generation from Herzen to the 1880s; others date 'classical populism' only from the 1870s or distinguish between it as an ideology and a revolutionary movement.

The populists, who were of the intelligentsia, were mainly students of various backgrounds, linked in small groups of which the Chaikovsky circle is one of the most important (1869–74). Their ideas, disseminated by the literary journals of the day and given much publicity by a persecuting government, derived directly from Herzen and Chernyshevsky and indirectly from Proudhon, Bakunin, and Marx. Herzen first advocated 'going to the people' and drew attention to the peasant commune (*mir*).

Their basic beliefs were the destruction of the tsarist autocracy and the centralized state apparatus, which were to be replaced by a loose federation of socialist self-governing units based on the commune. Central to populism is a faith in, and often idealization of, the peasant way of life and organization. This was developed, especially by Mikhailovsky, into a theory of economic development. Russia, through the commune, could bypass Western capitalism and pass from feudalism to socialism. The commune and co-operative workshop would make possible socialist development, using technology and some forms of industrialization without exploitation. This would ensure also the full development of individual personality, the other central aim of populism, and one which often conflicted with their desire for service to the community. This individualist, moral nature of populism was also emphasized by the other chief theorist of populism, P. Lavrov, who stressed the role of a critically thinking elite and their moral duty to achieve social justice and equality for the peasantry.

The 'going to the people' movement (*Khozhdenie v narod*) of the 1870s culminated in the summer of 1874 with a pilgrimage to the villages. The Bakuninists expected to create an immediate social upheaval, while the followers of Lavrov assumed a period of education. Others (and it was to these that the term 'populist' was first applied) preached the subordination of the intelligentsia to the peasantry and went to learn the true way of life. All groups assumed that the people would make their own revolution.

After the failure of 1874 there was an increased concentration on organization. Land and Liberty (*zemlya i volya*) was founded 1876, but split 1879 into The People's Will (*Narodnaya Volya*) and Black Partition (*Chernyi Peredel*). The former concentrated on terrorism and assassinated Alexander II in 1881. Their political aims, involving the seizure and use of state power, contrasted with classical populism's assumption of a social revolution and brought them nearer to the Jacobin wing of the movement, associated with the names of Nechaev and Tkachev.

The revolutionary movement declined in the 1880s, but the legal populists kept the economic theories alive in their debate with the Marxists.

F. Venturi, *Roots of Revolution* (London, 1960).
A. Walicki, *The Controversy over Capitalism* (London, 1969).
BJW

POPULISM in the US, agrarian political doctrine associated with the Populist (People's) Party. The emergence of populism and the party in the early 1890s reflected the growing discontent of mid-western and southern farmers with declining prices, poor credit facilities, and rising freight and warehousing costs. These conditions, especially after the disastrous harvests of the late 1880s, impelled the Farmers Alliances, Greenbackers, and other groups to political action, and resulted in the creation of the People's party (1891), which held its first national convention at Omaha (1892). The convention drew up a comprehensive programme which included such proposals as free coinage of silver and farm credit schemes designed to help the farmers; an eight-hour working day; immigration restriction, and the prohibition of labour spies to win the support of urban labour; the direct election of senators, and a secret ballot to democratize the political system. Of these, the most fertile politically was the silver issue, and after a vigorous campaign the Populist presidential candidate, Gen. James B. Weaver, polled over 1 million votes. However, the Populists were soon faced with problems common amongst third parties in the US. In those states where their ideas were popular, they were adopted by the major parties. Attempts to establish common cause with urban labour against Eastern finance capitalism foundered upon divisions within the socialist ranks, and the antipathy of Samuel Gompers of the American Federation of Labor. Although support for the party was extensive in 1894, and appeared to be even more so in 1896, its fate in fact rested on the attitude of the major parties on the silver issue. Hopes of a Populist monopoly of the free-silver plank were dashed at the Democratic convention at Chicago (1896), when the silver Democrats took control, the party declared for free silver, and nominated William Jennings Bryan. The Populists now faced two equally unpleasant alternatives. They could continue to fight the election as a third party, and thus ensure a Republican victory by splitting the silver vote, or they could abandon their separate identity in fusion with the Democrats. The party convention (1896) took the latter course and nominated Bryan, together with a Populist vice-presidential candidate. Bryan's defeat by the Republican, McKinley, virtually eliminated the Populists as an effective party, but Populism persisted into the 20th cent. Many of its demands and principles, except for free silver, were adopted by those mid-western progressives who sought the redress of agrarian grievances by the use of governmental power. Populist influences may also be detected in the rise of Huey Long in LA and in the introverted attitude to foreign relations of US senator Gerald P. Nye in the 1930s.

J. D. Hicks, *The Populist Revolt* (Minneapolis, 1931).
N. Pollack, *The Populist Response to Industrial America* (Cambridge, MA 1962).　　　　　DBS

POPULONIA, in northern Italy, noted Etruscan city uncharacteristically founded on the coast, opposite Elba. The literary tradition of a later settlement there (from Volaterrae) is contradicted by the archaeological evidence of its two cemeteries. The city was a centre of iron manufactures. In 282 BC the Romans decisively defeated the Boii there.

PORDENONE, ODORICO DI (d. 1331), Franciscan missionary whose account (1330) of his mission to India, Indonesia, Cambodia, and China added appreciably to European knowledge of the Far East.

PORDIRIATO (PORFIRIATE) in Mexico, period of dictatorial rule by Porfirio Díaz (1876–80, 1884–1911). Gen. Díaz rebelled twice (1872, 1876) before overthrowing Sebastian Lerdo de Tejada's civilian government. Díaz ruled through force and compromise, bringing peace to Mexico for the first time since its independence. The 'Porfirian Peace' was bought at the expense of the poor, who saw their living standards decline and their village lands fall to the wealthy creole elite and army generals. Foreign capital, particularly from the US and Britain, poured in and the process of industrialization began, favoured treatment being given to the governments that invested money. The Church too progressed, benefiting from Díaz's willingness to ignore the laws of the 1850s. The regime toppled under attack from agrarian revolutionaries and political idealists. Porfirism became a general name for the tendency among Latin American dictators to grant sweeping concessions to foreign capitalists and pursue a strong policy at home in order to maintain a favourable climate for foreign investment.

PORPHYRY (c. AD 230–303), Neoplatonist philosopher, a disciple and successor of Plotinus and the most serious opponent of Christianity in the ancient world. He was born of a pagan family and brought up at Tyre, where he had close associations with the Christians, in particular, with Origen. He became convinced by Plotinus while studying philosophy at Athens (c. 262) and embraced Neoplatonism, becoming a successful teacher and numbering Iamblichus among his pupils. He turned his scholarly equipment against the Church, not only in a special treatise in 15 books, but also in a chronicle of world history designed to refute the writings of Julius Africanus and others.

PORT ARTHUR, name given to the Chinese port of Lü-shun by Admiral Seymour, named after Lieut. Arthur of the British navy, in 1860 during the Arrow War. It was strategically located to guard the sea approach to Tientsin and Peking, and was a bone of contention between Russia and Japan. In 1898 Russia secured a lease of the port and strongly fortified it, only to lose it to the Japanese in 1905. In their turn, the Japanese lost it to the USSR in the Second World War. The Russians kept Port Arthur until 1955, when they returned it to China.

PORT MAHON (1708), principal port of the Mediterranean island of Minorca, captured (1708) by the British from the Spaniards in the War of the Spanish Succession. It contributed to Britain's naval supremacy in the Mediterranean for most of the 18th cent., though held by France (1756–62) and retaken by Spain (1782). It was captured again by Britain in 1798 and finally restored to Spain in 1802.

PORT ROYAL, Jamaican port which became a centre for naval ships and pirates. The British built a fort there (1656), known after the Restoration (1660) as Fort Charles. The island's capital grew up around it, becoming wealthy and notorious as the headquarters of numerous buccaneers. Following an earthquake, the best part of the town sank beneath the waters (1692). It was reconstructed but again destroyed, by hurricane and fire (1702–3); whereupon the seat of government was moved inland. The fort, however, retained its importance. Many 18th-cent. naval expeditions were assembled there and Lord Nelson was in command of the fort (1779). A coaling station there was abandoned when coalburners gave way to oil in the 1930s. The town was destroyed by a hurricane in 1951, and rebuilt yet again.

PORT ROYAL, BATTLES OF (1690, 1710), capture of the French fortress of Port Royal on the western coast of NS by a force of MA militiamen under their English commander, Sir William Phipps (11 May 1690). After being retaken by the French in 1691 and retained by them in the peace of Ryswick (1697), Port Royal was attacked three times by the English in the War of the Spanish Succession (1704, 1707, 1710), being captured again at the last attempt by Col. Francis Nicholson and Sir Charles Hobby and renamed Annapolis Royal in honour of Queen Anne.

PORTAGES, term (from the French, *porter*) originating in North America to mark short land passages in which boats and supplies were carried from one river basin to another. The most important portages were between streams draining into the Mississippi river and the Great Lakes–St Lawrence river systems.

PORTAL OF HUNGERFORD, CHARLES FREDERICK ALGERNON PORTAL, Viscount (1893–   ), British airman who served with distinction in the First World War as a fighter pilot in France. During the Second World War he was air-officer commanding-in-chief, Bomber Command (April–Oct. 1940), and chief of the air staff (1940–5). Besides directing the policy and operations of the RAF he took a prominent part in the formulation of British and Allied strategy. At Bomber Command during the battle of Britain he was the first advocate of the indiscriminate bombing of German towns; and as chief of the air staff he made such attacks official strategy. He directed the Allied bomber offensive 'Pointblank' and inspired the 'Thunderclap' attack on Dresden in Feb. 1945. Later, he was associated with the United Kingdom Atomic Energy Programme.

PORTALES PLAZAZUELOS, DIEGO JOSÉ VICTOR (1793–1837), Chilean businessman and politician, who exercised considerable control over the Conservative regimes which came to power in Chile by defeating the Liberals in 1830, and which purged the army, persecuted Liberals, and showed favour to business interests.

The influence of Portales Plazazuelos, who preferred to exercise control from behind the scenes, is also apparent in the conservative Chilean constitution of 1833, which lasted for over 90 years. He represented the *nouveau riche* merchant classes of Valparaiso and Santiago and insisted on the need for order, if commerce were to develop. He distrusted intellectuals and was impatient with the conservatism of the old, landowning elites. He was noted for his financial honesty and ruthless efficiency.

As minister of war, he favoured Chile's attack on the Peruvian–Bolivian Confederation (1836), which he felt was a threat to the balance of power on the Pacific coast. Chile defeated the confederation and broke it up.

PORTALIS, JEAN (1746–1807), French lawyer and politician, who, as part-architect of the *Concordat* and the *Code Civil*, helped to construct the Napoleonic system. After *Brumaire*, Napoleon I appointed him to the *conseil d'état* and the commission set up to draft the civil law code. Portalis worked hard to ground it in Roman law principles. He especially influenced sections of the code dealing with marriage and succession laws. As minister in charge of public worship and ecclesiastical affairs (1801), Portalis shaped the *Concordat*, and balanced appointments of 'non-juring' priests, who enjoyed papal favour, with preferments for the '*constitutionnels*'.

PORTE SAINTE-ANTOINE (2 July 1652), battle of the French wars of the Fronde, when royal troops under Turenne hemmed in the rebel force led by Condé in the Faubourg Sainte-Antoine, Paris. At the last moment the gates were opened by rebel supporters, allowing Condé's men to retreat with heavy losses into the city. The Ducs de Nemours and De la Rochefoucauld were among the wounded.

PORTEÑOS, nickname of the inhabitants of Buenos Aires, the port and capital of Argentina. *Porteño* municipal loyalty was clearly manifested in 1806–7, when, with little assistance from Spanish authorities, local leaders organized the defeat of the British expeditions of Beresford and Whitelocke. Encouraged by their success, the *porteños* increasingly resisted the reimposition of royal authority. The Argentine independence movement began in Buenos Aires in May 1810 with an open town meeting ('*cabildo abierto*') and a de facto seizure of power. In succeeding decades, however, conflict between Buenos Aires and the interior was the greatest obstacle to the unification of Argentina. *Porteños* demanded free trade and free movement of European capital, technology, immigrants, and ideas; the traditionalist interior, at a disadvantage through the facts of geography, resisted all these imperatives. The creation (1880) of a federal district under a federal constitution ostensibly removed the sources of strife; nevertheless, Buenos Aires' economic, political, and cultural hegemony proved irresistible.

PORTEOUS RIOTS (1736) in Scotland, occurred in Edinburgh following the execution of a smuggler named Wilson, who had robbed a customs collector, and resulted in the town guard under Capt. John Porteous firing on the crowd. Porteous, the leader, was tried for murder and sentenced to death, but was reprieved by Queen Caroline, wife of George II at that time Guardian of the Realm. This action incensed the Edinburgh mob, who lynched Porteous without inter-ference from the magistrates. The British government conducted an enquiry, but was faced by a conspiracy of silence. Punitive acts were, however, passed, Edinburgh being fined £2000, and the lord provost deposed. In addition, all ministers were required to invite their congregations to discover Porteous's murderers.

PORTER, DAVID DIXON (1813–91), US sailor who commanded the *Powhatan* on its abortive mission to relieve Fort Pickens, FL, at the beginning of the American Civil War. Porter was one of the planners of the New Orleans expedition (1862), commanded the Union Mississippi squadron (1862–4), and then the North Atlantic Blockading Squadron. Later he became superintendent of the US Naval Academy (1865–9), adviser to the secretary of the navy, and head of the Board of Inspection after 1877.

PORTES GIL, EMILIO (1891–), Mexican politician, minister of the interior (1924–8), provisional president (1928–30), and minister of foreign affairs (1934–6). His political career began as a deputy to the national congress (1916–20) and later he became governor of Tamaulipas (1920–4). He was appointed provisional president after the assassination of Álvaro Obregón. During his administration, which was subject to the control of the former president, Plutarco Elías Calles, the 'official party' was organized (*Partido Nacional de la Revolución*) and the Regional Confederation of Labour (CROM) ceased to be a major recipient of government favours.

PORTLAND, WILLIAM HENRY CAVENDISH BENTINCK, 3rd Duke of (1738–1809), British politician, who was an ally of Rockingham. He resigned as lord chamberlain on Rockingham's fall (1766), and was opposed to the Grafton ministry. He was suspected of being the author of the *Letters* of Junius. He became lord lieutenant of Ireland under Rockingham (1782) and first lord of the treasury in the Fox–North coalition, leading the Rockingham Whigs after the ministry fell (1783). After the outbreak of the French Revolution he allied himself with the Younger Pitt, whom he served as home secretary (1794–1801). He continued in office under Addington, but served Pitt, on his return, as lord president of the council (1804–5). After Pitt's death he led the opposition to the Ministry of All the Talents (1806–7) and on its defeat (1807–9) formed his own administration. The quarrel between Canning and Castlereagh weakened his authority and the stability of the cabinet.

PORTLAND, RICHARD WESTON, 1st Earl of (1st of 1st creation) (1577–1635), English politician, who was appointed joint commissioner, comptroller, and surveyor of the navy in 1618. He favoured the Roman Catholics, was sympathetic towards Spain, and was employed on several diplomatic missions, mainly concerning the Palatinate. He opposed the Duke of Buckingham over the Spanish War, but as chancellor of the exchequer he was compelled to find money for it without obtaining supplies from parliament. In 1628 he was appointed lord high treasurer. After Buckingham's death he was the politician with the most influence over Charles I, but was highly unpopular in the country at large. His unpopularity was increased by his urging the king to dissolve parliament and by his efforts to reduce expenditure, which led to peace with France (1630) and to parsimony at court, through which he incurred the hostility of Queen Henrietta Maria. He retained the king's support, however, until his death, despite his being attacked by Laud and Wentworth.

PORTLAND, HANS WILLIAM BENTINCK, 5th Earl of (1st of 2nd creation) (?1649–1709), Dutch favourite and adviser of William of Orange. In 1677 he was sent on a mission to England, partly to enlist English aid in ending the disastrous Franco–Dutch War, and partly to enter into preliminary negotiations for the marriage between William and Mary. Bentinck was sent to England again (1683), ostensibly to congratulate Princess Anne on her forthcoming marriage, but also to sound English opinion on public issues. He also served as a diplomat on the continent, negotiating the neutrality of the German princes during the British Revolution of 1688. He accompanied William on his invasion of England and also in his campaigns in Ireland and Flanders, being present at the battles of Boyne (1690) and Landau (1693). He was rewarded with an earldom and with liberal grants of land.

As Portland, he dominated the councils of his master, now William III, and for this reason was intensely unpopular in Britain, especially since William preferred his advice on British affairs to that of the British themselves. It was through Portland's informal discussions with Marshal Boufflers, circumventing the more formal plenipotentiary negotiations, that the basis of peace and the foundations of the treaty of Ryswick (1697) were drawn up. On the reopening of diplomatic relations with France, Portland was appointed ambassador to France and negotiated for William the Partition treaties (1698, 1700) in an attempt to maintain the peace of Europe in the face of a disputed Spanish succession. Portland was later unfairly accused by his enemies of neglecting British interests in these treaties.

With the accession of Queen Anne in 1702 his influence declined.

PORTLAND, BATTLE OF (18 Feb. 1653), naval engagement of the First Anglo-Dutch War (1652–4), fought off Portland on the south coast of England between a Dutch fleet under Tromp and De Ruyter and the English under Admiral Blake and Generals George Monck and Richard Deane. The English pursued a convoy of Dutch merchant ships and their escort eastwards, destroying 17 Dutch combat ships and 50 merchantmen, and themselves suffering comparable losses.

PORTO BELLO, BATTLE OF (22 Nov. 1739), British attack and capture of the Spanish settlement of Porto Bello on the isthmus of Panama, the haunt of Spanish coastguards, by a small force of six ships and 200 soldiers from Jamaica under the command of Admiral Edward Vernon.

PORTOLA, DON GASPAR DE (*c.* 1723–84), Mexican explorer, who led an expedition from Mexico into CA and became the first governor of the area. He established a *presidio* at Monterey. Father Junipero Serra accompanied him and began the work of establishing a chain of missions in CA.

PORTONOVO, BATTLE OF (July 1781), during the First Mysore War between 1500 British troops under Sir Eyre Coote and some 65,000 Mysoris under Hyder Ali. From an entrenched position Hyder blocked the British advance upon Cuddalore, but was forced to retreat with heavy casualties, estimated at 10,000 killed and wounded.

PORT-ROYAL DES CHAMPS, Cistercian convent situated south-west of Paris which became a centre of Jansenism in the 17th cent. through the influence of its abbess, Mère Angélique. In 1626 an outbreak of plague and the inadequacy of the accommodation drove the nuns from Port-Royal to a new home in the Faubourg St Jacques in Paris, where their abbess fell under the influence of the Abbé de St Cyran, who had been a fellow student of Jansen. From 1637 the old site at Port-Royal des Champs was inhabited by a group of men, some clerics, some laymen, under Mère Angélique's brother, Antoine Arnauld, who dedicated themselves to a life of prayer and study. They were joined after 1648 by some of the nuns from the Paris house and moved to Les Granges, a nearby farm, which became a centre for Jansenist education.

After the Jesuits had stirred up doubts about Jansenist orthodoxy, the nuns of Port-Royal des Champs were involved in a long controversy, during which they were placed under an interdict (1664–9), which ended with the peace of the Church (1668–9). After a respite, hostility towards the Jansenists was renewed in the late 17th cent., and in 1679 the pupils and lay persons were evicted from the convent, the nuns were forbidden to receive any more novices and were placed under the Paris house, now no longer a Jansenist stronghold. By 1705 only 25 nuns remained in Port-Royal des Champs and in 1708 Louis XIV obtained a papal bull ordering the convent's suppression. In 1709 the nuns were dispersed and the furniture and relics were taken over by the Paris house. The buildings were razed to the ground in 1710, the graveyards were desecrated, and the church demolished (1712).

PORTSMOUTH, LOUISE RENÉE DE KEROUALLE, Duchess of (1649–1734), principal mistress of King Charles II from her arrival in England (1670) until his death (1685). Her political significance was exaggerated by contemporaries, for although she influenced appointments, there is no evidence that she decided royal policy.

PORTSMOUTH, TREATY OF (5 Sept. 1905), which ended the Russo-Japanese War (1904–5). The choice of Portsmouth (NH) was determined by the request which Japan, the victor, though exhausted, had made for President Theodore Roosevelt's good offices. Although Japan's demands for an indemnity and northern Sakhalin were successfully resisted by Russia, the latter did cede southern Sakhalin and promised not to interfere in Korea. Most important of all, she handed over her lease of Port Arthur and the other rights she had acquired in southern Manchuria, thus laying the foundation for the later clash between Japan and the Chinese nationalist movement. Although the treaty aroused great public indignation in Japan, it prepared the way for an early Russo-Japanese reconciliation (1907) and for increased stability in Far Eastern international relations.

PORTSMOUTH, TREATY OF (15 Jan. 1948), Anglo-Iraqi alliance to replace a 1930 treaty, providing for co-ordination of defence. It was never ratified because of continuous demonstrations against it in Baghdad, which led to the fall of the prime minister, Salih Jabr. The demonstrations really reflected general opposition to the political manipulations of the Iraqi government and the reverses suffered in Palestine.

PORTUGUESE in East Africa. The Portuguese arrived in 1498, and for the next 200 years dominated the east coast from the Lamu Archipelago to Sofala, and also operated sporadically to the north and south of these limits. Barawa was sacked in 1505, and Inhambane and the island of Inhaca, opposite Lourenço Marques, occasionally visited. After the Portuguese sack of Kilwa and Mombasa in 1505, and Mombasa again in 1528, there was little opposition until the Turkish raids of 1586 and 1588, which were the cause of the construction of Fort Jesus at Mombasa, to take the place of the unfortified settlement at Malindi. In 1606 and 1608 Mozambique was attacked unsuccessfully by the Dutch. In 1652 began the long war with the Omani Arabs, during which Mombasa was lost in 1698 and the Portuguese northern limits pushed back to Cape Delgado.

The Portuguese exercised their authority through two captains, responsible to the viceroy of Goa: in the north from Kilwa and then Malindi (1512–93), and subsequently from Mombasa; in the south from Sofala and later Mozambique. The authority consisted of attempts to operate a commercial monopoly, and to pay for the control points by customs duties and licences. Only in the Zambezi valley, owing to the presence of gold, was any interest taken in administration or settlement but, because of the paucity of resources and occasional military success of the African inhabitants, these efforts were transitory or abortive. Their authority inland was restricted to the towns of Sena and Tete. Around these were feudal estates, ruled by mulatto barons, who derived more income from slaves than from gold or ivory. In 1752 Mozambique became independent of Goa, but it was not until late in the 19th cent. that an administration was set up which covered the whole territory.

PORTUGUESE in Morocco. The presence of the Portuguese in this region represented the first stage of their overseas expansion. The motivation, political, religious, or economic, of this expansion has been disputed, but following the capture of Ceuta (1415), Portugal seized Tangiers, Arzila, and Larache (1471), together with Arfa (1469), and obtained Spanish recognition of their influence on the Atlantic coast (1479). After the taking of the southern port of Massab (1488), a string of conquests (1505–19), beginning with that of Agadir, brought the rest of the seaboard largely under Portuguese control. Most of these conquests, however, were lost (1540–1) with the rise of the Sa'dians, while a major invasion was defeated at Al-Qasr al-Kabir (Alcazaequivir) (1578). Of those territories that were left, Ceuta, Larache, Arzila, and Tangier went to Spain and England (1640, 1661), and the last, Mazagan, fell to Morocco (1769).

PORTUGUESE in West Africa. Portuguese contact with West Africa began in the 14th cent. with voyages to the Atlantic islands, including the Canaries, followed in the next century by privateering raids on the Moroccan coast and exploitation of the Mauretanian fisheries. The major phase of exploration began in the reign of Duarte in 1433 and proceeded as follows: the rounding of Cape Bojador (1434), the Senegal river (1446), Sierra Leone (1460), Costa da Mina (1471), the Equator (1475), and the Congo river (1483). By the end of the 15th cent. Portuguese settlements had been established on the islands of Cape Verde and São Tomé, trading posts on the mainland at Arguin (1448), São Jorge da Mina (1482), and Benin (1485).

These enterprises were controlled by the rulers of Portugal, who claimed exclusive rights over all trade along the west African coasts. They had some success in diverting Ashanti gold to their trading posts on the Costa da Mina (Gold Coast); pepper yielded a sizeable revenue before the opening of the sea route to India; and São Tomé in the first half of the 16th cent. became a major source of sugar for Europe. All this commerce depended upon a traffic in slaves which began around the mid-15th cent. in Upper Guinea and later shifted its centre to Lower Guinea and the Congo with São Tomé as the operational centre; after 1530 there developed the transatlantic slave trade.

In order to promote trade and missionary activity, which was also under their patronage, Portuguese kings were generally anxious to cultivate good relations with African rulers, who in turn often found it advantageous to permit the Portuguese to trade in their territories. Few, however, welcomed Christian missionaries. The most notable exceptions were the rulers of the Congo, most of whom, from the beginning of the 16th cent. became at least nominal Christians. Nowhere, outside the Portuguese islands, did the new religion penetrate among the mass of the people.

From the beginning of the 17th cent. the Portuguese rapidly lost ground to the Dutch, who first took over their trade and then seized their forts on the Gold Coast. By 1650 Portugal retained influence only in the islands and the Cacheu-Farim area of Upper Guinea, where a mulatto population defended its interests. A revival towards the end of the century was inspired by a vastly expanded demand for slaves from Portuguese Brazil; this was met first by establishing a trading station on the Dahomean coast, and then, in the middle of the 18th cent., by a great expansion of the slave trade through Bissau. With the end of the slave trade the West African possessions of Portugal—Guinea, Cape Verde islands, São Tomé, and Príncipe—sank into backwardness for more than a century.

J. W. Blake, *European Beginnings in West Africa* (London, 1937).
C. R. Boxer, *The Portuguese Sea-Borne Empire* (London, 1969).   AFCR

PORTUGUESE REPUBLIC (1910). Despite the army's support, popular enthusiasm, and foreign goodwill, the creation of the republic introduced a period of unprecedented instability. Until Salazar's seizure of power in 1928, there were about one coup and three governments annually, as well as serious strikes and near anarchy. The abolition of the monarchy did nothing to solve Portugal's basic problem, the lack of a competent governing class. The last king, Manuel II (*reg.* 1908–10), had found no men capable of pursuing a policy of conciliation after the assassination of his father, followed by a period of martial law. Republicanism appeared to offer a fresh start, but responsibility for proving that it could work fell to a generation of politicians corrupted by habitual intrigue.

POSEIDIUM (AL MINA), ancient trading settlement at the mouth of the Orontes river in northern Syria, settled by Greeks from Euboea in the 8th cent. BC. It was probably here that the Greeks first came into direct contact with the East. The result was the adoption of the alphabet from the Phoenicians (8th cent.), the Orientalizing Period in Greek art (7th cent.), and possibly eastern influence on Greek literature, eg, Hesiod's *Theogony*. In the 7th cent. Aeginetans and eastern Greeks from Miletus and Rhodes seem to have replaced Euboeans as principal traders. The eclipse of the settlement (*c.* 600) is perhaps to be associated with the contemporary collapse of the Assyrian empire.

POSEIDONIA (PAESTUM), ancient Greek city in southwest Italy, near Salerno, founded by Sybaris in the 7th cent. BC. It flourished in the 6th–5th cents BC and is famous for its well-preserved Doric temples of that period.

POSEIDONIUS (*c.* 135–*c.* 50 BC), Greek Stoic philosopher, who settled first at Rhodes, where Cicero was his pupil (78) and Pompey the Great twice visited him, and then at Rome. Few fragments of his works, which included a history of Rome (*c.* 146–*c.* 79 BC), have survived.

POSITIVISM IN LATIN AMERICA, philosophical doctrine of the Frenchman, Auguste Comte (1789–1857), who contended that philosophical investigation should be limited to natural phenomena and attempted a classification of the exact sciences. Three stages of development governed history and science; and sociology, a term coined by Comte, was considered the most complex of all sciences. Comte's *Course of Positive Philosophy* appeared in six volumes from 1830 onward. During the last ten years of his life he elaborated a positivist religion which enjoyed some success in France.

The influence of positivism spread abroad, carried thither by Comte's disciples, such as Gabino Barreda of Mexico (1870s), and Benjamin Constant of Brazil (1880s). It became the official doctrine of the Mexican school system during the Porfirian dictatorship (1876–1911). In Brazil, Positivism influenced the military leaders of the republican movement through the military academy and is still influential today. In Argentina the doctrine became intertwined with socialism after the 1880s. Its influence was also felt at the same time among young radicals in Uruguay.

POSOSHKOV, IVAN (*fl.* 18th cent.), Russian merchant, industrialist, and writer, who shared Peter I's concern for the technical and economic development of Russia. He was a keen observer and critic of many aspects of Russian social and political life in the early 18th cent.

POST, PIETER (1608–69), Dutch architect of Haarlem, who built the Mauritshuis at The Hague for Count John Maurice of Nassau (1633–5) on Jacob van Campen's designs. Together they revolutionized Dutch architecture by their austere classical style.

POST BOY, in England, thrice-weekly newspaper published by Abel Boyer, established shortly after the expiry of the

Licensing Act (1695). The *Post Boy* became the most widely read of the Tory newspapers in Queen Anne's reign, with an average sale of 3000–4000 copies per issue between 1704 and 1712.

POST OFFICE ACT (1840) in Britain ensured cheap and efficient postage which accelerated communications in business and social relations. Revenue from the post office had been used to pay for the French Wars and charges remained high after the peace of 1815. In 1836 Rowland Hill published a scheme to abolish the method of charging postage according to the distance and the number of sheets. Instead, rates were to vary by weight from a uniform minimum of 1d, and prepayment of letters was to be made with postage stamps. Following a parliamentary enquiry, the act of 1840 embodied Hill's proposals. The result was a temporary but substantial fall in revenue and a sharp increase in the number of letters posted.

POTAWATOMI INDIANS, American Algonquian tribe, which supported the French against the British and took part in Pontiac's rebellion (1763). They sided with the British in the American War of Independence and fought the US until the treaty of Greenville (1795). The Potawatomi joined the British again in the War of 1812. They gradually sold their lands (1836–41) and most of them moved on a reservation in KS (1846), but some moved again (1868) to lands in OK.

POTEMKIN, GREGORY ALEKSANDROVICH, Prince (1739–1791), Russian politician, a favourite of Catherine II, who was viceroy of New Russia (1774–91) and Prince of Taurida. He was responsible for annexing the Crimea (1783) and developing a Black Sea fleet. Despite his sham 'Potemkin villages' (1787), erected to make an impression during a royal tour, his achievements in settling the area were real. His aims included the 'Greek Project' for re-establishing the Byzantine empire under the Grand Duke Constantine, and the creation of an independent kingdom of Dacia (to consist of Wallachia, Moldavia, and Bessarabia).

POTEMPA MURDER (9 Aug. 1932), killing of a Silesian communist named Pietrzuch by five SA men, who were subsequently sentenced to death (22 Aug.) under a practically simultaneous new law extending the death penalty to this kind of offence. Hitler's open support for the murderers, whose sentence was soon commuted, caused widespread revulsion and illustrates the pressure he was subjected to within the NSDAP in the period immediately preceding his achievement of power. The incident was typical of many acts of violence committed against both the left and the right following the end of the Weimar republic.

POTIDAEA, ancient Greek city-state founded by Corinth (*c.* 600 BC) at an important trading position on the Pallene isthmus in Chalcidice. It maintained unusually close links with its mother-city and, though overrun by the Persians in 480, rebelled successfully in the winter of 480–479 and 300 Potidaeans fought at Plataea (479). It joined the Delian League, but in 432, after intrigues with Perdiccas II of Macedon and the Corinthians, it rejected an Athenian ultimatum and rebelled. The subsequent Athenian siege was one of the immediate pretexts of the great Peloponnesian War, but no help came and it surrendered (429), the inhabitants being expelled and replaced by Athenians. It was refounded after Athens' defeat (404) and joined the Chalcidian League, but in 364 was won for Athens by Timotheus and again settled by Athenians. Philip II of Macedon took it (356) and gave it temporarily to the Chalcidian League, before he conquered that too (348). Cassander founded Cassandreia on its site in 316.

POTOCKI, IGNACY (1750–1829), Polish politician and chief member of the committee appointed by the Polish four-Year Diet to prepare a constitution. The constitution of May 1791 was a compromise between his republican views and those of Stanislas Augustus. After Kosciusko's insurrection Potocki was imprisoned in Russia (1794–6).

POTOCKI, STANISLAS KOSTKA (1755–1821), Polish politician, president of the council of state of the duchy of Warsaw (1807), and minister of education and church affairs in the Polish kingdom created by the Congress of Vienna (1815–20). He was dismissed from his ministry because of his anti-clerical writings.

POTOCKI FAMILY in Poland, famous for its political influence, which grew from the early 17th cent., especially in Moldavia, where the Potockis supported their cousins, the Moghilas. In the succession disputes of the 18th cent. the family were pro-French and pro-Prussian, and under the leadership of Theodore Potocki, Primate of Poland, and Joseph Potocki, Palatine of Ruthenia, they opposed the candidature of the Saxon house in favour of that of Stanislas Leszczynski. After Augustus III's election (1734) they sought his deposition, and also war on Russia, and one of the most famous of the line, Count Ignacy Potocki, joined Kosciusko in the war of independence against Russia (1794). The family remained prominent in the 19th cent.

POTOMAC, ARMY OF THE, Federal force formed to protect Washington during the American Civil War (1861). It was welded into an efficent army by Gen. McClellan, operated under successive commanders in VA, MD, and PA, and was under the field command of Gen. Meade when hostilities ended (1865).

POTOMAC INDIANS, major tribe of the Powhatan Confederacy, formerly living on the Potomac river in VA, US, where remnants of the tribe remain (1970). They were among the first to be encountered by European explorers. Their numbers were greatly reduced in wars between the Confederacy and the English colonists.

POTOSÍ, MINE OF, Bolivian mountain of silver ore, was discovered by an Indian in 1545. By the end of the colonial period, it had produced an estimated 60 million troy pounds (22,300,000 kgs) of silver and in the middle of the 17th cent. was supporting the largest city in Latin America. It stood at an altitude of over 12,000 ft (3660 metres), the extreme limit of human habitability. Labour conditions under the *mita* system were notoriously bad, but the mine produced much of the silver which financed Spain's power during the Habsburg era. About 1640, partly because of severe flood damage in 1626, production began to decline, and by 1800 the mine was surrounded by a mere village of some 8000 inhabitants. In 1600 its population had been 160,000.

POTSDAM, ancient town in Brandenburg, situated on the Havel river, south-west of Berlin. Having been in the 10th cent. a Slav settlement, it became in the 14th cent. a chartered town and in 1640 a garrison town. From the 18th cent. it developed as a commercial and industrial centre of Prussia, and it was here that the Hohenzollerns had their summer residence from the time of Frederick the Great, who erected many of its finest buildings, *eg*, the Sans Souci palace, a masterpiece of German rococo.

POTSDAM, EDICT OF (8 Nov. 1685), issued by Elector Frederick William I of Brandenburg, invited French Huguenots who were expelled after Louis XIV's renunciation of the Edict of Nantes to settle in Hohenzollern territories. As a result, some 20,000 immigrants sought 'safe and free retreat' which he promised, to the benefit of Brandenburg's industries.

POTSDAM CONVENTION (1910), agreement between Germany and Russia in which Germany promised to respect

Russia's monopoly of railways in northern Persia and Russia to tolerate German imports into the area and drop opposition to the Baghdad railway. Russia gained the greatest strategic advantage from the convention. Germany, having come to terms with France over Morocco (1909), was mainly concerned to undermine the Anglo-Russian entente and end the threat of war on two fronts from the alignment of France, Britain, and Russia against her. The agreement at Potsdam did mark a temporary trend in Germany's favour, but only until the renewal of the Moroccan crisis at Agadir (1911).

POTWALLOPER BOROUGHS in England, sub-divisions of the Scot and Lot boroughs, in which the franchise depended upon proof that the voter provided his own sustenance, was master of a fireplace at which he could cook it, and was in control of a doorway leading to his dwelling. It originated in the days of serfdom, when serfs and freemen mingled in urban areas, and when freemen occasionally took meals in public to prove that they were free and self-sustaining.

POUJADE, PIERRE (1920–), French political figure who was leader of the short-lived Poujadist movement in France. This represented essentially the protest of small shopkeepers and artisans against modern economic tendencies. The term 'Poujadism' is sometimes used to describe similar movements elsewhere. Poujade himself was a stationer in a small town, and founded his 'Union de Défense des Commerçants et Artisans' in 1954. The movement spread almost spontaneously, often taking the form of a refusal to pay taxes, and was strongest in the declining rural areas of central France. Over 50 Poujadist candidates were returned in the 1956 election, a partial reflection of popular disillusionment with the Fourth Republic. The violence of the movement alarmed some observers, but the Poujadist deputies made little political impact, and Poujadism disappeared as a serious force with the fall of the Fourth Republic. Poujade himself was never elected to parliament.

POUM (Partido Obrero de Unificación Marxista), in Spain. At the end of 1931 Andréas Nin and Joaquín Maurín left the Spanish Communist Party in protest against Stalin's persecution of Trotsky. Each founded revolutionary Marxist groups; Nin started Oposición Communista and Maurín Bloque Obrero y Campesino—an anticipation of the Popular Front. They were divided on the question of co-operation with other groups, but were reunited after the Feb. 1936 elections and founded POUM, which, like its two predecessors, was of Trotskyite tendencies.

When the Spanish Civil War broke out, POUM joined with the CNT in supporting the revolution, although POUM's members were divided from the anarchists by their belief in the need for workers to take over the powers of the state.

POUM's biggest problem was the hostility of orthodox communists, by whom it was regarded as heretical. Its newspaper, *La Batalla*, exposed the horrors and show trials of Stalinism and attacked Spanish communists for their support of the bourgeoisie. The POUM militia were starved of arms at the front, and Nin was forced out of the Catalan government. In April 1937, after the communists had suggested that POUM was collaborating with Franco, the militia was disbanded in the name of military efficiency, and POUM newspapers and radio stations outside Catalonia were seized.

On 3 May 1937 POUM and the CNT in Barcelona rose in protest against communist opposition, but their resistance was crushed. Communists in the government unsuccessfully demanded the dissolution of POUM, which was eventually disposed of by communists using their own methods. On 16 June Col. Orlov, the Stalinist police chief in Spain, ordered the arrest of all POUM leaders. The party was declared illegal, Nin was murdered, and the other leaders kept imprisoned until Oct. 1938, when they were tried.   PP

POUND, SIR ALFRED DUDLEY (1877–1943), British sailor who served in the First World War and was (1939–43) First

Sea Lord and chief of the naval staff in the Second World War. He was responsible for the policy, administration, and overall strategic direction of the navy, and for the conduct of operations in home waters and the Atlantic.

POUND, EZRA LOOMIS (1885–1972), US poet and critic, who studied in Europe (1906), taught briefly in IN, and went to Italy, where he published *A Lume Spento* (1908). On moving to England (1909), he attracted attention with *Personae* (1909) and *Exaltations* (1909). He remained in London until 1920, becoming the leading member of the Imagist group of poets, and was associated with various small magazines in which he championed writers such as Joyce, Eliot, and Yeats. His choice of poetic material became increasingly esoteric, as in *Ripostes* (1912), a translation of *The Sonnets and Ballate of Guido Calvacanti* (1912), and *Cathay* (1915), a translation from the Chinese based on the notes of Ernest Fenollosa. In 1915 he began his monumental *Cantos*, a long poem to which he continually added, employing a technique based on the Chinese ideogram. It depicts a fragmented voyage through American, European, and Chinese history in a search of a society that has not been desecrated and perverted by 'usury', Pound's term for capitalist economics. He eventually settled at Rapallo (1928), where he wrote *Make It New* (1934), *ABC of Reading* (1934), and *Guide to Kulchur* (1938).

Believing in the necessity of strong government as a bulwark against the 'usurocrats', he openly supported fascism, and during the Second World War broadcast fascist propaganda from Rome. He was charged in the US with treason, and being judged insane was committed to a Washington asylum (1945), where he produced the first of several collected editions of *The Cantos of Ezra Pound* (1948), *Money Pamphlets by £* (6 vols, 1950–2), detailing his own economic theories, *The Translations of Ezra Pound* (1953), and *The Literary Essays of Ezra Pound* (1954). He was released in 1958, returned to Italy, and continued to make additions to the *Cantos*, and published *Impact: Essays on Ignorance and the Decline of American Civilisation* (1960). Whatever the final verdict may be on his difficult, and perhaps over-ambitious, *Cantos*, Pound's reputation as the most important 20th-cent. US poet seems secure. As a pioneer of the New Poetry, his influence on other writers and critics is comparable to that of Emerson's a century before.

Eva Hesse, *New Approaches to Ezra Pound* (London, 1969). T. H. Jackson, *The Early Poetry of Ezra Pound* (Cambridge MA, 1968).   EFAL

POUNDMAKER (1826–86), Cree Indian chief in the Canadian North-West Territories, who during the North-West Rebellion, laid siege to Battleford, Sask. (March 1885), and defeated troops commanded by Col. William Otter at the battle of Cut Knife Hill (2 May 1885). He later had to surrender (26 May 1885).

POUSSIN, NICOLAS (1594–1665), French exponent of classicism in painting, who influenced the art and theory of painting in his own time. He was born in Normandy, went to Paris to become a painter, then to Rome (1624), where he remained virtually for the rest of his life. The greatest influences on his art were the Antique style and Raphael. He often chose themes from classical mythology and his pictures illustrate the theory of painting for which he became famous in his own time, the Heroic style. During his stay in Paris he painted decorations for the Grand Gallery of the Louvre and some designs for cartoons for Gobelin tapestries.

POWDERLY, TERENCE VINCENT (1849–1924), US labour leader, who started work as a railway switch tender at the age of 13. He became active in the Machinists' and Blacksmiths' Union (1871) and joined the Knights of Labor (1874). He was chosen as Grand Master Workman of the Knights (1879–93), which he made the largest labour organization in the US. He opposed strikes, preferring mediation and arbitration instead, and worked for reforms in the economic system that would benefit all working people. After resigning as head of the Knights, he was admitted to the PA bar (1894), served as US Commissioner-General of Immigration (1897–1902), and was chief of the Division of Information of the US Bureau of Immigration (1907–21).

POWELL, JOHN ENOCH (1912–   ), British politician, who became professor of Greek at Sydney University (1937–9) when only 25. On the outbreak of the Second World War he returned home and in the army rose from private to brigadier in five years. He entered parliament in 1950 as Conservative MP for Wolverhampton South West. He was then a staunch defender of Britain's imperial role, having been strongly influenced by his wartime service in India. In Jan. 1957 he became financial secretary to the treasury, but resigned this post early in 1958 (with the chancellor and the economic secretary) in protest against the refusal of the prime minister, Harold Macmillan, to cut government expenditure. He continued to champion free enterprise economy. In July 1960 he became minister of health, and entered the cabinet in 1962. He resigned at the end of 1963, after Home's appointment as prime minister.

While holding government office he had indicated no concern with the Commonwealth immigration question which subsequently preoccupied him. However, immigration was increasing in his own constituency. The success of the Conservative candidate's anti-immigration platform in neighbouring Smethwick, amid the Conservative electoral defeat of 1964, convinced him that the party rank and file looked for firmer leadership on the immigration issue. By 1965 he had abandoned imperial visions so far as to demand that Commonwealth immigrants should have alien status. He fared badly in the 1965 elections for the party leadership and subsequently became shadow defence minister under Heath. But he continued to take an independent line on economic, social, and foreign policies, demanding stricter controls on entry and voluntary repatriation of immigrants, and indicated that even second and third generation coloured immigrants should never be considered full British citizens. As a result, Heath dropped him from the shadow cabinet.

In the 1970 general election he still dissociated himself from the party line. He also accused government officials of deliberately concealing immigration statistics from the public. In 1970 his personal political following was still considerable. In opposing government policies on both immigration and the European Common Market, he championed opinions which both main parties had side-stepped.

POWELL, JOHN WESLEY (1834–1902), US geologist and explorer. After serving in the Union army during the American Civil War, he taught at IL Wesleyan College and IL Normal University. In 1869 he led an expedition, financed by Congress and the Smithsonian Institution, through the Grand Canyon of the Colorado river by boat. He made further explorations in 1871, 1874, and 1875, worked for the US Geological and Geographical Survey of the Territories (1875–9), and as director of the Geological Survey (1890–4) produced a series of topographical maps on the scale of four miles to an inch that established a scientific reputation for the Geological Survey. His major publications were *Explorations of the Colorado River of the West and its Tributaries* (1875), and a *Report on the Lands of the Arid Region of the United States* (1878).

POWERS, HIRAM (1805–73), US sculptor, who made portrait busts of many famous men, including Andrew Jackson and John Marshall (1834–6). His female nude, *Greek Slave* (1843), was one of the most celebrated statues of its day, and his statues of Franklin and Jefferson were placed in the US Capitol (1863).

POWHATAN INDIANS, confederacy of American Algonquian tribes united by a chief of the same name. The first permanent English settlement, Jamestown, was established in their territory (1607) and Powhatan's daughter, Pocahantes, married the Englishman John Rolfe. Wars with the colonists severely reduced their numbers, but some bands survive (1970) in VA.

POWYS, kingdom of central and north-east Wales. Its central position, proximity to England, and lack of natural boundaries meant that Powys was usually obliged to ally itself either with Gwynedd or with the Anglo-Norman invaders. The kingdom achieved a brief supremacy under Cadwgan ap Bleddyn (*reg.* 1088–1111), benefiting from the expulsion by King Henry I of the earls of Shrewsbury (1102). Family feuds and the abduction of Nest, wife of the constable of Pembroke, by Cadwgan's son, Owain, resulted in the intervention of Henry I and the loss of the kingdom's supremacy. In 1160 Powys was divided into two principalities. Gwenwynwyn, ruler of southern Powys, was expelled by Llywelyn I of Gwynedd and died in exile in 1216. But the machinations of his son Gruffydd, in league with Edward I of England, brought the defeat and death of the last important native ruler of Wales, Llywelyn II, and the English conquest in 1282–3.

POYARKOV, VASILI (*fl.* 1638–68), Russian Cossack explorer, whose discovery of the Amur river (1643–6) was followed by the Russian foundation of the fort of Albazin (1651) and the town of Nerchinsk at the confluence of the Shilka and the Nertcha (1658). The Amur valley was later lost to the Chinese by the treaty of Nerchinsk (1689).

POYNINGS, SIR EDWARD (1459–1521), English soldier and administrator, who was the leader of the Kentish rising of 1483 against Richard III and supported Henry VII in 1485. He was later lord deputy in Ireland (1494–6). The parliament which he assembled at Drogheda in Dec. 1494 enacted several important statutes, known subsequently as Poynings' laws. They made it impossible to convoke any Irish parliament except by the authority of the English government, and denied validity to any Irish enactments unless they were sanctioned by the English king's council. This legislation was repealed in 1782.

POZHARSKY, DMITRI, Prince (*fl.* 17th cent.), Muscovite nobleman who was created a *boyar* and became one of the two leaders of national resistance to the Polish regime of Tsar Vladislav during the time of troubles (1611–12). He raised a general levy of the people which drove back Chodkiewicz's forces and relieved Moscow (1612), and helped to organize the general council which elected Tsar Michael Romanov (1613).

POZSONY (PRESSBURG), DIETS OF (1687, 1712), meetings of the Hungarian diet at Pressburg, convoked by the Habsburg emperors. The first was called after Habsburg forces had recovered most of Hungary from Turkish control. The emperor Leopold's military successes enabled him to act from a position of strength. He agreed to confirm the Hungarian constitution subject to three important modifications: the hereditary right of succession in the Habsburg male line should be recognized; the constitutional right of resistance should be abolished; and the laws and privileges were to be observed in the light of royal interpretation. Furthermore, Leopold's son, Joseph, was crowned King of Hungary on 9 Dec. 1687.

The second diet was convoked by the Emperor Charles VI after the failure of Francis Rakoczi's rebellion to confirm the peace of Szatmar (1711). Charles was crowned king and swore to respect the rights, privileges, and laws of the Hungarian estates as well as the religious liberties of the Protestants. Croatia and Transylvania were not included in this agreement. The national defence system was to be strengthened by the creation of a standing army under the Crown, to be paid for by annual taxes, from which the

Magyar nobles were exempt. The diet recognized the hereditary rights of the Habsburg male line and Charles confirmed its right of election should the male line die out, but within a year he had privately promulgated the pragmatic sanction (19 April 1713), which was ultimately recognized by the Hungarian Diet in 1722.

PRADO, MARIANO IGNACIO (1826–1901), Peruvian soldier, dictator, and president of Peru (1876–9), who in 1865 seized power, which he retained for three years and promptly made war on Spain. He became president in 1876 and besides antagonizing aristocratic circles, had to face economic recession. When the Chilean war began (1879) his support dwindled and he retired to Europe.

PRADO Y UGARTECHE, MANUEL (1889–), Peruvian engineer, banker, and twice president of Peru (1939–45, 1956–63). In his first administration he settled a difficult boundary dispute with Ecuador. His major opponents, the youthful Popular American Revolutionary Alliance (APRA), reached agreement with him, and before he left office (1945) he legalized their party. On returning later to act as a compromise president between the military and APRA, he was faced with an empty treasury and depleted reserves of foreign currency. However, he reformed the national currency and raised funds from the sale of oil, by which the rich gained more proportionately than did the poor. Nevertheless, his supporters began to look elsewhere for leadership and when his term of office ended in 1963 he retired from public life.

PRAECELSAE DEVOTIONIS (1514), papal bull promulgated by Leo X, giving Rome's blessing to discoveries and conquests which the Portuguese might make, and bestowing on Portugal the right to all lands taken from heathen races in Africa, India, and all other lands reached by sailing eastwards.

PRAEFECTUS, Latin term, generally translated as 'prefect', for officers of middle rank in the Roman army and administration, chiefly in the imperial period; except for the senatorial prefect of the city of Rome, they were of equestrian rank. Most numerous were the prefects in command of units of *auxilia* but the most important prefects were the commander of the praetorian guard, the governor of Egypt, and the controller of the food supply of Rome. In the middle of the 3rd cent. AD prefects replaced senators as legionary commanders.

PRAEMUNIRE, STATUTES OF, in England, enactments designed to provide drastic penalties against the persons appointed to bishoprics or other Church benefices by the papacy in violation of the Statutes of Provisors, prohibiting such appointments. The offenders might be imprisoned at the king's pleasure and all their goods confiscated. There were three statutes (1353, 1365, and 1393) and were used only sporadically, but could be employed against any ecclesiastic in trouble with the king. The most famous use of them was against Cardinal Wolsey in 1529, destroying his position as a papal legate and menacing him with the loss of all his ecclesiastical possessions.

PRAET, AUGUSTE LOUIS DE FLANDRES, Sieur de (*fl.* 16th cent.), imperial diplomat for the Emperor Charles V in both England and France, and a trusted member of the imperial council. He concluded an alliance between Charles V, Henry VIII, Archduke Ferdinand, and the Constable Bourbon against France (Aug. 1523), but was later arrested (1524) and asked to leave England (1525) for conducting secret anti-English, pro-French intrigues. He was later used by Charles as a roving ambassador, *eg*, he attended the Regensburg negotiations (1541).

PRAETOR, ancient Roman magistrate, ranking below the consuls. The title, originally denoting the consul as leader of the army, was given to a new magistrate created in 366 BC as a subordinate colleague of the consuls. By 246 there were two praetors to administer justice between citizens and between aliens (or an alien and a citizen) respectively. The increasing number of provinces which needed governors led to the number of praetors being raised to four in 227 and six in 197. Sulla increased the number to eight and laid it down that during their year of office they should all remain in Rome as judges and in the following year should govern provinces as propraetors. This system was abolished by Augustus, who also reduced the number of praetors to 12 from Julius Caesar's total of 16. Although under Nerva the number rose to 18, the praetorship under the empire became, like the consulate, a largely honorary appointment.

PRAETORIAN GUARD, important in Roman history as the bodyguard of the Roman emperors. It was organized by Augustus on the precedent of the bodyguard of earlier generals. At first there were nine cohorts, and later 12, totalling some 6000 men. Tiberius concentrated them in a camp just outside Rome. As the only military force in Italy, they sometimes played a violent part in imperial history, *eg*, deserting Caligula and Nero, murdering Galba (69) and Pertinax (193), and 'auctioning' the imperial position to Didius Julianus (193). Septimius Severus doubled the number of the guards, but recruited them from provincials rather than Italians. Their pay and conditions were superior to those of legionaries, and their establishment served as a staff college and administrative school, though this was abolished by Constantine.

PRAGMATIC ARMY, allied army of British, Hanoverian, Hessian, and, later, Dutch troops, stationed in the Low Countries as an auxiliary force to assist the Austrians (1742) and commanded by George II in the War of the Austrian Succession. After defeating the French at Dettingen on the Main (27 June 1743), the army remained inactive, restricted by the fact that Britain and France were not officially at war until 1744, and by British public opinion, which favoured limited participation in the continental war. In 1744 the aged Marshal Wade assumed command against the French under Marshal Saxe, and later the Duke of Cumberland replaced him, until the 1745 rebellion necessitated the recall of British troops from Europe.

PRAGMATIC SANCTION, Habsburg family law privately drawn up on the orders of the Emperor Charles VI to alter the mutual succession pact made by the Emperor Leopold I in 1703 and to establish the undivided succession of his own heirs, male or female, throughout the Habsburg lands (19 April 1713). After his first-born son died in 1716, three daughters were born, in 1717, 1718, and 1724. Charles, fearing that he would never have a male heir, became concerned to secure recognition of the law to protect the rights of succession of his eldest daughter, Maria Theresa. In 1718 the imperial government had announced the law publicly and requested that it should be accepted by all the estates of the empire; by 1732 this had been achieved, subject to the guarantee that all the existing rights and privileges of the estates should be guaranteed. Meanwhile, by 1726 Spain and Russia had agreed to the Pragmatic Sanction, and were followed in 1731 by Britain and the United Provinces. Finally, in 1738, all the signatories of the third treaty of Vienna, including France, assented to it, leaving only Bavaria a non-signatory power. Despite these paper guarantees, however, after Charles's death (1740) Frederick II of Prussia repudiated his father's recognition of Maria Theresa's rights by the treaty of Berlin (1728) and claimed the Habsburg province of Silesia, which his armies promptly invaded (16 Dec. 1740), plunging Europe into the War of the Austrian Succession (1740–8).

PRAGUE, modern capital of Czechoslovakia, situated on the Moldau river, a tributary of the Elbe. It was, from the 9th cent., the historic seat of the dukes of Bohemia. In 973–4 it became a bishopric, already being the site of a castle and market, and by the 11th cent. it was the centre of considerable commercial activity through its situation at the heart of the country's road network. It was heavily settled with Germans by the late Premyslid and Luxemburg kings, and, as one of the largest cities in medieval Europe, became the leading cultural centre north of the Alps and the seat of a university (1348), whose most famous scholar was John Hus. The Týn Church in the Old Prague Square was the chief Hussite church of Bohemia, where until 1623 there was a statue of George of Podebrady (*reg.* 1458–71), the first non-Catholic king of western Europe, in whose reign Utraquism was established and the city enriched by churches and halls of the late Gothic style, *eg*, the Vladislav Hall in Prague castle (completed 1493). From the acquisition of the Bohemian Crown by the Catholic Habsburg emperors on the death of Louis II (1526), religious and political discontent grew until it burst out in the Defenestration of Prague (23 May 1618), which heralded the Thirty Years War. However, after the defeat of the Protestant king of Bohemia, Frederick of the Palatinate, at the battle of the White Hill outside Prague, and the public execution of Bohemian nobles and commoners in the Old Town Square (1621), German influences revived and the forces of the Counter-Reformation reimposed Catholicism. Prague was the scene of two Austrian military defeats in the wars of the mid-18th cent. (1741, 1757). By the mid-19th cent. it had become a centre of rapid industrialization and the revival of Czech nationalism, being chosen as the site of the Slav Congress (1848). But the revolutionary outburst of 1848 was harshly suppressed by the Austrian authorities under Prince Windischgratz, and Prague remained under Habsburg rule until 1919, when it became the capital of the newly established republic of Czechoslovakia. Prague was occupied by German forces (1939–45), but its citizens revolted against their Nazi overlords (May 1945), an event to be repeated 23 years later (Aug. 1968) against Russian occupying forces, but without success.

PRAGUE, PEACE OF (1635), German religious and political settlement which marked the climax of imperial authority in the 17th cent. and superseded the Edict of Restitution (1629). It was imposed by the Emperor Ferdinand II with the concurrence of the Elector John George of Saxony, and accepted by the majority of German princes, including the Calvinist Elector of Brandenburg, whose religion was not, in fact, given recognition by the peace, and it established that ecclesiastical territories were to be retained for 40 years by those who had possessed them in 1627 instead of 1552. Land disputes were to be settled in the imperial court or *reichskammergericht*, composed equally of Protestant and Catholic members. To enable the emperor to enforce the terms of the settlement and expel foreign armies from German soil, he was to possess an army financed by the estates of the empire, while all princely leagues and private armies were forbidden. To France and Sweden, allied since April 1635, the peace appeared as a defensive pact by the German states to challenge them. Sweden therefore continued to fight for territorial satisfaction, while Richelieu declared war on the Spanish and Austrian Habsburgs eight days before the peace was published. Thus it failed to end the Thirty Years War, which continued largely as a political struggle.

PRAGUE, SIEGE OF (1757), key campaign in Frederick II of Prussia's projected seizure of Bohemia, to which the invasion of Saxony (1756) was a prelude. Frederick hoped to capture the enemy magazines of northern Bohemia. Under Charles of Lorraine the Austrians, some 70,000 strong, occupied an entrenched position on the Moldau, and although the force of 60,000 Prussians successfully carried the enemy defences, the former were able to retreat into Prague. The battle before Prague on 6 May 1757 was bitter, both sides sustaining heavy losses. The Austrians lost Marshal Braun and 8000 men, while the Prussians suffered 14,000 casualties,

including Marshal Schwerin. Prussia's resources were further depleted by their defeat at Kollin, when Frederick failed to halt a relieving Austrian army under Marshal Daun. The Prussian siege of Prague was halted and the invasion of Bohemia abandoned.

PRAGUE, TREATY OF (1866), signed after the battle of Sadowa, marked the final Prussian victory over Austria in the struggle for predominance in Germany. It was the first effective step towards German unification under Prussian domination. By the terms of the treaty the German Confederation was dissolved, Hanover, Hesse-Cassel, Schleswig-Holstein, and Frankfurt-am-Main were annexed by Prussia, and Saxony joined the enlarged Prussia to form the North German Confederation. Austria was deprived of Venetia, which went to Italy, Bavaria, Württemberg, Baden, and Hesse-Darmstadt, allies of Austria, were left independent for fear of French intervention, but signed treaties with Prussia, under whose command their armies were to be placed in time of war.

PRAIRIAL LOI DE 22 (1794), law forced through the French Convention by Robespierre on 10 June, which led to an intensification of the Terror which followed the French Revolution. The law allowed the Revolutionary Tribunal to dispense with the hearing of evidence in defence of those brought before it, reducing its proceedings to ordering either an acquittal or death sentence. Fearful of the implications of the law, the anti-Robespierre groups within the Convention combined to destroy him before they could be brought before the tribunal.

PRAIRIE DU CHIEN, TREATY OF (1825), divided the old North-west Territory of the US among the Sioux, Chippewa, Sauk and Fox, Potawatomi, Winnebago, and Iowa Indians. The treaty provided the ground work for further treaties for cessions of land from individual tribes.

PRAIRIE SCHOONER, large canvas-covered wagon, developed and brought into common use in the overland trade between the US and Mexico after 1821. It was usually drawn by three to six yoke of oxen or by mules, and used extensively for transporting settlers and freight throughout the West between 1830 and 1870.

PRAISE OF FOLLY (1509), or *Encomium Moriae*, a satire by Erasmus in tribute to Sir Thomas More, denouncing scholastic philosophers, grammarians, lawyers, logicians, monks, idle and ignorant clergy, and all the entrenched enemies of reform. Erasmus reminds his readers of the spirit of divine simplicity in which St Paul advised men to become fools in order to be wise.

PRAJADHIPOK (1893–1941), King of Siam (*reg.* 1925–35), youngest son of King Rama V, who did not expect to succeed to the throne. Before succeeding his brother he served in the Thai army. He relied heavily upon the princes of his father's generation, but pressure for democratic reform grew, fed by the economic retrenchment of the late 1920s, and the revolution of 1932 ended royal absolution. Prajadhipok chafed at the new autocracy of the People's Party regime and in 1935 he abdicated. He died in exile in England.

PRAKRIT (lit. 'natural'), term indicating the spoken Indo-Aryan idioms of ancient India (in contrast to Sanskrit, the religious and literary language). Some forms of Prakrit were used in inscriptions, such as those of the Emperor Asoka, and others in the Indian theatre, where special types of Prakrit characterized different groups of the population.

PRAMBANAN, village in Java, Indonesia, east of Jogjakarta, which is particularly rich in architectural remains of the pre-Muslim past (*c.* AD 775–930), notably the huge Buddhist complex of 240 buildings at Chandi Sewu, the twin complexes of Cyandi Plaosan, the temples of Kalasan (dated AD 778), Sari, Banyunibo, the Ratubaka plateau, and the great Saivite complex of Lara Jonggrang, the main temples of which have been restored by the Archaeological Service of the republic of Indonesia, which maintains a field office at Prambanan. It is likely that Medang, the capital of ancient Mataram, was situated in the neighbourhood.

PRARTHANA SAMAJ, Indian society founded by Keshab Chandra Sen in 1869, whose activities were directed to social reforms, such as improved conditions for the depressed classes and the remarriage of Hindu widows.

PRASAD, RAJENDRA (1884–1963), Indian nationalist politician and president of India (1950–62), who, having been recruited by Gandhi during the Champaran campaign (1917), became his chief lieutenant in Bihar and a major force in the Congress, over which he presided four times (1932, 1934, 1939, 1947). From 1936 he was a member of the influential parliamentary sub-committee, and also minister of food and agriculture in the interim government (1946–7), but left the cabinet on becoming president of the Indian Constituent Assembly, of which he had been chairman since its formation in Dec. 1946. On the inauguration of the new constitution he was elected the first president of the republic.

PRASAT THONG (*reg.* 1630–56), King of Siam, usurper of the throne, after a series of manœuvres (1628–30). During his reign there were several revolts, and contacts with the western world increased, especially with the Dutch East India Co.

PRATIHARA DYNASTY, also called Gurjara-Pratihara, name of an ancient Indian royal family, the main branch of which controlled large parts of northern India (excluding Bengal) from Kanauj, UP (*c.* 815–1020 or later). Though formerly considered non-Indian in origin, it is now generally assumed that they, like other Rajput clans, were among the tribes of Mount Abu, Rajasthan, and had emerged as a ruling clan by the 7th cent. AD. They became especially powerful after the conquest by Nagabhata II of Kanauj (*c.* 815). The empire attained the peak of its power under Bhoja (?*reg.* 836–90) and Mahendrapala (?*reg.* 890–910). Unlike the practice in the Maurya and Gupta empires, the Pratiharas left the administration of vast areas to semi-independent princes, which led, in the 10th cent., to a quasi-feudal structure of the empire. From the middle of the 10th cent. decline set in till, in 1018, Kanauj was ransacked by Mahmud of Ghazni.

The Pratihara empire is important in several respects. As long as it stood firm it probably slowed down the expansion of Islam into southern Asia. The threat of the Muslims, however, made Hinduism more introverted, which is reflected in the increasing rigidity of the caste system. The empire is, in addition, important because of its art and architecture and Sanskrit literature.

PRATT, SIR ROGER (1620–84), English architect, who played a considerable part in the rebuilding of London after the fire of 1666.

PRATT, SIR THOMAS SIMSON (1797–1879), British soldier, who commanded forces in Australia (1856–61) and led the Taranaki campaigns (1860–1) against the Maoris in NZ.

PRAXITELES (*fl.* 4th cent. BC), Athenian sculptor, who worked in marble and bronze, specializing in youthful human figures, which include the surviving statue of Hermes and Dionysus from Olympia.

PRAYING INDIANS, American Indians of various tribes, particularly MA Indians, who became Christian converts and were gathered into congregations (1650–74). Most of them joined the Indian uprising (1675) known as King Philip's War and were either destroyed or dispersed with the main tribes of the area.

PREAH VIHEAR, Khmer (Cambodian) temple dating from the late 9th cent., situated on an overhanging cliff in the Dangrek mountains on the Thai–Cambodian border. It became the subject of a frontier dispute between the Thai and Cambodian governments, which was adjudicated in favour of Cambodia by the International Court of Justice in 1962.

PRECEDENCE, assumption of the correct rank or position by the representatives of European states or by an individual or a group of people within those states. In the 17th–18th cents precedence was regarded as a question of the utmost importance, both on an international and on a personal level. The problems of precedence bedevilled many of the peace conferences of the period, *eg,* the Münster and Osnabruck negotiations (1646–8), thus prolonging warfare. The assumption of the title of emperor by Peter I of Russia (1721) instigated interminable controversies. On a lower level, the *affaire du bonnet* in France (1716) was a noted case of disputed precedence. Such disputes are significant in that they, like the growth of diplomatic procedure, mark a stage in the development of a sophisticated political society in Europe.

PRECEDENCE, STATUTE OF (1539), in England, arranged the 'precedence' or order of sitting in the House of Lords, and provided for the presence there of the leading officers of the Crown, *eg,* lord chancellor, lord treasurer, lord privy seal, lord president, and principal secretary, as well as certain household officials, whether they were noblemen or not. This attempt to retain all the leading privy councillors in the Lords failed, for, except for the lord chancellor, who throughout the 16th cent. presided over the House, none of the officers attended unless they were peers. Many, however, sought election to the House of Commons instead.

PREDESTINATION, Christian doctrine relating to the bestowal of grace, the logical derivation of the concept of an omnipotent God, which asserted that some men were predestined or elected to gain eternal salvation by the gift of divine grace, while others were condemned to damnation. The doctrine originated in the teachings of SS Paul and Augustine, but was resurrected by Bucer and Calvin, giving their supporters the moral strength to survive persecution. Although most fully developed in Calvinism, the doctrine appealed to French Jansenism, which opposed the contrasting concept of man's free will to reject grace or to achieve it through good works, which was strongly upheld by the Jesuits.

PRE-EMPTION ACTS (1830–91), in the US, legislation providing for the sale of land in the public domain to bona fide settlers in the hope of curbing land speculation. Pre-emption meant the right of squatters on public lands to buy the land they had cultivated in advance of public auction. As the frontier of settlement moved west and settlers illegally occupied the land before it had been officially surveyed or offered for sale, strong popular pressures were exerted in Congress to grant pre-emption rights. The Pre-Emption Act of 1830 authorized such settlers to purchase up to a quarter section (160 acres—650,000 sq. metres) of unsurveyed public land at a minimum price of $1.25 an acre. This temporary measure was successfully renewed during the 1850s with respect to particular groups, and in 1841 a general Pre-Emption Act was passed, confirming the provisions of the 1830 act, with certain limitations and exceptions. It also included a provision whereby 500,000 acres (2000 sq. kms) of the public domain were to be given to each state for the provision of internal improvements, but this clause was repealed in the following year. The Pre-Emption Acts were finally repealed in 1891.

PREFECTS (1800), officials through whom Napoleon I chiefly exerted his authority over France as First Consul, then as emperor. The prefect was the chief administrator of the new provincial departments and in many ways was a throw-back to the pre-revolutionary *intendant*. Strictly controlled and appointed by the central government in Paris, he had the task of enforcing the Napoleonic codes, carrying out the government's economic policies, collecting taxes, and recruiting troops. The effectiveness of the prefects as centralizing agents throughout the 19th cent. depended inevitably on the attitude and policy of the governments themselves. Napoleon III used them as effectively as his uncle, especially as electoral agents to ensure a majority in the Chamber.

PRELIMINARIES OF PARIS (1727), terms of agreement reached between the major powers, reducing the recent tension between the two armed camps, France, Britain, the United Provinces, Sweden, and Denmark on the one hand, and Spain and the Emperor Charles VI on the other. An international crisis had arisen from the delays in the Congress of Cambrai (1721–4) and the unnatural reconciliation between Spain and the Habsburgs which led to the formation of the Alliance of Hanover. In 1727 Spain went so far as to declare war on the Hanoverian bloc, but the intervention of Cardinal Fleury, who mediated between Britain and the empire, produced the peace preliminaries which were signed in Paris.

PREMCHAND (1880–1936), Indian publisher and writer, born Dhanpat Rai, who used this pseudonym from 1910 to disguise his identity while still serving as a government teacher (1900–21), for his stories had political as well as social themes, to which the government took exception. He wrote constantly, in Urdu and (increasingly after 1916) in Hindi, and published 12 novels and some 300 stories. The best known of his novels is his last, *Godan* (1936) (*The Gift of a Cow*). He is regarded as the creator of modern Hindi fiction.

PREMYSLID DYNASTY, line of rulers of Bohemia and Moravia from at least the 9th cent. to 1306, descended from the legendary Przemysl. After the destruction of Svatopluk's Great Moravia by the Hungarians in 906, the Premyslids established a strong state based on Bohemia further westwards. They christianized the country and Boleslaw I contributed to the German victory over the Hungarians in 955, and became, like all his descendants, a dependent of the German rulers. By the 13th cent. they were the strongest princes in the empire. Silver mines provided them with great wealth and from the 11th cent. they encouraged German settlement. The dynasty made Bohemia a great state with a firm foundation of monarchical government, and aspired to conquer Poland, Austria, and Hungary. Their ambitions passed to the Luxemburg, and later the Habsburg, rulers of Bohemia.

PRENDERGAST, SIR HARRY (1834–1913), British officer who fought in the Indian Mutiny and commanded the British force that advanced virtually unopposed to Mandalay in the Third Burmese War (1885).

PREOBRAZHENSKY in Russia, regiment of royal bodyguards, founded by Peter I and called after a village situated on the Yauza river near Moscow, his childhood home. During the 18th cent. the regiment played a significant role in successive palace coups, which resulted in the succession of Tsarinas Anna (1730), Elizabeth (1741), and Catherine II (1762). It also supported the liberal provisional government in the early stages of the 1917 revolution.

PREROGATIVE, special discretionary rights of the Crown, normally outside the jurisdiction of the law, *eg*, right of dispensation and suspension of laws, which developed in the later Middle Ages and gave European monarchs considerable, if not absolute, political authority, especially during the 15th–18th cents. The royal prerogative in England was curbed by the revolution settlement (1688–1719) and was undermined in France when the 1789 Revolution brought the end of divine-right monarchy, whereas in Russia, Austria, and Prussia it survived until the downfall of the monarchies in those countries in the 20th cent.

PRESBYTERIANISM, branch of the Christian Church in which the theology of Calvin is emphasized through insistence on Calvinistic doctrine. It is administered by a General Assembly, Synods, Presbyteries, and Kirk-sessions in descending order of hierarchy. Ministers are elected by the people and ordained by the presbytery. Preaching plays an important part in worship, and ministers must be academic scholars of high standing.

In Scotland Presbyterianism is the state Church, although it claims a spiritual independence. Its origins in Scotland lie in the events of the 16th-cent. Reformation. In 1560 the influence of John Knox led to the establishment of a pattern that was broadly Presbyterian and assumed a stricter Presbyterian role under Andrew Melville in 1582. For a century (*c.* 1580–*c.* 1680) Presbyterianism and Episcopacy struggled in Scotland for dominance. The Stuart kings, James I and Charles I, ensured the influence of Episcopacy for a generation (1612–38). Subsequently, the Scots rejected bishops, partly because of their hostility to the Prayer Book introduced by Abp Laud.

During the Civil Wars and the protectorate Presbyterianism was the effective religious force in Scotland. The Restoration of Charles II (1660) brought about a bitter conflict in Scotland. Episcopacy was re-established and the loyalties of the nation seemed equally divided, with extremists on either side. The rejection by the entire Scottish episcopate of William III led to the return of Presbyterianism as the state Church (1690), a position entrenched by the Act of Union (1707), if weakened by the Disruption (1843).

Scottish Presbyterianism, divided on issues of establishment and patronage in the 19th cent., was almost entirely unified by the two unions of 1900 and 1929, only a remnant of the Free Church (1900) and United Free Church (1929) continuing to stand apart in very small numbers.

Scottish Presbyterianism has made a major contribution to missionary work overseas and to education.

There were signs in the 1960s of a growing reconciliation in spirit between Presbyterians and the Episcopal Church in Scotland, which survived the 1690 settlement and grew in strength after the repeal of the Penal Laws (1792) against it. Elsewhere Presbyterianism, partly as a consequence of emigration from Scotland, and partly owing to independent expressions of Calvinism, took firm roots in the US, Canada, South Africa, Australia, and New Zealand, as well as in Wales, Ireland, and England.

C. L. Warr, *Presbyterian Tradition* (London, 1933).
J. Moffatt, *The Presbyterian Churches* (London, 1928).
GMDH

PRESCOTT, WILLIAM HICKLING (1796–1859), US historian, who, in spite of defective eyesight, did a vast amount of research with the help of readers, and wrote *The History of the Reign of Ferdinand and Isabella* (1837–8), *A History of the Conquest of Mexico* (1843), and *A History of the Conquest of Peru* (1847); he also completed three volumes of a *History of the Reign of Philip II* (1855–8). His scholarship and powers of narration won him critical praise and a wide readership in Britain and America. He was the first US historian to employ Spanish archival material in the writing of Latin American history.

PRESIDENTS À MORTIER in France, senior judges of the *parlement* of Paris, who from the time of St Louis's coronation (1226) until the 18th cent. could be distinguished as presidents from the other magistrates by their *mortiers* or black velvet caps.

PRESIDIAL COURTS in France, royal tribunals established by edict in Henry II's reign (Jan. 1552) with limited authority between that of the *parlements* and the bailiwicks, each consisting of nine judges. They were competent to try certain lesser criminal offences and to judge those civil cases which came on appeal from the bailiwick and involved no more than 500 *livres* damages. They were intended to lessen the burden of appeal cases going to the *parlements*, and by the end of the 16th cent. some 65 courts had been set up. They declined in importance in the 18th cent., but survived until 1789.

PRESIDIOS in Latin America, frontier blockhouses manned by small parties of soldiers and used extensively by the Spanish, usually in conjunction with a mission, to pacify and convert the natives of northern Mexico and the American South-west.

PRESS GANG, military or naval squads which compelled men into military service. Such gangs were once common in France, Prussia, and England. The New Model Army in the English Civil War was largely raised by impressment. After 1688 the English parliament occasionally made use of this form of recruiting, the last general press being in 1779. Impressment for the royal navy was a prerogative of the Crown which was not exercised after the conclusion of the French Wars (1815).

PRESSBURG TREATY (1805), signed after Napoleon's defeat of Austria and Russia at Austerlitz. It marked the end of the Holy Roman empire and the creation of the Confederation of the Rhine. Austria was deprived of Venetia, Dalmatia, and the Tyrol, and Bavaria was strengthened.

PRESTES, LUÍS CARLOS (1898–), Brazilian politician and revolutionary of the 1920s. He led the communist revolt (1935), and was secretary-general of the Communist Party from 1946 onwards. He once served on the executive committee of the Comintern, and was (1970) noted for his consistent adherence to Soviet policy directives. He was also a senator (1945–8).

PRESTON, BATTLES OF (1648, 1715). In 1648, the battle of Preston was the decisive engagement of the second English Civil War. The Duke of Hamilton invaded England (8 July) with nearly 20,000 Scots. On 17 Aug. Oliver Cromwell with 9000 men attacked the Scottish flank, which stretched for 30 miles (48 kms), and drove the Scots and their English supporters into Preston. Hamilton crossed the Ribble river, leaving 4000 prisoners. In bad weather Cromwell pursued, and on 19 Aug. caught up with the Scottish foot at Winwick, about three miles (4 kms) from Warrington. After losing 1000 killed Gen. Baillie surrendered. Hamilton and 3000 horse fled, but were forced to surrender to John Lambert at Uttoxeter (25 Aug.). This victory and the surrender of Colchester (28 Aug.) ended the war.

The second battle of Preston, in 1715, was equally decisive in ending the cause of the first Jacobite rebellion. The supporters of the Old Pretender, James Edward, rose in revolt in northern England, under the leadership of James Radclyffe, Earl of Derwentwater, but failed to link up with the revolt in Scotland. They marched on Preston and occupied it, but surrendered to the royal army under Gen. Charles Wills after a vigorous resistance (14 Nov.). The revolt collapsed and Derwentwater and 29 others were executed (1716). Henceforth the Jacobite cause remained relatively insignificant until 1745.

PRESTONPANS, BATTLE OF (1745), near Edinburgh, fought between the Jacobites under Charles Edward Stuart and the Hanoverian troops of Gen. Cope. After a five-minute skirmish the government forces fled. The victory brought the Jacobites many new recruits and made possible the invasion of England.

PREVÉSA (PREVEZA), BATTLE OF (Sept. 1538), on the western coast of Greece. The Ottoman fleet under Khayr al-Din Barbarossa overcame a Christian armada of Venetian, Spanish, and Genoese vessels. The encounter marked the passing of the initiative in naval affairs in the Mediterranean to the Ottomans, in whose hands it remained until the battle of Lepanto (Oct. 1571).

PREVOST, SIR GEORGE (1767–1816), British soldier and colonial governor. He was governor of St Lucia (1798–1801), and of Dominica (1802–8), and lieutenant-governor of NS (1808–11). He returned victorious from an expedition against Martinique (1809), was made administrator of Lower Canada (1811), and governor-in-chief (1812), during which appointment he did much to conciliate the French Canadians. As commanding general of the military forces at Sackett's Harbour (28 May 1813) and Plattsburg (11 Sept. 1814), Prevost gave inadequate support to the naval forces and withdrew under fire. He was ordered to be court-martialled in Britain for his failure at Plattsburg, but died before the hearing.

PRÉVOST D'EXILES, ANTOINE FRANÇOIS, Abbé de (1697–1763), French writer and thinker, noted for his story, *Manon Lescaut*, which was part of the *Mémoires d'un homme de qualité* (1731).

PRÉVÔT in France, official, whose post as administrator of royal lands originated in the early Middle Ages. The acquisition of hereditary rights by the 11th cent. rendered the *prévôt* less effective as a royal agent, and during Philip Augustus's reign (1180–1223) he was replaced by the bailiff, though remaining as a judge of civil cases in the first instance. The *prévôt*'s competence was regulated by edicts of 1536 and 1559, by which time his office had become venal. It was eventually suppressed by edicts of 1734 and 1749. The *prévôt* of Paris had lost his hitherto important police functions to the lieutenant-general of police in 1667, but his court and the administrative area survived until 1789.

PRICE, GEORGE (1812–90), Jamaican planter and politician, who was a member of the Assembly and (until 1862) of the Executive Council. He left Jamaica in 1865, in protest at Eyre's conduct. In England he supported efforts to put Eyre on trial.

PRICE, RICHARD (1723–91), Welsh dissenting minister and writer, of radical views, whose *Review of the Principal Questions in Morals* (1756) led to his drafting a programme of economic and political reform for Lord Shelburne's consideration. His pamphlet on the national debt (1771) was influential in the Younger Pitt's subsequent adoption of the sinking fund. Price argued in favour of American claims to independence, and a sermon by him favourable to the French Revolution contributed to fears of sedition in Britain and was denounced by Burke.

PRICE, SIR UVEDALE (1747–1829), English landscape designer, who opposed the school of landscape design associated with Lancelot Brown. He travelled on the continent with the politician, Charles James Fox, and took the rugged grandeur of alpine scenery and the paintings of Salvator Rosa as models for his garden style. He published his ideas in *An Essay on the Picturesque* (1794).

PRICE REVOLUTION, inflationary economic phenomenon of the 16th and early 17th cents, which produced considerable changes in economic and social patterns. Whereas the late medieval economy had been relatively stable, that of 16th-cent. Europe changed drastically, notably through rapidly rising prices. General price indices worked out for France by Einaudi suggest that, taking prices in 1471–2 as 100, they rose to 111·5 (1473–86), then fell to 106·6 (1487–1514), to rise phenomenally thereafter to 161·5 (1515–54),

265·2 (1555–75), and finally 627·5 (1590–8), although the rise continued until the 1630s. This accords well with other estimates of a quadrupling of prices over the century, with land and food prices rising higher than the average.

The price rise has usually been ascribed to imports of bullion from South America, notably of silver from Potosí (1545), which poured into Spain and eventually, because of Spain's economic weakness, into the rest of Europe throughout the century, reaching a peak in the last decade and continuing into the following century. Certainly, this silver was a major cause of price inflation, partly through the operation of Gresham's Law, but recently historians have found that silver alone will not satisfactorily explain all aspects of the price revolution. The price rise began in the 15th cent. before the arrival either of West African gold or American silver, as, *eg*, in England, where food prices started to rise sharply (1480). Inflation in Spain, although showing a close connection with the arrival of bullion, continued at times when Spain was bereft of bullion, while it was not until quite late (1557) that the process of refining silver through mercury was introduced, so that the fullest impact of the silver imports did not come until the price rise was under way.

One factor, closely connected with bullion imports, which seems to have played a part in the price rise is the state of the financial organization, which was inefficient and encouraged speculation and state manipulation of coinage. As a result of this the value of the *livre tournois* fell by over 31 per cent in the first half of the 16th cent. (1493–1561). There is thus an element of truth in Malestroit's contention, in his argument with Bodin on the price revolution (1556–8), that prices had fallen in real terms. On the whole, Bodin was correct in his insistence on the effect of bullion and dearth. The latter is increasingly regarded as a result of a rapidly rising population which began in the 15th cent. and raised the European population from around 55 million in 1450 to about 100 million in 1600, often outstripping the growth of agriculture and industry, causing plague, hunger, and rapid inflation. An increase in population is not a complete explanation, for in France prices continued to rise when the population declined during the Religious Wars. It is in the combination of demographic growth, bullion imports, and speculation, all working together in a relatively static economy, that one must find the explanation for the price revolution.

Its effects were usually drastic, varying according to the inherent economic structure. Thus it stimulated English industry and agriculture, but virtually ruined Spain. Different classes were differently affected. Cultivators, merchants, and speculators could often gain, but those living on fixed incomes, whether nobles or urban artisans, were badly hit, losing a quarter of their purchasing power. The growing number of unemployed drifting into the towns and the thwarted aspirations of groups whose position was thus undermined, combined, particularly when exacerbated by war, to produce social and political unrest and dissension which often broke out in the 16th cent. and was to be a recurrent phenomenon in the 17th.

R. B. Wernham, *New Cambridge Modern History*, vol. 3, *The Price Revolution and the Counter Reformation* (London, 1968).
E. J. Hamilton, *American Treasure and the Price Revolution in Spain 1501–1650* (Cambridge, MA, 1934). CHC

PRIDE, THOMAS (d. 1658), English soldier in the Civil War, who commanded a regiment at Naseby (1645) and served with Oliver Cromwell at Preston (1648), Dunbar (1650), and Worcester (1651). On 6 Dec. 1648, under orders from the army council, he stood at the entrance of the House of Commons and arrested or excluded about 140 Presbyterian MPs—an episode known as Pride's Purge. Most of those excluded had continued to negotiate with Charles I after the second Civil War, in defiance of the army, and had opposed the trial of the king. The rest of the Long Parliament, known as the 'Rump', contained no more than 50 or 60 MPs. The purge enabled the army and its Independent supporters to push through the execution of the king and the establishment of the Commonwealth. Pride himself signed the death-warrant on King Charles I in 1649. Though he opposed the proposal to make Cromwell king, he accepted a place in Cromwell's upper house.

PRIDI PHANOMYONG (1900–   ), Thai politician, lawyer, and intellectual leader of Thailand's revolution (1932), who became prime minister in 1946. His radical economic schemes, drafted in 1933, frightened conservatives, who viewed him a communist and forced him briefly into exile. He later served as minister of the interior and foreign affairs, and as minister of finance. He was also regent for the absent king during the Second World War. During the Japanese occupation he covertly led the underground Free Thai organization, and engineered the overthrow of Phibunsongkhram in 1944. He was the power behind the post-war government, was held responsible for King Ananda's death (1947), and was again forced into exile. In China from the early 1950s onwards he became nominal head of the Thai Patriotic Front.

PRIESTLEY, JOSEPH (1733–1804), English scientist, educationalist, and dissenting minister. He was a tutor at Warrington Academy (1761), minister at Leeds (1767–73), literary companion to the Earl of Selburne, and minister at Birmingham (1780–91). He emigrated to PA in 1794 after his house and laboratory had been destroyed by a mob hostile to sympathizers with the French Revolution. As a chemist he made great advances in the study of gases. By using mercury in his pneumatic trough, he discovered a number of gases which are soluble in water, including sulphur dioxide, ammonia, and hydrogen chloride. He discovered oxygen in 1774, unaware that the Swedish chemist, Scheele, had also discovered the gas some two years earlier. He was the first to use carbon dioxide in the preparation of mineral waters. Priestley foreshadowed the application of utilitarianism in education, government, and society, notably in *Miscellaneous Observations Relating to Education* (1778).

PRIETO Y TUERO, INDALECID (1883–1962), Spanish politician, who became a deputy to the Cortes in 1918 and attracted the jealousy of Largo Caballero, which began a rivalry which was to divide socialism for the next 20 years.

In 1925 Prieto opposed Largo Caballero's entry into the Primo government lest collaboration with the dictatorship should taint the party. In 1930 he worked hard to ensure the formation of the republic and in the first republican government he was minister of finance and then (1931) of public works, following on the constructive work of the dictatorship. As leader of the reformist wing of the Socialist Party, he was in sympathy with the bourgeois Republicans. By 1933, when Azana's government was falling, he was ready to collaborate with the radicals to forestall a right-wing government, but Largo Caballero, having moved leftwards, was totally opposed to such co-operation.

The Asturian rising of 1934 widened the gap between them. Although Prieto bought arms for it, he was determined because of its failure never to identify himself with revolution again. Thus, throughout 1936, while Largo Caballero advocated extreme revolutionary action, Prieto became the solid realist. He helped Azana to create the popular front and after the elections he urged the UGT to stop the revolutionary disorders that were discrediting the government and use legal means to strengthen working-class power, pointing out that disorder was provoking middle-class fascism. He advocated a policy of agrarian reform based on irrigation, but refused to become prime minister lest this should cause the UGT to leave the popular front.

When the violence of right and left reached its peak in July 1936, he took a lead in demanding the distribution of arms to the workers to prevent the expansion of fascism.

When the Civil War began, he worked tirelessly for Giral's government, becoming (1936) minister of the air force and navy. He was persistently frustrated by Largo Caballero's slowness, bureaucracy, and personal animosity, and he acted against him in the cabinet crisis of May 1937, providing a decisive factor in Caballero's fall. Thereafter, as minister of defence, Prieto agreed with the communists on the need for efficient prosecution of the war, although—because of his resentment at increasing Russian interference—he began to weed out communists from key posts.

The communists retaliated by stimulating a campaign to demand his resignation. Teruel, on which Prieto had placed his hopes, was starved of arms and its fall shattered both his prestige and his confidence. He became convinced that all was lost and that a negotiated peace was necessary to save lives, and consequently was accused of defeatism. He resigned in April 1938. PP

PRIGG v. PENNSYLVANIA, 16 Peters 539 (1842), US Supreme Court case concerning the constitutionality of state legislation and of the federal fugitive slave law (1793). Prigg seized a runaway slave in PA and forcibly took him back to MA. On his return to PA, Prigg was indicted and convicted of violating a state act (1826). Justice Story, giving the majority opinion of a divided court, declared the PA statute unconstitutional. Since execution of provisions of the constitution was exclusively a federal power, he upheld the national legislation, while accepting that state courts could not be required to enforce it.

PRIME MINISTERS' CONFERENCE, THE AUSTRALIAN, extra-constitutional expedient evolved to handle administrative and political problems arising out of Commonwealth–state relations after Federation (1901), and also to facilitate discussions between the several states without the presence of the Commonwealth prime minister. The conference was criticized for producing more talk than action but it served a useful purpose despite the transfer of some of its financial functions to the Australian Loan Council, set up by the 1928 Financial Agreement, and the delegation of more distinctively administrative matters to conferences of appropriate ministers, especially after the Second World War.

PRIMITIVA ILLA ECCLESIA (1516), papal bull incorporating the terms of the Concordat of Bologna (1516) between Francis I and Pope Leo X and stipulating the approval of the agreement by both the Lateran Council and the French Church.

PRIMO DE RIVERA, JOSÉ ANTONIO (1903–36), Spanish lawyer, journalist, and politician, who advocated a Spanish regeneration through a nationalist revolution. In Oct. 1933 he founded the Falange Española as the organization through which to establish his own form of poetic nationalism. He wanted an authoritarian national reconstruction firmly placed within the context of eternal Spanish values. His central theme was 'harmony of classes and professions in one destiny'.

The Falange gained few supporters and (1934) he had to amalgamate the movement with the more crudely fascist Juntas de Ofensiva Nacional Sindicalista of Ledesma Ramos. The new movement, hardly more successful, took its Nazi-style practical content from Ledesma Ramos, while Primo provided an emotional tone of mystical exaltation with calls for personal sacrifice and talk of a national mission. By 1936 he was being forced to accept monarchist funds and see his movement become the free-lance agent of the right. Yet his major ambition remained to give the revolutionary aspirations of the left a nationalist bias.

In March 1936 he was arrested and imprisoned in Alicante. Reluctantly, on 29 June he gave orders for Falangists to join the generals' rising. He was condemned to death in Nov. and executed on the orders of the communist provincial governor, though there had been no official confirmation of the sentence by the government. After the Civil War his remains were transferred to the Valle de los Caidos, Spain's monument to the war dead.

Veneration of his memory was turned into a national cult. Every church carried the slogan 'José Antonio Presente' and his complete works became the bible of Serrano Suner's new Nationalist Spain. Ironically, he became, as it were, the patron saint of a cause that was far from the idealistic, national revolution which he had advocated. PP

PRIMO DE RIVERA, MIGUEL (1870–1930), Spanish soldier and dictator (1923–30), who thought he had a divine mission to replace the rule of professional politicians with 'intuitionism', the sympathetic government of a man of good sense, in touch with the common people. He failed to solve the problem of Catalan nationalism and his energetic attempts to reform local government and taxation had little result. But otherwise his paternalism produced solid achievements. He modernized labour relations, initiated a remarkable programme of public works, and consolidated Spain's Moroccan protectorate. But he found no solution to Spain's constitutional instability. The moment never seemed right for his frequently promised return to 'normality'. His disregard for judicial procedures prevented the politicians and intellectuals from becoming reconciled to his rule and his resignation, following the collapse of the peseta (1929) and the loss of the army's support, contributed ultimately to the downfall of the monarchy (1931).

PRIMROSE LEAGUE in Britain, party political organization founded in 1883 by the Tory Democrat Lord Randolph Churchill. It mobilized imperialist sympathies so as to attract voluntary election workers and mass support for the Conservative Party. Although somewhat vague in its doctrine, by 1910 it had attracted 2 million members, but their numbers declined as greater recreational opportunities occurred in succeeding decades.

PRINCE, THE, Machiavelli's best-known treatise and one of the most important works of political theory ever written. It was composed in 1513 and published in 1532. It was inspired by the expulsion of the French and the restoration of the Medici to Florence by force of papal and imperial arms (1512). It heralded the modern nation state by analysing the nature of secular government under the princely ruler and abandoning the theological basis of medieval political philosophy.

PRINCE, THOMAS (1687–1758), American clergyman and writer, who was pastor of the Old South Church in Boston (1718–58). He wrote *The Chronological History of New England* (1736–55), which started with the Creation and made the advent of the Puritans in America a part of God's design.

PRINCE EDWARD ISLAND, Canadian province, situated in the Gulf of St Lawrence. It was visited by Jacques Cartier (1534) and named Île-Saint-Jean by the French. After four attempts at colonization had failed, the island became a French royal colony (1725). A profitable fishery was established (1731), and when the British gained control (1758) the population had risen to 5000. In 1763 the island was divided into 67 plots, which were distributed by lottery, mainly to absentee British speculators. Although the land was granted on condition that it would be settled and the fishery developed, the proprietors did neither. The island was separated from NS and in 1769 its own provincial government and legislature were established. In 1851 George Coles achieved responsible government for the province, which, because of hostility to the proposal for the unification of the maritime provinces, did not enter into confederation with Canada until 1873.

PRINCE OF WALES, non-hereditary title of the eldest son and heir-apparent of the English monarch, first bestowed on the future Edward II at Caernarvon (1301). The eldest son becomes at birth Duke of Cornwall, but the monarch may, if and when he wishes, issue letters patent to create him Prince of Wales, and this has occurred regularly since Edward III bestowed the title on the Black Prince (1343).

When the English and Scottish monarchies were merged into the British monarchy in 1603, the Prince of Wales assumed also the dukedom of Rothesay, formerly the title of the Scottish heir-apparent.

PRINCEPS, Roman term, meaning 'leading citizen', used widely of the Roman emperors. In the republic it was conveniently used with reference to leading politicians, several of them in each generation, and was chosen by the first Emperor Augustus, who sought for a politically acceptable term to disguise the monarchical character of his rule and to avoid *rex* (king), which was hated by tradition, and *dictator*, which Julius Caesar had made unpopular. The term then came to be equivalent to *imperator* (emperor), though it never became a formal constitutional title. The abstract *principatus*, 'principate', was derived from it and used as an equivalent to 'reign'.

PRINCES OF THE BLOOD in France, collateral male relatives of the ruling sovereign, and next to the royal children and grandchildren, the leading members of the *noblesse de race*.

PRINCETON, BATTLE OF (3 Jan. 1777), engagement between British and American forces during the American War of Independence. After the battle of Trenton, patriot units, commanded by Gen. Hugh Mercer, clashed with a large British force under Gen. James Grant and Lord Cornwallis. Mercer was killed, but the British were then surprised and routed by the main American army under George Washington. The battle did much to restore colonial morale and marked a turning point in the war.

PRINCIPALITY OF WALES. King Edward I's settlement of Wales after the defeat of Llywelyn II in 1282 had legal and administrative, as well as military and economic, aspects. The lesser Welsh lords were imprisoned, but Powys retained its native ruler, who held the land of the king by feudal tenure. The lands held by Llywelyn were confiscated by the Crown. Some portions were granted as lordships, such as Denbigh, Ruthin, and Chirk, while the remainder became Crown land, not part of the realm. These areas were reorganized as shires on the English model, the *cantref* of Tegeingl becoming the shire of Flint and Llywelyn's principality of Gwynedd becoming the shires of Anglesey, Caernarvon, and Merioneth. The Crown already held Cardigan and Carmarthen, which were now recreated shires. Together these shires formed the principality of Wales (north and west) and were administered according to the terms of the Statute of Wales (1284). New administrative machinery and new officials were introduced. The king's Justice of North Wales (and the Justice of West Wales) presided over the high courts and the Court of Great Sessions; sheriffs were responsible for details of administration. English criminal law was introduced, making crimes offences against the state rather than against kindred and depriving the victim's kin of the right of vengeance and compensation. The custom of 'hue and cry' laid the obligation of capture on the people at large, not the kin alone. The Edwardian settlement was not revolutionary, as Welsh civil law was largely retained and the holding of land was little affected, but the authority of the state in enforcing law and order was firmly introduced. In 1301 the Crown lands in Wales were granted by Edward I to his eldest son with the title 'prince of Wales', a title held by the sovereign's eldest son ever since.

BFR

PRINCIPIA MATHEMATICA (*Mathematical Principles of Natural Philosophy*), Isaac Newton's great scientific treatise, which expounded his system of the universe. It was first wholly published in 1687. His aim was not limited to verify-ing the Copernican system, nor to synthesizing the developments in astronomy and mechanics from the time of Galileo and Kepler, but rather to set down his views of physics and celestial mechanics in the light of quantitative experimental method. Book I sets out the general theory of dynamics, especially the theory of the motions of bodies under the action of a centripetal force directed towards some point or body. Book II expounds the theory of fluids, and Book III applies the general theory of dynamics to the inverse-square law of gravitation and demonstrates the phenomena of the planets and their satellites, the moon and the tides.

PRINCIPIO COMPANY, early American iron works, established in MD in 1715 and owned by British capitalists and iron masters. It exported bar iron to Britain (1718). The company came to an end (1780), when MD confiscated British property within the state.

PRINTING, originally the process of reproducing texts by the use of movable type, and later of monochrome illustrations, originated in the Far East (AD 618), but developed independently in western Europe. Several factors combined to produce printing: the invention of the press; the introduction of cheap, strong paper, sufficiently thin to yield a satisfactory impression; the use of heavy ink; and, above all, of movable metal type. Engraving with metal plates or wood blocks was already known in the 14th cent. and the inventors of printing were essentially skilled metal workers. The discovery is usually attributed to Johann Gutenberg (c. 1398–1468), of Mainz, but he was only one of many working in different parts of Europe at about the same time (eg, William Caxton in England) to perfect the technique. Gutenberg was the first to print on a large scale. By the end of the 15th cent. printing presses were established throughout western Europe and between 1450 and 1500 at least 10,000 texts were printed. Thereafter printing had a profound effect on communications, and hence on the quality of life. It remained unchallenged by any other media until the invention of broadcasting in the 20th cent.

PRÍO SOCARRÁS, CARLOS (1903–   ), Cuban politician and president of Cuba (1948–52), who was leader of the *Auténticos* (the Authentic Party) in the 1940s. His government was expelled from office by the army, led by Fulgencio Batista.

PRIOR, MATTHEW (1664–1721), English diplomat and poet, whose first major role in diplomacy was to report to England the arrangements between William III and Louis XIV for the partition of the Spanish inheritance. In 1711 he was sent to Fontainebleau to communicate the 'Tory ministers' preliminary demands as a prerequisite for the conclusion of the war of the Spanish Succession. In 1712 he again went to France and remained in Paris until 1714. Upon his return to England, he was arrested by order of the new Whig government. Articles of impeachment were drawn up against him for his alleged part in the making of peace (1713) and he was held in custody (1715–17). A collected edition of his poems for private subscription had meanwhile been prepared by his friends and its appearance is said to have netted him some £4000. His poetry included 'Henry and Emma' and 'To a child of Quality'. As a poet he was a storyteller of lucidity and charm, whose poems were in contrast to much of the more weighty versification of his day.

PRISON ACT (1839) in Britain, established the uniform and improved treatment of prisoners. It followed the report of the parliamentary committee of 1835 and laid down that prisoners should be housed in separate cells, given productive work, allowed to read books, and talk at work or on exercise. Following the suggestions of James Mill, Romilly, and others, Peel, as home secretary, had ordered the payment of gaolers, regular inspection of and reports on prison conditions, and the grading of prisoners for instruction and work, but his instructions applied only to the prisons of the county justices in London and the larger provincial towns. A reform applicable to the whole prison system was needed. The abandonment of transportation led to further prison building and more detailed regulations (1865).

PRIVATEER, privately owned armed ship commissioned and authorized by a government to take reprisals against, or to prey upon, an enemy. The practice of issuing such commissions ceased as a result of the Declaration of Paris (1856), except in the US, which did not sign the declaration. The system was outlawed by the Hague Convention of 1907.

PROBUS, M. AURELIUS (*c.* AD 232–82), Roman Emperor (*reg.* 276–82), who was proclaimed by the eastern armies and recognized after the death of Florianus at Tarsus. He continued the work of restoration begun by Claudius and Aurelian, suppressing usurpations in Gaul and the east, campaigning successfully on the northern frontier, and crushing internal tribal revolts in Isauria and Egypt. It was said to be his ambition to restore peace and make armies unnecessary; but he was killed by his own troops at Sirmium and replaced by Carus.

PROCLAMATION LINE (1763), British rule which made the Alleghenies a boundary beyond which American white settlers were not allowed to go. The western lands were to be preserved for the Indians, but the Indians did not understand this policy, to which frontiersmen and land speculators were opposed, and it became a significant grievance between the North American colonies and Britain.

PROCLAMATIONS, STATUTE OF (1539), in England, attempt to settle doubtful points on the legality of proclamations by providing that the king, on the advice of his council, or the greater part of it, might issue proclamations having the full force of law. The king could also direct JPs to see they were carried out, and offenders against them could be punished by specified members of the council, sitting as a board. Neither Common Law nor statute could be infringed by a proclamation. It also provided that proclamations should 'not be prejudicial to any person's inheritance, offices, liberties, goods, chattels or life'. Though the statute accepted the legislative supremacy of parliament, its absolutist flavour led to its repeal in 1547.

PROCONSUL, ancient Roman term applied to a consul whose *imperium* was prolonged beyond his year of office. It was first used in the case of Q. Publilius Philo (326 BC) as a device of prorogation of *imperium* of consuls and praetors. It later became the regular method in the Late Republic of providing provincial governors. The proconsulship tended to become dissociated from the consulship and was conferred on private citizens, *eg,* Pompey in 77, 66, and 65, and Pompey's law of 52 fixed an interval of five years between magistracy and promagistracy. Under the Principate the term proconsul was applied to all governors of senatorial provinces.

PROCOPIUS (*c.* 500–70), Byzantine historian, who is the main narrative authority for the reign of the Emperor Justinian I. Procopius accompanied Justinian's greatest general, Belisarius, on his campaign as a legal adviser. His official histories described Justinian's wars and building enterprises. Different in character is the notorious *Secret History*, in which his patron, Justinian, and the latter's wife, Theodora, are depicted in a most unfavourable light. All modern historians of this period have been troubled by the problem of how far they can follow the testimony of Procopius.

PROCURATOR, financial and administrative official in the Roman empire, originally a term relating to Roman private law. Imperial procurators (*procuratores Augusti*) administered provincial revenues and the emperors' private property, and governed a few small provinces, *eg,* Judaea. From the

2nd cent. AD central government departments were headed by imperial procurators, who were grouped in three grades, according to their salaries.

PROGRESSIVE MOVEMENT in the US, reform movement in the late 19th and early 20th cents. It was essentially a response to the problems created by industrialization and urbanization. Big business, 'machine politics', city slums, and extremes of personal wealth and poverty were felt by progressives to be corrupting the traditional American ideal of political and economic democracy. To restore popular government and overthrow the power of political machines, progressives supported such reforms as direct primaries, the short ballot, the direct election of senators (established by the 17th Amendment to the US constitution, 1913), corrupt practices legislation, the initiative and referendum, and the recall of elected officials by public demand. On economic issues, however, there was less agreement among progressives. Some, including most Democrats and the supporters of Henry George's Single Tax movement, cherished the Jeffersonian ideal of a neutral, umpire state giving no favours to any class or interest. These sought, through such means, an anti-trust legislation and the abolition of privileged access to natural resources, to restore a state of competition in which opportunity was open to all. Others favoured direct government regulation of business and social welfare legislation. These divergent approaches were set forth, respectively, in Woodrow Wilson's New Freedom and Theodore Roosevelt's New Nationalism.

Progressivism made a political impact first at the city level, with the election of a number of reform mayors in the 1890s and 1900s. These mayors, of whom Tom L. Johnson, of Cleveland (1901–9), was the most famous, sought to eliminate corruption and subject private utility companies to more stringent regulation. The municipal reform movement culminated in the widespread adoption in the 1910s and 1920s of the commission and city manager forms of government. At the state level, progressive administrations, like that led by Robert M. La Follette in Wisconsin, introduced such reforms as maximum hours and minimum wages for women workers, industrial accident insurance, the abolition of child labour, and the establishment of commissions to regulate the rates and services of railroads and other public service corporations. At the federal level, the progressive movement was less successful, but, during the presidencies of Theodore Roosevelt (1901–9) and Woodrow Wilson (1913–21), legislation was enacted subjecting railroads, industrial corporations, and banks to public control.

The progressive movement never achieved a unified national organization and was notably diverse in its objectives and support. Although in the West and South it drew support from former Populists, the movement derived most of its strength from the professional and business classes of the cities and small towns. Revelations of corruption and injustice in various areas of business and politics by 'muckraking' journalists, such as Lincoln Steffens and Ray Stannard Baker, aroused public indignation, and this helped organized groups to promote specific reforms. Thus, while social workers and social gospel clergymen agitated for measures to alleviate the condition of the poor, progressive businessmen sought to promote efficiency through the conservation of natural resources and the rationalization of economic organization and political machinery. These different movements, skilfully harmonized by Roosevelt as the Progressive Party's presidential candidate in 1912, persisted in some form into the 1920s. But, as was shown by the comparative lack of success of La Follette's presidential campaign in 1924, reform was lacking in both political cohesion and public support after the First World War.

George E. Mowry, *The Era of Theodore Roosevelt, 1900–1912* (New York, 1958).
Arthur S. Link, *Woodrow Wilson and the Progressive Era, 1910–1917* (New York, 1954).   JAT

PROGRESSIVE PARTY of Canada, farmer-based political organization, founded in 1920 against high-tariff policies. The Progressive Party was supported by the Canadian Council of Agriculture. In 1921 it sent men to the Canadian House of Commons and, by holding the balance of power, succeeded in lowering freight rates. The so-called 'Ginger Group' which split from the Progressives (1924) led to the founding of the Co-operative Commonwealth Federation. The party held the balance of power until 1926, after which it declined in importance, electing only ten members to parliament in 1930. During this parliament the party merged with the Co-operative Commonwealth Federation.

PROHIBITION in NZ was largely a reaction to drunkenness in early colonial society. The NZ Alliance (1885) and other prohibitionist bodies mounted a political campaign in the 1890s for a 'direct vote' on the issues of 'continuance', 'reduction', and 'no-licence', but failed to secure a simple majority poll. In 1910 after some local triumphs for 'no-licence', the movement agreed to a national referendum with those who supported 'continuance'. Although they came near to securing a simple majority in 1919, support for prohibition fell away steadily until it reached no more than 20 per cent (1963).

PROHIBITION (1920–33) in the US, period when the 18th Amendment to the US constitution and the Volstead Prohibition Act were operative. Since the passage of laws in ME in 1846 and 1851, various pressure groups throughout the country had dedicated themselves to the passage of legislation interdicting the manufacture and sale of intoxicating liquors. By 1906, 18 states had at various times adopted state-wide prohibition laws, although only three retained them. More telling, however, was the increasing liberality with which state legislatures gave counties, cities, and towns a 'local option', or the authority to license, regulate, tax, or prohibit the sale of liquor within their particular jurisdictions. Increasingly, large areas of the US became 'dry' through local option. At the same time the Prohibition Party (founded 1869), the Women's Christian Temperance Union (founded 1874), the Anti-Saloon League (founded 1893), and numerous other national and local groups appealed for the passage of national legislation.

By Dec. 1917 a Congressional resolution proposing a prohibition amendment to the constitution had passed both Houses by the required two-thirds majority. By 1918 more than half the states had prohibitory liquor laws. By 16 Jan. 1919 the 18th Amendment to the constitution—the Prohibition Amendment—had been ratified by the necessary three-fourths of the states. It became operative on 16 Jan. 1920. On 27 Oct. 1919 Congress passed the Volstead Prohibition Act, over President Wilson's veto, prohibiting the sale and manufacture of liquors over one-half of 1 per cent alcohol.

Few issues in US history, including slavery and the Vietnam War, have proved as divisive as the adoption of prohibition. Despite the righteous motives of its sponsors, prohibition resulted in an era of wholesale avoidance of the law, in which widespread police and political corruption allowed criminals such as Al Capone to flourish. In 1931 the Wickersham Commission, headed by Attorney-General G. W. Wickersham, concluded that 'Few things are more easily made than alcohol' and that the prohibition laws were unenforceable. The 1932 Democratic National Convention reflected growing popular discontent with prohibition when it demanded the repeal of the 18th Amendment. By 5 Dec. 1933 Congress and three-fourths of the states had voted to end the 'noble experiment'.

Andrew Sinclair, *Prohibition: the era of excess* (London, 1962). Herbert Asbury, *The Great Illusion* (New York, 1950). FPK

PROKOP THE BALD (?1380–1434), Hussite priest and national leader of the extreme Hussite Taborites after the death of John Zizka. He was a clever diplomat and war leader, who changed the strategy of the movement to an offensive, invading German territories. He was killed at Lipany, where the Taborites were defeated by an alliance of the Catholics and moderate Hussites.

PROKOPOVICH, FEOFAN (1681–1736), Russian cleric, poet, and Abp of Novgorod (1724), whose greatest achievement was the drawing up of the Spiritual Regulation initiating the programme of Church reform and establishing the Most Holy Directing Synod, a new governing body of churchmen who replaced the patriarchate of the Russian Church (1721). Prokopovich became vice-president of this body.

PROME, on the Irrawaddy, 200 miles (322 kms) above Rangoon. Prehistoric Prome was known as Sri Ksetra. The present town, a river port, is an important centre of trade and communications. It is the terminus of the western main railway line out of Rangoon, on the western trunk road from Rangoon to Mandalay, and the starting point of a track over the Arakan range to Taungup on the coast.

PRONUNCIAMIENTO, in Spanish a pronouncement or declaration, and in Latin American politics a term used to refer to a revolt or call to arms against the government in power. The *pronunciamiento* often takes the form of a written manifesto which specifies the alleged failings of the regime which caused the revolt, and promises that such shortcomings will disappear when the rebels come to power.

PROPAGATION OF THE GOSPEL in Wales, commission which virtually ruled the country (1649–52) under the presidency of Maj.-Gen. Thomas Harrison. The commission, which treated Wales as a sort of missionary diocese, met peripatetically as two separate bodies, for north and south, each with its own officials. It was the only part of a general plan for the propagation of the Gospel for the whole of Britain which was ever put into practice.

PROPHESYINGS in England, conferences of the clergy devoted to systematic biblical exposition, established by Puritan preachers in the 1560s. They were a development of the 'conference' method of biblical study perfected by the Protestant humanists of Zürich and widely employed in the continental reformed churches. Held in market-town churches, they attracted popular interest and offered indoctrination and homiletic training to the more ignorant clergy. They were sometimes actively encouraged by bishops, and did much to propagate and establish the Anglican reformed religion in Elizabethan England. They reached their heyday in the reign of James I, when they could be found in most parts of the country. Their ultimate authority was based on a text of St Paul: 'Let the prophets speak two or three, and let the other judge . . . For ye may all prophesy one by one, that all may learn, and all may be comforted.'

PROPRIETARY GOVERNMENT, early European system of colonial rule. The English, French, and Dutch governments frequently made grants of land to favoured individuals or companies who became the proprietors. The proprietors were authorized to make laws, with the consent of the settlers, for the government of their colonies, appointing governors and convening elected legislative assemblies. Normally, a fifth of all precious metals mined in any colony were to pass to the Crown.

The first English grant (1606) was to the Virginia Co., which was promoted to settle the North American coast between Spanish FL and French-occupied NS. The London Co., a branch of the Virginia Co., settled Jamestown, VA (1607). Several subsequent grants were made in North America, the last being to William Penn (1692). A further grant to the Virginia Co. (1612) included Bermuda. In South America, Robert Harcourt received a grant (1613) over all lands between the Amazon and the Essequibo. His colony failed. The first English West Indian grant was to Ralph

Merrifield and some associates (1625) to settle St Kitts, Nevis, Montserrat, and either Barbuda or Barbados—islands 'lately discovered' by Thomas Warner, who was appointed lieutenant. Later, conflicting and overlapping grants were given to the Earl of Carlisle and the Earl of Montgomery. Carlisle's grant, the most valuable, included St Kitts, Nevis, Montserrat, Barbados, Antigua, Grenada, St Vincent, and St Lucia.

The French king granted proprietary rights over St Kitts (1626) to the Compagnie de Saint Christophe. In 1635 the Compagnie des Îles d'Amérique obtained rights over all French West Indian possessions. French proprietary government was, however, complicated by the king's appointment of a lieutenant-general who on occasion replaced the proprietors' governors with his own nominees.

In 1621 the proprietary rights in all Dutch New World settlements were granted to the Dutch West India Co. They established (1624) colonies in New Netherlands (NY). The Dutch North American colonies were captured by the English (1664), and renamed New York, after James, Duke of York, to whom they were granted. One by one, the North American colonies, except CT and RI, were subjected to royal government. In the West Indies all English and French proprietary colonies became royal in the second half of the 17th cent. Dutch New World colonies did not cease to be proprietary until the renewal of the West India Co.'s charter was refused in 1791.   RH

PROSCRIPTIONS, ROMAN, publication of a list of persons whose property was confiscated and who were outlawed and could be killed with impunity. Sulla (82–81 BC) and Octavian, Antony, and Lepidus (43–42) removed their political and personal enemies in this way.

PROTAGORAS (*c.* 485–411 BC), itinerant Greek sophist from Abdera and friend of Pericles at Athens. Though principally a grammar and rhetoric teacher, he is celebrated for his dictum that man is the measure of all things.

PROTECTORATE, CROMWELLIAN (1653–9), the government of the English republic under Oliver and Richard Cromwell ruling as Lord Protectors, with the assistance of a Council of State and a parliament. The protectorate was established after the failure of Barebone's Parliament by the Instrument of Government drawn up by the council of officers under John Lambert. On 16 Dec. 1653 Oliver Cromwell took the oath as Lord Protector, and in the next few months ruled by powers granted him in the Instrument, promulgating a series of controversial ordinances, *eg*, the establishment of a central committee of 'Triers' to investigate the qualifications of candidates for the ministry (March 1654), and of 'Ejectors' to remove 'scandalous, ignorant, and insufficient ministers and schoolmasters' (Aug. 1654). The first parliament of the protectorate (3 Sept. 1654) sought to amend the Instrument. Cromwell tried to bind the MPs by an oath of recognition, but nevertheless they prepared a constitutional bill to challenge his control of the army, his veto on legislation, and his income. On 22 Jan. 1655 Cromwell dissolved parliament.

Though the regime was based upon the army, Cromwell was determined to reduce the army establishment and strengthen the local militia. This he proceeded to do after the failure of Penruddock's rising (March 1655). The rule of the major-generals was instituted to co-ordinate military and local government, their expenses being defrayed by a tax of 10 per cent on Royalist estates. Though the major-generals tried to influence borough elections and the council of officers removed about 100 MPs, Cromwell's second parliament, which met on 17 Sept. 1656, was anti-military. The civilian Cromwellians, who wanted a return to a more conservative form of government, gained the leadership for a time. They threw out a bill for a decimation tax, a move which led to the ending of the major-generals' rule. On 23 Feb. 1657 they brought in a Remonstrance (later the Humble Petition and Advice) which called on Cromwell to accept the Crown. Though the offer was attractive, in that it promised to establish a more permanent and traditional regime, Cromwell finally rejected it (8 May 1657), after long negotiations, because he realized that the majority of the army would not support it. Parliament consequently deleted the kingship clause, accepted Cromwell's amendments, and established the second protectorate by the Humble Petition and Advice (25 May), which set up a more monarchical form of government; a second chamber was created in parliament and the protector was empowered to nominate his successor. Parliament was prorogued on 26 June 1657, to reassemble in its new form on 20 Jan. 1658. The new upper or 'Other House' removed from the Commons some of Cromwell's ablest supporters, while the new constitution enabled those 100 MPs excluded in Sept. 1656 to take their seats. The republican MPs thus admitted so criticized the 'Other House' that Cromwell dissolved parliament (4 Feb. 1658).

Despite such setbacks, Cromwell's government grew less militaristic during the last few months of his life, and the trend continued under his son Richard, who succeeded him on his death (3 Sept. 1658). Richard's parliament (Jan.–April 1659), though weakened by republican dissension, proved too anti-militaristic for the army, which forced Richard to dissolve it (22 April). Some of the army generals planned to keep Richard as titular protector, but the pressure of the rank and file, led by the junior officers, for the restoration of the Rump proved too strong. The Rump returned on 7 May and on the 25th Richard Cromwell resigned, thereby formally ending the protectorate.

G. Davies, *The Early Stuarts* (Oxford, 1937).
J. P. Kenyon, *The Stuart Constitution* (Cambridge, 1966). CJ

PROTESTANT UNION, alliance of Protestant German states under the leadership of the elector palatine for the defence of religious peace in the empire (1608). The union, which included Neuburg, Württemberg, Baden, Brandenburg, Ulm, Strasbourg, and Nuremberg, was formed through the initiative of Christian of Anhalt in answer to the annexation of Donauwörth by the Catholic Duke, Maximilian of Bavaria (1608), but in turn it provoked the creation of the Catholic League (1609). The Elector Christian II of Saxony refused to join the Protestant Union, which was further weakened by the serious rift between Lutherans and Calvinists, the suspicion of the cities for the princes, and the restraining influence of German constitutionalism. In 1617, on the eve of the Thirty Years War, Brandenburg left the union, and when the Bohemian crisis reached its climax (1620) it remained inactive. After Frederick of the Palatinate had been banned by Emperor Ferdinand II, the union's members assembled at Heilbronn to protest, but finally disbanded, never to reconvene, after agreeing to the Mainz Accord (14 May 1621).

PROTESTANTS TOLERATION EDICT (1787) in France. After the plight of French Protestants had been publicized in the Calas Affair (1762–5), religious equality for Protestants was proposed by Turgot during his ministry (1774–6), but this reform was not implemented until 1787, when Louis XVI agreed that they should be granted full civil rights, including that of entry into trades and professions from which they had hitherto been excluded, and also recognized the legitimacy of Protestant marriages registered with the local authorities. The edict was devised by Rabaut Saint-Etienne.

PROTESTATION (1529), signed by six German princes and 14 cities against the resolution (1526) of the Diet of Speyer to revoke the decree of toleration made at the Diet and to forbid the further secularization of Church lands. Their action gave Protestantism its name and led to the formation of the militant Schmalkaldic League (1531).

PROTOGEROV, ALEXANDER (1867–1928), Bulgarian soldier and IMRO leader, who commanded a Bulgarian unit against the Serbs during the First World War, served as food administrator of Bulgaria, and led the troops which suppressed the Radomir rebellion in 1918. In Nov. 1919 he was arrested by Stambuliski for his part in atrocities committed against the Serbs during the war, but escaped before his trial and fled to Italy. After the war Protogerov entered the ruling triumvirate of the Internal Macedonian Revolutionary Organization (IMRO). In April 1924 he identified himself formally with the communist party by signing the Vienna Manifesto, which attacked the Bulgarian government and aligned IMRO with the communists and federalists. Later, Alexandrov and Protogerov, who had initiated the negotiations with the communists, repudiated the manifesto. Alexandrov was shot, allegedly with the connivance of Protogerov, and in July 1928 Protogerov was himself killed by Mihailov, a rival leader.

PROTO-LITERATE PERIOD (c. 3100–2800 BC), period immediately after the invention of writing; it is characterized in Mesopotamia by the increased use of writing, the building of ziqqurats, and the use of cylinder seals.

PROUDHON, PIERRE JOSEPH (1809–65), French Socialist thinker, who expounded theories of anarchism and of trade unionism. He was a rival of Marx as a shaper of international socialism. In *Qu'est-ce-que la propriété?* (1840) he maintained that work is the only source of wealth, proposed the abolition of rent, interest, and profit, and advocated a kind of peasant proprietorship, and federal anarchism. The French delegates to the first International put forward his ideas, which were decisively defeated (1869) in favour of Marx's. But within France Proudhon's influence remained great, and he also influenced Bakunin, whose methods, however, were very different, and the Syndicalists.

PROVIDENCE COMPANY, formed in 1630 to finance the development of Providence Island, colonized in 1629 by an expedition sent out from England by the Earl of Warwick. Of the 26 members of the company, nearly two-thirds were members of the House of Commons or the House of Lords, and the company acted as an unofficial political organization which kept the opponents of Charles I's policies in touch with each other. Prominent members included John Pym, who was treasurer, Oliver St John, Lord Brooke, Viscount Saye and Sele, and Lord Warwick. With the conquest of the island by the Spanish, the members were left heavily in debt. The last known meeting of the company took place on 5 Feb. 1650.

PROVIDENCE ISLAND, or Santa Catalina, is situated in the Caribbean, 125 miles (201 kms) off the Mosquito Coast of Central America, its correct name being Old Providence. (It is not to be confused with New Providence in the Bahamas.) It was colonized by the English in 1629 and conquered by the Spanish in 1641.

PROVIDENCE PLANTATION, American settlement on Narragansett Bay created by Roger Williams (1636), who purchased the site from the Indians. William Coddington settled on the island of Aquidneck (1639) and founded Newport; Anne Hutchinson and her husband settled at Portsmouth (1642); and Samuel Gorton settled at Warwick (1643). These four settlements were joined under a charter from the English parliament (1644) and were called the Incorporation of Providence Plantations in Narragansett Bay in New England.

PROVINCE OF CANADA (1840–67), system of government created by the British Act of Union (1840). The act provided for a central and responsible government by merging the legislature of Upper and Lower Canada—renamed Canada West and Canada East. Government was exercised by the governor, and an Executive Council chosen by the legislature.

Economic difficulties and party and ethnic conflicts led to the termination of the Province of Canada and the establishment of a federated system under the British North American Act (1867).

PROVINCIAL COURTS ORDINANCE (1914) (as amended to 1922), in Nigeria, established provincial courts throughout the protectorate of Nigeria, though they were introduced in the Northern Provinces in 1900. They administered English law (besides customary law), but were presided over by Provincial Residents not necessarily qualified in law; nor were lawyers allowed to appear in the provincial courts. There were no rights of appeal to the Supreme Court in criminal cases, though such rights existed in certain categories of civil cases. The provincial court system, intended as it was to insulate the protectorate as much as possible from the 'inimical' influences of the Supreme Court, failed to achieve its political objective and probably retarded the development of the Nigerian legal system. The courts were abolished in 1933.

PROVINCIAL ESTATES in France, gatherings of representatives in the constituent provinces of the French monarchy. As general assemblies of the three estates of a province, they emerged during the 14th cent. in order to provide for consultation and defence, particularly by voting money to the French Crown, or their feudal lord, whom, as in Béarn or Burgundy, they originally served as estates-general. They had proliferated by the 15th cent., so that most regions including towns and districts, had provincial estates. Their powers and structure varied greatly from region to region, as had their origins. Existing mainly for voting subsidies, they were often consulted on diplomatic matters and were allowed to petition the Crown or publish edicts of their own. They were aristocratic and feudal in composition and only representative in the most general way. There was little attempt at election, and the peasantry was excluded everywhere, except in Normandy, the third estate being represented solely by the towns, while other orders such as the clergy were excluded by the estates of Dauphiné and Vivarais. Normandy and then Languedoc were the most democratic, with all three orders sitting and voting together. In some cases the estates maintained standing committees, or, as in Burgundy, took over responsibility for tax collection, but others could merely vote grievances, as in Provence. Their administrative record is much less significant than some authorities claim, and they were not greatly esteemed by the public.

When the monarchy began to turn against them, and particularly against the smaller estates, there was no opposition. At their height in the early 15th cent. there were over 30 provincial estates, ie, Albigéois, Anjoumois, Artois, Aunis, Auvergne, Béarn, Bourges, Brittany, Burgundy, Caen, Cambrésis, Castres, Comminges, Dauphiné, Douai, Flanders, Gevaudan, Guyenne, Languedoc, Lille, Maconnais, Marche, Navarre, Normandy, Périgord, Poitou, Provence, Quercy, Rovergue, Saintonge, Touraine, Velay, Venaissin, and Vivarais. Some, like Marche, were never called after this time, and many smaller ones were absorbed in the 16th cent. by the larger provincial estates. Many more were deliberately set aside by the cardinals: Auvergne (1624), Dauphiné (1628), Rovergue, Périgord and Guyenne (1630), and Normandy (1659). Provence was partially dismantled (1629) and only a revolt in Languedoc preserved some relics there (1632). By the 18th cent. there were only ten *pays d'états* left, and their ability to do anything more than make it slightly harder for the Crown to extract the full burden of taxation had vanished. They preserved some status and sometimes carried out public works as well as tax collection (where they did not commute their liabilities into a lump sum payment), but they were only a shadow of their former selves. The enthusiasm shown for them by late 18th-cent. reformers was based on myth, not reality. They had been systematically undermined by a combination of public indifference, their own shortcomings, and the determination of the Crown to centralize financial and administrative authority in its own hands.

G. Griffiths, *Representative Government in Western Europe during the Sixteenth Century* (Oxford, 1968). CHC

PROVINCIAL GOVERNMENT AND PROVINCIALISM in NZ, the shape and landscape of which largely determined that NZ should be settled at several points, and would require strong regional government in the early period. Two abortive provinces, New Ulster and New Munster, were proclaimed in 1846; more realistically the 1852 NZ Constitution Act established six provinces: Auckland, New Plymouth (Taranaki, 1858), Wellington, Nelson, Canterbury, and Otago. To these were added Hawkes Bay (1858) and Marlborough (1859), Southland (1861–70), and Westland (1873). Though the NZ General Assembly had over-riding powers, the system, quasi-federal in operation, was abolished in 1875–6, allegedly for being expensive, out-dated, and cumbersome, and also inequitable as between provinces. But provincialism and lesser forms of regionalism remained strong in NZ society and politics.

PROVINCIAL LEAGUES (1314–15) in France. The heavy financial exactions of Philip IV of France to pay for a fruitless war in Flanders, the oppressive government of officials in the localities, and the desire of many of the nobility to enjoy old rights, of which they had been deprived by the Crown, led to the formation of leagues of nobles in the French provinces. Such leagues were formed especially in the north and east in the last year of Philip's reign (1314). His son, Louis X, was left to deal with them. His first concession to the leagues was the removal and execution of his father's minister, De Marigny, who was sacrificed as a scapegoat for the royal financial policy. Then local charters of liberties were granted to the individual leagues to appease them. The chief factor enabling Louis to control this outburst was the lack of unity between the leagues.

PROVISIONAL GOVERNMENT (March–Oct. 1917) in Russia, brought into being during the night of 1–2 March 1917 as the result of an agreement between the provisional committee of the duma and the Petrograd soviet. The latter (which in fact controlled Petrograd) commissioned the former (which hardly existed outside the Tauride Palace) to form a government. Certain conditions were agreed—that a Constituent Assembly should be called to decide the future destiny of Russia, that local government should be democratized, and that political prisoners should be pardoned. Nothing was said about other matters of critical importance; *eg*, war and peace and the distribution of land. For its part, the Soviet helped to restore army discipline (Order No. 1) which provided that the military orders of the provisional government should be obeyed when they did not conflict with the Soviet's orders. The failure of the Soviet to seize power in March 1917 is puzzling. The probable explanation is that its leaders, Mensheviks and SRs, convinced of the literal truth of the Marxist interpretation of history, believed that it was impossible for socialists to take command of a 'bourgeois' revolution. The result was that Russia was saddled with 'dual power', resulting in inevitable conflict and dissension, weaknesses which allowed the party not represented at the birth of the provisional government—the Bolsheviks—to discredit both sides. The first cabinet was led by Prince Lvov and dominated by the foreign minister, Miliukov. Its members were mostly Kadets and Octobrists. It collapsed early in May because Miliukov published his intention of carrying on the war until the original annexationist aims of the Tsarist government had been attained. Lvov formed the First Coalition on 5 May; it contained six socialist ministers. This ministry collapsed after the 'July Days', when the Petrograd 'street' revolted against the government's war policy. On 24 July Kerensky formed the second coalition in which there was a majority of socialist ministers. Yet the

'right' tendency of this coalition was shown by the arrest of the Bolshevik leaders and the reintroduction of the death penalty at the front. The failure of Kornilov's 'putsch' brought down the second coalition and presaged the end of the provisional government: it had failed (*a*) to defend Petrograd against a right-wing plot; (*b*) to place itself upon a foundation of popular support, other than that provided by the Soviet; (*c*) to keep control over the borderlands which, by the autumn of 1917, had won a de facto autonomy; and (*e*) to prevent the peasants from helping themselves to the land. But the most serious developments of all were taking place within the Soviet. From about the beginning of Sept., in Petrograd, Moscow, and other large cities, the Soviets were shedding their moderate socialist leadership and turning to the Bolsheviks. Without Soviet support the provisional government was lost, a fact clearly demonstrated by the easy success of the Bolshevik revolution (24–5 Oct.). The final cabinet meeting of the provisional government was prolonged for several hours, not because the Winter Palace was gallantly defended, but because the Red Guards were unable to find their way about in its darkened corridors. At length a footman led the way and the ministers were taken into captivity.

A. F. Kerensky, *The Catastrophe: Kerensky's own story of the Russian revolution* (New York, 1927).
P. Miliukov, *Political Memoirs, 1905–17* (Ann Arbor, 1967).
GS

PROVISORS, STATUTES OF, in England, enactments aimed against the practice of papal appointment to English bishoprics and other Church benefices, papal 'provision' being the technical term for such appointments. The series started with a statute of 1306. That of 1351 forbade acceptance of a provision and a statute of 1390 forbade also the request for a provision. Under the so-called statutes of praemunire (1353, 1365, 1393) the beneficiaries from unlawful provisions were liable to imprisonment at the king's pleasure and confiscation of all their goods. This legislation was applied only sporadically, but it could be employed to overpower clergy in trouble with the king.

PRUDENTIUS (AURELIUS CLEMENS), Latin Christian poet (AD 348–*c.* 410), and provincial governor, whose work appeared in a collected edition in 405. They include the *Psychomachia*, an allegory on the battle for the soul, the *Contra Symmachum*, a defence of Christianity against paganism, the *Cathemerinon*, the 'Daily Round' of the Christian life, poems on the divinity of Christ and the origin of sin, and a collection of ballads on Christian martyrs, in which Prudentius shows a particular interest in the martyrs of Spain. His poetry was highly influential, and despite some rhetorical excesses possesses considerable lyric charm, metrical variety, and a wide cultural range.

PRUSSIA, Baltic duchy that lasted from the 12th cent. until 1701, when it became a German kingdom under the Hohenzollern rulers of Brandenburg, which it remained until the creation of the second German Reich.

The native Prussians were heathens of Slav stock. The conquest of their lands proceeded from 1226, when the Emperor Frederick II granted the area from the Vistula to the Niemen to the Grand Master of the Teutonic Order. The first German forts of Thorn and Kulm were founded on the Vistula (1231), whence the conquerors pushed on to the Frisches Haff, established the fortress of Elbing, and overran Ermeland and Samland. In 1252 Memel was established, and Königsberg in 1255. After the revolts of 1240 and 1261–1273 had been suppressed, the native Prussians were reduced to serfdom and the area was systematically colonized by German peasants and traders, who built villages and towns, numbering 93 by 1410, *eg*, Marienberg (1274).

In 1410 the ruling order of Teutonic Knights was soundly beaten at the battle of Tannenburg by the neighbouring kingdom of Poland, and during the rest of the 15th cent. Prussia was adversely effected by the series of Polish invasions, the depopulation of the countryside, and economic stagnation in the towns. The decisive defeat of the Teutonic order in the 13-year war with Poland (1453–66) led to the treaty of Thorn (1466), by which the Grand Master was forced to relinquish the western half of Prussia to Casimir IV and retain East Prussia conditionally on becoming a vassal of the Polish Crown.

From the late 15th cent. the grand mastership was held by successive German princes, powerful enough to avoid paying homage to the kings of Poland. In 1525 the Grand Master Albrecht of Hohenzollern was converted to Lutheranism and after dissolving the order and secularizing its property he became the first German Duke of Prussia, albeit as a Polish vassal. The duchy was inherited by his descendant, the Elector John Sigismund of Brandenburg, in 1618. By this period the creation by the nobility of large arable estates, worked by a servile peasantry, was well under way. Although Prussia suffered less than Brandenburg in the Thirty Years War (1618–48), the ports of Memel and Pillau were conquered by Gustavus Adolphus of Sweden (1626). However, the accession of the Elector Frederick William I (1640) laid the foundation of Prussia's gradual expansion. In 1648 he acquired East Pomerania, and by adroitly changing sides in the Northern War the Elector secured Sweden's recognition of his sovereign authority over his territories (treaty of Labiau, 1656). In 1657 Poland followed suit (treaty of Wehlau, 1657), and the peace of Oliva (1660) finally confirmed the ending of Prussian vassalage to Poland.

From this time Brandenburg-Prussia steadily rose to primacy among the German Protestant states. With imperial approval on 18 Jan. 1701 the Elector Frederick crowned himself King of Prussia. His successor, King Frederick William I (1713–40), acquired West Pomerania and the port of Stettin. Finally, under Frederick the Great, Prussia's prestige and territorial expansion were forged by the unifying factors of a strong standing army, with its *junker* officer class, ruthless economy in government, and a king dedicated to the service of the state. The wars of 1740–63 established Prussia's political parity with Austria. In addition to Silesia, first overrun in 1740, Frederick secured much Polish territory, including West Prussia (1772), Danzig, Thorn, Poznan (1793), and Warsaw (1795) from a partitioned and defenceless Poland.

Despite temporary alliances with Austria in the French Revolutionary and Napoleonic Wars (*eg*, 1792–5, 1813), when Prussia was defeated at Jena (1806) and shorn of her lands by France, Austro-Prussian rivalry for Germany's domination revived after 1815. The Congress of Vienna (1815) recreated the Prussian kingdom, with the addition of northern Saxony, Westphalia, and the Rhine province to compensate for the loss of the Polish acquisitions of 1795. The extensive economic, military, social, and educational reforms of the period 1799–1818 reinvigorated Prussia. The *Zollverein* (1834), the construction of a railway network, and the industrial revolution after 1850 prepared the way for Germany's absorption into Prussia, a move powerfully advocated by Prussians such as the historian Niebuhr. The success of Bismarck's 'blood and iron' policy fulfilled the process, and with France's defeat (1870) and Austria's exclusion from Germany, the kingdom of Prussia ceased to have an independent existence and became the dominating force of the German empire (1871).

F. L. Carsten, *The Origins of Prussia* (Oxford, 1953).
Hajo Holborn, *A History of Modern Germany 1648–1840* (London, 1965).   MKS

PRUTH CAPITULATION OF THE (1711), peace terms forced on Tsar Peter I by the victorious Turks under their grand vizier, Mehemet Baltadji, after the Russian surrender on the Prut river. Peter had rashly advanced into the Danubian provinces with an army of about 50,000 men, hoping for the help of the hospodars of Wallachia and Moldavia. Surrounded by a Turkish force five times their size, the Russians gave in to terms which deprived Peter of most of what he had gained in 1700, Azov, Taganrog, the Dnieper forts, and the right to a Black Sea fleet. In addition, Peter was not to intervene in Poland and Charles XII was to have free passage to Sweden.

PRYDE, JAMES (1869–1941), Scottish painter whose work included paintings of architectural ruins, and whose interest in the theatre led him to design theatrical posters.

PRYDYDD Y BYCHAN (1200–*c.* 1270), Welsh bard whose name literally means 'the little poet'. His compositions were printed in *Myvyrian Archaeology*.

PRYNNE, WILLIAM (1600–69), English pamphleteer, antiquarian, and politician, who was imprisoned for his opposition to the religious policy of Abp Laud. He was set free by the Long Parliament (1640) and his sentence was declared illegal. Because he favoured a national Church with the king as head, he opposed both Presbyterians and Independents, siding with the parliament against the army. Being opposed to the execution of Charles I, he was expelled from parliament by Pride's Purge (1648) and imprisoned (1650–3). He returned to his seat in 1660 and supported the Restoration. He was elected to both the Convention (1660) and the Cavalier Parliament (1661). Later, he served the cause of historians as keeper of the records in the Tower of London, saving many documents from destruction.

PRZERWA-TETMAJER, KAZIMIERZ (1865–1940), Polish poet and writer whose lyrics provided an effective picture of Polish life and legend, often by a return to the dialect of earlier centuries.

PSELLOS, MICHAEL CONSTANTINE (1018–*c.* 1078), Byzantine official, scholar, philosopher, and historian, who exercised much influence during the reign of Constantine IX (*reg.* 1042–54) and of his successors. His History (*Chronographia*), covering the years 1025–78, and his letters, treatises, and orations contain a wealth of information on the affairs of Byzantium during his lifetime.

PSEMTEK I (Psammetichus), Egyptian King (*reg. c.* 664–610 BC) and founder of the XXVIth (Saite) dynasty. He was a Delta prince who, with the help of Greek mercenaries, expelled the Assyrians, defeated the other Delta princes, and gradually gained control of the whole country.

PSKOV, ancient Slav frontier town at the southern end of Lake Peipus on the trading route to the Gulf of Finland. From the earliest recorded times it was linked with Novgorod and was subject to German and Swedish attacks from the 13th cent. Its political independence from Novgorod, officially recognized by the treaty of Bolotovo (1347), ended when Vassily III of Moscow suppressed its local code of justice and democratic city council and incorporated Pskov into Muscovy (1510). The town was later besieged by the Poles under Stephen Bathory (1581) and the Swedes (1613). It was the scene of Tsar Nicholas II's abdication (1917).

PSYCHO-HISTORY, relatively new and emerging area of historical study. It takes its rise from the psychoanalytic work of Sigmund Freud, starting primarily from his *Interpretation of Dreams* (1900), though it can, in fact, be based on theories other than the Freudian, *eg*, Jungian. Freud himself showed the way in such works as *Leonardo da Vinci* (1910) and *A Seventeenth-Century Demonological Neurosis* (1923). His collaboration with William C. Bullitt, *Thomas Woodrow Wilson* (1967), was published posthumously and must be looked upon as something of an aberration. Of more speculative interest is Freud's *Totem and Taboo* (1913) and *Moses and Monotheism* (1939), where psychoanalytic explanations are added to a general philosophy of history.

Freud's early work in psychoanalysis was limited in its

usefulness to historians by an over-emphasis on the *id*, by definition unavailable to usual historical investigation, and on early infancy, where historical materials are generally lacking. As a result, the earliest efforts at psycho-history tended to be superficial and to reduce their subjects to pathological specimens. Freud himself, however, moved increasingly to a concern with the *ego* (mainly conscious processes) and the *superego* (the internalized values of an individual, first derived from his parents and then from society). These efforts were furthered by others, such as his daughter, Anna Freud, in *The Ego and the Mechanisms of Defense* (1936), and Heinz Hartmann, *Ego Psychology and the Problem of Adaptation* (1939). With the work of Erik H. Erikson and his school, attention to the ego's interaction with the superego and to the sequence of psycho-sexual and psycho-social phases embodied in the individual life-history came into prominence. Thus, developments in psychoanalysis, concerned with conscious processes and continuing change in a social-cultural setting, prepared the way for a truer development of psycho-history.

Erikson himself did pioneer work in this new field with his book, *Young Man Luther* (1958), as well as in many articles, and eventually in *Gandhi's Truth* (1969). In such works he showed how study of the life-history of a great man could illuminate the general history of an entire period or people. The individual, solving his own problems, helped a whole generation to solve theirs. In addition to the work done by Erikson and his followers on life-histories, other scholars have been working in another part of psycho-history: family history. Here the required social context for individual development is provided, but necessarily in its historical dimension, for the family and its relationship to society changes over time. Such work points insistently to the fact that psycho-history does not *reduce* history to psychoanalysis, but can only be done well in relation, for example, to social, economic, and intellectual history, by *adding* psychoanalysis to history.

Group psycho-history has posed greater difficulties than life-history and family history, because of the lack of a firm basis for clinical observation—Freud's work was primarily with individuals—and because of the greater difficulty for historians of knowing what materials are relevant. The result has been that this section of psycho-history, intrinsically perhaps of greatest interest to the historian, still presents the greatest challenge. Studies of witchcraft, reactions to disaster, developing attitudes to autonomy, and similar phenomena point the way in this part of psycho-history.

Psycho-history, as a new area of history, has still many problems to face: what sort of analytic training does an historian need? What school of psychoanalysis or psychology is most useful to his purposes? How can one psychoanalyse a dead person—that is, verify one's theories and hypotheses? How does one integrate one's psychoanalytic findings with, for example, social and intellectual history? How does one integrate one's psycho-historical work with general historical explanation? These, and related questions, are now in the process of being answered by theoretical and empirical work. This new discipline of psycho-history has moved forward impressively in the period since 1960.

E. Erikson, *Childhood and Society* (London, 1950).   BM

PTOLEMY I SOTER (*c.* 367–282 BC), King of Egypt (*reg.* 305–282), Macedonian soldier, and friend of Alexander the Great, who founded a dynasty which ruled Egypt until 31 BC. He became satrap of Egypt (323) and survived efforts by Perdiccas and Antigonus Monophthalmus to remove him. In 305 he declared himself king. After Antigonus's death (301), Ptolemy acquired Phoenicia, Cyprus, and some other overseas territories. In 285 he shared his throne with his son (Ptolemy II Philadelphus), who undertook much of the administration. Ptolemy encouraged Greek immigration to Egypt, developed Alexandria, where he kept Alexander's body, as his new capital, and began the detailed economic

organization which Philadelphus developed. He also wrote a book, which does not survive, about Alexander's expedition.

PTOLEMY II PHILADELPHUS (308–246 BC), King of Egypt (*reg.* 285–246) and son and successor of Ptolemy I. He was joint king with Ptolemy I from 285, and spent his main energies in administering and developing Egypt's economic potential, particularly in taxation (illustrated by his 'Revenue Laws') and land reclamation (illustrated by the 'Zenon Papyri'). In international affairs his strong navy retained Ptolemaic supremacy in the Aegean. He fought the Chremonidean War against Macedonia and the First and Second Syrian Wars against the Seleucids, all of which were indecisive. He continued Ptolemy I's encouragement of Greek immigrants and shared his pride in Alexandria, where he built the Pharos lighthouse, the Museum, and the Library.

PTOLEMY III EUERGETES (*c.* 284–221 BC), King of Egypt (*reg.* 246–221) and son and successor of Ptolemy II. He regained Cyrene by marrying Berenice II, and fought the 'Third Syrian War' (246–241), in which Ptolemaic armies penetrated briefly into Mesopotamia and gained major cities in Syria, Asia Minor, and Thrace. Internal Egyptian difficulties may have prevented him from fully exploiting these successes. Under his rule, internal economic consolidation continued in Egypt.

PTOLEMY IV PHILOPATOR (*c.* 244–204 BC), King of Egypt (*reg.* 221–204), son and successor of Ptolemy III. He defeated Antiochus III of Syria at Raphia (217) using native Egyptian troops who, recognizing their military effectiveness, began a rebellion in upper Egypt which continued sporadically throughout the reign, disrupted the Egyptian economy, and weakened the central government.

PTOLEMY IX AULETES (d. 51 BC), King of Egypt (*reg.* 80–51), who was the illegitimate son of Ptolemy VIII. He was expelled by the Alexandrians (58), tried to buy his restoration from Julius Caesar, and was finally restored by Gabinius (55). On his death, he left Egypt to his children, Cleopatra and Ptolemy.

P'U YI, HENRY (1906–68), last Emperor of China (*reg.* 1908–1924, 1932–45), who succeeded his uncle with the reign-title Hsüan-T'ung; his father acted as his regent. After the fall of the Ch'ing dynasty (1911), he was permitted to live the life of an emperor until 1924, when he was evicted from the Winter Palace in Peking by Feng Yü-hsiang. The Japanese re-established him as Emperor of Manchukuo (1932–45), but he was never more than a puppet. At the end of the Second World War he was taken to the Soviet Union by Soviet troops who liberated Manchuria, and spent the next five years there. In 1950 he returned to China and underwent a prolonged political re-education, which he recorded in his autobiography.

PUBLIC ACCOUNTS, COMMISSIONERS OF (1667–70) in England, commission established by parliament to look into the expenditure of Charles II's government. The second Anglo–Dutch War (1665–7) had exposed the deficiencies of Charles's administration and the House of Commons strongly suspected large-scale fraud, especially in connection with seamen's pay. The Medway disaster forced Charles to agree to a commission for taking public accounts which would have the power to subpoena any royal servant and cross-examine him under oath, and have access to all records. The commission's reports to parliament were inconclusive, but they provided an invaluable precedent, taken up after 1688.

PUBLIC ACCOUNTS COMMISSION (1780) in Britain, appointed by Lord North. Its wide-ranging and thorough investigations were summarized in 15 reports which provided the basis for the Younger Pitt's reorganization of the administration.

PUBLIC HEALTH ACTS (1848, 1875, 1936) in Britain have been responsible for the improvement of standards of health by the prevention of disease through legislative measures.

Although improvement commissioners, municipal corporations, and local boards of health were empowered to look after public health during the first half of the 19th cent., little was achieved because of the expense involved and the inevitable interference with individual freedom. Public conscience, stirred by Edwin Chadwick's *The Sanitary Conditions of the Labouring Classes* (1842), was reinforced by several cholera epidemics. The miasmic theory of the cause of disease was generally held before the development of bacteriology, so the 1848 act aimed at improving the standards of water supplies, main drainage, sewage disposal, and street cleaning. It also set up a general board of health, which included Chadwick. It had power to create local boards on the petition of 10 per cent of the inhabitants of a locality. Once a local board had been set up, the central board had little power over its activities, and Chadwick's attacks on local vested interests which clashed with the needs for water, sewerage, and control over the sale of food made the central board unpopular. In 1858 it was abolished and its duties distributed among other government departments. Later, these were brought together under the local government board (1871), a department set up to deal with the growing problems of drainage, water supply, food inspection, and smoke pollution.

In 1872 the appointment of medical officers of health by local health authorities became compulsory. The first had been appointed in Liverpool in 1847, and John Simon became London's first medical officer of health in 1848. He was later medical officer to the general board of health (1855) and then to the local government board.

The 1875 Act continued to make it the duty of local authorities to enforce the safeguards of public health within their own areas. The 1936 act consolidated the 25 acts that had been passed since 1875 with the growth of medical knowledge.

The scope of the 1936 Act covered port health, sewerage, refuse disposal, nuisances, water supplies, infectious diseases, hospitals, maternity and child welfare, and public baths. In the field of public health it was reinforced by the Factory Acts and the Food and Drugs Act (1938) and superseded, in part, by the National Health Service Act (1946).   AMCGH

PUBLIC ORDER ACT (1937) in Britain, legislation rushed through parliament at the end of 1936 and which became law on 1 Jan. 1937. It was occasioned by the increasing disorders which had attended meetings of Sir Oswald Mosley's British Union of Fascists, especially the 'battle of Cable Street' in the East End of London on 5 Oct. 1936. The act removed the right to wear distinctive uniforms for political purposes and strengthened the authority of the commissioner of police in controlling, or if necessary banning, outdoor political meetings.

PUBLIC WORKS ADMINISTRATION (1933–9) in the US, agency established by the National Industrial Recovery Act to stimulate employment and capital investment through federal financing of public works. Through its 'pump priming' activity in the construction of roads, public buildings, and dams, such as Grand Coulee and Bonneville on the Columbia river, it was hoped to stimulate activity in the private sector of industry. Cautiously administered by the secretary of the interior, Harold L. Ickes, PWA none the less spent almost $6000 million before it was absorbed by the Federal Works Agency. It pioneered slum clearance until its housing programme was transferred to the US Housing Authority (1937), and PWA funds were also used to build naval vessels and improve military installations.

PUBLICANI, ancient Roman tax-collectors and public contractors, who bid every five years at public auctions held by the newly elected censors for the right to collect taxes in Italy and the provinces or to carry out public works. In the 1st cent. BC their activities in the provinces, especially in Roman Asia, were often oppressive, but in the early empire although they were still used to collect taxes, their greed was controlled by the emperor's procurators.

PUCKERING, SIR JOHN (1544–96), Elizabethan lawyer and politician, who held the offices of lord keeper of the great seal (1592) and speaker of the House of Commons (1584–6, 1586–7).

PUEA, TE, Princess (1884–1952), NZ Maori social leader and daughter of King Tawhiao, who played a leading part in encouraging both Maori arts and land development.

PUEBLA, BATTLE OF AND SIEGE OF (5 May 1862), engagement at the Mexican city of Puebla between Mexican and French troops, in which the Mexicans routed the French and the latter were forced to initiate a siege (1863), which was eventually successful. The French, under Gen. Laurencez, were marching towards Mexico City (1862), where they hoped to establish French hegemony. The Mexican general, Ignacio Zaragoza, led a poorly armed contingent of former *guerilleros*. Laurencez ordered an attack on a fortified hill and suffered over 1000 losses, whereupon the French fled to the coast.

A second French army, under Gen. Forey, arrived (1863) and besieged Puebla, which was defended by 30,000, under Gen. González Ortega. The city surrendered only when food and ammunition were exhausted.

PUEBLO INDIANS, term applied to Indians of the American South-west, who lived in permanent villages of stone and adobe dwellings. They were first discovered by the Spanish (1540), who exacted oaths of obedience and sent missionaries to them. A general Pueblo revolt (1680) restored Indian independence until the Spanish reconquest (1692). Apart from a minor revolt (1696) and a brief uprising (1847) by the Taos, the Pueblos have been peaceful. They occupy reservation lands given them under Spanish land grants, later confirmed by the US.

PUERTO RICO, West Indian island discovered by Columbus in 1493 and settled by the Spaniards in the period 1512–22 and fortified in the 1590s to protect the lucrative trade with Spain in gold and sugar from privateers. Despite various British attacks in the 18th cent., it remained under Spanish control until the peace of Paris (Oct. 1898), when it was taken by the US.

After 1898 the country passed through various constitutional changes. These included a military administration (1898–1900) and a period of rule (1900–17) by a US-appointed president with a nominated Executive Council. In 1917 came elective upper and lower chambers, and representation in the US Congress.

After the Second World War there emerged the Puerto Rican Commonwealth, or 'Associated Free State', a political arrangement between Puerto Rico and the US, arranged largely under the aegis of Luis Muñoz Marín and his Popular Democratic Party (PPD). The Commonwealth, embodied in the constitution of 1952, stated that Puerto Ricans could elect their own governor and internal and local representatives, and could send a resident commissioner to Washington, DC; external affairs for the island were to be conducted by the US. This system was weakened in 1968, when the governorship was won by the political party which favoured US statehood. Meanwhile, a party which favoured complete Puerto Rican independence also grew up in the 1960s.

PUEYRREDÓN, JUAN MARTÍN DE (1777–1850), Argentine soldier, diplomat, and administrator during the early years of the Platine independence movement. He was appointed (1816) by the Congress of Tucumán as supreme director of the United Provinces for a three-year term. He and (after

1817) the Congress ruled from Buenos Aires, where Pueyrredón came under bitter attack from liberal factions for his involvement in schemes to install a monarchy. He was successful in organizing a supply base for San Martín's Army of the Andes, but failed either to resist the Portuguese invasion of the Banda Oriental (Uruguay) or to suppress the assertive autonomism of the litoral *caudillos*. In 1819 Congress promulgated a centralizing and aristocratic constitution with which Pueyrredón was in sympathy. Believing, however, that it would be impossible to enforce, he resigned as supreme director.

PUFENDORF, SAMUEL VON, Baron (1632–94), German lawyer and historian, whose *State of the German Empire* (1667) written under the pseudonym Severinus de Mozambano, was an astute assessment of the imperial constitution. He was a prolific writer of works on jurisprudence and history, *eg*, he was commissioned to write the histories of Gustavus Adolphus and Charles Gustavus of Sweden (1677–88) and went to Berlin to write studies of the reigns of the Great Elector and Frederick III of Brandenburg (1688–94). In all his works he noted the pragmatism of politicians whose actions were based on *raison d'état*.

PUGACHEV, EMELIAN (1726–75), Don cossack and army deserter, who led a widespread peasant rebellion (1773–4) which resulted in the capture of Kazan and threatened Moscow. He proclaimed himself Peter III and set up a mock court with its own elected administration and propaganda. Behind the appeal to legitimacy was a revolutionary programme promising extermination of landlords and officials, abolition of serfdom, taxation, and military service, and the restoration of the old faith.

The extent of Pugachev's popularity indicates the social problems of the reign. He was supported by serfs, who believed rumours of their forthcoming emancipation; Ural (Yaik) cossacks, whose freedom had been curtailed; and Ural mine workers. Bashkirs, Tatars, and other minorities recently overrun by Russian expansion and subjected to Orthodox and Russian pressure also rallied to him. In 1774 he was betrayed, captured and executed, and the rebellion was ruthlessly suppressed.

PUGET, PIERRE (1622–94), French architect and sculptor, who worked in Genoa (1661–7) and spent several years in southern France, designing the portico of the Hôtel de Ville in Toulon and the Halle au Poisson and Hospice de Charité in Marseilles. His sculptures include the *Milo of Crotona* and the relief of *Alexander and Diogenes*.

PUGIN, AUGUSTUS NORTHMORE (1812–52), British architect, whose *True Principles of Pointed or Christian Architecture* (1841) was the major inspiration of the 19th-cent. Gothic revival.

PUGIN and NAMIN ('Northerners' and 'Southerners'), two factions in the Korean bureaucracy, which arose between the two groups centred upon policies with regard to the Japanese invasion of 1592–3, the appointment of a Crown Prince, and policy towards the defeated *Soin* ('Westerners'). By 1600 the *Pugin* were clearly predominant, but split into *Taebuk* (Great Northerners) and *Sobuk* (Small Northerners). In 1623 the *Taebuk* and their puppet king, Kwanghae-gun (1608–23), were overthrown in a coup organized by the *Soin*.

PUGLIESE, EMANUELE (1874–), general commanding the Rome garrison in 1922, who assured the Facta government that the *circa* 28,400 troops, despite pro-fascist sympathies among some, would resist any fascist assault if so ordered, and who took necessary defence precautions. The king did not test his judgement, but entrusted Mussolini with power.

PUJO COMMITTEE (1912) in the US, created by Congress to investigate the 'Money Trust'. A sub-committee of the House of Representatives Committee on Banking and Currency, chaired by Arsene Pujo of LA (1861–1939), held hearings at which J. P. Morgan and other financiers testified. The committee concluded that existing banking and credit practices resulted in a vast concentration of control of money and credit in the hands of a few men.

PULITZER, JOSEPH (1847–1911), US journalist, newspaper publisher, and politician, who emigrated from Hungary to the US (1864) and served briefly in the Union army. He was elected to the MO legislature (1869), became part owner of the *Westliche Post* (1871–3), and purchased the St Louis *Post* and *Dispatch*, combining them as the *Post-Dispatch* (1878). He also purchased the New York *World* (1883) and established the *Evening World* (1887). His newspapers attacked privilege and corruption, and, in competition with the Hearst newspapers, engaged in sensational 'yellow journalism' during the 1890s. In subsequent years the *World* returned to its former standards and became highly respected. In his will Pulitzer endowed a school of journalism at Columbia University and 14 Pulitzer prizes, to be awarded annually in journalism, letters, and music.

PULLMAN, GEORGE MORTIMER (1831–97), US inventor and industrialist, who developed the Pullman railway sleeping car (1858–65). He organized the Pullman Palace Car Co. (1867) and founded the company town of Pullman, IL.

PULLMAN STRIKE (1894) in US, against the Pullman Palace Car Co., after wage cuts among factory workers in the town of Pullman, IL. In response to an appeal by Pullman strikers, members of the American Railway Union refused to move trains carrying Pullman cars, and the ensuing stoppage quickly paralysed railroads throughout the North. The General Managers Association, acting for the railroads, refused to deal with the ARU and persuaded President Grover Cleveland and Attorney-General Richard Olney (over the protest of Gov. John Peter Altgeld) to issue an injunction against the strike leaders and authorize the use of armed force against the strikers on the grounds that the strike was obstructing delivery of US mails. Two thousand US troops were sent to Chicago (4 July 1894), the union lost control of the strikers, 12 people died in riots, and the strike was broken. Eugene V. Debs, president of the ARU, and other leaders were imprisoned for defying the injunction, based on a clause of the Sherman Anti-Trust Act (1890), which declared as illegal conspiracies to restrain trade and commerce. The Supreme Court upheld the convictions (In re *Debs* 158 US 564) on 'broader grounds' than the Sherman act, but the legislation came to be regarded as a weapon to be enforced against organized labour as much as against the trusts.

PULTUSK, BATTLE OF (12 April 1703), Swedish victory over the Saxons in the Great Northern War. After wintering in Poland, Charles XI of Sweden marched his army northwards until they came on a force of 10,000 Saxons at Pultusk, 51 kms north of Warsaw. As soon as Charles launched his attack the enemy fled, leaving 600 dead and 1000 prisoners.

PUNCH, British weekly magazine, begun by Henry Mayhew (1841) as a democratic journal. It lampooned the royal family until 1851, when its political comment and caricatures became less savage and it inclined more towards social satire. For some 70 years it was considered to be the leading humorous magazine and attracted to its pages many well-known satirical writers and artists, among them Thackeray, Tom Taylor, Charles Keene, Sir John Tenniel, W. S. Gilbert, and George du Maurier.

PUNIC WARS (264–241, 218–201, 149–146 BC), struggle between Rome and Carthage which made Rome mistress of the western Mediterranean and ended with Carthage's destruction. Before the 3rd cent., Rome had respected Carthage's trading monopoly in the western Mediterranean, but her conquests in southern Italy, and Carthaginian successes in Sicily, created an atmosphere of suspicion. The first war started when, on the invitation of the Mamertines, the Romans expelled a Carthaginian garrison from Messana. The Romans overran most of Sicily and their newly built fleet won remarkable victories at Mylae (260) and Ecnomus (256); despite losses in storms, Regulus' failure in Africa (255), and Hamilcar Barca's resistance at Eryx, Roman doggedness was rewarded with final victory off the Aegates islands (241). The Carthaginians agreed by the treaty of Catulus to evacuate Sicily and pay a heavy indemnity.

Rome's seizure of Sardinia, while the Carthaginians were fighting their own mercenaries (238), increased Carthaginian resentment and many, including Hamilcar Barca, architect of the new empire in Spain, may have seen this as preparation for another war with Rome. The Romans, preoccupied with the Gauls of northern Italy, recognized Carthaginian dominion south of the Ebro (c. 226); but later interference (221) caused Hannibal to attack Saguntum, 161 kms south of the Ebro (219), and this attack on an ally became an occasion for war (218). Hannibal surprised the Romans by crossing the Alps into Italy and defeating them with huge losses at the Trebia river (218), Lake Trasimene (217), and Cannae (216), but the Romans stood firm and most of their allies in Italy remained loyal. While the Scipios in Spain blocked the reinforcement route, they followed Fabius Maximus' strategy of avoiding pitched battles with Hannibal, and by making prodigious efforts to raise more legions and money they gradually regained some of the lost towns (eg, Capua, 211), and penned him in the south. The Carthaginians failed to exploit the defeat of the Scipios in Spain (211), Sicilian risings against Rome, where Marcellus recovered Syracuse (211), and Hannibal's alliance with Philip V of Macedon (215). The younger Scipio (later Africanus) expelled them from Spain (210–206), and, though Hasdrubal evaded him to reach Italy, his army was destroyed at the Metaurus river (207). Scipio now invaded Africa (204) and with the aid of the Numidian Massinissa finally defeated Hannibal, who had been recalled from Italy, at Zama (202). The terms agreed upon deprived the Carthaginians of their empire and made them virtually dependent on Rome. They obliged them also to submit constant territorial disputes with Massinissa to Roman arbitration, which was invariably unfavourable. Eventually the Carthaginians were provoked into making a counter-attack and the Roman Senate, which had become increasingly ruthless towards suspect allies, persuaded by Cato the Elder to see military ambitions behind Carthage's spectacular economic resurgence, declared the third war (149). Carthage was besieged and destroyed by Scipio Aemilianus; her territory became the Roman province of Africa (146).   PGW

PUNJAB, or land of the 'five rivers' in India, namely, the Jhelum, Chenab, Ravi, Beas, and Sutlej. Though strictly it includes the land between the Indus and the Sutlej, the term more recently was extended to the Jumna. Historically, it has been a corridor for invaders who have left behind many different races. In prehistoric times the Punjab contained in Harappa one of the twin capitals of the Indus civilization (c. 2300–1750 BC). It was the site of the early Aryan invaders (c. 1750 BC), and the *Rigveda* was probably composed there. About 500 BC parts became a Persian satrapy. Alexander (326–5 BC), penetrating as far as the Beas, found the Punjab peopled with war-like tribes. After his death the Punjab became part of the Indian Mauryan empire (312–c. 185 BC). Greek adventurers from Bactria set up kingdoms known from their aristic coins in the 2nd and 1st cents BC, the best-known being Menander. These were overrun in turn by the Sakas, the Pallavas, and the Kushans, whose empire extended from the Jumna to Central Asia (c. AD 50–200). During this time the Punjab was a centre of Buddhism, the Mahayana sect being patronized by the Emperor Kanishka. In the 4th and 5th cents AD the Punjab was part of the Hindu Gupta empire. In the later 5th cent. it was overrun by the Huns and

associated tribes, and the flourishing Buddhist culture was overthrown. From the ensuing turmoil there emerged (c. 7th cent. AD) the Rajput clans and tribes as the Jats and the Gujars.

In the 11th cent. the Turkish Muslim Mahmud of Ghazni (967–1030), after raiding India, annexed the Punjab. The Ghaznavids gave way to the Ghurids in 1186 and it was from Lahore that Muhammad Ghuri advanced to the conquest of north India (1191). During the Delhi sultanate (1206–1526) the Punjab was generally a frontier province, charged with the defence of India against the Mongols. It was devastated by Timur (1397–8). The Lodi governor, Daulat Khan, invited Babur the Mughal to India. The Punjab became a *suba* of the Mughal empire (1526–1756) with Kabul as the frontier province to the west.

Mughal authority was finally broken by the Afghan Ahmad Shah Abdali (*reg.* 1747–72) but power passed to the Sikhs, a militant religious community, from about 1767. After the battle of Panipat (1761) they spread over the Punjab and were organized into the kingdom of Lahore by Ranjit Singh (*reg.* 1792–1839). On his death (1839) the kingdom fell into confusion and was annexed by the British (1849) after two wars. Extensive irrigation in the late 19th cent. made the province prosperous, but communal tension was severe. In 1947 the province was divided between India and Pakistan and an estimated 500,000 died following massacres. The Pakistan province of the Punjab was merged with West Pakistan in 1956. The Indian Punjab, having lost Lahore, built a new capital at Chandigarh and became prosperous. But the Sikhs still wanted their own *suba* and this they achieved in 1968, the Hindu half of the state being named Haryana.

S. M. Latif, *History of the Punjab* (Calcutta, 1891).   TGPS

PUNJAB LAND ALIENATION ACT (1900), attempt under the viceroyalty of Curzon to protect the cultivators of the soil from eviction by money-lenders.

PURANAS, ancient Hindu texts, in Sanskrit, of an encyclopedic nature, containing sections on cosmology, geography, religion, law, tradition, and often other topics as well. There are 18 of these texts in all. There are many similar texts, these being known as Upapuranas.

Although the Puranas are traditionally assigned to a remote antiquity, it is thought by modern scholars that the actual extant texts are not older than the early cents AD, while most of them are considerably later. They incorporate, however, old traditions. Some Puranas contain long historical sections, usually in the form of prophecies. They are essentially genealogies of royal dynasties traced back to the sun or the moon. They are of very unequal value, so that modern historians are reluctant to use them as sources except when they are at least partially confirmed by more reliable sources (such as inscriptions), and then only for periods not too far removed from the supposed date of the Puranas concerned. The Puranas are, however, indispensable for the study of ancient Indian religion and related topics.

PURCELL, HENRY (1659–95), English composer, who was appointed organist of Westminster Abbey in 1679, and was made one of the organists of the chapel royal (1682). He published (1685) a set of 12 sonatas and composed an anthem for the coronation of James II and his queen in 1685. Later in 1685 he was also appointed harpsichordist for the king's private music. He attended the coronation of William and Mary (1689) and wrote the music for a birthday ode to Queen Mary, the first of six which he was to produce annually. In 1690 he wrote the music for five stage works, including the comedy *Amphitryon* by Dryden, with whom his association was renewed in the production of *King Arthur* (1691) and in *Cleomenes* (1692). One of his greatest achievements was *The Fairy Queen* (1692), an operatic adaptation of Shakespeare's *A Midsummer Night's Dream.* He wrote supporting music for more than half a dozen plays both in 1693 and in 1694, and for St Cecilia's Day 1694 he wrote a *Te Deum and Jubilate* for solo voices, chorus, and orchestra. Much of the solemn music performed at the funeral of Queen Mary (1695) was written by Purcell. It was heard again later that year at his own funeral. Purcell's vast output included operas, incidental music, secular cantatas, odes, songs, anthems, and instrumental pieces.

PURCHAS, SAMUEL (*c.* 1575–1626), English clergyman who collected material about travel and exploration and carried on the work of Richard Hakluyt. His book *Purchas his Pilgrimage* (1613) consists of primary accounts of voyages, mostly by Englishmen. His work, though not always reliable, is important to historians because it was compiled from manuscripts, some of which have since been lost.

PURE FOOD AND DRUG ACT (1906) in US, legislation designed to prevent the adulteration or mislabelling of certain food products, confectionery, and proprietary medicines. It was passed in response to public agitation resulting from Upton Sinclair's novel *The Jungle* and the lobbying of Dr Harvey W. Wiley. The act, although attacked by many business interests, was supported by many large food producers who wished to protect themselves from less scrupulous competitors.

PURITANS, ACT AGAINST (1593), in England, aimed principally against the Separatists, who refused to go to church and formed their own conventicles. It punished offenders with three months' imprisonment, followed by banishment if they were obdurate, and death if they returned. The hanging of three sectaries in the same year drove the Puritans into exile or underground, and a large Separatist congregation in London migrated to Amsterdam.

PURITANS IN AMERICA, English Protestants not in sympathy with the Church of England who settled in New England. The earliest of these groups, the Separatists, or Pilgrims, left England, went to Holland (1608), and eventually settled the Plymouth colony in New England (1620). The Puritans of Massachusetts Bay colony were a larger group; during the 'Great Migration' (1630–40) an estimated 20,000 came to New England. The Puritans established a Bible commonwealth, citizenship of which was restricted to church members. Starting with the Halfway Covenant (1662), which gave partial church membership to those without a religious experience, the ties between the Church and state were loosened and their theology was slightly liberalized. Puritans banned attendance at the theatre, church music, sensuous poetry, and the celebration of Christmas, and supported the witchcraft trials of Salem (1692). The Massachusetts General Lawes and Libertyes (1648) advocated many forms of freedom and protection of the individual, and the Puritans promoted education and preserved the humanist tradition. They have had a profound moral and intellectual influence on American culture.

PURITANISM, movement to 'purify' the Church of England, which began in the 1560s. The religious settlement of 1559 never satisfied men who in Mary's reign had worshipped in Geneva, Frankfurt, and other centres of radical Protestantism, and the 'vestiarian controversy', mainly suppressed by the Book of Advertisements (1566), was only the first wave of the attack. Puritanism was strengthened by the adherence of genuine moderates who felt that the official Church was dangerously lukewarm in its attitude to Rome and these fears were stimulated by Elizabeth I's excommunication (1570) and the Catholic plots of 1569–72. Presbyterianism, defined in Thomas Cartwright's *First Admonition to Parliament* (1572), was radical and positive in attacking episcopacy as a popish institution not sanctioned in scripture and in demanding the replacement of the prayer book by a directory of public worship on the Genevan pattern.

These proposals were taken up in parliament, but the queen resented the affront to her prerogative. Cartwright was forced to leave the country (1574), and with the systematic dispersal of its leadership militant Puritanism lost its immediate threat. But at once there was a new problem, with the spread after 1573 of 'prophesyings', informal meetings, to which laymen were sometimes admitted, to study scripture and improve the piety, preaching, and discipline of the clergy. Elizabeth viewed these as cells carrying on private worship independently of the Church and likely to infect it with Presbyterian ideas. From prophesyings developed (*c.* 1582) the 'classical' movement, inspired by the Presbyterian Field, an unofficial organization of local *classes* rising to provincial and national synods.

The final manifestation of Elizabethan Puritanism was the Independent or separatist movement, led by Browne and Barrow, which repudiated all connection between Church and state and asserted the independence of each individual congregation where two or three were gathered together in the Lord's name. This splinter movement was rejected by more orthodox Puritans, and the division in their ranks eased the work of suppression. The appointment of Whitgift as Abp of Canterbury (1583), the enforcement of articles requiring acceptance of the royal supremacy, the prayer book and the 39 Articles, and the rigorous use of the Court of High Commission gradually pushed the movement underground. The anti-episcopal Marprelate tracts (1587–8) were too scurrilous to be effective, and Whitgift's campaign ended with a severe act against conventiclers (1593) and the hanging of three extremists for alleged sedition.

But the victory was won at a high cost, both political and spiritual. Politically, Elizabeth's use of the prerogative to resist Puritanism exposed it to attack on a wide front. In almost every parliamentary session between 1566 and 1593 religion was the mainspring of disputes which eroded the Crown's authority. Conversely, men hostile to the government on other grounds joined the Puritans for tactical reasons, and the spread of Puritanism among the gentry was a significant feature of the reign. Basically the Puritans were loyal, since national disunity would open the gates to the Counter-Reformation, but something like an organized opposition developed in the Commons, and sharp debates about privilege created precedents for the following century.

Spiritually, the Church's quarrel with the Puritans deprived it of elements which would have reformed its inward condition. Puritanism was not a homogeneous movement, and not all its adherents were strict Calvinists; but in a broad sense it recruited thousands who wanted to give a visible spiritual content to the makeshift construction of 1559. The clergy were ill-paid and ignorant, and their status was worsened by the cynical secularization encouraged by the queen and her courtiers. Romish vestments and episcopacy were not the enemy so much as ignorance and apathy. The spontaneous demand for a 'preaching' ministry reflected one of the strongest psychological needs of the age, and if prophesyings had been allowed to stimulate the devotion and intelligence of the clergy, the Church might have retained the loyalty of many whom Whitgift was obliged to attack.

Morally and socially, Puritanism has been associated with a joyless spirit hostile to music and the theatre. This is a somewhat exaggerated picture, and it would be fairer to say that Puritanism brought to the English character a *gravitas* which at the time was badly needed. In their rich variety many of the great Elizabethans were alarmingly extravagant and unstable, and Puritanism, with its sober thoughts of the morrow, was a tonic to the national mind. Although its inherent fragmentation wrecked it as a political instrument in the 17th cent., it taught the English how to build an empire by patient labour rather than with the expectation of quick results. Puritan thrift provided the sinews of the Industrial Revolution, and Puritan piety kept alive the study of the Bible when public worship was forbidden, rallied to Wesley's defiance of 18th-cent. materialism, mitigated the evils of the factory system, and later helped to supply the Labour Party with its moral fervour.

A. F. Scott Pearson, *Thomas Cartwright and Elizabethan Puritanism* (Cambridge, 1925).

M. M. Knappen, *Elizabethan Puritanism* (Chicago, 1939).
MMR

PURNAVARMAN (*fl.* 5th cent. AD), King of Taruma in West Java, Indonesia, known from five Sanskrit inscriptions, three of which were discovered near present Bogor. One, found near present Jakarta, deals with a canal dug by order of the king presumably for irrigation and/or flood control. These inscriptions constitute the oldest written evidence of Java.

PURNEA (d. 1812), Brahman in the service of Haidar Ali of Mysore and *diwan* (finance minister) of Tipu Sultan. When the Hindu dynasty was restored in 1799 he was retained as *diwan* by the British until 1811.

PUROS, champions of radical social change in Mexico from the first republic (1823) to the reform movement (1855). They were mainly of mixed origins (*mestizos*) and opposed the creole landed families and the wealth of the Church.

PURUSHOTTAMA (d. 1497), the second King of the Gajapati dynasty of Orissa (*reg.* 1467–97), whose authority was challenged by his brother Hamvira. His reign was occupied by wars with Vijayanagar, the Bahmani kings of the Deccan, and their successors.

PURVEYANCE in England, right exercised by the English kings of compulsory purchase on credit of goods for royal use. Intended for the supplying of the royal court, it became a major abuse when it was employed to supply entire armies and navies or for continuous provisioning of royal castles. There were continued complaints against it. Magna Carta of 1215 tried to regulate it and there were further ineffective attempts at reform in 1300 and under Edward III. During the early 17th cent. it was an important grievance against the monarchy and was largely abolished in 1660.

PUSAN PERIMETER, line of defence in the south-east corner of Korea, held by the United Nations Command in the Korean War (Aug.–Sept. 1950).

PUSEY, EDWARD BOUVERIE (1800–82), English theologian and professor of Hebrew at Oxford (1828–82), whose contribution (1833) to the series of *Tracts* being published in Oxford by Newman and others identified him with the Oxford Movement. On Newman's acceptance into the Church of Rome, Pusey assumed unofficial leadership of the Tractarian party within the Church of England. He was suspended from preaching in the university church (1843–5) for a sermon on the real presence of Christ. He believed, and declared so in an open letter to John Keble in 1865, that union between the Church of England and the Church of Rome was possible, and only prevented by unofficial assumptions, devotions, and practices assumed by the contemporary Roman Catholic Church. For some Anglicans this might have been true, but Pusey's thought ignored the strength of the Evangelical party within the Church of England. Certainly, his hopes were vain after the definition of papal infallibility (1870). Pusey House, Oxford, notable for its library, is a memorial to his work.

PUSHKIN, ALEXANDER SERGEYEVICH (1799–1837), Russian poet and author of *Eugene Onegin, Boris Godunov,* and other works. He was of noble birth, and held various court sinecures. He was educated in the ideas of the enlightenment and was friendly with the Decembrists. He was exiled twice, but was protected by Nicholas I, who personally censored his works in his own interest. Later he became a moderate

westernizer and a historian. He is best described as a 'liberal conservative', who combined a reverence for Russian monarchy and traditions with a belief in an independent nobility and Western culture.

PUTTE, ERRYK VAN DER (1574–1646), Flemish scholar, historian, and writer on classical subjects. His *Statera belli ac pacis* (1633) recommended peace between the northern and southern provinces of the Netherlands.

PUYO (Chinese, Fuyü), ancient state of central Manchuria, from whose rulers the kings of Koguryo claimed descent. It was a rival of the Koguryo, and was generally allied with China. In 285–6 several of its ruling clan fled to Korea to escape an invasion by the Mu-jung Hsien-pi; these refugees became the ancestors of the kings of Paekche. Puyo itself was conquered by the Mu-jung in 346.

PYDNA, BATTLE OF (June 168 BC), decisive victory near the Macedonian coast in the Third Macedonian War. The Romans, under Aemilius Paullus, overcame Perseus of Macedon, who fled, but was captured at Samothrace; his kingdom was divided thereafter into four republics.

PYLOS, Mycenaean settlement in the south-western Peloponnese, surrounded by tholos tombs and famous as the site of 'Nestor's Palace', discovered on Epano Englianos in AD 1939. Owing to the absence of later settlement its excavated remains constitute the finest known example of a Mycenaean palace, built in the 13th cent. BC, and—surprisingly—unfortified. Most important are hundreds of Linear B clay tablets which were baked hard when the palace was destroyed by fire *c.* 1200 and were found by the excavators in the ruins of its archives. In the great Peloponnesian War (425 BC) the bay of Pylos, south of Nestor's Palace (mod. bay of Navarino) was the scene of an Athenian landing and naval victory which forced the Spartans to sue unsuccessfully for peace. The Athenians captured the island of Sphacteria and retained their footing there until 409.

PYM, JOHN (*c.* 1583–1643), English politician and leader of the opposition to Charles I in the Long Parliament. He entered parliament (1621) under the patronage of the 3rd Earl of Bedford and at once became an opponent of arbitrary government, eg, he was a promoter of the Protestation (18 Dec. 1621), one of the managers of Buckingham's impeachment (1626), and a leading supporter of the Petition of Right (1628).

As treasurer of the Providence Island Co. (1629–40) he moved among the leading members of the parliamentary opposition to Charles I during the 'eleven years' tyranny'. The company, partially a front for opposition meetings, provided a model of organization which was to come into its own under Pym in the Long Parliament. By the time of the Short Parliament (April–May 1640) the opposition was used to acting together and recognized Pym as its leader. Pym in this parliament denounced grievances with moderation and firmness. By the time of the calling of the Long Parliament (Nov. 1640) he was recognized as the leader of the Country Party—the opposition to the Court Party. He skilfully carried on the twin policies of the Country Party—the establishment of reforms and the ending of arbitrary government, by, above all, the impeachment of Strafford. Pym did not at first agree with the act of attainder which finally disposed of Strafford, but was persuaded by the enthusiasm of the majority of his friends.

Pym was no Puritan, but an adherent of the pre-Laudian Church of England, and in this he differed from most of his associates. He wanted reform, not the abolition of episcopacy, but when he became convinced of the political importance of the bishops, he voted for the Root and Branch Bill (May 1641).

He was a strong supporter of the Grand Remonstrance and his speech of 22 Nov. helped to secure its passing, though even his consummate political skill could not prevent the break-up of the Country Party. However, he retained his leading position in the realignment of parties during the winter of 1641–2. This was no doubt partly due to his being cited as one of the five MPs impeached for treason by Charles I (3 Jan. 1642), and he narrowly escaped arrest by fleeing to the safety of the city of London.

As leader of the emerging Parliamentary Party he naturally played a large part in the preparation for civil war, and in July 1642 was named as one of the 15 members of the committee of safety. He became the great organizer of the parliamentary forces in the field and of the matter of raising of taxes and providing supplies.

Pym, as leader of a middle party between the war and peace parties within the Parliamentary Party, tried to prevent a general war after the battle of Edgehill (Oct. 1642) by urging parliament to petition the king for negotiations, but Charles refused the petition. From then on Pym organized parliament for victory, *eg*, an excise on the sale of all goods was established, and in May 1643 negotiations were opened with the Scots for an alliance. The Solemn League and Covenant, accepted by parliament on 25 Sept. 1643, was Pym's last contribution to parliament's cause.

S. R. Brett, *John Pym, 1583–1643* (London, 1940).
J. H. Hexter, *The Reign of King Pym* (Cambridge, MA, 1941).   CJ

PYNCHON, WILLIAM (*c.* 1590–1662), English colonist, who emigrated to America (1630), founded Roxbury, and acted as treasurer of the Massachusetts Bay colony (1632–4). He moved to Springfield (1636) and became a magistrate, virtually ruling the colony himself. His warehouse at the head of deep water navigation on the Connecticut river handled much of the local fur trade. He returned to England (1652), partly because of differences with New England religious leaders.

PYRAMIDS, tombs of the kings of ancient Egypt. It is estimated that more than 80 were built. The earliest known, the Step Pyramid of Djoser (*c.* 2700 BC), at Saqqara, near Cairo, was copied by at least three of his successors, but pyramid building reached its zenith with the kings of the IVth dynasty. Senefru (*c.* 2620) developed the later most familiar shape by filling in the steps of his pyramid at Meodum to form smooth sides. Khufru (*c.* 2596), whose 'Great Pyramid' covered an area of over 13 acres (52,500 sq. metres) and was 481 ft (146 metres) high, Khafre (*c.* 2573), and Menkaure (*c.* 2507) all built at Giza. The kings of the Vth dynasty built at Abusir and those of the VIth dynasty at Saqqara, the latter kings inscribing their pyramids' inner chambers with texts that are of archaeological importance. Pyramid building then ended for a time until, during the period of the XIIth dynasty (*c.* 1991–1786), pyramids were built at Lisht and Illahun. After this period, except for a revival of pyramid building by later Ethiopian rulers, the kings chose secret rock-hewn tombs as their burial places. The pyramid was the central point of a large funerary area. Near the edge of the desert and accessible by boat during the inundation season was a chapel from which a walled-in causeway led to a funerary temple on the east side of the pyramid. Smaller pyramids close by were for wives and children. The origin of the pyramidal shape is not clear but it probably had a religious significance and was used only by the kings. Noblemen were entombed in flat-topped edifices.

Ahmed Fakhry, *The Pyramids* (Chicago, 1961).
W. Stephenson Smith, *The Art and Architecture of Ancient Egypt* (Baltimore, 1958).   JKG

PYRAMIDS, BATTLE OF THE (21 July 1798) (more accurately of Embaba, on the left bank of the Nile opposite Bulaq, some ten miles (16 kms) from the pyramids), where 25,000 French troops under Napoleon Bonaparte defeated the smaller Egyptian Mamluk forces of Murad Bey in the French Wars. The victory fatally weakened Mamluk power, established French control of Egypt, and marked the beginning of a new relationship between Europe and the Middle East.

PYRENEES, TREATY OF THE (1659), Franco-Spanish peace settlement concluded between Mazarin and Don Luis de Haro, ending the final phase of the Thirty Years War. Although its terms were not so favourable to Philip IV as those offered by France in 1656, they were reasonably moderate in view of Spain's successive military defeats (1643–59). Artois, Roussillon, and part of Cerdagne were ceded by Spain to France, but Mazarin agreed to the restoration of Catalonia, Franche-Comté, and France's Italian conquests, except Pinerolo. Furthermore, a marriage was arranged between Philip IV's elder daughter, Maria Theresa, and Louis XIV, full payment of her dowry of 500,000 *escudos* being a condition of the infanta's renunciation of all future claims to the Spanish throne. Spain had been isolated since co-operation between the Spanish and Austrian branches of the Habsburg family had broken down when Austria concluded the peace of Westphalia (1648), and the Pyrenees treaty thus marked the end of Spanish hegemony in Europe. It did not, however, end the Habsburg–Bourbon struggle, which was to be renewed over the Spanish succession, to which the Duke of Anjou, grandson of Louis XIV and Maria Theresa, laid claim (1700).

PYRRHONISM, form of Greek scepticism revived by Montaigne during the 16th cent., his supporters being known as the 'New Pyrrhonists'.

PYRRHUS OF EPIRUS (*reg.* 319–272 BC), Molossian King, who brought Epirus to its peak, and, inspired by the example of Alexander the Great, sought a western empire. After extending his kingdom in western and northern Greece, he accepted the overtures of Tarentum and invaded Italy. In defeating the Romans at Heraclea and Asculum (280–279), he achieved the original 'Pyrrhic victories'. Following inconclusive success against the Carthaginians in Sicily, he returned to Italy, but after heavy losses near Beneventum (275) he retired home. After attacking Macedon and Sparta, he was killed in Argos.

PYTHAGORAS (*fl.* 6th cent. BC), Greek mystic, mathematician, and philosopher, born at Samos. He fled (*c.* 530) from Polycrates' tyranny to Croton in southern Italy, where he founded a religious and philosophical order of considerable influence later in antiquity.

PYTHEAS (*fl.* 4th cent. BC), Greek explorer from Massilia (Marseilles), who sailed (*c.* 310–306 BC) through the Straits of Gibraltar, visited the tin mines of Cornwall, and circumnavigated Britain. His measurements of the sun's shadow were the first steps towards creating a network of longitudes and latitudes.

PYU INSCRIPTIONS at Pagan. The Myazedi inscriptions, dated 1113, record the same text in Burmese, Mon, Pali, and Pyu, giving the key to all that is known of the Pyu language.

QADESH, ancient city (Tell Neby Mend) of Syria on an important north–south route, and site of a battle (c. 1285 BC) between the Egyptians under Rameses II and the Hittites under Muwatallis. Despite Egyptian claims to victory, the battle seems to have been indecisive, or possibly even a Hittite victory.

QADI, judge trained in the Shari'a, ie, in the Sacred Law of Islam. According to the legal theorists, a *qadi* had to be male, free, adult, and in full possession of his faculties, Muslim in faith and irreproachable in character. His role was to decide cases in dispute, to act as guardian for orphans and minors, to supervise pious foundations (*awqaf*), and to appoint deputies (*na'ib*) empowered to act in his name. The *qadi*, during the golden age of the Ottoman empire, had also an important share in the transaction of government business at the local level.

QADI'ASKER (judge of the army), title given to two high officials in the Ottoman empire, the *Qadi'asker*s of Rumeli and of Anadolu. The *qadi'asker*s had a seat in the *Diwan* or Council of State and assisted the grand vizier in matters involving questions of law. Each *qadi'asker* was authorized to appoint the *qadis* (judges) and mosque officials acting within the area under his supervision.

QADIRIYYA, Muslim brotherhood founded by Abd al-Qadir al-Jailani (d. 1166), but drawing its inspiration from the teachings of Junaid (d. 909). Branches still exist in India, Anatolia, the Yemen, and most parts of Africa. The brotherhood became particularly popular in north Africa, where it shared the ground with the Tunisian-based Shadhiliyya order from the mid-13th cent. In Morocco it has suffered degeneration in many rural areas and has become a disguise for semi-pagan rituals. From the late 18th cent. it also had to face the challenge of the Tijaniyya order founded in Fez.

In West Africa the Qadiriyya brotherhood has played an important role in Islamization. It has also served the purpose of providing local foci in the form of the sheikhs and their initiated disciples for a religion that has little hierarchy or formal organization. Devotion to the founder and other saints of the order was a useful palliative for abandoned ancestor cults. Its main agents were the Kunta Arabs of the Tuwat–Timbuctoo area and the Moorish tribes of southern Mauritania. Kunta leaders received the order in the early 16th cent., supposedly through Al-Maghili and Al-Suyuti, though the precise links remain obscure, and it was propagated through the Bakka'i clan in the 17th and 18th cents. In southern Mauritania Sheikh Sidiya (1780–1868) and his grandson, Sheikh Sidiya al-Saghir (1862–1924), led an important Qadiriyya revival in the face of Tijaniyya encroachment.

The brotherhood is (1970) found all over West Africa, still competing for adherents with the Tijaniyya, and clashes occasionally break out between the two.

QADISIYA, AL-, south of the present Najaf and close to the site of the future garrison town of Al-Kufa. Here in AD 637 the Muslims, fighting against the forces of Sassanid Persia, won a decisive battle which gave them control over most of Iraq.

QA'IM, AL- (reg. AD 934–46), Fatimid Caliph, whose reign saw the Fatimid fleet active against the coasts of France and Italy and also against Egypt. A major revolt amongst the Zenata Berbers, under the Kharijite Abu Yazid, began in 943. The revolt met with such success that Al-Qa'im was driven to take refuge in Mahdiya. He died before the insurrection was suppressed, Berber resistance to the Fatimids continuing until 947, when Abu Yazid himself was slain.

QA'IM MAQAM, term used in Arabic and Turkish to denote an official subordinate to a provincial governor. In Persian it is used by certain ministers and is particularly associated with one individual, Abu'l Qasim, Qa'im Maqam (d. 1935), who was notable as one of the first great reforming ministers and as a significant Persian prose writer.

QAIRAWAN, first Muslim capital of the Tunisian area (Ifriqiyya), on the edge of the Tunisian steppe. It was abandoned as a seat of government (1057), and superseded first by Mahdiya and then Tunis; it remains notable principally for its mosque and law schools.

QA'IT BAY (reg. 1468–95), Mamluk Sultan of Egypt and Syria, who had been bought as a slave in the time of Sultan Barsbay (reg. 1422–38) and manumitted in the reign of Sultan Jaqmaq (reg. 1438–53). The main problem confronting Qa'it Bay was the expansion of Ottoman power in Asia Minor. He was involved (1465–72) in a conflict which led to the establishment—until 1480—of a prince subordinate to the Mamluks on the throne of Albistan, a small Turcoman state in the border zone of northern Syria. The Ottomans and the Mamluks engaged in a war (1485–91) for the control of Cilicia. This confrontation, although it ended in favour of the Mamluks, did little to ease their situation, the danger from the Ottomans remaining no less strong than it had been before.

QAJAR, ruling dynasty of Iran (1794–1925), which takes its name from a Turkoman tribe from north-east Iran, prominent during the Safawid dynasty. The dynasty was established by the eunuch Agha Muhammad (1742–97), who, after the death of Karim Khan Zand, set himself up in northern and central Iran, making Teheran his capital. He defeated the last Zand ruler, Lutf Ali Khan (1794), and was crowned shah (1796). Agha Muhammad was succeeded by his nephew, Fath Ali Shah, son of Husayn Quli Khan (1751–77). Fath Ali's reign (reg. 1797–1834) was marked by the establishment of the characteristic Qajar system of recruiting provincial governors from the royal family and by the loss of territory in Transcaucasia to Russia (treaties of Gulistan, 1813, and Turkomanchai, 1828). He was succeeded by his grandson, Muhammad Shah (reg. 1834–48), the son of Abbas Mirza (1789–1834). Muhammad was succeeded by his son, Nasir al-Din (reg. 1848–96), whose continuation of his father's eastward ambitions against Herat contributed to the Anglo-Persian War (1856). The latter part of Nasir's reign was marked by the growth of foreign indebtedness and interference in Iranian affairs, the reaction to which under his son and successor, Muzaffar al-Din (reg. 1896–1907), led to the granting of a constitution. Muzaffar was succeeded by his son, Muhammad Ali (reg. 1907–9), whose unsuccessful attempt to revoke the constitution led to his deposition; in 1911 he made an attempt to regain his throne. A regency was established (1909–14) until his son, Ahmad Shah (reg.

1914–25), attained his majority. Ahmad was forced into exile by Reza Khan (1923) and formally deposed (31 Oct. 1925). Reza Khan was elected first Shah of the Pahlevi dynasty (12 Oct. 1925).

P. Avery, *Modern Iran* (London, 1965).   MEY

QALAWUN (*reg.* AD 1279–90), Al-Malik al-Mansur Sayf al-Din, Mamluk Sultan, was of Kipçak origin. At the beginning of his reign he was faced with an invasion by the Mongols from Persia into Syria. The Mongol force, which included some Armenian, Frankish, and Georgian troops, was defeated at Hims in 1280. Qalawun also brought to virtual completion the long endeavour of Sultan Baybars (1260–77) to expel the Latins from Syria. The great fortress of Al-Marqab fell to Qalawun in 1285, and Tripoli in 1289. He spent large sums on repairing the fortifications at Aleppo and Damascus, the rebuilding of Tripoli, and the foundation of a great hospital (Al-Maristan Al-Mansuri) at Cairo.

QANSAWH AL-GHAWRI (*reg.* AD 1500–16), Mamluk Sultan, whose reign saw the Mamluks engaged in efforts to hold back the Portuguese in the Indian Ocean. With assistance in material and munitions from the Ottomans, Qansawh al-Ghawri sent to western India a fleet which overcame a Portuguese squadron off Chaul, but was itself defeated near Diu (1508–9). A second Mamluk fleet was despatched to the Yemen in 1516, though without a decisive result. In the same year Al-Ghawri marched into northern Syria, hoping to counteract, along the Taurus frontier, Ottoman intervention (1515–16), which had changed the situation there to the disadvantage of the Mamluks. At Marj Dabiq (Aug. 1516) the Ottomans, under Selim I, crushed the Mamluk forces, Qansawh al-Ghawri being slain in the rout and all of Syria falling to Sultan Selim.

QANUN-NAME, term used amongst the Ottoman Turks to denote a set of regulations (qanun) either of a general or of a limited (*eg,* a provincial) application. A qanun was not, in the strict sense, a legislative act, but rather an official statement of hitherto existing custom and practice.

QAPUDAN PASHA (QAPUDAN-I DERYA: the 'Captain of the Sea'), term denoting the high admiral of the Ottoman fleet, who exercised a general supervision over all matters of a naval and maritime character in the Ottoman empire.

QARA QOYUNLU, Turcomans who ruled over much of Persia, Al-Jazira, and Azerbayjan (AD 1375–1468). Their first important chieftain, Qara Yusuf, fled to the Ottomans before the advance of Timur Beg. After the death of Timur in 1405 he brought under his control Tabriz, Diyar Bakir, Iraq Arabi (1410), Qazwin, and Iraq Ajemi (1419). His successor, Iskandar, was defeated by the Timurid, Shah Rukh, in 1421, 1429, and 1434. None the less, he was able to retain possession of Azerbayjan. The power of the Qara Qoyunlu was at its height in the mid-15th cent. under Jahan Shah, who, from Azerbayjan, extended his influence over Iraq Ajemi, Fars, and Kirman. Jahan Shah lost his life in conflict with the rival Turcomans of the Aq Qoyunlu, whose able chieftain made an end of the Qara Qoyunlu domination (1468–9).

QARAWIYYIN (Kairwanian), mosque dating from the 9th-cent. settlement at Fez of émigrés from Qairawan. It is noted for its school, resembling the Egyptian equivalent Al-Azhar, as a seat of traditional Muslim scholarship.

QASR, AL-, AL-KABIR (Alcazarquivir), **BATTLE OF** (1578), in which a Portuguese army under King Sebastian, invading Morocco in conjunction with a deposed sultan, was routed by the reigning sultan, Abd Al-Malik. All three monarchs perished, giving the encounter the name of the battle of the three kings.

QATIF, TREATY OF (1915), Anglo-Saudi agreement guaranteeing the independence of Ibn Sa'ud, within frontiers to be agreed at the end of the First World War, in return for British control of Saudi foreign relations.

QAVAM AL-SULTANEH, AHMAD (1882–1955), Iranian landowner and politician who held several important ministerial appointments, including that of prime minister, on several occasions under the Qajar and Pahlevi dynasties. As prime minister (1946–7), he negotiated skilfully to remove Russian troops from Iran, crush the separatist movement in Azerbayjan, bring the Tudeh party under control, and deny Russia an oil concession in northern Iran.

QAYDU (*reg.* 1269–*c.* 1303), Mongol ruler in eastern Turkestan and parts of western Mongolia. As the grandson of Ögetei (d. 1241) he claimed the title of Great Khan, which was held by Khublai Khan. Qaydu united behind him many Mongols who were opposed to the increasing Sinification of the empire.

QAYS. The centuries before the rise of Islam saw the slow infiltration of tribal elements from Arabia into Iraq and Syria—among them the North Arabian and the South Arabian Kalb. An enduring sense of differentiation divided the northern from the southern Arabs. During the period of Umayyad rule (AD 661–750) there was a serious recrudescence of tribal animosities among the Arab warrior caste dominant within the Muslim empire. The numerous small feuds inherited from nomadic Arabia now came to life inside the restricted milieu of the Arab armies. The movement of troops from one garrison centre to another allowed the reviving antagonisms to fall into a new and fateful alignment, *ie*, to coalesce into two great factions coinciding with the line of cleavage between the North Arabian and South Arabian tribes. The names of Qays and Kalb—above all in relation to Syria, the main foundation of Umayyad rule, but now increasingly torn by tribal discord—came to be synonymous with the two major factions which, developing rapidly after the death of the Caliph Mu'awiya in 680, did much to bring about the fall of the Umayyads and fatally to impair the Arab ascendancy in AD 750.

QUADRILATERAL, four fortified towns in northern Italy (Peschiera, Verona, Mantua, Legnano), forming the strong point of the Austrian defence of Venetia in 1848 and 1859 during the struggle for Italian unification.

QUADROS, JÂNIO DA SILVA (1917–   ), Brazilian politician and president of Brazil (1961), whose meteoric political career culminated in a landslide election to the presidency on a programme of nationalism, administrative efficiency, and respect for human dignity. He resigned abruptly on 25 Aug. 1961 and his political rights were cancelled by the revolutionary government in 1964.

QUADRUPLE ALLIANCE (1718), treaty signed by Britain, France, and the Holy Roman empire, so called because the United Provinces were also expected to sign it. The alliance formed part of the great powers' scheme for collective security to enforce a stable European situation. The treaty provided for a territorial arrangement in Italy to be enforced despite Spain's Sardinian and Sicilian expeditions (1717–18). The emperor was to receive Sicily, Savoy was to receive Sardinia, Monferrat, and part of the Milanese, while Parma and Tuscany were assigned to the Spanish Infant. Finally, the emperor and Philip V were to recognize one another's titles and possessions, and the succession to the thrones of England and France, as established at Utrecht, was guaranteed. The principle of collective security was enforced on Spain by a British fleet at Cape Passaro (1718) and no major wars subsequently broke out in Europe until 1733.

QUADRUPLE ALLIANCE (1815), treaty, signed by Austria, Prussia, Russia, and Britain simultaneously with the second treaty of Paris (20 Nov.). This was Castlereagh's scheme to achieve 'repose' in post-Napoleonic Europe. The signatories agreed to maintain the 1815 Vienna and Paris treaties' provisions for 20 years, permanently to exclude the Bonapartes from France, and if necessary reinforce allied occupation troops there. Article VI envisaged periodic top-level meetings to discuss treaty problems and other matters of common interest. The alliance recognized the Great Powers' ascendancy and aimed at transmuting wartime co-operation into a permanent Concert of Europe. France joined the alliance (1818), but it was soon undermined by the divergent aims and outlook of England and the absolutist continental regimes, and the lack of any organization.

QUADRUPLE ALLIANCE (1834), between France, Britain, Spain, and Portugal. In recent dynastic conflicts the apparently constitutional candidates for the Spanish and Portuguese thrones, Isabella and Maria, had been supported by Britain and France. But each was suspicious of the other's intentions in the Iberian peninsula, and they hoped to lessen tension between themselves by forming an alliance to exclude the rival candidates, Miguel of Portugal and Carlos of Spain. An immediate conflict was averted, though the Carlist revolt continued in Spain. Britain and France even appeared temporarily as a liberal bulwark against Austria, Russia, and Prussia. But their fundamental suspicions of each other remained and flared up again in the 1840s over the question of the Spanish marriage.

QUAESTIONES, permanent criminal courts in ancient Rome. The first (*Quaestio de rebus repetundis*) was established in 149 BC to try cases of maladministration by provincial governors, and Sulla, Julius Caesar, and Augustus extended and systematized the *quaestiones*. Members of the jury were originally senators, but the composition of the *quaestio* on provincial maladministration became a political issue after its transference to the *equites* by C. Gracchus (123), a compromise being reached in 70 which lasted until Augustus. The *quaestiones* were presided over by a praetor and charges could be laid by any citizen. They disappeared in the first half of the 3rd cent. AD.

QUAESTORS, lowest of the ancient Roman career-magistrates. They were concerned chiefly with state-finance and at first (*c.* 500 BC) there were two, who acted as general assistants to the consuls. After being increased to four (421) they specialized, two supervising the treasury (*aerarium*) and the others, later, the finances of the consuls in their provinces. Sulla increased their number to 20, to develop provincial administration (81); they gained financial, judicial, and military experience under the governors of provinces, a practice which continued under the emperors in provinces administered by the Senate. The quaestorship was the normal qualification for entry to the Senate.

QUAKERS, English sect, properly called the Society of Friends, who received their colloquial title from a judge whom their founder, George Fox (1642–91), advised to 'tremble at the name of the Lord'. Fox, a Leicestershire cobbler, began his ministry (*c.* 1647) in the social and religious ferment of the Puritan revolution, although his ideas had much in common with the radical mysticism of pre-Reformation Germany. He taught that the essence of Christianity was the 'inward light' that dwells in every man and needs no minister, liturgy, sacraments, or external rites to sustain it. True faith consists in the word of scripture, but the believer needs the inspiration of the spirit to enable him to understand it and to direct his actions.

In its early days the movement was discredited by the adherence of 'ranters' and other extravagant sectaries who disrupted official services and advertised themselves by public demonstrations. Although Oliver Cromwell admired Fox personally, he could not prevent the punishment of anti-social extremists, and after the Clarendon Code (1661) the Quakers were further persecuted for refusing to pay tithes, since they disapproved of a paid ministry, and for holding their own private meetings instead of attending church.

Fox himself was imprisoned eight times, but he preached diligently all over Britain, and as his character matured he showed the qualities of a genuine leader. After 1656 he gave the society a skeletal organization of monthly and quarterly meetings and a hierarchy of ministers, elders, and overseers. In the 1670s the conversion of Robert Barclay and William Penn brought a further leavening of wordly sense, and the society gained prestige through the foundation of Pennsylvania (1682) by a band of settlers who, true to the Quaker creed of non-violence, went out unarmed and made treaties with the Indians which both sides respected.

The Toleration Act (1689) allowed the Quakers freedom of worship, and the right to make an affirmation, in place of the religious oaths which they abhorred. With Fox's death and the end of active persecution the movement lost its early proselytizing zeal. Like other dissenters, Quakers were still debarred from public office, and the army and navy were also closed to them because of their rejection of violence. They occupied themselves in commerce and philanthropy, and an American Quaker, John Woolman, gave a practical lead to the anti-slavery agitation by freeing the slaves on his plantations. Quakers also worked vigorously to achieve better conditions in prisons and asylums, the mitigation of the penal code, and abolition of the opium trade. To further their campaign for non-sectarian education they opened numerous Sunday schools where practical subjects were taught to children of any denomination.

The first Quaker sat in the British House of Commons in 1833, and with the gradual removal in the 19th cent. of all disabilities the society became less exclusive, abandoning its peculiar habits of speech and dress and entering fully into public life. Quakers have founded schools for adults, launched ambitious foreign missions, and honourably served the country through their work for the hospital and ambulance services in time of war, while the families of Rowntree and Cadbury pioneered schemes of social and industrial reorganization which anticipated the welfare state.

But the society has had its ideological difficulties, arising from the sort of conflict between conscience and authority that has always disturbed such highly individualistic movements. Rejecting any idea of systematic worship—Fox's name for a church was 'steeple-house'—a Quaker meeting at first consisted of a devotional silence which might be interrupted when a member felt himself to be stirred by the spirit within him. Inevitably, the prompting of the 'inward light' tended to be over-emphasized at the expense of the basic scriptural faith, and English Quakers debated this issue with characteristic honesty and thoroughness whan a small split occurred in the 1830s after the publication of *The Beacon* by a Manchester minister, Isaac Crewdson. To preserve a proper balance, scriptural readings, and even hymns, have been introduced into Quaker meetings. But the society still has no paid or ordained ministry, and administrative expenses have to be financed by charitable subscription.

Many Quakers followed the original pioneers to Pennsylvania to escape persecution. Although the society has flourished in the US, the doctrinal dispute was more serious there, and the movement was almost split in two by the secession (1828) of Elias Hicks, followed later by John Wilbur, who both asserted the pre-eminence of personal inspiration over scripture.

In 1970 there were fewer than 25,000 Quakers in Britain, and only about 110,000 in America. Yet the social and ethical influence of the society has been out of all proportion to its numerical strength.

A. N. Brayshaw, *The Quakers* (London, 1938).   MMR

QUALIFICATION BILLS (1696–7, 1703, 1710–11) in Britain, Tory and 'Country' party attempts to impose property qualifications upon members of the House of Commons. The first attempt in 1696 was vetoed by the Crown, while the second in 1697 failed to pass the Lords. The Tories revived the measure (1703) in the wake of their electoral triumph of 1702. Besides having to possess estates sufficient to support them, MPs had to be native born. Though supported by some 'country' Whigs, it was rejected by the Whig majority in the Lords. The 1710 bill, which finally became law in 1711, imposed an estate qualification for county MPs of £600 p.a., and of £300 p.a. for borough MPs. Its provisions did not extend to the four university seats, nor to the 45 Scottish seats. Neither were eldest sons of peers or heirs of country gentlemen of more than £600 p.a. to be included. The Tories, by this act, hoped to protect their constituencies from the competition of army officers and the younger sons of Whig peers. In this they failed, for the act affected both Whig and Tory alike, while the power of the political patron made strict enforcement impossible. By the 1715 election the act was a dead letter.

QUALIFICATION OF WOMEN ACT (1907). Although this act fell far short of the aspirations of the suffragettes, it ensured that in Britain women, already allowed on district and parish councils, would be admitted to membership and to all offices of the county and borough councils.

QUANG-TRUNG (1752–92), reign-title of a Tay-Son emperor of Viet-nam (*reg.* 1788–92), who was born as Nguyen Hue. He was one of three brothers who led the Tay-Son rebellion, which began in 1773. He played a prominent part in their intervention in the north, from 1786, and later proclaimed himself emperor there. In 1788–9 he defeated a Chinese attempt to reconquer Tongking. As a ruler he was energetic in the reorganization of administration, but was not strongly Confucian. His early death prevented many of his plans from coming to fruition.

QUAPAW INDIANS, American tribe formerly living along the Mississippi river in AR. They ceded their lands and retired to a reservation in OK (1877), where lands were allotted to them. Being dissatisfied with the apportionment, they carried out their own land reform, for which they obtained Congressional approval (1895)—the only tribe to do so.

QUARANTINE SPEECH (5 Oct. 1937) in the US, major policy statement by President F. D. Roosevelt in Chicago, IL, in which he warned of the dangers to the US inherent in the spread of war overseas. Speaking of the interdependence of nations, and the necessity for peace-loving nations to make a concerted effort against aggression, he used the metaphor of physical disease and said that when an epidemic starts to spread 'the community approves and joins in a quarantine of the patients in order to protect the health of the community against the spread of the disease'.

QUATRE BRAS, BATTLE OF (10 June 1815), fought at the end of the French Wars, about 30 kms south of Brussels, at the junction of two important roads. Wellington's troops prevented Ney from reinforcing Napoleon I, who beat—but failed to rout—Blucher's Prussians at Ligny, 13 kms to the south-east.

QUEBEC, oldest city in Canada, located at the confluence of the St Lawrence and St Charles rivers. The first European visitor was Jacques Cartier (1535–6). A fur-trading post was established at Quebec by Samuel de Champlain (1608) and it was made the capital of New France (1663). It was held briefly by the English (1629–32), but later defied their attempts at conquest (1690, 1711), though it eventually surrendered (1760) after the battle of the Plains of Abraham.

It was ceded to Britain in 1763, and was unsuccessfully besieged by an American force (1775–6). Quebec was the capital of British Canada (1763–91), of Lower Canada (1791–1840), and of the Province of Canada (1851–5, 1859–1865), and has been since 1867 that of the Province of Quebec. It was at the Quebec Conference (1864) that agreement was reached favouring a federated state of Canada.

The original English province of Quebec included all of Canada, exclusive of the Hudson's Bay Co. lands, and part of the modern US. As a result of nationalist and local jealousies, the territory was divided into Upper and Lower Canada (1791), the former corresponding closely to the modern province of Que. Responsible government was granted to Upper and Lower Canada (1841) and provincial autonomy was granted in the British North American Act, which also created the province of Que. (1867). The province includes the major cities of Quebec and Montreal and is the centre for the French-speaking population of Canada.

E. C. Woodley, *The Province of Quebec through Four Centuries* (Toronto, 1944).
M. De La Roche, *Quebec, Historic Seaport* (New York, 1944).
GS

QUEBEC ACT (1774) in Britain, extended the boundaries of the province of Que. to the Ohio and Mississippi rivers, restored French civil law, assured the maintenance of French governmental structure, and pledged toleration of the Roman Catholic religion in Que. The act aroused hostility in the British North American colonies as the extension of Que's boundaries to the Mississippi river jeopardized the trans-Appalachian land claims of several colonies and appeared to benefit French Catholics at the expense of British Protestants.

QUEBEC, BATTLES OF (1629, 1690, 1759, 1760, 1775–6). The French trading post of Quebec first surrendered to an English fleet under David Kirke (1629), after which it had an English garrison until its return to France (1632). Quebec withstood a siege by English and colonial troops led by William Phipps (5–9 Oct. 1690), for the French, forewarned of the expedition, strengthened their position so that the landing party was repulsed and the bombardment failed. In the French and Indian War, Quebec capitulated to the British after the battle of the Plains of Abraham (13 Sept. 1759), when James Wolfe, after a surprise attack, defeated the French under Montcalm. Both leaders were killed. The Duc de Lévis attempted to retake Quebec (28 April 1760), but retreated on the arrival of a British fleet. Quebec was ceded to Britain (1763) as part of New France. An American attempt to seize Quebec (Oct. 1775–May 1776) ended in failure when the British, under Sir Guy Carleton, beat off attacks by the troops of Generals Benedict Arnold and Richard Montgomery.

QUEBEC CONFERENCE, FIRST (Aug. 1943), during the Second World War (held under the code name Quadrant), between F. D. Roosevelt and Winston Churchill to discuss the implications of Mussolini's overthrow (July 1943). While the conference was in progress negotiations were going on which led to the Italian armistice. Strategic decisions were taken affecting hostilities in the Far East (including an attack on north Burma rather than Sumatra, as Churchill proposed). The invasion of northern Europe—Overlord—was also accepted by the Combined Chiefs of Staff at Quebec and a supplementary invasion (Anvil) discussed for a landing in the south of France by forces freed from the Italian campaign. Political matters under discussion included plans for a post-war international organization. Differing formulas were drawn up by the British and Americans for the degree of recognition which they were prepared to accord to the French Committee of National Liberation.

As the conference ended news arrived that Stalin had agreed to a conference of foreign ministers. This preceded the first summit meeting of the war at Teheran (Nov. 1943).

QUEBEC CONFERENCE, SECOND (Sept. 1944), during the Second World War, between F. D. Roosevelt (who summoned Morgenthau, secretary of the treasury, to attend) and Winston Churchill. It was notable especially for the acceptance of Morgenthau's plan for the 'pastoralization' of Germany, including the dismantling of the industries of the Ruhr and the Saar. (The acceptance of this proposal by Roosevelt and Churchill brought vigorous protests from their own advisers and ministers and the Morgenthau plan was then dropped.) It was also agreed that an Anglo-American committee of experts should work out details for Lend-Lease, on the assumption that Lend-Lease would continue after the defeat of Germany.

The conference was held in a mood of justified optimism with regard to the campaign against Germany and agreement was readily arrived at for the transfer of resources to continue the war against Japan.

QUEBEC EXPEDITION (1711), diversionary attack on French colonial possessions during the War of the Spanish Succession, mainly determined by political motives. These were the Tory 'Blue Water' policy, which favoured maritime and colonial war, and St John's attempt to ingratiate himself with Abigail Hill by choosing her brother, Gen. Hill, to command the project. The expedition failed, partly through the incompetence of Hill himself.

QUEBEC LIBERATION FRONT (Front de Libération du Quebec), French Canadian nationalist group, associated since its founding (c. 1963) with bombings in the province of Quebec. The FLQ attained international importance by kidnapping (5 Oct. 1970) James Richard Cross, senior British trade commissioner in Montreal, and (10 Oct. 1970) Pierre Laporte, Quebec minister of labour and immigration. The kidnappers demanded a ransom of $500,000, release of 26 'political' prisoners, and publication of the FLQ's manifesto. The Canadian government outlawed the FLQ and invoked the War Measures Act of 1914. Laporte was murdered (17 Oct. 1970) and Cross was released (3 Dec. 1970), his kidnappers being given safe passage to Cuba.

QUECHUAS, native peoples of the Andean area, who speak the language of the same name. The origin of the Quechua language is unknown, but it was spoken by the Incas, who fostered its spread throughout their empire. The Spanish missionaries likewise encouraged those natives who spoke other languages to speak Quechua, since a common language was of assistance to them in giving religious instruction. As a result, the Quechua language is spoken in the general area of the Inca empire from Ecuador to the province of Tucumán in Argentina. Indeed, the name Quechua, formerly designating a small district of central Peru, was given to the language of the Incas by the Dominican friar, Domingo de Santo Tomás, in his grammar. Continued use of the language no doubt sustains feelings of kinship among the natives, but Quechua-speakers do not think of themselves as 'Quechuas'.

QUEEN ANNE'S BOUNTY (1704) in England, royal proposals for an increase in the livings of impoverished clergymen. The Crown's income from first-fruits and tenths was to be used to supplement inadequate stipends, while all arrears of poor clergymen to the Crown were to be remitted. These proposals were given effect by an act of parliament (1704). The scheme was applicable only to the Church of England.

QUEEN ANNE'S WAR (1702–13), American counterpart of the War of Spanish Succession in Europe. The war consisted mainly of naval actions and privateering off the West Indies and frontier raiding around Carolina and New England. The British captured St Christopher (1702), but failed to take Guadeloupe (1703), and thereafter trade suffered from the attentions of privateers. Britain gave little assistance to the New Englanders in their war against the French in Canada, but a British contingent was present at the capture of Port Royal (Oct. 1710) which marked the loss of Acadia to the French. The war officially ended with the treaty of Utrecht (1713).

QUEENSBERRY, JAMES DOUGLAS, 2nd Duke of (Scottish) (1662–1711), Scottish politician, who held many offices in Scotland, but was deprived of them as a result of his association with the Jacobite intriguer, Lord Lovat. He was restored in 1705 and appointed (1706) a commissioner for the union with England, which he successfully helped to carry through. In 1708 he was appointed joint keeper of the privy seal. From 1709 he was the first holder of the new post of third secretary of state (for Scotland).

QUEENSLAND, Australia's second largest state. Its climate is semi-tropical and it is famous for its barrier reef and gold coast tourist resorts. It was officially separated from NSW in 1859. Like Vic., it was settled by pastoralists from the 'mother colony' and its early development centred mainly on wool. Gold, copper, coal, sugar, and tropical fruit provided the basis for further growth; then in the 1960s tourism, rich oilfields, and bauxite deposits brought a boom to the state. Qld politics, marked at the turn of the 19th cent. by a controversy over indentured Polynesian (Kanaka) labour, subsequently became notable for long periods of Labor Party dominance, the Australian Labor Party itself being largely dominated by the powerful but moderate Australian Workers' Union. Unified metropolitan local government distinguished the capital, Brisbane, from other Australian cities.

QUEENSTOWN HEIGHTS, BATTLE OF (13 Oct. 1812), British victory over the Americans in the War of 1812. Gen. Stephen van Rensselaer failed to induce his New York militia to cross the Niagara river into Canada to support a small US army detachment which had gained the Queenstown Heights, this led to the detachment's defeat and capture by the British, under Maj. Roger Sheaffe, who took over command when Maj.-Gen. Isaac Brock was killed during the battle.

QUEIROZ LAW (1850) in Brazil, named after its sponsor, the Brazilian minister of empire, Eusébio de Queiroz. The law, passed under British pressure, prohibited and effectively abolished the Negro slave trade between Africa and Brazil. Its passage reflected the growing anti-slavery feelings of educated Brazilians, and the monarchy's ability to enforce legislation detrimental to the economic interests of politically powerful coffee and sugar planters, who were the principal slave-owners. The slave traffic, which had begun across the south Atlantic in 1550, was finally suppressed in 1853. The Queiroz Law was the first major step towards Brazil's abolition of slavery itself in 1888.

QUEMOY AND MATSU, two groups of islands off the Chinese mainland which featured in US Far Eastern policy during the 1950s. After 1949, they remained under the control of the Chinese Nationalist government on Taiwan, but were claimed by the People's Republic of China. In Sept. 1954 Quemoy was bombarded from the mainland; the US, whose Seventh Fleet already guarded Taiwan, sought to safeguard the offshore islands without committing itself to military action. A Mutual Defence treaty was concluded with the Nationalists (Dec. 1954), which affirmed the US right of protection of Formosa and the Pescadores islands without specifically including Quemoy and Matsu. A Joint Congressional Resolution on Formosa (Jan. 1955) authorized military action at President Eisenhower's discretion, and secretary of state Dulles announced that such action would be taken if communist attacks were construed as a prelude to an invasion of Formosa. The Nationalists withdrew from the Tachen and Nanki islands to the north (Feb. 1955) and communist hostilities ceased a month later. A second crisis

(Aug.–Oct. 1958) was ended by US reaffirmation of the Formosa Resolution.

QUEREMISTAS, supporters of Getúlio Vargas in the 1945 presidential campaign in Brazil. Their aim was to ensure that Vargas remained president until a new national constitution was drafted. The name derives from their slogan, '*Queremos Getúlio!*' ('We want Getúlio!').

QUERÉTARO LITERARY SOCIETY in Mexico, group of intellectuals who organized themselves as admirers of the fine arts (1808) and plotted with some success for national independence. Their influence was felt during the Hidalgo revolt (1810).

QUESNAY, FRANÇOIS (1694–1774), French economist, who attacked mercantilist theories and whose ideas formed the basis of the physiocratic school. He was physician to the Duke of Villeroi and then to Louis XV, and also author of *Tableau Économique* (1758), *Maximes* (1758), and *Physiocratie* (1768), and a contributor to the *Encyclopédie* of Diderot and D'Alembert.

QUESNEL, PASQUIER (1634–1719), French cleric and writer of Jansenist persuasion, whose writings enjoyed widespread acceptance until an attack on his commentaries by the Abp of Paris drove him into exile (1681), mainly in the Spanish Netherlands. There he became associated with Antoine Arnauld and Jansenist ideas, but he was not formally condemned until the Jansenist Bp Noailles commended his *Nouveau Testament avec des Réflexions Morales* (1692), a version of a work which had already gone through many editions (since 1667). This eventually led to his condemnation by Rome and his arrest by the Spanish authorities (1703). He escaped to Holland and spent his last years defending his own and Jansenist ideas against the condemnation of the bull *Unigenitus* (1713), although his thinking was as much Bérullian as Jansenist.

QUETTA, town in Baluchistan, West Pakistan, commanding the Bolan route to the Indus valley. It was occupied by the British in 1877 because of the Russian advance towards Afghanistan. It suffered severely from an earthquake in 1935.

QUETZALCÓATL, ancient Mesoamerican deity, probably of Toltec origin, worshipped by the Maya of Yucatán as Kukulcán and by the Maya of Guatemala as Gucumatz. Translated literally the Nahua term meant 'feathered serpent'. Popular legend surrounds the figure who, apparently, had been a king among the Toltecs. The Spanish chroniclers maintained that the aborigines recalled him as a bearded white man who brought knowledge, religion, and peace. Quetzalcóatl then sailed away to the east, promising to return in the year *A Acatl* of the Mexican calendar.

The deity then appeared among the Maya as Kukulcán, also the bearer of knowledge and religion. The Spaniards arrived in the year *A Acatl*, a fact made much of by the Spanish chroniclers. Quetzalcóatl is often viewed as a legend descriptive of the sun in its movements.

QUEUILLE, HENRI (1884–1970), French doctor and politician, who entered parliament in 1914, and was a minister in numerous inter-war governments. During the Second World War he joined De Gaulle in London, then returned to politics. He was prime minister three times (1948–9, 1950, 1951), and established something of a record by being a minister without a break for six years (1948–54). Within the Radical Party he opposed the left-wing tendencies of Mendès-France.

QUEVEDO Y VILLEGAS, FRANCISCO GOMEZ DE (1580–1645), Spanish diplomat and prose satirist, who wrote *La Lora de Todos* (1635–6) and *La Vida del Buscon* (1626). He was a minister at Naples under the viceroy, the Duke of Osuna, on whose behalf he was involved in Spanish conspiracies in Nice (1613) and Venice (1618). After Osuna's downfall Quevedo was imprisoned (1620–3). Later he became a secretary to Philip IV (1632), then was imprisoned again in the monastery of San Marcos in Léon for his political criticisms (1639–43).

QUEZON, MANUEL LUIS (1878–1944), Filipino politician and president of the Commonwealth of the Philippines (1935–44), who fought against the US (1899–1901), and afterwards became a lawyer, then was fiscal of Mindoro, and later of Tayabas (now Quezon) provinces. He protected the poor and ignorant from exploitation by the rich and educated, and as governor of Tayabas strove for greater local autonomy. In 1907 he represented this province in the Philippine National Assembly, and was among those who led the fight for immediate independence. He was resident commissioner in Washington, DC (1909–16), where he successfully lobbied for the passage of the Jones Law (1916), which established the Philippine Senate. Quezon was elected first president of the Senate, wresting from S. Osmena the leadership of the Nacionalista Party in 1922. As leader, he was elected first president of the Commonwealth government in 1935. When the US entered the Second World War in Dec. 1941, Quezon left for the US, where the Commonwealth government functioned in exile. He died there on 1 Aug. 1944, two years before the Philippines won her independence from the US (1946), for which he had struggled all his life.

QUIBERON BAY, BATTLE OF (29 Nov. 1759), naval engagement off the coast of France during the Seven Years War. It was fought in a heavy gale between a British fleet of 33 ships, under Hawke, and 24 French ships, under Conflans. The French took refuge in Quiberon Bay, pursued by Hawke's fleet, who captured or sank all but four of the French ships.

QUIBERON BAY EXPEDITION (1795), disastrous attempt by a force of French émigrés to stir up a national revolt and restore the monarchy in the person of the Comte de Provence. In the reaction after the period of Robespierre Jacobinism there were widespread hopes that the republican government would restore the Bourbon monarchy, with constitutional limitations. This move was thwarted, however, by Provence's aggressive manifesto from Verona and by the untimely expedition which disembarked from British ships on the promontory of Quiberon in southern Brittany. Defeated by the republican forces under Hoche (July 1795), 428 French nobles were among 748 prisoners shot in the aftermath of the affair. The new constitution, produced by the Convention in Aug., was republican in character.

QUICK, SIR JOHN (1852–1932), Australian lawyer and politician, who was a federalist and Australian Natives Association leader. He successfully advocated an elected convention to frame a constitution for submission to popular vote. He wrote, with R. R. Garran, *The Annotated Constitution of the Australian Commonwealth* (1901).

QUICKSWOOD, HUGH RICHARD HEATHCOTE GASCOIGNE-CECIL, Baron (1869–1956), British politician, who entered politics in 1891. He was the author of *Conservatism* (1912), and *Conservative Ideals* (1926). In these he argued that 'Tory Democracy' was the most secure political guide for a social reformer, as well as a bulwark against revolutionary change. He was provost of Eton College (1936–44).

QUIEPO DE LLANO, GONZALO (1875–1951), Spanish soldier and political figure. At first he held Republican views, and in 1931 he conspired against the monarchy; he was also involved in the plot which resulted in the premature rising at Jaca in Dec., which was headed by Gálan and Hernández. He became head of the Carabineros (frontier police) under the Republic, but in 1936, angered by the ejection of his relative Alcalá Zamora from the presidency, he joined the military rising. In Seville, he made several arrests, disarmed the Republican assault guards, and occupied government buildings before rebel resistance could be consolidated. He crushed the general strike by a combination of propaganda and terror, *eg*, announcing over the radio that the Nationalist rising had been successful all over Spain and sending troops disguised as Moors into proletarian districts.

During the Civil War he ruled a militarily and economically independent empire in Andalusia, where he imposed a savage discipline—towards the end of 1937 20,000 workers had been killed in Seville alone. He stimulated agriculture by a system of loans to peasants, kept up exports of sherry, olive oil, and citrus fruits, and made deals with Italian and German concerns. In Jan. 1937 he led the Army of the South in its victorious attack on Málaga. But his independence and irresponsibility eventually lost him Franco's favour, and after 1939 he was excluded from power.

QUIETISM, doctrine of Christian perfection expounded by Miguel de Molinos, who held that perfection consists in passivity of the soul, and in the suppression of human effort so that divine action can have full play. This doctrine caused a serious theological controversy in the Catholic Church in Italy and France in the late 17th cent. Molinos was condemned in 1687 and his French follower, Mme Guyon, was likewise condemned (1689), while in 1699 the pope forbade the circulation of Fénélon's *Maximes* in which Mme Guyon **was** defended.

QUILOMBOS, Brazilian villages or settlements of runaway slaves. Such settlements, called *palenques* or *cumbes* in Spanish America, were a constant problem to slaveholders and the authorities, because they attracted increasing numbers of runaways. To prevent discovery and capture, *quilombos* were located as far as possible from Iberian population centres. The prevalence and size of such settlements have been frequently exaggerated, but some were populous and highly organized, and occasionally their activities constituted a serious menace. In the late 16th cent. bands of Panamanian runaways harassed Spanish trade in the isthmus and assisted English privateers, notably Drake. In Brazil, the most famous *quilombo* was that of Palmares.

QUINAULT, PHILIPPE (1635–88), French dramatic poet and librettist, who was patronized by Mme de Montespan and was popular with the young Louis XIV. He collaborated with the composer Lully in a large number of works, *eg*, the ballet-tragedy *Psyché* (1671).

QUINCY, JOSIAH (1744–75), American lawyer, who took an active interest in the political crisis that was developing between Britain and her American colonies. He wrote several articles for the press under various pseudonyms, strongly urging the colonial point of view. Nevertheless, he defended, with John Adams, the British soldiers accused after the 'Boston Massacre' (March 1770). In Sept. 1774 he visited Britain to try to prevent an armed conflict, but although he had discussions with Lord North, the British prime minister, and others, he accomplished nothing.

QUINN, JAMES (1819–81), Irish-born clergyman who pioneered the Irish dominance of the Australian episcopacy when he became the first Roman Catholic Bp of Brisbane (1861). He increased Catholicism in Qld through his own immigration scheme in 1862, and through strict supervision of church appointments and finance.

QUINQUEREME, standard Hellenistic and Roman warship of the 3rd–1st cents BC. It replaced the smaller trireme of the 6th–4th cents and had a crew of 300, with perhaps five men to each oar.

QUIPUS, knotted fibre cords used by the Incas, in conjunction with a rudimentary abacus, to keep numerical records.

QUIRINIUS, CENSUS OF (AD 6), assessment of the newly annexed Judaea by the Roman governor of Syria, P. Sulpicius Qurinius, the Cyrenius of St Luke 2 : 2.

QUIROGA, GASPAR DE (1512–94), Spanish cleric and Abp of Toledo, who, as a supporter of the royal prerogative in ecclesiastical matters, was appointed inspector of monasteries in Naples and Sicily by Philip II. He was also made president of the council of Italy, inquisitor-general, and finally a cardinal (1578). He was an orthodox moderate, protected intellectuals (*eg*, Arias Montano), and allowed the introduction of the Copernican system into Spanish education. He was also a patron of artists (*eg*, El Greco). In political matters he supported Antonio Perez and gave considerable financial backing to Philip II's foreign policy, especially his efforts to crush English Protestantism. Quiroga was deeply concerned for the reform of the diocesan clergy, the advancement of education, and the care of the poor. In 1582 he summoned a church council at Toledo to implement the Tridentine decrees, and afterwards prepared an Index of prohibited books (1583) and one of expurgated works (1584).

QUIROGA, VASCO DE (1470–1565), Bp of Michoacán, who was a member of the second Mexican *audiencia* (1530). He founded self-supporting Indian communities, based on the plan of More's *Utopia*, whose essential characteristics were widely copied elsewhere in the native mission villages.

QUIROS, PEDRO FERNANDEZ DE (*c.* 1560–1615), Portuguese sailor, who was Mendana's pilot. In a new voyage in search of a supposed east Pacific continent (1605–6) he eventually discovered the New Hebrides, where a storm—not mutiny, as alleged—parted him from his consorts. His many subsequent appeals to the Spanish king urging a second expedition helped to create the myth of the Great South Land, *Terra Australis Incognita*.

QUISLING, VIDKUN ABRAHAM LAURITZ JONSSØN (1887–1945), Norwegian soldier and politician. During the First World War he was attached to the general staff, but in 1918 became military attaché at Petrograd. He spent most of the next decade in Russia, meeting many important revolutionaries. In Jan. 1922 he was granted leave of absence to assist Nansen in his work for famine relief. He travelled widely in Russia, the Balkans, and the Near East, earning high commendation for his humanitarian work. He represented (1927–9) British interests at Moscow. After returning to Norway in 1929 he entered politics. Owing to his close connections with Russia he had been suspected of communist leanings, but in the election of 1930 he campaigned vigorously for the right-of-centre Agrarian Party, becoming minister of defence (1931–3) in the Agrarian Party government.

In 1933 he formed his own party, Nasjonal Samling (National Unification), which was nationalistic and xenophobic in character. It fared badly in the elections of 1933 and 1936 and gradually became fascist in outlook. In 1939 Quisling went twice to Germany, where through the good offices of Rosenberg he obtained financial and political backing for his party. During the early months of the Second World War he became involved in German plans for the invasion of Norway.

On 9 April 1940, when the invasion took place, he seized power, declaring himself prime minister. Opposition from influential personalities in both Norway and Germany led to his fall from office on 15 April. Despite this setback he remained leader of those prepared to collaborate with Germany and on 25 Sept. 1940 high-ranking members of his party became ministers, albeit responsible to Josef Terboven, the German *reichskommissar*. On 1 Feb. 1942 he became minister-president.

His wartime administration was both unsuccessful and unpopular, and after the collapse of Germany he was arrested, tried, and convicted of treason, for which he was shot. The high promise of his early years being forgotten, he is remembered only as the archetypal traitor and collaborator.

PMH

QUIT INDIA MOVEMENT (Aug. 1942), last of the major campaigns by the Congress against British rule. The movement was to have been a *satyagraha* campaign led by Gandhi, but it developed instead into a short-lived, violent revolt. With the failure of the Cripps Mission (April 1942) and a steadily worsening war situation, Gandhi gained support for his view that Britain should 'Quit India' and leave the country to meet the Japanese with non-violent non-co-operation. A Working Committee draft resolution, which threatened the start of civil disobedience unless there was an immediate transfer of power, was presented to a meeting of the All-India Congress Committee in Bombay on 7 Aug. 1942. The exact nature of the campaign had not been decided upon at this point and when the resolution was passed on 8 Aug. Gandhi expected to have time to negotiate with the government of India. In fact, the government had already decided on its course of action and the entire Working Committee was arrested early on 9 Aug. and placed in detention for the duration of the war. The movement was thus deprived of leadership and opposition to the arrests quickly became violent. Stern repressive measures by police and troops added to the fierceness of the disturbances, particularly in Bihar, the eastern districts of the United Provinces, Maharashtra, and Calcutta and Midnapore district in Bengal. Attacks on government offices and police stations, and on telegraph and railway systems were widespread and there was for a time severe dislocation of the war effort. In retaliation, some 100,000 arrests were made and massive collective fines imposed on whole villages. In all, several thousand people were killed or wounded. The main force of the revolt was spent by the end of the month, although there were still areas of disturbance in 1943 and some underground factions, in Satara and Midnapore districts in particular, were never eliminated altogether. This was the most serious challenge to British control that was made by the Congress, but without proper military resources such a conflict was bound to fail.

PDR

QUITMAN, JOHN ANTHONY (1798–1858), US soldier and politician, who served in the Mexican War and was governor of MS (1850–1). He was opposed to the Compromise of 1850, and was a vehement supporter of slavery and the doctrine of states rights. He served as a congressman from MS (1855–1858).

QUIVIRA, legendary Indian ruler, whose cities, encrusted with gold and precious stones, were sought by the 1540 Coronado expedition in present-day TX, OK, and KS.

QURAYSH, North Arabian tribe, which established itself at Mecca before the advent of Islam. The Quraysh acted as guardians of the sacred shrine, the Ka'ba, and also achieved importance as merchants, entering into trade relations with the Byzantines, the Abyssinians, and the Persians. Within Mecca the ruling element, known as the 'Quraysh of the Inside', consisted of prosperous merchants, bankers, and entrepreneurs. Of lesser prestige were the 'Quraysh of the Outside', embracing small traders, artisans, and the like. It was into the Banu Hashim, a clan of respectable status, though not included among the great families who controlled Mecca, that the Prophet Muhammad was born (*c.* AD 570–580).

QUTAYBA IBN MUSLIM (d. AD 715), governor of Khurasan (704–15). In a series of brilliant campaigns he captured Balkh (705), Bukhara and the neighbouring lands (706–9), and then Samarkand, with the region of Khwarazm (710–12). He also undertook a campaign (713–15) in the direction of Farghana.

QUTB SHAHI DYNASTY, ruling family of the state of Golkonda, India (1518–1687). The state was founded by a Turki officer who had been appointed as a governor by the Bahmani minister, Mahmud Gawan. After Gawan's death (1481) the officer withdrew from the Bahmani court, declared the state to be independent (1518) and assumed the title of Quli Qutb Shah. He lived to be 90 and died (1543) by his son's hand. The kingdom largely coincided with the old Hindu state of Warangal and remained generally aloof from the frequent Deccan wars, except the coalition against Vijayanagar (1563). In the 17th cent. the dynasty expanded southwards into the coastal Deccan while pressed by the Mughals from the north. It was extinguished by the Emperor Aurangzeb (1687).

QUTB-UD-DIN AIBEK (d. 1210), Turki military slave of Sultan Muhammad of Ghuri (d. 1206), who rose in rank and was eventually charged with the Indian campaign by Muhammad Ghuri after the defeat of Prithvi Raj at Tarain (1192). He took Delhi (1193) and later (with Muhammad's help) defeated Jai Chand of Kanauj and also took Gwalior and Ajmir (1197). He built the Quwwat-ul-Islam mosque at Mahrauli, Delhi, and began the Qutb Minar. His general, Muhammad Khilji, conquered both Bihar and Bengal (1193–1200) by a series of daring moves. On Muhammad Ghuri's death (1206), his successor declared Aibek an independent sovereign.

QUTUZ (*reg.* AD 1259–60), Al-Muzaffar Sayf al-Din, Mamluk Sultan, whose brief reign is notable for the defeat that the Mamluks inflicted on the Mongols at Ayn Jalud near Nazareth in a battle which marked the furthest limit of the Mongol advance into the Muslim world. Qutuz was killed by the Mamluk amir Baybars, who succeeded him on the throne.

QUWATLI, AL-, SHUKRI (1891–1967), Syrian nationalist politician from Damascus, who became leader of the National Bloc (1940), president of the Syrian republic (1943–9, 1955–8), and one of the chief architects of the United Arab republic (1958).

RABAT, city on the Atlantic coast of Morocco, originally a military foundation of the 12th cent. near Salé. It was developed in the 19th cent. at the expense of its neighbour and is now (1970) the modern capital of the country.

RABAUT SAINT-ETIENNE, JEAN (1743–93), French lawyer, Protestant minister, and politician in the French Revolution, who fought for Protestant rights and was the chief instigator of the edict granting equal civil rights (1788). As a deputy of the third estate he defended religious parity. In 1790 he played a large part in organizing the *gendarmerie*. He published *Almanach historique de la Révolution Française* (1791). He was guillotined at the end of 1793.

RABELAIS, FRANÇOIS (1494–1553), French novelist and satirist, who became a Franciscan (1520), but transferred to the Benedictines, as they were more receptive to humanism (1525). He was secretary to his abbot for a while, then became a secular priest (1528) and began to study medicine (1530), publishing a number of Italian treatises (1531) which were well received. He practised in Lyons (1532), where he wrote *Pantagruel*, a satire of a popular folk tale of the day which won him instant success and the condemnation of the Sorbonne (1532). He spent much of the next few years in Italy with members of the Du Bellay family and published a second book, *Gargantua* (1534), which reflected many of his own experiences. This too was condemned (1534), as was his *Tiers Livre* (1545), and he was forced into exile, although by then a master of requests (1542). His *Quatrième Livre* also attracted censure for its attack on the papacy (1552) and his fifth work (which was only partly his) was published posthumously (1564).

RABIH IBN FADLALLAH (*c.* 1845–1900), Sudanese soldier, who joined the merchant adventurer, Al-Zubair al-Ja'ali, in the Bahr al-Ghazal and rose rapidly to become commander of his patron's slave soldiers. At one time he was governor of what is now the Central African republic. After taking a leading part in the invasion of Darfur and in Sulaiman ibn Zubair's revolt against the Egyptian government, he set off for the west with 800 gunmen, by whom he was elected emir. In 1888 he accepted the Mahdiyya and corresponded with the Khalifa Abdullah and Hayat al-Din ibn Sa'id. He attacked Baghirmi (1892) and in 1893 overthrew the Shehu of Bornu, where he established a settled government in the name of the Mahdi. He was defeated and killed by the French at the battle of Kusseri (April 1900). Rabih was a gifted military and civil administrator who organized a highly disciplined army and established an efficient civil administration in Bornu.

RACCONIGI AGREEMENT (1909), between Italy and Russia, sprang from Italy's need for independent safeguards after the Bosnian crisis (1908) had revealed her weakness within the Triple Alliance. In an exchange of notes at Victor Emmanuel's country palace, Italy and Russia agreed to maintain the status quo in the Balkans and make no independent agreements with a third power. This directly contradicted an agreement, reached only a week before, in which Italy and Austria promised to make no exclusive agreements about the Balkans with a third power. The safeguards to Italy were largely offset by the dangers of sumultaneous commitment to two antagonistic powers and an atmosphere of general distrust.

RACE RELATIONS ACTS (1965, 1968), in Britain, legislative measures which made racial discrimination illegal in housing, employment, and such services as insurance and credit facilities. A Race Relations Board was established which acts as a supervisory and conciliatory body with power to bring cases before specially constituted county courts.

RACINE, JEAN (1639–99), French dramatic poet, whose early poems (1660) and first play (1664) enjoyed no great success, but in 1665 was awarded a small royal pension. This was increased after the production of his later plays, which included *Andromaque* (1667), *Britannicus* (1669), and *Phèdre* (1677), and eventually he was appointed to a lucrative venal office and the post of royal historiographer (1677). After this Racine left the theatre for some years and became one of the intimate circle of King Louis XIV, for whom he wrote accounts of his campaigns. In 1698 he was disgraced, partly because of his contacts with the Jansenist Port Royal. His last works were of a religious nature and do not compare with his earlier writings.

RADAR. Though the scientific principles on which radar is based were common knowledge from the late 19th cent., their application to the practical task of detecting aircraft or ships came only in the 1930s. Known initially in some countries as 'radio detection' or 'radio location', but from 1942 as radar (an abbreviation of 'radio detection and ranging'), the system is based on the pulsation of radio waves, the detection of their echo from objects, and measurements to calculate range and distance. The stimulus that gave rise to its simultaneous development in Britain, the US, Germany, and France was the need to discover some means of providing early warning of air attack to enable fighters to become airborne in time to intercept bombers. In Britain, Sir Henry Tizard's Committee for the Scientific Survey of Air Defence adopted the system pioneered by Sir Robert Watson-Watt of the National Physical Laboratory in 1935; by March 1939 a chain of 20 ('CH') stations had been constructed from St Andrews in Scotland down the east coast to Southampton. By the beginning of the Second World War the Germans had also developed a similar system based on their Freya and Wurtzburg installations. The fitting of radar in aircraft and ships was very largely a British achievement: limitations of space demanded a small, short-wave set which it was not possible to construct in large quantities until two physicists at Birmingham University, Boot and Randall, invented the resonant cavity magnetron in 1940. This discovery was shared with the Americans and gave the Allies an outstanding advantage in the war, when there emerged a great variety of uses for radar.

In air defence it played a crucial role in the defence of Britain, especially during the battle of Britain and the 'Blitz' and during the V1 and V2 attacks of 1944–5; conversely, Britain was forced to find ways of jamming the German radar system during her strategic bombing offensive against Germany. Radar was also used to control fighter operations from the ground, to direct anti-aircraft gunfire, as an air navigational aid (Oboe), and as a means of helping to locate targets in night bombing operations (H_2S). It was of decisive importance in the anti-submarine operations in the Atlantic and the Pacific: aircraft fitted with short-wave radar could locate surfaced U-boats at long range or at night, and the equipping of Allied aircraft with the centimetric radar sets in 1943 was responsible in large measure for the winning of the battle of the Atlantic that year. It was also used for ship-to-ship detection, notably in the pursuit of the *Bismarck* and in the closing night stages of the battle of Cape Matapan. Since the war there have been further refinements in equipment and techniques. Apart from its use in the field of civil aviation it plays a central role in the weapons and defence systems associated with nuclear missiles. NRB

RADBRUCH, GUSTAV (1878–1949), German lawyer and social democrat politician who belonged to the Hofgeismar group of right-wing socialists and favoured the adoption of nationalism as part of his party's policy. As justice minister (1921–2, 1923) he helped to draft the Decree for the Protection of the Republic (1922), which prescribed strong penalties for anti-republican activities, and to some extent limited freedom of expression. He resigned from Stresemann's coalition cabinet in Nov. 1923. Radbruch was also an academic jurist and published a standard textbook on jurisprudence.

RADCLIFFE AWARD (1947), continuous partition line proposed by the Radcliffe commission as the frontier of the two new states, the Indian Union and Pakistan, in the two provinces of the Punjab and Bengal. Under the chairmanship of Sir Cyril (later Lord) Radcliffe, the plan was carried through within six weeks, starting on 8 July 1947. On 16 Aug. 1947 the recommendation was accepted as the basis of partition by the leaders of the Indian National Congress and the All-India Muslim League.

RADEK, KARL (1885–1939), Russian politician, who was born Sobelsohn, of Jewish parents, at Lvov. He played a leading part in the Polish and German SD parties before 1914. In 1915 he was a member of the Zimmerwald 'left'. His clandestine contacts with the German government enabled him to help the transfer of Lenin from Switzerland to Petrograd and he accompanied Trotsky to the peace negotiations at Brest-Litovsk. After the First World War he became a leading member of the Comintern and was present at the Baku congress of the peoples of the east (1920). He was discredited in 1923, both because he dissuaded Brandler, a German communist leader, from starting a revolution in Saxony, and because of his 'Schlagetter' speech in which he encouraged right-wing groups in Germany to make common cause with the communists against the Versailles powers. In 1924 he was dropped from the central committee. Later he was involved in the fall of Trotsky and exiled to Tobolsk (1927). He was one of the first of the Trotskyite group to make his peace with Stalin, and he probably denounced Blumkin, the Trotskyite GPU agent, to Stalin. He was rewarded by being reinstated in the party and was given the job of writing on Soviet foreign policy for the press. He was tried in 1937 with the 'Anti-Soviet Trotskyite Centre'.

RADESCU, NICOLAE (1876–1953), Rumanian soldier and politician, who formed a government in Dec. 1944. He made a mistake in reserving the ministry of interior for himself, while allowing the communists, chiefly through Teohari Georgescu, to manage the day-to-day security matters. The communists continually harassed the government and in Feb. 1945 troops were involved in a shooting incident with communist demonstrators. The communists demanded Radescu's resignation and arrest. In the midst of chaos he sought asylum in the British embassy and eventually resigned (March 1945).

RADETZKY, JOSEPH (1766–1858), Austrian soldier and governor-general in Italy, who was famous for his training

methods. He won the battles of Custozza and Novara during the revolutions of 1848–9. Johann Strauss's famous *Radetzkymarsch* is dedicated to him.

RADFORD, ARTHUR WILLIAM (1896–), US sailor and pioneer in naval aviation, who served with the US navy in both World Wars. He became chairman of the Joint Chiefs of Staff (1953–7). In 1954 he argued for the use of tactical atomic weapons in Indo-China.

RADHAKANATA DEB, SIR RAJA (1794–1867), Indian leader of the orthodox Hindu community in Bengal, who opposed the Brahmo Samaj and social reform. He was interested in disseminating English education and in reviving Sanskrit learning. He wrote a comprehensive Sanskrit dictionary.

RADHAKRISHNAN, SARVAPALLI (1888–), Indian philosopher, diplomat, and president of India (1962–7). After being professor of philosophy at Calcutta University (1921–1939), Spalding professor of Eastern religions at Oxford (1936–52), and vice-chancellor of Benares Hindu University (1939–48), he became ambassador to the Soviet Union (1949–52). He returned to India to become vice-president (1952–62) and subsequently president. He published major works on classical Hindu philosophy and books which sought to explain Hinduism to European readers, *eg*, *The Hindu View of Life* (1927). In his *Eastern Religions and Western Thought* (1939) he attempted to reconcile Hindu and Western philosophy.

RADICAL CIVIC UNION (Unión Cívica Radical), Argentine Radical Party, founded in 1891 by Leandro Alem. Until the late 1880s the political domination—enforced by widespread fraud—of the oligarchy of landlords, bankers, and merchants who presided over Argentina's rapid economic development, went largely unchallenged. However, the subsequent business collapse, and the corruption and incompetence of Juárez Celman's administration, resulted in urban middle-class business and professional men demanding reforms. Under the leadership of the lawyer and politician Leandro Alem, they campaigned for honest government, civil rights, equitable taxes, and an end to the enrichment of political favourites. In a short revolt in July 1890 they overthrew Juárez Celman, who was replaced by a much more astute oligarch, Carlos Pellegrini. The Radicals remained in opposition (1891–1916), boycotting elections and entering into conspiracies. On Alem's suicide in 1896, the leadership of the RCU passed to his nephew, Hipólito Yrigoyen. In these years Argentina's urban population, already swollen by immigrants, expanded still further; demands for effective popular representation, which were supported by Socialists and Progressive Democrats, became at length irresistible. In 1912 a law was passed that ensured free secret manhood suffrage, and in 1916, in Argentina's first free national elections, Yrigoyen became president.

His term of office (1916–22) was followed by that of Marceló T. de Alvear (1922–8). Yrigoyen returned to office in 1928, but his second term was marred by corruption among his subordinates. Though incorruptible himself, he was aged and erratic and unable to cope with the effects of the worldwide economic crisis. In Sept. 1930 he was deposed during a military coup which enjoyed wide civilian support.

The 14 years of middle-class Radical rule were generally accounted a failure. Despite their nationalist rhetoric, the Radicals had done little to affect Argentina's traditional subservience to the demands of foreign markets or her dependence on foreign manufactures, and capital. Some social legislation had been enacted, but Yrigoyen had savagely repressed a general strike in 1919, and had repeatedly intervened in provincial affairs, thereby damaging Argentina's fragile federal structure. The Radicals had also shown a tendency towards factionalism, splitting into followers of

Yrigoyen ('personalists'), and his enemies ('anti-personalists'), who grouped themselves about Alvear.

After 1930, the Radicals, although remaining the largest middle-class political movement, were in power only twice for short periods. Arturo Frondizi of the Intransigent faction (UCRI) sought (1958–62) to restore the nation's economy and simultaneously to reincorporate Perónist labour into political life; he was deposed by implacably anti-Perónist army officers. A similar fate befell the less dynamic Arturo Illía, of the Popular faction (UCRP), who was removed in 1966 to make way for the openly militarist regime of Gen. Onganía. The historic shortcomings of the Radicals recapitulate in miniature the overall failings of Argentine liberal democracy.

P. G. Snow, *Argentine Radicalism: the history and doctrine of the Radical Civil Union* (Iowa City, 1965).   RCN

RADICAL PARTY in Italy, founded in 1878 by ex-republicans under the leadership of A. Bertani. It advocated advanced democracy within the monarchy. Moderates among its membership achieved some electoral success early in the 20th cent. and joined various governments, promoting educational reform, franchise extensions, and divorce plans, but disputes over the issues involved in the First World War led to their decline.

In 1955 E. Rossi and other progressive liberals founded a new Radical Party which promoted congresses, studies, and discussions for reforming centre-left policies, and supported some local councillors.

RADICAL REPUBLICANS in the US, anti-slavery Republicans, who viewed the restoration or 'reconstruction' of the Union after the end of the American Civil War as a congressional rather than a presidential prerogative. Described by their opponents and by many historians as collectively vindictive, profane, hypocritical, and ugly, such congressional Republican leaders as Thaddeus Stevens, Zachary Chandler, Henry Wilson, Benjamin Wade, and Charles Sumner believed that the former Confederate states had committed political suicide and were now in the condition of subject territories. They were determined to maintain the political supremacy of the Republican Party and to preserve legislation enacted during the war which gave help to Northern businessmen. Also, they wished to punish the 'treason' of secession. They had a real concern for the welfare of the freed Negro and viewed Negro suffrage as the *sine qua non* of reconstruction.

The radicals in Congress, regarding Lincoln's plan of reconstruction as too lenient, secured the passage of the Wade–Davis Bill (1864), which provided for congressional reconstruction with a majority of the electorate in any former Confederate state required to take an oath of loyalty to the Union before readmission. Lincoln vetoed the bill, but his successor, Andrew Johnson, attempting to continue Lincoln's programme, while simultaneously handing out wholesale pardons to former Confederates, met growing and skilful opposition from the radicals. This culminated in an attempt to impeach him which failed by only one vote (1868).

Congressional radicals saw the black codes enacted by the early post-war Southern legislatures as an attempt to fasten a perpetually servile status on the freedman. They accordingly made the destruction of these codes, together with aid to the freedmen, the cornerstones of reconstruction and secured the passage of a Civil Rights Bill, over Johnson's veto (1866), which forbade states to discriminate against citizens on grounds of race or colour. The 14th (1868) and 15th (1870) Amendments to the US constitution represented their final triumph.

In their conception of federal power, their egalitarianism and their recognition that the South, although prostrate, was neither contrite nor prepared to extend the Negro his constitutional rights, the radical Republicans were the innovators, idealists, and realists of their day. Thaddeus Stevens demanded 'a radical reorganization in Southern institutions,

habits and manners'. That this did not occur is the real tragedy of reconstruction.

W. R. Brock, *An American Crisis: Congress and Reconstruction, 1865–67* (London, 1963).
K. M. Stampp, *The Era of Reconstruction, 1865–1877* (New York, 1965).   JW

RADICALISM in Britain, desire to evaluate and alter political institutions and social conditions. In the second half of the 18th cent. it inspired an articulate minority of Whigs and dissenters to press for the reform of parliament, and, under the impact of the French Revolution, broadened into a movement of popular agitation which saw the reform of parliament as a means of changing society and bettering the lot of the working man. The London Corresponding Society (1792), in particular, pointed the way forward to the working man's politics of the 19th cent.

After being driven underground by government repression and losing support through the course of events in France, intellectual radicalism re-emerged early in the 19th cent. in the utilitarian philosophy of Bentham, and popular radicalism in the movement, led by Francis Burdett, William Cobbett, and Francis Place, which led to the Peterloo Massacre (1819) and culminated in the reform of parliament in 1832. In the reformed parliament a small group of radicals pressed for further reform, but they were not supported by the Whigs, who had given qualified support to radical aims before 1832.

The mid-19th cent. saw a divergence between those radicals who were involved in militant working-class politics and those of the Manchester school, who concentrated on financial rather than political reform. The Crimean War (1854) also stimulated conflicting radical attitudes, some radicals welcoming and others opposing it. Despite these differences there was a consistent radical trend towards the further reform of parliament, kept alive by the Little Charter movement and inspired by the 1848 revolutions in Europe and the Risorgimento in Italy. An upsurge of popular enthusiasm followed the American Civil War and Garibaldi's visit to Britain (1864), leading to the formation of the Reform League (1865) and helping to convert both Whigs and Tories to the need for reform. Radicalism played an important part in creating the climate in which the second reform bill was passed in 1867 and the conversion of both parties to policies of improvement and progress was the result of a century of cumulative radical protest.

S. Maccoby, *English Radicalism, 1762–85* (London, 1935).
S. Maccoby, *English Radicalism, 1786–1832* (London, 1955).
          SH

RADISHCHEV, ALEXANDER NIKOLAYEVICH (1749–1802), Russian revolutionary and critic of Catherine II, who is regarded as a founder of the Russian revolutionary movement. He was educated in the ideals of the Enlightenment and believed in equality before the law and in the right to happiness. His *Journey from St Petersburg to Moscow* (1790) coincided with news of the French Revolution, and revealed his moral indignation at the conditions of the peasants, which, he claimed, invited and justified revolt against the nobility. The book was an open indictment of autocratic rule and advocated constitutional monarchy and a legislative assembly. Radishchev was accordingly exiled to Siberia, but later was appointed by Alexander I to serve on a legal commission. His death, however, prevented him from doing so.

RADOWITZ, JOSEPH MARIA (1797–1853), Prussian soldier and politician, who sought, unsuccessfully, to bring about German military unification under Prussia. As a close friend of King Frederick William IV, he had great influence on Prussian policy, and in 1850 became foreign minister, and attempted to create a German union excluding Austria. After Olmütz he was dismissed.

RADSTADT, PEACE OF (1714), one of the treaties ending the War of the Spanish Succession. It was negotiated by

Marshal Villars on behalf of France, and Eugéne of Savoy on behalf of the emperor, and confirmed to France all the territories of Alsace, including Strasbourg and Landau, but restored all French conquests to the east of the Rhine. Recognition was given to the emperor's acquisitions of the former Spanish Netherlands, Milan, Sardinia, and Naples, as well as of fortresses and harbours on the coast of Tuscany. The electors of Cologne and Bavaria were also reinstated in their territories. However, the peace left Spain and the Emperor Charles VI still officially at war. Neither was satisfied, the emperor still coveting the Spanish Crown, while Philip V was determined to regain his former Italian possessions. Their enmity, which threatened the peace and stability of Europe, resulted in Stanhope's policy of collective security by alliances to prevent war.

RADZIWILL, KARL STANISLAUS (1734–90), Polish political figure who led opposition to the pro-Russian Czartoryski family. He opposed political concessions to non-Catholics and joined the confederations of Radom and Bar against King Stanislaus Poniatowski. He fled to Turkey, but was allowed to return after the First Partition of Poland.

RADZIWILL FAMILY, Lithuanian–Polish noble house, raised to the rank of princes of the realm in the 16th cent. Nicholas Radziwill (1515–65), known as 'the Black', prince of Nieswiez and governor of Vilna, became an ardent Calvinist, published a Polish translation of the Bible (1563), and helped to establish Protestantism strongly in Lithuania. Some of the family, however, returned to Catholicism under Sigismund III. The wealthy but eccentric Charles Stanislas (1734–90) opposed the election of Poniatowski as king (1764) and was therefore exiled. Prince Anthony Henry (1775–1833), who married a daughter of Prince Ferdinand of Prussia, was a musician and composer. His great-grandson, Prince Janus (1880–1967), supported Pilsudski after his coup (1926) and after 1930 served on the foreign affairs committee. His son, Stanislas (1914–   ), married Caroline Lee Bouvier (1959), sister-in-law of the US President John F. Kennedy.

RAEDER, ERICH (1877–1960), German sailor, who commanded a cruiser in the First World War and became chief of the naval command in 1928. He played a vital part (1933–9) in the reconstruction of the German navy. Raeder was a strategist of skill and vision whose ideas on the application of German sea power and the conduct of the Second World War as a whole were constantly blocked by Hitler, Göring, and Keitel. Hitler's declaration of war in 1939 found the German navy still weak, as Raeder had set 1944–5 as the date for completing its expansion. Hitler's decision to invade Norway was a direct result of Raeder's suggestions (Oct. 1939), but the latter's desire to defeat Britain by intensifying the naval war after the fall of France was frustrated by Hitler's refusal to strengthen the submarine arm, *eg*, in Sept. 1940 Germany had no more U-boats than in Sept. 1939. In 1941 Raeder wanted to concentrate a fleet in the Mediterranean instead of attacking Russia, but this was prevented by Hitler's strategic aims and by the failure to win Spain's co-operation. Raeder's position was undermined in May 1941, when his desire to cut off British trade led to the loss of the *Bismarck*; his resignation in 1943 followed a similar setback which led Hitler to order the paying-off of capital ships and consequently the abandonment of Raeder's conception of a balanced fleet. At the Nuremberg war trials he was sentenced to nine years' imprisonment (1946–55).

RAETIA, Roman province covering the Tyrol and parts of Bavaria and Switzerland, south of the Danube. It was annexed (*c.* 16 BC), but was garrisoned only by cohorts of *auxilia* till the late 2nd cent. AD. Its mountainous character inhibited urban development, but among the principal towns were Augusta Vindelicorum (Augsburg) and Castra Regina (Regensburg). From the 3rd cent. it was exposed to attacks by the Allemanni, who ultimately settled in most of it in the 5th cent.

RAFFLES, SIR THOMAS STAMFORD (1781–1826), British colonial administrator and founder of Singapore. He was of limited education, but outstanding ability, energy, and intellectual curiosity. He earned the attention of Lord Minto only three years after his appointment to Penang (1805), by his well-argued appeal against the planned destruction of Malacca by the British (1808). The governor-general used him as 'Agent-General for the Malay States' (1810–11) in preparing his attack on Java. Raffles gathered intelligence for him, negotiated with anti-Dutch Indonesian rulers, and began to formulate a grand design for a second British raj in South-East Asia.

After the British conquest, Raffles remained as lieutenant-governor of Java (1811–16). He initiated an impressive range of reforms, generally directed towards the substitution of direct rule and a liberal economic system for the Dutch use of Javanese regents in an exploitative economy. He attempted to make the village headman the basis of government, responsible for the collection of his novel land rent, which replaced the Dutch system of tribute through forced deliveries of produce. Raffles also attacked slavery, reformed justice and finance, and began the scholarly investigation of Indonesian society. In the short period allowed him, most of these reforms were only partially effected, and produced more disruption than profit to the East India Co., who therefore replaced him (1816). Nevertheless, his work laid the basis for a more efficient restored Dutch regime.

On being appointed lieutenant-governor of the decaying Bencoolen settlement (1818–24), Raffles continued his political and scientific activities, sending missions to Minangkabau, Nias, Palembang, and elsewhere. He frequently defied instructions in the hope of preventing the Dutch from reassuming their dominance of Indonesia. All his schemes were repudiated, however, except his occupation of Singapore island (1819), the immediate commercial value of which to Britain outweighed Dutch protests.

C. E. Wurtzburg, *Raffles of the Eastern Isles* (London, 1954).
AJSR

RAGHIB PASHA (*reg.* 1757–63), Ottoman Grand Vizier, who sought to maintain peaceful relations with the states of Europe. He concluded (1761) a pact of friendship with Prussia. At home he tried to restore the finances of the central regime and to bring the armed forces of the state into a more effective condition.

RAGLAN, FITZROY JAMES HENRY SOMERSET, 1st Baron (1788–1855), British soldier, who was commander-in-chief of the British forces in the Crimea (1854–5). He shared responsibility for the ill-fated Charge of the Light Brigade and for British incompetence in the conduct of the campaign. As a young man he fought in the Peninsular campaign and at Waterloo (1815).

RAGNAR LODBROK (d. *c.* 862), Viking leader who raided Paris in 848 and was bought off by King Charles of West Francia. He then harried in England and was reputedly captured and executed by King Aelle of Northumbria, whose father is believed to have been killed by Ragnar. The invasion of Northumbria in 867 by Ragnar's three sons bent on avenging their father led to the destruction of that kingdom and the death of King Aelle. Thereafter until 954 southern Northumbria was controlled by Viking rulers.

RAGUNATH RAO (RAGHOBA) (*fl.* 18th cent.), son of the second Maratha peshwa, Baji Rao I, and father of the last peshwa, Baji Rao II; he was himself peshwa (1773–4). An unsuccessful attempt by the Bombay government in 1775 to reinstall him as peshwa led to war with the Marathas until the treaty of Salbai (1782).

RAGUSA (DUBROVNIK), seaport of Dalmatia, founded at the time of the Slav invasions into the Balkan world. Ragusa, being at the end of the trade routes running from various parts of the Balkans to the Adriatic Sea, became an important centre of commerce. The town was dependent at first on the Venetians (1205–1358) and then on the Hungarians (1358–1526). After the battle of Mohacs in 1526 it paid tribute to the Turks, enjoying in return large commercial privileges within the Ottoman empire. Its large merchant marine became particularly important in the 16th cent., competing successfully with the Venetians.

RAIKES, ROBERT (1755–1811), English founder of the Sunday school movement. From 1757 he was the proprietor of the *Gloucester Journal*. Noting the plight of neglected children, he began, with Thomas Stock, the first Sunday school (*c.* 1780), the idea of which he successfully publicized.

RAILROAD LAND GRANTS in the US (1850–71), grants of public land other than the right of way and depot sites (1835–) to subsidize the construction of railroads. The terms of the initial land grant (1850) provided that alternate sections of land for six miles (9·6 kms) on either side of the right of way from Chicago to Mobile, AL, and from Cairo, IL, to Dubuque, IA, should be given to the states in which the public land lay and through which the railroad would pass. This land was to be sold and the proceeds used to build the railroad. The rapid completion of the Illinois Central Railroad (1856) gave a great impetus to land settlement and speculation. The success of this railroad stimulated a scramble for land grants, and 14·6 million acres (59,000 sq. kms) were given to railroads in 1856 and 5·1 million (20,600 sq. kms) in 1857. Altogether, 129 million acres (522,000 sq. kms) of public land were donated by Congress to the states (37·8 million—153,000 sq. kms) and to individual railroads (91·2 million—369,000 sq. kms) for the purpose of railroad construction. Most important and grandest in conception were the huge land grants to the four transcontinental railroads (1869–83). Those to the Union Pacific and Central Railroads (1862) were generous, but the Northern Pacific Railroad received a grant (1864) which was even more extensive, amounting to 39 million acres (158,000 sq. kms). The unprecedented liberality of Pacific railroad land grants was due largely to the difficult terrain through which the railroads were to pass, and to the political influences of their promoters in the US Congress.

Land grant railroads organized land departments and undertook strenuous advertising campaigns in the eastern US and in Europe to attract settlers, and their lands were sold on long-term credit at prevailing prices. Land reformers condemned land grants to railroads as contrary to the homestead principle and eventually succeeded in ending the policy (1871). However, the building of the railroads, and the land grant policy, made possible the rapid settlement of the American West.

Paul W. Gates, *History of Public Land Development* (Washington, DC, 1968).
Benjamin H. Hibbard, *A History of the Public Land Policies* (Madison, 1965).   AB

RAILWAYS in Australia. The dearth of navigable rivers and the vast distances made railways unusually important in Australia. By 1920, when the main era of tracklaying had ended, Australia ranked seventh in railway mileage and had, in proportion to population, a greater length of track than any other country. Nevertheless, much of the interior remained hundreds of miles from the nearest railway station.

While private companies built some railways, mostly to mining fields, the colonial (later state) governments dominated the railways. Mileage of government track increased from 23 miles (32 kms) in 1855 to 4000 (6440 kms) in 1881, to 16,000 (25,700 kms) in 1911, and to a total of just over 27,000 (43,500 kms) in the 1930s. As the capital cities were

ports, and already linked by steamships, the inter-capital railways came late; the first, between Melbourne and Sydney, was opened in 1883, but the transcontinental railway between Adelaide and Perth was not completed until 1917. Many of these inter-state railways were impaired by breaks of gauge, since NSW built 4 ft 8½in. (143 cms) track, Vic. and parts of SA 5 ft 3 in. (160 cms), and the remaining colonies 3 ft 6 in. (105 cms). The most inconvenient breaks were eliminated by standard gauge tracks in the 1960s, and by 1970 the same train could travel from Sydney to Perth.

RAILWAYS in Britain. The first railway with modern features, controlling its own rolling stock, relying on locomotives for traction, and open for public traffic in both goods and passengers, was the Liverpool and Manchester Railway of 1830. It created an enthusiasm for railway building which reached its highest levels in the 'railway manias' (1837–40, 1845–9). By 1852 the basic trunk system of Britain was complete and by 1870 most of the network was made. Amalgamations by then had reduced the number of companies to a little over 100 and some level of co-ordination between them had been established.

The British experience in railways was unusual in that it caused neither the specific development of new areas of settlement nor the impetus of the Industrial Revolution. But railways did alter the distribution of population and increased the scale of economic change. The cheap transport they provided made possible the chief characteristic of the late Victorian economy of geographical specialization. Railways were expensive to build, costing on average £40,000 a mile, and most systems had double tracks with built-up stations and bridges and used land that was expensive because it had already been developed. Consequently railways had a marked influence on the provision of both capital and labour. At the peak of the 'railway mania' of the 1840s they absorbed nearly 70 per cent of British capital investment. They led to the extension of the principle of limited liability, enlarged the size of the investing public, and caused the growth of provincial stock exchanges. Labour was involved not only in building them, with few mechanical aids, but also in working the system.

Though railways were initially built to transport goods, particularly coal, they made their early profits predominantly from passenger traffic. However, they increased the demand for coal, iron, steel, and building materials. Their effect on agriculture was delayed until the 1870s and in purely agricultural districts railways did no better than had canals.

Railway competition forced canal companies to lower their rates (only the efficient companies remained in business) and rapidly put an end to the system of stage-coaches and of long-distance road transport. As a result, turnpike trusts gradually ceased to operate, and in the second half of the 19th cent. the road system carried only local traffic, including the increasing serving railheads.

The speculative operations of early railway financiers, the dangers of monopoly, and the companies' demands for urban land led to early government intervention and control. Under the so-called 'Cheap Trains Act' (1844) fares were controlled and later the Board of Trade enforced standard methods of auditing and safety precautions. In the 1880s co-ordinated rates were laid down by parliament, but difficulties involved in changing these in a period of rising costs contributed to bad labour relations which lasted until 1914. Railways were effectively taken over by the government during the First World War and organized into four big amalgamations which continued afterwards.

Competition with road transport in general goods and in short-haul passenger routes led to an absolute decline in rail traffic between the wars and put an economic strain on the railways, whose overheads were very heavy. The Second World War again saw state control and a short period of profitability and was followed by nationalization, which had been under consideration as early as 1844.

The 1960s saw the closure of unprofitable local lines and

of some stretches of main lines where duplication, from the days of 19th-cent. competition in building, existed.

M. Robbins, *The Railway Age* (London, 1962).
H. J. Dyos and D. H. Aldcroft, *British Transport* (London, 1969).
                                                                    RMM

RAILWAYS in Canada. The first Canadian transcontinental railroad was the Canadian Pacific Railway. It had been originally mooted in the 1840s, but it did not become a serious proposition until British Columbia joined the Dominion of Canada (1871). Sir John Macdonald, the prime minister, after failing to obtain co-operation of two competing groups, issued the Canadian Pacific Railway Co. charter (1872) to a consortium of Montreal capitalists led by Hugh Allan. A Liberal MP, L. S. Huntingdon, declared that the offer of the charter to Allan had been accompanied by a request for contributions to Conservative Party funds. The ensuing 'Pacific Scandal' brought down the government, which was replaced by the Liberals under William Lyon Mackenzie (1873), who favoured the railway but did not initiate its construction. BC threatened secession and extracted a promise of the railway from the British colonial secretary. On his return to power (1878), Macdonald chartered a new company which chose a southerly route from Lake Superior, on grounds of economy, and the railway was completed in 1885. The CPR was the only railway company to escape nationalization and show a profit after the First World War.

In 1880 the Hudson Bay Railway was planned to connect the Canadian prairie provinces. Its construction began in 1910 and was completed in 1931.

In 1917 the National Co. was established to include all Canadian railways, apart from the Canadian Pacific. The management of the company was given to the Canadian Railway Board. Demand for nationalization of the railroads had come from farmers, but it was the financial failure of the Canadian Northern and Grand Trunk railroads which led the Conservative Party to propose government ownership.

Railways in Canada totalled 17,000 miles (27,350 kms) of track in 1900, and by 1970 represented over 40,000 miles (64,360 kms).

RAILWAYS in Europe. These became important later than those of Britain, were subject to more state participation and control, and were on the whole more important economically and politically, Britain being an island with a lively coastal traffic.

The Belgians began building railways in 1833, at first importing rails and locomotives from Britain, but soon developing their own railway construction industry, which exported to other European countries. Germany, Holland, and Scandinavia soon followed suit, allowing private capital to take the initiative, but retaining state control through short concessions. By 1860, Prussia controlled over half her national network. The real extension of the French railway network came with the Second Empire and the creation of the *Crédit Mobilier*. The Habsburg empire planned a state network with Trieste as an international port, but state finance was insufficient and the network was finally completed by Pereire and Rothschild capital.

Russia built her first, very short, railway in 1836, but most of her network was built after the establishment of an Anglo-French company (1857). The important transcontinental lines—the Trans-Caspian (1880–8) and the Trans-Siberian (1891–1903)—came at the end of the century. These lines made Russian penetration of Asia real as well as political.

Political motives were involved in the penetration of the Alps, the tunnels of Semmering (1854), Mont-Cenis (1858–1871), and St Gotthard (1882) reflecting the alliances and political preoccupations of the day. The Arlberg (1884) allowed France to bypass south Germany to reach Austria and south-east Europe.

The railways stimulated the economy of the countries concerned and only after 1860 were the military and strategic possibilities even considered. Politically they acted as a unifying factor. After 1860 a certain amount of economic colonialism was involved in the financial arrangements, and by this time Britain, whose finance and expertise had been important in the 1840s and 1850s, was more concerned with railways in India and South America.

In the middle of the 20th cent. European railways faced a decided challenge from road and air traffic in terms of both passengers and freight.   DMK

RAILWAYS in India were first seriously considered during the governor-generalship of Lord Dalhousie (1848–56). Dalhousie himself provided the pattern with his Minute of 1853, which was accepted by the British government. The first 200 miles (322 kms) of completed track proved so useful during the Indian Mutiny (1857–8) that even in the period of financial stringency following the mutiny there was general approval for large-scale developments. The motives for construction were both strategic and commercial.

By 1859 the construction of 5000 miles (8045 kms) of track was approved. By 1900 the main features of the system, with 25,000 miles (46,225 kms) of track, were complete. By 1939 some 43,000 miles (69,200 kms) had been built in British India. There were, in 1970, about 36,000 miles (58,000 kms) of track in India and over 7000 miles (11,300 kms) in Pakistan. The plan of development was the linking of the ports of Calcutta, Madras, Bombay, and Karachi with the hinterland, and a trunk line in northern India from Calcutta to Peshawar and links from Bombay to Calcutta and Delhi. From these feeder lines were developed as demand justified. At first a uniform gauge of 5 ft 6 in. (168 cms), intermediate between both the European and the US standard gauge, and the Russian gauge, was planned. But from 1869, for reasons of economy, a metre gauge was introduced whose lines, originally intended as feeders to the broad gauge, developed into a separate system. A few narrow-gauge (2 ft 6 in) (76 cms) lines were also built.

At first the government sought to control construction by means of private companies with guaranteed profits. But scarcity of capital and high costs made progress slow. From 1869 the government constructed its own lines and leased them to operating companies on improved terms with an option to take over at the expiry of the lease. This tendency developed steadily until by 1939 three-quarters of the railways were state-owned and about a half state-operated. In independent India the whole system has been nationalized. Criticism turned on high cost of construction, alleged extravagance by the operating companies, inefficiency, and unsuitability to Indian conditions. Against this was the undeniable fact that construction had been sound, enabling the railways to take increasing loads and survive the strains of the two World Wars. From 1900 there was an operational profit; after the criticisms of the Acworth Commission (1921) reorganization led to a unified system controlled by a Railway Board with an independent budget.

The system provided India with an economic skeleton upon which the flesh of commerce and industry could grow. Though originally intended mainly to provide means of egress for raw materials to the ports, the system also met the needs of internal trade. In the Second World War it proved able to meet the double strain of east-to-west traffic for the Burma campaign and north-to-south traffic for food distribution. The independent government of India after 1947 recognized the worth of the system by reopening closed routes, strengthening existing lines and building new ones.

J. N. Sahni, *Indian Railways, One Hundred Years, 1853–1953* (New Delhi, 1953).
N. Sanyal, *Development of Indian Railways* (Calcutta, 1930).
                                                                    TGPS

RAILWAYS in the Far East. The development of this form of transport in East and South-East Asia began only after

1860. The first railway there was a short line constructed by the Dutch in Java and opened in 1867; it was followed by further construction in the Dutch East Indies in the following decades. Other colonial governments in South-East Asia followed suit. The French built a short line in Cochin-China in 1881, and in 1890 began one in Tongking. The governor-general, Paul Doumer, anxious to develop railways in Indo-China in order to attract investment, conceived a plan to build over 1000 miles (1609 kms) of track in 1898: it had been more than carried out by the time French colonial rule was interrupted by the Japanese coup in 1945. After 1880 lines were also built by the British in Malaya.

Of the countries in the area that retained their independence, Japan was clearly in the lead. Lines were opened from Tokyo to Yokohama (1872) and Kobe to Kyoto (1877), but building began in earnest only in the 1880s. By 1890, Japan had 1449 miles (2330 kms) of track, and over 5000 miles (8045 kms) by 1910. Private capital played an important part in the early years, but in 1906 legislation was passed to nationalize the greater part of the system. Expansion continued under state control, and by 1930 there were over 17,000 miles (27,380 kms) of railway in Japan.

Siam, anxious to modernize its government and economy in the 1890s, built its first line in 1892–3, and by 1900 had established rail links between Bangkok, Lopburi, and Khorat. In 1909 an Anglo-Thai agreement permitted the construction of the line from Singapore to Bangkok.

It is remarkable that, by comparison with India and even with Japan, the railway came late to China. This was due partly to the existence of a very effective system of inland waterways for transport in most of its regions; but also to the suspicions of conservative officials, who did not wish to see foreigners build railways, yet lacked the capital to do so themselves. In 1863 a high official, Li Hung-chang, rejected a foreign proposal to build a line from Shanghai to Suchow; and when in 1876 a line was built between Shanghai and Wusung without authorization, it was immediately bought up by the Chinese government and destroyed. As a result, the first effective railway in China, linking Tientsin and the Kaiping mines, was not opened until 1888. A line from Peking to Tientsin was opened in 1896, but at the end of the century China had less than 250 miles (402 kms) of railways.

Changes came with the 'scramble for concessions' in China in the later 1890s. By the end of 1898 the government had been forced to sign agreements with Western powers permitting them to build over 5000 miles (8045 kms) of railways. These included the Chinese Eastern Railway across northern Manchuria and the Southern Manchurian Railway down to Port Arthur, which played an important part in the Russo-Japanese War. By the end of the Ch'ing period, China had over 6000 miles (9650 kms) of railways, then further development was interrupted by the war-lord period. It was not resumed until after 1927; by the time of the Japanese attack on China ten years later the total mileage had risen to nearly 10,000 (16,090 kms) The war meant further interruption, and consequently much still remained to be done in the 1950s, when the communist regime made great efforts to catch up. A line from Chungking to Chengtu was completed in 1952, and another linking Peking with Ulan Bator in 1955.

Apart from this work in China, railway-building has become less important since 1945, in this as in other areas of the world. The Far East has far fewer railways, in proportion to both space and population, than Europe, North America, or India and Pakistan. The railway has given way to the motor vehicle and to aircraft as the most important means of mechanized communication and transport.   RBS

RAILWAYS in the US. Five systems of transcontinental railroads from the Mississippi valley to the Pacific coast were built in the period 1869–93. With the exception of the Great Northern, all were constructed with the aid of federal land grants. The movement to construct a transcontinental railroad began in the 1840s, but the question became intertwined in sectional politics, for it was believed that the section securing the eastern terminus would have a perpetual economic advantage. The report of the Pacific Railroad Survey (1855) found four routes practicable, but failed to silence sectional controversy. After the outbreak of the American Civil War Congress agreed on the central route through South Pass. In 1862 the Union Pacific Railroad was chartered to build west from the 100th meridian to the western boundary of Nevada territory and the Central Pacific to build from the Pacific coast to the Missouri valley, or until it met the Union Pacific. Each railroad was granted its right of way, plus ten alternative sections of public land for each mile of track laid, and was given loans of between $16,000 and $48,000 per mile of track, depending upon the nature of the terrain. After two years of delay Congress was forced to double the land grant and relegate the government loans to a second mortgage. Construction started in earnest in 1866 and the great race began. The two railroads eventually met at Promontory Point, near Ogden, UT, on 10 May 1869. The Atchison, Topeka and Santa Fé Railroad was chartered in 1859, had reached CO by 1873, and after numerous reorganizations gained a right of way to San Francisco and Los Angeles in 1883. The Northern Pacific (1864) was to take the northern route from Lake Superior to Puget Sound. Construction did not begin until 1870, despite generous land grants, and it did not reach Portland, OR, until 1883 and Seattle, WA, until 1887. The Texas and Pacific Railroad (1871) joined the Southern Pacific in 1882 and forged another transcontinental route across the south-west. The Great Northern (1889), the only transcontinental railroad not to receive massive federal land grants, resulted from the reorganization by James J. Hill (1838–1916) of the St Paul and Pacific Railroad; it reached Seattle in 1893. Promotion of this route was noteworthy for the organized immigration sponsored by the company to settle the lands along the right of way.

Thereafter further railroad construction was slight. More track was laid down in the period up to the First World War, but subsequent investment lay in double-tracking and in the improvement of rolling-stock. Railroads suffered in the 1930s through the Depression and the advent of the motor car, while the post-Second World War era of domestic airline expansion offered a further challenge. But the major importance of the railroad as a conveyor of freight was sustained.   AB

RAINBOROUGH, THOMAS (d. 1648), English soldier and republican, who was a colonel under both Lord Fairfax and the Earl of Manchester in the Civil Wars and commanded a regiment at Naseby (1645). He played a prominent part in the Putney Debates (Oct.–Nov. 1647) of the army council. As a leader of the republican officers, he supported the Levellers' Agreement of the People and called for a democratic extension of the suffrage. He was in command at the siege of Pontefract Castle, and was later murdered by Royalists at Doncaster.

RAJA HAJI (d. 1784), Bugis warrior, who, as *Raja Muda* (viceroy) of Johor-Riau (1777–84), posed a serious threat to Dutch Malacca (1782–4) until his death during a siege of the city.

RAJA KECHIL (d. 1745), Minangkabau (Sumatra) adventurer, who seized the throne, first of Siak (c. 1713), then of Johor-Riau (1718), claiming to be the son of the assassinated (1699) Sultan Mahmud. His subsequent expulsion from Johor-Riau by Bugis warriors (1721) marked the beginning of Bugis ascendency in the sultanate.

RAJAGOPALACHARI, CHAKRAVARTI (1879–), Indian nationalist politician, and last governor-general of India (1948–50). As Gandhi's chief lieutenant in Madras, he was the dominant figure in the Madras Congress until the end of the 1930s. He was also a leading figure in the Working Committee until he resigned (1942), disagreeing with policy on the Pakistan question. He came back into Congress at the end of the Second World War and was a member of the Interim government (1946–7) before becoming, in succession, governor of West Bengal (1947–8) and governor-general. After his term as governor-general, he joined Nehru's cabinet as minister without portfolio and was later home minister (1951). He returned to Madras as chief minister (1952–4), but became increasingly critical of Congress's socialist policies and drifted away from Congress. He became, in 1959, one of the founders of the conservative Swatantra Party.

RAJAGRIHA (RAJGIR), earliest capital of the ancient Indian kingdom of Magadha (approximately present Bihar), situated about 50 miles (80 kms) south of Patna. It flourished in the time of Lord Buddha during the reigns of Bimbisara (c. 540–490 BC) and Ajatasatru (c. 490–460), but in the middle of the 5th cent. BC the capital was transferred to Pataliputra (Patna) and Rajagriha subsequently declined. Its huge walls, 25 miles (40 kms) long, still testify to its ancient greatness.

RAJASINHA II (reg. 1635–87), King of Kandy, Ceylon, who was an autocratic ruler of strong personality and marked ability. After defeating the Portuguese (1638), he negotiated with the Dutch in order to oust them, which he eventually did (1656). He was, however, angry when the Dutch took over the Portuguese possessions instead of handing them over to him, as agreed, but the Dutch claimed that Rajasinha had not paid his share of the campaign's cost. Thereafter his relations with them deteriorated.

RAJASINHA, SRI VIKRAMA (reg. 1798–1815), King of Kandy, Ceylon, was a Malabar by race. Some Kandyan chiefs intrigued with the British against him and in 1815 an expedition was sent to depose him. He was exiled to India and proved to be the last King of Kandy.

RAJASTHAN, state of the Indian union, formed (1948) out of the princely states of Rajputana. Jaipur is its capital.

RAJATARANGINI, River of Kings, name of the great chronicle of Kashmir, composed by Kalhana, son of a high court official, in c. AD 1150. It describes the history of Kashmir from the earliest times to that of its composition. It is based on a critical analysis of earlier chronicles and other texts, but Kalhana also made extensive use of official documents such as land grant deeds and foundation charters of temples. In the last part he writes also from personal knowledge. Though dealing with only a small part of southern Asia, the *Rajatarangini* has a richness of detail unequalled in ancient southern Asia except in Ceylon.

RAJK, LASZLO (1909–49), Hungarian politician, who joined the Communist Party and was imprisoned (1932–3). He then fought with the international brigade in Spain (1936–9). He was interned in France (1939–41), then taken to Germany, but was released as the result of the intervention of his brothers, members of the Arrow Cross movement. He returned to Hungary (1945), was appointed secretary-general of the Hungarian Workers (communist) Party, and minister of the interior (1946–8), then minister of foreign affairs (1948–9). He thus played a key role in the establishment of communist rule in Hungary. None the less, he was a victim of the first stage in the purge of communist leaders in the Soviet bloc. He was accused of being an employee of US and Yugoslav intelligence and tried in one of the most grandiose trials staged outside the Soviet Union. He was condemned and executed (Sept. 1949). His reputation was rehabilitated in 1956.

RAJPUTS (from Sanskrit *rajaputra*, 'prince'), Indian caste consisting of a large number (often fixed at 36) of royal clans organized along quasi-feudal lines in Rajputana (Rajasthan), India, where they constitute the dominant caste. The Rajputs distinguish themselves by a special way of life with a strong emphasis on honour and chivalry. Self-immolation of widows (sati or suttee) was more prevalent in Rajputana than anywhere else in India. As the Rajputs appear relatively late in Indian history—they are not attested before the 7th cent. AD—their emergence has often been associated with foreign invasions, notably that of the Central Asian Hunas (Huns) in the 6–7th cents AD. Although some foreign admixtures are likely, it now seems that the Rajputs were originally essentially Indian tribes in areas such as those around Mount Abu, which came into the fold of Hinduism at a relatively late stage.

A number of ancient Indian royal dynasties are of Rajput stock, notably the Pratiharas of Kanauj, the Cahumanas (Chauhans) in different parts of Rajasthan, the Chaulukyas (Solankis) of Gujarat, and the Yadavas of Devagiri.

Many Rajputs fought with distinction against the Muslims (11th–13th cents AD), and some, like the Chauhans, with remarkable valour, but internal divisions, especially rivalry between clans, affected the success of their resistance.

RAJYA SABHA, 'Council of States', the 250-member upper house of the Indian parliament, presided over by the vice-president of India. The members are elected indirectly by the state legislatures, except for 12 who are appointed by the president as representatives of the arts or professions. One-third of the members retire every second year. The Rajya Sabha has the same ordinary powers of legislation as the lower house, the Lok Sabha, but has no original financial powers and its amendments can be rejected by the lower house.

RÁKÓCZY, FRANCIS II LEOPOLD, Count (1657–1735), Prince of Transylvania (reg. 1704–35), Hungarian rebel leader, grandson of George Rákóczy II and Peter Zrini and stepson of Thököly, a gentle and reluctant organizer of the great revolt of 1703–11 against the Habsburg emperors, Leopold and Joseph. Brought up in Habsburg court circles and a Jesuit foundation in Bohemia, he became the most powerful magnate in north-east Hungary and was imprisoned for corresponding with Leopold's enemy, Louis XIV. He escaped to Poland, where he joined the rebel leader, Nicholas Berczenyi. In 1703 he returned to Hungary, when the Habsburgs were absorbed in the conflict over the Spanish Succession, raised a revolt against royal oppression which had intensified since 1689, and was declared Prince of Transylvania. With widespread support from nobles and Protestants, he issued a solemn manifesto (Feb. 1704) proclaiming the invalidity of the 1687 settlement, and negotiated with Louis XIV, Augustus of Poland, and Tsar Peter I. In 1707 Transylvania swore homage to Rákóczy and the Magyars dethroned Joseph and declared an interregnum. By 1708, however, having been saved by the battles of Blenheim (1704) and Turin (1706), the Habsburgs regained the initiative. In 1711 Rákóczy went to Poland for help, insisting on international guarantees for any Hungarian settlement, but the Diet abandoned him and negotiated the peace of Szatmar (1711), confirmed at Pozsony (1712), recognizing the Habsburg hereditary male right to the Crown. Despite an amnesty Rákóczy retired to Turkey, where he died over 20 years later.

RÁKÓCZY, GEORGE I (1591–1648), Prince of Transylvania (reg. 1630–48), who allied himself with Brandenburg, Sweden, and France to undermine Habsburg security in the Thirty Years War and finally forced the Emperor Ferdinand III to make the peace of Linz (1645), granting important religious and political guarantees. Transylvania's independence was, however, dissipated by his son, Prince George II (1621–60), whose rash entry into Charles X of Sweden's Polish schemes (1657) resulted in the annihilation of his forces by the Tatars and Poles and his defeat by the Turks at Klausenburg (1660).

RÁKÓCZY, noble Hungarian house, its most notable members being George Rákóczy I, Prince of Transylvania (reg. 1630–48); George Rákóczy II, Prince of Transylvania (reg.

1648–60), whose ambitions led the Ottoman Grand Vizier Mehemmed Köprülü to reassert Turkish control over Transylvania; and Francis Rákóczy, Prince of Transylvania (*reg.* 1704–35), who led a movement of resistance to the Habsburgs until 1711.

RAKOSI, MATYAS (1892–), Hungarian communist politician. In the First World War he was taken prisoner and carried on revolutionary activities among his fellow prisoners. With the end of the war he became a founder-member of the Hungarian Communist Party. In the communist government of Bela Kun (1919) he was vice-commissar of commerce, then commissar of production. He went to Moscow (1920) and worked with the Comintern, travelling in Europe and making use of his wide knowledge of languages in organizing communist parties. On returning to Hungary he was arrested (1924) and imprisoned; shortly after his release he was again imprisoned (1935). He was then (1940) returned to Russia under an agreement made between the two countries (at the time when the Nazi-Soviet pact was operative), whereby Hungary handed over a number of political prisoners in return for army banners captured in 1848. Rakosi stayed in Moscow during the Second World War and became a Soviet citizen, but returned (1945) to Hungary as a leading member of the 'Moscow group'. He was largely responsible for the establishment of communist rule under Stalinist direction—including the arrest and execution of Rajk and the torture and imprisonment of Kadar. He was secretary-general of the Hungarian Communist Party (1945–56) and prime minister (1952–3). The death of Stalin gravely weakened his position and he was replaced as prime minister by Imre Nagy. He tried to resist the growing demands for liberalization by making concessions while keeping power in his own hands, but eventually managed to secure Nagy's dismissal (1955). But the tide of liberalism proved too strong; he was dismissed from the post of first secretary (July 1956) and went to Moscow. He was expelled from the party (1962) and stayed in the Soviet Union.

RAKOVSKY, CHRISTIAN GEORGEVICH (1873–1939), Russian diplomat, doctor, historian, and revolutionary, who was born in the Dobrogea of an ancient aristocratic family. He studied medicine at Montpellier and later gained a European reputation for his medical writings. After the Bolshevik revolution Lenin sent him to the Ukraine, where he helped to reconcile nationalist groups to Bolshevik rule. Later, after the Red Army had entered Kiev, he became chairman of the Ukrainian council of people's commissars. As such he resisted Stalin's centralizing policy in 1923, claiming that the Ukraine should appoint its own diplomatic representatives abroad. He was (1923–5) Soviet envoy to Britain, negotiating a comprehensive series of agreements with Ramsay MacDonald's government, only to see most of them abandoned by Baldwin's. In 1925 he was moved to Paris as ambassador; this was regarded as the key post because the Soviet government wished to wean France away from the Locarno Pact. Again Rakovsky negotiated several interlocking agreements about debts, loans, and trade, but the whole effort collapsed when Poincaré returned to power and, on a trumped-up charge, secured the expulsion of Rakovsky from France (1927).

Rakovsky was Trotsky's closest political ally; when Trotsky fell, Rakovsky was exiled to Astrakhan, where he worked as a minor clerk in the Gosplan office. He tried to rally the exiled Trotskyites against Stalin: in his 'Letter to Valentinov' (1928) he put the case against compromise very clearly. He himself was the last of the Oppositionists to capitulate (1934), giving as his reason the need to present a solid front against Hitler. He was tried in March 1938 as a member of the 'Anti-Soviet bloc of rights and Trotskyites' and sentenced to imprisonment. There he soon died. He wrote many historical works, including *Metternich and his Age* (1912) and *Romania and Bessarabia* (1925).   **GS**

RALEIGH, SIR WALTER (*c.* 1552–1618), English soldier, courtier, writer, and explorer. He was a volunteer in the Huguenot armies at Jarnac and Montcontour (1569), fought in the Netherlands, and in 1578 joined the Atlantic expedition of his half-brother, Sir Humphrey Gilbert, who had received a patent to occupy any unappropriated territory he might discover. The voyage, although fruitless, stimulated Raleigh's interest in colonies and exploration. He afterwards helped to subdue the Desmond revolt in Ireland (1580).

On a mission to court (1581), he attracted Queen Elizabeth I's favour and, with Leicester's help, quickly achieved prosperity, receiving grants of land, valuable monopolies, and the wardenship of the Stannaries. But although the queen made him captain of her guard, she was mistrustful of his intransigence, his ambition, and his constant advocacy of war with Spain, and withheld from him the sort of responsible post that might have disciplined his great abilities.

Raleigh spent much of his time and considerable fortune in financing voyages of discovery. He sponsored Gilbert's fatal voyage to Nfld (1583) and, on inheriting his patent, sent out an expedition (1584) which settled on Roanoke Island, which he named Virginia. Efforts during the next few years to develop the settlement were costly and unsuccessful.

Raleigh helped in the preparations to meet the Spanish Armada (1588), but his favoured position at court was weakened by the rise of Essex, and in 1592 he was disgraced for seducing one of the queen's ladies, Elizabeth Throckmorton, whom he subsequently married. He was recalled by Elizabeth from a voyage he had undertaken with Frobisher and imprisoned in the Tower of London, where he studied stories about the legendary city of Manoa, fabled source of Peruvian gold. On his release, he sailed forth to establish a base in Trinidad, from which he attempted to explore the Orinoco (1595), describing his adventures in *The Discovery of Guiana* (1596).

He accompanied Essex to Cadiz (1596), but the quarrel between them was renewed during the Azores expedition in the following year and Raleigh's public career was virtually over. His interest in chemistry had already branded him as a sorcerer and atheist, and Essex and Robert Cecil assured James VI of Scotland that Raleigh was hostile to his accession in England. He was unjustly convicted of conspiring to give the throne to Arabella Stuart (1603) and with his wife and son he lived in the Tower, busy with writing and scientific research, until he was released in 1616 in the hope that he might restore the king's dwindling finances by discovering El Dorado. A condition that there should be no embroilment with the Spaniards was obviously impracticable, and on his return from an unhappy and unsuccessful voyage Raleigh was executed on the old treason charge of 1603.

Raleigh had a rare faculty of making enemies, and pride forbade him to conciliate them. He was perhaps greatest in the sphere in which he was least regarded by his contemporaries. Because he left no substantial body of verse, his poetry has been under-rated. Although even here he was incapable of sustained achievement, some of his poems were among the finest of the age: 'The Lie', 'The Pilgrimage', the ballad of *Walsingham*, the sonnet on 'the grave where Laura lay', and the lines he wrote on the eve of execution, 'Even such is time'. Imprisonment brought serenity, and his *History of the World* (1614), nominally from the Creation to 130 BC, but enlivened by modern instances, taught the wisdom of surrender to God's all-seeing judgements.

A. L. Rowse, *The Expansion of Elizabethan England* (London, 1955).

D. B. Quinn, *Raleigh and the British Empire* (London, 1947).   **MMR**

RALEIGH'S PATENT (1584), grant from Queen Elizabeth I of England, renewing Humphrey Gilbert's patent (1578), in Sir Walter Raleigh's favour (March 1584), which allowed him to colonize any lands not actually held or inhabited by Christian people.

RAM KHAMHAENG (*reg. c.* 1279–99), King of Sukhothai (Siam), who, through warfare and alliances, made his state into a major kingdom, extending north-eastwards into Laos, through central Siam, and southwards to Malaya. His one inscription (1292), in a new Thai script devised by himself, is remarkably clear and simple. He spoke as a father to his subjects, offering them justice, protection, free trade, and peace. His legend was important to King Rama IV in the 19th cent., who used it to justify his assumption of new royal roles.

RAMA, mythical hero, principal figure of the ancient Indian epic, the *Ramayana*. Rama was generally regarded as the ideal king in later tradition in India and in parts of South-East Asia.

RAMA I (1737–1809), King of Siam (*reg.* 1782–1809), founder and first king of the Chakri dynasty. His father was a high official of the Ayudhya kingdom and his mother partly Chinese. He was appointed (*c.* 1764) chief judge in Ratburi province. During the Burmese invasion (1766–7) he joined his younger brother in the service of Taksin, soon becoming the new king's minister of the North (Chakri) and his most effective general and leader of armies which expelled the Burmese. He established the new dynasty, and asserted Thai suzerainty in Laos, Cambodia, and the northern Malay states. A rebellion in the capital early in 1782 brought him back from campaigns in Cambodia to assume the throne of Siam, and his brother became his *uparaja*. He moved the capital to Bankok and reconstructed the royal court and administration. His ministers were chosen from men he had known in battle, among whom were the sons of old prominent families, and he established an easy working relationship with them. He was an accomplished poet and a patron of literature and the arts, and sponsored both an ecclesiastical convocation for the revision of the Buddhist scriptures and a commission for the first codification of Thai law, which produced the Three Seals Law (1805). His *uparaja* having died in 1803, he was succeeded by his son, Rama II. His official title was Phut-thayotfa Chulalok, the name Rama I being conferred on him by Rama VI.

RAMA II (1768–1824), King of Siam (*reg.* 1809–24), known chiefly for his poetry, was also an effective ruler during a disturbed period. He was the eldest son of Rama I by Queen Amarin. He was made *uparaja* in 1806 and succeeded his father. As king he was attentive to administrative detail and made several legal reforms. He cultivated good relations with Viet-nam, and maintained strong defences against Burma. The best-known of his poetic compositions are his versions of *Inao* and the *Ramayana*.

RAMA III (1788–1851), King of Siam (*reg.* 1824–51), who made Siam's first uneasy accommodations with the West. He was the eldest son of Rama II, but by a concubine, not a queen. Rama II's failure to name a successor to his *uparaja*, who died in 1817, left the choice of the new king in 1824 to the royal family and nobility of the court. They chose Rama III as the eldest of the princes, and one experienced in public affairs. He was sensitive to the problems of foreign trade and relations, which appears to have led him to accept the Burney treaty with Britain (1826). Good relations with the West being apparently secure, he felt free to devote his full attention to new problems in the east, following Chao Anu's rebellion in Laos (1826–8) and struggles with Viet-nam over Cambodia (1833–47). Western pressure was renewed in the late 1840s, but the king was probably unwilling to tie the hands of his successors, and he sent British and American envoys away empty-handed (1850).

RAMA IV (MONGKUT) (1804–68,) King of Siam (*reg.* 1851–1868), son of Rama II and Queen Suriyen. As a youth, while temporarily in the Buddhist monkhood, he was passed over by the accession council, which chose Rama III to be king in

1824. In these circumstances Prince Mongkut found it both politically expedient and intellectually satisfying to remain in the monkhood. His religious quest led him independently to a fundamental re-examination of Thai Buddhism and to the formation of what later became the Thammayut reform sect, based on a return to the first principles of the religion. As a monk he travelled widely throughout the kingdom, and studied Western languages and sciences with French and American missionaries. In 1851 powerful friends with similar inclinations, chief among whom were members of the Bunnag family, secured his claims to the throne. But being distrustful of them and uncertain of the loyalty of his younger brother, Mongkut had the latter named 'Second King', with the title Pin Klao, to rule as his equal; but this arrangement rapidly deteriorated. The Bowring treaty, which he concluded with Britain (1855), opened the kingdom to foreign trade and required the reorganization of the revenue system, a work accomplished under the able leadership of the *Kalahom*, Suriyawong (Chuang Bunnag). Difficulties with the West continued, with the bombardment of Trengganu by the British (1862) and the loss to France of suzerainty over Cambodia (1863). Throughout his reign, he was restrained by internal politics from attempting fundamental reform.

DKW

RAMA V (CHULALONGKORN) (1853–1910), King of Siam (*reg.* 1868–1910), who saw his country safely through the most dangerous phase of Western imperial expansion. He was the son of Rama IV and Queen Thepsirin, and by the mid-1860s was recognized abroad as heir-apparent. He succeeded his father when only 15 years old, and to begin with was dominated by the regent, Chaophraya Suriyawong. After visiting the Netherlands Indies, Malaya, and India, he secured control of the throne in 1873, and embarked immediately on fundamental administrative, financial, and legal reforms and the abolition of slavery, provoking opposition which crystallized in the Front Palace Crisis (1875). The price of its settlement was a postponement of his reforms until the leading figures of the old order had passed from the scene in the mid-1880s. Then, under the king's Western-educated younger brothers, a drastic reorganization of government began, and in 1892 cabinet government was introduced. These reforms were begun too late, however, to forestall a further loss of territory to France following the Paknam Incident (1893); and in later treaties with France (1904–7) and Britain (1909), Siam lost further territory in Laos, Cambodia, and the northern Malay states, in return for jurisdictional concession. However, the combination of an Anglo-French guarantee of the neutrality of central Thailand (1896), the astute diplomacy of Prince Devawongse, and an improved provincial administration led by Prince Damrong Rajanubhab, consolidated and secured the rest of the kingdom. During his reign, a modern educational system and bureaucracy were created and extensive railways were constructed. Chulalongkorn's reign, the longest in Thai history, ensured the preservation of Thai independence and laid the foundations of modern Thailand.

DKW

RAMA VI (VAJIRAVUDH) (1881–1925), King of Siam (*reg.* 1910–25), founder of modern Thai nationalism, who was the son of Rama V and Queen Saowapha. He was appointed Crown Prince (1894), studied at Oxford and Sandhurst, and returned to Bangkok (1903) to serve in military and cere-monial positions and as regent (1907–10) for his father. Young military officers, inspired by personal grievances and democratic dreams, planned a *coup d'état* against him early in 1912 which was forestalled by mass arrests. The king attempted to create an independent political following by establishing the para-military Wild Tiger Corps, and at his court gathered young men more receptive to his ideas than were his father's generation and their designated successors; but in doing so he alienated the army and the old princes. Though he was sympathetic to Western ideas, he did not believe his country to be ready for parliamentary democracy.

He was most immediately effective as a propagandist of Thai nationalism, as in his pamphlets, 'The Jews of the East', directed against the economically dominant Chinese minority; more than anyone, he was responsible for the rapid development of modern Thai literature and the stimulation of political change.

RAMADIER, PAUL (1888–1961), French lawyer, politician, and *président du conseil* in 1947, when the Communists were removed from the government. In 1928 he was elected Socialist deputy for the Aveyron department, but left the Socialist Party (1933) because of its unwillingness to cooperate with the Radicals in a government, and joining the newly formed Union socialiste et républicaine. His first cabinet post was as under-secretary of state for public works in Blum's first popular front government. He also served in Chautemps' fourth ministry (1938) and Daladier's third as minister of works, but resigned in 1938 over the government's intention to abolish the 40-hour week.

After voting against granting full constitutional powers to Pétain, he took part in the Resistance during the Second World War and rejoined the socialist party. After the war he formed his own ministry (Jan. 1947). His tenure of office was a vital one in the history of the Fourth Republic, for it was Ramadier who made the transition from the tripartite coalition of popular Republicans, Socialists, and Communists to the third force coalition of Socialists, popular Republicans, and various centre parties. His actions in dismissing the communist ministers without himself resigning forced the hesitant Socialist party into approving a 'Third Force' policy and thereby established the political pattern of the Fourth Republic.

Ramadier was minister of national defence in Queille's government (1948–9) and minister of economic affairs in Mollet's (1956–7), but after losing his seat in the elections of 1958 he retired from political life.

RAMAN, SIR CHANDRASEKHARA VENKATA (1888–1970), Indian physicist, who became director of the Indian Institute of Science in Bangalore and, after that, of his own Raman Institute. His major work was concerned with the scattering of light. The 'Raman effect' (1928), for which he was awarded the Nobel Prize in 1930, is the observation that light of a single frequency acquires weak components of different frequencies when scattered by material bodies.

His work in establishing a place for scientific research in the life of modern India must be considered at least as important as his own research.

RAMANANDA (*fl.* 15th cent.), *bhakti* saint and poet, who lived in Benares. He was brought up in the tradition of Ramanuja's Vaishnavism and introduced three innovations: he made no distinction between caste and outcaste, used the vernacular instead of Sanskrit, and substituted the cult of Rama and Sita for that of Krishna and Radha. The poet-mystic Kabir (*c.* 1440–1518) was his disciple.

RAMANATHAN, SIR PONNAMBALAM (1851–1930), Sinhalese politician, who was a member of a distinguished Tamil family in Ceylon. He was attorney-general (1890–7), and became prominent in the agitation for constitutional advance. He was elected to the 'educated Ceylonese' seat on the Legislative Council in 1910, and was a founder of the National Congress, which he left in 1921 owing to his disapproval of its proposals for Tamil representation on the council.

RAMANUJA, Indian philosopher (*c.* 1050–1130), who worked mainly at Srirangam near Trichinopoly, Madras state, India. The doctrine promulgated by Ramanuja, called Qualified Monism, combines the monism of Vedanta with intense devotion to Vishnu. It inaugurated a Vaishnavite revival in India and even in South-East Asia, notably at Angkor Vat, Cambodia.

RAMAYANA, ancient Indian epic in Sanskrit verse, ascribed to the legendary sage Valmiki, but dating back, in its present form, to the early centuries AD. Compared with the *Mahabharata*, the *Ramayana* is more compact and homogeneous; also, on the whole, more refined and poetic. It tells the story of Rama, eldest son of Dasaratha, King of Ayodhya (near present Faizabad, Uttar Pradesh). Owing to court intrigues Rama was temporarily barred from the succession and with his wife, Sita, daughter of Janaka, ruler of a neighbouring kingdom (Videha), and his younger brother, Lakshmana, left Ayodhya to live in exile in the Dandaka forest of central India. There Sita was abducted and carried off to the palace of a ten-headed giant (*rakshasa*) Ravana, king of the island of Lanka (identified with Ceylon). In his resolve to rescue Sita, Rama concluded an alliance with the monkeys, among whom Hanuman is the most prominent, discovered Sita's whereabouts, and, after long preparations, set out to conquer Lanka. These preparations included the construction of an enormous dam (later identified with the present Adam's Bridge from the Dhanushkodi peninsula in India to the Mannar peninsula in Ceylon), along which Rama's army invaded Lanka. After Ravana had been killed and Sita rescued, Rama returned triumphantly to Ayodhya, was consecrated king, and reigned happily thereafter.

Though it is likely that part of the story is based on real events it is impossible to reconstruct an historical nucleus that can be assigned to a definite period. It has been suggested that the *Ramayana* describes allegorically the expansion of Brahmanic civilization from the Gangetic valley to central and southern India. This, however, would explain only some aspects of the epic. On the other hand, the epic was no doubt composed to lay down norms of behaviour for Hinduism in its developing stages. Rama represents the ideal of kingship, Sita that of the chaste Hindu wife, while Lakshmana and Hanuman symbolize the devoted brother and the faithful ally respectively. As Rama is also an incarnation (*avatara*) of Vishnu, the religious aspect is present as well.

The influence of the *Ramayana*, in India and South-East Asia, cannot be over-rated. The story has been retold in many different forms and languages. It has inspired some of the greatest works of art and architecture. It was very popular in Java, where an Old Javanese *Ramayana* was composed in the 10th cent. Other ancient versions are known in, *eg*, Malay, Thai, Mon, and Laotian. Above all, the epic has set examples which were models of conduct through the ages and may therefore have exercised great influence upon events and developments.

Hari Prasad Shastri (trans.), *The Ramayana of Valmiki*,
    3 vols (London, 1952).   JG de C

RAMBOUILLET, HÔTEL DE, Parisian home of Catherine de Vivonne, Marquise de Rambouillet (1588–1665), with its famous *chambre bleue*, the setting for her *salons* and the fashionable social and literary centre of France in the generation preceding the *Frondes* (1618–49).

RAMEAU, JEAN PHILIPPE (1683–1764), French organist and composer of opera and ballet. His principal operas were *Hippolyte* (1732) and *Castor and Pollux* (1737). His *Treatise on Harmony* (1722), originating the conception of 'fundamental bass', was important in the development of musical style, and he composed cantatas and pieces for harpsichord.

RAMESES II (*?reg. c.* 1290–1224 BC), Egyptian King of the XIXth dynasty, who left many grandiose edifices, *eg*, at Abu Simbel, Abydos, and Thebes, and many inscriptions, boasting of his own achievements. He also replaces the names of his predecessors with his own on other buildings. Aiming to restore the empire of Thothmes III, he invaded Syria and met the Hittites at Qadesh (*c.* 1285), where he claimed a great victory, though it seems likely that the Hittites had the advantage. After a further 16 years of indecisive war, the two countries made peace; the Hittites were allotted northern

Syria; and the Egyptians southern Syria and Palestine. Rameses defended the Delta from Libyan invaders, and his reign seems to have been a period of some prosperity.

RAMESES III (*reg. c.* 1182–1151 BC), Egyptian King of the XXth dynasty, who defended Egypt against two Libyan invasions and, in a great sea and a land battle, saved Egypt from the Sea Peoples. Heavy expenditure on war and building had drained the royal treasury and resulting discontent led to Rameses' assassination.

RAMEZAY, CLAUDE DE (1659–1724), French soldier and colonial governor, who went to Canada (1685), where he served first against the Iroquois (1687), then at Quebec during the siege of William Phipps (1690). He was governor of Trois-Rivières (1690–9), and of Montreal (1704–24). He was also administrator of the government of New France (1714–16).

RAMILLIES, BATTLE OF (1706), fought in the Spanish Netherlands during the War of the Spanish Succession, between the armies, commanded by the Duke of Marlborough, and French forces, commanded by Marshal Villeroi. The French were decisively defeated. Following on this success, Marlborough overran much of the Spanish Netherlands, capturing numerous towns and fortresses.

RAMKRISHNA PARAMAHAMSA (1836–86), Bengali Brahman ascetic and spiritual teacher, who was inspired with an intense love of humanity and had a deep faith in the inherent truth of all religions. He was a priest at the temple of the goddess Kali at Dakshineswar, near Calcutta, where he spent years in meditation and prayer. He was regarded by many Indians as an incarnation of God. His chief disciple was Swami Vivekananda.

RAMKRISHNA MISSION in India, founded by Swami Vivekananda in 1897 to spread the teachings of Ramkrishna Paramahamsa and to help suffering humanity. It was an attempt to regenerate the Hindu social system by blending India's traditional spiritual disciplines with Western humanitarianism. It sponsored and ran schools, colleges, and hospitals, though an attempt to open schools for the untouchables was not very successful.

RAMNARAYAN TARKARATNA (1822–86), Bengali dramatist, social reformer, and professor of Sanskrit, whose *Kulin-Kula-Sarbbasva* (1854) is considered to be the earliest drama in Bengali.

RAMSAY, ALLAN (1685–1758), Scottish poet, a wigmaker of Edinburgh, who influenced Burns. He preserved many Scottish folk songs, published a dramatic pastoral, *The Gentle Shepherd* (1725), and a version of the old Scots poem 'Christ's Kirk on the Green'. He set up the first circulating library in Britain to encourage the arts.

RAMSAY, ANDREW MICHAEL (1686–1743), known as the chevalier de Ramsay, Scottish writer in France, who was converted to Catholicism by Fénelon and became tutor to the two sons of James Edward Stuart in Rome (1724–5). He was the author of an apologia for the philosophy of divine right, *Essay on Civil Government* (1719), a *Life of Fénelon* (1723), and *Les Voyages de Cyrus* (1727).

RAMSAY, SIR BERTRAM HOME (1883–1945), British sailor, who was responsible for planning the major Allied amphibious operations of the Second World War. On the outbreak of the war Ramsay became flag officer, Dover, a post from which he improvised the evacuation of the British Expeditionary Force from Dunkirk. He was subsequently responsible for the planning of the naval side of the Allied landings in North Africa (1942), Sicily (1943), and Normandy (1944). Under Eisenhower he commanded the naval

forces at D-Day and thereafter until his death in an air accident.

RAMSAY, SIR WILLIAM (1852–1916), British chemist, who, in association with Lord Rayleigh, was responsible for the discovery of the gas argon in 1894, and the remaining elements which form the group of rare or inert gases. He was awarded the Nobel Prize for Chemistry in 1904.

RAMUS, or PIERRE DE LA RAMÉE (1515–72), French philosopher, a Zwinglian, and anti-clerical scholar, who taught at the Collège de France (1551–62) and was known for his famous neo-scholastic Method, outlined in *Dialectica* (1543). He was killed in the St Bartholomew Massacre.

RAMUSIO, GIAMBATTISTA (1485–1557), Venetian diplomat, scholar, and traveller, known chiefly for the accounts of his explorations published in the *Raccolta Della Navigazioni a Viaggi* (1550–9).

RANADE, MAHADEV GOVIND (1842–1901), Martha Chitpavan Brahman, scholar, judge, and reformer. After entering the service of the British government he rose to be a judge of the Bombay high court (1893–1901). As a member of the Prarthana Samaj he opposed infant marriage and favoured both the remarriage of widows and female education. He was a supporter of the Indian National Congress.

RANCE, SIR HUBERT ELVIN (1898–   ), British soldier, who was director of civil affairs in the military government of Burma (1945–6), and governor (1946–8). Within a few days of his taking office as governor a police strike took place which marked the effective shift of power in Burma from British to Burmese hands. Rance effected the formal transfer peacefully and won the confidence of Aung San, and of U Nu. He was governor of Trinidad (1950–5).

RAND REVOLT in South Africa. In 1922 white gold-mine workers on the Witwatersrand struck because of attempts by mine owners to employ Africans in skilled occupations, thereby interfering with the colour bar which ensured the privileged position of the whites. The strike turned into a revolt in which nearly 250 lives were lost, and which Smuts suppressed by using regular troops and Afrikaner commandos. Subsequent South African governments guaranteed the privileges of the white industrial workers.

RANDOLPH, ASA PHILIP (1889–   ), US Negro labour and civil rights leader, who organized (1925) the Brotherhood of Sleeping Car Porters, a railway union. During the Second World War he was director of the March on Washington Movement, which led President F. D. Roosevelt to initiate the Committee on Fair Employment Practice (1941). He became the first Negro vice-president of the AFL–CIO (1957), and helped direct the 1963 civil rights march on Washington.

RANDOLPH, EDMUND JENNINGS (1753–1813), American lawyer and politician, who became VA's first attorney-general (1776–86). He was a delegate to the Continental Congress (1779–82), and governor of VA (1786–88). As delegate to the Annapolis and Philadelphia Conventions (1786–7) he drafted the Virginia Plan for the establishment of a federal government. He refused to sign the constitution of 1787, but later urged VA to ratify it. He was first US attorney-general (1789–93), and secretary of state (1794–5). In the dispute between Hamilton and Jefferson he tried to remain neutral. He opposed Jay's Treaty, and resigned after being accused of accepting bribes from the French. After becoming a leading VA lawyer he was chief counsel for the defence at Aaron Burr's trial for treason (1807).

RANDOLPH, EDWARD (1632–1703), British agent, sent 1675–6) to investigate violations of the laws of trade in

New England and to deliver a report on the colony. Though biased against the Puritans, the report had a basis of fact and was influential in the abrogation of the Massachusetts Charter (1684).

RANDOLPH, JOHN (1773–1833), US politician, who was a congressman from VA (1799–1813, 1815–17, 1819–25, 1827–9), and a senator (1825–7). His oratory sustained the political ideals of states' rights and the strict construction of the US constitution. He was US minister to Russia (1830–1).

RANDOLPH, PEYTON (1721–75), English-born lawyer, who was king's attorney for VA (1744–66) and a member of the House of Burgesses (1748–9, 1752–75). As a moderate he sought to end certain elements of British rule, but did not wish for complete independence. He presided over the VA conventions of 1774 and 1775.

RANGAKU (lit. 'Dutch learning), means by which knowledge of Europe and European science entered Japan after the relaxation of the ban on foreign books in 1720. Dutch traders being the only Europeans allowed to visit Japan, it was only through them and their books that Japanese scholars could learn of European developments. Western medicine attracted the greatest attention, but interest soon spread to military and political matters, and Honda Toshiaki, Hayashi Shihei, Satō Nobuhiro, and others sounded warnings about Japan's unpreparedness to meet possible threats from the West. Since the political implications of *rangaku* were sometimes inimical to the established order, the 'Dutch scholars' were occasionally persecuted, but their studies did much to prepare Japan to meet the Western challenge after 1853.

RANGITAKE, TE, or Wiremu Kingi (*c.* 1795–1882), NZ Maori chief, who vetoed an inferior chief's proposal to sell tribal lands at Waitara to Gov. Gore Browne (1859). Kingi's resistance precipitated the Taranaki War (1860–1).

RANGOON (originally known as Dagon), port on the Rangoon river, linked by canal to the mouths of the Irrawaddy. It was the capital of British Burma from 1852 and of all of Burma from 1886. Its present name, which means 'End of Strife', was given to it by Alaungpaya in 1755. Under the British Rangoon became an important port and grew speedily into a modern cosmopolitan city, predominantly Indian, Chinese, and European, the trade of Burma being mostly in their hands. After independence the expropriation of foreign traders greatly changed this.

RANJIT SINGH (1780–1839), ruler of the Punjab. In 1792 he succeeded his father as head of the Sukarchakia *misl* (branch) of the Sikh confederacy. His greatness lies in his welding of the discordant Sikh *misl*s of the Punjab into a stable kingdom at a time when Afghanistan was distracted by dynastic and political troubles. Ranjit Singh was astute enough not to quarrel with the British and by the treaty of Amritsar (1809) recognized that his co-religionists, the cis-Sutlej Sikhs, were under British protection. This treaty advanced the British frontier from the Jumna to the Sutlej. Between 1813 and 1821 Ranjit Singh annexed Attock, Kashmir, Dera Ghazi Khan, and Dera Ismail Khan. It was not until 1834 that Peshawar passed into Sikh hands.

RANKE, LEOPOLD (1795–1886), German historian at Berlin University, who was the founder of modern historical method. He taught that a historian should not judge, but only demonstrate, and he pioneered work on original source material and on understanding the past in its own terms, not those of the present.

RANKOVIC, ALEXANDER (1909–   ), Yugoslav political leader, who joined the Communist Party in 1928 and collaborated with Tito in reorganizing the party in 1938. He was a key figure in the Partisan resistance, being responsible for

intelligence and security. During the Second World War he built up the UDBA (security service), which became the source of his power in Yugoslavia, being virtually in control of security, judicial, and personnel matters within the party (1945–65). He used the UDBA as a vehicle for his ambitions to succeed Tito and implement his centralist policies, but his challenge to Tito led to his downfall. In 1966 he resigned his positions and was expelled from the party. His fall was not only a personal defeat, but a defeat for Serbian hegemony and bureaucratic centralism.

RANTZAU, VON, family of, noble family which originated in Holstein. One of its members, Johann (1492–1565), soldier and statesman, influenced Frederick I to accept the Danish Crown and spread the Reformation in Denmark. He was succeeded as governor of Schleswig-Holstein by his son, Heinrich (1526–98). His great-grandson, Josias (1609–1650), served in the armies of the Prince of Orange, Christian IV, Gustavus Adolphus, and the Emperor Ferdinand II. Eventually he entered French service in 1635 and became a marshal of France (1645).

RANULF FLAMBARD (d. 1128), English bishop and administrator, who rose to prominence under King William II (1087–1100), chiefly through his ability to procure money, and was rewarded in 1099 with the bishopric of Durham. At first disgraced by Henry I, he rendered the new king valuable services in securing the defection of the Normans to Henry's cause and was serving in the royal administration again by 1109. His later years were occupied with the completion of the nave of Durham cathedral, one of the earliest European churches with Gothic features.

RAPACKI, ADAM (1909–   ), Polish communist politician, who was associated with the Polish Socialist Party (PPS) before the Second World War. He fought in the campaign of Sept. 1939, during which he was taken prisoner, returning to Poland in 1945. He rapidly achieved an important position in the reconstituted PPS and was elected to the Central Committee in 1947 and the Political Committee in 1948. He was a strong supporter of Jozef Cyrankewicz, who advocated the union of the PPS with the Communist Polish Workers' Party. Rapacki held the posts of minister for marine affairs (1949–50) and minister for higher education (1950–1). In April 1956, when the Stalinist system was crumbling, he emerged as a supporter of Edward Ochab and became minister of foreign affairs. He showed ability in advancing the Polish cause, and won widespread respect in Western Europe. He lost his position in 1969, as a result of his opposition to Polish participation in the invasion of Czechoslovakia and to the anti-zionist campaign, which had resulted in a far-reaching purge of Jews and liberals in the ministry.

RAPACKI PLAN, proposal by the Polish foreign minister, Rapacki, presented to the General Assembly of the UN (Oct. 1957), for the creation of a zone free of nuclear weapons in Germany and Poland. The climate in which it was proposed was favourable to the extent that it coincided with a number of similar suggestions for 'disengagement' in Europe. But it was not suited to the strategy of the Western powers, because it depended on nuclear weapons as a balance to the more numerous land forces of the Soviet Union in Europe, and the plan was not taken up.

RAPHAEL SANZIO (1483–1520), one of the most outstanding and influential Italian painters of the High Renaissance. He went to Rome (1508) to undertake the fresco painting of the Vatican *Stanze* for Pope Julius II. The first and most remarkable is the *Stanza della Segnatura* (1509–11), whose four great pictures include *The School of Athens*, in which the monumental style of the Renaissance reaches perfection.

RASHID AL-DIN (*c.* 1247–1318), Muslim historian, physician, and politician in the time of the Mongol Il-Khan of Persia,

Abaka. His influence was at its height in the reigns of Ghazan Khan (*reg.* 1295–1304) and Uljaytu (*reg.* 1304–1 6), but he was dismissed from office after the death of Uljaytu and executed in 1318. He was the author of a chronicle, the *Jami al-Tawarikh*, written in Persian and devoted to the affairs of the Mongols.

RASHID ALI AL-GAYLANI (1892–1965), Iraqi lawyer and politician, who was four times prime minister. During the Second World War his ambiguous relations with the Axis powers in 1940 led to his resignation under British pressure (Jan. 1941). He was restored to power (1 April) by an army coup, when the regent and other pro-British politicians fled. Rashid Ali deposed the regent and established a new regime. Believing that the new government favoured the Axis, Britain intervened militarily, expelled Rashid Ali and his supporters (May 1941), and restored the government of Abd al-Ilah. Rashid Ali took refuge in Germany and later in Saudi Arabia. He returned to Iraq (1958), but was arrested and imprisoned for complicity in a plot against Kassim and exiled again (1961).

RASHID, MEHEMMED (d. 1735), official historiographer (waq'a'-i nuwis) to the Ottoman sultan, who became *Qadi* of Aleppo (1720), of Istanbul (1730), and of Anadolu (1734). He was the author of a valuable Ottoman chronicle which continues the work of Na'ima and covers the period 1660–1721.

RASHIDAS, family established in Hail (north-eastern Arabia), which, under Muhammad ibn Rashid (d. 1897), became the dominant power in central Arabia in the last quarter of the 19th cent., but subsequently became subordinated to the Ottomans and finally defeated by Ibn Sa'ud (1921).

RASHTRAKUTAS, ancient Indian royal dynasty (*c.* AD 750–973) which controlled the western Deccan from Manyakheta (Malkhed, *c.* 100 miles (161 kms) west of Hyderabad). They had been feudatories of the Chalukyas of Badami till Dantidurga made himself independent of his overlords, whom he subsequently defeated. For over two centuries the Rashtrakutas remained in control of a large empire. Some rulers, notably Govinda III (*reg.* 793–814) and Indra III (*reg.* 914–928), conducted campaigns into the Gangetic valley and southern India, but during the long reign of Amoghavarsha I (*reg.* 814–90) the empire enjoyed peace. The power of the dynasty came to an abrupt end when a branch of the Chalukyas regained supremacy.

The Rashtrakutas are important in the history of Jainism, which flourished under their patronage, also in Canarese (Kannada) literature, art, and architecture, especially the rock-cut temples of Ellora.

RASHTRIYA SWAYAMSEVAK SANGH in India, 'National Volunteer Group', founded in 1925 in Nagpur by Keshav Baliram Hedgewar (1889–1940), to provide a dedicated and efficient cadre of Hindu political activists. The uniformed *swayamsevak*s (volunteers), a tightly disciplined organization, drilled, exercised, and attended lectures on national problems. They numbered 500 until Hedgewar decided to expand the area of recruitment into north India; at the time of his death the *Sangh* had 100,000 members. 'Guruji' Madhavrao Sadashiv Golwalkar (1906–), who became leader after Hedgewar, had expanded the *Sangh* to 500,000 at the time of partition—in which the *Sangh* was active. The ban which followed Gandhi's assassination by a former RSS member caused a rapid falling away in membership, but after the ban was lifted (July 1949), Golwalkar was able to re-establish the movement, so that by the late 1960s it claimed 750,000 members. In this period it played a key role in the formation and running of the *Jana Sangh*.

RASKOL, schism within the Russian Orthodox Church between the reformers and the traditionalists or Old Believers,

provoked by the Nikonian innovations of the mid-17th cent. The rejection of the ancient ritualistic traditions of the *raskolniks* altered the relations between Church and state and affected the intellectual climate. Coinciding with increasing contact with western Europe, the *raskol* contributed to the end of old Russia.

'RASPUTIN', GREGORY YEFIMOVICH (*c.* 1872–1916), Siberian peasant and mystic, family name Novykh, who gained great influence at the Russian court of Nicholas II and Alexandra. Belonging to an esoteric sect of flagellants, he claimed powers of healing. Settling in St Petersburg, he gained royal favour through his supposed palliative effects on the Tsarevitch Alexis's haemophilia. The scandals of his private life earned him the name of Rasputin (debauchee) but his denouncers were silenced. By 1915 he and the tsarina virtually controlled domestic affairs. He became increasingly corrupt and autocratic until a group of ultra-conservatives including Yusupov and Pavlovich decided (Dec. 1916) to murder him to save the monarchy's reputation.

RASSEMBLEMENT DÉMOCRATIQUE AFRICAIN, independence movement formed in 1946, at Bamako (mod. Mali), as an inter-territorial organization for the whole of French West and Equatorial Africa. With Félix Houphouet-Boigny (afterwards president of Ivory Coast) as its chairman, and the Sudanese, Gabriel d'Arboussier, as its secretary-general, the RDA soon acquired a preponderant influence among African nationalists throughout French Africa (with the exception of French Somaliland), and claimed by 1948 to have some 700,000 adherents. Already, in 1946, RDA supporters had won 18 seats in the French National Assembly elected that year. Personal and ideological conflicts then deprived the RDA of its unity, and its decline was hastened by the *loi cadre* (1956), which provided for autonomous development of states within the colonial federations of West and Equatorial Africa, a constitutional change which opened the way to separate political independence for these states.

RASSEMBLEMENT DU PEUPLE FRANÇAIS (RPF) in France, political movement founded by De Gaulle in 1947 which expressed his dislike of the parliamentary system of the Fourth Republic and was designed as a mass movement rather than a conventional political party. It had striking success at first, gaining nearly 40 per cent of the vote in the 1947 municipal elections, and it seemed as if it might carry De Gaulle back to power. But in the 1951 parliamentary election its votes were fewer, and its 120 deputies were not enough to give it a dominating position. De Gaulle's policy of non-co-operation with governments tended to lead the RPF into destructive and irresponsible opposition, and caused the secession of the Action Républicaine et Sociale group (1952). Disillusioned by his followers' tendency to behave like conventional politicians, De Gaulle dissolved the group (1953). The deputies renamed themselves Républicains Sociaux.

RASTATT CONGRESS (1797–9), set up during the French Wars, after the peace of Campo Formio, to recognize the cession by the Prussian empire of the lands on the left bank of the Rhine to France. It was proposed that Prussian princes and landowners should be compensated for their losses out of secularized ecclesiastical lands. The congress broke up in 1799, its business uncompleted.

The quasi-voluntary cession of these lands to France was important because it ended the medieval social system and feudal land tenure and fragmentation in this potentially rich part of Germany, without, however, introducing democratic control. It was not possible to return to the *status quo ante* in 1815.

RATANA CHURCH, THE, in NZ, largest Maori religious movement, founded by T. W. Ratana, a faith-healer in 1920. Although initially Christian based, the movement soon evolved specifically Maori religious forms, and championed Maori grievances. It was linked with the NZ Labour Party (1931) and monopolized the four Maori parliamentary seats from 1943. Its adherents numbered 28,000 in 1970.

RATHENAU, WALTHER (1867–1922), German industrialist and politician, who grew up in the intellectual atmosphere of the wealthy German-Jewish bourgeoisie. In the years preceding the First World War he held leading positions in 86 German and 21 foreign firms, and also took an interest in the arts and public affairs. He became an outspoken critic of William II's rigid class structure, and wrote several short books on industrial society and its future development. But he was a reformist and patriot, not a revolutionary, and when war came in 1914 he soon realized that the Reich would soon run into economic difficulties unless its supplies and production capacities were co-ordinated. His proposals were taken up by the government and he was made head of the department for raw materials in the war ministry. When he left (March 1915) the foundations of Germany's economic mobilization for a long war had been established. He then devoted himself almost exclusively to steering his business empire through the difficulties imposed by the war. He was again drawn into politics in July 1920 as a member of the German delegation to the Spa reparations conference. He became a close adviser to Joseph Wirth, who, when made Reich chancellor in May 1921, asked him to be minister for reconstruction. In 1921 he became foreign minister, though reluctantly, and with forebodings that his political enemies might try to kill him. His part in making the Rapallo treaty (1922) made him more than ever the target of anti-semitism and nationalism and eventually he was murdered by members of a terrorist organization.

RATHENOW, BATTLE OF (25 June 1675), engagement at Rathenow on the Havel river between a force of Brandenburgers under Elector Frederick William and the Swedish army led by Charles XI. Surprised in their camp after a long march, the Swedes suffered a serious reverse, which was followed shortly afterwards by their defeat at Fehrbellin.

RATHMINES, BATTLE OF (2 Aug. 1649), victory of the Parliamentary forces garrison in Dublin, commanded by Col. Michael Jones, over the Royalist forces of James Butler, Marquis of Ormonde, south of the city. After repelling Ormonde's night assault, Jones led a surprise attack on the royalist camp, killing 4000 men and capturing 2000, together with Ormonde's artillery.

RATIO STUDIORUM, scheme of educational regulations first published by the Society of Jesus in 1591 but revised in 1599, and based on a report of six Jesuit educationalists (1584–6). It was based on theory and experience and covered all aspects of education, eg, curriculum, discipline, technique, and in advocating a general, liberal type of education ensured the supremacy of the Jesuits in this field until their suppression in 1773.

RATIONALISM, philosophical concept based on the guidance of reason and systematic thought, an offshoot of the natural philosophy of Descartes, Spinoza, and Newton which affected many European intellectuals from the late 17th cent. onwards, eg, Nicole, Arnauld, and Thomasius. The movement stressed the need for reform of taxation, justice, and administration, and attacked religious superstition and the tyranny of clerical authority, both Catholic and sectarian.

RATISBON or REGENSBURG, DIET OF (Sept. 1640–Oct. 1641), imperial Diet summoned by the Emperor Ferdinand III to rally the princes in the face of defeat by Swedish and French forces in the Thirty Years War. Ferdinand tried to achieve general acceptance of the peace of Prague, but failed after the Elector of Brandenburg made a truce with Sweden which persuaded the princes of the need for a general peace.

RATISBON or REGENSBURG, DIET OF (1653–4), imperial Diet held to define the nature and extent of the obligations of the German states to the emperor and the empire, arising from the peace of Westphalia (1648). On 17 May 1654 the Diet published its recess, known as the 'youngest recess', containing a new statute to regulate the Imperial High Court (*Reichskammergericht*) and alleviate the backlog of judicial work.

RATISBON or REGENSBURG, DIET OF (1663), imperial Diet, known as the 'Eternal' or 'Everlasting' Diet, which ended only with the dissolution of the Holy Roman empire in 1806. After 1664 it remained in existence as a congress of diplomats permanently in session, but no important political or constitutional legislation was promulgated except the law placing the defence of the empire in the hands of the ten Circles (1681). The final recess of the Diet was made on 24 March 1803.

RATISBON or REGENSBURG, TRUCE OF (1684), general armistice of 20 years' duration concluded between the empire and France. The proposal for a long-term truce with Louis XIV had been urged by Brandenburg and discussed at the Imperial Diet assembled in Ratisbon or Regensburg since 1683. Louis XIV acceded to the suggestion of a general truce after the relief of Vienna had strengthened the imperial position (Sept. 1683), but before its conclusion French forces were successful in the Netherlands and Luxemburg, thus assuring favourable terms for France. Louis XIV was left in possession of his conquests, including the *réunion* gains made since 1678. However, the truce was effective for only four years, and was ended by the French invasion of the Palatinate (1688) and the War of the League of Augsburg (1689–97), which undermined the prestige France had enjoyed at the time of the truce of Ratisbon.

RAUF BEY (Hüseyin Rauf Orbay) (1881–1964), Ottoman sailor and politician, who, with Mustafa Kemal, organized nationalist resistance in Turkey (1919). He was arrested and detained (1920–1) by British forces who had occupied Istanbul, being stationed in the vicinity under the terms of the Mudros armistice. Rauf Bey afterwards became prime minister (1922), but subsequently drew apart from Atatürk and formed the Progressive Republican Party (1924–5). He left for Europe after the proscription of the party in 1925, was sentenced *in absentia* for alleged complicity in a plot against Atatürk (1926), and returned to Turkey only after his death. Because of the Ottoman government's sympathy with the nationalists under Atatürk, who had clashed with Allied forces in Anatolia, the Allies decided to occupy Istanbul and force a change of government. They did so on 16 March 1920 and arrested a number of nationalist leaders who were serving as deputies in the Ottoman government, and put them in detention in Malta. Rauf was among them. They were released in 1921.

RAUPARAHA, TE (*c.* 1768–1849), NZ Maori, who dominated mid-NZ tribes by his ruthlessness and skill. His suspected treachery led Gov. Grey to arrest him (1846), thus destroying his *mana* (prestige).

RAUSCHENBUSCH, WALTER (1861–1918), US clergyman and theologian, who was pastor of the Second German Baptist Church in New York city (1886–97) and then taught at Rochester Theological Seminary (1897–1918). He was a strong advocate of the Social Gospel, and his teaching and writings, particularly *Christianity and the Social Crisis* (1907) and *A Theology for the Social Gospel* (1917), exercised great influence on Christian thought and progressive reform movements in the US.

RAUSCHNING, HERMANN (1887–   ), German politician, who was active in the German minority movement in Posen at the end of the First World War, and later became involved in nationalist politics in the Free City of Danzig, where he was leader of the Landbund and deputy NSDAP gauleiter (1932). After the Nazis came to power in Germany (1933), the Danzig Volkstag (assembly) was dissolved. Rauschning led the NSDAP in the ensuing elections, in which the party won an absolute majority, and he became president of the Danzig senate, *ie*, head of the government. Against the wishes of his vice-president, Greiser, and the gauleiter, Forster, he formed a coalition with the Centre Party and embarked on policies which showed a marked divergence from the official NSDAP line. Whereas the ultimate aim of the German and Danzig NSDAPs was to reincorporate the city into the Reich, Rauschning was strongly committed to preserving Danzig's independence, and resisted the attempted interference of the German NSDAP through its allies in the Danzig Party. At first his policy of rapprochement with Poland was supported by Hitler, for reasons of political expedience; but when he adopted an economic and financial programme based on a long-term recognition of the realities of Danzig's existing position, he provoked strong opposition in the extremist wing of his party and was denounced to Hitler and Hess as an anti-Nazi. His refusal to follow the German example in suppressing political opposition and introducing anti-Semitic measures in Danzig also led to his increasing isolation within his own government, and in Nov. 1934 he resigned. His experiences in this period, and especially the long and revealing conversations he had with Hitler in mid-1933 defending himself against his critics, led eventually to his complete rejection of Nazism. In 1936 he fled from Germany, and while in exile wrote several books attacking the regime and publicizing what he knew of the Nazi programme and philosophy. After the Second World War he lived in the US.

RAVAILLAC, FRANÇOIS (1578–1610), French assassin of Henry IV, who stabbed the king to death in his coach in the streets of Paris.

RAVENNA, port in north-east Italy. It was protected by marshes, and from 404 onwards it became the main residence of the Western Roman emperors. The presence of an important naval base added to their sense of security there. The successive barbarian rulers of Italy, Odoacer, and Theodoric, took it over as their capital and a second Germanic settlement sprang up to the east of the city. After the reconquest of Italy by Justinian I it became the seat of the Byzantine viceroys and remained the capital of Byzantine Italy until its conquest by the Lombards in the middle of the 8th cent. Ravenna is famous for its Gothic and Byzantine mosaics, particularly the portraits of Justinian and his wife, Theodora, in the church of San Vitale (*c.* 550).

RAVENNA, BATTLE OF (1512), French victory over the forces of the Holy League during the Italian Wars. After being driven from the siege lines around Ravenna (11 April) the French, under Louis XII's nephew, Gaston de Foix, overwhelmed the Spanish soldiery of the league, commanded by Pedro Navarro and the Marquis de Pescara. The French cannon and cavalry, supported by hired German pikemen and musketeers, won the day, but French rejoicing was muted when Gaston fell in the moment of triumph. His death encouraged the Emperor Maximilian and the Swiss cantons to join the anti-French coalition which by the end of 1512 had driven the French from Milan.

RAVENSBURG, German Rhenish county which, with that of Mark, was ruled by the Duke of Cleves-Jülich until 1609. It was claimed by John Sigismund, Elector of Brandenburg-Prussia, who took possession of it in 1614.

RAY, JOHN (1627–1705), English naturalist, whose descriptions of tours of English and Welsh countries included the first catalogues of local flora in Britain. His *Methodus Plantarum Nova* was the first step towards a natural system of plant classification. In the 1690s he also classified animals, birds, fishes, and insects. This cleared the way for Linnaeus's work. His *Historia Plantarum* (1704) described 11,700 species. In 1670 he published anonymously his *Collection of English Proverbs*.

RAYATWARI SYSTEM, one of the three main types of British land revenue settlement in India. The main principle underlying the system was direct dealing with the peasants, without recourse to go-betweens or farmers of revenue. Under British rule this was the predominant system in Madras, Bombay, and Burma.

RAYBURN, SAMUEL TALIAFERRO (1882–1961), US politician, member (1913–61), and speaker of the US House of Representatives (1940–7, 1949–53, 1955–61). He exercised great influence within the Democratic Party from the New Deal era until his death.

RAYDANIYYA, AL-, BATTLE OF (23 Jan. 1517), fought near Cairo. At the beginning of AD 1517 the Ottoman Sultan Selim I, having defeated the Mamluks at Marj Dabiq in Aug. 1517 and taken control of Syria, marched across the Sinai desert into Egypt. The Mamluks, under their sultan, Tuman Bay, had prepared a defensive position, armed with cannon, at Al-Raydaniyya. Here the Ottomans routed the Mamluk forces and advanced against Cairo, which fell to them after several days of street-fighting.

RAYLEIGH, JOHN WILLIAM STRUTT, 3rd Baron (1842–1919), British physicist, who was professor of physics at the Cavendish Laboratory, Cambridge (1879), and at the Royal Institution (1887). His work on the density of nitrogen led to the discovery, in association with Sir William Ramsay, of the inert gases. In 1904 he was awarded the Nobel Prize for Physics.

RAYMOND III (1152–87), Count of Tripoli, regent (1185–6) of the kingdom of Jerusalem in the name of the infant Baldwin V. He was politically well acquainted with the prevailing situation in the Muslim lands and was convinced of the need for the Latins to avoid a major confrontation with Salah al-Din (Saladin), who had united Egypt, Syria, and Al-Jazira into a formidable state ranged against the Crusaders. The death of Baldwin V and the accession to the throne of Guy de Lusignan deprived the count of his office of regent and brought to the fore at Jerusalem the faction inclined to war. The indiscipline of Renaud de Chatillon, lord of Kerak of Moab, precipitated a new conflict, which led to the destruction of the Crusading forces at the battle of Hattin in 1187—a disaster which undermined much of Raymond's pacific policy.

RAYMOND V (d. 1194), Count of Toulouse (*reg.* 1148–94), who was the creator of a centralized, effectively governed territorial state with its centre in the prosperous and culturally advanced region of central Languedoc. His predecessors in the period 1095–1148 had all been involved in crusades in Syria and had neglected their French lands. Raymond did the opposite, added considerably to the possessions of the counts, and left to his son, Raymond VI, one of the most powerful principalities of western Europe. This was viewed with apprehension by King Philip Augustus of France and his hostility was a major cause of the disasters that befell the Toulousan state under Raymond VI early in the 13th cent.

RAYMOND VI (d. 1222), Count of Toulouse (*reg.* 1194–1222), who inherited in Languedoc a powerful state from his father, Raymond V, but the predominance of the counts of Toulouse over the south of France aroused the hostility of King Philip Augustus of France, especially as Raymond was the nephew and ally of Philip's principal enemies, kings Richard and John of England. Disaster overwhelmed Raymond because he refused to support the persecution of the Albigensian heretics who were numerous in his lands. Raymond was himself orthodox, but knew that persecution would ruin many of his personal followers and would impoverish his subjects. The murder in 1209 of the papal legate in Languedoc provided the occasion for launching a crusade against the Albigensians. It was encouraged by Philip Augustus, its leader, Simon de Montfort, being Philip's vassal. Raymond, for rallying to the defence of his subjects, was excommunicated and deposed. The war lasted until Simon's death in 1218, inflicting immense destruction on Languedoc. Raymond died, still in possession of some of his lands.

RAZI, AL- (Rhazes), Abu Bakr ibn Zakariya (AD 850–923), born at Al-Rayy not far from Teheran, was the greatest of Arab physicians. His *Kitab al-Asrar* (*Book of Secrets*), translated into Latin, was an important source of chemical knowledge in Europe during the 12th–14th cents. One of his monographs (rendered into Latin at Venice in 1565) contains the first clinical account of smallpox. His greatest work was *Al-Hawi* (the *Comprehensive Book*), translated into Latin under the title of 'Continens'. It constituted an encyclopedia of medical knowledge, summarizing all that the Arabs had learned from Greek, Persian, and Hindu sources, with their own additions of new material.

RAZIN, STENKA (d. 1671), Cossack outlaw and leader of the great rebellion of 1667–71 against the oppressive nobility and corrupt and arbitrary officialdom of Tsar Alexis's reign (1645–76). With a horde of dissident Cossacks and dispossessed peasants, Razin established a fortified settlement on the Don and then marched across the Volga to harass the Caspian trade routes. They then turned against Moscow and seized Astrakhan, Saratov, and Samara (1670), reorganizing the government on Cossack principles and slaughtering the tsar's supporters. The rebellion spread through the Volga basin to Nizhni-Novgorod, but the Muscovite forces rallied at Simbirsk (Oct. 1670) and routed the rebels. Razin was seized by other Cossacks (April 1671) and brought to Moscow to be executed.

REA, PHILIP RUSSELL REA, 2nd Baron (1900–   ), British Liberal politician, who became (1955) president of the Liberal Party. In 1954 he headed the British parliamentary delegation to Burma and Indonesia and was a delegate (1957) to the Council of Europe in Strasbourg.

READ, GABRIEL (1824–94), Tasmanian prospector, who made the first major gold discovery in NZ at 'Gabriel's Gully', near Lawrence, Otago, in 1861.

READING, RUFUS DANIEL ISAACS, 1st Marquis of (1860–1935), British lawyer, politician, and diplomat, who was attorney-general in Asquith's government (1910–13) and lord chief justice (1913–21). He also held office as ambassador to Washington (1918–19), viceroy of India (1921–6), and briefly, as foreign secretary, in Ramsay MacDonald's National government (1931). His combination of the office of lord chief justice with that of British ambassador in the US was unique. He played a vital role in the closing months of the First World War, during which the US was involved as a combatant nation. His tenure of office in India was one of a calm and practical approach during the years in which the future government of India was being worked out.

REALISM. Medieval realism stood in opposition to nominalism and, like nominalism, entered medieval western thought through the works of Boethius. Plato had maintained that an essence (or idea) existed independently of manifestations of it in particular objects (*eg*, intelligence existed independently of intelligent beings). This is absolute realism or idealism. Aristotle maintained that although essence was separate from its manifestations, it could be apprehended only through those manifestations. This is moderate realism. Both the Platonic and Aristotelian forms of realism were known in the Middle Ages, but for all practical purposes medieval realism was the Aristotelian, moderate realism,

adopted and applied to theology by Thomas Aquinas and the medieval Aristotelians who based the whole structure of metaphysics and Thomist theology on it.

REALPOLITIK in Germany, policy of the possible, a term often used to characterize Bismarck's methods. The term was first coined by a former liberal, Ludwig von Rochau, in his book *Grundsätze der Realpolitik* (1853). Von Rochau did not advocate opportunism or power politics, but a policy of limited ends within practical reach, in contrast to the idealistic all-or-nothing approach of the Frankfurt Assembly. The word is an apt summary of Bismarck's realism and his refusal to be governed by ideologies. Many former liberals supported him, for his success in unifying Germany and, casting overboard hankerings for responsible parliamentary government, formed the National Liberal Party.

In many ways, *Realpolitik* harked back to the type of bargaining of the pre-revolutionary era. It would have been difficult to apply where an electorate had to be considered, and was less successful after 1871.

Realpolitik, and the consequent split in the German liberal ranks, was the first dissociation of liberalism and nationalism. The old liberals clung to the ideal of democracy. The new liberals considered themselves practical statesmen and hoped that, once national unity was achieved, parliamentary democracy would follow. Their hopes were raised by Bismarck's introduction of manhood suffrage for the North German Confederation, but by the end of the 1870s they had realized that representation without responsibility was a fraud. Thus the split marked the end of any effective German liberal party.

Otto Pflanze, *Bismarck and the Development of Germany, 1815–1871* (Princeton, 1963).   DMK

REASON OF STATE (*raison d'état* or *realpolitik*), political doctrine developed during the late 16th cent., an expression of the new motive force in international politics, *ie*, that the centralized sovereign state had superseded the ideal of medieval constitutionalism and that moral considerations had no place in determining international disputes. Foreshadowed in the cynical realism of Machiavelli's *Prince*, it was expounded more clearly by Giovanni Botero (1540–1617) in *Della Ragion di Stato* and was implied in Grotius's *De Jure Belli et Pacis*. The concept was written into international law at the time of the peace of Westphalia (1648) and has remained the dominant factor in subsequent international relations.

RÉAUMUR, RENÉ ANTOINE FERCHAULT DE (1683–1757), French scientific polymath, 'the Pliny of the eighteenth century'. Elected to the French Academy of Sciences at the age of 25, Réaumur was commissioned to prepare a report on the whole field of contemporary technology; the result was the celebrated *Description des Arts et Métiers*, published posthumously in 27 volumes. Meanwhile his own contributions to science were impressive in their range and quality. His researches into steel and tinplate manufacture put these on a scientific basis for the first time and led to the establishment of these industries in France. His six-volume *Mémoires pour servir à l'histoire des insectes* mark him as one of the founders of the science of entomology. He did pioneer work on the measurement of temperature; established for the first time the nature of the digestive process; and made important advances in many other fields. He contributed a great deal to the concept of an industrial society based on scientific research.

REBEC, BATTLE OF (1524), in Italy between the Imperialists, under the renegade Constable de Bourbon, who inflicted heavy losses upon the French, commanded by Guillaume Bonnivet. The chevalier de Bayard was one of those killed.

REBELLION LOSSES ACT (1849) in Canada, legislation to repay those whose property was damaged in the rebellion of

1837. The assent of Lord Elgin, the governor, to the measure in the face of public opposition was later regarded as a step towards responsible government in Canada.

REBELLION OF 1837 in Canada, insurrection led by William Lyon Mackenzie in Upper Canada and Louis-Joseph Papineau in Lower Canada, against the autocratic system of colonial government in Canada. Risings in Upper Canada were put down, but with help from US sympathizers Mackenzie set up a provisional government on Navy Island in the Niagara river and proclaimed a republic. Skirmishes and raids resulted in a number of prisoners being taken; 20 were executed, and the rest pardoned by 1845. In Lower Canada 12 *patriotes*, led by Papineau, adopted the Declaration of Saint-Ours, in which civil disobedience was advocated. Insurgents gathered at Saint-Denis and Saint-Charles, but were defeated and dispersed after bitter fighting. The second uprising was headed by American sympathizers (1838), but was likewise overcome. Twelve prisoners were executed, and more transported, but security for all was given by the Amnesty Act (1849).

REBOUÇAS, ANDRÉ (1838–98), Brazilian mulatto, civil engineer, and abolitionist, who took pride in being called the representative of the 'mulatto population' of Brazil. He spent two years (1860–2) in Europe, studying the construction of docks and railways. On returning to Brazil he built the first modern docks in Rio de Janeiro, Maranhão, Paraíba, Recife, and Bahia. As an ardent abolitionist, he proposed a form of agrarian reform for ex-slaves after their emancipation. He accompanied the Emperor Pedro II into exile, rather than accept the republic in 1889. After Pedro's death in 1891, he spent six years in Portuguese Africa, hoping to help in the liberation of the 'black continent'.

RECHBERG, JOHANN BERNARD, Count (1809–99), Austrian politician and foreign minister, who was a supporter of Austro-Prussian collaboration in German affairs. As foreign minister (1859) he assiduously sought friendship with Prussia and dual domination of the German Confederation. His relations with Bismarck, which were friendly, culminated in joint intervention in Schleswig-Holstein and war against Denmark. Because of his inability to obtain satisfactory terms from Prussia for relinquishing claims to Holstein, he was dismissed by Francis Joseph (1864) in favour of the Greater German party and an Austrian forward movement in Germany. Rechberg's policy of friendship with Prussia in political matters was inconsistent with his attempts to undermine Prussia's position in the Zollverein in concert with the South German states, but it was Austria's isolation in Europe and her financial weakness which rendered his efforts in both nugatory.

RECONQUISTA, reconquest of the Iberian peninsula after its occupation by the Moors in the 8th cent. The battle of Covadonga (718), which symbolizes the beginning of the *Reconquista*, was a minor encounter and the following years saw only minor forays into Muslim territory. The idea of a unified peninsula under Christian rule took root in the 9th cent. Thereafter the movement southwards became increasingly rapid, taking on more and more the character of a religious crusade, and reached a peak in the 13th cent. Christian domination was complete after the occupation of Granada in 1492. The various foci of resistance to Muslim domination produced the three major kingdoms of the peninsula in the later Middle Ages. By the 13th cent. Portugal reached its southern seaboard and Aragon conquered the area apportioned to it by the treaty of Almizra (1244), so that both states directed their energies to maritime expansion in the Atlantic and the Mediterranean respectively and evolved into states dominated by maritime interests. On the other hand Castile, which had to conquer a far larger area, became a crusading society and evolved religious and military values which guided Spain's conduct as a world

power in the 16th and 17th cents. The difficulty of populating its conquest in the south allowed the amassing of large estates by the nobility, which successfully delayed the emergence of stable centralized government and created a large landless peasantry, thus producing a major social problem still largely unsolved in 1970.

RECONSTRUCTION in the US, name given to the period of readjustment following the American Civil War. Presidential Reconstruction began with Lincoln's Proclamation (8 Dec. 1863), offering an amnesty to rebels and advancing the 'Ten Percent Plan', which was generous to whites, but ignored former slaves. The creation of 'loyal' governments within four of the Confederate states began in 1864, LA making the greatest progress. When Congress passed the Wade–Davis Bill (July 1864) to assert Congressional prerogatives and ensure genuinely reconstructed governments, Lincoln vetoed the bill. Despite early indications of a rigorous policy towards the South, Lincoln's successor, President Andrew Johnson, hoping to establish a national conservative coalition with southern support, adopted an indulgent attitude towards the former Confederacy. His proclamations (29 May 1865 onwards) promoted conservative control in the reorganization of southern states and provided no protection for the freedmen. With Congress out of session, Johnson was free to implement his policy, discounting the growing concern of Congressional leaders and other public figures.

When Congress reconvened (Dec. 1865), Johnson presented them with a *fait accompli*: the southern states were reorganized. Congress reacted negatively, refusing seats to members from those states, and early in 1866 attempted to supplement Johnson's programme by protecting freedmen with a strengthened Freedmen's Bureau (19 Feb. 1866) and a Civil Rights Bill (9 April 1868). Johnson tried to veto both. Congress then passed the 14th Amendment (16 June 1866), which, among other provisions, sought to guarantee the citizenship of the Negro, but it was not ratified by the requisite numbers of states until July 1868.

The existence in a number of southern states of 'Black Codes' that restricted the freedom of the emancipated Negroes helped to harden attitudes, and political tensions increased when Johnson openly broke with the Congressional majority and attempted through speeches, extreme use of patronage powers, and support for a new National Union Party, to influence the Congressional elections in 1866. He failed, and the Radical Republicans emerged in sufficient strength to implement their own programme.

A number of Reconstruction Acts were passed (1867–8), which sought to guarantee Negro suffrage, temporarily disfranchised some former Confederates, and divided the South into five military districts, each under martial law, pending acceptable reorganization. Most states had complied by 1868, all by 1870. With the acceptance by Congress and by the president of reorganized governments, the process of reconstruction was legally completed.

Following Congressional Reconstruction, all the southern states except VA underwent a period of Radical Republican dominance erroneously called 'Black Reconstruction'. While Negroes constituted a majority in the legislature of SC, their power in the South as a whole fell short of that warranted by their numbers. The period is often depicted as one of corruption, confiscatory taxes, and general misgovernment. While such allegations are correct in some cases (*eg*, LA and SC), others, notably MS, were honestly administered. Public education and other progressive programmes were initiated.

Opponents of the Radicals relied on appeals to white unity and terrorism to bring their governments down. The last Radical state governments fell to the Conservative-Democrat 'Redeemers' in disputed elections in 1876.

Kenneth M. Stampp, *The Era of Reconstruction, 1865–1877* (New York, 1965).
W. R. Brock, *An American Crisis: Congress and Reconstruction, 1865–1877* (London, 1963).   **PCP**

RECONSTRUCTION FINANCE CORPORATION (1932–57), in the US, federal agency established during the administration of Herbert Hoover to try to alleviate the Depression by federal 'pump-priming' loans to private banking, insurance, mortgage and loan associations, and railroads. Its activities were greatly expanded during the New Deal. Originally capitalized at $500 million, it had lent over $48,000 million and survived various reorganizations by the time its remaining functions were transferred to other federal agencies in 1957.

RECOPILACIÓN **(OF THE LAWS OF THE KINGDOMS OF THE INDIES),** compilation of laws for the governance of the Spanish American empire. Spain was the most legalistic of colonial powers, and work on the *Recopilación* was begun in 1570 to synthesize the huge mass of minutely detailed, conflicting, and frequently out-of-date legislation pertaining to Spanish America. Many worked at the task, notably Antonio León Pinelo, but its enormity and the Crown's penury prevented publication until 1681. The result was a four-volume code containing some 6400 laws. Unfortunately, the *Recopilación* was never revised to include later legislation. In the distribution and co-ordination of the statutes, the *Recopilación* lacks the organic character of a modern code, and is not free from inconsistency, contradiction, and error, but it is none the less one of the most humane and comprehensive codes published for any colonial empire.

RECUSANCY, religious nonconformity based on a refusal to acknowledge the supremacy of the ruling sovereign or to conform to the rites of the established church. The term is usually applied to the Roman Catholic population of England, Ireland, Scotland, and Wales from the Henrician reformation of the 16th cent. until the relief acts of the late 18th and early 19th cents.

RECUSANTS, ACT AGAINST (1581) in England, Elizabethan legislation, designed to extend the existing treason law to include all those who might persuade Englishmen to deny allegiance to Elizabeth I or to the Church of England, and to increase the recusancy fine to the prohibitive figure of £20. The act resulted from the influx of English Catholic missionaries from Europe who were dedicated to the country's reconversion to Catholicism, which began in 1577. Antipapal feeling in the Commons, first aroused by the provocative bull, *Regnans in excelsis* (1570), caused the government to strengthen its hand in convicting priests and preventing conversions. Further stringent legislation followed in 1585 and 1593.

RED ARMY in Russia. The Workers' and Peasants' Red Army was recruited in Jan. 1918 by a decree of the Bolshevik government. In March of the same year Trotsky became president of the supreme war council and people's commissar for war, a post he held until 1924. Under his guidance the Red Army was expanded from a volunteer force of 150,000 in 1918 to a conscript force of 5½ million in 1921. Faced with the need to suppress internal and external threats to Bolshevism, he brought into the Red Army 50,000 officers and 200,000 ncos of the old tsarist army: the first two commanders-in-chief, Vatsetis and Kamenev, were ex-colonels of the imperial general staff. After 1921, with the end of the Civil War and the signing of the treaty of Riga with Poland, the Red Army was reduced in size; in 1925 Trotsky's successor, Frunze, fixed its strength at 562,000, but by 1939 it had risen to 2 million, with Voroshilov as commissar (1925–40). In the early inter-war years it remained, as far as was practicable, a people's militia of workers and peasants, reinforced with cavalry, much as it had been during the Civil War; but with Russia's industrialization in the 1930s it was modernized and mechanized and by 1939 was more like other continental armies, being based on universal military service and maintaining a large reserve. A feature of the Red Army was the attachment of political commissars to every unit: this origi-

nated in an attempt to solve the inherent difficulty in a revolutionary regime of ensuring the army's loyalty, an essential with so large a number of tsarist officers in the Red Army during the Civil War. The political commissars were appointed by the Communist Party, and supervised the combatant commanders ('military specialists'), being at the same time responsible for supplies and for the morale and political education of the rank and file. In times of political calm they were reduced to the role of advisers, official emphasis being placed on the 'unity of command'; but during periods of uncertainty, such as followed Stalin's purges, theirs was an important office. In 1937 the old ranks up to that of colonel were restored, but although five marshals of the Soviet Union were appointed the rank of general was not reintroduced until June 1940 and the word 'officer' not until late in 1942. In May 1937 the Red Army first felt the effects of Stalin's purges, and it is estimated that by 1939 some 35,000 officers had been removed; the victims included three of the five marshals, among them Tukhachevsky, and the greater part of the High Command. This drastic measure greatly reduced the army's effectiveness as a fighting force and inhibited initiative in the officer corps; the poor showing of the Red Army in the Russo–Finnish War of 1939–40 and the tightening of discipline under Timoshenko, defence commissar from 1940, did little to restore it in time to meet the onslaught of the Germans in June 1941. The word 'Red' was officially dropped from the title of the Russian army in 1946.   NRB

RED BOOK in Sweden, red-covered liturgy based on the Catholic Mass, which was accepted by the clergy at a meeting in Stockholm (1577) under strong pressure from John III. It is uncertain how far the king was influenced by his foreign ambitions and how far by his sympathy with the Counter-Reformation. A Catholic mission to Sweden from Norway was expelled in 1583.

RED CLOUD (1822–1909), chief of the American Oglala Sioux Indians, who led the opposition to the building of the 'Bozeman Trail' through Sioux hunting grounds in the Big Horn Mountains to the gold regions of MT (1865). His tribe reached agreement with the US at the treaty of Fort Laramie (6 Nov. 1868).

RED CROSS (1864), national and international body founded in Geneva (Aug. 1864) for the protection and care of war casualties. It was inspired by Henri Dunant, who had been deeply moved by the plight of the wounded in the battle of Solferino. The International Committee of the Red Cross was founded in 1863, and a diplomatic conference drew up (1864) the first international treaty whereby governments agreed to care for the wounded of war, whether ally or enemy. The outcome of the conference was the first Geneva convention, signed by 26 nations, which guaranteed protection for the war wounded and the neutrality of hospitals bearing the Red Cross sign. The sign of a red cross on a white field was adopted as an emblem which could be easily recognized on a battlefield. New methods of warfare in the 20th cent. led to revisions and new conventions to protect victims of warfare at sea (1907), prisoners of war (1929), and civilians in time of war (1949).

RED FRIDAY (31 July 1925) in Britain, on which the prime minister, Stanley Baldwin, intervened in a dispute between the miners and the coalowners to arrange for the payment of a special subsidy to the industry for nine months and avoid a national strike over a wage claim.

The British mining industry was seriously damaged by the First World War and its aftermath. Coal exports reached a peak in 1913, but were interrupted by the war, and were never resumed in quantity because of the opening of coalfields in former export markets. At the same time, the conversion of shipping from coal to oil firing decimated the demand for bunker fuel, which particularly affected South Wales.

The effects of this crisis were first felt in 1921, when the owners locked out the miners to enforce wage reductions immediately the mines were released from state control. The miners had been promised support through the 'Triple Alliance' of railwaymen and transport workers, but on 'Black Friday' (15 April 1921) these two found reasons for not striking in sympathy with the miners, who had eventually to accept the reductions and returned to work in July. The crisis was temporarily alleviated by the French occupation of the Ruhr in 1923, which disrupted European coal production, but had returned in full force by 1925, when the owners demanded further reductions.

The miners saw 'Red Friday' as a triumph to offset 'Black Friday', but nothing changed during the nine months' period of grace, and at the end of it the General Strike broke out. Again, the miners eventually had to accept wage cuts when they went back to work in Nov. 1926.

RED JACKET (c. 1756–1830), American Indian orator and chief of the Seneca tribe, who fought with the British in the American War of Independence and received his name because of the jacket given him by the British. He visited President Washington (1792) as a representative of his people and through his oratory swung Senecan support to the US during the War of 1812. Although remaining at peace with the US, he frequently clashed with the government over the intrusion of white customs and religion among the Indians.

RED RIVER REBELLION (1869–70) in Canada. Alarmed by the transfer of Hudson's Bay Co.'s lands to the Dominion of Canada and by movements of white Protestant settlers into the Red River valley, Métis (half breeds) under Louis Riel prevented government surveys of Métis lands (Oct. 1869), and armed Métis, led by Joseph Lépine, forced the lieutenant-governor of the NWT to seek refuge in the US. Riel seized Fort Garry (Nov. 1869), formed a provisional government (Dec. 1869), and was appointed president. Métis demands for land rights and Catholic schools were rejected by the Canadian government and a British-Canadian military force, under Col. Garnet Wolseley, restored order in the NWT (Aug. 1870). Lépine and Riel were banished from Canada for five years.

RED SCARE in the US, period of national hysteria which reached its height in 1919–21. The scare had its immediate origins in the First World War, during which the US government, supported by patriotic groups like the American Legion and the National Civic Federation, attempted to suppress sedition by various means, including the passing of alien, espionage, and sedition acts, and the banning of certain publications from the mails. Partly because of the anti-war attitude of the Socialist Party and partly because of fears of Bolshevist subversion aroused by the Russian Revolution, the principal targets of government action were trade unions and radical political groups. The ending of the war saw no lessening of tension, which was maintained by bomb scares, strikes, the investigation of the Lusk Committee into Bolshevik activity, the founding of the American Communist Party, and the nation-wide raid on 'reds' by the Department of Justice, on the orders of attorney-general A. Mitchell Palmer.

RED SHIRT MOVEMENT in India, nickname, derived from the dark plum-coloured tunics worn by Khan Abdul Ghaffar Khan's volunteer organization the *Khudai Khidmatgar*, the 'servants of God'. It was founded in 1929, and organized in a military-style hierarchy with local branches under the control of a Central Afghan *Jirga* (council). Although originally intended as a social-work organization, the red shirts were involved in the civil disobedience movement (1930–2) and they formed the basis of Abdul Ghaffar's pro-Congress political control of the North-West Frontier Province until 1946. They also provided the basis for a scheme for a separate state of Pakhtoonistan in 1947. The new nation of Pakistan banned the movement.

RED TURBANS, Chinese rebel bands comprising members of the Triad and other secret societies, who ravaged Kwangtung province, particularly the area around Canton, in 1854–5. They wore red turbans, and swore to restore the Ming dynasty. The causes of their revolt were much the same as those that brought about the Taiping Rebellion: a bad harvest in 1852 and a severe trade recession in 1853 depressed the areas around Canton. As there was no genuine pretender to the Ming throne, to serve as a figurehead, the Red Turbans failed to achieve unity of purpose or of their operations. They quickly degenerated into plundering hordes, creating a free-for-all situation for other bandits and pirates as well. They were finally suppressed, after much bloodshed, by a combination of gentry-led militia, government troops, and mercenaries.

REDEMPTION TREATY (1649), financial agreement between Denmark and the United Provinces, whereby the latter were committed to paying the Danes 140,000 *riskdalers* per annum in return for the exemption of Dutch shipping from the Sound dues. This agreement, which destroyed Swedish-Dutch friendship and gave Denmark security from Swedish aggression, was later cancelled by the Rescissory treaty (1653).

REDEMPTORISTS, members of the Congregation of the Most Holy Redeemer, a religious order founded in 1732 at Scala, Italy, by St Alfonso Maria de Liguori, and approved by the papacy in 1749. Redemptorist foundations, dedicated to the sanctification of their members and preaching to the poor through parish missions, were established in northern Europe from the late 18th cent. and in America in 1832. A similar order of nuns was founded by De Liguori in 1731, which received papal recognition in 1750.

REDFERN, WILLIAM (c. 1774–1833) Australian 'emancipist' surgeon, transported to NSW in 1801 for his part in the Nore mutiny. He enjoyed the favour of Gov. Lachlan Macquarie, but suffered the humiliations commonly extended by Commissioner J. T. Bigge and 'exclusives' to pardoned convicts of proven quality. He was appointed assistant surgeon at Norfolk Island shortly after his arrival in NSW, was given a free pardon (1803), and appointed assistant surgeon in Sydney (1808). He later maintained a successful private practice in the colony.

RED-FIGURE POTTERY, decorative style which evolved in late 6th-cent. BC Athens, superseding Black-Figure ware and which maintained Athenian dominance in overseas markets. Natural red figures were left on a black-painted background and thin glazed lines gave greater freedom in detail.

REDING, ALOYS, Count (1755–1818), Swiss soldier during the French invasion (1798). He defeated the French at Morgarten and headed the supporters of the Swiss oligarchy until he was imprisoned by Ney. He resumed his political career after Napoleon's Act of Mediation (1803).

REDMOND, JOHN EDWARD (1856–1918), Irish politician and leader of the Irish Home Rule Party in the British parliament, who was elected MP for New Ross (1881). He remained loyal to Parnell after the split of 1890 and led the minority of the party which supported him. He was MP for Waterford (1891–1918) and was leader of the reunited party, which exercised pressure on Asquith's Liberal government, the existence of which depended on Irish votes in the House of Commons. Redmond believed in the achievement of his party's aims by any methods, except terrorism, and strove for peace in the period of virtual civil war before 1914. He was prepared to accept, at least temporarily, the exclusion of any North-Eastern counties which voted against Home Rule. He pledged support for the British war effort in the First World War, though this was opposed by extremist republicans, and he was deeply distressed by the Easter Rising in Dublin (1916).

REDONDA, West Indian island discovered and named by Columbus (1493).

REDUCCIONES (*reduções* in Portuguese), mission villages in colonial Latin America into which widely scattered natives were concentrated (lit. 'reduced') for purposes of religious instruction, training, and often to protect them from the demands of the civilian population. The most famous were those which the Jesuits established in Paraguay.

REDUCTION in Sweden, term used for the resumption of lands alienated by the Crown. The policy was supported by the lower estates, which resented the exemption of noble property from taxation, although the effect of the large Reduction made by Charles XI was to facilitate the establishment of absolutism.

REED, JOHN (1887–1920), US journalist, who contributed to radical magazines and joined the staff of *The Masses* (1913). He reported the Mexican revolution and the First World War, witnessed the October Revolution in Russia in 1917, became a friend of Lenin, and wrote propaganda for the Bolsheviks. After returning to the US he became a leader of the American Communist Labor Party (1919), but after being indicted for sedition he returned to the Soviet Union, where he died. His eye-witness account of the Bolshevik revolution, *Ten Days that Shook the World* (1919), is a classic.

REED, THOMAS BRACKETT (1839–1902), US lawyer and politician, who served in the House of Representatives (1877–99) and was speaker (1889–91, 1895–9). He secured the adoption of the Reed Rules of Procedure (1890) which increased the powers of the speaker and of committee chairmen in the interest of facilitating enactment of the legislative programme of the congressional majority party. He resigned in protest against the imperial policies that the US seemed to have adopted at the time of the Spanish–American War.

REED, WALTER (1851–1902), US military surgeon and bacteriologist, who served as head of the US army Yellow Fever Commission in Cuba (1900), whose investigations proved that the disease was transmitted by mosquitoes.

REEVES, SIR WILLIAM CONRAD (1821–1902), West Indian lawyer, who was the son of a Barbadian slave and a white father. He was appointed Barbados solicitor-general and elected to the Assembly (1874). He was later appointed attorney-general (1882) and chief justice (1886).

REEVES, WILLIAM PEMBER (1857–1932), NZ radical politician, historian, and poet, who entered parliament in 1887. He was strongly influenced by Fabian socialism and contributed substantially to the Liberal victory in 1890. As minister of labour (1892) in Ballance's cabinet, he introduced comprehensive labour reforms, notably the compulsory industrial arbitration act (1894). He was director of the London School of Economics (1908–19).

REFORM, ECONOMICAL, in Britain, one of the most conspicuous demands (1779–82) for the reduction of the influence of the Crown. The demand began in 1779, outside parliament, with a county petitioning movement similar but more widespread than that of 1769. The most prominent of the petitioning counties was not Middlesex, as in 1769, but Yorkshire, under Christopher Wyvill. The petitions demanded economy, an increase in the number of county MPs, and triennial parliaments. Through Sir George Savile, the Yorkshire movement was linked with the Rockinghamites in parliament,

though the latter's demands were confined to 'economy'. In Feb. 1780 Burke defined the petitioners' objective as 'the independence of parliament and the economic reformation of the civil and other establishments' and in April Dunning carried a resolution that 'the influence of the Crown has increased, is increasing, and ought to be diminished'. The Rockinghamite programme was implemented in 1782 with the passing of Burke's Civil Establishments Act, Crewe's Act, and Clerke's Act excluding contractors from the Commons. The other aims of the county petitioners were not mentioned.

It cannot be claimed that the 1782 reforms either effected economies or increased administrative efficiency—but this was not their primary aim. They may have made some small reduction in the influence of the Crown, but here the startling reduction came in the next half-century, and was effected by Pitt and his successors, whose prime object was to increase government efficiency.   BK

REFORM CLUB (1836) in Britain, formed as a headquarters of Whig and radical politics to counter the influence of the Conservative Carlton Club, and as a centre for party management and social gatherings.

REFORM LEAGUE in Britain, organization of respectable London working men and middle-class Liberal sympathizers founded in 1865 which, immediately before the 1867 Reform Act, mobilized popular support for 'registered and residential' manhood suffrage. Its leaders, eager to keep within the bounds of parliamentary legality, and to promote working-class Liberal candidates at the 1868 general election, were half-frightened of the masses they were leading.

REFORM PARTY in NZ, right-wing 'anti-socialist' party which represented the interests of NZ property-owners, who were primarily farmers. Many of them, alarmed by militant labour, turned from Ward's Liberal Party to Massey's opposition, called 'Reform' from 1909. Their original intention was the freeing of the civil service from political control by Liberals. The party, the first to be fully established in NZ, was formally constituted in 1912. Whether in, or sharing, power (1912–28), Reform put farming interests first and sought to strengthen imperial political and economic ties. In coalition (1931–5), the party became inextricably involved with Depression policies, and was dissolved (1936) into the National Party.

REFORMA, THE, in Mexico, reform movement (1855–67) which fostered laws attacking ecclesiastical and military privileges (*fueros*), and Church and village, corporately held, property. It represented a severe attack on the position of the oligarchy inherited from the colonial epoch (pre-1821). At the same time, it established a legal basis for the destruction of traditional villages throughout Mexico, in the futile hope of creating a class of independent yeoman farmers.

Support for the movement came from urban mixed (*mestizo*) population, who were largely of the middle class and had suffered from discrimination by the creole oligarchy. Having driven out the infamous dictator, Santa Anna, they sought to establish a constitutional regime which would permanently check the ambitions of Church and army. Economic growth was to be fostered by removing Church properties held in mortmain.

The revolution of Ayutla (1855), led by Gen. Juan Álvarez, brought the reformers to power. A moderate government was established under Ignacio Comonfort (1855–8). The *Ley Juárez* (1855) abolished ecclesiastical and military *fueros* or law codes, the *Ley Lerdo* (1856) limited corporate ownership of land; and a federalist constitution (1857), incorporating these measures, was adopted. Conservative reaction was immediate and violent. In the War of the Reform (1858–60) which followed, the conservative general, Zuloaga, seized the capital and Comonfort fled into exile. Benito Juárez assumed the liberal presidency and retreated to Veracruz.

As a result of the conflict the liberals enacted more drastic anti-clerical legislation. The Reform Laws (July 1859) expropriated all ecclesiastical property except Church buildings, suppressed all monasteries, nationalized all cemeteries, and made marriage a civil contract. The liberals won the war and Juárez emerged as president.

The conservatives turned to France for aid. Napoleon III sent troops, who drove Juárez from Mexico City (1863) and established Maximilian of Austria (1864–7) as Emperor of Mexico. Juárez held out in Chihuahua, and, at the conclusion of the US Civil War, Napoleon III withdrew his support. Having failed to mollify the clerical-conservatives, Maximilian, without support, was executed while Juárez was victorious. He was re-elected and ruled strongly until 1872.

W. V. Scholes, *Mexican Politics During the Juárez Regime, 1855–1872* (Columbia, MO, 1957). HDS

REFORMATION IN DENMARK, became established at the accession of Christian III (1536). There had been Lutheran teaching in Copenhagen since 1521, but the determining factor was the king's need of Church land. All the bishops were arrested and deprived of their sees, and new 'superintendents' were ordained by Buchenhagen (who was only in priest's orders). A Church Ordinance was approved by Luther and adopted in an amended Danish version (1539) for Denmark and Norway, the driving-force being Peder Palladius, bishop of Zealand (1537–60).

REFORMATION IN ENGLAND, process by which the Crown and parliament cut the spiritual, juridical, and financial bonds which linked the English Church to the papacy and established a national Anglican Church. Both causes and effects were religious, intellectual, social, and economic, and the process left few aspects of national life untouched.

The Reformation was not state-produced (Protestantism had affected important groups in English society years before) but state intervention was decisive. Growing anti-clericalism caused by ecclesiastical abuses (personified by Wolsey), as well as the activities of such Protestant groups as the Lollards, aided by the wide diffusion of propaganda made possible by the invention of printing, helped to cause the Henrician Reformation of the 1530s. The Reformation, however, must be distinguished from the advent of Protestantism in England. Though King Henry VIII's chief minister, Thomas Cromwell, and Abp Thomas Cranmer were attracted to Lutheranism, Henry himself retained Catholic views on dogma, apart from papal supremacy, as did most of his bishops and nobles. Henry's legislation sprang from the question of the royal annulment or divorce, which, though it did not cause the Reformation, certainly affected its timing.

Wolsey's failure to secure the annulment (1529–30) was followed by the Pardon of the Clergy (1531), the Supplication of the Commons against the Ordinaries, and the Submission of the Clergy (1532), which gave Henry control of the Church. Cromwell drafted a long series of acts replacing papal authority with royal supremacy. The dissolution of the monasteries followed in 1536 and 1539. Alongside this legislation the king ruled the Church through proclamations and injunctions.

A Catholic reaction set in (1539–40), led by Norfolk and Bp Gardiner. The Six Articles Act (1539) and the execution of Cromwell (1540) were followed by the King's Book (1543), a Catholic restatement of dogma. Henry's policy of reaction, however, was fitfully applied and in the country Protestantism advanced.

Edward VI had been educated as a Protestant, and during his reign Protector Somerset pursued far more liberal policies than Henry. He repealed the Six Articles Act, the oppressive Henrician treason laws, and allowed priests to marry (1549). The Acts of Uniformity (1549, 1552) established the Edwardian Prayer Book as the only legal form of worship. This book fused both Catholic and Lutheran liturgies into the rites of a national Church. Protestantism advanced

further under Northumberland. The Prayer Book was revised and the 42 Articles of Religion—a more Protestant interpretation of faith—were enforced.

In the reign of Mary I a further Catholic reaction took place. First, parliament abrogated Edward VI's statutes, restoring the 1547 situation. In 1554 parliament went further and restored the situation of 1529 by repealing Henry's anti-papal legislation.

In the Elizabethan Settlement (1559), royal supremacy was restored with Elizabeth I taking the title of 'Supreme Governor'. The second Prayer Book was re-established with a few amendments, and in 1563 the settlement was completed with a revised formulary of faith known as the 39 Articles, which received parliamentary confirmation in 1571. This settlement was an uneasy compromise between the radical Protestantism of the 1559 house of commons and the conservative Protestantism of Elizabeth. The compromise also led to the growth of the Puritan movement within the Anglican Church, and it became clear in the 17th cent. that the attempt at a comprehensive settlement had failed.

A. G. Dickens, *The English Reformation* (London, 1964). P. Hughes, *The Reformation in England* (London, 1950–4). CJ

REFORMATION IN FRANCE, although less pervasive than the religious revolution in Britain and Scandinavia, penetrated more deeply than in Italy or in Spain and gave rise to grave political conflicts within France during the later 16th and early 17th cents.

The reformed religion found a favourable climate of opinion in the humanism of scholars like Guillaume Budé, founder of the humanist Collège de France, and Jacques Lefèvre d'Etaples, who became the leader of a small group of moderate but orthodox reformers, including Briçonnet, Bp of Meaux, the mystic Gerard Boussel, Guillaume Farel, the future Protestant leader, and Margaret of Angoulême, sister of Francis I. From the 1520s Lutheranism crept into France, especially to the trading centres, eg, Lyons, where it found support among the lower classes, but the movement provoked little hostility from the Crown before 1525, although it was attacked by the theological faculty of the Sorbonne, the defender of orthodox Catholicism. The attitude of the monarchy was to prove fundamental to the course of the French reformation because, though anti-clericalism did exist, eg, in the works of Rabelais, nationalist opposition to Rome was irrelevant in a country where the Church enjoyed a large degree of Gallican independence and royal leadership. Although the circle at Meaux dispersed in 1525 to escape persecution and one of the few noble Protestants, Louis de Berquin, was burned in 1529, Francis I did not feel committed to a policy of persecution lest it jeopardize his political relations with the German Protestant princes.

However, in 1534 a radical change occurred in royal policy with the appearance of the anti-Catholic *placards* in Paris and the major French towns (Oct. 1534), which produced a bitter Catholic reaction. A series of persecuting edicts (1538–1543) and acts of extermination, eg, the massacre of 3000 Waldensians (1545), followed. French Protestantism was reinforced from the mid-1530s by the spread, among the lower classes of the Languedoc and the seaboard towns of Normandy and Brittany, of the ideas of John Calvin, himself a Frenchman though an exile in Geneva. Henry II none the less continued his father's harsh policies, setting up a special court, the chambre ardente, to deal with heresy, and issuing further repressive edicts, eg, that of Ecouen (1559).

From 1555 the reformation in France took a new turn, as trained Calvinist pastors infiltrated and a large number of the nobility, estimated at one-half by 1562, was converted to this more militant creed. The converts included highly influential figures, eg, the Prince de Condé, the Châtillon brothers, and Duplessis-Mornay, and, despite the execution for heresy of a leading magistrate, Anne Du Bourg, the Calvinists were strong enough to hold their first national synod in Paris in 1559.

The death of Henry II and the succession of three weak kings created a turbulent situation (1559–89), as a strong Huguenot noble faction vied with the aggressively Catholic house of Guise for influence over the Crown and power to decide the religious fate of France. The queen mother, Catherine de' Medici, at first tried conciliation at the Colloquy of Poissy (1561), in which Calvin's lieutenant, Theodore Beza, took a leading part, and she granted an edict of toleration (1562). However, when the massacre of Vassy precipitated the wars of religion the Crown alternated between recognizing the existence of the Huguenots, *eg*, by the pacification of Amboise (1563) and the peace of Monsieur (1576), and conniving at their extermination, *eg*, the St Bartholomew Massacre (1572). Although Henry IV's conversion to Catholicism (1594) vindicated the political necessity of French kings to conform to the religion of the majority of Frenchmen, the Edict of Nantes (1598) guaranteed the right of the militant Calvinist minority to exist within the French state. Despite the revocation of this protective law by Louis XIV (1685), a tiny but determined number of Calvinists has continued to flourish in France to the present day.

J. T. McNeill, *History and Character of Calvinism* (New York, 1954).
J. E. Neale, *The Age of Catherine de Medici* (London, 1963).

MKS

REFORMATION IN GERMANY, original source of the great religious revolution of the 16th cent. which gave rise to the reformed Protestant Churches and particularly to the Lutheran religion. The reformation began with the personal revolt of one man, Martin Luther (1483–1546), a German intellectual of peasant stock, who became an Augustinian friar and professor of theology at Wittenberg University. His initial concern was with his own sense of guilt which led him to embrace the doctrine of justification by faith alone (1513). In 1517 he protested in 95 theses against the practice of selling indulgences and was consequently ordered to recant unconditionally. This in turn prompted Luther to consider his attitude to papal authority, to church councils, and to the Holy Scriptures. Interviews between him and Cardinal Cajetan (1518) and a debate with Johann Eck (1519) only stimulated his own opposition; 41 propositions attributed to him were condemned by the papal bull *Exsurge Domine* (1520) and he was excommunicated (1521), though he defiantly burned the papal bull publicly in Wittenberg. In three famous manifestoes of 1520 he stated his fundamental beliefs. *Address to the Nobility of the German Nation* put forward a sweeping programme of Church reform. *On the Babylonish Captivity of the Church* attacked the hierarchical and sacramental system of the Church, and in *On the Liberty of a Christian Man* Luther asserted his doctrine of justification by faith. He then defied Emperor Charles V at the Diet of Worms (1521), and to escape from an imperial ban took refuge in Wartburg castle, where he translated the New Testament into German and wrote many pamphlets.

The implications of Luther's personal revolt now began to be widely felt in Germany. He had already won a response from scholars at Wittenberg, *eg*, Andrew Carlstadt and Philip Melanchthon, and from princes and knights, *eg*, Frederick, Elector of Saxony and Sickingen and Hutten. From 1521 his evangelical ideas spread to a number of imperial free cities, *eg*, Erfurt, Nuremberg, Magdeburg, Altenburg, and among the peasants of Swabia, Franconia, and Thuringia. While Luther was in hiding his radical supporters carried through fundamental reforms, *eg*, Carlstadt in Wittenberg abolished private masses and religious pictures, denounced celibacy and monastic vows, and introduced communion in both kinds and a vernacular liturgy. Luther sought to restrain, reform, and condemn lawlessness, rejecting an alliance with the rebellious peasantry (1524–5). Although he still led the growing body of reformers, his example had inspired a number of scattered extremist groups, whose beliefs were based on apocalyptic and mystical theology. Among these

prophets were Thomas Münzer, the peasant leader, spiritualists such as Hans Denck, Sebastian Franck and Caspar Schwenckfeld, and Anabaptists like Conrad Grebel and Melchior Hoffmann, through whom the millenarian tradition in Protestantism was established.

The fate of German Lutheranism, however, depended upon the ability of the Emperor Charles V to suppress its most loyal supporters, the German princes. From 1525 the new faith was embraced by Albert of Hohenzollern, Philip of Hesse, the Margrave of Brandenburg-Ansbach, the Prince of Anhalt, and the Dukes of Brunswick, Württemberg, and Saxony. Charles, preoccupied with the war in Italy and his enmity with Francis I of France, was forced to postpone action against the German reform movement. While Luther continued to lecture and write, therefore, his disciple, Melanchthon, drafted the Augsburg Confession (1530), which provided the basis of the Lutheran Church and the political doctrine of the Schmalkaldic League (1531). Another colleague, Johann Bugenhagen, organized the Lutheran Church in northern Germany. By 1529 Charles V and the Catholic princes in the imperial Diet were ready to withdraw their earlier concessions (1526), thus provoking the historic *Protestation* of the evangelical princes and cities which gave them the name of *Protestant*. However, the strength of the Protestant princes and the need for help against the Turks (1531) caused Charles to call a truce at Nuremberg (1532), which gave Lutheranism the vital breathing-space it needed to establish itself. Although moderate Protestants and Catholics hoped for a theological reconciliation at the conferences of Hagenau and Regensburg, a genuine compromise proved impossible, particularly on the doctrine of the eucharist (1541). In 1546 Charles was again in a position to employ force against the Protestants, and, helped by the defection of Maurice of Saxony, he defeated the Schmalkaldic League at Mühlberg (1547) and dictated the Interim of Augsburg (1548).

Protestantism, however, was again saved by the political intervention of Francis I, and Charles finally abdicated control of German affairs to his brother, Ferdinand. The peace of Augsburg (1555) recognized the religious stalemate in Germany and the existence of Lutheranism, acknowledging the legal rights of the Lutherans to their secularized lands. The clause, *cuius regio eius religio*, gave the German princes the authority to choose their subjects' faith, echoing the erastianism which Luther had championed.

The later 16th cent. marked two further developments in the German reformation. Calvinism was introduced from Switzerland and was embraced by a number of princes, *eg*, Frederick III, Elector Palatine, the house of Nassau, and the town of Bremen, although it did not supersede Lutheranism as it had done in France, Scotland, and the Netherlands. A bitter schism occurred, however, within the Lutheran fold between the Gnesiolutherans and the Philippists, supporters of Melanchthon, which resolved itself in the Formula of Concord (1577–80).

H. Holborn, *A History of Modern Germany: the Reformation* (London, 1965).
A. G. Dickens, *Reformation and Society in 16th century Europe* (London, 1966).

MKS

REFORMATION IN POLAND, process by which several reformed sects infiltrated into the Catholic kingdom of Poland in the half-century from 1520. By the end of the 17th cent. most of them had been eradicated by the forces of the Counter-Reformation. Reformist sentiment, existing from the 15th cent., and the growth of Cracow as a centre for Erasmian humanism in the early 16th cent., were factors influencing the development of Protestantism. The impact of the German reformation, however, came via the Livonian ports of Riga and Reval and was sustained by German merchants and preachers. Outbursts of iconoclasm and the spoliation of monasteries occurred (1523–5) through the influence of preachers like the Pomeranian German Andreas

Knopken. In 1526 King Sigismund I intervened to suppress such a disturbance in Danzig, dismissing the newly instituted Protestant town council, ordering the execution of 15 Lutheran leaders, and making apostasy punishable by death. The Lutherans were encouraged by the conversion of Duke Albert Hohenzollern of Prussia (1525), who fostered Protestantism in his capital of Königsberg, printing Lutheran literature for distribution in Poland. He also founded a Protestant university there (1544). They enjoyed too the protection of Queen Bona Sforza, wife of Sigismund I, and her humanist circle. Thus, at the time of Sigismund's death (1548) Protestantism had made limited headway among the Germans and intellectuals in Poland, despite intermittent measures against heresy, although it had little influence with the peasantry and the nobility. From the 1550s, however, Calvinism began to influence the nobility of the middle and lower rank. Traditionally anti-clerical—for they resented the Church's exemption from taxes and its excessive wealth—they also found the concept of lay elders attractive. In Lithuania and Little Poland this militant Protestantism made considerable ground, stimulated by the conversion of the Radziwills and the proselytizing of Jan Laski and Cruciger, the former Lutheran superintendent of Little Poland. In 1552 Sigismund II Augustus tried to enforce the heresy laws in the Diet but was forced to compromise. By this time another sect had become well established in the Torun, Posnan, and Leszno areas, the Bohemian Brethren, who had been driven from Habsburg Bohemia in 1548. A group of Anti-trinitarians, whose most prominent leaders were Laelius and Faustus Socinus, also found refuge in Poland in the 1550s. To defend themselves against the Jesuit counter-attack, the Lutherans, Calvinists, and Bohemian Brethren mutually guaranteed their confessional rights (1570) and imposed the idea of religious toleration on the Confederation of Warsaw (1573). Although Sigismund II and Stephen Bathory were liberal Catholic rulers, by the time of the latter's death (1586) Poland's 360 Jesuit priests and 12 Jesuit colleges had begun to pose a threat to the reformed Churches.

P. Fox, *The Reformation in Poland* (Baltimore, 1924).
S. Kot, *Socinianism in Poland*, tr. by E. M. Wilbur (Boston, 1957). MKS

REFORMATION IN SCOTLAND, essentially a Calvinist movement associated with the names of Knox and Melville, which took root among a section of the nobility and spread to the common people in the late 1550s and 1560s, a generation later than the religious revolutions in the rest of Europe. However, once Calvin's militant theology entered Scotland it forged a spirit of national self-determination that severed the traditional alliance with Catholic France.

Lutheran books first entered Scotland through the east coast ports in the 1520s, provoking a royal prohibition in 1525. Although Protestant ideas had a limited impact, as early as 1528 a prominent evangelical, Patrick Hamilton, who had studied at Wittenberg and Marburg, was burned at St Andrews. By the 1540s Protestantism had won converts among the nobles, lairds, and wealthy townspeople, to the extent that Cardinal Beaton ordered the burning of the learned reforming divine George Wishart (1546), whose death profoundly affected his follower, John Knox. While the English Reformation had proceeded with the Crown's support, James V and Beaton had rejected Henry VIII's proposals for a Scottish Reformation under the Crown (1536, 1541, 1542), and after James's death (1542) the regency government maintained a policy of defending Catholicism in alliance with France, a trend accentuated when Mary of Guise became regent (1554) in the absence of the young Queen Mary in France. Scottish Protestant refugees, including Knox, fled to Geneva to escape persecution, while the Catholic Abp John Hamilton tried to counter Protestantism in the three provincial councils of 1549, 1552, and 1559 by eliminating deep-seated abuses and producing a moderate Catholic catechism (1552).

A significant event in the Scottish Reformation occurred in Dec. 1557, when a number of Scottish nobles, calling themselves the lords of the congregation, banded together in an association or covenant, and no less important was the final return to Scotland (May 1559) of Knox, determined to propagate his Calvinist faith. By midsummer 1559 all central Scotland had been won over by the lords of the congregation, though the fate of Protestantism hung in the balance as the French forces of the regent retook Edinburgh and Stirling (Nov.–Dec. 1559). The Reformation was secured, however, when Elizabeth I decided to send naval and military assistance (1560), while the death of Mary of Guise (June 1560) and the conclusion of hostilities (July 1560) enabled the Scottish estates in the so-called Reformation parliament to pass legislation fundamental to the development of Calvinism. The mass was forbidden, papal authority abolished, and a Calvinist confession of faith adopted (Aug. 1560). Furthermore, a book of discipline was prepared by Knox (1560), provincial synods appointed (1562), and a revised form of Knox's Genevan liturgy accepted as the official book of common order.

Calvinism established itself in Scotland partly because of the Crown's weakness and the government of pro-French regents (1542–61). In the critical period after Mary of Guise's death and until Mary's return from France (1560–62) the Protestant lords took control of Scotland, and during the years of Mary's personal rule (1562–7) all sections of opinion were alienated by her irresponsible behaviour. Her abdication (1567) was followed by the confirmation of the anti-papal legislation of 1560 by the Scottish estates and the assumption of power by successive pro-English regents, *eg*, Murray, Lennox, Mar, and Morton, who preserved the Reformation changes.

On the other hand, the reformed faith faced some vicissitudes. Many of the Protestant nobility would not accept that the ministers of the reformed Church, or kirk, should have ultimate jurisdiction over ecclesiastical property, education, private morals, and conduct, and Knox's book of discipline, which would have devoted the wealth of the Catholic Church to the reformed Church, was not acceptable to the Scottish parliament of 1567. Thus many Catholic priests and monks remained in their livings and monasteries and only after 1572 were vacant episcopal sees filled by those of the reformed faith. Periodic attempts were made to stir up Catholic reaction, *eg*, through Esmé Stuart, Earl of Lennox. However, the basis of Scottish Presbyterianism was laid when in 1578 a second book of discipline was drawn up by the Genevan Calvinist Andrew Melville, which condemned the episcopacy and declared the parity of the ministry. It was adopted by the church assembly, but rejected by the estates and by James VI, who was determined to preserve the episcopacy in order to retain royal control over church and state. The long struggle between Crown and kirk opened in 1579, and in 1583 Melville, accused of treason, took refuge in England. The Black Acts were passed (1584), declaring the king to be the head of the Church and state and reinforcing the authority of the bishops and of parliament over the Church. Eventually a compromise agreement permitted the erection of presbyteries and enforced the subjection of the bishops to the general assembly (1586). In 1592 James VI made further concessions in the Golden Act, when parliament ratified the liberties and privileges of the kirk, which was given the right to call a general assembly. Although the Stuart kings detested thorough-going Presbyterianism and bolstered the episcopal system, they could not alter the fact that the reformed Calvinist Church had taken firm root in Scotland by the end of the 16th cent. Nevertheless, the 17th cent. saw constant changes of fortune for both episcopacy and presbyterianism, until the latter was successful in becoming the state Church after 1689.

G. Donaldson, *The Scottish Reformation* (London, 1960). MKS

REFORMATION IN SWEDEN, was introduced by Gustavus Vasa and confirmed by his youngest son, Charles IX.

Gustavus from his accession (1523) countenanced Lutheran teachers and attacked the wealth of the Church, but the decisive step was taken at the Riksdag of Västerås (1527), when its property was placed at the disposal of the Crown and the new teaching was sanctioned in principle. Though Lutheranism was zealously propagated by the brothers Petri and was popular in the towns, it caused unrest in country districts, where it seems to have taken a generation for the Bible and services in the vernacular to win general support. In the reign of John III (1568–92) the Counter-Reformation movement tried to gain a hold on Sweden, but in 1594, while the Catholic Sigismund III was king, the Meeting of Uppsala accepted the Augsburg Confession, which became a symbol of national unity.

REFORMATION IN SWITZERLAND, multifarious movement, the product of a spiritual receptiveness, first evident in Zürich, and particular political and social conditions. Switzerland in the 16th cent. consisted of a loose association of self-governing city-states and rural cantons, whose independent-minded and freedom-loving people had successfully rejected their Burgundian and Habsburg overlords. Economic stagnation and the collapse of Swiss military prowess at Marignano (1515) and at Bicocca (1522) had, however, created social tension. The appointment of Huldreich Zwingli (1484–1531), a cleric trained in the humanist tradition of classical Latin and Greek literature, as people's priest in the cathedral of Zürich (1 Jan. 1519) marked the beginning of the Swiss Reformation. He began to preach an exposition of the scriptures, stressing the importance of faith in the pursuit of salvation, and went on to demand a purification of religious ceremonies, particularly of the use of images, holy pictures, and church music, and the abolition of clerical celibacy (1522). Furthermore, in 67 articles of Jan. 1523, he attacked papal authority, the doctrine of transubstantiation, and the intercession of fasting, pilgrimages, and saints, which led to a public disputation at the request of the city council (29 Jan. 1523) where he trounced the ill-prepared Catholic authorities. In 1525 he achieved the culmination of his reforms with the abolition of the mass and its replacement by a commemorative service in the vernacular. Zwingli shared with Calvin the belief in the need for Church discipline through a theocracy of lay magistrates and pastors. However, his sacramentarian concept of the communion service, which he defended at the colloquy of Marburg (1529), failed to take root. He believed in the use of military force to protect the reformed Church, *eg*, he formed the Christian Civic League to counteract the Christian Union and led Zürich into two wars (1529, 1531) in the last of which he was killed.

The peace of Kappel (1531) established the principle and practice of religious coexistence in Switzerland. Despite Zwingli's death his reformed Church lived on through the work of his successor in Zürich, Heinrich Bullinger, who for 44 years worked for the unity of Swiss Protestantism. His First Helvetic Confession (1536) provided a common doctrine for the city magistrates of Zürich and Basle, with Zwinglian and Lutheran elements. His *Consensus Tigrinus* (1549) achieved conciliation with Calvin on the Lord's Supper and his second Helvetic Confession (1566) was adopted by most Swiss Protestants as the doctrine of their reformed Church.

Meanwhile Zwingli's influence had spread beyond the bounds of Zürich. His critical views of child baptism were taken up by a group of Swiss radicals (1525), *eg*, Conrad Grebel, Felix Mantz, Wilhelm Reublin, Baltasar Hubmaier, and Grebel's convert, George Blaurock, most of them ex-priests. Their practices of adult baptism by immersion and replacement of the mass by a simple commemorative service was sharply resisted by the city authorities. The threat of death by drowning, imprisonment, and banishment forced the Anabaptists to leave Switzerland (1526).

Less extreme evangelical doctrines penetrated other towns. Wolfgang Capito (1478–1541) had been active in Basle since 1520, but the arrival (Nov. 1522) of Oecolampadius (1484–1531) led to religious changes culminating in the introduction

of the reformed religion by the city council (1529). Through the influence of Zwingli's follower, Berthold Haller (1492–1536), the Berne council adopted the Reformation, proclaiming the abolition of the mass, the renunciation of images, and the dissolution of the monasteries (7 Feb. 1528). From there Protestant influence penetrated south-west Switzerland towards Geneva, which was encouraged by the Berne authorities to take an independent stand against the Catholic bishop of Geneva and the Duke of Savoy. Guillaume Farel, the fiery evangelizer of Neufchâtel, arrived in Geneva in 1532 and in public disputations (Jan. 1534, May, June 1535) demoralized the Catholic participants. The Genevan city council ordered first the suspension of the mass (Aug. 1535) and then (May 1536) the enforcement of the reformed doctrines.

It was Farel's assistant, John Calvin, who completed the Swiss reformation. Expelled with Farel by the council and exiled to Strasbourg (1538–41) when he came under Martin Bucer's influence, Calvin returned to Geneva as the leading pastor and from the acceptance of his ecclesiastical ordinances of 1541 established his austere, disciplined, and dedicated brand of Protestantism. With its new academy for the training of pastors (1559) under the headship of Theodore Beza (1519–1605), Geneva became the centre of Calvinist education and propaganda and the main refuge for exiled Protestants.

O. Farmer, *Zwingli, the Reformer, his Life and Work* (London, 1952).
J. T. McNeill, *The History and Character of Calvinism* (New York, 1954).   MKS

REFORMATION IN THE LOW COUNTRIES. The early development of Protestantism sprang from the mystical tradition which had produced the Brethren of the Common Life and the *devotio moderna*, as well as the reforming humanist spirit of Erasmus of Rotterdam. From the 1520s Lutheran and Anabaptist preachers found a ready response among the artisans and labourers of the old industrial towns of the Netherlands, and in 1523 the first Lutheran martyrs, Heinrich Voes and Johann Esch, were burnt in Brussels on Charles V's orders. Anabaptism was introduced by the itinerant missionary Melchior Hoffmann, but the early native leaders were Jan Matthys, a baker of Haarlem, and Jan Bockelson, a tailor of Leyden. From the 1530s Anabaptist communities spread in the Amsterdam, Kampen, Zwolle, and Derventer areas despite the bitter opposition of Lutherans and Catholics and repressive imperial edicts (1529, 1535, 1538). After the collapse of early Anabaptism at Münster the movement was revived in the Netherlands in the new Mennonite form. Menno Simons (d. 1561), a Catholic priest of Dutch Friesland, renounced his Church (1536) and devoted the rest of his life to establishing the pacifist Anabaptism from which the modern Baptist movement has evolved. In 1540 he published his *Foundation of Christian Doctrine* in Dutch, which became the basis of Mennonite teaching. Another Anabaptist leader was David Joris, who made many converts. Although some 1600 Protestants were martyred, including about 1000 Anabaptists, during the years 1523–55, the reformed Churches took root in the Low Countries. In the second half of the 16th cent. the more militant Calvinist faith gained ground. It was established in the southern provinces after the return of Guy de Bres to Antwerp and the foundation of Calvinist congregations in Tournai, Lille, and Valenciennes (1560), and was further strengthened by his *Confessio Belgica* (1561), which laid down doctrine and discipline. Calvinism had penetrated the northern provinces from John Laski's church at Emden in the 1540s, but from 1566, when the widespread iconoclastic rioting in Flanders produced a violent Catholic backlash, including the repressive regime of the Duke of Alva, a militant minority of Calvinists in the north assumed the leadership of the revolt against Philip II's government. Catholicism was reimposed upon the southern provinces, but by 1600 half the people of Holland

and Zeeland were Calvinist. Despite the bitter rift between moderate Arminians and the triumphant orthodox Calvinists (1609–18) their numbers continued to increase in the 17th cent. after the Synod of Dort (1619) had settled the doctrine of the Dutch Reformed Church.

G. R. Renier, *The Dutch Nation* (London, 1944).   WKS

REFORMATION OF MANNERS, SOCIETIES FOR THE, in England, voluntary associations of dissenters and members of the Anglican Church, formed in the period 1691–1740 to promote concern for social and moral reform. They were more negative and repressive than the contemporary Societies for the Promotion of Christian Knowledge (1698) and for the Propagation of the Gospel (1701).

REGALE in France, traditional royal right which existed in half the dioceses of France, by which the king could administer vacant bishoprics and draw revenue from them. Louis XIV tried to extend the right to the whole country (1675), provoking a controversy in which the Jansenists and the papacy were united, until the matter was exacerbated by the Gallican Articles (1682), and was merged in the defence of Gallicanism.

REGENCY BILL (1788) in Britain, embodying the younger Pitt's proposal to make the Prince of Wales regent, but not with full royal powers. The bill restricted his power of making peers and appointing officers, forbade him to dispose of any of the king's property, and gave the care of the king's person and household to the queen, assisted by a council on which no member of the royal family should sit. Parliament had legislated for a regency in 1765 on George III's own suggestion. In 1788 the king's illness prevented him not only from suggesting a regency, but also from giving his assent to the bill. Pitt therefore proposed that the royal assent should be signified by commission—a legal fiction, but a necessary one if the bill were to be passed.

The king fell ill in the autumn of 1788. Pitt hoped that the illness would be short. Fox and Burke claimed that the heir to the throne should automatically and immediately assume full royal power as regent. Pitt accused them of denying parliamentary sovereignty. They accused him of being the enemy of royal power. Before the crisis was resolved the king recovered (Feb. 1789), and the bill was withdrawn. A bill similar to Pitt's was introduced by Perceval's government when the king fell ill again (Dec. 1810), and passed in Feb. 1811, with the king's assent given by commission.

REGENSBURG or RATISBON, COLLOQUY AND DIET OF (1540–1), most spectacular attempt of the Reformation to heal the religious schism between Catholics and Protestants in Europe. The colloquy or discussion began at Hagenau (June 1540), was adjourned to Worms (Nov. 1540), and was finally deferred to the imperial Diet which was due to meet at Regensburg in April 1541, and at which Emperor Charles V was to be present. Charles arrived in Feb. 1541 when Catholic morale was high, having been boosted by Philip of Hesse's disgrace for committing bigamy. A committee of theologians, which included Melanchthon, Bucer, Pflug, Eck, Gropper, and the papal legate Contarini, was entrusted with the negotiations for theological unity. They agreed on a formula to define 'double justification' by faith and works, but it proved impossible to compromise on transubstantiation, papal authority, and the question of the veneration of saints. Luther refused to support Melanchthon and Pope Paul III Contarini, the agreement on justification by faith was rejected, and after a promising start the colloquy collapsed in failure. The recess issued in July 1541 referred the matter of religion to a general council of the Church, and the colloquy's failure convinced Charles V that only force could overcome the Protestants.

REGENTS in the Netherlands, ruling merchant class or *heeren*, who rose to power in the northern provinces of the Netherlands in the wake of their successful revolt against Spain (1568–1648), ousting the old Catholic oligarchy in the city governments of the Dutch republic. Although their wealth was made in trade and they remained an urban patriciate, by the later 17th cent. they were investing in land and fine country houses and had become an hereditary elite. This upper-middle class of Dutch society, which included families like the Bichers, Pels, De Graeffs, Trips, and De Geers, was associated with republican, anti-Orangist politics. They dominated the republic in the first two decades of the 17th cent. until the judicial murder of their leader, Oldenbarneveldt, and lost power in the period 1619–50, when the house of Orange and its supporters were in the ascendant. The regents, however, regained power in the years 1650–72 under the De Witts and again in the early 18th cent. under Heinsius. In religious terms they tended to be moderate-minded Calvinists of the Arminian mould, opposed to the rigidity of Gomarist Calvinism. Their open-minded, rational, and latitudinarian attitudes were revealed by their patronage of artists and their flexible economic policy, characterized by Pieter de la Court's work, *The Interest of Holland*.

REGIDORES, councillors who sat on the governing body (*cabildo*) of Spanish American urban centres. Municipal administration was their concern, *eg*, public works, police regulations, water supply, allocation of building sites and garden lots, and the management of municipal property. *Regidores* who were usually unsalaried, were elected for one-year terms by the *vecinos* (principal property-holders) of the town, but in practice the Crown often granted the office for life, or sold it with the right of inheritance, to chosen individuals. *Regidores* in any event were drawn from and represented the rich and powerful among their communities. With the *cabildo* itself, the office of *regidor* declined in importance as the colonial period progressed, but it was always eagerly sought after by prestige-hungry Creoles. Late in the colonial period, the office became important once more with the Bourbon efforts to revive the *cabildo*.

REGILLUS, LAKE, BATTLE OF (496 BC), near Tusculum, 32 kms east of Rome, claimed by Roman tradition as a decisive victory over the Latin League's challenge to Roman hegemony, though the subsequent treaty of Cassius (493) acknowledged the equality of the contestants.

REGIMINI MILITANTIS ECCLESIAE (1540), papal bull promulgated by Pope Paul III to establish the Society of Jesus, its founder, Ignatius Loyola, being empowered to make new constitutions. He was shortly after elected its first general (1541).

REGIONAL CONFEDERATION OF MEXICAN LABOUR (CROM), *Confederación Regional Obrera Mexicana*, founded in 1918 by Luis N. Morones, as a Mexican craft-union federation, the power of which was particularly apparent during the presidencies of Álvaro Obregón and Plutarco Elias Calles (1920–8). A group of 18 men (*Grupo Acción*) ran CROM during the 1920s. The leadership supported the presidency of Obregón (1920–4) and obtained both government recognition and political patronage. Independent unions were crushed in an attempt to create a totally dominant confederation. With official support from President Calles, Morones became the second most powerful figure in Mexico and the labour leaders became rich and corrupt. Employers were blackmailed and union rosters were padded. CROM lost government support after 1928 and gradually gave way to independent unions. A new confederation, the CGOC, soon replaced CROM (1932).

REGISTRATION OF VOTERS in Britain became necessary in 1832 because of the increased number of voters, and the 1832 Reform Act provided that the overseers of the poor who compiled the rate books should also compile the register. One aim of the Reform Act had been to reduce the cost of elections, but in fact expenses rose as more seats were contested and constituency parties and agents sought to get their supporters on the Electoral Register. The increase of the electorate both from natural causes and the 1867 Reform Act, together with the Ballot Act (1872), combined to make bribery and corruption futile, and finally in 1883 election expenses were regulated by law in accordance with the size and type of constituency, and strict rules about the type of expenditure allowed and the auditing of accounts were laid down.

REGISTRO SHIPS (or 'register ships'), employed by the early Spanish Bourbons for trade with Latin America after the breakdown of the Habsburg convoy system. Such vessels might be legally freighted only by members of the Cadiz *Consulado*, who still enjoyed a monopoly of American trade, and sailed singly for their Spanish American destinations. *Registro* ships were employed during much of the 18th cent., but were rendered unnecessary as the Cadiz *Consulado's* monopoly privileges were first curtailed in favour of joint-stock companies for specific American regions and then abolished altogether (1765–89) in favour of free trade between Spanish and American ports.

REGISTRY ACTS in Britain. To prevent illicit slave trading the abolitionist, William Wilberforce, introduced in parliament a bill (1815) requiring slave registration by all colonial slave owners. The West Indian lobby argued that the bill was unconstitutional, but agreed, if it was not pursued, to persuade the West Indian Assemblies to pass their own registration acts. This they eventually did, introducing a system of triennial returns operative between 1817 and 1832. In Barbados, confusion arose between the conceptions of registration and emancipation, leading to a slave revolt in 1816.

REGLAMENTO OF COMMERCE (12 Oct. 1778), decree which abolished the monopoly of Spanish American commerce enjoyed by the Cadiz merchants' guild. The other principal ports of Spain were permitted to engage in such trade, and a complex series of customs duties was replaced by a simple 7 per cent *ad valorem* duty. These concessions, originally granted (1765) to the Caribbean islands to encourage economic development, coincided there with the beginning of the sugar boom, and the result was an astonishing growth in the volume of trade and government customs duties. This encouraged the Crown to extend the privileges to certain selected regions, and finally, in 1778, to all of Spanish America, except Venezuela and Mexico. In 1789, when the success of the *reglamento* seemed conclusively proved, the latter valuable colonies were likewise included under its provisions. The decree was one of the most significant of the Bourbon Reforms.

REGNANS IN EXCELSIS (1570), papal bull promulgated by Pope Pius V proclaiming the excommunication of Queen Elizabeth I of England and absolving her subjects from their allegiance to the Crown. Though the work of a sincere Dominican, the bull proved a political blunder, partly because it was issued without the knowledge or agreement of the only Catholic prince capable of executing it, Philip II of Spain, and partly because it sought to impose upon English Catholics, hitherto mostly quiescent and unmolested, the choice between social, political, and economic proscription and spiritual damnation. Though the vast majority chose to risk the latter by remaining loyal to the Crown during the Spanish War, the queen's councillors could not take this for granted and in retaliation parliament imposed a series of increasingly stringent laws upon recusants (1571, 1581, 1585, 1593). The bull thus ended hopes of reconciliation and a comprehensive English Church.

REGULATING ACT (1773) in Britain, legislative measure which sought to control and improve the system of administration in the East India Co.'s possessions. Warren Hastings

became the first governor-general of Bengal; he was assisted by a supreme council of four (deciding by a majority vote). This was the major defect of the act, in that Hastings could be out-voted, and Philip Francis, the leader of a hostile majority, over-ruled him. The act also set up a supreme court of justice in Calcutta, but failed to define the relationship between that court and the council. Furthermore, the act lacked clarity in its declaration of Bengal's supremacy over the subordinate presidencies of Madras and Bombay. This hampered Hastings's foreign policy. These defects were remedied by later legislation.

REGULATORS, organized groups of American frontier settlers in the Carolinas, who began to protest (1768) against their lack of representation in the colonial assemblies. They were crushed by Gov. William Tryon's force at the battle of Almance (1771).

REGULUS (*fl.* 3rd cent. BC), Roman leader who, in the First Punic War, after victory off Cape Ecnomus (256 BC), invaded Africa with two legions, but was defeated and captured in 255 by the Spartan mercenary, Xanthippus. The story of his despatch to Rome from Carthage to negotiate peace, and his return to torture and death, is of doubtful authenticity.

REHNSKOLD, KARL GUSTAF, Count (1651–1722), Swedish soldier, who achieved some renown in the Zealand campaign against Denmark (1700) and in the battle of Narva (1700) against Russia before sharing command with Charles at Kliszow (1702) and winning another victory over the Saxons at Fraustadt (1706). After being captured at Poltava, he spent nine years as a prisoner in Russia (1718) before returning to Sweden.

REIBEY, MARY (1777–1855), née Haydock, an orphan, was transported to NSW for 'stealing' a horse at the age of 13. Her case illustrates the injustice suffered by many early convicts sent to Australia. She was more fortunate than some, for she married an Irishman, Thomas Reibey (1769–1811), who had sailed on the same transport and, later, in Sydney made a successful career in commerce and shipping. On his death, Mary (by then a hotel-keeper) administered and extended her husband's business, trained three of her sons, who became merchants in Tas., took two of her four daughters on a visit to England, and herself became respected for her active educational and religious work. A grandson, Thomas Reibey (1821–1912), became prime minister of Tas. and later speaker of its House of Assembly, after having been archdeacon of Launceston.

REICHENAU, WALTHER VON (1884–1942), German soldier. After serving in the First World War he was transferred to the general staff, then joined the war ministry (1929), and in Feb. 1933 was promoted to a senior post by the new minister, Blomberg. At the outbreak of the Second World War he was appointed commander of the 10th Army in the Polish campaign, and later commanded the 6th Army on the Western Front (1940), and in Russia (1941–2). He was made a field marshal in 1940. Although possessing some independence of judgement and a forceful personality, Von Reichenau was a Nazi supporter and admirer of Hitler, and turned against him only towards the end of his life after disagreements on strategy.

REICHENBACH, TREATY OF (1790), convention made between Austria and Prussia which prevented an escalation of the Austro-Russo-Turkish war. After the Prussians had made two anti-Russian treaties with Turkey and Poland (Jan. and March 1790) which threatened the security of Russia's ally, Austria, the Emperor, Leopold II, interceded personally to bring about better relations with Frederick William II of Prussia. Negotiations for a settlement opened at Reichenbach in Silesia in June. Prussia dropped her demand for the cession by Austria of Galicia to Poland, from which Prussia had hoped to gain Danzig and Thorn. Leopold agreed to make peace with Turkey through the mediation of Prussia, Britain, and the Dutch.

REICHENBACH TREATY (1813) between Austria, Russia, and Prussia marked the beginning of Austria's adhesion to the Fourth Coalition during the French Wars. Austria agreed to join the allied coalition if her proposals to Napoleon I for the dissolution of the duchy of Warsaw, the restoration to her of the Illyrian provinces, and the relinquishment of French conquests in North Germany, were refused. Napoleon refused to make these concessions and Austria declared war.

Metternich hoped to make an early peace with Napoleon to prevent Russia from entering western Europe. Britain was not prepared to make peace on these terms.

REICHSBANNER SCHWARZ-ROT-GOLD in Germany. The repeated attempts by right-wing forces to overthrow the Weimar republic led to the establishment (May 1924) of a Republican para-military organization, founded by Otto Hörsing at Magdeburg. The *Reichsbanner* aimed at attracting citizens who were prepared actively to defend the Weimar constitution. The organization grew rapidly and by the mid-1920s it had some 100,000 followers. But despite the support of a number of prominent middle-class politicians, the *Reichsbanner* never succeeded in becoming a genuinely multiparty organization. Most of its leaders and members were Social Democrats, and the right stigmatized it as 'Marxist'. The *Reichsbanner* was seldom of importance until the rise of the 'National Opposition' in 1930. With the appearance of massive anti-Republican para-military organizations, the association began to copy many of the techniques and principles of its opponents and furnished strong-arm squads to protect its members engaged in political activities. Hörsing was replaced by Karl Höltermann, and the *Reichsbanner* began to play an important role in the 'Iron Front', whose supporters risked their lives to fight the National Socialists in the streets. However, on 20 July 1932, the leadership hesitated to ask its members to defend the government against dissolution. Thus moral defeat came several months before annihilation. Repressive measures were taken against the *Reichsbanner* soon after Hitler's seizure of power, and a few months later the organization had ceased to exist. Nevertheless, its activities testify to the fact that the Weimer republic was not entirely 'a Republic without Republicans'.

REICHSKAMMERGERICHT, standing high court of justice of the Holy Roman empire, inaugurated by the Emperor Maximilian I (31 Oct. 1495) at the reichstag of Worms. The emperor was to nominate its president, who was to be assisted originally by eight nobles and eight doctors of law, approved by the reichstag, the running expenses being paid out of a general tax voted by the estates, the Common Penny. The court adopted Roman law principles and sat first at Frankfurt; later it moved to Speyer on the middle Rhine, away from Habsburg influence. It was organized in its final form by the Emperor Ferdinand I in the mid-16th cent., having then 24 judges, and its proceedings were reviewed annually by an appellate commission appointed by the reichstag. By the end of the 16th cent., however, the court was swamped with litigation and its machinery proved slow and clumsy. From 1588 the appellate commission lapsed and the court was increasingly bypassed by the *reichshofrat* or Aulic Council.

REICHSREGIMENT, name of an attempted reform of the German imperial constitution, introduced at the Diet of Worms in 1495. It was one of a series of repeated attempts made in the later Middle Ages to create some more effective federal institutions. In 1495 the German princes, led by Abp Berchtold von Henneberg of Mainz, created a permanent council which was to sit at Nuremburg, an imperial capital. Emperor Maximilian I soon deprived it of any effectiveness.

REICHSTADT AGREEMENT (1876), attempt by Austria and Russia to work out a common policy for the partition of the Balkans in the event of a Russian defeat of Turkey. By failing to honour the promise that Austria should gain a foothold in Bosnia-Herzegovina in the San Stefano treaty, Russia increased the suspicion between them, which was ultimately to lead to war. The agreement that Russia should take Southern Bessarabia from Rumania was also conveniently forgotten in the Russo-Rumanian military convention (1877), in which Russia guaranteed Rumanian territorial integrity, in exchange for a safe-conduct of Russian troops through Rumania en route for Turkey. Russia successfully claimed Southern Bessarabia in the Berlin Congress (1878), an example of the cavalier treatment of the Balkan states by the European powers, which eventually thwarted their ambitions by stimulating Balkan nationalism.

REICHSTAG, diet or assembly of the Holy Roman empire, representing the estates and consisting of three curias, the electors, the princes, and the free imperial cities of Germany. It was an unwieldy body of medieval origin which assembled only temporarily and at times specified by the emperor. None the less, by the end of the 15th cent. it had become the supreme executive power in the empire, with defined procedures. The emperor summoned the Diet, made specific proposals to the representatives, and then withdrew while the curias deliberated separately. They then consulted together under the presidency of the Elector of Mainz before conveying their unanimous decision to the emperor. With his approval the decisions were promulgated as law. At the Diet of Worms (1495) the Reichstag's functions were enlarged to include the determining of methods of tax collection, the maintenance of peace, the conduct of foreign policy, and the right to declare war. It reached its apogee in the 16th cent. when the Turkish threat necessitated frequent diets to make military and financial decisions, thus providing constant opportunity for the estates to ventilate their grievances. In 1555 the Reichstag delegated its authority to a working committee, the Reichsdeputation, which prepared legislation for the main Diet. Yet from the late 16th cent. the Diet was increasingly divided on religious grounds which inhibited members in making decisions. It took part in the negotiations leading to the peace of Westphalia (1648), which guaranteed its constitutional role. However, in reality it had long ceased to be an effective organ of imperial government and the essentials of sovereignty had passed to the individual princes. The right of the French and Swedish ambassadors to be represented at the Diet from 1648, with powers to intervene to defend 'German liberties', also increased the tendency towards particularism. From 1663 until its abolition in 1806 the Diet devolved into a permanent congress of ambassadors at Regensburg with no real executive authority.

REICHSTAG FIRE (1933) in Germany. The Reichstag, or parliament building, in Berlin was destroyed by fire on 27 Feb. 1933, less than a month after Hitler had become chancellor. The alleged incendiary, Van der Lubbe, was brought to trial together with the German communist, Torgler, and three Bulgarian communists, Dmitrov, Popov, and Tanev. Despite the political bias of the court, Dmitrov's brilliant defence secured the acquittal of all the defendants except Van der Lubbe, who was later executed. The question of whether the Nazis themselves were responsible for the fire remained in dispute; nevertheless, the new regime seized on the incident as a means of reinforcing its legality and further suppressing opposition. Up to this time the Nazis, with no absolute Reichstag majority and a minority of cabinet posts, had been obliged to use restraint in their political behaviour, especially *vis-à-vis* the Communist Party and other left-wing opponents. Coming less than a week before the important elections of 5 March, the fire was thus a welcome pretext for muzzling both the Socializische Partei Deutschlands (SPD) and the Kommunist Partei Deutschlands (KPD), the latter being effectively banned and thousands of its functionaries arrested. Two presidential orders issued on 28 Feb. suspended the basic constitutional freedoms in Germany, increased to draconian levels the penalties for many offences, and extended the concept of treason to cover any conceivable opposition to the regime. The extreme importance of the fire and the scare it was used to create, can be gauged by the fact that it was these orders, rather than the later Enabling Law, that introduced the permanent state of emergency and the abolition of the rule of law, and thus legalized the Nazi political terror.

REID, SIR GEORGE (1845–1918), Scottish-born Australian politician, who was prime minister of NSW (1894–9) and Australian prime minister (1904–5). He entered politics (1880) and became leader of the NSW Free Trade Party (1891). He was a central, if controversial, figure in the later stages of the federal movement, and a member of the first Commonwealth parliament, leading the free trade opposition (1901–8), except for his brief term as prime minister. He was the first Australian High Commissioner in London (1909–1916), and after his term of office he remained in Britain and became an MP.

REID, WHITELAW (1837–1912), US journalist and diplomat, who took part in the first presidential campaign of the Republican Party (1856), became a journalist, and reported the American Civil War for the *Cincinnati Gazette*. He was also librarian of the US House of Representatives (1863–6). After the war he speculated unsuccessfully in Southern cotton (1865–7), joined the *New York Tribune* (1868), and became managing editor the following year. He succeeded Horace Greeley as editor-in-chief and main proprietor (1872), continued the newspaper's attacks on political corruption, increased its reputation for authoritative journalism, introduced Linotype and other technical advances, and helped to introduce skyscrapers into New York with the new Tribune building (1873). He had been offered diplomatic appointments in Berlin in 1877 and 1881, and finally accepted the post of US ambassador to France (1889). He ran unsuccessfully as Republican vice-presidential candidate in 1892, and in 1898 took part in the Paris negotiations that ended the Spanish–American war. In 1905 he became US ambassador to Britain.

REINDORF, CARL CHRISTIAN (1834–1917), Ghanian missionary of the Basel Evangelical Society, who pioneered missionary work among the Ga people. He published *The History of the Gold Coast and Asante* (1895).

REINSURANCE TREATY (1887), agreement between Germany and Russia to maintain a benevolent neutrality in any conflict other than an Austro-Russian or Franco-German dispute. Germany was already in defensive alliance with Austria and the publication of the Dual Alliance in 1888, showing that in the last resort Germany would stand by Austria, followed by William II's failure to renew the Reinsurance treaty in 1890, meant that it was of short-term importance only, indicating Bismarck's desire to remain friendly with Russia. For Bismarck's commitment to Austria had opened up the very possibility he most feared—war on two fronts against France and Russia. Unwittingly he drew France and Russia closer together by the *Lombardverbot*, which, by forbidding the Reichsbank to accept Russian securities, led to a greatly increased French financial interest in Russia.

REITER, German horsemen, usually of the dispossessed knightly class, who fought as mercenary soldiers in the wars of the 16th cent., including the French civil wars, in which they took an active part on the Protestant side under their leader, John Casimir of the Palatinate.

REITH OF STONEHAVEN, JOHN CHARLES WALSHAM REITH, 1st Baron (1889–), Scottish-born, first director-general of the British Broadcasting Corporation who established the essential quality and standards of broadcasting in Britain. He served in the First World War and was seriously wounded. After the war he was engaged in private business then became general manager of the British Broadcasting Co. (1922). When the British Broadcasting Corporation was established (1927) he became director-general. He insisted on setting the highest standards, directing the BBC as an instrument for social betterment, and retaining its independence. He left the BBC to become chairman of Imperial Airways (1938) then served as minister of information in Chamberlain's government (1940) and then at transport, works and buildings, and works and planning under Churchill (1940–2). For the remainder of the war he was made director of Combined Operations material planning. After the war he held various posts of which the most important was that of chairman of the colonial Development Corporation (1950–1959). He was also appointed lord high commissioner to the General Assembly of the Church of Scotland.

He published his autobiography in two volumes: *Into the Wind* (1949) and *Wearing Spurs* (1966). The annual series of Reith lectures was established by the BBC (1947) in his honour.

RELIGION, FRENCH WARS OF (1562–98), intermittent politico-religious conflict lasting over 35 years and consisting of separate outbreaks of civil violence (1562–3, 1567–8, 1568–70, 1572–6, 1577, 1580, 1585–9, 1589–95, 1595–8). They began as a struggle between great noble factions, fortified by religious and feudal alignments, which went unchecked by a series of young and weak kings, and ended when one of the aristocratic contestants, Henry of Navarre, assumed the Crown and restored order in France through a policy of religious toleration and political moderation.

The spectacular spread of Calvinism in France (1555–9) heralded the wars and persuaded the queen mother, Catherine de' Medici, to abandon the repressive religious policy of Francis I and Henry II in the name of political good sense. Guided by a moderate chancellor, L'Hôpital, she summoned the Colloquy of Poissy (1561), which attempted to heal the religious schism by rational discussion, and agreed to the January edict, granting toleration to the Calvinists (1562). This apparent favour to the Huguenots (Calvinists) brought a violent reaction from the house of Guise, the champions of Catholicism, and the first civil war began with the massacre of a Huguenot congregation at Vassy (March 1562). Guise's forces occupied Paris and took control of the royal family, while the Huguenots rose in the provinces, their commanders, Condé and Coligny, establishing their headquarters at Orléans. The deaths of the opposing leaders, Anthony of Navarre and St André, and the capture of Montmorency and Condé, affected both sides and after the battle of Dreux (Dec. 1562) the war drew to a close, despite the murder of the Duc de Guise by a Protestant fanatic (Feb. 1563). A compromise was reached by the pacification of Amboise (March 1563).

The second war was precipitated by Huguenot fears of an international Catholic plot, which prompted Condé and Coligny to attempt a coup to capture the queen mother and King Charles IX at Meaux (Sept. 1567) and to seek military help from the German *reiters* under John Casimir of the Palatinate. Montmorency was killed at the battle of St Denis (Nov. 1567) and another compromise was patched up by the peace of Longjumeau (7 March 1568). It proved more in the nature of a truce, for in Sept 1568 the third war broke out. In an effort to reassert their authority, Catherine de' Medici and Charles IX had dismissed L'Hôpital (Sept. 1568) and restored the Guise faction to favour. The edicts of pacification were rescinded and Calvinist preachers faced expulsion from France, while plans were laid to seize Condé and Coligny. Although Condé was killed at the battle of Jarnac (1569) and the Huguenots were again defeated by the Duke of Anjou at Moncontour (1569), the Catholic forces failed to exploit these victories and the two sides concluded another compromise, the peace of St Germain (Aug. 1570).

Coligny now regained Charles IX's confidence and advocated a united French assault on Spain. His death, however, was connived at by the jealous queen mother, and by the Guises, who were anxious to avenge the old duke's death (1563). The murder of Coligny by minions of Guise and the massacre on the eve of St Bartholomew of some 3000 Huguenots gathered in Paris to celebrate the marriage of Marguerite de Valois to Condé's nephew, Henry of Navarre, was the prelude to the fourth civil war. In the provinces Huguenots fought for survival and openly resisted the authority of a tyrannical ruler, while the *Politiques*, *eg*, Damville and Alençon, joined forces to challenge extreme Catholicism. A general assembly of *Politiques* and Huguenots at Nîmes (Dec. 1574) declared the independence of the provinces of Languedoc, Provence, and Dauphiné and established religious toleration. Finally, in 1576, the peace of Monsieur brought another respite and gave the Huguenots freedom of worship outside Paris and other legal guarantees. From this time onwards the dominant issue in the wars was political rather than religious, as the rival leaders, Guise, Navarre, and Alençon, strove to exert the feudal power of the great nobility at the expense of the feeble royal administration. In this struggle the Catholic League, first formed in 1576 and revived in 1584, played an important part, but increasingly became a subsidized tool of Spain (treaty of Joinville, Dec. 1584).

Meanwhile, in 1576 the Estates-General met at Blois (Dec.) through the league's machinations. Henry III tried to control the league by claiming leadership (Jan. 1577), but was unable to prevent renewed fighting between Catholic and Protestant nobles who defied his authority. Deserted by the *Politiques*, the Huguenots were defeated (1577) and had to accept the curbing of their freedom in the Edict of Poitiers or Bergerac (1577). An uneasy peace followed (1577–84) with occasional outbursts of violence, until the death of Alençon (1584) created a critical situation. The nearest heir became the Huguenot leader, Henry of Navarre, who was unacceptable to the Catholics and the league, now under Guise leadership (1584). In the penultimate phase of the religious wars, the War of the Three Henries (1585–9), the League forced Henry III to revoke all previous edicts of toleration and pacification (treaty of Nemours, July 1585) and sought to exclude Navarre from the succession. Guise won popular support in Paris and humiliated the helpless king in the Day of Barricades (May 1588). In a last effort to restore his authority Henry III arranged the assassination of Guise and his brother (Dec. 1588), only to die himself in Aug. 1589.

Henry of Navarre, who now assumed the throne (1589), was faced with five more years of civil war against the armies of the league under the leadership of Mayenne and Parma, who championed the claim of the Cardinal de Bourbon. In 1594 Henry regained Paris, having renounced his Huguenot faith in favour of Catholicism, and the league was dissolved. In its final phase the war became a struggle against the Spanish forces upholding the claim of the Infanta Isabella, daughter of Philip II, and Elizabeth de Valois, who were driven from Burgundy and Picardy in 1598. The conclusion of the treaty of Vervins (1598), recognizing Henry IV, and the confirmation of religious toleration for the Huguenots by the Edict of Nantes (1598), brought the civil wars to a conclusion.

E. Armstrong, *The French Wars of Religion* (London, 1892). R. M. Kingdom, *Geneva and the Coming of the Wars of Religion* (Geneva, 1954).   JHS

RELIGION PRÉTENDUE RÉFORMÉE (RPR) or the so-called reformed religion, the name given in 17th-cent. France to the Calvinist or Huguenot faith which had been embraced by a minority of Frenchmen.

RELIQUARIES. The veneration of saints, especially of martyrs, appears at an early date both in the Eastern and Western Church, and legislation was passed which affirmed the doctrine of the veneration of saints and their relics. The performance of miracles was often credited to relics and this in turn led to an insatiable demand for them, resulting in the fabrication and sale of spurious relics to churches and private persons. A great increase in the popularity of relics resulted in the production of large numbers of metal reliquaries to house the sacred remains. Boxes, crosses, and caskets resembling miniature funerary monuments are among the most popular shapes, and these are often of precious metal studded with gems. Surviving examples give eloquent testimony to the skills of medieval metalworkers and jewellers.

REMARQUE, ERICH MARIA (1898–1970), German novelist whose earliest and most controversial books, *All Quiet on the Western Front* (1929) and *The Way Back* (1931), described the ordeals of the First World War and its aftermath without glamour or sentimentality. They sold several millions of copies and caused an outcry among German nationalists. In 1931 Remarque emigrated to Switzerland and in 1937 (his books having been officially burned in Nazi Germany) to the US, where he was naturalized in 1947. The themes of war, exile, and persecution continued to inspire his later work.

REMBRANDT VAN RIJN (1606–69), Dutch painter, whose works, especially in their use of chiaroscuro, influenced the development of Western painting. By 1631 he was established as the leading portrait painter in Holland, but he also painted historical scenes, as well as religious and mythological subjects. Over 60 self-portraits of Rembrandt have survived, among them some of his greatest masterpieces of psychological penetration. The end of the 1640s saw his greatest period as an etcher, usually of New Testament scenes, but after 1655 his activity in this direction declined. He left about 600 paintings, 290 etchings, and over 1400 drawings.

REMINGTON, FREDERIC (1861–1909), US painter and sculptor who specialized in depicting life on the Great Plains. His studies of Indians, cowboys, and soldiers in action helped to create the heroic image of the West.

REMÓN CANTERA, JOSÉ ANTONIO (1908–55), Panamanian chief of police (1949–52), and president (1952–5). He attempted to diversify Panama's economy in order to lessen her dependence on the Panama Canal.

REMONSTRANTS in Scotland, minority of extremist Covenanters in the Scottish general assembly (1650), called after the western remonstrance drawn up at Dumfries (17 Oct. 1650). They wanted the Scottish army to be purged and the rigid enforcement of the act of classes; but they ceased to be significant when their army was defeated by a detachment of the English sectarian army under Lambert (Dec. 1650).

REMONSTRANTS in the Netherlands, moderate wing of the Dutch Reformed Church, whose most eminent leader was Arminius, which criticised the intolerance of the extreme Calvinism of the Gomarists or Contra-Remonstrants, believing even in the freedom of the will. A period of theological and political conflict occurred in the years after the truce with Spain (1609–19), ending with the condemnation to death of a leading Remonstrant, Oldenbarneveldt, and the expulsion of the Remonstrant party from the Dutch Protestant Church at the Synod of Dort (1619).

RENAISSANCE, CAROLINGIAN, first revival in western Europe of learning and literacy after the period of the barbarian invasions and settement in the 5th–6th cents, which had virtually obliterated classical learning. Libraries had been destroyed, manuscripts had perished, and literacy maintained a precarious existence only among some of the clergy. Outside Italy, only in Ireland from the 6th cent. did classical Latin literature find an audience. From there it was taken to

Northumbria in the 7th and 8th cents and thence to the continent in the age of Charlemagne. Charlemagne gathered round him a band of scholars and writers, the Visigoth Theodulf, the Italians Peter of Pisa and Paul the Deacon, the Irishmen Clement and Dungal, the German Einhard (his future biographer), and the Englishman Alcuin. By his patronage of, friendship with, and encouragement of these men and by his decrees that every cathedral and abbey should maintain a grammar school, Charlemagne laid the foundations of medieval education. Alcuin was particularly connected with the development of the palace school while residing at the court (782–90). As abbot of Tours (from 796) he produced there a revised text of St Jerome's Latin Bible, which became the standard version of the scriptures. Another vitally important achievement of the Carolingian ecclesiastical libraries was the copying of several classical texts which would otherwise have been lost, including Caesar's *Gallic Wars*, part of Livy's *History of Rome*, Lucretius' *De Rerum Natura*, the *Annals*, *Germania*, and *Agricola* of Tacitus, and Virgil's *Eclogues*. The Carolingian scribes evolved the Carolingian minuscule, the careful script which forms the foundation of later handwriting and printing. Yet another momentous achievement was in the sphere of law. Various Germanic customary codes were written down and attempts were made (especially under Charlemagne's son, Louis) to replace primitive legal procedures by more rational use of witnesses and written documents, with particularly enduring results in Italy. The Carolingian renaissance added little that was new, but it revived the usage of correct Latin, rescued the education of the clergy from serious breakdown, and so extended the area influenced by this revival of learning that even the devastations of the Vikings and Hungarians in the 8th–9th cents were unable to wipe it out.   JG

RENAISSANCE, TWELFTH-CENTURY, term to describe the great flowering of medieval humanism. This period saw the birth of the universities—Paris, Bologna, and Oxford—the rediscovery of the logical and ethical works of Aristotle, which caused an intellectual revolution as radical as the scientific revolution of the 17th cent. It saw also the widespread use of the Gothic arch, one of the fundamental architectural innovations, and the birth of the systematic study of law, canon and civil. It produced a new naturalism in painting and sculpture which later spread to Italy and informed the work of Niccolo Pisano and the Tuscan painters. It was the age of Abelard, John of Salisbury and the new dialectic, of the troubadours and the Goliards and the wandering scholars who abandoned metrical poetry and invented rhyme and who produced the first completely secular poetry of the Middle Ages. It was the period of early polyphonic music. As a whole, the 12th cent. can be seen as the true renaissance of which the late medieval Italian renaissance was a continuation.

RENAISSANCE STYLE, term used for the profound change in architecture, sculpture, and painting which occurred in western Europe (mainly in Italy) in the 15th cent. Its introduction involved a revolution in observation and theory which was most marked in architecture and painting. The changes in architecture came first and were especially noticeable in the work of a group of Florentines, notably Brunelleschi (1377–1446) and Alberti (1404–72), who were inspired by the ruins of antiquity which they studied extensively in Rome. The republication of the ancient treatise of Vitruvius reinforced their advocacy of a return to classical standards in building, discontinued in the Romanesque buildings of the earlier Middle Ages. Measurements of ancient buildings were made and their proportions were imitated. The recovery of classical standards was incomplete, usually only the more 'finished' stonework and the classical decorative motifs being adopted. The Renaissance architects achieved also some remarkable feats of engineering, such as the placing of a dome on Florence Cathedral (1420–34), in imitation of the example of the Pantheon at Rome. Michelangelo's later design for the dome of St Peter's at Rome stems from his Florentine achievement.

The revolution in painting was independent of classical models and represented a combination of innovation by painters in the Netherlands and in Italy. The realism which was one of its main features probably grew out of subtle changes in attitude to the individual and the extension of lay patronage. There was also the new preoccupation with perspective which was based on the revolution in architecture. Masaccio (d. 1428), one of the most successful Florentine pioneers in the use of perspective, was a friend of the architect Brunelleschi. The great works of Renaissance sculpture owed their power to the combination of Roman inspiration in proportions and realism with the power of psychological expression derived from the religious medieval statuary. The Florentine Donatello (d. 1466), the greatest early Renaissance sculptor, was a friend of both Brunelleschi and Masaccio.   EBF

RENAUDOT, THEOPHRASTE (1586–1653), French doctor, who became physician to Louis XIII (1612), commissioner-general of the poor of Paris (1625), founder of the first Parisian labour exchange and of the first French newspaper, the *Gazette de France* (1631), and editor of the *Mercure Français* (1638–44). After being involved in a long court case with the Paris medical faculty (1640), he was deprived of the patronage of Richelieu and of Louis XIII and forbidden to practise in Paris by the *parlement* (1644), though his *Treatise on Diagnosis* (1642) had become a standard work.

RENDSBURG, DIETS OF (1525, 1542), assemblies of the Danish estates. The first was unable to persuade Frederick I to suppress the new Lutheran heresy in Denmark, and the second passed a special church ordinance extending the reformed church to the duchies of Schleswig-Holstein (1542).

RENÉE OF FRANCE, Duchess of Ferrara (1510–76), daughter of Louis XII of France and wife of Duke Ercole II of Ferrara. Her court became a well-known refuge for French Protestants, *eg*, Calvin, and humanists, *eg*, Fulvio Pellegrini Morato. She returned to France in 1559 rather than submit to her Catholic son, Duke Alfonso.

RENNER, KARL (1870–1950), Austrian politician and president of Austria (1945–50), who joined the Social Democrats and was elected to the Reichsrat (1907), soon acquiring the leadership of the moderates. He supported the empire, provided it reorganized itself on the basis of cultural autonomy for all races, and therefore backed the last emperor's abortive federalist scheme of 1918. When the Dual Monarchy collapsed he became the first chancellor of the Austrian republic in Nov. 1918. In Sept. 1919 he became foreign minister as well and signed the treaty of St Germain. At home his main concerns were the anti-Habsburg legislation, for whose passage through the Lower Chamber (Nationalrat) he was chiefly instrumental; he initiated social welfare programmes especially in Vienna and the establishment of a sound basis for the state's finances and economy. In June 1920 the coalition dissolved when the Christian Socialists walked out, but Renner continued to play a leading role in politics as head of the Social Democrats and as president of the Nationalrat (1931–3). He accepted the fait accompli of German annexation in 1938, although he deplored the methods used, and when the Austrian left grew restive he was for a time sent to a concentration camp. His anti-Nazi record meant that both Austrians and the occupying Red Army approved his heading the first post-war government in April 1945. After the socialists were defeated in the Nov. 1945 general election he was unanimously elected to the presidency.

RENNIE, JOHN (1761–1821), pioneer of civil engineering. His work included the East and West India Docks, Holyhead Harbour, and London Bridge, which was completed by his sons, George (1791–1866) and Sir John (1794–1874). His nephew, George Rennie (1802–60), was MP for Ipswich (1841–7) and governor of the Falkland Islands (1847–55).

RENOVACIÓN ESPAÑOLA, political group in Spain. The political right was shattered by the abdication of Alfonso XIII in April 1931. However, in May, some army officers and aristocrats met and founded the Círculo Monárquico. A cultural review, *Acción Española*, was also established, as was a society of the same name for the organization of lectures and seminars which became centres of monarchist opposition to the republic.

Under Antonio Goicoechea, monarchists infiltrated Gil Robles's moderate Acción Nacional, but their seditious activities, including their implication in the Sanjurjo rising, eventually forced Gil Robles to expel them. In March 1933 Goicoechea founded another party, Renovación Nacional, centred on Madrid. It never had many members and most of them were landowners, industrialists, or army officers of extremist views. Its chief aim was the regeneration of Spain by an authoritarian Catholic monarchy.

The party developed into something more modern in 1934, when Calvo Sotelo returned from exile to take over its leadership. Influenced by Salazar in Portugal and Maurras of Action Française, he pursued a militant anti-parliamentarian and fascist programme. Under his leadership, Renovación Española intensified the climate of violence in Spanish politics in 1935 and 1936 by inflammatory speeches and meetings.

An attempt was made to steal support from CEDA and the Falange by the creation of a National Block of the right, led by Renovación Española. It was hoped to install a monarchy after a totalitarian state had been established, but failed to achieve this aim. Nevertheless, Renovación Española played a key role in the polarization of politics after Feb. 1936. Calvo Sotelo became the unchallenged leader of the right and it seems likely that members of the party took part in and provided funds for the military rising of July. Thereafter, the party fused with the nationalist forces.   PP

RENTES in France, form of investment common in pre-revolutionary France. They should not be confused with the English 'rent', as they were virtually inalienable *rights* to a share in certain revenues, either from agriculture or, from the 16th cent., from various Parisian taxes. Sold either by individuals or by the state (1522), they proved popular and became a major element in French investment and government finance, so that the *rentiers*—as the body of investors were known—played a large part in French politics.

RENWICK, JAMES (1818–95), US architect, who employed Gothic and Romanesque elements in a highly personal and eclectic style. Among his notable buildings are the Smithsonian Institution, Washington, DC (1846), St Patrick's Cathedral, New York city (1853–87), and Vassar College (1865).

REPARTIMIENTO, name applied in colonial Latin America to two separate systems involving the native population. First, on the Caribbean islands in the early 16th cent., the *repartimiento* was equivalent to what later became the *encomienda* on the mainland. Second, in Mexico the *repartimiento* was a forced labour system similar to the Peruvian *mita*. The *repartimiento* was cumbersome to administer and could only be used to recruit unskilled labour on a rotational basis; also its operation suffered the catastrophic decline of the native population in the 16th cent. Early 17th-cent. legislation limited its operation to urgent public works, mining, and food production, but the two latter industries relied increasingly on peonage to create a permanent labour force. In 1632 the *repartimiento* was restricted to public works and mining, and thereafter was vital only to the former.

REPRESENTATION OF THE PEOPLE ACTS (ENGLAND) (1832, 1867, 1884), in Britain, succeeded in making parliament more sensitive to the wishes of the population, although manhood suffrage was not introduced until 1918.

The 1832 Reform Act was concerned chiefly with the redistribution of seats and standardization of franchise qualifications in order to end 'pocket' and 'rotten' boroughs. Small boroughs were disfranchised or reduced to single-member constituencies, 42 large towns were enfranchised, and the number of county members increased. A £10 household franchise was established in boroughs, and in the counties copyholders and long leaseholders were enfranchised, as well as tenants-at-will paying £50 a year. The act did not substantially alter the type of MP, but made parliament more responsive to the wishes of substantial sections of constituents.

The 1867 Reform Act extended the borough franchise to every householder paying rates who had lived there for one year, and introduced a £10 lodger franchise. In the counties the franchise was extended to £12 occupiers and £5 owners and long leaseholders. The act was accompanied by a redistribution of seats and the enfranchisement of the universities of London, Edinburgh, and Glasgow. The act enfranchised the urban working class, whose interests assumed a greater importance. The act also provided that parliament should not in future be automatically dissolved on the death of a sovereign.

The 1884 Reform Act, which applied also to Scotland and Ireland, reduced the £12 occupier franchise to £10 and extended household, lodger, and service franchises to the counties. By this act most agricultural workers received the vote and the way was prepared for the redistribution act of 1885, which merged boroughs of less than 15,000 inhabitants with their counties. This redistribution act also made towns of less than 50,000 inhabitants single-member constituencies and divided towns of more than 100,000 inhabitants into separate constituencies. No further franchise changes occurred until 1918.

These reform acts were more important than the introduction of manhood suffrage in some European countries because the British parliament had wrested from the throne control over legislature and executive before 1832. After the first Reform Act, the initiative and power moved steadily from the House of Lords to the House of Commons, culminating in the Parliament Act of 1911. Thus the movement was steadily in the direction of making government responsible to the will of the majority. No proposals for protecting minority rights or for proportional representation were entertained.   DMK

REPRESENTATION OF THE PEOPLE ACTS (IRELAND, SCOTLAND) (1832, 1868), in Britain, differed to a slight extent from those for England. In Scotland, the 1832 Reform Act increased the number of members fixed by the Act of Union from 45 to 53. The burgh franchise was extended to all £10 householders and the county franchise to all owners of property worth £10 a year, and to a few classes of leaseholders. The 1868 Reform Act (Scotland) increased the number of Scottish members to 60, and its other provisions were the same as those of the 1867 Reform Act (England).

In Ireland the 1832 Reform Act resulted in no disfranchisement, as 'rotten' boroughs had been disfranchised at the time of the Union. The number of Irish members was increased from 100 to 105, and the franchise taken from corporations and given to £10 householders. This resulted in a very narrow franchise, so in 1850 it was extended to householders rated at £8, remaining unaltered in 1868 in the counties, though the borough franchise was reduced to £4 and the lodgers' vote given. In the redistribution of seats in 1885 Ireland received preferential treatment in retaining 105 members, when with respect to her population the number should have been reduced to 91.

None of the above measures had great effect in Ireland, Englishmen from one of the two main parties representing Irish constituencies for as long as voting remained public. The Secret Ballot Act (1872) produced a dramatic change, as Irishmen no longer voted in accordance with the wishes of their landlords for fear of eviction, and the Irish party, originally under Parnell, became an important and often dominant factor at Westminster. DMK

REPRESENTATIVE THEORY in Britain, defines the relationship between MPs and their constituents. The theory that MPs were representatives, sent to parliament to discuss matters of common national interest, not delegates sent to carry out certain specific commands of their constituents, was accepted generally in the 18th cent. It was first notably stated by Algernon Sydney and frequently restated, *eg*, by Burke in his celebrated letter to his Bristol constituents (1774). The theory was based on a precise view of the nature of parliament: that it was a deliberative, not a legislative or constituent assembly. Therefore, MPs should come to it free from pressure and open-minded, and constituents should not seek to bind to a particular policy.

The opposite theory, though a minority one, was present all through the 18th cent. and was expressed in practice by a series of attempts by constituents to give their members instructions or to exact pledges from them. If not all those who tried to instruct their members were fully aware that they were endorsing a theory which implied a change in the nature of parliament, this awareness was at least present among late 18th-cent. and early 19th-cent. radicals.

The theory of representation stated by Sydney and Burke has never been explicitly rejected. But in the course of the 19th cent. practice came to be more and more divorced from theory: the circumstances of the passing of the 1832 Reform Act seemed to many people to endorse the opposite theory, and the strengthening of the executive and the growth of the party system after 1867 seemed to take all reality from the idea that MPs were free when they came to parliament to discuss and decide as seemed best to them. They were bound, however, in a new away—not by instructions from their constituents, but by party discipline. The old theory of representation is still, from time to time, stated, but parliament is clearly not now (1970) a deliberative assembly in the old sense any more than its members are representatives in the old sense. BK

REPTON, HUMPHRY (1752–1818), English landscape gardener who set out to 'improve' estates by emphasizing their picturesque qualities with clearings and planting, and by making houses and buildings an integral part of the whole. This involved architectural as well as landscape planning and to this end he collaborated with John Nash and, later, with his own sons.

REPUBLICAN PARTY in Italy (*Partito Repubblicano Italiano* —PRI). Mazzinians established a formal party in 1895, which was anti-monarchist, against industrial monopolies, and favoured local self-government. Its support was mostly in the north and by 1900 it had won 29 seats. The party provided independent 'Mazzinian' partisan groups (1944–5) during the Second World War and strenuously campaigned against the monarchy in liberated Italy. Though very small by 1945, it shared in the post-war coalitions. Notable ministers, such as Carlo Sforza and Ugo La Malfa, influenced the debates. They favoured the European Common Market, bureaucratic reorganization, agrarian reform, regionalism, and a revision of the Lateran Agreements.

REPUBLICAN PARTY in the US, major political party formed as a result of widespread dissatisfaction among many Whigs, Free Soilers, and Democrats over the expansion of slavery into the federal territories. Its formal beginnings are traced to a meeting in Ripon, WI (1854). Few democratic political parties have had a more successful beginning. Some 40 Republicans were elected to the US House of Representatives, several became governors and senators (1854), and in the 1856 presidential election the party emerged as a major force, with John C. Fremont carrying 11 northern states. The continuing crisis over slavery and organization of the west

contributed to Republican control of the House of Representatives (1858, 1860), and to the presidential victory of Abraham Lincoln (1860) on a platform opposed to the spread of slavery and advocating protective tariffs and free homesteads for settlers.

During the American Civil War the party became identified with national unity and freedom for the slaves and established itself as the dominant political party. Except for the victories of Grover Cleveland and Woodrow Wilson, it controlled the presidency until 1932. The basis of its strength was a fusion of northern and western interests, the isolation of the Democratic Party in the South, and vigorous policies of 'sound money', high tariffs, and national expansion.

In the 1920s, the party's internal divisions, stemming from the growth of progressivism between 1900 and 1910, were resolved in the return to 'Normalcy'. Republican presidential victories in 1920 and 1924 culminated in Hoover's landslide victory in 1928. Within a few months, however, the prosperity of the 'New Economic Era' collapsed and with the Great Depression the political fortunes of the Republican Party disintegrated. Their congressional majorities were eroded in the 1930 elections and in 1932 the Democratic Party controlled both houses of Congress. President Hoover suffered overwhelming defeat in the presidential elections, and further humiliations followed in 1934 and 1936. The party, forced to adjust itself to a new role, gradually recouped its congressional losses and by 1946 had regained control. The end of the Second World War, and President Truman's unpopularity, made Republicans confident of victory in 1948, but Truman's surprising success exposed its sectional and policy weaknesses. Although presidential victory came in 1952, it was primarily due to the personal appeal of Eisenhower, a fact emphasized by continued Republican losses in Congress (1952–60). Defeat in 1960 promoted a massive conservative reaction within the party, and nomination of Senator Barry Goldwater (1964) led to overwhelming electoral defeat.

Few Republicans after 1964 were optimistic about the future, but major divisions within the Democratic Party, and the emergence in 1968 of George Wallace as a strong third party candidate, created an unexpected opportunity. Richard Nixon, defeated Republican presidential candidate in 1960, sought to heal internal wounds and won the nomination and a narrow presidential victory, but the party's strength at other levels gave it no more than an opportunity to reassert itself as the majority party.

G. H. Mayer, *The Republican Party 1854–1966* (London and New York, 1964).
M. C. Moos, *The Republicans: a history of their party* (New York, 1956). JDL

REQUERIMIENTO (1510), document devised to give legal sanction to the Spanish conquests in America. The *Requerimiento* called upon the natives to submit peacefully and receive the faith. Every Spanish conqueror was required to read the document to the natives prior to hostilities.

REQUESENS Y ZUNIGA, DON LUIS DE (1528–76), Spanish diplomat and administrator, who was Spanish ambassador in Rome, councillor to Don John of Austria (1568–71), Spanish governor of Milan (1571–3), and governor-general of the Netherlands (1573–6). In the last position he succeeded the Duke of Alva, whose policy of ruthless military dictatorship had stimulated the revolt of the Sea Beggars. Requesens therefore tried moderate means to secure a reconciliation between the Spanish government and the rebels. On arriving in Brussels in Nov. 1573, his hand was strengthened by the defeat of the rebel forces at Mook Heide (April 1574). He advised a general pardon (June 1574), the suppression of the Council of Troubles, and the abolition of the hated sales tax, the Tenth Penny. Pacification, however, could only succeed if he could control the army, and the mutiny of the unpaid Spanish, Walloon, and German troops in Antwerp nullified his professed moderation. At a conference at Breda

(Feb. 1575) between his representatives and the deputies of the estates of Holland and Zeeland, he agreed to the withdrawal of Spanish troops and officials, but could not promise liberty of conscience. From this point his government was doomed to failure. Philip II's second bankruptcy (Sept. 1575) prevented adequate financial aid reaching him while his own health deteriorated.

REQUESTS, COURTS OF in England, offshoot of the king's council, which arose from 14th-cent. conciliar arrangements to expedite the supplications of the poor for legal redress, but which took shape as a court in King Henry VII's reign. In 1516 Wolsey established four conciliar committees to hear cases concerning poor men and Crown servants, and of these one—the committee in the White Hall—became the separately constituted court of requests by 1530. It was characterized by the speed and cheapness of its litigation and by a greater inclination to Roman law, and the use of written documents and witnesses, although it administered English common law. Under King Edward VI two permanent masters of requests were appointed and from 1562 they were aided by two unpaid, 'extraordinary' masters. In the later part of Queen Elizabeth I's reign the court came under attack from the common law courts, but although the court of common pleas declared that it had no power of judicature in the case of *Stepney v. Flood* (1599), the court of requests survived until 1642, after which the masters of requests ceased to sit.

RERESBY, SIR JOHN (1634–89), English politician, whose posthumous *Memoirs* (1734) and *Travels* (1813) described his continental journeys during the Interregnum (1648–60), his subsequent career as high sheriff of Yorkshire, and his uncertain allegiances during the political crises of the reigns of Charles II and James II.

RESCISSORY ACT (1661) in Scotland, measure which annulled all the acts of the Scottish parliaments passed since 1633, including those of 1641, a parliament at which Charles I had been personally present. It was disliked by Lauderdale, who regarded it as far too sweeping, and by the Presbyterians as, in effect, it restored episcopacy.

RESHID PASHA, MUSTAFA (1800–58), Ottoman Tanzimat reformer, who was chiefly responsible for the Hatti Sherif of Gülhane (1839) and for important administrative, legal, and financial reforms. He was grand vizier six times (1846–58).

RESIDENCIA, in colonial Spanish America a judicial review of an official's conduct at the end of his term in office. The process was required of all Crown-appointed bureaucrats to ensure high standards of conduct and efficiency and to maintain royal control over its agents abroad.

RESOLUTIONERS in Scotland, moderate majority in the Scottish general assembly, which passed the 'first public resolution' (14 Dec. 1650) in favour of allowing all who were not committed enemies of the Covenant to fight in the Scottish army, and was opposed to the western remonstrance of Oct. 1650.

RESPONSIBLE GOVERNMENT, name given to the British system of cabinet government when applied to the colonies. Early in the 19th cent., when the king still had an effective share in government, appointing his ministers and influencing their policies, it was impossible for a colonial governor to delegate his authority to a cabinet of colonists depending primarily on a colonial assembly for their ministerial positions. Responsible government was a new and radical departure in colonial history made possible by the new circumstances in the white-settler colonies from the 1830s onwards. They already had some form of representative assemblies, and

further advance was encouraged both by the propaganda of the Manchester School, which condemned colonies as expensive luxuries requiring aristocratic governors and garrisons of troops to maintain them, and by the constructive criticisms of Radicals like Edward Gibbon Wakefield, who pleaded for a systematic interest in colonization, and the work of Sir James Stephens at the colonial office.

Lord Durham's Report on the Affairs of British North America (1839), following his visit to Canada to report on uprisings there, was the manifesto of the advanced colonial reformers. He argued that Britain should avoid trouble by letting colonial affairs be managed by responsible ministers chosen from the colonists. Britain should retain her four major interests in the constitution, foreign relations, international trade, and the disposal of waste lands; the rest should all be transferred to the colonists.

The Canada Act (1840) did not fully implement Durham's radical suggestions, but it united the two provinces of Canada, which had been separated in 1791, and set up a bicameral legislature, a nominated legislative council, and an elected assembly. After 1846 Lord Grey, the Whig colonial secretary, gave the governors freedom to act on Durham's recommendations if they chose to do so. Canada and Nova Scotia formed cabinets from 1848 onwards. The British North America Act (1867) created a new, federal, and almost completely self-governing Dominion of Canada.

The way seemed clear for the concept of responsible government to be extended to all colonies, though questions were soon raised as to whether cabinet government was applicable throughout the empire, to India and Crown colonies, and whether Durham's definition of the four 'imperial' fields of government was permanently valid.

In mid-century the principle was gradually established that any colony which had a sufficient number of free European settlers to manage its affairs efficiently might qualify. The first responsible ministry in New Zealand took office in 1856 and colonies with responsible government were to form an imperial elite, an extra division in the complicated structure of the British empire.

Growing British enthusiasm for economy meant that all such colonies must accept certain responsibilities, even if against their own inclinations, *eg*, for defence. Despite humanitarian doubts about white supremacy, the presence of a large number of non-Europeans did not disqualify a colony from responsible government.

Responsible government was extended in the 20th cent. The Australian colonies formed the Commonwealth of Australia (1901), the Cape and Natal joined the ex-Boer colonies of Transvaal and the Orange Free State to form the Union of South Africa (1910). These older colonies or dominions were by 1914 in most respects like independent states, though there were still considerable legal and constitutional barriers to full sovereign status, which was virtually conceded by the Statute of Westminster (1931).   JRA

RESTITUTION, EDICT OF (1629), imperial edict promulgated by Emperor Ferdinand II in the flush of military success in the Thirty Years War. It ordered the restoration of all ecclesiastical property to those who owned it in 1555 and of all goods appropriated by German princes since the Edict of Passau (1552), involving two archbishoprics, 12 bishoprics, and 50 major convents. Thus Ferdinand hoped to recover all the German lands lost to Protestantism during the previous 75 years, and exclude recognition to Calvinism altogether. Habsburg and Wittelsbach candidates were soon imposed on seven bishoprics and Wallenstein's army of 100,000 enforced the edict on the smaller secular authorities, *eg*, Augsburg, where the Catholic bishop was restored and Protestantism forbidden, although only a tenth of the population was Catholic, while the leading Protestant princes, *eg*, John George of Saxony, protested weakly. The dismissal of Wallenstein (1630) and the intervention of Gustavus Adolphus of Sweden undermined the Restitution Edict, which was later superseded by the peace of Prague (1635).

RESTORATION, THE (1660), return of Charles II from the Dutch republic to England on 4 June. The Royalists maintained that he had been king ever since the death of his father, Charles I, on 30 Jan. 1649, but it was not until he came back to England that he effectively exercised the royal prerogatives. The Restoration Settlement was the working-out of a solution of the various problems that had arisen in England during nearly two decades of civil war and republican government.

RESTORATION DRAMA in England, collective description of plays written in the period from King Charles II's restoration (1660), to Queen Anne's reign (1702–14) and characterized by a reaction against Puritan severity. They were written for the amusement of the fashionable world surrounding the court and were performed at the King's theatre, which from 1663 was settled at the Theatre Royal in Drury Lane. The revived theatre was quite different from that of Shakespeare's day. The playhouses were roofed in, and the stage had artificial lighting, a drop curtain, and painted scenery. Women's parts were no longer taken by youths, but by actresses, *eg*, Nell Gwynne.

The best-known playwright of tragedy was Thomas Otway (1651–85), who wrote *The Orphan* (1680) and *Venice Preserved* (1682). The comedies of manners were characterized by witty conversation, plots of complicated intrigue, and characters who represented types rather than individuals— the fop, the rake, the coquette, or the boor. Their authors depicted the licentiousness, profanity, and ignorance of society rather than criticized it, though their purpose was to shock those who disapproved of such hedonism. William Wycherley's *The Country Wife* (1672) typified the cynical frivolity of early Restoration drama and William Congreve (1670–1729) produced its finest examples, in *Love for Love* (1695) and *The Way of the World* (1700). Sir John Vanbrugh, the architect (1664–1726), also belonged to the school, his best-known play being *The Provok'd Wife* (1697). The last Restoration dramatist was George Farquhar (1677–1707), author of *The Constant Couple* (1699) and *The Beaux' Strategem*, whose characters were drawn from a wider section of society. In the latter years of the 17th cent. condemnation of the comedies by wits and moralists increased, the most outspoken being Jeremy Collier's *A Short View of the Immorality and Profaneness of the English Stage* (1698). The revived drama of the mid-18th cent. was similar in plot, but less bawdy and superficial.

RESTRAINING ORDERS (1712), issued by Bolingbroke during the War of the Spanish Succession to the Duke of Ormonde, commander of the English troops in Flanders, requiring him not to use his forces against France. The orders, communicated to France but not to the English allies, were an attempt to force a peace settlement on to the latter.

RETIEF, PIETER (1780–1838,) leader of the Afrikaner Voortrekkers who migrated from the Cape Colony in 1837. He was killed by the Zulu king, Dingane.

RETZ, JEAN FRANÇOIS DE GONDI, Cardinal de (1613–79), French politician and prelate. His involvement in the Soissons plot (1640) earned him Richelieu's disfavour and he was refused the co-adjutatorship and succession to the Archbishopric of Paris, which was virtually a family possession, until after the cardinal's death (1643). He quarrelled with Mazarin (1648) and tried to use the *Fronde* to increase his own power and that of the Church. Though at first influential with the populace, he lost this support when he became a cardinal and tried to continue his intrigues after the collapse of the *Fronde* (1653). When arrested on the personal orders of Louis XIV (1653) he refused to surrender his rights to the archbishopric (1654) and eventually escaped to Italy. Driven out of Rome, he travelled through Europe before finally resigning his rights (1662). He was then permitted to live on his estates and was used on diplomatic missions in Italy by Louis (1665), but was never really accepted at court. He spent his last years writing his *Mémoires* and devoting himself to charitable works.

RÉUNION (2510 sq. kms), island in the Indian Ocean with 418,000 inhabitants. After 1946 it became a *département* of the French republic, with three representatives in the national assembly and two in the senate. A *préfet* governs (1970) the island.

RÉUNIONS, THE, annexation by the French Crown in the decade after the peace of Nymwegen (1678) of all dependencies of those lands acquired by France in the preceding half-century. To establish the legality of his action, Louis XIV ordered the setting up of special courts, the chambers of reunion, to determine the extent of France's just claims, *eg*, in Metz, Besançon, Breisach, and Tournai. The courts' decisions, whether disputed by another sovereign ruler or not, were enforced by military action, *eg*, Strasbourg was seized from the empire and Casale from Spain (1681). This *réunion* policy aroused increasing hostility throughout Europe, and at the peace of Ryswick (1697) many of the annexed territories were restored to their former rulers.

REUTER CONCESSION, vast economic concession granted by Iran to Baron Julius de Reuter in 1873. It included the rights to build railways, exploit mines, and establish a national bank. It was cancelled because of Russian opposition, although the bank concession ultimately bore fruit in the influential Imperial Bank of Persia (subsequently the British Bank of Iran and the Middle East).

REUTERN, MIKHAIL KRISTOFOROVICH, Count (1820–90), Russian politician and minister of finance (1862–78), who encouraged private credit institutions, introduced a uniform state budget, and tried unsuccessfully to make the rouble convertible. He followed a free trade policy unusual in Russia.

REUTHER, WALTER PHILIP (1907–70), US labour leader, who worked in the steel and automobile industries, including the Ford Motor Co. in Detroit, MI. After being discharged from Ford's (1933) because of his union activities, he spent two years travelling and working in Europe and the USSR. On his return to the US (1935), he became a leading organizer for the United Automobile Workers. As president of the UAW (1946–70) and the CIO (1952–5), he pioneered the guaranteed annual wage, made the UAW influential in social reform in the US, led the CIO into a merger with the American Federation of Labor (1955), and became a vice-president of the AFL–CIO and president of its Industrial Union Department. The merger did not heal the division between the old craft unions of the AF of L and the industrial unions of the CIO, and when the tension between the two became intolerable, Reuther withdrew the UAW (1968). Throughout the 1960s he was one of the most forward-looking, aggressive, and respected leaders of the US labour movement.

REVENGE, galleon of the Elizabethan royal navy, launched in 1575 at a cost of £4000. She measured 92 ft long and 32 ft in beam, according to Hawkins's specifications, and carried nearly 50 guns and 250 men. Considered by Drake to be the perfect warship, *Revenge* was chosen as his flagship for the Armada campaign (1588). She was the only royal ship to surrender to Spain in the Anglo-Spanish War (1585–1604), after a stand off the Azores under Sir Richard Grenville (1591).

REVENUE OF THE CROWN OF ENGLAND, financial resources of English monarchs, which were first handled by the exchequer in the 12th cent., and by the 15th cent. were divided into two categories, the ordinary revenues that belonged to the Crown by prerogative right or permanent grant, and the extraordinary revenues which were granted by parliament when the need arose. At various times the revenue was nandled by other departments of the royal household, *eg*, the wardrobe in the 13th cent., the chamber in the 14th and late 15th cents, and several minor courts in the 16th cent., *eg*, the duchy of Lancaster. However, from the late Tudor period there was a tendency to gather control of revenue into the hands of the lord treasurer, and this process was completed in the period 1660–85 with the centralization of receipts at the exchequer.

The ordinary revenues included rents from Crown lands, which were considerably increased from 1485 by inheritance, confiscation, and forfeiture, and were handled by the courts of general surveyors and augmentations; the traditional feudal incidents of aids, purveyance, pre-emption, relief, escheats, wardship, and the custody of the lands of widows and wards which were handled by the court of wards and liveries; the profits of justice fees for writs, fines, and penal profits, the ancient customs duties on wool, hides, and leather levied from Edward I's reign, and tunnage and poundage from King Edward III's reign, all of which were in the exchequer's hands. Finally, in the 1530s were added the ecclesiastical revenues of the courts of first fruits and tenths and augmentations, until their abolition in 1554. In Queen Elizabeth I's reign these ordinary revenues amounted to £200,000 per annum. To extract the maximum from the ordinary revenues the early Stuart kings enforced their feudal rights stringently. After the Restoration (1660) the Crown's feudal revenues were abolished by statute, though they had been stopped by parliamentary ordinance of 1643, and with them the court of wards. In return the Crown was granted in perpetuity £100,000 per annum from the excise, while King Charles II received for life the revenue from customs duties, valued about £400,000 per annum and £300,000 per annum from the excise, together with the revenues from the post office, stamp duties, and a hearth tax (from 1661), which were expected to yield £1,200,000 per annum. By 1697 it was recognized that it was no longer possible for the monarch to 'live of his own', and a distinction was drawn between the revenues of the Crown essential for the government of the realm and those required by the monarch to maintain the royal household. £700,000 per annum was ear-marked from tunnage and poundage to provide for the household through the civil list.

The extraordinary revenues consisted of taxation imposed with parliamentary consent. From the late 12th cent. a tax on movable property was raised from time to time which from King Edward III's reign became a fifteenth of a tenth, but as the assessment was fixed from the 14th cent. supplementary taxes or subsidies were raised, which from King Henry VIII's reign was a fixed levy on income from land and personal property. The subsidy remained the main direct tax under the Tudors. Occasionally a per capita tax or poll-tax was levied, *eg*, in 1380 and 1512. King Edward IV had demanded voluntary loans or benevolences, and though abolished by a statute of 1483 they were revived by Wolsey and occasionally by Henry VIII's successors. Finally, the Tudors levied additional duties on imports, known as impositions. Both benevolences and impositions were used to such a degree by James I and Charles I that bitter conflict occurred between parliament and the Crown over the extraordinary revenues in the first half of the 17th cent.

In 1660–85 tax-farming of revenues was abolished and they doubled in amount, as the Crown came to rely increasingly on customs and excise, supplemented by direct taxes which responded to the expanding economy. The large-scale wars of the period 1688–1714, however, created an unprecedented demand for revenue which could not be raised from direct taxes, *eg*, the land tax, stamp, house, and window duties, although their yield roughly doubled in the years 1688–97, nor from indirect taxes, *eg*, excise on both luxury and common commodities. The expenditure could only be met by heavy and ingenious borrowing by short-term exchequer bills and long-term loans. Britain's successful emergence from this and later periods of war rested, however, on the revolutionary credit machinery established in the 1690s, the Bank of England and the National Debt. In the 18th–20th cents new and revolutionary direct and indirect taxes have been created to swell the public revenue, *eg*, income tax, corn duties, road tax, death duties, and purchase tax. JHS

REVERE, PAUL (1735–1818), American silversmith, engraver, and folk-hero of the American Revolution. He took part in the Boston Tea Party (16 Dec. 1773), was courier for the Massachusetts Committee of Correspondence (1774), and rode from Charlestown to Lexington (18 April 1775) to warn local minute-men of approaching British troops, an exploit commemorated in Longfellow's poem 'Paul Revere's Ride'. He designed the first Continental currency and the first official seal for the new United States.

REVETT, NICHOLAS (1720–1804), British architect and draughtsman, who was a popularizer of Grecian architecture. With James Stuart, he travelled in Italy and Greece (1751–5) and published the first volume of *The Antiquities of Athens* (1762). The measured drawings which made the *Antiquities* so valuable, as the first accurate survey of Greek ruins, were Revett's. His subsequent expedition, with two others, to Asia Minor, was sponsored by the Dilettanti Society and resulted in *Ionian Antiquities* (1769–97).

REVIEWS in Britain were influential in forming public taste and opinions on artistic, political, and social questions from the beginning of the 19th cent. They appealed to an increasing educated middle and upper class readership, both in London and the provinces, and published contributions from the best writers and most influential thinkers in national life.

The *Edinburgh Review and Critical Journal* (1802–1929) was Whig in outlook at its inception, being well disposed to discussion of change in government and society, but increasingly hostile to innovation in the arts. Its contributors included Brougham, Sidney Smith, Carlyle, Hazlitt, and Macaulay. Having 10,000 subscribers initially, its editor was able to pay notable contributors for long articles which aroused public discussion. Its chief rival was the *Quarterly Review*, founded in 1809 by John Murray at the suggestion of Sir Walter Scott and Robert Southey, with Lockhart as its first editor. It had links with the Tory Party through Canning and Liverpool and it became increasingly conservative both in politics and the arts. The *Westminster Review* (1824–1914) was founded with the Support of Hazlitt, Leigh Hunt, and others to express a more radical point of view.

In the mid-19th cent. interest in the reviews declined in face of lessening political controversy and competition from illustrated magazines. It revived briefly with the *Fortnightly Review* (1865–1950). Under the editorship of John Morley (1867–82), it contained important articles on political, social, and artistic topics from such writers as J. S. Mill, Bagehot, Herbert Spencer, Huxley, Galton, Freeman, and Gardiner. Another influential periodical at this time was the *Saturday Review*, a conservative organ under the guidance of Lord Salisbury. VEC

REVILLAGIGEDO, FRANCISCO DE GÜEMES Y HORCASITAS, Count of (1682–1766), viceroy of Mexico. Under Revillagigedo, whose term began in 1746, the finances of the colony were reorganized, and economic conditions greatly improved, largely because of increased silver production.

REVOCATION ACT (1625) in Scotland, legislation at the beginning of King Charles I's reign, revoking all grants of Crown property made since 1540 and rescinding all dispositions of ecclesiastical property and conversions into temporal lordships. The purpose of this revocation was to enable Charles to make adequate provision for the augmentation of the stipends of the reformed clergy from Church lands and tithes.

REVOCATION OF THE EDICT OF NANTES, or Edict of Fontainebleau (22 Feb. 1685) by which Louis XIV cancelled the remaining privileges enjoyed by French Huguenots. Although theoretically allowing them liberty of conscience in their homes, the edict abolished all external signs of Calvinism as an established Church, such as pastors, marriages, and chapels. The edict was introduced partly on the suggestion of Le Tellier and others who felt that the *dragonnades* had weakened Calvinism to a point where a formal prohibition could be effective. This was acceptable to Louis XIV not only because of his dislike of religious dissidence, but because he wished to reduce the financial drain caused by conversions (which were rewarded by tax concessions) and because it would demonstrate his theological orthodoxy to the papacy, with which he was then in conflict. The revocation succeeded in driving Calvinism underground rather than destroying it and then only at the cost of strengthening its will to resist and of aiding Louis's European opponents, both economically and morally.

REVOLUTIONS, 1848, THE, occurred in western and central European countries including France, the German Confederation, the Austrian territories, and Italy. They were marked by civil and international strife and numerous governmental changes. In some, economic and political grievance, strengthened by the rise of liberalism and socialism, were evident; elsewhere demands for national freedom from alien rule were paramount.

In France, the Second Republic was proclaimed on the abdication of Louis Philippe. Socialists, led by Louis Blanc, were involved in the failure of National Workshops, which led to a reaction in favour of moderate government and the election of Louis Napoleon as president in Dec. In Germany, liberal constitutions were granted in many states, including Prussia, and in March the Vorparlament met in preparation for a National German Parliament. In Prussia, Frederick William forcibly regained control and a general reaction against liberals and their attempts at national unity occurred. Britain was not immune from disturbance, since 1848 saw the organization of the third Chartist petition by O'Connor; while in Ireland Smith O'Brien and the Young Ireland movement, as well as increasing violence between landlord and tenant, showed the power of economic hardship allied to growing nationalism.

Within the Austrian empire the position was most critical. Liberals gained control after the Vienna uprising, Metternich resigned and fled, and by the Vienna Edict, Ferdinand I granted a liberal constitution, while in Hungary a Magyar anti-Austrian revolution under Kossuth triumphed. The Austrian emperor fled to Innsbruck in May, but a Czech uprising in Prague was defeated by Windischgratz, and the Croats and Serbs with some Rumanian support rallied under Jellačič against the Magyars and in defence of their national rights. In Oct. the Hungarian and Austrian radicals made common cause, but were defeated in Austria, where Prince Felix Schwarzenberg restored order, aided by the new emperor, Franz Joseph. The Hungarians under Georgei were victorious until in May 1849, to forestall a Polish uprising, Tsar Nicholas offered Austria assistance and the Magyars were put down with much severity by Haynau and others. In Italy liberal constitutions were granted by Ferdinand of Naples, Leopold of Tuscany, and Charles Albert of Savoy. With the news of Metternich's fall, Austrian power crumbled before revolts in Milan, Parma, Modena, and Venice under Manin. With the defeat of the Sardinians by the Austrians under Radetzky at Custozza and Novara (1849), the revolutions collapsed. In Rome the French overthrew the republican constitution of Mazzini and Garibaldi and Pius IX was restored.

The revolutionaries of 1848 were unsuccessful except in inspiring widespread reaction among the ruling classes of Europe. Yet they foreshadowed the triumph of nationalism, if not of liberalism.

P. Robertson, *Revolutions of 1848* (Princeton, NJ, 1952).

VEC

REVUE DES DEUX-MONDES, French periodical, founded in 1829. After 1831, under the direction of Buloz, it acquired an enormous circulation and built up a reputation that enabled it to be one of the most effective critics of the Second Empire (1852–70).

REXISTS in Belgium, name applied to the neo-fascist party in Belgium. Its origins lay in two weekly newspapers founded by Léon Degrelle in 1932 and later known collectively as *Rex*. Degrelle hoped to use this journal to encourage the renovation of the Catholic Party, of which he was a member. But he was expelled for his extreme criticism and founded his own party, which took the name of his journal. Preaching the dangers of communism and capitalizing on the general discontent during the Depression, though trying not to become embroiled in the current linguistic quarrels, Degrelle attracted those who elsewhere responded to fascism. In the 1936 elections, the Rexists gained 21 seats. But this sudden success was short-lived. Degrelle's popularity waned that same year when it became known that he had secretly fraternized with Hitler, and support for the Rexists declined with the reorientation of Belgian foreign policy towards a position of independence (1936). Furthermore, the disruptive effect of the Rexists on Belgian politics stimulated the necessary reorganization of the Catholic Party for which Degrelle had earlier campaigned, and many Rexists returned to their traditional support for that party.

Though supporting Belgium's new foreign policy and declaration of neutrality (1939), the Rexists advocated coming to terms with Hitler in 1940. Sensing the possible dangers of a well-organized fascist party, the government arrested many Rexists and sent Degrelle to France. However, after the armistice he returned to Belgium and worked in close collaboration with the Nazis. Following the liberation of Belgium (Sept. 1944) many Rexists were executed as war criminals, but Degrelle had fled to Spain, where he was granted asylum. With the ending of the Second World War, the Rexists Party disappeared.

JL

REYES, ALFONSO (1889–1959), Mexican writer, poet, and diplomat, who was ambassador to Brazil (1930–6) and to Argentina (1936–7). He is one of the most celebrated essayists in the Spanish language.

REYES, RAFAEL (1850–1918), Colombian politician, soldier, and conservative president of Colombia (1904–9). His programme for economic reform was hampered by his difficulties with the Colombian congress and the national press. His attempt to recognize the independence of Panama, which had seceded from Colombia in 1903, precipitated a governmental crisis in 1909, and he resigned.

REYNAUD, PAUL (1878–1966), French politician and prime minister when France was defeated in 1940. His attempts to rally the French people and fight on were not supported by his colleagues, and he was forced to resign in favour of Pétain. Reynaud entered parliament in 1919, and became a leader of the independent conservatives and an expert on finance. In the 1930s he was the only politician to support De Gaulle's ideas on mechanized warfare, but could not get the army to accept them. As minister of finance in Daladier's government (1938–40) he introduced a stringent programme designed to concentrate resources on rearmament. It included higher taxes, cuts in public expenditure, and longer hours of work, undoing some of the reforms of the Popular Front. This programme, though unpopular, helped to bring an end to the Depression.

He opposed the Munich agreement and the spirit of appeasement, and was therefore a natural choice to succeed Daladier (March 1940). He prosecuted the war energetically, and sought to strengthen his cabinet after the German invasion by the inclusion of Pétain and Weygand. He also gave De Gaulle a minor post. When France's defeat became clear, Reynaud, supported by Churchill, tried to persuade the government to continue resistance in North Africa, but was outvoted by the supporters of an armistice, and resigned on 16 June.

He was interned by the Vichy regime, then deported to Germany. He returned to parliament after the Second World War.

REYNOLDS, GEORGE WILLIAM MacARTHUR (1814–1879) British journalist and radical politician, whose close knowledge of French culture influenced his career. He was an active Chartist for some years from 1848. His greatest achievement lay in popular journalism, and in his radical *Reynolds's Weekly Newspaper*, launched in May 1850.

REYNOLDS, SIR JOSHUA (1723–92), British portrait painter, and first president of the Royal Academy. He painted many notable men and women in England in the second half of the 18th cent. Visits to Rome and Venice (1750–2) influenced his work strongly. His aim was to combine native English tradition with the classical grand style and he hoped, through the Academy, to establish a British school of painting to compare with those of Rome and Bologna. After 1781, when he visited Holland, his own work was less consciously classical.

REZA SHAH (1878–1944), Iranian dictator and founder of the Pahlevi dynasty. As commander of the Persian Cossack Brigade he seized power (Feb. 1921), in conjunction with Sayyid Zia al-Din al-Tabataba'i, whom he expelled in May 1921. As minister of war (1921–3) Reza re-established internal security and built up the army. He became prime minister (Oct. 1923), deposed the last Qajar ruler, Ahmad Shah (Oct. 1924), and was himself elected shah (12 Dec. 1924). He abdicated (Sept. 1941) following the Anglo-Russian occupation of Iran and died in exile in South Africa. As ruler of Iran he modelled himself upon Mustafa Kemal Atatürk, the Turkish dictator, established strict political control, and carried through a policy of state-directed modernization. Politically he broke the power of the tribes and built up a strong bureaucracy; economically he promoted commercial and industrial development under state control, developed communications, especially the Trans-Iranian railway (1927–38) from Bandar Shapur on the Gulf to Bandar Shah on the Caspian, which was financed entirely from internal Iranian resources; socially he pursued a policy of secularizing law and education, greatly expanded the latter system, and enforced the adoption of Western clothing; ideologically he emphasized Iranian nationalism, which he attempted to assert in his foreign policy. Despite the repression, corruption, and economic and social hardship which accompanied his rule, his autocratic methods achieved remarkable success in transforming the nature of Iran.

MEY

RHEE, SYNGMAN (1875–1965), president of (South) Korea (1948–60). Until 1945 he campaigned, often bitterly, for US support for Korea against Japan. He had been president of the exiled Korean provisional government (1919–21) and always associated with it; but his personality was the most divisive factor in the violent factionalism which rendered it impotent. In 1945 he presented himself as embodying all Korean aspirations, and a massive personal following ensured his unopposed election in 1948 as South Korea's first president. He grew increasingly autocratic and incapable of dealing with the realities of Korea's situation, and his re-election in 1952, 1956, and 1960 was achieved by means increasingly fraudulent. In 1960 the April Revolution forced his resignation, and he lived in Hawaii, where he died.

RHEGIUM, ancient Greek colony in southern Italy (mod. Reggio) founded (*c.* 730 BC) by Chalcidians from Zancle and Messenians from the Peloponnese. In the 5th cent. its tyrant, Anaxilas (*reg.* 494–476), opposed Hippocrates of Gela and Gelon of Syracuse. He won Zancle (*c.* 490), renaming it

Messana, and later supported the Carthaginian invasion of 480. After Anaxilas' death continued hostility between Rhegium and Syracuse helped to provoke the Athenians to intervene unsuccessfully against Syracuse during the great Peloponnesian War in 427–424, but Rhegium only half-heartedly supported the Athenian expedition of 415–413. The colony was destroyed by Dionysius I (387), but soon rebuilt, and in time enjoyed good relations with Rome, becoming prosperous under the empire.

RHEIMS BIBLE, English translation of the Vulgate made by English Catholic exiles who had been expelled from Douai in the Netherlands by Requesens, its Spanish governor, and had settled at Rheims in France.

RHEINFELDT, BATTLE OF (1638), victory of the Protestant German forces of Duke Bernard of Saxe-Weimar over the imperialists under Count Savelli and Johann von Werth at the Rhine bridgehead east of Basle in the 30 Years War. After retiring from Rheinfeldt, Bernard retraced his steps and took the imperialists by surprise, capturing Von Werth. He then marched northwards to reduce Breisach.

RHETT, ROBERT BARNWELL (1800–76), US lawyer and politician, from SC, who was elected to the state legislature (1826), served in the US House of Representatives (1837–49), and succeeded John C. Calhoun as US senator (1850). An extreme advocate of states rights, he led the secessionist movement in SC and welcomed the Civil War. He was not given office by the Confederate government, and became a stern critic of Jefferson Davis.

RHINELAND, region in western Germany bordering France and the Low Countries and flanking both banks of the Rhine. After the First World War many in France demanded the annexation of the left bank to increase French security. Faced with Anglo-American opposition, however, the French government accepted instead (in the treaty of Versailles) the Allied occupation of the Rhineland (with provision for its termination, in three successive stages, over 15 years). In addition, Germany was to demilitarize the territory between its western frontier and a line drawn 50 kms to the east of the river and parallel to it. Meanwhile, the French in occupation of the Rhineland tried to stimulate the growth of a Rhineland separatist movement—an attempt which, although renewed when they occupied the Ruhr (1923), produced no durable result.

The signatories to the treaty of Locarno (including German) reaffirmed and guaranteed the permanent demilitarization of the Rhineland. Subsequently, German acceptance of the Young plan (1929) brought the end of Allied occupation five years ahead of the provisions of the Versailles treaty.

After Hitler's accession to power German troops were stationed in the Rhineland and minor military installations set up. Hitler then (7 March 1936) ordered German troops into the Rhineland in force, on the pretext that the Franco-Soviet pact invalidated the Locarno treaty. Although the crisis had been foreseen, none of the Locarno powers had made plans to counteract it. Italy secretly supported Hitler's action. Belgium's weak position offered the country no alternative but co-operation with Britain and France—although as a result of the Rhineland crisis the Belgian government declared its future neutrality. The French manned the Maginot Line, but decided to concert all further action with their co-signatories to the Locarno Pact, with whom they had frequent meetings in the following ten days. They had no military plans for a quick retaliatory action, but pressed for economic and even military sanctions, though their motive in so doing was probably to secure a future British commitment to France rather than effective action in the present. The British government, however, would not agree to any such proposals. The British public had some sympathy with German action in sending soldiers into German territory and the British government sought to exchange acceptance of the Rhineland remilitarization for some larger European settlement. They insisted, through months of discussion, on settlement by negotiation. However, faced by Germany's refusal to make any concessions and French anxiety about their own security they reluctantly agreed (at Eden's insistence) on staff conversations with France and Belgium as an additional measure of security pending a settlement. However, the scope of these talks was so limited as to deprive them of real value.

Debate among the Locarno powers continued into 1937, but the importance of the issue faded with the onset of the Spanish Civil War and a solution was thus found in a tacit acceptance of the fait accompli.

Subsequently the Rhineland crisis came to be regarded as the most favourable moment at which Hitler's aggrandizement might have been checked and the Second World War avoided. It was cited as an example of a mistake to be avoided, notably in justification of the Suez expedition (1956).

JK

RHODE ISLAND, British North American colony. Rhode Island was first settled at Providence by Roger Williams (1636), who had fled from MA after a religious dispute. The coast had been visited earlier by Miguel Cortereal (1511), Giovanni da Verrazzano (1524), and Adriaen Block (1614). Da Verrazzano was probably indirectly responsible for the name of the colony when he wrote that one of the nearby islands reminded him of Rhodes in the Mediterranean. Other religious refugees founded Portsmouth (1638), and Warwick (1634–47); Newport (1639) was an offshoot of Portsmouth. A charter was granted (1644) to the four settlements, which united to form the Colony of Providence Plantations. The colony's tradition of religious freedom was confirmed by Charles II's charter (1663), although Roman Catholics were deprived of suffrage (1664–1783). During the colonial wars (17th–18th cents) RI became a centre of privateering against the Dutch and French, and local forces were also raised for campaigns against the French and Indians. Growing discontent within the colony against British commercial legislation, particularly the Molasses Act (1733) and the various Navigation Acts, was reflected in the attacks on the *Maidstone* (1765) and the revenue sloops *Liberty* (1769) and *Gaspeé* (1772). The colony raised 1500 men to fight against the British after the battle of Lexington (1775) and declared its independence (4 May 1776), although only one important battle, that of Rhode Island (Aug. 1778) was fought in the area. RI did not immediately join the US, and was not represented at the 1787 Convention, though it eventually ratified the new constitution (29 May 1790).

Earl C. Tanner, *Rhode Island: a brief history* (Providence, RI, 1954).

AJS

RHODES, ALEXANDRE DE (1591–1660), French Jesuit missionary in East Asia, who spent two years in Goa (1619–1621) before going to Japan. But the difficulties experienced by the Jesuits in Japan led them to turn their attention to new fields. Rhodes was successively in Viet-nam and Macao. Later he was active in the Cochin-China area of Viet-nam (1640–5). He became convinced of the importance of an Asian priesthood, and after his return to Europe (1652) persuaded the pope to create the *Société des Missions Étrangéres* (1658). He ended his days as a missionary in Persia. He is remembered by Viet-namese Catholics for his work in propagating the Romanized script of their language, *quoc-ngu*.

RHODES, CECIL JOHN (1853–1902), South African politician, who went, on health grounds, to South Africa in 1870. He first tried cotton planting in Natal, but soon moved to the recently discovered diamond diggings, and began to amalgamate small-scale companies. His De Beers Co., which was founded in 1880, gained monopolistic control over the Kimberley diamond mines, and Rhodes made a fortune. He also acquired large gold-mining interests on the Witwaters-

rand, as head of the Consolidated Goldfields of South Africa. By the early 1880s Rhodes was taking part in Cape politics, and became prime minister in 1890, the year after his British South Africa Co. had been granted a royal charter (1889).

By means of the BSA Co. Rhodes sent white settlers into Mashonaland in 1890, and invaded Matabeleland in 1893. The territory north of the Zambezi was also under the company's control. Rhodes's power was at its height during the first half of the 1890s. He envisaged a federated South Africa under British rule, but governed by white men on the spot. White South Africa would extend its influence to the north, with a 'Cape to Cairo' railway linking British territories in South, Central, and East Africa. The main obstacle to the materialization of these dreams appeared to be the South African republic under Kruger. Rhodes encouraged plots to overthrow the republic, but the failure of the Jameson Raid (1896) led to his resignation as Cape prime minister. He died at Cape Town just before the end of the Anglo-Boer War.

Rhodes was a man of colossal energy and will-power, overbearing, and with strange quirks of character. In all his dreams for white South Africa, Africans had but one role—to provide cheap labour. He was a capitalist and imperialist of genius, but he failed even to attempt a solution of South Africa's greatest problem. He had returned to Britain to read for a degree at Oxford and in his will he established a number of scholarships tenable at the university for students of the British Empire, the US, and Germany.

J. G. Lockhart and C. M. Woodhouse, *Rhodes* (London, 1963).

T. O. Ranger, *Revolt in Southern Rhodesia* (London, 1967).

AEE

RHODES, Greek island in the south-east Aegean, possibly a Mycenean outpost, later settled by Dorian immigrants, who in turn colonized Asia Minor, Sicily (*eg*, Gela), southern Italy, and Spain. On being liberated from Persia (479 BC) it joined the Delian League, but seceded (412) and became a Peloponnesian base. Its separate communities joined together to build a new city (408), which though it became commercially prosperous, suffered from internal strife until its capture by Alexander the Great (332). On his death (323) it asserted independence, resisted Demetrius Pollorcetes' siege (305–304), and later supported Roman intervention against Philip V of Macedon (215) and Antiochus III of Syria (192), but it suffered economically from Roman support of Delos as a free port (167). It was important in the Middle Ages as the fortress of the Knights of St John of Jerusalem (AD 1309–1522). The knights occupied the island in 1309, establishing there a powerful fortress and a strong naval squadron. To the Christian world the knights represented a continuation of the 'crusade' against the infidel. To the Muslims Rhodes was a stronghold of pirates raiding the adjacent mainland and plundering the sea-borne traffic to and from Syria and Egypt. It was inevitable that, with the rise of the Ottoman state, the attacks from Rhodes should be ended. Mehemmed II, in 1480, sent a large force to take the island, but the attempt was unsuccessful. The Ottoman conquest of Syria and Egypt (1516–17) rendered the presence of the knights still more irksome. Finally, Sultan Suleiman laid siege to Rhodes and conquered it in 1522. Thereafter, it belonged to the Ottoman empire until 1912, when it passed to Italy, becoming part of Greece after the Second World War.

RHODESIA, territory in southern Africa whose African population contains (1970) a tiny minority of white settlers. European entry into the area came through early 19th-cent. missionaries and explorers, while the establishment of the British South Africa Co., financed by Cecil Rhodes, led to economic growth, land investment, railway-building, and a clamour by Europeans for responsible government. Thus, in

1923, Southern Rhodesia was annexed to the British Crown as a colony after a referendum had rejected union with South Africa.

Under the leadership, principally, of Sir Godfrey Huggins, the colony's fortunes prospered, particularly in tobacco, and its interests were represented at imperial conferences from 1935 onwards.

Southern Rhodesia was part of the Federation of Rhodesia and Nyasaland (1953–63). Thereafter it was known, after the break-up of the federation, as Rhodesia. It was refused independence by the British government, remaining a self-governing colony under a constitution devised in 1961 which, while giving a measure of political participation to the country's 4 million Africans, effectively retained political power in the hands of the 220,000 white settlers. The racial supremacist Rhodesian Front Party won the 1962 elections, and demanded independence from Britain. Successive Conservative and Labour governments in Britain refused to grant this on white Rhodesian terms. The Rhodesian leader, Ian Smith, promised Rhodesians that he would obtain independence and maintain white supremacy. African nationalist organizations were banned, and in the 1965 elections the Rhodesian Front Party won an overwhelming victory. Smith continued to negotiate with the British Labour prime minister Harold Wilson, until 11 Nov. 1965, when he promulgated a Unilateral Declaration of Independence (UDI). This began a revolt by the white settlers against Britain which was unresolved by 1970. Meanwhile Rhodesia, possessing de facto independence, had declared herself to be a republic in 1969.

Northern Rhodesia became a British protectorate in 1923 after the British South Africa Co.'s charter was terminated. It was a member of the Central African Federation (1953–1963), achieving internal self-government, thereafter, as Zambia. Zambia became an independent republic within the Commonwealth in 1964.   GMDH

RHODRI MAWR (*reg.* 844–77), King of Gwynedd, who later succeeded to the throne of Powys and to parts of south-west Wales. He thus united a large part of Wales under his single rule and, although the unity was short-lived, he established for later princes the ideal of a united kingdom. His success against the Danes, together with the unity he achieved, probably earned him the title 'Great'.

RHUDDLAN, STATUTE OF (1284), known also as the Statute of Wales, enactment made by King Edward I of England to settle the administration of Wales after his conquest of the principality in 1282–3.

RHYS AP GRUFFYDD (*c.* 1130–97), Prince of Deheubarth, south-west Wales (1155–97). By 1165 he had obtained control of the whole of Deheubarth and of Ceredigion further to the north, ejecting the Norman–Welsh marcher lords planted around his boundaries. With Owain, Prince of Gwynedd, he defeated King Henry II of England in 1165 and, after Owain's death in 1170, he was for the rest of his life the most important Welsh prince. Henry II sought his support against the Normans in Ireland, recognized him as ruler of Deheubarth, and appointed him the royal justice of South Wales. A temporary balance was thus struck between Norman and Welsh Wales, but Rhys's friendship with Henry opened the way for the ultimate growth of Norman penetration into South Wales.

RIBAR, IVAN (1881–   ), Yugoslav lawyer and politician, who was president of the Yugoslav constituent assembly which in 1921 laid the foundations of the new state. He later became vice-president of the Serbian Democratic Party, but at the outbreak of the Second World War he joined the Partisans. He was president of the Anti-Fascist Council of People's Liberation of Yugoslavia (AVNOJ), the political arm of the Partisan movement and of the Yugoslav pro-

visional parliament, and was later president of Yugoslavia (1945–58).

RIBAUT, JEAN (*c.* 1520–65), French Huguenot, who went to FL (1562) to establish a colony for Huguenot exiles. He claimed the territory for France and sailed for home, leaving a contingent on Parris Island, SC. Later the colony was abandoned, De Laudonniere having founded another Huguenot settlement on the St Johns river. Ribaut returned to Florida (1565) with five warships and engaged the fleet of the Spanish colonizer, Menendez de Aviles. A hurricane scattered the French fleet and the Spanish routed and killed Ribaut and most of the French settlers.

RIBBENTROP, JOACHIM VON (1893–1946), German diplomat and politician, who was foreign minister under the Nazis (1938–45). He joined the NSDAP shortly before it came to power, but by virtue of his experience and his ambition he rose quickly in the party hierarchy and soon eclipsed his main rival in the field of foreign affairs, Rosenberg. His pretensions to aristocratic status and to membership of international society were held in contempt by most other Nazi leaders but endeared him to Hitler, who found his contacts before 1933 useful and saw him an eminently suitable diplomatic representative for Nazi Germany afterwards. In 1934 he was given the task of achieving a diplomatic rapprochement with England, and for this purpose he created a private office, the *Dienststelle Ribbentrop*, which was financed by party funds and rivalled both the official foreign ministry under Neurath and Rosenberg's own private *Amt Rosenberg*. In 1935 he was posted to London as a special emissary for disarmament negotiations, and the Anglo-German naval agreement of that year was basically achieved by him independently of the German foreign ministry and embassy. His reward was to be appointed ambassador to Britain (1936), where his ostentatious behaviour attracted much hostile attention, *eg*, when he greeted the king with the Nazi salute at an official reception. In fact, Ribbentrop pursued, officially, a friendly policy towards Britain, but with little real conviction, and his own hostility (partly perhaps the result of his rejection by English society) came to the fore in German foreign policy when he became foreign minister (1938). By this time, Hitler felt sufficiently secure to challenge the reluctance of the High Command and the old foreign ministry corps to countenance his own expansionist foreign policy; in the showdown which followed Blomberg and Fritsch were removed from office, and Ribbentrop was recalled from London to replace Neurath at the foreign ministry. Ribbentrop fulfilled his duties with reckless cynicism, encouraging Hitler in his aggressive plans and arguing that Germany should exploit to the full the Western fear of war. In Aug. 1939 he went to Moscow to sign the Nazi–Soviet pact, which he regarded as his greatest personal triumph, and he was also responsible for the conclusion of the Tripartite pact the following year. As the Second World War proceeded, however, his influence began to wane, and by 1944 his authority was little more than nominal. He was tried as a major war criminal at Nuremberg, and executed in 1946.

The Ribbentrop Memoirs, ed. A. Bullock (London, 1954).

AJC

RIBEIRO, BERNARDIN (1482–1552), Portuguese poet and man of letters, author of the pastoral *Saudades*, better known by its opening words, *Menina e Moca* (1554).

RIBERA, JOSÉ (1588–1656), Spanish painter and engraver, who settled in Naples, where he came under the influence of Caravaggio. His work, *The Dead Christ*, reveals the stern naturalism which he observed in the Neapolitan master.

RICARDO, DAVID (1772–1823), British financier, economist, and politician, who was the chief founder of the classical school of political economy. With James Mill he formed the Political Economy Club (1821), was in close contact with Malthus, and sat in the Commons (1819–23). In his most important work, the *Principles of Political Economy and Taxation* (1817), he elaborated his theory of rent, examined the connection between rent, profit, and wages, and considered the incidence of taxation. Accepting, in the main, Adam Smith's labour theory of value and conception of the distribution of income, Ricardo based on them his subsistence theory of wages. He argued that any rise in wages above subsistence level would stimulate population growth, necessitate the cultivation of less fertile land, and therefore increase the cost of food. This would both reduce the real value of wages and, by encouraging demands for an increase in money wages, lead in the long run to a fall in manufacturing profits.

Ricardo saw political economy as a set of immutable laws which government should, on the whole, not seek to tamper with. He therefore advocated the repeal of the usury laws, the end of restrictions on the use of machinery and on wages, and the abolition of protective tariffs, especially the corn laws.   BK

RICASOLI, BETTINO, Baron (1809–80), Italian politician, who formed the provisional government of Florence, which, together with Modena, Parma, and Bologna, successfully demanded annexation to Piedmont in 1860, enabling the proclamation of a kingdom of Italy. As prime minister of Italy (1861–2, 1866–7), he attempted to resolve the antagonism between Church and state, but his premature introduction of a Free Church Bill (1867) caused his own downfall and an outcry which ended all hope of immediate reconciliation.

RICCI, MATTEO (1552–1610), Italian Jesuit missionary in India and China. He learned the Chinese language, studied Confucian ethics, and adopted Chinese manners. His knowledge of astronomy, mathematics, geography, and science aroused the curiosity of many Chinese scholars and officials, amongst whom Ricci made many friends. After 18 years in the provinces, he was permitted to go to Peking (1601) to seek imperial patronage. He never saw the emperor, but was allowed to rent a house and to carry on his work with Chinese financial support. Ricci was always careful to present himself first as a scholar and scientist, although he did make some converts among the highest officials of the Chinese empire. His sympathetic approach, however, laid the ground work of a controversy between his successors and the Holy See.

RICCI, SCIPIONE DE (1741–1810), Italian priest, who became Bp of Pistoia and a leading figure in the Jansenist movement in Italy where he instigated reform in the Tuscan Church under the patronage of Archduke Leopold. The synod of Pistoia, meeting under De Ricci's auspices in 1786, aroused the hostility of the other Tuscan bishops, who condemned its extreme Jansenist propositions. Popular opposition to his views drove De Ricci to resign his see in 1791. The pope condemned the synod (1794) and De Ricci was imprisoned (1799).

RICCIO, VINCENZO (1858–1930), Italian politician. While minister of posts (1914–16), he helped to neutralize opposition to Salandra's manœuvres to involve Italy in the First World War. In Facta's cabinet (1922), he made plans for Salandra's return to power, facilitated Fascist Party rallies, informed its leaders of government actions, impeded those who sought to curb fascist illegalities, and so aided Mussolini's take-over.

RICH, RICHARD RICH, 1st Baron (1496–1567), English lawyer and politician who held offices under Henry VIII, Edward VI, and Mary I. He was speaker of the House of Commons in 1536, solicitor-general, privy councillor, and chancellor of the Court of Augmentations (1540). On Edward's accession he was appointed lord chancellor in succession to Wriothesley (1547–51), and was later a member of Mary I's council (1553).

RICH, EDMUND (*c.* 1170–1240), English cleric, famous as a teacher and revered as a mystic and ascetic. He was elected Abp of Canterbury in 1233. He played a leading part in 1234 in ending a civil war between the supporters of Richard Marshal and Henry III. He was much involved in disputes with the papacy and the king, but was respected for his integrity. He was revered as a saint even in his lifetime and after his death there was an immediate demand for his canonization which took place only six years later.

RICHARD I (1157–99), King of England (*reg.* 1189–99), eldest surviving son of Henry II. In youth he was made ruler of Aquitaine, and exercised his martial talents against his rebellious barons, his brothers, and his father in turn. Succeeding to England in 1189, he at once prepared for the Third Crusade, recklessly auctioning all available offices and properties to finance the expedition. In the Holy Land he contributed to the capture of Acre and was victorious over Salah al-Din, but failed to take Jerusalem. In 1192, receiving news of the intrigues of his brother John, Richard left for home, but in Germany fell into the hands of his enemy the emperor. His subjects raised a vast sum for his release, but he returned to England only briefly in 1194, his energies for the remainder of his reign being devoted to defending and fortifying his French possessions. In 1199 he was killed while besieging the castle of a petty vassal. Regarded in his own day and since as the pattern of kingly strength and valour, and called Cœur-de-lion, he put adventure before kingship and politically achieved nothing lasting.

RICHARD II (1367–1400), King of England (*reg.* 1377–99), who succeeded his grandfather, Edward III, at the age of ten. His reign was a troubled one. The failing fortunes of the English in France, the turmoil caused by the Great Schism, the challenge to established beliefs by John Wycliffe and his Lollard followers, the long-term effects of the Black Death, and the heavy burden of taxation, which together precipitated the Peasants' Revolt of 1381, were all factors beyond his control. During his minority the realm was dominated by his uncles, especially John of Gaunt, Duke of Lancaster, and his first attempt at recovering royal authority led to the savage magnate opposition of the Lords Appellant, culminating in Richard's deposition at the end of 1387. He was soon reinstated as his enemies quarrelled about the succession, but his closest friends were executed by the appellants, led by Richard's uncle, Thomas, Duke of Gloucester. Richard took his revenge in 1397–9, executing Gloucester and other appellants or exiling them (notably his cousin Henry of Lancaster). Richard was a man of courage, as he showed in the Peasants' Revolt, of taste and refinement, of sound sense in foreign affairs, ending the war with France, but he lacked popular appeal and antagonized the nobility. In 1397–9 suspiciousness and fear drove him to arbitrary and unwise policies. Henry of Lancaster found it easy to convert his return from exile to claim his inheritance into a deposition of Richard in Sept. 1399. Early in 1400 Richard died in prison. It is possible that he was murdered.   JG

RICHARD III (1452–85), King of England (*reg.* 1483–5), one of the most controversial of English rulers. He was regarded until recently as one of the great villains of English history, the Tudors, who supplanted him, having encouraged a belief that he was a monstrous criminal, a view of him immortalized in Shakespeare's play. The youngest brother of King Edward IV, Richard was conspicuously loyal to him, sharing his exile in 1470–1 and contributing to his victories in 1471. Despite some disagreements the two brothers collaborated well during the remainder of Edward's reign and Richard acquired a solid reputation for administrative ability. On

Edward's sudden death in April 1483, Richard was named Protector of the kingdom during the minority of his young nephew, Edward V. Fear of the child's mother, Queen Elizabeth Woodville, probably explains Richard's speedy seizure and execution of her relatives and leading supporters. The enmities thus aroused made it dangerous for Richard to remain a mere Protector and in June he assumed the Crown, while Edward V and his brother were imprisoned. The two boys were probably dead by Oct. 1483, when the Duke of Buckingham, formerly Richard's supporter, started a rising in support of his own hereditary claims to the throne. This was crushed, but when Henry Tudor, the future Henry VII, the main Lancastrian claimant, landed in Wales in 1485, support for Richard dwindled. At the crucial battle of Bosworth (22 Aug.) some of his leading followers abstained from the conflict. Richard, fighting with desperate courage, was killed through the sudden treachery of Sir William Stanley (whom Henry VII distrusted so much that he had him executed in 1495).

RICHARD, TIMOTHY (1845–1919), Welsh missionary, philanthropist, and educationalist in China, who saw Western progress as part of God's plan, and sought to introduce it into China. After working for several years in Shantung, he went to Shansi in 1876 to conduct famine relief. He then engaged in literary and editorial work in Peking and Tientsin (1887–91). In 1891 he became the secretary of the Society for the Diffusion of Christian and General Knowledge among the Chinese, whose aim was to disseminate Western learning and ideas of reform. During the reform movement (1895–8) he regularly advised K'ang Yu-wei and Liang Ch'i-ch'ao. After the Boxer Rising, he was invited by the governor of Shansi to found a university and schools in that province, to be financed by the Chinese and controlled by the foreigners as a form of indemnity paid by that province for the massacre of missionaries within its boundaries. Despite his missionary background, therefore, Richard served as a source of inspiration for reformers and forward-looking officials of the declining Ch'ing empire.

RICHARD OF WALLINGFORD (1291–1336), English astronomer who was abbot of St Albans from 1326 where (in spite of being a leper) he made important contributions to mathematics and astronomy. He designed the great St Albans astronomical clock, the first clock known to have a mechanical escapement.

RICHARDSON, ARNOLD EDWIN VICTOR (1883–1949), Australian agricultural scientist, who became superintendent of agriculture in Vic. (1911), and dean of the faculty of agriculture and director of the new school of agriculture in Melbourne University (1920). Later, in Adelaide he was professor of agriculture and director of the Waite agricultural research institute (1924–37). He was also deputy chief executive officer and then chief executive officer (1945) of the Commonwealth scientific and research organization. He bred many varieties of wheat in Vic. and was regarded as a leading agricultural scientist and researcher.

RICHARDSON, HENRY HOBSON (1838–86), US architect, whose use of materials and emphasis upon functional realism profoundly influenced the development of American architecture. He was preoccupied with form, mass, and unity, adding to these Romanesque elements and in such buildings as the Town Hall and Library, North Easton, MA (1881), the Marshall Field Building in Chicago (1885–7) and the Allegheny Courthouse and Jail, Pittsburgh (1885–7), he sought an American idiom that would reflect the assertive energy of the industrial age.

RICHARDSON, SIR JOHN (1787–1865), Scottish naval surgeon, who accompanied Sir John Franklin as surgeon-naturalist on a Canadian expedition to Coppermine river (1819–22), and headed a party working from the Mackenzie

river to the Coppermine (1825–7), contributing natural history notes on both expeditions. He returned to the Arctic to search for Franklin (1848).

RICHARDSON, SAMUEL (1689–1761), English novelist, who was the son of a Derbyshire joiner and had little education. He established a printing press in London and was printer to the House of Commons. His three famous novels, *Pamela* (1740–1), *Clarissa Harlowe* (1747–8), and *Sir Charles Grandison* (1753–4), were among the first novels in the English language, and though didactic and somewhat sentimental, were immediately popular and had considerable influence on the writing of fiction.

RICHELIEU, ARMAND JEAN DU PLESSIS, Cardinal and Duc de (1585–1642), French statesman and for 18 years principal minister of Louis XIII, during which time he raised the monarchy to heights of unprecedented authority both within France and in the wider European context.

He was born in Paris of a lesser noble family from Poitou, and nominated Bp of Lucon by Henry IV (1606). He was elected by the clergy of Poitou to the Estates-General of Oct. 1614, where he attracted the attention of the queen mother, Marie de' Medici, and was chosen to present the final address of the French clergy. He remained in Paris, was patronized by the Concinis, became almoner to Anne of Austria (1615) and secretary of state (1616) before being exiled with Marie de' Medici to Blois (1617) and Avignon (1618). He negotiated the treaty of Angoulême (1619) which reconciled the queen mother to her son, Louis XIII. After the death of the royal favourite, Luynes (Dec. 1621), he returned to power, was created cardinal (5 Sept. 1622), and admitted to Louis XIII's council (29 April 1624). On the disgrace of the superintendent of finances, Charles de la Vieuville, Richelieu became Louis's principal minister (1624).

He proved an indefatigable servant of the French Crown, dedicated to the principle of *raison d'état*, his main aims being to secure universal obedience to the French monarchy and to raise its international prestige. These objectives required him to crush the rebellious nobility, cut down the privileges of the Huguenots, and carry out broad internal reforms, outlined in the *Testament Politique*, which would cleanse the financial system and revive the economy and overseas trade. To implement the reforms presented to the assembly of notables (1626–7) he required peace with Spain, which was secured by the treaty of Monson (1626). From 1627, when he became 'Grand Master, head, and superintendent of the commerce and navigation of France' he undertook a shipbuilding programme, though forced to raise a hired force of 67 ships initially. His complete programme of reform was, however, thwarted by internal divisions and international war. In 1627–8 he undertook the subjection of La Rochelle in order to curb English maritime interference and to crush the political and military independence of the Huguenots. He dealt equally ruthlessly with the recalcitrant nobility and peasantry, crushing the plots of Chalais, Boutteville, Marillac, Cinq Mars, and the Va-nu-pieds rising in Normandy. The construction of fortified strongholds and the practice of duelling were forbidden, as being conducive to lawlessness. To promote economic self-sufficiency encouragement was given to the manufacture of tapestry, glass, silk, linen, and woollen cloth, and privileges allowed to companies which established colonies in America, Africa, and the West Indies. Richelieu also believed in the prestige to be derived from cultural supremacy, and among his achievements was the founding of the Académie Française (1635).

In foreign affairs he sought, first, the defence of France by the occupation of key points along the borders with imperial and Spanish territories. He thus involved France in the War of the Mantuan Succession (1628–31) to garrison Pinerolo and Casale. Through diplomatic means he worked for the dismissal of Wallenstein, the general whose armies crushed the Protestant princes in the Thirty Years War

(1630). To undermine the power of the Habsburgs he prolonged this conflict, negotiating with the United Provinces, Gustavus Adolphus of Sweden (treaty of Barwalde, 1631), and after the king's death with Chancellor Oxenstierna and Prince Bernard of Saxe-Weimar, only finally declaring open war on Philip IV of Spain on the eve of the peace of Prague (1635). Before he died he savoured the triumph of French armies in the Spanish Netherlands, Lorraine, Alsace, and Roussillon.

Richelieu lived in sumptuous style in his great Paris residence of the Palais Cardinal, later the royal residence of the Palais-Royal, or in his favourite country house at Rueil. Hated by all classes for his cold authoritarianism, he nevertheless retained the goodwill of Louis XIII, for whom he created the modern French state.

C. J. Burckhardt, *Richelieu and his Age* (in course of translation), 3 vols (London, 1967–   ).   MKS

RICHELIEU, ARMAND DU PLESSIS, Duc de (1766–1822), French diplomat and politician, and a leading moderate in the reign of Louis XVIII. Before the Revolution (1789) he was a diplomat and entered Russia's service during the emigration, becoming prime minister partly at Russia's suggestion (1815). He signed the second treaty of Paris and later served as minister of foreign affairs, in which capacity he took part in the negotiations which led to the end of the allied occupation. He again became prime minister after the murder of the Duc de Berri (1820), but fell from office in 1821, being insufficiently extreme for the Ultras.

RICHERISM in France, anti-episcopal and 'presbyterian' attitude, which was widely adopted by the lower clergy during the last phase of the Jansenist controversy in 18th-cent. France. The movement took its name from Edmond Richer, who had put forward the idea that the government of the Church belonged to the whole community of pastors, of which the episcopacy was simply one order.

RICHMOND, CHARLES LENNOX, 8th Duke of (3rd of 4th creation) (1735–1806), British diplomat and politician, who was the uncle of Charles James Fox. He was ambassador at Paris and Southern secretary in the first Rockingham administration for three months in 1766. In the 1770s he emerged as a reformer in opposition to North, defending the actions of the American colonists (1775) and supporting economical reform (1779). He introduced into the House of Lords (1780) a bill proposing annual parliaments, manhood suffrage, and equal electoral districts. The bill gained no support, but is a landmark in the history of the reform movement. On the death of Rockingham (1782), the leadership of his group passed to Portland, and thereafter Richmond's taste for reform began to weaken. He entered Pitt's cabinet in 1784 as master-general of the ordnance and for the next 22 years was a supporter of Pitt's two administrations.

RICHMOND, CHRISTOPHER WILLIAM (1821–95), NZ politician and judge, who was minister for native affairs during the Taranaki War (1860–1). In his view Maori resistance was seen to be rebellion. He was later a judge (1862–95).

RICIMER (*c.* 420–72), chieftain of the Suevi, who was brought up at the court of the Emperor Valentinian III and after the latter's murder of Aetius (454) became one of the main powers behind the throne, setting up and then destroying a succession of emperors. In 461 he brought about the downfall and murder of Majorian, perhaps the ablest Western Roman emperor of the 5th cent. After storming Rome in 472, he appointed yet another emperor, Olybrius, but both men died later in the same year.

RICKMAN, JOHN (1771–1840), British economist and statistician, who prepared the first census (1800), a necessary basis for more efficient administration. He devised the methods to be employed and wrote the reports on the first four censuses (1801–31). He compiled the annual abstracts of the Poor Law returns (1816–36), and was also Clerk Assistant (1820–40) to the House of Commons, and prepared an index to the *Journals*.

RICKOVER, HYMAN GEORGE (1900–   ), US sailor, who (from 1949) directed the project to adapt a nuclear reactor for submarine power production. The advantage of a nuclear fuel supply was that a submarine could remain submerged for several months, as it would not need to surface to charge its batteries. The first nuclear submarine, the USS *Nautilus*, was launched in 1955. Subsequently, Rickover was responsible for the development of the Polaris intercontinental missile, which could be launched from a submerged nuclear submarine. These formed in 1970 a principal strategic armament of the Great Powers.

RIDDA, AL- ('apostasy'). The Arab tribes of the Hijaz and the Najd sought, in AD 632, to renounce their dependence on the Muslim state, holding that the death of the Prophet Muhammad in that year had severed the bond which thus far had united them in obedience to him and to the cause of Islam. It was this recalcitrance which later Muslim historians interpreted, misleadingly, as a rejection of the Muslim faith. Abu Bakr, the first caliph, was resolute to maintain the heritage of the Prophet and therefore used force in order to overcome the resistance of the tribesmen. The campaigns (632–3) of the Ridda war, being successful, brought together under the generals in command of the Muslim forces a large concentration of tribal warriors. It was in the logic of the situation that this concentration of strength should be used to some new purpose. Out of the Ridda conflict to restore Muslim control in central Arabia arose therefore at once, and without predetermination from Medina, the great campaigns against Byzantium and Sasanid Persia which led, during the next two decades, to the creation of a Muslim empire.

RIDGWAY, MATTHEW BUNKER (1895–   ), US soldier who held various staff appointments in the Second World War, commanded the 8th Army in Korea (1950–1), and replaced Gen. MacArthur (1951). He was Supreme Allied Commander in Europe (1952–3) and army chief of staff (1953–5).

RIDLEY, NICHOLAS (1500–55), English theologian, who became Bp of London. He had been esteemed at Cambridge for his learning and became chaplain to Abp Cranmer (1537) and master of Pembroke Hall and a royal chaplain (1540). It is said that (*c.* 1546) he converted Cranmer from a belief in the Real Presence. He was Bp of Rochester (1547) before succeeding Bonner at London (1550). He was a strong Protestant and assisted in the preparation of the Edwardian prayer books and destroyed the cathedral altars at Rochester and St Paul's; but he deplored the secularization of guild revenues and urged their application to schools and charity. He was imprisoned for supporting Lady Jane Grey (1553), and after being examined on his religious opinions, was condemned as a heretic and, with Latimer, burnt at Oxford during the reign of the Catholic Mary I.

RIDOLPHI, ROBERTO (1531–1612), Florentine banker, who settled in London (1555) and became deeply involved in Catholic intrigues to overthrow Queen Elizabeth I. After being arrested in the abortive northern plot of 1569, he tried to organize another rebellion (1570–1) by winning the support of the Duke of Norfolk, the Duke of Alva, and Philip II of Spain, but Burghley discovered the plans and in Ridolphi's absence abroad Norfolk was executed (April 1572).

RIEL, LOUIS (1844–85), Canadian revolutionary, who became leader of the Metis (half-breeds). They feared dispossession by incoming settlers, following the transfer of the

Hudson's Bay Co.'s lands to Canada. Riel organized the Red River Rebellion (1869–70), seized Fort Garry, and formed a provisional government (1870), demanding the incorporation of the Red River Country as an autonomous province of the Canadian federation. The Metis' list of rights was accepted and the area became part of the federation, as Manitoba (1870). Riel was elected to the federal parliament, but because of his activities during the rebellion was expelled from it in 1874. Later he was pardoned, but was exiled for five years. On his return he led Canadian resistance to the Metis and other settlers along the Saskatchewan river (1884), and again set up a provisional government. After three months of sporadic fighting, the North-West Rebellion was suppressed and the Metis and their Indian allies surrendered. Riel was tried and executed at Regina, Sask.

RIENZO, COLA DI (1313–54), Roman demagogue, who dreamed of reviving the glory of ancient Rome, thus becoming the victim of his classical education. During the absence of the papacy at Avignon he took advantage of factional strife to stir up a popular revolt against the nobility and acquired dictatorial powers, instituting a revolutionary government based on classical models. A rising of nobles in 1354 led to his murder.

RIGA, capital of Latvia, situated on the Dvina river. Its importance was established in the 13th cent. by Albert, Bp of Livonia, and it was a significant port in the Middle Ages as part of the Hanseatic League. Gustavus Adolphus of Sweden secured it in 1621 from the Poles. After unsuccessful attacks by the Russians (1656) and the Saxons (1700), it fell into Russian hands in 1710, becoming Russia's principal western port for the handling of Baltic trade. After the First World War, a Latvian nationalist government was established (1919) which included Livonia, and Riga became the capital. In 1940 the country became a constituent-republic of the Soviet Union.

RIGA TREATY (1921), peace treaty between Russia and Poland, establishing an agreed common frontier. After the end of the First World War, Poland had been unwilling to accept the eastern frontier proposed by the Allies, *ie*, the Curzon Line, which would have deprived her of the Ukraine and other areas to which she made historic claim. Taking advantage of the weakened state of the Soviet army after the civil war, Polish troops, led by Pilsudski, marched into Russia in the spring of 1920, and reached Kiev; in June the Russians counterattacked. By Aug. Tukachevsky's army was at the gates of Warsaw, but at the last moment the Poles regained the initiative and swept the Russians back again, pushing them 241 kms east of the Curzon Line and occupying Vilna en route. An armistice was signed on 18 Oct., and the peace treaty itself on 18 March 1921. Under its terms Poland secured a far more generous frontier than was provided by the Curzon Line, though still less than the claim she based on her 1772 borders; Russia renounced her claim to Galicia, and both countries agreed on a policy of mutual non-intervention. The treaty thus settled the Russo-Polish dispute, but did not fix all Poland's eastern boundaries, leaving the problems of Eastern Galicia and Vilna to be solved later.

RIGAUD, ANDRÉ (1761–1811), Haitian mulatto soldier and secessionist, who changed sides several times during the Haitian wars of independence. In 1810 he attempted to govern Haiti's southern peninsula as a separate state, but his regime was short-lived.

RIGAUD, HYACINTHE FRANÇOIS (1659–1743), French portrait-painter who received many commissions at the courts of Louis XIV and XV. He paid particular attention to the niceties and distinctions of rank, uniform, and position which were so significant in his times. His portrait of Louis XIV, with most of his other works, is in the Louvre.

RIGBY, RICHARD (1722–88), British politician and businessman, who became the Duke of Bedford's secretary in 1757, held minor office in Ireland (1759, 1765), and retained an interest in Irish affairs. After 1761 he was the chief spokesman and manager of Bedford's group in the Commons, supporting the Bute and Grenville administrations, and opposing the repeal of the Stamp Act, Wilkes, and various reform proposals. He held the lucrative post of paymaster of the forces (1768–84).

RIGHTS. Concept which has engaged the attention of historians and philosophers throughout the ages. Man has been seen to have both natural and legal rights which, in their turn, involve him in duties. Post-Renaissance thinkers became concerned with the nature of the individual in reaction to the more impersonal ideas of the Middle Ages. Philosophers such as Hobbes and Spinoza established an identity between rights and power while Locke related rights to the political needs of society. His influence affected the working-out of the English Revolution (1688) and had repercussions on both French and American thinkers in the late 18th cent. Jefferson's drafting of the American Declaration of Independence spoke of 'inalienable rights . . . among these are Life, Liberty and pursuit of Happiness'. While the gap between theoretical rights and practical politics remained profound in US society and elsewhere, the struggle had begun for political equality, and continued in the following two centuries. Successes included the abolition of slavery, large franchises and the rule of law. In the 19th and 20th cents rights became identified with equality-claims in areas less strictly political.

RIGHTS OF MAN, DECLARATION OF (1789), made by the French National Assembly on 27 Aug., effectively combined universal political principles, derived from the writings of the French Enlightenment and the example of the American Revolution, with the social and political interests of the French middle class. The declaration dealt a final blow to the privileged society of the *ancien régime* by providing security for property, freedom from arbitrary imprisonment, freedom of the press, and liberty of conscience.

RIGVEDA, oldest text of India (*c.* 1200–1000 BC), comprising over 1000 hymns in an archaic type of Sanskrit, addressed to many different gods. It represents the earliest state of Indian religion, reflecting a time when the Indo-Aryans lived in the Punjab in tribal and semi-nomadic conditions and were involved in conflicts with the earlier settled population.

RIIS, JACOB AUGUST (1849–1914), US author and social reformer. After a variety of jobs, he became a police reporter on the *New York Tribune* (1877) and then the *Evening Sun* (1888). This work convinced him that poverty was the pre-eminent cause of crime and he became an ardent social reformer. His books included *How the Other Half Lives* (1890), *The Children of the Poor* (1892), *The Making of an American* (1901), *Children of the Tenements* (1902), *The Battle with the Slums* (1902), and *Is there a Santa Claus?* (1904), besides a presidential campaign biography *Theodore Roosevelt, the Citizen* (1904). His work as writer and lecturer to achieve reform of tenement house conditions earned him fame as the 'great emancipator of the slums'. He was also an advocate of school reform, and was active in the movement to provide small parks and playgrounds in the cities.

RIKKOKUSHI, voluminous 'Six National Histories', compiled at the Japanese court (8th–9th cents) and written in Chinese. They were discontinued when Chinese influence ceased to be dominant.

RIKSDAG, Swedish Diet, originated in the 14th cent., but first became a true parliament in the Age of Freedom (1719–

1772). National assemblies drawn from different classes were used by the early Vasa kings to secure support for their policies. But in 1612 the accession charter of Gustavus Adolphus, while providing for due consultation with the Riksdag, also promised that the Crown would not burden its subjects by too frequent meetings. In 1617 the proceedings were regulated by an ordinance which fixed the number of estates at four and arranged that, in the event of their disagreeing with each other, final decisions would be taken by the king. Under the Form of Government set up in 1634 the Riksdag figured as an occasional counterpoise to the power of the nobles, but from 1680 until the death of Charles XII (1718) its authority declined.

Under the constitutional monarchy, however, the council became responsible to the triennial meetings of the Riksdag, and especially to its secret committee, from which the representatives of the peasantry were normally excluded.

RILEY, CHARLES OWEN LEAVER (1854–1929), Australian clergyman, who became Anglican bishop of Perth, WA (1895), and first archbishop (1914–29). He was chaplain-general of Australian forces during the First World War. The dioceses of Bunbury, Kalgoorlie, and North-west Australia were created under his auspices.

RINGATU, NZ Maori religious movement, combining Old Testament doctrines and Hauhau ritual, founded by Te Kooti (1867). It was an informal, almost quietist, church whose adherents numbered 6000 in 1970.

RINTELEN, ANTON VON (1876–1946), Austrian politician, who was a member of the conservative Christian Social Party, twice education minister (1926, 1932–3), and then ambassador to Rome (1933–4). He supported the German policy of *Anschluss* (incorporation) with Austria, and was personally implicated in the Nazi-inspired putsch of 25 July 1934, during which he was appointed 'chancellor'. After its failure he was sentenced to life imprisonment, but was later pardoned.

RIO BRANCO, JOSÉ MARIA DA SILVA PARANHOS, JÚNIOR, Baron of (1845–1912), Brazilian historian, diplomat, and politician. After a decade in politics, during which he published an abolitionist journal and wrote his first historical works, he was appointed consul in Liverpool. The position gave him ample time to pursue the study of Brazilian history, particularly documents concerning the frontiers of Brazil. In 1895 he became a national celebrity through his successful presentation of Brazil's case in the arbitration of the Misiones dispute with Argentina. Thereafter his career was identified with the peaceful settlement of Brazil's boundaries in the Amazon basin. He was foreign minister (1902–12).

RIO BRANCO, JOSÉ MARIA DA SILVA PARANHOS, Viscount of (1819–80), Brazilian politician and diplomat, who entered politics in 1848 as a liberal deputy from Rio de Janeiro, and became a conservative senator from Matto Grosso in 1862. He began his diplomatic career in 1851 as secretary of the Brazilian mission to the Río de la Plata. Thereafter, until the end of the Paraguayan War (1870), Rio Branco served variously as minister to Uruguay, navy minister, foreign minister, and chief Brazilian negotiator with the allies (Argentina and Uruguay), and with the defeated enemy. He was prime minister (1871–5), longer than anyone else in the Brazilian empire. He was responsible for the Rio Branco law (1871) providing for the gradual emancipation of slaves in Brazil.

RIO BRANCO LAW (1871) in Brazil, legislation which stipulated that children of slave mothers were born free, but that slave masters might work a child from the age of 8 to 21. It was a major step in the gradual abolition of Negro slavery in Brazil.

RIO DE ORO (Spanish Sahara), large segment of the western Sahara abutting on the Atlantic, with a population of nomadic Berbers of 35,000 and (in 1970) 5000 Europeans. Though Spanish interest on this coast dates from the 16th cent.; it was not until Franco-Spanish agreements of 1900, 1904, and 1912 that regular colonial administration was introduced here.

RIO MUNI, small enclave lying between Cameroon and Gabon on the western equatorial coast of Africa; it has a population (1970) of 250,000. It was visited by Spanish travellers in the 1880s, and awarded to Spain by a treaty signed in Paris in 1900. Spanish administration remained nominal, except along the seaboard, until the late 1930s. In 1968 Rio Muni became politically independent, together with Fernando Po and Annobón. In 1969 clashes took place between its people and the Spanish.

RIOM TRIAL (1942) in France, political trial at which the Vichy government tried to fix the blame for France's defeat in 1940 on the leaders of the Third Republic. The principal defendants were the former prime ministers, Blum and Daladier, and Gen. Gamelin. They were prejudged by being interned before the trial, but were allowed to defend themselves freely. They did so to some effect, showing that the pre-war governments had begun rearmament, and directing attention to the faults of the military administration in which Pétain had been prominent. The trial was suspended after a few months after pressure by the Germans, who had expected it to 'prove' France's responsibility for the war itself. The defendants remained in prison, and were later deported to Germany.

RIOS MORALES, JUAN ANTONIO (1888–1946), Chilean politician and president of Chile (1942–6), whose regime during the Second World War was beset by economic problems and had to depend on US aid.

RIOT ACT (1715) in Britain legislative measure passed to clarify the law relating to riots and to ensure the maintenance of law and order during the Jacobite crisis. Previously, as in *Dammaree's Case* (1710), any riot which damaged property could be construed as levying war against the king and as such was treasonable. To prevent excessive punishments for such crimes, rioters were usually found guilty and then pardoned. The new legislation was drawn up to end this ambiguity. The act provided that if 12 or more people were unlawfully and riotously assembled and did not disperse within one hour of a magistrate reading the riot act they were guilty of a felony. The act also indemnified any person who injured or killed rioters while helping to disperse them. In fact, the situation remained unsatisfactory, since magistrates refused to summon military aid without first reading the proclamation and then waiting for an hour.

RIPON, FREDERICK JOHN ROBINSON, 1st Earl of (1782–1852), British liberal Tory politician, who became an MP in 1806, and quickly showed his ability in commercial and financial matters. He held minor office (1809–17), and was president of the board of trade (1818–23). As chancellor of the exchequer (1823–7) he introduced progressive fiscal reforms, consolidating and reducing tariffs and proposing to modify the 1815 Corn Law (which he had introduced). His successful budgets led Cobbett to nickname him 'Prosperity Robinson'. He was a firm supporter of Catholic emancipation. In Canning's government (1827), as Viscount Goderich, he was secretary of state for war and the colonies and leader of the House of Lords. George IV made him prime minister in 1827 after Canning's death, but he could not manage his very mixed group of ministers and resigned (Jan. 1828) before meeting parliament. He served in Grey's reform ministry as secretary for war and the colonies (1830) and lord privy seal (1833), but resigned in 1834, with three other ministers, because of disagreement with Russell's Irish policy.

His liberal commercial views drew him to Peel, and in Peel's second ministry he was president of the board of trade (1841–3) and president of the board of control (1843–6).

RIPON, GEORGE FREDERICK SAMUEL ROBINSON, 1st Marquis of (1827–1909), British politician and viceroy of India (1880–4), who entered parliament as Liberal member for Hull (1852). He was appointed viceroy of India by the Liberal government in 1880, becoming the first Roman Catholic to hold the office.

Of all the viceroys he did most to make the British connection acceptable to educated Indian opinion. He sponsored a Factory Act, the first of its kind in India, and repealed Lytton's Vernacular Press Act (1878), which had muzzled the Indian press. In 1882 he decided to foster local self-government as a measure of political education, even at the cost of administrative efficiency, and larger powers were given to rural and urban boards. He re-established the Department of Revenue and Agriculture and appointed an Education Commission to spread popular education on a broader basis. He is, however, chiefly remembered for the Ilbert Bill (1883), by which he sought to permit senior Indian judges to try criminal cases in which Britons might be involved. This proposal exasperated the unofficial British element in Bengal and Bihar and it was considerably modified. The importance of the controversy is that it intensified racial antagonism.

Ripon went to India pledged to reverse his predecessor's policy towards Afghanistan. He began to make plans for a retirement from Baluchistan to Jacobabad, and even to the Indus, only to find that in face of the Russian advance towards Merv this was impossible. Not only was Baluchistan retained, but the Bolan railway was extended to Chaman. After his return to Britain he became first lord of the admiralty (1886) and secretary for the colonies (1892–5).

L. Wolf, *Life of the First Marquess of Ripon*, 2 vols (London, 1921).
S. Gopal, *The Viceroyalty of Lord Ripon, 1880–1884* (Oxford, 1953). CCD

RIPON, TREATY OF (1640), ended the second Bishops' War in England. It was negotiated by a commission of the council of peers whom Charles I had called to York on his defeat by the Scots. The terms of the treaty amounted to a royal surrender. The Scots were to remain in possession of Northumberland and Durham and were to receive £850 a day until matters in dispute were settled. The treaty implied that parliamentary assent was necessary for the final settlement, and the money granted the Scots ensured that a parliament would be called.

RIPPERDA, JAN WILLEM, Baron (1690–1737), Dutch-born diplomat, who entered the service of Spain and for a time dominated Spanish diplomacy. He was appointed Dutch envoy to Madrid after the War of the Spanish Succession, where he entered into intrigue with Alberoni, his advice to the United Provinces resulting in their refusal to sign the Quadruple Alliance (1718). On being converted to Catholicism, Ripperda entered the service of Spain and was put in charge of royal manufactures, producing various schemes to aid Spain's economic recovery. As a diplomat he was largely responsible for the *volte face* of Spanish foreign policy that resulted in the treaty of Vienna (1725) and alliance with the emperor. Following this success he was appointed foreign minister and for a time captivated Philip V and Elizabeth Farnese with his grandiose schemes. He was largely responsible for the siege of Gibraltar and with its failure he fell from power.

RISHIS, primeval Indian sages believed to be endowed with supernatural powers, which are attributed to concentration and asceticism. Though traditionally seven in number (*saptarshi*), many more are found in Sanskrit literature. Brahmin clans (*gotra*) are each traced back to one individual rishi (eg, Vasishtha, Gotama, Bharadvaja, etc.).

RISLEY, SIR HERBERT HOPE (1851–1911), British ethnologist and colonial servant, who was secretary in the home department, government of India (1902–9), and a member of the viceroy's council (1909–10). He published *The Tribes and Castes of Bengal* (1891), was responsible for the Indian census report (1901), and was influential in the determination of the electoral details of the Morley–Minto reforms (1909).

RISORGIMENTO, in Italy, literally, 'the Resurrection', a first term used by Bettinelli, in *Del Risorgimento d'Italia dopo il Mille*, a cultural history of Italy (1775), and since adopted by historians as a convenient word to describe the Italian movement of national regeneration which led to the political unification of the country in 1870.

The roots of the movement lay in the work of enlightened 18th-cent. rulers, Charles III of Naples, Leopold of Tuscany, and Joseph II in Lombardy, whose administrative and economic reforms helped to create a new, articulate official class of increasing political awareness. Throughout its course, the Risorgimento remained largely the preserve of the educated minority. Secondary influences were the French Revolution and the French occupation of Italy during the Napoleonic period. Italian Jacobins at first welcomed the improved efficiency and humanity of the French administration, but soon became disenchanted with the increasing exactions to feed the French war machine. After the peace of Campo Formio, patriots formulated the idea of Italian unity as a safeguard against French exploitation. Secret societies such as the Adelphi, the Carbonari, and the Federati were avowedly anti-French in their aims and attitudes.

Between 1815 and 1848 the chief characteristic of the Risorgimento was its regionalism. Its literary side flourished in Tuscany; new economic and scientific ideas were disseminated from Lombardy in journals with an increasingly wide circulation. Secret societies continued to be most active in Naples and Sicily and new political ideas emanated from Sardinia. The failure of the risings in Naples and Turin in 1821 revealed the shortcomings of existing societies and led to the foundation of Mazzini's Young Italy, which abandoned secrecy, was republican in its ideals, national in organization, and aimed at insurrection. It was opposed by theorists such as D'Azeglio and Gioberti, who advocated federation under papal or Sardinian leadership. The separatist development of the abortive 1848 revolutions in Italy reflected the diverse and discordant objectives of the period which preceded them.

After 1852 Cavour was the chief figure in the political unification of Italy, but the Risorgimento became Sardinian and annexationist at the expense of the populist and fusionist beliefs of Mazzini and Garibaldi. It was never accompanied by social and economic revolution. Once unification was complete, the peasants of central and southern Italy were abandoned to their poverty. Like so many nationalist movements, the Risorgimento has left a somewhat ambivalent legacy. The realities of transformism were a poor substitute for the fervent expectations aroused in the process of national revival.

S. B. Clough and S. Saladino, *A History of Modern Italy* (New York, 1968). SH

RITCHIE OF DUNDEE, CHARLES THOMPSON RITCHIE, 1st Baron (1838–1906), British Conservative politician, who was president of the local government board in Salisbury's ministry. He was responsible for the Local Government Act (1888) which created county councils. As chancellor of the exchequer he persuaded the cabinet to drop the corn duty. He was dismissed by A. J. Balfour (1903) for his extremist support of taxation for revenue only.

RITES CONTROVERSY, in the Roman Catholic Church, over missionary strategy in China in the 17th and 18th cents.

The controversy centred upon two issues: the use of Chinese terms to render Christian concepts, and the toleration by missionaries of ancestral worship and the worship of Confucius. Early Jesuit missionaries had adopted Matteo Ricci's policy of avoiding conflict with Chinese customs by using Chinese terminology and permitting Chinese converts to perform rites honouring ancestors and Confucius. However, not all agreed with this approach, particularly the Franciscans and the Dominicans, who came in the 1630s, and who, basing their experience in less culturally resistant lands like Mexico and the Philippines, opposed any concession to Chinese customs. The question was referred to Rome, and precipitated a dispute between the pope and the Chinese emperor. The controversy was finally closed by a papal bull in 1742 condemning the early Jesuit position. The Chinese emperors, hostile to the papal challenge to their power, began to persecute the missionaries, although a few of them were allowed to remain serving as astronomers, interpreters, and cartographers.

RITTENHOUSE, DAVID (1732–96), American mathematician, instrument-maker, and astronomer, who was president of the American Philosophical Society (1791–6) and made boundary surveys in many of the North American colonies.

RITUALISTS in England, Anglo-Catholics who introduced or reintroduced medieval or modern Roman Catholic practices into the Church of England. The clergy among them came from theological colleges which had been influenced by followers of the Oxford Movement. Ritualism was the subject of an enquiry by a Royal Commission (1867) which produced four reports, on vestments, incense, lights, the lectionary, and prayer book revision. The commission's proposals, though strongly criticized by High Churchmen, led to the Public Worship Regulation Act (1874) to suppress the growth of ritualism in the Church of England. The act, which was drafted by Abp Tait and supported by Queen Victoria, was passed only after drastic amendments and amid great protests. It fell into disuse after the imprisonment of four priests and the failure of the Protestant attack on Edward King, Bp of Lincoln, for illegal practices in divine worship (1888–92).

RIVADAVIA, BERNARDINO (1780–1845), Argentine soldier, diplomat, and liberal politician, who served as a soldier and administrator at Buenos Aires during the early years of the independence movement. He was engaged (1814–20) on diplomatic missions, mostly in Europe. There his doctrinaire rationalism was confirmed: he became convinced of the applicability of European models of efficient centralized administration to Argentinian problems of reform and development. His return to Argentina coincided with the fragmentation of the United Provinces of La Plata following the unsuccessful attempt (1819) to impose a 'unitary' (ie, centralist) constitution. In 1820, under the governorship of Martín Rodríguez, Rivadavia became one of the two ministers of government of the autonomous province of Buenos Aires. Within the provincial framework Rivadavia was able to implement many of his modernizing projects; he sought simultaneously to revive the larger Argentine federal union. In 1824 like-minded provincial delegates met in a constituent assembly in Buenos Aires. By 1826 his ambitions appeared to have met with success, for the assembly produced another centralist constitution embodying limited franchise, and elected Rivadavia president of the United Provinces. Rivadavia's arguments in favour of a strong central executive had been strengthened by military necessity, for by the end of 1825 Argentina was at war with Brazil over possession of the Banda Oriental (Uruguay). Nevertheless, the new regime provoked defiance from the autonomist *caudillos* of the interior, abetted by the autonomist party within Buenos Aires province, who objected to Rivadavia's attempt to federalize Buenos Aires city as the national capital. Hostility to Rivadavia mounted because of his

ambiguity towards an accord with Brazil that would have recognized Brazilian sovereignty in Uruguay. In July 1827 he resigned the presidency. The rest of his life he spent in exile.

The Rivadavian reforms disappeared in the nativist and localist reaction that followed, although many were to reappear decades later. The most important were: stimulation of European immigration, the founding (1821) of the national University of Buenos Aires, the first attempts to create a national bank, and the suppression of the ecclesiastical 'fuero,' ie, privileged legal jurisdiction, which implied also separation of Church and state. Other measures had more ambiguous or ironic consequences. The Baring Bros. loan of 1824 and the British commercial treaty of 1825 initiated a long history of governmental relationship with British commercial interests. The law of emphyteusis (provincial in 1822, nation-wide in 1826) sought to settle small farmers on the *pampa* on long-term rentals, while retaining public title to the land (which thus served as collateral for public obligations). It defied the contemporary requirement for extensive grazing lands, however. By the end of the 1820s some 21 million acres (85,000 sq. kms) were in the usufruct of some 500 individuals, almost all of them cattlemen; under succeeding regimes usufruct became possession. The creation of a powerful land-holding class, almost non-existent under the colony, was thus greatly accelerated. RCN

RIVALTO, PEACE OF (4 Sept. 1630), six-week truce negotiated by the papal embassy which included the young diplomat Mazarin, to provide a cessation of hostilities in the Valtelline dispute between France and Spain. It was superseded by the peace of Ratisbon (13 Oct. 1630).

RIVERA, DIEGO (1886–1957), Mexican artist of the post-revolutionary school of muralists, whose works captured the spirit and purpose of the revolution (1910–17). His works celebrated the Indian past and vilified the Spaniards, the Church, foreign capitalists, and large land-holders.

RIVERA, JOSÉ FRUCTUOSO (1790–1854), Uruguayan politician and first president of independent Uruguay (1830–4). He later led the 'colorado' faction in its protracted struggle against the Buenos Aires-backed 'blancos' of Oribe.

RIVETT, SIR ALBERT CHERBURY DAVID (1885–1961), Australian scientist, whose influence on the development of scientific research in Australia exceeded that of any other man of his time. He was chief executive officer of the Australian Council for Scientific and Industrial Research (1926–49). His rigorous standards set a lasting pattern of scientific integrity in Australian research work.

RIVOLI, BATTLE OF (1797), French victory during Napoleon I's Italian campaign in the French Wars. The Austrians under Alvinzi attacked the French position on the heights of Rivoli, but were overwhelmingly defeated and one division surrendered without fighting.

RIZZIO, DAVID (1540–66), Italian musician who became a favourite of Mary Queen of Scots, and her private secretary. He was murdered in Holyroodhouse, Edinburgh, at the instigation of the queen's husband, Lord Darnley.

ROANOKE COLONY, first English settlement in North America, based on a grant to Sir Walter Raleigh (1584). Between 1585 and 1587 225 settlers were brought to Roanoke Island, NC. When the colony was again visited (Aug. 1591), the settlers had disappeared and it is assumed that they were massacred by Indians or Spanish.

ROB ROY, nickname of **ROBERT MACGREGOR** (1671–1734), notorious Scottish freebooter, acting head of the Macgregor clan, who typified the lawlessness of the Scottish Highlands in the early 18th cent. After the seizure of his lands for debt by the Duke of Montrose (1712) he made war on society, resorting to cattle-raiding and extortion for a livelihood. He was nominally a Jacobite from 1691, was present at Glenshiel (1719), and later captured (1722).

ROBBIA, DELLA (FAMILY OF), Florentine artists who originated the technique of imposing polychrome glazes on terracotta reliefs and statues, mostly of a religious nature. Their work is extremely distinctive, the colours blue, yellow, and green being used, often with a border of flowers and fruit, in the cases of reliefs. The technique was secret, though it has been widely imitated down to modern times and become a traditional form of Florentine art. The greatest of the family was Luca (1399–1482), who was also a sculptor, the most notable of his works being the Cantoria or choir stand for Florence Cathedral (1431–7). Andrea (1435–1528) was his nephew and Andrea's sons, Giovanni (1469–c. 1529) and Girolamo (1488–1566), carried on the tradition.

ROBERT I THE FRISIAN (d. 1093), Count of Flanders (*reg.* 1072–93), whose rebellion against his nephew Arnulf III, Count of Flanders and Hainault, in 1071, destroyed the union between these two principalities and thus the chance of an outstandingly powerful state emerging in the Netherlands at an early date. Robert, who was Count of Holland in the right of his wife, relied in his rebellion on the support of the Flemish towns and on the rapidly developing maritime Flanders. Arnulf, in spite of being supported by his uncle, King William I of England, by Philip of France, and the feudal nobility of Flanders and Hainault, was defeated and killed at Cassel (Feb. 1071). This was the first display of the strength of the new urban and maritime elements in the society of Flanders, which, as again in 1127–8, assured the accession to Flanders of a count of their choice against the wishes of the feudal nobility.

ROBERT II (c. 1051–1134), Duke of Normandy (*reg.* 1087–1106), eldest son of William the Conqueror, who had been designated as his heir to Normandy, while his more effective younger brother, William Rufus, succeeded in 1087 to the English Crown. Robert showed himself to best advantage as one of the bravest and most unselfish leaders of the First Crusade (1096–9) and was one of the commanders responsible for the Christian conquest of Jerusalem in 1099. But in Normandy he was no match for his two formidable brothers, Kings William II and Henry I. The latter defeated and captured him at Tinchebrai in 1106 and detained him for the rest of his life.

ROBERT I (1278–1343), King of Naples (*reg.* 1309–43), most powerful Italian ruler of his day. He was a benevolent autocrat, who realized the poverty of his southern Italian kingdom and the limited nature of his resources, and aimed mainly at preserving the existing balance of power in Italy. In this he succeeded, but his attempts to reform his state were only moderately effective and under his successors the kingdom of Naples reverted to anarchy and misgovernment. He was a patron of artists and writers.

ROBERT I BRUCE (1274–1329), King of Scotland (*reg.* 1306–29), grandson of one of the many claimants to the Scottish throne on the death of the Maid of Norway (1291). He emerged in 1306 as the leader of the nationalist and anti-English party after years of service under Edward I, when he murdered John Comyn and had himself crowned King of Scotland. He gradually won control of Scotland and assured its independence by his victory at Bannockburn (1314). This was followed by an invasion of Ireland by his brother, Edward Bruce, and Robert's invasions of England, which culminated in a victory at Myton (Yorkshire) in 1319. In 1328, by the treaty of Northampton, the English recognized Scotland's independence and when Robert died in the following year he was succeeded by his son, David II.

ROBERT OF CHESTER (*fl.* 12th cent.), English natural philosopher who introduced Arabic mathematics and alchemy to Europe. Educated in Chester, Robert went to study under the Moors in Spain. He translated into Latin for the first time the Koran (1143) and Islamic treatises on alchemy (1144) and algebra. These influenced greatly the development of European science.

ROBERT OF MOLESMES, Saint (*c.* 1027–1110), French monk, who founded the abbey of Molesmes (1075). Dissatisfied with its lack of austerity, he moved to Cîteaux, which abbey he founded in 1098. At the request of his monks at Molesmes and on the order of the pope he returned there after 18 months. Thus, although he founded Cîteaux, he did not found the Cistercian order, which developed only after his departure.

ROBERTS OF KANDAHAR AND WATERFORD, FREDERICK SLEIGH ROBERTS, 1st Earl of (1832–1914), British soldier who served in the Indian Mutiny, and who won the Victoria Cross. In 1879–80, during the Second Afghan War, he undertook a march from Kabul to Kandahar, transporting 10,000 soldiers and 8000 camp-followers over 300 miles (483 kms) in 22 days. He was commander-in-chief in Ireland (1895–1899) before assuming supreme command (1899) in the Anglo-Boer War. His services were distinguished, and he was rewarded with an earldom. He led an Indian expeditionary force despatched to France in 1914.

ROBERTSON, JAMES (1742–1814), American politician, who settled (1771) in the Watauga valley. He became a leader of the Watauga Association and became well known as an Indian fighter and agent. He explored lands along the Cumberland river (1779) and led a frontier party to a settlement on the Cumberland, at present-day Nashville (1781). He represented Cumberland in the NC Assembly (1785–9). Later, he played (1786–9) an obscure part in Spanish efforts to detach TN from the US. He represented Davidson County in the TN Constitutional Convention (1796) and the state of TN in the US Senate (1798). In his later years he negotiated treaties with the Cherokee Indians (1798, 1807) and served as Indian agent to the Chickasaw Indians.

ROBERTSON, SIR JOHN (1816–91), Australian politician, who was three times prime minister of NSW. His (largely abortive) 'free selection before survey' legislation of 1861 was designed to break up large estates in the interest of agricultural settlement. He was a political rival of Henry Parkes and strongly opposed the early federal movement.

ROBERTSON, WILLIAM (1721–93), Scottish Presbyterian minister and historian, who was associated in Edinburgh with Allan Ramsay, Adam Smith, and David Hume. Robertson's historical method of generalization based on the patient accumulation of facts was first revealed in his *History of Scotland* (1759). He was made historiographer for Scotland (1763) and was principal of Edinburgh University (1762–92). His *History of the Reign of Charles V* (1769) brought him European fame. He is regarded as one of the founders of British historiography.

ROBERTSON, SIR WILLIAM ROBERT (1860–1933), British soldier, who rose from private to field marshal. He served in India in the 1890s, in the Anglo-Boer War and became (1915) chief of the general staff in the First World War. He directed all operations until he was dismissed by Lloyd George in Feb. 1918. His assessment of the future course of the war, in its final phase, proved accurate and three months later he became commander-in-chief in Britain before commanding the army of the Rhine (1919–20).

ROBERVAL, JEAN-FRANÇOIS DE LA ROQUE, Sieur de (*c.* 1500–60), French explorer, who was instructed (1540) by the French Crown to found a colony on the St Lawrence river in Canada, for which he received a subsidy and a number of prisoners, who were to form the basis of the population. The colony was established at Cap Rouge (1542), where Jacques Cartier had already erected buildings, and Roberval added a fort, France-Roy. He went up the St Lawrence, but failed to pass the Lachine rapids (1543). He returned with the colonists to France, and the failure of the colony discouraged French interest in Canada for 50 years.

ROBESPIERRE, MAXIMILIEN FRANÇOIS MARIE ISIDORE DE (1758–94), French political figure and lawyer, who was a deputy to the states general in 1789. He soon made his mark in the National Assembly, distinguishing himself among the radical deputies who wished to keep the French Revolution moving forward and preaching distrust of those who sought moderate and gradual progress. He opposed restrictions on the franchise, on a new martial law passed in 1789 to suppress disorders, and on anyone who attacked the radicalism of Paris, its mob, its clubs, and its journalists. He thus became one of the popular heroes of the capital, quickly establishing his reputation as an incorruptible friend of the people. He was assisted in this by the attention paid to his journalism and his speeches, which were delivered not only in the Assembly, but in the Jacobin Club. There he established an ascendancy which assured him a platform when (like all other members of the National Assembly) he was politically idle because he was ineligible to sit in the Legislative Assembly.

During the first months of 1791 he used the club to attack the policies of the government, above all that of taking France into war. Yet the outbreak of the French Wars in 1793 helped to give him and other radicals an opportunity to overthrow the monarchy. Increasing popular distress and discontent, judiciously encouraged, culminated in the rising of Aug. 10. In this Robespierre played no obvious direct part, but it opened a way for him to re-enter politics as a member of the Convention. His first months there were largely spent in a struggle with the Girondins, once his allies, now his enemies. After their fall he joined the Committee of Public Safety, and the year after this is the period of his ascendancy.

While the committee was collectively responsible for its decisions, Robespierre exercised a great and sometimes dominating influence in it because of his enthusiasm, his ability, and his energy. He was closely identified with the regime in the eyes of the outside world, above all, with the policies of the Terror. This was to contribute to his downfall. His ruthlessness led to growing alarm about where he might strike next. Gradually, a loose coalition of opponents formed in the Convention. On 27 July 1794 (the 9th *Thermidor* in the revolutionary calendar) he and his friends (including his brother) were arrested. After attempting suicide, Robespierre lay some hours a prisoner before a quick hearing by the Revolutionary Tribunal sent him to the guillotine the next day.

J. M. Thompson, *Robespierre*, 2 vols (Oxford, 1935).　　JMR

ROBETHON, JEAN DE (d. 1722), French Huguenot refugee, who left France after the revocation of the Edict of Nantes (1685), entering the secretarial service successively of the Dukes of Brunswick-Lüneberg, William III, George William of Celle, and the Hanoverian minister, Bernstorff. He was chosen by Elector George to accompany him to England as his private secretary on his accession (1714), and played an important role in English politics.

ROBIN HOOD, legendary English outlaw from Sherwood Forest, who by using his power to help poor people and fighting the corrupt sheriff of Nottinghamshire, became the subject of a popular 14th-cent. English romance. He is traditionally associated with the time of King John (*reg.*

1199–1216), but his real prototype may have flourished during the troubled reign of Edward II (*reg.* 1307–27).

ROBINSON, HENRY (1605–64), English merchant and author, whose remarkable output included works enunciating the principle of liberty of conscience (1643–4), propositions for legal reform (1651–3), and treatises on economic matters, eg, *Brief considerations concerning the Advancement of Trade and Navigation* (1649).

ROBINSON, JOHN (1650–1723), English cleric and diplomat, who had wide experience as an envoy in Stockholm, Danzig, and Hamburg, and was dean of Windsor (1707), Bp of Bristol (1710) and finally Bp of London (1713). Briefly appointed lord privy seal (1711), he became British plenipotentiary at the peace negotiations at Utrecht (1712–13), for which he was rewarded with the London see. He was a Hanoverian tory who supported the Protestant succession in the critical years, 1713–15.

ROBINSON, JOHN (1727–1802), British politician, who was secretary to the treasury (1770–82). He was a pioneer in electoral strategy and master-minded the constituencies for Lord North, organizing all his support. His careful analysis of MPs' and constituency opinions played some part in the Younger Pitt's victory in the general election of March 1784.

ROBINSON, SIR JOHN BEVERLEY (1791–1863), Canadian jurist, lawyer, and politician who was solicitor-general for Upper Canada (1815) and was elected to the House of Assembly (1821), where he opposed union with Lower Canada, and helped to safeguard Upper Canada's customs duties. He was chief justice of Upper Canada (1829–62).

ROBOT PATENT (1775), royal edict of the co-regency of Maria Theresa and Joseph II to restrict the nobility's control over the serfs by controlling the amount of serf labour (*robots*) owned by the peasantry. The Bohemian revolt (1772) prompted Joseph to raise the question of serfdom with the council of state and it was decreed that an adjustment of the *robots* should be negotiated between lords and serfs within six months (1774), a step which aroused serious opposition from the aristocratic estates. The Bohemian estates eventually suggested the commutation of some *robots* into cash payments. Realizing that this offered no solution to the penniless serfs, however, Joseph issued the *robot* patent (Aug. 1775) making the 1774 law compulsory and laying down a graduated scale of labour services depending on taxes paid, with a minimum of 13 days' labour per annum and a maximum of three days a week. Extraordinary harvest-time labour dues were also regulated and the *robots* were abolished for Sundays and holidays.

ROBSART, AMY (1525–60), wife of Robert Dudley, Earl of Leicester, whose sudden death at Cumnor Place, Oxfordshire (8 Sept. 1560), giving rise to rumours of her murder by her husband, the queen's favourite, curbed Queen Elizabeth I's infatuation and restored her political good sense. Henceforth the queen rejected involvement with the English nobility and sought suitors from among foreign royalty.

ROCA, JULIO ARGENTINO (1843–1914), Argentinian soldier and politician, who was twice president of Argentina (1880–6, 1898–1904). As war minister under President Avellaneda, Roca organized (1879–80) a sizeable expedition to the Río Negro valley, which, making use of new military technology, crushed for all time the war-making potential of the plains Indians. The conquered area was open to stock raising and speculation, and ultimately to colonization. Roca used the prestige thus won to vault to the presidency, and thereafter pursued his true vocation, politics. He presided over the consolidation of the power of the landowning oligarchy and of its political arm, the National Autonomist, or Conservative, Party. His first administration witnessed the

beginning of Argentina's first great economic boom (1882–9), with growth in immigration, railroads, agricultural and pastoral expansion, meat-packing, and public works. His second administration was chiefly occupied with settlement of the dangerous Chilean boundary dispute.

ROCAFUERTE, VICENTE (1783–1847), Ecuadorian writer and president of Ecuador (1835–9) who led the Liberals of Guayaquil against the Conservatives of Quito under Juan José Flores. In 1836, in a pact to lessen strife, Flores agreed to hand over the presidency to Rocafuerte, who returned the favour to Flores in 1839. Flores's second term was so repressive that in 1839 Rocafuerte led a revolt, the failure of which resulted in Rocafuerte being exiled.

ROCA–RUNCIMAN AGREEMENT (1933), commercial pact signed by the Argentine vice-president and the president of the British board of trade. It was renewed in 1936. Argentina's export economy, already gravely affected by falling prices and contracting markets, was further threatened in 1932 with the loss—through the Imperial Preference system—of her principal customer, Britain. The resultant negotiations assured Argentine beef a somewhat precarious place in the British market, in return for great concessions. Britain gained control of most of Argentina's meat-packing industry; tariffs on British manufactures were reduced; coal was imported free; and British capital was to be given 'benevolent treatment'. Gen. Justo's regime, fraudulently elected in 1932, was bitterly denounced by Argentine nationalists as '*vende-patria*', for its alleged favouritism to traditional landowning circles and their British clients at the expense of newer national Argentine interests.

ROCHEFORT, French Biscayan port, situated at the mouth of the Charente river, just south of La Rochelle, an important naval base for the French Atlantic fleet with dockyards and an arsenal established under Colbert. It was blockaded by the British in the Seven Years War (1757–8) and in the Napoleonic Wars (1804–5) and was the scene of Napoleon's surrender to the British warship *Bellerophon* (1815).

ROCHEFORT-LUÇAY, VICTOR HENRI, Marquis de (1832–1913), French extreme republican journalist, who became a nationalist. For his virulent attacks on the empire in *La Lanterne* he was exiled, and then rewarded with a place in the Legislature (1869). After siding with the Commune he was sentenced to life imprisonment, but escaped from New Caledonia (1874), and later resumed his journalistic and political career, supporting Boulanger (who sent him into exile again) and the anti-Dreyfusard cause.

ROCHES, GUILLAUME DES (*fl.* 12th cent.), hereditary seneschal of Anjou and Touraine, who, on the death of King Richard I of England in 1199, initially favoured the claims of Richard's nephew, Arthur of Brittany, in preference to Richard's brother John. He reluctantly accepted John's proclamation as king and in 1202 led John's army which captured Arthur, exacting, however, a promise that the captive and his followers would be well treated. On John's breach of this undertaking, followed by the murder of Arthur, Roches revolted, rapidly raising the leading men of Anjou and Touraine against John, whose loss of these provinces was followed in 1203 by a concerted attack of all his enemies in Normandy, which was lost in 1204.

ROCHES, PETER DES (d. 1238), bishop of Winchester, who was one of the ablest and most determined supporters of King John's attempted enforcement of his royal prerogatives. He acted as chief justiciar of England in 1213–15. He had to be dismissed as part of John's temporary surrender to the rebellious baronage in June 1215, but again came to the fore as one of the principal royalist leaders during the civil war in 1215–17. He was tutor to King Henry III during the earliest years of his reign and became his chief adviser in 1232–4.

His return to power raised the fear of a revival of the authoritarian policies of John and he was forced into exile in 1234.

ROCHESTER, LAURENCE HYDE, 4th Earl of (1st of 2nd creation) (1642–1711), English Tory politician, who became an MP in the Convention parliament (1660). In the next year he entered the Cavalier parliament, and in addition occupied a post in the royal household (1662–75). In 1679 he was appointed to a commissionership of the treasury, an office he retained until he was dismissed (1684). At this time he was one of the closest Anglican friends of James, Duke of York, and not without influence in the counsels of Charles II. He is reputed to have played a major part in the conclusion of the subsidy treaty with France in 1681, and in the same year to have advised the king to summon the new parliament to Oxford rather than to Westminster. That year he was ennobled as Earl of Rochester and was made lord treasurer, but removed in 1687. He was in touch with William of Orange, after whose arrival in England he and some 50 other peers and bishops advised James to summon a free parliament, but to no avail. In the debates in the Convention parliament he favoured the claims of Mary alone, but after the crown had been offered to William and Mary conjointly he was willing to swear allegiance to both. But he was not given office, nor was he immediately readmitted to the privy council. Not until 1700 was he given ministerial office, and then only the lord lieutenancy of Ireland. He made no haste to take up residence there, and early in 1702 William dismissed him. However, William died shortly afterwards, and Queen Anne decided to retain his services. Nevertheless, early in 1703 he resigned. In the House of Lords he continued to figure prominently but without exerting any real influence on the course of events. His opposition to the continental strategy of the government was fruitless and occasional conformity by dissenters was not made illegal as he wished. Yet Anne's growing dislike of her Whig ministers produced opportunities for the Tories and in the late summer of 1710 Rochester was appointed president of the council.   BM

ROCHET, WALDECK (1905–), French politician, who was elected communist deputy for Puteaux in 1936 and re-elected for Saône-et-Loire (1945) and for Seine-Saint-Denis (1967). He was president of the National Assembly's agricultural commission (1946–7), president also of the communist parliamentary group (1958–9), and assistant secretary-general of the party in 1961, becoming the obvious successor to Maurice Thorez. He was elected secretary-general in 1964 and led the party into co-operation with the Fédération de la gauche démocrate et socialiste (FGDS). Owing to illhealth his deputies were taken over in 1969 by Georges Marchais, who replaced him as secretary-general in 1970.

ROCKEFELLER, JOHN DAVISON (1838–1937), US industrialist, financier, and philanthropist, whose career is often regarded as a prime example of the American self-made man. He was born in New York and grew up in Cleveland, OH, worked in the produce commission business, and in 1859, with an English partner, established his own firm. In 1863 he became associated with oil refining, and within two years began to expand his interests in this new industry. With a series of partners, who included Samuel Andrews and Henry M. Flagler, he became the largest refiner in Cleveland and in 1870 organized the Standard Oil Co. with a capital of $1 million.

Under Rockefeller's meticulous organization, the company grew into the largest oil firm in the US, and came to be regarded as the prototype of the modern, efficient, and ruthless American business corporation. By the mid-1870s Standard Oil had taken over most of its competitors by means of price-cutting wars, the negotiation of favourable railroad rebates, and efficient commercial operations. By 1879 the company controlled some 90 per cent of the refining capacity of the US. In order to stabilize and consolidate its position, and enable Standard Oil of Ohio to operate legally in other states, a trust agreement was drawn up (1879) and perfected (1881), whereby all stock was controlled by a board of trustees. This new departure in business organization and control was challenged in the courts and in 1892 the Supreme Court of OH ordered the trust to be dissolved. Integrated control of the oil business was, however, still maintained by the Rockefeller interests through interlocking directorates between associated companies in different states, and in 1899 a new device was found with the establishment of Standard Oil of New Jersey—a holding company with a capital of $110 million that exercised overall control of the Standard Oil empire. This corporation, in turn, was ordered to be dissolved by the US Supreme Court (1911) and John Rockefeller formally retired from active leadership in the business, and from his other financial activities, which included railroad and steel investments. From the late 1890s he was primarily concerned with the distribution of much of his vast wealth in charitable and philanthropic ventures. He was a Sunday School teacher for much of his life, and while believing in the virtues of free competition and the survival of the fittest, also believed, like Andrew Carnegie, in the obligations of wealth and the moral worth of charity. He helped to establish Chicago University (1892), endowed the Rockefeller Institute for Medical Research (1901), the General Education Board (1902), and the Rockefeller Foundation (1913) 'to promote the well-being of mankind'.

Allan Nevins, *Study in Power: John D. Rockefeller, industrialist and philanthropist* (New York, 1953).
Ralph W. Hidy and Muriel E. Hidy, *History of Standard Oil Company (New Jersey): Pioneering in Big Business 1882–1911* (New York, 1955).   MW

ROCKEFELLER, NELSON ALDRICH (1908–), US politician and grandson of John D. Rockefeller, who entered government service as Co-ordinator of Inter-American Affairs (1940–4), and later served as assistant secretary of state for American Republic Affairs (1944–5). He is believed to have originated the concept of technical and economic aid that was embodied in President Truman's Point Four programme (1949–). He served as under-secretary for health, education, and welfare (1953–4), as a special assistant to the president on foreign affairs (1954–5), and was chairman of a committee on government reorganization (1952–8). He was elected as Republican governor of NY in 1958, and was re-elected in 1962, 1966, and 1970. He was a leading contender for the presidential nomination in 1960 and in subsequent elections, but his liberal political record proved incompatible with the conservative tendencies of the national Republican Party, and his political instincts proved less sure at national than at state level.

ROCKHILL, WILLIAM WOODVILLE (1854–1914), US diplomat, who held a variety of posts, particularly in Korea (1886–1887) and China (1905–9). He played an important role in shaping the policy of the Open Door in China, and in 1900 he was sent as special agent to China to settle difficulties after the Boxer Rebellion.

ROCKINGHAM, CHARLES WATSON-WENTWORTH, 2nd Marquis of (1730–82), British politician and landowner in Yorkshire and Ireland. He held minor offices (1751–62), and then went into opposition. He headed an administration for a few months on the fall of George Grenville (1765). At the same time Edmund Burke became his secretary, and began to develop the characteristic views of the Rockingham group. Rockingham repealed the Stamp Act (1766), but reasserted Britain's right to tax the colonies in the Declaratory Act. He thereby antagonized both King George III and the colonists and was dismissed in 1766. In the late 1770s Rockingham and his followers emerged as the principal critics of Lord North's administration. They spoke in favour of American independence and economical reform,

but showed a lukewarm interest in parliamentary reform. Their attack became formidable (1779–80) and on the fall of North (1782) George III was reluctantly forced to turn to them. As a result of the king's weakness at this point Rockingham was able to insist on carrying out his own programme, embodying economic reform and peace negotiations with America, regardless of the king's wishes. In spite of his short periods of office, Rockingham's name has survived because of the association of his followers with a clear-cut programme, which in fact owed much to the skill of Burke.

ROCOCO, ornamental style that characterized the arts in mid-18th-cent. Europe, especially in France and Germany. It originated in France during the Regency (1715–23) in reaction to the heavy formality and oppressiveness of Louis XIV's reign and was the last stylistic mode to belong solely to the aristocracy and upper classes in Europe. Its characteristics were the free play of fancy, and lightness, and gracefulness. The most extreme examples of Rococo in architecture are found in the churches in Bavaria and the châteaux of Frederick the Great at Berlin and Potsdam. In furniture Rococo is typified by the *Louis Quinze* style, and in painting by the works of Tiepolo, Boucher, and Watteau.

ROCROI, BATTLE OF (19 May 1643), defeat of the Spaniards under Don Francisco de Melo by the French army, commanded by the Duc d'Enghien in the later stage of the Thirty Years War. The battle was fiercely contested and at first the French left wing was repulsed, but Melo lacked cavalry and the French were able to break the Spanish line, killing 8000 infantry and taking 7000 prisoners and 24 cannon. The disaster destroyed the reputation for invincibility which the well-disciplined Spanish infantry had enjoyed for 100 years.

RODNEY OF RODNEY STOKE, GEORGE BRYDGES RODNEY, 1st Baron (1719–92), British sailor during the American War of Independence, who served with distinction under Hawke in 1747 and Boscawen at Louisburg in 1758. He commanded in the Caribbean (1761–74) and in 1781 captured the Dutch 'free' port of St Eustatius, but his most important victory was over De Grasse at the battle of the Saintes in 1782, which ended the French threat to the West Indies and won back control of the Atlantic.

RODÓ, JOSÉ ENRIQUE (1872–1917), Uruguayan essayist, whose *Ariel* (1900) was regarded as an ethical gospel by two generations of Latin Americans. It is cast in the imagery of Shakespeare's *Tempest* and it is a speculative analysis of the perils of democracy, reflecting the unease of intellectuals at the growing presence of the US in Latin America.

RODRIGUEZ–CHAMUSEDO EXPEDITION (1581), to the American south-west, led by two Spaniards, Augustin Rodriguez, a Franciscan friar, and a soldier, Francisco Sánchez Chamusedo. They failed to form settlements, but the expedition paved the way for a permanent Spanish occupation of NM (1597).

ROE, SIR THOMAS (1580–1644), English diplomat, who established a settlement in Guiana (1611–17), and, as James I's ambassador to the Mughal court, secured permission for English traders to live in Surat and trade with the interior of India (1616). He became ambassador at Constantinople (1621–8), during which time he wrote his *True and faithful relation of what happened in Constantinople*, and was eventually accredited to the emperor. He was the English observer at the Diet of Regensburg (1641).

ROEBLING, JOHN AUGUSTUS (1806–69), US civil engineer, whose first wire cable suspension bridge was built over the Monongahela at Pittsburgh (1846). This was followed by a railway suspension bridge at Niagara Falls (1851–5). Roebling also designed Brooklyn Bridge in New York (1869). He died after an accident on the site and the work was completed by his son, Washington Augustus Roebling (1837–1926).

ROEBUCK, JOHN ARTHUR (1802–79), British lawyer and radical politician, who was a Benthamite in sympathy, but too independent to become, as John Stuart Mill hoped, the leader of a parliamentary Radical party. He was MP for Bath (1832–7, 1841–7) and for Sheffield (1849–68, 1874–9). He made his mark at once with a plan (1833) for 'universal and national education', administered by a central education department under a cabinet minister. In weekly *Pamphlets for the People* he publicized his views on various issues, advocating further parliamentary reform, including reform of the Lords, support for the new poor law, and opposition to factory and all other restrictive legislation, including the Corn Laws. He had spent his youth in Canada and spoke on Canadian problems in the Commons. In 1855 his motion for an enquiry into the conduct of the Crimean War led to the fall of Aberdeen's government. He was chairman of the Administrative Reform Association (1856). In the 1870s he supported Disraeli's foreign policy. He published *History of the Whig Ministry of 1830* (1852) and other political works.

ROENTGEN, WILHELM KONRAD (1845–1923), German physicist, who in Nov. 1895 discovered a new type of radiation, which he called X-rays. Roentgen showed that the extent of penetration of a material by X-rays was dependent on its density. Thus, though rays passed readily through soft body tissue, they were absorbed by bone. Roentgen's first X-ray photograph was of his wife's hand, clearly showing her wedding ring. This technique soon revolutionized medical diagnosis. The discovery of X-rays also led to others of significance, *eg*, that of radioactivity by Becquerel, which transformed physical science. In 1901 Roentgen was the recipient of the first Nobel Prize in physics.

ROGER I (1031–1101), Count of Sicily (*reg*. 1072–1101) and youngest of the several sons of a Norman knight, Tancred d'Hauteville, who came to seek their fortunes in Italy. With his brother, Duke Robert Guiscard, he started conquering Calabria (1061) and in 1062 they extended their enterprises to Muslim Sicily. This was a dependency of a larger state in Tunisia which, because of internal disasters, was unable to give much help to the Sicilian Muslims. Roger's forces were usually quite small and he did not complete his conquest of Sicily till 1091. It was left to his son, Roger II, to use Sicily for reunifying all the Norman lands of his family in southern Italy.

ROGER II (1095–1154), King of Sicily (*reg*. 1130–54), who was the creator of the unified Norman kingdom of Sicily, combining both that island and the mainland of southern Italy. He was the son of Count Roger I, who had conquered Sicily from the Muslims. He was able to profit from the death (1127) of his cousin William, who ruled the Norman territories on the mainland, to reunite all the Norman territories of Italy. A friendly pope permitted his assumption in 1130 of the newly created Crown of Sicily, held in vassalage from the papacy. A host of enemies tried to dislodge Roger from his new kingdom. They included the German emperors, the pope, and even the great St Bernard, who organized a campaign against him. Roger, relying especially on his fleet, one of the best in the Mediterranean and commanded by George of Antioch, defeated all these attacks. In his last years his enterprises ranged far beyond Italy. In 1147–8 his fleet successfully raided Greece and after 1146 he also ruled part of North Africa (Tripoli and Tunis). Internally he perfected the Norman administration, beginning the unification of Arabic, Byzantine, and feudal institutions which in the later 12th cent. made Sicily into the most efficiently governed kingdom in western Europe. His court at Palermo was a fascinating centre of intellectual and artistic patronage and some of the most beautiful surviving Sicilian churches date in their present form from his reign.

ROGER OF SALISBURY (d. 1139), English bishop and administrator. Henry I made him his chancellor (1101–2), and left him in control of the government of England. His position thus anticipated the functions of the officials styled in the later 12th cent. as chief justiciars, though it is doubtful whether such a specific office existed in Roger's time. By tradition Roger was the main creator of the English exchequer. He maintained his position under Stephen until 1139 when that king, out of fear of his power, imprisoned him and shortly afterwards contrived his death. He left behind a dynasty of administrators, his great-nephew, Richard Fitz Nigel, acting as treasurer during most of the reign of Henry II. He is the author of the *Dialogue of the Exchequer*, which preserves some of the traditions about Roger's achievement.

ROGER OF WENDOVER (d. 1236), English monk, who was the first of a succession of important English monastic chroniclers writing at the abbey of St Albans. He is an important source for the history of the period 1200–35, though his hostility to King John has perplexed modern historians in their efforts to achieve a better understanding of his reign.

ROGERS, JOHN (*c*. 1500–55), English cleric and first of the English Protestant martyrs of the Marian persecution (1555–1558), who was burnt at the stake at Smithfield. He was converted to the reformed Protestant Church when travelling in Antwerp and Wittenberg, and wrote a complete translation of the Bible under the pseudonym of Thomas Matthews (1537). He was appointed prebendary of St Paul's during Edward VI's reign (1551) and on Mary Tudor's accession (1553) delivered an uncompromising attack on the Roman Catholic church at St Paul's Cross, for which he was imprisoned in Newgate and subsequently sentenced to death.

ROGERS, ROBERT (1731–95), American soldier, who commanded Rogers's Rangers, a group of NY and VT frontiersmen, in the French and Indian War (1754–63). He received the surrender of French posts on the Great Lakes and the Ohio river (1760). During the American War of Independence Rogers, uncertain of his loyalties, was first arrested by the Americans and then dismissed by the British.

ROGERS, WOODES (d. 1732), English sailor, financed by Bristol merchants, who preyed on Spanish shipping in the Pacific (1708–10). He was governor of the Bahamas (1718, 1729–32).

ROGGEVEEN, JACOB (1659–1729), Dutch sailor, who discovered and described Easter Island (1722), and later sighted Samoa.

ROGIER, CHARLES LATOUR (1800–85), Belgian journalist and politician, who was one of the fathers of Belgian independence. He led volunteers from Liège to Brussels and ensured the success of the Revolution as head of the Provisional government (1830). After independence he held a variety of offices, was twice prime minister (1847–52, 1857–1868), and an active deputy for most of his life.

ROHAN, HENRI, Prince de Leon, Duc de (1579–1638), Breton nobleman descended from the d'Albrets, which gave him a claim to the kingdom of Navarre until Louis XIII's birth (1601). He was the son-in-law of Henry IV's minister, Sully, and an energetic leader of the French Huguenots (1621–9). He rose to the fore as a soldier, rallying the Huguenot forces in the Saintonge, Upper Guyenne, and Upper Languedoc (1610–20), and after withstanding the royal siege of Montauban (1621), made the treaty of Montpellier (1622). With his brother, the Duke of Soubise, he organized the Huguenot revolts in La Rochelle and Languedoc (1625–9), but eventually submitted to the peace of Alais (1629). After several years' voluntary exile in Italy he entered Louis XIII's service and was one of the leading French generals in the

Thirty Years War. He commanded the successful French invasion of the Valtelline (1635), but was expelled by the Grisons (1637).

ROHILLAS (men of the hilly country), name given to Afghans who settled in Rohilkhand during Muslim rule. Under their chief, Daud Khan, their power increased after the death of Aurangzeb (1707). When the Marathas attacked Rohilkhand in 1771, Shuja-ud-daulah of Oudh agreed to help them for 40 lakhs of rupees. Later the Rohillas refused to abide by their pecuniary engagements. Warren Hastings agreed to help Shuja-ud-daulah to expel (though not to exterminate) the Rohillas, who were defeated, their leader, Hafiz Rahmat Khan, being slain (1774). After the war, Faizullah Khan was allowed to retain Rampur as a *jagir*. In 1801, on the cession of Rohilkhand to the British, the Rohillas were allowed to retain Rampur. It remained one of the Indian princely states until it was absorbed into Uttar Pradesh in 1950.

RÖHM, ERNST (1887–1934), German soldier and politician. Having reached the rank of captain in the regular army, he served in the Freikorps von Epp during the suppression of the Soviet regime in Munich in May 1919. He then joined Drexler's German Workers' Party (later NSDAP) and helped to organize the SA. After taking part in the Munich putsch (8–9 Nov. 1923), he was imprisoned, then released. During Hitler's imprisonment he was jointly in charge of the Nazi movement with Rosenberg. After a quarrel with Hitler in May 1925 over the future role of the SA, he left Germany to serve in the Bolivian army. In 1930 he was recalled by Hitler, who appointed him chief of staff of the SA. The last stage of this career began with Hitler's achievement of power in 1933. By the middle of that year, the SA numbered about 2½ million men; in Dec. Röhm joined the cabinet. But his growing ambition and his demands that the SA should be increasingly militarized alarmed the generals, who feared for the army's exclusive position and ideological autonomy, and also alienated Hitler, who was still dependent on the goodwill of the officer corps. Increasing tension in the summer of 1934 led to the purge of 30 June–1 July, in which Röhm was shot. The events of his later career provide an example of the bitter animosities with which Hitler's immediate entourage was racked.

RÖHM PURGE (30 June–1 July 1934) in Germany, brutal elimination, organized by Hitler, Himmler, and Göring, of the SA leaders, whose military ambitions and revolutionary ideas threatened Hitler's alliance with the army. The purge was carried out mainly by the SS, with the knowledge, but not the active assistance, of the army command. Besides Röhm, Heines, and some 50 other SA leaders, those killed included Von Kahr, Von Schleicher, Gregor Strasser, and many of Hitler's other rivals and enemies. The purge, which showed Hitler's initial need for military approval, also marked an important stage in the development of the SS.

ROJAS PINILLA, GUSTAVO (1900–), Colombian soldier and president of Colombia, who overthrew the constitutional but unpopular conservative president, Laureano Gómez, by a military *coup d'état* in 1953. For two years Rojas Pinilla's popularity remained high because he offered a respite to a country exhausted by rural violence and political conflict. By 1957, however, many Colombians felt that his regime had become worse than the one preceeding it, and he in turn was expelled from office by a *coup d'état*. After 1957 he attempted unsuccessfully to organize a political party and return to power.

RŌJŪ (lit. 'elders'), the senior council of the *bakufu* in Tokugawa Japan, composed generally of five of the more substantial *fudai daimyō*s. The council eventually became the main centre of power in the *bakufu*.

ROLAND DE LA PLÂTIERE, JEAN MARIE (1734–93), French politician, who was a leading Girondin and acted as French minister of the interior (1792). His wife, Jeanne Marie (1754–93), probably had more political influence. She was executed in 1793, and two days later her husband committed suicide, almost certainly avoiding a fate similar to hers.

ROLFE, JOHN (1585–1622), English colonist, who sailed to VA (1609), where, after experimenting with the native tobacco, he discovered new methods of cultivating and curing it and made tobacco the staple, profitable crop of VA. He married Pocahantes (1613), daughter of a local Indian chief, and thus ensured peace with the Indians for eight crucial years. After taking Pocahantes to England, where she died (1616), Rolfe returned to VA (1617) and was appointed (1621) to the Council of the VA colony. He was probably killed in an Indian attack.

ROLIN, NICHOLAS (c. 1380–1462), principal adviser of Duke Philip the Good of Burgundy (1419–67) at a time when the duke was one of the most important European rulers. As chancellor of Burgundy from 1422 onwards, Rolin was head of the Burgundian civil service and was also in charge of Burgundian diplomacy. Originally a simple burgess of Autun, he rose to immense wealth and his son John became a cardinal in 1448. Philip gradually lost confidence in him because of Rolin's abuse of power and financial corruption. His influence was over by 1459.

ROLLE, RICHARD (c. 1300–49), English author and mystic who lived as a hermit at Hampole, near Doncaster, and died during the Black Death. He was the author of several works which enjoyed considerable popularity, especially the Latin *Incendium Amoris* (*Fire of Love*), and a number of mystical songs and lyrics which are among the best medieval verse in English.

ROLLESTON, WILLIAM (1831–1903), NZ politician of liberal views but conservative associations, who was superintendent of Canterbury (1868–76). As minister of lands, he attempted unsuccessfully (1882–3) to introduce a liberal policy of 'perpetual lease'. He led the opposition against the Liberal government (1891–3).

ROLLIAD (1784), satirical verses written by a group of British parliamentary Whigs after their electoral defeat (1784). *Criticisms on the Rolliad*, originally published in the press, took the form of reviews of an imaginary epic, the *Rolliad*, in which a leading character was a real-life MP, John Rolle, who was a strong supporter of the ministry.

ROLLO OF NORMANDY (d. c. 933), Viking leader, probably of Norwegian origin, to whose warrior bands King Charles the Simple in 911 surrendered the territories on the coast of modern Normandy. Rollo died still a pagan. His descendants created in Normandy one of the strongest medieval French principalities.

ROMAN CATHOLIC CHURCH, THE, IN AUSTRALIA, began as the proscribed religion of Irish convicts transported to NSW after the Irish rebellion (1798). The colony's administration feared Catholic sedition and subversion, but an official chaplaincy was permitted from 1820. From 1835, under BP Polding, the Church grew rapidly in extent and liberties. The laity, occupying the lower social and economic levels, was predominantly Irish. English domination of the hierarchy was challenged from the 1850s, and by Cardinal Moran's time (1884–1911) had been completely replaced by an Irish hierarchy with a Roman training, itself to be challenged successfully in the 1920s by advocates of an Australian hierarchy. Tensions, sectarian and ideological, between Catholics (a quarter of the population) and the rest of the community were endemic. They came to a head in the educational conflicts of the 1860s and 1870s, from which emerged a secular and a Catholic system, which continued to be a divisive issue. Further public controversies arose over politics, Catholics, who tended to align themselves with the Labor Party from 1905, mostly opposing conscription (1916–17), supporting Irish independence (1916–21) and in the 1950s becoming bitterly divided among themselves over communist influence in the labour movement and over principles of Church-and-state relations. Particularly after the Second World War, the Catholic community became less homogeneous, under the impact of the large proportion of European Catholics in the million post-war immigrants, and as an increasing number of Catholics moved into higher socio-economic levels.

PJ O'F

ROMAN CATHOLIC RELIEF ACTS in Britain, which relieved Roman Catholics from some of their disabilities, illustrate the gradual decline in anti-Catholic feeling. The 1778 act allowed army recruits to take a simple oath of fidelity to the Crown, in place of an oath against transubstantiation. Popular reaction to the 1778 act was seen in the anti-Catholic Gordon Riots. The 1791 act was wider in scope. In 1788 Roman Catholics had memorialized William Pitt the Younger on the subject of their disabilities, and exhaustive enquiries (1788–1791) showed that Catholics no longer claimed that the pope had any jurisdiction in England, and thus allayed Protestant fears of their loyalty. This act (1791) removed certain limitations on Catholics and gave legal toleration to Catholic schools and churches. Though Catholic teaching and worship were no longer penalized, they remained subject to restriction; church steeples and bells, open-air worship, monastic orders, and the education of the children of Protestants in Catholic schools were forbidden.

In 1793 an act, applicable to Ireland, admitted Catholics to the franchise, the universities, and the professions. The 1829 act was the most decisive measure. At a crucial point in Anglo-Irish relations, it removed almost all disabilities. Those that remained, *eg*, the prohibition of public religious celebrations or the use of Anglican episcopal see titles by the Catholic hierarchy, were virtually a dead-letter. They were removed by an act of 1936. Thereafter Catholics were penalized only in that none might rule as the sovereign, nor be regent or lord chancellor, or present anyone to an Anglican benefice.

ROMAN QUESTION in Italy. Mazzini's declaration of a Roman republic (1849) was seen by him as an attempt to destroy Catholicism. But the heroic defence of Rome against the united forces of Catholic Europe was probably inspired more directly by the Romans' desire for the independence of their city. From now on the temporal power of the papacy could only be sustained by a French army of occupation. French defeat in the Franco-Prussian War (1870) was immediately followed by the entry of Italian troops into Rome.

This completed the unification of Italy, but it did not end the Roman Question, for the pope's unrelenting opposition to unification had driven most Italian nationalists to share Mazzini's anti-clericalism, which was reinforced by Pius IX's constant appeals to the enemies of Italy, both before and after 1870. The Law of Guarantees (1871), recognizing papal sovereignty within the Vatican and offering the pope an annuity, failed to modify his intransigence. In the *Non expedit* he refused to recognize the Italian state and forbade Catholics to participate in it. Although this was not cancelled until 1919, it was increasingly ignored. The effect of the Roman Question on foreign affairs created more problems than the relations between Church and state within Italy.

The inclusion of Rome in Italy was largely responsible for the Italo-French hostility (1870–82), which caused Italy to seek the protection of Austria and Germany in the Triple Alliance (1882). This was counterbalanced by the suspicions aroused in Europe by the Papal Decree of Infallibility, leading eventually to the diplomatic isolation of the papacy. But even this rebounded against Italy, when Bismarck held the Italian government responsible for the pope's role in the *Kulturkampf*. The Roman Question thus contributed to the

war scare of 1875 and increased Germany's contempt of Italy.

The problem was solved in the long term by the papacy finding itself a new international role, unrelated to temporal power. This was largely the work of Leo XIII, who, having failed to win the diplomatic support of France and Germany, concentrated on allying the papacy with social reform. This gained him international respect and made conciliation easier within Italy, though the Church did not formally recognize the kingdom of Italy until the Lateran treaty (1929).

C. Seton-Watson, *Italy from Liberalism to Fascism* (London, 1967).

SH

ROMANESQUE, basic architectural style of western Christendom from the 8th to the 12th cent. The style is essentially based on the round arch and it derives much from late Roman architecture. Its formative period was *c*. 950–1050 in France, when monasticism was at its height and it was monastic architecture—especially that of the Cluniacs, as exemplified by their monastery at Cluny (built 950–1043), with its substantial vaulting and twin belfries—which became the medium whereby the Romanesque style spread. The period 1050–1150 saw the development of high Romanesque, characterized by the absorption of Oriental and Byzantine influences and by increasing skills in construction and decoration. Spacious churches of entirely vaulted type were built and these have magnificent plans with ambulatories, radiating chapels, and impressive towers. The church at Cluny (built 1088–1130), with its early carvings, is a masterpiece of this period and other excellent examples exist at Tours, Conques, Limoges, and Santiago. In France Romanesque has its own distinctive style. Magnificent Romanesque churches were also built in Italy, but many were later demolished to make way for buildings in Renaissance or Baroque styles. This period also saw the development of local 'schools' in Germany, the Iberian peninsula, Palestine, and England. The Norman conquest saw the building of monumental churches in England, especially by the Benedictines, producing such masterpieces as the cathedrals of Durham and Ely. Smaller churches were also built in this style, an interesting example being Kilpeck church in Herefordshire, England, with its exuberant carvings. This architectural style also graced secular buildings, but the last great effort of Romanesque was in the buildings of the Cistercian order, which expanded all over Europe in the course of the 12th cent.

JD

ROMANOS I LEKAPENOS (*reg*. 920–44), Byzantine Emperor, as father of Helena, the wife of the Emperor Constantine VII, he was raised in 920 in the status of co-emperor. In the east his reign witnessed the successful campaigns of John Kurkuas against the Muslims, which marked the beginning of the Byzantine reconquests in Syria and Mesopotamia. At home Romanos initiated a policy of resistance to the great nobles, who strove to take over the small peasant estates owing military service, which constituted one of the main foundations of the armed strength of Byzantium. This attempt to protect the peasantry remained one of the main preoccupations of successive Byzantine emperors for over a century.

ROMANOS IV DIOGENES (*reg*. 1068–71), Byzantine Emperor, defeated and captured in battle against the Seljuk sultan Alp Arslan at Manzikert. This disaster meant the loss of much of Asia Minor to the Turks, but the main coastal areas and harbours still remained under Byzantine control, so that the economy of the Byzantine empire was not irretrievably ruined.

ROMANOV DYNASTY, ruling houses in Russia from the time of Michael Romanov's election to the throne by the *zemsky sobor* at the end of the Time of Troubles (21 Feb. 1613) to the abdication of Tsar Nicholas II in Pskov (March 1917). The direct male line ended with the death of Tsar Peter II in 1730.

ROMANOVNA, ANASTASIA (*c.* 1530–*c.* 1558), first wife of Tsar Ivan IV of Russia (married 1547) and mother of Tsar Fedor I. She was a member of the popular *boyar* family of Romanov, an offshoot of the ancient noble line of Koshkin. Her marriage into the Rurik dynasty helped to secure the Russian throne for her great-nephew, Michael, grandson of her brother Nikita (1613).

ROMANTICISM, term usually used by historians to denote a movement of thought and feeling, occurring in the 18th–19th cents in the Western world. It appears first to have been used in its modern sense, as a catchword for an aesthetic ideal and a philosophical movement, by Friedrich Schlegel in the periodical *Atheneum* (1798). Some historians, *eg*, A. O. Lovejoy, insist that one ought not to speak of 'Romanticism', as there is no unequivocal meaning to it, but only of Romantic periods and movements. Seen in these terms, one can refer to at least the following modern historical exhibitions of Romantic attitudes: a pre-Romanticism, in English literature, around the 1740s; a pre-Romanticism in France, circling around the influence of J. J. Rousseau; a fully-fledged Romanticism in the 1790s in Germany, where the term was invented; outbursts of Romanticism around 1801 in France (Chateaubriand) and in England (Wordsworth and Coleridge); and a second efflorescence in France around the second and third decades of the 19th cent., strongly influenced by the earlier German example.

Why fully fledged Romanticism occurred when it did requires a complicated answer. It seems to have been partly a response to (*a*) the failure of the French Revolution to fulfil its ideals; (*b*) the oncoming Industrial Revolution, with its dissolution of the bonds and connections of a rural society; (*c*) the neo-classical Enlightenment, which seemed to have exhausted the limited thoughts, sensations, and experiences at its disposal; and (*d*) the abstract, dissecting world of 18th-cent. science, with its dismissal of sensuous perception of the whole. Above all, Romanticism embodied a rejection of the staid, sober, rational, calculating values of the bourgeoisie, newly risen to power in modern society, and perceived by Romantics as purely philistine.

The causes or motives of Romanticism are, naturally, closely connected to some of its leading characteristics. Romantics emphasized a return to 'nature', conceived of as immediate sensations rather than a Newtonian abstraction; placed great stress on a longing for the infinite, on voluntarism, dynamism, and struggle, on diversity and particularity, and on holism and organism; embraced a concern with process rather than mechanism; sought a lost unity of man, society, and nature; glorified the primitive and the exotic; preferred analogy and metaphor to logical analysis; and, above all, stressed the emotions over reason.

Romanticism manifested itself with especial strength in two areas of note: aesthetics and politics. In the first, it stressed the artist's genius, creative imagination, and emotional spontaneity; as Wordsworth put it, art is 'the spontaneous overflow of powerful feelings'. Art became an index to personality, often created for oneself rather than for a public audience. 'Sincerity' was a prime criterion. In political Romanticism, the attack was on the bourgeois centre, with its rationalism, atomistic individualism, and moderate liberalism. Both conservative and radical political thinkers embraced Romantic values as they castigated bourgeois capitalism for its 'alienation' of man, its creation of a fretful urban life, its breaking of human ties and substitution for them of 'callous "cash payment"', its uprootedness, and its over-civilization. Conservative Romantics found a lost unity in the Middle Ages, with their supposedly stable, hierarchical Church and state. Radical Romantics appealed to a primitive folk communism in the past as a model for their projected communism of the future. Both glorified belonging to closely knit groups, and the end of alienating, artificial, contractual society.

It would be wrong to see Romanticism as at any time completely dominating the value-scheme of Western civilization. From the late 18th to the early 19th cent. onwards, however, it was in a constant dialectic with other value-patterns, such as Utilitarianism, Positivism, Realism, and so forth. In the arts, it seems to have lost ground in the middle of the 19th cent. to Realism, but then emerged again powerfully towards the end of the century in such forms as symbolism and dadaism. In sociology, it strongly combated Positivism, and stressed *Gemeinschaft* versus *Gesellschaft*. Above all, perhaps, it left a general legacy of deepened awareness of man's emotions and motives; without Romanticism it is difficult to conceive of a Nietzsche, and, indeed, of a Freud. Once brought into recognized existence around 1798, Romanticism became an imperishable part of modern historical consciousness.

Northrop Frye (ed.), *Romanticism Reconsidered* (New York, 1963).
John B. Halsted (ed.), *Romanticism* (Boston, MA, 1965).

BM

ROME, founded in 8th cent. BC through the amalgamation of Iron Age settlements on the seven hills. The traditional seven kings, from the founder, Romulus, to Tarquinius Superbus, are only legendary. The earliest known form of government was a monarchy, replaced, traditionally in 509 BC, by the republican system with two annually elected consuls. The early centuries of the republic were marked internally by the Struggle of the Orders between the Patricians and the Plebeians and externally by warfare against the Aequi, Volsci, Etruscans, Samnites, and Gauls, which led to Rome's gaining control of the Italian peninsula, a process completed by her defeat of Pyrrhus' invasion (281–272). The First Punic War (264–241) brought Rome her first overseas provinces, Sicily and Sardinia-Corsica, and hard-won victory in the Second made her the strongest Mediterranean power with interest in Africa and an empire in Spain (218–201). Greece was annexed after the Macedonian Wars (215–206, 200–196, 171–167, 149–146) and a war with Syria (192–189), and Carthage was finally destroyed in 146. The subjugation of the Greek East was later completed by Lucullus and Pompey in the Third Mithridatic War (74–62). At home the tribunate of Tiberius Gracchus (133) began a process of disintegration, which led through the increasing use of violence by Marius, Saturninus, Cinna, and Carbo and the effects of the Social War (90–88) to Sulla's capture of Rome and his dictatorship (82–79). The republican system, unable to sustain the ambition of war-lords like Sulla, Pompey, and Julius Caesar, backed by their client armies as voters or soldiers, was destroyed by Caesar's invasion of Italy (49) after the Gallic Wars. Caesar's dictatorship and his murder (44) led to further civil war between Antony, Lepidus, and Augustus, who eventually emerged as sole ruler of the Roman world after the battle of Actium (31). He restored internal stability and his reign (31 BC–AD 14) was the golden age of Roman literature, exemplified by, *eg*, Virgil, Horace, and Livy. He brought Egypt into the Roman empire, completed the conquest of Spain, and established the northern frontier on the Rhine and the Danube. In Asia his frontier policy was based not on conquest but on a ring of client kingdoms to protect the Roman provinces from Parthia. Principal later annexations included those of Cappadocia (AD 17), Mauretania (40), Britain (43), Thrace (46), Lesser Armenia (72), Arabia Petraea (105), Dacia (106), and Osroene (195); Armenia, Assyria, and Mesopotamia were also briefly occupied (115–117). Essentially, Augustus' policies and administrative system, although becoming progressively more rigid, survived until the barbarian invasions of the Goths, Franks, and Alemanni in the 3rd cent. AD, when the Persians under the Sassanian dynasty also attacked the eastern provinces. The recovery under Gallienus, Claudius Gothicus, Aurelian, and Probus (253–82) was completed in the establishment by Diocletian (284–305) and Constantine the Great (307–37) of a radically different system, designed to hold the empire together under a central authority. Although Constantine's successors, Constantius II, Julian, Valentinian, and Valens, on the whole successfully resisted barbarian pressure, Valens was killed and his army destroyed by the Visigoths at Adrianople (378) and Theodosius (379–95) was forced to allow them to settle in Thrace. In 410 the Visigoths under Alaric captured and sacked Rome, while Vandals, Alans, Sueves, and Burgundians occupied Gaul and Spain and in 429 the Vandals took Africa. Eventually in 476 the last western emperor, Romulus Augustulus, was compelled to abdicate and the German, Odoacer, was crowned King of Italy.

With the fall of the Roman empire in the west, imperial Rome was gradually replaced by papal Rome, although at first the civil administration remained virtually unaltered. The Lombard invasion of Italy (568–72) led to a resistance movement in Rome under the influence of the Church. The latter's prestige was greatly enhanced by the accession of Pope Gregory the Great (*reg.* 590–604), whose moral and political authority enabled the city and Church to withstand Lombard attacks, while at the same time he built up an ordered Church hierarchy under his control. The first developments leading to the creation of a papal state can be seen from this time.

By the 8th cent. the duchy of Rome owned extensive lands in central Italy and the pope was the head of a large administrative body possessing enormous revenues. In 751 the Lombard seizure of Ravenna led Pope Stephen II to appeal to Pepin, King of the Franks, to save Rome. Central Italy's connection with Constantinople being completely severed, the papacy now relied on Frankish protection. This precedent was followed by Pope Leo II, who, having antagonized the Romans, turned to Charlemagne for support and in gratitude gave the imperial crown to the Frankish king on Christmas Day 800. Thus was created the Holy Roman empire, an empire whose connections with Rome were to be very tenuous.

Saracen and Hungarian threats and internal strife led to anarchy in 10th-cent. Rome, with the emperors increasingly creating and deposing popes. The Germanic influence grew and during the papacy of Hildebrand (Gregory VII) disagreement between him and the Emperor Henry IV became acute. Then Rome itself was sacked by the Normans under Robert Guiscard. It was Pope Urban II who regained some papal prestige in 1096 when he launched the First Crusade.

The growth of free, independent communes throughout Italy now affected Rome, where the revolutionary Arnold of Brescia fought for a republic. By 1145 a compromise was reached, the Roman Commune was constituted, but the pope's spiritual role remained unchanged, and with Frederick Barbarossa's assistance, even enhanced, despite the creation of popes and anti-popes. The pontificate of Innocent III (*reg.* 1198–1216) made the papacy a European power of some force.

Roman politics in the 13th cent. frequently revolved round the rival ambitions of the Guelph and Ghibelline factions and the temporary removal of the papacy to Avignon led to a growth of self-government in Rome. The Great Schism (1378–1417) resulted in political repercussions throughout Europe, but with the pontificate of Martin V comparative order was restored and a period of reconstruction began. During the late 15th cent. many sumptuous buildings were erected, among them the Sistine Chapel. Under Julius II (*reg.* 1503–13) Bramante began the rebuilding of St Peter's, the work being completed under Michelangelo's direction. The development of the city followed, with the Spanish Steps and immediate environs growing up as the centre. The Reformation had a traumatic effect on the Church, but Rome itself continued to expand. In the 17th cent. Roman baroque art reached its peak in the work of Bernini and Borromini, and in the next century public gardens, fountains, palaces, and imposing church facades embellished the city.

With the 19th cent. Risorgimento the focal points of Italian politics shifted, but the aim of the leaders of the movement was to make Rome the capital of the new kingdom—and this it became in 1870. The gigantic monument to Victor Emmanuel was begun on the Capitoline Hill in 1885. Italian Unification had automatically meant an end to papal territorial power, which was now confined to the Vatican, which in 1929 was recognized by the Fascist regime as an independent sovereign state. Under Mussolini a rapid expansion of Rome's suburbs took place. The city developed as a centre of industry and commerce, closely linked with the hinterland which supplies many raw materials. After the Second World War commercial expansion continued and Rome's central position in the Italian peninsula, along with its capital and religious status, ensured its dominant role among the cities of Italy.

M. Grant, *The Climax of Rome* (London, 1968).
E. O'Neill, *Rome* (London, 1919).   DCE
                                                      MEB

ROME, SACK OF (1527), storming of the papal capital by the imperialists in the Italian Wars, in which the commander, Constable de Bourbon, was killed in the first assault (9 May 1527). After taking the city, the unpaid soldiery massacred around 8000 civilians and plundered the buildings in an orgy which deeply shocked Christian Europe. Pope Clement VII escaped to the castle of Sant' Angelo, where he held out until 26 Nov., and after signing a treaty with Emperor Charles V fled to Orvieto (7 Dec. 1527).

ROME AGREEMENT (7 Jan. 1935), name usually given to the Franco-Italian agreements of 1935, the high point of inter-war relations between the two powers. There had been conflict since 1919 over colonies in Africa, Mediterranean naval parity, and rivalry in south-eastern Europe over satellites and spheres of influence. The French had long wanted to improve relations with Mussolini, hoping to add Italy to their circle of allies around Germany. Mussolini, for his part, could only afford the luxury of a quarrel with France when his northern frontier was secure. This condition ceased to exist after the murder of Dollfuss in July 1934, which showed the extent of Hitler's ambitions in central Europe, and Italy was sufficiently alarmed to see the value of a detente with France. The German revival was thus the catalyst that brought the two powers briefly together. The major terms negotiated by Laval, the French foreign minister, and Mussolini were: slight frontier rectifications in Africa; a special protocol on the status of Italians in Tunisia; and a declaration on economic collaboration; concerning Europe—an agreement over Austria that was an unmistakable warning to Hitler and, even more clearly, a declaration condemning unilateral rearmament. The agreement had a dual importance: it marked a crucial step in the at least nominal resistance of the powers to German resurgence, culminating at Stresa. More crucially, there was a tacit division of interests in East Africa which left Italy with the opportunity for, at the least, the economic penetration of Abyssinia. Laval later denied his encouragement of Mussolini, but it now seems clear that the Rome Agreement was an essential prelude to the Abyssinian War. Mussolini's bellicosity while acting on this encouragement in the long run destroyed the power-grouping opposed to Hitler, and effectively doomed the rapprochement brought about by the agreement as a whole.   KM

ROME PROTOCOLS, agreement signed at Rome (7 March 1934) between Italy, Austria, and Hungary. The basic aim of Mussolini's foreign policy at this time was to safeguard Italy's prime gain from the First World War, the removal of a great power from her northern frontier. Therefore he had to support Austria against Nazi pressure. He had joined with Britain and France on 17 Feb. 1934 in declaring his political interest in Austria's independence and now brought to fruition long conceived plans for economic support of the struggling republic, which he rightly saw as the only viable alternative to 'Anschluss'—incorporation within the Third Reich. Throughout 1933 there had been frequent discussions between Dollfuss's government and the Italians, and Mussolini worked hard to build up some kind of Danubian economic organization to replace the Habsburg empire. The Little Entente countries were sceptical, suspicious of what might be an attempt to bring back the Habsburgs themselves; but Mussolini pressed on with his plans and in March 1934 Dollfuss and Gömbös of Hungary, who had good relations with the Italians, joined the dictator in negotiating the economic agreement. The protocols included a clause allowing for both economic and political consultation in future; a declaration of intention to increase economic contacts; and a specific Austro-Italian agreement by which Mussolini bound himself to accept as large a quantity of Austrian exports (notably timber) as possible. Detailed bilateral agreements were drawn up by the end of May 1934. Austria and Hungary undoubtedly benefited from these economic provisions, and political consultation was continued by Schuschnigg after the murder of Dollfuss. These protocols, along with Mussolini's reaction to the Dollfuss assassination, mark the high point in Italian support for Austria against Hitler. The economic agreements, unlike the political relationship, lasted down to 1938—and in Hungary's case beyond.   KM

ROME TREATIES (1957) established the European Economic Community and the European Atomic Energy Community. Drafts of the treaties were prepared by an inter-governmental committee set up at the Messina Conference (June 1955). The treaties were signed (25 March) by Belgium, France, German Federal Republic, Italy, Luxemburg, and the Netherlands. They came into force on 1 Jan. 1958.

ROME–BERLIN AXIS (1936–43), name given to the partnership of Germany and Italy, from a phrase in a speech of Mussolini's in 1936. Italy's initial reaction to Nazi Germany had been one of mistrust, because of German ambitions towards Austria; but Abyssinia and the Spanish War isolated Italy, who (1936–8) steadily drifted into the German orbit. The link, the key to Italo-German relations in this period, was a personal one: the mutual trust that existed, for most of the time, between the dictators. From Sept. 1937 Mussolini was convinced that Hitler would win a European war, and proved this in March 1938 by abandoning Austria. From late 1938 the story is one of increasing German domination of Italy and her foreign policy, interrupted by periods of strain and resentment within Italy, for the Axis was very much Mussolini's own policy, backed only by Farinacci among the top Fascist leaders. Relations cooled after Munich, but Mussolini felt he could restore Italian pride and equality of gains in the Balkans. In May 1939 Ribbentrop finally talked the Italians into a military alliance, the Pact of Steel—and although Mussolini at first kept out of the war, the prospects of aggrandisement and his faith in Hitler's success induced him to attack France in June 1940, again despite opposition from within his own party. Military incompetence now increased Germany's hold on Italy and demonstrated Mussolini's junior role. From autumn 1938 he had begun a half-hearted anti-Semitic policy, and after mid-1941 Italy was much more integrated into the 'New Order' domestically, especially in terms of labour service. This and successive military defeats served to undermine Mussolini's position and he fell in July 1943. This marks the end of the Axis, for now relations between Germany and Italy were purely those of conqueror and conquered, with Mussolini in the so-called Salo republic as a mere puppet of the Nazis.   KM.

RØMER, OLE CHRISTENSEN (1644–1710), Danish astronomer and discoverer of the finite velocity of light who spent ten years at the Copenhagen University before going to Paris. Here he observed that the eclipses of Jupiter's moons occurred slightly earlier or later than predicted when the earth was nearer to or further from the other planet. He realized that this must be due to the time taken by light to travel from the eclipse, and was able to deduce its velocity for the first time.

ROMILLY, SAMUEL (1757–1818), British Whig politician and criminal law reformer, whose attempts to reform the criminal law met with hostility in the early years of the 19th cent., when the political climate was not yet ready for Benthamite reforms. But his work, combined with that of Mackintosh and Fowell Buxton, laid the basis for the major revision of the law effected by Peel in the 1820s.

ROMMEL, ERWIN (1891–1944), German soldier, who joined the army in 1910. After a distinguished First World War career, he held important training posts (1921–38) and commanded the 7th armoured division in the Second World War during the campaign against France in May–June 1940. In Feb. 1941 he became commander-in-chief of the newly formed Afrika corps, with the task of remedying the setbacks inflicted on the Italians. After the reconquest of Cyrenaica in April 1941 and Tobruk and Benghazi early in 1942, Rommel invaded Egypt and by June had reached El Alamein. However, hampered by shortage of supplies and by unrealistic orders from Hitler, he had to retreat before Montgomery's counterattack in Oct., which led eventually to the loss of Libya and Tunisia to the British. He was recalled to Europe in 1943 to command Army Group B, first in Italy and then in France, where he organized the construction of the Atlantic Wall.

Although he had initially welcomed National Socialism and for a time enjoyed Hitler's confidence, Rommel became increasingly sceptical about Hitler's direction of the war. From 1943 onwards he established contact with the resistance movement, which planned to appoint him as provisional head of state after Hitler's overthrow. In July 1944 he demanded that Hitler should draw the appropriate conclusions from the military situation and determined to end the war in the West independently if necessary. All these plans failed owing to Hitler's survival of the 20 July plot and Rommel's own injury in an Allied air attack; when his links with the conspirators became known Rommel committed suicide on 14 Oct. 1944.   RJVL

ROMNEY, HENRY SIDNEY, Earl of (1641–1704), British Whig politician, who was envoy to The Hague (1681–5) and was later involved in the intrigues with William of Orange. He was secretary of state (1690–2), lord lieutenant of Ireland (1692–5), and master of the ordinance (1693–1702).

ROMNEY, GEORGE WILCKEN (1907–), US industrialist and politician, who became president of American Motors (1954–62), and governor of MI (1963–9) and sought the Republican presidential nomination (1968). In 1969 he was appointed US secretary of housing and urban development.

ROMORANTIN, EDICT OF (1560), French royal edict issued by Francis II through the influence of Chancellor L'Hôpital, to quell early signs of religious revolt. The responsibility for the legal processes of suppressing heresy were taken away from the lay judges and remitted to ecclesiastical judges, thus implying the desirability of procedural delay for appeal. The edict was resisted by the magistrates and was modified by a royal declaration of Aug. 1560.

ROMULUS, mythical founder of Rome, of which his name is a personification. To his imaginary reign (753–717 BC) are traditionally attributed the institution of Senate and Assembly, the first code of law, the amalgamation with the Sabines under Titus Tatius, and the division of the population into *curiae*, or alternatively tribes.

ROMULUS AUGUSTUS (*c.* 455–?), Emperor (*reg.* 475–6), conventionally regarded as the last of the Western Roman emperors who was elevated to the throne by his father, Orestes, and Odoacer, commander of the barbarian troops in Italy. He was soon deposed by Odoacer and died at an unknown date in a monastery.

RONCAGLIA, DIET OF (1158), meeting near Piacenza, in Lombardy, attended by most Italian barons, and representatives of the cities, and bishops from northern and central Italy, where the emperor Frederick I Barbarossa established for some years complete control over the Italian provinces of the empire and defined his imperial rights in Italy.

RONCESVALLES, site of an attack by Basques, in alliance with Muslims, on the Frankish army of Charlemagne retreating from an incursion into Spain (778). The Franks suffered severe losses and several of their subordinate commanders were killed, including Roland, margrave of the Breton march, whose death forms the basis of the *Song of Roland*, one of the most important epics current in medieval France.

RŌNIN (lit. 'wave-man'), name given to a Japanese samurai who left or lost his lord. After the end of the civil war of the 16th cent. the large number of dispossessed *rōnins* presented a threat to the Tokugawa *bakufu*, which was only removed by the failure of a *rōnin* rebellion plot in 1651. In the final years of the Tokugawa period *rōnins* again played an important role in Japanese politics, when numerous samurai left their *hans* to engage in anti-foreign and pro-imperial activities in Edo and Kyoto.

ROOKE, SIR GEORGE (1650–1709), English sailor and politician, who fought at the battles of Beachy Head (1690) and Barfleur (1692). He became MP for Portsmouth in 1698 and later led an Anglo-Dutch squadron to the Sound (1700), the entrance to the Baltic, having been entrusted with the delicate mission of restoring stability in that region. At the outset he jeopardized its success by assisting the King of Sweden to bombard Copenhagen and land troops on the island of Zealand. However, on instructions from England he modified his conduct. On the outbreak of the War of the Spanish Succession, Rooke was the naval commander of a combined operation against the Spanish port of Cadiz, but nothing was achieved. However, he learned of the impending arrival of a Spanish treasure fleet from the New World, and was able to redeem his reputation by shattering it at Vigo Bay. He took the Austrian archduke (whom the Allies recognized as King Charles III of Spain) to Lisbon (1704) and then went on to land a few troops at Barcelona, who were shortly afterwards re-embarked. His most outstanding exploit was the capture in 1704 of Gibraltar, which he defended against the French at the battle of Malaga. When he returned to England he was treated as a hero by the Tories, who exaggerated his naval triumphs in comparison with the military victory at Blenheim.

ROON, ALBRECHT, Count von (1803–79), Prussian soldier, politician, and minister of war (1858–73), who originated Prussian army reforms. He created the system of rapid mobilization that proved so effective in the wars against Austria (1866) and France (1870–1).

ROOSEBEKE, BATTLE OF (27 Nov. 1382), in Flanders, led to the crushing of one of the most determined urban rebellions against the count and the propertied classes of Flanders. The leaders of the rebellion were the men of Ghent, dominated by the weavers. The count, Louis de Male, sought the support of his son-in-law, Duke Philip the Bold of Burgundy, who managed to bring into Flanders a royal French army. The men of Ghent, remembering the leadership of James Van Artvelde in an earlier rebellion against the counts (1338–45), elected (1382) as their leader James's son, Philip (1340–82). He was no match for the better-equipped and better-led chivalry of France and was killed in a massacre of his followers at Roosebeke. Ghent's resistance was prolonged to 1385, when it was blockaded into submission.

ROOSEVELT, ANNA ELEANOR (1884–1962), wife of US president F. D. Roosevelt, author, champion of the underprivileged, and tireless worker for the United Nations and the cause of world peace. Born in New York, daughter of Elliott Roosevelt (1860–94) and niece of Theodore Roosevelt, she married her fifth cousin, Franklin (1905). Though at first preoccupied with raising their five children, she did much to keep her husband's political interests and ambitions alive after he was crippled by poliomyelitis in 1921, and she also became active in the NY state Democratic Party. During the presidential years she became a crusader for social and economic causes, for young people, and for civil rights. From 1935 she wrote a widely syndicated daily newspaper column, 'My Day'. As a delegate to the United Nations (1945–53), she served on the commission on human rights. Among her many writings are the autobiographical *This is My Story* (1937), *This I Remember* (1949), and *On My Own* (1958).

ROOSEVELT, FRANKLIN DELANO (1882–1945), US politician, who was elected to the presidency four times (1932, 1936, 1940, 1944), an achievement unique in American history, and who inaugurated the New Deal policies of the 1930s. He began his political career in the NY state senate in 1910, and was an early supporter of Woodrow Wilson, whom he served as assistant secretary of the navy (1913–20). He ran unsuccessfully as Democratic vice-presidential candidate in 1920, was then crippled by poliomyelitis (1921), and temporarily retired from public life. He returned in 1924 and 1928 to nominate Alfred E. Smith at the Democratic presidential convention, and succeeded Smith as governor of New York (1929–33). As a politician he displayed an acute awareness of urban workers' aspirations and helped to consolidate the Democratic rural–urban coalition. On becoming governor as the Depression was sweeping the country, he instituted a number of economic reforms and welfare programmes that foreshadowed his presidential policies. He was re-elected by a large majority in 1930 and emerged as a leading candidate for the Democratic nomination in 1932, and was chosen after a confused pre-convention battle in which he was forced to renounce his former advocacy of entry into the League of Nations. His campaign against Hoover was focused on the promise of a New Deal for the American people and emphasis on the 'forgotten man at the bottom of the economic pyramid'. In the first 100 days of his administration a wide-ranging programme of legislation aimed at recovery, relief, and reform was introduced. Although some of the legislation, including the Tennessee Valley Authority Act, was sustained by the US Supreme Court a number of New Deal policies, including the National Industrial Recovery Act and the Agricultural Adjustment Act, were declared unconstitutional. Following his landslide victory in 1936 Roosevelt attempted to reorganize the court in order to secure a compliant judiciary, but met with vehement and successful opposition. Although it helped to restore confidence, and to reshape the economy, the New Deal had qualified economic success, prosperity being restored only by the coming of the Second World War. Despite rejection of the League of Nations in 1932, Roosevelt's foreign policy was one of the 'Good Neighbor', of co-operation with other democratic nations in the interests of peace. Outside forces and domestic pressure from isolationists, who wished to insulate the US from war by discouraging contact with belligerents, stifled his tentative policy until the outbreak of war in 1939. Domestic opinion then began to change and in 1940 he was able to conclude the Destroyer Deal, in 1941 to secure passage of the Lend-Lease Act and to sign the Atlantic Charter, a declaration of war aims. After the Japanese attack on Pearl Harbor the US became a full belligerent and Roosevelt worked closely with Allied leaders in the conduct of the war and in planning for peace. He strongly supported the concept of a United Nations Organization but died suddenly just before the meeting of the San Francisco conference in 1945 at which UNO was founded.

J. MacG. Burns, *Roosevelt: the lion and the fox* (New York, 1956).

F. Perkins, *The Roosevelt I Knew* (New York, 1946).   DKA

ROOSEVELT, THEODORE (1858–1919), US politician and 26th president of the US. After being privately educated because of poor health and bad eyesight, which helped to make him a devotee of physical fitness and the 'strenuous life', he graduated from Harvard (1880). He had already begun writing *The Naval War of 1812* (published 1882), and his interest in history led later to biographies of *Thomas Hart Benton* (1886) and *Gouverneur Morris* (1888), and *The Winning of the West* (4 vols, 1889–96). As an independent Republican member of the NY state legislature (1882–4), he was an enthusiastic reformer, but alienated the Republican Party machine and failed to secure re-election (1884). After the death of his first wife, Alice Lee, he spent two years ranching in Dakota, then returned to contend unsuccessfully for the mayoralty of New York (1886). In 1889 he was appointed a Civil Service Commissioner by President Harrison and was later police commissioner for New York (1895–7), becoming closely identified with the cause of civic reform. As McKinley's assistant secretary of the navy (1897–1898) he was credited with making the fleet's dispositions on the eve of hostilities with Spain that led to Dewey's victory at Manila Bay. He resigned (May 1898) in order to fight in the war, and led the 'Rough Riders' in the Cuba campaign. After his success at San Juan Hill he became a popular hero and was elected governor of NY (1898). His reform programme alienated the Republican 'boss', Thomas C. Platt, who sought to relegate Roosevelt to obscurity by engineering his nomination to the vice-presidency (1900); but on the assassination of McKinley (1901) Roosevelt became president and was elected in his own right in 1904. His domestic and foreign policies were exaggerated by his penchant for self-publicity. The 'Square Deal' gave him a reputation for 'trust-busting' although he was less active in this area than his successor, William Howard Taft, and legislation such as the Pure Food and Drug Act (1906), while helping to strengthen the progressive movement, also had the support of business groups. His foreign policy, characterized as 'Big Stick' diplomacy, included support for the Panama revolt against Colombia (1903), and he antagonized Latin American susceptibilities by enunciating the Roosevelt Corollary to the Monroe Doctrine (1904). Concerned in the wider world with the protection of US interests, he sought to preserve the balance of power, and his part in promoting the treaty of Portsmouth between Russia and Japan (1905) helped to earn him the Nobel Peace Prize (1910). When he retired from the presidency (1909) he went big game hunting in Africa, but personal differences with his chosen successor, Taft, and a belief that the president was pursuing conservative policies, led Roosevelt to oppose Taft for the Republican presidential nomination in 1912. His failure resulted in the withdrawal of his progressive followers from the Republican Party and he campaigned unsuccessfully on a third party Progressive ticket on the platform of the New Nationalism. He supported US neutrality in 1914, but soon developed sympathy for the Allied cause and opposed President Wilson's policies. He died in 1919 during the developing crisis over the Versailles treaty.

G. S. Mowry, *The Era of Theodore Roosevelt 1900–1912* (New York, 1958).
W. H. Harbaugh, *Power and Responsibility: the life and times of Theodore Roosevelt* (New York, 1961).   WJR

ROOSEVELT COROLLARY in the US, extension of the Monroe Doctrine by President Theodore Roosevelt, enunciated in his annual message to Congress (1904) and later in a special message to the Senate (March 1905). It was occasioned by the chronic financial situation of Santo Domingo, and by the risk of foreign intervention to enforce the republic to honour its foreign debts. Roosevelt declared that whenever, through misgovernment or impotence, a nation failed to maintain civilized standards and conduct towards other nations, intervention by some 'civilized nation' might ultimately be required. He asserted that in the Western hemis-

phere the US could not ignore this duty of intervention, although only as a last resort when such misconduct by a Western nation had 'invited foreign aggression to the detriment of the entire body of American nations'.

ROOT, ELIHU (1845–1937), US lawyer and politician, who assisted the defence in the trial of 'Boss' Tweed (1873), but whose reputation was untarnished by the scandals of his time. He was active in Republican state politics, and an adviser to Theodore Roosevelt from 1895, although he held no public office until President McKinley appointed him as secretary of war (1899). He served until 1904, and reorganized the military establishment to meet new demands created by the 'imperial' responsibilities assumed by the US after the Spanish–American War. He was also deeply involved in the problems of Cuba, Puerto Rico, and the Philippines. He returned to the cabinet as Roosevelt's secretary of state (1905), helped to improve US relations with the Latin American republics, and negotiated the Root–Takahira Agreement with Japan (1908). He was an internationalist in outlook, and favoured the resolution of disputes by arbitration. He worked constantly for world peace, was president of the Carnegie Endowment for International Peace (1910–25), and was awarded the Nobel Peace Prize (1912). As US senator from New York (1909–15) his support of William Howard Taft destroyed his long friendship with Roosevelt. He was critical of Woodrow Wilson's neutrality policies and favoured intervention in the First World War on the side of the Allied Powers. He supported membership of the League of Nations, with reservations, and advocated American membership of the Permanent Court of International Justice, which he helped to establish at The Hague (1920–1).

ROOT AND BRANCH PETITION (11 Dec. 1640), London petition introduced into the House of Commons demanding the abolition of episcopacy, 'root and branch'. It was kept in abeyance until Feb. 1641, when a debate took place in which episcopacy was both attacked and defended. In March a bill was passed in the Commons to exclude bishops from the House of Lords, but the Lords rejected it (June 1641). In the summer of 1641 another Commons bill was introduced to abolish bishops, deans, and chapters 'root and branch', but this bill was dropped, the church party proving too strong. Early in 1642 popular indignation was strong against the bishops and an act to remove them from the Lords received Charles I's reluctant assent (13 Feb.). Finally, in 1643 an ordinance of parliament declared bishops, deans, and chapters abolished, while another confiscated their lands.

ROOT–TAKAHIRA AGREEMENT, (1908), exchange of notes between the US secretary of state and the Japanese ambassador in Washington regarding the western Pacific. The two powers agreed to maintain the existing status quo in the Pacific, respect each other's territorial possessions, maintain the Open Door, and by peaceful means support the independence and integrity of China.

ROSAS, JUAN MANUEL DE (1793–1877), Argentine cattleowner and dictator (1829–52), who founded a lucrative *saladero* (an establishment preparing salt beef for export), and for a time controlled the salt monopoly. Like other landowners, he recruited a private army, which the weakness of central government made a necessity for maintaining order on the turbulent Indian frontier.

Rosas became governor and captain-general of Buenos Aires province (1820–32), and headed a military expedition which stabilized, through treaties, the southern Indian frontier. In 1835 the provincial legislature invested him with dictatorial authority, which remained the basis of his power until 1852. He called himself a '*federal*', or provincial autonomist, and persecuted his 'unitary' enemies. Already in 1831, in the Litoral League, he had initiated a series of interprovincial pacts with the interior *caudillos*, which made Argentina a de facto confederation. He pursued an aggressive policy which resulted in an inconclusive war with Bolivia (1837–8), a French blockade of the Plata estuary (1838–40), a protracted intervention in Uruguay in support of Oribe's '*blanco*' faction (1838–51), and a joint Franco-British blockade (1845–8). Within Argentina, discontent with Buenos Aires' commercial dominance was exploited by Justo Jose de Urquiza, *caudillo* of Entre Rios province. At Monte Caseros on 3 Feb. 1852 forces under his leadership united with Argentinian exiles and Uruguayan and Brazilian contingents and routed Rosas's army. Rosas himself fled to England.

His regime had depended on force and on terror aroused by the secret society known as the '*mazorca*'. It represented the triumph of creole nativism over the liberal tendencies of the previous administration headed by Rivadavia. Encouragement of immigration and education was abandoned and the Church regained much of its former power. In socio-economic terms the Rosas period saw the ascendancy of the great cattle estates over the agricultural yeoman society envisaged by the Rivadavians. Despite Rosas's ostensible federalism, the growing preponderance of Buenos Aires' pastoral economy made it inevitable that the city and province would dominate any subsequent national organization, whatever its form.

RCN

ROSCA, or 'the screw', derogatory term applied by some Bolivians to the tin-mining triumvirate of Simón I. Patiño, Mauricio Hochschild, and Carlos V. Aramayo, who controlled much of Bolivia's tin mining as a 'state within a state' until their holdings were nationalized in 1952. By extension, Bolivians sometimes use the term Rosca to refer to the elite by which the country was dominated before the 1952 MNR-led revolution.

ROSE, GEORGE (1744–1818), British politician, who was a devoted political organizer for the Younger Pitt, holding office as vice-president of the board of trade and joint paymaster-general in Pitt's second administration (1804–6). He wrote pamphlets on financial subjects. His diaries and correspondence (2 vols, 1860) provide useful historical source material.

ROSEBERY, ARCHIBALD PHILIP PRIMROSE, 5th Earl of (Scottish) (1847–1929), British politician, who held office in Gladstone's second, third, and fourth administrations. As foreign secretary (1892–4) he was responsible for Uganda being declared a British protectorate and revealed strong imperialist views which he had developed during a visit to Australia (1883–4). In a speech at Adelaide he had used the term 'British Commonwealth'. Rosebery's imperialism, though enlightened, made him disliked by some fellow-Liberals. Nevertheless, he succeeded Gladstone as prime minister (1894–5), though Sir William Harcourt seemed the more obvious choice. His brief ministry's only achievement was the introduction, by Harcourt, as chancellor of the exchequer, of the 1894 budget, which included death duties and new principles in taxation. Rosebery, as a substantial landowner, was personally opposed to his government's policy. This detachment from Liberal thought became more marked. He resigned from the leadership of the party (1896) a year after going out of office. During the Anglo-Boer War he was broadly in sympathy with the Conservative government's policy, and would not identify himself with later Liberal policy towards Ireland. In consequence, he never returned to office, and for the rest of his life lived largely in Scotland. His interest in the turf (during his brief premiership his horses twice won the Derby) lost him nonconformist allegiance. He published several books, including *Pitt* (1891), *Napoleon, the Last Phase* (1901), and *Chatham, Early Life and Connections* (1910).

R. R. James, *Rosebery* (London, 1963).   GMDH

ROSECRANS, WILLIAM STARKE (1819–98), US soldier, diplomat, and politician, who rose during the American Civil War to command the Army of the Cumberland (1862), but was relieved after his defeat at Chickamauga (1863). He was appointed minister to Mexico (1868–9), and served as a congressman from CA (1881–5).

ROSENBERG, ARTHUR (1893–1946), German writer and politician, and editor of the *Volkischer Beobachter* (1921). He became well known as the chief ideologist of Nazism, and in *The Myth of the Twentieth Century* purported to anatomize the political and philosophical decline of Europe under the influence of Christianity, the Jew, and the French Revolution. Although he was originally Hitler's personal adviser on foreign affairs and head of the NSDAP foreign policy committee in the Reichstag, his authority lessened after 1933, his imprecise ideological dreams failing to match Hitler's own firmly conceived *Realpolitik*. In 1934 he was given an ill-defined authority over Nazi ideological policy, but found himself increasingly excluded from the real centres of power in the regime, and when Neurath left the foreign ministry (1938) he was passed over in favour of Ribbentrop. Rosenberg was strongly opposed to the Nazi–Soviet pact (1939), but after the Russian invasion and his appointment as commissioner for the east (1941), he hoped for a new chance to see his own policies realized. But his authority remained minimal and was constantly challenged by Himmler and Koch. Eventually he later lost confidence in Hitler and became appalled by the brutality of Nazi rule in the east. He was tried as a war criminal at Nuremberg and sentenced to death.

ROSES, WARS OF THE, dynastic struggle which raged intermittently in England (1455–85). The wars take their name from the red and white roses adopted as emblems by the rival houses of Lancaster and York. The ineffectual personality and mental breakdown of Henry VI (1453–4) had caused a crisis in the government at a time of final defeat in France and rising discontent at home. Richard, Duke of York, head of a collateral branch of the Plantagenet dynasty, rebelled in 1455, claiming first the protectorship of the realm, then the Crown itself. In 1460, following the capture of Henry VI at Northampton, York was accepted as heir to the throne, but fell at Wakefield later in the year. His claims passed to his son, Edward, who entered London in Feb. 1461 and was accepted as king by the city. After inflicting a crushing defeat upon the Lancastrians at Towton, he was crowned as Edward IV in June. Lancastrian resistance collapsed with the recapture of Henry VI in 1465. In 1470, however, having quarrelled with his most powerful supporter, the Earl of Warwick, Edward was forced to flee the country, whereupon Warwick restored Henry VI. Returning in 1471, Edward defeated Warwick at Barnet and Queen Margaret, wife of Henry VI, at Tewkesbury, and following these final blows to Lancastrian hopes Henry VI was put to death in the Tower of London. The right of the House of York to the throne was not further challenged in Edward IV's lifetime, but the usurpation and tyranny of his brother, Richard III, rallied support to the last representative of the otherwise extinct house of Lancaster, Henry Tudor. In 1485 Henry landed in Wales, and at Bosworth defeated and killed Richard III in the final battle of the Roses. The marriage shortly after, of Henry VII to Elizabeth of York, daughter of Edward IV, brought the rivalry of the two houses to an end. Beneath the dynastic conflict lay the desire, particularly of the towns and merchant classes, for strong and stable government, and victory in each phase went ultimately to the side which seemed the better able to promise this. The world of virtually independent magnates and private armies perished at Bosworth; the Tudor dictatorship was acceptable because it offered an alternative to misgovernment and feudal strife.

BP

ROSETTA STONE, stone tablet, discovered near Rosetta, Egypt, in 1799, bearing an inscription in Greek, Egyptian hieroglyphs, and demotic script, of a decree in honour of

Pharaoh Ptolemy, dated 196 BC. With the aid of the Greek version, Thomas Young and Jean François Champollion made great advances in the decipherment of Egyptian scripts.

ROSICRUCIANISM, unorthodox secret brotherhood, allegedly called after its 15th-cent. German founder, Christian Rosenkreutz. It was first revealed in two anonymous pamphlets (1614, 1615), thought to be the work of the German theologian Johann Valentin Andrea. The 17th-cent. movement purported to be broadly Christian and Reformed, though different from the established Protestant Churches, and its members were involved in alchemy and secret rituals, their ideas being perhaps linked vaguely with the iatrochemistry of Paracelsus and the mysticism of Boehme. During the 18th cent. the vogue for secret societies led to a revival of the name and ideals of rosicrucianism, associated with such men as the notorious Count Cagliostro (1743–95), the Italian charlatan. Later offshoots in 19th-cent. Germany and England have no historical continuity with the original movement.

ROSKILDE, PEACE OF (1658), peace treaty signed between Sweden and Denmark-Norway, ending the first phase of their conflict in the Northern War. Charles X of Sweden had brought his armies across Pomerania and into Denmark from the south, the hard frost making it possible for them to cross the Belt and threaten Copenhagen (Jan. 1658). The Danes were therefore obliged to sue for peace and cede to Sweden half the customs dues from the Sound, the island of Bornholm, Halland, Blekinge, and Scania on the Scandinavian peninsula, and the Norwegian provinces of Båhus, Herjedal and Jaemteland, and Trondheim. A further clause in the treaty cancelled the alliance between Denmark and the United Provinces, closed the Baltic to the Dutch fleet, and promised joint Scandinavian action against the Dutch. However, Charles X, suspicious of Denmark's intention to fulfil this clause, blockaded Copenhagen and the war was re-opened (1658).

ROSS, BETSY (1752–1836), US folk heroine, who is supposed to have made the first stars and stripes flag and to have suggested a five-pointed star because it could be cut with one clip of the scissors. According to family legend, for which no contemporary evidence exists, George Washington, Robert Morris, and George Ross, her husband's step-brother, called at Betsy Ross's upholstery shop in Arch Street, Philadelphia, with a rough design for a flag with six-pointed stars. She was later asked to make a flag embodying her suggestion. Whatever the truth of the story, a five-pointed stars and stripes was later adopted by Congress as the national flag (14 June 1777).

ROSS, SIR GEORGE WILLIAM (1841–1914), Canadian politician. As minister of education for Ont. (1883–99), Ross was responsible for important changes in the educational system. He entered politics as a Liberal (1872), was prime minister of Ont. (1899–1905), and leader of the opposition in the Senate of Canada (1910–14).

ROSS, JOHN (1790–1866), American Indian chief, who was elected the first president of the Cherokee republic (4 July 1827) and led the progressive faction of the Cherokees until his death.

ROSSBACH, BATTLE OF (5 Nov. 1757), fought in Thuringia between 80,000 French and Austrians under Marshal Soubise and 30,000 Prussians led by Frederick II. The allied army attacked the Prussians occupying the heights of Rossbach, but were repulsed by the Prussian cavalry under Seidlitz and lost 11 generals as prisoners in the ensuing flight. This was the first major defeat which Prussian forces inflicted upon French ones in the Seven Years War.

ROSSI, ERNESTO (1897–   ), Italian journalist and historian, who organized an anti-fascist clandestine network, 'Giustizia e Liberta', directed 'Partito d'Azione' partisan movements, wrote studies on fascism, and founded the Radical Party (1955). He was imprisoned for his political activities (1931–43).

ROSSLYN, ALEXANDER WEDDERBURN, 1st Earl of (1733–1805), British politician, who was called to the bar (1757), became an MP (1762), and was solicitor-general (1771) in Lord North's government. He joined Fox briefly (1784), served the Younger Pitt as lord chancellor (1793–1801), though he opposed his Irish policy, and supported Addington from 1801.

ROSTOVSTSEV, YAKOV IVANOVICH (1803–60), Russian soldier and a close associate of Alexander II. He was a liberal member of commissions involved in the emancipation of the serfs and was responsible for much of the detailed work that was involved.

ROTATION OF CROPS in Britain. Changing the crop burden of land is a necessary part of retaining or restoring fertility, as well, in some cases, as a means of giving an opportunity for the land to be cleaned. It has become a general principle of good farming to limit the number of successive grain crops. Skilful use of varying crops can also take advantage of their different growing timetables. In a sense, the traditional two- or three-field system, mixing grain crops and fallow, was a primitive rotation, but it was one of relatively low efficiency which left the land idle for long stretches of time. In the late 16th and 17th cents experiments were made in many parts of England both in the introduction of new crops and the varying handling of old ones, and some of the resulting 'courses' or rotations increased productivity. The most widespread and flexible of these was the system of 'up and down' husbandry, in which land was laid down under a temporary lay of grass for several years and then broken up for successive cereal crops. Another which spread in the 18th cent. is inaccurately referred to as 'the Norfolk system'; this, one of several popular rotations in Norfolk which used the new crop of turnips, was a succession of turnips, barley, clover, and wheat. For land suitable for turnips and able to stand this degree of extraction this course was beneficial, but its dominance in books on 18th-cent. agriculture implies an oversimplification of the situation. Successful rotations have always had to be suited both to the soil and climate of a district and to the economic pressures and possibilities affecting the farm as a whole. In 19th-cent. Scotland much use was made of the system of temporary grass, in a form of farming similar to 'up and down', and in the period after 1873 British agriculture as a whole, turning belatedly away from wheat, developed new rotations as it increased the quantity of fodder crops from arable land.   RMM

ROTHERMERE, HAROLD SIDNEY HARMSWORTH, 1st Viscount (1868–1940), British newspaper owner and politician, who was the younger brother of Lord Northcliffe. He founded the *Daily Mirror* (1908) and on Northcliffe's death (1922) he acquired the *Daily Mail*. Though nominally a Liberal, he advocated Protection, and for a time supported Mosley's British Union of Fascists. He was secretary of state for air (1917) and, in the 1920s and 1930s, gave Hitler favourable treatment in his newspapers.

ROTHSCHILD, MEYER ANSELME, Baron de (1743–1812), Jewish financier, founder of the famous bank at Frankfurt, and of the line of Rothschild. His five sons followed him into banking and established branches of the family in Frankfurt, Vienna, London, Naples, and Paris.

ROTOS (Spanish, lit. 'broken ones'), term used in Chile to identify the rural, landless poor, but by extension it sometimes refers to the poorer classes in general.

ROTTEN BOROUGHS in Britain, towns which, although their population and importance had long since declined, retained an ancient right to send members to parliament, *eg*, Cornish villages that were formerly prosperous through tin mining; Sarum, which had become no more than a walled mound; and Dunwich, which had been eroded by the sea. Their representatives were nominated by rich landowners, and the Younger Pitt was defeated in a measure (1785) to disfranchise 35 rotten boroughs on payment of £1 million to the proprietors. The two members for Grampound, in Cornwall, were transferred to Yorkshire (1821), and the Reform Act of 1832 abolished the representation of 56 boroughs having fewer than 2000 inhabitants. Altogether 143 seats were redistributed among the counties and the new industrial cities.

ROTUMA, small south-west Pacific island, discovered by Edwards in the *Pandora* (1791), inhabited by some 4000 light-skinned, sophisticated Micro-Polynesians. Clan rivalries exacerbated by sectarian competition led to war in 1871 and 1878, culminating in a plea for British annexation. In 1881 the island became a dependency of Fiji, where many islanders still (1970) live and work.

ROTURIER, French legal term derived from the Latin *ruptura* or broken land, denoting one who was a commoner and enjoyed none of the rights of nobility, such as exemption from the *taille*.

ROUCOUX, BATTLE OF (1746), French victory near Liège over the imperialists in the War of the Austrian Succession. Maurice de Saxe defeated a mixed force under Charles of Lorraine, which included a British contingent under Ligonier, and afterwards occupied Brabant.

ROUEN, TREATY OF (1517), treaty representing the auld alliance between France and Scotland, negotiated by the Duke of Albany and providing for mutual assistance against England and a marriage between James V and a daughter of Francis I. Although ratified by the Scots in 1521 and by Francis in 1522, the marriage clause was not implemented until 1537, when James married Madeleine de Valois. The bride died five months later and James then took Mary de Guise (1538) as his wife.

ROUGES, Canadian members of the *parti démocratique*, who gathered in 1848 around L. J. Papineau. They wanted to repeal the Act of Union, to enlarge the franchise, and be annexed by the US, although these views were later modified by contact with other political groups.

ROUGH RIDERS in the US, popular name for a volunteer cavalry force of Western cowboys and adventurers recruited by Theodore Roosevelt to serve in the Spanish–American War (1898). The Rough Riders, led by Leonard Wood and Roosevelt himself, were officially named the First US Cavalry Volunteers. Though regarded as something of a comic turn by Roosevelt's critics they distinguished themselves at the battle of San Juan Hill.

ROUHER, EUGÈNE (1814–84), French Bonapartist lawyer and politician, who became minister of justice (1849–52). He held a variety of offices during the Second Empire, being particularly concerned with economic affairs, and earning the nickname of the 'Vice-Emperor'. On the fall of the empire, he fled abroad, but returned as a deputy for Corsica (1872–81) and was an active leader of the Bonapartist party until 1879.

ROUILLE, ANTOINE LOUIS, Comte de Jouy (1689–1761), French administrator, who began his career as a councillor in the *parlement* of Paris (1711) and then passed into government service (1725), holding a variety of posts, including those of minister of the navy (1749–54) and of foreign affairs (1754–1757). In the latter capacity he negotiated the first treaty of Versailles (1755).

ROUND TABLE CONFERENCE (1887) in Britain, unsuccessful attempt, on the initiative of Joseph Chamberlain, to reunite the Liberal Party which had split after Gladstone's conversion to Home Rule for Ireland (1885). The failure to restore harmony confirmed the drift of the Liberal Unionists, including Chamberlain's radicals, to the Conservative Party, leaving the way clear for the socialists to capture the working-class vote and eventually replace the Liberals as the political alternative to conservatism.

ROUND TABLE CONFERENCE AGREEMENT (INDONESIA) (Dec. 1949), ended Indonesia's revolution against Dutch rule. It had been preceded by the Linggadjati Agreement (March 1947) and the Renville Agreement (Jan. 1948), both of which involved territorial and political concessions by the Indonesian republic in response to Dutch attempts to re-establish control after the Second World War. 'Police actions' in July 1947 and Dec. 1948 extended the area under Netherlands military occupation. However, these Dutch successes were counteracted by rising impatience at home with the war, and by US and UN pressure for withdrawal, and inability to keep occupied areas free of guerillas. The Round Table Agreement provided for a federal United States of Indonesia, of which the revolutionary republic would be only one part, but the other states collapsed as soon as Dutch support was withdrawn in 1950. Other economic and political terms were abrogated during the 1950s by the Indonesians in connection with the West Irian disputes.

ROUND TABLE CONFERENCES (1930–2), constitutional discussions in London between representatives of Britain, British India, and the Indian states, at which the basis of the Government of India Act (1935) was formulated.

The idea of a conference was put forward by Lord Irwin as part of his declaration on Dominion status (1929), which was designed to meet Congress's demands. It effectively superseded the Simon Commission and was initially welcomed by Indian political opinion. The first session of the conference (12 Nov. 1930–19 Jan. 1931) had no Congress representative, however, because the Congress leaders found the terms of reference unsatisfactory. The Delhi pact between Gandhi and Irwin, which ended the first round of civil disobedience (March 1931), brought Gandhi, accompanied by M. M. Malaviya and Mrs Naidu, to the second session (7 Sept.–1 Dec. 1931), but the renewal of civil disobedience shortly after Gandhi's return to India meant that the Congress took no part in the final session (17 Nov.–24 Dec. 1932). This lack of Congress representation was a serious blow to the conference because it was impossible that an acceptable constitution could be devised in the absence of the strongest Indian party. None the less, the delegates did represent a wide cross-section of the other parties, British and Indian, and there can be no doubt that the discussions had a considerable influence on the shape of Indian constitutional thinking and practice.

While the work of the conference was carried over between the three sessions, each had its own character. The first was the most significant in terms of discussion of principles. The conference worked, in this session, through a series of sub-committees, of which those dealing with the provincial constitution, franchise, minorities, and federal structure, were the most important. There was a large measure of agreement in favour of provincial autonomy in the first sub-committee, and on franchise it was agreed that while adult suffrage was the goal all that could be expected at this time was a substantial increase in the existing electorate. The minorities sub-committee, which had to handle the difficult problem of communal representation, was unable to reach any agreement, but its discussions made it clear that separate electorates would be the basic demand of all minorities and the Depressed Classes as well. The most significant work was that done by the federal structure sub-committee, because the question of a federation between British and Indian India was the key to the work of the whole conference. The sub-committee drew up plans for a bicameral federal legislature and for an executive which would be responsible to the legislature for all matters except defence and foreign affairs, of which the governor-general would continue to be in charge. This did not satisfy the Liberals such as Sapru, but they were forced to accept it as the only means of achieving any progress at all towards responsible government at the centre.

The first session ended on a hopeful note, but this was silenced by the second session. The demands which Gandhi brought from the Congress cut through the plans agreed to earlier. The Congress insisted on full responsible government at the centre and the right of secession—which they saw as the essence of Dominion status, a subject which the British managers of the conference had contrived to sidetrack in the earlier discussions. Gandhi's membership of the federal structure committee at this session was therefore largely nugatory, for neither side had anything effective to offer. Nor was he in a position to make any headway on the minorities committee, for the Congress's refusal to contemplate separate communal representation cut across the stand taken by the whole array of minorities' representatives. The session thus made no progress at all on the basic questions and the prime minister therefore announced that if the Indians could agree amongst themselves on the communal issue the government would announce its own award.

The specialist committees of franchise and finance questions visited India and reported in the first half of 1932 and the cabinet was reluctant to bother with a third session. But the Indian Liberals insisted, and so, after the announcement of the Communal Award in Aug., a final session was convened. The franchise was now settled and the communal question was out of the way, but there was ominous disquiet about the possibility of any progress towards federation. The effects of earlier British manœuvres were now becoming apparent, for, to the dismay of the Liberals, it was now clear that by linking the creation of central responsible government to the formation of the federation the government had given the princes an effective veto on India's future constitutional development.

C. H. Philips and M. D. Wainwright, *The Partition of India. Policies and Perspectives 1935–47* (London, 1970).
R. Coupland, *The Indian Problem, 1833–1835* (Oxford, 1968).
                                                                                    PDR

ROUSSEAU, JEAN BAPTISTE (1670–1741), Parisian-born poet of the French classical school, known for his cantatas, who was banished from France in 1712 for writing satirical couplets attacking prominent men of letters and lived in Switzerland, Austria, and finally Brussels, where he died.

ROUSSEAU, JEAN JACQUES (1712–78), French philosopher and herald of revolution, who made his name as a writer in 1750 with a prize essay on the effects of the arts and sciences on morals for the academy of Dijon. In 1759 he published *La Nouvelle Héloïse* and in 1762 *Émile*, which has had a profound effect on educational theory in the 19th and 20th cents. In it Rousseau proposed a new system of education based on the child's natural development towards moral and intellectual self-reliance, and on the power of example.

His *Contrat Social* (1762) expounded the theory of the surrender of the individual's natural rights to the whole of society under the sovereign direction of the general will. His writings, which included his *Confessions*, offended government, Church, and contemporary thinkers. He left France to avoid arrest and went to Berne, but was ordered to leave and at the invitation of David Hume he went to England (1766). Quarrels resulting from his tendency to paranoia caused him to return to France in 1767. The instability of his temperament made him his own worst enemy and though he continued to write prolifically he remained on the whole unhappy and permanently suspicious of those around him. Rousseau was one of the most passionate and eloquent writers of the age. His attack on the evils of society and his faith in the perfectibility of man, extolled in many memorable phrases, had a revolutionary influence throughout Europe.

During the French Revolution his *Contrat Social* had a powerful effect on the Declaration of the Rights of Man and was a personal inspiration to the Revolutionary leaders, especially Robespierre. Rousseau's political ideas, in which various inconsistencies may be discerned, have been used to champion both democratic and fascist states. In his theory of social contract he argued that since each individual receives in exchange for his surrender of liberty an inseparable part of the whole sovereign power of the community, he is ultimately as free as he was before entering the contract. He said little about law, since laws imposed by the general will cannot logically be unjust, and the day-to-day details of translating the general will into practice were ignored. Disciples of Rousseau declared that all men were equal and naturally good; that no monarch had any title to sovereignty; that all existing governments strove to monopolize sovereign power unjustly; that existing representative governments, such as that of England, were useless alternatives to his ideal city-state, since the English people were only free at the time of a general election. In England Rousseau's writings affected the Romantics and all later democratic reformers, though they shunned the ruthless application of his doctrines, such as the French Revolutionaries attempted.   JRA

ROUSSILLON, Catalan county of Rossello, situated in the north-east corner of that principality, first civilized by the Greeks and then the Romans, then occupied by the Visigoths and later part of Catalonia from the 9th cent. Roussillon was annexed by King Louis XI of France in 1463, then restored by Charles VIII to Ferdinand of Aragon by the treaty of Barcelona (1493). It was overrun by the French in the Thirty Years War (1639–42) and since the peace of the Pyrenees (1659) has been recognized permanently as a part of France.

ROUTHIER, SIR ADOLPHE-BASILE (1839–1920), Canadian lawyer. As a judge of the superior court of Que. he created a storm by his ruling (reversed by the Canadian Supreme Court) that clergy could guide their parishioners as they wished in political issues (1876). He later helped to organize the Ultramontane wing of the Canadian Conservative Party and wrote its manifesto.

ROUTIÉRS, in France, mercenary troops employed during the Hundred Years War. The name was especially used for bands of these men who were out of employment, when they ravaged the countryside on their own account. The plundering by mercenaries triggered off the peasant uprising north of Paris in 1358 (the *Jacquerie*). After the conclusion of the Anglo-French peace at Brétigny, whole armies of *routiérs* were unleashed, one of them even trying to hold the pope to ransom at Avignon. The prolonged war between France and England from 1415 to 1444 again produced huge bands of *routiérs*. King Charles VII tried to disperse them by incorporating the better soldiers into his newly organized permanent regular army, while others were given an amnesty and were ultimately disbanded.

ROUVIER, PIERRE MAURICE (1842–1911), French lawyer and financial expert, and politician, who served as a deputy (1871–1903) and held the ministries of commerce and finance on several occasions. He was prime minister in 1887, 1892, and 1905–6. In his third period of office he abandoned his policy of a Franco-German rapprochement because of Germany's policy in Morocco.

ROWELL, SIR SYDNEY FAIRBAIRN (1894–   ), Australian soldier, who commanded Australian forces in New Guinea in 1942 during the Second World War and subsequently served in the Middle East and Britain. He was chief of the Australian general staff (1950–4) and chairman of the Commonwealth Aircraft Corporation (1957–68).

ROWELL–SIROIS REPORT (1940), of a Royal Commission established (1937) to enquire into Canada's economic situation. The commission, under N. W. Rowell until his resignation (1938), and subsequently under J. N. Sirois, analysed the inequalities between geographical regions, and recommended a rearrangement of federal duties and responsibilities. Opposition from Ont., Que., and BC, prevented implementation of the report.

ROWLATT BILLS (1919) in India, legislation based on the report of Mr Justice Rowlatt's Sedition Committee (1918) appointed by the government of India. The committee, convinced of the serious threat of revolution, recommended the perpetuation of powers taken under the Defence of India Act (1915). The suggested legislation gave the government extraordinary peacetime powers to prosecute revolutionaries and to prevent revolutionary conspiracy. The normal legal procedure was to be modified with regard to trial, committal, and evidence. The government would retain powers to restrict the movement, residence, and activities of suspected persons and to search, arrest, and detain them. The substance of the recommendations was incorporated in two bills presented to the Imperial Legislative Council (Feb. 1919). They aroused a storm of protest and after being passed against the united votes of the Indian non-official members, one bill was enacted (21 March) as the Anarchical and Revolutionary Crimes Act (1919). As he had threatened to do during their passage through the Legislative Council, Gandhi organized a nation-wide *satyagraha* campaign against the act, which ended in the Amritsar massacre (April 1919). The act was never, in fact, used and it was eventually repealed by the new Legislative Assembly.

ROWNTREE, SEEBOHM (1871–1954), British manufacturer and philanthropist, who was a son of the York Quaker chocolate manufacturer and reformer, Joseph Rowntree. He was chairman (1925–41) of the family firm and his main social work was devoted to the study and alleviation of poverty. Organizations to which he devoted considerable time were the Nuffield Trust for Special Areas, the Outward Bound Trust, and the War on Want committee. His publications included *Poverty, a Study of Town Life* (1901); *Betting and Gambling, a National Evil*; *Land and Labour*; *The Human Factor in Business*; and *Poverty and the Welfare State*.

ROWTON HEATH, BATTLE OF (24 Sept. 1645), Parliamentary victory over the Royalists in the English Civil Wars. The Royalist cavalry under Sir Marmaduke Langdale, which was defending Chester, was attacked by Col. Poyntz's force, which on receiving infantry support drove the former from the field.

ROXAS, MANUEL (1892–1948), Filipino politician, last president of the Philippine Commonwealth, and first president of the Philippine republic inaugurated on July 4, 1946. In 1919 he was elected governor of Capiz and in 1922 representative of its first district in the Philippine Legislature. In the same year, as a protégé of Quezon and following the first contest between Quezon and Osmena for political leadership, Roxas became the speaker of the House of Representatives. He thus emerged as the third leading politician on the national scene. In 1941, Quezon sent his two rivals, Roxas and Osmena, on a mission to the US, the 'Osrox Mission', which resulted in the passage of the first Philippine Independence Act. Quezon objected to it, however, and the Philippine Legislature rejected it, but not without dividing the Nacionalista Party members into 'Antis', led by Quezon, and 'Ros', led by Osmena, and causing Roxas to be ousted from the speakership (1933). Having regained Quezon's trust after the coalition of the party's two wings in 1935, Roxas became Gen. MacArthur's aide and liaison officer between the Philippine Commonwealth and the US armed forces in the Far East. He held a number of government positions, including the office of the secretary of finance.

During the Japanese occupation of the Philippines, Quezon delegated practically all his powers to Roxas. As head of an espionage centre in Manila, Roxas continued to communicate with MacArthur, for which service he was exonerated from the charge of collaboration when the US army returned to the Philippines in 1946. Roxas won the presidency from Osmena in the April 1946 election. RBS

ROY, MANABENDRA NATH (1887–1954), Indian revolutionary leader, whose real name was Narendra Nath Bhattacharya. He was involved in revolutionary activities in Bengal until 1915, when he went to the US, where he changed his name, and then went to Mexico. There he became involved in communist activities and later associated with communist circles in Europe and the USSR. From the second congress of the Comintern (1920), until his expulsion in 1929, he played a significant part in the formulation of Comintern strategy in colonial areas, although he was often at variance with prevailing doctrines and his lack of success when sent to China (1927) led to his downfall. Throughout the 1920s he worked for the establishment of a communist party in India, sending emissaries there and writing constantly in Comintern periodicals and in his own paper, *Vanguard* (later called *Masses of India*). He was charged in the Cawnpore Conspiracy Case (1924), in his absence, and was eventually sentenced to six years imprisonment after his return to India in 1930. On his release in 1936, he tried to move into the Congress from his base in Dehra Dun, but had to resign in 1940 following disagreements over organizational matters and Congress policy on the war. Later, he promoted a new philosophy of 'Radical Humanism' and a new and unsuccessful Radical Democratic Party.

ROY, RAM MOHAN (1774–1833), Indian scholar and social and religious reformer, who was one of the first Indians to be influenced by the humanitarian spirit of western culture. He translated the *Vedanta* into Bengali and the *Upanishads* into Bengali and English. In these translations and other publications he praised the monotheistic doctrines of the *Upanishads* and protested against idolatry. In 1820 he published in Sanskrit and Bengali the *Precepts of Jesus*, in which he denied the divinity of Christ. This led to a bitter controversy with the Baptist missionaries at Serampore. At the same time he welcomed the humanitarian message of Christianity. In 1828 he founded the Brahmo Samaj, a theistic organization, 'for the worship and adoration of the Eternal, Unsearchable Immutable Being, who is the Author and Preserver of the Universe'. He claimed that his monotheistic form of worship could be followed by Hindus, Muslims, and Christians. He believed in the unity of God, discarded the worship of images, and rejected the divinity of Christ, but accepted his ethical teachings. He was not only a religious reformer but was opposed to all social evils, such as the caste system. He championed the cause of the emancipation of women and played a prominent part, with Bentinck, in the abolition of *suttee* (the burning of Hindu widows on the funeral pyres of their husbands). He also advocated the remarriage of widows. He was opposed to polygamy, Kulinism, child-marriage, human sacrifice, and infanticide. To vindicate his views he made use of the press and was one of the pioneers of Bengali journalism. As a politician he protested against the miserable condition of the peasantry and the economic drain from India to England.

Towards the end of his life he went to Britain to represent the grievances of the titular Mughal Emperor of Delhi, Akbar II. He was well received both there and in France.

N. S. Bose, *The Indian Awakening in Bengal* (Calcutta, 1960). CCD

ROYAL AFRICAN COMPANY, English trading company, founded in 1672 to succeed the Co. of Royal Adventurers (1661–72). Its shareholders included Charles II and the Duke of York. It acquired the former company's monopoly of

African trade, its West African forts and trading posts, and the right to supply slaves to the British West Indies. On being granted the further right to supply the Spaniards, it established depots at Barbados and Jamaica. The company maintained Gold Coast forts at Cape Coast Castle, the company's African headquarters, Kormantine, Winneba, and Accra. The company's fort on Bence Island, Sierra Leone, abandoned (1728), was subsequently restored by independent traders, whose claim to it was upheld. On the Gambia river, the company maintained a chain of inland 'factories' manned by agents from whom the slaves purchased were collected periodically by craft sent up the river from Fort James at its mouth. Though the company handled slaves principally, it also purchased other African produce—particularly gold and ivory. Despite its monopoly, modified in 1690, and the right to confiscate the vessels of interlopers, the company was unable to prevent unlicensed traders from trespassing. West Indian planters complained that the company's deliveries of slaves were insufficient and their prices too high. In 1698 the slave trade was thrown open to all comers, subject only to the requirement that they should pay 10 per cent of the value of their cargoes as a contribution to maintenance of the company's forts and garrisons. The company's revenues were stimulated when, by the treaty of Utrecht (1713), Spain was compelled to transfer the Asiento, for supplying to her colonies 4800 slaves per year for 30 years. Until 1721 slaves were purchased exclusively from the Royal African Co. A new company charter was obtained by the Duke of Chandos (1720), but in 1750 this charter was withdrawn by Act of Parliament, the company's forts being thereafter maintained at public expense.

R. K. Davies, *The Royal African Company* (London, 1957).
RH

ROYAL CANADIAN MOUNTED POLICE,

semi-military police force formed in 1873 to police the NWT, where the infiltration of lawless American traders was causing Indian trouble, and to help to settle Indians on reserves and to protect new settlers. The Mounted Police maintained law and order by their mobility, and established posts in strategic places, expanding towards the Arctic and westward. The prefix Royal was granted (1904) in recognition of the services of the police, whose motto since 1873 has been *Maintiens le droit*. In 1920 the Dominion Police of other parts of Canada were merged with the newly designated Royal Canadian Mounted Police. Although a federal force, subject to the Canadian department of justice, the RCMP in the 1950s and 1960s began to perform the function of provincial police in most parts of Canada.

ROYAL COMMISSIONS

in Britain, committees set up by the governments of the day to investigate problems and recommend new lines of policy for legislation. Early in the 19th cent. this work had been mainly carried out by Select Committees of the House of Commons. Royal Commissions had been used infrequently as in the Commission on the Common Law (1829), but in the 1830s the Whigs made much greater use of them. They included not only MPs but also experts in political economy and administration. Opinion outside the House of Commons was sounded and put to use. By 1849 more than 100 Royal Commissions had been set up and almost every major piece of social legislation brought in between 1832 and 1867 followed this type of thorough initial investigation.

The prototype was the Royal Commission for enquiring into the Administration and Practical Operation of the Poor Laws, set up by the prime minister, Grey, three months before the Reform Bill was finally passed (1832). The commission contained barristers, politicians, bishops, and economists. Its report (1834) showed the marked Benthamite influence of Edwin Chadwick, and of the Benthamites who conducted the local investigations in the provinces. It was issued in Feb. 1834, and in April Lord Althorp introduced the Poor Law Amendment Bill and in Aug. it passed into law. The way was paved for the age of the Blue Books, as the Commissions' Reports were called, which not only kept MPs informed, but were sometimes best-sellers. This use of Benthamite experts in the 1830s shaped a new climate of opinion favourable to social reform later in the century.

Notable Royal Commissions in the 1830s included that on Judicial Reform (1833), Municipal Reform (1835), and Church Reform (1835), each recommending a Benthamite approach towards greater efficiency and standardizing of procedures. Royal Commissions could also be used by governments as a delaying tactic for the consideration of difficult or embarrassing problems.

Poor law policy was wide enough to touch many other social questions and led to the effective national control of public health. The detailed examination of statistics, variation on local death rates, and the vigilance of local inspectors and professional men was a spur to action. Chadwick's masterpiece, the famous Report on the Sanitary Condition of the Labouring Classes (1842), with its scandalous revelations, led immediately to the appointment of the Royal Commission on the Health of Towns, which published its report in 1845, this being followed by the Public Health Act (1848) setting up a central Board of Health of three members, of whom Chadwick was one, and Local Boards on the lines of the poor law system. Thus by the end of the century Royal Commissions had become firmly established procedures for examining problems prior to legislation and were frequently used later, as on the Commission on Trades Unions (1867) and on the Poor Law and Relief of Distress (1909), which with its famous Minority Report did not result in legislation until 1929.
JRA

ROYAL FIFTH (QUINTO),

royalty collected by the Spanish Crown upon American production of precious stones, mercury, gold, and (especially) silver. The *quinto* was the most lucrative source of royal revenue in America and lasted, with certain exceptions, until the 18th cent., when it was cut to one-tenth.

ROYAL INSTITUTION

in London was founded (1799) by, among others, Sir Joseph Banks and Henry Cavendish, and financed by private subscription. Its purpose was the diffusion of knowledge by lectures in the field of applied science.

ROYAL MARRIAGES ACT

(1772), in Britain, stated that marriages of members of the royal family should not be valid unless they had the consent of the king in council or, if the parties were over 25, they had given 12 months' notice to the privy council. The act was occasioned by George III's fear of the effect on the dignity of the royal family of the marriages of two of his brothers, the Duke of Gloucester having married the illegitimate Lady Waldegrave, and the Duke of Cumberland a widow, Mrs Horton.

ROYAL NIGER COMPANY,

formerly the United African Co., formed in 1879 by George Goldie to obtain a monopoly of trade on the Niger; it was renamed (1886) when it secured political power through a royal charter. It established British politico-economic influence so firmly on the Niger that the area became part of the British empire.

ROYAL PARDON,

one of the ancient prerogatives of the English Crown which rested on longstanding custom and precedent. It was exercised personally and without restraint by sovereigns until the Act of Settlement (1701) rendered illegal the right to pardon under the Great Seal those facing impeachment by the Commons for political offences. The right to pardon judicial offenders remained, though it is now (1970) vested in the home secretary acting in the sovereign's name.

ROYAL PATRONAGE OF THE INDIES,

wide powers exercised by the Spanish Crown over the Latin American

Church, acquired most notably by papal bulls of 1501 and 1508. In return for making itself responsible for the maintenance of the Church and the conversion of the Indians, the Crown was given control over the administration of ecclesiastical taxation and nominated not only high Church dignitaries but the parish clergy as well. Papal bulls and decisions of church councils could not be published without royal approval, and the Crown further authorized the erection of all ecclesiastical institutions and set the limits of dioceses. In short, the Spanish king was literally the secular head of the American Church, a privilege which the Spanish Bourbons in the 18th cent., under the influence of French Gallicanism, claimed by virtue, not of papal concession, but of their own sovereignty.

ROYAL SOCIETY, THE, in London, for the improving of natural knowledge. A nucleus of members was in existence before its foundation in 1660. The 'Invisible College' had been formed (*c.* 1645) to discuss the new or experimental philosophy. Gresham College was the regular meeting place for the society, and Sir Robert Moray (or Murray) was its first president. In 1661 King Charles II became a member, and in 1662 the society was incorporated as the 'Royal Society'. The council of the Royal Society met for the first time in 1663, and in 1665 its first publication, *Philosophical Transactions*—the world's first regular scientific publication—appeared under the auspices of Henry Oldenburg, the society's first secretary. Since Charles II's reign the society has advised governments on scientific problems. Most distinguished British scientists have been elected as fellows.

ROYAL VETO, ancient prerogative of English monarchs, resting on custom and precedent, to quash parliamentary legislation. The right was much used by Queen Elizabeth I (*reg.* 1558–1603), *eg*, the 1571 bill to compel attendance once a year at the Anglican communion, and was asserted by her, *eg*, 27 Feb. 1593, when she was dealing with a recalcitrant Commons, though often the mere intimation of the monarch's displeasure was sufficient to render the veto unnecessary. The last occasion upon which it was used was in Feb. 1708, when Anne vetoed the Scottish Militia Bill.

ROYALISTS in England, those who supported and fought for King Charles I in the English Civil War. Royalists were the combination of the large minority of the Country party which deserted the Country leaders over the Grand Remonstrance (Nov. 1642), and the remnants of the Court party which had remained faithful to the king in 1640–2 and formed the old royalists. The Royalists were socially indistinguishable from the Parliamentarians, there being no significant difference in status, wealth, or occupation. The Royalist MPs however tended to originate more frequently from families with a record of parliamentary service.

ROYCE, JOSIAH (1855–1916), US philosopher, whose philosophy was a combination of rationalist metaphysics and empiricism, arising from a religious view of reality, which he welded into a comprehensive idealist theory. His moral philosophy centred on the notion of loyalty which he held to be the highest good, and he developed new and significant interpretations of Christianity.

ROYER-COLLARD, PIERRE PAUL (1763–1845), French lawyer and leader of the Doctrinaire school of politicians and philosophers after 1815. After the Revolution (1789) he came under suspicion and was ejected from the Commune (1792) and the *Conseil des Cinq Cents* (1797). He corresponded (1798–1803) with Louis XVIII, who later used him to control the press and education in the first Restoration (1814). He played a leading role as deputy and theorist of liberal monarchy until he was dismissed from the government by the Ultras (1820). He took part in the opposition to Charles X, and remained a deputy until 1842, but never regained his political influence. Many academics and poli-

ticians were influenced by his political and psychological theories.

ROZWI, Shona clan in modern Rhodesia which, under the leadership of the *changamires* or Rozwi dynasty, challenged the supremacy of Mwenemutapa and established (*c.* 1500) the second major centralized empire of the Shona peoples. The Rozwi political system was reinforced by a religious structure based on spirit mediums, the most powerful of whom probably lived at Great Zimbabwe. In the late 17th cent. the Rozwi effectively challenged the declining power of Mwenemutapa, and the rising power of the Portuguese, to create an empire whose political unity survived until the Ndebele raids of the 1830s, and whose religious influence remained strong when British colonial occupation took place.

RTISHCHEV, FEDOR MIKHAILOVICH (1625–73), Russian courtier of wealthy noble stock, close friend and trusted adviser of Tsar Alexis Romanov from his childhood days, who was a zealous champion of scholarship, education, and Western culture. He built the Andreevsky monastery near Moscow, where 30 learned monks from Ukrainian monasteries were installed to translate foreign books into Russian and to teach Greek, Latin, and Slavonic studies. Later, when clerical scholars from Moscow joined the community, it became a free academy of learning, to which government officials were encouraged to go, while Rtishchev himself studied Greek there. In addition to his educational interests, he served Alexis as a government administrator and diplomat, and was known as a wholehearted philanthropist, who fought for social justice and was responsible for government schemes and private acts of generosity to help the poor, sick, infirm, old, and enslaved.

RUBENS, SIR PETER PAUL (1577–1640), Flemish-born Baroque painter, architect, diplomat, and decorator. He was appointed court painter to the Spanish Governors of the Netherlands and set up a large studio with numerous assistants, from which came forth historical and religious allegories, portraits, and landscapes. These were often executed by assistants from sketches by Rubens, who provided the finishing touches. In England in 1629 he was knighted by Charles I, who commissioned a ceiling depicting the allegorical apotheosis of James I for Inigo Jones's Banqueting House in Whitehall. It remains the only ceiling by Rubens to survive, in beautiful juxtaposition to the classic serenity of the building. The vitality and imagination of Rubens's work, as well as his rich sense of colour, influenced generations of European artists from Watteau to Delacroix and Renoir.

RUBRUCK, GUILLAUME DE (*fl.* 13th cent.), Franciscan friar sent by King Louis IX of France on a mission to the Mongol Khan Mongu at Karakorum to secure his support against the Syrian Muslims (1253–4). Rubruck wrote a detailed and vivid narrative of his adventures. After his return he met the English scholar Roger Bacon and influenced Bacon's ideas.

RUDINI, ANTONIO DI, Marquis (1839–1908), Italian politician and leader of the right wing in Italy after 1886. He was prime minister twice (1891–2, 1896–8), each time in succession to Crispi. His main achievement in each ministry was to relieve international tension and restore some of the damage inflicted on Italy's reputation by Crispi. He renewed the Triple Alliance (1891), and following Italy's disastrous defeat at Adowa (1896) secured Eritrea, but indulged in no further colonial adventures. This policy improved relations with Britain, but Rudini was unable to overcome the hostility of France. Nor could he devise a remedy for Italy's acute financial difficulties and explosive social situation. By resorting to repressive measures and finally martial law he hastened the spread of anarchy. His coalition broke up after the death of Cavalotti.

RUDOLPH IV (d. 1365), Duke of Austria (*reg.* 1358–65), who was one of the most remarkable medieval rulers of Austria. In

1363 he added Tyrol with its rich silver mines to the Habsburg dominions. He did much for Vienna, his capital, being responsible for the building of the new cathedral of St Stephen's and, in 1365, founded a university there, the second oldest in Germany. He was the first Habsburg to use the title of archduke, his claim to the title being based on a forged document (*privilegium maius*) purporting to be a Roman imperial decree conferring on Austrian rulers special rights in the empire.

RUDOLPH II (1552–1612), Emperor (*reg.* 1576–1612), son of the Emperor Maximilian and the Infanta Maria, Charles V's daughter. He was elected King of Hungary (1572), and of Bohemia (1575). Then chosen as emperor in succession to his father (1576). He was educated by the Jesuits at Philip II's court in Spain, abandoned his father's tolerant outlook, and remained a devout Catholic sympathetic to the Counter-Reformation. Eventually he became a recluse and buried himself in the Hradschin palace in Prague, surrounded by his art collection and various astrologers and alchemists, who included Tycho Brahe and Johann Kepler. His interest in his political responsibilities diminished, he delayed interfering in the Cologne War (1583–9), and after 1594 he ceased to attend the Reichstag. His projected suppression of Protestantism in Hungary provoked the revolt of Stephen Bocskai (1604–6), after which he was forced to surrender Austria, Hungary, and Moravia to his brother Matthias's control (1608). In 1609 he was likewise compelled to grant the Letter of Majesty to his Bohemian subjects guaranteeing religious toleration, and after a struggle for power surrendered his authority in Bohemia, Silesia, and Lusatia to Matthias (1611). His conclusion of the peace of Sitvatorok with Turkey (1606) was his only notable achievement. He was succeeded in the imperial title by Matthias.

RUDOLPH I (1218–91), German King (*reg.* 1273–91), and founder of the Habsburg dynasty. He had taken part (1267–8) in the invasion of Italy by Conradin, the last Hohenstaufen opponent of Charles of Anjou, King of Sicily. But in 1273 Pope Gregory X, alarmed by the growing power of Charles in Italy, was anxious to re-establish a more effective German kingship and Rudolph, as member of a strong faction in southern Germany, seemed a suitable counterweight to Charles. Rudolph promised to abandon all German royal claims in Italy and he concentrated on restoring internal peace and better order in Germany. His main objective was the creation of a powerful principality for his own dynasty. By defeating King Ottokar II of Bohemia in 1278 he acquired for the Habsburgs the duchies of Austria and Styria, which henceforth formed the core of Habsburg power until 1918.

RUEIL, TREATY OF (12 March 1649), truce between the French government and court and the *Frondeurs*, which ended the first phase of the revolt of the *Fronde*. Threatened by the possibility of Spanish invasion and the militant Paris mob, the regent, Anne of Austria, confirmed the royal declarations of May, July, and Oct. 1648, granting concessions to the nobles and the magistrates. The court, which had lived at Richelieu's favourite residence of Rueil since Sept. 1648, returned to Paris.

RUFFIN, EDMUND (1794–1865), US agriculturalist and essayist, who demonstrated that the application of marl could restore the exhausted soils of the VA tide-water region. He propounded his views in *An Essay on Calcareous Materials* (1832). In 1833 he founded and edited (1833–45) an agricultural journal, the *Farmer's Register*. After initial opposition, his methods were adopted by a number of large planters and contributed to the resurgence of agriculture in VA, NC, SC, and MD. Ruffin was an ardent defender of slavery, an early advocate of secession, and presented the secessionist case in an essay, *Anticipations of the Future* (1860). As a member of the Charleston Palmetto Guard he fired the first shot against Fort Sumter (1861). He committed suicide on learning of the Confederate surrender at Appomattox (1865).

RUGARUGA, native mercenaries, who became increasingly common in central and southern Tanzania during the 19th cent. In the turbulent years following the Ngoni invasions and the extension of the coastal slave trade, they were prepared to attach themselves to any leader who could provide regular and substantial loot. Though apparently unprincipled themselves, they sometimes assisted in the creation of states in the interior.

RUHINDA (*fl.* ? 15th cent.), eponymous ancestral founder of the Hinda ruling clan in southern Uganda, and, by tradition, first King of Ankole and then of Karagwe.

RUIZ, SIMON (1525–97), Spanish merchant banker of the Castilian town of Medina del Campo, the prototype of the 16th-cent. businessman. He began his career as an importer of Breton linens and built up sufficient capital to make a fortune by speculating on the exchange. His business became an international concern, communicating with merchants in Lisbon, Antwerp, Lyons, and Genoa. From 1576 he lent money to Philip II to finance the Spanish army in Flanders, and he gave generously to charity, founding a hospital in his native town.

RUIZ CORTINES, ADOLFO (1891–), Mexican politician and president of Mexico (1952–8). From being governor of Veracruz (1944), he rose to be minister of the interior (1948), primarily through his friendship with Miguel Alemán. Under his presidency the honesty and efficiency of the bureaucracy showed signs of improvement.

RUKN AL-DAWLA, Abu Ali al-Hasan (d. AD 976), second of three brothers (Imad al-Dawla, Rukn al-Dawla, Mu'izz al-Dawla) who established the Buyid regime in Persia, Al-Jazira, and Iraq. By 943 he had gained control of the Jibal area in Persia (the ancient Media, later to be known as Iraq al-'Ajemi, Persian Iraq, and embracing Hamadhan, Al-Rayy and Isfahan). His position, in the face of continuing pressure from the Ziyarids and the Samanids, remained uncertain till *c.* 955–6.

RUM ('Rome')—expression used amongst the Seljuk Turks to denote at first the region of Sivas and Kayseri. It came thereafter to have a wider meaning, ie, to indicate the lands which had once constituted Byzantine Asia Minor, the lands of the 'Rhomaioi' or Romans (cf. the Seljuk Sultanate of Rum). At a later time the Ottoman beg was to become a sultan—the 'Sultan al-Rum'. The word is also to be found in the expression Rum-ili (the land of Rum), a designation in use amongst the Ottoman Turks to denote their territories in the Balkans. The peace of Berlin (1878) established the autonomous province of Rumelia, its capital being Plovdiv (Philippopolis), which was united with Bulgaria in 1885.

RUM ROW, chain of ships, many from the West Indies, which smuggled liquor into the US during the Prohibition era (1918–33).

RUMANIA, UNION OF PRINCIPALITIES (1859), occurred when both Moldavia and Wallachia chose the same governor, Col. Alexander Couza. The principalities, although under Turkish suzerainty, had enjoyed Russian protection since the treaty of Kuchuk-Kainardji (1770). Their occupation by Russia (1853) had been the subject of an ultimatum which was one of the causes of the Crimean War. By the Parish treaty (1856) Europe, not Russia, became the guarantor of their liberties of worship, legislation, and commerce. Rumanians expected this to lead to union and autonomy, and were supported by Napoleon III. After the election of Prince Cuza, the Powers recognized the union (1861).

RUMBOLD, SIR GEORGE MONTAGUE (1869–1941), British diplomat, whose career embraced experience in Tokyo, Teheran, Munich, and Madrid before 1914. Thereafter he served in Switzerland, Poland, and as ambassador to Turkey (1920–4). Here, with Gen. Harington, he exercised great restraint during the 'Chanak Incident'. After the Madrid embassy his last post was in Berlin (1928–33). His warnings against the rise of Nazism were frequent from 1930, but never totally pessimistic until Hitler achieved power early in 1933. Rumbold's warnings, distinguished by their accuracy and reasonableness, strengthened the case of the 'anti-appeasers' who gathered round Vansittart throughout the 1930s.

RUMFORD, BENJAMIN THOMPSON, Count (1753–1814), American scientist, who was a loyalist in the American War of Independence and moved to Britain, where his scientific research led to his election to a fellowship of the Royal Society (1779). He was adviser to the Elector of Bavaria (1783–95) and was created a Count of the Holy Roman empire in 1791. He is best known for showing the connection between mechanical energy and heat and his contribution to the establishment of the law of conservation of energy.

RUMP PARLIAMENT (1648–53, 1659–60) in England, residual members of the Long Parliament after the secession of the Royalist MPs and the expulsion of the Presbyterian MPs by the army in Pride's Purge (Dec. 1648). In June 1644 the Royalist MPs who had deserted were expelled and by-elections ordered. The MPs thus elected were known as 'Recruiters'. By 1653 less than 100 of the original 507 MPs were still on the rolls, and not all of these sat. During the Rump the representative character of the Long Parliament had gone and faction ruled. On 4 Jan. 1649 the Rump passed three resolutions: (*a*) the people were the ultimate residual of power; (*b*) the people had delegated this power to their chosen representatives; (*c*) legislation by the Commons alone, without king or lords, was legally valid. The Rump thereafter proceeded to try and execute King Charles I (30 Jan. 1649), abolish the House of Lords (19 March), and the monarchy (17 March), establish a council of state as the executive body, and declare England a Commonwealth (19 May). Because of its oligarchic nature, the Rump found it difficult to establish its authority in England. It retained the unpopular taxation of the war years, and failed to respond to any degree to the steady pressure from the army for social, political, and legal reforms. The Rump was particularly dilatory on the question of religion and abolition of tithes. After the army's victories at Dunbar (Sept. 1650) and Worcester (Sept. 1651) reforms were grudgingly approved, but the Rump's intention of maintaining itself in power soon became clear. The army petitioned that it should dissolve itself and institute elections (Aug. 1652). Cromwell, aware that the Rump was the only constitutional or legal authority left in England, refrained from taking action until he was forced to do so by the Rump. In April 1653 a bill was produced to make the tenure of sitting MPs perpetual. The Rump also proposed to dismiss Cromwell as commander-in-chief. On 20 April he therefore expelled the members and the Rump came to an end.

It was restored on the fall of the protectorate in May 1659. The rank and file of the army, backed by the junior officers, agitated for the return of the Rump during the last few months of Richard Cromwell's rule. The council of officers was forced to agree, and on 7 May the Rump was restored. During their enforced retirement the members had learnt nothing and they remained as obdurate as ever. Tension mounted between them and the army throughout the summer of 1659, and upon their refusal of the Derby Petition they were expelled by John Lambert (13 Oct.). Anarchy threatened England, and the army and republican leaders became discredited. Gen. Monck, the commander in Scotland, called for the restoration of the Rump, and it was finally restored by a bankrupt army on 26 Dec. 1659. It proved moribund and Monck, having marched into England, readmitted the MPs excluded by Pride in 1648 (21 Feb. 1660), swamping the old-guard republicans. The Long Parliament, as it now again became, dissolved itself and ordered a general election (16 March).

G. Davies, *The Early Stuarts* (Oxford, 1937).
J. P. Kenyon, *The Stuart Constitution* (Cambridge, 1966).
                                                          CJ

RUMPSTEAK CLUB in England, organization of Walpole's Whig opponents, sometimes called the Liberty Club, founded on 15 Jan. 1734. Its leading members were the Dukes of Bedford, Bolton, and Queensberry, and the Earls of Chesterfield and Marchmont and Viscount Carteret, and they met every Tuesday during parliamentary sessions to plan tactics.

RUNCIMAN OF DOXFORD, WALTER RUNCIMAN, 1st Viscount (1870–1949), British politician, who entered his father's shipping business, but soon turned to a political career. He became MP for Oldham in 1899, but lost his seat to Winston Churchill in 1900. He returned to parliament as MP for Dewsbury in 1902 and soon built up a reputation by forthright financial speeches. His first office was with the local government board, then in 1907 he became financial secretary to the treasury. A staunch Methodist, he yet won Anglican confidence at the board of education, to which he was appointed in 1908. Three years later he became president of the board of agriculture and fisheries, and in 1914 president of the board of trade, where he was in charge of shipping during the war. He showed considerable ability in economic warfare and in reviving the shipping industry. In 1916 he resigned from the government, with Asquith, and two years later lost his seat. He sat in the House of Commons for 13 years (1924–37) between the wars and briefly held office again as president of the board of trade.

In July 1938 the foreign secretary, Halifax, asked him to act as mediator in Prague between the Czech government and the Sudeten Germans, but he had little success, owing to Hitler's violently anti-Czech speeches, which only inflamed the situation. For a short period before the outbreak of the Second World War he became lord president of the council.

RUNDSTEDT, KARL RUDOLF GERD VON (1875–1953), German soldier, who joined the Prussian army in 1892. Both during and after the First World War he held staff appointments, and in 1932 became military commandant of Berlin. On the outbreak of the Second World War he commanded the army group south in the invasion of Poland. After serving with distinction against France, he became a field marshal (1940). In 1941 he commanded the army group south in the campaign against Russia, but was recalled owing to differences with Hitler over the conduct of operations. In 1942 he was appointed supreme commander in the west, but was replaced by Von Kluge in July 1944 after the Allied invasion. He was reinstated in Sept. but finally dismissed in March 1945 after the failure of the Ardennes offensive and in May he was captured by the Allies.

RUNES, ancient Germanic script, designed to be incised on wood, metal, or stone rather than written. Runes were used in Scandinavia from at least the 2nd cent. AD. The original number of runes was 24; this was reduced in Scandinavia by around 800 to 16, resulting in a system of some ambiguity. Judging from literary references, runes had strong pagan supernatural associations and did not present any serious rivalry to the Roman alphabet when this was introduced at the conversion to Christianity of the inhabitants of Scandinavia, though the runic script continued to be used at least until the 14th cent.

RUOTH (and variant forms), name used by the Luo people of Kenya for the chief who ruled over their traditional political unit, the *oganda*, of which there were about a dozen, each *ruoth* being advised by a council of elders. Its origins must be very old, since the same title in other forms occurs among peoples of the Luo language 'family' whose separation from a putative parent stock took place in a remote past: thus the word used for their king by the Shilluk of the Upper Nile (Republic of the Sudan) is *reth*. The *ruoth* of the Kenya Luo tended to acquire new political and even military powers during the troubled decades of the mid-19th cent., though their earlier functions may have been mainly ritual. This was a development of stronger chiefship that occurred among many East African peoples of that period.

RUPERT, Prince (1619–82), English soldier, a nephew of King Charles I, and Royalist cavalry commander in the English Civil War, often called Rupert of the Rhine or of the Palatinate. He was the son of King Frederick V Bohemia, the elector palatine, and of Elizabeth, daughter of James I of England. After his father had been expelled from Bohemia he settled with his family in the United Provinces. He joined Charles I in 1642 and was appointed general of the horse, soon building up a reputation as a skilful and courageous commander. His success in battle was unbroken till Marston Moor (July 1644). In Nov. 1644 he was appointed general of the king's army. Dissension grew between him and Lord Digby and prepared the way for Rupert's dismissal by Charles after he had been forced to surrender Bristol to Sir Thomas Fairfax (Sept. 1645). Being determined to defend his conduct over the surrender of Bristol, Rupert saw Charles in Oct. at Newark, where a Council of War acquitted him of charges of infidelity and cowardice. Convinced that the king's cause was lost after Naseby (June 1645), he left the country in June 1646, but was later reconciled with Charles and given the command of the Royalist fleet. However, by 1653 he had only one ship left. At the Restoration in 1660 he was given an active naval command in the Second Anglo–Dutch War. Though he did not meddle in politics, in his last years he was attracted by Shaftesbury's anti-Catholic policy.

RUPERT'S LAND, Canadian district which originally included Ungava, the Red River valley, the areas around Hudson and James Bays, and land south of the north branch of the Saskatchewan. These lands were granted to the Hudson's Bay Co. (1670), and named in honour of Prince Rupert, first governor of the company. Rupert's Land was sold to Canada (1869) for £300,000 and one-twentieth of the arable land. From Rupert's Land the province of Man. was created (1870), and the rest of the area absorbed into the NWT.

RURALES, Mexican rural police force used effectively by the dictator Porfirio Díaz (1876–80, 1884–1911) to establish and maintain peace in the countryside and to assure the security of the large land-holders.

RURIK, HOUSE OF, ruling dynasty of the first Russian state, founded by the Varanger prince Rurik, a Norse adventurer and pirate, who ruled South Jutland and Friesland and settled in Novgorod with his followers (*c.* 862), as recorded in the Russian Chronicle. His kinsman Oleg succeeded him and moved south to Kiev, and from then until the dynasty's extinction (1598) all the princes of the Russian principalities were descendants of Rurik, while the leading *boyar* families were descended from collateral relatives. The last of the direct line was the feeble-minded son of Ivan the Terrible, Fedor I (*reg.* 1584–98), who died without heir.

RUSE, JAMES (1760–1837), Australian 'emancipist' farmer in the NSW penal settlement. He was the first ex-convict to receive a land grant at Parramatta in conformity with Gov. Arthur Phillip's policy of making their first Australian settlement self-supporting.

RUSH, BENJAMIN (1745–1813), American physician, patriot, and social reformer, who helped to establish a society for the abolition of slavery (1774), was a delegate to the Continental Congress (1776), and a signatory of the Declaration of Independence. He played a prominent part in securing PA's ratification of the Federal Constitution (1787–8). His medical practice made him acutely conscious of the problems of poverty, and he established in Philadelphia the first free dispensary in America (1786). He advocated temperance, and supported educational and prison reform. William Cobbett's strictures on him in *The Rush Light* (1800) resulted from his excessive resort to bleeding and purges during the yellow fever epidemic (1793), but Rush saw the association between insanitary conditions and the spread of the disease. He also did pioneering work in the fields of psychiatry and experimental physiology.

RUSH, RICHARD (1780–1859), US lawyer, politician, and diplomat, son of Benjamin Rush. He was a Republican and enjoyed national office continuously (1811–29) as comptroller of the treasury (1811–14), attorney-general (1814–17), secretary of state (1817), minister to Britain (1817–25), and secretary of the treasury (1825–9). He negotiated important conventions with Britain (1817–18), which limited armaments on the Great Lakes, fixed the 49th parallel as the northwestern boundary between the Great Lakes and the Rockies, and arranged the joint occupation of OR which lasted for 28 years. After being defeated as the National Republicans' vice-presidential candidate in 1828, he ceased to hold office, though his public services continued. It was he who secured (1836–8) the Smithson bequest to the US, which was used to establish the Smithsonian Institution. After 1832 Rush favoured the Democrats, and under President Polk became US minister to France (1847–9).

RUSH–BAGGOT AGREEMENT (1817), Anglo-American treaty to limit armaments on the Great Lakes. It was drawn up by the American secretary of state, Richard Rush, and the British minister in Washington, Sir Charles Baggot. Both countries agreed to limit their warships to 100 tons, one each on Lakes Champlain and Ontario and two on the Upper Lakes, above the Niagara Falls. Castlereagh, the British foreign secretary, and John Quincy Adams and James Monroe on the American side supported the agreement, and in order that it might be binding on later administrations, and to allay British fears, the pact was ratified unanimously by the US Senate on 16 April 1818. The Rush–Baggot Agreement is considered a model of effective disarmament and has remained in force since 1817.

RUSK, DEAN (1909–   ), US politician, who held various posts in the war and state departments (1946–52), was president of the Rockefeller Foundation (1952–60), and became secretary of state (1961). He continued to serve under President Johnson and became particularly identified with US policy in Viet-nam.

RUSKIN, JOHN (1819–1900), British art critic and writer on social problems. Beginning as a defender of J. M. W. Turner and the pre-Raphaelites, in vol. I of *Modern Painters* (1834), he developed, in later volumes (1846–60) and in *Seven Lamps of Architecture* (1849) and *Stones of Venice* (1851–3), his theory of the connection between art and social and moral life. In *Political Economy of Art* (1857), he attacked contemporary art and society and thence was led, like Carlyle, to challenge the assumptions of the prevailing political economy, notably in his combative and independent-minded *Unto This Last* (1860). This was perhaps the most influential of his books, affecting not only socialistic thought, but the attitude of ordinary people to art and taste. Ruskin spent most of his fortune on various social experiments, including the revival of the hand-made linen industry in Langdale, the establishment of the Art for Schools Association, and the foundation of a drawing school at Oxford. Many of his later writings were books and pamphlets advocating a system of national education, the organization of workmen, old age pensions, housing reform, and nature conservation. His autobiography, *Praeterita*, was published at intervals (1885–9), but never finished.

RUSKIN COLLEGE (1899), founded in Oxford for the education of working men and women on broad lines. It was not originally part of the university, but its students were allowed to attend lectures. It is important in the education of trade union officials and workers in labour movements sent there with scholarships provided by unions or labour bodies.

RUSSELL, LORD JOHN RUSSELL, 1st Earl (1792–1878), British politician and Whig prime minister (1846–52, 1865–6), who entered parliament in 1813. His early career wavered between literature and politics. In 1819 he declared for parliamentary reform and in 1822 introduced an unsuccessful bill. Unlike Grey, he supported Canning's government (1827). He helped to confirm the Whig–nonconformist alliance by championing Test and Corporation Act repeal in 1828. He became famous in 1831–2 by introducing the three Reform Bills, which he was largely responsible for drafting. For Russell, reform was 'the safety-valve of society', and revolution could be averted by an aristocracy responsive to popular demands. He wished to revive the alliance between the Whigs and the people, but opposed a Whig–Radical alliance. As home secretary (1835–9), he introduced several valuable penal, prison, and educational reforms, and he led the Whig opposition in 1841–6. In his famous Edinburgh letter (Nov. 1845), he announced his support for the repeal of the Corn Laws, abandoning his earlier advocacy of a fixed duty. One of his reasons for condemning the Corn Laws was, characteristically, that they had been 'the source of bitter divisions among classes'. In Dec. 1845 he accepted the queen's commission to form a government, but after a fortnight admitted that he could not do so.

Russell's first ministry was too exclusively Whig in composition, and though keen to accompany Irish coercion with valuable land tenure reforms which would have anticipated Gladstone's 1870 Land Act, he failed to push them through. He guided Liberals towards Irish Church disestablishment, but in his anti-Catholic letter (1850) to the Bp of Durham and in his popular Ecclesiastical Titles Bill (1851) his rational religion temporarily overcame his genuine zeal for religious toleration. Russell's policies were as radical as Gladstone's, and he never lost touch with prominent reformers—Attwood, O'Connell, Bright. But he failed to weld Liberal MPs and their extra-parliamentary sympathizers into a national party. He often opposed Palmerston's aggressive foreign policy in earlier years, but his partnership with him when Palmerston became foreign secretary (1859–65) was harmonious. They were in agreement on the Italian question, and were both criticized for their handling of the Schleswig-Holstein problem. As prime minister (1865) after Palmerston's death, Russell's aim was to pass a second Reform Bill. He resigned on the defeat of his 1866 bill and relinquished the Liberal leadership to Gladstone.

Russell was in office during 1830–41, 1846–55, 1859–66. He constantly proposed reforms in government machinery, *eg*, the separation of the war and colonial offices (1854), though his exaggerated absorption in constitutional history sometimes reduced their utility. He could not compete with Palmerston for the Liberal leadership. He seemed an arch-Whig, more concerned with promoting civil liberty than with solving social problems, and his reputation was never again so high as in 1831–2. His Whiggish ideas bore fruit overseas. As colonial secretary (1839–41, 1855), he promoted colonial self-government, and in a famous despatch of 1860 he defended the Italian Risorgimento by invoking the principles of 1688. Although he was didactic and impetuous, his undoubted cultivation and his pronounced political and domestic morality strengthened the reputation of early Victorian Whig cabinets and enhanced their shrewdness in handling extra-parliamentary demands for reform.

Spencer Walpole, *The Life of Lord John Russell*, 2 vols (London, 1889).

A. Wyatt Tilby, *Lord John Russell* (London, 1930).   BHH

RUSSELL, BERTRAND ARTHUR WILLIAM RUSSELL, 3rd Earl (1872–1970), British philosopher and mathematician. By birth as much as by intellect, he represented a type of Whig tradition in British thought. He was a grandson of Lord John Russell, the Victorian prime minister.

Russell was educated privately before going to Cambridge and it was there that his best work as a philosopher was completed. The *Principles of Mathematics* (1903) was followed by *Principia Mathematica* (1910, with A. N. Whitehead) and *Problems of Philosophy* (1911). *Principia Mathematica*, a three-volume work, was Russell's *chef d'œuvre* and it was sometimes a disappointment to him that its reception as a definitive work was less than total. Underlying his philosophy at this period was the conviction that things could be reduced to their constituent parts and that they could be known by that which constituted them. While he rejected the tenets of French philosophy and adhered to the empiricism of the British school, the mathematical certainties of his thinking were only partly accepted in this country. It is likely that the most enduring elements of his pre-1914 writing have been his studies of logic and his efforts to clear away much of what he took to be semantic confusion in the discussion of philosophic problems.

After the outbreak of the First World War his interests turned more obviously to politics and history. He was a conscientious objector to military service, was deprived of his fellowship at Trinity College for this objection, and, finally, imprisoned for the same reason. This led him into association with members of the Independent Labour Party and through them into active Labour politics—he was twice Labour candidate for Chelsea in the 1920s—and he was to remain a member of the Labour Party, with a couple of spectacular interruptions, for the rest of his life.

He remained, too, a convinced socialist all his life, but not an uncritical one; after a visit to Russia he wrote *The Theory and Practice of Bolshevism* (1920), an attack upon the violence and intolerance of the Bolshevik government. The misuse of power and the encroachment of the state upon individual freedom were themes that he increasingly turned to in the 1930s. In *Freedom and Organisation* (1934) he looked at the history of Europe in the four decades before the First World War and in *Power* (1938) he studied more generally the nature of authority and control in the modern state.

Though never rejecting collectivism in economic and social life he was concerned with encouraging the liberation of the individual from unnecessary or inherited restraints. Thus he had advanced notions of education—at one time he ran his own school—and of sexual emancipation. (As evidence of the latter, he was married four times and, as his autobiography shows, he had a somewhat detached view of his wives.) In the 1950s he reverted to the anti-militaristic attitude of the First World War, becoming an energetic supporter of nuclear disarmament, upon which issue he again left the Labour Party.   RMCK

RUSSELL, THOMAS (1830–1904), NZ land speculator and politician, who promoted Maori land confiscation policies (1863–4) and founded some major NZ financial institutions.

RUSSELL, SIR WILLIAM HOWARD (1821–1907), Irish journalist and war correspondent. He reported on various conflicts, mostly for *The Times*, whose publication of his despatches from the Crimea (1854–5) describing the British army's living conditions contributed substantially to the fall of Aberdeen's ministry and to a subsequent improvement in arrangements for the army's welfare. In 1860 Russell founded the *Army and Navy Gazette*, which he edited (1860–1907).

RUSSELL, MAJORS AND WADDELL (1854–62) in the US, freight and transportation firm founded by William H. Russell (1812–72) and Alexander Majors (1814–1900), who were later joined by William B. Waddell (1857). Initially they were engaged in carrying supplies to US army posts in the Great Plains and Rocky Mountains. Later they expanded to dominate the western US freight business, but over-extended their resources in stage-coach lines such as the Central Overland, California, and Pikes Peak Express, and their financial ruin was completed by disastrous losses with the Pony Express (April 1860–Oct. 1861).

RUSSIAN CIVIL WAR (1917–21), provoked by the Bolshevik revolution and the dissolution of the constituent assembly. It was fought over the whole area of the former Russian empire and it was complicated by the intervention of Russia's former wartime allies and the national aspirations of the inhabitants of the peripheral borderlands. It created conditions of anarchy and starvation such as to give an advantage to the Bolsheviks with their superior discipline. Trotsky was the most important leader on the Red side; he organized the Red Army and he won the crucial battle of Sviazhsk (the 'Valmy' of the Russian Revolution). The Reds enjoyed the advantage of interior lines of communication and the control of the main industrial centres. The Whites lacked authoritative leadership, except for that of Wrangel, but even more significantly they lacked any common ideology other than a common hatred of Bolshevism. Thus it proved impossible to unite all the anti-Bolshevik forces. When Kolchak seized power he bitterly offended both the SRs and the Siberian separatists. Denikin could find little support from the Menshevik governments of the Caucasus; likewise the Ukrainian nationalists, Petliura and Makhno, distrusted the Great Russian chauvinism of the Whites. The equally powerful chauvinism of the Reds was partially concealed during the period of the Civil War by Lenin's apparently liberal attitude towards nationalism. It is unlikely that the Whites would have achieved even such success as they did had it not been for Allied and particularly British intervention. Allied troops and material were sent to Archangel, the Baltic states, Siberia, the Black Sea, and Central Asia. The Allies' motives were mixed. Before the defeat of Germany (Nov. 1918) it was hoped to establish an Eastern Front; after that date some western groups wanted to encourage the dissolution of the Russian empire and some Western statesmen wanted to prevent the spread of Bolshevism into Western Europe. The main fronts were the southern and the eastern; the year of military decision was 1919. Kolchak's thrust from the Urals was broken up by June; but Denikin swept on towards Moscow from the south. On 13 Oct. the White Guards approached Tula, the last town before Moscow. At the same time, Yudenich, based on Estonia and armed with British tanks, reached the suburbs of Petrograd. But Denikin was already over-extended and street fighting was more than Yudenich's small force could manage. The capital were saved and the Allies started to withdraw their support. The failure of the White cause was the signal for the Polish invasion of the Ukraine (1920). At first Pilsudski drove unhindered towards Kiev; but the Red Army under Tukhachevsky recovered rapidly and by the autumn was approaching Warsaw. This alarmed the Western governments which brought pressure to bear on Poland to make peace (treaty of Riga, 1921). Although further fighting was required to establish Bolshevik authority in the Caucasus and Central Asia, this brought the Civil War to an end. The new regime had managed to retain all the territory of the tsars with the exception of Finland, the Baltic states, parts of Belorussia and the Ukraine and Bessarabia.

D. Footman, *Civil War in Russia* (London, 1962).

R. Pipes, *The Formation of the Soviet Union: communism and nationalism, 1917–23* (Cambridge, MA, 1953).   GS

RUSSIAN MUSLIM CONGRESS (Sept. 1920). The main purpose behind this congress at Baku was to arouse the peoples of the east to revolt against imperialism, and especially British imperialism, in order to facilitate the allegedly incipient revolution of the European proletarians. Invitations were issued by the Comintern, which sent Zinoviev, Radek, and Bela Kun to preside over the meetings. There were 1891 delegates, including 235 Turks, but there were only three Arabs. Zinoviev struck a dramatic note when he urged the delegates to participate in a holy war in the first place against English imperialism! But if the delegates were united by their hatred of imperialism, they were at odds about almost everything else. Muslims and other members of eastern religious groups could hardly be happy about the Communist party's attitude towards religion. A petition was received on behalf of the '315 millions of the people of India' requesting aid against imperialism, but desiring the retention of domestic and religious habits. Another difficulty was caused by the status of 'bourgeois' nationalism; by no means all the enemies of Britain could be called 'proletarians'. The arrival of the former Young Turk, Enver Pasha, emphasized this difficulty. He was certainly anti-British: but he was opposed to Kemal (whom most of the Turks at the Congress supported) and worse still, was a notorious murderer of Armenians, and thus *persona non grata* to the 157 Armenian delegates. The congress did mark the renaissance, in a new form, of the traditional Russian awareness of the possibility of calling in the East to redress the balance of the West.   GS

RUSSIAN ORTHODOX CHURCH, derived from the Greek Orthodox Christian Church of Byzantium and imposed on the heathen Russian peoples by Prince Vladimir I (*reg.* 980–1015) after his own conversion (988) in order to strengthen his power over the new Kievan state through the Byzantine concept of absolutism instituted by God and supported by the Church. The Russian Church therefore acquired the doctrine, ritual, and distinctive culture of Byzantium, reflected in the religious paintings and icons adorning its churches and the importance of singing in religious services.

After the Tatar conquest of the 13th cent., the Church as well as the state was divided and in the reign of Ivan I, Grand Duke of Moscow (*reg.* 1328–40), that city replaced Kiev as the seat of the metropolitan, the chief prelate. The 15th cent. saw important developments in the Russian Church. After the Eastern Church and the Latin Church of Western Europe, which had broken apart in 1054, had been reunited at the Council of Florence (1439), the patriarch of Constantinople proclaimed this momentous event in Moscow's main cathedral, only to find reunion rejected by the clergy and the state. A new metropolitan of Moscow was elected by a council of Russian bishops convoked by Vassily II (*reg.* 1431–62) and from this time there were two metropolitans in Russia, one in Moscow and a Greek one for West Russia and Lithuania. The independence of the Muscovite Church became permanent when shortly afterwards (1453) the Turkish infidel captured Constantinople, making the metropolitan of Moscow effective protector of all Orthodox Christians. The marriage of Zoe, niece of the last Eastern emperor, to Ivan III, contributed to the doctrine of the Third Rome. In the reigns of Vassily III (*reg.* 1505–33) and Ivan IV (*reg.* 1533–84) the Church became economically and spiritually stronger and was the basis of the autocratic Russian state. The elevation of Metropolitan Job to the patriarchate of Russia (1589) recognized the Church's autonomy.

The decline of the importance of the Orthodox Church before the rising power of the state possibly dates from the great schism (*Raskol*) of the mid-17th cent. The modifications which Patriarch Nikon introduced in ritual initiated a violent rift between the Old Believers and the official Church, which remained until the present century. The Church of West Russia was also challenged by the Catholic Counter-Reformation which restored the Roman faith in large areas of Poland. Western European influences penetrated Russia from the later 17th cent., and received official encouragement from Peter I (*reg.* 1689–1725), whose reign greatly accelerated the secularization of culture and domination of the state over the Church. The process was symbolized by the abolition of the patriarchate (1721) and its replacement by a state commission, the Holy Synod. The Church was further weakened by the confiscation of its lands under Catherine II (1764), and its subordination was reflected in the words of Paul I, 'the tsar is the head of the Church' (1797).

During the 18th cent. the Old Believers split into different groups, but the suppression of dissent did not prevent the appearance of new sects, *eg*, the *Khlysty*. At the same time the state exploited the Church to extend its power in new directions, the assumption of political and spiritual leadership over Orthodox subjects in Poland and the Turkish Balkans, and the encouragement of Russian national sentiment. Orthodoxy was challenged in the 19th cent. by such movements as tolstoyanism among the intellectuals and Baptism among the masses. It was encouraged, however, by the more tolerant policy of the state, which began with the manifesto of 1905 giving religious freedom, and culminated in the restoration of the patriarchate (1917). After the Bolshevik revolution a decree of 23 Jan. 1918 severed the connection between Church and state and nationalized Church property, while further anti-religious legislation followed in 1921, and Patriarch Tikhon was deposed in 1923. Since then Russia's leaders have maintained intermittent religious persecution to prevent the growth of conflicting loyalties, despite the restoration of the patriarchate in the Second World War (4 Sept. 1943).

G. Vernadsky, *A History of Russia* (Yale, 1961).   MKS

RUSSIAN REVOLUTION (1905), year of disturbances which profoundly shook Russian government and society. Bloody Sunday (9 Jan. 1905), when a peaceful workers' demonstration was fired on while petitioning the tsar, is usually taken as the starting point. It was followed by widespread strikes and demonstrations in many parts of Russia.

The liberal constitutional movement which followed the founding of the Union of Liberation held a banquet in Nov. 1904 to publicize its demands for a constitution. After Bloody Sunday the tsar issued a rescript to Bulygin, the minister of the interior, promising an elected consultative assembly (Duma). This proposal, published in Aug., was rejected by the liberals. Meanwhile the trade union and professional movement had been growing and a Union of Unions was founded. The publication of the October Manifesto (17–30 Oct.), forced by Witte, the prime minister, on the unwilling Nicholas, who preferred a military dictatorship, marked the height of governmental concessions. It promised a constitution with full civil liberties and a wider franchise for the Duma, without whose consent no bill was to become law. Although a considerable concession, this fell short of providing a constituent assembly, and the constitutional movement split into Kadets and Octobrists.

The working-class movement in Jan. had been largely spontaneous and economic in aim. After Bloody Sunday the influence of revolutionary parties, especially the Mensheviks, increased. Strikes were increased rather than diminished by the Shidlovsky commission to investigate factory conditions, which only give the workers experience of electing delegates. A railway strike in Oct. developed into a general strike. In St Petersburg a soviet of Workers' Deputies, founded on workers' initiative and led by Trotsky, dominated Oct.

Peasant uprisings were widespread, being partly influenced by Socialist Revolutionaries, who also carried out a terrorist campaign. A Peasants' Union was founded at a congress in July and rural unrest continued well into 1906. Nationalist independence movements affected the whole empire from Finland to the Caucasus. Right-wing nationalist groups, like the Russian Monarchist Party and the Union of the Russian People, developed and the year was marked by severe pogroms.

The October manifesto ushered in a period of legalized trade union activity, and freedom of speech, press, and association, but apart from a Bolshevik uprising in Moscow in Dec., the movement slowly collapsed. Except for a few incidents such as the mutiny in the *Potemkin*, the armed forces remained loyal, and the end of the Russo-Japanese War (Aug. 1905) enabled troops to be used to crush the revolution. A large Anglo-French loan early in 1906 restored solvency and by the time the First Duma met many concessions were withdrawn.

The events of the year were described by Lenin as a dress rehearsal for later revolution. They had considerable influence on events in Persia and Turkey, as well as in Asia. They were followed by the Stolypin land reforms and the Duma period of semi-constitutional government.

S. Harcave, *First Blood* (London, 1964).

J. Keep, *The Rise of Social Democracy in Russia* (London, 1963).   BJW

RUSSIAN REVOLUTION (Feb. 1917), final scene in the collapse of the Russian monarchy. The authority of the tsar had been eroded since the military disasters of 1915. Matters had not been improved by the fact that Nicholas II had taken over personal command of the army and thus left political power in the hands of the empress and her favourites. Liberal members of the Duma, afraid that the war would be lost and anxious that, if it were to be won, it should not be won while the autocrat remained in power, promoted a whispering campaign against the royal family. It was alleged that they were pro-German and that the military disasters were the result of treachery, not inefficiency. Nicholas refused to compromise with the Duma Liberals and to appoint a cabinet which would meet with their approval. He continued to employ bureaucrats like Sturmer and Prince Golitsyn, who enjoyed the confidence of nobody but the empress. Even after the murder of Rasputin (Dec. 1916) he was not moved by the evidence of a Liberal plot (approved by several leading generals) to end the autocracy and to replace it with a constitutional monarchy. Events in Petrograd, however, overtook both the Liberals and the tsar. The winter of 1916–17 was unusually cold. There was little fuel and food prices increased by 50 per cent as a result of the breakdown of the transport system. Strikes and bread riots resulted on 22 Feb. when the employers declared a lock-out in the Putilov works which employed tens of thousands of the most militant workers. On the next day the socialist groups organized processions of women to demand bread; on 25 Feb. the strike was general in Petrograd and the workers had started to cross the ice on the Neva and to invade the fashionable and administrative quarters of Petrograd. It was time to use the troops of the swollen and unruly Petrograd garrison. But this undisciplined force, weakened by inaction and an easy prey to socialist agitators, refused to aid the police in keeping order. The turning point came on Sunday, 26 Feb. A company of the Volinsky regiment on duty along the Catherine canal opened fire on the police. The mutiny spread rapidly to all the other units and by nightfall on 27 Feb. Petrograd was no longer under the control of the government. The same process continued in Moscow and the other cities with very little bloodshed. During the days of the revolution Nicholas had been at the army's headquarters at Mogilev. He tried to rejoin his family at Tsarskoe Selo and also to get some loyal troops into Petrograd—a single disciplined unit would have been enough. But his efforts were foiled by the generals, who were in league with the Liberals. On 1 March the Imperial train arrived at Pskov and the generals demanded the abdication of the tsar. At first Nicholas proposed to preserve the monarchy by abdicating in favour of either his son or his brother, the Grand Duke Michael. But this solution, which would have been supported by the generals and the Duma Liberals, could not be put into effect because of the forces released by the February Revolution. The February Days had not placed the Liberal plotters in power; effective authority had fallen to the Petrograd Soviet of workers and soldiers.

W. H. Chamberlin, *The Russian Revolution, 1917–21* (New York, 1952).
G. Katkov, *Russia 1917: the February revolution* (London, 1967).
                                                                    GS

RUSSIAN REVOLUTION

RUSSIAN REVOLUTION (Oct. 1917), victory of the Bolsheviks and the beginning of the Soviet Union. As a result of the 'July Days' the Bolsheviks had been checked, their leaders being either imprisoned or driven into exile. Yet the failure of the other socialist parties to seize power, and of the provisional government to attend to the peace and land questions, the ambiguous relationship of Kerensky to the Kornilov putsch—all these factors tended to neutralize the Bolsheviks' defeat in July and to make it seem that their programme was the only one capable of translating the aspirations of the masses into reality. From the beginning of Sept. the Bolsheviks began to win majorities in Petrograd, Moscow, and other large city Soviets. It seemed certain that they would dominate the second All-Russia congress of Soviets, due to meet on 25 Oct. Lenin, still in hiding from the police, realized that the situation was both opportune and dangerous. The danger to the Bolsheviks was that they (like the Mensheviks and SRs) would sink in public esteem were they to sit idly by while their star was in the ascendant. Nevertheless, he had to work hard to persuade the central committee to opt for armed insurrection. Moderates like Kamenev and Zinoviev thought that it was madness to seize power by force when it had become obvious that the congress of Soviets would have a Bolshevik majority. The crucial vote was taken on 16 Oct., after which the details of revolution were left to Trotsky. He built upon the basis of the military revolutionary committee of the Petrograd Soviet, under whose control the Red Guards formed earlier to meet the threat of Kornilov were placed. Trotsky had little faith in his own forces, but luckily for him his opponents were even weaker. The provisional government was well aware of the preparations being made against it; it was obvious, for example, that the Smolny institute, the HQ of the Petrograd Soviet, was being turned into an arsenal. But Kerensky failed to prepare effective counter-measures, partly because such troops as he might have used had been won over to the Bolsheviks by the war of words which Trotsky knew so well how to wage, and partly because Kerensky hoped that he would be able to crush the Bolsheviks as easily as he had in July. When the insurrection began at 2 a.m. on 25 Oct. Kerensky could count on the loyalty of only a few military cadets and the women's battalion guarding the Winter Palace. By dawn the inexperienced Red Guards had captured all the points of importance except the Winter Palace. That was not 'assaulted' until the evening of 25 Oct. The women fled and suffered no casualties except that three were raped. While these events, which 'shook the world', went forward, the life of Petrograd was hardly disturbed. Shops and restaurants remained open and Chaliapin drew enthusiastic audiences to his performance in *Don Carlos*. In Moscow the Bolshevik revolution was not achieved with such ease: fighting ended only on 1 Nov. By that time the attempt of Kerensky to recapture Petrograd had been frustrated, not so much by the bayonets of the Red Guard as by the words of Bolshevik agitators. The Mensheviks and most of the SRs, outraged by the Bolshevik seizure of power, had walked out of the second congress of Soviets and Lenin and his companions were in the seats of power. The ease with which they had achieved their objective encouraged them to think that they were about to achieve the same result throughout Europe.

E. H. Carr, *The Bolshevik Revolution, 1917–23*, 3 vols (London, 1954).
J. Reed, *Ten Days That Shook The World* (New York, 1919).
                                                                    GS

RUSSIAN STATE BANK, created in 1860, was an attempt to solve the financial crisis resulting from the Crimean War. However, it was not made the official bank of issue.

RUSSIFICATION POLICY, official policy in the reigns of Alexander III and Nicholas II which is particularly associated with Pobedonestsev. It extolled the unity and expansion of the state, as opposed to loyalty to a monarch, as an essential part of nationalist beliefs. It also sought to impose Russian language, culture, and often religion, as well as administration, on all non-Russian minorities, whether loyal or not; anti-Semitism too was part of the policy. Its application resulted in the rise of a nationalist intelligentsia from Finland to the Caucasus.

RUSSO-CZECH TREATY (May 1935), mutual assistance agreement concluded between the USSR and Czechoslovakia, motivated by the growing threat from Nazi Germany. It committed each party to join France in aiding the other state were it ever attacked. Thus it complemented the Franco-Czech treaty (1924) and the recently signed Franco-Soviet pact. The treaty emphasized the divisions in the Little Entente, for neither Rumania nor Yugoslavia felt themselves threatened by Germany and both refused to conclude a similar agreement with the USSR. In the event, neither the USSR nor France came to the assistance of Czechoslovakia during the crisis of 1938, the treaty thus proving abortive.

RUSSO-FINNISH WAR (30 Nov. 1939–13 March 1940). After Russia's invasion of Poland in conjunction with Germany (Sept. 1939), the Soviet government took further measures to increase the security of its western frontiers. By 10 Oct. Estonia, Latvia, and Lithuania had been induced to accept Russian garrisons at key points on their territories. On 14 Oct. demands were presented to Finland for the cession of islands in the Gulf of Finland and areas on the Karelian isthmus to safeguard the approaches to Leningrad; the frontier further north was also to be rectified. These demands were, in strategic terms, comparatively moderate, and compensation was offered elsewhere, but the Finns were reluctant to cede territory which they regarded as an essential part of their homeland, and on 30 Nov., while negotiations were still in progress, the Russians attacked Finland.

At first they met with considerable setbacks. Expecting a popular rising against the Finnish government, they advanced in no great force, unprepared for serious resistance or a long campaign. Their logistic arrangements were poor, and the terrain and climate favoured the defence. They succeeded, however, in taking the Arctic port of Petsamo, the only route by which outside help could easily reach the Finns, but their main advance up the Karelian Isthmus was halted by the Mannerheim Line. A flanking attack north of Lake Ladoga also failed, as did two thrusts further north across the waist of Finland past Salla and Suomussalmi.

Finland's resistance to unprovoked aggression by a vastly stronger neighbour aroused widespread sympathy in the West. The French and British governments prepared to send troops to their assistance, hoping to secure, en route, the Swedish iron-ore deposits at Kiruna and Gällivare, and the Norwegian port of Narvik, through which the ore, on which Germany largely depended, was exported; they thought that this might lead to a German invasion of Scandinavia and large-scale fighting there, averting the threat of a repetition of the battles on French soil in the First World War, besides making possible the liberation of Poland. Difficulties with Norway and Sweden prevented the execution of this plan before Finland collapsed, and saved the Allies from disastrous involvement in war with Russia as well as Germany; but fear of such a move was one factor in Hitler's decision to invade Norway. The initial Finnish resistance also created an altogether exaggerated impression of Soviet military incapacity, and thus helped to bring about the German invasion of Russia.

On 1 Feb., however, the Russians began an assault on the

Mannerheim Line in overwhelming force. Within a fortnight they had reached Viipuri, which was encircled by troops advancing across the frozen Gulf of Finland. Further resistance was useless and on 13 March the Finns acceded to their terms. When Germany invaded Russia in 1941 the war was renewed; the Finns recovered their lost territory with German aid, but lost it all, and more, in 1944.   PJBD

RUSSO-JAPANESE AGREEMENT (1907), political agreement which contained secret clauses delineating spheres of influence—Japanese in Korea and South Manchuria, Russian in Northern Manchuria and Outer Mongolia.

RUSSO-JAPANESE WAR (1904–5), fought as a result of incompetent imperialist policies for which Nicholas II was chiefly to blame. Its origins are associated with Bezobrazov and his schemes for East Asian development and a timber concession on the Yalu river in Korea, which were opposed by Witte. After the latter's fall from power (1903), policy was confused. Russian troops remained in Manchuria, but Bezobrazov's influence declined. Despite opposition to war by the ministers of foreign affairs and war, and even by the tsar, negotiations with Japan failed. In Feb. 1904 without warning, the Japanese struck at the Russian fleet.

Admiral Alexeyev and Gen. Kuropatkin failed to co-ordinate the tactics of the army and navy. The war involved a series of disasters for Russia on land (Mukden) and at sea (Port Arthur and Tsushima), despite the navy's reinforcement by the Baltic squadron. Peace was negotiated by Witte at Portsmouth (US) in Aug. 1905. Russia lost the Liaotung peninsula, the South Manchurian railway, and southern Sakhalin, but paid no indemnity. In Russia, where the war had been bitterly opposed, it merged into the revolution of 1905.

RUSSO-POLISH PACT (1932), characteristic episode in early 1930s Soviet diplomacy, designed to lower the international temperature by demonstrating that the Soviet Union, 15 years after the Revolution, was fully occupied with its own problems and accepted the independence of the many states totally or partially composed of former Russian territory. Russo-Polish relations had been chequered ever since the Revolution, but began to improve about 1931. The first draft of the pact was produced in Aug. 1931; there was an exchange of armaments information in Sept., and the pact itself came into being in Jan. 1932. Its signature was delayed in the hope that a Russo-Rumanian agreement could be added, but this failed to materialize in time. The pact was eventually signed in July, and in Nov. a conciliation convention added. For Poland the pact represented a useful detente with Russia, and enhanced her bargaining power with Germany, her other potentially dangerous neighbour. The Poles always took it seriously, in that they always kept the Germans at arms' length, despite hints of partnership in an anti-Bolshevik crusade. Russia was also happy with the situation for a time, but the 1934 Polish–German pact awakened Soviet suspicions and relations grew progressively cooler, particularly after Poland repulsed Litvinov's attempts in 1934–5 to create an Eastern Locarno security system on the network of pacts of which the Polish one had been intended to provide the centrepiece. As the 1930s passed, it became clear that the key to Russia's security lay in Berlin, not Warsaw, hence the effective supersession of the Polish agreement by the Molotov–Ribbentrop pact (Aug. 1939).

RUSSO-SWEDISH WAR (1788–90), attack launched by Gustavus III of Sweden when Russia was already at war with Turkey. An advance against St Petersburg was halted by the Conspiracy of Anjala, a mutiny of noble army officers, who claimed that the attack required the prior sanction of the Riksdag. Danish intervention, however, enabled the king to rally the people to his side. The conspiracy was foiled, the Danish invasion checked, and an enhancement of the royal powers forced through the Riksdag against the will

of the nobles. After a Swedish naval victory at Svensksund (1790), the peace of Värälä restored the status quo.

RUSSO-TURKISH WAR (1735–9), started by Russia, whose armies attacked the Crimean Tatars (1735) and forced the Turks to declare war. Under Münnich and Lacey the Russians won some surprising successes, taking Azov (1737) and Ochakov and defeating the Turks near the Pruth at Stavuchany. In 1736, however, the Porte concluded a treaty with Persia, thus freeing the Turkish forces for the Balkans. Austria was induced to join Russia, according to the terms of their 1726 alliance, but deprived of the military genius of Prince Eugene their war effort was ineffective. Field Marshal Seckendorff was driven back from Serbia, and Königsegg and Wallis were equally unsuccessful, the latter being defeated by the Turks at Kroszka, near Belgrade (1739). Abortive negotiations had been initiated at Nemirov in 1737, but by 1739 Austria and Russia were ready to make peace. Russia merely retained Azov for her efforts, and Austria's surrender of almost all she had gained at Passarowitz (1718) was said to have hastened the Emperor Charles VI's death (1740).

RUSSO-TURKISH WARS (1768–74, 1787–92, 1806–12, 1828–1829, 1877–8). Russia's desire to dominate the Balkans for strategic, commercial, and ideological reasons led to a series of wars with Turkey. Russian aims and methods in the area varied, but eventual domination of the Balkans, Constantinople, and the Straits, after the collapse of the Turkish empire, was Russia's consistent policy.

The Russian government first considered rousing the Balkan Christians against Turkey during the war of 1768–74, when Russia overran Moldavia and Wallachia and her fleet was victorious in the Aegean. The treaty of Kuchuk-Kainardji (1774), often taken as the starting point of the Eastern Question, gave Russia the Kuban, Azov, Kerch, and, in the area between the Bug and Dnieper, a foothold on the Black Sea. The Crimea was declared independent, Russia was granted navigation rights in the Black Sea and passage through the Strait for merchant ships. An Orthodox church was opened in Constantinople, giving Russia vague rights over the Turkish Christians.

Russia's growing strength in the Crimea and conflict in the Caucasus again led to war in 1787. Catherine's original plans involved the overthrow of Turkey, the appointment of Grand Duke Constantine as ruler of Constantinople, and a new kingdom of Dacia. Conflict with Sweden, the defection of Austria, and British and Prussian opposition caused a diplomatic crisis. Nevertheless the treaty of Jassy gave Ochakov to Russia.

Partition of Turkey was also discussed by Alexander I and Napoleon at Tilsit during the Russo-Turkish War of 1806–12, when Russia gained Bessarabia. However, when, in the war (1828–9) which followed the battle of Navarino, the Russian army reached Adrianople in sight of Constantinople, a secret committee (1829) laid down the policy of preserving the weak Turkish empire as a contribution to Russian security. Instead, political influence over the South Slavs became Russia's aim, and the treaty of Adrianople gave Serbia and the Rumanian principalities autonomy under Russian protection.

This policy was adhered to despite the disasters of the Crimean War and the loss of Bessarabia. The Pan-Slavs of the 1870s challenged the methods of the foreign office, and aimed at solving the problem, including the straits question, by direct Russo-Turkish agreement and the creation of a Balkan federation under Russian control. The treaty of San Stefano, negotiated (March 1878) by Ignatiev after the war of 1877–8 (during the Near Eastern crisis, 1875–8), was the height of their achievement. After initial defeats at Plevna the Russian army had again reached Adrianople by Jan. 1878, despite much confusion over policy. The treaty of San Stefano was modified, in accordance with the policy of the foreign office of negotiating with the powers, and at the insistence of the great powers at the Congress of Berlin. Although a diplomatic defeat for Russia, the terms agreed to at Berlin marked an enormous advance on 1856 in terms of Russian influence over Bulgaria, and the independence of the South slavs. Russia regained Bessarabia and acquired Kars and Ardahan.

M. S. Anderson, *The Eastern Question* (London, 1966).
I. Lederer (ed.), *Russian Foreign Policy* (Yale, 1962).   BJW

RUSTAMIDS, of Tahert, Ibadi dynasty of the 9th cent. on the high plains of the central Maghrib. The circumstances under which the Abbasids overthrew the Umayyads (750) led in the desert areas of Tripolitania and Tunisia to the independence of the local population under the leadership of members of the Ibadi sect of Kharijites, some of whom came from the east. Defeated by an Egyptian army (761), under the Persian, Ibn Rustam, the Ibadi leaders emigrated westwards to found the city of Tahert, which in the 9th cent. held the allegiance of peoples on the southern fringes of Aghlabid Tunisia (Ifriqiyya) as far east as Tripoli. The city was an important commercial centre, trading east to Egypt and Iraq and south across the Sahara to the Niger bend. Its politics were characterized by quarrels over the power of the imam, and the dynasty was overthrown by the Fatimids (909), when the Ibadis of Tahert fled to Mzab in the Sahara, where their oasis colony still (1970) exists.

RÜSTEM PASHA (d. 1561), Ottoman Grand Vizier (1544–53, 1555–61), who married Mihr-u-Mah, the daughter of Sultan Suleiman and his consort Khurrem and showed himself to be an able administrator and politician. He was involved in intrigues which led to the execution of Mustafa, a son of Suleiman, in 1553, an event productive of so much tension that Suleiman deemed it wise to remove Rüstem Pasha from the grand vizierate. He regained the office in 1555.

RUTHERFORD OF NELSON, ERNEST RUTHERFORD, Baron (1871–1937), British physicist, who was the founder of nuclear physics. As a result of an outstanding series of experiments (1898–1909) he determined the nature of alpha particles, one of the three types of radiation given off by radioactive substances, and evolved the theory of both the radioactive disintegration of elements and the nuclear atom. For this work he was awarded the 1908 Nobel Prize for Physics. In 1919 he demonstrated the first artificial splitting of atoms with the transmutation of one element into another.

RUTHVEN, RAID OF (1582), in Scotland, political coup when the pro-English Protestant lords, led by the Earls of Mar and Gowrie and Lords Lindsay and Boyd, seized the youthful James VI at Perth and carried him off to Ruthven castle (Aug. 1582). James was held by the Ruthven raiders for ten months, while they overthrew the pro-French Earls of Lennox and Arran. The latter returned to power, however, after James's escape (June 1583).

RUTLAND, CHARLES MANNERS, 4th Duke of (1754–87), British politician, who held office under Shelburne (1782–3) and the Younger Pitt (1783–4), when he became lord-lieutenant of Ireland. He was one of Pitt's closest friends.

RUTLAND, JOHN JAMES ROBERT MANNERS, 7th Duke of (1818–1906), British politician, who formed the 'Young England' party with Disraeli, and became the first commissioner for works, and later postmaster-general.

RUTLEDGE, JOHN (1739–1800), American lawyer and politician, who served in the SC colonial legislature (1761–76) and was a delegate to the First and Second Continental Congresses (1774–6). He helped to draft the SC constitution (1776), was president of the state general assembly (1776–8), governor (1779–81), a member of Congress (1782–3), and was elected to the state chancery court (1784). As a prominent member of the Philadelphia Convention (1787) he sought to protect Southern interests. He was one of the first to be appointed an associate justice to the US Supreme Court (1789–91), and was chief justice of SC (1791–5). Though appointed by President Washington as chief justice of the Supreme Court (1795), he was rejected by the Senate for political reasons stemming from his opposition to Jay's treaty.

RUYTER, MICHIEL ADRIAANZOON DE (1607–76), Dutch sailor, who distinguished himself in the naval wars of the 17th cent. He was vice-commander of the Dutch escort fleet for the treasure convoy during the first Anglo-Dutch War (1652–4) under Tromp, defeated the Swedes at Nyborg (Nov. 1659) in the Northern War (1655–60), and again fought England in the second and third Dutch Wars (1665–7, 1672–8). In 1664 he was in African waters defending the Dutch slave trade, and he returned home by a devious route via America and Norway, to be appointed commander of the Dutch fleet at Texel. In 1666 he encountered the English fleet off Lowestoft and fought a bitter but drawn battle for four days (1–4 June). He took his revenge in the following year with a spectacular attack up the Medway which threatened London itself and resulted in the capture of the English flagship, the *Royal Charles* (17 June 1667). During the Anglo-Dutch conflict of 1672–4 there were four naval battles, all costly and indecisive, *eg*, Sole Bay (1672) and Texel (1673). After England withdrew from the War, De Ruyter concentrated on securing the Mediterranean from the French navy, but he was killed during the minor Dutch victory of Etna (1676).

RWANDA (26,338 sq. kms), republic in central Africa, with a population of 3 million, chiefly Hutu and Tutsi people. Before independence in 1962 Rwanda was part of the Belgian UN mandate of Ruanda-Urundi. The president and cabinet hold executive power, leading a legislative assembly of 44 members elected by adult suffrage.

RYAN, THOMAS JOSEPH (1876–1921), Australian lawyer and Labor politician, who was responsible for advanced social legislation as Qld prime minister (1915–19). He was later deputy leader of the Federal Labor Party.

RYAZAN, Russian principality and town, situated southeast of Moscow in the Oka basin, founded by the house of Chernigov and overrun by the Tatars in 1237. It was created a grand duchy under the Tatar Janibeg (1342–57), but later appealed to Moscow for help against the Tatars, accepting subordination in return. Half of Ryazan was bequeathed to Ivan III and the remainder was formally annexed by Vassily III of Muscovy in 1521, when the last independent prince was arrested for secretly negotiating with the Tatars. Later he fled to Lithuania.

RYDER, RICHARD (1766–1832), British lawyer and politician, who was judge-advocate-general (1807) and home secretary (1809–12) in Perceval's administration.

RYDZ-ŚMIGLY, EDWARD (1886–1941), Polish soldier, who was a leading figure in Pilsudski's Legionary Movement in Austrian Poland. He served with the Legions (1914–17) and became the commanding officer of the Polish Military Organization, the Pilsudski-ite underground in Russian Poland, at this time occupied by the Central Powers. In the People's Government established in Lublin in Nov. 1918 he held the post of minister of war. He took a prominent part in military operations during the next three years and participated in the Polish capture of Kiev (May 1920). In May 1921 he became an army inspector. After Pilsudski's death in May 1935 Rydz became general inspector, the designate commander-in-chief. Pilsudski's intention in proposing him for this office appears to have been his desire to keep the army out of politics, but inevitably, given the vast powers enjoyed by the general inspector, Rydz came to play an important political role. In Nov. 1935 he was made a marshal and in April 1936 was officially mentioned by the prime minister as 'the second man in the state' after the president. Neither in the military nor in the political sphere did Rydz prove a success. He bears a considerable responsibility for the failure to modernize the army and for its inadequate performance in Sept. 1939 at the start of the Second World War.

After the Polish defeat, Rydz fled to Rumania, an action which was widely condemned in Poland. He returned to Warsaw in 1941 and attempted to join the underground home army, but was refused on the grounds that he had compromised himself in the Sept. campaign.

RYE HOUSE PLOT, THE (1683), in England, allegedly a Whig plot. Rye House was a farmhouse belonging to Richard Rumbold at Hoddesden in Herts. According to the dubious evidence of Robert West, John Rumsey, and Josiah Keeling, there had been a plot to murder King Charles II in April 1683 at Rye House on his way back from the racing at Newmarket. The plot misfired because the royal party had returned early. None the less, certain prominent Whig leaders were arrested and one of them, the Earl of Essex, committed suicide in prison. Algernon Sidney and Lord William Russell were executed. The Rye House plot may be regarded as the royalist counterpart of the popish plot: in essence false, although certain of the details may well have been true.

RYMER, THOMAS (1646–1713), English historical scholar, who wrote the first serious study of English foreign relations, the *Foedera etc.*, published in 15 vols (1702–13).

RYMNIK, BATTLE OF (Sept. 1789), fought on the Rymnik river in Moldavia, near Martineşti. A combined Russian and Austrian force under the command of Count Suworow and the Prince of Coburg defeated the Ottoman Turks.

RYSWICK, TREATY OF (May–Oct. 1697), peace settlement that ended the War of the League of Augsburg (1688–97), negotiated with Swedish mediation by the representatives of Louis XIV of France, Charles II of Spain, William III for England and the Netherlands, and the Emperor Leopold I for the Habsburgs and the German princes. Louis made initial concessions which won the agreement of the maritime powers and Spain (20 Sept. 1697) and threatened to isolate the emperor. He agreed to recognize William III as King of England and Princess Anne as his successor. He promised to evacuate his troops from Spanish soil, *eg*, Barcelona, and to restore most of the lands annexed by his *réunion* policy since 1678, *eg*, Luxemburg. French commercial regulations were to be relaxed in favour of Dutch trade and a line of barrier fortresses in the Spanish Netherlands were to be garrisoned by Dutch troops as a guarantee against French aggression. Lorraine was to be restored to Duke Charles's son, Leopold Joseph, with the exception of Saarlouis, and free navigation on the Rhine guaranteed. The fortresses on the right bank of the Rhine, formerly 'reunited' by France, *eg*, Philippsburg, Kehl, Freiburg, and Breisach, were to be restored to the empire. In return, Louis received confirmation of his possession of Strasbourg and of the French interpretation of sovereignty over Alsace, and at the Catholic Elector Palatine's instigation the important 'Ryswick clause' guaranteed that no change should be made in the religious status of the lands surrendered by France, thus reopening the religious debate in the empire.

Ryswick coincided with the zenith of Leopold's European prestige, which was enhanced by the reconquest of Hungary from the Turks and his son's succession as King of the Romans and of Hungary, and was ostensibly a check to French expansionist ambitions in central Europe. To Louis, however, it gave France peace with honour and the chance to concentrate on the greater diplomatic prize of acquiring the Spanish succession for the Bourbon dynasty.

RYŪKYŪ ISLANDS, comprising Okinawa, Miyako, Amami-ōshima, and others, formed a kingdom which, according to traditions compiled in literary form when Japanese influence was predominant, was founded by Shunten (*reg.* 1187–?1237), a scion of the Japanese Minamoto clan. In the 14th cent. the Okinawan kingdom split into three principalities: Hokuzan, Chūzan, and Nanzan, but by 1429 these had been reunited by Shō Hashi, King of Chūzan, who founded the first Shō dynasty. After Shō Hashi's death in 1439, succession disputes and conspiracies brought his dynasty to an end, and a second Shō dynasty was founded, whose third ruler, Shō Shin (*reg.* 1477–1526), raised Okinawa to the peak of its prosperity.

With very little in the way of natural products, the kingdom could only flourish as a trading station on the routes between China, Korea, and Japan. The 15th and 16th cents, when Japan was politically divided, provided an opportunity for the Ryūkyūans, under the patronage of kings such as Shō Hashi and Shō Shin, to play a major role in this trade. It was at this period that the kingdom extended its control to Miyako and other outlying islands, while Shuri, the capital, was beautified with palaces and parks. However, the strategic position of Okinawa led to other external pressures. Already in 1272–4 King Eiso is said to have resisted Khublai Khan's demand for contributions towards the Mongol expeditions against Japan, while in 1592 Hideyoshi forced the Okinawan king to provide supplies for his forces in Korea.

The reunification of Japan spelt the beginning of the end of Okinawa's independent role, and in 1609 the islands were taken over by the *Daimyō* of Satsuma, in southern Kyūshū, who thereby assumed control over all contacts with China. Although kings continued to 'reign' in Okinawa for another two and a half centuries, the kingdom's internal administration was under close surveillance by Satsuma, who were unable however to prevent Commodore Perry from taking the Ryūkyūs in 1853–4 for use as a pawn in his negotiations with the *shōgun*. This incident led to growing Japanese pressure for direct annexation of the islands, and in 1879 the last king was deported to Tokyo and Ryūkyū placed under a prefectural administration. Most of the relics of the Okinawan kingdom, including the royal palaces and tombs, were destroyed during the battle for Okinawa in 1945, in which it has been estimated that some 47,000 Okinawan civilians perished. Thereafter the Ryūkyū were wholly or partly under US administration, but were scheduled to return to direct Japanese rule in 1972

George H. Kerr, *Okinawa, the History of an Island People* (Rutland, VT, 1958).   KHJG

RZECZPOSPOLITA, Polish–Lithuanian Commonwealth or federation of states which was created in the 16th cent. mainly through the efforts of the last of the Jagiellon rulers, Sigismund Augustus (*reg.* 1548–72). It consisted of the kingdom of Poland, the grand duchy of Lithuania, Ruthenia, Mazovia, royal Prussia, ducal Prussia, and Courland and Livonia, and was sealed by the Union of Lublin (1569). From 1572 the commonwealth was increasingly assailed by external enemies, the Cossacks, Russians, Swedes, and Turks, and suffered from constitutional difficulties which encouraged anarchy and prevented the growth of an absolute state on the general European pattern. None the less, despite the additional union with Saxony from 1697, the *rzeczpospolita* survived until the partitions of Poland (1772–95).

S

SA, in Germany, initials for *Sturmabteilung*, or Storm Division (also known as the Brownshirts), a uniformed arm of the NSDAP. Founded in 1921 as the *Ordnertruppe, ie,* a protection group for party meetings, it received the designation SA after the Hofbräuhaus brawl of Nov. 1921, and soon took on the appearance of a para-military formation. As a recognized volunteer unit the SA was eligible for arms and support from the German army, and thus was not entirely under Hitler's own control. In 1925–6 it was re-organized and placed under the command of Pfeffer, though its members were still mainly ex-army men. Hitler did succeed in strengthening party control over it and making it a political arm of the party rather than a military extension of the Reichswehr, but internal revolts such as those in Munich (1927) and Berlin (1930) showed that Hitler's authority was still contested.

Under Röhm's leadership (1931–4) the SA began to aim again at a more independent role, both in organization and leadership. Röhm saw his troops as the armed vanguard of a working-class revolution which he believed the NSDAP itself was too effete and bourgeois to accomplish. After 1929 the SA came into growing conflict with the elitist SS, founded (1925–6) as a unit of the SA, but now achieving independence under the energetic and ambitious Himmler.

With this background of conflict Hitler had good reason to decide upon the destruction of the SA (June 1934) as a political factor, the more so as the Reichswehr was beginning to resent the ambitions of this rival army. The so-called Röhm putsch of 30 June 1934, in which the SA leadership was summarily executed, eliminated the threat of a second, SA revolution. Although the SA survived under the new leadership of Lutze, its political importance was permanently broken.

SA DE NORONHA, CONSTANTINE DE (d. 1630), Portuguese captain-general of Ceylon (1618–20, 1623–30). He was a ruler of high character and ability, who gave better treatment to the people and remedied many of the abuses which had marred Portuguese rule. He took over the Tamil kingdom of Jaffna and the ports of Trincomali and Batticaoloa on the east coast. His successes alarmed King Senarat of Kandy, who suborned some of De Sa's Sinhalese officials. They induced De Sa to invade the kingdom with insufficient forces, then betrayed him. He was killed in the ensuing battle.

SA'ADABAD PACT (8 July 1936), Consultative non-aggression pact signed between Turkey, Iran, Iraq, and Afghanistan. It was inspired partly by fear of Italian ambitions in the Middle East.

SAAVEDRA, ALVARO DE CERON (d. 1529), Spanish navigator who twice failed (1528, 1529) to discover a viable return passage from the Moluccas to Mexico, an achievement reserved to Urdaneta (1565).

SABA, West Indian island located north-west of St Eustatius. It was occupied by the Dutch (1640) and still (1970) belongs to them. It was the last stronghold of the buccaneers.

SABAEANS, first millennium BC south Arabian tribal confederation in Yemen and Hadramauth. Its capitals were first at Kharibah, then at Marib. It established an elaborate system of government and derived profit from the carefully protected spice trade. The kingdom was divided (115 BC) between the Hamda tribe of the coast and the Himyar tribe of the uplands around Shabwa. The Himyarite state was eventually overthrown by the Abyssinians (AD 525).

SABAHEDDIN, Prince (1877–1948), Ottoman liberal politician, son of Damad Mahmud Pasha (1855–1903), who, after being involved in various political manœuvres, fled to Paris with his son, who later succeeded as leader of the liberal faction of the Young Turks. Sabaheddin founded the League for Private Initiative and Decentralization, advocating a loose federal structure for the Ottoman empire to be achieved with European assistance, in opposition to the exclusive, centralizing policies of Ahmed Riza. After 1908 he was prominent in Ottoman liberal politics, but was eventually forced into permanent exile (1913).

SABBATARIANISM, doctrine of those Christians who regard the first day of the week as the sabbath to be respected as a holy day according to the 4th commandment. The rigorous observance of the sabbath became a characteristic of Scottish Presbyterianism from the time of John Knox and of English Puritanism, and the Westminster Assembly of 1647 gave a classic statement of the concept. In the 19th–20th cents the doctrine has been promoted by societies urging strict Sunday observance laws.

SABINE, SIR EDWARD (1788–1883), British soldier and Arctic explorer, who served in North America during the War of 1812. He was appointed astronomer to Arctic expeditions led by John Ross (1818) and Edward Parry (1819–20). On these expeditions Sabine accumulated and recorded much scientific information, particularly in the field of terrestrial magnetism.

SABINI, ancient Italian race dwelling in the Apennines north-east of Rome, around Reate and Amiternum. The Romans absorbed elements of their population and culture in the Regal period (7th–6th cents BC), and by 449 had halted their aggressive incursions. They were conquered in 290 by Curius Dentatus, became full Roman citizens in 268, and were rapidly Romanized.

SABLAT, BATTLE OF (June 1619), first Habsburg victory of the Thirty Years War when the imperial forces of Ferdinand II overwhelmingly defeated the 3000-strong force of Ernst von Mansfeld near the village of Sablat in Bohemia.

SACCO–VANZETTI CASE (1920–7) in the US, trial and political controversy heightened by tension aroused by the 'Red Scare' (1919–20). Two Italian-born radicals, Nicola Sacco (1891–1927) and Bartolomeo Vanzetti (1888–1927), were arrested, tried, and convicted (1921) for the murder of a pay-roll guard during a robbery in South Braintree, MA (1920). The evidence against the accused contained serious weaknesses, and the judge and jury were thought by many to be prejudiced against the defendants because of their immigrant origin and radical activities. After world-wide protest the governor of MA appointed an investigating commission to review the trial and he himself headed a further enquiry. Both bodies found that the trial had been fair and upheld its verdict. Amid protest and demonstrations, the men were eventually executed (1927).

A number of literary works, including 'Justice Denied in Massachusetts', a poem by Edna St Vincent Millay (1927), *Boston*, a novel by Upton Sinclair (1928), 'Firehead', a narrative poem by Lola Ridge (1929), and *Winterset*, a play by Maxwell Anderson (1935), were inspired by the case.

SACHEVERELL, THE TRIAL OF DR (1710) in England, impeachment of a high church apologist by the Whig ministry. Henry Sacheverell (c. 1674–1724), fellow of Magdalen College, Oxford, and chaplain of St Saviour's, Southwark, preached in St Paul's Cathedral, London, in Nov. 1709 (the anniversary of William III's landing) a violent sermon affirming the doctrine of non-resistance to the Crown. Because they were attacked in the sermon, Godolphin and the ministers impeached him for seditious libel. The peers' verdict in 1710 was 69 for conviction, 52 for acquittal. Sentence of three years' suspension from preaching and the burning of the sermon followed. Sacheverell became the hero of the London mob and a factor leading to a replacement of the ministry by Harley and the Tories.

SACHS, HANS (1494–1576), German poet and mastersinger, a shoemaker of Nuremberg, who adapted the *Fastnachtspiel* or Shrovetide play to produce popular dramas with a Protestant bias.

SACHSENSPIEGEL or the *Mirror of the Saxons* was the earliest codification in the medieval German vernacular of the legal customs of a German region. It was drawn up (c. 1222) by Eike von Repgow. Already at that time much of it was archaic and obsolete, but it was regarded as binding law and is of great value to the study of early German institutions and language.

SACKVILLE OF DRAYTON, LORD GEORGE SACKVILLE (after 1770 **GERMAIN**), 1st Viscount (1716–85), British soldier and politician, whose army career was ended by his court-martial for disobedience while commanding the British contingent at the battle of Minden (1759). He was dismissed from the army and the privy council, but his standing in the Commons grew steadily in the 1760s and his speeches on America (1772–4) exerted great influence. In office, however, as secretary of state with particular responsibility for the American colonies (1775–82), he proved critical and uncooperative.

SACRAMENTARIANS, Evangelical followers of Zwingli of Zürich and Oecolampadius of Basle, who embraced the symbolical interpretation of the eucharist from 1524, in contrast to the Lutheran concept of consubstantiation. Oecolampadius's *De Genuina verborum Domini* (1525) became the sacramentarians' handbook, but they lost ground after the deaths of the two reformers.

SACRED WAR, FIRST, fought (c. 590 BC) by Thessaly, Athens, and Cleisthenes of Sicyon against Crisa on behalf of Delphi. Crisa, which was accused of levying tolls from visitors to Delphi, was destroyed and Delphi became the second seat of the Amphictyonic League. The Athenian contingent was led by Alcmaeon, whose son Megacles later (c. 570) married Agariste, daughter of Cleisthenes of Sicyon.

SACRED WAR, SECOND, name given to an incident in the first Peloponnesian War (?448 BC), when first a Spartan expedition secured Delphi for the Delphians, and then the Athenians returned it to the Phocians.

SACRED WAR, THIRD (355–346 BC), fought in central Greece between Phocis and members of the Amphictyonic League, led by Thebes. Inspired by Philomelus, the Phocians defied an Amphictyonic judgement whereby they were fined for cultivating sacred land (356) and on the declaration of war they seized the treasures of Delphi to raise a mercenary army. Their successes seriously weakened Thebes and enabled Philip II of Macedon to intervene first in Thessaly, where after a setback in 353 he defeated Philomelus' successor, Onomarchus (352), then in central Greece. The Athenians, who had stopped Philip at Thermopylae in 352, abandoned the Phocians in the peace of Philocrates (346) and Philip subjected them, gaining control of the Amphictyonic Council.

SADANOBU (1758–1829), Japanese *daimyō* and *bakufu* leader, who was the grandson of Tokugawa Yoshimune. He took the lead in introducing the *Kansei* Reforms (1787–93), the object of which was to restore the *bakufu*'s financial position by imposing economics and sumptuary laws, encouraging agricultural production, limiting foreign trade, and cancelling the debts of *bakufu* retainers. Though temporarily effective, these traditional measures weakened the *bakufu* by making it more difficult to tap the increasing wealth of the merchants, but they were relaxed when the opposition of the shogunal court forced Sadanobu to resign.

SADASHIVA BHAO (1730–61), Maratha soldier, commonly known as the Bhao Sahib, nephew of the second Maratha Peshwa Baji Rao and first cousin of the third Balaji Baji Rao. He won his reputation by capturing Sangola (1750). After winning the battle of Udgir (1760) against the nizam, he was sent to retrieve the Maratha fortunes in the north against Ahmad Shah Abdali, the Afghan. After preliminary successes he was cut off at Panipat from his lines of communication. He attempted to break out, but was defeated and killed and his army destroyed (14 Jan. 1761). The Marathas did not return to the north till 1770.

SA'DI, Shaykh Muslih al-Din (d. 1292), Persian poet whose best-known works are the Bustan, a series of moral and philosophical poems, and the Gulistan, a volume of anecdotes and maxims written in a rhyming prose. He was also the author of ghazals or short odes.

SA'DI, AL-, Abd al-Rahman ibn Abdulla (1596– c.1655), born in Timbuctoo of mixed Arab descent, whose *Ta'rikh al-Sudan* constitutes the major historical source for the Western Sudan.

SA'DIANS, first Sharifian dynasty of Morocco (1549–1659), arose from a family of marabouts, or holy men, claiming descent from the Prophet (whence the title Sharif), in southern Morocco, where they exemplified a feature of North African tribal society in which such marabouts have frequently exercised political power as arbitrators. When associated, as many of them have been, in tariqas or brotherhoods, their networks of *zawiya*s or lodges have often provided tribal groupings with political consciousness and purpose. In this case the stimulus appears to have been the establishment of the Portuguese on the southern coast.

During the first decades of the 16th cent. the Sa'dians wrested the leadership of the southern tribes from rival marabouts, took over Marrakesh (1525) and expelled the Portuguese from Agadir, Agouz, Safi, and Azemmour (1541–2). Under Muhammad al-Shaikh they then turned against the discredited Wattasids of Fez and obtained the Moroccan sultanate (1549–54), claiming the title of caliph and adopting Marrakesh instead of Fez as their capital. Immediately they clashed with the Turks of Algiers in an enduring rivalry which entered into the politics of the age of Philip II. Under Abd Allah (reg. 1557–74) dynastic quarrels led to a diplomatic involvement with Spain and the Ottoman empire, while the sultan endeavoured to repress the marabouts, whose agitation had been the background of the dynasty's rise. On Abd Allah's death, his brother, Abd al-Malik, seized the throne, with Turkish help, from his son, Al-Mutawakkil, who fled first to Spain, then to Portugal. A Portuguese invasion followed, but it was defeated at Al-Qasr Al-Kabir (Alcazarquivir) (1578). The new sultan, Ahmad al-Dhahabi (the Golden), played off the powers, including England, with an economy whose principal extravagance was the conquest of Timbuctoo. On his death (1603) further dynastic quarrels reduced the power of the sultanate. The extreme south, the centre, and the east of the country fell into the hands of marabouts; Salé and Rabat became a republic of Moorish exiles from Spain, and a pirates' nest. After 1626 the Sa'dians were reduced to Marrakesh, where the last of the dynasty was murdered (1659) some years before the triumph of its Alawid successor.   MB

SADLER, MICHAEL THOMAS (1780–1835), British tory politician and philanthropist. He was Evangelical leader of the Ten-Hours movement. He opposed Catholic emancipation and the Reform Bill, and decried laissez-faire economic principles as an encouragement to employers to exploit labour. His 1831 bill restricting factory working hours for nine to eighteen-year-olds to ten a day led to a distinguished committee of enquiry with himself as chairman. The Factory Act (1833), and a Royal Commission (which largely reinforced the committee's findings) resulted. Ashley became the factory reformers' parliamentary spokesman when Macaulay unseated Sadler at Leeds.

SADLER COMMISSION, Calcutta University Commission (1917–19), presided over by Sir Michael Sadler, vice-chancellor of Leeds University. The commission's report was concerned with every aspect of higher education in Bengal. Its most important recommendations were the replacement of the older affiliating type of university by a unitary, teaching, and residential type, and the creation of 'intermediate colleges' to teach for the intermediate examination separate from degree courses. It looked for the early establishment of Dacca University and the upgrading of district colleges into universities. The government of India commended its suggestions to provincial governments in 1920, but progress both of university reform and the new colleges was slow. The next major review of Indian university education, the Indian Statutory Commission's auxiliary committee on education which was chaired by Sir Philip Hartog (a member of the Sadler Commission), commented that it was unlikely that the unitary-type university would be able to meet India's needs and that the affiliating university would continue for many years. The changes in intermediate education were more controversial and by the time the Hartog committee reported little progress had been made.

SADOLETO, GIACOMO (1477–1547), Venetian cleric, who served as a papal administrator, being secretary to Pope Leo X, was created Bp of Carpentras (1517) and made his name as one of the leading humanist scholars of his day. He was one of the first members of the pious guild of the Oratory of the Divine Love (1517) and later carried out much-needed reforms within his diocese in accordance with enlightened Catholic opinion. Elevated to the cardinalate by Pope Paul III (1536), he was appointed by him to the papal reform commission (1536) which produced the *Consilium . . . de Emendanda Ecclesia* (1537).

SADOWA, BATTLE OF (July 1866), in Bohemia, fought between evenly matched numbers of Prussians and Austrians, which decided the Austro-Prussian War in Prussia's favour. Austria's losses of 25,000 compared with Prussia's 9000 have been attributed to Prussian use of the breech-loading rifle. Prussian use of railways for troop movements was novel but not decisive.

SADR DIWANI ADALAT, or chief-civil court of appeal, in India, established at Calcutta by Warren Hastings in 1772 to hear appeals from the provincial civil courts. It was presided over by the governor of Bengal and two members of his council, assisted by Indians. As in the provincial courts, Hindu and Muslim law was administered and the maulvis and Brahmans attended to expound their respective laws. Because of friction between it and the Supreme Court, established by the Regulating Act (1773), Hastings appointed Impey, the chief justice of the Supreme Court, as president of the Sadr Diwani Adalat. This was not rectified until the Declaratory Act (1781). In 1861, when high courts were established in Calcutta, Madras, and Bombay, the Sadr Diwani Adalat, together with the Supreme Court, was amalgamated with the high court of Calcutta.

SADR NIZAMAT ADALAT, in India, set up by Warren Hastings in 1772 to supervise the proceedings of the provincial courts of criminal judicature. At first it was established at Murshidabad, with an Indian as president, assisted by a chief Kazi, a chief mufti, and three maulvis. In accordance with his policy of centralization, Hastings had it removed to Calcutta but, in 1775, the hostile majority on his council placed it under the deputy nawab at Murshidabad. In 1790 Cornwallis transferred it once more to Calcutta, where it remained until 1861, when the Sadr Nizamat Adalat was merged into the high court of Calcutta.

SAFAWID, Muslim dynasty of Turkish or possibly Kurdish origin ruling Iran (1501–1736). The name derives from Sheikh Safi al-Din Ishaq (1252–1334), who founded a Muslim religious order (the Safawiyya) centred at Ardebil, south-west of the Caspian. Safi claimed descent from Ali, the Prophet's son-in-law, via the seventh imam, Musa al-Kazim. So, although the founder was himself Sunni, it is unsurprising that the order assumed a Shi'ite character, notably from the time of Sheikh Khwaja Ali (1392–1427). Under Sheikh Junayd (1447–60) the order became proselytizing and political in its aims and gathered support among the Turkish tribes of Asia Minor and Azerbayjan. These tribes (including the Ustajlu, Shamlu, Tekelü, Beharlu, Zul Qadr, Qadar, and Afshar) eventually became the basis of the support of Isma il I, who defeated the remnants of the preceding Aq Qoyunlu regime and made himself first Safawid ruler of Iran (*reg.* 1499–1504). His conflicts with the Ottomans and the Uzbegs established the broad limits of his domain. He was succeeded by his son Tahmasp I (*reg.* 1524–1576). At the beginning and end of Tahmasp's reign there was civil war among the Turkish tribes but the unity of the Safawid state was restored by Abbas I (the Great) (*reg.* 1585–1628), who captured Baghdad from the Ottomans in the west and Kandahar from the Mughals in the east. Under Abbas the evolution from a theocratic to a secular basis for the state, which had begun as early as the reign of Isma il, was carried much further. The successors of Abbas were his grandson Safi I (*reg.* 1629–42), Safi's son Abbas II (*reg.* 1642–66), and Abbas's son Safi, who took the name Suleiman (*reg.* 1666–94). Under Suleiman's son Sultan Husayn (*reg.* 1694–1722) Safawid control loosened and succumbed to an attack by the Ghilzay Afghans (1722). During the years 1722–1729 Iran also suffered Russian and Ottoman invasions, but unity was restored by Nadir Quli Khan Afshar, who, after being de facto ruler from 1732, deposed the last Safawid ruler in 1736. Some members of the Safawid dynasty continued as nominal rulers in certain parts of Iran until the end of the 18th cent.   MEY

SAFFAH, AL-, ABU'L'ABBAS (*reg.* 749–54), first Abbasid caliph, proclaimed in 749 at Al-Kufa in Iraq. The defeat of the last Umayyad caliph, Marwan II, in the battle of the Great Zab river (Jan. 750) marked a decisive moment in the great revolution which overthrew the house of Umayya and brought the house of Abbas to the throne. In Aug, 750 Marwan II was taken and killed at Busir in Egypt. The reign of Al-Saffah witnessed also the suppression of a revolt at Bukhara which sought to enforce the claim of the House of Ali to the caliphate.

SAFFARID, name of a Muslim dynasty originating in the Persian province of Sijistan and raised to prominence by Ya'qub ibn Layth al-Saffar (the Coppersmith). By the time of his death in 879 Ya'qub ibn Layth had extended Saffarid control over Sijistan, Kirman, and much of Khurasan. His brother and successor, Amr ibn Layth, strove hard to consolidate Saffarid influence over Khurasan and also over Fars. He came into conflict with the rising power of the Samanids, suffered defeat at their hands in 900, and, being sent as a captive to the Abbasid caliph, was executed at Baghdad (902), an event which marked the end of the Saffarid emirs as a major force in Persia and the adjacent lands.

SAGA, supreme art-form of medieval Iceland which represents a major contribution to world literature. It consisted of prose narrative describing a fairly complete sequence of events. The historical form common to most sagas was derived largely from the 12th-cent. historians and genealogists. Other, ultimately foreign, genres which influenced and were absorbed into the saga included saints' lives and romances. Many sagas drew on two major periods: the Icelandic 'saga age' (c. 10th cent.) and the legendary prehistory of other lands. These diverse sources are reflected in great variation of saga content, from the almost purely historical to almost pure legend and even deliberate 'fiction'. The contents of sagas may have been elaborated during a long period of oral transmission but the current view is that their literary form should be attributed to particular authors at the time when they were written down. Saga-writing proper was preceded by a period ending in the 12th cent., when the chief literary activity was the composition of complex skaldic poetry. The great age of saga-writing, mostly by unknown authors, was the 13th cent.

SAGASTA, PRAXEDES (1827–1903), Spanish politician, founder of the Spanish Liberal Party, and several times prime minister of Spain. His acceptance of the 1876 constitution and his willingness to operate the system of *caciquismo* (electoral management) in the interests of strong government, strengthened the monarchy during Maria Cristina's regency and enabled him to implement a programme of thoroughgoing liberal reforms (1885–90). But although these gave Spain the appearance of democratic monarchy they did not contribute to the urgent need for modernization of the economy or for social reform. Sagasta failed to see beyond the immediate political situation and did not broaden the basis of his party to meet the real needs of Spain.

SAGAULI, TREATY OF (4 March 1816), brought the Anglo-Nepalese War to an end. The Gurkhas ceded Garhwal and Kumaon and most of the Tarai. They withdrew from Sikkim and accepted a British resident at Katmandu.

SAGINAW TREATY (29 Sept. 1819), negotiated by the US official, Lewis Cass, with the Chippewa Indians. In return for an annuity of $1000, land was ceded to the US in the Saginaw Bay area of MI territory.

SAGUENAY, KINGDOM OF, mythical Canadian land said to lie between the Saguenay and Ottawa rivers and allegedly full of precious metals. Francis I sent two expeditions (1535, 1541) to Canada to search for the 'kingdom'. They resulted in considerable loss of life, but nothing of any value was found.

SAGUNTUM, ancient Spanish town 161 kms south of the Ebro, allied to Rome c. 227 BC. It was stormed by Hannibal 219 (this being the cause of the Second Punic War) and recaptured by the Scipios in 212. Later, it became a base of the Roman rebel Sertorius (expelled 75 BC), then a self-governing town (*municipium*) with citizen rights under Augustus.

SAHA, MEGHNAD (1893–1956), Indian politician and physicist who overcame a background of poverty to become professor of physics at Calcutta in 1921. His most famous work was in astrophysics, where the Saha equation describes the conditions in the hot atmospheres of stars and enables the astronomical observations of them to be interpreted. He was active in public life, a member of parliament, and instrumental in the development of modern science in India.

SAHAGÚN, BERNARDINO DE (c. 1500–90), Franciscan friar, whose *General History of the Things of New Spain,* compiled through the use of native informants, is vital to our knowledge of the daily life, religious customs, and beliefs of the Aztecs.

SAHAYDACHNY, HETMAN (d. 1622), Ukrainian Cossack leader who worked for the organization of the Cossacks into territorial units or regiments and for the replacement, by a registered class of native gentry, of the alien gentry class who had hitherto dominated the peasantry.

SAHLE SELASSIE (reg. 1813–47), King of the central Ethiopian province of Shoa and founder of its power. On inheriting the throne of Shoa, at a time when this province was largely isolated by the Galla from other Christian provinces of Ethiopia, then warring among themselves, he succeeded in greatly consolidating the Shoan realm. This he did partly by good government and partly by importing firearms. He was also interested in introducing foreign craftsmen, and sought to open contact with Europe, signing treaties of friendship and commerce with Britain and France in 1841 and 1843 respectively. He thus paved the way for the later successes of his grandson, Menelik II.

SAID IBN SULTAN (reg. 1806–56), Sultan of Oman and Zanzibar. Assisted by the British-Indian government, he defended his position against attacks by rival sheikhs, the Wahhabis, and the pirate Jawasmi of the Persian Gulf, but failed to conquer Bahrayn. From 1820 he was more interested in his East African than Arab dominions, and by 1837 had restored the whole coast to obedience. Under the protection of Britain, and financed by Indian merchants, he instigated the planting of cloves in Zanzibar and developed the trade routes into Africa. During his reign the coast enjoyed a prosperity probably more widespread than at any time in the past.

SA'ID HALIM PASHA, MEHMED (1863–1921), Ottoman politician and grandson of Muhammad Ali of Egypt. He was a prominent member of the Committee of Union and Progress and served as grand vizier (1913–17).

SA'ID PASHA (1822–63), Pasha of Egypt (reg. 1854–63) in succession to his nephew, Abbas I, youngest son of Muhammad Ali. Sa'id made important innovations by granting new land rights (1858), by his concession for the Suez Canal (1856), and by foreign borrowings.

SAIFAWA, one of the most famous dynasties of western Africa. Its early kings ruled over the original Kanuri state of Kanem, near Lake Chad, about 1000 years ago, while its last king held the throne of Bornu (successor-state to Kanem) until 1846: the name itself derives from that of Saif dnu Yazin, a 7th-cent. ruler of the Himyaritic state of Yemen in southern Arabia, from whom the Kanuri rulers claimed descent, though almost certainly without any basis of fact. The earliest Saifawa were chiefs of a number of small states in the Chad region from which the larger state of Kanem gradually crystallized, the power of these chiefs being founded in the alliance of a number of neighbouring groups who spoke one or other of the central Saharan languages. Ibadite traders from the Maghrib undoubtedly introduced the ideas of Islam to this region in the 8th and 9th cents, but the Kanuri kings accepted Islam, according to tradition, only towards the end of the 11th cent.

Saifawa influence spread far to the north under Dunama II (d. 1259), who made an alliance with the Hafsid king of Tunis and occupied the Fezzan. Kanemi power was then weakened by internal disputes following the death of Ibrahim Nikale (late 13th cent.); in about 1329 a subject people called the Bulala rose in revolt and drove the Saifawa out of Kanem, westward into Bornu (now north-eastern Nigeria). A second Kanuri empire under Saifawa rulers was established in Bornu by Ali Gaji in the 15th cent.; his son Idris Katagarmabe reoccuped Kanem, east of the lake, while Idris Alooma (d. *c.* 1619) again extended the empire's influence. This new empire grew wealthy under other strong rulers during the 17th cent. and its cities became centres of Muslim learning, although the end of that century brought renewed troubles from Desert Berbers (Tawreg) and from some of the empire's subject peoples.

In 1808 the ruling Saifawa *mai* (king) was driven from his capital by Fulani *mujahiddin* under Goni Mukhtar, but was restored by the aid of *Shehu* (Sheikh) Muhammad Amin al-Kanemi, who thereupon became the country's effective ruler. Its nominal Saifawa ruler, *Mai* Ibrahim (*reg.* 1818–46), attempted to regain his authority by alliance with neighbouring Wadai; this attempt failed, and Ibrahim and his son Ali were killed in 1846.

SAIGŌ, TAKAMORI (1827–77), Japanese soldier and political leader, who played an important part in the Meiji Restoration, but died opposing the Meiji government. Though by birth a samurai of low rank, his great stature and forceful character made him a leading figure in Satsuma in the 1850s, and although twice exiled he helped to establish the Satsuma–Chōshū alliance (1866). After commanding the imperial forces during the Restoration War, Saigō became unhappy about the new government's reform policies, and although he accepted office in 1870 the refusal of his boyhood friend, Ōkubo Toshimichi, to agree to a Korean expedition led to his resignation (1873). He returned to Satsuma Saigō and became the focus of many discontented samurai who wished to overthrow the government. When some of his followers attacked government forces (Feb. 1877) Saigō felt bound to support them, although he considered their attempt futile. His death by hara-kiri has earned him great admiration from later generations of Japanese, to whom it symbolizes his tragic failure to reconcile old values and new loyalties.

SAIGON, TREATIES OF, between France and Viet-nam (Annam) (1862, 1874). In June 1862 the Viet-namese emperor, Tu-Duc, ceded to France the three provinces of Cochin-China, which she had occupied in 1860; she also agreed to pay an indemnity of 20 million francs to France and Spain, and opened to French and Spanish merchants the ports of Da-Nang, Ba-Lac, and Quang-An. In 1863 the Viet-namese sent an embassy to France to try to obtain the return of the lost provinces, but in vain. By 1867 the threat to French control over them was so great that French troops annexed the three remaining provinces of Cochin-China; this annexation was not accepted by Viet-nam until 1874. Meanwhile, in 1873, a French force under Francis Garnier occupied Hanoi, but the French government decided to order its withdrawal.

By the second treaty of Saigon (March 1874) the Viet-namese ceded the whole of Cochin-China to France, opened for trade the ports of Qui-Nhon, Hai-Phong, and Hanoi, and agreed to tolerate Christianity. In return, the French recognized Viet-nam's independence, so long as the emperor respected French wishes in his relations with other powers. The French subsequently interpreted this as acceptance of a French protectorate.   RBS

SAILENDRA (lit. 'Lords of the Mountain'), name of a royal dynasty in ancient Java, Indonesia (*c.* AD 775–860), and Sri Vijaya, South Sumatra (*c.* 860–1025, or later). The origin of the Sailendra kings, who appear to have assumed authority in Central Java shortly after Sanjaya, is obscure. The older view of Indian origin has rightly lost support. Though some scholars connect the Sailendras with the dynasty in control of Funan (southern Cambodia) till the 7th cent. AD, it now seems likely that they were a purely Indonesian family.

The Sailendras were great patrons of Mahayana Buddhism and sponsored the building of numerous Buddhist monuments in Java, notably Borobudur. As rulers of Sumatra they continued the traditional policy of Sri Vijaya by encouraging trade and shipping, and preserving friendly relations with China. They were also in relation with Indian states, but a South Indian campaign against Sri Vijaya (*c.* 1025) caused great havoc. Though Sri Vijaya remained a strong power for over two centuries it is doubtful whether it continued to be governed by the Sailendras.

SAILING CRAFT in East Africa. For many centuries East Africa's good harbours, sailing conditions, and chances of trade have encouraged large fleets of local sailing craft and larger vessels trading from Arabia, Persia, and India. All these are commonly called dhows—a word said to come from the Swahili *dau*, a small sailing vessel—although Arabs do not use this word.

The earlier local vessels—such as the Lamu *mtepe*, still in use until recently—were built with stitched planks, the ribs being inserted afterwards. But the arrival of the Portuguese after 1497 caused a revolution in design, and the carvel-built, iron-fastened boat gradually came in. The larger vessels still prominent in the 'dhow harbours' of Mombasa and Zanzibar likewise show Portuguese or other European influences, having high, square sterns reminiscent of 16th-cent. European vessels. The Persian *baghla* has a finely carved stern, while the *sambuk* from the Red Sea may have multi-coloured paintwork round the stern, again reminiscent of a European custom. *Sambuks*, which arrive on the coast with the monsoon winds at the beginning of the year, are usually from 80 to 150 tons, with a single mast rigged for a large lateen sail. An earlier type of *sambuk*, with three masts, is no longer seen. The *boom* from Persia is a similar type, but has a long and steeply raked bow.

All these vessels are fully decked, with a triangular-shaped hatch on the hold, and a forward-raking mast wedged in the forward apex of the triangle. The smaller Somali-owned *sambuks*, the Lamu *mtepe*, and the Kenya *buti* and *jahazi* are often half-decked or open, with a deck-house formed by an arched roof of *makuti* or palm-frond thatch. Matting weather-screens are often placed along the sides. Round Mombasa a bowsprit is quite common, while a marked feature is the presence of *oculi* or 'eyes', painted discs nailed to either side of the bows, thought to guide the boat safely, or, in the case of fishing boats, to watch for shoals of fish. The *ngalawa*, a small sailing canoe made from a hollowed tree-trunk, and having a starboard-rigged outrigger, is still (1970) in use and may have a remote Indonesian origin.

G. L. Sullivan, *Dhow Chasing in Zanzibar Waters* (London, 1873).
J. Jewel, *Dhows at Mombasa* (Nairobi, 1970).   OWF

SAILLANT, LOUIS (1910–   ), French trade unionist and secretary of the World Federation of Trade Unions, which had (1970) its headquarters in Prague. He was an official in the CGT trade union movement in pre-war France, then organized clandestine trade union activities in the Resistance. He became president of the National Resistance Council, and a member of the Consultative Assembly (1944). He represented the CGT in the international negotiations which set up the WFTU and became its first general secretary (1945).

ST ALBAN, FRANCIS BACON, Viscount (1561–1626), English lawyer, philosopher, writer, and politician. In the constitutional struggles of the reign of James I he supported the Crown, believing good government to consist in a wise exercise of the royal prerogative, assisted by the judges as 'lions under the throne'. This made him unpopular with the parliamentary opposition and with the lawyers, particularly Sir Edward Coke, and his impeachment in 1621 on a technical charge of accepting bribes was largely an act of political revenge.

His fame as a writer chiefly depends on his *Essays*, masterpieces of compressed thought and expression, but his influence in his own time was as a leader of an intellectual revolution against older habits of thought. Rejecting the scholastic and humanist tradition of the universities, rooted deep in Aristotle, he said that knowledge should be freed from religious and emotional preconceptions and should be pursued in a spirit that was humble, modern, empirical, and scientific. His *History of Henry VII* (1622) was a pioneer work in another literary field. In substituting psychological and political analysis for the chroniclers' familiar aggregation of facts, it was one of the first 'modern' biographies.

He was the younger son of Sir Nicholas Bacon (1509–79), lord keeper, and a nephew of Burghley, but these connections failed to procure him a political career and he only made his name by turning on his patron, the Earl of Essex, after the latter's abortive rising (1601) against Elizabeth I. Under James's favour he became solicitor-general (1607), attorney-general (1613), lord chancellor, and Baron Verulam (1618) and Viscount St Alban (1621). Although his impeachment ended his political career, the savage penalties that resulted were only partially enforced and he was allowed to take his seat in the Lords.

Bacon's intellectual position was made clear in *The Advancement of Learning* (1606). The traditional disciplines of Rhetoric encouraged the mistake of studying words instead of things, and accordingly he proposed a new approach to the systematization of knowledge. Thought must be unshackled by forging new instruments of enquiry, and the *Novum Organum* (1620) introduced by the *Instauratio Magna Scientiarum*, was a blueprint for the renewal of knowledge and investigative method in every significant area. The *Novum Organum* itself austerely stipulated that man, being only the interpreter of Nature, should not theorize beyond the limits of his experience.

Bacon did not live to fulfil his theme. He died from a chill resulting from a characteristic experiment in inductive science when, in order to test the possibilities of refrigeration, he buried a chicken in the snow to see if this would preserve the body. In the posthumous *New Atlantis* (1626), a political fable set on an imaginary Pacific island, he demonstrated again the intellectual consistency of one who, at the age of 30, wrote that 'I have taken all knowledge to be my province'.

J. Spedding, R. L. Ellis, and D. D. Heath, *Life, Letters and Works*, 14 vols (London, 1857–74).
R. W. Church, *Bacon* (Oxford, 1884).   MMR

ST ALDWYN, MICHAEL EDWARD HICKS-BEACH, 1st Earl (1837–1916), British Conservative politician, who was one of the able young men given office by Disraeli, who appointed him Irish chief secretary (1874–8) and colonial secretary (1878–80), in which office he handled the Zulu Wars and defended Frere. He was leader of the House of Commons in Salisbury's caretaker government of 1885, and again in his ministry of 1886, but resigned in favour of Lord Randolph Churchill, with whom he had become closely associated. He was Irish chief secretary (1886–7) and chancellor of the exchequer in Salisbury's ministry of 1895. As such, he was responsible for financing the Boer War and, following Gladstone's precedent in the Crimean War, did so largely from taxation. On Salisbury's retirement (1902) he also retired and went to the House of Lords.

ST ANDRÉ, JACQUES D'ALBON, Seigneur de (*c.* 1505–62), French Catholic nobleman and marshal who, with Constable Montmorency and the Duc de Guise, formed a Triumvirate (April 1561) to destroy the Huguenots in France, with Spanish help. This action contributed to the outbreak of the first Civil War, in which, after taking Poitiers, St André was killed at the battle of Dreux (Dec. 1562).

ST ARNAUD, ARMAND JACQUES LEROY (1801–54), French soldier, who, after a distinguished military career in Algeria, organized the *coup d'état* for Napoleon III, was promoted marshal (1852), and commanded the French army in the Crimean War.

ST BARTHOLOMEW, West Indian island located south of Anguilla. It was first occupied by France (1648), ceded to Sweden (1784), and returned to France (1877).

ST BARTHOLOMEW'S DAY, MASSACRE OF (1572), in France, slaughter of French Huguenots in Paris on St Bartholomew's Day (24 Aug.), ordered by the King Charles IX at the instigation of his mother, Catherine de' Medici, on the occasion of the marriage of Marguerite de Valois and the Huguenot Henry of Navarre (18 Aug.). Catherine's jealousy of Admiral Coligny, the Huguenot leader, and her suspicion of his anti-Spanish policy, led her to take desperate measures and to approve a plot hatched by the Duc de Guise and his family to exterminate Coligny in revenge for the murder of Francis de Guise (1563). The planned attempt on Coligny's life failed (22 Aug.), but in the panic of realization that her complicity would be revealed, Catherine authorized the assassination of all the Huguenot leaders. She did not, however, foresee the mass slaughter which began in the early hours of 24 Aug. and continued for another month in the French provinces. Though the papacy and Philip II of Spain rejoiced, horror swept the Protestant countries, while French Huguenots abandoned their former policy of passive obedience and proclaimed the right of resistance.

SAINT CASTIN, JEAN VINCENT D'ABBADIE, Baron de (1652–1707), French soldier, who went to New France (1665) and took command of Fort Pentagoët, Acadia (1676). He married the daughter of a chief of the Abnaki Indians and became their war chief, leading them in raids on British forts (1690, 1696). He was forced to return temporarily to France (1701) because of his being involved in illegal fur-trading activities.

ST CLOUD in France, royal palace outside Paris built by a Parisian bourgeois, bought by Catherine de' Medici, and later remodelled as a château by Mansart (1678). Used by Marie Antoinette and Napoleon, it was destroyed in the battle of Bizenval (1871).

ST CYRAN, JEAN-ANTOINE DUVERGIER DE HAURANNE, Abbé de (1581–1643), French cleric who was one of the dominant figures of the French Counter-Reformation. Involved in the theological and political controversies of his time, he fell foul of both the Jesuits and Richelieu, particularly for his *Petrus Aurelius* (1631) which eventually led to his arrest by Richelieu (1638). Imprisoned at Vincennes in very harsh conditions, he was the sympathic object of a storm of protest particularly from the monastery of Port Royal, where he was spiritual director (1635). Eventually released (1643) he died a few months later, leaving to the world the great treatise of his intimate friend Jansen with whose ideas he has been inextricably linked by historians. However, he was Jansen's intellectual equal, not his pupil, and his ideas were those of orthodox Berullian Catholicism rather than those of a heretical party.

ST DENIS, BATTLE OF (1567), Catholic victory over the French Huguenots during the second Civil War (1567–8), when the forces of the Constable Montmorency, who was killed, defeated those of the Prince of Condé and his German allies.

SAINT DENIS EXPEDITION (1714–15), French trading expedition led by Louis Juchereau de Saint Denis (1676–1744), who founded a post at Natchitoches on the Red river in LA.

ST DIZIER, AGREEMENT OF (April 1561), understanding concluded in France between Mary Queen of Scots and Lord

James Stuart, acting on behalf of the Protestant lords in Scotland. The latter were willing to permit Mary and her attendants to hear private mass and to uphold her succession rights to the childless Elizabeth of England, provided she would accept the religious settlement of 1560–1 and their political guidance. For over three years after her return to Scotland (Aug. 1561) Mary adhered to this agreement.

ST EUSTATIUS, West Indian island occupied by the Dutch (1635). During the American War of Independence, while Holland was still neutral, the island was a thriving centre for trade with the rebellious colonies. After Holland went to war against Britain (1781), the British fleet, under Rodney, seized the island. It was returned to the Dutch in 1783.

ST FRANCIS INDIANS, mixed group whose members settled at the Catholic mission village of St Francis in Quebec after English settlers drove them from their tribal homes in New England. During the French and Indian War (1755–63) they raided the English colonies until a force under Robert Rogers burnt their village (1759), killing many and scattering the rest. Some of the St Francis joined the British in the American War of Independence and the War of 1812.

ST GABRIEL, small wooden ship built by Vitus Bering and his crew of 44 men for their first voyage of exploration from the Arctic coast of Kamchatka (1728). Her sails were hoisted on 13 July 1728 and the party sailed past the mouth of the Anadyr and reached the straits between Siberia and Alaska before turning back to Kamchatka.

ST GEORGE'S CAY, BATTLE OF (10 Sept. 1798), military victory for Britain and her colonists over Spain, following the latter's challenge to British occupation of the Bay of Honduras. The victory paved the way for the eventual British domination in what later became British Honduras.

ST GEORGE'S CHAPEL, Windsor, begun (*c.* 1476) by King Edward IV on the site of a former royal chapel and completed by Henry VII; there have since been substantial renovations and additions. Like King's College, Cambridge, and the royal chapel at Westminster, it was built in Perpendicular Gothic and has the characteristic vaulted interior, tracery, and thrusting buttresses. There is an impressive facade on the west front and a wrought-iron grille, made by John Tresilian, to enclose the tomb of Edward IV. It is the burial place of several British sovereigns.

ST GERMAIN, DECLARATION OF (1649), French edict prohibiting the import of English cloth into France which brought English retaliatory measures on French imports.

ST GERMAIN, PACIFICATION OF (1570), settlement between the King Charles IX of France and the Huguenots, the most favourable treaty secured by them to that date and the fruit of Coligny's overwhelming victory of Arnay-le-duc (15 June 1570) in the third Civil War. The edict of pacification (8 Aug. 1570) restored the status quo as existing on 1 Aug., the Huguenots were to be granted four towns of security, La Rochelle, Cognac, Montauban, and La Charité, and the restoration of their lands, honours, offices, and judicial and other privileges. The Crown agreed to pay off the *reiters,* German mercenaries who fought for the Huguenot cause. The peace was welcomed by the majority of the people, anxious for peace and economic recovery, but it proved only temporary because of the continued ambitions of the Guise faction and the intervention of Spain in French internal affairs.

ST GERMAIN, PEACE OF (1679), treaty ending the hostilities between Sweden and Brandenburg, which arose from Louis XIV's Dutch war, and mediated by the French king. Although the Swedes had been defeated by the Great Elector's forces, *eg* at Fehrbellin (1675), Brandenburg was allowed to retain only a strip of East Pomerania because of the pressure applied by Sweden's powerful French ally.

ST GERMAIN, TREATY OF (1632), Anglo-French treaty restoring to France those territories in Quebec and Acadia captured by the British companies operating in the area and activated by the Kirke brothers, the Canada Co. and the Nova Scotia Co. (1628–9).

ST GERMAIN, TREATY OF (1919), peace settlement signed between the Allied Powers and Austria at the end of the First World War. Although the war had been fought collectively by the Austro-Hungarian empire, the Allies formally acknowledged the separation of the two states and recognized the republic of Austria, now shorn of most of its former possessions. Disregarding the protests of the Austrian representatives to the Paris peace conference, the Allied Powers, in their endeavour to apply the principle of self-determination to the minorities of the former empire and protect their newly gained independence, deprived Austria of approximately one-third of its German-speaking population. Although the US president, Wilson, himself had been prepared to be less severe in the treatment of Austria, the French demanded the cession of the Sudetenland to Czechoslovakia on the grounds of the latter's security; and the Italian delegation insisted on the implementation of the secret agreements of the treaty of London (1915) by which Italy had been promised the South Tyrol and the Trentino. In addition, the treaty of St Germain ceded Dalmatia, Slovenia, and Bosnia-Herzegovina to Yugoslavia and Galicia and Bukovina to Poland and Rumania respectively. A clause similar to that in the treaty of Versailles effectively prevented Anschluss between Austria and Germany by stipulating that the unanimous consent of the League of Nations was required before such a union could take place.

The military terms limited the Austrian army to a long-term volunteer force of 30,000 and dismembered the former Austro-Hungarian navy, distributing part of the fleet among the Allies.

In signing the treaty Austria assumed responsibility for damage inflicted on the Allies, but although the total cost was left to be finalized by the Reparations Committee and some payments in kind were made, no money was ever paid. On the contrary, by 1921 the demands on Austria had already begun to relax and were finally cancelled in 1922 by a large financial loan to Austria from the League of Nations.

The dismembered state of Austria had been left in an unenviable economic position with a large proportion of its population living in Vienna and much of its former industrial and agricultural sources lost to its successor states. The enforced separation of Austria and Germany was particularly regretted and the issue underlay the friction between the two countries during the 1930s until Hitler successfully challenged the treaty and effected the prohibited Anschluss (1938).

WFK

ST GOTTHARD ON RAAB, BATTLE OF (Aug. 1664), victory of a numerically inferior force of French and Germans under the imperial commander, Montecuccoli, over the Turkish army of 100,000 men under Fazil Ahmed, hailed as the triumph of Christian arms over the infidel. Montecuccoli's army of 60,000 held a strong position behind the Raab river, some 80 kms east of Vienna, and they destroyed the Turkish horde as they crossed the river near the monastery of St Gotthard. Despite the victory, the Emperor Leopold confirmed the treaty of Vasvar, the terms of which were not unfavourable to Turkey.

ST HELENA, island in the south Atlantic of 100 sq. kms with a population (1970) of nearly 5000. It was discovered by the Portuguese and administered by the English East India Co. from the 17th cent. until it became a Crown colony in 1834. Napoleon I was imprisoned on the island from 1815 till his death in 1821. In 1968 the first elected members took their seats in the Legislative Council.

ST ISIDORE OF SEVILLE (570–636), Spanish scholar, who compiled an encyclopaedia, called *Etymologiae*, which set out to record the body of existing knowledge within a Christian framework. It was widely used as an educational work until the 13th cent.

ST JEAN DE MAURIENNE AGREEMENT (1917), tripartite agreement between Britain, France, and Italy, by which an area of the Ottoman empire surrounding Smyrna was to be ceded to Italy at the end of the First World War. The origin of the agreement lay in Italian anxiety at the news of the Sykes–Picot agreement (1916) on the division of interests in the Middle East between Britain and France. To be effective, the agreement required the signature of Russia, but the Revolution (Oct. 1917) prevented this. The agreement was significant, therefore, only as a contribution to Italy's sense of grievance after the war.

ST JOHN, OLIVER (*c.* 1598–1673), English lawyer and politician, who was chief justice of the court of Common Pleas during the Commonwealth. In 1630, with the Earl of Bedford, he was charged before the Star Chamber with the publication of seditious libel, but the case was dismissed. He was a member of the Providence Island Co., moved in Parliamentary opposition circles, and became well known in 1637 through his defence of John Hampden in his trial over ship money. In 1638 he married into the Cromwell family and became an intimate friend of Oliver Cromwell. As an MP in the Short and Long Parliaments he allied himself closely with the opposition leaders, Bedford, Pym, and Hampden. In order to try to win the support of St John's friends, Charles I appointed St John solicitor-general (Jan. 1641), but his loyalties and politics remained unchanged. He was active in Strafford's impeachment and attainder and in various opposition bills, *eg*, the Militia Bill. After Pym's death (Dec. 1643) he inherited for some time his role as leader of the middle party within the Long Parliament. In 1647 he supported the army in its quarrel with parliament, and in 1648 was appointed chief justice of the Common Pleas. He refused to act, however, at the king's trial (Jan. 1649). He was active during the Commonwealth and protectorate, being one of the commissioners responsible for the union with Scotland, and in 1657 he urged Cromwell to take the Crown. He was excluded from office at the Restoration, and in 1662 retired to the continent.

ST JOHN OF THE CROSS, Juan de Yepes (1542–91), Spanish mystic, who rebelled against the laxity of the Carmelite order and, with the encouragement of Theresa of Avila, set up a house for discalced friars to observe their strict rule (1568). Afterwards he was persecuted and imprisoned by his superiors. At Granada (1581) he made the acquaintance of Arabian mystics and wrote *The Dark Night of the Soul* and three other works setting forth a connected mystical doctrine. They describe the purgation of the soul from the dark night of the senses and the final purification of the spirit until after intense suffering it attains the transforming union with God. He was canonized in 1726.

ST JUST, LOUIS ANTOINE DE (1767–94), French politician, who was Robespierre's closest colleague, sharing both his political and his moral principles. For him the Jacobin dictatorship and the Terror were necessary steps towards establishing the 'Republic of Virtue'. As a member of the Committee of Public Safety, he was instrumental in destroying both Danton and Hébert. His missions to the front during the first year of the French Wars had an invigorating effect on the Rhine army, but his quarrels with Carnot over the conduct of the war did much to weaken the Jacobins in their last months of power. He was executed with Robespierre and Couthon, all three being victims of the coup of *Thermidor*.

ST KITTS (St Christopher's), British island in the West Indies ,discovered by Columbus (1493) on his second voyage to America. Thomas Warner established the first permanent settlement there in the name of the British Crown (1623). The island was referred to as 'The Mother Colony of the British West Indies' because the English used it as a base for colonization of other islands in the Caribbean. The French also established a settlement on the island (1623), and both settlements were nearly destroyed by the Spanish fleet (1629). After the fleet departed, the few remaining French re-established a colony and dominated the island until the British portions were later restored (1689). The British gained complete control of the island (1782) and in 1882 the islands of St Kitts, Nevis, and Anguilla were united under a common administration. In 1967 the three islands adopted 'associate status' with Britain, with the right to independence, at any time, if they so wished.

SAINT LAURENT, LOUIS STEPHEN (1882–1968), Canadian lawyer, politician, and prime minister, who was a recognized authority on constitutional law. He entered federal politics (1941) on being asked by the Liberal prime minister, Mackenzie King, to be minister of justice. He became secretary for external affairs (1946) and succeeded King as prime minister in 1948, continuing the policies of his predecessor. His term of office was notable for the relaxation of tensions between French- and English-speaking Canadians and for the welding of a close economic and military alliance with the US.

SAINT LAWRENCE SEAWAY, maritime highway connecting the Saint Lawrence river and the Great Lakes. The idea of a seaway was put forward in 1900 and became the subject of many US and Canadian commissions and reports (1921, 1926, 1927). In 1932 a treaty was signed between the US and Canada accepting the principle of building a seaway but, owing to opposition from American railroads and other interested groups, work did not begin until 1954. The seaway was officially opened by President Eisenhower and Queen Elizabeth II in 1959.

ST LEGER, SIR ANTHONY (1496–1559), English lord deputy of Ireland (1540–8, 1553–6) who pursued a policy of moderation and conciliation, persuading the Irish parliament to grant Henry VIII the style of King of Ireland and winning the allegiance of the tribal chiefs whom he also induced to acknowledge the royal supremacy. Though recalled (1548–1553), he was restored by Edward VI but finally dismissed by Mary I.

ST LUCIA, West Indian island discovered by the Spanish (1502) and settled by the British (1638). The island, with its excellent natural harbour, was a source of conflict between the French and the British. It was finally ceded to Britain (1814). In 1967 it adopted 'associate status' with Britain, with the right to independence, at any time, if it so wished.

ST MARTIN, West Indian island located between Anguilla and St Bartholomew. It was occupied by the French (1640–8) and divided between Holland and France (1648). The island is still (1970) divided between the two countries.

ST MARY'S CLYST, BATTLE OF (1549), victory of the English royal forces in the Civil War commanded by Lord Russell over the Devon rebels who attacked his army while on the way to relieve Arundel's siege of Exeter.

ST PETERSBURG, formerly the capital of Russia (1712–1918), called Petrograd (1914–24) and now Leningrad after Lenin, it is the second largest city of the USSR and a leading industrial centre. With its 360 bridges spanning the Neva river, it is regarded as one of the world's most beautiful cities and was founded by Peter the Great to serve as a 'window on Europe' (1703–12). Though sited on low and swampy ground at the mouth of the Neva, which resulted in the deaths of thousands of the artisans and craftsmen involved in its construction, the city grew rapidly in the 18th cent. as the main outlet for European trade. Its working-class population and the sailors of the nearby Kronstadt naval base played a leading part in the Russian Revolution (1917) but its people were to suffer great hardships in the ensuing civil war (1918–21) and during the Second World War, when it was besieged for 900 days by the German armies (1941–4). By 1950 the work of restoring a city largely destroyed by war was completed.

ST PETERSBURG TREATY (Aug. 1772), between Russia, Prussia, and Austria, which established the first partition of Poland, dividing between the powers about one-third of Polish soil.

SAINT PIERRE, JACQUES LE GARDEUR, Sieur de (1701–1755), French Canadian soldier, who served in various parts of French North America and built Fort La Jonquière (1751). As commander of Fort Le Bœuf he rejected a VA demand, presented by George Washington, that the French should withdraw from the OH valley (1753).

ST QUENTIN, BATTLE OF (Aug. 1557), victory of Philip II's forces commanded by Duke Emmanuel Philibert of Savoy and Count Egmont over the French and their German mercenaries under Constable Montmorency, who tried unsuccessfully to relieve the fortress of St Quentin in the Netherlands (10 Aug. 1557). The French were trapped in a narrow pass and were utterly routed, losing 15,000 killed, wounded, or captured, including Montmorency himself.

ST SOPHIA, Church of the Holy Wisdom, the metropolitan cathedral of Constantinople. It was built by the Emperor Justinian I. The work of construction, entrusted to Anthemios of Tralles and Isodoros of Miletus, was carried out mainly in 532–7. Isodoros the Younger completed it in 558–63. In terms of mechanical innovation St Sophia is outstanding and it is one of the supreme triumphs of Byzantine architecture. It comprises a vast aisled nave 76 metres long and 31 metres wide, superb galleries, the whole being dominated by an immense shallow dome. The building is uniquely bright, being flooded with light. The interior is richly decorated in coloured marbles and contains brilliant mosaics. After the Turkish conquest of Constantinople it was transformed into a Muslim mosque, but the mosaics were preserved.

ST STEPHEN, CROWN OF, in Hungary, holy crown, said to have been sent to King Stephen I of Hungary (c 967–1038) by Pope Sylvester II, subsequently the emblem of the traditional sovereign status of Hungarian kings.

ST THERESA ALTAR, Baroque representation of the ecstasy of St Theresa by Bernini in the church of Santa Maria della Vittoria, Rome (1644–7). Bernini carved St Theresa's transcendental experience in white marble, creating the illusion of sweeping, upward movement. The altar itself is a perfect synthesis of sculpture, architecure, and the principles of painting.

ST VINCENT, JOHN JERVIS, Earl of (1735–1823), British sailor and politician who served in the Seven Years' War, the American War of Independence and the French Wars. He took part in the capture of Martinique and Guadeloupe (1794) prior to his victory against the Spanish at St Vincent in 1797 in which he cut in half the enemy fleet. He restored order in the Navy after the mutiny of 1797 and then—when over sixty—entered politics as first lord of the admiralty (1801–4) in Addington's ministry. In office, he sought to bring about improvements in naval conditions and administration, in sympathy with views held by Admiral Nelson. He returned to active service in 1806 in charge of the Channel fleet, and lived to see the war concluded and the settlement made at Vienna.

ST VINCENT, island in the British West Indies discovered by Columbus (1498). It was granted by the English Crown to the Earl of Carlisle (1627) and to Lord Willoughby (1672). After being declared neutral (1748), the island was captured by the British (1762), by the French (1779), then restored to Britain (1783). In 1967 it adopted 'associate status' with Britain, with the right to independence, at any time, if it so wished.

ST WENCESLAS, TREATY OF (1517), truce between the Bohemian towns and the landed nobility, by which the burghers surrendered their monopoly of brewing and selling beer, while the nobles recognized their autonomy and confirmed their right to representation in the Diet, of which they had been deprived in 1500.

SAINTE-MENEHOULD, PEACE OF (1614), agreement between Marie de' Medici, regent of France, and the great nobles led by Condé, Longueville, Mayenne, Bouillon, and Vendôme, to end aristocratic grievances and prevent the outbreak of civil war. The queen mother conceded honours and large pensions, eg, Condé received 450,000 livres, and agreed to the summoning of the estates general.

SAINTES, BATTLE OF THE (9–12 April 1782), British victory by which Admirals Hood and Rodney destroyed the French fleet of De Grasse between Guadeloupe and Dominica. As a result of this victory, the British recovered their West Indian possessions, taken by the French during the American War in Independence (1775–83).

SAINT-GAUDENS, AUGUSTUS (1848–1907), Irish-born US sculptor, whose technical skill and imaginative perception, displayed in such works as *Hiawatha* (1871), *Farragut* (1881), the *Adams Memorial* (1891), and *Sherman* (1903), established him as one of the greatest sculptors of his time.

SAINTS, RULE OF THE, in England, extreme doctrine developed from Calvinism which stated that the rule of the prince should be replaced by the rule of a band of saints, ie, a chosen group of private men of proven holiness and virtue. The saint was the militant Christian activist, who not only participated in congregational government, but also tried to create the holy commonwealth. The allegiance of the saints was to God's Word and they tried to shape society accordingly. The saints became parliamentary intransigents, attacking the traditional hierarchy of Church and state. Their most extreme wing—the 5th Monarchists—believed that the execution of Charles I cleared the way for the inauguration of the millennium, when 'the saints of the most High shall take the kingdom, and possess the kingdom for ever' (Daniel 8 : 18). To them Barebone's Parliament was to be the instrument of their rule, and upon its demise they regarded Oliver Cromwell as an apostate.

SAINT-SIMON, HENRI, Comte de (1760–1824), French social theorist, who advocated social regeneration through economic rather than political progress. He was a member of the old nobility, but also an enthusiastic 1789 revolutionary and believed that capitalist development could be harnessed to create a new type of society. His followers welcomed the Second Empire and influenced its economic programme.

SAINT-SIMON, LOUIS DE ROUVROY, Duke of (1675–1755), French soldier, diplomat, and writer, who distinguished himself at the battles of Namur and Neerwinden. He was an exponent of aristocratic government and promoted the *Polysynodie* experiment (1716–18) to counteract the powers of the secretaries of state. In 1721 he was appointed French ambassador to Spain, but retired in 1723 to write his famous memoirs which throw much critical light upon political events during Louis XIV's reign and the regency of Philip of Orléans.

SAIONJI, KIMMOCHI (1849–1940), Japanese politician, the longest-surviving *genrō* (Meiji elder statesman) who held a key position in 20th-cent. Japanese politics. Though a court noble, he supported the people's rights movement after studying in France (1870–80), but was soon persuaded to enter the government. After holding several ministerial posts, he succeeded Itō Hirobumi as president of the *Seiyūkai* party (1903). He was twice prime minister (1906–8, 1911–12), but left active politics in 1913, though he later represented Japan at the Versailles peace conference. As the sole surviving *genrō* after 1924, Saionji was in a position to wield great influence, but although he tended to favour party cabinets he was more concerned to keep the emperor out of political controversy than to use his prestige to oppose military encroachment upon government.

SAISUNAGA DYNASTY, line of rulers of ancient Magadha (Bihar, India) (*c.* 550–350 BC), originally from Rajagriha (Rajgir), later from Pataliputra (Patna). It was founded by Bimbisara, a contemporary and patron of Lord Buddha.

SAITE DYNASTY (XXVIth, 664–525 BC), founded by Psemtek, the Prince of Sais, who united Egypt after the Ethiopian period. Syria–Palestine was lost, but the period was marked by considerable prosperity, the influx of foreigners, and an artistic revival modelled on the art of the Old Kingdom.

SAITŌ CABINET (26 May 1932–8 July 1934), cabinet which marked the end of party government in pre-Second World War Japan, formed by the moderate Admiral Saitō after the assassination of Inukai Ki. It included some politicians, but gave strong representation to the army and the bureaucracy. It was this cabinet which took Japan out of the League of Nations (27 March 1933).

SAKA ERA, ancient Indian era reckoned from AD 78. Its commencement probably marks the accession of King Kanishka of the Kushan dynasty. From the 7th cent. it extended to large parts of India and also spread to South-East Asia. Present attempts (1970) at recalling it in India have met with only limited success.

SAKALAVA, 17th–19th-cent. kingdom in western Madagascar, of African (Bantu) origins.

SAKARYA, BATTLE OF (24 Aug. 1921), decisive repulse of Greek forces by Turkish Nationalists, which won for Mustafa Kemal the title 'Ghazi'.

SAKDI NA, system of social and administrative status in Thailand, by which individuals were hierarchically ranked according to their nominal land holdings. It existed from the 15th to the early 20th cents. The term might loosely be translated as 'riceland power'.

SAKURA (*fl.* 14th cent.), freed slave who usurped the throne of Mali (*c.* 1300), and expanded the empire. He died while returning from a pilgrimage to Mecca.

SAKYAPA PERIOD, in Tibetan history. Phakpa (1235–80), Lama of Sakya monastery, acted as ruler of Tibet from 1254 under Khublai Khan's patronage. Making use of Mongol systems of administration and communications, successive Sakya Lamas ruled Tibet, entering into a 'priest–patron' relationship with Mongol emperors which formed the pattern for the role of the Dalai Lamas *vis-à-vis* the Manchus. Their reign was marked by wars against the Drikung Kargyüpa sect and internecine quarrels, and when Mongol backing weakened they were overcome by Changchup Gyeltsen in 1354.

SALABAT JANG (d. 1763), third son of the first Nizam of Hyderabad (*reg.* 1724–48). On the assassination of the second nizam, Nasir Jang (1750), he was passed over in favour of his nephew, Muzaffar Jang, but on the latter's murder (Feb. 1751) he assumed power with the help of a

French force under De Bussy. Salabat's weakness necessitated De Bussy's presence to maintain him. When Lally arrived from France (1758) to fight the British, De Bussy was recalled with his troops (1759). In spite of British support, Salabat was deposed (1762) by his more vigorous brother, Nizam Ali, and murdered during the following year.

SALAGA, important pre-colonial West African town in the kingdom of Gonja, where West African products were exchanged for those of North Africa in the trans-Saharan trade. It was also the main outlet for the pre-colonial kolanut trade from Ashanti to Hausaland.

SALAH AL-DIN (1138–93), Ayyubid Sultan of Egypt and Syria (*reg.* 1169–93), known to the Christians as Saladin. He shared in the campaigns which his uncle Shirkuh made against Egypt and in 1169, on the death of Shirkuh, assumed control of affairs at Cairo. Salah al-Din, in 1171, brought to an end the Fatimid regime in Egypt, when the last caliph, Al-'Adid, died. The likelihood of a conflict between Salah al-Din and his nominal overlord Nur al-Din, the Zangid prince of Damascus and Aleppo, was removed through the death of Nur al-Din in 1174. Salah al-Din then occupied Damascus, assigning Aleppo to Al-Salih Isma'il, the heir to the dead Nur al-Din. Not until 1183, on the demise of Al-Salih Isma'il, did Salah al-Din take over Aleppo. The years 1184–7 saw him engaged in the reduction of the small dynasties of Al-Jazira (Mesopotamia) to his obedience. He thus reunited—and joined to Egypt—the territories once subject to Nur al-Din.

Salah al-Din, after 1169, had been involved from time to time in hostilities with the Latin kingdom of Jerusalem. The decisive moment came in 1187, when at the battle of Hattin, not far from Tiberias in Galilee, Salah al-Din routed the Christian forces under the command of Guy de Lusignan. Most of Palestine, including Jerusalem and Acre, fell now to the Muslims. The Christians, in 1189, laid siege to Acre. Meanwhile, the disaster of Hattin and its consequences had aroused the princes of Europe to organize the Third Crusade, the main participants thereof being Philippe Auguste of France and Richard Cœur de Lion of England. The Crusade took Acre from the Muslims after a long and bitter siege (1189–91). Richard of England, in 1191, defeated the forces of Salah al-Din at Arsuf. He was unable, however, to recover Jerusalem and in 1192 made a peace with Salah al-Din. The great sultan died soon afterwards. The Ayyubid regime which he had created was destined to last until 1250. VJP

SALAMANCA, BATTLE OF (1812), Wellington's decisive defeat of Marmont. It led to Joseph Bonaparte's evacuation of Madrid and the crumbling of French power in Spain during the Peninsular campaign in the French Wars.

SALAMIS, BATTLE OF (Sept. 480 BC), Greek naval victory during the Persian Wars. After penetrating Thermopylae, the Persians overran Boeotia and Attica, most of the Athenians taking to their ships or crossing to Salamis, Aegina, or the Peloponnese. Some Peloponnesian contingents urged withdrawal, but the Greek ships, over half of which were Athenian and Aeginetan, remained between Attica and Salamis, where narrow waters could offset superior Persian numbers and mobility. The Persians, unable to split their fleet to attack the Peloponnese after losses in storms and fighting off Cape Artemisium, and anxious for a decision before winter, confidently attacked and were defeated. Though this rendered the Peloponnese safe, central Greece remained in Persian hands until the Greeks' victory at Plataea in 479.

SALANDRA, ANTONIO (1853–1931), Italian lawyer and politician, who became prime minister during the First World War. His government chose a policy of neutrality, but Salandra began to fear the consequences to Italy if, in the resettlement of Europe after the war, she failed to gain strategic or Italian-speaking territories, such as Trentino, Trieste, Dalmatia, and Albania. He resisted British and French blandishments to join the Allies in the First World War and encouraged his foreign minister, Sonnino, to negotiate with the Austrians on the possible rewards for Italy's continued neutrality. Simultaneously, Sonnino discussed the possibility of Italy's intervention on the British and French side. Despite warnings of public and parliamentary hostility to war, Salandra opted for the secret treaty of London (26 April 1915) and on 23 May declared war on Austria. His underestimation of the consequences resulted in nationalists and neutralists jointly ousting him in June 1916. After the war, hoping to be prime minister again, and with Mussolini as his ally, he undermined the Facta government. Later, Salandra served as subordinate to Mussolini, whom he represented at the League of Nations (1922–4).

SALBAI, TREATY OF (17 May 1782), ended the first Anglo-Maratha War. It virtually recognized the independence of Mahadaji Sindhia and secured peace with the Marathas for 20 years. It also left the British free to deal with Haidar Ali of Mysore.

SALCEDO, DIEGO DE (d. 1671), governor-general of the Philippines (1663–8), whose main concern was the establishment of friendly and commercial relations with neighbouring countries like Cambodia, Siam, and the Dutch East Indies. Investing in the trade with Batavia (now Jakarta) he imported not only goods but also Dutchmen, an arrangement which broke into the Manila merchants' monopoly of the galleon trade. During his five-year administration of the Philippines, he quarrelled with both civil and religious officials, and aroused the hostility of the merchants because of his monopoly of the Batavia trade. He came to grief as a result of the animosity of an Augustinian friar who, as Commissary of the Inquisition, could take into custody any person suspected of heresy. In Oct. 1668 Salcedo was arrested and charged for having traded with the Dutch heretics and familiarly consorting with them. He died on a galleon taking him to Mexico where he was to be tried by the Tribunal of the Inquisition. The Council of the Indies and the Tribunal of the Inquisition later condemned the Augustinian Commissary of the Inquisition and ordered him to be divested of his office and sent home for trial.

SALE OF OFFICES or venality, practice of European administration prior to the 19th cent., in which governments sold hereditary tenure of a wide variety of state employments. The practice was common in the Western empire and in Byzantium as well as in the Ottoman empire and many parts of the East. In Europe, following the Roman example, the Catholic Church often sold high offices. Canon Law allowed the holder of a benefice to resign his office in favour of another, a practice which usually concealed monetary payment, and the habit was copied in many feudal kingdoms. There office-holding was an attractive prospect as it conferred nobility and was rewarded by tax exemptions and by extortionate fees rather than by salary. It took root in France, where resignation of minor offices was common, although sale was officially forbidden until the end of the 15th cent. Then the Crown, because of its financial need, took to selling offices itself, often dividing or creating posts simply to sell them.

In the 16th cent., states had to make increasing use of secular administrators rather than ecclesiastical ones, and in an age of continuous and expensive warfare it could not raise the money to pay them properly and was forced to use offices as a means of raising capital, allowing the official to recoup himself at the expense of the public. It is estimated that 50,000 offices throughout the administration were created in France. The emergence of a large group of office-holders had considerable political implications. Having paid large sums for their positions, people wished to preserve them, both for the status they conferred and to recoup their investment. This tended towards hereditary tenure, denying the Crown control of its subordinates, while the insecurity of many officers left them open to the temptations of patronage by the great. However, for financial reasons the Crown granted security of tenure in France through the Paulette.

Generally the growth of venality was common, if not so marked as in France. In Spain, the Crown had sold minor offices in order to finance the Moorish wars and under Philip II it became a systematic process, despite the disapproval of the Cortes. The latter kept up their opposition till the time of Philip IV, by which time it had spread widely throughout the administration, though not in the army or the judiciary. The practice was known in England but neither the courts nor Crown were favourable and it never extended outside central government. Curtailed during the Interregnum, it returned with the Restoration, particularly in the army, but was eradicated from civilian life by late 18th-cent. reforms. Elsewhere venality seems to have been a late arrival, except in some Italian states, since in Holland it became public only in the 18th cent., while the Spaniards had to impose it on Belgium. Frederick II and other eastern rulers sold offices to finance their wars, but German officials never enjoyed the same privileges as those in the west. On the whole 18th-cent. rulers were politically opposed to the practice, so the Austrians curbed it in Belgium and even in France regulations were tightened (1771). Before this the practice had been assailed by critics alarmed at the loss in state authority it caused and the scope opened for corruption. This aspect can be exaggerated for often it was not so much corruption as a means of paying officers. Ownership of office could give officials an independence of favourites that they would not otherwise have enjoyed. None the less, it was not demonstrably an honest system and was abolished in revolutionary France, pushing Europe along the road to true bureaucratic administration.

K. Swart, *The Sale of Offices in the Seventeenth Century* (The Hague, 1949).   CHC

SALEM WITCHCRAFT TRIALS (1692), in America, religious hysteria in Salem. A group of young girls feigned hysteria and accused Tituba, a family slave, of witchcraft. Under flogging, Tituba falsely named two confederates, and a chain of accusation and counter-accusation began in which no one knew who would be accused next by the 'afflicted children'. Gov. Phipps set up a special court to try the accused, but the judges themselves became victims of the general panic. This led them to put 150 persons in prison and have 14 women and 5 men hanged. Later in the same year, the mania subsided, the special court was dissolved and prisoners released. The trial judge and the 12 jurymen later confessed their error and indemnities were granted to the bereaved families.

SALERNO, harbour in south-western Italy, which originated as a Roman colony (194 BC). It achieved its greatest importance as a centre of the Norman state (after 1071). A magnificent cathedral was started by the Norman, Duke Robert Guiscard, in 1076, and a university, famous for its medical faculty, was also founded there (c. 1150). The city was sacked by the Emperor Henry VI in 1194 as part of his conquest of the Norman kingdom. In the 13th cent. it was eclipsed in importance by Naples.

SALES, FRANCIS DE, Saint (1567–1622), Savoyard cleric who became Bp of Geneva and one of the outstanding figures of the French Counter-Reformation. He undertook an intense missionary campaign, preaching humility, love, and confidence in God's mercy, and writing works which were to have a profound effect upon the religious revival in France, *eg, Introduction to the Devout Life* (1608) and *Treaties of Divine Love* (1616). In 1602 he came to Paris, preached in the queen's own chapel and the fashionable parish churches, and was received into the religious circle of Mme Acarie (St Mary of the Incarnation), patron of the Carmelites and the Ursulines. Encouraged by this remarkable woman, he in turn had a great effect upon the nobles and members of the royal family, and gave valuable guidance and friendship to Jeanne de Chantal, founder of the Congregation of the Visitation (1610), Angelique Arnauld, St Vincent de Paul, and Pierre de Bérulle. In this way his influence was felt on all the new religious orders founded in early 17th-cent. France.

SALIH, AL-, NAJM AL-DIN AYYUB (*reg.* 1240–9), Sultan of Egypt and Syria whose reign witnessed, in 1244, the recapture of Jerusalem, which had been under Latin control since 1229. Al-Salih died at a critical moment when a new crusade from Europe, led by Louis IX of France, had taken the important town of Damietta in the eastern delta of the Nile.

SALIM, HADJI AGUS (1889–1954), Indonesian politician, and pioneer of Indonesia's independence movement. He was a modernist Muslim of Minangkabau (West Sumatra) origin and led the *Sarekat Islam* against the communists. Later he became a leader of the *Masjumi* party. He served (1947–9) as minister for foreign affairs.

SALIMULLAH, KHWAJA, Nawab Bahadur of Dacca (1884–1915), Bengal Muslim leader, who succeeded to the head of Bengal's foremost Muslim landed estate (1901). He helped to rally the community to the support of the British as a means of gaining political security. The formation of the new province of East Bengal and Assam (1905), with Dacca as its capital, was a manifestation of this security and in the anti-partition agitation which followed, Salimullah drew the Muslims together to protect their gains. He supported the Simla deputation to Minto (Oct. 1906) and took a leading part in the meeting in Dacca at the end of that year at which the All-India Muslim League was formed. The annulment of the partition of Bengal (1911) was a blow to his position and the strategy which he had devised, and after presiding at the Calcutta session of the league (1912) he retired from politics.

SALISBURY, ROBERT CECIL, 15th Earl of (1st of 4th creation) (1550–1612), English politician, son of William Cecil by his second wife, who was secretary of state (1596–1608), negotiated the accession of James I and became his principal adviser.

He was one of the commissioners sent to negotiate a peace in the Netherlands (1588) and although he was not given office until 1596, he was one of the Crown's active supporters in the Commons, defending the Crown's prerogative against attacks on its ecclesiastical jurisdiction and the granting of monopolies. In 1598 he went as envoy to France to try to deter Henry IV from making a separate peace with Spain.

On his father's death (1598) Cecil successfully resisted the attempts of Essex, Bacon, and Raleigh to reduce his influence and he was bitterly denounced by the Essex faction. At the same time he began secret negotiations to secure the succession for James VI of Scotland. Although Elizabeth I never officially sanctioned it, this was the only sensible and realistic course, and James's peaceful accession was largely due to his efforts.

James employed him to arrange the peace with Spain (1604), in which he failed to get permission for Englishmen to trade with the Indies. He was given a peerage (1603) and an earldom (1605), but from the Lords he was unable to exercise the same influence in debates and his elevation was fatal to his efforts to establish a working relationship between Crown and parliament.

He was industrious and subtle but he lacked the ability and integrity of his father. He resembles Clarendon in his failure to recognize or adapt himself to changing circumstances, and the solutions he proposed for the constitutional and financial issues in James's first parliament (1604–11) satisfied neither his master nor the opposition. Fortunately, however, James was in some awe of him, and his skill and experience had a sobering effect whose value became clearly evident after his death.

The judges' verdict in Bate's case (1606) encouraged Salisbury to issue a revised Book of Rates aimed at increasing the Crown's revenue while pretending to have a protectionist motive. The Commons and merchants were furious, and a tentative scheme to commute some of the Crown's traditional revenues for a fixed subsidy broke down in mutual mistrust and recrimination.

In foreign affairs Salisbury favoured a Protestant league against the Habsburgs, but he was at the same time drawing a pension from Spain, and James in any case preferred the role of arbiter to that of combatant. Salisbury's motives were devious and obscure, but he opposed the scheme to marry James's son to the Spanish infanta and supported the betrothal of Princess Elizabeth to the Protestant Elector Palatine.

He was obliged by James to surrender his father's mansion at Theobalds. He built Hatfield House instead but died heavily in debt before being able to live there.   MMR

SALISBURY, ROBERT ARTHUR TALBOT GASCOYNE-CECIL, 3rd Marquis of (1830–1903), British politician. As prime minister (1885, 1886–92, 1895–1902) he tactfully encouraged the adherence of Joseph Chamberlain and the Unionists to strengthen conservative forces at home, and maintained a policy of diplomatic non-alignment, sometimes known as 'splendid isolation', in the later period of Britain's imperial greatness.

As a young man he travelled within the empire, became an MP in 1853, and wrote for the *Saturday* and *Quarterly Reviews*. Although distrustful of Disraeli (also a member of the cabinet), he served as secretary of state for India under Lord Derby (1866), but resigned on account of the way household suffrage was introduced in the Reform Bill (1867). On succeeding his father in the house of lords, he tried to delay, but persuaded the lords to accept, Irish disestablishment (1868). In 1874 he resumed office as secretary for India under Disraeli, establishing the Indian public works department, developing railways and irrigation, and combating famine. On the Eastern Question again becoming critical (1876), he represented Britain at the Constantinople Conference and pressed for reform of the Turkish empire. In 1877, on becoming foreign secretary, he issued the Salisbury circular, which secured general agreement on the dangers of dismembering the Turkish empire. His negotiation of the preliminary Anglo-Russian agreement helped to ensure the success of the Congress of Berlin (1878). On Disraeli's death he succeeded him as leader of the Conservatives. He was opposed to electoral reform unless it was to be accompanied by redistribution (1884).

He became prime minister and foreign secretary in 1885, resuming power, with Unionist support, after the Liberal split on Home Rule. In 1895 and 1900 (the khaki election) he won electoral majorities. In domestic affairs he accepted the reformist tendencies of the Unionists and ensured the passing of the County Councils Act (1888), free education (1891), and the Workmen's Compensation Act (1897), which he had earlier opposed. He successfully faced a challenge from the Third Party and Lord Randolph Churchill, who resigned as chancellor of the exchequer over the budget (1886). He presided over the Jubilee celebrations and the colonial conferences of 1887 and 1897. In foreign policy he supported a united Bulgaria (1885), and concluded secret Tripartite Mediterranean agreements with Austria and Italy (1887), but refused to join the Triple Alliance. After the retirement of Bismarck (1890) Salisbury dominated European diplomacy and took a major part in mapping spheres of influence in Africa with Italy, Portugal, Germany, and France. He established the cabinet Committee of Defence (1895), and dealt with the Armenian massacres (1896), conflicts in British

Guiana and Venezuela (1895), which involved the US, and the Fashoda incident with France (1898). He resisted Chamberlain's advocacy of alliance with Germany, but the Boer War (1899–1900) and the Hague Conference (1899) suggested the danger of British isolation and after his retirement from the foreign office (1900) this was abandoned. Salisbury's resignation in 1902 ended a period of stability and opened the way for diplomatic and political change.

J. A. S. Grenville, *Lord Salisbury and Foreign Policy at the close of the 19th Century* (London, 1964).

SALK, JONAS EDWARD (1914–), US microbiologist, who developd a vaccine against poliomyelitis, which in 1952 he clinically tested with success. Within two years the vaccine was being produced in quantity. Subsequently, an alternative was developed by Albert Bruce Sabin (1906–), which could be taken orally. Since the mid-1950s, as a result of these vaccines, the incidence of poliomyelitis has diminished considerably.

SALLUST, C. Sallustius Crispus (86–*c.* 34 BC), Roman historian. After opposing Cicero in Milo's trial as tribune of the plebs (52), he was expelled from the Senate for alleged immorality (50) and joined Caesar, with whom he served with little success in the Civil War (49–47). As praetor he served in Africa and became governor of Numidia, which he was accused of plundering. Being disappointed in his political ambitions, he turned to history, writing monographs on Catiline's conspiracy and the Jugurthine War and the *Historiae* in five books, covering the years 79–67 BC and now extant only in fragments. Although containing many errors and distortions, Sallust's works present an important attempt to account for the disintegration of the Roman republic, and their harsh style was very influential.

SALMOND, SIR JOHN WILLIAM (1862–1924), NZ politician and solicitor-general (1911–20), who advanced legal standards in government, and contributed notably to the Washington disarmament conference (1921–2).

SALOME (*fl.* 1st cent. AD), daughter of Herodias, who danced before Herod Antipas and received as a reward the head of John the Baptist.

SALONAE (mod. Solin), capital of the Roman province of Dalmatia and birthplace of the Emperor Diocletian. It was destroyed by the Avars (*c.* AD 615). Extensive remains survive.

SALONS, in France, term used to denote informal gatherings for the purpose of social and cultural discussion, where they were one of the keystones of intellectual life. Their prototypes can be seen in the academies gathered around Charles IX but the first real salon—so called because it met in the salon or drawing room of the Marquise de Rambouillet in the rue St Thomas du Louvre—came a little later (1608). For many years she regularly received writers, courtiers, and other interested parties who came to dance, act, and to discuss or hear the latest writings and gossip of the day. Her practice was copied by many other hostesses, both then and in the 18th cent. Salons came to act as one of the major arbiters of cultivated tastes, and success there was necessary for public success and chairs in one of the academies. Towards the end of the 18th cent. they became more political and masculine in tone, a habit which continued into the 19th cent., as late as the time of Proust, by which time the growth of the mass media rather thrust them into the background. The term is also used in French to signify an exhibition of paintings.

SALSES, SIEGE OF (1639–40), border fortress on the Catalan-Roussillon frontier, first occupied by the French (July 1639) in the Franco-Spanish War of 1635–59 and then besieged by the Spanish forces (1639–40). Olivares ordered the mobilization of Catalan arms to assist in the siege and the Roussillon campaign, but despite the surrender of Salses by the French (6 Jan. 1640), Catalan hostility to the Madrid administration erupted into rebellion in the summer of 1640.

SALT MARCH (1930) in India, initial move in Gandhi's civil disobedience campaign. Gandhi left Sabarmati *ashram* on 12 March and walked, with some 70 *satyagrahis*, to Dandi, where he made salt from the sea (6 April). He hoped that his early arrest would bring an outcry which would force the viceroy to negotiate with him, but although Nehru was arrested (14 April), Irwin allowed him to go on in the hope that the movement would fizzle out. There were widespread demonstrations and boycotts and many regional leaders were arrested, but only when he threatened to raid the Dharsana salt depot was Gandhi apprehended (5 May). The Dharsana raid was carried out (21 May) and the All-India Congress Committee authorized the extension of the campaign into an attack upon a wide range of other regulations.

SALT TAX, duty existing in most European countries from the 16th cent. either as a definite tax or as a concealed tax through monopoly, its prevalence indicating the economic importance of a commodity essential to man's good health and used widely as a preservative for meat, fish, and for curing hides. In France it was known as the *gabelle* and was levied from the 13th cent., being regulated to the benefit of the Crown between the 15th and 18th cents. A salt tax was introduced in Bavaria in 1593, in Spain in 1631, and in Brandenburg in 1652 salt became a state monopoly. It was one of the indirect taxes existing in the United Provinces in the 17th cent., and was a state monopoly in Russia. In England the salt trade was also organized on a monopoly basis from Elizabeth's reign until the abolition of monopolies under the early Stuarts. In 1732 Sir Robert Walpole imposed a general salt tax which brought considerable opposition. As an imposition on a universally needed commodity, it was highly unpopular and tended to be replaced by more equitable taxes, *eg*, upon luxuries, from the 19th cent.

SALT TAX, in India. Under British rule salt, whether produced in India or imported, was subject to a duty which formed an important item of revenue. During the greater part of the 19th cent. it varied from province to province until 1882, when it was made uniform at $2\frac{1}{2}$ rupees per *maund* of 82 lb. This was reduced to one rupee in 1907. The tax was unpopular because it imposed an undue burden on the poorest classes. After 1947 the government of India abolished the tax but had to reimpose it because of a serious loss of revenue.

SALT TRADE in the Middle Ages. The demand for salt in Europe outstripped the supply as large quantities became necessary to help in preserving meat and fish. Mineral deposits of salt and salt springs were exploited in every part of Europe (*eg*, at Droitwich in England, Salins in Burgundy, Lüneburg in northern Germany, and Wieliczka in Poland). The largest and cheapest supplies came from the evaporation of sea water in western Europe and the Mediterranean. An important source of supply was the Bay of Bourgneuf on the western coast of France. From the later 14th cent. onwards great Hanseatic fleets, unable to trade in the Baltic in winter, sailed each autumn from Germany to fetch this 'Bay salt'.

SALT TRADE (Saharan). In the period 800–1600 salt was the most important commodity bartered for West African gold. It came from three main salt-pans: Awlil, near the south Mauritanian coast; Idjil (Fort Gourard), and Taghaza. From as early as the 11th cent. salt was taken from Awlil to the Senegal river and thence upstream by canoe. From Idjil it passed through the caravan towns to Walata, and from there to Mali or across to Timbuctoo. Taghaza may have been in operation as early as the 11th cent.; more certain references date from the late 13th cent., and in 1352 Ibn Battuta visited the flats, of which he left a sombre description.

Taghaza salt went mainly to the Niger Bend, and especially to Timbuctoo, where it was sent up-river to Jenne and bartered for gold dust from the forest zones. This salt was mined by slaves of the Massufa Sanhaja, whose caravans had the monopoly of transportation. Early in the 16th cent. Taghaza came under Songhay control. Later in the century the salt trade became a matter of dispute between Songhay and the Sa'dian sultans of Marrakesh and was a partial cause of their invasion of Songhay (1591). During the dispute new workings were opened up farther south of Taodeni and to this day an annual caravan bearing slabs of rock-salt arrives in Timbuctoo in Dec.

SALTER, JAMES ARTHUR SALTER, Baron (1881–), British civil servant, scholar, and politician. After a varied career in the public service (1904–34), where he specialized in economic matters, he was professor of politics at Oxford University (1934–44) and served as independent MP for the university (1937–50). He held minor office in Churchill's wartime government. As a Conservative MP after 1951 he was minister of state for economic affairs (1951–2). In this position he was largely responsible, with Lord Cherwell, for the abandonment of the 'Robot' plan to make sterling fully convertible and to introduce a floating rate of exchange.

SALTONSTALL, SIR RICHARD (1586–1658), English colonist and puritan, who was an original patentee of the Massachusetts Bay Co. (1629). With John Winthrop, Saltonstall led the migration to Massachusetts Bay (1630).

SALTYKOV, MICHAEL (*fl.*17th cent.), Muscovite nobleman, who concluded a famous agreement with Sigismund III of Poland at Smolensk in 1610 which was in effect a draft of a constitutional monarchy, upon which terms Sigismund's son, Vladislav, was to become tsar during the Time of Troubles.

SALUTATI, COLUCCIO (d. 1406), chancellor of Florence, who was largely responsible for making Florence the leading centre of early Renaissance humanism and for the teaching of Greek at Florence University.

SALVADO, DOM ROSENDO (1814–1900), Spanish Benedictine monk, who arrived in Western Australia from Italy (1846) with a fellow monk, the future Bp Joseph Maria Benedict Serra, and began missionary work among Aborigines at New Norcia, 80 miles (128 kms) from Perth. A lasting tribute to their work is the active Benedictine monastery at New Norcia, the Spanish architecture of which rises suddenly out of the Australian bush.

SALVEMINI, GAETANO (1873–1957), Italian historian and politician, who was a radical advocate of democracy and economic reform for southern Italy, of which he was a native. He was a critic of Giolitti's political 'system', *eg*, in *Il ministro della malavita* (1909), but failed to overcome the north's habitual indifference. In exile, during Mussolini's domination, he wrote anti-fascist books, *eg, Under the Axe of Fascism* (1936), and taught at Harvard (1933–48).

SALVIUS JULIANUS (c. AD 100–69), Roman jurist, who was entrusted (c. 130) by Hadrian with the revision of the praetorian edict. In his later works, especially his *Digesta*, Roman jurisprudence reached its highest point. The *Digests*, which were extensively commented on by later jurists and used by Justinian's compilers, are remarkable for their simplicity of language, the wide extent of the author's thought, and his preference for practical solutions of general benefit rather than for a strict adherence to the letter of the law.

SAMANID, name of a Muslim dynasty which first rose to importance at Samarkand and Bukhara in Transoxania. It was the Amir Isma'il ibn Ahmad (892–907) who established the power of the Samanids on a sure foundation, consolidating their influence in Transoxania and Khurasan. The dynasty attained the summit of its splendour in the reign of Nasr ibn Ahmad (*reg.* 913–43). Dynastic discord, the pressure of the Turkish Ilek Khans from the steppe lands of Central Asia, and the rise of a powerful Muslim state at Ghazna were factors which led to the decline and, in 999, to the collapse of the Samanid regime.

SAMARIN, YURY FYODOROVICH (1818–76), Russian Slavophile publicist and politician, who was a member of emancipation committees and was influential in the retention of *mir*. He later developed Pan-Slavist and nationalist ideas.

SAMGUK SAGI ('Historical Record of the Three Kingdoms'), Korean history written (1145) by Kim Pu-sik (1075–1151), a Neo-Confucian statesman of the Koryu dynasty. Kim Pu-sik modelled his work upon the *Shih-chi* of the great Chinese historian Ssu-ma Ch'ien (c. 140–90 BC), with the result that his book, which includes the history of Koguryo, Paekche, and Silla, is written with a strongly pro-Chinese bias and frequently incorporates lengthy passages from Chinese sources. Unfortunately, because of this 'scholarly' approach —which also includes the establishment of an artificially precise chronological framework for the Three Kingdoms Period—the *Samguk-sagi* soon eclipsed earlier Korean historical works in popularity. Consequently these ceased to be copied and have disappeared.

SAMGUK-YUSA ('Memorabilia of the Three Kingdoms'), Korean historical work written (c. 1270) in which legends and speculations concerning ancient Korea were collected by the Buddhist monk Il-yon (1206–89). Unlike the *Samguk-sagi*. the *Samguk-yusa* shows little trace of Chinese influence, and is particularly valuable as it contains a summary of an earlier chronicle, the *Karak-kukki* (1076), and deals with the history of Karak, a principality which does not receive separate treatment in the *Samguk-sagi*. The *Samguk-yusa* also includes a number of early Korean songs or poems spelt out phonetically in Chinese characters.

SAMNITE WARS, important episodes in Rome's conquest of Italy (343–290 BC). The First War was a brief Samnite challenge to Roman expansion in Campania (343–341). The Second, provoked by Roman advances to the Samnite frontiers, was fought for control of Apulia. Roman disasters at Caudium (321) and Lautulae (315) were followed by insurrections in Campania and Apulia, in Etruria (310–308), and among the Hernici (307) and the Aequi and the Paeligni (305). Only after these had been quelled did the Samnites make peace, by which they retained their independence. In the Third War (298–290) Samnites and invading Gauls joined at Sentinum, where Rome won a famous victory (295); the Samnites finally came to terms in 290, and were awarded Roman citizenship, but without the franchise.

SAMNITES, generic title of ancient Oscan peoples living in southern Italy between Latium/Campania and Apulia. They encroached (450–350 BC) on Campania and Lucania. After alliance with Rome against the Gauls (354), they clashed with her in the Samnite Wars (343–290). Though defeated, they remained fiercely independent. Pyrrhus and Hannibal found supporters among them, and they led the Italians against Rome in the Social War (90–88); in the subsequent Civil War they marched on Rome, but were defeated at the Colline Gate by Sulla (82 BC), who later sought to extirpate them. They gradually became Romanized.

SAMO (c. 620–58), ruler of the first recorded Slavonic state, was a merchant from northern France, who led a Slavonic rising against the Avars (c. 623). His state was probably centred in Moravia, to the east of Bohemia. The movements of the Croats and the Serbs into the regions which they occupy in modern Yugoslavia may have been connected with Samo's activities.

SAMOA (in the Pacific), discovered by Roggeveen (1722) and visited by Bougainville (1768) and La Pérouse (1787). The London Missionary Society (1830) won early success but failed to maintain peace in the face of succession struggles between the major Tupua and Malietoa families (1848–55). The factions meanwhile exchanged land for muskets, J. C. Godeffroy's acquiring 25,000 acres, the Polynesian Land Co. 300,000 acres—a development which led to the establishment of a central council of chiefs (*ta'imua*). A promising constitutional experiment (1873–6) under the US soldier, Col. Steinberger, was sabotaged by the powers, the struggle between the rival families being resumed with foreign help. In 1881 the Germans deported King Malietoa and installed Tupua Talasese with Brandeis as prime minister, the Samoans rallying round Mata'afa Iosefa. This situation ended in a naval débâcle in the hurricane of March 1889 in Apia harbour. International agreement for a Samoan government under Malietoa and adjustment of the land issue failed to allay local rivalries and in 1899 the US annexed Eastern Samoa while Germany held Western Samoa until 1914, when NZ occupied the group. Western Samoa ('C' Mandate, 1920) was accorded substantial independence in 1962.

SAMORI (*c.* 1830–1900), Manding leader, who created a vast but ephemeral empire along the upper reaches of the Niger and its tributaries, eastward to the middle Volta. Early in life he joined a local chief's army in the Kankan area. He achieved distinction as a warrior and soon created his own force. His subsequent campaigns, though fought in the name of Islam, had little basis in *jihad* law, but Samori's energy compensated for his lack of learning. In the first phase he subdued Kunadugu and made Bisandugu his headquarters (1866); he then took Kankan in eastern Guinea (1873) and proclaimed himself *almami*—head of the Muslim community. French intervention (1882) forced him to turn eastwards and in the 1890s he seized the Muslim Dyula towns of Kong, Bonduku, and Buna in the Ivory Coast. He attempted to advance over the Black Volta, but met stiff resistance from the British. In 1898 he was defeated by the French and later died in exile. In 40 restless years he had overrun vast areas of the West African interior. Destructive though his campaigns were, he always set up in his wake mosques, schools, and village and district administrations. His 162 administrative districts were grouped into ten provinces, but owing to French pressure he could never settle long enough to establish a centralized state.   JOH

SAMOS, Aegean island off Asia Minor, first settled by Greeks (*c.* 1000 BC). In the 7th–6th cents Samians reached southern Spain (*eg*, Colaeus in *c.* 635), were prominent as traders at Naucratis in Egypt (*c.* 600), settled in the Propontis (*eg*, Perinthus in *c.* 600), and as pirates roved widely about the Aegean. Rising prosperity resulted in Polycrates' tyranny (*c.* 535–522). Samos, subsequently controlled by Persia, joined half-heartedly the Ionian Revolt (499–494), was liberated in 479, and joined the Delian League (?478). After attempting another revolt from Athens (440–439), the Samians remained loyal, even after the Athenians' final defeat at Aegospotami (405), and briefly enjoyed Athenian citizenship, then fell to Lysander (404). In the 4th cent. Samos was recovered by Athens (365) and received Athenian settlers. After Alexander the Great's conquests it was eclipsed by Rhodes.

SAMUEL (*fl.* 10th cent.), Tsar of Bulgaria. After the death of the Tsar Symeon in 927, the first Bulgarian empire fell into decline and much of Bulgaria came under Byzantine rule in the reign of the Emperor John I Tzimiskes (*reg.* 969–976). In the region of Macedonia, however, Samuel assumed the title of tsar and overran Serbia and northern Bulgaria. A long and bitter conflict ensued between the Tsar Samuel and the Emperor Basil II (*reg.* 976–1025), who inflicted a terrible defeat on the Bulgarians in 1014. On receiving the news of this disaster Samuel died. The state that he had created broke down in 1018 and Bulgaria remained subject thereafter to Byzantium until the emergence of the second Bulgarian empire in 1185.

SAMUEL, HERBERT LOUIS SAMUEL, 1st Viscount (1870–1963), British politician and writer, born into a Jewish banking family. He entered parliament in 1902 as a Liberal MP. His parliamentary advancement was rapid, becoming under-secretary at the home office (1905) and entering the cabinet in 1909. During the First World War he was, in turn, postmaster-general, president of the local government board, and home secretary. After the war he served in Belgium and Palestine as high commissioner.

His most renowned political and industrial contribution in Britain was his work as chairman of the Royal Commission on the Coal Industry in 1925. His report contained many suggestions for a reorganization of the industry, but the collapse of the General Strike in 1926 saw the miners' conditions deteriorating. As leader of the Liberal Party (1931–5) he gave his support to Ramsay MacDonald's National government in 1931 and was appointed home secretary, resigning, however, in the following year because of opposition to the government's increasing drift towards protection. He then became leader of that section of the Liberals opposed to the National Liberals under Simon.

His literary works include *The War and Liberty* (1917), *Philosophy and the Ordinary Man* (1932), *Essay in Physics* (1951), and *In Search of Reality* (1957).

SAMURAI, term originally meaning 'servant' or 'attendant', which came to be applied generally to all the members of the warrior class of feudal Japan, replacing the earlier '*bushi*'. This warrior class emerged in the provinces as the central government declined and private estates became common (9th–11th cents). Its members, who frequently came from the local aristocracy, the descendants of the *uji*s (local ruling families) of the Yamato period (4th–7th cents), were well armed. By the 12th cent. most samurai fought on horseback with bows and arrows, curved swords, and light armour. In later centuries, particularly the 16th, an increasing number of samurai bore two swords and fought on foot. By the Tokugawa period the samurai class was divided hierarchically into many hereditary grades, sometimes reflecting different social origins, sometimes a samurai's outstanding service to his lord. At the top were the *shōgun*, the *daimyō*s, and their *karō*s (house elders); the latter usually received an annual stipend of over 1000 *koku*s (4960 bushels) of rice; at the bottom came the *ashigaru*s, foot soldiers, mainly of peasant origin, whose stipends could be as little as 20 *koku*s. After 1600 entry into the samurai class became almost impossible, as the Tokugawa rulers imposed a rigid class division, but although this system brought centuries of almost total peace and changed many samurai from soldiers into scholars or *han* bureaucrats, a conscious attempt was made to maintain the older samurai values, particularly that of unquestioning loyalty to one's lord. These values were sometimes strained in the later Tokugawa period, when the financial difficulties of *daimyō*s frequently caused them to reduce stipends, and the dissatisfaction of lower samurai played a large part in bringing about the Meiji Restoration (1868). After the Restoration, the samurai lost their position as a special legal class, retaining only the honorary title of *shizoku*, but their role in the creation of modern Japan was immense. Partly because of their large numbers (about 6 per cent the population), their high educational level, and their strong sense of loyalty, which made them especially susceptible to the appeal of nationalism, samurai played a dominant role in government, army, police, and education, and also provided many of Japan's leading entrepreneurs.

G. B. Sansom, *Japan, A Short Cultural History* (London, 1931).   RLS

SAN FRANCISCO CONFERENCE (April–June 1945), which drafted the Charter of the United Nations. It was sponsored by the four countries which had taken part in the preceding conference at Dumbarton Oaks (Britain, China, the US, and the USSR) and by France. It was attended by representatives of all those powers engaged in the Second World War as members of the wartime United Nations.

On the broad outlines of an international organization there was little disagreement—the ground had been prepared not only by the Dumbarton Oaks conference but also by discussions between Britain, the US, and the USSR at Yalta. It was agreed that an international, rather than supranational, organization should be established. It was accepted (although with some reluctance by the smaller powers) that the great powers should be given the major responsibility within the organization. It was agreed, too, that immediate enforcement action to counter aggression should be provided for. On this understanding the main structure of the United Nations was built. It was not given competence in matters of domestic jurisdiction. The Security Council was given a permanent membership of the five great powers and was in continuous existence so that (with the aid of a Military Staff Committee) it could act at very short notice.

In spite of the broad areas of agreement, differences remained on two main questions, the second of which almost led to a breakdown of the conference. The first issue was that of membership. In accordance with an understanding reached at Yalta the Soviet Union (which had proposed that all sixteen constituent republics of the USSR should be given membership) was given two additional seats, one for Ukraine the other for Byelorussia. The more important difference of view was over the use of the veto, in spite of the fact that the Western powers believed this issue, also, to have been settled at Yalta. The use of the veto when enforcement action was proposed was not in question; but the Soviet Union sought a more extended veto, available when the Security Council was seeking the peaceful settlement of a dispute. On this point Harry Hopkins (the late President Roosevelt's personal adviser) intervened directly with Stalin and secured his agreement to the formula (embodied in Article 27 of the Charter) that a party to a dispute could not use the veto against action designed to achieve the pacific settlement of a dispute. A further difference (which cut across the division between the Western powers and the Soviet Union) was over the question of trusteeship over dependent areas, but it too was resolved. The conference ended with the signature of the Charter (26 June 1945).   WK

SAN FRANCISCO EARTHQUAKE AND FIRE (18 April 1906), in the US, disaster which devastated 3000 acres in the heart of the city. The fire that followed the earthquake caused the greatest damage, raging through the central business district and residential areas for three days before it was finally brought under control. 497 city blocks, or about a third of the city, were razed to the ground. Property losses were estimated at $350–500 million, 500 people died and about 250,000 were rendered homeless. Under stringent building restrictions, reconstruction of the city progressed rapidly but on the old plan rather than to the grandiose new design prepared by Daniel Burnham.

SAN JACINTO, BATTLE OF (21 April 1836), last major engagement of the Texas Revolution. Gen. Sam Houston's 800 men defeated a larger Mexican force and captured Gen. Santa Anna, who then signed the armistice which led to Texan independence.

SAN JUAN HILL, BATTLE OF (1 July 1898), major military engagement of the Spanish–American War. Under Gen. William R. Shafter 18,000 US troops, including the Rough Riders led by Col. Theodore Roosevelt, successfully attacked Spanish defences on the hills above the city of Santiago, Cuba. Santiago surrendered after a short siege.

SAN MIN CHU I, in China, often translated as the 'Three People's Principles', was Sun Yat-sen's theory of nationalism, democracy, and 'people's livelihood'. It was first conceived in 1905 in skeletal form, and was fully expounded in a draft prepared in 1918–20 when Sun took refuge in the French Concession in Shanghai. The draft was subsequently destroyed in 1922. What we now have is the transcript of his 16 lectures on the subject delivered in 1924. Before 1912, Sun's nationalism was mainly restricted to anti-Manchu-ism. After 1922 it took on an anti-Western tinge, as the Western powers failed to support the cause of Chinese republicanism. Regarding democracy, Sun envisaged a three-stage progression: from military government, to political tutelage, and finally constitutional government. The 'People's Livelihood' drew heavily upon Henry George's ideas. It also advocated national ownership of major industrial enterprises. It was socialist, but anti-Marxist. The *San Min Chu I* became the doctrine of the Kuomintang, and was a basic text in school curricula in Nationalist China after 1928.

SAN STEFANO TREATY (3 March 1878), negotiated by Ignatiev at the end of the Russo-Turkish War. It represented the height of Pan-Slavist achievement, created a large Bulgaria under Russian influence, enlarged Montenegro, and gave Russia both territorial gains and an indemnity. Earlier drafts had envisaged Russo-Turkish defence of the Straits and an alliance. The treaty was revised at the Congress of Berlin in June 1878.

SANADS OF ADOPTION, granted after the Indian Mutiny to placate the princes who had become alarmed at Dalhousie's annexations in accordance with the doctrine of lapse. In future they had the right to adopt if there were no direct heirs.

SANCHI, in India, ancient Buddhist centre, north of Bhopal, Madhya Pradesh, India. The oldest monuments there are three *stupa*s, originally built in the time of Asoka (3rd cent. BC) but subsequently enlarged. Railings and gateways were added in the Satavahana period (1st cent. AD). The gateways are decorated with reliefs and sculpture, important for our knowledge of early Indian art and Buddhism of a more popular kind than that reflected by the texts.

SANCROFT, WILLIAM (1617–93), English theologian, who was a fellow of Emmanuel College, Cambridge, but was ejected through Puritan influence (1651) during the interregnum. On the restoration of Charles II (1660) he became a royal chaplain, master of Emmanuel (1662–5), dean of St Paul's Cathedral, London (1664–77), and Abp of Canterbury (1678–90). He refused to serve on the court of ecclesiastical commission when the Roman Catholic James II ascended the throne, and petitioned James, with six other bishops, against the second declaration of indulgence (1688). For this, he was imprisoned in the Tower of London, tried, and acquitted with his fellow bishops. Although he had taken this stand against James II, he was unable to accept William of Orange as the lawful king. He thus identified himself with the non-jurors, who scrupled to take an oath of allegiance to William and Mary. Sancroft was suspended (1689) and deprived (1690) of his archbishopric. In England the influence of Sancroft, seven other bishops, and about 400 priests, gave a modest strength to the non-juring tradition in the 18th cent. Non-jurors were suspect for their Jacobite sympathies and their belief in passive obedience to the sovereign. Although some consecration of bishops and ordination of priests took place, the natural course of death gradually minimized the ranks of the non-juring clergy.

SAND CREEK MASSACRE (Nov. 1864), slaughter of Black Kettle's and Little Antelope's band of Sioux Indians in CO by US militia. The Indians were caught unawares and 450 out of 700 were killed. Protests were raised in the eastern states and the massacre was denounced by Gen. Nelson A.

Miles as 'the foulest and most unjustified crime in the annals of America'.

SAND RIVER CONVENTION (1852), agreement by Britain that the Transvaal should be independent, provided there was no slavery. This condition was honoured only in name, the slaves being called 'apprentices'. The Transvaal Boers, who were extremely anti-British, formed the nucleus of the Afrikaner movement.

SANDALWOOD TRADE in the Pacific, centred on Mbua Bay, Fiji (1800–13), the Marquesas (1815), and Hawaii (1811–1828). Peter Dillon's rich find (1825) at Erromangan in the New Hebrides went unexploited until the discovery in 1840 of a new source at Gwahma (Guam), Maré Island, which stimulated a brief but blood-stained rush (1841–4). By 1844 the business was largely monopolized by James Paddon and Robert Towns, who (1846–59) conducted a small triangular trade in tea, sugar, and sandalwood which yielded useful if uncertain returns. The enterprise collapsed in 1867 with the simultaneous drying up of Chinese demand and island wood, but massive Australian imports of China teas continued unaffected until the late 1870s.

SANDBURG, CARL AUGUST (1878–1967), US poet and writer, who was influenced by Whitman. His verse includes 'Poetry' (1914), 'Chicago Poems' (1916), 'Cornhuskers' (1918), and 'The People, Yes' (1936). He was always ready to declare his liberal social position, his faith in America, and in the working man. In *The American Songbag* (1927), he attempted to define a folk-image of America. Abraham Lincoln, of whom he wrote a six-volume autobiography (1926–39), embodied for him the Mid-western values he held dear. He also wrote novels, children's stories, and an autobiography.

SANDERS, OTTO LIMAN VON (1855–1929), German soldier, who led a military mission to Istanbul (1913) and commanded certain Ottoman armies during the First World War, notably during the Dardanelles campaign (1915–16).

SANDOMIERZ, CONSENSUS OF (1570), mutual agreement of the three principal Protestant sects in 16th-cent. Poland, the Calvinists, Bohemian Brethren, and Lutherans, to counter the influence of the Catholic Reformers. They agreed to retain their own organizations and church services, but to hold general synods in common and prepare a joint catechism, though the consensus had broken down by the synod of Thorn (1595) when the Lutherans withdrew.

SANDWICH, JOHN MONTAGU, 4th Earl of (1718–92), British diplomat and politician, who held office three times as first lord of the admiralty (1748–51, 1763, 1771–82) and twice as secretary of state (1763–5, 1770–1). His reputation has suffered by his being in office during the defeats in the American War of Independence. He was, in fact, an efficient and reforming politician of considerable talent.

SANDYS, SIR EDWIN (1561–1629), English politician and colonist, who entered parliament (1604) and became an influential leader of the opposition to the Crown. He joined the Virginia Co. (1607) and became its treasurer and controller (1619). He was unsuccessful as treasurer, and was replaced (1621), but the company continued to fail and its charter was annulled (1624). His last years were devoted to the affairs of the East India Co.

SANGKUM RYASTER NIYUM, or 'People's Socialist Community', ruling political party in Cambodia (1955–70). It was created by Prince Narodom Sihanouk and its aim was to combine elements of socialism with the traditional Cambodian view of the state.

SANHAJA. The traditions of the Berber peoples of North Africa divide their ethnic groups into two main divisions, the Beranes and the Botr. Within the former are several subdivisions, among them the Sanhaja, who claim to have emigrated into North Africa from the Yemen. This view, though now largely discredited, may preserve a memory of some ancient connection between the inhabitants of North Africa and the Arabian peninsula. Even a sceptical Arab historian like Ibn Khaldun was tempted to attribute some truth to this widespread myth. The Sanhaja settled over many centuries in two main regions: the Kabyle mountains of northern Algeria and the middle Atlas of Morocco; and far to the south in the desert wastes of Mauritania and the central Sahara. The Kabyle and kindred northern Sanhaja groups in Morocco share the life and habits of the mountain Berbers of those regions, and although they boast of a common name have no apparent links with the southern Saharan groups, who differ in their dress, mode of life, and language.

Most of the southern Sanhaja claim descent from an ancestress, Tiski the Lame, and comprise three principal divisions. Their descendants are distributed over vast areas of the Sahara, and appear to have incorporated some ancient Libyan peoples mentioned by the classical authors. These three divisions of the Sanhaja, who formed the principal body of the Almoravid movement, were the Gudala, the Lamtuna, and the Massufa. The Gudala were originally located near the Atlantic coast but their descendants became dispersed as far east as Aïr. The Lamtuna were centred in the mountainous areas of the Adrar and Taganit in Mauritania, but later settled in the central Sahara. The Massufa were always the most widely distributed. Their descendants are to be found in Aïr, Mali, and eastern Mauritania.

Other Berber Saharans, such as the Lamta and the Hawara, were held to be of a different origin from these three groups, although they shared the same nomadic habits and a matrilineal social system, and their men wore the veil. Many Tuareg and Mauritanian Moorish tribes are Sanhaja. In Mauritania the term has become debased and indicates the tributary class, although Znaga Berber is still spoken by a few tribes respected for their scholarship. This dialect is probably a survival of the language once spoken by the Lamtuna, although owing to Arabization it will not survive long after 1970.

F. Rodd, *People of the Veil* (London, 1926).   HTN

SANITARY CONDITION OF THE LABOURING CLASSES, REPORT ON (1842), in Britain, most impressive and influential of the many reports on social problems prepared by Edwin Chadwick. It was based on information gathered through the poor law machinery, on his own reading and observations, and on comments from experts. The report, which set a new standard of comprehensiveness and rigour for such enquiries, showed the full gravity of the situation. The solution it urged was more controversial. It was influenced by the pythogenic (ie, atmospheric) theory of disease, and neglected to indicate the need for adequate food, pure water, and quarantine regulations. It advocated sanitary engineering rather than medicine as a remedy, and in so far as it promoted the more efficient disposal of sewage, it was beneficial. The report was designed as a manifesto for the public health movement and coloured its outlook up to and after the Public Health Act (1848).

SANJAQ, Turkish word meaning banner or standard, eg, of a particular beg. In the time of the Ottoman empire the word came to denote the territories under the control of the beg, ie, a province within the empire. Hence the expression 'Sanjaq Begi', the title accorded to a beg governing such a province.

SANJAYA (*reg. c.* AD 717–32), founder and first King of ancient Mataram, Central Java, Indonesia. His accession marks the beginning of an era, while 732 is the date of the Sanskrit inscription of Changal issued by Sanjaya.

SANJURJO SACANELL, JOSÉ (1872–1936), Spanish soldier, who in 1931 was head of the Civil Guard. His refusal to place the guard at the king's disposal ensured Spain's bloodless transition from a monarchy to a Republic, but the Republican government, aware of his right-wing sympathies, transferred him to the *Carabineros*, the frontier guards. In 1932 Sanjurjo was persuaded by Carlist friends and monarchists that he must save Spain from anarchy. The government got wind of his intention to plan a rising in Madrid, and the conspirators were rounded up (10 Aug.) and a declaration of martial law by Sanjurjo in Seville was rendered futile by a general strike of the city's workers.

After being captured while fleeing to Portugal, he was court-martialled and sentenced to death, but to avoid making him a martyr the government commuted his sentence to one of life imprisonment. Early in 1934 he and the other conspirators were pardoned and he retired to Portugal.

In 1936 another military conspiracy began, and as the senior general Sanjurjo was its natural figure-head. The plotting was done by others, but in Feb. 1936 he himself went to Germany, ostensibly for the Winter Olympics, but in reality to seek military help for the rising. After the army had seized power, it was intended he should be president of a military junta, but he was killed in an air crash.

SANKARACHARYA (*fl.* 9th cent. AD), Indian philosopher who systematized doctrines of the Upanishads into strict monism (Advaita, lit. = non-duality). Most of his activity belongs to the western Deccan, but it is impossible to reconstruct his life from the numerous legends.

SANKEY, JOHN SANKEY, Viscount (1866–1948), British lawyer and politician who first practised in South Wales and became involved in workmen's compensation cases. In 1914 he was elevated to the bench and became chairman of the enemy aliens advisory committee.

In 1919 he chaired the commission appointed to investigate conditions in the coal industry (Sankey Report), which after a long investigation recommended nationalization. To Sankey's disappointment this was not acted upon, but his views enamoured him to Labour MPs, many of whom expected him to become lord chancellor in 1924. He did, indeed, gain the Woolsack in 1929 during Ramsay MacDonald's second ministry. He was one of the few ministers choosing to stay in the government after 1931, which he did until Baldwin became prime minister in 1935.

As lord chancellor he had many political functions, especially important being his work at the imperial conference and the India round table conference. His interest in legal reform led him to appoint the law revision committee, from whose recommendations several useful pieces of legislation resulted.

SANKEY REPORT (1919) in Britain, name given collectively to the four reports on the mining industry published in June 1919, as the result of a royal commission under the chairmanship of John Sankey. In 1919 the two important industries still under government control after the First World War were the mines and railways. Fears of soaring prices and of miners' militancy which might lead to a resurrection of the pre-war 'triple alliance' of miners, railwaymen, and transport workers, led to the act of parliament setting up the royal commission. It was a unique body under a high court judge, representing owners and men. The recommendations ranged from total nationalization on the one hand to full private ownership on the other. This inevitable disagreement was used by Lloyd George, who offered some ideas for reorganization to the miners. They rejected these plans. Government control was prolonged, the miners maintained their existing wages and the seven-hour day was imposed by act of parliament. The industry was however still very divided and the reluctance to accept nationalization was resented by the miners' union.

SANKIN KŌTAI (lit.'alternate attendance'), system whereby all *daimyō*s in Tokugawa Japan (1635–1862) were compelled by the *bakufu* to spend alternate years in Edo and to leave their wives and children there. It was a key factor in maintaining an enduring peace, but it had the unanticipated effect of stimulating rapid commercial growth, especially in Edo and Osaka, and impoverishing the samurai class.

SANKORE, north-eastern quarter of Timbuctoo and traditional home of the city's scholars. Its heyday was the period 1450–1600, when Timbuctoo formed part of the Songhay empire. Scholars from many areas settled there to teach Islamic law, dogma, logic, Arabic, and the various Islamic sciences, which they taught in their houses and sometimes in the Sankore mosque. It was their activities that gave rise to the legendary fame of the 'University of Timbuctoo'. Many of the Sankore scholars were prolific authors, though few of their works have survived, except some of Ahmad Baba's (d. 1627) and the great *History* of Al-Sa'di (d. *c.* 1655). Soon after the Moroccan invasion (1591), many Sankore scholars were massacred by the soldiers and others were deported to Morocco. Islamic sciences are still (1970) imparted in the houses of Sankore.

SANS-CULOTTES (1789) in France, term originally used to describe the mass of the poorer classes in French towns at the start of the Revolution, and then applied more specifically to members of these classes who were politically active in Paris. They were not an industrial proletariat, but small shopkeepers, craftsmen, wage-earners, and the unemployed. Their main grievance, which made them intervene directly against the monarchy and successive Revolutionary governments, was the price of bread. Their wish for economic controls on food prices and a democratic system of government both in Paris and France as a whole brought them into temporary alliance with the Jacobins, whose dictatorship ultimately rested on their support. The governments which followed the Jacobins were finally able to bring the sans-culottes under control by using the regular army.

SANSKRIT, classical language of ancient India, based on the language of the religious texts of the Veda. Precise rules for correct use of Sanskrit were laid down in Panini's grammar (*c.* 5th cent. BC), and from the 2nd cent. AD it was used as an official language in royal edicts, etc. It remained essentially the language of religion, literature, and erudition, as well as a spoken language among some members of the highest classes of society.

SANTA CRUZ, ALBARO DE BAZAN, 1st Marquis of (1526–1588), Spanish nobleman and sailor, who distinguished himself at the battle of Lepanto (1571) and defeated the French allies of the Portuguese Pretender, Don Antonio, in the Azores (1582–3). He is credited with having suggested the English Enterprise to Philip II (1583) and organized the construction of the Armada, though he died (Feb. 1588) before its departure.

SANTA CRUZ, ALONSO DE (*fl.* 16th cent.), Castilian cosmographer who invented the spherical map.

SANTA CRUZ, chief seaport and capital of Tenerife, one of the Canary Islands, which was conquered by the Spaniards from the Portuguese in 1493. The town was founded in 1494 and was later the scene of Admiral Robert Blake's spectacular destruction of the Spanish treasure fleet (1657) and of Horatio Nelson's only naval failure when he lost his right arm (1797).

SANTA FÉ TRAIL (1821–80), oldest regular land route across the American Great Plains, from the Missouri valley southwest to Santa Fé. From Old Franklin, Independence, and Westport, the trail led to the Great Bend of the Arkansas, followed the river to Fort Dodge, and then forked. The more direct but more dangerous Cimarron Route across the high plains to the Sangre de Cristo mountains was used almost exclusively until 1845. The longer Mountain Route up the Arkansas and through Raton Pass to La Junta, where it converged with the Cimarron Cutoff, became popular during and after the Mexican War (1846–8). Pioneered by Missouri traders as a commercial route into the South-west and Mexico, the first wagon trains reached Santa Fé in 1824. Once established, the pattern of exchanging American cloth for Mexican specie and bullion continued unchanged until 1842–3 when Mexico imposed severe restrictions on American traders. After 1848 the trail again became a major freighting route into New Mexico and, with the discovery of gold in CA and CO, gained an additional role as a migration route to the West. Continually shortened in the 1870s as the railroads pushed westwards, the trail was finally superseded when the Atchison, Topeka, and Santa Fé Railroad reached Santa Fé (Feb. 1880).

SANTA MARTA, BATTLE OF (29 Aug. 1702), French naval victory in the West Indies in which Admiral Jean du Casse defeated a British fleet under John Benbow.

SANTALS, primitive tribes of the Santal Parganas in the Indian state of Bihar. Their language, Santali or Har, is a dialect of the Munda language Kherwari. They rebelled in 1855 against their oppressive landlords, but were suppressed by a strong military force.

SANTAYANA, GEORGE (1863–1952), Spanish-born US philosopher. Attracted towards Hinduism, he was opposed to the Protestant ethic of American and European culture and the phenomenological and analytical traditions of Western philosophy, but his own doctrines were very much a reaction against contemporary views. His philosophical development falls into two main periods. In *The Sense of Beauty* (1896) and *The Life of Reason* (1905–6) he considered philosophy to be a branch of psychology; but in the period from *Scepticism and Animal Faith* (1923) to his *Realms of Being* (1927–40), he felt the need to draw more rigorous ontological distinctions between different kinds of being.

SANTIAGO DE COMPOSTELA, town in north-western Spain, where the sepulchre of the apostle James was allegedly discovered in the 9th cent., and a major centre of pilgrimage for medieval Europe. The pilgrim route from France across northern Spain brought the emergent Christian kingdoms of the area into contact with European influences, particularly in the 11th cent., when French Cluniac monks set up communities along it and persuaded Alfonso VI of Castile to introduce the standard Roman liturgy into Spain in place of the Visigothic liturgy. This pilgrim route also played an important part in the spread of the Romanesque style of church architecture.

SANTINIKETAN ('abode of peace'), in India, Rabindranath Tagore's educational settlement near Bolpur in Bengal. In 1901 Tagore started a school modelled on the traditional *ashram*, in which he developed in a natural setting his ideas of education through crafts. He provided financial backing for the school and gave it his Nobel Prize money (1913). Later, he added an agricultural school and a 'Rural Reconstruction Centre' nearby at Sriniketan, where he developed co-operative institutions among the villagers. In 1921 he drew the whole settlement into his international university, Visva-Bharati, transferring to it all the properties and giving it the copyright of his Bengali works. It was recognized as a national university after independence (1947) and by 1970 had some 700 students.

SANUSIYYA, movement which originated with Muhammad al-Sanusi who founded (1837) a *tariqa* or Sufi brotherhood among the bedouin of Arabia. He attempted to introduce the order into Maghrib, his native region, but was deterred by French successes, and settled in Cyrenaica (1843), where he attracted a large following among the

bedouin tribes extending westwards into Tripolitania and southwards towards the Sudan. In 1856 he moved inland to the oasis of Jaghbub, which became the headquarters of the order. The *ikhwan* or brothers trained at Jaghbub were sent to the tribes, usually at their request, to found a *zawiya* or lodge, acting as marabouts or holy men, who had traditionally mediated in tribal disputes as well as performing their religious functions.

On the basis of tribal society the order thus built up a considerable organization of a political character, whose missionary efforts led to its extension under Al-Mahdi (1859–1902), son of the founder, into the central Sudan, with outposts as far away as Senegal. In 1895 Al-Mahdi moved south from Jaghbub to Kufra oasis, and in 1899 still further south to Qiru, to direct the work, but came into conflict with the French, who (1900–14) overran the southern desert to the border of the Anglo-Egyptian Sudan and eradicated the order there as a centre of active resistance. Al-Mahdi's successor, Ahmad, returned north to co-operate with the Turks against the Italian invasion of Tripolitania and Cyrenaica (1911). In Cyrenaica the order continued to resist after the Turks had withdrawn (1912), becoming less a religious organization than a political one, a process accelerated by Ahmad's relinquishment of its political direction to his cousin, Idris, after an unsuccessful attack on British Egypt (1916).

As de facto amir, Idris made terms with Italy and Britain (1917), while Ahmad left for Istanbul (1918). An uneasy condominium of Italians and Sanusiyya operated in Cyrenaica until 1922–3, when Idris accepted a Tripolitanian offer of allegiance to claim the amirate of Libya, and when the Italians attacked he retired to Egypt. In the partisan warfare of the second Italo-Sanusi War (1923–32) the organization of the order was wiped out, and the country was colonized by Italy in the 1930s. Tribal sentiment, however, remained focused on Idris, whom the British recognized as amir on the outbreak of the Second World War, and who recruited a Cyrenaican force round the Sanusi flag. This became the nucleus of the post-war Libyan state, which translated the Sanusi leader into a king and completed the evolution of the order into a political movement. With the deposition of Idris (1969), Libyan nationalism seemed likely (1970) to find a modified basis.

E. E. Evans-Pritchard, *The Sanusi of Cyrenaica* (Oxford, 1949).   MB

SÃO THOMÉ, island in the Gulf of Guinea discovered by Portuguese sailors in the 1470s and used by Portugal as a convict settlement and a source of sugar. The demand for slave labour to work the sugar plantations resulted in the island becoming an important entrepôt for the slave trade in the 16th–17th cents.

SAPRU, SIR TEJ BAHADUR (1875–1949), Indian nationalist politician, chiefly notable for his contribution to Indian constitution-making (1917–42). He was a leading Congressman in the United Provinces (1906–17), a founder-member of the National Liberal Federation, and twice its president (1923, 1927). He sat in the UP legislative council (1913–16) and the Imperial legislative council (1916–20) and later was law member of the government of India (1920–2). There was no important stage in the Indian constitution-making process in which he was not involved. He was in contact with Montagu during his visit (1917) and a member of the Liberal deputation to the Joint Select Committee on the 1919 bill. He was also a member of Lord Southborough's franchise committee (1919) and, as law member, helped to inaugurate reforms. In 1924 he was one of the 'minority' of the Muddiman Committee which, in a dissenting report, called for a speedy amendment of the constitution. As a leader of the Simon boycott campaign, he was one of the leading authors of the nationalist constitution presented to the All-Parties Conference in the Nehru Report (1928). Then, although he rejected the work of the Simon Commission, he worked closely with Lord Irwin, the viceroy, and was the outstanding Indian representative at the Round Table Conferences (1930–2). He later took part in the work of the Joint Parliamentary Committee on the new reforms scheme. He was disappointed by the lack of progress that was made with the federation scheme in the late 1930s, and in the politically deadlocked years of the war he made an effort, with the Non-Party Conference (1941), to find a solution to the difficulties. His appeal for action in 1942 led to the despatch of the Cripps Mission. While he remained a greatly respected elder statesman, he was not in a position to find solutions to the intractable problems of the later 1940s.   PDR

SARACEN, name given, in the classical authors of the first three centuries AD, to an Arab tribe located in the Sinai area. The word came thereafter, amongst the Christians, to denote the Arabs—and, after the rise of Islam, the Muslims—in a general sense, being applied above all to the Muslims ranged against the Latin Crusaders in Syria, Palestine, and Egypt during the 11th–13th cents.

SARAGAT, GIUSEPPE (1898–), Italian politician and president of Italy (1964–), who, from the 1920s onwards, led the struggle for democratic socialism without communist ties. In exile in France he led the Unitary Socialist Party (PSU) and joined with Nenni's Partito Socialista (PSI) in 1930 to organize resistance. During the Second World War he was a key socialist leader. He was a minister under Bonomi (1944), ambassador at Paris (1945–6), and was elected president of the Constituent Assembly in 1946. He resented Nenni's communist links and broke away in 1947 and formed the Social Democrat Party (PSDI), working with Christian Democrats. He was deputy prime minister under De Gasperi (1947–9), under Scelba (1954–5), and under Segni (1955–7). In 1964 he became foreign minister. Following Segni's resignation, he was elected president (Dec. 1964) after 21 ballots, when the Christian Democrats relented in his favour. He encouraged centre-left policies and socialist unity, provided that communists were excluded. He also favoured an improvement in the climate of European unity in the late 1960s.

SARAGOSSA, strategically important Aragonese fortress which was twice besieged by French forces (1808, 1809). Palafox held each street against Lannes (1809) at tremendous cost.

SARAJEVO, capital of the Balkan province of Bosnia, and scene of the crisis which precipitated the First World War. On 28 June 1914, during an official visit to the city, the Austrian Archduke Franz Ferdinand and his wife were assassinated by Gavrilo Princip, a member of a secret nationalist group, Young Bosnia, which was itself supported by the 'Black Hand', a Serbian terrorist organization. The Austrians accused the Serbian government of complicity in the murder, which they considered to be the culmination of several years of provocation by Serbia. The accusation was never proven, but Austria was anxious to take advantage of the situation in order to reassert her flagging authority over the Balkans. Her policy was to have far-reaching consequences. Encouraged by the Kaiser and his military chief, Von Moltke, that Austria could rely on Germany's support, the Austrian foreign minister, Berchtold, and chief of staff, Conrad, favoured immediate punitive action, a pre-emptive war to restrain the growing threat from Serb nationalism which, supported by Russia, was undermining Austria's position in the Balkans. But in the complicated system of the Austro-Hungarian empire, the caution advised by Tizsa, the Hungarian foreign minister, had to be taken into account and an ultimatum was accordingly addressed to Serbia (23 July), though its tenor was calculated to lead to its being rejected. Despite the humiliating demands made on it, the Serbian government accepted practically all the

terms. Vienna, however, was not prepared to negotiate, summarily dismissed Serbia's reply and broke off diplomatic relations with her (25 July). Belated advice from London and Berlin failed to halt the train of events. On 26 July Austria mobilized against Serbia and declared war two days later. By 4 Aug. the powers of Europe had also mobilized, and the First World War had begun.   JK

SARATOGA, BATTLE OF (Oct. 1777), surrender of the British and the turning point during the American Revolution. The British general, John Burgoyne, surrendered his army of over 5000 men to Horatio Gates on condition that they were allowed to return to England after promising not to take any further part in the war. As a result of the American success France decided to ally itself with the US.

SARAY, Persian word meaning 'palace', used to denote the capital of the Altun Ordu or Golden Horde. It was founded in the time of Batu Khan, the first prince (d. 1256) of the Altun Ordu. Saray is perhaps to be located at Tzarev, on the Akhtuba, which branches off from the Volga river. Timur Beg sacked the town in 1395. It was ravaged again in 1472 and in 1480. Thereafter it fell into ruin.

SARBAH, JOHN MENSAH (1864–1910), Ghanaian lawyer and nationalist leader, whose writings include *The Fanti Customary Laws* (1897) and *Fanti National Constitution* (1906). He was a key figure in the founding of the Aborigines' Rights Protection Society (1897) and served on the Legislative Council (1901–10).

SARDA ACT (1928), in India, name given to the controversial Child Marriage Restraint Act which was introduced in the Indian Legislative Assembly by Rai Sahib Har Bilas Sarda from Ajmer. The act raised the marriageable age for girls from 12 to 14 years and also provided that boys under 18 years should be treated as children for marriage purposes. Penalties were provided for those contracting or performing child marriages and parents or guardians were liable to prosecution for allowing their children to be married.

SARDIS, in western Turkey, 77 kms east of Izmir, in antiquity the seat of the kings of Lydia and of the Persian satraps of western Asia Minor. It was the first city to mint gold and silver coins. Athenian participation in sacking it during the Ionian Revolt (499 BC) provoked the Persian expedition against Athens in 490.

SAREKAT ISLAM ('Islamic Union'), first Indonesian mass party. It was formed in 1911 by Javanese merchants and quickly became a general protest movement, attracting villagers who were no longer satisfied with the traditional leadership. However, government pressure soon demoralized its adherents. In 1921 the movement split into a 'Red' wing, led by the Indonesian Communist Party, and a 'White', under the leadership of U. S. Tjokroaminoto and Hadji Agus Salim; the latter sought an orientation towards religious concerns. The communists were expelled in 1923 and took most of the membership with them. After several reorganizations, the White group became the Islamic Union Party of Indonesia (PSII), which continues (1970) as a minor religious party.

SARGENT, JOHN SINGER (1856–1925), US painter, who lived and worked for 40 years in London, where his work became immensely fashionable. Among his best-known paintings are his portraits (in the Tate Gallery) of the Wertheimer family and of Mme Gautreau, and his mural, *The History of Religion*, in the Boston Public Library and Art Museum.

SARGON OF AKKAD (c. 2334–2279 BC), founder of the kingdom of Akkad, the first Semitic state of Mesopotamia, whose life is surrounded by legend. At first a servant of the

King of Kish, he later formed his own state around the city of Agade, which he probably founded. He is reputed to have built an empire by conquering all of southern Mesopotamia, south-west Persia, including Elam, and regions as far north and west as the Lebanon and the Taurus mountains, ruling his empire with the help of Akkadian city governors. He retained the Sumerian religion, but used Akkadian together with Sumerian in official inscriptions.

SARGON II (*reg.* 721–705 BC), Assyrian King at the height of Assyrian power, who spent most of his reign in a struggle against rebellion, which was fostered in Syria–Palestine by Egypt, in Babylon by Elam, and in the northern areas by Urartu. In 714 Urartu was invaded and crushingly defeated, and by 710 most of the Zagros area and Syria–Palestine, excepting Judah, was in Sargon's hands. Babylon, which had been taken by a Chaldean chief in 720, was reconquered in 710. By the end of his reign the empire was larger and more secure than ever before. He founded his own capital at Dur-Sharrukin (mod. Khorsabad).

SARIT THANARAT (1908–63), Thai politician and prime minister of Thailand (1959–63), who came to prominence in 1947 as an active participant in the coup which led to Phibunsongkhram's return to power. By 1954 he was commander-in-chief of the army. He was a rival of Phao Siyanon for the succession to Phibun. In the 1957 elections he remained aloof, then aligned himself with popular opposition to Phao and Phibun and led the coup which overthrew them in 1957. Because of ill-health he left Thailand temporarily, and on his return he set up a military dictatorship. He attracted broad support and encouraged rural economic development and education.

SARKAR, SIR JADUNATH (1870–1961), Indian historian whose working life was spent mainly at Patna. His critical study and collation of Persian manuscripts gave a new dimension to Indian historical study, especially that of the Mughal field. His chief works are *The History of Aurangzeb* (5 vols, 1912–25) and *The Fall of the Mughal Empire* (4 vols, 1932–50).

SARKAR, derived from two Persian words signifying 'the head' and 'business'. In India it was used as a synonym for authority, the state, and the East India Co. It was also a Mughal administrative term for a district or sub-division of a *suba* or province. Many Hindu officials, especially in Bengal, suffixed the word as a surname.

SARKARS, NORTHERN, THE, five districts stretching along the east coast of India from the borders of Orissa to the Guntur district south of the Kistna river. Their organization dates from the Muslim occupation. In 1750–3 all the Sarkars were granted in *jagir* (a tenure carrying rights to revenues) to the French general, De Bussy, to maintain his troops, which were supporting the Nizam of Hyderabad. The French were ejected (1759) by a British force under Col. Forde, and British occupation was confirmed by the Emperor Shah Alam in 1765. The nizam was compensated and his claims finally commuted for a money payment (1823). These districts are now (1970) part of the Indian state of Andhra Pradesh.

SARMATIANS, ancient Indo-European nomadic people first mentioned by Herodotus (5th cent. BC) as neighbours of the closely related Scythians in southern Russia. From the 3rd cent. BC they moved from east of the Don and in the 1st cent. BC their two chief branches, Roxolani and Iazyges, settled north of the lower Danube. Both became clients of Rome in the 1st cent. AD, but later joined in the barbarian raids on the empire.

SARMIENTO, DOMINGO FAUSTINO (1811–88), Argentine soldier, educationalist, writer, diplomat, and president (1868–74) of Argentina. At the end of a varied career he could have been considered the quintessential enlightened and Europeanizing Argentine of the 19th cent. As a young man he joined the distinguished company of Argentines exiled by Juan Manuel de Rosas. In Chile in the 1840s he was a journalist, then, as protégé of President Manuel Montt, he founded, directed, and taught in Chile's first normal school. In 1845 the Chilean government sent him to Europe and North America to study educational methods. In the US, he became friendly with the educationalist, Horace Mann, whose methods he later adapted to Argentine conditions. He fought among the victors at Caseros (1852), which ended Rosas's tyranny. In the 1850s he served as Buenos Aires senator and head of public instruction, and became governor of San Juan province. Thereafter he served as minister to Chile and Peru (1864) and to the US (1865–8), whence he returned to Argentina to assume the presidency (1868) to which he had been elected *in absentia*. As president he stimulated immigration, commerce, agriculture, and communications. His dominant passion, however, remained education; his slogan was, 'to govern is to educate'. He organized primary education, founded normal schools, and attracted foreign scholars to strengthen the universities. He remained absorbed in this work under his successor, Nicolás Avellaneda, and also served as senator, director of Buenos Aires' public instruction, editor of the influential *El Nacional*, minister of interior, and national superintendent of schools.

His collected works fill 52 volumes. They include important essays on immigration and other subjects of public importance, and his *Civilization or Barbarism: the life of Juan Facundo Quiroga* (1845), is a classic exploration of the relations between environment, culture, and political authority. He concluded that 'barbarism' must be conquered by urban enlightenment and frontier stagnation give way to material progress. America, in fine, must be educated by Europe. The imperatives enunciated by him as a theoretician were, of course, those that he implemented as a politician.

A. W. Bunkley, *The Life of Sarmiento* (Princeton, 1952).

RCN

SARNATH, in India, important ancient Buddhist centre, north of Varanasi (Benares). Here was the ancient Deer Park, the site of Lord Buddha's First Sermon, commemorated by the Dhamekh *stupa*. Most of the remains belong to the Gupta period (5th–7th cent. AD). Owing to the harmony and perfection of their shape the Buddha images of Sarnath rank among the most splendid examples of Buddhist art.

SARPI, FRA PAOLO (1552–1623), Venetian monk, historian, and theologian, who wrote a history of the Council of Trent remarkable for its hostility to the papacy. He also made his name by championing his native republic against Pope Paul V in the bitter dispute over clerical immunities and papal jurisdiction (1606–7), being excommunicated by the pope and seriously wounded by assassins (1607).

SARRANT, ALBERT (1872–1962), French politician and *President du Conseil* at the time of remilitarization of the Rhineland. He was a member of one of the most eminent Republican families in France. His father was mayor of Carcassonne and his brother, Maurice, editor of the influential provincial paper *La Depêche de Toulouse*. In 1902 he was elected Radical Socialist deputy for the Aude *département*. Most of his political career was concentrated on colonial questions and he was twice governor of Indo-China (1911–14, 1916–19). In Indo-China Sarrant accomplished several badly needed reforms including a complete renovation of the civil service.

During the inter-war period he was minister of colonies (1920–4, 1932–3). He was minister of the interior in Poincaré's cabinet (1926–8) and in Doumergue's cabinet (1934). His first attempt to form his own government lasted only three weeks (Oct. 1933) because of the precarious financial situation in France. His second administration (1936) was the result of the lack of a stable majority in the National Assembly, and as a caretaker government was ill-suited to deal with the German invasion of the Rhineland on 7 March 1936. As a spokesman for those Radicals who desired to restrict alliances only to the Centre parties he faded into the background during the Popular Front. After the Second World War he was elected to the assembly of the French Union and became its president in 1951.

SARSFIELD, PATRICK (*c.* 1650–93), Irish soldier who served James II at Sedgemoor (1685) and in the Catholic reorganization of the Irish army (1686–8). He accompanied James to France (1688) and to Ireland (1689), successfully defended Limerick against William III's forces (1690) but surrendered the town after a two-month siege (13 Oct. 1691). He then joined French service in accordance with the treaty of Limerick (1691) but was mortally wounded at the battle of Landen (1693)

SARTRE, JEAN-PAUL (1905–   ), French writer and philosopher who was an influential figure in post-war France both through his writing and by his personal interventions in politics as a 'committed' intellectual. His first novel appeared in 1938, but the bulk of his literary work was published in the 1940s. His novel trilogy *The Roads to Freedom* (1945–9) depicted the mood among young intellectuals on the eve of the Second World War, in which he fought. After his release from prison he published clandestinely in the Resistance press, and wrote plays which were produced in occupied Paris. His philosophical work *Being and Nothingness* (1943) introduced the philosophy of existentialism to France, and had a deep influence on the younger generation in the post-war years. As presented by Sartre, existentialism denied any meaning in life external to the individual, but stressed the responsibility of individuals for the choices which they made and the consequences of their actions. It implied the need for political activism and social responsibility. In later works Sartre sought to combine the existentialist view of the individual with a Marxist theory of society and history.

Sartre founded and directed the review *Les Temps modernes* (1946), and exercised a continuing political influence through articles and essays. His ideal of democracy and socialism made him generally hostile to the Western form of liberal democracy. He consistently opposed the US and its foreign policy, and sympathized with the aspirations of the 'Third World'. His political stance and his interest in Marxism often brought him into close sympathy with the Communist Party, but he never became a member, and broke with it sharply after the 1956 Hungarian rising. He insisted on remaining independent of all political parties, though he was one of the founders of the short-lived *Rassemblement Démocratique Révolutionnaire* movement (1948).

In the 1960s he opposed French policy in Algeria, championed the Cuban revolution, denounced American intervention in Viet-nam, and sympathized with the extreme left opposition to the Fifth Republic. He was chairman of the International War Crimes Tribunal on Viet-nam set up by the Russell Foundation (1966).

M. Cranston, *Sartre* (Edinburgh, 1962 and, as *Jean-Paul Sartre*, New York, 1962).
P. Thody, *Jean-Paul Sartre: A Literary and Political Study* (London and New York, 1960). RDA

SASKATCHEWAN, province in western Canada, originally the name of an administrative district of the North-West Territory, which became a province of Canada in 1905. It was part of a grant made by King Charles II to the Hudson's Bay Co. (1670). Expeditions to the area were made by Henry Kelsey (1690–2), the La Véreyndre brothers (1750), and Samuel Hearne (1774). The last led to the establishment of the Cumberland House community, a fur-trading post and

the first permanent white settlement in Sask. Until their merger (1821), the Hudson's Bay Co. and the North-West Co. were rivals for control of the fur trade in the area. Sask. was transferred to Canada (1869) and became part of the North-West Territory (1875). The settlement of Sask. was stimulated by the completion of the Winnipeg–St Paul Railroad (1878) and the Canadian Pacific Railroad (1885); towns such as Regina, Medicine Hat, and Calgary grew along the railroad lines. Early in the 20th cent. immigrants arrived from central and eastern Europe.

Sask. has the largest agricultural area of any Canadian province and farming issues, such as wheat prices, tariffs, and freight rates, dominate its provincial politics. The Liberal party was in power (1905–29), then formed a coalition with the Conservative Party (1929–34), and again became the majority party (1934–44). The Liberals were swept from power by the Commonwealth Co-operative Federation (1944), a social democratic party led by T. C. Douglas and supported largely by rural votes. The Liberals returned to power in 1964.

J. F. C. Wright, *Saskatchewan: history of a province* (Toronto, 1955). RU

SASSANID, dynasty and period of Iranian history (*c.* 224–651). The dynasty came to power when Ardashir, a lord of Fars, revolted against and defeated (*c.* 224) the last Parthian king, Artabanus V. The Sassanians claimed to be the true Persian successors of the Achaemenids. At its height their empire stretched from Mesopotamia and Syria in the west to north-west India in the east. The Sassanians inherited the Arsacid organization of government, which was local and feudal. Strong rulers were able to maintain their authority by increased centralization of power, but under weak kings, especially in the 5th cent., the nobility grew in strength. Chosroes I in the 6th cent. restored the power of the monarchy and government was firmly centralized under ministries. From his reign onwards there was a movement of power away from the great nobles towards the lower nobility, the priesthood, the army, and the bureaucracy. Towards the end of the period, the bureaucracy and the army had become more powerful than the kings and the lower nobility had become petty rulers and had built their own castles. During the Sassanian period Zoroastrianism became the national religion, established under Shapur I in the 3rd cent. by Kartir, who organized the priesthood, had temples built, and attacked rival religions. The Christian Church grew stronger, especially in Armenia and Transcaucasia, despite persecution. After the conversion of Constantine, the Iranian Christians were suspected of being pro-Roman, but after their break with the Byzantine Church (424) and their later adoption of a contrary position to Constantinople on Nestorianism, the position of Iranian Christians improved. Although the court was wealthy and in the early centuries there may have been economic prosperity, it seems that the later centuries could not have been prosperous. There were continuous and costly wars, crushing taxation, and state interference in business. The introduction of Zoroastrianism led to the division of the people into four separate classes: the warriors, the scribes, the priests, and the common people, whose position seems to have deteriorated.

For a time the Kushans controlled the trade routes to the east, and the destruction of frontier towns like Hatra during the wars with Rome also closed some of the western trade routes. The Sassanians ended the centuries of Roman victories over Parthian Iran. Shapur I is particularly remembered for his defeat and capture of the Emperor Valerian. Under later kings the Romans redressed the balance, but by then the Iranians were less interested in western conquests. In the east there was constant trouble from nomads and from the two empires, first the Kushan and later the Ephthalite, which were established on the eastern frontiers. The Sassanians founded a number of towns (eg, Feruzabad, Bishapur, and Gundeshapur) and it was a period of rich culture, influenced by Greek, Roman, and Oriental models, though there was also a steady development of Iranian art, as well as a revival of former traditions and cultures. The national epics were written down, music and games like chess and polo became popular, and for the court, at least, it seems to have been a brilliant and luxurious age, but one which disintegrated rapidly when faced with the onslaught of the Muslim Arabs in the middle of the 7th cent.

A. Christensen, *L'Iran sous les Sasanides* (Copenhagen, 1944).
                                                                                          JKG

SASTRI, VALANGIMON SANKARANARAYANA SRINI-VASA (1869–1946), Indian social worker, politician, and diplomat, who joined G. K. Gokhale's Servants of Indian Society (1907) and succeeded him as president of the society (1915–27). In politics he was convinced of the importance of the Montagu–Chelmsford reforms, and was one of the leaders of the moderate group which broke with Congress (1918) and formed the National Liberal Federation. He was a member of the Madras and then of the Imperial legislature (1913–20) and of the new Council of State (1921–5). His most important work after 1920 lay in the international field, in negotiations concerning the status of Indian communities domiciled in other parts of the empire. He raised the question of Indians in South Africa at the Imperial Conference (1921) and in 1922 was sent by the government of India to Australia, New Zealand, and Canada to report on the condition of Indians there. In 1923 he led a delegation to present the case of the Kenya Indians to the British government. He was a member of the Round Table Conference between India and South Africa (1926–7) and became India's first High Commissioner in South Africa (1927–9). After his return, he appeared before the Joint Select Committee on East Africa (1931) to present the Indians' point of view, was a member of the second Round Table Conference in South Africa (1932), and visited Malaya (1936) to investigate the condition of Indians living there. He served on the Indian Railways Committee (1921–2) and the Royal Commission on Indian Labour (1929) and he attended the first two sessions of the Round Table Conference (1930–1). He was vice-chancellor of Annamalai University in Madras (1935–40).   PDR

SASTROAMIDJOJO, ALI (1903–   ), Indonesian politician and prime minister (1953–5, 1956–7). As chairman of the Nationalist Party (1955–66), he co-operated closely with Sukarno, and consequently was deposed when Sukarno fell from power.

SATAVAHANA DYNASTY (*c.* 50 BC–AD 200), line of rulers of the northern Deccan (present Maharashtra and Andhra Pradesh, India), known mainly from inscriptions and Puranas, with capital at Pratisthana (Paithan). They were the most powerful Indian empire at a time when most of northern India was controlled by foreigners. The Satavahana empire reached the peak of its power during the reigns of Gautamiputra Satakani and Vasisthiputra Pulumavi (2nd cent.). It disintegrated when their subordinates (such as the Ikshvakus of Andhra Pradesh) made themselves independent (beginning of the 3rd cent.).

Among the important foundations of the period are the Buddhist caves of Nasik, Karle, and Kanheri, and the great *stupa* of Amaravati.

SATI, burning of Hindu widows on the funeral pyres of their husbands. The Greeks had found it prevalent in the Punjab as early as the 4th cent. BC. Unsuccessful attempts were made to suppress *sati* before the days of British rule. At first the British tolerated it for fear that attempts at its suppression would lead to rebellion. Eventually, in 1829, Bentinck declared it illegal in the Bengal Presidency. It would be wrong to give all the credit to Bentinck, for the writings of William Carey and the Baptist missionaries at

Serampore and the pamphlets of Ram Mohan Roy all had a profound effect. Dalhousie was chiefly responsible for its abolition in the Indian states.

SATRAPS OF UJJAIN (*c.* AD 125–400), rulers of one of the branches of Scythians (Sakas) which invaded the Indo-Pakistani sub-continent (1st cent. BC), moved southward and finally settled down in Malwa (capital: Ujjain). After a few generations they became thoroughly Indianized. The earliest rulers probably acted as governors of the Kushan emperors and so used the title of satraps, which was continued even after their successors had made themselves completely independent (*c.* AD 125). Their greatest ruler was Rudradaman, whose Girnar (Surashtra) inscription (AD 150) is the oldest known document written entirely in pure Sanskrit. It deals with the repair of an ancient irrigation reservoir, the dykes of which had collapsed and caused havoc to the surrounding countryside. The power of the satraps came to an abrupt end when the area was conquered by Candra Gupta II (*c.* 400) and incorporated into the Gupta empire.

SATRAPY, administrative unit of ancient Iran. It was adopted by Cyrus II and developed by Darius I, under whom the satrapy was based on existing national or political boundaries, but there were also vassal kingdoms which were not satrapies. The number of satrapies varied through redistribution and occasional rebellions, but satrapies tended to become smaller in size and increase in number under the Achaemenids. Each satrapy was governed by a satrap, a man of high birth, usually appointed for life, though in some periods the office became hereditary. The satrap was the highest judicial authority, and was also responsible for communications and the collection of taxes. He was assisted by a secretary and a commander of the soldiers. Under the Seleucids the satrapies appear to have been more independent of the central government, while under the Parthians there were only a few satrapies among many petty principalities. In the Sassanian period the provinces were again divided up and governed by officials from the nobility, or later by military governors, directly responsible to the central government.

SATSUMA, *han* (autonomous domain) of feudal Japan. It was located in south-western Kyushu, and was ruled by the Shimazu family from the Kamakura period until 1871, when it became Kagoshima prefecture. Although subdued by Hideyoshi (1587) and reduced in size by Ieyasu after the battle of Sekigahara (1600), Satsuma retained its autonomy and pride. It maintained a larger proportion of samurai than other *han*s and established control over the Ryukyu islands (1609). In 1868 Satsuma played the leading part in overthrowing the Tokugawa *bakufu* and thereafter its samurai filled many important positions, especially in the navy.

SATURDAY EVENING POST in the US, weekly illustrated magazine (1821–1969). In 1897 the long-established but struggling journal was bought by Cyrus H. K. Curtis (1850–1933), the successful publisher of *The Ladies' Home Journal* (1883–   ). Curtis appointed George Horace Lorimer (1867–1937) as editor-in-chief, and the *Post* became one of the most popular magazines of the time. By 1922 its average circulation was over 2 million, and this had trebled by 1963. Aimed at middle-class America, and with a conservative and business orientation, it uncritically accepted traditional American values and institutions that were regularly depicted on its covers by the artist Norman Rockwell (1894–   ). Because of financial difficulties the magazine was suspended in 1969.

SATURNINUS, L. APPULEIUS (d. 100 BC), Roman revolutionary demagogue. As tribune (103) he bid for Marius' support by proposing a law to give his veterans land in Africa, as well as a corn law and a treason law. Metellus Numidicus tried to exclude Saturninus from the Senate (102), but he was re-elected tribune for 100, when he proposed a wide-ranging colonial law to attract the support of army veterans. At the consular elections Saturninus' associate, Glaucia, stood as a candidate, although praetor in office, and had a rival murdered. The Senate called on the consuls to take action and Saturninus was suppressed by Marius and afterwards lynched.

SAUK INDIANS, American tribe, first mentioned by the French (c. 1640) as living in MI. Inter-tribal warfare forced them to flee to Green Bay, and after a battle with the French (1733), the Sauk became united with the Fox tribe and settled in the upper Mississippi valley. A Sauk band living near St Louis signed a treaty (1804) ceding all claim to territory in WI, IL, and MO. Anger among the rest of the tribe culminated in the Black Hawk War (1832). The Sauk ceded their last lands in IA (1837) and moved to KS. In 1867 they accepted a tract in Indian Territory.

SAUL (reg. c. 1022–1000 BC), first Israelite King, who united the Hebrew tribes against various surrounding peoples, and defeated the Ammonites, and the Philistines, though his defeat of them was not conclusive. His personal animosity towards the popular future king, David, led to continual internal troubles and he lost the support of the priests. When the Philistines again attacked (c. 1000) Saul was defeated and killed.

SAULT-STE-MARIE, Canadian mission founded (1688) by the Society of Jesus as the first permanent white settlement in MI. Straddling the St Mary's river, which connects Lakes Superior and Huron, its strategic location made it a centre for the fur trade. The North-West Co. built a lock canal round the rapids at Sault-Ste-Marie (1798), which was destroyed by the US in the War of 1812. After it was rebuilt, the discovery of the vast Mesabi iron-ore range (1890) required the expansion of the Sault-Ste-Marie water-way.

SAUSSURE, HORACE-BÉNÉDICT DE (1740–99), Swiss naturalist, traveller, and writer. He was a keen Alpinist and promoted the first ascent of Mont Blanc; in the third ascent (1787) he himself took part. He was made a fellow of the Royal Society for his researches on hygrometry.

SAVA OF SERBIA (fl. 13th cent. AD), national figure and saint in Serbian history, who was the youngest son of the Serbian ruler, Stefan Nemanya. His most important achievements were his share in the foundation of the monastery of Hilendar on Mount Athos, and the organization of the Serbian Church as an autonomous ecclesiastical unit within the patriarchate of Constantinople (1219). He was himself its first archbishop. In addition to being a man of deep piety and sincere devotion to the monastic life, he was also an excellent organizer, an energetic traveller, and an able writer. His works include a biography of his father.

SAVAGE, MICHAEL JOSEPH (1872–1940), NZ politician and first Labour prime minister, who came from Australia in 1907. He was deputy leader of the parliamentary party (1923–33) and became its leader in 1933; Labour's victory in 1935 was popularly credited to him. As prime minister he was revered as the embodiment of social welfare and justice.

SAVANG VATTHANA (1907–   ), King of Laos (reg. 1959–   ), eldest son of Sisavangvong, who became crown prince in 1941 and succeeded his father in 1959.

SAVARKAR, VINAYAK DAMODAR (1883–1966), Indian revolutionary and later Hindu Mahasabha leader. As students, Savarkar and his brothers set up a number of groups dedicated to revolutionary activities. The most extensive was the Abhinava Bharat Society (New India Society) (1904), which was not dissolved until 1952. In 1906 Savarkar went to

London, having won one of Krishnavarma's political scholarships. His Free India Society did a great deal to recruit members for terrorist activities at India House and to procure arms and technical knowledge on bomb-making. Savarkar also wrote a good deal, notably a history of the Indian Mutiny, *The First Indian War of Independence.* From June 1907 India House was under his control, but the assassination of Sir Curzon Wyllie (1909) brought the circle there to an end and the arrest of his elder brother was followed by his own arrest and extradition to India, where he was sentenced to two terms of transportation for life and sent to the Andamans (1911–21). Later, he was imprisoned at Ratnagiri and Yeravada (1921–3) and then interned in Ratnagiri town until 1937. While in gaol Savarkar wrote his basic treatise on Hindu nationalism, *Hindutva,* and, after 1924, assisted the Hindu Sabha's *shuddhi* and *sangathan* (proselytization and unity) campaigns.

His release from restrictions in 1937 enabled him to take a more active part in the Hindu Mahasabha, of which he was president until 1944. He was the most able and determined leader that the Mahasabha ever had, but was not physically strong enough, nor experienced enough in modern political organization to be able to establish the Mahasabha as a viable alternative to Congress. The apparent implication of Mahasabha members in Gandhi's assassination (1948) threw a great deal of suspicion on him, but he was acquitted at a trial in 1948–9.   PDR

SAVERY, THOMAS (1650–1715), English engineer and inventor of an unsophisticated pumping engine (1698). With his knowledge of Dutch he had translated one of Coehoorn's books on military engineering, and by his experiment with steam pressure in the pump contributed to the development of the steam engine, particularly Thomas Newcomen's invention.

SAVIGNY, FRIEDRICH KARL VON (1779–1861), German lawyer, who created the German historical school of law. He traced the origin of law to the customs and traditions of the community, not to the deliberate will of the legislator.

SAVILE, SIR GEORGE (1726–84), British politician, who was MP for Yorkshire (1759–83). He opposed general warrants (1763) and was invited to join Rockingham's administration (1765), but refused, preferring to remain independent. In the 1770s he supported the American colonists (1775). He was a notable advocate of religious toleration and in 1772 spoke in favour of the Feathers petition for relief from subscription to the Thirty-nine Articles. In 1778 he introduced the Roman Catholic Relief Act, as a result of which his house was burned in 1780 by the Gordon Rioters. In 1779 he was prominent in the Yorkshire Association, and provided the link between it and the Rockingham party, which he now supported. During the 1770s he had moved from independence to opposition.

SAVINGS BANK ACT (1828), in Britain, reflected a change in public opinion about the benefits of Savings Banks. In the 1817 act they were regarded as a valuable means of keeping down the poor rate, as were friendly societies, and were consequently given a favourable position. Their money was to be invested in the Commission for the Reduction of the National Debt at a fixed rate of interest of over $4\frac{1}{2}$ per cent. Under this encouragement the number of banks expanded rapidly, but as the general rate of interest was falling this led to a loss to the exchequer. By the late 1820s it was realized that labourers, the main recipients of poor relief, were not for the most part in a position to use the banks and there seemed little reason for the state to subsidize small savings. Pressure by Joseph Hume for government economy led to the Savings Bank Act, which reduced the rate of fixed interest and also the limit on the size of deposits allowed. The act did not prevent there being still some financial loss to the state, nor did it include regulations to prevent fraud.

SAVO ISLAND, BATTLE OF (9 Aug. 1942), naval engagement between Allied and Japanese forces in the Solomon Islands campaign during the Second World War. The Japanese inflicted serious losses on a combined US–Australian fleet with negligible damage to themselves, and US forces on Guadalcanal were left temporarily without naval support or adequate supplies.

SAVONAROLA, JEROME (1452–98), Florentine monk, who abandoned (1474) a secular career to enter the Dominican order. In 1491 he became the prior of the strict, observant convent of St Marco at Florence. He had immense influence as a preacher, his fervour, sincerity, learning, and austerity of life winning him a large and devoted following. A feature of his preaching which proved a fatal handicap was that he was prone to making prophecies. They were often merely well-meant threats of disasters to come if the Florentines did not abandon their evil ways, but they encouraged his enemies to denounce him as a false prophet. After the overthrow of the rule of the Medici in 1494 a more democratic republic was set up at Florence. Savonarola was supported by the popular party, while the hitherto predominant corrupt rich oligarchy looked with dismay at this intrusion of an honest fanatic. By 1495 Savonarola had drifted into a conflict with Pope Alexander VI. He aroused dismay by ignoring the papal excommunication in 1497. The threat of a papal interdict on Florence encouraged his enemies to recapture power. After the election of a hostile government at Florence, he was seized by a mob, tortured, and executed as a heretic.

SAVOY, originally a transalpine state centred on the area from Lake Neuchâtel to the Middle Isère in the 4th cent. but which by the 9th cent. included the region around Chambery. From the 14th cent. it was associated with the Italian duchy of Piedmont and from the 18th cent. with the kingdom of Sardinia until its final annexation by the second French Empire (1860).

In the 10th cent. the county of Savoy became part of the kingdom of Burgundy or Arles, which in 1032 was claimed by the German Emperor Conrad II, supported by Umberto the Whitehanded, the founder of the modern house of Savoy. In the reign of Count Amadeus V, who was recognized as a feudal prince of the Holy Roman empire (1313), Chambery again became the capital of Savoy. From the mid-14th cent. the state underwent a century of consolidation and expansion. Amadeus VI, known as 'the Green Count', a strong-willed ruler, took Gallipoli from the Turks (1366–7), mediated the peace of Turin between Venice and Genoa (1381), and obtained the cession of all the Angevin rights in Piedmont. Amadeus VII, 'the Red Count', annexed Nice in 1388, while Amadeus VIII acquired Annecy (1405), Saluzzo (1413), the lands of the Achaea family (1418), and Vercelli (1427). He looked to the emperor for support in counteracting the power of France and Burgundy and was granted the title of duke by Sigismund (1416). He created new institutions to centralize his lands, unified the legal system (1430), and after abdicating in favour of his son Louis (1440) became Pope Felix V and used his position to acquire the vacant see of Geneva (1444).

By the mid-15th cent. Savoy was a substantial state stretching from Lake Neuchâtel to the Mediterranean, but from the accession of Duke Louis I (*reg.* 1440–65), with his frivolous wife and corrupt ministers, the duchy began to decline in importance. Successive family conflict and weak rulers undermined the state, which suffered grave losses in the Italian Wars of the early 16th cent. Under the pro-Habsburg Charles III Savoy and most of Piedmont were overrun by French forces, a Swiss revolt overthrew the Savoyard cardinal-bishop of Geneva (1533) and defeated the Savoyard forces (1535), and his rival Federico Gonzago of Mantua acquired Montferrat from Charles V (1536). The reconstruction of Piedmont-Savoy began under Emmanuel Philibert (1528–80) (*reg.* 1553–80), joint victor of St Quentin (1557), to whom France restored the two duchies by the treaty of Cateau-Cambrésis (1559). In 1563 he also regained Turin, and throughout his reign he worked to build a modest fleet, a standing army, and an efficient absolutist administration. His successor, Charles Emmanuel I dreamed of winning a foreign crown for himself, not least the French (1590), and he received the French-speaking territories of Bresse, Bugey, and Valromey in return for Saluzzo at the treaty of Lyons (1601), but his attack on Geneva failed (1602) and he ruined Savoy's economy by becoming involved in two unsuccessful wars over Montferrat, one against Spain (1613–18) and the other against France (1627–30), in which the major powers fought to control the 'Spanish road' to the Netherlands, running through Savoy. Victor Amadeus I recovered Savoy from the French and obtained a third of Montferrat (treaty of Cherasco, 1631) but his state became a dependency of France. Victor Amadeus II added considerably to Savoy's possessions and prestige by his policy of opportunism. He won Pinerolo in the War of the League of Augsburg (1689–1697) and added the remainder of Montferrat and Sicily by the treaty of Utrecht (1713), with the title of king, though he was forced by the great powers to exchange Sicily for the less fertile Sardinia (1718). From this time Savoy became a subordinate part of the Sardinian kingdom, though the real seat of power was in Piedmont.

The French Revolutionary and Napoleonic Wars were catastrophic for Savoy. Victor Amadeus III was forced to cede it with Nice to the French (1796), Charles Emmanuel IV's brief reign (*reg.* 1796–8) ended in abdication, while his successor, Victor Emmanuel I, retired to Sardinia (1806). In 1815 Savoy was returned to him, and in the age of dawning nationalism and liberalism Sardinia-Savoy was the only Italian state with a semblance of independence from Austrian domination. Victor Emmanuel II and his able minister Cavour proceeded to unify Italy, but the price paid for the creation of the Italian kingdom was the cession of Savoy and Nice, confirmed by plebiscite, to Louis Napoleon of France (1860). The house of Savoy, however, continued to reign in Italy until 1946 when Victor Emmanuel III abdicated and a republic was declared.　　　　　　　　　MKS

SAVOY CONFERENCE (April–July 1661) in England, between Anglicans and Presbyterians, who were prepared to accept a modified form of Episcopacy on the lines traded by James Ussher, Abp of Armagh, before the Civil War. The aim of the conference, held at the Bp of London's lodgings in the Savoy, was to work out forms of worship and belief. It failed completely because the bishops offered only limited concessions, while Richard Baxter, leader of the Presbyterians, was inflexible and could do nothing against the rising tide of Anglicanism. Before the conference ended the Cavalier Parliament had met and begun to take decisions which led to the triumph of Anglican uniformity.

SAW, U (1900–48), Burmese lawyer, politician, and journalist who formed (1938) the Myochit Party and raised the Galon Tat, a private army for political purposes. He became minister for forests and agriculture (1939) and prime minister (1940), although the Myochit Party had no absolute majority and was not even the largest single party. He visited Britain during the Second World War, but failed to obtain from the government a promise of dominion status after the war. On his way back to Burma he was arrested by the British for treacherous communications with the Japanese and was interned. On his release after the war, he returned to Burma and made an unsuccessful attempt at a political comeback. He was later charged with instigating the assassination of Aung San and six other cabinet ministers on 19 July 1947, for which he was convicted and hanged.

SAWBRIDGE, JOHN (1732–95), British politician and one of the series of 18th-cent. aldermen of the city of London who, as MPs for the city, vigorously opposed the government. He pressed for parliamentary reform, especially for annual parliaments, and attacked the government's American policy. He welcomed the Feathers Petition (1772), but, following his constituents' wishes, opposed the Roman Catholic Relief Act (1778). He was a founder-member of the Society of Supporters of the Bill of Rights (1769) and usually supported John Wilkes, whom he succeeded as lord mayor of London in 1775.

SAXO GRAMMATICUS (*c.* 1150–*c.* 1216), Danish historian who was probably the secretary to Abp Absolom (d. 1201), at whose instigation he wrote a huge history of the Danes. It contains much interesting material but must be used cautiously.

SAXONS, Germanic tribes from the Elbe–Rhine area, first mentioned by Ptolemy, who began raiding Roman Britain in the 3rd cent. Population pressures, fears of political or religious persecution, and desire for plunder led to piratical raids contemporaneously with Angles and Jutes. In defence the Romans built the Saxon Shore forts on southern and eastern coasts and appointed officials to repulse the threat. The 5th-cent. Roman withdrawal from Britain gave the invaders their chance and, admitted at first as federati to help the British, their permanent settlement followed.

Pagan worshippers of Woden, Nerthus, and Thor, their first foothold was in Kent, then by the late 5th cent. Aelle of Sussex became the first English bretwalda. Their advance through southern Britain was briefly halted at the battle of Mount Badon. Essex, Middlesex, Surrey, and southern Mercia all developed under Saxon influence, but the kingdom of Wessex, founded traditionally by Cerdic and Cynric in the Thames, Berks, and Wilts area was to be of greatest significance in English history. The battle of Dyrham (*c.* 577) marked the Saxon advance to the west coast. Acceptance of 7th-cent. Roman Christianity brought England closer to Europe and the reign of Ine of Wessex (*reg.* 688–726) saw further expansion and unique social legislation.

In 829 Mercia was overrun by Egbert of Wessex after his victory at Ellendun and under Alfred (*reg.* 871–900) the serious Viking challenge was withstood. Henceforth the *Anglo Saxon Chronicle* records significant events showing how the West Saxon dynasty became the focus of English nationalism. By the 10th cent. Saxon society was highly developed; Christianity strengthened under Edgar and Dunstan; law and order and local government well entrenched.

Renewed Viking attacks in Aethelred II's reign brought serious danger to England and in 1016, with the accession of Cnut, Saxon England fell under Danish rule. The ending of this dynasty in 1042 saw Saxon kings enter their last phase. Edward the Confessor's reign witnessed the rise of great earls, the most ambitious being Godwin of Wessex, whose son Harold, defeated by the Normans in 1066, was the last Saxon ruler. Over successive centuries Norman–Saxon assimilation gradually took place.

F. Stenton, *Anglo Saxon England* (Oxford, 1947).
G. O. Sayles, *The Medieval Foundations of England* (London, 1948). MEB

SAXONY, term applied to different areas of northern Europe at varying periods. The Saxons were a Germanic people occupying the modern region of Holstein from the 2nd cent., but who inhabited a large area of marshy waste spanning the upper Ruhr, Ems, Weser, Aller, and Lower Elbe rivers at the time of their conquest by Charlemagne in the 8th cent. Saxony was part of the inheritance of Charles's grandson, Louis the German, at the treaty of Verdun (843), and during the unsettled period of the Viking and Magyar invasions the duchy rose to prominence through the leadership of the Liudolfinger dynasty, from whom the Saxon kings of Germany sprang. This Saxon line ruled the German empire from Henry I's accession (919) to Henry II's death (1024) and began the drive to absorb the Slav peoples of eastern Europe. In 961 the Saxon ducal title was transferred to Herman Billung, whose family retained it until 1106, despite

the destruction of Saxon resistance to the Emperor Henry IV at Langensalza (1075). The title of Duke of Saxony and the Billung allodial lands passed in 1106 to Lothar of Supplinburg, who defeated the Emperor Henry V at Welfesholz (1115) and succeeded to his title also (1125). But on the downfall of his grandson, the Welf duke Henry the Lion, in 1180, the extensive lands of Saxony were dismembered by the victorious Emperor Frederick I.

In 1180 the Saxon lands west of the Weser were conferred, as the duchy of Westphalia, on the Abp of Cologne, while those east of the Weser were bestowed, with the ducal title, on Bernard of Anhalt, son of Albrecht the Bear of Brandenburg. From 1180, therefore, until the extinction of the male line (1422) the term Saxony denotes the two small and separate areas, one around Lauenburg on the right bank of the lower Elbe and the other around Wittenberg on the middle Elbe; for on the death of Bernard's son, Albert (1257), who first received the electoral title from the emperor, Saxony was split between his sons, John I and Albert II. After family disputes, Albert II's son, Rudolph I, was recognized as Elector of Saxe-Wittenberg by the Golden Bull of 1356, although the Saxe-Lauenburg line continued to claim the duchy and electorate for two more centuries.

On the death of Albert III of Saxe-Wittenberg (1422) the Emperor Sigismund I endowed Frederick of Wettin, margrave of Meissen, with the electorate of Saxony (1423). His Wettin lands, Meissen, Lusatia, and Thuringia, lay further south from Wittenberg, and included the most flourishing mining region of Germany. By the treaty of Leipzig (1485) this powerful Saxon state centred on the middle Elbe was partitioned between Frederick's two grandsons, Ernest and Albert, Ernest taking the Saxe-Wittenberg inheritance and most of Thuringia, with the electoral title, and Albert the Meissen lands and the ducal title. It was Elector Frederick the Wise who made Saxony the cradle of the Reformation, by protecting Martin Luther and adopting the Lutheran faith himself (1524). His brother John was a co-founder of the Protestant League of Schmalkalde. On the other hand Duke George 'the Bearded' of the Albertine line opposed the religious changes, crushed the German peasantry at Frankenhausen (1525), and joined the Catholic League of Nuremberg (1538). His work, however, was undone by his successors, his brother Duke Henry, and his nephew, Maurice, who adopted Protestantism. In 1547 Elector John Frederick I was humiliatingly defeated at Mühlberg by the imperial forces and his electoral title and lands were bestowed by Charles V upon his Albertine cousin, Maurice. The long political quarrel between the Ernestine and Albertine branches of the Saxon house were now translated into theological terms, in a quarrel between the Gnesiolutherans and the Philippists. The Ernestine prince John George tried unsuccessfully to recover his electoral title with the help of an unscrupulous adventurer, Grumback, but was imprisoned for 28 years, leaving the Albertine family in possession of the Saxon electorate.

Under Elector Augustus, in the 16th cent., Saxony enjoyed considerable prosperity, Leipzig developing as a great centre of the arts. It was the long reign of his grandson, John George I (*reg.* 1611–56), which marked the decline of Saxony's role as the leading Protestant state before the rising power of Brandenburg. He played an equivocal part in the Thirty Years War (1618–48), and though he secured Lusatia (1635), the creation of the separate duchies of Saxe-Weissenfels, Saxe-Merseburg, and Saxe-Zeitz for his younger sons weakened the electorate for his pro-Habsburg successors, John George II (*reg.* 1656–80) and John George III (*reg.* 1680–91). Meanwhile, in 1635–6 the Welf descendants of Henry the Lion negotiated plans to consolidate their possessions in Lower Saxony, the former Saxon lands of the lower Elbe, by creating the duchies of Brunswick-Wolfenbuttel, Luneburg-Celle, and Hanover.

Under the Catholic elector, Frederick Augustus (*reg.* 1694–1733), brother of John George IV (*reg.* 1691–4), Saxony acquired the elective crown of Poland, thus enhancing his prestige and forging a close connection with Catholic Austria, but Saxony lost the reputation of Protestant leadership acquired at the Reformation and became involved in a series of wars in the 18th cent. Frederick Augustus III gave up Saxony's Polish aspirations and promoted industrial prosperity, but became a client of Napoleon I, for which he received the title of King of Saxony at the peace of Posen (1806) and Grand Duke of Warsaw (1807) and the lands of Lower Lusatia. At the Congress of Vienna (1815), however, he lost two-fifths of his territories to Frederick William of Prussia, including Lusatia, northern Thuringia, and Wittenberg. Anthony Clement and Frederick Augustus II faced the first revolts of the industrial artisans and bourgeoisie of Dresden and Leipzig in 1848–9. After conceding to the insurgents' demands for a provisional government pledged to liberal reforms (1848), Frederick Augustus fled from Dresden, but was restored later by Prussian troops (1849). When John I supported Austria in the Seven Weeks War (1866) Prussian forces overran his country, forcing him to pay an indemnity and to merge Saxony in the North German Confederation under Prussia (1866) which in turn became part of the German Reich of 1871. Under Albert I (*reg.* 1873–1902) and George I (*reg.* 1902–4) the Social Democratic Party made considerable progress. During the First World War Saxony contributed substantially with men and materials to the German war effort, but the Kaiser's defeat led to revolution (2 Nov. 1918) and the abdication of Frederick Augustus III. On 1 Nov. 1920 Saxony adopted a republican constitution as a free state within the Weimar republic. A coalition of Social Democrats and Communists under Erich Zeigner was overthrown by German forces sent by the German chancellor Stresemann (1923), after which moderate Social Democrats held power until 1929. The Nazi Party controlled Saxony from 1933 until the Soviet occupation (1945) at the end of the Second World War, after which the state was incorporated into the German Democratic Republic.

G. Barraclough, *The Origins of Modern Germany* (Oxford, 1946).
H. Holborn, *A History of Modern Germany* (London, 1965).
MKS

SAY, JEAN-BAPTISTE (1767–1832), French economist and counterpart of the Scotsman, Adam Smith, whom he criticized for treating theory and fact in the same book. Say's law of the market attempted to establish the interdependence of supply and demand, since every supply of goods involves a demand. Thus an increase in the productivity of labour (*eg*, by machinery) necessarily increased purchasing power to match it, and any supposed over-production would be temporary and local.

SAYBROOK PLATFORM (1708), revision of the ecclesiastical policy of the English colony of Connecticut which stressed 'consociation' (rule by Councils) in contrast to the Cambridge platform, favouring autonomy of individual churches. The adoption of the Saybrook platform made church policy and government effectively Presbyterian in character.

SAYE AND SELE, WILLIAM FIENNES, 1st Viscount (1582–1662), English politician and opponent of King Charles I. He was one of a small group of peers who worked with parliamentary leaders in the Commons during the 1620s and 1630s against the royal policy. At his seat, Broughton Castle, near Banbury, secret meetings took place during the 1630s at which opposition tactics were probably planned. He was basically a moderate. Though supporting parliament in the Civil War he opposed the execution of Charles I and retired from political activity during the Commonwealth. He welcomed the Restoration.

SAYF AL-DAWLA, Abu'l-Hasan 'Ali (*reg.* 945–67), Amir of Aleppo who met sustained Byzantine offensive directed against northern Syria and Al-Jazira (Mesopotamia), an offensive he was able to slow down, but not to overcome. The serious reverses which he suffered in battle during the last years of his life foreshadowed the imminent reduction (969) of Aleppo to the status of a Byzantine protectorate. He was the patron of the Arabic poet Al-Mutanabbi.

SAYYID, Arabic word meaning lord or prince. The term was often used of persons descended from the House of the Prophet Muhammad, descendants who enjoyed a special respect and formed a privileged group under their own 'marshal', *ie*, the Naqib al-Ashraf.

SAYYID AHMAD KHAN (1817–98), Indian lawyer and educational reformer, one of the most important Muslims of the 19th cent., whose family had held important offices under the Mughal emperors. He entered the service of the East India Co. in 1837, and later became a judge (1855–76). During the Indian Mutiny he did much to save British lives and afterwards strove to persuade the government that Muslims were not primarily responsible for the Mutiny, which he did partly through his book, *The Causes of the Indian Revolt* (Urdu version, 1859, English translation, 1877), and through a pamphlet, 'The Loyal Mohammedans of India' (1860). He also wrote a commentary on the Bible to show Muslims that, despite serious differences, Christianity was not so foreign to their own beliefs as they imagined. He advocated the social progress of Muslim women, which led to a breach between himself and orthodox Muslims and endangered his life.

He realized that Indian Muslims would have to come to terms with the West, politically and culturally, that English education was a valuable qualification for government service, and that by abstaining from it Muslims had become subordinate to the Hindus, who had taken their place in the administration of the country. He laid great stress on the necessity for teaching Western science through Urdu translations and through the medium of English. This led to the formation of the Scientific Society of Ghazipore (1863). After a visit to England in 1869 Sayyid's respect for European civilization increased. He played a major part in establishing the Anglo-Oriental College at Aligarh (1875), without which Indian Muslims would have lagged far behind the Hindus. He also started a Muslim Educational Conference, which developed a network of branches throughout Muslim India. In 1887 he came out openly against the participation of Muslims in the Indian National Congress, which he regarded as primarily a Hindu body.

G. F. I. Graham, *Life and Work of Sir Syed Ahmed Khan* (London, 1907).
W. C. Smith, *Modern Islam in India* (London, 1946).   CCD

SAYYID DYNASTY, In India, whose members doubtfully claimed descent from the Prophet Muhammad. They replaced the moribund Tughluq dynasty (1414) until they themselves were replaced by the Afghan Lodis (1451). Only the first of their four rulers, Khizr Khan, was of any note. As governor of Multan on behalf of Taimur's successor, Shah Rukh, he marched to Delhi when the nobles there elected Daulat Khan Lodi to the throne. His reign was occupied in suppressing rebellions. So were those of his three successors, Mubarak Shah (1421–32), Muhammad (1434–44), and Alam Shah, with ever-diminishing success. The last ruler handed over power to Bahlul Lodi and retired to Badaon.

SAZONOV, SERGEI DMITRIEVICH (1861–1927), Russian diplomat and politician, who served in the embassy in London (1904–6) and at the Vatican (1906–9), and was foreign minister (1910–16).

SCABINUS, Latin term for a man with a special position in a Frankish folkmoot (court of a county or its sub-divisions) in the 8th–9th cents. In such a court the king's official representative, the count or his subordinates, awarded the verdict on the advice of doomsmen (*scabini*) who knew the local customs. Before the reign of Charlemagne (*reg.* 768–814) the counts selected on each occasion their own doomsmen. To check the abuse of justice by the counts Charlemagne insisted on the appointment in each county of permanent *scabini*, acting for life, and selected them on the advice of royal envoys (*missi*) whom he regularly sent on missions throughout his kingdom. The counts resented the existence of this body of independent *scabini* and, after the decline of power of Charlemagne's successors in the 9th cent., these permanent doomsmen were gradually changed into feudal dependants of the counts. A public court of the county was thus transformed into the private, feudal court of the count. Public justice disappeared in most of France after the 9th cent.

SCADDAN, JOHN (1876–1934), Australian politician, who, as Labor prime minister of WA (1911–16), pursued optimistic land settlement policies and ventures in state socialism. He broke with his party over conscription (1917) and was a member of non-Labor WA governments (1919–24, 1930–3), being minister for unemployment during the years of economic depression.

SCALA family in Verona (*c.* 1260–1387), dynasty of Italian despots who rose to power as supporters of the imperialist party and successfully avoided the violent overthrow of republican institutions in Verona while enjoying all the realities of supreme rule. Martino I (*c.* 1260–77) was the first effective ruler of Verona. By exploiting the great strategic importance of Verona and the immense agrarian prosperity of its regions, the family made it into one of the most powerful north Italian states. The greatest ruler of the dynasty was Cangrade, in the 14th cent., the patron of Dante. The rule of the Scala was ended in 1387 by the Visconti dukes of Milan, most of their state falling ultimately (after 1402) to Venice.

SCANDINAVIAN SHIPPING in the Middle Ages. A major cause of Viking expansion in the 8th–11th cents was that they possessed the first reliable ocean-going ships known in north-western Europe. By not later than the 8th cent. Norsemen had equipped their ships with keels, masts, and sails. Of shallow draught, they could enter shallow estuaries. The surviving 9th-cent. Gokstad ship could be rowed by 32 oars and had an effective mast and sail which would enable it to sail close to the wind. It could probably have taken 70 people besides cargo. Warships were larger and narrower. The Norwegian king Olaf Tryggvason (d. 1000) was said to possess a warship of 68 oars carrying more than 200 warriors.

SCANDINAVIANISM, movement towards unity among the governments and peoples of the Scandinavian peninsula and Denmark. It was strongly supported by the universities, and, in 1848, caused a Swedish garrison to be sent to Fünen as a deterrent against a Prussian invasion. Close ties of language and culture were counterbalanced by divergent political and economic interests.

SCANIA (SKÅNE), southern extremity of the Scandinavian peninsula, taken by the Swedes from the Danes in 1658 and retained in spite of Danish invasions during the Scanian War (1676–9) and the Great Northern War (1700–21).

SCANIAN WAR (1676–9), attempt by the Danes to regain territory lost to Sweden on the Scandinavian mainland. Their invasion of Scania was at first successful, but after defeats at Halmstad and Lund (Dec. 1676), the Danes kept the campaign going chiefly with Scanian irregulars. Meanwhile, Danish naval victories under Niels Juel, gained with Dutch support, deprived the Swedes of Gotland and their

possessions in Germany. France, however, insisted in 1679 on a return to the status quo.

SCAPA FLOW, large natural anchorage in the Orkney Islands, 15 miles (24 kms) long and 8 miles (12 kms) wide. It was used as a British naval base during both World Wars. After the First World War a large part of the surrendered German fleet was interned, and on 6 June 1919 scuttled there on the orders of Admiral von Reuter. Scapa Flow was not properly fortified against submarine attack and the torpedoing of the battleship *Royal Oak* in the Second World War (14 Oct. 1939) showed that its natural complexity was not by itself an adequate safeguard. The base was closed in 1956.

SCARBROUGH, RICHARD LUMLEY, 1st Earl of (*c.* 1650–1721), English soldier and politician, who was a member of the abortive expedition to Tangier (1680), and had a principal share in the Duke of Monmouth's capture after Sedgemoor (1685). He opposed the rule of James II and was one of the seven men who signed the invitation asking William of Orange to invade England (31 June 1688). He served at the battle of the Boyne (1690), and later in Flanders. After the treaty of Ryswick (1697) he retired from military service, but became (1706) a commissioner for the Union with Scotland and held various other political posts under Anne and George I.

SCARLATTI, DOMENICO (1685–1759), Italian composer, who studied and wrote in Rome, Lisbon, and Madrid, and left some 500 compositions for the harpsichord, which were important in the development of the sonata form.

SCHACHT, HJALMAR (1887–1970), German politician and banker, who, as currency commissioner (1923), had the task of stabilizing the mark after Germany's catastrophic inflation. In Dec. 1923, as president of the Reichsbank, he steered Germany through the crisis, partly because his excellent relations with British financiers ensured him foreign support. However, after publicly opposing the Young Plan in 1929, he resigned (March 1930). His growing political ambitions helped him to accommodate his views to the changing political climate of the 1930s, and he began to lend open support to Hitler. In 1934 he became his acting economic minister, and as plenipotentiary for war production he wielded major economic power in Germany until about 1936, when the Four-Year Plan for rearmament introduced a new factor. Anxious above all to maintain a stable currency and a high level of exports, and worried by the inflationary threat of unbridled government expenditure, he resigned as minister (1937) and Reichsbank president (1938), being replaced in both posts by Funk. In 1946 he was one of the principal defendants at Nuremberg, but was acquitted; a sentence imposed later by a denazification court was quashed (1949), and, until his retirement, he was active in banking (1953–63).

SCHALL VON BELL, JOHANNES ADAM (1591–1666), German astronomer and missionary who was a Jesuit, spending his entire missionary career in China. In 1622 he was sent to Peking to learn the language, and soon made himself known at court by calculating several eclipses. In 1630 he was given a position in the Calendrical Bureau, and two years later was permitted to celebrate mass in the palace for a modest group of converts. Just before the collapse of the Ming dynasty, he was asked to cast guns for use against the Manchus. Despite his assistance to the Ming, the first Manchu emperor, Shun-chih, continued to employ him as the court astronomer. For several years (1651–7) Schall was close to the emperor, who gave him high honours and permitted him to build a church in Peking. However, in 1657, the emperor became a Buddhist, and in 1664 Schall was thrown into prison as a result of charges made by an antiforeign astronomer. He was released in 1665, but died the following year.

SCHANZER, CARLO (1865–1953), Italian politician, who held various offices (1906–22) and was a delegate to the League of Nations. He was Italy's representative at the Washington naval talks (1921–2), at which Italy achieved parity with France, and he negotiated the 1922 settlement with Yugoslavia over Fiume, Zara, and Italian citizens in Dalmatia. He presided over the Geneva settlement of Austrian finances (Oct. 1922).

SCHARNHORST, GERHARD VON JOHN DAVID (1755–1813), Prussian soldier who fought in the French Wars and, in 1807, assumed responsibility, with Gneisenau, in re-organizing the Prussian army. This was a major factor in Napoleon I's defeat at Leipzig in 1813 although Scharnhorst did not live quite long enough to see this battle.

SCHECHTER v. US, 295 US 495 (1935), US Supreme Court case in which the National Industrial Recovery Act (1933) was unanimously declared unconstitutional. The case involved an appeal by slaughterhouse operators from a conviction for violating codes of fair competition for the live poultry industry in New York city. The conviction included violation of the code's wages and hours provisions. The opinion of Chief Justice Hughes was based on three main grounds: that, despite the grave national emergency, the extraordinary authority granted under the legislation was prohibited by the Tenth Amendment; that the act illegally delegated legislative power; and that the poultry code under review attempted to regulate intra-state commercial transactions and so exceeded the federal commerce power, Schechter's business having only an indirect effect on inter-state commerce.

SCHEELE, CARL WILHELM (1742–86), Swedish chemist who discovered oxygen independently of Joseph Priestley, but whose discovery was not published until 1777 in his *Chemical Treatise on Fire and Air*. He was the first to isolate chlorine gas and discover important naturally occurring organic compounds, including tartaric, citric, malic, lactic, and uric acids, glycerol, and lactose.

SCHELLENBERG, WALTER (1900–52), German lawyer, soldier, and security chief. As deputy leader (1939) and later leader (1942–4) of Bureau VI of the *Reichssicherheitshauptamt* (RSHA), he was in charge of the foreign intelligence service under Himmler. He planned the Venlo incident in Nov. 1939, whereby the Germans tried to implicate the British secret service in an attempt on Hitler's life. Like certain other SS officers, he was not wholly sympathetic to Hitler and his ideology, regarding the extermination of the Jews as a particularly misguided (though not immoral) policy. He put his faith in Himmler and in an ideal of austere and heroic leadership which he believed the SS should incorporate; he wanted to purge the SS of corrupt fanatics and establish Himmler's supremacy in a new Germany. Towards the end of the Second World War he encouraged Himmler to resist Hitler openly, and arranged his meetings with Bernadotte in April 1945, in the hope that an alternative to unconditional surrender could be negotiated with the Allies. After the failure of these plans and Germany's collapse, he fled to Sweden, but was later tried at Nuremberg and sentenced to six years' imprisonment.

SCHELLENBERG, THE, fortress situated on a hill dominating the east side of the town of Donauwörth on the Danube, which was occupied by the Franco-Bavarian army under D'Arco and stormed successfully by the allied forces of Louis of Baden and the Duke of Marlborough in the War of the Spanish Succession (2 July 1704). Both sides suffered heavy casualties, but Marlborough went on to win Blenheim.

SCHIFF, JACOB HENRY (1847–1920), US financier and philanthropist, who came to the US from Germany in 1865, became a broker, and joined the powerful investment firm of Kuhn, Loeb and Co. (1875). He played an important part in floating American securities on the European market and in financing railroad development in the US. He was a founder of the American Jewish Committee (1906).

SCHIFFER, EUGEN (1860–1954), German lawyer and liberal politician, who was *Reich* finance minister (1919), and minister of justice and vice-chancellor (1919–20, 1921). He resigned from the left-liberal German Democratic Party in Oct. 1924 because he felt that it was moving too far to the left. Thereafter he strove actively but in vain to effect the union of all liberal middle-class parties in the Weimar republic. He was a co-founder of the Liberal Democratic Party in Berlin in 1945 and head of the central administration of justice in the Soviet occupation zone, resigning in protest from the latter position in 1948 and refusing the offer of the presidency of the supreme court of the German Democratic Republic.

SCHILLER, JOHANN CHRISTOPH FRIEDRICH VON (1759–1805), German poet, dramatist, and historian of the early Romantic school, whose works include *The Robbers* (1781), *Don Carlos* (1787), *History of the Thirty Years War* (1791–2), *Wallenstein* (1800), *Mary Stuart* (1801), and *William Tell* (1804).

SCHISM ACT (1714), in Britain, legislative measure passed by the last (Tory) parliament of Queen Anne in its only session. It was one of the measures (the Occasional Conformity Act was another) favoured by extremists of the Church of England so as to stamp out Dissent. The act stated that Roman Catholics and Dissenters had been evading the requirements of the Act of Uniformity for teachers to sign a declaration expressing conformity to the liturgy of the Church of England and non-resistance to the sovereign and to obtain episcopal licences. Those convicted of breaking this law were to be imprisoned for three months. Furthermore, stringent conditions were laid down for the granting of licences: applicants were to have taken the Anglican sacrament within the previous year, to have sworn the oaths of allegiance, abjuration, and supremacy, and to have made the declaration against Transubstantiation: a duly qualified teacher who subsequently attended a conventicle was thereby to be disqualified. Provided they fulfilled the other obligations, teachers of the young at home or at the universities were not, however, required to be licensed. Nor did the act extend to teachers of reading, writing, and arithmetic or to what was then called navigation. The whole Act was to apply to Ireland also. It received the royal assent, but on the very day when it was due to take effect Queen Anne died, and her successor, George I, did not take any steps to enforce it. It was repealed in 1719.

SCHLABRENDORFF, FABIAN VON (1907–), German lawyer and a representative of the conservative-nationalist arm of the anti-Nazi resistance. Before the Second World War, he helped to establish opposition cells in the provinces, and in 1939 tried to warn British politicians of the folly of appeasement. During the war he worked with the military opposition on the Eastern Front, and played a key part in the unsuccessful attempt to assassinate Hitler in March 1943. He was arrested after 20 July 1944, and narrowly escaped execution.

SCHLAGETER, ALBERT LEO (1894–1923), German underground fighter against French occupation of the Ruhr in 1923. On 15 March 1923 he led an attack on a railway bridge at Calcum. He was arrested, tried by a French military tribunal and executed on 26 May. His execution aroused tremendous indignation in Germany and was particularly exploited by nationalist groups eager for stronger action against the French. The communists also tried to take up Schlageter's case in their own interests. On 20 July 1923 Karl Radek told the Executive Committee of the Comintern that counter-revolutionary nationalists like Schlageter should be honoured for their bravery and efforts made to win them over to the communist camp. Attempts to exploit this 'Schlageter line' by the German Communist Party did not, however, prove successful.

SCHLANGE-SCHÖNINGEN, HANS (1886–1960), German nationalist politician of the Weimar period, who was elected a Deutsche National Volks Partie (DNVP) member of the Reichstag in 1924, but resigned from the party in 1930 in protest against its leader Hugenberg's dictatorial attitude to the 'freedom law', *ie*, the proposed referendum over the Young Plan and Germany's war-guilt. He turned to the Agrarian Party, and was one of the few members who backed Brüning against the Harzburg front in Oct. 1931. As national commissionar for eastern aid, he did important work for agricultural reconstruction during the Depression (1931–2).

SCHLEITHEIM CONFESSION (1527), Anabaptist document, otherwise called the 'Brotherly Union of a number of Children of God concerning Seven Articles', probably the work of Michael Sattler and approved by a gathering at Schlatt, near Schaffhausen, in north Switzerland. This creed represented the views of the majority of Europe's Anabaptists and was widely circulated in the 16th cent.

SCHLESWIG-HOLSTEIN, two duchies whose possession was contested between Denmark and the rising power of Germany. As Duke of Holstein, whose population was German, the King of Denmark was a member of the German Confederation, but his duchy of Schleswig, peopled in the south by Germans but in the north by Danes, lay outside the confederation and was regarded by the Danes as indissolubly attached to their kingdom. This main dispute between nationalities was complicated by a dynastic difficulty, in that the Danish Crown was due to pass through female descent to Christian of Glücksburg, whereas the Salic Law recognized in the duchies gave a better claim there to the dukes of Augustenburg. Moreover, the European powers were interested in the dispute, especially Britain and France, for the sake of the balance of power, and Prussia for the sake of prestige and, later, aggrandisement.

In 1848–50 three campaigns between the Danes and the rebels, backed by the Prussian and other German forces, ended in the submission of the duchies to the Danish Crown and their acceptance of Christian as their future sovereign in a form of union which at least left Holstein in the German Confederation. Though this arrangement had the approval of the powers in the treaty of London (1852), Christian, on his accession in 1863, accepted a constitution which incorporated Schleswig in Denmark, whereupon the Augustenburg claims were revived with the support of Germans in both duchies. Bismarck, who afterwards alleged that 'from the beginning he kept annexation steadily before his eyes', brought Prussia with Austria into a war against Denmark, which was originally launched as a federal execution (Dec. 1863). Since British and French intervention was confined to the conference table, the duchies were quickly wrested from Danish hands, shared temporarily between Prussia and Austria (Convention of Gastein), and finally made the prize of victory in the Austro-Prussian War.

No more was heard of the Augustenburg claim or (after 1878) of a proposed plebiscite for fixing an equitable frontier in North Schleswig.

L. D. Steefel, *The Schleswig-Holstein Question* (Cambridge, MA, 1932).   TKD

SCHLICK, ANDREAS, Count (1569–1621), Bohemian politician who was leader of the Bohemian Protestant nobility in the revolt against the Habsburgs (1619–21). He was captured in Prague after the battle of the White Mountain and executed.

SCHLIEFFEN PLAN in Germany. Count Alfred von Schlieffen, chief of the German general staff (1891–1905), was responsible for a plan which did much to bring about the outbreak of the First World War, and to determine its course.

Germany's strategic problem was that in a long war her resources, and those of her ally, Austria, were bound to prove inferior to those of the Franco-Russian Alliance, probably supported by Britain. Schlieffen proposed to take advantage of Germany's central position and Russia's great distances, few railways, and poor organization, to crush France with the whole of the German army before Russia could be ready to act in the east. By using reserve troops in the first line, a decisive short-term superiority could be achieved over the French and British. The direct Franco-German frontier was short, mountainous, and heavily fortified, making it unsuitable for offensive operations; and the French intended to attack there to reconquer Alsace-Lorraine. Schlieffen therefore decided that the main German advance should pass through neutral Belgium and swing south round Paris to drive the French armies against the frontier fortifications and destroy them.

Schlieffen's plan was modified, and its eventual execution directed by his successor, the younger Moltke, to whom Germany's failure to achieve a decisive victory in 1914 is usually attributed: but the original plan had its weaknesses. It took no account of the possibility of the Russians launching an offensive before they were fully prepared to do so, in order to assist their allies, or of the ability of the French to extend their left wing (with troops withdrawn from Lorraine) faster—by using the railway—than the Germans could outflank it by marching. It made impossible demands on the endurance of the German infantry, who were exhausted, and had outrun their supplies by the time they reached the Marne. While the confusion which then prevailed in the German command must be attributed first to Moltke's personal inadequacy, it is doubtful whether, with the means of communication available, anyone could have controlled so far-flung and complicated a manœuvre.   PJBD

SCHMALKALDIC ARTICLES (1537), evangelical confession drawn up by Martin Luther at the request of the princes of the Schmalkaldic League to provide a statement of Protestant doctrine as the basis of discussion at a future general council of the Church. The articles were in fact superfluous because the princes declined to attend a council.

SCHMALKALDIC LEAGUE, defensive alliance of the Protestant princes and cities of the Holy Roman empire which emerged in 1531 under the leadership of Philip, landgrave of Hesse, and John, Elector of Saxony, to provide military protection for its members, should they be attacked by the Catholic forces of the Emperor Charles V on account of their Protestant faith. The league was named after the little town on the borders of Saxony and Hesse where its assemblies frequently took place, and its original members, in addition to Hesse and Saxony, were the dukes of Brunswick and Lüneberg, Prince Wolfgang of Anhalt, the counts of Mansfeld and the cities of Strasbourg, Ulm, Constance, Reutlingen, Memmingen, Lindau, Biberach, Isny, Lübeck, Magdeburg, and Bremen. It was later joined by Gottingen, Goslar, Einbeck, Hamburg, Rostock, Augsburg, Frankfurt, and Hanover. The league proved its strength over the restoration of Duke Ulrich of Württemberg (1534), but it finally collapsed when its forces were shattered at Mühlberg (1547).

SCHMALKALDIC WAR (1546–7), conflict between the League of Schmalkalde and Charles V, the result of the emperor's determination to have a showdown with the Protestant princes and cities. Charles had made careful preparations before inciting the league to war. He made peace with France at the treaty of Crespy (1544) and alliances with the pope, Paul III, and the Catholic Duke Albert of Bavaria (June 1546), and finally enticed the support of Maurice of

Saxony with the promise of the Saxon electorate (Oct. 1546). He then challenged the league by declaring 'His imperial Majesty means to restore unity, peace and justice in the Empire'. The league held discussions through the winter of 1545–6 and rallied its troops under Sebastian Schärtlin von Burtenbach, preparing to dominate the Danube basin and threaten the Tyrol. Charles V took the initiative, however, and with fresh troops from Italy and the Netherlands swept through the Danubian cities by the end of 1546. Duke Ulrich of Württemberg was expelled from his duchy, although reinstated on a fine of 300,000 guilders and the restoration of Catholicism in his duchy. In the spring of 1547 the emperor marched northwards to crush John Frederick of Saxony. At the battle of Mühlberg (24 April 1547) the Spanish infantry destroyed the armies of the Schmalkaldic League. John Frederick was captured, his lands overrun by his treacherous cousin, Maurice, and Archduke Ferdinand, and Philip of Hesse, who sought the emperor's mercy, was likewise made a prisoner.

SCHMERLING, ANTON (1805–93), Austrian politician, who was head of the Frankfurt provisional government in 1848, and Austrian minister of the interior (1860–5). He was responsible for the liberal-centralist constitution (*Februarpatent*), which was violently opposed by non-German federalists and the Hungarians.

Schmerling was a liberal, a 'Greater German', and a centralist, and had considerable support among these three groups, as well as among civil servants, Sudeten Germans, German nationalists, and Hungarian Old Conservatives, as well as the Hungarian 1848 party. Naturally he could not please them all, and in fact succeeded in pleasing none. By 1864 Francis Joseph, seeing his country menaced externally by France, Sardinia, and Prussia, and on the verge of revolt at home, decided to compromise with the Hungarians. Schmerling was dismissed (July 1865) before the creation of the Dual Monarchy in 1867.

SCHMIDT, GUIDO (1901–   ), Austrian civil servant and politician of strongly nationalist views. He was a close colleague of Schuschnigg, who appointed him state secretary in the foreign ministry after the Austro-German agreement of July 1936. He held this post until Feb. 1938, when he became foreign minister until the *Anschluss* with Germany in March 1938. He co-operated closely with the Germans, and was on good terms with Göring. After the war he was tried for treason in connection with the events leading to the *Anschluss*, but was acquitted (1947).

SCHMIDT, PAUL (1899–1970), German foreign ministry official, best known for his work as Hitler's translator. With his knowledge of English, French, Italian, and Spanish, Schmidt officiated at most of the major confrontations between Hitler and foreign diplomats. His reports on these meetings, and his memories of Hitler's behaviour and statements, make his post-war writings an important source of information on the period.

SCHOBER, JOHANNES (1874–1932), Austrian civil servant and politician of strongly nationalist and conservative views, who was police chief in Vienna, where he forestalled the communist uprising of 1919. He became chancellor and foreign minister in a non-party bourgeois government in 1921, and had to acquiesce in the transfer of Austrian territory to Hungary and Czechoslovakia under the settlements after the First World War. In the intervals of his political career he returned to his post as police chief, and was responsible for vigorously suppressing the disorders of July 1927, thereby forfeiting socialist support. He became chancellor again in Sept. 1929 and achieved some success in coping with the effects of the Depression. By 1930, however, he had quarrelled with his main political supporters, Seipel's Christian Social Party and the pan-German *Heimwehr*, and was forced out of office. He lent his name to the *Landbund*

political bloc, and contested the 1930 elections on the issues of law and order, afterwards joining the new government as foreign minister. In March 1931 he negotiated the abortive customs union with Germany, forbidden under the Versailles treaty and strongly opposed by France. This failure renewed antagonism in discussions on the tactics of Austro-German union and reopened the rift between Seipel and Schober, who was forced to resign (1932).

SCHOELCHER, VICTOR (1804–93), West Indian politician, who successfully proposed the abolition of slavery in the French colonies, with compensation for slave owners (1848). He served as a representative from the French West Indies to the French National Assembly (elected in 1848) and served again in the Third Republic (1871).

SCHOLAE PALATINAE, a corps of elite troops established (*c.* AD 324) in the time of Constantine the Great attached to the person of the emperor and placed under the command of the *Magister Officiorum*. At a later date one of the corps constituting the armed forces of the Byzantine central regime was called *scholae* and was entrusted to an officer called *domestikos*, who often acted as general-in-chief of the Byzantine armies. By the late 10th cent. the *scholae* were replaced by other guards, especially the Varangians recruited into the service of Byzantium after 988.

SCHOLASTICISM, term first used derisively in the 16th cent., which refers to the medieval 'schools' and universities and is used in two senses. The first sense is as a description of the medieval mode of study; the reliance on logic and dialectic to the almost complete exclusion of observations and experiment as the means of acquiring and extending knowledge. In the second, and obviously connected, sense it describes the attitude of mind which produced the attempts at making one great synthesis of all knowledge with theology, buttressed by philosophy, as the centre to which all other areas of knowledge were attached. To the medieval scholar, knowledge (*scientia*) was indivisible and ultimately all knowledge was only of God and his works; hence those characteristic products of scholasticism, the encyclopaedic *Summae* and, even, *Summae Summarum*.

SCHOLZ, ERNST (1874–1932), German politician, who was Reich economics minister (1920–1). He led the right wing of the German People's Party (DVP) and made constant difficulties for Stresemann within his own party. As chairman of the DVP and its parliamentary group after Stresemann's death in 1929, Scholz manœuvred the party towards the extreme nationalist right.

SCHOMBERG, FREDERICK HERMAN, Marshal de (1615–1690), French soldier who was created marshal in 1675 but resigned his commission in protest against the persecution of Huguenots. He entered the service of William of Orange, serving in England and Ireland, where he was killed at the battle of the Boyne (1690).

SCHOMBURGK LINE, result of a survey (1840) by Sir Robert Schomburgk (1804–65), which established a boundary between British Guiana and Venezuela. The line was unacceptable to Venezuela until the settlement of 1897.

SCHÖNBORN, JOHN PHILIP, Count von (1605–73), member of the German family of Schönborn who produced numerous ecclesiastical princes and commissioned much fine baroque architecture in Franconia and Vienna in the 17th–18th cents. After military service against the Turks, he became Prince-Bp of Würzburg (1642) and then Electoral Abp of Mainz and arch-chancellor of the empire (1647), playing an important part in the peace conference at Münster (1647–1648). After Westphalia he strove to preserve peace and the neutrality of the empire, formed the Rhenish Federation (Dec. 1652) and contrived the election of Leopold I as emperor (1658) on specific terms (the capitulation of election). In 1663 he became Bp of Worms, and in his last years patronized the young philosopher, Leibniz.

SCHONBRUNN, imperial palace designed by Fischer von Erlach for King Joseph I of Hungary. It was begun in 1696. Extensive rebuilding has reduced the architectural value of what was a fine example of Northern Baroque style.

SCHOUTEN, WILLEM CORNELISZOON (d. 1625), Dutch navigator who sailed (1615) via Le Maire's strait (Cape Horn) in search of Quiros's eastern Pacific continent. Passing north-west along northern New Guinea, he discovered New Ireland.

SCHRÖDER, GERHARD (1910–), West German lawyer and politician. After the Second World War, during which he served on the Russian front, he held various local administrative posts in North Rhine–Westphalia and in 1947 resumed his law practice in Düsseldorf. He was directly involved (1947–53) in the reorganization of the West German iron and steel industry and played a part in the introduction of co-determination in the industry. In 1949 he was elected to the Bundestag as a Christian Democrat and became successively minister of the interior (1953–61), of foreign affairs (1961–6), and of defence (1966–9). He distinguished himself chiefly as foreign minister in Erhard's government, when he introduced a more active eastern policy which marked the first significant departure from the conservative attitudes of the Adenauer era. The Hallstein doctrine was allowed to lapse with regard to Eastern Europe; trade missions were established in Poland, Hungary, Bulgaria, and Rumania, full consular and diplomatic relations being the next objective. Obstruction to the new initiatives came not from the opposition party, the SPD, but from conservative forces within the CDU/CSU, particularly from Strauss and his supporters. This *Ostpolitik* laid the foundations for the intensified efforts in this direction of the grand coalition after 1966 and of the socialist–liberal coalition after 1969. In 1966 Schröder was a candidate for the succession to Erhard, but the opposition of Strauss's wing of the CDU/CSU nullified his chances.

SCHRÖDINGER, ERWIN (1887–1961), Austrian physicist and discoverer of wave mechanics in subatomic physics. While professor of physics at Zürich he published (1926) his papers on wave mechanics, the most easily visualized form of quantum mechanics. This describes the behaviour of sub-atomic particles by means of the 'Schrödinger equation', which gives them their observed wave-like properties. He shared the 1933 Nobel Prize for Physics with P. A. M. Dirac.

SCHUBERT, CARL VON (1882–1947), German foreign official and diplomat, who was appointed state secretary in the foreign ministry by Stresemann in 1924 in succession to Ago von Maltzan, whose views on foreign policy ran counter to Stresemann's. He was an ardent and efficient exponent of the policy of fulfilment and, when Stresemann was ill, represented him in discussions in Geneva and elsewhere. In 1930 he became Germany's ambassador to Rome.

SCHULENBURG, FRIEDRICH WERNER VON DER (1875–1944), German diplomat, who as ambassador at Moscow (1934–41), tried to further a policy of rapprochement with the Soviet Union. He was strongly opposed to the German declaration of war on Russia (1941), and offered his services as negotiator when Russia made cautious peace soundings in 1942. He became deeply involved in the anti-Nazi resistance, and was nominated as foreign minister in Goerdeler's proposed cabinet. He was arrested and executed after the failure of the July Plot (1944).

SCHULENBURG, FRITZ-DIETLOF VON DER (1902–44), German civil servant, who was executed for his part in the anti-Nazi resistance. He was born into an aristocratic Prussian family, and modelled his civil service career on the upright traditional principles of the idealized Prussian bureaucracy. He found it hard to come to terms with the Weimar republic, which he regarded as an unstable substitute for a strongly organized and administratively self-reliant state. For this reason he gave his allegiance to the rising Nationalsozialistische Deutsche Arbeiterparte (NSDAP) (1931), although he had already explored other alternatives to the existing political system, including the Kommunist Partie Deutschlande (KPD). While an active party member he worked for a policy of comprehensive administrative reform and decentralization, *ie, Reichsreform*, which he, in common with a group of other civil servants and political figures, believed could be best achieved under a strong Nazi regime. By 1937, however, he realized that he had been mistaken in his conviction that Nazism would solve Germany's political problems, and he had become aware of the brutal policies being pursued in her name. He supported plans to overthrow the regime, and was chosen by Goerdeler as a possible interior minister in a post-putsch government.

SCHULENBURG, JOHANN MATTHIAS, Count von der (1661–1747), German soldier of an old noble family from Altmark, who served in the Northern War against Charles XII (1705), fought with Eugène at Malplaquet (1709), and who defended the Adriatic against the Turks in the Venetian–Turkish War (1714–18), in which the Austrians successfully intervened (1716–18).

SCHUMAN, ROBERT (1886–1963), French lawyer and politician who was one of the architects of European integration. The dominating aim of his life, Franco-German reconciliation, was related to his personal background. Born into a family from Lorraine, he studied in Germany, and started his career as a lawyer in German Lorraine. After the return of Alsace-Lorraine to France he became a deputy for the area, sitting for the Christian Democrat PDP party and specializing in Franco-German questions. He had a minor post in the Reynaud government (1940), and supported Pétain for a short period. But he was later deported to Germany, and worked in the Resistance after his release. He returned to parliament after the Second World War as a leader of the new MRP party. He was prime minister twice (1947–8, 1948), but his period of office as foreign minister (1948–52) was more fruitful.

He signed the Atlantic Pact for France (1949), then announced the 'Schuman Plan' (1950), which led to the creation of the European Coal and Steel Community. This plan, inspired by Jean Monnet, marked the beginning of the economic integration of Western Europe. He also introduced the plan for a European Defence Community, but growing opposition to this in France led to his resignation. He played little part in French politics after this, but was first president of the European Parliamentary Assembly (1958), and president of the European Movement (1955).

SCHURMAN COMMISSION (1899), or First Philippine Commission, created by the US president, McKinley, and headed by J. G. Schurman, then president of Cornell University. It was intended to reassure the Filipinos of America's 'benevolent' intentions and so dissuade them from further armed resistance to the establishment of American sovereignty in their country. After investigating existing conditions, the commission was to recommend to the US president the kind of government to be formed. It conducted public hearings in Manila but its work was interrupted by the Philippine–American war, which broke out on 4 Feb. 1899. Its report to the president, in Jan. 1900, concluded that the Filipinos, though of a 'well-endowed race', were unprepared for independence; American authority had to be enforced to guide and protect the people. The commission recommended the setting up of a centralized government at Manila; a bicameral legislature, with the lower house to be popularly elected; some degree of autonomy in the provinces, with American consultants advising members of town councils; provisions for a civil service system and a free public elementary school; and the replacement of military rule by a civil government as soon as peace was restored.

SCHURZ, CARL (1829–1906), German-born US politician, soldier, and writer, who was active in the German revolutionary movements of 1848–9, was proscribed, and emigrated to the US (1852). He settled in WI in 1856 and became an active Republican, who was valued for his appeal to German immigrants. He campaigned for Abraham Lincoln, was appointed US minister to Spain (1861–2), and then, at his request, brigadier-general of volunteers in the Union army. He was always radically opposed to slavery, strongly favoured emancipation, and in 1865 recommended Negro suffrage to President Johnson. After editing newspapers in Detroit and St Louis, he served in the US Senate (1869–75), and became a prominent Liberal Republican, being noted for his advocacy of civil service reform. In 1877 President Hayes appointed him secretary of the interior, where he pursued enlightened Indian policies. After 1881 he returned to journalism, remained a spokesman for liberal reform, and opposed American expansionism and the war with Spain (1898). He wrote a *Life of Henry Clay* (1887) and his *Reminiscences* (3 vols, 1907–8) form a valuable memoir of his times.

SCHUSCHNIGG, KURT VON (1897–), Austrian lawyer and politician whose family traditions and early life were marked by a potent combination of Catholicism, loyalty to the Habsburgs, and pro-Germanism, and these also dominated his political career. After the First World War he became a lawyer in Innsbruck. He was drawn into politics by an admiration for the Catholic Social leader, Seipel, coupled with a hatred for the left and a mistrust of the extreme right. He served as minister of justice (1932–4) under Buresch and Dollfuss. With the latter he shared anti-parliamentarian, clerical, and semi-corporatist viewpoints. He organized the 'non-party' Fatherland Front and became its official head in 1934—an organization designed to draw support away from the Nazis and to act as the militant arm of the vaguely conceived Christian Corporatist state that he and Dollfuss desired. After Dollfuss's murder in July 1934 he became chancellor. The problem of Germany dominated his tenure of office, both as a matter of foreign affairs. and as a domestic concern, since the Austrian Nazis were ceaselessly active, while his own government was divided over how to deal with Hitler. The foreign minister, Guido Schmidt, worked secretly, like many others, for German annexation; while Schuschnigg lacked the popular appeal that might have rallied support against Nazism. From early 1936 fear of invasion was continuous, and since Mussolini's loyalty seemed doubtful, he tried to come to terms with Hitler in July. On the surface, Hitler seemed to have guaranteed Austrian integrity, but the real gains were Germany's, by forcing crypto-Nazis into the Austrian government and isolating Austria diplomatically. By early 1938 tension had increased and he was persuaded to visit Hitler at Berchtesgaden only to receive what amounted to an ultimatum for a fully Nazified government in Vienna. He half accepted it and then tried to use a plebiscite as a means of rallying public opinion. This provoked armed intervention by Hitler and Seyss-Inquart replaced Schuschnigg, who was arrested. It was probably thanks to the influence of Mussolini that he was treated with a surprising degree of mildness and survived the Second World War. He moved to the US, becoming professor of government at St Louis (1948–67) and now (1970) lives in Innsbruck.   KM

SCHÜTZ, HEINRICH (1585–1672), German composer who studied law at Marburg and music at Venice before becoming the *kapellmeister* to the Danish court (1633–5) and then director of music at the electoral court of Saxony in Dresden (1641–72). His best-known works are his four vocal settings of the passion story.

SCHUTZBUND (Defence Union) in Austria, para-military formation of the Austrian Social Democrat Party, founded in 1923 and led by Julius Deutsch. A series of confrontations between it and the rival right-wing Frontkämpfer culminated (July 1927) in a major battle in Vienna, where a general strike had been called in protest against the right-wing bias shown by law courts. Vienna's police chief, Schober, refused to enlist Schutzbund co-operation in suppressing these disorders, thus preventing any reconciliation in the future. In succeeding years the Schutzbund was kept under pressure from the fascist Heimwehr and the constant threat of a right-wing coup, but was dogged by persistent police and judicial bias against it. On 31 March 1933 the organization was dissolved by the government, on the spurious pretext that all party militias were to be disbanded. Its members began arming themselves clandestinely, but too late, for many of their leaders were arrested before the rising of Feb. 1934. A year later the leaders were given severe prison sentences and the Schutzbund effectively ceased to exist. It failed to prevent the counter-revolution in Austria mainly because it had not followed through the logic of its structure and situation by seizing a dynamic initiative in crises; instead it chose to work as a pressure group, a role irrelevant to the critical problem of defending Austrian democracy.

SCHWAB, CHARLES MICHAEL (1862–1939), US steel industrialist, who was president of the Carnegie Steel Co. (1897–1901) and first president of the United States Steel Corporation (1901–3). He resigned (1903) to direct the Bethlehem Steel Corporation (1903–13), which became the largest independent rival to US Steel. During the First World War he was in charge of shipbuilding for the US Shipping Board Emergency Fleet Corporation.

SCHWABACH ARTICLES (1529), statement of 15 articles of Protestant doctrine drawn up as the result of the Marburg Colloquy and at the instigation of Philip of Hesse, who wanted to forge a united Protestant front. The articles, however, merely confirmed the theological differences between the Lutherans and Zwinglians, especially over the eucharist.

SCHWARZENBERG, FELIX, Prince (1800–52), Austrian diplomat, politician, and minister, who was a protagonist of Habsburg leadership in central Europe. He was called to power in 1848 after a career in diplomacy and the army and was chiefly responsible for the bloody repression of the Hungarians, for the dissolution of the Kremsier Reichstag, and for the centralized absolutism introduced in 1851. He also imposed the Olmütz Convention on Prussia. His death ended the brief period of Austrian domination in European affairs.

SCHWEIGAARD, ANTON MARTIN (1808–70), Norwegian politician who was a free trader championing the reduction of tariffs as an encouragement to trade. By the end of the 19th cent. his policies had been vindicated and the nation's economy had expanded considerably.

SCHWENCKFELD, CASPAR VON (1489–1561), German radical reformer of aristocratic birth, privy councillor to the Duke of Leignitz in Silesia, where he led the Lutheran reformation in the 1520s. Exiled to Strasbourg, where he spent five years (1529–34), he passed the remainder of his life wandering around Germany. He was one of the earliest apostles of religious toleration.

SCHWERIN, OTTO VON (1616–79), German politician descended from a medieval Pomeranian baronial family which produced a line of administrators and soldiers, he was president of the privy council of Brandenburg (1658–79) under the Elector Frederick William I.

SCIONE, ancient Greek city-state founded by Achaeans (*c.* 700 BC) on the Pallene peninsula of Chalcidice, in the north-west Aegean. It was depopulated after a siege in the great Peloponnesian War (421) by the Athenians, who slaughtered the garrison, but reconstituted by the Spartans in 404.

SCIPIO, P. CORNELIUS the Elder (d. 211 BC), Roman consul (218) and first general to confront Hannibal in the Second Punic War, initially at the Rhone and later in northern Italy at the Ticinus and the Trebia, where the Romans were defeated. In 217–211 he campaigned in Spain with his brother, Cnaeus, preventing the reinforcement of Hannibal, but after victory at Ibera (215) and the recapture of Saguntum (212), both Roman armies and generals were destroyed (211).

SCIPIO AEMILIANUS, P. CORNELIUS (185–129 BC), Roman soldier, politician, and literary figure, and son of Aemilius Paullus. After service at Pydna (168) and in Spain (151), he fought at Carthage as military tribune (149), and after being specially elected consul, ended the siege and destroyed the city (147–146). Henceforward, as a dominant figure at Rome (censor 142), he supported the policy of increasing ruthlessness in Spain, where he took command in his second consulship and destroyed Numantia (134–133). He was also active in eastern diplomacy, leading a peripatetic embassy in 140–139. In domestic politics he was essentially conservative, opposing the Gracchan agrarian and constitutional agitations until his death. He combined this traditional attitude with a liberal appreciation of Greek culture, and gave his name to the Scipionic Circle, with which Panaetius, Polybius, and Terence were associated.

SCIPIO AFRICANUS, P. CORNELIUS (236–?184 BC), Roman soldier, famous for his victories in the Second Punic War. After serving with distinction against Hannibal in Italy 218–211), he was appointed to command in Spain at the age of 25, having held only the aedileship. Introducing new legionary tactics, he captured New Carthage (209), defeated Hannibal's brother, Hasdrubal, at Baecula (208), and routed the remaining Carthaginian armies at Ilipa (206) to make Spain a Roman province. After training an army as consul in Sicily (205), he crossed to Africa, where with the aid of Massinissa's Numidian cavalry he won victories in the Great Plains against Hasdrubal Gisgo (203) and decisively against Hannibal at Zama (202).

After arranging the peace he returned home a legendary figure, invested with the title of Africanus. For years he dominated the Senate with his philhellenic policies, becoming censor and *princeps senatus* (199) and consul again (194). But his talents were military rather than political or diplomatic. He pleaded unsuccessfully for the retention of a Roman force in Greece to counter the threat of Antiochus III of Syria, and failed to resolve the Carthage–Massinissa territorial dispute (193). He joined his brother, Lucius, in Asia in the successful war against Antiochus (190–189), but the subsequent treaty of Apamea was harsher than he wished. Subsequently the brothers were attacked at Rome by Cato the Elder and his followers, including the Petillii; Lucius was fined for peculation (187), and when Publius himself was threatened with indictment, he withdrew to Liternum, where he died.

H. H. Scullard, *Scipio Africanus* (London, 1970).   PGW

SCIPIO NASICA CORCULUM, Roman politician, who was twice consul (162, 155 BC) and censor (159). He fought at Pydna (168) and completed the reduction of Dalmatia (155). Politically, his fame rests on his persistent but unavailing opposition to Cato the Elder over the destruction of Carthage.

SCOPES TRIAL (1925), in the US, trial of John T. Scopes, a high school biology teacher in Dayton, TN, on charges under a state law which banned the teaching in state schools and colleges of any other theory of evolution than the biblical account of creation. The law was the achievement of a fundamentalist anti-evolution movement which had gained considerable support in the Southern Protestant 'Bible Belt' states, and had already brought about the dismissal of six professors from Tennessee University for teaching the principles of scientific evolution. Scopes was defended by Clarence Darrow, counsel for the state being William Jennings Bryan, who also took the witness stand as an expert on the Bible. Although Scopes was found guilty, and the constitutionality of the statute was later upheld by the state Supreme Court, his sentence was set aside on a technicality and any encouragement which the anti-evolutionists may have gained from the conviction was more than offset by the ridicule attached to Bryan for the ignorance he showed of elementary science.

SCOT AND LOT BOROUGHS in England, parliamentary seats in which the franchise depended on the payment of the poor rate or church rate, the equivalent of the medieval scot and lot tax, or simply on the condition, other than residence, that the voter was self-sustaining and had not been a charge on the poor rate. This meant that the franchise was in the possession of the inhabitants generally, as distinct from burgage holders, corporations, or freemen. A six-month residence qualification imposed by a 1786 act was the only unifying element in the franchise. There were 59 such boroughs before 1832.

SCOTS, ORIGINS OF, Irish invaders who colonized the west coast of Britain in the late Roman period. In the late 5th cent. they established the kingdom of Dalriada (Argyll) in western Scotland, which was ultimately destined to unite the whole of Scotland. The Scots were largely Christian by the late 6th cent. and their religious centre at Iona was regarded with great veneration by the whole of Christian northern Britain. In late 7th cent. Dalriada was for a time conquered by the English Northumbrians (until 685) and they were under Pictish domination during much of the 8th cent. Dalriada emerged as the dominant power in Scotland under Kenneth Mac Alpin, who combined descent from both Scottish and Pictish ruling dynasties and conquered the Picts in the 830s. His successors were able to avoid conquest by the Norsemen and in the early 10th cent. to impose the usages of the Scottish Church on the Picts.

SCOTT, ROSE (1847–1925), Australian politician, who became corresponding secretary of the Womanhood Suffrage League (1891). She later instructed women on non-party lines in how to exercise their newly acquired voting rights. She was a convinced pacifist, and also campaigned for legislation protecting women and child workers.

SCOTT, THOMAS ALEXANDER (1823–81), US railroad executive who was president (1874–80) of the expanding Pennsylvania Railroad. During the American Civil War he organized railroad operations for the Union government.

SCOTT, SIR WALTER (1771–1832), Scottish lawyer and writer whose novels, published anonymously under the name 'Waverley', appeared almost annually from 1814 onwards. They included *Waverley* (1814), *Ivanhoe* (1819), and *The Fortunes of Nigel* (1822). He was forced to write prolifically to meet debts incurred by the publishing firm with which he was associated. He also wrote works of a dramatic, antiquarian, and poetic nature. He represented a major influence in Scottish literary circles and in the European Romantic movement as a whole.

SCOTT, WINFIELD (1786–1866), US soldier who fought in the War of 1812 and later helped to modernize the army. He became general-in-chief in 1841 and won fame during the Mexican War, particularly after taking Veracruz and Mexico City (1847). In 1852 he ran unsuccessfully as Whig candidate for the presidency. At the outbreak of the Civil War he remained loyal to the Union. He retired from high command in Nov. 1861.

SCOTTISH EPISCOPAL CHURCH, independent province of the Anglican Communion. Of the 14 ancient sees some are united and there are now (1970) seven dioceses. The bishops elect one of their number as *primus episcopus*.

The origins of the Scottish province are to be found in the last years of the Roman occupation of Britain, and in Christian missionary work begun by St Ninian in the 4th cent. and continued by St Columba and others. In the 11th cent. the Celtic Church was reorganized according to western practice, religious Orders introduced, and a complete diocesan system established, but there was never a metropolitan and no one see had primacy over others until the end of the 15th cent., when archbishoprics were established at St Andrews and Glasgow.

During the Reformation, controversy between Episcopalians and Presbyterians on Church government began (1560) and lasted intermittently until 1690. Episcopacy was restored in 1610 and apostolic succession maintained, and, after a period of Presbyterianism (1638–61), was again established in 1661. The final disestablishment of Episcopacy took place in 1690 because the bishops declined to give their allegiance to King William III in the state prayers. Penal laws severely limited the ministry of Episcopal clergymen until they were repealed in 1792. In 1764 a Scottish Liturgy emerged similar to that now (1970) used. It formed the basis of the American Protestant Episcopal Communion Office.

In the 19th and 20th cents closer understanding between the Scottish Episcopal Church and the Church of England led to statutes being passed in 1840 and 1864 recognizing Scottish Orders in England. The influence of the Oxford Movement led to the reintroduction in Scotland of vestments and ritual. In the 20th cent., with greater financial resources, the Church has been associated in missionary work at home and overseas, and in matters involving social and moral responsibility. By 1970 the Scottish Episcopal Church and the established Presbyterian Church of Scotland had achieved a closer relationship than at any earlier time since the Reformation.

F. Goldie, *History of the Episcopal Church in Scotland* (London, 1951).

G. Donaldson, *Scotland: Church and State through sixteen centuries* (London, 1960).   GMDH

SCOTTISH MARCH, ill-defined borderland between England and Scotland. The border on the west could wander from Carlisle to the Ribble and in the east from the Tees to the Forth. From the capture of Berwick by Edward I in 1296, the border hinged on Berwick and Carlisle. The march was the buffer between the two countries, as the Welsh March was between England and Wales, and the grant of palatine powers to the Bp of Durham by the Conqueror paralleled the grants on the Welsh border. The border was particularly fluid in the 12th cent. and stable in the 13th but after the great Scottish victory at Bannockburn (1314) it was again very exposed. From about that time two officers, called wardens, were given responsibility for security of the western (Cumberland) and eastern (Northumberland) marches of England. This responsibility was later (*c.* 1490) vested in the Council of the North.

SCOTTISH NATIONALISM can be traced back to the 1880s, when the demand arose for 'Home Rule All Round', *ie*, for devolution of the sort proposed by Gladstone for Ireland to be extended to all parts of the United Kingdom, including Scotland. The present-day Scottish National Party dates from 1928, but it had only one political success, a wartime by-election, until the 1960s, although over 1 million Scots showed vaguely nationalist sentiments by signing the Scottish Covenant of 1950–1. The SNP's membership and organization improved greatly after good by-election results in 1961 and 1962, and the party had, after 1964, for the first time enough electoral credibility to profit from the Labour government's unpopularity. This was important for its victory at the Hamilton by-election (2 Nov. 1967) and its striking success at the 1968 local elections, when it won more votes than any other party. Other reasons for its success were less closely connected with disillusionment with the Labour government. Some of its support came from former Conservatives who voted Nationalist as the only way to keep Labour out. And in local elections, the SNP profited not so much from 'swing' of Labour voters to it as from differential abstention: Labour and right-wing voters stayed at home, while people who had never before voted in local elections came out to vote Nationalist. This was a fragile basis for support, which crumbled in 1969 and 1970. In the 1970 general election the Nationalists lost Hamilton, and seemed to have been transformed from an urban to a rural protest party, with several good results culminating in victory in the Western Isles. Their future success may depend on rural by-election opportunities for the expression of discontent.   IM

SCOTTISH OFFICE, created in the form of a Scottish secretary and office by the Conservative government of Lord Salisbury in 1885, though the pressure for it came from Scottish politicians of the Liberal Party, particularly Lord Rosebery. It was at first based on London and, though it soon controlled the work of the Scottish education department and had a miscellaneous collection of other functions, it could not control from London the various Edinburgh-based central boards (for instance that supervising the poor law). The creation of a base waited until the inter-war period. The Scottish secretary, who had been in the cabinet since the 1890s, became a secretary of state in 1926, and the boards were gradually grouped under him, making four departments in all (home, health, education, and agriculture) in St Andrews House in Edinburgh.

SCRATCHLEY, SIR PETER HENRY (1835–85), British soldier, who served in the Crimean War and in India and became (1877) adviser to Australian governments on defence questions. He was special commissioner to New Guinea after the declaration of a British protectorate over the south-eastern part of the island in 1884.

SCRIPPS, EDWARD WYLLIS (1854–1926), US newspaper magnate who built up a publishing empire which controlled 28 newspapers in 15 states and a news service that became the United Press Association.

SCROGGS, SIR WILLIAM (*c.* 1623–83), English lord chief justice (1678), notorious for the cruelty and partiality with which he sentenced 21 men to death during the Popish Plot trials (1678–80). He was then impeached by the Commons but removed from office by King Charles II after parliament's dissolution and given a rich pension.

SCROPE, RICHARD (d. 1405), English cleric who was son of the first Baron Scrope of Masham, chancellor of Cambridge (1378), Bp of Coventry (1386), and, finally, Abp of York (1398). He came to share the misgivings of his friends, the Percies, about Henry IV and raised an army against him. He was persuaded to disband his force and was then arrested, tried, and executed (1405). The questionable nature of the proceedings against him and his own high reputation led him to be popularly venerated as a saint and increased the discontent against Henry IV.

SCUDÉRY, Mademoiselle **MADELEINE DE** (1607–1701), French writer of popular romances, who first entered the literary society of Mme de Rambouillet's salon in Paris in 1630, but whose own literary career began with *Ibrahim ou l'Illustre Bassa* (1647). Her most famous novels were *Artamène ou le Grand Cyrus* (1648–53) and *Clélie* (1654–61), which won her popularity at Louis XIV's court.

SCULLIN, JAMES HENRY (1876–1953), Australian politician and prime minister (1929–32), who twice sat in the

Commonwealth parliament (1910–13, 1922–49). His accession to office as prime minister coincided with the impact of the economic depression. With only minority support in the Senate he could not carry the major constitutional and banking measures and other legislation necessary for tackling the depression along lines acceptable to his cabinet, his party, and the trade union movement. With the Labor movement split, he retained office and was forced to implement many deflationary policies until the ALP was defeated in the election of 1932. Because of ill-health he yielded the party leadership to Curtin in 1935, but retained his seat. He declined office in the Labor governments of 1941–9, but gave invaluable support and advice to the ministries of Curtin and Chifley.

SCULPTURE, African, whether for ritual, commemorative, or decorative purposes, is a living art in much of the continent and has its roots in great antiquity. Wood sculpture, often of outstanding artistic distinction, has been common in many of the forest areas, while much metal and terracotta work of similar virtue was done in various parts of West Africa. Sculpture in stone has ranged from the monoliths of Axum (c. AD 300) to the 'bird-figures' of Zimbabwe (c. 1500), while smaller stone figures have occurred in widely separated regions, and also in later times. Much good work was also done in ivory, notably at Benin and along the west and east coasts. The best of all this work has combined a daring plasticity with respect for form in highly original styles. It can be said that sculpture has been one of the central arts of Africa.

SCURVY, common fatal disease among sailors during long sea voyages in the 16th–18th cents, caused by vitamin C deficiency in the diet. Its prevention was studied by a Scots physician, James Lind (d. 1794), who served in the British navy in the 1740s and whose *Treatise of Scurvy* (1754) and *Essay for preserving the Health of Seamen* advocated green vegetables, fresh fruit, and lime juice. In 1795 rations of lime juice were made compulsory by the British admiralty for serving sailors.

SCUTAGE, in England, feudal payment (from Lat. *scutum* = a shield) customarily fixed at two marks (£1·33) on a knight's fee, which from about 1100 could be given instead of performance of knight service. By the 13th cent. it was more usual in England to pay scutage than to perform the service. The right to collect was formally abandoned by the English Crown in 1340.

SCYTHIANS (Persian, Saka), name loosely used in antiquity to denote any nomads from the Steppes, but properly for an Indo-European nomadic people of mixed ethnic origin, who moved from east of the Altai Mountains into south Russia (9th cent. BC). They drove the Cimmerians from the Caucasus and north of the Black Sea into Urartu and Asia Minor, set up a kingdom, centred probably in Azerbayjan, and for a few decades dominated the surrounding region. Attacked by the Medes (625), some Scythians settled in the area between the Caspian and Aral Seas, while others withdrew to the region between the Carpathians and the Don which had been dominated by Scythians since c. 700. They exploited its fertility to trade wheat for Greek artefacts with Greek colonies on the Black Sea coast, who supplied it to the homeland, especially Athens, where mercenary Scythian archers formed the police force. The Greek historian Herodotus (5th cent. BC) describes many of their strange customs, especially elaborate burial ceremonies involving the ritual killing of wives, servants, and animals. The Scythians were skilful horsemen and they frustrated invasions over the Danube by the Persian king Darius I (513) and by Alexander the Great's general Zopyrion (c. 325), but after 300 were driven out by Celts from the west and Sarmatians from the east and disappeared from history.

SEA BEGGARS, Calvinist rebels who fled from the Duke of Alva's repression in their native Netherlands and turned into privateers, *Gueux de mer*, under La Marck, harrying shipping between Spain and the Netherlands from their havens in Emden, La Rochelle, and Dover (1569–72). Their expulsion from English ports (March 1572) and their seizure of Brill initiated the conquest of Holland and Zeeland from Spanish rule.

SEA PEOPLES, people from the Aegean shores and islands, who invaded the coasts of Asia Minor, Syria, and Palestine (c. 1200 BC), causing considerable disturbance in the area. They were defeated (c. 1174) by Rameses III at the frontiers of Egypt, and many, including the Philistines, settled on the coast of Canaan.

SEABURY, SAMUEL (1729–96), American clergyman and Bp of CT, who became the first presiding bishop of the US Protestant Episcopal Church. He had supported the Loyalists before 1776 and was imprisoned for attacking the Continental Congress. He later accepted the new US government. After the securing of independence (1776), it was no longer possible for a bishop to seek consecration at the hands of English bishops, since an oath of allegiance to the British Crown would be required. Seabury was therefore consecrated at Aberdeen in 1784 by Scottish bishops who, since the Revolution of 1688, had rejected allegiance to the Crown.

SEALANDS, DYNASTY OF, rulers who were known as kings of the Sealand, the marshy ground at the head of the Persian Gulf. They seem to have been contemporaries of the early Kassites who conquered Babylonia after 1595 BC.

SEALS, ROYAL, in England. Originally there was only one royal seal—that later known as the Great Seal—which already existed in the time of Edward the Confessor. From at least the mid-12th cent. it was in the custody of the chancellor with an exchequer duplicate in the charge of his deputy, the chancellor of the exchequer. This seal was large, had two faces with a portrait of the king seated on one side and on horseback on the reverse, was normally used pendant, *ie,* hanging from the document, and was used—eventually used only—for all very important and formal documents, such as treaties and charters. By the end of the 12th cent. with the departmentalization of government, the need was felt for other less grand seals which were known as the small seals. The griffin seal belonged to the chamber. More important was the privy seal, kept in the wardrobe and originally the private seal of the king, which replaced the great seal when that became formalized. In the course of the 13th cent. the wardrobe became a great office of state and the privy seal, which was separated from it and under an independent keeper from 1311, a seal of state. So there appeared in the mid-14th cent. a third small seal, the signet, kept by the king's *secretarius* (secretary) from which originated all the modern departments of government.

SEARCH, RIGHT OF, disputed issue of maritime law in which the European, Scandinavian, and, later, American governments questioned Britain's right, in time of war, to seize and search neutral shipping, in order to enforce a blockade or confiscate war contraband. Britain's naval supremacy and geographical command of European commerce meant that a concerted effort was needed to check the searches. During the American War of Independence, the lawlessness of British privateers and the frustrations of countries which stood to make a profit from the carrying trade provoked the formation of the League of Armed Neutrality (1780), to which Britain was bound to submit, since one member, Sweden, was her major source of naval supplies. But the British response to the formation of a similar league in 1800 was the sinking of the Danish fleet in Copenhagen (1801), after which a code was drawn up for the searching of merchant ships. This was particularly resented by the US, who declared war on Britain in 1812, after a British ship opened fire on the *Chesapeake* for its refusal to submit to a search.

Two attempts were made in the maritime clauses of the peace of Paris (1856), which Britain signed, and the Declaration of London (1909), which she refused to ratify, to allow the free transit of shipping, except obvious contraband, in time of war. But the legal arguments were somewhat artificial, for a strong naval power, attempting to enforce a blockade, would lose the advantages of its naval supremacy if it eschewed the right of search. This was tacitly admitted by the US during the First World War, when, although technically a neutral power until 1917, they did not act to prevent the gradual tightening of Britain's blockade of Germany.   SH

SEATON OF SEATON, JOHN COLBORNE, 1st Baron (1778–1863), British soldier and lieutenant-governor of Upper Canada (1829–36), who put down the rebellion of 1837, and in 1839 became governor-in-chief of British North America.

SEBASTIAN I (1554–78), King of Portugal (*reg.* 1557–78), posthumous son of Prince John (1537–54) and grandson of King John III (*reg.* 1521–57), whom he succeeded as a young child. During his long minority Portugal was governed by his grandmother, Catherine of Habsburg. Sebastian was dedicated to the idea of a crusade against the infidel Turk and led a disastrous campaign to North Africa, being killed, together with the flower of the Portuguese nobility, at the battle of Alcazarquivir (4 Aug. 1578). His death left Portugal to his aged uncle, Cardinal Henry, and hastened the extinction of the Aviz dynasty and of Portuguese political independence.

SEBETWANE (*c.* 1800–51), chief of the Fokeng or Kololo, who left their lands on the South African high veld during the Mfecane (Time of Troubles) in the 1820s, and after long journeyings settled north of the Zambezi in the 1840s. There Sebetwane conquered the Lozi and established a kingdom over them. His son, Sekeletu, succeeded him, but Kololo domination over the Lozi rapidly disintegrated. However, the Lozi continue to speak the Sotho language of the Kololo.

SEBUKTEGIN (d. 997), Turkish slave (ghulam) prominent in the service of the Samanid amirs. In 977 he established himself as effective master of Ghazna in eastern Afghanistan. With the Samanid regime falling into decline he was able to extend his influence over Khurasan. None the less, until his death in 997, he was content to regard himself as a vassal of the Samanids. His able conduct of affairs prepared the ground for the reign of his son, Mahmud of Ghazna.

SECESSION MOVEMENTS, THE, US, threats or attempts by dissatisfied sections or minority groups to withdraw from the federal union. Secession became a reality in 1860–1, but a secessionist tradition had existed in America since colonial times, the Pilgrim Fathers being 'the first outspoken secessionists'. The right of a people to alter or abolish any form of government which became despotic was asserted in the Declaration of Independence and the American War of Independence was, essentially, a secessionist struggle. From the early national period to the great sectional crisis of the 1850s the union was to be threatened by separatist movements. The secession of the Southern slave states in 1860 was the culmination of a pervasive theme in American development.

Democratic Republicans opposed to Federalist legislation, particularly the Alien and Sedition Acts (1798), posed the first serious threat of secession. The moderate views of Thomas Jefferson prevailed and the crisis passed, but the Kentucky and Virginia Resolves (1798), based on concepts of state sovereignty and the compact theory of the constitution, were to provide a reference for later secessionist appeals. The Federalists, in turn, were also to contemplate secession as the means of redressing their grievances. Alarmed by the Louisiana Purchase (1803), the 'Essex Junto' planned a confederacy consisting of New England and New York, justifying their actions by states rights arguments similar to the Kentucky and Virginia Resolves, but this move was blocked by Alexander Hamilton. Extremists in the Hartford Convention (1814–15), another Federalist protest against Republican policies, including the War of 1812, which they delighted in calling 'Mr Madison's War', favoured secession, but the treaty of Ghent (1814) brought a temporary halt to secessionist agitation.

Further threats of secession, by both the North and the South, were provoked by the slavery issue which dominated national politics from the 1820s to the Civil War. The South considered the possibility of seceding over the admission of MO to the union when the balance between free and slave states appeared about to be upset; the disputed tariffs of 1828 and 1832 and the possible exclusion of slavery from the Mexican cessions after the War of 1846–8 further hardened extremist opinion in favour of Southern separatism. In the North, John Quincy Adams believed that the free states would secede if TX were annexed and William Lloyd Garrison urged that there should be 'No Union With Slaveholders' and Northern secession from the union to absolve the section from giving constitutional sanction to slavery.

Although the nullification crisis and the Nashville Convention (1850) produced strident calls for Southern secession, the slave states were unprepared to act in concert. But after Lincoln became the Republican presidential candidate (1860), Southern governors and congressmen openly advocated secession, should he be elected. Eleven states were subsequently to secede from the union and form the Confederate States of America. The SC secession convention declared (20 Dec. 1860) that 'the union now subsisting between South Carolina and other states, under the name 'United States of America' is hereby dissolved'. Lincoln rejected the logic of secession, and in his inaugural address (4 March 1861) declared that the union was perpetual. For him, secession was synonymous with rebellion, and this belief sustained the Union's cause during the Civil War.

Paul C. Nagel, *One Nation Indivisible: the union in American thought, 1770–1861* (Oxford, 1964).
R. A. Wooster, *The Secession Conventions of the South* (Princeton, 1962).   JW

SECESSION REFERENDUM (1933) in western Australia. Deep-rooted discontentment over the effects of Federation on the western third of Australia, which in 1901 had entered the Commonwealth against the wishes of most colonists, was brought to a head by the hardships of the economic depression, most severely felt in this predominantly agricultural state. Increased powers of the Commonwealth government and persistent 'dumping' by Vic. and NSW manufacturers were among grievances exploited during an ably organized referendum campaign in 1933. But a vote of 138,653 in favour of secession, against which only 70,706 voted, failed to induce the British parliament to intervene. Concessions from Canberra (including the setting up of the Commonwealth Grants Commission), combined with recovery from the Depression, had eased discontent by the late 1930s. After the Second World War social services, improved communications, mineral discoveries, increased immigration, and a vigorous and varied state development programme in the 1950s and 1960s, ended the secessionist movement.

SECKENDORF, FRIEDRICH HEINRICH, Count (1673–1763), German soldier and diplomat, and nephew of the politician and historian, Veit Ludwig von Seckendorf (1626–92) by whom he was brought up. He joined the imperial army in 1694, serving in the War of the Spanish Succession, the closing stages of the Northern War, *eg*, at Stralsund (1715), and in the Turkish War under Prince Eugène (1717–18).

Appointed imperial plenipotentiary to the Prussian court (1725), he successfully detached Prussia from the League of Hanover (1727) before undertaking diplomatic missions to Dresden (1728), the United Provinces (1731), and Denmark (1732). In 1731 he was appointed imperial governor of Philippsburg, negotiated the treaty of Loewenwolde (1732), and fought in the War of the Polish Succession, defeating the French at Klausen (1735). While leading the imperial advance into Serbia during the Turkish War of 1736–9 he was driven back decisively and was subsequently arrested by the imperial government and imprisoned for three years (1737–40). Although released by Maria Theresa (1740) he entered Bavarian service in the War of the Austrian Succession (1740–8), negotiating the treaty of Fussen (1745). He was captured by the Prussians in the Seven Years War (1756–63), later ransomed, and died in retirement at the age of 90.

SECKER, THOMAS (1693–1768), English cleric from a dissenting background who became Bp of Oxford (1737–58) and Abp of Canterbury (1758–68). He was tolerant towards Methodists and deplored the circumstances which had led them to part company with the Church of England.

SECLUSION, ACT OF (1654), in the Netherlands, legislation passed by the estates of Holland, which debarred the Prince of Orange (the future King William III of England) and his descendants from holding office in that state. It was exacted by Oliver Cromwell from Jan de Witt as the price for ratifying the treaty of Westminster (1654) and it aroused opposition in the other states of the United Provinces. It was repealed in 1660.

SECOND ATHENIAN CONFEDERACY, alliance of Greek city-states, mostly in the Aegean, organized by Athens (378 BC) in support of Theban opposition to Spartan imperialism. The Athenians, hitherto restrained by the King's Peace (387–386), trod warily, excluding the Asiatic Greeks, subjects of Persia, and promising in the charter to avoid the unpopular features of the 5th-cent. Delian League (eg, tribute, garrisons, cleruchies). The confederacy, which had gained about 70 members by 374, won naval battles against Sparta off Naxos (376) and Corcyra (375), but general peace settlements in 375–374 and 371 failed and further warfare from 369 against Thebes—which had defected with some other allies—put an increasing strain on both the Confederacy's resources and Athens' liberalism. But, despite the Athenians' failure in the Social War (357–355) to prevent the secession of Chios, Cos, and Rhodes, the other allies remained loyal until the Confederacy was dissolved after Philip II of Macedon's victory at Chaeronea (338).

SECOND BOOK OF DISCIPLINE in Scotland, foundation of Scottish Presbyterianism, drawn up in 1578 by Andrew Melville, the Scottish Calvinist, who returned from Geneva in 1574, in which the episcopacy was condemned and the doctrine of the parity of ministers was clearly stated.

SECOND ESTATE in France, nobility, or second of the three social orders until 1789, who possessed certain financial and judicial privileges in common, eg, exemption from the personal *taille*, as well as social prestige.

SECOND FRONT. The opening of a 'second front' against Germany in the Second World War became a major point of debate among the Allies with the entry of Russia and the US into the war in June and Dec. 1941 respectively. Stalin was vociferous in his demands that British and US forces should establish a second front on the European mainland as soon as possible in order to relieve the pressure on Russia. The US chiefs of staff tended to favour operations in the Pacific against the Japanese, but were over-ruled by Roosevelt, a firm believer in dealing with Germany first; subsequently Gen. Marshall, US chief of army staff, proposed the launching of a cross-Channel invasion, probably landing on the Cherbourg peninsula, in either 1942 or 1943. This scheme was vehemently opposed by Churchill and the British chiefs of staff, who were more familiar with the complexities and dangers of amphibious warfare and were aware of the hazards of attempting such a plan with resources so limited that the initial bridgehead could easily be contained. The British argued for an indirect approach to Germany, using Allied superiority at sea for landing in North Africa and then attacking Italy via Sicily, thus ensuring that German resources were as widely committed as possible before a cross-Channel invasion was launched. After much controversy the British plan prevailed, despite Stalin's hostility and the suspicions of the US chiefs of staff: the North African landing took place in Nov. 1942, the invasion of Sicily in June, and of Italy in Sept. 1943, and the opening of the second front, proper, came in June 1944 with the D-Day landings in Normandy. NRB

SECOND WORLD WAR (1939–45). This began raggedly in the sense that China and Japan had been at war since 1937, while Soviet Russia was attacked only in June 1941. Nor did the war become truly world-wide until the US were forced in by the Japanese attack on Pearl Harbor on 7 Dec. 1941. Conventionally, the Second World War began when Germany invaded Poland on 1 Sept. 1939. Britain and France, though pledged to assist Poland, held back until 3 Sept., when the British House of Commons forced war on a reluctant government, and France followed suit. No serious attempt was made to help Poland, which was overrun by the end of Sept. and partitioned between Germany and Soviet Russia. Then came the 'phoney' war, with little activity except an ineffective blockade. In Nov. Soviet Russia attacked Finland. On 13 Dec. three British cruisers crippled the German *Graf Spee*, which was then scuttled.

(a) *1940*. The British and French governments planned to help Finland, but this became unnecessary because peace was arranged between Finland and Soviet Russia on 12 March. The British then prepared to mine Norwegian waters, but were anticipated by a German invasion of Denmark and Norway on 9 April. British troops were sent to Norway and had to be withdrawn after a series of defeats. This caused the fall of Chamberlain. Churchill, who was in fact responsible for the Norwegian campaign, formed a real National government on 10 May. On the same day German troops invaded Holland and Belgium. On 15 May the Germans broke through the French lines at Sedan and a week later they reached the sea, cutting off the Allied forces in Belgium. The bulk of the British and some French were withdrawn from Dunkirk after losing their heavy equipment. France was defeated and surrendered on 25 June. Italy declared war against Britain and France on 10 June. Germany prepared to invade England, but the German air force was defeated in the battle of Britain, which ended on 15 Sept. German night raids (the Blitz) continued throughout the winter. In Nov. Italy attacked Greece, but was repulsed. In Dec. the British army in Egypt won a great victory over the Italians and overran Cyrenaica.

(b) *1941*. In March Lend-Lease was instituted, thus ensuring US supplies to Britain. The Italian fleet was defeated at Cape Matapan. In April Germany invaded Yugoslavia and Greece. British troops were sent to aid Greece, but were compelled to withdraw after heavy defeats. German forces under Rommel enabled the Italians to reconquer all Cyrenaica, except for Tobruk. In May the Germans captured Crete by air landings. On 27 May the German battleship *Bismarck* was sunk in the Atlantic. On 22 June Germany attacked Soviet Russia without warning. The Russians suffered catastrophic defeats and lost much territory, until they halted the Germans at the gates of Moscow in Dec. On 7 Dec. Japanese aircraft attacked the US navy at Pearl Harbor and sank much of it. Germany and Italy declared war on the US, and Britain declared war on Japan. Immediately afterwards, *Prince of Wales* and *Repulse* were sunk off Malaya by the Japanese.

(c) *1942*. The Japanese took Singapore in Feb., and then overran Burma and the Dutch East Indies. Their naval forces were halted by the US at the battle of the Coral Sea in May and defeated at the battle of Midway in June. German and Italian forces advanced into Egypt in July. The Germans launched a new Russian offensive and reached the outskirts of Stalingrad, which they failed to take. On 23 Oct. Montgomery won the battle of El Alamein and began a victorious march across North Africa. British and US forces landed in French North Africa on 7 Nov. The Germans occupied all France, and the French fleet at Toulon was scuttled. On 19 Nov. the German forces besieging Stalingrad were cut off and on 31 Jan. 1943 they surrendered.

(d) *1943*. Allied victories now began in earnest. All resistance in North Africa ceased on 12 May. The Russians won the greatest tank battle of all time at Kursk in July. On 10 July the Allies effected a landing in Sicily. Mussolini was overthrown on 25 July, but Allied delays enabled the Germans to occupy most of Italy before Allied forces invaded the Italian mainland on 3 Sept. Italy surrendered on 7 Sept., but Mussolini was rescued by the Germans and set up a Fascist Social Republic in the north. In Nov. Churchill, Roosevelt, and Stalin met at Teheran and agreed on strategy to defeat Germany.

(e) *1944*. On 22 Jan. Allied forces landed at Anzio, but were pinned down by the Germans, and Rome was not taken until 4 June. On 6 June British and US forces landed in Normandy. The British maintained a prolonged battle in front of Caen, which enabled the Americans to take Cherbourg and break out of the Cotentin peninsula in July. A German counter-offensive towards Avranches was repulsed, and the Germans were encircled. On 25 Aug. Paris was liberated, and a provisional government set up under De Gaulle. All Russian territory was liberated, but the Russians were checked before Warsaw, and a Polish rising there was suppressed by the Germans. In Sept. Belgium was liberated. British forces failed, however, to take Arnhem. In Dec. a German counter-offensive in the Ardennes was defeated.

(f) *1945*. Greece was liberated and a communist movement there was suppressed by British troops. In March the Allies began their last offensive across the Rhine. Hitler and his wife died in circumstances that have never been clarified on 30 April. Mussolini and his mistress were shot by Italian partisans. The Russians took Berlin. Germany surrendered unconditionally on 8 May.

Preparations were made to invade Japan. On 6 Aug. the first atomic bomb was dropped on Hiroshima. On 8 Aug. Soviet Russia declared war on Japan. A second atomic bomb was dropped on Nagasaki. On 14 Aug. Japan agreed to unconditional surrender, in fact being allowed to retain the Mikado. The Second World War officially ended on 2 Sept. 1945. There was total victory for the three major Allies—Britain, Soviet Russia, and the US. But, as the Potsdam conference had already indicated in July, Allied unity did not survive the end of the war.

J. F. C. Fuller, *The Second World War 1939–1945* (London, 1949).

L. L. Snyder, *The War: a concise history 1939–1945* (London, 1962).   AJPT

SECRET BALLOT IN AUSTRALIA. Adopted by Vic. and SA in March 1856, the 'Australian' or 'Victorian' ballot was subsequently accepted throughout Australia, the US, and the British Commonwealth. The principle of voting by secret ballot was adopted by radicals in both colonies throughout the 1850s and, though vigorously denounced by conservatives as 'unmanly', was introduced in time for the elections to the first parliaments in Vic. (1856) and SA (1857).

SECRET SERVICE FUND, in Britain, annual allowance, fixed at £3000 each in 1707, paid to the secretaries of state by the treasury to cover the cost of rewarding spies and intelligence agents, a service which received an impetus in the 18th cent. through fears of Jacobitism. On occasions additional sums were issued to the agents concerned or to the secretary of state. The widespread belief that there was a large-scale and costly secret service organization through which ministers could manipulate patronage—now regarded by historians as an exaggerated charge—led to the Civil Establishment Act (1782).

SECRETARY FOR THE NORTH in Britain, one of the two British secretaries of state in charge of foreign affairs, who looked after the northern department or province, which normally consisted of the Holy Roman empire, Holland, Scandinavia, Poland, and Russia. Until 1706 the junior secretary held the northern department. After that date the two assumed equal status until the accession of George I, when the northern department became more important. Under George III they reassumed an equal status.

SECRETARY FOR THE SOUTH in Britain, secretary of state in charge of the southern department, normally consisting of France, Switzerland, Italy, the Iberian peninsula, and Turkey (plus Ireland, the colonies, and the Channel Islands). Domestic affairs were common to the secretaries for both the north and for the south, and no attempt was made to separate their functions.

SECTIONALISM IN US HISTORY, concept, given classic expression by Frederick Jackson Turner, that geographic, economic, social, and political divisions within the US have affected its historical development. Turner maintained that: 'Our politics and our society have been shaped by sectional complexity and interplay, not unlike what goes on between European nations. Sections are more important than states in shaping the underlying forces in American history.' Certainly, sectional differences and tensions were evident in the colonial and Revolutionary periods, and sectional interests were considered in the framing of the constitution and in the compromises effected between Northern and Southern economic interests. Washington attempted to balance sectional interests in the selection of his cabinet, while the economic policies of Alexander Hamilton, supported by the New England states but opposed by the South, aggravated sectional feeling. By the early 19th cent. the meaningful sections were those of the North-East or 'North', the West, and the South. Economically, the North-East was emerging as an industrial region, in which manufacturers, merchants, and a working class predominated. The West was an agricultural section, but also one of nascent industrialism. The South, even more than the West, was an agricultural section producing staple crops for export. Thus, before 1860, the salient feature of the US economy was the concentration of different economic activities in different geographical sections. Politically, the East favoured protection, and federal support for internal improvements, and opposed, initially, territorial expansion. The South generally favoured the converse, as did the West, and at first the two sections formed an uneasy alliance in national politics, but the slavery issue transcended sectional economic alignments and emphasized sectional differences. Thus, the question of slavery's extension into the territories broke the South–West alliance, since westerners did not wish to compete with slave labour in the territories, and contributed to the East–West realignment which brought the Republican Party into power (1860). Similarly, the South, which had joined the other two sections in condemning slavery as an evil came, after 1830, to defend it as a 'positive good' and became a self-conscious section dedicated to maintaining the slave system. The shift in the South from nationalism to extreme sectionalism is epitomized by the career of John C. Calhoun. Sectional conflict, with slavery as its fundamental cause, resulted in the American Civil War; the aftermath of the war, Reconstruction, can be seen as a short-lived attempt to form a working alliance between the North and the South through the Negro vote.

With the 'reconstruction' of the union, rapid industrialization, and America's emergence, early in the 20th cent. as a world power, sectionalism became less acute in US politics, but was to reappear in such essentially regional protests as the Greenback, Granger, and Populist movements, and in southern resistance to civil rights legislation. Sectionalism and nationalism have co-existed in American development and the US remains, in many respects, as much a confederation of sections as a union of states. The sectional approach to US history, if pressed to extremes, however, can lead to a minimization of other factors in American growth such as class conflict, group conflicts *within* sections, and to a neglect of politics and issues at the state level.

F. J. Turner, *The Significance of Sections in American History* (New York, 1932).
Merrill Jensen (ed.), *Regionalism in America* (WI, 1965). JW

SECULAR GAMES, ancient Roman celebrations of the end of one era and the beginning of another, held in 348, 249, and 146 BC. Augustus celebrated them in 17 BC, and Claudius in AD 47 for the 800th anniversary of Rome, Domitian in 88, Septimius Severus in 204, and Philip in 248 for the 1000th anniversary of the city, following Claudius' calculations.

SECURITIES AND EXCHANGE COMMISSION (1934–) in the US, federal agency charged with the administration of legislation over the financial and securities markets designed to protect the investor and the public. The five members of the commission are appointed by the president of the US, subject to the advice and consent of the Senate, and serve for staggered terms of five years.

SECURITY, ACT OF (1704) in Scotland, legislative measure passed by the Scottish parliament in 1703 but which only received royal assent on the refusal of supply (Aug. 1704). The act laid down that on Queen Anne's death without issue the estates were to name a successor to the Scottish throne from the Protestant descendants of the Stuart house, but this was not to be the same person as the successor to the English Crown, unless steps were taken and approved, guaranteeing the Crown, parliament, Presbyterian Church, justice, and economic prosperity of Scotland. This act challenged the English government to renew attempts at a constitutional settlement between the two countries. This was finally achieved in 1707.

SEDAN, BATTLE OF (1870), battle in the Franco-Prussian War in which Marshal MacMahon and Napoleon III were encircled with a large part of the French army, and had to surrender (2 Sept. 1870). This marked the end of the Second Empire in France.

SEDDON, RICHARD JOHN (1845–1906), NZ politician and prime minister, who became an MP in 1879, championing Westland interests. After joining Ballance's Liberal cabinet as minister of public works (1891), he showed unexpected talents as an administrator. As acting prime minister on Ballance's death (1893), he withstood a challenge from Stout, virtually Ballance's choice, and was confirmed as Liberal leader. A second challenge from Stout on the difficult issue of Prohibition was narrowly but skilfully defeated. His success at the 1893 elections confirmed his ascendancy, and enabled him to press forward with Liberal reforms, the work primarily of McKenzie, Reeves, and Ward. His greatest legislative achievement was the marathon passage of Old Age Pensions (1898). To head off Labor discontent, he founded the Liberal–Labor Federation (1899), a shadowy organization subservient to himself. Many 'Conservative' opponents came to see him as an effective check to radicals, and his demonstrative role at Imperial Conferences—together with NZ's notable contribution to British Boer War forces—made him widely accepted in both Britain and NZ. Soon after his fifth electoral success (1905), he died.

R. M. Burdon, *King Dick* (Christchurch, 1955). WJG

SEDGEMOOR, BATTLE OF (6 July 1685), end of Monmouth's Rebellion and the last battle fought on English soil. On 11 June 1685 the Duke of Monmouth landed at Lyme Regis, Dorset, to lead a revolt against his Roman Catholic uncle, James II. Having failed to take Bristol, Monmouth, with nearly 4000 men, fell back on Bridgwater, where he was confronted by a royal army of 2500 men under the Earl of Feversham and his cavalry commander, John Churchill (later Duke of Marlborough). Faced with mass desertions from his army, Monmouth decided on a night attack, but the rebels lost their way and in the ensuing confusion Monmouth's army was routed. He fled, but was captured three days later and executed on Tower Hill (15 July); his followers suffered the vengeance of Judge Jeffreys and his 'Bloody Assize'.

SEDITIOUS MEETINGS ACT (1795) in Britain, with the Treasonable Practices Act (1795), was part of the Younger Pitt's campaign of anti-Jacobin repression. It prohibited for three years, except under the licence and control of the magistrates, meetings of more than 50 people, and public lectures.

SEECKT, HANS VON (1866–1936), German soldier who, after a distinguished career as a staff officer in the First World War, became head of the German Army Command (1920–6). In the critical period between Nov. 1923 and March 1924 he was given emergency constitutional powers to deal with the Munich putsch and other disturbances. He was also (1933–5) military adviser to Chiang-Kai-Shek.

His appointment to supreme command was crucial both for the German army and for the Weimar republic. As a Prussian officer, he found it hard to adjust himself to the post-war situation: he realized that an immediate restoration of the monarchy was impracticable, yet disliked democracy and abhorred the republic and its supporters. His aim was to rebuild the army as an exclusive unit dedicated to efficiency and traditional 'national' values remote from party politics, and he set out to overcome some of the restrictions imposed in 1919 at Versailles, which he did by temporary co-operation with the Russians and by making the Reichswehr into a highly trained nucleus for the much larger army which Germany would need if ever she were to revise the peace treaty by force.

Like many senior officers, Von Seeckt regarded National Socialism as a potentially revolutionary movement with aims quite different from those of traditional conservatism; he was not impressed by Hitler, whom he met in March 1923. But his right-wing bias and his ambiguous attitude to the republic were an important step towards the army's increasing involvement in politics in the period leading to Hitler's achievement of power. RJVL

SEELEY, SIR JOHN ROBERT (1834–95), British historian and professor of modern history at Cambridge (1869–94), whose powerful book, *The Expansion of England*, did much to foster popular enthusiasm for imperialism. He was a specialist on Napoleon and on the rise of Prussia; he believed in rule by the strong, and was a member of the Imperial Federation League. His other writings included *Ecce Homo* (1865), a controversial biography of Christ.

SEGESTA, in north-western Sicily (51 kms south-west of Palermo), ancient city of the native Elymians, which, despite its remoteness from the chief Greek foundations, became hellenized to an unusual degree, adopting the Greek script for its language and coinage similar to that of the Greek, and building a Greek theatre and the first stage of a Doric temple. It became involved in Greek history, with important consequences, when in 415 BC its appeal for help against Selinus led to the disastrous Athenian expedition, whose failure profoundly affected the issue of the great Peloponnesian War. Its subsequent appeal to Carthage (410) led to the successful Carthaginian invasions of 409–405 and to its own subjection. It regained some prosperity under the Romans.

SEGNI, ANTONIO (1891–   ), Italian politician and president of Italy (1962–4), who was the founder of Christian Democracy (DC) in Sardinia (1944). He made his reputation as agricultural minister under De Gasperi, by introducing moderate land redistribution (1949–50). His own government (1955–7) (with Social Democrats and Liberals) was noted for increasing state involvement in industry, and for the treaty of Rome. During his minority DC government (1959–1960) there were serious Alto Adige border troubles with Austrian minorities, which, as foreign minister (1920–2), he began to settle, but was then elected president.

SEGREGATION IN THE US, physical separation of whites and blacks, either by law or custom, dating generally from the late 19th cent. During slavery, by its very nature, the two races frequently came into close contact and the position of the Negro was rigidly defined. But the existence of segregationary practices have been discovered in some antebellum cities. As early as 1816, New Orleans enacted an ordinance segregating Negroes from whites in places of public accommodation, and Negroes were generally excluded from Northern schools, or provided with separate facilities. During Reconstruction, occasional laws and tacit de facto segregation was evident in several former Confederate states, notably SC. By 1878 most Southern and border states had given legal sanction to segregation in education. The earliest Southern 'Jim Crow' law affecting accommodation in railroad cars was enacted in TN in 1881, but following the Supreme Court's 'separate but equal' decision in *Plessy v. Ferguson* (1896), segregation in public transport increased rapidly. Yet only after 1900 was segregation rigidly and uniformly applied throughout the South, affecting such institutions as prisons, hospitals, factories, and state homes for the old, the deaf, and the blind. In the North also, despite legislation designed to uphold the intention of the 14th Amendment, Negroes were, in practice, usually kept separate from whites. By 1900, the American Federation of Labor was admitting unions to membership which practised segregation. During the 1920s and 1930s, segregationary laws were extended to cover transport by taxi cabs and buses—airlines found it impractical to institute segregation. In 1933 TX prohibited 'Caucasians' and 'Africans' from wrestling or boxing together; in 1937 AR required segregation at race tracks. In 1944 the sociologist Gunnar Myrdal observed: 'Segregation is now becoming so complete that the white Southerner practically never sees a Negro except as his servant and in other standardized and formalized caste situations.' Military segregation, practised in the US armed forces during the Civil War, the First World War, and the Second World War, was prohibited by President Truman's executive order of 1948, but the order was only gradually implemented. The widespread residential segregation in most American cities in 1970 was largely a consequence of the Negro's depressed economic status, and was accomplished without the need for legal sanction. Despite the Supreme Court's 1954 decision that segregation in public schools was inherently unequal, it set no deadline for desegregation and recalcitrant Southern governors effectively nullified the court's ruling. Moreover, educational segregation was not confined to the South, and 'the slow retreat of de jure segregation in Southern schools was paralleled by an advance of de facto segregation of schools in cities in the North. With legal segregation ended, the US remained in 1970 a fundamentally segregated society, leading the National Advisory Commission on Civil Disorders (1968) to conclude: 'Our nation is moving towards two societies, one black, one white —separate and unequal.'

C. Vann Woodward, *The Strange Career of Jim Crow* (Oxford, 1966).
Gunnar Myrdal, *An American Dilemma: the Negro problem and modern democracy* (New York, 1962).   JW

SEGU, town on the upper Niger river and centre of a Bambara state (*c.* 1750–1861). It was occupied by the French (1891) and is now (1970) in the republic of Mali.

SÉGUR, LOUIS-PHILIPPE, Comte de (1753–1830), French diplomat of the *ancien régime*, who, having been minister to Russia (1784–9), was one of the few aristocrats willing to appear at the court of Napoleon I, although he had no political influence there.

SEHESTED, HANNIBAL (1609–66), Danish politician, son-in-law of King Christian IV, who was a governor of Norway (1642–51), where he showed much independence. After a period of disgrace, he helped in 1660 to set up the autocratic monarchy and collegial administration in Denmark, and in his last years led missions to the English and French courts.

SEI, SHŌNAGON (*fl.* 10th cent.), Japanese court lady and writer, whose most famous work, translated as *The Pillow Book of Sei Shōnagon*, gives a vivid and perceptive glimpse of Heian court society.

SEIGNELAY, JEAN-BAPTISTE COLBERT, Marquis de (1651–90), French politician and son of the great Colbert, under whom he was trained for government service. He succeeded his father as secretary for the marine and commerce (1683) and continued to build up a powerful French navy which was able to challenge the English fleet at Beachy Head (1690).

SEIPEL, IGNAZ (1876–1932), Austrian politician, scholar, and Catholic priest, who belonged to the conservative Christian Social Party, and was a parliamentary deputy from 1919. As federal chancellor (1922–4), he was responsible for the stabilization of Austria's currency and economic reconstruction after the inflation. He retired from office shortly after an attempt on his life. During his second chancellorship (1926–9), he pursued a fiercely anti-socialist policy which sharpened Austria's internal political conflicts. In 1929 he left his party, but held office again briefly as foreign minister (1930).

SEISACHTHEIA, ancient Greek 'shaking off of burdens', the term later applied to Solon's supposed liberation of enslaved peasants and the *hectemoroi* in 594 BC by cancelling debts and prohibiting future loans on the security of the person.

SEISSER, HANS VON (1874–   ), German soldier, who was commander of the Bavarian Landespolizei and a participant in the Munich putsch of 1923. He belonged, with Von Kahr and Von Lossow, to the anti-republican triumvirate which hoped to exploit the chaotic situation of 1923 to achieve greater independence for Bavaria, using Hitler and other extremists as their instruments. He frequently acted as intermediary between Hitler and the Bavarian government.

SEIYŪKAI, Japanese political party established in 1900 by Itō Hirobumi on the foundations of the Jiyūtō. It had a majority in the Japanese Diet for many years and played a large part in breaking down the monopoly of office held by the *genrō* and their protégés. Its greatest success was the establishment of a Seiyūkai cabinet (1918) under Hara Kei, but after his assassination (1921), no outstanding leader emerged and the party found itself increasingly in opposition to a Kenseikai or Minseitō cabinet. Seiyūkai criticism of the Minseitō's moderate foreign policy after 1928 contributed to the discrediting of party government, as did numerous cases of corruption in which members of the Seiyūkai were involved.

SEIZE MAI (1877) in France, unsuccessful attempt by MacMahon to induce a royalist majority in the Chamber by administrative pressure.

SEJANUS, LUCIUS AELIUS (d. AD 31), prefect of the praetorian guard under the Roman Emperor Tiberius, and an efficient defender of public order. Though long trusted by Tiberius, he probably murdered his son, Drusus (23), and also encompassed the ruin of several members of the imperial family involved in real or imaginary plots. He fell from power and was executed for aspiring to the principate himself.

SEJARAH ('family tree, genealogy'), term used in Malay for dynastic tradition, indicating literary works recording such traditions about the Muslim kingdoms in Indonesia and Malaysia from the 15th cent. These works describe the reigns of kings and other events in chronological order, and include, besides historical data, legends, and stories, and are partly didactic. The best known is the *Sejarah Melayu*, the oldest extant version of which dates back to 1612. Other texts of the same type are *Sejarah Banten*, which describes the history of the West Javanese sultanate, founded in the beginning of the 16th cent., and *Hikayat Raja-raja Banjar dan Kotawaringin*, which deals with the sultanate of Banjarmasin, Borneo.

SEJM in Poland, parliamentary institution consisting of the king, an upper house or senate, whose members were the bishops and archbishops and heads of the leading aristocratic families in their capacity as the Crown's chief officials, and a lower house of representatives of the *szlachta* or lesser nobility. This representative body emerged in the late 15th cent. and by the early 16th cent. had the right to elect the monarch and to make laws. Until 1529 the senate had 87 members and after Poland's union with Lithuania (1569) 140, by which time the lower house had 158. After the extinction of the powerful Jagiellon dynasty (1572) this legislative body began to decline in importance, as the 16th-cent. rule that unanimity was essential for legislative decisions was accepted. The first instance of the disruption of the *sejm* by this *liberum veto* was in 1652, and in the Saxon period (1697–1763) out of the 28 *sejms* held, 23 were wrecked through this constitutional machinery, mostly to the advantage of Poland's European neighbours. The long-needed reform of the Polish constitution (1791) carried out by the great *sejm* of 1788–92, ended, with the institution itself, in the 2nd and 3rd partitions (1793, 1795).

SEJONG (*reg.* 1418–50), fourth King of the Korean Yi dynasty, who is credited with the invention of *Han'gul*, the official script of Korea. He was a zealous reformer, who initiated measures to stop raiding by northern tribes and to put down Japanese piracy. He was hostile to Buddhism, which had exerted a strong influence under the preceding Koryo dynasty, and he disbanded most of the Buddhist monasteries, banishing monks from the capital.

SEKHUKHUNE (*reg.* 1861–82), Chief of the Pedi people of the north-eastern Transvaal, who withstood Zulu, Ndebele, and Swazi raids in the 19th cent. Under Sekhukhune, the Pedi chiefdom, organized on the Zulu model, extended its control over neighbouring Africans and resisted Boer attempts at taxation. In 1876 they repulsed a Boer commando, one of the factors which led to the British annexation of the Transvaal (1877). Sekhukhune was eventually conquered by British troops under Sir Garnet Wolseley (1879). After a brief exile, he returned to his people, but was murdered by his brother in 1882.

SEKIGAHARA, BATTLE OF (1600), most important battle of Japan's internal history, won by Tokugawa Ieyasu over an alliance of mainly south-western *daimyō*s. It made possible land confiscation on a large scale and provided a firm basis for Tokugawa rule.

SELANGOR WAR (1866–73), between rival Malay chiefs (and after 1870 also between rival Chinese societies) for control of the tin-rich Klang river valley in Selangor. Although fighting ended (1873) in the victory of Tengku Kudin and Yap Ah Loy, it created the climate of anarchy which prompted the British to intervene in the state (1874).

SELBORNE, ROUNDELL PALMER, 1st Earl of (1812–95), British Liberal lord chancellor, who opposed Irish Home Rule (1886). He became successively solicitor-general (1861), attorney-general (1863–6), and lord chancellor (1872–4, 1880–5). He fostered the Judicature Act (1873) and the Married Women's Property Act (1882), and published a defence of the Church of England against disestablishment (1886).

SELBY, WILLIAM COURT GULLY, 1st Viscount (1835–1909), British politician who, as speaker of the House of Commons (1895–1905), established the tradition that an efficient speaker shall be re-elected to the office irrespective of party. He was a Liberal MP, yet was unanimously re-elected by the Commons while it had a large Unionist majority (1895).

SELBY, BATTLE OF (1644), engagement in the English Civil War which broke the royalist hold imposed on Yorkshire after Adwalton Moor (1643). The position of the royalists, under the Marquis of Newcastle, was threatened by the Scots from the north and a parliamentary army from the south. Newcastle sent Lord John Belasyse to fend off the southern force, but his army was routed at Selby on the Ouse river, south of York (11 April). Belasyse lost over 1000 men and all his artillery and baggage. The Scots and Parliamentarians then besieged York.

SELDEN, JOHN (1584–1654), English lawyer, legal antiquary, politician, and oriental scholar. As an MP he assisted in the preparation of the protestation on the rights and privileges of the House of Commons (1621) and was committed to the Tower. Later he was involved in the impeachment of Buckingham and in drawing up and carrying the Petition of Right (1628). His opposition to the royal government reached its apogee when he was one of the MPs responsible for the passage in the Commons of resolutions against the illegal levying of tonnage and poundage. He was again sent to the Tower with Eliot and others. In the 1630s he inclined to the court and seems to have secured favours from Charles I, to whom he dedicated his *Mare Clausum* (1635) against the freedom of the seas. This book had been written earlier but James I had prohibited its publication. In 1640 Selden was elected to the Long Parliament, and in 1643 was a member of the Westminster Assembly of divines. He took the Solemn League and Covenant (1646), and was voted £5000 compensation by parliament for his sufferings under the monarchy (1647). His collection of Oriental mss passed on his death to the Bodleian Library, Oxford.

SELEUCIDS, dynasty of Macedonian kings founded by Seleucus I Nicator in the 4th cent. BC, who ruled a kingdom based on Syria and Mesopotamia which, under Seleucus I, stretched from India to the Aegean. During the 3rd cent. Iran was mostly lost to the Parthians and Asia Minor to Pergamum; and although Antiochus III briefly gained control, the kingdom's core became Syria when Iran again slipped away and Asia Minor was forbidden to Antiochus by Rome in the treaty of Apamea (188). Antiochus III also recovered Coele Syria (200), long in dispute with the Ptolemies, but the Jewish Maccabees' rebellion caused serious difficulties there (after 166). Nevertheless, the Seleucids maintained themselves as Roman clients until Syria became a Roman province (64 BC).

SELEUCUS I NICATOR (c. 358–281 BC), Satrap of Babylonia after the death of Alexander the Great. Expelled by Antigonus Monophthalmus (315), he returned with Ptolemy's support (311), proclaimed himself king and re-established Macedonian control in Iran, though he ceded the Indian provinces to Chandragupta for some elephants (c. 304). A member of the coalition against Antigonus, he fought at Ipsus (301) and gained a Mediterranean coastline in Syria and Cilicia, but did not win Asia Minor until he defeated Lysimachus at Corupedion (281). Seven months later he was assassinated while crossing to Europe to claim Lysimachus' vacant throne. An ardent city-builder, Seleucus' numerous foundations included Antioch-in-Syria and Seleucia-on-Tigris.

SELF-DENYING ORDINANCE (1645) in England, obliged members of both houses of the Long Parliament to resign all their offices, military and civil. The original ordinance which developed out of the quarrel between the Earl of Manchester and Oliver Cromwell proposed that no member of either house should hold any office. This would have meant the removal of Cromwell as well as Manchester, but it was thrown out by the Lords. The New Model army removed the men from Manchester's army, and in consequence the direct attack on him was dropped. The new ordinance, accepted by the Lords on 3 April, required all members of either house to surrender their offices within 40 days. Manchester and Essex had, in fact, resigned on 2 April. The ordinance, which had no objection to members being reappointed, enabled Cromwell to become lieutenant-general of the New Model.

'SELF-STRENGTHENING' in China, term describing China's effort to strengthen itself against foreign encroachment in the late 19th cent. After China's defeat in the *Arrow* War, and after the suppression of the Taiping rebellion, a few officials began to realize the need to build up China's military power along Western lines. Self-strengthening began, therefore, with the creation of the Kiangnan Arsenal, the Foochow Navy Yard, and the ordnance industry in general. In 1872 the China Merchant's Steam Navigation Co. was established to recapture the coastal and Yangtse river carrying-trade from foreign firms. These efforts were followed by mechanized coal mining and a few short telegraph lines in the 1870s. The railway also made a modest beginning in the 1880s. However, owing to the inertia of tradition, institutional failures, corruption, shortage of funds, and the lack of directive from Peking and of co-operation among provinces, none of these efforts produced the desired result. 'Self-strengthening' finally came to a dismal end in the Sino–Japanese War (1894–1895).

SELIM I (c. 1470–1520), Ottoman Sultan (*reg.* 1512–20), called Yawuz (often rendered into English as 'Grim', though the word had in Turkish the sense of 'Inexorable'). Selim I, during the reign of his father, Bayezid II, was appointed to be sanjaq begi of Trebizond. Hoping to ensure his own succession to the throne, Selim sailed across the Black Sea in 1511 to Kaffa in the Crimea. With aid from Mengli Giray, the Khan of the Krim Taters, Selim marched into the Balkans, only to suffer, at Corlu, in battle against his father Bayezid, a defeat which left him no choice but to flee to the Crimea for refuge. The fact that Ahmed, the son of Bayezid and the chief rival of Selim, took over much of Asia Minor in 1511 and the fear that Ahmed might seek aid from Safawid Persia led, in 1512, to the return of Selim from the Crimea and to the abdication of Bayezid II. Selim, now sultan, defeated and killed his brother Ahmed in 1513. The growth of Safawid influence, religious and political, among the Turcoman tribes in Asia Minor threatened to undermine Ottoman control of that area. Selim then turned against Persia, crushing the forces of Shah Isma'il at Caldiran in 1514. The measures which followed the battle of Caldiran altered profoundly the conditions hitherto prevailing in the border lands between the Ottoman empire and the Mamluk sultanate of Egypt and Syria. In 1516 the Mamluks, under Qansawh al-Ghawri, marched into northern Syria, seeking to restore the situation to their own advantage. At Marj Dabiq in 1516 the Ottomans routed the Mamluk forces and overran Syria. Further battles at Gaza in 1516 and at Raydaniyya in 1517 led to the Ottoman

conquest of Egypt and to the fall of the Mamluk sultanate, a triumph which gave to the Ottoman empire large new resources and to the Ottoman sultan a vast prestige as Khadim al-Haramayn, the Servitor of the Sacred Cities of Mecca and Medina. Selim I died in 1520 at a moment when he was about to undertake a campaign against the Knights of St John at Rhodes, the great fortress which later surrendered to his son, Suleiman, in 1522.   VJP

SELIM II (1524–74), Ottoman Sultan (*reg.* 1566–74), the major event of whose reign was a new war against Venice and Spain. Ottoman forces, invading Cyprus (under Venetian rule since 1489), besieged and took Nicosia in 1570 and Famagusta in 1571. Venice, meanwhile, entered into an alliance with Spain against the Ottomans. At Lepanto in Oct. 1571 a Christian armada won a great battle which resulted in the almost complete destruction of the Ottoman fleet. Lepanto, though hailed throughout Europe as a most glorious triumph against the Infidel, was destined to be a hollow success. The Ottomans, during the winter of 1571–2, undertook a vast deployment of their resources and built a new fleet as powerful as the one lost at Lepanto. At the same time discord was rife among the Christians. Venice desired to preserve as much as possible of her old imperium in the Levant; Spain was preoccupied with the affairs of the western Mediterranean. The Christian allies failed, under these circumstances, to exploit the opportunities which Lepanto had offered to them. In 1573 Venice, finding the war fruitless and onerous, sought peace and yielded Cyprus to the Ottomans. Spain continued the conflict in North Africa, and in 1573 her forces took control of Tunis. The Ottomans, however, seized the town in 1574—a success which marked the emergence of a third Muslim corsair state on the African shore (the other two being Algiers and Tripoli) and was also the last notable event in the war.

SELIM III (1761–1807), Ottoman Sultan (*reg.* 1789–1807) who came to the throne at a time when the Ottoman empire was at war (1787–92) with Austria and Russia—a conflict which ended in the peace settlements negotiated at Sistova with the Austrians in 1791 and at Jassy with the Russians in 1792. Selim III was eager to reform the Ottoman state on European lines. The complex of reforms which he strove to introduce is known as the Nizam-i Jedid. One of his main endeavours was to modernize the armed forces of the Ottoman empire and, above all, to create new regiments recruited, trained, and equipped in accordance with the methods current in Europe. Through his reform programme, he aroused much opposition amongst the conservative elements around the throne, eg, amongst the Janissaries and the 'ulama. A wave of reaction led to the deposition of Sultan Selim in 1807 and to the accession of Mustafa IV as the representative of the reaction. The powerful a'yan of the Danube, led by Bayrakdar Mustafa Pasha, carried out in 1808 a counter-offensive which dethroned Mustafa IV, but not in time to save Selim III, who was executed before the a'yan could liberate him from confinement.

SELINUS, ancient Greek city-state in south-west Sicily, 11 kms south-east of Castelvetrano, founded from Gela (c. 628 BC). In the 6th and 5th cents the Selinuntines, who derived great prosperity from agriculture and apparently enjoyed the friendship of Carthage, with which they traded, built a series of Doric temples, of which impressive ruins survive. Their pressure induced their northern neighbour, Segesta, to call in the unsuccessful Athenian expedition of 415–413, but they themselves succumbed to Carthaginian invasion in 409. The city, after being temporarily recovered by Dionysius I (368), reverted to the Carthaginians, who destroyed it in the First Punic War, transferring its inhabitants to Lilybaeum (250).

SELJUK. Islam had made progress in the steppe lands of Central Asia during the time of the Samanid amirs who ruled

(AD 874–999/1004) over Khurasan and Transoxania. Pressure from the east began to set in motion the Turkish tribes known as the Oghuz. The disintegration of the Samanid state allowed these Turks (now Muslim) to penetrate across the Amu Darya (Oxus) into Khurasan. This advance was to bring them into conflict with the Ghaznawid sultan, Mas'ud, who suffered a decisive reverse in battle against them at Dandanqan in 1040. There was, along the north-eastern frontier of the Muslim empire, a power vacuum which the Turks alone could fill. Among them the Seljuk house (not of royal descent and endowed therefore with no claim to the title of khan) had risen to prominence as condottiere soldiers, recruiting Turkish troops to serve the Ghaznawids in their numerous campaigns, eg, against India. The term Seljuk, in relation to the Turks, has thus no ethnic meaning (cf. the designation 'Oghuz'); it is of dynastic significance only.

Advancing across Persia into Iraq, the Seljuk Turks subdued the eastern lands of the Muslim empire to their own control, entering Baghdad in 1055. The Seljuk sultanate so established was at the summit of its power during the reigns of Alp Arslan (reg. 1063–72) and Malik Shah (reg. 1072–92). In general the Seljuks took over the bureaucratic and administrative system elaborated in the earlier centuries of Muslim rule, leaving the conduct of affairs in the hands of great dignitaries like the famous vizier of Malik Shah, ie, Nizam al-Mulk (d. 1092).

The Seljuk sultanate was to last for about 100 years—until the death of Sanjar in 1157. Of the factors which contributed to its decline two are of particular importance. It was the tradition of the Turkish tribes to regard power as inherent not in one man alone, but in the whole of the royal house. There existed, under the 'Great' Seljuk sultans, a number of subordinate Seljuk regimes, eg, of Kirman, Syria, Asia Minor, and Iraq. Dynastic discord between and within these states and also the ambitions of the atabegs (the officers appointed to act as guardian and tutor of the young Seljuk princes) did much, after the death of Malik Shah, to weaken the edifice of Seljuk rule. A further source of trouble was the tension existing between the nomadic Turks and the settled populations. It was incumbent on the Seljuks to maintain order in the territories subject to them and thus to curb the indiscipline of the nomads. The effect to achieve this aim often led to hostilities with the Turkish tribes, a conflict which was partly responsible for the disintegration of the Seljuk empire.　　　　　　　　　　　　　　　　　　　　VJP

SELJUKS OF RUM. After the decisive battle of Manzikert (1071) the Seljuk Turks overran most of Asia Minor. The Byzantines, under Alexios I Komnenos, began to force back the Turks eastward, a *riconquista* which came to an end when in 1176 the Seljuks, under Kilij Arslan II (reg. 1155–1192), routed the forces of the Emperor Manuel at the battle of Myriokephalon. The years of the Byzantine counter-offensive witnessed also a prolonged conflict between the Seljuks and a rival line of Turkish begs, the Danishmends, for control of central and eastern Asia Minor. This confrontation was resolved in favour of the Seljuks during the reign of Kilij Arslan II. The repulse of the Byzantines and the absorption of the Danishmend territories led to the emergence of a powerful Seljuk sultanate of Rum, with its centre at Konya. This state attained its apogee in the time of Sultan 'Ala al-Din Kaykobad I (reg. 1220–37), a period of great splendour and prosperity. At the battle of Kösedagh (1243) the Mongols inflicted a severe defeat on the Seljuks of Rum. The sultanate fell into an increasing dependence on the Mongol Il-Khans of Persia. Although deprived, above all after 1277, of effective power, Seljuk princes continued to reign at Konya until 1308.

SELLASIA, BATTLE OF (222 BC), decisive victory near Sparta of Antigonus III Doson of Macedonia over Cleomenes III of Sparta which re-established Macedonian power in Peloponnese.

SELOUS, FREDERICK COURTNEY (1851–1917). South African trader, who emigrated from London (1871), traded north of the Limpopo, and led the pioneer column of white settlers into Rhodesia (1890).

SELVES, JUSTIN GERMAIN CASIMIR DE (1848–1934), French politician and foreign minister during the Agadir crisis (1911), whose diplomatic inexperience was revealed in his suggestion that French or British ships should draw up alongside the German gunboat *Panther*. Both cabinets refused to implement his proposal, but his exaggeration of German demands possibly contributed to British willingness to back France.

SELWYN, GEORGE AUGUSTUS (1809–78), English cleric who became New Zealand's first Anglican primate and was consecrated bishop of the newly-formed diocese of NZ in 1841. He arrived in the colony at a difficult stage in Church development: Anglican missionaries had long worked independently among Maoris; struggling European colonists lacked proper pastoral care. The situation called forth all his great administrative abilities and physical resources. In protracted journeys (1842–3), he visited all parts of settled NZ by sea and land. Much of the Pacific lay in his diocese, and he made four cruises of Melanesia (1847–51). He was a strong defender of Maori rights, and had great influence in native policy. Though Maori–European reconciliation was his aim, he ultimately confessed defeat on this issue. Returning to England, he was enthroned as Bp of Lichfield in 1868.

SEMAKOKIRO (d. *c.* 1814), King (*kabaka*) of Buganda in Uganda during the early years of the 19th cent., who encouraged long-distance trade with the East Coast, especially trade in imported cotton goods.

SEMAUN (1899–), Indonesian politician, who was responsible for developing communist influence within the Sarekat Islam movement. He was chairman of the Indonesian Communist Party (1920–3), pursuing a relatively moderate and nationalist line until 1923, when he was exiled.

SEME, PIXLEY KA ISAKA (1880–1928), African lawyer, politician, and journalist, who was one of the founders of the South African National Congress in 1912, and of the newspaper *Abantu-Bathno*. He was legal adviser to the Swazi royal family and was closely connected with Swaziland's opposition to incorporation into South Africa.

SEMINOLE WARS (1816–18, 1835–42) in the US, struggles between Seminole Indians and US troops in FL and southern GA and AL. Most Seminole Indians lived in Spanish FL, where their numbers were augmented by Negroes fleeing from the US and living with the Seminoles both as slaves and freemen. Pressure from the state of GA persuaded the US to send Col. D. L. Clinch into FL, to attack the Seminole and their black allies and return runaway slaves to their owners (July 1816). Clinch, joined by about 200 Creeks under William McIntosh, attacked Fort Apalachicola, where about 330 Indians and blacks had taken refuge. The fort was blown up (26 July) and 270 of them were killed, the rest being taken captive. Reprisals from the Indians and blacks along the GA border followed. A small army under Gen. Andrew Jackson was given instructions to pursue those who were hostile across the FL border. Jackson moved into FL (April 1818), burnt a number of towns and captured a few slaves, bringing eastern FL under US control and thus ending the first Seminole War (May 1818).

The Adams-Onis Treaty (22 Feb. 1819) gave ownership of FL to the US, bringing the Seminole Indians for the first time under US jurisdiction. The question of runaway slaves finding haven among the Seminoles continued to irritate whites in the vicinity and led to the second Seminole War. According to the treaty of Payne's Landing (9 May 1832), the Seminoles were to be removed to the Indian

Territory, but, under the leadership of Osceola, they killed Wiley Thompson, the Seminole agent, and four other whites (28 Dec. 1835). This incident started a war which lasted for seven years. A few hundred Indian and black warriors fighting from the cover of swamps and everglades held off regiments of US regulars, volunteers, and friendly Indians. Bloodhounds were used to track the elusive enemy and a flag of truce was violated to capture Osceola (3 Dec. 1837). After the death of about 1500 soldiers and the expenditure of between $30 million and $50 million the US ceased formal military operations (Aug. 1842). The second Seminole War was the fiercest of all the Indian Wars and its end marked the removal of the last resisting Indians from east of the Mississippi river. Only a few hundred Seminoles remained deep in the FL everglades. Many of them were removed by later US action (1856) and only a tiny remnant of the Seminole nation was left in its native home.

E. C. McReynold, *The Seminoles* (Norman, 1967).   DHP

SEMIRAMIS (*fl.* 9th cent. BC), mother of Adad-nirari III, Assyrian king (*reg.* 810–783), and his regent for five years. She may have been Babylonian and brought Babylonian culture to Assyria. In time, she acquired a legendary and improbable reputation for beauty, cruelty, and alleged achievements, such as the conquest of Egypt and of India.

SEMITIC, word coined (1781, by derivation from Shem, son of Noah) by A. L. Schlözer to describe a group of languages (now usually regarded as part of the larger Hamito-Semitic family) which includes Akkadian (Assyrian), Canaanite (Hebrew, Phoenician, etc.), Aramaic, Arabic, and Ethiopic. Subsequent attempts, *eg*, by Ernest Renan, to give this essentially linguistic term a cultural or racial significance have been unconvincing. It has, however, been persuasively argued, especially by L. Caetani, that the original Semitic speakers were nomads or semi-nomads of the Syro-Arabian desert, who expanded, peacefully or otherwise, into the Fertile Crescent from the earliest times. Recent research has caused Caetani's explanation of this movement in terms of the progressive desiccation of Arabia to be virtually abandoned and has strengthened the concept of continuous peaceful expansion at the expense of the older theory of a succession of cataclysmic invasions.

SEMPACH, BATTLE OF (1386), site of the defeat of an Austrian army by Lucerne and the Forest Cantons in which Duke Leopold III of Inner Austria was killed. It was a terrible blow to Austria and ended attempts to win back the central Swiss area by force.

SEMYONOVSKY, in Russia, guards regiment, formed in the 1690s by Peter I from the colony of foreign officers quartered at the village of Semyonovsky outside Moscow, which he frequented as a youth. Later the regiment became recruited almost exclusively from the metropolitan nobility and remained one of the supreme royal regiments until 1917.

SENA DYNASTY, rulers of ancient Bengal, India (*c.* 1097–1223 or later). They came originally from Karnataka (present Mysore) and rose to prominence during the decline of the Palas (second half of the 11th cent.), and developed into the predominant power in Bengal during the reign of Vijayasena (*reg.* 1097–1160). The last great ruler was Lakshmanasena (*reg.* 1178–1206), but in the last years of his reign important parts of the kingdom came under control of the Muslims under Bakhtyar Khalji. From then the Senas persisted for some time as a local power in south-east Bengal.

The Sena kingdom was one of the last great Hindu states in northern India. Mahayana Buddhism, patronized by the Palas, declined in favour of Saivism and Vaishnavism, which inspired great works of art and literature. Jayadeva's *Gitagovinda*, describing Radha's love for Krishna in lyrical stanzas, is among the greatest masterpieces of Sanskrit literature.

SENADO DA CÂMARA, Brazilian town council at the lowest level of colonial government. Every town and its hinterland (*termo*) was administered by a *câmara*, whose members were in part elected by the leading citizens (*homens bons*), in part hereditary, and in the 18th cent. more and more often appointed by the Crown. Voting members, whose number varied, included one or two presiding officers (*juizes ordinário*), several aldermen (*vereadores*), a procurator (*procurador*), and sometimes additional officers. The *câmaras* enacted municipal legislation, licensed businesses, administered municipal property, provided public services, fixed prices of basic commodities, and levied taxes to defray their expenses. In the 18th cent. much of their power over prices and taxes was taken from them by the Crown.

SENANAYAKE, DON STEPHEN (1884–1952), Sinhalese landowner and politician, who entered politics in Ceylon after being put in detention during the religious riots of 1915. He became a member of the legislative council (1924) and of the state council (1931), when he was elected minister of agriculture and lands. In 1936 he succeeded Sir Baron Jayatilaka as vice-president of the council and became the undisputed leader of the movement for constitutional reform, which he was largely responsible for securing. He became Ceylon's first prime minister under the Soulbury constitution (1947), and of independent Ceylon soon afterwards, an office which he held until his death. He also held the portfolios of foreign affairs and defence. He was a knowledgeable and enthusiastic promoter of better agriculture. As prime minister he helped to improve relations between the island's communities.

SENANAYAKE, DUDLEY (1911–), Sinhalese politician and prime minister of Ceylon. He was elected to the state council in 1936, and to the House of Representatives in 1947, when he was appointed minister of agriculture and lands. On the death of D. S. Senanayake, his father (1952), he was, in accordance with the latter's wish, appointed prime minister. Two years later, partly because of ill-health, he resigned. On returning to politics in 1957 he again led the United National Party, then in opposition. In the March 1963 general election his party was returned with the largest number of seats and he formed a government. But it was almost immediately defeated in the House of Representatives, and in the election which followed in July Mrs Bandaranaike's party was returned. In the next election (1966), however, the UNP obtained a majority and he again became prime minister. Deterioration in the island's economic position made his task difficult. His efforts were largely concentrated on increasing food production, and had some success. He did away with the crippling subsidy on the retail price of imported rice.

SENATE in Russia, originally a provisional institution of nine members with supreme executive functions, set up by Peter I to act in his absence on the Pruth campaign (1711) and charged with the duties of controlling the judicial system, government expenditure and revenue and with supervising the whole administration. The Senate thus replaced the old *Boyars*' Duma and later acquired responsibility over the administrative colleges established in 1718, becoming a permanent, semi-legislative body. Its work, however, was strictly supervised by the tsar's agents, and many of its functions were taken over (1727) by the supreme privy council in Catherine I's reign. Catherine II divided the Senate into six departments, and it was reorganized again by Alexander I (1802), and shorn of political authority, but it survived as an institution until 1917.

SENATE, NAPOLEONIC (1799) in France, body of 80 co-opted life members instituted under the Consulate and continued under the Empire, which was responsible for selecting those elected indirectly for membership of the two legislative bodies. Although it was potentially capable of displaying some political independence, the Senate merely acted as a vehicle for strengthening Napoleon's personal power.

SENATE, ROMAN, aristocratic council of ancient Rome, which, although only an advisory body with no constitutional powers, effectively governed until the 1st cent. BC. It was traditionally founded by Romulus and was originally a council of the heads of leading families which advised the king. In the late regal period the patricians (*patres*) contrived to monopolize membership of the Senate and the magistracies, an exclusiveness which increased after the expulsion of the kings (509 BC). When the plebeians gained admission to the magistracies during the Struggle of the Orders, they also entered the Senate, being known as *conscripti*. In the earlier republic the Senate numbered 300 and was recruited every five years by the censors. Sulla (82–81) increased the number to 600 and made the automatic recruitment of quaestors as the only means of entry. Julius Caesar (46–44) further increased the membership to 900 and it subsequently became even larger before the Emperor Augustus reduced it to 600 (29–28). Since the Senate contained magistrates and ex-magistrates and was the only public body in more or less permanent session, it acquired, especially during and after the Second Punic War (218–202), wide powers, which were undermined in the late 2nd and 1st cents BC by politicians appealing to the sovereignty of the people, but Augustus restored the dignity of the Senate, but in the Late Empire it became a largely decorative body, especially after Constantine's foundation of a Senate at Constantinople.   DCE

SENATUS CONSULTUM ULTIMUM, ancient Roman so-called 'last decree of the Senate', couched in the form of let the consuls [and, sometimes, other named magistrates] see that the state takes no harm'. It was not a declaration of martial law or an emergency suspension of the constitution, since the Senate as an advisory body had no power to act thus. At most, it gave the magistrates the moral support of the leading men in the state. It was first passed against C. Gracchus (121 BC), and employed frequently in subsequent years, for the last time in 40 BC.

SENECA THE ELDER (*c.* 55 BC–AD 38), Roman writer on rhetoric. Fragments of his works survive.

SENECA THE YOUNGER (*c.* 5 BC–AD 65), Roman politician, philosopher, and son of Seneca the Elder. After studying philosophy and rhetoric, he entered the Senate. After being exiled to Corsica for alleged adultery with the Emperor Claudius' niece, Julia Livilla (41), he was recalled in 49 and made tutor to Nero. When Nero became emperor in 54, Seneca co-operated with Burrus in the running of the empire, Nero being uninterested. After Burrus' death in 62, Seneca retired and devoted himself to writing, but was forced to commit suicide for alleged complicity in Piso's conspiracy. The great wealth he acquired in office damaged his reputation, but after his retirement Nero's government declined. A number of his literary works survived, including some Stoic essays and tragedies, the latter being influential in the European Renaissance.

SENECA INDIANS, American tribe of the Iroquois confederacy, formerly living in western NY state. They fought in the Iroquois wars against the Huron, Erie, and other tribes and supported the British against the French in the French and Indian War (1755–63). Because they were pro-British in the American War of Independence, US forces burnt their villages and crops (1779). Some of the Seneca subsequently remained in NY, others fled to Ont. The so-called Seneca of Sandusky, which incorporated remnants of all Iroquois tribes, ceded their lands in OH (1837) and moved to Indian territory, where they were given lands in OK (1902).

SENEF, BATTLE OF (1674), drawn battle near Charleroi in the Dutch War (1672–8), between a 45,000-strong army under Condé and a mixed force of 60,000 Spaniards, Flemings, and Germans under the Prince of Orange. When Orange retreated towards Le Quesnay, exposing his flank, Condé attacked the Allied vanguard, but the Dutchman took up a strong position at Senef and the two armies fought for 17 hours without a significant result. It was Condé's last battle.

SENEFRU (reg. 2620–2596 BC), Egyptian King whose raids into Nubia and Libya, and annexation of Sinai brought great wealth to the country. He built himself at least two, and possibly three, pyramids, at Meidum and Dahshur.

SENEGAL (197,722 sq. kms) in West Africa, formerly a province of French West Africa. The population (1970) of 3,600,000 includes Wolof, Fulbe, and Serer groups. After independence in 1960 a new constitution (1963) established a presidential system of government.

SENEGAMBIA, West Africa, for long the name given by Europeans to the coastland and river estuaries enclosing the area between the south bank of the Gambia river and the north bank of the Senegal river. In 1970 this area comprised the countries of Senegal and Gambia. European contact began here with Portuguese exploring and trading voyages in the middle of the 15th cent. and after; later, the area was of trading and exploring interest to the French, Dutch, and British. Here they found useful commercial partners with the kings and leading men of a large range of coastal states, ranging from those of the Wolof in the north to those of the Mandinka and other small states around the course of the Gambia. During a brief period of British supremacy, the area was administratively united as the province of Senegambia (1765–83), an early experiment in Africa in British Crown colony government; its administrative centre was at St Louis, Senegal.

SENGHOR, LEOPOLD SEDAR (1906–), Senegalese writer, politician, and president of Senegal, who was a founder of the influential Presence Africaine (1947), and devoted most of his life to the political development of Senegal. He was elected (1945) to the constituent assembly of the Fourth French Republic as a deputy for Senegal and joined the French Socialist Party (SFIO), but held aloof from the more radical Rassemblement Démocratique Africain. He was re-elected in 1946, and formed a new party, the Bloc Démocratique Sénégalais, in 1948, as a breakaway from the SFIO; this evolved in various ways and in 1958 fused with other parties. Senghor became president of an independent Senegal in 1960. With President Houphouet-Boigny of the Ivory Coast, he conceived the future in terms of close Franco-African relations and in the 1960s enjoyed the homage of successive French governments.

SENGOKU PERIOD, century of Japanese history (*c.* 1467–1590) when central authority disappeared and the whole country was almost constantly ravaged by war. Eventually the most outstanding of the new *daimyōs*, Oda Nobunaga, Takeda, Hōjō, and Mōri, together with some older ones, such as Uesugi and Shimazu, were able to challenge the national leadership, often making use of firearms of European type and new tactics. Nobunaga was the most successful of these challengers and his re-establishment of central authority was completed by his general, Hideyoshi, and his ally, Ieyasu. Their achievement brought peace, but it also ended an era of great social mobility.

SENI PRAMOJ (1905–), Thai lawyer, diplomat, politician, and leader of the opposition Democrat Party. As ambassador to the US during the Second World War he refused to present Thailand's declaration of war, and helped to form the Free Thai underground movement. After serving as prime minister (1945–6) he returned to private law practice. In 1968 he assumed the leadership of the Democratic Party, on Khuang Aphaiwong's death, and in 1969 was elected to the new parliament.

SENIOR, NASSAU WILLIAM (1790–1864), British economist, lawyer, and journalist, who was professor of political economy at Oxford (1825–30, 1847–52). He was a member of the poor law commission (1833) and wrote its report. His *Outline of the Science of Political Economy* (1836) showed him to be one of the first British economists to see the value of a commodity as deriving not from the work involved in producing it, as Adam Smith and Ricardo maintained, but from subjective judgement of its utility. He did not share the unlimited faith of his predecessors in automatic adjustments of the market. In his lectures, his essays on *The Poor Law* (1834) and *The Factory Act* (1837), and his contributions to the *Edinburgh Review* he accepted the necessity of state intervention, but was concerned that this should not hinder the working of economic forces.

SENNACHERIB (*reg.* 704–681 BC), Assyrian King, who spent most of his reign suppressing revolts in various parts of his empire. A revolt in Palestine and Phoenicia, encouraged by Egypt, was quelled in 701. Repeated rebellions in Babylonia were finally ended in 689, when Babylon was taken and sacked. Elam, which had encouraged the Babylonian troubles, was attacked twice, but with only partial success. Sennacherib's most lasting memorials were his buildings and other public works, particularly the city of Nineveh, which he enlarged and rebuilt.

SENNETT, MACK (1884–1960), Canadian-born US film producer and director, whose Keystone comedies (1912–16) transformed burlesque slapstick into cinematographic art. Using camera tricks such as double exposure and fast motion, he created sequences for his famous bathing beauties and Keystone Kops in which the absurd moved into fantasy, and helped to introduce comedians such as Charlie Chaplin, Buster Keaton, and W. C. Fields.

SENTINUM, BATTLE OF (295 BC), decisive victory during the Third Samnite War of the Romans under Fabius Rullianus and Decimus Mus over a coalition of Samnites and invading Gauls.

SEPARATE ELECTORATES, in India, were widely used in 20th-cent. Indian constitutions as a system of ensuring the representation of a specified social, religious, or ethnic group by the provision of constituencies for which only members of that group can be electors and stand as candidates. They are to be distinguished from reserved seats, for which only a specified candidate can be returned but for which the whole electorate votes. The first general application of the system was in the separate electorates which were provided for the Muslims in both the imperial and provincial legislatures under the Morley–Minto reforms (1909). The Congress was opposed to the system at that time, but its acceptance of the scheme in the Lucknow pact (1916) helped to reinforce it, and as a result Muslims were given an increased proportion of seats under the Montagu–Chelmsford reforms (1919). In the 1919 reforms, moreover, other communities put forward claims for similar privileges. Only the Sikhs in the Punjab were given separate electorates, but 'non-Brahmans' in Madras and Bombay were given sizeable blocs of reserved seats within the 'general' (*ie*, Hindu) constituencies and smaller groups such as Indian Christians, Anglo-Indians (Eurasians), and Scheduled Castes were given nominated representatives. Under the 1935 act, Anglo-Indians, Indian Christians, and even Europeans were given separate electorates. The Scheduled Castes, led by B. R. Ambedkar, were also given separate electorates in the Communal Award (Aug. 1932), but this was subsequently changed to reserved seats by the Poona pact (Sept. 1932). In the constitution of independent India, separate electorates were discontinued, although some reserved seats were retained for Scheduled castes and tribes.   PDR

SEPARATION OF CHURCH AND STATE (1905) in France, disestablishment of the Roman Catholic Church. The anti-clerical opposition to the privileged position conferred by the Concordat (1801) on the Church was given an additional fillip by the vigour of some Catholics in the anti-Dreyfusard cause. There was considerable controversy between Church and state over the position of religious orders (1901), the appointment of bishops, and a state visit to the King of Italy (1904), and Combès introduced a bill to end state support and control of the Church, giving control not to the hierarchy but to associations of interested Catholics. This was passed (1905) against intense opposition which forced the state to drop some of the provisions of the act when it became law. Eventually the Church found some advantage in being free of state interference.

SEPARATION OF POWERS, constitutional doctrine, especially favoured in the 18th cent., which aimed at securing the liberty of the subject. The legislative, executive, and judicial organs of government were distinguished, and suggestions for their separation included rules that the same person should not hold power in more than one organ, or that one organ should not control or interfere with the functions of another, or that one organ should not exercise the functions of another.

The doctrine was first notably expressed by Montesquieu in *Esprit des Lois* (1748), where he described and commented on the British constitution. Though he used 'executive' to denote only the power to execute matters of war and diplomacy, he referred to the legislative, executive, and judicial powers of government and stressed the danger of arbitrary rule where laws are enforced and enacted by the same body, especially if the executive consists of one man who is not responsible to the judicature or a representative assembly. Montesquieu noted the triumph as a legislative power of the English parliament by the Bill of Rights (1689), while the monarch maintained executive power and the judiciary its independence. In reality, the British constitution worked by a system of checks and balances rather than by separation of powers. The Act of Settlement (1701) had excluded ministers from the Commons, but this provision was repealed (1705), and the growth of the cabinet system by which the monarch governed through ministers responsible to parliament dealt a blow to the attainment of separation of powers in Britain. Though the personal influence over parliament through patronage which George III and other sovereigns enjoyed faded with the passing of economic reform and the growth of democracy after the 1832 Reform Act, separation of powers in Britain came to mean only the maintenance of an independent judiciary, and Bagehot saw the constitution as dominated by the executive (1867).

The Declaration of the Rights of Man (1789) in France and the constitution of the United States (1789) were more clearly influenced by the doctrine. Under the latter a cabinet of heads of government departments is responsible to the president alone and not to Congress, neither the president nor any member of the cabinet can be a member of Congress, and the president can veto, but not enforce acceptance in Congress of, legislation. The judiciary is independent, though it has the power to declare laws invalid if they infringe the constitution.   VEC

SEPEIA, BATTLE OF (*c.* 494 BC), in the eastern Peloponnese, near Argos, ended in defeat by the Spartans, under Cleomenes I, of the Argives, who lost 6000 dead and were effectively neutralized for the Persian invasions of 490 and 480–479.

SEPTEMBER THIRTIETH MOVEMENT (*Gestapu*), Indonesian military clique which, on 1 Oct. 1965, under the leadership of Lieut.-Col. Untung, kidnapped and killed members of the Army general staff, declaring that they had anticipated a plot to overthrow President Sukarno; the president, however, failed to endorse this action. Gen. Suharto used the occasion to take control of the military situation and then to seize political power. Army leaders accused the Indonesian

Communist Party of sponsoring Untung's move, which was used to justify the party's violent elimination. Sukarno remained in office until March 1966, but the Oct. coup marked his real fall from power.

SEPTENNIAL ACT (1716), in Britain, legislative measure replacing the Triennial Act (1694) and enabling parliaments to sit for seven years. Opponents claimed it was unconstitutional to extend an existing parliament, but for the Whigs it was a matter of expediency: to reduce riots which accompanied elections at a time of Jacobite disturbances.

SEPTIMIUS SEVERUS, L. (146–211), Roman Emperor (*reg.* 193–211), who was the founder and outstanding member of the Severan dynasty. Proclaimed by the army when governor of Pannonia upon Pertinax' death at Rome, he overcame his rivals in a series of civil wars—Didius Julianus at Rome (193), Pescennius Niger in the east (194), and Clodius Albinus, whom he had for a time recognized as Caesar, in Gaul (196). He married the Syrian Julia Domna and asserted the continuity with the preceding Antonine dynasty by promoting to the rank of Augustus his sons, Domna, Caracalla (in 198), and Geta (209). Although celebrating Secular Games at Rome in 204, he spent little time there, conducting campaigns in the east (195–6, 197–8), where he annexed the new province of Mesopotamia, travelling in Egypt and the Balkans (199–202) and finally campaigning in Britain (208–11). African by birth, he visited his native city of Leptis Magna in 203, and embellished it with grandiose new buildings. Severus did not enjoy good relations with the Senate, and was regarded as a harsh and vindictive emperor, while his stationing of legionary troops near Rome also caused resentment; but by his administrative and military measures, and by careful economy, he secured stability for the empire after a time of extravagance and political uncertainty. He died at York and was succeeded jointly by his sons.

SEPTUAGINT, most influential of the Greek versions of the Hebrew Old Testament and the one usually quoted by New Testament writers. Jewish tradition ascribed it to Ptolemy Philadelphus (285–246 BC), but internal evidence indicates that it was the work of several Alexandrinian Jewish translators over a long period.

SEPULVEDA, JUAN GINES DE (1490–1573), Spanish theologian, Aristotelian scholar, and historiographer royal (from 1536), who was involved in a renowned, but inconclusive, debate with Bartholome de Las Casas in Valladolid (1550) over the legality of the Spaniards' treatment of the American Indians. He believed that conquest should precede conversion but the more humanitarian views of Las Casas gradually won favour with the Crown.

SEQUANI, Gallic tribe in Roman times, who inhabited modern Franch-Comté and part of Burgundy; their capital was at Vesontio (mod. Besançon). Having invited Ariovistus to help them against the Aedui (71 BC), they lost a third of their territory to him and appealed to Julius Caesar (58), who ended Ariovistus' encroachments. But when he compelled the Sequani to give up captured Aeduan territory, they joined Vercingetorix' rising (52). Augustus enrolled them in the province of Gallia Belgica, which Diocletian enlarged by adding Helvetia and part of Germania Superior, calling it Provincia Maxima Sequanorum.

SEQUIER FAMILY in France, who held official positions in the 16th and 17th cents. Founded by a Parisian businessman in the early part of the 16th cent., the family entered the *parlement* of Paris in the person of a grandson Pierre I (1504–1580), who became a baron and a royal councillor, while other members of the family held further offices, particularly under Henry IV. The most distinguished member of the family was Pierre I's grandson Pierre V (1588–1672) who

began his career as a *conseiller au parlement* (1612), and then passed into royal service as a *maître des requêtes* (1618) and *intendant* (1621). He inherited a presidency in the *parlement* (1624) which began the accumulation of a large fortune which grew while he became keeper of the seals (1633) and finally chancellor (1635) and duke (1640). He served Richelieu and Mazarin loyally, playing a large part in maintaining public order, and died an immensely wealthy man, though also a cultivated and devout one. He left only daughters who married into the old nobility, but the family was continued, though on a less notable level, by other branches such as that of St Brisson.

SEQUOYA (Sequoyah) (*c.* 1770–1843), American Indian scholar, who developed an alphabet of 85 characters (1809–1821) for writing the Cherokee language. He taught it to Cherokees in AR (1821), in OK (1828), and in Mexico. The Cherokee council approved the alphabet (1821) and newspapers and books were printed in it.

SEQUOYA LEAGUE, organization founded (1902) in CA by Charles Lummis. Its object was to improve the lot of American Indian tribes through its own programmes and by bringing pressure to bear on US government departments and on Congress.

SERAMPORE, town in West Bengal on the right bank of the Hugli river, opposite Barrackpore. Originally a Danish settlement, it was purchased by the East India Co. in 1845. It was the scene of the labours of the Baptist missionaries Carey, Marshman, and Ward.

SERAPIS (or SARAPIS), ancient Egyptian god, whose cult originated at Memphis and was used by Ptolemy I in an attempt to link Egyptian and Greek religion. Though Egyptians reverted to the old cult, the new one achieved wide influence among Greeks, though it was later overshadowed by that of Isis.

SERBO–BULGARIAN WAR (1885). Serbia had failed to gain compensation for Bulgarian gains in the Balkan crisis of the 1880s. She therefore planned an ill-conceived and unsuccessful attack which provoked an invasion of Serbian territory. This was only halted by Austrian diplomatic intervention. The war confirmed Serbia's dependence on Austria, but, since Russia had also disapproved of Bulgaria's access of territory, Bulgaria's victory proclaimed her independence of Russia, temporarily swinging the balance of power in the Balkans in Austria's favour.

SERFDOM in Europe. Over the greater part of western Europe from the 8th to the 14th cents a servile peasantry attached to the estates of landlords, who were regarded as the owners and masters of its members, was one of the main classes of society. Its origins were diverse. Some peasants were descendants of slaves who had belonged to Roman owners, or were men who had been captured in wars. Others were landless or impoverished freemen seeking the protection of lords. Servile peasantry in many cases included landholders, formerly free, who had been forced into a condition of dependence by conquest or other means of compulsion.

The economic purpose of serfdom was to assure landlords of a body of dependent labourers to cultivate their estates, while in return the lords tolerated the serfs' possession of sufficient land holdings and other goods to permit the survival of them and their families. In much of France, the Netherlands, western Germany, and Italy, serfdom began to decline in the 12th cent. and had largely disappeared by the end of the 13th cent. Landlords were giving up direct exploitation of their estates and ceased to need servile labour. The widespread colonization of new lands encouraged the mass flight of serfs, and to avoid this landlords had often to emancipate them voluntarily. In England, where the landlords enjoyed a specially effective protection of the common law created by King Henry II and his sons, serfdom, under the special name of villeinage, persisted more tenaciously until the late 14th cent. and remnants of it lingered on as late as the 17th cent. In eastern Germany and the Slavonic lands further to the east, populations were too small to allow landlords to create a class of serfs before the 15th cent. Thereafter a special type of particularly oppressive serfdom evolved in these lands, and endured until the 19th cent.   EBF

SEROV, IVAN ALEKSANDROVICH (1905–), Russian official responsible for some of the harshest actions of the Soviet security agencies at the time of the Second World War. He joined the Communist Party in 1926 and received military training, then transferred (1939) to security work. He was appointed commissar for internal affairs in the Ukraine, where, while Khrushchev was first secretary of the Ukrainian Party, he was responsible for security operations (including deportation) in the territory newly annexed from Poland. He was then appointed first deputy commissar for state security and deputy and first deputy commissar for internal affairs of the USSR (1941). In this capacity he was responsible for the massive deportations first from the Baltic states then from those areas of eastern and southern Russia where nationalist and religious opposition to Russian communist rule might be stimulated by the German invasion (the peoples concerned were the Balkars, Chechens, Crimean Tatars, Ingushes, Kalmyks, Karachays, and Volga Germans). After the war he was deputy supreme commander of Soviet forces in Germany (1945–7) responsible for security among Soviet citizens living abroad and the armed forces. After Stalin's death he was appointed chairman of the committee of state security (1954–8). He went to Britain to prepare for the visit there of Khrushchev and Bulganin (1956) but as a result of British public protest was excluded from the visit itself. He was appointed chief of military intelligence (1958) but was removed from this post as a result of the Penkovksy case (1963).

SERRA, JUNIPERO (1713–84), Spanish-born American pioneer and missionary, who worked among Indians in Mexico City. In 1769 Serra and five Franciscans accompanied a military expedition under Portola and founded a mission at San Diego, the first of a chain of 21 founded by Serra on the Californian coast between San Diego and San Francisco. Under his leadership substantial progress was made in livestock breeding, harvesting, and workshop construction.

SERRANO, FRANCISCO, Duke de la Torre (1810–85), Spanish soldier and politician of progressive sympathies. He fought against the Carlists (1833–9) and helped to overthrow the regency of Queen Cristina (1840). He was minister of war under Lopez and Olozaga, captain-general of Granada (1848), became a marshal in 1856, and was captain-general of Cuba (1859–62); on his return to Spain he was created Duke de la Torre. He helped O'Donnell to put down the insurrection of 22 June 1866, but was banished (1868) with other military notables of the Liberal Union. On returning from exile, he took command of an army which routed Isabella's troops at Alcolea and forced the queen herself into exile. He was appointed regent (1869) in the provisional government and first prime minister of the new monarchy (1870), but resigned (1871) because he was unable to keep his coalition government together. He was connected, though not as a principal, with the 1873 plot against the first republic, and in 1874 he was regent until the restoration of the Bourbons.

SERRANO SUÑER, RAMÓN (1901–), Spanish lawyer and politician, who became a deputy in the Cortes and rose to be head of the JAP (*Juventud de Acción Popular*), the youth movement of the CEDA. During the violence in 1936 he moved to the right and in April merged the JAP with the Falange. When the army rose in Madrid in July, he was captured and imprisoned.

In April 1937 he escaped to Salamanca, where he became the principal political adviser to Gen. Franco, his brother-in-law, for whose new state he tried to find a political formula. He rejected the existing parties and suggested instead the creation of a unified party based on the Falange. On 19 April, Franco forcibly merged the Falange and the Carlists into a new party, of which Serrano Suñer became secretary-general. Henceforth, he became the great political manager of Nationalist Spain. His first task was to 'transform an insurrection into a political enterprise'. This he sought to do by creating a new one-party state, the corporative state of Falangist Spain, which favoured landowners and businessmen and had a clerical bias.

In the first regular cabinet of Nationalist Spain he was minister of the interior. Although completely dependent on Franco, he virtually ruled the country and had vast power. In Jan. 1939 the ministries of public order and of the interior were merged under him, and in March the Court of Political Responsibilities was created, under his presidency, to try all those who had opposed the 'National Movement' since 1 Oct. 1934. He maintained his position throughout the Second World War, during which time he was sympathetic to the Germans. Thereafter, he took little part in politics and in his retirement wrote his political memoirs, *Entre Hendaya y Gibraltar*.

SERTÃO (SERTÕES), Portuguese term often translated into English as 'backlands'. It refers to empty, unexplored, uncultivated, or underdeveloped areas in the interior of Brazil, particularly to the semi-arid inland regions of the north-east.

SERTORIUS, Q. (*c.* 121–72) BC), Roman soldier, whose stand in Spain undermined the authority of the Senate after Sulla's reforms. Having served under Marius against the Teutones (102) and under Didius in Spain (98), he was quaestor (91) and fought with Marius and Cinna in their capture of Rome (87). He was praetor in 83, but fled to Spain and then to Mauretania when Sulla invaded Italy. After returning to Spain he established himself as an independent war-lord among the Lusitanians, where he was joined by many Roman fugitives. He withstood the attacks of all the Roman generals, including Pompey, sent to suppress him, but was eventually murdered by his lieutenant, Perperna, and some other officers.

SERVAN-SCHREIBER, JEAN-JACQUES (1924–), French journalist and politician, pursuing policies of radical but non-socialist reform. He worked for the daily *Le Monde* after service in the Second World War, then founded his own weekly, *L'Express* (1953). *L'Express* was the organ of the reforming prime minister Mendès-France, and Servan-Schreiber himself became one of the leading 'Mendesists' in the Radical Party. In later years *L'Express* was noted for its opposition to the Algerian War, acting as a voice of conscience for the whole French left. Under the Fifth Republic, Servan-Schreiber tried unsuccessfully to promote a coalition of the centre and non-communist left against De Gaulle. In 1969 he resigned the direction of *L'Express* to become general secretary of the Radical Party, seeking to repeat Mendès-France's attempt to reinvigorate the party. He won a striking by-election victory at Nancy (1970), using American-style tactics new to France, but lost a later by-election at Bordeaux. He wrote *The American Challenge* (1967), describing American economic penetration of Europe.

SERVANTS OF INDIA SOCIETY, founded in Poona (1905) by G. K. Gokhale and three followers. The society's aim was to unite and train a group of men who would devote themselves entirely to the political and social advancement of India. The members pledged themselves to live only on the small allowance which the society gave them and not to work for their own advancement. By 1909 the society had some 20 members and less than 30 half a century later, but this small group included men who made significant contributions to Indian development in a number of fields. Gokhale remained president until his death (1915). His successors were V. S. Srinivasa Sastri (1915–27), G. K. Deodhar (1927–1935), and Hriday Nath Kunzru (1935–). A number of other social service organizations were founded by members of the society, including the Poona *Seva Sadan*, the Allahabad *Seva Samiti*, and the *Seva Samiti* Boy Scouts Association.

SERVETUS, MICHAEL (MIGUEL SERVETO Y REVES) (1511–53), Spanish-born physician and theologian who lived mostly in Strasbourg and Vienne in Switzerland. He studied medicine at Paris University and discovered the pulmonary circulation of the blood, but is better known for his anti-trinitarian views which brought him the hostility of Catholics, Lutherans, and Calvinists alike. In 1531 he published his *De Trinitatis Erroribus*, denying the trinity, and he also wrote a bitter attack upon Calvin's *Institutes*. The fullest expression of his theology, however, appeared in his *Christianismi Restitutio* (1553), of which all but three of the 1000 copies were destroyed. Forced to flee from the Catholic Inquisition at Vienne, where he had quietly practised medicine for some years, he was arrested and tried by the authorities in Calvin's Geneva on a charge of heresy and subsequently burnt at the stake (1553).

SERVICIOS in Spain, traditional grants or subsidies voted by the Castilian Cortes in the 16th–17th cents, ostensibly as a temporary measure to meet an emergency. In 1504 Ferdinand of Aragon had asked for a regular *servicio* every three years, a demand renewed by Charles V in 1523, in whose reign the subsidy became an ordinary tax, payable by the *pecheros* or commoners, the nobility enjoying the privilege of exemption. In 1591 the *servicio* was fixed at 405,000 ducats p.a. granted every three years by the Cortes. By the 18th cent. it constituted only $2\frac{1}{2}$ per cent of the royal income of Castile and was finally abolished in 1795.

SERVIUS TULLIUS (*reg.* 578–535 BC), traditionally sixth King of Rome, whose reign marks a Latin interruption in the Etruscan domination of the Tarquins. His Servian constitution changed the basis of citizenship from birth qualification to property census, in order to meet mounting military commitments. Five classes were created, each sub-divided into centuries. From this military reform sprang the Comitia Centuriata, which evolved into a political assembly. The so-called Servian Wall is a 4th-cent. construction, but Servius may have constructed earthworks round the city. He also built the temple to Diana on the Aventine.

SESMARIA, land grant given by the Portuguese government in the 16th cent. and thereafter to encourage the colonization of Brazil. *Sesmarias* tended to be large in size and encouraged the growth of latifundia.

SESOSTRIS, Greek form of Usertsen (occasionally Senusret), the name of three kings of the XIIth dynasty in Egypt. Classical writers confused the achievements of these three rulers and associated them with only one king, whose deeds were magnified until he was regarded as the greatest king known to history.

SESTOS, ancient Greek city-state on the west shore of the Hellespont (Dardanelles), founded by Aeolians from Lesbos in the 7th cent. BC. Though small, it was in an important position, and was held at various times by Persia, Athens, and Sparta. In 338 it fell to Macedon.

SETI I (*reg. c.* 1309–1291 BC), Egyptian King of the XIXth dynasty, who waged a campaign against the Hittites which resulted in a peace treaty giving Egypt control of Palestine and part of Syria. Seti built fine temples at Abydos and Kurna and the Hypo-style Hall at Karnak.

SETON, ELIZABETH ANN BAYLEY (1774–1821), US religious, known as Mother Seton, founder of the American Sisters of Charity, who pioneered charitable work in New York, married a merchant there, and after his death was converted to Roman Catholicism (1805). She moved to MD, where she was influenced by Bp John Carroll, and opened a free parochial school for girls in Baltimore (1808); in 1809 she formed a community called the Sisters of St Joseph. This, known after 1812 as the Sisters of Charity of St Joseph, was the first native American religious order. She was beatified in 1963.

SETON, ERNEST THOMPSON (1860–1946), Canadian writer, artist, and naturalist, whose interest in youth work led him to found the Woodcraft League (1902). He was chief of the Boy Scouts of America (1910–15), and was a prolific writer of books on wild-life and woodcraft, illustrated by himself.

SETTHATHIRAT (1533–71), King of Chiengmai (*reg.* 1545–1549), and King of Laos (*reg.* 1548–71). He was drawn into warfare between Siam and Burma, and despite numerous setbacks withstood a Burmese attack on his new Laotian capital at Vientiane (1565). He never surrendered his independence or his dream of Laotian unity.

SETTLEMENT, ACT OF (IRELAND) (1652), in England, legislative measure which attempted to settle the land question at the end of the Irish Rebellion to the satisfaction of the English conquerors. It laid down what classes of landowners should forfeit their estates, and its penalties extended to virtually the whole population. Four classes of person were excepted from pardon for life and estate: (*a*) all who had taken part in the rebellion before the establishment of the Confederacy; (*b*) all Catholic ecclesiastics who had aided the rebellion; (*c*) all who had been responsible for killing civilians, or had killed English soldiers; (*d*) all those still in arms who had failed to submit within 28 days. One hundred and four persons were excepted from pardon by name, *eg*, Ormonde. All other persons, except those who had helped the English, were to suffer partial forfeiture of their estates according to their degree of delinquency. Those who had surrendered on terms were to have the benefit of their articles of surrender.

The act did not provide machinery to carry out the forfeitures, and the execution of the act was left to Charles Fleetwood and the English parliamentary commissioners. After the act was published little was done, as further legislation was felt to be needed. The scheme known as 'transplantation' to Connaught was finally adopted, whereby delinquents were to receive lands of equivalent value to the lands they were entitled to retain by the Act of Settlement.

SETTLEMENT, ACT OF (IRELAND) (1662), in England, legislative attempt to settle the Irish land question at the Restoration. Piecemeal restoration of land had been attempted immediately after Charles II's return, and commissioners had been established (Nov. 1660), but statutory authority was lacking. The Irish parliament (1661) was dominated by ex-Cromwellians and had little sympathy for any scheme which would mean the loss of their lands. In April 1662 the English council decided on a bill, which was accepted by the Irish parliament in May. It gave statutory authority to the royal commissioners, who formed a court of claims to administer its terms. All land confiscated since 23 Oct. 1641 was vested in the Crown as a trustee for (*a*) confirmation to the Adventurers and soldiers of land held by them on 7 May 1659; (*b*) payment of arrears due to officers who had served with Ormonde before 5 June 1649; (*c*) restoration of various classes of dispossessed landowners. Cromwellian settlers of lands which were restored to others were to be compensated with lands of equal value. Three types of person were entitled to restoration: (1) those who had served Charles abroad (ensign men); (2) those who had accepted and kept the terms of the peace of 1646 or 1649 (article men); (3) those who had been innocent of rebellion (innocents).

The court of claims was overwhelmed with claims from the innocents, and there was not enough land to go round. The rivalry between Cromwellians and 'innocents' eventually led to Blood's conspiracy to overthrow the government (May 1663), which failed. The Act of Settlement had to be modified by the Act of Explanation which confiscated one-third of the Adventurers' and soldiers' land, but there was still insufficient to meet all claims.

SETTLEMENT, THE ACT OF (1701), in England, legislative measure which was an integral part of the Revolution Settlement. In accordance with the Bill of Rights (1689), when Queen Mary died on 7 Jan. 1695 King William continued to rule as sole monarch. As there were no children of their marriage, he would be succeeded upon his death by Princess (later Queen) Anne. However, after Anne the succession was to have passed to any surviving heir of hers, but her only surviving son, William, Duke of Gloucester, died on 30 June 1700, very shortly after his eleventh birthday. This was referred to by William in his speech from the throne opening his fifth parliament in January 1701. A bill was introduced and this Act of Settlement received the royal assent on 23 June 1701 as an Act for the Further Limitation of the Crown and Better Securing the Rights and Liberties of the Subject. It therefore amplified the Bill of Rights. Three of the points covered had been proposed in 1689, including the Hanoverian Succession. After reaffirming that no Roman Catholic was eligible to rule and that subjects of a ruler who became a Roman Catholic were absolved from their allegiance, the act named the Electress Sophia of Hanover (who was the grand-daughter of James I) and her heirs as next in line of succession after Anne. She or they were to take the prescribed coronation oath and recite and sign the declaration against transubstantiation, and additionally join in communion with the Church of England. If England were to be ruled by a foreigner, she was not automatically to become involved in a war on behalf of that person's native country. In future a monarch was not to go outside the British Isles without the consent of parliament. Matters concerning the government of England appropriate to discussion in the privy council were to be transacted there and resolutions taken were to be signed by those in favour. No foreigner was to be eligible to be a privy councillor or a member of parliament or to enjoy an office of trust under the Crown or to receive any grant of land from the Crown. No person holding an office of profit or receiving a royal pension was to be eligible to be a member of parliament. Judges were to hold office during good behaviour or *quandiu se bene gesserint*. No royal pardon was to be sufficient to halt proceedings under an impeachment. Not all of these reforms were put into effect, and those concerning the travelling of the monarch and transactions in the privy council were repealed in 1716.   BM

SETTLEMENT LAWS in England, were, like other developments in the English poor law, parliamentary measures that legalized an existing situation hitherto unrecognized in law. In 1662 an act was passed to prevent paupers of parishes which failed to give them relief from moving into parishes that were more observant of the Elizabethan poor law. Incomers who seemed likely to need relief could be sent back to the parishes from which they came. Though this act removed an injustice in some parishes, it created a serious threat to the mobility of labour. To meet this problem a legal structure, based on further enactments and case law, was gradually built up which made possible a system of conditional movement, supported by certificates from the parish of legal settlement, and extending also to the children of a migrant. This meant that legal settlement might be a very artificial concept, and removal could involve considerable hardship. In 1795 parishes were forbidden to refuse incomers unless they had already been in receipt of poor relief, but since this measure coincided with the start of the 'speenhamland' system of supplementing wages out of poor relief in agricultural areas, it probably had little effect.

SEVASTOPOL, SIEGE OF (Oct. 1854–Sept. 1855), during the Crimean War. The delay of the British and French in taking advantage of their success in the battle of the Alma enabled the Russian engineer, Gen. Todleben, to fortify the town, which withstood the Allies for almost a year.

SEVEN DAYS, BATTLES OF THE (26 June–2 July 1862), series of engagements which concluded the Peninsular campaign of the American Civil War. Gen. Lee's brilliantly conceived but poorly executed strategy forced the Union army, under Gen. McClellan, to abandon its advance on Richmond.

SEVEN OAKS, BATTLE OF (19 June 1816), engagement, at Seven Oaks, Canada, between a raiding party of French half-breeds and Indians organized by the North-West Co. and Robert Semple, governor of Assiniboia. The defeat of Semple and his men forced the abandonment of the Red river settlement.

SEVEN YEARS WAR (1756–63), general European conflict which grew out of the undeclared world-wide struggle between France and Britain that began in North America in 1754, and the 16-year-old Austro-Prussian struggle for control of Silesia.

The background to the war is to be found in the 'Diplomatic Revolution' which aligned Austria, France, Russia, Sweden, and Saxony against Prussia, Britain, and Portugal. The immediate cause, however, was Frederick II's invasion of Saxony (29 Aug. 1756), which he considered the best means of defence against an imminent Austro-Russo-Saxon attack. Frederick thus made Prussia the focal point of a European war which was characterized by wide fluctuations of fortune and numerous major battles.

After laying siege to the Saxon army under the Elector Augustus III, Frederick failed to take Prague (May–June 1757) and was defeated by the Austrians at Kollin (18 June 1757). Meanwhile, Britain was unable to offer help because of the French defeat of Cumberland's Army of Observation at Hastenbeck (26 July 1757) and its disbandment by the Convention of Kloster-Seven (8 Sept. 1757). A Russian army invaded East Prussia and defeated the Prussians at Gross-Jägersdorf (30 Aug. 1757), while the Swedes invaded Pomerania (Sept. 1757) and the Austrians reached Berlin (16 Oct. 1757). Prussia's desperate position was retrieved by Frederick's brilliant victories over the Franco-Imperial alliance at Rossbach (5 Nov. 1757) and Leuthen (Dec. 1757), and from April 1758 Frederick was further helped by the presence of an Anglo-German army on his western flank, commanded by the able Prince of Brunswick. However, Prussia was still hard-pressed, for Frederick's armies had been seriously depleted by the bitter fighting of 1757. Yet once again he moved against the Austrians. He cleared Silesia by taking Schweidnitz (16 April 1758), but was forced to raise the siege of Olmütz after running short of supplies (July 1758). Frederick's army was diverted to meet the Russian advance under Fermor, whose army he defeated in a bitter battle at Zorndorf (Aug. 1758). But he found himself faced with a Swedish invasion of Prussian Pomerania and was defeated by the Austrians at Höchkirch (10 Oct. 1758).

Meanwhile, in the west, Brunswick drove the French from Westphalia, Hanover, Brunswick, and Hesse and defeated them at Crefeld (23 June 1758). The French, under Soubise, counter-attacked at Cassel and Sönderhausen (23 July 1758), but were routed at Minden (1 Aug. 1758). In 1759 Choiseul planned a double invasion of Britain by 40,000 Frenchmen encamped in Flanders and Brittany, but British naval superiority triumphed at Lagos (19 Aug. 1759) and Quiberon Bay (Nov. 1759).

In the same year, Frederick's financial and military position deteriorated further, and Prussia's total destruction appeared imminent as the Russians took revenge on him at the battle of Künersdorf (13 Aug. 1759). Saltykov, however, failed to follow up this victory by reinforcing the Austrian forces, who took Leipzig, Torgau, and Dresden and defeated the Prussians at Naxen in the autumn of 1759. Throughout 1760 Frederick managed to sustain his war effort. Though the Austrians under Loudon defeated the Prussians at Landschüt (23 June 1760), he retained most of Saxony, and with inferior numbers defeated the Austrians again at the battles of Leignitz (15 Aug. 1760) and Torgau (3 Nov. 1760). Austria also felt the financial strain, her French subsidies having been cut by half since 1759, and the Anglo-French struggle in Hesse, Hanover, and Westphalia had reached stalemate. Prussian fortunes were at their lowest by the end of 1761, Frederick having lost Silesia, East Pomerania, and much of Saxony. The death of the Tsarina Elizabeth (5 Jan. 1762) saved Prussia from total defeat. Her successor, Peter III, withdrew the Russian armies from Germany after making peace, while the Swedes followed suit (May 1762). Even Peter's murder (July 1762) and Catherine II's accession did not revive the Austro-Russian alliance. Austria was defeated at Freiberg and Burkersdorf (21 July) and the recapture of Schweidnitz secured Silesia for Prussia. Maria Theresa, now isolated, concluded peace terms with Prussia at Hubertusburg (15 Feb. 1763), while the overseas campaigns between Britain and France, aided by Spain, her ally of the Family Compact (15 Aug. 1761), were ended by the peace of Paris (10 Feb. 1763).   MKS

SEVEN YEARS WAR OF THE NORTH (1563–70), destructive and indecisive conflict between Denmark and Sweden. Its main cause lay in the ambitions of the two young kings, Frederick II of Denmark–Norway and Eric XIV of Sweden, and its main result was acceptance of the division of Scandinavia into two kingdoms, as established in 1523. The Danes (who had Lübeck and Poland as allies) captured the Swedish west coast fortress of Älvsborg (1563) and their army of mercenaries under Rantzau won a victory at Axtorna (1565). Frederick then advanced across Sweden to Norrköping, but fell back for want of support. The remaining land operations consisted of merciless ravagings of frontier districts in Denmark and Norway, as well as in Sweden. At sea the new Swedish navy, under Henrik Horn, gained control of the Baltic by its successes at Bornholm (1565) and Öland (1566). In 1568 civil war in Sweden resulted in the displacement of Eric by John III, whereupon the King of Poland, who was John's brother-in-law, made peace, and hostilities ended two years later with the mutual restoration of conquests (peace of Stettin).

SEVENTH-DAY ADVENTISTS, evangelical denomination which worships on the seventh day—Saturday—and whose members believe in the second coming of Christ. It embraces the Millerites, followers of William Miller (1782–1849), a New York farmer who successively preached that the world would end in 1843, 1844, and then on some indefinite date in the future. It is active in education and medicine, and, in the US, has a total membership (1970) of more than 400,000.

SEVERUS ALEXANDER (c. 208–35 AD), Roman Emperor (reg. 222–35), originally Alexianus, son of Julia Mamaea, who was adopted (221) as M. Aurelius Alexander by the Emperor Elagabalus, after whose murder Alexander was proclaimed by the praetorian guard. He took the name of Severus to recall Septimius Severus. He tried to correct the excesses of Elagabalus and was well regarded by the Senate; but his reign was marred by the excessive influence of his mother, and by military indiscipline, both at Rome and in the provinces. His eastern campaign (231–3) was only moderately successful, and was interrupted by a crisis on the northern frontier, where, at Moguntiacum (mod. Mainz) on the Rhine, he and his mother were murdered by soldiers, who proclaimed Maximinus as emperor.

SEVIER, JOHN (1745–1815), American soldier and politician, who led TN militiamen to victory over the British at King's Mountain (1780) and later led the movement which set up a separate state of Franklin, of which he became the governor. This project, however, ended in failure (1788) and in his being denounced as a disturber of the public peace. As an advocate of the new Federal constitution, Sevier won a full pardon and election to the NC senate (1789). He became first governor of TN (1796–1801) and was re-elected (1803–1809). He served in Congress (1811–15).

SEVILLE, ancient city of Andalusia, captured from the Visigoths by the Umayyad Turks in the 8th cent. and remaining under Islamic control until 1248. As the seat of an archbishopric and a university in the 13th cent. it rose to importance as a great port and commercial centre by the 15th cent. As the home of the Casa de la Contratación (House of Trade) through which it controlled the monopoly of trade with the New World, Seville became a boom town in the 16th cent. and by 1588 was Spain's largest city. Decline set in during the 17th cent., however, partly because of the contraction of the American trade and also through Olivares's repeated confiscation of the silver imports and the disastrous outbreak of plague (1649) which killed half the population. By the 1680s Seville had been overtaken by Cadiz and had ceased to be the bullion centre of Spain.

It gained political importance in the 20th cent. as a city of political extremes. Dock-workers and agricultural workers were politically active through the CNT and the UCT and even in the Communist Party. At the same time, Seville was one of the few places where the early Falange took hold. Thus, throughout the Second Republic, Seville was in a political turmoil. In April 1931 the town declared for a republic. In July of the same year a CNT general strike was put down by troops after CNT headquarters were shelled and 30 people killed. In Aug. 1932 Seville was the scene of Sanjurjo's unsuccessful rising. In 1933 there was much dockside violence.

In 1936, despite the strength of its working-class militants, Seville quickly fell to the military rebels, so its many beautiful Moorish buildings survived intact. Queipo de Llano took the civil government by surprise with only a handful of men and some artillery. The working-class districts resisted to the end, but on July 20 troops arrived from Morocco. The unarmed workers were quickly subdued, many being put to the sword. Thereafter, Seville remained securely in the Nationalist zone.

SEVILLE, TREATY OF (1729), agreement between Spain, France, England, and the United Provinces, which created a volte-face in Spanish foreign policy and ended Ripperda's attempts at an Austro-Spanish rapprochement. Elizabeth Farnese of Spain guaranteed a halt to the siege of Gibraltar and the restoration of English ships seized in the Indies and of trading privileges of English merchants in Spain. In return France and England agreed that Spain should send 6000 troops to support Don Carlos's succession to Parma and Tuscany.

SEWALL, SAMUEL (1652–1730), American judge and writer, who was a member of the governor's court of New England throughout most of his life. Though without legal training, he served (1692) as a judge of the superior court of the colony. He sat on the bench specially commissioned for the Salem witchcraft trials (1692) and was the only one of the nine judges publicly to admit his error (1697). He wrote the first anti-slavery tract in America, 'The Selling of Joseph' (1700), and others on Indians, politics, and religion, but is chiefly remembered for his *Diary* covering the period 1674–1729, with a gap between 1677 and 1685, which vividly portrays the man and his period.

SEWARD, WILLIAM HENRY (1801–72), US lawyer and politician who became active in the popular movements which swept through western New York in the 1820s. He was a member of the state senate (1830–4), forcefully opposed the policies of the Jacksonians, and finally led the Anti-masons into the newly formed Whig Party. He was soon recognized as party leader in NY and was elected governor (1838). He supported large expenditures on internal improvements, proposed widespread humanitarian reforms, opposed slavery, and advocated the setting up of state-supported Catholic schools for the growing immigrant population. Deciding that his views were too advanced for public opinion, he declined renomination (1842), but continued to be politically active while still pursuing a successful career at the bar.

He was elected to the US Senate (1848) at a time of heightening sectional crisis, and tried to hold the national Whig Party together, but refused to compromise on slavery. On 11 March 1850 he denounced Clay's proposals for a settlement and threatened to appeal to 'a higher law' than the constitution. He opposed the Kansas–Nebraska Bill (1854) and, when the Whig Party collapsed, joined the new Republican Party (1855). While maintaining his anti-slavery attitude in what he declared (25 Oct. 1858) to be the 'irrepressible conflict' between North and South, he became the leading candidate for the Republican presidential nomination in 1860, but was defeated by Abraham Lincoln.

He was appointed secretary of state in 1861, but his attempts to devise means of averting a civil war weakened his own position and strengthened Lincoln's. He became a faithful cabinet officer and an important conservative influence within the administration. Although seriously injured on the night of Lincoln's assassination, he continued to serve as secretary of state (to 1869), advised conciliatory treatment of the defeated South, and wrote many of President Andrew Johnson's messages vetoing Radical Reconstruction measures. In actively supporting the president, Seward divided himself from his party and his former supporters.

His main achievements after 1861 lay in the critical field of foreign affairs. His finesse and firmness as secretary of state were largely responsible for preventing European intervention in the Civil War. In the *Trent* affair of 1861 he coolly conciliated Britain without antagonizing American prejudices. Later, his protests stopped Britain building cruisers for the Confederacy. At the end of the war he secured the withdrawal of French troops from Mexico, and in 1867 purchased AK ('Seward's Folly') for $7,200,000. As an ardent expansionist, he worked unsuccessfully for the acquisition of the Danish West Indies and Hawaii.

G. G. Van Deusen, *William Henry Seward* (New York, 1967).

F. Bancroft, *The Life of William H. Seward*, 2 vols (New York, 1900).   DJR

SEWELL, HENRY (1807–79), NZ politician and the country's first prime minister, who was a member of the first NZ parliament and of FitzGerald's 'mixed executive' (1854). He formed the first administration under responsible government (1856) and held ministerial office frequently thereafter until 1872.

SEX DISQUALIFICATION (REMOVAL) ACT (1919), in Britain, legislative measure which stated that there must be no disqualification by sex or marriage from exercising any public function or from being appointed to or holding any civil or judicial office. This was to apply also to civil professions, incorporated societies, and jury service. The act was in many ways complementary to the women's suffrage movement. One or two reservations applied to the civil service (overseas postings), and to the proviso that at the judge's discretion all-male or all-female juries could be constituted. The act was a considerable advancement in the status of women.

SEXAGENARY CYCLE. The Chinese calendar was based on a luni-solar system of 12 months, with the addition of an intercalary month when necessary. Great attention was paid by imperial governments to the regulation of the calendar, and state officials were responsible for calendrical reckoning,

correction, and promulgation. Since the 2nd cent. BC years have been designated in short series, according to the *nien-hao* system. In addition, years have been enumerated by means of the 60 terms of the sexagenary cycle. This is formed by combining two terms, *ie*, Chinese characters, drawn cyclically from two series of respectively 10 and 12 characters. The two sets are found in the oracle bone inscriptions of *c.* 1400–1100 BC; their origin is uncertain, but both may bear a symbolic significance in Chinese folklore and mark the early stages of Chinese mathematical skills.

SEYCHELLES, archipelago in the Indian Ocean (400 sq. kms) which, with neighbouring islands, became a British colony in 1814. It was occupied and settled by the French in the 18th cent., when its spice plantations attracted migrants and slaves from East Africa, Mauritius, India, and China. The constitution of 1967 provided for adult suffrage to elect the governing council and the governor to be president.

SEYMOUR OF SUDELEY, THOMAS SEYMOUR, Baron (*c.* 1508–49), English diplomat, soldier, and administrator who served in embassies to France, Hungary, and the Netherlands, and fought in France before becoming lord high admiral (1547). He was brother to the Protector Somerset and to Queen Jane, third wife of Henry VIII. He himself married Henry VIII's widow (and sixth wife), Katherine Parr (1547). A year later she died and he was attainted on the orders of the Earl of Warwick for making overtures to Princess Elizabeth, the future queen. On Warwick's orders he was executed for treason.

SEYMOUR, SIR EDWARD (1633–1708), English politician descended from Protector Somerset, who was a High Church Anglican and Tory. He was treasurer of the navy (1666–73), speaker of the House of Commons (1673–80), and after supporting William III's cause (Nov. 1688) became lord of the treasury (1692–4). Queen Anne appointed him comptroller of the royal household (1702) and a cabinet minister, but later dismissed him (1704) for persistently obstructing the policies of Godolphin and Marlborough.

SEYMOUR, HORATIO (1810–86), US lawyer and politician who exercised a moderating influence in NY state politics. He served in the NY assembly (1842, 1844–5) and helped to reconcile conflicting wings of the state Democratic Party, was governor of NY (1853–5, 1863–5), was briefly considered as a compromise Democratic presidential candidate in 1860, and was the unsuccessful Democratic nominee in 1868). He strongly opposed the corrupt political machine of 'Boss' Tweed and supported the moderate reformer Grover Cleveland.

SEYSSEL, CLAUDE DE (1450–1520), Savoyard cleric and Abp of Turin who entered the service of the French Crown, whose powers he celebrated in the *Grand'Monarchie de France* (1519).

SEYSS-INQUART, ARTHUR VON (1892–1946), Austrian laywer, politician, and Nazi leader, born in the Sudetenland and educated in Vienna. He was a First World War colleague of Schuschnigg, and, both being lawyers, their contacts continued into the 1920s. It was characteristic of the naive Schuschnigg to trust Seyss-Inquart because of their friendship and the strongly avowed Catholicism they apparently shared, and this eased the Nazis' path to power in Austria. During the 1930s Seyss-Inquart was never a fully committed Nazi—he was a member of the group of fellow-travellers who called themselves 'betont Nationaler', 'pronounced nationals'—but he, and particularly Glaise-Horstenau, were more than just a respectable front for the Nazis and they acted as much more positive instruments of Hitler's will (1937–8). He became a counsellor of state in 1937 and used his influence to encourage disorder, designed to produce internal chaos in Austria and therefore necessitate German intervention. Hitler's demands of Feb. 1938 included Seyss-Inquart as minister of interior, and the Austrian government agreed. When Schuschnigg tried to escape from his false position by invoking public opinion against German annexation the Nazis intervened: President Miklas was forced into making Seyss-Inquart chancellor, on 11 March, so that the German army could legitimately be 'invited' into Austria to restore order. His chancellorship was brief—on 13 March Austria was incorporated into Germany and he became governor. From now on he was just one of many Nazi 'hatchet' men. In Oct. 1939 he became Frank's deputy in charge of the general government of Poland, and in May 1940 Reich commissioner for the Netherlands, being particularly industrious in implementing slave labour programmes. He retained Hitler's trust until the end and in the Führer's testament was nominated foreign minister. He was captured in May 1945, tried at Nuremberg, and executed in Oct. 1946.

KM

SFORZA, CARLO, Count (1872–1952), Italian diplomat and politician, who, as under-secretary (1919–20) and minister (1920–1) of foreign affairs, promoted friendly Italian leadership of the new Balkan states. He infuriated Italian nationalists by guaranteeing Albania's independence (Aug. 1920) and by agreeing to a free state of Fiume in the Rapallo treaty with Yugoslavia (Nov. 1920). He was ambassador to Paris (1921–2), but resigned over Mussolini's foreign policy and became his leading opponent. In 1924 he made an unsuccessful bid to have Mussolini arrested or dismissed. For this he was exiled and while abroad spent his time in writing anti-fascist articles and books. He returned to Italy in 1943 to lead the republican campaign for the king's dismissal as a fascist collaborator and to head the commission set up to purge ex-fascists (1944). As foreign minister (1947–51), he inspired De Gasperi's government with ideas for European co-operation and unity.

SFORZA, FRANCESCO, Duke of Milan (d. 1466), son of a professional *condotierre*. He became one of the most accomplished commanders of his time, especially as a military organizer. In 1441 he married the only daughter of his master, the last Visconti Duke of Milan, Filippo Maria (d. 1447). On Filippo's death Sforza's long-matured plans for succeeding him at first misfired, as a republic was unexpectedly proclaimed at Milan (the Ambrogian republic). Supported by his friend Cosimo de' Medici, the richest Italian banker and the virtual ruler of Florence, Sforza captured Milan in 1450 after a siege. He concluded a general peace with Milan's neighbours in 1454 and thereafter gave the Milanese state one of the periods of greatest peace and prosperity in its history, which endured under his successors down to the beginning of the foreign invasions of northern Italy in 1499.

SFORZA, LUDOVICO, Duke of Milan (d. 1508), who was effective ruler of Milan after 1479 on behalf of his nephew, whom he ultimately displaced. He was invested as duke in 1494 by the Emperor Maximilian, who married his niece. He encouraged the French invasion of Italy in 1494, but later played a leading part in their expulsion (1495). He was defeated and captured in 1500 by Louis XII of France and died in captivity.

SHACKAMAXON, TREATY OF (23 June 1683), agreement between the English colonizer William Penn, and a delegation of Delaware Indians led by Tammany. The treaty sanctioned the purchase by Penn of land within the present Bucks County, PA, and was the beginning of Penn's friendly relations with the Indians.

SHACKLETON, SIR ERNEST HENRY (1874–1922), British explorer, who joined Scott's Antarctic expedition (1901), then commanded the British expedition (1907–9) which penetrated to within 100 miles (161 kms) of the South Pole.

He led the *Endurance* expedition (1914–17) and became director of equipment and transport to North Russia (1918–1919). He died on an expedition with Rowett and was buried in South Georgia.

SHAFTESBURY, ANTHONY ASHLEY COOPER, Earl of (1st of 1st creation) (1621–83), English politician, commonly regarded as 'the first Whig'. He was elected to the Short Parliament (1640) but failed to secure re-election to its successor, the Long Parliament. At the outset of the first Civil War he was uncommitted to either side but by early 1643 had definitely opted for the Royalist cause, only to change his allegiance a year later. He was one of those selected for the Nominated Parliament (1653). He served for a while on the executive Council of State and was elected to both the first and second Protectorate parliaments. Whereas he was in favour of the assumption of kingship by Cromwell, he opposed the idea that the upper chamber should be treated as a House of Lords. He was prominent immediately before the Restoration (1660), after which he was created Baron Ashley (1661) and given a minor government post. He was appointed to the Treasury Commission (1667) and became celebrated as one of the Cabal, being particularly interested in the colonies and trade. He was created Earl of Shaftesbury (1672) and made lord chancellor, a post in which he proved himself both fair and enlightened. In the following year he appeared to betray his own tolerant principles by supporting the proposed Test Act, and certainly he thereby incurred the hostility of Charles II who dismissed him in 1673. Thereafter he was permanently in opposition to the King. He was sent to the Tower of London by the House of Lords for contempt (1677). After obtaining a writ of *habeas corpus*, he fought an unsuccessful action in King's Bench, one of his arguments being that his committal had been contrary to fundamental law. Shaftesbury had still to reach the peak of his political career. Following his release and the opportune Popish Plot disclosures, from his Green Ribbon Club he created an embryonic political party, the members of which were nicknamed Whigs by their political opponents. Shaftesbury's primary object at this time, the statutory Exclusion of the heir-presumptive, James, Duke of York (which would have been contrary to that very fundamental law which Shaftesbury had so recently invoked) and the substitution of the Duke of Monmouth, was not attained. None of the three Exclusion Bills became law, but his Habeas Corpus Act did, and momentarily, for a few months in 1679, Shaftesbury again held ministerial office as president of the council. When Charles II had triumphed over the Whigs their leader was accused of treasonable activities and imprisoned in the Tower. But when he was indicted, the grand jury of the county of Middlesex refused to return a true bill against him. Upon release he fled to the Dutch republic (1682).

K. H. D. Haley, *The First Earl of Shaftesbury* (Oxford, 1968).

BM

SHAFTESBURY, ANTHONY ASHLEY-COOPER, 7th Earl of (1801–85), British politician and philanthropist, who sat in the House of Commons as Lord Ashley until 1851. He was concerned mainly with child labour and the plights of lunatics and factory workers, and gradually identified himself with the evangelical movement. He held minor offices under Wellington and Peel, but from 1841 shunned executive responsibility so as to free himself for philanthropic work. He helped to promote legislation to prohibit chimney sweeps from employing climbing boys (1840), and to exclude women and children from the mines (1842), and curb factory hours (1847), which measures were later extended. But his strictures on laissez-faire implied no repudiation of voluntary action or personal independence. He was against state-subsidized housing, and his abiding paternalism was incompatible with working-class enfranchisement and trade unionism.

He was alarmed at the spectre of revolution and believed that social catastrophe could be avoided only if rich and powerful individuals interested themselves in the welfare of the poor. During the 1850s he was active in many evangelical (and sometimes sectarian) societies that favoured housing, sanitary, and sabbatarian reforms, and he built a model village on his own estate in Dorset.

His diary sheds a strange light on his public success, but it is an unhappy document—riddled with details on self-doubt, illness, money difficulties, and family problems. He was totally out of sympathy with his times. He consistently opposed rationalism and ritualism, believed that franchise extension in 1867 would lead to expropriation of private property, and saw nothing good in Cobden's Little England. His outlook condemned him to political impotence, which he mildly resented.

He was too ready to impute selfish motives to his critics. Posterity can admire his courage and compassion, but can also see how his partisan standpoint caused so many good men to oppose him.

J. L. and B. Hammond, *Lord Shaftesbury* (London, 1936).
G. F. A. Best, *Shaftesbury* (London, 1964).   BHH

SHAH, Persian word meaning 'king'—cf. the related forms 'shahinshah', a title accorded to the Sassanids, and 'padishah', often used of the Ottoman sultan. The word is also found as an element in personal names—cf. the Ayyubid Turan Shah or the Mughal Shah Jahan.

SHAH ALAM (1728–1806), regal title of Prince Ali Gauhar, the eldest son of the Emperor Alamgir II. On his father's assassination (1759), he assumed the Imperial Crown in Bihar. He tried to reassert his authority in Bengal, but was defeated at the battle of Buxar (1764). He granted the *diwani* of Bengal, Bihar, and Orissa to the East India Co. (1765) and kept court at Allahabad. In 1772 he returned to Delhi, where his fortunes revived under Mirza Najaf Khan (d. 1781). He then fell under the power of the Maratha chief, Madhu Rao Sindhia (1785), was blinded by the Rohilla Ghulam Qadir (1788), and restored by Sindhia. He passed under British protection when Lord Lake captured Delhi (1803).

SHAH JAHAN (1593–1666), fifth Mughal Emperor of India (*reg.* 1627–58), and third son of the Emperor Jahangir. During his reign the empire reached its zenith. On his accession he murdered all the Mughal male collaterals, but his administration was benevolent and efficient. He lost Kandahar to the Persians, but continued to advance in the Deccan. The absence of great wars and rebellions made India prosperous. Shah Jahan was a great builder and patron of the arts. He rebuilt the fort at Agra and erected the Taj Mahal (1630–48) there in memory of his favourite wife, Mumtaz Mahal. He built Shahjahanabad (1638–48), with its Jama Masjid (1644–58) at Delhi. He was deposed by his third son, Aurangzeb (1658), and was confined in the Agra fort till his death.

SHAHBANDAR (from the Persian, meaning 'harbourmaster'), official in most Muslim ports in the Indian Ocean and South-East Asia, charged with levying duties, conducting the king's trade, and supervising foreigners.

SHAHEINAB, neolithic site on the left bank of the Nile, 30 miles (48 kms) north of Omdurman. Decorated pottery, bone harpoons, and stone gouges were characteristic artefacts.

SHAKA (*c.* 1787–1828), illegitimate son of Senzenghakona, chief of the small Zulu people living between the White Mfolozi and Upper Mhlatuze rivers in south-east Africa. In 1816 Shaka usurped the position of his brother and became chief of the Zulu, having already made his name as an outstanding warrior in Dingiswayo's Mthethwa army. He applied the Mthethwa military system to the Zulu, conscripting all men under 40 into age-set regiments under the command of his own appointees. These soldiers could marry only with his permission. The drill, discipline, and mobility of his troops, together with his surprise tactics, enabled him to conquer and absorb most of the peoples of Natal and Zululand. The decisive moments in this were his absorption of the Mthethwa on Dingiswayo's death (1818) and his victory over the Ndwandwe in 1819. Though he arose in a period of increasing military conflict, Shaka's concept of 'total war' made his conquests far more devastating than those of his predecessors and they had repercussions over a vast area of South, Central, and East Africa. Within the Zulu state all power was concentrated in Shaka's hands, giving him far more extensive powers than the traditional chiefs in this area.

In 1824 the first British traders were welcomed at Shaka's capital. He was anxious to learn about the settlement at the Cape and to acquire firearms. Though their accounts are probably exaggerated, they arrived at a time when Shaka's terrorization was alienating his people. This was particularly so after the death of his mother, Nandi, in 1827, when many Zulus were killed in a wave of mass hysteria. In 1828 he was assassinated by his half-brothers. Despite the sadistic aspects of his rule, in ten years he had created a large empire out of the fissiparous chiefdoms of Natal and Zululand. This continued to be the most powerful African state in Southern Africa until the last quarter of the 19th century.

J. D. Cooper, *The Zulu Aftermath* (London, 1966).

SHAKERS, American religious sect, more correctly known as 'The United Society of Believers in Christ's Second Appearing'. It was founded by 'Mother' Ann Lee, of Manchester, England, who brought a small following to America (1774). This group settled in Lebanon, NY (1787), and by 1794 ten more communities, grouped into bishoprics under New Lebanon, were established in NY and New England and in the first quarter of the 19th cent. spread as far as IN. They believed in a dual deity, the male principle being manifest in Jesus and the female in Mother Ann Lee. Confession, celibacy, sex equality, and common property were among their beliefs.

SHAKESPEARE, WILLIAM (1564–1616), English poet and dramatist, born at Stratford-upon Avon, Warwick, where his father was a respected tradesman and civic officer. By 1592 William was known in London as an actor and playwright. The success of his two romantic poems, 'Venus and Adonis' (1593) and 'The Rape of Lucrece' (1594), did not divert him from the theatre and after 1594 he was a leading member of the Chamberlain's Men, owners of the Globe (1599) and of an indoor theatre at Blackfriars (1608). His sonnets were printed in 1609, and the First Folio, containing 36 plays, in 1623, *Pericles* being added in the third edition of 1664. Shakespeare bought New Place, the largest house in Stratford (1597), and increasingly spent more time away from London. He drew most of his dramatic plots from chronicles, novels, and other popular sources, and though the plots are not in themselves remarkable, he was a consummate dramatist. The universalizing agent is his poetry, which transforms the immediate situation and makes his characters spokesmen for all mankind. Coleridge defined his supreme attributes as *music* and *concentration*: the melody which brings delight and makes the words memorable, and the metaphorical compression which fuses diverse elements in a single act of illumination and discovers their underlying unity.

SHALMANESER III (*reg.* 858–824 BC), Assyrian King, who spent most of his reign fighting in the area from the Mediterranean to the Persian Gulf, but with only partial success. He failed to defeat conclusively the growing power of the Medes and Urartians and his reign ended in internal revolt.

SHAMANISM, religion of northern and central Asia, centred on a wizard or priest (shaman) who it was believed could communicate with dead ancestors and act as an intermediary with the spirits thought to inhabit natural phenomena, *eg,* mountains, rivers, and, especially, the sky (Tengri). Shamanism was the religion of the early Mongol rulers, but their descendants abandoned it in favour of Islam and Buddhism.

SHAMSHI-ADAD I (*reg. c.* 1814–1781 BC), Amorite chief, who took the throne of Assyria from his brother and founded the first Assyrian empire. He conquered Mari and controlled all of northern Mesopotamia. He has left many valuable letters to and from his sons and other rulers.

SHAMSHI-ADAD V (*reg.* 823–811 BC), Assyrian King, who succeeded Shalmaneser III during a period of civil war. Having subdued the revolt, he spent the rest of his reign in restoring his authority in the vassal states in the north and north-east, and in Babylonia.

SHAMYL (*c.* 1796–1871), Avar leader of a Murid movement which opposed Russian control over Daghestan (1834–59). He had a reputation for ruthlessness and military genius.

SHANG KINGDOM, established in the Yellow river area, traditionally from 1766 to 1122 BC, and later called Yin. About 1900 literary references to the existence of this kingdom were confirmed dramatically by archaeological evidence at An-yang. The cultural standard of the kingdom was sufficiently well advanced to permit some degree of social organization and political direction, together with the practice of writing. The system of fraternal succession by the kings came to be replaced by a patrilineal system.

SHANG YANG (d. 338 BC), politician of the kingdom of Ch'in, whose forceful realist policies were based on legal principles and contributed decisively to the emergence of Ch'in as the strongest of the pre-imperial states that were to form the first Chinese empire. Shang Yang was involved in political intrigues and died the death of a criminal.

SHANGHAI CAMPAIGN (1932), Japanese offensive against China, in which civilians were bombed for the first time. The campaign was one of the more important incidents in Japan's undeclared war against China (1931–7), but was short and inconclusive. During the course of it, the Shanghai area of Chapei was bombed and heavy civilian casualties inflicted.

SHANGHAI INTERNATIONAL SETTLEMENT, created in 1863, was a large area outside the Chinese city of Shanghai leased in perpetuity by foreign nations, which paid modest ground-rents to the Chinese government. It had its beginning in 1843 when the British set up their concession. The Americans quickly followed suit, and in 1863 joined with the British to form the International Settlement, which was now inhabited by other foreign nationals. The French, however, maintained their own separate concession to the west of the Chinese city. The International Settlement was outside Chinese jurisdiction and free from Chinese taxation. It had its municipal council representing British and American interests, with the former dominating. Because of the security and opportunities offered by the settlement, many Chinese took up residence there, and many more came there in times of crisis. To deal with this mixed population, a Mixed Court was established in 1864, with a Chinese magistrate and a foreign consular 'assessor', to hear cases between Chinese and cases in which Chinese were defendants. The settlement was also the seat of the British Supreme Court for China and Japan, handling appeals from all her consular courts. In 1899 the area of the settlement was tripled (as was the French Concession), and completely overshadowed the Chinese city. In 1915 the foreign population in the settlement was 18,519 (7387 Japanese, 5521 British, and 1448 Americans). There were some 700,000 Chinese who paid tax but were without representation in the Municipal Council. After protests during the 1920s, the Chinese were in 1930 allowed

five as opposed to the nine foreign councillors. With the establishment of the Chinese People's Republic the settlement came to an end.   DP

SHANGHAI PURGE (April 1927), purge of Chinese communists from the Kuomintang, launched initially in Shanghai. Shanghai was taken by Kuomintang forces in March 1927, with the aid of the city's active, communist-led labour unions. Shortly afterwards Chiang Kai shek ordered a purge of communists within the Kuomintang. The purge, planned in secret with the probable help of Chiang's friends in the Shanghai secret societies, turned into a bloodbath, as thousands of people were slaughtered by their erstwhile Kuomintang allies. The Communist Party was crippled by the loss of many of its urban activists, in Shanghai and in other cities to which the purge was extended.

SHANN, EDWARD OWEN GIBLIN (1884–1935), Australian economic historian, who was one of the few writers to detect significant similarities between economic trends in Australia in the late 1880s and 1920s. His *Boom of 1888–90 and Now* (1927) was an influential contemporary document, while his *Economic History of Australia* (1930) was then the most comprehensive survey and analysis in that field. He was economic adviser to the Bank of New South Wales during the Depression years.

SHANS, Thai–Chinese race closely related to the Siamese and the most numerous minority race in Burma. The Shans occupy the high plateau on the east of Burma, though small groups have penetrated into northern Burma and Assam. Remaining in their mountain fastnesses and inhabiting a country of small valleys, the Shans have retained their racial identity and a high degree of separatism, with numbers of small states each until recently having its own ruling chief. The chiefs were known as Sawbwas, Myosas, or Ngwegunhmus, according to rank. Of the states, Hsipaw, North Hsenwi, Yawnghwe, and Kengtung were the most notable, each having its own miniature—but long—history.

Shan chiefs in various combinations dominated Upper Burma from the fall of the Pagan dynasty (1287) until the rise of the Toungoo dynasty under Tabinshweti (*reg.* 1531–50) and Bayinnaung (*reg.* 1551–81) From this time a theoretical Burmese suzerainty was established over the Shan states, though its effective extent varied greatly from time to time in accordance with the balance of power between Burmese and Shans. When the British annexed Upper Burma (1886) they found the Shan chiefs technically subject to the Burmese, but in fact they were very largely independent so long as they paid their tribute. The British held themselves to have inherited this constitutional position, though it required some spirited, if miniature, operations to enforce it. The chiefs were then confirmed in their offices and allowed to continue to govern their states, subject to the payment of tribute and provided that their administration attained certain modest standards of decency and competency.

The quasi-federal constitution of Burma after independence made provision for a Shan state with a right of secession after ten years and subject to certain procedures. The danger of secession was one of the causes of the military coup in Burma in 1962, and the revolutionary government then lost no time in removing the chiefs, except for Kengtung, and incorporating the Shan state into Burma. There is now (1970) a widespread Shan nationalist movement using neighbouring Thailand as a base.

G. E. Harvey, *History of Burma* (London, 1925).
F. N. Trager, *Burma: from kingdom to republic* (London, 1966).   FSVD

SHAPUR I (*reg. c.* 240–72), Iranian King, who inherited from his father, Ardashir, the newly formed Sassanian empire and by his military successes completely changed the relationship of Iran with its neighbours. In the east he occupied the Indus valley and brought the Kushan empire under his suzerainty. Most of Transcaucasia was conquered and in the west the Romans ceded Mesopotamia and Armenia (244). In 259 the war with Rome was resumed and at the battle of Edessa the Emperor Valerian and 70,000 men were captured. The latter were settled throughout the empire and employed on public works such as bridge- and road-building. At home, Shapur founded towns, eg, Bishapur and Gundeshapur, encouraged literature by commissioning the translation of Greek and Indian works, and patronized the religious teacher Mani.

SHAPUR II (*reg*. 309–79), Sassanian King, who restored Iranian prestige (which had declined after the death of his namesake, Shapur I), by annexing the Kushan empire, recovering Armenia from the Romans, and successfully defending the frontiers from nomad attacks.

SHARECROPPING in the US, term used to describe a farming system, well developed in the southern states after the American Civil War, whereby a tenant farmer who owned neither tools nor livestock normally received a half of the cotton or tobacco crop in return for his labour in the fields. Prevalent among emancipated Negroes, sharecropping produced a fragmented landscape of fields and dwellings. Few sharecroppers could maintain themselves until the crops were in, and credit was provided in exchange for a lien on the tenant's share of the growing crop. The system meant that sharecroppers were rarely able to extricate themselves from a state of economic bondage. As late as 1936 about 60 per cent of southern plantations were worked by sharecroppers, but after 1940 the system began to break down under the impact of mechanization which encouraged the consolidation of holdings.

SHAREEF REPORT (1939) in India, report of a committee appointed by the Bihar provincial Muslim League to enquire into the condition of Muslims in Bihar under the Congress ministry (1937–9). Its charges against the Congress administration were even more strongly worded than the earlier Pirpur Report and it put forward the view that Muslims might be forced to migrate from Bihar because of the intolerable conditions which, it claimed, discriminatory policies had created in the province.

SHARI'A, Sacred Law of Islam. The Shari'a rests on the revelation of Allah enshrined in the Koran. It stands also on the Sunna or practice of the Prophet Muhammad and on the Hadith or traditions. Out of these three basic elements was elaborated, during the first centuries of Islam, the corpus of the sacred law. The Shari'a embraces the whole life of a Muslim, religious, political, social, domestic, and personal. Of the prescriptions which it enjoins on him not all are equal in binding force. The actions of a Muslim are divided into five categories—obligatory, meritorious, indifferent, reprehensible, and forbidden. Islam recognizes four distinct schools of law (madhhab, pl. madhahib) as valid in their interpretation of the Shari'a—the Hanafi, the Shafi'i the Maliki, and the Hanbali madhahib.

SHARIF (pl. Ashraf), Arabic word meaning noble or exalted. It came to denote the descendants of the Prophet Muhammad and also of his uncles Al-'Abbas and Abu Talib. Under the Abbasid caliphs the Ashraf had over them a naqib or marshal, of their own selection.

SHARIF HUSAYN IBN ALI (*c*. 1853/6–1931), King of the Hijaz (*reg*. 1916–24), who was an Arab politician of ancient Meccan family. As Amir (or Sharif) of Mecca (1906–16) he built up his personal position in the Hijaz and (1916) with Arab nationalist and British support proclaimed a revolt against Ottoman rule. As King of the Hijaz he alienated the Saudi family which eventually expelled him from Arabia. His assumption of the caliphate (1924) received little support.

SHAR-KALI-SHARRI (*reg. c.* 2217–2193 BC), last Sargonid King of Akkad, whose reign saw the break-up of the empire. Elam became independent, and there were revolts in Sumer and wars with the Lullubi, Guti, and northern nomads.

SHARP, GRANVILLE (1735–1813), British philanthropist and advocate of parliamentary reform, who was an important figure in the anti-slavery movement, opposed the press-gang, and was one of the founders of the British and Foreign Bible Society. He was associated with the Wyvill and the Yorkshire reform movement and with the Society for Constitutional Information, and supported the cause of the American colonies. He published tracts on parliamentary and social reform.

SHARP, JAMES (1613–79), Scottish cleric who was Abp of St Andrews and Primate of Scotland, reputedly thus rewarded for his share in negotiating the Restoration of King Charles II and the episcopacy to Scotland. Originally a professing Presbyterian, he was deported to London with other ministers (1651–2), and chosen by the more moderate party in the kirk to plead their cause with Oliver Cromwell. Sent by Monck to Breda in 1660, he apparently had a change of religious heart, and was later responsible for the ejection of Presbyterian ministers in the south-western counties of Scotland and a series of repressive measures (1663–5) which led to the Pentland Rising (1666). His severity to the rebels only increased popular hatred towards him, and on 13 May 1679 he was hacked to death by 12 outlawed Covenanters who waylaid his coach near St Andrews.

SHARPEVILLE, African location near Vereeniging in the Transvaal (South Africa), where on 21 March 1960 police fired on a 10,000-strong demonstration against the pass laws organized by the Pan-African Congress; 67 Africans were killed and 186 injured. The episode aroused world-wide opposition to South Africa's racial policy.

SHASHANQ I (*reg. c.* 945–924 BC), Egyptian King of Libyan origin, founder of the XXIInd dynasty. Little is known of his foreign relations, but he attacked Gezer, which he gave to Solomon, King of Israel, who had married his daughter, and also attacked (*c.* 930) and sacked Jerusalem, much of the loot from which he presented to the temples at Thebes.

SHASTRI, LAL BAHADUR (1904–66), Indian politician and prime minister of India (1964–6), who devoted himself to nationalist political activity in the Congress and in Lajpat Rai's Servants of the People Society, of which he became president. He had a considerable reputation as a Congress organizer, his experience extending from his handling of the Allahabad District Congress Committee (1930–6), his secretaryship of the United Provinces' Agrarian Reforms Enquiry Committee (1936), his work as the Congress electoral organizer in UP (1945–6), and, at the national level, in the first three general elections after independence. This reputation was carried over into his career as a state and central cabinet minister. He was elected to the UP Legislative Assembly and became minister for police and transport. Nehru brought him to Delhi as general secretary of the Congress (1951) and put him in the central cabinet after the elections (1952). He was in turn minister for railways (1952–6), transport and communications (1957–8), commerce and industries (1958–61), and home affairs (1961–3). His skill as a mediator during his term as home minister gave him great influence in the government, and although he resigned with other ministers under the 'Kamaraj Plan' (1963) he came back within six months to help Nehru in his last illness. After Nehru's death in May 1964, Kamaraj ensured Shastri's selection as his successor. His major task as prime minister was to negotiate with President Ayub Khan at Tashkent in Jan. 1966 to halt the war between India and Pakistan which had begun in the previous Sept. He died in Tashkent shortly after concluding the Tashkent Declaration.   PDR

SHAW, GEORGE BERNARD (1856–1950), Irish dramatist and writer. After some unsuccessful years as a novelist he became established in London as a music critic and a commentator on socialism. He joined the Fabian Society in 1884 and edited *Fabian Essays on Socialism* (1889). In the 1890s his career as a playwright was launched with *Arms and the Man, Candida, You Never Can Tell*, and, in the US, *The Devil's Disciple*. His famous plays followed at regular intervals up till the Second World War, *eg, Man and Superman* (1903), *John Bull's Other Island* (1904), *Major Barbara* (1905), *The Doctor's Dilemma* (1906), *Androcles and the Lion* (1913), *Saint Joan* (1923), *The Apple Cart* (1929), and *Geneva* (1939). Meanwhile, his political opinions found an equally important public in books such as *The Intelligent Woman's Guide to Socialism and Capitalism* (1928) and *Everybody's Political What's What* (1944). He was a controversial figure throughout his long life who faced in his writings and public utterances hypocrisy, and social evils, *eg*, slum landlordism. The impact of his technique lay in his use of satire and his appeal to the intellect.

SHAW, PERCY (1890–   ), English inventor, in 1934, of the reflecting roadstud, the 'cat's eye', which enabled motorists to drive in thick fog. Its usefulness became fully established during the Second World War because of its ability to reflect light in the direction of origin, rather than, as other devices did, scatter light upwards for aircraft to spot. The cat's eye became widely used in many countries.

SHAWBAK, AL-, Crusader fortress located in Transjordan, south of the Dead Sea. To the Latins it was known as Mons Regalis (Montréal). Baldwin I built this famous castle in 1115 in order to command the desert routes leading from Damascus southward to the Hijaz and to Egypt. Al-Shawbak fell to the Muslims after their great triumph over the Christians at the battle of Hattin in 1187.

SHAWNEE INDIANS, North American tribe of Algonquian linguistic stock, whose early history is obscure. They were definitely located (*c.* 1670) in TN and SC, then began moving northward (*c.* 1674), the various bands being united in the Ohio river valley (*c.* 1760). The Shawnee were French allies in the French and Indian War (1755–63) and joined the British in the American War of Independence (1775–83). They signed the treaty of Greenville (1795), with the US, but many followed the Shawnee medicine man known as the Prophet, whose uprising was crushed at the battle of Tippecanoe (1811). His brother, Tecumseh, led the tribes who sided with the British in the War of 1812. After living on various reservations, the Shawnee took lands in OK (1890).

SHAYBANID, name given to the descendants of Shayban (Sibagan), a son of Jōchi, who held an apanage in western Siberia. Under Abu'l Khayr Khan (*reg.* 1428–68) the Shaybanids (or Uzbeks) moved southwards into Turkestan. Abu'l Khayr was defeated, but his grandson, Muhammad Shaybani (1451–1510), also invaded Turkestan (1500) and established the Shaybanid khanate (1500–99). This was consolidated under Ubaydallah (*reg.* 1533–9), who fought continued but ultimately unsuccessful wars against the Safawids of Iran. Under Abdullah Khan II (*reg.* 1583–98) the khanate enjoyed a last burst of vigour and large areas of north-eastern Iran were plundered, but after his death power passed to the Janid dynasty. The Shaybanids had, however, provided the political framework for the consolidation of Uzbek predominance in Turkestan.

SHAYKH AL-ISLAM. It was not uncommon for a Muslim jurisconsult or mufti of some note to be addressed as a 'shaykh al-Islam'. The mufti of Istanbul acquired in the course of time a position of pre-eminence amongst the 'ulama of the Ottoman empire. To him in particular the title of Shaykh al-Islam was accorded from the reign of Sultan Suleiman Kanuni (*reg.* 1520–66) onward. The mufti of Istanbul often had to issue a legal decision (*fetwa*) on matters of great importance—cf. the *fetwa*s of Abu'l Su'ud authorizing a war against Cyprus in 1570; of Abd Allah Efendi allowing the establishment of a Turkish printing press in 1727; and of Es'ad Efendi supporting the reforms (Nizam-i Jedid) of Sultan Selim III (*reg.* 1789–1807).

SHAYS REBELLION (1786–7) in the US, popular insurrection in MA, in protest at the failure of the state legislature to issue paper money and take measures to prevent foreclosure for debt at a time of declining farm prices and specie shortage. Mob disturbances in Northampton, Worcester, and other towns were followed by confrontation between the state militia and some 500 militant farmers led by Daniel Shays (1747–1825) at Springfield (Sept. 1786). Attempts to raise federal forces were inhibited by lack of funds. An attack by Shays on Springfield was repulsed by state forces (Jan. 1787) and the uprising was finally crushed in Feb. 1787, Shays fleeing to VT. The state legislature passed some measures to relieve the economic situation, and Shays was pardoned in June 1788, but the importance of the Shays rebellion is in the impetus that it gave to the movement for strengthening the powers of the federal government.

SHEEP FARMING IN NEW ZEALAND, the country's chief source of wealth since 1840, was an offshoot of Australian pastoralism. The pioneers, C. R. Bidwill (Wairarapa) and the Deans brothers (Canterbury), imported sheep from NSW in 1843. The open tussock grasslands from Hawkes Bay to Otago were quickly occupied by squatters, and by 1861 sheep totals reached 2·8 million. Australian sheepmen (called 'Shagroons' in Canterbury) set an example of flock management, and NSW squatting laws were adopted in NZ (1849–   ); the Australian disease 'scab' was not eliminated, however, till 1892. NZ dependence on British wool prices became apparent as flock numbers reached 13 million (1880). Attempts to export preserved meat (1869–   ) and the 'boiling down' of carcases had limited success, but the introduction of refrigeration (1882), especially through the efforts of W. S. Davidson, opened new UK markets. Expansion was slow in the depression till about 1895, but swifter thereafter (3·6 million carcases, 1905). The challenge of growing meat markets was met by the breeding of dual-purpose sheep, notably the Corriedale breed, principally by James Little from 1866. On their success the reputation of 'Prime Canterbury' and of NZ mutton generally was established in Britain. Pasture improvement gradually raised NZ's sheep population to 60·3 million in 1970, when the volume of all mutton exports was 470,000 tons (478 million kgs), and of wool 680 million lbs (309 million kgs). Dependence on sheep farming lessened markedly after 1945, but it remained NZ's greatest source of overseas income.   WJG

SHEHUS OF BORNU, title taken by the Al-Kanemi family when they established themselves as de facto rulers of Bornu. The first Shehu, Muhammad al-Amin, was succeeded by his son Umar (*reg.* 1837–81), a scholar like his father, who neglected state affairs. In 1846 Umar was faced by a revolt of the last Saifawa Mai, aided by Wadai, and in 1853–4 he was temporarily deposed by his brother, Abd al-Rahman. He was succeeded by three of his sons in turn, Bukr (*reg.* 1880–4), Ibrahim (*reg.* 1884–5), and Hashim (*reg.* 1885–93). The last was defeated by Rabih and executed soon afterwards by his more energetic nephew, Kiyari ibn Bukr, who was then captured and executed by Rabih. Since the partition of Bornu at Rabih's death there have been two Shehus, one at Maiduguri and the other at Dikwa (technically an emir).

SHELDON, GILBERT (1598–1677), English cleric who became Abp of Canterbury. As warden of All Souls College, Oxford

(1626–48), he was ejected by parliament for his royalist activities. He regained the wardenship in 1659, and was Bp of London and master of the Savoy (1660–3). The Savoy Conference (1660) was held in his lodging. He was Abp of Canterbury from 1663 and chancellor of Oxford University from 1667. The Sheldonian Theatre, Oxford, was built (1669) at his expense.

SHELEPIN, ALEKSANDR NIKOLAYEVICH (1918–), Russian politician who joined the Communist Party in 1940. His success in political work brought very rapid advancement; he was a political commissar during the Finnish War (1939) then rose rapidly in the Komsomol, working in the Moscow Komsomol instead of serving at the front (1940–3) then being appointed secretary of the Komsomol central committee (1940–52) and first secretary (1952–8). He was made a member of the central committee of the CPSU (1952). He succeeded Serov as chairman of the state security committee (1958–61). He strongly supported Khrushchev and was prominent in pressing the attack on the anti-party group. When Khrushchev introduced his reform of the party structure he was appointed head of a newly formed Party–State Control Committee and made a deputy chairman of the council of ministers in 1962.

He thus became a powerful figure who had pursued his whole career in the central government of the Soviet Union, with contacts in both party and state apparatus (including those built up in the Komsomol) as well as a network of acquaintance and knowledge through the security system. He played an important part in Khrushchev's overthrow, but his subsequent fate was that of a powerful man who has failed to reach the top post. He was promoted to full membership of the Presidium, but shortly afterwards the Party–State Control Committee was remodelled and renamed (People's Control Committee) prior to Shelepin's replacement at its head. At the same time he gave up his deputy chairmanship of the council of ministers (1965). He was then (1966) appointed as chairman of the Central Trade Union Council, a post which, having little political responsibility, was seen as representing a demotion.

SHEN CHIA-PEN (1840–1913), Chinese official in the Ch'ing empire. In 1904 he was given charge of legal reform in an attempt to abolish extraterritoriality. However, owing to conservative opposition, his reform was too mild to bring about basic changes in China's legal system. Just before his death, he served as minister of justice in Yüan Shih-k'ai's cabinet.

SHENANDOAH, THE, cruiser flying the flag of the Confederate States of America which sailed into Port Phillip (Australia) in Jan. 1865. Sir Charles Darling, governor of Vic., allowed it to undergo repairs, despite US consular protests. The *Shenandoah* was also allowed to recruit men. These incidents involved international litigation after the American Civil War which cost the British government a considerable sum. The case also had some importance in establishing precedents in international arbitration.

SHENG HSUAN-HUAI (1844–1916), Chinese official of the Ch'ing dynasty who managed government-supervised industrial enterprises. Before the fall of Li Hung-chang in 1895 Sheng was closely associated with Li, and most of the latter's modernization enterprises were initiated, directed, or managed by him. They included the China Merchant's Steam Navigation Co., the Imperial Telegraph Administration (1881), and the Shanghai Cotton Cloth Mill. After 1895 Sheng was asked by Chang Chih-tung to direct the construction of the Peking–Hankow Railway, as head of the Imperial Railway Administration. He also took over the management of the Han-Yeh-P'ing Coal and Iron Co. in 1896. Sheng regarded communication as of primary importance in the modernization of China, and it was his attempt to nationalize the railways that sparked off the 1911 Republican

Revolution. In the field of diplomacy he was best known for his neutralization of South China during the Boxer Rising. He was also the founder of China's first modern bank (the Imperial Bank of China, 1897), and the Peiyang College (Tientsin, 1886) and the Nanyang College (Shanghai, 1897), which produced many Chinese engineers. During the last years of the Ch'ing dynasty, Sheng's power suffered considerably at the hands of Yuan Shih-k'ai, and after the 1911 revolution he lost all political power, though retaining control over the China Merchant's Co., the Han-Yeh-P'ing Co., and his cotton mills.

SHENSTONE, WILLIAM (1714–63), English melancholic minor poet and garden designer, who coined the term 'landscape gardener'. Associated with the prospects in his gardens were contrived poetic allusions and inscriptions. Many of Shenstone's precepts were adopted and developed on a much more extensive scale by Lancelot Brown.

SHEPILOV, DIMITRIY TROFIMOVICH (1905–), Russian politician who was political commander in the Ukraine under Khrushchev during the Second World War. He was appointed head of the propaganda section of the central committee of the CPSU (1948) and editor of *Pravda* (1952–5). As Khrushchev established his dominance Shepilov rose rapidly, being made a secretary of the central committee (1955), foreign minister and candidate member of the Presidium (1956) and secretary of the central committee, again, in 1957. As foreign minister he was responsible for the expansion of Soviet interests into the Middle East. In spite of being a supporter of Khrushchev he joined the anti-party group and as a result was purged after the leadership crisis (June 1957).

SHEPPARD, KATHERINE WILSON (1848–1934), NZ Women's Christian Temperance Union leader, who was prominent in the campaign for women's suffrage, enacted in 1893.

SHEPSTONE, SIR THEOPHILUS (1817–93), South African politician, who acted as interpreter during 'the war with the Xhosa in 1835. After six years as British resident in Kaffraria, he came to Natal in 1846, where until 1875 he acted as chief intermediary between the colonists and the African population, either as 'Diplomatic Agent to the Native Tribes' or as secretary for native affairs. Faced with the problems of administering the Africans of Natal, their social organization shattered by the *Mfecane* and without their traditional chiefs, Shepstone evolved Natal's policy of segregation and 'indirect rule'. With considerable administrative skill, he was able to settle the Africans on lands especially set aside for their occupation and to govern them according to customary law. The more progressive aspects of his policy were never implemented and the reserves became increasingly poverty-stricken and over-populated. He was responsible for the British annexation of the Transvaal in 1877, part of the wider British scheme for the confederation of South Africa.

SHERBRO, name given to a coastal area of Sierra Leone, West Africa, and of the people living there. These people are themselves Bulom in origin, and the name derived probably from that of one of their chiefs. They were early partners with Europeans in the coastal trade of their country, and long governed themselves with local chiefs before becoming part of the British protectorate of Sierra Leone, and thus part of the modern country of that name.

SHERBROOKE, ROBERT LOWE, Viscount (1811–92), British Liberal politician, who lived in Australia as a barrister and was a member of the NSW Legislative Council. He returned to Britain, became an MP (1852), and a *Times* leader-writer. As vice-president of the committee of the council on education (1859–64), he insisted on the payment of teachers according to their pupils' examination results. He refused to support parliamentary reform (1866) and his speeches during the reform debates (1866–7) showed his apprehension about advancing democracy and the tyranny of an ignorant majority. Yet he showed a distaste for privilege, superstition, ignorance, class prejudice, and sentimentality. He was a pioneer user of the typewriter and of the bicycle. His rigid faith in political economy made him resist T. H. Green's new 'constructive' Liberalism, and his period in office as chancellor of the exchequer (1868–73) and as home secretary (1873–4), was noticeable for its doctrinaire parsimony.

SHEREMETIEV, BORIS PETROVICH, Count (1652–1719), Russian *boyar* and soldier who served Peter the Great. As commander of the Cossack cavalry at Narva (1700) he shared responsibility for the defeat, but later vindicated himself against the Swedes at Eristler (1701), Hammelshof (1702), and Poltava (1709). He was with Peter as the commander-in-chief at the capitulation of the Pruth (1711).

SHERIDAN, PHILIP HENRY (1831–88), US soldier, who graduated from West Point (1853), served in the West before the Civil War, commanded cavalry in the western theatre (1862–3), and led the cavalry of the Army of the Potomac (1864–5). He was a harsh military governor of LA and TX (1867) and was removed to command on the frontier (1867–1870). He became army commander-in-chief (1883–8).

SHERIDAN, RICHARD BRINSLEY (1751–1816), English dramatist and politician. Among his plays the best-known are *The Rivals* (1775), *The Duenna* (1775), and *The School for Scandal* (1777). He entered parliament in 1780, and after holding various minor posts, became under-secretary for foreign affairs. He used his power of rhetoric to good effect in the impeachment of Warren Hastings of which he, with Burke and Fox, was one of the leading instigators. He was an outspoken opponent of the Younger Pitt's anti-Jacobin legislation and a faithful adherent of the Prince of Wales's set.

SHERIFF (shire reeve) in England, in origin, an official of the West Saxon kings in charge of the king's estates in the shire. He emerged as the chief administrative official in all the English counties in the course of the 10th cent., when the Anglo-Saxon *ealdormen*, who had administered particular shires, were replaced by regional earls. The sheriff was henceforth the king's chief financial, legal, and military official in the shire; he was president of the shire court, accounted for royal revenues, maintained law and order, and led the shire levy to war. The Anglo-Saxon sheriff was usually of thegnly class. Immediately after the Norman conquest his Norman successors were usually mightier personages entrusted with the formidable castles built at the chief county towns and normally owning considerable estates in the county. The office tended to become hereditary and its power became exorbitant. King Henry I, in an attempt to place limitations on it, replaced the baronial sheriffs with 'new men' of lower class and with less lands. The same policy was pursued by Henry II and his sons. The rise of the exchequer as a royal accounting office diminished the danger of large-scale embezzlement of royal assets and the institution of regular visits by royal justices itinerant ensured still further that a close watch would be kept on the sheriff. By the late 12th cent. coroners existed in all counties, keeping an independent record of matters concerning the Crown, and the Great Charter of 1215 debarred the sheriff from acting as royal judge in his own county. The revenues administered by the sheriff in the 13th cent. were reduced as other types of officials took over some of their fiscal functions. Thereafter the office tended to be held for short periods, usually a year, by local county gentlemen, who derived considerable prestige from it, but not much profit. JG

SHERIFFMUIR, BATTLE OF (1715), indecisive Scottish battle in the Jacobite rebellion (fought on the same day as the battle of Preston) between 3500 men under Argyll, supporters of the Hanoverian cause, and 9000 Jacobite Highlanders under Mar. Although Argyll's left wing was routed by the Macdonalds, the rest retired in good order, while Mar withdrew to Perth.

SHERMAN, JOHN (1823–1900), US politician, who served as a congressman (1855–61) and senator (1861–77, 1881–97) from OH, and as secretary of the treasury (1877–81). He was an authority on financial matters and drafted the Sherman Anti-Trust Act (1890). He was appointed secretary of state by President McKinley (1897) but resigned in 1898 because of ill-health and opposition to the war with Spain.

SHERMAN, WILLIAM TECUMSEH (1820–91), US soldier, who was superintendent of the Alexandria Military Academy (1859–61). During the Civil War he succeeded Gen. Grant as commander of the Army of the Tennessee (Sept. 1863) and of all Union forces in the western theatre (March 1864). His seizure of Atlanta (Sept. 1864) and his punitive march through the Carolinas (Nov. 1864–April 1865) hastened the end of hostilities, but intensified the bitterness of the South. He commanded the division of the Mississippi (1865–9) and was army commander-in-chief (1869–83).

SHERMAN SILVER PURCHASE ACT (1890) in the US, legislation, named after Senator John Sherman, of OH, providing for the monthly purchase of 4,500,000 ounces of silver by the US Treasury in exchange for treasury notes acceptable as legal tender. As the notes were redeemable in gold or silver, pressure was placed upon the nation's gold reserves, and the act contributed to the panic of 1893. It was repealed (1893) as part of the government's attempt to restore confidence in the economy.

SHI'A. In AD 661, on the death of Ali, the cousin and son-in-law of the Prophet Muhammad, Mu'awiya, of the House of Umayya, became caliph. Among the Arabs who dominated the Muslim empire there now emerged a 'legitimist' opposition, religio-political in character, which held that the caliphate should be vested in the descendants of Ali and his wife, Fatima, the daughter of the Prophet. This opposition was much strengthened when, in 680, Al-Husayn, a son of Ali, was slain at Karbala, thus providing the Shi'a cause with a martyr. The mawali, *ie*, the new converts to Islam, failing to win from the Arab elite within the Umayyad state that full and equal status which was their due as Muslims, began to give their allegiance to the Shi'a. These mawali elements brought into the Shi'i faith religious ideas deriving from their Christian, Jewish, and Zoroastrian antecedents, *eg*, the Messianic idea of a Mahdi withdrawn into concealment, but destined to reapppear in the world and to restore at last the reign of true justice on earth—an idea which found forcible expression in Iraq during the revolt (685–7) of Al-Mukhtar against the Umayyad regime. An extremist sect within the Shi'i movement, the Hashimiyya, was to become in the course of time a potent propagandist and subversive machine directed against the Umayyad line. It had a large role in the rebellion of 750 which overthrew the Umayyads. This revolution carried to the throne a prince, Al-Saffah, not of Alid, but of Abbasid descent. The Shi'a continued therefore to be active, opposing now the Abbasid caliphate and fomenting numerous revolts in the empire. Among the adherents of the Shi'a some—the Ithna Ashariyya or Twelver Shi'a—followed a moderate line of belief, differing in no vast degree from the orthodox or Sunni form of Islam. Others took a more extreme view, holding the descendants of Ali to be of more than human status and the sole authoritative repositories of the true Muslim religion. The extremists gave their allegiance to Isma'il, the son of the Imam Ja'far al-Sadiq (d. 765). Out of the Isma'ili movement was to come the Fatimid caliphate established in Ifriqiyya through the efforts of Abu Abd Allah al-Shiʻi and Ubayd Allah al-Mahdi and later transferred to Egypt in AD 969. Also connected with the Ismaʻilis were the Qaramita or Carmathians, who controlled the Bahrayn area during the 10th–11th cents. The Shiʻa found its most abiding support in Persia and is still (1970) the official faith of that land.   VJP

SHIDEHARA, KIJŪRŌ (1872–1951), Japanese diplomat. Japan's moderate diplomacy in the 1920s is generally associated with his name. After representing Japan at the Washington Disarmament Conference (1921–2), Shidehara endeavoured, as foreign minister (1924–7, 1929–31), to preserve Japan's treaty rights in China without resorting to force; but the rise of the Chinese nationalist movement and the dissatisfaction of the Japanese army made his task impossible, and the Wakatsuki cabinet in which he served was forced to resign soon after the outbreak of the Manchurian Incident (18 Sept. 1931).

SHIH HUANG-TI, title of the first emperor of the Ch'in dynasty, who reigned from 221 to 210 BC.

SHIHAB, FUʻAD (CHEHAB) (1903–), Lebanese soldier and politician, who belonged to an old Maronite family. As commander-in-chief of the Lebanese army (1945–58) he played a discreet role in refusing to allow the army to be used either by Bishara al-Khuri or Camille Chamoun in furtherance of their political aims. As president (1958–64) in succession to Chamoun, he restored internal stability and enlarged the role of the state in Lebanese life.

SHILOH, BATTLE OF (6–7 April 1862), costly engagement in western TN during the American Civil War. Gen. Grant's Union army was surprised by 40,000 Confederate troops under Gen. Albert S. Johnston. Despite initial success Johnston was forced to retreat, each side having lost over 10,000 men.

SHIMABARA RISING (1637–8), rebellion in Kyūshū Island, southern Japan, by over 20,000 Christians, mainly peasants, against oppressive taxation and religious persecution. It was put down with enormous bloodshed.

SHIMONOSEKI, TREATY OF (17 April 1895), ended the nine-month war between Japan and China, and gave Japan not only Taiwan, a freer hand in Korea, and a large indemnity, but also possession of most of the Liaotung peninsula in southern Manchuria. Russia, however, supported by Germany and France, and claiming to act in the interests of peace, advised Japan to renounce the latter provision (23 April). This 'Triple Intervention', though accepted by Japan (30 April), was regarded as a national humiliation and strengthened the determination of Japan's leaders to increase her military strength.

SHINGAKU, Japanese religious sect, founded by Ishida Baigan (1685–1744). It was influential among merchants, to whose activity it gave moral justification while stressing the need for high ethical standards.

SHINGANHOE in Korea, formed in 1927, became the largest and most effective nationalist organization in Korea under Japanese occupation. Its central leadership was conservative, but many of its local leaders were communists. The Comintern's instructions (1928) to communists to disassociate themselves from bourgeois nationalist movements in colonial countries led to the Shinganhoe's dissolution in 1931, and to right-wing nationalists' regarding the communists as their chief enemy.

SHINQIT, ancient name for Mauritania, but more particularly the Adrar town of Shinqiti, which was built in 1261. To its principal peoples, the Aghlal and the Idaw Ali, Mauritania owes some of its most outstanding scholars.

SHINTŌ (lit. 'The Way of the Gods'), the indigenous religion of Japan. Although it possesses a considerable mythology in which divine ancestry is attributed to the Japanese imperial line, Shintō has no real theology or philosophy. Originating as the nature worship of an agrarian people, with trust rather than fear the dominant emotion, it venerated natural phenomena of exceptional power or beauty as *kami* (superior). In its ceremonies fertility and purification rites were of prime importance; in its social aspect Shintō stressed reverence for the *ujigami* (clan ancestral deity) of each *uji* (clan) and inculcated obedience to the *uji* chief. These practices were of importance politically to the Yamato dynasty, which, as it extended its power throughout Japan, established its own ancestors as the chief deities. Because of this, and because it expressed fundamental Japanese attitudes and feelings, Shintō survived the spread of Buddhism (6th–8th cents). It was, however, affected by Buddhism. The teaching of Kūkai, the founder of *Shingon* Buddhism, led to the identification of local Shintō deities with *bodhisattva*s, and many of the thousands of Shintō shrines were maintained by Buddhist priests. After the Meiji Restoration the government attempted to separate Shintō from Buddhism, hoping to use the Shintō myths concerning the founding of the country to reinforce patriotism and loyalty to the imperial dynasty. This 'State Shintoism', which was officially declared to be not a religion, was strongly emphasized in government propaganda in the 1930s. It was abolished by the Occupation after the Second World War, but popular Shintō survived, and there were still 68,000,000 adherents of the various sects in 1970.   RLS

SHINWELL, EMMANUEL SHINWELL, Life Baron (1884–), British politician who entered parliament in 1922, holding office in the two Labour administrations of Attlee (1945–51).

SHIP MONEY in England, tax whose levy by King Charles I without the consent of parliament helped to bring about the breakdown of his government, and the calling of the Long Parliament. The tax originated with the Plantagenet kings, who exercised the right of requiring ports and maritime counties to furnish ships or money in time of war. Though several statutes had made non-parliamentary taxation illegal, the levying of ship money in time of war had never totally died out, eg, James I levied £40,000 on London and £8550 on other ports without difficulty (1619). In 1628 Charles I demanded £173,000, but withdrew the writs because of opposition. In 1634 he again issued writs to the ports to provide ships against a possible future danger. London claimed exemption, but there was no opposition on constitutional grounds and £80,000 was collected. Writs for £200,000 were issued to inland, as well as coastal, counties and towns in 1635. Opposition forced Charles to consult the judges, and 10 out of 12 agreed that in times of national emergency, of which the Crown was sole judge, ship money could be levied all over the country. A third writ of 1636 made it clear that Charles intended to convert ship money into a permanent tax without parliamentary authority. Viscount Saye and Sele and John Hampden refused payment and a test case, which lasted six months, was heard in 1637. Out of 12 judges only 7 found for the king. This narrow defeat for Hampden encouraged others, and local government ceased to respond to royal command. The complete defeat of ship money was attested by the collection figures for 1640: of £214,400 demanded, only £43,417 was paid. An act of 1641 made ship money illegal.   CJ

SHIP OF THE LINE, traditional battleship of the English navy from the Elizabeth period to the 20th cent. which superseded the round ship of the medieval navy still predominating in Henry VIII's reign. The 'line' ship was built in a ratio of roughly 3 : 1 of length to beam and carried armament which fired broadsides. Grenville's *Revenge* was perhaps the first proper 'line' ship and the *Victory* was the best 19th-cent. example.

SHIPPEN, WILLIAM (1673–1743), English politician who was a country tory under Queen Anne, opposed the Mutiny Bill in 1718 and attacked standing armies as instruments of oppression. Throughout the supremacy of Sir Robert Walpole he opposed the government consistently, sometimes single-handedly. He and Walpole, however, had respect for each other, and in 1741 Shippen refused to support the cabal which was trying to oust Walpole.

SHIPPING in the Middle Ages must be divided into the Mediterranean and northern types. In the south the galley, propelled by oars, was the type of ship mainly used in antiquity. It remained in use in the Mediterranean throughout the Middle Ages, but with considerable improvements: a steering rudder was introduced by the 13th cent. More important still was the appearance, by the late 13th cent., of larger and heavier merchant galleys which travelled normally under sail, but were also capable of being rowed in an emergency or when navigating in shallow waters. When built with exceptional care, as in the Venetian state Arsenal, they were the safest vessels produced by a medieval ship-builder. For 60 years after 1437 not a single Venetian merchant galley was lost at sea. Ordinary sailing vessels were also used in the Mediterranean, equipped with two masts and carrying a variety of sails. But the main region of superior sailing ships was in the Atlantic and the North Sea. The tough, very seaworthy round ships of 13th-cent. Flemish and German merchants created a tradition of shipbuilding capable of gradual improvement and increasing sophistication. In the 14th and early 15th cents shipbuilders of the Atlantic seaboard (probably in northern Spain) produced a combination of the best features of the sailing ships from both the Mediterranean and northern seas. The ultimate result were the caravels and the galleons which enabled the Europeans to undertake distant explorations in the later 15th and 16th cents. Without this revolution in the build and rigging of sailing ships (spreading mainly between 1425 and 1475) the regular voyages to Asia and America could never have been undertaken.   EBF

SHIRAKAWA (1053–1129), Japanese emperor (*reg.* 1072–86), who consolidated the practice of *insei* (cloister government), begun by his father, Go-Sanjō, by controlling court and governmental affairs during the 43 years following his abdication.

SHIRAZI, name adopted by most of the Swahili-speaking Muslims of the East African coast, whether urban or rural, and whether of partly Arab or partly Persian origins, so as to distinguish themselves from the later Omani or other intrusive Arab families, as well as from other Africans. The primary centre of settlement is believed to have been in southern Somalia, the Shungwaya of tradition, and to date back to the 9th cent. or earlier. From this area, beginning in the late 12th cent., secondary settlements were established at Mombasa, Pemba, Zanzibar, Mafia, Kilwa, and on the Comoro Islands.

SHIRE IN ENGLAND originated in the Anglo-Saxon kingdom of Wessex in the late 8th cent. and soon became an important instrument of local government. Some shires were mere territorial units; former independent kingdoms like Kent or Sussex; others were tribal divisions within an old kingdom like Norfolk or Suffolk in East Anglia, others still were territorial groupings round a large town, *eg*, Dorset, which centred on Dorchester.

Under Alfred (*reg.* 871–99) their political, military, and judicial importance expanded under *ealdormen* and shire reeves and by the early 11th cent. all England south of the Tees was divided into shires, each sub-divided into hundreds or wapentakes. The Normans and Angevins maintained this administrative unit and under them the knights and lesser gentry played an increasing role in shire government. With the evolution of parliament in the 13th cent. knights were summoned as representatives of the shires or counties and thus their importance was still recognized in the more centralized government which was developing. Shires (or counties) remained the unit of local government in Britain through the succeeding centuries, though by 1970 various evidence suggested they might give way to larger adminis-trative regions.

SHIRKUH (d. 1169), Abu'l-Harith Asad al-Din, uncle of Salah al-Din (Saladin), soldier who served Nur al-Din, the Zangid lord of Aleppo and Damascus. He made three campaigns against Egypt (1164, 1167, 1169), the last of which gave him control of affairs at Cairo as the vizier of the last Fatimid caliph, Al-'Adid. Shirkuh died two months after his assumption of the office of vizier, the dominance that he had won in Egypt falling now to Salah al-Din.

SHIRLEY, JAMES (1596–1666), English poet and dramatist who served in the Civil War. His numerous works included *The Traitor* (1631) and *The Cardinal* (1641). He wrote little during the period of the Commonwealth and subsequently died from the effects of exposure during the Fire of London.

SHIRLEY, WILLIAM (1694–1771), English lawyer and colonial official, who emigrated from England (1731) to Boston, where, as advocate-general, he represented English imperial interests and enforced the trade acts. As governor of MA (1741–55) he settled the land-bank controversy, secured appropriations for defence from the general court, devised the seizure of Louisborg (1745) from the French, and took part in the negotiations (1749–53) over the boundary between New England and French North America. He replaced Gen. Edward Braddock as supreme commander of the British North American forces (1755), but the failure of the Niagara expedition led to his being recalled to England (1756). He was governor of the Bahamas (1759–70).

SHIRLEY v. FAGG (1675) in England, case by which the House of Lords established its right to act as a court of appeal. Thomas Shirley appealed to the Lords against a Chancery decree in favour of Sir John Fagg, MP, and the Commons took this as a breach of privilege. Several people involved in other cases, and Fagg himself, were imprisoned by the Commons. Both houses stood firm, but in the prorogation of parliament (Nov. 1675–Feb. 1677) the case was quietly dropped, and the appellate jurisdiction of the Lords was not questioned again.

SHITAB RAI (d. 1773), Hindu officer in the Nawab of Bengal's administration. As deputy governor of Bihar he sought to forestall famine (1769) but the Calcutta government failed to act. Later accused of corruption by the British, he was acquitted after a short trial but died the same year.

SHIVAJI (1627–80), Maratha leader and hero, son of Shahji Bhonsle, a *jagirdar* of the Bijapur state in the Deccan, India. In 1659 he scattered a Bijapur army under Afzal Khan after murdering him at an interview with an instrument known as 'the tiger's claw'. In 1660 the new Mughal emperor sent an army against him, but without success until Raja Jai Singh forced him to submit (1665). Shivaji twice plundered the Mughal port of Surat (1664, 1669). A fruitless journey to Agra and interview with Aurangzeb (1666) ended with a secret flight. Operations against the Mughals were resumed (1670), from which time dates the imposition of *chauth* on non-Maratha territory. Sivaji declared himself independent at Raigarh (1674) and then turned southwards. He claimed his father's lands, took the fortress of Gingi, and secured a half-share of the rich Tanjore state from his brother.

His success rested on his organization of the Maratha people and state and his original methods of warfare. He started with the largely homogeneous Maratha people. He united these with the intellectual Brahmans and low-caste Prabhus by patronizing the casteless *bhakti* cult and his slogan of defence of the homeland (*desh*), religion (*dharma*), and the cow against the Muslim invader. He organized his kingdom efficiently with an equitable land system. He used guerrilla tactics in war, moving rapidly with light horse and relying on speed and surprise for success. He financed his wars and enriched the kingdom by plunder from raids and the institutions of *chauth* and *sardeshmukhi*, respectively one quarter and one tenth of the revenue of any district overrun. Shivaji's exploits, leadership, and organization gave the Maratha people a sense of unity and purpose they had never previously experienced. They responded by making him their national hero.

S. N. Sen, *Siva Chhatrapati* (Calcutta, 1920).
V. N. Sarkar, *Shivaji and his Times* (Calcutta, 1919).   TGPS

SHOCKLEY, WILLIAM BRADFORD (1910–), US physicist who, together with John Bardeen (1908–) and Walter Houser Brattain (1902–), developed (1948) the transistor at the Bell Telephone Laboratories in the US. This device, which has since revolutionized electronics, exploits the properties of semi-conducting materials, such as silicon and germanium. The transistor can do all the operations of a conventional radio valve, but since the 1950s has replaced it because of its advantageous compactness, reliability, and performance.

SHŌGUN, title held by most feudal heads of government in Japan. An abbreviation of *Sei I Tai Shōgun* (Barbarian-Conquering-Great-General), it originated during the wars against the Ainus (8th–11th cents). After Minamoto Yoritomo received the title (1192) it was inherited by his successors and by the heads of the Ashikaga *bakufu* (1338–1573). Both Nobunaga and Hideyoshi were prevented by their birth from becoming *shōgun* but Tokugawa Ieyasu was able to claim Minamoto ancestry and he and his descendants held the office (1603–1867) until the restoration of imperial rule.

SHOLES, CHRISTOPHER LATHAM (1819–90), US developer of the typewriter, who worked as a printer and journalist in WI, helped to invent numbering machines, and, with associates, patented a typewriter (1868). His machine, bought and perfected by the Remington Arms Co. (1873), helped to revolutionize office work.

SHŌMU (701–56), Japanese emperor (*reg.* 724–49), who greatly encouraged the growth of Buddhism by establishing an official monastery in each province and erecting in the capital a bronze statue, 53 ft (16 metres) high, of Vairocana.

SHONA, name loosely applied to the peoples of Rhodesia who have been least influenced by the 19th-cent. Ngoni invasions. Shona culture is tentatively thought to be associated with immigrant groups who introduced stone building traditions into Rhodesia from the 11th cent. From the 15th cent. they became notable for their experiments in the political organization of the Mwenemutapa and Rozwi empires. Apart from the major groups of the Karanga, Rozwi, and Korekore, the peoples of Manyika, Kiteve, and Tawara are culturally and linguistically related to the Shona.

SHOP STEWARDS, in Britain, elected representatives of trade union members on the factory floor who handle local grievances. The first union to write shop stewards into its constitution was the Amalgamated Society of Engineers (forerunner of the AEU, now the AEF) before the First World War, and the historical importance of shop stewards lies mainly in their role in engineering during that war. In 1915 the union executives signed an agreement abjuring strikes and restrictive practices for the duration of the war.

This caused a rift with the rank-and-file membership who resented 'dilution', *ie*, the introduction of unskilled or female labour, and who later in the war frequently became involved in dispute over the exemption of skilled men from conscription. Led by the shop stewards, they staged a number of unofficial strikes as on Clydeside in March 1916 and nationally in May 1917.

The stewards themselves were often men of avowedly revolutionary aims, though the grievances they represented were basically conservative. Outside observers, such as Lenin, mistakenly assumed that the shop stewards were the harbingers of a revolutionary mass movement; but after a last fling in Jan. 1919, the shop stewards' movement collapsed with the wartime conditions that had brought it about.

Though the political role of shop stewards did not re-emerge, they became industrially more important as they spread to other industries, and were most important in 1970 in areas such as the motor industry, where bargaining was invariably conducted at plant level over a complex multitude of rates.   IM

SHORT, AUGUSTUS (1802–83), first Anglican Bp of Adelaide (1847), who founded St Peter's Cathedral (1869), and St Barnabas Theological College (1881). He led the way in establishing Australian church government by consensual compact (1855) and established the Anglican bishopric of Perth (1857). He was first vice-chancellor of Adelaide University (1872–6) and its second chancellor (1876–83).

SHORT PARLIAMENT (1640) in England, summoned by King Charles I, on the advice of Strafford, to demand subsidies to fight the Scottish army assembled in the north as a protest against the prayer book, But Pym made a decisive speech enumerating the country's grievances against the government, which included religious 'innovations', illegal taxation, and the neglect of parliament, and the commons resolved that 'till the liberties of the house and kingdom were cleared, they knew not whether they had anything to give or no'. They rejected Charles's offer to abandon ship money in return for 12 subsidies, and scorning any further conciliation, he rashly dissolved the parliament after only three weeks.

'SHORTEST WAY WITH THE DISSENTERS', in England, pamphlet written by Defoe (1702) parodying the violence of Anglican extremists and advising the extermination of nonconformists. Defoe's irony was initially taken seriously so that when the hoax was discovered Defoe was pilloried and imprisoned by the furious Anglicans.

SHORTHAND, the practice of writing legibly by signs at a rate near to that of speech so as to record it verbatim. It is of importance in preserving speeches, *eg*, as a true record of parliamentary or legal proceedings, and in the efficient conduct of official and commercial business. A form of shorthand was known in ancient Greece and Rome; modern shorthand in England dates from 1588, when Timothy Bright published his *Characterie: an Arte of Shorte, Swifte, and Secret Writing by Character*. The idea was taken up by John Willis, who put forward a system based on the alphabet (orthographic), but omitting vowels and silent letters (1602). A similar system by Shelton (1630) was used by Samuel Pepys in his diary, perhaps indicating its use in the civil service of that time. In 1767 Byrom, in his *Universal English Shorthand*, introduced a popular scheme involving the use of strokes in writing and representing the vowels by dots. This was improved by Samuel Taylor (1786), whose scheme was widely adopted in Europe and assisted the publication of parliamentary debates in England. By classifying language scientifically Sir Isaac Pitman developed simpler abbreviations based on phonetics in *Stenographic Sound Hand* (1837); another modern system, devised by John Robert Gregg (1888), was widely adopted in the US. As a result, many stenographers were trained for work in government, the law, and business, and an occupation provided for women in the 20th cent.

SHOSHONEAN INDIANS, American family of tribes formerly occupying a territory in the American West from the Rocky Mountains to the Sierra Nevada range, extending to the WY plains and the Pacific coast, and including such disparate tribes as the Comanche and the Hopi. Contact with Europeans had a profound effect on most of the tribes. The Comanche and Shoshoneans of WY became raiders (c. 1700) after obtaining horses from the Spanish and guns from the French. The traditional life of the Shoshonean tribes in southern CA was permanently disrupted by Spanish missionaries who settled among them after 1770. Last to be affected were the tribes of the inhospitable Great Basin, including the Northern and Southern Paiute, Ute, and Gosiute, who were overtaken by white settlements in the last half of the 19th cent.

SHŌTOKU TAISHI (574–622), Japanese prince, scholar, and politician, who played a large part in introducing Buddhism and Chinese theories of government into Japan. As regent (573–622) during the reign of the Empress Suiko, he co-operated with the Soga family, to which he was closely related, in strengthening the Yamato dynasty. An outstanding scholar, he wrote highly respected Buddhist commentaries and encouraged the building of temples. Of more direct political relevance were his introduction of court ranks (603), which took precedence over older hereditary titles and strengthened the growing concept of a bureaucracy of merit, and his '17 article constitution' (604), which further propagated Chinese political and ethical concepts. He also paved the way for the great changes of the later 7th cent. by sending official missions to China.

SHOVELL, SIR CLOWDISLEY (1650–1707), English politician and sailor, who served in the Second and Third Anglo-Dutch Wars. He was in the Mediterranean for many years, usually commanding his own vessel against the Barbary Corsairs. In 1698 he was first elected to parliament for Rochester, the seat for which he was re-elected in four successive general elections. In the War of the Spanish Succession one of his first tasks was to escort back to England the treasure ships captured by Rooke at Vigo Bay. After commanding in the Mediterranean in 1703, he assisted Rooke in the capture of Gibraltar the next year, and fought at the battle of Malaga. Along with the Earl of Peterborough, he was responsible for the fall of Barcelona in 1705. He commanded the Anglo-Dutch fleet off the coast of Provence (1707), supporting the forces of the Duke of Savoy and of the Holy Roman emperor (under Prince Eugène), advancing to Toulon, which came under siege and which he heavily bombarded. The siege was abandoned, however, and he successfully covered the withdrawal of the Allied troops before sailing back to England, but his flagship, the *Association*, and two other ships were wrecked off the Scilly Isles. Many of the sunken valuables have recently been recovered.   BM

SHŌWA PERIOD (25 Dec. 1926–), reign of the present (1970) Japanese emperor, Hirohito, whose official title is *Shōwa Tennō*. The literal meaning of *Shōwa*, 'enlightenment and harmony', has borne little relation to events, however. Economic hardship and many plots and assassinations, followed by military encroachments on political and social life, and Japan's disastrous drift into war with China and the US, gave currency to the term '*kurai tanima*' ('dark valley') to describe most of the period before 1945. Japan's rapid economic progress since the early 1950s has not alleviated the social and cultural problems caused by modernization.

SHRADDHANAND, SWAMI (1856–1926), Indian politician and educationalist. Lala Munshi Ram, as he was before he became a *sanyasi* (1917), was mainly concerned with Arya Samaj activities in the Punjab until that time. His most notable work was the creation of the Kangri *Gurukula* at Hardwar (1902), a school and college designed to give boys a traditional Hindu education. He gave up the governorship of the *Gurukula* when he became a *sanyasi* and turned increasingly to political activities, first in the *satyagraha* campaigns (1919–21) in Delhi and the Punjab, then the Akali agitations in the Punjab, and finally the *shuddhi* and *sangathan* campaigns of the Hindu Mahasabha from 1923 onwards. In his last years he also took up the cause of untouchables and, being dissatisfied with Congress policies, formed the *Dalit Uddhar Sabha* to work for the improvement of their position.

SHREWSBURY, CHARLES TALBOT, Duke of (1st of 1st creation), (1660–1718), English politician, who became earl in 1668. He was brought up a Roman Catholic, but under the influence of Abp Tillotson he became an Anglican in 1679 and in the reign of James II he resisted all persuasion to return to the Catholic faith. He entered into the conspiracy against James II and was one of the 'Immortal Seven' who signed (30 June 1688) the letter inviting William of Orange to invade England. Shrewsbury went to Holland in Sep. 1688 and returned with William in Nov. He was appointed secretary of state for the northern department (1689), became disillusioned with the growing party strife and resigned in 1690. He was suspected of Jacobite sympathies and was dismissed from the privy council with Marlborough (1692), and became active in opposition, criticizing the government's conduct of the war and bringing in the Triennial Bill. He became secretary of state for the southern department in 1694 and was created Duke of Shrewsbury. He was appointed lord chamberlain in 1699, resigning on health grounds in 1700.

He lived abroad (1700–7), chiefly in Rome. Returning to England, he gradually became alienated from his old Whig associates, and in 1710 allied with the Tories, becoming lord chamberlain (1710–4). In 1713 he became lord lieutenant of Ireland, and on the dismissal of Harley, Queen Anne appointed Shrewsbury lord treasurer (30 July–11 Oct. 1714). When Anne died (1 Aug. 1714) Shrewsbury helped to secure the Hanoverian succession. He became lord chamberlain again, resigning in 1715.   CJ

SHREWSBURY, JOHN TALBOT, 4th Earl of (1st of 2nd creation) (c. 1384–1453), English soldier, whom Joan of Arc defeated at Orléans and captured at Patay (1429). He was the commander of the English army that tried to recover Gascony in 1453. It was an unbalanced army, comprising too few knights and men-at-arms and a disproportionate number of archers and ordinary infantry. It was destroyed by the French and Talbot was killed.

SHREWSBURY, BATTLE OF (20 July 1403), victory of King Henry IV of England over the rebel Henry Percy (Hotspur) and his uncle, Thomas, Earl of Worcester. The rebels had tried to capture young Henry, Prince of Wales, but this was forestalled by the arrival of the king, who joined battle with them before Owain Glendower could arrive to help the Percies. Hotspur was killed.

SHUISKY, VASILI, Tsar (*fl.* 17th cent.), Russian prince, who was the *boyars*' candidate for the position of tsar during the Time of Troubles. In May 1606 he led the revolt of the *boyars* to overthrow the false Dmitri in Moscow, and was forthwith nominated tsar by his fellow conspirators, agreeing to certain constitutional limitations upon his autocratic power. The peasant revolt of Bolotnikov and Polish intervention in support of a second false Dmitri followed. Shuisky called on Sweden for help, thus provoking Sigismund III of Poland to declare war. After Sigismund besieged Smolensk (1609) he was deposed by a revolt of the gentry led by Liapunov (1610), was forced to become a monk, and was taken as a prisoner to Sigismund in Warsaw (1611).

SHULGI (c. 2094–2047 BC), King of Ur at the height of its power under the Third Dynasty. He brought Assyria and

Elam under his control, defended the eastern frontiers by diplomacy and military expeditions, completed new buildings, and improved the economy and administration of the empire.

SHUN-CHIH, reign-title of Fu-lin (*reg.* 1638–61), first Emperor of the Ch'ing dynasty (1644–61). Fu-lin was chosen head of the Manchu state on the death of his father, Abahai (1643), and when the Manchus conquered China the following year he was proclaimed Emperor of China. However, real power was exercised by Dorgan (1612–50), one of the two prince regents, who must be credited with laying the foundations of Manchu rule. After 1650, power fell into the hands of Dorgan's rivals; Fu-lin himself began to be active in government affairs, but initially was much handicapped by his lack of knowledge of the Chinese language. Fu-lin was also religiously inclined, and was very close to the Jesuit missionary Adam Schall von Bell before he became a devout Buddhist in 1657.

SHUO-WEN, China's first dictionary, completed in AD 121. The book lists over 9000 characters in a systematic fashion, explaining their meaning and pronunciation, and reproducing written forms that had been used in contemporary inscriptions. In describing the usage of the characters, the work often cites from texts that have now been lost, and thus forms a valuable source of data for students of Chinese literature and history.

SHUVALOV, PYOTR ANDREYEVICH, Count (1827–87), Russian politician and diplomat, who opposed emancipation and whose influence at home was reactionary. While ambassador in London he showed great diplomatic talent in averting an Anglo-Russian war (1878). As working head of the delegation at the treaty of Berlin he was responsible for Russia's acquisition of considerable gains.

SHWEDAGON, best-known and most venerable of Burma's countless pagodas. The Shwedagon stands on the most southerly spur of the Pegu Yomas, or hills, in the northern outskirts of Rangoon. Buddhists fix the date of its foundation as 588 BC. It certainly dates from far back in prehistory. The original structure has from time to time been encased in a fresh layer of bricks and regilt to attain its present imposing size and beautiful shape. It is said to cover relics not only of Gautama, but of three preceding Buddhas, and is a great place of pilgrimage.

SIAK SULTANATE, Malay state in Eastern Sumatra, independent of Riau-Johore since the time of Raja Kechil (1721). It flourished in the late 18th cent., when its suzerainty reached as far northward as the fertile Deli-Langkat region. Siak's acceptance of Netherlands Indies' sovereignty (1858) provided the legal basis for the Dutch advance into the more important northern states, where Dutch tobacco plantations soon flourished.

SIAN INCIDENT (1936) in China, kidnapping of Chiang Kai-shek by subordinates, who believed his resistance to Japanese aggression was not firm enough. He was seized at Sian in north-west China by Manchurian officers who were bitter about the loss of their homeland to the Japanese, and he was held until he agreed to form a united front with the communists. Chang Hsüeh-liang, the Manchurian leader, assumed responsibility for his arrest, and returned with him to Nanking. He himself was arrested, and not released until 1961.

SIBERIA, RUSSIAN CONQUEST OF, epic expansion of the Muscovite state in the 16th–20th cents, which opened up the vast region of northern Asia between the Urals and the Pacific, from the Arctic Ocean in the north to China and Mongolia in the south. From the 12th cent. Novgorod merchants had traded in furs with the tribes of the lower Ob

river, but it was not until 1581 that Yermak Timofeevich, a mercenary of the great merchant family of Stroganov, led his Cossack band on an expedition up the Chusovaya river, defeated the Mongol khanate, and opened up the conquest of Siberia. From Yermak's death (1585) the expansion proceeded rapidly. The Cossacks used the river systems of the Ob, Yenisei, and Lena, establishing fortified towns (*ostrogs*), eg, Tobolsk (1587), Tomsk (1604), Yakutsk (1632), Okhotsk (1649), and Irkutsk (1652), and imposing tributes of furs on the natives. In the Amur region alone the Russians were checked by the Chinese army and by the terms of the treaty of Nerchinsk (1689) withdrew their claims to southern Siberia. It was not until 1858 that the Amur became the frontier between Russia and China. In 1699 Kamchatka was taken and in 1756 the Altai area was annexed. Meanwhile the exploration was put on a systematic, scientific basis when the Russian Academy of Sciences organized several expeditions, mainly to northern Siberia and the Far East, eg, the second expedition of Vitus Bering, whose party included the historian Müller, the botanist and chemist Gmelin, the natural historian Steller, and the astronomer De Lisle. In the 19th cent. geographical discovery was taken over by the Imperial Russian Geographical Society and certain Siberian businessmen. Although the original motive for conquest had been the acquisition of furs, by the 18th cent. the mining of silver and copper in the Altai region was started, while silver and lead were found in the Nerschinsk area. Forced labour was used by the state, which until 1763 administered the annexed areas through the Siberian office in Moscow, and latterly in St Petersburg. The full industrial potential of Siberia has only been realized in the present century.

G. A. Lensen (ed.), *Russia's Eastward Expansion* (New York, 1964).   MKS

SIBIR, Turko-Mongol khanate centred on the Irtysh–Tobol basin, its capital being near modern Tobolsk. It was founded in the 15th cent. by the Shaybanid Ibek, disrupted by the expedition of the Cossack adventurer Yermak (d. 1585), and eventually incorporated into the Tsarist empire under Boris Godunov (*reg.* 1598–1605). The descendants of the last khan, Kuchum (d. *c.* 1601), reigned as Khans of Kazimov (1614–1681).

SIBYLLINE ORACLES, collection of oracles written by Jews and Christians between *c.* 150 BC and the 4th cent. AD in imitation of the pagan 'Sibylline books', to present Jewish and Christian doctrines to the pagan world.

SICELIOTS, comprehensive term for all Greeks living in ancient Sicily, as distinct from non-Greeks, eg, Sicels, within Sicily and other Greeks outside Sicily. It perhaps was first used by Greek Sicilian nationalists in the 5th cent. BC, eg, Hermocrates of Syracuse.

SICELS, pre-Greek inhabitants of ancient Sicily. Though of uncertain origin, they were possibly Indo-European-speaking intruders from Italy and conquerors of the earlier non-Indo-European Sicans and Elymians from Africa and Spain. They occupied principally central and eastern Sicily and came *c.* 730 BC into close contact with the first Greek colonies. In general, early relations were good, except at Syracuse, where Sicels were killed and enslaved by the Greek settlers. Increasing domination of Sicel communities by Greeks, and especially Syracusans, provoked the unsuccessful nationalist movement led by Ducetius (*c.* 460–440). Subsequent attempts by the Sicels, supported by Athens (415) and Carthage (405), to preserve their autonomy were finally frustrated in the 4th cent. by Dionysius I's extensive interference in Sicel affairs.

SICILIAN ENTERPRISE. In 1254 Pope Innocent IV offered the Sicilian throne to Edmund of Lancaster, younger son of the English King Henry III, in return for payment of the papal debts, standing at 135,000 marks. Henry was enamoured of the scheme and also subsequently threatened with interdict if he withdrew from it. The English baronage and clergy deplored the scheme and finally (April 1258) not only refused aid for it but made the demands for reforms that began the period of baronial revolt (1258–65).

SICILIAN EXPEDITION (1718), launched by Spain against the Duke of Savoy in an attempt to recover former Spanish possessions in Italy. Though the expedition was successful Britain refused to allow an upsetting of the balance of power and peace and the Spanish fleet was destroyed at Cape Passaro (1718) by Admiral Byng.

SICILIAN VESPERS, War of the (1282–1302), derives its name from an uprising at Palermo, capital of Sicily, at the hour of vespers, on 30 March 1282. The rising was the culmination of years of resentment by the Sicilians against the rule of a Frenchman, Charles of Anjou, who, since his conquest of the kingdom of Sicily in 1266, had distrusted the islanders and moved his capital to Naples on the Italian mainland. Sicily was the most heavily exploited of his dominions and the rising at Palermo was followed by the massacre of Frenchmen throughout Sicily. From the start the rising was supported by King Peter III of Aragon, husband of a daughter of Manfred, the last Hohenstaufen ruler of Sicily, who was killed by Charles in 1266. Manfred's former associates played a vital part in the ensuing war, especially John of Procida, chancellor of Aragon, and Roger de Loria, a naval commander, who assured the command of the sea to the Sicilians. The war was protracted because Charles of Anjou had been introduced into southern Italy by the papacy and a succession of popes regarded the crushing of the Sicilian revolt as of utmost importance. Crusades were preached against the Sicilians and their allies, leading to the invasion of Aragon (1285) by Charles's nephew, King Philip III of France. This ended in disaster as Loria annihilated the supporting French fleet and Philip III died during the retreat from Spain. Thereafter the war continued mainly in Italy and ended in 1302 through the exhaustion of all the belligerents. Henceforth Sicily remained an independent kingdom under the Aragonese dynasty, but southern Italy suffered damage from which it did not recover for centuries.
MH

SICKINGEN, FRANZ VON (1481–1523), German knight and mercenary soldier, a native of the Rhineland who fought for various causes, eg, against the Venetians for the Emperor Maximilian (1508) and against Württemberg for the Swabian League (1518). He also served Charles V against the French (1521), but from 1520 worked with Ulrich von Hütten to establish the Lutheran reformation and create a Protestant league of knights. While under the imperial ban he was besieged in his castle of Landstühl by the forces of Trier, Hesse, and the Count Palatine and was killed there.

SICYON, ancient Greek city-state in the north-east Peloponnese 16 kms west of Corinth, traditionally settled by Dorians from Argos c. 1000 BC. Early in the 6th cent. its tyrant, Cleisthenes, asserted Sicyon's independence of Argos and extended its influence into central Greece. After Sparta's expulsion of the last Orthagorid tyrant, Sicyon entered the Peloponnesian League (c. 550) and was not again of political significance until, through its citizen Aratus, it participated in the power of the Achaean League (3rd cent.). It produced, however, painters and sculptors of merit, eg, Lysippus in the 4th cent.

SIDGWICK, HENRY (1838–1900), English philosopher and economist, who was an advocate of university education for women and pioneered this cause successfully at Cambridge.

SIDI IFNI, small Spanish enclave on the Moroccan seaboard. Though Spanish presence here dates from 1476, when a Canary Islands adventurer, Diego Garcia de Herrera, established a small trading fort named Santa Cruz de Mar Pequeña, it was not until 1860 that Spain was able to include Sidi Ifni within its empire under the treaty of Tetouan. Spanish possession was reconfirmed, within slightly modified frontiers, by a Franco-Spanish treaty of 1912. In 1969 the enclave was handed over to Morocco. Its population (1970) was 50,000.

SIDMOUTH, HENRY ADDINGTON, 1st Viscount (1757–1844), British politician, who became prime minister in 1801, after King George III had refused to support the Younger Pitt's plans for Roman Catholic emancipation, to which Addington was opposed. Addington shared fairly general doubts about the wisdom of continuing the French Wars, and his administration negotiated the peace of Amiens in March 1802. On the resumption of war in 1804 he was replaced by Pitt. In the 'Ministry of all the Talents' (1806–7) he was lord privy seal. As Viscount Sidmouth he held office as home secretary (1812–21) and became a target for attack by Cobbett, Hunt, and the popular radicals, because of his reputation for severity in the suppression of radical activity and his use of spies and *agents provocateurs*.

SIDNEY, ALGERNON (1622–83), English politician who served in the parliamentary armies during the Civil War, and in Ireland under his brother, the lord lieutenant. Though nominated as a commissioner for Charles I's trial, he took no part. As a member of the 1651 council of state, he disapproved of Cromwell's assumption of power and retired to Holland, returning in 1659. In exile on the continent till 1677, he returned and joined the intrigues of the 'country' party, and looked to Monmouth for the succession. After Shaftesbury's death (1682), he worked closely with Monmouth, Russell, Essex, and Hampden, and was charged with treason on discovery of the Rye House Plot (1683). Tried before Judge Jeffreys, he was found guilty and beheaded.

SIDNEY, SIR PHILIP (1554–86), English soldier, diplomat, politician, and poet, who went on diplomatic missions to France, Germany, and the Netherlands, where he was made governor of Flushing (1584). He was mortally wounded fighting the Spaniards at Zutphen, and his personal charm and chivalry, his enthusiasm for literature and exploration, and his romantic death seem to epitomize the Elizabethan age. Sidney was anxious to naturalize classical metres in English, and *The Apologie for Poetrie* (1580, pub. 1595, after Sidney's death) was a critical discussion of lasting value, despite its failure to realize the possibilities of poetic drama. His sonnets to Penelope Devereux (1580–4) were collected as *Astrophel and Stella*, and *Arcadia* (1580 et seq.), a prose romance containing pastoral eclogues, was written for the amusement of his sister, the Countess of Pembroke.

SIDON, one of the principal Phoenician towns, famous for its glassware and embroideries. It was captured by Assyria (677 BC) and from then was only periodically independent between conquests by the great powers.

SIDQI PASHA, ISMA'IL (1875–1950), Egyptian industrialist and politician, once a member of the Wafd Party. He later became a supporter of King Fu'ad and, as prime minister (1930–4), when he was called the 'strong man of Egyptian politics', he abolished the old Egyptian constitution and remodelled a new one. His 1946 agreement with the British minister, Ernest Bevin, on the British evacuation of Egypt was rejected by the Egyptian parliament.

SIEGE WARFARE in Europe, investment of fortified strategic towns, the most common pattern of warfare in the 17th cent., when decisive battles were relatively rare because of the cost of maintaining a large, armoured body of cavalry with which they could be won. The siege, as perfected by Turenne,

Charles of Lorraine, and William III, was cheaper and more reliable, depending for its success upon the skill of military engineers of whom the two most eminent were Vauban and Coornhert. The War of the League of Augsburg (1689–97) marked the climax of European siege warfare. From the end of the 17th cent. the invention of the bayonet, the replacement of the firelock by the flintlock, and the development of the artillery heralded the return of the pitched battle which was effectively exploited in the 18th cent. by Marlborough, Eugène, Charles XII of Sweden, and Frederick the Great of Prussia.

SIEGECRAFT in the Middle Ages. Castles and fortified towns played a prominent role in medieval warfare. Medieval wars of the 11th–14th cents largely resolved themselves into a series of interminable sieges. Before the 12th cent. most castles were made of timber on a rock or artificial mound and could be formidable fortresses, though vulnerable to fire. With the coming of stone castles of increasing elaboration in the 12th–13th cents the besiegers tended to be at a strong disadvantage. To achieve success they either had to starve the garrison out or break into the castle at the cost of heavy casualties. One way of gaining entry was by filling in ditches surrounding the castle and wheeling up a movable tower to the wall, discharging large bodies of assailants directly on to the ramparts. Another alternative was the breaching of the walls, followed by an assault through the breach. The techniques used for effecting a breach, particularly the machines for hurling projectiles (the ballista and the mangonel), were derived from classical antiquity. The mangonel especially, which was used to hurl large stones against a section of the walls, was so effective that it continued in use for long after the introduction of siege guns. The most efficient way of bringing down a wall or a tower was by undermining. This was impossible only when a castle was built on a solid rock and most difficult if it was surrounded by water. The introduction of siege artillery in the 15th cent. ended the superiority of defence over attack. As early as 1450 Charles VII of France had such an effective siege train that he captured all the English-held castles in Normandy in one year.

SIEGFRIED LINE. In the First World War this was known as the Hindenburg Line. In the Second World War it was Hitler's 'West Wall'. Work on it began after the reoccupation of the Rhineland in 1936 and continued intermittently until 1944; by then a continuous belt of field fortifications extended down Germany's frontier from north of the Ruhr to Switzerland. This position, though extremely strong in some places, was probably of greater psychological than practical significance for both sides. In the autumn of 1944 it was on this line that the German armies retreating from France halted and regrouped. The line, combined with Allied logistical difficulties and strategic errors, seriously delayed the invasion of Germany. In the spring of 1945, however, it was rapidly penetrated at several points, though not without hard fighting.

SIEMENS, SIR CHARLES WILLIAM (1823–83), German-born English engineer, who in collaboration with his brother Friedrich (1826–1904) in the early 1860s improved Bessemer's process of steel making. They developed an open-hearth furnace in which the air blast was preheated by a heat-regeneration process and introduced the use of controlled additions of iron ore (oxide) to remove excess carbon. This later development coincided with the use of scrap iron by Pierre Emil Martin (1824–1915) to dilute the carbon. By 1900 the steel production in the world by the Siemens–Martin open-hearth furnace, as it became known, exceeded that from Bessemer converters.

SIEMENS, WERNER (1816–92), German industrialist, pioneer of electro-technology, and brother of Sir Charles Siemens. In 1844 he became superintendent of the Berlin artillery workshops and in 1848, in spite of official scepticism, set up the first telegraph in Germany, between Berlin and Frankfurt am Main. His most important discovery was the principle of the dynamo in 1866; from then on, he became one of the leading figures of the new electrical industry, which played a crucial part in Germany's economic development and urbanization. Like Alfred Krupp and Emil Rathenau, Siemens combined scientific knowledge and inventiveness with a shrewd business sense and also with enlightened social ideas; like them, too, he was the head of a distinguished family. His son, William (1855–1919), greatly enlarged his father's firm and achieved further advances in telegraphy, electric lighting, and engineering.

SIENA, Italian city-republic in southern Tuscany. In the Middle Ages it was one of the principal rivals of Florence and was distinguished by the fierce and war-like spirit of its citizens. In the 13th cent. it was briefly one of the leading Italian banking centres, its chief family of Bonsignori being the richest Italian financiers of the period 1250–90. Lack of important industries made it difficult for Siena to retain a position of first rank in the business world and this in turn adversely affected its political power. It was finally conquered by Florence in 1555. The greatest glory of Siena springs from the patronage extended to a long succession of great artists. Duccio di Buoninsegna (d. *c.* 1318), Ambrogio Lorenzetti (d. 1348), one of the pioneers in the inclusion of landscape, and Simone Martini are among the most important Italian painters of the 14th cent. Siena's stupendous cathedral would have been one of the biggest in Italy if the plague of 1348–9 had not stopped its expansion. A distinctive school of painters and sculptors continued to work at Siena in the 15th and 16th cents, the painters being particularly notable as fine decorators.

SIERRA, JUSTO (1848–1912), Mexican writer, politician, and liberal reformer, who, as education minister under Porfirio Díaz, re-established the Autonomous University (1910). Under the influence of Positivism he became a supporter of a dictatorial regime.

SIERRA LEONE (78,000 sq. kms) in West Africa, formerly a British protectorate which became an independent member of the Commonwealth in 1961. The population (1970) of 2,180,300 included Mende, Temne, and Creole people. A house of representatives of 66 is elected by adult suffrage and is led by a prime minister and cabinet with executive power.

SIETE PARTIDAS, LAS, in Castile, legal treatise compiled under the supervision of Alfonso the Wise in the 13th cent. in an attempt to bring greater legal uniformity to his kingdom and to affirm the supremacy of the monarch in the state. It drew heavily on Justinian's Code of Civil Law and the Spanish *Fuero Juzgo*. Although it was used in appeal cases before 1348, it was not formally promulgated until that date and eventually had a great influence on Spanish legal thought.

SIEVERSHAUSEN, BATTLE OF (1553), battle of the German religious wars, where Maurice, Elector of Saxony, destroyed the Brandenburg army of Margrave Albert Alcibiades, though he died two days later from wounds received in the action.

SIEYÈS, EMMANUEL JOSEPH (1748–1836), French abbé and politician during the Revolution. He had a decisive influence on the formulation of middle-class demands at the meeting of the estates-general through his pamphlet *Qu'est-ce que le Tiers État?* (Jan. 1789). Though at first a constitutional royalist, he eventually voted for the execution of the king (1793). He favoured restriction of the franchise to substantial citizens, but was able to avoid involvement in the political struggles of 1793–4 and survived the Terror. In May 1799 he was made a director and used his position to plan a *coup* *d'état* against the Directory itself. In the Brumaire coup he hoped Bonaparte would allow him to set up a system which would provide 'authority from above' with 'confidence from below'. Too late, he realized that this was not to be, but his ideas did have some influence on the Consulate and he co-operated with Napoleon in the Senate. His association with the emperor forced Sieyès to live in exile (1815–30) after Napoleon's fall.

SIFFIN, BATTLE OF (July 657), located north of Al-Raqqa, on the west bank of the Euphrates. The armies of Mu'awiya and of Ali met in conflict. The battle ended without a decisive result, an appeal being made from the sword to arbitration. Representatives of Mu'awiya and Ali met later at Adhruh in Jan. 659 to consider the issues under dispute.

SIFTON, SIR CLIFFORD (1861–1929), Canadian politician, who became a member of the Man. legislature in 1888 and served until 1896 as provincial attorney-general and then as minister of education. He was the leading figure in the settlement of the Man. schools controversy. In 1896 he was elected to the Canadian House of Commons and was minister of the interior (1896–1905). He introduced (1897) a measure to extend responsible government to the NWT. In 1905 he resigned over the education clauses of the Autonomy Bills. He led a revolt against the Liberal prime minister, Sir Wilfred Laurier, because of the US–Canada Reciprocity treaty (1911). In the subsequent election his campaign against the treaty was one of the causes of the Liberals' defeat.

SIGER OF BRABANT (*c.* 1240–*c.* 1281), French philosopher who taught at Paris, where he was the leader of a group of Aristotelians who were deeply influenced by the commentaries on Aristotle of the Arabic scholar Averroes. Siger's teaching led to his condemnation for heresy (1275–7). He was murdered while on a visit to the pope in connection with his condemnation.

SIGEUM, ancient Greek settlement that controlled the entrance to the Hellespont (Dardanelles), established by the Athenians probably *c.* 600 BC and later strengthened (*c.* 540) by Peisistratus against attacks from Mytilene. In the 5th–4th cents possession of Sigeum remained vital to Athens' control of the Black Sea corn trade.

SIGISMUND (*reg.* 1410–37), German Emperor of the Luxemburg dynasty, whose principal base was in Hungary. His claims to the inheritance of Bohemia after the death of his elder brother Wenceslas (d. 1419) were nullified by the national Bohemian revolt. Sigismund had been responsible for inviting John Hus, the Bohemian religious leader, to the church council of Constance and had provided him with a safe-conduct, but had failed to save him subsequently from trial and burning. Thereafter all attempts to reconquer Bohemia through a series of Catholic crusades against the Hussite heretics ended in disaster.

SIGISMUND II (1520–72), King of Poland (*reg.* 1548–72), son of Sigismund I. He was the last representative of the direct male line of the Jagiellon dynasty. As a child of 10 Sigismund was elected and crowned king in succession to his father, though his reign in Poland did not begin until his father's death in 1548. Meanwhile he had been made Grand Duke of Lithuania (*reg* 1544–8). His reign was marked by internal tension and external expansion. During his lifetime the Reformation spread rapidly in Poland and in 1555 he granted freedom of worship to all Protestants, with the result that Poland became a refuge for the most radical sects, *eg,* Anabaptists, Bohemian Brethren, and Antitrinitarians. From the first *sejm* of 1548 he was in conflict with the rising *szlachta* class who gradually won control of the legislature and executive. In 1561 he accepted the integration of Livonia into Poland, the ruling Grand Master, Gerhard Kettler, having sought Polish aid against the Russian tsar, Ivan IV. This brought Sigismund into conflict with the tsar, whose forces seized Polotsk in 1563. To strengthen Lithuania and Poland in the war against Russia (1561–70) Sigismund allied himself with Denmark (1563) and Sweden (1568) and finally, by the union of Lublin (1569), converted the personal union between his grand duchy and his kingdom into one constitutional state, consisting of Poland, Lithuania, West Prussia, White Russia, and the Ukraine. This multi-religious, multi-lingual commonwealth was the final achievement of his reign. MKS

SIGISMUND III (1566–1632), King of Poland (*reg.* 1587–1632) and King of Sweden (*reg.* 1592–9), who was the son of John III of Sweden and of Catharine, sister of Sigismund II of Poland. He was brought up in the Catholic religion of his mother. This made him unacceptable as King of Sweden, where he was strongly opposed by his uncle, Duke Charles, who had the support of the Riksdag. Although the Council sided with Sigismund, he was defeated at Stångebro (1598) and deposed in 1599 by the Riksdag. His family's claim to the Swedish throne was not formally abandoned until 1660.

In 1592 Sigismund married a daughter of Archduke Charles of Styria, which brought him into closer relations with the emperor and the pope. He established the Uniate Church in Poland, but failed in his efforts to reduce the power of the nobility. Abroad, his armies defeated the Swedes at Kirkholm in Livonia (1605) and occupied Moscow (1610). Nevertheless, Sigismund had no lasting success against Russians, Turks, or Swedes, and at the Truce of Altmark (1629) he surrendered Livonia to his triumphant cousin, Gustavus Adolphus.

SIGUENZA Y GÓNGORA, CARLOS DE (1645–1700), Mexican intellectual, who was professor of mathematics at Mexico University, royal cosmographer, astronomer, historian, poet, and critic. His reputation extended to Europe, and he was perhaps the most brilliant Mexican savant of the colonial period.

SIJILMASA, once the major northern caravan terminus for the western Sahara; located in the Tafilelt region of southern Morocco its ruins cover an area of over 20 sq. miles (51·8 sq. kms). Founded in the 8th cent. by the Banu Midrar, it was a flourishing centre of Kharijite Islam. For a short time early in the 10th cent. it was controlled by Ubaidallah, the Fatimid Mahdi. Zenata Berbers seized the city as clients of the Umayyad caliphate of Cordoba, but were never popular, and when Sijilmasa was captured by the Almoravids (1055) there was little opposition. For many centuries the city was nominally under successive Moroccan dynasties, although it remained semi-independent and was a centre of sedition. It retained its commercial supremacy until the 14th cent., when its importance slowly declined. Tafilelt replaced Sijilmasa between 1515 and 1540, and the oasis fell into ruins, although in the 17th cent. the region as a whole was to be the cradle of the Alawid Shurafa dynasty of Morocco.

SIKANDER, SIR HYAT KHAN (1892–1942), Punjab Muslim politician, who was a member of Fazl-i-Husain's Punjab National Unionist Party from 1921, when he first entered the Punjab Legislative Council. He built a strong position of leadership in the Punjab by the time provincial autonomy was introduced (1937). He was chairman of the provincial 'Simon' committee (1928) and received his reward from a grateful government in appointment as Revenue Member (1929) and acting governor (1932, 1934). He became a deputy-governor of the new Reserve Bank of India (1935) but with Fazl-i-Husain's death in 1936 he returned to lead the Unionists to a substantial election victory (1937) and become chief minister. Initially hostile to Jinnah and the league, he compromised so as to keep Unionist control on provincial matters and maintained an uneasy alliance with Jinnah until his death.

SIKH WARS, between the British and the Sikhs of the Punjab (1845–6, 1848–9). The death of Ranjit Singh (1839) was followed by years of misrule. Fearing a British attack, the Sikh army crossed the Sutlej on 11 Dec. 1845. They were defeated in four fiercely contested battles—Mudki and Ferozeshah (Dec. 1845), Aliwal (Jan. 1846), and Sobraon (Feb. 1846). After this the Punjab became a British protectorate with Sir Henry Lawrence as resident. The murder of two British officers at Multan led to the second war. After the indecisive battle of Chillianwalla (13 Jan. 1849), the Sikhs were routed at Gujrat (21 Feb. 1849). There then followed the annexation of the Punjab.

SIKHS, or disciples, originally a religious brotherhood who broke away from Hinduism in the days of Nanak (1469–1539), their first religious leader or guru. Nanak was a quietist who stressed the unity of God and opposed caste distinctions. His successor, Guru Angad (d. 1552), began to write the *Adi Granth* or Sikh scriptures. He is said to have invented the Gurmukhi script, often erroneously described as a language. To Guru Ramdas (d. 1581) is due the foundation of the golden temple at Amritsar built on a plot of land which was the gift of Akbar, the Mughal emperor. Guru Arjan (d. 1606) enlarged the *Adi Granth*. He was tortured to death on Jahangir's orders because he unwisely gave shelter to Jahangir's fugitive son, Prince Khusru. Under the next guru, Har Govind (d. 1645), the Sikhs became more militant and fought against Shah Jahan. Guru Tegh Bahadur was put to death (1675) by Aurangzeb because he refused to accept Islam. It was under Govind Singh (d. 1708), the tenth or last guru, that the Sikhs were transformed from a religious brotherhood into a strong military power. After this the Sikh brotherhood was known as the *Khalsa* or Pune. The Sikhs were not an ethnic group, for anyone could become a Sikh. To distinguish them from other groups Govind Singh ordered the use of what is known as the five Ks: the *Kes* (unshorn hair); the *Kachh* (short drawers); the *Kara* (iron bangle); the *Kirpan* (sword); and the *Kangha* (hair comb). The growth of Sikh power in the Punjab was the result of Muslim religious and political persecution and was facilitated by the weakness of the late Mughals after the death of Aurangzeb in 1707. After the death of Ahmad Shah Durrami, in 1773, they were able to consolidate their power in the Punjab. Later came the development of the Sikh community after 1857, the rise of the Akali Sikhs, the treatment of Sikhs who attempted to settle in other parts of the Commonwealth, and the splendid record of the Sikh regiments of the Indian army. The partition of 1947 was followed by a Sikh exodus from Pakistan to India.

J. D. Cunningham, *A History of the Sikhs* (Oxford, 1918).
M. Macauliffe, *The Sikh Religion*, 6 vols (Oxford, 1909).
                              CCD

SIKKIM, princely state and protectorate of the republic of India, situated in the eastern Himalayas between Nepal and Bhutan. Its highest peak is Kanchenjunga (28,140 ft—8700 metres), one of the highest mountains in the world. The state's population (about 136,000 in 1970) consists chiefly of Nepalese, Bhotias, and Lepchas. The state religion is Buddhism. According to local tradition, the ancestors of its rulers came from Tibet in the middle of the 17th cent. Till the end of the 18th cent. Sikkim was a dependency of Tibet, though subject to invasion from Nepal. British relations with Sikkim began in the Gurkha War of 1814–16, after which the British restored to Sikkim the territories wrested from her by the Nepalese. In 1835, in return for an annual pension of 3000 rupees, the raja granted the site of Darjeeling to the British. The prevalence of slavery in Sikkim led the British to intervene once more. In 1849, the raja, hoping to enforce his claims to runaway slaves, kidnapped Dr Campbell, the superintendent of Darjeeling, and Dr Hooker, the famous naturalist, who were then travelling in Sikkim. Because of this the Sikkim *tarai* was annexed and the raja's pension stopped. Further kidnapping of British Bengali sub-

jects for the purpose of slavery led to another British expedition and by a treaty of 1861 the raja had to make restitution. In 1863 he was granted an allowance of 6000 rupees, which was increased to 12,000 in 1873. In 1888 Tibetan forces which had invaded Sikkim were expelled, and then a British political officer was stationed at Gangtok, the capital, to advise the maharaja. By the Anglo-Chinese Convention of 1890, Sikkim was acknowledged to be a British protectorate. At the same time, the frontier between Sikkim and Tibet was defined. In 1914 the maharaja placed the resources of his state at the disposal of the British. After 1947 British paramountcy over Sikkim lapsed. In 1949 Indian troops were sent to Sikkim at the ruler's request to restore order. By the treaty of Dec. 1950, Sikkim was declared an Indian protectorate and in return for an annual subsidy of 30,000 rupees India was to control her foreign relations and be responsible for her defence. At the same time, India was given permission to construct railways, aerodromes, and wireless stations.

J. Morris, *Living with Lepchas* (London, 1938).
C. U. Aitchison, *Treaties, Engagements and Sanads*, vol. 12 (Calcutta, 1931).   CCD

SIKORSKI, WLADYSLAW (1891–1943), Polish soldier and politician. Before the First World War, as an officer in the Austrian army, he co-operated with Marshal Pilsudski's Legionary Movement. During the war he quarrelled with Pilsudski over the Polish problem, for which he himself advocated an Austro-Polish solution by which Russian Poland would be incorporated into Austro-Hungary; Pilsudski wanted complete independence. After 1918, Sikorski served in the Polish army and became chief of the general staff (1921–2). His relations with Pilsudski improved and as prime minister (Dec. 1922–May 1923) he had the marshal's support. But their relations grew cool again on account of Sikorski's proposals for reorganizing the army's high command while he was minister of war (1924–5). He neither supported nor opposed Pilsudski's coup of May 1926, but remained deeply suspect to Pilsudski's supporters and was forced to retire from the army in 1928. He then became a convinced opponent of Pilsudski, and later he strongly attacked the loosening of Poland's links with France and the regime's failure to modernize the army. He was one of the creators of the liberal-democratic 'Morges Front'.

After Poland's defeat in Sept. 1939 at the start of the Second World War, Sikorski became prime minister of the government-in-exile and supreme commander of the Polish forces. His death in an air crash off Gibraltar has been attributed both to sabotage by right-wing Poles and to communists, but was probably the result of an accident.

SILES, HERNANDO (1841–1942), Bolivian lawyer, politician, and president of Bolivia (1926–30), who headed the nationalist party. Economic difficulties led to his overthrow.

SILES SUAZO, HERNÁN (1914–), Bolivian politician and president of Bolivia (1956–60), who led the street fighting which brought the National Revolutionary Movement (MNR) to power in 1952 during the Bolivian National Revolution. He then handed over the presidency to Victor Paz Estenssoro. In 1956 Siles was himself elected president. During his term of office attempts were made to combat inflation and stabilize the revolution. His enemies accused him of having become a conservative and in 1960 he was succeeded by Paz Estenssoro, with whom he broke soon afterwards. In 1964 the MNR was expelled from power.

SILESIA, Slav province lying in the basin of the upper and middle Oder, bounded by the Sudeten mountains to the south-west. By the 10th cent. it was disputed between the Premyslid dynasty of Bohemia and the Piast rulers of Poland, but after Mieszko I of Poland acquired it from the Bohemians (989–92) it remained a Polish province until 1335. Early in this period Christianity reached Silesia from Germany, the first bishopric being established in 1000 at Smogorzow. The province became a possession of the elder branch of the Piast house from the restoration of Boleslav I and Mieszko II with imperial support, but from this time it was subject to increasing colonization by German settlers. Under Duke Henry I of Breslau (*reg.* 1201–38), known as 'the Bearded', and his son Henry II (*reg.* 1238–41) attempts were made to link Silesia with the Polish kingdom in a union which would give Silesia predominance, but after Henry II's death in battle against the Mongols (1241) the province was gradually sub-divided into 16 small principalities under Piast dukes, who owed allegiance to the Polish Crown.

From 1327 John of Luxemburg, King of Bohemia (*reg.* 1313–46), successfully extracted homage from a number of Silesian princes. Following the devastation of Poland by the Teutonic invasions (1331–2) and the death of Ladislas the Short (*reg.* 1306–32) the young successor to the Polish throne, Casimir (*reg.* 1333–70), renounced his sovereignty over the Silesian Piasts to John of Bohemia at the Congress of Visegrad (1335). Thus from 1335 Silesia accepted the overlordship of Bohemia, a fact confirmed by Charles IV's annexation of the province in 1369. Relations between Silesia and Bohemia were not always friendly, *eg*, in 1425–35 Silesia was ravaged for siding with the Emperor Sigismund (*reg.* 1419–37) against the Bohemian Hussites. After the extinction of the Luxemburg dynasty (1458) most of the Silesian princes recognized the suzerainty of George Podiebrad (*reg.* 1458–71), though many of the towns resisted in favour of Matthias Corvinus of Hungary, who ruled most of Silesia from 1469 until his death (1490), and was the creator of the Silesian constitution. He overrode the independent rights of the Silesian princes, imposed general taxes and summoned a states general almost annually from 1474. In 1490 Silesia reverted to Vladislav Jagiello (*reg.* 1450–1516), King of Poland and Bohemia and from 1491 also King of Hungary. On the death of his son, Louis, at Mohacz (1526) the lands of the Crown of St Wenceslas, including Silesia, passed to his brother-in-law, Archduke Ferdinand of Habsburg, the future emperor and the first of the successive Habsburg rulers of Silesia.

At the Reformation Lutheranism swept much of Silesia, especially the principalities of Liegnitz and Brieg, and despite the Jesuit order's efforts to restore Catholicism it remained the most Protestant part of the Habsburg lands. The province repudiated the election of Archduke Ferdinand as King of Bohemia and supported the candidature of the Protestant elector Palatine, Frederick (1618), and was considerably devastated in the Thirty Years War, losing 20 per cent of its population. From 1627 it became a part of the hereditary dominions of the Habsburgs, but at the peace of Westphalia (1648) religious freedom was guaranteed, as it had been confirmed by the Letter of Majesty (1621).

During the 17th and 18th cents the mining, woollen, and linen industries were developed, making Silesia the richest of Austria's provinces and Wroclaw (Breslau) the business centre of the Habsburg empire. Coveted by Brandenburg from 1675, when the Emperor Leopold I pocketed the duchies of Liegnitz, Brieg, and Wohlau—despite the claims of the Elector Frederick William—it was invaded by the forces of Frederick the Great (1740) in defiance of the Pragmatic Sanction which precipitated the War of the Austrian Succession. It was retained by Frederick by the treaties of Breslau (1742) and Dresden (1745), and despite the Austrian reoccupation in 1760 and the fact that Maria Theresa and Kaunitz made the recovery of the province the linchpin of Habsburg foreign policy from 1742 to 1780, remained a part of Prussia from the treaty of Hubertusburg (1763) until 1921.

Under Prussia the Protestant majority enjoyed effective religious freedom, and underwent a renewed Germanization programme, efficient administration and economic development, *eg*, of the coal industry. After Napoleon's downfall the province was retained by Prussia and merged with Saxon Lusatia (1815) until it became part of the German Reich (1871). Its possession was disputed at the end of the First World War between Poland, Czechoslovakia, and Germany, but despite a majority of German votes in the plebiscite the new frontiers gave Poland three-quarters of the coalfields and two-thirds of the steel-producing areas of Silesia. The Cieszyn region was divided between Poland and Czechoslovakia and Lower Silesia left to Germany (Oct. 1921). This settlement was overthrown by the Hitler regime in Sept. 1939, Polish Silesia being annexed to Germany, but at the Potsdam Conference at the end of the Second World War German Silesia, except the Neisse area, reverted to Poland.

MKS

SILICEO, JUAN MARTINEZ (1486–1557), Spanish cleric who became Cardinal Abp of Toledo (1546), where he led the movement in favour of Spanish racial purity directed against the *conversos* or those of Jewish origin. In 1547 he instituted the Toledo statute, eliminating from ecclesiastical appointments all who were of mixed blood, a law ratified by the Crown in 1556.

SILK INDUSTRY in the Middle Ages. In the 6th cent. silkworms were brought from China to the Byzantine empire and Constantinople became the greatest European centre for the manufacture of fine silk. In Italy the industry was first established in Sicily. The capture of skilled silk workers by the Sicilian king, Roger II, during his invasion of Greece in 1148, was intended to expand the industry. In the 13th cent. Lucca in Tuscany became the most important Italian centre for fine silks. Until the 16th cent. no important silk industries developed north of the Alps, and throughout the later Middle Ages the Italians virtually monopolized the silk trade in north-western Europe, silk probably being their most valuable export.

SILK ROADS, term applied somewhat loosely to the communication lines that led from China to Central Asia. The routes led from Tun-huang round the northern and southern sides of the Takla Makan desert, passing by way of oases and small communities, and joining together near the Pamir mountains. From the time of Chang Ch'ien, diplomatic and commercial contacts have been made along these routes between China and the western world, but for long trade was conducted by middlemen, without direct contact between Chinese and Mediterranean merchants. Travellers along these routes brought Buddhism to China in the early days of the Christian era and included some pilgrims visiting the home of Buddhism in India. By the T'ang (AD 618–906) and the Sung (960–1279) periods, merchants from the Middle East were coming this way far more frequently than previously; some of the early western travellers such as Marco Polo and the missionaries from Europe travelled on this route to China.

SILK TRADE, luxury trade imported into western Europe from the Middle East by the Crusaders. Sericulture was established by the Moors in Sicily and southern Spain in the Middle Ages and the production industry established in medieval Florence, Genoa, Milan, and Venice by the princely houses, whence the cloth was exported to England, France, and Germany. With the decline of the Italian towns in the 16th cent. silk production continued in Spain, with Toledo the chief centre, France, Italy, and Flanders being the main importers. The suppression of the Alpujarras revolt in the 1560s, however, ruined the Morisco economy based on silk and Philip II's taxation of the exported woven silks furthered the decline. Meanwhile silk weaving had been started at Tours in France in 1480 with the encouragement of Louis XI, and Francis I also transposed the industry from Milan to the Rhone valley (1520). Sully encouraged the industry at Lyons but it was really Colbert's introduction of premiums for mulberry trees which entrenched sericulture in the Rhone and made Lyons the great centre for the modern silk industry of France. The industry was introduced into England in the

14th cent., but received its first encouragement from the immigration of skilled Flemish weavers during the Spanish–Netherlands war (1568–1648). James I was interested in the industry and tried to introduce it to the New World (1609). However, it was not until the late 17th cent. that the English silk trade received the considerable impetus of the immigration of around 40,000 Huguenot weavers, driven by religious persecution from France. Many settled in the Spitalfields area of London and established silk production there. In the 18th cent. silk became one of England's leading industries, helped by the stringent prohibition of silk articles from France and bounties to English silk. It was also stimulated by the introduction of the silk-throwing machine, which had been smuggled into England from Italy by John Lombe (1716). He and his brother Thomas built factories on the Derwent, and Macclesfield and London remained the two leading centres of the English industry.   MKS

SILLA, ancient state established among the Han tribes of Chin-han in south-eastern Korea. Although the traditional histories place its foundation in 57 BC, there is no contemporary evidence for its existence before the first Silla embassy to China in 377. Even after this the neighbouring states of Koguryo and Paekche tended to shut off this part of Korea from direct contact with China, so that Silla long remained something of a cultural backwater. Harassed by Paekche and the Japanese Yamato state, the kings of Silla in this period were clients of Koguryo. However, in the 6th cent. Silla shook off Koguryo's control, annexing Karak in 532 and defeating Paekche in 554; at the same time its rulers adopted Buddhism as the state religion.

Silla was the major beneficiary from the wars fought by the Chinese Sui and T'ang dynasties in Korea, and after the destruction of both Paekche and Koguryo in the mid-7th. cent. it united most of Korea south of the Taedong under its control. This was the 'golden age' of Silla history; its ships dominated the trade routes between China and Japan, and Silla monks travelled as far afield as India. However, attempts to take over administrative institutions of a Chinese type, such as the examination system, ended in failure, and after the end of the direct royal line in 780 a long period of increasing disorders ensued. The country was taken over and divided by competing bandit leaders, of whom the most famous was Kung Ye. In 935 the last nominal king of Silla abdicated in favour of Wang Kon, Kung Ye's former lieutenant, who established his own dynasty, called Koryo.
                                                                                       KHJG

SILLMAN, BENJAMIN (1779–1864), US chemist, naturalist and geologist at Yale University, who did much to popularize and establish the academic and laboratory teaching of science. He published an *Elements of Chemistry* (1830–1), was the founder and editor of the *American Journal of Science* (1818–), and helped to establish the Yale Department of Philosophy and the Arts (1847) out of which grew the Sheffield Scientific School.

SILURES, native tribe of ancient descent in south Wales, who, under Caratacus, opposed the Roman invasion. After some success (AD 51–2) their resistance was checked (58) and broken (74). Caerwent (Venta Silurum) became their administrative centre.

SILVA, JOSÉ ASUNCIÓN (1865–96), Colombian poet, an early 'modernist', whose work is dominated by pessimism and a gentle despair.

SILVA, JUAN DE (1567–1616), Dutch official who became governor-general of the Philippines (1609–16). When he arrived in the Philippines, the Dutch East India Co. had designs on the Moluccas, then garrisoned by Spanish and Portuguese troops. The Dutch, pursuing this aim, carried out recurring blockades of Manila and attacks on Iloilo in the southern Philippines. A blockade of Manila could keep the Chinese junks from bringing in silk and other goods for the Manila–Acapulco trade, which was the country's lifeline as a colony. The new governor prepared an armada for the colony's defence, and later engaged in an offensive war with the Dutch. He channelled most of the colonial treasury funds into this venture, and built the biggest fleet ever assembled in the Philippines. But this involved recalling some men from key strategic posts, and withdrawing artillery from Mindanao. Consequently the colony's defences were weakened and the impoverished condition of the country continued to deteriorate. Despite De Silva's victory in the sea battle of Playa Honda, he was unsuccessful in his ambitious naval campaign of 1616 which he planned to undertake with the help of a Portuguese flotilla from Goa, but the Portuguese failed to rendezvous with De Silva's fleet at Malacca, where he died. The Dutch then combined with the Muslims of Sulu, in southern Philippines, to strike at the Spanish bases, and continued to threaten Manila and other parts of the country until the peace of Westphalia (1648).   JMS

SILVA, RUY GOMEZ DE, Prince of Eboli (1516–73), Portuguese grandee, favourite and confidant of Philip II of Spain and member of the Council of State, whose marriage to the ambitious Dona Ana de Mendoza (1559) resulted in the consolidation of the Mendoza faction at court over the rival Alba faction. After his death the leadership of the Eboli 'peace' party was assumed by his widow and by Antonio Perez.

SILVA PÔRTO, ANTÓNIO FRANCISCO FERREIRA DA (*fl.* 19th cent.), Portuguese trader, who pioneered the expansion of ivory routes into the Zambezi and Congo basins from the Atlantic coast.

SIMCOE, JOHN GRAVES (1752–1806), British soldier who served as commander of the Queen's Rangers in the American War of Independence. As first lieut.-governor of Upper Canada (1792–4), he invited settlers to emigrate here and founded the provincial capital of York (later Toronto). He was governor of San Domingo (1794–7) and was appointed commander-in-chief in India (1806) but died before he could take up the appointment.

SIMEON, CHARLES (1759–1836), English evangelical divine who spent the greater part of his working life as incumbent of Holy Trinity, Cambridge (1783–1836), and exercised a strong personal influence over undergraduates. He was a founder of the Church Missionary Society (1797).

SIMLA, Himalayan hill station in the Punjab and former summer capital of the British government of India. It was acquired by the British after the Gurkha War of 1815–16. After Lord Amherst, the governor-general, spent the summer here in 1827 it became important as a sanitarium. Lord William Bentinck and others followed his example, but it was not until 1864 that the annual migration became an official routine. After Indian independence (1947) it ceased to be a summer capital.

SIMLA DEPUTATION (1 Oct. 1906), Indian Muslim deputation led by the Aga Khan, which presented Lord Minto with an address outlining Muslim political demands. The address put forward two basic claims: first, that Muslims should be given representation as a community through separate electorates in which only Muslims would vote; and second, that, because of the 'political importance' of the community, this representation should be greater than that provided on a strict proportion of the population. The Muslims were adamant in wanting elected and not nominated representatives, but they claimed that there was no chance of a Muslim being elected by the Hindu 'majority' unless he was prepared to make himself dependent on Hindu votes, which would make an unsatisfactory representative of the the Muslim community. They also asked for a guaranteed

Muslim share of appointments in the civil services and the judiciary.

Minto did not make any specific commitments about Muslim representation, but in his reply was sympathetic to their demands and gave firm support to the proposal for separate electorates in the discussions which led to the 'Morley–Minto reforms' (1909). Hindus were dismayed by the outcome of the deputation's demands and later alleged that the deputation had been engineered by the government in an effort to nullify any political gain which the other reforms might bring. There was certainly official help and support for the deputation, and it is clear that it did represent a genuine concern by the conservative Muslim leadership both for the community's interests and their own position within it.   PDR

SIMMS, WILLIAM GILMORE (1806–70), US author and poet whose reputation rests upon his many romances of the early South, notably 'The Yemassee' (1835). The depredations of civil war and changes in post-war literary taste left him impoverished and neglected.

SIMNEL, LAMBERT (c. 1477–1534), English impostor, who was taken to Ireland to impersonate the Earl of Warwick, Edward IV's nephew, then imprisoned in the Tower. He was crowned in 1487 and gained the support of the Earl of Kildare and the Abp of Dublin. Joined by the Earl of Lincoln and Lord Lovell they invaded Lancashire, but were defeated by Henry VII at Stoke (1487). Simnel was taken into Henry's household, where he rose to be royal falconer.

SIMON, JOHN ALLSEBROOK SIMON, 1st Viscount (1873–1954), British Liberal, lawyer, politician, and author of the Simon Report on India (1930), which recommended an increase in responsible government in the provinces and indirect election to the central legislature. Becoming an MP in 1906, he was attorney-general (1913–15) and home secretary (1915–16), resigning from Asquith's Coalition government in conscientious opposition to conscription. He asserted that the General Strike (1926) was illegal, though this was much disputed. He led the National Liberals in the MacDonald government and held office throughout the 1930s. As foreign secretary (1931–5) he supported disarmament, though he was blamed for the failure of the international disarmament conference (1934). He visited Adolf Hitler in 1935 in Germany, and, as home secretary (1935–7) and chancellor of the exchequer (1937–40), he supported Neville Chamberlain and appeasement. He upheld Munich (1938) but firmly accepted the necessity for the Second World War, becoming lord chancellor in the war cabinet (1940–5). He was among the last Liberal politicians to hold office in an administration.

SIMON, SIR JOHN (1816–1904), English doctor and pioneer of public health. As medical officer of health for the city of London he was responsible for the successful working of the Public Health Act (1848), a task which he continued, despite opposition, as medical officer of the local government board (1855–76). His writings include *English Sanitary Institutions* (1890).

SIMON, RICHARD (1638–1712), French cleric and writer. Having entered into a controversy with the Port Royalists and the Benedictines, his *Histoire critique du Vieux Testament* was banned and destroyed by a decree of the council of state (1679). The *Histoire* was finally published in Rotterdam (1685).

SIMON COMMISSION, Indian Statutory Commission (1927–1930) which was chaired by Sir John Simon. Appointed under the provisions of the Government of India Act (1919) that there should be statutory commissions at 10-yearly intervals to review progress, the commission consisted of seven members of parliament, the most notable of whom in addi-

tion to Simon was the Labour MP Clement Attlee. The commission held discussions and took evidence during two visits to India (Feb.–March 1928; Oct. 1928–April 1929) and a sitting in London (June–July 1929), amassing 14 volumes of evidence from governments and individuals and producing (May 1930) a two-volume report comprising a survey of conditions and detailed recommendations for the future constitution.

While it was a most competent piece of work, the report was politically a dead-letter even before it was written. The composition of the commission was a blunder by both the government of India and the India Office, for it offered a direct insult to Indian political leaders by insinuating that Indians were incapable of participating in the formulation of their own constitution and by emphasizing parliament's self-assumed right to determine the manner and pace of India's constitutional progress. The result was that the Congress, the Liberals, the Hindu Mahasabha, the Jinnah-led Muslim League, and the Khilafat Conference all refused to co-operate in any way. This did not stop the commission operating and there were, in fact, many groups which did come before it because they felt that their interests would be jeopardized if they did not make representations to a body charged with making constitutional changes, but this did not alter the fact that the nationalist movement was absent from the discussions. The government made efforts to repair the mistake by appointing an Indian Central Committee (under Sir Sankaran Nair), and provincial 'Simon' committees to sit with the commission and hold discussions with it. But these committees were a poor second best as a representation of Indian views about the future of the constitution. Indeed, packed as they were with landlords and others with special vested interests, they gave a misleading impression of what Indians would be prepared to accept for the future.

In its recommendations the commission was prepared to move towards provincial autonomy but it suggested that the provincial executive should be chosen by the governor and include, if he wished, officials and others from outside the legislature. It thought, too, that it would be impracticable to base the franchise on adult suffrage and it saw no alternative to communal representation for minorities. At the centre, the commission, which was firmly convinced of the inevitability of federation between British India and the Indian states, felt that the central legislature must be merely an indirectly elected legislature representing the federating units and not the people directly through territorial constituencies. Any firm proposals about this federal legislature, it believed, would have to wait until federation had become a fact. Until it did so, a Legislative Assembly and Council of State could continue for British India and the Governor-General in Council could continue as the executive government at the centre, with a consultative 'Council of Greater India' being set up to consider matters of common interest. At both the centre and the provinces, the head of the administration would retain powers to safeguard security, peace, and tranquillity and the rights of the minorities and the services. Defence, it suggested, would almost certainly remain an imperial, rather than an Indian, concern for the foreseeable future.

In all of this the commission's thinking fell a long way short of Indian nationalist expectations by the late 1920s as outlined in the Nehru Report (1928). As it was, the report was nullified even before its publication, by the efforts made by Lord Irwin in Oct. 1929 to retrieve the situation by making clear to the nationalists that the government would not be bound by what Simon suggested and that, instead, the whole matter would be discussed at a Round Table Conference in 1930.

S. Gopal, *The Viceroyalty of Lord Irwin, 1926–31* (London, 1957).

S. R. Mehrotra, *India and the Commonwealth, 1885–1929* (London, 1965).
                                                          PDR

SIMONETTA, CICCA (d. 1479), secretary to Francesco Sforza, Duke of Milan and chief co-architect, together with the duke, of Sforza power in the state of Milan. He was the real ruler of the city during the minority of Duke Giangaleazzo. He was resented by the Milanese nobility as a low-born foreign Guelph, and was executed by Ludovico Sforza to win support on his accession to the duchy.

SIMONY, buying or selling of something spiritual for a temporal price, derived from Simon Magnus (Acts 8 : 18) who tried to buy from the apostles the power of conferring the gifts of the Holy Ghost. Condemned by the Church from the 5th cent., it became endemic in western Europe in the 9th–10th cents, and was a major object of attack by Pope Gregory VII. The practice of buying benefices or ecclesiastical preferment continued, however, and was bitterly criticized by Martin Luther in the early 16th cent. After the secularization of Church property by the Protestant churches and the Catholic reformation of the post-Tridentine period the practice gradually disappeared.

SIMOVIĆ, DUŠAN (1882–1962), Yugoslav airman and politician who led the *coup d'état* in Yugoslavia (March 1941) during the Second World War. He was commander of the air force when plans were made to overthrow Cvetkovic's government after it signed the Tripartite treaty. He became prime minister after the coup. His government sought to maintain a neutral policy towards Germany and to strengthen Yugoslavia's ties with the Soviet Union. A treaty of friendship and non-aggression was concluded with the Soviet Union (5 April 1941) the day before Germany attacked Yugoslavia. When war came Simović went into exile with the king and royalist government. After the war he returned to Yugoslavia.

SIMPSON, SIR GEORGE (1787–1860), Scots-born Canadian fur-trader who arrived in Canada as a clerk in the Hudson's Bay Co. (1809) and rose to become (1891) governor-in-chief of the company.

SINAN, called Qoja Mi'mar Sinan (AD 1490–1578), Ottoman soldier and architect, born at Kayseri of Christian Greek parents. He entered the service of the sultan through the devshirme, was enrolled in the corps of Janissaries and fought during the campaign of 1514 against Persia and at the sieges of Belgrade (1521) and Rhodes (1522). Under Suleiman Kanuni (*reg.* 1520–66) and Selim II (*reg.* 1566–74) he was responsible for the construction of numerous mosques, colleges, palaces, baths, aqueducts, hospitals, etc., ranging in location from Bosnia to the Hijaz. Amongst his most famous achievements are the two mosques known as the Süleymaniye and the Selimiye.

SINAN PASHA, QOJA (d. 1596), five times Ottoman Grand Vizier (*reg.* 1580–2, 1589–91, 1593–5, 1595, 1595–6), of Albanian descent, who entered the service of the Ottomans through the devshirme. He commanded the forces of the sultan in the Yemen (1569), at Tunis (1574), and against Persia (1580). The last years of his life saw him involved in the great conflict of 1593–1606 between Austria and the Ottoman empire. Sinan Pasha took the Hungarian fortress of Györ (Raeb) in 1594, but was unsuccessful in his campaign of 1595 against Wallachia.

SINARQUISM, or *sinarquismo,* contraction of the Spanish for 'without anarchy', a Mexican fascist movement, founded in 1936. Sinarquism taught that an authoritarian government was required to restore the order and prosperity which New Spain had enjoyed during the colonial era. Catholic principles were to be the basis for the new state and anti-clericalism, communism, and liberalism would be stamped out. Sinarquism looked with favour upon Franco's Spain, while it was hostile to the US.

One million Mexicans allegedly belonged to the movement (1941), which soon split into two factions (1944), the Popular Force Party and a non-political body. Many peasant supporters were brought into the PAN (*Partido de Acción Nacional*) during the 1950s. In 1970 Sinarquism was of little importance in Mexico.

SINCLAIR, SIR JOHN (1754–1835), Scottish agriculturist, politician, and economist, who was one of the last important figures in the spread of 'improvement' and the agricultural revolution, and a founder of the board of agriculture. He held office as president of the board (1793–8, 1806–13). He was involved in economic controversy over the bullion question in 1810 and after, arguing for the maintenance of paper currency as a means of expanding the money supply to the needs of an expanding economy.

SINCLAIR, UPTON (1878–1968), US writer, who produced over 100 books. He won international fame with *The Jungle* (1906), a novel about conditions in the Chicago stockyards, which advocated socialism for their amelioration. Public reaction to the book helped to instigate President Theodore Roosevelt's pure-food legislation. Throughout his life Sinclair was a crusader for the under-privileged. He narrowly missed winning the governorship of CA (1934), after establishing EPIC (End Poverty in California), an organization which united unemployed workers and progressives, and continued to exercise political influence within the state. At the end of his life he wrote *The Autobiography of Upton Sinclair* (1962).

SIND, in Pakistan, region of the lower Indus valley and its delta. It was a principal site of the Indus civilization (*c.* 2250–1800 BC) and was conquered by the Persians (*c.* 500 BC), then traversed by Alexander (325 BC). Sind was later conquered by the Arab general Muhammad-bin-Kasim (AD 712) and became mainly Muslim. It remained outside the mainstream of Indian life until it became a Mughal province (1592–*c.* 1750). With the Mughal break-up Sind was divided among a number of chiefs or amirs who owed allegiance to the Durrani Afghan shahs. After the British had failed to replace Shah Shuja on the Afghan throne, in the first Afghan War, they seized Sind (1843) and incorporated it in the Bombay Presidency. It became a governor's province (1935) and is now (1970) a part of West Pakistan. Its chief city is the port of Karachi, for some years the Pakistan capital.

SINDHIA, HOUSE OF, Maratha ruling family of Gwalior, founded by Ranoji Sindhia in the time of Peshwa Baji Rao I. After Ranoji's death in 1745 the most important member of the family was Mahadaji Sindhia, whose power increased after the third battle of Panipat (1761). It was with his help that Warren Hastings brought the first Anglo-Maratha War to an end by the treaty of Salbai (1782). Until his death in 1794 Sindhia sought to consolidate his power in Hindustan by controlling the Maratha peshwa. His successor, Daulat Rao Sindhia (*reg.* 1794–1827), was defeated by Wellesley during the Second Maratha War (1803). Because of internal dissensions British military intervention was necessary in 1843. After this the rulers of Gwalior remained faithful to the British connection.

SINDOK (*reg.* c. 929–947), King of Java, who probably married into the royal family of ancient Mataram, Central Java, occupied some of the highest posts, and finally succeeded to the throne. He subsequently transferred the capital to east Java, probably in the Brantas delta south-west of modern Surabaya. The reasons for this transfer (and the ensuing neglect of Central Java) are not clear, but it seems that economic considerations, notably the control of trade and shipping in eastern Indonesia, played an important part.

SINGAPORE, island of, 217 sq. miles (561 sq. kms) separated by a narrow strait from Malaya. Its population in 1970 was over 3 million, and since the 19th cent. it has been a focus of Far Eastern trade. Its prospects as a colony were recognized by 16th-cent. European explorers, but it was not until 1819 that it was established as a free port by Sir Stamford Raffles, who secured the derelict island, which formally became British in the treaty of London (1814). In 1826 it became part of the Straits Settlements. Its expansion in the 19th cent. was rapid and considerable and its role as the great *entrepreneur* of the east gave it strategic importance, especially as a naval base. This led to its seizure (1942) by Japan in the Second World War. After the war Singapore embarked on a separate political life independent of the rest of the Malay states.

During the 1950s Singapore's politics were unstable and mistrust existed between her population, largely of Chinese, and the Malays in the Malaysian Federation. A conference in London (1956) discussed the idea of a Malaysia embracing Singapore and though this scheme failed, an agreement in 1957 led to a brief (1963–5) Malaysian Federation. Meanwhile, internal self-government had been secured in 1959. Singapore ceded from the Federation in 1965 through a lack of political goodwill all-round, and became (1965) an independent state within the Commonwealth, adopting a republic constitution, with a president, and a cabinet responsible to a legislature of 58 members.

SINGAPORE, FALL OF, to the Japanese (1942). As the base for the British Far Eastern Fleet in the Second World War, Singapore was rapidly developed after the outbreak of hostilities in the Pacific into an 'impregnable citadel' from which to resist Japan's southward advance. The surrender of Lieut.-Gen. Percival and 85,000 men to the numerically inferior forces of Lieut.-Gen. Yamashita, after a ten-day siege (15 Feb. 1942), therefore came as one of the most spectacular and unexpected defeats in British history. Japanese superiority lay in control of the air, greater mobility under Malayan conditions, and the orientation of Singapore's defences towards the sea rather than towards the mainland from which the Japanese attack developed after their two-month campaign in Malaya.

SINGER, ISAAC MERRITT (1811–75), US inventor and developer of the sewing machine, which he patented in 1851.

SINGLE WHIP REFORM, series of measures gradually introduced in China during the 16th cent. in order to strengthen the economy and to bring some degree of uniformity into the system of tax collection. In the preceding century or so this had been based on a property classification of individuals or families, or a quantitative classification of land. Such classifications had become obsolete, with a consequent falsification of records and evasion of responsibilities; and while the government was failing to collect sufficient revenue and the peasantry were suffering unjust extortion, a large number of minor taxes had been introduced, leading to increasing complexity and some economic disruption. The changes that were later known as the Single Whip Reform were brought about by officials in different areas to regularize and clarify the situation. Different items of land-tax and obligations for service were amalgamated under a single, or very few, headings. The classification of individuals was simplified; regular dates were specified for the collection of tax; there was a general tendency for dues to be paid in silver rather than in kind and for hired labour, paid by the government out of tax receipts, to replace a dependence on corvée labour to which males had been subject.

SINGOSARI or Singhasari, also called Tumapel, village eight miles (12 kms) north of Malang, East Java, Indonesia, once the site of an ancient capital (AD 1222–92). Its founder, Ken Angrok, established himself in this area in revolt against the empire of Kadiri. The greatest figure of Singosari was Kertanagara (1268–92), who was killed during a counter-revolution by the viceroy of Kadiri, Jaya-katwang, shortly before the arrival of a Chinese expeditionary force.

SINHA, SATYENDRA PRASANNA SINHA, 1st Baron (1864–1928), Indian politician, under-secretary of state for India (1919–20), and the first Indian to be raised to the British peerage. He was advocate-general of Bengal (1907–9) and was the first Indian to join the viceroy's executive council, when he became law member (1909). As president of Congress (1915), he called for a clear lead from Britain on reforms, and after a second period as advocate-general in Bengal (1917–19),' he entered the House of Lords as under-secretary of state, his task being to help Montagu to pilot such reforms through parliament. He was appointed governor of Bihar and Orissa (1920–1), being the first Indian to be head of a local administration. He also served on the judicial committee of the privy council (1926–8).

SINHALA MAHA SABHA in Ceylon, movement founded in 1937, whose main objective was the revival of Sinhalese language and culture and the promotion of the Buddhist religion. It merged with the United National Party in 1947.

SINKING FUND ACT (1786) in Britain, legislative measure to reduce the amount of the national debt by setting aside part of current revenue to accumulate at interest. The first sinking fund was established by Sir Robert Walpole in 1717 and the national debt fell from £54 million in 1717 to £46 million in 1739. The major wars of the 18th cent. all entailed increases in the debt, and the project of a sinking fund was revived by the Younger Pitt in 1786. Pitt's act set aside £1 million annually to be transferred to an independent body of commissioners for reducing the national debt. The commissioners were to buy up stock which would accumulate interest, which in turn would be used to buy more stock. As the interest as well as the capital annually transferred came from the taxpayer, a more economical system might have been the immediate cancellation of the stock, but this point was obscured by the contemporary popularity of Richard Price's writings.

The prolonged period of the French Wars after 1793 destroyed the benefits of the sinking fund. As interest rates rose during the war, new loans were being floated which carried higher interest than the stocks being bought by the commissioners. After 1815, when the government was under strong pressure to reduce war taxes, it became increasingly hard to produce a surplus for the sinking fund, and the attempt was abandoned in 1829. Thereafter no regular arrangement for the reduction of the national debt existed until Stafford Northcote introduced a new sinking fund in 1875, which provided for a regular surplus to be devoted to the purchase of debt stock. The burden of the national debt was much less heavy by the end of the 19th cent., partly because there had been no major wars, other than the Crimean War, and the capital of the debt had not been increased, and partly because of the great growth of national wealth in the 19th cent. The question of a sinking fund appeared very much more urgent in the 18th cent. than it did in the time of Northcote.

E. L. Hargreaves, *The National Debt* (London, 1930).
John Ehrman, *The Younger Pitt: the years of acclaim* (London, 1969). LMB

SINN FEIN, in Ireland, 'Ourselves Alone', Irish republican party founded by Arthur Griffith (1902) to achieve peacefully political and economic independence on the lines of Deak and List. He was superseded by more fiery leaders in 1914 like Connolly, Pearse, Plunkett, and Ceant. Their dramatic but abortive Easter Rising in Dublin (1916), followed by their executions together with the hanging of Casement, gave Sinn Fein its popular martyrs. From 1917, with De Valera leading, the party swept all Ireland, except Ulster, winning 73 seats in the 1918 elections, although 36 candidates including De Valera were in gaol. The 'Troubles' grew more violent, the Sinn Feiners refusing to come to Westminster and establishing their first Irish Republican parliament (the Dail) in Dublin (1919). The party disintegrated in 1922, moderates like Griffith accepting the Irish Free State, but De Valera resisting by setting up a new Republican army, claiming to continue Sinn Fein traditions in his new organization, 'Fianna Fail', 'Soldiers of Ireland'.

SINO-JAPANESE WAR (1894–5), brought about by the rivalry between China and Japan in Korea, was the first major conflict between the two nations. Under increasing pressure from the West and from Japan, in the 1860s and the 1870s Korea, like China, had adopted a policy of 'self-strengthening'. But the Korean court at Seoul was divided between those who wished to follow the Chinese way and those who wanted to copy the Japanese model. In 1884 the pro-Japanese radicals, with the help of Japanese legation guards, staged a coup leading to a direct clash between Chinese and Japanese forces, and the latter's defeat. However, in the ensuing negotiation it was agreed that in future China and Japan would notify each other before sending troops to Korea (the Li–Ito Convention, signed by Li Hung-chang and Ito Hirobumi). The following decade saw the expansion of Chinese influence in Korea but without the much-needed reforms and modernization. At the same time, the Japanese became increasingly uneasy about Chinese ascendancy and feelings ran high when a pro-Japanese Korean reformer was assassinated in 1894. In that year, the anti-foreign and anti-government *Tonghak* movement broke out into rebellion, and the Korean court asked for Chinese military aid. The Chinese then suppressed the *Tonghak*s; but the Japanese, invoking the Li–Ito Convention, none the less sent troops to Korea and demanded sweeping reforms which would lead to Japanese domination. The Chinese refused and war was declared.

The Japanese, who had modernized far more successfully than the Chinese, quickly drove the latter out of Korea and invaded Manchuria. But the decisive battle was fought at sea, off the Yalu river, in which the Chinese suffered serious losses. The Japanese subsequently took Port Arthur and practically destroyed the rest of the Peiyang fleet, and the Chinese were forced to negotiate the treaty of Shimonoseki.

The Sino-Japanese War thus marked the end of Chinese suzerainty over Korea, the failure of their self-strengthening movement, and the rise of Japan as an imperialist power in East Asia.   DP

SINOPE, ancient Greek settlement on the southern shore of the Black Sea, founded by Miletus in the 7th cent. BC and of central importance in Black Sea trade throughout antiquity. In the 5th cent. it came under Athenian influence (434), but later re-emerged after Phanaces I's conquest (183) as the residence of the kings of Pontus. After its subsequent conquest by Rome (70) it remained prosperous under the empire.

SINOPE, BATTLE OF (30 Nov. 1853), destruction of the Turkish fleet by the Russian Admiral Nakhimov during the Russo-Turkish War which preceded the outbreak of the Crimean War. It was unfairly denounced as a 'massacre' in Britain.

SINO-SOVIET DISPUTE, conflict between the two major communist powers which came into the open in 1959. To outside observers the conflict took the form of ideological argument and mutual accusation as China attacked the 'revisionism' of the Soviet Union. Khrushchev attempted a revaluation of the Leninist view of the inevitability of war at the twentieth party congress (1956) and stressed the dangers of nuclear war. At the same time he sought a rapprochement with the US. The Chinese rejected Khrushchev's view and held that 'US imperialism holds nothing but venom for the peace efforts of the socialist camp headed by the Soviet Union'. At the same time China sought to advance more rapidly towards the achievement of a socialist society and denounced the conservatism of Soviet policies.

The ideological debate was carried on at long range, meetings of the communist parties of the two countries and of the world communist movement being used as the principal forums. The debate divided the world communist movement, but the Soviet Union succeeded in maintaining its supremacy. In Europe a single country, Albania, was able (through its geographical position) to escape from Russian control and form close links with China.

Underneath the open ideological conflict there lay a clear difference of interests between the two powers. The intensity of the dispute may have been due initially to the refusal of the Soviet Union to share its nuclear capability with China. In addition there was conflict over territorial claims, of minor importance. This led (1969) to frontier clashes on Damansky (Chenpao) island in the Ussuri river and along the Amuri and Ussuri rivers in Sinkiang. Open conflict was however avoided and negotiations successfully conducted between the two powers.

D. S. Zagoria, *Sino-Soviet Conflict* (Princeton, 1962).   WK

SINZHEIM, BATTLE OF (June 1674), French victory over the imperialists in Alsace, when Marshal Turenne surprised and defeated his adversary in a pitched battle with inferior forces during the last campaign of his life.

SIOUX INDIANS (Dakota), tribe of American Indians, who were the most numerous of the Great Plains tribes and were considered the outstanding horsemen among American Indians. Originally the Sioux were forest people who lived around the head of the Mississippi river. During the first half of the 18th cent., French traders moved up from the south-east and equipped the Chippewas, bitter enemies of the Sioux, with firearms. Being unable thereafter to hold their own against the Chippewas, the Sioux drifted westward. There are seven main divisions of the tribe, of which the Tetons account for about two-thirds. The Tetons, like many other Sioux, are divided into sub-divisions, such as the Oglalas, Hunkpapas, and Brulés. The Santee, or eastern Sioux, are another major division, and were the first group to make contact with Europeans (*c.* 1640).

Sioux and white relations were relatively peaceful until the attack on Fort Laramie, WY (19 Aug. 1854). The continuous advance of whites, pushing the Sioux further west, began a long struggle against white encroachment, which included the Sioux Uprising (1862), the Fetterman Massacre (1866), the battle of the Little Big Horn (1876), and the Massacre at Wounded Knee (1890). Among the Sioux leaders in their wars against the US were Little Crow, Red Cloud, Crazy Horse, and Sitting Bull. Gradually the Sioux were all moved to reservations in MN, MT, NB, ND, and SD, where they now live (1970).

R. B. Hassrick *et al.*, *Sioux: life and customs of a warrior society* (Norman, 1964).   PCP

SIOUX UPRISING (Aug. 1862), outbreak of the Santee Sioux in south-western MN, US. The uprising began when a party of Indians murdered some whites (the 'Acton Massacre', 17 Aug. 1862). The fear of white vengeance, combined with unease among the Sioux because of a cut in annuities and rations, caused Little Crow to lead a force of warriors against white settlers. White troops defeated the Indians at Wood Lake (23 Sept.) and Camp Release (27 Sept.) and effectively ended the outbreak. The Sioux surrendered and 38 were hanged (26 Dec. 1863); afterwards the remainder were removed to the Dakota Territory. This Indian uprising, the most serious during the American Civil War, marked the end of the Santee Sioux as a unified tribe.

SIPAHI, Persian word meaning 'soldier' (whence French, spahi, and English, sepoy). Among the Ottoman Turks the word was used to denote in general the horsemen who held 'fiefs' in the provinces of the empire and came to war at the call of the sultan. It acquired in the usage of India, especially during the 18th and 19th cents, the sense of native troops used as foot-soldiers.

SIPPAR, city of Sumeria, situated at modern Abu-Habba, and a prosperous trading centre. Important historical and literary texts from the old Babylonian and Chaldean periods have been found there.

SIQUEIROS, DAVID ALFARO (1898–), Mexican soldier, painter, and muralist, who advocated a national popular art. He fought in the Mexican revolution (1914–17) and in the Spanish Civil War (1936–9). He was imprisoned in Mexico (1962–3) for his political beliefs.

SIRAJ-UD-DAULAH (*c.* 1737–57), Nawab of Bengal (*reg.* 1756–7), who succeeded his grandfather, Alivardi Khan. He soon attacked the British merchants in Calcutta on the charge of fortifying the city without permission against the French. He took Calcutta (20 June) but was not personally responsible for the Black Hole incident. On Clive's recapture of Calcutta he made peace with the East India Co. Distracted by dangers from the British, French, and Afghans in the north, he alienated support and fell to a conspiracy supported by Clive. After the battle of Plassey (June 1757) he fled but was captured and executed.

SISAK (SISSEK), BATTLE OF (June 1593), at a Croatian fortress near the confluence of the Kulpa and Sava rivers. The Christian levies of Inner Austria and Croatia defeated the Ottoman forces under the command of Hasan, Pasha of Bosnia, a battle which marked the beginning of a great conflict (1593–1606) between the Ottoman empire and Austria.

SISAL, fibrous plant whose fibres are used in making twine and rope. During the colonial period in eastern Africa, sisal was an important cash and estate crop. Synthetic fibres in the 20th cent. much reduced sisal's value.

SISAVANGVONG (*reg.* 1904–59), King of Laos, reigned throughout almost all the period of the French protectorate. His loyalty to the French brought him the extension of his sovereignty beyond the kingdom of Luang Prabang to include all of Laos (1941). The post-second World War challenge of young nationalists and ambitious princes strengthened his position *vis-à-vis* the French, and Laotian independence under a constitutional monarchy was granted in 1949. He was succeeded by his son, Savang Vatthana.

SISMONDI, LÉONARD (1773–1842), Swiss historian and economist, who spent much of the revolutionary period in Italy. He wrote a *History of the Italian Republics* (16 vols, 1807–18). As an economist, he criticized the classical school and was one of the first economists to see the possibility and the dangers of over-production.

SISOWATH (*reg.* 1904–28), King of Cambodia, half-brother of his predecessor, Norodom (*reg.* 1860–1904). He was notable for his pro-French attitude during that king's reign. As king, himself, he was willing to accept many changes which the French wished to make, but which Norodom had resisted. Institutionally, his reign was an important turning-point in the development of modern Cambodia.

SISTOVA, PEACE OF (1791), whereby Austria and the Ottoman empire brought to an end the state of war existing between them since 1787. Austria relinquished the territories which her forces had overrun in the course of the war, retaining only the town of Orsova, together with a small area of land extending along the Unna river in Croatia.

SITTING BULL (*c.* 1834–90), American Indian leader, of the Hunkpapa Teton division of the Sioux Indians, who was active in the Sioux wars of the 1860s and 1870s. He was a leader with Crazy Horse of the Sioux who defeated Col. Custer at the battle of the Little Big Horn (1876). After the surrender of the main body of the Sioux (Oct. 1876) he

escaped to Canada. He returned to the US (1881) after being offered an amnesty.

SIVA, one of the most widely and most ardently worshipped Indian gods. Although the antecedents of Siva worship can be traced back to Vedic times, real Sivaism (or Saivism) is attested from the early centuries AD. In iconography he is represented as three-eyed and four-armed, holding different attributes such as trident and rosary. He is, however, also worshipped in the shape of a *linga*, originally a stylized *membrum virile*. A typically South Indian representation of Siva is that as 'King of the dance' (*Nataraja*).

SIX ACTS (1819), in Britain, legislation passed after the 'Peterloo Massacre' in the belief that there existed a widespread revolutionary conspiracy to overthrow the government. The first act prohibited meetings to train people to use arms; the second gave JPs powers to issue warrants to search for arms; the third reduced procedural delays in prosecutions for misdemeanours. The fourth strengthened the law against seditious assemblies by forbidding the holding of meetings of more than 50 people to discuss grievances, except in the parish where the summoner resided. The fifth gave the courts power to order the seizure of copies of libels in the hands of convicted persons; and the sixth subjected political pamphlets to stamp duty. The government's belief in a widespread conspiracy, though probably mistaken, was not surprising in view of the evidence it had, and there was certainly widespread unrest, though this was mainly the result of distress. Opposition to the acts in parliament was not great, though some were criticised as being too severe.

PR

SIX ARTICLES, STATUTE OF (1539), in England, legislative measure which defined by an act of parliament a dogma decreeing Catholic orthodoxy. It was a triumph for King Henry VIII's conservative bishops, led by Gardiner, over Thomas Cromwell and Cranmer. The articles asserted the doctrine of transubstantiation, the need for auricular confession, the sanctity of monastic vows, communion of one kind, the holding of private masses, and the illegality of clerical marriage. The act also established the powers of episcopal courts to initiate trials for heresy without presentment by jury. Although it halted the progress towards Protestantism, the act was only occasionally enforced, *eg,* the trial of Anne Askew, during Henry's reign. It was repealed by Edward VI's first parliament at Somerset's instigation (1547).

SIX DYNASTIES in China, general term for the period 222–589. Apart from the short reunification of 265–316, China was ruled by a number of short-lived dynasties operating in limited areas of the north or south. In the north, a series of 16 houses founded mostly by non-Chinese leaders was followed by a period of some stability under Northern Wei. In the south six dynasties were designated by Chinese historians as being the legitimate holders of imperial power. Chinese culture was enriched during this period of dynastic disunity owing to ethnic admixture, the shift of the court and Chinese population to the south, experiments in political institutions, innovations in economic practice, the growing hold of Buddhism, the development of new forms of literature and the creations of Chinese sculptors.

SIXTUS IV (*reg.* 1471–84), Pope, whose pontificate saw the building of the Sistine Chapel and began the rebuilding of St Peter's. His main concern was for the advancement of his three nephews. Giuliano della Rovere (later Julius II) and Pietro Riario were made cardinals while Girolamo Riario, in his efforts to create a principality for himself, involved Sixtus in the infamous Pazzi conspiracy against the Medici (1478) followed by a war against Florence.

SIXTUS V (1521–90), Pope (*reg.* 1585–90), whose pontificate was notable for administrative reforms in the government of the Church and establishing the Vatican Library. He established the number of cardinals at 70. During his reign Anglo-Spanish relations culminated in war. In the hopes of winning England back to the Catholic faith, Sixtus encouraged Philip II's proposed invasion with his Armada (1588). While the cause of the Counter-Reformation was his closest concern, he was realist enough to appreciate the political jealousies between the great Catholic powers of France and Spain.

SJAHRIR, SUTAN (1909–66), Indonesian politician and prime minister of the revolutionary Indonesian republic (1945–7). In 1948 he broke with the socialist leader Amir Sjarifuddin to form the pro-Western Indonesian Socialist Party. In 1960 the party was banned, and from 1962 until his death Sjahrir was confined on Sukarno's orders.

SJARIFUDDIN, AMIR (1907–48), Indonesian politician, who was a Christian of Batak (Sumatran) origin. He led the Gerindo Party in the 1930s and the Socialist Party during the 1945–9 Indonesian revolution. He was prime minister (1947–8), when his fall revealed a polarization between left and right in the revolutionary republic. In Aug. 1948 he declared his adherence to the Indonesian Communist Party, under the leadership of Musso. He was shot following a clash in Sept. 1948 between government and communist forces.

SKALDIC POETRY, earliest literary genre peculiar to Scandinavia, dating from the 9th to the 11th cents and composed chiefly in Norway and Iceland. Its metre and diction were complex, the effect being comparable to musical counterpoint. It was primarily courtly in function, to praise a ruler and composed for him by his professional poets. Its complexities of metre and diction prevented later falsification and it is an important historical source.

SKANDERBEG (ISKENDER BEG), *ie*, George Kastrioti (1405–68), of a noble house, influential in the region around Krujë. Handed over to the Ottoman Turks as a hostage, George Kastrioti was educated at Edirne (Adrianople) as a Muslim. In 1443, during the course of an Ottoman campaign against the Hungarians, he abandoned the service of the sultan, went to Krujë, declared himself to be a Christian and thereafter led the Albanian resistance to the Ottomans— a task which filled the rest of his life. Skanderbeg sought aid from Naples and was for a time engaged as a soldier fighting on behalf of the Aragonese against the Angevins. He also made an entente with Venice when the Signoria, in 1463, became involved in a war with the Ottoman empire which lasted until 1479. The Albanians, under the guidance of Skanderbeg, repulsed major Ottoman attacks on Krujë in 1450, 1466, and 1467. Skanderbeg died at the beginning of 1468, but Krujë itself did not fall to the Ottomans until 1478.

SKELTON, JOHN (*c.* 1460–1529), English poet who was tutor to Prince Henry (King Henry VIII). His patron was Wolsey. Later he attacked the cardinal in *Colyn Cloute*, a general satire on the clergy, *Speke, Parrot*, and *Why come ye nat to courte?* To avoid imprisonment he took sanctuary in Westminster Abbey, where he died. Much of his poetry survives and one of his plays, *Magnificence*.

SKINNER v. THE EAST INDIA CO (1668–70), in England, dispute between the two houses of parliament over the question of the original jurisdiction of the House of Lords in civil suits. In 1666 Thomas Skinner, a London merchant, petitioned King Charles II, asserting he could gain no redress from the East India Co., which had injured his property. The House of Lords found in favour of Skinner, but the company complained to the House of Commons, which declared the Lords' proceedings illegal. The dispute dragged on for a year until Charles advised the two houses to stop proceedings. As a result the Lords abandoned claims to original jurisdiction in civil suits.

SKOBELEV, MIKHAIL DMITRIYEVICH (1843–82), Russian soldier noted for his feats during the conquest of Kokand (1875–6), of the Turkomans (1881), and during the Russo-Turkish war (1877–8).

SKOPIN-SHUISKY, MICHAEL VASILIEVICH, Prince (1586–1610), Russian *boyar* and soldier who was the nephew of Tsar Vasili Shuisky. He negotiated a Swedish alliance to bring military aid to his uncle against the second false Dmitri (1609), and with the help of De la Gardie's contingent drove the rebels from their camp at Tushino. He then triumphantly occupied Moscow, before dying suddenly under suspicious circumstances.

SKRZYŃSKI, ALEXANDER (1882–1931), Polish politician and diplomat, who had been a member of the Austrian diplomatic service. He entered the Polish service after independence and held the office of minister in Bucharest. He was twice foreign minister (1922–38, 1924–6) and represented Poland at Locarno. He was head of a coalition government (1925–6). After the coup of May 1926, he played no part in politics.

SKULSKI, LEOPOLD (1878–1969), Polish politician, who before the First World War was active in the *Sokol* movement (a political-gymnastic organization), and was (1916–19) mayor of Lodz. In the first parliament in independent Poland, his right-centre National Peasant Union held an important position and he headed a coalition government (1919–20); he was also minister of the interior (1920). In the elections of 1922 his party did badly and he played little part in politics thereafter.

SKURATOV-BELSKY, MALYUTA (d. 1570), Russian henchman and leading *oprichnik* under Ivan IV, who reputedly smothered or strangled the Metropolitan Philip in the Tver 'Otroch' monastery on Ivan's orders (23 Dec. 1569), but was himself executed with his fellow *oprichnik*, Basmanov, at Ivan's instigation.

SLANKAMEN, BATTLE OF (Aug. 1691), on the right bank of the Danube where Ludwig von Baden, commanding the forces of the Emperor Leopold I, routed the Ottoman Turks, the Grand Vizier Mustafa Köprülü being slain in the course of the battle.

SLANSKY, RUDOLPH SALZMANN (1901–52), Russian politician who joined the Communist Party and became a member of the central committee (1928) and a deputy in the Czechoslovak parliament (1935–7). He went to the Soviet Union (1938) and during the Second World War was active with Soviet partisans. He returned to become secretary-general of the party (1945), delegate to the Cominform (1947), and deputy prime minister (1951). He was then arrested and tried together with Vladimir Clementis in the last major trial of the Stalin era, and one that was marked by its anti-Semitism. He was executed but his reputation was later rehabilitated (1963).

SLATER, SAMUEL (1768–1835) founder of the American cotton-spinning industry, who emigrated from Britain (1789), carrying with him memorized details of textile machinery. In partnership with Almy and Brown, of RI, he built a cotton-spinning factory at Pawtucket (1793). He later set up his own firm, and established several mills in RI, CT, and MA.

SLAUGHTERHOUSE CASES, 16 Wallace 36 (1873), case in which the US Supreme Court interpreted the 14th Amendment to the constitution for the first time. The LA state legislature having granted a virtual monopoly of the slaughterhouse business in New Orleans (1867), it was claimed in the state courts that this was a violation of the 14th Amendment. The LA supreme court held that it was a legitimate exercise of state police power. The Supreme Court considered the case on appeal, especially a claim that the action violated the privileges and immunities clause of the 14th Amendment, and in a divided opinion, refused to accept the claim. A distinction was made between those privileges and immunities accruing to an individual as a state citizen and as a national citizen, only the latter being protected by the 14th Amendment. Traditional common law rights and state bills of rights were solely under the protection of the states, and the privileges and immunities clause did not restrict state power to regulate private property interests within their boundaries. The court also rejected the plaintiff's claim that he had been deprived of property without due process of law. Four of the justices dissented from this narrow interpretation of the 14th Amendment on the ground that there had been a violation of the plaintiff's rights on both counts; this view later gained majority support.   JDL

SLAVE DYNASTY, THE (1206–90), of Delhi, so-called because its members came from the class of Turkish military slaves. The dynasty was founded by Qutb-ud-din Aibek, the lieutenant of Sultan Muhammad of Ghur, in his conquest of north India. On Muhammad's death (1206) his successor declared him an independent sovereign. On his death (1210), his son, who proved incapable, was replaced by another slave, his brother-in-law, Iltutmish (*reg.* 1210–36). He recovered Gwalior and Bengal, put down many rebellions, and added Malwa and Sind to the sultanate. Above all, he held at bay Chingiz Khan (d. 1227), who had reached the Indus in pursuit of the Sultan of Khwarizm. He nominated as his successor his daughter Raziyya, who held her own (*reg.* 1236–40) until she was deposed by the nobles. After two short reigns a younger son of Iltutmish, Nasir-ud-din, succeeded (*reg.* 1246–66); he appointed his father-in-law, Ulugh Khan Balban as minister. On Nasir's death Balban became sultan (*reg.* 1266–86). Besides repressing rebellions he preserved north-west India from the Mongol menace, and refortified Lahore (1270). His son Muhammad defeated the Mongols in 1279. Muhammad having died in 1285, his son Qaiqabad (*reg.* 1286–90) succeeded Balban and the dynasty ended with Qaiqabad's murder in 1290. The Slave dynasty was a bastion of defence against the Mongols, sheltering refugee kings and men of letters.

A. B. M. Habibulla, *The Foundation of Muslim Rule in India* (London, 1945).   TGPS

SLAVE REVOLTS, in the West Indies. Slave insurrections occurred frequently in the islands between the 16th and 19th cents. They were a serious danger to the Europeans on the islands and the fear of slave revolts was a contributory factor to the cruel and inhuman punishment given recalcitrant slaves by their owners. Cuba suffered more slave revolts than any other Caribbean island. The first recorded revolt (1533) was mild, but later the blacks sacked Havana (1538). The most serious revolts on the island occurred during the 18th and 19th cents. On one occasion (1727) 300 slaves revolted and only the widespread use of Spanish troops prevented more blacks from joining the rebellion. Slave insurrections in Cuba ended only with the abolition of slavery (1886). Slave plans to revolt were uncovered in Barbados in 1649, 1676, 1693, and 1702. Jamaica was plagued with at least 12 slave revolts during the 18th cent. The Maroons—free Negroes in the Blue Mountains—fought a guerrilla war with the English (1734–8), and elicited some support from the slaves. During the most significant revolt (1760) slaves of several estates turned on their masters. Before the insurrection was quelled, 60 whites and some 400 blacks had been killed. Antigua was racked by a crisis (1736) when a slave conspiracy was discovered, the leaders of which were severely punished. Fighting between the French and their slaves on Martinique and Guadeloupe occurred (1792–3) and forced many blacks to flee the islands. The most serious and best organized insurrection of the 18th cent. was on Santo

Domingo (1791). The entire northern part of the island was embodied in a revolt which lasted two months, 2000 whites and 10,000 blacks being killed. Out of this revolt the African-born slave Jean-Jacques Dessalines (*c.* 1758–1806) emerged and proclaimed himself Emperor of Haiti (1804), which became the first independent nation in the Caribbean.

There were several 19th-cent. revolts in the British West Indies. In Barbados an Easter Sunday revolt in 1816 destroyed 60 estates, but only one white was killed. The black rebels suffered heavy loss of life. Nearly 13,000 slaves revolted in the Crown colony of Demerara (1823), but again the blacks suffered most. On the eve of emancipation a slave revolt in Jamaica was suppressed by the use of militia (1831). The abolition of slavery in the 19th cent. brought to an end the continual outbreak of slave insurrections in the Caribbean.

J. H. Parry and P. M. Sherlock, *A Short History of the West Indies* (London, 1956).
P. M. Sherlock, *West Indies* (New York, 1966).   TC

SLAVE TRADE across the Atlantic had three main phases. The first began with Portuguese exploration of the West African coast during the 15th cent. From seizing a few individuals found near the coast, the Portuguese soon turned to trading for slaves, which they sold in Europe or put to work in their Atlantic island colonies.

A second phase was introduced by the demand for labour in the developing American colonies of Spain and Portugal. African slaves reached the Caribbean islands by way of Lisbon, until in 1532 the Portuguese began to permit direct shipment of cargoes from Africa to the Americas. By the second half of the century demand and profit had so increased that English and French interlopers entered the trade, the first English slaving voyage being that of Hawkins in 1562. The Dutch joined in at the beginning of the 17th cent., sending their first cargo to Trinidad in 1606. By the middle of the century the English and Dutch had become the principal suppliers of slaves to the West Indies and North America. Their source of supply was Upper Guinea and the Niger Delta, while Portuguese and Brazilians supplied Brazil mainly from Angola.

The third and most intensive period of the slave trade began in the 18th cent. as a result of the rapid development of the plantation system in North America and the Caribbean, and of mining in Brazil. Existing slave markets were expanded and new ones added, in particular those of the so-called Slave Coast (Whydah, Badagry, Porto Novo, and Lagos). Legal prohibitions on the slave trade after 1807 took effect only gradually, and it was not until after 1850 that it finally petered out.

The Atlantic slave trade brought about one of the greatest forced migrations in history, which has had profound effects upon the ethnic composition and culture of Brazil, North America, and the Caribbean. In Africa many areas suffered severe depopulation from constant slave raiding.

D. P. Mannix and M. Cowley, *Black Cargoes, a History of the Atlantic Slave Trade* (London, 1963).
Basil Davidson, *Black Mother* (London, 1961).   AR

SLAVE TRADE IN AFRICA. The export and import of servile labour dates back to very early times in Egypt and North Africa, and became gradually more extensive throughout the rise of Islam and the European Middle Ages. By the 11th cent. there was a steady annual export of men and women from the Sudan (both west and east) to the Maghrib and Al-Andalus in the west and to Egypt and parts of southern Europe in the east, while a correspondingly steady import of non-Christian (and sometimes Christian) Europeans, mainly Slav and neighbouring peoples, reached Egypt and the eastern Maghrib. These European exports dwindled and stopped during the Late Middle Ages, but African exchanges of servile labour continued within the continent, mainly as an export from the Sudan, until the 19th cent., and a small trickle of slaves still reaches Saudi Arabia every year.

Though very long in duration, this overland slave trade almost certainly had a far smaller socio-economic impact upon Africa than the shorter but much more intensive Atlantic slave trade. The number exported annually was limited by the nature of the employment for which the slaves were destined. With the solitary exception of southern Iraq in the 9th cent., where a plantation economy using African slaves flourished briefly, servile labour in North Africa, as in the Sudan, was almost always used in various forms of domestic or personal work, including military service in special bodyguards, by men of power and wealth who required servants who stood outside traditional kinship networks and whose purely personal loyalty might thus be more reliable. As the records of Al-Andalus and Fatimid Egypt clearly show, these servants were invariably expensive, were much prized by their owners and were endowed with rights and privileges such as chattel slaves could seldom or never hope for. They came, moreover, from economies which had little or no use for slave labour, and were for the most part 'rightless persons' captured in raiding warfare or sentenced for serious offences in the courts. As in Africa south of the Sahara, these 'rightless persons' could often work themselves to freedom, marry into their owners' families, possess personal property, and carry on business dealings on their own account.

The nature of this overland slave trade changed somewhat in later centuries. It had always been liable to occasional cruelty, as in the making of eunuchs, but it developed some of the violent characteristics of the oversea slave trade, and probably increased in volume. It certainly increased in volume in East Africa, where a 19th-cent. slave trade from the interior began feeding the clove plantations of Zanzibar after 1818, the sugar plantations of Mauritius somewhat later, and, until the 1880s, even the transatlantic plantations, where large numbers of slaves were no more than chattels. In earlier times, by contrast, the records of the East Coast trade speak rarely or not at all of slave exports, although it is certain that small numbers of enslaved Africans did service in many parts of Asia, including China, during the European Middle Ages.

Basil Davidson, *The Africans* (London, 1969)   BD

SLAVE TRADE, SOCIETY FOR THE ABOLITION OF, in England, humanitarian pressure group launched by Quakers and others under the leadership of Granville Sharp, who had championed Somersett's Case (1772), and Thomas Clarkson. They won over William Wilberforce as their parliamentary spokesman, who greatly influenced the Younger Pitt. Attempts at reform were defeated in the climate of the French Revolution but the society triumphed in the Abolition of the Slave Trade Act (1807).

SLAVERY, ABOLITION OF, in British colonies. The abolition of the trade was the first step. It was attained in Britain by Quaker, evangelical, and humanitarian pressure in 1807, when it was enacted that no ship should engage in the slave trade from British territory. Many powerful individuals were implicated in the 'Atlantic triangle', which involved the shipment of slaves from Africa to America, but from the mid-18th cent. Quakers began to organize opposition to it. In 1772 Somersett's Case decided that a slave became free on reaching British soil, and in 1783 a Quaker anti-slave trade association was formed. This grew into William Wilberforce's non-denominational society, founded in 1787, and rapid progress was made until 1792. The movement was subsequently discredited by its Jacobin contacts but was revived after 1805 through support from the Clapham Sect and increased Whig influence in the government. By the act of 1807 the trade was formally abolished.

Slavery itself was virtually abolished in 1833 as a result of the efforts of Wilberforce and Sir Thomas Buxton, and the influence of women, nonconformists, evangelical Anglicans, and above all Quakers. The planters received £20 million compensation, and existing slaves were apprenticed for seven years. Further pressure ensured the complete abolition of slavery in 1838. Other nations followed Britain's example— France in 1848, the US in 1863, and Spain in 1886. The need for enforcement of the abolition required much British naval activity and justified colonial annexation. The anti-slavery movement developed new pressure-group techniques, set moral limits to the freedom of trade, and upheld middle-class moral leadership.   BHH

SLAVERY IN THE GREEK AND ROMAN WORLD. The enslavement of fellow-citizens by creditors was ended at an early stage of political development (*eg*, at Athens by Solon in 594 BC, at Rome in 4th cent BC), and that of fellow-Greeks after conquest (*eg*, Messene by Sparta in 7th cent., Melos by Athens in 416 BC) was rare and reprehensible; but the morality of using foreign slaves, whether acquired by conquest or through trade, was rarely questioned before the rise of Christianity, despite real feelings for their own slaves as fellow-humans evidently shown by individual masters. In most Greek cities, especially Athens, and in Rome the use of such slaves was widespread, particularly in households and in industries, where it undoubtedly helped to inhibit technical advance.

SLAVERY IN LATIN AMERICA. During the early decades of Iberian conquest and settlement, Indians were frequently enslaved, but after *c.* 1550 legal servile status applied, with certain exceptions, only to imported Africans, who arrived in large numbers during the late 16th cent. and thereafter, and were used primarily in the export agriculture and extractive sectors of the economy. The Brazilian sugar boom of the 16th–17th cents and the 19th-cent. coffee boom were dependent upon black slave labour. The gold and diamonds which poured from Brazil in the 18th cent. were likewise extracted by the African. In Spanish America, black slaves were extensively employed in the cultivation of Venezuelan cacao and coffee, Cuban and Mexican sugar, and Peruvian wine, wheat, and cotton. Everywhere in Latin America were to be found black artisans, servants, stevedores, sailors, and (in times of emergency) militiamen.

Some historians have judged Latin American slavery to have been more benign than Anglo-Saxon slavery in North America and the Caribbean, and have attributed the difference to the greater institutional presence of the Iberian state and the Catholic Church. In fact, both slave systems were equally harsh at different points in time, and largely in reaction to economic trends rather than legal and institutional pressure. In Latin America, however, the essential humanity of the slave, with loose regulations concerning manumission and large numbers of free blacks, was more readily tolerated than in English America. Latin Americans could view the world in the hierarchical terms of Catholicism, and assign to the blacks an inferior station without denying their humanity. Free blacks could be tolerated, since they formed a part of the labour force, and even race mixture could be informally sanctioned, since skin colour was viewed in hierarchical rather than in absolute terms; the whiter the skin, the more socially acceptable the person. But education and money could buy social whiteness, since the Iberians, accustomed to the cultural conglomeration that was the Mediterranean, could reconcile dark skin and high status.

For these reasons, slavery survived for longer in Latin America than in the US. The logic of egalitarianism did not press for its abolition. More persuasive was England, whose navy stopped the slave trade and whose thinkers condemned slavery as morally wrong without necessarily considering the black as an equal. Agitation for the abolition of slavery in Latin America, where it occurred, was often strident but never led to bloodshed. Brazil, in 1888, became the last country in the Western Hemisphere to abolish slavery.

Laura Foner and Eugene D. Genovese (eds), *Slavery in the New World* (Englewood Cliffs, NJ, 1969).

Gilberto Freyre, *The Masters and the Slaves: a study in the Development of Brazilian civilization* (New York, 1956).

FPB

SLAVERY IN THE US dates from the colonial period when white indentured servants and imported Africans were held in bondage. By the close of the 18th cent. Negro slavery was a legal institution in the 13 colonies and was implicitly recognized in the Federal constitution (1787). The development of the Southern plantation system, the invention of the cotton gin (1793), westward expansion in the early 19th cent. into areas suited for cotton cultivation and the factor of racial prejudice combined to strengthen slavery in the American South both in custom and in law. By 1800, through legislative or judicial action, slavery had been virtually abolished in the North, where it was seen to conflict with fundamental American principles and was never economically essential, but it was to remain the South's 'peculiar institution' until the 13th Amendment (1865) ended slavery in the US.

Slaveholdings were concentrated in areas best suited for the cultivation of cotton, sugar, rice, tobacco, and hemp, and were proportionately more numerous in the lower than in the upper South. In 1860 nearly half of the South's total slave population (4 million) was in the cotton states, and of the total white population (8 million) only 384,884 were slave owners, with nearly 90 per cent owning less than 20 slaves. It was the planter aristocracy, those families (about 10,000) owning more than 50 slaves, which provided the political and social leadership of the ante-bellum South. Primarily regarded as property, slaves could be bought and sold and their condition was hereditary. The Southern slave codes prohibited the instruction of slaves in reading and writing, set restrictions on the movement of slaves, codified punishments for slave crimes, and generally revealed an increasing opposition to emancipation in any form. These laws were often evaded in practice but the slave remained, in essence, an individual held down by force. On farms and plantations slaves were classified as house slaves and field hands, subject to strict supervision. By 1850, 400,000 slaves lived in urban centres, engaged in a wide range of occupations including industrial employment.

Slavery was both economically profitable and psychologically necessary for the white South, which elaborated a detailed and ingenious defence of the system as benefiting both races. Contemporary observers and later historians have given conflicting estimates of slavery, examining such categories as slave clothing, food, shelter, and discipline. Certainly the relations between masters and slaves were so complex and varied as to allow no easy generalizations. However, there is evidence that slaves resented their status, often feigning illness or performing dilatory work, although rarely rising to organized revolt. The disruption of family life under slavery, widespread miscegenation and the tensions of the regime undoubtedly caused enduring psychological harm to blacks. Politically, the issue of slavery extension into the US territories dominated American life from the 1850s to the Civil War. Lincoln's Emancipation Proclamation (1863) and the 13th Amendment freed the slaves, but after the Civil War a caste system gradually replaced slavery as the characteristic feature of Southern society.

K. M. Stampp, *The Peculiar Institution: Slavery in the Ante-Bellum South* (New York, 1956).

John White and Ralph Willett, *Slavery in the American South* (London, 1970).

JW

SLAVOPHILISM, philosophical movement of the 1840s and 1850s which emerged from the discussion circles of the 1830s in which opposition was expressed to the ideas of Chaadaev and Belinsky and those who became known as westernizers.

The slavophiles were basically a small group of interrelated noble families centred on Moscow and their country estates. Their most important members were A. Khomyakov, an outstanding orthodox theologian, the Kireyevsky brothers, and the Aksakov brothers. They combined an early interest in the German romantics with a study of Russian history and a deep nationalism and reacted against the westernizers' belief that Russia must continue the policies of Peter I and follow western paths of development. They based their ideas on the uniqueness of Russia's history and civilization and a messianic belief in its future greatness.

Unlike the proponents of official nationality, they abhorred the Russia of Nicholas I and opposed bureaucracy, censorship, and serfdom. They aimed at reform to restore an idealized pre-Petrine system of society. Orthodoxy as a religion and a basis of society was fundamental to their views and they extolled its conciliar practices and stress on family life. In their concern with agricultural development they greatly admired the peasant commune and communal way of life, which they contrasted with western individualism.

Politically they wanted what they believed was the Muscovite system of autocracy—a monarch who accepted autocratic power from the people as well as God, ruling in harmony with the traditions and interest of the people and aided periodically by a *zemskii sobor*. All government was evil, the tsar's assumption of authority was a sacrificial act, and bureaucracy and censorship were unnecessary western innovations. Authority was personal and patriarchal and based on custom, not law.

Samarin and Koshelyov held political posts and their ideas had some influence on the Emancipation Act. Mainly they were concerned with Russia, but the Moscow Slavonic Benevolent Committee (1858) supported the cultural and religious activities of the south slavs and their ideas are best known from Khomyakov's Message to the Serbians (1860). Ivan Aksakov was to link their ideas to the more political and nationalistically aggressive Pan-Slavism.

P. K. Christoff, *An Introduction to Nineteenth-Century Russian Slavophilism, A Study in Ideas*, vol. 1 (The Hague, 1961).

N. V. Riasanovsky, *Russia and the West in the Teaching of the Slavophils* (Harvard, 1952).

BJW

SLAVS, Southern. The collapse of the empire of the Huns after 455 set in motion a series of Slav migrations from the area between the Dnieper and Oder rivers. They are believed to have been among the invaders who menaced Constantinople in the time of the Emperor Anastasius, who built new walls around the city to keep them out. The Danube frontier was stabilized by the Emperor Justinian (*reg.* 527–65), but the entry into Europe of another Asiatic horde, the Avars (*c.* 560), drove several Slavonic tribes southwards across the Danube. During the late 6th cent. most of the Balkan lands, except some coastal districts, were overrun by Slavs. Those who settled in Greece were gradually hellenized in the 7th and 8th cents. The labours of St Cyril and St Methodios during the years 862–5 initiated a movement of conversion which brought the Slav peoples living further to the north into dependence on the Orthodox Church. In the course of time Slav states made their appearance, and some of them attained great prominence, *eg*, the First Bulgarian Empire (the Bulgars having been assimilated to the Slavs), which was at its height under Symeon the Great (*reg.* 893–927); the Second Bulgarian Empire, founded in 1185 and conquered two centuries later by the Ottoman Turks; and Serbia, which reached its apogee under Stefan Dusan (*reg.* 1331–55) and was thereafter incorporated into the Ottoman empire during the years 1389–1459.

SLIM, WILLIAM JOSEPH SLIM, 1st Viscount (1891–1970), British soldier who joined the army in 1914, and after service in the First World War transferred to the Indian army in 1920. In 1940 he was a brigade commander in the 5th Indian Division's actions in Eritrea and in the following year commanded the 10th Indian Division in Syria, Iraq, and Iran. He returned to India in 1942 and for the remainder of the Second World War was engaged in the war against the Japanese, commanding the 14th Army from 1943. The Japanese offensive of 1943 towards India was halted by his forces in Assam in the battles of Kohima and Imphal, and from Dec. of that year the 14th Army conducted a brilliantly conceived and handled campaign which had driven the Japanese out of Burma by May 1944. This campaign revealed Slim's greatness as a commander and as a leader of men; he mastered the logistic problems posed by the difficult mountainous and jungle terrain, relying on self-sufficiency and air-dropped supplies to provide the tactical mobility necessary to match that of the Japanese. His strategic and tactical insight is well illustrated by the battle for the crossing of the Irrawaddy (Feb.–March 1945). He was commander-in-chief (1945–6) of all Allied land forces in South-East Asia, and in 1948 was appointed chief of the imperial general staff in succession to Field Marshal Montgomery. He was briefly deputy chairman of the British Railway Executive and was governor-general of Australia (1953–60). In 1964 he became governor of Windsor Castle.

SLIVNITZA, BATTLE OF (1885). Bulgaria, despite Russia's withdrawal of all its senior officers from the Bulgarian army, inflicted a decisive defeat on Serbia, forcing Milan of Serbia into dependence on Austria, while establishing their own independence of Russia.

SLOANE, SIR HANS (1660–1753), English physician, naturalist, and collector of a herbarium, 50,000 books, 3500 volumes of manuscripts, 32,000 coins and medals, classical antiquities, etc. By his will the collections were offered to the nation for £20,000. Parliament accepted the offer and Sloane's Collections (with the Harleian and Cottonian Libraries) became the British Museum.

SLOCUM, JOHN (1841–1909), American Indian who 'died' in 1881 and went to heaven. On the strength of this experience, he founded his own form of Christian sect in Puget Sound, Washington. The Indian agent had him arrested but on his release he established his own church (1892) and attracted a group of Indian followers.

SLUTER, CLAUS (d. 1406), Dutch sculptor, who entered (1385) the service of Philip the Bold, Duke of Burgundy, for whom he produced the sculptured doorway of the Chartreuse de Champol near Dijon.

SLUYS, BATTLE OF (June 1340), off the Flemish coast. An English fleet, commanded by Edward III, captured all but 24 out of a French fleet of about 200 ships. This was the first great English victory of the Hundred Years War and gave them control of the Channel for a generation.

SMALL SWORD SOCIETY, in China, off-shoot of the Chinese Triad Society, a loosely organized secret society whose aim was to 'overthrow the Ch'ing and restore the Ming.' Its membership was drawn mainly from the fringe elements in a Confucian society. Its most noteworthy achievement in modern history was the seizure of the walled Chinese city of Shanghai in Sept. 1853, following upon a revolt of the Small Sword Society of Amoy (May–Nov. 1853). But because of ideological differences, their hoped-for alliance with the Taipings did not come about. The uprising was finally crushed by Ch'ing forces, aided by Westerners in Shanghai; but only after 17 months in which they gave proof of their administrative ability under difficult circumstances.

SMALLPOX, acute infectious disease caused by a virus, which killed rich and poor alike until the mid-18th cent. From 1760 inoculation began to have significant results but vaccination evolved by Dr Jenner (1749–1823) in 1796 is the best means of prevention.

SMILES, SAMUEL (1812–1904), English writer whose moral treatises, especially *Self-Help* (1859) and various industrial biographies, helped to create the enterprising, self-reliant, and ambitious character demanded by early capitalism. For Victorian slum-dwellers his exhortations were often unrealistic, but his socialist critics exaggerated the materialism and selfishness involved in his militant individualism.

SMIRKE, SIR ROBERT (1781–1867), British architect, who designed many late Georgian public buildings in London. His style was predominantly a plain and spacious classical, his best-known building being the British Museum.

SMITH, ADAM (1723–90), Scottish economist and author of *The Wealth of Nations* (1776). He is often called the father of political economy which he defined as 'the art of managing the resources of a people and of its government'. Smith lectured at Edinburgh (1748–50) and was professor of moral philosophy at Glasgow (1752–64). His book *Theory of Moral Sentiments* (1759), which inspired Charles Townshend to appoint him travelling tutor to his stepson, with a pension for life, enabled Smith first to travel in France (1764–6) and then to retire and devote himself to political economy. In France he met Quesnay, Turgot, and other physiocrats. They must be added to Francis Hutcheson (who had lectured to Smith at Glasgow) and David Hume as influences on *The Wealth of Nations* (1776). The book was at once accepted as authoritative and five editions were published in Smith's lifetime. Its basic tenets were concern for the liberty of the individual, and belief that self-interest, if allowed free play, would produce beneficent results. It followed that the less the government interfered the better, and that free trade and the free working of economic laws should be substituted for restrictive mercantilism. Smith used his theories to make detailed and informed criticisms of contemporary commercial and industrial legislation rather than, as the physiocrats did, to construct a logical deductive system. This concrete element in his work, coming at a time of commercial and industrial transition, is one reason for his great influence on his contemporaries, on the succeeding generation of classical economists, and on 19th-cent. legislation.

BK

SMITH, ALFRED EMANUEL (1873–1944), US politician. Born in a tenement on New York's Lower East Side, he rose through city and state politics to become governor of NY (1919–21, 1923–9). He was an Irish-American Roman Catholic and an opponent of prohibition, and he came to symbolize the values of the modern American city. His defeat as Democratic presidential candidate in 1928 has often been attributed to his religion. However, Herbert Hoover's identification with the nation's prosperity would probably have defeated any contender, and the votes Smith lost in the prohibitionist, Protestant, rural areas were partially compensated for by those he gained among urban immigrant groups, who were to form an important element in Franklin Roosevelt's later Democratic majorities. Although he first achieved prominence as sponsor of safety legislation in NY state after the Triangle fire (1911), Smith's economic views were generally conservative and, as a member of the American Liberty League (1934), he was a prominent opponent of the New Deal.

SMITH, SIR CHARLES KINGSFORD (1897–1935), Australian airman, one of a group who, after service in the RFC during the First World War, made contributions to the experimental inter-continental flights and competitions in the 1920s and 1930s which gradually conditioned Australian governments, investors, and the general public to a realization of the potential revolution in civilian communications. With

Charles Ulm (1897–1934) he crossed the Pacific by air in the *Southern Cross* (1928) and they also crossed the Tasman Sea and the Australian continent in a non-stop flight from near Melbourne to Perth. Earlier, the brothers Sir Ross Macpherson Smith (1892–1922) and Sir Keith Macpherson Smith (1890–1955) had won the Australian government's £10,000 prize (1919) for a flight from London to Australia within 30 days. While such aviators blazed the sky-trails, they had little *immediate* and personal success in establishing stable and continuing commercial services.   FA

SMITH, GOLDWIN (1823–1910), English historian and writer. He campaigned actively for the reform of Oxford University, and was one of two secretaries to the Royal Commission on the university (1850–2). He was a member of the Newcastle Commission on education (1858) and in the same year was appointed regius professor of modern history at Oxford. He left to become professor of history at the newly founded Cornell University in 1868, and spent the rest of his life in the US and Canada. There he advocated Canadian independence and political union with the US. He became counsellor to the Canada First group and president of their National Club. His main work in Canada was literary and editorial. He founded the *Canadian Monthly and National Review* (1872), the *Telegram* (1874), the *Bystander* (1880), and the *Week* (1883).

SMITH, HERBERT (1862–1938), British mining official who was miners' president during the crucial period of the 1920s. He entered a pit at the age of ten and soon took an active part in the miners' movements and West Riding politics. For 46 years he was an official of the Yorkshire Miners' Association, and their president from 1906. In 1910 he unsuccessfully stood as Labour candidate for Morley, but won recognition for his rescue work in the Whitehaven pit disaster of that year.

In the events of 1921 he fully supported the miners' strike action and shared their disappointment over the 'betrayal' of 'Black Friday' in April. He sought a national pool of miners' wages to equalize rich and poor mining areas. As president of the Miners' Federation of Great Britain, he led his men in the events leading to the 1926 General Strike, holding out vigorously against owners' local agreements and any lengthening of miners' hours. As president of the International Miners' Federation, he had visited Russia in 1924, and was, until his death, still active in mining rescue operations.

SMITH, JEDEDIAH STRONG (1798–1831), US fur trader and explorer who was one of the most famous of the Mountain Men of the 1820s, the first American explorer of the Great Basin of the Rocky Mountains, and the first American to cross the Sierras into CA. He opened up the South Pass route from WY into the Rocky Mountains (1824), pioneered a trail from Salt Lake across the Mohave Desert to the San Joaquin valley of CA (1826), and returned through OR and ID to Pierre's Hole, WY (1828–9). He then moved south to trade along the Santa Fé Trail and was killed by Comanche Indians.

SMITH, JOHN (1580–1631), English soldier, explorer, and writer, who left England for the colonies as a soldier and, after an adventurous eight years, which he recounted in his *True Travels* (1630), he returned to England (1604) to join the band of colonists which, under the auspices of the Virginia Co. of London, landed at Jamestown (1607). He was captured by Indians while trying to procure food for the hard-pressed colony, and claimed that his life was spared only after the intervention of Pocahantes, the chief's daughter. Having been injured by a gunpowder explosion (1609), he returned to England and published his first primary contribution to cartography, 'A Map of Virginia' (1612). In 1614, he brought a valuable cargo of fish and furs from New

England and wrote *A Description of New England* (1616), coining the name of the region.

SMITH, JOHN (1735–1824), US Baptist minister and politician, who was elected one of the first two US senators from OH (1803). His association with Aaron Burr's conspiracy led to his resignation from the Senate (1807).

SMITH, JOSEPH (1805–44), US founder of Mormonism, who was brought up in western NY, a centre of fervent revivalism. Experiencing a series of divine revelations, the semi-literate Smith allegedly discovered (1827) and translated plates of gold inscribed with ancient characters which told how the 'true' church, now defunct, had come to America long before Columbus. In 1830 he published *The Book of Mormon* and founded the 'Church of Jesus Christ of Latter-Day Saints'. Early converts other than Smith formulated its doctrine and ecclesiastical organization, but his revelations were responsible for the rules concerning abstinence (1833) and polygamy (1843). Hostility to the growing sect forced Smith and his followers to move westwards to OH and MO, and then eastwards to Nauvoo, IL (1839). Here Smith's growing megalomania and political dictatorship, together with the sanctioning of polygamy, aroused dissension within the community, as well as opposition from outside. After being arrested on charges that included polygamy and the suppression of civil liberties, Smith and his brother were murdered by a mob in Carthage, IL (27 June 1844).

SMITH, SYDNEY (1771–1845), English clergyman, who was a founder of (1802) and a prolific contributor to the *Edinburgh Review* and lectured on Moral Philosophy at the Royal Institution (1804–6). He supported Catholic Emancipation and parliamentary reform. His reputation rests principally on the extravagant wit of his conversation, letters, and reviews.

SMITH, SIR THOMAS (1558–1625), English merchant, who was connected with important London trading companies and was a promoter of colonial settlements. After 20 years as governor of the East India Co., he became treasurer of the London Co. for the colonization of Virginia.

SMITH, THOMAS SOUTHWOOD (1788–1861), English unitarian minister, doctor, and sanitary reformer, who was a Benthamite and took particular interest in public health and housing. He helped to found the *Westminster Review* (1824). With Chadwick, he was a member of the 1833 factory enquiry and was active in the movement for sanitary reform. He was a founder of the Health of Towns Association (1844) and the medical member of the Board of Health (1848).

SMITH, WILLIAM HENRY (1815–91), British politician and businessman, son of the founder of Messrs W. H. Smith, booksellers in the Strand, who secured the privilege of selling books at railway stations (1849). He became Conservative MP for Westminster (1868) and served in Disraeli's government (1874–80) as secretary to the treasury and first lord of the admiralty. As secretary for war in Lord Salisbury's cabinet he successfully opposed Lord Randolph Churchill's budgetary proposals for economies (1886) and replaced him, on his resignation, as leader of the House of Commons (1887–91).

SMITH ACT (1940), in the US, alien registration act, drafted by Congressman Howard W. Smith of VA, that strengthened existing legislation and made it unlawful to advocate or teach the overthrow of government in the US by force or violence or to become a member of any group committed to such ends. Its constitutionality was upheld by the US Supreme Court in *Dennis v. United States* (1951).

SMITH SQUARE, in London, for a brief period the headquarters of all three British political parties, its attraction being that it is barely 400 yards from the Houses of Parliament. Conservative Central Office has been there since 1958; the Labour Party since 1928, when Transport House was opened as the joint headquarters of the party and the Transport and General Workers' Union, and the Liberal Party (1965–8), until financial stringency forced them to move elsewhere.

SMITHFIELD, area in the north of the city of London, known for its modern meat market and the site of a medieval market from 1183. In the Middle Ages it was the scene of jousting tournaments but in the 16th–17th cents was associated with the execution of the victims of religious persecution, *eg*, in Mary I's reign (1553–8) the 'fires of Smithfield' accounted for about 273 Protestant martyrs.

SMITHSONIAN INSTITUTION (1846–), in Washington, DC, for the increase and diffusion of knowledge, founded under the will of an Englishman, James Smithson (1765–1829), with an endowment for its upkeep. Its original Gothic buildings on the Mall (1847–55) were designed by James Renwick. Associated with the Smithsonian are the Museums of Natural History and Arts and Industries, the National Gallery of Art, the Freer Gallery, the Bureau of Indian Ethnology, and the Astrophysical Observatory.

SMOLENSK, ancient Slav settlement at a strategic intersection of routes on the upper Dnieper river, captured by Rurik's successor, Oleg, in 880. By the 13th cent. it had become a flourishing city and capital of the principality, but in the 14th cent. West Russia, including Smolensk, became subject to the Grand Duke of Lithuania, though enjoying considerable autonomy. In 1514 it was taken by the Muscovite grand duke, Vassily III, but was occupied by the Poles during the Time of Troubles and was retained by Poland by the truce of Deulino (1618). Muscovy tried but failed to recover it on the renewal of war with Poland (1632–4), but finally won back the principality in the war of 1654–67. Smolensk was retained by Moscow at the treaty of Andrussovo (1667). The city was taken by Napoleon and he retreated through it after the Moscow campaign (1812). The Germans just reached Smolensk in their advance of spring 1918 and again occupied it during the Second World War, when it was the scene of one of the bitterest battles of the war (July–Sept. 1941). It was reoccupied by the Russians in Oct. 1943 and reverted finally to the USSR.

SMOLENSK, BATTLES OF (Aug. 1812, July 1941). The first battle was fought in the French Wars. The French defeated the Russians, whose command was disunited. Gen. Berclay de Tolly retreated after initial heavy casualties and was replaced by Kutusov.

Smolensk was also the scene of a battle in the Second World War when Russian forces failed to hold German troops under Gen. Fedor von Bock, who were carrying out Hitler's invasion, 'Operation Barbarossa', to overrun Russia.

SMOLLETT, TOBIAS GEORGE (1721–71), Scottish novelist and journalist, whose first novels, *Roderick Random* (1748) and *Peregrine Pickle* (1751), were racy, picaresque, and ferociously satirical. He founded the *Critical Review* (1756), and edited the *True Briton* (1762), and wrote a *Complete History of England* (1758). His last and greatest novel, written after ten years of ill-health and inactivity, was *Humphrey Clinker* (1771).

SMUTS, JAN CHRISTIAAN (1870–1950), South African soldier and politician. In 1898 he became state attorney of the Transvaal (South African republic). As a general during the Anglo-Boer War (1899–1902) he showed himself to be courageous and enterprising, leading commando raids deep into the Cape Colony. He helped to draft the terms of the peace treaty of Vereeniging, being responsible for the section which denied franchise rights to Africans in the former republics. He was opposed to the importation of Chinese labour into the gold-mines of the Transvaal, and was Botha's right-hand man when Het Volk Party came to power in that colony in 1907.

Smuts played a major role in the formulation of the constitution of the Union of South Africa, which was established in 1910, and held a variety of ministerial posts under Botha, who was the first prime minster of the Union until his death in 1919, when Smuts became prime minister. In 1924 he was ousted from office by Hertzog's National Party. During Smuts's first administration there was considerable racial tension, which was not alleviated by his repressive measures. In 1933 his party and Hertzog's formed a coalition government, Smuts being deputy prime minister. He became prime minister again in 1939, after a disagreement with Hertzog over South Africa's participation in the Second World War. He remained in office until the United Party's electoral defeat by the new National Party in 1948. Until his death he was leader of the opposition.

Smuts was not only a South African politician, but a major world statesman. In 1916, as Allied commander in East Africa he successfully opposed the German forces there and rose so high in British esteem that in 1917 he was invited to join the war cabinet; only 15 years earlier he had fought bitterly against the British in South Africa. He played a considerable part in the establishment of the League of Nations and of the mandated territories under the league. During the Second World War he was a close adviser to Churchill and other Allied leaders. Towards the end of the war he became alarmed by the threat of Russian expansion, having less faith in the United Nations Organization than he had had in the league during its early years; nevertheless, he drafted the preamble to the UNO's charter on human rights.

Smuts was also a philosopher of note (in 1926, he published *Holism and Evolution*), and a botanist. His dominating intellect did not always make him popular with his political colleagues, and he lacked the common touch. His breadth of vision was more attuned to the world stage than to the affairs of South Africa, and his loftiness prevented him from understanding either the force of Afrikaner nationalism or the virulence of racism in South Africa. In spite of his ideals about human existence, he did little, while in office, to improve the lot of the black majority of the South African population. It could be said that he lacked realism, and a sense of the increasing seriousness of the problems of his age. His genius was Victorian in its individuality and scope, and seemed out of place by the mid-20th cent.

W. K. Hancock, *Smuts*, vol. 1, *The Sanguine Years, 1870–1919* (Cambridge, 1962).
W. K. Hancock, *Smuts*, vol. 2, *The Fields of Force* (Cambridge, 1968).   AEA

SMYRNA, ANCIENT, Greek city in Asia Minor established (*c.* 1000 BC) by Aeolian refugees from central Greece; later (*c.* 700) it was won by the Ionian League. Recent excavations have revealed Smyrna's development from a humble, primitively fortified settlement of a few hundred huts (9th–8th cents) to a well-built town with a fine wall (*c.* 600). After its destruction by the Lydian King, Alyattes (*c.* 600), Smyrna was not rebuilt until *c.* 320. Under the Roman empire it was one of the most prosperous cities in the province of Asia.

SNOUCK HURGRONJE, CHRISTIAAN (1857–1936), Dutch oriental scholar and professor of Islamic law at Leyden University, known for his studies of the Meccan pilgrimage and Atjehnese Islam. As adviser to the Netherlands East Indies government (1889–1906) he helped the Dutch to achieve victory in the Atjeh War through his understanding of the Atjehnese social structure, and he was influential in formulating colonial policy towards Islam.

SNOWDEN, PHILIP SNOWDEN, Viscount (1864–1937), British politician who joined the Labour movement via the

ILP and never had trade union experience. He soon became an expert on national finance and the drink question. He opposed the First World War and championed conscientious objectors, but the Russian Revolution strengthened the democratic aspect of his socialism. In the early 1920s his vigorous attacks on Bolshevism helped to free the British Labour Party from continental influences. As chancellor of the exchequer in the 1924 Labour government he produced a Gladstonian budget. He had no sympathy with the General Strike, and was popular in the city of London as chancellor in the 1929 Labour government. His connections with the National government after 1931, however, damned him with the Labour Party, and he ended his career unhappily.

SNOWY MOUNTAINS SCHEME, network of mountain tunnels, reservoirs, and power-stations in south-eastern Australia. It was begun in 1949 and diverts waters from the Snowy, a short river flowing to the Pacific Ocean, into the long inland-flowing Murray and Murrumbidgee rivers. The scheme, which lies between Sydney and Melbourne, supplies them both with electricity and also supplies water to the irrigation settlements on the interior plains. The project was directed (1949–67) by Sir William Hudson, a New Zealand engineer (1896–), who had worked on British hydro-electric schemes.

SO or SAO of Bornu in Nigeria, legendary race of giants said to have been tricked and defeated by the Kanuri. Research suggests that So was a general term for the aboriginal inhabitants.

SO CHAEPIL (1866–1951), Korean soldier and reformer. As head of the Korean Military Academy, he forced through the reforms of 1884, which were reversed within days by the Min family, supported by Chinese troops. All So's family was killed, and he fled to the US. He returned to Korea (1896–7), and founded Korea's first popular newspaper and the Independence Club. He returned again (1947–8), and held honorary office in the Korean provisional government.

SOANE, SIR JOHN (1753–1837), British architect, who designed the Bank of England (1788–1833), and held a number of government posts, including that of architect to the board of works (1814–32). He built many public buildings and churches. His personal style, uninfluenced by Greek or Gothic revival, gives him a unique position in English architecture. He presented his London house, now the Soane Museum, and his collection of antiquities and paintings, to the nation (1833).

SOBHUZA (*reg. c.* 1815–36), chief of the Dhlamini clan, who founded the Swazi nation, comprising the Nguni and Sotho peoples north of the Pongola river (South-East Africa) during the *Mfecane*.

SOBIESKI, JOHN III (1624–96), King of Poland (*reg.* 1674–1696), Polish magnate and soldier who was elected to the throne in succession to Michael Wisniowiecki. After being educated by the Jesuits he toured western Europe, went on a diplomatic mission to the Porte and entered military service in 1648. He fought against the Tatars and the Cossacks (1651–2) and with the Swedes (1654–5). In 1665 he was made commander-in-chief of the Polish army and married Princess Zamoyski, formerly Marie Casimire de la Grange d'Arquien, who encouraged his pro-French sympathies. Sobieski became involved in intrigue against Wisniowiecki (1669–72) but then (1672–6) he concentrated on checking the Turkish threat against Poland, *eg*, he won a brilliant victory at Choczim (11 Nov. 1673), which made him the favourite candidate for the throne (1674). In the first years of his reign he pursued a French alliance and aimed at the recovery of East Prussia from Brandenburg, but after 1679 he became increasingly pro-Habsburg as he sought to create a league of Christian countries against the Turkish infidel. The climax of his career came on 12 Sept. 1683 when he raised the siege of

Vienna with a greatly inferior force of Poles and checked the Turkish advance into western Europe. Despite the ingratitude of Emperor Leopold I he succeeded in forging a Holy League of Poland, Venice, Austria, and the Holy See (1684), but in his later campaigns to reconquer Moldavia, Wallachia, and the Ukraine (1684–91) his efforts proved fruitless. He made peace with Russia (1686) by confirming the concessions of the 1667 truce, but his last years were clouded by internal conflicts between the pro-French faction led by his wife and the pro-Habsburg nobles, who paralysed the meetings of the Diet and prevented constructive policies.

SOBRAON, BATTLE OF (10 Feb. 1846), in which Gen. Gough gained a decisive victory over a strongly entrenched Sikh army near Ferozepore. Sikh losses were estimated at about 10,000 men. The battle was followed by the British occupation of Lahore and the end of the first Sikh War.

SOCAGE TENURE in England, originally peculiar to the English Danelaw. It was freehold tenure of land by a peasant. The peasant, called a sokeman, made suit of court (OE *soc* = court) to his lord but was himself free and could dispose of his land as he chose. After the 12th cent. it came to denote any lay land tenure which was free and not burdened with feudal military service.

SOCIAL CREDIT PARTY in Canada, reformist movement, deriving its inspiration from the social and economic theories of Clifford Douglas, which were popularized by the United Farmers of Alberta and by William Aberhart, a high-school principal from Calgary, during a series of religious broadcasts. Aberhart, who modified Douglas's theories and promised a redistribution of wealth, founded the Social Credit Party, which won the 1935 Alta provincial election. Aberhart consequently became prime minister. The main acts of the Social Credit government, *eg*, the Social Credit Measures Act (1936), the Alberta Credit House Act (1936), and the Alberta Social Credit Act (1937) were either disallowed by the federal government or declared unconstitutional. Although the party ruled Alta from 1935 onwards and captured BC in 1952, it had only a limited success in the other provinces. In 1935 the party won 17 seats in the federal parliament, but none in 1958. Owing to the rise of the party in Que., it won 30 seats in 1962, but only 24 in 1963.

SOCIAL CREDIT PARTY in NZ, formed in 1953 when the effects of inflation became apparent to consumers, small businessmen, and farmers. Its predecessors were the Country Party (1922–38) and the Douglas Social Credit Movement of the 1930s. The party contested elections from 1954 as a third party opposed to the National and Labour parties. It achieved at its best 14·48 per cent of the votes and one seat (1966).

SOCIAL DEMOCRATIC FEDERATION (1881) in Britain, founded by Henry Hyndman, partly to counteract the National Liberal Federation, which appeared to be attracting working-class support; it was originally known as the Democratic Federation. Subsequently it drew its strength from socialist intellectuals, and tended to be dogmatic and sectarian. Its original programme was based on a Chartist type of radicalism and on land nationalization. Prominent socialists, among them William Morris and Eleanor Marx, joined the movement, which in 1883 adopted a socialist programme of public ownership of the means of production. Quarrels about Hyndman's leadership led Morris and others to secede and join the Socialist League in 1884; at the same time the Federation added the word 'Social' to its name. The third Reform Act, the trade depression of 1886, and the Liberal split over Home Rule, opened political opportunities to the SDF, which organized demonstrations that culminated in Bloody Sunday (1887). Thereafter the movement lost ground, except in some parts of London. It showed no more than 'benevolent neutrality' towards the Independent Labour

Party when it was formed in 1893. In 1900 the SDF joined the Labour Representation Committee but, characteristically, seceded 18 months later.

SOCIAL DEMOCRATIC LABOUR PARTY in Russia, founded at Minsk in March 1898 by the uniting of several Marxist groups. It included revisionists, economists, and political Marxists of widely differing trends, and at its second congress in 1903 it split into Menshevik and Bolshevik factions.

SOCIAL DEMOCRATIC PARTY in Germany, created by the fusion of Lassalle's General German Workers' Association, founded in 1863, and Liebknecht and Bebel's Social Democratic Workers' Party, founded in 1869. The former sought parliamentary democracy and the institution of producer co-operatives run by the state; the latter was a Marxist socialist party, committed to revolution. They agreed on a common programme at Gotha (1875), which was subsequently condemned by Marx, though his condemnation was not published.

Bismarck's introduction (1878) of anti-socialist legislation compelled the party to break the law in order to hold meetings, and this produced a more revolutionary approach. When the laws lapsed, the Erfurt programme (1891) officially adopted Marxism as the maximum objective, but sought in the meantime a more democratic government and an improvement in the lot of the working class.

The easing of its legal position gradually produced tension in the German Social Democratic Party, which however did not lead to an actual split because the virtual extinction of the Liberal Party under Bismarck left the party as the sole advocate of the working class. The Erfurt programme had been Marxist, and the improvement in the condition of the workers, together with increased prosperity, did not seem to accord with the Marxist thesis of increasing misery and unemployment under capitalism. To Eduard Bernstein it seemed that capitalism was set for almost indefinite expansion and that wealth was being better distributed; therefore socialism should come about by a voluntary decision of the people, and revolution, which would be disruptive of economic improvement, should be opposed.

Bernstein's revisionism was not of practical importance at the time he put it forward, as all sections of the party agreed that the time was not ripe for revolution and that they should press instead for responsible parliamentary government, the development of trades unions and co-operatives, and increased security and benefits for the workers. It was, however, the origin of the division in principle which resulted eventually in the organization of socialism and communism in two separate parties.

German Social Democracy was influential in the Second International chiefly because of the party's strength in the German Reichstag. In 1881, the party polled a mere 300,000 votes, but by 1890 it took 20 per cent of them, and by 1903 nearly one-third. Socialist parties from other countries therefore paid considerable attention to the Germans' organization and thought, though at the same time deriding them for the contrast between their numerical strength and their lack of power.

Carl E. Schorske, *German Social Democracy 1905–17* (Harvard, 1955).

Arthur Rosenberg, *Democracy and Socialism* (London, 1939).

DMK

SOCIAL GOSPEL, movement in American Protestantism which emphasized the need for social improvement rather than individual salvation. It emerged in the late 19th cent. as a response to the challenge presented both to Christian values and to the traditional position of the churches by industrialization and urbanization. The politics of Social Gospel clergymen ranged from mild reformism to outright socialism, but all agreed in condemning the inhumanity of contemporary capitalism. The movement, usually associated with liberal theology, was centred in theological seminaries and urban churches and was strongest in the Episcopalian and Congregational denominations. Walter Rauschenbusch's *Christianity and the Social Crisis* (1907) was an outstanding statement of the radical Social Gospel, and the formation of the Federal Council of Churches in 1908 gave the movement an institutional forum. Although usually associated with the Progressive era, the Social Gospel has remained an important element in American Protestantism.

SOCIAL SECURITY in NZ, originated in the Old Age Pensions Act (1898), which established the principle of society's responsibility for the deserving indigent. Those eligible had to be not less than 65 years old, and the maximum annual payment was £18. In 1899 stringent means tests reduced the original recipients to 7487. Pensions were later increased and the categories of eligibility extended to include widows with children (1911), disabled miners (1912), and the blind (1924). In 1926 a small, restricted family allowance was introduced. The Labour government revised and increased the old age and invalidity pensions (1936) and made means tests less severe. The Social Security Act (1938) embodied the principle that 'benefits' (no longer pensions) could be claimed by right of citizenship. It also eliminated the elements of 'charity' and 'insurance' and defined its aims as comprehensive protection from social misfortune. This act's innovations included medical benefits—free consultations, drugs and hospital treatment, and child benefits (50p per week). By 1968, revised social security and health benefits absorbed 8·1 per cent of the national income.

SOCIAL WAR, GREEK (357–355 BC), unsuccessful attempt by the Athenians to retain three allies in the Second Athenian Confederacy—Chios, Cos, and Rhodes. Disturbed by recent Athenian actions, *eg*, the sending of cleruchies to Samos and elsewhere, and encouraged by Mausolus of Caria, these three had seceded and were joined by Byzantium. Though the Athenians prevented the movement from spreading, they were defeated at Embata (356) and made peace, when an attempt to raise money by assisting a rebellious satrap provoked the Persian king, Artaxerxes III, to threaten intervention. The war distracted the Athenians' attention from the rise of Philip II of Macedon and seriously weakened their capacity to fight him.

SOCIAL WAR, ROMAN (90–88 BC), rebellion of Rome's Italian allies (*socii*) to secure equal status with Roman citizens. It was caused by the murder of Livius Drusus the younger. Most of central and southern Italy rebelled and established a separate state, Italia, with a capital at Corfinium. The campaigns of 90 were disastrous for Rome, but in 89 political concessions drew the teeth of the rebellion, Pompeius Strabo captured Asculum, and by 88 only the Lucanians and Samnites were still under arms. They were defeated by Sulla, whose capture of Nola ended the war. Roman citizenship was then extended to the inhabitants of all Italy south of the Po river.

SOCIALISM, as a coherent doctrine and as a basis for political action, is the product of industrialism as it first arose in Britain, Germany, and France, and later spread to the US and Russia. Socialism has had three main phases. In the first and most virulent it represented the bitter reaction of rural individuals, used to a paternalistic society, against a newer, harsher, and disciplined type of employment in factories. Complaints were made of a cruel, selfish system which set men against men instead of allowing them to live in brotherhood, and they blamed their hunger not on a bad harvest—an 'act of God'—but on rich employers paying them off; the result being the inexplicable paradox of starvation existing while the means of production lay idle. In this first phase most socialists simply wanted to overthrow the system, their socialism sometimes being combined with demands for democratic rights, sometimes being mixed with nationalist sentiments, and sometimes emerging in the aftermath of a war. During this period socialism assumed several different forms and drew on a wide variety of ideologies. There were traces of Christianity in its doctrine of love and mutual help. The English Utilitarian philosophers, with their emphasis on the greatest happiness of the greatest number, also had an influence, as did Rousseau's extreme democracy, Tom Paine's *Rights of Man*, and Hegel's philosophy of history, *ie*, that newer and higher forms of society are bound to succeed each other.

The socialist doctrines that had been evolved by the mid-19th cent. were of two main kinds and concentrated on two methods of achieving their objectives. One was a political doctrine that accepted the state and, sometimes, industrialism, but protested against the injustice of the existing organization of both. The first mass movement in Britain that subscribed to these views was Chartism (1838–48), its rather diffuse democratic doctrines being systematized and given a German philosophical backing by Marx and Engels in and after 1848. The other doctrine tended to ignore the state and to argue that no regulating machinery was necessary, that working men were capable of taking over and running industry in the interests of the people, the means of achieving this kind of socialism usually being mass membership of a trade union and a general strike. This doctrine, originated in Britain by Robert Owen, was developed on the continent by Proudhon and St Simon. This first phase of socialism ended in Britain after 1848 and in France and Germany after 1871. Echoes of it were heard elsewhere as industrialism moved east and west across Europe and America; its one success was when Lenin and his Bolshevik Party took advantage of the collapse of the state machine in Russia in 1917.

The second phase came as the working classes began to forget their experiences before the Industrial Revolution and became used to an industrial society. Then socialist movements began to concentrate on improving the workers' conditions within the system, as well as retaining the distant objective of taking over the state. In this period, trade unionism began to be closely allied with the emergent political parties of the left, the German Social Democratic Party rising rapidly after 1880, and French socialists likewise working their way to prominence through the National Assembly; in Britain the Labour Party was founded in 1900.

The problem that faced these parties and trade unions was how far they were prepared to co-operate with non-socialists in running a capitalist state system. In Russia there was a split on this issue between the Mensheviks and the Bolsheviks, both of which parties were illegal up to the First World War. In the US the total socialist vote reached a maximum of 1 million in 1912, but it was in Germany, in the 'Revisionist Controversy', that the issue was chiefly discussed. The problem was then obscured by the First World War, by the achievement of socialism of a non-democratic type (communism) in Russia, and by the struggle against fascism which occurred during the 1930s and early 1940s.

The third phase of socialism appeared after 1945. By this time the system adopted in Russia had spread throughout Eastern Europe in the wake of the victorious Red Army and active communist parties existed in China, Indonesia, and other parts of Asia and in South America. The communist or soviet form of socialism had no time for democracy (of which there was no tradition in Russia) and believed that the working class should control all aspects of society and run all industry through its party leaders. Though this system appeared to have adjusted itself to Russian needs and was adapted to an agrarian society in China by Mao Tse-tung (who had conquered all the Chinese mainland by 1948), it came to have less and less attraction for Western nations. There were revolts against the system in Hungary in 1956 and in Czechoslovakia in 1968, both being repressed by Russian invasions. Elsewhere in Europe, socialist parties'

acceptance of democratic principles has become the normal practice.

In Scandinavia, socialist parties have held power for long periods—in Sweden since 1932. In Britain the Labour Party had two short periods of office (1924, 1929–31) and two longer periods (1945–51, 1964–70). The overthrow of the capitalist system, which objective was abandoned by all these socialist parties in their formative years, has not been forgotten so much as bypassed. Increasingly it has been accepted that capitalism has developed into a managerial system where ownership of the large combines is not important, though the problem of controlling these centres of power, whether owned by capitalists or by the state, is still acute. Modern Western socialism adheres to the old doctrines that society ought to be organized in the general interest, that the apparatus of the state should be used to promote equal treatment for all, and that brotherhood rather than mutal exploitation should be the aim of government. These objectives are to be achieved by an elaborate welfare system; an egalitarian pattern of education; control of the major power centres; and a reasonable rate of economic growth which will help to cover the cost of achieving these aims. Though these Western socialist parties have many achievements to their credit, they can no longer claim that the working classes give them unswerving support and they have accepted that they must be prepared to win or lose power according to their record as governing parties.

Sir Alexander Grey, *The Socialist Tradition* (London, 1944). N. McKenzie, *Socialism: a short history* (London, 1949).

JMac

SOCIALISM IN ONE COUNTRY in Russia, slogan which lay at the heart of the dispute between Stalin and Trotsky in the 1920s. The Bolshevik Revolution (1917) was carried out with the expectation that revolution would follow very quickly in the rest of Europe, particularly in Germany. When this expectation was not realized Lenin reached the conclusion that a socialist society could be constructed in Russia, in spite of its economic backwardness and its encirclement by capitalist powers. In the struggle for power following Lenin's illness (1922–3) and death (Jan. 1924) Stalin held to the doctrine of *Socialism in one country* while Trotsky, together with Kamenev and Zinoviev, attacked Stalin, arguing that the successful accomplishment of the socialist revolution in Russia was dependent on the overthrow of capitalism, by revolution, outside Russia.

The ideological dispute was one element of the struggle between Trotsky and Stalin in which the attacks on Stalin's accumulation of power were as important as the doctrinal polemic. The Trotskyists were decisively defeated at the 14th Party Congress (Dec. 1925) and again at the 15th Congress (Dec. 1927) before which Trotsky and Zinoviev were expelled from the party.

SOCIALIST LABOR PARTY in the US, originated (1877) from the New York Workingmen's party (1874). In the 1890s Daniel De Leon emerged as the party's leader, but his revolutionary brand of socialism drove many of the less militant members to join Eugene Debs's Socialist Party of America in 1901.

SOCIALIST LEAGUE (1884) in Britain, splinter group which broke away from the Social Democratic Federation (SDF), William Morris being its leading light. Its ideology was revolutionary and contemptuous of reform through parliament. Its membership came to include an increasing number of anarchists. It was a small movement and after a few years it began to disintegrate. Morris himself resigned from it in 1890.

SOCIALIST PARTIES in India. Social democratic political organization in India began with the formation of the Congress Socialist Party in 1934, which remained a splinter group within Congress until after independence (1947). It had some influence on Congress social and economic policy, *eg*, in the agrarian programme adopted at Faizpur (1936), and the election manifesto for the 1937 elections. Although they refused to take portfolios in the Congress ministries, several important socialists sat in the Legislative Assemblies with the Congress. The communists used the CSP branches as convenient points of entry for their strategy of using a 'united front from below' to infiltrate Congress in the 1930s, but the war precipitated a showdown and the communists were expelled from the CSP. The Quit India movement (1942) gave the socialists important opportunities for organization and action and they were active both in the revolt in August and later in guerrilla campaigns led by Jayaprakash Narayan.

Relations within the Congress were always difficult for the socialists and in 1948 they broke away and established the Socialist Party as an alternative to that of the Congress. The party attracted less support than had been hoped for, and was unable to match the Congress in terms of organization or resources. Signs that there were socialist stirrings within Congress itself came with the formation of the Congress Democratic Front (1950) by J. B. Kripalani, and this group's eventual breakaway and emergence as the Kisan Mazdoor Praja Party (Peasants, Workers, and People's Party) (1951). Although there was talk of a merger between the KMPP and the Socialist Party, this did not occur until after the first general elections (1952). The Socialist Party was the more successful of the two in the elections, but between them they won 21 Lok Sabha seats and some 200 state assembly seats, and when after the elections they merged and became the Praja Socialist Party they formed the third largest all-India party after Congress and the communists.

The subsequent history of the socialist parties is one of constant splits and mergers and of defections by leaders. The first leader to resign was Jaya Prakash Narayan, who left socialism in 1952 to devote himself to Vinoba Bhave's *sarvodaya* movement. He was followed by J. B. Kripalani (1959), who became a freelance Gandhian socialist, and Asoka Mehta (1964), who moved into the Congress and to a place on the Planning Commission, taking a good many of his followers with him. A more important breakaway, because it led to the foundation of the present two-socialist-party system, occurred in 1956, when Ram Manohar Lohia, the leader of a sizeable group, formed a socialist party that aimed to maintain that 'equidistance' between Congress and communists which Lohia believed was the proper position for such a party. Despite this breakaway, the PSP maintained its position in the 1957 elections at both the national and the state level, but when in 1962 the 'Lohia Socialists' entered the elections they began to undermine the PSP's position. The merger of the PSP and the Lohia Socialists (1964) into the Samyukta Socialist Party (United Socialist Party), was short-lived and in the following year a new PSP emerged. By the late 1960s the SSP, led by Lohia, was the more energetic and more successful party, exploiting populist themes such as Hindi chauvinism in such a way that after the 1967 elections it had become a major force in several north Indian states. The PSP, maintaining a more orthodox social democratic line, began to lose votes and seats, and though it maintained some strength in particular states, it looked as though it could no longer merit serious consideration as an all-India party.

W. H. Morris Jones, *The Government and Politics of India* (London, 1964).
M. Weiner, *Party Politics in India* (Princeton, 1957).   PDR

SOCIALIST PARTY in France (Section Française de L'Internationale Ouvrière; SFIO). It refers first to the United Socialist Party formed in 1905, then to the 'social democrat' party after the creation of the Communist Party in 1920. The SFIO was at the peak of its influence at the time of the Popular Front (1936) and immediately after the Second World War.

The SFIO was formed by a union of the orthodox Marxist wing of French socialism, led by Guesde, with the 'reformists', led by Jaurès. Jaurès quickly became the dominating personality of the party, and its political strength increased until in 1914 it had over 100 seats in parliament. The SFIO opposed the march to war, but when war came its leaders, including Guesde, joined the 'Sacred Union' coalition government. The strains of war, and the Russian Revolution, led to growing pacifist feeling within the party, and it left the coalition in 1917. The old division between reformists and revolutionaries also reappeared, and at the Congress of Tours (1920) the majority voted to join the Third International, and became the Communist Party.

The new SFIO was, at first, weak, but under the leadership of Blum it soon built up its strength. It remained faithful to its old principles by refusing to take office in 'bourgeois' governments, though it joined with the Radicals in electoral alliances, *eg*, the Cartel des Gauches of 1924. The creation of the Popular Front alliance with Radicals and Communists gave the SFIO a chance to hold power on its own terms. The Socialists were the dominant partners in Blum's Popular Front government (1936–7), and their ideas were reflected in its social reforms.   RDA

SOCIALIST PARTY in Indonesia (PSI), established in 1948 as the result of a split in the Socialist Party between the followers of Amir Sjarifuddin and Sutan Sjahrir. The faction led by Sjahrir entered the Hatta cabinet of 1948 and participated in the first post-revolutionary governments. Its principal support came from the Western-educated Djakarta elite, whose high social position and occupation of key administrative posts gave it an important role, in spite of its small numbers. The PSI did not attempt to attract mass support, but relied on popular recognition of its talents for its electoral appeal, a miscalculation proved by its poor showing in the elections of 1955. In the politics of the 1950s the PSI aligned itself with the Masjumi party against the Nationalists and Communists; internationally, it adopted a pro-Western position. In 1960 it was banned for refusing to accede to 'Guided Democracy'.

SOCIALIST PARTY in Italy (Partito Socialista Italiano; PSI), founded in 1895, was successful in parliamentary elections, but in 1912 its membership split into 'maximalists', who wanted a revolution, and 'reformists' (notably Bissolati), who were prepared to work with non-socialist organizations. The PSI's opposition to Italy's involvement in the First World War provoked Mussolini to defect to right-wing radicalism. After the war, 'maximalist' leaders expected a communist revolution, but failed to exploit political and economic crises. Their extremism frightened uncommitted Italians towards fascism, while equally unconstructive 'reformists' refused to strengthen the machinery of government by participating in coalitions. While fascist violence increased, the PSI fell apart. In Jan. 1921 a group of members who accepted Lenin's 'Twenty-One Conditions' formed the communist party (PCI). In Oct. 1922 Turati's 'reformists' were expelled from the PSI and formed the Unitary Socialist Party (PSU).

The PSI was banned in 1926. Many members joined the PSU in exile in 1930 and in 1934 made collaboration pacts with the suppressed PCI. PSI and PSU socialists combined in the Partito Socialista Italiano di Unita Proletaria (PSIUP) (1943–7) and participated in governments of national liberation and reconstruction. Saragat's social democrats opposed any links with the PCI, and formed their own party, named at first the PSLI, then the PSDI, and remained in alliance with the Christian Democrats. Nenni's remaining majority socialists, now in opposition, renamed themselves the PSI, and came to emphasize reformist, pro-NATO, and Common Market policies. After 1963 they joined Christian Democrat centre–left coalitions. This link was opposed by 26 left-wing deputies, who created the pro-Chinese PSIUP. The PSI and PSDI became united in 1966–9 as the PSU, but mutual recriminations followed electoral setbacks in 1968, and the PSI resumed its separate identity.   CFB

SOCIALIST PARTY in Spain (Partido Democrático Socialista Obrero), founded in Madrid in May 1879 by members of the labour aristocracy, mainly printers. Its leader was the president of the Printers' Association, Pablo Iglesias, who was to build up and organize the party virtually single-handed. From him, the party acquired its austere and moralistic tone. Influenced by the French socialist Guesde, Iglesias gave the party a severe attitude of intransigence to bourgeois parties, through the newspaper *El Socialista* of which he was editor.

In the beginning, development was slow and recruitment was confined to Madrid, Bilbao, and Asturias. However, the party's campaign against the Cuban War brought it an influx of support and after the defeat of 1898 its criticisms of the rottenness of the Restoration system also increased its popularity. In 1909 Iglesias dropped his intransigence and the party allied with the Republicans against government reaction, inefficiency, and conscription for the Moroccan war. This immediately secured Iglesias a seat in the Cortes. The Socialist party continued to grow and in 1917 it participated in the ill-fated reform movement which progressed to a revolutionary general strike and a savage military repression.

By this time Iglesias was failing with ill-health and new leaders were rising, such as the liberal intellectual Julian Besteiro and the equally liberal and cosmopolitan Indalecio Prieto, as well as the proletarian unionist Largo Caballero. This heralded divisions in the party. In 1920–1 the party discussed the question of joining the Third International. A deputation was sent to Russia and returned with mixed impressions. The party was divided, but for perhaps the last time in his life Iglesias intervened decisively in favour of remaining apart. The more left-wing socialists split off to form the Communist party.

In 1925 the socialists decided to collaborate with the Primo de Rivera dictatorship in order to increase membership, while the anarchists were outlawed. In 1930 the party agreed to support a Republican government. Three socialists —Prieto, Largo Caballero, and the intellectual Fernando de los Rios—participated in the first Republican government. But the party was dividing. A moderate reformist wing, under Prieto and Besteiro, was growing more convinced of the need to collaborate with the Republicans, while a left-wing group, under Largo Caballero and his young advisers Luis Araquistain and Alvarez del Vayo, felt that all-out revolution was the only way to fight fascism.

This division split the party until the end of the Civil War. In Oct. 1934 Largo Caballero encouraged the Workers' Alliance, which was the backbone of the Asturian rebellion. The experience of 1934 encouraged the left in their revolutionism, but provoked in the Prieto camp a desire for more moderate courses. In 1936 the Socialist Party participated in the Popular Front, but after the elections Largo Caballero's group refused to join the government and went over to revolutionary strikes, while Prieto called for collaboration to strengthen the republic.

Divisions were partly hidden by the outbreak of the Civil War. Both groups joined the Caballero government of Sept. 1936. Feeling that the needs of the revolution must be secondary to the needs of the war, the moderate socialists, especially Prieto and Negrin, tended to collaborate with the communists. This led in the cabinet crisis of May 1937 to the virtual eclipse of the left wing. The resignation of Prieto in April 1938 marked the similar fate of the moderates. After the war, the party functioned in exile under the leadership of Prieto.   PP

SOCIALIST PARTY OF AMERICA, formed in 1901 by an alliance between Eugene Debs' Social Democratic Party and dissidents of the Socialist Labour Party. Its maximum membership of 118,000 (1912) was greater than that of any other socialist party in the US and in 1920 Debs, who was four times socialist presidential candidate, polled over 900,000 votes. The SPA, which was essentially non-violent and anti-syndicalist, aimed at the introduction of a socialist commonwealth through parliamentary means. Anti-radical feeling during and after the First World War damaged its prospects, and despite the able leadership of Norman Thomas after 1926 it never again achieved its pre-war membership. By the 1950s it had virtually disappeared as a national party.

SOCIALIST REVOLUTIONARIES PARTY in Russia (SRs), founded in 1901 from populist groups. Its combat detachment relied on terrorism and political assassination to attain its ends. The party's programme included a democratic republic, a federative state, and the socialization of land, based on the *mir* and equalization of land holdings. The party encouraged peasant uprisings (1902–6) and was influential in the Peasants' Union (1905), the Soviet, and the first Dumas. The right wing, 'people's socialists', opposed terrorism which was discredited by the scandal of Azev, the double-agent (1908). The left wing, 'maximalists', aimed at the socialization of industry. The two groups were also divided during the First World War over the issue of defence versus internationalism. Under their leader, V. M. Chernov, the SRs were influential in both the Soviet and the Provisional governments (1917) and gained a majority in the Constituent Assembly (Jan. 1918). The left-wing SRs joined the Bolshevik government after Lenin's land decree (Nov. 1917) and remained as part of it until the peace of Brest-Litovsk (March 1918). Chernov joined the Samara government. SR hostility resulted in assassinations, the wounding of Lenin (1918), and attempted uprisings during the Civil War.

SOCIALIST UNION OF GERMAN STUDENTS (SDS, German abbreviation for Sozialistischer Deutscher Studentenbund). Originally the official student group of the post-war West German Democratic Party (SPD), the SDS became the most influential left-wing student organization of the 1960s.

Friction between the SDS and the SPD accumulated in the 1950s because of continuing disagreements over German rearmament, support of NATO, and contacts with East Germany, and the differences became unbridgeable after the 1959 Bad Godesberg party conference, where the revisionist right and centre in the SPD emerged victorious. In 1960 the party created a second student organization, the Sozialistische Hochschulbund (SHB), and in 1961 the SPD declared membership in the SDS incompatible with party membership and withdrew all subsidies to the group. The formation of the grand coalition government by the SPD and CDU/CSU in 1966 brought an intensification of SDS activity and increasingly frequent, often violent, clashes with university administrations, city governments, and police. Although a small minority group in the universities, because of its activism and its talented and vocal leadership, the SDS emerged as the vanguard of the so-called 'extra-parliamentary opposition'. The SDS hope was to mobilize sufficient popular support to create a viable political force which would, unlike the SPD, be true to socialism and could revolutionize society. Violence involving the SDS reached its apex in 1967 after the tragic killing of a Berlin student by police during a demonstration against the Shah of Iran. Concentrating attention on the need for university reform, on protest against the conservative Springer press empire, and against the projected insertion of an emergency clause in the constitution, the SDS unceasingly organized demonstrations and disruptions, acting hereby as a catalyst to left-wing student activity, and receiving at least the moral support of a widening student public. The attempted murder of the SDS leader Rudi Dutschke in 1968 resulted not only in another spasm of considerable violence but also in the adoption of increasingly radical and often conflicting views by the successors of the incapacitated Dutschke. The SDS quickly split into rival factions, splintered, and by the end of the 1960s had lost most of its former resonance.   ME

SOCIALIST UNITY PARTY of Germany (Sozialistische Einheitspartei Deutschlands; SED), ruling party in the former five-party system of East Germany, the German

Democratic Republic. The party was formed in 1946 by the fusion of the Communist Party (KPD), led by Wilhelm Pieck, and Otto Grotewohl's faction of the East German section of the Social Democratic Party. Power was initially concentrated in an 80-member *Vorstand* (executive) elected by party congresses in 1946, 1947, 1950, 1954, 1958, 1963, and 1967, and three party conferences in 1949, 1952, and 1956; it was replaced in 1963 by a central committee. The Politburo ranked above this executive after 1949. In 1968 the Politburo had 15 full members.

In 1963 its membership demonstrated continuity with the SED's pre-Second World War origins, containing three social democrats and 11 pre-1933 communists.

In 1948 the SED proclaimed that it would be a 'party of a new type'; meaning that after the early compromise between certain communists and social democrats, the SED was to become an orthodox communist party in all but name. There are three periods in its history: that of 'anti-fascist democracy' (1945–52); a period of 'building socialism' (1952–1958), and, from 1958, a period of socialist consolidation. By 1970 the party's membership, which is predominantly working class, was more than 1·8 million, *ie*, some 15 per cent of the adult population.

SOCIÉTÉ SAINT-JEAN BAPTISTE, LA, name of two French-Canadian societies, one in Montreal (founded in 1834), the other in Quebec (founded in 1843) in honour of St John the Baptist, the patron saint of Canada. They sponsored a programme of lectures, scholarships, and an annual book prize, and published a French-language almanac. They owned several substantial banks and insurance companies.

SOCIETY FOR ENFORCING THE KING'S PROCLAMATION AGAINST IMMORALITY in Britain, set up in 1787 by Hannah More and the Clapham Sect, to enforce King George III's proclamation of 1786, illustrating the growing importance of the Evangelical movement. The society's legalistic attitude to morality was to become typical of Victorian Britain.

SOCIETY FOR PROMOTING CHRISTIAN KNOWLEDGE, founded in London in 1698. It is the oldest Anglican missionary society, and exists to promote Christian knowledge both at home and abroad. Its early achievements included in the 18th cent. the establishment of many charity schools. By the 20th cent. the society had become a world-wide organization chiefly engaged in publishing and distributing Christian literature in many languages.

SOCIETY ISLANDS (in the Pacific), hub of Polynesia, are traditionally divided into two groups, the Leeward (Rai'atea), the religious centre, and the Windward (Tahiti), the political. The latter was ruled (*c.* 1750) by independent chiefs owing loose allegiance to a paramount ceremonial chief (*ari'i nui*). Two successive *ari'i nui*, Pomare I and II, sought to seize temporal authority, aided by possession of the insignia of the war god Oro, and by visiting Europeans, *eg*, Wallis (1767), Bougainville (1768), Cook (1769, 1774, 1777), Bligh (1788–9), Vancouver (1791), London Missionary Society missionaries, and various traders. In 1815, after tribal conflict, the diseased and dwindling population finally accepted literacy and Christianity with Pomare II as king, but on his death (1821) the kingdom lapsed into semi-anarchy and antinomianism. In 1843 Admiral Dupetit-Thouars took advantage of the exclusion of two Picpus priests by the pro-British Queen Pomare IV to establish a French protectorate, the Leeward Islands securing their independence in 1847. The influential LMS was gradually stifled, being eventually replaced (1862) by the Paris Evangelical Society, which preserved the Protestant predominance. Chinese cotton pickers, introduced by William Stewart in 1861, who increased from 1000 to 6655 by 1951, notably modified the original Tahitian stock. In 1880 Pomare V ceded the kingdom under pressure, the Leeward Islands also being annexed in 1887. A consultative

body established in 1884 was long settler-dominated. After the Gaullist coup in 1945 minority representation was granted to literate French-speaking Tahitians who have been increasingly vocal in the new Territorial Assembly of French Polynesia which was established in 1956–7.

SOCIETY OF JESUS, order of regular clerks of the Catholic Church, founded by St Ignatius Loyola in Paris (15 Aug. 1534) and officially authorized by Pope Paul III in 1540 with Ignatius as its first general (1541). The society initially undertook charitable work but later concentrated on theological study, spiritual direction, preaching, foreign missions, and education. Its firm organization and crusading zeal made the Jesuits the ideal instrument of the Counter-Reformation and they greatly influenced the post-Tridentine Church. By the 18th cent., however, the order had undergone a certain spiritual decay and the Jesuits' emphasis upon free will was attacked by the Jansenist wing of the Catholic Church. They were finally expelled from Portugal (1759), France (1764), and Spain (1767) before being officially suppressed by Pope Clement XIV on 21 July 1773. Before the end of the 18th cent. steps were taken to restore the order, which was finally effected by Pius VII on 4 Aug. 1814.

SOCIETY OF SEASONS in France, secret republican society, set up by Auguste Blanqui to oppose the July Monarchy by force, following the suppression of the more moderate society of the Rights of Man (1834). The failure of the society's armed rising of 1839, through lack of popular support, had the effect of discrediting secret societies in general, in favour of more open opposition to Louis Philippe.

SOCIETY OF THE FRIENDS OF THE FATHERLAND in Spain, economic organization founded in 1765 by a Basque nobleman, the Count of Penaflorida, under Charles III's patronage, to encourage the country's agriculture, commerce, industry, arts, and science. Branches of the society were founded in all the major towns and flourished until the French invasion of 1794. The society had an important influence on the economic recovery of Spain in the second half of the 18th cent.

SOCIETY OF THE RIGHTS OF MAN in France, moderate republican society founded in 1830 in opposition to the July Monarchy. It grew rapidly after staging a rising in sympathy with the silk workers' strike of 1834. Both the rising and the strike were forcibly suppressed by the government, which was provoked into declaring collective bargaining illegal.

SOCIETY OF WEST INDIAN MERCHANTS in Britain, organization representing the interests of British West Indian merchants, which became particularly effective when it joined with the Society of West Indian Planters and Merchants in London (after 1783) to form the West Indian Lobby in parliament. It proved one of the most effective parliamentary lobbies in Britain, and was in the vanguard of those seeking to maintain both the slave trade and slavery itself.

SOCINIANISM, pacifist and anti-trinitarian teachings of Lelio Sozzino (1525–65) and his nephew Fausto Sozzini (1539–1604), natives of Siena and religious radicals who settled in Poland, the former in 1564, the latter in 1579. Here they exercised considerable influence among the unitarian Anabaptists who became known as Socinians, and were centred on the city of Rakow.

SOCOTRA (3625 sq. kms) island off Cape Guardafui with a population of 6000 Arabs. It was formerly a part of the sultanate of Mahri, and after 1968 was part of the Peoples' Republic of South Yemen.

SOCRATES (469–399 BC), Athenian philosopher, known only from the works of others, *eg*, Plato and Xenophon, whose career marked the transition from physical speculation to moral philosophy and scientific argument with accurate terminological definition. Convinced of his own wisdom in recognizing his total ignorance, he used 'Socratic irony' to expose false beliefs and assumptions of others before making positive constructions from first principles. In a troubled age he was to philosophers a serious figure, a source of entertainment to the young, of ridicule to comedians, and of subversion to the establishment, which caused his trial and capital sentence for introducing strange gods and corrupting youth.

SOE, THAKIN (*fl.* 20th cent.), Burmese communist, a member of the Thakin party, who was interned (1940) for anti-war activities. In 1946 he formed the 'Red Flag', a more extreme communist party, which rebelled against the Anti-Fascist People's Freedom League (AFPFL) and the government.

SOFALA, from a Semitic root meaning 'low'. It was the name of a small Arab settlement about 30 kms south of Beira, through which, from the 9th cent. onwards, gold that was mined or washed from rivers in the highlands of Karanga and Butua (now Rhodesia), was exported. The Portuguese built a fort and established a trading centre there, which was reasonably prosperous in the first quarter of the 16th cent., but subsequently declined with the development of Mozambique as the southern Portuguese headquarters.

SOFIA COUP (1923), in Bulgaria, overthrew the peasant-orientated regime of Stambuliski. The coup was planned by the opposition, which despaired of ousting Stambuliski by constitutional means after he had won a resounding victory in the elections of April 1923. The leading force behind the plot, in which the army and others collaborated, was IMRD. The coup was planned by Volkov and Velcev, of the Officers' League, and Z. Tsankov and Ivan Mihailov, of IMRO. The conspirators used troops of the Sofia garrison to force their way into the palace. King Boris, of whose complicity in the coup nothing is known for certain, recognized the rebels as the new government. At once IMRO bands were unleashed against Stambuliski's supporters and many were brutally murdered. Stambuliski himself was captured, tortured, forced to dig his own grave, and then killed. The Communist Party was much criticized for its passivity during the coup. Tsankov became prime minister of the new government, which reversed Stambuliski's policies on social reform and reconciliation with Yugoslavia over the question of Macedonia which had inspired the coup.

SOGA, family in early Japanese history. It was closely concerned with the introduction of Chinese and Korean practices and the strengthening of the Yamato dynasty's authority, but eventually it attempted to usurp the throne and was overthrown. Soga interest in new governmental techniques resulted from the family's hereditary responsibility for the imperial treasury and its contacts with Chinese scribes. It was the first to support Buddhism, then associated with continental progress, and when, after some setbacks, the new religion was officially adopted at court, following Soga-no-Umako's military victory over the Mononobe and Nakatomi families (587), Soga influence became supreme. Umako's successors, Emishi and Iruka, abused their position, however, by assuming imperial prerogatives, and a *coup d'état* was staged by their rivals which destroyed Soga power (645).

SOGDIA, ancient country between the Oxus and Jaxartes rivers, which was conquered successively by Iranians, Greeks, and Arabs (7th cent.). The Sogdians, who spoke an Iranian language, lived on oases, *eg*, Bukhara and Samarkand. Their society was well organized and they had extensive irrigation schemes. They were merchants, trading with areas as distant as China and Asia Minor.

SOIL CONSERVATION AND DOMESTIC ALLOTMENT ACT (1936) in the US, legislation which formed part of the New Deal agricultural policy. Partly designed to replace the Agricultural Adjustment Act (1933) which had been declared unconstitutional by the Supreme Court, the act attempted to re-establish farm income by making payments to farmers who reduced their acreage of soil-depleting crops and practised conservation techniques.

SOISSONS, CONGRESS OF (1544), scene of the conference between the Emperor Charles V and Francis I following the former's successful campaign in northern France (July–Sept. 1544) and of the drawing up of the terms of peace embodied in the two treaties of Crespy.

SOISSONS, CONGRESS OF (1728–29), protracted peace conference between the great powers, Britain, Spain, the Habsburg empire, and France, negotiated by the chief minister of the latter country, Cardinal Fleury, following the Anglo-Spanish naval war of 1727 which threatened to develop into a major European conflict. The congress led to the signing of the treaty of Seville (Nov. 1729).

SŌKA GAKKAI in Japan (lit. 'Value-creating Study Association'), Japanese Buddhist sect. It has enjoyed a more sensational success than any of Japan's other new religions, its adherents numbering at least 13,500,000 in 1967. Founded in 1931, its appeal lies in the sense of belonging which its intense methods of proselytism and discipline give, especially to the urban masses. Though based in part on the teaching of Nichiren, its present leader, Ikeda Daisaku, has adapted Sōka Gakkai ideas to contemporary realities by stressing the value of material possessions, and he has greatly increased his organization's political significance by establishing a political party, the Kōmeitō. The latter won 47 seats in the 1969 general election. Although its stated policies were moderate, it was considered (1970) by some as a potential threat to Japanese democracy.

SOKOTO, town in north-eastern Nigeria, founded by Muhammad Bello (1819). It was the seat of the Sokoto caliphs (1817–1903).

SOLANDER, DANIEL (1733–82), Swedish naturalist, who went to London on the advice of Linnaeus and eventually attracted the attention of Sir Joseph Banks. He sailed as a scientist in *Endeavour* and subsequently became Banks's secretary and librarian, assisting him in collecting, and in cataloguing and publishing his findings.

SOLE BAY, BATTLE OF (May 1672), naval victory of the Dutch under De Ruyter over the Anglo-French fleet under the Duke of York and the Comte d'Estrees which was surprised at anchor in Sole or Southwold Bay. Technically indecisive, the allied fleet none the less suffered heavily from the Dutch fireships and was unable to take the offensive for over a month.

SOLEMN ENGAGEMENT OF THE ARMY (1647), in England, first formal intervention of the army into politics in the Civil War. The army intervened on the plea that it was more representative of the nation than the Presbyterian junto ruling the Long Parliament. It was the beginning of the army's attempt to represent itself as having a mission, even a mandate. On 5 June officers and men subscribed not to disband until their claims for arrears had been met and the constitution of Church and state had been settled to their liking.

SOLFERINO, BATTLE OF (1859), between France and Austria in northern Italy, was technically a French victory, but the huge losses suffered by both sides contributed to their willingness to agree to an armistice. Piedmontese hopes of further gains from Austria were thus disappointed.

SOLIDARITÉ FRANÇAISE, small French fascist party of the 1930s. It was led by Jean Renaud, but the real sponsor was the millionaire industrialist François Coty. The movement stood for little except the use of violence, and failed to attract a large membership.

SOLIS, JUAN DIAZ DE (c. 1470–1516), Portuguese sailor who sailed with Vicente Yanex Pinzon, the discoverer of Brazil (1497–8, 1508–9), was appointed pilot-major of Spain on Vespucci's death (1512) and finally set out to find a passage to the East Indies via America which resulted in the discovery of the Rio de la Plata (1515–16). He was killed by Guarani Indians when he landed near the mouth of Panama.

SOLOMON (reg. c. 961–922 BC), Israelite King, who succeeded his father, David. In general, he preserved David's empire. Its core was Palestine and stretched from Dan to Beersheba; the rest comprised uncertain areas of authority in southern Syria, and the desert east of the Jordan and southwards towards Al-Arish and Aqaba, although his power in Edom to the south-east and in southern Syria weakened and the coastal cities of Phoenicia and Philistia remained independent. Solomon's reign was a time of great prosperity in Palestine owing to his control of wealthy trade routes and exploitation of important copper mines. He built the great temple in Jerusalem. After his death the kingdom was divided into Israel and Judah.

SOLOMON ISLANDS (in the Pacific), group of high malarious islands inhabited by Papuo-Melanesian and Polynesian peoples, traditionally divided into small, ancestrally dominated clans. Discovered by Mendana in 1568, the islands were 'lost' for 200 years until identified by Buâche (1781) and D'Entrecasteaux (1793). Early Marist fathers (1846–7) were expelled, contact thereafter being maintained by whalers, traders, labour recruiters, and the Melanesian Mission and, after 1870, British naval vessels. In 1877 the group came under the partial jurisdiction of the Western Pacific High Commission, finally passing to Britain by the Berlin agreement (1886) which led to a protectorate (1893) extended (1897, 1898) to take in Rennell and Bellona, and the Santa Cruz group, with C. M. Woodford as first resident (1896). Woodford's mild regime, partly financed by revenue from Burns, Philp, and Levers' Plantations gradually brought results, aided by a new local interest in missions which bore the burden of education and medical work. In 1936–7 the group was divided into eight administrative districts with an advisory council, a promising experiment suspended by war and Marching Rule. In 1960 the government established central institutions in Honiara, enlarged and liberalized in 1967 in preparation for responsible self-government and independence in the late 1970s.

SOLOMONIC RESTORATION (1270), establishment by the Emperor Yekuno Amlak of Ethiopia of a line of rulers claiming descent from Solomon and the Queen of Sheba.

SOLON, legendary Athenian law-giver, reformer, and poet; traditionally archon in 594 BC and founder of the Athenian democracy. Details of his reforms and quotations from his poems and laws first appear in 4th-cent. political speeches and treatises. He supposedly solved a situation of general indebtedness, bondage, and enslavement of the poor by the rich by abolishing debts, thus liberating the *hectemoroi* (sixth-parters), by redeeming slaves, and by forbidding the future security of debts on the person (*seisachtheia*). Androtion (c. 345) maintained, rather obscurely, that Solon reduced interest rates by increasing the size of coins. In his constitutional reforms he is said to have divided political privilege according to carefully defined income groups—*pentacosio-medimni* (over 500 measures), *hippeis* (over 300), *zeugitae* (over 200), and *thetes* (under 200). *Pentacosiomedimni* and *hippeis* were eligible for the archonship, whereas *thetes*

could participate only in the *ecclesia* and the *heliaea*. He retained the Areopagus, but added a council (*boule*) of 400 and allowed appeal to the *heliaea* from decisions of the archons. Some features of the tradition, *eg*, his supposed reform in 594 of Athenian coinage (first introduced *c*. 520), are clearly later fabrications and it is possible that practically all our evidence, including even the poems attributed to him, represents the aspirations of various Athenian political groups of the late 5th–4th cents.

W. G. Forrest, *The Emergence of Greek Democracy* (London, 1966).   JDS

SOLVAY, ERNEST (1839–1922), Belgian chemist who was responsible for the successful development of the industrial process which bears his name. In this process, sodium carbonate is produced cheaply, by the interaction of brine, ammonia, and carbon dioxide.

SOLVYCHEGODSK in Russia, town situated near the confluence of the Dvina and Sukhona rivers, an important fur depot and centre for salt production in the 16th cent., when it was the capital of the large private commercial empire of the Stroganovs. It declined from the 18th cent. when St Petersburg superseded Archangel as the chief northern port of Russia.

SOLWAY MOSS, BATTLE OF (Dec. 1542), English victory by a band of 500 borderers led by Thomas Dacre and John Musgrave over a larger Scottish invading force in the marshes of Solway Moss. Although casualties were light, hundreds of Scots, including many nobles, surrendered and the news of the rout resulted in the death of James V of Scotland.

SOMALI PEOPLE and CULTURE. The Somali number about 3·5 millions and inhabit the Horn of Africa (Somali republic, Eastern Ethiopia, and Territoire Français des Afars et des Issas). They fall into three broad divisions: the Northern, the Hawiyya, and the Sab. The Northern Somali, more than half the total, are divided into three large clans, namely the Dir, the Isaq, and the Darod, and these into numerous tribes and smaller patrilineal groups (*rer*). They are pastoral nomads, grazing cattle, sheep, and goats over scant pastures on the central plains. The basis of their economy is the camel, both for its practical value and as the unit of wealth and prestige. Among them live three 'out-caste' groups, the Tomal (smiths), Yibir (sorcerers), and Midgan, who perform various menial tasks; these groups are descendants of pre-Somali inhabitants of the Horn.

The Hawiyya, who spearheaded the southern push of the Somali in the 14th cent., now (1970) inhabit the area of the Shibeli valley. In their territory lies Mogadishu, the capital of the republic formed in 1960, a city with a millennium of history. The Sab, composed of the Digil and Rahanweyn clans, are agriculturalists of the Benadir coastal area between the Shibeli and Juba rivers.

The Somali are Muslims of the Shafi'i school, but like most nomads are fiercely proud of their traditional institutions. Outside the towns it is Somali customary law, rather than the strict *shari'a* code, which is the dominant regulating force. Like the desert Arabs, they express themselves most typically in poetry, which is often set to music. The Somali language, spoken by all groups, but with wide dialectal differences, belongs to the Kushitic family of the western Red Sea and Horn, though it has absorbed much Arabic vocabulary. Until recently it was rarely written, owing to the lack of an agreed orthography, but now a modified form of Roman script is officially accepted.

During the colonial period three European powers divided most of Somali territory: the British, who established a protectorate over the northern region in 1887, but ceded the Hawd to Ethiopia in 1894; the French, who took an enclave centred on Djibuti a year later; and the Italians, who took the southern and coastal region in 1894. Under the drive of several local nationalist parties, Somali sovereignty was restored in 1960 to British Somaliland, which then became fused with ex-Italian Somalia when the latter, a week later, emerged from the UN Trusteeship status awarded to it at the end of the Second World War.

I. M. Lewis, *Peoples of the Horn of Africa* (London, 1955).
I. M. Lewis, *A Pastoral Democracy* (London, 1961). RP

SOMALI, REPUBLIC OF (638,000 sq. kms), in the Horn of Africa, formerly British and Italian Somaliland. It gained independence in 1960. A National Assembly of 123 members is elected by adult suffrage every five years, and a president every six years. Somali people form almost the entire population (1970) of 2,500,000.

SOMASCHI, order of clerks regular, founded in 1532 by the Venetian ex-soldier Girolamo Miani (1481–1537), dedicated to charitable works, especially the care of orphans, and centred on the little town of Somascha, near Bergamo, where Miani died of the plague. The society was then maintained by Miani's chief follower, Angelo Marco Gambara, first received papal confirmation in 1540, and though temporarily united with the Theatines (1547–55) reverted to an independent society before being elevated to the status of a full religious order (1568). Although small in membership, it enjoyed a considerable reputation in the later 17th cent. for educational work.

SOMBART, WERNER (1863–1941), German economist, who, with Arthur Spiethoff and Max Weber, was one of the last exponents of the German historical school of economics. His *Der moderne Kapitalismus* (1902) traces the origins and development of capitalism.

SOMERS, JOHN SOMERS, Baron (1st creation) (1651–1716), British lawyer and Whig politician who first became well known as defending counsel in the trial of the seven bishops (1688). He joined the opposition to James II, played a leading part in drafting the Declaration of Right, and was rewarded by William III with the posts of solicitor-general (1689), attorney-general (1692), lord keeper (1693), and finally lord chancellor (1697).

Somers was one of the few Englishmen to gain the trust and favour of William III, whom he persuaded to remain in the country after the Commons had disbanded the Dutch guards (1698). However, a Tory-dominated House of Commons demanded Somers's impeachment (1701) for affixing the Great Seal to a blank commission (1698) authorizing unnamed negotiators to sign a Partition treaty, and Somers was only saved by his favour in the House of Lords. As a member of the Whig Junto, he contributed to the growth of the Whig's party organization and did a great deal to ensure co-ordination among the junto's members, thus helping to provide a united leadership. Somers also brought an intellectual aura to the junto by his patronage of such men as Locke, Newton, and Addison.

Largely because of his involvement in party politics, Queen Anne disapproved of Somers and he remained in the political wilderness until 1708. However, he was among those who drafted the Regency Act (1706) and the Act of Union (1707). After the Whigs' election triumph in 1708, Anne was forced to accept him in her ministry as lord president of the council. He played a leading part in foreign affairs, presenting the famous *No Peace Without Spain* motion to the House of Lords (1707) and supporting the War of the Spanish Succession until the Whig ministry collapsed (1710). He then resigned with his colleagues, despite the efforts of Harley and Queen Anne—who had revised her opinion of him—to retain his services.

Somers did not reappear at the privy council until shortly before the Queen's death, when he advocated the Hanoverian Succession. However, as he had insured himself by cor

respondence with St Germain, and as George I had no intention of allowing the junto to dominate, Somers was not named as one of the lord justices to rule until the king's arrival, nor was he appointed to high office in the first ministry of George I. AW

SOMERS, SIR GEORGE (1554–1610), English sailor and explorer, who took part in several buccaneering voyages in search of Spanish treasure ships (1595–1603). He was instrumental in founding the South Virginian Co. (1606) and after James I granted a charter to the company (1609), Somers was named admiral of the association. As commander of a fleet taking settlers to VA (1609), his ship was wrecked in what later became known as the Bermuda Islands, which Somers claimed for England. He remained there for ten months, then sailed to VA. Intending to return to England, he made another voyage to Bermuda, where he died.

SOMERSET, EDMUND BEAUFORT, 2nd Duke of (1st creation) (1406–55), a grandson of John of Gaunt, Duke of Lancaster (in a junior, originally illegitimate line). On succeeding to the family dukedom in 1444, he inherited the position of one of the leading councillors of King Henry VI from his uncle, Cardinal Henry Beaufort (d. 1447). With his associates in the council, especially the Duke of Suffolk, he was the target for attack by a group of magnates out of power, led by the heir to the Crown, Richard, Duke of York. Suffolk was impeached and murdered in 1450. In the parliament of 1451 Somerset was blamed by York for the loss of Normandy (1449–50). When Henry VI lapsed into insanity in 1453 Somerset was imprisoned in the Tower of London by York's faction. He was released on the king's recovery in 1454 and was thereafter the leader of the royalists. It seemed to York and his impetuous ally, Warwick, that only violence could restore them to power. They attacked the king at St Albans in 1455 and after a quick victory captured and murdered Somerset. This was the start of the Wars of the Roses.

SOMERSET, EDMUND BEAUFORT, titular Duke of (*c.* 1439–71), the son of King Henry VI's chief adviser, who had been murdered by the Yorkists after the battle of St Albans (1455). Edmund's brother was executed in 1464 by the Yorkist king, Edward IV. Edmund fled abroad and became the leader of the Lancastrian exiles. After the restoration of Henry VI in 1470–1, he was in charge of bringing reinforcements from France and led the last Lancastrian army that resisted Edward IV at Tewksbury and was annihilated (6 May 1471), Edmund himself being killed. In 1485 Henry Tudor, the son of Edmund's sister, Margaret, recovered the Crown for the Lancastrians as King Henry VII. Beaufort was regarded as a duke by Lancastrians, although the family's titles and estates had been forfeited under attainder by the Yorkists in 1465.

SOMERSET, EDWARD SEYMOUR, 5th Duke of (1st of 3rd creation) (1506–52), English soldier and politician who was Lord Protector of the Realm under his nephew, Edward VI (1547–9). Eldest son of Sir John Seymour and brother of Jane, third wife of King Henry VIII, he first rose in the king's favour through his relationship to the queen, serving on diplomatic missions and as commander of the successful Scottish campaign of 1544. With Cranmer he promoted Henry's marriage to the mildly Protestant Katherine Parr (1543) and on the king's death brought his young nephew to London to be crowned and was created Protector by the late king's executors and Duke of Somerset by the new council (Jan. 1547). His first problem was to deal effectively with the old alliance between France and Scotland, and he personally led the English forces, 17,000 strong, to the resounding victory at Pinkie (Sept. 1547). His subsequent moderation towards the Scots, voiced in *An Epistle or Exhortation* (1548), was, however, interpreted as weakness. The young queen, Mary, was shipped to France to marry the dauphin Francis in defiance of the treaty of Greenwich

(1548) and Henry II besieged Boulogne and reinforced the French garrisons in Scotland.

Meanwhile Somerset proceeded cautiously with the promotion of Protestantism. He ended the persecution of Protestants under the Six Articles, ordered a new ecclesiastical visitation, dismissed Wriothesley, the leading Catholic layman in the council, and imprisoned Bps Bonner and Gardiner. The first parliament of the protectorate repealed much of the repressive legislation of Henry's reign, including the Six Articles. Another Chantries Act (1548) confiscated endowments providing for prayers for the dead, communion of both kinds, and the appointment of bishops by royal letters patent introduced. Finally the Act of Uniformity (1549) enforced the use of Cranmer's book of common prayer on Whit Sunday 1549. The last act gave rise to a serious revolt in Cornwall, followed by another outburst of popular discontent in Norfolk, known as Ket's rebellion (1549). Somerset had been aware of social unrest caused by depopulation and inflation. Influenced by the ideas of the Commonwealth party he had issued a proclamation against enclosures and instituted an enquiry into the breach of existing laws. His good intentions did not reach the disillusioned masses and were scorned by the propertied classes. His family's name had been tarnished by the execution for treason of his brother, Thomas (March 1549), and he submitted to the aristocratic opposition, being committed to the Tower (14 Oct. 1549). However, his political rival, Warwick, was not yet strong enough to dispose of him, so Somerset was released early in 1550 and reinstated by the council. The uneasy truce lasted until Warwick, created Duke of Northumberland in Oct. 1551, had established his faction in royal favour. Somerset was again arrested, tried on trumped-up charges (Dec. 1551), and executed (22 Jan. 1552).

W. K. Jordan, *Edward VI: the young king* (London, 1969).
W. K. Jordan (ed.), *Chronicles and Political Papers of King Edward VI* (Cornell, 1966).   MKS

SOMERSET, CHARLES SEYMOUR, 10th Duke of (5th of 3rd creation (1662–1748), English Whig politician who (1682) married Elizabeth, daughter of the Earl of Northumberland, who brought his immense estates. As a supporter of the Prince of Orange in 1688, and Master of the Horse in 1702, he was in favour under Queen Anne and in 1711 his wife replaced the Duchess of Marlborough as Mistress of the Robes. In the crisis on Anne's death (1714), he acted with Argyll, Shrewsbury, and other Whigs who, by insisting on their right to be present in the privy council, secured the Hanoverian succession.

SOMERSET, ROBERT CARR, 6th Earl of (1st of 3rd creation) (*c.* 1585–1645), Scottish politician and favourite of King James VI and I, who was introduced at court (1607) and was soon lavished with honours and favours. As Viscount Rochester (1611), he was the first Scot to sit in the House of Lords. His influence over James was paramount, though he never had complete control over royal patronage or decided the major issues of royal policy. He was largely responsible for bringing James's court into disrepute. In 1615 he was implicated in the murder of his friend, Sir Thomas Overbury, which had occurred two years earlier. He was condemned to death for the murder, but was pardoned by the king and thereafter lived in strict retirement.

SOMERSETT JUDGMENT (1772) in England, adjudication by Lord Mansfield (June 1772) which established that the state of slavery was not known in English law. The Court of Session in Scotland delivered a similar judgment in the case of *Knight v. Wedderburn* (Jan. 1778).

SOMME, BATTLE OF THE (1 July–18 Nov. 1916), fought in the First World War and one of the bloodiest battles in history. After many months' preparation and six days' bombardment a series of frontal attacks in close formation on strong German positions lasted for nearly five months and involved 55 British and 20 French divisions. Joffre expected a battle of attrition, but Haig hoped for a break-through and kept five cavalry divisions in reserve to exploit it. The Germans say that on 15 Sept. their front was in fact broken, but the British never noticed. The Allies lost 600,000–800,000 men, the British 400,000–500,000; the Germans 540,000–650,000.

Tanks were used for the first time. They achieved little, owing to small numbers, technical difficulties, bad tactics, and unsuitable terrain, but Haig was convinced of their value and ordered them in large numbers.

SOMNATH, ancient port in Saurashtra, India, famous for the ancient, probably Jaina, temple. It was destroyed by Mahmud of Ghazni (AD 1024) and subsequently rebuilt and destroyed several times. The present ruins give only a vague idea of its ancient splendour.

SOMOZA, ANASTASIO (1896–1956), Nicaraguan politician, president, and dictator of Nicaragua (1937–56). He was commander of the National Guard (1934) that killed the rebel, Augusto César Sandino. His election as president (1936) was virtually unopposed and established an authority, through his family, that still ruled in 1970. After 1947, there was a succession of puppet presidents, but Samoza dominated the national legislature and censored the press through the manipulation of a new constitution (1950). Various attempts to assassinate him failed; meanwhile an opposition group grew up around Pedro Joaquín Chamorro Cardenal, a member of an old conservative family. Under Somoza various social reforms were introduced, including a labour code, an income tax, social security, and a National Development Institute (INFONAC).

In 1956 Somoza was murdered and it was suggested after his death that his personal fortune amounted to over $100 million, accumulated from coffee, cattle, airlines, shipping, and other national concerns. It was arranged that his sons should take over the government, and one of them, Luis Somoza Debayle (1922–67), assumed the presidency, his younger brother, Anastasio Somoza Debayle (1925–), retaining control of the National Guard.

The dictator himself had several times interfered in the affairs of neighbouring states, especially those of Costa Rica, yet in the 1950s the economy he created in Nicaragua, with US co-operation, was the most flourishing in Central America.   VCP

SON NGOC THANH (1906–), Cambodian journalist and politician, who was partly a Viet-namese. In 1936 he founded a Cambodian-language newspaper which criticized the French protectorate. In 1942, after organizing an anti-French demonstration by Buddhist monks, he fled to Bangkok, and was then taken by the Japanese to Tokyo. In 1944 he returned to Phnom Penh and became foreign minister under King Norodom Sihanouk; soon afterwards he staged a coup and made himself prime minister. He became leader of the *Khmer Issarak* movement which aimed at Cambodia's independence. In 1945, he was arrested by the French and forced to live in France thereafter. In 1951, however, he returned to Cambodia and was welcomed as a hero. In 1952 he disappeared from Phnom Penh and joined a *Khmer Issarak* group near the Thai border, where he remained until late 1954. King Sihanouk prevented him from returning to Cambodian politics following the Geneva Agreements, and he again went into exile in Thailand.

SONDERBUND (1845), defensive pact formed by seven Swiss Catholic cantons—Lucerne, Uri, Schwyz, Underwalden, Zug, Fribourg, and Valais—against a reform of the 1815 federal pact and a reduction of cantonal sovereignty. Swiss radicals, who were demanding closer political and economic union, and more civil and political freedom for individuals, identified Catholic monks and the Jesuits in particular as their chief opponents. Dissolution of Aargan's monasteries on one hand, and Lucerne's transference of higher education to the Jesuits on the other, enflamed public opinion. The radical cantons' anti-Jesuit demonstrations, which culminated in an abortive invasion of Lucerne (March 1845), were the immediate cause of the Sonderbund's formation. It was declared unconstitutional by the Diet's Protestant majority, and civil war followed.

SONGHAY people, living on the banks of the Niger river from Jenne to Gaya and on the adjacent plains of the area south of Ansongo. Their language, for long unclassified, has recently been assigned to the Nilo-Saharan family as a separate branch. Songhay origins are obscure, but it is clear that the modern Songhay form an amalgam of many earlier groups, some traditionally fishermen, others hunters and farmers. Before the 15th cent. the Songhay were chiefly confined to the area south of Ansongo, with Gao as a northerly outpost for the trans-Saharan trade. Their history as a political unit goes back to the Za (or Dia) dynasty of uncertain antiquity (perhaps 8th cent.); Saharan nomads (Berber or Zaghawa) are said to have had a hand in establishing a petty state based on Kukiya. The 15th Za was converted to Islam early in the 11th cent., though the religion assumed little importance until the 16th.

In the 13th–14th cents Mali had intermittent control of the Niger Bend up to Gao, but a son of the 27th Za, held hostage in Mali, managed to escape and found a new dynasty, the Sunnis. During the rule of the penultimate Sunni, Ali (*reg.* 1464–92), Songhay expanded rapidly and absorbed areas of eastern and northern Mali, then in decline. The Askia dynasty (1493–1591) saw Songhay at the height of its political and economic power—a vast, though amorphous, state, with an economy based on riverain agriculture and control of the southern termini of the trans-Saharan trade. In 1591 a small Moroccan force defeated the army of the Askias and founded a fragile state based on Timbuctoo. The remnants of the Askia dynasty set up a small independent state in the nuclear Songhay area (Dendi) towards the borders of modern Nigeria. The whole area fell piecemeal to the French in the 1890s and is now (1970) divided between the republics of Niger and Mali.   JOH

SONINKE people of north-western Mali, related to the Manding. They played an important role in Western Sudanese history, principally as architects of the ancient Ghanaian empire.

SONNENFELS, JOSEPH EDLER VON (1732–1817), Austrian administrator, friend of Joseph II, and one of the chief exponents of cameralism.

SONOY, JONKHEER DIETRICH (1529–97), Dutch nobleman, Sea Beggar, and diplomat who was one of William of Orange's most loyal supporters in the Dutch revolt. He led the seizure of Enkhuizen (1572) and was appointed governor of the northern quarter of Holland by William (1572), showing a cruel indifference to the plight of Dutch Catholics. He was finally dismissed in 1588 for supporting Leicester as governor-general.

SONS OF LIBERTY in America, secret society formed to oppose the British Stamp Act (1765). Their activities resulted in the resignation of all stamp agents and the enforcement of a boycott on British imports. Royal officials were summoned to 'Liberty Trees' to give an account of their conduct to the people. The Sons of Liberty continued to harry Crown officials until the outbreak of the American Revolution.

SONTHONAX, LÉGER FELICITÉ (1763–1813), French politician of the Revolutionary era, who was appointed a commissioner to Santo Domingo by the French national assembly in 1792. He dominated the government of the colony and issued a proclamation freeing the slaves in Santo Domingo. Certain features of his edict were used later as the basis for the British Abolition of Slavery Act (1833).

SOONG CH'ING-LING (1890–), Chinese political figure, widow of Sun Yat-sen, and sister of Mme Chiang Kai-shek. She married Sun Yat-sen in 1914. After his death (1925) she devoted herself to trying to preserve what she believed to be the true spirit of his teaching. She quarrelled bitterly with Chiang Kai-shek, his successor and her brother-in-law. After 1949 she became a vice-chairman of the Chinese People's Republic.

SOONG MEI-LING (1901–) (Mme Chiang Kai-shek), Chinese political figure and younger sister of Soong Ch'ingling. She married Chiang when he was already established as Kuomintang chief (1927). Her charm of manner was of value to her husband in his negotiations, especially with the US.

SOONG, TSE-WEN (1891–), Chinese economist and government official, who was trained as an economist in the US. He held office intermittently under the Kuomintang (1927–45), but was never allowed enough authority for him to carry out genuine economic reforms.

SOPHIA, Dowager Electress of Hanover (1630–1714), youngest daughter of Elizabeth Stuart, the daughter of James I, and Frederick, the Elector Palatine. It was rumoured that she would marry King Charles II of England, but instead she married Ernest Augustus, first Elector of Hanover.
Sophia was named in the Act of Settlement (1701) as heiress of England after the death of the future Queen Anne. Though she had an inferior claim to numerous Catholic Stuarts, her Protestantism made her the nearest Stuart descendant eligible to assume the Crown. She died three months before Queen Anne, leaving her son, George Lewis, to succeed (1714) as King George I.

SOPHIA ALEKSEEVNA (1657–1704), third daughter of Tsar Alexis, who instigated a rising among the *streltsi* on the death of her brother Fedor II (1682) and assumed the regency of Russia for her half-brothers Ivan and Peter, being effective ruler from 1682–1689. In 1689 Peter forced her into a Moscow convent and became tsar, but in 1698 she was imprisoned on suspicion of inciting the great rebellion of the *streltsi* while Peter was abroad.

SOPHIA (ZOË) PALAIOLOGOS (*fl.* 15th cent.), niece of the last Byzantine emperor, Constantine XI Palaiologos, who in 1472, became the second wife of Ivan III of Muscovy. Their marriage was favoured by the pope, whose ward she was, as an attempt to revive the union between the Catholic and Orthodox Churches. Under her influence Russian court ceremonial developed many Byzantine features, the autocratic power of the ruler became intensified, and Ivan III assumed the title *Samoderzhets* (autocrat) of All Russia. These events exercised a decisive influence on the development of the Russian monarchy and the theoretical conception of Moscow as the 'Third Rome' and heir of Byzantium.

SOPHISTS, name originally given in ancient Greece to the independent teachers who appeared in the second half of the 5th cent. BC offering instruction for payment on a variety of subjects, especially rhetoric (*eg,* Gorgias, Protagoras). Generally rationalist in religion and ethics, they were often unpopular. Those who condemned Socrates regarded him as a Sophist.

SOPHOCLES (*c.* 496–406 BC), second of the three great Athenian tragedians and a political figure, being elected *strategos* twice and special commissioner (*proboulos*) in 412. Seven of his plays, surviving from some 120, show innovation in introducing a third actor to increase personal and dramatic interest at the expense of the chorus, and in the use of painted scenery and the abandonment of the trilogy. Sophocles, a master of dramatic tension, excelled in portraying the conflicting demands of duty and man's approach to ineluctable fate, while high-lighting a defect in character, as seen in Antigone's stubborn insistence on her brother Polynices' divine right of burial despite Creon's official decree (the *Antigone*), and in Oedipus' haughty approach to, and unwitting murder of, his father, Laius, and subsequent marriage to his mother, Jocasta (the *Oedipus Rex*).

SORANZO, GIOVANNI (d. 1328), Doge of Venice, whose reign saw the recovery of Venetian influence and prosperity. He was responsible for Venetian expansion on to the Italian mainland, made necessary by the need for a commercial outlet and control over food-producing areas. This marked the end of an era of predominantly maritime preoccupations and the beginning of Venice's deeper involvement in Italian politics.

SORBONNE, popular name for Paris University. The university grew out of the cathedral and other church schools of the 12th cent. Originally controlled by a representative of the bishop and regarded with disfavour by the townspeople, the schools developed into a largely self-governing academic community of masters and the students dependent on them, protected by pope and king, and which was the leading intellectual centre of western Christendom (*c.* 1260). The university was divided into a number of nations, representing the various areas from which students were drawn, which played a large role in organizing academic life. There were some colleges, including one founded to give lodging to 12 poor students by Robert de Sorbon, chaplain to St Louis (1257). Its numbers grew to 360 and gradually it took on a teaching function, particularly in theology, so that it was often identified with the Faculty of Theology. Finally the Sorbonne came to monopolize chairs in theology and the faculty held its meetings in the Sorbonne (1554), by which time it had lost its residential character. By then the university had lost much of its lustre due to the Great Schism and the Reformation. It played a large part in political and theological disputes, acting as a profoundly conservative and Thomist force, so that it was suppressed by the Revolution (1792). Only partially restored thereafter it fell on bad days and did not revive until the Third Republic, by which time the Faculty of Theology had been suppressed (1885), and a whole new range of disciplines and buildings installed. Housing a vast proportion of the French student body it came under great pressure in the mid-20th cent. and became once more a centre of radical thought and action (1968), and in an attempt to meet the pressure of numbers the university was decentralized across the Paris sub-region (1970).   CHC

SOREL, GEORGES (1847–1922), French engineer and politician, who was an exponent of syndicalism. He combined the Marxist theory of a class struggle with Nietzsche's belief in violence as a medium of change, to justify a revolutionary trade union movement, in which the unions would use the general strike as an instrument of proletarian revolution and themselves provide the basis on which society could be rebuilt. In the long term, Sorel's views had more influence on the right than on the left, for his appeal to irrationalism and violence was one of the bases of fascism in the 1930s.

SORSKY, NIL (*c.* 1433–1508), Russian monk, who spent his early monastic life at Mount Athos in Greece, where he was influenced by the Hesychast movement. He returned to Russia and became a champion of the eremitic form of monastic life, the goal of which was mystic union with the Godhead. He also became the leading exponent of the 'Non-possessors', who attacked the wealth and property of the Church.

SOSHANGANE (*fl.* 19th cent.), opponent of Shaka, the Zulu king, who fled from the Natal–Zululand area with his followers to the hinterland of southern Mozambique; there he established the kingdom of Gaza. His grandson Gungunyana, who was defeated by the Portuguese in 1895, was the last of the independent African monarchs in southern Africa to be overcome by the whites.

SOTO EXPEDITION, DE (1539–43), Spanish exploration in North America. Hernando De Soto (*c.* 1500–42) landed in Tampa Bay, FL, in May 1539. After exploring parts of FL (1539–40), he wandered over the present states of GA, NC, SC, AL, and possibly TN. He reached the Mississippi river (March 1541), crossed it, and explored AR and OK. On De Soto's death, his successor, Luis de Moscoso, led the party down the Mississippi and after building ships sailed to Pánuco in Mexico (Sept. 1543).

SOULBURY COMMISSION (1945–6), sent out by the British government to consider Ceylon's advance to near independence. It consisted of Lord Soulbury (1887–1971), a former minister, Frederick Rees, and Frederick Burrows, a leading trade unionist. It was disliked by the board of ministers, who had wanted direct negotiations with the British government and who therefore refused to give evidence before it. However, means were found to convey their views to the commission, whose report tallied largely with the constitutional proposals made earlier by D. S. Senanayake. The report recommended a constitution on the 'Westminster model' with a senate of 30 members, half elected by the House of Representatives and half nominated; a House of Representatives of 101 members, 95 elected and 6 appointed to represent interests otherwise inadequately represented; and a cabinet of ministers in sole charge of their departments and responsible to parliament. There were, however, a few limitations, including external affairs, defence, and amendment of the constitution. There were also provisions to so delimit constituencies as to give fair representation to minority communities.

The commission's report was accepted by the British government and by the Ceylon state council. Elections were held in Aug. 1947 and the new constitution came into operation. But at the opening of parliament the governor announced that full independence was being conceded, and it was granted in Feb. 1948.

SOULIGNAVONGSA (*reg.* 1637–94), King of Laos, who restored peace to Lan Xang after a period of dynastic conflict. His reign was the golden age of Laos, and its last period of peaceful unity. The execution of the crown prince after an amorous intrigue left the king without direct heirs, and after his death the kingdom was divided into three parts.

SOULT, NICOLAS (1769–1851), French soldier, who rose from being a private to become (1847) marshal-general of France. His greatest success was at Austerlitz, but this was followed by an inglorious role in the Peninsular War. He routed the English at Corunna, but was himself driven out of Portugal after a pointless delay at Oporto. After a period as viceroy of Andalusia, which he spent in looting art treasures, Soult assumed command of the army of Spain, but was too late to fight more than a rearguard action before Wellington pursued the French beyond the Pyrenees. His incompetence as chief of staff helped to ruin Napoleon I's chances at Waterloo. But this and his constant pursuit of personal ambition were forgotten in France after 1815, for he outlived all but one of the original marshals to become one of Louis Philippe's prime ministers (1832–4).

SOUND DUES, charges levied by Denmark on traffic through the strait between Zealand and Scania, instituted in 1429 as a payment on each ship and extended to cargoes in 1567. These dues were cherished by Danish kings as a personal revenue. All powers trading with the Baltic resented their exaction, from which the Swedes secured exemption in 1613–1720 (and their Baltic provinces, 1645–1720), while the Dutch were allowed to compound temporarily for a lump sum (1649–53). This had a significant effect on English foreign policy in the 17th cent. The dues continued to be levied until 1857, when this abolition removed a four-centuries-old impediment to Baltic trade. The US having refused to continue payment, the dues were commuted for about £3 million. The result was a serious loss to the Danish Crown, but a gain to Copenhagen in competing for trade against Hamburg.

SOUPHANOUVONG, Prince (1912–), leader of the communist Pathet Lao insurgents in Laos. Trained in civil engineering in Paris, he built bridges and roads in Viet-nam (1938–45) and married a Viet-namese. He was defence minister in the nationalist provisional government in Vientiane (1945–6) and foreign minister of the Free Lao exile government in Bangkok (1947–8). But he broke with his colleagues to join cause with the Viet-Minh and with their aid organized the Pathet Lao in 1950. Temporary reconciliations brought him into the national government (1957–8) and again after the Geneva Conference (1962–3), but he has led his troops against the government continuously since 1963.

SOUSA, JOHN PHILIP (1854–1932), US bandmaster and composer, who was conductor of the US Marine Band (1880–92) and wrote over a 100 marches, including 'Semper Fidelis' (1888), 'The Washington Post' (1889), and 'The Stars and Stripes Forever' (1897).

SOUSTELLE, JACQUES (1912–), French scholar and politician who was, at first, a close follower of De Gaulle, but later opposed him violently on the question of Algeria. He established his reputation before the Second World War as an ethnologist and an expert on the civilizations of Central America. He joined De Gaulle in London in 1940, and occupied various posts under him in Algeria and at the Liberation. He entered parliament and was a minister in De Gaulle's government (1945–6), but resigned from politics when De Gaulle left power. He then became general secretary of the Gaullist RPF movement (1947), and returned to parliament in 1951.

He was appointed governor-general of Algeria by Mendès-France. In this post (1955–6) he became popular with the European population, and the defence of their interests became his main political role. He was a leading member of the 'Algeria lobby' in the last years of the Fourth Republic, and in the 1958 crisis went to Algiers and helped persuade the insurgent settlers to support De Gaulle. He became a minister after De Gaulle's return to power, but was dismissed because of his open sympathy with the 1960 Algiers rising. As De Gaulle's intention of giving independence to Algeria became clear, Soustelle joined the extreme right-wing opposition. He left France in 1961 when threatened with prosecution, but returned in 1968.

SOUTH AFRICA, REPUBLIC OF (1,223,000 sq. kms), formerly the Union of South Africa in the British Commonwealth. It declared republican status and left the Commonwealth in 1961. The population (1970) of 19 million included Xhosa, Zulu, Sotho, Tswana, and other groups. Of the population in 1970 19 per cent were European settlers, and there were substantial groups of Asians and 'Cape coloureds'. Europeans over 18 years old had the vote for an all-white house of assembly and senate. They also elected the president. The Coloureds of Cape province over 21 years old voted for their own representative councils.

SOUTH AUSTRALIA, Australian state founded in 1836 mainly by British nonconformists; it had no convict settlements. Its pastoralists were not significant politically, and its early expansion depended mainly on wheat. It was the granary of Australia (1850–80) and also produced wool, copper, and wine. Irrigation schemes and large deposits of iron ore (Australia's main source of supply until the 1960s) helped to sustain the primary sector in the 20th cent. Secondary industry grew slowly until government policy encouraged them in the 1930s.

SOUTH CAROLINA, former English colony in North America, first visited by Spaniards (1521) and settled by them for a brief period under Lucas Vazquez de Ayllón (1526). The Spaniards erected a fort on Parris Island (1566) and for 20 years thwarted all attempts by French Protestants to settle there. In 1629 Charles I granted all territory between the 31° and 36° parallels to Sir Robert Heath, who named the area Carolina in Charles's honour, but no settlement occurred and the same territory was granted by Charles II (1663) to the 'Carolina Proprietors'. A second charter (1665) extended the area to the 29° parallel in the south and to the 36° 30′ parallel in the north, for which area the proprietors were to legislate 'by and with the advice, assent, and approbation of the freemen', but the proprietary board adopted John Locke's feudalistic Fundamental Constitutions. The first permanent English settlement at Albemarle (1670) moved across the Ashley river (1680) to the modern site of Charleston, and settlement by English dissenters from Barbados, and French Protestants spread, mainly along the coast. The northern part of the territory was neglected by the proprietors and regarded as inhospitable by settlers. During the proprietary rule (1670–1719) the settlers refused to pay quit-rents and rejected the Fundamental Constitutions, and in 1693 the Commons house elected by the settlers secured the right to initiate legislation. However, the proprietors vetoed popular laws and failed to assist in the wars with the Indians, and in 1719 the Commons house usurped control of the colony. The British government appointed royal governors for North and South Carolina (1712) and purchased the proprietors' land titles (1729). Royal rule (1720–75) coincided with a period of prosperity based on trade in deerskins, rice, and indigo and Charleston's trade with the Indians. The Commons house, modelling itself on the British House of Commons, grew in power and influence and by 1760 the royal council had virtually ceased to exercise any control over legislation. The dispute over the Wilkes Fund (1769–75), involving the Commons' right to control the purse, resulted in delegates going to the Stamp Act Congress (1765). In 1774 a provincial congress sent delegates to the Continental Congress and assumed control of the colony, and when the royal governor dissolved the assembly and fled (15 Sept. 1775), royal rule ended, and a State Constitution for SC was signed in March 1776.

D. D. Wallace, *History of South Carolina*, 4 vols (New York, 1934). WM

SOUTH CAROLINA EXPOSITION AND PROTEST (1828), states-rights statement drafted by John C. Calhoun for the SC legislature in response to the 'Tariff of Abominations' of 1828. However, as Calhoun admitted, the disputed tariff was the occasion rather than the cause of the exposition, for it was slavery which really needed theoretical protection against federal interference.

SOUTH DAKOTA, 40th member state of the US, admitted in 1889. This north central region, first explored by the Vérendrye brothers (1742–3, passed to Spain (1762), reverted to France (1800), and was sold to the US under the Louisiana Purchase (1803). Permanent settlement began along the Missouri river at Yankton (1859), and Dakota Territory —then including ND, SD, and parts of WY and MT— was established (1861). Discovery of gold in the Black Hills (1875), which were surrounded by land granted to the Sioux tribes by the treaty of Laramie (1876), led to increased settlement and conflict with the Indians. The Sioux massacred Gen. Custer's force at the battle of the Little Big Horn (1876), but the revolt was crushed at the battle of Wounded Knee, which ended the Messiah War (1890). Large numbers of immigrants from northern and central Europe settled in the territory during the 1880s, and both

SD and ND achieved statehood in 1889. Although SD is the largest US producer of gold, the state's economy has long been dominated by the cultivation of cereal crops in the north-west, mixed farming in the James river valley, and cattle raising in the west. Agrarian discontent led to support for the Farmers' Alliance (1884) and the Populist Party of the 1890s.

SOUTH PASS, most renowned of the passes across the continental divide in the US, is a broad level valley at an elevation of 7500 ft, lying at the southern end of the Wind River mountains in south-central WY. It was probably discovered by white traders in 1807–8, and was first effectively traversed in 1824 by a fur-trading party under Jedediah Smith. Capt. Bonneville took the first wagons through the pass in 1832. Because of the easy and gradual approach to the pass from the east it became the gateway through the Rockies for the great emigrant trails to OR and CA. The first transcontinental railroad was laid through South Pass in 1869.

SOUTH SEA BUBBLE (1720) in Britain, financial crisis resulting from the collapse of the South Sea Co. In 1719 the company proposed to take over three-fifths of the national debt—some £30 million. The company was to pay immediately £7 million and in return accept 5 per cent interest until 1727 and thereafter 4 per cent, together with trading privileges. The company gambled on a rise in the value of its own shares and a fever of speculation followed. The shares of the company rose from 130 per cent to over 1000 per cent in six months, and other companies followed this example. In an effort to suppress their rivals the company itself spread alarm, causing panic selling and the bottom to fall out of the market. In an effort to stem the disaster Sir Robert Walpole produced a plan for £18 million of the company's stock to be transferred in equal shares to the Bank of England and the East India Co. Walpole's supremacy was assured by the political effects of the Bubble, which involved many ministers with accusations of bribery.

SOUTH SEA COMPANY in Britain, established in 1711 by Harley as a Tory alternative to the Whig financial establishments and to incorporate £9 million worth of the floating debt into company stock. In return the company was to enjoy a monopoly over South Sea trade and over concessions gained from Spain upon the resumption of peace.

SOUTH SEAS EVANGELICAL MISSION, THE, founded by Florence Young (1856–1940), who established the non-sectarian Queensland Kanaka Mission (1886), later extended to northern Qld (1899). After service with the China Inland Mission (1890–1900) Florence Young pioneered the Solomon Islands branch of the mission at Malu'u and One Pusu, Malaita (1904), in the interests of returning converts repatriated from Australia. The mission finally established a firm foothold on the island (also at Guadalcanal and San Cristoval), though its native clergy played a leading role in the Marching Rule movement (1943).

SOUTH WEST AFRICA was captured from Germany by South African forces in the First World War and, under the treaty of Versailles, became a League of Nations territory mandated to South Africa. A considerable number of German settlers remained there. The remnants of Herero, Nama (and other smaller Khoikhoi peoples), and the larger Ovambo tribe, were allocated 'reserves'. The South African government regarded South West Africa as an extension of South Africa, and settled several thousand poor white Afrikaners in the central highland region. After the Second World War South Africa refused to place the territory under United Nations trusteeship, and in most respects ruled South West Africa as a fifth province of the Union/Republic. Apartheid legislation was applied to the territory, Ovamboland was designated to become a **Bantustan**, and from 1949 whites elected their representatives to the South African parliament (as well as to a local Legislative Assembly). There were 75,000 whites in the territory in 1970 and 500,000 non-whites. African nationalist movements were banned, but operated in exile; they renamed South West Africa Namibia.

In 1961 Ethiopia and Liberia, as African member states of the old League of Nations, asked the International Court of Justice at The Hague to condemn aspects of South Africa's activities in South West Africa as violations of the mandate, but in July 1966 the court finally concluded that the two applicants had no legal right or interest in the subject matter of their complaints. All efforts by the United Nations to assert authority in South West Africa failed.   AEA

SOUTHAMPTON, HENRY WRIOTHESLEY, 4th Earl of (3rd of 2nd creation) (1573–1624), English soldier, courtier, and patron of writers, among them John Florio, Nashe, Gervase Markham, and Barnabe Barnes. Shakespeare's *Venus and Adonis* (1593) and *The Rape of Lucrece* (1594) were dedicated to him, and he is thought by some to have been the 'Mr W. H.' of the sonnets. He served with Essex on his voyages to Cadiz and the Azores (1596–7), was master of the horse in Essex's Irish army (1599), and was sentenced to death for his part in the Essex rising (1601). The sentence was commuted and on Elizabeth I's death he was released from prison and subsequently interested himself in colonial projects in VA and the East. Later he led a troop of volunteers in the Thirty Years War.

SOUTHAMPTON, in England, one of the safest natural harbours in the British Isles, which made it into one of the principal ports of medieval England and the main starting-point for modern transatlantic voyages. The town was established on its present site in the 11th cent. as the harbour for the Old English royal capital at Winchester and developed as the chief centre for the import of French wines. It reached the height of its importance in the century after 1380, when the Italian trading fleets made it their chief port of call in England, bringing spices and essential chemicals for the textile industry in exchange for wool from the Cotswolds and cloth from southern England. The financial centre of Italian business was in London, but it was safer for Italian merchants to channel their commodities through Southampton, where the Italians could also count on a friendly municipality. After *c.* 1500 the town declined, only to revive with the coming of the railways in the 19th cent. It suffered considerably from bombing in the Second World War.

SOUTH-EAST ASIA COLLECTIVE DEFENCE TREATY (Sept. 1954), signed at Manila and sometimes called the 'Manila treaty', intended to provide for the security of South-East Asia following the Geneva agreements. It had been an objective of US diplomacy for some time, and had been resisted by the British government until the Indo-China war could be brought to an end. The signatories to the treaty were Australia, Britain, France, New Zealand, Pakistan, Philippines, Thailand, and the US.

The signatories undertook to act 'to meet the common danger' in the event of aggression in the treaty area, and to consult if the integrity or political independence of a state in the area should be threatened (Art. LV). The area of the treaty was defined as South-East and South-West Asia, but did not include 'the Pacific area north of 21 degrees 30 minutes north'—a latitude which runs just south of Formosa (Art. VIII). A protocol to the treaty includes in the treaty area 'the States of Cambodia and Laos and the free territory under the jurisdiction of the State of Viet-nam'.

The treaty was accompanied by a declaration on the part of the US government that its reference to armed attack in Article IV applied 'only to Communist aggression', although it undertook to consult in the event of any other form of aggression.

A further document accompanying the treaty was the 'Pacific Charter', being a declaration of adherence to the principles of the UN Charter and the principle of equal rights and self-determination of peoples.

In common with the North Atlantic treaty the treaty established an Organization, with a Council and a secretary-general (from 1957) and a Military Planning Office in Bangkok (also from 1957). In practice the organization has not become effective. The French government, strongly critical of US policy in Viet-nam, withdrew increasingly from the organization; Pakistan has also disagreed with the other members and participated intermittently in the work of the organization which, in any case, came to be increasingly overshadowed by the Viet-nam War.   WK

SOUTHERN CHRISTIAN LEADERSHIP CONFERENCE in the US, civil rights organization established in 1957 by Martin Luther King to spread the philosophy and techniques of non-violent, direct-action protest and civil disobedience. SCLC engaged in protest marches against de facto segregation and discrimination, sponsored voter education and registration projects, the training of Negro leaders, and economic boycotts. Ralph Abernathy became president of SCLC after King's murder in 1968.

SOUTHEY, ROBERT (1774–1843), English poet and man of letters, who was a founder of, and a regular contributor to, the *Quarterly Review* (1809–38), and wrote a biography of Nelson (1813).

SOUVANNA PHOUMA, Prince (1901–), Laotian politician and prime minister of Laos, who served in the Vientiane provisional government (1945–6), and when the French reoccupied Laos fled with it to Bangkok. National reconciliation when Laos became independent induced him to return there in 1949. He was minister of public works (1950–1) and prime minister in 1951–4, 1956–8, 1960, and again after 1962. His policies of neutrality and national union proved difficult to maintain in the face of foreign interference.

SOUZA, MARTIM AFFONSO DE (c. 1500–64), first Portuguese governor of Brazil, who dislodged the French from Pernambuco, and in the south founded São Vicente (1532), the first permanent settlement in Brazil, and Piratininga, near modern São Paulo.

SOUZA, THOMÉ DE (c. 1510–64), Portuguese governor and captain-general of Brazil, who sharply restricted the power of the *donatarios* and worked closely with the Jesuits to unify the struggling colony. He is considered the true 'founder of Brazil'.

SOUZA, WASHINGTON LUIZ PEREIRA DE (1870–1957), Brazilian politician and president of Brazil (1926–30), who made his reputation as an administrator in municipal and state posts in São Paulo, including those of the prefect of the city of São Paulo and the governor of the state. He was senator from São Paulo (1924–6) and was returned unopposed as administration candidate for the presidency. As president, Souza ended the rebellions that had gone on since 1922, and launched a highway-building programme, but failed in his effort to stabilize the nation's finances. His economic programme was ruined by the world-wide Depression of 1929 and Brazil's successive bumper coffee crops in 1929–30. He was deposed by the revolution of Oct. 1930 that brought Getúlio Vargas to power and remained in voluntary exile until 1947.

SOVIET OF WORKERS' DEPUTIES (1905), established in St Petersburg at the height of the revolution in Oct. (Soviet being the Russian word for council). It was a workers' movement for the co-ordination of strikes and included members of the Shidlevsky commission and of various revolutionary parties. It existed for six weeks, and its member-ship, of which Trotsky was the most outstanding figure, was about 500.

SOVIET–FINNISH TREATY (1948) of mutual assistance which obliged Finland to resist aggression on the part of 'Germany or any state allied to [her]' with the help, in case of need, of the Soviet Union. Finland undertook no commitment to help the Soviet Union if it were attacked.

SOVIET–FINNISH TREATY (1955), renewal of the mutual assistance treaty of 1948 which included provision for the evacuation by the Soviet Union of the naval base of Porkkala (leased under the peace treaty of 1947). The treaty was important as part of the detente of 1955, when the new Soviet leadership signed the Austrian treaty and effected a reconciliation with Yugoslavia.

SOYER, ALEXIS BENOÎT (1809–58), French chef at the Reform Club in London, who, during the Crimean War, visited the British zone with the government's permission, but at his own expense, to inspect the army's feeding arrangements, of which there had been much criticism. His subsequent recommendations resulted in a general and permanent improvement in army catering. He wrote several books, mainly with the aim of educating the poor in matters of diet and cookery.

SPAAK, PAUL-HENRI (1899–), Belgian politician and lawyer who played a major role in Belgian politics from his election as a Socialist deputy in 1932. He was minister of transport and posts (1935) and foreign minister (1936), a position which he subsequently held several times until his retirement in 1966.

As foreign minister he sought a realistic foreign policy 'exclusively and wholly Belgian', and played an important part in the reorientation of Belgian policy to a position of independence—as opposed to neutrality, formally pronounced by parliament in Oct. 1936. He was elected prime minister in May 1938, and was again foreign minister in 1939 until the outbreak of the Second World War, although he retained his position during the government's exile in London (Oct. 1940–Sept. 1944). Returning to Belgium at the end of the war, he held the posts of prime minister and foreign minister jointly (1946–9) and was a principal opponent to the return of King Leopold III.

In the post-war period his interest in international co-operation was paramount. He headed the Belgian delegation to the San Francisco Conference (1945) and was the first president of the United Nations General Assembly (1946). Deeply committed to the idea of European unity and active in encouraging the development of the Common Market, he ratified the Benelux treaty (1948), and acted as president of the Consultative Assembly of the Council of Europe (1949–1951). He returned to the foreign ministry (1954) and was instrumental in joining Belgium to NATO, at which he was later secretary-general (1957–61). In April 1961 he formed a Coalition government between the Christian Socialists and his own Socialist Party, once again acting as foreign minister.   JL

SPAIN, ROMAN, originally the two provinces in the east and south, Hither Spain (Hispania Citerior) and Further Spain (Hispania Ulterior), organized in 197 BC after the expulsion of the Carthaginians in the Second Punic War (206). Severe fighting in the 2nd cent., especially against the Lusitanians and Celtiberians, made these provinces secure, but the whole Iberian peninsula was not subdued until Agrippa's campaign in 19 BC. Hither Spain then became Hispania Tarraconensis and Further was divided into Baetica, southern, and Lusitania, western. Spain's chief value to Rome at first lay in its mines but, with its rapid romanization, which had begun early round cities such as Gades, Corduba, and Tarraco, it produced some eminent Roman writers of the 1st cent. AD, *eg*, the Senecas, Lucan, Martial, and later, the Emperors Trajan,

Hadrian, and Marcus Aurelius, as well as excellent legionaries. The province was invaded by the Vandals in AD 409 and eventually occupied by the Visigoths (from 461).

SPANGENBERG, AUGUSTUS GOTTLIEB (1704–92), Prussian-born leader of the Moravian Church or Unitas Fratrum in the later 18th cent. After serving as assistant to Count Zinzendorf at the Moravian brethren's community at Herrnhut in Saxony (1733) he went on three missions to America (1735–9, 1745–9, 1751–3), before returning to Herrnhut, where he became the dominating figure from 1762 to his death.

SPANISH CIVIL WAR, THE (1936–9). From the spring of 1936 army officers, enraged by the Republic's military reforms, its sympathy with regional autonomy and its failure to maintain public order, were plotting a rising. The assassination of Calvo Sotelo on 13 July was the spark which set events moving. Garrisons rose at Melilla in Morocco on July 17–18 and on the following day garrisons revolted everywhere. In the south the towns of Cordoba, Granada, Cadiz, and Seville fell to the rebels. In the north they took all of Galicia, a large part of Leon, and part of Asturias. Catalonia was saved for the Republic by the prompt action of the Barcelona workers, who forestalled Gen. Goded's coup. The old traditional Castilian towns of Salamanca, Valladolid, Burgos, and Segovia fell, as well as Pamplona and Zaragoza. The attempted rising in Madrid failed when the armed working classes stormed the Montaña barracks. Toledo's garrison remained temporarily besieged in the Alcázar. Valencia remained in Republican hands. The Basque provinces divided: Vizcaya and Guipuzcoa sided with the Republic to safeguard their autonomy; Alava and Navarre with the Nationalists to protect the Church and traditional society.

Thus, the attempted rapid coup was transformed by the resistance of the working classes into civil war. For the Nationalists it became a crusade to save Spain and Catholicism from foreign revolutionary elements. They were supported by the Church and most of the wealthier classes. The army, the Civil Guard, and the Assault Guard largely adhered to the right. The Republic counted on a few loyal officers and on the untrained but enthusiastic working-class militias. Many people supported the side in whose territory they found themselves. Both sides were fighting for causes which had enthused them during the Republic: the right for an authoritarian state of order, property, and religion; the left for social revolution.

The Nationalists enjoyed the advantage of troops and military supplies from Italy and Germany. These played a crucial role in the Nationalist victory, especially at the end of July, when German and Italian aircraft facilitated the ferrying of the Army of Africa to Spain, thus allowing the Nationalists to sweep through Andalusia and Estremadura. The Republic received aid from Russia, in sufficient quantities to save Madrid but not to win the war, and from Mexico to a lesser extent. Britain and France set up a Non-Intervention Committee to minimize the danger of international conflict. Ignored by the fascist powers, the committee had the practical effect of depriving the Republic of its international rights as a legally constituted government to buy arms.

The Republican zone witnessed a revolutionary take-over of the economy in the early weeks of the war. Industry and agriculture were enthusiastically collectivized by the working class and revolutionary militias hastily formed. Neither collectivization nor the militias represented the most efficient use of the Republic's limited resources, and to steal thunder from the other parties the communists called for the efficient prosecution of the war by concentrating power in the hands of the government, which they were at the same time infiltrating. This was the central dilemma of the war for the Republic—its greatest strength was working-class enthusiasm, but workers' militias were indisciplined and inefficient, and it did not suit the foreign policy of Russia, on whom the Republic depended for arms, that the revolution triumphed in Spain. Using the lever of arms, the communists gained increasing power, managing successively to eliminate the POUM, to oust Largo Caballero from the government, and to reduce the power of the CNT by depriving their militia of arms.

In the Nationalist zone the predominance of the army precluded internecine quarrelling. The accidental deaths of Sanjurjo and Mola left Franco as undisputed leader, a position which he had effectively acquired through his command of the Moroccan army, the strongest part of the Nationalist forces. His position was strengthened further after April 1937, when Serrano Suñer unified the Falange and the Carlists into the unified party, FET y las JONS, as a prelude to building the new Spain, a vaguely corporative and Catholic one-party state.

For most of the war the Nationalists held the initiative. Franco aimed to reduce the Republic to total unconditional surrender by a war of attrition and so occasional Republican offensives briefly snatched back the initiative. In Aug. 1936 the Nationalists took Badajoz, thereby uniting their Southern conquests with their northern bases. In Sept. they took Irun and San Sebastian. They then began a major push on Madrid which would probably have fallen had they not made a detour to relieve the besieged Alcazar in Toledo. This breathing space allowed the reinforcement of Madrid with the International Brigades. The siege of Madrid began on 6 Nov. and on the 7th the government moved to Valencia, leaving the city under Gen. Miaja. Thereafter, the Nationalists hung everything on taking Madrid, but the courage of the *Madrileños* and the arrival of Russian arms enabled it to survive to the end.

Early 1937 was costly for the Republicans. In Feb. Malaga fell unnecessarily through internal treason and dissent. In the spring two Nationalist attempts to cut the roads out of Madrid were defeated at Jarama and Guadalajara, the latter against Italian troops, but with crippling losses. In April began perhaps the decisive campaign of the war, the conquest of the north. Enjoying almost total air superiority, the Nationalists attacked the 'iron ring' of defences round Bilbao. Lack of food and poor support saw the city fall on 19 June. Santander fell on 25 Aug., Gijon on 21 Oct., so the Nationalists had the use of all the north's industry.

In July the Nationalists had considered a major push on Madrid but this was stopped by a Republican offensive on Brunete, which while briefly successful involved huge losses. In the winter of 1937–8 a further Republican offensive at Teruel suffered the same fate of rapid success followed by crippling losses in defence of earlier gains. In the autumn of 1937 Franco decided to take Valencia and it was in an attempt to stop his advance that the Ebro offensive was launched in July 1938. Initially successful, the offensive destroyed the Republican army. In Dec. the Nationalists began to sweep north and on 26 Jan. 1939 Barcelona fell and thousands of refugees fled to France.

When the Nationalists turned south for a big attack on Madrid, which was virtually without food and heating, Col. Casado formed a Council of Defence to negotiate a surrender. Supporters of Negrín and the communists revolted and there was heavy fighting for a week. The victorious Nationalists entered Madrid on 28 March after a war in which nearly 1 million people had died.　　　　PP

SPANISH IN NORTH AFRICA. The Spanish presence in North Africa grew out of the association between Morocco and Muslim Spain. After the fall of Granada (1492), Spain seized Melilla (1497), then occupied various stations and cities, including Oran and Bougie eastwards along the Mediterranean coast until Tunis was taken (1535). By the end of the 16th cent. possessions east of Oran had been lost to the corsairs, but acquisition of the Portuguese empire (1580–1640) provided compensation to the west. By the end of the 18th cent. Spain was left only with stations on the coast of the Rif, notably Ceuta and Melilla. The Spanish protectorate of northern Morocco (1912) provided territory inland. With French aid against the rebel Abd al-Karim (1926) it was subdued and incorporated into independent Morocco (1956).

SPANISH MARRIAGES QUESTION (1846) increased the friction between France and Britain after the Straits Convention (1841). Britain was anxious to postpone the marriages of Isabella of Spain and her sister, the Infanta, and to avoid a match between Isabella and the son of Louis Philippe, King of France. After Palmerston's failure to exclude the French from the negotiations, it was agreed that Isabella should marry the allegedly impotent Francis of Cadiz, and her sister the Duke of Montpensier, Louis Philippe's son. This interference in the affairs of Spain demonstrated Spanish weakness in Europe and further undermined the confidence in the regime.

SPANISH MYSTICS, school of religious thinkers in 16th–17th-cent. Spain, one of the most striking phenomena of the Catholic Counter-Reformation. The literary outburst of mystical works, dominated by the two outstanding Carmelites, St Theresa of Avila and St John of the Cross, began with the reformer Garcia de Cisneros but included numerous important figures, including St Ignatius Loyola, Luis de Granada, St Peter of Alcantara, and Luis de Leon.

SPANISH NETHERLANDS, provinces of Brabant, Limburg, Luxemburg, Flanders, Artois, Hainault, Holland, Zeeland, Namur, Walloon Flanders, Tournai, Mechlin, and Overyssel, which from the 14th cent. were part of the lands of the dukes of Burgundy but passed to the Spanish Crown through the succession of Philip the Fair to the Burgundian inheritance (1482) and to the throne of Castile (1504). His early death (1506) transferred these lands to his son, Archduke Charles of Habsburg, though they were ruled by regents Margaret of Habsburg and Mary of Habsburg in Charles's name. In this period the Spanish Netherlands enjoyed moderate prosperity centred on the great commercial metropolis of Antwerp, and wise government, as well as the addition of Friesland (1515–1524), the lands of the Bp of Utrecht (1528), Groningen and Drenthe (1536), and Guelders (1543). On Charles V's abdication (1555) the Spanish Netherlands were at first ruled by their new sovereign, Philip II, who continued his father's policies of unification, centralization, and the eradication of Protestant heresy. The opposition which Philip aroused among the higher nobility and clergy grew more radical under his regent, Margaret of Parma (1559–67), and social discontent due to inflation and a slump in the textile industry gave Calvinist extremists the opportunity to stir up rebellion. Alva's reign of terror (1567–73) inaugurated the Dutch revolt (1568), and by 1576 the united Netherlands pledged themselves to expel the Spanish troops. The rift between Catholics and Protestants, however, disrupted this brief unity and by 1579 the Netherlands had divided between the Union of Arras under the Spanish Crown and the Union of Utrecht, led by Holland. A long struggle ensued during which Parma reconquered the southern provinces for Spain, though the lands north of the Rhine and Meuse were recovered by the Dutch through the genius of Maurice of Nassau. A truce of 1609, largely confirmed by the treaty of Münster (1648) after another period of warfare (1621–48), established the independence of the seven northern provinces, leaving Spain with the remaining 10 southern provinces of the Netherlands. Of these, most of Artois was later acquired by France by the treaty of the Pyrenees (1659), while Brabant and Hainault were claimed by Louis XIV on behalf of his wife, the elder daughter of the Spanish king, Philip IV, and the War of Devolution (1667–8) left France in possession of some Netherlands fortresses, including Lille. However, the combined naval and military power of the maritime countries under William III baulked Louis's attempts to dominate the Spanish Netherlands which became the main area of operations in both the Wars of the League of Augsburg (1689–97) and the Spanish Succession (1702–13). Efforts to negotiate the succession to the Spanish empire broke down, though the terms of the Partition treaties (1698, 1700), which apportioned the Spanish Netherlands to Archduke Charles of Habsburg, were eventually fulfilled by the treaty of Utrecht (1713), when the Spanish Netherlands became the Austrian Netherlands in compensation for the Bourbon acquisition of the Spanish throne.   MKS

SPANISH REPUBLIC (1873), short-lived experiment in republicanism, following the flight of Isabella (1868) and the abdication of Amadeo of Savoy. The failure of the radical attempt to create a constitutional monarchy left no alternative but a republic, for which there was an equal lack of popular support. The Federalists made a bid for power under the leadership of Pi y Margall, but the extremism of some federal leaders, combined with a Carlist revolt, caused the new republic to degenerate swiftly into military dictatorship, culminating in the restoration of Alfonso XII (1875).

SPANISH REVOLUTION (1854), explosion of popular fury against Queen Isabella, which marked a permanent decline in the prestige of the Spanish monarchy. The military dictatorship of Narvaez had collapsed in 1851, only to be replaced by the reactionary ministry of Bravo Murillo. Hitherto the queen's ministers had incurred most of the blame for the continued political instability, but when she reacted to a liberal petition demanding a return to constitutional government by declaring a state of siege in Madrid and expelling the opposition leaders from the country, she herself was revealed as an enemy of the constitution. The revolutionaries, led by O'Donnell and joined by Espartero, forced her to capitulate and the two generals embarked on an unsuccessful attempt at democratic reform.

SPANISH ROAD, trans-European land route from Milan to the Netherlands, which ran through the Alps and down the Rhine valley to Franche-Comté and contained certain strategic points, *eg*, the Valtelline pass, Breisach, and Luxemburg. Vital for the communications system of the Spanish Crown from the 1580s, when English and Dutch pirates closed the normal sea routes to Flushing, and threatened increasingly by French power in the 17th cent., it played an important part in the strategy of Habsburg–Bourbon wars until the Netherlands were severed from the Spanish Crown in 1713 at the treaty of Utrecht.

SPANISH SAHARA (266,000 sq. kms) in western Sahara, formerly known as Rio de Oro and Sekia el Hamra. It was recognized as a province of Spain in 1958 and a governor-general ruled thereafter on behalf of Spain. The population in 1970 was 68,400, chiefly nomadic people belonging to Berber and Arab groups.

SPANISH SECOND REPUBLIC (April 1931–July 1936). The April 1931 elections showing a Republican victory in the towns, Alfonso XIII left Spain on 14 April. The Revolutionary Committee formed at the pact of San Sebastian became the provisional government of the Republic. Huge problems concerning regional separatism, industrial and agrarian unrest, the army and the Church, all left unsolved by the monarchy, had to be faced. Tacitly accepted, except by the extremes of right and left, the Republic yet lacked enthusiastic supporters for its task of introducing reforms acceptable to the left without alienating the upper classes, the army, and the Church. Church burnings and monarchist conspiracies in May indicated the enormity of the task.

The ruling Republicans showed sensitivity to little except their own doctrinaire anti-clericalism. Thereby estranging the moderate conservatives, the government had to rely on the Socialists, who saw the Republic as a mere prelude to revolution. Dec. 1931 saw the appearance of a partisan constitution, which described the state as 'a democratic republic of workers of all classes', countenanced regional autonomy, disestablished the Church, and declared the subordination of all property to national interests. The conservative classes were thus forced into opposition to the Republic itself.

Right-wing groups were also upset by the reforms of Azaña's government. The army was enraged by the 1931 military reforms and even more by the Catalan autonomy statute of Sept. 1932. The Agrarian Law of the same date infuriated landowners, yet was so riddled with loopholes that it barely helped the peasants. Right-wing opposition grew, embodied in *Renovación Española* and CEDA. Its potential temper was revealed by Sanjurjo's attempted coup in Aug. 1932. Equally the left regarded the Republic as a betrayal. Thus there were enormous problems of public order. Jan. 1932 saw an anarchist uprising and the CNT encouraged constant strikes and disturbances. Governmental violence in their suppression, especially at Casas Viejas in Jan. 1933, discredited Azaña's regime. In the summer he had to resign.

In the consequent elections in Nov. left-wing disunity helped the right wing to victory. The Radical, Alejandro Lerroux, formed a centre-right government with the support of CEDA. There followed the so-called two black years, the *bienio negro*, during which the legislation of the previous two years was reversed. The propertied classes took advantage of power to lower wages and sack leftist workers. A crisis was reached in Oct. 1934, when three CEDA ministers joined the government. The frustrated left rose in Catalonia and Asturias. Put down with great violence, the Asturian rising prefigured the civil war. Thereafter, the left was determined on revolution, the right on authoritarian government. After a period of government instability and persecution of the left, the *bienio* ended with financial scandals.

Unified into the Popular Front, the left won the Feb. 1936 elections. Chaos reigned. Peasants seized land in the south. The extreme right—the Falange—engaged the Socialists in street gun-fights. Attempts at compromise were lost in the spiralling polarization. Army officers were plotting to restore order when the terrorism culminated in the murder of the rightist leader, Calvo Sotelo, on 13 July. This was the signal for their rising and the Civil War began on 18 July.   PP

SPANISH SUCCESSION, WAR OF THE (1702–13). The origins of the war lay in the rival claimants disputing the inheritance when the line of the Spanish Habsburgs came to an end with the death of Charles II (1700). Louis XIV and William III, the leaders of the two European coalitions, had tried to prevent a war by negotiating the Partition treaties (1698, 1700). But Louis, by acceptance of the last will of Charles II, which bequeathed the whole empire to Louis XIV's grandson, Philip of Anjou, aroused the hostility of William III.

Only the Holy Roman emperor, a rival claimant, refused to recognize the French claimant, Philip V, as King of Spain, but by a series of blunders Louis XIV caused the formation of the Grand Alliance (1701) which declared war on France (1702). The war aims of the allies were several. Austria fought to gain some territorial compensation, in particular Italy. The maritime powers, England and the United Provinces, fought to protect their commercial and colonial interests in Spain, the Indies, and the Mediterranean by preventing French domination in those areas. In addition these powers fought to prevent the territorial aggrandizement of France, especially towards the strategic Spanish Netherlands. Control of this area was vital to the security of the maritime powers. Thus another war aim was the right for the Dutch to garrison a barrier of fortresses in the Spanish Netherlands. Finally there was an ideological conflict between the limited monarchy system of government of England and the divine right absolutism of France. This led England to demand French recognition of the sovereignty of Anne and of the Protestant Succession as established by the Act of Settlement (1701).

The various auxiliary powers of the Grand Alliance fought as mercenaries and to gain territory. One auxiliary however—Portugal—insisted on an extension of the allied war aims. In the Methuen treaty (1703) Portugal urged that Philip V should be replaced by the Austrian candidate, Archduke Charles. This *No peace without Spain* was to prolong the war, since the allies refused to make peace at The Hague (1708) and at Gertruydenburg (1709) unless it was enforced.

The war was fought in a number of theatres. In the Spanish Netherlands the allies were supreme, Marlborough's successes enabling an invasion of France. Similarly, in Italy, Prince Eugène of Savoy expelled the French. In Germany the electors of Bavaria and Cologne were expelled and the French armies held at the Rhine. At sea, allied maritime supremacy enabled the capture of the Spanish Mediterranean islands and limited France to privateering. Only in Spain did the allies fail. Philip V emerged as a national leader to expel the allies in spite of the occupation of Madrid (1706, 1710). Charles's accession to the Habsburg empire (1711) ended his chance of gaining Spain, since the allies feared his large empire would threaten the balance of power of Europe. The withdrawal of English forces enabled a French military recovery led by Villars and enforced a peace settlement. Thus at the peace of Utrecht France made a partial diplomatic recovery though most of the allied war aims were fulfilled. The war, in both its geography and its issues, anticipated much of the 18th-cent. Anglo-French conflict.

H. Kamen, *The War of Succession in Spain, 1700–15* (London, 1969).   AW

SPANISH–AMERICAN WAR (1898) was initiated by the US and fought ostensibly to end civil war in Cuba and free the island from Spanish rule. But it also manifested the Americans' desire to consolidate their strategic position and extend their economic penetration to the Caribbean area. The reluctance of two US presidents, Cleveland and McKinley, to intervene in the Cuban civil war (1895–8) was offset by humanitarian and jingoistic sentiments in the country, stimulated by the popular press. Although Spain offered (1897) limited autonomy to the insurgents and suspended hostilities, the destruction of the USS *Maine* in Havana harbour (15 Feb. 1898) exacerbated the demand for intervention, and McKinley asked Congress (11 April) for authority to end the civil war. Spain broke off diplomatic relations with the US (21 April) and on 25 April Congress declared a state of war to have existed since 21 April. On 1 May a US squadron, under Commodore Dewey, entered Manila Bay in the Philippines and destroyed the Spanish fleet. In July the US army stormed the heights overlooking Santiago, Theodore Roosevelt's 'Rough Riders' taking part in the assault on San Juan hill. Admiral Cervera's fleet was forced into the arms of the American blockade, and Wake Island and Puerto Rico were occupied. In the ensuing peace negotiations in Paris, Spain ceded Puerto Rico, Guam, and the Philippines to the US, and relinquished all claims to Cuba, whilst the US paid Spain $20 million for possession of the Philippines.   DBS

SPARKS, JARED (1789–1866), US editor and historian, who published and edited the *North American Review* (1823–9). He was editor of *The Diplomatic Correspondence of the American Revolution* (12 vols, 1829–30), *The Writings of George Washington* (12 vols, 1834–7), and *The Works of Benjamin Franklin* (10 vols, 1836–40), and he pioneered the collection of US historical documents. He was professor of history at Harvard (1839–49), of which he became president (1849), but he resigned (1853) because of opposition to his efforts to introduce new methods.

SPARRE, ERIK (1550–1600), Swedish nobleman who opposed the future King Charles IX. As the confidant of John III he was involved in arranging Sigismund's candidature for the Polish throne, but fell into disfavour with John and later with Duke Charles, whom he opposed in the council and in his writings, such as *Pro lege, rege, et grege* (1587). He eventually joined Sigismund, by whom he was surrendered to Duke Charles after the defeat at Stångebro, and was executed at Linköping.

SPARTA, territorially the largest, and for centuries the most powerful, ancient Greek city-state, founded (*c.* 1000 BC) by Dorian intruders in the south-eastern Peloponnese. By *c.* 800 four villages in the Eurotas valley had coalesced to form a single state ruled by two royal families, the Agiads and the Eurypontids. During the 8th cent. this state, having won control of the Eurotas valley and conquered Messenia (*c.* 735–715), soon afterwards achieved through the definitive 'Lycurgan' reforms its classical form. The conquered territory, with the exception of that owned by the *perioeci*, was divided equally between all adult Spartan males and worked on their behalf by the much more numerous conquered helots. The state's dependence upon the secure subjection of the helots produced a unique systematization in political, social, and economic life of traditional features of primitive Dorian tribalism, *eg*, the simple division of power between kings, council (*gerousia*), and assembly (*apella*) and especially the exclusively military education of Spartan males from their sixth to their thirtieth years. Despite the failure of subsequent attempts at territorial expansion against Argos and the Arcadians in the 7th and early 6th cents, and a Messenian revolt (*c.* 650), it is shown by archaeological remains and the poetry of Terpander and Alcman that Sparta shared fully in the orientalizing cultural renaissance of the 7th cent. For a while the state, though dedicated to war, remained open and gay. Repeated military failures against Tegea led the ephor Chilon (*c.* 556) to initiate a significant change in Spartan foreign policy. Henceforward the Spartans no longer sought territorial expansion by conquest, but more subtle domination by alliance. Their consequent position at the head of the Peloponnesian League, which eventually comprised all the Peloponnese except Argos and Achaea, enabled Cleomenes I to humble Argos at Sepeia (494); but earlier attempts to intervene beyond the Peloponnese in Samos (525) and Athens (508) were less successful. Nevertheless, Sparta's influence throughout Greece made her the natural leader against Persia in 480–479. After the Persian Wars, Argive revanchism, emergent Arcadian nationalism, a disastrous earthquake (464), and a second Messenian revolt (464–455), at first impeded the Spartans' opposition to the rapid growth of Athenian power, but they gave their allies enough help in the First Peloponnesian War (459–446) to contain Athenian encroachment. They fought the great Peloponnesian War (431–404) supposedly to defend Greek freedom against the 'tyrant city' of Athens, but Athenian encouragement of Messenian unrest and fear of Argos impelled them to make peace temporarily in 421. Soon afterwards they defeated the Argive coalition at Mantinea (418), but renewed fears of Athenian ambitions prompted them to support Syracuse against Athenian attack (414) and to occupy Decelea in Attica (413). Persian money, Lysander's energy, and Athenian political instability finally secured Sparta's victory. After 404 the Spartans quarrelled with their chief allies, Thebes and Corinth, and Agesilaus' pan-hellenic crusade against Persia (396–395) was frustrated by general Greek opposition to Spartan domination. Despite victory in the Corinthian War (395–386), specious support for city-state autonomy, renown among contemporary intellectuals as the ideal of political stability, and the seeming elimination by *c.* 380 of all opposition, Sparta was defeated by Thebes at Leuctra (371) and lost Messenia (370). The full citizens decreased disastrously in number, but their kings, *eg*, Agis III and Areus, obstinately opposed all later Macedonian attempts to effect their complete subjection. Finally, the constitution was radically reformed by Agis IV (*reg.* 244–241) and Cleomenes III (*reg.* 236–222) and until Nabis' defeat by the Roman Flamininus (*reg.* 195–192), Sparta tried unsuccessfully to recover her past glory under the banner of revolution. As Rome's ally against the Achaean League in

146, Sparta subsequently prospered under the Roman empire as a tourist attraction, though a travesty of its former self, which was ended by the Goths in AD 395. The modern town of Sparta was built on the ancient site in 1834.

H. Michell, *Sparta* (Cambridge, 1964).
W. G. Forrest, *A History of Sparta 950–192* BC (London, 1968).   JDS

SPARTACUS (d. 71 BC), Roman gladiator of Thracian origin who raised a slave revolt in Italy (73), gathered an army of 90,000, and defeated five Roman armies before he was brought to bay and destroyed by Crassus.

SPEAKER, THE, in England. A unified House of Commons comprising knights of the shire and burgesses meeting together emerged in England by 1332 at the latest. It is probable that at first it had no permanent chairman and small deputations of members acted as spokesmen when appearing before the king. A speaker elected for the entire duration of a parliament first appears for certain in 1376, when Peter de la Mare acted as the leader of the Commons in the exceptionally turbulent 'Good Parliament'. Thereafter a continuous succession of speakers can be traced, elected by the Commons. The speaker presided over their debates and acted as their spokesman to the monarch, enjoying a privileged freedom of speech in discharge of his functions. By the later years of King Richard II the office came to be filled by royal nominees and thereafter until 1642 he remained primarily a royal servant. In later centuries the speaker was essentially a parliamentarian and the office became one of great distinction, its holders being noted for their total impartiality and personal dignity.

SPECIAL JURIES ACT (1730) in Britain, legislative measure which empowered judges to swear in a jury with a higher property qualification, arising from the acquittal of one Francklin, a printer of Bolingbroke's *Craftsman*, by a jury chosen by a Tory sheriff (1729). In accordance with the act, Francklin was subsequently convicted by a special jury (1731).

SPECIE CIRCULAR (1836) in the US, directive issued by President Jackson that all future payments for public land were to be made in gold and silver. At a time of inordinate speculation in western lands and a mania for internal improvements in the states, the circular was intended to stabilize the currency and curb speculation. However, the economy had already been weakened by the crop failure of 1835, which produced an adverse balance of trade, and the need for specie to pay foreign creditors. In addition, the failure of several British mercantile houses towards the end of 1836 cut back the demand for US cotton. Thus the circular, although effective in damping down land speculation, undermined confidence in the circulating paper currency and contributed to the panic of 1837.

SPECTATOR, THE. English periodical edited by Richard Steele and Joseph Addison which appeared briefly (1711–12, 1714) at the start of the 18th cent. It was non-political in its approach, seeking to entertain, and to create new standards in public taste.

SPEECH FROM THE THRONE in Britain, constitutional device enabling the policy of the British monarch to be presented before both houses at the opening of each new parliamentary session. Following the Revolution of 1688 it was increasingly used by royal ministers as a means of bridging the gap between the executive and the legislature. In the 20th cent. it incorporates the government's projected legislative programme.

SPEED, JOHN (*c.* 1552–1629), English historian and cartographer. His important works were the *Theatre of the Empire* *of Great Britain* (1611), a series of 54 maps of England published individually since 1607, and the *History of Great Britain under the Conquests of the Romans . . . to . . . King James* (1611).

SPEELMAN, CORNELIS (1628–84), Dutch soldier and governor-general of the Dutch East India Co. (1681–4), who led an expedition against the Maccasarese (1667). He later led (1677) the Dutch forces which put down the rebellion of Trunadjaja in Java, and succeeded in establishing Susuhunan Amangkurat II as the new ruler of Kartasura.

SPEENHAMLAND SYSTEM in Britain, arose from a decision of the justices of the peace of Berkshire in their quarter sessions at Speenhamland in 1795, a year of food shortage and high prices, that the poor rate in Berkshire should be used to supplement wages on a scale regulated by the price of bread. The scale, which ensured a man the cost of three gallon loaves for himself and one for each dependant every week, was worked out on the assumption that a third of a man's wages went on food. Because the problem of food shortage and low wages was general in rural areas, and because of the strong disinclination of government or justices to fix wages, the scale was adopted by many parts of the country, and though it never had legislative sanction it is reasonable to speak of it as a 'system'.

In the period after the French Wars the high cost of poor relief led to pressure to reorganize the English Poor Law. The Royal Commission set up in 1832 to examine the working of the Poor Law made no systematic analysis, but implied in its report that a system of Poor Law allowances to supplement wages was still generally in use. In fact, recent research suggests that by then Poor Law allowances of this kind were only found in the wheat-raising south-east of England, and were only available for large families. The general belief in the widespread use of the Speenhamland system lay behind the Poor Law Amendment Act of 1834, which established central supervision of the Poor Law and attempted to abolish out-relief.

Opponents of the Speenhamland system argued that it encouraged early marriage and thereby large families, and that it held down the level of wages. There is no evidence that it had either of these effects. The birth rate seems to have been slightly higher in industrial counties than in those where the Speenhamland system was applied, perhaps because of the selective immigration of young adults, and the low level of wages in the wheat-growing areas continued long after 1834. One unfortunate effect of the system was to bring the ordinary working labourer within the action of the laws of Settlement, which could be used to prevent mobility of labour.

J. D. Marshall, *The Old Poor Law, 1795–1834* (London, 1968).
J. R. Poynter, *Society and Pauperism* (London, 1965).   RMM

SPEER, ALBERT (1905–), German architect, politician, and armaments minister, who was a relatively early associate of the Nazis, having joined the NSDAP in 1931. His designs for the staging of mass meetings in 1933 set the style for the public ceremonial of the Nazi regime, with its pretentious magnificence and pomposity, and brought him to the notice of Hitler. In 1934 he was commissioned to design the Nuremberg stadium and was appointed to an official party office. He was made responsible for the planned reconstruction of Berlin, for which he designed the new Reich chancellery (1937). His close personal contacts with Hitler gave him a high status in the Third Reich, though he held no major political office until his appointment as minister for armaments and munitions in 1942. Under his supervision the German economy was turned over to capacity war production, and the output of armaments trebled (1942–4). In 1945, when Germany's defeat in the Second World War was inevitable, he tried to resist Hitler's policy of national

self-immolation, and refused to carry out orders for the destruction of industrial plant before the advancing Allied troops. Only his exceptional relationship with Hitler saved him from arrest or execution, though he was dropped from the government that was named as successor to the Führer. Speer was sentenced to 20 years' imprisonment at the Nuremberg trials, and was released in 1966.

SPEIDEL, HANS (1897–), German soldier, who served in both the First and Second World Wars. In the second he served on the Eastern Front and later in the West as a chief of staff under Rommel. He was imprisoned (1944–5), being suspected of resistance activity, then was tried, but was acquitted. After the war he played an important part both in West Germany's military reconstruction, as government military adviser (1951–5), commander-in-chief (1955–7), and special adviser (1963–4), and in NATO as commander of land forces (1957–63).

SPEKE, JOHN HANNING (1827–64), British soldier and explorer, who explored in the Himalayas and Tibet. He later accompanied Burton on an expedition sponsored by the Royal Geographical Society to discover the source of the White Nile. He found and named Lake Victoria Nyanza and declared it to be the source, though without proof. On a second expedition with Grant, he found and named the Ripon Falls. Burton contested his conclusions.

SPENCE, CAROLINE HELEN (1825–1910), Australian political figure and writer who was among the first Australian women to play an active part in politics. She was concerned primarily with electoral reform, championed proportional representation, and won a considerable reputation as a platform speaker.

SPENCE, WILLIAM GUTHRIE (1846–1926), Australian trade union leader and politician, born in the Orkneys, emigrated from Scotland to the Victorian goldfields (1853), and became secretary of the Amalgamated Miners' Association (1878). In 1886 Spence began organizing the shearers and by 1890, as president of the Amalgamated Shearers' Union and AMA secretary, was the leading trade unionist in Australia. He was a Labor MP in NSW from 1898 and in the Commonwealth parliament (1901–19), except for a short break in 1917. He became postmaster-general (1913) but, in 1916, left the Australian Labor Party over the conscription issue.

SPENCER, GEORGE JOHN SPENCER, 2nd Earl (1758–1834), British politician. As Viscount Althorp he was a Whig MP for Northampton (1780) and Surrey (1782), holding minor office under Rockingham. As Earl Spencer, he joined Pitt's administration in 1793. He was first lord of the admiralty (1794–1801), being in office during the naval mutinies of 1797, the battles of Camperdown and St Vincent, and was partly responsible for the advancement of Nelson. Dockyards and ships of the line were put into first-class condition after a period of neglect. He left office with Pitt in 1801, later serving briefly as home secretary under Fox (1806–7). In retirement Spencer laid the foundations of the great collections of books that later became the John Rylands Library.

SPENCER, JOHN POYNTZ SPENCER, 5th Earl (1835–1910), British politician who was lord lieutenant of Ireland in Gladstone's first ministry (1868–74), and supported Irish Church disestablishment and land legislation. In Gladstone's second ministry (1880–5) he became lord president of the council, with responsibility for education, but in March 1882 he again went to Ireland as lord lieutenant, the previous lord lieutenant, Cowper, and chief secretary, Forster, having resigned in opposition to the Kilmainham treaty. The day after his arrival in Dublin his new chief secretary, Lord Frederick Cavendish, was murdered in Phoenix Park. Thereafter Spencer was spokesman for firm policies in

Ireland. He remained loyal to Gladstone in the Home Rule split of 1886, and became first lord of the admiralty in Gladstone's fourth ministry (1892–4).

SPENCER, HERBERT (1820–1903), British engineer, philosopher, sociologist, and educationist who pioneered evolutionary theory. After a period as railway engineer (1837–41) he became an active journalist. His first books were *Principles of Psychology* (1855), *Education* (1861), *First Principles* (1862), and *Principles of Biology* (1864). Thereafter he devoted himself to the massive collection of material and data leading to his *Descriptive Sociology* (1881). In the 1890s he returned to philosophical writing in which his influence on individualism, pacifism, and biological thinking was profound and world wide.

SPENCER, SIR WALTER BALDWIN (1860–1929), Australian biologist and ethnologist whose publications described pioneer work in central and northern Australia. He was special commissioner for aboriginals and chief protector in the Northern Territory (1912).

SPENDER, SIR PERCY CLAUDE (1897–), Australian lawyer, diplomat, and politician who held several portfolios in the Menzies Liberal–Country Party administration in the Second World War (1939–41) and on Labor's defeat in 1949 had two years as minister for external affairs when he was primarily responsible for initiating the Colombo Plan (1950). He then became Australian ambassador in Washington, DC (1951–8). In 1958 he became a justice of the International Court of Justice at The Hague, becoming president (1964–7).

SPENSER, EDMUND (*c*. 1552–99), English poet, who published his pastoral *Shepherd's Calendar* (1579), beginning in the same year *The Fairy Queen* (1589–96), an allegory regarded as the greatest English poem since Chaucer's *Canterbury Tales*. His other works included *Astrophel* (1586), an elegy on his friend Philip Sidney, *Colin Clout's Come Home Again* (1595), and *Epithalamion*. Spenser reluctantly spent several years in Ireland, where he was secretary to the lord deputy (1580). Further books of *The Fairy Queen* may have been lost when his home at Kilcolman Castle was destroyed in an affray, and he returned to London to die in poverty.

SPERANSKY, MIKHAIL MIKHAILOVICH, Count (1772–1839), Russian politician, who was Alexander I's principal adviser (1807–12). In an early memorandum (1802) he gave vent to his moral indignation at the condition of the peasantry and Russian backwardness and corruption. He was apparently opposed to serfdom, but envisaged a long process of education before action could be taken. He advocated primogeniture and an independent nobility. As a practical administrator with experience of educational, bureaucratic, and legal reforms he submitted to Alexander in 1809 his *Introduction to the Constitution of the Laws of the State*. His aim was the abolition of the arbitrary nature of autocracy and the introduction of an absolute monarchy, on the *rechstaadt* pattern, within a legal framework and with an efficient bureaucratic machinery. The draft divided the legislative, judicial, and administrative functions of government and divided society into three estates: the nobility, the middle class, and the peasantry. All were to be equal before the law and to have civil rights according to their status. The legislative was to express public opinion through elected juries and a four-tier system of noble-elected assemblies culminating in a state Duma. This was to meet annually and to be consultative, having no legislative powers. There was to be an independent judiciary headed by the Senate, and the executive was to consist of co-ordinated ministries with ministers answerable to the Duma for the emperor's acts, but not responsible to it.

Although the most comprehensive attempt at reform within the system, the *Introduction* achieved little. A council of state (1810) and a system of ministries were the only

parts of it that were implemented, except for minor financial and administrative reforms. Although far from a constitution, it is possible that Speransky saw it as eventually moving Russia towards a constitutional system of monarchy.

He was opposed by Karamzin and Arakheyev, and as a result of political and personal intrigues was disgraced and banished (1812). He became governor of Penza (1816) and governor-general of Siberia (1819), where he carried out an important reform of Siberian administration. His greatest achievement was the codification of laws (1833), by which time he was an upholder of autocracy.

M. Raeff, *Michael Speransky, Statesman of Imperial Russia 1772–1839* (The Hague, 1957).
L. Schapiro, *Rationalism and Nationalism in Russian Nineteenth Century Political Thought* (Yale, 1967). BJW

SPERRY, ELMER AMBROSE (1860–1930), US inventor, who held over 400 patents and made significant contributions to various technologies. His most important work was that from 1896 on the properties of the gyroscope, which resulted in the development of a gyroscopic compass (1910) and gyroscopic stabilizers for ships (1913) and aircraft (1914).

SPEYER, DIETS OF (1526, 1529), meetings of the German estates at the imperial diets held to attempt to bring about a religious settlement in Germany. The absence of the Emperor Charles V in Granada during the summer of 1526 resulted in a compromise settlement being agreed by the estates (Aug. 1526). A recess or decree of toleration was issued which ignored the Edict of Worms (1521) and left to each prince and city the duty of deciding their religious affinity in accordance with their conscience. At the second diet (March 1529) the Protestant side suffered a severe setback. At the instigation of the Archduke Ferdinand, the 1526 recess was repealed, the 1521 edict was to be enforced and no further secularization of Church lands was to take place. This diet drew a sharp reaction from the six Lutheran princes and 16 reformed cities of Germany who signed a Protestation, affirming their right to follow their religious convictions, a document which gave the name of 'Protestant' to its adherents.

SPEYER, TREATY OF (1544), settlement between the Netherlands and Denmark, granting the Netherlands full rights of trade and passage in the Baltic. This restoration of peaceful relations, vitiated since 1523 by the Emperor Charles V's support for his dethroned brother-in-law, Christian II of Denmark, and later for his niece, Dorothea, provoking Lübeck's interference in the Baltic, was vital for Dutch mercantile prosperity.

SPICE ISLANDS, Molucca group of islands in the Far East, including Tidore, Ternate, Amboina, and the Banda Isles, source of the much-coveted oriental spices, especially cloves, first discovered by the Portuguese (*c*. 1514), who made a treaty with the Sultan of Ternate. A Spanish-financed expedition commanded by Sebastian del Cano reached the islands in 1521 but in 1529 the Emperor Charles V ceded the Spanish claim to the Portuguese for 350,000 ducats (treaty of Saragossa). In the later 16th cent. a series of vigorous native sultans caused the Portuguese settlement in Ternate considerable trouble, although they were reinforced by Spanish troops after the union of the two countries (1580). However, as the Dutch East India Co. began to monopolize the spice trade they gradually occupied the Moluccas (1621–63), which became part of the Dutch empire in the Far East until the 20th cent.

SPICE TRADE in the Middle Ages. It was difficult to preserve foodstuffs for long in medieval Europe and food was heavily spiced whenever possible. Medieval Europe obtained its supplies of spices from Asia: from the 12th cent. onwards their import became the preserve of the Italians. By the late Middle Ages the Venetians largely monopolized the trade in pepper, the most important spice of all, by securing special privileges in Egypt. The Portuguese sea voyages to Asia intercepted this traffic at its source in India and Indonesia and after 1500 there was a great increase in the quantities of spices available on the European markets.

SPIEGEL, LAURENS PIETER VAN DE (1737–1800), Grand Pensionary of Holland (1787–95), who secured the post on the restoration of the Stadtholdership (1787) as the man most likely to popularize the rule of the House of Orange and the hereditary principle. He negotiated the defensive Triple Alliance between Britain, Prussia, and Holland (1788), attempted many reforms, and nationalized the possessions of the West India Co.

SPIEGHEL, HENDRIK LAURENSZOON (1549–1612), Dutch merchant and Catholic poet, who promoted the use of the pure Dutch language in literature, as in his two major works, the *Dialogue of Dutch Literature* and the *Mirror of the Heart*.

SPINET, keyboard stringed instrument in which the strings were plucked by a quill, widely used in the 16th–18th cents. It was probably called after Spinetti, who adapted the early harpsichord to the oblong shape usually associated with the spinet.

SPINNING JENNY in Britain, one of the crucial developments that inaugurated the Industrial Revolution. It was invented *c.* 1764 by James Hargreaves, as a hand device for spinning eight soft cotton threads at once. By 1780 it had been enlarged to include over 80 spindles and Samuel Crompton combined its principle with rollers to produce the 'mule', which could make stronger threads, suitable for both weft and warp. The mule and the larger jennies were too big for use at home, and so began the change-over from cottage industry to factory system. The jenny also overcame a bottleneck in production and consequently changed the price structure of the textile industry.

SPINOLA, AMBROGLIO (1569–1630), Genoese nobleman who entered Spanish military service (1602), replacing Archduke Albert as commander-in-chief in the Low Countries (1604), and proved to be a soldier of genius. After winning successes against Prince Maurice at Ostend (1604), Grol, and Oldenzaal (1605) he worked with the archdukes for a military truce with the northern provinces, realizing that the Spanish government were not prepared to grant the money needed for an all-out military campaign. After the Twelve Years' truce was signed (1609), he spent his private fortune on improving the Spanish army and planning for the renewed war with the Dutch. In 1614 he occupied Aix-la-Chapelle and Wesel (Cleves) in retaliation against the Dutch–Brandenburg seizure of Jülich. While Frederick of the Palatinate was ensconced in Bohemia Spinola seized the key fortresses along the Spanish supply line from Milan to Flanders, occupying the Rhenish Palatinate (1620). He followed this by bluffing the Protestant Union into disbanding their army by the Mainz Accord (1621). The crowning point of his military career, however, was the capture of Breda from the Dutch (1625), a feat immortalized in Velasquez's famous painting. As the Dutch campaigns deteriorated into a war of attrition, and supplies of money were not forthcoming, Spinola championed a policy of peace, but was over-ruled by Philip IV's minister, Olivares, and resigned his command (1627), withdrawing from the Netherlands. In 1629 he was appointed governor of Milan and died during the siege of Casale.

SPINOZA, BARUCH (1632–77), Dutch philosopher of Portuguese–Jewish émigré descent. His deep and early interest in optics, the new astronomy, and Cartesian philosophy resulted in his being excluded from the Sephardic Jewish community of Amsterdam (1656), after which he sought a living in Haarlem as a grinder and polisher of lenses. In 1660 he moved to Leyden and began to correspond with Oldenburg, Huygens, and Boyle, but in 1663 he went to Voorburg

near The Hague and finally to his native Amsterdam, where he died at the comparatively young age of 44 (21 Feb. 1677). Spinoza declined the chair of philosophy at Heidelberg offered to him by Elector Charles Louis of the Palatinate, preferring independence and solitude. He wrote on many subjects: theology, pure philosophy, and political theory. All but his *Tractatus Theologica-Politicus* (1670) were published after his death, and that work was banned by the civil authorities (1674), by which time he was assailed as a thorough-going atheist. He shared with Hobbes a belief in the need to find a rational explanation of the universe, the great importance attached to power and their pessimistic view of human nature. In the *Tractatus Theologica-Politicus* he regarded direct democracy as the most natural form of government, but his unavailing protest against the murder of the De Witt brothers (1672) led to a modification of his political views, and his earlier belief that 'the true purpose of the state is liberty' gave way to 'the function of the state is purely and simply to guarantee peace and security, it follows that the best state is that . . . in which their [*ie,* men's] rights are inviolate' (*Tractatus Politicus,* his great unfinished work). His principal works of philosophy were the short treatise *De Intellectus Emendatione* and his *Ethica,* in which he expounded his fundamental pantheism and metaphysical determinism based on his development of Descartes's philosophy.   JHS

SPIRACH, BATTLE OF (Nov. 1703), victory of the French under Marshal Tallard over the allied force commanded by the Prince of Hesse-Cassel in the War of the Spanish Succession. The prince's efforts to relieve the besieged city of Landau on the upper Rhine failed, and after his inferior numbers were defeated by Tallard Landau fell to the French.

SPIRITUAL EXERCISES, course of meditations upon the life and death of Christ, devised by Ignatius Loyola. It was first printed in Rome in 1548 but had been substantially completed by 1543 and was the fruit of Loyola's religious experience at Manresa in 1522–3. The *Exercises* provided the means of leading the soul to sanctity and heroic resolve and as such became an instrument of immense spiritual power, as well as prolonging the medieval tradition that meditation should be an integral part of the devout life of both clerics and laymen, into the modern Catholic Church.

SPIRITUAL REGULATION (1721), long document drawn up by Prokopovich initiating Peter I's programme of Church reform in Russia and setting up the Holy Synod as the new governing body of the Russian Church.

SPITALFIELDS, district of London north of the Tower. Its name is derived from the fact that the land belonged to the hospital, or 'spital', of St Mary Without Bishopsgate, founded in 1197.

SPITHEAD MUTINY (1797) in Britain broke out among the sailors of the Channel fleet under Lord Bridport, lying at Spithead (April 1797). The identity of the leaders remains obscure, but their organization and discipline was unquestioned and they promised to put to sea if the enemy should appear. When the Admiralty agreed to the sailors' requests for better food, medical attention, and that wages should be increased from the rates established at the Restoration to 1s per day, the strike subsided. However, apparent delay brought a second outbreak on board the man-of-war the *London,* when Admiral Colpoys and his captain were confined by the men. Only a royal pardon distributed to each ship by Lord Howe and the passing of an Act of Parliament to raise wages brought an end to the mutiny (10 May).

SPLENDID ISOLATION, term applied to the British policy of diplomatic non-involvement in the 1890s. It was used by Viscount Goschen (1896), quoting from a speech of G. E. Forster in the Canadian parliament. While associated with Lord Salisbury, the aim of retaining a free hand for British diplomacy was traditional in the Victorian era, though international contacts in defence of national interests were always maintained. The increasing power of Germany, Japan, and the US and the competition for African colonies among European powers changed the situation. Salisbury opposed binding international commitments, but he was willing to co-operate with the powers of the Triple Alliance (1882) when mutual interests were involved. He resisted Joseph Chamberlain's advocacy of a German alliance (1898–1901), but Lansdowne and Grey, his successors in the post of foreign secretary from 1900, abandoned Splendid Isolation by forming the Triple Entente (1907).

SPLITTER, BATTLE OF (Jan. 1679), overwhelming defeat of the invading Swedish army under Field Marshal Horn by the Brandenberg army commanded by the elector Frederick William I, during the Dutch War. Horn was taken prisoner and the remnants of the Swedish army fled to Riga. Louis XIV, Sweden's ally, mediated the peace of St Germain, ceding a strip of Swedish Pomerania to Brandenburg (1679).

SPOILS SYSTEM, in the US, political practice whereby political loyalty was the prime qualification for appointment to public office. The term went into general use after a speech by US senator William L. Marcy of NY (1832) in which he declared that 'to the victors belong the spoils.' President Andrew Jackson, who believed in the principle of rotation of office, has been charged with introducing the system nationally, but he replaced no greater percentage of office-holders than some of his predecessors and wholesale removal of incumbents only came with the Whig accession to power in 1841. Thereafter the system became entrenched. A professional civil service began to be introduced after the Pendleton Act (1881) but the spoils system continued to be widely practised, and came to include manipulation of public office for private gain.

SPORTS, BOOK OF (1618) in England, declaration of James I in favour of certain sports which could be played after Sunday church services. It was the result of an attempt to suppress Sunday games in Somersetshire, and was based on a declaration issued to Lancashire magistrates in 1617 and extended to the whole country in 1618. It was read in every parish church, and aroused fierce opposition among some Puritans. It was reissued in 1663. John Milton accused the book of encouraging men to 'gaming, jigging, wassailing, and mixed dancing' (1641).

SPORTULA, Roman term originally meaning gifts in kind or money by patrons to their dependants. Later it meant the fees or perquisites exacted by officials for the transaction of business.

SPOTSWOOD, ALEXANDER (1676–1740), English soldier and governor of Virginia (1710–22), who encouraged settlers and led explorations westwards (1716).

SPOTSYLVANIA COURTHOUSE, BATTLE OF (10–12 May 1864), major engagement during the Wilderness campaign in the American Civil War. Union forces drove into VA but were checked with heavy losses near Fredericksburg by Lee's outnumbered Confederate forces.

SPOTTISWOODE, JOHN (1565–1639), Scottish churchman and chancellor, who was Abp of Glasgow and then of St Andrews. He took part in the coronation of Charles I at Holyrood (1633) and supported the efforts of both James VI and I and Charles I to secure episcopacy in Scotland. He sympathized with Charles's introduction of a new liturgy into Scotland, though he was not as closely identified with its drafting as were other Scottish bishops.

SPRECKELS, CLAUS (1828–1908), German-born San Francisco merchant and sugar refiner and founder of a sugar empire on Maui, Hawaii, who exercised influence there until 1886.

SPRING AND AUTUMN ANNALS (CH'UN-CH'IU), one of the Chinese classics, whose compilation was attributed to Confucius. This chronicle of the state of Lu covers the period 722–481 BC. It is couched in terse terms and had been interpreted as an attempt to formulate moral judgements on past actions for the guidance of contemporary rulers.

SPRUANCE, RAYMOND AMES (1886–), US sailor and diplomat in the Second World War, who led the Fifth Fleet in the invasion of the Gilbert and Marshall Islands (1944–5). He later served as US ambassador to the Philippines (1952–1955).

SPURIUS CASSIUS (d. 486 BC), negotiator of the first treaty between Rome and the Latins (493 BC), the *foedus Cassianum.* He became consul, and was killed for supporting the agitation of landless peasants.

SPURS, BATTLE OF THE (1513), English victory at Guinegate over a French force trying to raise the siege of Thérouanne. Thérouanne and Tournai were taken, and a 'perpetual peace' (1514) was sealed by the marriage of Henry VIII's sister, Mary, to Louis XII of France. The peace proved ineffective and war was resumed in 1521.

SQUADRISMO in Italy, policy and action of Italian Fascist squads organized for violence. Nationalist-inspired youths, ex-servicemen, and unemployed workers were organized (1920) in Trieste to attack Slovenes. They spread through Venezia-Giulia and Emilia, violently attacking socialist and Catholic institutions and individuals. They forcibly took over municipal councils, meeting with little governmental or socialist resistance, and were sometimes aided by local police and soldiers. In 1922 squads seized Fiume and Trentino. Their success, especially in strike-breaking, forced anti-socialist policies on Mussolini, but his continuing control of north-central Italian municipalities ensured his success in Oct. 1922. The squads, after being slowly disciplined and organized nationally, were incorporated (1923) into the Fascist Militia (MVSN). They lost independent power after a final wave of intimidation (1923–5). Local leaders (*ras*), *eg*, Arpinati, Balbo, Farinacci, and Grandi, remained powerful in Mussolini's government and party.

SQUADRONE, THE, in Scotland, group of politicians representing the Presbyterian country interest and loosely allied with the Whigs. They gained office in 1704 but were removed after the Capt. Green affair and their failure to settle the Hanoverian Succession in Scotland. After the Act of Union (1707) the Squadrone formed an independent interest, though they relied increasingly on the Whigs.

SQUARE DEAL, in the US, phrase characterizing the domestic policies of President Theodore Roosevelt, used by him in a 4th July speech in Springfield, IL, in 1903, and frequently thereafter. It expressed his concept of fair play between groups of interests and mutual obligation between classes. Inherent in the policies of the Square Deal was the role of the federal government as arbiter between conflicting social and economic forces and as guardian of the public welfare.

SQUATTERS in Australia. In early 19th-cent. Van Diemen's Land and in NSW 'squatting' meant landholding without legal tenure. It also implied anti-social, even criminal behaviour. As, however, the squatter in NSW was in fact by the 1820s and 1830s a man tending sheep or cattle outside the restricted areas of settlement and as the wool so produced became an increasingly important staple export, to be a 'squatter' became a mark of economic, social, and political distinction in Australia. With the mid-century growth of self-government and responsible government, control of the colony of NSW passed increasingly into the hands of the squatter-pastoralists who dominated its legislative councils. This fact produced its own reaction: under attack by smaller agricultural settlers and urban manufacturers and trade unionists, 'squatter' became an emotive term of Australian politico-social abuse, sometimes ideologically confused with 'capitalist' and 'reactionary' and giving rise to the derivative word 'squattocracy'—against which Liberal-Radicals and Labor politicians fought, jointly and severally, around the turn of the century.

SRI KSETRA, SARIKSHETRA, or THAREKHETTARA, old Prome, prehistoric capital of the Pyu Kings (c. 7th–8th cents AD). Remains of circular city walls and broad moats are traceable.

SRI LANKA FREEDOM PARTY in Ceylon, founded by S. Bandaranaike in 1951 when he broke away from the United National Party. It won the general elections of 1956 and July 1963. Its declared policy was to bring the Sinhalese language and the Buddhist religion to the foremost position in the country.

SRI VIJAYA, ancient Indonesian empire (c. 780–1275), its capital being in or near present Palembang (south Sumatra) and a secondary centre in Kedah (Malaya). For nearly five centuries Sri Vijaya controlled trade and shipping through the Straits of Malacca and the Sunda Straits, and dominated vast parts of Sumatra, the Malay peninsula (including the Kra isthmus), and western Java. The rapid rise of Sri Vijaya can be regarded as the culmination of a long tradition of seaborne trade along the east coast of Sumatra. In addition to its own important hinterland, this coast provided easy access to the Straits of Malacca and the Java Sea. The main factor that determined its success over its rivals must, however, have been the energy of its population.

A small number of inscriptions, dated AD 683–6, show some basic features of the empire: the use of Old Malay as the official language, the prevalence of Mahayana Buddhism, and the presence of a hierarchy of officials bound by oath to the king.

Throughout its history Sri Vijaya was in friendly relations with the Chinese, for whom Sri Vijaya was a power capable of maintaining some stability and security of shipping in South-East Asia. Its political and economic importance was matched by its cultural significance as a great centre of Buddhist scholarship which attracted famous Buddhist pilgrims.

Between the 9th and the 11th cents there was keen rivalry with Java, which led to intermittent warfare. In 1025, however, Sri Vijaya suffered a devastating raid by the South Indian Cholas. The main consequence of this was the establishment of a balance of power with Java, where a strong state had emerged under Airlangga. Sri Vijaya, though no longer as powerful as before, remained in control of shipping in the western part of the archipelago, whereas Javanese supremacy was gradually established in the eastern part.

This stability lasted for about two centuries. A Chinese account of 1225 shows Sri Vijaya as still a great power, although a few details may indicate the beginning of its decline. Important parts of the Malay peninsula had become independent by the middle of the 13th cent. and Sri Vijaya began to disintegrate not long afterwards and ceased to exist as an important state before c. 1275.

It is difficult for the historian to explain the causes of the decline of this once powerful empire. The expansion of Javanese influence in western Indonesia during the Singhasari period, the Thai expansion which ended Sri Vijayan influence on the peninsula, and the beginnings of Islam in north Sumatra, are no doubt important factors, although they do not explain what really happened. There may well have been internal factors, such as rebellions, about which we

have no information. It may also be significant that the decline of Sri Vijaya coincides chronologically with that of the Pagan empire in Burma, the Khmer empire in Cambodia, and the Polonnaruva kingdom in Ceylon. The latter half of the 13th cent. is apparently a period during which the old order in South-East Asia broke down.

O. W. Wolters, *Early Indonesian Commerce* (Cornell, 1967).
                                                                    JG de C

SS, in Germany, (initials for *Schutzstaffel*, began in 1925 as a small personal bodyguard for Hitler, selected from the Sturmabteilung (SA) and was led, after 1929, by Heinrich Himmler. It was still ultimately subordinate at that time to the SA command and remained relatively insignificant until the Röhm purge (June–July 1934), in which its members played a leading part. It then grew rapidly more important, some of its units being given military equipment and training, and increased its scope still further with Himmler's appointment to command of the police in 1936. Its many branches included the fully armed SS-Verfügungstruppe, which was at Hitler's personal disposal; the Totenkopfverbände, which was in charge of the concentration camps; and the SD (Sicherheitsdienst) which, under Heydrich, gradually extended its security operations to all aspects of German life and also to foreign espionage. The SS numbered 240,000 in 1939 and 900,000 by 1945, when it included the fully military Waffen-SS, based, after 1943, on conscription. It was one of the organizations of which membership alone was declared a criminal offence by the victorious allies after the Second World War (treaty of London, 8 Aug. 1945).

The SS was one of the most formidable of all totalitarian organizations, embodying Nazi racialism, anti-traditionalism, and—in its most extreme form—a determination to exterminate opposition. Its absolute subordination to the arbitrary will of the Führer ('Our honour is loyalty') undermined the foundation of law upon which the German state had traditionally been based. Like other Nazi organizations, its development depended to a large extent on personalities rather than on abstract policy and its activities ranged from the murder of Jews and political prisoners to cultural developments. It served to a considerable degree as a means of social advancement for middle-class lawyers, civil servants, and academics whose main interests lay elsewhere.   RJVL

SSU-MA CH'IEN (d. c. 90 BC), Chinese official and historian, who continued the work started by his father of compiling China's first major work of history the *Shih-chi* or Historical Records. The book, in 130 chapters, claims to cover the whole history of humanity until the reign in which the author lived, that of Han Wu-ti (*reg.* 141–87). However, most of the book concerns the Han period (206–c. 90). It is regarded as the first of the standard histories and its form was adapted in subsequent works. Ssu-ma Ch'ien was personally punished for his bold defence of an unsuccessful Han general.

SSU-MA KUANG (1018–86), Chinese official and historian of China, who expressed bitter opposition to the innovations suggested by Wang An-shih as a means of reforming Sung institutions and administrative practice. During a period of political eclipse he devoted himself to the production of a single comprehensive history of China for the period 403 BC–AD 959. With his team of collaborators he used the material found in the various parts of the standard histories and elsewhere to compile a strictly chronological account of events. His intention was to avoid the inconsistencies of those sources and their artificial, and somewhat misleading, division of periods simply according to dynastic rise and fall. The resulting work, the *Comprehensive Mirror for Aid in Government*, extends to 294 chapters and provides a far more clearly understood record of incidents than do the standard histories, where information relevant to a particular event is often dispersed among several chapters. The scholarship of the authors is demonstrated in a set of critical notes published with the work, giving reasons for their choice of one of several alternatives or their preference for one source as against another.

STADTHOLDER in the Netherlands, provincial official of the sovereign states of the Netherlands, who in Burgundian times had represented the absent sovereign ruler. In the era of the Dutch republic the incumbent of the stadtholderate of Holland, Zeeland, and most of the other provinces was invariably a Prince of Orange who therefore endowed the position with considerable status. The *stadtholder*'s executive functions were somewhat ambiguous, but included the right of electing urban magistrates, appointing several provincial officials, and granting pardons or remission of sentences.

STADTLOHN, BATTLE OF (Aug. 1623), imperialist victory under Tilly over the Protestant forces of Christian of Brunswick in the Thirty Years War. Christian fled to the Netherlands, leaving Tilly in undisputed control of Austria and Bohemia, and forcing Frederick of the Palatinate to sign an armistice with the emperor.

STAFFARDA, BATTLE OF (Aug. 1690), French victory over the Spanish and Savoyard troops of Victor Amadeus, fought by the abbey of Staffarda, south of Pinerolo in the War of the League of Augsburg. Catinat followed up his victory by taking Saluzzo and Susa.

STAFFORD, GRANVILLE LEVESON-GOWER, 1st Marquis of (1721–1803), British politician and a member of the 'Bloomsbury Gang'. He served as lord privy seal (1755–7), lord chamberlain of the household (1763–5), and lord president of the council (1767–79). He at first favoured severity against the American colonists, but resigned in protest against the continuance of the American War of Independence and the incompetence of Lord North. He refused to form an administration on the fall of Shelburne (1783), preferring to support and serve under the Younger Pitt as lord president of the council (1783) and lord privy seal (1784–94).

STAFFORD, SIR EDWARD WILLIAM (1819–1901), NZ politician who was three times prime minister. He entered parliament in 1855, and headed the first ministry to achieve much-needed executive stability (1856–61). He negotiated the 'Compact of 1856', regularizing the provinces' revenue, but further difficulties with them prompted him to introduce the New Provinces Act (1858). The ministry's policy in the Taranaki crisis (1859–60), at first popular, proved inconclusive, and led to his defeat (1861). He returned to office in 1865, and his political skill was demonstrated in the retention (with Grey's collaboration) of British troops at British expense while not disavowing 'self-reliance'. He fell from office in 1869 but was prime minister again in 1872.

STAHL, GEORG ERNST (1660–1734), German chemist, physician, and pupil of J. J. Becher, who popularized the concept of phlogiston which dominated 18th-cent. chemical thought. He also introduced the doctrine of vitalism in physiology, which he enunciated in *Theoria Medica Vera* (1707).

STAHLHELM (lit. 'steel helmet') in Germany, para-military organization founded in 1918 at Magdeburg by a group of ex-soldiers led by Capt. Franz Seldte. It became one of the most influential organizations of its kind in Weimar Germany, and had between 300,000 (1926) and 500,000 (1930) members. The Seldte wing, which was moderately nationalist, had good connections with the Deutsche Volkspartie (DVP) and its leader, Gustav Stresemann. However, by 1924 a radical faction under the leadership of Theodor Duesterberg had grown powerful enough to manœuvre the *Stahlhelm* into a position of violent anti-republicanism which jeopardized the protection hitherto offered by Stresemann. The *Stahlhelm* participated actively in the plebiscite against the Young Plan in 1929. In 1930 the Seldte wing made a short-lived

attempt to steer the *Stahlhelm* back on to a more moderate course of collaboration with President Hindenburg, its most prominent honorary member. But finally Duesterberg's policy of reckless opposition to the Brüning presidential government proved so persuasive that the *Stahlhelmers* were soon to be found among the organizers of the Harzburg Front (1931). In March 1932 Duesterberg was a presidential candidate, opposing both Hindenburg and Hitler. Paradoxically, the radical wing then became increasingly sceptical of the Nationalsozialistische Deutsche Arbeiterpartei (NSDAP) and its willingness to accept other anti-Republicans as equal partners, and on 30 Jan. 1933 Duesterberg acquiesced reluctantly in Seldte's entry into Hitler's cabinet. While Seldte collaborated faithfully, Duesterberg came to regret having approved a Nazi-led government and embarked on a course which, from Hitler's point of view, was obstructive. At the end of April 1933 Duesterberg was removed from his post as second *Bundesführer* (lit. 'league leader'). Seldte was now free to start liquidating the *Stahlhelm*, a protracted process which ended with the dissolution of the rump *Nationalsozialistischer Frontkampferbund* (lit. 'league of fighters in the National Socialist front') in Nov. 1935.   VRB

STAHREMBERG FAMILY, Austrian noble family, counts of the empire, who served the Habsburgs ably as soldiers, administrators, and diplomats. Count Ernst Rüdiger von Stahremberg (1638–1701), governor of the city of Vienna, distinguished himself in its defence against the Turkish besiegers (July–Sept. 1683) and afterwards became president of the Imperial War Council (*Hofkriegsrat*) until his death. His stepbrother, Count Thomas Gundaker Stahremberg (1663–1745), became president of the cabinet (*Hofkammer*) in succession to Count Salaburg at a critical point of the War of the Spanish Succession (1703) and served as a principal adviser to the Emperors Leopold, Joseph, Charles VI, and Archduchess Maria Theresa, in matters of defence and finance. Count Guido Stahremberg (1654–1737), a cousin of Ernst Rüdiger, was a capable soldier and rose to be field marshal and commander-in-chief of the Austrian forces in Spain (1709–13). He became the rival and personal enemy of Prince Eugène, under whom he had served against the Turks at Zenta (1697) and in Italy (1701–4).

STAIR, JOHN DALRYMPLE, 2nd Earl of (Scottish) (1673–1747), British soldier, politician, and diplomat. In a distinguished military career he served in the War of the League of Augsburg and the War of the Spanish Succession, obtaining high rank through the patronage of William III and Marlborough. Recalled from the war by the Tories (1711), he entered politics, sitting as a Scottish representative peer. He was prominent in making preparations for the accession of George I in Scotland. He began his diplomatic career as ambassador to Augustus II, elector of Saxony (1707). His most important office was as ambassador to Paris (1715). He maintained close relations with the regent Orléans, aiding Stanhope's system of alliances and securing the expulsion of the Pretender from France. On his recall (1720), he re-entered politics in opposition to Sir Robert Walpole, thereby losing many of his sinecures. He was later a field marshal (1742), served at Dettingen (1743), and commanded government forces during the Jacobite Rebellion (1745).

STAKHANOV MOVEMENT, in Russia, propaganda device used under Stalin to increase the output of workers and peasants. A coal miner, A. Stakhanov, was the prototype of a specially picked worker, given advantageous conditions, who achieved an exceptionally high output which was then taken as a standard or example for other workers. It then proved simpler to invent accounts of similar achievements and (as was revealed after Stalin's death) this practice was in fact adopted.

STALIN, JOSEPH VISSARIONOVICH (real name, Dzhugashvili) (1879–1953), Russian politician and dictator, who, in succession to Lenin, established the communist system of government, dominated the world communist movement, led the Soviet Union during the Second World War, and directed the extension of communist rule to eastern Europe.

He became (1899) an active revolutionary as a member of the Social Democratic Party. He was imprisoned in Batum (April 1902), then deported to Siberia, whence he escaped. While in prison he was elected to the executive committee of the Caucasus Federation of the Social Democratic Party. After his escape he joined the Bolshevik wing of the party. During the 1905 revolution he remained in the Caucasus, spreading Leninist doctrine and organizing revolutionary action. He met Lenin for the first time at the party conference at Tammerfors, Finland (1905). He attended the party conferences held in Stockholm (1906) and London (1907) and took issue with Lenin on agricultural policy, advocating the sharing of land amongst the peasants rather than Lenin's programme of nationalization. During this time he was commonly known by the pseudonym *Koba*, meaning 'the Indomitable' in the Turkish vernacular of Batum. He continued to organize illegal activities, particularly robberies which enriched the party funds. He became leader of the Bolsheviks in Baku, but was repeatedly arrested and exiled to Siberia. When the Bolsheviks finally split from the Mensheviks (1912) he was recruited by Lenin to the central committee of the Bolshevik Party. He became first editor of *Pravda* (1912) and began to use (from early 1913) the pseudonym *Stalin*, meaning 'Man of Steel'. He wrote *Marxism and the National Problem* (1913) in which he set out his own (and Lenin's) arguments in favour of self-determination for oppressed nations. After the abdication of the tsar (March 1917), he rallied to Lenin's side when the latter reached St Petersburg and urged the immediate capture of power; he organized Lenin's escape and was a dominant figure at the sixth party congress (July 1917).

After the success of the Bolshevik revolution Stalin was appointed Commissar for Nationalities (1917–23) and Commissar for the Worker-Peasant Inspectorate with supervisory functions over the whole of Soviet administration (1919–23). He proclaimed the independence of Finland in Helsinki (Nov. 1917) in accordance with his views in *Marxism and the National Question*, but thereafter maintained that the right to secede from Russia did not extend to non-Bolshevik governments. He ordered the invasion of Georgia (Feb. 1921) and the overthrow of the Menshevik government there. He played an important part in the direction of the Civil War, and developed an intense enmity with Trotsky as a result.

During this time he steadily increased his power within the Bolshevik Party, as one of five members of the Politbureau and the only liaison officer with the Orgbureau. The control which he built up was further increased by his nomination, with Lenin's support, to the post of general secretary to the central committee (April 1922). This was the only position he held until he took over the premiership (1940), the chairmanship of the state defence committee (1941), the ministry of defence, and the supreme command of the armed forces (1941). Lenin became increasingly offended by Stalin's rudeness and high-handedness, but his illness and death (Jan. 1924) enabled Stalin to consolidate his position.

Through the 1920s Stalin, by ruthless political manœuvring, rendered his rivals impotent. He first allied himself with Zinoviev and Kamenev against Trotsky. During this period he adopted the policy of 'socialism in one country', arguing, against Trotsky, that the communist revolution could be achieved in Russia without the necessity of socialist revolution in the rest of the world. He then (1925) joined forces with the right (Bukharin, Rykov, and Tomsky) against his former allies. Trotsky, Zinoviev, and Kamenev were expelled from the party (1927). Stalin's control was now complete, and extended over the world communist movement through the apparatus of the Comintern.

Stalin imposed his distinctive pattern on Soviet Russia. In the first five-year plan (1928–34) he carried through the forced collectivization of agriculture and directed the industrialization of the country, with particular emphasis on heavy industry, exploiting forced labour drawn from the land. The industrial growth of the Soviet Union in this period remains unsurpassed, but it was achieved at the cost of the collapse of agricultural production and vast human suffering. He directed purges of the party, starting from the pretext of the murder of Kirov (1934), for which Stalin himself, it was later said, was responsible. Through the purge nearly all the old Bolsheviks were removed, confessing to supposed crimes in a series of state trials. The purge was extensive enough to constitute a reign of terror in which the security organs came to dominate the party. This was accompanied by an increasingly rigid control of communist orthodoxy (which took on a nationalist tone in the face of the German threat) and the growth of a 'cult of personality', idolizing Stalin, which reached its fullest crescendo during and after the war.

When Germany attacked Russia (1941) Stalin took personal responsibility for the conduct of the war. He stayed in the Kremlin as the German armies advanced on Moscow and the government moved to Kuibyshev. He directed the movement of industry behind the Urals. As the war resulted in the formation of the 'Grand Alliance' he entered into close contact, by correspondence, with Roosevelt and Churchill. The latter he received in Moscow (Oct. 1944) while all three met at the wartime conferences of Teheran (Nov. 1943) and Yalta (Feb. 1945) and at Potsdam (July–Aug. 1945).

At the end of the war Stalin presided over the extension of Russian frontiers to correspond very closely with those of Tsarist Russia, and the establishment of communist rule in Eastern Europe. He enforced loyalty to himself and his own communist model, expelling Tito from the Cominform. In the last years of his life it appeared likely that a new purge was in preparation, distinguished by a strong element of anti-Semitism. Stalin also appeared to be preparing a reversal of foreign policy to escape from the constraints of the Cold War when he published the *Economic Problems of Communism* and summoned the nineteenth party congress (1952). Whatever his plans, they were cut short by his death.

J. V. Stalin, *Works* (Moscow, 1946).
I. Deutscher, *Stalin* (London, 1949).   WK

STALINGRAD, BATTLE OF (Aug. 1942–Jan. 1943), crushing German defeat on the Russian front in the Second World War. Hitler's strategic aims in 1942 were Leningrad, and the capture of the Caucasus oilfields. The northern portion of his Southern Army was ordered to take Stalingrad so as to provide protection for the thrust into the Caucasus, by blocking the Volga–Don bottleneck. In fact, as Russian resistance stiffened and Hitler began to invest increasing emotional capital in the need to seize the city, this strategically subsidiary battle began to take priority, thus baulking the almost successful attempts to conquer the oilfields and ensuring an even greater moral blow when Paulus's Sixth Army, attacking Stalingrad itself, was destroyed. The campaign had begun well enough with the armoured drive to the Volga, but once the German troops faced street fighting and attrition in the most adverse circumstances, from mid-Sept., the advantage began to pass to the Russians. The German general staff was well aware of the dangerous position as winter approached, since their long, exposed flank, linking Stalingrad and Voronezh, was only defended by Hungarian, Rumanian, and Italian forces. Hitler refused to retreat and gave the Russians full opportunity for a devastating counteroffensive, planned by Zhukov on 19–20 Nov. By 23 Nov. Paulus was cut off. A German attempt to break through to him failed because of Paulus's timidity in refusing to disobey Hitler's order to stay where he was, and the weakness of Manstein's relieving army. Early in Jan. the German forces in the Caucasus pulled back towards Rostov, and there was now no hope for the Sixth Army—Rokossovsky's final assault beginning on 10 Jan. crushed the frozen, starving

Germans and Paulus surrendered on 31 Jan. The total loss to the Wehrmacht was about 300,000 men killed or captured; but even more, it was a huge psychological blow—thus Stalingrad is often seen as the decisive turning point of the war.   KM

STAMBULISKI, ALEXANDER (1879–1923), Bulgarian politician, Agrarian leader, and chief of the reform administration after the First World War. He entered parliament (1908) and became party leader in 1911. He was arrested in 1915 for opposing Bulgaria's participation in the war. After Bulgaria's defeat, he and the Agrarian Party achieved power and formed the nucleus of the coalition of Oct. 1919. Stambuliski represented Bulgaria at the Paris Peace Conference and signed the treaty of Neuilly. He returned to Bulgaria and led his party in the 1920 elections, at which it won an overwhelming victory. The communists offered the only opposition and an agreement was reached between the two parties. The reform government redistributed the land to the peasantry, replaced military service with labour service, initiated judicial reforms, sought reconciliation with neighbouring states, and tried to curb the power of IMRO. But Stambuliski's authoritarian methods and the government's favouritism towards the peasants stimulated considerable opposition. IMRO was particularly incensed by the government's passivity towards Macedonia. The opposition combined in 1923 to overthrow the regime in a bloody coup in which Stambuliski himself was tortured to death.

STAMP ACT (1765), in Britain, levied a duty on all American colonial newspapers, pamphlets, commercial papers, cards, and dice in order to secure a colonial contribution to the increased cost of garrisoning the frontier, a task made urgent and expensive by Pontiac's Conspiracy (1763). It followed closely upon the Sugar Act (1764), a similar revenue measure, and was met with widespread and violent opposition from the colonies, who raised the issue of taxation without representation and entered into Non-Importation Agreements as a reprisal. London merchants led a movement for repeal of the Stamp Act in 1766, but the Declaratory Act, passed in 1766 by Rockingham's administration, affirmed the principle of such taxation.

STAMP ACT CONGRESS (1765) in America, a protest congress called by the MA house of representatives, which regarded the British Stamp Act (1765) as a threat to self-rule in the colonies. Nine colonies responded and 27 delegates met in New York (Oct. 1765). They protested to King George III and parliament against recent taxes on the ground that taxation without representation violated a basic British constitutional principle. They argued that they could be taxed only by their local assemblies, as distance precluded colonial representation in the British parliament. The Congress was a significant step in the development of the spirit and agencies of national unity.

STANDARD HISTORIES OF CHINA, sometimes termed dynastic histories. A total of some 26 historical compilations covers the history of China during the imperial period (221 BC–AD 1910). Beginning with the earliest, the *Shih-chi*, these works were at first compiled by individual scholars or officials, often working under the patronage of the government. But from the T'ang period onwards the work was entrusted to a commission appointed by the state, which was often superintended by a senior and highly respected statesman. Each one of the standard histories is, in principle, concerned with a single dynastic period, except for the *Shih-chi*. But while uniform coverage is not complete for the whole period, for some dynasties two standard histories were compiled. In undertaking responsibility for this work, governments were able to make use of historical records as a means of showing that they legitimately possessed the Mandate of Heaven and were authorized to govern China.

The form of these histories was first set in the *Shih-chi* and has been followed in principle by its successors. Terse imperial annals describe actions of the emperor or those in which he was concerned and may include the text of some imperial decrees. Sets of tables list the principal officeholders of state, members of the imperial house, and members of the nobility. Essays discuss topics such as state institutions, economics, law, state ceremonies, and religion; and biographies, which often extend to half the work, trace the careers, achievements and family relationships of officials, military leaders or other prominent persons; sometimes the texts of their more important submissions to the emperor are incorporated. The biographies also include chapters which concern the foreign peoples with whom the government had come into contact.

A long process of compilation based on a series of notes and records preceded the production of the Standard Histories, whose form gives some scope for biased treatment, *eg*, in the selection of subjects for the biographies, or in the inclusion or rejection of surviving reports made by officials. By convention, short notes of appreciation were appended at the end of the chapters, thereby allowing the compiler some room for criticism.

W. G. Beasley and E. G. Pulleyblank (ed.), *Historians of China and Japan* (Oxford, 1961).   ML

STANDING ARMY CONTROVERSY in England, between the executive, in the form of the king, and parliament in the 17th cent. over who was to control the army and whether there was to be one in peacetime. James I, Charles I, and Charles II hoped to fight a successful war and at the end to establish a permanent army. Their policies were bitterly unpopular in parliament, and the control of the army was one of the main causes of the Civil War. The Militia Act (1661) vested the control of the army in the king. The fear of a standing army under James II helped to cause the Revolution of 1688. The Bill of Rights (1689) stated that the keeping of a standing army in time of peace without the consent of parliament was unlawful. Parliamentary control was finally confirmed by the Mutiny Act (1689), which is re-enacted every year. The controversy continued into the 18th cent. and in 1718 William Shippen attacked standing armies as instruments of oppression.

STANDING BEAR (1829–1908), American Ponca Indian chief, who opposed the removal of his tribe from northern NB to Indian Territory (Jan. 1877). On a tour of the eastern US he told of his tribe's troubles and won attention and sympathy which resulted in a US Senate investigation (1880) that upheld his claim. He and his people were allowed to return to their old reservation.

STANDING CLOSER ASSOCIATION COMMITTEE, in the West Indies, organization established at Montego Bay, Jamaica (1947), to study the prospects of a British West Indian federation and to draw up a federal constitution. The subsequent report issued by the committee (1953) was placed before a second conference (1956) and accepted with some modifications. The West Indian Federation was formed in 1958. It excluded British Guiana and British Honduras, which had rejected the conference's reports. The Federation collapsed in 1962.

STANDISH, MILES (c. 1584–1656), English soldier, who accompanied the Pilgrim Fathers (1620) to America, where he dealt with the Indians and supervised the building of a fort. As agent for the Plymouth Colony he negotiated loans and property rights in England (1625) and jointly with John Alden founded the town of Duxbury, MA. (1637).

STANFORD, LELAND (1824–93), US lawyer, businessman, politician, and railroad promoter, who established himself as a merchant and served as governor of CA (1861–3). As president of the Central Pacific Railroad (1861–93) he was both energetic and successful in securing public land grants and loans to finance construction. He served in the US Senate (1885–93), and was also president of the Southern Pacific Railroad (1885–90). In 1885 he endowed Leland Stanford University, CA, as a memorial to his son.

STANG, FREDERICK (1808–84), Norwegian politician who headed a ministry in the years 1861–80, assuming the title of 'prime minister' in 1873 when the new King of Sweden and Norway, Oscar II, accepted this Norwegian claim to a further expression of national independence.

STANHOPE, JAMES STANHOPE, 1st Earl (1673–1721), British soldier, diplomat, and politician. He served in Spain during the War of the Spanish Succession, being present at the capture of Barcelona (1705), Madrid (1706), and Port Mahon (1706). He was largely responsible for the campaign of 1710 with the victories at Almenara and Saragossa and the disaster at Brihuega, where he was captured. After returning from Spain he devoted himself to Whig politics, in particular the safeguarding of the Hanoverian Succession. On the accession of George I he became secretary of state for the southern department (1714–16). He was one of the few Englishmen to advocate European involvement and for this reason was in high favour with the German court. Thus with the split in the Whig party (1717) and the fall of Townshend and Walpole, Stanhope (with Sunderland) rose to lead the ministry, becoming first lord of the treasury and chancellor of the exchequer (1717–18), and secretary of state for the northern department (1716–17, 1718–21).

His foreign policy was based on the belief that the peace of Utrecht (1719) was a failure and he aimed to restore British prestige and end the diplomatic isolation of the previous Tory ministry. By building up a system of alliances he hoped to gain continental recognition of the Protestant succession and deprive the Jacobites of foreign support. In addition, he wished to enforce the wider policy of collective security to ensure peace and stability in Europe and allow the great powers to make an economic recovery after the wars of Louis XIV. Thus he negotiated the Triple Alliance (1717) and the Quadruple Alliance (1718). It is probable that he saw his system of collective security as a temporary solution for the economic needs of Europe and not as a semi-permanent system of peace and reconstruction, as envisaged by Sir Robert Walpole. He was willing to enforce European stability by a limited war if necessary. In two areas in particular, the Baltic and the Mediterranean, he used British naval strength to maintain a balance of power and prevent the escalation of war. In the Baltic, though he was careful to support the Hanoverian ambitions of George I, he managed to patch up differences between Prussia and Hanover and attempted, unsuccessfully, to preserve some balance between Russia and Sweden. Similarly, in the Mediterranean, he used British naval supremacy to crush the ambitions of Alberoni and enforce a status quo between Spain and Austria.

In his domestic policy he was a champion of one-party government to assure a Whig supremacy. Thus he supported the Septennial Act (1716) and the Peerage Bill (1719) to assure the dominance of the existing ministry. However, he did pursue a liberal religious policy resulting in the repeal of the Occasional Conformity and Schism acts and, but for the Church opposition, he would have supported the measures to restore civil liberties to dissenters. He had little involvement in the scheme to liquidate the national debt which resulted in the South Sea Bubble, nor was he involved financially. While defending the government's policy over this crisis in the House of Lords he suffered a stroke and died.

B. Williams, *Stanhope: A Study in Eighteenth-century War and Diplomacy* (Oxford, 1932).   AW

STANHOPE, CHARLES STANHOPE, 3rd Earl (1753–1816), British radical politician and scientist, who married Lady Hester Pitt, sister of William Pitt the Younger. He was active in the county petitioning movement (1780) and as MP for Chipping Wycombe (1780–6) he introduced proposals, some of which Pitt supported, for the better regulation of elections. After 1784 Stanhope grew increasingly critical of Pitt's policy and in 1786 was the chief critic of the Sinking Fund. He was a supporter of the French Revolution, to Edmund Burke's criticism of which he published an answer advocating recognition of the French republic (1794). For five years (1795–1800) he withdrew from parliament, claiming to be in a 'minority of one'.

In 1772 Stanhope became a Fellow of the Royal Society and took out patents for steam vessels in 1790 and 1807. He also invented a microscopic lens, a stereotyping process, and calculating machines, and planned a canal from Holsworthy, Devon, to the Bristol Channel.

STANISLAS AUGUSTUS PONIATOWSKI (1732–98), King of Poland (*reg.* 1764–96), was related on his mother's side to the Czartoryskis and was a lover of Catherine II of Russia. He was elected King of Poland through her influence, reigning throughout the period of its gradual dismemberment by Russia, Austria, and Prussia.

He travelled widely in Britain, France, Germany, and Russia before becoming king. He was an industrious intellectual and under his aegis Poland underwent a remarkable artistic and intellectual revival in the spirit of the Enlightenment. He inaugurated a programme of political reform and soon clashed with Catherine, who preferred to see the continuation of anarchy in Poland. With his encouragement the various *sejms* (diets) (1764–8, 1775) prepared the way for the Great *Sejm* of 1788–92, whose main achievement was the constitution of May 1791, for which Stanislas shared responsibility. The 11 articles of the new constitution laid down that government should consist of three powers, the legislature, the executive, and the judiciary, the executive power being vested in the king in council and the legislature or *Sejm* consisting of chambers of deputies and of senators, which were to be renewed every two years. The status of the *szlachta* (privileged class) and the municipalities were guaranteed, and the protection of the law was to be given to the peasantry. Steps were taken to centralize government and to deal more efficiently with finance, education, defence, and the bureaucratic administration.

Stanislas also tried to promote industry on his private estates and on Crown lands, but Polish economic development in general was hampered by lack of capital and disastrous commercial treaties with Prussia (1775), Russian hostility, and the steady losses of territory through the partitions of 1772 and 1793. The ignominious dismemberment of Poland which Stanislas was unable to prevent has marred his reputation, which suffered also from his ability to compromise and accept rather than fight inherent weaknesses. After the third and final partition arranged between Poland's three neighbours, Stanislas abdicated (1796), his act of abdication being formally recorded in the Convention of St Petersburg (1797).   MKS

STANISLAW OF SZECZEPANOW, Saint (1030–79), patron saint of Poland, who owed his canonization to an unhistorical legend of a saintly bishop murdered by an evil king, Boleslaw II. The historic Boleslaw was a leading supporter of Pope Gregory VII, while his opponents, including Bp Stanislaw of Cracow, relied on the support of the German emperor, Henry IV. Boleslaw executed the bishop for treasonable conspiracy but this provoked revolts and he had to flee from Poland in 1079. The movement for canonization of Stanislaw developed at Cracow in the 13th cent. and was satisfied by Innocent IV in 1253, while the real circumstances of the bishop's death were overlooked.

STANLEY, ARTHUR PENRHYN (1815–81), British theologian, who was a pupil of Thomas Arnold, headmaster of Rugby School, whose *Life and Correspondence* he published (1844). As professor of ecclesiastical history at Oxford and later as dean of Westminster, he led the broad church party within the Church of England and fostered good relations with other Christian denominations.

STANLEY, SIR HENRY MORTON (1841–1904), journalist, explorer, and politician, Welsh-born, but American by adoption, who visted Africa as a correspondent for the *New York Herald* during Napier's Ethiopian expedition. He was next commissioned by the same newspaper to find David Livingstone, then believed to be lost, and achieved fame by doing so. In 1873 he accompanied Wolseley's expedition against the Ashanti, continuing meanwhile to write copiously of his experiences. His most important mission was to the Congo. He made a hazardous trans-African journey (1874–7) from Bagamoyo on the coast of Tanzania to Boma at the mouth of the Congo, greatly adding to European knowledge of the region. On returning, he offered to open up the Congo commercially for Britain, but the offer was refused. However King Leopold II of Belgium availed himself of it and for five years employed Stanley to sign 'treaties' with Congo chiefs and to help in establishing the 'Congo Free State'. In 1892 he again became a British citizen, and later an MP (1895–1900). Of his many books, *Through the Dark Continent*, describing his journey through the Congo, is the best known.

STANLEY, SIR WILLIAM (d. 1495), English soldier, who was involved in the Wars of the Roses. At the battle of Bosworth (1485) his private army watched the fight from afar, then, seizing a chance to fall upon King Richard III's flank, did so and killed him, making Henry Tudor king. But Henry VII feared Stanley and in 1495 had him executed, ostensibly for corresponding with Yorkist exiles.

STANMORE, ARTHUR CHARLES HAMILTON-GORDON, 1st Baron (1829–1912), British politician and colonial servant, who joined the colonial service in 1858 and became successively governor of New Brunswick (1861–6), Trinidad (1866–70), Mauritius (1870–4), Fiji (1874–80), New Zealand (1880–2), and Ceylon (1883–90). He fostered indigenous values, notably in Fiji.

STANSFELD, SIR JAMES (1820–98), British politician who sat in parliament (1859–95) and who advocated Italian unification. His first presidency of the Local Government Board (1871–4) secured some sanitary legislation. After 1874 his rare combination of moral idealism and practical political sense enabled him to broaden the recruitment of Josephine Butler's unpopular movement against the Contagious Diseases Acts and to tackle the doctors on their own medical and statistical ground. His management of the 1877–82 parliamentary enquiry ensured the repeal of the acts in 1886, when he again briefly became president of the Local Government Board.

STANTON, EDWIN McMASTER (1814–69), US lawyer and politician, who became US attorney-general in President Buchanan's cabinet (Dec. 1860). As Lincoln's secretary of war (1862–5) he was an efficient and honest administrator, but his arrogance and small regard for individuals made him widely unpopular. He supported radical policies towards the South after the Civil War, and his dismissal from office in defiance of the Tenure of Office Act (1867) led to the attempt to impeach Johnson, on whose acquittal (1868) Stanton resigned. President Grant appointed him to the US Supreme Court (1869) but he died before taking his seat.

STANTON, ELIZABETH CADY (1815–1902), US campaigner for women's rights. She married Henry B. Stanton (1805–87) in 1840 and insisted that the word 'obey' be omitted from the service. With Lucretia Mott she organized the Seneca Falls convention (1848) that issued a declaration of women's rights, and after 1851 was associated with Susan B. Anthony's campaigns for female suffrage. She was first president of the National Woman Suffrage Association (1869) and president of the National American Woman Suffrage Association that resulted from the merger of two competing national organizations in 1890.

STAPLE OF WOOL. From 1294 onwards attempts were made by medieval English kings to control the vital wool export by regulating the towns at which English raw wool could be marketed. This was a useful diplomatic counter in dealings with foreign powers and, at first, the staple migrated between various towns of the Netherlands and northern France. The conquest of Calais in 1347, which was repopulated with Englishmen, led to a fairly permanent establishment of the staple there from 1363 onwards. The company of wool exporters who controlled it were able to preserve thereby a monopoly control over the trade and administered the customs on wool. In return they financed the defence of Calais and advanced loans to the Crown. This arrangement ended only with the capture of Calais by France in 1558.

STAPLETON, WILLIAM (d. 1686), English colonial official, who was governor-in-chief of the British Leeward Islands in the West Indies, where he protected British interests against buccaneers and European enemies.

STAR CHAMBER, COURT OF, in England, kings' council sitting as a court and inheriting the old jurisdictional authority which the council exercised on the king's behalf. It possibly took its name from the stars depicted on the ceiling of the main room at Westminster in which it met. Its origins are not clear, but by the 1530s it had become a separate court. The privy council and the Star Chamber were two aspects of essentially the same body of men, and after 1540 these aspects were embodied in distinct institutions. Contrary to popular belief, there was no connection between the Star Chamber and the body created by the confusingly named 'Pro Camera Stellata' Act (1487). The Star Chamber Court rested on no statute, but derived from the immemorial authority of the king's council to receive petitions and grievances. Under Henry VII it heard cases between parties and acted as the king's state tribunal, suppressing violence and keeping great men in order. It virtually lapsed on Henry's death, and it was probably Wolsey who revived its authority. It only became a distinct court after Wolsey's fall and in 1540 it acquired its own clerical organization; it was, however, at all times the council sitting as a court. Long before the Stuarts the membership consisted simply of the privy council and the two chief justices.

The court met only in term time and usually for two days a week. It continued to use conciliar procedures: cases began upon petition and the accused, being summoned by writ of subpoena, had to answer on oath. There was no jury and proceedings were in English. Punishments were arbitrary, including imprisonment, fines, the pillory, whipping, branding, mutilation, but not death. The court did useful work in enforcing law where other courts were subject to corruption, and it was relatively speedy, flexible, and complete in its work. Consequently throughout the 16th cent. and until the Civil War it was very popular with litigants. Sir Edward Coke described it as 'the most honourable court (our parliament excepted) that is in the Christian world'.

There were no new developments under the Stuarts, and though it retained its popularity in some quarters the Star Chamber became increasingly unpopular amongst some leading sections of society. Its employment by Charles I to enforce unpopular policies, particularly in ecclesiastical matters, made it increasingly hated by the parliamentary and Puritan opposition to Charles's government. In the 1630s it meted out severe and unpopular punishments to such people as Lilburn and Prynne, and it became increasingly besmirched by its association with the Laudian hierarchy. In the absence of parliament it was used by the government to enforce its proclamations, particularly those concerning fiscal and social policies. Its comparative success in enforcing a centralized economic policy ensured its unpopularity with the landed classes, especially when it became involved in ship money. In 1640 John Pym accused the Star Chamber of becoming 'a court of revenue'. As a consequence it fell foul of the Long Parliament and was abolished in 1641. It was not re-established at the Restoration in 1660.

G. R. Elton, *The Tudor Constitution* (Cambridge, 1962).
J. P. Kenyon, *The Stuart Constitution* (Cambridge, 1966).

CJ

'STAR SPANGLED BANNER', US national anthem. Composed by Francis Scott Key to the tune of the popular drinking song 'To Anacreon in Heaven', it was written during the British bombardment of Fort McHenry, Baltimore (13–14 Sept. 1814), during the War of 1812. Although quickly established as a patriotic song, it was not officially adopted by Congress as the national anthem until 1931. The name is also applied to the US national flag, the Stars and Stripes.

STARHEMBERG, ERNST RÜDIGER VON (1889–1956), Austrian nationalist politician, who served in the First World War and later with the *Freikorps*. He was involved in the rise of Nazism in Germany and in both the Kapp putsch (1921) and the Munich putsch (1923), but broke with the Nazis soon afterwards. Returning to Austria, he became active in the *Heimwehr*, a militant nationalist organization with fascist leanings, of which he became the leader in 1930, thereby splitting the organization into his own pro-German wing and a pro-Italian group associated with the Christian Social Party. The bloc failed however to win support in the ensuing elections and in 1931 Starhemberg made secret appeals to Mussolini for arms and finance, in exchange for which the *Heimwehr* was committed to a pro-Italian policy. As the Austrian nationalist movement polarized more and more along German-Nazi and Italian-fascist lines, Starhemberg attached himself more closely to the Italian side, and as vice-chancellor (1934–6) pursued a pro-Mussolini policy against mounting Nazi influence in Austria. By 1936 Schuschnigg had ousted Starhemberg, whom he expelled from his government. The *Heimwehr* was banned and Starhemberg's political career was thus brought to an end. He left Austria and did not return until after the Second World War.

STARK, JOHN (1728–1822), American frontiersman, who served with Rogers' Rangers in the French and Indian War (1754–63) and during the American War of Independence. He defeated British forces at the battle of Bennington (1777).

STATE, THE. The word the 'State' in the sense in which it is normally understood today (1970) is generally said to have been first used by Machiavelli. Many of its features were developed by the monarchies of the 16th and later centuries. But it was only in 19th-cent. Europe, after the French Revolution, that the concept became central to political theory, and that the full range of the modern State's claims and responsibilities was established.

Authority which had been largely personal and acquired by inheritance was recognized as being an attribute of an abstraction called the 'State'; and even though monarchy continued until 1918 and even later, to be the normal form of government in Europe, the monarch's own powers were those conferred upon him by law in virtue of his position as 'head of State'. His subjects were better described as citizens, since, like those of republics, their duties were also prescribed by the laws of the particular State to which they belonged.

The distinctive privileges and duties hitherto attributed to particular classes or groups within society disappeared; all were subject to taxation to meet the financial needs of the State, and in nearly all European States compulsory military service became the normal thing. During the 19th cent. the State took upon itself increasing responsibilities for the health and material and moral welfare of its citizens, most obviously in laws governing the conditions of labour, in the provision of education, and in the setting up of systems of social insurance. Even where a degree of autonomy was retained by the churches, the State established through its own legislation the demarcation lines between secular and spiritual authority.

The range of services provided by the State, and the demand for efficient and unbiased administration, led to the development out of earlier beginnings of civil services or bureaucracies, entrance to which depended increasingly upon objective tests of merit rather than prescriptive right. The recruitment of diplomatic and of naval and military officers was affected more slowly by the same general tendency towards professionalization, and the elimination of aristocratic privilege. In the administration of justice the lay element, as represented, *eg*, by the English justice of the peace, played a less important role by comparison with the professional judiciary.

The development of the State in these respects had two major political consequences. The importance to the citizen of the matters now dealt with by the State reinforced the demand for a representative element in the governmental system; and by 1914 in nearly all European countries, as well as in the US, an elected legislature played an important role; in many countries the effective Executive itself became dependent upon a majority in the legislature, and thus ultimately upon the electorate. In order to provide an ideological basis for obedience to the State's demands in place of the older ties of personal loyalty, emphasis was placed upon the relationship between each State and the nation of which it was held to be the political embodiment; the national flag, the national anthem, and other symbolic devices were used to enhance the impressiveness of State occasions. It became common in political discourse to talk of the 'nation-state' or even to use 'state' and 'nation' indifferently, as in a phrase like 'international law'.

Where the State was, for historical reasons, the political expression of a multi-national conglomeration, as in the Austrian or Russian empires, the sentiment of nationality worked against the State, which could at best only be identified with the largest or most powerful of the nations concerned. The demand that all States should be nation-states and that it was only the nation that gave legitimacy to the State gave rise to the explosive doctrine of national self-determination, the main source of conflict, and of the reshaping of the map of Europe between the end of the French Revolution and the end of the Second World War.

The legal doctrine of sovereignty upon which the State based its claims upon its own citizens made it difficult to envisage any superior system of obligation, so that the contacts between citizens of different States and the relations between nations were more fully subordinated to the requirements of the State than in previous periods when the structure of authority had been looser and more multifarious.

The identification of the State with the status quo meant that its capture or overthrow was an essential precondition of any major and immediate change in the distribution of wealth or social advantages, and this produced the Marxist interpretation of the State as the organ of the possessing classes only, rather than of the entire nation. But until the Tsarist Russian empire crumbled under the impact of military defeat the modern State proved capable of holding its own in the face of any force except that of nationalism.

H. J. Laski, *The State in Theory and Practice* (London, 1935).
A. D. Lindsay, *The Modern Democratic State*, vol. 1 (only volume published) (London, 1943).

MBEL

STATE MONOPOLIES in China. Control of the iron and salt industries was taken over by the Chinese governments from private hands *c.* 120 BC, and thereafter officials were responsible for manufacture and distribution. The monopolies have not been imposed regularly and their form has been far from constant. At times the production of alcoholic spirits or tea was subject to state monopoly. In the latter part of the T'ang period the Salt Commission rose to be one of the principal financial organs of state, raising revenue through the sale of salt to merchants, who then distributed it, at a profit, to the public. A more sophisticated system embodying the issue of licences was operated in the Ming and Ch'ing periods.

STATE SECURITY in Russia, system in the Soviet Union which has undergone some structural change, and many changes of name since the Bolshevik Revolution. It was first called the Cheka (1917) then renamed State Political Administration or GPU (1922) or OGPU (1924). It became the People's Commissariat of Internal Affairs, NKVD (1934), which was then divided into two agencies, one the NKVD and the other the People's Commissariat of State Security, NKGB (1943). When the 'commissariats' were all renamed 'ministries' these became MVD and MGB (1946). They were reunited (1953) and then separated again, the title MVD remaining and its fellow agency being the Committee of State Security or KGB (1954). The MVD was then replaced (1960) by agencies of the same name in each of the republics (1960); they were renamed Ministries of Protection of Public Order, MOOP (1962). They were once more centralized and a USSR ministry established under the same name (1966) for two years when it once more became the MVD (1968). The KGB meanwhile (since 1954) had remained unchanged.

The functions of intelligence and counter-intelligence, surveillance, detention, and punishment have thus been carried out by a network of organizations grouped under a single or dual department. In addition these organizations have carried out industrial operations in the employment of forced labour, although this diminished after Stalin's death. In the later period of Stalin's rule the security agencies became more powerful than the Communist Party and were controlled only by Stalin and his immediate assistants—a state of affairs condemned by Krushchev in his secret speech (1956). After that point the security agencies were demoted. While retaining great prestige and privilege, they were no longer all-powerful.

R. Slusser and S. Wolin, *The Soviet Secret Police* (New York, 1957).
F. C. Barghoorn, 'The Security Police' in *Interest Groups in Soviet Politics* (ed. H. G. Skilling and F. Griffiths) (Princeton, 1970).   WK

STATES GENERAL of the Netherlands, central organ and most important federal institution of the united provinces of the Netherlands, a body descended from the Burgundian institution. It was not a sovereign body, for sovereignty lay with the estates of the seven provinces of Holland, Zeeland, Gelderland, Utrecht, Friesland, Overyssel, and Groningen, who sent a delegation to the states general, meeting at The Hague daily, including Sundays, for two or three hours. Unanimity was necessary for a decision committing all the members of the states general. Acting as the representative of the union, the states also had the important duties of conducting foreign policy and defence, deciding on federal taxation and nominating the captain-general and admiral-general of the union, though these offices were usually held by the Orange family. At the revolution of 1795 it was replaced by a representative body of the people with a personal voting system, although the name 'states general' was applied to a new representative institution of two chambers established by the constitution of 1814.

STATES REORGANIZATION COMMISSION (1953–5) in India, appointed to report on the question of reorganizing the states of India on linguistic lines. It recommended a considerable rationalization of the 27 states which then existed, and the creation of two new states—Mysore and Kerala—

on a linguistic basis. However, it recommended against the division of Bombay into Marathi- and Gujarati-speaking states and the division of the Punjab between Hindi and Punjabi speakers. These recommendations were carried out in the States Reorganization Act (1956), but there was considerable discontent in both Bombay and the Punjab, and eventually Bombay was divided (1960) into Maharashtra and Gujarat, and Punjab and Haryana were formed (1966).

STATES RIGHTS in the US, political slogan and constitutional doctrine that evolved from colonial particularism and a 'strict construction' reading of the US constitution that upheld the powers of the states against those of the federal government. The classic constitutional basis of states' rights under the constitution is the 10th Amendment (1791): 'The powers not delegated to the US by the Constitution, nor prohibited by it to the States, are reserved to the States respectively, or to the people.' States' rights theories were expressed in the Kentucky and Virginia Resolves (1798), the Webster–Hayne debate (1830), and in Southern statements of state sovereignty prior to the Civil War. At some point, every major US political party has endorsed states' rights principles. In recent years, states' rights have been invoked by Southerners opposed to civil rights legislation. In the 1948 presidential election, Southern Democrats, protesting the party's strong civil rights platform, nominated Gov. J. Strom Thurmond of SC for the presidency on a States' Rights ('Dixiecrat') ticket. More generally, US parties, pressure groups, and sections frequently invoke states' rights maxims whenever their economic or material interests appear threatened.

STATILIUS TAURUS, T. (*fl.* 1st cent. BC), Roman soldier and consul (37, 26 BC), who fought for Octavian against Sextus Pompey (36), in Africa (35), Illyricum (34–33), at Actium (31), and in Spain (29). He was appointed prefect of Rome when Augustus visited the western provinces in 16.

STATIONERS' COMPANY in London, trade guild of printers and publishers in existence since 1403. It received its royal charter from Mary I (1557), partly for the better tracking down of heretical writings. It soon became, with government encouragement, the all-powerful organ which controlled the English book trade. Its part in censorship ended when the Licensing Act lapsed in 1695, while its control of the printing trade lapsed in 1785 when the London printers negotiated a wage agreement with a compositors' trade union.

STATUTE OF WESTMINSTER (1931) in Britain, legislative measure which gave legal recognition to the dominion parliaments within the British empire as self-governing entities owing an allegiance only to the Crown. The dominions were no longer bound by the colonial laws validity act (1865) which had rendered void laws repugnant to Westminster legislation. The movement towards the statute stemmed from the imperial conferences of 1926 and 1930.

STATUTES in England. In origins a statute was a written text which had the effect of modifying or altering the unwritten common law and those whose authority derived primarily from its general acceptance (which is why Magna Carta is regarded as the earliest statute of the realm). Since the time of Edward I, a statute has in practice been an Act of Parliament and remains in force, even though obsolete, until repealed.

STATUTORY CIVIL SERVICE in India, attempt by Lytton's government (1879) to evade the increasing demand for further Indianization of the Indian civil service. The members of the new service were to be Indians of good family, nominated by the local governments and appointed on probation by the government of India. This failed to satisfy the aspirations of educated Indians; not only was the pay less than that of the Covenanted civil service, but members of the upper classes showed no eagerness to join. It was abolished in 1885.

STAUDINGER, HERMANN (1881–1965), German founder of polymer chemistry. His studies from the 1920s helped to provide a basis for the industrial developments in plastics and synthetic fibres, which occurred particularly during and subsequent to the Second World War.

STAUFFENBERG, KLAUS SCHENK VON (1907–44), German soldier, who was a leading member of the anti-Nazi resistance. He came from an aristocratic Catholic family and began his career in a cavalry regiment. Although at first he was swept along in the surge of nationalist enthusiasm after 1933, he rejected the brutality of Nazism. Having witnessed SS barbarism in Russia, he became active in the anti-Nazi resistance (1942). As a member of the Kreisau Circle, he came into contact with socialist opponents of Nazism and got a more practical insight into the nature of the political alternative to Hitler than many of his more conservative army colleagues. After being severely wounded in North Africa, he returned to the general staff in Sept. 1942, and from then on was closely linked with plans for killing Hitler. Being present with him at military conferences, he was ideally placed to attempt his assassination, and it was Stauffenberg who on 20 July 1944 planted the bomb in Hitler's conference room. Assuming that the attempt had succeeded, he returned to Berlin to take over the direction of the coup there. The same evening, after the collapse of the plot, he was summarily executed together with three other leaders.

STEAM ENGINE. The early 18th cent. steam engine, designed in Britain by Thomas Newcomen, was an atmospheric apparatus whose use involved a high waste of energy. It could be profitably used only where coal was very cheap, *ie*, in draining coal-mines. By developing a separate condenser, James Watt in the 1760s produced an engine four times as efficient, and later added a device for rotary motion. As a result, steam power became an economic form of energy for many industries. Improved technology in the 19th cent. made possible the further economy of high-pressure engines.

STEELE, SIR RICHARD (1672–1729), English journalist, politician, and dramatist who published, in conjunction with Joseph Addison, the *Tatler* (1709–11) and the *Spectator* (1711–12). Despite their brief duration (the *Spectator* enjoyed a brief revival in 1714) the influence of the papers was considerable and sought to establish new standards in literary taste and public attitudes. In 1713 Steele entered parliament and for the next 10 years his writings took on a strong political flavour. The last of his comedies, *The Conscious Lovers*, appeared in 1722.

STEELE, SIR SAMUEL BENFIELD (1849–1919), Canadian soldier and police official, who was a member of the Red river expedition (1870–1). As a sergeant-major in the North-West Mounted Police he travelled extensively in the west, setting up posts there (1873–5). He rose to be superintendent (1885) and during the North-West rebellion (1885) he formed Steele's Scouts and served in the army as a cavalry major. After the Klondike gold-rush, he became police commander in the Yukon and BC (1898), saw active service in South Africa (1901–6), and returned to Canada (1907) as a major-general in the Canadian army. He was inspector-general from 1914 to 1918.

STEEN, JAN (1626–79), Dutch painter, a native of Leyden and an innkeeper by trade, whose works showed his insight into his subjects, who were largely drawn from the lower-middle class in the Netherlands. His works include *The Music Lesson, The Christening Feast, Tavern Company*, and *The Doctor's Visit*.

STEFAN DUSHAN (d. 1355), Ruler of Serbia (*reg.* 1331–55), under whom medieval Serbia reached its greatest territorial limits; these included the former Byzantine territory of Albania, Epirus, Thessaly, and most of Macedonia. In 1345 Dushan assumed the title of tsar, this being the first step in an ambitious design to capture Constantinople and from there to rule a revived Greco-Serbian empire in place of the Byzantine empire, then rapidly declining; but this idea was frustrated by Dushan's sudden death. He is famous for his *Zokonik*, a comprehensive legal code, the first of its kind to be promulgated by a Slav ruler in the Balkans.

STEFAN NEMANYA (d. 1200), Grand *Zhupan* of Rascia (*reg.* 1169–96), the founder of the medieval Serbian state, which was ruled by his descendants until the late 14th cent. He united the Serbs of Rascia and Zeta under his rule and established his independence of the Byzantine empire, to which the Serbs had previously been nominally subject. In 1196 he abdicated and entered the monastery of Studenica, which he himself had founded. Later, he went to Mount Athos, and together with his son Sava founded there the Serbian monastery of Hilendar.

STEFFENS, JOSEPH LINCOLN (1866–1936), US journalist, author, and reformer. As managing editor of *McClure's Magazine* (1902–6), he helped to make it famous for 'muckraking' attacks on corruption in business and public life. His exposures of corruption in urban government were collected in *The Shame of the Cities* (1904), and *The Struggle for Self Government* (1906). He was a defender of the rights of labour, and was active in the defence of the alleged syndicalist dynamiter of the *Los Angeles Times* building (1911). His radical views were reinforced by visits to Mexico (1914, 1916) and to Russia (1917, 1919). Until the Great Depression, Steffens hoped for peaceful evolutionary progress in the US, but thereafter he believed that only revolution would be effective and that communism was 'inevitable'.

STEICHEN, EDWARD (1879–), US photographer who helped to develop photography as an art. He worked with Alfred Stieglitz, was head of the Photographic Division of the Army Air Service during the First World War, directed the Navy Photographic Institute during the Second World War, and was director of photography at the Museum of Modern Art (1947–62). His Family of Man exhibition (1955), a photographic portrayal of the human condition, was shown throughout the world.

STEIN, GERTRUDE (1874–1946), US writer, whose salon in Paris became a focus for American expatriate writers and artists after the First World War. In her work she experimented with form and language, and influenced a whole generation of writers including Sherwood Anderson, Ernest Hemingway, and F. Scott Fitzgerald. Her most enduring work is *Three Lives* (1909) and *The Autobiography of Alice B. Toklas* (1933).

STEIN, HEINRICH FRIEDRICH KARL VON (1757–1831), Prussian reformer of the nation's social, military, and administrative system, who entered Prussian service in 1780 and until 1804 was responsible for the Westphalian mines and (from 1787) the internal tax system. He then became minister of state for finance, manufactures, and trade. He was dismissed in 1807, but recalled 10 months later, after Tilsit, and introduced his chief reforms, the emancipation of the peasants and the abolition of restrictions on landownership (1807), the reform of municipal government (1808), and the modernization of the central administration (1808). Because an indiscreet letter of his was intercepted, he had to flee Napoleon's wrath (Dec. 1808) and remained in hiding for three years. In 1812 Tsar Alexander appointed him his adviser and he was subsequently put in charge of administering lands conquered from the French, which did not endear him to the Prussian king. He took part in the Vienna

Congress as a representative of the tsar and in opposition to Metternich. In retirement he founded (1819) a society to preserve the records of the German past which published the *Monumenta Germaniae*.

He was no democrat. His plans for reform were designed primarily for administrative efficiency, and secondly as a bulwark against revolution. He wanted to educate and strengthen the economy of the small landowner and burgher, but he left a franchise based on property ownership. He showed no interest in national unity. The fall of Stein, and the failure to complete his plans for reform, cannot therefore be blamed for the subsequent authoritarian nature of the Prussian state. On the other hand, his administrative reforms and the tradition of efficiency he established were in no small part responsible for the subsequent growth of the economic and administrative power of Prussia.

G. S. Ford, *Stein and the Era of Reform in Prussia* (London, 1922).
W. M. Simon, *The Failure of the Prussian Reform Movement, 1807–19* (New York, 1955). DMK

STEINBECK, JOHN ERNEST (1902–69), US novelist. In *The Pastures of Heaven* (1932), a collection of stories about the farming community of a small CA valley, he found materials and themes that were to characterize much of his later work. *The Grapes of Wrath* (1939), his most famous novel, tells the story of the Joads, a family of dispossessed OK dirt-farmers who move to CA in search of work; it won a Pulitzer Prize in 1940. His success continued with *Cannery Row* (1945), *The Pearl* (1947), and *East of Eden* (1952). In 1962 he received the Nobel Prize for Literature.

STEINKIRK, BATTLE OF (Aug. 1692), bitter engagement in the Netherlands during the War of the League of Augsburg between the allied force of English, Dutch, and German soldiers under William of Orange and the Prince of Waldeck and the French under Luxembourg. After several hours of heavy fighting the English daybreak attack on the French camp was repulsed, but William withdrew his army in good order.

STELLER, GEORG WILHELM (1709–46), German naturalist and explorer who accompanied Vitus Bering on his expedition to northern Asia (1737) and on his second voyage to the Alaskan coast (1741–2). He explored Kamchatka (1740–1, 1742–4) and wrote accounts of his travels and the fauna, including the species later known as Steller's sea cow and sea lion.

STENGEL, CHARLES DILLON (1890–), US baseball player and manager. After playing with several National League teams, he became one of the great major league managers of recent times with the Brooklyn Dodgers (1934–7), Boston Braves (1937–43), and most notably with the New York Yankees (1949–60), where he won ten league championships and seven World Series. He came out of retirement to manage the New York Mets (1962–5), and was elected to the Baseball Hall of Fame in 1966.

STEPHEN (1097–1154), King of England (*reg.* 1135–54), third son of Stephen, Count of Blois and Chartres, and of his wive, Adela, daughter of William the Conqueror, was brought up in the household of his uncle, King Henry I of England. A temporary illness prevented his sailing (Nov. 1120) with his cousin William, who was drowned in the White Ship. Henceforth he spent much time at the court of his uncle, Henry I.

In 1125 Stephen married Matilda of Boulogne, thus strengthening his position across the Channel. In that year his cousin Matilda, widow of the Emperor Henry V, returned to England as a serious contender for her father's succession. In 1127 and 1133 Stephen, possibly under pressure, headed the nobles swearing fealty to her as heir to the throne. On the death of Henry I (Dec. 1135) Stephen crossed from Wissant, was joined in allegiance by many lay and ecclesiastical magnates, and crowned in Westminster. Insecure on his throne, the new king soon became obliged to make many concessions which weakened his position.

In Sept. 1139 Matilda, with her half-brother Robert of Gloucester, landed in England and was treated chivalrously by Stephen; shortly afterwards the period of anarchy began. Stephen rarely followed up his opportunities and the Bristol–Gloucester–Wallingford areas fell to Matilda. The king himself was captured at Lincoln by Ranulf of Chester in 1141, to be released in the same year in exchange for Earl Robert, who had been captured at Winchester.

Gradually the king recovered nominal control, but great magnates such as Geoffrey de Mandeville ruled vast areas virtually unchallenged. In 1153 Henry, Matilda's son by her marriage to Geoffrey of Anjou, came to England and won obvious support. The death of Stephen's son, Eustace, made the king lose heart and seek a truce: Stephen, by the treaty of Wallingford (Nov. 1153), should remain king for life, and be succeeded by Henry. In Oct. 1154 the king died at Dover. Brave, generous, and affable, Stephen had rarely commanded the respect needed in a most complex situation, and his entire reign was threatened by insecurity. MEB

STEPHEN BATHORY, elected Prince of Transylvania (1571) and King of Poland (1575). A highly intelligent and cultured man, whose interest in humanism sprang from his education at Padua, he was also a gifted soldier and powerful monarch. Under his leadership (1576–86) Poland enjoyed both military glory and political prestige. Although an ardent Roman Catholic he showed remarkable tolerance, believing that the Tridentine reforms should be imposed by example and not by force. To divert Poland's energies from religious quarrels he embarked upon war against the traditional enemy, Muscovy. In 1578 he routed the forces of Ivan the Terrible at Wenden, and after four years of military success forced him to accept a humiliating truce (1582), ceding all non-Swedish Livonia to Poland. Muscovy's eclipse, accelerated by the death of Ivan in 1584, left Poland supreme in eastern Europe.

Meanwhile, Stephen became involved in a grandiose crusade against Turkey to enable Poland to unite with Hungary and Muscovy in a vast Eastern empire, but he died suddenly before it was launched.

STEPHEN II (*reg.* 752–7), Pope, in whose pontificate Rome was threatened by the Lombards. His appeal to the Byzantine emperor for help was rejected and Stephen appealed (753, 754, 756) to the Frankish king Pepin. This marked the end of papal recognition of the overlordship of Constantinople and the beginning of Frankish influence in Italy, turning into conquest in 774.

STEPHEN THE GREAT (*reg.* 1457–1504), Vaivoda of Moldavia, who waged a long struggle to preserve Moldavian independence against Hungary, Poland, and the Ottoman empire. His effort ultimately failed as the Ottomans first occupied the fortresses of Kilya on the Danube and Ak Kerman on the Dniester (1484) and subsequently asserted a general control over the principality (1503).

STEPHEN BOCSKAY (1557–1606), Vaivoda of Transylvania. Disliking the Habsburg policies designed to diminish the power of the Hungarian estates and the rights of the Hungarian Protestants, he made common cause with the Turks during the last years of the war of 1593–1606 between the Ottoman empire and Austria. In 1605 the estates of Transylvania elected him to be their vaivoda, a choice which the Ottoman Sultan Ahmed I hastened to approve. Bocskay, in June 1606, was able to negotiate with Austria, at Vienna, an agreement which ensured to the Hungarians their political and religious privileges and to himself a formal recognition as Vaivoda of Transylvania. This agreement was confirmed at the peace of Zsitvatorok in Nov. 1606. Bocskay died in Dec.

STEPHEN, JAMES (1758–1832), British lawyer and politician, who was a leading opponent of the slave trade. He practised law in the island of St Christopher's (1783–94), whence he sent information about the slave trade to William Wilberforce. He published *Slavery in the West India Colonies delineated* (1824–30), and lived to see the slave trade abolished, though not slavery itself.

STEPHENS, ALEXANDER HAMILTON (1812–83), US lawyer, planter, politician, and vice-president of the Confederate States of America (1861–5), who served in the US Congress as a Whig (1843–59). He supported the Compromise of 1850 and the Kansas–Nebraska Act (1854), and opposed secession, but accepted GA's decision to leave the Union. As Confederate vice-president, he became leader of the opposition to Jefferson Davis, whom he publicly accused of trying to establish a military dictatorship. He himself opposed such necessary war measures as conscription, impressment of supplies, and the suspension of *habeas corpus*. In 1865 Stephens attended the abortive peace conference at Hampton Roads, VA. He was elected to the US Senate (1866), but as a 'rebel' was prevented from taking his seat; he served later in the House of Representatives (1873–82) until his election as governor of GA. His *Constitutional View of the Late War Between the States* (1868, 1870) is a sensational but laborious justification of secession, based on theories of state sovereignty.

STEPHENS, ALFRED GEORGE (1865–1933), Australian literary critic and the first Australian of major stature in this field. His best work was done as a newspaper and magazine editor, especially while literary editor of the Sydney *Bulletin* (1896–1906).

STEPHENS, JOSEPH RAYNER (1805–79), British Chartist who was a Wesleyan minister from 1829, but was suspended (1834) for advocating disestablishment. Active in the factory movement, he was drawn into Chartism by his indignation at the new poor law. He never sympathized with the Chartists' political objectives, but his eloquent and extremist speeches caused him to be imprisoned (1839–40). He championed miners' trade unionism. With his remarkably detailed knowledge of Lancashire customs, personalities, and dialect, he lent weight and continuity in the North of England to the concept of Tory Radicalism from the 1830s to the 1870s.

STEPHENSON, ROBERT (1803–59), British pioneer railway engineer, who, with his father, developed the first effective locomotive, the *Rocket*. He became one of the great developers of the early railway system, and built the London and Birmingham line and other trunk lines, the Menai Straits bridge, and the Royal Border bridge at Berwick. He did a great deal to establish that the British railway system would be set up on the principle of using locomotives and adopting 'standard' gauge.

STEPINAC, Cardinal (1890–1960), conservative and nationalist Croatian Catholic leader, who before the Second World War was Abp of Zagreb. The proclamation of the independent Croatian state he called a 'splendid opportunity of furthering the Croat and Holy Catholic cause'. He never disassociated himself from the Ustase regime in Croatia. After the war he was brought to trial on charges of collaborating with the Germans and supporting the Pavelić regime, and sentenced to 15 years' imprisonment. He was released in 1951, stripped of his ecclesiastical rank, and exiled to his native village. In 1952 Pope Pius XII caused a major conflict with the Yugoslav government by elevating Stepinac to the rank of cardinal. Marshal Tito of Yugoslavia at once severed relations with the Vatican. Six years after Stepinac's death, in 1966, relations were restored as part of a major agreement.

STERLING AREA came into existence (as the sterling bloc) when Britain left the gold standard (1931) and a large number of countries decided to stabilize their currencies in terms of sterling. During the Second World War the sterling area diminished in size, including only the British Commonwealth (but not Canada), Eire, Egypt, Sudan, Iraq, Jordan, and Iceland. From being a loose association it became one which the British and the Commonwealth used to the maximum advantage in the conduct of the war. At the end of the war Britain found itself in debt to members of the sterling area (and to outside countries with accounts in sterling)—India and Egypt holding the largest sterling balances, as a result of British spending in those countries for military purposes. US pressure and British optimism combined to make sterling convertible (July 1947) but the consequent drain on the reserves led to the abandonment of convertibility five weeks later. From Dec. 1958 convertibility was restored and the sterling area became increasingly less important, although sterling remained a reserve currency (a status which successive governments actively tried to maintain).

STERN GANG, British name for a Zionist underground military group, founded by Abraham Stern (1907–42) in 1940, when he left Irgun because of its decision to suspend anti-British activities during the war. The Stern Gang remained active until 1948 and is believed to have been responsible for the murders of Lord Moyne (1944) and Count Bernadotte (1948).

STETERBURG, BATTLE OF (Sept. 1553), imperial victory over the forces of Albert Alcibiades, margrave of Brandenburg-Culmbach during the closing stage of the German wars of the Emperor Charles V. A second defeat for the margrave in 1554 forced him to flee to France, but the emperor realized that military victories had not solved the religious division in Germany.

STETTIN, PEACE OF (1570), ended the Seven Years War between Denmark and Sweden by restoring the pre-war frontiers. Sweden, however, paid a large sum for the return of Älvsborg.

STETTINIUS, EDWARD REILLY (1900–49), US industrialist and politician, who resigned the chairmanship of United States Steel (1939) to become chairman of the War Resources Board (1939–40), lend-lease administrator (1941–3), and undersecretary of state (1943–4), before succeeding Cordell Hull as secretary of state (1944), He accompanied President F. D. Roosevelt to the Yalta Conference (1945), was retained as secretary for a short time by President Truman, and led the US delegation to the San Francisco Conference (1945). He served as US representative to the UN (1945–6).

STEVENS, BERTRAM (1872–1922), Australian literary and art critic, who was founder and editor (1916–22) of *Art in Australia*.

STEVENS, THADDEUS (1792–1868), US lawyer and politician, who was a leading advocate of 'radical Reconstruction' after the American Civil War. As an opponent of slavery, he led a campaign for Negro suffrage in PA (1826), served in the US House of Representatives as a 'free-soil' Whig (1849–53), and helped to organize the Republican Party in PA. He returned to Congress in 1859 and became chairman of the powerful Ways and Means Committee, the dominant member of the Joint Committee of Fifteen, which framed the 14th Amendment, and chaired the committee which prepared impeachment charges against President Andrew Johnson. Being in favour of a 'hard' Reconstruction policy, he demanded the punishment of former Confederates, 'a radical reorganization of Southern institutions, habits, and manners', and that the former Confederate states be treated as territories subject to Congressional jurisdiction. He also argued that once economically secure, the freedman must be given the vote. A consummate politician and formidable speaker, Stevens had only a small personal following in Congress, and his Reconstruction plans were frustrated. His will stipulated that he was to be buried in a cemetery where both whites and blacks might be interred. JW

STEVENS, WALLACE (1879–1955), US lawyer, businessman, and poet, who practised in New York, where his poetry began to appear. His works included 'Harmonium' (1923), 'Ideas of Order' (1935), 'The Man with the Blue Guitar' (1937), 'Notes Towards a Supreme Fiction' (1942), 'Esthétique du Mal' (1945), and 'Collected Poems' (1954). In *The Necessary Angel: essays on reality and the imagination* (1951) he expounded his ideas about the importance of poetry in the modern world. Although his poetry attracted little attention during his lifetime, its subsequent revaluation has established him as one of the greatest of modern American poets.

STEVENSON, ADLAI EWING (1900–65), US lawyer, politician, and diplomat, who was admitted to the IL bar (1926) and practised law in Chicago. During the Second World War he was an assistant to the secretary of the navy (1941–4), an adviser at the San Francisco conference (1945), and a US delegate to the United Nations (1946–7). He served as governor of IL (1949–53) and was twice nominated as presidential candidate of the Democratic Party (1952, 1956), but was heavily defeated on both occasions. In the troubled years of the early 1950s he sought to bring an element of reason to political debate. In 1961 President Kennedy appointed him as US ambassador to the United Nations, where, despite occasional misgivings about American policy, he remained until his death.

STEVIN, SIMON (1548–1620), Flemish mathematician and engineer, quartermaster of the northern states' army and adviser to Maurice of Nassau on matters of fortification and military engineering. He devised a type of decimal system and was one of the founders of 17th-cent. mechanics. Though a Catholic, he settled at the Protestant Leyden University and wrote in Dutch rather than his native language.

STEWART, ALEXANDER TURNEY (1803–1876), US merchant, who emigrated to the US and opened a lace shop in New York city (1823). By 1850 he had become the largest dry-goods merchant in the city, and in 1862 opened a new establishment at Broadway and Ninth Street in New York which was the largest retail store in the world.

STEWART, DOUGLAS (1913–), NZ poet, dramatist, and critic who settled in Australia in 1938. His books, connected mainly with Australian life, and usually romantic in attitude, included *The Dosser in Springtime* (1946), *The Birdsville Track* (1955), *Rutherford* (1962), *Ned Kelly* (1942), *The Fire on the Snow*, and *The Golden Lover* (1944).

STEWART, HAROLD FREDERICK (1916–), Australian poet who (1944) collaborated with James McAuley on the 'Ern Malley' poems, the best-known hoax in Australian literary history. His own work included *Phoenix Wings* (1948) and *Orpheus and Other Poems* (1956).

STEWART, WILLIAM DOWNIE (1878–1949), NZ politician, who was a member of Reform cabinets (1921–8). He was minister of finance during the Depression (1931–5). Rather than devalue NZ currency, he resigned.

STIEGLITZ, ALFRED (1864–1946), US photographer who made photography a fine art. He discovered the potential of the camera whilst studying in Germany (1881) and exploited it as a creative medium. A founder of the Photo-Secession movement (1902) and of Gallery 291 in New York (1905), his interest in the arts extended beyond photography. He helped to introduce modern French painting into the US,

and was a patron of young American artists such as John Marin and Georgia O'Keefe.

STIERNHIELM, GEORG (1598–1672), Swedish poet at the court of Queen Christina, who was the 'father of Swedish poetry'. His 'Hercules', a didactic poem in hexameters, was published in 1658. Stiernhielm also made important contributions to philology, history, mathematics, and philosophy.

STILICHO (*c.* 350–*c.* 408), Vandal, who was supreme commander of the armies of the Western Roman empire (395–408). He foiled the Visigothic invasion of Italy led by Alaric (401–2) and destroyed a great host, consisting of various Germanic tribes, which irrupted into Italy in 405. But in order to defend Italy he denuded the Rhine frontier of troops and in 406 Gaul was invaded by a combination of Germanic and Sarmatian tribes, who later on passed into Spain. These provinces could never be fully reconquered by the Romans and from Spain the Vandals were subsequently able to invade north-west Africa (429) and to conquer this granary of Italy. In 408 Stilicho was murdered through treachery by his jealous and suspicious master, the Emperor Honorius. His death left Italy defenceless and encouraged a fresh invasion by Alaric and his Visigoths. Bypassing the imperial court at Ravenna, they advanced on Rome, which they sacked, being the first foreign enemy to do so for nearly 800 years.

STILWELL, JOSEPH WARREN (1883–1946), US soldier, who served in China, where he became Chiang Kai-shek's chief of staff and commander of US forces in the China–Burma–India theatre (1942). He was recalled after conflict with Chiang (1944) and commanded the US 10th Army on Okinawa (1945).

STIMSON, HENRY LEWIS (1867–1950), US lawyer and politician, who began his public career as a US attorney (1906–9), was Republican candidate for the governorship of NY (1910), and secretary of war to President Taft (1911–13). In 1927 he was appointed special representative to Nicaragua, and then governor-general of the Philippines (1927–9); after which he became secretary of state to President Hoover (1929–33). Relations between himself, a New York patrician, and Hoover, a self-made Quaker engineer, were never close, and Stimson was unable to share Hoover's confidence in moral sanctions or disarmament. Faced with an international economic crisis and Japanese aggression in the Far East, he was prepared to go further than Hoover on the European debt question and towards collective security to contain Japan. His final period of office was as secretary of war in F. D. Roosevelt's cabinet, where he remained throughout the Second World War, during which he advised President Truman to use the atomic bomb. He retired a month after Japan's surrender (1945).

STIMSON DOCTRINE (1932), in the US; policy of non-recognition of gains made by force, invoked in response to Japanese aggression in Manchuria (1931). Although named after secretary of state Henry L. Stimson, the doctrine more nearly expressed the thinking of President Hoover. Its concept of a moral sanction against aggression was derived from a note to Japan by secretary Bryan in 1915, but it also represented a logical development from the moral-legalism of the Nine-Power treaty (1922) and the Kellogg–Briand pact (1928). Japanese success in establishing the puppet state of Manchukuo (1932) was a direct affront to the doctrine, and exposed the bankruptcy of US policy, while that policy's virtual endorsement by the League of Nations marked the downfall of collective security and gave encouragement to other potential aggressors.

STINNES, HUGO (1870–1924), German industrialist who built up a large complex of coal-mining, ship-owning, and other commercial interests, partly as a result of opportunities presented during and after the First World War. On 9 Oct. 1918 he was empowered by representatives of heavy industry to negotiate an agreement on post-war labour relations with the German trade unions. On 12 Nov.—when the German empire had already collapsed in revolution—the employers and the unions made an agreement under which unions were recognized as representing the interests of labour, factory committees and labour exchanges were to be set up and the employers accepted the eight-hour day, albeit with reservations. In return the employers were secured against union pressure for the socialization of industry at a time when the political power of labour seemed very strong. After the revolution Stinnes himself joined Stresemann's German People's Party (DVP) and was elected to the Reichstag in 1920. He was a violent opponent of the Versailles treaty and caused a sensation at the conference in Spa, July 1920, when he launched an outspoken attack on Allied policies. He was not, however, averse to negotiations with the French over reparations deliveries if these might benefit the German coal industry. The industrial boom during the inflation period until 1923 had seen him expand his industrial activities to an impressive extent. However, his death in April 1924 coincided with the deflation which followed the revaluation of the mark, and his successors had to dismantle a large part of his entrepreneurial empire.   AJN

STIRLING, SIR JAMES (1791–1865), British sailor who was the founder and first governor of WA, administering the colony (1829–39) following his voyage of investigation in 1827. He retained his interest in the colony's welfare after he returned to active duty in the royal navy.

STIRLING, BATTLE OF (Sept. 1297), in central Scotland. The Scots had been under English control since Edward I of England's campaign of 1296. In the king's absence abroad, the English army, under the Earl of Surrey, was defeated by a largely peasant force led by William Wallace.

STIRRUPS, item of equestrian equipment not essential for a horseman but giving a tremendous advantage to a cavalryman wearing heavy chain mail or other armour and fighting with a long lance, sword, and shield. It is not certain who introduced them into western Europe and when. They were apparently used by the Sarmatians and the Goths in southern Russia in the 3rd cent. AD. They appear to have been adopted by the Frankish cavalry by the 8th cent. Henceforth the heavily armoured cavalry, using stirrups, was to form an elite of European armies for most of the Middle Ages.

STOCKDALE v. HANSARD (1837) in Britain, one of the most important conflicts between the House of Commons and the courts of law on the subject of parliamentary privilege. The court ruled that the House of Commons could not, by resolution, extend privilege to a paper, published by its order, which contained defamatory matter, and the Commons rejected the court's ruling. The position was clarified by the Parliamentary Papers Publication Act, which gave privilege to all papers orderd to be printed by either house.

STOCKHOLM, capital of modern Sweden. The city grew up (*c.* 1251–5) around a castle founded by Birger Jarl, ruler of Sweden. It has a splendid natural harbour and it was founded to promote commerce with the German Hanseatic merchants. It became the chief German colony in Sweden and the centre for the shipment of Swedish copper, the chief Swedish export. It had a population of around 6000–7000 in 1500 and became the capital of the independent kingdom of Sweden re-established by the Vasa dynasty in 1523.

STOCKHOLM BLOOD BATH (1520), execution in the market place of about 90 persons, including two bishops and six members of the Council, by means of which the Danish King Christian II tried to safeguard his reconquest of Sweden. The victims were charged as heretics on account of the deposition of Abp Trolle, so that an amnesty given in Christian's name need not apply.

STOCKHOLM CONFERENCE (Sept. 1917), intended as the third conference of the Second International (following those at Zimmerwald, 1915, and Kienthal, 1916). It was organized in an atmosphere of crisis following the March revolution in Russia. On returning from St Petersburg French and British socialists (Longuet, Pressemane, and Henderson) successfully urged their reluctant parties that they should participate in the conference, but their governments refused them passports. As a result, only the German and Russian socialists, of the major powers, together with Swiss, Finns, Poles, Rumanians, Norwegians, Austrians, and Swedes attended. The failure of the conference served Lenin well in Russia, assisting the Bolsheviks' bid for power as the party that would end the First World War.

STOCKHOLM, TREATIES OF (1719–20), forming part of the settlement between Sweden and her enemies in the Great Northern War, were negotiated under the influence of the British minister, Carteret. By the treaty of Nov. 1719 Bremen and Verden were ceded to Hanover, and by that of Jan. 1720 Pomerania west of the Peene (including Stettin and the islands of Usedom and Wollin) was ceded to Prussia. In return, the Swedish government received some financial compensation, support for its dynastic settlement, and a British alliance to strengthen its hand in dealing with Denmark and Russia.

STOCKING FRAME, English invention of the late 16th cent., usually attributed to William Lee. It was the basis of the highly capitalized stocking industry which expanded rapidly from the mid-17th cent. around the Nottingham area to satisfy the domestic market.

STOCKMAR, CHRISTIAN FRIEDRICH, Baron von (1787–1863), German physician and adviser to Prince Leopold of Coburg, Queen Victoria's uncle, and tutor to Leopold's nephew Albert, whom she married. Stockmar was sent to London by Leopold in 1837. He remained there until 1841, when Albert himself became Victoria's chief adviser. His advice on personal matters was disinterested and sensible, but on constitutional matters it was coloured too much by his continental background, *eg*, he encouraged Victoria in Nov. 1852 to think that she had a right to prevent Palmerston from leading the House of Commons. Luckily she did not act on his advice. In 1848 Stockmar represented Coburg at the Diet of Frankfurt, where he supported the idea of Prussia as head of a united Germany.

STOCKPORT CORRESPONDING SOCIETY, in England. The Corresponding Society of London, an early radical group, had established affiliated associations in many of the provincial towns, notably at Stockport in Cheshire, by 1793. The Stockport society worked for manhood suffrage, annual parliaments, cheaper government, and a simpler legal system. The society was a forerunner of Chartism.

STOCKTON, ROBERT FIELD (1795–1866), US sailor and politician, who served in the War of 1812 and later in the Mediterranean. Whilst serving with the Pacific squadron at the outbreak of the war with Mexico (1846) he exceeded his instructions, captured Los Angeles, and proclaimed himself governor and commander-in-chief in CA. After a Mexican rebellion against US rule Stockton joined forces with Gen. Stephen W. Kearny and completed the subjugation of CA. He appointed John C. Fremont governor but this was contested by Kearny, who was made governor on instructions from Washington. Stockton resigned from the navy (1850) and served briefly as US senator from NJ (1851–3).

STODDARD, SOLOMON (1643–1729), American clergyman who, as pastor of Northampton, practised 'Stoddardianism', whereby the Lord's Supper was a 'converting ordinance'.

STOICS, school of philosophers founded (*c.* 300 BC) by Zeno of Citium and named after the Athenian Stoa Poikile (assembly hall) where he taught. They attained their greatest influence at Rome and through their contribution to Christian thought. Believing that virtue came from knowledge and that reason was nature's guiding principle, they aimed to live according to nature, ignoring pain and pleasure as irrelevant to happiness. Their passive and fatalistic outlook yielded to a more positive attitude with the spread of Roman dominion in the Mediterranean and Near East, for a government whose rule transcended national boundaries and engendered belief in universl natural law was compatible with stoic doctrine on the brotherhood of man, and the Roman sense of public duty coincided with the stoic ideals of personal virtue. The stoics' belief in social equality made hard for them the substitution of imperial for republican rule at Rome and their opposition to the Emperors Nero, Vespasian, and Domitian was voiced by men such as Paetus Thrasea and Helvidius Priscus, but benevolent emperors reconciled them to 'the rule of the best man' and the Emperor Marcus Aurelius (d. AD 180) was a stoic.

STOJADINOVIC, MILAN (1888–1961), Yugoslavian politician, who was appointed prime minister by Prince Paul in 1935. At first he pursued a conciliatory policy, releasing political prisoners and relaxing police pressure, but no attempt was made to resolve the lingering constitutional crisis. He governed through the Yugoslav Radical Union, which comprised Serbian, Muslim, and Slovene elements. In 1937 he sought to appease the Croats by negotiating a concordat with the Vatican, but the indifference of the Croatian leaders and the opposition of the Orthodox Serbians led him to drop the enterprise. His foreign policy was marked by a move away from traditional allies and alliances, particularly France and the Balkan and little ententes, and the forging of close relationships with Bulgaria, Italy, and Germany. Opposition to his regime mounted as he employed 'fascist' techniques in elections and increasingly harsh disciplinary measures against his opponents. He was replaced in 1939 by Cvetkovic. During the Second World War he was interned by Britain and her allies on Mauritius and later he emigrated to Argentina, where he died.

STOKES AFFAIR (1911), diplomatic crisis over an Iranian attempt to appoint a British officer to command the treasury gendarmerie. Russia opposed the appointment and Britain vetoed it.

STOLBOVA, PEACE OF (1617), ended the Russo-Swedish War which had developed out of Jacob de la Gardie's occupation of Moscow (1610) and the attempt to place a Swedish candidate upon the Russian throne. The first Romanov tsar, Michael, ceded Ingria and Kexholm, thus accepting Russia's exclusion from Baltic, though not from Arctic, waters.

STOLLHOFFEN, LINES OF (1707), Marshal Villars' brilliant disruption of the German Rhine defences in the War of the Spanish Succession, when he stormed and captured the imperialist lines commanded by the incompetent Marquis de Bayreuth (22 May 1707). The French captured 50 imperialist guns and overran south-west Germany.

STOLYPIN, PYOTR ARKADEYEVICH (1862–1911), Russian politician, governor of Grodno (1902) and Saratov (1903), minister of the interior (1906), and prime minister (1906–11). His policy combined firm repression of revolution with reform from above. After failure to get Octobrists to join the government, he dissolved the Duma, changed the electoral law (1907), and introduced reforms through emergency decree. His agrarian reforms broke up the commune (*mir*). Hereditary land tenure by heads of families was established

and peasants were encouraged to leave or dissolve the commune and establish smallholdings (*hutor*), enclosing their land and abolishing strips. Stolypin's aim was the establishment of a prosperous conservative Kulak class and agricultural improvement generally. He increased the resources available to peasant land-banks and encouraged education and migration to Siberia. Although the ultimate value of his policy is debatable, by 1914 it had had considerable success.

STONE, HARLAN FISKE (1872–1946), US lawyer, who was appointed US attorney-general by President Coolidge (1924), and then an associate justice of the US Supreme Court (1925). He was quickly identified as a liberal on social issues and dissented from the majority in a number of cases in which New Deal legislation, such as the Agricultural Adjustment Act (1933), was invalidated. He was a consistent advocate of judicial self-restraint in cases involving social legislation and was a strong defender of individual liberties, though he upheld restrictions imposed during the Second World War on US citizens of Japanese origin (1943). He served as chief justice (1941–6).

STONE, LOUIS (1871–1935), Australian novelist, whose novels *Jonah* (1911) and *Betty Wayside* (1915) were among the first to make a realistic study of urban life in Australia.

STONE CLASSICS, inscriptions of the Chinese classics on stone tablets. These were engraved to provide a permanent and orthodox text for scholars, who were able to make rubbings from the stone as their own personal copies. Material specimens still survive of the first project for this work (AD 175), which has been repeated on a number of occasions.

STONEHENGE in Wiltshire, circular grouping of large standing stones aligned on the midsummer sunrise and forming an integral part of a monument with a surrounding bank and ditch. The appearance of Stonehenge as we know it is the result of three phases of building and reconstruction, the last and most extensive of which, characterized by the unique use of stone lintels, may be assigned to the Wessex Culture of the Early Bronze Age. Specific technical refinements, such as the use of the mortice-and-tenon joint, point to the influence from the contemporary eastern Mediterranean that is already apparent in other features of the Wessex Culture. The association in popular belief between Stonehenge and the Druids has arisen out of a hypothesis first put forward in the 17th cent. AD, and has no basis in fact.

STORY, JOSEPH (1779–1845), US lawyer and politician, who served in the MA state legislature (1805–8, 1811) and in the US House of Representatives (1808–9). He was appointed by President Madison to the US Supreme Court (1811), and his decisions in admiralty and prize cases during the War of 1812 were notable expositions of international law. Though overshadowed by Chief Justice Marshall, he was an ardent nationalist. After Marshall's death he continued to uphold a broad construction of the constitution, and in cases such as *Prigg v. Pennsylvania* (1842) reasserted the pre-eminence and exclusiveness of federal power. His *Commentaries on the Constitution of the US* (1833) is a classic interpretation.

STOSS, VEIT (?1440–1553), Gothic sculptor, whose main works in wood were the altar-piece in the church of Our Lady in Cracow, his native town, and several altars and the great Rosary in the church of St Laurence in Nuremberg.

STOUGHTON, WILLIAM (1631–1701), American colonial official and lieutenant-governor of MA (1692–1701), who presided as chief justice and prosecutor over the Salem witchcraft trials (1692), where he insisted on the admission of 'spectral evidence'.

STOUT, SIR ROBERT (1844–1930), NZ lawyer and politician, who came from the Shetland Islands to Dunedin in

1863 and entered parliament in 1875. He opposed abolition of the provinces and advocated the formation of a Liberal Party. Later, in coalition with Vogel, ostensibly his political opponent (1884–7), Stout precariously held office as prime minister amid factional confusion. He advocated social reform, the labour movement, and that the Liberal Party should be more effective. He expected to succeed Ballance as Liberal prime minister, but Seddon thwarted him (1893). By espousing Prohibition, he threatened both Liberal unity and Seddon's leadership. Subsequently he accepted the chief justiceship from Seddon, which he held for the rest of his career (1899–1926).

STOWE, HARRIET ELIZABETH BEECHER (1811–96), US novelist, whom the Fugitive Slave Law (1850) inspired to write *Uncle Tom's Cabin* (1852), with the intention of showing 'the best side' of slavery 'and something faintly approaching the worst'. The book, which antagonized the South and stiffened anti-slavery sentiment in the North, is said to have caused Lincoln to call Mrs Stowe 'the little lady who made this great war'. Despite its melodrama and sentiment, the book is a finely drawn picture of the working, tensions, and dangers of slavery, and its popular image as a work of anti-Southern propaganda probably resulted from the many stage versions of it that were performed in the US. Mrs Stowe's visit to Britain in 1853 was a triumphal tour. She wrote *The Key to Uncle Tom's Cabin* (1853) in an attempt to refute accusations of prejudice. Her other works included the anti-slavery novel, *Dred: a tale of the great dismal swamp* (1856), and a number of New England tales, such as *Oldtown Folks* (1869).

STRACHAN, JOHN (1778–1867), Canadian clergyman and educationalist, who became the first Bp of Toronto (1839). He obtained a royal charter for the establishment of King's College (1827) and Trinity College (1851) in Canada.

STRACHEY, EVELYN JOHN (1901–63), British politician, who entered parliament as a Labour MP (1929). He resigned in 1931 to become one of the founders of Sir Oswald Mosley's New Party. Subsequently, he broke with Mosley, and identified himself with the pacifist left wing of the Labour Party. Despite this, he served in the RAF during the Second World War, and afterwards held office in Attlee's administration as minister of food (1946–50) and secretary of state for war (1950–1). He wrote several books on politics.

STRADIVARIUS, ANTONIO (c. 1644–1737), Italian maker of stringed instruments, born at Cremona, where he was apprenticed to Amati. He gradually discarded his master's style and after 1700 worked on original lines, making violins unsurpassed for tone and elegant workmanship. The 'Bossier' and the 'Alard' were his most famous models. His work was continued by his sons, Francesco (1671–1743) and Omobono (1679–1742).

STRAFFORD, THOMAS WENTWORTH, 1st Earl of (1593–1641), English politician, whose early career in parliament was one of opposition to the government of Charles I. In the 1625 parliament he opposed the granting of supplies until grievances were dealt with. By 1628 he had become the acknowledged leader of the Commons, and tried to promote a bill of rights to secure the liberties of the subject, but finally accepted Coke's expedient of a Petition of Right. Wentworth, however, did not join Eliot's attack on Buckingham, but tried to act as mediator between Crown and parliament. As a result, he was created a baron (July 1628) and was appointed president of the council of the north (Dec. 1628). His vigorous administration centred on his assertion of the council's jurisdiction as a prerogative court. At this time began his friendship with William Laud, Bp of London (Abp of Canterbury in 1633). Together they cor-

responded over the instituting of 'thorough' in the king's government.

In 1631 Wentworth was appointed lord deputy of Ireland, though he did not leave England until 1633. He took to Ireland the same vigorous determination to crush faction and rule for the king's benefit, and thus the state's, as he had pursued at York. Though successful in managing the Irish parliament, he aroused the opposition of the native Roman Catholics and of many Protestant settlers, particularly the Earl of Cork. His rule brought prosperity to Ireland, but was resented in England, particularly among the country opposition, who feared his authoritarian government would soon envelop England. Charles I, however, did not fully support Wentworth, often giving ear to his detractors at court. However, the disastrous First Bishops War forced Charles to seek Wentworth's advice, and he returned to England (Sept. 1639) to become one of the king's inner council. He persuaded Charles to summon parliaments in England and Ireland in order to obtain supplies. In Jan. 1640 he was created Earl of Strafford. He returned to Ireland and successfully managed the Irish parliament, but the Short Parliament in England (April–May 1640) proved unwilling to grant supplies and Strafford reluctantly agreed to its dissolution. He now came to the conclusion that Charles was entitled to use emergency powers to defend England. The unwillingness of the other councillors to follow such a vigorous policy meant that not only was the Second Bishops War a catastrophe, but that all the odium fell on Strafford, who became the most hated man in England, marked down for destruction by the country when the Long Parliament met (Nov. 1640). On 11 Nov. he was impeached and charged with attempting to subvert the fundamental laws of the kingdom. He defended himself so successfully at his trial that it had to be abandoned and the opposition resorted to an act of attainder. Charles, under pressure, signed Strafford's death warrant, and on 12 May 1641 he was executed on Tower Hill.

H. F. Kearney, *Strafford in Ireland* (Manchester, 1959).
C. V. Wedgwood, *Thomas Wentworth, first Earl of Strafford* (London, 1961).   CJ

STRAITS QUESTION, international diplomatic problems arising out of rights of passage through the straits of the Dardanelles and the Bosphorus between the Mediterranean and the Black Sea. The question first acquired significance following the treaty of Kuchuk-Kainardji (1774) which conceded (*inter alia*) freedom of navigation for Russia on the Black Sea and passage for merchant ships through the straits. Following the economic devlopment of the Ukraine, control of the straits, in one form or another, became a vital aim of Russian foreign policy, which other European powers, notably Britain, sought to frustrate. In 1833 the treaty of Unkiar Skelessi was thought (wrongly) to give Russia free passage through the straits. In his 1840–1 diplomacy Palmerston secured international recognition of the ancient Ottoman rule closing the straits to all foreign warships while the Ottoman empire was at peace (Straits Convention, 13 June 1841). The regime of the straits, as it was described, continued to be a source of international tension, especially in 1878, but it survived until 1918, when the Ottoman defeat and Russia's temporary eclipse allowed the Allies to establish control of the straits. The treaty of Sèvres (1920) proposed that they should be controlled by an international commission and should be opened to all vessels (including warships) of all nations. This proposal was modified by the Straits Convention (24 July 1923), which allowed free passage for all merchant vessels and for warships of under 10,000 tons in time of peace; it also established an International Straits Commission at Istanbul. This was abolished by the Montreux Convention (1936), which restored control of the straits to Turkey. These post-First World War changes in the regime of the straits were consistently opposed by Russia, who regarded them as a threat to the security of her Black Sea coast, and who made a determined effort in 1946 to induce Turkey to alter them.

C. Phillipson and L. N. Buxton, *The Question of the Bosphorus and the Dardanelles* (London, 1917).   MEY

STRAITS SETTLEMENTS, three British establishments, Penang, Malacca, and Singapore, in the Straits of Malacca. Penang was acquired from Kedah in 1786 (and the adjacent strip of mainland in 1800), Singapore from Riau-Johor in 1819, and Malacca from the Dutch in 1824. In 1826 the two latter were united with Penang, then the fourth Presidency of India, which was soon reduced to an East India Co. Residency under Bengal (1830).

Although Britain's strategic desire for a naval base east of the Bay of Bengal, and for control of the Malacca Straits, played a large part in the foundation of both Penang and Singapore, the major importance of the settlements in practice was commercial. Singapore in particular was ideally situated at the intersection of international as well as local South-East Asian trade routes. It quickly overshadowed the other two settlements, and in this century has been the leading South-East Asian port.

The Straits Settlements became a British Crown colony (1867) as a result of a lengthy agitation by Straits interests, rule from India being resented. One grievance was soon remedied when Britain began a policy of intervention in the peninsular Malay states (1874), which increased the commercial and political importance of the Straits Settlements. After the Pacific War (1941–5) Penang and Malacca were federated with Malaya, while Singapore, with its predominantly Chinese population, followed a separate path.   AJSR

STRALSUND, BATTLES OF (1628, 1715), Pomeranian port, besieged by Wallenstein's imperialist troops (July 1628) during the Thirty Years War. Although defended only by the inhabitants and a small force of Swedes and Scots, the siege had lasted 11 weeks before Wallenstein withdrew. It was besieged again in the Great Northern War by a Prusso-Danish force of 36,000 men under Frederick William III and Frederick IV. The attackers seized the nearby island of Rugen and Charles XII of Sweden was severely wounded when trying to retake it. He fled to Sweden (1715), leaving the garrison in Stralsund to surrender.

STRÄNGNÄS RIKSDAG (1523), electoral assembly by which Gustavus Vasa was chosen as King of Sweden. Similar national meetings to organize support had been held by Sten Sture the Younger.

STRASBOURG, strategic town of the upper Rhineland, situated at a crossroads of routes from France to central Europe and from Italy to the Netherlands. Originally a Celtic settlement, known to the Romans as Argentoratum, it was the scene of a great battle between the Emperor Julian and the Germanic tribes (357) resulting in a Roman victory. In the 5th cent. it became Frankish, and after the collapse of Charlemagne's empire became part of the East Frankish kingdom. The early medieval history of Strasbourg revolved around the struggle between the bishop and the citizens, which resulted in the latter's victory at the battle of Oberhausbergen (1262). Meanwhile, under Philip of Hohenstaufen, Duke of Swabia (*reg.* 1198–1208), it had become an imperial free city, a status it was to enjoy for over 500 years. Strasbourg played a distinctive part in the Reformation. A natural ally of the Swiss confederation in the later Middle Ages and a centre for the printing press, it readily accepted Protestantism under the leadership of Jacob Sturm von Sturmeck (1523) and until 1534 became a refuge for reformers of all sects, *eg,* Capito, Bucer, Schwenckfeld, Carlstadt, Servetus, and later, Calvin. In 1534 the city acceded to the Lutheranism of the Augsburg Confession and around 2000 non-Lutheran Protestants were driven out, though it joined the Schmalkaldic League and survived the collapse of that union (1546). In 1609 Strasbourg joined the Protestant Union, but it was recognized as neutral in the Thirty Years War, and remained part of the empire when Alsace was ceded to France (1648). In 1681 it was seized by Louis XIV with the support of its bishop, the pro-French Von Furstenburg, though its annexation did much to forge the anti-French League of Augsburg. The treaty of Ryswick (1697) confirmed its possession by France, however, and it remained French until 1870. At the French Revolution the privileges which it had enjoyed as a free town were abolished and the episcopal lands annexed. Strasbourg was the scene of bitter fighting in the Franco-Prussian War (1870–1) and after its garrison surrendered (28 Sept. 1870) it became German until the end of the First World War (1918), when it reverted to France. In 1944 the city suffered heavily from Allied bombing, but after its liberation from the Germans (23 Nov. 1944) once again became a part of France.   MKS

STRASSER, GREGOR (1892–1934), German politician, who joined the Nazi movement (1920) and after the Munich putsch virtually took over what remained of the party during Hitler's imprisonment (1924). As a Reichstag deputy and organizational leader of the NSDAP in north Germany, Strasser held a position only less powerful than Hitler's own, and by the middle of 1925 began to challenge his leadership in earnest. With his brother Otto, Goebbels, and other north German Nazis, Strasser represented the more radical 'socialist' wing of the movement, which was opposed to Hitler's opportunism, his disregard of policy and principle, and his autocratic leadership. Strasser attempted to introduce a counter-organization, with an alternative party programme which emphasized social reform and had a national-bolshevist flavour. At a meeting in 1926, however, his breakaway movement was rejected and Hitler's line overwhelmingly endorsed. Despite this setback, Strasser remained a powerful figure in the party; but although he was propaganda leader (1925–8) and organizational leader (1928–32), his disagreements with Hitler were never fully reconciled. The final break came in Dec. 1932, when he resigned all his party offices in protest against Hitler's refusal to form a coalition cabinet. He retired from the political field until 1934, when Hitler apparently tried to recover his support by offering him a ministry. Strasser rejected this overture; two weeks later, on 29 June, he was one of the victims of Hitler's purge of the Nazi opposition.   AJC

STRASSER, OTTO (1897–   ), German politician, who joined the NSDAP in 1925 and was active, with his brother Gregor, in the north German radical wing of the party. He edited the *Berliner Arbeitszeitung* and joined in the attempt to unseat Hitler and introduce a more radical note into the Nazi programme (1926). He ended his association with Hitler in 1930 over an industrial strike and shortly afterwards was driven from the party. He founded the Union of Revolutionary National Socialists or 'Black Front', which was involved in the abortive SA revolt in Berlin (1931). In 1933 he left Germany, thereby saving himself from almost certain death in the 1934 purge. He returned to Germany in 1955.

STRATEGIC AIR COMMAND (SAC) in the US, chief striking wing of the US air force, developed during the reorganization of armed services that followed the National Security Act (1947). It established headquarters at Offutt Air Force Base, NB, and deployed a massive striking power consisting of nuclear-armed bombers and ballistic missiles.

STRATEGOS, ancient Greek word for general, who was often a political as well as military leader. This was especially true at Athens, where a board of 10 of equal status elected annually by popular vote, normally one from each tribe, superseded in importance the nine archons from 487 BC. Requiring expertise in war, finance, and diplomacy, they were exempt from normal limitations on re-election, both Cimon and Pericles holding office continuously for long periods in 5th cent. A *strategos* was also the principal official of the Aetolian and Achaean Leagues and in the Hellenistic monarchies *strategoi* were regional controllers. The title was also accorded to the official at the head of the armed forces and of the local administration in each theme of the Byzantine empire.

STRATFORD, JOHN (d. 1348), Bp of Winchester (1323–33) and Abp of Canterbury (1333–48), who incurred Edward II's anger by accepting a papal appointment to Winchester, and played a part in Edward's deposition (1326–7). He obtained Edward III's favour and became his chief minister. The king gradually grew to distrust him, and in 1340 dismissed him, ostensibly for failing to finance the war against France.

STRATHCLYDE emerged as a British frontier state in the late Roman period (late 4th and early 5th cents) with a capital at Dumbarton. It was subject to attack from Picts, Irish Scots, and English Northumbrians, and was a very vulnerable state. Though British kings continued to rule on the Clyde until the early years of the 11th cent., Strathclyde became increasingly subject to Scottish pressure and finally came to form part of the Scottish kingdom.

STRATHCONA AND MOUNT ROYAL, DONALD ALEXANDER SMITH, Baron (1820–1914), Canadian businessman and politician, who joined the Hudson's Bay Co. (1838) and saw service in Quebec and Labrador. He rose from being chief trader (1852) to become a governor of the company (1899). He bought the St Paul, Minneapolis and Manitoba Railway, a vital link in western transportation, and personally rescued the Canadian Pacific Railway from ruin at the risk of his own fortune (1880). He was president of the Bank of Montreal (1882–7), served in the Canadian House of Commons (1871–80, 1887–96), and was Canadian high commissioner to London (1896–1913).

STRATTON, BATTLE OF (May 1643), Royalist victory over the parliamentary forces in Cornwall during the English Civil War. Sir Ralph Hopton's royalists attacked the parliamentary position at Stratton Hill and after severe fighting defeated Gen. Chudleigh's forces, capturing the general, 1700 men, 13 guns, the baggage, and the munitions.

STRAUSS, FRANZ JOSEPH (1915–   ), West German politician, who was a co-founder member of the executive (1946), general secretary (1949), and deputy chairman (1952) of the Christian Social Union. He was elected to the Bundestag in 1949, and in 1953 joined Adenauer's cabinet as minister for special tasks. In 1955 he became the minister responsible for atomic affairs, and in 1956 became minister of defence, in which capacity he built up the West German armed force into a first-rate military instrument. One of his most important achievements was the firm civilian control which he established over the army. During the *Spiegel* affair (1962), in which its publisher and several of its editors were arrested on dubious charges of treason, Strauss made some inconsistent statements in parliament, and the public outcry which followed led to his resignation and a reshuffling of the cabinet. He became an adamant critic of Erhard's government and especially of the foreign policy of Schröder, to whose conciliatory and flexible eastern policy he objected strongly. Arguing that US power had its limits, he expressed sympathy with many of De Gaulle's views, particularly for the idea of a more 'European' policy in world affairs. As a 'king-maker' in the election of Erhard's successor in 1966, Strauss was rewarded by Kiesinger with the finance portfolio, which he retained until 1969.

STREETON, SIR ARTHUR (1867–1943), Australian landscape painter whose high-key palette and handling of distance typified the so-called 'Heidelberg school'.

STREICHER, JULIUS (1885–1946), German National Socialist politician and radical anti-Semite, who became active in radical right-wing politics and journalism and in 1922 founded the Nuremberg branch of the NSDAP, thus opening Protestant North Bavaria to National Socialism. After imprisonment for his part in the Munich putsch (Nov. 1923), he entered the Bavarian Landtag and became Gauleiter of Mittelfranken (1924–39). During the Third Reich he played a prominent part in the campaign against the Jews but was disgraced after a scandal in 1939. After being captured by the Russians, he was executed at Nuremberg (16 Oct. 1946) for crimes against humanity.

STRELTSI, in Russia, semi-professional, semi-military class stationed in Moscow and the other main Russian towns from the reign of Ivan IV (*reg.* 1533–84) to that of Peter I (*reg.* 1689–1725), whose power was broken by the latter after their Moscow revolt of 1697.

STRESEMANN, GUSTAV (1878–1929), German politician who entered Ernst Bassermann's National Liberal Party which helped him to gain a Reichstag seat in the 1907 elections. Despite political setbacks, he soon became one of the party's front-benchers and during the First World War succeeded Bassermann as leader of the National Liberal Reichstag faction. He advocated far-reaching annexations and unlimited submarine warfare and collaborated (1917) with Ludendorff and extreme right-wing forces to bring about Chancellor Bethmann Hollweg's downfall. When the monarchy collapsed, Stresemann's long record of anti-democratic nationalism prevented him from joining the left-liberal DDP. He therefore founded the DVP, trying to make it a rallying point for the right-wing bourgeoisie which resented the 1918 revolutionary settlement. He continued to profess monarchism without abandoning his pragmatic approach to politics. He realized that, for economic reasons alone, Germany ultimately depended on international co-operation. With his approval, the DVP joined the Fehrenbach government in 1920 and in 1921 he was mentioned as a potential candidate for the chancellorship. He did not become chancellor until Aug. 1923, but during the three months in which he governed was confronted with the pernicious problems of galloping inflation, Ruhr occupation, separatism, and right-wing attempts to overthrow the republic. After his fall from power on 23 Nov. 1923, he rejoined the newly formed cabinet as foreign minister. In this position he achieved his greatest successes. In 1924 he negotiated the Dawes Plan, followed a year later by the Locarno Pact and Germany's entry into the League of Nations in 1926. His policy of reconciliation and fulfilment brought him the Nobel Peace Prize (together with Aristide Briand) and the reputation of a great European. But his private papers indicate that he remained what he had always been: a patriotic German. The 'Spirit of Locarno' and the solution of the reparations question were to him a means of securing for Germany the breathing space needed for recovery. His policies were to provide the country with a new power base from which to resume its struggle for 'equality'. There is little doubt that to Stresemann this meant regaining the Reich's hegemonial position in Europe. Most Germans misunderstood the long-range implications of his 'European' strategy, and right-wing agitation against his policies helped to create a political climate in which many Germans began to seek someone promising a short cut to the re-establishment of 'equality'.

H. L. Bretton, *Stresemann and the Revision of Versailles* (Stanford, 1953).
H. A. Turner, *Stresemann and the Politics of the Weimar Republic* (Princeton, 1963).   VRB

STRZELECKI, SIR PAUL EDMUND DE (1797–1873), Polish explorer and scientist, who left Poland in 1830, travelled widely, and visited Australia (1839–43). There he undertook a geological survey, exploring parts of Van Diemen's Land, Gippsland, and the Australian Alps, in which he named Mount Kosciusko. His *Physical Description of New South Wales and Van Diemen's Land* (1845) was published in London, where he was engaged in famine relief and encouraged immigration to Australia.

STRICKLAND, WALTER (d. *c.* 1657), English politician and diplomat, who was an agent of the Long Parliament to the states general of the United Provinces (1642–8, 1649–50). He was sent to negotiate an alliance with Holland in 1651, but failed. As an MP, he was a member of several of the Commonwealth and protectorate's councils of state. In 1657 he was summoned to Cromwell's House of Lords, and opposed the introduction of the Humble Petition and Advice.

STRICT CONSTRUCTION OF THE UNITED STATES CONSTITUTION, recurrent doctrine to limit the powers of the Federal government to those specifically laid down by the constitution of 1787 and its subsequent amendments. This interpretation has been appealed to throughout US history by minority and sectional groups who have believed their interests to be threatened by an uncircumscribed exercise of national power. Thus Thomas Jefferson, opposing incorporation of the Bank of the United States in 1791, argued that the bank bill was unconstitutional because it was not authorized by the enumerated powers of Congress, and because congressional power to 'make all laws necessary and proper for carrying into execution' its delegated powers covered laws which were indispensable and not merely convenient for that purpose. The strict construction doctrine was also used by defenders of slavery, who argued that the constitution nowhere empowered the Federal government to restrict or destroy that institution, and in more recent times it has been frequently appealed to by opponents of increasing federal intervention in the social and economic life of the nation.

STRIKES IN NEW ZEALAND. The first great industrial upheaval in NZ was the 1890 maritime strike, which spread from Australia. The newly formed Maritime Council (1889), conducting the strike to show trans-Tasman solidarity, was defeated by non-union labour, government action, and lack of public sympathy. NZ's most bitter industrial conflict, the 'Red' Federation of Labour, professedly syndicalist, sought to break the arbitration system in the Waihi (1912) and waterfront (1913) strikes, but employer-formed ('scab') unions and special police helped defeat the strikers. NZ's third labour–capital crisis was the waterfront strike (1951). A militant trades union congress attempted to wrench Labour out of the arbitration system, allegedly not controlling post-war inflation. Stringent emergency regulations, denounced as 'Fascist', greatly curbed strike action. The geographical division of labour between several centres, and the small scale of NZ industry underlay all three reverses.

STRODE, WILLIAM (1598–1645), English politician, who became a leader of the opposition to the rule of Charles I in 1629. He was imprisoned by Charles (1629–40), which made him bitter towards the government but a martyr to the opposition. He was the first to propose control by parliament of ministerial appointments and the militia (Nov. 1640). He played a leading part in the prosecutions of Strafford and Laud, and was one of the five members whom the king tried to arrest (3 Jan. 1642).

STRODE'S CASE (1512), in England, granted the House of Commons formal recognition that, as part of the high court of parliament, they were privileged against inferior courts. Richard Strode, a Devonshire MP, had promoted a bill hostile to the tin interests of his county, and had been imprisoned and fined by the Stannary Court. An act was passed declaring that action in parliament could not be made the basis of prosecution in other courts.

STROESSNER, ALFREDO (1913–), Paraguayan soldier and president, who assumed office in 1965 after an election in which he was the only candidate. He was 're-elected' several times. His regime, which was criticized as being dictatorial and repressive, led many Paraguayans to live in exile, especially in Argentina. Stroessner was (1954–70) strongly supported by the Paraguayan army and the so-called 'Colorado' or 'Red' Party. Though some economic progress was made in the 1960s, many felt that no serious attempt could be made to solve Paraguay's many problems while he remained in power.

STROGANOV, PAVEL ALEKSANDROVICH (1772–1817), Russian politician, and a member of Alexander I's Unofficial Committee. He was educated in France, where he visited Jacobin clubs. He returned to Russia convinced of the need to use autocratic powers to reform Russian society and improve the conditions of the peasantry.

STROGANOV FAMILY in Russia, wealthy family of Novgorodian extraction who became great merchant entrepreneurs trading in fish, grain, and furs, and large-scale industrialists producing salt, iron, potash, and tar. The family business centred on Solikamsk and Solvychegodsk. In the closing years of the 16th cent. they patronized the Cossack explorers of Siberia, *eg*, Yermak, and the school of icon painters.

STRONG, CHARLES (1844–1942), Australian theologian and social reformer, who was minister of Scots Church, Melbourne. He was deposed for heresy by the Presbyterian Church of Victoria (1883), became first minister of a free religious society, the Australian Church, and conducted his ministry from an impressive building erected in the heart of the city by his supporters in 1885. A trust to support the study of comparative religion, founded in 1957, honours his life and work.

STRONG, JOSIAH (1847–1916), US Congregational minister, who believed that the US had a mission to expand its influence throughout the world. He also expressed a belief in the ethnic superiority of American civilization, and the necessity for 'imperialism' in *Our Country* (1885) and *Expansion* (1900), books which had considerable contemporary impact. He founded The League for Social Service (1898), campaigned for the prevention of accidents, and is credited with coining the slogan 'Safety First'. His other works include *Religious Movements for Social Betterment* (1900) and *The Challenge of the City* (1907).

STROSSMAYER, JOSEPH GEORGE (1815–1905), Croatian Roman Catholic bishop and theologian, leader of the Pan-Slav movement in Austria-Hungary, and opponent of papal infallibility. His nationalist sympathies were particularly evident in his concern for Slavonic education and his opposition to Hungarian political dominance. He was one of the last European bishops to promulgate the decree of papal infallibility (1870).

STRUENSEE, JOHANN FRIEDRICH (1737–72), German-born Danish physician and political figure, who governed Denmark for nearly two years on the principles of enlightened despotism. While practising in Schleswig-Holstein he became court physician to the degenerate King Christian VII and the lover of his young queen, Caroline Matilda. Having gained an ascendancy over the Danish king, whose powers were absolute, he removed the principal officials and carried out sweeping reforms of the legal system, serfdom, the censorship, the administration of Norway, and much else. But his hasty methods, contempt for national feeling, and illicit relations with the queen enabled his enemies, headed by the queen dowager, to overthrow him and have him barbarously executed for high treason.

STRUGGLE OF THE ORDERS, term given to the internal conflict between patricians and plebeians in the first two centuries of the Roman republic (*c.* 500–287 BC). The roots of the conflict lay in political privilege (only patricians could attain magistracies or priesthoods), social exclusiveness (intermarriage being forbidden), and economic oppression. The plebeians' gradual victory is attributable to their organization into a separate corporation within the state. They established their own assembly (*concilium plebis*) which passed its own resolutions (*plebiscita*), kept its own records, and had its own officers (plebeian tribunes, plebeian aediles). When necessary a general strike (*secessio*) was organized to extort political or economic concessions during national crises.

The main stages were: (*a*) Secession in 494 (outcome uncertain); (*b*) *Lex Publilia* (471), by which plebeian assembly and two tribunes were recognized; (*c*) publication of the Twelve Tables and the Valerio–Horatian Laws (450–49), probably recognizing tribunes' sacrosanctity and those *plebiscita* approved by the Senate; (*d*) *Lex Canuleia* (445), permitting intermarriage; (*e*) Licinio–Sextian Laws (367), introducing economic palliatives and opening the consulship to plebeians; (*f*) *Leges Publiliae* (339), making one censor automatically plebeian, and strengthening the centuriate assembly; (*g*) *Lex Ogulnia* (300), opening priesthoods to plebeians; (*h*) *Lex Hortensia* (287), giving *plebiscita* the force of law. Henceforward the orders were increasingly close-knit, and patrician blood had a purely social cachet.   PGW

STRUVE, PYOTR BERNGARDOVICH (1870–1944), Russian economist and leading thinker among legal Marxists in the 1890s, who edited *Liberation* (*Osvobozhdenie*) (1902–5). As a member of the second Duma, he contributed to *Vekhi* symposium (1909) and opposed the Bolshevik revolution.

STRYDOM, JOHANNES GERHARDUS (1893–1958), South African politician and second prime minister of the nationalist government in South Africa (1954–8). He was an extreme upholder of white supremacy.

STUART, ARABELLA (1575–1615), next, after James Stuart (VI of Scotland), in succession to the English throne. Though her claim was slight, Arabella was English-born, and her supporters claimed common law forbade aliens to inherit English land. After a number of plots centred around her and her marriage to William Seymour, another claimant, Arabella was imprisoned.

STUART, SIR CHARLES (1753–1801), British soldier, who served in the American War of Independence and was appointed (1794) to the command of the military forces in the Mediterranean in the French Wars. He captured Corsica (1794) and commanded the army of defence in Portugal (1796–8). He later captured Minorca (1798) and made an expedition to Sicily (1799) to reorganize its defences against French invasion.

STUART, GILBERT (1755–1828), US portrait painter, who went to London, studied under Benjamin West (1777–82), and rapidly found acclaim in both London and Dublin. He painted the portraits of many famous Americans, including three studies from life of President George Washington.

STUART, JAMES (1713–88), British architect and interior decorator, popularly known as 'the Athenian'. With Nicholas Revett, he visited Athens (1751–3), where he measured and drew architectural remains. His book *The Antiquities of Athens* (1762) made him famous as a pioneer of classical archaeology as well as a major influence on 18th-cent. taste. He achieved some success in the Grecian style as an architect, his work finding important expression at Nuneham Mansion, Oxfordshire, where he designed interior mouldings and a classical temple in the garden.

STUART, JAMES EDWARD (THE OLD PRETENDER) (1688–1766), son of King James II and Mary of Modena, whose birth opened up the prospect of a British dynasty of Catholic Stuart monarchs, was the final threat to the religion and liberties of many Englishmen, and helped to provoke the Revolution of 1688. He was smuggled to France in Dec. 1688. The Old Pretender's claim to the throne was ignored by the Convention (1689), though for all Jacobites he became the rightful heir.

Recognized as King of England by Louis XIV (1702), he was used by England's enemies to embarrass her government for the next two decades. He led the attempted invasion of Scotland (1708), but was prevented from landing. He fought with the French army at Oudenarde (1708) and Malplaquet (1709), but was driven out of France by the terms of the treaty of Utrecht (1713).

James Edward's cause was an important factor in British politics in the last years of Anne's reign and he might have succeeded her but for his personal loyalty to Catholicism. He landed in Scotland during the Jacobite Rebellion (1715), but after six weeks travelled to Rome, where he remained for the rest of his life.

STUART, JAMES EWELL BROWN (1833–64), US soldier, who served in KS and, after accepting a Confederate commission (1861), rose to command the cavalry of the Army of northern VA (1862). After making a number of daring and brilliant raids behind the Union lines, he was mortally wounded during the Wilderness campaign (11 May 1864).

STUART, JOHN McDOUALL (1815–66), Australian explorer who joined the South Australian survey department (1838). He made four journeys (1858–62) from Adelaide, reaching the centre of Australia in 1860 and opening a route to Van Diemen's Gulf on the north coast in 1862.

STUART (or STEWART), HOUSE OF, royal line inheriting the throne of Scotland (1371) through Robert II, and the throne of England (1603) through James I of England and VI of Scotland. The family name derived from the office of High-Steward given in heredity to Walter Fitz-Alan by David I. Robert II, by his marriage to Marjorie, daughter of Robert Bruce, succeeded his uncle by marriage, David II, after the latter's death without male issue. The Stuarts gained the English throne through marriage, James VI being descended from James IV and Margaret Tudor, daughter of Henry VII.

The Stuart line in both countries came to an end with the death of Anne (1714) since the Jacobite line was excluded from the succession by parliamentary act. Subsequently, Jacobite rebellions (1715, 1745) upheld the Stuart cause against the Hanoverians, but by 1760 their bid had totally ended. Stuart claims to the throne were renounced by Cardinal Henry Stuart, grandson of James II and VII. Direct descendants of the Stuart line still exist.

STUDENT NON-VIOLENT COORDINATING COMMITTEE in the US, militant civil rights organization formed in 1960 by college students 'to build a social order of justice permeated by love'. It sent field workers into the South to stimulate voter registration and protest against segregated lunch-counters. It gradually became a more radical movement and advocated 'Black Power'.

STUKELEY, THOMAS (*c.* 1525–78), English adventurer, who served as a mercenary in the French army and under the Duke of Savoy, and from 1558 engaged in buccaneering. He surrendered and was pardoned by Queen Elizabeth I (1565). He then entered the service of Spain and commanded three galleys under Don John of Austria at the battle of Lepanto. He was killed while commanding the centre of the Portuguese army at the battle of Alcazar.

STUKELEY, WILLIAM (1687–1765), English antiquary and cofounder and first secretary of the Society of Antiquaries (1718). His publications included *Itinerarium Curiosum*

(1724) and *Stonehenge* (1740). He was especially interested in Druidism.

STURE, STEN (*c.* 1492–1520), Regent of Sweden and a champion of its independence from Denmark. He was the son of the regent, Svante Nilsson, whom he succeeded (1512), adopting the noble name of Sture to win supporters. By popular propaganda and devious manœuvres he acquired authority over the Council and the Church. He postponed a breach with Denmark as long as possible, and then repulsed two expeditions (1517, 1518) by which King Christian II sought to secure the Swedish throne. He was fatally wounded in a battle against a third Danish force.

STURE, SVANTE (1517–67), Swedish nobleman and son of Sten Sture. He enjoyed the special favour of Gustavus I, and King Eric XIV made him marshal of the realm (1560) and governor of Estonia (1562). He was, however, recalled from Estonia in disgrace (1564) and with others of his family was murdered in prison after being accused of treachery.

STURLA THORDARSON, name of two major Icelandic chieftains of the end of the republic. The earlier, Hvamm-Sturla (1116–83), was the first of the family of the Sturlungar to attain great power. His sons dominated Iceland for the half-century after his death. The second Sturla, his grandson (1214–84), was also a writer. He was the author of the most important parts of Sturlunga saga, the great history of the end of the Icelandic republic.

STURM, JACOB (1489–1553), German burgomaster and a leader of the reformation in Strasbourg, who advised the city council to join the Augsburg Confession in 1534. He took part in the Diet of Regensburg and had to sue for pardon for his city from the emperor after the defeat of the Schmalkaldic League at Mühlberg (1546).

STURM, JOHN (1507–89), German scholar and educationalist, who became the rector of the Protestant gymnasium or humanist academy at Strasbourg (1538). The academy's fame rests partly on its combination of classical proficiency and moral training of a Protestant sectarian form, and partly on its effect on education throughout Europe, *eg*, Calvin's foundation of the Geneva academy under Beza (1559) and probably the Jesuit colleges owed their constitutions to Sturm's ideas. In 1581 he was driven from Strasbourg by Lutheran intolerance but was ultimately allowed to return.

STURT, CHARLES (1795–1869), Australian soldier, explorer, and public servant, who, while exploring the lower Macquarie river, discovered the Darling, and in 1829 followed the Murrumbidgee and Murray rivers to Lake Alexandria, thus solving the question of the oceanic outlet of the Murray–Darling system. He overlanded cattle along the Murray to Adelaide in 1838 and subsequently held several positions in the SA public service. He led an expedition (1844–6) into central Australia which discovered Cooper's Creek and extensive deserts.

STURZO, LUIGI (1871–1959), Sicilian priest and politician, who secured the Vatican's permission in 1918 to launch a national Christian democrat party, Partito Popolare (1919). As the party's secretary he became its extra-parliamentary leader (1919–23). He moderated between extreme factions, but in 1922 he came to favour socialist collaboration against the fascist movement, and thus lost the support of the Vatican and the right wing of the party. This compelled him to resign and he eventually went into exile (1924–46).

STUYVESANT, PETER (*c.* 1592–1672), Dutch governor of the New Netherlands (1647), who had previously directed the Dutch West India Co's colony at Curaçao. His authoritarian rule failed to prevent the people of New Amsterdam from making a 'remonstrance' to the states general and achieving independent municipal government (1653). He surrendered the New Netherlands to the British (1664) and retired to his NY farm.

SU TUNG-P'O, literary title of Su Shih (1037–1101), Chinese official and man of letters, whose father, Su Hsün, and younger brother, Su Che, were also writers. He served in a variety of official posts both in the central government and the provinces. He was opposed to the reforms proposed and partly instituted by Wang An-shih and expressed systematic criticism in reports to the emperor. As a result, his career as an official suffered several setbacks and he spent long periods away from the cultural life of K'ai-feng, the capital city. While playing his part as a member of a Confucian-based society and civil service, he was subject to Buddhist influences, particularly those of Ch'an (Jap. Zen) Buddhism; and his descriptive accounts of the world of nature reveal his growing appreciation of Tao thought. Su Shih was an acknowledged master of the old-style prose, in which he set out to expound his political views logically and clearly, and to describe scenes and anecdotes vividly. As a poet he wrote with profusion and a complete mastery of form.

SUAREZ, FRANCISCO (1548–1617), Spanish Jesuit theologian and political philosopher, whose many works included the famous handbook of scholastic metaphysics, *Disputationis Metaphysicae*, the *Defensio Fidei*, attacking the Church of England, and the *De Legibus*, setting down the principles of natural and international law. He was the greatest figure in that revival of Thomist scholasticism which was a characteristic of the Catholic Reformation.

SUBANDRIO (1915–), Javanese diplomat and politician, who headed the London office of the revolutionary Indonesian republic (1947–9), and then became Indonesia's first ambassador to Britain. As foreign minister (1959–65) he played a key part in formulating Indonesia's radically anti-Western attitude during 'Guided Democracy', particularly its 'Confrontation' with Malaysia. He was first deputy prime minister (1963–5) and was widely regarded as Sukarno's probable successor, but the army's leaders disliked and feared him. He was imprisoned when Sukarno fell.

SUBASIĆ, IVAN (1892–1955), Yugoslav politician, who provided a link between the government-in-exile and the Partisans during the Second World War. He was ban of Croatia after the conclusion of the Sporazum and became (1944) prime minister of the government-in-exile. In exile he remained aloof from other political figures and expressed sympathy for the Partisans. Shortly after his appointment he had a series of meetings with Tito at which it was agreed that the two groups would co-operate and the people would decide the future form of government in Yugoslavia. In Nov. 1944 the two concluded an agreement providing for the establishment of a regency and the holding of a plebiscite. The regency was set up in March 1945 and Subasić became minister of foreign affairs in the provisional government. But he resigned later in the year in protest against the way in which elections were to be held, and retired from political life.

SUBLET DE NOYERS, FRANÇOIS (1588–1645), French administrator, who served under Richelieu in several capacities, particularly as secretary of state for war (1636–45).

SUBMARINE. Successful experiments with submersible craft date from the early 17th cent., but it was not until the late 19th cent. that technical skills were sufficiently far advanced to make possible the construction of a workable submarine. Among the early pioneers were the Dutchman Cornelius Drebbel (1620s) and the Americans David Bushnell (in the American War of Independence) and Robert Fulton (in the French Wars). A handpropelled submersible, the *Hunley*, sank the Federal corvette *Housatanic* in Charleston Harbor during the American Civil War. Out of the many experiments in the closing years of the 19th cent. there emerged a design by the American, J. P. Holland, which combined the characteristics of the submarine as it was to remain for much of the first half of the 20th cent.: powered by an internal combustion engine (originally petrol, later diesel) on the surface, and under water by electric motors run from storage batteries; fitted with a periscope to assist navigation; armed with torpedoes, and sometimes a gun for surface action. The US navy took delivery of a quantity of these boats in 1900, and the British admiralty ordered them for the royal navy in 1901. Though the design and construction of submarines improved immeasurably in the following years, they remained fundamentally the same, submersibles rather than true submarines, for they had to surface at regular intervals to recharge their batteries. It was not until 1944 that the Germans developed the schnorkel, which enabled the vessel to remain submerged while recharging its batteries. In 1954 the first true submarine was launched, the USS *Nautilus*, nuclear-propelled, of unlimited range, high under-water speed, and the ability to remain submerged for an indefinite time; the royal navy launched its first nuclear submarine, HMS *Dreadnought*, in 1960. During the 1960s the US and British navies introduced the nuclear missile-carrying Polaris submarines into service.

Submarines first made a major impact during the First World War, especially in the Germans' offensive against British and Allied merchant shipping; briefly in 1915 and again from 1917 they resorted to unrestricted submarine warfare in an attempt to blockade Britain, forcing the royal navy to divert more of its resources to anti-submarine warfare and to reintroduce convoys and escorts for merchant shipping. A similar pattern established itself in the Second World War: the German U-boat fleet comprised the main part of its navy and was employed in a determined attempt to cut British sea-borne communications in the long-drawn-out and fiercely contested battle of the Atlantic; British submarines were used against Italian shipping in the Mediterranean, and American submarine operations in the Pacific accounted for nearly 90 per cent of the Japanese merchant marine. They were also employed against warships, sometimes with spectacularly economical results, *eg*, the sinking of the aircraft carrier *Ark Royal* by U 81 in the Mediterranean in 1941.   NRB

SUBMISSION OF THE CLERGY (1532) in England, Convocation's surrender of the Church's legislative independence to the Crown. In 1530–1, threatened with the penalties of Praemunire, Convocation had paid a fine for receiving Wolsey as legate and acknowledged Henry VIII as their supreme head, 'so far as the law of Christ allows'. In 1532, in reply to the Commons' 'supplication against the ordinaries', Convocation agreed to make no new laws without the king's licence and to submit existing canons for his approval. This submission meant that the English clergy would be powerless to prevent a breach with Rome, and Sir Thomas More resigned as chancellor on the following day. The surrender was embodied in a statute (1534) which also transferred appeals in ecclesiastical suits from the archbishops' courts to the king in Chancery.

SUCCESSION, STATUTES OF (1534, 1536, 1543) in England, legislative measures which reflected the progress of King Henry VIII's marital inclinations and administrative necessities. The act of 1534 declared his first marriage, with Catherine of Aragon, to be invalid and vested the succession in the issue of Anne Boleyn, his now lawful spouse. It prescribed severe penalties for anyone who opposed the marriage and its issue, by deed, word, or writing, and empowered the king to exact an oath of adherence to all its provisions. This oath was attached to the statute in the following session, and together with the Treasons Act (1534) it could be construed as demanding on pain of treason the subject's acceptance of royal supremacy and the rejection of the pope. It was to be a test of complicity in Henry's actions, and More and Fisher were among its victims.

The ups and downs of Henry's connubial life necessitated further acts in 1536 (to annul the two previous marriages and vest the succession in the issue of Jane Seymour) and 1540 (to dissolve the 'pretensed' and fruitless marriage with Anne of Cleves). The statute of 1543 entailed the succession upon Edward, son of Jane Seymour, and his children; next upon Catherine of Aragon's daughter Mary, who by implication had been declared illegitimate in 1534; and finally upon Anne Boleyn's daughter, Elizabeth. Henry reserved the right to change this order of succession in his will. In fact, he did not, and it was the act of 1543 which Northumberland attempted to set aside on Edward VI's death in 1553.

SUCCESSORS, WARS OF, generic title for the military struggles of Alexander the Great's marshals, which lasted for more than 40 years after his death (323 BC). Each attempted to carve up Alexander's empire for his own advantage. The chief participants were Antigonus Monophthalmus, Seleucus Nicator, Ptolemy Soter, Lysimachus, and Cassander; the most important result was the emergence of the three main hellenistic kingdoms, Ptolemaic Egypt, Seleucid Asia, and Antigonid Macedonia.

SUCRE, ANTONIO JOSÉ DE (1795–1830), Bolivian soldier and president of Bolivia, who was one of Bólivar's lieutenants and distinguished himself in the campaign to free Ecuador, Peru, and Bolivia from Spanish domination. He led an advance force by sea and seized the port city of Guayaquil, then marched into the interior towards Quito. On the outskirts of the city he routed the Spanish forces on the slopes of Pichincha (24 May 1822), thus paving the way for Bólivar's triumphant entry.

Sucre later assisted Bólivar during the Peruvian campaign. By 1824 Bólivar held power in Lima, but royalist forces still controlled the highlands, and Sucre was entrusted with the task of dislodging them. He won the battle of Junin (6 Aug.), and for their next encounter the rival armies met on the high plateau near Ayacucho, and on 9 Dec., despite the royalists' superiority in men and guns, Sucre won a decisive victory. The Spanish lost some 2000 men, and the viceroy and his chief aids were taken prisoner. Sucre's victory marked the virtual end of the wars for Spanish American independence.

He next led his army into Upper Peru (mod. Bolivia) and supported the founding of an independent nation there, of which he became president for a two-year term (1826–8). He proved an excellent administrator, but conditions in Bolivia were too chaotic for him to remedy them. In 1828, when his term of office was not quite completed, he was confronted by a mutiny of his own troops, uprisings by ambitious *caudillos*, and an invasion from Peru led by Gamarra. He was forced from power and later assassinated in Colombia.

Guillermo A. Sherwell, *Antonio José de Sucre* (Washington, DC, 1924).   FPB

SUDAN, EGYPTIAN CONQUEST. The systematic conquest of the northern Sudan by the forces of Muhammad Ali (1820–1) was followed by the establishment of a regular Turco-Egyptian administration. As a result of a major southward expansion under the Khedive Isma'il (*reg.* 1863–1879) the Equatorial province of Bahr al-Gazal and Darfur was added, as well as Suakin and Massawa on the Red Sea coast. Egyptian rule was ended by the Mahdist revolt (1881–5).

SUDAN, REPUBLIC OF (2,506,000 sq. kms) in north-central Africa, with a population of 13,500,000, comprising Arab, Nuer, Dinka, Azande, and several other groups. It was

formerly the Anglo-Egyptian Sudan and secured independence in 1956. After the coup of May 1969 a military government took over.

SUDANESE NATIONALISM. With the emergence of a group of Western-educated Sudanese, especially in the civil service, demands for a greater share in government were put forward. In 1943 two parties were formed—the radical Ashiqqa Party (led by Isma'il al-Azhari, linked with the influential Mirghani family and the Khatmiyya sect, and favouring union with Egypt) and the moderate Umma Party (supported by the Mahdi family and its religious supporters, the Ansar, and favouring the gradual achievement of complete independence). A series of British concessions followed. An Advisory Council, including elected Sudanese members, was set up (1944) and transformed (1948) into a Legislative Assembly with members from the northern and southern Sudan, which elected the Sudanese leader (Abdullah Beg Khalil of the Umma Party) of the newly created Executive Council. Britain still reserved control of certain matters, notably foreign relations. The problem of the Egyptian claim to the Sudan, which had been a major difficulty, was resolved by the Anglo-Egyptian agreement (12 Feb. 1953), which promised Sudanese self-determination after a three-year transitional period of self-government. In the parliamentary elections of 1953 the National Unionist Party won a majority and its leader, Azhari, became prime minister (Jan. 1954). Sudanization of all services was accelerated (1954–5), producing as a by-product the 1955 revolt in the southern provinces. The last British forces were evacuated (Nov. 1955), and the Sudan was declared independent (Dec. 1955), opinion having swung against union with Egypt. The Republic of the Sudan was proclaimed on 1 Jan. 1956. MEY

SUDBURY, SIMON (d. 1381), English cleric who became Bp of London (1361), Abp of Canterbury (1375), and chancellor (1380–1). He was a close ally of Duke John of Gaunt and a special target of the peasants (many of whom were his Kentish tenants) in their revolt of 1381. He fell into their hands and was beheaded in the Tower of London. He was an upright prelate and a conscientious royal servant. His death high-lighted the unpopularity of the royal government and the upper clergy.

SUDRAS, lowest of the four great classes of the Hindus since the beginning of the 1st millennium BC. They comprise numerous castes, some of which are 'clean' (ie, whose members cause no pollution to those of higher castes), others 'unclean' and subject to different degrees of discrimination.

SUEBI, early German tribal name, used first of a tribe on the Main river, which invaded Gaul (c. 72 BC), but later extended to include the inhabitants of a large part of Western Germany, who later appear as separate tribes, eg, Allemanni, Quadi, and Marcomanni. The Quadi, under the earlier name, joined the Vandals in the invasion of the empire in AD 406 and set up an independent kingdom in north-western Spain which lasted until the 6th cent. The Allemanni remained east of the Rhine and bequeathed the name of the Suebi to Schwaben.

SUETONIUS PAULINUS (fl. 1st cent. AD), Roman governor of Britain (AD 58–61). After crushing Mauretanian resistance, he was sent by the Emperor Nero to overcome Welsh opposition. He defeated the Silures and Deceangli (58–9) and turned to Anglesey (60), the Druids' stronghold, but Boudicca's revolt diverted him. He made a hasty but fruitless bid to rescue London, and after it and Verulamium had been destroyed, he overwhelmed the rebels, inflicting, so it is said, 80,000 casualties for the loss of 400 men. His ruthless devastation of rebel territory aroused excessive antagonism and after an imperial enquiry he was recalled to Rome.

SUETONIUS TRANQUILLUS, GAIUS (c. AD 75–140), Roman biographer, who became secretary to the Emperor Hadrian. His most famous literary work, Lives of the Caesars, consisted of a series of short biographies, ranging from Julius Caesar to Domitian. The material for each life is organized under categories, eg, ancestry, education, accession, character of government, and virtues and vices. Though hardly comparable with modern biographies, the Lives contain within a short compass much valuable information, but also unreliable scandal.

SUEZ CANAL. Although it had been discussed from an early period, the construction of a canal to link the Mediterranean with the Gulf of Suez did not become feasible until the development of steam navigation and the realization that the Red Sea was not, as had been thought, substantially higher than the Mediterranean. Sa'id Pasha gave a concession for the construction and operation of a canal to Ferdinand de Lesseps on 20 Nov. 1854 (revised 5 Jan. 1856). De Lesseps formed the Suez Canal Co. (1858) and the canal was opened in 1869. Britain, which, under Palmerston's inspiration, had steadfastly obstructed the work for political reasons, now took advantage of the financial difficulties of Khedive Isma'il to buy his shares in the Canal Co. for £4 million (1875). Although financially profitable, the purchase had more symbolic than political importance because the control of the company remained in the hands of the predominantly French directors. Real control of the canal, however, belonged to the power which controlled Egypt and it has been argued that the security of the canal was the principal element in the British decision (1882) to intervene in Egypt. The international importance of the canal was recognized by the Constantinople Convention (29 Oct. 1888), which proclaimed the right of free transit ('in time of war as in time of peace, to every vessel of commerce or of war without distinction of flag'). Although the canal had been expected to benefit Mediterranean ports it was British shipping, which averaged two-thirds of the total tonnage, that predominated from the beginning. Once established, the canal carried some 7 per cent of the world's trade before 1945; with the increase in oil shipments the amount rose thereafter to 15 per cent. Economically the canal was important in stimulating the export of bulk cargoes of foodstuffs and raw materials (especially from new plantation and mining industries) from Asia and Australasia to Europe, and the export of manufactured goods from Europe.

The canal also was important militarily in that it made rapid troop movements possible and thus facilitated European control of Asian and East African territories, as well as furthering Ottoman and Egyptian ambitions in the Red Sea area. The military and economic importance of the canal in British eyes made its control a major problem in Anglo-Egyptian negotiations (1919–53). The 1953 agreement provided for British evacuation of the Canal Zone base with a provision for its reactivation. But the nationalization of the Canal Co. and the subsequent Suez War (1956), which led to temporary closure of the canal, restored complete Egyptian control until the June War (1967) closed the canal.

C. W. Hallberg, The Suez Canal (New York, 1931).
D. A. Farnie, East and West of Suez (Oxford, 1969). MEY

SUEZ WAR (1956), unsuccessful attack on Egypt by Israel, Britain, and France. The episode had two points of origin: Israeli-Egyptian hostility, which had been exacerbated by the raids of Egyptian-trained commandos into Israel; and Anglo-French fears of the challenge posed by Nasserism to their own position or that of their protégés in North Africa and the Middle East. The decisive event was the Egyptian nationalization of the Suez Canal Co. (26 July 1956), which itself was immediately provoked by the US refusal (19 July) to finance the Aswan Dam because of Egypt's increasing orientation towards the USSR since the Sept. 1955 agreement by which Egypt purchased arms from Czechoslovakia. The loss of control over the management of the canal was thought to menace the security of West European oil supplies and a plan was immediately prepared for an Anglo-French military occupation of the Canal Zone. The US secretary of state, John Foster Dulles, urged restraint and a conference of maritime nations was summoned in London (Aug.) to establish an international authority to operate the canal. Egypt subsequently rejected the conference proposals, which were transmitted by Robert Menzies. In Sept. Dulles put forward a new proposal for a Suez Canal Users' Association, but, as it soon became apparent that the US would take no action to enforce either the conference or the SCUA proposals, Britain and France reverted to their military project, for which preparations were maturing. The dispute was also referred to the United Nations. In late Sept. and early Oct. the military plan was modified to accommodate Israeli participation and the new plan elaborated in discussions during Oct. The Israeli attack was launched on 29 Oct. Britain and France issued an ultimatum calling on Israel and Egypt to withdraw on either side of the canal and followed this by air attacks on the Canal Zone. Paratroops were dropped on Port Said and Port Fuad (5 Nov.) and the Anglo-French invasion fleet arrived on 6 Nov. On the same day Britain and France agreed to a cease-fire. British and French forces were evacuated (22 Dec.) and Israeli forces in March 1957. The episode constituted a major victory for President Nasser and a major defeat for Britain and France, whose influence in the Middle East was thereafter seriously impaired. The Anglo-French withdrawal was due to opposition at home and abroad, and threats of Russian intervention, but most of all to US opposition. An important factor in achieving the withdrawal was UN intervention under the leadership of the Canadian foreign minister, Lester Pearson, which resulted in the rapid formation of the UN Expeditionary Force to supervise the withdrawal and later act as a buffer along the Israeli border. This buffer and the opening of the Gulf of Aqaba represented useful gains from the episode for Israel.

Hugh Thomas, *The Suez Affair* (London, 1970).
Kennett Love, *Suez: the twice-fought war* (London, 1970).

MEY

SUFFOLK, WILLIAM DE LA POLE, 1st Duke of (1st creation (1396–1450), grandson of Michael de la Pole, the chancellor of Richard II's reign. He became a favourite of Henry VI and of Henry's French wife, Margaret, whose marriage he had negotiated, but was otherwise extremely unpopular. The price of the marriage was the surrender to the French in 1444 of Maine, thus exposing the southern frontier of Normandy. In 1447 Suffolk procured the arrest of Henry's heir, Humphrey, Duke of Gloucester, who died soon afterwards. The arrest was a notable example of his violent and arbitrary methods and he was also hated for supporting a group of unscrupulous and lawless followers and lesser officials. The resumption of the war by the French led to disasters (1449–50). Suffolk was impeached in parliament, charged with treason, and mysteriously murdered on his way to exile.

SUFFOLK, CHARLES BRANDON, 4th Duke of (1st of 2nd creation) (c. 1484–1545), English soldier and close friend of King Henry VIII, whom he served as a soldier and counsellor for over 30 years. After fighting at the battle of Flodden (1513), he was created Duke of Suffolk. On the accession of King Francis I, he was sent to France to congratulate the king on Henry VIII's behalf. While there he courted and secretly married Mary, the young widow of Louis XII and Henry's favourite sister. The king forgave this breach of etiquette and Suffolk continued his career as a royal general, though his flamboyant but pointless expedition to France in 1523 compared badly with his success at Flodden. After Wolsey's downfall he was consulted by Henry on political matters, though he had little ability in this direction. He commanded the forces that invaded France in 1544.

SUFFOLK, MICHAEL DE LA POLE, 5th Earl of (1st of 3rd creation) (1330–89), the son of William de la Pole, the richest 14th-cent. English merchant, whose wealth had enabled him to acquire large estates. Michael had been trained for a military career and was a personal follower of King Edward III. His great wealth and ability made him an unusual member of the aristocracy and he was summoned as a magnate to parliament after 1385. He became chancellor in 1383 and the young king, Richard II, developed a marked personal attachment to him. This caused much antagonism and he was blamed for the mishandling of the Scottish war of 1385. He was impeached by his enemies in the parliament of 1386 and only a flight abroad in 1387 saved his life. He died in exile. His perceptive remarks in parliament (in 1383) about the causes of the Peasants' Revolt in 1381, which he attributed to general misgovernment, lack of justice, and oppression of officials, reveal him as a royal minister of unusual intelligence and honesty.

SUFFOLK RESOLVES (1774), economic sanctions against Britain planned by a meeting of American colonists from Suffolk County, MA, as a reprisal for the 'Intolerable' Acts. The Resolves were carried by Paul Revere to Philadelphia, where they were endorsed by the Continental Congress.

SUFFRAGETTES in Britain. The women's suffrage movement originated in the 1860s, declined in the 1880s, but revived after 1897 as the National Union of Women's Suffrage Societies. The suffragists' revival owed much to their rivals the suffragettes, organized after 1903 in the Women's Social and Political Union—for their self-advertising tactics broke the press silence on feminism, exposed opponents' bigotry, and brought fulfilment and companionship to many lonely women. The suffragettes repudiated Victorian Liberalism only because in no other way could they break into the male-dominated world of politics. Literary influences were not important, for Mrs Emmeline Pankhurst the suffragette leader was no intellectual, and her movement never produced a manifesto to supersede J. S. Mill's *Subjection of Women*. WSPU strategy ensured that by Sept. 1910 some 500 suffragettes had been imprisoned, and in 1912 Mrs Pankhurst described 'the argument of the broken pane' as 'the most valuable argument in modern politics'. Here was a foretaste of the 'direct action' now so fashionable among reformers.

Unfortunately newspaper 'stunts' required a conspiratorial strategy which, when combined with the forceful Pankhurst temperament, accentuated the suffragette movement's authoritarian structure. A semi-totalitarian atmosphere was created in which criticism became disloyalty, and critics (notably the founders of the Women's Freedom League in 1908, the Pethick-Lawrences in 1911, and Sylvia Pankhurst in 1913) were expelled. This mistaking of means for ends could never procure the economic sophistication and political maturity which women's long-term interests required. Furthermore, the WSPU was drifting away from its early Labour Party allegiance, whereas during a period of Liberal supremacy only a democratic feminist campaign could succeed. Middle-class spinsters had long dominated the feminist movement, and had promoted what Eleanor Rathbone called a 'me too feminism' which stressed women's fitness for male roles. Feminists had therefore opposed special factory legislation for working women, and had neglected the importance of industrial welfare and family allowances. Christabel Pankhurst's leadership took this trend further. The WSPU, by attacking the sporting facilities and sexual habits of men, drifted towards sex-war.

Sylvia Pankhurst (1882–1960) therefore broke off from the WSPU to found the East London Federation in 1913. Whereas her sister Christabel had always played down class-war and played up sex-war, Sylvia restored the original left-wing affiliation, and raised mass feminist support in London's East End. Her processions and deputations induced Asquith to declare in June 1914 that 'if the change has to come, we must face it boldly, and make it thorough-going and democratic'. At the outbreak of the First World

War, Emmeline and Christabel Pankhurst disbanded the WSPU and moved into recruiting work. In 1918 the enfranchisement of women over 30 owed something to fears of a revived WSPU, but was also a response to NUWSS political influence, to Sylvia Pankhurst, and to women's war work. Nor can women's subsequent advancement be credited solely to feminists. The employment opportunities created by modern bureaucracy and technology, together with the birth-control techniques which so many feminists detested, have done far more than enfranchisement for the emancipation of 20th-cent. women.

E. Sylvia Pankhurst, *The Suffragette Movement* (London, 1931).   BHH

SUFI, from the Arabic *suf*, meaning wool: cf. *tasawwuf*, the wearing of the woollen robe, *ie*, to devote oneself to the mystical life—to the career of a sufi. Sufism, at first an expression of a personal faith, mystical in character, developed during the 9th and succeeding centuries into a religious and social movement organized in dervish brotherhoods, sometimes associated with craft guilds, and enjoying much support amongst the mass of the people. The Sufis, though not overtly heretical in their beliefs, found themselves aligned in general against the formalism of Sunni or orthodox Islam. It was to be the task of Al-Ghazali (1059–1111) to achieve a measure of reconciliation between the doctrines of the Sunni faith and the mysticism of the Sufis.

SUFYAN, ABU (*c*. 565–653), of the Arab tribe of Quraysh, prominent in the opposition to the Prophet Muhammad both before and after the *Hijra* of 622. He had a notable share in the campaign of Uhud (625) against the Muslims and also in the attack which the Meccans undertook thereafter against Medina (627). His son Mu'awiya was to win the caliphate for the house of Umayya, holding the throne himself during the years AD 661–80.

SUGAR ACT (1764) in Britain, legislative measure specifically designed to raise revenue for the Crown in the American colonies. The act, devised by George Grenville, lowered the duty on molasses, but raised the duty on foreign refined sugars and increased the subsidy on British sugar supplied to the colonies. Grenville made molasses smuggling unprofitable, secured monopoly control of the American market for the British, and instituted a good revenue raiser. It prompted a debate on the right of the British parliament to tax for revenue purposes, which crystallized into widespread opposition after the Stamp Act (1765), whereupon the sugar duty was reduced, but it continued to raise revenue for the Crown.

SUGAR TRADE. Honey was the only sweetener available locally in medieval Europe. After the First Crusade sugar began to be imported from Syria, where large plantations of sugar cane were developed in the Latin states. In the 14th cent. the Venetians financed sugar production in Cyprus while the Genoese distributed Sicilian sugar. In the 15th cent. it was transplanted by the Portuguese to the Atlantic islands, especially Madeira, with the financial help of the Genoese, who marketed it all over western Europe. It was quite natural for the Portuguese to extend its cultivation into Brazil in the 16th cent. and from there it spread to the West Indies. Subsequently, until the 19th cent., the sugar trade was an important aspect of Europe's colonial economy.

SUGER (d. 1151), French cleric and scholar, who was a childhood friend of King Louis VI of France (d. 1137). He became his chief adviser and biographer. As abbot of St Denis (1122–51), the principal royal abbey of France, he was one of the leading French prelates. He remained the chief adviser of Louis's successor, King Louis VII, and acted as regent of the kingdom during the latter's absence on crusade in 1147–9. He rebuilt the church of St Denis as the first complete example of the new Gothic style and it became the model for this type of architecture. He saw outward splendour as an essential feature of worship and expressed this conception in his abbey church.

SUHARTO (1921–), Indonesian politician and second president of Indonesia, who was born in the Jogjakarta area of Java. He joined the Royal Netherlands Indies army (KNIL) and during the Japanese occupation served in the Fatherland Defence Corps (PETA), which provided the core of the Indonesian army's leadership for the revolution of 1945–9. He served in the Diponegoro (Central Java) Division and later commanded it (1956–9). In 1961–2 he headed the military forces assigned to the West Irian dispute and also the army components in the Malaysia 'Confrontation' of 1963–5.

As head of the Army Strategic Command (Kostrad), he controlled key military units; moreover, as the senior general on active service he held command of the army whenever its regular commander was absent. He did not belong to the group of more Westernized officers headed by Gen. Nasution, who led the army in quiet but determined opposition to Sukarno. This detachment from the mainstream of military leaders explained Suharto's exclusion from the attacks on army leaders in the 'September Thirtieth Movement'. In response to the movement, Suharto proclaimed himself emergency commander of the armed forces; but Sukarno, anxious to prevent so powerful and strong-willed a man from becoming military chief, rejected his claim. Suharto then turned against the president, who was never able to regain the initiative. In March 1966 Suharto assumed presidential powers, and a year later took the presidential title for himself. His contest with Sukarno and Indonesia's desperate economic situation impelled him away from the militant anti-imperialism of 'Guided Democracy'. His 'New Order' ended Indonesia's 'Confrontation' with Malaysia, encouraged foreign investment, and sought to depoliticise and stabilize the country under indirect army rule.   RTM

SUHRAWARDY, HUSSAIN SHAHEED (1892–1963), Bengal Muslim leader and prime minister of Pakistan (1956–7). He was initially a Swarajist member of the Bengal Legislative Council (1924), but moved towards the Muslim League and by the late 1920s had become its secretary. He was minister for civil supplies in Nazimuddin's government (1943–5), and in 1946 displaced him as chief minister. He campaigned with Gandhi against the communal violence in Calcutta before partition and tried unsuccessfully to sponsor a scheme for a 'united sovereign Bengal'. After partition he stayed in Calcutta for some time to help to solve communal problems there. He was the founder of the Awami League Party in East Pakistan and became leader of the opposition in the National Assembly (1955) and prime minister in 1956.

SUI DYNASTY (589–617), first authority to bring about the reunification of China as one empire since 316. The dynasty has been criticized for its oppressive methods and extravagance. Its achievements lay in its establishment of strong government, which prepared the way for the more permanent unification of T'ang, and in reasserting Chinese prestige in central Asia. Although Sui overtaxed China's military strength by fighting large-scale campaigns in Korea, long-lasting economic benefits followed the building of the Grand Canal.

SUKARNO, ACHMED (1897–1970), Indonesian politician and first president of Indonesia. He began life as an architect and then became involved in the nascent secular nationalist movement. In 1927 he helped to establish an association that became the Indonesian National Party (PNI), which adopted a non-co-operative attitude towards the colonial government. His oratory attracted popular adherents to the party and also the attention of the Netherlands Indies authorities, who in 1929 arrested him for revolutionary activities. During his imprisonment (1929–31) the PNI split into the elite New PNI and the mass-oriented Indonesia Party (Partindo). Sukarno, failing to reunite them, followed his populist inclinations and assumed the leadership of the Partindo. In 1933 he was arrested again, and was kept in exile until the Japanese invasion in 1942. During the Second World War he, together with Mohammad Hatta, led Indonesian nationalists in co-operating with Japan. On 17 Aug. 1945, while they were hesitating over their response to the Japanese collapse, Sukarno and Hatta were kidnapped by radical youths, who demanded that they should declare independence. Sukarno became president of the new republic and steered it through its 1945–9 revolution against the returning Dutch.

In the post-revolutionary period Sukarno's role was at first limited, for the parliamentary system of government and the 'administrative' style of its leaders did not allow him much scope. However, as the parliamentary government struggled with factionalism, disagreement on post-revolutionary aims, and regional dissent, Sukarno became increasingly an arbiter of elite disputes and a rallying point for the masses. He called for 'Guided Democracy' and in 1959 this was brought about by the substitution of presidential for parliamentary government. Sukarno stressed the importance of internal unity and the revival of the revolutionary spirit, and pursued an increasingly radical foreign policy to promote these ends. His regime mixed populist and pre-colonial symbols; towards the end of his rule, as all governmental decisions came to depend on him, he increasingly used the style of the traditional Javanese rulers. At the same time he allowed more prominence to the Indonesian Communist Party, which alarmed the army and other right-wing circles. In 1965, after the attempted coup by the 'September Thirtieth Movement', he was removed from power by Gen. Suharto, who formally replaced him as president in March 1967.

B. Dahm, Sukarno and the Struggle for Indonesian Independence (Cornell, 1969).

Cindy Adams, Sukarno, an Autobiography (Indianapolis, 1965).   RTM

SUKEBATOR

SUKEBATOR (1893–1923), Mongolian soldier and politician. After the demobilization of the Mongol army by the Chinese in 1920 he took part in the organization of a revolutionary group in Urga. This group eventually merged with another, with Choibalsang among its members, to form the nucleus of the Mongol People's party. In 1920 he went with six other revolutionaries to Russia, with the approval of the Jebtsundamba Khutuktu, to seek help against the Chinese. He stayed in Irkutsk, where he received military training. His great achievement was the recruitment and arming of the partisan army which took Khiakta (Altan Bulak) from the Chinese in March 1921. Sukebator was minister of war in the government of Oct. 1921. Early in 1923 he fell ill and died. Later it was said that he had been poisoned by counter-revolutionaries, but this story has now been dropped from his official biography.

SUKHOTHAI, early kingdom in north central Thailand, and the first Thai state to extend over the plains of central Siam. It began as a tributary of the Angkorian empire, and seized its independence in c. 1219, proclaiming open hostility to all that its Cambodian overlords had stood for. It attained its greatest extent under King Ram Khamhaeng, reaching by 1292 as far as Nakhon Si Thammarat (Ligor) and Luang Prabang. Its early success was a product of careful diplomacy which ensured the neutrality of Chiengmai, Lavo, and China and left it free to expand to the north-east and south at the expense of Angkor. However, the political change which it stimulated encouraged other Thai princes similarly to challenge Angkor; and by the mid-14th cent. its southern provinces had been taken by Ayudhya. After Ayudhya had reduced Angkor Sukhothai came under increasing pressure and in 1378 was forced to accept the suzerainty of Ayudhya.

Although temporarily able to reassert its independence under King Maha Dhammaraja III in 1400, Ayudhya firmly abolished the old state in 1438, putting its provinces under a Thai prince in Phitsanulok.

The significance of Sukhothai in Thai history is its important role in the dissemination of Theravada Buddhism, and its example of simple, paternal government, which was respected by Ayudhya and was revived by King Mongkut, who in 1833 rediscovered Ram Khamhaeng's inscription of 1292. The extensive ruins of Sukhothai remain, 350 kms north of Bangkok.   DKW

SULAYHID, name of a dynasty ruling over much of the Yemen in nominal dependence on the Fatimid caliphate in Egypt. The Sulayhid regime, established (notably in the years AD 1061–5) by Ali ibn Muhammad, of the tribe of Hamdan, endured (with Dhu Jibla as its main centre) until 1138.

SULEIMAN (1495–1566), Ottoman Sultan (reg. 1520–66), known to his people as Qanuni (the Giver of Laws) and to the Europeans as Il Magnifico, the Magnificent Sultan. His long reign was a time of restless and far-reaching endeavour. Suleiman carried out three campaigns (1534, 1548, 1554) against Safawid Persia—campaigns which consolidated Ottoman control over large areas of eastern Asia Minor (the regions of Erzurum and Lake Van) and achieved also the conquest of Iraq, Baghdad falling to the sultan in 1534.

Further to the south, in the lands bordering the Indian Ocean, the Ottomans sustained a long-drawn conflict with the Portuguese. The building of a fleet able to operate in and beyond the Red Sea imposed on the Ottomans a large and continuing expense—all the requisite materials and armament had to be carried from Asia Minor to Egypt and thence overland to Suez. No doubt the halting of the Christian advance was due in great measure to the weaknesses inherent in the situation of the Portuguese. None the less, the Ottomans contributed much to the final result—taking control of Aden in 1538 (the year when Khadim Suleiman Pasha led his famous expedition to attack the Portuguese at Diu in western India); establishing a new province of Habeş (Abyssinia) at Massawa and Sawakin to counter an entente between the Portuguese and Christian Ethiopia; and conducting in the Persian Gulf a series of naval campaigns against the Portuguese in 1551–3 and 1559.

More important still was the Ottoman naval offensive in the Mediterranean. Algiers, under the protection of the sultan and through the genius of Khayr al-Din Barbarossa, emerged by 1529 as a powerful corsair state on the North African shore. The Ottoman conquest of Tripoli in 1551 and their occupation of Tunis in 1574, after the death of Suleiman, brought into being a second and a third corsair regime. An end was thus made of the aspiration cherished in Spain since the fall of Granada in 1492, ie, to subject North Africa to Christian rule. Elsewhere the Ottomans, during the years 1537–40, conquered the last possessions remaining to Venice in the Morea and, at the battle of Prevesa in 1538, wrested from a combined Venetian–Spanish fleet a naval initiative which was to endure until the Christian triumph at Lepanto in 1571. Only at Malta did the Ottomans suffer a notable reverse, their assault on this strategic fortress being repulsed with much loss in 1565.

The reign of Suleiman witnessed also a stubborn conflict between the Ottomans and the Habsburgs, with the lands along the middle Danube as the main theatre of war. In 1521 Sultan Suleiman took Belgrade and in 1526, at Mohácz, crushed the Hungarians in the most brilliant of his victories, the Hungarian king, Lajos II, losing his life in the course of the battle. The legal heir to the Hungarian throne, the Habsburg Ferdinand of Austria, now sought to gain control of his inheritance. Suleiman established the vaivoda of Transylvania, John Zapolya, as a vassal prince at Buda and then tried to eliminate Austria as a factor in the Hungarian imbroglio, undertaking to this end a direct (though unsuccessful) assault on Vienna (in 1529) and a further raid into Austria during the Güns campaign of 1532. On the death of Zapolya (1540) Suleiman appointed John Sigismund, the infant son of Zapolya, to be vaivoda in Transylvania and also, in the great campaigns of 1541 and 1543, brought the Hungarian lands along the middle Danube (Belgrade–Buda–Esztergom) under direct Ottoman rule. Three Hungaries now existed in place of the old kingdom—Habsburg, in the north and west; Ottoman, in the centre; and (dependent on the sultan) Transylvania in the east. Suleiman himself died in his tent before the walls of the Hungarian fortress of Szigetvár in 1566. His reign saw the rich unfolding of all that was most characteristic of Ottoman civilization.   VJP

SULEIMAN ÇELEBI (*fl.* 15th cent.), a son of the Ottoman Sultan Bayezid I (*reg.* 1389–1403). After the battle of Ankara (1402) Suleiman Çelebi ruled over the Balkan provinces of the Ottoman empire from Edirne (Adrianople) until his death in 1411.

SULH, AL-, FAMILY, Sunni Muslim Lebanese family. Riyadh al-Sulh (d. 1951) was one of the main architects of the Lebanese National Pact and, as the ally of President Bishara al-Khuri, was the dominant Sunni politician (1943–1951). His brother, Sami al-Sulh (1890–1968), was also several times prime minister and enjoyed a similar eminence in association with President Camille Chamoun until 1958.

SULLA, L. CORNELIUS (138–78 BC), Roman soldier and politician, who came from a depressed patrician family. He was quaestor (107) under Marius in the Jugurthine War, when his capture of Jugurtha began his rivalry with Marius, under whom he also served against the Cimbri and Teutones (104–102). He was praetor in 93, governed Cilicia in 92, and returned to Rome to take command in the Social War. As consul (88) he obtained the command in the First Mithridatic War, but when Marius had it abrogated he appealed to his legions and marched on Rome, which he captured. After victories over Mithridates in Greece and Asia (87–84), he invaded Italy, where his enemies had regained power, and defeated them in civil war (83–81). He was dictator (81–79), holding a proscription of his enemies and passing a series of measures designed to restrict the political power of the people and tribunes and to restore control of the state to a senatorial oligarchy protected by a ring of veteran colonies around Rome. His political reforms were swept away within nine years, but his reorganization of legal procedures was more lasting.

SULLIVAN, LOUIS HENRI (1856–1924), US architect, whose belief that 'form should follow function' helped to liberate American architecture from the Beaux Arts traditions of the classical revival. After 1893 he experimented with steel-frame structures. In the Wainwright buildings, St Louis, MO (1890–1), the Guaranty building in Buffalo, NY (1894–5), the Bayard building, New York (1897–8), and the Carson, Pirie, Scott Store, Chicago, IL (1899–1904), his interplay of vertical and horizontal elements with decorative facings of brick, sandstone, and terracotta, were classic statements of the new American aesthetic.

SULLY, MAXIMILIAN DE BETHUNE, Duc de (*c.* 1559–1641), Huguenot soldier, politician, and administrator. The second son of a noble Huguenot family, originally from Flanders, whose property was confiscated (1569), he escaped the massacre of St Bartholomew (1572) and trained for the Huguenot army which he joined on the death of his father (1574), although two of his brothers fought on the Catholic side. He fought successfully in the Midi and rose to be one of Henry of Navarre's leading gunners and advisers. After Henry became king he was confirmed as a *conseiller d'état* and later admitted to the *Conseil des Finances* (1596), where he soon made his mark by touring the provinces enforcing

royal debts and thereby providing the money and supplies necessary for the siege of Amiens (1597). He also provided the first real statements of government finances for some time and was soon the acknowledged head of the royal financial machine (1598) as well as a trusted member of Henry's inner cabinet.

Sully enjoyed the king's complete confidence and held a large number of offices: superintendent of finances, grand master of artillery, superintendent of buildings, *grand voyer* and governor of Poitou and the Bastille, etc. He also served as envoy to England (1603), mediator with the Huguenots, and commander of the army in the campaign against Savoy (1601). Ambitious and energetic, he made himself felt in all these fields, particularly in finance and works. He was not an original financial thinker and made no sweeping changes, contenting himself with making the existing system work and succeeded in building up both an annual surplus and substantial reserves. Contrary to certain beliefs, he also supported Henry IV in his attempts to revive French manufactures. In the field of public works he did much to reorganize French fortifications and to rebuild roads and bridges after the devastation of the Religious Wars, so that he must be regarded as one of the founders of the engineers of *Ponts et Chaussées*, the French road-building corps. Created a duke and peer (1606), he supervised the preparations for the German campaign (1609) Henry was planning before his assassination, but found himself out of place in the spendthrift and Catholic court of Marie de Medici and he soon retired (1611). He was called on to mediate with the Huguenots on several occasions but was neglected by subsequent governments, although he was eventually made a marshal of France (1634). He spent his last years developing his estates, having written his memoirs, *Économies Royales*, early on (1612–13) in his retirement.

D. Buisseret, *Sully and the Growth of Centralized Government in France* (London, 1968).   CHC

SULPICIUS RUFUS, P. (*c.* 121–88 BC), Roman politician, quaestor (93), and *legatus* of Pompeius Strabo in the Social War (89). As tribune (88) he advocated the equitable registration of the newly enfranchised Italians and supported Marius, securing the transfer to him of Sulla's command in the campaign against Mithridates, but was killed after Sulla captured Rome.

SULTAN, a word occurring in the Koran and in the Hadith with the sense of 'power'. It became a title given to Muslim princes ruling in sovereign independence over the territories subject to them, *eg*, to the Seljuks, the Mamluks, and the Ottomans. Amongst the Ottomans it was not the sultan alone who held this title, but also the princes and princesses of the imperial house. The title was also accorded at times (above all in the Ottoman empire) to religious figures of note, *eg*, to sheikhs renowned as mystics.

SULTAN AGUNG (*fl.* 17th cent.), Ruler of the Central Javanese kingdom of Mataram (*reg.* 1613–45). He is traditionally believed to have been the third of his line, after Panembahan Senapati (?*reg.* 1584–1601) and Panembahan Seda Krapjak (*reg.* 1601–13), and is the first Javanese monarch of whom descriptions by Europeans exist. In a series of expeditions he extended the authority of Mataram throughout most of Java and Madura. His relations with the Dutch East India Co., which established Batavia in 1619, were reasonably amicable until he besieged the Dutch post there, unsuccessfully, in 1628–9.

He introduced the Islamic lunar calendrical system in 1633, although the years continued to be numbered in the Javanese era, based originally on the Hindu Saka era. In AD 1641 he abandoned the title Susuhunan for that of Sultan, which he is said to have received from Mecca.

SULTAN GALIEV (*c.* 1880–*c.* 1929), Muslim politician from Kazan who joined the Communist Party (Nov. 1917) and played an important part in the Russian Revolution. He advocated the formation of a Muslim Communist Party, an Islamic and Turkish socialist republic within the USSR, and, ultimately, the formation of a Colonial International to direct the revolution of colonial peoples against Europeans, including Russians. He was arrested in 1923–4 and again in Nov. 1928, after which he disappeared.

SULTAN b. SAQAR (d. 1866), most powerful of the pirate sheikhs in the Persian Gulf during the first quarter of the 19th cent. He succeeded his father at Ras al Khaima in 1803 as chief of the Qawasim. On 29 April 1806 he made a treaty with the government of Bombay, promising to respect the East India Co.'s property and flag. Dispossessed by the Wahhabi power, he escaped to Muscat and was re-established at Sharja on the Pirate Coast in 1814. There he gradually resumed his ascendancy over the Qawasim, whose increasing lawlessness led to the destruction of their strongholds by an expedition from Bombay under Sir William Grant Keir (1819–20). Thereafter, as the sultan's intelligence and influence could not be denied, he was recognized by the government of India as paramount sheikh on the Pirate Coast.

SULTANATE OF DELHI (1206–1526), name of the north Indian Muslim empire between the first conquest (1192) and the Mughal conquest. From 1192 to 1206 Muslim India was part of the Turkish Ghurid empire, Qutb-ud-din Aibek being viceroy. During this time Delhi, Uttar Pradesh, Bihar, and Bengal were conquered and the last traces of Buddhism destroyed. The empire was powerful until Taimur's invasion (1398). The Slave dynasty (1206–90) entrenched itself in north India, repelled Mongol invasions from the north-west, and provided an asylum for Muslim refugees. In India it was an army of occupation which combined fanaticism with dependence on Hindus for administration. Ala-ud-din (*reg.* 1296–1316) of the Khilji dynasty (1290–1320) defeated the Rajputs, annexed Gujarat, and directed raids to the far south. The Tughluq dynasty expanded briefly to south India to Madurai under Muhammad Shah (*reg.* 1325–51) but lost the Deccan to a Muslim revolt (1347). After Firoz Shah's (*reg.* 1351–88) death the empire declined until overwhelmed by Taimur's destructive raid (1398). The Tughluqs were succeeded by the Sayyids (1414–50), claiming Arab descent, who ruled only a shrinking area around Delhi. They were succeeded by the more vigorous Afghan Lodis, who reconquered the kingdoms of Jaunpur, Bihar, and Malwa before falling to the Mughal Babur at Panipat (1526). Under the Turkish sultans the empire was a military bureaucracy operating through Hindu subordinates. Afghan rule was a loosely knit military confederacy which collapsed at the first defeat. The sultanate's function was to preserve India from the Mongols and acclimatize Islam in India. The sultans were prolific builders and developed many varieties of Indo-Muslim architecture.

Ishwari Prasad, *History of Medieval India* (Allahabad, 1933).
                                                                                    TGPS

SULU SULTANATE, Muslim centre in the southern Philippines. The capital, Jolo, in the Sulu archipelago, was brought into contact with Islam from the 14th cent., when it was a centre of Chinese and Malay trade. The sultanate was already in existence at the time of the first Spanish attack (1578), and it grew more powerful, at the expense of Brunei, in the 17th cent. Despite repeated military expeditions, alternating with treaties of friendship, the Spanish did not establish authority over Sulu until 1878. With the transfer of its legitimate trade to European centres, Sulu became politically unimportant, and was used as a centre for piratic raids in Borneo, Mindanao, and the Visayas. From the 17th cent. Sulu claimed suzerainty over coastal North Borneo. The cession (or in the Philippine view, lease) of these rights to the British North Borneo Co. (1878) formed the crux of the Philippine claim to Sabah from 1962.

SUMAGURU KANTE, chief of the Sosso people who built an empire on the ruins of ancient Ghana. He was defeated and killed by Sundiata (*c.* 1240) and his territory incorporated into Mali.

SUMER, most southerly part of ancient Mesopotamia and the site of a very early civilization. The origins of the Sumerian people, *ie*, people who spoke the Sumerian language, are unknown, but remains of settlements have been found at Eridu (5th millennium BC) and at Al-Ubaid (4th millennium BC). By the 3rd millennium the country had at least 12 separate city-states: Kish, Sippar, Akshak, Larak, Nippur, Adab, Umma, Lagash, Bad-tibira, Uruk, Larsa, and Ur. Each state consisted of the city and the land and villages around it and each had its own deity, to whom the land was thought to belong. Consequently the temple became the central institution and the ruler was considered to be the god's representative, although quite early in Sumerian history the functions of ruler and priest became to some extent separated. The cities were continually at war with each other, one city sometimes achieving temporary ascendancy over the others, eg, Kish (*c.* 2760), Ur (*c.* 2630), Lagash (*c.* 2550), Uruk and Adab (*c.* 2450), Mari (*c.* 2400), Umma (*c.* 2360), Uruk (*c.* 2260), and Ur (*c.* 2113–2004). Except for the last period, when Ur controlled the whole of Mesopotamia, the city-state system prevented Sumeria from becoming a great political power and it was frequently under the control of other people, eg, the Elamites (*c.* 2530), Akkad (*c.* 2334–2193), and the Guti (*c.* 2250–2120). It was basically an agricultural country, though there was some trading, and was nevertheless a complex and civilized society with bureaucracies, legal codes, division of labour, and a money economy using standardized pieces of metal. Sumer developed the system of cuneiform writing, a mathematical system based on a unit of six, controlled irrigation with canals, dams, and reservoirs, and had an elaborate art, literature, and theology.

The Sumerian pantheon consisted of a large number of deities of varying importance, each with human qualities and a special task. Each city had its own deity, some being worshipped throughout Sumeria. An, whose temple was at Urak, was the god of the heavens and king of the other gods, but Enlil, the deity of Nippur, became in time the most important god and his approval was required for all rulers of Sumer and Akkad. Sumeria had a profound cultural and religious influence on the rest of Mesopotamia and beyond, and although the Sumerians as a separate, independent people ceased to exist after the Amorite invasions of *c.* 2000 BC, their culture and religion were adopted, with only few changes, by the Amorites, Kassites, Assyrians, and Chaldeans who followed them.

S. N. Kramer, *The Sumerians* (Chicago, 1963).   JKG

SUMERIAN KING LIST, list of Sumerian rulers of various kingdoms, from mythical kings of the 3rd millennium BC to Sin-Magir (*?reg. c.* 1827–1817) of Isin.

SUMMONER, or apparitor, in England, a petty officer of a court, civil or ecclesiastical, who cited or warned people to appear at the court. Ecclesiastical summoners in particular acquired an evil reputation, immortalized in Chaucer's satiric treatment in the *Canterbury Tales*.

SUMNER, CHARLES (1811–74), US lawyer and politician. His denunciation of the Mexican War contributed to his defeat when running for Congress (1848), but he was elected to the US Senate in 1851. Before the Civil War he supported such reform movements as those for temperance, world peace, women's rights, and abolitionism. In 1856 he delivered a two-day oration in the Senate, castigating the South in general, and Senator Andrew P. Butler of SC in particular, for its 'crime against Kansas'. Two days later Sumner was attacked in the Senate chamber by Butler's nephew, Congressman Preston Brooks, and his injuries kept him away from the Senate for over three years. He was an efficient chairman of the Senate Committee on Foreign Relations during the Civil War, and supported most administration measures, but was critical of Lincoln's slowness in issuing an emancipation proclamation. After Appomattox he became a leading Radical Republican and supported the impeachment of Andrew Johnson. On Reconstruction he refused to compromise, and viewed Negro suffrage as the essential condition for Southern readmittance to the Union.

SUMNER, WILLIAM GRAHAM (1840–1910), US clergyman, who became interested in social and economic questions, and took up the recently created chair of political and social science at Yale (1872). His early work, typified by *What Social Classes Owe to Each Other* (1883), combined evolutionary theories and classical economics in a violent attack on socialism, protectionism, and all forms of government intervention in what he saw as the self-regulating and natural evolution of capitalism. An increasing admiration for Herbert Spencer turned him away from economics towards anthropology and social science. His studies of the evolution of social institutions and customs, *Folkways* (1907), and the posthumous *Science of Society* (4 vols, 1927–8) exerted considerable influence on the development of the social sciences.

SUN HSING-YEN (1753–1818), Chinese scholar, bibliophile, and calligrapher, who was a native of Kiangsu. His work was mainly in compiling local gazetteers, and in editing and establishing more correct versions of ancient texts, the intelligibility of which had suffered after centuries of miscopying and misprinting.

SUN K'O (1895–   ), Chinese politician also known as Sun Fo, son of Sun Yat-sen and active in Kuomintang politics (1923–49).

SUN YAT-SEN (1866–1925), Chinese politician who was leader of the 1911 Revolution and of the Kuomintang ('Nationalist Party') in China. A Cantonese from Hsiangshan district, in his early years he received a Western education and medical training in Honolulu (1879–82) and Hong Kong (1884–94). It was in Hong Kong that he became a Christian and interested himself in Western theories of popular sovereignty and anti-Manchuism. After his failure to convert Li Hung-chang to his reformist proposals in 1894, he turned to a revolutionary cause, which led to his flight to Japan (1895). He spent the next 16 years organizing revolution from outside China. The Hsing-chung Hui ('Revive China Society') had already been founded in Honolulu in 1894; he now established a branch in Yokohama (1895), then embarked on a tour of the US and Britain to preach revolution. It was in the British Museum that Sun became acquainted with Western socialist thinking and the ideas of Karl Marx and Henry George.

During the Boxer Rising (1900) Sun once again approached Li Hung-chang (now governor-general of Kwangtung and Kwangsi) in the hope of realizing a Cantonese secessionist movement, but to no avail. He then intensified his revolutionary activities, concentrating on recruiting student support, and establishing branches of his Hsing-chung Hui in South-East Asia and Europe. In 1905, helped by Japanese liberals, Sun struck an alliance with other revolutionary leaders (Huang Hsing and Sung Chiao-jen) and formed the T'ung-meng Hui ('United League'), dedicated to the expulsion of the Manchus and the establishment of a Chinese republic. Thus prepared, Sun and his associates staged risings in south China from their base in Hanoi. These risings, though unsuccessful, helped to revive nationalist aspirations in colonial Indo-China, leading to Sun's expulsion by the French. The British in Malaya and the Japanese soon followed suit, and Sun left for Europe and North America, leaving the planning of revolution to Huang Hsing and Hu Han-min.

The revolutionaries finally succeeded in overthrowing the Manchus, and on 1 Jan. 1912 Sun was elected provisional president of the new republic; but only to resign three weeks later in favour of Yüan Shih-k'ai, who, because of military resources at his disposal, was then regarded as the only man capable of holding the fragmented nation together. As Yüan's dictatorial ambitions soon became clear, Sun denounced him and encouraged provincial governors to rebel against him (1913). The so-called Second Revolution, however, failed to challenge Yüan's supremacy, and Sun sought asylum in Japan. While in Japan, he reorganized the KMT, a rather loosely organized political party created in 1912 at the initiative of Sung Chiao-jen, turning it into a tightly knit group under his personal control, well suited to his revolutionary needs.

After the death of Yüan Shih-k'ai (1916), China collapsed into warlordism, and the Peking government, which claimed legitimate control over the nation, came under the dictatorial Tuan Ch'i-jui. Sun's aim therefore was to unify the country under a representative government. His opportunity came in 1920, when pro-Sun elements seized control of the Canton government and elected Sun president-extraordinary. By early 1923 he had eliminated most of the dissident elements, and established a military government, for purposes of national unification. Disenchanted with the policies of the Western democracies, Sun now turned to the Soviet Union for aid, and undertook to co-operate with the Chinese Communist Party. The KMT was also reorganized, after the Soviet model but with Sun's *San Min Chu I* ('Three People's Principles') firmly established as its aims. In order to train cadets he set up the Whampoa Academy (1924), with Chiang K'ai-shek as commandant. Thus, although Sun died the following year, the groundwork for national unification was firmly laid.

Though he was not much respected during his lifetime, a cult of Sun Yat-sen grew up rapidly after his death. He was honoured in 1940 by the National Government as the 'father of the country', and in 1949 by the Communist government as the pioneer of the revolution.

Lyon Sharman, *Sun Yat-sen, his life and its meaning* (New York, 1934).
Harold Z. Schiffrin, *Sun Yat-sen and the Origins of the Chinese Revolution* (Berkeley & Los Angeles, 1968).   DP

SUNA II (d. 1856), King (*kabaka*) of Buganda in Uganda, who encouraged Zanzibari traders to settle at his court, their firearms being exchanged for slaves and ivory.

SUNDAY, WILLIAM ASHLEY (1862–1935), US evangelist who became a professional baseball player in Chicago, Pittsburgh, and Philadelphia (1883–91), worked for the Chicago YMCA (1891–5), became an evangelist (1896), and was ordained as a Presbyterian (1903). A vehement fundamentalist, he is believed to have preached to some 80 million people in his highly organized revival meetings, and to have made up to 6000 converts a month.

SUNDAY OBSERVANCE in Britain, controversial issue first raised during the 17th cent. Later, it was most influential during the 19th cent., when sabbatarianism combated the widespread contemporary drunkenness and employers' continuous pressure to extend working hours. Humanitarianism inspired Lord Shaftesbury's sabbatarianism as well as his factory legislation. Temperance pressure helped curtail Sunday drinking hours in England, and incorporated Sunday closing into Scottish and Welsh culture after 1833 and 1881 respectively.

Sunday observance, as the badge of religiosity and therefore of respectability, was championed by the Anglican evangelical Lord's Day Observance Society founded in 1831. Embattled against railways and materialism, the society fought a losing battle with the National Sunday League, founded by London artisans in 1855. The league's excursions and its success in getting the public art galleries and museums opened on Sunday afternoons from 1896 steadily eroded the traditional Sunday, and the work was completed in the 20th cent. by two World Wars, the motor car, radio, television, and mass spectator sport. Nevertheless, the concept of Sunday Observance remained strong (1970) in parts of Scotland and Wales.

SUNDAY SCHOOL SOCIETY (1785) in Britain, organized and co-ordinated the Sunday schools which provided the poor child with religious education. The idea appealed to parents and employers because it enabled children to work six days a week and yet acquire the rudiments of literacy. It exercised a civilizing influence on the labour force and constituted the first example of mass elementary education in England, establishing it on a religious basis.

The first Sunday school was probably started by a Methodist minister in High Wycombe, but the institution was publicized by Robert Raikes of Gloucester in his own newspaper and the *Gentleman's Magazine*. The resulting Society for the Establishment and Support of Sunday Schools in the Different counties of England was run through committees composed equally of churchmen and nonconformists, with the aim of assisting laymen and clerics in setting up Sunday schools until they could become financially independent. By 1787 there were 250,000 pupils. The society's rules were that children should be instructed in reading from the Bible and prayer book, but should not learn writing or arithmetic on the sabbath, and were to be taken to church or chapel during school. Teachers were at first paid a small fee, but with increased voluntary effort this became unnecessary. Evangelicals such as Sarah Trimmer and Hannah More were often appointed visitors and subscribed or raised funds for their schools. The society split when nonconformity became suspected of association with French revolutionary activity and the Church of England withdrew, thus destroying the interdenominational character of the Sunday school movement and foreshadowing the sectarian bigotry of later educational debate.   VEC

SUNDERLAND, ROBERT SPENCER, 3rd Earl of (2nd of 2nd creation) (1641–1702), English politician who entered the House of Lords (1661) in the Cavalier Parliament. In the 1670s his services were used mainly in diplomatic missions to Madrid and Paris. His first spell of ministerial office was (1679–81) as secretary of state, first for the north, then for the south, but he was dismissed after advocating the debarring of James, Duke of York from the succession in favour of William of Orange during the debates on the Second Exclusion Bill. But he obtained office again, perhaps largely owing to the influence of the Duchess of Portsmouth: he was secretary of state again, first for the north and then for the south, until 1688. Somehow he had made himself acceptable to the very man whom he had so recently been seeking to exclude from the succession. He had also become a Roman Catholic. But in 1688, prior to the landing of William of Orange in England, James dismissed him from office. He fled to the Dutch republic, even before James had reached France, and did not return to England till 1690. He abandoned his Roman Catholicism, but even though he was one of the exceptions to the amnesty of 1690 he was not prevented from taking his seat in the House of Lords again in 1692. Never after the Glorious Revolution (1688) did he hold ministerial office, yet he was certainly not without influence. His unofficial advice to William III may well have been decisive in certain of the ministerial changes before the end of the reign.

J. P. Kenyon, *Robert Spencer, Earl of Sunderland* (London, 1958).   BM

SUNDERLAND, CHARLES SPENCER, 4th Earl of (3rd of 2nd creation) (1674–1722), British Whig politician, who married Anne (1700), daughter of John Churchill, Duke of Marlborough. His marriage was a political event of importance for through it Marlborough was drawn towards the Whigs.

Sunderland was appointed secretary of state for the south (1706–10) through the influence of his mother-in-law, becoming the first member of the Whig Junto to obtain office. His influence increased in 1708 with the return of a Whig majority and the entry of fellow members of the Junto into office. He was disliked by Queen Anne, dismissed in June 1710, and in Aug. a Tory majority in the Commons swept the Whigs from office. In 1711 Sunderland was attacked in the Lords over the conduct of the war in Spain, but an effort to impeach him failed. He allied himself with Nottingham in opposition to the ministry and moved the Occasional Conformity Bill against his former friends, the dissenters. Though a strong Hanoverian supporter, he failed to regain the secretaryship on George I's accession. He did hold several offices, however, *eg*, lord lieutenant of Ireland and lord privy seal, but had no real authority. After joining with Townshend and later Stanhope, he fomented dissension within the ministry, and succeeded in replacing Townshend as secretary for the north (1717). He was later lord president of the council (1718–19) and first lord of the treasury (1718–1721). Because he founded the South Sea Co. (1720), he became implicated in the crash of 1721 and was forced by public clamour to resign his treasury post, being replaced by Sir Robert Walpole. He continued to have influence with George I as groom of the stole.

SUNDIATA (*fl.* 13th cent.), also called Mari-Jata, who freed Mali from the yoke of Sumaguru Kante, the Sosso chief (*c.* 1240). Under him the various Malinke chieftaincies were first united into the basis of the Mali empire. Defeat of the Sosso enabled Mali to gain control of the caravan termini of the southern Sahara and facilitated exportation of its gold. Under Sundiata the empire expanded rapidly to the south and west and it is probable that the lands of the Niger flood-plain were added at this stage. Oral tradition records Sundiata as being the great Manding hero, a powerful warrior and magician.

SUNG CHIAO-JEN (1882–1913), Chinese politician and follower of Sun Yat-sen, who organized the Kuomintang after the 1911 Revolution. Yüan Shih-k'ai regarded the Kuomintang as a threat, and in 1913 had Sung, its main organizational leader, assassinated.

SUNG DYNASTY, more correctly Northern Sung (960–1126) and Southern Sung (1127–1279). Despite political and military weaknesses, the reunification of China after some two centuries of ineffectual government and dynastic disturbance ushered in a period of cultural brilliance, technological advance, and economic development. The Sung house was throughout subject to pressure from the northern peoples and was obliged to purchase security at the cost of money or materials. After losing control in the north-west to the Hsi-hsia people, the dynasty was eventually forced to yield place in the north-east and east, as far as the Huai river, to the newly arisen Chin dynasty. From 1127 the Sung house was established at Lin-an, until it was expelled by the Yüan (Mongol) dynasty.

The situation of the Sung dynasty in the Yangtse area extended China's cultural influence conspicuously in regions that had not previously been greatly affected by the activities of Chinese officials, scholars, and men of leisure. Rice cultivation was improved by the efforts of both government and landowners and the adoption of new methods of irrigation. With increasingly specialized production, trade prospered and new commercial cities arose to meet its needs. Printing, which had been developed from the 10th cent., allowed the introduction of paper currencies, and this was accompanied by credit arrangements.

During the Sung period the Chinese civil service reached its highest point of complexity, with an unprecedentedly large number of official posts. The high prestige of the civil servant ensured a sufficiency of candidates for government service and laid down the cultural standards to which townsmen and countrymen aspired. As effective government was coming to depend more and more on the co-operation between officials and the semi-official leaders of the clans and guilds, some statesmen took steps to promote the social stability of the family system. Technological inventions transformed many aspects of daily life, eg, the production of textiles, water and road transport, and ceramics. Explanatory manuals, compendia of scientific data, and de luxe editions of literary works are included in the work of the Sung printing houses. New styles and techniques of printing were created, and a new impetus given to Chinese philosophy by intellectual movements known collectively as Neo-Confucianism.

J. Gernet, *Daily Life in China on the Eve of the Mongol Invasion* (London, 1962).   ML

SUNJO (1790–1834), King of Korea (*reg.* 1800–34), whose reign was marked by violent persecutions of Christianity, and by popular revolts, provoked by the Andong Kim family.

SUN–JOFFE AGREEMENT (1923), agreement between Sun Yat-sen and Adolf Joffe, of the Comintern, which initiated co-operation between the Kuomintang and the Chinese Communist Party, and laid the foundations for the work of Soviet advisers in the Chinese revolutionary movement. In 1923 Sun's career was at a low ebb; he turned to the Soviet Union in desperation after being scorned by the Western powers.

SUNJONG (1874–1926), King of the Yi dynasty of Korea (*reg.* 1907–10). He was deposed at the time of the Japanese annexation in 1910.

SUNNA, Arabic word meaning custom or usage. There is frequent reference in the religious literature of Islam, *eg*, in the Hadith, to the sunna of the Prophet Muhammad, *ie*, to the deeds and practices which marked his career. The word came in the course of time to denote also the orthodox form of the Muslim faith, standing in contradistinction to the Shi'a, the name given to the most notable of Islamic heterodoxies. To the orthodox Muslim the sunna of Muhammad afforded a standard of conduct which complemented the injunctions of the Koran.

SUNNI ALI (*reg.* 1464–92), Ruler of the Sunni dynasty of Songhay, who expanded the state from its original homogeneous nucleus on the eastern Niger Bend to a large multi-ethnic state reaching round the Niger to beyond Jenne and along the Saharan fringes to Walata. His capital was at Gao, and there were other residences at Kabara (the port of Timbuctoo) and in Tindirma (south-east of Lake Faguibine).

Muslim written sources portray Ali as a cruel and vicious tyrant, while Songhay oral tradition lauds him as a semi-divine hero. Certainly his treatment of Timbuctoo scholars (1468) was harsh, but he was equally harsh towards all who opposed him. Though denounced by some scholars as a pagan, he in fact held a very fine balance between the forces of Islam and traditional religion in his new empire. His successor tried to ignore the Islamic force and was quickly ousted by the leader of the Muslim faction, Askia Muhammad.

SUNNI DYNASTY of Songhay, totalling some 19 rulers, was founded by Ali Golom (*c.* 1275). Ali is said to have been the son of a Za ruler of Kukiya, forced into the service of the Mali sultan. Given a command along the Niger, he soon established his independence. Under his successors Mali again made northern Songhay tributary, but its authority was unstable.

Little is known of the Sunni dynasty until near its end. The antepenultimate ruler, Sulaiman Dandi, was powerful enough to raid provinces of north-eastern Mali and his successor, Sunni Ali, established his control to beyond Jenne.

The dynasty closed in 1493 with the brief reign of Sunni Baro, who was defeated by Askia Muhammad, himself perhaps related to the Sunnis.

SUNTHON PHU (1786–1855), Thai poet and author of long sections of the epic poem, 'Khun Chang Khun Phaen', and of much love poetry.

SUPPILULIUMAS I (*reg. c.* 1380–1346 BC), founder of the Hittite empire. After an early failure against his enemy, Mitanni, he prepared for another campaign by conquering or allying himself with the local tribal rulers and then (*c.* 1360) he invaded Mitanni, sacked the capital, advanced into Syria, which had been under Mitannian rule, and reduced at least the northern states to vassalage. A period of disorder in Mitanni enabled him to mount a final campaign in Syria (*c.* 1354) in which Carchemish was conquered and the government of the whole area reorganized firmly under Hittite control. Shortly afterwards continuing disorder finally allowed him to reduce Mitanni to a state of vassalage.

SUPREMACY, STATUTES OF (1534, 1559), in England, legislative measures which asserted the Crown's supreme authority over the English Church. King Henry VIII's act (1534) was largely declaratory. In 1531 he had used the threat of Praemunire to extract from the clergy an admission that he was their 'singular protector, only and supreme lord, and, as far as the law of Christ allows, even supreme head'. The next year, in pretending to adjudicate upon complaints made against the clergy by the Commons, he declared that, through their oath of allegiance to the pope, the clergy 'be but half our subjects' and won a formal submission in which they surrendered their right of independent legislation. Further measures (1532–4) stopped all payments to Rome, transferred ecclesiastical appeals to the Crown, and outlawed all foreign jurisdiction by forbidding the hearing of appeals in the papal courts.

The Act in Restraint of Appeals (1533) stated that 'by divers sundry old authentic histories and chronicles . . . this realm of England is an empire . . . governed by one supreme head and king'. The pope having already been deprived of his legislative and judicial powers, the Act of Supremacy merely recorded an established fact, declaring that the king 'shall be taken, accepted and reputed the only supreme head in earth of the Church of England called *Anglicana Ecclesia*'. The only novelty in the act was to give the Crown the power of ecclesiastical visitation, indicating that the attack on the monasteries was already being planned.

Royal supremacy was thus claimed to be the resumption of ancient rights usurped by the Bp of Rome, whose pretended authority in the temporal sphere properly belonged to the Crown. Although these measures were all embodied in statute, the royal supremacy was personal, not parliamentary. The episcopal or administrative powers of the Church were inherent in the monarch by virtue of an office that was divinely ordained. Although he did not exercise priestly functions and delegated his spiritual authority to others, ultimate responsibility for the doctrine and government of the Church was solely his.

Mary I restored ecclesiastical supremacy to the pope, and Elizabeth I's act of 1559 had to be drafted three times before parliament would accept it. There being some doubt whether a woman could be supreme head, it declared her 'supreme governor . . . as well in all spirititual or ecclesiastical things or causes as temporal'. It enabled a High Commission court for the correction of errors and abuses to be set up, and required all lay and ecclesiastical officials to take an oath acknowledging the queen's supremacy and renouncing foreign allegiances.

Because of its personal character, royal supremacy was disliked by some Protestants as well as Catholics. If the ruler were 'godly', well enough; but if he or she were not, it could prove a very unsatisfactory arrangement. For most of her reign Elizabeth had to defend her supremacy as belonging exclusively to the royal prerogative, in opposition to the Puritan contention that it was shared with parliament. Her insistence provoked the frustrated zealots to attack the prerogative on other matters besides religion.

G. R. Elton, *The Tudor Constitution* (Cambridge, 1960).
MMR

SUPREME BEING, CULT OF (1794), in France, Robespierre's attempt to reconcile the majority of Catholics with the French Revolution, while giving expression to the religious ideas of Rousseau. He hoped that it would meet the charges of atheism levelled against the republic because of the attacks on organized religion by the Hébertists, but it merely produced suspicion on all sides. Although the Convention had formally adopted this new civic religion on 7 May 1794, it died with Robespierre.

SUPREME COURT OF JUDICATURE ACT (1873) in Britain, legislative measure passed by Gladstone's Liberal administration, as a consolidation of a legal field full of medieval survivals. It was an excellent piece of drafting by Lord Selborne, the lord chancellor. Previously there were two legal systems, the common law, administered in one set of courts, and equity, which over-rode it, in another. The act combined the two, declaring that they should be administered concurrently in every court by every judge, and that in cases of conflict equity should prevail. All existing courts were remodelled, Queen's Bench, Common Pleas, Exchequer, Chancery, High Court of Admiralty, Court of Probate, Court of Divorce and Matrimonial Causes were all united to form one Supreme Court of Judicature. The London Bankruptcy Court was later incorporated into the system (1883).

The act abolished the appeal jurisdiction of the House of Lords. This led to an outcry. Lord Cairns's Amending Act passed by the Conservatives (1876) restored the final appeal to the Lords past the appeal court, constituting the Lords' tribunal as it exists today (1970).

The Judicature Act was the foundation of the modern unified legal system. A number of subsidiary acts were passed. In 1881 the Crown, which was empowered under the act to make further changes by Orders in Council, merged the Common Pleas Division and the Exchequer Division into the Queen's Bench. In 1925 the whole series of acts was consolidated in the Judicature Act but the basis of the system established (1873–5) remained unchanged in 1970.
BHH

SUPREME COURT, OF THE US, highest court in the federal judicial system. The US constitution gives the court original jurisdiction in all cases affecting ambassadors, other public ministers and consuls, and those in which a state shall be a party, and appellate jurisdiction in all other cases coming before it, with such exceptions and under such regulations as Congress shall make. Its judicial powers are defined by the US constitution, statutes, and its own precedents, but a combination of convention and necessity has extended its influence. The Supreme Court can, but does not always, consider any case involving questions of federal law, and such cases may come on appeal from lower federal courts, from state courts, by writ of error or writ of *certiorari*. This exercise of judicial review can extend to important matters such as the meaning of a legislative statute, the constitutionality of a presidential action or the meaning of a particular clause of the US constitution, and the court is the final arbiter on questions concerning the nature of the federal system, and the respective authority of different levels of government.

The political potential of the court is revealed in formal matters, such as its composition. Since 1869 it has consisted of a chief justice and eight associate justices, but its size is determined by statute. It was initially fixed at six (1789), then five (1801), seven (1807), nine (1837), ten (1863), and seven (1866), and some of these changes were the result of political

attempts to affect the balance of opinion on the court. Justices are appointed by the president of the US subject to the advice and consent of the Senate. Senate opposition has led to the withdrawal of nominations, and the Senate has also rejected outright some nominees. The court is subject to limitations imposed by the constitution, and by others which are self-imposed. It can only consider cases for which it has constitutional authority, will only consider cases in which there is a genuine conflict between litigants, and will not give advisory opinions.

The history of the court reflects its political role. Originally considered a body of little or no influence, the political potentialities of a skilful use of judicial power were revealed during John Marshall's term as chief justice (1801–35), while the political effects of court opinions were demonstrated by the *Dred Scott* case (1857) and *Plessy v. Ferguson* (1896). The full political value of the ability to interpret the constitution was shown in a number of decisions involving state and national legislation in the 1880s and 1890s, and during the 1930s, when the decisions of the court stimulated a constitutional crisis. Since the 1930s the court, exercising judicial self-restraint, has been reluctant to challenge the constitutionality of acts of Congress, but became a source of political controversy in the 1950s and 1960s by its vigorous defence of civil rights and individual liberties.

S. Krislov, *The Supreme Court in the Political Process* (London & New York, 1965).
C. Warren, *The Supreme Court in United States History*, 2 vols (Boston, 1960).
JDL

SUPREME COURT PACKING PLAN, in the US, proposal made by President Franklin D. Roosevelt to reform the federal judiciary (1937). Frustrated by Supreme Court decisions invalidating major parts of his New Deal programme on grounds of its unconstitutionality, Roosevelt introduced a Plan for the Reorganization of the Judicial Branch into Congress (5 Feb. 1937). Under the guise of improving judicial efficiency, the plan permitted the president to increase the Supreme Court bench with up to six new justices by appointing an additional member for each incumbent failing to retire within six months of attaining the age of seventy. Circuit and district court benches were to be increased in size, and their work supervised by a proctor. The bill met with strong criticism in the press and with vigorous bipartisan opposition, led by Burton K. Wheeler of MT, in the Senate. Chief Justice Hughes effectively dismissed Roosevelt's accusation of inefficiency in a public letter addressed to Senator Wheeler. When the court sustained a Washington minimum wage statute (29 March), and upheld the constitutionality of the Wagner Act (12 April), and when Justice Van Devanter announced his retirement (18 May), the political reasons for reorganizing the Supreme Court seemed to disappear. The death of Senate majority leader Joseph Robinson of AR (14 July) finally removed any possibility of successful passage of the comprehensive bill. Only a minor act reorganizing the lower courts was passed.
ICP

SUR DYNASTY, THE, of Delhi (1540–55), established by Sher Shah, an Afghan chief of Bihar, who took advantage of the Mughal Homayun's weakness and after twice defeating him at Chausa (1539), and Kanauj (1540) drove him from India. Sher Shah in five years consolidated his power and outlined a revenue and administrative system which provided a blue-print for the Mughal Akbar. After his death before Kalanjar (1545) his son Islam Shah succeeded, but on his death (1554) the dynasty broke into factions and was ejected by Homayun (1555).

SURAJ MAL (d. 1763), Jat chieftain and Raja of Bharatpur (*reg.* 1756–63), who was the ablest of the Jat chiefs. Taking advantage of Mughal weakness, he seized Agra in 1761. He was defeated and killed while opposing Najib-ud-daula, regent of Delhi.

SURAKARTA, also called Solo, in central Java. After 1745 it was the seat of the Susuhunans, who carried the name Pakubuwana. In 1755 the kingdom was split, one half going to the sultans of Jogjakarta. In 1757 a further division gave a portion of the lands of Surakarta to the Prince Mangkunegara and his descendants. The area is now (1970) incorporated into the republic of Indonesia.

SURAPATI (d. 1706), Javanese soldier and rebel leader in east and central Java, said to have been originally a Balinese slave in the service of the Dutch. In the late 1670s he led a group of soldiers in rebellion against the Dutch, and ultimately found support at the Javanese court of Amangkurat II (*reg.* 1677–1703). In 1686 he slaughtered a Dutch force sent to Kartasura to arrest him. He then fled eastwards to Pasuruan, while the Dutch withdrew the remnants of their garrison from Kartasura. Javanese troops sent out against Surapati had no success, possibly an intentional outcome. He then extended his domain in eastern Java and Balambangan, where his descendants were to hold out until 1777. Subsequent efforts by the Dutch East India Co. proved more successful, and in 1706 Dutch troops severely wounded Surapati in an attack upon Bangil.

SURINAM (Dutch Guiana), in South America. The coast of Guiana, discovered by the Spaniard Alonso de Hojeda (1499), was first settled by the Dutch over a century later, but was destroyed by the Spaniards (1613). English settlers (1630) were displaced by equally unsuccessful Frenchmen (1640). English planters from Barbados settled there (1650), but by the treaty of Breda (1667) the territory was awarded to the Dutch, who then surrendered NY. The English seized Surinam (1799), surrendering it to the Batavian republic at the peace of Amiens (1802). In 1804 the English recaptured it, finally returning it to the Dutch by the treaty of Paris (1816). Dutch Guiana developed a plantation economy based on sugar, coffee, cocoa, and cotton. The plantations were worked by African slave labour, and after the abolition of slavery (1863) Dutch planters introduced indentured servants, chiefly from India and Indonesia. In the interior escaped slaves, known as Djukas or Bush Negroes, formed their own groups, along with a small Amerindian population. Surinam was governed by the Dutch West India Co. until renewal of its charter was refused in 1791; it then became a Crown possession. The growth of political parties, based on ethnic divisions, led, after the Second World War, to expansion of the franchise (1949) and to internal self-government (1954).

SURJI-ARJUNGAON, TREATY OF (30 Dec. 1803), ended the war between Daulat Rao Sindhia and the East India Co. Sindhia ceded his territories in the Ganges–Jumna *doab* and accepted a British resident at his court.

SURMAN, JOHN (*c.* 1689–1724), English colonial official and servant of the East India Co., who led an embassy to the Mughal court of Farrukhsiyar (1714–17). Because no English merchant knew Persian, he had as a colleague an Armenian, Khwaja Sarhad, friction with whom hindered the mission. Nevertheless, aided by a cure effected by William Hamilton, a surgeon who had been attending the emperor, the mission obtained *farman*s (mandates) granting the company additional land round Calcutta and confirming its freedom from internal dues. The award, though contested by the Nawab of Bengal, was a landmark in the company's history.

SURVIVANCE, in France, practice which developed in 16th-cent. France and continued until 1789, of resigning office in favour of a close relative, while continuing to hold the position jointly, with royal dispensation, for the duration of life. This procedure evolved to preserve offices within a family by insuring against sudden death.

SURYAVARMAN, name taken by two important kings of Angkor, Cambodia. The first of them (*reg.* 1011–50) built the Ta-Keo temple, and was probably responsible for extending the hydraulic system of Angkor. He was powerful enough to intervene in a conflict between Champa and Dai-Viet, on the side of the former (*c.* 1030). Suryavarman II (*reg.* 1113–50) was the builder of Angkor Wat. Unlike other kings of Angkor, he was a Vishnavite Hindu rather than a Saivite. In 1116 he sent envoys to China. In 1128, 1132, and 1136 his armies invaded Dai-Viet, but were driven back. In 1144–5 a Khmer attack on Champa was more successful, culminating in the sack of Vijaya, the Cham capital.

SUSA, ancient city at the junction of a number of roads on the Khuzistan plain. It was the capital of Elam and later a capital of Persia in Achaemenid times (*c.* 559–330 BC).

SUSA, PEACE OF (April 1629), Anglo-French peace treaty, following the collapse of English naval support for the French Huguenots' rebellion at La Rochelle. Deserted by Charles I, the Huguenot leader, the Duc de Rohan, therefore signed a treaty with Philip IV (3 May 1629) promising Spanish military aid for the rebels in southern France.

SUSLOV, MIKHAIL ANDREYEVICH (1902–   ), Soviet politician and Communist Party official, often regarded as one of the most doctrinaire communists of the Khrushchev period. He joined the Communist Party in 1921, and rose rapidly during the great purge, being secretary of the Rostov Oblast committee (1937–9), then the Stavropol territorial committee (1939–41). He joined the central committee (1941), served as a political officer during the Second World War, then was appointed to a commanding position in Lithuania (1944–6) where he was responsible for bringing the country under Soviet rule. He was then appointed head of the agitation and propaganda department of the central committee (1946), becoming a secretary of the central committee in the following year (1947). He took over leadership of the Cominform on the death of Zhdanov (1948) and continued to play an important part in relations with foreign parties, particularly at the world communist meetings in Moscow (1957, 1960). In addition, he served for a time as editor of *Pravda* (1949–50). He is reported to have taken an active part in the attack on the 'anti-party group' (1957), but he remained independent of Khrushchev, and took an ideological stand against him. He is said to have led the indictment against Khrushchev when the latter was ousted from power (1964).   WFK

SUSLOV, NADIA (1843–1918), pioneer Russian woman doctor, daughter of a freed serf whose master, Count Sheremetieff, paid for her education. She was trained at St Petersburg and in Switzerland, built up a large practice, and fought for the social and economic liberation of women in Russia.

SUSNEYOS (*reg.* 1607–32), Emperor of Ethiopia. Having come to power with the support of descendants of Portuguese musketeers, he wrote to Philip III of Spain proposing an alliance and the despatch of Spanish musketeers to fight his Muslim and Gala enemies. In 1621 he announced his willingness to become a Catholic and revealed his conversion in 1626, when he tried by force to impose Catholicism on his subjects. This leading to rebellion and civil war, he established religious toleration and abdicated in 1632.

SUSPENDING POWER in Britain, by which the king claimed the right to nullify parliamentary statutes entirely. Thus it was a more far-reaching assertion of royal authority than the dispensing power, and if conceded could have destroyed parliament's legislative authority. Charles II and James II tried to use this power to resolve religious conflicts, *eg*, Charles's Declarations of Indulgence (1662, 1672), but parliament compelled Charles to withdraw both. On 17 April 1688 James II reissued his Declaration of Indulgence of a year before, adding to it an order that it should be read in every church in the kingdom. Abp Sancroft and six bishops petitioned against this, and the questionable use of the suspending power, since the declaration meant that the Test Act and the oaths of allegiance and supremacy were not to be applied to office-holders. In 1689 the Bill of Rights declared that 'the pretended power of suspending of laws, or the execution of laws, by regal authority, without consent of parliament, is illegal'.

SUSSEX PLEDGE (4 May 1916), undertaking given by Germany that henceforth her submarines would not destroy merchant vessels without warning and safety provisions. Arising from the sinking of an unarmed French cross-channel steamer, it marked the temporary success of the US diplomatic campaign against U-boat warfare which began with the 'Strict Accountability' note of 10 Feb. 1915.

SUSUHUNAN, hereditary title of a number of rulers of the house of Mataram, also sometimes called Sunan. After 1755 the title was used exclusively by the rulers of Surakarta, with the name Pakubuwana. The title is Javanese, meaning 'he who is honoured'.

SUTEJ, JURAJ (1889–), Yugoslav lawyer and politician, who was a leader of the Croat Peasant Party and became minister of finance in the Cvetkovic government of 1939–41. During the Second World War he served in all the governments-in-exile. In 1945 he joined the provisional government of Yugoslavia as minister of trade and industry. But, together with Subasií, he resigned his post in protest against the conduct of the 1945 elections.

SUTRAS, Sanskrit texts of ancient India consisting each of numerous aphorisms reduced to the utmost brevity for mnemotechnic reasons. Most of these texts deal with ritual, law, Sanskrit grammar, and philosophy.

SUTTER'S FORT, stronghold and residence erected by John Augustus Sutter (1803–80) on his lands in the lower Sacramento valley of CA (1841). For many immigrants in the 1840s it marked the end of the California Trail across the Sierras. When gold was discovered near the fort (Jan. 1848) hundreds of squatters moved in, most of the fort was dismantled, and Sutter ruined.

SUTTON HOO SHIP BURIAL, discovered in Suffolk in 1939. The ship was 85 ft (26 metres) long and 14 ft (4·3 metres) wide. The treasures in the grave were many and varied and suggested that this was the cenotaph of a king, possibly Raedwald (c. 617).

SUVOROV, ALEKSANDER VASILEYEVICH, Count (1730–1800), Russian soldier who was victorious in the Seven Years War, and, later, against the Turks and against Napoleon I. His crossing of the Alps (1799) became a legend in military history.

SUZUKI, KANTARŌ (1867–1948), Japanese sailor and politician, who was appointed prime minister (April 1945). He presided over the cabinet which accepted unconditional surrender.

SVATOPLUK OF MORAVIA (d. 894). The collapse of the Avar empire after 791 led to the emergence of a Great Moravian state ruled by a native dynasty, of which Svatopluk was the most powerful member. He replaced (c. 870) his uncle Ratislav, under whom a form of Christianity, using a Slavonic liturgy, had been introduced from Constantinople by St Cyril and St Methodius. Though unfriendly to Methodius, Svatopluk spread the Slavonic rite to his conquests in modern Hungary, Bohemia, and southern Poland. After 892 he had to resist attack by the nomad Hungarians instigated by the German King Arnulf. They completely destroyed the Moravian state in 906, so that even the site of Svatopluk's capital cannot be rediscovered.

SVEIN HARALDSSON (*reg.* 986–1014) (Forkbeard), Danish king, son, and successor of Harold Bluetooth. Having supplanted his father, he extended Danish power in Scandinavia by throwing off any Swedish authority that may have been imposed (c. 980) and he was the motive force behind the confederacy which destroyed Olaf Tryggvason of Norway (c. 1000). Abroad, he extended the scope of Viking activities to full-scale conquest, especially in the England of Aethelred the Unready. He was acknowledged as King of England late in 1013 and died there, leaving his claims to his son Cnut.

SVERDRUP, JOHAN (1816–92), Norwegian politician and lawyer who advocated democratic reforms and liberal principles. He brought the cabinet into actual membership of the Storthing (Parliament) in 1884, so giving the country 'responsible government'. His Liberal administration (1884–1889) fulfilled many of his aims, *eg*, trial by jury and a widened suffrage but split on the issue of the power of the clergy in local government. In foreign affairs he was regarded as indifferent to the growing cause of complete independence from Sweden.

SVERRE SIGURDSSON (d. 1202), King of Norway (*reg.* 1184–1202), who claimed descent from the otherwise extinct Yngling royal dynasty, challenged the predominance of the Church in Norway, and appealed to the old concept of kingship by popular election as against kingship by divine right. With Swedish help, after a civil war (1177–84), he drove out the bishops and King Magnus V. He radically reformed Norwegian government and sharply defended the principle of secular supremacy against the Church. But his son King Hakon III was subsequently reconciled with the papacy.

SVYATOSLAV I (d. 972), Prince of Kiev and its last pagan ruler, who fought successfully against the Khazars, and unsuccessfully in Bulgaria. He was driven out of Bulgaria by the Byzantine emperor, John I Tzimiskes, in 971 and killed by an ambush of Pecheneg nomads on his way back to Kiev.

SWABIAN LEAGUE, association of 22 imperial cities of Germany, princes, prelates, and the knights' league of Swabia, founded in 1488 at Esslingen to counteract the Swiss and the Wittelsbach rulers of Bavaria. Tyrol and Württemberg joined from the outset, the states of Palatinate, Mainz, Trier, and Baden soon acceded, while Hesse, Bavaria, Ansbach, and Bayreuth eventually became members. The league established a federal council and an army of 13,000 men, who helped to rescue the future Emperor Maximilian I from captivity in the Netherlands shortly after its formation (1488). It became the mainstay of Habsburg authority in south-west Germany during Maximilian's reign, and remained active during the early part of Charles V's reign, *eg*, when Ulrich of Württemberg seized Reutlingen (1519) the league expelled him and sold the duchy to Charles V (1520). Under George Truchess the league's forces co-operated in the overthrow of Franz von Sickingen (1523) and the suppression of the Peasants' War (1524–25). Its members, however, became divided on religious grounds and, despite Charles V's attempts to revive the league, by 1536 it had become defunct.

SWABIAN WAR (1499), conflict between the Swiss and Maximilian I, who was allied to Constance and the Swabian League. It was the last war fought by the Swiss to maintain their independence and ended in the peace of Basle, by which Maximilian I tacitly recognized Switzerland's independence.

SWADESHI MOVEMENT in India, often linked with the boycott of British goods, which aimed at encouraging the manufacture and use of Indian-made goods such as cloth, soap, sugar, etc. Adopted as one of the basic agitational strategies against the partition of Bengal (1905), the Swadeshi (lit. 'of our own country') movement spread rapidly in Bengal and into other provinces. Bonfires were made of foreign cloth, shops were picketed, and those that continued to sell foreign goods were threatened with a boycott. Indian mills and factories were able to meet some of the demand thus created and a stimulus was given to many new industries—notably perhaps the Tata Iron and Steel Co. (1907). Swadeshi shops and volunteer salesmen sold locally produced goods and for a time patriotic fervour induced many people even to pay higher prices for them. While moderate Congressmen distinguished sharply between the Swadeshi movement to promote Indian industries and the boycott movement to redress the Bengal grievance, more extreme Congressmen saw both Swadeshi and boycott as weapons with which to beat Britain and achieve *swaraj*. Conflict over this question split the Congress at Surat in 1907.

SWAHILI CHRONICLES, record oral traditions, written down in the 19th cent., some specifically by or for Europeans. The most important are the various versions of the Pate chronicle and the Lamu, Kilwa, and Mombasa chronicles. Two of the Pate versions are in English; the Mombasa chronicle is in English and French; the others have survived, as they were written, in Swahili. The Pate chronicle is a dynastic history and begins with the arrival of the Nabahani, allegedly in AD 1204. In fact, they did not reach East Africa until the end of the 16th cent. The Lamu chronicle describes the arrival of Syrians in the 7th cent. and their conflict and eventual union with earlier immigrants from the Yemen. It then leaps to the 18th cent.

The Kilwa chronicle describes the arrival of the Shirazi and then leaps likewise to the 18th cent. The Mombasa chronicle, on the other hand, begins with the building of Fort Jesus by the Portuguese in the late 16th cent. and then moves to the 18th cent. The Pate chronicle, in which reference is made to the Portuguese, is the only one susceptible of correlation with other sources, which are much confused.
· For the 18th cent. the value of these chronicles is considerable, both for the detail recorded and for the way of life depicted. Some of the texts may include material which was probably written originally in Arabic. Their description of events earlier than the middle of the 18th cent. is questionable, but among the fantasies there are certainly recollections of facts, such as the making of the ivory horn of Pate, which would otherwise have been lost.

SWAHILI CULTURE, Arabo-Muslim culture, using a Bantu-African language and containing Persian, Indian, and probably Indonesian elements, as yet little understood. The African contribution is to be found in the music and dancing, and in inheritance and marriage customs, which are sometimes contrary to Islamic law. It is a culture arising from settlements of traders from Arabia and founded at least as early as the 9th cent. of the Christian era. It extended along the shores of the Indian Ocean from Mogadishu in Somalia to Sofala in Mozambique, and included the off-shore islands of Pemba, Zanzibar, Mafia, and the Comoros, and the north and north-west coasts of Madagascar as far south as Majunga and Bueni. The literature consists of poems, secular and religious, which in their present and written form belong to the 18th cent., although earlier material is incorporated in some of them. The spoken language originated many centuries earlier. The architecture, consisting of mosques, houses, and tombs, built of coral-rag and rubble, red earth and lime, is in the Islamic tradition, but has well-defined local features, of which the most striking are the tall tomb pillars, which do not occur elsewhere in the Muslim world. Another peculiarity of the coastal culture were the dhows made of planks tied together with coconut fibres, with a swan-neck prow and a lateen sail of coconut matting, called *mtepe*; these were in use until *c.* 1920. Local crafts include the making of carved musical horns in ivory or wood, and woodwork in the form of carved doors in Indian style, ornamental locks, chairs inlaid with horn and ivory, and stools for grating coconuts. A fine standard of needlework is shown in the embroidered white cotton caps.

SWAINSON, WILLIAM (1809–84), NZ politician, who was attorney-general (1841–54) in the crisis (1854) over responsible government, which he opposed, fearing European encroachment on Maori land.

SWAMMERDAM, JAN (1637–80), Dutch naturalist and doctor of medicine of Leyden, famous for his anatomical and physiological studies of insects. Among his discoveries made with the help of simple biconvex lenses were the life-cycle of the may-fly and that the embryo of the insect is pre-formed in the egg.

SWAN, SIR JOSEPH WILSON (1828–1914), British physicist and chemist, who started (1848) to investigate the use of a carbon filament for an incandescent electric lamp. However, progress was prevented by the state of other fields of technology and it was not until 1878 that Swan was able to demonstrate publicly a reliable carbon filament lamp. These soon gained popularity in Britain and in 1881 the House of Commons was lit by them. Edison had produced a similar bulb at about the same time, but unlike Swan had obtained patents. In 1882 Edison lost a patent infringement action against Swan but they settled their differences and formed a joint company in Britain in 1883.

SWANSEA, seaport of Glamorganshire, Wales. The name stands for Sweyn's 'ey' or inlet and may be derived from Sweyn Forkbeard, who visited the Bristol Channel. The earliest known form of the name appears as Sweynesse in a charter of *c.* 1184. The town grew up around the castle built by Henry de Newburgh (*c.* 1099), which was finally destroyed by Owain Glendower. In the Civil War the town was royalist until the summer of 1645. Coal had been mined since the Middle Ages, but became important in the 18th cent. when copper smelting expanded. The docks were expanded in the 19th cent. for the shipment of coal from South Wales. The university college was founded in 1920, and in 1970 the town was the headquarters of British tin-plate and zinc production.

SWARAJYA PARTY, in India, or 'Self-Government Party', formed by a group of Congressmen led by C. R. Das, Motilal Nehru, and Vithalbhai Patel following the collapse of non-co-operation (1922). They aimed to re-establish Congress control of the legislatures and, by a programme of 'uniform, continuous and consistent obstruction', to force the government to negotiate further concessions. Anxious to minimize their break with the Gandhian movement, the 'pro-changers' called their policy 'non-co-operation from within', but their opponents ('no-changers') blocked their plans at the Gaya session (1922)—of which Das was president —and resolved to campaign against any such group at the elections. Das thereupon resigned the presidency and the Swarajists formed their party outside Congress, although they all remained members of the movement. Negotiations over 1923 softened the conflict and a special session in September gave permission for congressmen to contest the elections that year and agreed that it would suspend all agitation against 'council entry'.

The 1923 elections made the Swarajists the largest party in the central assembly and in several provinces but only in the Central Provinces and Bengal were they able to bring the legislatures to a halt. And despite their favourable position Gandhi was not reconciled to their activities until (Nov. 1924) he gained an agreement that they would carry out the 'constructive programme' in return for endorsement as Congress's legislative wing. Opposition within the party to the policy of obstruction led to the resignation of the 'Responsive Co-operationists' from Central Provinces and Bombay (1926) and this group, allied with Malaviya's Hindu nationalist 'Independent Congress Party', opposed the Swarajists in the 1926 elections on the grounds that they were insufficiently active in the defence of Hindus. The party's position was greatly weakened as a result and it operated less effectively until the walk-out in May 1929 which brought its activities to an end. It was revived in the aftermath of civil disobedience to conduct the Congress campaign for the central assembly elections (1934). With Gandhi's blessing it had some success but it was weakened to some extent by the opposition of the Malaviya-led 'Congress Nationalist Party' which campaigned for decisive opposition to the Communal Award. PDR

SWASTIKA, or hooked cross, one of the most ancient of religious symbols or charms, which is found in many countries, from India (Sanskrit *svasta*, luck) to Mexico. In European mythology it represented Thor's hammer or the wheel of the sun and became closely linked with the revival of Germanic legends and beliefs at the end of the 19th cent. As a result of this, it was used by many of the extreme right-wing movements which emerged in Germany after the First World War and was chosen by Hitler as the symbol of National Socialism. In Sept. 1935 it became Nazi Germany's official national emblem.

SWATANTRA PARTY in India, main conservative party, formed in 1959 by a merger of regional groups representing businessmen, well-to-do farmers, and landholders, former rulers of princely states, and led, in the main, by dissident Congressmen, the most notable of whom was C. Rajagopalachari. Its constituent groups account for its strength in certain regions and also for its 'free enterprise' policies, which call for an end to state control over industry and opposition to co-operative farming and radical land reform. In its first electoral contest (1962) the party emerged as the second largest opposition party. It further improved its position in 1967, becoming the major partner in a coalition government in the state of Orissa.

SWAZI, nation formed out of Sotho- and Nguni-speaking peoples, situated between modern Zululand, Portuguese East Africa, and the Transvaal, by the Dhlamini royal clan of the Ngwane people, who moved across the Pongola river during the Mfecane (*c.* 1815). Organized on similar lines to the military kingdoms of northern Zululand, the Ngwane conquered existing peoples in the area relatively easily and incorporated them under their traditional authorities. The age-regiment system, and the appointment of territorial chiefs subject only to the Swazi king, created a measure of central control and loyalty.

Throughout the 19th cent. the Swazi royal family developed their skill in diplomacy, which they first used in dealing with the Zulu kings. Later they used it to ward off Boer, Portuguese, and British rule by playing off one side against another, though at the expense of very considerable loss of land. In 1894 they came under the jurisdiction of the South African republic. After the Anglo-Boer War, Swaziland became a British protectorate. Until the 1950s the British government considered the future of Swaziland to lie in its incorporation into South Africa. This was strongly resisted by the Swazi, despite their economic dependence on South Africa and the presence of a large number of white settlers in their territory. In 1968 Swaziland became an independent state within the British Commonwealth. Its king is executive head of state and appoints the prime minister and cabinet from a House of Assembly and senate which are elected by adult suffrage. All adult male Swazis advise the king direct through the National Council.

SWEDENBORG, EMMANUEL (1688–1772), Swedish philosopher, scientist, and mystic. He wrote books on a large range of subjects—algebra, calculus, navigation, astronomy, and chemistry—before publishing his monumental *Opera Philosophica et Mineralia* (1734), which was followed by his *Philosophical Argument on the Infinite*, and anatomical and physiological studies, *Economy of the Animal Kingdom* and *The Animal Kingdom*. By 1743 he was becoming convinced of his direct access to the spirit world and gave up his scientific work to carry out spiritual and psychical research.

He moved to London, and in 1754 underwent a religious conversion as a result of which he became the prophet of a new apocalyptic religion from which the New Jerusalem Church sprang.

SWEDISH AFRICA COMPANY (1649–67) built Cape Coast Castle (1652), which they lost to the English in 1664.

SWEDISH CONSTITUTION (1809) was set up after Gustavus IV had been deposed as the result of a widely supported coup. A committee of the four estates allocated the executive power to the Crown, operating through ministerial heads of departments; the legislative to the *Riksdag*, with provision for quinquennial sessions and acceptance for most purposes of a majority of three estates; and the judicial to irremovable judges, including an *ombudsman* as a safeguard against the encroachments of bureaucracy. It remained in force in 1970.

SWEDISH DIET, or Estates General, body constituting the *Riksdag* or 'Day of the Realm'. After its formation in 1435 it met occasionally at times of crisis (*eg*, at Västerås in 1527), but was more fully organized by Gustavus Adolphus (1617). It levied new taxes and expressed the views of the different estates on royal policy, and in 1634 its decisions were given the force of law. It acquired supreme power under the 1719 constitution. The four estates of nobles, clergy, burgesses, and peasants met triennially, but deliberated and voted separately and only members of the first three were regularly eligible for the all-powerful Secret Committee, which appointed the ministers. The so-called Age of Freedom after 1719 was racked by party quarrels between the more aristocratic 'Hats' and the more popularly based 'Caps', which had the support respectively of France and Russia. The Hats drove the country into the Seven Years War as the ally of France, while the Caps weakened the defences of Finland and approved the first partition of Poland to suit the Russians. In 1772, however, the *coup d'état* of Gustavus III resulted in the subordination of the Diet, which was to meet only when the sovereign chose, and the abolition of the parties.

SWEDISH EAST INDIA COMPANY, founded in 1731, traded chiefly with Canton. Large profits were earned on tea and chinaware, but the company declined after the 1780s and was abolished in 1813.

SWEDISH POMERANIA, including Stralsund and Rügen, was reunited in 1815 with the portions previously ceded to Brandenburg–Prussia. In 1805–7 it had served as a base for unsuccessful operations in the French Wars against Napoleon I, and was briefly in Danish hands (treaty of Kiel) before it was acquired by Prussia in exchange for Lauenburg.

SWEDISH SOUTH SEA COMPANY, founded in 1626 by a Dutch adventurer at Gothenburg. It made unsuccessful attempts to trade or colonize in regions controlled by Spain. Its ships also conveyed the first Swedish expedition to the Delaware.

SWEDISH WEST INDIA COMPANY, founded in 1786 to trade from St Barthélemy. It was abolished in 1805.

SWEDISH-DUTCH COMMERCIAL TREATY (1681), gave the Dutch 'most-favoured nation' treatment (as in 1659–67) and caused Sweden to abandon privileged companies and increase foreign rights of access to her ports. In 1691, however, she protected her own foreign trade by a treaty of armed neutrality with Denmark which was designed to counter the Anglo-Dutch blockade of France.

SWEELINCK, JAN PIETERSZOON (1562–1621), Dutch composer and one of the greatest of the early organists, who founded the distinctive North German school which later included Buxtehude and J. S. Bach. He studied in Venice and later became organist of the Old Church, Amsterdam (1581–1621), and composed mainly church music and organ works.

SWETTENHAM, SIR FRANK ATHELSTANE (1851–1946), British colonial administrator in Malaya, who made his career in the pioneering days of British rule in Selangor and Perak (1874–96). He championed the plan to federate the first four protected Malay States under a resident-general in Kuala Lumpur, and became himself the first resident-general (1896–1901). He established the Federated Malay States (FMS) as a relatively centralized and autonomous political unity. As governor of the Straits Settlements and high commissioner for the Malay States (1901–4), he pleaded for the extension of British influence at the expense of Siamese in the northern Malay states of Trengganu, Kelantan, Patani, and Kedah. These efforts were partially rewarded in the Anglo-Siamese treaty of 1902.

SWEYN II, ESTRITHSON (*reg.* 1064–76), King of Denmark. Shortly after Cnut's death in 1035, his great kingdom, comprising much of Scandinavia and England, dissolved and for a while Denmark came under Norwegian rule. Sweyn II, a nephew of Cnut, ended this Norwegian rule after a long war (1047–64). He founded a new Danish kingdom on western European lines and in close association with the Church.

SWIFT, GUSTAVUS FRANKLIN (1839–1903), US industrialist who pioneered methods of shipping refrigerated meat in the 1870s. His firm, Swift and Co. (1885), expanded purchasing, marketing, processing, and shipping facilities in the US and abroad and by the late 1890s controlled a huge vertically integrated empire. In 1902 Swift combined with the Armour and Morris companies to form the National Packing Co., the 'Beef Trust', which was dissolved by the US Supreme Court (1905).

SWIFT, JONATHAN (1667–1745), Irish cleric and author who was first employed in the household of Sir William Temple. Whilst there he wrote *The Battle of the Books* (1704) and *A Tale of a Tub* (1704). During Queen Anne's reign he frequently visited England on behalf of the Church of Ireland, and made the acquaintance of writers such as Addison and Steele. At first he was willing to be known as a Whig but eventually disclaimed the appellation. By the end of 1710, when Godolphin had fallen from power, he was on the closest terms with the Tory leaders Harley and St John, and was contributing scathing and vituperative articles to the Tory newspaper *The Examiner*. He stated forcefully and cogently the case for peace during the War of the Spanish Succession in the greatest of his pamphlets, 'The Conduct of the Allies' (1711). Meanwhile, the ecclesiastical promotion which he obtained from the Tories in 1713, the deanery of St Patrick's, Dublin, was most disappointing. Queen Anne had refused to make him a bishop. Swift regarded his return to Ireland as virtually a banishment. He spent the rest of his life there, apart from two brief visits to England. He wrote one further major pamphlet 'The Public Spirit of the Whigs' (1714), but after the death of Anne and the eclipse of the Tories his heyday as a political writer was over. In Ireland he turned his literary energies to a variety of subjects, even denouncing the exploitation of his fellow-countrymen over the affair of Wood's Halfpence in *Drapier's Letters to the People of Ireland* (1724). By that time he was writing *Gulliver's Travels*, published in 1726.

SWISS CONFEDERATION, evolved gradually out of a defensive alliance of a number of otherwise autonomous communities in central Switzerland. The conclusion of a perpetual alliance of the three Forest Cantons south of Lake Lucerne in 1291 is usually regarded as the first step in the growth of the confederation, though this was probably only a renewal of an earlier agreement. The opening up of a route through the St Gotthard pass, south of Lake Lucerne, in the 13th cent. brought a new prosperity to this region. It also increased the danger of exactions by territorial lords. The most serious threat came from the Habsburgs, who, from being merely the leading Swiss magnates, became in 1273 kings of Germany. The confederation of 1291, while affirming a demand to be tried solely by native judges, did not claim independence from the Habsburg rule, but the confederates gradually drifted into open hostility towards this dynasty. In 1315 they won their first great victory at Morgarten in resisting a Habsburg attack. Emperor Louis the Bavarian recognized the confederation as an autonomous unit within the German empire and the Habsburgs did so in 1355. By then it had expanded through the adhesion of other cantons and the support of the richest Swiss towns of Berne and Zürich. Another Habsburg offensive in 1386 ended in a Swiss victory at Sempach, which was followed by further territorial annexations by the confederation. In the later 15th cent. the Swiss infantry became the terror of their neighbours. In 1476 they defeated the invasion of Switzerland by Charles of Burgundy and killed him at Nancy (1477). Italian states eagerly recruited the Swiss into their service during the Italian wars (1499–1525). By then the confederation numbered 13 members, but it was a very loose combination of virtually autonomous cantons. The appearance of Protestantism at first menaced the unity of the league, but the victory of the Catholic cantons over the Protestants of Zürich at Kappel in 1531 and the death there of Zwingli, Zürich's religious 'prophet', inaugurated an era of tacit tolerance between the two religions within Switzerland (1542).

MH

SWISS CONFEDERATION (1848) represented both a successful compromise between native advocates of a unitary state and upholders of traditional cantonal sovereignty, and a hopeful symbol to liberals and democrats everywhere. The Radicals' quick success in the Sonderbund War (1847), and the temporary distraction of Europe's great powers by revolutions, made 1848 propitious for constitution-building. In two months the Revision Commission prepared a draft which each canton except Fribourg submitted to a referendum, which was approved by a substantial majority.

A bicameral legislature, in which the National Council represented nation-wide opinion, and the Council of States upheld cantonal interests, partly pacified traditionalists. The legislature elected the executive seven-man Federal Council, whose permanence gave Swiss policies more consistency. The federal government could stop internal disputes and amend the cantons' constitutions. Its assumption of all diplomatic and some military responsibilities reinforced national unity and removed opportunities for foreign intervention. Cantons could no longer contract to supply mercenaries to other countries.

The confederation's new financial independence necessarily strengthened its position. Federal control of ports, coinage (based on the French franc), customs (internal tolls were abolished), and weights and measures, necessitated standardization and greater national prosperity, as did the rapid though haphazard growth of railways. The existence of a republican government elected by manhood suffrage, in a country where three national languages and two religions coexisted peacefully and citizens were guaranteeed civil liberties, posed a challenge to conservative Europe. Switzerland carefully preserved its neutrality during and after the 1848 upheavals, despite protests over the asylum given to refugees such as Mazzini and Richard Wagner. Britain consistently supported the new confederation, notably in its dispute (1848–56) with Prussia over Neuchatel.

MRB

SWISS MERCENARIES, infantry soldiers of the Swiss cantons, whose hired labour in the service of the German emperors, French kings, Sforza dukes of Milan, and the papacy constituted the Swiss confederation's chief export in the period of the Italian Wars. The military reputation of the Swiss infantry was established by their victories over the Burgundian cavalry at Grandson and Morat (1476). Until 1510 they were employed by Louis XII in his conquest of northern Italy, but took part in the imperial victory at Novara (1513) and helped to drive the French out of Italy.

However, their reputation for invincibility was profoundly shaken by their defeat at Marignano (1515) after which the Swiss mercenary leader Matthias Schinner signed a perpetual peace with France (1516). After being shattered by the imperial artillery at Bicocca (1522) these hardy and well-disciplined infantrymen were superseded on European battle-fields by the Spanish *tercios*.

SWITZERLAND, CIVIL WAR IN (1847), fought between the Catholic Sonderbund and those cantons (which were a majority) that advocated constitutional revision and a stronger, liberalizing central government. The war ended after 25 days in a victory for the latter. The out-numbered Sonderbund expected Austrian and French help, but the swift victory of the Diet's troops under Dufour forestalled its arrival. Traditional cantonal rivalries, which the Sonderbund upheld, weakened their military efforts. They paid the war's costs and installed new cantonal administrations. Palmerston supported the Diet against belated pressure from the other great powers. The war marked the beginnings of Switzerland's true national independence and unity, and a widespread European revolutionary upsurge.

SWOPE, GERARD (1872–1957), US businessman, engineer, and government adviser, who held various positions in the electrical engineering industry (1893–1922), and became chairman of the International General Electrical Co. (1922–1933) and a director of many other companies. He served on various government committees during the 1930s, *eg*, the Industrial Advisory Board of the NRA.

SYBARIS, ancient Greek colony in southern Italy near the mouth of the Crati river, Calabria, founded (*c.* 720 BC) from Troezen and Achaea. In the 6th cent. it and its colonies, *eg*, Paestum, controlled Etruscan trade, and Sybarite wealth and luxury became proverbial. The colony was destroyed by Croton in 510 and, after two failures to resettle the original site, Thurii was founded nearby in 443.

SYBOTA, BATTLE OF (433 BC), off south-east Corcyra (Corfu), one of the incidents leading to the great Peloponnesian War. The intervention of ten Athenian ships to save the Corcyreans from defeat by the Corinthians, who withdrew when 20 more appeared, was regarded by the Corinthians as an act of war.

SYDNEY OF ST LEONARDS, THOMAS TOWNSHEND, 1st Viscount (1733–1800), British Whig politician, who sympathized with Chatham rather than Rockingham. He served in minor capacities under Rockingham and Chatham in the 1760s, defended Charles Townshend's duties, taxing the American colonies (1767), but went into opposition over the Middlesex election controversy (1769) and became a leading member of the opposition to North's government. He was secretary at war in Rockingham's second administration. Under Shelburne (1782–3) he was home secretary, and as the government's chief spokesman in the Commons defended the terms of the peace treaty with America. He was home secretary again (1783–9) under the Younger Pitt, but was never one of Pitt's inner circle of advisers.

SYKES, SIR MARK (1879–1919), British writer and politician, who conducted the British negotiations with France which culminated in the Sykes–Picot agreement (1916). He played an important part in the formulation of British policy towards the Ottoman empire in the First World War.

SYKES–PICOT AGREEMENT (1916), Anglo-French agreement on spheres of influence in the Arab Middle East, after the First World War. It provided for French control of coastal Syria, Lebanon, and Mosul, British control of Mesopotamia (together with Haifa and Acre), and an international administration in Palestine. Elsewhere, Britain and France were to recognize an independent Arab state or states, in the northern area of which France, and in the southern Britain, would have certain economic and other rights of priority. The agreement, which was subsequently modified, became the subject of great controversy because of its conflict with Allied promises to the Arabs, *eg*, in the Husayn–McMahon correspondence.

SYLVESTER II (*reg.* 999–1003), Pope, who was one of the most learned scholars among medieval popes. His knowledge of music, astronomy, and mathematics made him a legendary figure. His work on the abacus became a standard text and he is the reputed inventor of the astrolabe. He was well known at the German imperial court under Otto II and Otto III, the latter making him Abp of Ravenna (998) and securing his election to the papacy. Otto's premature death (1002) was soon followed by that of Sylvester before he had a chance to accomplish much as pope.

SYLVESTER (*fl.* 16th cent.), Russian priest of the Blagoveshchensky Cathedral, court chaplain to Ivan IV, and a trusted member of the tsar's Chosen Council (1547–60). He eventually fell foul of the tsar, partly for openly championing the succession of Prince Vladimir against Ivan's son, Dmitri, when Ivan was thought to be dying (1553), and partly for advocating the conquest of Crimea rather than the Baltic provinces (1558). Accused by Ivan of plotting to deprive him of his authority, he was banished to the monastery of Solovestsk on the White Sea (1560).

SYMEON (*reg.* 893–927), Tsar of Bulgaria, under whom the first Bulgarian empire was at the summit of its splendour. The tsar, having brought under his control most of the Balkan lands, sought to subdue Constantinople itself. His resources did not suffice, however, and he failed to take Constantinople in 913 and 924. After his death, internal dissension did much to weaken the Bulgarian state and thus to lessen the danger confronting Byzantium.

SYMMACHUS, Q. AURELIUS (*c.* AD 340–402), Roman senator and orator, known through his collection of private letters and administrative reports, which he submitted to the emperor as prefect of Rome (384–5). He was a fervent supporter of state paganism. In his petition for the restoration of the Altar of Victory and priestly salaries (384) he was defeated by Ambrose of Milan, but continued to enjoy great prestige and, especially in the last years of his life, political influence. His writings were in his own day highly regarded, and are of great value to the social and political history of his age.

SYNCHRONOUS HISTORY, chronicle from the 7th cent. BC (apparently the preamble to an Assyro-Babylonian treaty), which surveys the relations of the two states from the early 15th to the early 8th cents.

SYNDICALISM, early 20th-cent. social theory, influenced by Proudhon rather than Marx, which advocated the replacement of the state by a syndicalist organization of society. Direct action, particularly strikes, were to be the means of doing so. The term is derived from the French *syndicat* and the movement grew out of French trade unionism with its localized character. It was led by Fernand Pelloutier, who from 1893 was secretary of the Confédération Générale du Travail, which in 1902 amalgamated with the Fédération des Bourses de Travail. Pelloutier tried to persuade workers to ignore political parties, and to show their solidarity by a general strike, using sabotage and violence to destroy capitalism. The theorist of the movement was Georges Sorel, who published *Réflexions sur la violence* (1908).

Although syndicalism was peculiarly French, it was found in other countries: in England (1910–14). Tom Mann was its spokesman; in the US the Industrial Workers of the World was founded in 1905 and suppressed in 1918, and in Italy syndicalism remained a force until the rise of Mussolini. In every country except Spain syndicalism had died down by the early 1920s. In Spain, with its anarchistic traditions, and particularly in Catalonia, syndicalism remained strong up to and during the Civil War. It was suppressed by Franco. PR

SYNOD OF ST FOY (May 1594) in France, one of a number of Huguenot assemblies held at a small town in the French *département* of the Gironde. A regional synod once sat there (1561) and after the Edict of Nantes a group of delegates met there to negotiate with the court (1601). The main meeting associated with St Foy called after the abjuration of Henry IV when the Huguenots were irritated by the king's slowness to grant them toleration and curtail the bias of the lower courts. A meeting of delegates revived the old political organization of the churches, on firmer and more democratic lines, and brought pressure on Henry by talking of looking for another protector such as the Elector Palatine. The king was forced to let the Synod meet more or less continuously, but finally conceded the Edict of Nantes only under threat of renewed hostilities.

SYNOECISM, ancient Greek term for the unification of several adjacent, but previously autonomous, communities into a single state with common citizenship. Often, as the term implies, this involved a new concentration of previously scattered population. The most famous synoecism was the creation of the Athenian state, supposedly by Theseus but in fact by Peisistratus, out of Athens and the surrounding communities of Attica (*c.* 545 BC). Athens' example was followed in the 5th cent. by the synoecism of Elis and of Mantinea (*c.* 470).

SYPHAX (*c. reg.* 213–202 BC), King of the Masaesylii, who reigned at the start of the Second Punic War over a region of Numidia corresponding approximately to modern Algeria. After fighting against the Carthaginians, he later joined them against Rome and was defeated by Massinissa, King of the Massylii. He was carried prisoner to Rome in 202 BC.

SYRACUSE, in eastern Sicily, in antiquity the principal Greek city-state on the island, founded by Corinth (*c.* 730 BC). It overcame hostile native Sicels, reducing some to serfdom, and its prosperity, derived from agriculture, is shown by its mid-6th cent. temple-building. It was temporarily overshadowed by Gela under Hippocrates (*c.* 499–*c.* 491), but flourished again under the 'tyrants' Gelon and Hiero I, who, after leading the successful resistance to Carthaginian invasion (480), subjected the other Greek cities of eastern Sicily. The democracy established in 466 abandoned their imperialism, but its revival after victories over the Etruscans (*c.* 453) and the Sicel Ducetius (450) prompted Leontini and Rhegium to seek Athenian help. Although, ignoring both Spartan expectations and Athenian provocation, the Syracusans remained neutral in the great Peloponnesian War, their further aggression, *eg,* against Leontini (422), provided an excuse for an Athenian attack, which almost succeeded (415). The Syracusans' destruction of their besiegers, a triumph for Hermocrates and their Spartan general, Gylippus, radically altered the course of the war in Sparta's favour, but within a few years they themselves nearly succumbed to internal strife and Carthaginian invasion, which engulfed Selinus, Acragas, and Gela (408–405). Syracuse was saved by Dionysius I, who while ruling ruthlessly as 'tyrant' (*reg.* 405–367) fought four wars with Carthage and enlarged the city, extending its power over Sicilian and Italian Greeks. But the Carthaginian menace survived him and threats to Syracuse's existence were fought off by Timoleon (344–343), who restored freedom and prosperity after the anarchy following Dionysius II's quarrel with Dion; by Agathocles (312–306), who re-established 'tyranny', became master of Greek Sicily and kept Syracuse stable until 289; and by Pyrrhus of Epirus in an interlude during his war with Rome (278–275). Eventually, Hiero II (*reg.* 270–*c.* 216) became Rome's ally in the First Punic War and acquiesced in Roman rule of Sicily. On his death in the Second Punic War Rome's

enemies made Syracuse Carthage's ally, but it was besieged and sacked by Marcellus (211). Syracuse remained the principal city of Sicily under the Romans. It was plundered by the Franks (*c* AD 280) and held by the Arabs (878–1085). TTBR

SYRIA, ROMAN, territories between the Euphrates and the Mediterranean, organized as a province by Pompey in 64 BC and later ruled by the emperors through legates with a garrison of four legions. It was a key province and guarded the neighbouring client-kingdoms, which were gradually absorbed as provinces, Syria Palaestina (AD 70), Arabia (105), Mesopotamia (195), and the frontier with the Parthians (Persians), who invaded Syria four times between 231 and 260, and Palmyra. After Diocletian's restoration (284–305), it enjoyed 200 years of peace and prosperity, exporting wine and olive oil and transmitting Asian caravan trade. Antioch, the chief city, was famous for both pagan and Christian learning, Berytus for its school of law, and Baalbek as a centre of pagan worship.

SYRIAN MASSACRES (1860). In 1858 a revolt of Maronite peasants against their Maronite landlords broke out in north Lebanon, then spread to Maronite peasants living under Druze landlords in south Lebanon, giving the struggle a sectarian character. The Druze, with the apparent agreement of local Ottoman officials, retaliated (May 1860). In four weeks an estimated 11,000 Christians were killed and nearly 100,000 made homeless. The massacre subsequently spread to Syria and nearly 5500 Christians were killed in Damascus. Order was restored by Fuad Pasha, who punished the officials responsible.

SYRIAN NATIONAL BLOC (Kutla al-Wataniyya), founded in 1928 out of the People's Party (1925) by Syrian nationalists opposed to French rule. The bloc formed the 1936 government and dominated Syrian politics (1943–7). After 1947 it split into the National Party (Al-Hizb al-Watani), based on Damascus, and the People's Party (Hizb al-Sha'b), based on Aleppo and Homs.

SYRIAN NATIONALISM. In the 19th cent. the term 'Syria' was normally used to denote the area covered by the modern states of Syria, Lebanon, Israel, and Jordan. This area was sub-divided into several Ottoman provinces. The development within it of various ideas of greater autonomy within or independence from the Ottoman empire form part of the history of Arab nationalism. Specifically, Syrian nationalism begins rather with the conquest of the area (1917–18) by the Allied forces under Allenby and the establishment of temporary administrations under British, French, and Arab control. The eastern area, centred on Damascus, was placed under the rule of Faysal, who attempted to rally Arab nationalists who were opposed to French claims in Syria. Faysal summoned the Syrian Congress (1919) which issued the Damascus Programme (2 July 1919), a demand for an independent united Syria, which would include the Lebanon and Palestine. Compromise between French and Arab ambitions proving impossible, the Syrian Congress declared Syria's independence, with Faysal as 'King of United Syria' (7–8 March 1920). The San Remo Conference decided (22 April 1920) to award the Syrian mandate to France. After an ultimatum (9 July), France occupied Damascus and overthrew Faysal's government (battle of Maysalun, 24 July 1920). French policy in Syria was characterized by attempts to divide the country for administrative purposes while retaining overall control. This led to the detachment of Greater Lebanon and Alexandretta (Hatay), but other attempts to create separate units failed because of determined Syrian opposition in the form of riots and rebellion against French rule in Jebel Druze and a large area of southern Syria (1925–6). Subsequently, French policy moved towards self-government. In 1928 a Constituent Assembly was elected, providing a focus for nationalist politicians to create the National Bloc. France refused to accept the nationalist's constitution, which proclaimed a united Syria, and issued her own constitution (1930), under which a parliament was elected (1932). Negotiations for a Franco-Syrian treaty were opened, but broke down. In 1936 the National Bloc organized a general strike. Negotiations were reopened which, after the formation of the Popular Front government in France, resulted in a Franco-Syrian treaty (Sept. 1936) promising Syria independence. This treaty was not ratified by France. In June 1941 British and Free French forces invaded Syria, overthrew the Vichy regime, and recognized Syria's independence (Sept. 1941). After new elections a nationalist government was formed and Shukri al-Quwaytli became president of the Syrian republic (Aug. 1943). The Free French authorities were still unwilling to concede complete independence and the issue was finally settled by armed British intervention (May 1945) which forced France to give way. Syrian independence was formally recognized in April 1946.

S. H. Longrigg, *Syria and Lebanon under French Mandate* (Oxford, 1958).

A. L. Tibawi, *A Modern History of Syria, including Lebanon and Palestine* (London, 1969).   MEY

SYRIAN REVOLUTIONS. The achievement of independence transferred power in Syria to the wealthy landowners and professional men who had dominated the Syrian nationalist movement since 1926. Riven by factions and still fascinated by concepts of a Greater Syria and Pan-Arabism, they proved unable to provide stable government, especially under the strains of the Palestine War (1948–9). By 1949 internal order could only be preserved by the army, which carried out a coup (30 March 1949) under the leadership of the commander-in-chief, Col. Husni al-Za 'im (1894–1949), who inaugurated a new constitution and was elected president (July). But he himself became the victim of a second army coup (13 Aug. 1949) led by Col. Muhammad Sami al-Hinnawi (1898–1950). Hinnawi's policy of union with Iraq aroused opposition which culminated in a third coup (19 Dec. 1949) led by Col. Adib al-Shishakli (1909–64). At first Shishakli was content to allow the older politicians to govern, but increasing friction led to him and the army assuming direct control (29 Nov. 1951). He ruled Syria until his overthrow during yet another coup (25 Feb. 1954), which began in Aleppo and was followed by an attempt to restore civilian government. The 1954 elections were again dominated by the older politicians, but were marked by substantial gains by parties of the left, especially the Ba'th Party, which won 17 seats and secured influences out of all proportion to its parliamentary strength. Subsequent governments moved steadily to the left, and the Ba'th, the communists, and fellow travellers strengthened their positions. The rivalry between these groups played an important part in producing the union with Egypt (Feb. 1958). The United Arab Republic broke up after a coup by Syrian army officers (28 Sept. 1961), which reflected unavoidable economic difficulties, and also Syrian resentment of Egyptian domination. Civilian government was temporarily restored, but again overthrown by an army coup (8 March 1963) supported by the Ba'th, which followed a similar coup in Iraq (8 Feb.). The Ba'thist officers suppressed attempted counter coups by pro-Egyptian elements (April and July 1963) and Gen. Amin al-Hafiz emerged as the dominant personality.

1963 marked a significant change in Syrian revolutions. Earlier revolutions had usually involved little more than changes of personnel but, from 1963, increasingly left-wing policies of nationalization and land reform were adopted. By 1965 the state controlled most industry and foreign trade and one-quarter of the country's arable land. In addition, the army became increasingly politicized and, within it, minority groups, especially the Alawis, Druze, and Isma'ilis, played a vital role. The cycle of subversion and repression led to

increasing tension and another coup (23 Feb. 1966) by radical Ba'thists. The dominant figures in the new regime were two Alawis, Salah al-Jadid and Hafiz al-Asad, the latter of whom triumphed in a new coup on 13 Nov. 1970.

P. Seale, *The Struggle for Syria* (Oxford, 1965).

G. H. Torrey, *Syrian Politics and the Military* (Ohio, 1963)   MEY

SYRIAN WARS, series of six wars fought between the Seleucids of Syria and the Ptolemies of Egypt in the 3rd and 2nd cents BC over that part of Phoenicia, rich in naval supplies and expertise, which the ancient world called 'Coele Syria' and which included Tyre and Sidon, the Jordan valley, and the mountains of the Lebanon. Before the first war Coele Syria was Ptolemaic, and remained so after each of the first four (c. 276–272; 260–255; 246–241; 219–217): only in the fifth (201–200) did it change hands, when Antiochus III defeated Ptolemy V's general, Scopas, at Panion. The sixth war (170–168) was a pre-emptive invasion of Egypt by Antiochus IV. Rome stopped him from keeping Egypt, but he retained Coele Syria.

SZATMAR, PEACE OF (1711), settlement negotiated between the imperial commander, Count Palffy, representing the Habsburg emperor Charles VI, and Count Karolyi, representing Francis Rakoczi, leader of the Hungarian rebels, after the failure of the latter's prolonged rebellion of 1703–11. The treaty initiated a long period of stability and peace for Hungary. The Habsburgs offered a general amnesty and agreed to convoke a diet at which Hungarian grievances could be aired. They secured two fundamental points, confirmation of the hereditary right of their male heirs to the Hungarian crown and the separation of the border states, *eg*, Transylvania and Croatia, from Hungarian influence. However, traditional Hungarian liberties were confirmed, the rights of Hungarian Protestants recognized, the privileges of the landowners and the sacrosanctity of the Diet preserved. In accordance with these terms, Charles VI was crowned king at Pressburg in 1712.

SZEKELS, war-like nomadic people of Asiatic origin, probably close to the Magyars, who arrived before the main Hungarian migration at the end of the 9th cent. After the Magyar conquest of Hungary the Szekels were settled in large numbers on the borders, where they acted as border troops, their largest concentration being in eastern Transylvania.

SZIGETVÁR, Hungarian fortress situated to the west of Pécs (Fünfkirchen) which fell to the Ottoman Turks in Sept. 1566. A little before the end of the Christian defence Sultan Suleiman the Magnificent died in his tent before the walls of the fortress.

SZILARD, LEO (1898–1964), Hungarian-born US physicist, who, with Enrico Fermi, developed the atomic pile (1942). After 1945 he became a leading advocate of the civil control of atomic energy.

SZLACHTA in Poland, general term denoting the numerous upper class of Polish society from the 15th cent., including great magnates and lesser gentry. They had considerable political influence through the local assemblies and the lower house of the *sejm*, nearly all possessed land and were *bene natus et possessionatus*, and they monopolized positions in the Church, the legal system, and the legislature, though they lost many of their privileges, *eg*., freedom from taxation and military service, in 1791. Though some were converted to Calvinism or Utraquism in the Reformation, by the 18th cent. most were Catholics.

TABARI, AL-, Abu Ja'far Muhammad ibn Jarir (839–923), wrote on a wide range of subjects, *eg*, on the Koran, on grammar, and on lexicographical matters. His fame rests on the *Ta'rikh al-Rasul wa'l-Muluk,* a chronicle arranged in annalistic form. The *Ta'rikh* begins with the patriarchs, prophets, and princes of the earliest times, continues thereafter with the Sasanids of Persia and then relates the affairs of the Prophet Muhammad, of the first caliphs and of the Umayyad and Abbasid dynasties to the year 915.

TABINSHWETI (*reg.* 1531–50), King of Toungoo who conquered Pegu, the delta, Martaban, and Prome. He transferred his capital to Pegu in 1539, partly because of the greater wealth of Pegu and its surrounding rice lands and partly in order to win the support of the Mons. He then turned north and occupied Pagan. Two disastrous campaigns followed against Siam. Tabinshweti had raised Toungoo from comparative unimportance to a potential kingdom of Burma. The potentiality was realized by his successor, Bayinnaung.

TABLE OF RANKS in Russia, register of social grades classified according to the type of service rendered to the Russian state, one of the social reforms introduced by Peter the Great (24 Jan. 1722) which aimed at replacing the old nobility of birth by a new nobility, a bureaucratic hierarchy based on ability.

TABORITES, extreme wing of the Bohemian Hussite movement, named after the town of Tabor and founded near Prague in 1420 by millenarian enthusiasts. They were strongest in the rural areas and drew their main support from the lower orders. It was not a unitary or organized movement. Some fanatics certainly wished to prepare for the second coming and preached a primitive communism. Its members fought for the 'Law of God' and preached the abolition of almost the whole visible Church, drawing heavily on scripture. Organized for war, the 'warriors of God' revolutionized warfare and swept all before them. Their power was broken at the battle of Lipany (1434) by an alliance of Catholic lords and moderate Hussites. Thousands were killed during and after the battle. In many respects the Taborites anticipated the peasant millenarian movements which grew up in Germany at the time of the Reformation.

TACHÉ, ALEXANDRE-ANTONIN (1823–94), Canadian Roman Catholic archbishop and political leader, who was sent to the Red River country as a missionary (1845). He developed great sympathy for the Métis, who risked losing their lands and hunting and fishing rights through the transfer of authority from the Hudson's Bay Co. to Canada (1869). He served as an unofficial mediator between the government and the Métis, but was in Rome when the Red River Rebellion broke out (1869–70). He returned at the request of the Canadian government and was influential in restoring order. After the North-West Rebellion (1885), however, he was no longer able to condone rebellion, and he countenanced the execution of the Métis leader, Louis Riel (16 Nov. 1885). In his last years he took an important part in the Man. separate-school controversy.

TACITUS, CORNELIUS (*c.* AD 55–118), Roman historian, who had a senatorial career and was a lawyer, a consul (97), and a governor of Asia (112). His works all post-date the death of the Emperor Domitian (96), whom he hated. There survive: *Agricola*, a brief memoir of his father-in-law, Julius Agricola, important for an account of his campaigns in Britain; *Germania*, a monograph on the geography and tribes of Germany; *Dialogue de Oratoribus*, on the decline of oratory; books I–V of the *Histories*, including a detailed account of the events of 69 (Year of the Four Emperors); and books I–VI and XI–XVI of the *Annals*, covering substantial parts of the reigns of the Emperors Tiberius, Claudius, and Nero. Tacitus was pessimistic about certain aspects of Roman history and society and disliked most of the emperors. In his works complicated emotional attitudes appear; nevertheless the *Histories* and *Annals* constitute a masterpiece of Roman literature and the most important single source for the history of the 1st cent. AD.

TACITUS, M. CLAUDIUS (*c.* AD 200–76), Roman Emperor (*reg.* 275–6), who was proclaimed after the death of Aurelian and chose his brother, Florianus, as praetorian prefect. He successfully fought the Goths in Asia Minor (276) but, after a reign of only six months, was murdered by his troops. Shortly afterwards Florianus, who had claimed the succession, was killed at Tarsus and Probus proclaimed emperor. Tacitus attempted to resist the increasing militarism of the Roman government; but the story of his protection of the works of the historian Tacitus, and of his claim to be descended from him, is fictitious.

TACKING in England, constitutional device to consolidate a controversial matter to a vital money bill in order to push the former through the House of Commons. It was employed by the High Church Tories in 1704 in an effort to push through an Occasional Conformity bill against dissenters, but it was discredited because the majority of MPs, the Crown, and the Lords felt that it was a highly partisan and unconstitutional weapon.

TACNA–ARICA DISPUTE, between Chile and Peru, arose over the use of the Atacama Desert, a strip of land, over 500 miles long, on the coast from Arica, Peru, to the central valley of Chile, a harsh, arid area between the Andes and the Pacific, whose boundaries the Spaniards never marked out. After independence, Peru claimed Tacna, Arica, and Tarapacá in the north. The central region, Antofagasta, was claimed by Bolivia as a corridor to the ocean. No clear boundary was defined south of Antofagasta. Until the middle of the 19th cent. this caused no dispute, then the marketable value of nitrates was suddenly discovered as a necessary ingredient of explosives, especially dynamite. The Atacama Desert contained great nitrate reserves, and Chilean entrepreneurs invaded the area with large forces of workers to mine nitrates and borax. Two agreements formed the basis of multi-national claims. An agreement between Chile and Bolivia (1866) allowed Chile to extend her border to the 24th parallel and to share with Bolivia the revenues from the section between the 23rd and 25th parallels. In the port of Antofagasta a colony of Chileans sprang up and they extended their operations from there into Tacna and Arica. In 1873 Peru and Bolivia made a secret treaty providing for mutual defence if Chile should try to extend political control over the region, while Bolivia agreed not to raise the rates at which it taxed Chilean entrepreneurs. Peru nationalized the nitrate deposits, however, and Bolivia raised the taxes (1878). Soon afterwards the Chilean government despatched troops to occupy Antofagasta in retribution and the dispute quickly degenerated into war between the three nations. Chile won all the territory involved except Tacna, which was retained by Peru.   VCP

TADMEKKA, southern Saharan trading town, linked, in its heyday (9th–11th cents), to centres in southern Tunisia and central Algeria. It has been tentatively identified with a site at Es-Souk in Mali.

TAEWONGUN, or Korean Prince Regent, title of Yi Ha-ung (1820–98), grandson of King Yongjo. In 1864 he seized power and put his son, Kojong, on the throne. He successfully challenged the traditional powerful families, but continued the persecutions of Christians, notably in 1866 and 1871. French and US retaliatory actions made him turn for help to Japan, where he saw the Meiji Restoration as having similar objectives to his own. This led China to support the family of Queen Min, which in 1873 resulted in the Taewongun's downfall. In 1894 he allied himself with the Tonghak revolutionaries, but the murder of Queen Min by the Japanese in 1895 led to his final exclusion from power. Although there is still much to be learnt about him, the Taewongun was clearly the most outstanding political figure in 19th-cent. Korea.

TAFAWA BALEWA, SIR ALHAJI ABUBAKAR (1912–66), Nigerian politician and the country's first prime minister. He was born in Bauchi, northern Nigeria, took office in 1957, and led Nigeria to independence in 1960. During the upheavals of post-independence politics, he strove to achieve national unity. He was killed in a *coup d'état* (Jan. 1966).

TAFF VALE JUDGMENT (1901) in Britain, judgment affecting trade unions. In 1900 there was a strike on the Taff Vale Railway and some 'blacklegs' sent down from London were induced by pickets of the Society of Railway Servants to break the contract of service they had made before they set out. The manager of the railway sought an injunction against the society to stop picketing. The injunction was granted by the high court, dismissed by the court of appeal, and finally restored (1901) by the House of Lords.

Under the Trade Union Act (1871), the property of the trade unions had been vested in trustees, and it was assumed that the unions themselves could not sue or be sued. The Taff Vale case ended this situation. Henceforth any union which attempted strike action would be liable for heavy damages. The case produced a strong demand for amendment of the law, which in turn contributed to the growing support for the Labour Representation Committee (1901–6). The law was amended by the Trades Disputes Act (1906).

TAFILELT, region of south-eastern Morocco, beyond the High Atlas, noted for the former city of Sijilmasa, and place of origin of the present Alawid dynasty of Morocco.

TAFT, ROBERT ALPHONSO (1889–1953), US lawyer and politician and son of President Taft. He began his political career in the OH House of Representatives (1921–6) and senate (1931–2). In 1938 he was elected to the US Senate, where he became a leading opponent of the New Deal. His main legislative achievement was the Taft–Hartley Act (1947). In foreign affairs he was an inveterate anti-interventionist before Pearl Harbor, and in the post-war years worked consistently to limit US commitments overseas. He became known as 'Mr Republican', a man respected for his intellect and integrity, but was disappointed in his ambition to become president. He was passed over in favour of Willkie in 1940, and Dewey in 1948, but seemed assured of the Republican nomination in 1952. But the extremism of the McCarthyite fringe of his supporters, and the fear that his appeal was too narrow, alienated both moderates and pragmatists who turned instead to Eisenhower.

TAFT, WILLIAM HOWARD (1857–1930), US politician and 27th president of the US and chief justice of the US Supreme Court. After serving as US solicitor-general (1890–2), he became a federal circuit court judge (1892–1900). As president of the Philippine Commission (1900) and as civil governor of the Philippines (1901–4) he encouraged economic and social development in the islands and his growing reputation led President T. Roosevelt twice to offer him an appointment on the US Supreme Court. As US secretary of war (1904–8) he became one of the president's closest advisers, and further enhanced his reputation as an administrator and conciliator, particularly through his part in initiating construction of the Panama Canal and mediating in Cuban affairs (1906). He reluctantly accepted nomination by the Republican Party as Roosevelt's successor and easily defeated the Democratic candidate, William Jennings Bryan, in the election of 1908. During his presidency Taft's conciliatory, middle-of-the-road policies on the tariff question, conservation, and the trusts alienated both the liberal and conservative wings of the Republican Party. He initiated more anti-trust actions than his predecessor, but his dismissal of Gifford Pinchot following the Ballinger–Pinchot quarrel over conservation policies led to a break with Roosevelt, who believed that Taft had betrayed him. His renomination in 1912 produced a split in the Republican Party, with Roosevelt running on a third party Progressive ticket, and Taft was overwhelmingly defeated by Woodrow Wilson. Taft then became professor of constitutional law at Yale, served on various commissions during the First World War, and in 1921 was appointed chief justice of the US Supreme Court by President Harding. The office gave him great personal satisfaction, and further opportunities for the expression of his moderate philosophy. He reformed judicial procedures to relieve the courts of a mass of litigation that threatened to swamp them, and was largely responsible for the 'Judges' bill (1925) which empowered the Supreme Court to limit the number of cases heard. He was generally conservative in his judicial attitude, but dissented from the majority opinion that held a minimum wage law for women unconstitutional in *Adkins v. Children's Hospital* (1923).

H. F. Pringle, *The Life and Times of William Howard Taft*, 2 vols (New York, 1939).
A. T. Mason, *William Howard Taft: Chief Justice* (New York, 1965).   WJR

TAFT COMMISSION (1900) in the US, or second Philippine commission, formed by President W. McKinley and presided over by Judge W. H. Taft. It differed from the first Schurman Philippine commission in being composed only of civilians and was vested with legislative and certain executive functions. Its brief included the 'benevolent assimilation' of the people of the Philippines, and its first task was to gather information on the condition and needs of the country. As soon as an area was pacified, the commission co-operated with the military authorities in establishing civilian control. On 4 July 1901 the civil government was inaugurated, with Taft as its first governor. The Philippine commission continued as the new government's law-making body. Among the laws passed by the Second Philippine commission were those establishing the municipal and provincial governments, the public school and civil service systems, the Philippine constabulary, and the purchase of friar lands which were sold to tenants on easy terms of payment.

TAFT–HARTLEY ACT (1947) in the US, labour legislation, named after its sponsors, Senator Robert A. Taft, of OH, and Congressman Fred A. Hartley, of NJ. It was passed by the Republican 80th Congress over the veto of President Truman. The act was the result of post-war industrial unrest and conservative hostility to the privileged position that labour was felt to have enjoyed since the New Deal. The act's provisions included prohibition of the closed shop and union contributions to political campaigns, establishment of an 80-day 'cooling-off' period before strikes threatening 'national health or safety' could take place, and required a non-communist affidavit from union leaders.

TAGANROG, Russian town and seaport of modern Rostov, situated on the northern shores of the Sea of Azov and founded in 1698 by Peter I as a naval dockyard and fortress. After being surrendered to the Turks by the humiliating capitulation of the Pruth river (1711), it became Russian again in 1739, but did not expand rapidly until the Sea of Azov and the Crimea were freed from Turkish control. In the 19th cent. it developed as an exporting centre.

TAGAUNG, KINGS OF, legendary Burmese rulers from the 8th cent. BC, whose capital was on the upper Irrawaddy.

TAGHAZA (Mali), salt pans in the central Sahara, whose output was bartered for gold on the southern savannah fringes. Control of Taghaza was the cause of the Moroccan invasion of Songhay (1591).

TAGLIACOZZO, BATTLE OF (1268), brought about the defeat of Conradin, last of the Hohenstaufen, who invaded Italy from Germany in 1267 in a bid to recapture the Neapolitan possessions of his ancestors from Charles of Anjou. Conradin's initial victory was turned into defeat when the concealed Angevin reserve attacked his forces, which were demoralized by their success. Conradin was executed and Charles ruled henceforth without future challenge from Germany.

TAGORE, ABANINDRANATH (1871–1951), Indian painter, who led the revival of painting in the 20th cent. which drew upon classical Indian models, particularly medieval miniatures. He and his followers became known as the 'Bengal' School or the 'Revivalists'.

TAGORE, DEVENDRANATH (1817–1905), Indian scholar and religious leader, known to his followers as the Maharshi (Great Saint), who founded the *Tatwabodhini Sabha* in 1839 and propagated his views by means of a Bengali newspaper, the *Tatwabodhini Patrika*. He was a member of the Brahmo Samaj and as a result of his work branches of it were formed outside Calcutta. In 1866, the younger members of the Brahmo Samaj, led by Keshab Chandra Sen, formed a new society, being desirous of more radical reforms.

TAGORE, DWARKANATH (1794–1846), Indian philanthropist and reformer, who was a supporter of the Brahmo Samaj, and advocated the abolition of *sati* and freedom of the press. He twice visited Europe.

TAGORE, RABINDRANATH (1861–1941), Bengali poet, writer, painter, and educationist, called *Gurudeva* (Reverend Teacher), who belonged to one of the most important of 19th-cent. Bengali families. His first book of poems (1881) attracted attention in Bengali literary circles and by the 1890s his reputation was established. His later work ranged over various other fields—songs, plays and dance dramas, novels, short stories, essays, and lectures. In all he published 251 Bengali volumes, many of which were translated into English, French, and German.

Up to 1912 he wrote exclusively in Bengali and was known only to Bengali readers. In that year, however, the publication of his own English translations of a selection from *Gitanjali* (*Song Offering*) brought him fame and in the following year the Nobel Prize for Literature. From then onwards his travels, lectures, and involvement in public affairs were constant. He was not, however, prepared to involve himself closely in politics. He had taken some part in the *Swadeshi* movement in the agitation against the partition of Bengal (1905–7), but had withdrawn in protest against the violence it engendered and he never lost his suspicion of political agitators, and especially revolutionaries. His Indian patriotism, however, was never in question. He was awarded a knighthood in 1915, but relinquished it after the Amritsar massacre (1919) and when, as the first unofficial speaker to be invited, he gave the convocational address at Calcutta University (1936), he insisted on speaking in Bengali. He was emphatic that international co-operation rather than 'selfish nationalism' was the prime need. This led him to oppose *satyagraha* and steadfastly to decline support of Gandhi's spinning campaign, although he maintained a personal friendship with him. There were memorable public exchanges between them in 1921 and 1925, although for the most part they 'agreed to disagree'. Much more controversial were Tagore's novels which dealt with political life, *Ghare Baire* (*The Home and the World*, 1915) which was about the *swadeshi* movement, and *Char Adhyay* (*Four Chapters*, 1934), about the revolutionary movement. Both raised storms of protest in Bengal because of Tagore's unpopular opinions.

Critics agree that his use of the Bengali language and landscape in his lyric verse, and his exploration of prose forms, make him one of the founders of modern Bengali literature. His importance lies in his having made Western readers aware of India in the years 1912–30.

K. Kripalani, *Rabindranath Tagore, a biography* (New York, 1962).
Rabindranath Tagore, *Collected Poems and Plays* (London, 1936).   PDR

TAGORE, SATYENDRANATH (1842–1923), first Indian to pass into the Indian civil service (1864). He was a poet and wrote several books in Bengali.

TAHARQA (*reg.* 688–663 BC), Kushite King, who was one of the XXVth dynasty Pharaohs of Egypt. He defended Egypt against Assyrian attacks.

TAHIR IBN AL-HUSAYN (c. 775–822) founded the Tahirid line of amirs in Khurasan. Tahir, during the last years of the Abbasid Caliph Harun al-Rashid (*reg.* 786–809), fought against the rebel Rafi' ibn Layth in Transoxania. He commanded the forces of Al-Ma' mun against Al-Amin in the civil war of 809–13. Tahir became governor of Khurasan in 821, acting thereafter in virtual independence of the caliph at Baghdad.

TAHIRID, name given to the amirs descended from Tahir ibn al-Husayn, who established in Khurasan (821–2) an autonomous regime in loose dependence on the Abbasid caliphate. This regime flourished during the years 822–62. The rise of the Saffarids led, however, to a rapid breakdown of Tahirid rule, the decisive date being the year 873, when the Saffarid Ya 'qub ibn Layth seized Nishapur, the capital of the Tahirid amirate.

TAHITI DISPUTE began when a British missionary and consul opposed French Catholics' attempts to start missions. The arrival of Dupetit-Thouars's frigate (1838) brought many of the islanders to France's side. Dupetit-Thouars subsequently tried to convert the 1842 French protectorate into an outright conquest, and the British official who resisted the attempt, was imprisoned. Louis-Philippe's government implicitly condoned Dupetit-Thouars's actions, but finally (1847) agreed that Tahiti should merely be a French protectorate. (It became a French colony in 1880.) The affair caused intense mutual ill-feeling in France and Britain.

TAHMASP I (1514–76), second Safawid Shah of Persia (*reg.* 1524–76) in succession to his father, Isma'il. He was involved in warfare with the Ottoman Turks, who extended their control over much of eastern Asia Minor (notably the regions of Erzurum and Lake Van) in 1534 and 1548–9 and also wrested Iraq from Persia in 1534–5. After a third campaign in 1554 the Ottomans made a peace with the Safawids concluded at Amasya in 1555. The Ottoman prince Bayezid, being in rebellion against his father, Sultan Suleiman, took refuge with Shah Tahmasp in 1559, but was handed over in 1561 to the Ottomans in return for a large payment in cash. Tahmasp, during the last years of his reign, had to face the incursions of the Uzbeg Turks from Transoxania into Khurasan. His death occurred at a time of growing tension between the Turcoman and Caucasian elements in the service of the Safawid regime.

TAHTAWI, AL-, RIFA'A BADAWI RAFI (1801–73), Egyptian educational reformer, translator from European languages, and political philosopher. He was the first writer to emphasize the concept of Egyptian territorial patriotism.

TAI CHEN (1724–77), Chinese scholar and philosopher of the Ch'ing period. As a leading mentor of the School of Empirical Research, Tai shared much of the principles and methodology of the School of Han Learning, but his approach was far more vigorous and thorough and his interests far more extensive. He contributed overwhelmingly to research methodology, linguistics, the calendar, and mathematics, and also to waterworks. He also evolved a 'philosophy of feeling', suggesting that the fulfilment of human desires is the realization of truth and righteousness, thus challenging the position of the Sung Neo-Confucianists.

T'AI, MOUNT, situated in east China (mod. Shantung province). It became one of China's sacred mountains and was an object of veneration from early in the imperial period. The conduct of the worship of heaven and earth at the summit was a means whereby an emperor could acquire spiritual support for his burden, assert his temporal authority, and consolidate his legitimate right to rule. By reporting his activities to these supernatural powers he could form a mystical union with heaven and earth and pray for their blessing on his future actions. The ascent was, however, only made some half-dozen times by an emperor of China, the first occasion being in 219 BC and the last in AD 1008.

TA'IF, TREATY OF (1934), Saudi Arabian–Yemeni agreement providing for the withdrawal of Saudi Arabian forces from occupied Yemeni territory in return for an indemnity. The treaty was followed by a boundary commission which established (1936) a stable frontier between the two states.

TAIHŌ CODE (701), most famous of Japan's compilations of administrative and penal laws. It was based on Chinese models and completed the work of the Taika Reform.

TAIKA REFORM in Japan, early political revolution which ranks as one of the two main turning points in Japanese history. Beginning as a *coup d'état* in 645, against the Soga family by Prince Naka no Ōe (later the Emperor Tenchi) and Nakatomi (later Fujiwara) Kamatari, it developed into a far-reaching change of governmental structure. Building on the innovations of Shōtoku Taishi and the knowledge of China gained in the previous half-century, the reformers issued an edict (646) proclaiming their intention of (*a*) abolishing private holdings of rice-land and of agricultural labour; (*b*) allotting to peasants specified amounts of land which would be changed every six years; (*c*) establishing a regular taxation system covering not only rice and other products, but also *corvée* and military service; (*d*) dividing the country into provinces to be administered by centrally appointed governors; (*e*) improving roads; and (*f*) building a permanent capital. These were not the only innovations proposed by the new rulers, who had already adopted the era name of *Taika* ('Great change'). They also took over from China a new central government structure, modified only by the addition of a *Shintō* ministry (*Jingikan*) ranking equally with the Grand Council of State (*Daijōkan*) and by the omission of the examination system as the pathway to office. The final element of the reform was the introduction of legal codes.

Although in traditional historiography most of these changes were regarded as having taken place within a few years, it is now clear that they were only put into general effect gradually. That the reformers were successful at all was due to a combination of factors. Externally, the prestige of Chinese institutions was greatly enhanced by the splendour of the T'ang empire and by Japan's inability to assist the Korean kingdom of Paekche against Chinese forces. Internally, the trend towards *uji* (clan) disintegration led many *uji* chiefs to acquiesce in the changes because they confirmed their local authority. In the longer term, however, and especially after the establishment of the capital at Nara, the effect of the Taika Reform was to shift the balance of power decisively in favour of the central aristocracy.

J. W. Hall, *Government and Local Power in Japan, 500–1700* (Princeton, 1966).   RLS

TAILLE (PERSONAL) in France, important direct tax levied by the French monarchy from the 15th cent. to 1789. It applied to most of France, excluding Guienne, Dauphiné, Languedoc, and Provence, and was assessed on a person's possessions at the arbitrary discretion of the collector. In practice it bore heavily on the peasantry, since the first, second, and many sections of the third estate were exempt.

TAILLE (REAL) in France, most important direct tax levied by the French monarchy from the 15th cent. until 1789, applied to members of all three estates living in the 'pays de taille réelle', *ie*, the Midi and south-west of France, and raised on 'common' land. It was less arbitrary and more efficient than the personal *taille*.

TAINE, HIPPOLYTE ADOLPHE (1828–93), French historian and philosopher, who maintained in his *Les Origines de la France Contemporaine*, that the French Revolution did not destroy the underlying continuity of French institutions. He was the leading spokesman for the pessimistic determinism which replaced the romanticism of the first half of the 19th cent.

TAIPING REBELLION (1850–64) in China, peasant-based rebellion, which brought about the biggest civil war in world history, raging over 16 provinces and taking a toll of 20–30 million lives. It had its origins in a group of socially discontented elements and misfits led by Hung Hsiu-ch'üan, himself a frustrated aspirant to office and a Hakka. (The Hakkas, as newcomers to south China, were much discriminated against by the older settlers.) In the late 1840s Hung and his relative, Feng Yün-shan (1822–52), organized their followers into the 'God Worshippers Society', based on Hung's defective conception of Christianity, at Thistle Mountain, Kwangsi. The deteriotion of dynastic administration and widespread economic hardship, partly caused by the shift of trade to Shanghai after the Opium War, led to the growth of anti-Manchu feelings, particularly in south China. The God Worshippers, therefore, quickly became an anti-dynastic movement. In 1850, with a following of some 10,000, they broke out into rebellion and in Jan. 1851 proclaimed the 'Heavenly Kingdom of Great Peace' (*T'ai-p'ing T'ien-kuo*), hence the name Taiping.

The rebels were forced to abandon their base in Kwangsi in mid-1852. They moved quickly through Hunan, briefly held the city of Wuchang, then moved rapidly down the Yangtse river, capturing Nanking, where they established their Heavenly Capital (1853). After settling at Nanking, the Taipings developed their government according to Hung's Christianity. The state was to be theocratic, encompassing all aspects of life, with Hung as the Heavenly King. Land was to be distributed equally, but private ownership was prohibited—all surplus had to be surrendered to the public storehouses. There was also to be unity of civil and military administration: farmers were soldiers, officers were administrators, preachers, judges, and teachers. The Taiping kingdom was a highly hierarchical society, with groups of 25 families as the basic social unit. Religious indoctrination was an important function of the state, and the annual civil service examination, based on Taiping religious teachings, served as a lure to religious studies. The movement was extremely puritanical: opium-smoking, tobacco, wine, prostitution, polygamy, gambling, foot-binding, and the sale of slaves were all prohibited. The sexes were to be equal, but in all public functions they were strictly segregated.

From Nanking, two major expeditions were launched in 1853 to conquer the rest of China. But the narrowness of their ideological appeal and the shortage of personnel prevented the Taipings from establishing permanent control and executing their land programme in the areas they conquered. These failures were compounded by weaknesses at the top. Hung had now withdrawn from active government, entrusting the kingdom to divine guidance. This led to a struggle for power among his subordinate kings. The ambition of Yang Hsiu-ch'ing finally brought about a bloody purge which liquidated most of the able leaders (1856). The Taiping cause declined rapidly from this date and came to a tragic end in July 1864.

Despite its initial success, the strong anti-Confucian bias of the Taiping movement rendered it unacceptable to the Chinese as a whole. In the end, it was the armies organized by such Confucian officials as Tseng Kuo-fan, Tso Tsung-t'ang, and Li Hung-chang, which suppressed the rebellion. Nevertheless, the Taiping Rebellion is an important event in modern Chinese history, embodying many revolutionary aspects which became a source of inspiration for later revolutionaries like Sun Yat-sen.

F. Michael, *The Taiping Rebellion, History and Documents*, vol. 1 (Seattle, 1966). DP

TAIRA CLAN, Japanese feudal family whose struggles with the Minamoto clan hastened the emergence of feudal government in Japan and inspired many heroic stories. The family was descended from the Emperor Kammu (*reg.* 781–806), and some Tairas acquired provincial positions and gained the allegiance of local warrior cliques. Their suppression of provincial revolts and employment by retired emperors in Kyoto increased their prestige and power, and when Tairas and Minamotos supported opposite sides in two court disputes (1156, 1159) the former emerged triumphant. During the following two decades the Taira leader, Kiyomori, no longer supported but controlled the court. Concentration on Kyoto affairs, however, weakened the Tairas' control over their warrior following and when Minamoto Yoritomo raised eastern Japan in revolt (1180) Taira power rapidly collapsed.

TAIRA KIYOMORI (1118–81), Japanese feudal leader, who was head of the Taira clan at the height of its power. After his defeat of the Minamoto family, Kiyomori became the unchallenged military master of Kyoto, using his power to secure high office, as well as many governorships and estate proprietorships for his family and followers. By marrying his daughters into the imperial and Fujiwara lines he further extended Taira influence in the traditional Fujiwara manner, eventually arranging the succession of his infant grandson as the Emperor Antoku. He had little difficulty in suppressing Fujiwara plots, but he was unable to prevent the reassertion by Yoritomo of Minamoto control over most of the eastern warriors (1180–1), and his death hastened the Tairas' rapid collapse.

TAIRŌ, high *bakufu* office in Tokugawa Japan, usually translated as 'regent' or 'great councillor'. It was used by Ii Naosuke in 1858–60 to assert authoritarian control over reformist *daimyōs*.

TAISHŌ PERIOD (30 July 1912–25 Dec. 1926), in Japan, reign of Yoshihito, officially known as *Taisho Tennō* (Great Righteousness Emperor). His mental incapacity necessitated the appointment in 1921 of Crown Prince Hirohito as regent. During this period Japan saw her position as a great power confirmed by the Versailles peace conference, but her diplomatic problems were added to by the ending of the Anglo-Japanese Alliance (1922), by the increased naval strength of the US in the Pacific, and by the emergence of Chinese nationalism, the leaders of which resented Japan's 'Twenty-One Demands' (1915) and threatened her Manchurian position. During this period Japan's economic strength grew quickly, though unevenly, most of her increased productivity and larger markets being secured during the First World War. The war also affected Japanese politics, since the prestige given to democratic government by Allied success contributed to the phenomena—party cabinets and the popularization of liberal and radical ideas—which have led historians to use the term 'Taishō Democracy' to describe the 1920s.

TAIT, ARCHIBALD CAMPBELL (1811–82), Scottish-born cleric of Presbyterian upbringing, who became Abp of Canterbury (1868–82). He had succeeded Thomas Arnold as headmaster of Rugby School (1842–9) and became dean of Carlisle (1849–56) and Bp of London (1856–68). He identified himself with the evangelical tradition in the Church of England and upheld the case for its continued establishment, while recognizing that the Church of Ireland should be disestablished.

TAIWAN (FORMOSA), island about 100 miles (161 kms) off the coast of Fukien province, China, which had its first contact with China under the Sui dynasty (581–618), but the first Chinese settlers did not appear until the 15th cent., pushing the aborigines away from the plains. From 1624 onwards it was gradually occupied by the Dutch, who in turn were driven away by Cheng Ch'eng-kung (Koxinga) in 1662. After the fall of Cheng, the island became a part of the Ch'ing empire (1680), administered as part of Fukien. In 1885 Taiwan became a separate province, but was soon taken by the Japanese as part of the spoils of the Sino-Japanese War (1894–5). Taiwan was returned to China at the end of the Second World War, and after 1949 was the only part of China controlled by the Nationalists under Chiang Kai-shek.

TAJ MAHAL, mausoleum built by the Mughal emperor, Shah Jahan (*reg.* 1627–58), for his favourite wife, Mumtaz Mahal (1592–1631), beneath which both lie buried. It consists of a central domed structure of marble with inlaid ornamentation, which stands on a spacious platform, flanked by two smaller buildings, one of them a mosque; at each corner of the platform is a minaret. The tomb and its satellite buildings are set in a garden, access to which is through a stately entrance. The whole edifice was completed in 1645 at a cost of £300,000, the architect being Ustad Isa. Suggestions that its design was influenced by European models are erroneous. It is considered the masterpiece of Mughal architecture.

TAKAHASHI, KOREKIYO (1854–1936), Japanese politician, who was three times finance minister and held office as prime minister (1921–2). He negotiated important foreign loans during the Russo-Japanese War and hastened Japan's industrial recovery from the Depression by adopting an inflationary policy. He was assassinated in the 26 Feb. 1936 mutiny by army extremists.

TAKAMINE, JOKICHI (1854–1922), Japanese-American biochemist and industrialist, who in 1887 founded the chemical fertilizer industry in Japan. He carried out his most important scientific work, however, in his private laboratory in 1901, ten years after he had taken up permanent residence in the US. Takamine was the first, albeit unknowingly, to isolate a pure hormone (adrenalin) from natural sources, in this case from the suprarenal glands. Subsequently, it was soon identified and then synthesized by other workers.

TAKEDDA, important centre of commerce and Islamic scholarship, west of the Aïr massif where copper was mined and smelted (14th–15th cents). It has been tentatively identified with a site at Azelik in the Niger republic.

TAKLA HAYMANOT (*fl.* 13th cent.), Ethiopian *Abuna*, or bishop, who helped to overthrow the usurping Zagwé dynasty and to replace it by the Solomonic line.

TAKSIZ (*reg.* 1767–82), King of Siam, who reconstructed the Siamese state after the destruction of Ayudhya by the Burmese. He was the half-Chinese adopted son of an official of the Ayudhya government and was governor of Tak (Phraya Tak; given name, Sin) at the time of the fall of Ayudhya in 1767. He fled the old capital, raised an army in the south-east of the country, and by the end of 1767 had defeated the Burmese armies remaining in central Siam. After moving the capital to Thonburi, opposite Bangkok, where Chinese traders imported food which sustained the state through its first years, he defeated other contenders for the throne. By 1770 he had restored the capital's control over rebellious provinces, and by 1776 had driven the Burmese from Chiengmai and the north. His armies, commanded by Gen. Chakri, then made further conquests, expanding the state into Laos and Cambodia. In the late 1770's Taksin grew increasingly arbitrary and vindictive; convinced that he had divine powers, he alienated the support of the élite. A minor rebellion against his officers at Ayudhya early in 1782 grew into a serious revolt, and none came to his aid. Hastening back from campaigns in Cambodia, Chakri arrived in Thonburi as the city fell and was made king on 6 April 1782, as Rama I. Taksin is said to have been executed shortly afterwards, although one school of Thai historians claims that he lived until 1825 in a mountain retreat in southern Siam.   DKW

TAKU FORTS in China, situated at the mouth of the Peiho guarding the riverine approach to Tientsin and Peking, were the site of many engagements between China and the Western powers. During the Arrow War, they were taken by the Anglo-French forces (1860), who occupied them until 1865. There were attempts to modernize the forts in the following decades, but during the Boxer Rising Taku was once again taken by the invading forces (17 June 1900). Together with other military installations guarding the seaward approach of Peking, the forts were dismantled in accordance with the Boxer Protocol (1901).

TALAS, site in Central Asia of a battle fought in 751 between Arab and Chinese forces. The defeat of the latter marked the limit of the Chinese westerly advance during the T'ang period.

TALAT PASHA, MAHMUD (1874–1921), Turkish politician and member of the committee of union and progress. With Enver and Jamal Pashas he was a member of the triumvirate which dominated the Ottoman government (1913–18). He served several times as minister of the interior and was grand vizier (1917–18).

TALAUVE, PILIMA (d. 1812), chief *adigar* (minister) of the last King of Kandy, Ceylon, who intrigued with the British against the king. Later he raised a rebellion, but this failed and he was executed.

TALAVERA, BATTLE OF (1809), in the French Wars. It was fought on the Tagus river during the Peninsular campaign. Wellington defeated Joseph Bonaparte's forces, but being short of supplies had to retreat into Portugal to avoid defeat by Ney's and Soult's combined armies.

TALBOT, THOMAS (1771–1853), Irish-born Canadian colonist, who obtained a grant along Lake Erie from the British government. He founded the Talbot settlement of 6000 colonists and 29 townships and served as its governor for nearly 50 years.

TALBOT, WILLIAM HENRY FOX (1800–77), British politician and inventor, who retired (1834) from a very brief political life and started to experiment with photography. In 1841 he patented the Talbotype process, which was significantly better than the analogous method developed simultaneously by Daguerre. The required exposure was considerably reduced and it introduced the negative–positive principle, still the basis of present-day photography. Talbot published the first book illustrated with photographs (*The Pencil of Nature*, 1844–6), pioneered flash photography of fast-moving objects (1851), and invented photoglyphy (1852). He was also a distinguished mathematician and decipherer of Assyrian Cuneiform inscriptions.

TALIB PASHA IBN SAYYID RAJAB, SAYYID (d. 1929), Iraqi politician, who represented Basra in the Ottoman parliament (1908–14), during which time he became the most prominent Arab nationalist in Iraq and organized the Basra Reform Committee. He was head of the provisional Iraq government (1915–20) and aimed at supreme power, but was mistrusted by the British and deported (1921).

TALIESIN (*fl.* 6th cent.), Welsh poet, whose works are the earliest known examples of Welsh poetry, surviving in 13th-cent. copies. As poems of eulogy or lament for his patrons, they begin a tradition which runs through medieval Welsh poetry.

TALIKOTA, BATTLE OF (23 Jan. 1565), between the forces of the Hindu Raja of Vijayanagar and those of four Muslim Deccan sultans. The Hindu leader, Ramaraja, was killed and Vijayanagar sacked and destroyed. Vijayanagar itself never recovered, but the state continued from other centres till 1640.

TALLAGE, originally a feudal tax levied on towns and on peasant tenants by a feudal overlord. The term came to be applied to any aid which was imposed and not granted. In England, royal tallage from towns and royal demesne estates began to arouse increasing opposition in 13th cent., culminating in an attempt in 1297 to secure the abolition of all arbitrary royal taxation. The royal tallage was finally abolished in 1340. The taxes exacted by lords from their servile tenants were also called tallages and the liability to these exactions was regarded in England as one of the tests of servile (unfree) status.

TALLARD, CAMILLE D'HOSTAN, Comte de (1652–1728), French soldier and diplomat, who was ambassador to London (1697–1702) and took part in the negotiations of both Partition Treaties (1698, 1700) between Louis XIV and William III.

On the outbreak of the War of the Spanish Succession he commanded forces in Alsace. At first he was successful, heavily defeating the imperial forces of the Prince of Hesse-Cassel at Spirbach (1703) and capturing Landau. In the following year he was sent to reinforce France's Bavarian ally after Marlborough's march to the Danube. At Blenheim (1704) he was decisively defeated, and after being captured, was sent to England, where he remained a prisoner until 1711. After Louis XIV's death he was appointed to the Council of Regency and became a minister of state (1726).

TALLEYRAND-PERIGORD, CHARLES MAURICE DE (1754–1838), French politician, whose astuteness and sceptical detachment enabled him to serve and survive successive regimes. He was appointed Bp of Autun (1788), represented his clergy in the states general, and supported the formation of the national assembly. He recommended secularization of Church property (Oct.–Nov. 1789) and the issue of *assignats*, and advocated a science-based educational curriculum. Pius VI excommunicated him (1791) for helping to launch the Civil Constitution of the clergy. As a diplomat, Talleyrand failed (1791–2) to preserve peace with Britain, and was exiled there and in the US after the convention discovered his correspondence with Louis XVI (Dec. 1792).

Through Barras's patronage he became foreign relations minister (1797–9), in which capacity he approved the Campo Formio peace terms, and the Egyptian expedition of 1798, but resigned adroitly before Brumaire. After being reinstated by Napoleon I, he drafted the Luneville peace terms (1801) and supported the Concordat. Napoleon condoned his venality and ambivalence because of his success in bringing about major changes in Italy, Germany, and Switzerland. The renewal of war with Britain (1803) was disliked by Talleyrand, who always valued Anglo-French relations. However, he was unable to limit Napoleon's schemes to what was politically feasible, and after 1805 his influence waned. On being excluded from the Tilsit discussions (1807), he resigned, and thereafter, although Napoleon sometimes consulted him, he prepared for the emperor's overthrow.

After Napoleon's abdication it was Talleyrand's tenacity and resourcefulness that prevented chaos. He won the tsar's support for a Bourbon restoration and kept the provisional government on a moderate course. The first treaty of Paris (May 1814), allowing France the 1792 frontiers, was a triumph largely due to him. At the Congress of Vienna he upheld the principles of legitimacy and the balance of power. He skilfully penetrated the discussions between the now disunited Great Powers and fully participated in them. After Waterloo (1815) he opposed the terms of the second treaty of Paris, but the elections of that year encompassed his dismissal and for 15 years he remained in retirement. Then, having sensed the collapse of Charles X's authority, he was ready with support for Louis-Philippe (July 1830). As ambassador in London (1830–4) he negotiated with Palmerston over Belgium's independence. Talleyrand's reputation was marred by his greed, cynicism, and treachery, yet his patriotism, political moderation, and diplomatic genius benefited France and Europe.

A. Duff Cooper, *Talleyrand* (London, 1932).
Crane Brinton, *The Lives of Talleyrand* (New York, 1936).

TALLIS, THOMAS (*c.* 1510–85), English musician and composer, who was organist at Waltham Abbey until its dissolution (1540). He became a gentleman of the Chapel Royal and won, jointly with Byrd, the royal monopoly of music printing. He wrote eight tunes for Parker's Psalter (1567), and many anthems and motets.

TALON, JEAN (?1625–94), French administrator, who was the first intendant of French Canada (1665–8, 1669–72). During his earlier term of office he conducted the first census of the colony, built a brewery, settled immigrants, and set up villages in Quebec. It was through his efforts that the colony was established on a sound economic basis. During his second term he extended the colony's boundaries and, with the governor, the Comte de Frontenac, planned the exploration of the Mississippi river and the establishment of forts to control trade on Lake Ontario. He encouraged both trade and industry, imported craftsmen, stimulated shipping on the lake, and built ships. At the end of his second term he returned to France and became *secrétaire de cabinet* to Louis XIV.

TALON, OMER (1595–1652), French lawyer and politician, who was *avocat-général* in the *parlement* of Paris, and a leader of the *parlementaire* opposition to Mazarin's policies before and during the *Frondes* (1648–52).

TAMBRALINGA, area and ancient kingdom on the Kra isthmus in southern Thailand, first mentioned in an Indian source (2nd cent. AD). It later came under the control of Sri Vijaya (8th cent. AD) and remained so till the 13th cent. In 1230, however, Tambralinga had become independent under Chandrabhanu, King of the Javakas, who twice launched an expedition against Ceylon (1247, 1270), presumably in quest of relics of Lord Buddha. The first expedition led to temporary occupation of part of the island, but the second appears to have been unsuccessful. No more is heard of Tambralinga after this event. The area was incorporated into the Thai empire before the end of the 13th cent.

TAMIHANA, WIREMU TARAPIPI (*c.* 1802–66), NZ Maori chief who was rebuffed in presenting grievances to Gov. Gore Browne (1857). He concluded that Maoris must establish their own government, and secured the election of Te Wherowhero as Maori king, but in the Waikato War (1863–4) he urged conciliation.

TAMIL MAHAJANA SABHA in Ceylon, founded by Tamils and led by the brothers Ramanathan and Arunachalam after they had broken away from the Ceylon National Congress (1921), being dissatisfied with the place suggested for the Tamil community in the plans for constitutional reform.

TAMILNAD, state of the republic of India, bounded on the north by Andhra Pradesh and Mysore and on the west by Kerala. The official language is Tamil, but Malayalam and Telugu are also spoken. Its history roughly corresponds to that of the old Madras Presidency.

TAMMANY (Tammanen) (*c.* 1620–93), American Indian. Little is known of Tammany, except that he was a sachem of the Delaware and signed the treaty of Shackamaxon (1683). He was widely respected among the Indians as a man of good judgement and integrity and his fame extended to the whites, who made up legends about him and facetiously established him as 'St Tammany', the 'patron saint' of America during the War of Independence. Tammany societies were formed as patriotic and charitable institutions. The best-known of these societies was the one in New York city founded by William Mooney (1786) which developed into a powerful political body whose central executive office was called Tammany Hall.

TAMMANY HALL in the US, headquarters of the New York county democratic committee and a term that became more generally current in American politics to signify local 'boss' and 'machine' control of the political process. Patriotic societies known as the Sons of Tammany were founded during the American Revolution, named after an Indian chief of the Delaware nation who was believed to have welcomed William Penn when he arrived to found his Quaker commonwealth. The Society of St Tammany, with rituals based on Indian customs, was formally organized in 1789 as a patriotic and social organization, but by the early 1800s had become a political club for Jeffersonian Republicans (later Democrats). It was one of a number of such clubs in New York city, although more powerful than most, until William Marcy Tweed turned it into the dominant political organization after 1860. The power of Tammany came to extend beyond New York city into the state government, and it exercised an important, and occasionally decisive, influence on the national Democratic Party until 1932.

TAMWORTH MANIFESTO (1834) in Britain, address to Sir Robert Peel's constituents in Tamworth, which came to be regarded as an election manifesto for the whole Tory Party. It did not outline a programme, but referred to specific issues, including the reform of municipal corporations, ecclesiastical property, and tithes, with which Peel's minority government had been faced. Its chief feature was its recognition of the Reform Act of 1832 as irrevocable and its appeal to middle-class desires for order and efficient government.

TAN CHENG LOCK (1883–1960), spokesman of the Malaya-born Chinese between the two World Wars, and founding president of the Malayan Chinese Association (1949–58). He rallied Chinese support for an independent, non-communist Malaya.

T'AN SSU-T'UNG (1865–98), Chinese philosopher and one of the six martyrs of the 'Hundred Days' Reform'. He was a native of Hunan. Although he was the son of a high official, T'an's nonconformism led him into a wide range of intellectual pursuits, embracing Christianity, Buddhism, and Taoism, as well as Confucianism. He was extremely influenced by the writings of Wang Fu-chih, and was nationalistic and advocated the establishment of a Chinese republic. During the 'Hundred Days' Reform' he even proposed the assassination of the empress dowager, Tz'u-hsi. T'an's extremism and his martyrdom made him a far greater hero to the new generation of Chinese in the early 20th cent. than was his master, K'ang Yu-wei.

TANAGRA, BATTLE OF (457 BC), in Boeotia during the First Peloponnesian War, a tactical victory of the Spartans and their allies over the Athenians and theirs. The Spartans, who had been blockaded in central Greece, withdrew to the Peloponnese, but two months later the Athenians defeated the Boeotians at Oenophyta.

TANAKA, GIICHI (1863–1929), Japanese soldier and politician, by birth a Chōshū samurai. He served as chief-of-staff in the Manchurian army during the Russo-Japanese War and as war minister under Hara Kei (1918–21), when he was responsible for Japan's ill-fated Siberian expedition. In 1925 he was invited to become leader of the disorganized *Seiyūkai* party, and when the Wakatsuki cabinet fell (1927), he became prime minister and foreign minister. The notorious 'Tanaka Memorial' attributed to him at this time is no longer considered genuine, but he did adopt a much stronger attitude than his predecessor towards China. His efforts to defend and extend Japanese interests were badly co-ordinated, however, and his despatch of troops to Shantung aroused Chinese hostility. Tanaka's cabinet fell in July 1929 because the army refused to punish officers who had assassinated Chang Tso-lin, war-lord of Manchuria.

TANDON, PURUSHOTTAMDAS (1882–1962), Indian nationalist politician, who took a leading part in the non-co-operation and civil disobedience campaigns and as speaker was an influential figure in the United Provinces' Legislative Assembly (1937–50). He resigned in order to contest the Congress presidential election (1950), as Sardar Patel's nominee. He was conservative and a strong protagonist of Hindi, and his victory was taken as a defeat for Nehru. After Patel's death (1950) he was urged to resign from the presidency and did so in Sept. 1951. Later he became a member of the *Lok Sabha* and then of the *Rajya Sabha*.

TANEY, ROGER BROOKE (1777–1864), US lawyer and politician, who was admitted to the MD bar in 1799. He was a Federalist state legislator (1799–1800), but broke with the Federalists in 1812. He was a state senator (1816–21), and after 1824 a supporter of Andrew Jackson. He resigned his post as MD's attorney-general (1827–31), to become US attorney-general under Jackson, and defined Jackson's constitutional position with regard to his veto of the bill to recharter the Bank of the United States (1832). Taney's recess appointment by Jackson as secretary of the treasury was rejected by the Senate (1834) and his nomination as associate justice of the US Supreme Court was rendered void by being postponed indefinitely (1835), but his nomination as chief justice a year later was confirmed despite opposition. He modified the nationalist emphasis of the court under Marshall, tended to emphasize the importance of community, as well as property, rights in *Charles River Bridge v. Warren Bridge* (1837), and in a series of decisions revised judicial interpretations of the commerce clause. His attitudes towards slavery and state rights were reflected in *Dred Scott v. Sandford* (1857), where he used a strict interpretation of the constitution to declare invalid the Missouri Compromise and the 1850 Compromise, and refused to accept that Negroes were US citizens. During the American Civil War he strongly protested against the infringement of civil rights, challenging Lincoln's suspension of *habeas corpus*.   JDL

T'ANG SHAO-YI (1860–1934), Chinese politician, who from having been an imperial scholar-bureaucrat became a republican politician after the 1911 Revolution. He was closely associated with Sun Yat-sen and the Kuomintang, and was a prime minister of the Chinese republic (March–June 1912).

T'ANG DYNASTY (618–906), period in which Chinese strength was reasserted, institutions of government made more complex, and effective and cultural activities promoted. Building on the examples left by its predecessors such as Wei and Sui, the T'ang dynasty operated a system of central government designed to separate administrative responsibilities among a number of organs and officials, both to secure working efficiency and to prevent the growth of power concentrations. The dignity of officials and their influence in the countryside was enhanced by the growing prestige of the civil service, and this was deliberately fostered by the government's emphasis on education, its promulgation of the Confucian texts, its reinforcement of social hierarchies, and, above all, by its operation of the system of examinations. The scholar–civil servants who came to prominence in this way contributed markedly to China's cultural enrichment during the reign of Hsüan-tsung (712–55), gave rise to new habits of writing in prose and poetry, and demanded the services of engineers, painters, and craftsmen for the building and embellishment of suitable palaces. At the same time the needs of government stimulated the production of voluminous historical and encyclopedic works to support the authority of the dynasty and the civil service.

Attempts, not entirely successful, were made to practise on a universal scale schemes for the equitable distribution of land and collection of tax and for the efficient maintenance of the army up to strength. Such projects failed because of a shortage of reliable and efficient officials, and the need to employ foreign leaders in positions of high responsibility at the frontiers. At the centre, political power could sometimes be monopolized by individual statesmen, with a resultant factionalism, court intrigue, and the subordination of imperial to personal needs. These weaknesses led to the outbreak of the An-Lu-shan rebellions from 755, after which T'ang power was never restored to its former strength. Before then, however, Chinese influence and military power had been extended deeply into central Asia, to the discomfiture of the Turkish (T'u-chüeh) or other confederacies, but the limit of T'ang expansion was marked by the defeat of the Chinese forces by Arabs at Talas, in 751. In the meantime T'ang had intervened in the Korean peninsula; models of T'ang government were adopted in Japan from 645 and diplomatic and cultural missions came thence to China to study T'ang cultural and political achievements. In addition large numbers of foreigners reached Ch'ang-an and other cities to establish trading interests. Both Buddhism and Taoism were at times favoured by T'ang emperors, and the practice of foreign religions such as Manichaeism and Nestorian Christianity was tolerated. But in 845 Buddhist establishments suffered very seriously from the dissolution of monasteries and the enforced return of large numbers of monks and nuns to lay life. This oppression was due to economic motives rather than ideological reasons.

E. Reischauer, *Ennin's Travels in T'ang China* (New York, 1955).   ML

T'ANGKU TRUCE (1933), truce concluded between China and Japan which ended recent hostilities and amounted to an abject surrender by the Chinese. Much of north China was virtually abandoned to Japan, under the Kuomintang policy of appeasing Japan while concentrating on the suppression of internal enemies, notably the Chinese communists.

TANGULAN RISING (Dec. 1931) in the Philippines, revolt against agrarian oppression, staged by members of a secret society called *Tangulan* (meaning 'fortress' or 'defence'), also referred to as *Kapatiran Anak ng Bayan* (Association of the Children of the Country), founded in Bulacan in Dec. 1927. The *Tangulan* had an estimated membership of over 12,000 in the various provinces of Luzon and the city of Manila. Like the Sakdal movement, the *Tangulan* looked to Japan for help. The immediate cause of the *Tangulan* Rising was the government's harshness towards any organization suspected to be seditious. Some 150 members, reportedly aiming to take Manila by midnight, were rounded up by the Manila police; others were apprehended by the Philippine constabulary at Caloocan, Rizal province. The rising can be viewed as a symptom of the discontent with existing social conditions, depression, and unemployment.

TANK. Though the idea of a 'land-ship' was referred to by many writers before the 20th cent., the tank became a practical possibility only with the invention of the internal combustion engine and caterpillar tracks. Essentially, a tank is a mobile armoured weapon-carrier, and the impetus for its development came at the beginning of the First World War with the need to find some means of overcoming the deadlock created by the trench system. The man most closely connected with the evolution of the tank was a British officer, Lieut-Col. Swinton, who pressed the idea on a reluctant War Office.

In the British cabinet, Winston Churchill alone was enthusiastic; he had earlier been interested in the idea of the armoured car and had charged Capt. Murray Sueter, head of the Royal Naval Air Service, with investigating the extent to which the American Holt caterpillar tractor, used for hauling heavy artillery, might be exploited as a means of crossing trenches. After much debate and many experiments William Tritton, managing director of Foster's of Lincoln, and Lieut. W. G. Wilson of the RNAS produced a vehicle which successfully carried out trials early in 1916. The War Office ordered 100 of them, and in Sept. 1916 the tank made its first appearance in battle on the Western Front. Apart from design problems there was the difficulty of devising the best operational technique for their use: in 1916 they were used in small numbers as an infantry support weapon, and it was not until the battle of Cambrai in Nov. 1917 that they were used en masse as a means of providing mobility. By the end of the First World War a technique for their use was being worked out by some progressive officers, notably Col. J. F. C. Fuller; others, such as Liddell Hart, De Gaulle, and Guderian developed this technique in the years between the wars.   NRB

TANNA (in the Pacific), active volcanic island in the southern New Hebrides (pop. 12,000) discovered by Cook (1774) and long notorious for its vigorous resistance to Christianity (1842–1903). In 1943 the island attracted further notice when the entire populace suddenly decamped to join an anti-mission cargo cult, 'John Frum' which still (1970) exercised a notable political influence.

TANNENBERG, BATTLE OF (1410), the defeat of the Teutonic Order by the combined forces of the Poles and the Lithuanians (called the battle of Grunwald by the Poles). This marked the end of the order's supremacy in the eastern Baltic. After another prolonged war in 1453–66 the Poles recovered Pomerania from the order, thus gaining access to the Baltic. The order ceased to exist in 1525, when what remained of its territories was turned into a secular state adhering to the Protestant religion.

TANNENBERG, BATTLE OF (26–31 Aug. 1914), fought in East Prussia during the First World War. A Russian march on Berlin, designed to relieve the pressure on the French, was decisively defeated, and the way opened for Germany's later successes in the East, and the making of the reputation of her generals, Hindenburg and Ludendorff.

The Russian plan was that their First Army should engage the German Eighth Army with an attack across Germany's eastern frontier, while their Second Army advanced from the south to attack the German flank and rear. Their forces lacked the mobility and organization necessary to execute such a manœuvre across bad terrain and advanced before their preparations were complete; but they achieved sufficient success to bring about Prittwitz's relief on 21 Aug. by Hindenburg, whose chief of staff was Ludendorff. Shortly thereafter Moltke withdrew two corps from the Western Front to reinforce the East; they arrived too late to play any part at Tannenberg, but were missed on the Marne.

Hindenburg and Ludendorff put into effect a plan to retrieve the situation which had been devised by the Eighth Army staff and inspired by Col. Max Hoffman. Taking advantage of the lack of co-ordination between the Russian armies and the slowness of their advance, of their ability to intercept and decipher Samsonov's radio orders to his subordinates, and of the excellent East Prussian railway system, they withdrew their whole army from contact with Rennenkampf and rushed it south to attack Samsonov simultaneously on both flanks. By the end of Aug. his entire army had virtually been destroyed, after which Rennenkampf was defeated in his turn, and driven out of East Prussia. In all, the Russians lost about 250,000 men, and much irreplaceable war material.

TANTIA TOPI (1819–59), Maratha Brahman, who was one of Nana Sahib's commanders during the Indian Mutiny. He was responsible, with Nana Sahib, for the massacres at Cawnpore. After several defeats he was captured in April 1859, tried, and executed.

TANTRISM, form of Indian religion, Buddhism and later also Hinduism (notably Sivaism), which prescribes or authorizes practices considered unorthodox or sinful according to the prevalent trends. Among some sects these practices included magic and witchcraft, or even ritual sexual intercourse and the eating of meat. Such rites were based on the assumption that established religions had banned them merely on account of the potency of their effects. Tantric influence on Indian political and cultural developments was no doubt considerable, but is difficult to assess. It certainly contributed to the decline of Buddhism in north India from the 9th cent. AD. Its influence in ancient Khmer and Javanese civilizations is much better attested.

TANUCCI, BERNARDO, Marquis di (1698–1785), Tuscan-born politician and lawyer, who served the kings of Naples and Sicily in the mid-18th cent. A lawyer by training, he advised Don Carlos on legal matters and modified Neapolitan legal procedure to make it less brutal and restricted the feudal privileges of the nobility. During the minority of Ferdinand of Naples he acted as regent (1759–67) and though his influence declined somewhat after Maria Carolina became queen (1768), he remained chief minister until his dismissal in 1776. He was a patron of letters and a critic of ecclesiastical abuses, *eg*, he refused to pay the traditional tribute owed by Naples to acknowledge its feudal subjection to Rome.

TANUMA, OKITSUGU (1719–88), *bakufu* politician in Tokugawa Japan. Although little more than a middle-ranking samurai by birth, Tanuma secured the favour of the 10th *shōgun*, Ieharu (*reg*. 1760–86), and rose to high office and power. Unlike most *bakufu* leaders, his attempts to restore Tokugawa finances were not reactionary. Instead of repressing commercial activity he encouraged it, increasing *bakufu* profits on existing monopolites and introducing new ones. Tanuma's methods were open to criticism, however, both on grounds of corruption and as a departure from tradition, and on Ieharu's death (1786) he was disgraced.

TANZANIA AFRICAN NATIONAL UNION (TANU), formed in Tanganyika in 1954 under Nyerere's leadership. TANU's objective was the creation of a national consciousness and preparation of the country for independence. It was opposed to the alienation of African land, and was active in the promotion of trade unions and co-operatives. Though membership was open only to Africans, collaboration was sought with Europeans and Asians who were ready to back the campaign for independence. Then, as later, TANU proved a party of evolution which stood for peace, equality, and harmony between racial groups.

TANZANIA, REPUBLIC OF (350,000 sq. miles—937,060 sq. kms), in East Africa, formerly the British UN mandate of Tanganyika and the sultanate of Zanzibar and Pemba under British protection. In 1964 Zanzibar and Pemba joined Tanganyika, which became independent in 1961, to form the republic of Tanzania. Nyamwezi, Chagga, Gogo, Hehe, and other groups formed in 1970 the population of 12,231,000. The president holds executive power and is elected by adult suffrage, as is the National Assembly of 204 members. Tanzania belonged in 1970 to the British Commonwealth.

TANZIMAT (reorganization), name applied to a period of Ottoman history (1839–76) which was characterized by important reforms. These fall into two categories. The first includes those which promised to all Ottoman citizens equality, justice, and a greater share in government. The best-known of these reforms are the great edicts (Hatts) of 1839 and 1856, and the 1876 constitution. Because many of these reforms were not carried out, and the timing of their announcement coincided with periods of pressure upon the Ottoman empire, when the Ottomans required European help, many writers have dismissed the Tanzimat as mere window-dressing. Such a judgement disregards the second, much more important category of reforms, which were designed to centralize and modernize the governmental structure of the Ottoman empire. These reforms, first attempted under Selim III (*reg.* 1789–1807), really took shape under Mahmud II (*reg.* 1808–39). They began with the object of transforming the Ottoman army into a disciplined professional force established on European lines. The cost of this in money and trained personnel forced the Ottoman government to increase its control over other institutions in society and led to a transformation of administration and a great growth in the power of the central government. It also led to important changes in education and law, by which these institutions were gradually removed from religious control and remodelled to resemble the systems which had developed in Europe. Although the Tanzimat reformers failed in their main objective of preserving the empire, since they were always unable to persuade the Balkan Christians to abandon their desire for independence and to ward off foreign intervention, and although they failed to create a real sense of Ottoman citizenship, they did reshape Ottoman government and society and pave the way for the further development of Turkey and other successor states.

B. Lewis, *The Emergence of Modern Turkey* (Oxford, 1961). R. H. Davison, *Reform in the Ottoman Empire, 1856–76* (Princeton, 1963).   MEY

TAOISM, term used to denote both one of China's most important ways of thought and one of her religions. As a way of thought, Taoism relates the transient human and natural activities of this world to the permanent principle of *Tao*, The Way, thus seeking constant, if undefinable, values that are not invalidated by the weakness of the human intellect or powers of perception. The theme was first enunciated in the *Tao-te ching* and the *Chuang-tzu*. Taoist religion is traced to the 2nd cent. AD, and its subsequent popular appeal was based partly on claims to prolong life by the practice of certain rites, by invoking magical and mysterious powers and ensuring harmony between an individual and the forces of the universe. The ideas of a Taoist religion have been expressed by a number of writers and painters; it has sometimes enjoyed imperial patronage and has been propagated by an established leadership in its many temples. By its practice of alchemy Taoist religion promoted the growth of scientific enquiry in China at an early stage.

TAO-KUANG REIGN (1821–51), the reign-title of Min-ning (*reg.* 1782–1851), the sixth emperor of the Ch'ing dynasty in China. He came to the throne at a time when the empire's population had reached 400 million and the finances were in a state of depletion. He consequently adopted a policy of retrenchment and limited military activities, but was unable to combat corruption and his traditional training prevented him from assuming a reformist role. His inability to tackle either the adverse balance of foreign trade or the debilitating effects of the opium trade revealed his lack of imagination and courage. His vacillation between war and peace during the Opium War, coupled with inability to cope effectively with its results, speeded up the process of dynastic decline. When he died, he left to his successor, Hsien-feng, a crumbling empire in a state of unrest and rebellion.

TAOS REBELLION (1847), revolt of Indians instigated by Mexicans living in Taos, NM. Gov. Charles Bent and other Americans were killed (17 Jan. 1847) and US troops were sent from Santa Fé early in Feb. to put the rebellion down.

TAO-TE CHING, Chinese classic, formerly attributed to Lao Tzu, said to have been a contemporary of Confucius (5th cent. BC). It is now believed to be an anthology of sayings and poems, perhaps compiled in the 4th or early 3rd cent. BC. The anthology casts doubt on the value of human emotions and judgements, rejecting both a materialist standpoint and an attempt to organize human society too rigidly. The book urges man to act in conformity with *Tao*, the principle underlying the natural and human world, and the means whereby contradictions may be resolved. At a later stage, teachers of Taoism sought to fasten authority for their doctrines on to the *Tao-te ching* or Lao Tzu.

TAQIZADEH, SAYYID HASAN (d. 1970), Iranian lawyer, politician, and intellectual from Tabriz, who played an important role in the constitutional movement (1906–9) and in the drafting of the Iranian constitution. He left Iran after the 1909 counter-revolution and edited *Kaveh* (1916–21). He returned to Iran to take a prominent part in the reforms of Reza Shah, but again went into exile. In his last years he became the doyen of Iranian politics and president of the senate (1950).

TARAIN, BATTLES OF (1191, 1192), decisive episode in the Muslim conquest of India. When Muhammad of Ghur invaded India he was met by Rajput Prithviraj, the Cahumana (Cauhan) king of Ajmer and Delhi, and defeated at Tarain, some 100 miles (161 kms) north of Delhi. The next year, however, Muhammad returned and, in the second battle of Tarain, decisively defeated Prithviraj, who was taken prisoner and later executed.

TARANTO, BATTLE OF (1940), Fleet Air Arm attack on the Italian navy. Following the broad outline of a plan conceived before the beginning of the Second World War, and after one postponement, Swordfish aircraft from the carrier HMS *Illustrious* attacked the Italian fleet as it lay at anchor in Taranto harbour in south-east Italy on the night of 11 Nov. 1940. Two flights, of twelve and nine aircraft respectively, took off from the carrier 273 kms south-east of Taranto, three hours apart. The first flight caught the Italians by surprise, and torpedo and bomb attacks were delivered against the ships in the inner and outer harbours as well as against shore installations. Despite the failure of several torpedoes to detonate, one battleship was sunk and two others so badly damaged that they were out of action for some six months; all this was achieved for the loss of two aircraft and one life. The success of the operation was a triumphant vindication for the hitherto controversial Fleet Air Arm, and demonstrated the importance of the aircraft carrier in naval warfare. The Italians temporarily moved their fleet away from Taranto to the less vulnerable harbours of their west coast; this, together with the reduction in their battle-ship strength, greatly decreased their operational effectiveness in the critical months that followed. There is evidence that the Japanese had the attack on Taranto in mind when they planned theirs on Pearl Harbor in Dec. 1941.

TARAWA, BATTLE OF (20–3 Nov. 1943), engagement between US and Japanese forces during the Second World War that marked the beginning of the US counter-offensive against Japanese positions in the central Pacific. Tarawa, in the Gilbert Islands, was taken after direct assault by US Marines.

TARBELL, IDA MINERVA (1857–1944), US journalist and writer, who was the daughter of an independent oil producer. She was editor of *McClure's Magazine* (1894–1906) and wrote a series of articles on the Standard Oil Trust, published in 1904 as *The History of the Standard Oil Company*. She described the savings resulting from the elimination of com-petition in the oil industry, the minimum of waste in Stan-dard's operations, and the devotion of John D. Rockefeller. But she also exposed the questionable business practices, bribery, fraud, and intimidation resorted to or condoned by Standard, and to her discomfort was regarded as a 'muck-raker'. She later published a study of the industrialist Elbert H. Gray.

TARDIEU, ANDRÉ (1876–1945), French journalist and poli-tician, whose advocacy of a 'technocratic' programme of economic modernization and social reform failed to win acceptance in the 1930s. He entered parliament in 1914, and later collaborated closely with Clemenceau. He was in charge of Franco-American war co-operation (1918–19), then an adviser at the peace negotiations. On returning to political life, he became a leader of the moderate right and was a minister in several governments. As prime minister (1929–30, 1930, 1932) he attempted to make the French economy more dynamic and efficient by means of public investment, while introducing measures of a welfare-state nature. Something was achieved in the field of health and social security, but his economic policy was strongly opposed in orthodox circles. In foreign affairs he supported the policies of Briand, and advocated an international air force under League of Nations command. He was a member of Doumergue's national unity government (1934), but retired from politics when he lost his seat in the 1936 election.

TARENTUM, Roman name of the ancient Greek city of Taras, in southern Italy (mod. Taranto), founded by Sparta (*c.* 700 BC) for the natural sons born to Spartan women in the first Messenian War. Though sympathetic towards Sparta and Syracuse in the great Peloponnesian War, it avoided arduous commitment and early in the 4th cent. under the philosopher Archytas achieved great prosperity, reflected in its splendid gold coinage. Thereafter it tended to seek over-seas aid against its Italian neighbours, and after provoking Rome to war over Thurii relied unsuccessfully on Pyrrhus of Epirus, and was subjected (272). It was plundered by the Romans after being betrayed to Hannibal (209), and lost importance to Brundisium (Brindisi) as the port of departure to Greece.

TARIFF BOARD, THE AUSTRALIAN, was established in 1921, to advise the Commonwealth government on necessary modifications and applications of its protectionist policy. Public hearings and representation of academic and farming interests were designed to assist the board in avoiding or correcting abuses but, while there were some ameliorative

and 'scientific' results, successive Commonwealth govern-ments resisted the board's alleged attempts to become more than an advisory body.

TARIFF OF ABOMINATIONS (1828) in the US, legislation devised by supporters of Andrew Jackson, who hoped to secure his election to the presidency in 1828 by presenting him to the North as a protectionist and to the South as a free trader. They introduced a bill with duties on raw materials higher than those on manufactures, expecting that New England would join with the South in defeating it, and thus discredit the John Quincy Adams administration in the eyes of the North. Jackson would then be able to appeal to the protectionists in the Middle States, whose votes, with those of the South, would decide the election in his favour. The plan misfired, enough New Englanders voting for the bill to secure its passage.

TARIFF REFORM in Britain, attempts to reintroduce pro-tection in the period 1895–1906. The motives for reform were more political than economic. They came from the desire of Joseph Chamberlain, as secretary of state for the colonies, to provide some formal structure for the empire, which would bind together the self-governing dominions and Britain. He wanted to see a system of 'imperial free trade' and a governing council of the empire: he also wished to place the burden of supporting the navy more fairly on those who benefited from its protection. Since the dominions already had protective tariffs, imperial free trade involved the intro-duction of differential tariffs for imports to Britain. In one way or another the scheme would have raised the costs of raw materials. It was put forward unsuccessfully at the 1902 imperial conference, and Chamberlain continued to cam-paign for it until 1906, when a stroke finished his political career. The Tariff Reformers found that Free Trade had still a religious aura in the eyes of the British public, and because of this they had to abandon any intention to put duties on food, so that only an emasculated programme was put forward at the general election of 1906. Even this form produced a serious split within the Conservative Party, and was a major reason for the striking Liberal success of that year. Though Tariff Reform was a political failure, it encouraged discussion and criticism among politicians and economists and produced lines of economic thinking that were revived in the inter-war Depression.   RMM

TARIQ IBN ZIYAD, Berber client of the invading Arabs, who led the Muslim armies into Spain (711) to overthrow the Visigothic kingdom and give his name to Gibraltar (*Jabal Tariq,* Tariq's mountain).

TARQUINIA, oldest of Etruscan cities, founded by Tarchon 96 kms north-west of Rome, renowned for its painted tombs and extensive cemeteries, which still survive. After the wan-ing of Etruscan power, it showed benevolent neutrality towards Rome's advance northward, and alliances were struck in 351 and 308 BC. Encouraged by Gallic successes to revolt in 284, it was reduced and thereafter held the status of *socii* until the 1st cent. BC.

TARQUINIUS PRISCUS (*reg.* 616–579 BC), traditionally fifth King of Rome and first Etruscan king (masking the reality of Etruscan domination). There is no need to deny his historicity, but the civil and military achievements ascribed to him (building of the Capitoline temple, the circus, and the sewage-system, and operations against the Latins) are inextricably entangled with those of Tarquinius Superbus.

TARQUINIUS SUPERBUS (Tarquin the Proud) (*reg.* 534–509 BC), seventh and last King of Rome, whose reign repre-sents a renewal of Etruscan domination, during which sub-stantial building was achieved at Rome, and Gabii and Suessa Pometia were captured. The traditional story of his overthrow by L. Junius Brutus and the liberation of Rome, which followed the rape of Lucretia, is legend.

TARSUS, birthplace of St Paul, situated at the mouth of the Cydmus and controlling the route across the Taurus from Syria to Asia Minor. It was first settled in the 5th millennium BC, and became successively the capital of Cilician kings and Persian satraps, and was significantly hellenized in the 5th and 4th cents, before it passed to Alexander the Great and then to the Seleucids. After being annexed by Pompey (66), it was granted freedom and immunity by Antony, and became the provincial capital of Roman Cilicia (*c.* AD 72), remaining important into early Byzantine times. A property qualification for citizens' rights disenfranchised most workers in its famous linen industry.

TARTAGLIA, NICCOLO (1500–57), Italian mathematician of the Renaissance, who applied the impetus theory to ballistics and published the first Latin translation of Archimedes (1543).

TARTE, JOSEPH ISRAEL (1848–1907), Canadian journalist and politician, who was editor and later owner of *Le Canadien* (1874–93), a member of the Quebec legislature (1877–81), and owner of the Liberal newspaper *La Patrie* (1897–1907). He was associated in his early years with the Ultramontane wing of the Conservative Party but left the party after publishing disclosures that led to a government scandal (1890–1). He joined the Liberal Party and became chief lieutenant to Wilfrid Laurier and a powerful critic of Conservative policy on the Man. schools issue. He was elected to parliament (1896) and appointed minister of public works (1896–1902) in Laurier's cabinet, but was dismissed when he infringed party discipline to campaign for higher tariffs (1902).

TARTESSUS, region and town in southern Spain, an important ancient centre for trade in raw metals from northern Europe to the East and legendary for its wealth. After early contacts with the Phoenicians (*c.* 1000 BC), it welcomed the first Greek trader, Colaeus of Samos (*c.* 635), and the Phocaeans who followed. Its friendliness towards Greeks may have been the cause of its destruction, perhaps by Carthaginians (*c.* 500).

TARUC, LUIS (1913–), Filipino politician and first leader of the Filipino *Hukbo nang Bayan Laban sa Hapon* (*Hukbalahap* or *Huk*), the 'People's Army Against Japan'. At first he was drawn towards the Sakdal movement and he went to Laguna, where the Sakdalistas were very active. He failed to find work there, and became disenchanted with Sakdalism. He therefore returned to Pampanga in 1935, after corresponding with the lawyer Pedro Abad Santos, who had founded the Socialist Party in the Philippines, and became acting secretary of that party in 1936. He was soon organizing political conferences, writing editorials for the party paper, and leading strikes, boycotts, and demonstrations. When the Socialist and Communist parties merged in 1938 to form the Communist Party of the Philippines, Taruc became a member of its loosely knit presidium. He organized the loosely knit peasants into more cohesive groups: the *Aguman Ding Madlang Talapagobra* (General Workers' Union) for the Pampanga peasants, and the *Pambansang Kaisahan ng Magsasaka* (National Union of Peasants) for the Tagalog-speaking peasants. When the Japanese invaded the Philippines in 1942 it was easy for Taruc to organize the members of these two groups as guerrilla fighters. On 29 March 1942 he formed the *Hukbo nang Bayan Laban sa Hapon*. While the Philippines were being liberated, he was imprisoned by the Americans, being released in Sept. 1945. Returning to Pampanga, he resumed the leadership of the *Hukbalahap*, and in the 1946 election won a congressional seat, representing the second district of Pampanga under the banner of the Democratic Alliance. But he was removed from his seat in Congress after charges of election fraud, and fled to the hills. He appeared briefly in Manila in June 1948 to meet President E. Quirino, who had proposed an amnesty for Taruc and his men. But he returned to the hills after the proclamation of the amnesty and remained an outlaw until his surrender in April 1954. He was given the maximum sentence of 12 years imprisonment for rebellion, and four life sentences in addition, but pardoned by President F. E. Marcos in Sept. 1968. Since then Taruc has been active in campaigning for reforms as a lecturer at the Jesuit Ateneo de Manila University and in co-operation with such groups as the Christian Socialist Movement, which have been working for reforms in Philippine society.

L. Taruc, *He Who Rides the Tiger. The story of an Asian guerrilla leader* (London, 1967). JMS

TASCA, ANGELO (A. ROSSI) (1892–), Italian syndicalist, who became a communist follower of Gramsci and his *Ordine Nuovo* group. After working for the Comintern, he was denounced by Stalin (1928) and expelled from the Italian Communist Party in 1929 for opposing Russian policies, and advocating links with socialists. He moved to France and, as A. Rossi, became a leading socialist, anti-fascist propagandist, and journalist. As a French citizen, he was a resistance fighter during the Second World War. He later wrote critical studies of the French Communist Party.

TASCHEREAU, ELZÉAR-ALEXANDRE (1820–98), Canadian Catholic priest who was for 30 years connected with the Quebec Seminary. As rector of Laval University he supported the university in its conflicts with the conservative Ultramontane clergy, but maintained a position of moderation in the struggles between the conservative clergy and leaders of liberal opinion. He was appointed Abp of Quebec (1871) and became, in 1886, the first Canadian cardinal.

TASHKENT DECLARATION (10 Jan. 1966) in India, agreement between Lal Bahadur Shastri and Ayub Khan which ended the Indo-Pakistanian war of 1965. Fighting began in the Rann of Kutch, a barren area of mud-flats on the Gujarat–Sind border, in April but in June forces were withdrawn under an agreement by which Pakistan's claims to territory in the area were submitted to arbitration. The tribunal adjudged (Feb. 1968) the greater part of the area to be Indian territory, but awarded a small pocket of land to Pakistan.

In Aug. 1965 the conflict shifted to Kashmir and the Punjab. Guerrillas from Pakistan's 'Azad Kashmir' region crossed into Indian Kashmir and later Pakistan deployed armoured units in Jammu, in the south. Indian forces then crossed the Punjab border and moved towards Lahore and Sialkot. Heavy, though inconclusive, fighting continued until a UN-sponsored cease-fire took effect (23 Sept.). Shortly before this, the USSR had offered facilities in Tashkent for a conference and this began on 4 Jan. 1966, with Kosygin, the Soviet prime minister, personally offering his good offices in the negotiations. He secured, at the last minute, a declaration which brought about a withdrawal to the positions occupied by both sides before 5 Aug. 1965 and agreed to take steps to improve relations. Kashmir, the real bone of contention, was mentioned but no solution about its future was offered. The declaration was not well received in Pakistan, and Indian reactions were muted by the death of Shastri only hours after he had signed the declaration.

TASMAN, ABEL JANSZOON (1603?–59), Dutch navigator sent in search of the South Land (Australia) who discovered Van Diemen's Land (southern Tasmania) (1642) and the western edge of Staten Land (NZ) in 1643. In a new voyage (1644) he missed Torres Strait but disposed of the alleged passage leading south from the Gulf of Carpentaria.

TASMANIA, Australia's island state, settled in 1803 after French scientific expeditions had aroused British suspicions.

Convicts, bushrangers, whalers, sealers, and a 'black' war, made the early history of 'Van Diemen's Land' turbulent, but in the 1830s and 1840s, when the whaling industry ceased and many pastoralists moved to Vic., economic growth slackened. Neither the discovery of copper at Mount Lyell (1883), nor development of an apple export industry in the 1890s, ensured sustained prosperity. Tas. relied consistently on Commonwealth aid, although hydro-electricity, minerals, and an expanding paper and tourist industry promised a happier, late-20th-cent. future.

TASSO, TORQUATO (1544–95) Italian poet of the late Renaissance and son of the poet Bernardo (1493–1569). He was patronized by the Dukes Vicenzo Gonzago of Milan and Alfonso II d'Este of Ferrara, for whose courts he wrote the epic masterpiece of the first Crusade, 'La Gerusalemme Liberata' (1575) and the pastoral play *Aminta* (1581), respectively.

TATA FAMILY in India, Parsi merchant family of Bombay, the most important industrial entrepreneurs in 20th-cent. India. The family's early activities were in the Far Eastern trade under Nusserwanji Tata (1822–86) and his son Jamsetji Nusserwanji Tata (1839–1904). Having been ruined in the Indian slump after the American Civil War, they retrieved their position from profits made in supplying a punitive expedition to Abyssinia (1867) and re-entered the China trade. Jamsetji, however, always used his capital to gain a foothold in the cotton industry. He made a profitable conversion of the Alexandra Mill in Bombay (1871) and then went on to build a new mill at Nagpur, the 'Empress' (1877), and to recondition mills in Bombay (the '*Swadeshi*', 1886) and Ahmedabad (the 'Advance', 1900). These mills were the key to the family's fortune.

In the 1890s Jamsetji began to diversify his interests. He purchased landed property in Bombay and entered the Bombay money market, began the building of the Taj Mahal Hotel (finished in 1915), and promoted sericulture in Mysore state. He had less success in his attempt to start a shipping line in competition with the P & O Co. and in the promotion of land reclamation schemes, but he did lay the basis for the Tata Iron and Steel Co. and the companies which were to erect hydro-electric plants in the Western Ghats behind Bombay. He did the initial work in clearing the way for prospecting and enlisting American expertise for the steel industry, but it was left to his eldest son, Dorabji Jamsetji (1859–1932), who did much of the prospecting himself, to raise the capital on the Bombay market and to direct the establishment of the plant at Jamshedpur in Bihar. TISCO began operations in 1911 and by the 1960s was producing two million tons of steel. Dorabji also took charge of the hydro-electric project. He headed the Tata Hydro-Electric Supply Co., which built the dams at Lonavla (1911), Walwhan (1912), and Shirawta (1920), and which began to supply power to Bombay in 1915.

Dorabji, his younger brother, Ratanji Jamsetji (1871–1918), and their cousin, R. D. Tata, expanded Jamsetji's original firm, Tata and Sons (1887), to Tata Sons and Co. (1907) and brought in further capital in 1917 when Tata Sons Ltd was registered. Dorabji was chairman of this group which by 1920 had 22 constituent companies, including, besides the cotton, steel, power, and real estate concerns already mentioned, oil mills for soap manufacture (1917) and the New India Assurance Co. (1919). Before the Second World War the group added printing (1930), domestic aviation (1932), cement (1936), engineering (1937), chemicals (1939), and, after the war, locomotives and automobiles (1945), international aviation (1948) and sundry electrical, engineering, and chemical concerns in the 1950s. After Dorabji's death this vast industrial empire was headed by Jamsetji's nephew, Sir Nowroji Bapuji Saklatvala (1875–1938), and then by R. D. Tata's son, Jahangir Ratanji Dadabhai Tata (1904–   ). J. R. D. Tata, the first pilot to qualify in India, had been the pioneer of Tata Airlines (1932), later renamed Air-India

Ltd, and Air-India International (1948), and after these were nationalized (1953) he remained as chairman.

From the time of Jamsetji Tata, a proportion of the enormous wealth acquired by the family has been applied to educational and philanthropic use in India. Jamsetji established a fund to help Indians study overseas (1892) and followed this by allocating the income from his Bombay properties as the basis for the Indian Institute of Science, which was built in Bangalore (1906). Trust funds set up by Sir Dorabji Tata (1932) provided for the foundation of the Tata Institute of Social Sciences (1936) and the Tata Institute of Fundamental Research (1945), and other trust funds established by Sir Ratanji and Sir Doranji's widow were applied to support medical and scientific research and the promotion of social welfare work.

F. R. Harris, *Jamsetji Nusserwanji Tata, A Chronicle of His Life* (London, 1958).
J. L. Keenan, *A Steel Man in India* (London, 1945).   PDR

TATAR, Muslim Turkish peoples who formed the majority of the population of the Golden Horde and its successor states in southern Russia and the Ukraine (13th–18th cents). The name was also born by a Mongolian tribe exterminated by Chinghiz Khan at the beginning of the 13th cent.

TATISHCHEV, VASILI NIKITICH (1686–1750), Russian historian, geographer, mining engineer, administrator, and patriot, who rose to prominence in Peter I's reign. He was involved in the Volynski circle and opposed the German influence of ministers such as Biron and Ostermann in the Empress Anna's reign (1730–40). He urged the government to promote the use of the Russian language and in 1729 began his great Russian history (completed 1739, pub. 1768–1769).

TATLER, THE, in England, single news sheet started in 1709 by Richard Steele and published by him, with Joseph Addison's help, every other weekday until 1711. It was largely non-political and intended to civilize public taste.

TAUFA'AHAU (George Tupou I) (1797–1893), high chief of Ha'apai, Tonga, who adopted Wesleyanism. After bitter struggles with reactionary Tongatapu chiefs (1830–40) he assumed the vacant Tu'i Kanokupolu title ('Tongan 'shogun',) finally suppressing the superior ceremonial chief, Tu'i Tonga (1869). He established a well-run independent constitutional state and died universally respected.

TAUNTON, HENRY LABOUCHERE, Baron (1798–1869), British politician who, as president of the board of trade (1839–41, 1847–52), carried responsibility for the repeal of the navigation laws (1849). He was later secretary for the colonies (1855–8) and presided over the commission, appointed in 1861, which enquired into the endowed grammar schools. The result was the Endowed Schools Act (1869). Although the report was huge, little was achieved for secondary education, either by the commission or the act, until the 20th cent.

TAUSEN, HANS (1494–1561), Danish cleric and scholar, called 'the Danish Luther', who was one of the leading protagonists of the Danish reformation. He became acquainted with the Flemish humanists at Louvain (1522), was inspired by Luther at Wittenberg (1523), and left the order of Knights' Hospitallers to become official Lutheran chaplain to Frederick I (1526). He was the first Danish priest to marry and to use the vernacular in services. In 1536 he became lecturer in Hebrew in Copenhagen University and in 1542 was appointed Bp of Ribe.

TAVERA, JUAN PARDO DE (1472–1545), Castilian cleric, cardinal-archbishop of Toledo from 1534, and one of the

Emperor Charles V's most trusted counsellors in Spain. Though he held rather narrow views and openly opposed Charles's universalist policies, especially his imperialist interests in Italy, he was appointed chief adviser to Empress Isabella and later to the young regent Philip during Charles's absences abroad.

TAWFIQ (1852–92), Khedive of Egypt (*reg.* 1879–92) in succession to his deposed father, whose authority was impaired by nationalist opposition and European financial control. In 1882 he lost effective power to Urabi Pasha. Tawfiq supported the British intervention and subsequently was obliged to carry out the policies of the British consul-general, Lord Cromer.

TAX-FARMING in Europe, system of tax collection practised in many European countries, and particularly in France, in medieval and early modern times. In the case of France, it originated in the early Middle Ages when the Capetian kings were merely feudal lords of the Île de France and unable to establish their own mechanism for tax collection. They therefore farmed out the collection of such dues as they claimed to those who were willing and able to undertake their collection. The contract—or *ferme* in the French—involved a down payment by the financier roughly comparable to the estimated revenue, which assured the Crown of its income much earlier than it would have otherwise received it, but which left the financier at liberty to extract as much as he could, in order to maximize his profit. The practice of farming was common to many feudal landlords and the Church as well as the Crown. The latter began by farming out estate revenues, but later went on to farm out taxes as well. The collection of taxes over a much wider area demanded a much more complex organization, and gradually permanent administrations developed for the collection of taxes, particularly indirect taxes, which were loaned to the financiers who won the regular auctions for the tax farms. During the 16th cent. the major indirect taxes, the *gabelle*, the *traités*, the *aides*, and the *domaines*, each acquired one farm instead of the several farms previously favoured by the Crown, and in one area a variety of taxes were brigaded together as the Five Great Farms (1581). This policy was carried to its logical conclusions by Colbert, who combined all the individual tax farms into one general farm (1681) for which a whole team of financiers had to bid and which required a massive organization on very modern lines to collect the money. The contract price was originally about 64 million *livres*, which represented half all government revenues (1685), and though this fell during the wars of Louis XIV it eventually rose to 144 million *livres* (1786). The success of the *ferme* encouraged Frederick II of Prussia to entrust the collection of many excise duties to a French tax farmer called De Launay (1786), who was paid a percentage of the takings. Elsewhere, however, *eg*, in Tuscany (1768), tax farms were gradually disbanded, as they did not allow the state sufficient control over the process and yield of tax collection. Even in France Necker and other finance ministers interfered more and more with the *ferme*, bringing it increasingly under direct control and paving the way for the revolutionary governments to take over tax collection themselves.

G. A. Mathews, *The Royal General Farm in Eighteenth-Century France* (New York, 1958).   CHC

TAXILA or Takshasila, important archaeological site, about 20 miles (32 kms) north-west of Rawalpindi, West Pakistan, with ruins of three ancient cities: Bhir Mound, Sirkap, and Sirsuk. It is situated in a relatively fertile valley at the meeting point of ancient trade routes connecting the Indo-Gangetic valleys with both Kashmir and Iran. Extensive excavations by Sir John Marshall have revealed its political, economic, and cultural importance (especially as a Buddhist centre) from the 5th cent. BC. It declined towards the end of the 5th cent. AD after invasions by the Hephthalite Huns.

TAYLOR, JAMES HUDSON (1832–1905), English missionary and founder of the China Inland Mission, who went to China in 1832 as the first representative of the China Evangelization Society. In 1856 he began to work independently, and ten years later founded the China Inland Mission, adopting a fundamentalist approach, to compete with the Catholic missions in the interior of China. Beginning with 13 missionaries in 1866, the mission eventually grew into the largest of all mission agencies in China; at the time of his death, it had 828 missionaries.

TAYLOR, JOHN (1753–1824), US lawyer and politician, who served in the VA House of Delegates (1779–85, 1796–1800) and as US senator (1792–4, 1803, 1822–4). He was opposed to the constitution of 1787 because he believed it gave inadequate guarantees of individual liberties and states' rights. He was a leading critic of Hamilton's financial policies, and introduced resolutions into the VA state legislature (1798) to limit federal power by a 'strict' interpretation of the US constitution. His views were propagated in numerous pamphlets and tracts, notably *An Inquiry into the Principles and Policy of the Government of the United States* (1814). He was an early advocate of scientific farming and some of his articles on the utility of manuring, the rotation of crops, and other new methods of agriculture were collected in *The Arator* (1813).

TAYLOR, MAXWELL DAVENPORT (1901–), US soldier and diplomat. After service in the Second World War and in Korea he became army chief of staff (1955). He resigned (1959) after disagreements over strategy, but later became the military representative of President Kennedy (1961–2), chairman of the joint chiefs of staff (1962–4), and ambassador to South Viet-nam (1964–5).

TAYLOR, RICHARD (1805–73), British clergyman, who was a missionary in NZ (1839–66) and exerted great influence both among Maoris and with whites on questions of native policy. He wrote prolifically on NZ and on Maori life.

TAYLOR, ZACHARY (1784–1850), US soldier and 12th president of the US, born in VA. He entered the army in 1808 and became a major in the War of 1812. His long military career was relatively uneventful until he achieved national fame in the Mexican War, when he was over 60. In 1845 President Polk sent him into TX to protect the disputed border with Mexico. When war broke out Taylor defeated the Mexicans at Palo Alto (1846) and drove them across the Rio Grande. He then conquered the northern provinces of Mexico, winning a major battle against Santa Anna at Buena Vista (1847).

Taylor, who was popular with his men, earned the nickname of 'Old Rough and Ready'. His military fame attracted the attention of politicians and in 1848, despite his total lack of political experience, the Whigs ran him as their presidential candidate. He defeated the Democrat, Lewis Cass. His short term of office was dominated by the problems of the newly acquired CA and the south-west. To organize them as territories would have reopened the slavery debate in Congress, and Taylor tried to avoid this by seeking their direct admission as states. Congress resisted this and debated other plans. The deadlock was broken by Taylor's sudden death, which opened the door for the Compromise of 1850.

TAYLOR GRAZING ACT (1934), in the US, legislation named after Congressman Edward T. Taylor, of CO (1858–1941), which ended the free, unregulated, and common use of the vacant, unappropriated, and unreserved lands of the public domain in the West. In order to prevent further deterioration of the range and to stabilize the ranching industry, the secretary of the interior was authorized to establish grazing districts and issue grazing permits to the forage resource. The act, a major piece of land legislation and an important part of the conservation programme of the New Deal, affected about 20 per cent of all land in the 11 Western states.

TAY-SON REBELLION, beginning in 1773, an important turning-point in Viet-namese history. It began in Qui-Nhon province, as a revolt against the Nguyen rulers of central Viet-nam: its leaders were three brothers, who had the family name of Nguyen, but were unrelated to the ruling clan. The three, who had the support of a number of Chinese residents of the area, began their campaign in 1773 and rebels were almost ready to capture Hue, when in Jan. 1775 it fell to a Trinh army marching south from Hanoi. The Trinh and the Tay-Son brothers, after inconclusive fighting, partitioned central Viet-nam in 1777; whereupon the Tay-Son were free to deal with the Nguyen survivors in the far south. In 1786 serious internal conflict in Tongking led the Tay-Son brothers to intervene there. The Le dynasty, and the Trinh, were overthrown, and a Chinese army which intervened in 1788-9 was driven out. One of the Tay-Son brothers proclaimed himself emperor at Hanoi, as Quang-Trung (*reg.* 1788-92), and another claimed the title of emperor at Qui-Nhon: Thai-Duc (*reg.* 1778-93). Their successors, however, were not able to maintain their position. By 1790 Nguyen Anh had recovered control of Saigon, and after several campaigns lasting ten years succeeded in conquering the whole of Viet-nam in 1801-2.

TCHAD (1,284,000 sq. kms) in north central Africa became independent in 1960. It was formerly part of French West Africa. The constitution of 1962 made the president head of state, with a council of ministers to assist him. A legislative assembly is elected for a five-year term by adult suffrage. The population (1970) of 3,500,000 included Arab, Bulala, Teda-Daza, and other elements.

TE UA, TUWHAKARARO HAUMENE (*fl.* 19th cent.), NZ Maori prophet, who founded Hauhauism (1862), a short-lived warrior cult based on the Old Testament and aimed at the ejection of Europeans.

TEA ACT (1773) in Britain, legislative measure which permitted the East India Co. to sell tea directly to America and to set up its own agencies there. In effect, it made the company a monopoly with power to collect the tea duties. The result was widespread agitation and the famous 'tea parties', most significant of which was that at Boston in 1774.

TEACH, EDWARD ('Blackbeard') (d. 1718), English privateer during the War of Spanish Succession, who turned pirate on the Spanish Main and was killed in an action with royal navy frigates off VA.

TEA-DRINKING in Europe. This social habit, first mentioned in European literature by Ramusio (1559), was well established in Holland by the mid-17th cent., when it began to establish itself also in England, that other maritime power with trading connections with the Far East. Tea-drinking occurred in fashionable coffee houses, but remained less popular than coffee-drinking while the price remained higher. In 1706 54,600 lbs of tea were imported by the English East India Co. from China, the price being almost £1 per lb, but by 1750 the amount had risen to 2,325,000 lbs, the price then being 5s per lb. It grew more popular still when the custom of taking afternoon tea with cakes became a fashionable habit in 19th-cent. upper- and middle-class circles.

TEAPOT DOME in the US, one of several scandals involving senior members of President Harding's administration (1921-1923). In 1921 the secretary of the interior, Albert Fall, persuaded the president to transfer control of naval oil reserves at Teapot Dome, WY, and Elk Hills, CA, to the interior department. In April 1922 Fall secretly leased the areas to private oil companies owned by Harry F. Sinclair

and Edward L. Doheny. At a Senate enquiry, Fall explained that he had leased Teapot Dome to Sinclair in the interests of national preparedness, and was about to lease Elk Hills to Doheny. A Senate investigating committee found that at the time of the Teapot Dome negotiations, Fall had received from Sinclair $223,000 in government bonds, $85,000 in cash, and a herd of pedigree cattle, and that Doheny had lent Fall $100,000. In 1927 the government won a suit to cancel the leases, and although Sinclair, Doheny, and Fall were acquitted of charges of conspiracy to defraud the government, Fall was convicted (1929) of bribery, fined $100,000, and sent to jail for a year (1931-2).

TECUMSEH (1768-1813), American Indian chief of the Shawnee tribe, who attempted to confederate all the western and southern tribes to oppose the white advance and hold the Ohio river as a permanent boundary (1805-11). Defeat at the battle of Tippecanoe (Nov. 1811) ended the hopes for confederation.

TEDDER, ARTHUR WILLIAM TEDDER, 1st Baron (1890-1967), British airman in the Second World War. He was appointed commander-in-chief RAF Middle East command in 1941, where he made a vital contribution to the success of Allied operations in North Africa by developing techniques of tactical air support for army action, and, in late 1942, by establishing a close liaison between British and American forces. As deputy supreme commander to Eisenhower in the invasion of Europe (1944-5) he had overall responsibility for all air operations before and after the D-Day landings. He was chief of the air staff (1946-50).

TEGEA, ancient Greek city-state in Central Peloponnese, Sparta's immediate northern neighbour, which after resisting a sustained attempt at conquest became the first state linked with Sparta in the series of alliances which became the Peloponnesian League (*c.* 550 BC). Though they joined the Argives against Sparta and were defeated (*c.* 470), the Tegeates were generally loyal allies, *eg*, in the troubles after the peace of Nicias (421) and the battle of Leuctra (371). Remains of Tegea's famous 4th-cent. temple of Athena are still visible.

TEH WANG (1902-), Mongolian nationalist and leader of the Inner Mongolian independence movement, whose hostility to Inner Mongolia's Chinese overlords led him in the 1930s to co-operate with China's enemy, Japan. His ambition to establish a semi-independent state under Chinese suzerainty was eventually realized by the Chinese communists; but Teh himself was disgraced for being a collaborator.

TEHERAN CONFERENCE (28 Nov.-1 Dec. 1943), first of the Second World War conferences between Roosevelt, Churchill, and Stalin. It ended a period of coolness which resulted from the postponement of the opening of a second front in Europe and mutual suspicions between the Soviet Union and the West about the possibility of a separate peace. The conference was remarkable for the close relationship which Roosevelt appeared to establish with Stalin. It was particularly important from a military point of view, since it resulted in agreement on the opening of a major Western offensive in France (code-name Overlord). Churchill pressed for a Mediterranean strategy, and there was much discussion of the possibility of bringing Turkey into the war; but he received no support from Roosevelt and his suggestions were met with suspicion by Stalin.

There were also wide-ranging political discussions, although they did not end in definitive agreement. Roosevelt outlined his plans for a post-war international organization based on the concept of 'Four Policemen' (the US, the USSR, the UK, and China) and in the course of the discussion said that US troops would not be available to enforce security in Europe. Stalin showed considerable anxiety about the continuance of danger from Germany; Churchill spoke of his intention not to surrender the British empire, and asked Stalin what his post-war territorial ambitions were, to which Stalin replied that it was not yet time to talk of such matters. Suggestions were put forward for the dismemberment of Germany, and it was agreed to refer the matter to the European Advisory Commission, set up the previous month at the foreign ministers' conference. There were practical discussions of arrangements for the implementation of the Italian armistice (so that the Russians could take their share of the Italian navy and merchant marine) and less decisive talk about the Polish government and frontiers, in the course of which Stalin announced his intention of annexing Königsberg, at which neither Roosevelt nor Churchill demurred. At the end of the conference a declaration on Persia was issued, promising further aid to that country and giving a commitment to the 'independence, sovereignty, and territorial integrity of Iran'.   WFK

TEHERAN TREATY (25 Nov. 1814), Anglo-Iranian agreement negotiated (1809) by Sir Harford Jones, but twice amended before its ratification. It ended French influence in Iran, which became Britain's ally in the defence of India. The British obligation to aid Iran if she were attacked was later cancelled in return for a financial payment (1828).

TEL-EL-KEBIR, BATTLE OF (13 Sept. 1882), in which a British/Indian force of 20,000, commanded by Sir Garnet Wolseley and acting under authority from the Khedive Tawfiq, defeated an Egyptian force of 10,000–15,000 under Arabi Pasha. British casualties were about 400. The Egyptian dead numbered about 4000. The victory inaugurated the period of British control in Egypt.

TELEPINUS (*reg. c.* 1525–1500 BC), Hittite King, who established safe, defensible frontiers and issued an edict which endured until the end of the empire and laid down precise laws of succession and rules of conduct for the king and nobles.

TELESCOPE, optical instrument used to view distant objects, probably first invented by a Dutchman, Hans Lippershey (*c.* 1608), an improved version of the instrument being produced by Galileo (1609), which proved to him the truth of the Copernican theory of the universe. Later scientists to refine the telescope further were Kepler, Huygens, and Newton.

TELFORD, THOMAS (1757–1834), Scottish civil engineer, who, after working in Edinburgh as a mason, went to London in 1782. By 1786 he had become a surveyor of public works for Shropshire, where he planned architectural improvements in Shrewsbury and built bridges over the Severn river, including the iron bridge at Buildwas. As surveyor, engineer, and architect on the Ellesmere Canal (1793), he built aqueducts over the Ceirog valley (1796–1801) and over the Dee (1795–1805). In Scotland, after 1803, he built roads, bridges, and harbours, and also the Caledonian Canal. His work in England included the Shrewsbury to Holyhead road and the two suspension bridges, at Conway and across the Menai Straits. He also built the Gotha Canal between the Baltic and the North Sea (1808–10). He was a founder and first president of the Institute of Civil Engineers.

TELL EL-AMARNA, site on the Nile, about 190 miles (305 kms) south of Cairo, of the capital of Egypt under Amenhetep IV (*reg. c.* 1367–1350 BC). After his death it was abandoned and soon fell into ruins. It was the site of the discovery (1891) of a large number of tablets bearing the correspondence of Amenhetep III and Amenhetep IV with neighbouring kings.

TELLER, EDWARD (1908–   ), Hungarian-born US physicist, who, as a refugee from Nazi Germany, settled in the US in 1935. During the Second World War he worked on the uranium bomb project at Los Alamos, NM. In the early

1950s Teller was a principal protagonist for the development of the even more powerful hydrogen fission bomb (H-bomb), which other scientists, notably Oppenheimer, were reluctant to support in view of the devastating capacity of existing nuclear weapons. As he was responsible for important technical developments which made the device practical, Teller is often called the father of the H-bomb. The first H-bomb was exploded in the Pacific in 1952, from whence the world entered the thermonuclear age.

TEMENGGONG, high Malay official, who usually exercised police or military functions. In the Riau-Johor empire the title was borne by the local ruling family in Singapore-Johor who, after 1824, became independent rulers of Johor.

TEMPERANCE MOVEMENT, in Britain, 19th- and early 20th-cent. crusade against alcoholic liquor. It began in the late 1820s as an attempt to form an association of abstainers, but this approach was too timid for provincial nonconformists, who advocated total abstention. In the 1840s in Ireland Father Theobald Mathew was spectacularly successful in his advocacy of temperance.

The Manchester-based United Kingdom Alliance, founded in 1853, promoted prohibition with increasing effect and politicized the movement, which gained great influence in the Gladstonian Liberal Party. By the 1890s the movement had acquired a champion in the cabinet, Sir William Harcourt. But by the early 20th cent. the increased respectability of dissent limited its popular appeal. The movement's sectarianism had always been a hindrance, but in its heyday it united the radical idealism of the labour aristocracy with the progressive anti-establishment zeal of militant dissent.

TEMPLAR, KNIGHTS, Order of the Poor Soldiers of Christ of the Temple, founded *c.* 1119, probably by two French knights, Hugh des Payens and Godfrey of St Omer, with the purpose of protecting and guiding pilgrims from the coast to Jerusalem. The order grew rich on endowments throughout Europe and increased its wealth through the banking and money-lending facilities it offered. With the fall of Jerusalem (1187) the order lost its reason for existence, while it became both feared and envied. Philip IV of France, desperate for funds, took advantage of the secrecy of the order to conduct a virulent and unprincipled campaign of calumny against it. Pope Clement V was in so weak a position that he was eventually compelled to surrender and dissolve the order (1314).

TEMPLE, RICHARD GRENVILLE-TEMPLE, 2nd Earl (1711–79), British Whig politician, who was a brother-in-law of the Elder Pitt. He succeeded to his mother's peerage in 1752 and became lord privy seal in Pitt's wartime ministry (1757–61); he resigned with him over Bute's peace policy. Temple, who was a patron of John Wilkes, author of the notorious *North Briton* article attacking Bute's actions (1763), was dismissed from his lord lieutenancy of Buckinghamshire for refusing to remove Wilkes from his parliamentary seat in the county. He has been suggested as the possible author of the *Junius Letters*.

TEMPLE, FREDERICK (1841–1902), British cleric and educationalist, who became Abp of Canterbury (1896–1902). After a fellowship at Balliol College, Oxford, he became principal of Kneller Hall teachers' training college (1849–55), inspector of training colleges (1855–7), and headmaster of Rugby school (1857–69). He also served on the Taunton commission on secondary education, contributed 'The Education of the World' to *Essays and Reviews* (1860), stimulated the movement which led to the Oxford 'Locals' Examinations being founded, and helped to establish secondary schools in the west of England. He was Bp of Exeter (1869–85) and of London (1885–96), showing a liberal approach to various issues, *eg,* Darwinism, and was tolerant towards Tractarianism, although opposed to it. He published *Religion and Science* (1884).

TEMPLE, SIR WILLIAM (1628–99), English politician, diplomat, and author who was employed in various continental negotiations, culminating in the Triple Alliance (1668) with Holland and Sweden. In 1668 he was appointed ambassador at The Hague. The treaty of Dover (1670) led to his recall. In 1674 he negotiated the treaty of Westminister with Holland, and had his embassy to The Hague renewed after declining the post of secretary of state. He was largely responsible for the marriage of Mary, the future James II's daughter, and William of Orange. Having been instrumental in the peace of Nymwegen (1679), he retired, refusing office under William III. He wrote several political essays and *An introduction to the History of England* (1695).

TEMPLE, WILLIAM (1881–1944), English cleric, and son of Abp Frederick Temple, who was Bp of Manchester (1921–9), Abp of York (1929–42), and Abp of Canterbury (1942–4). He became headmaster of Repton School, Derbyshire, while still under 30—his successor there, Geoffrey Fisher, subsequently succeeding him in the see of Canterbury. His experience at Manchester gave him an insight into industrial and social problems, and he was actively identified with the Workers' Educational Association, and with issues raised by strikes and unemployment. His thoughts on these matters appeared in *Christianity and Social Order* (1942). As archbishop, he inaugurated the British Council of Churches and pointed the way towards Church unity, but his death cut short the career of a man whose influence after the Second World War might have been profound.

TEMPLEWOOD, SAMUEL JOHN GURNEY HOARE, Viscount (1880–1959), British politician, who came from a family of merchant bankers. After being private secretary to the colonial secretary, Alfred Lyttelton, in 1905, he represented Brixton on the London County Council (1907–10). He was Conservative MP for Chelsea (1910–44). Between the wars he occupied almost every senior cabinet office and was one of the most influential leaders of his party. As air minister (1922–4, 1924–9) he was the first to occupy a cabinet seat in the right of that department. As secretary of state for India (1931–5) he was responsible for the Government of India Act, which paved the way for Indian self-government. During his short period as foreign secretary in 1935 his political career was almost ruined and his reputation irreparably damaged by his association with the Hoare–Laval pact, by which it was proposed that Mussolini's invasion of Abyssinia should be recognized as legitimate and most of that country ceded to Italy. During the furore which followed, Hoare resigned, but was recalled to the cabinet in the following year as first lord of the admiralty and remained in the government until 1940. As first lord, he secured a considerable expansion of the naval building programme and discussed with Winston Churchill the form that this should take. As home secretary (1937–9) he showed a special interest in penal reform. He was lord privy seal in the war cabinet (1939–40) and again air minister in 1940, when Churchill sent him as special ambassador to Spain, with the political task of keeping that country out of the Second World War.

TEMPSKY, GUSTAVUS FERDINAND VON (1828–68), Prussian soldier of fortune, who fought, prospected, and explored in America before leading his own Rangers in the NZ Maori wars (1863–8).

TEN ARTICLES OF RELIGION (1536), in England, first formulary of faith in the Church of England, issued by King Henry VIII's government in July 1536 and enforced by Cromwell's Injunctions of Aug., making the articles binding upon clergy and laity alike. They constituted a compromise between orthodox Catholic belief and the reformed religion of Luther, retaining the sacraments of the eucharist,

penance, and baptism, and conforming to traditional Catholic views of good works, but rejecting prayers to the saints and for the dead. This compromise was superseded in 1537 by the Bishops' Book, which revived the four other sacraments of the Catholic Church.

TEN RESOLUTIONS, statement of policy on Canadian colonial affairs, passed in the British parliament (1847). Among its provisions was a refusal of the colony's demands for responsible government and an elected legislative council.

TEN THOUSAND, EXPEDITION OF (401–400 BC), march from Babylonia to Trapezus (Trebizond) on the Black Sea by a Greek mercenary contingent in the army which Cyrus the younger had led from Western Asia Minor to challenge his brother, Artaxerxes II, for the Persian throne. In a battle at Cunaxa the Greeks were victorious, but Cyrus was killed and their own leaders subsequently lured to their death by Tissaphernes. The Greeks, however, elected new generals, among them Xenophon, whose *Anabasis* records the expedition, and fought their way through the mountains of Armenia in winter. Though the achievement of the Ten Thousand was exaggerated by Greek orators and marred by depradations in Greek cities between Trapezus and Byzantium, their resilience provides a fine example of the Greek spirit of self-disciplined freedom.

TEN YEAR RULE in Britain, cabinet decision first informally adopted (1919) by Lloyd George's coalition government on the promptings of Winston Churchill, then secretary of state for war and air. The cabinet gave instructions that the service estimates should be framed on the assumption 'that the British Empire will not be engaged in any great war during the next ten years and that no expeditionary force will be required'. This rule was restated informally to the chiefs of staff each year between 1925 and 1927 by the Conservative government, and in 1928 Churchill, then chancellor of the exchequer, persuaded the cabinet and the committee of imperial defence to establish it permanently. It remained in force until March 1932, when events in the Far East led to its abandonment. In the immediate aftermath of the First World War, when there was necessarily a reduction in armaments and the international scene appeared relatively settled, the rule was justifiable, but the long-term effects of its continuation were disastrous (ironically it was Churchill, as prime minister in the Second World War, who was to feel its effects most strongly). In the early 1930s the armed forces were dangerously weak, morale was low, and there was little money available for research and development to assist any of the three services, and armament factories had been adapted to other activities or were so understaffed that when the first steps towards rearmament were taken they were unable to meet the demands made on them.   NRB

TENASSERIM, river and town in southern Burma—more generally, that part of Burma east and south of the Salween river. Until 1765, except for the period 1551–81, Tenasserim was part of Siam, thereafter it was included in Burma. Its importance derived from the fact that it controlled the overland route from the west to Siam, cutting out the long, expensive, and dangerous journey round the Malay peninsula.

TENG HSIAO-P'ING (1902–), Chinese politician, communist leader, and party organizer, who made his career as a political organiser, and in the party secretariat. In 1954 he became secretary of the party, a position of enormous power. His organizational skills, and his dislike of uncontrolled radicalism, as favoured by Mao Tse-tung, brought him close to Liu Shao-ch'i, but into conflict with Mao. During the Cultural Revolution (1966) he disappeared from the Chinese leadership, with Liu and many other party organizers, but has not been personally vilified to the same extent as Liu.

TENISON, THOMAS (1636–1715), Archbishop of Canterbury (1694–1715), whose latitudinarian outlook and moderation towards dissenters made him a favourite of William III, but Queen Anne was hostile to him, partly because he was politically a Whig, and she took her ecclesiastical advice from Abp Sharp of York. Tenison was active in opposition to the Occasional Conformity bills and in support of the union with Scotland (1707). He was also strongly in favour of the Hanoverian succession, and he lived long enough to crown George I.

TENNENT, WILLIAM (1673–1745), Irish-born Presbyterian clergyman, who emigrated to Philadelphia (1717), where, as pastor of Neshaminy, PA (1726), he established 'Log College' (1727) to train evangelicals. It later became the centre of the 'Great Awakening'. 'Log College' supporters united with others to establish (1746) the College of New Jersey (Princeton).

TENNESSEE VALLEY AUTHORITY (1933–   ) in the US, federal agency to develop and conserve the resources of the Tennessee river valley. It was a central part of the New Deal programme of the 1930s, and was based on earlier progressive proposals for harnessing the Tennessee river, but embodied a much wider concept of regional rehabilitation, embracing parts of seven states, and covering an area of over 41,000 square miles (160,000 sq. kms). The authority controlled the river and its tributaries by a series of more than 20 major dams, many of which also produced hydro-electric power that was sold to consumers and provided a 'yardstick' for private utility companies' pricing policies. Conservation projects were started and modern farming techniques introduced. The TVA was a notably successful example of co-operation between the federal government and state and local authorities, and its constitutionality was upheld by the US Supreme Court in *Ashwander v. TVA* (1936).

TENNIS COURT OATH (1789) in France, taken on 20 June in a tennis court at Versailles by the deputies of the French third estate after they had been locked out of their assembly hall. The deputies had declared themselves to be the National Assembly and by the oath they bound themselves 'never to separate . . . until the constitution of the kingdom is established and affirmed on a sound basis'.

TENNYSON, ALFRED TENNYSON, 1st Baron (1809–92), English poet who won the Chancellor's medal for English verse at Cambridge (1829), and became poet-laureate (1850) after the death of Wordsworth. Subsequently, he wrote the 'Charge of the Light Brigade' (1854).

TENOCHTITLÁN, Aztec capital founded (*c.* 1325) on an island in Lake Texcoco in the valley of Mexico. The splendour of the city increased in proportion to its influence in the Triple Alliance with the lake cities of Texcoco and Tlacopán, and by *c.* 1500 Tenochtitlán was the dominant partner in an alliance which controlled most of central Mexico. Upon the Spanish arrival (1519), Tenochtitlán was a great city, linked to the shore by causeways and drawing drinking water by aqueduct from the hills of Chapúltepec. Cortés, who described Tenochtitlán as 'the most beautiful city in the world', none the less decided to destroy it during his final campaign in 1521 to crush Aztec resistance. At the time of his victory the process was almost completed, and the rest of the city was razed to make way for the present capital of Mexico.

TEOTIHUACÁN, huge pre-Columbian ceremonial centre north of Mexico City, built by little-known peoples. It was rebuilt at least once for religious reasons, but was abandoned in the 10th cent. at the height of its glory. Crop failure, religious conflict, and revolt have all been advanced to explain its abandonment.

TEPE YAHYA, in the Soghun valley, south of Kerman in Iran, site of an ancient civilization with written records dating back to *c.* 3000 BC.

TER HEIDE, BATTLE OF (Aug. 1653), naval engagement of the first Anglo-Dutch War, otherwise known as the battle of Scheveningen, at the opening of which the Dutch admiral, Martin Harpertszoon Tromp, was killed.

TERAUCHI, MASATAKE (1852–1919), Japanese soldier and politician, who was governor-general in Korea after its annexation (1910) and three times war minister. His only cabinet (1916–18) was noted for its financial support of the Chinese war-lord, Tuan Ch'i-jui.

TERBORCH, GERARD (1617–81), Dutch painter, who produced genre pictures and fashionable portraits, characterized by his great skill at rendering textures. He studied under his father and Pieter Molyn at Haarlem and visited England, Italy, and Germany, where he was inspired to paint the conference leading to *The Peace of Munster* (1648). From 1654 he lived at Derventer, of which he became burgomaster. Among his best-known pictures are *The Reading Lesson*, *The Concert*, *The Guitar Lesson*, and *The Smoker*.

TERCEIRA, BATTLE OF (1582), Spanish naval victory in the Azores, when a powerful fleet under the Marquis of Santa Cruz destroyed a French fleet commanded by the Florentine condottiere, Filippo Strozzi, supporting the Portuguese claimant to the throne of Portugal, Don Antonio, prior of Crato. Don Antonio was defeated again in 1583, enabling the Spaniards to complete the conquest of the Azores.

TERCIO in Spain, standard regimental unit of the Spanish army first introduced in 1534, which established the reputation for invincibility which the Spanish infantry enjoyed from the Italian Wars to the Thirty Years War. Originally consisting of 3600 men, of whom 1500 were pikemen, 1600 swordsmen, and 500 arquebusiers, its size was reduced to 1200–1600 men later in the 16th cent. In battle formation the pikemen formed protective squares round the swordsmen, who were supported by the arquebusiers and artillery.

TERENCE (P. Terentius Afer) (*c.* 195–159 BC), one of Rome's two famous comic dramatists, an African by origin. As a member of the cultural circle of Scipio Aemilianus he exploited the increasing taste at Rome for the comedy of manners in the Greek style. Six of his plays have survived.

TERJAN, BATTLE OF (1473), in eastern Asia Minor, where the Ottoman sultan Mehemmed II routed the forces of the Aq Qoyunlu chieftain, so making innocuous the entente established in 1472 between Venice, Cyprus, the Knights of St. John at Rhodes, and the Aq Qoyunlu Turcomans, then ruling over much of Persia, and Asia Minor.

TERNATE SULTANATE, North Moluccas, principal centre of the 'spice islands' (15th–17th cents). Two small volcanic islands, Ternate and its neighbouring rival Tidore, were the original source of cloves. By the 15th cent. each had become the centre of a rival network of loyalties throughout the Moluccas, the Ternatan federation being stronger and more explicitly Islamic. Ternate was one of the major objectives of early European expansion; the Portuguese made Ternate their base in Eastern Indonesia (1512–75), as did the early Dutch (1607). However, the Dutch later ordered the destruction of all clove trees in Ternate (1651), as they found Amboina a more convenient source.

TERRA, GABRIEL (1873–1942), president of Uruguay (1930–8) who, in 1933 during the world-wide economic crisis, assumed dictatorial powers. His heavy-handed measures proved relatively successful, and he withdrew from the presidency in 1938; whereupon Uruguay's representative democracy was soon restored.

TERRA AUSTRALIS INCOGNITA, mythical concept of classical writers that a great inhabited continent existed in the south seas. The idea was revived by 16th-cent. voyagers in the Pacific, but was proved erroneous by Capt. James Cook's circumnavigation of New Zealand and confirmation of the existence of Torres Strait (1770), as well as by his subsequent voyage of 1773–4 to the fringe of the Antarctic ice-barrier.

TERRAY, Abbé (1715–78), French controller-general of finances for the last years (1769–74) of Louis XV's reign, whose drastic expedients improved the budgetary position in pre-revolutionary France. His first action in office was to repudiate a part of the national debt and suspend payment on treasury bonds and loans. Realizing that France could ill afford a war of revenge against England, he contributed to Choiseul's downfall (1770) by opposing his bellicose attitude in the Falkland Islands dispute. After Maupeou's abolition of the *parlements* (1771) Terray proceeded with certain long-needed reforms. He put into effect Machault's improved method of assessing and collecting the *vingtième*, reformed the *capitation* tax in Paris, and gathered in an additional 20 million *livres* by a tax lease negotiated with the Farmers-General (1774). Despite these measures, he bequeathed an annual deficit of 37 million *livres* to his successor, Turgot, whom Louis XVI appointed on his accession (1774).

TERRE NAPOLÉON, name given by the French navigator Capt. Nicolas Baudin to the southern coast of Australia, between the head of the Great Australian Bight and Wilson's Promontory, in the discovery and charting of which he had, however, been anticipated by Capt. Matthew Flinders.

TERROR, REIGN OF (1793–4) in France, systematic execution of political opponents during the French Revolution, which probably claimed as many as 40,000 victims. The aim of the official Terror in Paris from Sept. 1793, when the Convention decreed 'terror the order of the day', was to eliminate all counter-revolutionary and anti-Jacobin elements. But 'suspects' brought before the Revolutionary Tribunal and guillotined included those suspected of currency frauds and selling on the black market, as well as aristocrats, clergy, and rival politicians. The Terror in Paris itself was comparatively mild compared with its exercise in areas in the provinces, where there was civil war and prisoners were executed en masse.

TERTULLIAN (*c.* AD 160–220), rigorist North African Church Father and the founder of Latin theology. He was born at Carthage and was well trained in Roman rhetoric and law. After his conversion to Christianity (*c.* 205) he wrote apologetic works defending the faith and also works attacking Jews, heretics, and pagans, as well as moral and ethical works. He became a Montanist (*c.* 207) and vigorously attacked the Catholic Church for its laxity, criticizing Callistus, Bp of Rome, for his views on sin and penitence. He exercised a profound influence on the theological vocabulary of the Latin Church and was the first to apply the term 'Trinity' to the three divine persons.

TESCHEN, TREATY OF (1779), settlement negotiated at Teschen in Austrian Silesia between Austria, Prussia, the Elector Palatine, and the Elector of Saxony at the end of the short and indecisive War of the Bavarian Succession. Russia, represented by Prince Repnin, and France by Breteuil, acted as mediators in the settlement, which took two months to negotiate. Austria received the Innviertel, that area of Bavaria bounded by the Inn, Danube, and the Salza rivers, and gave up her claim to the rest of the electorate; a meagre gain, indicating the effective strength of Prussian opposition to the Habsburgs. Austria also agreed not to oppose the union of the Hohenzollern territories of Ansbach and Bayreuth with Brandenburg. The Elector of Saxony was compensated financially for his claims in Bavaria.

The treaty gave Russia a new prestige in German politics,

comparable with the role of arbiter enjoyed by France after Westphalia (1648).

TESSÉ, RENÉ DE FROULAY, Comte de (1651–1725), French soldier and diplomat, who served in the later wars of Louis XIV, and became ambassador to Spain (1723–5).

TESSIN, CARL GUSTAF (1695–1770), Swedish politician and diplomat, son of the younger Nicodemus Tessin. He was a leader of the moderates in the Hat party in Sweden and became marshal of the realm (1738), ambassador in Paris (1739–42), and chancellor (1747–52). As palace superintendent and founder of the Academy of Art, he introduced rococo influences.

TESSIN, NICODEMUS, THE YOUNGER (1654–1728), Swedish architect, who succeeded his father (of the same name) as palace architect in 1681, and embellished Stockholm with many buildings worthy of the Swedish Age of Greatness.

TEST ACT, THE (1673), in Britain, legislative measure of King Charles II's Cavalier parliament. When parliament met in 1673 it insisted that Charles should withdraw his Declaration of Indulgence, and then proceeded to pass the Test Act, which received the royal assent on 8 April. All existing and future holders of office under the Crown were to swear the oaths of allegiance and supremacy, take the sacrament according to the usage of the Church of England, and to sign a declaration against transubstantiation. Those who refused were debarred from being executors of wills, guardians of minors, and suitors in courts of law. This act remained in force until 1828. A further Test Act (1678) required MPs and peers to make affirmations of religious belief. In effect, Roman Catholic peers were thus prevented from sitting in the Lords.

TEST AND CORPORATION ACTS, REPEAL OF (1828), in Britain, important stage in the development of equal civil rights in England. The Test Act (1673) had been designed to exclude Roman Catholics and dissenters from public offices, and the Corporation Act (1661) excluded them from corporations. Annual indemnity acts from 1729 had relieved those dissenters who had failed to qualify under the acts, by taking communion according to the rites of the Church of England. Repeal, which would give the dissenters a formal equality of status, was proposed by Lord John Russell, of the opposition, and Peel, Huskisson, and Palmerston accepted it when they found that the Commons generally were in favour of it. A declaration 'on the true faith of a Christian', which continued to exclude Jews from office, was substituted for the sacramental test. The immediate effect of the repeal was to strengthen the case for Roman Catholic Emancipation in the following year.

TESTAMENT POLITIQUE, memoirs of Cardinal Richelieu, first published in the Dutch republic in 1688, which reveal the political ideas of this great minister of Louis XIII.

TET OFFENSIVE in Viet-nam, major turning point in the Viet-nam War, in Jan.–Feb. 1968. It began with a series of attacks on 48 towns and bases in South Viet-nam, timed to achieve the greatest surprise at the Viet-namese New Year holiday. It also included major operations in Saigon and Hue. At Saigon, the communists occupied the American embassy compound for several hours, and held out for many days at certain key points, before order was restored. At Hue, they held the citadel and imperial palace from 31 Jan. till 24 Feb., before withdrawing. The offensive was followed by periods of intensive fighting initiated by the communists during 1968–9, though without the same degree of surprise. One of their objectives was to inflict a high rate of casualties on American forces.

TETE and **SENA**, commercial emporia on the lower Zambezi river, Mozambique, the first about 515 kms from the Indian Ocean, the second about 257 kms. Originating probably in Swahili–Shona entrepôts for trade with the Indian Ocean, they were settled by the Portuguese in *c.* 1550, and became bases for Portuguese military penetration, commercial activities, and the establishment of settlers on *prazo* estates.

TETON INDIANS, American tribe, the main division of the Dakota Sioux, first encountered by the French (1680) in MN, before they moved west of the Missouri river. Under their chiefs, Crazy Horse, Red Cloud, and Sitting Bull, they took part in all the Indian wars of the Northern Plains, notably the battle of the Little Big Horn (1876) and the final Sioux uprising (1890), which culminated in the battle at Wounded Knee. The Teton were allotted lands in SD (1868), where they still (1970) live.

TEUTOBURG FOREST, BATTLE OF (AD 9), between the Ems and Weser rivers in Germany, defeat of the Romans under P. Quinctilius Varus by the German, Arminius. Three legions were lost and Roman expansion east of the Rhine was ended.

TEUTONES, Germanic tribe of Roman times living originally on the coast of Holstein, who migrated and joined the Cimbri in their attempted invasion of Italy. They were annihilated by Marius at the battle of Aquae Sextiae (102 BC).

TEUTONIC ORDER, one of the military orders founded in the 12th cent. to defend the Christian territories in Palestine and Syria, its full title being the order of the Knights of St Mary's Hospital at Jerusalem. After Jerusalem was lost by the Christians (1187) the order migrated to Europe. In 1226 the grand master, Hermann von Salza, with the encouragement of his friend, the Emperor Frederick II, introduced the order into eastern Europe at the invitation of the Polish duke, Conrad of Masovia, who wanted its help against the pagan tribes of Prussians and Lithuanians to the north and east of his lands. In the course of the 13th cent. the order conquered a compact territory forming modern East Prussia, while a related Order of the Knights of the Sword was conquering much of modern Latvia and Estonia. In the 14th cent. the Teutonic Order of East Prussia became a great menace to all its neighbours, to Christian Poles as well as pagan Lithuanians. This brought about the union of Poland and Lithuania in 1386 and the defeat of the Teutonic Order at Tannenberg in 1410 by the combined Polish and Lithuanian armies. The Teutonic Order ceased to exist in 1525, when its grand master, Albert of Brandenburg, became a Lutheran and proclaimed himself a lay ruler.

TEWKESBURY, BATTLE OF (4 May 1471), marked the end of the Lancastrian cause in England. After defeating the Earl of Warwick at Barnet, King Edward IV (*reg.* 1461–83) marched against the second Lancastrian army, led by Queen Margaret of Anjou, which had just arrived from France, and annihilated it. Margaret's son, Prince Edward, was killed in the battle.

TEWODROS (or THEODORE) II (1818–68), Emperor of Ethiopia (*reg.* 1855–68), who was born in the western province of Qwara during a period of disunity in Ethiopia. He was called Kassa and was the son of a minor chief. By military prowess he made himself the master of Wara, whereupon Queen Menen, the mother of the ruler of Gondar, then the capital, sent an army to crush him. The expedition failed, and Kassa was allowed to marry the Queen's grand-daughter, Tewabetch. By 1854 he was the ruler of Gondar and Amhara, and in 1855 defeated his principal rival, Wube of Tigre, and proclaimed himself Tewodros, a significant choice, as legend said that a sovereign of this name would rule justly, conquer Islam, and capture Jerusalem.

Tewodros dreamed of reuniting the empire and restoring its greatness. He attempted to conquer the different provinces, crush the nobles, reorganize taxes, and expropriate Church land, as well as to abolish the slave trade and convert Muslims and pagans to Christianity. He tried to create a paid army directly loyal to himself to replace the feudal levies, who looted the countryside and obeyed only their own immediate masters. He had rifles smuggled through the Sudan and Massawa, both under hostile Ottoman rule, obliged Protestant missionaries in the country to cast cannon for him, and built roads for this artillery. He also sought to develop relations with Europe, to exchange embassies with foreign powers, and to import gunsmiths and other craftsmen. He accordingly wrote to Queen Victoria, but his letter remained unanswered, so he decided to force the British government to listen by arresting the British envoy and other Europeans, thus provoking the British government in 1867 into sending an expedition against him. The British, who had the co-operation of the ruler of Tigre, advanced rapidly against his mountain fortress of Magdala; Tewodros, unable to repulse the invaders, killed himself on 13 April 1868.

S. Rubenson, *King of Kings, Tewodros of Ethiopia* (Addis Ababa, 1966).

R. Pankhurst, *Economic History of Ethiopia 1800–1935* (Addis Ababa, 1968).   RP

TEXAS, 28th member state of the US, admitted in 1845. In 1519 Alonso de Piñeda sailed along the Gulf coast of this south-western region and it was also explored by Cabeza de Vaca (1528–36) and Coronado (1541). Spanish interest was reawakened by La Salle's short-lived French settlement on Matagorda Bay (1685), and an expedition under Alonso de Léon established a mission at San Francisco de Los Tejas (1690). Permanent settlement began at San Antonio de Bexar (1718). The region passed to Mexico (1821), which licensed Stephen Austin to settle 300 American families along the lower Brazos river (1821); during the next 15 years over 25,000 Americans followed. These TX settlers, rebelling against Santa Anna's dictatorship (1835), established a provisional government, and, despite the loss of the Alamo, defeated the Mexicans at San Jacinto (1836). Under the governorship of Sam Houston (1836–45) TX became an independent republic. In 1845, at its own request, it was annexed to the US. Its annexation provoked the Mexican–American War (1846–1848), which resulted in an extension of the US–TX border with Mexico to the Rio Grande. The state of TX seceded from the US (1861), but there was little fighting within its borders during the Civil War, and it was readmitted to the Union (1870). In the late 19th cent. cattle ranching dominated TX's economy, but, although farming has since been diversified and cotton is grown on a large scale, the state's prosperity is now heavily dependent upon the exploitation of its vast mineral resources. Oil was discovered at Spindletop (1901), and the east TX oilfield was in 1970 one of the largest in the world.   ICP

TEXAS RANGERS, American force of mounted law enforcement officers, first organized in the 1820s, when TX was still a province of Mexico. They were reformed by Samuel Houston in 1840 and used mainly against Indians and Mexican marauders. Without uniform, and with the six-shooter as their chief weapon, they helped to introduce the rule of law in TX and gained an impressive reputation for courage and integrity, particularly during the troubled period that followed the American Civil War.

TEXAS v. WHITE, 7 Wallace 700 (1869), US Supreme Court case involving an action by TX to recover title to certain US bonds formerly state property, but sold by the Confederate state government during the Civil War. Its significance lies in the opportunity provided for Chief Justice Chase to assert the Lincoln theory of secession. He argued that the US was an indissoluble union of indissoluble states. Secession therefore did not destroy the state of TX, nor the obligations of

Texans as US citizens. The Confederate state government was therefore no more than an illegal combination. He went on to support the view that the constitutional right of guaranteeing republican government rested with Congress.

TEXCOCO, city on the lake of the same name in the valley of Mexico and partner in the 15th-cent. triple alliance (with Tenochtitlán and Tlacopán) which dominated most of central Mexico. Shortly before the arrival of the Spaniards, Texcoco was reduced to near-vassal status by Tenochtitlán.

TEXEL, BATTLE OF (1653), indecisive naval engagement of the first Anglo-Dutch War, between an English fleet under Monk and a Dutch fleet under Van Tromp. The arrival of Blake from the Thames with 18 additional ships broke the Dutch, who nearly lost their flagship, the *Brederode*.

THAELMANN, ERNST (1886–1944), German politician and chairman of the German Communist Party. Starting as an unskilled worker in the docks and shipyards of Hamburg, he became known for his socialist radicalism. When the German Socialist Party split during the First World War he joined the break-away Independents and rose (1919–20) to the leadership of the new party's Hamburg branch, which became the most radical of all the party locals. In Oct. 1920 he went with the majority of his party into the United Communist Party, where he again became a leading figure on the left wing. When the left came to power in the Communist Party in 1924, he was one of the inner circle of the party leadership. He broke (1926) with his rebellious past and followed the Comintern's change of line to a more moderate policy. The Comintern (now in Stalin's hands) in turn installed Thaelmann as party leader and maintained him in office against several challenges until 1933. Though he was surrounded by more clever men, his position was bolstered by his personal popularity among the party's following. He was the Communist Party's candidate for the presidency of the Reich in 1925 and 1932, and chief German representative of the party's stark intransigence of the years 1929–33, when the refusal of the communists to co-operate with the social democrats and other parties helped to paralyse the political system and prepare the way for Hitler. In May 1933 he was arrested by the Nazis and remained for over 11 years in solitary confinement. He was executed in Buchenwald in Aug. 1944.

THAGS, gangs of professional murderers who moved about India in the guise of peaceful travellers or as pilgrims and ascetics. They felt no remorse for their crimes, which they thought pleasing to the Hindu goddess Kali. They generally strangled their victims with a handkerchief or scarf in the form of a noose. They were protected by otherwise respectable Indians who shared their spoils. Thagi was probably at its worst in the early 19th cent., though it had existed from very early times. The gangs were hunted down (1831–7) by Capt. William Sleeman.

THAI–JAPANESE PACT (Dec. 1941) brought Thailand into the Second World War on the side of the Japanese, and was accompanied by declarations of war against Britain and the US. Although Japanese policies and war aims had a certain attraction for the prime minister, Phibunsongkhram, and although the two countries had been drawing closer together for several years, the alliance was essentially the product of Japanese force. It temporarily restored to Thailand territories previously lost to Britain and France, and preserved the country's independence, as well as some degree of internal autonomy.

THAILAND–BURMA RAILWAY, constructed under Japanese military supervision during the Second World War to link Bangkok and Rangoon. It was completed in 1943. So many European prisoners of war and Asian forced labourers died in its construction that it became known as the 'railway of death'.

THAKIN or DOBAMA PARTY, in Burma, which was communistic in outlook, was formed in 1936 with Aung San as its secretary-general and Thakin Nu as treasurer. The party was proscribed (1940–1), but 30 of its members escaped to Japan and became known as the Thirty Heroes.

THALES (*fl.* 7th cent. BC), traditionally the founder of ancient Greek philosophy, who was active at Miletus. He believed that all matter was composed of water and supposedly predicted the solar eclipse of 28 May 585.

THAMES, BATTLE OF (5 Oct. 1813), also known as the battle of Moraviantown fought in the War of 1812–14 between the US, under Gen. W. H. Harrison, and a combined British and Indian force under Col. Henry A. Proctor and Tecumseh, at the Thames river bridge, near Fairfield, Ont. The British were defeated and Tecumseh was killed.

THAN TUN, THAKIN (1915–68), Burmese politician and communist member of the Thakin party, who was one of the Thirty Heroes. He held office in Ba Maw's government under the Japanese, became general secretary of the Anti-Fascist People's Freedom League (1945–6), and was the leader of its communist wing. When Thakin Soe rebelled in 1946 Than Tun and the 'White Flag', or less extreme communists, at first continued to support the AFPFL and the government. In 1948, however, they also rebelled. After 20 years in the 'underground' Than Tun was shot dead by one of his own guerrillas, who had found himself listed by his leader 'for elimination'.

THANGBRAND (*fl.* 10th cent.), apostle of Iceland, probably of German origin, who was sent there by King Olaf Tryggvason to convert the population. He stayed there for three years, then returned to Norway (c. 999), having given and taken much offence, but also having baptized some notable chieftains. On his dismal report, Olaf decided to take more drastic measures against the Icelanders, the threat of which was enough to cause Icelandic Christians to make another— and this time successful—attempt to convert their countrymen (c. 1000).

THANOM KITTIKACHORN (1911–), Thai soldier and politician, who rose to the command of the vital First Army (Bangkok) in 1954. He worked closely with Sarit Thanarat, standing in for him as prime minister in 1958. He was deputy prime minister and minister of defence in Sarit's government (1959–63) and became prime minister on the latter's death in Dec. 1963.

THANT, U (1909–), Burmese diplomat and third holder of the office of secretary-general of the UN. He entered the Burmese ministry of information (1947) as a civil servant, joined the Burmese delegation to the UN (1952–3), returned to government service in Rangoon, and was then appointed Burmese permanent representative to the UN. He was elected secretary-general (1961) after the death of Hammarskjöld and in the middle of the Congo crisis. He proved less positively active than was Hammarskjöld, but established his authority by the integrity of his neutralism and his devotion to the organization.

THAPSUS, BATTLE OF (46 BC), in the Roman Civil War of 49–45. Julius Caesar defeated the Pompeian forces in North Africa under Cato the younger, Metellus Scipio, and King Juba II.

THASOS, ancient Greek island city-state in the Northern Aegean, founded from Paros (c. 710 BC) and itself the founder of Neapolis and other colonies on the Thracian coast. At an early stage it became prosperous through trade and from mining on the island and the adjacent mainland. In 492 it submitted to Persia, but was freed *c.* 479 and joined the Delian League. After a quarrel with Athens over the mainland mines and Athens' proposed colony on the Strymon (465), it was subjected (463). It remained prosperous, however, after paying in 446 the highest annual tribute, 30 talents, and a later rebellion (411–409) was half-hearted. In the 4th cent. it was again Athens' ally until it was subdued by Philip II of Macedon (340).

THATON, capital of the Mon kingdom before the founding of Pegu, supposedly in AD 825. Thaton was a centre of trade and religion, but was conquered by Anawrahta (1057) and monks and scriptures were removed to Pagan.

THEATINE ORDER, religious order of regular clerics, founded in 1524 by four members of the Oratory of Divine Love, of whom the two most famous were Gaetano Thiene and Gian Pietro Carafa, then Abp of Brindisi, and later Pope Paul IV. The name 'Theatine' was taken from the Latin form of one of Carafa's bishoprics, Chieti. The order consisted of a body of pastoral priests who took monastic vows, but lived and worked in society, with the purpose of setting the highest example of behaviour for the regular clergy. They concentrated on preaching and the cure of souls and became an important spiritual influence in the Catholic Church of the early Reformation period, despite the fact that they remained few in number. Driven to Venice after the sack of Rome (1527), the order returned to Rome in 1557.

THEBES, capital of ancient Egypt from *c.* 2134 BC, which reached the height of its importance in *c.* 1575–1194. It was situated on the Nile, with the temple complexes of Luxor and Karnak, and the royal funerary areas on either side of the river. The city was destroyed by Ashurbanipal (*c.* 664).

THEBES, in central Greece, the chief city-state of Boeotia in antiquity and briefly in the 4th cent. BC the rival of Athens and Sparta for the leadership of Greece. Archaeology and legend, *eg*, the story of Oedipus, show it to have been a Mycenean stronghold. In *c.* 1000 BC it was occupied by Boeotian invaders from the north-west. The Thebans, who were prosperous enough never to have organized overseas colonies, avoided 'tyranny' and violent revolution, but attempts to dominate Boeotia brought them into conflict with Athens, which allied itself with Plataea (519) and punished with defeat the Thebans' support for Cleomenes I of Sparta (506). In the Persian Wars, after fighting at Thermopylae, the Thebans surrendered to Xerxes (480) and fought for Mardonius at Plataea (479). The Spartans, however, decided not to punish traitors and were looking to Thebes as a counter-poise to Athens' expansion in the first Peloponnesian War when the Athenians won control of all Boeotia (457). The Thebans, though apparently not prominent in the risings and victory at Coronea which liberated Boeotia (447), remained implacably hostile to Plataea and Athens, and persuaded the Spartans to attack Plataea in the great Peloponnesian War (429) and to execute the prisoners when it surrendered (427). Then, after inflicting an important defeat on the Athenians at Delium (424), they helped Corinth and other Spartan allies to render the peace of Nicias ineffective (421–420). The Thebans, who by now were predominant in the Boeotian confederacy, profited from the pillaging of Attica (413–404), but after failing to secure Athens' destruction (404) they became increasingly estranged by Spartan imperialism, and in 395 joined Corinth, Argos, and Athens in the Corinthian War against Sparta, defeating Lysander at Haliartus (395) and frustrating Agesilaus at Coronea (394). The King's Peace (387–386) however enabled the Spartans to make the Boeotian cities independent of Thebes and in 382 they treacherously seized control of Thebes itself. Its dramatic liberation (Dec. 379) began Sparta's decline. With Athenian support, Spartan invasions were defeated and at Leuctra (371) a powerful army organized by Epaminondas and Pelopidas defeated Sparta's final attempt to destroy the Boeotian confederacy. Epaminondas invaded the Peloponnese in support of Sparta's former allies, penetrated Laconia, and crippled Sparta by refounding Messene; and when Pelopidas secured Persian approval for a favourable peace settlement Theban supremacy seemed assured. But Athenian opposition, the alienation of Thebes' Peloponnesian allies, divisions at home, and the ineffectiveness of Persia frustrated these hopes and a further victory at Mantinea was nullified by Epaminondas' death (362). Defeats in the third Sacred War (355–346) further weakened the Thebans and encouraged co-operation with Philip II of Macedon, but in 339 they joined the Athenian coalition which he defeated at Chaeronea (338). The Boeotian confederacy was now dissolved and Thebes garrisoned, and in 335 Alexander the Great destroyed the city after an attempted revolt. It was refounded by Cassander (313), but never regained its importance. The poet Pindar was Thebes' only notable contributor to Greek culture.   TTBR

THEGN, in Anglo-Saxon England, a term signifying a nobleman. *Thegns* served in the retinues of the kings and formed the backbone of the army, the *fyrd*. They were often considerable landowners and, towards the end of the Saxon period, the holders of private courts. As a class, they were either destroyed or depressed into tenant status by William I.

THEME, BYZANTINE, system of regional military administration, instituted in the 6th cent. by Justinian I. Civil and military government had hitherto been separate, but under the new system the army commander of each region (*strategos*) was entrusted also with supreme authority over civil administration. The system was evolved in Asia Minor because of constant warfare with the Persians and, later, the Arabs. Regiments of regular troops known as *themata*, each commanded by a *strategos*, were permanently stationed in vulnerable districts and these areas came to be called *themes*. In the 8th cent. Leo the Isaurian extended the system to Europe. By the 9th cent. there existed 25 *themes*. The *strategos* enjoyed almost unlimited power in his *theme*, but was appointed and could be dismissed at the emperor's pleasure. This thematic structure worked reasonably well until the middle of the 11th cent.

THEMISTIUS (*c.* AD 317–89), Greek philosopher and rhetorician, who rose to an influential position in eastern Roman society. Despite his paganism, he enjoyed the favour of successive Christian emperors, being made proconsul of Constantinople by Constantius II and commissioned to enrol new eastern senators; he also became tutor to Theodosius' son, Arcadius, and prefect of Constantinople (384). He was a colleague and friend of Libanius and was equally devoted to Greek culture, being famous for his philosophical writings, of which a commentary on Aristotle survives, together with speeches delivered on various public occasions.

THEMISTOCLES (d. *c.* 462 BC), leader of Athens' resistance to Persia after the victory at Marathon (490). His development of the navy saved Greece in the second invasion (480–479), made possible Athenian leadership and later control of the Delian League, and led at home to the further extension of democracy. After Miltiades' death (489), with the Persians expected to return, Themistocles strengthened Athens' will to resist by ostracizing suspected partisans for Persia and prepared its defences by fortifying the Piraeus, so as to replace the open anchorage at Phalerum. He also enlarged the fleet and after Aristides' ostracism diverted Laurium silver production to purposes of public defence. During the invasion he was prominent in the war-councils of the Greeks, especially in the fleet, where he ensured naval successes at Artemisium and, by subterfuge, at Salamis (480). After the Persian retreat he out-manœuvred the suspicious Spartans by constructing defensive walls at Athens, but lost influence as the Athenians would not confront Persia and

Sparta simultaneously. As a result, he was ostracized (*c.* 472) and finally discredited by implication in the disloyal activities of the Spartan regent, Pausanias. Ironically he eventually found refuge with Artaxerxes in Persia.

THEOBALD, Count of Champagne (d. 1152), brother of King Stephen of England, who avoided getting involved in Stephen's wars in England and Normandy. His chief preoccupation was assuring good government and internal peace to his subjects. Under his rule the periodic fairs held at his capital of Troyes and the other towns of the counts of Champagne first began to acquire international importance as the meeting place between the men of the Netherlands and merchants from southern and eastern France. He not only gave his special protection to merchants attending his fairs throughout his own domains, but intervened to secure justice for anybody connected with the fairs in other parts of France. This policy ensured a great future for the fairs of Champagne and a steady rise in income for Theobald and his successors.

THEOBALD OF BEC (d. 1161), archbishop of Canterbury, who was a conciliator, especially in the troubles of Stephen's reign, and was largely responsible for the development of the study of canon law in England. He was a noted patron of scholars. Among those who lived in his household were the Italian jurist Vacarius, John of Salisbury, and Thomas Becket, whom he advised Henry II to appoint as his successor at Canterbury.

THEODORA (d. 548), wife of the Emperor Justinian I. During the revolt against his rule at Constantinople in 532, the emperor and his advisers were prepared to flee, but Theodora rallied them, summoned loyal troops, which were led by Belisarius, and with terrible bloodshed the revolt was put down. Theodora tried to moderate Justinian's tendencies to persecute the monophysite heretics in Egypt and Syria, and after her death his religious policy became savagely intolerant.

THEODORE I LASKARIS (*c.* 1175–1222), Byzantine Emperor (*reg.* 1208–22), who established a Byzantine succession state at Nikaea in north-west Asia Minor after the fall of Constantinople to the Fourth Crusade in 1204. His successors reconquered Constantinople in 1261.

THEODORE I (*c.* 1690–1755), King of Corsica (*reg.* 1736–8), who, as a German adventurer called Baron Von Neuhoff, was an agent in the Gyllenborg–Alberoni plot to restore the Stuarts in Britain (1717). He was crowned King of Corsica in 1736 before being driven out by the Genoese in 1738. He was exiled to London and died there.

THEODORE (602–90), native of Tarsus in Asia Minor, who was sent by the pope to England. He became Abp of Canterbury (668–90), and successfully established the authority of Canterbury over the Church in England. He travelled widely, created an efficient pattern of dioceses, held important councils, and issued canonical decrees. With his friend Hadrian, whom he had brought to England and made abbot of St Augustine's, he established at Canterbury a distinguished centre of learning.

THEODORE STUDITES, Saint (759–826), abbot of Studios, one of the most resolute opponents of Iconoclasm in the reign of Pope Leo V (*reg.* 813–20). He was the author of polemical treatises against Iconoclastic doctrines.

THEODORIC (*reg.* 474–526), King of the Ostrogoths, whose invasion of Italy in 488 was sanctioned by the Byzantine emperor Zeno. By 493 he was master of Italy. He was the first Ostrogothic ruler who could be properly described as a monarch and he issued a number of written laws and enforced them. His reign gave Italy a relatively peaceful period.

The Roman civil service continued to function and, although the Ostrogoths were Arian Christians, they received full cooperation from the indigenous inhabitants. His splendid mausoleum survives at Ravenna. Ten years after his death the Byzantine emperor Justinian attacked his kingdom and ultimately conquered it by 552 after 16 years of warfare.

THEODOSIUS I (AD 347–95), Roman Emperor (*reg.* 379–95), last ruler of the unified empire, which was divided at his death between his sons, Arcadius in the east and Honorius in the west. He was recalled from Spain, promoted after the death of Valens at the battle of Hadrianople (Aug. 378), and concluded a treaty settling the Goths within the Roman empire (382). In 386 he made peace with Persia. After defeating the western usurper Magnus Maximus (388), he returned to the east (391), but was obliged to march again to the west to deal with the pretender Eugenius, whom he defeated at the battle of the Frigidus river (394). Shortly afterwards, he died at Milan. From the beginning of his reign, he declared himself to be a pious Christian and introduced legislation against heresies and paganism. In 389 and 390 he had two confrontations with Ambrose of Milan, at the second of which he was forced to perform public penance for ordering a massacre at Thessaloniki.

THEODOSIUS II (*reg.* 408–50), Eastern Roman Emperor who succeeded his father, Honorius, as a child. His long reign was one of the decisive periods in Byzantine history, as it became probable that this part of the empire, unlike its Western neighbour, would survive permanently despite barbarian attacks. No Germanic or other barbarian tribes were allowed to establish themselves in any of the main provinces of the Eastern state. The personal contribution of Theodosius to this policy is not easy to assess. His government seems to have become unusually popular because of its well-meant efforts to protect the population from oppressions by the great magnates. An important codification of the Roman Law in 438 was part of this policy. When in the 440s the Hunnish King Attila invaded the Balkans, he met with determined resistance, and after 450 he turned his armies against the Western empire, where he met more demoralized populations. In the West he was defeated by the resistance of German tribes rather than by the Romans.

THEODOSIUS (d. 1074), Saint, abbot of the Kievan Monastery of Caves, and one of the outstanding figures in Russian monasticism. Under him the Monastery of Caves was moved above the ground and its daily life regulated according to the 'Rule' of the monastery of Studion in Constantinople.

THEOPHILOS (d. 842), Byzantine Emperor (*reg.* 829–42), whose reign saw the last notable attempt to enforce the Iconoclast doctrine on the Byzantine Church and the discontinuance of this policy after his death marked its final failure. Much of the reign was spent in conflict with the Muslims, Palermo in Sicily falling to the North African state of Ifriqiyya in 831 and Ankara and Amorion in Asia Minor to the caliph of Baghdad in 838.

THEOPHRASTUS (*c.* 370–*c.* 285 BC), Greek philosopher, and student of Aristotle. He is often known as the father of botany because he classified plants on the basis of their perennating forms and textures (woody, herbaceous, etc.). This primitive system made possible more generalized and developed discussion. In his *Historia Plantarum* he roughly classified and described 480 kinds of plants. He succeeded Aristotle as head of the Peripatetic school at Athens, where he taught and wrote on physics and philosophy.

THEOPOMPUS (b. 376 BC), Greek historian, politician, and pupil of Isocrates at Athens. Fragments of his writings still extant on Greek history (411–394) and on Philip II of Macedon reveal an unusual detachment and sympathy with Philip and Alexander the Great.

THEOSOPHICAL SOCIETY in the US, founded in 1875 by Mme H. P. Blavatsky. Her doctrine derived from various sources, but principally from Buddhism, emphasized the universal brotherhood of man, and a belief that all religions were variants of one underlying religion. Theosophy was also concerned with occultism, and Mme Blavatsky maintained that psychic phenomena had been manifested in her presence. In Britain her best-known disciple was Mrs Annie Besant.

THERA, volcanic Aegean island (mod. Santorin), originally the site of a Minoan settlement, which has been identified by some with the legendary Atlantis. It was obliterated by a massive eruption (c. 1475 BC) which caused widespread destruction as far away as Crete. Later (c. 900) it was occupied by Dorian Greeks from Sparta. Lasting drought (c. 630) led to the despatch of a colony to Cyrene. In the Hellenistic period it achieved some importance as a Ptolemaic naval base.

THERAMENES (d. 404 BC), Athenian politician, who helped to establish the oligarchic regimes of the Four Hundred (411) and the Thirty Tyrants (404), but came to oppose the extremists of both. He organized the moderate democratic constitution which replaced the Four Hundred, and then participated in the restored radical democracy and in its war effort against Sparta. After failing to rescue some shipwrecked sailors at Arginusae (406), he prosecuted the *strategoi* in order to escape blame. Following Athens' defeat at Aegospotami (405), Theramenes was twice envoy to Sparta. He negotiated the surrender that ended the great Peloponnesian War, and was elected to the constitutional reviewing commission which usurped power as the 'Thirty Tyrants'. Again alarmed by their excesses, he advocated a broader constitution, but was charged with conspiracy by Critias and executed.

THERESA OF AVILA, Saint (1515–82), Spanish Catholic reformer, of Castilian parentage, who entered a Carmelite convent in her native town (1533). She devoted herself to the contemplative life and to correcting the relaxed discipline of the religious orders. In the face of conservative opposition she obtained permission to found a small convent at Avila dedicated to strict Carmelite observance, and in 1567 was given authority to establish similar foundations elsewhere. With the help of St John of the Cross she also established her rule among the Carmelite friars. Theresa was a woman of great energy and a sincere and kindly personality, and her reforms helped to check the spread of Protestantism in Spain and to inspire the Counter-Reformation. Her writings include *The Way of Perfection*, a spiritual autobiography (1565), and *The Castle of the Soul*, a guide to the contemplative life (1577). Theresa was canonized in 1622, her feast falling on 15 Oct., and in 1814 she was declared patron saint of Spain.

THERMIDORIANS (1794), group of French Revolutionary politicians, who joined together to overthrow Robespierre and his supporters in the *coup d'état* of 9 *Thermidor* (27 July). Among them were former associates of Robespierre and other confirmed terrorists, like Fouché and Barras, as well as members of the Convention who had been sickened by the Terror. Their immediate aim was their own safety and the destruction of Robespierre, which they achieved by persuading the Convention to reassert its control over the Committee of Public Safety. Until the establishment of the Directory (1795), France had no effective executive and was ruled by these men through the Convention. Their main task was to dismantle the machinery of the Terror and Jacobin dictatorship and to destroy the power of the *sans-culottes* and the Paris Commune. In doing so, they achieved the ascendancy of the upper middle classes.

THERMOMETER, instrument to measure heat, pioneered by Galileo with his air thermoscope. The German instrument-maker Gabriel Daniel Fahrenheit (1686–1736) invented the first genuine thermometer, consisting of mercury in glass with a graduated scale of temperatures (1714). The French scientist Réamur (1683–1757) also invented a scale, and the Swedish astronomer Anders Celsius (1701–44) proposed one from which the centigrade scale was adapted.

THERMOPYLAE, BATTLE OF (480 BC), valiant but vain defence of the coastal pass into central Greece by 300 Spartans, under King Leonidas, and some 7000 of their Greek allies, against the Persian invaders under King Xerxes. It is uncertain whether the Greek resistance was intended to be permament or was merely to gain time while the Isthmus of Corinth was strengthened, Attica evacuated, and the Persian fleet engaged off Cape Artemisium. After two days of unsuccessful frontal attacks the Persians turned the position by approaching along a mountain path. Leonidas and the Spartans fought to the death and their courageous example inspired the Greeks to later victories.

THERON (d. 472 BC), Tyrant of Greek Acragas in southern Sicily (*reg.* 488–472), father-in-law of Gelon of Syracuse, and his ally against the Carthaginian invaders (480). Theron's expulsion of Terillus from Himera led to the invasion and he himself was under attack at Himera when Gelon's army arrived to overwhelm the Carthaginian army. Theron maintained Acragas' prosperity, but his successor was soon overthrown and democracy established.

THESEUS, legendary King of Mycenaean Athens, whose association with Minos of Crete, where he killed the Minotaur, may possibly reflect the subservience of Mycenaean Athens to Minoan Crete. Much of the legend is attributable to 6th–5th-cent. Athenian propaganda. Peisistratus (c. 545 BC) emphasized Theseus' supposed synoecism of Attica to justify his own nationalistic programme, and soon after 477 Cimon brought Theseus' bones from Scyros to Athens, emphasizing his connection with Delos to support Athenian leadership of the Delian League. By 400 Athenian democrats had even established Theseus as the founder of Athenian democracy.

THESPIAE, small ancient Greek city-state in Boeotia, 16 kms west of Thebes. It was, with Plataea, the only Boeotian state not to surrender to Persia (480 BC). Its opposition to Theban domination led to the demolition of its walls in 423 and its subjection in 372.

THESSALONIKI (or SALONIKA), leading Greek seaport, originally founded in 315 BC, which became, after Constantinople, the second most important economic centre in the Byzantine empire and, as such, was a target for frequent attacks by foreign invaders, enduring many sieges. One of the most extraordinary incidents in its history occurred in 1342, when it passed under the control of religious and social revolutionaries known as the Zealots, who governed it as an independent commune until 1350. The town fell to the Ottoman Turks in 1430. In modern times it was for a time the headquarters of the Committee of Union and Progress, which ultimately carried out the Young Turk Revolution of 1908. The town became part of Greece in 1912.

THESSALY, fertile area of north-eastern Greece, famous in antiquity for horse-breeding, but rarely with political importance to match its natural resources. The Thessalians occupied the area in c. 1,000 BC and by 600 had formed a loose confederacy. They were the strongest military power in Greece, during and after the First Sacred War (c. 590). Weakened thereafter by the rivalries of the chief cities, Larisa, Pharsalus, and Pherae, and the persistent power of aristocratic families (eg, the Aleuadae of Larisa), the Thessalians fell behind the developing city-states to the south. They either actively supported or failed to oppose the Persian invasion of 480–479 and, despite the potential value of their cavalry, played little part in the Peloponnesian Wars

(459–404). Thessaly was briefly united under Jason of Pherae (*c.* 375–370), who built up a strong army, but lapsed again into internal strife between local 'tyrants' and fell an easy prey to Philip II of Macedon (352). Thessaly was ruled by Macedonian kings until Rome's victory in the Second Macedonian War (196) and was then organized into a new league of cities, which survived at least to the 3rd cent. AD.

THETES, ancient Athenian 'wage-labourers', defined in terms of income (under 200 measures) by Solon (594 BC) as the poorest class of citizens. He supposedly restricted their participation in government to membership of the *ecclesia* and *heliaea* (later *dicasteria*). After the decline in power of the archons and the Areopagus (500–462), such membership gave the *thetes* considerable, often overwhelming, political influence under the radical democracy (461–404). Two revolutionary attempts to deny *thetes* these rights in 411 and 404–403 proved unsuccessful. There are, however, indications that in the growing political apathy of the 4th cent., *thetes* were increasingly less concerned to attend the *ecclesia* and serve in the *dicasteria*.

THIBAW, MIN (1858–1916), last King of Burma (*reg.* 1878–1886), who was the younger son of Mondon by a lesser queen. In 1885, resenting British disapproval and the British presence in Lower Burma, and counting on the moral support of the French, Thibaw accused a British company, the Bombay-Burmah Trading Corporation, which had been granted a contract to export timber, of felling and removing more than twice the amount on which it had paid royalties. Accusations were also made that Burmese officials had been bribed and that the company had not paid its Burmese employees. The company was found guilty of the charges. Possibly they were justified, but essentially they were a pretext for withdrawing the concession from the Bombay-Burmah Trading Corporation and giving it to a French syndicate. But the British, believing that the French were secretly negotiating a treaty with the Burmese that would give them not only trading rights, but also military concessions, and that they had promised to supply arms, demanded that the Burmese should reopen the case. This they refused to do. Whereupon the British delivered an ultimatum, to which Thibaw made no reply, and on 14 Nov. 1885 the British invaded Upper Burma. The French did not intervene, the Burmese made virtually no resistance, and within a fortnight Mandalay was occupied. Thibaw was deported to Ratnagiri on the Bombay coast, where he died.

D. G. E. Hall, *Burma* (London, 1950).
J. F. Cady, *A History of Modern Burma* (New York, 1958).
FSVD

THIERS, LOUIS ADOLPHE (1797–1877), French politician, lawyer, journalist, historian, and president of France. As a journalist he supported, in the *National*, Louis-Philippe's accession (July 1830).

His first two brief periods as prime minister (1836, 1839) were ended by Louis-Philippe's refusal to follow more active policies, first in Spain and then in Egypt. Thiers fell after bringing France to the brink of war over Muhammad Ali's claims to Syria. He was succeeded by Guizot (1840), a more conformable agent for a king who wished to rule, not merely to reign. He was reappointed (Feb. 1848), but it was too late to save Orleanism. In Dec. 1848 Thiers supported Louis Napoleon's presidential candidature, wrongly believing the Orleanists could make him their tool. After Louis Napoleon's coup (Dec. 1851), he was arrested and briefly exiled, partly because he did not sympathize with Napoleon's further ambitions. On his return he resumed his historical writing (1851–63). In 1863 he became an opposition deputy for a Paris division and demanded more political liberalization. In 1870 he predicted France's defeat by Prussia.

After the Second Empire's overthrow, he refused to join the government of national defence and, instead, fruitlessly sought foreign mediation for France. Elections in Feb. 1871 produced the overwhelmingly conservative Bordeaux assembly, which (sitting later at Versailles) proclaimed Thiers chief of the executive power. He failed to prevent Prussia's annexation of Alsace-Lorraine, but in return for allowing Prussian troops to enter Paris, France kept Belfort and her war indemnity was reduced.

Thiers's determination to assert his government's authority over Paris (March 1871) helped to provoke the Commune into insurrection. Its members, remembering Thiers as the oppressor of Parisian working-class demonstrators (1834), blamed him for the carnage which accompanied the Commune's suppression (May). In 1871 he was elected president of the republic and represented order and continuity at a time when French morale was low. His support for a republic as the type of regime least likely to divide France dismayed his monarchist supporters, but helped to make republicanism respectable among the bourgeoisie. His personal ascendancy ended (May 1873) with his overthrow by disgruntled monarchists. By Sept. France had paid off her indemnity to Prussia, whose troops withdrew, and Thiers was proclaimed 'Liberator of the Territory'.

C. Pomaret, *Monsieur Thiers et son Siècle* (Paris, 1948).
J. M. S. Allison, *Thiers and the French Monarchy* (Boston, 1926).
MRB

THIETMAR (d. 1018), bishop of Merseburg, who held one of the principal east Saxon bishoprics and wrote an important chronicle, which is the main source for the reigns of Otto II, Otto III, and Henry II and for the great Slavonic revolts in the east during that period.

THIEU-TRI (*reg.* 1841–7), reign-title of the third Emperor of the Nguyen dynasty in Viet-nam, who continued, less successfully, the policies of his father, Minh-Mang. In 1847 the French, angered by his persecution of Christianity, made an attack on Da-Nang, near Hue, news of which may have hastened his death.

THIN RED LINE, THE, description of the Highland Brigade as it awaited the oncoming Russian cavalry at Balaclava in the Crimean War. The actual reference, by *The Times* correspondent, W. H. Russell, was to 'that thin red streak tipped with a line of steel'.

THINITE, period of ancient Egyptian history (1st and IInd dynasties, *c.* 3100–2700 BC), when the country was united, and its capital was This. Hieroglyphic writing developed and a high artistic standard was achieved.

THIRD DEPARTMENT OF IMPERIAL CHANCERY (1826–1880) in Russia, body in charge of state police, security, and censorship. It was founded after the Decembrist uprising (1826) to ensure public safety and prevent subversion and maladministration. Its informers and military police, who had wide arbitrary powers, became the core of Nicholas I's government.

THIRD ESTATE in France, social category in pre-revolutionary France denoting a wide range of people of varying wealth outside the privileged noble and clerical orders. The term covered wealthy members of the bourgeoisie, *roturiers*, and even the serfs, all of whom bore the burden of royal taxation, and was first used at the meeting of the estates general at Tours (1484).

THIRD *VINGTIÈME* in France, renewal of the first and second *vingtième* by the controller-general, the *abbé* Terray, in an edict of Nov. 1771. This provided for a direct tax of 3/20ths on all sources of income, including land and feudal dues.

THIRD WORLD, term which became current in the 1960s, derived initially from the French and distinguishing the rest of the world from the 'two worlds' of the 'US bloc' and the 'Soviet bloc'. Used imprecisely, it generally refers to countries which lack industry and are in consequence poor—although neither Spain nor Greece is usually included, but Kuwait may be, while the status of Israel is uncertain. The academic value of the term is negligible, given the infinite variety in the societies it covers; but it has considerable emotional appeal. Certain problems are thought of as common to the Third World—poverty, need to expand the industrial base, maldistribution of wealth—and certain themes—opposition to imperialism, development, socialism—recur in references to the Third World. Pejorative terms are hardly ever used in reference to the Third World and some of the 18th-cent. concepts of the noble savage recur in the discussion of its problems, sufferings, and virtues.

THIRTY HEROES OR COMRADES, THE, in Burma, members of the Thakin Party who escaped to Japan (1940–41). They returned with the Japanese invaders to raise Burmese guerrillas.

THIRTY TYRANTS, group of Athenian oligarchs (404–403 BC), who, after Athens' defeat in the great Peloponnesian War, were elected to be constitutional review commissioners. Led by Critias and Theramenes and encouraged by the Spartan Lysander, they suppressed democratic institutions and usurped power. They also eliminated democratic politicians, confiscated property indiscriminately, thereby alienating responsible moderate opinion, and, after temporizing over Theramenes' demands for a published list of citizens, executed him. Soon afterwards, faced by Thrasybulus and democratic leaders who had regrouped at Phyle to recapture the Piraeus, their rump withdrew under an amnesty to Eleusis (403), where they were killed (401).

THIRTY YEARS PEACE (446–445 BC), agreement which ended the first Peloponnesian War between Athens and Sparta and its allies. The Athenians gave up places they still held in the Peloponnese and on the isthmus of Corinth, though Aegina remained tributary and both Athens and Sparta were free to deal with their allies as they wished. The peace ended in 432, the Spartans agreeing to regard it as transgressed by Athenian actions against Corinth, Megara, and Aegina, and the great Peloponnesian War began.

THIRTY YEARS WAR (1618–48), most complex and specifically German phase of that long and diffuse struggle for the balance of power in Europe between the Bourbon kings of France and the Habsburg dynasty in Spain and the empire (1618–1715). This general conflict was the renewal of an earlier struggle involving the Valois and Habsburgs in the age of the Italian Wars (1494–1559), which had been interrupted by the French Wars of Religion and Spain's involvement with the revolt of the Netherlands.

While France recovered under Henry IV two urgent problems faced the Habsburgs in Germany. One was the recognition of Calvinism, which had spread rapidly in the later 16th cent., but had not been accepted by the peace of Augsburg (1555). A confrontation between this military creed and a Catholic Church, reinvigorated by the Tridentine decrees and the Jesuit order, seemed imminent and was foreshadowed by the formation of the Protestant Union under the Elector of Brandenburg and the Catholic League under Maximilian of Bavaria (1609–10). In one sense, therefore, the general war sparked off by the Bohemian revolt (1618) could be called the greatest of the German wars of religion, which ended with the toleration of Calvinism on equal terms with Lutheranism (1648). The second German question to be resolved was the underlying constitutional conflict between the imperial government and the princes and cities of the empire. This began with the revolt of the Bohemian and Austrian estates against the absolutism of Ferdinand II, which produced the election of Elector Frederick V of the Palatinate to the Bohemian Crown (1619) and the Bohemian

War of 1619–21. This revolt ended disastrously, with Frederick's defeat by the forces of the Catholic League at the battle of the White Mountain (Nov. 1620), in which the Lutheran Elector of Saxony concurred, and was followed by the total subjugation of Bohemia, Moravia, and Upper Austria. The enigmatic role played in the years 1620–48 by the princes, especially of Saxony, Brandenburg, and Bavaria, can be explained in terms of their belief in German constitutionalism. Moreover, the intervention of Gustavus Adolphus of Sweden (1630) purported to restore the liberties of the German princes which were undermined by the Emperor Ferdinand II's Edict of Restitution (1629). This edict was later superseded by the peace of Prague (1635), but the monarchical powers assumed by Ferdinand at this, the apex of his success, were eroded in the later years of the war. The peace of Westphalia (1648) upheld the independence of the princes and strictly limited the power of the emperor.

However, if the Thirty Years War began as a complex German conflict it developed into a series of wars located all over Europe, fought for widely different reasons and linked only by the participants' association with or hostility to the Habsburg family. The fate of Frederick of Bohemia was partly sealed by the Spanish troops under Spinola, who overran the Palatinate and occupied the left bank of the Rhine in a short war of 1620–2 to keep open the vital Spanish road between northern Italy and the Spanish Netherlands. The attempt to retain control of this transcontinental route caused two other minor wars, the struggle for the Valtelline (1620–39) and the War of the Mantuan Succession (1628–31). Spain's involvement in these wars was based on Philip IV's desire to triumph over the rebellious northern provinces of the Netherlands, whose 12-year truce with Spain expired in 1621. To the Dutch therefore the Thirty Years War is merely one phase of the Eighty Years War of Independence which began in 1568. Despite the early successes of Spinola, eg, the capture of Breda (1625), and the death of Maurice of Nassau (1625), the Dutch held their ground and inflicted crippling blows on Spain's naval power (eg, 1628, 1639), finally gaining recognition of their sovereignty at the end of the war (1648).

The defeated and deposed Frederick V took refuge with his co-religionists in The Hague (1621) and sought financial and military aid from other Protestant princes, thus extending the scope of the war. When Christian of Brunswick and Ernst von Mansfeld failed to contain the Catholic forces (1621–4) the princes of the Lower Saxon circle approached Christian IV of Denmark as Duke of Holstein, while Frederick appealed in vain to his father-in-law, James I of England (1625). Bethlen Gabor, Calvinist prince of Transylvania, likewise intervened against the Habsburgs to a limited extent (1624, 1626), but Danish support collapsed at Lütter (1626), after which Christian withdrew from the war (1629). To counteract the victories of the imperial forces under Tilly and Wallenstein, Gustavus Adolphus was encouraged to invade Pomerania and Mecklenburg (1630–1). Armed by French subsidies and with devastating success he defeated Tilly at Breitenfeld (1631) and swept through northern Germany and the Rhinelands. After Gustavus' death at Lützen (1632) Chancellor Oxenstierna consolidated a Protestant alliance of German princes under Swedish leadership (the Heilbronn Confederation, 1633) but their subsequent defeat at Nördlingen (1634) threatened the survival of the Protestant cause.

At this point (1635) France, hitherto embroiled with Spain in the Valtelline and Mantua, and committed only to diplomatic intrigue (1629–30) and financial subsidies (1631) against the Habsburg emperor, now intervened openly in the Thirty Years War to undermine the political hegemony of the Habsburgs. Richelieu negotiated alliances with Sweden and the United Provinces, declared war on Spain, and hired the services of Bernard of Saxe-Weimar (1635). The intervention of France enabled Sweden to recover the military initiative in northern and central Germany through the victories of Baner and Torstenson (1636–43), while Bernard overran

Alsace (1637). Spain's war effort after 1640 was hampered by revolts in Catalonia and Portugal and her reputation for military invincibility eroded by the battles of Rocroi (1643) and Lens (1648).

Meanwhile peace negotiations had started in the Westphalian towns of Münster and Osnabrück against a background of indecisive campaigning in Germany. Although the Bavarian generals, Von Mercy and Von Werth, inflicted several defeats upon France (1643–5), Maximilian's lands were twice devastated by French troops (1646, 1647). However, it was the longstanding enmity between Denmark and Sweden over the domination of the Baltic and lower Elbe and Weser rivers which helped to prolong the war in the 1640s. Torstenson occupied Schleswig-Holstein and Jutland, defeating Gallas and the imperial army which went to the support of Denmark (1644). The collapse of Spain and the consequent isolation of the Emperor Ferdinand III finally brought the German war to a halt by the treaties collectively known as the peace of Westphalia, although the Franco-Spanish conflict continued until 1659 and the Baltic War until 1660.

Historians have not always agreed on the social and economic effects of the Thirty Years War in Germany, although it seems that it accelerated the economic depression where it was already under way before 1618 and affected some areas much more adversely and directly than others. Yet, however disastrous in material terms, the flowering of the German baroque in the 17th cent. disproves the suggestion of spiritual and intellectual decline.

C. V. Wedgwood, *The Thirty Years War* (London, 1938).
H. Holborn, *A History of Modern Germany: The Reformation* (London, 1959). JHS

THIRTY-EIGHTH PARALLEL, divided Korea into North and South by a decision of the Potsdam Conference in 1945. The proposal came from the US, apparently ignorant of an identical proposal made to Russia by Japan in the Lobanov–Yamagata talks of 1896.

THIRTY-NINE ARTICLES (1563) in England, Confession of Faith of the Church of England, based upon Cranmer's 42 Articles of 1552, and passed by Convocation in 1563, thus completing the Elizabethan Church settlement. The Articles provided a definition of doctrine with sufficient latitude to accommodate Catholics and moderate Protestants and to unite the country behind the throne. Although the Commons tried to enforce this confession by act of parliament in 1566, it was not until 1571 that it received statutory sanction and was enforced upon the Anglican clergy.

THOMAS, GEORGE HENRY (1816–70), US soldier, who served in FL in the Mexican War (1846–8) and was an instructor at West Point (1851–4). He remained in the Union army after the secession of the South and fought in the Shenandoah valley and KY campaigns (1861–3). At the battle of Chickamauga (Sept. 1863) he commanded the left flank of Rosecrans's Army of the Cumberland and his firm stand under pressure made him known as the 'Rock of Chickamauga'. After replacing Rosecrans, he served in Sherman's Atlanta campaign (1864) and again in TN. He was urged to stand as a presidential candidate in 1868, but refused to do so.

THOMAS, JAMES HENRY (1874–1949), British trade union official and politician, who began his career as a railwayman and was active in the Amalgamated Society of Railway Servants (later the National Union of Railwaymen). He was a leading figure among those pressing the union to support an independent party—the Labour Party—because they felt that the Liberals could no longer look after trade union and working-class interests. His main activities in politics were industrial. On 'Black Friday' (15 April 1921) he managed to ease the railwaymen and transport workers out of their commitment to strike in sympathy with the miners.

He was colonial secretary in the 1924 Labour government, and in that of 1929, initially, minister with responsibility for unemployment. In this he was unsuccessful, and in 1930 became dominions secretary. On staying with Ramsay MacDonald when the National government was formed in 1931, he was expelled from the Labour Party and the NUR, but remained dominions secretary till his political career was ended by an alleged budget leak in 1936.

THOMAS, NORMAN MATTOON (1884–1968), US Presbyterian minister, journalist, and socialist leader. For seven years he served as a minister in East Harlem. During the First World War he was a pacifist and in 1918 joined the Socialist Party. He was founder and editor of *The World Tomorrow* (1918–21), was actively concerned with industrial problems, and stood as socialist candidate for the governorship of NY (1924). After the death of Eugene Debs in 1926, he became leader of the US Socialist Party and stood as its presidential candidate six times (1928–48). Although there was little chance of his being elected, he did not think his efforts vain. He made the principles of the democratic Left familiar, and in his last years he spoke throughout the US in opposition to the country's role in Viet-nam and in support of civil liberties.

THOMASON, JAMES (1804–53), British colonial official, who served in the East India Co. He was magistrate and collector of Azamgarh (1832–7), secretary to the government of the North-Western Provinces (1837–42), and their lieutenant-governor (1843–53). His period of office was noted for the completion of the land settlement and the registration of tenures. It also saw the beginning of primary education, the extension of irrigation, improvement in roads and communications, and the instruction of Indians in civil engineering.

THOMPSON, DAVID (1770–1857), Canadian fur trader, explorer, and geographer, who served in the Hudson's Bay Co. (1784–97). In 1796 he made an expedition to Lake Athabasca by a new route via Reindeer and Wollaston lakes and the Black river. In 1797 he joined the rival North-West Co. in order to combine fur trading with surveying. He explored the headwaters of the Mississippi river (1797–8), built the first trading post on the Columbia river (1807), and was the first European to travel its full length (1811). He left the west (1812), settled near Montreal, and prepared a map of the western regions (1812–14). He was engaged by the International Boundary Commission (1816–26) to survey the Canadian–US border from St Regis on the St Lawrence river to Lake of the Woods. Although regarded as a very great geographer, he spent his last years in poverty and obscurity.

THOMPSON, SIR JOHN SPARROW DAVID (1844–94), Canadian politician and prime minister of Canada (1892–4), who began his political career as a Conservative member of the NS legislature (1877) and became attorney-general (1878) and prime minister (1882). After his government fell (1882), he served as a judge of the provincial supreme court until his appointment as minister of justice in Macdonald's government (1885). He defended the government in several political–religious controversies, including those that followed the execution of Louis Riel (1885) and the passage of the Jesuits Estates Act (1888–9), and he completed the codification of the Canadian criminal laws (1892). He acted as legal adviser in the negotiations for the Bayard–Chamberlain treaty (1888), and, as prime minister, was one of the representatives of Britain in the Bering Sea fishery disputes with the US (1893).

THOMPSON, THOMAS PERRONET (1783–1869), British soldier, journalist, and politician, who took part in the Peninsular War and in various expeditions in British India. He later published articles on political and economic matters, expressing utilitarian views, advocating Free Trade, and attacking the Corn Laws. His 'Catechism on the Corn Laws' (1827) was a major instrument of propaganda against the laws until 1846. He edited the *Westminster Review* (1829). As an MP he played an active part in trade debates.

THOMSON, SIR JOSEPH JOHN (1856–1940), English physicist. The discovery of X-rays (Roentgen) promoted investigations of the cathode rays which produced them. In 1897, at the Cavendish Laboratory, Cambridge, Thomson showed that they were charged particles, with a mass only a small fraction of that of hydrogen, the lightest atom known. He eventually called the particles 'electrons', using the word proposed by G. J. Stoney (1826–1911) for a hypothetical unit of electric current. Thomson demonstrated that electrons were universal constituents of matter and thereby founded the field of subatomic physics. The work of the research group under his leadership made the Cavendish Laboratory world famous. Thomson was awarded the Nobel Prize for Physics in 1906 and it is noteworthy that in addition seven of his research assistants subsequently were so honoured.

THOREAU, HENRY DAVID (1817–62), US Transcendentalist writer, who ran a private school founded on the liberal principles of Bronson Alcott. Under the influence of Emerson he became closely associated with the Transcendentalists and published articles in *The Dial* and other magazines. He was a keen amateur naturalist and retired from society for a time (1845–7), and lived in close communion with nature, putting into practice many of the Transcendentalists' ideas. In 1849 he published an essay on 'Resistance to Civil Government' (later known as 'Civil Disobedience'), asserting the superiority of the individual to the state, and maintaining that conscience, not law, is the only true moral arbiter. In 1854 he published *Walden*, his most famous work, in which he advocated simplicity, economy, and extreme individualism. His lecture on 'Slavery in Massachussetts' (1854) reflects his increasing involvement in the anti-slavery movement and he became a champion of the abolitionist, John Brown. Accounts of his expeditions and observations on nature were published as *Excursions* (1863), *The Maine Woods* (1864), *Cape Cod* (1865), and *A Yankee in Canada* (1866). His collected *Writings* (1906), include the *Journal* that he kept from 1837.

Henry S. Canty, *Thoreau* (Boston, 1939).
Sherman Paul, *The Shores of America: Thoreau's inward exploration* (IL, 1958).

THOREZ, MAURICE (1900–64), French politician and leader of the French Communist Party for 34 years, during a period when it played an important political role. He was active in the socialist movement from an early age, and joined the new Communist Party on its formation (1920). He became a full-time official, and rose rapidly in the hierarchy, entering the Political Bureau in 1925. In 1930 he was appointed general secretary. From 1934 he took up the idea of a Popular Front with other left-wing parties, and played a major part in bringing the alliance about, though he refused to join the Popular Front government formed after the 1936 election. In 1939, when the Communist Party was declared illegal, he deserted from the army and went into hiding, then escaped to Russia, where he spent the Second World War.

He returned to France in 1944, and resumed leadership of a party which enjoyed great prestige because of its Resistance record, and which was shortly to gain mass electoral support. This made him an important political figure. He was a minister under De Gaulle (1945–6), then vice-prime minister in the 'tripartite' governments which relied on communist participation. He lost office with the other communist ministers in 1947, and the party entered a period of permanent opposition.

Despite periods of illness, he remained the party's leader until his death. There were many internal crises, but the party retained the support of both working-class voters and intellectuals. The French party under him was noted for its stress on orthodoxy and its intellectual rigidity, and it accepted 'destalinization' after 1956 only reluctantly.   RDA

THORKELL THE TALL (d. *c.* 1024), Danish Viking leader, who was one of the subordinate commanders who led raids on England under King Sweyn of Denmark in 1009–12. He was unable to prevent his men from murdering Abp Aelfeah of Canterbury in 1012 and this challenge to his authority led him to desert to the English. But after 1014 he supported Cnut, Sweyn's son, in his conquest of England and was possibly the most important of Cnut's followers. He was regent of Denmark (1023–4).

THORNE, ROBERT (d. 1527), English merchant and geographer, who urged King Henry VIII to promote voyages of exploration in search of the north-east and north-west passages to the Far East and himself helped to finance Sebastian Cabot's voyage of 1526. His activities had an influence upon John Rut's voyage (1527), Chancellor and Willoughby's attempts to find a north-east passage (1553), and even Hudson's polar explorations (1607).

THOROUGH, in England, word originally used in the private correspondence of Thomas Wentworth, Earl of Strafford, and William Laud, Abp of Canterbury, to mean administrative efficiency achieved by driving through all opposition and by carrying out intensive enquiries. The implications of this policy were important in the conflict between King Charles I and parliament.

THORPE, JOHN JEREMY (1929–   ), British Liberal politician and lawyer. In 1959 he was elected MP for North Devon and later became treasurer of the Liberal Party (1965–7), in which capacity he did much to improve the party's finances. In 1967 he was elected leader of the Liberals and became a privy councillor.

THOTHMES I (Tuthmosis) (*reg. c.* 1528–1510 BC), Egyptian King of the XVIIIth dynasty, who inaugurated the territorial expansion of Egypt during the New Kingdom. He incorporated Nubia in an administrative district with southern Egypt, under an official called the 'prince of Kush'. A campaign in the east took him to the Euphrates. He was the first king to build his tomb in what became known as the Valley of the Kings.

THOTHMES II (Tuthmosis) (*reg. c.* 1510–1490 BC), Egyptian King of the XVIIIth dynasty, about whom little is known, except that he put down a revolt in Nubia and conducted a campaign in Palestine.

THOTHMES III (Tuthmosis) (*reg. c.* 1490–1436 BC), Egyptian King of the XVIIIth dynasty. Until 1468 the affairs of Egypt were directed by the regent, Queen Hatshepsut. On her death Thothmes started a career of conquest in western Asia, defeating the Syrian princes at Megiddo (*c.* 1457), conquering Palestine and Syria, and crossing the Euphrates to defeat the King of Mitanni. He received tribute from the rulers of Babylon, Cyprus, Nubia, the Hittites, Assyria, and the Phoenician cities, giving much of his wealth to the priesthood of Amen and erecting many buildings and monuments all over Egypt. Administering the empire by native princes under Egyptian officials he brought the area from Nubia to the Euphrates firmly under Egyptian control.

THOUVENEL, ÉDOUARD (1818–66), French politician and foreign minister (1860–2), who negotiated the commercial treaty with Britain (1860) and tried unsuccessfully to withdraw France's Roman garrison.

THRACIANS, ancient Indo-European people who lived north of the Aegean. Though Greek colonists settled along the coast from *c.* 700 BC, the Thracians remained comparatively backward, split into independent tribes. The Odrysians, whose king, Sitalces, proved an ineffective ally to Athens in the great Peloponnesian War, achieved a degree of dominance in the 5th cent., but in the 4th inter-tribe rivalry led the southern Thracians to succumb to Philip II of Macedon. Lysimachus extended Macedonia's control, but after his death (281) most Thracians became independent and despite the Romans' annexation of Macedonia (148), were not subdued by them until *c.* 12 BC, to be annexed after a period of client-status in AD 46.

THRANE, MARCUS MÖLLER (1817–90), Norwegian journalist who 'felt a personal responsibility for improving matters'. He organized co-operative shops and established workmen's associations, making claims similar to those of the Chartists in England. He won support from peasant cottars and small farmers, and the social disturbances he created led to his imprisonment (1851–8). Subsequently he visited the US, to which he had encouraged many Norwegians to emigrate. Although he played no major role after his imprisonment, his work pioneered the growth of the Labour Party in Norway.

THRASEA PAETUS (d. AD 66), Roman senator and Stoic, who was consul in 56 and influential until 62. He made several unsuccessful protests against Nero's excesses and was ordered to commit suicide.

THRASYBULUS OF STIRIA (d. 389 BC), Athenian democratic politician and soldier, who did much to thwart the oligarchic revolutions of the Four Hundred (411) and the Thirty Tyrants (404–403) and to effect Athens' resurgence after the great Peloponnesian War. In 411 he organized successful opposition in the fleet at Samos to the oligarchic revolutionaries at Athens and his defeat of the Peloponnesian fleet at Cynossema helped to ensure the restoration of Athenian democracy. In 403, during the oligarchic regime of the Thirty Tyrants at Athens, he regrouped exiled democratic partisans in Boeotia and, attacking from Phyle, defeated the oligarchs and Spartan troops at Munychia. In 395 he supported alliance with Thebes in the Corinthian War and in the naval revival captured Byzantium (390), where he imposed transit dues, and Lesbos (389). He was killed in a raid on Aspendos.

THREE BISHOPRICS, city-bishoprics of Metz, Toul, and Verdun, situated in the strategically important duchy of Lorraine, originally ecclesiastical principalities of the Holy Roman empire, but occupied by French forces after they had been promised to King Henry II by the Protestant German princes in return for military help against the Emperor Charles V (1552). By the treaty of Cateau-Cambrésis they were ceded to Henry as vicar-general of the empire (1559), but during the Thirty Years War France claimed full sovereignty over the bishoprics, which was recognized by the treaty of Münster (1648). To strengthen France's Rhine frontier, Louis XIV sought to annex temporal dependencies of the bishoprics through the chamber of *réunion* formed by the *parlement* of Metz, but his ambitions were not fulfilled until the reversion of all Lorraine and Bar to France in the mid-18th cent.

THREE KINGDOMS, period of Chinese history (220–80). After some decades of instability, the eastern Han dynasty lost power of rule in 220, and the three kingdoms of Wei, Shu-Han, and Wu were established respectively in the north, west, and south of China. Each kingdom claimed authority for its ruling house, and their geographical divisions corresponded partly to divisions of economic resources. The three kingdoms' period ended with the short reunification of the western Chin dynasty.

THREE SEALS LAW in Thailand, major recodification of traditional law, accomplished under King Rama I in 1805.

The official manuscripts of the law, containing some provisions 450 years old, bore the seals of the three major ministries, *Mahatthai, Kalahom,* and *Phrakhlang.*

THROCKMORTON, FRANCIS (1554–84), English conspirator and Catholic sympathizer, who was engaged in treasonable intrigues with exiled papists on the continent (1580). He returned to England (1583) to act as agent in a conspiracy aimed at a French invasion of England to release Mary Queen of Scots. He was arrested, tried, and executed (10 July 1584).

THROCKMORTON, SIR NICHOLAS (1515–71), English diplomat and politician. As a sympathizer with Protestant reforms, he was suspected of complicity in Wyatt's rebellion (1554), but was acquitted. He rose rapidly under Queen Elizabeth I, becoming ambassador to France (1559–64), where he was a strong supporter of the Huguenots, and ambassador to Scotland (1565, 1567), where he became a personal friend of Mary Queen of Scots. Consequently he fell under suspicion of sympathizing with the rebellion of the Northern Catholics (1569) and was imprisoned for a time.

THUCYDIDES (d. *c.* 400 BC), ancient Athenian historian, who projected a history of the great Peloponnesian War (431–404), of which he wrote eight books covering the years to 411. They were complex and terse in style, and penetrating in intellect and in causal analysis. He innovated a chronological system of numbering summers and winters from the onset of the war, and was one of the earliest continuous prose writers, who profoundly influenced subsequent historiography. He was exiled (424–404) for failure as the general at Amphipolis. Emphasizing the virtues of research and impartiality, he approached participants on both sides in the writing of his history, which he regarded as a work to be 'a possession for ever' and a practical guide for future politicians.

THUCYDIDES (*fl.* 5th cent. BC), Athenian politician, who, like his father-in-law, Cimon, opposed radical democracy. He challenged Pericles' leadership, and especially his policy of using allied war contributions for Athens' building programme. He was ostracized in 443.

THUGUT, JOHANN (1736–1818), Austrian politician, foreign minister (1793), and chancellor (1794–1800), who secured important territorial concessions from Turkey and Poland, but resigned after successive Austrian defeats by France in the French Wars.

THUKU, HARRY (1895–), Kenyan political figure, who became a treasury clerk (1919) and helped to create the East African Association and the Young Kikuyu Association (1921). His arrest in 1922 caused disturbances in Nairobi, but put an end to his radical efforts.

THULE, furthest northerly geographical limit mentioned by the ancient Greeks and Romans. It is vaguely defined, but probably indicates the Shetlands, which were viewed by Agricola's Roman fleet (AD 84).

THÜNEN, JOHANN HEINRICH VON (1783–1850), German economist, who anticipated the opportunity cost principles later stated by Wieser. His *Der isolierte Staat* is a pioneering study of the importance of the disposition of productive factors.

THURII, ancient Greek city in southern Italy, near the mouth of the Crati river, Calabria, founded in 443 BC by Athens to replace Sybaris. It was sturdily independent and refused help to the Athenian expedition to Sicily (415–413) and later successfully resisted Dionysius I of Syracuse (*c.* 375), but under pressure from the native Lucanians a

Roman garrison was invited. Its expulsion by the Tarentines led to war between them and Rome, and to Rome's conquest of southern Italy, after the unsuccessful intervention of Pyrrhus of Epirus.

THURLOE, JOHN (1616–68), English secretary of state under the Commonwealth and protectorate, who was appointed secretary to the parliamentary commissioners at Uxbridge (1645) and secretary to the council of state (1652). In this post he also had control over the intelligence department and the posts. His spy system was extremely efficient and was the envy of many contemporary governments. He was appointed to Oliver Cromwell's second council (1657), and was one of the inner ring of advisers to Richard Cromwell. He proved indispensable to each successive government in 1659–60 and retained his position until the Restoration (1660), which he had resisted. He was arrested for high treason (May 1660), but was soon freed and performed his last service by writing several papers on foreign affairs for the Earl of Clarendon.

THURLOW, EDWARD THURLOW, 1st Baron (1731–1806), British lawyer and politician, who entered parliament in 1765 and became prominent at the bar. He became solicitor-general (1770), attorney-general (1771), and lord chancellor (1778). He was regarded as a constitutional authority, and his anti-American and generally conservative views won him the confidence of King George III. He sat in successive cabinets (1778–83), watching proceedings and intervening on the king's behalf. The Fox–North coalition (1783) caused him to be dismissed, but he returned as lord chancellor with the Younger Pitt (Dec. 1783), having in the meantime been the intermediary who had advised the House of Lords to reject Fox's India Bill. Thurlow remained in Pitt's cabinet, in his old role, until 1792. Their relations, at first cordial, steadily worsened, as a result of Thurlow's unco-operative character. In May 1792 Pitt and Grenville procured his dismissal, by asking George III to chose between Thurlow and themselves. The incident is often regarded as a land-mark in the development of the prime minister's control over the membership of his cabinet.

THURMOND, JAMES STROM (1902–   ), US politician. While governor of SC (1947–51) he ran as Dixiecrat candi-date for the presidency (1948). He became a US senator in 1955. In 1964 he left the Democratic Party to support Barry Goldwater's presidential campaign, and subsequently be-came a key figure in the Republican Party's 'southern strategy'.

THURN, HEINRICH MATTHIAS, Count (1567–1640), Bohe-mian knight, leader of the more radical Protestant nobles who instigated the defenestration of Prague (1618) and com-manded the Bohemian army which attacked Vienna (1619). After the disastrous battle of the White Mountain (1620) he fled into exile with Frederick V and spent many years intriguing unsuccessfully against the Habsburgs, for a while commanding a Swedish force under Gustavus Adolphus, during which time he fought at Leipzig (1631) and Lützen (1632).

THYSSEN, FRITZ (1873–1951), German industrialist, who was general director of the August Thyssen foundries in Oberhausen, and chairman of the supervisory board of directors of the steel trust Vereinigte Stahlwerke. He was one of Hitler's first financial supporters from the ranks of heavy industry. He was involved in organizing passive resist-ance in the Ruhr in 1923 and met Hitler personally through Ludendorff. He was impressed by the Nazi leader's virulent nationalism, and, although himself a member of the German National People's Party, he made a substantial contribution in gold marks to Nazi coffers. In sympathy with Hitler's vituperative anti-communism, and believing that National Socialism in power would restore the monarchy and perhaps

introduce corporatism, he began to work actively for Hitler after 1929 and became a member of the NSDAP in 1931. He arranged for Hitler's famous speech to the Industry Club in 1932 and later in the year urged Hindenburg to appoint Hitler as chancellor.

In 1933 he became economic adviser to the Ruhr *Gauleiter* and in Nov. a deputy in the plebiscitary Reichstag, but became increasingly disillusioned because Hitler took neither monarchism not corporatism seriously. He was outraged by the Nazi–Soviet pact of Aug. 1939, and on the outbreak of the Second World War he went first to Switzerland and then to Paris. His assets in Germany were confiscated by the state. In 1940 he was turned over to the Nazis by the Vichy regime and imprisoned for the duration of the war.

A German denazification court demanded after the war that he pay a fine amounting to 20 per cent of the value of his property. But he claimed that he was destitute, and the fine was not paid.   ME

TIAHUANACO, great pre-Columbian ruins just south of Lake Titicaca in modern Bolivia, noted for massive, cut-stone masonry buildings and for equally massive relief sculpture. Its inhabitants held sway in the Andean area during the 6th–11th cents.

TIBERIUS (42 BC–AD 37), Roman Emperor (*reg.* AD 14–37), a member of the patrician Claudian family, who became stepson of Octavian (later the Emperor Augustus). He served Augustus in many important military commands, particu-larly in Germany (9–7 BC, AD 4–6) and Pannonia (12–9 BC, AD 6–9). He was forced into an unhappy marriage (11 BC) with Augustus' daughter Julia, whose two sons by her former marriage to Agrippa were marked out as the emperor's prospective successors, but was rescued from this invidious position by their deaths, and was reluctantly recognized by Augustus as his heir. Tiberius sought to follow the policies of Augustus, and in particular the latter's advice to maintain the existing imperial frontiers. The provinces' prosperity continued to increase under peaceful conditions and Tiberius was much concerned to ensure an honest administration. In Rome and Italy, however, Tiberius' reputation suffered, because his withdrawn and proud manner alienated both the Senate and the masses. A number of senators perished after being tried for *maiestas* (treason), for which he was held responsible, sometimes unjustly. His aloofness became worse on his son Drusus' death (23) and after subsequent intrigues involving Agrippina the Elder and the praetorian prefect, Sejanus. He spent his later years on Capri, still fully con-cerned in imperial government, while the atmosphere in Rome itself was one of suspicion and unease.

TIBFARILLA, BATTLE OF (1056–7), last battle between the Lamtuna followers of Abdullah ibn Yasin and his former Gudala allies. It was probably decisive in establishing the political supremacy of the Lamtuna over the Almoravid movement.

TIDORE SULTANATE, clove-producing island and sultanate in the Moluccas (Indonesia). As the rival of its stronger neighbour, Ternate, Tidore was a convenient base and a source of cloves for the Spanish (1522–9) as an alternative to the Portuguese in Ternate, and for the Portuguese them-selves after their expulsion from Ternate (1575).

T'IEN-T'AI, important school of Far Eastern (Mahayana) Buddhism. It was founded in China by the monk Chih-I (538–597), its principal sacred text being the *Lotus Sutra* (*Saddharma pundarika Sutra*). The sect places special em-phasis on meditation, and the worship of Sakyamuni. Its Japanese counterpart, the Tendai sect, was founded by Saicho (also called Dengyo, 766–822), and still (1970) flourishes. It has an important offshoot in the Nichiren sect.

TIENTSIN, TREATIES OF (1858), signed by China with Britain and France, to conclude the Arrow War. In addition to indemnities, the Chinese conceded the following: the right of foreign ministers to reside in Peking, which was previously not allowed under the tribute system; the right of foreigners to travel in the interior of China; and the opening of ten new treaty ports. Ratification of the treaties in 1859 was obstructed by the Chinese. This led to a renewal of hostilities in 1860 and the Peking Convention, which increased the indemnities, added Tientsin as a treaty port, the cession of Kowloon to Britain, and the right of Catholic missionaries to own properties in the interior of China. The treaty ending the war of 1884–5 between China and France was also signed at Tientsin.

TIENTSIN MASSACRE (21 June 1870) in China, culmination of an anti-Christian riot, in which 21 foreigners were killed by a mob at Tientsin. The target was a Catholic orphanage which had been offering a premium for each child presented, thus providing a ready market for Chinese kidnappers. The high mortality rate within the orphanage, due to the nuns' interest in baptizing sick and dying children, further confirmed the popular Chinese notion that behind high walls and closed gates children were bewitched, mutilated, and their hearts and eyes extracted for making medicine. In the heat of the riot the French consul and his chancellor fired at the Chinese magistrate, missed, and killed his servant. The mob retaliated by killing the Frenchmen, two priests, ten sisters, seven foreign residents (some by mistake), and a number of Chinese converts; they also destroyed several churches and the French consulate. Foreign gunboats soon appeared, and the Chinese, under pressure, succumbed to foreign demands; they punished the culprits, paid a compensation of 400,000 taels, and sent a mission of apology to France.

TIEPOLO, GIOVANNI BATTISTA (1696–1770), Venetian Rococo painter and interior decorator, one of the last in the great era of Italian painting. He is famous for huge frescoes and ceiling paintings in palaces and churches all over Europe.

TIERNEY, GEORGE (1761–1830), British politician, who was leader of the Whig Party (1798) against the Younger Pitt when Fox and his followers withdrew from the Commons, and also in the period 1817–21. He held office as treasurer of the navy and privy councillor under Addington (1802–4) and was later president of the board of control (1806) and master of the mint (1827–9).

TIGELLINUS, OFONIUS (d. AD 69), one of the Roman Emperor Nero's praetorian prefects (62–8), whose influence is said to have been wholly bad. He took no part in the events that led to Nero's fall, and was forced by Otho to commit suicide.

TIGLATHPILESER I (*reg. c.* 1115–1077 BC), Assyrian King, who was responsible for a brief resurgence of Assyrian power by destroying the invading Mushki army, conquering the lands around his northern frontiers—during one campaign he reached the Phoenician coast—and checking an invasion by the Aramaean nomads.

TIGLATHPILESER III (*reg. c.* 745–727 BC), Assyrian King, who restored the power of Assyria after a period of weakness. In many campaigns against Urartu, the Aramaean tribes, in Palestine, Syria, Iran, and Babylonia, he brought under his control the area from the frontiers of Egypt to the Persian Gulf. Administrative reforms strengthened his royal authority at the expense of the nobility and conquered territories were governed by Assyrian officials responsible to the king. A standing army, levied mostly in the provinces, replaced the traditional levy of Assyrian peasants conscripted for the annual campaign. He started the policy of mass deportations from conquered territories which became the common practice of later Assyrian rulers.

TIGRANES I (*reg.* 96–55 BC), King of Armenia, who after acquiring control of the Seleucid empire from the Euphrates to the sea, supported his father-in-law, Mithridates VI of Pontus, against Rome, but was defeated by Lucullus (69–68) and Pompey (66).

TIJANIYYA, Muslim brotherhood, founded by Ahmad ibn Muhammad al-Tijani (1737–1815), spiritually linked to the Khalwatiyya. Its chief strength lies in North and West Africa. Its distinctive features include a strict ban on belonging to any other brotherhood; prohibition of smoking; the clasping of hands in prayer (contrary to prevailing Maliki practice); and acceptance of any de facto temporal government. This latter rule meant that its members could accept French colonial rule and even collaborate with French officials. Thus, in Algeria, the Tijanis opposed the resistance movement of Abd al-Kader in the 1830s and even joined forces with the French against him.

The most important manifestation of the Tijaniyya has been in West Africa. Its spread there, though originally promoted peacefully from Algeria, was largely due to the militant efforts of a Tokolor scholar, Al-Hajj Umar (d. 1864). His *jihad* against the Bambara and Fulani populations of the upper Niger led to Tijani teachings being imposed on a largely Qadiri population. In Nigeria the order probably dates from Al-Hajj Umar's stay in Sokoto in the 1820s before his *jihad* and nowadays it probably has as many adherents as the Qadiriyya. The headquarters of the West African Tijaniyya in 1970 were at Kaolack, Senegal, where its spiritual head, Ibrahim Nyas, lived. His followers were to be found in almost every West African country from the Gambia to the Cameroons.

TIKULTI-NINURTU I (*reg. c.* 1244–1208 BC), Assyrian King, the last in a line of strong rulers. He waged successful campaigns in the north and west of Assyria, attacked Babylonia, defeated the Kassite king, and took Babylon. He was murdered by his sons and Assyria entered a period of weakness.

TILAK, BAL GANGADHAR (1856–1920), Indian nationalist politician, journalist, and writer, known as *Lokamanya* (revered by the people). Although never president of the Congress, and despite the fact that he was defeated on the several occasions on which he attempted to gain control of the Congress Party, Tilak was a major force in the Indian nationalist movement (1890–1920). He took a leading part in the publication of the Marathi weekly, *Kesari*, and the English weekly, *Mahratta*, and by the 1890s he was in editorial control of both. Being convinced of the need for broad-based support, he developed a specifically Hindu nationalism on which his influence was to rest. His imaginative political use of local traditions in the festivals for the diety *Ganapati* (1893) and the Maratha national hero, Shivaji (1896), as a means of mobilizing popular support and creating a militant, nationalist ideology, and his emphasis on *Hindutva*, 'Hindu-ness', the organic links between Hindus in all parts of India, were at variance with the elite and reformist conceptions of those who controlled the Congress at that time. Not surprisingly, he was disappointed with the Congress and anxious either to reform it or to replace it with a more militant organization which would preserve rather than weaken the cultural basis of the Hindu 'nation'. His attempt to take over at the Poona session (1895), however, failed. He was arrested because of his apparent connection with the outbreak of terrorist activity in Poona in 1897, and imprisoned (1897–8) for 'sedition'.

After his release, he resumed his nationalist activities. He maintained links with revolutionary groups in India and London and, when the partition of Bengal provided a readymade cause, his 'New Party' came increasingly to the fore, demanding more militant action, *eg* through the boycott and the *swadeshi* programme, in order to obtain immediate independence outside the empire (*swaraj*). A split within the Congress was narrowly averted in 1905–6, but when the 'moderates' insisted on electing their own presidential nominee at the Surat session (1907), there was an open breach and most of the 'New Party' left the Congress. And in 1908 the 'moderates' rewrote the Congress constitution to keep them out. The next year, too, Tilak and other military leaders were imprisoned.

During the six years that he was in detention he was not idle, and his scholarly, if esoteric, works on Hindu history and philosophy, which had begun with *Orion* (1893) and *The Arctic Home of the Vedas* (1903), were brought to their conclusion in his *Gita Rahasya* (*The Secret Meaning of the Gita*, 1915) which stressed the politically useful, activist doctrines which he found in the *Bhagavad Gita*. On his return to Maharashtra he formed the Indian Home Rule League (1916), which operated in Maharashtra and effectively restored and reinforced his political influence there. From 1916 he began to move back into Congress and, while far from adopting the 'moderate' position which he had scorned a decade before, propounded, in conjunction with the reforms discussed earlier (1917–20), the strategy of 'responsive co-operation', under which Congressmen would use the legislatures while pressing for further concessions. He was opposed to Gandhi's non-co-operation programme in 1920 and formed the Congress Democratic Party to put his own policies into effect. Ironically, he died on the day (1 Aug.) on which Gandhi began non-co-operation, and his policies were swept aside by the following which Gandhi had marshalled. His responsive co-operationist ideas were, however, to be influential in the Maharashtrian action in the Swarajya Party after 1923.

S. Wolpert, *Tilak and Gokhale. Revolution and Reform in the Making of Modern India* (Berkeley, 1961).

D. V. Tahmankar, *Lokamanya Tilak, Father of Indian Unrest* (London, 1956).   PDR

TILDEN, SAMUEL JONES (1814–86), US lawyer and politician, who was prominent in NY Democratic politics after 1841, and also built up a substantial fortune through his law practice. At the outbreak of the Civil War, he advised Stanton to crush the South, but thereafter led Democratic 'constitutional opposition' to centralized government and supported presidential Reconstruction. Tilden was largely responsible for breaking the Tweed and Canal 'rings' in NY in the 1870s, was governor of NY (1875–6), and the Democratic presidential candidate in the disputed election of 1876. His estate, left in trust to the city of New York, was used to help found the New York Public Library (1895).

TILE, NEHEMIAH (d. 1891), Wesleyan minister, who founded the Thembu National Church in South Africa with Ngangelizwe, the Thembu chief, as its head. Despite its limited base, Tile's church found supporters outside the Thembu people, and influenced the Independent Church movement on the Witwatersrand. Tile also acted as political adviser to the Thembu chiefs at a time of increasing pressure from the Cape colonial government.

TILLETT, BENJAMIN (1860–1943), British trade union leader and politician. Shocked by the conditions of dock workers, of whom he was one, he helped to organize them into a union and was one of the leaders of the 1889 London dock strike which achieved a minimum payment of 2½p (6d) per hour for dockers. It was on Tillett's initiative that the National Transport Workers' Federation was formed. He travelled extensively abroad as a member of the International Federation of Ship, Dock, and River Workers. He became interested in the political aspects of the Labour movement and became an alderman of the London County Council (1892) and was one of the founders of the Independent Labour Party, and of the Labour Party. At his fifth attempt he entered parliament in 1917 as Labour MP for Salford, Lancs.

He was (1921–31) a member of the general council of the Trades Union Congress and its chairman in 1928.

TILLEY, SIR SAMUEL LEONARD (1818–96), Canadian politician, who entered politics as a reformer and served in the NB assembly as a Liberal (1850–1, 1854–6, 1857–67) and as head of the provincial government (1861). He supported confederation and represented his province in the Charlottetown and Quebec confederation conferences (1864), but his policies led to his defeat by anti-confederation forces (1865). He served in the Canadian parliament (1867–73) and became the first minister of customs and excise for the new Dominion (1867). He served also as lieutenant-governor of NB (1873–8, 1885–93). He returned to parliament (1878) and entered Macdonald's government as minister of finance, in which capacity he introduced a policy of tariff protection.

TILLICH, PAUL (1886–1965), German Protestant theologian, who held (1924–33) chairs of theology and philosophy at various German universities, including Frankfurt. He was a founder-member of the small circle of Religious Socialists, who attempted to effect a reconciliation between the Church and the German socialist movement, which was strongly anti-clerical. In 1933 he was deprived of his university post by the newly established Nazi regime. He moved to the US, where he became a professor at the Union Theological Seminary, New York, and later at Harvard University. He was one of the most influential figures of 'modern theology'. Like Karl Barth and Dietrich Bonhoeffer, he sought to interpret traditional Christian belief in a way which would be intelligible to a secular society. He gave prominence to the idea that God was to be found not in abstract, philosophical concepts, but in personal experience, in the 'depths of being'.

TILLMAN, BENJAMIN RYAN (1847–1918), US politician, who was spokesman for Southern rural interests. He became champion of poor white farmers, was Democratic governor of SC (1890–4), and US senator (1895–1918). He was a vehement supporter of white supremacy and preached class warfare, but in the interests of his poor white constituents he supported educational and other reforms.

TILLON, CHARLES (1897–   ), French politician who was a prominent communist in the French Resistance during the Second World War. In the First World War he served in the navy, and was imprisoned for his part in the Black Sea mutiny against French intervention in Russia (1919). He then became an official in the trade union movement and of the Communist Party, and was elected to parliament in 1936. He fought in the Spanish Civil War. After Russia had entered the Second World War, he organized and led the Francs-Tireurs et Partisans, one of the most active Resistance movements. At the Liberation he became minister of air under De Gaulle, and remained in the government until the dismissal of the communist ministers (1947). He was deprived of office in the Communist Party in 1952 after disagreements with the leadership, but was later reinstated.

TILLOTSON, JOHN (1630–94), archbishop of Canterbury (1691–4), who was present at the Savoy Conference (1661), where he was identified with the Presbyterians. In 1670 he became dean of Canterbury, and gained influence over Princess Anne, who followed his advice in regard to the settlement of the Crown on William and Mary. He was made clerk of the closet to William III and dean of St Paul's, London. On his advice the king appointed an ecclesiastical commission for the reconciliation of the dissenters.

TILLY, JOHAN TZERCLAES, Count (1559–1632), Flemish soldier, who learned the art of war under the Duke of Parma and led the armies of the Duke of Bavaria (1610), the Catholic League (1618), and finally the emperor (1630) in the Thirty Years War. His decisive victories at White Mountain and Prague (1620) dissipated Frederick V's hopes of retaining the Bohemian Crown. He separated the forces of Mansfeld and Baden, defeating the latter at Wimpfen (1622), he expelled Christian of Brunswick from the Palatinate and defeated him at Stadtlohn (1623), and went on to beat the Danish armies at Lütter (1626). With Wallenstein, he forced Christian of Denmark to sign the treaty of Lübeck (1629) and succeeded Wallenstein as commander-in-chief of the imperial armies in 1630. In a life of military achievements only the atrocities following the storming of Magdeburg (May 1631) stained his reputation. He met Gustavus Adolphus at Breitenfeld, and in a later encounter by the Lech river (April 1632), was mortally wounded.

TILOKA (*reg.* 1441–87), King of Chiengmai in northern Thailand, who was the contemporary and rival of Borommatrailokanat of Ayudha, and the greatest of the kings of Lanna. After forcing his father to abdicate in 1441, he usurped the throne and extended his control over northern Thailand. He provoked a war with Ayudhya which dragged on throughout his reign, neither side being successful. He was a harsh and strong ruler yet a great patron of Buddhism and must be credited with the flourishing of Lao culture and Buddhist scholarship during the period of his reign.

TILSIT MEETING (25 June 1807), resulted in an agreement during the French Wars between Napoleon I and Alexander I which ended the conflict between them, whereby Prussian losses and the Grand Duchy of Warsaw were both recognized. A secret alliance envisaged an Anglo–Russian war if Russian mediation between France and Britain failed, and French aid to partition European Turkey if Napoleon's mediation between Turkey and Russia failed.

TIMAR, name given, amongst the Ottoman Turks, to a particular grant of revenue from land—a grant intended to maintain the timar *sipahisi*, or *sipahi*, together with his retinue, as an efficient soldier in the service of the sultan. The minimum grant was known as a *kilij* (sword). Good service to the state would bring to the *sipahi* additions (*terakki*) of revenue, the maximum annual yield being 19,999 akches. Promotion above that level took the *sipahi* into the ranks of the *zu'ama* (sing. *za'im*), *ie*, of horsemen holding a *zi'amet*. As his annual revenue increased in amount, so the *sipahi* would be expected to bring with him to war a proportionate number of his own soldiers (*jebelü*). The status of *sipahi* was not hereditable, though, in practice, it was not unusual for a 'fief' to be granted to one or more sons of a dead *sipahi*—not, however, the grant which his father might have held at the time of his death, but an *ibtida* timari, a 'beginner's fief'. Recruitment into the *sipahi* class was made from various sources, *eg*, from the *sipahi* families in existence, from men serving in the central regime of the empire, and from soldiers distinguished for their conduct in battle. The timar system was established in most, but not in all, the provinces of the Ottoman empire, *eg*, not in Egypt, Iraq, the Crimea, or North Africa. It went into gradual decline in the 17th cent. and was abolished in 1831.

TIMBER PREFERENCE in Britain, one of the most important and most long-lasting elements in the mercantilist system of trade regulation. In the 18th cent. European timber paid duties on entry to Britain, and colonial timber from British North America received a bounty. In practice, while home-produced timber was still a significant element in shipbuilding and house building, and shipping costs were high, this preference was not of great significance. The French Wars saw the consumption of the main reserves of the home supply, and in 1811 the duty was doubled, resulting in a big discrimination against European, *ie*, Scandinavian, timber. Timber was the biggest single import in the post-war period and the leading raw material which contributed to the exchequer. The revenue from it in the 1820s was approximately £1½ million a year. The duty was thus important in every way and had a marked effect on price, since it fixed the cost of timber by the cost of bringing in Canadian supplies. Since timber was the main raw material used in shipbuilding, and an important one in the building of houses, factories, and railways, the duty placed a burden on all these activities.

Timber preference survived two other important elements in the mercantilist structure, the Corn Laws and the Navigation Laws, but in 1851 the duties were halved. The preference survived until 1860 and the duty until 1866.

TIMBUCTOO, town of some 8000 inhabitants in the republic of Mali, situated 8 kms from Kabara, which is its port during the Niger flood season (Nov.–March). At the height of the floods small boats can reach Timbuctoo itself on an arm of the Niger. The present population (1970) consisted of Songhay (Arma—descendants of the Moroccan invaders of 1591—and Gabibi, commoners), Bela serfs of the Tuareg, and a floating population of Arab traders and nomads and Tuareg.

The town grew up in the late 11th cent. as a summer camp for Tuaregs, who came down from Arawan to graze their flocks by the Niger. Probably in the late 13th cent. Timbuctoo was incorporated into the Mali empire. With the decline of Mali in the late 14th cent. it grew in importance; trade routes from North Africa shifted eastwards from the Walata axis to make Timbuctoo a major caravan terminal. Being linked by water to Jenne, the entrepot for the forest gold, the town grew prosperous as intermediary in the gold and salt trade. This urban growth, with its international links, formed a favourable milieu for the growth of Islamic scholarship; during the 15th–16th cents Timbuctoo housed a cosmopolitan community of scholars.

By 1433 Malian control had ended and for the next 35 years the town was ruled by Tuareg through a resident governor. When Sunni Ali, the Songhay ruler, captured the city (1468) during his rapid eastward expansion, most scholars fled to Walata and those who remained were harshly treated. Timbuctoo remained part of the Songhay empire throughout the 16th cent. and was specially favoured by most of the Askias (1493–1591). The Askias had their own civil governor (*Timbuktu-koi*) and revenue collector (*Timbuktu-mondio*), but the city's religious judge (*qadi*) enjoyed wide liberty of action.

After the Moroccan conquest (1591), Timbuctoo became the capital of the pashas, but their rule marked a period of commercial and intellectual decline. Their ineffectual administration laid the city open to attacks from the Bambara and Tuareg, particularly from the late 17th cent. In 1826 the Fulani leader, Ahmad Lobbo, of Masina took the city, but it became semi-autonomous again under the Kunta chief, Ahmad Al-Bakka'i, from 1846. The city was finally taken by the French in 1893.

F. Dubois, *Timbuctoo the Mysterious* (London, 1897).
H. Miner, *The Primitive City of Timbuctoo* (New York, 1965).
JOH

TIMBUCTOO PASHAS. After the first defeat of the Songhay at Tondibi (1591), Judar Pasha, commander of the Moroccan force, made for Timbuctoo after only a brief stay in the Songhay capital, Gao. There he built a fortified quarter and the city became the seat of the pashas' government. The pashas were able to subdue Jenne and install a caid there, as they did at Gao, but they controlled little beyond this stretch of the Niger.

The rule of the pashas was fraught with internal strife and their administrative and military weakness led to continual Tuareg and Bambara incursions. After 1612 pashas were appointed by their forces without reference to Morocco and in 1660 Pasha Hamu cut all links with his sultan in Marrakesh. In 1727 Timbuctoo became a tributary of the Bambara of Segu and from 1787 the pashas became pawns of the Tuareg.

TIME OF TROUBLES (1591–1613) in Russia, confused period of Russian history, characterized by dynastic uncertainty and civil strife, which followed the death of Tsarevich Dmitri (1591) and lasted until the accession of Michael Romanov. Social discontent and economic depression were already widespread by the time of Ivan IV's death (1584). The reign of his son, Fedor I (1584–98), a weakling and a bigot, was the prelude to the chaos which began with the assassination of his half-brother and heir, Dmitri, the last descendant of the Rurik dynasty (1591). On Fedor's death his widow, Irene, to whom he had bequeathed the realm, declined the Crown and entered a convent (1598). The *zemsky sobor* proclaimed as tsar Fedor's brother-in-law, a leading *boyar*, Boris Godunov, although his authority was restricted by *boyar* claims to a share in government, by widespread famine (1601–3), and by the appearance of a pretender, claiming to be the dead Dmitri, who won the support of the oppressed peasantry and the Cossacks (1603). The civil war was further complicated by the intervention of foreign powers. Sigismund III and the Polish nobility gave Dmitri moral support and he was betrothed by a Polish princess, Marina Mniszek. After Tsar Boris's sudden death (April 1605) the false Dmitri entered Moscow (June) and was elected tsar (July 1605), but he proved unable to control the *boyars* or the discontented populace and fell victim to a *boyar* revolt led by Vasili Shuisky, who was elected tsar by popular acclamation (1606). Vasili sought to conciliate the *boyars* and agreed to rule with their advice, but a Cossack rising in south Russia led by Bolotnikov disturbed his rule and the appearance of a second false Dmitri (1608), who established his camp at Tushino, caused the nobility to waver in their allegiance to him. Vasily turned for help to Charles IX of Sweden, while their mutual enemy, Sigismund III of Poland, claimed the Russian throne and ordered his armies to advance on Moscow. In 1609 they reached Smolensk and defeated the Russo-Swedish forces at Kluchino (1610). Vasili was dethroned and taken back to Warsaw as a prisoner, while the conservative faction of *boyars* offered the throne to Sigismund's son, Vladislav, on confirmation of their privileges. Shortly afterwards, the false Dmitri was killed by an avenging tatar (1610). A national revolt against Poland was thereupon initiated by Patriarch Hermogen. A Russian army of Cossacks and gentry appeared before Moscow, but its unity disintegrated. Another army was raised by Prince Dmitri Pozharsky and a merchant of Nizhni-Novgorod, Kusma Minin (1612), which advanced on the capital, defeated a Polish army, and forced the Moscow garrison to surrender. The *zemsky sobor* elected a new tsar. Rejecting a Swedish candidate, the estates chose a great-nephew of Ivan IV, the 17-year-old Michael Fedorovich Romanov, whose accession inaugurated the Romanov dynasty and ended the Time of Troubles (Feb. 1613).   MKS

TIMES, THE (1785), in Britain has held a pre-eminent position among British newspapers for much of the last 150 years. It was founded by John Walter as the *Daily Universal Register* in 1785 and he changed its name to *The Times* three years later. In the French Wars Walter recognized the public demand for war news, and began to lay the foundations of the paper's pre-eminence in foreign reporting which distinguished it in the 19th cent. John Walter II, who succeeded him, insisted on the paper's independence of governmental subsidies and further enhanced its reputation. Under two successive editors, Barnes and Delane, the paper acquired a circulation and standing which far out-distanced its rivals. Its greater circulation in turn enabled it to finance fuller reporting of home and foreign news, and in early Victorian Britain it exercised a strong influence on the formation of opinion. This predominant position was weakened by the ending of newspaper stamp duties. By the 1850s these had been reduced to a flat rate on all papers of 1d, including postage. After 1855 *The Times*, a larger and heavier paper, was burdened with higher postal charges than its rivals, and it began to lose ground to the other London dailies, and even more to the provincial dailies founded at that time. By the 1870s it had been overtaken in circulation by the *Daily News*

and the *Daily Telegraph* and by the end of the century eclipsed by the *Daily Mail*.

   Though it retained its standing as a 'quality paper', it encountered serious financial difficulties. In 1908 it was bought by Lord Northcliffe, who restored it to prosperity. On his death in 1922 it was sold to John Walter, the former proprietor, and Col. J. J. Astor, an American millionaire, who provided the money. Geoffrey Dawson, its editor, exercised great influence during the inter-war years, supporting Baldwin, especially over the Abdication of King Edward VIII. In 1967 the paper was bought by Lord Thomson of Fleet and became closely associated with *The Sunday Times*.

The History of the Times, 4 vols (London, 1935–54).   LMB

TIMOFEEV, IVAN (*fl.* 1613), Russian government clerk and publicist, who at the beginning of Michael Romanov's reign (1613–45) wrote an account of the Time of Troubles.

TIMOLEON (d. *c.* 330 BC), liberator of Syracuse and preserver of Greek Sicily, who was sent from Corinth in 344 with a small force to save the Syracusans from the internecine struggle between would-be 'tyrants' which had continued since the failure of Dionysius II (357) and from Carthaginian attack. After hard fighting with the 'tyrant' Hicetas and the Carthaginians, Timoleon freed Syracuse in the autumn of 343. He defeated a new Carthaginian invasion of Sicily at the Crimisus river (341) and after making peace with Carthage (339) expelled 'tyrants' from other cities, restored Gela and Acragas, and at Syracuse devised a new 'mixed' constitution, after which he retired from public life (*c.* 337).

TIMOSHENKO, SEMEN KONSTANTINOVICH (1895–), Russian soldier and marshal of the Soviet Union. During the First World War he took part in revolutionary activities among the soldiers, then joined the Red partisans (1918) and trained irregulars from whom a Red Army regiment was eventually formed. During the Civil War he was attached to Badyenny's cavalry regiment and fought on the Polish front (1920). Between the wars he held various military commands. He replaced Voroshilov as commissar for defence (1940) and introduced modern training methods and stricter discipline in the Red Army. He took part in the Soviet occupation of Poland (1939) and held a command in Karelia in the Finnish War (1939–40). His subsequent commands during the war against Germany were not very successful.

TIMOTHEUS (d. 354 BC), Athenian soldier, who won allies for the Second Athenian Confederacy in northern Greece (375) and helped to ensure Athens' naval supremacy over Sparta in the Ionian and Aegean seas. After infringing the peace with Sparta (374), he maintained his command until he ran short of funds, when Iphicrates superseded him (373). On being restored to favour (366), he supported the Persian satrap, Ariobarzanes, in revolt and expanded Athens' control in the Aegean, provoking allied discontent, but failed to capture Amphipolis and burnt his fleet on the Strymon to prevent its capture (360). He was appointed commander in the Social War (357), but was unsuccessful at Embata (356).

TIMUR (1336–1405), Central Asian, Turkish, Muslim conqueror, known because of his injured leg as 'the Lame', hence Tamerlane. He first became known as a military adventurer, having attracted a band of followers and was by 1369 supreme in Transoxania. After consolidating his power in Turkestan with campaigns against Khurasan and Mughulistan (1370–80), he began a career of foreign conquest. He led a campaign in Iran (1380–8, 1392–4); two major campaigns against the Golden Horde (1388–91, 1395), from which that state never fully recovered; an invasion of India, culminating in the sack of Delhi (1398–9); a campaign against the Mamluks of Egypt and Syria (1399–1401), during which he sacked Damascus; and a campaign against the Ottoman sultanate in which he defeated and captured

Bayazid I at the battle of Ankara (1402). At the time of his death he was marching against China. His remarkable military success rested on the power of the Turkish horsemen of Central Asia, but more was needed to establish the basis of a durable empire. Timur made little attempt to set up permanent governmental machinery after his conquests, being usually content to install vassal rulers. He himself never took the title of Great Khan, preferring to rule in the name of puppet Chingizide rulers. His empire was an uneasy compromise between the nomadic Turko-Mongol and the settled Muslim elements. Although his campaigns were fought in the name of Islam, they were usually against fellow Muslims and religion was habitually subordinated to plunder as a motive. Central Asia, and especially his capital, Samarkand, became prosperous through the booty he accumulated, industries were established by imported artisans, and fine buildings were constructed. After his death, his descendants, the Timurids, rapidly lost authority everywhere except in Central Asia.   MEY

TIMUR SHAH (c. 1745–93), Ruler of Afghanistan (reg. 1772–93). He was the second son and successor of Ahmad Shah Durrani and ruled in preference to his elder brother, Sulayman. During his reign the capital was transferred from Kandahar to Kabul. Although Timur held the Durrani empire together, the signs of future collapse became visible during his lifetime.

TIMURIDS, name given to the descendants of Timur (1336–1405), who was succeeded by his son Shah Rukh (reg. 1405–47). Rukh removed the capital to Herat from Samarkand, which was left in the charge of his son, Ulugh Beg (d. 1449), who patronized writers and scientists and constructed a celebrated observatory. The tolerant liberalism of Ulugh Beg and his followers clashed with the strict fundamentalism of the popular Islamic dervish orders. Abu Sa'id (reg. 1451–1469) was forced to make concessions to orthodoxy, although Herat witnessed the last Timurid cultural efflorescence under Sultan Husayn Bayqara (reg. 1470–1506). But, weakened by domestic strife, the Timurids eventually succumbed to the Shaybanids, who made themselves masters of Central Asia early in the 16th cent. The last notable Timurid, Baber, took refuge in Afghanistan, whence he launched the invasion of India which established the Mughal dynasty there. Timurid rule in Central Asia, politically undistinguished, was noteworthy for its cultural brilliance revealed in its architecture, painting, and Persian and Chaghatai Turkish literature.

TIN TUT, U (1895–1948), Burmese politician and senior member of the Indian civil service in Burma, who resigned (1946) from the ICS to take up politics and became member for finance and revenue and, after independence, minister for foreign affairs (1948). He retired from politics to become inspector-general of auxiliary forces. He was assassinated in 1948.

TINDAL, MATTHEW (c. 1657–1733), English philosopher, the first of whose two larger works, *The Rights of the Christian Church Asserted Against the Romanish And All Other Priests Who Claim An Independent Power Over It* (1706), is a defence of Erastianism. The author, publisher, and printer were prosecuted, but by 1709 the work had reached a fourth edition. His *A Defence of the Rights of the Christian Church* (1709) was burnt by the common hangman, with Sacheverell's sermon (1710), and remained an object of denunciation for many years. His second large work was *Christianity as Old as the Creation* (1730).

TING LING (1907–   ), pseudonym of Chiang Ping-shih, Chinese writer, whose messianic and romantic writing, combining feminist and revolutionary strands, was influential in the 1930s and 1940s. She was closely associated with the Communist Party, but her fiery temperament brought her into conflict with the communist literary establishment, and she disappeared from the scene in the mid-1950s.

TIPPECANOE, BATTLE OF (7 Nov. 1811), US Indian struggle fought on the west bank of the Wabash river in IN. Gen. Harrison with 900 troops defeated and dispersed the Shawnee Indians, bringing to an end plans for a confederation of all western and southern tribes.

TIPPERMUIR, BATTLE OF (1644), royalist victory in Scotland during the Civil Wars, when the marquis of Montrose and 3000 Scottish royalists defeated a force of Covenanters under Lord Elcho twice the size and occupied Perth.

TIPPU TIP, Hamed bin Muhammed el Murjebi (c. 1837–1905), Swahili trader in eastern Africa, who established an empire in the eastern Congo before surrendering it to the Belgians. He was the greatest of the east coast caravaneers in the 19th cent. and pioneered routes into the Congo. His prime interest was in ivory, but his requirements of labour to man his trading stations and settlements caused him to become extensively involved in slave-trading as well. During negotiations in 1887 with H. M. Stanley and King Leopold he briefly succeeded in gaining the governorship of the Eastern Congo under European suzerainty.

TIPU SULTAN (1750–99), Ruler of Mysore (reg. 1782–99) and son of Haidar Ali, who succeeded his father (1782) during the Second Mysore War (1780–4) with the British, which ended with a mutual restoration of conquests by the treaty of Mangalore. The Third Mysore War (1790–2) ended with the treaty of Seringapatam (1792), when Tipu was forced to cede half of Mysore. The final war with Tipu (March–May 1799) occurred during Wellesley's governor-generalship. Tipu was defeated and killed at Seringapatam. Wellesley formed a small central kingdom of Mysore and restored the ancient Hindu dynasty. What was left was divided between the nizam and the British.

TIRADENTES CONSPIRACY, first serious outbreak against Portuguese authority in Brazil, centred in the mining province of Minas Gerais. The 1788 rebellion was led by Joaquim José da Silva Xavier, a jack-of-all-trades, including dentistry, whose popular name, 'Tiradentes' ('tooth-puller'), stuck to the rebellion. The rebels' grievances were genuine. The province's production of gold and diamonds was declining, and the Portuguese Crown hoped to keep its revenues stable by raising taxes and lowering wages, thus worsening the workers' economic conditions. As a leader of the ensuing conspiracy, Tiradentes articulated these grievances, but also urged the abolition of slavery, the establishment of factories, the creation of a university, and Brazilian independence. The uprising was quickly crushed, its leaders captured, and Tiradentes beheaded (21 April 1792).

TIRAILLEURS SÉNÉGALAIS (Senegalese Rifles), were African troops raised in maritime Senegal by Faidherbe after 1859 for use in colonial conquest and 'pacification'. Their small numbers were soon enlarged by recruitment elsewhere, and Tirailleurs were committed in many theatres, such as Madagascar, Morocco, and the western Sudan, and, in Europe, in the Crimean and Franco-Prussian campaigns, though only in small numbers in the latter.

There was intensive recruitment during the First World War of both conscripts or volunteers, in all the African territories of the French empire, and some 160,000 Tirailleurs fought on the Western Front during those years; about 24,000 of these were officially reported killed. Tirailleurs continued as an important fighting element in the French army until 1960; most of them then returned to countries which had become independent, and were dispersed or absorbed into new national forces.

TIRHAKHAH (*reg. c.* 689–664 BC), Nubian King of Egypt of the XXVth (Kushite or Ethiopian) dynasty, whose early years appear to have been prosperous. He was twice driven from Egypt by the Assyrians (671, 667) and died in Napata.

TIRIBAZUS (d. *c.* 355 BC), Persian satrap at Sardis in 392 BC, whose co-operation with the Spartan Antalcidas in the transference of Persian support from Athens to Sparta in the Corinthian War led ultimately to the King's Peace (387). He later commanded against Evagoras of Cyprus (*c.* 381–379).

TIRIDATES (*reg. c.* 248–211 BC), King of Parthia, who occupied that country (*c.* 248), annexed Hyrcania (southeast of the Caspian Sea), and founded his capital at Arsak. Later, with expansion further westward, he moved the capital to Hecatompylos on an important trade route.

TIROL, SILVER MINES OF, large-scale processing plants, centred on Schwaz, which were a major source of European silver in the Middle Ages. Capitalist exploitation of deep veins began in the 15th cent., when south German financiers, especially the Fuggers and Welsers, began to mine the silver. They provided security for enormous loans raised by the Habsburgs.

TIRYNS, important centre of ancient Mycenaean civilization in the eastern Peloponnese 8 kms south-east of Argos. Its well-planned palace with good sanitation and frescoes (14th–12th cents BC) was first excavated by Schliemann and Dörpfeld in 1884. Despite the construction in the 13th cent. BC of massive fortifications, including well-protected steps to a nearby spring, the palace did not escape the widespread destruction of Mycenaean sites (*c.* 1200 BC). It was subsequently of little importance and was absorbed by Argos in the 5th cent.

TISSA DEVANAMPIYA (*reg. c.* 250–210 BC), King of Ceylon, who was converted to Buddhism by Mahinda, son or brother of Asoka, and was the first truly historical ruler of the island.

TISSAPHERNES (d. 395 BC), Persian soldier and administrator, known in Greek history because of his unscrupulous diplomacy as satrap in Sardis during and directly after the great Peloponnesian War. After the Athenian disaster in Sicily (413), he outbid Pharnabazus, satrap of Hellespontine Phrygia, in encouraging Athens' allies to revolt and Sparta's navy to take action. He used the exiled Alcibiades, however, to weaken both sides, and withheld the support promised to the Spartans. His policy was frustrated by Darius II, who ordered his son, Cyrus, to achieve a victory for Sparta. On Darius' death (404), Tissaphernes supported Artaxerxes II against Cyrus' rival claim and treacherously lured the Greek commanders to death after the battle of Cunaxa (401). Returning to the west, he provoked Sparta into war by threatening to subdue the Asiatic Greeks (400), but after military failure was executed.

TISZA, KOLOMAN, Count (1830–1902), Hungarian politician and prime minister of Hungary (1875–80), who welded the radical and moderate parties into a parliamentary oligarchy, which ruled exclusively in the interests of the Magyars. By ignoring or withdrawing concessions made to non-Magyars by previous governments, Tisza failed to promote a policy of conciliation, which was vital if Hungary was to overcome the problem of her mixed nationalities and achieve stability. By ignoring the fate of the Austrian part of the empire, except to extort financial concessions favourable to Hungary, his government ensured that the Ausgleich would not succeed in its aim of maintaining the tottering structure of the Habsburg empire intact.

TITHE, ancient due payable to the established Christian Church and dating back to biblical times. By the 6th cent. the practice of setting aside a tenth of one's income as God's property was established and became obligatory as the Christian Church spread over Europe, but the tithe was never levied by the Orthodox Church. After the Reformation the imposition of tithes continued for the benefit of the reformed Churches and under English law was payable for the maintenance of the parish priest. Opposition to this tax was widespread and was a common motive in peasant revolts. It was abolished in France at the Revolution (1789), in Ireland in 1871, and Italy in 1887. In England it was commuted for a rent charge by the Tithe Act (1836), but the Tithe Act (1936) abolished this also.

TITIAN (TIZIANO VECELLI) (*c.* 1487–1576), one of the greatest painters of the Venetian school. In 1516 he painted the *Bacchus and Ariadne* and about the same time *Sacred and Profane Love,* portraying the Venetian ideal of feminine beauty, of which he was so great an interpreter. In 1533 he became Charles V's court painter. He visited the imperial court at Augsburg twice (1548–9, 1550–1) and painted Charles V many times. After the emperor's abdication he worked for Philip II, for whom he painted mythological compositions.

TITO, JOSIP BROZ (1892–   ), Yugoslavian politician and president of Yugoslavia, born at Kraguvac in Croatia. As a machinist and locksmith he became involved in trade union affairs while still a young man. During the First World War he served in the Austro-Hungarian army and was captured by the Russians. He spent five years in Russia (1915–20), and fought in the International Red Guard during the Civil War. During this period he was indoctrinated with communist tactics. On returning to Yugoslavia he became leader of the Croatian Metal Workers Union and an active member of the communist underground. He was arrested in 1928 and spent the next five years in prison. On his release he went to Spain, where he fought in the Civil War. In 1934 he joined the central committee of the Yugoslav Communist Party, then in considerable disarray. Three years later, on instructions from the Comintern, he was appointed secretary-general of the party and was charged with its reorganization. The party at this time was riven by internal dissent and harried by the police. Tito, operating from Zagreb, began to put new life into it by improving its organization and recruitment. When Yugoslavia was invaded by the Axis armies, he led the communists' resistance and began to lay the foundations of a new state. The partisans, who attracted the bulk of Yugoslav patriots, became the most successful resistance force in Eastern Europe. A political arm (AVNOJ) was established in 1943, which became a provisional administration and later a provisional government. At this time Tito began to differ from Stalin, who wanted to slow down the pace of the Yugoslav revolution in order to appease his Western allies. Tito pretended to co-operate with the royalist government-in-exile, but all power in Yugoslavia was in the hands of the communists, under whose leadership the country had been liberated. In 1945 he became president of Yugoslavia and a communist republic was established. In 1948 he found himself at loggerheads with the Kremlin; Stalin feared his influence in Eastern Europe and the threat of Yugoslavia's power in the Balkans, and Tito objected to Russian interference in his country's affairs. The split marked the birth of national communism and Tito's second triumph over foreign domination and dictatorship. After 1948 he tried to strike a balance between centralization and decentralization. At first he endorsed Djilas's proposals, but felt compelled to curb his excesses when Djilas's criticisms of the regime went beyond bounds. In 1966, after a prolonged stalemate, the advocates of decentralization won a victory, Rankovic, a close associate of Tito's, being dropped from the leadership. Tito also sought to resolve the country's nationality problem (he himself is universally regarded as a Yugoslav), but national differences and animosities persisted. He had emerged by 1970 as a world statesman of considerable prominence. His policy of non-alignment, seeking a balance between the international communist movement and the capitalist powers, earned him respect in all capitals.   JMK

TITOKOWARU (d. 1888), NZ Maori warrior chief, who led Taranaki Hauhaus in successful guerrilla warfare, and in two victories (1868) against NZ government forces.

TITTONI, TOMMASO (1855–1931), Italian diplomat, politician, and president of the senate (1919–29). As foreign minister (1903–9), he faced growing irredentist demands for territories, mainly at Austria's expense, but still sought to maintain cordial relations with Austria, Italy's Triple Alliance partner since 1882. He also developed alternative links with Balkan countries, *eg*, Serbia and Bulgaria, and with France and Russia. Finally, he accepted the Russo-Italian 'Racconigi Agreement' (1909), though it was contrary to the policy of the Triple Alliance, for maintaining the Balkan status quo or else altering it jointly. During his second period as foreign minister in 1919, he was badgered by the irredentists and sought a compromise solution at talks in Paris on Fiume and Dalmatia, but his former allies were unco-operative. He temporarily reduced international tension by the Tittoni-Venizelos Agreement (1919), a compromise with Greece over rival claims in Albania and the Dodecanese, though Albanian events in 1920 forestalled the agreement's implementation.

TITULESCU, NICOLAE (1882–1941), Rumanian politician and diplomat, who became a prominent figure in the League of Nations. He began his political career in the Liberal Party, but served in the coalition governments of all shades as minister of finance (1917–21). He was a delegate to the Paris Peace Conference in 1919–20, and was permanent Rumanian representative at the League of Nations (1920–36). He was also ambassador to Britain (1922–7). He was twice minister of foreign affairs (1927–8, 1932–6). As a staunch defender of the post-war settlement, he championed collective security as the best means of preserving it. He played an important part in both the Little and Balkan Ententes and sought a rapprochement with the Soviet Union. In 1930–1 he served as president of the League of Nations. His dismissal from the foreign ministry in 1936 signalled a major shift in Rumanian policy, away from collective security and close ties with France towards a conciliatory and unequal relationship with Germany.

TITUS (AD 39–81), Roman Emperor (*reg.* 79–81), elder son of the Emperor Vespasian, who carried on the siege of Jerusalem in 69, when his father was proclaimed emperor, and brought it to a conclusion. During his two years as emperor he was generally popular and belied a reputation for extravagance and cruelty. Without dissipating the imperial finances he acted generously and took active measures to relieve distress caused by the eruption of Vesuvius in 79.

T'I-YUNG, Chinese phrase which became important during the late 19th cent., as China responded to Western intrusion. Often translated as 'Chinese learning for the essential principles, Western learning for the practical applications', it is an abbreviated form of a phrase made famous by Chang Chih-tung in the 1890s to justify Westernization as part of his reform programme. *T'i* ('substance') and *yung* ('function') were terms drawn from Neo-Confucian metaphysics, and originally stood for the ontological and functional aspects of the same reality. In so far as Western learning and Chinese essential principles are not correlatives of the same entity, Chang was distorting the original *t'i-yung* concept, applying it unphilosophically to cover up a compromise dictated by harsh necessity.

TIZARD, SIR HENRY THOMAS (1885–1959), British physical chemist and organizer of radar defence of Britain in the Second World War. Earlier (1933) he had been appointed chairman of the Committee on Scientific Survey of Air Defence. Here, with remarkable skill and foresight, he turned radar from a scientific possibility into an equipped and organized reality in time for the battle of Britain. Winston Churchill, however, preferred Lord Cherwell as his scientific adviser and Tizard returned to work at Oxford University in 1942.

TJOKROAMINOTO, UMAR SAID (1883–1934), Javanese nationalist, who founded Indonesia's first mass party, the Sarekat Islam. He was a skilful and popular orator, whose style was consciously copied by Indonesia's first president, Sukarno. Though Tjokroaminoto's approach to politics was essentially populist, government pressure and the communist challenge within the Sarekat Islam caused him to emphasize the Islamic nature of the party. In the less controversial role to which this move confined him he was unable to maintain his popularity, and in the late 1920s he was replaced by a new generation of secular nationalists.

TKACHEV, PYOTR NIKITICH (1844–86), Russian politician, revolutionary, and Jacobin, who was associated with Nechaev and influenced by Marx. In *The Tocsin*, published in Geneva (1875–81), he emphasized the need for a disciplined, centralized, revolutionary elite to seize and use state power to establish socialism based on the commune and to halt further capitalist development in Russia.

TLAXCALA, in Aztec Mexico, the one city of the central plateau which retained its independence. Some experts claim that the Aztecs tolerated Tlaxcalan independence because the city was a source of captives for sacrifice, since at regular intervals the two sides engaged in ritual warfare for the purpose of obtaining sacrificial victims. Others maintain that the Aztecs were in fact never able to conquer the Tlaxcalans and made the best of a bad situation. In any event, Cortés exploited the enmity between the two by first defeating the Tlaxcalans and then drawing them into an alliance. When driven from Tenochtitlán after the *Noche Trieste* defeat, the Spanish used Tlaxcala as refuge, and the Tlaxcalans were indispensable auxiliaries during the final siege of the Aztec capital. As a reward, the Spanish Crown gave them privileged status, including, for a time, exemption from the payment of tribute.

TLEMCEN, city of western Algeria, established in the Middle Ages as an important political and commerical centre dominating the route to Morocco.

TOBACCO CONCESSION, monopoly of the curing and sale of the Persian tobacco crop granted to a British company in 1890. A widespread agitation under religious leadership, which involved a boycott of tobacco, forced the government to cancel the concession (1892). The incident is usually regarded as marking the beginning of the Persian constitutional movement.

TOBAGO, West Indian island, first sighted by Columbus in 1498. The Dutch, who settled there in 1628, were expelled by Carib Indians in 1630. On returning in 1633 they were executed by the Spaniards. Courlanders (Latvians) who settled there the next year were ousted (1639) by English settlers, who were themselves expelled by Caribs in 1640. Later, Courlanders and Dutch both established colonies, but in 1658 the latter ousted their rivals. The Dutch colony was destroyed in 1672 by an English force, but the island was returned to the Dutch in 1674; then in 1677 it was captured by the French and in the following year was recognized as theirs. By agreement it was reserved for Caribs, then in 1763 was transferred to Britain.

With the development of plantations slave revolts began to occur (1770–1, 1774). In 1781 the island capitulated to the French, then was captured by the British (1793), who restored it to the French, and in 1803 captured it again. British ownership was confirmed in 1814. In 1831 legal discrimination against free coloured people was removed and slavery abolished. Tobago was under the governors of Barbados (1833–85), and later shared the Windward Islands' governor until the island was annexed to Trinidad in 1889. It remained in 1970 part of the independent nation of Trinidad.

TOBAR DOCTRINE (1907), policy enunciated by the Ecuadorian, Carlos R. Tobar (1856–1920), under which it was suggested that a certain degree of interference or moral pressure by the American nations in the affairs of a straying member should be permitted if one of the American republics should succumb to a dictatorial or unconstitutional regime. Tobar suggested that in such cases the weapon of non-recognition should be used.

By the mid-1930s the doctrine was a dead letter, but its principles were still invoked by some American nations from time to time, *eg*, Betancourt's government in Venezuela (1958–64).

TOCQUEVILLE, ALEXIS HENRI CHARLES MAURICE CLEREL, Comte de (1805–59), French civil servant, politician, and writer, whose *De la Démocratie en Amérique* (2 vols, 1835) became the classic description of Jacksonian America. In 1831 he went to the US to study the American penal system. With his friend, Gustave de Beaumont, he travelled for 18 months throughout the US, and extended his brief into a thorough-going analysis of the nature of American institutions and the national character. A perceptive social observer, he traced the interaction of ideas of democracy, revolution, and individualism with environmental forces and inherited historical experience, making a complex analysis of elitism, egalitarianism, and statism that is still relevant to the American experience today. On his return to France he became active in politics, was elected to the French Chamber of Deputies (1839), became an opponent of Louis Napoleon, and served intermittently until his retirement from public life in 1851. In *L'Ancien régime et la révolution* (1856), his other major work, De Tocqueville applied his thesis of the levelling implications of democracy to the period of the French Revolution.

TODAR MAL, RAJA (d. 1589), Indian soldier and revenue minister of the Mughal Emperor Akbar, whose revenue settlements became a pattern for the whole Mughal empire. After 'settling' Gujarat (1574–5) he was appointed diwan (1580) and carried through his revenue *bandobast* in northern India. It included measurement, classification of soils, and fixation of demand according to price levels. He also changed the revenue language from Hindi to Persian, with far-reaching results.

TOGLIATTI, PALMIRO (1893–1964), Italian politician and leader of the Italian Communist Party (PCI) (1926–64), who used various pseudonyms, *eg*, Palmi, Ercoli, Alfredo, and Correnti. He was the chief supporter of Gramsci, in the *Ordine Nuovo* group, in creating the PCI in 1921, opposing Bordiga's faction to control the party by 1925. After being briefly imprisoned (1925), he went to Moscow, became a Comintern member, and in 1926 de facto leader of the PCI from abroad. He was the Comintern's chief political representative in Spain (1937–8), where he undermined non-communist republicans. After 1934 he promoted unity-of-action pacts with Nenni's socialists (PSI), which in 1943 became the basis for combined action. By 1944 he was the PCI's undisputed leader. He disappointed many partisans by rejecting revolutionary tactics, co-operating with Badoglio and the monarchy, and postponing constitutional arguments. He held posts in successive cabinets (1944–6), undermined National Liberation committees and the Action Party, and established the PCI as a mass party to rival Christian Democracy. Though his bid to win control via the ballot-box failed in 1946, he rejected the northern Italian workers' call for revolution which followed an attempt to kill him in July 1948. After Stalin's death he more readily accepted the faction which demanded an 'Italian road to socialism', and,

following Khrushchev's 1956 revelations, he enunciated openly the theory of 'polycentrism': the right of communist parties to pursue different, autonomous paths to socialism without central (Soviet) domination. But he justified Soviet policies, towards Poland and Hungary (though offering different explanations for the 1956 revolts) and rapidly curbed PCI dissidents. By 1962 he had moved to a reformist position, from which he slowly rebuilt the PCI's prestige, while still attacking Socialist parties as 'non-socialist'. He also criticized Russia's attitude towards China as being destructive of communist unity, as was seen in the Yalta Testament released on his death. His comparative moderation and flexibility over domestic issues attracted non-ideological supporters to the PCI, whose serious internal conflicts were masked only by his rigid insistence on party discipline.

C. F. Delzell, *Mussolini's Enemies* (Princeton, 1961).
D. L. M. Blackmer, *Unity in Diversity: Italian communism and the communist world* (Cambridge, MA, 1968).   CFB

TOGO, SHIGENORI (1882–1950), Japanese politician and diplomat, who was foreign minister under Tōjō Hideki (1941–3) and Suzuki Kantarō (1945). He was sentenced to 20 years' imprisonment by the Tokyo Tribunal (1948), despite a record of moderation. His reminiscences were translated as *The Cause of Japan* (1956).

TOGO, REPUBLIC OF (56,600 sq. kms), in West Africa, formerly a UN trust territory administered by France and Britain which became independent in 1960. Cabrai, Ewe, and many other peoples formed (1970) a population of 1,586,000. The constitution was suspended in 1967 after an army coup. The president and the cabinet hold executive power, but future elections were promised in 1970.

TO'JANGGUT REBELLION (1915), anti-British peasant revolt in Malaya. The rebels, excited by an unpopular land tax, held the Pasir Puteh district of Kelantan for about three weeks.

TŌJŌ, HIDEKI (1884–1948), Japanese soldier and politician. It was his cabinet which took Japan into the Second World War. His administrative ability, belief in economic planning, and membership of the *Tōseiha* ('Control' Faction) brought him steady promotion until he became war minister (1940). In Oct. 1941 he was appointed prime minister in the hope that he would be able to resist the army's demands for war. He was instructed by the Emperor to reappraise Japan's policy, disregarding an Imperial conference decision of 6 Sept. 1941 to declare war if negotiations with the US were not immediately successful. Tōjō, however, shared the army's view that Japan must take military action before economic sanctions exhausted her oil supplies and he was willing to gamble on American reluctance to fight a major war over east Asia. Another imperial conference (5 Nov.) approved a plan to complete war preparations early in Dec., and when the US adopted an uncompromising attitude in the Hull note (26 Nov.), Tōjō ignored the objections raised at a meeting of elder statesmen (29 Nov.) and from an imperial conference secured a decision (1 Dec.) to begin hostilities.

Despite the success of the Pearl Harbor attack, however, Japan lacked the resources, particularly in shipping, to withstand the American counter-attack. Tōjō was unable to achieve complete co-operation between the army, the navy, and the big industrialists, and by July 1944 military defeat and economic collapse had undermined confidence in his leadership. Though never a dictator, Tōjō made himself a figurehead to an unusual extent for a Japanese and he strongly resented criticism. When, however, he failed to secure support for a new cabinet and was informed that the emperor desired his retirement, he yielded. He was condemned to death as a major war criminal and executed (1948).

R. J. C. Butow, *Tojo and the Coming of the War* (Princeton, 1961).   RLS

TOKAY, BATTLE OF (Sept. 1527), victory of the Habsburg forces of Archduke Ferdinand, King of Bohemia and Hungary, over the Hungarian claimant, John Zapolyai, who had been elected king by the nationalist party in Nov. 1526. The defeated leader was forced to take refuge in the mountains of Transylvania (1527–38), while Ferdinand established his authority over the western third of Hungary.

TOKELAU ISLANDS (Union group), four small Polynesian South-western Pacific atolls, discovered by Roggeveen (1722), Byron (1765), and others. After the Peruvian slaving episode (1861) Nukuono accepted Catholicism, and Atafu accepted Protestantism while Fakofu adopted both. These three became a British protectorate (1877) but the southern islet, Olosenga, fell to the US, being occupied by Eli Jennings of New Bedford (1856). The Tokelau proper were incorporated in the Gilbert and Ellice colony in 1916, transferred to NZ (1925) at British request, and annexed to NZ (1946). In 1964 the Tokelauans opted for retention of NZ citizenship and were progressively resettled within NZ.

TOKHTAMISH, Mongol Khan of the White Horde (1378–95), who made himself ruler (1381) of the Golden Horde, re-established its authority over the northern Slav states, and attacked Moscow (1382). His quarrel with Timur (*reg.* 1369–1405) over control of Transcaucasia precipitated Timur's invasions of the territory of the Golden Horde (1389–91, 1395), during which Tokhtamish's power was effectively destroyed.

TOKHTU KHAN (*reg.* 1291–1313), Ruler of the Golden Horde and son of Möngka-Temür (Timur) (*reg.* 1267–80). He broke the power of the great vassal, Noghay (d. 1299), and resumed an expansionist policy in the Caucasus.

TÖKÖLY, IMRE, Count (1656–1705), Protestant Hungarian nobleman and leader of the Hungarian patriots in exile (*kurucok*), who led the revolt against Emperor Leopold (1678–99) in Hungary and Transylvania. In 1670 Tököly's father was executed for conspiracy against the emperor and he took refuge in Transylvania, where he was elected commander of the nationalists. From 1678 he began to drive the Habsburg forces out of northern and western Hungary and forced Leopold to negotiate the treaty of Sopron with the Hungarian nobility (1681), restoring the Hungarian constitution and promising to convoke the Diet and remedy grievances. In 1682 Tököly married Ilona Zrinyi, widow of Francis Rakoczi I, and joined forces with the Turkish pasha at Buda, whence they embarked together on the reconquest of the rest of Hungary. At the end of 1682 Leopold sued for a truce with Tököly, leaving him master of eastern Hungary. However, the defeat of the Turks before Vienna (1683) initiated the Habsburg reoccupation of Hungary and Tököly's forces were driven back. Although he defeated the imperial army at Zernyest (1690), he barely escaped from the battlefield of Zalankemen and after the peace of Carlowitz (1699) he retired to Constantinople, where he died.

TOKUGAWA SHOGUNATE, central government of Japan (1603–1867), which gave Japan two centuries of peace, but at the cost of isolating the country from the outside world. The key to the Tokugawa shogunate's success lay in its control of most of the strategic centre of the country, its imposition of a rigid hierarchical class system, and its *sankin kōtai* system which forced *daimyō*s to spend at least half their lives in Edo. Having increased considerably in administrative complexity since its establishment by Tokugawa Ieyasu, the shogunate experienced continual financial difficulties from the early 18th cent. But its eventual downfall was caused by its unwillingness to share its power, after the opening of Japan by the West (1854–8) had caused the leading *daimyō*s to demand a genuinely national government. By the time the last *shōgun* agreed to a *daimyō* confederation (1867), the *bakufu* had incurred the bitter enmity

of Satsuma and Chōshū, and it not only lost its monopoly of power but was abolished.

TOKYO EARTHQUAKE (1 Sept. 1923), greatest natural disaster in Japanese history. It extended to Yokohama and Shizuoka and resulted in an estimated 132,807 casualties, dead or missing, and the destruction of 576,262 houses.

TOLAND, JOHN (1670–1722), Irish political philosopher. His *Christianity not mysterious* (1696) was burned by the public hangman for its rationalism, and in several works he debated the comparative evidence for canonical and apocryphal scriptures. He won the favour of Sophia of Hanover, for whom he wrote an *Account of the Courts of Prussia and Hanover* (1705).

TOLEDO, DON FRANCISCO DE (*c.* 1515–84), Castilian nobleman and Spanish colonial administrator. As viceroy of Peru (1569–81) he established Spanish royal administration in that country under the council of the Indies. He introduced the Inquisition into Peru and Philip II's celebrated code of laws (1573).

TOLERATION, RELIGIOUS, in Europe, concept that men of all faiths should worship freely and coexist peacefully within one state. Medieval Europe had been broadly united in one orthodox Christian faith, although the unorthodox minorities, *eg*, Albigensians, Hussites, and Wycliffites, experienced uncompromising persecution. The Protestant Reformation of the early 16th cent. first raised the question of toleration in an acute form. A few radical reformers, *eg*, Schwenckfeld and Franck, advocated religious toleration in the early 16th cent. but they were isolated figures, for the immediate effect of the Reformation was to provide fresh stimuli to bigotry and to encourage the suppression of dissidents, Catholic or Protestant, *eg*, Calvin's persecution of his fellow Protestant, Servetus. However, when it became apparent that neither repression nor confessional reunion could be achieved in the empire, the original seat of the Reformation, the German princes came to terms with the Emperor Charles V in the peace of Augsburg, which recognized the coexistence of Catholicism and Lutheranism on the principle of *cuius regio euis religio* (1555), an agreement which marked the first official step towards religious toleration in Europe. The idea that different sects could be respected within one state was, however, still a rare concept, confined broadly to Transylvania, Poland, where it was enshrined in the Confederation of Warsaw (1573), and the Netherlands, where it was expressed in the Pacification of Ghent (1576). Toleration was still anathema to both Geneva and Rome, the most violent clash between these two Churches occurring in France during the Wars of Religion, but contributing to the outbreak of the Thirty Years War in Germany. Out of this conflict emerged a measure of toleration in France, the Edict of Nantes (1598), and the extension of *cuius regio* to Calvinism in Germany (1648); but in the 17th cent. France reverted to the principle of religious conformity in the belief that toleration of a multitude of sects would lead to political weakness, as it had done in Poland and the empire. Outbursts of religious fanaticism also occurred in the predominantly Protestant countries in the 17th cent., *eg*, the execution of Oldenbarneveldt by the Gomarists (1619), but in the course of this century Europe moved slowly towards the toleration of all creeds, including Judaism, *eg*, in the United Provinces, Brandenburg, and to a lesser extent the empire of Maximilian II and Rudolph II, stimulated by the rationalism of Bodin, Grotius, and Bayle, whose *Commentaire Philosophique* (1681) made the rare appeal for toleration of atheists. In England, where antitrinitarian and Catholic dissenters were penalized socially and politically until the 19th cent., religious persecution had died out by 1700. One early advocate of general toleration was Roger Williams, founder of Rhode Island (1631), and in the mid-17th cent. the Baptists and Independents appealed for the toleration of all Protestants.

Though conformity was legally entrenched after the Restoration (1660), latitudinarian views grew more general, and were reflected in John Locke's *Letter on Toleration* (1689). The Toleration Act of 1689 granted religious freedom to trinitarian Protestants. The Catholic countries of Europe, where absolute monarchy and the repressive forces of the Counter-reformation, *eg*, the Inquisition, were entrenched, were slower to accept toleration. The Moriscoes were driven from Spain in 1609, the Huguenots from France in 1685, where religious persecution continued until the mid-18th cent., *eg*, the Calas Affair. By this time the impact of the Enlightenment was undermining the dominant influence of the Catholic Church, producing a more flexible attitude to life, so that on the eve of the French Revolution religious toleration was spreading and had been introduced in France (1787) and in Austria (1781).

W. K. Jordan, *The Development of Religious Toleration in England*, 4 vols (London, 1932–40).
J. Lecler, *Toleration and the Reformation*, tr. by T. L. Westow, 2 vols (London, 1960). MKS

TOLERATION ACT, the (1689), in Britain, legislative measure passed by the Convention parliament of William and Mary exempting Protestants dissenting from the Church of England from the penalties of certain laws, the most important of which were those enjoining attendance at Sunday service in the local parish church and the Conventicle Act (1670) prohibiting attendance at dissenting chapels. The Toleration Act exempted from prosecution and punishment all Protestants who were registered and certified as having sworn the oaths of allegiance and supremacy and made and signed a declaration against transubstantiation; or, in the case of those who scrupled to take oaths (such as Quakers), who had made and signed the declaration against transubstantiation and also one of fidelity to William and Mary and signed a profession of Christian belief in the Trinity and in the inspiration of the scriptures. Furthermore, dissenting ministers were also to be exempted from the penalties prescribed by the Act of Uniformity, the Five Mile Act, and the second Conventicle Act, provided that they gave their approbation of and signed 35 and part of a 36th of the 39 Articles; except that those who scrupled to baptize infants were excused from the wording of the relevant article. The Toleration Act specifically excluded from relief Roman Catholics and also all those who denied the doctrine of the Trinity, either in writing or in printing. It did not repeal any existing legislation, so that such measures as the Corporation Act and the Test Act remained law. Thereby Roman Catholics continued to be debarred from most public offices owing to requirements which they were unable to fulfil.

TOLERATION ACT (1712) in Britain, legislative measure passed by the Tory majority in parliament following the riots and persecution of episcopal clergymen in Scotland, which stemmed in turn from the appeal of the Rev. James Greenshields to the British House of Lords (1711). The act, which gave legal recognition to the Scottish Episcopalians, aroused serious alarm among many Scots, who feared the undermining of the official Presbyterian Church and a Jacobite restoration inspired by the Episcopalians. The act created a further strain on the relationship between England and Scotland during the early years of adjustment to the Act of Union (1707).

TOLERATION ACT (1719) in Britain, legislative measure to end the tests which had hitherto debarred Irish nonconformists from civil and military service to the British Crown.

TOLMIDES (d. 447 BC), Athenian soldier, who in the first Peloponnesian War ravaged Peloponnesian territory. By capturing Corinthian Chalcis and settling the base of Naupactus, he established Athenian forces in western Greek waters (456–455). His death in battle at Coronea in Boeotia marked the end of Athens' land imperialism which preceded the Thirty Years Peace with Sparta (445).

TOLPUDDLE MARTYRS (1834) in Britain, six farmworkers at Tolpuddle, Dorset, who were transported for swearing men into a trade union lodge. They intended to join Robert Owen's recently founded Grand National Consolidated Trade Union, which had organized a huge but unsuccessful demonstration. The respectability of the martyrs, five of whom were Wesleyans, ensured that they served only three of their seven years' sentences. The event showed how limited were the Whigs' sympathies with the working-class allies who had been so useful to them in 1831–2, and thereby nourished Chartism. The incident also ended the prospects of unskilled trade unionism for fifty years.

TOLS, type of traditional Sanskrit academy in medieval Bengal and Bihar, comparable with the ancient *ashramas*. They were founded by Brahman *gurus* (teachers), who each attracted a number of disciples. The latter normally entered a *tol* only after they had already acquired elementary knowledge. Some of the *tols* developed into colleges in the 19th cent.

TOLSTOY, DMITRI ANDREYEVICH, Count (1823–89), Russian conservative politician. He was minister of education (1866–80), a noted disciplinarian, and one who emphasized the value of the classics. Under his aegis the number of educational institutions increased. In 1882 he was appointed minister of the interior. His conservative reorganization of the administrative machine involved the replacement of justices of the peace by land captains.

TOLSTOY, LEV NIKOLAYEVICH, Count (1828–1910), Russian novelist and thinker, who served in the army in the Caucasus and the Crimean War. His greatest works were *War and Peace* (1869) and *Anna Karenina* (1877). The first developed his theory of history, stressing the importance of a mass of obscure individuals rather than 'great men'. He was interested in peasant education and agricultural improvement, and he devoted his energies after the publication of *Confession* (1882) to educational experiments in his school at Yasnaya Polyana, and the formulation of his religious beliefs, for which he was excommunicated by the Orthodox Church. His advocacy of communal agricultural labour, a simple peasant existence, and non-violence, and his opposition to organized government, brought him numerous disciples. In 1891 he organized famine relief and aided the Dukhobor emigration to Canada.

TOLTECS, Mexican peoples who, in the 10th–11th cents, established a formidable state centred at Tula in modern Hidalgo. The Toltecs were noted for their military prowess, for their skill as builders, and for their worship of the feathered-serpent god, Quetzalcoatl. They greatly influenced the Aztecs and the Mayas.

TOLUY (d. 1232), fourth and youngest son of Chingiz Khan, who, as the so-called hearth child, inherited the central part of his father's dominions in Mongolia.

TOMPION, THOMAS (1639–1713), English horologist and 'father of English watchmaking', who made notable advances in clockmaking, and helped to invent both the cylinder escapement and the balance-spring wheel that together made flat watches possible.

TONDIBI, BATTLE OF (12 March 1591), at which the Songhay army was defeated by the forces of Al-Mansur, Sa'dian sultan of Morocco.

TONE, THEOBALD WOLFE (1763–98), Irish lawyer and patriot, who founded the republican Society of United Irishmen to agitate for Irish independence. During the

French Wars he took part in an unsuccessful French expedition (1796) to invade Ireland and secure it from the British. In 1798, on a similar expedition, he was captured and condemned to death by a court-martial. He escaped his sentence by suicide.

TONGA in the Pacific, discovered by Schouten (1616) and revisited by Tasman (1643) and Cook (1773–4, 1777). It was originally inhabited by Polynesians and ruled by a supreme priest-king, Tu'i Tonga. His secular powers passed in turn to two new title-holders, Tu'i Ha'a Takalaua (*c.* AD 1470) and Tu'i Kanokupolu (*c.* 1600), the latter's line long maintained firm peace. In 1799 the reigning Tu'i Kanokupolu was eliminated in a power struggle by Finau of Vava'u (d. 1809), all the ceremonial titles temporarily lapsing. About 1820 the late Tu'i Kanokupolu's son, Taufa'ahau (1797–1893), set about restoring his family's fortunes, after 1831 as an adherent of the Wesleyan Mission (founded in 1822). In 1837–40 he overthrew the powerful Ha'a Havea chiefs of Tongatapu and later, as Tu'i Kanokupolu, he overthrew a heathen–Catholic combination under Tu'i Tonga, Laufilitonga, whose title he assumed (1867) and abolished (1869). Putting aside his earlier Fijian aspirations, he devoted himself thereafter to the establishment of an independent state. In 1885 he thus broke with the Australian Wesleyan Conference and set up a Free Church. In 1890 he finally agreed to the appointment of a British official, Basil Thomson (1861–1939), to reform the government. In 1900–1 his successor, George Tupou II (d. 1918), agreed to a measure of British protection and in 1905 accepted certain constitutional limitations in the interests of good government. His successor, Queen Salote, with her husband, Prince Tungi, as prime minister, contributed much to Tongan stability. She was succeeded (1965) by Taufa'ahau Tupou IV, a descendant of all three ancient royal lineages, whose reign thus far (1970) has been marked by numerous fruitful innovations for the good of his people. GSP

TONGHAK RISING, culmination of popular protests in Korea in the 19th cent. arising from the imposition of heavy taxes at Kobu, in the south-west, late in 1893. The peasants used the organization of their Tonghak (now called Chondo-gyo) religion to present their protests against the powerful landowning families. Fighting flared up in April 1894, and the court called for Chinese help. Japan denounced this as a breach of the Tientsin treaty of 1885, and Chinese and Japanese troops landed in Korea in June, thus beginning the Sino-Japanese War. After defeating the Chinese in Korea, the Japanese helped to quell the rising, in which more than 300,000 people were killed. The Japanese success led to the promulgation of reforms which the pro-Japanese progressives had been demanding. Paradoxically these coincided with some of the Tonghak demands, but they became largely ineffective after King Kojong asserted control of the court in 1895.

TONGIN and **SOIN** ('Easterners' and 'Westerners'), factions among the Confucian bureaucrats of Korea, which originated during the reign of King Sonjo (1567–1608) and were named from the residences of their leaders in the capital. The *Tongin,* or 'idealist' faction, founded by Kim Hyo-won (1545–90), in 1584 displaced the *Soin* or 'conservatives', led by Sin Ui-gyon (1535–87), brother of the queen dowager. Later, the *Tongin* divided into the *Pugin* and *Namin,* and were ousted in 1623 by a *coup d'état* organized by the *Soin.*

TONGKING, European name applied to the northern part of Viet-nam, and in particular to the French protectorate established over the area in 1883, which formally came to an end in 1945. The name derives from the Sino-Viet-namese Dong-Kinh, meaning 'Eastern capital'.

TØNNING, most important fortified town of the dukes of Holstein-Gottorp. It was besieged by the Danes in 1700, but was not captured until the operations of 1713, when the Swedish general, Stenbock, had taken refuge there from the Russian–Saxon forces which drove him out of Germany after his victory over the Danes at Gadebusch (1712).

TONTI, HENRI DE (?1650–1704), Canadian soldier, fur trader, and explorer. He was born in France, of Italian parents, entered the French army in 1668, and lost his right hand in action in Sicily (1677). He went to Canada as an aide to Robert La Salle (1678) and after supervising the building of La Salle's ship, *Griffon* (1679), he accompanied him on his exploration of the Mississippi river. He helped to build Fort Saint-Louis-des-Illinois and was left in charge while La Salle made his fatal attempt to reach the mouth of the Mississippi by sea. Tonti later led the expedition down the Mississippi to search for La Salle (1696).

TOOKE, JOHN HORNE (1736–1812), British clergyman, radical, and philologist. He was the son of a London poulterer, John Horne, and assumed (1782) the surname Tooke from a rich eccentric who adopted him as his heir. Tooke became a clergyman in 1760, but resigned his living in 1773. He was Wilkes's chief supporter during the 1768 Middlesex elections and a founder of the Society of Supporters of the Bill of Rights. He quarrelled with Wilkes and left the society in 1770 because its aims were not wide or radical enough. He came back into radical politics in 1781, when he joined the Society for Constitutional Information, and soon became one of its most prominent members. He advocated associations and encouraged the formation of the London Corresponding Society (1792). In 1794 he was one of the radical leaders indicted for treason and acquitted. He was twice an unsuccessful candidate for parliament (1786, 1797), and though elected in 1801, was excluded by the Clerical Disqualification Act. He retired to Wimbledon, where his Sunday parties of politicians and literary men were celebrated. His book, *The Diversions of Purley* (1782), expounds his ideas on philology.

TOOMBS, ROBERT AUGUSTUS (1810–85), US lawyer, politician, and Confederate leader, who served in the state assembly (1837–40, 1842–4) and in the US House of Representatives (1845–53). He was originally a Whig, devoted to sound financial policies, but left the party when it adopted 'Northern principles' in 1849, though he supported the Compromise of 1850 and consistently sought to harmonize sectional differences. As a US senator (1853–61), he supported the Kansas–Nebraska Bill (1854) and strove to prevent the disintegration of the Democratic Party. In Dec. 1860 he supported secession and helped draw up the Confederate constitution (1861). He served briefly as Confederate secretary of state (1861), and as a brigadier on the VA front (1861–2), but was an unwilling subordinate and became an awkward and recalcitrant opponent of Jefferson Davis's regime. After a brief post-war exile. Toombs resumed his law practice and became an opponent of the Reconstruction governments and of corporate monopolies.

TOOTH RELIC OF LORD BUDDHA (*Dalada*), the most famous of all the relics, brought from India to Ceylon (4th cent. AD), where it became the most glorious symbol of the Buddhist state. During invasions it used to be hidden in remote mountain areas, then reinstalled in the capital as soon as safety was restored. The Tooth Relic, associated with many miracles, always had its own temple with special ceremonies and an annual festival with processions (*perehera*). It is at present enshrined in Kandy.

T'O-PA, Mongolian people who founded the northern Wei dynasty in China (386–439).

TORBAY in England, harbour in south Devon, scene of the landing of William of Orange and his army of 12,000 Dutch English, Scottish, and other Protestant supporters (5 Nov.

1688), which led to the defection of James II and the Revolution of 1688–9.

TORCH, OPERATION (1942), in the Second World War, Allied amphibious landing in North Africa. In July 1942 the Allies abandoned the idea of opening a second front on the European continent in 1942 or 1943, and decided instead to land troops in North Africa with the object of clearing North Africa of Axis troops before embarking upon an invasion of Italy. Gen. Eisenhower, then virtually unknown, was selected to command the operation, and Admiral Cunningham the naval forces. American and British forces were to occupy neutral Vichy French Morocco and Algeria before moving eastwards into Tunisia. Three widely separated landing points were selected: Casablanca, on the Moroccan Atlantic coast, and Oran and Algiers inside the Mediterranean. The planning and execution of so complex an operation undertaken so far from Britain and the US was a masterly achievement, particularly at this stage of the war. The landings took place on 8 Nov., coinciding with the later stages of Montgomery's successful offensive at El Alamein in Egypt. All three forces met with initial resistance, fierce in some places, but within three days the Vichy French leader in North Africa, Admiral Darlan, was persuaded to end the fighting. The landings led to a massive Axis reinforcement of Tunisia and to the German occupation of Vichy France. The subsequent movement of troops eastwards into Tunisia started promisingly with the quick occupation of the ports of Bougie and Bone, but strong resistance during the winter delayed their advance, and North Africa was not cleared of Axis troops until May 1943.   NRB

TORCY, JEAN-BAPTISTE DE COLBERT, Marquis de (1665–1746), French politician, son of Charles Colbert, Marquis de Croissy, nephew of Colbert, cousin of the Marquis de Seignelay, and son-in-law of Arnaud de Pomponne, whom he succeeded as secretary of state for foreign affairs (Sept. 1699), to become Louis XIV's last foreign minister (1699–1715). In 1680 Torcy entered the diplomatic service as his father's personal secretary and gained valuable experience on diplomatic missions to Portugal, Denmark, Hamburg, Berlin, Ratisbon, Vienna, Rome, Naples, and London. In 1689 he won a permanent place in the highest administrative circles when his father was granted the right of *survivance* on his secretaryship. In 1691–2 Torcy accompanied Louis XIV to the battlefields of the Netherlands as his personal secretary, and in 1698 took an important part in negotiating the partition treaty with William III. Yet in 1700, by which time he was sole minister in charge of foreign affairs, he advised Louis to accept the terms of Charles II of Spain's will, which ultimately led to France's involvement in the War of the Spanish Succession. He was sent by Louis to The Hague to negotiate the peace preliminaries of May 1709, and after these failed he skilfully directed the secret negotiations with the Tory government in Britain which led to the peace of Utrecht (1713).

TORDA, DIET OF (1567), meeting of the Transylvanian Diet which granted religious toleration to all sects, including the growing anti-trinitarian movement, to which Ferenc David, the leader of the Transylvanian Calvinists, and John Sigismund, Prince of Transylvania, had recently been converted.

TORDENSKJOLD, PEDER WESSEL, Baron (1691–1720), Norwegian sailor who fought against the Swedes, defeating them in 1715 at the battle of Dynekilen and, again, in 1719 off the coast of Baahuslen. His victories ended a long period of Swedish aggression against Norway and Denmark. He died in a duel.

TORDESILLAS, TREATY OF (1494), agreement reached under papal supervision which apportioned Atlantic exploration between Spain and Portugal. The dividing line, longitude 46° 37′ W, resulted in Portugal's securing Brazil (not yet discovered at that time) and gave Spain a claim to the rest of the Americas. The treaty, and its counterpart, that of Zaragossa (1529), established the principle of the Spanish and Portuguese monopolies of empire which the English, Dutch, and French were to challenge in the 16th and 17th cents.

TORGAU, BATTLE OF (3 Nov. 1760), Prussian victory against the Austrians under Count Daun, which gave Frederick II possession of Saxony during the Seven Years War. Although the Austrians occupied a strong position, Gen. Ziethen led the Prussian army to the heights of Torgau under cover of darkness and seized the Austrian batteries.

TORGAU, FORMULA OF (1576), statement of Lutheran doctrine compiled at a conference held at Torgau at the instigation of Augustus of Saxony, an amalgamation of the 11 articles of James Andreae's *Swabian Concord* (1574) and the *Formula of Maulbronn*, commissioned earlier in 1576 by Augustus. Largely the work of Melanchthon's followers, the Torgau formula was later abbreviated by Andreae into the *Epitome* of the *Formula of Concord*, which was published in German in 1580.

TORGAU ALLIANCE, league of the Protestant German princes of Hesse, Saxony, Prussia, Lüneburg, and the reformed cities of the empire, led by Duke John of Saxony and Philip of Hesse (1525) which opposed the enforcement of the Edict of Worms and won a decree of toleration at the Diet of Speyer (1526). Similar Protestant leagues were resurrected in 1551 and 1591 to counter the Catholic threat.

TORRE, MARTINO DELLA (d. 1264), Tyrant of Milan, leader of the popular party against the pro-German nobility, led by the archbishop, being elected 'Ancient of the People' in 1258. His family, as rulers of Como and Novara, helped the Milanese after their defeat by the Emperor Frederick II at Cortenuova (1237), and thus won great popularity. Torre's regime provided the model for later despotic rulers of Milan, among them, the Visconti.

TORRENS LAND SYSTEM in Australia, takes its name from Sir Robert Richard Torrens (1814–84), the South Australian, prime minister, who introduced (1857) a greatly simplified system for registering land transfers. It was adopted by all other Australian colonies and NZ in the 1860s and 1870s, and the system subsequently spread to North America and Britain, and also influenced various European and colonial communities.

TORRES, CAMILO (1766–1816), Colombian politician and federalist leader in the struggle for independence against Spain, and head of the new independent government (1815–16). Bolívar placed him in the presidency, but the Spanish troops reconquered most of the area the following year, captured Torres, and executed him.

TORRES, LUIS VAEZ DE (d. c. 1615), Spanish sailor, who discovered (1606) the channel which bears his name between the north of Australia and New Guinea.

TORRES RESTREPO, CAMILO (1929–66), Colombian priest and revolutionary, who became involved in the new social Catholicism while studying in Belgium. On returning to Colombia his views became increasingly radical and he joined Marxist guerrilla groups fighting in the countryside. He was killed by government forces.

TORRES VEDRAS, BATTLE OF (1810), Wellington's reply to Napoleon's massive invasion of Portugal during the Peninsular War. He staged a tactical withdrawal before Massena's forces, retreating to Lisbon behind the superbly fortified Torres Vedras lines. Lack of supplies forced the French to withdraw, enabling Wellington to take the offensive in 1811.

TORRICELLI, EVANGELISTA (1608–47), Italian physician and mathematician, amanuensis to Galileo (1641), who worked out the fundamental principles of hydro-mechanics and produced the first barometer (1643). He also improved the telescope and the microscope.

TORRINGTON, ARTHUR HERBERT, 3rd Earl of (1st of 2nd creation) (1647–1716), English sailor, who commanded in the Mediterranean (1680–3) and earned the favour of the Duke of York (later James II), but he refused to support James's proposal for the repeal of the Test Act and was dismissed from the office of master of the robes. He entered into the conspiracy to dethrone James and carried over the invitation (30 June 1688) to William of Orange to invade England. He commanded the invasion fleet, and after the Revolution was named first lord of the admiralty. He fought the battle of Bantry Bay and was created Earl of Torrington in 1689. In 1690 he refused to engage the French fully at Beachy Head and retired to the Thames. At a subsequent court-martial he was acquitted, after expounding the strategy of the 'fleet in being' to protect England from invasion.

TORRINGTON, GEORGE BYNG, 1st Viscount (1663–1733), British sailor, who fought at the battles of Beachy Head (1690), Malaga (1704), and Cape Passaro (1718). Squadrons under his command captured Gibraltar (1704) and scattered the invasion fleet of the Pretender off Scotland (1708). Byng started his career in the army, but transferred to the navy, becoming admiral of the fleet in 1718 and first lord of the admiralty (1727–33). He was created Viscount Torrington in 1721. His Whig inclinations greatly affected his career. Whenever the Tories were in power promotion came slowly and he was dismissed by a Tory government for suspected Hanoverian inclinations (1714). With the accession of George I his career again prospered.

TORSTENSON, LENNART (1603–51), Swedish soldier who, at the age of 15, was harness-bearer to Gustavus Adolphus, who sent him to study artillery in the Netherlands (1623) and gave him command of that arm in 1630. His health was ruined as a prisoner-of-war (1632–3), but in 1641–5 he returned to service as commander-in-chief in succession to Banér. His victories included the second battle of Breitenfeld (1644) and Jankau (1645). He invaded the Imperial Crown Lands on three occasions and in the Danish War he overran the whole of Jutland (1644).

TORTURE, USE OF, widely practised part of legal procedure against criminals in European countries, derived from Roman law and revived as a device to establish guilt in the later Middle Ages. It was condemned by the leaders of the 18th-cent. Enlightenment, *eg*, Montesquieu, Voltaire, and Beccaria, and had been abolished by the end of the 18th cent., *eg*, in the Emperor Joseph II's criminal code of 1787, though savage punishment of offenders continued throughout the 19th cent. In the 20th cent. totalitarianism brought the return of torture, primarily as an instrument used against political offenders.

TORY DEMOCRACY in Britain, slogan used by late-Victorian Tory politicians seeking a mass following. It seemed an imposture to Gladstone and Rosebery, who saw the Liberal Party as the working man's party, but the factory movement of the 1840s illustrates the traditionalist anti-Benthamite and anti-puritan affinities that existed between the Tory gentry and radical working men. Disraeli, J. E. Gorst, and Lord Randolph Churchill capitalized on this tradition, which was the basis of later 20th-cent. working-class support for the Conservative Party.

TORY PARTY in England, one of the parties in English politics from the late 17th cent. The original Tory Party developed in the Exclusion Crisis in the early 1680s, and the name became current at that time. Used pejoratively, Tory originally meant an Irish Catholic bandit. The Tories were the supporters of hereditary succession, the royal prerogative, divine right, and non-resistance. Above all, they were loyal to the privileges of the Church of England. Under James II the Tories had the choice of seeing a Catholic monarch gradually destroy the privileges of the Anglican Church or resisting and abandoning their theory of divine right and submission to the royal prerogative. The majority chose to defend their Church. Some refused to renounce James II and became Jacobites.

Though an equal partner with the Whigs in the 1688 Revolution, the Tories were greatly transformed by the experience, which left the party almost destitute of political theory. Most Tories accepted William III with reluctance. They could not transfer the old reverence for kingship to a foreign Calvinist. Consequently they drifted into opposition, the rank and file expressing hostility to the king's foreign policy, to the concessions to dissenters, to the expansion of the central administration, and to the creation of a system of public credit. They regarded themselves as defenders of the landed interest against the Whig moneyed interests. Socially, the great majority of the party were landed gentry and squires. They claimed that they were defending the interests of the nation against the court. Indeed, under William, the party struggle was not one of Tory against Whig, but 'Country' against 'Court'.

The Tory–Whig rivalry was renewed under Queen Anne. The succession problem had revived the positive aspects of Toryism. James II died (1701) and Anne, with a strong hereditary claim, succeeded the childless William (1702). The future equivocal attitude of the Tories to the Hanoverian succession, however, was to divide the party and to prove its undoing. Under Anne, the Tories objected to the French war, which involved foreign alliances and a heavy burden of taxation. They had to emphasize their religious principles to cover up their differences over the succession. As the natural Church party, the Tories could rely on the cry of 'the Church in danger' to rally support and damage their opponents.

Despite the support of Queen Anne and a natural majority in the nation, the Tory Party remained divided. First, the party since 1688 was based on a philosophy creating fundamental contradictions, and it was further divided over the succession, including both Jacobites and Hanoverians. Second, it lacked unified leadership. The prominent Tories disagreed as much as the rank and file. The older Tories grouped around Nottingham and Rochester faced the newer Tories around Harley and St John. While Nottingham was committed to Hanover, Harley and St John dabbled in Jacobite intrigues. Lastly, the Tory squires resisted party pressures whenever possible and the party lacked the strong organization of the Whigs.

The factious nature of the party proved disastrous in 1714. Despite the Tory majority in both houses of parliament, there was only one Tory minister (Nottingham) in George I's first ministry. The leading Tories were impeached after the Whig election victory in 1715, and the consequent flight of Bolingbroke (formerly St John) and Ormonde to the Pretender strengthened the smear of Jacobitism which was to keep individual Tories out of office for 30 years. By the mid-18th cent. the party as such no longer existed, and even the name Tory meant little when 'connection' was all-important in politics.

The name 'Tory', used to denote principles both practical and respectable, was revived by George Canning, a disciple of William Pitt the Younger. In the 1830s and 1840s the Tory Party was transformed by Sir Robert Peel into the Conservative Party.

K. Feiling, *A History of the Tory Party, 1640–1714* (Oxford, 1924).
G. Holmes, *British Politics in the Age of Anne* (London, 1967).
                                                                    CJ

TORY RADICALISM in England, ideas of certain Tories in the 1830s seeking to solve the 'condition of England' question, harness working-class disillusionment with the Great Reform Bill (1832) which had denied them the vote, and to counter-attack Whig reforms.

The Tory Radicals were a collection of sincere, erratic, often colourful individualists with no coherent philosophy or organization, except an uneasy resistance to 'progress' and a desire to help the working class, with whom they felt a natural sympathy. This was reflected in the crusade for Factory Reform launched by men like Richard Oastler and Michael Sadler, which won the support of the Tory Lord Shaftesbury. Oastler, steward to a Yorkshire landlord and a Tory by instinct and conviction, was an Evangelical, who had turned from the abolition of slavery in the empire to the cause of the white factory slaves in the North.

Tory Radicals bitterly opposed the utilitarian philosophy of Jeremy Bentham, with its centralizing administrative creed, which dominated the 1830s and 1840s. Their nostalgia, like Cobbett's, for a Golden Age of 'Altar, Throne and Cottage', rejected the harsh, impersonal New Poor Law and its 'efficiency', preferring the old, neighbourly system of poor relief. John Fielden, Tory MP for Oldham, who ruled his factories like a benevolent despot, fought a rearguard action against the introduction of the Registration of Births, Marriages, and Deaths Act (1836) into his village of Tod-morden, and kept out the union workhouse for a generation. Carlyle in his attack on 'Mammon worship' increased both Tory and working-class hostility to the Philistine newly rich middle class and their Whig allies in parliament.

Disraeli as a young politician, expressed some Tory Radical aims in his election manifestoes. The old Toryism was worn out. The new party must be a coalition between Tories and Radicals, willing to accept reforms like secret ballots, triennial parliaments, governmental economy, and improvement of living conditions. The general election (1841) in which the Whigs were beaten showed the value of the working-class support to the Tories, Lord Shaftesbury gaining much sympathy for the Factory Reform cause, and John Walter, Tory editor of *The Times*, wresting Nottingham from the Whigs with powerful Chartist help.

Tory Radicalism proved short-lived. The Tories once in power (1841–6) under Peel were hostile to violent Chartism and opposed to trade union progress; Shaftesbury achieved some reforms, but not a ten-hour day, from his party. Concern for the welfare of the people, acceptance of the use of state action as a factory legislation, and the extension of the vote continued and greatly shaped the ideas of Tory Democracy later promoted by Disraeli when he was prime minister.   JRA

TOSA, *han* (autonomous domain) of feudal Japan which played an important role in the Meiji Restoration. Tosa samurai founded the earliest Japanese political parties.

TŌSEIHA (lit. 'Control Faction'), important group of high-ranking officers in the pre-Second World War Japanese army. Its conflict in the early 1930s with the 'Imperial Way' Faction had important repercussions on Japanese politics. The *Tōseiha*'s main concerns, army mechanization, and an economy mobilized for war, were not fully achieved, however, until after the unsuccessful mutiny (26 Feb. 1936) in Tokyo, which discredited radicalism and traditionalism within the army and made politicians less inclined to resist *Tōseiha* demands, for fear of leadership passing into the hands of officers more hostile to the existing social and political order.

TOSTIG (d. 1066), younger brother of King Harold II of England, with whom he quarrelled in 1065. He encouraged Harold's enemies to invade England in 1066. Tostig landed in Yorkshire with the army of King Harald Hardrada of Norway. Harold II defeated and killed them both at Stamfordbridge (25 Sept. 1066), but during his campaign in Yorkshire William of Normandy was able to land unopposed in Sussex. Harold II returned south by forced marches but his exhausted and depleted army was destroyed by the Normans at Hastings.

'T'OTHERSIDERS', name given by established Western Australians to allegedly fly-by-night migrants from the eastern colonies, especially Vic., during the gold-rushes of the 1890s. To the 't'othersiders' the locals were conservative and unenterprising 'sandgropers'. With the passage of years both terms were heard less often, especially after many of the migrants of 1894–1903, approximately 125,000, had settled permanently in wheatbelt districts and other parts of the rapidly developing colony of WA, whose decision to enter the 1901 Commonwealth of Australia was appreciably influenced by 't'othersider' pressure.

TOTILA (d. 552), King of the Ostrogoths (*reg.* 541–52). After the death of Theodoric, Italy was torn with strife between a Roman and a Gothic party, which culminated in an invasion of Italy by a Byzantine army under Belisarius in 536. The Goths were successively defeated until Totila was elected king. He proved a formidable leader, driving the Byzantines from the mainland of Italy and even recovering Sardinia, Corsica, and parts of Sicily and Dalmatia by 550. A much larger Byzantine army under Narses defeated Totila, who was killed at Taginae. With his death the Gothic cause was lost in Italy.

TOULON, BATTLE OF (July 1707), joint amphibious and military attack during the War of the Spanish Succession by a combined Anglo-Dutch fleet under Sir Clowdisley Shovell and an army of Piedmontese and Austrians under Eugene and the Duke of Savoy. The allies sank eight French ships in the harbour and destroyed about 130 houses, though Marlborough's Grand Design to take the naval base failed.

TOULON, BATTLE OF (Feb. 1744), naval engagement off Toulon between a British blockading fleet commanded by Admiral Matthews and the combined Franco-Spanish fleets in the War of the Austrian Succession. The Bourbon fleets made for the shelter of Spanish ports and the battle was regarded in England as a national disgrace, for which Matthews and four captains were court-martialled and cashiered. Nevertheless, it ended Franco-Spanish co-operation in the Mediterranean.

TOULON EXPEDITION (1793), British naval expedition sent to reinforce the French royalists against the republicans' besieging force (29 Aug. 1793), made memorable by the first appearance of Napoleon as the latter's artillery commander. Invigorated by Danton's Committee of Public Safety, the French republican army, under Gen. Dugommier (1736–94), captured Toulon's land defences (18 Dec.) and the small British garrison under Lord Mulgrave withdrew in Admiral Hood's ships.

TOULON SCUTTLE (27 Nov. 1942), destruction of most of the French Mediterranean fleet during the Second World War after the German invasion of the unoccupied zone of France on 11 Nov. 1942. Under the armistice of 1940 Southern France and the French fleet had remained under the control of the Vichy government, but the Anglo-American invasion of North Africa on 8 Nov. prompted Hitler to alter this by force. After vain efforts by the French admiralty to negotiate the establishment of a neutral area, Admiral de Laborde ordered the scuttling. Of 225,000 tons of shipping, only 25,000 remained.

TOULOUSE, BATTLE OF (1814), culminating episode of the Peninsular War, when Wellington broke Soult's remaining forces in south-western France.

TOUNGOO DYNASTY of Burma, founded in 1531 by Tabinshweti. Until 1635 the capital was Pegu, and thereafter

Ava. Its most famous king was Bayinnaung. The dynasty was overthrown by Alaungpaya (1752).

TOURÉ, AHMED SÉKOU (1922–), Guinease politician and president of Guinea. He was active in organizing trade unions in French-speaking West Africa, became secretary of a posts-and-telegraphs union in 1945, and worked closely with the French trade union movement (CGT). As a founding member of the Rassemblement Démocratique Africain he became secretary of its Guinea branch, the Parti Démocratique de Guinée (PDG) in 1952, and emerged as one of the most effective nationalist leaders of the French-speaking colonies. In 1958 he became president of independent Guinea after the PDG, under his shrewd guidance, had secured a majority of votes for a negative response to President de Gaulle's offer of continued membership in a French-controlled community of states. Touré was able, even in the face of stiff French opposition, to uphold his country's new status. In the 1960s he steered the politics of Guinea into socialist paths of development, and maintained his own and the PDG's radical convictions.

TOURNAMENT, THE, originally a form of practice in the art of fighting as a knight. It was intended to give the knight proficiency and ease in the special circumstances of fighting on horseback in association with other knights charging in a close formation. The earliest recorded mentions of tournaments date from the middle of the 11th cent. and they appear to have evolved in France. With the elaboration of the chivalric code and the ideal of knighthood from the 12th cent. onwards, the tournament came to be less of a practical and and more of a social and sporting event. It developed into a series of single combats encompassed with elaborate rules. Being an occasion where there was a great concourse of nobility, tournaments were, especially in troubled times, suspect as giving cover to treasonable meetings. Thus the tournament was not always looked on with favour by kings and in England, for example, from the time of Richard I, was forbidden, except when specially licensed.

TOURNEFORT, JOSEPH PITTON DE (1656–1708), French systematic botanist, whose classificational method was superseded by that of Linnaeus. He is regarded as the father of the modern concept of the genus as the smallest practical unit of classification, with species as variants. His genera, accepted by later botanists, include, among many others, *Fagus* (Beech), *Salix* (Willow), and *Populus* (Poplar).

TOURS, CONGRESS OF (1920), congress of which the French socialist movement split into rival communist and socialist parties, permanently weakening the left. Like other socialist parties, the French SFIO had to decide whether to join the new Russian-led Communist International, which involved accepting the '21 conditions' laid down by the Bolsheviks. These conditions especially condemned 'reformism' and 'centrism', towards which there had always been strong leanings among French socialists. At Tours the partisans of adherence to the Third International were led by Marcel Cachin, the opponents by Léon Blum. The majority voted for adherence, and became the Communist Party. The minority (about one-third) retained the name SFIO, but the old party organization, including the newspaper *L'Humanité*, passed to the majority. A similar split followed at the Lille congress of the CGT trade union movement (1921).

TOUSSAINT L'OUVERTURE, PIERRE-DOMINIQUE (real name François Breda) (c. 1743–1803), Haitian revolutionary leader and national hero. As a slave Toussaint joined the uprising against the French, led by Jacques Vincent Ogé. In 1795 he reached an understanding with the French under which most of the island passed into his de facto control. Slavery was abolished and Toussaint helped the French to expel Spanish and British invading forces. His regime was troubled, however, by revolts. The mulattoes in the south

were defeated (1801), and Toussaint proclaimed the nation's independence. Napoleon I promptly sent a French expeditionary force to Haiti under Gen. Leclerc and with it went many of the mulatto leaders who, after opposing Toussaint, had taken refuge in France.

Leclerc captured Toussaint by a subterfuge (1802). He was sent to prison in France, where he died the following year. Leclerc's expedition was gradually defeated by yellow fever and black guerillas. It was finally expelled by Jean Jacques Dessalines in 1803, and Haiti's independence was proclaimed on 1 Jan. 1804.

Toussaint's deeds and personality inspired many poets and novelists in Europe and America.

TOWNSHEND OF RAYNHAM, GEORGE TOWNSHEND, 1st Marquis of (1724–1807), British politician, who supported the Elder Pitt and the Grenvilles, and then Bute. As lord lieutenant of Ireland (1767–72) he obtained various concessions, including limitations on the duration of the Irish parliament, security of tenure for Irish judges, and the introduction of *habeas corpus*. He later served Lord North as master-general of the ordnance (1772–82).

TOWNSHEND, CHARLES (1725–67), British politician, whose fiscal policy contributed to the revolt of the American colonists. He was lord of the admiralty (1754), secretary for war (1761), and president of the board of trade (1763). He resigned in opposition to Grenville, but resumed office as paymaster of the forces (1765–6) and became chancellor of the exchequer and leader of the Commons under Chatham (1766–7). By imposing duties on lead, glass, paper, painter's colours, and tea imported into America from Britain, Townshend sought to raise sorely needed revenue under the guise of regulating trade, the colonists having repudiated the British right to impose direct taxation, as defined by the Stamp Act (1765).

TOWTON, BATTLE OF (29 March 1461), most savage battle of the Wars of the Roses. It assured the retention of the English throne by Edward IV and drove Margaret of Anjou and her son Edward into exile.

TOYNBEE, ARNOLD (1852–83), British social reformer and economist, whose work among the poor in the East End of London was commemorated by the opening of Toynbee Hall (1884), the first important university settlement. His pioneering book, *The Industrial Revolution of the eighteenth century in England* (1884), based on his lectures to working-class audiences, gave currency to the term 'industrial revolution'.

TOYNBEE, ARNOLD (1889–), British scholar, whose classical background and study of international relations he combined in an attempt to develop a new theory of history and civilization. During both World Wars he was actively involved both in Near- and Middle-Eastern policy in intelligence work and at the foreign office.

In 1919 he was appointed professor of Byzantine history and modern Greek language and literature at London University and later was director of studies at the Royal Institute of International Affairs (1925–55). He contributed and supervised the writing of many of the annual *Surveys of International Affairs*, and also wrote prolifically on the Near and Middle East, on Greek civilization, on travel, and on religion.

He is best known for his huge *A Study of History*, the first volume of which appeared in 1934 and the last in 1961. This is essentially an old-fashioned piece of historical writing in which Toynbee is looking for recurring patterns in historical development and of constant and repeating forces in the rise and fall of civilizations. He has posited several theories to explain these patterns.

Though *A Study of History* has received much popular praise, it has been less well received by professional historians, who argue that the only civilization meeting Toynbee's pattern is the Graeco-Roman and who suggest that much of the rest of the *Study* is more than commonly informed by personal values and prejudices.

TOZAMA, name meaning 'outside the group', applied to those *daimyōs* in Tokugawa Japan who were neither retainers of the Tokugawa house before 1600 nor descendants of Ieyasu.

TRACTATUS THEOLOGICO-POLITICUS, one of the major works of the political philosopher Baruch Spinoza, published in Holland in 1670, in which he set out his views of the state, championing the concept of direct democracy and freedom in the famous phrase, 'the true purpose of the state is liberty'.

TRACY, ALEXANDRE DE PROUVILLE, Marquis de (1602–1670), French soldier, who was lieutenant-general of the French territories in North America (1663–7). He was responsible for a decisive campaign against Iroquois tribes which forced the Indians to make peace with the French (1666–7).

TRADE, ACT FOR THE ENCOURAGEMENT OF (1663), in Britain, legislative measure which enacted that European goods for English plantations must be shipped in England and in English ships. It supplemented the Navigation Act of 1660, which did not prevent direct trade between the plantations and European ports in colonial ships.

TRADE AGREEMENTS ACT (1934) in the US, legislation introducing a reciprocal trade policy that formed the cornerstone of the tariff liberalization programme of the secretary of state, Cordell Hull. Under the act the president of the US was authorized to lower tariffs by up to 50 per cent through executive agreement with foreign nations. Bilateral agreements under the act were subject to the 'most-favoured-nation' principle, and so came to have multi-lateral effects. The principles of the act were renewed in subsequent legislation.

'TRADE DIVERSION POLICY', THE AUSTRALIAN (1936), major blunder by A. J. Lyons's government in attempting to offset its failure to increase Australia's exports to Japan and the US. By imposing quotas and tariff restrictions on imports from these countries it was hoped to 'divert' imports to better export customers, notably in Britain. Hostile reactions overseas and domestic criticism brought about a rapid reversal of the policy. Its adverse effects were soon minimized as political considerations came to dominate Australia's relations with both the US and Japan.

TRADE UNIONISM. The urge for wage-earners to form trade unions, those 'continuous associations for the purpose of maintaining or improving the conditions of their working lives', in the classical definition of Sidney and Beatrice Webb, is a characteristic feature of modern industrial society. Trade unionism had its origins in Britain, not, as was once claimed, in the medieval craft gilds, but in 18th- and in some cases 17th-cent. combinations of journeymen designed, even before the growth of factory trades, to preserve craft skills, to raise wages, and to improve working conditions. It grew into a movement of political and social significance in the climate of the Industrial Revolution and, after repression in the earlier part of the 19th cent., achieved a measure of legal and social acceptance in the 1870s, by which time it had also begun to develop in the continent of Europe, and particularly in Germany. Today (1970) the labour force in Britain is some 40 per cent organized into trade unions, and greater or lesser degrees of organization are to be found in other countries.

During the past quarter of a century trade unionism has spread from manual to white-collar workers, and in the same period a gap has grown up between the social democratic trade unions of the West and the state-dominated trade unions of the Soviet bloc, symbolized by the breakaway of the former from the communist-dominated World Federation of Trade Unions and the foundation of the International Confederation of Free Trade Unions in 1949. This break has not, however, prevented such liaison as is possible through a common association in the International Labour Organization, founded in 1919 as a tripartite government, employer, trade union body to improve international labour standards. Western trade unions, while to a greater or lesser degree Marxist in inspiration (and least of all so in Britain and Canada), have generally evolved through the regulation of wages and condition by collective bargaining. Following the United States pattern, this has involved, in the case of Canada, a degree of political disengagement and a role as an 'institution against industry'. In Western Europe the tendency has been for trade unions, while pursuing their bargaining role, to be increasingly institutionalized and accepted as part of the framework of a pluralistic social and political system. In such situations trade unions have come to accept the fact of a large measure of private ownership of capital, while it has been in turn accepted by other institutions that they may properly seek, whether by direct negotiation or by relationships with political parties, to affect changes in income distribution and social provisions offered by the state.

In most countries tensions between governments and trade unions have tended to grow in the 1960s. It is too early in 1970 to say whether the era of Western type 'consensus' trade unionism is over, but there are signs that the aims of trade unions and governments have begun to diverge. At the centre of differences is the issue of inflation and the role played by wage demands in raising price levels; associated with this is the question of productivity and the desire of strong trade unions to regulate the supply of labour in the interests of their members. In Britain the character of trade unionism changed during the 1960s as its leadership appeared to act less as a group involved in the development and application of public policy as a collection of individuals primarily concerned to pursue the sectional interests of their rank-and-file members. The apparent shift in collective bargaining from national or industry-wide level to shop floor negotiation associated with this change of attitude was noted by the Donovan *Royal Commission on Trade Unions and Employers' Associations* which reported in 1968, and given as the reason for stoppages and disorder in some British factories. The commission recommended strengthened machinery for the reform of voluntary collective bargaining arrangements, particularly at company and plant levels. At the same time the Conservative Party, in a policy statement entitled *Fair Deal at Work*, advocated a more unorthodox approach to the situation in the form of a legal framework for British industrial relations having some resemblance to that developed in the United States of America which was immediately taken up by the advent of the Heath administration to office in 1970. This has exacerbated the already existing conflicts between government and trade unions in Britain, since the latter have declared themselves wholly opposed to this approach to industrial relations problems and declared their unwillingness to co-operate in pursuing it.   AM

TRADE UNIONISM IN THE UNITED STATES. The first labour union to be formed was that of the Journeymen Shoemakers (1792). After 1833 the rising prosperity of the northeast and the industrialization of this area caused an increase in the growth of Labour organizations. Trades unions, that is federations of all the organized trades in a single community, were formed in 12 northern cities. In 1837 these sent delegates to organize a National Trades' Union. However, the panic of 1837 destroyed this early growth, and the subsequent years of hardship tended to encourage the growth of co-operatives following the line of Robert Owen's experiment. Unions tended to be restricted to the area within municipal boundaries. After the Civil War the development of a national economy made this local organization out of date, and national craft unions of skilled workers became increasingly popular. By 1870 there were 30 such unions with a total membership of over 290,000.

In 1869 a new organization arose, the Noble Order of Knights of Labor. This organization accepted all workers regardless of race or sex, and by 1889 it numbered over 1 million. Because the Knights refused to distinguish between the skilled and the unskilled, it became an organization of the unskilled, for skilled craftsmen were reluctant to join. The Knights advocated a system of worker-owned factories to end the division between worker and employer, and they campaigned for an eight-hour day, arbitration instead of strikes, and government ownership of railroads, telephones, and telegraphs. Their own internal dissensions destroyed them after they had lost public confidence as a result of the bomb explosion in Chicago in 1886 at one of their protest meetings. The Knights were not responsible, but the public became suspicious of all radical movements.

In their place grew up the American Federation of Labor (AF of L), founded in 1881, an organization of craft unions. The AF of L concentrated on improving its members' wages and conditions of work by peaceful means, and what it achieved was as much the result of organizational skill as of any other factor. By 1904 it had 1,676,000 members. However, the AF of L did not include unskilled workers.

In the early 20th cent. there was increasing industrial unrest and violence. These troubles militated against the unions, who lost much public sympathy. This was a misfortune, for in President Theodore Roosevelt these had had their first friend in the White House, who was prepared to use the power of the federal government to achieve parity between management and unions. Fear of the growing power of the unions led in 1902 to the formation of the National Association of Manufacturers whose aim was the destruction of unions. It was partially successful, for by 1909 membership of the AF of L was down to $\frac{1}{4}$ million.

Mention must be made of the Industrial Workers of the World—the IWW, formed in 1905. This was an extreme left-wing orgnization advocating the use of violence and class war to achieve its aim, which was to seize control of industry. The IWW virtually disappeared in 1920 after the Palmer Raids of 1919 directed against Bolsheviks.

The presidency of Wilson saw some improvement in labour conditions, while the AF of L believed in the use of political action to improve conditions of labour they refused to form a Labor Party. American unions prefer to avoid any close association with either party, but tend to find themselves more in sympathy with the Democratic Party than with the Republican.

The years of the New Deal saw two important changes—the passage of the Wagner Act (1935) and the Fair Labor Standards Act (1938) together with the emergence of the Congress of Industrial Organization (CIO).

New Deal legislation, in the form of the National Recovery Act (NRA), had set up a National Labor Relations Board to deal with disputes arising from the NRA. Then the Supreme Court declared the NRA invalid, the Wagner Act set up an independent National Labor Relations Board to deal with unfair practices. The Fair Labor Standards Act (1938) put 'a ceiling over hours and a floor under wages', providing for a maximum working week of 40 hours and a minimum wage of 40 cents an hour. It also virtually eliminated child labour.

The CIO was a large-scale break-away from the AF of L by workers who felt that the latter was too timid and conservative. Under the leadership of John L. Lewis of the United Mine Workers, the CIO returned to the Knights of Labor's policy of industrial unions, and succeeded in establishing unionism in the steel, motor car, and textile industries which had hitherto resisted it. To establish closed shops, the CIO adopted a policy of sit-ins. These led to violence in 1937 and 1938, which lost the CIO much public support.

During the Second World War the unions made, and kept, a no-strike pledge, but after the war strikes took place of

sufficient seriousness for the federal government to take over the mines.

In 1947 the Taft–Hartley Act was passed. This outlawed closed shops, provided for a 60-day cooling-off period, and an 80-day injuction against strikes that might endanger national health or safety.

In 1959 Congress passed a Labor Act setting up codes of practice for labour, and provided for federal supervision of the internal affairs of unions.

In 1955 the AF of L and the CIO merged, their joint membership being 17 million; 25 per cent of the labour force, but over 50 per cent of 'blue-collar' workers.   JCB

TRADES UNION ACT (1913) in Britain, legislative measure which permitted trade unions to raise contributions from their members for political purposes provided they kept their political fund separate from their other funds. Union members were allowed to contract out of paying the political levy by making a written statement. Such levies could only be established after a favourable ballot of members. The act was passed in some measure in return for Labour support for Lloyd George's National Insurance Bill and it helped to restore Labour Party finances, even though trade union leaders resented some of its restrictions.

TRADES UNION ACT (1927) in Britain, legislative measure which reversed the provision of the Trades Union Act (1913) allowing trade unions to set up a political fund from which those opposed to it could contract out of payment. The 1927 act substituted the principle of contracting in by those who wished to pay (a position again reversed in 1946). In addition, it banned trade unions among established civil servants.

The 1927 act was an outcome of the General Strike (1926) and, while it weakened the finances of the Labour Party, it strengthened the links between the party and the trade unions.

TRADES UNION ACT (1946) in Britain, legislative measure which repealed the *Trades Union Act* (1927). The act restored the position established by the measures of 1906 and 1913, and boosted Labour Party funds by allowing 'contracting out' of the trade union political levy in place of 'contracting in.'

TRADES UNION AND DISPUTES ACT (1906) in Britain, legislative measure made necessary by the decision of the House of Lords in 1901 in the Taff Vale case, which laid the funds of a trade union open to civil damages for the acts of its officials, in this case for the loss caused to a railway company by a strike. The decision meant that no union could afford to organize a strike, and drove the trade union movement to take an active part in politics. The result was a sharp rise in Labour representation in parliament in the 1906 election. The price of Labour support for the Liberal government was seen to be social reform and the restoring to trade unions of the right to an effective strike. The act gave the trade unions in law the immunity from civil actions for damages that they had had in practice before 1901.

TRADES UNION CONGRESS in Britain, founded in 1868 and accepted in the late 19th cent. as the central authority for labour policy. The first congress was held in Manchester in 1868, having been summoned by the local Trades' Council, and larger congresses, at Birmingham in 1869 and in London in 1871, followed. Impending legislation by the Liberal government gave point to the 1871 meeting, and the congress appointed a Parliamentary Committee to watch events in parliament. From that time the TUC was chiefly concerned with legislation, like other contemporary pressure groups. It avoided direct intervention in trade disputes, and was not strongly concerned with independent labour representation, though it supported the Labour Representation Committee of 1900. Nor was it much concerned with the internal affairs of the movement, such as the relationship between rival unions, or the relative merits of different forms of wage structure. In policy, it was dominated by the largest unions. In 1921 the TUC was reconstituted, the General Council, assisted by a paid secretariat, replacing the old Parliamentary Committee.

The first Labour government of 1924 paid little attention to the TUC and its demands for a high employment level and adequate wages. Two years later the General Strike collapsed when the Miners' Federation refused to accept the ultimate authority of the TUC General Council, which thereupon called off the strike, leaving the miners to fight alone. Ensuing Conservative legislation; the enforcement of the 'contracting in' system; the dissociation of the civil service unions from the TUC; and the declaring of general strikes to be illegal, seriously damaged the movement.

Throughout the economic difficulties and rearmament debates of the 1930s lip-service was paid to TUC ideas for stronger government action. Massive union demonstrations and lobbyings were organized to focus attention on the poverty of the workers, but it was not until Ernest Bevin became minister of labour in Churchill's ministry in 1940 that the TUC had an active voice in government.

In the 1945 general election, 120 trade union-sponsored candidates were elected and the TUC played an important advisory role in the Labour government's nationalization and health service schemes. Throughout the 1950s and 1960s new legislation relating to contracts of employment, retraining schemes, and redundancy payments were all subjected to close TUC scrutiny before presentation to parliament.

By 1968, its centenary, 163 unions were affiliated to the TUC, which was increasingly attracting white-collar workers. Bitter clashes, however, divided the TUC from Wilson's government, and prices and incomes policies and trade union reform became very delicate issues. These quarrels continued when Heath's government in 1970 introduced the Industrial Relations Bill.   MB
                                                            MEB

TRADES UNIONS IN NEW ZEALAND began among skilled workers, an 1878 act giving them legal status. The first union congress met in 1885, but depression checked unions' growth. 'New unionism', launched in 1889, was destroyed in the 1890 maritime strike. W. P. Reeve's Arbitration Act (1894) revived labour organization, registered unionists numbering 23,000 in 1901. By 1908 Australian militants were denouncing arbitration, thus causing a moderate–militant split. The 1912–13 strikes ended in the militants' defeat, and in restriction of strike action (1913). Post-war depression brought union membership to low levels (71,000 in 1933), but revived confidence in arbitration. The Labour government's 'compulsory unionism' (1936) quickly raised the total to 254,000 (1939). Post-war inflation renewed the moderate-militant split, but the 1951 waterfront strike brought further curbs on militancy. In 1961 the National government introduced 'voluntary' unionism, but this made little significant change. In 1966 unionists numbered 366,000; the union average was 973.

TRADESCANT, JOHN (d. *c.* 1637), English traveller, naturalist, and gardener to King Charles I of England and Queen Henrietta Maria. He established a physic garden and museum, the contents of which formed the basis of the Ashmolean Museum at Oxford. His son, John Tradescant (1608–62), collected plants from North America and is credited with introducing many species, including Lilac, False-acacia, and Occidental plane, to Britain. Father and son are commemorated in the common genus *Tradescantia*.

TRAFALGAR, BATTLE OF (21 Oct. 1805), fought off the south-west coast of Spain during the French Wars. The battle had been preceded by a British pursuit of the French across the Atlantic to the West Indies. The French intention had been to draw off British shipping from the English Channel to make a military invasion of Britain possible. In the event, the invasion plan was called off. The fleets which had crossed the Atlantic both ways in the summer met in Oct. Nelson, in command of the British, implemented his plan to divide Villeneuve's French fleet by cutting through its line. The battle was brief but fierce, ships interlocked by their rigging engaging in close combat. Nelson was mortally wounded on his flagship, *Victory*, and his death marred a victory which secured British control of the seas and contributed to the ultimate fall of Napoleon—though armies, rather than navies, were to be the essential instrument of this.

TRAJAN (M. Ulpius Traianus) (AD 53–117), Roman Emperor (*reg.* 98–117), who was born at Italica in southern Spain and had a distinguished military career under Domitian. In 97, when governor of Upper Germany, he was adopted by the elderly emperor Nerva, whom he succeeded shortly afterwards. Above all a soldier, Trajan made the first major attempts to expand the Roman empire since Claudius' invasion of Britain. Dacia was annexed in two campaigns (101–2, 105–6), and proved of some strategic and economic benefit to the empire, but his attempt (113–17) to annex Armenia and Mesopotamia failed after initial successes. His provincial administration was equitable and paternalist in tone. In Italy he developed the *alimenta* scheme to increase the population. Substantial public works were undertaken in various regions, particularly in Rome, where Trajan's Forum was the most notable. He was popular with all sections of the community and later generations agreed with the title *Optimus Princeps* (Best of Emperors) conferred on him in his own lifetime.

TRAJAN'S COLUMN, monument in Rome, erected to celebrate the Emperor Trajan's conquest of Dacia (AD 106). It is 38 metres high and decorated with a spiral relief depicting the Dacian campaigns, probably on the basis of Trajan's own account.

TRAMWAYS (OUTRAMWAYS), first developed in Britain, by James Outram (1776), when, as adviser to the Duke of Norfolk's colliery at Sheffield, he laid L-shaped cast-iron rails spiked to cross sleepers. Tramways were used for cheap public transport in the US from New York to Harlem (1832) and in Britain at Birkenhead (1860). At first trams were drawn by horse and then by cable, but Henry Pinkus in the US pioneered traction by electricity (1840), and George Green patented the dynamo method (1891), which was cheaper and more reliable. The Tramways Act (1870) placed the building of tramways in Britain, for which confirmation by act of parliament was needed, under the control of the board of trade. Trams remained a cheap form of transport in the 20th cent. As late as 1948 a $\frac{1}{2}$d fare was charged in Dundee, Scotland. Nevertheless, laid tracks proved inconvenient in the face of increasing traffic. By 1970 trams had almost disappeared although they were still retained in some European cities, *eg*, Copenhagen.

TRAN DYNASTY, reigning dynasty of Viet-nam (1225–1400). The Tran family rose to power early in the 13th cent., and in 1225 was strong enough to depose the previous dynasty, the Ly. The leading figure in this coup, Tran Thu Do (1194–1264), did not seize the throne for himself, but installed his infant nephew as emperor, himself acting as regent. His example was followed by subsequent generations, and for a time it became standard practice for the Tran emperor to abdicate in his prime and hand the throne to his heir, in order to ensure a smooth succession. It was only in the later 14th cent., when this practice declined, that the Tran clan began to lose authority to court factions. The more powerful monarchs of the dynasty were responsible for institutional reforms to strengthen the kingdom and its resources. In the period 1281–8 its strength was tested by attacks from China, which were successfully resisted under the leadership of Tran Hung Dao: once again, the Vietnamese agreed to send tribute, but prevented the imposition of direct rule from China. The 14th cent. saw a renewal of conflict with Champa, especially after a succession dispute in Viet-nam in 1369 as a result of which one of the parties sought Cham aid. The Chams made a series of attacks (1371–84) on Viet-nam, and Hanoi was sacked by them on three occasions. The Viet-namese recovery was led by Ho Quy Ly, whose power increased from about 1389, until in 1400 he was strong enough to depose the Tran and establish a short-lived dynasty of his own. It was ostensibly in order to restore the Tran that the Chinese invaded Tongking in 1407, but after conquering it the Ming imposed direct provincial government on the Viet-namese. Following the eventual defeat of the Chinese in 1427, a Tran prince was briefly restored to the throne, only to be deposed to make way for the Le dynasty. The Tran period, like that which preceded it, was more Buddhist than Confucian, and several Tran emperors were patrons of the 'Bamboo Forest' sect. During the 14th cent., however, Confucianism gained in strength, and the number and importance of Confucian scholars at court increased.   RBS

TRAN HUNG DAO (d. 1300), Viet-namese soldier, a relative of the imperial clan, who emerged as commander-in-chief of Dai-Viet in 1283, after the first invasion by armies of Khublai Khan. Despite some success, the Chinese were forced to retreat, and further invasions in 1284–5 and 1287–8 were likewise defeated. Tran Hung Dao's most famous victory was at Bach-Dang in 1288. After his death a cult was founded in his honour, which became one of the most important elements in the popular religion of Tongking.

TRANSCASPIAN RAILROAD, from Krasnovodsk to Tashkent, begun (1880) in connection with the Russian campaign against the Turkomans and subsequently extended to the Oxus (1885–6), Samarkand (1888), and finally Tashkent (1898), the major part of the work being directed by M. N. Annenkov. The railroad was of great importance in the economic development of Turkestan, although it was later partially superseded by the Tashkent–Orenburg Line (1900–1906) and the Turk–Sib (1930).

TRANSCAUCASIAN REPUBLIC, independent democratic federative republic of Transcaucasia, proclaimed (22 April 1918), with Nikolai Chkheidze as president and Akakii Chkhenkeli as prime minister. The republic broke up (26 May 1918) under Ottoman pressure, when Georgia declared its independence with German protection, leaving the other constituent parts (Armenia and Azerbayjan) to form themselves also into independent republics.

TRANSCENDENTALISM in the US, term usually applied to the central beliefs of the members of the Transcendental Club (c. 1836–60), focused on Emerson's house in Concord, MA. Originally called the 'Hedge Club', its first meetings were held to coincide with the visits of Frederic Henry Hedge (1805–90), an authority on German culture. Its members, who held open forums on a variety of religious, philosophical, and literary subjects, were strongly influenced by German transcendental philosophy, especially that of Kant. Thus they became known as the Transcendentalists and, in addition to Emerson and Hedge, included such other New England intellectuals as Thoreau, Margaret Fuller (1810–50), Amos Bronson Alcott (1799–1888), William Ellery Channing (1818–1901), Theodore Parker (1810–60), George Ripley (1802–80), Jones Very (1813–80), and Elizabeth Peabody (1804–94). Characterized by their eclectic tastes and willingness to discuss any new ideas, the Transcendentalists were also influenced, in varying degrees, by Swedenborg, Carlyle, the Cambridge Platonists, Coleridge, and other English Romantic poets, and by the *Bhagavad Gita* and the *Upanishads*. Transcendentalism can thus be seen more accurately as an attitude of mind than as a conscious philosophical or literary movement. Central to all its exponents, however, is an emphasis on Man's innate divinity, and on his individual worth, a fervent belief in the superiority of intuitive to sensory perception, and an optimistic faith—arising from the Unitarian background of many of the group—in Man's ultimate perfectibility. Therefore, while Thoreau and Emerson stress the Transcendentalist's primary emphasis on individual fulfilment and self-improvement, much consideration was also given to the possibilities of reform through social action and many of the group were deeply involved in contemporary reform movements, especially the cause of anti-slavery. With others, Ripley established Brook Farm (1841–7), a utopian settlement in the Boston suburb of West Roxbury, and Alcott initiated a similar, but less successful, community at Fruitlands (1843). Alcott, who was committed to improving education, also founded an experimental school in Philadelphia (1830–4), described in *Record of a School* (1835), and the famous Temple school, run on Pestolozzian principles of child-centred education. Although frequently castigated by his contemporaries, he had considerable influence on the development of progressive education. Finding it difficult to place their work in existing magazines, the Transcendentalists founded *The Dial* (1840–4), which remains the best source for the writings of the lesser-known members. Its first editor, Margaret Fuller, an ardent feminist, and author of *Woman in the Nineteenth Century* (1845), was succeeded by Emerson in 1842, who made it a coherent organ of the movement. Although geographically limited to Concord, Transcendentalism was a major intellectual force, and an important influence on such writers as Whitman, Melville, Hawthorne, and Emily Dickinson. Its finest expression is found in Thoreau's *Walden*, and in the essays of Emerson.

Harold C. Goddard, *Studies in New England Transcendentalism* (New York, 1960).
Perry Miller, *The American Transcendentalists* (New York, 1957).   EFAL

TRANSJORDAN, CREATION OF. Until 1923 Transjordan was never a separate political entity. Although made part of the British mandated area (1920), it was not incorporated with the Palestine administration. In Nov. 1920 Abdullah ibn Husayn (1880–1951) arrived in Ma'an (then part of the kingdom of the Hijaz), ostensibly en route to the aid of his brother, Feisal, against France. Abdullah entered Amman (2 March 1921) and (29 March) agreed with Winston Churchill, the British colonial secretary, to establish a government in Transjordan, having abandoned his wider ambitions. British advisers and a subsidy were supplied and the arrangement was formalized in the Anglo-Transjordan agreement (April 1923), by which Britain recognized the authority of the amirate.

TRANSPORTATION, CONVICTS, to Australia. During the 80 years following the foundation of NSW in 1788 as a penal settlement, Australian colonies received about 137,000 male and 25,000 female prisoners. After c. 1820 most convicts were 'assigned' to work for private employers, who became responsible for their food and shelter. Their masters could report them to the magistrates for summary punishment, and persistent misbehaviour might result in a return to government service.

'Government men' were employed on public works, especially road building. Up till 1820 many were so employed on their arrival; thereafter, most of those doing so were 'under punishment'. After 1826 they were sometimes sentenced to work in chains, or as a more severe punishment would be sent to a penal settlement, such as Norfolk Island, Moreton Bay (Brisbane), or Port Arthur in Van Diemen's Land (Tas.).

The British government objected to the cost of maintaining those who were not assigned; on the other hand, it often argued that assigned service, though economical, was an insufficient punishment. For this reason it would have liked to work all the men in gangs for a time after their arrival; it planned to do this by the 'probation system', introduced into Van Diemen's Land in 1842, but this proved more costly than had been expected and broke down because of the large numbers sent to the colony and the difficulty of supervising the probation gangs.

Up to this time transportation had been an important factor in the British penal code, and about one-fifth of those convicted at assizes were transported. These were nearly all common prisoners, the number of 'politicals' being only about 1000.

Although more expensive than expected, transportation represented, in the form of open confinement, an interesting experiment in penology. As a deterrent, the lot of the assigned convict was far more irksome than was believed in Britain, but ignorance of Australian conditions, and difficulties in administration, weakened the faith of the British authorities in its efficacy. In the end, the expensive failure of the probation system and the building of penitentiaries at home caused the British government to abandon transportation in 1852, except for sending long-term prisoners to WA. Largely because of economic depression, this colony had asked for convicts in 1850 and by 1868 had nearly 10,000 men usefully employed on public works.

By 1850 the system had become very unpopular in the eastern Australian colonies. Convicts had undoubtedly helped economic development at first, for they supplied cheap labour and a market for colonial produce, while expenditure by the British government was an important 'invisible export'. But the morally lowering influence of convicts aroused great concern among the free population; rivalry between 'emancipists' and 'exclusives' hindered political and social development, and before 1850 escaped convicts often became bushrangers.

L. L. Robson, *The Convict Settlers of Australia* (Melbourne, 1965).
A. G. L. Shaw, *Convicts and the Colonies* (London, 1966).
                                                                AGLS

TRANS-SIBERIAN RAILWAY, built 1891–1904. It originally reached Vladivostok via Manchuria, a line wholly in Russian territory being completed only in 1916. It greatly facilitated the economic development and colonization of Siberia.

TRANSUBSTANTIATION, Catholic doctrine that the whole substance of the bread and wine are changed at the act of consecration into the whole substance of the Body and Blood of Christ, only the external appearance or 'accidents' of the bread and wine remaining. The doctrine was defined as a matter of faith by the Lateran Council of 1215, confirmed by the Council of Trent during the 16th cent., and became one of the fundamental and irreconcilable differences between the Catholic and Protestant Churches.

TRANSVAAL, province of South Africa. Much of the Transvaal was settled by Khoikhoi and Bantu-speaking peoples from at least the 10th cent. AD. In the 1820s it was invaded by the Ndbele of Mzilikazi, and in the late 1830s by white farmers trekking up from the Cape Colony. In 1837 the whites defeated the Ndbele, who withdrew north of the Limpopo. The white Afrikaners (Boers) were formally granted their independence by Britain in 1852. The British occupied the Transvaal from Natal in 1877, but retreated after a minor defeat at Majuba (1881). The independence of the South African republic was ensured by the Pretoria (1881) and London (1884) conventions. If Britain had realized the huge mineral resources of the Transvaal, a greater effort might have been put into retaining control of the territory. As it was, gold was discovered on the Witwatersrand in 1886.

This discovery changed the history of the whole of South Africa: the Transvaal became the economic heart of the subcontinent. Non-Afrikaans-speaking whites flocked to the Rand, as did large numbers of Africans, without whose cheap labour the low-grade gold ore could never have been exploited. Kruger's treatment of the 'foreign' whites, the Uitlanders, was used by Britain as a pretext for waging the

Anglo-Boer War (1899–1902). Large areas of the Transvaal were devastated by British forces before the war came to an end with the peace treaty of Vereeniging. The territory became a Crown colony, and in 1906 was granted self-government, under Louis Botha's Het Volk ministry. In 1910 the Transvaal joined the Union of South Africa, the constitution of which was largely the work of Smuts, Botha's right-hand man. Botha became prime minister of the new Union. The Transvaal, one of the four provinces, continued to dominate 20th-cent. South Africa, politically and economically.
                                                                AEA

TRANSYLVANIA COMPANY, name adopted in 1774 by Richard Henderson's Louisa Co. of American land speculators and under which it acquired (1775) from the Cherokee Indians the territory subsequently known as KY. The company sponsored settlement and much pioneering work, but its petition for sovereignty over the 'Transylvania Colony' was rejected by the Continental Congress (1778), the issue being finally settled when KY became a state (1792).

TRASIMENE, LAKE, BATTLE OF (217 BC), in central Italy in the Second Punic War. It was a Roman disaster in which two legions under Flaminius were ambushed and massacred by Hannibal. In the ensuing crisis the Romans appointed Q. Fabius Maximus dictator, but none of their allies went over to Hannibal.

TRAVENDAL, TREATY OF (1700), removed Denmark-Norway from the first coalition against Charles XII of Sweden. The signatories were Frederick IV and Sweden's ally, the Duke of Holstein-Gottorp, to whom the Danish king promised the evacuation of his territory and concession of the disputed *jus armorum*. As Frederick also undertook not to act 'like an enemy' towards Sweden, Britain and the Netherlands as guarantors of the treaty, used the presence of their fleets to induce Charles XII to evacuate Zealand.

TRAVERSE DES SIOUX, TREATY OF (23 July 1851), negotiated between the US government and the Sisseton and Wahpeton bands of the Sioux Indians. In return for land in southern MN, northern IA, and eastern SD, the US agreed to pay $40,000 cash and $68,000 annually for 50 years. The non-fufilment of this treaty was a cause of the Sioux War of 1862.

TREASONABLE PRACTICES ACT (1795) in Britain, legislative measure which extended the law of treason to cover writing, printing, speaking, or preaching in such a way as to encourage hatred or contempt of the king or constitution. With the Seditious Meetings Act of the same year it gave a powerful weapon to the Younger Pitt's administration in its attack on Jacobinism at home, in the years following the French Revolution.

TREASURE FLEETS, convoys of Spanish ships which in the 16th–17th cents sailed from Seville or Cadiz to bring to Europe the gold and silver bullion mined in the Spanish New World colonies. By the 1560s this transatlantic trade had been organized into two convoys a year. The *flota* sailed to Veracruz in the Gulf of Mexico in April or May and the *galleones* left Spain in August for the Caribbean ports of Nombre de Dios and Cartagena. After wintering in America, the two fleets united at Havana in March for the return voyage to Spain, the convoy system acting as a protection against the attacks of Dutch, French, or English privateers.

TREASURY, THE, in England, department of government responsible for economic policy and co-ordination, the control of public expenditure, and for the efficient running of the civil service. The chancellor of the exchequer is the political head, though the prime minister is first lord of the treasury.

The department developed in the royal households of the Saxon and Norman monarchs. The office of lord high treasurer dates from Norman times and was one of the great medieval offices of state. The first step in the development of the treasury as a public department was the appointment of Sir Henry Maynard (d. 1610) as a secretary. Under the early Stuarts the treasurership was often put into commission for a short period. Though a temporary measure, the entrusting of duties to a board had the important effect of stimulating the need for a secretary and regular procedures. In 1667 King Charles II appointed a new type of commission, which did not include any of the principal privy councillors, except the chancellor of the exchequer, with Sir George Downing as its secretary. He was responsible for the organization of the first real system of treasury records and of the necessary administration which went with them. The practice of putting the treasurership into commission and of making that commission independent of the privy council led to the rise of the first lord of the treasury as the leading minister of the crown. It also began the slower development whereby the chancellor of the exchequer became the effective head of the treasury.

In the 17th cent., when the treasury was in commission, the exchequer—the medieval accounting department—became part of the responsibility of that commission, and it became accepted that the chancellor could act for the treasury board. It was not until the mid-18th cent., however, when the first lord of the treasury became preoccupied with the wider functions of prime minister, that the chancellor became the working head of the treasury, and even in the 19th cent. the office did not necessarily carry cabinet rank.

The last lord treasurer, the duke of Shrewsbury, resigned in 1714, and the office has been in commission ever since, but no meeting of the treasury board for the transaction of ordinary business has been held since the mid-19th cent.

In the 19th cent. the treasury developed as parliament's principal instrument for the control of expenditure. Estimates of civil departments were presented to parliament by the treasury from the 1820s. It was laid down (though not by statute) in 1861 that the estimates of departments must be approved by the treasury before being presented to parliament. The Exchequer and Audit Departments Act (1866) gave the treasury statutory control over all expenditure for the first time, creating the post of comptroller and auditor-general.

The modern structure of the treasury probably owes more to Gladstone than to anyone else. As chancellor of the exchequer for 10 years and prime minister for 12, he established a unified system of government administration spreading outwards from the treasury, based on a reformed civil service and the 1866 act. The post of permanent secretary to the treasury was created in 1867, and in 1919 the holder was formally recognized as head of the civil service.

In 1947 the treasury assumed responsibility for the co-ordination of economic policy, a role it temporarily lost on the creation of the Department of Economic Affairs in 1964.

S. B. Baxter, *The Development of the Treasury, 1660–1702* (London, 1957).
Lord Bridges, *The Treasury* (London, 1964).   CJ

TREBIA, RIVER, BATTLE OF (218 BC), in northern Italy, south-west of Piacenza, first large-scale engagement of the Second Punic War, in which Hannibal's cavalry superiority destroyed over 20,000 men under P. Cornelius Scipio the elder and Sempronius Longus.

TREBIZOND, city in Asia Minor. In 1204 Alexios and David Komnenos, two grandsons of the Emperor Andronikos I (*reg.* 1183–5), with the aid of King Thamar of Georgia (*reg.* 1184–1212), took Trebizond and established there a separate regime. David Komnenos extended the influence of the new state westwards to embrace Sinope, Herakleia, and Amastris. This attempt at expansion was, however, brought to an end when the Byzantines of Nikaea, under Theodore I Laskaris, seized Amastris and Herakleia in 1214. The state of Trebizond, restricted thus in territorial extent, flourished as a commercial centre located at the end of an important trade route running from Persia through Erzerum to the Black Sea coast and as a major exporter of alum. Yielding tribute to the Seljuks and later to the Mongols and to Timur Beg, the regime of the Komnenoi endured until Sultan Mehemmed II conquered Trebizond in 1461.

TREDEGAR IRON WORKS in the US, rolling mill near Richmond, VA. It was built in 1836, bought by Joseph Reid Anderson (1848), and, operating with slave labour, produced high-quality iron. It was the Confederacy's sole manufacturer of heavy artillery during the Civil War, and afterwards supplied munitions of the US government.

TREGARDT, LOUIS (1783–1838), Boer farmer, who established (1834) a settlement beyond the colonial frontier in the eastern Cape. In the following year he left the Cape, before the main body of Voortrekkers, for the Zoutspansberg mountains in the northern Transvaal. Further trekking brought his party to the east coast.

TREITSCHKE, HEINRICH VON (1834–96), German author of the monumental *History of Germany in the 19th Century* (1st vol. 1879), whose work influenced a generation of Germans to idealize their race, to see Prussia as the inevitable and rightful dominator of the other German states, and to denigrate those, such as the Jews and the British, who were to be considered an obstacle to the rising power of Germany.

TRELAWNY, EDWARD (1699–1754), English soldier and colonial governor. He was governor of Jamaica (1738–63). Recognizing the impossibility of defeating the Maroon Negroes, he concluded two treaties of peace with their leaders (1739), conceding lands and freedom. In 1742 he led a force from Jamaica to support a march on Panama across the isthmus from Porto Bello, but on this plan being abandoned, he withdrew. Commanding 350 men, he helped capture Port Louis in Santo Domingo (1748). When hostilities with Spain ended (1748) he proposed a colony on the Mosquito coast of Central America where slavery would be prohibited. The plan was approved and a superintendent appointed (1750), but it was abandoned because of Spanish opposition.

TRENCHARD, HUGH MONTAGUE TRENCHARD, 1st Viscount (1875–1956), British airman, first Chief of the Air Staff, and 'father' of the Royal Air Force. He began his career in the army in 1893, and took an early interest in aviation. By 1914 he was deputy commandant of the Central Flying School. On the outbreak of the First World War he was appointed to command the military wing of the Royal Flying Corps, and in 1915 was transferred to the command of the RFC in France. In this capacity he was a persistent advocate of the independent role of the aircraft, as opposed to its use in tactical support for military operations, and pioneered the first steps towards the strategic bombing of Germany. With the decision to create an independent Royal Air Force in April 1918, following the 1917 Smuts Report, Trenchard was appointed first Chief of the Air Staff, but a clash with the new secretary of state for air, Lord Rothermere, led to his resignation and posting as commander of the new long-range independent bombing force designed to raid Berlin and other important German targets. In 1919 he was reinstated as Chief of the Air Staff and remained in office until 1929. In these ten years he created the peacetime Royal Air Force, emphasizing its importance in an independent strategic bombing role to the exclusion of other functions, and the need for its co-operation with the army and navy, which had wide repercussions in the early years of the Second World War. He was also deeply interested in training, and founded the RAF College at Cranwell. He was Commissioner of the Metropolitan Police (1931–5), during which time he founded the Hendon Police College.   NRB

TRENGGANU SULTANATE, in eastern Malaya. Under Sultan Mansur (1740–94) Trengganu was an important centre for Chinese and Malay trade, and the focus of Malay attempts to shake off Bugis predominance. Thereafter Trengganu generally followed an isolationist policy, which kept it free of both Siamese and British control until the appointment of a British resident in 1910.

***TRENT* AFFAIR** (1861), diplomatic crisis between the US and Britain during the American Civil War. Capt. Charles Wilkes of the USS *San Jacinto* seized two Confederate commissioners, James Mason and John Slidell, bound for Britain aboard the British ship *Trent* (8 Nov. 1861). Hostile British reaction, viewing the seizure as an abuse of neutral rights at sea, was eventually placated by a note from the US secretary of state (26 Dec. 1861), which 'cheerfully liberated' the commissioners because Wilkes had failed to take his prize to port for adjudication. The influence of Prince Albert softened the original demands made by Lord Palmerston, British foreign secretary, and prevented a serious clash between the two nations.

TRENT, COUNCIL OF, most decisive general council of the Christian Church of modern times, summoned by Pope Paul III to the imperial city of Trent by a papal bull of 22 May 1542 and charged with the task of achieving the reformation of the Church, the definition of dogma, and the reunion of Christendom.

The Emperor Charles V had long pressed for an oecumenical council to be assembled in Germany to heal the religious schism within the empire. Fearful of a revival of extreme conciliarism, Paul had resisted his demands until the failure of the Reform Commission and of the Regensburg Colloquy, and the growth of Protestantism within Italy itself forced his hand. Political cross-currents in Europe, above all the rivalry between the houses of Habsburg and Valois, had also contributed to its delay. Paul had contemplated a council as early as 1536 and his bull of 1542 named 1 Nov. 1542 as the date of the first session, but renewed fighting between France and the empire postponed the opening until 13 Dec. 1545, which only 31 bishops and some 50 theologians attended.

This first period of eight sessions (1545–7), which was marked by the influence of reformers such as Marcello Cervini and Reginald Pole, proved constructive in the elaboration of dogmatic definitions. The council rejected the Protestant emphasis upon the scriptures and upheld the view that the authentic version, the Vulgate, should have equal validity with the apostolic tradition. Moreover the Protestant emphasis on original sin was also rejected and the Catholic doctrine of justification by faith and good works was re-affirmed, as was the efficacy of the traditional seven sacraments. The sacramental doctrines of baptism and confirmation were more clearly expounded than hitherto. In the field of ecclesiastical reform less was achieved. The ancient canons on pluralism and non-residence were confirmed, but no machinery for enforcement was established. At this point (Feb. 1547) the pope adjourned the council to Bologna and its work was further interrupted by a quarrel between him and Charles V. After defeating the Schmalkaldic League of Lutheran princes, Charles independently sought a reconciliation with them through the moderate Interim of Augsburg (May 1548).

Paul III's successor, Julius III (*reg.* 1550–4), wanted an accommodation with the emperor, so he recalled the council to Trent and it duly assembled for a seond period of six sessions (May 1551–April 1552). Under the firm guidance of Marcello Crescenzi the delegates clearly restated the doctrine of transubstantiation and stressed the importance of oral confession. The defeated Protestants who attended during this second period made sweeping demands for increasing episcopal authority and the 14th session ended in deadlock and confusion.

The succession of Paul IV to the Holy See (1555) shattered the hopes of reformers, since Paul had no faith in conciliar

traditions. It was his successor, Pius IV (*reg.* 1559–64), who recalled the council for its third and final period of 11 sessions in Jan. 1562, to meet the rising threat of a more militant Protestantism—Calvinism—which had entrenched itself in France. These final sessions were attended by a large Spanish contingent led by Pedro Guerreno, a French delegation, which included Charles de Guise, Cardinal of Lorraine, some small delegations, among which the Polish Cardinal Stanislas Hosius stood out, and the dominating Italian group, led by the legate Cardinal Giovanni Morone. Bitter divisions arose over the source of episcopal authority, despite early agreement over the sacrificial character of the Mass and the true veneration of saints. Morone skilfully guided the council towards the subject of 'the cure of souls'. Pluralism was again forbidden, reforms were imposed on religious orders, regular diocesan visitations were demanded and provision laid down for the establishment of a seminary in every diocese to ensure the adequate education of the clergy. The remaining tasks of revising the Index, and authorizing of a new catechism, breviary, and missal, were left to the pope. The final session closed on 4 Dec. 1563, and the council's decrees were confirmed by papal bull in Jan. 1564 and implemented by a special commission formed in Aug. 1564.

The original purpose of the council—to heal the religious schism in Europe—was abandoned by the theologians at Trent. Instead, their achievements were perhaps two-fold: they clarified Catholic doctrine to arm future generations with the certainty of religious truth, and they created the modern papacy. The price of these developments was the abandonment of that liberal humanism of men like Erasmus, which had characterized the early Catholic reformation.

H. Jedin, *History of the Council of Trent*, 2 vols (London, 1957, 1961).
H. J. Schroeder, *Canons and Decrees of the Council of Trent* (London, 1941).   MKS

TRENTON, BATTLE OF (26 Dec. 1776), important engagement between British and American troops in the American War of Independence, fought at Trenton, NJ. George Washington led 2400 Patriots across the Delaware river, surprised and routed the Hessian garrison under Col. Joham Rall, and captured over 900 Hessians, while sustaining casualties of only four wounded. This victory, together with that at Princeton (3 Jan. 1777), led to the recovery of western NJ and gave new life to the patriot cause. Frederick the Great called Washington's manœuvres in NJ the most brilliant military campaign of the century.

TRENWITH, WILLIAM ARTHUR (1847–1925), Tasmanian politician and trade unionist, who pioneered the political labour movement in the colony. As Victorian MP (1889–1903) he had ministerial experience in non-Labor governments, broke with the increasingly disciplined Labor Party (1901), and sat in the senate of the Commonwealth parliament (1903–10).

TRÉSAGUET, PIERRE (1716–96), French civil engineer, who was responsible for the introduction of improved and cheaper methods of road construction at a time when the European road system was being rebuilt and extended. In addition, he was the first to recognize, and also to demonstrate, the importance of regular road maintenance. Previously the practice had been to neglect roads until they fell into serious disrepair. His methods became adopted by most European engineers, including Thomas Telford (1757–1834) in Britain.

TRÉSOR DE L'ÉPARGNE, in France, fiscal agency created by Francis I (1523) to unite collection and control of all royal revenues, previously divided into ordinary (estate) and extraordinary (taxation) levies. Established at Paris (1532), it became a potent instrument of financial centralization and was eventually reformed and reorganized by Colbert into the *Trésor Royal* (1668).

TREVELYAN, SIR CHARLES EDWARD (1807–86), British civil servant, who was Lord Macaulay's brother-in-law and shared his Wig utilitarian views. After 12 years (1826–38) in the Indian civil service Trevelyan returned to Britain and was assistant secretary to the treasury (1840–59). In 1853, the year that the Indian civil service was opened to competitive examination, Gladstone appointed Trevelyan and Sir Stafford Northcote to enquire into methods of entry into the civil service. Their report (1854) recommended that civil servants in the higher grades should be recruited by examination consisting of subjects studied at the older universities, that the examination should be the same for all departments, and that it should be conducted not by heads of departments but by independent commissioners. Trevelyan returned to India as governor of Madras (1859), was recalled (1860), and returned again as finance minister (1862).

TREVELYAN, SIR GEORGE OTTO (1838–1928), British civil servant, politician and biographer of his uncle, Lord Macaulay. He was a Liberal MP, and held a great variety of secretaryships—to the admiralty, Ireland, Scotland, and the chancellorship of the duchy of Lancaster.

TREVERORUM (properly Colonia Augusta Treverorum), Roman name of modern Trier, taken from the Treveri, a powerful Celtic tribe of the Moselle basin. The Roman city was founded early in the 1st cent. AD and probably received colonial status from the Emperor Claudius (AD 41–54). After replacing Rheims as residence of the governor of Gallia Belgica it became the financial and economic centre of most of the Rhineland and achieved great prosperity. In the 4th cent. it was the residence of the praetorian prefect of the Gallic provinces and sometimes of emperors; in the 5th it was sacked several times by the Germans, but traces of urban life survived. Several important Roman buildings remain, including baths, a basilica, a former imperial palace, and the so-called *Porta Nigra*.

TREVIRANUS, GOTTFRIED REINHOLD (1891–), German sailor and Reichstag deputy (1924–30), when he founded a splinter group, the Volkskonservative Vereinigung. He joined forces with a group of other former Deutsche National Volks Partei (DNVP) politicians to form the Konservative Volkspartei. He served as minister in the Brüning cabinet until 1932 and later left Germany.

TREVITHICK, RICHARD (1771–1833), British engineer and inventor. Having developed early high-pressure non-condensing steam engines in Cornish mines, he produced the first steam carriage for passengers at Redruth in 1801 and the first steam locomotive for use on rails in South Wales in 1804. His inventions, coming just after the expiry of Watt's patent (1800), began to break down Watts's view that steam could not be applied to locomotion.

TRIAD SOCIETY in China, also known under the names of 'Heaven and Earth Society', and 'Hung League', was an anti-Manchu secret society. According to the society's own tradition it was created in 1674 in Fukien. Most probably however it originated in Taiwan, then moved to Fukien and subsequently spread over most of south China. Various branches of the Triad Society assumed different names at different times, and after 1800 they frequently raised their standard against the Ch'ing dynasty. Two major risings occurred in the early 1850s: those of the 'Red Turbans' in Kwangtung and the 'Small Sword Society' at Shanghai and Amoy. During the 19th cent. the Triads also established branches in overseas Chinese communities, *eg*, in CA, Siam, Australia, and British Malaya. When abroad, the Triad Society lost much of its political meaning, and assumed the nature of a Friendly Society. Towards the end of the 19th cent. the Triads inside and outside China worked with Sun Yat-sen for the overthrow of the Manchu dynasty. Mao Tse-tung also made use of Triad leaders in the late 1920s.

TRIAL OF CONTROVERTED ELECTIONS (GRENVILLE'S) ACT (1770) in Britain, legislative measure which established an impartial and more efficient machinery for making decisions in disputed election cases, and a possible method of franchise reform. The House of Commons won the right to try controverted elections in 1604, and retained it until 1868, when, by act of parliament, it was handed over to the judges. The method of trial varied, but always involved consideration and final decision by the whole House, and took up much time at the beginning of each parliament.

Decisions revealed the Commons' attitude to the ministers rather than the merits of the elections: Walpole's 'loss' of controverted elections in 1741 was followed by his resignation in 1742. Under Grenville's act each disputed election was tried by a committee of 13, chosen by lot, with power to examine witnesses on oath and make a final decision. The act was made permanent in 1774. Several pre-1832 statutory reforms in the borough franchise were based on suggestions from Grenville committees, *eg*, Cricklade (1771), New Shoreham (1781). The system lasted until 1868, with small alterations in the size and method of constituting the committees (1841, 1842).

TRIANGLE FIRE (26 March 1911), in the US, disastrous fire at the Triangle Shirtwaist Factory in New York city, in which 147 women workers died, exposing the inadequacy of fire regulations. The tragedy led to the appointment of a Factory Investigating Commission and a revision of the state factory code (1912–14).

TRIANGULAR TRADE, commerce between Britain's American colonies, Africa, and the West Indies. Ships from New England ports carried goods to Africa, where part of the cargo, mainly rum, was bartered for Negro slaves. The slaves, together with the rest of the cargo, were then shipped to the West Indies and traded for the sugar and molasses used in the production of rum in New England. Each leg of the run was made to yield a profit, the 'Middle Passage' usually being the most profitable.

TRIANON DECREES (1810) in France, by which special tribunals were set up to eliminate contraband trade with Britain. They helped to provoke an economic crisis in Britain, illustrating the severe pressure that Napoleon I's continental system could exert on her economy, when rigorously applied.

TRIBONIAN (*fl*. 6th cent.), Constantinople lawyer, who was appointed by the Emperor Justinian I as head of the commission entrusted with the revision and codification of Roman Law. The resulting Code of Civil Law (523–33) was one of Justinian's most influential achievements and remained until modern times the main collection of Roman Law known in Europe.

TRIBUNE, MILITARY, senior officers of the ancient Roman legions, each of which had six tribunes usually assigned to administrative duties rather than tactical command. Under the empire the military tribunate was held by young men starting a senatorial or equestrian career.

TRIBUNE OF THE PEOPLE, ancient Roman official created (493 BC) by the plebeians to protect them from patrician oppression. Eventually numbering ten, they acquired very wide powers from the plebeian threat of revolution, including that of veto over the acts of all other magistrates, and the right of personal inviolability. After the end of the Struggle of the Orders they retained their revolutionary powers, which were revived in the late 2nd cent. by, *eg*, Tiberius and Gaius Gracchus, Saturninus and others, and, although briefly restricted by Sulla (81–80), contributed considerably to the political chaos of the Late Republic. Augustus accepted tribunician power (23), as did later emperors, and the office declined in importance until it was abolished by Constantine.

TRIBUTE LISTS, ATHENIAN, accounts of quotas for Athens' treasury of $\frac{1}{60}$th of the annual contributions of member of the Delian League, published annually and inscribed on tablets on the Athenian Acropolis. Many fragments survive, constituting a valuable source for Athenian imperial history; 253 fragments from two marble blocks cover the years 454/3–432/1 BC, others the period to 415/4, when a trade tax replaced the former system of contributions.

TRIBUTE SYSTEM OF CHINA, Western term used to describe the traditional system of relationships between the Son of Heaven (the Chinese emperor) and other states. Originally formulated in Chou times, after the creation of a centralized territorial empire under the Han (founded 206 BC), the system underwent many refinements, as Chinese experience within and without the empire increased. The system was based on the concept that the Son of Heaven occupied a pivotal position in the universe, maintaining order among mankind and harmony between humanity and the rest of the cosmos. Relations within the system were hierarchical and personal and centred round the Son of Heaven, who embodied human civilization. Tribute relations were therefore essentially ritualistic. A non-Chinese ruler, after presenting a symbolic tribute of local products, would receive a patent of an appointment, a Chinese noble rank, receive presents (usually of greater material value) from the Son of Heaven, perform the kotow in the latter's presence, and use the Chinese calendar. The Chinese empire under the tribute system was therefore one without any equal neighbours, and although it was not imperialistic it permitted no true international relations. The system was thus anathema to the Western concept of international relations, and under increasing Western and Japanese encroachment after the Opium War the system gradually collapsed; it was preserved until 1911 only among a few tribute states, mainly in north and central Asia.

TRIBUTES, annual capitation tax levied upon the native peoples of colonial Spanish America, first imposed by Columbus on Hispaniola in 1495. Tribute became universal on the mainland, where many native peoples were accustomed to paying such exactions to their own overlords. In the 16th–17th cents tribute was paid either to the Crown, in token of overlordship, or to individuals under the *encomienda* system. Originally paid in a wide variety of commodities, tribute gradually consisted of money and (sometimes) maize. In the beginning, the *encomenderos* demanded all the tribute they could exact, but after *c.* 1550 the Crown increasingly standardized and lowered the amount, and, with the gradual decline of the *encomienda* system, tribute came to be monopolized by the government. Although regulations and exemptions varied from colony to colony, tribute was ordinarily paid by adult natives of both sexes until the age of 50–5.

TRIBUTUM, ancient Roman tax, originally a war-tax levied intermittently on citizens and regarded as a loan and sometimes repaid, *eg,* in 167 BC when it was abolished. After 167 the term was applied only to provincial taxation in those provinces which paid a fixed tribute. Under the empire *tributum soli* was levied on land, *tributum capitis* on other forms of property. Until Diocletian's reign Italy was exempt, but all provincials, whether Roman citizens or not, paid *tributum* unless expressly exempted as individuals or communities.

TRIER, imperial city on the site of the Roman settlement of Augusta Treverorum, from which Trèves, the French version of its name, is taken. It was the seat of the medieval Rhenish archbishopric, whose prince was also a member of the imperial college of electors from the 13th cent. Trier's position on the Moselle near Luxemburg gave it a prominent role in Franco-German relations, particularly in the reign of Louis XIV, when its lands were occupied by the French (1673, 1688–9, 1705). In 1803 Trier's right of election was abolished by the final recess of the empire, and in 1815 as part of the Rhenish province its lands were absorbed into Prussia.

TRIER, TREATY OF (1632), treaty of neutrality arranged by Richelieu and signed by the electoral-archbishopric of Trier, France, and Sweden in the Thirty Years War. The agreement, which contributed to the collapse of the Catholic League, gave France the coveted right to occupy the Rhine fortresses of Ehrenbreitstein and Philippsburg, while the Spanish troops were ejected from Trier itself.

TRINH CLAN, most powerful family in north Viet-nam from the later 16th cent. till 1788. Like their rivals the Nguyen, the Trinh came from the province of Thanh-Hoa. They first emerged as a powerful group in the troubled years of the early 16th cent. When Mac Dang Dueg seized the throne at Hanoi in 1527, they withdrew and helped the Nguyen to restore the Le at Thanh-Hoa in 1532. From 1545 there was continuous rivalry between the Trinh and the Nguyen, and by 1573 the former had emerged as the stronger. They virtually controlled the Le court, so that when the Le were restored as emperors at Hanoi, it was Trinh Tung who became effective ruler. On his death in 1623 he was succeeded by Trinh Trang, who ruled until 1657. The position established by the clan was thus one of hereditary control, not unlike that of the Japanese *shōgun*; but they never felt strong enough to seize the throne for themselves. Their rule continued until 1787, when the last of them was overthrown after the Tay-Son rising had spread to Tongking. The Trinh period saw a revival of Buddhism, and a corresponding decline in the importance of Confucian scholars; Trinh Cuong (*reg.* 1709–29) and Trinh Giang (*reg.* 1729–40) were notable patrons of Buddhism. The later 17th and 18th cents also saw the growth of Christian missionary activity in Viet-nam, and the number of Catholics increased, despite periodic persecutions.   RBS

TRINH–NGUYEN WARS, in 17th-cent. Viet-nam. Rivalry between the Trinh and Nguyen clans began about 1545, when they were jointly supporting the Le dynasty against the Mac. In 1600, after the country had been reunited under Le rule, the conflict between them forced Nguyen Hoang to withdraw to the country around Hue, as semi-independent governor of Central Viet-nam. The conflict developed into open warfare in 1627, when the Nguyen refused a request for tribute by the Trinh, and defeated an invasion of their territory by northern forces. In 1630–4 the Trinh made an all-out effort to conquer the provinces controlled by their rivals, but failed. There were further campaigns in 1642–3, 1648, 1655–7, 1660–2, and 1672–3, but although a small amount of territory changed hands from time to time, the Trinh were unable to gain a lasting victory, and made no further attempt to control the south from 1673 until 1774. Although they had greater resources, they were fighting far away from home and against well-trained armies who were defending their own land; this goes far towards explaining the Nguyens' successful resistance.

TRINIDAD, island in the West Indies, first settled by Yaio or Arawak Indians. It was claimed for Spain by Christopher Columbus in 1498. The next Spanish visit, a slave-trading raid (1510), so displeased the king that he directed the viceroy to ensure the Amerindians protection. In 1530 Antonio Sedeno was appointed captain-general of Trinidad for life. Arriving (1531), his relations with the Amerindians became hostile and the Spanish were forced to leave. Spanish efforts to retake Trinidad (1532–3) failed and not until 1569–70 did Juan Troche de Leon overcome Amerindian resistance. An English settlement (1632) was captured by the Spanish governor Don Diego Lopez de Escobar (1633), and the settlers were executed. After a massacre of whites (1699), the Spaniards killed the Amerindian males and enslaved their women and children. From 1783 Spain encouraged immigration and so many Frenchmen were admitted that by 1786 they dominated local government. The island surrendered to the British under Sir Ralph Abercromby (1797) and was ceded to Britain by the treaty of Amiens (1802). Following the capitulation, disabilities against free coloured people were introduced, but protests (1823) led to their removal (1829). Unlike British colonies acquired earlier, Trinidad was not allowed an elected assembly. The governor's advisory council was given (1831) limited legislative functions. In 1837 a revolt of Africans, freed from a slaver and enlisted as soldiers, was crushed. British conquest stimulated the growth of sugar plantations, but abolition of the slave trade (1808) restricted the labour supply. Small numbers of Chinese (1806), North American Indian (1814), and Portuguese (1834) immigrants, and 134,000 indentured labourers from India (1845–1917), were imported. Oil was discovered (1866) and commercial production began (1909). In 1889 Tobago was united with Trinidad. In the 1920s and early 1930s Arthur Cipriani, a radical member of the legislature's elected minority, won popular support by agitating for the island's self-government. From riots in 1937 Tubal Uriah Butler emerged as a popular leader and trade unions were firmly established. Following adult suffrage (1946), the legislature (1950) and Executive Council (1956) were given elected majorities and a restricted cabinet government was allowed (1959). The People's National Movement, founded in 1956 by Eric Williams, became the dominant political party. The island was part of the West Indian Federation (1958–61) and became internally self-governing in 1961 and independent in 1962.

Eric Williams, *A History of the People of Trinidad and Tobago* (London, 1964).   RH

TRINITARIANS, believers in the Christian doctrine of the Trinity, *ie*, of God as one being in three Persons: Father, Son, and Holy Ghost. The term is also applied to members of the Order of the Most Holy Trinity, a mendicant order founded in 1198, distinguished for its austerity and devoted to freeing Christian slaves from Muslim captivity.

TRIPARTITE DECLARATION (May 1950), signed by Britain, France, and the US in an attempt to stabilize the Middle East after the establishment of the state of Israel. The three governments undertook to limit the supply of arms to the Arab states and Israel and to require assurances, before providing arms, that the purchaser did not intend any act of aggression. The three governments also undertook, if they found 'that any of the states was preparing to violate frontiers or armistice lines', to act within and outside the UN to prevent such violation. The limitation on armaments worked well for a few years, but the system began to break when the French government moved towards an alliance with Israel against Nasser, and it collapsed with the sale of Soviet arms to Egypt (1955).

TRIPARTITE PACT (1940), signed between Japan, Germany, and Italy (27 Sept. 1940) at the height of the German success in the Second World War. Germany and Italy recognized Japan's 'leadership in the establishment of a new order in Greater East Asia' in return for a reciprocal undertaking on the part of Japan. Mutual obligations of assistance were exchanged in the event of any one of the contracting parties being attacked 'by a power at present not involved in the European war'. The pact was of little practical importance. Germany did not concert with Japan its attack on the Soviet Union, nor Japan its attack on Pearl Harbor with Germany. Under the terms of the treaty Germany was not obliged to assist Japan, but Hitler assured Matsuoka (March 1941) that 'If Japan got into a conflict with the US, Germany would take the necessary steps'. Consistently he declared war as soon as the Japanese attack was made.

TRIPARTITE TREATY (July 1838), between the British, Ranjit Singh, and Shah Shuja, who was to be restored as

Amir of Kabul on condition that he renounced all claims on Sind. Ranjit was also to be confirmed in his possessions along the Indus.

TRIPLE ALLIANCE (1668), short-lived diplomatic venture of King Charles II of England. A treaty was concluded between England and the Dutch republic in Jan. 1668, and this was adhered to by Sweden in the following May. It was intended to provide terms of mediation for a peace between France and Spain, who were fighting the War of Devolution, in which the extent of French successes had aroused anxiety, particularly in the Dutch republic. Secretly the English and Dutch pledged themselves to take up arms against Louis XIV if he refused to make peace with Spain on the terms suggested. In fact, peace was made between France and Spain in the treaty of Aix-la-Chapelle (May 1668). It is unlikely, however, that the magnanimous terms granted by Louis at that particular time were the result of pressure exerted by the Triple Alliance. Louis had reason to think that he would shortly gain more than he was now exacting from Spain, for in Jan. 1668 he had signed with the Emperor Leopold I the partition treaty, by which, upon the death of Charles II of Spain, his dominions were to be shared between Louis and Leopold—a settlement which never came into operation, as Charles's death did not occur until Nov. 1700. Louis was willing therefore to end the fighting against Spain, though he was well aware of the existence of the Triple Alliance, and his anger seems to have been directed chiefly against the Dutch, who were technically bound to him by treaty. He never forgave them. During the next few years he sought successfully to isolate them from their allies.

TRIPLE ALLIANCE (1717), between France, Britain, and the United Provinces, preserved European peace until 1731 and lasted nominally until 1744. It provided mutual guarantees of the British and French successions as laid down at Utrecht (1713), while France also undertook to refuse aid to Jacobites and to destroy the Dunkirk fortifications.

TRIPLE ALLIANCE (1788), series of treaties concluded between Britain, Prussia, and the United Provinces.

The death of Frederick II of Prussia (1786) paved the way for an Anglo-Prussian rapprochement. In Sept. 1787 the Prince of Orange, *stadtholder* of the United Provinces, and brother-in-law of the new Prussian king, Frederick William II, was restored to his former authority by a Prussian army with British assistance, thus defeating the pro-French 'Patriot' party. From this joint action came an Anglo-Prussian convention (Oct. 1787), partly inspired by fear of Russian expansion in the Near East, which was followed by a defensive alliance between the two powers (August 1788), guaranteeing the integrity and constitution of the United Provinces. Meanwhile, the Dutch had made treaties of alliance with Britain and Prussia (April 1788).

The three powers showed their solidarity by intervening to restore the status quo in the Baltic (1789) and in the Habsburg empire (1790). Anglo-Prussian friendship grew cool, however, when the Polish Partition reunited Austria, Prussia, and Russia, to the exclusion of Britain and the Dutch (1793).

TRIPLE ALLIANCE (1815), defensive alliance between Britain, Austria, and France, designed to curb Russian influence on the Vienna settlement. The alliance reflected Britain's fear that Russia might replace France as the aggressive power in Europe. Castlereagh, the British foreign minister, was determined to establish a strong power on the Rhine as a buffer against France. Russia wanted to keep Germany weak and divided, fearing that too powerful a neighbour might threaten Russia. By involving France, Castlereagh flattered Talleyrand and made Russia more willing to compromise. But, in deference to Russia, an enlarged Prussia was to provide the defence against France, leaving the other German states loosely grouped in a confederation under

afterwards royalist officers kidnapped him and demanded the restoration of the monarchy, whereupon his government fell.

TSANKOV, GEORGI (1913–), Bulgarian communist politician, who joined the central committee in 1950 and the Politburo in 1951. He was minister of the interior (1951–62). In this post he acquired sufficient power to threaten Zhivkov's supremacy and consequently was purged with other would-be rivals at the eighth party congress in 1960.

TS'AO K'UN (1862–1934), Chinese war-lord of the early Republican period, who was associated with the Chihli Clique, and was briefly president of China (1923–4).

TS'AO TS'AO, Chinese soldier (d. AD 220), whose early career was spent in the last decades of the Han dynasty, when the rivalries of eunuchs and the families of imperial consorts, the youth and weakness of the emperors, and the loss of purpose at court had led to the failure of governmental authority and the decay of dynastic power. He was one of the most able soldiers of the day, and featured in the bids for power that finally led to the establishment of the three kingdoms in 220. In that year, Ts'ao Ts'ao's son, Ts'ao P'ei, set himself up as King of Wei in northern China. In addition to his importance politically and historically, he has been portrayed as an heroic figure in fiction, romance, and drama.

TSAR, title of the Russian rulers introduced in 1547 by Ivan IV (1533–84) and in use until the Russian revolution of 1917. Derived from the Latin word *Caesar* meaning emperor, the term was intended to express the highest form of dominion, parallel with the Holy Roman emperor of western Europe.

TSARSKOYE SELO, Russian equivalent of Versailles, a magnificent collection of palaces, churches, monuments, and gardens built in the 18th cent. and situated 32 kms south of St Petersburg on high ground above the swamps. It was the summer resort of the imperial court until 1917.

TSCHERNEMBL, GEORGE ERASMUS, Baron von (d. 1626), Protestant nobleman of Upper Austria, a champion of the nobility's independence against the sovereignty of the ruler, who challenged the rights of Archduke Ferdinand to succeed to the Bohemian throne in 1619–20.

TSENG KUO-FAN (1811–72), Chinese politician, soldier, and scholar. After routine appointments as a metropolitan official, he was made junior vice-president of the Board of Ceremonies. Similar positions during the next few years gave him a wide knowledge of state affairs, which proved to be invaluable when he was charged with the organization of militia to fight the Taipings in his native province (1853). Initially he deployed his militia (later to become the famous Hsiang or Hunan army) to fight local bandits in order to gain experience. In 1854 he was confident enough to campaign outside his province, driving the Taipings out of Wuchang; in 1855 he established his camp at Nanchang, Kiangsi, engaging the rebels on the Yangtse river. Despite the aid of a capable personal staff and his well-trained militia, his early campaigning years were full of obstacles and humiliating defeats, and he twice attempted to commit suicide. Fearing that his provincial army might become too powerful, the throne forced him to rely on local rather than government financial support, which was often reluctantly and tardily provided. However, in 1860 most of his difficulties were removed when he was appointed governor-general of the Liang-Kiang provinces, and Imperial Commissioner for the suppression of the Taipings, in South China; the throne was thus finally forced to recognize the decrepit state of the imperial troops, which suffered serious losses that year. With new power vested in him, Tseng Kuofan was able to bring capable personnel into the scene: Li Hung-chang to campaign in Kiangsu, Tso Tsung-t'ang in Chekiang, and Shen Pao-chen (1820–79) in Kiangsi,

guarding his rear and providing some of his military supplies. Thus assisted, he was finally able to destroy the Taipings in 1864.

After the Taiping Rebellion he concentrated on the rehabilitation and the restoration of traditional scholarship in the Liang-Kiang provinces. He was soon called upon to suppress the Nien rebels in Shantung; but after more than a year's unsuccessful campaign, he was replaced by his protégé, Li Hung-chang, while he returned to Liang-Kiang. In 1868 he was appointed governor-general of Chihli, but his incumbency was cut short by anti-foreign elements, who were dissatisfied with his handling of the Tientsin Massacre (1870). Once again, he returned to his Liang-Kiang post, which he held until his death.

W. J. Hall, *Tseng Kuo-fan and the Taiping Rebellion* (New York, 1964).
Gideon Ch'en, *Tseng Kuo-fan: pioneer promoter of the steamship in China* (Peiping, 1935).   DP

TSETSE FLY, genus *Glossina*, are present in 22 species and in varying intensity over some $4\frac{1}{4}$ million square miles (10,900,000 sq. kms) of tropical Africa. Always a major obstacle to the growth and spread of tropical populations, as well as to the introduction or use of cattle for food or draught purposes, tsetse are the carriers of trypanosomes (microscopic unicellular Protozoa) which infect human blood with the disease of sleeping sickness and the blood of hoofed cattle with that of the similarly fatal disease of nagana. All or most of the fly's species transmit nagana; five of them, on present knowledge, carry sleeping sickness. The latter results from two species of trypanosome, known as 'Gambian' and 'Rhodesian' (*Trypanosoma gambiense* and *T. rhodesiense*) carried respectively by the *palpalis* group of fly species and the *morsitans* group. The former are generally riverine in habitat, while the latter live in woodland savannahs; only nagana, on present knowledge, is in general carried by the forest species.

Tsetse appear to have been present in large regions of tropical Africa—though not necessarily in their present distribution or intensity—since the earliest times of human evolution there. They have long been extinct everywhere else in the world, but Miocene shales in North America have yielded fossil tsetse of some 50 million years ago, and it has been suggested that tsetse-carried trypanosomiasis may have destroyed North America's prehistoric horses and camels. It can be convincingly argued that few and perhaps no other African pests have had so profoundly destructive an effect upon the nature of human and bovid development in the African tropics.

A serious Uganda epidemic of trypanosomiasis in 1903 led to the establishment of a Sleeping Sickness Bureau by British doctors and scientists. Much research and devoted observation in the field by British and other workers since then, but with important break-throughs in the last two or three decades, has tracked the tsetse's habits and defined its behaviour in detail; and these are now well known. Such knowledge has led to repeated and partially successful efforts to reduce the fly's incidence.

T. M. Nash, *Africa's Bane: the tsetse fly* (London, 1969).
                                                                                          BD

TSO CHUAN, historical text covering the period 722–464 BC and included in the Chinese classics. The work is anecdotal and has for long been treated as a commentary on or amplification of the events recorded in the *Spring and Autumn Annals*. However, it was in all probability compiled as an independent piece of writing, some time before 300 BC.

TSO TSUNG-T'ANG (1812–85), Chinese soldier and politician. His knowledge of geography and military strategy brought him to the attention of the governor of Hunan, who in 1852 gave him full responsibility in all military affairs against the Taipings. Because of his success, the throne ordered him to recruit an army of 5000 Hunanese to campaign in Kiangsi and Anhwei provinces (1860). Repeated success led to rapid promotion: he was commander-in-chief of government forces in Chekiang (1861), governor of Chekiang (1862), and governor-general of Fukien and Chekiang (1863). After the fall of the Taiping kingdom he devoted much energy to rehabilitation and education, while continuing his suppression of Taiping remnants in Fukien. Tso recognized the superiority of Western arms and technology. During his campaigns against the rebels he made use of an Anglo-French army; he also experimented with a locally built steam boat. In 1866 he founded the Foochow Navy Yard, engaging some 40 French engineers for the construction of modern warships and the training of Chinese engineers and naval officers.

Before he could complete his programme of rehabilitation and modernization in Fukien and Chekiang he was appointed governor-general of Shensi and Kansu (north-west China) to suppress the Muslim Rebellion there. He was delayed on his way by the Nien Rebellion, which he helped to suppress; and only late in 1868 was he at last able to begin his campaign against the Muslim rebels. For the next 12 years Tso remained in north-west China, conducting his campaign with absolute dedication and reorganizing the provincial administration as territory was recovered. To obviate the difficulties and the expense of long supply lines, he encouraged the local cotton industry, established a modern cotton and woollen mill, and used the leisure hours of his soldiers to farm unused land. By 1874 Shensi and Kansu were recovered, and Tso was made a Grand Secretary; the following year he was ordered to continue the suppression of rebellion in Chinese Turkestan, the remotest part of the Chinese empire. The situation was complicated by the Russian occupation of Ili, and by the existence of Yakub Beg's regime, which the British were supporting as a possible buffer against Russian expansion. Tso therefore proposed a 10-million-tael loan, but it was opposed by Li Hung-chang and Shen Pao-chen, who wished to use China's resources for maritime defence. Tso eventually obtained the necessary funds, which enabled him not only to complete the recovery of Chinese Turkestan (1878), but also to adopt a strong position against the Russians, thus securing a favourable settlement of the Ili dispute. In 1880 Tso was appointed a Grand Councillor and a member of the Tsungli Yamen, but his honesty and outspokenness made him ill at ease among the effete officials of the capital. In 1882 he was given a high provincial appointment, and during the Sino-French War was appointed Imperial Commissioner for maritime defence in Fukien, where he died.

W. L. Bales, *Tso Tsung-t'ang, soldier and statesman of Old China* (Shanghai, 1937).

Gideon Ch'en, *Tso Tsung-t'ang, Pioneer promoter of the modern dockyard and the woollen mill in China* (Peiping, 1938).   DP

TSONG KHAPA (1357–1419), founder of the Gelugpa sect of Tibetan Buddhism, who studied in central Tibet (1374–1397) under teachers of various sects, and taught at the Kadampa monastery of Reting (1397–1409). He then founded his own monastery of Ganden, near Lhasa. He wrote a large number of doctrinal works, and won great renown for his insistence on the strict maintenance of monastic discipline and encouragement of learning. Regarded as a second Buddha, he does not become reincarnated in this world.

TSUNAYOSHI (1646–1709), fifth Tokugawa *shōgun*, who was especially noted for his patronage of Confucian teaching.

TSUNGLI YAMEN, institution founded in China in 1861 on the recommendation of Prince Kung, for the purpose of handling foreign affairs, and the most important institutional innovation of the T'ung-chih Restoration. It was not a 'foreign office', as it was often referred to in Western literature, for it had no decision-making power. On the other hand its recommendations were often accepted by the Grand Council, the highest authority in the bureaucracy, because its leading ministers were also Grand Councillors. Foreign relations apart, the Tsungli Yamen was also instrumental in introducing or supporting modernization projects: the T'ung-wen Kuan, telegraphy, railways, mining, maritime defence, postal service system, education, etc. But the power of the Tsungli Yamen was limited by the fact that provincial officials continued to handle foreign affairs; moreover, its ministers were overworked, since each held at least one other important office, and most of them were ignorant of the West. The personal decline of Prince Kung from 1869, and the death of the most capable minister of the Tsungli Yamen, Wen-hsiang (1818–76), signalled its decline. The rise of Li Hung-chang from 1870, the creation of the Board of Admiralty (1885), and the ever-present manipulation by the Empress Dowager Tz'u-hsi, also diminished its role. In 1901 the Tsungli Yamen was replaced by a proper foreign office (*Wai-wu-pu*), as stipulated in the Boxer Protocol.

TSUNYI CONFERENCE (1935), meeting which marked the advent of Mao Tse-tung to full power over the Chinese Communist Party. At a meeting of the CCP Politburo in the early stages of the Long March, he was appointed to the newly created post of chairman of the Politburo.

TSUSHIMA, BATTLE OF (27 May 1905), naval battle of the Russo-Japanese War. Admiral Tōgō's decisive victory over the Russian Baltic fleet safeguarded Japanese supremacy at sea and greatly reduced Russian hopes of military victory.

TU FU (712–70), Chinese poet, who served as a minor official and during the An Lu-shan rebellion spent a long period in flight and wandering about. Most of his work is in the highly schematic form of modulated poetry, of which he was a recognized master. In contrast with Li Po's Taoist point of view, Tu Fu's approach is that of a Confucian philosopher, anxious to improve mankind by means of moral training.

TUAMOTU ARCHIPELAGO, THE, extensive SE–NW atoll barrier (Eastern Pacific) discovered by Quiros (1606) and definitively surveyed by Caillet (1884). In the 18th–19th cents local sea-rovers from Anaa and Fakarava occasionally penetrated as far west as Tahiti, where many accepted Christianity. Pearl-shellers laid the basis for a French protectorate (1847) though early Catholic priests at Fai'ite and Anaa (1849) were driven out by Mormon adherents, Anaa being pacified only in 1861. In 1880 the group was annexed by France, which thus acquired Makatea's rich phosphates (exhausted in 1966) and the modern nuclear test site at Mururoa.

TUAN CH'I-JUI (1865–1936), leader of the Anfu clique in the war-lord period of modern Chinese history (1911–25).

TUAREG, nomad Berber people numbering in 1970 some 500,000, with semi-settled groups near Timbuctoo, Agadez, and Ghadames. They wander in areas of the central Sahara, where there are salt mines, caravan routes, and seasonal pasturage. They speak *Tamahaq*, a Berber language, and use *Tifinagh*, a script derived from Punic and other Libyan scripts, to make rock inscriptions and documents, though today it is almost forgotten. Many lettered Tuareg have a knowledge of Classical Arabic, and some of their groups have contributed to Islamic scholarship in West Africa.

Tuareg society is based on a class structure consisting of warriors, religious teachers, tributaries, slaves, and artisans, each having its own fixed status and mutual interdependence within the community. The Tuareg are monogamous, custom permitting a freedom between the sexes prohibited in most Arab and Muslim societies. Several of their customs, *eg*, the wearing of a face veil by men, but not by women, have been adopted by neighbouring societies.

TUBMAN, HARRIET (1821–1913), born a slave in MD, US, who escaped to Philadelphia in 1849 and became the most famous and daring agent of the underground railroad. John Brown called her 'Gen. Tubman', and she led scores of fugitive slaves to freedom. She was an effective anti-slavery speaker, and served as a nurse and Union spy during the Civil War. Later she worked for Negro education in NC.

T'U-CHÜEH, Turkish people from Central Asia. In the second half of the 6th cent. they built up a powerful confederacy and rose to a position of dominance over peoples such as the Juan-juan, whom they conquered in 552, and the Hepthalites. The T'u-chüeh were active as far west as Bokhara and Samarkand, and at times controlled the land communications between China and the Byzantine empire. In 581 they split into two major groups, of which one acknowledged the suzerainty of the Chinese Sui dynasty. It was with the help of T'u-chüeh forces that Li Yüan and his son, Li Shih-min, were able to found the T'ang empire in 618. Thereafter Chinese territory became subject to raids of the eastern T'u-chüeh, who sometimes penetrated to the gates of Ch'ang-an city. By a vigorous show of bravery and by his persuasive powers, Li Shih-min succeeded in throwing them back (630). T'ang policy was to maintain the division between the two groups, and the Chinese finally defeated the western T'u-chüeh in 657–9.

TUCHÜN, Chinese military title, used by military governors of provinces at the height of the Chinese war-lord era (*c.* 1916–28). The term was often used synonomously with 'war-lord' by westerners living in China.

TUCUMÁN, CONGRESS OF (1816), assembly of provincial delegates which declared Argentine's independence from Spain. It sat in Buenos Aires and acted as a provisional government. It met under the external threat of Spanish reconquest; internally, bitter strife raged between the Buenos Aires centralists and the autonomists of the interior (the littoral provinces, in fact, met simultaneously in a rival congress summoned by Artigas). After naming Pueyrredón as Supreme Director, the Tucumán congress acceded to the entreaties of Generals Belgrano and San Martín for immediate independence in order to promote unity in the face of a military crisis. The congress also throughout its existence deliberated schemes (supported by the generals) to create a constitutional monarchy under Inca or Brazilian royalty, for which it was denounced by liberals. In 1819 it promulgated a centralizing and aristocratic constitution which could not be enforced. The regime dissolved in anarchy the following year.

TUDEH PARTY in Iran, left-wing political group, with strong communist leanings, founded in 1941 after the relaxation of political control following the abdication of Reza Shah. Under the leadership of Sulaiman Muhsin Iskanderi (d. 1944) it expanded rapidly and, in Aug. 1946, three Tudeh Party members were admitted to the cabinet, only to be manœuvred out in Oct. The Tudeh Party was suppressed in 1949, but was revived during Musaddiq's prime ministership (1951–3), and adopted a much more radical programme. The party was again crushed in 1954–5 and in 1960 reverted to a more liberal programme.

TUDOR, HOUSE OF, in England, royal family of Welsh descent which ruled England and Wales from 1485 to 1603. Owen Tudor, the first well-documented member of the family, was descended from Edryfed Vychan of Tregarnedd in Anglesey, a steward of Llywelyn, prince of North Wales in 1232. Owen Tudor, also known as Owen ap Meredydd, lived with, and probably married, Catherine of Valois, widow of King Henry V of England. They had five children, in-cluding two sons, Edmund and Jaspar. Owen, fighting for his stepson, Henry VI, was captured and beheaded by the Yorkists at the battle of Mortimer's Cross (1461). His eldest son, Edmund (*c.* 1430–56), was created Earl of Richmond in 1453. He was declared of legitimate birth and in 1455 married Margaret, daughter of John Beaufort, Duke of Somerset. His only son, later King Henry VII, was born three months after his death (1457).

Edmund's younger brother, Jasper (*c.* 1431–95), was created Earl of Pembroke in 1453. He fought for Henry VI at St Albans (1455) and fled the country after Mortimer's Cross. After an abortive invasion of Wales (1465), he forfeited his earldom by attainder. He returned in 1470 with the Earl of Warwick, and after the defeat of Tewkesbury (at which he was not present) he took his nephew Richmond (the future Henry VII) to Brittany. He returned again in 1485 with Richmond, and after Bosworth Field was created Duke of Bedford and restored to his earldom, and in 1492 became earl marshal. He left no legitimate issue, but his illegitimate daughter, Helen, is said to have been the mother of Stephen Gardiner, Bp of Winchester.

Henry VII married Elizabeth, daughter of Edward IV. Their eldest son, Arthur, died in 1502. His younger brother thus succeeded as Henry VIII in 1509. By this time the dynasty was secure. Henry VII had based his claim to the Crown on conquest. He had no royal ancestry on the male side, and could only claim to represent the Lancastrian line through his mother, Margaret. She was the last of the Beauforts, John of Gaunt's illegitimate descendants who had been legitimized by the pope and Richard II. An insertion, of doubtful validity, in Henry IV's confirmation of Richard's grant had denied their right to succeed to the Crown. Henry VII had, however, successfully asserted his claim and by careful government secured the Crown for his progeny. The strength of the dynasty was shown when Henry VIII's three legitimate children (Edward VI, Mary I, and Elizabeth I) succeeded him without difficulty.

Henry VII had two daughters, Mary who married Louis XII of France and Charles Brandon, Duke of Suffolk, and Margaret who married James IV of Scotland and Archibald Douglas, Earl of Angus. From Mary's union with Brandon were descended Lady Jane Grey, who claimed the throne in 1553, and Catherine Grey, from whom the dukes of Somerset were descended. From Margaret's union with James IV were descended James V, Mary Queen of Scots, and James VI, who succeeded as King of England in 1603 when the direct Tudor line died out. From Margaret's union with Angus were descended the earls of Lennox and Lord Darnley, father of James VI of Scotland and I of England.

G. R. Elton, *England under the Tudors* (London, 1955).
C. Morris, *The Tudors* (London, 1950).   CJ

TU-DUC (1829–83), reign-title of the last independent Emperor of Viet-nam (*reg.* 1847–83), who inherited the throne as a youth. His reign was one in which power lay with a succession of officials. The emperor himself was a noted Confucian scholar, but unlike contemporary rulers in South-East Asia, notably Rama IV of Siam and Mindon of Burma, he had no interest in Western ideas. Catholic missionaries continued to be expelled or executed throughout the 1850s. Such Viet-namese voices as were raised in favour of Western learning, *eg*, that of Nguyen Truong To, were unheeded at Hue. During Tu-Duc's reign Viet-nam lost ground steadily to the French. In 1860 the latter seized Saigon and three surrounding provinces, and forced them to secede under the first treaty of Saigon (1862). In 1867 the French seized three more southern provinces. Added to this external pressure was the factor of repeated court conflicts, with significant plots and revolts in 1851, 1864, and 1866, and an uprising in Tongking in 1862–4. The impression is one of a gradual decline in effectiveness. In 1873 Francis Garnier led a force to Tongking and captured Hanoi; although it was withdrawn, Hue had to accept the second treaty of Saigon (1874). The

French returned to Tongking in 1882. By the time of Tu-Duc's death they were ready to impose a protectorate on Viet-nam, which was accepted in the treaty of Hue (1883–4).

TUGHLUQ DYNASTY, THE (1320–1414), founded by Ghazi Malik, a Qaraunah noble, who executed the usurper, Khusru Khan. His regnal title was Ghiyas-ud-din (*reg.* 1321–5). He restored order, subdued the Hindu raja of Warangal, and suppressed a rebellion in Bengal. He built the fortress city of Tughluqabad, near old Delhi. He was probably murdered by his son Muhammad Shah (*reg.* 1325–51), an erratic genius who tried currency experiments, moved the capital to Daulatbad (1327) and back, and attacked the north hill country. In his reign the empire began to break up with the revolt of Madurai (1335), Bengal (1337), and the Deccan (1347). He died while suppressing revolt in Sind. His nephew, Firoz Shah (*reg.* 1361–88), restored the situation, though he could not recover Bengal or the Deccan. He was a great builder and restorer, and constructed irrigation canals. He built a new city at Delhi (Firoz Shah *Kotla*), adorned with an Asoka pillar. After his death, disputed successions distracted the empire; his grandson Mahmud (*reg.* 1394–1413) was defeated at Delhi by Timur (1398), who sacked the city and completed the disintegration of the empire. Delhi and the Punjab were left desolate by this visitation. On Mahmud's death the diminished state of Delhi was seized shortly afterwards by Khizr Khan Sayyid.

TUGHRIL BEG, Rukn al-Din Abu Talib Muhammad (*reg.* 1038–63), first of the Great Seljuk sultans, whose effective control over Khurasan was assured to Tughril Beg when (1040) the Seljuks crushed the forces of the Ghaznawid Sultan Mas'ud at the battle of Dandanqan. Moving westward thereafter across Persia, the Seljuks entered Baghdad in 1055, making an end of the Buyid regime there. It was not until 1060 that the Seljuk hold on Baghdad was secure. When Tughril Beg died he left the throne to Alp Arslan, a son of his brother, Chaghri Beg.

TUGWELL, REXFORD GUY (1891–), US political scientist, and one of the original members of F. D. Roosevelt's Brains Trust. He helped to draft the Agricultural Adjustment Act (1933) and served as assistant secretary and under-secretary in the department of agriculture (1933–7). He was appointed governor of Puerto Rico in 1941 and after the Second World War taught at Chicago University.

TUKHACHEVSKY, MIKHAIL NIKOLAYEVICH (1893–1937), Russian soldier and marshal of the Soviet Union, who entered the cadet corps of the Imperial Russian Army in 1911. He served in the First World War as an officer, was taken prisoner (1915), tried unsuccessfully to escape, but eventually succeeded in reaching Russia (Oct. 1917), where he joined the Bolsheviks. He was given a command and was brilliantly successful. In the Civil War he fought against Kolchak and commanded the Red Army against Poland (1920). He was responsible for the suppression of the Kronstadt mutiny and the Tambov rising (1921). In 1922 he was appointed head of the Military Academy. He was strongly opposed to Trotsky's plans for the reorganization of the Red Army and was responsible for its development along strict military lines. He was deputy chief of staff (1924) then chief of staff (1925–8). In 1931 he was appointed Voroshilov's deputy commissar for Military and Naval Affairs and deputy chairman of the Revolutionary Military Council. During the great Stalinist purge he was accused of contact with the Germans in the pursuit of a military conspiracy and was executed without trial (June 1937). He was rehabilitated (1958) during Khrushchev's period of power.

TULA, capital of the Toltecs in pre-Columbian Mexico. It is representative of Mesoamerican sites which made the transition from ceremonial centres to cities to be lived in and defended by military societies.

TULA in Russia, provincial town situated in the Oka basin on the southern borders of old Muscovy, the centre of the earliest iron-mining and smelting industry in Russia and basis of the armament industry until the late 17th cent. By 1725 the depletion of iron ore and wood for charcoal smelting affected its pre-eminence, and it was superseded by newer developments in the Urals and St Petersburg regions. Tula remained a centre for the manufacture of cutlery and hardware in the 19th cent.

TULIP ERA (lale devri), name given to a period in Ottoman history (1718–1830) characterized by a literary and artistic efflorescence and the beginnings of a European style of modernization, which included the introduction of printing (1724) and military reforms, and was ended by a conservative revolt (1730) and the execution of the grand vizier, Ibrahim Pasha.

TULL, JETHRO (1674–1741), English lawyer and farmer, who studied European farming practices which led him to pioneer soil cultivation in Berkshire through aeration and the sowing of seed in rows (as opposed to broadcasting it). His book, *Horse-hoeing Husbandry* (1733), spread his ideas.

TULLUS HOSTILIUS (*reg.* 673–642 BC), third King of Rome, by tradition, who destroyed Alba Longa, probably in retaliation for an attack on Rome. The Curia Hostilia, where the senate met, may date from his reign.

TULSIDAS (1532–1623), Hindi poet of the Rama cult, who lived in Benares. His version of 'Ramayana', the 'Ramcharitamanasa', exercised an incalculable influence on north Indian Hindus.

TULUNID, name given to a line of amirs ruling over Egypt and Syria during the years 868–905. The first of these amirs, Ahmad ibn Tulun (*reg.* 868–84), soon added to his command of the armed forces in Egypt an effective control over the revenues of the province—revenues which he strove to increase through a wise and careful administration. With the resources available to him he was able to recruit a strong army and to extend his influence over much of Syria. Ahmed ibn Tulun was fortunate in that the government of the caliph at Baghdad was involved in a long and bitter conflict (868–883) with the Zanj and had therefore little time to spare for events in Egypt. Khumarawayh (*reg.* 884–96), the son and successor of Ahmad ibn Tulun, was able to negotiate with the caliph an agreement which, in return for an annual tribute to Baghdad, recognized Tulunid rule over Egypt, Syria, and the adjacent territories. After the murder of Khumarawayh in 896 the Tulunid regime fell into a rapid decline as a result of continuing feuds and intrigues among the generals and dignitaries around the throne. In 905 troops under the command of Muhammad ibn Sulayman, acting in the name of the Caliph al-Muktafi (*reg.* 902–8), entered Egypt and made an end of the Tulunid amirate.

TULUVA DYNASTY, THE (1505–65), third and most famous of the four dynasties of the Hindu empire of Vijayanagar. It was founded by Narasa Nayak, first the minister of Saluva Narasimha (*reg.* 1486–92), and then regent for his sons. Narasa's son, Vira Narasimha, seized the throne (*reg.* 1505–9) and, later, his half-brother, Krishnadeva Raya (*reg.* 1509–29), became the greatest of the Vijayanagar kings. The splendour of his court was described by the Portuguese, Domingos Paes (1522). From *c.* 1542 power was exercised by the minister, Ramaraja, in the name of the last Tuluva king, Sadasiva. After the battle of Talikota (1565) Ramaraja's brother, Tirumula, usurped the throne.

TUNG CHUNG-SHU, Chinese writer and philosopher, who formulated the earliest scheme of state Confucianism. This incorporated veneration for Confucius, attention to the lessons of some early texts, a belief in heaven's active participation in human affairs, and a belief in the theories of *Yin-yang* and the Five Elements.

T'UNG-CHIH REIGN (1862–75), reign-title of Tsai-chun (*reg.* 1856–75), eighth emperor of the Chinese Ch'ing dynasty, the only son of the Hsien-feng emperor and his favourite consort Tz'u-hsi (who was empress dowager after 1861). As the T'ung-chih emperor was a minor, actual power was held by Tz'u-hsi and the other Empress Dowager Tz'u-an (senior consort of the deceased Hsien-feng). Even after he came of age early in 1873, he was not permitted to exercise real power. Resenting Tz'u-hsi's meddling with his public and private life, and misled by certain eunuchs and officials, he found consolation in Peking's pleasure quarters which led to his death, officially of smallpox, but probably of syphilis. Although his reign-title had given the T'ung-chih Restoration its name, he had little to do with its failure or success.

T'UNG-CHIH RESTORATION (1862–74) in China, term that refers to the government's efforts to restore the Confucian social and political order which had obtained before the Opium War. As the efforts were made mainly by provincial officials, there was no overall programme for the empire, although the common Confucian background of the individuals concerned did produce a large area of agreement on aims and methods. Generally, the Restoration was characterized by the suppression of rebellions and the restoration of civil (especially local) government, by a wide search for new talent and the revival of civil service examinations, and by the rehabilitation of the traditional economy. The general tone was one of conservatism. Even the 'self-strengthening' movement, which began as part of the Restoration, and the modest attempts to modernize China's foreign relations (*eg*, creation of the Tsungli Yamen and the T'ung-wen Kuan), were intended to defend the Confucian order against Western incursions, although they had wider implications and consequences. Initially, the Restoration was helped by the 'co-operative policy' of the foreign powers, but the Tientsin Massacre (1870) led to the resumption of the 'gunboat policy'. The exhilarating feeling of a dynastic revival was also dampened by the self-seeking empress dowager, Tz'u-hsi, who dominated the court.

TUNG-LIN PARTY in China, so-called 'Party of the Eastern Grove', a political group which had its origins in the Tung-Lin Academy. It was founded in 1604 by a group of scholar-officials who had been dismissed from government. The Ming dynasty, already corrupt and in decline by this time, was dominated by a powerful eunuch, Wei Chung-hsien (1568–1627). Influenced by the iconoclastic individualism of the philosophy of Wang Yang-ming, the Tung-lin scholars attacked the corrupt government and the autocratic Wei. During 1620–3 the Tung-lin partisans rose briefly to power, thanks to the influence of a friendly eunuch. But Wei fought back, and the Tung-lin members were punished severely in the ensuing purge. Although numbering over 300 members at its peak, the Tung-lin Party was not a political party in the modern sense. Its members came from various provinces, many of them had no group consciousness, and they had no unity of policy except that of restoring a moral, Confucian government. Thus the party enjoyed the praise of later historians, although it was part of the political fragmentation that characterized the end of the Ming dynasty.

T'UNG-MENG HUI ('United League') in China, revolutionary organization that was instrumental in the overthrow of the Ch'ing dynasty and the establishment of the republic. It was founded by Sun Yat-sen and Huang Hsing in 1905. During the following years it established branches among overseas Chinese communities (South-East Asia, US, etc.) for fund-raising and other revolutionary purposes. Its radical programme soon attracted many members from among the followers of the reformists Liang Ch'i-ch'ao and K'ang Yu-wei. The T'ung-meng Hui boasted such leaders as Sung Chiao-jen, Hu Han-min, as well as Sun and Huang. During the latter part of the 1900s it infiltrated the Ch'ing 'New Army' and staged numerous risings in south and central China. It finally succeeded in 1911 and, in the following year, absorbed several other parties to form the Nationalist Party (Kuomintang).

T'UNG TIEN, title of a Chinese encyclopedic work completed in 801. It was undertaken to assist civil servants in the conduct of their duties, to help candidates for the examinations, and partly as a proud record of the validity and achievements of Chinese institutions. The book is divided into large sections which correspond with different aspects of government, *eg*, economic practice; the system of recruiting officials; the functions of the civil service; the conduct of rites and music; the armed forces; state punishments; administrative geography; and frontier defence. Each chapter includes extracts from works such as the Standard Histories and also from books which may now have been lost. The extracts are set out in chronological order and describe the growth of institutions and practices from the earliest and mythical periods until the contemporary T'ang dynasty. The *T'ung-tien* is the first of a series of encyclopedic compilations of this type and is a most valuable source for the history of the T'ang period.

T'UNG-WEN KUAN in China, often translated as 'Interpreters' College' or 'College of Foreign Languages', was created in 1862 under the Tsungli Yamen to train interpreters to help in handling China's foreign affairs. It employed Western as well as Chinese teachers. From 1866 Western science, international law, and political economy were also taught, and a printing office was created to publish works in these fields. In 1902 it was absorbed into the Imperial University.

TUN-HUANG, provincial unit and town at the extreme northwestern edge of China (mod. Kansu province). Official posts were first established there in *c*. 100 BC, but since then the area has from time to time been outside Chinese control. Archaeological sites and caves have revealed valuable evidence, in material and documentary form, of Chinese administration from the Han period onwards, together with remnants of early Buddhist and other texts.

TUNIS, BEYS OF, rulers of Tunisia since the 17th cent. The bey, an officer controlling the patronage of the government of the Ottoman province, ousted the dey, a military officer, from effective power. A monarchy was firmly established when a general took the title in order to found the Husainid dynasty (1705–1957). In the 19th cent. the beys tended to look towards France for support at home and abroad, getting into debt as they attempted to modernize the regime. On the pretext of a threat to Algeria, France exercised wide powers of supervision from 1881, which culminated in a colonial regime. To retain their throne, the beys remained complaisant. Following independence in 1956 the Tunisian monarchy was suppressed in 1957.

TUNISIA (164,150 sq. kms) in North Africa, formerly a French protectorate which became independent in 1956. Berber and Arab groups made up a population (1970) of 4,457,800.

TUNISIAN CRUSADE (1270), second crusading venture of King Louis IX of France. His brother Charles, King of Sicily, persuaded him to direct it against Tunisia, which menaced Sicily. After landing outside Tunis, the crusading army was ravaged by plague, from which St Louis died (Aug. 1270). The Crusade had to be evacuated and some of its survivors went to Palestine, where the whole expedition should have gone in the first place.

TUNJUR, people scattered from Sudan to Bornu, whose main centre is in Kanem (near Lake Chad). In the late 16th and early 17th cents they ruled over what are now Darfur and Wadai, before being driven from the first by Sulayman Solong, and from the second by Abd al-Kerim.

TUNNAGE AND POUNDAGE in England, customs duties on wine and wool, developed in the Middle Ages and consolidated under Edward III, which were granted by parliament to the Tudors and James I for life. A general resistance to these duties grew under the Stuarts, and in 1625 the House of Commons reviewed the whole field of customs and only granted tunnage and poundage to Charles I for a year. Charles continued to collect them without parliamentary sanction and in 1626 parliament declared his action illegal. The privy council in turn declared the taxes independent of parliamentary control, and in 1628–9 the controversy grew fierce, culminating in two resolutions of the Commons condemning the levying of tunnage and poundage without the consent of parliament. Tunnage and poundage remained a grievance until the Civil War. In 1641 the Tunnage and Poundage Act gave Charles the taxes for two months only, and it was renewed at two-monthly intervals until July 1642. In 1697 tunnage and poundage was incorporated into the civil list.

TUNSTALL, CUTHBERT (1474–1559), English cleric, who became master of the rolls (1516), dean of Salisbury (1521), Bp of London (1522), keeper of the privy seal (1523), and Bp of Durham (1530). During the Reformation he remained a Catholic while believing in passive obedience to the civil power. Though friendly with Somerset and Cranmer, he was in a difficult position under Edward VI, and was imprisoned by Northumberland, tried for treason, and deprived of his bishopric (1552). He was restored under Mary I, but refused to take the oath of supremacy on the accession of Elizabeth I and was again deprived (1559).

TUPAC AMARU II (JOSÉ GABRIEL CONDORCANQUI), Marquis of Oropesa (1742–81), leader of perhaps the most serious native rebellion in Spanish American history. Although of Inca lineage and a member of the native nobility, Condorcanqui was also a Spanish-educated *mestizo* of considerable wealth who had been shown high favour by the Crown. Some historians attribute his rebellion to a genuine sympathy with the plight of the native masses, but others contend that he was angered by alleged slights by the colonial authorities. In 1780, taking the name of the last Inca emperor, Condorcanqui led a native revolt which dominated much of the Peruvian highlands. He insisted on loyalty to the king, but the Creole upper classes refused to join him, and the Crown suppressed the revolt with great difficulty and much bloodshed. Condorcanqui was executed in a frightful manner.

TUPPER, SIR CHARLES (1821–1915), Canadian doctor, politician, and prime minister, who left a successful medical practice in NS to enter politics as a member of the provincial assembly (1855) and took a leading role in the confederation movement against Joseph Howe. He was elected a Conservative member of the House of Commons (1867–84), and served the cabinet as president of the council (1870), minister of inland revenue (1872), and minister of customs (1873). As the first minister of railways and canals (1879–84), Tupper organized the department and introduced the bill giving the Canadian Pacific Railway its charter (1881). He served also as Canadian high commissioner in London (1884–7, 1888–96) and finance minister in Macdonald's cabinet (1887–8). He became secretary of state under Sir Mackenzie Bowell (1896) and upon Bowell's resignation was prime minister for a brief period until the Conservative defeat, after which he led the opposition until his retirement (1900).

TURABA, BATTLE OF (1919), defeat of Hijazi troops under Abdullah by Saudi (Ikhwan) forces, which marked the beginning of the contest between the Hashemites and Saudis for supremacy in Arabia.

TURATI, FILIPPO (1857–1932), Italian politician and co-founder, with Anna Kuliscioff, of the Italian Socialist Party (Partito Socialista) in 1891. He was leader (1896–1926) of its reformist deputies. His willingness to support non-socialist ministers, notably Giolitti, on conditions facilitated the development of the Socialist Party. But his reformism, gradualism, and opposition to violence alienated the party's maximalists. He helped to prevent factory seizures (Aug. 1920) and general strikes leading to revolutionary attempts, but he refused to join non-socialist coalitions. This led Mussolini to have him expelled from the PSI as a reformist. He then started the Unitary Socialist Party in 1922, courageously defying fascist intimidation before being smuggled out of Italy to France in 1926.

TURCOMAN, generic term designating the nomadic tribes, Turkish in their origin, who followed the pastoral mode of life remoted from the settled areas and towns, *eg*, the tribal elements to be found in Asia Minor and in Persia. The word should not be confused with Türkmen (the name of a particular tribe); nor with Turk (denoting, in Ottoman usage, the population, Turkish in speech and Muslim in faith, settled on the soil of Asia Minor).

TURDETANI, ancient tribe of south-western Spain, chiefly known for a revolt against Rome in 197 BC and put down by Cato the Elder.

TURENNE, HENRI DE LA TOUR D'AUVERGNE, Viscount de (1611–75), French marshal and soldier, who was brought up a Protestant and learned the art of war from his uncle, Maurice of Nassau, in the Dutch War of Independence (1625–30). He took service in the French army in 1630 and rose to be supreme commander of the French armies in the Thirty Years' War (1643), after his victories over the Spaniards at Casale and Montferrato (1640), and his reconquest of Roussillon (1642). Though routed at Marienthal by the imperialists (1645), he conquered Trier and shared the Bavarian campaigns with the Swedish armies (1645–8). He joined the *Frondeurs* in the first phase of the civil wars of the *Fronde* (1649) but after being defeated at Rethel (1650), he withdrew to Flanders, until, on becoming reconciled with the court, he turned against Condé and the rebellious nobility (1652), forcing them to retire from France. He went on to conquer much of the Spanish Netherlands and defeated Condé again at the battle of the Dunes (1658). In 1667 Turenne commanded the French armies in the Spanish Netherlands, and in 1668 was converted to Catholicism. He led the triumphant French campaign against Holland (1672) and held his ground against the forces of Montecuccoli and the Elector of Brandenburg (1673). In the course of the Dutch War he crushed the Brandenburgers at Colmar, and laid waste the Palatinate and Alsace.

TURGENEV, IVAN SERGEYEVICH (1818–83), Russian novelist, author of *Sportsman's Sketches* (1847–52), which drew attention to the humane qualities of the Russian peasantry; of *Rudin* (1855); and of *Fathers and Children* (1862), whose hero, Bazarov, became the prototype of Nihilism and was violently criticized by the radicals. Although a friend of Herzen, he eventually quarrelled with him, Herzen's idealization of the Russian peasant seeming unrealistic to Turgenev, who argued that Russia must follow a European pattern and that the task of the intelligentsia was to transmit civilization to the peasantry.

TURGHUD ALI RE'IS (d. 1565), known to the Christians as Dragut, a famous corsair, trained under Khayr al-Din Barbarossa. After service at the sea battle of Prevesa (1538) he was captured on the coast of Corsica in 1540 and remained a prisoner in the hands of the Genoese until Khayr al-Din ransomed him in 1544. In 1551 he captured Tripoli from the Knights of St John, establishing there a second corsair regime on the North African shore (the first of the corsair states was Algiers).

TURGOT, ANNE ROBERT JACQUES, Baron de l'Aulne (1727–81), French politician, philosopher, and finance minister, who, as a disciple of the Physiocrats, tried to effect radical reforms in pre-revolutionary France. He believed in 'a fully articulated theory of progress' and wrote a famous economic treatise, *Réflexions sur la formation et la distribution des richesses* (1766). After being highly successful as the intendant of the Limousin (1761–74), he was appointed minister of marine (July 1774), and then controller-general (Aug. 1774) by Louis XVI. At first he showed a certain political naïveté in supporting the recall of the *parlements*, the chief obstacle to financial reforms affecting the privileged classes. He began his ministry by introducing some improvements in the collection of the *taille* and by reducing pensions and sinecures. He relaxed restrictions on the corn trade, introduced by Terray, appointed the great scientist, Lavoisier, to take charge of the manufacture of gunpowder in the new *regié des poudres*, and abolished the private monopoly of the postal service, which he made a public system. He also proposed fundamental changes in the education system to train all children in citizenship, and advocated a certain degree of decentralization of government, state protection for the poor, and the reorganization of the army and the ministry of war. By 1775 he had reduced national expenditure by some 66 million *livres* and the interest on loans from 8,700,000 to some 3 million *livres*.

The climax of his programme of economic reform came with the Six Edicts (Jan. 1776). The earlier laissez-faire edicts concerning the corn trade were to be extended to include Paris, and a number of unnecessary offices in the markets and quays of the capital were to be abolished. The restrictive guilds which controlled many industries (*jurandes*) were to be abolished and the peasants' labour services (*corvée*) replaced by a general tax levied on all landowners for the maintenance of roads. These relics of medieval society had been the object of physiocratic attack and the preamble to the edicts contained a general condemnation of privilege.

Turgot's work was attacked by powerful vested interests, the financiers, the *parlements*, and the *dévot* party. The Six Edicts had to be registered by a *lit de justice* (March 1776), though Parisians and peasantry alike celebrated the new measures of freedom. His position, however, was being undermined by the other ministers, Saint-Germain, Vergennes, Miromesnil, and even Maurepas. In May 1776 Louis XVI dismissed him and by the summer many of his reforms had been suspended.

Douglas Dakin, *Turgot and the Ancien Régime in France* (London, 1939).
B. C. A. Behrens, *The Ancien Régime* (London, 1967).
MKS

TURIN, BATTLE OF (Sept. 1706), imperial victory of Prince Eugène against the French who were besieging the Savoyard capital under La Feuillade in the War of the Spanish Succession. Eugène brought his army 322 kms from the Adige river to force the besiegers' fortifications. Marshal Marsin was mortally wounded and captured, while Italy, saved from the French, fell under Austrian domination.

TURIN, TREATY OF (1696), secret peace agreement between Count Tessé, representative of Louis XIV of France and the Savoyard finance minister, Giambattista Gropello, representing Victor Amadeus, Duke of Savoy. In return for Savoy's defection from the allied cause in the War of the League of Augsburg, Louis XIV allowed Savoyard troops into Casale and Pinerolo. This undermined the allied war effort and forced the emperor and Spain to accede to the neutrality of Italy.

TURIN CANON, ancient Egyptian king-list, dating from the time of Rameses II (*reg. c.* 1290–1224 BC) and now in the Turin Museum. It gives a list of kings, starting with Menes, with the length of life and reign of each.

TURKEY COUP (1960), army coup on 27 May against the government of Adnan Menderes and his Democratic Party, who were accused of adopting repressive policies to ensure their continuance in power. Opposition also came from those who were opposed to the inflationary economic policies, the modification of the secularizing Republican Party policies, and Menderes's political interference with the army. The coup was led by Gen. Cemal Gürsel, who subsequently became president (26 Oct. 1961). Menderes was executed and many Democrats imprisoned after trial. In 1961 a new constitution was introduced, elections held, and government returned to civilian hands, the army junta having defeated attempts by Colonels Alparslan Türkesh and Talat Aydemir to establish permanent military rule.

TURKISH INDEPENDENCE. The defeat of the Ottoman empire in the First World War and the Allied plans to partition it provoked a strong reaction in Anatolia, which was inflamed by the Greek landing at Smyrna (May 1919). This hostility was exploited by Mustafa Kemal (1881–1938), who arrived at Samsun (19 May 1919), ostensibly to demobilize Ottoman forces, and resigned his commission when recalled by the Ottoman government. Working through the Association for the Defence of the Rights of Eastern Anatolia (founded 3 March 1919), he summoned congresses at Erzerum (July–Aug.) and Sivas (Sept. 1919), which formulated the aims embodied in the Turkish National Pact. The Ottoman government, under Ali Reza, made concessions to the Nationalists (Oct. 1919), who won a majority in the elections in Dec. However, in March 1919, the Nationalist MPs in Istanbul were arrested and the Ottoman government, under Allied pressure, opposed the Nationalists, who now summoned in Ankara their own parliament, the Grand National Assembly (April 1920). The Nationalists defeated the Ottoman forces sent against them and then confronted their main adversary, Greece, whom they repulsed at Inönü (April) and the Sakarya river (Aug. 1921) and finally expelled from Smyrna (Sept. 1922). Observing these events, France, Italy, and eventually Britain (armistice of Mudaniya, 11 Oct. 1922) decided to withdraw from the area. By the treaty of Lausanne (24 July 1923) the Nationalists, now recognized as the legal government of Turkey, achieved international recognition of the independence they had won. MEY

TURKISH NATIONALISM. Until the 19th cent. Turks regarded themselves primarily as Muslims. The word 'Turk' in the Ottoman empire was reserved for the Anatolian nomad or peasant and had connotations of uncouthness, while 'Turkey' was used only by Europeans. The Ottoman reformers of the 19th and early 20th cents, while retaining the Islamic bond for Muslims, stressed the concept of common allegiance to the Ottoman dynasty (Ottomanism). With the gradual dissolution of the Ottoman empire and the impact of European ideas of linguistic nationalism the concept of Turkism began to develop at the end of the 19th cent., when it was strongly reinforced by the advent of Pan-Turk émigrés from Russia. After the 1908 Young Turk revolution, various societies (the Turkish Society, 1908; the Turkish Hearth, 1912) and periodicals (*The Turkish Homeland*) were founded, which elaborated ideas of Turkish nationalism. The movement was aided by emphasis on primary education, which led to new interest in the simpler form of Turkish spoken in Anatolia. Despite the growing interest in Turkism, however, the dominant ideology of the Ottoman empire until its collapse in 1918 remained a mixture of Islam and Ottoman centralization. The loss of the Arab provinces in 1918 led to a close correspondence between the Ottoman empire and the area inhabited by Turkish speakers. Even so, the so-called nationalist movement (1919–23) still drew its main strength from traditional Muslim hostility to infidel interference with Islamic lands. It was only gradually, under the guidance of Mustafa Kemal, that the name 'Türkiye' was first adopted (1921), the republic created (1924), and through the rewriting of history and the remodelling of language the idea of Turkish nationalism slowly disseminated. MEY

TURKISH WARS, phrase understood to embrace the successive confrontations between the Ottoman empire and its chief Christian rivals—ie, Venice, Austria, and Russia—during the 15th–19th cents. During the Middle Ages Venice had acquired a rich imperium in the Levant. The rise of the Ottoman Turks led to a series of wars, with the Venetians intent on defending their overseas possessions and the Turks determined to take them under their own control: 1463–79 (Ottoman conquest of Negroponte); 1499–1503 (Venetian enclaves in the Morea, eg, Modon, Koron, Navarino, fall to the Ottomans); 1537–40 (end of Venetian rule in the Morea); 1570–3 (Ottoman conquest of Cyprus); 1645–9 (Ottomans take Crete from Venice); 1684–99 (Venetian reconquest of the Morea); and 1714–18 (Venice forced to relinquish the Morea to the Turks).

The reign of Sultan Suleiman saw the destruction of the old Hungarian kingdom at the battle of Mohácz in 1526. That kingdom passed to the legal heir through marriage, the Habsburg Archduke Ferdinand of Austria. During the years 1527–40 Suleiman, regarding Hungary as his own by right of conquest, maintained at Buda, as a king dependent on himself, John Azpolya, formerly vaivoda of Transylvania. After 1540 three Hungaries emerged—Habsburg, in the north and west; Ottoman along the middle Danube (Belgrade–Buda–Esztergom); and Transylvania, east of the Tisza river, under a vaivoda owing allegiance to the sultan. There was little change in this situation during the conflict of 1593–1606, which represented for the Ottomans perhaps their last real chance to continue their advance against Europe on a large scale. Their offensive ended, however, in virtual defeat. At the peace of Zsitva-Torok in 1606 the Ottoman sultan had to recognize the Habsburg emperor as his equal. The revival of Ottoman aggression under the Köprülü viziers after 1656 committed the armies of the sultan to a dangerous course, since the Austria of Leopold I had been raised during the 16th and 17th cents to the status of a great power. The war of the Sacra Liga (1684–99), which followed the Ottoman siege of Vienna in 1683, ended in the peace of Carlowitz, the Ottomans now ceding their Hungarian possessions to the Habsburg emperor, with the exception of Temesvar, which itself fell to the Austrians in the brief war of 1716–18. Subsequent confrontations in 1737–9 and again in 1787–92 made little change in the situation that had existed between the Ottoman empire and Austria since 1699 and 1718.

The first conflict of note between Russia and the Ottoman empire, a border conflict in the Ukraine, came in 1678–81. Peter the Great, entering the war of Sacra Liga, took Azov in 1696. His campaign against the Ottomans in 1711 ended, however, in defeat on the Pruth river. Not until 1736–9 did Russia undertake a major offensive designed to extend her influence southwards, at the expense of the Turks, in the lands adjacent to the Black Sea. Although the Russians gained considerable success in the field, the diplomatic manœuvres which led to the peace of Belgrade in 1739 gave them little reward for their vast expenditure on the war. Far more advantageous to Russia was the conflict of 1768–74. By the peace of Kuchuk-Kainardji the Russians achieved substantial territorial gains and also a plausible excuse for subsequent intervention in the affairs of the Ottoman empire. The settlement of 1774 was only a prelude to the Russian annexation of the khanate of the Crimea in 1783. A new war in 1787–92 brought additional territories to Russia along the coast of the Black Sea, and in yet another war in 1806–12 she advanced her frontier to the Pruth river and the Kilya mouth of the Danube. Later hostilities between the Russians and the Ottomans in 1828–9, 1853–6 (the Crimean War), and 1877–8 represent important phases in the 'Eastern

Question' so prominent in the political and diplomatic annals of the 19th–20th cents.

D. Vaughan, *Europe and the Turk* (Liverpool, 1954). VJP

TURKOMANCHAI TREATY (22 Feb. 1828), Russo–Iranian agreement ending the war (1826–8), which had opened with an Iranian attack, provoked by the Russian occupation of Gokcheh in defiance of the treaty of Gulistan (1813). By the treaty, Iran ceded territory in Azerbayjan to Russia, establishing the Arras frontier, and agreed to pay a large indemnity. A commercial agreement signed at the same time afforded a basis for additional Russian influence.

TURK–SIB RAILWAY, linking Turkestan with the Trans-Siberian railway at Novosibirsk, via Alma Ata and Semipalatinsk, begun in 1912–13 and completed in 1930. It was intended to make possible increased cotton cultivation in Turkestan by facilitating imports of cheap Siberian wheat, and it became an important agency of Soviet influence in eastern Turkestan.

TURNER, SIR GEORGE (1857–1916), Australian lawyer and politician in pre-Federation Vic. As prime minister of the colony, he was responsible for the financial measures needed for Vic's recovery from the depression of the early 1890s. He gave cautious support to Federation in 1900, and was several times Commonwealth treasurer and a member of the House of Representatives (1901–6).

TURNER, WILLIAM (d. 1568), English theologian and botanist, who inquired into plants from a scientific point of view. He introduced lucerne as a fodder crop from the continent, and his *Herbal* promoted the study of botany in England.

TURNER INSURRECTION (21 Aug. 1831) in the US, last and most serious of three Negro slave revolts in the American South. It was preceded by the Gabriel insurrection in VA (1800) and the Vesey plot in SC (1822), and was led by the semi-educated Negro preacher, Nat Turner (1800–31). Over 50 slaves rebelled and murdered 55 white inhabitants of Southampton County, VA. The slaves were hunted down and captured, and 17 of them were hanged, including Nat Turner (11 Nov. 1831). Southern reaction was intense, and led to severely repressive slave codes and demands for fugitive slave laws.

TURNER'S FRONTIER THESIS OF AMERICAN DEVELOPMENT, general theory to explain the 'uniqueness' of the American character, enunciated by the US historian, Frederick Jackson Turner (1861–1932). In its popular connotation, the frontier means a line separating, at any given moment, the settled regions from those not yet organized. This phase of the American experience was declared ended by the director of the US Census (1890). Alternatively, frontier has been defined as the region on either side of the furthest line of settlement which has a population of only 2–6 inhabitants per square mile. A third meaning of the term has been the process by which old patterns of life and ideas undergo continuous adaptation to new requirements. In this process land is settled in a succession of economic stages, including fur trading, cattle grazing, mining, farming, and urban development. Frontier has also been used as a metaphor for early social and economic evolution, particularly applied to the time-span of the first two to three decades of development and as a metaphor for new opportunity. From these ideas of the frontier, Turner, writing during the late 19th and early 20th cents, developed a theory which shaped much American historical writing. He stated his hypothesis in a seminal paper, 'The Significance of the Frontier in American History', read to a meeting of the American Historical Association in Chicago (1893), when he claimed that 'the existence of an area of free land, its continuous recession, and the advance of American settlement westward', explain American development. According to Turner, the peculiarity of the US and its institutions resulted from the influence of a changing environment as the expanding population crossed and pioneered a continent over the course of three centuries. He reiterated this thesis in later writings, such as *The Frontier in American History* (1920) and *The Significance of Sections in American History* (1932), often paying marked attention to the part which he claimed the frontier had played in stimulating the growth of American democracy. Turner was very much a product of his age, and his writings were thus both deterministic and Darwinian. His hypothesis rests on its general plausibility rather than upon proof, but although the theory and its component parts have been subject to constant attack since the 1920s, it still provides a useful approach to US history.

R. A. Billington, *Westward Expansion* (New York, 1960).
M. Curti, *Frederick Jackson Turner* (Mexico, 1949).   MW

TURNHOUT, BATTLE OF (Aug. 1597), victory of Maurice of Nassau and his cavalry over the forces of Archduke Albert in the Netherlands, which enabled the Dutch to complete the conquest of the eastern provinces and take Rheinberg, Grol, and Oldenzaal, setting the seal on their independence from the Spanish Crown.

TURNIPS, root vegetables, the use of which as an integral part of a four-year crop rotation was attributed to Viscount Townshend (nicknamed 'Turnip' Townshend) of Norfolk in the 1730s. They had, however, been introduced into English agriculture as a fallow field crop from the mid-17th cent. and helped to improve the fertility of the soil as well as to provide a valuable winter feed for cattle.

TURNPIKE TRUSTS, in Britain, started in the reign of King Charles II, but their main period of development was in the second half of the 18th cent., particularly 1750–70 and the years around 1800. The trusts, set up by parliament, were responsible for the care and maintenance of roads, in place of the parishes, which otherwise had this duty. They were allowed to receive parish funds and raise tolls for these purposes and could also make their own arrangements for collecting other sums for road improvement, and, as landowners and local businessmen were often members of the trusts, they had a strong economic interest in the efficient upkeep of the roads.

The trusts, though regulated as regards standards of road care and level of tolls by the General Highway Act (1767), never provided a real road 'system' and this was one of the weaknesses of the arrangement. At their most extensive, in 1837, there were more than 1000 separate trusts, which maintained about 22,000 miles (35,200 kms) of roads—somewhat less than a sixth of all those in the country. Some areas had very few turnpike roads, others were well routed; the level of maintenance also varied greatly. In a few cases trusts were under fraudulent management, but usually local patriotism, which was one of the motives for creating them, prevented this, though it did not necessarily prevent muddle and incompetence. There was, however, little regulation of the use of funds or methods of accounting and most trusts found it difficult to set aside enough money for repairs after paying the interest on their capital. By 1837, though their total revenue from tolls was £1½ million, many trusts were in difficulties.

Turnpike trusts did in fact achieve a great improvement in the state of the roads, and so had an important influence on the agriculture and industrial development of the late 18th cent. They made possible the elaborate system of stage and mail coaches which gave the country relatively fast, if expensive, means of travel and communication. The introduction by the railways of a faster, cheaper, and more comfortable means of travel caused a substantial drop in the trusts' revenue and eventually they became insolvent. Efforts were made, in some cases with success, to return the functions of the trusts to the parishes, and an act of 1835 allowed parishes to set up Highway Boards. But not until the 1860s was it recognized that local government needed mandatory acts, and by then the trusts were almost totally decayed. Britain could no longer be said to have a road system. The railways had taken over long-distance traffic and it was not until the ubiquity of the motor car made new national arrangements essential that a planned road system was reintroduced.

RMM

TUSCARORA INDIANS, American tribe first encountered in NC (*c.* 1650) by European settlers, who appropriated their lands and sold them as slaves. This treatment of them precipitated two wars (1711, 1713), in which the Tuscarora were defeated. They took refuge among the Iroquois of NY, mainly the Oneida, and were made members of the Iroquois League (*c.* 1722). The majority were loyal to the colonies in the American War of Independence and suffered at the hands of Indian allies of the British. The Oneida sold the lands they gave the Tuscarora (1785), making them homeless until they were given a small grant in western NY (1797), where a few remained in 1970.

TUSHINO in Russia, village on the north-western outskirts of Moscow, site of the camp of the second false Dmitri and his Cossack and Polish followers (1608–9) during the Time of Troubles. It was destroyed by the Poles after the Pretender fled to Kaluga seeking protection from the Swedish allies of Tsar Vasili Shuisky.

TUSKEGEE INSTITUTE in the US, industrial school for Negroes, established in 1881 by the state legislature in AL. Its first principal, Booker T. Washington, had to contend with inadequate facilities and white hostility, but successfully instructed students in the building of school premises and the provision of basic services for the institution and the surrounding white and black communities.

TUTANKHAMUN (*reg. c.* 1347–1339 BC), Egyptian King of the XVIIIth dynasty, who restored the worship of Amen, ending the heresy introduced by Amenhetep IV. His tomb, found intact in 1922 by Howard Carter, revealed immense treasures which have aided the study of Egyptian ceremonial rites and arts.

TUTORA, BATTLE OF (Sept. 1620), victory of the Turks over the Polish–Moldavian forces commanded by Zolkiewski on the Pruth river, the first direct clash between Poland and Turkey since Varna (1444). However, the Turkish advance was checked near Khotin (1621) and the brief war ended with a return to the status quo.

TUTTLINGEN, BATTLE OF (1643), imperial victory over the French in Württemberg during the Thirty Years War. The Bavarian generals, Franz von Mercy and Johann von Werth, surprised the French forces under the Count de Guébriant at their camp near Tuttlingen, drove them back, and recovered Rottweil, thus avenging the recent imperialist disaster at Rocroi (1643).

TUWAT, oasis region in south-western Algeria, first mentioned by Ptolemy. Never conquered by the Romans, Vandals, or Byzantines, these oases commanded a major trans-Saharan route, and were probably converted to Islam in the 8th cent. After being subdued by the Almoravids, they regained their independence, but were again subjugated by the Marinids of Fez in 1315.

In the 15th cent. they enjoyed a semi-independent status and great prosperity, based on their date groves and the Saharan caravan trade. They included over 200 villages and towns, among them several belonging to Jewish communities; these were greatly reduced through persecution under Al-Maghili in 1492.

Much of the region was restored to Moroccan control in 1588, but by the early 17th cent. was governed by a vassal emir. In 1667 Tuwat was again placed under a Moroccan governor. Later, it was ruled by France, and in post-colonial times the discovery of natural gas promised in 1970 to restore the oases' former prosperity.

TUXTEPEC, PLAN OF (1876) in Mexico, successful revolutionary plan which was proclaimed by Porfirio Díaz against the government of Lerdo de Tejada. Díaz insisted on 'effective suffrage and no re-election' and demanded the president's resignation. He had rebelled unsuccessfully under a similar plan, that of La Noria, four years earlier. Government forces drove Díaz into exile, but he soon returned and defeated Lerdo's supporters (Nov. 1876). He was installed as president (May 1877) and governed dictatorially in defiance of the slogans of the Plan of Tuxtepec (1876–80, 1884–1911).

TWA, pygmoid African people, speaking languages of the Bantu family, and most commonly found (1970) in the forest country of south-west Uganda, Rwanda, and in the Ituri forest of eastern Congo. Before the expansion of the major Bantu-speaking societies in East Africa, they probably dominated much of the open country, possibly connecting with similar hunting-gathering peoples further south. As effective bowmen, they were sometimes brought into military alliances, but never into durable political subordination.

TWEED, WILLIAM MARCY (1823–78), US political figure, identified with corruption in New York city. He was elected alderman in 1851, and four years later captured control of Tammany Hall. By manœuvring himself and his henchmen into key positions in the city's administration, Tweed and his associates (1865–71) robbed its treasury of an estimated $200 million. The Tweed 'Ring' proper was formed on 1 Jan. 1869 and within 30 months had cost the city between $30 million and $60 million. In 1870 *Harpers Weekly* and the *New York Times* began a campaign against Tweed which brought to light proof of his corruption. An investigating Committee of Seventy, which included Samuel J. Tilden, discovered evidence which led to Tweed's arrest, trial (1873), and sentence of twelve years' imprisonment. This was reduced on appeal, but in 1876 he was recommitted and died in prison.

TWEEDALE, JOHN HAY, 1st Marquis of (Scottish) (1626–1697), politician who successfully rode the political upheavals in Scotland in the second half of the 17th cent. Siding first with Charles I (1642), he fought against the royalists at Marston Moor (1644) and became a commissioner for Scotland in the London parliament (1659). Although he became a privy councillor after the Restoration (1660), he was later deprived of his post as president of the council (1674), but was readmitted in 1682 and served both James II and William III, until his dismissal for his part in promoting the Darien Scheme (1696).

TWEEDSMUIR, JOHN BUCHAN, 1st Baron (1875–1940), British author and politician, who was born in Scotland. He was Lord Milner's private secretary in South Africa (1901–3), and then became a literary adviser and limited partner of the publishing firm of T. Nelson (1907) and a prolific writer of biographies, historical works, and adventure novels, the most famous of which was *The Thirty-nine Steps* (1915). During the First World War he served as director of the department of information (1917–18). He was elected a member of parliament for the Scottish Universities (1927–35), and later was governor-general of Canada (1935–40), where he showed a strong interest in French-Canadian culture and helped to consolidate Canadian–American relations.

TWELVE TABLES, first codified law at Rome, published in 451–450 BC by the Decemvirate under Appius Claudius. They marked an important stage in the Struggle of the Orders, since codification restricted manipulation of the law by patrician oligarchs. Mainly emphasizing rights in civil law, the Tables attained venerable status in the late republic, being learnt by heart at school, and some stipulations remained as long as Rome herself.

TWELVE YEARS TRUCE (1609–21), cessation of hostilities between Spain and the insurgent northern provinces of the Netherlands which formed a break in the 80-year-long revolt of the Netherlands. The truce was concluded by the deputies of Philip III of Spain and the estates of the United Provinces (9 April 1609), meeting at The Hague under the mediation of England and France. The military achievements of the opposing commanders, the Duke of Parma and Maurice of Nassau, had split the Spanish Netherlands in half by the end of the 16th cent. and had created a military stalemate which neither side could break. In addition, the Spanish economy could no longer sustain the military effort needed to support an indefinite war. On his own initiative the sovereign prince of the Netherlands, Archduke Albert of Austria, therefore concluded an armistice with the Dutch, which Philip III refused to ratify. However, the new Spanish commander, Ambroglio Spinola, realizing the impossibility of victory without adequate supplies, continued negotiations with the rebel estates, whose moderate leader, Oldenbarneveldt, likewise wanted peace. The truce of 1609, which the Duke of Lerma's government in Spain reluctantly accepted, gave the United Provinces de facto recognition. During the truce the Dutch enjoyed great economic prosperity and consolidated their gains in the Far East at Portugal's expense, while Spain merely received a respite from the financial pressures of war. The *pax hispanica* was threatened by the emergence of the Contra-Remonstrant party in Holland (1617–19), the deaths of Archduke Albert and Philip III (1621) and the rise to power in Spain of Balthasar de Zúñiga and his nephew, the future Count of Olivares, who was pledged to aggressive policies which would revive Spanish hegemony in the world. Thus when the truce finally expired (9 April 1621) it was not renewed. By the treaties of Westphalia which ended the Thirty Years War (1648) the terms of the 1609 truce were broadly confirmed and legal recognition was granted to the sovereign United Provinces.

TWENTY-FOUR ARTICLES (1583) in England, ecclesiastical code published by Abp Whitgift prohibiting 'prophesyings', reinforcing existing regulations about clerical dress, enforcing acceptance of the Prayer Book, and upholding the authority of the bishops and the 39 Articles. The court of commission for ecclesiastical causes was entrusted with the task of enforcing these articles upon the Elizabethan clergy, which did much to silence the opposition of the Puritans.

TWENTY-ONE DEMANDS (1915), series of Japanese demands on China, chiefly concerning the disposal of German concessions in China. Yuan Shih-k'ai accepted the demands. At the Versailles Conference (1919) the full extent of his concessions, and the backing they had received from the powers, was revealed, and provoked a storm of protest in China, the start of the May 4th Movement.

TWENTY-SIXTH OF JULY MOVEMENT (1953) in Cuba, political movement led by Fidel Castro Ruz, and named after the unsuccessful attack made on that day on the Moncada barracks by Castro and his associates.

Members of the movement invaded Cuba under Castro's leadership in Dec. 1956, and conducted a guerrilla war against the regime of Fulgencio Batista. At that stage the Twenty-sixth of July programme spoke of a return to constitutional government and a general mild reformism.

Castro and the movement reached power in 1959 and gradually the aims of both became radicalized. Nationalization of the sugar industry, purging of dissidents, a deterioration of relations with the US, a radical programme of land reform, and closer economic ties with the USSR were prominent features of the new policy.

The original Twenty-sixth of July Movement was gradually merged with the Cuban Communist Party. In 1961 the first amalgam was named the Integrated Revolutionary Organizations (ORI). In 1963, after a severe purge, the party was renamed The United Party of the Socialist Revolution (PURS), and in 1965 it became the Communist Party of Cuba (PCC).

TYABJI, BADRUDDIN (1844–1906), Indian judge and reformer, the first Indian to be called to the English bar (1867) and the first Indian Muslim judge of the Bombay high court. He acted as president of the Indian National Congress at Madras (1887) in opposition to Sayyid Ahmad Khan's boycott of the Congress. He advocated higher education for Indian women.

TYDINGS–McDUFFIE ACT (1934) in the US, legislation named after Senator Millard Tydings, of MD, and Congressman John McDuffie, of AL, that provided for independence of the Philippines after 12 years, the removal of US military posts, and settlement of the future status of US naval bases by negotiation. The act was unanimously accepted by the Philippine legislature.

TYL EULENSPIEGEL, legendary German folk tale of the pranks of a 14th-cent. peasant, the earliest surviving edition, published in Strasbourg, dating from 1515. It was translated into many languages and won immense popularity throughout Europe for its earthy humour and irony, becoming a model for popular satire.

TYLER, JOHN (1790–1862), US politician and tenth president of the US, who served in the VA House of Delegates (1811–16, 1823–5), the US House of Representatives (1817–1821), and the US Senate (1827–36). He was governor of VA (1825–7). An anti-Jackson Democrat, he was drawn into the emerging Whig Party in the mid-1830s and received the Whig vice-presidential nomination in the campaign of 1840. On the death of President Harrison (1841), Tyler became the first president of the US by right of succession. He soon clashed with Henry Clay and other Whig leaders over the Whigs' nationalist programme and the whole cabinet, with the exception of the secretary of state, Daniel Webster, resigned (Sept. 1841). Thereafter his presidential term was one of solid, if unspectacular, achievement. He ended the Seminole War (1842), reformed the navy, encouraged negotiation of the Webster–Ashburton treaty (1842), and began negotiations for the annexation of TX. He supported the presidential nomination of James K. Polk (1844), worked for compromise between North and South (1860–1), and when this failed gave his allegiance to the Confederacy.

TYLER, WAT (d. 1381), English leader of the Kentish peasants in their revolt against the government. His origins are unknown, but he maintained a remarkable hold over his followers. He was murdered by the lord mayor of London while parleying with King Richard II and his death ended the rising in London.

TYNDALE, WILLIAM (c. 1490–1536), English theologian and translator of the Bible, who studied at Cambridge under Erasmus. He was soon in trouble for heretical opinions and went to London to seek the support of Bp Tunstall for a vernacular Bible. Failing in this, he left for Hamburg (1524) with the protection and financial help of the Merchant Adventurers. He visited Luther at Wittenberg, and his translation of the New Testament, completed at Cologne and Worms, was on sale in London in 1526, and circulated widely despite the clergy's efforts to suppress it. In 1525–9 he was in Antwerp working on the Old Testament, and he wrote *The Obedience of a Christian Man* (1528), asserting the complete authority of scripture and royal supremacy over the Church. He engaged in controversy with Thomas More, and attacked Wolsey in *The Practice of Prelates* (1530). The reformers would have welcomed him in England, but he was arrested in Antwerp (1535) and executed after 18 months' imprisonment. His translations formed the greater part of Matthew's Bible (1537), and the Authorized Version (1611) owed much to his literary genius and accurate scholarship.

TYPHUS, closely related group of diseases characterized by the onset of fever, skin eruptions, and toxaemia, of which the classic strain is the louse-borne epidemic typhus, first recognized in 15th-cent. Granada and intermittently prevalent in devastating epidemics in Europe and the British Isles in the 17th–19th cents. Always associated with filth, poverty, war, famine, and overcrowded conditions, such as were found in prisons and refugee camps, it disappeared from western Europe with the improvement in living conditions, except for a brief reappearance in the Nazi concentration camps, but it remained prevalent in Poland, Russia, and Rumania in the early 20th cent.

TYRANNICIDE, legal right of resistance to, and *in extremis*, murder of a tyrannical ruler, first advocated by John Knox in the 1550s, but popularized by Huguenot writers after the St Bartholomew Massacre (1572). In the 1580s the theory was championed by Catholic writers, eg, the Jesuit Bellarmine, and by the Catholic League, though support for the concept declined after 1593, as France wearied of assassination and civil war.

TYRANNY, ANCIENT GREEK, illegal autocracy, as distinct from hereditary kingship (*basileus*), that first appeared in ancient Greece, perhaps partly in imitation of oriental, especially Lydian, monarchy, in the dynamic, revolutionary, and orientalizing atmosphere of the 7th–6th cents BC. The earliest tyrants in mainland Greece usually came from the fringe of the ruling nobility and exploited local discontent to establish their own power, eg, Pheidon (c. 670) among the emergent hoplites at Argos; Cypselus (c. 650) and Cleisthenes (c. 600) among non-Dorians at Corinth and Sicyon respectively; and Peisistratus (c. 550) among outlying regions and the poor in Attica. Polycrates of Samos (c. 530) was little more than a successful pirate. In Asia Minor most Greek tyrants held their position by either opposing, eg, Thrasybulus of Miletus (c. 600), or supporting, eg, Artemisia of Halicarnassus (c. 480), the dominant eastern power. In the west significant tyranny appeared later than elsewhere. The Carthaginian threat strengthened Gelon and Hieron at Syracuse (485–465) and later Dionysius I (*reg.* 405–367). All tyrants were nationalist and most, with the notable exception of Gelon and Hieron, enjoyed popular, but not aristocratic, support. They tended to build and coin profusely, encouraged poetry and the fine arts, and promoted urbanization. In fact, ancient Greece showed its greatest vigour under the political extremes of tyranny and radical democracy.

TYRCONNELL, RORY O'DONNELL, 1st Earl of (1st creation) (Irish) (1575–1608), younger brother of 'Red Hugh' O'Donnell, who tried to raise a rebellion in Ireland against the English. After the defeat of Kinsale (1601), he signified his allegiance to the lord deputy, Lord Mountjoy, and went to London with Hugh O'Neill, Earl of Tyrone, where James I created him Earl of Tyrconnell (1603). The English terms for a settlement in Ireland satisfied neither him nor Niall Garve, then chief of the O'Donnells. Tyrconnell began negotiations with Spain, which however led to his sudden departure with Tyrone from Ireland (Sept. 1607), an event known as 'the flight of the earls'. He went to Rome, where he died. In 1614 he was posthumously attainted.

TYRCONNELL, RICHARD TALBOT, 3rd Earl of (Irish) (1st of 3rd creation) (1630–91), Irish Jacobite. In the English Civil War he served the royalists, escaping to Spain after the fall of Drogheda (1649). In 1655 he was arrested in London for plotting against the protectorate, but escaped. After the Restoration (1660) he was employed in the household of the Duke of York (later James II). He went into exile following his arrest during the Popish Plot. James appointed him commander-in-chief in Ireland and made him Earl of Tyrconnell in 1685. As lord deputy (1687), he led the Jacobite forces in Ireland against William III. After the siege of Limerick had been raised by William's forces (1690), Tyrconnell fled to France, to return in 1691. It was too late to affect the Jacobite cause and he died at Limerick.

TYRE (Sur), Phoenician city, built on an island. It exported famous purple-dyed textiles and in the 10th cent. BC was the leading Phoenician city. From the 7th cent. BC onwards it was conquered by a series of great powers. It enjoyed occasional prosperity until its destruction by the Egyptian Mamluks (AD 1291).

TYRE, SIEGE OF (332 BC), exploit of Alexander the Great, who stormed the city, situated on an offshore island, despite ferocious resistance.

TYRONE, HUGH O'NEILL, 3rd Earl of (Irish) (1st creation) (c. 1540–1616), Irish patriot, who became leader of the O'Neill clan in 1593, being the son of Matthew, reputedly an illegitimate son of Conn, Earl of Tyrone. In 1585 he had attended the Irish parliament as Earl of Tyrone. He posed as the Catholic champion and sought help from Spain against the English. He was formally pardoned by Elizabeth I in 1598, but two months later destroyed an English force at the battle of the Yellow Ford. He failed to follow up his victory and signed a truce with the Earl of Essex (1599). He was finally defeated at Kinsale (1601) and submitted to the English. James I confirmed his title and estates (1603). Tyrone soon became dissatisfied with his treatment, and anticipating arrest fled with Tyrconnell to Rome (1607). This famous event, known as 'the flight of the earls', was the end of Tyrone's career. He was attainted for high treason by the Irish parliament and his honours were forfeited (1613). He died in Rome.

TYRTAEUS, ancient Spartan poet, contemporary with the Second Messenian War (c. 650 BC). His interpretation of the so-called Lycurgan constitution shows that he supported the later reaction to the earlier democratic reforms that followed the First Messenian War.

TZ'U-HSI, Empress Dowager (1835–1908), de facto ruler of China from 1861 until her death. Often referred to in Western literature as 'The Old Buddha', she once claimed that she had more power than Queen Victoria. Beginning as a low-ranking concubine of the Hsien-feng emperor, she owed her meteoric rise to her good looks and the fact that she bore the emperor his only son. When the latter, still a minor, ascended to the throne as the T'ung-chih emperor (1862), she became the empress dowager and quickly removed all opponents and institutional blockages. Thus the way was cleared for a co-regency with Empress Dowager T'zu-an (1837–81), the senior consort of Hsien-feng. As T'zu-an was neither able nor ambitious, Tz'u-hsi practically dominated the court. The only person who stood in her way was Prince Kung, her brother-in-law, whom she feared. However, in 1865 she deprived him of his special status as prince regent on charges of corruption, and further manipulations in 1869 restricted his activities even more. Tz'u-hsi's career was almost ruined in 1875 when the T'ung-chih emperor died without issue. The dynastic law of succession prescribed that the successor be chosen from the next generation below the deceased, which would make Tz'u-hsi an 'empress dowager-grandmother', twice removed from the legal source of power. Instead, she autocratically chose a three-year-old nephew of the deceased, thus maintaining her regency. The death of Tz'u-an, her co-regent, removed another obstacle. Her crowning success came in 1884, when the entire Grand Council and four members of the Tsungli Yamen, both headed by Prince Kung, were removed on the pretext that they had mishandled the war against France. That this was a vendetta against Prince Kung was evident, in that no change of policy was effected afterwards. After 1884 Prince Kung's power dwindled rapidly.

In 1889 the Kuang-hsü emperor came of age and assumed personal rule, and Tz'u-hsi therefore retired. But to ensure her control over policy making, she forced the emperor to marry a cousin of her choice and she used her favourite eunuchs and officials to effect general supervision. Thus hampered, the emperor's attempt at reform in 1898 was aborted, and he ended up in compulsory confinement. She attempted to dethrone the emperor, but was thwarted by the foreign powers; in revenge, she secretly gave support to the fanatically anti-foreign Boxer Rising. After the Boxers were suppressed, she finally recognized the need for reform and adopted much of the programme of the 'Hundred Days' Reform' which she had opposed in 1898. The most important reforms were the abolition of the traditional examination system, the establishment of modern schools, and the sending of students abroad (mainly to Japan). She died one day after the death of the emperor, whom, according to unverified accounts, she murdered.

J. O. P. Bland and E. Backhouse, *China under the Empress Dowager* (London, 1910).   DP

U2 INCIDENT (May 1960), pretext for the Russian withdrawal from the summit conference which was to have begun in Paris (16 May 1960). The U2, a high-flying US reconnaissance plane, was shot down over the Soviet Union (1 May). The pilot (Francis Gary Powers) survived and confessed to being engaged in an espionage operation—of which the plane and its equipment gave ample evidence. Similar reconnaissance flights had been carried out for four years, and the Soviet government was aware of them. President Eisenhower did not try to conceal the character of the U2 flight. The matter was made into a major incident by Khrushchev, who withdrew from the Paris conference before it had effectively started. Since there was nothing new or unknown in the U2 flights and since it would have been possible to conceal, at least for the time being, that one had been ended in this way, it is generally assumed that Khrushchev was glad to find an opportunity to withdraw from a conference which was unlikely to bring him any substantial gains, particularly on the status of Berlin.

UBAID, site near Ur, which gives its name to a period of proto-history (4th millennium BC), characterized by village societies, engaged in agriculture and fishing, using clay and stone tools and producing a distinctive pottery found all over Mesopotamia, but particularly in the south.

UBAYD ALLAH AL-MAHDI (*reg.* 910–34), first of the Fatimid caliphs, who was raised to power through the successful propaganda of the Da'i Abu Abd Allah al-Shi'i among the Kitama Berbers in Ifriqiyya. With the support of the Kitama the Fatimids took Kayrawan in AD 909, overthrowing the regime of the Aghlabid emirs hitherto dominant there. Ubayd Allah entered Al-Kayrawan in 910 and assumed the status of a caliph. His reign witnessed a number of fruitless attempts to take over Egypt.

UBICO, JORGE (1878–1946), Guatemalan soldier, who became president and dictator of Guatemala (1931–44) and extended his tenure in office by plebiscite (1935) and later through the actions of a cowed constitutional congress. He ruled through brutality and censorship, handled government efficiently, and posed as the friend of the Indian masses. He was one of a triumvirate of generals who toppled the confederationist government of Guatemala in 1921. Once in power he centralized government, modernized the army, used press censorship and government spies to a degree heretofore unknown to Guatemalans, and exiled or imprisoned his opponents. To deal with the effects of the world Depression he supported the established, foreign-controlled coffee and banana industries. In the hope of winning US approval, he confiscated the holdings of German coffee planters and aided the United Fruit Co., an American firm, in gaining control of Guatemalan railways. Despite his stated friendship for the Indians, they suffered under his leadership. He compelled them by law (1933) to work two weeks a year without pay on highway construction if they could not pay a small tax, and then he published a vagrancy law that required all Indians to work at least 150 days a year, each carrying a special booklet marked by employers. The law was rigidly enforced because it made a cheap source of labour readily available. His dictatorship ended when students, labour, and army elements demonstrated publicly against him. He resigned rather than oppose the uprisings, leaving the government in the hands of one of his lieutenants, who was himself deposed, ushering in the Guatemalan revolution led by the educator Juan José Arévalo.   VCP

UDAIPUR, TREATY OF (1817), by which the Rajput state of Udaipur (Mewar) came under British protection during the Indian governor-generalship of the Marquis of Hastings.

UDALL, NICHOLAS (1505–56), English cleric, who was headmaster of Eton (1534–41) and of Westminister (1554–6). He was a humanist scholar who translated Erasmus and selections from the Bible, but is chiefly remembered as a playwright, especially for his rollicking comedy, *Ralph Roister Doister* (1567), which influenced later English writers of comedy.

UGANDA, inland territory in East Africa of 243,000 sq. kms with a population (1970) of 8 million. It was invaded in the 16th cent. by Hamitic tribes from the north-west. Arab and Swahili traders, together with European missionaries and the British East Africa Co., came in the 19th cent., and in 1893 the territory became a British protectorate. In 1962 Uganda became an independent member of the Commonwealth, and five years later (1967) a republic within the Commonwealth. The president sits in the national assembly of 82 members, to whom the cabinet is responsible.

UGANDA PEOPLE'S CONGRESS emerged from the earlier Uganda National Congress, which had become preoccupied with Baganda affairs and thus failed to win nation-wide support. It was founded by Milton Obote in March 1960, and its members took a leading part in the London constitutional conference on Uganda's future in the same year. By skilful manœuvring between various contending parties, notably the Democratic Party and the Baganda Kabaka Yekka, the UPC emerged supreme, and Obote became the first prime minister of an independent Uganda in Oct. 1962, and afterwards the first president of the Uganda republic.

Succeeding years were occupied in a political struggle for constitutional unity. A split in the UPC was defeated by Obote in 1965–6, and this was quickly followed by deposition of the *kabaka*, the Buganda king, in a violent coup. A new constitution of 1967 achieved the UPC's aim of securing a unified country without the complications of hereditary monarchs and 'feudal' power-groups. Subsequently the party's programme emphasized the interests of the ordinary peasant, for which it pledged itself to further measures.

UGARIT (mod. Ras Shamra), ancient city on the Syrian coast. Excavations have revealed five main phases of occupation extending from Neolithic times until the city's destruction by the Sea Peoples (12th cent. BC). Writings in an alphabetic, cuneiform script, related to Phoenician, have been found there.

UIGHURS, people from Central Asia. After breaking away from the control of the western Turks, the Uighurs helped Li Shih-min, the second T'ang emperor, to launch campaigns against the Turks in 639–40 and 647–8. As a result, Chinese power was established in the Tarim basin. Apart from short periods, the Uighurs remained in alliance with the T'ang dynasty and helped materially to restore law and order during the An Lu-shan and other rebellions that started in 755. For these services they were able to extort valuable materials such as silk from China, which was now too weak to refuse such demands. The Uighurs had adopted Manichaeism as their official religion, and, as distinct from other peoples of Central Asia, had evolved a native script for their language.

UITKOMST CULTURE, one of the two Iron Age cultures found in the southern and central Transvaal, its main focus being between the Magaliesburg and the Witwatersrand. Characterized by stone-walled settlements, it is very similar both to the neighbouring 'Buispoort culture' and to Rhodesia's possibly related Leopard's Kopje culture. The earliest site to be dated so far is Melville Kopje (AD 1060-). It survived until the 19th cent.

UJI in Japan, early social unit. Usually translated as 'clan', it was more accurately an extended family which controlled the agricultural communities in its area. These dominant families had been brought, by the mid-4th cent., to acknowledge the suzerainty of the Yamato dynasty and were ranked in accordance with their relationship to the dynasty and their local importance. They early developed the practice of erecting large burial mounds, but by the 7th cent. an increasing number of smaller mounds were appearing, suggesting that the authority of some *uji* chiefs was disintegrating. The Taika Reform (*c.* 645–700) ended direct *uji* control of the provinces, but the new district officials came mostly from old *uji* families.

UJJAIN (Ujjayini or Ujjeni), town in Madhya Pradesh, India, situated along a main road connecting the west coast (Gulf of Broach) with the Gangetic valley. Originally the capital of the kingdom of Avanti (5th–4th cents BC), it became the seat of a viceroy in Asoka's empire and later the capital of the Western Kshatrapas (*c.* AD 50–400). It remained a great cultural centre till long afterwards.

UJJAIN, SATRAPS OF (*c.* AD 125–400), rulers of one of the branches of Scythians (Sakas) which invaded the Indo-Pakistani sub-continent (1st cent. BC), moved southwards, and finally settled in Malwa (capital: Ujjain). After a few generations they became thoroughly Indianized. The earliest rulers probably acted as governors of the Kushan emperors and so adopted the title of satrap, which continued in use even after their successors had made themselves completely independent (*c.* AD 125). Their greatest ruler was Rudradaman, whose Girnar (Surashtra) inscripton (AD 150) is the oldest known document written entirely in pure Sanskrit. It deals with the repair of an ancient irrigation reservoir, the dykes of which had collapsed and caused havoc to the surrounding countryside. The power of the satraps came to an abrupt end when the area was conquered by Chandra Gupta II (*c.* 400) and incorporated into the Gupta empire.

UKRAINE in Russia, one of the 15 constituent republics of the USSR, formerly known as Little Russia, which lies across the southern steppe of European Russia and is centred on the ancient town of Kiev. The region was occupied in the mid-6th cent. by a number of Slavic tribes, but from the 9th cent. was overrun by the Varangians or Russi, under whose dukes the frontier provinces or *ukraina* of Kiev, Chernigov, and Pereyaslavl were forged into the first Russian state. From the 10th–11th cents Kievan Rus extended northwards and westwards towards Poland, but its expansion was halted by the Tatar invasions (1237–41) which devastated the lands of Kiev and paved the way for its occupation by the rising power of Lithuania. In 1362 Grand Duke Olgerd of Lithuania made himself master of a large part of the Ukraine, which from the 15th cent. was peopled by growing communities of free cossacks, or peasant outlaws.

The mid-16th cent. was a turning point in the history of the Ukraine. By the union of Lublin (1568–9), which created the great commonwealth of Poland-Lithuania, hitherto only linked by personal ties, the Ukrainian provinces of Kiev, Volynia, and Podolia were transferred from Lithuania to Poland. In the course of the next half-century Stephen Bathory, the Polish king, tried to transform the free communities of the Ukraine into a militia of registered cossacks. Serfdom intensified as the cossacks were brought more closely under the control of the Polish aristocracy, and from 1596 the Ukrainians felt their adherence to the Orthodox Church was being undermined by recognition of the new Uniate Church, a fusion of Catholic and Orthodox.

From 1620 the Ukrainian cossacks took part in a series of unsuccessful risings against Poland, which came to a climax with the career of the dynamic *hetman*, Bogdan Khmelnitsky. To avoid defeat and servitude at the hands of the Poles, he finally appealed to Tsar Alexis to defend the Ukraine (1651), and by the treaty of Pereyaslavl (1654) the cossacks recognized the suzerainty of the tsar in return for a guarantee of their rights and privileges. This historic agreement, however, did not immediately settle the future of the Ukraine, which became a battleground for the Poles and Russians (1655–67), ending with the partition of the Ukraine between its two powerful neighbours (treaty of Andrussovo). The cossack lands on the right bank of the Dnieper were returned to Poland and those on the left bank, together with Kiev, to Russia.

During the next 40 years the cossacks sought first to unite with the Turks against the Poles and then to exploit the hostility between Sweden and Russia in order to salvage their independence, but after Peter I's victory at Poltava (1709) the Ukraine fell gradually under Russian control, and by the end of the 18th cent. this process was complete. Ukrainian nationalism was reborn in the mid-19th cent., when 30 patriots in Kiev founded the secret Brotherhood of St Cyril and St Methodius, but its members were arrested and deported (1847). After the tsarist government forbade the use of the Ukrainian language in schools (1876), Lvov, in the western Ukrainian province of Galicia, became the centre of the nationalist movement. In the First World War the region was overrun by the Germans (1915), who supported the separatist movement (1917–18) and concluded a separate treaty of Brest–Litovsk with the Ukraine (March 1918). German troops drove out the short-lived Bolshevik regime in the Ukraine (Feb.–April 1918), but withdrew again after the armistice of 11 Nov. 1918, leaving the Ukraine to the mercies of the Russian Civil War (1919–20). Exploiting this situation, the armies of Poland occupied Kiev (May 1920), and though expelled by the Red Army, secured several million Ukrainians for Poland by the treaty of Riga (1921). The remainder of the Ukraine became absorbed in the USSR in 1923, while the Polish areas of Little Russia were regained after 1945.

G. Vernadsky, *Bohdan, Hetman of Ukraine* (New Haven, 1941).
M. Hrushevsky, *A History of Ukraine* (New Haven, 1941).
JHS

ULAMA, plural of the Arabic word *alim*, which denotes one who has *ilm*, ie, knowledge or learning. In the course of time the expression *ulama* came to designate the theologians and canonists expert in the Shari'a, the Sacred Law of Islam. Among the *ulama* are to be numbered the *qadi*s or judges and the *mufti*s or jurisconsults of the Muslim world.

ULATE BLANCO, OTILIO (1895-), Costa Rican politician and president of Costa Rica (1949–53), who founded the National Union Party, a group of wealthy opponents of organized social welfare. During his presidency the national legislature was controlled by social reformers who issued a new constitution (1949) that replaced the army with a national police force, banned the Communist Party, instituted new taxes, nationalized the banks, and established a civil service system. Nevertheless Ulate Blanco's presidency ended with a treasury surplus and he retained leadership of his party. He stood for office again after the following term, but was defeated by a social reform candidate.

ULBRICHT, WALTER (1893–), German politician and effective ruler of East Germany from 1945. He joined the German Socialist Party in 1912, and took up a position on the left of the party in opposition to the First World War, and after being mobilized was imprisoned for trying to desert. He joined the German Communist Party as soon as it was formed (1919) and was appointed to the central committee (1923). He was elected to the German Reichstag (1928–33), then, on Hitler's advent to power, he left Germany and went to the Soviet Union, where he remained (1933–45), working with the Comintern. During the Second World War he was engaged in propaganda work among German prisoners.

He returned to Germany with the Soviet armies (1945) at the head of the 'Ulbricht group' of communists, whose task was to re-establish German municipal government in such a way as to retain power in communist hands behind a facade of officials who, often, were non-communists. He was a member of the Saxony Anhalt Diet (1946) and president of the Economic Committee of the German People's Council (1948). Effective power remained, however, with the Socialist Unity Party, formed in 1946 from a merger between the Communist Party and the Social Democrat Party with the backing of the Soviet Union. At first, Ulbricht held a secondary position as vice-chairman, officially subordinate to the Communist Pieck and the Social Democrat Grotewohl; but he appears to have been the key man from the first. He was appointed general (later first) secretary of the Socialist Unity Party (1950). He was also made first deputy prime minister (1949–60) and then chairman of the newly created Council of State (1960–71). He thus distinguished himself by his political longevity through the vicissitudes of change in the communist world, where he held a particularly exposed position. He adapted his actions and opinions to changes in Soviet policy and retained a strong belief in the leadership of the Soviet Union in the communist world. His methods of rule resembled in some respects those of Stalin. On the other hand, the German Democratic Republic has maintained a security system without the terror which characterized Stalin's rule in Russia. His influence with Soviet leaders remains a matter of speculation. It is said that he played an important part in the Berlin crisis (1958–61) and it is certainly the case that the interests of the German Democratic Republic were served by the building of the Berlin wall to stop the massive flight of refugees to the west. He is also reported to have been influential in urging Soviet action against Czechoslovakia (1968).

D. Childs, *East Germany* (London, 1969).   WK

ULJAYTU (reg. 1304–16), Il-Khanid Ruler in Iran (capital, Sultaniyah), noted for his patronage of the arts, especially architecture. He fought campaigns in Khurasan, but his only raid into Syria ended in failure (1313) after he was unable to obtain European support for an attack on its Mamluk rulers.

ULLA, BATTLE OF (1546), Lithuanian victory over the Russians during the Northern War (1558–83). With the victory at Orsha, the Lithuanians thus retaliated for Ivan IV's seizure of Polotsk on the Dvina (1563), but they failed to follow up their victories further.

ULLSWATER, JAMES WILLIAM LOWTHER, 1st Viscount (1855–1949), British lawyer, politician, and speaker of the House of Commons (1905–21), who entered politics as Conservative MP for Penrith (1886–1921). After holding a succession of junior offices, he became deputy speaker in 1895. He was elected speaker in 1905 and was appreciated by all for his imperturbable temper, friendly manners, and lively wit. His responsibilities were heavy in a difficult parliamentary period. There was conflict between the Liberals in the Commons and the Conservatives in the Lords, tension over Home Rule, and repeated scenes were provoked by Irish affairs and the First World War. As speaker he presided fairly and tactfully over the conference of party members dealing with the vexed question of electoral reform. He retired in 1921, but continued a life of active public service on royal commissions and in local government.

ULM, BATTLE OF (1805), Austrian defeat in the French Wars by Napoleon I, which was followed by Vienna's first capitulation in history.

ULM, TREATY OF (1620), armistice between the Catholic League and the Protestant Union of German states at the beginning of the Thirty Years War, by which both parties agreed to respect the other's territories (3 July 1620) at the instigation of the French. The latter's hopes of thus protecting the Palatinate, whose elector, Frederick V, had rashly assumed the Bohemian Crown (1619), were, however, soon dashed by Spinola's invasion of the Rhenish Palatinate.

ULPIAN (DOMITIUS ULPIANUS) (d. AD 223), Roman lawyer from Tyre in Syria, whose numerous legal textbooks, monographs, and commentaries became authoritative sources of law and survive in extensive citations in the *Digest* of Justinian. He became praetorian prefect under Severus Alexander (222).

ULRIKA ELEONORA (1688–1741), Queen of Sweden (reg. 1718–20), who was Charles XII's younger sister and successor, but abdicated in favour of her consort, who became Frederick I.

ULSTER, originally an ancient kingdom of the Gaelic Celtic pentarchy in Ireland, but in modern times the six counties of Tyrone, Londonderry, Antrim, Down, Armagh, and Fermanagh, the partially self-governing union of northern Ireland which is an integral part of the United Kingdom of Britain.

From about the birth of Christ to the 3rd cent. Ulster was the greatest of the five kingdoms of Ireland and stretched southwards to the Boyne and the middle Shannon. From the 4th cent. it contracted before the rising house of Conn, the high kings of Ireland, and the sons of Niall of the Nine Hostages, whose raiders seized the future St Patrick and brought him to Ireland, and founded a new state variously called *Aileach*, Ulster or the kingdom of the north (c. 400). It was from Patrick's mission in Ulster that St Columba evangelized the Picts of Scotland in the 6th cent. Ulster resisted invading viking Norsemen in the 9th–10th cents and by 1000 had expanded to include present-day Monaghan, Louth, Armagh, and Down, but during the anarchy that preceded the Norman invasion its kings were involved in a long struggle with their rivals in Munster. In 1177 John de Courcy, younger son of a Somerset knight, led the conquest of eastern Ulster by defeating the king, Rory MacDonlevy, at Downpatrick, and from 1205 the title of Earl of Ulster was held by the De Lacys and the De Burghs (1264–1333), then through Lionel, Duke of Clarence, it passed to the Mortimers (1368–1423) and thence through Richard, Earl of Cambridge, to the house of York and the English Crown in the person of Richard's grandson, Edward IV. But for practical purposes Ulster remained independent of English rule under its noble line of O'Neill, descendants of Niall of the Nine Hostages. In 1541 Conn O'Neill accepted Henry VIII as King of Ireland, promising to attend the Irish parliament and to hold his lands by knight-service in return for the title of Earl of Tyrone, but his son, Shane 'the Proud', was an uncompromising opponent of English legal and religious innovations and his name was attainted on his death by Elizabeth I in 1567. After a generation of peace the northern chiefs rebelled against the English Crown (the Tyrone War of 1594–1603) under the great Hugh O'Neill, Earl of Tyrone, and sought Spanish help. The rebellion was finally overcome by Lord Mountjoy and O'Neill submitted to James I (1603), renouncing his title, lands, and authority, and a new chapter was opened in the history of Ulster.

This began with the 'Flight of the Earls', when the 99 leading men of Ulster departed Ireland forever in voluntary exile (1607), the royal confiscation of the six counties of Tyrone, Donegal, Derry, Armagh, Cavan, and Fermanagh, and the settlement of 500,000 acres (2023 sq. kms) by English and Scots under the articles of Plantation (May 1609). The city of London was granted all the northern part of county Derry, with its vast woods and rich fisheries. The Protestant colony grew slowly, but by 1641, when the next great rebellion occurred, the Protestants owned 3 million (12,140 sq. kms) of the 3½ million (14,160 sq. kms) acres of the six counties. Owen Roe O'Neill commanded the Ulster rising against this injustice, while his kinsman, Sir Felim O'Neill, led the notorious massacre and dispossession of some 10,000 Protestant planters (1641). As the English civil wars progressed, Charles I sought Irish aid, and royalist sympathy was strong in Ulster, even among the established Presbyterian Church (1642), when the Independents triumphed in England. But vicious repression by Cromwell's subordinate, Sir Charles Coote, crushed resistance to parliament in Ulster (1649–51). Under the Cromwellian 'Act of Settlement' (1652) the Catholic gentry were transplanted to Connaught or to Barbados and Presbyterians of royalist sympathy to Munster. Altogether 11 million acres, (44,500 sq. kms) were earmarked for the Adventurers and the rank and file of Cromwell's army, and the restoration of the monarchy by Cromwellian leaders (1660) insured against a wholesale restoration of dispossessed Catholics. The latter's hopes were raised by James II (*reg.* 1685–88) and only the Protestant strongholds of Derry and Enniskillen proclaimed for William of Orange (1688). The siege of Derry by Catholic forces lasted from 17 April to 30 July 1689 and once Ulster was under William III's control the Presbyterians looked hopefully for religious toleration and political security. William encouraged Huguenot refugees to establish a linen industry in Ulster, but the Presbyterians were denied political power, both local and central, as indeed were the Catholics, by the High Church Anglican establishment of Anne's reign. In the 18th cent. thousands of Ulstermen emigrated to America to seek political and religious equality, while Protestant nationalists, hostile to English management of the Irish parliament and to restrictive economic measures, joined with Catholics in supporting the Patriot Party and the United Irishmen. However, desperate competition for the available farms in Ulster and religious differences produced bitter feuds, *eg*, the battle of the Diamond (1795) and the institution of the Orange order 'to maintain the laws and peace of the country and the Protestant Constitution, and to defend the King and his heirs as long as they shall maintain the Protestant ascendancy'. Ulster seethed with discontent, but was disarmed by Gen. Lake (1797) on the eve of the great rebellion of 1798.

After the Union (1801) Ulster, through its capitalized industries, enjoyed greater prosperity than southern Ireland, and the predominantly Protestant, Scots-descended population of north-east Ulster strongly resisted Gladstone's attempts to introduce Home Rule (1886, 1892) for fear of a Catholic ascendancy, *eg*, serious rioting occurred in Belfast between Catholic and Protestant workmen (1886). Protestant Ulstermen, led by Sir Edward Carson, swore to the Solemn Covenant in defence of the Union (1912), but the First World War postponed the implementation of Home Rule (1914). By the end of the war it was clear that to force Ulster to sever the union was politically impossible, and Lloyd George's Amending Act (1920) allowed the six counties of Ulster, in which the Protestants had a total majority, to vote themselves out of an independent Ireland. The first parliament of Ulster met at Stormont in 1921 and Ulster's boundary with the Irish Free State was settled in 1925. Ulster then enjoyed internal stability until the 1960s, when the much-increased and more vocal Catholic population raised the issue of equal civil rights within a society based on a Protestant ascendancy. By 1970 sectarian bigotry and Catholic and Republican extremism had led to civil disorders which offered the prospect of reawakening the buried issue of Irish reunion. MKS

ULSTER COVENANT (1912), pledge devised by Sir Edward Carson in Belfast whereby 2000 Ulster demonstrators, after a religious service, undertook 'to stand by each other to defend their cherished position of equal citizenship in the United Kingdom and to use all necessary means to defeat the setting up of a Home Rule Parliament in Ireland'.

ULSTER MASSACRES (1641) in Ireland, episode in the great Irish rising of 1641 against the Stuart government and the Jacobean Plantations in Ulster, when some 10,000 Protestant English and Scots planters were massacred by the native Catholics, led by Sir Felim O'Neill. The widespread cruelties aroused great bitterness in England and a desire for revenge lay behind Cromwell's savage reprisals at Drogheda (1649) and the setting up of a high court at Dublin to try those involved, *eg*, O'Neill.

ULSTER VOLUNTEERS, resistance movement formed by the Ulster Party (Jan. 1912), after the magistrates had given Sir Edward Carson's party permission to drill as part of their campaign of opposition to Asquith's Home Rule policy. In April 1912, when Carson and the British Conservative leader, Bonar Law, took the salute at a review of 80,000 Ulster Volunteers in Belfast, the Conservative Party came close to fostering armed rebellion. The formation of the Volunteers was countered by the creation of a private army of Irish nationalists. The government was compelled to impose an embargo on the importation of arms into Ireland, but the Volunteers evaded this by gun-running, which brought them over 30,000 rifles and ammunition (April 1914). Civil war between the two armies was postponed by the outbreak of the First World War.

ULTRAMONTANISM, belief in the ultimate authority of the Catholic Church and that it supersedes loyalty to the state. It was particularly in evidence in 19th-cent. France, being encouraged by Pope Pius IX's decree of Papal Infallibility (1870), and contributed to the *Kulturkampf* in Germany (1870s). But despite its association with periods of reaction in politics, the long-term result of the ultramontane movement was to free the papacy from its dependence on civil powers and give the Catholic Church a new freedom of action, which has been exploited by its missionaries and enabled the pope to emerge as an international figure.

The liberating potentialities of ultramontanism were first foreseen by Lammenais in the 1840s. He envisaged the Church espousing the cause of constitutional liberty and becoming the spearhead of moral regeneration. Instead, French Catholics during the Second Empire reverted to their traditional conservatism. They welcomed Pius IX's stand against liberalism and progress and during the Third Republic fought a bitter, but unsuccessful, battle for the Church's control of education. Under Leo XIII, however, the papacy came to terms with its diplomatic isolation and loss of temporal power and, although some ultramontanes insisted on a narrowly conservative interpretation of papal infallibility, Leo himself led the Church in the direction of Christian Democracy. Individual Catholics looked to the pope as their spiritual leader, but found no cause for conflict with the state, since the aim of their involvement in politics was to create a more just and compassionate society, not to further the claims of the Catholic Church.

But ultramontanism had given rise to a conflict between clericals and anti-clericals that could not easily be eradicated by a change of emphasis at the top. Another of its legacies to the 20th cent. was the intense veneration of the papacy which was a feature of modern Catholicism, although this was less evident by 1970.

A. R. Vidler, *The Church in an Age of Revolution* (Cambridge, 1961).

E. E. Y. Hales, *Pio Nono* (Oxford, 1954).   SH

ULTRA-ROYALISTS in France, reactionary party led by Louis XVIII's brother, the Comte d'Artois, which tried to dominate French politics after 1815. In so doing, they destroyed the restored Bourbon dynasty which they revered. Believing in Divine Right, Ultras sought the eventual destruction of the 1814 Charter, compensation for émigrés, and restoration of the Catholic Church's political and educational influence and of the old territorial aristocracy's position. Their propagandists, who included De Maistre, Lamennais, and Chateaubriand, asserted that a regenerate France could arise from a semi-mystical devotion to the 'union of Throne and Altar'. Their secret, Jesuit-influenced society, *Les Chevaliers de la Foi* (dissolved 1826), fostered these ideas.

Ultras were responsible for Ney's execution and for the White Terror in southern France, which claimed two to three hundred Republican, Bonapartist, and Protestant victims (1815). Their extremism embarrassed Louis XVIII in his efforts to introduce conciliatory policies. Despite their 1815 electoral triumph, he preferred to govern through moderates. Ultra-royalist influence revived after the assassination of the Duc de Berri, Artois's son (1820). Villèle's ministry (1821–8), while restoring France's finances and international prestige, also carried out much of the Ultras' programme, particularly after Artois's accession as Charles X (1824). The Church regained control of education, and about 70,000 émigrés, or their heirs, were indemnified, by a conversion loan, which incensed the *rentiers*. Intermittent press censorship and an anti-sacrilege law increased the Ultras' unpopularity, as did a premature dissolution of the Chamber of Deputies (Nov. 1827). Polignac's ministry (April 1829–July 1830) provoked a revolution whose quick success showed how little national support the Ultras had.   MRB

UMAR I (*reg.* AD 632–44), Umar ibn al-Khattab, the second Caliph of Islam. Tradition asserts that he became a Muslim some years before the Hijra of AD 622. On the death of the Prophet Muhammad in 632 Umar ibn al-Khattab had a notable share in the choice of Abu Bakr as the first *khalifa*. His reign witnessed the campaigns of conquest which gave to the Muslims possession of a vast empire—*eg*, the campaigns of Ajnadayn and the Yarmuk in Syria, and of Al-Qadisiya and Nihawand in Persia. It witnessed also the Muslim occupation of Egypt. The fact that Umar I was able to exert effective control over the new-won territories and to establish the foundations of an imperial regime affords convincing evidence of his great abilities as a statesman and administrator.

UMAR II (*c.* AD 682–720), Umar ibn Abd al-Aziz ibn Marwan, Umayyad Caliph (*reg.* AD 717–20), who spent much of his life at Medina, becoming governor of the Hijaz in the time of the Caliph al-Walid I (*reg.* 705–15). His reign was notable for a series of reforms. Converts to Islam sought to pay the lesser rate of land taxation (*ushr*) imposed on Muslims rather than the higher rate (*kharaj*) levied on non-Muslims, with the result that the state suffered a serious loss of revenue. In AD 719 Umar II ordained that Muslim proprietors of land should pay only the *ushr* taxation, but that henceforward no transfer to *kharaj* land to Muslims would be legal. Should a Muslim acquire such land, he would be obliged to give to the state the *kharaj* due from it. A final solution was not, in fact, to be found until the reign of the Caliph Hisham (724–43), when a legal fiction was devised to the effect that the land, and not the owner, paid *kharaj*. All *kharaj* land now paid the full taxation irrespective of the religion or descent of the proprietor. Umar II also tried to ensure for the new converts (*mawali*) who served in the armed forces of the Umayyad state (*eg*, in Khurasan) a rate of payment equal to that of the Arab warriors.

UMAR IBN SA'ID AL-FUTI, known as Al-Hajj Umar (*c.* 1794–1864), was born at Halwar in Senegal, received a traditional Muslim education, and early in life was initiated into the Tijaniyya brotherhood. Soon afterwards, he left for Mecca, where he was for three years under the tutelage of Muhammad al-Ghali, a disciple of Al-Tijani, the founder of the brotherhood. Al-Ghali invested him as his representative (*khalifa*) for West Africa. On his return, Umar passed through Bornu and then spent several years in Sokoto, where the explorer Clapperton saw him in 1826. In Sokoto he met and disputed with Al-Bakka'i, the Qadiri leader from Timbuctoo, who later called for a holy war against him. Umar took part in some of Muhammad Bello's campaigns and gathered booty and experience. He also married one of Bello's daughters.

By 1838 Umar was in Masina and from there he visited Segu, Kangaba, and Kankan, finally settling at Dinguiraye in central Guinea (1845). There he gathered disciples and by 1854 had enough support to declare a *jihad*. His first moves were against Kaarta in north-western Mali, but he soon came up against the French, who broke his blockade of the town of Medina (1857). Unable to advance towards his native Futa Toro, he turned eastwards into Bambara country and took Segu (1861). He then attempted the capture of Masina, but the strongly Qadiri-oriented population, joined by Al-Bakka'i's forces, defeated him and he was killed. After his death, the state he had created was plagued by internal squabbles and though his son Ahmad remained titular head until 1893, he ended up by fleeing to Sokoto in the face of a French advance and administrative disintegration.   JOH

UMAR KHAYYAM (d. *c.* 1132), Persian mathematician, astronomer, and poet, born at or near Nishapur in Khurasan, whom the Seljuk Sultan Malik Shah invited (1074) to assist in the reform of the calendar. His fame as a poet rests on his ruba'is or quatrains, well known through the 'Rubaiyat' of Edward Fitzgerald (1809–83), first published in 1859. Umar Khayyam lived to a great age, certainly well over 100 years.

UMARI, AL-, IBN FADLALLAH (d. 1349), came from a family in the service of the Mamluk sultans of Egypt. His encyclopedic *Masalik al-Absar* contains a valuable description of the empire of Mali.

UMAYYAD, Arab Muslim dynasty (661–750) established by Mu'awiya I (*reg.* 661–80), during the civil wars which followed the death of Uthman (656). Under the Umayyads, the capital of the Muslim empire moved to Damascus, from which city Mu'awiya and his successors (of whom the most notable were Abd al-Malik (*reg.* 685–705), Al-Walid (*reg.* 705–15), and his great viceroy, Hajjaj (d. 714), and Hisham (*reg.* 724–43)), directed campaigns which spread Muslim rule into North Africa (under Uqba ibn Nafi), Spain, Transoxania (under Qutayba ibn Muslim), and Sind, and twice besieged Constantinople. The Umayyads also established the bureaucratic machinery necessary to govern the Muslim empire and facilitated the spread of Arabic and Islam in the conquered territories. Within their empire the Umayyads faced two great challenges. The first was the demand advanced by the new non-Arab converts to Islam (the *mawali*) for equality with the Arab warrior elite which dominated the Umayyad regime, and the second was the ancient Arab tribal rivalries now transplanted to the garrison towns of Syria and Iraq which tended to coalesce into a division between northern and southern Arabs. Discontented elements eventually united under the leadership of the descendants of Abbas, the Prophet's uncle, the Umayyads were overthrown and almost exterminated, and the Abbasid regime was established (750). One Umayyad, Abd al-Rahman, escaped to Spain to establish an independent Umayyad dynasty (756–1031).

UMAYYAD RULERS OF MUSLIM SPAIN (Al-Andalus), dynasty founded in 756 by Abd al-Rahman I, Al-Dakhil, who had fled from the massacre of the Umayyads of Damascus after the Abbasid revolution of 750. Muslim invasion from Morocco in 711 had overthrown the capital of the Visigothic kingdom, Toledo, and brought the peninsula under Arab control, save for the mountain populations of the north. North African Berbers then began taking the highland country of the centre and the south, while the towns, and the political power they gave, fell to groups of Arab soldiery led by aristocratic families. Abd al-Rahman's major task, ruling from his capital at Cordoba, was to master this factious nobility. Later, during the 9th cent., the influence of the nobles declined as Islam and an Arabic culture spread to the native population, and brought the rise of a more homogeneous people.

The first Umayyad ruler, or amir, was followed by Hisham I (d. 796), and Al-Hakam I (d. 822), who continued along lines laid down by Abd al-Rahman I. Under Abd al-Rahman II (d. 852) there came a large increase of central power: the amir ruled as a despot in Abbasid fashion, and disposed of a considerable bureaucracy as well as a militia of slave origin; Cordoba grew into a rich and splendid, if often turbulent, metropolis. The dynasty reached its peak as a military empire in the 10th cent. Abd al-Rahman III (d. 961) rebuilt the central authority after an interval of chaos (912), and proclaimed himself caliph in rivalry to the claims of the North African Fatimids (929). His sphere of influence extended over Christian Spain and the western Maghrib. The Umayyad system, and its state, began to disintegrate in the 11th cent. after the death (1002) of the great vizier Almanzor (Al-Mansur: the Victorious); and the dynasty ended in 1031 during protracted civil war, being followed by the local regimes of the *muluk al-Tawa'if*.

W. M. Watt and P. Cachia, *A History of Islamic Spain* (Edinburgh, 1965).

UMBERTO II (1904–), King of Italy (*reg*. 1946). As a professional soldier in the Second World War he commanded army groups. When King Victor Emmanuel III abdicated, Umberto succeeded him, but a plebiscite, resulting in a majority of 54 per cent in favour of a republic, led to his going into exile in Portugal. In 1947 he was banned from Italy for life.

UMMA, city of Sumeria on the Shatt-el-Hai, frequently in conflict with Lagash, whose water supply it controlled. Its ensi, Lugal-zagge-si (*c*. 2400–2371 BC), conquered Sumer and claimed to have conquered all Mesopotamia and Syria.

UMMA, Arabic word used in the Koran in the sense of 'people' or 'community'. At first the Prophet Muhammad envisaged the new faith of Islam as addressed above all to the inhabitants of Mecca and in particular to his own tribe, the Quraysh. He came thereafter, especially during the years of his dominance at Medina (AD 622–32), to think of Islam as directed towards the Arabs in general and even to all mankind. Muhammad created at Medina a form of organization theocratic in character, but transcending the limitations inherent in such exclusive concepts as tribe and race; an organization which, resting on the profession of the Muslim faith, was capable of indefinite expansion to include all men irrespective of their origin and heritage—racial, religious, or cultural.

UNAM SANCTAM (1302), papal bull of Pope Boniface VIII, which was the most extreme statement of papal superiority, if not supremacy, over temporal rulers. In it spiritual power had authority over temporal power and the highest spiritual power under God (*ie*, the papacy) had authority over all other spiritual powers.

UN-AMERICAN ACTIVITIES COMMITTEE in the US, committee of the House of Representatives, created as a special committee under the chairmanship of Martin Dies (1938). It became a standing committee (1945), extended its investigations of un-American and subversive activity in the US, and was denounced by liberals for alleged recklessness in bringing charges of communism against both individuals and organized groups, for its indifferent legislative record, and for usurping the functions of the FBI. Its influence and activities declined in the late 1960s, and in an attempt to change its image and emphasis it became known as the House Committee on Internal Security (1969).

UNAMUNO JUGO, MIGUEL DE (1864–1936), Spanish writer and politician, who was made professor of Greek at Salamanca University in 1891, where he remained for the rest of his life, becoming the senior figure of the so-called 'generation of 1898'. His books and articles propounded an anguished personal philosophy and revealed a disturbing questioning of Spain's isolated and anachronistic position in the modern world.

His publications gave him an international reputation. *En Torno Al Casticismo* (1895) was infused with the Castilian pessimism prevalent in most of his work and which had an enormous intellectual influence in Spain. His existentialist novel, *Paz En La Guerra* (1897), was followed by *Vida de Don Quijote y Sancho* (1905), in which he examined the work of Cervantes. *Del Sentimiento Trágico De La Vida* (1913) was the fullest expression of his philosophy of anguish and doubt. This, together with his last great work, *La Agonía del Cristianismo* (1925), was aimed at exalting the need for individual integrity and at the same time sowed spiritual doubt.

Besides occupying a central position in Spain's intellectual life, Unamuno from time to time also entered the political scene. In 1924 he was deported to the Canary Islands for his attacks on Primo de Rivera. He also regularly criticized the decadent monarchy. He was an independent Republican deputy (1931–3) to the Cortes, but withdrew from politics in despair at the republic's inability to keep public order. At first he supported the military rising of 1936 in the hope of its putting an end to chaos. Ultimately, he was repelled by the violence and atrocities of the war. On 12 Oct. 1936, in a public lecture on the *Día de la Raza*, a celebration of the Hispanic race, he denounced the Nationalist general Millán Astray. Thereafter, he was kept under house arrest until his death.   PP

UNCLE SAM in the US, sobriquet for the US government and people, and name given to a cartoon figure of a tall man, dressed in striped trousers, jacket emblazoned with stars, and a top hat decorated with stars and stripes, created by Seba Smith (1792–1868). During the War of 1812 meat barrels marketed by Samuel Wilson (1766–1854), a contractor from Troy, NY, carried the initials US. The story spread that they stood for 'Uncle Sam' Wilson, and the contractor's honesty, thrift, and patriotism were such that the initials came to symbolize not just the country, but the national character.

UNCLE TOM'S CABIN (1852), novel about American Negro slavery by Harriet Beecher Stowe. It was first serialized in *The National Era* (1851–2), and subsequently published as a book, its appearance coinciding with a public outcry over the Fugitive Slave Act (1850). Dealing in simple, human terms with the misfortunes of a noble and devout Negro slave, Uncle Tom, it succeeded in arousing anti-slavery sentiment where hundreds of more overtly political treatises had failed. Within two weeks of its publication in book form, it sold 10,000 copies and 300,000 copies within a year. For a time it was the most popular book in America, and greatly helped the Abolitionist cause.

UNCONDITIONAL SURRENDER in the Second World War. The unconditional surrender of Germany, Japan, and Italy was adopted as the official war aim of the Allies in Jan. 1943 at the Casablanca Conference attended by Winston Churchill and President Roosevelt. The words themselves were first used publicly by Roosevelt at a press conference; although he later claimed they were spontaneous, it now seems they were the result of mature thought. The policy of demanding unconditional surrender has been one of the most strongly criticized of all the decisions of grand strategy in the Second World War. In Germany's case, its critics argue, the opposition to Hitler within Germany was dispirited, and his position was strengthened when it became known that the war was to be fought to a finish and that the Allies had abandoned any earlier distinction between Nazism and Germany. It is also argued that, given the fanatical nature of Nazism, unconditional surrender necessarily involved the total destruction of Germany, which could only be achieved by an Anglo-American invasion from the West in conjunction with a Russian advance from the East, and it was this that left Russia in a position of dominance in Eastern and Central Europe. Those who approve the demand for unconditional surrender argue variously that it was unlikely that either Germany or Japan would have surrendered without total destruction, that the case of Italy demonstrated that the existence of the official policy did not prevent Badoglio's government from negotiating terms, and that in the circumstances of Jan. 1943 it was essential for the Allies to reassure Stalin of their determination not to accept a compromise peace. In the case of hostilities in Europe, Badoglio's government surrendered on negotiated terms on 3 Sept. 1943; the German armies fighting in Italy surrendered unconditionally on 2 May 1945, those in north-west Europe to Montgomery on Lüneburg Heath on 4 May, and the general surrender of all the armed forces was signed at Rheims on 7 May.

It is also argued that insistence on unconditional surrender of the Japanese without admitting the continued status of the emperor prolonged the war in the Far East and made the use of the atomic bombs necessary. Admiral Suzuki's peace party came to power in April and made an initial request for mediation to the Russians on 12 July 1945, but the Allied powers formally repeated their demand for unconditional surrender from the Potsdam conference on 26 July, without mentioning concessions about the emperor. Japanese vacillations were terminated only with the dropping of the atomic bombs and Russia's entry into the war: on 15 Aug. the emperor announced to the nation the decision to surrender in accordance with the Potsdam terms and on the understanding that the emperor's status would not be prejudiced. This the Allies accepted, and the formal instrument of unconditional surrender was signed on board the USS *Missouri* on 2 Sept.   NRB

UNDERGROUND RAILROAD in the US, name given before the American Civil War to the secret system of routes and hiding places used by fugitive slaves from the South heading for the free states or Canada. The term, originally 'Underground Road', supposedly dates from 1831, when a master, after unsuccessfully pursuing a slave across the Ohio river, remarked that he 'must have gone off on an underground road'. The Underground Railroad of legend was an efficient and highly organized network of 'conductors' and 'stations' which transported thousands of slaves to freedom. In reality, it was often a haphazard enterprise and the loss of slaves by its operations was relatively slight. But the publicized activities of such 'conductors' as John Brown, the Quaker, Levi Coffin, and the escaped slave, Harriet Tubman, alleged to have gone South 19 times and to have led more than 300 slaves to safety, effectively dramatized the slavery issue. The Underground Railroad was an illegal operation, since it violated federal fugitive slave laws.

UNDERHILL, FRANK HAWKINS (1889–1966), Canadian historian and journalist, who was founder and editor of *Canadian Forum* (1919) and a founder of the League for Social Reconstruction (1932).

UNDERWOOD TARIFF (1913) in the US, legislation named after its sponsor, congressman Oscar W. Underwood, of AL (1862–1925), which significantly lowered protective tariffs for the first time in 60 years. Overall average rates were cut from 57 per cent to 29 per cent, and to make up for losses in revenue a modest income tax was introduced. The passage of the bill was a notable achievement for the new administration of Woodrow Wilson.

UNEMPLOYED WORKMEN ACT (1905), in Britain, legislative measure enabling local authorities to assist the unemployed out of the rates after investigation by local Distress Committees. It represented official recognition of the poor law's irrelevance to the unemployment problem.

UNEMPLOYMENT INSURANCE ACT (1911), in Britain, legislative measure which was Part II of Lloyd George's National Insurance policy. It compelled about 2,250,000 low-paid workers in trades especially subject to fluctuating employment levels to insure themselves. Weekly payments of $2\frac{1}{2}$d entitled them to a maximum of 15 seven-shilling weekly benefits in a year. Employers (who stamped and retained workers' cards) and the government contributed equal amounts to the fund. Benefits were withheld if unemployment derived from a trade dispute, misconduct at work, or refusal of reasonable employment. Labour exchanges administered the scheme, whose contributory basis annoyed socialists.

UNIACKE, RICHARD JOHN (1753–1830), Canadian politician, born in Ireland, who emigrated to Canada, where he became solicitor-general of NS (1781). He served as a member of the NS House of Assembly (1783–93, 1798–1806) and attorney-general of NS (1797–1830). He advocated Canadian confederation in his pamphlet 'Observations on the British Colonies in North America with a proposal for the confederation of the whole under one government (1826).

UNIATES, CHURCH OF THE, religious movement of those who supported the union under the Pope of the Orthodox and Catholic churches of Poland-Lithuania, as established by the synod of Brest (1596). Although orthodox rites were retained by the Uniate Church, many Orthodox supporters continued to oppose the union, especially in the Ukraine.

UNIFORMITY, ACT OF (1549) in England, legislative measure of King Edward VI's reign enforcing the use of the moderate Protestant Prayer Book drawn up by Abp Cranmer. It ordered the exclusive use of the new book, but imposed only mild penalties upon priests who disobeyed this injunction, and none on absenting laymen. Although designed to win the support of the moderate masses, it proved ineffectual and was repealed by Mary I in 1553.

UNIFORMITY, ACT OF (1552) in England, legislative measure of Edward VI's reign which enforced the use of Abp Cranmer's revised (1552) Prayer Book, which was unequivocally Protestant in character. It instituted severe penalties for failure to use the book, enforced attendance at the prescribed services, and asserted that the Church's liturgy and ceremonial depended upon parliamentary authority. This, like the first act of uniformity, was repealed by Mary I (1553).

UNIFORMITY, ACT OF (1559) in England, legislative measure which was one of the two principal statutes of the Elizabeth church settlement, enacted to enforce the use of the 1559 Prayer Book, which though a slightly modified version of the 1552 book, was distinctly Protestant. The act was passed by a strongly Protestant House of Commons conscious of the authority of parliament on liturgical matters, but it passed the Lords with a majority of only three, all the spiritual peers voting against it. To enforce the laity's attendance at church services a weekly fine of 12d was introduced for recusants, while for refusing to use the Prayer Book the clergy faced six months' imprisonment for a first offence and life imprisonment for a third.

UNIFORMITY, ACT OF (1662) in England, imposed the Book of Common Prayer and the liturgy of the Church of England upon all ordained preachers and teachers, thus forcing about 2000, or one-fifth of all the beneficed clergy, from the Church. It was approved by the Anglican-dominated Cavalier Parliament elected in April 1661, which, because of the fifth Monarchists' uprising in Jan. 1661, was opposed to any compromise. The act imposed a declaration on all in holy orders embodying (*a*) a repudiation of the Solemn League and Covenant; (*b*) a denial of the right to take up arms against the king; and (*c*) an undertaking to adopt the liturgy of the Church of England as established by law. The act implied a recognition for the first time that the Church of England did not command the loyalty of all English Protestants. It was also far from producing uniformity, and the Conventicle Act (1664) formally accepted the existence of a separate Protestant community. Thus the word 'Nonconformity' had technical significance in English religious definition thereafter.

UNIGENITUS (1713), papal bull of Pope Clement XI promulgated after pressure from King Louis XIV of France, condemning 101 propositions of the *Reflexions Morales* (1699) of the Jansenist, Pasquier Quesnel. Far from suppressing the longstanding Jansenist controversy within the French Church, after Louis's death (1715) it provoked an appeal to a future general council of the Church by several bishops (1717) and divided the French clergy into 'constitutionaries' who supported the bull and 'appellants' who received support from the *parlement* of Paris. The Jansenist issue was thus prolonged until the mid-18th cent.

UNION, ACT OF (1707) in Britain, legislative measure providing the statutory link between England and Scotland. After the Stuart Restoration (1660) the short-lived legislative union between England, Scotland, and Ireland came to an end, though the personal union of the crowns was resumed. Edinburgh and Dublin were allowed their separate parliaments again, but whereas Ireland was constitutionally subordinate to England (1660–1801), Scotland was united with England by an Act of Union (1707), when an underlying community of interests between the two kingdoms triumphed over divergent opinions and Great Britain was established under a single Crown. Even in William III's reign (1700), the English House of Lords had given approval to a bill authorizing the Crown to appoint commissioners to negotiate a union, but the Commons did not do so. Queen Anne took the initiative (1702), and after many false starts two sets of commissioners were appointed. They met for the first time in April 1706. Their Articles of Union formed the basis for the acts passed by both English and Scottish parliaments.

As from 12 May 1707 there was to be a unitary state, Great Britain, consisting of England and Scotland, of which Anne was to be the queen. Thereafter, the succession was to pass to Sophia or her issue. The separate parliament at Edinburgh was extinguished, but the Scots were to be represented instead at Westminster. Along with the English MPs, there were to be 45 Scottish members, and 16 representative Scottish peers were to sit with the English peers. There was to be free trade between the two countries, and England's colonies were to be open to the Scots on equal terms. The Scots were to retain their own legal system. The established Church of England was to remain Anglican, while in Scotland, Presbyterian became the state church, though in order to qualify for government office in England

Scotsmen had to take the Anglican sacramental test if called upon to do so.

The immediate aftermath of the act showed that no legislative measure could eradicate past mistrust between the two nations. There was a major test of its ecclesiastical and legal implications when the case of James Greenshields was heard in the House of Lords. Greenshields was an episcopalian clergyman who was disciplined by the presbyterian authorities for using the Anglican prayer-book in public. He appealed successfully to the English upper house—permitted so to do by article 19 of the terms of the act. His action led to the Toleration Act of 1712, though episcopalians knew little of its benefits for the rest of the cent. The whole affair did nothing to smooth sensitive Scottish feelings, while the economic benefits which the smaller nation had anticipated were half a generation in coming.

G. S. Pryde, *The Treaty of Union of Scotland and England (1707)* (London, 1950).

UNION, ACT OF (1840), in Britain, legislative measure which created the Province of Canada by reuniting Upper and Lower Canada, as recommended in the Durham Report after the rebellion of 1837.

UNION, ACT OF (1910), in Britain, legislative measure which created the Dominion of South Africa. After the Anglo-Boer War and the subsequent period of reconstruction, the leading proponents of union between the British colonies in South Africa (Cape, Natal, Orange Free State, and Transvaal) were Smuts, an Africaner general, and Merriman, a Cape liberal. A National Convention of white representatives met in Durban in 1908 to devise a constitution. In its final form this constitution established a strong unitary state. The four colonies became provinces with residual powers. As a sop to particularism, the capital was divided, Pretoria becoming the executive, Cape Town the legislative, and Bloemfontein the judicial centre.

One of the crucial issues that split the white colonies before union was the franchise. The Cape 'colour-blind' constitution enabled a number of the more affluent Africans and Coloured people to vote. In the Transvaal and Orange Free State only white males had the vote under constitutions granted by the British government in 1906 and 1907 respectively. Some of the Cape politicians wanted their system extended to the whole of South Africa, as did the British government, but the 'northern' leaders, both English- and Afrikaans-speaking, would not consent. The outcome was a compromise, whereby non-whites retained access to the franchise in the Cape, although they lost the right (never exercised) to elect their own candidates.

The Union parliament was for whites only. Cape Africans were removed from the common roll in 1936, and Coloured people in 1956. No non-whites participated in the making of the Union. The British high commissioner, Lord Selborne, intervened behind the scenes to encourage the entrenchment of the Cape franchise, and to prevent the immediate incorporation of Basutoland, Bechuanaland, and Swaziland. Rhodesia also remained outside the Union. A deputation of non-whites visited Britain to protest against the constitution, but the act became law in 1909 with only slight Liberal and Labour dissent in the British parliament. Union was established on 31 May 1910. The most notable change in the constitution when South Africa became a republic in 1961 was the substitution of a president for the British monarch.

L. M. Thompson, *The Unification of South Africa, 1902–1910* (Oxford, 1960).
N. Mansergh, *South Africa 1901–1961. The price of magnanimity* (London, 1962). AEA

UNION, EDICT OF (1588), in France, terms of agreement between King Henry III of France and the Catholic League by which Henry was forced to consent to the appointment of the Duc de Guise as lieutenant-general of the realm and to nominate Cardinal de Bourbon as next in line of succession (July 1588). This royal concession was forced on Henry after the humiliating Day of the Barricades (1588) and added to his hatred of the Guise family.

UNION DÉMOCRATIQUE ET SOCIALISTE DE LA RÉSISTANCE (UDSR)

in France, small political party, formed in 1945, which played a modest part in the politics of the Fourth Republic. It was the only party to have its origins directly in the Resistance movements, whose spirit it tried to embody and perpetuate. Because of its central political position, it in fact tended to attract men of different views and to lack consistent principles; until the formation of the Gaullist RPF movement (1947) it included many Gaullists. Under the leadership of René Pleven (1947–53), the UDSR moved in a conservative direction supporting governments of the centre. But the movement's next leader, François Mitterrand, stressed its socialism and it worked closely with the black African deputies in the French parliament. Mitterrand's opposition to the return of De Gaulle (1958) caused Pleven and others to leave the party, and it had little electoral success under the Fifth Republic. Mitterrand was a candidate of the united left in the 1965 presidential election, and the UDSR was part of the left 'Federation' formed for the 1967 parliamentary election. Mitterrand later became leader of the 'Convention of Republican Institutions'.

UNIÓN GENERAL DE TRABAJADORES

in Spain. The history of the Socialist trade union, the UGT, is closely linked to that of the Socialist Party. It was founded in 1888 and grew out of the Madrid Printers' Federation. Although based in Barcelona, its main support was among building workers and typographers in Madrid. It was never successful in Catalonia, and in 1899 the UGT moved its headquarters to Madrid. It was led and virtually created by Pablo Iglesias and was a typical social-democratic reformist union, moderate and disciplined, and fiercely opposed to electoral corruption. Its growth was slow, membership rising from 3355 in 1888 to 8848 in 1893. It then dropped, but increased again after the Socialists' stand against the Cuban War and by 1899 had reached 15,264. Moreover, the UGT was finding support among the shipyard and foundry workers of Bilbao and the miners of Asturias. By Feb. 1905 it had 56,905 members. The introduction of the *Casa del Pueblo*—a workers' library and social centre—in many towns after 1908 helped to increase recruitment.

Despite government persecution, the UGT continued to grow, especially after 1909, when it took a lead in the campaign against the Moroccan War. Thereafter, co-operating with the Republican parties, it became more of a political force. This change was accentuated during the First World War, although numbers remained steady at around 100,000. Wartime inflation increased union militancy, which was reflected in the general strike of Dec. 1916. The UGT was also to the fore of the national reform movement of the following year. Although its strike was suppressed by the army, a moral victory was gained, since in Feb. 1918 the imprisoned strike leaders were elected to the Cortes.

After weathering the storm which split Spanish socialism on the issue of union with the Communist International, the UGT made considerable gains during the 1920s. Iglesias, after long illness, died in 1925 and was succeeded by Largo Caballero, who, being obsessed by fear of the anarchists, took a post in Primo de Rivera's corporative labour organization. By administering industrial arbitration boards, the *comités paritarios*, so as to favour the UGT, Largo consolidated the union's strength; so much so that the coming of the Second Republic found the Socialists the most powerful anti-monarchical group.

Largo became minister of labour in Azaña's government and again used his position to favour the UGT; its numbers continued to increase under the republic. From being less than 300,000 in 1930, they rose in 1932 to 1 million and to 1,250,000 in 1934. Half of these members were rural workers recruited by the Union's agrarian offshoot, the Federación Española de Trabajadores de la Tierra. The influence of the FETT'S landless labourers, together with general disappointment with the inadequacy of the republic's social reform, drove the UGT to extremism. Socialist miners were the backbone of the Asturian rising of 1934. Uniting itself with the Popular Front, the UGT refused to collaborate with the Republicans after the Feb. 1936 election victory and was in the forefront of violent strike action in 1936. During the Civil War the Union was prominent in Madrid, Asturias, and Bilbao, although in Catalonia it fell almost immediately under the control of the communists.   PP

UNION INTER-COLONIALE,

association of nationalist leaders of countries of the French empire, formed in Paris in 1921 by Nguyen Ai-Quoc (Ho Chi-Minh), Jean Ralaimongo, a Malagasy leader, and others. Its periodical, *Paria*, had considerable influence in early nationalist circles, including those of French West Africa.

UNION OF ARMS

in Spain, plan of the Spanish minister, the *Count* of Olivares, to strengthen Spain for her imperial role by establishing Castilian uniformity throughout the land and by creating, in particular, a common army of 140,000 men, to be raised and equipped by all the provinces of the Iberian peninsula. This was in order to relieve the economic strain imposed upon Castile by the demands of the Thirty Years War and required the kingdoms of Catalonia, Aragon, Portugal, and Naples to contribute and pay 16,000 men each. The idea was first proposed to Philip IV in a memorandum of 1624 and despite provincial opposition was published by decree in Castile on 25 July 1626. Although Aragon and Valencia agreed to make a regular financial contribution, Catalonia refused both money and men, and Olivares's persistent efforts to harness the Catalans to the scheme, particularly after the successful French invasion of Catalonia (1639), merely precipitated the great revolt of Catalonia (1640). Dislike for the plan also contributed to unrest in Portugal, which also broke into revolt in 1640.

UNION OF GERMAN SOCIALIST STUDENTS

(Sozialistischer Deutscher Studentenbund), originally the official student group of the West German Social Democratic Party (SPD), and later the most influential left-wing student organization of the 1960s.

Friction between the SDS and the SPD increased in the 1950s because of continuing disagreement over German rearmament, support of NATO, and contacts with East Germany, and after the 1959 Bad Godesberg party conference, where the revisionist right and centre in the SPD emerged victorious, the differences became unbridgeable. In 1960 the party created a second student organization, the Sozialistische Hochschulbund (SHB) and in 1961 the SPD declared membership in the SDS incompatible with party membership and withdrew all subsidies to the group. The formation of the grand coalition government by the SPD and CDU/CSU in 1966 brought an intensification of SDS activity and increasingly frequent, often violent, clashes with university administrations, city governments, and police. Although the SDS forms only a small minority in the universities, because of its activism and its articulate leadership it emerged in the vanguard of the so-called 'extraparliamentary opposition'. The SDS's hope was to mobilize sufficient popular support to create itself as a viable political force which would, unlike the SPD, be true to socialism and would revolutionize society. Violence involving the SDS reached its apex in 1967 after the killing of a Berlin student by police during a demonstration against the Shah of Iran. Concentrating attention on the need for university reform, on protest against the conservative Springer press empire, and against the projected insertion of an emergency clause in the constitution, the SDS organized continuous demonstrations and disruptions, acting thereby as a catalyst to left-wing student activity, and received at least the moral support of a widening student public. The attempted murder of the SDS leader, Rudi Dutschke, in 1968, resulted in another spasm of violence and in the adoption of increasingly radical and often conflicting views by the successors of the incapacitated Dutschke. The SDS quickly split into rival factions, splintered, and by the end of the 1960s had lost most of its former authority. ME

UNION OF RUSSIAN PEOPLE (Black Hundreds), conservative organization in Russia founded in 1905, which aimed at achieving mass support for the monarchy by appealing to extreme nationalist, anti-Semitic, and anti-intellectual sentiment.

UNION OF THE CROWNS (1603), when James VI of Scotland also became James I of England. This 'regal union' did not unite the two countries. Though they shared the same monarch, they had their own parliaments and privy councils, their own laws and law courts, their own national churches, their own taxation system, and to some extent their own foreign policy. The 1604 articles of union were opposed in England, and rejected by the English parliament. The Cromwellian union (1652–60) was imposed by force upon the Scots and did not survive the Restoration. Despite another attempt by Lauderdale (1669–70), political union was not finally achieved until 1707. Even then, Scotland retained her own legal system and national (Presbyterian) Church.

UNION OF UTRECHT (1579). alliance of the Netherlands provinces of Holland, Zeeland, Utrecht, Drenthe, Gelderland, Overyssel, Friesland, and Groningen, concluded in 1579 to counter the Walloon Union of Arras, to promote the war against Philip II wholeheartedly, and to defend Calvinism. The Union was followed in 1581 by the repudiation of Philip's sovereignty and shared power between the states general and the house of Orange-Nassau, and eventually formed the basis of the federation which was called the Republic of the United Netherlands, recognized by the peace of Westphalia (1648).

UNION OF WALES AND ENGLAND, ACT OF (1536) in England, legislative measure incorporating the old principality of Wales into England. The marcher lordships were dissolved, annexed to the existing English and Welsh counties of Shropshire, Hereford, Gloucester, Glamorgan, Carmarthen, Pembroke, and Merioneth, and the rest divided into five new counties, Monmouth, Brecknock, Radnor, Montgomery, and Denbigh. English law and the whole system of local administration was extended to Wales, whose shires and boroughs were to send 24 MPs to parliament. The ground had been prepared from 1534, when Thomas Cromwell secured the appointment of his friend Rowland Lee to the presidency of the council in the marches. In the following years, equipped with new statutes, *eg*, the 1534 act transferring murder and felony trials from the marcher lords' lands to the English county sessions, Lee established law and order in Wales and the marches. A general act 'for recontinuing of certain liberties and franchises heretofore taken from the Crown' assisted him by subjecting the whole nation to the royal writ.

UNIONE ITALIANA DEL LAVORO (UIL) in Italy, small trade union federation founded in 1914 with syndicalist and war interventionist policies. After 1922 it became violently republican and anti-fascist. A new UIL emerged in 1950, federating unions which wished to avoid Communist- (CGIL) or Catholic- (CSIL) dominated federations. It was in 1970 the smallest of three federations, and was increasingly associated with the Social Democrat Party.

UNIONIST PARTY in Britain, name given to the Conservative Party together with those Liberal opponents of Gladstone like Joseph Chamberlain, who left the Liberals after the split over Home Rule (1886). The party was known as the Conservative and Unionist Party until the settlement of Ireland (1922). It was in power from 1886 to 1892 and 1895 to 1905, and joined in the Coalition cabinets (1915–22).

UNITARIANS, opponents of the orthodox doctrine of the Trinity as an undivided unity of divine nature who stress the human personality of Christ. The movement in Europe can be traced back to Servetus and Laelius and Faustus Socinus in the 16th cent. In England, unitarian views were promoted by John Biddle and Thomas Firmin in the 17th cent. The movement gained ground with the Toleration Act (1689) and spread both inside the Church of England and among dissenters, including men of social and intellectual distinction such as the Duke of Grafton and Joseph Priestley, the scientist and philosopher, who was a unitarian preacher, but opposed the institution of a separate church. In 1773 Theophilus Lindsey resigned his living at Catterick and opened the first unitarian chapel in London. After the full legalization of unitarianism (1813), the British and Foreign Unitarian Association was founded (1825), but no authoritative confession of faith was issued. In the US some New England puritanism developed on unitarian lines and influenced the Harvard divinity school from its foundation (1816) until it became unsectarian (1870). Ralph Waldo Emerson guided the movement towards rationalism and humanitarianism, and in 1910 unitarians joined the International Congress of Free Christians and Other Religious Liberals.

UNITARIOS in Argentina, party of political centralization during the early decades of Argentine independence. The centralizing faction saw Buenos Aires as the funnel for 19th-cent. European enlightenment and the hub from which Argentina's economic potential could be exploited. To ensure this they demanded a centralized national administration, liberal and modernizing in its programmes, elite in its composition. These *unitaries* were opposed by the *federales*, upholders of provincial liberties and traditional customs, and leaders of a populist resistance to Europeanization and authoritarianism. The *federales* frustrated *unitario* constitutions in 1819 and 1826, and drove the arch-*unitario*, Rivadavia, into exile. The *unitarios* were persecuted savagely by Rosas. The durable 1853 constitution succeeded, however, in reconciling the two factions to more parliamentary forms of conflict.

UNITARY SOCIALIST PARTY in Italy (Partito Socialista Unitario, or PSU), founded by reformists, under Turati and Matteotti, who were expelled from the Partito Socialista (PSI) in 1922 for rejecting demands by the Comintern and seeking non-socialist collaboration against fascism. The PSI became the clearest defender of democratic liberties and joined the 'Aventine' secessionists from parliament in 1924, but failed to persuade others to force the king to dismiss Mussolini. The fascists dissolved the USP in Nov. 1925. Some exiled members, under Saragat, joined the PSI in 1930, but many social democrats resigned from the party in 1947 and subsequently joined Christian Democrat coalitions. They united with PSI socialists as the Partito Socialista Unificato (PSU) (1966–9) to facilitate centre-left government, and retained this title when PSI socialists again left the party, blaming social democrat moderates for the coalition's shortcomings in reform, and for the electoral setbacks in 1968.

UNITED ARAB REPUBLIC, political unit formed by the union of Egypt and Syria (5 Feb. 1958), with Abd al-Nasser as president. The UAR originated in a general desire for Arab union, always strong in Syria, and the fear of members of the Ba'th and other Syrian politicians that, without Egyptian support, they might be displaced by a left-wing coalition that would include communists. Most Syrian politicians would have preferred a loose federation, but Nasser who thought union premature, insisted on close control. Egypt thereafter (1958–61) established strict political control over Syria; allegations of economic exploitation of Syria by Egypt seem unfounded. Syrian resentment at the country being excluded from power was enhanced by economic difficulties resulting from prolonged drought and led to an army coup (28 Sept. 1961) and the ending of the union. This was accepted by Egypt on 5 Oct. 1961, although Egypt retained the name of the United Arab Republic. During the lifetime of the UAR it was open to all Arab states to join, but only Yemen entered into a loose association (March 1958) called the United Arab States, which was terminated in Dec. 1961.

UNITED EAST INDIA COMPANY OF THE NETHERLANDS (1602–1798), formed as a chartered company (1602) with a capital of £540,000. It concentrated on the spice trade of Indonesia and had its headquarters at Batavia in Java (1619). After 1641 it controlled both the Moluccas and Malacca. The company ejected its English rivals (1623) at the 'massacre' of Amboina. The Dutch entered the Indian trade in order to use Indian textiles to pay for Indonesian spices. They had factories in Bengal, on the Coromandel coast, at Surat, and on the Malabar coast, where they tried to establish a pepper monopoly. They also took control of Ceylon because of its cinnamon. The company declined in the 18th cent. owing to heavy overheads and decreasing resources in Europe. From c. 1780 it lost the important carrying trade to the British.

UNITED EMPIRE PARTY, in Britain, founded jointly by Lord Beaverbrook and Lord Rothermere at the end of 1929, and devoted itself to the cause of Empire free trade. It purported to be a political party in its own right; in fact, at least from Beaverbrook's point of view, it was to be more of a pressure group within the Conservative Party to convert it to Empire free trade and remove Baldwin from the Conservative leadership. In Oct. 1930 an Empire free trader (though not a member of the United Empire Party) defeated the official Conservative candidate in South Paddington, but in March 1931, at a by-election for Westminster St George's, Baldwin delivered an attack on the press lords and the United Empire candidate was badly defeated. Beaverbrook thereafter withdrew his support and the party soon disappeared, partly because some of its policies were adopted in the Ottawa agreements (1932).

UNITED FARMERS' PARTIES in Canada, political movement which developed through the United Farmers' Movement (1918–22), reflecting the Canadian farmers' dissatisfaction with both the Liberal and Conservative governments' failure to respond to a demand for lower tariffs on farm machinery and agricultural implements. The parties led to the founding of the Progressive Party (1920) by T. A. Crerar. The United Farmers' parties carried three provincial elections (Ont., 1919; Alta, 1921; Man., 1922) and elected 64 Progressive Party members to the Canadian House of Commons, where the party held the balance of power between the Liberals and Conservatives. By 1924 the Progressive Party was nearly defunct, but the United Farmers of Alta continued to exert national influence until their merger with the Co-operative Commonwealth Federation (1932), and the United Farmers of Man. controlled their provincial government until 1958.

UNITED FRUIT COMPANY, exporter of fruit, oils, woods, sugar, and quinine from plantations throughout the Caribbean region and northern South America. It was formed in 1899 after some years of competition among American entrepreneurs in Central America for control of the export of fruit, especially of bananas. Shortly afterwards, huge plantations appeared along the Caribbean coast, Ecuador, and Colombia. The company influenced the politics of countries

in which it was established. It acquired cheap lands and paid few taxes, and its workers received poor wages and were subject to discriminatory treatment. As a result of demands for better social conditions, coupled with growing nationalism among the workers, UFCO, as it is known, raised its workers' wages and improved their working conditions and facilities. Most of UFCO's plantations in Ecuador were sold and the company also lost holdings after agrarian reform laws were issued in Guatemala (1952) and Cuba (1959).

UNITED GOLD COAST CONVENTION (UGCC) in Ghana, political party founded in 1947 mainly by J. B. Danquah. It was the first local party to make self-government its avowed objective, and proved too middle class to have a mass appeal. It lost ground to the Convention People's Party and was dissolved in 1952.

UNITED IRISHMEN movement started by the lawyer Wolfe Tone (1763–98), initially to instigate parliamentary and religious reforms. Stimulated by English repression, Jacobin ideas, and hopes of French military aid, the movement plunged into the rebellion of 1798, which was ruthlessly put down after the defeat of Vinegar Hill. Wolfe Tone committed suicide in prison. The rebellion strengthened the Younger Pitt's view that some Act of Union combining Catholic relief was essential.

UNITED MALAY'S NATIONAL ORGANIZATION (UMNO), strongest constituent of the ruling Alliance Party in Malaya/ Malaysia. As the product and vehicle of the strong Malay opposition to the Malayan Union scheme (1946), UMNO united for the first time all shades of articulate Malay opinion except the pro-Indonesian left. After its success in annulling the Malayan Union (1948), UMNO adopted the goal of *merdeka* (independence). Its popular founder and first president, Dato Onn bin Ja'afar, believing that this could only be achieved through a multi-racial party, resigned to form such a party in 1951. However, under the leadership of Tunku Abdul Rahman UMNO defeated Onn's party at the first municipal elections (1952), helped by an electoral pact with the Malayan Chinese Association (MCA). This successful ad hoc arrangement quickly grew into the Alliance Party, in which UMNO, MCA, and the Malayan Indian Congress jointly contested elections, sharing seats and cabinet portfolios on the basis of their voting strength.

Unlike its two partners in their communities, UMNO always enjoyed the electoral support of the majority of Malays, which enabled it to dominate successive Alliance governments. Tunku Abdul Rahman and Abdul Razak continued to be prime minister and deputy prime minister respectively, while ministries such as those of education and home affairs, which dealt with matters involving racial sensibilities, remained in UMNO hands. Nevertheless, within UMNO pressure has been exerted to prevent the compromise of Malay interests by the leadership, notably over relations with Singapore (1965), the national language bill (1967), and, most acutely, during the 1969 racial troubles.   AJSR

UNITED NATIONAL INDEPENDENCE PARTY (UNIP) in Zambia, formed in 1959 by Kenneth Kaunda and other nationalist leaders as a means of winning independence for Northern Rhodesia. It achieved its first main objective in 1964, with the creation of Zambia, and remained in 1970 a strong modernizing force. Its only organized political opposition came from the African National Congress, formed in 1948, led by Harry Nkumbula, and supported by conservative elements in the Barotse and other chiefdoms. But this opposition had little of the vigour associated with UNIP's leadership.

UNITED NATIONAL PARTY in Ceylon. When the new constitution for Ceylon was approved in 1947 there were only two small organized political parties, both parties of the 'left'. The followers of D. S. Senanayake, including J. L.

Kotelawala, set about organizing a party, and at the 1947 general election this party won the largest number of seats (42) in the House of Representatives. With the aid of some independent members, Senanayake was able to form a government. After his death in 1952 the party, led by his son Dudley, won a handsome majority in the general election, and remained in power until 1956, when it was heavily defeated. However, it regained office at the 1965 election. Its leaders were drawn from the English-educated elite, and this helped to make it unpopular. They were frequently accused of corruption and nepotism, alleged neglect of Sinhalese interests, and for being too Westernized.

UNITED NATIONS, international organization for the maintenance of peace and security and the promotion of international welfare, set up by the signatories of the Charter of the United Nations (26 June 1945) which came into force on 24 Oct. 1945. The term United Nations was used for the wartime alliance against Germany, Italy, and Japan and plans for the post-war organization were worked out between the Allies in meetings between the heads of the great powers and at the San Francisco conference (April–June 1945).

The main structure of the UN follows, with certain important changes, that of the League of Nations. Each member country is represented in the General Assembly, where each has one vote. Under the charter, the prime responsibility for security is given to the Security Council, which has five permanent members—Britain, France, China, US, USSR, and, since 1965, ten (originally six) members elected for periods of two years. The charter's concept was thus that of a large assembly which would provide a forum for debate and a means of defusing tense international situations, while the Security Council would be instantly on call, empowered to take rapid decisions and back them up through a Military Staff Committee and forces made available by member nations. (In practice the Staff Committee, although formally established in Feb. 1946, remained inoperative and no forces were assigned to it.) However, such action required the affirmative votes of seven members (since 1965, nine), including the concurring votes of the permanent members. Since, by the time the UN met, the wartime alliance had given way to the Cold War, the UN was hamstrung, except in circumstances when the great powers, opposed to each other on Cold War issues, happened to be in agreement (or in the unique circumstance of the outbreak of the Korean War, when the Soviet Union was boycotting the organization in protest against its failure to recognize communist China). The balance between the General Assembly and the Security Council has therefore changed over the years at the same time as the membership has grown with the accession to independence of new states. Membership of the UN has remained a desirable concomitant of national independence —in contrast to membership of the League of Nations, for the league never succeeded in becoming a world-wide organization.

The charter established two other councils, elected from the General Assembly. The Economic and Social Council (ECOSOC), which has 27 members, is responsible for coordinating UN policy in economic, social, and cultural fields, its establishment under the charter being an indication of the importance which the founders of the UN attached to these questions as underlying the stability of world politics. Its work has been concerned primarily with the gathering of information, particularly of a statistical kind, and the coordination of the activity of the specialized agencies. It works through a series of commissions, some of them subject commissions (population, statistics, human rights, narcotics) and the others regional commissions—the Economic Commission for Europe (ECE), for Asia and the Far East (ECAFE), for Latin America (ECLA), and for Africa (ECA). In addition, two special bodies have been established under the aegis of the ECOSOC: the United Nations Development Programme (UNDP—founded Nov. 1965), which brought together the Expanded Programme of Technical Assistance and the UN

Special Fund; and the United Nations High Commissioner for Refugees, with headquarters in Geneva (established 1950), which is responsible for the 'international protection' of refugees.

The second council, the Trusteeship Council, has, by the nature of its work, had a role of diminishing importance. Its responsibility under the charter is to assist the political, economic, and social development of UN Trust territories. These consisted of the League of Nations' former Mandated territories (except South-West Africa, which South Africa, as the Mandatory power, refused to concede). In 1968 only two Trust territories (New Guinea, under Australian administration, and the Pacific islands, under US) remained. Despite the diminishing role of the Trusteeship Council the self-government of colonial territories has been one of the major subjects of debate and division within the UN, with the anti-colonialist side basing its case on Chapter XI of the Charter, entitled 'Declaration Regarding Non-Self-Governing Territories'.

The UN has brought under its aegis the World Court, now known as the International Court of Justice. The statute of the court is annexed to the charter and its members (15 judges elected for nine years) are chosen by the General Assembly and the Security Council. However the court retains its independence from the UN.

I. L. Claude, *Swords into Plowshares* (New York, 1956).
H. G. Nicholas, *The United Nations as a Political Institution* (London, 1962). WK

UNITED NATIONS RELIEF AND REHABILITATION ADMINISTRATION (UNRRA) grew from a plan first conceived in the British ministry of economic warfare (1941) and was established by agreement between 44 states, including the Soviet Union (Nov. 1943). Its purpose was to provide relief in the form of food, clothing, and shelter as the Second World War came to an end. Its activities were financed largely by the US, Britain, and the Commonwealth, but it was warmly accepted by all participating nations, and with the increasing tension of the post-war years it brought considerable aid into Eastern Europe. It was wound up in 1948 and replaced by the Marshall plan, which was effective only in Western Europe, an indication of the deepening divisions caused by the Cold War.

UNITED NATIONS RELIEF AND WORKS AGENCY (UNRWA), organization established in 1949 in accordance with the Clapp mission's recommendations to provide relief and economic assistance to Palestinian Arab refugees.

UNITED NATIONS SPECIAL COMMITTEE ON PALESTINE (UNSCOP), 11-national investigatory committee, established in 1947, which recommended, by a majority, the partition of Palestine; a minority sought a federal union in Palestine.

UNITED PARTY in Australia, launched as the major non-Labour party in May 1931 under the leadership of J. A. Lyons, a former Tasmanian Labour prime minister and Commonwealth prime minister (1931–9). Its formation reflected the diminished prestige of the Nationalist Party and the desire of civic reform movements to prevent the dissemination of J. T. Lang's radical policies introduced to combat the effects of the Depression. The party's formal organization remained incomplete and anomalous, the older title of 'United' being retained in Qld until 1936 and in Tas. and WA until 1945, and there being no provision for a federal conference. Internal discontent culminated in the party's gradual disintegration (1941–5). It was replaced by Menzies's 'Liberal' party.

UNITED PARTY OF NEW ZEALAND, formed in 1927, mainly by A. E. Davy, as a non-Labour opposition to Reform. It won office in 1928, but the Depression forced it into a coalition (1931) with Reform. The United Party dissolved into the National Party in 1936.

UNITED PARTY OF SOUTH AFRICA, formed in 1934 by the fusion of Smuts's South African Party and J. B. Hertzog's Nationalists. The United Party governed South Africa under Smuts during the Second World War, but lost the 1948 elections to the Purified Nationalists led by Dr J. Malan. The UP failed to provide white South Africans with a consistent racial policy, and as the official opposition party it lost more and more ground to the Nationalists at each election, until 1970, when it regained a few seats. By the 1960s it had become almost entirely the party of English-speaking white South Africans, though some of these supported the predominantly Afrikaner Nationalists. The UP's racial policy differed only in theory from the Nationalists' policy of apartheid. The leader of the United Party from 1956 was Sir D. P. de Villiers Graaff.

UNITED PRESS INTERNATIONAL (1958–), world's largest news service, formed by the amalgamation of the Scripps–Howard United Press (1907–) and the Hearst International News Service (1909–).

UNITED SOCIALIST PARTY OF CATALONIA (Partito Socialista Unificat de Catalunya) in Spain, formed shortly after the outbreak of the Spanish Civil War. Although theoretically socialist it was effectively controlled by the communists. It was affiliated to the Comintern, a Comintern delegate, Erno Gerö, was attached to it, and communists were in charge of its organization, its press, and its internal security. Its secretary-general, Comorera, was a member of the central committee of the Spanish Communist Party. The PSUC espoused the cause of the middle classes and included in its ranks many ex-members of the *Esquerra* and *rabassaires*. It infiltrated the Catalan police and pursued a policy of organized terrorism against anarchists and the POUM. The militias were disarmed in favour of regular formations and the anarchist-held fronts were starved of arms.

The PSUC's minister of supply, Comorera, put an end to revolutionary requisition and collectivization. In Jan. 1937 he abolished bread rationing, which caused considerable hardship to Barcelona's working-class population. In May, Rodriquez Salas, the PSUC's police chief, visited Barcelona's central telephone exchange, which had been occupied by the CNT. This was a provocation which brought to a head the smouldering discontent of the POUM and the CNT against the pressure of the PSUC. For three days there was fighting in Barcelona. When order was restored, the episode was used by the communists to discredit the POUM and the CNT which were virtually destroyed. But, until the end of the Spanish Civil War, the PSUC remained the strongest power in Catalonia.

UNITED STATES INFORMATION AGENCY (1953–), branch of the US government, the aim of which is help to achieve US foreign policy objectives by influencing public opinion in foreign countries. It evolved from the Office of War Information (1942–5) and the post-war information and cultural services of the Department of State. The libraries and other facilities provided by its overseas arm, the United States Information Service, fulfil educational and propaganda functions.

UNIVERSAL NEGRO IMPROVEMENT ASSOCIATION, Negro protest movement, founded by Marcus Garvey in Jamaica (1914) as the Universal Negro Improvement and Conservation Association and African Communities League. Its real development followed formation of the New York 'division' (1917) after Garvey's migration to the US (1916). The UNIA aimed to arouse Negro self-respect through 'regeneration of Africa', encouraging migration of Negroes to their African 'homeland'. Branches appeared in many American cities, the British West Indies, Canada, Central

America, and parts of West Africa. Its influence, which gradually assumed international proportions, exceeded that of all previous American Negro organizations, but declined after Garvey was imprisoned (1925) for allegedly using the US mails to defraud. On his release he was deported (1928), and tried to run the UNIA from Jamaica (1929–34) and London (1935–40). However, few branches survived his death in 1940.

UNIVERSAL POSTAL UNION (founded in 1874 as the General Union of Posts) became the UPN in 1878. It was based on the first International Postal Convention, which guarantees to every member state the full use of postal services with arrangements for uniformity of classification and standards. In 1968 it became a specialized agency of the UN.

UNIVERSALISTS, American religion, founded by John Murray (1741–1815), who emigrated from London to MA in 1770. The Universalists were non-Trinitarians, who opposed Calvinist doctrines of predestination. Murray joined Elhanan Winchester, of PA, and Caleb Rich, of NH, to form the Universalist Church (1790). Universalists spread into rural areas of New England and NY. After 1805 the movement was led by Hosea Ballou (1771–1852), who preached the doctrine of a loving God. In 1961 the Universalists merged with the theologically related Unitarians to form the Universalist–Unitarian Association.

UNIVERSITIES grew out of the schools which in the 11th and early 12th cents became famous as places of higher learning, usually in one subject, though sometimes in more (*eg*, Bologna for law, Montpellier for medicine, Paris for logic and theology). The medieval name for a university was *studium generale* or place of general resort, which made it distinguishable from schools, such as Chartres (and even the Paris of Abelard) by three things: first, a university was a place to which students from anywhere could study; second, it was organized into a number of faculties and offered a certain range of subjects; third, it held a charter (usually a papal bull) to issue licences to teach everywhere (*ius ubique docendi*), ie, to grant degrees. There were students' universities and masters' universities; Bologna, the earliest university, was a students' university, ie, one where the student body was the ultimate authority. Paris, Oxford, and most other universities were controlled by the masters. These organized themselves on the pattern of trade guilds into an association called a *universitas* (the whole body of masters). It was during the Renaissance that this term was transferred from the corporation of masters to the institution itself. In the centuries that followed, universities emerged as centres of higher education in the arts and sciences.

UNIVERSITY EXTENSION in Britain, mid-19th-cent. movement to make higher learning more accessible to all classes of society. Lectures as a means of adult education were recommended by William Sewell in *Suggestions for the Extension of a University* (1850). At the instigation of James Stuart, a syndicate was established at Cambridge (1873) to supply lecturers for mechanics' institutes and other bodies, who ran at their own cost 12-week courses on history, literature, economics, science, etc. Oxford and London joined the scheme and a joint universities' board was established (1876). Local colleges were later affiliated, and thus the growth of university colleges in provincial centres was stimulated. Following the final report on adult education of the Ministry of Reconstruction (1919), university extra-mural departments were established.

UNIVERSITY TESTS ACT (1871) in Britain enabled every man at Oxford and Cambridge to take degrees or hold offices, except of a theological nature, without subscribing to articles of faith or attending religious worship. Religious services and instruction within the university were preserved, but the act diminished the dominance of the Anglican Church in university life.

UNKIAR-SKELESSI, TREATY OF (8 July, 1833), Russo-Ottoman defensive alliance, containing a secret clause closing the Straits to warships of all nations when the Ottoman empire was at peace. The treaty, which was the outcome of Russian assistance to the Ottomans against Muhammad Ali of Egypt, was generally thought to give Russia control over Ottoman policy and was a major factor in the development of British hostility to Russian policy in the East.

UNTOUCHABLES, term applied to a number of caste groups which, because of their unclean occupations, were considered by 'caste Hindus' to be ritually polluting. They were placed under various social restrictions and were generally menial servants or labourers. Their separation from 'caste Hindus' gave them their other common title of 'outcastes'. Economic changes and the growth of towns gave greater opportunities to members of these groups and from the turn of the 19th cent. organized efforts were made to improve their status. Caste associations were formed and groups often provided with a new name and 'history' in order to throw off older disabilities. By the 1920s such associations were beginning to co-operate at both a regional and national level under the general name of 'Depressed Classes'. Leaders of this Depressed Class movement, the most notable of whom was Dr Ambedkar, believed that they had to act as a united body separate from the caste Hindus, if they were to improve their position. They tended, therefore, to resent attempts by others to start 'uplift' work among the Depressed Classes ('Harijans' or 'people of God', as Gandhi called them). They pressed, too, for separate electorates and succeeded in achieving this aim in the Communal Award (1932). Gandhi's opposition to this move, however, produced the Poona pact (1932), under which the separate electorates were replaced by reserved seats within the general (Hindu) constituencies. The term 'Scheduled Castes' derived from this decision because it was necessary for electoral purposes to 'schedule' castes eligible to stand and vote for such reserved seats. Ambedkar's new all-India organization (1942) was called the Scheduled Castes Federation.

The Indian constitution (1950) formally abolished untouchability and made discrimination on grounds of untouchability illegal. At the same time, it was decided that the Scheduled Castes needed continued help and support to improve their position within the community and consequently seats in legislatures, scholarships, and appointments in the civil and armed services were reserved for them, while a Commissioner for Scheduled Castes and Tribes (the latter being the 'aboriginal' peoples of India) was appointed. PDR

UNYANYEMBE, in central Tanzania, one of the most successful of the Nyamwezi trading states during the 19th cent., whose rulers numbered forceful characters such as Fundikira (d. *c.* 1858) and Mnwa Sele (d. 1865), and whose contemporaries or rivals included other enterprising trader-kings, such as Nyungu ya Mawe (d. 1884), of Ukimbo. Like its neighbours, Unyanyembe was important in the long-distance trade between the East African interior and the coast.

UPANISHADS, relatively short Sanskrit texts of ancient India, of which there exist some 300 in all. The oldest of these date back to about the 5th cent. BC. They generally deal, in the form of dialogues between a teacher and a pupil, with basic problems of existence. They have had great influence on Indian thought up to the present time.

UPARAJA, in Thailand, office of the heir-apparent, instituted in the latter half of the 16th cent. to secure regular succession to the throne. During the Chakri dynasty, from 1782, the position was usually filled by the king's younger brother. It was abolished on the death of the last uparaja,

Wichaichan, in 1885, when it was replaced by a Western system of succession, eventually codified in law.

UPHAM, CHARLES HAZLITT (1908–), NZ soldier, who was awarded the Victoria Cross and bar for gallantry in Crete (1941), and in the western desert (1942), the only Second World War serviceman so honoured.

UPPER VOLTA (274,000 sq. kms) in West Africa, formerly a province of French West Africa, which became independent in 1960 as a republic ruled by military decree. In 1970 the population of 4,955,000 included Mossi, Bobo, Gourounsi, and Senufo peoples.

UPPSALA in Sweden, mentioned in the 9th cent. as being famous for its great heathen temple. The first cathedral of the bishops of Uppsala was built there (*c.* 1100). After its destruction by fire it was rebuilt in 1273 on a new site, that of the modern city, which became the ecclesiastical capital of Sweden. The kings of Sweden were crowned there.

UPPSALA, SYNOD OF (1593), in Sweden, meeting of clergy with the Council and other nobles, which settled the basis of the Swedish Church. It adopted the Augsburg Confession, together with the three creeds and the Swedish church ordinance of 1571. Duke Charles accepted the omission of any concession to the Reformed (Calvinist) Church in order that he might secure a united front against King Sigismund.

UQAYLID, name given to a line of Arab emirs. The Banu Uqayl, descended from the tribe of Amir ibn Sa'sa'a, rose to prominence at Mosul, when the Hamdanid regime fell into decline, the first notable member of the house being their chieftain Abu'l-Dhawwad Muhammad ibn Musayyid (d. AD *c.* 996). Uqaylid influence was at its height in the time of the emir Muslim ibn Quraysh ibn Badran (*reg.* 1061–85). It weakened thereafter owing to dynastic discord and because of the intervention of the Seljuks, who made an end of Uqaylid rule at Mosul in 1096. Another branch of the Uqaylid house held Ja'bar and Al-Raqqa during the years AD *c.* 1086–*c.* 1168.

UQBA IBN NAFI IBNABD AL-QAYS AL QURAYSHI AL-FIHRI (d. 683), Muslim soldier, who led the Muslim forces operating in Ifriqiyya (the region of modern Tunisia). Uqba ibn Nafi founded an important garrison town at Al-Kayrawan (670). He was dismissed from his command in 675, but was restored to it in 682. He then began a march westward into the Maghrib, penetrating to the neighbourhood of Tangier and thereafter moving southwards into Morocco, and through the Atlas mountains, to the sea. He was killed in battle against the Berbers on the edge of the Sahara, near modern Biskra.

UR, Sumerian city (mod. Muqqayr) on the Euphrates, which existed throughout the history of ancient Mesopotamia. During excavations from 1922 onwards by Sir Leonard Woolley many important relics, texts, and inscriptions dating from early times (*c.* 3000 BC) until the Seleucid period (*c.* 300 BC) were found. The city had its greatest period under the Third Dynasty (usually abbreviated to Ur III), (*c.* 2112–2004), founded by Ur-Nammu (*reg. c.* 2112–2095), who was followed by Shulgi (*reg. c.* 2095–2047), Amer-Suen (*reg. c.* 2047–2038), Su-Sin (*reg. c.* 2038–2029), and Ibbi-Sin (*reg. c.* 2029–2004). Many texts show that there was considerable prosperity and great building activity at the time. Ur-Nammu built canals, public and religious buildings, and many ziqqurats, including the one at Ur. Centralized government enabled Ur to control an extensive Sumerian empire which finally collapsed under the attacks of the Amorites in the west and the Elamites in the east. Later, attempts were made to restore the city, notably by the Kassite and Chaldean kings, but it fell into ruin (*c.* 316 BC) when the Euphrates changed its course.

URALS in Russia, mountain range dividing Russia and stretching from north to south between Muscovy and the western Siberian plain. The Urals, first discovered by the Novgorod empire *c.* 1200, were found in the 16th cent. to be rich in copper and iron deposits. From Peter I's reign they produced 40 per cent of Russia's iron ore and became the leading mining and metallurgical region of the world. By 1800 they had been found to contain valuable minerals, *eg*, jasper, quartz, topaz, amethyst, asbestos, marble, gypsum, mineral oil, salt, saltpetre, gold, silver, and lead.

URARTU, ancient and powerful kingdom of Armenia, which developed after the uniting of several tribes into a small principality around Lake Van in the 9th cent BC. Backed by prosperous agriculture and wealth from copper and iron mines, the country grew more powerful, attaining its apogee during the reigns of Ishpuini, his son Menua, and his grandson Argistis I (late 9th and first half of the 8th cents BC), when Urartain power extended over Transcaucasia and the Lake Urmiah region and into northern Syria. Conflict with Assyria began at an early period and in 714 Urartu suffered a disastrous defeat at the hands of the Assyrian ruler Sargon. Following a temporary revival, the Urartian state finally succumbed to the attacks of the Medes (early 6th cent.). Recent excavations of city walls, temples, warehouses, and irrigation canals and the discovery of stone and metal goods and numerous cuneiform inscriptions on rocks and tablets (showing a language related to Hurrian, but not yet fully understood) have demonstrated the importance of the Urartian civilization.

URBAN II (*reg.* 1088–99), Pope, who was prior of Cluny before being elected to the papacy. His pontificate marked the zenith of the period of the Gregorian reforms, especially by his summoning of the First Crusade at the council of Clermont in 1095. The success of this crusade in recovering Jerusalem was a great papal triumph.

URBAN V (*reg.* 1362–70), Pope, who, although a Frenchman, was determined to return the papacy to Rome from Avignon. Cardinal Albornoz having restored order in the papal states, Urban left for Rome (1367) despite strong opposition from his cardinals and the French king. He was forced to return to Avignon because of new disturbances and died shortly afterwards. His successor, Gregory XI, made a fresh attempt to return to Rome, thereby causing a disastrous schism in the church after his death.

URBAN VI (*reg.* 1378–89), Pope. When Gregory XI, who had insisted on the return of the papacy from Avignon to Rome, died in Italy in 1378, there was an overwhelming demand among the Romans that the papacy should remain in their city. Urban VI, previously Abp of Bari, was elected on 10 April 1378 in a conclave threatened and eventually disrupted by a Roman mob, which demanded an Italian pope. The choice seemed a good one. Urban had been an efficient chancellor to Gregory XI and was held in high esteem as a theologian and as a man, but after his election he seemed to become unhinged and began to act in a violent, tyrannical, and unbalanced way that dismayed the cardinals. In Aug. a majority of them left Rome and in Sept. declared his election invalid on the grounds of the pressure of the mob, which inhibited a free election. They elected Cardinal Robert of Geneva, as Clement VII, and thus began the Great Schism. Urban continued to act in a manner scarcely rational and at least five cardinals and a bishop were done to death for opposing him.

URBAN VII (1521–90), Pope (*reg.* 1590), who was previously Abp of Rossano. He was elected to succeed Sixtus V, but reigned for only 12 days.

URBAN VIII (1568–1644), Pope (*reg.* 1623–44), whose long pontificate marked the climax of the Italian baroque. He was a cultured man, who wrote poems and sonnets in Latin and Greek and was the patron of Bernini and Borromini. He presided over the inauguration of the new St Peter's in Rome (18 Nov. 1626) and the building of the Palazzo Barberini. Among his achievements were the revision of the Catholic breviary (1631) and the founding of the College for the Propagation of the Faith, a testimony to his crusading spirit. Although he longed to lead a war against heretics and infidels, his early years as papal nuncio to France contributed to his strong pro-French and anti-Habsburg policies on the international scene, and thus he tried to undermine the imperial leadership of Catholic Germany. His efforts at peaceful mediation in the Thirty Years War (1635, 1638) came to nothing. He established his own family among the Roman aristocracy and extended papal influence in Italy by the acquisition of the duchy of Urbino. He is remembered as the denouncer of Jansenism, whose bull, *In Eminenti* (1642), condemning the *Augustinus*, opened a prolonged religious controversy.

URBAN COHORTS, ancient Roman force stationed partly in the city, partly in neighbouring towns, and consisting of three cohorts, each 1000 strong, commanded by tribunes. Originally part of the Praetorian Guard, they acquired a separate existence with the appointment of L. Piso as the first permanent prefect of the city *c.* AD 13. In AD 23 Tiberius concentrated the Praetorians and the Urban Cohorts, which remained, however, under the command of the city prefect, in one large barracks at Rome. With the Praetorians they formed an elite corps, receiving higher pay than ordinary soldiers. They were abolished by Constantine the Great.

URBINO, fortified city in the mountains of central Italy, one of the best natural fortresses of that country. In the 14th and 15th cents Urbino became the capital of the great warrior dynasty of the Montefeltro. Its most notable member, Duke Federico (*reg.* 1444–82), built one of the most splendid Renaissance palaces in Italy. It was designed by a succession of great architects, including Luciano Laurana and Francesco di Giorgio. Outstanding painters and sculptors were employed to decorate it, among them Piero della Francesca, Ucello, and Fiamberti. Urbino continued as the centre of a brilliant court in the 16th cent., Baldassare Castiglione's famous dialogue of *The Courtier* taking place in the ducal palace. The ruling dynasty died out in 1626 and Urbino was annexed by the papacy.

URDU, mixed language of Hindi and Persian, deriving its name from the Turkish word meaning 'a camp'. The language arose out of Hindu contacts with the Muslim Turks who used Persian for official and literary purposes from *c.* 1200. It has a Hindi syntax with a strong infusion of Persian and Arabic words. The formative process was hastened by the decision (*c.* 1580) to keep local records in Persian instead of Hindi. The language was widely used by the Hindus and Muslims around the Muslim courts of north India and the Deccan. It developed a large literature, including both prose and verse. It is, as well as Bengali, an official language of Pakistan.

URFÉ, HONORÉ D' (1568–1625), French writer, who fought in the French religious wars and later settled in Savoy, where he wrote the pastoral romance, *L'Astrée* (1607–27), regarded as the first French novel, which was rapturously received by French literary society. It helped to establish a new ideal of courtly gallantry and love, reflecting D'Urfé's own romantic life story.

URIBURU, JOSÉ FÉLIX (1868–1932), Argentine soldier and political leader, who had championed the German cause in the First World War. He led the 1930 military revolt which destroyed civilian middle-class rule and sought to impose an authoritarian, nationalist, and corporatist regime, but was frustrated by traditionalist military politicians, who instead restored the old oligarchic order.

UR-NAMMU (*reg. c.* 2112–2095 BC), founder of the Third Dynasty of Ur, who restored the supremacy of the Sumerians in Mesopotamia. He inaugurated construction work on ziqqurats and canals, cleared existing waterways, restored trade, drew up a code of laws, and brought a period of prosperity to his city.

URQUHART, DAVID (1805–77), British diplomatist and politician, who was with Stratford Canning's mission to Constantinople in 1831–2 and was made secretary to the Greek embassy in 1836. He was recalled in 1837 for his open hostility to Russia. As an MP he spoke and wrote in favour of Turkey and denounced Palmerston. His attacks on Palmerston's foreign policy made him, from time to time, an ally both of Bright and the radicals and of Disraeli.

URQUIZA, JUSTO JOSÉ DE (1800–70), Argentine provincial *caudillo* and president of Argentine (1854–60). As governor of Entre Rios province after 1842, he reacted to Buenos Aires's increasing economic domination of the Argentine Confederation by rallying the forces that overthrew the dictator, Juan Manuel de Rosas, at Monte Caseros on 3 Feb. 1852. Urquiza became president of the Confederation under a new constitution promulgated on 1 May 1853. Buenos Aires, however, dissociated itself from the new regime, which chose the city of Paraná as its capital. Under Urquiza, international commercial treaties were concluded, the Paraná and Uruguay rivers opened to world trade, and attempts made to stimulate agriculture and pastoral life. Tension with Buenos Aires led to hostilities in 1860–1. Buenos Aires's victory at Pavón (1861) ensured that Buenos Aires, restored to the republic, would also become its capital and economic hub. Urquiza was murdered by his political rivals in 1870.

URRUTIA LLEÓ, MANUEL (1901–), Cuban lawyer, judge, and provisional president of Cuba, whose anti-Batista attitudes and judicial fairness led Fidel Castro Ruz to propose him as provisional president of the Cuban republic in Jan. 1959. Within a matter of months friction between Urrutia and Castro caused the former to resign.

URSINS, MARIE-ANNE DE LA TRÉMOUILLE, Princess des (1642–1722), French-born princess who dominated the government of Spain in the critical years of the War of the Spanish Succession. She fulfilled her political ambitions, when, through the influence of Mme de Maintenon and the Duchess of Burgundy, she was appointed *camarera-mayor* to the 14-year-old Princess Marie Louise of Savoy on her marriage to Louis XIV's grandson, Philip of Anjou, the future King of Spain. She greatly influenced the young monarch, guiding his pro-French administration, until the death of Marie Louise (1714). She was exiled to France soon after Philip's marriage to Elizabeth Farnese (Jan. 1715), and later retired to Genoa and then to Rome.

URSULINE ORDER, greatest and earliest teaching order for women in the Catholic Church, founded in 1535 by St Angela Merici and fostered in its early years by Pope Paul III. Initially it was devoted to the spiritual regeneration of girls and to charitable works, but it developed into an educational order from the end of the 16th cent., after the first school was established in Parma (1595).

URUK (mod. Warka), Sumerian city and home of Gilgamesh, which gave its name to a culture dated *c.* 3300–3100 BC, characterized by pottery made on a wheel, cylinder seals, mosaic decoration, and the first appearance of writing.

US STEEL CORPORATION (1901–), the first thousand million dollar corporation in the US and one of the largest steel companies in the world, created by the merger of eight large specialized companies into a vertically integrated holding company. This grand consolidation of the industrial interests of Andrew Carnegie, Henry Clay Frick, and Elbert H. Gary was arranged by the financier J. P. Morgan, and in 1906 US Steel created a vast modern steel-making complex at Gary, IN, which reasserted its pre-eminence in the industry. Although subjected to anti-trust investigations in 1911, US Steel continued to grow both by the acquisition of related firms and by expansion. In 1970 it produced a quarter of the total US output of steel, although its share of the market had declined since 1911.

US v. BUTLER, 297 US 1 (1936), US Supreme Court case invalidating the Agricultural Adjustment Act (1933). Justice Roberts, in a 6–3 decision, while upholding the power of the federal government to tax and spend for the general welfare, refused to validate the processing tax levied under the act, on the grounds that the use of such money by the federal government to regulate agricultural production violated the Tenth Amendment. In a dissenting opinion, Justice Stone attacked both the constitutional logic of the majority and the action of the court in striking down the legislation.

US v. DARBY, 312 US 100 (1941), US Supreme Court case involving a federal prosecution to enforce minimum wage standards. Justice Stone, speaking for a unanimous court, upheld the provisions of the Fair Labor Standards Act (1938), since the commerce power was complete and Congress could regulate intra-state activities where they had a substantial effect on inter-state commerce.

US v. E.C. KNIGHT CO., 156 US 1 (1895), US Supreme Court decision limiting implementation of the Sherman Anti-Trust Act (1890). The case involved a government suit to dissolve the American Sugar Refining Co., which controlled over 90 per cent of the resources for manufacturing refined sugar in the US. Chief Justice Fuller denied the government's claim, arguing that the act was directed only against combinations in inter-state commerce and did not invalidate combination in production. His distinction between 'direct' and 'indirect' effects on commerce established an important precedent and a stumbling-block to attempts at regulation by the federal government.

USEFUL KNOWLEDGE SOCIETY in Britain, founded in 1827 by Lord Brougham. It published cheap and informative literature, including the *Penny Cyclopaedia*, and a series of pamphlets on technical subjects and political economy, partly designed to combat radical propaganda.

USERTSEN I (Senworse) (*reg. c.* 1971–1928 BC), Egyptian King of the XIIth dynasty, who traded with Phoenicia and invaded Nubia, probably to secure trade with the Sudan and supplies of gold. He exploited mines and quarries, and built extensively, especially at Thebes, Tanis, and Heliopolis.

USERTSEN III (Senworse) (*reg. c.* 1878–1843 BC), Egyptian King of the XIIth dynasty, who annexed Lower Nubia to the second cataract, building fortresses and establishing garrisons for its defence. He campaigned in Palestine, and reached Shechem. During his reign royal power grew at the expense of that of the provincial nobles.

USES, STATUTE OF (1536) in England, legislative measure passed by the Reformation parliament after five years' delay which was designed to protect the Crown's prerogative rights and curb the evasion of feudal incidents by those who had the 'use' of property legally owned by another person. The 1536 act declared that lands in use were to be regarded as the full property of those who profited by them. This was met with opposition from a section of the gentry.

USHAKOV, SIMEON (1626–86), Russian painter, whose technique was distinctly Western and who painted pictures on religious themes rather than the traditional icons.

USSELINCX, WILLEM (1567–1647), Dutch writer, who advocated Dutch colonization in the Americas, and is credited with inspiring the establishment of the Dutch West India Co.

USSHER, JAMES (1581–1656), Irish scholar, who was professor of theology at Trinity College, Dublin, Bp of Meath (1620), and Abp of Armagh (1625). In his earlier years he was a bitter opponent of Catholicism, and headed the list of 12 Irish prelates who signed a protestation against toleration for Catholics (1626). In 1640 he went to England and the great Irish rebellion of 1641 prevented his returning to Ireland again. His *Chronologia Sacra* (1660) is the standard chronology for early editions of the English Bible.

USURY, lending of money for interest (assured profit). From earliest times the Christian Church, basing itself on Scripture, condemned the practice and scholastics reinforced this by the Aristotelian argument that money was sterile and could not breed money (as developed by Aquinas). Nevertheless, money-lending at interest was common practice in the Middle Ages, though the interest was usually disguised. Transactions involving risk were not usurious and a frequent method was to combine loans with transactions involving different currencies, interest being concealed in exchange rates which were subject to fluctuations and hence involved risk. The prominence of bills of exchange as commercial documents partly originated in this. In the 16th cent. Calvin accepted interest on loans between businessmen, while condemning it if it were charged to poor men for subsistence loans, while the Catholic Church continued ineffectively to reiterate its general condemnation.

UTAH, 45th member state of the US, admitted in 1896. The region between the Rocky Mountains and the Sierra Nevada was probably visited by Coronado's expedition (1540), and was crossed by the Spanish missionaries, Domínquez and Escalante (1776). It was explored by American fur traders, among them James Bridger (1824) and Jedediah Smith (1826–7). The first Mormons, led by Brigham Young, settled at Salt Lake City (1847), and were followed by others who irrigated and cultivated Salt Lake valley. The area was ceded to the US by Mexico in 1848, and a provisional government was established (1849), which sought admission to the US as the state of Deseret. This was refused and the area was organized as Utah Territory (1850). Brigham Young served as the first territorial governor (1850–7), but friction with the Federal government led to his replacement and to occupation by Federal troops (1857–62). Subsequent economic and political rivalry between Mormons and 'Gentiles' crystallized in a dispute over the Mormon practice of polygamy. Under pressure from Washington, the Mormon Church disavowed the practice (1890), and statehood was achieved in 1896. Intensive mixed farming and cattle raising long dominated UT's economy, but mining, particularly of copper, oil, and uranium, and the development of a sophisticated weapons industry since the Second World War, increased the state's prosperity.

UTE INDIANS, war-like American tribe, formerly occupying a large area of CO, and parts of UT and NM. They were first encountered by the Spanish (1776). They ceded their lands to the US in a series of treaties and settled on reservations in UT and CO.

UTENBOGAERT, JAN (1557–1644), moderate Dutch Calvinist theologian and leader of the Remonstrant party. After being court chaplain to Maurice of Nassau at The Hague, he left the United Provinces when Arminianism was condemned by the synod of Dort (1719), and established a Remonstrant brotherhood at Antwerp (1619–21). Later, he was driven into exile and went to Paris (1621).

UTEVE (QUITEVE), important trading kingdom of central Mozambique, controlling the Shahili and Portuguese gold routes from Sofala to Manyika and the inland plateau from the 15th to 17th cents.

UTHMAN (*reg.* 644–55), Uthman ibn Affan, the third Caliph, whose accession represented a triumph for the old oligarchic elements dominant at Mecca before and during the life of the Prophet Muhammad. Uthman, once he was caliph, made numerous appointments from these Meccan families to high office in the Muslim empire—a course of action which aroused discontent. More significant still was the fact that the personal weakness of Uthman as caliph gave a free rein to the anarchic tendencies of the Arab warriors which, hitherto, success in war had held in check. Now, with the tide of conquest beginning to ebb, those tendencies found expression in defiance and intrigue against the regime of Uthman. A number of prominent personalities became involved in this conflict, among them A'isha (the wife of the Prophet Muhammad), Talha and Al-Zubayr, two Meccans of great influence, Amir ibn al-As, the conqueror of Egypt, discontented because of his removal from the control of that province, and Ali, the cousin and son-in-law of the Prophet. In June 656 mutinous troops from Egypt, who had come to Medina to make known their grievances, attacked and wounded Uthman mortally, an event which weakened seriously the religious and moral prestige attached to the office of caliph.

UTHMAN DIQNA (d. 1926), Sudanese follower of the Mahdi from Suakin, who mobilized the support of the Beja tribes of eastern Sudan (Kipling's Fuzzy-Wuzzies) in 1883 and became one of the principal leaders of the Mahdist state.

UTHMAN IBN FUDI (1754–1817), called in Hausa Usumanu dan Fodio, Fulani scholar and reformer from Maratta in north-west Nigeria. His ancestors had emigrated from Futa Toro in the mid-15th cent. and his clan, the Banu Al, were noted for their piety and scholarship. From 1774 he began to make preaching tours from a base in Degel, assisted by his brother Abdullah, and visited many parts of Gobir, Zamfara, and Kebbi. On returning to Degel (1793), he continued teaching and receiving disciples and pupils who constituted his 'Community'.

Relations with the Gobir sultans had been declining since 1789; foreseeing the possibility of an armed struggle in his bid for Islamic reform, Uthman advised his community to arm itself. Repressive edicts by the Gobir sultan Nafata and his successor Yunfa (1802) widened the breach, and when the latter attacked an ally of Uthman's at the turn of 1804, Uthman made a formal withdrawal (*hijra*) to Gudu beyond Yunfa's jurisdiction. There his followers proclaimed him leader of a *jihad* against the king of Gobir and then against the other Hausa rulers. Many early victories were won, but Gobir resistance was not broken finally until the fall of Alkalawa (1808). Meanwhile, Muslim leaders in Kano, Katsina, Daura, and Zamfara had sworn allegiance to Uthman, whom his son, Muhammad Bello, had portrayed as the precursor of the Mahdi. Campaigns had also extended southwards to Borgu, Yauri, and Bauchi. In 1812 Uthman divided administrative responsibility between his brother Abdullah, who had the western provinces, and his son Bello, who commanded the east. Uthman, never a military leader, retired to a life of scholarship and guidance of the Community until his death (1817).

Apart from inspiring a successful *jihad*, Uthman was important as a scholar, teacher, and mystic. His teaching created a climate for Islamic reform and as leader of the Qadiriyya brotherhood he could command loyalty and obedience. His great erudition, displayed in over 100 works in Arabic, ensured support from scholars and gave him the ability to enunciate and defend an Islamic ideology and set up a state administration.

D. M. Last, *The Sokoto Caliphate* (London, 1967).   JOH

UTICA (mod. Utique, Tunisia), ancient Phoenician and Roman city. Though now some miles inland, in antiquity it was a coastal site and was first settled by the Phoenicians, probably in the 8th cent. BC. Among Phoenician colonies it was second in importance only to Carthage and retained formal independence in the Carthaginian empire. After escaping destruction during the Third Punic War (149–146 BC) by its timely surrender to Rome, it became the capital of the Roman province of Africa. It received municipal rights from Augustus, but declined in importance when his new foundation of Carthage became the provincial capital. Substantial remains of the Roman town survive.

UTILITARIANISM in Britain, ethical theory that action is right if it achieves the greatest good of the greatest number, which influenced the kind and degree of reform in 19th-cent. Britain. The idea of the greatest good or happiness is found in Richard Cumberland's *De Legibus Naturae* (1672), and is echoed in the work of other writers, notably William Paley, who applied utilitarian principles to religious belief. The use of the term *utilitarian* is first found in the work of Jeremy Bentham, who defended utilitarianism as a moral theory in *Principles of Morals and Legislation* (1789), postulating that man's pursuit of pleasure and avoidance of pain is a prime motive in human conduct, but invoking the doctrine of sanctions against those who pursued their own selfish pleasures to the detriment of society. J. S. Mill, in his *Utilitarianism* (1863), rejected psychological hedonism. Instead, he gave fullest expression to the idea of the greatest good of the greatest number as a justification for [action. His ideas were further developed by G. E. Moore in *Principia Ethica* (1903).

Bentham's writings were influential in obtaining a climate favourable to reform, since he aimed to destroy Blackstone's insistence on the sanctity of tradition in English law. For him, the law was a set of rules with a given purpose, which could be altered or erased if the rules ceased to be useful and ceased to lead to the happiness which was the aim of society as well as the individuals who comprised it. Utilitarian philosophers convinced the influential classes of the need for reforms which would lead to peace and order in society because they did not threaten private freedom or property, but merely tried to prevent any one class from damaging the interests of another. Among the statesmen affected by utilitarian ideas were Peel and Brougham. Utilitarianism led to the codification of the law and to reforms in the penal system (1822–9), to the Poor Law Amendment Act (1834), and the Municipal Corporations Act (1835), as well as to changes in educational curricula and the use of endowments. The Reform Act (1832) can also be seen as transferring political power to those of the middle class who were able to identify themselves with the greatest good of the greatest number.

L. Stephen, *English Utilitarianism* (London, 1900).
J. Plamenatz, *The English Utilitarians* (Oxford, 1958).   VEC

UTOPIA, satirical work of the English humanist Sir Thomas More, published in Latin in 1516. In it the ideal planned society was depicted as one in which men were rigorously disciplined and private property and the money economy were abolished.

UTPALA DYNASTY, line of rulers of Kashmir (855–1003), founded by Avantivarman (*reg.* 855–83), whose reign was generally peaceful and prosperous. His successor, Sankaravarman, is, however, mainly remembered for the oppressive taxation which he introduced. The most remarkable figure is Queen Didda (*reg.* 958–1003), who was married into the dynasty, but became a queen in her own right after the early death of her husband. Didda re-established and maintained a strong central authority, which was often challenged by local chiefs.

UTRAQUISTS, religious movement in Bohemia, Poland, and Hungary which stemmed from the moderate wing of the Hussites. The main doctrine of the movement was communion in both kinds for the laity (in Latin *sub utraque parte*), which was won in Bohemia by the 'Compacts' of 1436. It was powerful in Prague University and maintained the episcopate while fostering some use of the vernacular in worship. After 1485 the Utraquists were the state Church of Bohemia and remained so until the Reformation and later.

UTRECHT, PEACE OF (1713), settlement ending the War of the Spanish Succession, with the treaties of Utrecht (1713), Radstadt, and Baden (1714).

France and Spain recognized the legal authority of Queen Anne and of the Hanoverian Succession as established in the Act of Settlement, and France agreed to expel James Stuart, the British Pretender, from French territory. In addition, Philip V of Spain was forced to repudiate his claim to the French throne to ensure that the Crowns of France and Spain were never united. In the event of the deaths of Louis XIV and his great-grandson, the future Louis XV, the Crown was to pass to the Duke of Orléans.

The settlement also brought about a number of territorial changes, partly designed to create strong barrier states on the borders of France. France retained Alsace and Strasbourg, but restored all conquests on the right bank of the Rhine. Philip V retained Spain and the Indies, but lost his other European possessions. The emperor, Charles VI, gained the Spanish Netherlands, Sardinia, Milan, Naples, Mantua, and the Tuscan ports, making the Habsburgs the dominant power in Italy. Victor Amadeus of Savoy received Sicily, more favourable boundaries with France, and recognition as heir-presumptive in Spain if Philip's line failed. The United Provinces gained the right to garrison a barrier of towns and fortresses in the Spanish Netherlands and Spanish Guelderland. Portugal gained the right to navigate the Amazon, as well as satisfaction over disputed claims to the Cap du Nord district between French Guiana and Brazil. In Germany, the electors of Bavaria and Cologne were restored, while the Elector of Brandenburg-Prussia gained Spanish Guelderland and recognition of his title as King of Prussia.

Most gains were made by Britain. From France, she gained Acadia, Hudson Bay, Nfld, and St Kitts, and thus became the leading colonial power in North America. From Spain she gained Gibraltar and Minorca, and so became the dominant naval power in the Mediterranean. To ensure her maritime supremacy, French naval bases at Dunkirk and Mardyk were to be destroyed. Finally, she made commercial gains, including the right of the South Sea Co. to send a ship each year to the Indies, and the lucrative Asiento slave trade.

Though the peace of Utrecht brought about the cessation of hostilities, it left a number of problems unsettled. Spain and the emperor did not come to terms, and Anglo-French colonial rivalry was exacerbated. However, the settlement offered the European powers a chance of economic recovery after the wars of Louis XIV.   AW

UVAROV, SERGEI SEMYONOVICH (1786–1855). Russian politician, minister of education (1833–49), president of the academy of Sciences (1818–55), privy councillor, and senator. His report on education (1832) for Nicholas I first enunciated the principles of official nationality (autocracy, orthodoxy, and nationality) which marked the reign. As an educated man, anxious to develop learning, he increased the number of educational institutes, laid the foundations of a modern educational system, and encouraged oriental and technical studies. All education, however, was uniform and reflected the principles of official nationality, and mass education was discouraged. The curricula favoured Russian history and the classics, the aim being to produce right-minded subjects for the Russian empire uncorrupted by European influences.

UXBRIDGE, NEGOTIATIONS AT (1645) in England, between representatives of King Charles I and the Long Parliament at a crucial stage in the Civil War. The propositions offered to the king had originally been drawn up under Scottish influence and were virtual terms of surrender. Parliament proposed that the king should take the Covenant, assent to the abolition of episcopacy and the Prayer Book, and to the establishment of Presbyterianism, agree that the militia and navy should be controlled by parliament and Scottish commissioners, and also to an act which would make void the Irish Cessation and enable parliament to prosecute the war in Ireland without hindrance from the king. The negotiations lasted from 31 Jan. to 22 Feb. 1645. Charles's rigidity on the Church question and his slipperiness over the militia exasperated the Scots and the peace party in parliament. The failure of the negotiations enabled Oliver Cromwell and his party to force the New Model ordinance through the Lords, and assured them of the continued active support of the Scots in the Civil War.

UZBEG KHAN (*reg.* 1312–41), Khan of the Golden Horde in succession to his uncle, Tokhtu, whose reign saw a great extension of Islam in the Horde and is usually regarded as its golden age, being a period of strong government and flourishing economic life.

UZBEK, name applied to the nomadic Turko-Mongol peoples of the Shaybanid horde, inhabiting modern Kazakhstan in the 14th cent., who subsequently migrated into Turkestan and became the leading community in Transoxania under the Shaybanid dynasty in the 16th cent.

and its successor the Janid (1599–1785). In this period much Uzbek settlement in the agricultural areas took place and intermingling with the existing Iranian and Turkish inhabitants. In the late 18th cent. three new Uzbek dynasties appeared: the Mangits in Bukhara (1785–1920); the Khungrats in Khiva (1767–1920), where they replaced the last Shaybanid rulers; and the Mins in Kokand (1798–1876). The Uzbeks were conquered by Russia in the second half of the 19th cent., although the last Uzbek rulers survived under Russian protection until 1920. In 1924 most of the Uzbek areas of Central Asia (including Khiva, Samarkand, Bukhara, Kokand, and Tashkent) were united to form the Uzbek SSR.

UZOI (Turkish Oghuz), Turkish people which moved westward from the lands north of the Black Sea in the wake of the Pechenegs. The Uzoi, in 1064, carried devastation far and wide through Bulgaria, Macedonia, and Thrace. Disease weakened them thereafter. Of the remnants of this horde some withdrew beyond the Danube, while others found employment as troops in the service of Byzantium.

UZUN HASAN (d. 1478), chieftain of the Turcoman confederation known as the Aq-Qoyunlu, or White Sheep, and located in the region of Diyar Bekir. In 1466–7 he broke the resistance of the rival Turcomans, the Qara-Qoyunlu, or Black Sheep, then led by their able chieftain, Jihan Shah, and took over most of western and central Persia. He later attempted to bring Asia Minor into dependence on himself. After an initial success against the Ottomans near Terjan (not far from Erzinjan), the Aq-Qoyunlu suffered defeat at Otluk-Beli (Bashkent) in 1473.

V

VACA DE CASTRO, CRISTÓBAL (*c.* 1492–1558), Spanish official, who was sent to investigate the rule of Francisco Pizarro in Peru. Arriving in 1541 after the latter's murder, he defeated the rebellion of Diego Almagro the Younger, and brought momentary peace to the area by dissuading Gonzalo Pizarro from forcibly claiming his dead brother's authority.

VAHRAM V (Arabic, Bahram) (*reg.* 421–439), Sassanian King of Iran, who was a hunter, poet, and musician and a favourite subject of Persian literature and art. His reign saw a continuance of the tendency for the monarchy to lose power to the feudal nobility, as he avoided clashes by surrendering some of his prerogatives. He conducted a successful campaign against the Ephthalites. Renewed persecution of the Christians led to an unsuccessful war with Byzantium and the Christians were granted freedom of worship. The Iranian Christians decided on independence from the Byzantine Church (424) and thus removed from themselves the old suspicion that they were Roman sympathizers.

VAI, predominantly Muslim people who occupy the western province of Liberia. They are noted for having invented their own system of writing, in 1814, in a script which has over 200 characters.

VAIDA-VOEVOD, ALEXANDRU (1872–1950), Rumanian political leader, first in Transylvania and later the Rumanian kingdom, who was one of the leaders of the Rumanian National Party. In 1918 he delivered a dramatic speech in the Hungarian parliament at Budapest declaring the intention of the Transylvanian Rumanians to secede from the Austro-Hungarian empire and unite Transylvania with Rumania. He served on the governing council of Transylvania (1918–19) and became prime minister of Rumania after the elections of 1919. His government completed the negotiations for the peace settlement by signing the minority treaty, but fell when its agrarian reform law proved unacceptable. Vaida-Voevod was minister of the interior (1928–30) in Maniu's National-Peasant government and, after Maniu's resignation again served as prime minister (June–Oct. 1932, Jan.–Nov. 1933); he then resigned because of a difference of views with Titulescu over relations with the Soviet Union. He was above all a nationalist, and his nationalism, which grew into chauvinism, split the National-Peasant Party. He maintained relations with the Iron Guard while in the government in an effort to harness their national zeal and opposition to communism. He left the party in 1934, when his scheme to reduce and eventually eliminate non-Rumanians from the civil service ('numerus Valachis') was rejected. He formed an extreme nationalist and semi-fascist political group and continued to collaborate with the royalist dictatorship and right-radical elements.   JMK

VAISALI (VESALI), ancient town, north-west of Patna, Bihar, India, originally the capital of the confederacy of the Licchavis, a republican tribe. It grew into a major Buddhist centre (from the 5th cent. BC) and was also a major administrative centre during the Gupta period (*c.* AD 320–550), as reflected by the discovery of a large number of official seals. It declined soon afterwards.

VAISHNAVISM or Vishnuism, one of the great religions of India, centred around the worship of Vishnu. Though many individual elements can be traced back to Vedic times, the full development of Vaishnavism is not attested before the 2nd cent. BC. Compared with other forms of Hinduism, Vaishnavism strongly emphasizes complete non-violence (including a ban on animal sacrifice) and absolute devotion (*bhakti*), adoration (*puja*) being a means of achieving liberation of the soul. It also developed its own philosophy, implicit in the *Bhagavadgita*, but fully elaborated by Ramanuja. In Vaishnava ritual, chant played an important part, while *bhakti* stimulated the growth of a rich iconography, with representations of Vishnu in different forms and including images of Lakshmi, Garuda, etc. As Vishnu was also a kind of divine prototype of kings he enjoyed royal patronage of many dynasties (*eg,* the Guptas). He was worshipped more in northern than in southern India, where Saivism has prevailed.

VAISYAS, in ancient India, originally: 'people of the tribe' (*vis*); later, the third of the four classes (*varna*), into which the population was (theoretically) divided, comprising many castes of free farmers, traders, and craftsmen.

VAKATAKAS, ancient Indian royal dynasty (*c.* AD 300–500) ruling in the northern Deccan (parts of Madhya Pradesh and Maharashtra), from *c.* 400 as subordinate allies of the Gupta dynasty of northern India.

VALABHI, ancient city in Saurashtra (Kathiawar), India, capital of the Maitraka dynasty (*c.* AD 490–743). Though most of the kings were Saivites, the city was also an important Buddhist centre, especially in the 7th cent. It was destroyed in a raid by the Arabs of Sind led by Junaid.

VAL-DE-GRÂCE, baroque church and convent in the faubourg St-Jacques in Paris endowed by Anne of Austria, which became the repository of the hearts of the French royal family. Anne commissioned François Mansart to build this spiritual haven (1645–67).

VALDES, ALONSO DE (*c.* 1490–1532), Spanish humanist philosopher and Latin secretary to the Emperor Charles V. In 1527 and 1528 he wrote two popular dialogues, *Mercurio y Caron* and *Lactancio y el arcediano*, attacking clerical abuses, justifying the sack of Rome on the grounds of Pope Clement VII's perversity, and upholding the universality and Christian spirit of the imperial ideal. After being deprived of Charles V's patronage on the latter's departure for Italy (1529), he was tried for heresy in his absence and died in Vienna.

VALDES, HERNANDO DE (1483–1568), Spanish inquisitor-general (1547–66), Dominican priest, and Abp of Seville, who inspired the censorship law prohibiting the reading of the Scriptures in Spanish (1551), the new and severe Index of 1559, and the revised constitution of the Spanish Inquisition (1561). As a defender of orthodoxy he crushed the Lutheran groups at Valladolid and Seville in a series of *autos da fé* (1559, 1560), but his most celebrated victim was Carranza, Abp of Toledo, whose unjust imprisonment for over seven years (1559) was engineered by Valdes.

VALDES, JUAN DE (*c.* 1500–41), Spanish humanist and religious leader, brother of Alonso de Valdes, secretary to the Emperor Charles V. He escaped to Italy in the emperor's train (1529) to avoid the anti-Erasmian movement in Spain, which subsequently convicted him of heresy and prohibited his works. He became imperial agent in Rome and from 1534 settled in Naples, where he was the guiding spirit of a group known as the *Valdesiani*, humanist mystics, mostly of aristocratic birth. He sought the regeneration of the Catholic Church from within and died within its fold, but his ideas, expressed in works, *eg, Dialogue of Christian Doctrine*, influenced people such as Aonio Palearo, Bernardino Ochino, and the Italian Nicodemists.

VALDIVIA, PEDRO DE (?1500–53), Spanish conqueror of Chile, who enriched himself in the conquest of Peru and became lieutenant-governor of the country. His first expedition was plagued by Araucanian hostility, but Valdivia managed to found Santiago (1541) and to hold his own. After returning to Peru in 1547 for reinforcements, he assisted in the defeat of Gonzalo Pizarro, and was confirmed in the governorship. He returned to Chile with more men and supplies and extended his power, particularly in the south, despite intense Araucanian opposition. In 1553, however, he was killed in an Indian ambuscade led, according to legend, by his Araucanian rival, Lautaro.

VALENCIA, eastern province and city of Spain, forming part of the Mediterranean seaboard of the Iberian peninsula. It was Roman in origin, but was taken by the Visigoths in 413 and by the Moors in 714 and remained a Moorish kingdom from 1010 to 1238. In 1238 James I of Aragon added it to his lands, but Valencia retained its traditional institutions, *eg,* the Cortes. The 15th cent. was the golden age of Valencia, when the eclipse of Catalonia resulted in the rise of Valencia city as the financial capital of the Levantine provinces. United with Castile under Ferdinand and Isabella (1479), it became part of the Habsburg possessions under Charles V (1519) and was the setting for the radical social movement of the *Germania* (1519–22). In 1525 Charles gave the large Moorish population of Valencia the choice of conversion or expulsion, and by 1609 there were some 135,000 Moriscos in the province, constituting about one-third of the population. Philip III's decision to expel these people, whose ancestral links with the Turkish infidel were feared to be perfidious, had a disastrous effect upon Valencia's economy (1609–14). Yet paradoxically, in the War of the Spanish Succession (1701–13) Valencia supported the Habsburg candidate, Archduke Charles, and was summarily deprived of its laws and liberties by the successful Bourbon claimant, Philip V. Valencia's textile industry, however, enjoyed a boom under Philip, who allowed the replacement of the crushing system of sales taxes by a single salt tax in the province (1717). After being held by the French in the closing stages of the Peninsular War (1812–14), it was the scene of rebellion against the reactionary Ferdinand VII (1819, 1820) and of re-emergent regionalism. Liberal revolts followed in 1835 and 1848, as elsewhere in Europe. In the Spanish Civil War (1936–9) Valencia fought for the republican cause, but after the fall of Barcelona (Jan. 1939) was unable to resist Franco's regime.

VALENCIENNES, Flemish town, originally a 7th-cent. foundation, famous for its lace-making industry. It belonged to the counts of Hainault (1047–1433) and the dukes of Burgundy (1433–1677). In 1677 it was captured by French forces, and retained by Louis XIV by the treaty of Nymwegen (1678), after which it was fortified by Vauban. It remained French except for brief enemy occupations in 1793–4, 1815, 1914–18, and 1940–4.

VALENS, FL. (AD 328–78), Roman Emperor (*reg.* 364–78), as eastern colleague of his brother Valentinian I. He was victorious against the Goths (369) and conducted a war against Persia, but after admitting the Goths into the Roman empire (376) he was defeated and killed by them at the battle of Hadrianople. He was succeeded by Theodosius.

VALENTINIAN I (FL. VALENTINIANUS) (AD 321–75), Roman emperor (*reg.* 364–75), who was proclaimed after the death of Jovian and chose his brother Valens as his colleague. He devoted himself to military restoration and fortification in the west, particularly on the Rhine and Danube frontiers. A rigorous and scrupulous emperor, he attempted to uproot corruption from the administration and supported the peasant classes against exploitation. From 370 he sanctioned prosecutions of Roman senators on charges of adultery and magic arts; but despite an unfavourable reputation earned by these activities Valentinian was a strong and devoted military ruler, to whom the empire owed much. He died on campaign at Brigetio in Pannonia (mod. Bregenz) and was succeeded jointly by his young sons, Gratian and Valentinian II.

VALENTINIAN II (AD 371–92), Roman Emperor (*reg.* 375–92), as son and joint successor of Valentinian I. He was deposed by the usurper Magnus Maximus (387), but was restored by Theodosius. His adviser, Arbogast, later turned against him and Valentinian was found hanged (May 392). Arbogast then proclaimed the usurper Eugenius.

VALENTINIAN III (419–55), Roman Emperor (*reg.* 425–55), who was incapable of effective government and distrustful of his ablest servants. In 454 he killed with his own hands the greatest of them, Aetius, who had saved the West from the Huns. In 455 Valentinian was in turn murdered by the usurper, Petronius Maximus. Thereupon, the Vandals sent a fleet from Africa from which troops landed outside Rome and sacked the city.

VALENZUELA, FERNANDO DE (1636–89), Spanish minister of Charles II of Spain (1669–77), who won the favour of Marianna of Austria, the queen regent (1669), and held power by pandering to popular demands for cheap food and entertainment. In 1677 he was overthrown by a revolt of the grandees in favour of Don Juan José and was exiled to the Philippines. He died in Mexico (1689).

VALERA, EAMON DE (1882–), Irish politician, born in New York, was sent to Ireland in 1885 upon his father's death. After graduating from Dublin he became a mathematics teacher and also active in the Nationalist cause. In the Easter Rising of 1916 he was captured and afterwards sentenced to death, but because of his American birth not executed, as were other leaders in the revolt. In 1917 he was released from jail, and then elected to parliament as a Sinn Fein member. In 1918 he was rearrested and imprisoned in England, but managed to escape, and fled to the US, where he worked for the Irish cause. Throughout this period his stature within the movement increased, and in 1919 he was elected president of the Dail.

He returned to Ireland in 1921 and led the delegation that negotiated the Anglo-Irish treaty, at first directly but later through plenipotentiaries. There were probably two likely reasons for this: it gave the negotiators an excuse to play for time; and it also gave De Valera a chance to repudiate the settlement when this was seen to be unsatisfactory. So it proved: in Jan. 1922 he opposed the treaty, and when it was approved by the Dail he led the Republican insurrection that followed (1922–3). The Republicans' opposition to the 1922 constitution kept them out of effective political power until 1927, when De Valera led a group of moderates (the Fianna Fail) back into political life. In the 1932 elections they triumphed over Cosgrave's Coalition ministry, and De Valera's three decades of political predominance began. Cosgrave had accomplished the task of reconstruction after the Civil War; Fianna Fail now set about severing the link with Britain. The repudiation of the old land annuities, payable to British shareholders, was the first step (1932); then followed the reconstruction of the constitution (1936–7), and the declaration of an all-Irish state (Eire) in 1937. The British economic offensive, after the repudiation of land annuities, began to crumble as danger loomed in Europe. In 1938 both sides agreed to a peace formula, the British giving up the Irish naval bases they had retained after 1922. Nevertheless, in 1939 Eire declared her neutrality when the Second World War broke out, De Valera rigidly continuing the policy of economic and political nationalism started in 1932.

In 1948 he was defeated in the general election, and Fianna Fail thereafter alternated with a series of weak coalition ministries formed by J. A. Costello. The last ministries of De Valera's career (1951–4, 1957–9) showed his continued popularity, but failed to contain the growing discontent with Irish economic problems, in particular agriculture and emigration. In 1959 he was elected president of Eire and re-elected in 1966. **GD**

VALERIAN (P. LICINIUS VALERIANUS) (*reg.* AD 253–60), Roman Emperor, who was proclaimed by the army in Raetia and chose as his colleague his son Gallienus, who succeeded him. Of the internal events of his reign little is known except his persecution of the Christians (from 257). Foreign affairs were dominated by wars, conducted by his generals against invasions of Goths on the Danube and Franks in Gaul, and by himself against the aggressive Persian king, Sapor (Shapur) I. In these, Valerian enjoyed some success, freeing Syria from Persian occupation and preparing an invasion of Persia. In 260, however, he was captured by the Persians and remained their prisoner until his death.

VALERIO-HORATIAN LAWS (449 BC), passed at Rome after a secession of the plebeians. The clauses are disputed. Tribunes' rights were probably legally recognized. *Plebiscita* were probably given binding force if approved by the Senate. But it is doubtful if a citizen's right of appeal against a magistrate was upheld in this legislation.

VALIESSAR, TRUCE OF (1659), temporary Russo-Swedish peace concluded at Valiessar, near Narva. Tsar Alexis was left in possession of Dorpat, which his troops had taken in 1656, but in the definitive peace settlement signed at Kardis (1661) he relinquished all Russia's conquests in Livonia.

VALLA, LORENZO (1407–57), Italian humanist, who excelled as a destructive critic, his aim being to create a new science of exact Latin and Greek philology based on a profound knowledge of correct classical usage. He analysed a large range of texts, literary, legal, philosophical (especially those of Aristotle), and religious (especially the Greek New Testament) in an attempt to elucidate the exact meaning that their authors intended to convey. Besides his superb linguistic attainments he brought to this task a knowledge of the classical institutions and history which he regarded as the essential background to the understanding of any author. Valla's *Elegances of the Latin Language*, a collection of learned comments on correct Latin usage, became a favourite book of the humanists. He is also remembered for two works the influence of which had important religious consequences: while he was acting as a secretary to King Alfonso of Naples the king, who was at war with Pope Eugenius IV, asked Valla to write an anti-papal treatise. He obliged by proving that one of the main documentary foundations for the papal claims to secular authority in Italy was an early medieval forgery. This treatise, *The False and Lying Donation of Constantine*, is a model of humanistic scholarship. It was first printed in Germany in 1517 and influenced Luther in his revulsion from the Roman papacy.

The last important task of Valla's lifetime, left unfinished at his death, was an attempt to recover an improved version of the New Testament and thus provide a guide for a revised edition of the Bible nearer to the original manuscripts. Erasmus printed these *Annotations on the New Testament* in 1504. They provided a model for his own New Testament of 1516 and decisively influenced all subsequent biblical study. Valla had done this work under papal patronage, having been invited to Rome by the humanist pope Nicholas

V. But in 1559 Erasmus's edition was put on the Index of Prohibited Books by the papacy, it being regarded at Rome as one of the sources employed by the Protestant schismatics. **EBF**

VALLANDIGHAM, CLEMENT LAIRD (1820–71), US lawyer and politician. As a leading Civil War Peace Democrat he argued against coercing the Confederacy back into the Union and refused to vote for any war measure. He was arrested, tried for treason (1863), and sentenced to imprisonment, but instead was banished to the Confederacy by Lincoln. Escaping to Canada, where he received *in absentia* the Democratic nomination for the governorship of OH, he returned to the US in 1864 and later supported liberal Republicanism.

VALLEY FORGE in the US, site of George Washington's winter quarters (19 Dec. 1777–19 June 1778) after the loss of Philadelphia during the American War of Independence. Valley Forge was of strategic importance, on the west bank of the Schuylkill river, 22 miles (35 kms) north-west of Philadelphia, and was also a good defensive position, but unexpectedly early and heavy snowfalls and a deficient commissariat subjected Washington's force of 11,000 men to severe hardship. Only personal loyalty to their general, and the retraining initiated by Baron Von Steuben, kept the army together.

VALMIKI, legendary ancient Indian ascetic and poet, traditionally regarded as the author of the *Ramayana*, but not a clearly historical figure.

VALMY, BATTLE OF (20 Sept. 1792), artillery duel fought near the Franco-Belgian frontier between a French force under Dumouriez and the Prussians under the Duke of Brunswick. The latter withdrew at nightfall, giving the appearance of a French victory, which was celebrated enthusiastically in Paris and encouraged the revolutionary fervour of the Convention.

VALOIS, CHARLES, Count of (d. 1325), French soldier and younger brother of King Philip IV of France, who spent much of his career in a vain search for a royal crown in either Germany or Italy. In 1328 his son succeeded Philip's sons as King of France (becoming King Philip VI—*reg.* 1328–50). His own importance lay in his success as leader of French armies in Gascony during the wars against England (1294–7, 1323–4). He was responsible for the destruction in 1301 of the political faction to which Dante belonged at Florence and for Dante's life-long exile, during which he wrote his *Divine Comedy*.

VALOIS, HOUSE OF, ruling dynasty of France from 1328, from the accession of Philip VI, formerly Count of Valois, nephew of Philip the Fair and cousin of the three Capetian kings who preceded him, until the death of Henry III in 1589. During the 14th–15th cents the direct male line of Philip VI ruled successively, *ie,* John II (*reg.* 1350–64), Charles V (*reg.* 1364–80), Charles VI (*reg.* 1380–1422), Charles VII (*reg.* 1422–61), Louis XI (*reg.* 1461–83), and Charles VIII (*reg.* 1483–98), while France was involved in the Hundred Years War with England, from which it emerged with a revitalized monarchy. On Charles VIII's death without heirs (1498), the Crown passed to Louis XII (1498–1515), of the Orléans branch of the Valois dynasty and great-grandson of Charles V. On Louis's death without male heirs (1515), the succession went to Francis of Angoulême, Duke of Valois and son of Charles of Angoulême, who, like Louis XII, was descended from Louis of Orléans. Francis I (*reg.* 1515–47) married Louis XII's daughter, Claude, and was in turn succeeded by their son, Henry II (*reg.* 1547–59), who continued his father's determined struggle against the powerful Habsburg dynasty of Spain and the empire. After Henry's death (1559) the Crown passed successively to his three childless sons, Francis II (*reg.* 1559–60), Charles IX (*reg.* 1560–74), and Henry III (*reg.* 1574–89), with whom the dynasty ended.

VALOR ECCLESIASTICUS in England, tax book incorporating the valuation of all ecclesiastical property, carried out with great efficiency and speed by commissioners appointed by Thomas Cromwell as a prelude to the dissolution of the monastic houses (1535).

VALPÓ, BATTLE OF (1537), defeat of a mixed force of German, Bohemian, and Austrian soldiers by the Ottoman frontier begs and their horsemen near the Hungarian fortress of Eszék (mod. Osijek).

VALTELLINE, valley of the upper Adda in Lombardy, now part of Italy, except for the side valley of Poschiaro, which belongs to Switzerland. In the late 16th–17th cents this area assumed critical importance as the key to control of the direct route between Milan and the Tyrol, a route vital to the Habsburgs, whose possessions lay in Italy and the Netherlands, as well as Spain and Austria. At the Reformation the population of the Grisons, the south-eastern part of Switzerland occupied by the *Graubunden*, became Protestant, and at the same time they acquired authority over the Valtelline, which had hitherto belonged to the Visconti rulers of Milan. This situation invited the interference of France, which, from Francis I's reign (1515–47), acquired the role of protector of the Grisons, while Spain posed as defender of the Catholic Valtelline. Beneath the religious conflict lay the political and military issues of domination of western Europe. Thus from 1618 for 20 years there was constant strife, during which the region was twice occupied by the Spaniards, twice by the French, and twice brought under papal trusteeship. In 1639 the valley was restored to the Grisons on condition that the Catholics there had freedom of worship (perpetual peace of Milan). In 1797 the Valtelline became incorporated into the Cisalpine republic, in 1805 into Napoleon's kingdom of Italy, and in 1815 into the Austrian-controlled duchy of Lombardy, whence it passed to Piedmont-Sardinia (1859). The area of the Grisons became Swiss in 1803.

VALUYEV, PYOTR ALEKSANDROVICH Count (1814–90), Russian politician and minister of the interior (1861–8), who supported the emancipation of serfs and social reforms. His proposal (1863) that the creation of the *zemstva* should be followed by a central representative institution, including *zemstva* delegates, with consultative powers over legislation, was refused.

VAN ARTEVELDE, JAMES (d. 1345), cloth merchant of Ghent, who became (1337) ruler of Flanders when the count was driven out. The Flemings had risen because King Edward III of England had cut off vital wool supplies. Van Artevelde secured the re-entry of wool and induced the Flemish towns to recognize Edward III in 1340 as King of France. His son, Philippe (d. 1382), led a rising by Flemish weavers, centred on Ghent. He was killed with many of his followers by the French army at Roosebeke.

VAN BAERLE, CASPAR (1584–1648), native of Antwerp, who was a classicist, humanist, and a leading Remonstrant. He was expelled from Leyden University after the Synod of Dort (1619), and later taught at the Athanaeum Illustre at Amsterdam.

VAN BUREN, MARTIN (1782–1862), US politician and eighth president of the US, who became active in Republican politics, served in the state senate (1812–20), and was attorney-general of NY (1816–19). On becoming a US senator in 1821 he maintained a close interest in NY politics, and was a member of the influential 'Albany Regency'. As an opponent of the administration of John Q. Adams, he became a leading campaigner for Andrew Jackson, and was rewarded with the secretaryship of state (1829). In this office he became Jackson's closest adviser, advocated the 'spoils system', and was successful in settling the longstanding dispute with Britain over West Indies trade, and with France over claims arising from the French Wars. After resigning in 1831 to allow Jackson to reorganize his cabinet, he was appointed minister to Britain, but the Senate rejected the nomination. He supported Jackson's opposition to the Bank of the United States and his stand during the nullification controversy, and was elected vice-president (1832). Retaining Jackson's confidence, he was the president's chosen successor (1836). As president (1837–41) his main tasks were to hold the Northern and Southern wings of the party together in the growing crisis over slavery, and to shore up the economy following the panic of 1837, but his efforts were unsuccessful and in the 1840 election he suffered a crushing defeat. His opposition to the annexation of TX probably cost him the Democratic nomination in 1844. He accepted nomination by the Free-Soil Party (1848), but without success, and supported the Compromise of 1850 and the Democratic Party in the election of 1852, but was opposed to the repeal of the Missouri Compromise and became disillusioned with Presidents Pierce and Buchanan. After the outbreak of Civil War he placed his confidence in the abilities of President Lincoln.

                                                                                    DBS

VAN DAM, PIETER (1621–1706), company solicitor of the Dutch East India Co., who represented the conservative opposition to the colonizing policy of Van Goens, the governor of Ceylon.

VAN DIEMEN, ANTHONY (1593–1645), Dutch colonial official and governor-general of the Dutch East India Co. (1636–45), who controlled the Molucca islands. He rediscovered Van Diemen's Land, later renamed Tasmania by the English after its actual discoverer, Abel Janszoon Tasman. He died in Batavia.

VAN DORP, JONKHEER PHILIPS (1587–1652), Dutch sailor, who was appointed admiral of Holland by Frederick Henry of Orange (1629) but was dismissed for incompetence in 1636.

VAN DYCK, SIR ANTHONY (1599–1641), Flemish painter, appointed court painter to King Charles I of England (1632), who executed portraits of the royal family. He was born at Antwerp, where he studied under Rubens, and later worked in Italy. His early interest was mostly in religious and historical subjects, but in England he found portrait-painting more remunerative and he set a fashion for the grand manner in portraiture which influenced English art for the next 200 years.

VAN DYCKVELT, EVERHARD VAN WEEDE (1626–1702), Dutch diplomat and nobleman of Utrecht, who was sent by William of Orange to England in 1687 on an unofficial visit to make contact with the English nobility and assess their attitude to William's succession rights. He was also used by William on other delicate diplomatic missions, *eg*, to sound out the burgomasters of Amsterdam on the use of the Dutch fleet and army in an invasion of England (1688), and to put out peace feelers to Louis XIV through an intermediary in Brussels (1693). Later, he was one of the chief Dutch negotiators for the peace of Ryswick (1697).

VAN EYCK, HUBERT and JAN (*fl.* 15th cent.), Flemish painters, who were possibly brothers, from Masseyck in Limburg. Hubert (d. 1426) is assumed to be the elder. Whether he painted part of the famous Ghent altarpiece (*Adoration of the Lamb*) is in dispute. At least ten signed and dated works of Jan are known (1432–41), including the Arnolfini Marriage. Jan was the founder, with Campin, of the school of Flemish painters. His use of natural surroundings and a naturalistic style was highly influential and he was responsible for major developments in the technique of oil painting, especially the use of transparent glazes to preserve the colour and surface.

VAN GOENS, RYCKLOF (1619–82), Dutch colonial official and governor-general of the Dutch East India Co. (1678–81), who as a boy went to the Indonesian archipelago and served there in a number of capacities. On five occasions he went on embassies to the court of Amangkurat I of Mataram, and the journals of his embassies are an important source of knowledge on the situation in Central Java. The rebellion of Trunadjaja was brought to an end during his governor-generalship.

VAN HEEMSKERK, JACOB (1569–1607), Dutch navigator, who explored the north seas while searching for the northeast passage (1595–8). He was made admiral of the Dutch fleet and was killed in a battle with the Spaniards off Gibraltar (25 April 1607).

VAN HELMONT, JOHANN BAPTISTA (1577–1644), Flemish philosopher and follower of the iatro-chemist, Paracelsus. He introduced the term 'gas' and distinguished between the non-inflammable carbon dioxide (*gas sylvestre*) and the inflammable methane (*gas pingue*). He published *Febrium Doctrina Inaudita* (1642) and *Ortus Mediciniae* (1648), in which he outlined a new natural philosophy, contending that there were only two elements, air and water.

VAN HEMBYZE, JAN (1513–84), burgomaster of Ghent, who led the revolution which established popular government and Calvinism in the city under a committee of defence (Oct. 1577) which lasted until his flight before William of Orange's entry into Ghent (Aug. 1579). He returned later (Aug. 1583) and began to collaborate with the Spanish governor, Parma, but was seized (March 1584) and executed by his fellow citizens for treachery (Aug. 1584).

VAN HEUTSZ, J. B. (1851–1924), Dutch colonial servant and soldier. He brought to an end the Atjeh War at the turn of the century by abandoning a defensive strategy and mounting a mobile, aggressive campaign. He was governor-general of the Dutch East Indies (1904–9), representing a regime that endorsed the consolidation of Netherlands control and the improvement of government efficiency.

VAN HOGENDORP, GIJSBRECHT KAREL (1771–1834), Orangist leader and 'father' of the Dutch constitution (1813). The democratic Patriots, who had failed to oust their ruling Orange family, welcomed the French invasion of the Netherlands and collaborated with Napoleon until they became disillusioned by his military reverses (1812–13). Hogendorp seized this opportunity to initiate an Orangist revolt in The Hague, which resulted in the restoration of William VI, Prince of Orange. Hogendorp was largely responsible for building up the new state, giving it a constitution, in which an elected states general was to control the king, and successfully seeking union with Belgium to provide a buffer state against France. The union (1815) made William King of the Netherlands.

VAN HOUT, JAN (1542–1609), Libertinist secretary of the town of Leyden, whose defence against the Spaniards he helped to organize (1574). In addition he was an historian and poet, writing in Dutch and giving patriotic encouragement to the younger poets of Leyden, Haarlem, and Amsterdam.

VAN KNUYT, JAN (*fl.* 1646–8), Dutch diplomat, who was an ally of the pro-French Orange party and a close friend of *stadtholder* Frederick Henry. He was a plenipotentiary at the Münster–Osnabruck negotiations that led to the peace of Westphalia (1646–8).

VAN LEUWENHOECK, ANTONY (1632–1723), Dutch scientist and fellow of the Royal Society (1680), originally a draper of Delft, who became the pioneer of modern microscopy, as well as being a considerable anatomist and entomologist. He wrote over 100 scientific papers for the Royal Society and more than 20 for the Paris Academy of Sciences. He increased the magnification of the microscope 300-fold, confirmed Malphighi's demonstration of the blood capillaries (1668), and gave the first accurate description of the red blood corpuscles (1674). In 1677 he described and illustrated the spermatozoa of animals. His other achievements include the investigation of the structure of teeth, the crystalline lens, a human muscle, plant organisms, and the life-cycles of the flea, eel, and aphides.

VAN LINSCHOTEN, JAN HUYGHEN (1563–1611), Dutch traveller and writer, who was employed in the service of the Portuguese archbishops of Goa (1583–9) and after returning to Amsterdam wrote an *Itinerario* (1595–6), a geographical description of the world, including an account of the Portuguese empire (1592). His knowledge was invaluable to the Far Eastern expedition of Cornelis Houtman (1595).

VAN LOO, CHARLES ANDRÉ (1705–65), French artist, who, after studying in Rome, settled in Paris as a portrait painter and sculptor, becoming a chief painter to Louis XV and a member of the Academy (1735). Among the celebrities whose portraits he produced were Diderot and Helvétius. His vigorous, colourful, and majestic style gave rise to a new French verb, *vanlooter*.

VAN MANDER, KAREL (1548–1606), Flemish painter, poet and author of the *Schilderboeck* (Book of Painters, 1604), in which he described artistic society in the Netherlands at the turn of the 16th–17th cents.

VAN MEETKERKE, ADOLF (1528–91), Flemish member of the estates general and councillor of state during the governor-generalship of the Earl of Leicester (1585–7).

VAN MOOK, HUBERTUS JOHANNES (1894–), Dutch colonial official, who served as head of the Netherlands East Indies government during the Indonesian revolution (1945–1949).

VAN NASSAU-SIEGEN, JOAN MAURITZ OF NASSAU (1604–79), Dutch colonial official and governor of the Brazilian possessions of the Dutch West India Co. He greatly extended Dutch territory and made every effort to conciliate his Portuguese subjects. Upon his return to the Netherlands he was prominent in military and diplomatic affairs in northern Europe.

VAN OLDENBARNEVELDT, JAN (1547–1619), Dutch politician and leader of Dutch independence from the Spanish Crown who, became pensionary of Rotterdam (1576) and helped to promote the union of Utrecht (1579). He persuaded the estates of Holland (1585) after William the Silent's death. On becoming grand pensionary of Holland (1586) he opposed the Earl of Leicester's policies as governor-general, especially over the issue of Dutch trade with Spain, and his initiative helped to found the Dutch East India Co. in 1602. In 1596 he achieved a diplomatic success by renewing the alliance with England and France, but from the beginning of the 17th cent. he became the leader of the Republican Party, opposed to the war-like policies of Maurice of Nassau. Oldenbarneveldt was the architect of the 12-year truce with Spain concluded in 1609. In the religious conflict between the Remonstrants or Arminians and the Gomarists this moderate Calvinist sided with the former party. After Maurice openly joined the Gomarists (1617) he ordered the arrest of the grand pensionary (1618), who was tried for treason, condemned, and executed.

VAN RIEBECK, JOHAN (1618–77), Dutch colonial official, who founded a base at the Cape of Good Hope after a career in the East Indies. During his time at the Cape he laid the foundations of the colony, taking crucial decisions which allowed East India Co. servants to become settlers and to import slaves for their labour requirements.

VAN RUENVEENE, PHILIP (PHILIPPUS ROVENIUS) (c. 1574–1651), Catholic archbishop of Utrecht, who was invested with the title at the request of the Catholics of the northern Netherlands, including Bp Jansen, his close friend. A native of Zwolle in Overyssel, he served as a priest in the Oldenzaal region during the 12-year Truce, becoming vicar apostolic of the northern Netherlands in 1614 and Abp of Philippi in 1622. Driven into hiding in 1626, he survived the occupation of Utrecht by the Dutch forces and a sentence of treason passed on him in 1640, and did much to prevent the decline of Catholicism in the northern Netherlands during the early 17th cent.

VAN RUYSDAEL, JACOB (1628–82), Dutch landscape painter, who taught Hobbema, and whose serious and austere vision of nature is illustrated by such paintings as *The Mill* and *The Shore at Scheveningen*.

VAN SWIETEN, GERHARD (1700–72), Dutch-born Catholic, who was personal physician to Empress Maria Theresa. He was educated at Leyden University, and became the head of the medical faculty at Vienna (1749). He advised the Habsburgs on the reform of the universities to curtail the pervading influence of the Jesuits and to educate students in the light of scientific progress made in the 17th–18th cents.

VAN TROMP, CORNELIS (1629–91), Dutch sailor, who shared the glory of De Ruyter's four-day battle off the Downs (June 1666) and won fame against the combined Anglo-French fleets in the Dutch War (1672–8), *eg*, off Schoneveld (June 1674), despite his personal conflict with the republican De Ruyter.

VAN TROMP, MARTIN HARPERTSZOON (1598–1653), Dutch sailor, who defeated the Spaniards twice in 1639, at Gravelines and the Downs in the Dutch War of Independence. In the First Anglo-Dutch War (1652–4) he lost two ships to Blake in a battle off Dover, but took his revenge off Dungeness in Nov. 1652, after which he is reputed to have hoisted a broom to the masthead of his flagship, the *Brederode*, to indicate that he had swept the Channel clear. In Feb. 1653, however, Blake attacked a Dutch convoy and in a three-day running battle with Tromp from Portland to Gris-Nez he destroyed over 50 Dutch merchantmen and some 17 warships, Tromp suffered a further blow in an engagement off the Gabbard (June 1653), in which he nearly lost the *Brederode*. On 31 July 1653 he was killed in a battle off Scheveningen in which Monk routed his fleet.

VAN VLIET, JEREMIAS, (*fl.* 17th cent.), Dutch colonial official and superintendent of the Dutch East India Co.'s trading establishment in Thailand (1633–40). He was the first Dutch governor of Malacca (1641–4) and the author of two accounts of Thailand.

VANBRUGH, SIR JOHN (1664–1726), English baroque architect and dramatist of the Restoration school of comedy. He was the grandson of a Protestant refugee from Ghent, was educated in France, and imprisoned briefly in the Bastille (1690–2). On returning to England, he became a staunch Whig. His first success as a playwright came with *The Relapse* (1696), which was followed by *The Provok'd Wife* (1697). He also won fame as the architect of Castle Howard (1702) and was appointed comptroller of royal works (1702). In 1705 he was commissioned by Queen Anne to design Blenheim Palace at Woodstock, the nation's memorial to the Duke of Marlborough. In 1704 he became Clarencieux King-of-Arms.

VANCOUVER, GEORGE (1757–98), British sailor, who accompanied Capt. James Cook on his voyages of discovery. He was given command of his own expedition (1790) to the north Pacific coast to arrange the return of British property seized by the Spanish at Nootka Sound, Canada, and while exploring the coastline of BC he disproved the theory of channels between the Hudson Bay and the Pacific Ocean. During that voyage he circumnavigated the globe, surveying the south-west coast of Australia and exploring numerous Pacific islands.

VANDALIA COLONY, unsuccessful American land scheme, based on a proposed grant of 24 million acres (197,120 sq. kms) to the Grand Ohio Co. Opposition from rival British and American colonial speculators and the start of the American War of Independence (1775), prevented the formation of the colony.

VANDALS, Germanic tribe, belonging to a group of Germans settled in eastern Europe in the 1st cent. AD. They were apparently defeated by the Goths early in the 4th cent. and were allowed by the Romans to settle in the Danube valley. Pushed westwards by the Hunnish invasions, they invaded Gaul in 406, passed into Spain, and, under their king, Gaiseric, crossed into Africa in 428–9. By 439 Carthage, the last free city of the Roman province of Africa, was taken by the Vandals, who henceforth controlled one of the main corn-growing regions of the Mediterranean world. Gaiseric, almost alone among the Germanic leaders, established a powerful fleet which dominated the western Mediterranean. A successful raid in 455 resulted in the brief capture of Rome, which was plundered. Gaiseric's successors were weaker men and the Vandals, being Arians, remained estranged from their Catholic subjects. In 533 the Byzantine general Belisarius overthrew their last king, Gelimer, in a brief campaign and the Vandals vanished from history.

VANDENBERG RESOLUTION (1948) in the US, Senate resolution supporting US participation in regional collective security agreements. It was introduced by the Republican senator, Arthur Vandenberg, of MI, one of the main architects of bipartisan foreign policy. Its easy passage removed fears that the Senate might frustrate collective-security arrangements with the Brussels pact countries, and prepared the way for the negotiation of the North Atlantic treaty (1949).

VANDERBILT, CORNELIUS (1794–1877), US business entrepreneur and financier, who made a fortune in the competitive steamboat business in the New York area after 1812. He established a transcontinental route to CA through Nicaragua, following the gold-rush of 1849, and in 1862 began to develop railroad interests. He failed to gain control of the Erie Railroad (1868), but built the New York and Harlem Railroad into the New York Central system.

VANE, SIR HENRY (1589–1654), English politician, known as the 'elder'. He was an MP from 1614 and became one of Charles I's advisers (1630). He was successively a commissioner of the admiralty (1632), for the colonies (1636), one of the privy councillors appointed to manage the affairs in Scotland on the outbreak of the Bishops' War (1639), and secretary of state (1640). He was appointed to the latter post on the wishes of Queen Henrietta Maria and the Marquis of Hamilton in opposition to the Earl of Strafford. In the Short Parliament (April–May 1640) Vane demanded supplies and proposed that the king should give up ship money in exchange for 12 subsidies. At Strafford's impeachment he stated that Strafford had advised the king in the privy council to employ Irish troops against England. Though accused of treachery by most of the court, he nevertheless accompanied Charles I to Scotland (Aug. 1641), but was later dismissed from all his offices (Nov. 1641). He joined the parliamentary opposition and was employed in several offices and committees, becoming a member of the Committee of Both Kingdoms (1644). At the negotiations at Uxbridge (1645) parliament demanded a barony for him from Charles. In 1650 the Rump refused to appoint him to the council of state, and in 1654 he was MP for Kent in Cromwell's first parliament.   CJ

VANE, SIR HENRY (1613–62), English politician, known as the 'younger', being the son of Sir Henry Vane the elder. Having acquired strong Puritan views early in life, he emigrated to MA of which he became governor (1636–7). On his return to England he was appointed joint treasurer of the navy (1639). He was a strong opponent of royal policy in the Short and Long Parliaments. As a leading commissioner for an alliance with the Scots (1643) and a strong opponent of Presbyterianism, he succeeded in toning down the terms of the Solemn League and Covenant. Though a leading independent, he withdrew from the Commons after Pride's Purge (6 Dec. 1648) and was absent until after the king's execution, of which he did not approve.

In 1649 he was appointed to the Commonwealth council of state and served on innumerable committees. He continually advocated religious toleration and opposed a state Church. His intimate friendship with Cromwell ended when the latter forcibly dissolved the Rump (April 1653). Under the protectorate he was imprisoned for a short while for suspected subversion (Sept.–Dec. 1656). At about this time he wrote his famous political tract, 'A Healing Question' (1656), in which he attacked the army—yet as an MP in Richard Cromwell's parliament (1659) he allied himself with the army in restoring the Rump and ending the protectorate. He was appointed to both the committee of safety and the council of state (May 1659) and virtually managed foreign affairs. After Lambert had expelled the Rump (Oct. 1659), Vane sought to reconcile the various factions within the army. Consequently he was suspected by the Rump when it returned again (Dec. 1659) and was expelled from the House. After being imprisoned at the Restoration, he was excepted from the indemnity bill by parliament. Though not a regicide, he was considered too dangerous a politician to be let to live, and in 1661 parliament demanded his trial for treason. He was executed in 1662.

J. Willcock, *Life of Sir Henry Vane the Younger* (London, 1913).   CJ

VANSITTART, ROBERT GILBERT VANSITTART, Baron (1881–1957), British diplomat, who served at embassies in Paris, Teheran, Cairo, and Stockholm, and in the foreign office in London. For four years he was private secretary to Lord Curzon, then foreign secretary, and in 1930 he became permanent under-secretary for foreign affairs. Through studying Nazism and talking to Hitler he became a violent opponent of Germany's policies. In an open clash with Neville Chamberlain he took up a very vigorous stand for a civil servant. As a result, in 1938 he was given less responsibility and in 1941 he retired with a peerage. After 1945 he turned his attention to attacks on communism. His publications included *Black Record* (1941), *Lessons of My Life* (1943), and his autobiography (1958).

VAN'T HOFF, JACOBUS HEINRICUS (1852–1911), Dutch physical chemist, famous for his theories on stereochemistry, which emphasized the three-dimensional arrangement of atoms in space. His *Études de Dynamique Chimique* (1884) led to the osmotic theory of solutions.

VA-NU-PIEDS, Norman peasant rising against royal fiscal policy (1639–40), which broke out in July 1639 because of threats to introduce the *gabelle* into the hitherto free region round Avranches. Taking their name from a probably legendary salt-worker who was forced by poverty to go bare-

foot, the rebels raised an army 5000 strong which caused the Crown much alarm before the rising was repressed by Gassion and Séquier.

VARANASI (Benares), holy city of the Hindus in the Benares division of Uttar Pradesh. The Hindu kingdom dates back to about 1200 BC. It formed part of the kingdom of Kanauj, but was conquered by Muslim invaders towards the end of the 12th cent. AD. When the Mughal empire disintegrated it was annexed by the nawab-wazir of Oudh, then ceded to the East India Co. in 1775. Warren Hastings's treatment of Chait Singh of Benares was one of the chief charges brought against Hastings at his impeachment. The raja of Benares remained faithful to the British during the Mutiny. In 1911 Benares was recognized as an Indian state, but was merged with Uttar Pradesh in 1949.

VARANGIANS. The Byzantine emperor Basil II (*reg.* 963 1025), in order to crush a dangerous military revolt, obtained from Vladimir of Kiev in 988 a force of some 6000 troops, who were destined to become the so-called Varangian guard attached to the person of the emperor. Later, adventurers from Scandinavia joined this force, including at one time Harald Hardrada, subsequently King of Norway (d. 1066). After the Norman conquest of England many English fugitives entered the Varangian guard and formed a predominant element in it late in the 11th cent.

VARELA IGLESIAS, JOSÉ ENRIQUE (1891–1951), Spanish soldier and right-wing politician, who persuaded Gen. Sanjurjo in 1932 that the country was ripe for revolt. After the failure of the Sanjurjada (Aug. 10), Varela began to work with the Carlists. He trained the Carlist militia, the *Requetés*, in Navarre while disguised as a wandering priest under the name of Pepe. He was prominent among the military plotters of 1936, meeting Mola and Franco in Madrid to finalize the strategy of the rising in each province. When the Civil War broke out he captured Cadiz with 600 men. He helped Franco to ferry Moors and legionaries across the Straits of Gibraltar and was made field commander of the army of Africa. After advancing into Andalusia and taking the Andalusian centre, he turned northwards towards Toledo to relieve the besieged garrison of the Alcazar. In Nov. 1936 he commanded the unsuccessful siege of Madrid. Thereafter, he was prominent in many Nationalist operations. In July 1937 he withstood the Republican counter-offensive on Brunete. He then helped in the Aragon offensive of March 1938. After the war he became minister of war.

VARENNES, FLIGHT TO (1791), by the French king, Louis XVI, and his family on 20–5 June, in an attempt to escape from the French Revolution in the hope of being able to suppress it by joining Austrian troops across the border and then appealing to the European rulers to intervene. The monarchy never recovered from the failure of this plan and the return of the royal family to Paris as prisoners.

VARGAS, GETÚLIO DORNELES (1883–1954), Brazilian politician and president (1951–4), who was the outstanding political leader of his generation in Brazil, and was identified with the broad political, economic, and social changes carried out, largely under his aegis, after 1930. He first attracted national attention as leader of his state's delegation in congress (1923–6), served as finance minister under President Washington Luiz Pereira de Souza (1926–8), and was governor of Rio Grande do Sul (1928–30). He was an unsuccessful candidate in the presidential elections of March 1930 and headed the revolutionaries who seized power in Nov. of that year. Vargas ruled without constitutional or congressional restraint until 17 July 1934, and as constitutional president, elected by the constituent assembly, until 10 Nov. 1937, when he set up the *Estado Novo*, or New State, with himself as dictator-president. When the dictatorship was overthrown by *coup d'état* on 29 Oct. 1945, he retired to his estate in Rio Grande do Sul. He was elected to both houses of congress from several states in the Dec. 1945 elections, but remained in semi-retirement until the 1950 presidential campaign, which he won. He took office on 31 Jan 1951. Unable to satisfy the demands of his followers and under constant attack by his critics, he lost the confidence of the armed forces. He took his own life on 24 Aug. 1954 rather than resign from office.

VARNA CRUSADE (1444) started as one of the most promising attempts to break the power of the Ottoman Turks in the Balkans and, had it succeeded, it might have saved Constantinople from capture nine years later. It was led by the young King of Poland and Hungary, Vladislav, who was decisively defeated at Varna in Bulgaria after the papal legate, Cesarini, persuaded the reluctant king to break a temporary truce with the Turks. Both Vladislav and Cesarini were killed.

VARRO, M. TERENTIUS (116–127 BC), Roman scholar and antiquarian, who was praetor and served in Illyricum (78–77), under Pompey in Spain (c. 76–71), and against the pirates (67). He was pardoned by Caesar after fighting with Pompey in the Civil War (49), and was appointed keeper of Caesar's proposed public library. Outlawed by Antony (43), he survived the civil wars and devoted himself to study. Varro wrote on Roman history, jurisprudence, rhetoric, literary history, philology (his work on the Latin language survives in part), agriculture (extant), architecture, music, and medicine. He also wrote a number of encyclopedic works and a collection of satirical essays.

VASA, HOUSE OF, from 1523 to 1818 provided every Swedish sovereign but two. From the accession of Gustavus I in 1523 the Vasas made the history of Sweden the history of its kings.

VASCONCELOS, JOSÉ (1882–1959), Mexican writer, politician, educationalist, and presidential candidate (1929), who entered politics (1910) as a supporter of Francisco I. Madero and joined the Carranza movement against Huerta, and later became rector of the national university and minister of education (1920–4), in which capacity he reorganized the Mexican educational system and created numerous new libraries and schools throughout the republic. His ministry patronized the artists of the mural renaissance. His foray into politics as an opponent to Calles (1924–9) resulted in a brief period of exile. Among his best-known works was his lengthy autobiography *Mexican Ulysses* (1963) originally written in 1935.

VASILY III IVANOVICH (1479–1533), Grand Duke of Muscovy (*reg.* 1505–33), and son of Ivan III and his second wife, Zoe (Sophia) Paleologus, niece of the last Emperor of Constantinople. He completed his father's task of rounding off the Muscovite empire, which thus extended from Chernigov to the Gulf of Finland, to the White Sea and to the Ural mountains. He waged two wars against Poland-Lithuania and incorporated into Muscovy the ancient principalities of Pskov (1510), Smolensk (1514), Ryazan (1517), and Starodub and Novgorod-Seversk (1523), though he was checked at Orsha (1514) by the Poles. A greater problem than the latter were the Crimean Tatars, who invaded Muscovy in 1521 and were halted only by Vasily's allies, the Astrakhan Tatars. Vasily was hated by the *boyars* because of his autocratic government, which was strengthened by the support he received from the Metropolitan, Daniel. With Daniel's sanction he divorced his first wife, Solomonida, who was barren, and married Helen Glinsky, of Lithuania (1525). He died leaving a three-year-old son, Ivan, to succeed him.

VÁSQUEZ, HORACIO (1860–1936), Dominican politician and president of Dominica (1899–1902, 1902–3, 1924–30), who organized the National Party, which he used as his personal political machine. His regime was overthrown in 1930 by Rafael L. Trujillo and his followers.

VASSY, MASSACRE OF (1562), in France, killing of some 30 Huguenot worshippers in a congregation at Vassy by retainers of the Catholic leader, the Duc de Guise, in defiance of the royal edict of toleration (Jan. 1562). The incident precipitated the first War of Religion in France (1562–3).

VÄSTERÅS, DIET OF (1527), in Sweden, marked the start of the reformation of the Swedish Church. The estates met the king's financial requirements by granting him the lands of the Church, though the nobles were entitled to recover whatever lands they had donated since 1454. This increased the Crown's properties from 5 to 25 per cent. Provision was also made for the Word of God 'to be preached purely'.

VASVAR, TRUCE OF (1664), treaty between the grand vizier of Turkey and Emperor Leopold I establishing a 20-year truce between the two powers. Although this agreement followed the great Turkish defeat at St Gotthard, Leopold was willing to recognize the sultan's suzerainty over Transylvania, his possession of Nagyvarad and Zerinvar, and the cession of the fortresses of Neuhäusel, Nitra, and Léva in western Hungary to Turkey, as well as paying an indemnity of 200,000 florins. Leopold contended that Habsburg resources were inadequate to expel the Turks from Hungary and he was also anxious about the possibility of a crisis over the Spanish succession. To the Hungarians, however, the truce seemed an act of treachery in breach of the constitution and an invitation to further unofficial Turkish aggression upon Christian territory.

VATICAN COUNCIL, THE (1869–70), had in its agenda 'modern errors', such as pantheism and rationalism, and the definition of the infallibility of the pope. The latter was defined by the bull *Pastor Aeternus* and provoked lively discussion, both as to its truth and the wisdom of promulgating it at that time. The council adjourned because of the Franco-Prussian War and consequent occupation of Rome by Italian troops, and was not reconvened until 1963.

VATTAGAMANI (*reg. c.* 89–77 BC), King of Ceylon, who re-established Sinhalese authority after 15 years of Tamil rule. The texts of the Buddhist Pali Canon (the *Tripitaka*), which had been orally transmitted from the time of the Buddha, were committed to writing during his reign.

VAU, LOUIS DE (1612–70), French architect and landscape gardener, who worked on the Tuileries, the Louvre, and Vincennes for Mazarin. He created his masterpiece for Fouquet at Vaux-le-Vicomte (1655–61). His success led Louis XIV to commission him to build Versailles and his ideas were the inspiration for much of the later work there.

VAUBAN, SEBASTIEN LE PRESTRE DE (1633–1707), French soldier and military engineer, who rose to high rank through merit and service. After serving under Turenne at the siege of Lille (1667), he became an adviser to the war minister, Louvois, and commissioner-general of fortifications (1678). He was the first engineer to be appointed a marshal of France (1703). He conducted the sieges in all Louis XIV's wars. His greatest achievement was the system of fortifications carried out in Flanders and Artois (mainly between 1667 and 1672). His defensive ideas dominated warfare in the later 17th cent. Basically, Vauban suggested defensible frontiers, without enclaves, protected by linear fortifications based on great works at key points. Thus, besides the 55 sieges he directed, he built 33 fortresses and repaired a further 300. Towards the end of his life he became concerned with France's financial position and argued in his *Projet d'une Dîme Royale* (1707) in favour of tax reform.

VAUCANSON, JACQUES DE (1709–82), French inventor of the first mechanical loom, who spent much of his great skill and ingenuity in making automata, elaborate mechanical toys. His looms, dating from 1745 onwards, were the first suitable for power operation.

VAUCELLES, TRUCE OF (1555), final peace concluded between the Emperor Charles V and the Valois monarchy of France before the emperor's abdication from the imperial throne. It proved to be only temporary because of the machinations of the anti-Habsburg pope, Paul IV, who provoked further hostilities (1556–8) in Italy and the Netherlands between Henry II and Philip II of Spain.

VAUDREUIL, PHILIPPE DE RIGAUD, Marquis de (1643–1725), French colonial official and governor of French Canada (1703–25), who went to Canada as commander of the colonial troops (1687). He became successively administrator (1688) and governor of Montreal (1699). He led expeditions against the Iroquois Indians (1689–97) and assisted in the defence of Quebec (1690). He was governor of New France (1703–25) and was afterwards made a marquis. His administration was marked by repeated raids on New England settlements and by economic depression. After a period in France (1714–16) he returned to Canada and, with Bp Saint-Vallier, helped to establish 82 parishes in New France.

VAUDREUIL-CAVAGNAL, PIERRE DE RIGAUD, Marquis de (1698–1778), French soldier and colonial official, who became governor of Three Rivers (1733). As governor of Louisiana (1742–53) he encouraged agricultural settlement in the Upper Mississippi valley and made peace with the Indians. He was appointed governor of New France (1755), but quarrelled with Montcalm over the strategy for the defence of French Canada, and as a result was placed under Montcalm's command. After Montcalm's death (1759), Vaudreuil again became senior officer and eventually capitulated to the British (1760). He returned to France in that year and was imprisoned in the Bastille for maladministration, but was acquitted of the charge.

VAUGHAN, HENRY (1622–95), Welsh religious poet, self-styled 'the Silurist', who practised medicine in his native South Wales. His published works included *Poems* (1646), 'Silex Scintillans', pious meditations and poems (1650–5), 'The Mount of Olives', devotions in prose (1652), and 'Thalia Rediviva: the pastimes and diversions of a country muse' (1678).

VAUGHAN, WILLIAM (1577–1641), Welsh poet and colonial organizer, who bought an interest in Nfld and sponsored a party of Welsh settlers at Cambriol, Trepassy Bay.

VAUXHALL GARDENS, in England, first known as New Spring Gardens, were laid out in 1661 on a site north of Harleyford Road in the borough of Lambeth, London, and frequented in the 17th cent. by such men as Samuel Pepys and John Evelyn, the diarists. The gardens, reconstructed and improved from 1728 by Jonathan Tyers and his sons, were fashionable in the 18th–mid-19th cents. They were closed in 1859.

VAUX-LE-VICOMTE, in France, château of Nicolas Fouquet, near Paris, perhaps the most important French building of the mid-17th cent. and regarded as a forerunner of Versailles. It was designed by Le Vau on the plan of the Palazzo Barberini, and started in 1657. Its décor was by Le Brun and Poussin and its gardens laid out by Le Nôtre.

VAZQUEZ DE LECA, MATEO (1542–91), Spanish administrator, who was secretary to Philip II. He espoused the enemies of Antonio Perez, whose downfall he engineered (1578), replacing him as chief royal secretary (1579). He won the king's confidence and was the chief member of Philip's administrative committee, the *junta de noche* (1585), until his death.

VEBLEN, THORSTEIN BUNDE (1857–1929), US writer and economist, who was managing editor of the *Journal of Political Economy* (1896–1905) and taught at various universities. He was a severe critic of laissez-faire capitalism and the Social Darwinist ethic. His reputation was based on *The Theory of the Leisure Class* (1899), an attack upon business values and methods and the ideology of wealth. His later works include *The Theory of Business Enterprise* (1904), a critical discussion of the business cycle and price system, *The Engineers and the Price System* (1921), which argued that technologists were best fitted to direct industry, and *The Higher Learning in America* (1918), a critique of universities controlled by businessmen. His ideas, drawn largely from European sources, were instrumental in weakening the hold of neo-classical economic theory in the US and in laying the foundations for the institutional school of economics.

VECTIGAL, ancient Roman term denoting an indirect tax, also applied to revenue and rents from state property. Under the republic, the only indirect taxes proper were harbour and customs dues (*portoria*) and a 5 per cent tax on manumitted slaves. *Vectigalia* were greatly increased in the empire and included a 1 per cent tax on sales by auction, a 5 per cent tax on inheritances, other than from close relations, and a 4 per cent tax on the sale of slaves. Until the time of Diocletian, the inhabitants of Italy, being exempt from *tributum*, paid only *vectigalia*, which were collected first by companies of *publicani*, then from the 2nd cent. AD by single contractors and later by state officials.

VEDA (in Sanskrit lit. knowledge, wisdom), used mainly to indicate the oldest religious texts of India, regarded as revealed wisdom (*sruti*). In its narrow sense, often referred to as 'the (Four) *Veda*s', it comprises the four great 'collections' (*Samhita*) of hymns, chants, ritual formulas, and spells: *Rigveda, Samaveda, Yajurveda,* and *Atharvaveda*. Of these, the *Rigveda* is the oldest (*c.* 1200–1000 BC). They represent a vast body of texts, handed down orally by a succession of teachers and pupils and finally written down (some time after AD 500). As these texts are metrical and have been held in great awe, the tradition turned out remarkably accurate, as appears from internal criteria.

In a wider connotation, *Veda* includes also numerous ancient prose texts on the theological and cosmological exegesis of the Samhitas, *eg*, the *Brahmana*s, and treatises discussing different aspects of the doctrines, including their philosophical and esoteric significance (*Aranyaka*s and *Upanishad*s). More loosely attached to the *Veda* are the auxiliary disciplines (*Vedanga*), such as the systematic treatment of public and domestic rituals (*Srauta-* and *Grihyasutras*), grammar, metrics, and even geometry. These later Vedic texts are difficult to date, but seem to belong to roughly 1000–500 BC. They contain a wealth of information on political, social, and cultural history. Their analysis, helped by the results of archaeological excavations in the Indo-Gangetic valleys, has recently made great progress. In general terms, they reflect the gradual expansion of literate civilization from the Punjab down the Gangetic valley to Bihar, and southward to Malwa. This expansion was accompanied by the transformation of tribal units into larger, predominantly monarchic, states, while Vedic religion began to adopt some typical features of Hinduism (emphasis on caste, rebirth, non-violence, etc.).

Louis Renou, *Vedic India* (Calcutta, 1957). JG dec

VEDANTA (in ancient India, 'end [or essence] of the Veda'), term used to denote the *Upanishad*s and the philosophical system based thereon. The latter was first enunciated in cryptic aphorisms by the saint Badarayana, who was a legendary figure, and fully elaborated by Sankaracharya. Vedanta was subsequently developed and partly transformed by later teachers, notably Ramanuja, Madhva, Nimbarka, and Vallabha. The basic doctrine is that of the fundamental identity (lit., non-duality, *advaita*) of the individual soul (*atman*) and the absolute (*brahman*), an identity which is obscured by ignorance (*avidya*) or illusion (*maya*). While *advaita* is absolute for Sankara, it is qualified for the later Vedantins. Vedanta has had great influence on Indian thought all through the centuries until the present time and has favoured the rise of certain Indian attitudes about the illusory nature of the world around us. It may also have conditioned some Western attitudes towards India.

VEGA, CARRIO LOPE FELIX DE (1562–1635), Spanish poet and dramatist of the Spanish baroque. In his early life he served the Crown, taking part in the Portuguese campaign of 1580 and the Armada of 1588. Later, he became secretary to the Duke of Alva and eventually took holy orders (1614), and became an officer of the Inquisition. In all his works he showed respect for the Crown, the Catholic Church, and the human personality. He was phenomenally prolific, and is credited with having written some 1500 plays, of which about 440 are in print. These included historical plays, eg, *No Judge like the King* and *A Certainty for a Doubt*, cloak-and-dagger comedies, eg, *The Gardener's Dog*, and dramas, eg, *Dorotea*.

VEGA, JUAN DE (*fl.* 1543–57), Spanish politician, who was appointed imperial envoy to the Holy See (1543–6) by the Emperor Charles V, and then viceroy of Sicily (1547–57), when that province was being constantly harassed by raids by Turkish corsairs, eg, Dragut. His task was to organize Spain's naval and military defences in the eastern Mediterranean.

VEII, 24 kms north-west of Rome, most southerly of the Twelve Cities of the Etruscan League and the first to be destroyed by Rome (*c.* 396 BC). Etruscan Veii was a notable artistic centre, and the site itself is remarkable for the surviving evidence of Etruscan engineering skill in collecting and dispersing water.

VELASCO IBARRA, JOSÉ MARÍA (1893–), Ecuadorian politician, lawyer, and president of Ecuador (1934–5, 1944–7, 1952–6, 1960–1, 1968–), who was supported, at various times, by conservatives, liberals, socialists, and communists. The basis of his political power lay in his popularity with Ecuadorian voters. At various times he was an economic conservative, and a radical; he reached power by *coup d'état* and by constitutional election, and served his constitutional term as president. Twice he suspended the constitution and ruled as a dictator. Recurrent problems with the Ecuadorian military establishment had, by 1970, removed him from power three times. A regular feature of his presidencies was his strong nationalism and an emphasis on Ecuador's perennial boundary dispute with Peru.

VELASQUEZ, DIEGO RODRIGUEZ DE SILVA Y (1599–1660), Spanish court painter to Philip IV, who was noted for his portraits of the royal family. In return for their numerous portraits he was rewarded with many favours: in 1633 he became constable of the royal household and court, in 1652 chief steward of the palace, and in 1659 he was knighted. He accompanied Philip on various military campaigns and journeys. *The Surrender of Breda*, painted in 1634 and depicting Justin of Nassau surrendering to Spinola, is in reality an extraordinary galaxy of portraits. This picture was one of a series celebrating victorious Spanish campaigns. With few exceptions he painted purely secular pictures with a technique that made him a forerunner of 19th-cent. Impressionism.

VELÁZQUEZ, DIEGO DE (*c.* 1460–1524), Spanish conqueror of Cuba, who began the conquest and settlement of Cuba in 1511, and showed exceptional administrative ability during his long rule. While slave-raiding and trading along the Honduras coast, his men found evidence of the highly developed mainland peoples, and Velázquez sent expeditions in 1517–18 to reconnoitre the coasts of Yucatan and the Gulf of Mexico. Encouraged by the evidence which these expeditions discovered, in 1519 Velázquez fitted out a much larger expedition and appointed his ex-secretary, Cortés, as commander. At the last minute Velázquez changed his mind, but Cortés left Cuba in clandestine haste to make the Mexican conquest his own. Velázquez sought to reassert his own authority through the Narváez expedition and through petitions to the crown, but failed.

VELČEV, DAMYAN (1883–1954), Bulgarian soldier and politician who assisted in the coup of 1923 which overthrew Stambuliski's regime. Afterwards, he grew increasingly distressed about the terror, inefficiency, and instability which the partnership between IMRO and the army introduced into Bulgarian public life. In 1930 he formed the Military League and became associated with Zveno. Together they combined, under Velčev's leadership, to precipitate the coup of May 1934. A government was formed, but Velčev's strained relations with King Boris caused it to fall within a year. Despite this, the government made several significant achievements: IMRO was liquidated, relations with the Soviet Union were restored, steps were made towards a reconciliation with Yugoslavia, and socio-economic reforms were undertaken. Velčev remained the power behind Zveno and a figure of importance in the army. Under his leadership, Zveno joined the Fatherland Front and co-operated with the Communist Party after the war. In 1944 he became minister of national defence, but was dismissed (1946) as the communists asserted their authority. He later became minister to Berne.

VELDE, WILLEM VAN DE (1633–1707), Dutch painter, of an Amsterdam family of artists, known for his seascapes and marine battle scenes, eg, *The Gale*. From 1677 he lived in London, taking service with King Charles II as court painter, and he died in Greenwich. His works served as models for Turner and other British marine painters.

VELLETRI, BATTLE OF (1744), indecisive engagement in central Italy between the Austrian forces of Maria Theresa and the 'Gallispan' armies of Louis XV and Philip V during the War of the Austrian Succession. The Austrians retreated northwards after the battle to support their ally, Charles Emmanuel III of Savoy, but the Gallispan commanders were divided by quarrels and achieved little in 1744.

VELLORE MUTINY (1806) in India, massacre by local Madras sepoys of most of their officers and a large number of European soldiers. The chief cause was the sepoys' belief that they were going to be converted forcibly to Christianity.

VENDÉE, LA (1793), in France, rising against the Revolutionary government in Paris. It was the most serious of the provincial revolts and was instigated by priests and aristocrats, while the peasants revolted in March against government attempts to conscript them. The revolt soon spread to most of western France, and although the rebels were defeated at Chollet (Oct.) La Vendée continued to be subject to periodic risings until Napoleon made a determined effort to end the disaffection by removing the conservative peasantry's main grievance, the persecution of the Church by successive Revolutionary regimes.

VENDÔME, LOUIS-JOSEPH, Duc de (1654–1712), French soldier, who took part in the invasion of Holland (1672), and later served under Turenne. He captured Barcelona (1697), and fought in the indecisive battle of Luzzara in Italy (1702). He was recalled to Flanders (1706) and defeated at Ramillies

(1708). Later, he was victorious in Spain at Brihuega and Villaviciosa (1710).

VENETI, ancient tribe which migrated into Italy (*c.* 1000 BC) occupying the area between the head of the Adriatic and the Alps, which had its capital at Patavium (Padua). The Veneti were hostile to the Gauls and supported Rome during the Gallic invasion (387) and the Second Punic War (218–202). They achieved Roman citizenship in 49 BC.

VENETIAN GLASS, one of Venice's main industries from the 10th cent. From 1291, it was located on the neighbouring island of Murano to eliminate the risk of fire in Venice. From the later 15th cent. the production of enamelled glassware, introduced by the Barovier family, grew in importance, but the industry's greatest achievement was the development of clear, colourless glass which was the basis of the export trade. From the late 16th cent., when enamelling was out of fashion, elaborate clear glass was produced. The demand was enormous in Europe until the production secrets spread to France, Spain, Portugal, and the German states, although it continued to inspire the international style in glass known as *Façon de Venise.*

VENEZUELAN ORGANIZING COMMITTEE FOR INDEPENDENT ELECTIONS (Comité Organizador Pro-eleccion Independiente), political party organized by Rafael Caldera in 1945 to oppose government policies, particularly those relating to the Church. It was in line with world-wide Christian Democratic tendencies, but less radical than Venezuela's Acción Democrática and Rómulo Betancourt on social questions. Though the name was officially changed to the Social Christian Party, it was still referred to as before. Following its suppression under the military dictatorship (1952–8), COPEI was reorganized. Rafael Caldera represented the party in the presidential elections of 1958, 1963, and 1969. He was victorious in 1969, although his party failed to receive a majority either of the popular vote or in the congress.

VENICE, for some 500 years (1100–1600) the richest maritime state of the Mediterranean. The city, built on islands interspersed with canals, is one of the most beautiful in the world, unique in its architecture. The Venetian state grew out of a confederation of 12 communities peopled by fugitives escaping from various barbarian invasions of the mainland (5th–6th cents.) During a war against the Franks the capital of the confederation was moved to Rialto, at the centre of modern Venice (*c.* 810), because of its inaccessibility to attackers. At the end of that war Venice was recognized as a dependency of the Byzantine empire and it developed henceforth as one of the few Italian cities privileged to trade in Byzantine lands. In 1082, in return for naval help to the Byzantines, Venice secured exemption from all the Byzantine taxes. The First Crusade opened up to the Venetians trade with Syria (after 1100). Competition with other Italians in the eastern Mediterranean led to growing Venetian resentment at the Byzantine tolerance of these rivals. Venice played the decisive part in diverting the Fourth Crusade to Constantinople, which ended in its capture (1202–4). The Black Sea was now opened up to the Venetians and they acquired a splendid collection of bases on the mainland and the islands of Greece. Thereafter, until the rise of Turkish power in the 15th cent., the Venetians had the lion's share of trade in the eastern Mediterranean; they specialized in spices and other luxuries which their fleets distributed to western Europe. Internally, Venice developed an exceptionally stable government. A merchant aristocracy ruled, but the rest of the population had ample opportunities for prospering; good order and justice were assured and the government protected the poorer classes from undue exploitation. But by 1500 Venice had acquired a large state on the Italian mainland which it could defend only with difficulty. The Portuguese, after reaching India (1498), tried to ruin the Venetian trade

in spices, and Turkish power spread (1517–25) to the whole of North Africa. Venice survived these challenges and the resultant internal upheavals, but by the 17th cent. it was ceasing to compete on even terms with its leading commercial rivals. It lived on its past prosperity and as an attractive centre for foreign visitors, which remained its chief distinction from the 18th cent. onwards.   EBF

VENIZELOS, ELEUTHERIOS (1864–1936), Greek politician and chief protagonist of the republican–royalist feud after the First World War. He was a Cretan who took part in the Cretan revolt (1896) against Turkey and became minister of justice when Crete gained autonomy. His defiance of the commissioner of Crete, establishment of a rival government, and proclamation of union with Greece (1897–8) made him a popular hero on the island. After the *coup d'état* of 1910 the Military League in Athens invited him to become their political adviser. He consequently went to Greece and at once proposed a revision of the constitution by a popular assembly. This plan was accepted and Venizelos won a seat in the assembly. In Oct. 1910 he became prime minister of Greece and announced that the constitution would be revised, but that the dynasty would be retained. That same year he formed the Liberal Party and also strengthened his position at the polls. The revised constitution was accepted in June 1911. In the First World War Venizelos was in open conflict with the throne. He sided with the Entente and hoped to intervene against the Central Powers, which King Constantine supported. At first, the Allies themselves rejected Venizelos's offers to intervene because the Russian government wanted a free hand in the Straits. In 1915 the king vetoed intervention and Venizelos resigned. Later he regained power, but resigned again a year later when the king refused to assist the Salonika expedition. A constitutional crisis ensued. A royalist government was formed after the elections of 1916 and Venizelos formed an extra-parliamentary opposition. In Sept. he proclaimed a revolution from Crete and in Oct. moved his government to Salonika, where it quickly received recognition by the Allies, who forced Constantine to abdicate, and in June 1917 Venizelos became prime minister once again. In July Greece intervened, he undertook the Anatolian adventure, and represented Greece at the peace conference (1918–20). With the treaty of Sèvres Venizelos won a great triumph, but on his return to Greece he was ousted by the electorate. After this he left Greece for eight years. He returned in 1928 and again became prime minister and leader of his party. He was twice prime minister after his return (1928–33, Jan.–March 1933). His rule was marred by corruption, dissension, and depression, but, above all, by a growing feud between republicans and royalists. Venizelos was accused of collusion in the attempted republican coups of 1933, when he narrowly escaped assassination, and 1935. The victory of the monarchy in the plebiscite of 1935 came at the close of his career and he died the next year.   JMK

VENLOO, TREATY OF (1543), peace that ended the War of the Guelders' Succession (1542–3), by which the emperor Charles V imposed a drastic settlement upon Duke William of Cleves. After Düren, Jülich, and other towns had been taken by imperial troops, William had to surrender Guelders, which he had inherited in 1538, and renounce Protestantism in his lands. This triumph enabled Charles to concentrate upon Cleves' French and German allies in the larger Habsburg–Valois confrontation.

VENN, JOHN (1759–1813), English clergyman who was a founder-member of the Church Missionary Society and the Evangelical rector of Clapham, whose parishioners included William Wilberforce, Granville Sharp, and Hannah More.

VENTÔSE, LAWS OF (1794) in France. Although never implemented, they were intended by some of the French Jacobin leaders, including St Just, to ensure *sans-culotte*

support for the government by the free distribution of confiscated estates and property.

VERACRUZ, Spanish settlement in Mexico established on the site of Cortés's landing when he came to conquer that country in 1519. It became the main point of convergence of the Spanish silver trains, and its port, San Juan d'Ulloa, the destination of the annual *flota* or bullion fleet in the 16th–17th cents.

VERACRUZ INCIDENT (1914) in the US, occupation by US forces of the port of Veracruz, stemming from a Mexican refusal to salute the US flag with 21 guns at Tampico, and the US desire to prevent the landing of the German vessel *Ypiranga*, which was carrying guns for Victoriano Huerta.

VERCELLAE, BATTLE OF (101 BC) (near mod. Vercelli, northern Italy), decisive defeat of the Cimbri by the Roman army under Q. Lutatius Catulus and Marius.

VERCINGETORIX, Celtic chieftain, who led a rising against Julius Caesar in Gaul (52 BC) and after at first being defeated adopted the tactic of destroying Caesar's supply lines and bringing him to battle on unfavourable ground. After being defeated and blockaded in Alesia, he surrendered and was killed after Caesar's triumph (46).

VERDUN, BATTLE OF (1916). In Feb. 1916, during the First World War, the German chief of staff, Falkenhayn, launched a major offensive against the old fortress of Verdun, lying in an awkwardly exposed salient on the Western Front, with the object of bringing the French army to battle and destroying it. The attack opened on 21 Feb. Within four days Fort Douaumont fell, but the French, now under Pétain, fought back heroically under conditions of great difficulty; none the less on 9 June Fort Vaux fell, and by 23 June the Germans had almost reached the heights overlooking the town. The British offensive launched on the Somme on 1 July and designed in part as a diversion, together with Brusilov's action on the Russian front and the heavy casualties being suffered by the Germans, led to a gradual easing of the situation. By the end of 1916 the French had with great difficulty recaptured much of the lost ground, though the whole action had cost them many divisions. The Germans suffered equally and, as a result of the failure of the attack, Falkenhayn was replaced by Hindenburg and Ludendorff.

VEREENIGING, TREATY OF (31 May 1902), brought the Anglo-Boer War (1899–1902) to an end. The Boers capitulated and their republics lost their independence, but Africans were specifically excluded from any future franchise which the new British colonies of the Transvaal and the Orange River might be granted.

VERELST, HENRY (1734–85), British colonial official in the East India Co.'s service, who was nominated by Lord Clive to succeed him as governor of Fort William in Bengal. During his term of office (1765–7) he tried to work Clive's system of dual government in co-operation with the deputy nawab, Muhammad Reza Khan, but he lacked firmness in dealing with the company's servants.

VERGENNES, CHARLES GRANIER, Comte de (1717–87), French politician and diplomat, who served as ambassador at Constantinople (1754–67) and later as secretary of state for foreign affairs (1774–87). As ambassador to the Porte he helped to patch up the breach in Franco-Turkish friendship, created by the Franco-Austrian treaty of Versailles (1756), by playing on Turkish fears of Russia. Thus he not only restored Franco-Turkish relations, but contributed to the hostility which erupted into the Russo-Turkish War (1768–1774).

Influenced by the humanitarian ideals of the Enlightenment, he pursued a policy of peace and stability in Europe, which enabled France to direct her resources towards America during the war of revenge upon Britain (1778–83). He thereby achieved his objects of restoring French prestige after the Seven Years War and of reducing Britain's colonial might to a level of parity. Reconciliation with Britain was sealed by the Pitt–Vergennes trade treaty of 1786.

VERGIL, POLYDORE (*c.* 1470–*c.* 1555), Italian historian and divine, who spent most of his life in England, becoming a naturalized subject in 1510. After being educated at Bologna and Padua, he was sent to England as a deputy-collector of Peter's Pence for the Holy See (1501), and became prebendary of Lincoln (1507) and of St Paul's (1513). In 1525 he published the first genuine edition of the historian Gildas, but his greatest work was the *History of England*, published in Basle (1534). In 1550 he returned to Italy, where he died.

VERITABLE RECORDS in China. In compiling the Standard Histories, the Chinese history commissions used a number of series of notes that had been made partly for purposes of administration, partly as an account of the emperor's action, and partly to record decisions of state. The commissions in their turn produced several drafts at successive stages of their work; and of these the *Veritable Records*, or *Shih-lu*, were in effect the penultimate version. As Chinese practice has been to destroy the different types of record at the point when they have been superseded by their successor, only fragments of the *Veritable Records* remain.

VERMEER, JAN (1632–75), Dutch painter specializing in portraying the quiet pursuits of ordinary people. He lived in relative obscurity and was a totally forgotten master until 1866. The few paintings of his that remain mostly depict solitary people engaged in tranquil occupations—sewing, playing the virginals, map-making, etc., in sunlit rooms.

VERMILION SEA, alleged by the American Sioux and Assiniboine Indians (1678–9) to be a bright red sea where white men lived. It is now believed that this referred to the Gulf of California.

VERMONT, disputed territory in North America, located largely between the Connecticut river and Lake Champlain, the first European to visit the area being Samuel de Champlain (1609). The first permanent French settlement was Fort St Anne (1666) and the earliest British post was Fort Dummer (1724). British expeditions to remove the French (1690, 1709, 1711) failed and the French established Forts St Frédéric (1731) and Carillon (1756, later renamed Ticonderoga), which they used as bases to raid British settlements in New England and NY. During the French and Indian War (1755–63), the British constructed Forts William Henry (1755) and Edward (1755), and British and colonial troops under Sir Jeffrey Amherst drove the French from VT. The British colonies of NH and NY claimed VT and gave land grants to their citizens. An appeal to the Crown had no practical effect, as armed settlers protected their land grants. During the American War of Independence VT declared itself an independent commonwealth (1777), elected a governor and legislature, annexed sections of NY and NH (1778, 1781), and entered into negotiations with Britain to obtain self-government. With the end of the war (1783), VT settled her disputes with her neighbours and agreed to become the 14th state of the US (1791).

M. B. Jones, *Vermont in the Making* (Cambridge, MA, 1939).
RCR

VERNACULAR PRESS ACT (1878), passed during the Indian viceroyalty of Lord Lytton. It imposed restrictions on newspapers published in Indian languages. This led to great agitation and the act was repealed by Lord Ripon in 1882.

VERNACULAR, USE OF THE, printing of literary works in the mother tongue, which began in the Renaissance period with the development of the printing press and the emergence of national languages and was given impetus by the Protestant Reformation. At first, scholars translated the Scriptures and edited classical and traditional stories in the vernacular to appeal to those not educated in the classics, but from the late 17th cent. Latin was displaced by the vernacular as the sole diplomatic language.

VERNEY, SIR RALPH (1613–96), English politician from Buckinghamshire whose voluminous and invaluable correspondence is preserved at the family seat of Claydon House. His father was the royalist standard-bearer at Edgehill, but he fought for the parliamentarian cause, though a sincere Anglican. He endured exile (1643–53) and imprisonment (1655), but was reconciled to the restoration of Charles II (1660), and as a member of the Convention parliament (1689) later welcomed William III and Mary as the defenders of English liberties.

VERNON, EDWARD (1684–1757), English sailor and politician, who entered the navy in 1700, afterwards serving in the West Indies and the Baltic. In 1739 he commanded an expedition sent to destroy Spanish West Indian settlements and shipping. After taking Porto Bello and Chagre (1740), he attacked Cartagena and Guantanamo (1741). He was promoted admiral in 1745, and given command of the ships in the North Sea. After a public quarrel with the British admiralty, largely over his terms of appointment, he resigned at his own request (1746). Subsequently he spoke on naval questions in the House of Commons.

VERNON, THOMAS (1654–1721), English politician and law reporter, famous for his *Reports of Cases decided in Chancery 1691–1718*, first published in 1726–8.

VERONA, CONGRESS OF (1822), which met to discuss revolutions in Spain, Greece, Italy, and South America, effectively marked the end of the system of periodic high-level personal diplomacy inaugurated in 1815. The Duke of Wellington, working to the instructions of Castlereagh, the British foreign minister, repudiated the projected French intervention in Spain, which Russia, Austria, and Prussia supported in varying degrees. Canning, appointed as foreign secretary after Castlereagh, underlined Britain's estrangement from the Alliance's 'system', whose disruption derived from Alexander I's vagaries and French ambitions, as well as British dislike of the principle of 'moral solidarity', implying Great Power action against revolutionary movements.

VERONESE, PAOLO (*c.* 1528–88), Venetian painter, who depicted the luxurious worldliness and sensuousness of the Venetians under the guises of biblical and historical allegory. He was called before the Inquisition in 1573 for taking licence in this way with religious subjects.

VERRAZANO, GIOVANNI DA (*c.* 1480–*c.* 1528), Italian sailor and explorer, who led a French expedition to the New World. He followed the North American coast north from near Cape Fear in NC to Cape Breton. During this voyage he discovered New York and Narragansett bays. He sailed again in 1528, but failed to return.

VERRES, C. (d. 43 BC), Roman governor of Sicily (73–70 BC), who was notorious for his rapacity. His prosecution by Cicero so overwhelmed Verres that he went into exile at Massilia before the case was completed. He was proscribed and killed in 43.

VERRI, PIETRO (1728–86), Milanese merchant, public servant, and economist, whose writings contain early approaches to the concepts of equilibrium and of demand-elasticity.

VERROCCHIO, ANDREA (1435–88), Florentine painter and sculptor, whose painting, distinguished by sweetness of expression and feeling of movement, was inherited by his pupil, Leonardo da Vinci. As a sculptor he desired to emulate Donatello, but his effects were less profound, though more elaborate. Some of his work foreshadowed baroque art.

VERSAILLES, small town outside Paris, which is famous for the vast royal château around which it grew up. The château is one of the most monumental achievements of classical art and architecture and a legacy of the personality of Louis XIV. It was copied by princes throughout Europe in the 17th and 18th cents.

Versailles was originally a hamlet in marshy country where Louis XIII had a hunting lodge. When Louis XIV assumed power (1661) he used Versailles as a setting for some of his entertainments, such as *Les Plaisirs de l'île enchanté* (1664) and their success led him to establish a permanent residence (1668). Colbert had urged him to rebuild the Louvre, but Louis had unpleasant memories of Paris during the *Fronde* and preferred to move to a setting on the lines of Vaux-le-Vicomte, which would be appropriate to his style of monarchy.

The architect was Vau, who was assisted by Le Nôtre, the landscape gardener, and Lebrun the artist was put in charge of the château's embellishment. The first château, completed by D'Orbay after Vau's death, was a three-storeyed edifice into which the lodge was fitted. The work proceeded slowly during the Dutch War, but the court moved there permanently soon after (1681). Extensive modifications were made during the next decade, when Mansart extended the château, adding such features as the *Galerie des Glaces*, destroying some of Vau's balance but making it more impressive. An annexe was added to house all the ministries, and a chapel (1699–1710), as well as two satellite residences, Marly (1682) and the Grand Trianon (1687). The former was Louis's favourite abode, to which he could retire from the publicity of Versailles. The whole complex cost more than 100 million *livres*, a not insignificant fraction of the national budget, and required the employment of thousands of labourers, many of whom died in the effort to create gardens out of the swamps. It was also the greatest source of artistic patronage in Europe, the impressive suites of rooms being sumptuously, if formally, decorated, often with Louis's favourite themes of Apollo and martial glory. The buildings, which included an orangery, a zoo, and theatre, were surrounded by acres of formal gardens full of classical statuary, irrigated and embellished by a complicated system of fountains, lakes, and canals.

But Versailles was more than merely a château surrounded by gardens: it was a way of life. It housed a vast staff, offered residence—often none too comfortably—to a great many courtiers, and embraced the central government as well as the court. In Louis XIV's time the whole of this organism centred round the king, who lived a totally public life amidst a court which was subjected to etiquette and regulations of almost Byzantine complexity. All this was done to mark the monarch off from his people, to create and symbolize the aloof power which Louis believed essential for government. Versailles was an allegory of power as well as a work of art, and one which had considerable repercussions on French society.

After the death of Louis XIV (1715) Versailles was not used so often and the Revolution forced the royal family to abandon it (1789). Under the Third Republic it housed the national assembly and the senate (1870–9). Today it is a museum and showplace, although it is occasionally used for public events.

I. Dunlop, *Versailles* (London, 1970).
G. Ziegler, *Everyday life at Versailles in the Seventeenth and Eighteenth centuries* (London, 1969). CHC

VERSAILLES, TREATY OF (1 May 1756), concluded between France and Austria. It marked the first breach in Franco-Prussian relations since 1741. The alliance was the achievement of Kaunitz, who, from the conclusion of the War of the Austrian Succession (1748), had worked for the political isolation of Prussia and the friendship of France. Franco-Austrian negotiations, which began in Aug. 1755, made little headway until the news broke of the Anglo-Prussian Convention of Westminister (Jan. 1756). France appeared to have been deserted by Prussia and Louis XV's council of ministers therefore authorized a convention of neutrality and a defensive alliance with Austria, together known as the First Treaty of Versailles. Louis promised not to attack Austrian territory, while Maria Theresa agreed to remain neutral in the Anglo-French War. Except for the latter, each country would support the other with 24,000 troops or a monthly subsidy if attacked by a third party.

VERSAILLES, TREATY OF (1 May 1757), second Franco-Austrian alliance, concluded exactly a year after the first, defensive treaty of Versailles. The immediate cause of this offensive agreement was Frederick II of Prussia's invasion of Saxony (1756-7) during the Seven Years War (1756-63), which stimulated Austria to press for a renewal of co-operation. By the second alliance, France committed herself to considerable involvement in the European war, agreeing to maintain an army of 105,000 men in Germany and a German mercenary force of 10,000 men, and to pay Austria an annual subsidy of 12 million florins. In return for demanding the restoration of Silesia to Austria, France was to receive four cities in the Austrian Netherlands, the remainder being granted to Louis XV's son-in-law, Don Philip of Parma, while that duchy was to revert to Austria.

VERSAILLES, TREATY OF (March 1759), third Franco-Austrian treaty and second offensive alliance between these two powers in the Seven Years War. Choiseul, increasingly preoccupied with the struggle with Britain, cut French subsidies to Austria by half and thus reduced her military support in Germany to 100,000 soldiers. He also refused to guarantee the restoration of Silesia to Austria as a war aim and renounced the arrangement by which Don Philip exchanged Parma for the Austrian Netherlands. This reduction in the French European commitment alleviated Frederick II of Prussia's critical position in 1760.

VERSAILLES, TREATY OF (28 June 1919), peace settlement concluded at the end of the First World War between the Allied Powers and Germany. By its terms Germany lost one-eighth of her pre-war territory and one-tenth of her population. France regained Alsace-Lorraine; Eupen and Malmédy were ceded to Belgium, and northern Schleswig to Denmark. The Saar was placed under international control pending the outcome of a plebiscite to be held after 15 years; in the meantime its valuable coalfields were ceded to France as compensation for the damage inflicted on her own. To the south, a small area was incorporated into the new Czech state, but union between Austria and Germany was forbidden without the unanimous consent of the League of Nations. In the east, Germany was divided by a 'corridor' designed to give Poland access to the sea at Danzig, which became a Free City linked economically and in its foreign relations to Poland. Lithuania absorbed Memel, and the future of Upper Silesia was left to be decided by a referendum in 1921. Finally, the League of Nations, whose Covenant was incorporated into the treaty, assumed responsibility for all Germany's overseas possessions.

The military and economic terms were equally severe. Ostensibly as a prelude to general disarmament, military service was abolished in Germany and the production of heavy armaments prohibited. Her army was limited to 100,000 men and her navy to 16,000. The Rhineland was demilitarized and was to be occupied by Allied troops for up to 15 years. The treaty held Germany responsible for the war and required her to pay reparations to the Allies. The total cost was set in 1921 at £6,600,000,000, but the loss of territory and the internationalization of her waterways dealt a grave blow to Germany's economy and seriously restricted her ability to pay.

Germany's power to moderate these terms had been negligible. Excluded from the peace conference, she had been permitted to submit only one set of proposals, which had been ignored. The Allies allowed Germany five days in which to accept the terms and, under duress, the Weimar Assembly finally agreed to what Germany hereafter considered to have been a *diktat*, and signed the treaty on 28 June 1919. Germany's hostility to the treaty was increasingly reflected in both Britain and the US by a feeling that the terms were excessively severe: only France continued to insist on their strict application, particularly after the US Senate failed to ratify the treaty.

By its very severity the treaty of Versailles sowed the seeds of its own undoing. Harsh and unrealistic, it demanded of Germany more than was feasible or possible, and paid little heed to the idealistic principles of the '14 Points' on which it was allegedly based. Whilst its excesses remained unmoderated, the treaty could only exacerbate post-war tensions and the next 20 years were witness to its unfortunate consequences. Although revision began peacefully under Stresemann, the vestiges of Versailles were finally undermined by the new and virulent German nationalism which the treaty itself had done much to foster.

W. M. Jordan, *Great Britain, France and the German Problem* (New York, 1943).
H. Nicolson, *Peacemaking 1919* (London, 1964).   JL

VERULAMIUM, Roman municipium in Britain (later St Albans) of some 200 acres, founded in c. AD 49 near the Catuvellaunian Prae Wood settlement, commanding northern and north-western routes from Londinium. It was burnt down in Boudicca's revolt in 60 and again in c. 155. Later it underwent reconstruction and was enclosed by a wall and masonry gates (c. 250).

VERVINS, PEACE OF (1598), Franco-Spanish treaty concluded on the initiative of Archduke Albert of Austria and through the mediation of the papal nuncio. It ended the war which Henry IV of France had started in 1595. The French regarded it as 'the most advantageous treaty that France had concluded for 500 years', and the settlement substantially confirmed the terms of the peace of Cateau-Cambrésis (1559) between France and Spain. Philip II agreed to give up Calais and Spain's other conquests in Picardy and Brittany, thus restoring France's territorial integrity which had been undermined in the preceding years of civil war.

VERWOERD, HENDRIK FRANSCH (1901-66), South African politician, who was born in Holland and went to South Africa in 1910. He entered Nationalist Party politics in the 1930s through the *Broederbond* and his editorship of the party newspaper, *Die Transvaaler*. In 1948 he entered parliament as a senator and in 1950 became minister for native affairs. He systematically applied his policies for the complete social segregation and retribalization of Africans. Although these were based on the discriminatory policies of previous South African governments, he vastly extended their scope and ramifications. In 1958 he became prime minister and led South Africa into a republic and out of the British Commonwealth. In 1966 he was assassinated.

VESALIUS, ANDREAS (1514-64), Flemish-born physician, whose great work, *De Humani Corporis Fabrica* (1543), inaugurated the modern study of anatomy. He was professor of surgery at Padua, Bologna, and Basle, and court physician to the Emperor Charles V and Philip II of Spain, having begun as an admirer of Galen, whose works he edited (1541). Yet the depth and precision of knowledge of human physiology contained in his excellently illustrated book started a scientific revolution which was to reject Galen's ideas. In 1564 he was sentenced to death by the Inquisition for body snatching and dissecting, but the verdict was commuted to a pilgrimage to Jerusalem, and he died on the island of Zante on the return journey.

VESPASIAN (T. Flavius Vespasianus) (AD 9–79), Roman Emperor (*reg.* 69–79), first of the Flavian dynasty. Of relatively humble origins, he rose through his competence as a soldier and commanded a legion in Claudius's invasion of Britain in 43. After a period of obscurity, Nero appointed him commander of the army sent to put down the Jewish revolt (66). In July 69 the legions of Egypt and Syria proclaimed him emperor against Vitellius and after the latter's defeat and death he was recognized universally. His main achievement as emperor was the restoration of stability and confidence to the empire after the disastrous Year of the Four Emperors (69). As he had two adult sons his succession posed no problem, and his government therefore concentrated on the exercise of caution and economy. After the suppression of the Batavian and Jewish revolts, the imperial defences were strengthened and provincial administration tightened. Vespasian practised strict economy in state and private expenditure, and his example of frugality set a new social precedent which contrasted with the extravagances of Nero's reign, and he died generally esteemed.

VESPUCCI, AMERIGO (*c.* 1451–1512), Italian explorer, whose Christian name came to be applied to the Western Hemisphere. In the early days of exploration, he made several voyages to the New World in the service of both Spain and Portugal. The most notable was the 1499 voyage along the Venezuelan coast, during which Vespucci was subordinate to Alonso de Ojeda. Convinced that what he had seen could not be Asia, Vespucci wrote his famous *Mundus Novus* letter, which circulated in Europe in 1503. Among those who read it was the German cartographer Waldseemüller, whose 1507 atlas labelled the New World 'America'. The name stuck, and in his own time Vespucci's fame eclipsed that of Columbus. In 1508 the Spanish Crown appointed Vespucci chief pilot (*piloto mayor*), and under his direction a hydrographic bureau and school of navigation was developed at Seville.

VESTIARIAN CONTROVERSY in England, dispute which broke out in 1566–7 over the wearing of the ecclesiastical dress prescribed in Abp Parker's *Advertisements* of March 1566. It was the first indication of the dissatisfaction of the Puritan element within the Anglican ranks with the Elizabethan church settlement.

VESUVIUS, MOUNT, volcano near Naples, whose most famous eruption (24–5 Aug. AD 79) buried Pompeii and Herculaneum in mud and lava, effectively preserving much of both towns for rediscovery in modern times. Pliny the Younger vividly described the death of his uncle, Pliny the Elder, who visited the scene and perished assisting fugitives.

VETERA (mod. Birten, near Xanten, Holland), site of a Roman legionary fortress on the Rhine. It was first occupied in *c.* 16 BC and was a base for Augustus' and Germanicus' invasions of Germany. Up to AD 69 it frequently held two legions. It was destroyed in the Batavian revolt (AD 69), but was soon rebuilt to accommodate one legion. Under Trajan a colony (Ulpia Traiana) was built nearby. The fortress was destroyed by the Franks (*c.* 276) and little is known of the later history of the site.

VETULONIA, one of the 12 cities of the Etruscan League, situated near Grosseto, 164 kms north-west of Rome. Rich in the Oriental type of 'circle tombs' characteristic of Etruscan civilization, it reached its zenith in the 7th cent. BC, probably deriving its great wealth from its proximity to the metal-rich region of north-western Etruria, centred on Massa Marittima. The Romans' tradition that their ancestors had adopted the insignia of their kings and magistrates from Vetulonia is supported by the discovery there of the only surviving example (dated to *c.* 600 BC) of *fasces*, the axe and bundle of rods carried by the attendants of the higher magistrates at Rome. Vetulonia declined in the 6th cent., but revived under Roman rule after 300 BC.

VIC, PEACE OF (1632), settlement forced by Richelieu upon Charles, Duc de Guise and Lorraine, for championing the cause of Louis XIII's rebellious brother, Gaston of Orléans. The latter had sought refuge in Lorraine after the Day of Dupes (1631) and married Charles's sister, Margaret (3 Jan.), although he abandoned her and fled to Brussels as French armies marched on Nancy. On 6 Jan. Charles came to terms with France, ceding Lorraine's border strongholds.

VICEROY OF INDIA, title of the governor-general after 1858. It occurs first in Queen Victoria's Proclamation of 1858 but had no statutory sanction and its origin was due to usage and convention. The viceroyalty ceased with independence in 1947.

VICEROYALTIES, largest territorial divisions of the Spanish American empire. In Habsburg times there were two viceroyalites. One was that of New Spain (1529), comprising all territory from Central America north, and the West Indies and the Philippines, centred in Mexico City. The second, centred in Lima (1544), encompassed Spain's South American possessions, and the Peruvian viceroy was of higher rank than his Mexican counterpart. Except in military matters, in practice neither viceroy exercised more than nominal authority outside the *audiencia* district of which he was president. Under the Bourbons, two new viceroyalties were created. That of New Granada (1739) was composed of roughly modern Panama, Ecuador, Colombia, and Venezuela, while that of Buenos Aires (1776) encompassed modern Paraguay, Argentina, Uruguay, and Bolivia.

VICEROYS, chief officers in the Spanish American empire, in whom was vested final responsibility for administration and warfare. The viceroy's theoretically wide powers were limited in practice by the Crown's consistent efforts to centralize decision-making in Madrid, particularly where expenditures were concerned, and by the necessity to consult with the *audiencia* before important action was taken. Viceroys served for a varying number of years and were paid handsome salaries. Many came from Spain's noblest and most distinguished families, although in the 18th cent. military experience and prior American service were also important. Most viceroys tended to be able men, and some (Mendoza, Toledo, the younger Revillagigedo) were extraordinarily so. After 1763 the office existed in Portuguese Brazil, but with more limited powers.

VICHY GOVERNMENT (1940–4), in France, regime, headed by Marshal Pétain, set up in France after her defeat by Germany in the Second World War. The regime began on 10 July 1940, when the parliament of the Third Republic voted full powers to Pétain, then prime minister under the existing constitution. In the new 'French state' Pétain held both legislative and executive powers, and no independent political institutions existed. His government had already signed the armistice dividing France into occupied and unoccupied zones. In principle, Vichy's authority extended to both, but it was only in the unoccupied zone in southern France it had any real freedom of action. Under the armistice it kept control of the navy and a lightly armed army. The regime also retained authority over French North Africa and the overseas colonies (though the latter were successively to go over to De Gaulle).

The internal history of the regime falls into two phases, separated by the German occupation of the whole country in 1942. In the first phase those in power were torn between defiance of Germany and collaboration based on the acceptance of her victory. Laval, the real creator of the regime and at first its dominant figure, supported collaboration, and this policy was symbolized by Pétain's meeting with Hitler at Montoire (Oct. 1940). But Pétain dismissed Laval in Dec. 1940, and a brief anti-German interlude followed under Flandin. Collaborationism returned, however, with the appointment of Darlan (Feb. 1941). In April 1942 Laval himself returned to power, and was head of government for the rest of the regime's existence.

The first phase was the period of the 'National Revolution', when conservatives who blamed France's defeat on the corrupting influence of democracy tried to regenerate France on lines indicated by the official slogan 'Work, Family, Fatherland'. The regime's policies, inspired partly by Catholicism and partly by the doctrines of Maurras, included the promotion of youth movements, anti-Semitic legislation, and the corporatist organization of peasants and industrial workers.

The occupation of the whole of France deprived the regime of any real autonomy. It was forced into ever closer collaboration with the Germans, and had to acquiesce in the plunder of French resources and the sending of French forced labour to Germany. The aged Pétain ceased to have much control over the government, which came to include men who were openly pro-Germans, like Darnand and Déat. In its early years the regime had undoubtedly been supported by most Frenchmen, but after 1942 its original claim to be protecting France from the excesses of direct German rule became less valid, and the Resistance became a serious force. The Vichy regime ended with the Liberation, when Pétain and Laval were carried off to Germany.

The Vichy episode caused many problems of conscience, and created bitter and long-lasting political divisions. After the war, there was a strong reaction against it, and those connected with it were tried and punished, but recent judgements have been more discriminating.

R. Aron, *The Vichy Regime, 1940–44* (London, 1958).   RDA

VICKSBURG, in the US, city situated on bluffs to the east of the Mississippi river and the scene of a major American Civil War campaign. With the fall of New Orleans (April 1862), Vicksburg became the chief Confederate stronghold on the Mississippi. It was unsuccessfully attacked by Admiral Farragut's fleet (May–June 1862), and Gen. Sherman's assault on Chickasaw Bluffs, supported by Admiral Porter's gunboats, was repulsed (29 Dec. 1862). Gen. Grant abandoned attacks on the city from his base at Memphis, circled to the west of Vicksburg, recrossed the Mississippi to the south, and drove two Confederate brigades out of Port Gibson (1 May 1863). His subordinate generals, Sherman and McPherson, forced Confederate Gen. Johnson to retire from Jackson, TN (14 May), while Grant turned westwards and pinned Gen. Pemberton's 32,000 troops within the defences of Vicksburg. After two costly assaults (19 and 22 May) Grant's army, eventually numbering 70,000, besieged the city, which surrendered on 4 July. With the fall of Fort Hudson (9 July 1863) Union control of the Mississippi was assured, and the Confederacy divided. Federal victories at Vicksburg and Gettysburg (3 July 1863) marked a turning point in the Civil War.

VICO, GIOVANNI BATTISTA (1668–1744), Italian philosopher and lawyer, who was regarded as the most original thinker in 18th-cent. Italy. In 1697 he became professor of rhetoric in Naples University, where he produced a novel philosophy of history, *Principii d'una Scienza Nuova* (1725), an attempt to discover the laws common to the evolution of all society.

VICTOR AMADEUS I (1587–1637), Duke of Savoy (*reg.* 1630–1637), son of Charles Emmanuel I. He married Christine, sister of Louis XIII (1620), and therefore, after becoming duke (1630), he tended to take a pro-French line during the Thirty Years War. He signed a secret treaty with France, agreeing to surrender the valuable fortress of Pinerolo in

return for part of Montferrat after the peace of Cherasco had officially neutralized the fort (1631). Later, he campaigned with the French until 1636.

VICTOR AMADEUS II (1666–1732), first King of Savoy (*reg.* 1675–1730), son of Charles Emmanuel II. He succeeded to the throne at the age of nine, but his mother governed for him, usually in the interests of France, until, at 16, he took over the government himself. He then broke with France and went over to the allied side in the War of the League of Augsburg (1693). Later he returned to the French side, having failed to secure the rewards he desired (1696, 1701). When the War of the Spanish Succession began to go against France, he changed sides yet again (1703) and was eventually recompensed with the kingdom of Sicily (1713), which he was forced to exchange for Sardinia by the terms of the Quadruple Alliance (1718). Thus was established the kingdom of Sardinia-Piedmont which he endowed with modern institutions and ruled with a considerable degree of benevolence. Having abdicated in 1730 in favour of his son, Charles Emmanuel III, he later changed his mind, and tried to reverse his decision, but he was arrested and imprisoned.

VICTOR AMADEUS III (1726–96), King of Sardinia (*reg.* 1773–96), succeeded his father, Charles Emmanuel III. He married a daughter of Philip V of Spain, patronized the arts and sciences, and instigated improvements to the army. Two of his daughters having married brothers of Louis XVI of France (whom the revolutionaries had set aside), he joined the anti-French coalition in 1792, but was unable to prevent the Revolutionary armies from overrunning his territories in 1792 and 1794. After Napoleon I's offensive of 1796, he surrendered Savoy and Nice to France in order to achieve peace.

VICTOR EMMANUEL II (1820–78), King of Italy (*reg.* 1861–78). As ruler of Piedmont, Victor Emmanuel had worked with Cavour to create a united Italian state under Piedmontese leadership. The mutual respect between the king and Garibaldi reconciled many republicans to the monarchy and his moderation and good sense were an important factor in establishing the new state. Although, after 1870, parliament gained strength at the expense of the monarchy, Victor Emmanuel exercised considerable authority, especially in foreign affairs. His visits to Germany and Austria (1873) reduced the tension caused by Franco-Italian hostility and his personal regard for the pope moderated the influence of anti-clericalism. The king attracted an emotional loyalty from his subjects that was not accorded to his successors.

VICTOR EMMANUEL III (1869–1947), King of Italy (*reg.* 1900–46), whose reign began hopefully. He gave Giolitti unstinting support and played an active part in formulating foreign policy, seeking to free Italy from exclusive dependence on the Triple Alliance. He controlled the crisis following the announcement of the treaty of London (1915), which resulted in Italian intervention on the side of the Allies. But after the First World War he was less decisive in his reaction to fascism. He did not personally support Mussolini, but his passive attitude made him his accomplice. He kept his own throne at the expense of the future of the monarchy, which fell after his abdication (9 May 1946) and a plebiscite (2 June 1946).

VICTORIA (1819–1901), Queen of Britain (*reg.* 1837–1901), Britain's longest-ruling sovereign, who restored the prestige of the monarchy and provided a pattern of ordered family life and strict morality that was a model for the Victorian middle classes, whose prejudices she shared and reinforced. Despite her determination and her devotion to public affairs, her inability to influence politics decisively showed that the contradictions inherent in constitutional monarchy had finally been resolved.

The queen's dependence on her prime minister, Melbourne, in the first years of her reign gave way after her marriage (1840) to complete devotion to Albert, the prince consort, who reinforced her desire for propriety. The royal couple were well informed and had a good grasp of the business of state; moreover they believed that the sovereign retained some prerogative in foreign affairs, a belief which caused conflict with Palmerston. In general, although the queen could express disapproval and occasionally influence the choice of individual ministers, in the last resort she could influence neither policy nor the composition of the government.

The death of Albert in 1861 led to a long period of withdrawal from public affairs that was not appreciated by the queen's subjects. The efforts of her prime minister, Gladstone, during the 1870s to bring her back into the mainstream of national life were a factor in the queen's increasingly difficult relationship with Gladstone. By contrast, she felt closely drawn to Disraeli, through whose inspiration she became empress of India (1877). At her jubilees of 1887 and 1897 there were nation-wide demonstrations of affection and reverence. She was mourned as the symbol of the age to which she gave her name and the dignified figurehead of the British empire. Her children had married into foreign royal houses, and she had become the matriarchal figure of Europe.

Elizabeth Longford, *Victoria R.I.* (London, 1964).
F. M. Hardie, *Political Influence of Queen Victoria 1861–1901* (London, 1963). S.H.

VICTORIA, GUADALUPE (MIGUEL FERNÁNDEZ FELIX) (1789–1843), Mexican politician and first president of the republic (1824–9). Throughout the struggle for national independence he was consistently a republican, having joined Father Hidalgo's abortive movement in 1810, and he persisted in his rebellion until Augustin Iturbide's monarchical plan of Iguala (1821) offered the republicans a chance to obtain independence through co-operation.

Victoria suffered persecution again during the period of Iturbide's empire (1821–3) and joined in the revolt against him. He defeated Nicolás Bravo for the presidency and initiated a neutral administration, attempting to forestall conflict between the aristocratic and popular factions within creole society. Popular anti-Spanish local revolts threatened his regime (1827) and an official persecution of the peninsular Spaniards was undertaken. A popular revolt on behalf of Gen. Vicente Guerrero forced Victoria from office in 1829.

VICTORIA, Australia's second most populous state, settled in the 1830s by pastoralists from Tas. and NSW. Immigrants attracted to the rich goldfields in the 1850s remained to help to shape Australian attitudes towards coloured immigration and protection. Vic.'s growth after 1860, based on wool, gold, the building industry, and manufacturing, was equalled only by that of free-trade NSW. Irrigation works led to successful, though erratic, agricultural development in the 20th cent., and secondary industry flourished from the 1940s, with future expansion promised by oil and natural gas deposits in Bass Strait. A traditional, if exaggerated, rivalry persisted between Sydney and the rapidly expanding but more sedate Vic. capital, Melbourne, Australia's commercial centre, at least until the 1960s.

VICUÑA MACKENNA, BENJAMIN (1831–86), Chilean historian, journalist, and politician, who spent many years in political exile and wrote voluminous and numerous histories of Chile and prominent Chileans.

VIDYASAGAR, ISWARCHANDRA (1820–91), Indian educationalist and social reformer, who was professor of Sanskrit in Calcutta. Although an orthodox Hindu, he advocated the remarriage of Hindu widows and believed in Western education.

VIEIRA, ANTÔNIO (1608–97), Brazilian Jesuit and writer, who became involved in every controversial issue of his times in Brazil and Portugal and was an uncompromising opponent of Indian slavery. His published *Sermons* and *Letters* place him among the leading 17th-cent. Portuguese prose stylists.

VIENNA, city established on the site of a Roman military settlement, which became the capital of the east German march formed in 10th cent. to protect Bavaria. Its margraves of the Babenberg dynasty (extinct 1246) made it into a wealthy city and it became the capital of the Habsburgs in 1278. By the 14th cent. it was second in size and wealth only to Cologne among German cities, and as its Habsburg masters achieved imperial dignity and created a great state, so Vienna prospered with them. The disintegration of the Habsburg empire in 1918 left Vienna as the huge capital of a little Austrian state and it never recovered its 19th-cent. eminence.

VIENNA AWARD (Nov. 1938), settlement of the Czech–Hungarian frontier by Germany and Italy. It formed the third stage in the disintegration of Czechoslovakia when, after Munich and the transference of Teschen to Poland, Hungary also gained considerable territory along her southern borders. These moves were to a large extent co-ordinated by Hitler but, as usual, he was able to turn existing problems to his own advantage. Prague and Budapest had been in dispute since 1919, almost 1 million Hungarians having been included in Czechoslovakia. From Aug. 1938 Hitler put pressure on Admiral Horthy, Regent of Hungary, to participate in at least a threat of military action against the Czechs, but Hungary was militarily weak, wary of the Little Entente, and merely publicized its claims before the Western Powers. In Sept. Horthy demanded a plebiscite, and Western weakness rather than German insistence had encouraged him to raise his terms. Advised by Britain to capitulate, the Czechs suggested a mixed commission of experts, and a conference met at Komarno early in Oct. The Hungarian delegates demanded an ethnic frontier as indicated by the 1910 census, and plebiscites in the rest of Slovakia and Ruthenia. They plainly hoped that the populations of these areas would voluntarily join Hungary. Talks broke down because the Czechs resisted this proposal and Hungary appealed to the Four Power signatories of Munich and mobilized along the Czech frontier. Germany and Italy prevented the dispute from spreading, but did not consult Britain and France, and agreed to arbitrate late in Oct. Their award disappointed the Hungarians because Hitler now preferred to keep Slovakia united, as a reliable satellite. A purely ethnic frontier was established, giving Horthy 31,100 sq. kms and about 1 million people, and, drawn up by such criteria, it was not surprising that enormous economic dislocation resulted. KM

VIENNA AWARD (1940), second indication of Germany's control of south-eastern Europe which, after Munich, became political as well as economic. The award settled a dispute between Hungary and Rumania which in the summer of 1940 had threatened to explode into war. The Soviet occupation of Bessarabia and Ukrainian Bukovina in July had triggered off a scramble for Rumania by Bulgaria and Hungary. Bulgaria settled for modest territorial gains in the south, but Hungarian aims were more grandiose: they had demanded most of Transylvania, and were prepared to back up their claims with force. The issue was of European importance because south-eastern Europe was regarded by both Russia and Germany as their sphere of influence. While fruitless talks went on between the Hungarian and Rumanian governments, in mid-Aug. Hitler was involved in the battle of Britain, thus his policy was the reverse of fishing in troubled waters. He wanted a peaceful settlement, so that Russia could not be given the excuse to march in and seize the crucial Rumanian oilfields. Therefore he threatened all the participants with an end to military supplies and economic contacts, if they did not compose their differences. In late

Aug. Ribbentrop and Ciano summoned the two claimants to Vienna to force them to accept Hitler's compromise; Rumania was to lose 113,000 sq. kms of Transylvania and 2½ million people. Manoilescu, the Rumanian delegate, had to be threatened with war before he would agree, and Teleki of Hungary was hardly more amenable; but on 30 Aug. the agreement was signed. The prime result was the abdication of King Carol of Rumania and a period of political chaos, exactly what Hitler had hoped to avoid, but the Germans moved swiftly and forestalled Russia's possible intervention by occupying the Ploesti oilfields in Oct. Axis influence in south-eastern Europe was now predominant.   KM

VIENNA (or SEYMOUR) CLAUSE (1702), additional clause in the treaty of the grand alliance nations clarifying the English war aim of 'security'. Ex-King James II died on 16 Sept. 1701, only nine days after the signing of the grand alliance. Louis XIV recognized James's son as King of England, Scotland, and Ireland, and treated him as such. He had recognized William as King of England at the peace of Ryswick, but he now referred to Anne (as he had done consistently) simply as the princess of Denmark. To many Englishmen it seemed that Louis was telling them whom they should have for their monarch. Hence on 21 Jan. 1702 a resolution of the House of Commons, moved by Sir Edward Seymour, requested that a new clause should be inserted into the treaty of grand alliance. The Seymour clause stated that peace should not be made before reparation had been obtained for William for this great indignity to himself and the English nation. It was agreed to without trouble by the Dutch, but the emperor proved most reluctant.

VIENNA CONFERENCE (1853) produced the Vienna Note, in which Britain, France, Austria, and Prussia drew up a list of the concessions they thought Turkey could safely make to Russia, to end the drift towards war, following Russia's occupation of the Danubian principalities and the arrival of British and French fleets at Besika Bay. Britain and France were anxious that if it came to war in the Crimea, Austria and Prussia would be involved, but both these countries were bent on neutrality. Turkey's rejection of the note caused Russia to interpret it to support her claim to protect Turkish Orthodox Christians. Britain and France then felt forced to take action independently of the Central Powers to show that their intention to bolster up Turkey against Russian encroachments was serious.

VIENNA CONFERENCE (1855), abortive attempt to end the Crimean war following the death of Nicholas I and the fall of Aberdeen's administration in Britain. The failure of the conference was mainly due to the aggressive policy of Palmerston in Britain and the continued reluctance of Austria to be drawn into the war. Austria demanded a Franco-British guarantee of her territory before she would run the risk of a Russian invasion. Palmerston proposed to neutralize the Black Sea. The failure to reach a compromise meant that there was no alternative to the resumption of hostilities.

VIENNA, CONGRESS OF (1814–15), meeting of European plenipotentiaries to settle outstanding territorial questions after the defeat of Napoleon I and after the first peace of Paris, whose eight signatories invited all countries taking part in the French Wars to the Congress. The main work was done by the 'Four' great powers of the Quadruple Alliance, which became the 'Five' by the admission of France (Jan. 1815). The chief problems to be discussed concerned Poland, Saxony, Germany, Italy, and Switzerland and the main disagreement was over the Polish–Saxon question. In Jan. 1815 Austria, France, and Britain signed a secret alliance against Prussia and Russia. This exercise in brinkmanship made negotiation possible and it was finally agreed (Feb. 1815) that Prussia should have some Saxon territory and that under the tsar's protection a kingdom of Poland should be created with a population of just over 3 million people. Austria received

compensation in Italy for her loss of the Netherlands; the German Confederation was set up; and the perpetual neutrality of Switzerland guaranteed.

The aims of Metternich, Castlereagh, and Talleyrand were primarily to create balance of power in Europe and to ensure that no country be left so unsatisfied that it would resort to war. They were also concerned at Russia's westward advance, but because of Frederick William III's support for the tsar could do little to curb it. The Final Act of the Congress, at its only plenary session, took place on 9 June 1815. Seven of the eight convening powers signed it, and the minor powers adhered to it.

The Vienna settlement came in for severe criticism after the middle of the 19th cent. because it was said to ignore the national aspirations of the peoples concerned and to perpetuate autocracy. To the statesmen at Vienna, liberalism and nationalism were temporary phenomena arising from the political heresy of the French Revolution, for all were European rather than national in outlook. Concern for the governed was shown in the guarantees for the national minority of the enlarged Holland and some liberalism in the order to each sovereign in the German Confederation to grant a constitution to his subjects. Another advance was due to the intermittent use of the principle of legitimacy, which recognized right, not might, as the basis of sovereignty. The greatest injustices—Norway to Sweden, Finland to Russia, Lombardy and Venetia to Austria—were rewards and compensations to victors, and only the last-mentioned occurred at Vienna.

In the 20th cent. criticism has been extended to the German settlement. At the time, Talleyrand warned of the dangers of strengthening Prussia, and others pressed Metternich to restore the Habsburgs as emperors of Germany. The subsequent eclipse of Austria by Prussia came about largely because of economic growth factors which changed the patterns of political power in a way that the statesmen at Vienna could hardly have been expected to foresee. The Vienna settlement remained virtually unchanged for 40 years, and no major European war occurred for nearly a century, and this may be considered the measure of its success.

Harold Nicolson, *The Congress of Vienna* (London, 1946).
                                                                              DMK

VIENNA, OTTOMAN SIEGES OF. The first Ottoman siege of Vienna occurred in 1529 during the reign of Sultan Suleiman Qanuni. Bad weather hindered the march of the Ottomans, and Suleiman did not reach Vienna until 27 Sept. (having left his large siege guns behind), when the campaign season was almost over. The town had been furnished, meanwhile, with a strong garrison and ample supplies and all Ottoman attempts to storm the walls were repulsed. On 15 Oct. the sultan began a long and difficult withdrawal to Buda and Belgrade and thence to Istanbul.

The second Ottoman siege of Vienna was undertaken in 1683 during the reign of Sultan Mehemmed IV. Qara Mustafa Pasha, the grand vizier, at the head of a powerful and well-equipped force, reached Vienna on 14 July and selected the southern sector of the walls as the main object of attack. The Christian defence, under Graf Stahremberg, was skilful and vigorous. North of the Danube, Charles of Lorraine held back the sultan's Hungarian allies and kept open the routes along which aid might come to the fortress. Meanwhile, troops from the German principalities and also from Poland (under the soldier-king, John Sobieski) began to gather for the liberation of Vienna. Qara Mustafa had failed to maintain a close watch over the western approaches to the city and on 12 Sept. the Christian relief forces attacked the Ottomans from the Kahlenberg ridge and broke into their camp before the walls of the beleaguered city. The rout of the Ottomans was complete. The rescue of Vienna was the prelude to the long war of the Sacra Liga (1684–99), which saw Austria, Venice, and Poland ranged against the Ottoman empire.   VJP

VIENNA REVOLUTION (1848), stimulated by a similar event in France, began with a mob demanding Metternich's resignation. This was followed by demonstrations and riots. In April, the establishment of a Constituent Assembly was promised and the court fled to Innsbruck. The Assembly proved overwhelmingly moderate and completed the emancipation of serfs by abolishing private justice and labour dues. When Kossuth appealed to the assembly to mediate between him and the monarchy, it sent troops against him. More disorders occurred in Oct., so court and assembly both moved to Olmütz. The radicals were defeated by Windischgrätz and Jellačič, Schwarzenberg took over the government, and in Dec. the Emperor Ferdinand abdicated in favour of his nephew, the 18-year-old Francis Joseph. This marked the end of the revolution, though the assembly sat until it was dissolved in March 1849.

VIENNA, TREATY OF (1515), agreement between Sigismund I of Poland and the Emperor Maximilian I of Habsburg, concluded on 22 July after a preliminary arrangement had been reached at Pressburg on 20 May. Hostilities were ended between Poland and the empire, the Habsburgs abandoned their Muscovite allies, and the problems of the Teutonic Order were settled. The Vienna negotiations also resolved the question of the Hungaro-Bohemian succession. King Louis Jagiellon of Hungary-Bohemia was married to Maximilian's grand-daughter, Mary, while his sister, Anne, was betrothed to Maximilian's grandson, Archduke Ferdinand. This double arrangement proved very important on the death of Louis at Mohacz (1526). The crowns of Hungary and Bohemia passed to Habsburg control, where, despite intermittent resistance, they remained for nearly 400 years.

VIENNA, TREATY OF (1719), agreement concluded between the Emperor Charles VI, George I of Britain and Hanover, and Augustus II of Saxony-Poland (Jan. 1719), guaranteeing Poland's frontiers and deciding that Peter I of Russia should be forced to evacuate Mecklenburg and Poland, which his troops had invaded in 1716.

VIENNA, TREATY OF (1725), negotiated between the Emperor Charles VI and Philip V of Spain, ending the Spanish and imperial adhesion to the Quadruple Alliance (1718). Philip V undertook to guarantee the Pragmatic Sanction and to support and give trading concessions to the Ostend Co. In return, the emperor promised to support the recovery of Gibraltar and Minorca, but acknowledged no obligation to fight for them and agreed to support the investiture of Don Carlos in the Italian duchies. In addition, a vague promise of the marriage of Don Carlos to an archduchess was discussed, though no details were agreed. Thus Philip V gained nothing more than he was already entitled to by the Quadruple Alliance, but undertook new and onerous obligations. However, the boastings of the Spanish negotiator, Ripperda, convinced Britain and France that the treaty included secret clauses directed against them and resulted in their counter-alliance under the treaty of Hanover (1725).

VIENNA, TREATY OF (1731), negotiated between the Emperor Charles VI, Britain, and the United Provinces, by which Walpole hoped to maintain European peace, gaining Austrian acceptance of the succession of Don Carlos to the Italian duchies. The emperor agreed to withdraw imperial troops and admit Don Carlos to Parma and Piacenza. In addition, he agreed to invest George II with Bremen and Verden and to suspend the operations of the Ostend Co. In return, Britain and the United Provinces guaranteed the Pragmatic Sanction and imperial possessions.

The treaty of Vienna marked the end of Britain's close alliance with France inagurated by Stanhope (though the alliance did not formally lapse until 1744) and a return to the old system of William III, namely close co-operation with the emperor and the Dutch.

VIENNA, TREATY OF (1738), ratifying the provisional peace signed to end the War of the Polish Succession (1735). Augustus III of Saxony was recognized as King of Poland, Stanislaus Leszczynski having renounced the throne 'voluntarily and for the sake of peace', and receiving as compensation Lorraine and Bar, which on his death were to go to France (annexed 1766). The kingdom of the Two Sicilies was given to Don Carlos, who restored Parma and Piacenza to the emperor. The emperor also regained the Milanese, with the exception of Novara and Tortona, which were awarded to Charles Emmanuel of Sardinia. In return, Sardinia and France guaranteed the Pragmatic Sanction. The treaty thus established a Spanish Bourbon dominance in southern Italy and Habsburg dominance in northern Italy, extended French defensible frontiers, and emphasized the diplomatic isolation of Britain, who played no part in the negotiations after being the arbiter of Europe for two decades.

VIENNA TREATY (1864), after the Austro-Prussian victory over Denmark, replaced the treaty of London (1852). Denmark ceded Schleswig, Holstein, and Lauenburg to Prussia and Austria, and agreed to accept any subsequent arrangement for the territories. Prussia hoped to annex them, and Austria hoped for compensation in Silesia and a guarantee of her remaining Italian possessions. Settlement was effected by the Convention of Gastein (1865). The treaty marked the turning-point in the struggle between Austria and Prussia for domination in Germany.

VIET-CONG, name by which supporters of the Front for the Liberation of South Viet-nam were known, principally by their opponents, during the 1960s. It means literally 'Vietnamese Communists', and was originally introduced by the South Viet-namese government some years before the creation of the front in 1960, in order to differentiate between the communists and the Viet-Minh front, which had included many non-communist nationalists.

VIET-MINH, abbreviated form of the political front which won Viet-namese independence from the French in 1954; its full name was Viet-Nam Doc-Lap Dong-Minh: Viet-nam Independence League. It was formed in May 1941, at a conference of the Indo-Chinese Communist Party in Cao-Bang province, North Viet-nam, and was throughout its existence dominated by its leading communist members, notably Ho Chi Minh, Pham Van Dong, and Vo Nguyen Giap.

VIET-NAM WAR, conflict between communists and anti-communists in Viet-nam during the 1960s, which led to large-scale US involvement from 1965. Two views exist regarding the origins of the war: the communists considering it to be an 'internal' rebellion against American activity in South Viet-nam, beginning about 1958–9; the Americans insisting that North Viet-nam committed 'aggression' against the South by infiltrating men and supplies across the 17th parallel. It is clear that by 1963 the North was sending in and supplying increasing numbers of guerrilla troops, while the Americans by the end of that year had troops in Viet-nam as military 'advisers'. During 1964 the war went very much in the communists' favour, so that by early 1965 the Saigon government and army were in a state of near-collapse. A major defeat of Saigon government forces occurred at Binh-Gia, east of Saigon in Jan. 1965. American policy was already geared for a possible intervention in greater strength. In Aug. 1964 the Gulf of Tonking Incident had been followed by bombing raids on North Viet-nam and by a US Congress resolution empowering President Johnson to take any necessary action. On the basis of that resolution, in March 1965 he implemented a policy of regular bombing raids on the North, which lasted, with a few short interruptions, till 1968. In July 1965 the US began to send in combat troops, and the ground war in the South moved into a new phase of 'escalation'. By the end of 1967 there were over

500,000 US troops in Viet-nam, together with contingents from South Korea, Australia, the Philippines, and Thailand; there were also 40,000 American forces in the latter country. The communists responded to the new situation by obtaining greater military aid from the USSR, including fighter-planes and ground-to-air missiles, and by sending their own regular troops to fight alongside the guerrillas in the South. In Jan. 1968, when the situation seemed to have reached an impasse, the communists launched their 'Tet offensive', with attacks on 48 towns and bases in the South, one of which penetrated the US embassy compound in Saigon. The offensive failed to end the war, but it gave the communists sufficient confidence to enter into negotiations with the Americans in Paris in May 1968, in return for a limitation of the bombing of the North. In Nov. 1968 these negotiations grew into a full-scale peace conference when the US halted its bombing of the North completely. The war nevertheless continued throughout 1969, both sides claiming great progress, but neither achieving victory. In April 1970 the conflict spread to Cambodia, which had long been a 'sanctuary' for communist troops, South Viet-namese and American forces both invading the country.   RBS

VIGER, DENIS-BENJAMIN (1774–1861), French Canadian politician and journalist, who founded *Le Spectateur* (1813) and was a member of the Lower Canada legislature (1808–1830). He was sent to Britain to place French-Canadian grievances before parliament (1828) and served as the London agent for Lower Canada (1831–5). Although he took no part in the rebellion of 1837, he was arrested on suspicion of complicity (1838) and spent 18 months in jail without being charged or tried. He later lost the support of his fellow nationalists because of his support of the non-partisan policies of the governor, Sir Charles Metcalfe. He served in the legislature of Upper Canada and on the Executive Council (1848–58). He firmly supported the view that French Canada was Britain's principal defence against American infiltration of the colony and must go to any lengths, even rebellion, to maintain its cultural independence.

VIGEVANO, CONVENTION OF (1696), agreement concluded between Victor Amadeus of Savoy, the Emperor Leopold, and Charles II of Spain, following the secret treaty of Turin between Savoy and France. The convention, which was accepted immediately by Louis XIV, provided for the neutrality of Italy for the rest of the War of the League of Augsburg, allowing Austrian troops to withdraw from Italy to deal with the Turks.

VIGLIUS AB AYTTA VAN ZUICHEM (1507–77), Dutch lawyer and loyal servant of the Spanish Crown and of the Catholic Church. He was appointed president of the council of justice by the Emperor Charles V (1549); he was also chancellor of the Order of the Fleece and adviser, under Granvelle, to the regent of the Netherlands, Margaret of Parma. He later co-operated with the Duke of Alva and was imprisoned by the estates of Brabant for his pro-Spanish activities (1576).

VIGNOLA, GIACOMO BAROGGIO DE (1507–73), Italian Renaissance architect, whose work had a profound influence on Italian and French ecclesiastical architecture. He studied at Bologna and was appointed a papal architect in 1551, succeeding Michelangelo as chief architect of St Peter's in 1564. Two of his best-known achievements are the Villa Giulia, which he designed (1550–5), for Pope Julius III, and the church of the Gesu, which has a cruciform plan of a nave with side chapels. He was also a writer of architectural theory, *eg, The Rule of the Five Orders* (1562).

VIGO, BATTLE OF (1702), Anglo-Dutch naval victory over the French at the onset of the War of the Spanish Succession. A Spanish treasure fleet, with a French convoy commanded by Châteaurenault, put into Vigo Bay in northern Spain, where it was surprised by an allied force. The French set fire to the ships after most of the cargo had been unloaded, but the entire Franco-Spanish force was either destroyed or captured. This encouraged Portugal to enter the war on the allied side.

VIJAYABAHU I (*reg.* 1055–1110), King of Ceylon, who was only loosely connected with the earlier kings of Anuradhapura, but achieved prestige and glory as a leader who united the Sinhalese in their struggle against the South Indian Cholas. He liberated the island in 1070 by taking the capital, Polonnaruva, and then kept it united until his death. He took a great interest in promoting irrigation and the Buddhist religion.

VIJAYANAGAR, EMPIRE OF (1336–1565), Hindu kingdom embodying Telugu and Canarese forms of Hinduism, and controlling most of India south of the Kistna and Tungabhadra rivers for more than two centuries. The capital, Vijayanagar, was built (1536–43) about 30 miles (48 kms) west of Bellary, south of the Tungabhadra. The empire's exact origin is disputed, but it is certain that it was established as a reaction against the Muslim invasion of the Deccan under Ala-ud-din Khilji and the recoil of Muhammad Tughluq from Warangal (1335–6). The founders were two brothers, Harihara (*reg.* 1336–54) and Bukka (*reg.* 1354–77), former officers of overthrown Hindu kingdoms, who organized an empire on a bureaucratic basis covering all south India. Their governors were *nayak*s or deputies, who were supported by imperial garrisons and military colonies. Controlling the rich trade with south-east Asia and the Middle East, they had large resources. They were engaged in constant wars with the Bahmani Muslim kingdom of the Deccan and, after its break-up, with its successor states.

The first dynasty was replaced by the Saluvas (1486), who gave way to the Tuluvas (1503–65). Krishnadeva Raya (*reg.* 1509–29) was the greatest Vijayanagar ruler, taking Raichur and its *doab* from the Bijapur sultan. From 1542 power passed to Ramaraja, whose policy of interference in Deccan wars led to a coalition of four sultans and eventually to his overthrow at Talikota (1565). Vijayanagar was sacked and never recovered. Ramaraja's brother, Tirumala, founded the Aravidu dynasty (*c.* 1570) at Penugonda. Venkata II (*reg.* c. 1586—1614) moved to Chandragiri and was the last ruler of any note.

R. Sewell, *A Forgotten Empire* (London, 1900).
H. Heras, *The Aravidu Dynasty of Vijayanagar* (Madras, 1927).   TGPS

VIKING, word of disputed etymology, normally used in the sense of 'Scandinavian pirate' and applied to describe Norsemen during the great age of Scandinavian expansion overseas (*c.* 800–*c.* 1066). The main causes of the Viking expansion were probably two-fold: rapid population growth and technological advances in the development of ships.

VILLA, FRANCISCO or 'PANCHO' (DOROTEO ARANGO) (1877–1923), Mexican politician from Durango, who at one time possessed the most powerful military band in the republic (1913–15). Though his revolutionary programme was never clear, he was favourably inclined towards the agrarians and he offered protection to the foreign mine operators in the north. His principal base of operations was Chihuahua. Here he recruited his famous cavalry (*dorados*) among the cowboys of the desert plains.

He had fled from peonage as a boy in Durango and became a prominent cattle rustler in the north. Francisco I. Madero offered him a pardon and summoned him to the revolution (1910). Villa supported Madero unswervingly and after his assassination he defied Victoriano Huerta and joined forces with Venustiano Carranza. The seeds of discord were apparent in the new alliance and Villa soon found Carranza favouring Álvaro Obregón in the drive for Mexico City. A clash between Obregón and Villa was seemingly unavoidable. Villa enlisted the aid of Emiliano Zapata of the south, but with little result. Obregón shattered Villa's forces at the battle of Celaya (1915).

The US had withdrawn its support from Villa, favouring Carranza instead. Villa sought to avenge himself while embarrassing Carranza by raiding Columbus, New Mexico (1916). He continued to raid in the north until Obregón revolted against Carranza (1920). Villa then retired to a ranch in Durango. Later he was murdered in an ambush (1923) which many believed to be the work of Plutarco Elías Calles's henchmen.   HDS

VILLA GUISTI, near Padua, used as a headquarters by the Italian supreme command in 1918. It was here that Austro-Hungarian delegates negotiated and signed the armistice terms ending the Italian campaign in the First World War. Italy thereafter took 'defensive' control of Austrian territory, including Dalmatia.

VILLAFRANCA (1859), armistice between France and Austria following the French victory at Solferino. France had been fighting in support of Piedmont's ambition to drive the Austrians out of northern Italy and the armistice secured Lombardy for Piedmont, but without the strategic Quadrilateral forts. Austria was left in control of Venetia and promised that the deposed rulers of Tuscany and Modena would be reinstated. Cavour regarded the armistice (confirmed at the peace of Zürich) as a betrayal, but Napoleon III had never been anxious to see Piedmont become over-powerful and he was anxious not to provoke Prussia, who had mobilized 460,000 men. Any agreement could only be temporary until the Italian question was solved. Villafranca was abrogated in 1860, when the Central Duchies, including Tuscany and Modena, were annexed by Piedmont.

VILLAFRANCA, BATTLE OF (Sept. 1515), victory of Francis I's French army over the Milanese troops of Duke Massimiliano Sforza in the Lombardy plain of Italy. It was the prelude to the French victory over the Swiss at Marignano.

VILLALAR, BATTLE OF (April 1521), defeat of the *Comuneros* forces by the royal army of Charles II (Emperor Charles V) under the constable of Castile, assisted by the Castilian nobility, near Toro, on the borders of Old Castile and Leon. The rebel leaders, Juan de Padilla, Juan Bravo, and Pedro Maldonado, were captured in the battle and executed on the following day, while resistance in the towns, except Toledo, collapsed forthwith.

VILLANOVANS, people represented from the 9th cent. BC in the Iron Age cemeteries of northern Italy (Villanova itself is a suburb of Bologna) and of Etruria. Biconical ossuaries are the most typical feature of Villanovan material culture in both areas. From the first half of the 8th cent. the Villanovans of south Etruria were open to influences from the eastern Mediterranean, which ultimately resulted in the transition from the Iron Age to the orientalizing period and so eventually to Etruscan civilization. No discussion of Etruscan origins is complete without adequate reference to the native element constituted by the Villanovans who preceded them.

VILLARD, HENRY (1835–1900), German-born US journalist, western railroad promoter, and financier, who emigrated (1853), settled in IL, and worked for the New York *Staats Zeitung* and the *Cincinnati Commercial*, covering the political rise of Abraham Lincoln. He was also a war correspondent for the *New York Herald* and the *New York Tribune* (1861–3). He was involved in western railroads after 1873 and became president of the Northern Pacific (1881–4). He also helped to found the Edison General Electric Co. and held majority control of the New York *Evening Post*.

VILLARD, OSWALD GARRISON (1872–1949), US newspaper proprietor and editor, who inherited ownership of the *New York Evening Post* and *The Nation* from his father. He advocated a policy of commitment to the principles of 19th-cent. liberalism—laissez-faire, free trade, anti-imperialism, and the defence of civil liberties. Although hostile to the progressive movement, he played a leading role in the foundation of the National Association for the Advancement of Colored People (NAACP) in 1909. The unpopularity he incurred as a result of his intransigent opposition to American intervention in the First World War led him to sell the *Evening Post* in 1918 and to assume the editorship of *The Nation* (1918–32), which became the leading liberal intellectual weekly of the 1920s. In the 1930s Villard remained a prominent advocate of isolationism and he joined the America First Committee in 1940.

VILLARROEL, GUALBERTO (1908–48), Bolivian soldier and president of Bolivia, who seized power in 1943 and with the support of the radical National Revolutionary Movement (MNR) began to implement a series of reforms. These reforms, and his suppression of dissent, caused an uprising at La Paz which brought about his death. The MNR regarded him as a martyr and national hero.

VILLARS, CLAUDE LOUIS HECTOR DE, Duc de (1653–1734), French soldier and politician. At the outbreak of the War of the Spanish Succession he commanded the French forces on the Rhine and defeated the Elector of Baden at Friedlingen (1702), when he became a marshal of France, and again at Höchstadt (1703). After differences with his co-commander, the Elector of Bavaria, he resigned his commission and was recalled to France, where he crushed the Huguenot revolt of the Camisards. Restored to his command on the Rhine, he stormed the fortified lines of Stollhofen (1707) and overran a large part of southern Germany.

After service in Italy he commanded the main French forces in northern France (1708). He proved himself the ablest French commander of the war, conducting a vigorous defence which culminated in checking the allies at Malplaquet (1709). He subsequently defeated Prince Eugène at Denain (1712). After the war he was appointed to the council of Regency (1715) and became a minister of state (1724).

VILLAVICIOSA, BATTLE OF (Dec. 1710), engagement around the village of Villaviciosa in eastern Castile between the Franco-Spanish forces of Philip V, commanded by the Duc de Vendôme, and the Habsburg forces of Archduke Charles, led by Field Marshal Stahremberg. Vendôme had beaten Stanhope at Brihuega the day before, and though Stahremberg was left in possession of the field, he retreated with his army to the last Habsburg stronghold of Barcelona.

VILLEDA MORALES, RAMON (1908–), Honduran physician and politician, who became president of Honduras (1957–63). Having served as ambassador to the US, he entered politics, but ended his career in exile. A return to constitutional government led him to campaign for the presidency, to which he was elected in 1957. His six-year term of office was considered to be progressive, and he and the Liberal Party enacted a new labour code and a social security law and protected national trade unions. His government also mediated between the unions and foreign fruit companies, such as the United Fruit Co., and under a new constitution the suffrage was expanded and a unicameral legislature introduced. But the government also granted virtual autonomy to the army and towards the end of Villeda's presidency certain army officers grew dissatisfied with his moderate reforms, and a few months before his term of office ended they overthrew him (1963).

VILLEHARDOUIN, GEOFFREY DE (d. *c.* 1213), marshal of Champagne, who went on the Fourth Crusade (1202–4).

His history of the *Conquest of Constantinople* is the most detailed account of the crusade.

VILLEINAGE in England, legal term for the special type of serfdom prevalent in medieval England. Over the greater part of western Europe from the 8th to the 14th cents a servile peasantry attached to the estates of landlords, who were regarded as the owners and masters of these men, was one of the main classes of society. In England, under the precociously developed legal system of King Henry II (*reg.* 1154–89), the serfs were denied the protection of the royal courts in all matters of property. This was the origin of the peculiarly English tenure in villeinage, whereby a man's title to the holdings he was cultivating might be tacitly recognized by his lord, but was ignored by the common law of England. The economic purpose of villeinage was to assure landlords of a body of dependent servile labourers, who cultivated the estates of their masters while, in return, the lords tolerated the possession by these villeins of sufficient land-holdings and certain goods to permit the survival of these men and of their families. When (*c.* 1350–1450) English landlords gave up the direct exploitation of most of their estates and leased them away, they usually commuted for money at the same time the labour services of their villeins, who had disappeared as a special class by the 17th cent.

VILLÈLE, JEAN, Comte de (1773–1854), French ultra-royalist politician, whose ministry (1821–8) re-established sound finance and France's international position while following other policies which hastened Charles X's downfall. Villèle failed to curb or satisfy the more intransigent Ultras. Anti-clericalism fed on the 1825 sacrilege law (which was never enforced), growing Church control of education, and press censorship. Financial compensation of émigrés by a conversion loan (1825) angered the bourgeoisie. Villèle disliked France's Spanish intervention (1823) supporting Ferdinand VII, but gained some credit from it. Chateaubriand's dismissal from the foreign ministry (1824) caused ultra-royalist rifts which, with growing liberal opposition reflected in the 1827 elections, led to Villèle's resignation.

VILLEROY, FRANÇOIS DE NEUFVILLE, Duc de (1644–1730), French soldier and politician, who served in Italy during the War of the Spanish Succession, where he was defeated by Prince Eugène at Chiari (1701) and captured at Cremona (1702). Later, he was decisively defeated by Marlborough at Ramillies (1706). He was never again employed as a soldier, but was appointed minister of state (1714) and to the council of Regency (1715).

VILLERS-COTTERETS, ORDINANCE OF (1539), one of the basic texts of French administration under the *ancien régime*. The work of Chancellor Poyet, it regularized judicial procedures, including the legalizing of torture, prevented artisans from combining to raise wages, and—perhaps most important of all—insisted on the keeping of parish registers and on the use of French as the official language of the courts and the administration throughout the country, even in areas where a dialect was still normally employed.

VILLIERS, CHARLES PELHAM (1802–98), British politician and pioneer of Free Trade, whose aristocratic connections were invaluable to the Anti-Corn Law League because he could influence opinion in the world of politics. As MP for Wolverhampton (1835–98) he introduced annual free trade motions (1838–45). As president of the Poor Law Board (1859–66), he rationalized London's poor law administration and relieved the effects of the Cotton Famine in Lancashire through administrative improvements and public works schemes.

VILLMERGEN, WARS OF (1656, 1712), religio-civil wars in Switzerland, indicating the unsatisfactory nature of the second peace of Kappel (1531). In the first war (1656) Berne and Zürich declared war on the Catholic cantons of Uri, Schwyz, Unterwalden, Lucerne, and Zug after Protestant families in Schwyz had been persecuted. A Bernese force was repulsed at Villmergen (Jan. 1656) and the peace of Baden (March 1656) did nothing to heal religious divisions.

The second war (1712) occurred over a minor incident when Berne and Zürich supported the Toggenburgers against the Catholic abbot of St Gallen. Preliminary peace negotiations at Aarau were denounced by the pope and the Catholics renewed their attacks, but were defeated by the Bernese at Villmergen (July 1712). The peace of Aarau (Aug. 1712) secured parity of religious rights and the abbot of St Gallen granted greater political and religious freedom to the Toggenburg.

VILVALDO BROTHERS (*fl.* 13th cent.), members of a leading Genoese family who in 1291 sailed from Genoa in search of a sea route to India. Despite a search by Ilgotino Vilvaldo for his father, their fate remains unknown. The knowledge of their voyage influenced Columbus.

VIMY RIDGE, BATTLE OF (9–14 April 1917), First World War campaign, fought in France, 8 kms north of Arras, its purpose being to draw German reserves away from the main French offensive on the Aisne. All four divisions of the Canadian Corps, together with the 17th Corps of the British 3rd Army, fought along a 6·4 km front, sustaining 11,000 casualties, and captured the position, which had remained in German hands during most of the war, despite repeated Allied offensives (1914, 1916). It was the most spectacular Canadian achievement of the war.

VINCENNES, in France, royal castle in the suburbs of Paris. Originally a hunting lodge, it was a favourite residence of St Louis and was developed in the 15th cent. as a major fortress with a fine keep and chapel. It ceased to be a royal residence under Louis IX, by whom it came to be used as a prison. It was partly remodelled by Mazarin and now (1970) serves as a barracks and repository for military archives.

VINCENT, STÉNIO JOSEPH (1874–1959), Haitian lawyer, journalist, and president of Haiti (1930–41), who began his presidency under the supervision of US marines, but in 1935, after they had been withdrawn, began a new term of office under a new constitution. In 1941 he helped to arrange the election of his successor, Elie Lescot, who set out to continue Vincent's policies.

VINCENT DE PAUL, Saint (1576–1660), French divine renowned for his zeal and charity, who founded the Congregation of Priests of the Missions (1625), better known as the Lazarists, whom Urban VIII recognized in 1632, as well as the noble Sisterhood of Charity (1634). He was almoner to Queen Marie de' Medici (1608) and later became almoner-general to the galleys (1619). Among his other achievements was the founding of the Paris Foundling Hospital.

VINDEX, GAIUS JULIUS (d. AD 68), Romanized Gaul, who, as governor of Lugdunensis, began a revolt which eventually overthrew Nero. Moved more by dislike of Nero's rule than by Gallic nationalism, he called on Galba to proclaim himself emperor, but his own irregular levies were crushed by the Rhine legions and he himself committed suicide.

VINDICIAE CONTRA TYRANNOS, Huguenot treatise produced in the turbulent period of the French Wars of Religion, expounding a theory of government by contract rather than divine right and justifying the right of resistance. It was published anonymously in 1579, but is usually attributed to Philippe Duplessis-Mornay.

VINEAM DOMINI (1705), papal bull promulgated by Pope Clement XI under pressure from Louis XIV of France, condemning Jansenism by forbidding mental reservations when taking the formulary of Clement IX.

VINGTIÈME in France, direct tax based on the earlier *dixième* (1710). It was introduced by Machault (1749) as a universal 5 per cent levy on incomes from property, *rentes*, feudal rights, and business and office holdings. Although it was emasculated as well as evaded by the privileged classes, it remained the most efficient and just form of taxation then available and further *vingtièmes* were levied in times of financial stringency (a second in 1756, a third in 1760–3). The rolls on which the *vingtièmes* were based are a valuable source for the social historian.

VINLAND, name of the southern-most of three landfalls made by Norsemen on the east coast of North America during the course of voyages from Iceland and Greenland *c.* AD 1000. It is mentioned in manuscripts known as *Hauk's Book*, the *Saga of Eric the Red*, and *Flatey Book*, of the 14th cent. and therefore antedates Christopher Columbus by almost 200 years. Leif Ericson, son of Eric the Red, sailed from Greenland in 1002 and after two landfalls to the south-west came to a third, where there was no frost, grass was covered with dew, the days and nights were of more equal length than in Greenland, or even Iceland, and the sun was higher in the sky on the shortest day. A German member of the crew explored the country and came back with vines and grapes, which he recognized from similar plants that he had seen in his homeland. This landfall was therefore called Vinland. There was also wild corn. The native inhabitants were named by the Norsemen *skraelings*, and had many characters recognizable as those of Red Indians. A map drawn *c.* 1440 was found and published in 1965, which shows Greenland and the three landfalls in North America (Vinland, Markland, and Helluland) depicted as an isolated island in the Western Atlantic ocean. It raised some unenlightened controversy, and there can be no doubt of the Norsemen's discovery of North America, as is further established by the discovery (1959) of a Norse grave and settlement in Nfld, in process of excavation.

VINNIUS, ANDREW (*fl.* 17th cent.), Dutch engineer and businessman, who lived in Russia in the mid-17th cent. and established the famous ironworks at Tula (1632), which became the basis of the Russian armaments industry.

VINSON, FREDERICK MOORE (1890–1953), US lawyer and politician, who served as a congressman (1923–9, 1931–8), resigning to become associate justice of the US court of appeals for the District of Columbia. He was director of the Office of Economic Stabilization (1943–5), a federal loan administrator (1945), and director of the Office of War Mobilization and Reconversion (1945), until his appointment as US secretary of the treasury (1945). He was chief justice of the US Supreme Court (1946–53).

VIRGIL, P. VERGILIUS MARO (70–19 BC), Roman poet, born at Andes near Mantua in Cisalpine Gaul and educated at Cremona, Milan, and Rome. He lost his estates in the confiscations of 42, but perhaps recovered them after appealing to Octavian. Under the patronage of Maecenas he became closely associated with Augustus and his family. His works are the pastoral 'Eclogues' (42–37 BC), the 'Georgics', an hexameter poem in four books on agriculture, dedicated to Maecenas (37–29), and the 'Aeneid', an epic poem about the origins of the Roman people, suggested by Augustus, who followed the progress of the work with deep interest and forbade its destruction after Virgil died before putting the finishing touches to it (29–19).

VIRGIN ISLANDS, group of West Indian islands sighted and named by Columbus (1493). The Spaniards expelled Carib Indians from some islands (1555), but did not settle. The islands provided a refuge in the 16th and 17th cents for pirates. Dutch settlers on Tortola (1648) were replaced by Englishmen (1666). The Danish West India Co. settled St Thomas (1671) and St John (1716). English settlers on St Croix were ejected by the Spaniards (1650), but an English settlement was made on Virgin Gorda (1680). French settlers occupied (1657–96) St Croix and, in 1733, France sold the island to the Danes. English migrants from Anguilla to Crab Island (1717) had their settlement destroyed by the Spaniards (1718). The British Leeward Islands governor annexed Tortola in 1762 and the British-controlled islands became part of the Leeward Islands colony. In 1801 and 1807–15 Britain occupied the Danish islands. Denmark sold her Virgin islands to the US (1917). The US islands have limited home rule. The British islands were separated from the Leewards in 1956, and remained (1970) British colonies.

VIRGINIA, former English colony in North America, first sighted in 1584 during an English exploration of the North American coast under a patent secured by Sir Walter Raleigh. After Raleigh's failure to establish a colony on Roanoke Island (1585), the Virginia Co. of London received a charter (1606) to found a colony. An initial settlement was made at Jamestown (1607) by Capt. John Smith. A new charter (1609) set the colony's boundaries as 200 miles north and 200 miles (322 kms) south of the mouth of the James river and westward to the Pacific Ocean. The reorganization of the colony under the new charter put most of the control in the hands of the governor. Two actions beneficial to Virginia were Gov. Thomas Dale's (1611–16) modification of the colony's communal system to allow individual property ownership and John Rolfe's tobacco-curing discovery (1612), which made the plant a profitable export. The introduction of slaves (1619) by a Dutch ship and the expansion of the plantation system increased the importance of tobacco. A new charter which the Virginia Co. received in 1612 increased the colony's independence and led to the calling of the first English colonial legislative assembly (1619), the House of Burgesses, under Gov. George Yeardley.

VIRGINIA, ARMY OF NORTHERN, Confederate field force in the eastern theatre of the American Civil War, originally comprising the armies of eastern VA and NC under Gen. Johnston. It was named by Gen. Lee when he assumed command (1 June 1862), and reorganized into three corps after the battle of Chancellorsville (May 1863). Numbering at its peak over 90,000 men, it fought in all the major engagements in the eastern sector until the surrender of its remaining 8000 at Appomattox (9 April 1865).

VIRGINIA CITY in Nevada, largest and most famous of US mining towns, was established as a mining camp on the eastern slope of Mount Davidson when the Comstock Lode was discovered (1859). By 1861 Virginia City had been transformed into a booming town, complete with a stock exchange and an opera house. The introduction of underground mining techniques for gold and silver in 1873 helped to sustain its precarious prosperity, and it reached its maximum population of 25,000 in 1876. When the price of silver fell in the early 1880s, and deepening shafts meant uneconomic mining, Virginia City went into a rapid decline. By 1890 it was almost a ghost town.

VIRGINIA INDIAN COMPANY (1714–17), American colonial company given control of trade with Indian tribes by Gov. Alexander Spotswood of VA.

VIRGINIA PLAN (1787) in the US, resolution for the reorganization of the US government proposed at the Philadelphia Convention. It was prepared by the VA delegation, led by James Madison, and introduced by Edmund Randolph, and ostensibly proposed amendments to the Articles of Confederation, but in reality recommended their replacement by a new constitution. It called for the establishment of a strong central government supreme over the states and operating directly on the people. The government would comprise an executive and judiciary and a bicarmeral legislature apportioned according to population, thus strengthening the power of the large states. Although challenged by the New Jersey Plan, the resolution provided a basis for discussion and its principles, though modified, were reflected in the constitution.

VIRGINIA RESOLVES (1769), American colonial protest adopted by the VA House of Burgesses against British taxation. It was introduced by George Washington and expressed the belief that only colonial legislatures could levy colonial taxes and censured the British for their reaction to MA's protest. Once the VA burgesses had passed these resolves, the other colonial legislatures followed suit.

VIRIATHUS (d. 139 BC), Spanish guerrilla leader prominent in the insurrection of the Lusitani against Rome (154–138). After humiliating a series of Roman generals and armies, he won independence for his people (141), but the Senate withdrew its agreement, and Servilius Caepio bribed Viriathus' friends to murder him (139).

VISBY, capital of the Swedish island of Gotland. It was an important centre of Baltic trade in Viking times, as is shown by finds of English and Arabic coins, but it really achieved its fame from the 11th cent. AD onwards as a commercial intermediary between east and west. It was one of the wealthiest towns in the Baltic region until 1361, when Waldemar IV of Denmark defeated the Gotland levies in a great battle fought outside the walls of Visby.

VISCONTI, GIOVANNI (1339–54), archbishop of Milan, who re-established his family as the effective lords of Milan, which in 1349 led to their recognition as hereditary rulers of the city. He extended the Viscontis' control over much of northern Italy, and was a noted patron of the arts and literature and befriended Petrarch.

VISCONTI, OTTONE (d. 1295), archbishop of Milan, founder of Visconti despotism in Milan and first Visconti archbishop of the city. Though the Visconti later temporarily lost control over Milan, they re-emerged as its hereditary rulers in the mid-14th cent.

VISCONTI dynasty were originally Lombard nobles whose prominence at Milan dates from 1277, when Ottone Visconti became its archbishop. They were consistently pro-imperialist, and were opposed by the pro-papal party and suffered strange vicissitudes before establishing themselves permanently as lords of Milan (after 1329). Lombardy was an immensely wealthy and fertile region and the Visconti came to control all of central Lombardy and at times many adjoining regions as well. These diverse possessions they tried to convert into a centralized state. The greatest ruler of their house was Gian Galleazzo III, who in 1395 purchased the title of Duke of Milan from the emperor. In his last years he controlled most of northern and central Italy and only his sudden death from plague (1402) frustrated his dream of re-establishing a kingdom of Italy. Under his sons (1402–47), who were the last male Visconti, Milan once again became the centre of a mainly Lombard state, but continued to be the capital of the most densely populated and prosperous region of Italy.

VISHNU, one of the major gods of Hinduism from the time of the *Rigveda*, worshipped under many names (Hari, Narayana, Krishna, Govinda, etc.). Iconographically he is represented (from the 1st cent. AD) in various forms, most typically standing, four-armed and holding a shell (*sankha*) and a wheel (*chakra*) as attributes. Associated with Vishnu are Lakshmi, the goddess of prosperity and royal sovereignty, and the mythical bird Garuda.

VISIGOTHS, western branch of the Germanic Goths settled in southern Russia in the 3rd–4th cents AD. They were pushed into the Roman empire by the Huns (*c.* 376). At first they were settled by the Roman government south of the Danube, but they rebelled against the Romans' exactions and annihilated the forces of Emperor Valens at Adrianople in 378. Thereafter they wandered through the provinces of the Roman empire without meeting effective opposition. Their king, Alaric, took them into Italy and they sacked Rome in 410, being the first barbarians to do so for 900 years. After 415 they were settled chiefly in southern France and played a decisive part in defeating the invasion of France by Attila and his Huns (453). By that time they had become Arian Christians. After being defeated by the Catholic Frankish king, Clovis, in 507, they were confined chiefly to Spain. But the Visigothic state there was never fully accepted by the subject Spanish populations and was rent by recurrent civil wars. It fell prey to the invading Muslim forces from North Africa, which crossed into Spain in 711 and speedily overran most of the country except for a remote corner in the north-west.

VISITA, in colonial Spanish America, investigation which might include an entire viceroyalty or which might be limited to a single province or official. *Visitas* were generally instituted because of serious emergencies or charges of mismanagement, and were carried out by *visitadores*, who made recommendations for action to the Crown.

VISSCHER FAMILY, Dutch merchant family from Amsterdam which produced three remarkable poets in the 16th–17th cents. Roemer Visscher (1547–1620) was, with Spiegel and Cornhert, one of the founders of the Dutch language. His home in Amsterdam was a centre for artists and men of letters, *eg*, Vondel and Hooft. His elder daughter, Anna Roemers (1584–1651), was called by Vondel 'la Sapho hollondaise'. Poetess, musician, painter, and linguist, she was a friend of Jacob Cats, and as a convert to Catholicism, an opponent of the long war of independence between the northern and southern provinces of the Netherlands. Her younger sister, Maria Tesselschade Roemers (1594–1649), likewise a convert, was well known as a singer and poet, and wrote charming romances, *eg, Complainte de Phyllis*.

VITELLIUS (AD 15–69), Roman Emperor (*reg.* 69), son of Claudius' chief adviser, who was placed in command of Lower Germany by Galba in 68, and proclaimed emperor by his troops on 2 Jan. 69. His army overcame Otho, but Vitellius was defeated by Vespasian's army at Cremona and killed at Rome.

VITORIA, FRANCISCO DE (1480–1546), Spanish political philosopher and Dominican theologian, who made a significant contribution to the development of Salamanca University as the intellectual centre of 16th-cent. Spain. He was known for his treatise, *Relectiones de Indis*, which defended the American Indians and expounded a rudimentary concept of modern international law.

VITRUVIUS POLLIO, M. (*fl.* 1st cent. BC), Roman architect and military engineer, whose extant treatise in 10 books, *De Architectura*, written after service under Julius Caesar in Africa (46) and dedicated to Augustus, was highly influential in the Italian Renaissance.

VITTORINO (RAMBOLDONI DA FELTRE) (*c.* 1378–1446), Italian humanist and teacher, who, in 1423, undertook to be tutor to the children of the Gonzaga dukes of Mantua in Lombardy on condition that he had complete freedom to experiment. His school, attached to the Gonzagas' palace, accepted gifted children from all levels of society. Science and mathematics were taught as well as the arts. The study of the classics was encouraged, new humanistic techniques were used, and freshly discovered texts introduced. Greek was taught alongside Latin. Sports were an important feature of the school and it was distinguished by its enlightened attitude to the development of the whole personality of its pupils. Corporal punishment was banned. The school served as a model for the best European Renaissance schools and greatly influenced the educational ideas of Erasmus.

VITTORIO VENETO, BATTLE OF (Oct. 1918), last battle on the Italian front in the First World War. In the autumn of 1918 the Italian high command was under strong pressure from the Supreme War Council and the British commander on the spot, Lord Cavan—aided by the Italian deputy chief of staff Badoglio—to go over to the offensive. Diaz, the commander-in-chief, would have been prepared to wait for Austria to collapse internally; but political considerations, *eg*, the need to be an actively victorious power at the peace conference, as well as the speed of the Habsburg disintegration, made him change his mind. His plan was to shatter the Austrian line at the junction of its mountain and Piave river fronts. Cavan was given the command of the 10th Army (one Italian, one British corps) to hold the right (Piave) flank. The key assault was to be made in the left centre by the Italians against Monte Grappa, and in between the two lay the 12th Army, French troops under Graziani. In fact, the Monte Grappa position held and the decisive break-throughs were made by the British and French on 27 Oct. They forced their way across the river between 23 and 27 Oct., then swept aside the crumbling Habsburg forces, weakened by lack of German aid, hunger, poor morale, and large-scale desertion, and pushed forward on an axis of advance aimed at Vittorio Veneto, the Austrian headquarters. The retreat turned into a rout, except for a sharp rearguard action on the Monticano on 29 Oct., and the Allied pursuit, led by cavalry, armoured cars, and aircraft, prevented any more substantial resistance. Vittorio Veneto was reached on 30 Oct., the Tagliamento by 2 Nov., and on the same day the Austrian forces in the north, on the Trentino front, surrendered. A full armistice was granted on 4 Nov.

VIVALDI, ANTONIO (*c.* 1675–1741), Venetian violinist and composer, whose violin concertos established his European reputation and a new musical form, which J. S. Bach later arranged for the clavier and organ.

VIVEKANANDA (1863–1902), Indian philosopher, pupil of Ramkrishna Paramahamsa and organizer of the Ramkrishna Mission. In 1893 he attended the World Congress of Religions in the US. He believed that India could conquer the world by means of her spirituality.

VIVES, JUAN LUIS DE (1492–1540), Spanish-born humanist philosopher and educationalist, and friend of Erasmus, whose cosmopolitan views he shared. He spent his adult life in France, England, and the Low Countries, finally settling in Bruges after being driven from England for opposing King Henry VIII's divorce from Catherine of Aragon. While in England he became an Oxford fellow and was tutor to Princess Mary. Among his best-known works are *De Tradendis Disciplinis* (1531), a remarkable treatise on education, and *Linguae Latinae exercitatio* (1538), advocating the acquisition of fluent and stylish Latin as the basis of the grammar school curriculum.

VIZCAINO, SEBASTIEN (d. *c.* 1606), Spanish merchant and explorer who founded a short-lived colony at La Paz (1597) in lower CA. He discovered Monterey Bay and continued north of Cape Mendocino, where after sighting a large river which was called the River of the West, later identified as the Columbia, his fleet was struck by a violent storm and he was forced to sail for home. No further exploration of the CA coast was made for 160 years.

VLADIMIR I (d. 1015), Prince of Kiev (*reg.* 980–1015), who was the son of Svyatoslav I. His decision to accept Christ-

ianity under the jurisdiction of the Patriarch of Constantinople, signalized by his own baptism in 988, was a shrewd political decision designed to end Russia's cultural isolation and strengthen his own position as a ruler. His conversion resulted in a marked increase in Byzantine influence in the spheres of art, literature, and law, which played an important part in the cultural development of Kievan Russia. He also extended Russian territory to the west, fought successful campaigns against the Volga Bulgars and the Pecheneg steppe nomads, and founded a number of cities.

VLADIMIR MONOMACHOS (d. 1125), Prince of Kiev (*reg.* 1113–25), one of the ablest rulers of Kievan Russia and a man of sincere piety, military capacity, and the gift of leadership. He was responsible for a number of successful campaigns against the Polovtsi steppe nomads, who frequently raided the Russian land, and for acts of social legislation designed to improve the condition of the poorer members of the population. His *Testament*, written for the guidance of his sons, ranks as a notable contribution to Old Russian literature.

VLADISLAV VII JAGIELLO (1456–1516), King of Bohemia (*reg.* 1471–1516) and of Hungary (*reg.* 1490–1516), eldest son of Casimir IV of Poland. He was dominated by an assurance of a Habsburg succession in his lands in the event of his having no legitimate male heir (1491). His son, Louis, succeeded to both thrones.

VLADISLAV IV VASA (1595–1648), King of Poland (*reg.* 1632–48), son of Sigismund III. He achieved many successes on the international scene, although his reign was a prelude to Poland's decline in the second half of the 17th cent. As a youth he served in the campaigns against Muscovy (1610–12, 1617–18) and was proclaimed Tsar of Russia in 1610, until the Polish forces were driven out of Moscow in 1612 and the Romanov dynasty acquired the Russian throne. After succeeding his father, he renewed hostilities with Russia, achieving a victorious peace (1634) which confirmed the extensive territorial gains awarded to Poland under the truce of Deulino (1618) in return for abandoning his claims to the tsardom. In the same year (1634) he concluded a brief but successful war with the Turks (1633–4) and in 1635 signed the treaty of Stuhmsdorf with Sweden, restoring to Poland the Prussian towns seized by Sweden and providing for a 26-year armistice. Vladislav refused to give up his claims to the Swedish throne, however, and still hoped for the restoration of Livonia. From this time he vacillated between a French and Habsburg alliance in the Thirty Years War. In 1633 he had renewed the Austrian treaty (1613) and in 1637 he married a daughter of the Emperor Ferdinand II, Archduchess Cecilie Renate of Habsburg, but by 1645 he turned to France by marrying, secondly, Louise Marie de Gonzague, Princess of Nevers. A Catholic of wide and tolerant views, he sanctioned an Orthodox hierarchy besides the Uniate one, but he met with constant opposition from the *sejm*, which hampered his great design, the renewal of Poland's traditional role as defender of Christendom against the Turks. He left unsolved the problem of Swedish expansion in the north and Ukrainian independence in the south-east, and his death coincided with the greatest and most successful of the Cossack rebellions, under Bogdan Khmelnitski (1648).

VLOTHA, BATTLE OF (Oct. 1638), imperialist victory in the Thirty Years War, fought on the Weser river between Count Hatzfeld's force and a small army under Charles Louis, the young Protestant elector palatine. The elector's brother was captured, his army, raised with English money, was destroyed, and he made his escape from the battlefield.

VO NGUYEN GIAP (1912–), North Vietnamese soldier and politician. He joined a revolutionary political party (*c.* 1927) while still a boy and for this was arrested by the French authorities and spent some years in prison. He next appeared in the mid-1930s as a student at Hanoi University, where he met and collaborated with Pham Van Dong and other communists. In 1940 he fled to South China to escape being arrested again, and in the following year helped to found the Viet-Minh, and soon emerged as its leading military specialist. He was responsible for creating a small Viet-Minh army, which in Aug. 1945 was powerful enough to take control of Hanoi. Vo Nguyen Giap became interior minister in Ho Chi Minh's provisional government, and in 1946 was left in charge of it while Ho and Pham Van Dong attended the Fontainebleau conference. In that same year he took steps to eliminate non-communist nationalists in Tongking, and prepared for the inevitable conflict with the French, which began in Dec. 1946. During the Indo-China War (1946–54) he led the Viet-Minh armies and was responsible for the strategy which culminated in the French defeat at Dien-Bien-Phu in May 1954. After the Geneva Agreement (1954) he became deputy prime minister and defence minister in the Hanoi government, and remained for many years one of the most powerful leaders of the Democratic Republic of Viet-nam.   RBS

VOETIUS, GYBERTUS (1589–1676), Dutch theologian and minister of the reformed Calvinist faith, who was professor of theology at Utrecht (1634–76). An inflexible and intolerant Gomarist, he opposed Arminianism, Cocceianism, and Cartesianism and prevented the assimilation of the Catholic towns of the Southern Netherlands into the north, *eg*, Hertogenbosch (1629). His principal works included *Selectae disputationes theologicae* and *Politica ecclesiastica* (1663–76).

VOGEL, SIR JULIUS (1835–99), NZ politician and prime minister, who entered politics as a strong provincialist in 1863. He became chief spokesman of Fox's ministry (1869–1872) at a crucial juncture: the Maori Wars were dying away and a depressed NZ needed a fresh stimulus. In 1870 he announced comprehensive and ingenious schemes of public works and immigration, to be financed by British loans. Unfortunately, his plans were swept away in a provincial scramble for grants. Though NZ's parliament and administration proved unequal to the task of allocating and spending the British loans prudently, 140,000 immigrants and over 1000 miles (1609 kms) of railways were acquired in the decade of 'Vogelism'. Although from 1870 onwards he was effective head of government, he was actually prime minister only in 1873–5 and 1876. Later, he became agent-general in Britain (1876–80). He took office in the ill-starred Stout–Vogel ministry (1884–7) primarily to retrieve his failing commercial enterprises. Expectations of prosperity restored by his confidence and ingenuity were dashed in a debt-ridden NZ and he was defeated. Soon afterwards, he retired to Britain. Among his many expansive policies, Vogel advocated a Pacific sub-empire for NZ, and imperial federation. The contrast between his public vision and his private scheming, in a faction-ridden political system, endowed him with an equivocal reputation, but 20th-cent. opinion tends to blame the system rather than the man.

VOGTEI in Germany, term best translated as 'protectorate' or 'stewardship', *ie*, the protectorate over a town, district or, most often, an abbey or church, enjoyed by a nobleman in medieval Germany. The vogtei was in the gift of medieval German kings and was extremely lucrative, as its holder took payments for his 'protection'. Many great families, including the Habsburgs, began their climb to power through the acquisition of Vogteien. During the Investiture Contest in the 11th–12th cents many who held this office were able to carry out a virtual secularization of church lands in their care.

VOITINSKY MISSION (1920), Soviet mission to China, led by G. N. Voitinsky, who met Sun Yat-sen and other Chinese leaders, and discussed possible forms of co-operation.

VOLATERRAE (mod. Volterra), one of the twelve cities of the Etruscan League and the capital not only of the metal-rich region of north-western Etruria, but also of a large agricultural zone. It seems to have developed rather late in the Etruscan period, becoming prosperous only in the 4th cent. BC through a flourishing local production of red-figured vases, stone funerary stelae, and, later still, of characteristic alabaster cinerary chests carved with mythological scenes. In the civil war between Sulla and the supporters of Marius in the 1st cent. Volaterrae was the last stronghold of the Marians and fell after a two-year siege (80 BC).

VOLGA RIVER, great arterial river of the USSR, 3710 kms in length. It rises in the Valdai hills of the Central Russian Uplands and flows into the Caspian Sea at Astrakhan. It is an important navigable waterway, abounding in fish, and provides the essential link between the cities of Baltic Russia and the Caspian region. From the late 16th cent., when the Muscovites seized control of it from the Tatars, it was the main communication network of the developing Russian state.

VOLPI DI MISURATA, GIUSEPPE, Count (1877–1947), Italian industrialist and politician, who was a supporter of fascism, and finance minister (1925–8). His deflationary, protectionist, state-interventionist measures cut budget deficits and allowed a temporary lira revaluation, though Mussolini over-ruled him in selecting a higher fixed parity in Dec. 1927. During his governorship of Tripolitania (1921–1925) the Libyan coast was reconquered.

VOLSCI, Italic mountain people who descended on Latium and the regions south-east of the Alban hills in the 6th cent. BC. The legend of Coriolanus, a Roman renegade who led the Volsci against Rome in 491 BC, doubtless reflects contemporary pressure on Rome by the Volsci and from the Samnites of Campania. The Volsci, together with the Aequi, were defeated by Rome's Latin allies in 431, and by 304 they were at last reduced to such total submission to Rome that virtually all trace of their original civilization was obliterated.

VOLSINII, one of the twelve cities of the Etruscan League, described by ancient writers as one of the oldest and wealthiest. It is usual to assume that Fanum Voltumnae, the religious centre of the league from the late 5th cent. BC, was near Volsinii. Fanum Voltumnae has yet to be found; Volsinii has been identified with both Orvieto and Bolsena. The latter is more likely to have been the site of the city as refounded by Rome in 264 BC, whereas the 6th–5th-cent. Etruscan cemetery at Crocefisso del Tufo, Orvieto, is both older and richer than any remains yet found at Bolsena.

VOLSTEAD ACT (1919) in the US, legislative measure providing for the enforcement of Prohibition. It was introduced by Andrew J. Volstead, of MN, and was passed by Congress (28 Oct.) over President Wilson's veto. It defined intoxicating liquor as that containing one half of one per cent alcohol by volume, and prescribed penalties for violation of the 18th Amendment, but permitted the manufacture of beer, on condition that its alcohol content was reduced to the permitted level before sale.

VOLTA, ALESSANDRO, Count (1745–1827), Italian physicist and inventor of the electric battery. On being dismissed (1799) for political reasons from his post as rector of Pavia University he went to Paris, where he announced his discovery of the 'Voltaic pile'. Previously, the scientist Galvani had observed the twitching of dissected muscles when touched with dissimilar metals forming a circuit; he correctly identified this phenomenon as electrical, but wrongly ascribed the source of electricity to the muscle. Volta disagreed, and his experiments led to his electric cell. He demonstrated this to Napoleon I, who reinstated him as rector in Pavia. Volta's batteries, the prototypes of all modern ones, made possible for the first time scientific experiments with strong continuous currents. The unit of electrical potential is named after him.

VOLTAIRE (FRANÇOIS MARIE AROUET) (1694–1778), French writer and thinker. While articled to a lawyer, he frequented literary circles and began writing. He made a name for himself by his wit, which also earned him first exile (1716) and then a period in the Bastille (1717–18). On being released he published his first major work, a play, *Oedipus* (1718). This and his first epic poem, the *Henriade* (1723), were both successful, but his free-thinking views brought him into conflict with society, hence his second period in the Bastille, his duel with the Chevalier Rohan-Chabot, and his exile in England (1726–8).

His period in England had a marked effect on him, and not merely in *Les Lettres Philosophiques* (1734), which confirmed his reputation and helped to establish him in the role of a humanitarian and social critic. He was also engaged at this time on his first historical work, on Charles XII of Sweden, and in popularizing English ideas (particularly religious tolerance) and literature in France. His *Les Lettres Philosophiques* and his personal affairs led him into further trouble with authority, which he circumvented by travelling first to Germany and then to Cirey in Champagne, where he established himself with his mistress, Mme du Châtelet (1734). While there he became involved in popularizing scientific thought, and also began a correspondence with Frederick II of Prussia (1736). For a while he regained favour at court, but eventually had to leave France altogether (1749) when he again became involved in further public debate, this time in part over Machault's tax reforms.

His belief in the necessity for a strong constitutional monarchy in France can be seen in his major historical work *Le Siècle de Louis XIV* (1755). By then he was living at Les Délices near Geneva. Although continuing to produce plays, poetry, and letters, his interests at this stage became more serious partly due to the impact of the Lisbon earthquake (1755), which led him in *Candide* (1758), one of his famous *contes*, to attack the prevailing revealed religious philosophy, urging a more rational and just society, based on applied knowledge and freedom for the educated. These themes can be found in his *Essai sur les Mœurs* (1756), the *Dictionnaire Philosophique* (1764), and in his contributions to the *Encyclopédie*. He also continued to involve himself in the affairs of France, defending both Calas (1762) and La Barre (1766), as well as attacking the *parlement* of Paris for its reactionary attitude.

He kept up a voluminous correspondence with savants throughout Europe, many of whom he entertained at his model estate at Ferney on the French–Swiss border (1758), enjoying an ever-growing reputation, which eventually earned him a triumphal return to Paris (1778) a few months before his death. He left behind him 15 million words, including over 20,000 letters.

T. Besterman, *Voltaire* (London, 1969).
H. N. Brailsford, *Voltaire* (London, 1963).   CHC

VOLUNTEER MOVEMENT (1859) in Britain, revival of the local volunteer forces, which had sprung up in Britain during the French Wars, in an attempt to strengthen the forces available for home defence, at a time when Napoleon III was suspected of anti-British intentions. The volunteers enjoyed both royal and literary patronage and survived until they were reorganized on a national basis and merged with the Territorial Army in 1908.

VOLYNIA, province of western Russia, part of the Ukraine and within the USSR after 1945. The principality was subdued by the Kievan state until it briefly secured independence in the mid-12th cent., only to be devastated by the Mongols in the mid-13th cent. and conquered by the grand duke of Lithuania. In 1569 it was transferred by Sigismund Augustus from Lithuania to Poland and was incorporated into Russia at the second and third Partitions of Poland (1793, 1795), then following the fate of the Ukraine.

VONDEL, JUSTUS VAN DEN (1587–1679), Dutch poet of the golden age of Dutch literature and a humanist who sympathized with the liberal Calvinists of his day, *eg*, Grotius, Oldenbarneveldt, and Vossius. Though originally a Calvinist, he rejected the doctrine of predestination as an unpardonable limitation upon man's free will. He wrote many polemics during the sectarian disputes of the 1620s, *eg*, 'Palamedes' (1625), and he dedicated his tragedy, 'Gijsbrecht van Amstel' (1637), to Grotius. His early works reveal the influence of Renaissance ornament and classical learning, but his finest poems were produced in his later years, after his conversion to Catholicism (1641), *eg*, his great religious epic, 'Lucifer' (1654). The last 20 years of his life were spent in comparative poverty, although he was much venerated by the literary world for the quality and quantity of his work, and greatly influenced German baroque poetry.

VOODOO, predominant religion of Haiti and a synchretic blend of African religions and Christianity, which developed its own hierarchy, churches, rites, and sacraments. It was condemned as barbaric and shameful by many Haitian presidents, and suffered persecution and proscription several times. A few presidents have supported it, either because they believed in it or because it was a useful means of social control. It met with great hostility from both Catholics and Protestants, and sensational versions of its rites and beliefs have been a favourite subject for novels and travel accounts. Today Voodoo is the religion of the rural poor and the urban lower classes of Haiti.

VOORTREKKERS in South Africa, 'those who travelled before', the name given to the Boer farmers who left the British colony of the Cape from *c*. 1837 to found independent republics in the interior of South Africa.

VORAGINE, JAMES OF (*c*. 1230–98), a Dominican writer and Abp of Genoa (1292). His fame rests on his *Golden Legends*, a collection of stories of miracles, which enjoyed great popularity in the Middle Ages and inspired numerous cycles of religious paintings, especially in Italy.

VORONEZH in Russia, fortress town on the upper reaches of the Don, first established in 1586 and greatly expanded under Tsar Peter I (1689–1725) as a centre of the Russian shipbuilding industry. It was here that the first Russian fleet was built (1695–6) for the Turkish campaign. Voronezh continued to prosper as the focal point of trading routes from western Europe and along the valley of the Don.

VORONTSOV, MIKHAIL SEMYONOVICH, Count (1782–1856), Russian governor-general of New Russia and viceroy of the Caucasus, where he failed to defeat the Murid sect led by Shamil, which waged a holy war in Daghestan. He was an Anglophile and a supporter of Uvarev.

VOROSHILOV, KLIMENTY YEFREMOVICH (1881–1969), Russian soldier, politician, and marshal of the Soviet Union. He emerged as a leading military figure from the Bolshevik political elite, having joined the Bolshevik faction of the Russian Social Democratic Party in 1903. Until the Civil War he was mainly involved in underground work, when not in prison or exile. In 1918 he organized the 5th Ukrainian Red Army, based on Tsaritsyn, in close co-operation with Stalin, the local political commissar, and formed an alliance with him which, strengthened by their mutual opposition to Trotsky, was to continue almost until Stalin's death. He was appointed commissar for defence in 1925 and joined the Politburo in Jan. 1926. Because he was not content to be in total agreement with Stalin his position involved him in many disputes, *eg*, when he backed Blyukher, who opposed collectivization in the areas threatened by Japan. He was also widely regarded as favouring closer relations with Germany in the mid-1930s. These attitudes were related to his awareness of Soviet military weakness. In his later political career he headed the Control Commission in Hungary (1945–7), and was Soviet head of state (1953). He retired in 1960.

VORTIGERN (*fl.* 5th cent.), British noble of the Cornovii claimed by Bede to be Gildas's 'Proud Tyrant' in south-east Britain in the mid-5th cent. Despised by the monk Gildas as a Pelagian heretic, Vortigern is criticized for inviting ships' companies of Saxons under Hengest and Horsa to come as *federati* to protect Britain from Picts and Scots. Landing at Ebbsfleet, Kent (*c.* 449), the Saxons served the Britons for a few years then revolted against them, defeating Vortigern and the Britons at Aylesford. Thus the Saxons gained a vital foothold in southern Britain 150 years after the withdrawal of the Roman legions.

VOSSIUS, GERHARD JOHANNES (1577–1649), Dutch humanist philosopher and philologist, whose Arminian views, expressed in his *Historia Pelagiana* (1618), caused him to lose his post as professor of theology at Leyden University. He moved to England and became a prebend of Canterbury Cathedral. In 1632 he returned to the Netherlands to become professor of history at the Amsterdam Athanaeum. Among his chief works are *Aristarcus, De Historiciis Graecis*, and *Commentaria Rhetorica*.

VOTCHINA in Russia, hereditary estates of the old Russian nobility, which preceded the *pomestya* or estates granted in recompense for service to the state.

VOTE OF NO ADDRESSES in England, parliamentary resolution breaking off all negotiations with King Charles I (17 Jan. 1648) after he had entered into a treaty with the Scots (the Engagement, Dec. 1647) from his refuge at Carisbrooke. The king's rejection of parliament's latest proposals (Dec. 1647) caused the Independents and Presbyterians to draw closer together, and both houses resolved that they would neither make further addresses to Charles nor receive any from him. In Feb. 1648 the Commons agreed to publish a declaration in defence of their vote and military preparations for the second Civil War were expedited.

VOYAGEURS, Canadians who paddled the large canoes used in the fur trade. In the Red River Expedition (1870), they served Gen. Wolseley, who later applied to Canada for a corps of voyageurs to assist him in his Nile expedition to relieve Gordon at Khartoum (1884). A corps of 386 lumbermen and Caughnawaga Indians enlisted in six months and served in the Sudan under Col. Frederick Denison.

VRIES, HUGO DE (1848–1935), Dutch plant physiologist and hybridist. Having prepared monographs on various cultivated plants for the Prussian government in the 1870s, he turned his attention to heredity and variation. He rediscovered and confirmed (1900) the results of the work performed by Mendel on heredity. As a result of later work he proposed that evolution takes place through large mutations in his *Die Mutationstheory* (1901–3), but 20th-cent. research has reduced the scope of application of his hypotheses.

VULCI, 88 kms north-west of Rome, near Montalto di Castro, one of the twelve cities of the Etruscan League. It is chiefly remarkable for the quantity and quality of imported Greek vases found there by Lucien Bonaparte and others from 1828 onwards. It has been estimated that by 1856 more than 15,000 tombs had been opened, and they have yielded more imported Attic pottery of the 6th and 5th cents than any other single Etruscan site. Vulci, whose history is scarcely mentioned in the literary sources before its conquest by Rome in 280 BC, was also an important centre of artistic production in its own right, specializing from the 6th cent. onwards in stone-carving and bronze-working.

VULGATE, St Jerome's translation of the Bible, completed in AD 404 to settle differences of text in Old Latin manuscripts. It is the translation most widely used in the West and is the official version of the Roman Catholic Church.

VYASA, name of a legendary poet of ancient India, traditionally the author of the great epic the 'Mahabharata', but not a clearly historical figure.

VYKHOVSKY, IVAN (*fl.* 17th cent.), anti-Russian Cossack leader who succeeded to the position of *hetman* after Bogdan Khmelnitski's death (1657). He negotiated the treaty of Hadziacz with the Poles (1657–8) and induced a war with Russia, but when his unreliable ally, the khan of Crimea, deserted him, he fled to Poland (1659), to be replaced as *hetman* by Yury Khmelnitski.

VYSHINSKY, ANDREY YANUAREVICH (1883–1955), Russian lawyer and politician, who joined the Social Democratic Party (1902) and stayed with the Mensheviks after the split in the party (1903) until after the Bolsheviks established themselves in power (1920). From being a lecturer at Moscow University he rose to be its rector. After his appointment as procurator of the Russian Federal Republic, which inaugurated his career as an outstanding state prosecutor—he was procurator of the USSR (1935)—he became a deputy prime minister (1939). He was public prosecutor in the Metro-Vickers trial (1933) and in many of the show trials of the 1930s. He served under Molotov as deputy minister for foreign affairs (1940–9) and was then appointed minister (1949–53). Thus he played a prominent role in the conferences and diplomacy of the Cold War after 1945, but was allowed no initiative or independence in doing so. After Stalin's death he was again deputy minister (1953–5).

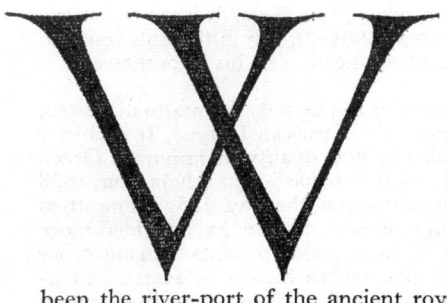

WAD BEN NAWA, major site of the Meroitic civilization which flourished along the Sudanese Nile before *c.* AD 350. Believed to have been the river-port of the ancient royal city of Naqa (near Meroe, about 120 miles—193 kms—north of modern Khartoum), Wad ben Nawa has been found by excavation to contain the ruins of a palace, two temples, and other buildings. One temple was of the time of Netekamani, and a brick with the cartouche of Queen Amanishakhete was discovered in the palace.

WADAI, Muslim sultanate in Chad republic, founded by Abd al-Kerim b. Jame, (*c.* 1635), who drove away his father-in-law, Dawud, the last Tunjur sultan. Abd al-Kerim was a scholar of Nile valley origin who claimed Abbasid descent. He studied in Baghirmi and Bornu. Under his immediate successors, wars were waged against Darfur and Baghirmi and in the late 18th cent. most of Kanem was taken from Bornu. Sabun conquered (*c.* 1815) Baghirmi and opened a direct trade route to North Africa via Kufra. His successors allied themselves with Muhammad Ali of Egypt. Muhammad Sharif formed close links with the Sanusiyya. In the later 19th cent. the state was threatened by the Mahdists, then by Rabih, and finally by the French, who occupied the capital, Abeche, in 1909.

WADAN, town in Mauritania founded in 1141 or 1329 by two Muslim scholars. The Portuguese established an entrepôt there (1487), as the town controlled the routes to the Ijjil salt mines and the Sudan.

WADDELL, RUTHERFORD (1849–1932), NZ social reformer, whose revelations about sweated labour in Dunedin (1888) led to a royal commission (1890).

WADDINGTON, WILLIAM HENRY (1826–94), French diplomat of British origin, who was ambassador to Britain (1883–93). As French plenipotentiary at the Berlin Congress (1878), he persuaded Lord Salisbury to allow France a free hand in Tunisia if Britain took Cyprus, a decision which drove Italy into the Triple Alliance.

WADE, BENJAMIN FRANKLIN (1800–78), US lawyer and politician, who was admitted to the OH bar (1827) and served as state senator (1837–9, 1841–3) and circuit court judge (1847–51), but resigned on being chosen as US senator from OH (1851–69). He became a leader of the Radical Republicans, and was joint sponsor of the Wade–Davis Bill, which sought to impose severe conditions on the readmittance of seceded states to the Union (1864). As President *pro tempore* of the Senate (1867–8), he strongly supported the impeachment of President Andrew Johnson, whom he would have succeeded had his impeachment been successful.

WADE, GEORGE (1673–1748), English soldier of Irish stock, who rose to become a field marshal (1743) and a member of the privy council. As commander of the royal forces in Scotland after the 1715 Jacobite rebellion, he was responsible for the construction of a network of roads (1720–1730). In 1744–5 he commanded in the Netherlands, but with little success. On returning to England he was unable to stop Prince Charles Edward's advance (1745) and was superseded by the Duke of Cumberland.

WADE, SIR THOMAS FRANCIS (1818–95), British diplomat and Sinologue, who was sent to China in 1841 during the Opium War. His tenacious memory and love of languages enabled him to master the Chinese language quickly. As an interpreter he served in the army and then in the supreme court in Hong Kong (1845), and worked with Sir John Francis Davies, superintendent of trade and governor of Hong Kong (1846), and with Lord Elgin during the Arrow War. In 1855 he was appointed Chinese secretary at Hong Kong, and also served in that capacity at the British legation at Peking in 1861. He became the British minister to Peking in 1871. As a diplomat, his reputation was increased by the settlement of the Chefoo Convention (1876), and by the mediation between China and Japan over Taiwan (1874). He encouraged modernization in China, so long as it was not strong enough to challenge British interests. After his retirement from the foreign office (1883), he was made the first professor of Chinese at Cambridge University (1888). His system of transliterating Chinese, slightly revised by Herbert A. Giles, is still used by a large number of scholars (1970).

WADE–DAVIS BILL (2 July 1864) in the US, Congressional attempt to provide an alternative to Lincoln's plan for reconstructing the Union at the end of the American Civil War. Named after its sponsors, Benjamin F. Wade, US senator from OH, and Congressman Henry W. Davis, MD, the bill stipulated that a seceded state could only be reorganized after a majority of the citizens had taken an oath of loyalty and its constitution had been approved by president and Congress. Lincoln's veto of the bill hardened Radical Republican opposition to presidential reconstruction.

WADGAON, CONVENTION OF (1779), signed by a retreating Bombay army which had attempted to intervene in Maratha affairs. Under the convention all territories acquired since 1773 were to be restored to the Marathas. It was promptly disowned by the civil authorities.

WAFD, Egyptian political party founded in 1918 under the aegis of Zaghlul Pasha. It was formed as a delegation (wafd) to present Egyptian demands for independence to Britain. Britain's refusal to recognize the Wafd or allow its representatives to go to London led to an agitation and the arrest and exile of Zaghlul and others (8 March 1919). In riots and demonstrations which followed, the Wafd emerged as the body most clearly representative of Egyptian opinion, capable of preventing any Anglo-Egyptian agreement unacceptable to itself, though unable, despite its success in subsequent elections, to achieve any progress in government because of the opposition of the court and because of its own contradictions. The Wafd's opportunity came in 1936, when the prime minister, Mustafa al-Nahhas, who had succeeded Zaghlul in 1927, negotiated the 1936 treaty with Britain, the power of the court being at that time temporarily reduced. Subsequently the Wafd was excluded from power by Faruq, only to be restored by British intervention (1942–4). Its association with the British, combined with allegations of corruption, lost the Wafd some of its popular support, while the changing economic and social climate in Egypt increasingly made its landlord leaders obsolete. The last Wafd government (1950–2) ended in disaster with the burning of Cairo (26 Jan. 1952). It was dissolved with other parties on 17 Jan. 1953.

WAGNER, ROBERT FERDINAND (1877–1953), US lawyer and politician, who served as NY state senator (1909–18), justice of the New York supreme court (1919–26), and senator from NY (1927–49). He became an influential figure in the Democratic Party, particularly during the New Deal years, and sponsored much liberal social legislation, including the National Industrial Recovery Act, the Social Security Act, the National Labour Relations Act (often called the Wagner Act), the Railway Pension Law, and the US Housing Act (1937).

WAGRAM, BATTLE OF (1809), victory by Napoleon I over Austria in the French Wars. It was followed by the treaty of Schönbrunn, by which Austria ceded territory containing 3½ million inhabitants, had to pay a heavy indemnity, and furnish Napoleon with troops.

WAHHABI, religious and political movement (known as the Wahhabiyya) which first came to prominence in Arabia during the 18th–19th cents. Muhammad ibn Abd al-Wahhab (1703–1792), of Uyayna, a small town in the Najd, was educated as a member of the *ulama* at Medina and Basra. He adhered to the strict Hanbali school and preached an austere interpretation of the Muslim faith which he derived from the teaching of Ibn Taymiyya (13th–14th cents). Expelled from Uyayna in 1745 on account of his insistent call for a return to the practices of primitive Islam, Muhammad ibn Abd al-Wahhab found a refuge at Dar'iyya under the protection of the local emir, Muhammad ibn Sa'ud. The co-operation of these men led to the formation of a powerful Wahhabi state in Arabia.

The Najd, and in particular the emirate of Riyad, was reduced to obedience in the years 1746–73. Wahhabi control was then extended over the region of Al-Ahsa in 1773–93. There followed a period of far-flung raids, in 1793–1805, against Iraq and the Hijaz. Wahhabi forces under the Sa'udi emir Abd al-Aziz rode northward in 1802 and sacked Karbala, the famous centre of Shi'i pilgrimage in Iraq. On the western edge of Arabia Mecca fell to the Wahhabiyya in 1803 and Medina in 1805.

The expansion of the Wahhabi state called forth a reaction from the Ottoman sultan, Mahmud II, who instructed the Pasha of Egypt, Muhammad Ali, to undertake a war of reconquest, which led to the recapture of Mecca and Medina (1812–13) and the subsequent advance of Egyptian forces into the Najd and the fall of Dar'iyya (1816–18). Muhammad Ali evacuated Najd in 1824, the rule of the Sa'udi emirs being restored there—an event which was to make possible the emergence, 100 years later, under the leadership of Abd al-Aziz ibn Sa'ud, of the present (1970) kingdom of Sa'udi Arabia.

H. St J. Philby, *Saudi Arabia* (London, 1955).   VJP

WAIRAU AFFRAY in NZ, clash between NZ Maoris and European settlers in Marlborough (1842). Rangihaeata and Te Rauparaha, Ngati Toa chiefs, disputed European land claims and obstructed surveyors. An ill-organized punitive expedition from Nelson, after confused parleying, was routed, leaving 22 Europeans dead. Gov. Fitzroy held Maori resistance to be justified, to the indignation of the settlers.

WAITANGI, TREATY OF (1840). Fearing Maori–European clashes, a reluctant British government despatched Capt. William Hobson (1839) to treat with Maori chiefs for the voluntary cession of sovereignty. With missionary assistance, Hobson secured (6 Feb. 1840) the adherence of 45 northern chiefs to a three-clause 'treaty', guaranteeing Maori lands and granting Maoris British citizenship. Though without legal status, the treaty was the moral and political condition

of British possession, proclaimed on grounds of cession, discovery, and settlement.

WAITE, MORRISON REMICK (1816–88), US lawyer and chief justice of the US Supreme Court. He became well known through the AL claims case (1873), and was appointed chief justice in 1874. After *Munn v. Illinois* (1877) he was concerned with interpretation of the 'due process of law' clause of the 14 Amendment to the US constitution. He upheld the power of the states to regulate property 'clothed with a public interest', but also, as in *Stone v. Farmers' Loan and Trust Co.* (1886), he saw limitations upon the power of the states, in that the 'power to regulate is not a power to destroy'. *Santa Clara County v. Southern Pacific Railroad Co.* (1886) is noteworthy for Waite's acceptance that a corporation is a person in law.

WAKATSUKI, REIJIRŌ (1866–1949), Japanese politician, who was twice prime minister. His first cabinet (1926–7) encountered the opposition of the conservative privy council, and his second (April–Dec. 1931) fell because it was unable to achieve a diplomatic solution of the Manchurian Incident which would satisfy both the army and public opinion.

WAKE, WILLIAM (1657–1737), English cleric and scholar, who was rewarded for his loyalty to the Protestant succession and the Whig party with the archbishopric of Canterbury (1716). As chaplain to the English ambassador in Paris he quarrelled with Bossuet, but later (1717–20) was involved in discussions for a proposed union between the Anglican and Gallican Churches. After opposing the repeal of the Occasional Conformity and Schism Acts he lost favour with the Whig ministry.

WAKE ISLAND, atoll in the central Pacific between Hawaii and Guam which was annexed by the US after the Spanish-American War (1898). It has strategic and commercial importance as a naval and air station, and during the Second World War it was occupied by the Japanese.

WAKEFIELD, EDWARD GIBBON (1796–1862), British colonial reformer, who in 1829, while imprisoned at Newgate for abducting an heiress, published a *Sketch of a Proposal for Colonizing Australasia* and *A Letter from Sydney*. He elaborated these in *England and America* (1833) and *A View of the Art of Colonization* (1849), in which he stated the essential principles of 'systematic colonization'. A superfluity of capital and labour might be transferred from a restricted field of employment in Britain and applied—by selling colonial land at a 'sufficient price' and expending the proceeds on emigrants selected from the British labouring classes—to supply the deficiencies of colonies where vast tracts of fertile land lay unproductive for want of capital and labour combined in correct proportions. Wakefield was indefatigable in seeking to translate his theories on colonization into practical terms. He assisted in planning the colony of SA and visited Canada twice: in 1838, as assistant to Lord Durham, and during 1841–4 when he was elected to the House of Assembly. He later became wholly occupied with colonization in New Zealand, where he lived (1853–62).

WAKEFIELD, GILBERT (1756–1801), British clergyman and classical scholar, who adopted Unitarian views and taught (1779–83) at the Warrington Academy. He edited Virgil's 'Georgics' (1788), Horace (1794), and Lucretius (1799), and wrote a diatribe against Edward Porson, the leading contemporary classical scholar. Wakefield's political opinions, like those of his brother Thomas, vicar of Richmond, Surrey, were radical, and he was a bitter critic of William Pitt the Younger. He was imprisoned (1799) for writing a seditious pamphlet.

WAKLEY, THOMAS (1795–1862), British doctor and politician, who founded the *Lancet* (1823) as an organ of radical medical opinion. This was a landmark in medical journalism. Wakley was MP for Finsbury (1835–52). He made his mark in the Commons with the defence of the Tolpuddle martyrs (1835), bitterly attacked the new poor law, sympathized with the Chartists, and supported the ten-hour factory movement and sanitary reform. He worked hard to improve the standing of the medical profession, introducing bills for the registration of medical practitioners (1846, 1847), giving evidence to the 1847 select committee, and writing articles in the *Lancet*. After 1852, when he retired from parliament, he turned his energies to a campaign against adulterated food.

WALATA, small cultural centre in south-east Mauritania, which started as a caravan station in the late 13th cent. The mixed origins of its population, probably never more than 3000, stimulated cultural life, while its unique domestic architecture, furniture, and painted decor suggest influences derived from Muslim Spain, Morocco, and Egypt. After 1500 other nomads, Arab and Berber, came to settle there. Saints and scholars were buried in Walata until recent times, when Nema replaced it as a regional capital.

WALCHEREN EXPEDITION (1809), unsuccessful British expedition to Scheldt, in the French Wars, with the object of diverting Napoleon's armies and restoring trade with Europe. Troops landed on the island of Walcheren, a centre for the contraband trade with Europe, but failed to push towards Antwerp and after a few months evacuated Walcheren. In 1810 the kingdom of Holland was annexed to France.

WALCOURT, BATTLE OF (Aug. 1689), Dutch victory in the Spanish Netherlands over Louis XIV at the outset of the War of the League of Augsburg (1689–97), when the Prince of Waldeck's cavalry overcame the French army, commanded by Marshal d'Humières.

WALD, LILLIAN D. (1867–1940), US social worker and social reformer, who trained as a nurse at the New York Hospital, pioneered public health nursing in the US, and in 1895 founded a settlement house in Henry Street, on New York's Lower East Side. Like Jane Addams's Hull House in Chicago, the Henry Street settlement provided an opportunity for middle-class young people to live among and help immigrant slum-dwellers. In common with many settlement workers, Lillian Wald was led into political activity by her desire to reform social conditions. She participated in the organization of the Women's Trade Union League (1903) and the National Association for the Advancement of Colored People (1909). In 1912 she joined Theodore Roosevelt's Progressive Party and publicly supported Alfred E. Smith (though disagreeing with his anti-prohibition stand) in 1928 and Franklin D. Roosevelt in 1936. Like her friend, Jane Addams, she was strongly opposed to war and was the first president of the American Union Against Militarism (1915–17).

WALDECK, GEORGE FREDERICK, Prince of (1620–92), German soldier and diplomat, who worked in imperial and Dutch service and became a confidant of William III of Orange. He fought at the battle of St Gotthard (1664) and the Turkish siege of Vienna (1683) and was rewarded by Emperor Leopold with the rank of field marshal and the title of prince of the empire (1682). In 1686 he was sent by William of Orange to arouse the German princes against Louis XIV of France and in 1689 he was appointed William's deputy by the states general. In William's absence abroad he defeated the French at Walcourt (1689), but was himself defeated at Fleurus (1690) and fought his last engagement at Steenkirk (1692).

WALDECK-ROUSSEAU, RENÉ (1846–1904), French politician and prime minister of France (1899–1902), who restored the authority of the government of the Third Republic threatened by an alliance of clerical, military, and monarchist factions during the Dreyfus Affair. His firm measures succeeded in controlling right-wing extremists in the army and the Church. But this was only possible with the support of all the pro-Republican elements, including the socialists and the anti-clericals. Waldeck-Rousseau wanted to avoid further bitterness and therefore refused to head the anti-clerical majority in 1902, an illustration of the republic's dilemma—that the only alternative to weak, middle-of-the-road coalitions, incapable of authoritative government, seemed to be extremes of the right or left.

WALDEGRAVE, JAMES WALDEGRAVE, 1st Earl (1685–1741). British diplomat, whose mother was an illegitimate daughter of King James II. Though educated in France as a Jacobite, he switched his allegiance to the Hanoverian regime and to Sir Robert Walpole in particular, becoming a diplomat first in Vienna (1727–30) and then in Paris (1730–40).

WALDEGRAVE, SIR RICHARD (d. 1410), English politician, who was speaker for the Commons (1381–2) in the first English parliament to assemble after the Peasants' Revolt of May–June 1381. He delivered a remarkable speech, warning parliament that similar revolts would occur unless the prevalent misgovernment and lack of justice were checked. He may almost certainly be identified with Chaucer's 'perfect gentle knight' in the *Canterbury Tales*.

WALDEMAR I (*c.* 1133–82), King of Denmark (*reg.* 1157–82), who, on achieving royal power in 1157 brought unity to Denmark after a prolonged period of civil wars. In association with Bp Absalon of Roskilde, who subsequently became the primate of Denmark, he re-established a powerful kingship based on the Church. He was the first Danish ruler to secure in his own lifetime the crowning of his heir, the future King Cnut IV. Waldemar's chief objective was the destruction of the Wendish pirates and, with the support of Absalon, this developed into a crusade to convert these heathen Slavs. By 1182 their centres at the mouth of the Oder were all conquered, Christianity was being established among them, and Denmark controlled a long stretch of north German coastline.

WALDEMAR II (1170–1241), King of Denmark (*reg.* 1202–41), in the first part of whose reign Danish territorial expansion reached its height and Denmark became the greatest power in the Baltic. By 1219 Waldemar had conquered and converted to Christianity a part of Estonia. But an attack by his German vassals in combination with the cities of north Germany led to a disastrous defeat at Bornhöved (1227) and Denmark lost most of her German territories. His last important achievement was the codification of Danish law (1241), known as the Jutland Code.

WALDEMAR IV ATTERTAG (*c.* 1321–75), King of Denmark, (*reg.* 1340–75), who ended the domination of the German counts of Holstein over part of Denmark and reunified the kingdom. His measures to limit the power of the German Hanseatic merchants, culminating in the conquest of the rich Hanseatic city of Visby on Gotland, led to a Hanseatic attack in conjunction with a great league of Denmark's other enemies. In this war (1367–70) the Danish islands were overrun, and by the peace of Stralsund (1370) he had to recognize the complete freedom of Hanseatic trade. But under his daughter Margaret (d. 1412) Denmark was again to become a great power and was united for a time with Norway and Sweden.

WALDSEEMULLER, MARTIN (*c.* 1480–1518), German cartographer, who is credited with being the first person to call the New World 'America'. He applied the name to the South American continent in his *Cosmographie Introductio* (1507), based on an account of the travels of Amerigo Vespucci.

WALES, ACTS CONCERNING (1536, 1543), in England, legislative measures whereby the principality of Wales was fully united with England. The union was part of the process by which, after the Reformation, Thomas Cromwell consolidated the king's authority in those regions where some independence remained. In 1536 it was decided to appoint JPs for Wales and Chester for the first time. Some weeks later the Act of Union ended the marcher lordships by joining some with existing Welsh and English counties and creating five new ones. English law and administration were extended to Wales, which henceforth was to send 24 members to parliament. In 1543 the broad policy of the first act was underlined and worked out in detail. Together they brought Wales under the direct rule of the central government, gave Welshmen equality before the law, and, by facilitating the introduction of the Reformation into Wales, secured tranquillity in the west.

WALEWSKI, ALEXANDRE Comte (1803–77), French politician, who was foreign minister at the time of Napoleon III's tortuous diplomacy during and after the Crimean War. His habitual duplicity, combined with that of Napoleon, did much to lower the standards of international morality in the 19th cent. His main achievement was a short-lived Franco-Russian entente created by France's willingness to modify Palmerston's designs on Russia in the peace of Paris (1856). But he did not succeed in checking Napoleon's Italian adventures, for the king did not even inform him of the pact of Plombières (1859), which was designed to provoke war with Austria. Walewski persuaded Russia to remain neutral in the ensuing conflict, but his increasing conservatism and inability to dominate Napoleon led to his resignation in 1860.

WALI, Arabic word used to denote either religious figures noted for their mystical knowledge of God or, more commonly, the governor of a province (cf. the Arabic *wilaya*—to rule). It acquired in the course of time a territorial sense, *ie*, a province (cf. the Ottoman *eyalet, vilayet*).

WALI, name given in Java to Muslim divines traditionally credited with the conversion of Java to Islam in the late 15th and 16th cents. They are commonly said to have been nine in number, each with the title Sunan. Historical materials concerning these figures are not entirely reliable, but it appears that the Islam taught by them was of a mystical and eclectic nature, possibly connected with the Sufi movement within Islam.

WALID I, AL-, *ie*, Al-Walid ibn Abd al-Malik (*c.* AD 670–715), Umayyad Caliph (*reg.* 705–15), whose reign was a second age of Muslim conquest. It witnessed the campaigns of Tariq ibn Zayyad and Musa ibn Nusayr against Visigothic Spain, of Qutayba ibn Muslim in central Asia, and of Muhammad ibn al-Qasim against Sind.

WALI-ULLAH SHAH (1703–62) of Delhi, Indian Muslim divine, who tried to find a new basis for Indian Islam in the Mughal disintegration of the 18th cent. He sought to return from the jurist's formalism to the traditions (*hadith*) of the Prophet and their interpretation by *ijtihad* (speculative understanding) instead of imitation (*taqlid*). He also sought to reconcile the *sufi* schools with orthodoxy and to rally Muslims on a religious war against the Marathas. He translated the Koran into Persian and his two sons rendered it in Urdu. His school influenced the 'Whabi' movement of Patna, the Deoband theological school, and Sayyid Ahmad Khan.

WALKER, JOHN (1780–1859), English apothecary, who invented (1827) and then sold the first friction matches, at 50 for 1s. The match was struck by gripping the head in a piece of sandpaper supplied with it and then withdrawing it rapidly.

WALKER, WILLIAM (1824–60), US lawyer and adventurer, whose interest in schemes to occupy parts of Mexico and Central America by force won him international attention as a

'filibuster'. His efforts to form a government in Nicaragua resulted in his execution by a Central American firing squad. He invaded Baja California, Mexico (1853), and proclaimed an independent republic made up of that state and neighbouring Sonora. Mexican troops forced him from the country, whereupun he turned to Nicaragua. With a group of 58 men, he captured the major city of Granada and established yet another republic, with himself as commander-in-chief of the army and Patricio Rivas, a Nicaraguan, as provisional president. Walker's rule ended when he fled the country after arousing the anger of all factions in local politics. A few years later he invaded Central America again, but a Central American 'National Army of Liberation' comprising forces from Nicaragua, Costa Rica, and El Salvador, supported by the firm of Cornelius Vanderbilt, an American entrepreneur with interest in an isthmian railway, defeated him. He was forced to flee once more and returned to Honduras (1860), where he was captured by the British authorities, who turned him over to the Honduran government. He was executed in the same year.

WALL, RICHARD (1694–1778), Irish Catholic émigré from County Waterford, who worked in Spanish diplomatic, military, and political service. He took part as a volunteer in the Spanish naval defeat off Cape Passaro (1718), fought in Lombardy, Naples, and the West Indies, and assisted at the peace negotiations at Aix-la-Chapelle (1747–8). He was Spanish ambassador in London (1748–52), but in 1752 became lieutenant-general and succeeded Carvajal as foreign minister, and then Ensenada as secretary of state (1754). He was a favourite of Ferdinand VI and Charles III, but the pro-French faction at court worked against him and he was unable to prevent the anti-British family Compact (1761).

WALLACE, ALFRED RUSSELL (1823–1913), British naturalist, who observed, while in the East Indies, the distinct geographical separation of Australasian and Asian species. This, coupled with a knowledge of Malthus's *Essay on the Principle of Population*, led him to write an essay *On the tendency of Varieties to depart Indefinitely from the Original Type*. This proposed natural selection as part of the mechanism of evolution. It was found to be so similar to Darwin's hypotheses that they presented a joint paper to the Linnean Society in 1858. Subsequently he was subordinate to Darwin in the development of evolutionary theory, although he founded the modern science of zoogeography in *Geographical Distribution of Animals* (1876) and published a comprehensive book on Darwinism in 1889. Later he attempted to differentiate between men's body and soul as he could not accept that man had evolved entirely from lower animals.

WALLACE, GEORGE CORLEY (1919–), US politician, who, as governor of AL (1963–6), attracted attention by his attempt to prevent desegregation of the state university. As a third-party candidate for the presidency in 1968 his exploitation of the issue of 'law and order' gained him significant support outside the Deep South, and provided the biggest challenge for many years to the major political parties.

WALLACE, HENRY AGARD (1888–1965), US journalist, agricultural expert, and politician, who, in 1910, became associate editor, and was later editor, of the influential periodical *Wallace's Farmer*, and won wide recognition as an agricultural economist and geneticist. At a time of declining farm income he was a devoted supporter of the farmers' cause and in 1933, although nominally a Republican, accepted appointment as secretary of agriculture in President F. D. Roosevelt's administration. After the collapse of the original Agricultural Adjustment Administration, he sponsored the 'Ever Normal Granary' plan of 1938, designed to stabilize prices by stock-piling part of the crop in good years. He was elected vice-president in 1940, but lost the 1944 nomination to Harry Truman. When Truman succeeded Roosevelt, Wallace served as secretary of commerce but was asked to resign in 1946 for publicly challenging too administration's foreign policy, which he believed to be the strongly anti Soviet. In 1948 he ran as presidential candidate for the new Progressive Party.

WALLACE, SIR WILLIAM (d. 1305), Scottish soldier, who emerged as the leader of the fight for Scottish independence. In 1297 he won a victory at Stirling Bridge, but was defeated the following year at Falkirk. He continued his activities against the English until he was betrayed and executed.

WALLAS, GRAHAM (1858–1932), British writer on political and social questions, who joined the Fabians in 1886, became a university extension lecturer (1890), and was on the staff of the London School of Economics (1895–1923). He resigned from the Fabian Society in 1904, being opposed to their support of Joseph Chamberlain's tariff policy, and with the passage of time he became less interested in the reform of institutions and more concerned with general questions of man in society. He was author of *Human Nature in Politics* (1908), and *Our Social Heritage* (1921).

WALLENSTEIN, ALBRECHT EUSEBIUS WENZEL VON (1583–1634), Duke of Friedland and Mecklenburg, Prince of Sagan, Czech commander-in-chief of the imperial forces, and the dominant figure in the empire during the first half of the Thirty Years War (1618–48). Born in Bohemia of a minor Protestant noble family and orphaned when young, he was converted to Catholicism as a youth. In 1614 he acquired vast estates in Moravia on the death of his wife, a rich widow whom he had married in 1609. He contributed to Archduke Ferdinand's campaign against Venice (1617) and on the outbreak of the Bohemian revolt (1618) raised a private army for Ferdinand and repeatedly lent him money. After the expulsion of Frederick from Bohemia (1620) Wallenstein enriched himself with the confiscated property of defeated nobles and built up a virtually independent principality in northern Bohemia centred on the town of Gitschin. In 1623 he married Isabella von Harrach, daughter of one of Emperor Ferdinand's closest advisers, and in the same year was created Count of Friedland. In 1625 the emperor accepted his offer of 20,000 men for the war in Germany and he soon became commander-in-chief in the empire. His military successes were based partly on his superior organization and partly on his insistence that occupied areas should feed and pay for his army. He trapped the Protestant forces of Ernst von Mansfeld at the Elbe bridgehead at Dessau (1626), and prevented their juncture with Bethlen Gabor. He then occupied the mark of Brandenburg as a preliminary to seizing the whole Baltic seaboard (1627). In 1628 Ferdinand bestowed on Wallenstein the titles of Duke of Mecklenburg and 'General of the Baltic and Oceanic Seas' and sold him the Silesian principality of Sagan. Wallenstein however failed to take Stralsund (Aug. 1628), though his victory at Wolgast (1628) forced Christian of Denmark to come to terms with the empire (1629). Relations between him and Ferdinand grew strained because of his opposition to the Edict of Restitution (1629) and he faced the opposition of the German Catholic princes led by Maximilian of Bavaria and their intrigue with Father Joseph, the French agent at the Regensburg diet. On 13 Aug. 1630 Ferdinand agreed to dismiss Wallenstein, who retired to his estates of Friedland. During his retirement he negotiated with Gustavus Adolphus of Sweden for the creation of an independent Bohemia under his leadership, but the Swedish king's victory at Breitenfeld (1631) forced the emperor to recall Wallenstein on his own terms, namely complete military authority as commander-in-chief (1632). He cleared Bohemia of the Saxon army and invaded Saxony, but was forced to retreat after being defeated at Lützen (Nov. 1623). Degenerating now in mind and body, he incurred the hostility of the Cardinal-Infant Ferdinand of Habsburg and the emperor's son, Ferdinand of Hungary, reopening negotiations with the Elector of Saxony and Bohemian Protestant exiles, and later with

Gustavus Adolphus, and plotting to acquire the Bohemian Crown and achieve revenge for his dismissal in 1630. The emperor learned of his double-dealing and won over Wallenstein's lieutenants, Piccolomini and Gallas. Wallenstein won his last victory at Steinau against the Swedes and Saxons (Oct. 1633) and retired to Pilsen, where he rallied his officers (12 Jan. 1634). On 24 Jan. 1634 the emperor signed a secret order dismissing him and on 18 Feb. issued a public proclamation of his treason. Hoping to contact the Protestants under Bernard of Saxe-Weimar, Wallenstein moved to Eger, where his faithful officers were murdered by Scottish and Irish mercenaries led by Col. Butler. Wallenstein himself was killed by another Irishman, Capt. Walter Devereux (25 Feb. 1634).

F. Watson, *Wallenstein, Soldier under Saturn* (London, 1938).
JHS

WALLER, EDMUND (1606–87), English poet and politician, best known for his lyric, 'Go, lovely Rose'. He was related to Oliver Cromwell and John Hampden and played an equivocal part in politics during the mid-17th cent. Though involved in a royalist plot (1643), he was allowed to emigrate to France for betraying his confederates and on payment of a fine of £10,000. He returned to England in 1651 and was later one of the managers of Clarendon's impeachment (1667). He wrote panegyrics on both Cromwell and Charles II.

WALLER, SIR WILLIAM (1597–1668), English soldier and politician in the Long Parliament, who was one of the instigators of the New Model Army. He won several successes in the Civil War, eg, the battle of Cheriton (1644), but was defeated also, eg, at Roundaway Down (1643) and Cropredy Bridge (1644). He gave up his command under the Self-Denying Ordinance (1645), was a Presbyterian leader in parliament, opposed to both Cromwell and the army, and was twice imprisoned for favouring compromises with the royalists (1648–51, 1659–60), though he was not rewarded by them at the Restoration (1660).

WALLHOF, BATTLE OF (1626), decisive Swedish victory over the Poles, which enabled Gustavus Adolphus to turn his attention to Prussia.

WALLINGFORD HOUSE PARTY in England, group of leading officers of Oliver Cromwell's army, led by John Lambert and Charles Fleetwood, after whose London residence they were named. During the last years of the protectorate they opposed the civilian Cromwellians in parliament, especially over the offer of the Crown to Cromwell, and after his death they were instrumental in ending the protectorate and restoring the Rump.

WALLIS, JOHN (1616–1703), English mathematician, Savilian Professor of Geometry at Oxford (1649–1703), and a founder of the Royal Society. His most important work, *Arithmetica Infinitorum* (1656), arrived at results from which the binomial theorem and differential and integral calculus were later developed.

WALLIS, SAMUEL (1728–95), British sailor, who discovered the Society Islands, including King George's Island (later Tahiti), on a voyage through the Pacific (1767–8), his account of which was first published in 1783. He also fought in the Seven Years War, and held the post of extra commissioner of the navy (1782–3, 1787–95).

WALLIS (UVEA) (in the Pacific), Polynesian island, discovered by Schouten (1616) and Wallis (1767). Wesleyan native teachers and Marist priests had little initial success, Père Chanel being martyred on nearby Futuna on 28 April 1841. After two 'religious' wars, the people finally accepted Catholicism in 1849. The island became a French protectorate in 1844, a full colony in 1917, and, in 1959, a voluntary member of the Union française.

WALPOLE OF WOLTERTON, HORATIO, 1st Baron (1678–1757), English politician and diplomat, brother of Sir Robert Walpole. He was secretary to the treasury (1715–17, 1721–4) and envoy to the states general of the United Provinces (1716) and later became British ambassador to France (1724–30). After tiring of Chauvelin, he returned to England as cofferer of the household (1730). From 1734 to 1740 he was ambassador to the states general.

WALRAS, LÉON (1837–1910), French economist, founder of the Lausanne school, who elaborated mathematically a theory of general economic equilibrium, *ie*, the mutual dependence of all elements in the economic system.

WALSH, FINTAN PATRICK (1896–1963), NZ trade union leader, who dominated the Federation of Labour from the 1940s until his death.

WALSINGHAM, SIR FRANCIS (1532–90), English politician, who, as a student at King's College, Cambridge, acquired the uncompromising Protestantism which guided his public and private life. After studying languages abroad (1550–2), he came to London to begin a legal career, but his religious views made it politic for him to return to Europe during Mary I's reign. His continental experience proved useful when he later set up an espionage system in the major European cities.

Walsingham entered the Commons in 1559, and Burghley soon recognized his abilities. After he had given warning of the Ridolfi plot he was sent to Paris (1570) to resist Guise influence at the French court and to discuss a marriage between Elizabeth and Anjou, the future Henry III. Probably the marriage scheme was not taken very seriously by either side, but Walsingham skilfully negotiated a mutual defensive alliance at Blois (April 1572), only to see his delicate policy wrecked by the massacre of St Bartholomew in Aug.

As secretary of state (1573–90) he was still occasionally employed on diplomatic missions (Netherlands 1578, France 1581, Scotland 1583), but in foreign affairs his advice was seldom regarded, since he sided with Leicester, against Elizabeth I and Burghley, in urging an aggressive Protestant alliance with the Huguenots and the Dutch rebels against a possible combination between Catholic France and Spain. Elizabeth was always unwilling to undertake a positive commitment of this kind. On the other hand, Walsingham's vigilance did enable him eventually to trap his arch-enemy Mary Queen of Scots. After her execution (1587) he regarded a Spanish invasion as inevitable and did what he could to make adequate preparation.

Although Puritan in his religious sympathies, he was sceptical of the benefits of private zeal. He upheld the queen's prerogative as a focus of unity and preferred to 'have all reformation done by public authority', consoling the radicals with the assurance that truth would prevail in its own good time, which would be most speedily hastened by discipline and patient instruction. Colonization was another means of spreading the truth, and he was always interested in overseas ventures. Hakluyt, whom he assisted financially, dedicated his *Voyages* to him.

His only material rewards for 40 years of public service were a knighthood (1577), the chancellorship of the Duchy of Lancaster (1578), and certain patents which declined in value through inflation, so that he died in debt. Elizabeth seldom gave titles to those faithful servants who could best assist her by their presence in the Commons. His career is an instructive illustration of the basic principles of Elizabethan government. Although she mostly ignored his advice, Elizabeth kept him at court because she valued his professionalism and loyalty.

C. Read, *Mr Secretary Walsingham and the Policy of Queen Elizabeth* (Oxford, 1925).

MMR

WALSINGHAM, THOMAS (d. *c.* 1422), English cleric and last of a succession of important English monastic chroniclers writing at the abbey of St Albans. He provides the chief narrative sources for the turbulent period from 1376 to 1422, though his anti-Lollard prejudice has probably distorted understanding of the religious history of this period.

WALTER, HUBERT (d. 1205), English administrator, who preserved and consolidated the effective and developed system of government created in England by King Henry II. He was a nephew of Henry's chief justiciar, Ranulph Glanville, and first came to prominence in preserving the royal government during the absence of King Richard I on a crusade. He became Abp of Canterbury in 1193 and also the chief justiciar, being the first man to combine these two offices. In 1198 he exchanged the justiciarship for the position of chancellor and carried out important reforms in the chancery, initiating in 1199 the series of chancery rolls on which were copied the more important documents issued by the king. He was prominent in assuring the accession of King John in 1199.

WALTER, JOHN (1739–1812), British journalist and founder of *The Times*. He began the *Daily Universal Register* in 1785 primarily to review home and foreign affairs, and to report parliamentary debates. In 1788 the paper was renamed *The Times*. His son, John Walter II (1776–1847), built up the paper to its pre-eminent position in mid-Victorian Britain, and was succeeded in turn as chief proprietor by his son, John Walter III (1818–94). The family maintained its connection with the paper until recent times. Both the son and grandson of the founder sat in parliament.

WALTHAM BLACK ACT (1722) in England, legislative measure of a penal nature passed during Walpole's premiership to meet a temporary outbreak of lawlessness in Waltham Forest: any man found disguised or with his face blackened was guilty of a felony and liable to be put to death. It was extended (1726) and severely applied by the Earl of Hardwicke, the attorney-general.

WALTHAM SYSTEM in the US, name given to the concentration of all processes of spinning and weaving of textiles in the same factory. The system, first established by Francis Cabot Lowell at Waltham, MA (1814), was quickly and successfully introduced into other New England mill towns and marked an important stage in development towards modern factory production.

WALTON, IZAAK (1593–1683), English author, who set up in London as an ironmonger (1614) and became the friend of literary men and ecclesiastics. He passed his later years with Bp Morley at Farnham and with his own son-in-law, a prebendary of Winchester. He wrote five *Lives* (1640–78), of Hooker, Donne, Sir Henry Wootton, George Herbert, and Bp Sanderson, which combine affection with scholarly diligence, but his larger fame rests upon *The Compleat Angler*, or *The Contemplative Man's Recreation* (1653). It quietly affirmed the continuity of essential things. The book linked Anglicanism and angling in a manner edifying to both and delightful even to those who practise neither. The fifth edition (1676) contained an addition by the angler-poet, Charles Cotton.

WALWYN, WILLIAM (1600–*c.* 1680), English merchant and radical pamphleteer, who propagated communistic ideas based on the teachings of primitive Christianity, which greatly influenced the Leveller movement in London. In his *Compassionate Samaritane* (1644) he also advocated religious toleration for Separatists and Anabaptists.

WAN AHMAD (*reg.* 1863–1914), ruler of Pahang, Malaya who came to power through a civil war (1857–63) against his brother, Mutahir, and frightened the British by seeking Siamese moral support. Although his change of title from Bendahara to Sultan (1882) symbolized his assertion of full independence from Riau-Johor, he was obliged to accept a British agent (1887) and later a resident (1888). This prompted an anti-British rebellion (1891–5), towards which his sympathies were ambiguous.

WANAMAKER, JOHN (1838–1922), US merchant and pioneer in modern retailing, who opened a men's haberdashery store in Philadelphia (1861) and, in 1877, opened a department store that grouped a number of separate departments under one roof. An active Republican, he became US postmaster-general (1889–93).

WANAX, Mycenaean Greek for 'lord', appearing thus on Linear B tablets and later in Homer. It was clearly the term for the Mycenaean palace monarch, *eg*, Agamemnon. Beneath the *wanax* stood the *lawagetas* (commander-in-chief), *telestai* (barons), and *hepetai* (counts).

WANDIWASH, BATTLE OF (Jan. 1760), in the Seven Years War, fought about half-way between Madras and Pondicherry in south India. The British defeated the French and subsequently captured Pondicherry, their chief settlement (15 Jan. 1761).

WANG AN-SHIH (1021–86), Chinese politician and author. Conscious of the weaknesses of the Sung empire, he suggested positive schemes for the reform of government institutions and economic practice, to meet the newly emerging needs of a prosperous commerce and the growth of towns. His proposals, which were too radical to win acceptance, may be studied in his essays.

WANG CHING-WEI (1884–1944), Chinese politician, who was prominent during the 1920s and 1930s. His fame was established before the 1911 Revolution, when he unsuccessfully attempted to blow up the prince regent. During the next decade he worked closely with Sun Yat-sen. In 1925, when Sun died, Wang expected to succeed him as leader of the Kuomintang, but was thwarted by Chiang Kai-shek, who controlled the military side of the Kuomintang. The following year (1926) Wang was forced into exile, the first of several ignominious retreats from China which marked the next decade of his career. Although he held several high offices in the Kuomintang government, there was bitter rivalry between him and Chiang, who invariably got the upper hand. Wang frequently acted as the focus of opposition to Chiang within the Kuomintang; his prestige as Sun's favourite disciple ensured that though often outpointed by Chiang, he was never destroyed politically. After the outbreak of the Anti-Japanese War (1937), a superficial unity was imposed at the top of the Kuomintang, but Wang was given no personal power. In 1939 he abandoned the Kuomintang government in west China, and in 1940 became the head of the Japanese puppet regime in Nanking. His motives in doing so are still obscure; it is possible that he hoped to arrange a separate peace with the Japanese, or that he believed that he would be able to mitigate the oppressive treatment which most of occupied China received from the Japanese. He was unsuccessful; the Japanese allowed him no greater authority than the Kuomintang had done. He died in 1944, before the end of the war. He and his colleagues have since been regarded as belonging to the lowest form of traitor, both by the Kuomintang and by the Communist Party. This attitude has precluded any serious study of one of the most fascinating of 20th-cent. Chinese politicians.   DCML

WANG CH'UNG (27–*c.* 100), Chinese rationalist philosopher, who protested against contemporary belief and superstition, and explained the operations of the natural and human world on rational principles, refusing to believe in the interference of heaven or the survival of human beings after death.

WANG FU-CHIH (1619–92), Chinese scholar, philosopher of history, and Ming loyalist, who was one of the three great thinkers of the Ming-Ch'ing transitional period. Attacking the metaphysics of Chu Hsi and the subjectivism of Wang Yang-ming, he maintained that the world consisted only of concrete things (including techniques and institutions). He inveighed against the quietism of Buddhism and Taoism, and against fatalism and the cyclical interpretation of history, because they misguided human behaviour and contributed to a false world view. Progress, as revealed by history, could be achieved if the people were given the will and power to exploit human and natural resources. Therefore, government must be benevolent, property fairly distributed, and the economy left to its own devices. In these matters, history serves as a guide and the historian must be honest and avoid sweeping generalizations. In China's relations with her neighbours, peaceful coexistence should be advocated, as different peoples have different cultures. Wang was therefore opposed to the Manchu conquest of China. During his lifetime he wrote more than 70 works, most of which were not published until 200 years later owing to their anti-Manchu nature.

WANG KUO-WEI (1877–1927), Chinese classical scholar and ultra-royalist, who was a native of Chekiang. While studying Japanese and several Western languages in Shanghai in 1898, he was exposed to the influence of the philosophies of Kang Yu-wei, Schopenhauer, and Nietzsche, which was partly expressed in his theory that literature should be 'for the description of life'. In 1906, when serving as a junior official of the newly founded board of education, he developed an interest in Chinese poetry and the drama of the Sung and Yüan dynasties. His works on the latter have never been completely superseded. After the Republican Revolution (1911) he moved to Japan, abandoned his literary interests, and devoted himself to the study of oracle bones, tortoise shells, bronze inscriptions, and bamboo strips unearthed at Tunhuang and Anyang, combining the best traditional scholarship with modern techniques. A pioneer in the use of these materials, he made considerable contributions to modern scholarship in ancient Chinese history.

As a royalist, he stayed away from the new republic until 1916, and became a tutor of P'u-yi, the last Ch'ing emperor, in 1923. His loyalty to the latter was such that he felt it appropriate to seek P'u-yi's authorization before accepting a professorship at Tsinghua University (1925). In 1927, when Chiang Kai-shek's troops threatened north China, he drowned himself in Kunming Lake in the Summer Palace.

WANG MANG (*fl.* 1st cent.), founder of the short-lived Chinese dynasty called Hsin (8–23), which marked an interregnum in Han dynastic rule. He was a relative of an imperial consort's family who usurped the throne.

WANG MING (1907–   ), pseudonym of Ch'en Shao-yü, Chinese communist politician, who studied in the Soviet Union, and came to be more Soviet than Chinese in his political position. This attitude brought him into conflict with Mao Tse-tung and other nationalist-communists, especially after he won control of the Chinese Communist Party headquarters (1931). Mao was not able to establish his own authority over the CCP until the Tsunyi Conference (1935), and even then he frequently had to face challenges from Wang and his pro-Soviet associates. Wang eventually returned to the Soviet Union and was resurrected in the 1960s as a pro-Soviet 'Chinese leader' in the Sino-Soviet dispute.

WANG YANG-MING (1472–1529), also called Wang Shou-jen, Chinese philosopher, who studied the writings of Chu Hsi (1130–1200), but disagreed with his views on the 'investigation of things'. He therefore developed his own 'idealist' philosophy, which was especially important in the later 16th and 17th cents.

WANGHIA, TREATY OF (July 1844), signed by Ch'i-ying and Caleb Cushing, representing the Chinese and US governments respectively; it opened formal relations between the two nations. In addition to the provisions of the treaty of Nanking, the treaty of Wanghia (Wang-hsia) also specified the prohibition of the opium trade, extra-territoriality, 'most-favoured-nation' treatment, the right to maintain churches and hospitals in the five treaty ports, and treaty revision after 12 years. The last stipulation was one of the causes of the Arrow War, as the Chinese were reluctant to discuss further concessions in 1854.

WAQF (pl. *awqaf*), Arabic word meaning 'a pious foundation'. According to the Shari'a the aim of the foundation must be pleasing to Allah, *ie*, it should serve religious or social ends acceptable to the Muslim faith, *eg*, the establishment of mosques, madrasas, hospitals, bridges, aqueducts, etc. A valid *waqf* is perpetual in character, comes into force at once and is irrevocable. The administration of the *waqf* is entrusted to a nazir or superintendent, who receives payment for his services. It is not excluded that the office of nazir should be vested in the founder himself and in his descendants. The qadi (judge administering holy law) had the right to supervise the management of the *awqaf* within his legal jurisdiction. *Waqf* grants became the basis of the financial independence of the ulema and the control and confiscation of *waqf*s a major objective of reforming Muslim governments in the 19th and 20th cents.

WAR COMMUNISM in Russia, system of government adopted by Lenin and the Bolsheviks during the Civil War. As a result of the chaotic conditions which followed the Bolshevik Revolution (Oct. 1917) and in accordance with their doctrine the Bolsheviks established a system of highly centralized control, direct control of the economy, including the appropriation of all industrial and agricultural products and their distribution by the government, rationing, the provision of basic services free or at minimal cost, and the payment of wages on an egalitarian scale. Production fell disastrously during this period until 'war communism' was abandoned and the New Economic Policy adopted (1921).

WAR DEBTS. By the end of 1920, when US loans in particular ended, a complex creditor–debtor relationship entangled Britain, France, Italy, Belgium, and some minor powers with the US. The Allies in the First World War had tended to regard American loans as the US contribution to the cause of victory while the US government regarded them as definite commercial loans, not gifts—as President Coolidge remarked, 'They hired the money, didn't they?' Both groups hoped Germany would bear the cost of the war, but it soon became obvious that this was impossible. Britain was at the centre of the tangle, owing the US £850 millions, but herself being owed nearly £2000 million by her allies and ex-allies. Altogether the US had lent £2500 millions and wanted it back with interest. The US government fought hard to block an overall settlement, as requested by Britain, and also against the idea of a general cancellation of all inter-Allied debts, but demanded separate settlements and resisted, this time unsuccessfully, the connecting of debts with German reparation payments. Thus in the 1920s Britain received £65 millions from her debtors and paid £300 millions to the US, while obtaining £120 millions from Germany. What kept the system of payments going during this period was the US willingness to finance German recovery—American loans found their way back home via the debtor powers who in turn squeezed Germany. The flow stopped from 1929 when US investment in Central Europe dried up, and payment could only have continued if the debtors had exported goods and services—this was impossible, so in 1932–3 President Hoover's one-year moratorium on payments was followed by the defaulting of all the US's debtors except Finland, and all remaining inter-Allied debts were cancelled. In 1962 the US treasury announced that $19·7 billion remained unpaid.   KM

WAR HAWKS in the US, name given to members of the US 12th congress (1811–13) who urged war with Britain. They were mainly young men from the South and West, strong nationalists who suspected Britain of encouraging Indian attacks on American settlements along the southern and north-western frontiers, and resented British infringements of America's neutral rights on the high seas. As expansionists, they advocated the annexation of Canada and FL. Prominent among them were Peter Porter, of NY (1773–1844), John C. Calhoun, of SC, and Henry Clay, of KY. When Clay became speaker of the House of Representatives in the 12th congress the War Hawks became more influential than their numbers perhaps warranted.

WAR OF 1812, conflict between the US and Britain that lasted two and a half years, having emerged from a longer period of strained relations. The US, while profiting commercially from the French Wars (1793–1815), had also suffered many invasions of its asserted rights as a neutral nation. The British blockade of Europe and Napoleon's 'continental system' was enforced with increasing harshness by powers locked in a struggle too desperate for strict observance of international law. After the failure of Jefferson's Embargo and other efforts at economic coercion of the belligerents, many Americans regarded war as the only alternative to surrender of their national honour.

The decision to fight Britain rather than France can be explained in a number of ways. Superior naval power had made Britain the more frequent offender; British impressment of sailors on American ships had inflamed public feeling in the US; British intrigue was blamed for a new Indian uprising in the North-west; Canada constituted a ready military target and a prize worth winning; the political party in power, the Jeffersonian Republicans, had been consistently more hostile to England than to France; and the British were the traditional and logical enemy in a 'second War for Independence'.

President Madison's request for a declaration of war received congressional approval in June 1812, but only by a vote of 19 to 13 in the US Senate and 79 to 49 in the House of Representatives. The strongest opposition came from the commercial states of the North-east, whose maritime rights were presumably at stake. Thus, a divided and ill-prepared US began hostilities against a nation that was much more powerful, but war-weary and preoccupied elsewhere.

American expectations of an easy victory were quickly dispelled. Detroit and several other North-west forts fell to British–Canadian forces in the summer of 1812. US offensives at Niagara and Lake Champlain failed ignominiously. By the end of the year the British navy was establishing a blockade of American ports. In 1813 the naval victory of Capt. Oliver H. Perry on Lake Erie enabled the US to retake Detroit, but a new drive towards Montreal came to nothing. Napoleon's defeat and abdication in the spring of 1814 released British troops for service in North America. While a diversionary force raided and burned Washington, an invading army of about 10,000 marched southwards along the Lake Champlain route. It was forced to withdraw, however, after Thomas Macdonough destroyed British naval power on the lake. The scene of action then shifted to LA, where Sir Edward Pakenham landed a large army of veterans in Dec. The ensuing battle of New Orleans (8 Jan. 1815) ended in a decisive victory for the American forces, commanded by Andrew Jackson. Unknown to participants in the battle, negotiators at Ghent had signed a peace treaty 15 days earlier. Its terms simply restored the *status quo ante bellum*, and so, despite Jackson's closing flourish, neither nation emerged from the war indisputably victorious.

Bradford Perkins, *Prologue to War* (Berkeley, CA, 1961). Reginald Horsman, *The War of 1812* (New York, 1969). DEF

WAR OF THE FARRAPOS, or Ragamuffins, in Brazil (1835–45), was an unsuccessful federalist rebellion, led by

Bento Gonçalves da Silva, with the object of achieving political autonomy, or perhaps independence, for Rio Grande do Sul. It was the last serious provincial revolt against the central authority of the Brazilian monarchy.

WAR OF THE PACIFIC (1879–83), fought between Bolivia, Chile, and Peru for control of the nitrate-producing fields in the Atacama desert, where the three states meet. The ill-defined border of the area became a matter of dispute when Chilean entrepreneurs moved into the region, Bolivian and Peruvian developers being unable to do so. Bolivia and Peru agreed (1873) to resist Chile's efforts to exercise political control of the region, and when Chile responded to Bolivia's failure to uphold a promised tax schedule by occupying Antofagasta, a Bolivian-owned port, Bolivia declared war upon Chile, which was fought on land and at sea. Chile and Peru seemed at the start to have equal naval resources; Bolivia's army and navy were both weak. Chile took the offensive early, and captured or destroyed the leading men-of-war of the Peruvian navy. Afterwards Peru was forced to await an invasion of her shores. The conflict on land was confused by the introduction of foreign arms and by poor co-ordination between Peru and Bolivia. At the end of the first year of the war Bolivia withdrew from a confrontation with Chile, surrendering the province of Antofagasta. Chile later went over to the offensive in Peru, captured Tacna, and marched upon Lima. Chilean forces sacked the city (1881) and organized a military government. The Peruvians retreated to the Andes and for two years refused to concede defeat. Then by the treaty of Ancón (1883) Chile agreed to evacuate all of Peru except Tarapacá, Tacna, and Arica; the two latter provinces were to be occupied and used by Chile for ten years; a plebiscite would then determine the future of the coastal area. As a result of the war, Chilean power increased, the elite of Peru were demoralized, and Bolivia lost its outlet to the sea. The plebiscite was never held, but by the terms of a 1929 settlement Arica became Chilean and Tacna was returned to Peru.

WARANGAL, capital of the Kakatiya dynasty (*c.* 1000–1323), some 100 miles north-east of Hyderabad, India. It flourished especially under Ganapati (*reg.* 1199–1262). The most remarkable feature of his reign was the promulgation of a 'safety charter' protecting the cargoes of shipwrecked vessels from seizure. The city has impressive fortifications. It fell to the Muslims in 1323, when the last Hindu ruler, Prataparudra II, was defeated.

WARD, ARTEMUS (1727–1800), American soldier in the American War of Independence. Early in the war he assumed command of the MA troops and was appointed second-in-command of the Continental Army (17 June 1776) under George Washington, but ill-health forced his premature resignation (1777). He was active in MA political affairs, and served as a Federalist representative to the US Congress (1791–5). 'Artemus Ward' was also the pen name of the American humorist, Charles Farrar Browne (1834–67).

WARD, EDWARD JOHN (1899–1963), Australian politician, formerly a tramway worker, who was a member of the Australian Commonwealth parliament for East Sydney (1931–63), and became minister for labour and national service (1941–3) and for transport and external territories (1943–9). 'Eddie' Ward, a rabble-rousing Laborite of the old school, was one of the few members of post-war parliaments who was sometimes successful in tackling the Liberal prime minister, R. G. Menzies, inside and outside the House of Representatives.

WARD, SIR JOSEPH (1856–1930), NZ politician who was twice prime minister. He joined the Liberal cabinet (1891), becoming colonial treasurer (1893). Dubious banking transactions led to resignation (1895) but he returned to office (1899) and became Liberal prime minister (1906). A strong advocate of imperial unity, he promoted military and naval preparations, NZ presenting Britain with a cruiser (1909). He laboured cleverly but deviously to maintain Liberal unity, but after the close-matched 1911 election could not prevent Reform victory (1912). In the National government (1915–19), Ward was Massey's deputy, travelling with him to imperial and peace conferences. Although defeated (1919) while attempting Liberal revival at Labour and Reform expense, he unexpectedly returned to power as head of the United cabinet (1928) but was soon incapacitated for work, resigning in 1930.

WARD, LESTER FRANK (1841–1913), US official and economist, who served in the Union army during the Civil War, in the US treasury department (1865–81), and as a government geologist and palaeontologist (1881–1906). He was a founder of American evolutionary sociology, urged systematic socio-economic planning, and argued against prevailing laissez-faire doctrines. His works included *Dynamic Sociology* (1883) and *Glimpses of the Cosmos* (6 vols, 1913–18).

WARDELL, ROBERT (1794–1834), British lawyer and journalist, who helped to found the first NSW independent newspaper, the *Australian* (1824). He was a fighter for freedom of the press and of the individual, and supported 'emancipists'. He was also a successful advocate in colonial courts.

WARDHA SCHEME in India, system of Basic National Education suggested by Gandhi in Oct. 1937. He envisaged a seven-year school programme based on craft or manual work which would become self-supporting by the sale of the goods produced. A conference at his Wardha *ashram* gave its support to the idea and a committee under Zakir Husain drew up a syllabus on these lines. A *Hindustani Talimi Sangh* or Education Board was established by the Haripura session of Congress to promote the scheme. Congress governments in office from 1937 to 1939 started to implement it—notably in the Central Provinces, where it was officially termed *Vidya Mandir* ('temple of learning') but it caused considerable Muslim apprehension.

WARDROBE, THE, in England, one of the most important offices of government in the 13th and 14th cents. Originally a sub-department of the royal chamber, it emerged as the chief financial and secretarial office of the household after 1232. Its officials were in constant contact with the king, and besides furnishing a body of reliable executive agents the wardrobe often provided some of the king's most influential advisers. The highest offices of state were staffed frequently by former wardrobe officials. Under forceful rulers like Edward I and Edward III, the wardrobe was exceptionally important and in wartime it supervised the financing of military operations. The office declined in political importance and governmental activity in the 15th cent. for reasons which remain obscure.

WARDS, COURT OF, in England, department of state, formed as a result of Thomas Cromwell's reform of the financial administration during King Henry VIII's reign, although the court itself was established by an act of parliament (1540) after that minister's downfall. Its purpose was to collect and handle the feudal income of the Crown, for which it had its own officials, seals, and location in Whitehall, Westminster. In 1542 it became the court of wards and liveries by the addition of the surveyor of liveries. Unlike the other financial courts of Cromwell's creation, it remained structurally independent of the exchequer in the later Tudor period, but William Cecil's retention of the mastership (1561–96) ensured its close connection with that court. Its abolition was proposed in the Great Contract (1610) and Charles I's exploitation of wardship in the 1630s resulted in its closure by order of parliament (1646), which was confirmed by acts of parliament in 1656 and 1660.

WARDSHIP in England, right of a feudal lord to the custody of the heirs of his tenants while they were under age, and of their lands. He enjoyed the revenues of these, but was obliged to keep them properly stocked and to provide suitably for the heir. A feudal lord also had the right to choose a husband for an heiress.

WARFUSÉE, RENÉ DE RENESSE, Count of (*fl.* 17th cent.), politician of the Southern Netherlands and president of the Brussels council of finance under Philip IV of Spain. With Count van den Bergh he conspired unsuccessfully to promote a rising against the Spanish Crown, its object being the secession of the French-speaking Walloon provinces to France and the Dutch-speaking areas to the Dutch republic (1632).

WARHAM, WILLIAM (*c.* 1450–1532), English cleric and lawyer, whom King Henry VII created successively master of the rolls (1494), Bp of London (1501), Abp of Canterbury (1503), and lord chancellor (1504). His influence declined with the rise of Wolsey, who replaced him as chancellor in 1515. A close friend of the English humanists, *eg,* Colet, Grocyn, and Linacre, he disapproved of heresy and Henry VIII's divorce, but tolerated the Henrician reformation.

WAR-LORD in China, name given to the many military commanders who ruled greater or smaller parts of China during the early Republican period. The war-lord era was at its height between 1916 and 1928. War-lords were eradicated after the communist take-over of China (1949).

WARNER, SETH (1743–84), American soldier, who, with Ethan Allen, resisted an attempt by the province of NY to exert authority over VT (1763). He took part in the surprise attack on the British post of Fort Ticonderoga (1775), and played a major part at the battle of Bennington (1777), when the arrival of his regiment turned the battle in the Americans' favour.

WARNER, SIR THOMAS (*c.* 1575–1649), English colonizer, who obtained the backing of a London merchant, Ralph Merrifield, to colonize the smaller Caribbean islands. After reaching St Kitts in 1624 his settlers remained with consent of the Carib Indians. St Kitts, Nevis, Montserrat, and Barbados were granted (1625) to Merrifield and his associates, Warner becoming the king's lieutenant. In 1626 Warner brought 100 new settlers to St Kitts and after establishing working relations with the French they massacred the Caribs. The Earl of Carlisle, who in 1627 received a grant which included St Kitts, appointed Warner governor for life. In 1643 parliament appointed him lieutenant-general of the Caribee islands.

WARREN, EARL (1891–   ), US lawyer and politician. He was deputy city attorney of Oakland (1919–20), deputy district attorney and later district attorney of Alameda County, CA (1920–39), chairman of the Republican State Central Committee (1934–6), and a Republican National Committeeman (1936–8). He was also attorney-general of CA (1939–43) and governor (1943–53), in which office he became an important figure in Republican national politics and was the party's vice-presidential candidate (1948). He was appointed (1953) chief justice of the US Supreme Court by President Eisenhower and his opinion in *Brown v. Board of Education* (1954) marked the beginning of a period of a liberal interpretation of the constitution, and a willingness to deal with questions previously avoided or left untouched by the court.

WARREN, JOSEPH (1741–75), American physician and revolutionary, who became active in various political clubs,

and was a member of the committee which requested Gov. Thomas Hutchinson to remove the British troops after the 'Boston Massacre' (1770). He helped to organize opposition to the British and wrote the 'Suffolk Resolve' which he sent to the Second Continental Congress (1774). He served in the Continental Army and was killed at the battle of Breeds Hill (1775).

WARREN COMMISSION (1963–64) in the US, commission appointed by President Johnson to investigate the murder of President J. F. Kennedy. The commission, consisting of seven members, under the chairmanship of Earl Warren, chief justice of the US Supreme Court, reported that it found no evidence of a conspiracy and decided that Lee Harvey Oswald alone had been responsible for the crime.

WARRI, Niger river port in southern Nigeria. It developed as a trading station for the export of palm produce in the 1880s, and became the seat of British administration (1891–1960) of what is now Delta Province. Today Warri is the headquarters of the same province of Nigeria's Mid-western State, a cosmopolitan town that is fast growing into an oil-rich city.

WARRING STATES (CHAN-KUO), period of Chinese history. The term is usually applied to the period 403–221 BC, when the large number of small estates of early China were being merged to form seven major kingdoms (Ch'in, Ch'u, Ch'i, Yen, Han, Wei, and Chao). Considerable fighting took place during the period owing to the rival pretensions of the states. The period is noted for the formulation of the basic systems of Chinese thought and political ideas, the growth of trade and cities, the development of iron, and the evolution of writing and art forms.

WARRISTON, ARCHIBALD, JOHNSTON, titular Lord (Scottish) (1611–63), Scottish presbyterian lawyer and politician, who took an active part in Anglo-Scottish political and religious negotiation (1639–43). He was appointed king's advocate by Charles I (1646), but later lost his offices and was reduced to poverty (1650–2). In 1661 he was condemned to death and forfeiture for holding office under Cromwell. He escaped to Hamburg and then to Rouen, but was extradited and, despite illness, was hanged in Edinburgh (July 1663). His title was a courtesy one.

WARSAW, BATTLE OF (1656), three-day battle for the Polish capital during the Northern War of 1655–7. The combined forces of Charles X of Sweden and Frederick William I of Brandenburg defeated the Poles under John Casimir (28–30 July 1656) for the first time and occupied the city, but the victory proved indecisive, for Emperor Leopold came to the aid of Poland, the Brandenburgers withdrew to Prussia rather than remain in the vast Polish plains, and Sweden was threatened first by the Dutch and then by Denmark.

WARSAW, BATTLE OF (Aug. 1920). On 11 Nov. 1918 Pilsudski was declared head of the government of an independent Poland, for which he claimed the frontiers of the old kingdom of Poland before the First Partition in 1772: the line of the Dvina and Dneiper, east of the 'Curzon Line' on the Bug recommended by the League of Nations. To realize these aspirations the Poles seized Vilna from Lithuania and went to war with the Ukrainians in Galicia in 1919, but they hesitated to intervene in the Russian Civil War until it had become clear that the victorious Bolsheviks would be no more favourable to their pretensions than the Tsarists. Thereupon, on 25 April 1920, they attacked Russia in the south, taking Kiev at the beginning of May. They now occupied most of the disputed territory, but were rapidly driven from it by the advance of Bolshevik forces, nearly double their own strength (about 200,000 men), under Tukhachevsky to the north and Yegorov to the south of the Pripet marshes. By

July Budenny's cavalry had driven them back to Lvov in the south. On 14 July Tukhachevsky captured Vilna; he crossed the Bug on the 22nd and took Brest-Litovsk on 1 Aug. The Poles prepared to stand on the line of the Vistula and Dneister in front of Warsaw and Lvov. Tukhachevsky proposed to turn their flank from the north, while Yegorov guarded the Russians' weakened centre; Yegorov however refused to co-operate, and on 16 Aug. Pilsudski attacked to the north-east from south of Warsaw, penetrating the Russian's weak centre and threatening their communications and the flank of Tukhachevsky's manœuvre. By the 25th the Russians had been driven back in confusion east of Brest-Litovsk, sustaining very heavy losses. Pilsudski proceeded to win further victories on the Niemen and the Shara, while Sikorski advanced in the south. On 10 Oct. an armistice was agreed and on 18 March 1921 the treaty of Riga recognized Polish frontiers which, though not on the Dvina and Dneiper, were far to the east of the Bug. The battle of Warsaw may perhaps have saved central Europe from Bolshevik domination; it certainly created inter-war Poland.

WARSAW, CONFEDERATION OF (1573), compact designed to preserve the religious liberty of the Polish nobility, whatever their faith, agreed to by the Convocation Diet on the occasion of the election to the throne of the Valois candidate, Henry, duke of Anjou, and formally confirmed on 11 May 1573.

WARSAW, GRAND DUCHY OF (1807–12), created from the Polish territories of Prussia by the treaty of Tilsit between France and Russia. It was seen by Napoleon I as a useful base for a future invasion of Russia, and welcomed by the Poles as the possible nucleus for the re-creation of Poland. The duchy remained loyal to Napoleon throughout its short existence, even though it was forced into the confederation of the Rhine and had to conform to Napoleon's economic system and contribute a large number of troops to the invasion of Russia (1812). These sacrifices to Polish national aspirations were in vain, since the duchy reverted to Prussia after the retreat from Moscow.

WARSAW, TREATY OF (1705), settlement between Poland and Sweden, imposed on the newly crowned Swedish candidate to the Polish throne, Stanislas Leszczynski, by the victorious Swedish king, Charles XII. It indicated the political and economic subjection of Poland to Sweden, eg, Sweden was free to recruit and garrison fortresses in Poland, Swedish merchants were exempted from most Polish customs duties, and the ports of Swedish Livonia were to enjoy the monopoly of the Russian export trade to western Europe.

WARSAW, TREATY OF (1717), compromise settlement between Augustus II, King of Poland and Elector of Saxony, and the leaders of the Confederation of Tarnogrod, ratified by the 'Dumb Diet'. Most of its terms remained a dead letter, but it represented a humiliation for Poland, for it benefited Russia, the mediator of the treaty, far more than the Polish state. All royal decisions were to be subject to the approval of a majority of senators, Saxon guards and officials in Poland were to be strictly limited, the army was to be restricted to a mere 24,000 men, the state's revenues were to be dealt with by a budget, and religious toleration to Protestants was curtailed. The Russian ambassador won two concessions: the retention of Livonia and the occupation of Courland (1718).

WARSAW PACT, name generally given to the Eastern European Mutual Assistance treaty, signed on 14 May 1955 by Albania, Bulgaria, Czechoslovakia, the German Democratic Republic, Hungary, Poland, Rumania, and the USSR. The treaty formed part of an attempt by the Soviet leadership, after Stalin's death (March 1953), to put the relationship of the USSR and the countries of Eastern Europe on a new, apparently more contractual basis. At the same time, it was a riposte to the signature of the Paris agreements and the inclusion of the German Federal Republic in NATO (1954).

The terms of the treaty were phrased in the most respectable international language, with frequent reference to the UN and the expression of an intention, 'in agreement with other States desiring to co-operate in this matter', to promote the 'general reduction of armaments and the prohibition of atomic, hydrogen, and other weapons of mass destruction' (Art. 2). The signatories pledged themselves to mutual assistance and agreed to set up a joint command and a Political Consultative Committee.

The Warsaw pact organization formed a useful framework for the conduct of Soviet military policy in Eastern Europe, although the dominance of the Soviet Union limited the reality of co-operation. Albania ceased to take part in its activities after she broke off relations with the Soviet Union (1961) and withdrew from the pact in protest against the Soviet invasion of Czechoslovakia (1968). Rumania frequently refused to participate in Warsaw pact manœuvres and dissented from declarations made by the Consultative Committee regarding international affairs, eg, over the Middle East war (1967) and North Viet-nam (1968).

WARTIME ELECTIONS ACT (1917) in Canada, legislative measure regulating the franchise, devised by Sir Robert Borden's government as an insurance against possible electoral defeat as a result of opposition to Canada's participation in the First World War. The bill, together with the Military Voters Act, gave the vote to all men in the Canadian armed forces and to wives, widows, and other female relatives of men serving overseas, disfranchised conscientious objectors, all people of enemy-alien birth, those who normally used an enemy-alien language, and all who had been naturalized after 1902, with the exception of women relatives of men serving overseas.

WARWICK, RICHARD NEVILLE, 16th Earl of (1st of 2nd creation) (1428–71), one of the principal protagonists in the Wars of the Roses, in which he earned the nickname, 'the King-maker'. Feuds with rivals of his family (the Percies), who supported the ineffective King Henry VI, induced him to join his uncle, Richard of York, in a bid for power. Warwick caused the first battle of the civil war (St Albans, 1455), at which Henry VI was captured. Hostilities restarted in 1459, but the army brought by Warwick from Calais would not fight against the king. A vengeful proscription of the Yorkists followed. In an attempt to recover their confiscated estates they invaded England again from Calais in 1460. This time the royal army, through treachery in its ranks, was destroyed at Northampton. But Warwick had no intention of replacing Henry VI by York and was dismayed when Richard of York made a bid for the Crown at a parliament. This split in the Yorkist faction led to the recognition of York as the only heir of Henry VI and shortly afterwards York was killed by the royalists. Warwick now had no choice but to support York's son, Edward, in the ensuing civil war and to accept him as King Edward IV. The Yorkists won the campaign of 1461, but already in that year Edward had made attempts to build up a personal group of supporters that might counterbalance Warwick. Recurrent dissensions led to Warwick's alliance with Clarence, Edward's younger brother, and in 1469 they suddenly turned on Edward, executing his closest collaborators. In Oct. 1470 Edward fled for his life to the Netherlands, while Warwick reinstated Henry VI, ruling with the support of his former royalist enemies. Edward's return soon revived the latent divisions in this uneasy coalition. Warwick was killed by Edward at the battle of Barnet (1471), his capacity to fight being undermined by the unreliability of his army. EBF

WARWICK, ROBERT RICH, 23rd Earl of (2nd of 7th creation) (c. 1580–1658), English sailor and Puritan colonial administrator, who procured a patent for the Massachusetts colony (1628), managed the Bermudas Co., and was a shareholder of the Providence Co. in the Caribbean. He was critical of King Charles I's government and opposed forced loans, ship money, and Laud's ecclesiastical policy, and so became estranged from the court. He was responsible for bringing the navy over to the Parliamentary side in the Civil War and was lord high admiral (1643–9). He was removed from his post on the dissolution of the House of Lords (1649).

WASHINGTON, BOOKER TALIAFERRO (1856–1915), US Negro educationist, born a slave in VA, who worked his way through Hampton Institute and became a teacher in Malden, WV (1875–7). He returned to Hampton as a member of the staff (1879–81). Chosen to organize a normal school for Negroes at Tuskegee, AL (1881), he travelled widely about the US soliciting funds and support for Tuskegee Institute, and became accepted by whites as the spokesman of Negroes in America. His policies of vocational education and gradual adjustment for Negroes as expressed in his 'Atlanta Compromise' speech (1895) and embodied in the curriculum at Tuskegee, came under attack from Negro intellectuals, who feared that such a philosophy would condemn blacks to perpetual manual labour, but Washington continued to be the confidant of white presidents and the channel of white philanthropy towards blacks until his death.

WASHINGTON, GEORGE (1732–99), American planter, soldier, and first president of the US, who was descended from English stock who had moved to Virginia in the 17th cent. He was employed as a surveyor (1748–52) until he inherited his brother's plantation of Mount Vernon. In 1753 Gov. Robert Dinwiddie of VA sent him to order the French from OH country lands claimed by VA and to cement relations with the Iroquois Indians. The French refused the VA ultimatum and Washington returned to VA (1754). In 1754 he was despatched with a militia detachment to build a fort on the forks of the Ohio river. As the French had already constructed Fort Duquesne on the site, he built Fort Necessity at Great Meadows, PA. He defeated a French and Indian war party, but in turn was surrounded at Fort Necessity and forced to surrender. In the following year he accompanied Gen. Edward Braddock on his ill-fated expedition against the French. Following Braddock's defeat near Fort Duquesne he retreated with the remnant of the British–VA force and returned to his life as a planter. During the Seven Years War (1756–63) he was commander of the VA militia and responsible for defending the colony's frontier and he joined Gen. John Forbes's troops in an expedition against Fort Duquesne (1758). The French abandoned the fort, and Washington, feeling the main danger to the frontier had passed, resigned his commission (1758), married a wealthy widow, Martha Dandridge Custis (1759), and settled down on his plantation. He was elected to the VA Assembly in 1758 and chiefly concerned himself with efforts to obtain land allotments for veterans of the French and Indian War. He was chosen as a VA delegate to the First (1774) and Second (1775) Continental Congresses. Appointed by Congress to lead the Continental Army, he took command of the colonial troops at Cambridge, MA (15 June 1775). With the aid of cannon captured at Ticonderoga, Washington forced the British to evacuate Boston (17 March 1776). Later in the year British army and naval forces under Gen. William Howe and Admiral Lord Richard Howe defeated his army in the NY area (Sept. 1776), forcing him to retreat through NJ and into PA. During the winter of 1776–7 Washington buoyed American hopes with brilliant victories at Trenton (25 Dec. 1776) and Princeton (3 Jan. 1777).

Washington's defeats at Brandywine (11 Sept. 1777) and Germantown (3–4 Oct. 1779) assured British control of Philadelphia. He took up winter quarters at Valley Forge near Philadelphia, where much of his army faded away, and he had to face indifferent support from the Continental Congress and an unsuccessful attempt to replace him as commander-in-chief by Horatio Gates. Fortunately the British ignored Washington's army and by the spring of 1778 it was better trained and heartened by news of an alliance with France. Sir Henry Clinton, who replaced Howe, abandoned Philadelphia and marched overland towards New York. Washington's army met the British at Monmouth, NJ (28 June 1778), where, after an indecisive battle, Clinton was able to finish his march to New York.

Washington helped plan, but took no military part in, the campaigns in the West and South (1779–81), but in the autumn of 1781 he led a combined Franco-American army which forced Lord Cornwallis to surrender 8000 British soldiers at Yorktown (19 Oct. 1781). With the cessation of hostilities (19 April 1783), he resigned his commission and returned to Mount Vernon.

During the years of peace which followed Washington rebuilt his plantation and travelled in the West. He chaired the Mount Vernon Conference to settle disputes between VA and MD over navigation of the Potomac river (1785). Washington attended the Annapolis Convention (1786) and was chosen chairman of the Constitutional Convention in Philadelphia (1787). His position at the convention gave public confidence in the new constitution and undoubtedly aided in its ratification in the state conventions (1788).

He was elected first president of the US in 1788, and was re-elected four years later. As president, he was critical of political divisions, but in general he assumed a Federalist stance and supported the policies of his secretary of the treasury, Alexander Hamilton. He backed military campaigns to open the OH country against hostile Indians and maintained a policy of neutrality in the war between France and Britain. His last public duty was commander-in-chief of an army being raised to meet a threat from the French (1798).

Douglas Southall Freeman, *George Washington: a biography* (New York, 1948–54). RCR

WASHINGTON, STATE OF, in the US, 42nd member state of the US, admitted in 1889. The Pacific north-west was claimed for Spain by Bruno Heceta (1775), and American claims were based upon Robert Gray's discovery of the Columbia river (1792) and upon the Lewis and Clark expedition (1805). The British also laid claim to the area following Capt. Cook's visit to Nootka (1778), and although John Jacob Astor's Pacific Fur Co. founded Fort Okanoga (1811) and Fort Spokane (1812) the region was dominated by the British Hudson's Bay Co. Joint occupancy by the US and Britain was established by the convention of 1818, US title to the area south of the 49th parallel was recognized by the Oregon treaty (1846), and Oregon Territory was established (1848). Although the settlement begun near Walla Walla by Marcus Whitman (1836) was destroyed by Indians (1844), the increasing population north of the Columbia river led to the formation of Washington Territory (1853). The territory was extended to include present-day ID and parts of MT and WY when OR attained statehood (1859), but the creation of Idaho Territory (1863) established the borders with which WA was admitted to the US (1889). Completion of the Great Northern Railroad (1892) and the discovery of gold in AK (1896) led to further settlement and enlarged Seattle's trade with AK and the Far East. Lumbering, shipbuilding, fishing, and agriculture contribute to WA's economy. The exploitation of the Columbia river's vast hydro-electric potential since the 1930s and the rising importance of aerospace industries since the Second World War added to the state's prosperity. ICP

WASHINGTON CONFERENCE (1921–2), international conference for the limitation of naval armaments and adjustment of Far Eastern questions, called on Anglo-American initiatives in Nov. 1921. Representatives of the US, Britain, and the Dominions, Japan, France, Italy, the Netherlands, Portugal, Belgium, and China met in Washington, DC, and the conference resulted in three major agreements. A Five-Power ten-year treaty (later extended to 15 years) reduced naval tonnage in capital ships to a ratio of $5:5:3:1 \cdot 75:1 \cdot 75$ for the US, Britain, Japan, France, and Italy respectively, while island fortifications in certain areas of the Pacific were limited to the status quo. A Nine-Power treaty bound the signatories to the principle of the Open Door and the territorial integrity of China. A Four-Power (US, Britain, France, and Japan) treaty ended the Anglo-Japanese Alliance and pledged the signatories to consultation in the event of aggression in the Far East.

WASHINGTON'S FAREWELL ADDRESS (17 Sept. 1796), in the US, address to the American nation by President George Washington, first published in the Philadelphia *Daily American Advertiser* (19 Sept.). Washington announced that he would not seek re-election to the presidency and then commented on national affairs. He spoke of the necessity of a strong union, and warned against the dangers of sectionalism and of divisive party politics. Stressing the difference in interests between the US and Europe, he justified his neutral policies towards warring European nations, and advocated the extension of US commercial interests overseas, but warned the country against making political connections and permanent alliances with foreign powers.

WASIT, city in Iraq situated between Al-Kufa and Basra, and built *c.* 702–5 to hold troops from Syria. It was the main support of the Umayyad regime, and thus limited the turbulence of the older garrison cities in Iraq, *ie*, Al-Kufa and Basra.

WASSMUSS, WILHELM (1880–1931), German diplomat, who organized tribal guerrilla operations against the British in southern Iran (1915–18) during the First World War.

WATAUGA SETTLEMENT, American frontier settlement started by William Bean (1769) on the Watauga river in TN. The settlement joined with others to form the Watauga Association (1772) and paved the way for the opening of the American south-west.

WATERFORD GLASS, heavy, deeply cut flint glass produced by English and Irish manufacturers in factories in the Waterford and Cork areas of southern Ireland after they were driven from England by the excise duty imposed on English glass in the period 1745–1825. The name is still applied to the heavier type of cut glass, in contrast to the thinner glass evolved in England in the mid-18th cent.

WATERLOO, BATTLE OF (18 June 1815), resulted in Napoleon's final defeat and ended his gamble of the Hundred Days. Although Blücher's Prussian army appeared at a decisive moment in the battle, it is debatable whether its appearance was crucial in ensuring the victory of Wellington's British troops.

WATERWAYS in Europe, inland networks of rivers, lakes, and canals which were important as a cheap and effective means of transport from the early Middle Ages, the Roman road system having decayed. Their economic importance reached its peak in the 18th cent. before the large-scale improvement of roads and the invention of railways. The Netherlands, France, Germany, Poland, and Russia all enjoyed natural navigable waterways. The Low Countries were the first western European power to develop these waterways, flooding having stimulated reclamation schemes and dyke- and canal-building, which gave the Dutch a superiority in engineering science. In France the exploitation of water transport began after the Civil Wars. Sully, Henry IV's minister, brought all navigable rivers under the royal domain and checked the creation of new obstructions,

eg, weirs or mills. The Vesle, Vienne, Eure, Ourcq, and Vilaine rivers were made navigable in stretches and projects were considered for uniting the Mediterranean with the Garonne or the Seine. The Seine–Loire canal was opened in 1642 and studies were made for a Saône–Rhône canal and a Saône–Yonne canal, although neither was built until the eve of the French Revolution (1789). Under Colbert, however, the Rhône–Garonne canal was completed (1684), linking the Mediterranean and Atlantic.

Elector Frederick William I of Brandenburg stimulated canal-building in the north German plain, *eg*, the Oder–Spree canal was completed in 1669. The Rhine was also made safer for navigation by the blasting of rocks. Charles IX of Sweden cut a 3·2-km canal to initiate the linking of Gothenburg with the Baltic. Britain lagged behind the continent in canal-building, the great era of construction being the second half of the 18th cent. Rivers had been used for transport of goods from Tudor times and the canal network was built around the natural river system, *eg*, the Aire–Calder Navigation. However, James Brindley's Bridgewater Canal (1759–61), which started the canal mania, was built without recourse to rivers.

In Russia the natural river systems were exploited from earliest times. In the 9th cent. the East Slavs established a north–south trading route by water, stretching from the Baltic to the Black Seas via the Neva, Volkhov, Lovat, and Dnieper rivers with their connecting portages. This route joined the other great waterway, the Volga, which flows into the Caspian and provides the trade route to Persia and the orient. Many towns, *eg*, Novgorod, Pskov, Polotsk, Smolensk, and Kiev, developed on these waterways and Moscow's access to rivers leading in all directions was one factor of its rise. The conquest of Siberia was made possible only by the natural and fortuitous series of parallel rivers linked by portages. Under Peter I canal construction was started in order to replace the portages, *eg*, the Vyshniy–Volochok canal (1720) was constructed to link tributaries of the Volga and Volkhov. While canals have declined in importance elsewhere in Europe, they have continued to be built in Russia to the present century, *eg*, the Volga–Don canal was completed in 1952.   MKS

WATSON, JOHN CHRISTIAN (1867–1941), Australian politician, first Labor prime minister of Australia (1904) and parliamentary leader (1901–7), who was the originator of the tactic of alliance with the protectionist Liberals led by Alfred Deakin. However, his party's 1905 Melbourne Conference prevented the alliance from being extended into a more far-reaching inter-party arrangement and Watson was also unsuccessful in opposing Labor's 1908 innovation of elected cabinets. He nevertheless secured the compulsory military training plank in the party's platform at the 1908 Brisbane Conference, as he had previously influenced adoption of the Australian Navy and Commonwealth Bank policies (Sydney, 1902). He gave place to Fisher as parliamentary leader (1907), retired from parliament in 1910, and later left the party (1916) over the conscription issue.

His great achievement was the respect which his personal integrity and skilful leadership won for Labor in the early Commonwealth parliaments.

WATSON, RICHARD (1737–1816), British cleric and scholar who was professor of chemistry (1764) and divinity (1771) at Cambridge, and later Bp of Llandaff. He attempted to refute Gibbon with his *Apology for Christianity* (1776) and Paine with his *Apology for the Bible* (1796).

WATSON, THOMAS EDWARD (1856–1922), US lawyer, politician, and one of the leaders of southern Populism, who became the spokesman for poor farmers in opposition to the commercial and industrial interests that dominated the state Democratic Party. He served one term as a US congressman (1891–3), was vice-presidential candidate of the Populist Party in 1896 and its presidential nominee in 1904. Although a strong advocate of agrarian reform, he reflected rural prejudice against Negroes and foreigners, supported the Ku Klux Klan, and opposed entry into the First World War. He was elected to the US Senate in 1920.

WATT, JAMES (1736–1819), British engineer, who discovered (1764) the cause of the Newcomen engine's waste of power, and in 1769 patented his own steam engine. His partnership with Matthew Boulton and William Murdoch in Birmingham (1775–1800) enabled him to experiment further and he produced a series of mechanical improvements. He became a Fellow of the Royal Society (1785) and in the 1790s engaged in much litigation to protect his patents. He retired in 1800 and devoted himself to mechanical and chemical research.

WATTASIDS, of Fez, sultans of Morocco (1471–1554). Beginning as viziers of the last feeble Marinids, they were driven from Fez (1459), only to return to the vacant throne as sultans at a time when Portuguese acquisitions on the coast had roused popular hostility, under religious leadership, against the government. Muhammad al-Shaikh was able to impose some stability around Fez by appointments of his followers and by courting religious opinion, but after his death (1504) the Sa'dians rose in the south and captured the initiative from the Wattasids, who were unable to resist European encroachments. The Sa'dian's capture of Agadir (1541) precipitated the conflict. In spite of its turning for help to Spain and the Turks, the dynasty was extinguished (1554).

WATTEAU, JEAN ANTOINE (1684–1721), French painter, who developed the pictorial convention of the *fête galante*, and whose style influenced the entire European Rococo movement. Born in Valenciennes, then a Flemish town, he was apprenticed there as a painter. He arrived in Paris in 1702 and worked under Claude Gillot, painter of subjects from the Italian *Commedia dell' Arte*. Gillot and Rubens (especially in his Marie de' Medici series) were the two great influences on Watteau's art.

WATTERSON, HENRY (1840–1921), US journalist. As editor of the Louisville (KY) *Courier-Journal* (1868–1918) 'Marse Henry' achieved national fame by expressing his pungent views in colourful language. He was prominent in the Liberal Republican movement which sponsored Horace Greeley's presidential candidacy in 1872, and, although generally a supporter of the Democratic Party, he was critical of Grover Cleveland, opposed William Jennings Bryan in 1896, and broke with Woodrow Wilson over the League of Nations.

WATTIGNIES, BATTLE OF (1793), French victory in the French Wars, when a conscript army under Jourdan attacked the Austrians under the Prince of Coburg, forcing them to raise the siege of Maubeuge.

WATTS, ISAAC (1674–1748), English theologian and hymn-writer, who became famous as a Dissenting preacher at Mark Lane in London (1702–12) and was the author of sacred poems, metrical psalms, and hymns, including 'O God, our Help in Ages Past'.

WAVELL, ARCHIBALD PERCIVAL WAVELL, 1st Earl (1883–1950), British soldier, who served in both World Wars and was appointed commander-in-chief in the Middle East in 1939, with a vast area of responsibility and very limited resources. In 1940–1 he liquidated Italy's East African empire and invaded and overran Cyrenaica, but the arrival of the Germans on the scene in March 1941, at the same time as the reinforcing of Greece by the British, led to a dispersal of his resources. Because of this, he suffered setbacks and was relieved of his post in June 1941 and was appointed commander-in-chief in India, where he was almost immediately called upon to face the Japanese attack on Malaya and Burma. He was viceroy of India (1943–7) and in this role made a contribution to the final stages of Indian independence, which his successor, Mountbatten, saw to their conclusion.

WAVERLEY, JOHN ANDERSON, 1st Viscount (1882–1958), British civil servant and politician, who became home secretary in Churchill's wartime government and was designated to succeed him as prime minister should both he and Eden be killed. He entered the colonial office in 1905 after taking a degree in science at Edinburgh. In 1913 he was secretary of the National Insurance Commission and in 1917 permanent secretary at the ministry of shipping. In 1919 he was appointed chairman of the board of inland revenue. As under-secretary for Ireland (1920–2) he was responsible for the maintainance of law and order, and helped to frame the Anglo-Irish treaty of 1921. As permanent under-secretary at the home office from 1922 he planned emergency powers and organization, and supervised their application during the General Strike of 1926.

In 1932 he was the first civil servant to be appointed governor of Bengal, India's most turbulent province, where he gave first priority to the suppression of terrorism. He was hated by the nationalists and survived an assassination attempt. In 1937 he refused the high commissionership of Palestine; later he was elected National government MP for the Scottish Universities. As lord privy seal in 1938 he organized civilian defence against enemy air attack and inspired the production of the 'Anderson shelter' for home use.

He joined Churchill's government as home secretary and minister for home security and was responsible for internment of aliens. As a member of the war cabinet he was responsible for the conduct of the war on the home front. He piloted Pay As You Earn income tax through the House of Commons; and supervised British participation in the atom bomb project.

In opposition after the war, he was a critic of the welfare state. He was created Viscount Waverley in 1952.   MC

WAY, SIR SAMUEL JAMES (1836–1916), Australian lawyer and politician who was chief justice of SA (1896–1915). Earlier, he combined a large practice with membership of the SA house of assembly. On leaving politics and the bar for the Supreme Court bench, he became the first Australian to be appointed to the judicial committee of the privy council (1897).

WAYNE, ANTHONY (1745–96), US soldier, who served in the War of Independence and became famous as 'Mad Anthony' after his storming of Stony Point on the Hudson (1779). He also fought in the Southern campaigns, and against the Creek Indians in GA (1782). A strong nationalist, he returned to the army as major-general (1792), and defeated the Indian tribes of the North-west at the battle of Fallen Timbers (20 Aug 1794), a victory that led to the treaty of Greenville (1795).

WAZIR (cf. the anglicized form 'vizier'), a term of Persian origin. Under the Abbasid caliphs the wazir was the head of the imperial administration, *eg*, the wazirs of the house of Barmak. The office was also important in Fatimid Egypt, where the wazir al-sayf (the vizier of the sword), from the time of Badr al-Jamali and Al-Afdal, controlled all affairs of state, military as well as civil. Nor was the vizierate less influential when the famous Nizam al-Mulk directed the administration of the Seljuk empire in the reign of Malik Shah. Four viziers held office during the golden age of the Ottoman Turks, the first among them being the grand vizier (sadr-i a'zam). Later, the rank of vizier was often accorded to various dignitaries high in the service of the Ottoman state.

WAZIRIS, fierce Pathan tribes on the Afghan frontier of Pakistan. The Mahsud Waziris inhabit the heart of Waziristan, but the Darwesh Khel are also found in Afghanistan. These tribes were constantly at war with the British (1849–1947).

WEAVER, JAMES BAIRD (1833–1912), US lawyer and politician who served in the Union Army during the American Civil War, and was internal revenue commissioner in IA (1867–73). He left the Republican Party because of its connections with big business, being opposed to its monetary policy. As a 'Greenback' supporter of paper money he was elected to the US House of Representatives (1878, 1884, 1886) and was the unsuccessful presidential candidate of the Greenback Party in 1880. Weaver helped to organize the Populist Party, and as Populist candidate for president (1892) received a popular vote of 1 million and 22 electoral votes. In 1896 he advocated Populist fusion with the Democratic Party and supported William Jennings Bryan.

WEBER, MAX (1864–1920), German sociologist and advocate of social imperialism, whose work, *Die protestantische Ethik und der Geist des Kapitalismus* (1904–5), argued that the religious struggle from which protestantism emerged was fundamental in the development of the capitalist mentality. As a methodologist of the social sciences he was a pioneer. He used the hypothetical approach to explain social phenomena; that is, he subtracted certain elements from the real situation and then compared it with the hypothetical one. In this way he dispensed with classical methods of explanation, based on causality.

WEBLEN, THORSTEIN BUNDE (1857–1929), American economist. In *Absentee Ownership* (1884) and *The Theory of the Leisure Class* (1891) he criticized the passivity of the *rentiers* and their extravagant spending. In *The Theory of Business Enterprise* (1904) and *The Place of Science in Modern Civilization* (1919) he opposed the classical and neo-classical approach to economics, wishing to free it from its rationalistic and hedonistic framework. He believed that economists should analyse the development of the various institutions of the capitalist system without judging it as a system which might be superseded.

WEBSTER, DANIEL (1782–1852), US lawyer, orator, and politician. As a young Federalist lawyer in Portsmouth he constantly opposed Jeffersonian policies which were hostile to the Federalists' mercantile interests. As US congressman (1813–17) he opposed the War of 1812, strove to embarrass its prosecution, and criticized nationalist legislation passed after the war. After moving to Boston in 1816, he built up a lucrative legal practice and appeared before the US Supreme Court in the *Dartmouth College* case (1819), *McCulloch v. Maryland* (1819), *Gibbons v. Ogden* (1824), and many others. His arguments were marked by a conservative regard for property and a Hamiltonian attitude to the constitution. He won much respect for his legal prowess and powerful eloquence, and served again as congressman (1823–7), and then as US senator from MA (1827–41).

As New England began to develop industries and to co-operate politically with western nationalists, Webster's politics underwent a transformation. In 1828 he became a protagonist of protective tariffs, which he had opposed in 1816 and 1824. He denounced Southern particularism and demolished the doctrine of nullification in a classic reply in the Senate to Robert Hayne (1830), when he declared himself for 'Liberty *and* Union, now and forever, one and inseparable'.

After supporting Jackson in the Nullification crisis, he turned against him during the controversy over the Bank of the US. As Senate spokesman for the bank, he sought its recharter and condemned Democratic financial policies, which he later blamed for the Panic of 1837. As a leader of the new Whig Party and a presidential candidate in 1836,

he campaigned for William H. Harrison (1840), was appointed US secretary of state (1841–3), and successfully resolved border disputes with Britain.

On returning to the US Senate in 1845, he opposed the extension of slavery, whether by the annexation of TX or by territorial conquests in the Mexican War, and supported the Wilmot Proviso. In the crisis of 1850, however, he deserted the Northern Whigs and advocated sectional compromise. His Seventh of March speech, pleading 'for the preservation of the Union', earned him the wrath of anti-slavery New England and the applause of its businessmen. To further the cause of compromise and unity he became Fillmore's secretary of state (1850–2), but was refused the presidential nomination in 1852.

C. M. Fuess, *Daniel Webster* (Boston, 1930).
R. N. Current, *Daniel Webster and the Rise of National Conservatism* (Boston, 1955).   DJR

WEBSTER, NOAH (1758–1843), US lexicographer, philologist, and journalist. While teaching at Goshen, NY, he began work on his 'Blue-Backed Speller', published as *A Grammatical Institute of the English Language* (3 parts, 1783–85). Asserting that 'America must be as independent in *literature* as she is in *politics*, as famous for *arts* as for *arms*', the 'Spelling Book' was instrumental in standardizing pronunciation and spelling in American, as distinct from British forms. By 1837 it had sold 15 million copies and over 70 million by 1890. Being concerned to promote copyright legislation in the 13 states, Webster was an ardent Federalist and published *Sketches of American Policy* (1785) in which he advocated a stronger union. He edited the *American Magazine* (1787–8), and *American Minerva* and *Herald* (1793–1803), and wrote articles on American history, banking, and statistics. Webster's *A Compendious Dictionary of the American Language* (1806) enlarged into *An American Dictionary of the English Language* (2 vols, 1828), of 70,000 words, established his international reputation as a lexicographer. In 1864 the *Dictionary* was generally adopted in schools and colleges throughout the US.

WEBSTER–ASHBURTON TREATY (1842), Anglo-American treaty negotiated by the US secretary of state, Daniel Webster, and the British envoy, Lord Ashburton, that settled a longstanding boundary dispute between ME and NB. The two countries also agreed to maintain naval squadrons off the African coast to suppress the slave trade.

WEBSTER–HAYNE DEBATE (19–27 Jan. 1830) in the US, one of the most important debates held in the Congress, involving the conflicting concepts of American nationalism and states' rights. It began when Senator Robert Hayne (1791–1839), of SC, criticized a proposal for restricting the sale of public lands. Subsequently he expounded the doctrines of nullification and states' rights formulated earlier by John C. Calhoun in the *South Carolina Exposition and Protest* (1828). Daniel Webster of MA, in his Second Reply to Hayne, defended congressional supremacy and attacked Southern nullification and compact theory doctrines as absurd and unconstitutional. Webster's famous peroration concluded strikingly that 'Liberty and Union' are 'one and inseparable'. Thousands of copies of Webster's address were quickly circulated throughout the US and greatly strengthened national sentiment in the North and West.

WEDDERBURN, SIR WILLIAM (1838–1918), Scottish politician, who entered the Indian civil service (1860) and served in Bombay (1860–87). After his retirement, he became president of the Indian National Congress (1889, 1910) and served as a Liberal in the House of Commons (1893–1900), heading the Indian Parliamentary Committee.

WEDEMEYER, ALBERT COADY (1897–), US soldier, who succeeded Gen. Stilwell as commander of US forces in

China (1944–6). His report on China (1947), in which he recommended US aid to Chiang Kai-shek, was not published until 1951 and its alleged suppression heightened controversy about US policy in Asia.

WEDGWOOD, JOSIAH (1730–95), British potter. His distinction as an early industrialist came both from technical improvements, in uniformity, style, and texture, in the pottery he made, and from his organization of the work on a much larger scale than in the past. Though the pottery industry can hardly be considered to have achieved an industrial revolution in his time, Wedgwood's attention to costing and marketing show him to have been a leading entrepreneur.

WEED, THURLOW (1797–1882), US editor and politician, who helped to organize the Anti-masonic Party in New York in the late 1820s. In 1830 he became editor of the *Albany Evening Journal* and used his paper to encourage the formation of the Whig Party. With his associates, William H. Seward and Horace Greeley, he dominated the Whig Party in NY state, gaining a reputation as a cynical but able and professional party manager. He later became a Republican and tried to secure the presidential nomination in 1860 for his friend Seward, but during the American Civil War he supported Lincoln.

WEEMS, MASON LOCKE (1759–1825), American clergyman and author, who spent eight years as an Episcopal minister in MD before becoming a travelling preacher and book salesman. He is best known for his anecdotal biography, *The Life and Memorable Actions of George Washington*, in the fifth edition of which (1806) appears the story of the hatchet and the cherry tree.

WEHLAU, TREATY OF (1657), agreement between John Casimir of Poland and Frederick William Elector of Brandenburg (Sept. 1657). Poland ceded the Prussian town of Elbing and the sovereignty of East Prussia to Brandenburg. The treaty was followed five months later by the offensive treaty of Bromberg against their common enemy, Sweden.

WEI, Chinese kingdom of the Warring States period, ending in 230 BC; to be distinguished from the dynastic title of three houses in the Six Dynasties period.

WEI DYNASTIES (northern Wei 386–439; western Wei 535–556; eastern Wei 534–50). Northern Wei was founded by the To-p'a family, who were one of the Hsien-pei peoples of Central Asia; it lasted longer than any other dynastic house between the Han and T'ang periods. Limited to north China, but extending into Central Asia, the dynasty was maintained by the service of Chinese officials, and saw the introduction of a new system of taxation.

WEI YÜAN (1794–1856), Chinese historian and geographer, a native of Hunan province. After editing a massive collection of government documents in 1827 for the guidance of the empire's administrators, Wei became a leading proponent of the 'school of statecraft', advocating a unity of knowledge and action in government. His deep concern over China's foreign affairs during the Opium War led to his close association with Lin Tse-hsü. Using materials on foreign countries turned over to him by Lin, he compiled the first significant Chinese work on the West, dealing with the history, geography, and politics of the Western nations, the manufacturing of modern arms and warships, and the methods of handling foreign relations. His slogan, 'learn the superior techniques of the barbarians to control the barbarians', influenced many leading officials of the 'Self-strengthening Movement'.

WEI-HAI-WEI, naval base at the north-eastern end of the Shantung promontory of China, fortified by Li Hung-chang after the Sino–French War (1884–5). It was captured by the Japanese during the Sino–Japanese War (1894–5), but the Japanese were unable to take permanent possession of it because of pressure from the Western powers. In 1898 the British secured a 25-year lease of Wei-Hai-Wei which, however, was not returned to China until 1930.

WEINGARTEN, TREATY OF (April 1525), agreement between the peasantry of Swabia and George Truchsess von Waldburg, leader of the forces of the Swabian League. The latter conceded some of the peasants' demands contained in the Twelve Articles of Memmingen, which had led to the Peasants' War in Swabia (1524–5), but the concessions were revoked after the peasant armies had been destroyed in the Franconian and Thuringian risings (1525).

WEISER, JOHANN CONRAD (1696–1760), German explorer, who migrated to America, lived with the Iroquois Indians (1713–14), and learned their language and customs. His diplomatic tact and knowledge were crucial in averting war between the colony of Pennsylvania and the Iroquois.

WEIZMANN, CHAIM (1874–1952), leader of the Zionist movement and first president of Israel, who was born in western Russia, the son of a timber merchant. He was educated at a secondary school in Pinsk, then went to Germany and studied first at Darmstadt (1892), then at the Charlottenburg Technische Hochschule (1893). He worked with future Zionists, attended the second Zionist Congress (1898), and then became a teacher in Geneva (1901). His particular type of Zionism, combining vision with empiricism, had already taken shape and he gathered round him a group of his contemporaries who formed the 'Democratic fraction' within the movement. At the Zionist Congress (1903) he took a decisive stand against acceptance of Britain's offer to establish a Jewish state in Uganda. He left Switzerland and accepted a post at Manchester University.

In 1907, after visiting Palestine, he became more than ever convinced of the need to develop colonization there as the accompaniment of political pressure to secure international acceptance of the Jewish case; at the same time his acquaintance with England confirmed him in his attachment to that country. He held no official position, but a combination of circumstances led to his becoming recognized as the most influential leader of the Zionist movement—the force of his personality, the decisive advantage which Britain could offer the Zionists as a result of the war, and the introduction which he secured, initially through C. P. Scott, to members of the British government. At the invitation of the government he left Manchester in 1916 and worked on the production of acetone in the admiralty laboratories in London. As a result of the contacts he established, he played a decisive role in securing the Balfour Declaration from the British government.

He went to Palestine in 1918 as head of the Zionist Commission, and at Aqaba he met Emir Feisal; he also laid the foundation stone of the Hebrew University, to which he attached the greatest importance, seeing it as part of the realization of the Zionist ideal. He was among those who presented the Zionist case to the Paris peace conference. He was elected president of the World Zionist Organization in 1920 and head of the newly created Jewish Agency in 1929.

His policy was based on his regard for Britain and belief that Zionist objectives could be achieved through influence on British decisions. The discrediting of this belief by British action twice led to his defeat—after the Passfield White Paper, followed by the 17th Zionist Congress (1931), and again after the Second World War (1946). After the first of these defeats, he worked to establish the Rehevoth (later Weizmann) research institute. The crisis caused by Hitler's rule in Germany brought him back to the presidency (1935). Before and during the Second World War he devoted all his energies to furthering the various needs of Jews and

Zionists—admission of refugees, recognition of the Zionist cause, and the creation (as in the First World War) of a Jewish brigade (established in 1944) within the British army. Eventually his dominance came to be challenged by those, particularly Ben Gurion, who despaired of the hopes he attached to British policy; they pressed successfully for the adoption of the Biltmore resolution (1942). After his resignation, Weizmann went to live in New York, hoping to influence the UN debate on the Palestine question (1947), and he had a decisive influence on Truman's policy. From the US he strongly urged the creation of the state of Israel, which, partly as a result of his prestige, was immediately recognized by the US. Ben Gurion's government offered Weizmann the presidency. He returned to Israel and went to live at Rehovoth. Ill-health and age limited the part he could play in the government of the country, but he maintained his close interest in events until shortly before his death.

C. Weizmann, *Trial and Error* (London, 1949).
Chaim Weizmann, ed. M. W. Weisgal and J. Carmichael (London, 1962).   WK

WEIZSÄCKER, ERNST FREIHERR VON (1882–1951), German diplomat. After serving in the navy, he joined the diplomatic service in 1920. In 1936 he became head of the political department of the foreign office, and two years later Ribbentrop appointed him his state secretary. He genuinely wished to preserve peace in Europe and was sympathetic to the opposition elements in the foreign office and the army, who secretly urged the British government to stand up to Hitler over Czechoslovakia. Apart from this, he remained a loyal functionary of the Nazi regime. His hopes for a peace settlement, after the Polish campaign, then after the fall of France, and even as late as 1943, were due to a mixture of naiveté and nationalistic sentiment. In 1943, at his own request, he became ambassador to the Vatican, where he remained, fearing prosecution after the end of the Second World War, until Aug. 1946. He was arrested in 1947 and was one of the chief defendants in the Wilhelmstrasse trial at Nuremberg. He was sentenced to seven years' imprisonment as a war criminal, but was released prematurely in Oct. 1950.

WELD, SIR FREDERICK ALOYSIUS (1823–91), NZ politician, who, as prime minister, was the chief advocate of colonial 'self-reliance' in suppressing the Maori rebellion (1864–5). Thereafter, he was successively governor of WA, where he promoted self-government (1869–75), Tas. (1875–1880), and the Straits Settlements (1880–7).

WELD, THEODORE DWIGHT (1803–95), US abolitionist, who was inspired by the evangelist Charles G. Finney, and was converted to abolitionism by Charles Stuart. After 1830 he devoted himself entirely to the anti-slavery cause. An eloquent preacher, his principal converts to abolitionism were the New York philanthropists Arthur and Lewis Tappan, the former slaveholder James G. Birney, and Harriet and Henry Ward Beecher. At Lane Theological Seminary in OH, supported financially by Arthur Tappan, he trained students as field agents for the American Anti-Slavery Society. Faced by opposition from Lyman Beecher, president of Lane, to anti-slavery agitation within the college, Weld withdrew with his followers (1834) and 'abolitionized' Oberlin College, OH. From 1836, with an augmented group of agents known as 'The Seventy', Weld preached the gospel of immediate emancipation throughout the North. He became adviser to the anti-slavery Whigs in Congress (1841–3), and secured the support of John Quincy Adams. In 1839 he published (anonymously) *Slavery As It Is*, a massive indictment of slavery, compiled from newspaper accounts and travellers' observations.

WELFS, South German noble family who rose to great power in the late 11th cent., Welf IV becoming Duke of Bavaria in 1070. In the first half of the 12th cent. they inherited the lands of the leading Saxon families and, by combining the duchies of Saxony and Bavaria, became the main rivals of the Hohenstaufen dynasty for the German kingship. This caused recurrent civil wars. Henry the Lion, the greatest member of the family, for a time achieved a compromise with his cousin, Emperor Frederick Barbarossa, and this enabled Henry to concentrate on expansion into the lands east of the Elbe river. A revival of conflict with Frederick led to Henry's expulsion and the Welf duchies were given to other houses. Henry's son, Otto IV, was briefly emperor (*reg.* 1208–14), and the family's personal possessions became the centre of the duchy of Brunswick (created in 1235). They became electors of Brunswick (Hanover) and in the 18th cent. kings of England.

WELLES, GIDEON (1802–78), US journalist and politician. As editor of the *Hartford Times* (1826–36) and a member of the CT state legislature (1827–35) he supported Andrew Jackson and held a number of state and federal offices (1836–49), but left the Democrats over the slavery issue and helped to organize the Republican party. He served as secretary of the navy (1861–9), created an efficient naval force, and in the cabinet was a spokesman for moderation and a supporter of presidential Reconstruction.

WELLES, SUMNER (1892–1961), US diplomat, who served as secretary in the US embassy in Tokyo (1915–17) and in Buenos Aires (1917–19), and then returned to the state department (1920), where he became head of the division of Latin American affairs (1921–2). After resigning from the department, he represented the US at several Latin American conferences and helped to formulate and implement what was later known as the 'good neighbor' policy. His service as assistant secretary of state for Latin American affairs (1933–7) ceased on his appointment as ambassador to Cuba (April–Dec. 1933). A close associate of President Franklin D. Roosevelt, he was promoted under-secretary of state (1937), but increasingly difficult personal relations with secretary of state Cordell Hull led to his resignation in 1943.

WELLESLEY OF NORRAGH, RICHARD COLLEY WELLESLEY, Marquis (Irish) (1760–1842), brother of the 1st Duke of Wellington and governor-general of India (1798–1805). In 1793 he became member of the board of control for India under the presidency of Dundas. On arriving in India as governor-general in April 1798, he found that the non-intervention policy of his predecessors, Cornwallis and Shore, had brought about a collapse of British prestige, while French military adventurers had acquired great influence at the Indian courts. Tipu, the Sultan of Mysore, was anti-British and had secretly sent agents to Poona, Hyderabad, Delhi, the Rajputs, Nepal, Kabul, and Mauritius, and he had also incited the Malabar chiefs to rebel. War was declared on Tipu, who was defeated in May 1799. Wellesley formed a small central kingdom of Mysore and restored the ancient Hindu Wodeyar dynasty; what was left was divided between the Nizam of Hyderabad and the East India Co. From this time onwards Mysore was effectively under British control. Tanjore, Surat, and the Carnatic were also placed under British administration. The ruler of Oudh was compelled (1801) to surrender Rohilkhand, Farrukhabad, Mainpuri, Etawah, Cawnpore, Fategarh, Allahabad, Azimgarh, Basti, and Gorakhpur. The chief justification for Wellesley's Oudh policy was strategic necessity, for Oudh was a source of weakness on an exposed frontier, but his efforts to persuade each member of the Maratha confederacy to subscribe to a separate subsidiary alliance ended in failure. He subsequently made war on the Maratha princes (1803–4). In 1805 he was recalled and his policy of pursuing British strength underwent some criticism in parliament.

Wellesley was foreign secretary (1809–12) in Perceval's

administration and twice lord-lieutenant of Ireland, where he sought to alleviate famine problems.

P. E. Roberts, *India under Wellesley* (London, 1929). CCD

WELLINGTON, ARTHUR WELLESLEY, 1st Duke of (1769–1852), British soldier and politician. Wellington never lost a battle, nor even a gun, and his qualities of iron control, attention to detail, and unyielding determination earned him the soubriquet of the 'Iron Duke'. He established his military reputation by a victory over the Maratha Confederacy in India (1803) and secured it in the long and arduous struggle against the French in the Iberian Peninsula (1808–14). At Vimiero, his tactics of lining up the infantry on the reverse slope of a hill proved to be a winning formula. English squares in such circumstances were superior to French columns, as was decisively illustrated at Waterloo.

Once Wellington was cleared of responsibility for the Convention of Cintra, he returned to the Peninsula with 20,000 men (1809). He saved Lisbon behind the lines of Torres Vedras (1810), painfully consolidated his position, and eventually, after the victory of Vittoria, drove the French out of Spain, giving immense impetus to the allied war effort, and faced Napoleon with the embarrassment of war on two fronts. Finally, at Waterloo (1815), the French emperor was decisively defeated.

Wellington's career in politics was less assured. As prime minister (1828–30) he spoilt Canning's Near Eastern policy and presided over the disintegration of the Pittite coalition which Liverpool had so ably kept together. His transparent honesty and candid speech were not always an asset, as was shown by his defence of the unreformed constitution in 1830, which precipitated the break-up of his party. As leader of the House of Lords he showed an acute awareness of the effect of the Reform Act (1832) on the constitution and insisted that the Lords must not flout the wishes of the Commons. The repeal of the Corn Laws owed much to him.

From 1842 to 1850 his stubborn refusal, as commander-in-chief of the British army, to overhaul the machine which had defeated Napoleon I, may have contributed to its pathetic performance in the Crimean War. But at his death, his lack of political imagination was forgiven and the veneration of the hero of Waterloo by the entire nation was unequivocal.

E. Longford, *The Years of the Sword* (London, 1969).
G. Davies, *Wellington and his Army* (London, 1954). SH

WELLINGTON, PROVINCE OF, in NZ. Though the NZ Co. settlements of Wellington and Wanganui (1840) were ill-adapted to NZ conditions, local Maoris were relatively few and the population grew to 3700 (1842). Bidwill, Clifford, and Weld established sheep-runs in the Wairarapa (1844). When proclaimed a province (1853), Wellington's population was about 6000. In 1859 Hawkes Bay separated from Wellington and became a new province. Palmerston North was founded in 1870.

WELLS FARGO AND COMPANY in the US, freighting firm organized by Henry Wells (1805–78), William Fargo (1818–81), and others in 1852 to function as the Western branch of the powerful American Express Co. By 1855 it had either bought out or eliminated most of its competitors, and dominated Western expressing. In the decades after the Civil War it provided a regular armed delivery service to the mining and lumber camps of the West and was the major agency for transporting bullion to Eastern markets. Wells Fargo also had extensive overseas operations. In 1918 it merged with other agencies to form the American Railway Express Co.

WELSBACH, CARL AUER VON, Baron (1858–1929), Austrian chemist, who invented the incandescent gas mantle, patented in 1855, which renewed interest in gas as an illuminant at a time of increasing competition from elec-

tricity. He also invented the alloy, Auer-metal, as well as the cigarette- and gas-lighter flint.

WELSER FAMILY, in Germany, house of merchant bankers of Augsburg whose wealth and fame was established by Bartholomew Welser (1488–1561). The family started as dealers in the metals and fustians of central Europe with a business in Antwerp and began to lend money to Emperor Charles V for his French wars and the imperial election (1519). They grew into the greatest German banking firm after the Fuggers and were granted the right to conquer and develop their own commercial empire in Venezuela (1528), though they suffered great losses when the charter was revoked (1546). They also traded with the colonists through an agency in Santo Domingo, possessed silver mines in Mexico, and financed, among other voyages, that of Pedro de Mendoza to the Rio de la Plata. Most of their ventures were failures, and by 1560 Spain had reverted to the custom of closing American enterprise to all foreigners. By the early 17th cent. the business was affected by inflation, speculation, and the decline of the German towns and in 1614 the banking house collapsed.

WELSH CASTLES. After the death of Llywelyn II and the loss of Welsh independence, Edward I maintained his hold on north Wales by building castles in strategic positions and creating boroughs around them. Conway and Caernarvon were new castles (1283); others, at Harlech, Criccieth, and Bere, were older Welsh strongholds rebuilt and strengthened. A new fortress was begun at Beaumaris after the revolt of 1294–5. Other castles were built at Flint, Rhuddlan, and Denbigh, while the Welsh castles at Ewloe, Deganwy, Dolwyddelan, and Dolbadarn were strengthened. Edward's castles were large structures completed at considerable cost over a period of years and are masterpieces of military architecture in conception and workmanship. Where site conditions allowed, the castles were 'concentric', consisting of circuits of walls within walls with ample provision for cross-firing, and were difficult of access. The most elaborate example is at Beaumaris.

WELSH INDIANS, legendary linguistic heirs of a Welsh prince called Madoc, who, according to a story of the Welsh bards, landed with his followers in America (1170). Several Welsh settlers in the 18th cent. claimed to have met Indians speaking Welsh, including the Tuscarora, Modoc, Hopi, Comanche, Pawnee, and, particularly, the Mandan. Extensive investigation has failed to prove that any traces of European languages exist in any native American languages.

WELSH MARCH. The first phase of the Norman invasion of Wales was not undertaken by the king, but was the result of private campaigns by individual lords, encouraged by the king, to win new lands. The Norman lord took over the territory of the Welsh lord whom he had conquered with that lord's rights and privileges. The Welsh lords had been petty kings and the marcher lords inherited their rights of collecting dues and services, setting up their own courts and systems of law and administration. The marcher lordships therefore exercised royal rights both by inheritance and by right of conquest. The king had no rights touching succession, but could confiscate the lordship in special circumstances and might arbitrate on appeal to him. Marcher lordships introduced foreign elements, castles, boroughs, and manors, into the fertile areas, the 'Englishries', but elsewhere in the 'Welshries', Welsh life continued. The marcher lordships were an ever-present threat to native Welsh rulers, but their independence, power, and rights, including the waging of private war, were a source also of disquiet to the king. At the time of the Edwardian Settlement of Wales the marcher lordships, like the principality of Wales, were not part of the realm. Edward I attempted to curb the power of the marcher lords, but their special rights were not abolished until the March and Principality of Wales were absorbed into the realm by the Act of Union of England and Wales (1536).

WELSH NATIONALISM. The 1880s saw a revival of Welsh nationalist sentiment, contemporary with Gladstone's first Irish Home Rule Bill. Cymru Fydd (roughly, Young Wales), led by Tom Ellis and Lloyd George, became an important pressure-group in the Liberal Party, but faded out in the late 1890s. The modern Plaid Cymru (Party of Wales), founded in 1927, was an amalgam of political and literary 'cultural' nationalists, which it still (1970) remains. Political success came when it won the Carmarthen by-election (July 1966). Its challenge was weaker in the 1970 general election, and it lost its one seat, though it still recorded some good results. The appeal of nationalism is strongest in Welsh-speaking, chapel-going, Sunday-closing rural north and west Wales, representing the protest of a threatened rural culture. If it was less successful in establishing itself in the urban south, it may be partly because there are unresolved tensions, for instance over the status of the Welsh language, between rural and urban Plaid Cymru supporters.

WEN I-TO (d. 1946), Chinese poet and scholar, who is chiefly known for his strenuous opposition to Kuomintang intellectual repression in the late 1940s. His murder by Kuomintang gunmen (1946) accelerated the drift of Chinese intellectuals away from the Kuomintang.

WENCESLAS II, King of Bohemia (*reg.* 1278–1305), and the last effective Premyslid ruler. As a Habsburg puppet, after the killing of his father, Ottokar II, by Rudolph of Habsburg at the battle of Marchfeld, he was allowed to retain only Bohemia and Silesia. In 1300, with Habsburg encouragement, he became King of Poland. His successor, Wenceslas III, was assassinated during a campaign against Polish rivals and the Premyslid dynasty became extinct.

WENCESLAS, Saint, Duke of Bohemia (d. 936), patron saint of Bohemia. About 929 he surrendered his lands to Henry the Fowler, received them back as a fief of the empire, and became Duke of Bohemia. He was a pious man and was murdered by his brother. His cult was fostered by the Emperor Charles IV.

WEN-HSÜAN, or Anthology of Literature, compiled by Hsiao T'ung (501–31). This work is the largest extant early collection of pre-T'ang prose and poetry. Designed to assemble specimen examples of fine writing, the anthology has enjoyed high prestige and has widely affected the growth of Chinese literature. The contents are arranged under three main headings: prose, poetry, and *fu* or rhymed prose, and these are sub-divided according to different literary genres. The collection is of particular value for the preservation of the somewhat artificial parallel styles of the Six Dynasties' Period which were later discarded; for the collected works of writers who lived before the age of printing; and for letters and documents that are of historical as well as literary importance.

WENSLEYDALE PEERAGE CASE (1856), in Britain, unsuccessful attempt to depart from the long-customary hereditary basis of the summons of peers to parliament. In order to strengthen the appellate jurisdiction of the House of Lords, Queen Victoria issued letters patent creating Sir James Parke, a retired judge, Baron Wensleydale for his life only. The House of Lords agreed with its Committee of Privileges that he was not entitled to sit on these terms. Victoria therefore created him a hereditary baron. Life peerages have formed part of many proposals for the reform of the House of Lords. There were a number of precedents between 1377 and 1758, but after the decision of the Lords in 1858 the only life peers were those created under the Appellate Jurisdiction Act (1876), four lords of appeal in ordinary (increased to nine in 1947).

WENTWORTH, BENNING (1696–1770), American colonial official, who became New Hampshire's first royal governor (1740–65). He supported New Hampshire's military efforts against the French, and New Hampshire troops participated in the attacks on Louisbourg (1745, 1758). He resigned (1765) after being accused of nepotism.

WENTWORTH, PAUL (1533–93), English politician and Puritan propagandist, who, in 1566, made one of the earliest assertions of parliamentary privilege when Queen Elizabeth I ordered the Commons to cease petitioning her about the succession after she had assured them of her intention to marry. She withdrew her command when Wentworth initiated a debate on the supposed violation of the liberties of the house. Wentworth realized that to alter the 1559 Prayer Book and religious settlement, which were upheld by the prerogative, he must assail the prerogative at every point.

WENTWORTH, PETER (c. 1524–96), English politician and Puritan propagandist, elder brother of Paul, who was similarly determined to promote a Puritan reformation by using parliamentary privilege to attack the royal prerogative. He entered parliament in 1571 and at once rebuked Sir Humphrey Gilbert for subservience to the Crown and defied Abp Parker's plea that in religion the Commons should submit to the bishops and the council. The Commons committed him to the Tower (1576) for complaining of the 'rumours and messages' of royal displeasure that stifled parliamentary debate. In 1587, Queen Elizabeth I imprisoned him for demanding a definition of the Commons' privileges when they were forbidden to discuss Cope's bill for a Presbyterian reformation. He went to the Tower for a third time (1593), and died there, after renewed propaganda about the succession. Although his immediate motives were narrowly religious, Wentworth was a forthright champion of parliamentary rights and his career anticipated the struggles of the Stuart period.

WENTWORTH FAMILY in Australia. D'Arcy Wentworth (c. 1762–1827), an Irish doctor, was principal surgeon and superintendent of police in the penal settlement of NSW, having arrived in Sydney in 1790. He commanded the sympathy and regard of many 'emancipists' and the respect of most governors.

His natural son, William Charles Wentworth (1790–1872), a lawyer, politician, and landowner, took part with Blaxland and others in the crossing of the Blue Mountains in 1813. Later, in England as the champion of Gov. Lachlan Macquarie against the 'exclusives', he began a long period of political radicalism during which he became identified with the defence of 'emancipists' and agitation for colonial self-government which culminated in the 1842 constitutional reforms. He also published *A Statistical, Historical and Political Description of the Colony of New South Wales . . .* (1819), the first book to be published by a native of Australia. After his return to NSW in 1824, he was associated with the journalist Robert Wardell (1794–1834) in launching the *Australian* newspaper. As an elected member of the NSW Legislative Council (1843), Wentworth became a champion of pastoral interests and individualism. Though his last years were spent in England, he continued to be honoured in the late 19th and 20th cents as a great Australian patriot who had done more than any other to win self-government for his country and to strengthen its native institutions, *eg*, its first university, Sydney, which he helped to found in 1850.

His great-grandson, William Charles Wentworth (1907–), held Commonwealth office as minister for social services and aboriginal affairs (1968) in Gorton's Liberal administration.

WERGELD. In Anglo-Saxon England, in common with Germanic Europe as a whole, a man's wergeld was the price at which his life was valued. In England, a nobleman's life was generally valued as worth that of six peasants. This sum had to be paid by his killer if a man were slain.

WERTH, JOHANN VON (*c.* 1600–52), German soldier, who rose through imperialist (1622) and then Bavarian service (1630) to become a general under Maximilian of Bavaria in the Thirty Years War (1618–48). He distinguished himself at Nordlingen (1634) and was successful in Picardy (1636), but was captured by Bernard of Saxe-Weimar at Rheinfelden (1638). He was held a prisoner by the French (1638–42), but later defeated them at Mergentheim (1645) and defended Bavaria from the French and Swedes (1646). In 1647 he left Maximilian's service in favour of that of Emperor Ferdinand III.

WESBERRY v. SANDERS, 376 US 1 (1964) in the US, Supreme Court case that invalidated a GA statute apportioning congressional election districts. A consequence of the state action was that the largest district contained a population three times that of the smallest. The court argued that the requirement in Article 1 of the constitution, that representatives to Congress be chosen 'by the people of the several states', meant that as nearly as possible the vote of an individual in a congressional election should be worth as much as that of any other individual.

WESLEY, CHARLES (1707–88), English evangelist theologian, hymn-writer, co-founder of the Methodist movement, and younger brother of John Wesley. He established the Holy Club in Oxford, a group of fellow students who gathered together for fasting, charitable works, and regular observance of the sacraments, and who were derisively called the 'methodists' because of their regular religious routine (1729). He accompanied John to Georgia on a missionary campaign (1735), but returned in 1736 because of failing health. None the less, he was an active itinerant preacher (1739–56). In later life he disagreed with his brother over the latter's doctrine of perfection (1762) and over the ordination of presbyters (1784).

WESLEY, JOHN (1703–91), English clergyman who was the originator of Methodism. The influences of his earlier years led to a critical conversion from which his achievements flowed.

His father, Samuel, was a scholarly High Church Tory, but it was largely from his mother, Susanna, that Wesley derived his love of learning, unaffected piety, and personal discipline. At Oxford University he emerged as leader of the Holy Club, a group of men on a serious quest for holiness. As chaplain to the Georgia colonists in America (1735–7) he experienced a deep sense of failure. The bearing of the Moravians there, and of Böhler, whom he met in England, made him question the status of his own Christian commitment. On 24 May 1738, while attending a meeting in Aldersgate Street, London, Wesley experienced an evangelical conversion, following which a deep consciousness of authentic faith initiated his mission to Britain.

His outstanding achievement was the establishing of Methodism. In the face of much hostility he was able to win, then organize, his converts into societies whose rapid and widespread growth indicated his effectiveness as preacher, administrator, and pastor. His theology was marked by two emphases rooted in his experience: the doctrine of Christian Perfection indicated that in a serious striving for holiness the faithful man would not be disappointed, and that of Assurance affirmed that an authentic faith was confirmed to the believer by the inner testimony of the Holy Spirit. His care for learning issued not only in the founding of Kingswood School, but also in a flood of books.

He did not seek to found but to revive a Church. Actions such as his ordaining preachers appeared irregular, but he believed himself a faithful member of the Church of England.

He transformed religious life in Britain, and influenced the strength and direction of social and political currents.   PD

WESSEX, GODWIN, Earl of (d. 1053), rose to power under Cnut. Subsequently his daughter married Edward the Confessor. In 1051 he quarrelled with Edward and was driven out of England. He was readmitted in 1052, since his followers would otherwise have caused a civil war.

WESSEX, one of the leading Anglo-Saxon kingdoms. It probably developed through the combination of two originally separate units, the Thames valley Saxons and the Saxons who entered England through Hampshire and Wiltshire. These groups had combined by the 6th cent., and in the 7th cent. areas further to the west in Dorset, Somerset, and Devon were conquered and colonized. In 825 Egbert, King of Wessex, was the first to shake off permanently the supremacy of Mercia. The Viking invasions later in the 9th cent. destroyed all the Anglo-Saxon kingdoms except Wessex, which under Alfred (*reg.* 871–99), repelled all Norse attacks. Under Alfred, Wessex developed into the main sanctuary of Anglo-Saxon culture. From it originated in the later 10th cent. the movement for monastic reform and the educational and artistic developments (especially the art of manuscript illumination) known as the 10th-cent. English renaissance. Under Alfred's successors Wessex conquered the rest of England, including the districts settled by the Vikings (the Danelaw), so that after 954 the kings of Wessex ruled over a unified English kingdom.

WEST, BENJAMIN (1738–1820), American painter, born near Philadelphia, who studied in Italy (1760–3) before settling in London. His historical canvases, notably *The Death of General Wolfe* (1771), earned him contemporary fame. He became (1772) historical painter to George III, and was a founder and second president of the Royal Academy. His work greatly influenced that of numerous American painters.

WEST, JOHN (1809–73), Australian divine and journalist, who was a Congregational minister in Launceston, Tas., from 1839 until he became editor of the *Sydney Morning Herald* (1854). During his ministry he founded the Anti-Transportation League. His *History of Tasmania* (1852) revealed him as a historiographer of quality.

WEST, NATHANAEL (1903–40), pseudonym of Nathan Wallenstein Weinstein, US writer, who was associate editor, with William Carlos Williams, of *Contact* magazine. His best-known novel, *Miss Lonelyhearts* (1933), is the story of a journalist's involvement in the lives of those who write to his paper for advice. After his next work, *A Cool Million*, (1934), a savage story on the Horatio Alger theme, West went as a script-writer to Hollywood. There he wrote a few scenarios and another novel, *The Day of the Locust* (1939), which describes the demoralizing atmosphere of life in Hollywood. His bitter, grotesque writing attracted little attention during his lifetime, but has become popular with a later generation.

WEST AFRICAN FRONTIER FORCE, established in 1899 by F. D. Lugard to meet French competition on the Niger. In 1901 the Frontier Police forces of the Gold Coast and Sierra Leone were merged with it, though most recruits continued to serve only in the regiments of their own territories. The force was used initially to conquer, and to enforce British rule in, the different territories. Thereafter, it was used in emergencies to support the police in maintaining law, order, and internal security.

During the First World War the WAFF fought the Germans in the Cameroons, Togo, and East Africa. In the Second World War the force was expanded from 8000 to 146,000 for the defence of West Africa and the liberation of Ethiopia and Burma. The demobilization of the bulk of the troops brought some technical skills into civilian life, as well as much frustration, which was a significant factor in the emergence of nationalist politics in the post-war years. The colonial regiments of the WAFF became the nuclei of the national armies of Sierra Leone, Ghana, and Nigeria.

WEST AFRICAN STUDENTS' UNION became, after the collapse of the West African National Congress, the most important pan-West African political organization of the inter-war years. Its London hostel, financed by Marcus Garvey and run by Ladipo Solanke, was an important centre for the political evolution of West African students, the leaders of the post-war independence movements.

WEST COAST HOTEL CO. v. PARRISH, 300 US 379 (1937) in the US, case in the Supreme Court in which Chief Justice Hughes, in a 5–4 majority decision, sustained a Washington state minimum wage law. The decision, over-ruling the precedent of *Adkins v. Children's Hospital* (1923), opened the way for further decisions sustaining federal social legislation.

WEST FLORIDA, British North American province (1763), bounded on the east by the Appalachicola river, on the south by Lake Pontchartrain and the Gulf of Mexico, on the west by the Mississippi river, and on the north by 31°. The northern boundary was changed (1764) to 32° 30′. In 1783 West Florida was transferred to Spain. A dispute over the northern boundary with the US was settled by the Pinckney treaty (1795) at 31°. By the Mobile Act (1804) the US Congress authorized President Jefferson to take over West Florida. Nothing happened until American settlers there seized the Spanish fort at Baton Rouge (1810) and requested annexation by the US. President Madison ordered the territorial governor of LA to assume control of a portion of West Florida (1810); the territory of Mississippi gained the remaining portions. Spain relinquished all claims to West Florida in the Adams–Onis treaty (1819).

WEST INDIA COMPANY, DUTCH, colonial trading company, incorporated in 1621. The company obtained a monopoly of African and American trade and proprietorship of Dutch possessions in America. It was empowered to make war and peace, appoint officials, and legislate for their possessions, and was required to maintain 16 large and 14 small ships. Until it was overtaken by English merchants the company dominated the slave trade. After the Dutch lost their North American colonies to England (1664), the company still maintained its Guiana settlements, and established Caribbean colonies on St Eustatius (1634), Curaçao, Bonaire, Aruba (1634–5), Saba (1640), and St Martin (1648). The company also held Pernambuco (1630) and other Brazilian settlements until it was expelled from them (1654). Eventually the company got into financial difficulties and was dissolved (1674), then reconstituted (1675). When renewal of its charter was refused in 1791 its colonies were vested in the state and the company was again dissolved (1794).

WEST INDIA COMPANY, FRENCH (Compagnie de l'Occident), a trading and colonizing company conceived by Jean-Baptiste Colbert in imitation of the Dutch West India Co. It was incorporated in 1664. The company had all proprietary rights in French American and West African possessions. It was granted a 40-year monopoly of all trade with the colonies, except the Nfld fisheries. Its capital came from the French government and private investors. The company was not profitable and was unable to meet the demand of the French West Indian colonies for Negro slaves. Colbert, yielding to the colonists' clamour for free trade, closed down the company's trading activities (1674) and its rights and privileges reverted to the Crown. In 1719 what remained of the company's assets was fused with the Compagnie des Indes Orientales to form the new Compagnie Française des Indes.

WEST INDIAN ENCUMBERED ESTATES COURT ACT (1854), in Britain, legislative measure which each West Indian colony was free either to adopt or reject, giving merchant consignees to whom planters were indebted priority over other mortgagees, settlements, and claims. This facilitated many estates passing into merchants' hands. Four West Indian colonies rejected the act, which was repealed in 1886.

WEST INDIAN FEDERATION, federal state which embraced the British Caribbean colonies of Antigua, Barbados, Dominica, Grenada, Jamaica, Montserrat, St Christopher–Nevis–Anguilla, St Lucia, St Vincent, and Trinidad and Tobago. The federation was created under the British Caribbean Federation Act (1956) and the West Indies (Federation) Order in Council (1957). It came into being with the holding of federal elections (1958), the federal legislature and executive council meeting in Trinidad. Sir Grantley Adams of Barbados was its first and only prime minister. The federal constitution gave the federal government little authority and a meagre budget, the governor-general enjoying extensive reserve powers. The British government was, however, committed to advance the federation to dominion status. Conferences attended by representatives of the unit governments, the federal government, and the British government were convened (1959, 1960, 1961) for the purpose of drawing up a new constitution to be introduced in 1962. Strong differences of opinion emerged between the representatives of the two largest units. N. W. Manley, the Jamaican prime minister, insisted that taxation should be under each unit's control and should not pass to the federal government. Dr Eric Williams, prime minister of Trinidad and Tobago, insisted on federal control of taxation but, fearing an influx of migrants to Trinidad from the smaller islands, demanded that immigration should remain under unit control. Despite attempts to find a compromise at the London conference (1961), the Trinidad and Tobago government was unable to accept the terms of the final draft and in a referendum the Jamaican electorate rejected federation. The British government accepted that the federation was defunct in 1961. It was wound up legally under the West Indies Act (1962) and the West Indies (Dissolution, etc.) Order in Council (1962).

WEST INDIAN LOBBY, colloquial name applied to a pressure group of West Indian planters, agents, and merchants bent on influencing British government policy. The lobby secured the passage of the Molasses Act (1733), defeated proposed increases in the sugar duty (1743–4), and prevented the retention of Guadeloupe in preference to Canada at the treaty of Paris (1763). It was alleged (1766) that 'upwards of forty' members of parliament were West Indian planters or their descendants. The reduced importance of West Indian trade in the late 18th cent. caused a decline of the lobby's influence. Though sugar duties had been increased to finance the American War of Independence, the lobby was unable to prevent further increases (1787, 1791), nor could it prevent the abolition of the slave trade (1807).

WEST INDIAN SUGAR. In the late 17th and early 18th cents the West Indies were turned predominantly into sugar plantations, with a resulting drop in the white population and a heavy investment in slaves. The European demand for sugar was high and mercantilist controls by the colonial powers kept up prices. Sugar was an important re-export commodity for Britain and was supported by a drawback. In the late 17th cent. one-third of British imports went on to Europe and in the early 19th cent. between a fifth and a sixth of a much larger production. European dependence on British sugar, and the British conquest of French colonies, led to sugar being one of the main commodities that defeated the Continental System. Large amounts were smuggled into Europe and sold at high prices.

The relative prosperity of the sugar plantations in the 18th cent. ended in the 19th. The liberation of the slaves in

British colonies was accompanied by inadequate compensation, and freed slaves did not like working regularly. A selective duty, favouring 'free grown' sugar, was introduced in the 1830s and sustained prices until its abolition in 1854. In the period that ensued, world production of sugar increased and various European governments, in the interests of self-sufficiency, offered subsidies for home-grown beet sugar, with unfortunate effects on colonial prices. Britain forced the moderation of this policy in 1903 by imposing a tariff on sugar supported by a selective bounty, but the West Indies remained an area of chronic poverty.

WEST INDIAN UNOFFICIAL CONFERENCE, name adopted by popular leaders from the eastern Caribbean British colonies for their meeting in Dominica (1932) at which self-government within a West Indian Federation was advocated. Representatives from Antigua, St Kitts, Dominica, St Lucia, Barbados, and Trinidad attended. At the same time, Grenada's representative, T. A. Marryshow, was in London urging similar demands.

WEST IRIAN DISPUTE, conflict between the Dutch and the Indonesians over the disposition of Netherlands New Guinea following the Indonesian revolution of 1945–9. The Round Table Conference Agreement (1949) had left that part of the former Netherlands East Indies under Dutch occupation, as a concession to Netherlands nationalist feeling; in the succeeding decade the Netherlands devoted considerable attention to developing the area as an example of constructive colonial effort. The Indonesians, however, considered 'West Irian' an essential part of their state, and as the nationalist temper rose during the 1950s increasing emphasis was placed on forcing its concession. In 1957 Dutch residents were expelled from Indonesia and Netherlands-owned property was nationalized, and in 1961 military harassment of colony began. The US entered the dispute as a mediator favourable to the Indonesian side; as a result partly of this, and partly of pressure by Dutch businessmen anxious to restore relations with Indonesia, the Netherlands agreed in Aug. 1962 to relinquish control. After interim UN rule, West Irian was handed over to the Indonesians in May 1963, on the understanding that in 1969 the Irianese would be allowed to choose whether they wished to continue under Indonesian rule. Mismanagement, economic stringency, and the contempt with which Indonesians tended to regard the local Papuan population led to a series of uprisings under both Presidents Sukarno and Suharto. However, as all non-Irianese parties to the dispute were agreed that the territory should remain in Indonesian hands, no international objections were raised when the 1969 'act of free choice' was made a purely symbolic one.   RJM

WEST POINT, New York, site of the US Military Academy, on the west bank of the Hudson river, north of New York city. It was an important military post during the American Revolution, and troops have occupied West Point continuously since 1778. The academy was founded by Act of Congress in 1802. Graduates receive a bachelor of science degree, are commissioned second lieutenant, and have traditionally formed an elite officer corps in the US army.

WEST VIRGINIA, in the US, 35th member state of the US, admitted in 1863, and originally forming the north-western part of the state of VA. The area was settled by Scots–Irish, Germans, and English colonists who had moved westwards from NJ, MD, and eastern VA during the early 18th cent. Seeking economic expansion, they pressed for internal improvements and liberal banking facilities, and were aided by the completion of the National Road from Cumberland, MD, to Wheeling (1818). However, the population felt its interests increasingly prejudiced by lack of proportional representation in the VA General Assembly, which was dominated by the slave-holding Tidewater region. Accordingly, when VA seceded from the Union (April 1861) 40 north-western counties broke away and formed a loyalist government at Wheeling (June 1861). A state of Kanawha was created (Aug. 1861), and was admitted to the US as the state of WV (1863). Industry expanded rapidly after the Civil War, often at the expense of social justice, and the state experienced bitter labour troubles in the late 19th and early 20th cents. Since the Second World War its economy has depended upon its chemical and metal industries, production of natural gas, and upon coal production, declining though this is. WV has suffered from high unemployment and a low per capita income.

WESTERN AUSTRALIA, Australia's largest, most thinly populated, and most isolated state. Development of the original Swan river settlement (1829) was confined mainly to the coastal south-west, and responsible government was retarded until rich gold discoveries in the 1890s attracted to Coolgardie and Kalgoorlie thousands of 't'othersiders'. In the early 20th cent. immigrants stimulated the wheat and wool trades. A mineral boom in the 1960s, based on iron ore, and including also nickel and bauxite, fostered northern development and secondary industry. Rural progress, accelerated by technological and scientific advances of the 1920s, was extended in the 1950s and 1960s to light lands north of Esperance, on the Australian Bight.

WESTERN DESIGN, term used to describe English plans for colonial expansion in the mid-17th cent. Oliver Cromwell's schemes for capturing Spanish Caribbean and American mainland possessions were based on misinformation about Spain's strength, published (1648) in a book by a renegade English Catholic, Thomas Gage. In 1654 Cromwell despatched 2500 troops to the Caribbean under Gen. Robert Venables and a further 4100 troops were recruited in the West Indies. The force was transported in a fleet commanded by Admiral William Penn, who carried sealed orders that were to be opened in Barbados. The expedition was defeated at Española (April 1655), but managed to seize Jamaica (May 1655), which was poorly defended. Subsequently, Penn and Venables spent a month in the Tower of London (Sept. 1655) as punishment for their lack of success, though they had secured Jamaica, which remained a British possession.

WESTERN EUROPEAN UNION, defence organization in Western Europe which originated with the Brussels treaty (March 1948) and was extended after the collapse of the European Defence Community (1954). The Brussels treaty provided for a 'Western Union' based on a strengthening of economic, social, and cultural ties and provision for mutual assistance in the event of attack. It was signed by Belgium, Britain, France, Luxembourg, and the Netherlands. The Western Union was, however, overshadowed by NATO, while plans for a much closer military integration which would permit West German rearmament were also worked out. The collapse of these plans when the French Assembly rejected the EDC treaty was followed by intensive British diplomacy to meet a number of immediate needs, of which the most important was to bring the German Federal Republic into NATO. The Brussels treaty was revised to permit the adherence of Italy and Germany and the Organization which it had established became the Western European Union, with a Council and an Assembly. At the same time, protocols were signed which limited the maximum strength of land and air forces in Europe, ensured a minimal British commitment, and forbade the German Federal Republic to manufacture atomic, biological, or chemical weapons or such armaments as missiles or strategic bombers. An agency for the Control of Armaments was set up to enforce these provisions.

Subsequently the Council of WEU agreed (1957) to British withdrawal of part of its forces from the continent of Europe and (on various occasions since 1958) has agreed to the removal of many of the restrictions on German armaments production.

WESTERN PACIFIC HIGH COMMISSION, THE, established in 1877 to control the activities of British nationals in extra-territorial waters. Hampered by lack of adequate funds and transport, the office gradually became more effective with the establishment of resident deputy commissionerships in the Gilbert and Ellice Islands (1892), the British Solomon Islands (1897), and the New Hebrides (1902). The high commissioner was relieved of the Fiji governorship in 1952 and located, with his court, at Honiara, British Solomon Islands Protectorate, in 1953.

WESTERN UNION (1856–) in the US, telegraph company based upon an earlier company organized (1851) to build a telegraph line from Buffalo, NY, to St Louis, MO. By 1860 it had extended its lines to the Mississippi valley and absorbed most of its competitors. The first transcontinental telegraph was completed on 24 Oct. 1861, thereby ruining the Pony Express. Western Union's attempts to develop a complementary telephone service were abandoned when it lost a number of patent infringement suits in the 1870s, and it then devoted itself exclusively to the telegraph. Acquisition of its major rival, the Postal Telegraph service of the International Telephone and Telegraph Co., in 1943 consolidated Western Union's position as leader in the field.

WESTINGHOUSE, GEORGE (1846–1914), US engineer, who, in 1869, took out the first of over 100 patents for an air brake and founded the Westinghouse Air Brake Co. This device, which was soon adopted, greatly increased the safe speed of trains, as it enabled the driver to apply simultaneously the individual brakes on all coaches and wagons. Westinghouse later (1886) formed the Westinghouse Electric Co. and developed a single-phase, high-voltage, alternating current system for light and power, particularly using equipment designed by Nikola Tesla (1856–1943). In competition, Edison meanwhile had committed himself to the use of direct current. After a bitter struggle Westinghouse, however, won the crucial victory by securing contracts to illuminate the World Fair at Chicago and develop the Niagara Falls power on an a.c. basis.

WESTMINSTER in Britain, known for its abbey, and as the seat of British government. The abbey, dedicated to St Peter, was documented in 785, but the present church is basically of the 13th–16th cents, although it was begun under Edward the Confessor and consecrated in 1065. With two exceptions, every English monarch has been crowned at the abbey from William I onwards and many are buried there. A royal palace is known to have stood nearby, at least since Cnut's reign. This extremely important royal residence figures prominently in English medieval history, and was extensively used until 1512. Little remains of the Palace of Westminster other than Westminster Hall, which was the place of the chief law-court of England until the 18th cent., and St Stephen's Chapel.

WESTMINSTER, TREATY OF (1527), agreement confirming an alliance between England and France, the provisions of which were contrary to English popular opinion. Mary, daughter of King Henry VIII, was to marry the widower, Francis I, and the two countries were to present a united front against Charles V if he should refuse to come to terms with them. It was followed by the sack of Rome (1527) and war with Charles (Jan. 1528).

WESTMINSTER, TREATY OF (1654), ended the first Anglo-Dutch War. The Dutch conceded the honouring of the English flag in English waters and agreed to pay an indemnity for English merchant losses in the Far East and for the massacre at Amboina. The other main provision, designed to discourage Dutch support of the exiled Stuarts and to exclude the house of Orange from public affairs in the United Provinces, was in the long run ineffectual.

WESTMINSTER, TREATY OF (1674), ended the Third Anglo-Dutch War. Under the treaty New York, taken by the Dutch in 1673, was returned to the English; the salute claimed by the English was recognized to extend to an area rather wider than hitherto, though differently defined; a sum of about £180,000 was to be paid to the English; there were no territorial changes, and no question arose of Charles II obtaining those parts of the Dutch homeland agreed by him with Louis XIV in 1670 in the secret treaty of Dover.

WESTMINSTER, TREATY OF (1716), mutual alliance, negotiated between Britain and the emperor whereby Britain guaranteed the existing rights and territories of the emperor, but refused to support his claims to Spanish and Savoyard territory. In return, the emperor guaranteed the Hanoverian Succession and offered his support to George I's various electoral interests in the Baltic. This treaty, one of Stanhope's alliances, strengthened British diplomatic prestige and the existing balance of power in the Mediterranean. The emperor's Italian possessions were granted the protection of an English fleet against Spanish invasion, while imperial resources were diverted towards war against the Turks.

WESTMINSTER ASSEMBLY (1643–7), in England, convened by the Long Parliament to consider a new form of liturgy and church government to replace episcopacy and the Prayer Book. As the Solemn League and Covenant (1643) promised a Presbyterian structure in return for the Scottish military alliance, the dominant group in the assembly was Presbyterian, but their dedicated zeal alarmed the Independents, who favoured toleration, and also the parliamentary assessors, who were unwilling to surrender the state's authority in religion to Presbyterian elders, however godly. The ascendancy of the army after 1646 defeated the assembly's efforts, but they did draw up a rigid scheme of Presbyterian discipline for every parish, a directory of public worship to replace the Prayer Book, and the Westminster Confession of Faith, still the standard formulary for English-speaking Presbyterians.

WESTMINSTER CONVENTION (1756), Anglo-Prussian agreement to secure the neutrality of the German states in the Anglo-French struggle just beginning. The agreement was sought by Frederick II of Prussia, who feared that the Anglo-Russian Convention of St Petersburg (1755) might result in a concerted attack on Prussia by Britain, Russia, and Austria. The convention had important repurcussions. France was made willing to enter a defensive alliance with Austria (first treaty of Versailles) and at the end of the year Russia, seeing the Anglo-Russian agreement undermined, joined the Austro-French alliance.

WESTMORLAND, RALPH DE NEVILLE, 1st Earl of (1st of 1st creation) (c. 1364–1425), member of the important Neville family, which had large estates in Yorkshire, Durham, and on the Scottish border. He was created earl by King Richard II to counterbalance the leading northern family, the Percies. In 1399 Henry of Lancaster deposed Richard II, largely with the help of the Percies. As king, Henry IV became alarmed by the power of these over-mighty subjects. In 1403 the Percies rebelled, seeking the Crown for one of themselves, and Westmorland rendered decisive help to Henry IV by detaining one of the two Percy armies in the north, while Henry destroyed the other main Percy army at the battle of Shrewsbury. Thereafter, Westmorland helped Henry to put down further northern uprisings, which ended with the killing of Northumberland, the head of the Percies, in 1408. Westmorland's most important grandsons were the Yorkist kings, Edward IV and Richard III, and their cousin, the Earl of Warwick ('the King-maker').

WESTON, THOMAS (*c*. 1575–*c*. 1644), English merchant and adventurer, who helped to finance the first voyage of the *Mayflower*. After hearing that the *Mayflower* had arrived safely in America, he outfitted the *Fortune* with 35 colonists and sent them to the Plymouth colony. He himself migrated to America, and became a member of the VA House of Burgesses (1628).

WESTPHALIA, DUCHY OF (1180–1806), principality consisting of the dioceses of Paderborn and Cologne, granted by the Emperor Frederick I to the archbishops of Cologne in 1180. It formed the western portion of the great duchy of Saxony, split up on the fall of Duke Henry the Lion in that year.

WESTPHALIA, PEACE OF (1648), series of treaties, collectively ending the hostilities of the Thirty Years War (1618–1648), excluding those between France and Spain, which was to determine the basis of the balanced European states system that continued until the French Revolution.

Abortive peace initiatives had been made by Pope Urban VIII (1635, 1638), and after sporadic meetings between the representatives of France, Sweden, and the empire at Hamburg (1638–41), a preliminary treaty was signed (25 Dec. 1641), providing for two simultaneous conferences at Münster and Osnabrück in Westphalia. This treaty was ratified by Louis XIII and the Emperor Ferdinand III in 1642. There were no provisions for a truce, however, and as the war fluctuated, the protagonists delayed or pressed for peace negotiations, which did not begin in earnest until mid-1645.

In international terms the peace marked the triumph of the Bourbons in France and the Vasas in Sweden over the Austrian Habsburgs. Although the war between France and Spain was to continue until 1659, Ferdinand III agreed to deny his Spanish cousin, Philip IV, military assistance and safe passage for his troops to France's eastern frontier. He also recognized the independence of the Swiss confederation from the empire. Though Spain had not yet reached her nadir, Philip IV's recognition of the independence of the United Provinces was a measure of Spain's decline during the 80-year struggle. The treaties of Münster and Osnabrück not only accorded France and Sweden valuable territorial gains, but made them guarantors of the German constitution, with the right to be represented at the imperial Diet by an ambassador who could intervene in defence of the 'German liberties'. The way was cleared for France's hegemony under Louis XIV.

These provisions profoundly affected the emperor's position within the German empire. The Habsburg concept of a strong, supranational empire dominating Europe was shattered as imperial institutions were deprived of political significance and the emperor himself became another monarch whose 'reserved rights' did not raise him above his neighbours. The particularist interests of the German princes were enshrined in the terms of the peace. They could decide their own and their subjects' religion, levy standing armies, conduct their own independent foreign policies, and control legislation and taxation, while the nature and extent of the estates' obligations to the emperor and empire were postponed for future discussion (held in 1653). By the cession of the Upper Palatinate and the electoral title to the Duke of Bavaria, and the three bishoprics of Magdeburg, Minden, and Halberstadt, with east Pomerania, to Brandenburg, the negotiators initiated the equilibrium of sovereign, absolutist monarchies in Germany.

The peace also indicated the extent to which religion had become a secondary motive of politicians and enshrined the concept of the *raison d'état* and political balance. Official recognition was extended to the Calvinist creed and both Protestant and Catholic leaders ignored the protests of Pope Innocent X against those clauses which were hostile to the Catholic Church. A secular concept of international relations finally replaced the medieval idea of a universal religious authority acting as arbiter of Christendom.   MKS

WETTINS, German dynasty which rose to prominence in the Middle Elbe region in the 11th cent. In 1088 they became margraves of Meissen and thereafter steadily increased their possessions until in 1423 they acquired the Saxon lands and electorate. Their wealth was based on large silver and lead mines.

WEYDEN, ROGER VAN DER (*c*. 1400–64), Flemish painter of the 'northern renaissance', who was a pupil of Robert Campin at Tournai and settled (*c*. 1432) at Brussels, where Hans Memlinc was one of his pupils. Van der Weyden's works, such as the Bishop Rolin's *Last Judgement* at Beaune (*c*. 1445) and the *Altar of the Virgin* (*c*. 1440) are marked by a tragic pathos and psychological subtlety which marked a major advance in art and deeply influenced later painters, not only in the Low Countries but in Germany and Italy also.

WHABI MOVEMENT in India, militant Islamic reform movement in the early 19th cent. in India, but without any real connection with the Wahabis of Arabia. Its chief leader was Sayyid Ahmad of Bareilly, a disciple of Shah Abdul Aziz of Delhi. He established himself in the Swat valley and waged a holy war against the Sikhs of the Punjab (1826–31). Karamat Ali of Jaunpur, another disciple of Abdul Aziz, was opposed to extreme measures. The Faraizi movement in east Bengal, founded by Haji Shariatullah of Faridpur, and often confused with Wahabism, was more economic than religious and was known chiefly for its instigation of a revolt of the Muslim tenantry in Bengal against the exactions of their Hindu landholders.

WHAMPOA, TREATY OF (24 Oct. 1844), first treaty signed between China and France which provided for the free propagation of Catholicism in the five treaty ports and the toleration of Chinese converts. The 'most-favoured-nation' treatment enabled the French to enjoy all the privileges granted to the US and Britain under the treaties of Wanghia and Nanking.

WHAMPOA ACADEMY, Chinese military academy, opened in 1924, whose first head was Chiang Kai-shek. It trained officers along Soviet lines, at first with Soviet instructors. The Whampoa graduates transformed many Kuomintang units from war-lord rabbles into effective forces, which played a key role in the Kuomintang unification of China. Whampoa graduates later made up the military elites of both the Kuomintang and Chinese communist armies.

WHARTON, THOMAS WHARTON, 1st Marquis of (1648–1715), British Whig politician, who entered the House of Commons (1673) as MP for Wendover and later held the county seat of Buckinghamshire. He supported the Exclusion movement and opposed James II in the parliament of 1685. He welcomed the Revolution of 1688, joining William of Orange at Exeter, and is credited with the authorship of the words of the revolutionary song 'Lillibullero'. He was rewarded by William III with the post of comptroller of the household (1689–1702) which made him the principal link between the king and the Commons.

Wharton devoted himself to building up the Whig Party's organization, and with his inheritance to the family title (1696) he began to group parliamentary seats under his patronage. He was dismissed by Queen Anne, and led the Whig opposition during the Buckinghamshire election case (1700–4) and later promoted the treaty of Union with Scotland (1707). With the fall of the Whigs he was prominent in opposition to the treaty of Utrecht and the Schism Bill.

WHARTON, EDITH (1862–1937), US novelist. The characters of her polite world consider themselves as bastions against the intrusive forces of democracy, and a break with conventional standards usually leads to tragedy, as in *Ethan Frome* (1911), a study of New England farming people. Her other books include *The Touchstone* (1900), *The Valley of Decision* (1902), and *The House of Mirth* (1905). From 1907 she lived in Paris and her experiences of the First World War enter into *Fighting France, From Dunkerque to Belfort* (1915), *The Marne* (1918), and *A Son at the Front* (1923). In *The Age of Innocence* (1920), which is generally considered to be her best novel, she returned to the world she knew from the inside and wrote ironically of New York society.

WHATELY, RICHARD (1787–1863), English scholar, economist, and cleric, who taught at Oxford and became first professor of political economy at Trinity College, Dublin (1832). He presided over a commission on the condition of the Irish poor (1833–6) and was Abp of Dublin (1831–63). In his preaching and writing he advocated social and educational reforms.

WHEATLEY, JOHN (1869–1930), Scottish politician, whose first political activity was to start (1906) the Catholic Socialist Society, which paved the way for the transition of the Irish vote in Glasgow from Liberal to Labour. During the First World War, as leader of the Labour group in Glasgow Corporation, he exercised a moderating influence on the industrial militancy of Red Clydeside. On his election to parliament in 1922 he became leader of the left-wing Clydeside group of ILP members, though his intellectualism was very different from the emotional appeal of his lieutenant, James Maxton. In the 1924 Labour government Wheatley was minister of housing; from a study of the 1917 Royal Commission's report on Scottish housing he concluded that under private enterprise houses would never again be built for letting at rents the working-class could afford to pay, and his Act introduced generous subsidies for council-house building.

He became disillusioned with orthodox Labour after 1924, although his views differed also from those of the conventional left, whose enthusiasm for nationalization he did not share. But his one attempt to shift Labour leftwards, using Maxton and A. J. Cook as his spokesmen, failed (1928).

WHEELER, BURTON KENDALL (1882–), US lawyer and politician, who was elected as a Democrat to the US Senate (1922). He was the Progressive Party's vice-presidential candidate (1924), and supported most of the New Deal's domestic programme in the 1930s, but like many western Progressives, he was an inveterate isolationist. He was a leading member of the America First movement before Pearl Harbor, and his views were little changed by the Second World War, though pressure of public opinion led him to vote for US membership of the UN (1945).

WHEELWRIGHT, WILLIAM (1798–1873), US-born railroad pioneer in South America, who was also active in steamship and telegraph development. He created the Chilean Copiapó–Caldera railroad (1849–52), the Rosario–Córdoba line, and the Trans-Andean (Buenos Aires–Santiago), completed in 1910.

WHIG PARTY, in Britain, parliamentary party which emerged during the later 17th cent. It was the dominating force in politics in the first half of the 18th cent. and survived into the 19th, eventually evolving into the Liberal Party.

The name originated as a term of abuse during the debates over the exclusion of James, Duke of York, from the succession (1679–80). Those who opposed the ministers of King Charles II organized petitions against the prorogation or dissolution of parliament and were called Petitioners, or Whigs, a shortened form of Whiggamores, or Scottish Presbyterian rebels, hostile to the established regime. These critics of Charles II's government, the heirs of the Country Party, led by the Earl of Shaftesbury, based their political principles on the old legal maxim that 'the king can do no wrong', interpreting it to mean that the king's ministers

should be responsible for public acts and that they should be accountable to parliament. The Whigs thus became the defenders of parliamentary government, ministerial responsibility, and Protestantism. Although Charles II successfully evaded the application of these concepts and crushed Whig leadership in the aftermath of the Rye House Plot (1683), the 1688 Revolution, which deposed his Catholic brother, James II, was a triumph for Whig principles. The Whigs' association with the Toleration Act (1689) also gave them a reputation for religious moderation and the financial expedients evolved by the Whig Junto after 1693, eg, the Bank of England, established their reputation for sound economic policies. During Queen Anne's reign (reg. 1702–14) the Whigs were united in their committal to the War of the Spanish Succession against Louis XIV, and even more by their adherence to the Protestant succession. They therefore enjoyed political power to the exclusion of the Tories, who appeared as crypto- if not actual Jacobites, once George I came to the throne (1714). Under Walpole the Whig monopoly of office was strengthened and the Tories were of little political significance. As a party of great landowners, supported by the dissenters, capitalists, and townspeople, the Whigs were entrenched as the epitome of Protestant nationalism.

In the reign of King George III the Tory principles of monarchical authority were revived and the Whigs strove to restrict the king's participation and influence in government, eg, by Burke's Economical Reform Bill. Under Charles James Fox they pressed for parliamentary reform and received support from the more radical elements in politics, eg, John Wilkes. However, the fear of revolutionary principles similar to those adopted in France (1789) drove many former Whigs into the Tory ranks, eg, Edmund Burke, leaving a small group under Fox to champion the unpopular causes of freedom and international peace and the humanitarian movement for the abolition of the slave trade. Although the Whigs were out of office in the post-war period (1815–27), they still received the support of the merchant and manufacturing classes and took the first steps towards a reform of government, law, and society in the 1830s, eg, Earl Grey's major act for the reform of parliament. But the Whigs were an aristocratic and wealthy upper middle-class party and already more radical thinkers, eg, Bentham and Mill, were laying the foundations of liberalism, which superseded Whiggism as a viable political force after Lord John Russell's ministry of 1846–52. MKS

WHIG PARTY in the US, major political party during the Jacksonian era. The success of the Democrats in 1828 and 1832 spurred opposition politicians on to try to unite the various opposition groups, such as the National Republicans, Anti-masons, and certain States Rights elements, into a new coalition party. The Bank War (1832–4) gave men like Henry Clay and Thurlow Weed an opportunity to whip up sentiment against President Jackson, whom they accused of high-handed behaviour and 'executive usurpation'. The term 'Whig', usually attributed to a suggestion of James Watson Webb, editor of the *New York Courier and Enquirer*, came to be used from about 1834, although the party was not fully organized at national level until 1840, when William Henry Harrison was elected to the presidency. United chiefly by hostility to Jackson during the 1830s, the party lacked any clear programme and in the 'Log Cabin' election of 1840 tended to avoid serious issues and to concentrate on creating a popular image of their candidate and abusing the Democrats. In the 1840s they tended to be associated with nationalistic attitudes.

Although the Whigs included some able leaders, like Henry Clay, Daniel Webster, and William H. Seward, the only Whig presidents were the military leaders William H. Harrison and Zachary Taylor, both of whom died in office. By 1850 the party was seriously divided by the slavery question, Conscience Whigs sympathizing with free soil ideas, while Cotton Whigs supported slavery. The party fared badly in the 1852 election, when it adopted another military leader,

Winfield Scott, as a candidate for the presidency, and it was finally destroyed by the divisions aroused by the Kansas–Nebraska Bill (1854).   MJH

WHIMSICAL TORIES in England, group of Tory MPs and peers, dedicated to the Hanoverian succession and the Protestant Church, and opposed to appeasement to France. They emerged as a distinct political entity under the leadership of Sir Thomas Hanmer and the Earl of Anglesey in the last years of Queen Anne's reign. The breach between the Oxford ministry and the Elector of Hanover caused them to criticize the Tory leadership (1711–12), but the proposed treaty of commerce with France stimulated their opposition (1712–13).

WHINFIELD, JOHN REX (1901–66), English chemist. Carother's discovery of nylon stimulated interest in the possible production of synthetic fibres from other classes of chemical substance. In 1941, with J. T. Dickson, Whinfield discovered Terylene, a polyester fibre, made from terephthalic acid and ethylene glycol. From its industrial development after the Second World War by Imperial Chemical Industries and Dupont grew a new branch of the textile industry. The possible uses of Terylene appeared to be endless, as it blended particularly well with natural fibres, such as wool.

WHISKEY REBELLION (1794) in the US, revolt of farmers in western PA, mainly against Hamilton's Excise Act (1791). Federal officials were attacked by the mob and the crisis served as a test of the president's power to call out the militia to enforce federal law. The militia from four states, including PA, obeyed the call and the rebels were routed.

WHISTLER, JAMES ABBOTT McNEILL (1834–1903), US painter, born in MA and educated in St Petersburg, Russia, where his father was an engineer. He returned to the US (1849) and went to the US Military Academy, but was dismissed (1854). In 1855 he went to Paris, where he associated with the French Impressionists, and later settled in London. Harmony rather than contrast is a marked characteristic of his work, as is seen in the series *Arrangements, Harmonies, Nocturnes*, and *Études* (1865–77), and the quality of his 400 etchings ranks him among the greatest masters of the genre. He was well known for his caustic wit and eccentric dress, and was author of *The Gentle Art of Making Enemies* (1890).

WHITAKER, SIR FREDERICK (1812–91), NZ politician, lawyer, financier, and land speculator. As prime minister of NZ (1863–4) he implemented a 'thorough' policy of suppressing Maori rebellion and confiscating Maori land.

WHITBOURNE, SIR RICHARD (c. 1579–1626), English adventurer and sailor, who was instrumental in the colonization of Nfld through his book *Discourse and Discovery of Newfound-land . . .* (1620). He fought against the Spanish Armada (1588) and was sent to Nfld to settle disputes between colonists and fishermen (1615), during which he was empowered to set up the first court on the island.

WHITBREAD, SAMUEL (1758–1815), English radical politician, who supported every liberal cause, including Catholic and Negro emancipation and parliamentary reform. He vociferously opposed the French Wars.

WHITBY, SYNOD OF (664), held to decide whether the Northumbrian Church should adopt the Roman Easter or maintain the Celtic usage. King Oswin's declaration in favour of Rome symbolized the ending of the influence of the Celtic clergy, who had been the first to introduce Christianity into Northumbria. This made possible the ultimate unification of the English Church under the Abp of Canterbury.

WHITE, ANDREW DICKSON (1832–1918), US educationist, politician, and diplomat, who served in the NY state legislature (1864–7), and, with Ezra Cornell, was instrumental in gaining a land grant charter for Cornell University (1865). He became the first president of Cornell (1867–85) and was a founder and first president of the American Historical Association (1884). He served as US minister to Germany (1879–81), to Russia (1892–4), as ambassador to Germany (1897–1902), and led the American delegation to The Hague Conference (1899).

WHITE, SIR CYRIL BRUDENELL BINGHAM (1876–1940), Australian soldier, who, with Gen. Bridges, organized the Australian Imperial Force, and as its chief of staff until May 1918 did much to promote its reputation and efficiency. He was chief of staff (1919–23) and was recalled to the post in 1940.

WHITE, EDWARD DOUGLASS (1845–1921), US lawyer, politician, and chief justice of the US Supreme Court. He served in the Confederate army, practised law, sat in the LA state legislature (1874–8) and on the state supreme court (1879–80), and was a US senator (1891–4). As associate justice of the US Supreme Court (1894–1910), and chief justice (1910–21), he showed a strong sense of nationalism, but also a firm belief that constitutional guarantees of individual liberties and state prerogatives should be preserved. Best known for enunciation of the 'rule of reason', distinguishing between legal and illegal combinations in restraint of trade in anti-trust cases, he dissented in *Lochner v. New York* (1905) and wrote the majority opinion in the case of *Wilson v. New* (1917) by which the Adamson Act was upheld.

WHITE, GILBERT (1859–1933), South African-born Australian cleric, who migrated to north Qld (1885) and founded the missionary diocese of Carpentaria (1900–15). He established two aboriginal mission stations and eventually became the first Bp of Willochra, SA (1915–25). By prodigious pastoral journeys he established the Church in large areas of the Australian bush and through his books, public utterances, and verse, was an influential figure in Australian life.

WHITE, JOHN (*fl.* 16th cent.), English artist and colonial pioneer, who was a member of the first Virginian settlement on Roanoke Island (1585–6) and leader of Raleigh's second abortive settlement (1587), returning to Virginia in 1590 to find no trace of his colonists. He made water-colour drawings of Indian life on the Atlantic coast and maps of the Virginian coastline.

WHITE, WILLIAM ALLEN (1868–1944), US journalist and author, who was brought up in the parochial environment of KS in the 1870s and 1880s, and, despite a limited education, became one of the most influential newspaper editors of his time. He was editor and owner of the Emporia, KS, *Gazette*, which achieved national recognition through his editorials. His attitude on social and political issues was progressive, and he strongly supported Theodore Roosevelt, both as Republican president (1901–9) and Progressive candidate for the presidency (1912). He also supported Wilson's progressive measures and attacked the conservative policies of Harding and Coolidge, but in the 1930s he condemned much of the New Deal as a corruption of progressive principles. In foreign affairs he was an internationalist, supporting American participation in the League of Nations (1919–20) and becoming chairman of the Committee to Defend America by Aiding the Allies (1940–1). His many works include *The Real Issues and Other Stories* (1896), *A Puritan in Babylon* (1938), and *The Autobiography of William Allen White* (1946).

WHITE CITIZENS' COUNCILS in the US, Southern anti-Negro organizations, centred in Mississippi, that emerged during the 1950s and were particularly opposed to the Supreme Court's school desegregation decision (1954). The councils officially decried violence, advising members to adopt economic reprisals and other social pressures against Negro, or white, civil rights activists.

WHITE HOUSE, THE, official residence of the president of the US in Washington, DC, at 1600 Pennsylvania Avenue NW, one and a half miles from the Capitol. The original house, sited according to Pierre-Charles L'Enfant's plans for the District of Columbia, was designed by James Hoban (c. 1762–1831) and was still unfinished when its first occupant, President John Adams, took up residence in Nov. 1800. The house was burnt by the British during the War of 1812, but was rebuilt by Hoban (1814–17). The north and south porticos were added by Benjamin Latrobe in the 1820s. The interior was rebuilt by McKim, Mead, and White in 1902, and considerable reconstructions were carried out between 1948 and 1952, when the balcony was added to the south portico. Originally referred to as the President's Palace, later as the President's House and the Executive Mansion, it was commonly known as the White House because of its exterior of painted sandstone, and was officially so designated in 1902.

WHITE LOTUS SOCIETY, Chinese secret society (not to be confused with the Lotus School of Buddhism), which probably originated in southern China in the 12th cent. Towards the end of the Ming dynasty, it rose against misgovernment. Under the Ch'ing it vowed to destroy the Manchus, and began a major rebellion in 1796 in the north-western and upper Yangtse provinces, which was suppressed only in 1804. It is said that the Nien rebels (1853–68) can be traced back to the White Lotus Society.

WHITE MOUNTAIN or HILL, BATTLE OF (Nov. 1620), first decisive battle of the Thirty Years War, a victory for the imperial forces of the Emperor Ferdinand II and the troops of the Catholic League of Duke Maximilian of Bavaria under Count Tilly over the Protestant levies of Frederick V of Bohemia under Christian of Anhalt. The battle ended in the rout of Anhalt's army and the flight of Frederick and his queen, Elizabeth, from Prague into permanent exile. It was followed by widespread confiscation of Protestant estates, repression of the Protestant religion, and the enforcement of imperial authority in Bohemia and Upper Austria.

WHITE MUTINY, name given to (a) a mutiny of the European officers of the East India Co. in Bengal in 1766; (b) a mutiny of the company's European officers in Madras in 1809; and (c) the mutiny of the company's European troops in 1859. British officers became mutinous in 1766 because they had been deprived of certain allowances, called *batta*. The 1809 mutiny in Madras also resulted from a reduction of allowances and because most of the staff appointments were held by officers in the king's service. Great discontent was caused in 1859 by the decision to amalgamate the company's European troops with the forces of the Crown. About 10,000 men took their discharge.

WHITE PLAINS, BATTLE OF (28 Oct. 1776), engagement during the American War of Independence. Gen. Howe's 20,000 British soldiers advanced up the East river and Long Island Sound and attacked 13,000 strongly entrenched American troops under Gen. Washington. The attack was repulsed, but Washington withdrew northwards, and Howe turned south to take Fort Washington on Manhattan Island.

WHITE TERROR in France, unleashed in 1794 against the Jacobins and their supporters after the fall of Robespierre. Largely confined to the French provinces, it took the form of unsystematic brutal massacres. The name was also applied in 1815 to a Catholic Royalist reaction in Southern France after Napoleon I's Hundred Days. Its victims included Protestants and republicans and prominent Bonapartists, who suffered particularly in Marseilles and the Gard *département*. La

Bourdonnaye, ultra-royalist minister of the interior, made little effort to curb the outrages which seriously damaged Louis XVIII's effort to reconcile France's hostile factions.

WHITEHEAD, ROBERT (1823–1905), English engineer, who in 1866, at his works at Fiume on the Adriatic, developed the underwater torpedo, the first guided missile. Subsequently, rights of construction were purchased by the main naval powers. The weapon's effectiveness was demonstrated by the Japanese during their attack on the Russian Fleet off Port Arthur in 1904.

WHITELOCKE, BULSTRODE (1605–75), English lawyer, politician, and diplomat, who was ambassador to Sweden (1653) under Oliver Cromwell. He was dismissed by him for opposing changes in courts of chancery (1655), but served under Richard Cromwell as president of the council of state and keeper of the great seal. After being pardoned under the Act of Oblivion, he lived in peaceful retirement after the Restoration (1660).

WHITELOCKE, JOHN (1757–1833), British soldier, who commanded the 1807 expedition to retake Buenos Aires from the Spaniards. He met with stubborn resistance and abandoned the undertaking, an action for which he was court-martialled and dismissed from the service.

WHITFIELD, GEORGE (1714–70), English preacher and leader of the Calvinistic wing of the Methodist revival, under the patronage of Selina, Countess of Huntingdon. Whitfield, a member of the Oxford Methodist 'Holy Club', began to emerge as a preacher even before his ordination. On the first of seven visits to America (1738) he preached out of doors, and later persuaded John Wesley to do the same. Their co-operation lapsed (1741) after theological disagreements over predestination, but they remained friendly. Although Whitfield lacked Wesley's organizing genius, his work anticipated many Wesleyan features. His influence on American religious revival was considerable.

WHITGIFT, JOHN (c. 1530–1604), English cleric, who, as Abp of Canterbury, served Queen Elizabeth I and crowned James I. He held Calvinist views on doctrinal matters, which he expressed in the Lambeth Articles (1595). He was also a champion of episcopacy and ecclesiastical discipline, and dealt severely with Presbyterians.

WHITLAM, EDWARD GOUGH (1916–   ), Australian lawyer, politician, and leader of the Australian Labor Party in the Commonwealth parliament from 1967. As deputy leader of the opposition from 1960, he faced a task similar to that which the wartime Labor prime minister, John Curtin, had performed successfully between 1935 and 1941 in reuniting his party and preparing it for office. Despite powerful extra-parliamentary hostility, notably in Vic., he made substantial progress after 1969.

WHITMAN, WALT(ER) (1819–92), US poet, who began his career as a printer (1835), then became a school teacher (1836–8), and later editor of the weekly *Long Islander* (1838–1839). After holding a number of minor editorial jobs, he became editor of the *Brooklyn Daily Eagle* (1846–8). Meanwhile, he published mediocre poetry and fiction in local magazines. Eventually his political views as an ardent free-soiler cost him his job, and he went to New Orleans (1848), where he worked briefly on the *Crescent*. On returning to Brooklyn, he edited a free-soil journal, the *Freeman* (1848–9), but resigned from the paper in order to devote more time to writing. *Leaves of Grass*, a collection of poems published anonymously (1855), showed the influence of Emersonian ideas, but Whitman combined the Transcendentalist emphasis on the importance and divinity of the individual with democratic ideals of freedom and equality that were his own. The unorthodox form of the verse and its down-to-earth honesty attracted little attention, despite the encouragement of Emerson and many enthusiastic reviews that Whitman himself wrote anonymously. Undeterred, he produced an enlarged edition (1856), in which he acknowledged his authorship, and printed Emerson's comments as a recommendation. While continuing with his writing, he also edited the Brooklyn *Times* (1857-9). A third edition of *Leaves of Grass* (1860) included two new sections, 'Calamus' and that later known as 'Children of Adam', and the poem 'Out of the Cradle Endlessly Rocking'. During the American Civil War he was a volunteer nurse in army hospitals and recorded his experiences in *Drum-Taps* (1865), the sequel to which contained the famous lament for Lincoln, 'When Lilacs Last in the Dooryard Bloom'd'. In 1866 a favourable biography of him by W. D. O'Connor, *The Good Gray Poet*, improved his reputation, which from then grew rapidly, both at home and abroad. Despite increasing ill-health, he continued to amend *Leaves of Grass* and wrote *Democratic Vistas* (1871), his best-known prose work. His later work includes collections of poetry and prose, among them *Two Rivulets* (1876) and *November Boughs* (1888), the autobiographical *Specimen Days* (1882), and revised and enlarged editions of *Leaves of Grass* (1876, 1881-2, 1882, 1888-9, 1891-2). Whitman is regarded as the most important US poet before the 20th cent. and his all-encompassing style, pioneering what later came to be called 'free verse', profoundly influenced the evolution of American poetry.

G. Wilson Allen, *The Solitary Singer* (New York, 1955).
Francis Murphy (ed.), *Walt Whitman* (London, 1969).

EFAL

WHITNEY, ELI (1765-1825), US inventor. After graduating from Yale University in 1792 he went to Savannah, GA, with a view to becoming a teacher. There he learnt of the urgent need for a machine to clean green-seed cotton and within ten days had designed a cotton gin which would enable a worker to increase his output by half. This device transformed cotton-growing into a big business, but it had unfortunate side effects in that it caused a revival of slave labour in the cotton plantations. A second major invention followed Whitney's securing of a government contract in 1798 for manufacturing rifles. Previously every rifle (and, in fact, every device consisting of more than one part) had been made by hand, each part being individually fitted. Whitney machined his parts with such precision that every component was replaceable. He may thus be called the originator of mass production.

WHITTIER, JOHN GREENLEAF (1807-92), US poet. His interest in local history, evident in his first book, *Legends of New-England in Prose and Verse* (1831), soon developed into an awareness of social injustice and he became an ardent Abolitionist (1833). He edited such anti-slavery journals as the *Pennsylvania Freeman* (1838-40) and the *National Era* (1847-60) and was a founder-member of the Liberty Party (1840). Much of the poetry he wrote during this period is included in *Poems Written During the Progress of the Abolition Question* (1838) and *Voices of Freedom* (1846). After *Home Ballads, Poems and Lyrics* (1860), his work showed a growing concern with Nature. *Snow-Bound* (1866) is generally regarded as his finest work.

WHITTINGTON, SIR RICHARD (d. 1423), English merchant. As a London mercer, he dealt in expensive textiles and supplied the households of two kings, Richard II and Henry IV, to whom he acted as one of his principal bankers. His fortune of some £6000 was used by his executors to establish various benefactions—to the London Guildhall, and to hospitals, schools, and almshouses. This is probably the origin of the Dick Whittington legend, commemorated to this day in one of the most popular of British pantomimes. His

mythical cat was first introduced in the Elizabethan version of this pantomime.

WHITTLE, SIR FRANK (1907-), English inventor of the first British jet-propulsive unit. After entering the RAF as a boy apprentice, he trained as a pilot, then qualified as an engineer and began research into the application of gas turbines for the jet-propulsion of aircraft, for which he took out patents in 1930, but the first jet-propelled flight, by the Gloster E28/39, forerunner of the Meteor, was not made until May 1941. Whittle, who remained closely connected with the subsequent development of jet propulsion, retired from the RAF in 1948.

WHITWORTH, SIR JOSEPH (1803-87), English engineer, who introduced the machine tools and methods which revolutionized workshop practice. Before 1830 a working tolerance of $\frac{1}{16}$ inch was good, but within a decade Whitworth's equipment enabled this to be reduced to $\frac{1}{1000}$ inch. This is still the accepted accuracy of conventional machining operations. In 1841 Whitworth suggested the establishment of a uniform system of screw threads. This was introduced and is still (1970) used, being known as the British Standard Whitworth (BSW) system. In the 1870s his firm became considerably interested in armament development and in 1893 amalgamated with that of Sir William Armstrong (1810-1900).

WICKERSHAM COMMISSION in the US, National Commission on Law Observance and Enforcement, established by President Hoover (May 1929) under the chairmanship of the former attorney-general, George W. Wickersham. Its findings on Prohibition (Jan. 1931) branded the 'great experiment' a failure, but recommended its retention, perhaps in a revised form. The commission published 13 other reports on general problems of law enforcement.

WIESBADEN AGREEMENT (Oct. 1921), Franco-German arrangement for the payment of reparations, negotiated after the First World War by Loucheur and Rathenau. Germany had had great difficulty in raising the first instalment of the schedule of payments drawn up at the London Conference (May 1921). This called for the transfer of gold to the Reparations Commission's account. The Wiesbaden Agreement was an attempt to find other means of payment, namely deliveries in kind, through commercial agreements between French and German private concerns. It was also proposed that a private German corporation should be established to facilitate direct reconstruction of the devastated areas by deliveries to French individuals who had suffered damage. The agreement was nullified in Nov. 1921 by the Reichsmark's collapse, which raised the question of a German demand for a reparations moratorium. It was in any case unpopular with French industrialists, who wished to restrict German imports.

WIESER, FRIEDRICH VON (1851-1926), Austrian economist, and a member of the 'subjective school', who contributed to the development of the 'opportunity cost principle', which defined the cost of a commodity as the ratio between its price and that of other commodities which could be produced with the same outlay.

WIGGLESWORTH, MICHAEL (1631-1705), American theologian and poet, whose poem 'The Day of Doom' (1662) described a Calvinist version of the Last Judgement and went through numerous editions.

WILBERFORCE, SAMUEL (1805-73), English clergyman, son of William Wilberforce. He was made Bp of Oxford—a strategically important diocese—in 1845. There he established a pattern for Anglican diocesan bishops by his energy in administration reforms, his preaching, and his work in the House of Lords. Within Oxfordshire he founded Cuddesdon

College for ordinands (1854) and Culham College for school-masters (1852). He consistently championed the Anglican *via media*. On the one hand, he was critical of the Church of Rome, and respected evangelicals for their lively conscience and their sense of mission, yet he was also in sympathy with the Oxford Movement's scholarship, and shared its view of the historic nature of the episcopate. This non-party attitude earned him a distrust that was intensified by his vacillation during the Hampden controversy (1847). In 1869 he was appointed Bp of Winchester.

WILBERFORCE, WILLIAM (1759–1833), English politician and reformer, who fought for the abolition of slavery. After being converted to evangelical christianity, he set up the Society for the Reformation of Manners (1784) and became a leader of the Clapham sect, contributing to the *Christian Observer* and issuing his *Practical View of the Prevailing Religious System*, an attack on latitudinarianism (1797). Although conservative in politics, he campaigned against the slave trade, and founded the Abolition Society (1787). As an MP he used his influence with his friend, William Pitt, to promote a bill to abolish the slave trade (1792), but it had no success. Wilberforce's speeches in the Commons and Clarkson's campaign in the country resulted in the abolition of the trade in the British empire (1807), but Wilberforce still carried on with his campaign and founded the Anti-Slavery Society (1823). By his efforts slavery itself was abolished in the British empire in 1833.

WILD GEESE, nickname of those Irish Jacobites who in the 18th cent. emigrated to serve in the Irish brigades of the armies of France, Spain, and Austria.

WILDER, THORNTON NIVEN (1897–   ), US writer, who became internationally famous with his novel, *The Bridge of San Luis Rey* (1927). His reputation rests mainly on his plays, which include *Our Town* (1938), *The Skin of Our Teeth* (1943), and *The Matchmaker* (1954).

WILDERNESS, BATTLE OF THE (5–7 May 1864), during the US Civil War in the wooded Wilderness area west of Fredericksburg, VA. Gen. Grant had tried to get his Union forces clear of the region before making an assault on Gen. Robert E. Lee's Army of North Virginia, but Lee chose to engage him in the Wilderness, where it was hoped that the terrain might neutralize Grant's numerical superiority. Lee inflicted some 18,000 casualties on the Union forces for a loss of 10,000 Confederate troops, but the battle was inconclusive and led to those of Spotsylvania and Cold Harbor.

WILDERNESS ROAD, American frontier trail, marked (1775) by Daniel Boone through the Cumberland Gap and into KY. The road was crucial to the opening up of the West.

WILDMAN, JOHN (*c.* 1621–93), English Leveller politician and lieutenant to John Lilburne, who put forward the doctrines of religious liberty, political equality, and individual freedom, *eg*, his *Agreement of the People* (1647) demanded manhood suffrage, frequent parliaments, and freedom of conscience. Besides being a fanatical politician, he was a shrewd businessman and speculated profitably in forfeited royalist estates (1649). After being imprisoned in 1655 for conspiring to overthrow Cromwell, he suffered a like fate under the Restoration government (1661–7), and was associated with Algernon Sidney and the republicans, again being imprisoned in 1683–4. At James II's accession he was one of Monmouth's chief agents, but escaped to the Dutch republic at the outbreak of the rebellion (1685). He was postmaster-general under William and Mary, and knighted by William in 1692.

WILFRID OF YORK (d. 709), Northumbrian noble, who took the lead in championing the Roman usage concerning Easter at the Synod of Whitby (664). He became Bp of York shortly afterwards. In 678 he was expelled by the King of Northumbria and his vast diocese was partitioned by Abp Theodore, as head of the English Church. While in exile, Wilfrid preached to the Frisians and converted the men of Sussex to Christianity (680). He was a pioneer in the introduction of Benedictine monasticism into England and was a munificent patron of artists.

WILKES, JOHN (1727–97), English politician, whose activities introduced a new element into politics. In the 1760s he waged three notable battles with the governments of George III—on the question of general warrants (1763–4), the Middlesex election (1769), and the reporting of parliamentary debates (1771). All three might be called popular causes, though Wilkes's violent invective alienated moderate opinion, including that of Pitt, and was at times too extreme even for Temple, Wilkes's patron. His outstanding influence on politics, however, came from the steps he and his supporters took towards the organization of public opinion out of parliament: the petitions to parliament and the Bill of Rights Society in 1769. In parliament, he did little to further radical causes and was never a leader. After 1780, when he condemned the Gordon riots, he turned away from radicalism altogether and became a supporter of Pitt's government. He was lord mayor of London in 1774.

WILKINS, JOHN (1614–72), English divine and scientist, who took a leading part in the foundation of the Royal Society (1662). In 1638 he became a chaplain in London and was associated with the circle of experimental philosophers at Gresham College. He wrote one of the earliest scientific fantasies, *Discovery of a World in the Moon* (1638). During the Civil War he sided with parliament and afterwards married Oliver Cromwell's sister (1656). He became warden of Wadham College, Oxford, but in 1659 moved to the mastership at Trinity College, Cambridge, which he had to surrender at the Restoration. He was the first secretary of the Royal Society (1662) and in 1668 became Bp of Chester. He had friends on both sides in the Civil War and had a profound influence on the study of science at Oxford.

WILKINSON, JAMES (1757–1825), US soldier, who during the American War of Independence rose to the rank of brigadier-general, as much through his skill as an intriguer as through his military prowess. He was compelled to resign as clothier-general because of irregularities in his accounts (1781), and later, while living in KY, negotiated with the Spanish authorities in LA, to whom he promised the west's secession in return for financial assistance. After being ruined by speculation, he rejoined the army (1791) and fought against the Indians on the north-west and southern frontiers. He became an associate of Aaron Burr, and was appointed governor of Louisiana Territory (1805–6), but betrayed Burr and was the chief prosecution witness at his trial for treason (1807). He fought without distinction in the War of 1812 and at the time of his death was speculating in TX land grants.

WILKINSON, JOHN (1728–1808), English businessman and ironmaster, who played an important part in the industrial expansion of the second half of the 18th cent. He set up an iron works at Broseley, Salop, and during the French Wars executed large government orders. In peacetime, too, his business thrived; his patent (1774) for boring cannon was applied to metal cylinders; he installed the first of Boulton and Watt's new engines at his works at Bradley; and he stimulated the use of iron for bridges, machine-parts, and small boats. He was the most conspicuous of those employers who relieved the dearth of coin (which encouraged the truck system) by issuing tokens. Those that he began to issue in 1787 at first circulated only locally, but later, when made redeemable in London and Liverpool, were used by other employers to pay wages.

WILLAMETTE VALLEY in the US, fertile area in OR, which was the magnet for large-scale overland migration in the 1840s along the Oregon Trail. It was first settled in the 1830s by French-Canadian employees of the Hudson's Bay Co., Methodist missionaries, and American fur traders, and by 1846 the valley's population included some 6000 American farmers. It was their agitation for self-government which led eventually to the favourable resolution of the Oregon question and the establishment of Oregon Territory (1848).

WILLCOCKS, JOSEPH (d. 1814), Irish-born Canadian journalist and politician, who founded the radical *Upper Canada Guardian*; or, *Freeman's Journal* (1807–12) in Niagara, Ont., the first newspaper in the province. Willcocks was a member of the Upper Canada legislature (1803–12). He fought for Canada at the battle of Queenston Heights, but deserted to the Americans (1813) and became head of a troop of 'Canadian volunteers' and later a colonel in the American army. He was killed in action at Fort Erie.

WILLCOCKS, SIR WILLIAM (1852–1932), British engineer, who designed the first Aswan Dam (1898) and devised the first comprehensive irrigation plan for Iraq (1911).

WILLIAM OF HOLLAND (d. 1256), Count of Holland, emperor-elect (1247–56), and a minor count of the German empire. He was deliberately elected as anti-king, in opposition to the Hohenstaufen ruler, Conrad IV, by the papal party in Germany because of his unimportance. He was first elected by the three Rhenish archbishops alone, and he based his power chiefly on the Rhenish cities. He was killed in battle against the rebellious Frisians.

WILLIAM V, Duke of Cleves (1516–92), son of Duke John III, who succeeded to the territories of Julich, Berg, Mark, Guelders, and Cleves (1539) and thus ruled a potentially powerful secular principality astride the Lower Rhine which was of considerable strategic value to the Habsburgs of Spain and Austria. His long reign (*reg.* 1539–92) began with the religious conflict between the Catholic and reformed Churches in 16th-cent. Europe and ended with the triumph of the Counter-Reformation. It started inauspiciously with his defeat by Charles V's imperial forces in the War of the Guelders Succession (1542–3), after which William was forced to repudiate Protestantism in his lands and renounce his claim to Guelders. During the second half of the 16th cent. both Calvinism and Lutheranism spread among his subjects, but William held to the Catholic faith, as did his son and heir, John William. From 1566 he suffered from prolonged mental illness which enabled the Catholics to gain ground in the government, but his son's madness (1590) and his own death left Cleves to become a battleground between relatives belonging to both religions, with conflicting claims to the regency and succession, a situation aggravated by financial chaos and the irresponsible occupation by Spanish troops.

WILLIAM I (1797–1888), King of Prussia (*reg.* 1861–88) and first German Emperor (1871). His life-long interests were the army and Prussia, and as soon as he became regent for his brother (1858) he adopted Roon's proposals for army reform, and appointed him war minister (1859). To solve the constitutional crisis arising from the abolition of the *Landwehr* and the extension of military service from two to three years, the king appointed Bismarck as minister-president, to govern without parliamentary support. Bismarck persuaded the king to take the lead in the expansion of Prussia, but William always retained the mastery in their relationship. His attachment to the throne of Prussia and the principle of legitimacy caused him to accept the title of German emperor only with reluctance when it was offered by the princes.

WILLIAM II (1859–1941), Emperor of Germany (*reg.* 1888–1918), son of Frederick III and of Victoria, daughter of Queen Victoria of Britain. The defect of a withered arm did not prevent his having a thorough-going military education before ascending the throne at the age of 29 after his father's brief reign of three months. He soon clashed with his chancellor, Bismarck, who had dominated European politics for a quarter of a century, and dismissed him in 1890. For the next 24 years he identified himself with the growth of Germany in military and naval terms and disturbed the temper of European relationships by indiscreet public statements, *eg,* on the occasion of the Kruger telegram (1896) and the Tangier incident (1905). In the uneasy years before the First World War he did little to preserve harmony with France, Russia, or Britain, and a personal hostility existed between him and King Edward VII.

Consequently, his actions and personality were contributory factors in the outbreak of war. He subsequently played the part of a war-leader, as the rulers of Prussia had done in the past, but real decision-making was taken out of his hands. Internal revolt in Germany in Nov. 1918 caused his abdication (9 Nov. 1918) two days before the armistice.

He fled to the Netherlands and a brief attempt followed to have him tried as a war criminal. In the event, there were more important issues to consider at Versailles than the fate of the Kaiser, who lived on at Doorn till his death. He published his *Memoirs* (1922) and *My Early Life* (1926).

WILLIAM I (*c.* 1027–87), King of England (*reg.* 1066–87), who was the illegitimate son of Robert I, Duke of Normandy. William was a boy when his father died and Normany a turbulent province under pressure from the Duke of Anjou and the King of France. By 1066, however, William had annexed Main and the French Vexin and began to introduce feudal tenure into Normandy. He saw himself as the nearest blood relative of Edward the Confessor, and apparently firmly believed that Edward had recognized him as his heir. He maintained also that Harold, Earl of Wessex, had sworn to uphold his right to the English kingdom. It is not possible to determine the truth of these claims, but they were accepted by Pope Alexander II, who gave William his blessing for the invasion of England, which resulted in the defeat of King Harold at Hastings on 14 Oct. 1066. English resistance to the Conqueror was only partial. Most Anglo-Saxons seem to have been prepared to accept the verdict of Hastings. What resistance there was was maintained, particularly in Northumbria, until the early 1070s and threatened the success of William's venture. However, opposition was systematically suppressed and the English disinherited or depressed to the status of tenants. A new alien aristocracy, predominantly from Normandy, was enriched with confiscated land now held from William by feudal tenure. The degree to which feudal tenure had been introduced by 1087 is difficult to determine, but there was probably still a need for clarification of precise obligations when the Conqueror died. William maintained the old English administrative system, though he abandoned the use of the Anglo-Saxon language. During his reign, with the co-operation of Lanfranc, Abp of Canterbury, the reform of the English Church on continental lines began. Norman abbots and bishops were appointed and Norman liturgies introduced. But William would not allow papal interference in the affairs of his new kingdom. Towards the close of his reign he instigated the great survey of England known as Domesday Book (1086).

D. C. Douglas, *William the Conqueror: the Norman impact upon England* (London, 1964).
R. A. Brown, *The Normans and the Norman Conquest* (London, 1969). DPK

WILLIAM II (*c.* 1056–1100), King of England (*reg.* 1087–1100). After 1095 he also administered Normandy. His reign saw the development of royal administration and the increased exploitation of the rights of the Crown, which tended to make the king unpopular and distrusted. An intelligent, witty man, but ruthless, cynical, and delighting in warfare, he had the makings of an oppressive tyrant. He was killed while hunting in the New Forest, and may have been murdered by his brother Henry, who immediately seized the Crown. Henry's first act was to issue a coronation charter promising to avoid his brother's abuses, which provides interesting evidence about malpractices current under William Rufus.

WILLIAM III (1650–1702), King of Britain (*reg.* 1689–1702), posthumous son of William II of Orange and his wife, Mary (1631–60), daughter of King Charles I of England. He was born at The Hague and was orphaned at the age of ten. After an Anglophile environment during his childhood, under his governor, Frederick van Nassau-Zuylestein, his education was taken over by the states of Holland on De Witt's initiative (1666), although the Eternal Edict (1667) safeguarded the state from an Orange monopoly of offices. In 1668 William gained his first political experience, being recognized as a member of the states of Zeeland, and in 1670 he entered the Council of State. On the eve of the war with Louis XIV (1672–8) he was appointed captain-general by the states general, but with limited authority, and withdrew his forces behind the natural water defences of Holland before the advancing French armies. In this national emergency the states of Zeeland and Holland proclaimed him *stadtholder* (1672), later on an hereditary basis (1674), and the states general withdrew their conditions upon the offices of captain and admiral-general, which also became hereditary (1674, 1675). His leadership in the crisis of 1672–4 made William a national hero. Treaties with the emperor, Spain, Lorraine, and Denmark and the withdrawal of England from the French alliance enabled the Dutch republic to survive. William captured Bonn (1673), but fought a costly and indecisive battle at Senef, near Charleroi (1674), but failed to take Maastricht (1676), and was defeated near Cassel (1677). He showed great perseverance, however, and after an Anglo-Dutch defensive treaty (March 1678) had sealed his marriage to Mary, daughter of James, Duke of York, Louis XIV came to terms with the Dutch (Treaty of Nymwegen, 1678).

William regarded this settlement as a defeat for the Dutch and the following decade was a period of frustration as he helplessly watched the republic, the empire, and Spain surrender to appeasement politics before Louis XIV's *réunion* system, *eg*, the Truce of Ratisbon (1684). However, Louis's revocation of the Edict of Nantes (1685) stimulated an anti-French coalition, and William's uncle, Frederick William of Brandenburg, signed a defensive alliance with the Dutch (1685), while the empire, Spain, and the German states became united in the League of Augsburg (1686). In that year William sent his adviser, Everard van Weede, to England to assess the country's hostility to his father-in-law, James II. By 1687 he had decided to intervene in England and persuaded the states to supply adequate forces. An invitation to William to overthrow James was delivered by Admiral Herbert (later Earl of Torrington) (July 1688) and signed by seven English statesmen, and France's preoccupation in the destruction of the Palatinate (1688) gave him the opportunity to take Louis by surprise. Thus, in Nov. 1688, equipped with an army of some 13,000 Dutch and German soldiers and a fleet of about 50 ships, William left the republic and landed at Torbay in Devon. James's flight and abdication enabled him to take control of the country with the minimum of trouble and on 23 Feb. 1689 William and Mary were declared joint rulers and accepted the Declaration of Rights.

The revolution against the Stuarts also spread to Scotland, and despite some Jacobite resistance, William and Mary were declared the rightful monarchs of Scotland (21 May 1689). If William's reputation in Scotland was soured by the massacre of Glencoe and the failure of the Darien scheme, his political intentions were sound, *eg*, he permitted the establishment of the Presbyterian Church by law (1690). Ireland, too, presented him with problems, for here Catholicism was entrenched. However, his victory at the Boyne (1 July 1690) initiated the complete conquest of Ireland,

though he left in 1691 to assume command in the Netherlands. The War of the League of Augsburg proved fairly indecisive, *eg*, though he lost at Steenkirk (1692) and Neerwinden (1693) he recaptured Namur (1695). By 1699 he had won Louis's recognition of his royal titles and the mutual restoration of French and Dutch territories.

William now foresaw the looming problem of the Spanish Succession, which had prompted Louis's reasonableness in the Ryswick negotiations (1697). With his trusted adviser, William Bentinck, Duke of Portland, he negotiated the first Partition treaty with Louis XIV (1698) and when this was thwarted by the death of the electoral prince of Bavaria (1699), he negotiated another settlement with his old adversary to prevent another European holocaust (1700). Only when Louis repudiated this second Partition treaty, not only accepting Charles II's will in his grandson's favour, but indicating his intention to create a unified Bourbon bloc which would dominate western Europe, did William undertake the creation of the Grand Alliance of the Maritime Powers and the empire for the final reduction of Louis XIV (1701), the diplomatic triumph of his life. William died early in 1702, following a fall from his horse, and was succeeded by his sister-in-law, Anne. His staunch Protestantism and lack of political partisanship (he favoured neither Whigs nor Tories in principle) should have endeared him to the English people, but his morose and reserved character masked his sterling qualities. His close friendship with the grand pensionary, Heinsius, had ensured the co-operation of the Maritime Powers. Though a soldier of only moderate ability, he understood military and political strategy and fought tenaciously to defend the European states system from the hegemony of France.

S. B. Baxter, *William III* (New York & London, 1966).
Nesca A. Robb, *William of Orange, a personal portrait*, 2 vols (New York & London, 1962, 1966). JHS

WILLIAM IV (1765–1837), King of Britain (*reg.* 1830–7), whose reign helped to define the role of the king in a constitutional monarchy. During the Reform Bill crisis (1831) William gave a vague promise to create enough new peers to prevent the House of Lords blocking the bill, but he then accepted Grey's resignation in preference to creating 50 peers to force the Lords to consider the disfranchising as well as the enfranchising clauses. This caused such an outburst of popular fury that the king had to give way.

In 1834 he allowed his dislike of radicalism to influence the choice of government. He accepted Melbourne's half-offered resignation so readily that it amounted to a dismissal. But royal influence was no longer effective. Wellington and Peel replaced Melbourne, but were unable to win a majority and had to resign in 1835.

WILLIAM I (1772–1843), King of the Netherlands (*reg.* 1840–1843), who presided over the unsuccessful attempt to unite Holland and Belgium (1815–30). As a hereditary *stadtholder* of Holland, William did not have sufficient detachment to understand Belgian resentment at his autocratic policy of imposing a state system of education and generally imposing a Dutch influence on the Belgian provinces. Yet Belgium benefited far more than Holland from the king's personal interest in economic policy, which earned him the nickname of the 'merchant king'. Support from Belgian industrialists did not, however, counteract hostility from Belgian liberals, who successfully fought for their independence in 1830. Nor was William's belief in autocratic government for long acceptable to the Dutch, who in 1840 forced him to abdicate in favour of his son.

WILLIAM II (1792–1849), King of the Netherlands (*reg.* 1843–9), came to the throne after the abdication of his father and restored the popularity of the monarchy by encouraging the restoration of trade and commerce and allowing the introduction of a new, liberal constitution in 1848.

WILLIAM THE LION (*c.* 1142–1214), King of Scotland (*reg.* 1165–1214), who, in 1176, secured from the papacy a declaration placing the Scottish Church under immediate papal control and thus freeing it from any dependence on the English Church. His reign witnessed the steady feudalization north of the Forth. William himself was forced in 1174 to recognize the overlordship of King Henry II of England, after being captured during a raid into Northumberland. He was freed from this feudal homage by Henry's successor, Richard I (1189), but the period of Henry's suzerainty over Scotland formed one of the main foundations for the subsequent claim of King Edward I to the overlordship over Scotland.

WILLIAM I (d. 1166), King of Sicily (*reg.* 1154–66), whose father, Roger II, had been the first to unify the Norman possessions in the south of Italy. His ruthless rule, which inevitably produced a reaction under his less formidable successors, was marred by repeated rebellions of towns and the feudal nobility, especially in his mainland territories. His suspicion and cruelty earned him the nickname of 'the Bad'. His chief importance lay in his sustained support of the popes in their struggle against the German emperor, Frederick Barbarossa. In 1165 William restored Alexander III, the greatest of the 12th-cent. popes, to Rome. William II, his successor, by adhering to the same policy, ensured the eventual victory of Alexander over Frederick.

WILLIAM I, Prince of Orange, Count of Nassau (1533–84), eldest son of Count William of Nassau-Dillenburg and Juliana of Stolberg, was known as William the Silent and was the first *stadtholder* and founder of the Dutch republic. He was born at Dillenburg, and succeeded to the principality of Orange on the death of his cousin, René de Chalon (1544), and to the county of Nassau in 1559. From 1544 he was educated at the court of Mary of Hungary, regent of the Netherlands, and in 1548 was appointed a page to the, Emperor Charles V. He married, first, Anne of Buren (1551), second, Anna of Saxony (1561), third, Charlotte of Bourbon (1575), and lastly, Louise de Cologny (1583), who altogether bore him three sons and nine daughters. In 1555 he became a councillor of state and knight of the golden fleece and after being appointed by Charles V as a commander of the imperial army, he fought in the Franco-Spanish War of 1556–9. In 1559 Philip II of Spain, sovereign ruler of the Netherlands, appointed him *stadtholder* of Holland, Zeeland, and Utrecht.
William opposed Philip II's policies of religious persecution of Protestantism and exploitation of the Netherlands for Spain's benefit, of which Cardinal Granvelle was the instrument. He formed a league of the nobility which forced Granvelle's departure from the Netherlands (1564), but he tried to restrain the more militant members of the aristocracy, mediating between the regent Margaret of Parma and those nobles who had signed the Compromise (1565–6). After the outburst of Calvinistic iconoclasm he tried to arrive at an agreement to ensure religious freedom to the Protestants. However, frustrated by Alva's arrival (1567), he left for Dillenberg and was officially deprived of his offices by Philip. He then began to plan a war of liberation from the Spanish Crown by the invasion of the Netherlands with the help of German and French Protestants. His campaign of 1568, however, was a failure and he then moved slowly towards an alliance with the Calvinists. He returned to Holland in 1572, after the Sea Beggars had started their reconquest from the coastal towns, and was acknowledged as *stadtholder* of that province. Though at first the rebels were repulsed, they won some successes, *eg*, Leyden (1574), and in 1576 William welcomed the union of the Netherlands against Spain in the Pacification of Ghent. However, under Don John of Austria and the Duke of Parma the Spaniards recovered much ground, and for the next five years William sought to promote the Duc d'Alençon as sovereign ruler of the Netherlands, in the hope that a Catholic French prince would appeal to all sections of the population (1578–83). Reluctantly he accepted the independence of the northern, Calvinist-dominated pro-vinces in the Union of Utrecht (1579), and became the first *stadtholder* of the union. In June 1580 Philip declared William an outlaw, to which William replied with his famous *Apology*. After Alençon's departure following the disastrous French Fury (1583), William accepted the hereditary title of Count of Holland and Zeeland, but on 10 July 1584, a few days before his official installation, he was murdered at Delft.

C. V. Wedgwood, *William the Silent* (London, 1944).   MKS

WILLIAM II OF NASSAU, Prince of Orange (1626–50), son of Frederick Henry of Orange-Nassau and grandson of William the Silent, who succeeded to all his father's offices, including that of *stadtholder* of the United Provinces (1647). Despite the peace of Westphalia, he sought to renew war with Spain in alliance with France and to intervene in the English Civil War on behalf of King Charles I, whose daughter, Mary, he had married (1641). He became involved in a conflict with the regents of Holland over the reduction of the armed forces (1649–50) and lost the support of the states general by his autocratic methods and his foreign policy. His death from smallpox (6 Nov. 1650) enabled the pacific and commercial policies of republicanism to triumph (1650–72).

WILLIAM V (1748–1806), *Stadtholder* of Holland after the death of his father, William IV, in 1751. His unpopularity, following Holland's economic losses in the American War of Independence, stimulated opposition to the hereditary stadtholderate from both conservative patriots and democratic reformers. The democratic seizure of Utrecht, however, rallied the patriots in support of the *stadtholder* and led to the emergence of the Orangist party. William's apathy hardly merited such support, for he made no attempt to regain his office after fleeing from the French in 1795.

WILLIAM LOUIS, Count of Nassau (1560–1620), Dutch Calvinist statesman, eldest son of John, Count of Nassau and nephew of William the Silent. He co-operated with his cousin, Maurice of Nassau, in the military campaigns against the Duke of Parma after William's death (1584) and was appointed *stadtholder* of the three most northerly provinces of the Netherlands, Friesland (1584), Groningen, and Drente (1594). He also encouraged Maurice to harry the Remonstrants (1618) in the religious conflict with Oldenbarneveldt.

WILLIAM OF MALMESBURY (*c.* 1090–*c.* 1143), English historian and one of the main authorities for English history of the 10th cent. He was more than a simple chronicler and tried to impose a pattern and unity upon his material. Besides the histories of the English kings and a contemporary history, *Historia Novella* (1125–42), he also wrote a church history and the lives of certain saints. His history of the abbey of Glastonbury is a remarkable example of his critical and sensible handling of traditions abounding in miraculous elements.

WILLIAM OF TYRE (*c.* 1130–*c.* 1187), historian of the Latin states in Syria and Palestine. He was himself born in the East, and became a leading adviser to the kings of Jerusalem, and also Abp of Tyre. His history deals with events after 1160 in which he directly participated. It conveys the special outlook of the men bred in the East, who regarded co-existence with the Muslims as a normal way of life, in contrast to the fanaticism of Crusaders on their brief incursions from Europe.

WILLIAM OF WYKEHAM (1324–1404), English cleric, who was the keeper of the privy seal (1363–7), chancellor (1367–1371, 1389–91), Bp of Winchester (1366–1404), and one of the leading political figures of his time. His fame rests chiefly, however, on his twin foundations of Winchester College

(1378–94) and New College, Oxford (1379–86), and his rebuilding of the nave of Winchester Cathedral.

WILLIAMS, ELEAZAR (1788–1858), American Indian missionary, who was the half-breed son of a St Regis Indian. He fought for the US in the War of 1812 and became a missionary to the Oneida Indians in 1815. He translated the Book of Common Prayer into the Iroquois language and moved with the Oneida to the Green Bay region of WI, where he started an Indian school. He left the reservation after being charged with duplicity in some land schemes. About 1838 Williams began to claim that he was the lost son of Louis XVI and Marie Antoinette, saying that he had been kidnapped and brought to the US as a baby. This claim was never given much credit, although it received a great deal of publicity.

WILLIAMS, HENRY (1782–1867), English sailor, who became an Anglican missionary, having arrived in NZ in 1823. He put conversion before education and demanded genuine adherence from Maori converts, among whom he gained considerable influence. His fear of uncontrolled European influence on the Maoris prompted him to promote British sovereignty (1840), and subsequently he mediated between the two races. In 1846 he was falsely accused by Gov. Grey of land-grabbing, and was not exonerated until 1855.

WILLIAMS, SIR JOSHUA STRANGE (1837–1915), NZ judge, who became first president of the NZ arbiration court (1895), an experiment in industrial relations to whose success he made a substantial contribution.

WILLIAMS, ROGER (c. 1603–83), English clergyman and colonist, famous as an apostle of religious toleration and democracy. He first went to America in 1630, but he clashed with the Puritan theocracy in MA and moved to Providence (1636), where he founded the Rhode Island settlement and became president of the colony (1654–7), for which he had secured a charter (1644). Rejecting all sects (1639), he practised the basic Christian tenet of charity, eg, to the American Indians and the Quakers.

WILLIAMS, TENNESSEE (1914–), adopted name of the Mississippi-born US dramatist, Thomas Lanier Williams. His plays include *The Glass Menagerie* (1944), *A Streetcar Named Desire* (1947), *Sweet Bird of Youth* (1959), and *The Night of the Iguana* (1961). They deal with sexually obsessed characters searching for love in a lonely, violent world.

WILLIAMS, WILLIAM (1800–78), English clergyman, who became a bishop (1859–76) in NZ. He published the first Maori New Testament (1837) and a Maori dictionary and grammar (1844).

WILLIAMS, WILLIAM CARLOS (1883–1963), US poet, who maintained an uneven friendship with Ezra Pound, which began when they were both students at Pennsylvania University. Although Williams subscribed in part to the tenets of both Imagism and Objectivism, he set himself against a literature which bred on literature, and was often hostile to both Pound and Eliot. He stood for an aggressively American poetry of vivid observation. After the 1940s his reputation grew steadily, largely through the publication of his long five-part poem, 'Paterson' (1946–58). He wrote many stories and essays, a few novels and plays, and a volume of autobiography. His major works include *Collected Later Poems* (1950), *Collected Earlier Poems* (1951), *The Desert Music and Other Poems* (1954), and *Journey to Love* (1955).

WILLIBRORD (658–739), Northumbrian missionary, who started work among the Frisians in 690 and was largely responsible for their conversion. He was supported by the Carolingians, and after Charles Martel had recaptured Utrecht in 719 Willibrord permanently established a bishopric there. Alcuin wrote his life.

WILLINGDON, FREEMAN FREEMAN-THOMAS, 1st Marquis of (1866–1941), governor-general of Canada (1926–31), and viceroy of India (1931–6). As governor of two Indian provinces, Bombay (1913–19) and Madras (1919–24), he took a progressive line during a period of reform, of which he was a firm advocate, and maintained good relations with the moderates in Bombay. In Madras he supervised the opening phase of the Montague–Chelmsford constitution and was fortunate in having the dominant Justice Party from which to select his ministers. So effective was the work of his government in this period that he was able to argue that Madras should have unilateral responsible government forthwith.

The governor-generalship of Canada was less onerous, the appointment of high commissioners under the terms of the Imperial Conference (1926) having relieved the governor-general of most of the post's important diplomatic and political duties. Not so the viceroyalty of India, to which Willingdon returned in 1931. In contrast to the relatively optimistic atmosphere of his earlier Indian regimes, the years of his Indian viceroyalty were both difficult and unsatisfactory and, experienced and determined though he was, he could make no effective changes in the climate of opinion. He arrived in time for a renewed round of civil disobedience (1932) and his period of office therefore began with the 'ordinance raj' by which the agitation was put down. His viceroyalty continued largely as a holding operation while the constitutional discussions dragged on. So protracted were they that Willingdon did not see the new act introduced.

WILLISON, SIR JOHN STEPHEN (1856–1927), Canadian journalist. As editor of the *Toronto Globe* and the *Toronto News* (1890–1902), he was a leading promoter of imperial federation.

WILLKIE, WENDELL LEWIS (1892–1944), US lawyer and politician. After military service in the First World War he became an industrial and utility lawyer. His struggle against the Tennessee Valley Authority earned him the reputation of a leading business opponent of the New Deal. In 1940, backed by the influential New York *Herald Tribune* and an enthusiastic amateur campaign, he secured the Republican presidential nomination while still a registered Democrat. Although defeated by Franklin Roosevelt, Willkie polled six million more votes than any previous Republican candidate. In *One World* (1943) he argued the need for international co-operation and collective security. He was less influential inside than outside the Republican Party, but partly under his pressure the party moved away from its pre-war isolationism. After being defeated in the WI primary he withdrew from the 1944 campaign.

WILLOUGHBY OF PARHAM, FRANCIS WILLOUGHBY, 5th Baron (c. 1613–66), English colonial governor, who was appointed lord lieutenant of Lincolnshire (1643). His relations with Cromwell becoming strained (1644), he was impeached (1647) and fled to Holland (1648). When the Downs fleet deserted parliament (1648) he became a royal vice-admiral. He was appointed governor of Barbados (1649) and when confronted by parliament's fleet (1651) he negotiated a treaty conceding Barbados to parliament. He was imprisoned in England (1655, 1666) for taking part in royalist conspiracies. After the Restoration he was reappointed as governor of Barbados, then of St Kitts, Nevis, Montserrat, and Antigua, and granted half their Crown revenues. He and Lawrence Hyde were granted all Surinam, excluding a 30,000-acre (121 sq. kms) royal reservation. He died at sea attempting to recapture St Kitts from the French.

WILLOUGHBY, SIR HUGH (d. 1554), English soldier and navigator, veteran of the Scottish wars, and commander of a force of ships sent to find the north-east passage to China and India (1553). The ships were scattered by storms and Willoughby, in the *Bona Esperanza*, landed in Lapland, where he and the crew perished during the Arctic winter (1553–4).

WILLOUGHBY DE ERESBY, PEREGRINE BERTIE, 13th Lord (1555–1601), English soldier born in Cleves, who came to England after the Marian persecution had ended and after diplomatic service (1582–5) became renowned for his exploits in the Netherlands (1586–9). He fought in Brabant and at Zutphen (1586), replaced the Earl of Leicester as supreme commander of the English forces (1587), and defended Bergen from the Spaniards (1588). After embarrassment caused by the friction between the English and Dutch governments he was recalled to England, but later led an expedition to Normandy in support of Henry of Navarre (1589–90). He was governor of Berwick-on-Tweed (1598).

WILLS'S COFFEE HOUSE in London, famous resort of literary critics, poets, and patrons at the turn of the 17th–18th cents, situated near Covent Garden. Until his death (1700) it was dominated by John Dryden, whom Alexander Pope was brought to see there as a boy, and after 1700 Addison continued Dryden's tradition.

WILMINGTON, SPENCER COMPTON, Earl of (*c.* 1673–1743), British politician, who entered parliament in 1698, and subsequently became speaker of the House of Commons (1715–27), paymaster-general (1722–30), lord privy seal (1730), and first lord of the treasury (1742–3).

WILMOT, LEMUEL ALLAN (1809–78), Canadian politician and lawyer, who was a member of the House of Assembly (1836), where he upheld the Liberal Party's policy of responsible government. As a member of the Executive Council (1843), he resigned with his colleagues in revolt against the policies of the lieutenant-governor, Sir William Colebrook (1846). He was later attorney-general of NB (1848).

WILMOT PROVISO (1846) in the US, amendment added to a money bill during the Mexican War by Congressman David Wilmot, a Pennsylvanian Democrat. It proposed the prohibition of slavery in any territory acquired from Mexico. The Proviso was rejected by the Senate, but was reintroduced in later sessions and became a rallying cry of the anti-slavery forces, receiving substantial support from Northern politicians. Replying for the South in 1847, John C. Calhoun denied that Congress had the power to prohibit slavery in the territories.

WILSON, SIR ARNOLD TALBOT (1884–1940), British soldier and politician, who became a political officer in Persia (1908–13) and in the Middle East (1914–20), where he played a major role in the negotiations which led to the creation of Iraq. While serving as an air gunner—at the age of 56—in the Second World War, he was shot down. At the time he was an MP.

WILSON, ERNEST HENRY (1876–1930), English plant collector, who is credited with collecting almost 3500 species of plants in China alone, of which some 900 were new to science. He joined the staff of the Arnold Arboretum in the US and became its keeper (1927).

WILSON, SIR HENRY HUGHES (1864–1922), British soldier and politician, who rose rapidly in the army during the First World War. He was of Protestant Irish stock and expressed pronounced views against Bolshevism and the Sinn Fein movement after the war. As MP for North Down (1922), he visited Ireland and made a series of strongly anti-Irish speeches. He thus became regarded as an arch-enemy by Sinn Fein, and on his return was murdered on the steps of his London house.

WILSON, HENRY LANE (1857–1932), US diplomat, who was ambassador to Mexico (1909–13) and considered friendly to US investors in Mexico. He supported the *coup d'état* of Victoriano Huerta against Francisco I. Madero (Feb. 1913). Later, he refused to intercede with Huerta to save Madero's life.

WILSON, HORACE HAYMAN (1786–1860), British doctor, linguist, and historian who joined the medical service of the East India Co. in 1808. He was the greatest Sanskrit scholar of his day and became the first Boden Professor of Sanskrit at Oxford (1833). He published many scholarly works.

WILSON, JAMES (1805–60), Scottish financier and politician who served as an MP and was appointed finance member of the Indian viceroy's Executive Council in 1859. He remodelled the whole system of Indian finance, introduced a paper currency, and imposed an income tax. He wrote several books on economics and edited *The Economist*.

WILSON, JAMES HAROLD (1916–   ), British politician, prime minister, and leader of the Labour Party, who was a civil servant at the ministry of fuel and power during the Second World War and was elected to parliament in 1945.

In 1947, after a few months as secretary for overseas trade, he became president of the board of trade at the age of 31. As a minister he was closely connected with the negotiation of GATT and with the post-war export drive. But it was the manner of his departure from the cabinet rather than his membership of it that made his name. In April 1951 he resigned from the government with the minister of labour, Aneurin Bevan, in protest against an increase in social service charges, which the chancellor of the exchequer, Hugh Gaitskell, had introduced to pay for the rearmament programme.

This resignation tended to place Wilson on the left of the party, though he was never a Bevanite in the sense that word came to be understood. He felt that the broad unity of the party was what mattered and he opposed Gaitskell whenever he felt that the latter's actions were endangering that unity. Thus, for the most part, Wilson was an active member of the party leadership during the years of opposition (1951–64), being spokesman on both finance and foreign affairs. His position, indeed, was so much of the centre that on Gaitskell's death in 1963 he was elected to the party leadership.

As leader of the opposition (1963–4), he attempted to deflect its forces away from divisive arguments over socialism by promoting Labour as the party of efficiency and technological change: these were to be the themes of his first government, which took office in Oct. 1964. Though in power with only a bare parliamentary majority, he led his ministry with characteristic self-confidence, and at the election of 1966 Labour was returned with a greatly increased majority.

Thereafter the government's legislative programme was restricted because of a series of financial crises and the decision (July 1966) to defend the existing exchange rate of the pound. From then, until Nov. 1967, when the pound was devalued, the government appeared to lose control of its financial policies. The consequences were sluggish economic growth, falling consumer demand, and, towards the end, a severe inflationary tendency. Despite all this Wilson's government could claim considerable successes. There was no significant reduction in social expenditure, which remained at a high level, the social services were strengthened, withdrawals from costly overseas commitments were begun. An array of official boards and institutions was established to encourage industrial efficiency, heavy state investments were made in private industry, and substantial assistance to encourage business amalgamations.

Some recovery and a spectacular improvement in the balance of payments did not prevent the defeat of the government in June 1970. Wilson was re-elected leader of the Labour Party in opposition.

WILSON, JOSEPH HAVELOCK (1858–1929), British politician, and founder of the National Union of Seamen (1887). He was its leader in its battles with the Shipping Federation in the 1890s.

WILSON, WOODROW (1856–1924), US politician and 28th president of the US (1913–21). He was educated at Princeton and Johns Hopkins universities and afterwards became a university teacher of history and political science. His most notable work was *Congressional Government* (1885), in which he criticized the American political system for its separation of executive from legislative responsibility and leadership. After achieving national prominence as a reforming president of Princeton (1902–10), he entered politics in 1910, when he was elected governor of NJ. Although his statements on public matters had led his political sponsors to assume that he was a conservative, he proved to be a progressive governor, persuading an unwilling legislature to pass a series of electoral and economic reforms. This helped him to win the Democratic presidential nomination in 1912, when the Republicans' strength had been weakened by Theodore Roosevelt's breakaway Progressive Party, and Wilson became the second Democrat to be elected president since the Civil War. In a remarkable exercise of executive leadership, he secured from the 63rd Congress (1913–15) legislation enacting the chief features of his reform programme, the 'New Freedom'.

With the outbreak of the First World War in Aug. 1914, he became increasingly concerned with foreign policy. His outlook on international affairs, like the New Freedom, was largely shaped by traditional liberal principles. As his attitude towards the Mexican Revolution had shown, he believed it was America's mission to promote her democratic ideals in the world. Appalled by the European war, he sought to end it through American mediation. While firmly opposing Germany's submarine campaign as an inhumane infringement of American rights, he was anxious to keep the US out of the war, and his success in doing this helped him to secure re-election, though by a narrow majority, in 1916. When, after Germany's resort to unrestricted submarine warfare (1 Feb. 1917) and the Zimmermann telegram, he reluctantly led the US into the war (6 April 1917), he justified American intervention primarily on the grounds that 'the world must be made safe for democracy' through the overthrow of autocratic regimes and the establishment of a permanent peace. He set forth (notably in his 14 points, 8 Jan. 1918) a programme for a new world order based upon such principles as open diplomacy, free trade, national self-determination, and a League of Nations to provide collective security against aggression. These ideals won the support of liberals in Europe as well as the US, but the Paris peace conference of 1919 (which he attended in person) fell short of realizing them, despite the establishment of the League of Nations. Wilson's hope that the US would join the League was obstructed by a resurgence of American isolationist sentiment, which was exploited by his Republican opponents in the US Senate under the leadership of Henry Cabot Lodge. Wilson's refusal to compromise over the terms of America's entry into the League of Nations contributed to the Senate's rejection of the treaty of Versailles (19 March 1920). While campaigning for the league in the autumn of 1919, Wilson suffered a stroke which largely incapacitated him for the rest of his period of office.

John M. Blum, *Woodrow Wilson and the Politics of Morality* (Boston & Toronto, 1956).
Arthur S. Link, *Wilson* (Princeton, 1947).   JAT

WILTSHIRE, THOMAS BOLEYN, 12th Earl of (1st of 6th creation) (1477–1539), English diplomat, and father of Queen Anne Boleyn, who served his future son-in-law, King Henry VIII, as ambassador to the Low Countries (1512) and Spain (1522). He also negotiated the preliminary arrangements for the Field of the Cloth of Gold (1519–20) while on the embassy to Francis I. In 1529 he was created Earl of Wiltshire.

WIMA KADPHISES (*fl.* 1st cent. AD), Kushan King, who extended his kingdom by conquests in western India, north of the Oxus river, and westwards into the Parthian empire.

WIMPFEN, BATTLE OF (May 1622), in the Thirty Years War between 14,000 Palatinate troops under George Frederick, Margrave of Baden, and the Bavarian and Spanish troops of the imperialist army under Tilly and Cordova, while the former were crossing the Neckar. Despite the steady artillery fire and brilliant cavalry charges of the Palatine forces, their infantry were routed by the imperialists, who captured their guns and baggage and drove the margrave to Stuttgart as a fugitive.

WINCHELSEA, ROBERT (*c.* 1240–1313), English cleric, who became Abp of Canterbury in 1294 against the wishes of King Edward I, and later drifted into a long series of conflicts with the Crown. He led the opposition to the wartime taxation of the clergy in 1296–7, and to Edward's corrupt but forceful chief minister, Walter Langton, in 1301. Edward I forced him to leave England and in 1305 procured his suspension by Pope Clement V. Edward II, on his accession in 1307, reversed many of his father's policies and recalled Winchelsea to England. But the archbishop soon became one of the leaders of opposition to the Crown and co-operated with the Lords Ordainer in imposing serious restrictions on Edward II.

WINCHESTER, WILLIAM PAULET, 1st Marquis of (*c.* 1485–1572), English politician, who held a variety of posts under four different monarchs, becoming lord president of the council (1546–50), keeper of the great seal, under the Duke of Somerset (1547), lord high treasurer (1550–72), and speaker of the House of Lords (1559, 1566). He was a careful trimmer, was distrusted by the Protestants, and opposed the attempt to make Jane Grey queen. Under Elizabeth I he counselled moderation, disliking Cecil's policies.

WINCHESTER, OLIVER FISHER (1810–80), US arms manufacturer, whose New Haven Arms Co. (1857–) developed repeating rifles that were widely used in the American Civil War. In 1866 he introduced the Winchester rifle, whose reliability and ease of operation quickly made it a standard weapon.

WINCHESTER, in England, seat of the West Saxon episcopal see from early in the second half of the 7th cent. AD, and capital of the West Saxon and early kings of England. Under Alfred the city was a centre of learning and was the seat of Cnut's government. In the late Saxon and early Norman periods it was, with London, the twin capital of England. Through its proximity to Southampton it became of great commercial importance, reaching the zenith of its prosperity *c.* 1100. However, by the late 12th cent. London emerged as the undisputed capital.

WINCHESTER, STATUTE OF (1275), English legislative measure which attempted to improve the maintenance of law and order. Criminals were to be pursued by the local community, highways were to be made safe, and town gates closed at night. All free subjects were to keep arms and armour, according to their rank, for the defence of the peace.

WINCKELMANN, JEAN-JOACHIM (1717–68), German archaeologist and antiquarian, who wrote *Reflections on the Imitation of Greek Sculpture and Painting* (1756), and the first modern *History of Ancient Art* (1764). He examined the remains of Herculaneum and Pompeii (1758), produced a treatise on ancient architecture (1762), and was appointed superintendent of Roman antiquities and librarian or scriptor in the Vatican (1763).

WINDEBANKE, SIR FRANCIS (1582–1646), English politician and secretary of state (1632–40), who was one of King

Charles I's closest pro-Spanish, pro-Catholic advisers in the council. His promotion to high office was largely due to his friendship with Richard Weston, Earl of Portland. After the arrest of Abp Laud and Strafford, Windebanke fled to Calais (1640). He died in Paris, a convert to the Catholic Church.

WINDHAM, WILLIAM (1750–1810), British politician, who sat in the House of Commons from 1784 until his death. He held minor office in the Fox–North coalition and opposed Pitt's government until after the outbreak of the French Wars. He was then secretary of state for war and the colonies (1794–1801), but resigned with Pitt. He did not support Pitt's second ministry, but turned back to Fox and again held office as secretary of state for war and the colonies in the 'Talents' ministry (1806–7). Windham was one of the managers of the impeachment of Warren Hastings (1788–95), and he also planned the invasion of the Vendée (1795). His army reforms (1806–7), aimed at abolishing Pitt's volunteer system and introducing short-term enlistment, were inefficiently planned and executed.

WINDISCHGRÄTZ, ALFRED, Prince (1787–1862), Austrian soldier and politician, who was leader of the conservative federalists in the Austrian upper house (1861). He suppressed the revolution in Prague (1848), and as supreme commander of Austrian troops outside Italy, captured Vienna and attacked the Hungarians.

WINDMILL, BATTLE OF (Nov. 1838), involving Americans who crossed the St Lawrence river, invaded Prescott in Upper Canada, and took possession of a windmill at Windmill Point. Retreat was cut off by Canadian militia, and 160 Americans were captured.

WINDOW TAX in Britain, first imposed in 1696, as a substitute for the hearth tax, to defray the cost of recoinage. Under the Younger Pitt, the tax made an important contribution to the national revenue. In 1782 he imposed a tax of 1s. per window, which rose sharply after the tenth window, and was trebled in 1797. Houses with fewer than seven windows were exempted in 1792, the exemption being extended in 1825 to houses with less than eight windows. The tax was reduced in 1823 and abolished in 1851, when it was replaced by an extension of the house duty. The tax did not extend to Scotland.

WINDSOR, TREATY OF (1506), procured by King Henry VII of England when Philip of Flanders was wrecked on the Dorset coast. The treaty promised Philip England's support against his father-in-law, Ferdinand of Spain, in return for the person of the Earl of Suffolk, who, as nephew of Edward IV, was a troublesome Yorkist claimant. The treaty also contained the commercial agreement known as the *Malus Intercursus*, which would have exempted English merchants from Flemish tolls. But Philip died later in the year and the only permanent result of the treaty was the surrender of Suffolk, who was imprisoned and died in the Tower of London (1513).

WINDSOR, TREATY OF (1522), between King Henry VIII of England and the Emperor Charles V, following a conference at Bruges in the previous year. Henry promised to invade France, the common enemy, Charles was betrothed to his daughter Mary, and Wolsey received vague assurances of support when the papacy fell vacant. But the English raids on France were unproductive, the new pope was Clement VII (1523), and Henry gained nothing from the emperor's eventual victory over the French.

WINDSOR CASTLE, at Berks in England, royal castle which owes its foundation to William I, who built a motte on the hill overlooking the Thames (*c.* 1070). Further work was carried out by successive kings, particularly Henry II, who built the circular keep, and Henry III. Edward III spent vast sums of money on the castle, transforming it into a

fortified palace. It has remained a favourite royal residence until the present time (1970). St George's Chapel, begun by Edward IV, ranks next to Westminster Abbey as an English royal mausoleum.

WINDWARD ISLANDS, British West Indian islands which, though they were separate colonies, shared the same governor. From 1833 to 1885 St Lucia, St Vincent, Grenada, and Tobago were subject to the governor of Barbados, all being known as the Windward Islands. An attempt to federate them into a single colony on the Leeward Islands pattern, involving abrogation of the Barbados constitution, led Barbados planters to form a 'Defence Association' (1876). The federation proposal was then abandoned. After being separated from Barbados (1885), the four islands were placed under a Windward Islands governor. Tobago was annexed to Trinidad in 1889, and Dominica was transferred from the Leewards to the Windwards in 1940. The Windward Islands entered the West Indian Federation (1958) as separate units. Each is now (1970) a state in association with the United Kingdom.

WINE TRADE IN THE MIDDLE AGES. Medieval wines deteriorated quickly, turning into vinegar. Consequently wines that were more than a year old fetched very low prices and each year's production had to be sold rapidly. Huge quantities of wine were disposed of throughout Europe every year and from the 13th cent. onwards many varieties competed with each other in the main European markets. Italians and Catalans shipped sweet wines from the Mediterranean; Gascon, English, and German fleets distributed wine from Gascony and wines from inland French regions and from the Rhineland were transported overland and by river. Because of the risks and high costs of the medieval wine trade it tended to be handled by many non-specialized merchants, as simply one of their many enterprises. Specialized wholesale dealers in wine did exist (*eg*, the London guild of vintners), but the more prosperous among them also invested heavily in other commodities. Wines were distinguished by the regions from which they came. In commercial records there are no mentions of more specialized brands, or of wines from particular localities.

WINGATE, CHARLES ORDE (1903–44), British soldier who served in the Sudan and explored the Libyan desert (1928–1933), and trained and led guerrilla forces during the Arab revolt in Palestine (1936–8). On the outbreak of the Second World War he organized Ethiopian and Sudanese irregulars against the Italians in East Africa, winning the support of Wavell, who, as commander-in-chief in India, enabled him to put his ideas into practice against the Japanese in Burma (1942–4). Wingate believed fanatically that the only way to defeat the Japanese was by attacking their supply depots and communications with 'long-range penetration groups'. These were to be mixed forces of British, Ghurka, and Burmese troops specially trained and equipped for jungle warfare, operating far behind the enemy lines, and supplied from the air. These ideas were not original, and it has been suggested that by March 1944, when Wingate was killed in an air crash, his Chindits were diverting too large a portion of the British effort from the orthodox forces which alone could defeat the Japanese in the field. The Chindits played a useful part in the early days but their contribution to the decisive battles of 1944, Kohima and Imphal, was small. They had however some psychological significance, demonstrating that British troops could operate in the jungle as effectively as the Japanese and enabling the British to act aggressively at a time when, and in a theatre where, they lacked the resources for an orthodox offensive.

WINGATE, SIR FRANCIS REGINALD (1861–1953), British soldier and administrator. He was transferred to the Egyptian army (1883) and, as director of military intelligence, played an important part in the conquest of the Sudan (1896–9).

As commander-in-chief of the Egyptian army and governor-general of the Sudan (1899–1916) he laid the foundations of the administration there. As high commissioner of Egypt (1917–19) he was largely responsible for the organization of the Arab revolt and for the first negotiations with the Wafd party.

WINNEBAGO INDIANS, American tribe encountered by the French (1634) on Green Bay in WI. They were first allies of the French, then of the British. By 1840 they had ceded all their lands, and the US government moved them several times before giving them a reservation in OK (1865).

WINSLOW, EDWARD (1595–1655), English colonist, who travelled to America in the *Mayflower* (1620). He gained the Indians' friendship for the Pilgrims, and helped to organize the New England Confederation (1637), on which he served as Plymouth's representative. He returned home to serve Oliver Cromwell during the Commonwealth.

WINSLOW, EDWARD (1746–1815), Canadian soldier and politician, who joined the British forces during the American War of Independence. He went to Halifax with the Loyalists (1783) and became a member of the executive council of NB. He was appointed to the provincial supreme court (1806) and was president (administrator) of NB from 1808 until his death.

WINSTANLEY, GERRARD (1609–52), English politician, leader of the 'True Levellers' or 'Diggers', and pamphleteer. Originally a cloth merchant, he was famous as the instigator of an experiment in agrarian communism at Cobham in Surrey (1649). He wrote many political and religious tracts, *eg,* 'The Law of Freedom' (1651), upholding the right of common people to free land.

'WINTER KING', THE, name given to Elector Frederick V of the Palatinate and King of Bohemia after his brief reign (4 Nov. 1619–8, Nov. 1620) had ended with the disastrous battle of the White Mountain.

WINTHROP, JOHN (1588–1649), English lawyer and colonist who joined the Company of the Massachusetts Bay, becoming governor of the company (1629) and emigrating to New England in 1630. He was at the centre of the political and religious conflicts of the early years of the colony. He opposed expanding the electorate and any liberalizing tendencies in New England Calvinism. His *Journal* (1630–49) is the basis of all historical work on New England.

WIRTH, JOSEPH (1879–1956), German politician and Reich chancellor (1921–2), who began his political career in 1913 as a deputy in the Lower Chamber of Baden and was later elected to the Reichstag as a representative of the Centre Party. After 1918, he became a leading figure in the party, acting as Reich minister of finance from March 1920 to Oct. 1921, when he became chancellor. After having played a key role in the making of the Rapallo treaty, he was forced to resign (Nov. 1922). In Brüning's cabinet he was minister of the interior (1930–1). After the National Socialists' seizure of power he emigrated to Switzerland. For a brief period after the Second World War he reappeared in politics as a member of the Bund der Deutschen (lit. League of Germans).

WISCONSIN, 30th member state of the US, admitted in 1848. The area to the south-west of the Great Lakes and north of the Mississippi was first explored by Jean Nicolet (1634). It was annexed by France (1671), and was dominated by French fur traders even after it passed into British possession (1763). Although the region was ceded to the US (1783), British troops were not withdrawn until after the War of 1812, and American control was only established with the garrisoning of Fort Howard at Green Bay and Fort Crawford at Prairie du Chien (1816). At first it formed part of the North-west Territory (1787–1800), then became part of Indiana Territory (1800–9), Illinois Territory (1809–18), and Michigan Territory (1818–36). Settlement spread with the discovery of lead ore in the south-west (1822) and the suppression of the Indians during the Black Hawk War (1832). Wisconsin Territory was established (1836), and a flow of settlers from New England and immigrants from Germany and Norway led to statehood in 1848. WI was the chief wheat-producing state in the US until 1870, then the growth of dairy farming and of industrialization strengthened its economy. During the early 20th cent. WI supported the Progressive movement, and the La Follette family dominated its local politics.

WISE, HENRY ALEXANDER (1806–76), US soldier and politician, who was elected to the US House of Representatives as a Jacksonian Democrat (1833). Being devoted to the doctrine of states rights, he became alienated from Jackson and Van Buren and became a Whig and then a Tyler Democrat. He refused President Tyler's offer of the secretaryship of the navy, and was rejected by Congress as minister to France, but served as US minister to Brazil (1844–7). He was prominent in VA state politics and served as governor (1856–60); he was firmly opposed to the spread of 'Know Nothingism'. He preferred to fight for Southern rights within the Union, but supported secession in 1861 and served with credit as a Confederate general in the defence of Richmond and during the final retreat to Appomattox.

WISHART, GEORGE (*c.* 1513–46), Scottish divine, who was one of the leading agents of the Scottish reformation. Originally a schoolmaster at Montrose, he spent the years 1539–43 in Germany, Switzerland, and England. After returning to Scotland (1543) he was arrested by Cardinal Beaton (1545), convicted of heresy by convocation, and burned at St Andrews (1546). His death profoundly affected John Knox and thus contributed to later events in Scotland.

WITANAGEMOT, in Anglo-Saxon England, meeting of the *witan* or wise men of the kingdom with the king. Its composition was possibly at the king's complete discretion, but the known assemblies consisted of prelates, lay notables (*ealdormen* and *thegns*), and royal clerks. As far as is known, it had no defined powers, but kings found it desirable or necessary to hold these assemblies.

WITBOOI, HENDRIK (d. 1905), chief of the Witbooi Nama in south-west Africa during the period of German colonial rule. In his early years he raided the Herero relentlessly, but in face of the German threat concluded peace with them in 1892. In 1893 and again in 1904–5 he led the Witboois in resistance to the Germans. He was killed in 1905.

WITCHCRAFT, in Europe, practice of the magical arts, sometimes with evil intent, but equally often associated with innocent people who deviated from the social norm. Witchcraft, which had been condemned by the medieval Church as a work of the devil, became the object of frenzied persecution in the 16th and 17th cents. The promulgation of the bull *Summis desiderantes* by Pope Innocent VIII (1484) and the publication of a manual of procedure for the Inquisition, the *Malleus Maleficarum,* by Heinrich Institorus and Jacob Sprenger (1487–8), initiated the wholesale burning of witches in Europe. After the Reformation both Catholic and Protestant countries alike perpetrated a vicious persecution of witches in the name of orthodoxy. King Henry VIII of England introduced an act declaring witchcraft and sorcery to be felonies without benefit of clergy, and this law was confirmed by acts of 1563 and 1603. Persecution was widespread in the German states, France, England, Scotland, and North America in the 17th cent., but was eventually checked by the spread of toleration and rationalism. Colbert halted the process in France, and English and Scottish legislation against witches was repealed in 1736, although the practice of burning had died out in England by 1712 and in Scotland in 1722.

WITH, WITTE CORNELISZOON DE (1599–1658), Dutch sailor, who took part in the Danish–Swedish War of 1643–5, the First Anglo–Dutch War of 1652–4, and the Northern War of 1655–60. He commanded the second relief fleet sent to Brazil (1647–8) and after his evacuation of the colony on the Recife was tried for cowardice, but acquitted. After Tromp's death, he led the Dutch fleet to victory off Terheide (10 Aug. 1653), but was killed in battle in the Sound.

WITHER, GEORGE (1588–1667), English poet and pamphleteer, famous for his satires, *eg*, 'Abuses Stript and Whipt' (1613), pastoral and religious poetry. After becoming a Puritan, he raised a troop of horse for the Parliamentary cause (1642), but was later imprisoned for his satire on the Restoration parliament (1661–3). His best verse was collected in *Juvenalia* (1622).

WITT, CORNELIS DE (1623–72), Dutch politician and brother of the grand pensionary, Jan de Witt, who served as deputy to the states general, accompanying De Ruyter during several naval engagements with England, *eg*, the attack on the Medway (1667). After being falsely accused of planning the assassination of William, Prince of Orange, he was imprisoned in Gevangenpoort and sentenced to banishment, but was murdered with his brother by Orange partisans (20 Aug. 1672).

WITT, JAN DE (1625–72), Dutch politician, who was appointed grand pensionary of Holland (1653), an office which he endowed with the significance it had previously enjoyed only under Oldenbarneveldt. He was a son of Jacob de Witt, burgomaster of Dordrecht, and became leader of the States party in opposition to the house of Orange, believing that the regents, who were the provincial magistrature, should hold the highest authority in the republic. In making peace with England (1654), he agreed to the Act of Seclusion, excluding the Orange family from its ancestral offices, and although the act was annulled at the Restoration (1660) and he was forced to consent to the adoption of Prince William of Orange as a Child of State during the Second Anglo–Dutch War, he ensured that the prince should not be *stadtholder* as well as captain-general (Eternal Edict, 1667). In 1662 Witt negotiated a French alliance and in 1658 intervened in the Baltic War to help Denmark against Sweden. He mediated the Concert of The Hague (1659) and presided over the naval victories against England (1666–7) which led to a compromise in the treaty of Breda (1667). However, opposition to his foreign policy grew as Dutch isolation became apparent, and in face of the French invasion of 1672 the country rallied to the house of Orange. De Witt resigned, and two weeks later he and his brother Cornelis were murdered by a mob of Orange partisans (20 Aug. 1672).

WITTE, SERGEI YULYEVICH, Count (1849–1915), Russian politician, who was associated with the rapid industrialization of Russia in the 1890s. After having spent some time in railway administration, he established a railway department in the ministry of finance (1889) and in 1892 became minister of communications, then finance minister (1892–1903). He was influenced by List and Bismarckian Germany and the 'Witte system' aimed at making Russia a great European imperial power, for which, Witte argued, rapid industrialization was essential. As minister of finance, he put Russia on the gold standard and balanced the budget. His ministry became in effect the centre of Russian government, almost a state within a state, with unusually wide powers of administration. In a memorandum of 1899 he argued the need for a centralized, planned economy, these aims being widely publicized.

Russia's industrial growth, which reached a rate of 9 per cent in the 1890s, was based on the rapid expansion of a railway network, of which the Trans-Siberian line was only a part. Being financed by large loans from France, and relying, as he did, on imported machinery and expertise, Witte was able to do without a mobile labour force, nor did he need an expanding market. Though his protectionist tariffs and high taxes impoverished the peasantry, he was aware of the need for peasant reform. He advocated the abolition of the commune, and although his committee on agriculture (1902) achieved little, it laid the foundations for the Stolypin reform.

Witte's policies were devised to achieve imperialist expansion in the Far East by peaceful economic penetration of Manchuria; an agreement with China (1896) enabled him to build the Chinese Eastern Railway and establish a Russo-Chinese bank.

He called his policy State Socialism and in 1897 passed labour laws establishing an $11\frac{1}{2}$-hour working day. As a proponent of modernization and westernization of society from above, he regarded the *zemstvo* as incompatible with autocracy and laid the blame for the 1905 revolution on the lack of social reforms. But his enemies accused him of ruining the peasantry and of tying Russia to the French alliance through establishing conditions of financial dependence and in 1903 he was dismissed. His Far Eastern policy was allowed to drift, with the result that the Russo–Japanese War broke out. At the end of the war, which he had opposed, Witte was recalled and negotiated the peace of Portsmouth with the Japanese (Aug. 1905) and advised the tsar to issue the October Manifesto. As prime minister (1905–6) he negotiated with Shipov to get Octobrists into the government, but he resigned before the first Duma met.

T. H. Von Laue, *Sergei Witte and the Industrialization of Russia* (Columbia, 1963).
S. Witte, *Memoirs* (ed. A. Yarmolinsky) (New York, 1921).
               BJW

WITTELSBACH DYNASTY, German ducal and later royal house, founded by Otto of Wittelsbach, the supporter of the Emperor Frederick Barbarossa, who bestowed on him the Welf duchy of Bavaria in 1180. The family took their name from the castle of Wittelsbach in the county of Scheyern and originated from the line of Liutpold of Bavaria (d. 907), military lord of the Bohemian march. Three German emperors belonged to the dynasty.

In 1215 the Rhenish Palatinate was added to the Bavarian duchy and after Duke Louis II (*reg.* 1253–94) the dynasty divided into two distinct lines. The Rhinelands were ruled by Rudolph I and his descendants of the elder branch of the Wittelsbachs, while Bavaria was ruled by Louis II's younger son, Louis who became the Emperor Louis IV. Under him the Wittelsbachs added the margravate of Brandenburg, which they held from 1324 to 1373, the counties of Tyrol (1342–63), Holland, Zeeland, and Hainault (1345–1433). Later the Zweibrucken family, a branch of the Rudolph line, also reigned in Sweden (1654–1718). The family rapidly divided into many branches, some of which were extinct by the Reformation, though the Bavarian Wittelsbachs introduced primogeniture as late as 1578. The 16th-cent. dukes of Bavaria remained true to the Catholic Church, but under Frederick III Calvinism was introduced into the Palatinate in the 1560s, and reaffirmed by Frederick IV. The latter's son, Frederick V, was driven out of the Rhenish Palatinate by Duke Maximilian of Bavaria, his Catholic Wittelsbach relative of the younger branch of the family (1623). The Lower Palatinate was restored to Frederick's son, Charles Louis, in 1633, but the peace of Westphalia (1648) confirmed the retention of the Upper Palatinate by Maximilian the Great, who acquired the title of elector. He was succeeded in turn by Ferdinand Maria (*reg.* 1651–79), Maximilian II Emmanuel (*reg.* 1679–1726), Charles Albert, the imperial candidate, and Maximilian Joseph (*reg.* 1745–77), after whom the direct line died out. The duchy of Bavaria then passed to the Palatinate in accordance with the treaty of Pavia (1329) and as confirmed by the late Elector of Bavaria (1774), but Charles Theodore of the Sulzbach Wittelsbachs also died without heir (1799) and was succeeded by Maximilian Joseph of the Zweibrucken branch, whose electoral title was raised to the royal dignity by the treaty of Pressburg (1805). He ruled as King Maximilian I (*reg.* 1806–25) and his descendant, Louis III (*reg.* 1913–18), was the last of the reigning Wittelsbachs, being deposed in favour of a republic (1918).   MKS

WITTENBERG, CONCORD OF (May 1536), doctrinal articles representing a statement of faith of the South Germans and Swiss which were acceptable to the Lutherans. The concord was drafted by Melanchthon at a congress of evangelical theologians headed by Luther and Martin Bucer, which was held at Wittenberg.

WITTENBERG, UNIVERSITY OF, springboard of the Protestant Reformation. It was founded in 1502 by Frederick the Wise of Saxony and had four faculties, theology, law, medicine, and arts. By 1518, when its famous professor of biblical theology, Martin Luther, was becoming a celebrity, it had 22 professors and about 600 students, and in the course of the years 1520–60 some 16,000 students attended lectures there. Among them were Hans Tausen, Olavus Petri, Michael Agricola, and George Wishart, who together provided an immense missionary force for the establishment of Lutheranism. Other eminent scholars who lectured at Wittenberg included Andrew Carlstadt, the radical reformer, and Philip Melanchthon, the humanist, who wrote the *Loci Communes* while teaching theology at the university.

WITTENBERG ARTICLES (1535), doctrinal statement, the result of discussion at Wittenberg between representatives of the Church of England, led by Bishops Fox and Heath and Robert Barnes, and the Protestant League of Schmalkalde. The articles were to be the basis of a united front between the Anglicans and Lutherans at the forthcoming general council of the Church, but they were forgotten when plans for the council failed to materialize (1536).

WITTENWEIER, BATTLE OF (30 July 1638), victory of the Protestant forces of Bernard of Saxe-Weimar over the imperialist commander, Count von Goetz, and his Bavarian troops in the Thirty Years War. The battle dashed Habsburg hopes of dividing the Bernardine and French armies and of preventing their capture of Breisach.

WITTSTOCK ON THE DOSSE, BATTLE OF (4 Oct. 1636), Swedish victory during the Thirty Years War. The battle was fought on the banks of a tributary of the Havel river in Brandenburg, between Marshals Baner and Torstensson on the one hand and a Saxon imperial army on the other. This success heralded a Swedish revival and enabled Sweden's armies to penetrate to the borders of Saxony and Thuringia.

WOAD TRADE IN THE MIDDLE AGES. Until the introduction of Asiatic indigo into Europe in the 16th cent., European dyers had to use a dye derived from the woad plant as their sole source of blue colour and as an essential ingredient of black. The processing and distribution of woad were specialized occupations and its cultivation, which required care and involved much expense, became highly localized. In the 13th cent. the best woad came from Picardy and was distributed by merchants in Amiens. In the later Middle Ages the Genoese introduced Lombardy woad into England and the Netherlands. Between *c.* 1480 and 1560 Languedoc was one of the chief sources of fine woad, and as a result its capital, Toulouse, became one of the most prosperous towns in France.

WÖHLER, FRIEDRICH (1800–82), German chemist, who became (1836) professor of chemistry at Göttingen University. His artificial synthesis of urea in 1828 led the way to further syntheses of organic compounds, and so destroyed the old 'vital force' theory of formation of such compounds. He was the first to isolate aluminium in a pure state, and also the elements boron and silicon.

WOLFE, JAMES (1727–59), English soldier, who was the son of a general who had fought under Marlborough. He was commissioned in his father's regiment of marines, the 44th Foot, and fought at Dettingen and in Scotland (1745–6). In the Seven Years War he was quartermaster-general in the Rochefort expedition (1757), then was sent to America as a brigadier (1758), where he took part in the attack on Louisburg (1758). After a brief return to England (1759), he was sent out again as a commander of a force of some 9000 men to take Quebec. He led his men to a landing place 1½ miles above the city, from which they ascended the wooded cliffs under cover of darkness, taking the French by storm (10 Sept.). Both he and the French commander, Montcalm, were mortally wounded in the battle, which resulted in Quebec's surrender on 18 Sept.

WOLFF, CHRISTIAN VON, Baron (1679–1754), German philosopher and mathematician, who popularized the philosophy of Leibnitz and developed a deductive rationalistic system based on natural law. In 1706 he went to Halle University as professor of mathematics and natural philosophy, but was driven out by Frederick William I, acting on the advice of the pietistic faculty of theology (1723). From Halle, Wolff moved to Marburg, where he remained until he was recalled to his old university by Frederick the Great (1740).

WOLFF, SIR HENRY DRUMMOND CHARLES (1830–1908), British politician and diplomat, a member of the Fourth Party, and founder of the Primrose League. As a diplomat (1859–64, 1878–80, 1887–1900), he played a prominent part in Middle Eastern affairs and was responsible for the arrangements under which the Ionian isles were transferred to Greece, and for the organization of Eastern Rumelia. He also acted as British envoy in Persia, Rumania, and Spain. As a politician he defended Disraeli's purchase of the Suez Canal shares (1875), joined the Fourth Party in copying Irish obstructive methods in opposition (1880), and concluded a convention with the sultan for the occupation of Egypt.

WOLFRAM VON ESCHENBACH (*fl.* 12th cent.), German poet, who came to prominence in the flowering of literature during the civil wars after the death of Henry VI. His epic, 'Parzifal', was an outstanding work of the period. He expressed a remarkable tolerance towards Muslim infidels.

WOLGAST, BATTLE OF (Sept. 1628), victory of Wallenstein's forces over Christian of Denmark in the Thirty Years War. The imperial levies descended on the Danes outside Wolgast on the sandy Pomeranian coast, forcing Christian to flee and sue for peace, and compensating for Wallenstein's failure to take Stralsund (July–Aug. 1628).

WOLMAR, DIETS OF (1522, 1526, 1554), meetings of the Livonian estates, held in the central town of Wolmar, which were concerned with the progress of the Reformation in the Baltic state. Lutheranism reached Livonia in 1521, and at the 1522 Diet representatives of the towns and knights united against the Catholic bishops. At the Diet of 1526 the estates suggested that the grand master of the Teutonic Knights should secularize Livonia, as Duke Albert of Hohenzollern had secularized Prussia, but this he refused to do. However, the Reformation had triumphed by 1554, when the Diet proclaimed general religious toleration in Livonia.

WOLOF PEOPLES (approx. 1½ million), who live between the Senegal and Gambia rivers and speak a West Atlantic language related to Fulani and Serer. They are mostly Muslims and form a major element in Senegal's population. They first became known through the Venetian, Cadamosto (1455), who visited Kayor, which, like other Wolof states (Walo, Baol, Saloum), recognized the suzerainty of the Bur-ba of Jolof. In the 16th cent. Jolof lost its pre-eminence and was ravaged by the Fulani chief, Koli Tenvella. The Wolof were reunited in the 19th cent. by Lat Dior, *damel* of Kayor, attempting to resist French expansion.

WOLSELEY, GARNET JOSEPH WOLSELEY, 1st Viscount (1833–1913), British soldier, who served in the Second Burmese War (1852–3), the Crimean War (1855), and the Indian Mutiny (1857–8), and was at the siege and capture of Lucknow. In 1860 he went to China as assistant quarter-master-general to the Anglo-French expedition. In Canada (1861) he was sent with troops to the Red River settlement in the North-West Territories to make it a part of the dominion of Canada. In 1871 he became assistant adjutant-general at the war office and thereafter took a leading part in effecting army reforms. He commanded an expedition into Ashanti (1873) and burned the capital, Kumasi. He was high commissioner of Cyprus (1878), served in South Africa (1879), and led the expedition to relieve Gen. Gordon at Khartoum (1885). He was commander-in-chief of the British forces (1895–1900).

WOLSEY, THOMAS (*c.* 1473–1530), English cleric, politician, and chief minister (1515–29) to King Henry VIII, who took his degree at Oxford at the age of 15 and proceeded to a fellowship of Magdalen. He rose rapidly, becoming dean of Lincoln (1509) and almoner to Henry VIII (1509), and as a privy councillor (1511) directed the preparations for war against France (1512–13). By 1515 he was lord chancellor and Abp of York. In 1517 he became a cardinal, and in 1518 papal legate *a latere*, a position which was made permanent in 1524. Thus he held the highest offices in Church and state and through his administrative ability and his love of power he acquired the wealth, pomp, and luxury of one second only to the king.

His domestic policies were vindicated by his judicial successes. He contributed to the establishment of a regular court of chancery and gave authority and definition to the court of Star Chamber. He thus repressed feudal jurisdictions and concentrated power in the Crown. He tried unsuccessfully to tackle the problem of rural depopulation by appointing commissioners in 1517, 1518, and 1526 to enquire into enclosures completed since their prohibition in 1488. His reversal of illicit enclosures failed to solve the underlying economic problem of inflation and unemployment, resulting from the rise in population, nor did it endear him to the gentry, who, like the poorer classes, bitterly resented his financial expedients of forced loans and benevolences (1524–8).

Wolsey professed to want ecclesiastical reform in accordance with humanist demands, but his own way of life exemplified the weaknesses in the Church which reformers most criticized, namely pluralism, non-residence, simony, nepotism, and the marriage of priests. While he paved the way for the unification of the Church in England by wielding his legatine authority over the two provinces of York and Canterbury, he undermined its allegiance to Rome and its popular image. His subservience to papal interests in pursuit of his personal ambitions of elevation to the Holy See (1521, 1524) resulted in disaster for England's foreign policy and led ultimately to his downfall.

Wolsey tried to cut an important figure in the international scene and to use England's position to defend the papacy and hold the balance between the Valois and Habsburg monarchs. His apparent triumphs, *eg*, the treaty of London (1518), the Field of the Cloth of Gold (1520), and the conference of Calais (1521), proved hollow successes, however, for he could not prevent Francis I and Charles V from coming to terms when events suited them, *eg*, the treaty of Noyon (1516) and the peace of Cambrai (1529), and England was not of sufficient significance to prevent the military hegemony of first one and then the other, *eg*, Francis I's domination of

Italy after Marignano (1515) and Charles V's supremacy over France and the papacy after Pavia (1525), the sack of Rome (1527), and the occupation of Naples (1528). Wolsey's reversal of foreign policy, *eg*, alliance with France and war with Charles V (1528–9), achieved nothing and only underlined the failure of his greatest diplomatic test, the annulment of Henry VIII's marriage to Catherine of Aragon, Charles V's aunt. Wolsey conducted the negotiations with Pope Clement VII and sat with Cardinal Compeggio on the papal commission (1528), but could master neither Compeggio's nor Catherine's intransigence. The revocation of the case to Rome was followed by his dismissal from the chancellorship and indictment for praemunire (Oct. 1529), and a year later he was arrested for treason. He died at Leicester on his journey southwards from York to London to face this charge. Just before his death he had founded Christ Church, Oxford —in his lifetime, Cardinal's College.

A. F. Pollard, *Wolsey* (London, 1905).
J. J. Scarisbrick, *Henry VIII* (London, 1968).   MKS

WOLVERHAMPTON, HENRY HARTLEY FOWLER, 1st Viscount (1830–1911), British politician. As mayor of Wolverhampton he reformed the town, as Chamberlain had done in Birmingham, and became a prominent Liberal MP (1880–1910). He was responsible for the Local Government Act (1894) which established urban and district councils within the counties and made them more democratic, with control over housing, sanitation, etc. He also set up parish councils in rural districts.

WOMEN'S SOCIAL AND POLITICAL UNION, in Britain, Manchester-based women's Labour Party organization founded by Mrs Pankhurst in 1903. It was authoritarian in structure, and organized on a non-party metropolitan basis. In struggling to enter the male world of politics its members adopted violent tactics which later damaged their cause, but before 1910 they usefully publicized it.

WOOD, FERNANDO (1812–81), US politician and businessman, who was elected mayor of New York three times (1854, 1856, 1859), but being pro-Southern in his views during the secession crisis, he proposed (Jan. 1861) that New York should become a free city. He denounced the war and joined Clement Vallandigham in organizing the 'peace' Democrats. He served as US congressman from NY (1863–5, 1867–81).

WOOD, GRANT (1892–1942), US painter, who portrayed the plain people of his state in such pictures as the famous *American Gothic* (1930). With Thomas Hart Benton of MO (1889–) he was one of the leaders of a Middle Western regional movement that focused on the realities of ordinary life in the American hinterland.

WOOD, HENRY WISE (1860–1941), Canadian farm leader, who joined the United Farmers of Alberta (1909), of which he was later president (1916–31). He favoured co-operative ventures but opposed, unsuccessfully, the efforts of the United Farmers of Alberta to enter politics.

WOOD, LEONARD (1860–1927), US doctor, soldier, and administrator, who was seventh American governor-general of the Philippines (1921–7). He became a colonel of the Rough Riders in the Spanish–American War, then military governor of Cuba, and was an unsuccessful contender for the Republican nomination in 1920. In 1921 he became a member of an investigatory mission sent by the US president to the Philippines; one of its findings was that the Filipinos were not yet ready to become independent of the US government. Filipino nationalist leaders protested against this conclusion, having enjoyed an expanded autonomy under the Filipinization policy of the preceding administration of Gov. F. B. Harrison (1913–21). As governor-general, despite the opposition of the Filipino leaders, Wood maintained harmonious relations during the first year of his six-year administration. New opposition came with the cabinet crisis of 1923, which resulted from Wood's interference in what the Filipinos considered a domestic affair and led to the resignation of all the Filipino departmental secretaries. Wood attached little importance to the Council of State, formed earlier by Gov. Harrison in order to centralize the leadership of the Filipino participation in government. He abolished the board of control, a government agency Harrison had created to administer and supervise the government-owned corporation and which had permitted the two Filipino members to outvote its American chairman. By frequently exercising his power of veto, he continued to provoke the opposition of Filipino legislators. He did, however, make some positive contributions to improving conditions, among them the restoration of the financial stability of the Philippine government; improvements in public health and sanitation, as well as in the administration of justice, and the acceleration of public works projects. He also took the initial steps towards the formation of a Philippine army for the defence of the Philippines.   JMS

WOODCOCK, GEORGE (1904–), British trade union leader and general secretary of the Trades Union Congress (1960–9). During his tenure of office the TUC became less of an oppositional and more of a governmental pressure group, as was shown, for instance, by the full formal incorporation of trade unions into the structure of economic planning and management from 1961 onwards.

WOOD'S EDUCATION DESPATCH (1854), drafted by Sir Charles Wood while president of the Board of Control for Indian Affairs (1852–5), imposed on the government of India the duty of organizing the educational system from the primary school to the university. The educational efforts of the East India Co. had been in accordance with the filtration theory and they regarded any attack on mass illiteracy as Utopian, believing that the first step was to educate the literary classes and let education filter down through them to the masses. But class and caste distinctions were serious obstacles to filtration. A realization of this had prompted Sir Charles Wood's despatch, which advocated grants in aid and training for teachers. It was followed by the creation of universities and technical institutions, and increased attention being paid to vernacular education. The cause of female education was viewed sympathetically in the despatch and a policy of strict religious neutrality was enjoined in government educational institutions.

WOOD'S HALFPENCE (1722–4), notorious episode surrounding the English ironmaster William Wood (1671–1730) and the Duchess of Kendal, ex-mistress of George I, which aroused serious opposition in Ireland to the selfish domination of that country by England's politicians. The duchess sold to Wood for £10,000 the patent which she had obtained from the English treasury to coin £100,800 worth of copper halfpence and farthings for Ireland (1722), a transaction which was expected to produce a profit of at least £36,000 when an additional patent for the American colonies was included. When the terms were known a storm burst in the Irish parliament, fanned by Swift's *Drapier's Letters* (1724). Despite the assurance by the master of the Mint, Sir Isaac Newton, that the coins were up to standard, the patents were withdrawn because of popular indignation.

WOODSWORTH, JAMES SHAVER (1874–1942), Canadian socialist politician, who was ordained in the Methodist ministry (1901), and served in Winnipeg, where he developed strong sympathy for the problems of the immigrant and worker. He became field secretary of the Canadian Welfare League (1913) and founded the Bureau of Social Research (1916). As a socialist and pacifist he lectured on social conditions, helped to organize the Non-Partisan League (1918), and participated in the Winnipeg general strike (1919). He

was a Labour member in the Canadian House of Commons (1921–42), a founder of the Co-operative Commonwealth Federation (1932), and its president until 1940. His pacifist convictions caused him to reject his party's decision to support the Second World War.

WOODVILLE, ELIZABETH (d. 1492), daughter of a parvenu English noble, Lord Rivers. Her marriage to King Edward IV was regarded, both by the aristocracy and the people, as a misalliance. This, and the promotion of her relatives, made her extremely unpopular with most of the king's entourage, and fear of her family may have played a decisive part after Edward's death in Richard III's decision to usurp the throne from Elizabeth's son, Edward V.

WOODWARD, ROBERT BURNS (1917–), US chemist, who synthesized complex organic compounds, starting only with simpler compounds, which could be made from the elements (carbon, hydrogen, oxygen, and nitrogen). The preparative routes, therefore, have not involved the use, at any stage, of an intermediate derived from living organisms. In 1944 he succeeded in synthesizing quinine, which Perkin had attempted to do nearly a century earlier and instead produced the aniline dyes. Notable syntheses for which Woodward and his school were responsible were steroids, such as cholesterol (1951), the steroid hormone, cortisone, the alkaloid, strychnine (1954), reserpine, the first of the tranquillizing drugs (1960), chlorophyll, the plant pigment (1960), and a tetracycline antibiotic (1962). For these achievements, particularly the synthesis of chlorophyll, Woodward was awarded the 1965 Nobel Prize for Chemistry.

WOOL STAPLE, in England. From 1294 onwards attempts were made by medieval English kings to control the vital wool export by regulating the towns at which English raw wool could be marketed. This was a useful diplomatic counter in dealings with foreign powers and, at first, the staple migrated between various towns of the Netherlands and northern France. The conquest of Calais in 1347, which was repopulated with Englishmen, led to a fairly permanent establishment of the staple there from 1363 onwards. The company of wool exporters who controlled it were able to preserve thereby a monopoly control over the trade and administered the customs on wool. In return, they financed the defence of Calais and advanced loans to the Crown. This arrangement ended only with the capture of Calais by France in 1558.

WOOL TRADE IN THE MIDDLE AGES. The manufacture of woollen cloth was the most important industry of medieval Europe. Sheep were kept in large numbers everywhere, but only certain varieties of wool were regarded as suitable for making the best types of cloth. Wool from some hilly parts of England and Wales was accepted in the 13th cent. as the best in Europe and the great textile centres of the Netherlands and Italy bought huge quantities. Fleeces produced by some 10 million sheep were being exported annually from England c. 1300. Another type of fine wool came from Spain, deriving from a species of sheep originally imported from North Africa. In the later Middle Ages the supply of English wool for the continental industries dwindled, as the bulk of it came to be absorbed by the growing English industry, and Spanish wool increasingly took its place. Just as the Spanish exploitation of the wool trade is a central issue of English history in the 13th and 14th cents., so the predominance of the Spanish association of wool producers, the MESTA, is a central feature of Castilian life in the late Middle Ages and beyond.

WOOLMAN, JOHN (1720–72), American Quaker and anti-slavery leader, whose early experiences of the slave trade convinced him that slavery was a denial of the Christian religion. A visit to Virginia in 1746 reinforced his abolitionist views. He also opposed any form of military conscription, as well as taxation for military purposes. His *Journal* (1774) and an essay, 'Some Considerations on the Keeping of Negroes' (1754), were important contributions to the abolitionist literature in America. His immediate impact was greater in England than in his own country.

WOOLWICH in England, Thames site of the royal dockyard built by King Henry VIII for the construction and repair of the fleet, and of England's oldest military and naval arsenal (1720). The Royal Military Academy was erected there (1741–5) and the dockyard, which had declined from the early 18th cent., was closed in 1869.

WOOLWORTH, FRANK WINFIELD (1852–1919), US pioneer in cheap mass retailing, who established his first successful 5 and 10 cent store in Lancaster, PA (1879). When F. W. Woolworth Co. was incorporated (1911), he owned over 1000 such stores and was a multi-millionaire.

WORCESTER, THOMAS DE PERCY, 2nd Earl of (1st of 2nd creation) (*c.* 1343–1403). As steward of the household to King Richard II of England, he deserted his master in 1399 and joined his Percy relatives in making Henry of Lancaster king. He was suspected of being a leading instigator of the rebellion of the Percies against Henry IV in 1403. He allegedly concealed from his nephew Henry Percy (Hotspur) an offer of reconciliation from the king before the battle of Shrewsbury, in which Hotspur was killed. Worcester himself was captured and later executed.

WORCESTER, JOHN TIPTOFT, 4th Earl of (1st of 4th creation) (1427–70), English politician, who combined an active political career as a leading supporter of King Edward IV with the more unusual interests of studying at Oxford and in Italy. He was Edward's treasurer, but in a sudden rebellion by the Earl of Warwick against Edward he was captured and executed.

WORCESTER, BATTLE OF (3 Sept. 1651), end of King Charles II of England's attempt to gain the English throne with Scottish aid. Despite the defeat of Dunbar (3 Sept. 1650) the Scots crowned Charles II (1 Jan. 1651). While Cromwell captured Edinburgh and marched for Perth, Charles and his Scottish army of 16,000 men, under David Leslie, marched into England. Cromwell captured Perth (2 Aug. 1651), and then pursued Charles, cutting him off from his base. On 3 Sept. 1651 Cromwell, with 20,000 men, attacked the Scots at Worcester. Charles's army was destroyed and he fled into exile. Monck was sent to Scotland to subdue resistance there, which he had succeeded in doing by May 1652.

WORCESTER v. GEORGIA, 6 Peters 515 (1832), US Supreme Court case involving the state of GA's conviction of Samuel Worcester for residing on Indian lands without a state licence. The decision of Chief Justice Marshall developed an earlier opinion in *Cherokee Nation v. Georgia* (1831), holding that the Cherokee nation was a distinct political community with territorial boundaries within which GA laws had no force and which GA citizens had no right to enter without permission. GA refused to appear before the court, or to accept the decision. President Jackson's refusal to implement Marshall's decision was the occasion of his famous statement: 'John Marshall has made his decision; now let him enforce it.'

WORDSWORTH, WILLIAM (1770–1850), English poet, who made a major contribution to the romantic movement. At first stimulated by the French Revolution (1789), he later became fearful of the excesses of the Reign of Terror and proved a firm patriot in his country's war with France (1793–1815). By the end of his life he had become almost a reactionary in his political outlook. These changing moods were reflected in his poetry, while his techniques in composition

showed a rejection of 18th-cent. classical verse-patterns which heralded the era of Romantic writers such as himself, Scott, and Coleridge. The appeal to nature and to the imagination expressed in supple, lyrical form and simple language first emerged in *Lyrical Ballads* (1798) (with Coleridge). There followed *The Prelude* (1805, but published posthumously) and *The Excursion* (1814). He wrote many brief patriotic sonnets, *eg,* 'Upon Westminster Bridge' and 'England, 1802', and some prose work. He lived much of his life in the English Lake District, the grandeur of whose landscape was in harmony with his emotional approach to writing.

WORKERS' EDUCATIONAL ASSOCIATION (1904) in Britain, founded by Albert Mansbridge, who, encouraged by the growth of elementary education, wished to promote the higher education of working men through an alliance of working-class organizations and university extension movements. Among the earliest branches were those at Derby, Rochdale, and Ilford (1904–5). They were supported by the Trades Union Congress, the Co-operative Union, and the Working Men's clubs among other bodies. The WEA worked on the assumption that the adult student should co-operate in his own education and a system of tutorial classes of no more than 30 students was developed by 1907, when a conference at Oxford decided to sponsor such groups, in which university teachers were to take part. The course was to consist of lectures and discussions, as well as the writing and reading of essays, and R. H. Tawney's assistance assured success. In 1908, a joint committee, consisting of equal numbers of members of the university and working-class nominated by the WEA, met at Oxford and this pattern was repeated elsewhere under the co-ordination of a joint advisory committee (1909).

By 1914 the WEA was running 152 classes with 3110 students. Progress was halted by the outbreak of the First World War, but a report on adult education by a committee of the ministry of reconstruction (1919) advocated grants to the WEA and other organizations for the provision of courses less advanced than those of the university extramural departments, and the number of students grew.

In 1920 the TUC and WEA set up the Workers' Educational Trade Union Committee, which encouraged the teaching of economics and industrial history. In spite of financial difficulties during the depression of the 1930s, psychology and other popular subjects were added to the curriculum. Though the WEA tried to avoid propaganda in education, its members realized that knowledge was a prerequisite to social and political advance.

M. D. Stocks, *The WEA, the First Fifty Years* (London, 1953).   VEC

WORKERS' PARTY, in Germany, Deutsche Arbeiter-Partei, a precursor of the Nazi Party. In 1918 a Munich locksmith, Anton Drexler, was influential in setting up a 'Committee of Independent Workmen', later called the 'Political Workers' Circle', which became in Jan. 1919 the German Workers' Party. The new organization was a beer-hall discussion group of some 40 members, whose first chairman was the journalist Karl Harrer. Hitler first attended one of its meetings on 12 Sept. 1919. He soon became a committee member and a spokesman for the party and gradually attracted larger audiences. He also organized right-wing propaganda, as well as the party's first mass meeting on 24 Feb. 1920 at which its new name was announced—the National Socialist German Workers' Party (NSDAP), subsequently known as the Nazi Party.

WORKMEN'S COMPENSATION ACT (1906), in Britain, legislative measure which consolidated the 1897 and 1900 acts, extending to a further 6 million employees, including shop assistants and domestic servants, employers' liability to pay compensation for accidents at work. For the first time industrial diseases were included. An employee received benefit equal to half his wages one week after disablement, or from the day of injury, if his disablement lasted more than a fortnight. Labour MPs succeeded in substantially increasing the scope of the bill during its passage, but disliked its partial denial of compensation to a workman guilty of 'serious or wilful misconduct'.

WORKS PROGRESS ADMINISTRATION (1935–9), in the US, agency that formed part of the New Deal's attack on unemployment during the Depression. WPA reflected the view of its administrator, Harry Hopkins, that speed was essential and by mid-1936 had put over 3 million men to work. Although frequently attacked for inefficiency, for useless 'make-work' projects, and for political corruption, WPA's achievements were impressive. For an expenditure of $11,000 million it built over 650,000 miles (1,050,000 kms) of road, thousands of public buildings, bridges, and other public works, and employed creative and professional people through activities such as the Federal Writers' and Federal Theatre Projects. Reorganized as the Works Projects Administration in 1939, it became part of the Federal Works Agency until its liquidation in 1943.

WORLD FEDERATION OF TRADE UNIONS, founded at the end of the Second World War. With the onset of the Cold War it soon split. The existing International Federation of Trade Unions (founded 1901) was dissolved (1945) and the new federation was formed, which included all the members of the IFTU, except the American Federation of Labor, and the Russian trade unions. The communists, who dominated the French and Italian unions, made a vigorous bid to dominate the WFTU, with the result that the British TUC and the American Congress of Industrial Organizations took the lead in breaking away and establishing (Nov. 1949) the International Confederation of Free Trade Unions.

WORLD HEALTH ORGANIZATION, specialized agency of the UN established in 1958 with the aim of raising the standard of health throughout the world, which it does through advisory services and technical assistance. It had in 1970 125 members, including the Soviet bloc.

WORLD'S COLUMBIAN EXPOSITION (1893), international exhibition held in Chicago, IL, to celebrate the 400th anniversary of the discovery of America by Christopher Columbus. The 'White City' fair, planned by Daniel H. Burnham, was predominantly 'classical revival' in style, Louis H. Sullivan's Transportation Building being one of the few to reflect a new American architecture.

WORMS, CONCORDAT OF, in Germany, compromise agreement made in 1122 between the Emperor Henry V and Pope Calixtus II, which ended the great investiture contest. The emperor was to invest a bishop or abbot with his feudal lands and titles and the Church was to invest him with the symbols of his spiritual office, the ring and the cross. The choice of bishops and abbots was retained, in practice, by the emperor, who thus secured what mattered most to him.

WORMS, DIET OF (1495), scene of an attempted reform of the structure of imperial government. The Emperor Maximilian I, in need of the empire's aid against France, was forced to permit the estates to debate reform, under the leadership of the Elector of Mainz, Von Henneberg. The Diet produced major legislation, proclaimed the eternal peace, the erection of an imperial supreme court, the first regular imperial tax and the apparatus to administer it, and a plan for a permanent council of princes to administer the empire. Some of these reforms endured, but nothing could make the empire into an effective state.

WORMS, DIET OF (1521), first meeting of the estates of the German empire under the young Emperor Charles V. Be-

sides the usual constitutional and financial matters, the Diet was to consider the future of Martin Luther, already condemned as a heretic and excommunicated by papal bulls of 1520 and 1521. The Diet was opened on 27 Jan. 1521, but Luther attended under a safe conduct on 17–18 April, defending his fundamental difference with the Church in a famous speech traditionally ending with the words, 'Here I stand; I can do no other; God help me; Amen.' He was none the less condemned by edict (May 1521).

WORMS, DIET OF (1545), inconclusive conference of the German estates, summoned by the Emperor Charles V to discuss the religious schism in the empire in accordance with his promise made at the Diet of Speyer (1544). It opened on 14 Dec. 1544, but made little headway, and in May 1544 Charles became involved in negotiations with the papal legate, Cardinal Farnese, for reopening war with the Protestants. The pope's military preparations provoked suspicion among Catholic representatives and anger from the Protestants, so Charles refrained from action and the Diet ended with the prospect of further dispute.

WORMS, DISPUTATION OF (1540), theological conference between Protestant and Catholic princes, ministers, and scholars, presided over by the imperial minister, Granvelle. Its purpose was to find a compromise settlement which would end the religious schism in the empire. It was originally to have been held at Speyer, but was transferred to Hagenau and then adjourned to Worms (25 Nov.). In a private meeting, Martin Bucer and Wolfgang Capito made some progress with Gerard Veltwyk and Johann Gropper on the question of original sin, and in the general discussions there was some understanding on the work of the Holy Spirit. Although the talks eventually broke down, the text of the conference was the basis for further negotiations at the Diet of Regensburg (1541).

WORMS, EDICT OF (1521), imperial condemnation of Martin Luther, drawn up by the Emperor Charles V, signed by the electors of Mainz, Trier, Cologne, and Brandenburg, and agreed by a reduced representation at the Diet of Worms (6 May 1521). It denounced Luther as a heretic, placed him under the imperial ban, and called on all members of the Diet to suppress his ideas.

WORMS, TREATY OF (1743), alliance negotiated by Lord Carteret between Britain, Savoy-Sardinia, and the Habsburgs to ensure the balance of power in Italy and the Mediterranean during the War of the Austrian Succession. The treaty secured the allegiance of the equivocal Charles Emmanuel of Savoy against the Bourbon powers of France and Spain, by promising that Britain would pay a subsidy of £200,000 a year to him and of £300,000 to Maria Theresa of Austria. After pressure from Carteret, Maria Theresa agreed to cede part of the Milanese and Piacenza to Charles Emmanuel, and in the event of the Bourbons being driven out of Naples and Sicily, the latter was also to be ceded to Savoy and Naples to Austria. The agreement seemed a triumph for Carteret at the time, but it soon provoked a Franco-Spanish treaty, Genoese support for the Bourbons in Italy, and Frederick the Great of Prussia's re-entry into the war (1744).

WOUNDED KNEE, BATTLE OF (29 Dec. 1890), fought at Wounded Knee Creek in SD, US, after a band of Sioux had been captured and ordered to disarm. There was some resistance and the 7th US Cavalry opened fire, killing over 200 Indians. This was the last important battle between Indians and US troops.

WRANGEL, CARL GUSTAF (1613–76), Swedish soldier and sailor. At sea he defeated the Danes at Fehmarn (1645) and fought a skilful, though unsuccessful, battle against the Dutch in the Sound in 1658. On land he served as commander-in-chief in Germany, where he co-operated with

Turenne (1646–8), stormed Fredriksodde (1657), and in 1674–5 conducted the campaign against Brandenburg up to the battle of Fehrbellin, which was fought in his absence.

WRATISLAW, JOHANN WENZEL VON, Count (1669–1712), Bohemian noble and diplomat in Habsburg service, who was appointed imperial ambassador to England in 1700 and, with Marlborough and the grand pensionary, Heinsius, was responsible for the forging of the Grand Alliance (1701) and the close co-operation which brought the allied success against France in the War of the Spanish Succession, *eg,* he advocated the combined operation against Bavaria and France which led to the Blenheim campaign.

WRATISLAW II (1061–92), Premyslid ruler of Bohemia (*reg.* 1085–92), who incorporated Moravia into his possessions. He was a faithful ally of the Emperor Henry IV and in 1085 was rewarded with the title of king, which was to last for his lifetime.

WREN, SIR CHRISTOPHER (1632–1723), English scientist and architect, who became a notable geometer and in 1661 Savilian Professor of Astronomy at Oxford. He was a charter member of the Royal Society and in 1681 became its president. His association with architecture effectively began in 1665 with his appointment as a commissioner for the restoration of St Paul's Cathedral. After the fire of London the following year, the cathedral was rebuilt to one of his designs. He became surveyor-general of public works in 1668 and subsequently devoted his efforts increasingly to architecture. He resigned the Oxford chair in 1673 and this really marked the end of his scientific work. In all, he designed over 100 buildings in London and elsewhere.

WRIGHT, FRANK LLOYD (1869–1959), US architect, whose domestic buildings emphasized the use of organic materials and were characterized by a dominant horizontal line with balanced geometrical masses enclosing open interlocking spaces. The strong influence of Mayan and oriental architecture may be seen in his Imperial Hotel, Tokyo (1916–22).

WRIGHT, SILAS (1795–1847), US lawyer and politician, who was an influential figure in NY state politics, a member of the 'Albany Regency', and an inveterate enemy of privileged minorities. He served in the state senate (1824–7), in the US House of Representatives (1827–9), as comptroller of NY (1829–33), US senator (1833–44), and governor of NY (1845–7).

WRIGHT, WILBUR (1867–1912) and **ORVILLE** (1871–1948), US inventors, who became interested in aviation through the experiments of the German gliding pioneer, Otto Lilienthal. Starting in 1900, they tested a series of gliders embodying an advanced control system they had invented, which was based on ailerons, *ie,* movable wing-tips. Other improvements were derived from experiments with models in their own wind tunnel. In 1902 they built and mounted a petrol engine in a larger version of the glider to drive two airscrews. With this machine they made the first airplane flight in history, on 17 Dec. 1903 at Kitty Hawk, NC. Successive flights by the two brothers lasted 12 and 59 seconds and were watched by five spectators. At the time this event did not create much interest. The Wright brothers, however, continued to make larger and more powerful machines and in 1905 made a 24-mile (38·6-km) flight lasting half an hour. Thereafter, public interest in aviation grew, particularly after the first flight across the English Channel in 1909.

WRONG, GEORGE MACKINNON (1860–1948), Canadian historian who devoted his life to the gathering of sources of information on Canadian history. He founded the *Review of Historical Publications Relating to Canada* (1897–1917), and was the editor of the *Canadian Historical Review.*

WU (*reg.* 690–705), Chinese Empress, the only woman who succeeded in founding her own dynasty and ruling China with full imperial authority (690–705). Her reign has been characterized as one of intrigue, oppression, and cruelty.

WU, kingdom situated in south China during the period ending 473 BC; it was also the name of one of the Three Kingdoms (222–80).

WU P'EI-FU (1878–1939), Chinese war-lord and leader of the Chihli Clique in early Republican China. His political acumen, concern for good government, and close relations with foreign powers enabled him to establish a relatively long lasting hegemony in northern and central China. He was eventually defeated by the Kuomintang (1927) and retired to study Buddhism.

WU SAN-KUEI (1612–78), Chinese soldier and founder of the short-lived Chou dynasty (1673–81). In 1644 he was charged with the defence of the Ming dynasty and given command of a large force in Liaotung. Caught between the invading Manchus and the advancing rebel forces of Li Tzu-ch'eng, Wu invited the Manchus to join him. After the establishment of the Manchu Ch'ing dynasty, he was given the title of prince, and proceeded to suppress a number of rebellions in northern and western China. At the time, a number of Ming princes were continuing their war of resistance, among whom Prince Kuei was the most powerful, controlling seven provinces in southern and south-west China in 1648. The destruction of Prince Kuei's regime earned Wu the title of prince of the blood of the first degree and jurisdiction over Yunnan. Soon, Wu established a satrapy virtually independent of the Ch'ing government, extending his control over Kweichow, Hunan, Szechuan, Shensi, and Kansu. Two other Chinese generals also enjoyed similar power in Fukien and Kwangtung. Mindful of their growing power, the Ch'ing government ordered their removal (1673). In reaction, Wu rebelled and proclaimed the Chou dynasty; and the others followed suit. Owing to strategical errors, Wu failed just at a time when success was probable. He died while in retreat and was succeeded by his grandson. The rebellion, known as the 'Rebellion of the Three Feudatories', was suppressed in 1681.

WULFSTAN (d. 1023), English scholar, who became Abp of York. He was one of the greatest literary figures of the 10th-cent. West Saxon renaissance and a legalist who exercised decisive influence on the royal legislation under Aethelred II. He wrote the *Sermo Lupi ad Anglos* (*Sermon of Wulfstan to the English*), in which he condemned the shortcomings of Anglo-Saxon society under Aethelred.

WULFSTAN (d. 1095), English scholar, who became Bp of Worcester and the only Anglo-Saxon bishop permanently retained by William the Conqueror. He rebuilt Worcester Cathedral and part of his church still survives as a crypt underneath the modern cathedral. His transcripts of the muniments of his see are an invaluable source. His devotion to pastoral work and his reputation for sanctity led to his canonization.

WUSTERHAUSEN, TREATY OF (1726), Austro-Prussian agreement by which Frederick William I of Prussia abandoned the Hanoverian alliance with Britain and France in favour of friendship with the Emperor Charles VI, and agreed to guarantee the Pragmatic Sanction. Frederick William was annoyed by delays over the Prussian–Hanoverian double marriage and misled by Charles VI's apparent sympathy for the Prussian succession in Jülich and Berg. He was also influenced by the recent (Aug.) defensive alliance between Catherine I of Russia and the emperor. The Wusterhausen agreement was transformed into a formal alliance in Dec. 1728.

WYATT, SIR FRANCIS (*c.* 1575–1644), English colonist, whose investment in the London Co. (1620) helped save the Virginia colony, and led to his appointment as the royal governor of Virginia (1639–42).

WYATT, SIR THOMAS (*c.* 1503–42), English courtier and poet, whose father held office under the first two Tudors. He was himself employed on missions abroad, a fact which encouraged his study of European literature. He was an admirer of Petrarch and, with Surrey, introduced the sonnet into England; but his finest satires and lyrics, *eg,* 'Forget not yet the tried intent', were in the native tradition.

WYATT, SIR THOMAS (*c.* 1521–54), English soldier and rebel leader, son of the poet of the same name. He joined the Earl of Surrey's volunteers and served in Flanders, *eg,* at Landrecies and Boulogne (1543–50). He led a rebellion in Kent, inspired by Protestantism and nationalist resentment over Mary I's proposed marriage to Philip II of Spain, and led his 3000 men as far as Fleet Street, London, before surrendering to government forces (Jan.–Feb. 1554). He was executed for high treason.

WYCHERLEY, WILLIAM (1640–1716), English dramatist, who excelled in the artificial and licentious comedy popular after the Restoration. After being brought up in France, he came to London to study law, but preferred a life of gaiety and fashion. His best comedies, *Love in a Wood, The Gentleman Dancing-Master, The Country Wife,* and *The Plain Dealer,* were produced in 1671–4. It has been argued that Wycherley was at heart a moralist who portrayed debauchery to make it appear ridiculous.

WYCLIFFE, JOHN (1330–84), English cleric, who, by his writings, started an important heretical movement. He was a theologian of considerable learning, cogency, and sincerity, though his activities reveal a certain lack of understanding of the world around him. His writings strongly disputed the divine origin of the authority of the papacy, demanded the provision of vernacular Bibles accessible to all lay people, and based the Christian doctrine exclusively on the Scriptures. He reduced the number of acceptable sacraments, most notably denying the real presence of Christ in the bread and wine of the mass. He was thus rejecting the doctrine of transubstantiation, a fundamental tenet of the Catholic faith. He was originally favoured by John of Gaunt, Duke of Lancaster, for Gaunt's own political ends, but when the implications of Wycliffe's ideas were fully realized by the duke, Wycliffe had to retire to his rectory. He was, however, sheltered from serious persecution and died at his house. His ideas were discredited by the Peasants' Revolt (1381), which many people ascribed, quite unjustifiably, to the seditious effect of his teachings. The most important consequence of Wycliffe's activities was the provision of English Bibles by his followers, the second of the two versions thus produced being a remarkably good translation. Deprived of academic leadership, his movement turned into a popular religion (known as Lollardy), which anticipated many of the features of 16th-cent. English Puritanism.

WYNENDAEL, BATTLE OF (28 Sept. 1708), Anglo-Dutch military victory over the French in the War of the Spanish Succession. In this short but sharp engagement, in which the French under Gen. La Motte attacked an allied convoy in Wynendael Woods, near Thornhout in the Spanish Netherlands, the allied commanders, Generals John Webb, William Cadogan, and Cornelis Nassau-Woudenberg, defeated a superior force.

WYNTER, SIR WILLIAM (d. 1589), English sailor who commanded (1559) the fleet sent to the Firth of Forth to prevent French reinforcements reaching the Marian party in Scotland. As surveyor of ships and master of ordnance, he dominated the navy board until John Hawkins's appointment as treasurer (1578). He took part in the Armada campaign (1588).

WYOMING, 44th member state of the US, admitted in 1890. The mountainous and high plain region embracing the headwaters of the North Platte, Yellowstone and Colorado rivers, and including South Pass, was the preserve of Indians and American fur traders in the early 19th cent. A Rocky Mountain Fur Co. party went through South Pass (1823–4), and Capt. Bonneville led the first wagons over the Rockies in 1832. Fort Laramie was established as a fur-trading post (1834), and, together with Fort Bridger (1843), became a depot on the Oregon Trail. Fur trading declined after 1840, but excitement over small discoveries of gold near South Pass (1867) and the completion of the Union Pacific Railroad (1869) increased settlement. Parts of WY were incorporated in Oregon Territory (1848–53), Utah Territory (1850–1868), Washington Territory (1853–63), Nebraska Territory (1854–68), Dakota Territory (1861–3, 1864–8), and Idaho Territory (1863–8). Wyoming Territory was established in 1868. Women were allowed to vote (1869) and served as jurors (1870). Expanding settlement, causing conflict with the Indians until the late 1870s, led to statehood (1890). During the late 19th cent. cattle-ranching was pre-eminent, but the harsh winter of 1886–7 and the success of sheep farming diminished its importance within the state. Since the Second World War WY's economy has largely depended on the mining of oil, natural gas, uranium, and large reserves of coal and iron ore, but the tourist trade, focused on Yellowstone and Grand Teton national parks, also makes a significant contribution to the state's income. ICP

WYOMING MASSACRE (3–6 July 1778), in America, massacre of nearly 300 American settlers in the Wyoming valley of Pennsylvania by British troops and Iroquois Indians. Gen. George Washington despatched an expedition which destroyed the war-making power of the Iroquois nation (1779).

WYTHE, GEORGE (1726–1806), American lawyer and politician, who served in the Virginia House of Burgesses (1754–5, 1758–68). He helped to draft the Virginia Resolutions (1765) opposing the Stamp Act. He also signed the Declaration of Independence (1776), and served in the Continental Congress (1776). Wythe assumed the 'professorship of Law and Police' at the College of William and Mary (1779), where he made important contributions to American jurisprudence. He strongly supported the ratification of the Federal constitution (1787–8).

WYVILL, CHRISTOPHER (1740–1822), English landowning cleric who advocated parliamentary reform and religious toleration. He led the Yorkshire Association (1779), whose parliamentary reform petition (1780) provided a focus for criticism of Lord North from many different quarters. After the petitioning movement collapsed, Wyvill persisted in his demands for redistribution of seats and shorter parliaments. Although disliking French revolutionary excesses, he supported Fox's and Whitbread's attacks on the French Wars. He advocated Catholic emancipation and, with Burdett, Cobbett, and Cartwright, encouraged the Hampden Clubs (from 1811 onwards), which sought enfranchisement of all taxpayers and abolition of income tax.

X Y COMPANY in Canada, common name of the Canadian New North-West Co., founded 1798, whose bales of furs were marked X Y. The company was reorganized (1803) as Sir Alexander Mackenzie and Co. and absorbed by the North-West Co. (1804).

XYZ AFFAIR (1797–8), diplomatic incident between the US and France that worsened relations between the two countries and led to undeclared naval warfare (1798–1800). C. C. Pinckney, Elbridge Gerry, and John Marshall, American commissioners sent to France by President John Adams to try to resolve outstanding differences, were asked by French representatives, whom they called X, Y, and Z, for a substantial loan and bribes before serious negotiations could be entertained. Their reply, 'No, no not a sixpence', and the slogan attributed to Pinckney, 'Millions for defense but not one cent for tribute', became popular American rallying cries and stimulated American national feeling.

XANTEN, PEACE OF (1614), settlement which concluded the Jülich–Cleves succession crisis. Wolfgang William of Neuburg, who had become a Catholic and married the sister of Maximilian of Bavaria, head of the Catholic League in Germany, was involved in military conflict with his rival claimant, the Calvinist John Sigismund of Brandenburg (1613–14). In a compromise of which the states-general of the United Provinces were guarantors, Wolfgang William received Jülich and Berg, John Sigismund Cleves, Mark, and Ravensburg, and the privileges of the estates of these territories were confirmed.

XANTHIPPUS (*fl.* 5th cent. BC), Athenian politician, and father of Pericles. He was ostracized in 484, but recalled for the Persian invasion (480). He commanded successfully at Mycale (479) and Sestos (478).

XAVIER, FRANCIS, Saint (1506–52), Spanish Jesuit missionary, 'the apostle of the Indies', who was the son of a Basque nobleman. He became a professor at Paris University at the age of 22, and Ignatius Loyola was one of his pupils. The master was converted by the pupil, and Xavier was one of the six original Jesuits who took their vows in Paris (1534).

He preached at first in Rome and then throughout Italy, and through his work in hospitals and the poorer quarters of the big cities he at once stood out as a man with an extraordinary capacity for friendship and communication. When John III of Portugal chose him to lead a mission to the Christian settlers in India, Xavier began his evangelizing work among the crew of the ship that took him there. On reaching Goa in 1542, he revived the flagging worship of the European colonists and at the same time brought Christianity to the natives. He addressed himself particularly to the children, explaining God through symbols they could understand. Then he made the long journey to the Pallava people, who fished for pearls off Cape Comorin, learning their dialect, and building chapels. Later, he returned to them with helpers brought from Goa.

Xavier next moved to Travancore, where he encountered some Brahman opposition, and then on to Malacca (1545) and the Malay peninsula. Malacca, a cosmopolitan town where merchants of all countries met, he found 'the wickedest place in the world', and he was welcomed by those who suffered from the corruption of the Portuguese officials. He made his headquarters in a hospital, working among the children and the sick, and he built a school. His influence was remarkable. By 1557 Malacca had a bishop, and Catholic Christianity was so deeply rooted that it survived the persecutions during the later Dutch occupation.

From Malaya Xavier went to Japan (1549–51), and by 1600 there were half a million Christians in that country. He then proposed to convert the vast empire of China, but obstacles were put in his way and he died on the island of Sancian, near Canton, before he could set foot on the mainland. His body was brought back to Malacca and buried there, but it was later taken to the cathedral at Goa. He was canonized in 1622.

Xavier was not a systematic missionary. Taking the whole of the East as his parish, he moved too quickly to consolidate his work, and his method of mass conversion was perhaps too indiscriminate to be permanently effective in all the places that he visited. But it has been well said of him that 'no man has opened so many doors', and he always tried to perpetuate his work by building schools and training local leaders whom he could trust to continue what he had begun.   MMR

XENOPHANES of Colophon (b. *c.* 570 BC), Ionian Greek philosopher, who challenged the accepted social values, religious beliefs, and historical traditions of his time. Denouncing anthropomorphism, the immoral heroic legends, and Homeric and Hesiodic tales of the gods, he initiated the ancient controversy between philosophy and poetry. He believed in a supreme divine intelligent, but incorporeal, being which controlled all things. In cosmology he thought that all things originated in elemental earth and water and that qualities, *eg*, sweetness, were relative in their sensation.

XENOPHON, (*c.* 430–*c.* 355 BC), Athenian aristocrat, a prolific writer and an associate of Socrates, best known for the *Anabasis*, describing the march of the Ten Thousand in Cyrus's attempted coup in Persia, and the *Hellenica*, a history of Greece (411–362). Becoming disenchanted with democracy and the Thirty 'Tyrants' oligarchic regime (404–403), he eschewed politics and joined Cyrus's expedition (401–399) by invitation. After its failure he helped to lead the Greek contingent back to Byzantium. Enjoying an active life, he served in Asia Minor against Persia with the Spartan King Agesilaus, whose discipline and command he admired. Thereafter he lived in exile at Scillus and Corinth, returning to Athens late in life. His practical interests, more appreciated by Romans than Greeks, show in discourses on education, leadership, horsemanship, cavalry command, estate management, and public revenues.

XERXES (*reg.* 486–465 BC), Achaemenid King of Persia, who succeeded Darius I after 12 years as viceroy of Babylon. His first task was to suppress the revolt which had started in Egypt before Darius' death and in 482 he had to deal with a rebellion in Babylon. In both cases the opposition was put down with great severity, in contrast to the policy of earlier Achaemenids, who had behaved in conquered lands as native rulers rather than as conquerors. He was persuaded, probably against his inclination, to go to war with Greece. His army was comprised of soldiers from 46 'nations', fighting in national groups, living off the land, and supported by a fleet, also of mixed nationality. The northern Greeks submitted while the other Greek states formed a league under Sparta which was defeated at Thermopylae. Attica was invaded and Athens captured, but Xerxes' fleet was destroyed at Salamis (480). He returned to Persia and his army under Mardonius was defeated at Plataea (479) and the fleet defeated at Mycale. Finally, in 466 a united Greece defeated the Persians on the banks of the Eurymedon. Persia's foothold in Europe was lost, but it is unlikely that the failure of the Greek campaign was so great a disaster to Persia as the Greek historians believed. The period was, in fact, for Persia one of economic prosperity, an increasing use being made of money, and Xerxes' great interest seems to have been building. He finished Darius' palace at Susa and continued the construction of Persepolis with a colossal hall, palace, and other buildings, richly decorated with fine sculptured reliefs. He was assassinated in 465.   JKG

X-GROUP in Africa, name given to a culture of Nubia which belongs to the period after the decay of Meroitic power, probably from about the 5th cent. AD to the mid-6th. The culture is known mainly from royal burials at Ballana and Qustul, mound graves which contained splendid grave goods, some being direct imports from Byzantine Egypt, and others showing Meroitic characteristics, such as crowns with the ram's head and plumes of Amun, the eye of Horus, or the winged disc. The pottery was finely made and much like Meroitic, but the designs were simpler and more crudely painted. The culture had a strong remnant of Meroitic civilization in it, though it seems that the art of writing had been lost.

In Nubia the power of Meroe had waned and Egypt was under Roman domination. Classical writers report that two peoples were infiltrating into Nubia south of the Roman frontier at the first Nile cataract, the Nobadae, and the Blemmyes. Whether or not either of these peoples was responsible for the X-Group culture is not known. Procopius informs us that c. AD 297 Diocletian introduced the Nobadae into the area south of his frontier in the hope that they would act as a buffer between his lands and the raiding Blemmyes. Later, Blemmyes and Nobadae joined forces and made sporadic raids on Egypt, now Christianized, until in 452 the general Maximinus was sent to quell them. They had to sue for peace and accept humiliating terms, but were allowed to continue their Egyptian style of pagan worship at the temple at Philae and clearly were not completely subjugated. About 540 a king of the Nobadae was converted to Christianity, as was much of the northern Sudan.

Few settlements of the X-Group people are known, but graves, in addition to those at Ballana and Qustul, have been found at many places between the first and fourth Nile cataracts.

W. B. Emery, *Egypt in Nubia* (London, 1965).
A. J. Arkell, *History of the Sudan to 1821* (London, 1961).
                                                                            MS

XHOSA, name of a Bantu-speaking people in the Cape Province of South Africa. Archaeological and genealogical evidence suggests that these people have been in the eastern Cape for a very long time; written evidence of shipwrecked white sailors from the 16th cent. shows that the main tribal groups, the Xhosa, Thembu, and Mpondo, were then *in situ*. Many of these people mixed with San or Khoikhoi, who introduced the characteristic clicks into Xhosa.

The Xhosa first met the white farmers (Boers) of the expanding Dutch East India Co. settlement at the Cape in the 18th cent. The first conflicts between the settlers and the Xhosas began in the 1770s. They increased rapidly in scale, and have been designated by white South African historians as the 'Kaffir Wars': the ninth, and final, war was fought from 1877 to 1878. This 100 years of African resistance to white incursion is unprecedented in the continent's history, and has been largely unrecognized in terms of achievement. The Xhosa at first took on the irregular forces or 'commandos' of the Dutch company; in the 19th cent. they took on regular British troops. In the course of this great struggle the Africans lost much of their land to the whites—most of that on the western side of the Kei river. But the Transkeian territories, which were reserved for African use by the Cape and subsequently by the South African governments, remained the land of Africans very largely because the whites could not wrest it from them. It was the Transkei which in 1963 was declared by the South African government to be the first Bantustan to be set up in pursuance of the policy of apartheid. In the early 1960s renewed fighting between African peasants (Mpondo) and white troops broke out, and in 1970 the Xhosa of the Transkei still lived under a state of emergency.

C. W. De Kiewiet, *A History of South Africa, Social and Economic* (Oxford, 1941).   AEA

XIENG KHOUANG, former principality in north-eastern Laos, which was in existence by the 8th cent. It maintained a precarious existence by playing off its neighbours, especially Luang Prabang and Viet-nam, against each other, and was incorporated into the kingdom of Laos only during the 19th cent. As the chief town of the Plain of Jars, it has continued to be of major strategic importance in the Indo-China wars, and was the scene of a major battle in 1970.

XOXE, KOCE (d. 1949), Albanian politician and communist leader, who was closely associated with Yugoslavia and with plans for its unification with Albania. Throughout the 1930s he organized, with Hoxha, discussion groups from which the Albanian Communist Party emerged. Before and during the Second World War he was the key figure in attempts to forge close links with the Yugoslavian Communist Party, his position in the Albanian party being dependent upon the relationship between the Albanian and Yugoslav parties. After the war he became deputy prime minister and minister of the interior. In 1947-8 he put forward proposals for the unification of Albania and Yugoslavia and saw to it that those who opposed the scheme were purged. But Tito's disgrace and expulsion from the Cominform upset Xoxe's plans and ruined his career. He attacked Tito and Yugoslavia's policy, but it was too late: in Nov. 1948 he was arrested and in June 1949 was tried and executed.

X-RAY DIFFRACTION, technique for crystal structure analysis. Essentially, a beam of X-rays is scattered (diffracted) by the atoms in the crystal. From the diffraction pattern, recorded on film, the position of atoms or ions in the crystal can be deduced. The technique was discovered by Von Laue in 1912 and further developed by W. H. and W. L. Bragg.

YADAVA DYNASTY, rulers of Devagiri (mod. Daulatabad), a remarkable stronghold near Aurangabad, Maharashtra, India (*c.* 1200–1312). The family first became known in the 11th cent., but then as subordinates of the Chalukyas, from whom they had made themselves independent by the end of the 12th cent. Their greatest ruler was Singhana (*reg.* 1210–1247), who controlled present Maharashtra and led campaigns into neighbouring areas. The Yadava kingdom came to an end when Devagiri was conquered by Malik Kafur for Sultan Al-ad-Din of Delhi. The impressive fortifications still give an idea of the power of the ancient kingdom.

YAGHMORASAN IBN ZAYYAN (d. 1283), founder of the dynasty of the Banu Abd al-Wadd at Tlemcen, who made himself independent of the Almohads, whose vassal he had been. He defended his power against the Hafsids of Tunis on the one hand and the Almohads of Marrakesh and the Marinids of Fez on the other, in order to confirm Tlemcen as the political and commercial capital of western Algeria.

YAGODA, GENRIKH GRIGORYEVICH (1891–1938), Soviet security chief, who was responsible for the first stage of the Stalinist purges. He made his career in the security service. joining the GPU in 1924 and becoming commissar for internal affairs, or head of the NKVD, in 1934. He was Stalin's principal agent in the purge which was unleashed after the murder of Kirov, and organized the trial of Zinoviev and Kamenev. He was replaced in Sept. 1936 by Yezhov, then appointed commissar for posts and telegraphs, but later arraigned in a show trial and shot.

YAKIMA WAR (1855–8), fought in eastern Washington and northern ID by two groups of Indians against white settlers and US troops. The war began when Yakima Indians under Kamiakin killed some prospectors and an Indian agent. The Indians were forced to submit to reservation life.

YAKUB BEG (*c.* 1820–77), Muslim adventurer from Khokand (Russian Turkestan), who, prompted by Muslim risings in Chinese Turkestan (modern Sinkiang province), took much of the Tarim basin and proclaimed himself *beg* ('chief') of an independent Muslim state in defiance of the Ch'ing (1865). In an attempt to forestall Russian expansion in Turkestan, the British supported Yakub Beg and urged the Ch'ing government to recognize his regime. The Chinese, under the vigorous leadership of Tso Tsung-t'ang, finally crushed Yakub Beg's regime (1877).

YAKUTSK, Russian city situated on the Lena river in eastern Siberia, founded as a fortified outpost in 1632. It became the chief fur-collecting centre of 18th-cent. Siberia.

YALTA CONFERENCE (Feb. 1945), second and more important of the meetings which Churchill, Roosevelt, and Stalin held during the Second World War. It settled little and provided much ground for subsequent dispute. It took place when victory in Europe was assured, so that strains in the wartime alliance were very obvious. Roosevelt was under considerable stress through fatigue and ill-health. Churchill's attempt to limit communist influence struck a discordant note with Roosevelt's optimism, which was sustained by that

of Harry Hopkins, his personal adviser. Much of the conference was taken up with the Polish question—both the territorial settlement and the composition of the government. The Western leaders agreed that Poland should move westwards, absorbing German territory and ceding territory in the east to Russia; but they were not prepared for this to extend as far as the western Neisse, as Stalin wanted. With regard to the government, Stalin conceded that the 'Provisional Government which is now functioning in Poland' (based on the communist committee in Lublin) should be reorganized 'on a broader democratic basis' and that 'free and unfettered elections' should be held. In addition, the US introduced a 'Declaration on Liberated Europe', presumably to counter the agreement which Churchill and Stalin had made for a division of their interests in southeastern Europe (Oct. 1944). The declaration, which Stalin accepted with little comment, expressed the interests of the three powers in liberated countries with the objective of instituting economic recovery, representative government, and free elections.

A substantial measure of agreement was reached on proposals for the United Nations Organization. Stalin accepted the American view of a limited veto in the Security Council—limited, that is to say, when the council was engaged in seeking the peaceful settlement of a dispute. (Despite this, the Soviet delegation to the San Francisco conference returned to Stalin's earlier demand for a complete veto.) It was accepted that the USSR should have three seats on the council and agreement was reached, in spite of Churchill's reluctance, on trusteeship provisions.

It was agreed that France should be given an occupation zone in Germany, and one in Berlin (in both cases carved out of the British and US zones), as well as a seat on the Control Council. But on the other principal German question, that of reparations, differences remained. Stalin pressed for a sum of $20,000 million, of which half should go to the Soviet Union. In the end Roosevelt, though not Churchill, agreed that this should be accepted 'as a basis for discussion'.

Stalin and Roosevelt also discussed questions arising from the Japanese war. Stalin reaffirmed that Russia would enter the war against Japan. An agreement was reached—to which Churchill assented—on the maintenance of the status quo in Outer Mongolia and the restoration of former Russian rights in Sakhalin, Dairen, and Port Arthur and the Chinese-Eastern and South-Manchurian railways, together with the handing over of the Kurile islands to the Soviet Union. Roosevelt undertook to secure the concurrence of Chiang Kai-Shek to this agreement, and Stalin to make an alliance with the nationalist government of China.   WK

YAM ZAPOLSKY, PEACE OF (1582), settlement mediated by the Holy See which ended the Livonian War between Poland-Lithuania and Muscovy (1558–82). A ten-year truce was arranged, and while Velikie Luki was restored to Ivan IV, he was forced to renounce his claims to Livonia and Polotsk, which were confirmed as being in the possession of Stephen Bathory of Poland.

YAMAGATA, ARITOMO (1838–1922), Japanese soldier and politician, who was chiefly responsible for the creation and shaping of the modern Japanese army and wielded great political influence during the first two decades of the 20th cent. He was born of low samurai rank in Chōshū and played an important role in *han* military affairs before and during the Meiji Restoration. On being appointed vice-minister of war in the new Meiji government, he immediately visited Europe (1869–70) to study military organization and was largely responsible for the establishment of a conscript army (1873), a fundamental step in the creation of an effective government, but in later years he made several changes which diminished civilian control over the services. During the Sino-Japanese War (1894–5) he commanded an army in Manchuria, while in the Russo-Japanese War (1904–5) he served as chief of staff; but although still active militarily, he had become even more significant politically. As home minister (1885–9), he adopted strong measures against the political parties and during the 1890s, when he was twice prime minister (1889–91, 1898–1900), he attempted to exclude the parties from power. Although his ultra-conservative views did not prevail, largely because of Itō Hirobumi's opposition, Yamagata's political stock rose steadily. After 1900 his influence rivalled Itō's and after the latter's death in 1909 he became unquestionably the most important *genrō* (elder statesman). No major decision could be reached without his acquiescence and it was generally his advice which determined who should be prime minister. Yamagata was thus able to delay the emergence of party cabinets, but at the same time his presence reduced the likelihood of open military opposition to government policies.   RLS

YAMAMOTO, GOMBEI (1852–1933), Japanese sailor and politician, who, after a distinguished naval career, twice served as prime minister (1913–14, 1923–4), but although his first cabinet was supported by the *Seiyūkai* and introduced some useful reforms, his second was an unpopular non-party ministry and was short-lived.

YAMASEE WAR (1715–16), began when a band of American Yamasee Indians attacked a settlement in south-eastern SC, killing about 90 whites. An uprising of most of the Indians from St Augustine, FL, to Cape Fear, NC, followed and was put down only when the Yamasee were driven into FL. The Yamasee War provided an argument in favour of the establishment of GA as a buffer colony between SC and FL.

YAMATO, region in central Japan, south of present-day Kyoto. It was the base from which the imperial dynasty unified Japan (4th cent.) and established the first Japanese state, a loose confederation of local ruling families, over which the power of the Yamato court gradually increased. The origins of the Yamato dynasty are obscure. Those scholars who believe it to have been indigenous mostly regard it as having descended from Himiko, the Queen of Yamatai, a powerful local kingdom mentioned in a 3rd-cent. Chinese history, though some place Yamatai in Kyūshū and argue that the dynasty moved to Yamato later. Others hold that it originated in Manchuria, established itself in Korea, and, after crossing to Japan at the head of a large band of well-armed mounted warriors, fought its way eastwards until it reached the Yamato plain. This view is supported by the fact that the Yamato dynasty was actively involved in the struggles between the Korean kingdoms (4th–7th cents) and actually controlled Mimana, in southern Korea, for many years; but scarcity of written evidence makes definite conclusions impossible.

YAMEN, office and residence of an official in imperial China. The term can sometimes refer to the office alone, as in the case of the Tsungli Yamen.

YANACONAS, hereditary Indian servitors in Peru, originating perhaps in Inca times. *Yanaconas* and their families were bound either to the land or to the service of a particular master. The Spanish Crown made an unsuccessful effort to abolish the institution, which survived until very recent times.

YANCEY, WILLIAM LOWNDES (1814–63), US lawyer and politician, who supported slavery and states' rights and wrote the Alabama Platform (1848) in reply to the Wilmot Proviso. In 1860 he led the withdrawal of Southern extremists from the Democratic presidential convention. After Lincoln's election, he wrote the Alabama secession ordinance.

YANDABO, TREATY OF (24 Feb. 1826), concluded the First Burmese War. Burma secured peace with the British by ceding Arakan and Tenasserim, by accepting a resident at Ava, and by paying an indemnity.

YANG DI PERTUAN AGONG, synthetic Malay title for the sovereign of Malaya/Malaysia since independence (1957). He is elected in rotation from among the nine Malay rulers.

YANG HSIU-CH'ING (d. 1856), Chinese soldier, who was commander-in-chief and 'prime minister' of the Taiping Rebellion in China. By origin, he was a charcoal-maker from Kwangsi. When the Taiping kingdom was proclaimed, he was made the 'Eastern king'. He was responsible for much of the military and administrative successes of the Taipings. But he was also ambitious, claiming divine revelations to justify his authoritarian behaviour. He was eventually eliminated by the other Taiping kings in 1856.

YANG-SHAO, neolithic site on the south bank of the Yellow river, characterized by painted pottery and dating from *c.* 2000–1500 BC.

YANKEE, term applied variously to residents of New England, the northern US, or the US in general. Its origin may be either Indian or Dutch, and it was originally meant as an insult.

YAO, people of northern Mozambique who pioneered and managed the ivory trade from Zambia and Malawi to Kilwa and Zanzibar from the 17th cent.

YA'QUB AL-MANSUR, Almohad ruler (*reg.* 1184–99), who took his title, 'the Victorious', from his defeat of Castile at Alarcos (1195), the principal triumph of a successful reign in Andalus and the Maghrib.

YA'QUB IBN KILLIS (*fl.* 10th cent.), Jew from Baghdad, who became a convert to Islam. Under the Fatimid Caliphs Al-Mu'izz (d. 975) and Al-'Aziz (d. 996) he reorganized the financial and administrative structure of Egypt on lines which remained effective throughout most of the Fatimid era. He also did much to stimulate and enlarge the commercial and manufacturing resources of Egypt.

YA'QUB IBN LAYTH AL-SAFFAR (d. 879), Persian leader, who brought much of Persia under the control of the Saffarid regime. He was master of Sijistan in 867, and in 870 reduced the regions of Balkh and Kabul to dependence on himself. In 873 he extended his influence over most of Khurasan. After falling out with the Abbasid caliph in Iraq, he marched against Baghdad, but was repulsed and withdrew in Khuzistan.

YAQUI INDIANS, American tribe formerly living along the Yaqui river in Sonora, Mexico, first encountered by the Spanish (1531), who made three attacks on the tribe (1609–1610), but were defeated each time. The Yaqui made a peace treaty (1610) and received Spanish missionaries, but staged a series of rebellions between 1740 and 1901. The Mexican government undertook to overcome the Yaqui permanently (1906–7) by deporting large numbers to Tehuantepec and Yucatan. Some remained in Sonora.

YARMUK, BATTLE OF (636), beside a river flowing from the Hawran into the Jordan, below the Sea of Galilee. The Arabs inflicted a great defeat on the Byzantines, which brought Syria and Palestine under Muslim rule.

YAVORSKY, STEPHEN (1658–1722), Russian divine and Metropolitan of Riazan and Moscow, who was appointed by Peter I to be 'temporary guardian of the Pontifical throne' after the death of Patriarch Adrian (1700). But he gradually lost influence with the creation of the senate (1711) and the rise to power of his opponent, Theofan Prokopovich.

YAYOI CULTURE, period of Japanese pre-history, named after an archaeological site in Tokyo. Beginning in Kyūshū (c. 300–250 BC), *Yayoi* culture introduced rice cultivation into Japan. Though it quickly spread eastwards, the limited archaeological evidence points to a fairly small number of immigrants rather than a massive wave. During the *Yayoi* period contacts with the continent increased, bronze, and later iron, implements being introduced into Japan. Techniques of pottery-making improved, although artistically *Yayoi* pottery is generally considered inferior to *Jōmon* pottery. Politically and socially the *Yayoi* period marked great changes. A 3rd-cent. Chinese account of Japan reveals a society which had become extremely authoritarian and hierarchical, and the appearance of large burial mounds indicates an increasingly powerful ruling class. The general prevalence of such mounds by AD 300 has led historians to treat the following four centuries as a new period, the *Kofun* (Ancient Tomb) period.

YAZDAGIRD III (*reg.* 632–51), last Sassanian King of Iran, who was unable to unite the rival factions or to control the power of local military governors, so that his empire was already disintegrating when the Arabs invaded (637) and gradually conquered the country. He was assassinated in 651.

YAZID I (642–83), Umayyad Caliph (*reg.* 680–83), son of Mu'awiya. On his accession to the throne, trouble broke out in the Hijaz. Al-Husayn, a son of the Caliph Ali, moved from the Hijaz to Iraq and, at Karbala in 680, lost his life in fighting Umayyad forces under the command of Ubayd Allah ibn Ziyad—an event of great importance for the future, since it gave a martyr to the Shi'a cause. The Hijaz itself turned to overt rebellion under Abdalla ibn al-Zubayr. Syrian troops led by Muslim ibn Uqba crushed the Medinese at the battle of Al-Harra in 683. The Syrians, commanded by Husayn ibn al-Numayr, laid siege to Mecca in the autumn of the same year, but withdrew northwards into Syria on the arrival of the news that the Caliph Yazid had died.

YAZIDI, name given to a Kurdish sect, inhabiting principally the areas around Mosul, the Jabal Sinjar, and Diyarbekir. Their faith is a syncretism of elements perhaps Christian in origin, with elements from Islam and other religions once flourishing in the lands of the Middle East. The Yazidis have both a spiritual head (*mir-i shaykhan*) and a secular head (*mirza bey*).

YAZOO LAND FRAUDS in the US, scandal involving the sale, under a GA state law (1795), of much of the land now comprising AL and MS to four land companies for $500,000. Revelations of bribery within the state legislature excited agitation against the law, and it was rescinded in 1796. The Yazoo claimants denied GA's right to annul the sale, and after the state had transferred its western claims to the US (1802), and the US Supreme Court's decision in *Fletcher v. Peck* (1810) that revocation of the initial grant impaired the obligation of contract, Congress paid compensation of over $4 million (1814).

YEAR OF THE FOUR EMPERORS (AD 69), crisis in Roman history in which Galba, Otho, Vitellius, and Vespasian were successively emperors. The death of Nero (68) ended a dynasty which had ruled the empire for a century and, with no fixed rule of succession existing, struggles for power were determined by military support. Galba was overthrown by the praetorian guard, inspired by Otho; Otho was defeated at Cremona by the legions of Germany in Vitellius' interest, while the latter's forces were overwhelmed in a later engagement at Cremona by the Danubian legions, which supported Vespasian. The crisis revealed the military basis of the emperors' power, the weakness of the Senate, which could only approve each successive claimant, and also the corporate feeling of the various army groups and their officers, and it endangered the empire itself, as the Batavians used the occasion to attack the Roman position on the Rhine. Stability was restored by Vespasian.

YEARDLEY, SIR GEORGE (*c.* 1587–1627), English colonist. After emigrating to Virginia (1609) he twice served as its governor (1618–21, 1626–7) and summoned the first English colonial representative assembly (1619).

YEHA, village in the northern Ethiopian province of Tigre, and capital of the first Sabaean settlers after 500 BC.

YEH-LU CH'U-TS'AI (1190–1244), descendant of the Liao dynastic family. Through serving the Chin (Jürched) empire, he had become expert in Chinese administration and put his gifts at the disposal of the Mongol conquerors, into whose hands he fell (c. 1215). He is said to have persuaded them of the value of retaining China as a prosperous agricultural community rather than as a devastated land devoid of produce.

YEKUNO AMLAK (*reg.* 1270–85), Emperor of Ethiopia and founder of the Solomonic dynasty which reigned until modern times.

YELLOW FORD, BATTLE OF (Aug. 1598), Irish victory of the Tyrone rebellion (1594–1603), when the men of O'Neill and O'Donell defeated some 4500 English soldiers under Sir Henry Bagenal on the Ulster border at the Blackwater. Bagenal was killed, a third of his army destroyed, and the remainder were driven back on Armagh.

YELLOW RIVER (Hwang Ho), known as 'China's Sorrow', second largest river in China (2700 miles; 4,344 kms). Originating in the Tibetan plateau, it cuts across the loess region in almost right-angled bends before it runs towards the sea. As it enters the North China Plain 500 miles from the sea, it deposits large amounts of silt (sometimes as much as 46 per cent by weight), building its bed up to over 20 ft above ground level at times. The river therefore has to be kept in its channel by dikes. A break in the dikes, which has been made frequently, floods several hundred square miles, covering the area with silt and rendering the land uncultivable for several years. Occasionally the river has changed its course, with similar disastrous results. Thus, from 1194 to 1852, it entered the sea south of Shantung peninsula, but from 1852 to 1938 on the north. The change of course in 1938 was made deliberately to check the Japanese invasion. In 1947 the river was redirected to its northern channel, where it remains today (1970). The Yellow river has been a major preoccupation of all Chinese governments, past and present, and inability to control it has often led to serious political consequences. Its frequent flooding (1882–98) has caused much social unrest, and contributed to the rise of the Boxer Movement and the weakening of the Ch'ing dynasty. A flood in 1887 took an estimated toll of 900,000 lives.   DP

YELLOW TURBANS. In AD 184 a rebellion broke out in eastern China under a leader of a Taoist religious sect, whose popular following looked to his powers as a faith healer. The rebellion formed one of the factors accompanying the decay and end of the Han dynasty. The term Yellow Turban derives from the headdress worn by the rebels.

YELLOWSTONE NATIONAL PARK in the US, first and largest national park to be established in the US (1872), a region of mountain and plateau, covering 3500 square miles in ID, MT, and WY. It includes the Grand Canyon of the Yellowstone river and numerous hot springs and geysers, one of which, 'Old Faithful', erupts on average every 60 minutes and rises to a height of 100 ft.

YEMEN REVOLUTIONS. Yemen became independent following the Ottoman defeat (1918), when the Zaydi Imam, Yahya ibn Muhammad (d. 1948), took possession of Sana. From the beginning, there was opposition to his conservative and autocratic rule from the Shafi'is of the coastal area, certain tribal groups and other Zaydi Sayyid families who were jealous of the Hamid al-Din family. A revolt (Feb. 1948) led by the Wazir family resulted in the assassination of the imam, but it was suppressed by his son and successor, Imam Ahmad (*reg.* 1948–62). Ahmad survived an abortive army revolt led by Al-Thulayya (1955), a tribal revolt (1960), and an attempted assassination at Hudayda (1961). New revolutionary ideas from Egypt were now increasingly influencing army officers and, immediately after the accession of Imam Muhammad al-Badr, son of Ahmad, the Yemeni Free Officers, led by Col. Abdullah al-Sallal and supported by the urban population, some intellectuals, and tribal confederations hostile to the imam, carried out a successful coup (26 Sept. 1962). Al-Badr escaped and rallied support among the Zaydi tribes of northern and central Yemen. The Republicans sought help from Egypt and the Royalists from Jordan and Saudi Arabia. A major war followed, punctuated by efforts to achieve a negotiated settlement. Agreement on the withdrawal of Egyptian and Saudi forces was reached at Jidda (Aug. 1965), but was not implemented until after the Khartoum conference (Aug. 1967), which followed the June war. The Egyptian withdrawal was completed by Jan. 1968. President Sallal was deposed (Nov. 1968), but the republic survived.　　　　　　　　　　　　　　　　　　MEY

YEN, kingdom of the Warring States period in China, which ended in 222 BC.

YEN CHING, former name of Peking, the Chinese capital. The name Yen originally referred to a state which flourished in that area in the later Chou period (771–222 BC).

YEN FU (1853–1921), Chinese scholar, who was a pioneer in the introduction of Western political, social, and economic ideas to China through his role as a translator and publicist. Impressed by the wealth and power of the West, Yen turned his attention to British political systems, economic institutions, social philosophy, and legal concepts.

In 1895 he decided to propagate his ideas through translation. The next 15 years saw his translation into Chinese of Huxley's *Evolution and Ethics* (1900), Smith's *Wealth of Nations* (1900), Mill's *On Liberty* (1903) and *Logic* (1905), Spencer's *A Study of Sociology* (1902), and Montesquieu's *De l'esprit des lois* (1909). Yen's choice of titles reflected his preference for struggle, progress, and government by impartial law. These ideas were also expressed in his essays. Although progressives were much indebted to his ideas, his overall influence was limited, partly because of his deliberately literary and abstruse style, but mainly because he urged caution at a time when young intellectuals were moving towards radicalism. His association with Yüan Shih-k'ai further alienated him from the mainstream of Chinese history. Nevertheless, he must be credited with a monumental contribution to Sino-Western cultural exchange.

B.I. Schwartz, *In Search of Wealth and Power, Yen Fu and the West* (Cambridge, MA, 1964).　　　　　　　　　　DP

YEN HSI-SHAN (1883–1960), Chinese war-lord, who controlled his native province, Shansi, from shortly after the 1911 Revolution until 1949. After 1928 he was nominally subordinate to the Kuomintang, but continued his idiosyncratic style of rule.

YEN K'O-CHÜN (1762–1843), Chinese scholar, who was the chief pioneer in the study of the much-neglected *Shuo-wen* (*Explanation of Writing*), a dictionary containing some 9000 Chinese characters compiled *c.* AD 100. In 1808 he launched into a monumental 'complete collection' of prose literature from the Han to the Sui dynasties (206 BC–AD 618), supplementing extant texts with inscriptions from stone and bronze, and other rare works. The project took 27 years to complete. Much of his time was devoted to establishing more satisfactory texts for works of antiquity which had suffered through centuries of copying and misprinting. Modern Chinese scholarship owes much to Yen, who produced some 70 books.

YENAN, small town in China's Shensi province, headquarters of the Chinese communist movement (1936–47). This period is often known as the Yenan period.

YEN-BAY REVOLT, abortive rising against the French in Feb. 1930, organized by the Viet-Nam Quoc-Dan Dang (Viet-nam Nationalist Party). A plan for a three-pronged revolt misfired, but the leaders at the Yen-Bay army post went ahead with their plan, permitting the French to suppress the movement with ease.

YENESEI, Siberian river which rises on the borders of Mongolia and flows northwards into the Arctic Ocean. It was first discovered by the Russians in the early 17th cent. The subjection of the river basin was ensured by the founding of Krasnoyarsk (1628). With its tributaries, the Upper, Stony, and Lower Tunguska rivers, the Yenesi provided vital water communications for the Siberian fur traders.

YENIKAL'E, Ottoman fortress commanding the Strait of Kerch, which unites the Sea of Azov with the Black Sea. The Ottomans had to cede Yenikal'e to the Russians in 1774.

YERMAK (d. 1585), Cossack renegade and explorer, who took service with the Stroganov family and penetrated beyond the Urals, thus initiating the conquest of Siberia (1581). He sailed up the Chusovaya and the Tura and reached the Irtysh, defeating the local tribes of Ostiaks and Voguls, from whom he extracted tributes of furs (1582–4). After enduring appalling hardship with his men in the Siberian winters, he was drowned in the Irtysh after enemy tribesmen had surprised his camp.

YEZHOV, NIKOLAI IVANOVICH (1895–*c.* 1939), Russian politician, who was director of Stalin's purges. He joined the Communist Party in 1917 and, with Stalin's backing, reached the Central Committee in 1927. In 1935 he headed the Party Control Commission, a post in which he could familiarize himself with the role for which Stalin had cast him. In Sept. 1936 he superseded Yagoda as commissar for internal affairs (NKVD); this was the moment at which the 'Yezhovshchina' (that is, the most terrible period of the purges) began. Yezhov started by purging the NKVD, and especially its senior ranks. The growing camp population was grimly amused to find that the new arrivals were those very NKVD officers who had recently sat in judgement upon them. Yezhov did not forget the NKVD officers serving abroad. Those who could not be lured home were murdered wherever they were serving (*eg*, Reiss in Switzerland). In addition to providing an enormous number of humble victims, Yezhov was charged with two special tasks: first, to purge the high command of the army and secondly to prepare the victims of the great show trials. During 1937 his influence was considerable. He received the Order of Lenin and the town of Yezhovo-Cherkesk was named after him. He became a candidate member of the Politburo, but by the summer of 1938 he was already in decline: Beria was appointed deputy commissar of the NKVD and he, not Yezhov, handled the purge of the Komsomol. After a brief tenure of the commissariat of water transport it was announced (Dec. 1938) that Yezhov had fallen. Stalin had decided to conclude the purges and Yezhov was a useful scapegoat. He was probably shot in 1939.

YI SUN-SIN (d. 1598), Korean sailor, who succeeded in retaining command of the seas round the peninsula during the period of Hideyoshi's invasion (1592-7) and became a national hero. He is famous for his innovation of 'turtle ships', ie, vessels with an iron superstructure to protect the archers and riflemen. He was killed in action against the Japanese evacuation fleet in Oct. 1598.

YI DYNASTY, founded by Yi Songgye, a general of the last rulers of Koryo, which ruled Korea from 1392 to 1910, a period which saw a much closer imitation of Chinese institutions, including the extension and perfection of the examination system (although entrance to the examinations was restricted to the scholar-gentry class). During the first century of the Yi, under such kings as Sejong (1418–50), the inventor of *Han'gul* script, Buddhism was severely restricted and Confucianism reigned supreme, while the dynasty extended its control in the north to the Yalü and Tumen rivers, the present boundaries of Korea. At this time the Koreans played a leading part in Far Eastern trade, and there are records of embassies from the kings of Ryūkyū.

From the end of the 15th cent., however, a long series of faction struggles within the scholar-gentry began, which eventually paralysed the administration, particularly under Chungjong (*reg.* 1506–1544) and Sonjo (*reg.* 1567–1608). This period saw the struggle between *Tongin* and *Soin*. In the midst of this factional strife came the invasions of Korea by Hideyoshi's armies, in 1592–7; these were among the most serious foreign incursions Korea had to face, and caused incalculable damage and loss of life. For the rest of its existence the dynasty dragged on in a state of near collapse, a condition which in the 19th cent. was exacerbated by repeated natural disasters, extensive banditry, disputes over the introduction of Christianity, and pressure from the western powers, who joined Japan in her efforts to force the opening of Korea to foreign trade in the 1870s. After the Russo-Japanese War, Japan gained a predominant position in Korea, and in 1910 deposed the last Yi ruler and annexed the country.   KHJG

YIN-YANG. Since the Warring States period, Chinese philosophers have used these two terms to express the two complementary forces or qualities whereby the universe was thought to have been created and maintained in operation. The terms are explained, materially, as female, dark or cold (*yin*), and male, light or warm (*yang*); the two forces are interlocked, being dependent on each other and giving way to each other's dominance according to a cosmic cycle. The explanation of the world in these terms is first attributed to Tsou Yen, whose school of naturalist philosophers grew up in east China from *c.* 300 BC. The concept was soon associated with the analysis of the material world as being formed of the five elements (*wu-hsing, ie,* wood, metal, fire, water, and earth), each one of which played a dominant part in changing the seasons of nature, characterizing the items of creation, and effecting movements in the world of heaven, nature, and man. When, in the Han period, the government felt the need to formulate theories which would support their exercise of temporal authority, political and moral theories were so framed as to include the concepts of *yin-yang* and the five elements. At the same time, these concepts had a firm hold on the popular mind, being invoked as reasons to explain mortality, sudden disaster, or good fortune. These concepts could not be dissociated from the practice of divination, and

were frequently exploited by governments seeking portents or omens which could be used in propaganda. Both *yin-yang* and the five elements are frequently symbolized in the designs of Chinese artists; and the stress on the number five in this connection led to the enumeration of other qualities or objects by five (eg, colours, directions, planets).   ML

YNGLING, DYNASTY OF, Norwegian kingdom of Vestfold, which came under the rule of the Yngling family in the 7th cent. AD. They created a powerful kingdom which was ultimately responsible for the unification of Norway in the late 9th cent. In a poem known as the 'Ynglinga Tal', part of which is preserved in the Ynglinga Saga, the story of the early Yngling kings is related, the family being traced back to the prestigious Swedish rulers at Uppsala. The notable grave mounds of the Borre group and the Oseberg and Gokstad ship-burials are possibly connected with members of the Yngling family.

YOHANNES IV (*reg.* 1871–89), Emperor of Ethiopia, a religious man and great patriot, who repulsed Egyptian, Dervish, and Italian invasions.

YORK, RICHARD PLANTAGENET, 3rd Duke of (1411–60), head of the junior branch of the Plantagenet family and chief landowner after the King of England, who came to the fore during the crisis in the government produced by the personal and mental incapacity of Henry VI. His claims to the Protectorship were bitterly resisted by the queen's party, and in 1455 he took up arms in order to assert them, and so began the Wars of the Roses. By 1460 success in battle led York to claim the throne itself, his justification being a maternal descent from Edward III superior to the king's own. Parliament compromised by acknowledging him as Henry's heir, but before the year was out he was killed at Wakefield. He was the father of Edward IV and Richard III.

YORK, FREDERICK AUGUSTUS, 11th Duke of (1763–1827), British soldier and second son of George III, who commanded the army in Flanders (1793–5) and held the new office of commander-in-chief (1798–1809). Though unsuccessful in the field, he was a good administrator and took military discipline and efficiency out of the hands of the secretary at war, thereby greatly improving morale and training. Under his auspices the new model Rifle Brigade (1800) and the Royal Military College (1802) were formed.

YORK, city of great strategic importance from Roman times onwards, which became the capital of the English kingdom of Northumbria. The first Christian minster in northern England was established here by King Edwin in *c.* 627 and it became the seat of the northern archbishopric. In the 8th cent. it was a famous centre of learning under Alcuin. After the Norman conquest the city remained capital of northern England, reaching the peak of its medieval prosperity early in the 14th cent. as an important inland harbour and a major centre of the wool trade. On a number of occasions between 1298 and 1339 it was the seat of the royal government, being used as a base for the wars against Scotland. Like the rest of northern England, it suffered a temporary decline in the late Middle Ages. It became a university city in 1962.

YORKE, CHARLES (1722–70), British lawyer and politician, who was solicitor-general (1756–61) and attorney-general (1762–3), in which capacity he advised moderation in Wilkes's case. He was an associate of Rockingham and again became attorney-general (1765–7), interpreting the Navigation Acts liberally and drafting a constitution later adopted for Quebec (1774). On Camden's dismissal (1770), Yorke deserted Rockingham to become lord chancellor at George III's urgent request. His death brought about the fall of Grafton's administration.

YORKE, CHARLES PHILIP (1764–1834), British lawyer and politician, who opposed Catholic emancipation and legal reform. He served as secretary at war (1801–3), home secretary (1803–4), and first lord of the admiralty (1810–12). His attempt to exclude the press from the Walcheren debate led to violent controversy (1810).

YORKTOWN, SURRENDER AT (19 Oct. 1781), capitulation of British troops under Lord Cornwallis to American and French forces under George Washington and Rochambeau, which ended military operations during the American War of Independence. The loss of naval control of Chesapeake Bay to a French fleet under De Grasse had weakened the British position on the Yorktown peninsula of VA, and the arrival of allied land forces precipitated the surrender of the British.

YORUBA-speaking people, numbering 11 to 12 million, occupy principally the Western, Lagos, and Kwara states of Nigeria, as well as Ketou, Save, and Porto Novo in south-eastern Dahomey. The Yoruba are closely related to the Fon, Ewe, and other Aja-speaking peoples of Dahomey and Tongo, and distinctly Yoruba-speaking groups still exist as far west as Atakpame in northern Togo. As a result of dispersal through the slave trade, Yoruba culture forms an important element in the Creole culture of Freetown and Bathurst (Gambia) and there are important survivals of Yoruba culture in Cuba and Bahia (north-eastern Brazil). In the heartland, the Yoruba comprise the Oyo, Ife, Egba, Egbado, Ijesha, Ijebu, Ekiti, Igbomina, Owe, Ondo, Owo, Akoko, and Ikale sub-groups. Culturally, they have ranged from the horse-riding Oyo of the savannah to the Ekiti and Ondo of the evergreen forests, and to the Ijebu and Ikale of the waterside. Other cultural differences have resulted from the contact of some with Benin to the east and others with Nupe and Borgu to the north. Yet culturally and linguistically the Yoruba have remained basically homogeneous.

Linguists claim that the Yoruba language is probably some 4000 years old in its present location. Little work has so far been done on the prehistory and early history of the Yoruba people. Their oral histories go back only to the establishment of the present ruling dynasties in the different kingdoms to which the Yoruba were divided. All the dynasties claim to have originated at Ile-Ife, which seems, between AD 900 and 1200, to have been the centre where the characteristic Yoruba culture developed—a monarchical system of government with a divine king; an urban social life on a scale unique in tropical Africa; the Sky God and a pantheon of divinities; and a distinctive art style.

The claim of a common origin at Ife by all the ruling dynasties helped to structure the relationship between the different rulers and in this way, to some extent, made up for the absence of political unity. This seems to have minimized internal wars until the 19th cent., when the Oyo empire collapsed, the Oyo pushed southward, and a series of wars ensued. These wars resulted in several slaves—often from the same village—finding their way to Brazil and Cuba or, on being freed by the British, to Freetown and Bathurst. Hence the significant survival of Yoruba culture in those places.

Islam was introduced into the Old Oyo empire perhaps as early as the 17th cent., but it did not spread far until the 19th cent., in the middle of which Christian missions came. Islam and Christianity are now well-established, but the traditional religion remains the main custodian of Yoruba cultural values. Yoruba became a written language in the 19th cent. Yoruba literature, of which some of the best known examples are Ifa divination chants and hunters' songs, is still largely oral and is extremely rich. Yoruba blue indigo cloth has long been famous for its quality.

S. Johnson, *The History of the Yorubas* (London, 1969).
A. Ojo, *Yoruba Culture* (London, 1966).   JFAA

YOSHIDA, SHIGERU (1878–1967), Japanese diplomat and politician, who played a large part in shaping post-war politics in Japan. He was a career diplomat and was arrested during the Pacific War for his part in organizing a peace party. He escaped the Occupation purge and was well qualified to become prime minister, a position he held five times. He won considerable popularity by opposing some of the more extreme Occupation policies, and after 1952 was responsible for revising the most radical American reforms, although it was his government which tied Japan to the US by the 1951 security treaty. He continued to influence Japanese policies even after he was forced out of office (Dec. 1954).

YOSHIDA, SHŌIN (1830–59), Japanese samurai, whose life and teaching exerted a great influence on several Meiji leaders. He was an ardent patriot and opened a school in Chōshū where such young samurai as Itō Hirobumi and Aritomo Yamagata listened to his idealistic views on politics. He planned to put his ideas into practice by assassinating a *bakufu* official (1858), but was arrested and executed.

YOSHIMASA (1436–90), 8th Ashikaga Japanese *shōgun*, whose rule was marked by extravagance and weakness. He was, however, an outstanding patron of the arts. It was his decision to abdicate which led to the Onin War (1467–77) and the eclipse of Ashikaga authority.

YOSHIMITSU (1358–1408), 3rd Ashikaga Japanese *shōgun*, whose rule brought to an end the long war between the Southern and Northern Courts (1336–92). Yoshimitsu himself was an outstanding patron, not only of the arts, but also of Zen Buddhism. After abdicating (1394) he remained in control and was responsible for increasing trade with China, though he has been blamed by some Japanese historians for accepting a tributary relationship with the Ming dynasty.

YOSHIMUNE (1684–1751), 8th Tokugawa Japanese *shōgun*, who was by birth a Tokugawa collateral *daimyō*. He had had experience of *han* government before being chosen to fill the ruling position when the main shogunal line failed (1716). Taking firm control of the *bakufu*, he attempted to solve its financial and administrative problems by a series of conservative measures, which had only a limited success owing to the complexity of the Japanese economy during the 17th cent.

YOSHINO PERIOD (1336–92), half-century of Japanese history when, as a result of an imperial succession dispute, two rival courts existed in Japan, the 'Northern', in Kyoto, and the 'Southern', which was compelled to take refuge in the mountainous Yoshino region south of Kyoto. The dispute itself became submerged in a much more general struggle between feudal lords for land and power. It was thus ended only when the Ashikaga shogunate had achieved national supremacy. The compromise solution of alternate succession which the shogunate arranged (1392) was never put into practice, however, and no later emperor came from the Southern line.

YOSHINOBU (KEIKI) (1837–1913), 15th and last Tokugawa Japanese *shōgun*, who attempted to preserve Tokugawa power by making radical governmental changes, but when it proved impossible to maintain *bakufu* supremacy he did not resist the Meiji Restoration. Before becoming political director of the *bakufu* (1862), Yoshinobu had favoured participation in government by the great *daimyōs*. After 1864, however, he supported those *bakufu* officials who wished to restore Tokugawa authoritarianism, and taking advantage of the pro-*bakufu* sympathies of Léon Roches, the French minister, he secured French assistance in military training and dockyard construction. A proposed French loan failed to materialize, however, and the emergence of a powerful anti-*bakufu* movement centred on Satsuma and Chōshū caused Yoshinobu to return the shogunal powers to the emperor (9 Nov. 1867) and work for a *daimyō* confederation. When this plan was rejected, Yoshinobu yielded rather than allowing Japan to become involved in a civil war.

YOUNG, ARTHUR (1741–1820) British agricultural journalist. In his lifetime his reputation rested on his *Annals of Agriculture* (1784–1809), a journal for agricultural improvers, and on his position as secretary to the old Board of Agriculture. Since his death more value has been placed on the journals of the tours which he undertook round Britain, Ireland, and France in the 1770s and 1780s. He had an easy style and a quick eye for points of contrast in social as well as economic features.

YOUNG, BRIGHAM (1801–77), US Mormon leader and colonizer of UT, who was converted to Mormonism in 1832 and became an active missionary. By 1838 he was senior member of the Church's administrative body. After the murder of Joseph Smith (1844), Young became head of the Church, rallied it in its hour of despair, and gave it a cohesive organization. In 1846–7 he led the mass Mormon migration to Deseret, the distant, isolated and barren valley of the Great Salt Lake. When in 1850 Congress organized Utah Territory, he was appointed governor and remained effective ruler of the settlement even after his dismissal in 1857. The survival, prosperity, and continued dominance of UT by Mormons owned much to the tight control Young exercised over its early development. He authorized polygamy and himself had some 20 wives and 56 children.

YOUNG, OWEN (1874–1962), US lawyer, businessman, and government adviser, who was chairman of the board of General Electric (1922–39). He was the US representative at the Reparations Conference (1924) and devised the Young Plan (1930), which established a schedule of reparations payments to be made by Germany.

YOUNG, THOMAS (1773–1829), English physicist, physician, and founder of the wave theory of light who was elected a Fellow of the Royal Society at the age of 21 for his work on the accommodation of the eye.

Since Newton's time, light had been considered to be particulate in character; the fact that light does not bend round obstacles was thought fatal to any wave theory. Young demonstrated by theory and experiment that light was in fact a wave motion with an extremely short wavelength, a view which remained undisputed until the present century.

He pursued several careers, in science, medicine, and public life; and contributed considerably to the problems of deciphering Egyptian hieroglyphics.

YOUNG ENGLAND, 19th cent. romantic movement within the Conservative Party, which sought to reassert the importance and ideals of the aristocracy as paternalistic agents of social justice, being used by Disraeli to undermine the leadership of Sir Robert Peel. Its leaders included George Smythe and Lord John Manners, who were influenced by F. W. Faber to revolt against liberal laissez-faire ideas and the dominance of the manufacturing classes. They held that a peaceful social and spiritual revolution could be accomplished in Britain by the landed upper classes in league with the working class and radicals. Disraeli supported Young England from 1842 and based his novel *Sybil* on its ideas, encouraging its members in their discontent with Peel. In 1845–6 the group broke up in disagreement over the Maynooth grant and the repeal of the Corn Laws, which Smythe supported and Disraeli and Manners opposed.

YOUNG IRELAND, Irish nationalist movement, modelled on Young Italy, which bridged the gulf between the moderation of O'Connell and the violence of the Fenians. The movement, led by Smith O'Brien, put forward a programme of national regeneration, with an emphasis on the cultural heritage of the Irish language, which became typical of 19th- and 20th-cent. nationalism. It also gave vent to such hatred of England that it became unlikely that Irish discontent could ever be cured by English benevolence. However, Young Ireland never secured broad popular support and its abortive rising in 1848 led to the arrest of most of its leaders.

YOUNG ITALY (1831), society founded by Mazzini, after the failure of the 1830 revolution in Italy, to rouse the whole of Italy in the cause of independence and to persuade the rest of Europe to give support to this aim. Mazzini was anxious to supersede the influence of the Carbonari, with its secrecy, limited aims, and aristocratic bias, and he kept only the names of members secret. Such was the appeal of Young Italy, which devoted a large proportion of its funds to propaganda, that by 1833 it numbered 60,000 supporters throughout Italy. It was of major importance in rousing apathetic sections of Italian society to positive enthusiasm for the *Risorgimento* and generating sympathy for Italy abroad.

YOUNG MEN'S BUDDHIST ASSOCIATION in Burma founded in 1906. The movement, originally inspired by the YMCA, developed political aspirations and became the nerve centre of Burmese nationalism. In 1921 it converted itself into the General Council of Burmese Associations.

YOUNG MEN'S CHRISTIAN ASSOCIATION (YMCA) in Britain, Evangelical organization founded by Sir George Williams (1821–1905) to provide an urban rendezvous for young men living in lodgings. It grew out of Bible and prayer meetings in 1844 and was complemented from 1855 by women's organizations performing a similar purpose. These became united in 1877 to form the Young Women's Christian Association.

YOUNG OTTOMANS, name used to denote a group of 19th-cent. critics of the Ottoman government. They included Namik Kemal, Mehmed Bey, Ziya Pasha, Ibrahim Shinasi, and Ali Suavi. After producing pamphlets attacking the Ottoman authorities, they fled to Paris and London (1867–1871), where, after functioning for a short period as a group under the patronage of Mustafa Fazil (1830–71), the Young Ottomans broke up and followed their own paths. Two (Namik and Ziya) later became involved in the 1876 constitutional movement. The real importance of the Young Ottomans lies in their development of a radical critique of the Ottoman Tanzimat and the inspiration they provided for later revolutionaries, *eg*, the Young Turks.

YOUNG PLAN (1930), schedule of German reparations payments which on 17 May 1930 superseded that of the 1924 Dawes Plan. The latter had been an interim settlement designed to restore international political and financial confidence. Its success led Germany to hope for a definitive reparations settlement, together with the Allied evacuation of the Rhineland zone, which had been occupied as a sanction against German defaults. An international committee of experts met at The Hague in Feb. 1929 under the chairmanship of Owen D. Young, of the US. Unlike the committee that formulated the Dawes Plan, it included a German delegation. Its report was presented on 7 June, and completed at the second Hague Conference in Aug. 1929 and Jan. 1930.

The Young Plan abolished the foreign controls established over German finances under the Dawes Plan, returned to Germany securities which had been taken into Allied hands, and transferred from the Allies to Germany the responsibility for converting reparations payments into foreign currencies. It also abolished the Reparations Commission, and, effectively, Allied powers to exercise sanctions against default; any dispute over payments was to be referred to the Permanent Court of International Justice at The Hague.

The plan imposed annuity payments on Germany, divided into two parts, conditional and unconditional. The unconditional payments were ultimately to total 700 million Reichsmarks, and to be furnished by a direct tax on Germany's railways. The conditional payments could be postponed for up to two years; the sum due for transfer into foreign currencies could be paid for the interim in Reichsmarks into the newly created Bank for International Settlements. From Sept. 1929 to March 1966 Germany was to pay an average annuity of 1·99 billion Reichsmarks. From 1966 to 1987 she was to pay annuities of 1·7 billion Reichsmarks to cover the cost of inter-Allied debts. Up to one-third of each annuity could be paid in material goods.

The Young Plan was strongly opposed by Nationalist groups in Germany, which resented the fact that the Rhineland evacuation was not to be immediate and that Germany was to pay a share of the occupation costs. This opposition and the strain of international negotiations were partially responsible for Stresemann's death in Oct. 1929. The onset of economic depression led to The Hague Agreements' being superseded by the 1932 Lausanne Agreements. These relieved Germany of Young Plan payments for three years. By 1935 Hitler was in power and all the agreements had become a dead letter.   ASJ

YOUNG POLAND (1831), democratic nationalist society, founded by the eminent Polish historian, Joachim Lelewel, its members being drawn from the thousands of Poles exiled in Europe after the unsuccessful 1830 rebellion against Russia. Unlike the aristocratic nationalists, who sought the diplomatic co-operation of the European powers, Young Poland, modelling its activities on the Young Italy movement, attempted vainly to recreate a Polish state by fomenting further insurrections.

YOUNG TURK REVOLUTION (1908), revolt against the autocratic power of the Ottoman sultan, Abdülhamid II. It began (July 1908) in the IIIrd Army in Macedonia, in the form of a demand for the restoration of the 1876 constitution, to which Abdülhamid agreed (24 July), after it became plain that his other troops would not suppress the revolt. The revolt was led by an organization known as the Committee of Union and Progress, which received encouragement and propaganda from a similar body organized by Ottoman émigrés in Europe. Civilians were also involved. A parliament was summoned, but the revolutionaries were content to leave government to established officials and to try to control its personnel and policies from outside. The success of the revolution was menaced by a counter-revolution (13 April 1909), which demanded the restoration of the Sharia, but it was eventually suppressed by the IIIrd Army under Mahmud Shevket Pasha. Abdülhamid, who had supported the counter-revolution, was deposed. Thereafter, although ultimate power remained with the army, the Committee of Union and Progress gradually came to dominate the government and introduce a policy of radical reform of government and society in order to try to prevent the further diminution of the empire. In 1913 the CUP achieved complete dominion under the triumvirate of Enver, Talat, and Jamal Pashas.

YOUNG WALES, name of a Welsh nationalist party proposed by Lloyd George (1895) and of a monthly magazine started by John Hugh Edwards. In 1894 Gladstone's Irish Home Rule Bill aroused the hopes of Scottish and Welsh nationalists. His subsequent resignation and replacement by Rosebery as leader of the Liberal Party, together with the disarray of the Welsh nationalist parties, led Lloyd George to declare his Young Wales proposals and the new magazine offered him a platform for his views and enhanced his popularity. His belief that the Anglo-Boer War was a more important issue than Welsh Home Rule led to his breaking with its editor (1898), and although he continued to protest his nationalism until Wales was secured as a liberal stronghold, the issue was dropped after the electoral victory of 1906.

YOUNGHUSBAND, SIR FRANCIS EDWARD (1863–1942), British soldier, diplomat, and explorer, who joined the army in 1882. In 1890 he was transferred to the Indian political department. He travelled extensively and explored the Karakoram range and the Pamirs. In 1892 he was appointed political officer in Hunza and later in Chitral, and was resident in the Maratha state of Indore (1902–3). He commanded the expedition (1903–4) sent by Lord Curzon to Tibet to counteract supposed penetration by the Russians. From 1906 to 1909 he was resident in Kashmir. After his retirement he founded the World Congress of Faiths (1936). He was closely involved in the planning of three Everest expeditions.

YPRES, JOHN DENTON PINKSTONE FRENCH, 1st Earl of (1852–1925), British soldier. Although a cavalry officer of limited staff experience, he distinguished himself in the Anglo-Boer War and was appointed chief of the imperial general staff in 1912. He resigned in 1914 over the Curragh Mutiny, but the outbreak of the First World War found him commander-in-chief of the British Expeditionary Force. He was temperamentally and intellectually unsuited to the complex and arduous task he was called upon to undertake, and was relieved of his command in Dec. 1915, to be succeeded by Sir Douglas Haig.

YPRES, BATTLES OF (1914, 1915, 1917), Belgian town which was the scene of three battles in the First World War.

(a) (20 Oct.–11 Nov. 1914). After the Aisne positions were consolidated in Sept. 1914, the British and the Germans launched simultaneous offensives in Flanders, each aiming at turning the other's flank before the trenches could be extended northwards. These attacks met head on outside Ypres, where the British regular troops, though they suffered extremely heavy losses, withstood the Germans' superior numbers and artillery, enabling the trench-line to be extended to the sea, and creating the famous Salient, a tongue of land commanded on three sides by German-occupied heights in which British and Dominion forces sustained one-quarter of all their casualties in the whole war.

(b) (22 April–24 May 1915). A limited German attack was intended to divert Allied reinforcements from their offensive in Artois and Champagne. The experimental use of chlorine gas for the first time on the Western Front led at first to considerable success against the French, but reserves were not available to exploit it and British and Canadian troops stabilized the situation.

(c) (22 July–20 Nov. 1917). In this offensive Haig aimed, first, to extricate the British armies from the Ypres Salient by capturing the whole of the ridge between Armentières and Dixmude, which dominates the Flemish plain; then to drive the Germans from the Belgian coastline, and specially from the ports of Ostend and Zeebrugge, to which the admiralty attached exaggerated importance as submarine bases; and finally, to cut the vital railway through the Liège gap and turn the flank of the German position in the west. He hoped thus to win the war before the Germans could take advantage of their successes in Russia to resume the offensive in France, and long before tanks and American troops would be available in decisive numbers. At the very least, pressure on the Germans would be maintained and their attention diverted from the French armies, exhausted and dispirited after the failure of Nivelle's spring offensive.

The British had no decisive superiority in men or guns, and, as the German positions overlooked theirs, could not achieve surprise. After the battle of Messines the Germans were allowed two months to recover and perfect their system of 'elastic' defence, which depended on numerous pillboxes, strong counter-attack forces held well back, and the lavish use of mustard gas and phosgene. The British bombardment, which began on 22 July, reduced the clay soil, in which the water-table lay only a few feet below the surface even before the usual autumn rains, to a liquid mud whose unique nastiness is legendary, and which rendered movement on the battlefield difficult for men, and largely impossible for supplies, tanks, and guns. The offensive, directed first from Gen. Gough's Fifth Army headquarters, and then from Plumer's Second, began on 31 July; further attacks were made on 16 Aug.; on 20 and 26 Sept.; on 4, 9, 12, 22, and 26 Oct.; and on 4 and 10 Nov. It rapidly became apparent that clearing the ridge would only deepen the Salient and that there was no hope of a break-through towards the coast, but the fighting was continued in order that more Germans should be killed, British reserves being used who might have been better employed in exploiting the success at Cambrai. With the capture of Passchendaele on 6 Nov. the fighting was allowed to peter out. The ridge was largely in British hands—though the position was untenable and was rapidly overrun during the Germans' spring offensive in 1918. The French may have been saved, and the Germans were certainly shaken, but 300,000–400,000 British and 50,000 French troops were killed, wounded, or captured, as against about 250,000 Germans.   PJBD

YPSILANTI, ALEXANDER, Prince (1783–1828), leader of an ill-conceived Greek revolt against Turkey in Moldavia, which led to his imprisonment and precipitated a more serious Greek revolt in the Morea (1821).

YRIGOYEN, HIPOLITO (1852–1933), Argentine politician, who was leader of the Argentine Radical Party. He began his career as a schoolmaster, a part-time stock-raiser, and was also a minor public functionary, and a politician, in which capacity he was a painstaking organizer with none of the panache of the traditional *caudillo*. His few public speeches were pretentious, moralizing, and obscure. Nevertheless, he was somehow able to persuade his followers—and apparently himself—that he was a man of destiny. In 1891 he followed his uncle, Leandro Alem, into the Radical Civic Union. In 1896 Alem committed suicide and Yrigoyen succeeded him as leader of the union. The Radicals attained a vast following among the rapidly expanding urban middle classes; they were, however, barred from power by the fraudulent methods with which the landowning oligarchy maintained its dominance. During these years Yrigoyen worked tirelessly to create a political machine. The Radicals' long period of opposition left them, however, ill-prepared to assume power, which they did in 1916, following free national elections held in consequence of the Roque Sáenz Peña Law of 1912.

Yrigoyen became president (1916) amidst jubilation and inflated hopes. His neutrality towards the belligerents in the First World War, although denounced in some quarters as pro-German, resulted in fact from his being an isolationist nationalist. He devoted much energy to establishing the Radicals as Argentina's majority party by manipulating powers of appointment and intervention in provincial affairs, with unfortunate consequences, for the Radicals were apt spoilsmen and thus the weak federal structure was further undermined. Yrigoyen's identification of the Radical cause with himself alienated many talented men from the party and in time provoked a schism between his followers ('personalists') and those of Marceló T. de Alvear ('anti-personalists'), whom Yrigoyen chose as his successor to the presidency for the 1922–8 term. The first administration's accomplishments were few and ambiguous. Some social legislation was enacted, but the general strike of 1919 was suppressed only with bloodshed. Despite much nationalist rhetoric, little was done beyond the creation of a public petroleum monopoly (YPF) to alter Argentina's traditional dependence on foreign markets, manufactures, and capital. Indeed, in the prosperous 1920s the Radicals' interests and values were not very different from those of the traditional oligarchs. Nevertheless, in 1928 Yrigoyen was re-elected president by an overwhelming majority. However, he proved unable to restrain his rapacious subordinates or to cope with the economic crisis which beset Argentina in 1929–30. In Sept. 1930 he was deposed by a military coup which enjoyed wide civilian support. After being imprisoned, he was released and died almost penniless in 1933. His funeral called forth massive demonstrations from a populace burdened with an unrepresentative militarist government. However, it is clear in retrospect that it was precisely Yrigoyen's failings as a statesman that cost Argentina its best opportunity to establish a firm representative liberal democracy.   RCN

YUAN SHIH-K'AI (1859–1916), Chinese soldier, who became the first president of the Chinese republic. He came under Li Hung-chang's patronage when the latter assigned him to the task of training the Korean army, to counter rising Japanese influence there (1882). After suppressing an insurrection, staged with Japanese backing, and following the Li-Ito Convention (1884), he was appointed Chinese resident in Korea and directed all the important affairs of that government. From 1885 to 1893 he was the most powerful person in Korea, but he failed to modernize the country along Western lines. His Korean career ended with China's defeat in the Sino-Japanese War.

During the reform movement of 1895–8 he showed much sympathy for the reformers. When the 'Hundred Days' Reform' was in danger of failure, the reformers placed considerable hopes on the support of Yuan, who was then in charge of training a new army of 7000 men. His failure to give support hastened the collapse of the reform. He soon became the Empress Dowager Tz'u-hsi's favourite, and in 1899 was appointed governor of Shantung. Throughout the Boxer Rising he showed good sense of judgement, punishing the fanatic rebels severely, and with the southern provincial leaders (eg, Li Hung-chang, Chang Chih-tung), he declared most of China neutral, thus absolving the empress dowager from personal disgrace when foreign troops defeated the Boxers.

On the death of Li Hung-chang, Yuan was appointed his successor as governor-general of Chihli (1901–7), the most powerful provincial post. However, in the subsequent institutional reforms Yuan was gradually eased out of power. The new ministry of the army, created in 1906, robbed him of four out of six of his Peiyang divisions. He was then removed from his power base to serve as grand councillor and minister of foreign affairs the following year. Eventually, after the death of the empress dowager, he was forced to retire (1909) only to be recalled in 1911 to save the dynasty from the revolutionaries. He returned on condition that he was given command of the army and the navy, as well as the premiership—conditions which made him the most powerful man in the empire.

Bargaining with the revolutionaries from this position of power, he secured a promise of the presidency, then induced the Emperor P'u-yi to abdicate. He installed his men in the most important ministries and thus dominated the cabinet, then disbanded the 50,000 troops under Huang Hsing, the 'Napoleon' of the Revolution. When his opponents, the Kuomintang (Nationalist Party), won the parliamentary elections, he arranged for the murder of its leader, Sung Chiao-jen. The revolutionaries eventually rose against him (the 'Second Revolution'), but were dispersed by Yuan's superior forces, supported by British loans and munitions. Thus, having rid himself of serious opposition, Yuan began to pursue his monarchical dreams. The constitution was revised, making him president for a ten-year term, subject to unlimited renewals, and empowering him to choose his successor. Encouraged by the Japanese after his acceptance of the infamous Twenty-one Demands (1915), he seized the throne and named 1916 the first year of his reign, ironically called 'Glorious Constitution'. This aroused serious opposition: military governors sympathetic to the republic rose, the constitutionalists led by Liang Ch'i-ch'ao condemned him, several provinces declared their independence, and two of his leading generals, Tuan Ch'i-jui and Feng Kuo-chang, refused to obey orders. The Japanese, who had given him vague encouragement at first, now stood aloof. Thus opposed, Yuan withdrew his monarchical claims (March 1916) and died soon afterwards.

Jerome Ch'en, *Yuan Shih-K'ai, 1859–1916: Brutus assumes the purple* (London, 1960).   DP

YÜAN DYNASTY (1280–1367). During the 12th cent. Mongol tribes from Central Asia under the leadership of Chingiz Khan penetrated as far as Poland and Hungary, inflicting harsh punishment on those who dared to resist their advance. The Yüan or Mongol dynasty was founded in China after some 30 years' effort which was directed to the east, and was the first of China's foreign dynasties to extend its dominion south of the Yangtse river. After defeating the southern Sung dynasty, the Mongol conquerors sent military and naval missions or diplomats to attempt further advances in Viet-nam, Burma, Java, and Japan, but these were not so markedly successful.

The Mongol government of China was based on traditional Chinese models, modified by an attempt to retain the distinction between the Mongol conquerors and their Chinese subjects. The structure of the central government and the institutions of the T"ang and Sung empires was largely maintained, but in provincial government a new departure was made by the organization of China in 12 major provinces. These co-ordinated the work of the 300 or so smaller administrative units evolved previously. While the instinctive reliance of the Mongols on military power contrasted with the traditional Chinese emphasis on cultural ideals as a means of establishing effective government, the Mongols were obliged to accept a number of social conventions and political methods of the Chinese in order to secure the services of Chinese officials. These however were supplemented by the employment of non-Chinese, particularly Muslims from Central or Western Asia; and the traditional Chinese examination system was not maintained regularly.

Marco Polo, one of the best-known European visitors to China, served the Yüan government as an official, and wrote a descriptive account of what he saw during his travels both before and after the Mongol conquest. Economic developments included the more widespread use of paper money and the construction of the second system of waterways, to be known as the Grand Canal. The capital city was established at the site of Peking, which was built anew for the purpose. Cultural changes included the development of the drama and the Chinese novel, whose appeal was directed to a more popular audience than one which depended solely on traditional classical texts.

E. O. Reischauer and J. K. Fairbank, *East Asia, the Great Tradition* (London, 1960).   ML

YÜEH-CHIH, Central Asiatic people. During the 2nd cent. BC they were displaced from pasture grounds in Kansu by the Hsiung-nu. Driven west, they were divided into two main communities, of which one was settled in Bactria. In *c.* 135 BC the Chinese sent Chang Ch'ien west to secure an alliance with the Yüeh-chih against the Hsiung-nu, but the mission was unsuccessful. In the 1st cent. AD the Yüeh-chih people split into five groups, of which one was established in a dominant position and gave rise to the Kushana empire of northern India.

YUGANTAR, 'New Era', sometimes spelt *Jugantar*, a Bengali revolutionary newspaper, started in March 1906. It became the most vigorous voice of Bengali terrorism and by 1907 was said to have a circulation of 7000. The press was seized and the editor imprisoned in July 1907, but publication did not finally cease until 1908. The name continued to be used afterwards to denote a major terrorist group in Calcutta.

YUGOSLAV CONCORDAT, papal agreement signed on 25 July 1935, but not brought before parliament until 23 July 1937. Despite its obtaining a majority, the government withdrew the bill in Jan. 1938 because of the storm of protest that it caused. Religious susceptibilities were important and the Serb Orthodox Church excommunicated most of the government. But political feeling was as deep, both Croat and Serb liberals realizing that the intention had been to secure the Catholic Church's support against communism and to detach the more conservative Catholic Croats from their peasant leader, Maček. However, Maček's position was strengthened in Oct. 1937 through an alliance with Serb Democrats, and that of the government was weakened.

YUGOSLAVIA *COUP D'ÉTAT* (1941), precipitated by the readiness of the Cvetkovic government to agree to the passage of German troops across Yugoslavia to assist the Italian invasion of Greece. The coup (27 March 1941) overthrew the regency of Prince Paul, and declared Prince Peter (whose 18th birthday was in Sept. 1941) to be of age. A new government was formed under Gen. Dusan Simovič. Winston Churchill said in the House of Commons that the Yugoslavs had 'saved the soul and the future of their country'. Hitler reacted by invading Yugoslavia. The army surrendered, but partisan warfare followed and Tito emerged as the partisans' leader.

YUGOV, ANTON (1904–   ), Bulgarian politician and communist leader, whose fall from power marked Zhivkov's final triumph. During the Second World War, when many Bulgarian communists were in the Soviet Union, Yugov helped to manage the party's affairs from inside Bulgaria. In 1944 he was named minister of the interior and organized the People's Militia, which he used as an instrument for a brutal campaign of terror. Yugov experienced a number of ups and downs in his career. In the early years of the regime he held a variety of posts: minister of the interior (1944–9), minister of industry (1950–1), and minister of heavy industry (1951–2), but despite his having served on the Politburo since 1937 he looked like rising no further. At the beginning of his second period as deputy prime minister (1949–50, 1952–6), he revived his political fortunes by intervening dramatically in the Plovdiv strike. During the 1950s he began to emerge as a claimant to supreme power and a clear rival to Zhivkov within the party. But at the 8th party congress in 1962, Zhivkov, without warning, charged Yugov with a string of offences and stripped him of all his offices.

YUKON TERRITORY, part of Canada between AK and the NWT. Robert Campbell explored it (1840–50), built Frances Lake trading post and Pelly Banks post, and discovered the upper reaches of the Yukon river. The Hudson's Bay Co. ceded the territory to the Crown and Canada acquired it by licence (1870) and incorporated it in the NWT. Rich gold deposits, discovered on Bonanza creek in 1896, precipitated the Klondike gold-rush (1898). The Yukon Act (1898) made it a separate territory with Dawson as its administrative centre. It was governed by an appointed council and sent one member to the Canadian parliament (1905). A renewal of interest in the YT came with the building of the Alaska Highway (1942). The Canol Pipe Line (1944) brought crude oil from the District of Mackenzie to be refined at Whitehorse, which became the administrative headquarters of the YT.

YUMAN INDIANS, group formerly occupying a large area of the American south-west and northern Baja California, including the Cocopa, Diegueño, Havasupai, Maricopa, Mohave, Tonto, Walapai, Yavapai, and Yuma. Most of them came under US control at the end of the war with Mexico (1848) and by 1886 had been gathered on to reservations.

YUNG WING (1828–1912), also called Jung Hung, Chinese official, who was the first Chinese graduate of an American university and an early advocate of the introduction of Western learning into China. He was a native of Kwangtung and, after being educated at a missionary school, was sent with the help of foreign funds to the US to continue his studies. After graduating at Yale University in 1854, he returned to China, where he became an interpreter, then went into the tea trade in the Shanghai area. In 1864 he was sent abroad by Tseng Kuo-fan to buy machinery for the projected Kiangnan Arsenal. On his return he urged Tseng to send Chinese students abroad to study, an idea that materialized in 1872 in the form of the China Education Mission. While in the US Yung went on a mission to Peru to look into Chinese labour conditions there (1874), and in 1878 he set up the first Chinese legation in the US. Owing to conservative opposition in China, as well as to US immigration restriction on Chinese and the discrimination of West Point and Annapolis academies against Chinese candidates, the Education Mission was abolished in 1881. Being unable to secure a satisfactory government appointment in China, Yung returned to the US, but in 1895 he was invited by Chang Chih-tung to serve on his staff. However, his proposals for the establishment of a modern national bank and a railway from Tientsin to Chinkiang were thwarted by Sheng Hsuan-huai. After the 'Hundred Days' Reform' (1898) Yung left China, and after sojourning briefly in Hong Kong, returned to the US and there wrote his autobiography, published in 1909.   DP

YUNGAY, BATTLE OF (Jan. 1839), fought near Lima, Peru, between troops of the Peruvian–Bolivian Confederation and separatist forces of Chile and Peru, led by the Peruvian general Ramón Castilla. The confederation forces were defeated and the government was dissolved.

YUNG-CHENG (1723–36), reign-title of Yin-chen (*reg.* 1678–1735), Third Emperor of the Chinese Ch'ing dynasty. On coming to the throne after years of intrigues and factional struggle, Yin-chen's first acts were to reduce the power of his contending brothers, to punish his opponents, and to publish a treatise condemning factions. The Jesuits, who had participated in the struggles, were, with few exceptions, deported. Jealous of his power, Yin-chen spied on almost everybody of consequence in the empire and tried to control the thought and behaviour of the country by circulating imperial maxims and expositions. Literary works were closely scrutinized and court records expurgated. Though despotic, and sometimes cruel, the Yung-cheng emperor was able and conscientious. He reformed the empire's finances and increased official salaries in order to eliminate corruption. His strict enforcement of the law kept the bureaucracy in line, and thus laid the foundation for the splendours of the Ch'ien-lung reign.

YUNG-LO, reign-title of the third Ming Emperor (*reg.* 1403–24), the achievements of whose reign included the adoption of Peking as the capital city, after extensively remodelling and rebuilding it on an ambitious scale; the despatch of expeditions against the Mongols; the sponsorship of maritime voyages; and the improvement of the canal system. Promotion of scholarship resulted in the compilation of the *Yung-lo ta-tien,* or Encyclopaedia of the Yung-lo period. The work, which was too large to print, was produced in manuscript, over 2000 scholars being engaged. The book was intended to include extracts from all the principal works on history, geography, government institutions, and philosophy. Only a small fraction of the original work and its two copies survives.

YUSUF BIN HASAN (b. *c.* 1606), King of Mombasa, was installed in 1626 by the Portuguese, who dominated the city from their fortress, named Jesus; they believed that Yusuf, whom they had educated at Goa (his baptismal name was Jeronimo Chingulia), would prove a convenient puppet. On becoming king, Yusuf reverted to the Muslim faith, attacked the Portuguese, took Fort Jesus from them and held it until 1632.

YUSUF IBN TASHFIN (d. 1106), cousin of the Abu Bakr ibn Umar, who assumed the leadership of the Almoravids after the deaths of Yahya ibn Umar and of the founder of the movement, Abdullah ibn Yasin. Yusuf and his cousin were joint conquerors of Morocco, and founded Marrakesh (*c.* 1069). After conquering western Algeria he was invited by the Abbasid ruler of Seville, Al-Mu'tamid, to rescue what remained of Muslim Spain. After landing at Algeciras, he defeated Alfonso VI in the battle of Al-Zallaqa (1086). A dispute then arose between Yusuf and Abu Bakr over the Almoravid leadership. Yusuf retained control of Morocco and Spain, while Abu Bakr returned to the Sahara and the Sudan, where he died some time after 1087. Following his successes in Spain, Yusuf, supported by eminent theologians, deposed the Muslim princes there, who had sought his help, captured Granada (1090) and Seville (1091), and exiled Al-Mu'tamid to Morocco.

ZABARELLA, FRANCESCO (1360–1417), Italian cardinal. As a canon lawyer whose works enjoyed a wide and long circulation he played a leading part in obtaining the convocation of the council of Constance (1414–17), which ended the Great Schism.

ZACCARIA, BENEDETTO (c. 1240–1307), Genoese sailor and merchant, who, in return for helping a Byzantine emperor to recapture Constantinople (1261), secured a monopoly of the best alum available to the European woollen industry from mines in Asia Minor. Zaccaria's ships distributed the alum in western Europe and he himself promoted the inauguration of a regular sea-route to England and Flanders. The Vivaldi brothers, his associates, tried in 1291 to sail from Genoa to India. Zaccaria commanded the fleet which in 1284 captured Pisa, Genoa's great rival.

ZACHARIAS (*reg.* 741–52), Pope, whose pontificate was marked by his support and patronage of St Boniface and his missionary work in Germany, by the re-establishment of direct contact, through Boniface's efforts, with the Frankish Church, and, above all, by his recognition of Pepin the Short, the first of the Carolingian kings of the Franks.

ZAFRULLAH KHAN, CHAUDHURI (1893–), Pakistani diplomat, lawyer, and Punjab politician, who was a member of the viceroy's executive council (1935–41) and a judge of the Indian Federal Court (1941–7). After partition, he was foreign minister of Pakistan (1947–54) and was his country's chief spokesman at the United Nations in the dispute over Kashmir. He became a judge of the International Court of Justice at The Hague in 1954 and has been a member of that court since then, except for a term of three years as Pakistan's chief representative at the UN, during which time he was president of the General Assembly (1962–3).

ZAGHAWA, semi-nomadic people living on both sides of the northern Chad–Sudan frontier. Classical Arab geographers frequently mentioned them as a nomadic people in the region extending from the Niger to the Sudan, and regarded them as the ancestors of the Saifawa.

ZAGHLUL PASHA, SA'D (c. 1857–1927), Egyptian lawyer and politician. He was minister of education (1906–10) and of justice (1910–13), then in 1918 he became leader of the Egyptian nationalist movement through what became the Wafd Party. He led the radical opposition to the British occupation and the political influence of the Egyptian Crown. In 1923 he was prime minister.

ZAGWE dynasty, line of usurping Ethiopian emperors, who, from the 12th to the 14th cent., ruled in the province of Lasta.

ZÄHRINGEN dynasty in Germany. The Emperor Henry IV (d. 1106) granted the dynasty an imperial *Vogtei* (protectorate) over central Switzerland and they formed an important unitary state in that south-western corner of the German empire. The family died out in 1218 and the Habsburgs, who were their leading supporters, ultimately succeeded to their inheritance, and thus began their ascent to power which culminated in the election of Rudolf Habsburg as emperor in 1273.

ZAIBATSU in Japan, literally 'financial clique', name given to the score of huge industrial combines which dominate the modern Japanese economy. With some exceptions, most of these combines rose to importance during the Meiji period (1868–1912), when they received subsidies and contracts from a government which urgently wanted to make Japan an industrial power. By the 1920s *zaibatsu* domination of the profitable modern sectors of industry and of banking was beginning to cause resentment and unpopularity among small businessmen and peasants, and the chief executive of Mitsui, the largest *zaibatsu*, was murdered (1932). *Zaibatsu* influence over the government and over political parties safeguarded them against attack, however, and their economic importance meant that during the war period (1937–45) they were treated with respect by the military–bureaucratic leadership. After 1945 the Occupation broke up the great combines, but after 1952 most of them reappeared in a modified form.

ZAKIR HUSAIN (1897–1969), Indian Muslim educationist and president of India (1967–9), who took a leading part in the foundation of the Jamia Millia Islamia, the National Muslim University, in Aligarh (1920). In 1926, he became shaikh or vice-chancellor of the Jamai, which had by then removed to Delhi. He retained this post until 1948, when he became vice-chancellor of Aligarh Muslim University (1948–57). After his retirement from Aligarh he was first appointed governor of Bihar (1957–62), then vice-president of India (1962–7), and eventually became president in the most seriously contested of all Indian presidential elections to date. In 1937 he was a leading adviser on Gandhi's Basic National Education Scheme.

ZALUSKI, JOSEF ANDREAS (1702–74), Polish divine and scholar, who was Bp of Kiiovie. With the help of his brother, Andreas Stanislas Zaluski, grand chancellor of Poland, he collected a library of 300,000 books and 10,000 mss, which they presented to the Polish nation (1747). It was taken by the Russians from Warsaw to St Petersburg in 1795.

ZAMA, BATTLE OF (Oct.–Nov. 202 BC), in the Second Punic War, final victory in Africa of the Romans, under Scipio Africanus, over the Carthaginians, under Hannibal. The site is disputed, but probably lay about 14 kms south of Le Kef between Naraggara (Sidi Youssef) and Zama Regia (Jama). The entire Carthaginian army of 35,000 was killed or captured, though Hannibal himself escaped, and Carthage accepted Roman terms.

ZAMBIA (746,000 sq. kms), republic in central Africa, formerly the British protectorate of Northern Rhodesia, which became independent in 1964. The president and National Assembly are elected by adult suffrage every five years. There is only one official political party. Bemba, Barotse, Ngoni, and other groups make up the population (1970) of 3,780,000, 3 per cent of which in 1970 was European.

ZAMBOS, term used in Spanish America to designate persons of mixed African and Indian blood. Miscegenation between the two groups, though frowned upon by the Spanish Crown in colonial times, proceeded apace, and the physical type is still common in certain regions, *eg*, coastal Peru and Ecuador.

ZAMFARA, former kingdom in northern Nigeria and one of the *banza* Hausa states. It was tributary to Bornu and Kebbi in the period *c*. 1715–56, and became one of the most powerful states in Hausaland.

ZAMINDARI ABOLITION, in India, schemes for the dispossession of the landholders (*zamindars*) which formed an important part of the programme of land reforms introduced in India after independence. The programme stems from schemes formulated by the Congress in the 1930s under Congress Socialist Party pressure and published in the Faizpur agrarian programme (1936) and the election manifestos of 1937 and 1946. Although the provisions vary, as do the names of landholders, in different states, the general pattern is remarkably similar. There has not been a general expropriation of landholders. Rather, the title of lands leased to tenants has been transferred to those tenants under a new tenure which brings the ex-tenant into direct relationship with the state. And lands which the former landlord continues to hold are held under a more or less similar title. The similarity of their relationship to the state is manifest in the fact that both now pay land revenue directly to the state, where formerly the tenant paid rent to the landlord. In all states, except Kashmir, landholders were given compensation for the lands which were taken from them, but not at full market rates. The earliest legislation was challenged in the courts by the landlords and the government of India amended the constitution to ensure that such legislation was not held to be contrary to the fundamental rights laid down in the constitution. The former landlords continue to hold lands which were recorded as being under their own cultivation and these are often quite extensive. *Zamindari* abolition lessened rather than eliminated the disparities within the Indian agrarian system.   PDR

ZAMOYSKI, ANDREW, Count (1800–74), leader of the 'white' conservative party in Russian-dominated Poland. He represented the serf-owning gentry, whose intransigence frustrated the emergence of a united nationalist movement in Poland. He feared the social policies of the 'white' radical nationalists almost as much as he hated the Russians, yet he failed to co-operate with Wielopolski's attempt to strengthen Poland by collaboration with Alexander II (1862–3).

ZAMOYSKI, JOHN (1541–1605), Polish politician, who was grand chancellor of Poland and was married to a cousin of Stephen Bathory, King of Poland, whom he first served. On the king's death (1587), Zamoyski secured the election of Sigismund Vasa and defeated the Habsburg candidate, Archduke Maximilian, at the battle of Byczyna (1588). To stimulate Poland's economy he organized his own vast estates for the production of corn, beef, and fish, and established industrial enterprises, *eg*, iron foundries. He also established over 60 villages and advocated the production of luxury goods to make Poland self-sufficient. Being a tolerant Catholic, he permitted Armenian and Greek churches in his domain. His relations with Sigismund deteriorated after 1592, when he instigated the summoning of a parliament to check Sigismund's intrigues with the Habsburgs. In a later Diet (1605) he accused Sigismund of violating constitutional liberties and of trying to create an absolute monarchy. Being a loyal supporter of Polish interests, Zamoyski sought to extend his country's influence in the Danube area, *eg*, by securing the accession of favourable candidates as hospodar of Moldavia (1595) and of Wallachia (1600).

ZANARDELLI, GUISEPPE (1826–1903), Italian politician, who was leader of the 'pure' left and held office in several governments before becoming Victor Emmanuel III's first prime minister (1901–3). He was devoted to the cause of freedom of conscience and was responsible for the abolition of capital punishment and recognition of the right to strike. He believed, with Giolitti, that the masses could only learn responsibility through the exercise of political power. But his most individual contribution to Italian politics was his acceptance, after a personal visit to Basilicata (1902), that the misery and poverty of the south was the responsibility of the whole nation, which could only be discharged by direct government action. His career was overshadowed by that of Giolitti, who replaced him in 1903.

ZANE'S TRACE in the US, pioneer road running through south-eastern OH in 1796 blazed by Ebenezer Zane (1747–1812). It ran from Wheeling, WV, via Zanesville and Chillicothe, to the Ohio river at Maysville, KY. For a generation Zane's Trace was the chief route of land travel through south-eastern OH, and the section between Wheeling and Zanesville later became part of the Cumberland (National) Road.

ZANGI, IMAD AL-DIN (1084–1146), Atabeg of Mosul, whose father, Aqsunqur, had been in the service of the Seljuk Sultan Malik Shah. Zangi became governor of Wasit in 1122–3 and of Mosul in 1127. Aleppo came under his control in 1129. In 1139 he attempted unsuccessfully to seize Damascus. In 1144, however, he achieved a notable success when he captured Edessa from the Latin Crusaders. He was succeeded in Mosul and Aleppo by his son, Nur al-Din.

ZANJ, name given to a rebellion in Arabia among the Negro slaves employed during the 9th cent. in the salt marshes near Basra. In Sept. 869 they rose in revolt under a certain Ali ibn Muhammad, and in 871 Basra fell to the rebels. Al-Muwaffaq, the brother of the Abbasid Caliph al-Mu'tamid (*reg.* 870–92), eventually drove them out of Khuzistan and forced them back on their main base at Al-Mukhtara, which was stormed in July 883. This brought the revolt to an end.

ZANZIBAR and PEMBA, islands of the old sultanate of Zanzibar. Zanzibar, known as Unguju, was originally occupied by the Hadimu, a Bantu people akin to the Zegua of the mainland. Pemba, known as Al Hadhra, 'the green island', was inhabited by a similar stock. Both islands received Arab and, according to local belief, Persian immigrants at least as early as the 9th cent. AD, and were converted to Islam. The immigrants included Dabuli, from Debul in Sind, Diba from the Maldive Islands, and Shirazi, originally from Persia, but possibly already colonialized after a 300-year residence in Shungwaya, at the south end of the Somali coast. The Shirazi rulers of Zanzibar in the 13th cent. called themselves sultans, and issued a copper coinage similar to that of their kinsmen at Kilwa. The rulers of Pemba, at times as many as four, were sheikhs of no great importance, although Pemba was a much-needed source of food for the whole coast.

In the 16th and 17th cents both islands were under Portuguese domination, which was interrupted by frequent rebellions. Pemba was seized by the Sultan of Mombasa in 1605, and later in the century received an influx of settlers from Pate. After the expulsion of the Portuguese in 1698, the two islands were governed from Zanzibar, but in 1746 the rebel Mazrui governor of Mombasa took Pemba, which was held by Mombasa until 1823, when it was retaken by the governor of Zanzibar. In the 19th cent. Zanzibar became the commercial and diplomatic capital of most of east and central Africa and, with Pemba, the source of most of the world's supply of cloves. In 1963 the British protectorate, proclaimed in 1895, was terminated. In 1964 the sultanate was overthrown and a republic proclaimed, which almost at once became united with Tanganyika as a self-governing part of the republic of Tanzania.   BD

ZAPATA, EMILIANO (1880–1919), Mexican agrarian revolutionary of Anenecuilco, Morelos, who led a rising against the illegal usurpations of oligarchic landholders (*latifundistas*) throughout his native state (1909–19). He became the actual as well as the symbolic leader of agrarian revolutionaries throughout Mexico during the great revolution (1910–17). Since the era of the Reform (1855–67), landowners had been expanding their holdings at the expense of village lands and during the Porfirian dictatorship (1876–1911) this tendency reached alarming proportions. The courts countenanced illegal seizures and even penalized villagers who brought charges.

Zapata and his followers began modestly, pulling up cane and tearing down fences around Villa de Ayala. Soon his forces grew, his prestige and authority spread throughout the south, and the landowners were in full flight. But the national revolutionaries (Madero, Carranza, González) little understood or cared about the southern movement. Zapata co-operated for a time (1914) with Francisco Villa, but he chose not to risk his forces in a co-ordinated national undertaking. He carried out his own land reform in the south and reinforced village (*pueblo*) institutions, but his gains were constantly jeopardized and frequently destroyed by forces sent into Morelos by the national revolutionaries.

In the Plan of Ayala (1911), Zapata set out his demands for immediate agrarian reform and expropriation of the lands of enemies of the revolution. His plan was substantially reproduced in Article 27 of the federal constitution of 1917. Only after 1917, when he became increasingly concerned about possible US intervention in Mexico, did he consider compromising with leaders who had not placed agrarian reform first among Mexican needs.

Following Zapata's betrayal and murder, his followers supported the overthrow of Carranza by Alvaro Obregón, who generally favoured the agrarian cause. The heritage of the *Zapatista* movement has included an extensive agrarian reform throughout Mexico, frequently carried out on a communal (*ejidal*) basis.

John Womack, *Zapata and the Mexican Revolution* (New York, 1969).   HDS

ZAPOLYAI, JOHN (1454–1540), King of Hungary (*reg.* 1526–40), who was a Hungarian nobleman, *voivode* or governor of Transylvania. He was the national candidate for the Hungarian throne after the death of Louis II and was crowned king at Stuhlweissenberg, receiving the support of the Turks against the Habsburg candidate, Archduke Ferdinand, who was also crowned. Finally, in 1538 Zapolyai agreed to the tripartite division of Hungary and the succession of Ferdinand after his own death, receiving the principality of Transylvania.

ZAPOROZHIE, region of the Dnieper basin, derived its name from the Russian meaning of 'beyond the cataracts', where the midstream islands protected by rapids originally formed the impregnable stronghold of the Ukrainian or Zaporozhie Cossacks from the 16th cent. It was stormed by Peter I's troops in 1709, and destroyed under Catherine I.

ZARIA, Zazzau or Zegzeg, town and emirate in Northern Nigeria, one of the *Hausa Bokwai*. Its early history is obscure. The city, the latest of a series of capitals, was traditionally founded by Zaria, the sister of Queen Amina, in the 15th or 16th cent. Originally it was much more extensive and included Kufena Hill, where many early remains have been discovered. The present smaller *enceinte* was possibly built in the 18th cent. The state is said to have reached its greatest extent under Amina, daughter of the founder of a new dynasty. According to Leo Africanus, it was conquered by Songhay. Later, wars were fought with Kano and Katsina, it was raided by the Jukun, and became tributary to Bornu, accepting a resident, perhaps in the 17th cent. The old dynasty was driven away and founded the emirate of Abuja at the time of the Fulani *jihad*. In the 19th cent. the throne rotated among three Fulani families. Zaria emirate was occupied by the British in 1901.

ZARUTSKY, IVAN, ATAMAN (d. 1614), leader of the Don Cossacks during the Time of Troubles in Muscovy. He defeated Tsar Vasili Shuisky's troops on the Volkhov (1608), marched on Moscow, and with Prince Trubetsky and Liapunov, whom his Cossacks later murdered, was elected head of the provisional government by the citizen army (1611). After Michael Romanov's election as tsar (1613), he and Tsaritsa Marina retired with the Cossacks to Astrakhan (1614), but were ousted and pursued by Muscovite forces. They were seized by the *streltsi* and brought to Moscow, where Zarutsky and Marina's son, Ivan, were executed (1614).

ZAYDI, name given to those adherents of the Shi'a who gave their allegiance to the descendants of Zayd ibn Ali, the grandson of Al-Husayn, who was killed at Karbala in AD 680. The Zaydi Muslims established two states, one in Persia, the other in the Yemen. Al-Hasan ibn Zayd founded an independent regime (*c.* 864–1126) in the region south of the Caspian Sea. A Zaydi imamate was also created (*c.* AD 900) in the Yemen under the guidance of Yahya ibn al-Husayn, a grandson of Al-Qasim al-Rassi (d. 860), who had played a large part in the formulation of the Zaydi doctrines. This imamate in the Yemen still survived in 1970.

ZEALOTS. Byzantine territories in Europe, suffering from frequent warfare, harsh taxation, and the dominance of an aristocratic class small in number, but endowed with large estates and privileges saw, in the time of the Palaiologoi, the growth of a 'proletariat', both on the land and in the towns. The animosities thus evoked of the poor against the rich broke out into bitter violence during the years of the civil war (1341–7) between John V Palaiologos and John VI Kantakuzenos. At Thessaloniki the social and economic discords assumed the form of a revolutionary movement, the adherents of which—the Zealots—seized control of the town in 1342, established a government virtually independent of Constantinople, and carried out a programme of expropriation directed above all against the nobles and the Church. With the end of the civil war in 1347 the prospect before the Zealots became more and more unfavourable. A ruthless suppression of all dissidence enabled them to survive for some years, but in 1350 their regime broke down and Thessaloniki renewed its obedience to the emperor at Constantinople.

ZEBRZYDOWSKI, NICHOLAS (*fl.* 17th cent.), Polish nobleman, Palatine of Cracow and instigator of the civil war in Poland known as Zebrzydowski's rebellion (1606–7). Fearing Sigismund III's apparently pro-Habsburg policies and the loss of aristocratic privileges and liberties, Zebrzydowski allied himself with the Protestant party, led by Prince Janusz Radziwill, though himself a devout Catholic. The rebellion was suppressed at Guzow (1607), but a general amnesty was granted (1609).

ZEEBRUGGE, harbour on the Belgian coast, where the ship canal from the inland port of Bruges reaches the sea; another canal links Bruges with Ostend. After its capture by the Germans in 1914 this port-complex became an important naval base. During the First World War submarines based at Bruges accounted for almost half the total losses of merchant shipping in the North Sea and the Western Approaches in 1917–18. Destroyers based at Bruges greatly facilitated submarine operations by frequent attacks on British patrols in the Dover Straits. Plans for blocking Zeebrugge and Ostend were discussed in British naval circles from Nov. 1916, but postponed until the failure of Haig's offensive at Ypres, which had as one of its subsidiary objectives the recapture of the Flanders ports. The attempt was made on 23 April 1918 by naval forces under the commander at Dover, Vice-Admiral Roger Keyes.

The principal objective was Zeebrugge, where, under the cover of smoke screens laid by coastal motor boats, three blockships were to be sunk in the canal entrance, while the batteries and harbour installations on the Mole—the massive stone breakwater protecting the harbour—were to be destroyed by landing parties from the old cruiser *Vindictive* and two Mersey ferry boats; an old submarine filled with explosives was to be used to demolish the viaduct linking the Mole to the mainland so as to prevent the German forces there from being reinforced. Only this last part of the operation went according to plan: the smoke blew the wrong way; the *Vindictive* reached the Mole at the wrong place, and though the landing force displayed considerable gallantry and suffered heavy casualties, it was unable to silence the batteries or to destroy any important installations; two of the blockships reached the canal entrance under heavy fire, but did not succeed in closing it completely (which was probably impossible). At Ostend a similar operation failed utterly, as did a second attempt on 10 May. German operations from Bruges suffered no more than temporary inconvenience. But the success claimed for the raid, and the daring and heroism with which it was executed (11 VCs were awarded), provided a useful boost to Allied morale during the German spring offensive.   PJBD

ZEELAND, sea-girt, Dutch-speaking province of the Netherlands, consisting of the islands off Brabant and including the ports of Middelburg, Flushing, and Zierickzee. The *stadtholder* was traditionally a prince of Orange until the 18th cent. and, with Holland, Zeeland became the centre of resistance to the Spanish Crown from the time that the Calvinist Sea Beggars seized control (1572). In 1648 it became a component state of the United Provinces.

ZELA, BATTLE OF (47 BC), Julius Caesar's defeat of Pharnaces, son of Mithridates VI of Pontus, at modern Zile in Turkey. Caesar summed up his victory in the famous phrase *veni vidi vici* ('I came, I saw, I conquered'), displayed, perhaps on a picture, at his triumph in 46.

ZELAYA, JOSÉ SANTOS (1853–1919), Nicaraguan politician, who was president and dictator of Nicaragua (1893–1909). He created the Nationalist Party and formulated its policies on reformist, anti-clerical lines. When the government came off badly in a border dispute with neighbouring Honduras, Zelaya seized the opportunity to declare a revolution. He was joined by university students, youthful army officers, and politicians, who brought him to power. Among the domestic reforms he carried out in his early years were the introduction of civil marriage and of secular teachers in schools, commercial and industrial changes, and the building of a railway from the heavily populated west coast to the sparsely settled Caribbean region. Incorporation of the eastern region into the rest of the country was one of his principal aims, and helped to formulate his foreign policy. His hatred for Britain was based on a clash with her government and local citizens, which was settled only when he agreed to pay damages. Later, he attacked British merchants, who encouraged a revolution against him (1909). Finally, the US threatened him, causing him to leave the country rather than to submit to an invasion. Earlier he had urged the other Central American states to join him in a confederation, but they refused to do so. Various conferences were held to discuss the matter and on two occasions war resulted between them. Zelaya fought both El Salvador (1902) and Honduras (1906), but to little avail. Conferences held at San José, Costa Rica (1906), and Washington (1907) failed to stem his zeal and eventually the US stepped in forcefully to stop him. His were the last efforts made to achieve a confederation of Central American states by military methods.

M. Rodriguez, *Central America* (Englewood Cliffs, 1965).
F. D. Parker, *The Central American Republics* (London & New York, 1964).   VCP

ZELO DOMUS DEI (1648), papal bull promulgated by Innocent X condemning the compromise settlement concerning ecclesiastical territories and reservations embodied in the peace of Westphalia.

ZEMSHCHINA, meaning 'the Land', term denoting those areas of west and south Muscovy which were divided from the *oprichnina* by Tsar Ivan IV from *c.* 1565 and continued to be administered in the traditional way.

ZEMSKI SOBOR, in Russia, council of the land or general assembly of the Muscovite state which existed from the mid-16th to the late 17th cent. It was first summoned by Tsar Ivan IV in 1550 to rally support for the Crown against the great magnates, and was a broadly representative body of men of all ranks, divided into two sections, the elected members and the administrative officials. The formation of the elected section was somewhat complex because of the variety and heterogeneity of the electoral units, and the nucleus of the *sobor* was the administrative section, consisting of members of the two supreme institutions, the *boyars'* council with the secretaries of the various government departments, the holy synod of the patriarch, the metropolitan and bishops. However, the composition, competence, and procedures were not rigidly established, and the *sobor* functioned both as a legislative and as an advisory body. It gained considerable importance as a stabilizing influence during the Time of Troubles, being responsible for the elections of Boris Gudonov (1598) and Michael Romanov (1613) to the throne. Michael continued to consult the *sobor* frequently in the first part of his reign and his son, Alexis, also used it, *eg*, to consider the nation's grievances and introduce a new code of laws (1649) and to debate the question of the Cossacks' submission to the tsar (1651–3). From 1654 to 1682, however, the *sobor* was never summoned and its role diminished as the Romanov dynasty consolidated its grip upon Russia. Peter I summoned it for the last time in 1698 to try his half-sister, Sophia.

ZEMSTVO (pl. *zemstva*), in Russia, district and provincial legislative assemblies consisting of elected representatives of nobles, townsmen, and peasants which were established (1864) as part of Alexander II's reforms. Their formation was welcomed by the liberal gentry as the first step towards representative government. However, restrictions on their powers were later introduced (1866–7) and in 1890 peasant representation was virtually abolished and the ministry of the interior's control increased. The *zemstva* performed valuable services in connection with public health, primary education, agriculture, and communications. The 'third element' (employed experts) became influential in the radical movement and professional organizations.

The *zemstva* formed an important basis for liberal constitutionalism and the right-wing *zemstvo*-gentry advocated a consultative national assembly, while the left wing followed I. I. Petrunkevich in demanding full constitutional government. Eventually the movement split between Kadets and Octobrists. A union of *zemstva* established in 1914 performed medical and supply work during the First World War.

ZEN, Japanese name of the school of *Mahayana* Buddhism, known in China as *ch'an* (Sansk. *dhyana*). The word means 'meditation' and the school or sect is characterized by its belief in the attainment of sudden enlightenment by concentrated meditation, rather than through the use of any particular scripture. The *ch'an* school was established in

China by the monk Bodhidharma (460–?534), and developed strongly in the 7th and 8th cents, when it produced such famous patriarchs as Hui-Neng (638–713) and Shan-Hui (670–762). Zen was introduced into Japan by the monk Yeisai (1140–1215), who founded the *Rinzai* sect; another Zen sect, the *Soto*, was founded by Dogen (1199–1253). This form of Buddhism was also important in Viet-nam down to the 13th cent. It has largely died out in China and Viet-nam, but still flourished in 1970 in Japan, where there are over 20,000 Zen temples.

ZENATA, name of a former nomadic Berber people of the central Maghrib.

ZENO (*reg.* 474–91), Roman Emperor in the East. He was an Isaurian soldier, originally named Tarasicodissa, but was rechristened Zeno by Leo I, whose sister Ariadne he married. On being promoted, he was charged with responsibility for ridding the Eastern empire of its overbearing Gothic troops, which he succeeded in doing. Shortly after Leo's death Zeno ascended the throne. During his reign the Western empire ended, although the fiction of a single emperor reigning over a reunited empire was maintained. However, Zeno never attempted to exercise power in the West. He proved a reasonably capable prince, who sought among other things to resolve the religious disputes which disturbed the peace of the empire.

ZENO OF ELEA (b. *c.* 490 BC), Greek philosopher of the Eleatic school, a pupil of Parmenides, who was regarded by Aristotle as originating dialectic by drawing opposite conclusions from opponents' premises. Arguing with the support of the famous paradoxes, *eg*, Achilles and the tortoise, that space and time are neither infinitely divisible nor composed of indivisible units, he attacked the Pythagoreans for confusing geometrical points and spatially extended units and upheld Parmenides' monism.

ZENO MAP, forgery produced by an Italian, Antonio Zeno (1558), supposedly recording an Arctic voyage made in the 14th cent. by one of Zeno's ancestors. Greenland is drawn as an extension of northern Norway, forming a large bay in which Iceland is located. The island of Frisland is also located in this bay, and there are broken coastlines of two land masses shown to the west. The explorers Martin Frobisher (1576) and John Davis (1585) used Zeno's map.

ZENOBIA, SEPTIMIA (*fl.* 3rd cent.), Empress, who, after the death of her husband, Odaenathus (266 or 267), ruled the Eastern empire established by him. She extended her realms to Syria, parts of Asia Minor, and Egypt, but after initial recognition was attacked by the Roman emperor Aurelian and defeated at Antioch and Emesa (272). While attempting to escape from the besieged city of Palmyra to fetch help from Persia, she was captured, taken to Rome, and paraded in triumph by Aurelian, but was apparently allowed to live there with her family. Palmyra itself, for long an important caravan city and the centre of a distinctive and flourishing culture, was captured and destroyed by Aurelian.

ZENTA, BATTLE OF (Sept. 1697), on the Tisza (Theiss) river, south of Szagedin, in Hungary. Prince Eugène of Savoy, commanding the forces of the Emperor Leopold I, inflicted a defeat on the Ottoman Turks which brought to an end the war of 1683–99 between Austria and the Ottoman empire.

ZEPPELIN, FERDINAND VON, Count (1838–1917), German inventor of the dirigible airship, first launched in 1900, which caught the imagination of the German people, but failed to prove its worth in the First World War, since it was easily shot down.

ZETLAND, LAURENCE JOHN LUMLEY DUNDAS, 2nd Marquis of (1876–1961), British politician and author, who was secretary of state for India (1935–40). His basic Indian experience came from his membership of the Islington Commission on the public services in India (1912) and his period as governor of Bengal (1916–21), during which he took a generally progressive line on reforms, but a firm line with the nationalist politicians with whom he had to deal. He was a member of the Round Table Conferences (1930–2) and of the Joint Parliamentary Committee on Indian reforms (1933–4), having by this time succeeded (1929) his father as Lord Zetland. His appointment as secretary of state ensured that there was a knowledgeable friend of India to guide the new constitution. He seemed to have been aware sooner than the viceroy, Lord Linlithgow, of the importance of dealing with Muslim fears of the federation scheme and, after the outbreak of the Second World War, of making some radical move to win the co-operation of the Indian parties. His own record of his Indian experiences is in his autobiography, *Essayez* (1956). He was also the author of several books dealing with his travels in Asia and of a biography of Lord Curzon.

ZEUGITAE (ancient Greek 'teamsters'), at Athens, defined in terms of income (200–300 measures) by Solon (594 BC) as the lower middle class of citizens. Important magistracies were closed to the *zeugitae* until they were made eligible for the archonship (457) soon after Ephialtes' reforms. Most *zeugitae* were hoplites and tended towards conservatism as the lower class of *thetes* won increasing influence under the radical democracy. Their support was sought in both the reactionary attempts at revolution in 411 and 404–403.

ZHDANOV, ANDREY ALEKSANDROVICH (1896–1948), Russian Soviet leader and close associate of Stalin, who joined the Bolsheviks (1915) and rose in the party, first in Nizhni-Novgorod (1424–34) and then in Leningrad (1934–44). He was first secretary of the Leningrad party organization (1934), secretary of the central committee (1934), a candidate member of the Politburo (1935) and then a full member (1939). He was from 1934 the leading spokesman on doctrinal questions and was responsible for the imposition of the 'socialist realist' style in the arts and the attack on Western influences in the arts and scholarship.

He was poised, at the end of the Second World War, to make a bid for the succession to Stalin, after whom he ranked third in the list of secretaries to the central committee. He was the principal exponent of the hard line which characterized Soviet policy at the beginning of the Cold War, propagating the doctrine, *eg*, on the 29th anniversary of the Bolshevik Revolution (7 Nov. 1946), of the increasing split of the world into socialist and imperialist camps. He was closely associated with the establishment of the Cominform (Sept. 1947).

His sudden death (31 Aug. 1948) was followed by a ruthless purge of his associates in the Leningrad organization. Zhdanov himself was not attacked, but his associates were condemned on bogus charges. Subsequently, Zhdanov's death was ascribed to the supposed 'plot' of Jewish doctors against the Stalinist leadership (1952). The Leningrad purge was attributed by Khrushchev to the head of the security service, Abakumov, who was executed (1954), and later (1956) to Malenkov.   WK

ZHIVKOV, TODOR CHRISTOV (1911–   ), Bulgarian politician, who was first secretary of the Bulgarian Communist Party and prime minister of Bulgaria. In 1928 he joined the Young Communist League and in 1932 the Communist Party. By 1934 he was secretary of the third area committee in Sofia and a member of the Sofia district party committee. In 1941 he appeared as a leader of the Sofia party and the partisan resistance, and in 1943 became the chief organizer of resistance in the region of Botevgrad and deputy commander of the Sofia zone. After the communists seized power in 1944, Zhivkov advanced steadily in the party's hierarchy. In 1945 he became a candidate member of the central committee and three years later a full member. He joined the secretariat of the central committee in 1950 and the Politburo in 1951. He was especially powerful in Sofia, where, after 1948, he held senior posts in the party. He was elected first secretary of the central committee at the sixth party congress in March 1954, though the real power remained in the hands of Chervenkov. Zhivkov, meanwhile, gathered his strength. Georgi Chankov, a major rival, was ousted in 1957, and in 1961 Chervenkov himself was purged. Zhivkov's triumph was completed in 1962 with the dismissal of Yugov as prime minister and his own assumption of the office. Zhivkov was, in 1970, the epitome of the *appartchik* in power.

ZHUKOV, GEORGIY KONSTANTINOVICH (1896–   ), Russian politician and marshal of the Soviet Union, who played an important part in the leadership crisis in 1957. After joining the Bolshevik Party and the Red Army (1918), he was attached to a cavalry brigade under Timoshenko. After the First World War he held various commands, and attended Frunze Military Academy (1928–31). He was later sent to China with a Soviet military mission and was then given command against the Japanese army on the Mongolian–Manchurian frontier (1939). During the Second World War he was chief of the general staff, then deputy commissar of defence and deputy supreme commander in chief. He played a decisive part in many of the major operations of the war, including the defence of Moscow, the battle of Stalingrad, the relief of Leningrad, and the advance to the west. He received the German surrender in Berlin on 8 May 1945 and was appointed to lead the Soviet Control Commission in Germany (1945–6). He was then removed to an obscure military command by Stalin (1946–52), but re-emerged after the latter's death as deputy minister of defence (1953–5) and then became minister (1955–7). He also became a candidate member of the Presidium of the central committee (1956)—the first professional soldier to do so. In the struggle for power (June 1957) he supported Khrushchev and materially helped him to rally support in the central committee. As a result, he was promoted to full membership of the Presidium, but shortly afterwards (Oct. 1957) was deprived of office on the grounds that he had sought to undermine the position of the Communist Party in the armed forces.

ZHUTOVIĆ, SRETEN (1910–   ), Serbian politician, who took the side of the Kremlin in the Soviet–Yugoslav dispute in 1948. He had long been a member of the Communist Party, and had organized the Serbian uprising in 1941, being Tito's deputy in the Partisan movement. In 1948, when trouble arose between Tito and Stalin, Zhutović sided with the latter. He was imprisoned, but soon afterwards he recanted and in 1951 was released. Some time later he was reinstated in the party and in 1970 worked in Belgrade.

ZIETHEN, HANS JOACHIM VON (1699–1786), Prussian soldier, who served under Frederick the Great. He was appointed commander of a regiment of hussars (1741), promoted to major-general (1744), and won the battle of Hohenfriedberg (1745) in the War of the Austrian Succession (1740–8). His record in the Seven Years War was equally distinguished. He served at Prague, Kolin (1757), Leuthen and Liegnitz (1760), and was responsible for the victory at Torgau (1760).

ZIMBA RAIDERS. Zimba was the name given to the 'people of Marundu', a section of the Marawi. A northward-raiding 'Zimba' horde attacked Kilwa in 1588–9 and are said to have eaten a large part of the population. After doing this again at Mombasa, they were destroyed by other raiders, the Segeju.

ZIMBABWE, GREAT, impressive group of stone buildings north of the Limpopo river in southern Africa. Although the site of Great Zimbabwe has been intermittently occupied since about the 3rd cent., stone buildings were not begun until after the 11th cent. They are tentatively associated with Shona occupation. The finest period of Zimbabwe architecture, with regular stone-walling and intricate chevron patterns worked into the structure, date from Rozwi (Shona) occupation (*c.* 1440) and after it, when the Great Wall and the conical tower were built. Zimbabwe was probably sacked by the Ndebele (*c.* 1830).

ZIMMERMANN TELEGRAM (19 Jan. 1917), note from the German foreign secretary to the German minister in Mexico, proposing an alliance with Mexico in the event of war between Germany and the US, and suggesting that Mexico should recover 'the territory lost by her in Texas, New Mexico, and Arizona'. It also suggested bringing Japan into the alliance. The telegram was intercepted by British intelligence and when published in America (1 March 1917) helped to create sentiment in favour of war with Germany.

ZIMMERWALD CONFERENCE (1915), first meeting of representatives of socialist parties, *ie,* members of the second international, after the outbreak of the First World War. It was attended by Lenin and Zinoviev, who used it as a platform from which to urge that the so-called imperialist war be turned into a civil war, and sought to bring about a split which was to lead to the establishment of the third international. Of the 38 delegates only seven supported Lenin. The majority's view was expressed in a manifesto drafted by Trotsky, which called for a general campaign against governments to compel them to end the war and to avoid anything that might lead to a division. A committee was set up which called a further meeting (Kienthal) and tried to organize a third (Stockholm).

ZINOVIEV LETTER (1924), allegedly the cause of the British Labour Party's defeat in the 1924 general election. It purported to be a letter from Grigori Zinoviev, the chairman of the Communist International, to the British Communist Party, and it called for an armed struggle against capitalism and seditious propaganda among the forces. It was published four days before polling day, together with an official foreign office protest to Russia.

The letter was almost certainly forged by White Russians in Berlin, and its publication was due largely to official and unofficial pressure from members and ex-members of the secret service. (The Conservative Central Office, which believed it to be genuine, paid £5000 to the presumed bearer of a copy to Britain, though no copy ever came to that office.)

The letter's effect on the 1924 election result has been disputed. The Labour vote was higher than that in the previous election, but the Liberal vote collapsed, and the Liberals' 159 seats were reduced to 40—the main cause of the massive Conservative majority which resulted. The importance of the letter may have lain in persuading those who would otherwise have voted Liberal, or abstained, to vote Conservative, and thus to sharpen the two-party polarization of British politics. The letter could effectively 'smear' Labour if—and only if—electors believed the Labour and Communist parties to be substantially the same. This view was already highly implausible by 1924, but a biased press may have conveyed this impression to marginal voters, and thus helped to make a heavy increase in the Conservative vote.

ZINZENDORF, JOHAN CHRISTIAN, Count (1738–1813), Austrian minister to the Emperor Francis II and councillor of state from 1792. He served as president of the Commission for the Commutation of Labour Services (1789) and was an advocate of laissez-faire economic theory. He provided a liberal voice of reason in the Habsburg empire.

ZINZENDORF, NICHOLAS LUDWIG, Count von (1700–60), Protestant nobleman of Upper Austria, who created the community of the Moravian Brethren at Herrnhut in Saxony (1722). Here he gave refuge to the Bohemian brethren, German Pietists, and other sectarians, established a Moravian liturgy (1727), and was consecrated a bishop of the Moravian Church (1737), which became one of the great missionary forces of the 18th cent. He also wrote some 2000 religious poems.

ZIONISM, movement to create a national home for the Jews in Palestine, which originated as a reaction to anti-Semitism and an alternative to revolutionary socialism for the beleaguered Jews of 19th-cent. Europe.

Zionism was the first concerted attempt by the Jews to establish a national as opposed to a religious identity. It attracted international attention through the publication of two pamphlets, *Auto-emancipation*, the work of Pinskev, an Odessa Jew, and *Der Judenstaat*, by the Austrian, Herzl. These provided much of the stimulus for the first Zionist Congress at Basel (1897).

The proposed purchase of land in Palestine aroused world-wide support, especially in the US, and appeared to gain substantial diplomatic support in the Balfour Declaration (1917). But Britain had also, in the Sykes–Picot agreement (1916), apparently supported Arab predominance in the area. Britain was given the task of resolving this dilemma when Palestine became a British mandate in 1919, but failed to get Arab agreement for a partition before 1939. The Second World War created an atmosphere in which zionism gained much sympathy. The United Nations drew up a scheme for partition and eventually took over the mandate (1948). By now the Jews were present in sufficient strength in Palestine to wage their own war for national independence against the Arab League, after which the New State of Israel was proclaimed under the presidency of Chaim Weizmann. The achievement of the Jewish nationalists stimulated Arab nationalism and contributed to the instability of Middle Eastern politics by introducing Arab–Israeli antagonism into the area.

ZIQQURAT, type of step tower built in most of the ancient Mesopotamian cities. Standing on a terrace, they rose in huge steps, built of brick and with temples at top and bottom. Their purpose is unknown, but they seem to have been religious buildings with some special significance.

ZIRIDS, dynasty from the mountain peoples of the central Maghrib, who were left in charge of the eastern Maghrib on the departure of the Fatimids (972). After warfare in the west, they abandoned their homeland to a collateral line, the Hammadids (1016), restricting themselves to Ifriqiyya (Tunisia), of which the capital was Qairawan. To avert discontent in Qairawan and the provinces, Mu'izz (*reg.* 1016–1062) changed his allegiance from the Shi'ite Fatimids to the Sunnite Abbasids (1048). A quarrel with Hilali Arab tribes, however, led to his defeat at Haidaran (1052) which precipitated the disintegration of his state. The sultan emigrated to Mahdiya (1057), where the dynasty enjoyed a reduced prosperity, in spite of a sack of the city by Pisa and Genoa (1087), in charge of a coastal dominion until its extinction by the Norman Roger II of Sicily (1148), made final by the Almohad conquest (1160).

ZIWA CULTURE, Iron Age culture of the first millennium AD in eastern Rhodesia, similar to and contemporary with the Gokomere culture with variations of pottery style and technique.

ZIYA GÖKALP (*c.* 1875–1924), Ottoman writer who, after 1908, came increasingly to advocate Turkism or Turkish nationalism in place of Ottomanism and Islam as the basis of the Ottoman state. After 1918 his views became the chief intellectual foundation of the Turkish republic. His slogan was 'We belong to the Turkish nation, the Muslim religious community and the European civilization'.

ZIYA PASHA (1825–80), Young Ottoman writer and advocate of a limited constitution, who later made his peace with the government and became governor of Syria (1876–80).

ZIYAD IBN ABIHI (d. *c.* 677), governor of Basra (665) and later of Al-Kufa also, where he acted as the vicegerent of the Umayyad caliph, Mu'aniya, over all the eastern provinces of the Muslim empire—provinces which he controlled with a remarkable and ruthless skill.

ZIYARID, name given to a line of emirs who ruled over Persian Iraq, Jurjan, and Tabaristan during the 10th and 11th cents AD. They often found themselves in conflict with the Samanids and also with the Buyids. In 1077 the Seljuk Sultan Malik Shah made an end of the Ziyarid regime.

ZIZKA, JOHN (*c.* 1360–1426), member of the Bohemian lower gentry. All but the last seven years of his life were insignificant and gave no indication of his future greatness. After a career as a military leader in Bohemia and abroad, he rose to be national leader of the Hussite extremist Taborites. Between 1419 and his death, although blind, he defended the Hussite movement against internal and external enemies by a defensive strategy. He revolutionized warfare and made significant contributions to military practice. His use of armoured wagons and firearms made the Taborite armies the scourge of their enemies. He seems to have been moved by deep religious conviction and an intense hatred of 'enemies of the Lord', notably king Sigismund.

ZOG, ZOGU AHMED (1893–1961), King of Albania (*reg.* 1928–39), son of a tribal chieftain of the Mati region of central Albania. Several of his ancestors had risen to high positions in the Ottoman bureaucracy. Zog himself was educated in military schools at Monastir and Istanbul. During the Balkan Wars he returned home to defend the lands of his family. He served in the Austro-Hungarian army during the First World War, but towards the end of it he was interned in Vienna. Zog was a member of the Popular Party, as was Fan Noli. He was minister of the interior in the government formed in 1920 and also held the post of commander-in-chief of the armed forces. When the Popular Party formed a government in Dec. 1921, Zog retained his posts. In March 1922 his decision to disarm the lowland tribes and his refusal to support the irredentism of the highlanders to Kosovo led to a rebellion. Fan Noli resigned, but Zog remained and quelled the revolt. In Dec. he became prime minister. Noli and others left the party in opposition to his government and in the 1924 election Noli was defeated. A right-wing government was formed round the landowner, Shevket Verlazi, but it soon was overthrown. Zog, who was the power behind Verlazi's government, fled to Yugoslavia and Noli assumed power. Zog went to Belgrade, where he planned his return. In Dec. 1924 he led a Yugoslav–Albanian force into Tirana and seized power. Noli fled to Italy, Albania was declared a republic, and Zog was made president. A constitution promulgated in March 1925 concentrated power in his hands. He relied increasingly upon Italy, militarily, economically, and politically. Although this partnership was economically beneficial, it was merely a cover for Italian ambitions in the Adriatic. Zog's position in Albania grew stronger and in 1928 the country was proclaimed a kingdom and Zog its king. He introduced many reforms, but his authoritarian rule caused considerable resentment. More important. Albania was increasingly the prisoner of Italy, and when Italy eventually decided to annex Albania there was little Zog could do to prevent it. In 1939 he and his wife, the Hungarian countess, Geraldine Apponyi, then bearing his heir, fled Albania before the Italian invaders. Zog fled to Greece and eventually to the US, where he died in 1961.

ZOLA, ÉMILE (1840–1902), French author, who used the novel as a vehicle for socialist propaganda and for the examination and indictment of society under the Second Empire. None of his prodigious literary output achieved such fame as his newspaper article 'J'accuse' (1898), which drew public attention to the Dreyfus case and rallied liberal and radical support in defence of the Third Republic against military and clerical extremism.

ZOLKIEWSKI, STANISLAS (d. 1620), Polish aristocrat, and grand hetman, who served Sigismund III of Poland loyally, especially during the Russian Time of Troubles. He defeated Zebrzydowski's rebellion at Guzow (1607) and led the Polish armies in Russia (1610). After winning a victory at Klushino near Smolensk (July 1610), he advanced towards Moscow, which he took after reaching agreement with a considerable section of the *boyars*. He engineered the election of Prince Ladislas of Poland as tsar in succession to Vasili Shuisky, on condition that the rights of the Orthodox Church remained inviolate, but when he realized that Sigismund III wanted the Russian throne for himself, Zolkiewski resigned his command and returned to Warsaw, bringing Shuisky and his brothers as prisoners. He helped to arrange the truce of Deulino (1618) and led the Polish advance into Moldavia when the Turks threatened to start a new war with Poland, but he was killed in battle near Cecora.

ZOLLVEREIN (1834–66), Free Trade association, mainly within the German Confederation, but excluding Austrian lands. It advanced the economic development of the area and helped to confirm Prussian leadership.

The need for a customs union arose from the chaotic political fragmentation, especially in the centre of the Confederation, and the failure to implement Article 19 of the Final Act of the Congress of Vienna, which provided for easing inter-state communications in the Confederation as a whole. The movement started when Prussia rationalized her own administration by transferring the collection of customs, excise, and tolls from the interior to her frontiers and making agreements with enclaves within her territory for a customs union and a division of the tax-yield on a basis of population ratio. In 1828 Hesse-Darmstadt joined the union, and in southern Germany Bavaria and Württemberg formed a similar union. In 1829 the two unions reached agreement and the construction of north–south main roads began. In 1831 Hesse-Cassel, which separated the eastern and western territories of Prussia, was then in economic difficulties, and so agreed to join Prussia in order to eliminate tolls on goods passing from east to west. She was followed in this move by Saxony and Thüringen in 1833.

The Zollverein was administered by representatives of member states, whose decisions had to be unanimous. For this reason, changes in Zollverein tariffs were normally only possible when treaties came up for renewal. The underdeveloped economies of the German states were dependent to a considerable extent on income from the Zollverein, which was divided in proportions favourable to non-Prussian states, and hence Prussia was able to ensure ratification of new agreements as a condition of renewal of treaties. The size of the customs union favoured road and rail developments (1840–65), which opened up new areas to industrial exploitation and made possible favourable commercial treaties with foreign countries.

Austria was not in a position to apply for membership before 1850 because she had not attained internal free trade. After Olmütz she made strenuous efforts to join, but was frustrated, partly because of her protectionist policy, and partly because Prussia did not want to relinquish her dominant position. Austria's subsequent efforts to detach equally protectionist South German states were unsuccessful.

After the Austro-Prussian War, a new Zollverein was created, consisting of the North German Confederation and the South German states. In 1871 it was superseded by the German empire.

The Zollverein was for Prussia a necessary administrative consequence of the allocation to her of Rhineland territory. It caused, rather than resulted from, the growth of German national feeling. Hindsight has made some historians see in it a calculated plot to exclude Austria from Germany and to ensure Prussian hegemony. This only appears to be true after 1850, when difficulties were deliberately created to prevent Austria's admission. The existence of the Zollverein and 40 years of administrative co-operation certainly facilitated the creation of the German empire, while the economic strength it gave to Prussia made unification feasible.

W. O. Henderson, *The Zollverein* (London, 1939).
A. H. Price, *The Evolution of the Zollverein* (Michigan, 1949).
                                                                                    DMK

ZORNDORF, BATTLE OF (Aug. 1758), Prussian victory over the Russian army under Fermor during the Seven Years War. Frederick II attacked the Russians, who were entrenched near Custrin in Brandenburg, and caused them to abandon their siege, both sides suffering heavy losses.

ZOROASTRIANISM, religion developed from the teachings of Zoroaster (*c.* 6th cent. BC), which was adopted by the Achaemenid kings of Iran. It declined under the Seleucids, but was revived by the Parthians and became the state religion under the Sassanians. After the Arab invasions (7th cent. BC) it declined again, but survives in some forms to the present day. Zoroaster taught of one supreme, beneficent god, Ahura Mazda, who possessed certain attributes, In time, these attributes were worshipped separately, with other gods, *eg*, Mithra, Anahita, and there developed a number of practices and rites, notably the preservation of fire as a sacred symbol of good. The sacred book of Zoroastrianism is the *Avesta*.

ZRINYI FAMILY in Hungary, noble family whose most famous representative was Miklos II Zrinyi (1620–64). In 1647 he was appointed *ban* or viceroy of Croatia by the Emperor Ferdinand III, but his main purpose in life was to drive both the Habsburgs and the Turks from his native land. He wrote essays on political and military science, but is best known for his *Szigeti Veszedelem* (1645–6), the first and finest epic of Hungarian literature, in which he recounted the heroic defence of the fortress of Szigetvar against the forces of Suleiman II by his own great-grandfather, Miklos I Zrinyi (1566). In 1664 he was killed by a wild boar and his estates passed to his brother, Peter, who became involved in intrigues with the Turks and French against the Emperor Leopold, for which he was arrested (1670) and executed (April 1671).

ZSITVA-TOROK, PEACE OF (1606), brought to an end the war of 1593–1606 between Austria and the Ottoman empire. The Ottomans acquired two Hungarian fortresses, Eger (Erlau) and Kanizsa, but in return had to accept the discontinuance of the tribute which the emperor had hitherto paid to the sultan, and also to recognize the emperor as the equal of the sultan.

ZULU EMPIRE, one of the most powerful African kingdoms in southern Africa in the 19th cent., created by the conquests of Shaka out of the numerous Nguni chiefdoms between the Pongola river in the north and the Umzimkulu in the south. Shaka's successors consolidated the internal structure of the Zulu state, so that to this day and despite its ultimate defeat, its subject peoples identify themselves as 'Zulu'. With the arrival of the Voortrekkers and the British the southern frontier of the kingdom was pushed back to the Tugela river. In 1879 the Zulus were defeated by the British and in

1887 Zululand became a British crown colony. It was annexed to Natal in 1897 and in 1970 formed part of the republic of South Africa.

ZULU WAR (1879), begun by Sir Bartle Frere against Disraeli's wishes, resulted in the British being defeated at Isandhlwana and the death of the Prince Imperial, who was killed while on a reconnaissance. Frere feared a blood-bath in a clash between the Transvaal Boers and the Zulu military kingdom. In 1876 Britain had annexed the Transvaal, whose leaders assented through fear of the Zulus under Cetshwayo. His defeat and deportation after the Zulu War made the Boers restive under British control and led to the Transvaal Rising (1881), whereby the Boers regained their independence, but continued to hate Britain.

The war caused great outcry in Britain and was partly responsible for discrediting Disraeli's 'forward' policy and for the Conservative electoral defeat of 1880.

ZUMÁRRAGA, JUAN DE (1468–1548), archbishop of Mexico, previously an obscure Franciscan friar who by chance impressed Charles I. He arrived in Mexico in 1528 and was appalled by the conditions which prevailed under the cruel and corrupt first *audiencia*. With great personal courage, he forced their removal almost single-handed. He co-operated with their successors, notably Viceroy Mendoza, and used his position as Protector of the Indians to defend native dignity, and was especially active in the founding of schools for them. He was equally tireless in suppressing the remnants of native religion, and it was Zumárraga who grudgingly accepted the miracle of Our Lady of Guadalupe. He was realistic enough not to oppose the *encomienda* system, and urged perpetual grants in order that the Spanish might act more paternally towards their charges. He also introduced the first printing press into Latin America (1534).

ZUNI INDIANS, Pueblo tribe of the American south-west, first encountered (1540) in northern AZ by Spanish explorers searching for the legendary riches of the 'Kingdom of Cibola'. The Spanish put them under the care of missionaries (1598) and established a mission among them (1629). They took part in the general Pueblo uprising (1680) and after reconquest by the Spaniards (1692) built a new pueblo at their present location in NM.

ZÚÑIGA, DON BALTHASAR DE (d. 1622), Spanish politician and diplomat, who became a favourite of the young Philip IV of Spain. As Spanish ambassador at the imperial courts of Rudolph II and Matthias I (1608–17), he was largely responsible for the creation of the Catholic League (1609) and tried to build up a strongly pro-Spanish party in the empire. He hoped for the succession of a hispanophile Habsburg to the Bohemian Crown and to the empire, who would secure the Spanish road to the Netherlands for Philip III. In 1617 he was succeeded by the Count of Onate and returned to Spain, where he became the spokesman of the 'war party' in the council of state. In 1621 the deaths of Archduke Albert of the Netherlands and of Philip III enabled him briefly to press his bellicose policies upon Philip IV, who had already fallen under the influence of Zúñiga's nephew, Gaspar de Guzman, the future Count of Olivares.

ZÚÑIGA, JUAN DE (c. 1490–1546), Spanish cleric, tutor, and confessor to Philip II of Spain. A loyal and pious servant trusted by Charles V, he guided Philip's moral supervision and advised him during his father's absence from Spain.

ZURARA, GOMES EANNES DE (*fl.* 15th cent.), historian of the Portuguese explorations in the earlier 15th cent., including the voyages organized by Prince Henry the Navigator down to 1448. His narrative is a trustworthy contemporary source.

ZURAWNO, PEACE OF (1676), marked the end of the Polish–Ottoman War, begun in 1672. Poland yielded to the Ottomans the province of Podolia in the Ukraine, including the fortress of Kaminiec. The Cossacks of the western Ukraine were to come under the protection of the sultan.

ZÜRICH, imperial free city occupying an important position on the route through the St Gotthard pass in the central Alps, which was opened up in the early 13th cent. By the 14th cent. it was the largest town in Switzerland, a centre of textile manufactures, and the capital of an expansionist city state. Zürich became one of the most powerful members of the independent Swiss confederation formed in the 14th–15th cents. After 1521, it became the focal point of Swiss Protestantism under the influence of Zwingli (d. 1531). In 1970 it was the chief commercial centre of Switzerland.

ZÜRICH, PEACE OF (1859), formal treaty between Austria and France, confirming the arrangements made at Villafranca to end their conflict in northern Italy. Napoleon III had agreed that while most of Lombardy should go to Piedmont, the duchies of Tuscany and Modena, which had rebelled during the war, should have their pro-Austrian rulers reinstated, but not by force. Before the peace of Zürich it was obvious that this was impractical. The formal treaty, in fact, marked the end of the temporary friendship between Austria and France.

ZÜRICH BIBLE, THE, work of a group of distinguished Swiss Protestant scholars who supported Zwingli, *eg*, Leo Jüd, Conrad Pellicanus, and Theodore Buchman (Bibliander). It was partly the result of Zwingli's advocacy of prophesyings or biblical readings with analytical interpretations.

ZURITA, JERONIMO (1512–80), Spanish chronicler, who wrote the history of Aragon in his *Anales de la Corona de Aragon* (1562–79).

ZUSMARHAUSEN, BATTLE OF (May 1648), one of the last battles of the Thirty Years War, at which Franco-Swedish forces under Turenne and Wrangel defeated the Bavarian-imperialist army near Augsburg. Melander, the imperialist commander, was mortally wounded, and though Montecucoli brought the remnants of their forces back to Landsberg Bavaria was again overrun.

ZUTPHEN, BATTLE OF (1586), Spanish victory in the Dutch War of Independence, famous as the battle in which Sir Philip Sidney was mortally wounded. The English expeditionary forces in Gelderland, commanded by the earls of Leicester and Essex and Lord Willoughby, besieged Zutphen, held by Spain since 1572, and tried to cut off a Spanish force sent to take supplies to the garrison, but they were themselves overwhelmed.

ZUYDER ZEE, BATTLE OF (Oct. 1573), naval victory of the Dutch Sea Beggars off Enkhuisen, when 30 Spanish ships, under the command of the Count of Bossu, were attacked and fled after Bossu, his flagship, and six other vessels had been captured.

ZUYLESTEIN, WILLIAM HENRY, Count (1645–1709), Dutch diplomat and soldier, cousin of William of Orange, whom he served as ambassador extraordinary, making a political reconnaissance in England (1685–8). He was created master of the robes (1689) and Earl of Rochford (1695), and received property in Ireland for his services.

ZVENO (the Link), Bulgarian reformist organization, founded in June 1927 by Dimo Kazasov after his expulsion from the Socialist Party. Originally it consisted of some 300 intellectuals and enjoyed the support of young army officers. It published a journal called *Zveno*, which was read by another

2500 intellectuals. By 1934 Col. Kimon Georgiev was the leader of Zveno. He was a friend of Damayan Velcev, leader of the Military League, and co-operated with him in the coup of 1934 and headed the government that was formed afterwards. Zveno's programme was one of national regeneration through authoritarian rule. The government destroyed IMRO and undertook various reform projects. But it soon ran into trouble with the king and was forced to resign. Zveno never held power under the royal dictatorship, but emerged as a political force during the Second World War. Both Velcev and Georgiev were keen to co-operate with the communists in the resistance and led Zveno into the popular front and later into the Fatherland Front. In 1945 the communists abandoned Zveno, but both Velcev and Georgiev were rewarded with positions under the new regime.

ZWAANENDAEL COLONY (1631–2), American colony near Delaware Bay, founded by the Dutch West India Co. A fort was built there and crops planted, but eventually the colonists, under Capt. Pieter Hayes, were massacred by Indians (1632).

ZWANGENDABA (d. 1845), leader of the Jere ethnic group of the Nguni-speaking southern Bantu, and one of those Ngoni warrior-chiefs who moved northwards (from northern Zululand) under pressure from Shaka. By 1835 he and his followers had crossed the Zambesi; later they moved northwards into Tanzania. Their subsequent impact on East African history was considerable.

On their long march from the south, the Ngoni developed a capacity to absorb heterogeneous alien groups while preserving their own identity. This allowed for strong military leadership. Their northward invasions undoubtedly had destructive effects, but should be seen in the wider context of constructive political change. In building their six small but powerful states they set an example in organization which others profitably followed. The rise of other leaders, such as Mirambo and Kasungu, owed much to Ngoni influence.

ZWICKAU PROPHETS, radical members of the Protestant reformation, who were the precursors of Anabaptism. These bearded extremists, who were textile weavers from the town of Zwickau on the Saxon–Bohemian border, came to Wittenberg in 1522, and in Luther's absence impressed Carlstadt and the authorities with their attacks on infant baptism and claims of heavenly visions.

ZWIDE (d. 1819), chief of the Ndwandwe people, who built up a confederacy north of the Mfolozi river in Zululand (South Africa) at the beginning of the 19th cent. He was the main rival of Dingiswayo, whom he killed in 1818, and Shaka, who defeated him in 1819. Commanders of his conquered armies led the people who became known as the Ngoni in Central and East Africa.

ZWINGER PALACE, electoral palace at Dresden commissioned by Augustus of Saxony, King of Poland, and built in the baroque style during the period 1711–22 by Matthäus Daniel Pöppelmann (1662–1736), the German architect.

ZWINGLI, ULRICH (1484–1531), Swiss Protestant reformer and first great leader of the Reformation in Zürich. After being ordained, he became parish priest at Glarus (1506) and later, as chaplain, accompanied the Swiss troops on two Italian campaigns, during which he was present at the battles of Novara (1513) and Marignano (1515). During this period he joined a circle of humanists and became deeply impressed by Erasmus. In 1516 he moved to the benefice of Einsiedeln and two years later to the cathedral of Zürich, to which he had been elected People's Priest (Dec. 1518).

Until 1520, Zwingli was officially a papal pensioner and the only indications of his growing antipathy towards the Church was his denunciation of the Franciscan indulgence-seller, Samson (Aug. 1518), and his absorption in the newly-translated Scriptures, with their revelations of current deviations from primitive Christianity. On 1 Jan. 1519 he announced his intention of preaching an exposition of St Mark's Gospel in the Great Minster, and in 1522 he petitioned the Bp of Constance to permit clerical marriage and soon afterwards espoused a widow. His theological position was embodied in the 67 articles which were presented to the city council of Zürich (19 Jan. 1523), in which he attacked the authority of the pope, the doctrine of transubstantiation, the intercession of saints, and the efficacy of fasts and pilgrimages. After a public disputation with the vicar-general of the Bp of Constance, the articles were accepted by the council and Zwingli's right to preach was endorsed. Later, in 1523, he asked for the abolition of the mass, and though this was not granted until 12 April 1525 the council had in the meantime ordered the removal of organs, relics, and images and the dissolution of monastic houses (1524). In 1525 his simple commemorative service of communion, in both kinds replaced the mass. He produced a reformed liturgy, including a new baptismal order, and the early morning choir service was replaced by the office of 'prophesying', ie, a service of biblical exposition (1525).

From 1525 he was drawn increasingly into theological controversy. He upheld the authority of the lay magistracy against the Anabaptists, whose views on re-baptism he found untenable, and stressed the concept of a theocracy which he handed down to Calvinism. Although he agreed with Luther's teaching on the doctrines of justification, predestination, and communion of both kinds for the laity, the Colloquy of Marburg (1529) revealed the irreconcilable difference in their concept of the nature of the eucharist. Zwingli's principal fear, however, was of a union of the Catholic cantons with the Habsburgs in a crusade to exterminate Swiss Protestantism. By 1528 he had organized the Christian Civic League, but was restrained from using force against the Catholic Christian Union (1529). In 1531 he instigated economic sanctions against the Catholic cantons, which provoked a declaration of war on Zürich. Zwingli accompanied the city's Protestant forces as chaplain on the battlefield of Kappel and was killed in the conflict, leaving the fate of Zürich in the capable hands of Bullinger.

O. Farmer, *Zwingli the Reformer, his Life and Work* (London, 1952). MKS